Britannica
Book of the Year

PAGE 3

Britannica
World Data

PAGE 609

1985
Britannica
Book of the Year

Encyclopædia Britannica, Inc.
Chicago
Auckland/Geneva/London/Manila/Paris/Rome
Seoul/Sydney/Tokyo/Toronto

THE UNIVERSITY OF CHICAGO

The Britannica Book of the Year is published with the editorial advice
of the faculties of the University of Chicago.

CONTENTS: Britannica Book of the Year

609   CONTENTS: Britannica World Data

Calendar 1985

JANUARY

1 New Year's Day
1 200th anniversary of *The Times,* renowned London newspaper
1 250th anniversary of the birth of Paul Revere, folk hero of the American Revolution
4 25th anniversary of the death of Albert Camus, French political theorist and 1957 Nobel laureate in literature
21 U.S. federal holiday honouring the Rev. Martin Luther King, Jr., civil rights activist
24 20th anniversary of the death of Winston Churchill, Britain's leader during World War II
26 Proclamation of the Republic of India (1950)

FEBRUARY

6 Waitangi Day, commemoration of the 1840 treaty that established British sovereignty over New Zealand and recognized the rights of Maori tribes
14 St. Valentine's Day
20 Chinese New Year's Day
20 Ash Wednesday; the first day of Lent in Western Christian churches
23 300th anniversary of the birth of George Frederick Handel, German-born composer of such masterpieces as *Messiah*
25 Tenth anniversary of the death of Elijah Muhammad, leader of the Nation of Islam (Black Muslims)

MARCH

8 75th International Women's Day
10 100th anniversary of the birth of Tamara Karsavina, great Russian ballerina and partner of Vaslav Nijinsky
17 St. Patrick's Day, national holiday in Ireland
21 20th anniversary of the Selma–Montgomery civil rights march in Alabama
21 300th anniversary of the birth of Johann Sebastian Bach, German organist and composer of many of the masterworks of Western music for keyboard, voice, and orchestra
25 Independence Day in Greece (1821)

APRIL

6 First day of the Jewish feast of Passover
7 Easter in the Western churches
14 Easter in the Eastern churches
26 Union Day in Tanzania (1964); commemoration of the amalgamation of Tanganyika, Zanzibar, and Pemba Island into a single nation
28 40th anniversary of Mussolini's death. He was shot to death near Azzano while trying to flee Italy in disguise. Two days later Adolf Hitler, his World War II ally, committed suicide in Berlin
28 In Japan, celebration of the emperor's birthday (1901)

MAY

1 May Day; International Labour Day
12 Mother's Day in the U.S.
14 20th anniversary of the death of Frances Perkins, first woman named to a Cabinet post by a U.S. president
17 Constitution Day in Norway (1814)
21 50th anniversary of the death of Jane Addams, U.S. social reformer and co-recipient of the 1931 Nobel Prize for Peace
22 Centenary of the death of Victor Hugo, French poet, dramatist, and novelist; his works include *Les Misérables* and *The Hunchback of Notre Dame*
23 First day of Ramadan, the ninth month on the Islamic calendar. Muslims observe a month-long fast, which is one of the "five pillars" of their Islamic faith
27 Memorial Day in the U.S.

JUNE

5 75th anniversary of the death of William S. Porter. After serving time in an Ohio penitentiary for embezzlement of bank funds, he published widely popular short stories under the pen name O. Henry
8 Official celebration of the birthday (1926) of Queen Elizabeth II
16 Father's Day in the U.S.
22 Id al-Fitr, Islamic festival marking the end of the fast of Ramadan
25 35th anniversary of the start of the Korean War, which ended in July 1953 after an estimated five million persons had been killed

JULY

4 Independence Day in the U.S. (1776)
6 450th anniversary of the death of Sir Thomas More. The former chancellor of England was imprisoned in the Tower of London, then beheaded on the orders of King Henry VIII
12 50th anniversary of Alcoholics Anonymous
14 Bastille Day, French holiday commemorating the successful storming of the medieval fortress in Paris in 1789. The event marked the start of the French Revolution
26 Establishment of the Republic of Liberia (1847)
28 Independence Day in Peru (1821)

AUGUST

1 Founding of the Swiss Confederation (1291)
13 75th anniversary of the death of Florence Nightingale, founder of the nursing profession
14 50th anniversary of the signing of the U.S. Social Security Act
25 Independence Day in Uruguay (1825)
27 20th anniversary of the death of Le Corbusier (Charles-Edouard Jeanneret), Swiss-born architect, city planner, painter, and author
29 10th anniversary of the death of Eamon De Valera, U.S.-born politician who helped found the Republic of Ireland. He spent more than 20 years as prime minister and 16 as president during his half century of public life

SEPTEMBER

4 20th anniversary of the death of Albert Schweitzer, accomplished musician and respected theologian, who became a doctor in 1913 so he could care for the needy in equatorial Africa
12 National Revolution Day in Ethiopia (1944). Emperor Haile Selassie had ruled the country for 44 years before being deposed. After his deposition he was confined to a three-room mud hut in an army barracks but was permitted to return to the palace and die with dignity
16 Rosh Hashana, Jewish New Year's Day
23 Unification of the Kingdom of Saudi Arabia (1932)
25 Yom Kippur, Jewish Day of Atonement
27 Islamic New Year's Day

OCTOBER

7 Centenary of the birth of Niels Bohr, Danish physicist and 1922 Nobel laureate. His son, Aage, shared a Nobel Prize for Physics in 1975
14 Thanksgiving Day in Canada
23 35th anniversary of the death of Russian-born entertainer Al Jolson. He starred in *The Jazz Singer,* the first feature film (1927) with synchronized speech and music
23 75th anniversary of the death of King Chulalongkorn, the long-reigning king of Siam (now Thailand), whose wide-ranging social revolution profoundly affected virtually every aspect of Siamese life, both public and private
24 United Nations Day

NOVEMBER

1 Algerian Revolution (1954)
3 Independence Day in Panama (1903)
7 Anniversary of the Bolshevik Revolution (1917), which ended the rule of the Russian tsars and brought Lenin to power as the head of a Communist state
15 Children's Shrine Visiting Day in Japan. Parents take seven-year-old daughters, five-year-old sons, and three-year-old boys and girls to a Shinto shrine to thank the tutelary deities for good health and pray for future blessings
20 75th anniversary of the death of Leo Tolstoy, Russian novelist, whose fame derived from such enduring classics as *War and Peace*
28 Thanksgiving Day in the U.S.
29 Proclamation of the Socialist Republic of Yugoslavia (1945)

DECEMBER

1 Beginning of Advent
2 Formation of the United Arab Emirates (1971); the federation includes seven largely autonomous emirates on the Arabian Peninsula
8 First day of Hanukka, Jewish Feast of Lights; it commemorates the rededication of the Second Temple of Jerusalem in 164 BC
12 Independence Day in Kenya (1963)
25 Christmas Day
28 National celebration of the birthday (1945) of Birendra Bir Bikram Shah Deva, the king of Nepal

Letter to the Reader

This volume represents an epochal undertaking. It reflects the first organic change in encyclopaedia yearbooks since those annual supplements were originally devised as a means of keeping an encyclopaedia up-to-date. For readers long familiar with the *Britannica Book of the Year,* a guide to the new additions presented here, and to the substantial reorganization of the contents, is essential. To new readers, a welcome and an introduction to this new work are due.

In the 1985 *Encyclopædia Britannica,* volatile statistical information about the nations of the world has, so far as possible, been removed from the *Macropædia* volumes and concentrated in a new book called *Britannica World Data,* which is contained within this volume. Annually revising hundreds of pages scattered across the alphabet in the *Macropædia,* so as to update constantly changing economic and other short-lived statistics, has been a manifest impossibility. It was partly to relieve this problem—though it could not be fully cured—that the *Book of the Year* was created in 1938. Now that *Britannica World Data* is *the* locus of such information, each subscriber's set may be updated annually to an extent never before possible, by the simple expedient of adding or replacing this one volume.

In recent years it has been our practice to reprint in the *Book of the Year* one or two newly revised *Macropædia* articles. Henceforward the number of pages devoted to that updating function will be larger, as it is here.

Macropædia articles have been noted for their annotated bibliographies of important books in the fields they address. A new bibliographic element is introduced in this volume: immediately following the revised *Macropædia* articles appear thoughtful reviews of several recently published books whose impact on their fields is profound; these reviews update related *Macropædia* bibliographies.

The order in which articles appear has been changed in this *Book of the Year* in response to reader suggestions, to accord more closely with the manner in which the *Macropædia* is organized, and for other reasons. The most conspicuous element in this reorganization is the relocation of all the narrative articles about the nations of the world, withdrawing them from an all-embracing alphabetical order (AERIAL SPORTS, AFGHANISTAN, AFRICAN AFFAIRS . . .) and grouping them in a single "superarticle," WORLD AFFAIRS. It is organized by modern geopolitical regions, so that, for instance, the reader turning to the region Middle East and North Africa will find there the subarticle *Middle Eastern and North African Affairs,* followed by sections on all the countries of the region in alphabetical order. At the beginning of the WORLD AFFAIRS article is an alphabetical table of contents to the whole article, including all the countries, the several regional affairs commentaries, *Dependent States, United Nations, Commonwealth of Nations,* and *Political Parties.*

As the *Sporting Record* pages in the *Micropædia* bring together all statistical data about records in sports, so the SPORTS AND GAMES article in the *Britannica Book of the Year* groups all such activities in one superarticle. Moreover, a three-page *Sporting Record* section has been added to update the *Micropædia,* and this follows SPORTS AND GAMES. Thus the text article (SPORTS AND GAMES) tells the story of how the new records were set, while *Sporting Record* brings together the year's new records themselves.

Both of the foregoing superarticles fit into the structure of the Year in Review section, which begins with the CHRONOLOGY OF EVENTS of the year, followed by PEOPLE OF THE YEAR (biographies of the men and women who shaped it, including Nobel Prize winners, plus obituaries of noted people who died in 1984). Under Events of 1984, which appears next, are all the articles and superarticles, alphabetically organized and ranging from AGRICULTURE AND FOOD SUPPLIES to WORLD AFFAIRS.

As longtime readers of the *Book of the Year* will recognize, certain titles within this section have been changed. In most cases, this has been done to make the title more explicit or up-to-date or to bring it into line with the *Macropædia* article it updates. For example, COMPUTERS has become INFORMATION PROCESSING AND INFORMATION SYSTEMS; DEFENSE has become MILITARY AFFAIRS. Other titles have been combined; *e.g.,* CRIME AND LAW ENFORCEMENT and PRISONS AND PENOLOGY are now one article with the heading CRIME, LAW ENFORCEMENT, AND PENOLOGY. Certain articles have been relocated within other articles having related subject matter. Thus, FISHERIES and FOOD PROCESSING are now sections within the article AGRICULTURE AND FOOD SUPPLIES; STOCK EXCHANGES is a section of ECONOMIC AFFAIRS. The *Ceramics* section of the old article MATERIALS SCIENCES is now under INDUSTRIAL REVIEW, and the *Metallurgy* section is under MINING AND METALLURGY. And a new article, HUMAN RIGHTS, has been added.

In case of confusion, readers are urged to consult the Index, and longtime readers who do so will find that all the valuable material the *Book of the Year* has always provided is still there, and at the same length. Finally, a new feature has been added. At the end of most articles—and in some cases, sections of articles—is a reference indicating which *Macropædia* article the Year in Review article, or section, updates. Thus readers who wish to pursue the subject in greater depth can turn immediately to the relevant article in the *Macropædia.*

The entirely new *Britannica World Data* follows the *Book of the Year.* They are separated by 12 pages of Flags of the Nations in full colour. After *Britannica World Data* appears a brief identification of contributors to the *Book of the Year,* and then the Index to the whole volume. This year's Index differs from its precursor in two important respects. First, it refers the reader to the articles in five previous editions of the *Book of the Year* instead of two, as has been our practice. Second, Feature Articles and Special Reports from preceding years are also indexed, which has not been the case in the past.

The Index is a suitable topic on which to conclude this letter, for one urgent suggestion to the reader bears repeating whenever possible: always consult the Index first. It is especially important to do so in a volume as dramatically changed as this. By far the most frequent complaint we receive is that a reader has been unable to find a subject—because, it turns out, the reader has not consulted the Index or did not read the brief instructions on using it that appear at the top of its first page.

The major changes described here have been carefully planned and executed in the hope that you, the person for whom this book is created, will find it more useful than ever before. That hope is shared by all the Britannica people who have had a part in producing it.

Bruce L. Felknor
Director of Yearbooks

Our Disintegrating World
The Menace of Global Anarchy

BY GEORGIE ANNE GEYER

World War II has been *the* watershed event of our times, the measure by which we mark our most recent human passage through this world. Its horrors—then the heroic rebuilding of whole societies and the consequent freeing from colonial rule of half the population of the world—touched virtually every human being on Earth.

In the developed and underdeveloped worlds alike, the war marked a break with man's whole history. After 1945 the ideas that "progress" was somehow inevitable and that the future of the modern world would be one basically of cohesion and coherence were assumed for the first time by human beings who before had lived out their lives in fatalistic acceptance. Man was proceeding toward a more developed, technological, and egalitarian future, and nothing, now, could stop him.

Yet, the most salient if unrecognized truth of the last quarter of the 20th century is the fact that those optimistic and often utopian assumptions have proved to be totally misguided.

What has happened instead in the 1970s and 1980s—indeed, in the very "1984" in which the writer George Orwell prophesied that mankind would be locked into an inhuman totalitarian prison of mind and body—is that the world is quietly but relentlessly being rent by a slow-motion disintegration.

Many countries whose structural and spiritual cohesion was taken for granted have been breaking apart like fissiparous human social particles into their component parts: tribes, clans, religious fundamentalisms of every faith, city gangs, death squads, terrorist movements, guerrilla movements, and narrow and rabid self-interest groups.

The borders assigned—often by colonial powers after World War II, usually without regard to the tribal and religious realities of the exploited regions—are no longer holding. The laws of international behaviour that were so painfully hammered out, beginning in feudal times when the nation-state began to emerge in Europe, are not recognized or obeyed by the new "irregular" powers of this new world. The international organizations that were to save mankind after the horrors of World War II either have turned into organizations presiding over the debate on the new decomposition or have been transmogrified into self-interest groups themselves. Paradoxically, as power passed to the powerless, more and more people seemed to become more unempowered.

Finally, war itself changed. Before World War II, in

modern times at least, warfare had "developed" to the point where it was overwhelmingly traditional, conventional, regular, hierarchical, and vertical in command structure. The armies of the Great Powers fought wars in which military hierarchies directed regular armies against other regular armies. After the end of World War II, all of that changed. There have been no more "world wars" since 1945, but there are dozens and dozens of small, nonconventional, irregular wars going on all over the world and taking more and more millions of civilian lives than ever before.

Yet, despite these changes of incalculable consequence to the sanity and health and future of the world, few have wanted to recognize that mankind is, indeed, living in a new and different world. Then, suddenly, important voices began to be heard:

• In his 1982 report to the United Nations, the Peruvian-born UN secretary-general, Javier Pérez de Cuéllar, put the institutional breakdown afflicting the world in the clearest and most unmistakable terms. "I believe that we are at present embarked on an exceedingly dangerous course," he said soberly, "one symptom of which is the crisis in the multilateral approach in international affairs and the concomitant erosion of the authority and status of world and regional inter-governmental institutions. Above all, this trend has adversely affected the United Nations, the instrument that was created specifically to prevent such a self-destructive course. Such a trend must be reversed before once again we bring upon ourselves a global catastrophe and find ourselves without institutions effective enough to prevent it.

"I cannot disguise my deep anxiety at present trends, for I am absolutely convinced that the United Nations is indispensable in a world fraught with tension and peril. Institutions such as this are not built in a day. They require constant constructive work and fidelity to the principles on which they are based."

• Analyzing what is in effect a parallel internal breakdown within the United States, former U.S. secretary of state Henry Kissinger told me in the spring of 1984, sitting in his office in a modern glass building in New York: "I think that America is almost approaching Argentine conditions in foreign policy. By this, I mean that, if you look at Argentine history over the last 50 years, every new government had about 53% support and then lost it by acting like a government. There has been an inherent tendency toward paralysis because the country was so profoundly divided. I think in the field of foreign policy we're beginning to approach that condition. I think what will surely happen is that the crisis of confidence will accelerate because we will look incapable of mastering events. And then the question is, who will emerge, a serious leader or a demagogue? And I don't have the answer to that.

"Our structural problems, I think, are, one, the disintegration of the relationship between the presidency and the

Georgie Anne Geyer is a syndicated columnist and television panelist on world affairs, the winner of many awards for distinguished international reporting and commentary. From the summer of 1983 through all of 1984, she conducted the interviews with world leaders that are reflected here—hard questions that do not have satisfactory or comforting answers.

11

Congress, which is accentuated by the disintegration of congressional leadership. As a result, a consensus has to be built on each issue. This gives incentives to each pressure group to make alliances with other pressure groups even if they are not interested in the specific topic. Number two is the organization of the executive branch by which policy emerges through an adversary process. That makes the outcome, even within the executive branch, almost accidental. Third, and most important, there is something wrong with the philosophy with which we approach foreign policy as a nation. And there is a crisis in our perception of what our role should be and what our vital interests are."

• Speaking of still another side of the breakdown process, Jacques de Larosière de Champfeu, the managing director of the International Monetary Fund, says, "The widespread growth of public debt that we are witnessing is unprecedented, even though certain countries—as, for example, Germany in the 1920s and the United States in the 1930s and early 1940s—have experienced it before. In my judgment, that growth is unsustainable over the long run. Thus, either it is stopped by coordinated and rational policies, or it will be stopped, as in the past, by a new burst of inflation with all the social, political, and economic disarray that accompanies it. What is at stake here is . . . the soundness of institutions."

• Perhaps no one has characterized the entire worldwide process of disintegration in more compelling words than U.S. Pres. Jimmy Carter's national security adviser, Zbigniew Brzezinski. In his memoirs and in interviews with me, he has said, "The factors that make for international instability are gaining the historical upper hand over the forces that work for more organized cooperation. The unavoidable conclusion of any detached analysis of global trends is that social turmoil, political unrest, economic crisis, and international friction are likely to become more widespread during the remainder of this century.

"Moreover, in the years ahead regional conflicts not involving the major powers are likely to become more threatening. Already in the late '70s and early '80s, regional conflicts have acquired immunity from effective international containment. As American power receded, it became more difficult to terminate local conflicts quickly. More generally, the combination of demographic pressures and political unrest will generate, particularly in the third world, increasing unrest and violence. Much, or maybe even most, of this will be internal, but it will inevitably impose major strains on international order. Moreover, it is almost a certainty that an increasing number of third world states will come to possess nuclear weapons, and some are likely to use them in the course of a conflict.

"The menace confronting humanity, in brief, is not Soviet hegemony, but global anarchy."

• Father Theodore Hesburgh, the president of the University of Notre Dame, addressed the religious aspect of breakdown, sitting in his gracious office on the beautiful Indiana campus on a glorious fall day, as he told me, "I see a much more apocalyptic thing coming as we get near the year 2000. Fundamentalists write me that what God wants is an apocalyptic time with the skies burning. I expect you saw the same thing in the year 1000. This is the second millennium in our history. Will we make it through to the third?

"It's been a difficult time," he went on thoughtfully, "probably the most difficult period mankind ever had. We've never before been able to wipe out humankind."

• Finally, Mahboolbul Haq, a Pakistani economist who was formerly a high official of the World Bank, ruminated

about the developing world to me one day in his office in Islamabad, but with a note of hope. "Disintegration?" he asked, and at the same time stated, "Yes, I think the third world is going through a new phase. After having closed off colonialism from outside, now it is starting to close it off from within.

"The struggles are for democracy, for finding that particular political system that fits the genius of the people. It almost at times appears like anarchy; but sometimes it is anarchy that leads to change. It is still better to have anarchy than feudalism. When stability is purchased at any cost, it only ends up with more extremism. The Western democracies, after all, found their inner spirit through experimentation. Cromwell's head foisted . . . rotten boroughs . . . the rape of girls . . . Charles Dickens would have easily given up on England!

"My feeling is that healthier societies are emerging because of these power struggles."

So there are many paradoxes here. Perhaps most of the indisputable trends so apparent in today's world are not merely negative in terms of human development, human rights, and human happiness. Perhaps some of them are positive indeed. Let us, then, look first not so much at regions—for the compelling factor in these new developments is precisely the fact that the patterns so dramatically and distinctly cross borders, cultures, and regions—but at the patterns themselves. Each area of change becomes a metaphor for what is happening with often eerie similarity elsewhere.

National Disintegration: The Example of Lebanon. Lebanon, before it began to disintegrate into warring clans in the mid-1970s, had been a small paradise of a country. With its glorious green mountains, dotted with rich Christian, Muslim, and Druze villages, descending to the azure blue of the Mediterranean, it had worked out a special social compact among its sectarian members.

By the 1980s it had become hell in a small place. Its hatreds imploded. Christians killed Muslims without quarter. Muslims killed Christians with a ferocity unknown since the Crusades. Druze and Palestinians entered the dark fray, until at any one time there were as many as 53 "irregular" armies fighting in Lebanon. Indeed, the "Lebanon syndrome" became the metaphor for irregular warfare and purposeless killing in our times.

What had happened here? The tragedy was played out in four stages. First, the country had been held together by a 1943 pact hammered out between the country's traditionally warring sects and clans which gave each side a part of the power. For 35 years it worked quite beautifully. Second, the balance began to unravel—at first, only underneath the surface—when the Muslim birthrate in the late '60s began to surpass that of the Christian population. Third, the change in the balance of internal power was known by everyone, but no one said anything about it for fear of upset or upheaval. Fourth, the explosion came in 1970 and 1971 when the Palestinians thrown out of Jordan in the war with King Hussein poured into Lebanon, thus destroying whatever was left of the crucially important population balance. At that point, the country was doomed.

When I returned to Beirut in the spring of 1977, I wanted to know what the war had been like—really like, inside. "What is striking here," a member of the French architectural team that was then trying to redesign the city said, standing in the midst of this perverse devastation and shaking his head, "is that it is as if there were a willful and deliberate effort to destroy."

Umayam Yaktin, one of a group then studying the

"Lebanon syndrome" for the American University of Beirut, told me, "Both sides wanted to kill innocent people. All the hospitals were hit—from all sides. I could go into Freud—that people were born with innate aggressive impulses—but I think it's more than that."

What the world was seeing, actually, was a totally new kind of war. Once the various sides saw that no group could win, at any cost, each side began to bomb its own people, to hit its own neighbourhoods with artillery, and to bomb theatres in which its own people were watching movies. The American general Andrew Goodpaster told me this was "irrational warfare."

Whatever title one wanted to give it, it was not really war; it was the breakdown of war. And it catapulted the foreign correspondent—as well as all the other "in-between people," like diplomats, businessmen, missionaries, Red Cross people—into a new kind of danger that we thought was impossible in "modern" times.

In these dark new wars, there were no borders. There were no recognized civilians—indeed, the "civilians" became the deliberate targets. There were no respected neutrals. Red Cross trucks and hospitals were deliberately hit, instead of being protected. Children fought and were killed, without second thoughts.

What had happened in the postcolonial period was the breakdown of the Great Powers' ability to keep even the minimal peace they had kept before. With this had come an almost total dismissal of such niceties as the "rules of war" and the "rules of noncombatancy" that had been built up over the centuries. To die in Spain's civil war was to be a hero to the generations. To die in Beirut's was coming to be to die without benefit of clergy, embassies, or even public note.

Iran and the Revolution of Return to the Past. When I saw the Ayatollah Ruhollah Khomeini in Paris in December of 1978, he sat regally but menacingly on a Persian carpet in the little French summerhouse where he was staying. An enormous man in a dour black robe, he sat with his hands folded in his lap, staring beyond me at some unseen vision. Then he did something he had not done before, in all of his talks with people—he called for a jihad or "holy war" in Iran against the shah of Iran and his followers.

"Yes," this man, who had lived for years in exile in Iraq, said, "we consider this war as a holy war, and by that we mean for the sake of Islam and for the sake of God and for the liberty of our people. That is why it is a holy war, and it will continue until the abdication of the shah, the eradication of the monarchy, and the end of foreign domination of our affairs and the establishment of an Islamic republic. We will not stop short of that, and the people will not accept anything short of that."

Within months of that interview and that brief respite between Khomeini's exile in Iraq and his return to a turbulent Iran, the supposedly "all-powerful" imperial shah-in-shah of Iran had been overthrown and exiled, and a 77-year-old man, who spoke the social and political language of the 7th century, not only ruled Iran but threatened the entire adjacent and even distant Muslim world with a revolution that would carry people back into history 1,300 years!

As Iran broke into an ancient fury of religious fanaticism, as thousands were executed for "crimes against God," as girls on the street were flogged for wearing lipstick, and finally as boys of 9 and 12 were sent to the front lines of a seemingly endless war with Iraq to die as "martyrs," a new "Shi'ah internationalism" became the overpowering fear of the moderate Muslim world. The moderate Muslim regimes feared, now, the breakdown of their own societies, as Khomeini introduced new wild cards into the already skewed deck of the Middle East: a return to the "purity" of the Muslim past and a concomitant destruction of all those within Islam who did not agree with the rites of purification!

In December of 1980, King Hussein of Jordan, whose moderation and rationality had long earned him many enemies among extremists on all sides in the Middle East, sat in his handsome office in the palace in Amman and spoke to me of what was happening. "What we see is a very sinister dimension," he said, shaking his head. "Khomeini's attempt is to create a regional conflict and divide the whole Middle East. It would have effects far broader than only in Iran. In my view, it is criminal. It would have created conditions that we have not experienced even in Lebanon or Northern Ireland. We are talking about total breakdown, not only in terms of

". . . something he had not done before . . . he called for a jihad or 'holy war' in Iran against the shah of Iran and his followers." Within months of his call for a holy war, Iran was ruled by Ayatollah Ruhollah Khomeini—"a 77-year-old man, who spoke the social and political language of the 7th century."

In Peru the Sendero Luminoso or "Shining Path" movement hopes to create conditions in which a revolution may flourish. The author states that the Sendero Luminoso was "anarchistically killing in the name of a 'hidden Inca'. . . who would reappear and restore the long-vanished Inca empire in a pure new world." Quechua-speaking Indians—who live in the rugged highlands and have long been alienated from the Spanish-speaking capital and lowlands—are among their prospects for recruitment.
COVER—GAMMA/LIAISON

societies breaking down, but in terms of old wounds being opened. For the moment, it has been averted. For the moment, these sinister objectives were averted."

At that time, the war between the ayatollah's new/old Iran and neighbouring secular, Ba'thist-socialist Iraq was only three months old. Khomeini had been sending agents to subvert the harsh Iraqi regime, wanting and intending to overthrow Iraqi strongman and president Saddam Hussein at-Takriti, a former underground terrorist himself, as he had overthrown the shah and as he thought he had overthrown Jimmy Carter. "He sent hundreds of agents," Iraqi Foreign Minister Tariq Aziz told me that December, of Khomeini. "We had to hang most of them. We're a very well-organized society."

The war raged on, unabated, and with all calls to the world from Iraq to end it unheeded, until 1984. Khomeini attacked with hundreds of thousands of often-unarmed children and adults in "human waves" reminiscent of medieval times. The idea was to force an opening in the militarily professional and modern Iraqi lines; the concomitant idea was that, then, the 51% of Iraq that is Arab Shi'ah would rise in sympathy with the Iranians. But the Iraqi lines—dug in east of Basra and in the south with great sand walls, a flooded desert, and 95 km (60 mi) of fortifications and men—somehow held.

That year, Khomeini began—just began—to rejoin the world he had spurned. Iran just started to talk again to the outside world. Time after time, announced "final offensives" east of Basra never came. Meanwhile, the massive use of Iranian schoolchildren as the front lines of the "human waves"—not to speak of their use to clear minefields—horrified the world.

For the moment at least, this particular and metaphoric "Return to the Past" revolution and war seemed to be beginning to moderate.

But the "Return to the Past" movements and revolutions were not to be found only in Khomeini's Iran. Not at all! They were beginning to spring up all across the globe and in totally unrelated cultures. Always, the central illuminating idea was that of returning to the "purity" of the past. Thus, finally, would man be purified and saved! But, if you believe that, then those who oppose that purification must of course be eliminated.

So there was the Pol Pot "purification" in Kampuchea, with as many as three million of seven million Kampucheans brutally murdered. There were the Islamic "fundamentalists" who killed Egyptian Pres. Anwar as-Sadat—they, too, believed in such "purification"—which of, course, included assassinating anybody who dealt with the infidels. There was the new Sendero Luminoso or "Shining Path" movement in Peru, which was anarchistically killing in the name of a "hidden Inca" buried under a mountain who would reappear and restore the long-vanished Inca empire in a pure new world. There were the Sikhs in India who assassinated Prime Minister Indira Gandhi in October 1984, demanding their own state and, again, a return to the "pure" Sikh religion of the past. There was every new form of Christian fundamentalism arising in the United States, and even in Judaism—in Israel—it was the return-to-the-Orthodox and to the biblical claims of thousands of years ago that provided the most compelling new form of political/religious expression.

All over the world, psychiatrists and sociologists were analyzing these new movements which the politicians and the theologians had created; none did so with more coherence than Sari Nasir of the University of Jordan: "We find the educated young across the Arab world really organizing themselves into study groups and discussion groups where they seem to talk more and more about fundamentalism. It is the first time in the Arab world when you find young people defying their parents, the regimes, the parties, everybody. They act in a very serious way. They are not going out into the streets and shouting. Their anger is being contained and expressed in planning for the future.

Females, paradoxically, are most active in these movements. Women in the Arab world have always looked at the man as the stronger entity, the person who could do something. The women now are saying that 'we can help by finding answers that you can't find.' It is a silent revolution. It gives them a feeling of self-confidence, of self-actualization, of control. It is also a reaction to the older generation—we failed. If you put the whole thing in one word, in one concept—it is the injustices that have been done to the Arab world.

"You see, frustrations disorganize people and render

them helpless—then it makes them acquire new methods and reorganize, and that is what is happening."

Muhammad as-Sherif, the editor of the prestigious Amman newspaper *Al-Dustour,* added that same day, simply but cogently, "We are living in a time of the correction of history."

What was fascinating to study was the way in which these various movements, popping up and brooding and stirring in so many different and remote-from-one-another countries at the same time, had so many similar social contours. Whether with the Islamic fundamentalists who murdered President Sadat or the Turkish boys who massively joined terrorist movements of the far right and the far left during the 1970s, the profile of the individual was that of a boy—or girl—from the very poorest and most backward area who came or was lured to the big city. There, afraid and alone, he—or she—eventually joined an extremist group that provided a reason for existence and relieved some of the terrible tension of facing modernity.

The Sikh experience in India afforded sociological explanations for still another part of the ominous puzzle. In the Sikhs' homeland of the Punjab, the Sikh extremism that culminated but did not end with Prime Minister Gandhi's death began when social changes started to threaten the power of the conservative Sikh clerics and their historic version of the faith. Secularized life-styles had been spreading among the young. More and more young men were shaving off their sacred beards and refusing to wear the hallowed Sikh turban. In effect trying to salvage their interests in a time of feared change, the clergy reacted by trying to ignite a new fundamentalism. However, their efforts—and even those of the once-radical independence party, the Akali Dal—soon were overshadowed by ultraradical Sikhs led by the ferocious Jarnail Singh Bhindranwale. When he and his men took over the Sikhs' sacred Golden Temple, they made its sanctuary one for murderers and terrorists who could not (they thought) be touched. (*See* WORLD AFFAIRS [South Asia]: *India.*)

The pattern: the acts of the fanatics were able to overwhelm and control the acts of the moderates and destroy the centre. And that precisely is another part of the pattern of social change—first the reaction of the traditional leaders to change, then the rise of the fanatics—that one sees in so many countries in the grip of chance and change today.

And all of these spiritually irredentist movements were and are closely related to all the other changes taking place in a structurally disintegrating world.

The Breakdown of Borders. Father Hesburgh sat in his office at Notre Dame and mused about the future of the world. "The sleeper issue of the next 20 years," he said thoughtfully, with deep concern in his voice, "is going to be massive illegal immigration—not only from Mexico and the Caribbean to the United States, but everywhere! I can see a famine in India and millions of Indians would just put packs on their backs and start walking north. I can see millions going from China to Siberia. . . ."

As he talked, the picture he drew with his words was that of ancient times: when massive migrations of peoples searching for farmland and water and surcease from their enemies threw the world into boiling chaos; when Turkic tribesmen moved west into south-central Europe, Anatolia, and the Arab world; when the Mongols spun out ferociously in all directions to conquer the great civilizations of the known world; when the Huns sailed down the Volga to conquer an already traumatized Mother Russia. And many in the world were quite cognizant of this deadly serious part of the disintegration quotient.

By the 1980s West Germans who had recruited Yugoslav and Turkish "guest workers" were offering them $10,000 a family to go home—and few were accepting the offer. India began building a 1,900-km (1,200-mi) barbed-wire fence between a Bangladesh overflowing with a crowded and increasingly miserable humanity and the Indian state of Assam, where hundreds of Bangladeshi immigrants had been slain by angry Assamese. In 1983 Nigerians brutally attacked scores of illegal Ghanaian immigrants whom they had earlier welcomed to do the harshest work. In Venezuela officials said that "if war came with Colombia, it would be because of the more than two million Colombians in Venezuela illegally." One high official said, typically, "They are destroying all the social progress we have made."

The syndrome, then, was everywhere, but it was most

Margaret Thatcher and Indira Gandhi were both targets of assassins in 1984, and Gandhi was their victim—after her punitive raid on the most sacred shrine of the Sikh religion, the Golden Temple at Amritsar, where Jarnail Singh Bhindranwale (right photo, centre front, wearing a white shawl over dark robes) was martyred by government troops.

dramatic—and ultimately most dangerous—in the United States. Ironically, this was "the" country in the world (outside of a few isolated nations, like Australia and New Zealand) that was historically spared the pain of the great invasions of peoples, of the wars that went with them and of the struggles they engendered. America was isolated by the great oceans that surrounded it: Was!

By the 1980s the United States was the only highly developed country in the world sharing a long undefended border with an underdeveloped and overpopulated country. Moreover, Mexico was not only dealing with economic breakdown and one of the world's worst cases of indebtedness, its population was booming—and dooming it. By a conservative estimate, six million illegal aliens, most of them Mexicans, were already in the United States, living in a kind of underworld in which they could be preyed upon by anyone and without recourse to the law. (There could well be as many as 12 million, analysts say.) Moreover, Mexico's population was expected—conservatively—to double from 60 million in 1980 to 120 million at the turn of the century. Illegal aliens were pouring across the porous and largely uncontrolled and undefended border; illegals were voting in many places; and all the indicators pointed to severe internal dislocations and conflicts just over the horizon. Moreover—and this is typical of the new era, too—the United States was politically unable to move, even to protect its right of citizenship and to protect its own culture, because the disintegration and fragmentation within its own political process was already so far advanced!

Turkish "guest workers" in West Germany were urged to go home—but continued to look through the want ads to find jobs rather than return to the difficult labour markets of their homeland. Bonuses to leave reached $10,000 per family.

Meanwhile, all of the American peripheries were virtually under siege from people escaping the growing poverty of the rest of the world—and also from international conspirators and terrorists. In Miami, for instance, the U.S. Immigration and Naturalization Service in 1983–84 apprehended hundreds of Sikh separatists, most of whom had been behind the iron curtain and had thousands of dollars on their persons. Many admitted that they had been told to go to the Sikh community in California and "stay underground" until "instructions came." The Indian government believed this was in conjunction with Sikh extremist plans to assassinate Indian diplomats in the United States.

Meanwhile, a congruent development was the extraordinary and pitiful growth in the number of refugees. In 1959 there were more than two million refugees in the world—that was World Refugee Year. Twenty-five years later there were ten million refugees receiving international assistance, the largest such figure in modern history.

In short, the last quarter of the 20th century was witnessing, in every area of the globe, the most severe types of dislocation imaginable.

The Rise of Irregular Warfare. And war changed.

In World War II power and might were used traditionally, conventionally, and vertically, if you will. Great armies opposed great armies, usually in traditional set-piece battles, although there certainly were jungle and guerrilla fights. But after 1945—even though countries like the United States, in particular, continued to respond in traditional military ways—warfare changed completely. It became "irregular," and massively so; and by that I mean fighting by guerrillas, terrorists, death squads, and gangs not generally connected to constituted governments and institutions.

Consider a few telling figures:

By 1984 there were no fewer than 40 wars raging across the globe, involving 45 different "nations" or, better said, "entities" of various forms. Of the 80 wars that began after 1945, only 28 took the traditional form of fighting between the regular armed forces of two or more states. Fully 46 were civil wars, insurgencies, or guerrilla contests, with the remaining 6 being riots and coups d'état. In World War I 17% of the casualties were civilians; in World War II, 45%; in Korea and Vietnam, 70%. Secretary-General Pérez de Cuéllar, one of the men who have carefully kept note of all of these changes in the world, announced to the UN in 1984 that conventional weapons had caused "some 20 million deaths in wars since 1945, almost twice as many of those civilian as military." He called the syndrome abroad in the world the "new anarchy," and he depicted it as "armed force, both overt and covert, used and increasingly justified as a legitimate means of obtaining national objectives."

There were Palestine Liberation Organizations, Baader-Meinhof gangs, Red Armies, South African liberation movements, Khmer Rouges, every form of Lebanese militia, death squads from Guatemala and El Salvador to Indonesia, street gangs in the United States taking on new military and political forms, the fear of "vigilantism" in the cities of the industrialized world as law and order broke down, and the continuing reliance on traditional "vertical" power forms on the part of the Great Powers, even though all the new threats involved "horizontal" power. There were even, in the United States, civilians donating money to and supporting the anti-Sandinista *contra* guerrillas in Nicaragua and Irish-Americans supporting the Irish Republican Army—the age of the individual's rent-a-guerrilla was at hand!

Overpopulation and unemployment in Ghana sent many domestic workers to Nigeria during that country's oil boom. When austerity threatened, the Ghanaians were packed home in a forced exodus.
FRANCOLON—GAMMA/LIAISON

Overpopulation and Its Consequences. At this same moment in mankind's history, still another change of watershed dimensions was occurring—the Earth's population was spinning out of control and, for the first time in man's long march out of savagery, out of balance with the soil, water, and other resources that must maintain it.

Some facts from a specialist on population, J. Joseph Speidel of the Population Crisis Committee in Washington, D.C.: "Is population growth a problem?" he asks, then answers, "Yes. The world is now just barely able to feed, clothe, and house the 4.8 billion people it holds. In some areas of the globe, basic necessities are not available to significant portions of the population. If we continue to add 80 to 90 million people a year until the end of the century, world resources and the people who need them will be on a disastrous collision course—with no winners.

"Why is world population growing so fast?" he asks, and answers, "In its simplest terms, the answer is that more people are being born than are dying—and that in many nations in the developing world, fully half their population was born since Lyndon Johnson was president of the U.S. in 1964. Using the U.S. as a yardstick, population will double in 100 years. Asia, on the other hand, will double in 38 years, Latin America in 30 years, and Africa in just 24 years. Not coincidentally, most of the fastest growing countries are also the poorest, with the highest infant and maternal mortality rates, worst health conditions, most illiteracy, and most fragile and scarcest natural resources."

Some other ominous observations:

Between 1980 and the year 2000, 700 million new jobs will have to be created—more than currently exist in the entire industrialized world. According to the International Labour Organization, there are some 300 million people underemployed or unemployed in the non-Communist less developed world—about 40% of the total work force. Some 55 million children under age 14 worldwide are forced to work for a living. In Brazil alone, 11 million abandoned children eke out a living on the streets of Rio de Janeiro and other cities. Up to 70% of agricultural labour in the third world is performed by women, but discrimination and growing labour surpluses lessen their participation in the modern economy. In the third world there are 72 dependents for every 100 working-age persons; in industrialized nations, the ratio is 54 to 100. This third world "dependency ratio" dampens prospects for economic growth.

In short, what the world was facing was not only the fact that the world's population was "growing" but the final Malthusian fact that the Earth's surface and substance simply no longer could provide for the numbers. There might still be empty spaces—as U.S. Pres. Ronald Reagan averred in his October 1984 presidential debate, to the consternation of family-planning analysts and environmentalists—but they were the Gobi Desert or the Himalayas or the wastelands of Siberia. They were empty because they were uninhabitable. The problem loomed like a great phantom leading the pack of all the other related problems for it made answers impossible.

Science fiction writer Isaac Asimov, a specialist on demography, warned, "Population growth at current rates will create a world without hope, gripped by starvation and desperation. It will be worse than a jungle because we have weapons immensely more destructive and vicious than teeth and claws."

Some further facts:

The average number of children born to a woman in Kenya is eight, which means that that country's population could catapult from 20 million today to 83 million in the year 2025. Bangladesh's fertility rate is 6.3 children per woman, which means that 266 million people—or nearly three times the present population—could be squeezed into an area the size of the state of Wisconsin by 2025. With a fertility rate of 4.7, India will become the world's most populous country by about the year 2045, with 1.5 billion people. Meanwhile, the developed world will be going in a quite different direction. Russian women now have an average of 2 children each (for non-Russian women in the U.S.S.R., the figure is 4.9); U.S. women have 1.9 children; Western European women, 1.8 children.

But out-of-control population growth means more—much more—than sheer crowding. It means that there is simply not enough food, health care, education, and housing. And it means still more. As populations increase exponentially, people plow up more and more acres of fragile land; as less land is available for farming, farmers abandon soil-saving practices to try to produce more food in the short term. Billions of tons of soil are lost each year as producers struggle to meet current needs, with no eye to the future at all.

One of the most accurate and thoughtful keepers of the tally on the Earth's resources is the Washington-based Worldwatch Institute. The president of Worldwatch, Lester R. Brown, recently announced that excessive soil erosion, unless arrested, will soon lead to higher food prices and persistent pockets of famine. "As demand for food climbs, the world is beginning to mine its soils, converting a renewable resource into a nonrenewable one," he warned. "Grave though the loss of topsoil may be, it is a quiet crisis, one that is not widely perceived. And, unlike earthquakes, volcanic eruptions, or other natural disasters, this disaster of human origin is unfolding gradually." But while even developed countries like the Soviet Union and the United States are losing topsoil at an alarming rate, the worst cases are in the less developed world. Haiti, for instance, has so little topsoil left—after decades in which farmers simply moved down from the mountains to the lower reaches as they destroyed the land—that there may be no arable land at all (!) by 1987.

The growing human plight of the world's great cities can be seen in Calcutta, in Chongqing (Chungking), and in Jakarta, but it can be seen especially in Mexico City. Once an elegant Hispanic queen of cities, with great sweeping boulevards and formal parks and lovely restaurants, Mexico City today is called by many observers an "urban apocalypse." Today, there are 15 million people there—by the turn of the century there will be 33 million or even 45 million in the once-pastoral Valley of Mexico alone! Already, the horrors are everywhere. The city is covered by a constant fog of pollution that makes flying into it like descending into a mist of human excrement. More than two million of the city's "residents" have no running water; more than three million have no sewerage facilities, so tons of fecal matter are left in the gutters. Poor Mexicans fleeing the impoverished countryside sit on steps, homeless and hopeless. So many scavenge for food in the garbage dumps that they are organized into unions. What is more, Mexico City has lost nearly 75% of its woodland in the past quarter century, and this reduces the water supply even as more water is needed. It is a cycle of horror without end—and it, too, is a metaphor for what is going to be happening in many cities, particularly in the third world.

But this problem, like all the others, does not end short of the political—it feeds directly into the political questions and equations of the immediate future. Given what is coming—unemployed youths roaming the streets in countries where half the population often is under 18 years of age, with no prospect of job formation, hungry, and looking to irregular leaders to lead them in new and as yet unpredictable movements—there is little question that even more political explosions are on the immediate horizon.

Consider some further and more precise indicators:

Throughout the world, more than 100 social, political, religious, and ethnic groups are now organized militarily, threatening some 52 sovereign states. More guerrilla wars are being waged today than ten years ago. Terrorism and assassination increase constantly. Mercenaries—indeed, small "armies" of them—are available not only to nations but to individuals and groups. Arms are pouring into the third world.

Allan E. Goodman, associate dean of the Georgetown University School of Foreign Service and former deputy director of the U.S. Central Intelligence Agency, summed up to me what he foresees because of population growth and its related problems. "Indicators point toward the kind of change and ensuing desperation that can only lead to further chaos," he said. Then he mentioned "the frustration of most revolutionary and irredentist causes and thus the upgrading of their terrorist methods, the nihilism of the middle-class young in Europe and Japan, instability within the Western industrial democracies, direct threats to national security from international terrorism and nuclear proliferation."

In the '80s, he said, "the unexpected and irrational are going to manifest themselves in combinations of events and problems so bizarre that we will underestimate both their probability and their impact. In such a world . . . the capability of governments to promote legitimacy, development, and political participation will be in short and precious supply. Most states will find the 1980s full of enough surprises to cause rethinking of conceptions of national power and the threats to—as well as the requisites of—security."

Finally, the multitudes, the growing agricultural problems, and the political breakdown mean hunger, famine, and death. It is already happening in Africa—from the Sahel and the Horn to Angola and Mozambique. One hundred fifty million people in Africa face starvation. That is the final chapter of the overpopulation story.

The Burden of Debt. What has happened to the world, economically, in this period is such an explosion in world debt that $800 billion is owed by less developed and developed countries alike. The world suddenly finds itself

Their poverty has forced these people to scavenge for food in a garbage dump in Mexico City. These scavengers are so numerous that they are organized into unions.

"Finally, the multitudes, the growing agricultural problems, and the political breakdown mean hunger, famine, and death. One hundred fifty million people in Africa face starvation."

DAVID BURNETT—CONTACT

in a position where nobody has the answer. The common but vague threat or prediction is "breakdown," but what could that really mean?

Perhaps no one has analyzed the situation more cogently than Larosière, who predicted, in the summer of 1984, a worldwide "debt explosion" that can be contained only if governments increase their revenues faster than the cost of the interest they have to pay, either by raising taxes or by cutting spending or both. "The debt explosion is not limited to a few countries, but rather is a worldwide phenomenon," Larosière pointed out in a watershed speech in Innsbruck, Austria, before the 40th congress of the International Institute of Public Finance.

"A phenomenon that may never have occurred before on such a scale is before us," he said. "Over the past two decades, several factors brought about an attitude of fiscal laxity on the part of policymakers of many countries. For a variety of reasons, the traditional stigma attaching to fiscal deficits and growing public debt gave way to a certain nonchalance on the part of policymakers. . . ."

He then went over "only a few" of the contributing factors. "The prevailing mood of the time created high expectations of the role that governments should play with respect to income maintenance, job creation, and income distribution. . . . People came to feel that they had almost a natural right to cheap or free health care, transportation, communications, and so forth. The disparity between the private cost of using these services and the social cost of providing them introduced enormous and growing burdens on the budget. Because the beneficiaries of these services represented large and politically powerful groups, while those who opposed them were less numerous and less concentrated, the political process generally favoured their expansion."

Other factors, he pointed out, included the sharp increases in the price of oil at the end of 1973, when oil price raises caused many governments "to borrow their way through the crisis rather than to pursue less popular adjustment policies. What has happened, then, is the fact that the combination of growing public debt and high real rates of interest has made interest payments by far the fastest growing component of public expenditures in most countries."

As to what exactly would—or could—happen if the world's debts were called in and the countries could not pay them, Friedrich Levcik of Vienna, a specialist on the debt crisis who is often consulted by endangered governments and banks, gave several suggestions. When I spoke to him in his pleasant office overlooking a leafy Viennese park, he warned repeatedly that the Western world must not push the highly indebted Eastern European countries to the wall. "I have warned them that Eastern Europe would only put the iron curtain down and start to pursue economic warfare," he said, "with great resultant harm to their populations, with rationing, Stalinist models, and a new cold war. For selfish reasons, they got their countries more and more dependent upon the West. Now they have to go on importing, if they want to use the facilities. They were so impressed with the Western performance, they thought it could go on forever. . . ."

What would happen if, say, Poland, one of the most indebted countries, were to go bankrupt? That was something that had not happened since before World War II—and it was one of the causes leading to World War II.

"It could mean some banks would go bankrupt," this thoughtful, white-haired man told me. "Then the government steps in, and the Western taxpayer has to pay. All the assets of the Poles would be seized. Even if Polish firms exported, those exports could be seized. What little trade remained would be completely on a barter basis, without money involved. Commodities would be swapped at the borders."

A return to feudal times? He nodded in assent. "Yes, that is possible," he agreed. Then he added, "It would be simply incredible."

As yet, no country had "collapsed." Still, nobody knew what to do—or what might come. And economic collapse—or even the threat of it—both exacerbated and lay at the core of all the other disintegrative threats.

Even the world's industrialists were concerned. Ford Motor Co. chairman Philip Caldwell, certainly one of the world's foremost spokesmen for industry, warned in a speech in September 1984 at the Massachusetts Institute of Technology, "We must stop pretending there is no problem. Huge trade imbalances are wreaking havoc all over the world, threatening the underpinnings of national economies everywhere. Their very real social costs—to individuals and communities—may well create political instability, and sooner than we think."

Institutional Breakdown and "Compassion Fatigue." Asked whether the United Nations had gone the "way of the League of Nations," U.S. historian Barbara Tuchman responded, "It certainly seems headed in that direction. It can't control affairs but is beset by cliques of the third world nations, and decisions are based on artificial and unreal voting patterns."

A former secretary-general of the United Nations, Kurt Waldheim, charges that the United Nations "threatens to become increasingly irrelevant in the real world. Its vitality is being sapped." He scolded those in the third world who back extremist resolutions that achieve nothing, and he scolded the major powers because "the habit of international cooperation is waning through their neglect or adamance." His final analysis is that the key to the problem lies in the contradiction in the UN Charter between the organization's first purpose—to maintain international peace and security—and its principle of "the sovereign equality of all its members," for the effect of that principle is to deprive the UN of any real authority.

What had happened to the international system? To the internationally agreed rules of combat and of legitimacy? What had happened to the United Nations itself, changing it from the "hope of the world" in the days immediately after World War II to a quarrelsome body that could accomplish very little in the real world?

First of all, 51 nations were original members in 1945. By 1984 there were 159 members, 32 of which had fewer than a million citizens. No one foresaw that.

What is more, during and after the furious process of decolonization, the countries of the third world first tried to form regional federations. These broke down, and the little new countries turned to the UN for recognition and perks and a forum to flaunt their nationalism.

By 1984 the United Nations was totally different from when it was founded by the Great Powers as a vehicle for world peace. It is a United Nations of blocs. There are the Soviet bloc, the Arab bloc, and the nonaligned bloc, which constitutes a voting majority in the General Assembly all by itself.

"Blocs," Jeane Kirkpatrick, the U.S. ambassador to the UN, told a Georgetown University audience in June 1982, "function in the United Nations very much like political parties in a legislature," complete with alliances and trade-offs on certain issues. But in this system, she observed further, "the United States is like a country without a party." It is an observer in a group called WEOG, which incongruously means West Europeans and Other Governments and includes Japan, Canada, Australia, and New Zealand. But this bloc, unlike the other blocs, does not vote together.

Other critics were even more tart in their analysis. *New York Times* columnist Flora Lewis wrote, "It is unrealistic at this stage of human contrariness to expect microdot countries and the lords of empty lands to coalesce and renounce their sovereign titles."

The overwhelming problems in the world are leading to a new lethargy and exhaustion in the international organizations and in the "aid" mechanisms of the developed world. And this lethargy and exhaustion are coming to be called "compassion fatigue" and "aid

(LEFT) FLANDRIN/ARAL/REZA—SIPA/SPECIAL FEATURES; (RIGHT) JAMES PICKERELL—BLACK STAR

"The post-World War II period also saw the massive and hemorrhagic breakup of the great colonial empires of the European powers. . . . It was a new world that did not respond to the European and American power and social configurations." At right, U.S. troops on a search and destroy mission in Vietnam. " 'There are no borders left,' an Afghan resistance fighter told me." Above, Afghan resistance fighters prepare to execute a captured enemy.

fatigue." The words are heard more and more around organizations like the World Bank, the U.S. Congress, the U.S. Immigration and Naturalization Service, the United Nations, and other bodies that must deal with the third world's distress. Not only are there not enough food and seeds and aid money to go around, there are not enough social workers and technicians to go around, given the burgeoning population in a world of shrinking resources. What these social workers and aid personnel are feeling is simply exhaustion—and they talk more and more about people's compassion becoming exhausted because they can no longer see the possibility of real progress.

This may represent the final danger—that the developed countries will try to close down or withdraw into their own developed "worlds," leaving the third world alone with its problems.

Why Is It Happening? Why should all these distinct but related developments have come together in the second half of the 20th century? Why have these threats of world breakdown emerged in precisely the era when man has achieved more scientific breakthroughs and knowledge than in all his previous history? Why was the road to progress so much more tortuous than it had seemed in those halcyon days after 1945?

What happened really is quite simple. The post-World War II period also saw the massive and hemorrhagic breakup of the great colonial empires of the European powers. Often they broke up into supposedly modern "nation-states," which would soon come to be seen as quite simply unnatural for peoples who still thought of themselves in terms of tribes, of clans, of religions, or of islands. At the same time, the Great Powers' ability to "keep peace" in the world broke down because the industrialized nations were themselves psychologically and structurally fragile on the inside.

The first class of postcolonial leaders in the less developed world swept to power in the '50s and early '60s, when a historic sea change was taking place in the relations between peoples and nations. Euphoria was the emotion of the day, and men and women long oppressed rightfully reveled in their new freedom. The problem was the expectation that these former colonies would almost automatically become "developed" nations, for was it not the colonial experience alone that had held them back?

The first postcolonial leaders—the fathers of these fragile but hopeful new nations and peoples—expressed that intense spirit of hope. They were men like Sukarno of Indonesia, Jawaharlal Nehru of India, Gamal Abdel Nasser of Egypt, and Ho Chi Minh of Vietnam. They were immensely able and often eloquent, but sometimes it seemed as if they believed they could develop their countries through rhetoric and charisma alone.

But all did not progress as expected. As the colonial empires dissolved, many of the new nations began what was to be one long period of slow-motion collapse, often marked by internal warfare. It was a new world that did not respond to the European and American power and social configurations of nation, state, or party. It should have come as no surprise that it soon began to devolve into its old and historically "normal" structures of tribe, clan, revolutionary cell, or extraterritorial religious movement.

"There are no borders left," an Afghan resistance fighter told me one shrouded night in Peshawar, on the Pakistan-Afghan border, as he stared at the immense mountains that separated him from Afghanistan. And I remembered then that Mohandas Gandhi had predicted many years ago, during India's classic fight for independence from Great Britain, that "the subcontinent will come to be divided by languages, not by international boundaries."

A new stage arrived. Since modernization did not immediately "work" or worked ineffectively or counterproductively, people began turning in on themselves and, sometimes, trying to return to their pasts. What was going on inside the struggling countries of the world—in particular, the third world—during this period? What do its leaders, planners, and thinkers think about it?

One of the most hardheaded analysts of the development process is Sherif Latfy, an Egyptian developmentalist who is the leading adviser to the sultanate of Oman. That country has one of the most balanced and successful development programs in the world, despite the fact that the young Sultan Qabus ibn Sa'id set his kingdom on the road to modernity only in 1970, when his medieval old father was overthrown and he began to move—judiciously—toward carefully chosen modern forms.

"The 'thing' will always be there," Latfy told me, sitting in his simple office in the picturesque old capital of Muscat. The "thing" was the imbalance that came, inexorably, when countries put themselves into this kind of pressure cooker of social change.

"If it were not 'Islam,' it would be called something else. It is simply something that comes with modern life. The frustration becomes bigger in the developing countries. You find people are frustrated with change—or without it. The more development you do, the more frustrated people become. Hundreds of years ago, no one knew what development was or what life in the U.S. was. The more development, the more impossible life becomes. What do you do? There is no economic solution to it. I can say, in many cases, what the world should have done, but no matter what you do, there often is no fixed answer. How to go through the transitional period? No one really knows.

"Look at the men who killed Sadat. These are the people brought to school by the government—so naturally they are going to blame the government for everything."

Everywhere in the third world, even in the most balanced and productive of situations, the conflict is there. Faisal Bashir, the first Saudi Bedouin to gain a Ph.D., announced himself to me one day in the elegant marble palace that is the Saudi Arabian Ministry of Development. "Here I am," said the slim young man with the immensely bright and intelligent eyes, "deputy planning minister of Saudi Arabia trying to implement the policy that will destroy the life that made me. From a human element, it's true. I'm working against the forces that created me. One more generation and it will end. Now, when we talk about nomadism, it is not the nomadism I remember. My father has a truck—he carries water in it to the sheep."

Then he paused and a look of deep sadness came over his face. "In your terms, I'm a great success," he said slowly, "a symbol of the Saudi Arabia Bedouin boy from the barren desert." Now his eyes gleamed like black olives. "You are wrong. Sometimes I think I'm a great failure in the world. I was raised to be the next leader of the tribe. What am I now? A technocrat trying to find the way to spend $236 billion a year." He paused, then summed up, "I act against all the forces that created me."

At the same time, Mahmoud Saffir, deputy minister of education of Saudi Arabia, explained how the kingdom was judiciously adopting only certain elements of change—ones that, it was hoped, would not prove too jarring to the hallowed old ways. "We don't want to accelerate the pace of modernization," he told me. "We are taking it

The late psychoanalyst Heinz Kohut made these comments while speaking with the author about countries where change has been unsuccessful: "Change is experienced as an agent of someone else. Discontinuity arouses tremendous anxiety. . . . they are at that stage of development where their goals are compatible with dying. Ours are not."

JAMES NACHTWEY—BLACK STAR

easy because we would cut the roots of the society and be nowhere. We do not want to borrow anything from abroad that is incompatible with our traditions. But there is no contradiction whatsoever between being developed and believing in Islam. The place where we might get head-to-head lies in the timing of a certain change. It is up to you to pull the hand of society with the first or the second gear. Our people are willing and ready to accept any changes as long as they do not destroy our roots. We get challenges from our students coming back from overseas with certain appealing ideas. They would like to do everything overnight. We tell them that all can be done, but in the proper time. The dimension of time and the dimension of space are all important, and in some kind of harmony. So far, we have been successful."

In the countries where change has not "been successful," where it has been so volcanic that it caused whole societies to explode socially, politically, and psychologically, the desperate frustrations often were turned against the outside agents of change. No one has explained this better than the late psychoanalyst Heinz Kohut of Chicago. Kohut spoke to me once at length about the tension in the less developed countries—countries like Iran, or Nicaragua, or China—that arises when they pit themselves against a country like the United States, which is often both the inspirer of change and the thwarter of it.

"The specifics of that tension arise from the attempt to change a national/cultural/religious 'self' into something that seems not to be it," he said. People in various Islamic countries, for instance, were clearly repressed and backward. They were clearly living a demeaning kind of existence leading to low self-esteem.

"Then came the shah in Iran, Ataturk in Turkey, Nasser in Egypt. In order to make their people more capable of self-respect, the message is 'Modernize!' But if the changes made are made abruptly, within one or two generations, that threatens the continuity of the ethnic self. It is much like the individual self. We were once children—then adolescents—then mature adults. When a person feels discontinuous, that is a terribly painful feeling. You do not hang together. People will do almost anything to avoid that.

"What happens when it is not within the capacity of people to change is that they want to overthrow those who forced them to move. Change is experienced as an agent of someone else. Discontinuity arouses tremendous anxiety. So when someone comes like Khomeini or Yasir Arafat, with something of a 'new world,' there is a sense of tremendous healing. They do anything for it, so long as the sense of continuity is reestablished.

"The riches that oil wells give does not give them self-esteem—that can only come from being master of one's own fate. Then there is a degree of sadism that is mobilized—give them [the foreign agents of change] a dose of that medicine that they inflict on others. They feel shamed by us, so they need to shame us. And they know that they can have tremendous power over us, because they are at that stage of development where their goals are compatible with dying. Ours are not. We can't say we'll do the same to you. We are at a totally different stage of selfhood in dealing with them. It is important to give them a sense of respect so they don't need to shame us."

Then he summed up what the West, by existing and by simply being the agent suggesting change, does to the less developed countries: "We took a picture of their poverty."

But all of the changes and all of the struggles were not in the less developed world. What remains uncanny in recent history is the fact that many of the changes are extraterritorial and cross borders and cultures and even economies.

George Ball, who served as undersecretary of state under Presidents Kennedy and Johnson, told me of the particularly American form of power fragmentation: "The old system and structure built up in the past world system served us particularly well. We went all those years without a war.

"A parable: There is a village in a valley, and they are constantly confronted by floods. The townspeople build a dam. Then a new generation comes along and that dam is an affront to ecology. The young say there is no need for it because there hasn't been a flood for 20 years. Then it really is the Age of Aquarius.

"One can say what he wants about the Eastern Establishment," he went on, responding to the internal changes that have taken place in the U.S. from the time when a relatively small group of people with similar ideas ran foreign policy, "but they had an understanding. What has happened today reminds me of Pascal, when he said that what is truth on one side of the Pyrenees is not truth on the other. I suggest that today we substitute the Rockies for the Pyrenees. Those Americans who suggest removing troops from Europe almost all come from the American West. They are the people the farthest possible away from the situation. What we are seeing is the shift of American political and economic power westward— and that is the key to why our foreign policy situation is so bad today.

"Foreign policy has become totally episodic. There is no sense of the structural whole. What is important one day—the Falklands war, or the civil war in El Salvador—

because of the limitation of the visual TV image every night is unimportant the next. It has destroyed the ability of the American people to have a solid structural view of the world."

Still others—intellectuals—attribute the fragmentation inside the U.S. today to a "loss of memory" and to the "loss of a sense of history."

"Since World War II," James Billington, historian and director of the Woodrow Wilson International Center for Scholars at the Smithsonian Institution in Washington, D.C., told me, "America has been shying away from the traditional system of transmitting values. It has lost the sense that the legacy of the past is intrinsically deserving of respect in its own right. This is partly as a result of the stresses and struggles of the late '60s.

"We have had a tremendous erosion within the history departments. There are two groups: one, the ideologues who view history as a foraging ground for lessons to impose on the people, and two, the more subtle and indulged methodologists, who are interested in methodology rather than ideology. They take social science techniques for the whole body of knowledge. Theirs is an irrelevant foraging.

"Virtually nobody is immersed in simply the authentically different aspects of the past—and this is particularly insulting to the dead. They can't answer back and say, 'None of the above!' So, as a result, there is a tremendous thirst for perspective, for history, for context, among ordinary people. And the intellectual leadership that should have offered it is not very responsive. As a result, historic thirst is satisfied by British TV or pop writers."

So, there are many elements to the change. There are those like French Pres. François Mitterrand, who told me, when I asked him what the greatest danger in the world today was: "I would say the arms race . . . and hunger in the world . . . and at the same time the slippage between the industrialized world and the developing world. Yes, dangers of war and of destruction."

A Ray of Hope. But are there not also elements of hope? Elements of redemption? Elements of broader empowerment?

Mahboolbul Haq certainly thinks there are. He indicates that—after the first stage of decolonization with its charismatic leaders and the economic disasters that

followed—the world is entering the next stage, the stage of serious, nonparanoid, and sober economic thinking and planning. He told me, "The ideological war in the third world has been won by the West without its realizing it. The third world found it ideologically fascinating to think that by turning Communist they would wean themselves away from those who dominated them. But now you find a new maturity coming, a greening of the independence movements and a liberating of the developing countries from the bitterness and finding fault ever with the outsiders. Our intellectuals have been realizing how much the problem is at home, and that socialism and Communism do not offer quick solutions. China is repudiating some of the regimentation. For third world peoples, what matters is whether we can feed ourselves.

"Ideology began to settle in the '70s along pragmatic lines. It was a greening of the liberation movements, but the West has not realized it and comes out quite boorishly when it doesn't need to. The West has further won by the fact that the Russians fumbled so clearly in the third world in the last three or four years. Their image was destroyed by their actions in Afghanistan and Kampuchea and by not helping the PLO. But unfortunately they are being rolled back at a time when America became very aggressive. The phases have not overlapped.

"We don't feel despondent. We are concerned about lack of structure."

A leader who is positively buoyant about his country and its prospects is Sultan Qabus of Oman. "We have no fear of the exporting of movements such as Khomeini's," he told me in 1981. "Nothing can be exported to this country that we do not want." He laughed lightly. "We have thousands of years of history and we are sure of ourselves. We do not easily allow ourselves to be driven into something we don't want. I'm very confident. Even the youngest person in this country is very aware of his tradition."

When I next interviewed him, in 1983, his only concern was that now, in a country that had emerged from medieval times only in 1970, he was wearied trying to keep up with the newly perceived needs of his 1.5 million people. "It is really frightening, really," he said, half in irony and half in deadly earnest. "You plan your

Gradual modernization is seen as progress in some of the developing world. In China, for example, the arrival of personal checks is one aspect of economic liberalization.

The brisk prosperity of Singapore is legendary throughout Southeast Asia. The large amount of construction creates jobs, and the completion of new commercial space houses new jobs. The economy is exemplary.

hospitals and schools, and you find that the demand is always more. We very quickly need a hospital with 500 beds. It is a must. But the planning—and knowing what you're planning for. . . ." He shook his head at this new phase.

Another world citizen who traces positive steps is Japan's Nobuhiko Ushiba, one of the small group of "wise men" who work to solve problems between Japan and the U.S. "It is very different today from prewar times. Today we have a forum in which to get together to discuss differences. That is the biggest difference—that and the existence of instant communications. Before the war, our leaders had never met each other. Nobody exchanged direct views, particularly the U.S. and Japan. Compared to now, that is extraordinary, because today we have so many channels. Sometimes, of course, communications come too rapidly. Foreign affairs interfere with domestic affairs. This will increase and be dangerous—we will have to have the wisdom to stop at the right time."

Ushiba's own prime minister, Yasuhiro Nakasone, spoke to me of the new world when I interviewed him in the prime minister's elegant office in 1983. "The Earth has shrunk very much," he told me, almost poetically, "and the water in the Bay of Tokyo is directly connected to the Potomac River."

U.S. Secretary of State George Shultz told me in the fall of 1983, "There are plenty of problems around and deeply disintegrative forces. I can describe plenty of areas of disintegration, particularly the tactics of terrorism with more and more governmental units behind it. But there is the other side of the coin." Had the world turned some kind of corner? "The imagery of the corner is too sharp," he responded. "Maybe a tidal image is better. It is sweeping along." Then he pointed out, in terms of

this "tidal image" of change, that democracy was again growing throughout the world, that in Latin America, for instance, there were, in 1984, 24 countries that were either democracies or headed toward democracy; there were only eight dictatorships, either of the right or of the left. Moreover, some parts of the world almost seemed to have singled themselves out for spectacular forms of development. No area was more notable, in this respect, than the countries of Asia that lay around the rim of the Pacific.

For the new leaders of the new nations after World War II, Earl Foell, the editor in chief of the *Christian Science Monitor,* wrote, "There was a smorgasbord of choices to get in on the feast. They could join the American or West European economic spheres—trade, aid, loans, educational opportunities. Or they could sample the Russian promise, the more Spartan wave of the future. Later they could choose the heretical Chinese version of Marxist aid— perhaps a Tanzam Railway—if they suspected Moscow's brand of being just another version of white imperialism. Or, they could listen for a higher bid from Taiwan— perhaps ingenious agricultural aid that produced not one, not two, but three rice crops a year.

"Guinea, Ghana, Indonesia, and Egypt experimented with the Soviet-brand product, then rejected it. India alternately gazed toward Khrushchev's Moscow, then Galbraith's America."

Then came the "chopstick states." "Almost unnoticed in Moscow and Washington," he wrote, "the Third World is no longer forced to select from a smorgasbord whose three main dishes are American stew, Soviet goulash, or nonaligned vegetarian. It now has before it the economic growth example of Korea, Malaysia, Singapore, Taiwan, Thailand and even a glimmer of hope from high-tech factories in North Borneo. What beckons is a version of the American-Japanese entrepreneurial, free-enterprise, competitive, incentive system. But a system practiced in smaller nations that other 'new' nations can identify with: practiced by nonwhites; practiced by peoples whose exported movies do not show an impossible dream of luxury apartments, swimming pools, and Aston Martin car chases."

From the mid-1970s to the mid-'80s, the rapidly industrializing Pacific countries had an average annual growth rate of 7.6%—roughly three times that of the nations of the European Communities. Their average per capita income ranged from $1,910 in South Korea, to $2,505 in Taiwan, to $5,340 in Hong Kong, to $5,910 in Singapore.

The Pacific rim countries were not alone. From Guinea and Mozambique, to Egypt, to Jamaica, to China— countries were searching, pragmatically this time, not for the glory they sought in the first heady stage of decolonization but for the new age of economic reality. The same thing was happening in the peripheries of the Soviet Union, where Hungary, for example, was already deeply into a highly successful economic liberalization, East Germany was beginning one, and China was in a full phase of "decommunization."

When I visited China for the second time in October 1984, Chen Ruifen (Ch'en Jui-fen), vice-president of the Institute of Foreign Affairs in Beijing (Peking), told me of the Chinese economic liberalization that had been taking place from 1978 onward. "We are putting all of our energies into economic construction. We are not wasting our energies in the old political campaigns that only violate society."

What was happening throughout Chinese society was

truly extraordinary. From 1978 on, Chinese leader Deng Xiaoping (Teng Hsiao-p'ing) and his group had gradually but systematically built incentives into an increasingly free-market-oriented "socialist" society. The people's commune—the basic and most sacred unit of Chinese Communism under Mao Zedong (Mao Tse-tung)—was abolished by the new constitution in January 1983, and the new units were called townships. Now every Chinese farmer could have his own piece of land and could do with it what he wanted; he needed only to pay a tax to the state at the end of the year. In October 1984 those reforms were confirmed by extending the "responsibility system" to urban industries. Moreover, Deng had separated Communist Party functions from all administrative and economic functions—those now lay in the hands of the managers and administrators. Along the coast, meanwhile, 4 economic zones and 14 economically open cities were set aside and developed as entry points for foreign technology. It was a remarkable change, and it illustrated, perhaps more than anything else, this new post-postcolonial period and what its imperatives were.

Bo Yibo (Po Yi-po), a veteran of the Long March and second to Deng on the powerful Party Advisory Commission, told me in 1983 of these "new Communists" of this new China: "They do accept the theories of Marx, Engels, Stalin, and Mao—but not with dogmatism. Instead, they have worked in line with the actual conditions of China. My view is that by the turn of the century China will still be on the road to socialism. But even then, economically speaking, the Chinese people will only be comparatively well off."

But this restraint in painting rosy pictures of success was far from universal in the developing world. Many of the wildest dreams of a new national glory have collapsed in the wreckage caused by a problem hardly anyone is willing to talk about. One person, at least, is.

In many ways, Singapore is the most interesting intellectually of all the "new" countries because it is a small area that, in order to progress, had to incorporate many new and challenging ideas, such as a state limit on children. Singapore, independent only since 1965, when it shed its British colonial status, is one of those artificially created countries—but one that has definitely "worked."

What is more, it is one whose leaders often lecture the rest of the third world.

For instance, Goh Keng Swee, Singapore's then deputy prime minister and minister of education, spoke in 1984 in London, stating cogently that "What holds developing countries back is not inadequate aid or trade, but their failure to establish competent organs of public administration and their failure, also, to develop durable and enlightened social and political institutions." He went further. He was so daring as to refer to the economic connection between corruption and public debt: an unmentionable!

"When large sums of money are lent to governments of developing countries which are notoriously corrupt and whose civil servants are conspicuously incompetent, there will be a problem in getting the money back. Yet, in the burgeoning literature on the sovereign debt problem, you can find no reference to this issue. The reason, I suppose, is that these are not matters to discuss in polite society, not even when hundreds of billions of dollars are at stake."

But more than hundreds of billions of dollars were at stake; the survival of civilization as we know it was at stake. The forces for survival were powerful, but even as they gathered strength, moving from World War II and colonialism, to the postwar period of decolonization, to the heady time of the charismatic leaders, and finally to the more pragmatic time of economic rationalization, so did their adversaries, corruption and the disintegrative impulses that have dominated recent history. It was the era of "the state" that swept developed and developing countries alike in this epoch—and it seemed to be coming to an end.

The great Roman Catholic thinker Pierre Teilhard de Chardin once wrote, "The age of nations is past. It remains to us now, if we do not wish to perish, to set aside the ancient prejudices and build the earth."

Many were indeed striving to build that Earth—in different ways—but it was also clear that for many the price of setting aside ancient prejudices was too high. Which destiny would prevail in a seeking and turbulent world was a question that could only begin to be answered at the beginning of 1985.

Yet the bright signs cannot hide the ugly intractability of war and the dissolution it brings. And that defines the shape of the cataclysm that may be yet to come.

FROM "THE CLIMATIC EFFECTS OF NUCLEAR WAR," BY RICHARD P. TURCO *ET AL., SCIENTIFIC AMERICAN,* VOL. 251, NO. 2. DRAWING BY IAN WORPOLE

Nuclear Winter
Its Discovery and Implications

BY STEPHEN H. SCHNEIDER

Why would someone living near Times Square, Trafalgar Square, or Red Square care about the long-term environmental consequences of a large-scale nuclear war? Indeed, would it make much difference to the populations of the combatant nations whether the climate got hot or cold after blasts and radioactivity had killed the bulk of their nation's people? But before asking whether "nuclear winter" should make any difference, we should first see what it is and why this newest controversy concerning the use of nuclear weapons did not arise until almost 40 years after the first "atom bomb" was dropped on Hiroshima.

Early Clues. No recent topic in the atmospheric sciences has been more talked about, more controversial, and—to many—more important than nuclear winter. The notion arises from the possibility that massive amounts of smoke that could be generated by thousands of fires following a nuclear holocaust could be transported long distances by the atmosphere and block solar energy from reaching the Earth's surface.

Nearly 25 years ago a brief article appeared in the *Bulletin of the Atomic Scientists* warning of massive fires that might occur in the wake of nuclear blasts. Indeed, nuclear strategists had long debated whether blast or fire or radioactivity effects were the principal destructive mechanisms of nuclear warfare. There were a few very early attempts to estimate the weather and climatic consequences of nuclear war in the 1960s, but none of these was based on sophisticated analyses. They had very weak conclusions, and they languished in relative obscurity.

Then, in the early 1970s, the potential effects of stratospheric ozone depletion from nitrogen oxides produced by high-flying aircraft were discovered independently by two atmospheric chemists, Harold Johnston of the University of California at Berkeley and Paul Crutzen of the University of Stockholm, who was then a postdoctoral fellow at the University of Oxford. Since large nuclear blasts can inject massive amounts of these pollutants—which can act as catalysts to destroy ozone—into the stratosphere, the U.S. National Academy of Sciences (NAS) was asked by the U.S. Arms Control and Disarmament Agency to assess the long-term, worldwide consequences of nuclear war. Although completely excluding fires and some other important issues (*see* Stephen H. Schneider and Randi Londer, *The Coevolution of Climate and Life*, 1984, for a longer history of this assessment), the NAS report, which was published in 1975, did focus attention on a new global-scale element that might plague survivors in the aftermath of nuclear war: a drastic ozone reduction, lasting for at least several years. Since ozone in the stratosphere helps to filter out most of the Sun's harmful ultraviolet rays and prevent them from reaching the Earth's surface, any significant reduction in this trace atmospheric gas could be damaging to many forms of life.

This 1974 effort also attempted to assess the climatic consequences of some rather modest dust injections into the stratosphere that the study's climatic effects group was told could be kicked up by nuclear explosions. Based on the estimate of dustiness the group was given to work with—a stratospheric dust veil comparable to that produced by a large volcanic eruption—the 1974 study could predict only a moderate cooling in the aftermath of a large-scale nuclear war. Although such a cooling of the Earth's surface would affect combatant and noncombatant nations alike, its predicted magnitude was too small to be remotely comparable in seriousness to the direct blast and radioactivity effects, which already were well-known threats of nuclear war.

The NAS report was subsequently attacked by environmental scientists Paul and Anne Ehrlich and John Holdren in their book *Ecoscience* for missing the atmospheric effects of fires and firestorms, which, they suggested, could have climatic significance. Although this group and others had speculated on possible weather and climatic effects of nuclear-war-induced smoke injected into the air, no one had really attempted to calculate just how much smoke might be injected into the air in a big nuclear war, at least until 1982.

The Crutzen-Birks Calculations. In 1980 *Ambio,* the environmental journal of the Royal Swedish Academy of Sciences, commissioned a series of studies of nuclear war. One of those asked to take part was Paul Crutzen, who was then director at the Max Planck Institute for Chemistry in Mainz, West Germany. Crutzen was joined by John Birks, a chemist affiliated with the University of Colorado. They first reexamined the stratospheric ozone issue, basing their estimates of the amount of chemicals produced in nuclear fireballs that could enter the stratosphere on a hypothetical war scenario developed by a panel of experts that *Ambio* had assembled.

Crutzen observed that the *Ambio* scenario assumed that the military strategies and new weapons systems available in the early 1980s implied shifts to a greater number of smaller-yield nuclear weapons than had been the case a decade earlier, when the NAS report was issued. Since it takes a large individual explosive yield to produce fireballs that can reach high into the stratosphere, where most ozone is located, this shift in military technology had significantly reduced the amounts of nitrogen oxides that a nuclear war might inject into the stratosphere. So it appeared that the ozone reduction from a large-scale war fought in the 1980s would probably be less than in one fought with 1970s weapons systems. Nevertheless, Crutzen and Birks looked further.

Stephen H. Schneider is head of the Visitors Program and deputy director of the Advanced Study Program at the National Center for Atmospheric Research at Boulder, Colo. Since the nuclear winter theory was first put forward, he has been one of the atmospheric scientists most frequently asked to assess the prospects that it poses for our planet and its survival.

Simulated nuclear war: brightest spot on the U.S. East Coast is an air burst over New York City. Most of the other major cities are already afire, their smoke climbing high over the Atlantic.

ILLUSTRATIONS, ©1983 JON LOMBERG

Since Crutzen and Birks did know about the large fires that would probably be associated with nuclear attacks, it was logical to examine the kinds of pollutants that big fires typically inject into the air. As a working hypothesis, they assumed that a million square kilometres (386,000 sq mi) of forested areas near war targets could burn—all within a few weeks' time. This area is about ten times larger than the area that burns annually as a result of wildfires—which occur randomly throughout the entire year. The gases and smoke generated from these fires, from blowouts in natural gas and petroleum wells, and from the fireballs themselves would seriously pollute the *lower* atmosphere—perhaps creating toxic smog akin to that in Los Angeles or Mexico City today—on a hemispheric scale. The action of sunlight on the smoke could, they reasoned, make a so-called photochemical smog toxic enough to kill many crops.

But to make this massive-scale smog would take sunlight and, toward the end of their study, they suddenly realized that the particles of soot and other materials in the smoke plumes from the forest fires alone would block out a substantial fraction of the sunlight, preventing it from reaching the lower atmosphere and thus eliminating much of the driving force behind this post-nuclear-war smog factory. But if the smoke particles were so abundant that they could shut off the processes that make smog, would not that imply darkness at the Earth's surface? This was the birth of the nuclear winter idea, although it took several more steps and some additional scientific efforts to develop the concept more fully. From their smoke pall calculations, Crutzen and Birks postulated that the sky could darken for weeks to months—perhaps eliminating photosynthesis of green plants long enough to devastate crops. They also recognized the potential for climatic effects, though they did not calculate any explicitly. They mentioned the potential importance of the burning of urban centres, but a quantitative analysis of this was left for subsequent studies. The Crutzen-Birks study soon led to several national and international investigations of the atmospheric aftereffects of nuclear war.

TTAPS and Controversy. To calculate the climatic effects of unprecedented disturbances like a nuclear smoke cloud takes a climatic theory—actually a mathematical model of how the Earth's climate works run in large computers. A group of National Aeronautics and Space Administration (NASA) scientists—including two of astronomer Carl Sagan's former students—had already built a simple climate model to estimate the effects of a thick, high-altitude cloud of debris from a hypothesized collision between the Earth and a giant asteroid some 65 million years ago, which physicist Luis Alvarez and co-workers speculated might have caused the extinction of the dinosaurs. Since the NASA scientists' model already existed, the tough remaining job was to extend the Crutzen-Birks estimate of how much smoke would get into the atmosphere.

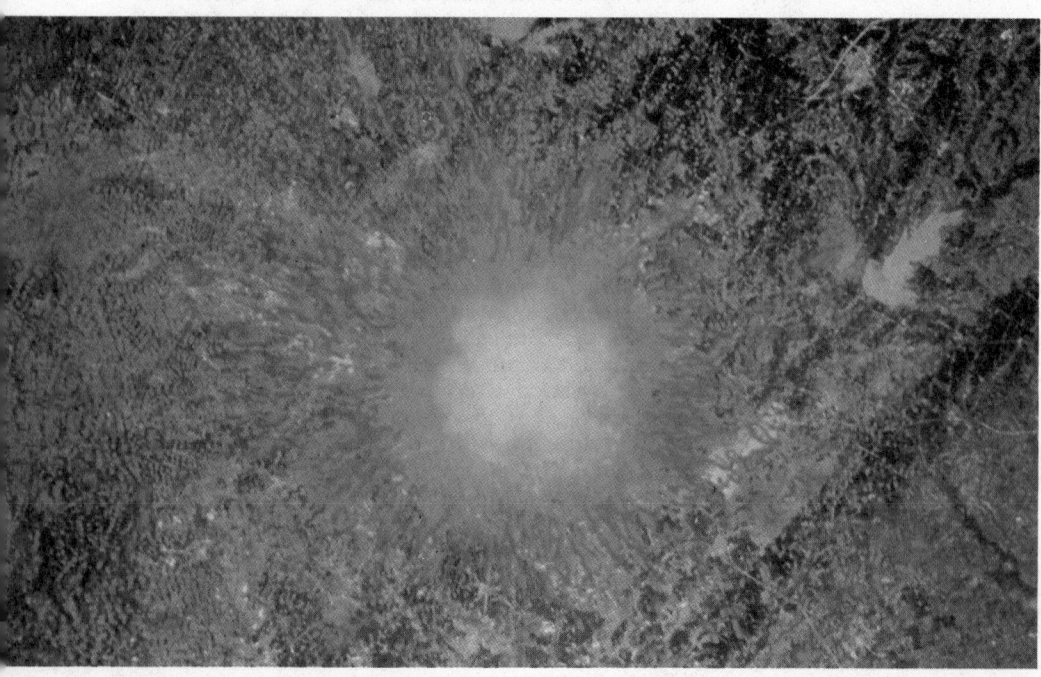

Each airburst over a city ignites various stores of flammable materials throughout the area, and each of the smaller fires contributes its column of smoke or toxic gases.

Within hours, or at most a few days, the first of the fallout drifts down over downwind areas—in this case Western Europe and North Africa.

©1983 JON LOMBERG/BRIAN KNOLL

Richard Turco, an atmospheric chemist, reexamined the Crutzen-Birks calculations and reduced their forest-burning estimates, but he added a quantitative dimension to the main ingredient—smoke from burning cities. This, he estimated, would put several hundred million tons of sooty smoke high into the atmosphere, where it could last at least for weeks. Eventually the now-famous TTAPS (Turco, Owen Toon, Thomas Ackerman, James Pollack, and Carl Sagan) article appeared (*Science*, Dec. 23, 1983), in which the term nuclear winter was coined, based on the continental-scale subfreezing temperatures they calculated. The possibility that smoke or dust produced in the mid-latitudes of the Northern Hemisphere could be transported by its own heating out of the zone of injection was speculated on by Sagan, based on an analogy to observations of Martian dust storms in which small regions of dust were sometimes seen to spread rapidly about the planet. A group of 20 biologists led by Paul Ehrlich, a Stanford University biologist, reckoned that the possible global spread of sooty smoke in high concentrations could cause decreased light levels and temperatures severe enough to induce massive extinctions, perhaps even of humans.

These dramatic and controversial works published in late 1983 received worldwide media attention—unlike the Crutzen-Birks discovery. But attention also went to bitter critics like physicist Edward Teller, who attacked both the TTAPS assumptions for smoke injection amounts and their very crude climatic model. The TTAPS assumptions about the soot input from burning cities after a major nuclear exchange were independently confirmed and extended by Crutzen and colleagues, who also pointed out the particular importance of fires in fossil fuel depots. These have a very large component of soot in their smoke plumes relative to most other materials found in urban areas. Thus the subsequent Crutzen calculations actually increased the smoke injection estimates over those made by TTAPS.

The TTAPS paper predicted land-surface cooling of 20 to 40 or more degrees Celsius (36° to 72° F) for up to many months from such nuclear smoke clouds. Although the authors were aware of many of their model's deficiencies, TTAPS was criticized, nonetheless, for a number of reasons. First, they used a so-called one-dimensional, radiative-convective climatic model, whereas the real world is, of course, three dimensional. Then, the TTAPS model was applied to either an all-land or an all-ocean planet and neglected the important effects of heat transported from oceans to land, which might ameliorate the land-surface cooling from the nuclear smoke. Finally, TTAPS used annually averaged solar radiative input, ignoring the potential effects of seasonality on the results. There are other criticisms that could be directed at TTAPS, such as their neglect of interactions between perturbed atmospheric conditions and smoke transport and removal, or their inability to treat important smaller-scale effects, such as fire plumes and their role in creating thunderstorm-like clouds that might wash out some of the initial smoke before it got very far in the atmosphere.

These latter criticisms apply to all climatic modeling of nuclear winter to date, but the first three difficulties mentioned above have been examined in the context of more complex, so-called three-dimensional, general-circulation models. Two such studies had been published as of 1984, a Soviet study by V. V. Alexandrov and G. L. Stenchikov (the AS study) and an American effort by C. Covey, S. H. Schneider, and S. L. Thompson (the CST study) at the National Center for Atmospheric Research (NCAR).

New Findings—New Uncertainties. The CST three-dimensional-model results significantly modified the one-dimensional TTAPS findings. Along with TTAPS and the Soviet work, it helped to provide the scientific support needed to conduct several major national and international assessments of the overall nuclear winter problem, including a second NAS study of the long-term atmospheric effects of nuclear explosions. At the request of this NAS study panel, then in progress, CST used a scenario for a large-scale nuclear-war-induced smoke cloud. The three-dimensional model's results confirmed, denied, and extended TTAPS.

Like TTAPS, CST found significantly reduced light and surface temperatures in mid-continental regions under the assumed high-altitude sooty smoke cloud. CST also observed that the smoke could be lifted by its own heating into the stratosphere, where it could more easily spread out of the war zone, at least in the summer or spring seasons. (But, as mentioned earlier, the CST model is not yet able to move or remove smoke interactively; thus Covey, Schneider, and Thompson have not yet been able to determine with confidence what might actually happen to the smoke cloud after injection. Work on this problem is under way.) However, CST also found that the magnitude of surface cooling under the smoke cloud was

Cities burn, and forests, and centres of petrochemical production and storage, and their plumes of smoke rise and spread through the atmosphere.

ILLUSTRATIONS (LEFT, BELOW, AND OPPOSITE), ©1983 JON LOMBERG

comparable to TTAPS only in mid-continental areas and in the summer. Along coasts the cooling was less by, perhaps, a factor of ten. Moreover, in the three-dimensional CST model there was a great seasonal dependence to the cooling—TTAPS made only a mean annual calculation—with CST's average land-temperature drops ranging from about half the TTAPS finding in the summer to very little in winter.

The most important CST result, however, was the discovery of the possibility that even a few days of dense smoke high overhead could drop surface temperatures on land below freezing, depending on location and meteorological conditions. Moreover, such a transient "quick freeze" could be exported by the lottery of wind directions—a sort of weather roulette—to almost any place in the hemisphere where the nuclear blasts had taken place, even if the overall size of the nuclear smoke cloud was many times less than that hypothesized by TTAPS or the NAS study. The plausibility of such rapid transient surface cooling was reinforced by a one-dimensional set of calculations of J. T. Kiehl and V. Ramaswamy at NCAR. Their study was designed to provide better calculations of the flow of radiant energy within the atmosphere than were available from the very simple treatment of these processes used by CST.

This possibility of quick freeze—it is too soon to say how certain it is—is both scientifically interesting and charged with major policy implications. It also cancels one implication of TTAPS. TTAPS postulated the existence of a "threshold" for nuclear winter—at a "modest" 100-megaton war in which major city centres were struck by a thousand 100-kiloton bombs. This scenario represents the use of about 1% of global nuclear arsenals. The implication is that wars in which total megatonnage above 100 is exploded on cities could trigger a nuclear winter. This threshold concept has led to conflicting policy implications. Whereas Carl Sagan said it implies that nuclear weapons stockpiles need to be reduced on both sides by a factor of 20 or more in order to drop below the TTAPS threshold, a U.S. Department of Defense official countered that the TTAPS threshold suggests that one side could launch a 99-megaton first strike on the other side, but the victims could not fire back without crossing the threshold. Fortunately, planners could stop thinking up such pathological threshold scenarios, because they arise only in the context of a one-dimensional model such as the one used by TTAPS. The three-dimensional models, with more realistic regional geography and dynamics included, show it is more likely that there would be a spectrum of probabilities and consequences, ranging from a higher

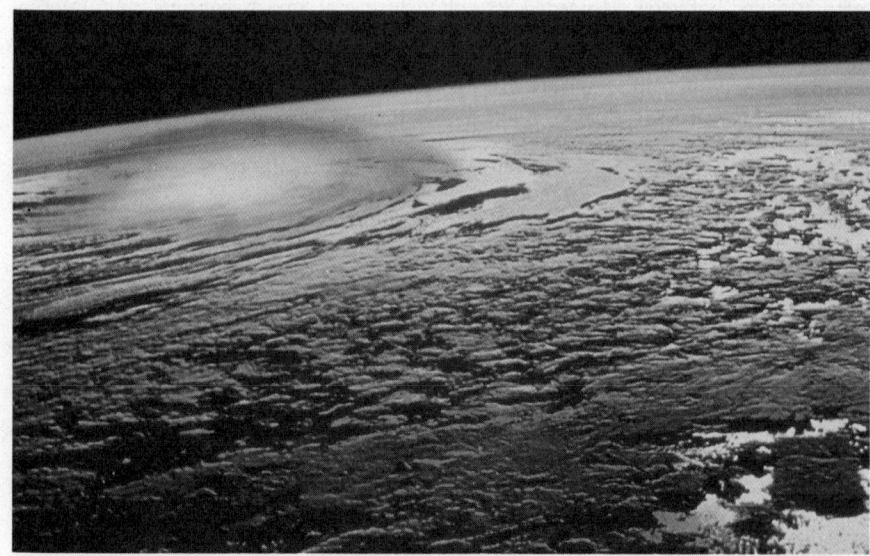

Meanwhile, the largest of the fireballs has already reached into the stratosphere and begun catalyzing the destruction of the ozone layer.

probability of transient quick freezes to a lower chance of a more devastating global-scale nuclear winter lasting for months—the scenario that so concerned the 20 biologists.

The greatest uncertainties surrounding the long-term climatic effects of nuclear smoke clouds arise not from the climatic models themselves but from the assumptions used to drive them. In particular, what no climatic model can explicitly calculate is the height to which a plume of smoke will rise over a city consumed by a firestorm. If the bulk of the smoke is injected above a few kilometres of altitude, this smoke will remain above the bulk of the water vapour in the atmosphere. The lifetime of the smoke, in turn, depends on how effective that water is in washing out the smoke. Thus the biggest questions in the theory of nuclear winter occur at the local scale: How much smoke will initially get how high? How much smoke will be removed and spread by atmospheric motions in the next few days as hundreds of plumes of smoke follow twisted and interlocking paths over distances of a few hundred kilometres (the so-called mesoscale problem)?

If, as Crutzen and Birks, TTAPS, the second NAS report, AS, and CST assumed, there are still some few hundred million tons of smoke spread high in the atmosphere a week or so "postwar," then the likelihood of severe climatic effects on a hemispheric to global scale is high. On the other hand, if there were a great deal more initial washout of smoke, either because the plume did not rise as high as is presently anticipated or because there was more rainfall, then the likelihood of global-scale nuclear winter would be lower, although the possibility of transient quick freezes would remain. It is simply too soon to estimate these relative probabilities, although there is some theoretical and experimental evidence that can be brought to bear on the problem of estimating how much smoke might get how high in the first few hours following the exchange of many nuclear weapons against a variety of targets.

Tracking Smoke Clouds. In World War II there were several firestorms associated with bombing. Large fires were started in Japan by the only two nuclear weapons ever exploded on cities. In addition, a number of firestorms were created by conventional bombing attacks, most notably in Dresden and Hamburg, Germany. What is known about the plumes from these fires? Does such knowledge tell anything about what might happen after nuclear explosions over modern cities? The answers to these questions are fuzzy. Hiroshima, for example, burned on a very humid summer day, and although the ensuing fire consumed nearly all combustible materials on the ground and created a tall column of smoke over the burned-out city, a gigantic cloud also formed from which an oily "black rain" fell. Thus at least some of the smoke material was washed out in the first few hours after the fire. Exactly how much remained is not known, for no careful measurements were made of the smoky aftereffects of the Hiroshima fire. Hamburg also seems to have created a tall column of smoke and some sort of cloud as well, but there was apparently much less black rain. The Dresden firestorm plume was observed to have moved at least to the North Sea, and little black rain was reported.

In addition to the few cases of World War II firestorms, there have been observations of large forest fires. The

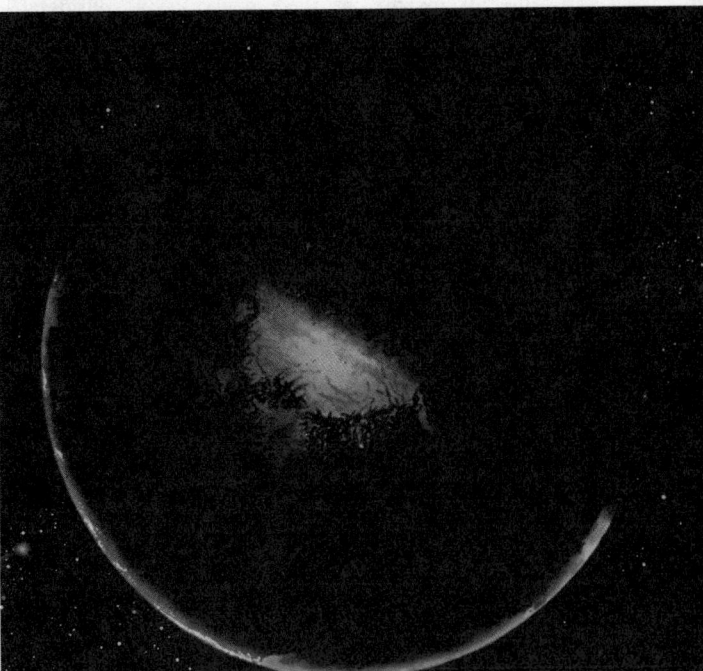

This series of views of nuclear war shows Earth oriented with Europe at the bottom, North America at left, and the U.S.S.R. on the nighttime side. (Top) Nuclear explosions dot the hemisphere. (Centre) The smoke from the massive fires set by the explosions begins to cover the Earth. (Bottom) After a few days the planet is shrouded with a blanket of soot and dust.

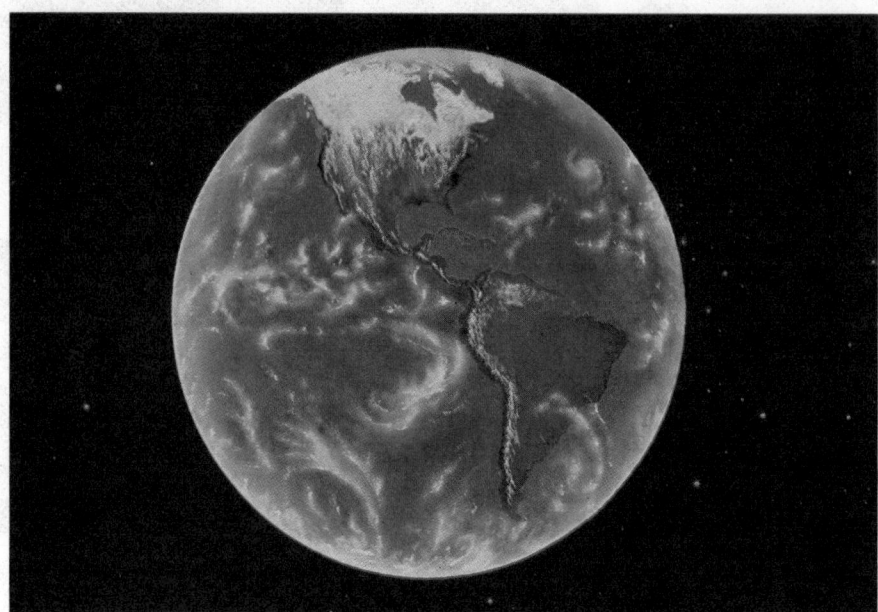

At last the dust settles, after a matter of months. It reveals a surface still frozen here and there and defoliated everywhere.
©JON LOMBERG

best documented took place in Alberta in the summer of 1950. The smoke plume from this fire could be clearly traced for days, and it was so dense that when it passed over Cleveland, Ohio, and Detroit on September 24 it darkened the sky to the point that lights were needed for afternoon baseball games. Temperatures were also several degrees below expected levels in Washington, D.C. This same cloud was observed by a Royal Air Force pilot over England several days later at a height of 9–12 km (c. 5–7 mi)! Clearly, when meteorological conditions permit, smoke from massive fires can rise very high and last for a long time in the atmosphere. What is most difficult to determine is whether the smoke columns from any one burning target would most closely resemble those at Hiroshima, Dresden, Alberta, or yet some other case.

One way to estimate how high smoke plumes would rise and how much smoke might be washed out immediately following a large fire is to build a mathematical model of the atmosphere on a scale of a few kilometres. Such so-called cumulus cloud models are available, and one was applied by Colorado State University meteorologist William Cotton to a hypothetical fire in which the city of Denver was "burned." Cotton chose a typical day in June for his fire, so there would be a considerable amount of moisture in his model's atmosphere, and some washout of smoke could be simulated. What resulted from this computer experiment was a firestorm in which soot and other tiny particles reached very high into the atmosphere. Quite surprisingly, nearly half of the soot produced was injected into the model's stratosphere, where presumably it would be above most atmospheric water vapour and thus unlikely to be removed quickly. Overall, his model removed only several percent of the injected soot. Although this cloud-scale model suffers from a large number of still-uncertain assumptions, it dramatically reinforced the concern expressed by earlier investigators about the plausibility of nuclear winter.

Nuclear Winter and Policy. What are the policy implications of the nuclear winter theory? It is obvious that a prolonged period of continental-scale freezing following a big nuclear war would make an already horrendous situation much worse. (Even a few days of frosts in the wrong places at the wrong times could be devastating.) Even though the threshold of nuclear winter

probably does not exist—and the worry that it makes a first strike more inviting thus becomes a nonworry— this raises a fundamental issue that has caused concern among a number of the scientists who first studied nuclear winter. That is, might their discoveries reveal something that would actually increase the likelihood of nuclear missiles being used? For instance, CST found that a war in summer would cause twice the surface cooling of the same war in spring. However, a winter war would drop surface temperatures very little, at least in the northern latitudes where temperatures were already below freezing. "Have we now told them when to push the buttons?" the scientists wondered.

It did not take long for the CST researchers to discount that concern. First, while the temperature effects in winter might be relatively small, it could be argued that relatively less smoke washout in that season might allow sufficient amounts of smoke to remain high up in the atmosphere long enough to affect springtime temperatures, a critical time for crops. Second, the immediate consequences of nuclear blasts and radioactivity have so far been sufficient to deter nuclear adventurism—in winter or any other season. So the presumed results of nuclear war are at least as bad as before nuclear winter was discovered and perhaps significantly worse, even for a winter war. But this line of thinking raised a serious issue that still cannot be entirely dismissed.

Suppose that nuclear winter is a real possibility and that it is accepted as such by nuclear strategists on both sides. Suppose also, however, that for some scenarios the climatic aftereffects are believed to be markedly worse for one side than for the other. If this were to be accepted by planners, then such a nuclear winter scenario could actually increase the probability of nuclear war, for it would imply an advantage to one side. Despite this possibility, it is unlikely that nuclear winter research itself will increase the probability of war. For example, to date no research groups have reported any smoke and dust aftermath scenario that leaves one side with a clear advantage. Everything produced so far makes the impact of nuclear war on both sides worse—from marginally so to catastrophically so (to say nothing of the noncombatants!).

Moreover, even if research could uncover some rare case in which one side seemed to be much less damaged by the ensuing smoke and dust clouds than the other, there are simply too many uncertainties in a chain of events that starts with warfare and ends up with the transport of uncertain quantities of smoke around the planet by winds to give planners much confidence in any detailed scenario. Miscalculation and uncertainty conspire against the credibility of any individual prediction of climatic aftereffects of a large-scale nuclear war. In other words, although we may have considerable confidence in the general statement that a spectrum of negative aftereffects are possible and even likely, no one who is knowledgeable about the issues can say with confidence that any one chain of events would transpire. In fact, there is a very good chance that unforeseen consequences would occur. Thus, if one side attempted to fight a particular nuclear war that might give them a climatic advantage when the explosions were over, they would be taking a considerable risk that miscalculation could put them in an unforeseen disadvantageous position. There is a significant probability that climatic aftereffects would be worse than expected for both sides. It is, therefore, unlikely that such aftereffects would give one side a meaningful edge, sufficient to tempt them to start pushing buttons. At least, that is what most researchers currently believe.

A New Factor in Arms Control. No question in our times could be more important: How can we reduce the probability that any of this will ever happen? Some say, freeze new weapons deployment. Others want more weapons deployed—"peace through strength"—ostensibly to obtain a reduction in weapons later on. Still others want different kinds of weapons systems. Among the latter are the so-called Star Wars defense systems or penetrator missiles that burrow into the enemy's hardened targets. These would replace the missiles currently deployed, which are set to explode at the surface or in the air—thus causing the raising of dust and smoke into the atmosphere that led to the concern over nuclear winter in the first place.

If we—or they—altered existing technologies or targeting policies to avoid deliberately starting big fires or kicking up large quantities of dust, this could make a big difference in helping to prevent a nuclear winter. But such a policy could also make nuclear war itself more thinkable, and thus perhaps more probable, even if less devastating. And who is to guarantee that the "losers" of such a limited exchange of penetrator warheads would not, out of desperation, throw what nuclear weapons they had left at the same old targets—*i.e.,* cities? (And for the foreseeable future both sides would have plenty of missiles left—enough to ensure the virtual destruction of any meaningful postwar civilization for the opponent, as well as enough to raise tens of millions of tons of dust, smoke, and toxic chemicals into the atmosphere.) Thus any attempt to circumvent the risks of nuclear winter by purely technical fixes would be likely to create yet another set of dangers.

What nuclear winter represents, then, is an opportunity to reexamine the policies—and the mind-set—that made this newest category of potential horrors so prominent. That mind-set is based on a combination of factors, ranging from real or imagined fears of a potential adversary's strength or intentions to the belief that one's

own security is enhanced by being the first to have new weapons systems to the simple greed of those who benefit financially or professionally from the production or deployment of massive numbers of new or existing weapons systems. If the nuclear winter discoveries can help lead to a reexamination of these factors, they could have a major impact on the probability of nuclear war.

But nuclear winter is not a proven entity, only plausible theory. How then, some ask, could policy be made on such an uncertain basis? Some of the most fundamental issues remain in doubt. For instance, although there are historical examples of large quantities of smoke entering the atmosphere as a result of fires, the amount of smoke that would rise from a thousand burning cities, how high it would go, and how far it would spread can never be definitively estimated—even by the most sophisticated computer models—until a thousand real cities burn. In other words, some elements of the theory of nuclear winter may be unverifiable.

In response, others point out that military and strategic planning is based on scenarios of political or military conflicts with probabilities well below that for nuclear winter. Uncertainty is an unavoidable element of all strategic planning. The more relevant question, they would argue, is whether the world can afford to take the risk of experiencing nuclear winter without making some effort to reduce the chance of its occurrence. To be sure, the large research programs now being considered in the U.S. and elsewhere can help to narrow uncertainties and thus put decision making related to nuclear winter on a firmer factual basis. But at what stage does "uncertainty"—that venerable excuse to delay action—become a device to avoid changing the current policies of the nuclear powers? These are the kinds of arguments that have accompanied the scientific findings on nuclear winter.

The arms race has been sustained in large measure by the belief that we—or they—are strategically better off with a technical advantage, even if it exists only on paper and even though it is inevitable that the other side, in response, will soon catch up and perhaps surge ahead. This is fundamentally a political, not a technical, issue. Thus any modifications to this conventional wisdom will have to come from fundamental changes in the political relationships between nuclear powers, not merely from technical adjustments to the numbers or deployment of nuclear weapons—although the latter could be important first steps toward a political climate conducive to serious arms reductions and more stable deployment strategies.

What nuclear winter issues add to the arms-control debate is an extension to the global scale of the already well-traveled conclusion that strategic nuclear weapons as now deployed constitute deterrence by mutual suicide. Nuclear winter also warns any noncombatant nations or terrorist groups contemplating a deliberate attempt to start a superpower nuclear war that they are not immune from devastating consequences. As to the criticism that nuclear winter is an uncertain theory and any talk of policy implications is premature, the following question could be asked: Would one agree to play Russian roulette just because it was not certain whether one, two, three, four, or five chambers were loaded?

The purpose of this section is to introduce to continuing *Book of the Year* subscribers selected *Macropædia* articles or portions of them that have been completely revised or written anew. It is intended to update the encyclopaedia, and particularly the *Macropædia,* in ways that cannot be accomplished fully by reviewing the year's events or by revising statistics annually, because the *Macropædia* texts themselves—written from a longer perspective than any yearly revision—supply authoritative interpretation and analysis as well as narrative and description.

In the massive restructuring of *Encyclopædia Britannica* for 1985, many sets of general articles on related topics have been taken out of purely alphabetical order and brought together under the larger headings that unite them. For example, the article on deserts and that on aquatic ecosystems have been assembled with other related articles under ECOSYSTEMS. The two new general articles presented here, however, are among the many on discrete topics that do not lend themselves to this kind of consolidation, and they appear in the new *Macropædia* as individual articles. They are CENSORSHIP and HUMAN RIGHTS. Each is an entirely new and up-to-date treatment of the subject by an eminent authority.

The 1985 reorganization of the *Britannica* also removed all but a few biographies from the *Macropædia,* relocating them in the *Micropædia* with thousands of shorter ones. The three biographies presented here, however, are among the relative handful on figures of such immense importance that they demanded inclusion in the *Macropædia*. These are Michael FARADAY, the 19th-century British chemist and physicist who made major contributions to the understanding of electricity and magnetism and to the foundations of electromagnetic theory; Antoine-Laurent LAVOISIER, the brilliant 18th-century Frenchman who founded modern chemistry; and Max PLANCK, the great German theoretical physicist who originated the quantum theory and whose work, bridging the 19th and 20th centuries, revolutionized the understanding of what goes on inside the atom. All three of these new biographies replace older and shorter ones.

Macropædia articles have been noted for their bibliographies, in which Britannica contributors or other authorities have supplied annotated lists of salient works of scholarship on the topic at hand. This feature continues in the restructured *Britannica,* and the complete bibliographies from the encyclopaedia accompany CENSORSHIP and HUMAN RIGHTS. Unfortunately, in order to accommodate the third of our new biographies, it was necessary to omit bibliographic material from all three. However, an entirely new bibliograhic feature appears at the end of this section. In it six recently published books that already have had substantial impact on their fields of learning are reviewed by scholars, beginning at page 57. [EDITOR]

Censorship

To censor is to act so as to change or suppress thoughts or actions considered contrary to the common good. This article discusses censorship and its relation to government and the rule of law.

The article is divided into the following sections:

Concerns relevant to censorship

THE STATUS OF "INDIVIDUALITY"

Censorship, as a term in English, goes back to the office of censor established in Rome in 443 BC. That officer, who conducted the census, regulated the morals of the citizens counted and classified. But, however honourable the origins of its name, censorship itself is today generally regarded as a relic of an unenlightened and much more oppressive age.

Illustrative of this change in opinion is how a community responds to such a sentiment as that with which Protagoras (*c.* 485–410 BC) opened his work *Concerning the Gods:*

About the gods I am not able to know either that they are, or that they are not, or what they are like in shape, the things preventing knowledge being many, such as the obscurity of the subject and that the life of man is short.

This public admission of agnosticism scandalized Protagoras' fellow Greeks. Such statements would no doubt have been received with hostility, and probably with social if not even criminal sanctions, throughout the ancient world. There are few places in the modern world, on the other hand, where such a statement cannot be made without the prospect of having to endure a pained and painful community response. This change reflects, among other things, a profound shift in opinion as to what is and is not a legitimate concern of government.

Whereas it could once be maintained that the law forbids whatever it does not permit, it is now generally accepted—at least wherever Western liberalism is in the ascendancy—that one may do whatever is not forbidden by law. Furthermore, it is now believed that what may be properly forbidden by law is quite limited. Much is made of permitting people to do with their lives (including their opinions) as they please, so long as they do no immediate and evident (usually physical) harm to others. Thus, Leo Strauss has observed, "The quarrel between the ancients and the moderns concerns eventually, and perhaps even from the beginning, the status of 'individuality.' "

All this is to say that individualism is made much of in modernity. The status, then, of censorship today very much depends on the standing of government itself and of legitimate authority, revealing but one aspect of the tension between "the individual and the state."

REQUIREMENTS OF SELF-GOVERNMENT

One critical source of the contemporary repudiation of censorship in the West depends on something that may be distinctive to modernity, an emphasis upon the dignity of the individual. This respect for individuality has its roots both in Christian doctrines and in the (not unrelated) sovereignty of the self reflected in state-of-nature theories about the foundations of social organization. Vital to this approach is the general opinion about the nature and sanctity of the human soul. This general opinion provides the foundation of a predominantly new, or modern, argument against censorship—against anything, in fact, that interferes with self-development, and especially such self-development (or, better still, "self-fulfillment") as a person happens to want and to choose for himself. This can be seen in terms of liberty—the liberty to become and to do what one pleases.

The old, or traditional, argument against censorship was much less individualistic and much more political in its orientation, making more of another sense of liberty. According to that sense, if a people is to be self-governing, it must have access to all information and arguments that may be relevant to its ability to discuss public affairs fully and to assess in a competent manner the conduct of the officials it chooses. Thus, "freedom of speech," which is constitutionally guaranteed to the people of the United States, first comes to view in Anglo-American legal history as a guarantee for the members of the British Parliament assembled to discuss the affairs of the kingdom.

In the circumstances of a people actually governing itself, it is obvious that there is no substitute for freedom of speech and of the press, particularly as that freedom permits an informed access to information and opinions about political matters. Even the more astute repressive regimes today recognize this underlying principle, in that their ruling bodies try to make certain that they themselves become and remain informed about what is really going on in their countries and abroad, however repressive they may be in not permitting their own people to learn about and openly to discuss public affairs. Whether anyone who thus rules unjustly, or otherwise improperly, can be regarded as truly understanding and hence truly controlling his situation is a question not limited to these circumstances.

"FREEDOM OF EXPRESSION"

The shift from the more political to the more individualistic view of liberty may be seen in how the constitutional guarantees with respect to speech and the press are typically spoken of in the United States. Restraints upon speaking and publishing, and indeed upon action generally, are fewer than at any time in the history of the country. This absence of restraints is reflected as well in the very terms in which these rights and privileges are described. What would once have been referred to as "freedom of speech and of the press" (drawing upon the language of the First Amendment to the Constitution of the United States) is now referred to as "freedom of expression."

To make much of freedom of expression is to encourage a liberation of the self from the constraints of the community. It may even be to assume that the self has, intrinsic to it or somehow available to it independent of any social guidance, intimations of what it is and what it wants. Thus, liberation may be seen in the currently fashionable insistence upon "doing one's own thing"—which can include a reliance upon standards and objectives that are solely one's own. It is difficult, in such circumstances, to avoid a radical subjectivism that tends to result in a thoroughgoing relativism with respect to moral and political judgments. One consequence of this approach is to identify an ever-expanding array of forms of expression that are believed to be entitled to immunity from government regulation.

On the other hand, if the emphasis is placed upon the more traditional language, "freedom of speech and of the press," the requirements and prerogatives of a self-governing people are apt to be made more of. This means, among other things, that a people must be prepared and equipped to make effective use of its considerable political power. (Even those rulers who act without the authority of the people must take care to shape their people in accordance with the needs and circumstances of their regime. This kind of effort need not be altogether selfish on the part of such rulers, since all regimes do have an interest in law and order, in common decency, and in a routine reliability or loyalty.) It should be evident that a people entrusted with the power of self-government must be able to exercise a disciplined judgment: not everything goes, and there are better and worse things awaiting the community and its citizens.

What is particularly difficult to argue for, and to maintain, is an arrangement that, while it leaves a people clearly free politically to discuss fully all matters of public interest with a view toward governing itself, routinely disciplines and otherwise prepares that same people for an effective exercise of its considerable freedom. In such circumstances, it is tempting for a people to take the case for, and the rhetoric of, liberty one step further—and thus to insist that no one should try to tell anyone else what kind of human being he should be. Yet, cannot it be said that only they are truly free who know what they are doing and who choose to do what is right? All others are, in varying degrees, prisoners of illusions and appetites, however much they may believe themselves to be freely expressing themselves.

True freedom

There are, then, two related sets of concerns evident in any consideration today of the forms and uses of censorship. One set of concerns has to do with the everyday governance of the community; the other, with the permanent shaping of the character of the people. The former is more political in its methods, the latter is more educational.

History of censorship

It should be instructive to consider how the problem of censorship has been dealt with in the ancient world, in premodern times, and in the modern world. Care must be taken here not to assume that the modern democratic regime, of a self-governing people, is the only legitimate regime. Rather, it is prudent to assume that most of those who have, in other times and places, thought about and acted upon such matters have been at least as humane and as sensible in their circumstances as modern democrats are apt to be in theirs.

ANCIENT GREECE AND ROME

It was taken for granted in the Greek community of antiquity, as well as in Rome, that citizens would be formed in accordance with the character and needs of the regime. This did not preclude the emergence of strong-minded men and women, as may be seen in the stories of Homer, of Plutarch, of Tacitus, and of the great playwrights. But it was evident, for example, that a citizen of Sparta was much more apt to be tough and unreflective (and certainly uncommunicative) than a citizen of Corinth (with its notorious openness to pleasure and luxury).

The scope of a city's concern was exhibited in the provisions it made for the establishment and promotion of religious worship. That "the gods of the city" were to be respected by every citizen was usually taken for granted. Presiding over religious observances was generally regarded as a privilege of citizenship: thus, in some cities it was an office in which the elderly in good standing could be expected to serve. A refusal to conform, at least outwardly, to the recognized worship of the community subjected one to hardships. And there could be difficulties, backed up by legal sanctions, for those who spoke improperly about such matters. The force of religious opinions could be seen not only in prosecutions for refusals to acknowledge the gods of the city but perhaps even more in the frequent unwillingness of a city (no matter what its obvious political or military interests) to conduct public business at a time when the religious calendar, auspices, or other such signs forbade civic activities. Indicative of respect for the

Power of religious opinion

Origin of freedom of speech

proprieties was the secrecy with which the religious mysteries, into which Greek and Roman men were routinely initiated, were evidently practiced—so much so that there does not seem to be any record from antiquity of precisely what constituted the various mysteries. Respect for the proprieties may be seen as well in the outrage provoked in Sparta by a poem by Archilochus (7th century BC) in which he celebrated his lifesaving cowardice.

Athens, it can be said, was much more liberal than the typical Greek city. This is not to suggest that the rulers of the other cities did not, among themselves, freely discuss the public business. But in Athens the rulers included much more of the population than in most cities of antiquity— and freedom of speech (for political purposes) spilled over there into the private lives of citizens. This may be seen, perhaps best of all, in the famous funeral address given by Pericles in 431 BC. Athenians, he pointed out, did not consider public discussion merely something to be put up with; rather, they believed that the best interests of the city could not be served without a full discussion of the issues before the assembly. There may be seen in the plays of an Aristophanes the kind of uninhibited discussions of politics that the Athenians were evidently accustomed to, discussions that could (in the license accorded to comedy) be couched in licentious terms not permitted in everyday discourse.

The limits of Athenian openness may be seen, of course, in the trial, conviction, and execution of Socrates in 399 BC on charges that he corrupted the youth and that he did not acknowledge the gods that the city did but other new divinities of his own. One may see, as well, in the *Republic* of Plato an account of a system of censorship, particularly of the arts, that is comprehensive. Not only are various opinions (particularly misconceptions about the gods and about the supposed terrors of death) to be discouraged, but various salutary opinions are to be encouraged and protected without having to be demonstrated to be true. Much of what is said in the *Republic* and elsewhere reflects the belief that the vital opinions of the community could be shaped by law and that men could be penalized for saying things that offended public sensibilities, undermined common morality, or subverted the institutions of the community.

The circumstances justifying the system of comprehensive "thought control" described in Plato's *Republic* are obviously rarely to be found. Thus, Socrates himself is recorded in the same dialogue (and in Plato's *Apology*) as complaining that cities with bad regimes do not permit their misconduct to be questioned and corrected. Such regimes should be compared with the regimes in the age of the good Roman emperors, the period from Nerva (*c.* AD 30–98) to Marcus Aurelius (121–180), the golden times, said Tacitus, when everyone could hold and defend whatever opinions he wished.

ANCIENT ISRAEL AND EARLY CHRISTIANITY

Much of what can be said about ancient Greece and Rome could be applied, with appropriate adaptations, to ancient Israel. The stories of the difficulties encountered by Jesus, and the offenses he came to be accused of, indicate the kinds of restrictions to which the Jews subjected themselves with respect to religious observances and with respect to what could and could not be said about divine matters. (The inhibitions so established were later reflected in the manner in which Moses Maimonides [1135–1204] proceeded in his publications, often relying upon "hints" rather than upon explicit discussion of sensitive topics.) The prevailing watchfulness, lest someone say or do what he should not, can be said to be anticipated by the commandment "You shall not take the name of the Lord your God in vain; for the Lord will not hold him guiltless who takes his name in vain" (Ex. 20:7). It may be seen as well in the ancient opinion that there is a name for God that must not be uttered.

It should be evident that this way of life—directing both opinions and actions and extending down to minute daily routines—could not help but shape a people for centuries, if not for millennia, to come. But it should also be evident that those in the position to know, and with a duty

to act, were expected to speak out and were, in effect, licensed to do so, however cautiously they were obliged to proceed on occasion. Thus, the prophet Nathan dared to challenge King David himself for what he had done to secure Bathsheba for his wife (II Sam. 12:1–24). On an earlier, perhaps even more striking, occasion, the patriarch Abraham dared to argue with God about the terms on which Sodom and Gomorrah might be saved from destruction (Gen. 18:16–33). God made concessions to Abraham, and David crumbled before Nathan's authority. But such presumptuousness on the part of mere mortals is possible, and likely to bear fruit, only in communities that have been trained to share and to respect certain moral principles grounded in thoughtfulness.

Nathan the Prophet

The thoughtfulness to which the Old Testament aspires is suggested by the following counsel by Moses to the people of Israel (Deut. 4:5–6):

Behold, I have taught you statutes and ordinances, as the Lord my God commanded me, that you should do them in the land which you are entering to take possession of it. Keep them and do them; for that will be your wisdom and your understanding in the sight of the peoples, who, when they hear all these statutes, will say, "Surely this great nation is a wise and understanding people."

This approach can be considered to provide the foundation for the assurance that has been so critical to modern arguments against censorship (John 8:32): ". . . and you will know the truth, and the truth will make you free." Further biblical authority against censorship may be found in such "free speech" dramas as that described in Acts 4:13–21.

It should be remembered that to say everything one thought or believed was regarded by pre-Christian writers as occasionally irresponsible or licentious: social consequences dictated a need for restraint. Christian writers, however, called for just such saying of everything as the indispensable witness of faith: transitory social considerations were not to impede, to the extent that they formerly had, the exercise of such a liberty, indeed of such a duty, so intimately related to the eternal welfare of the soul. Thus we see an encouragement of the private—of an individuality that turned eventually against organized religion itself and legitimated a radical self-indulgence.

ANCIENT CHINA

Perhaps no people has ever been so thoroughly trained, on such a large scale and for so long, as the Chinese. Critical to that training was a system of education that culminated in a rigorous selection, by examination, of candidates for administrative posts. Particularly influential was the thought of Confucius (551–479 BC), with its considerable emphasis upon deference to authority and to family elders and upon respect for ritual observances and propriety. Cautiousness in speech was encouraged, licentious expressions were discouraged, and long-established teachings were relied upon for shaping character. All in all, it was contrary to Chinese good taste to speak openly of the faults of one's government or of one's rulers. And so it could be counselled by Confucius, "He who is not in any particular office has nothing to do with plans for the administration of its duties" (*Analects* [*Lun yü*], 7:14). It has been suggested that such sentiments have operated to prevent the spread in China of opinions supportive of political liberty.

Confucius

Still, it could be recognized by Confucius that "oppressive government is fiercer than a tiger." He could counsel that if a ruler's words are not good, and if people are discouraged from opposing them, the ruin of the country can be expected (*Analects,* 13:5). Blatant oppressiveness, and an attempt to stamp out the influence of Confucius and of other sages, could be seen in the wholesale destruction of books in China in 231 BC. But the Confucian mode was revived thereafter, to become the dominant influence for almost two millennia. Its pervasiveness may well be judged oppressive by contemporary Western standards, since so much depended, it seems, on mastering the orthodox texts and discipline.

Whether or not the typical Chinese government was indeed oppressive, effective control of information was lodged in the authorities, since access to the evidently vital public archives of earlier administrations was limited to a relative few. In addition, decisive control of what was thought, and how, depended in large part on a determination of what the authoritative texts were—something that has been critical in the West, as well, in the establishment of useful canons, both sacred and secular. Thus, Richard McKeon has suggested, "Censorship may be the enforcement of judgments based on power, passion, corruption, or prejudice—political, popular, elite, or sectarian. It may also be based on scholarship and the use of critical methods in the interest of advancing a taste for literature, art, learning, and science."

MEDIEVAL CHRISTENDOM

Among the heirs of Greece (through Rome) and of Israel were the Christians of varying professions. Perhaps the most dramatic form of censorship in Christendom was that displayed in the development by the Roman Catholic Church of the *Index Librorum Prohibitorum,* a list of proscribed books, the origins of which go back (in a primitive form) to the 5th century AD and which continued to have official sanction well into the 20th century. The most spectacular instance of the silencing of a thinker of note may well have been the restrictions placed upon Galileo in 1633.

The orthodoxy protected by an institution such as the *Index* probably had to be a system of thought in which much was made of certain books, particularly if other publications should seem to challenge in significant respects the teachings of the canonical texts. This must have become even more acute a problem when means became available, especially after the invention of printing, to produce and distribute books in large quantities.

The establishment of a fairly precise orthodoxy led to a perhaps unprecedented recourse to creeds. Thus, for example, the Nicene Creed was promulgated in AD 325. It was devised to fend off a heretical threat to Christian doctrine—and it led, partly because of a unilateral change in wording made by the Western church, to the Schism of 1054 between Eastern Orthodoxy and Roman Catholicism.

Thus, it very much mattered which doctrines people were taught and what came to be believed—and this was largely determined, as it usually is, by the action of some authority, ecclesiastical or temporal. Similar developments can be seen in the Islāmic world down to this day.

It is difficult to distinguish religious and nonreligious elements in the more celebrated controversies of the medieval Christian world, just as it is today among Islāmic peoples. The persecutions of witches—which ranged across much of western Europe from the 14th to the 18th century and cost hundreds of thousands, if not millions, of lives—can be understood as due to any number of political, social, and psychic disturbances as well as to strictly religious differences.

Joan of Arc and Thomas More

The trials of Joan of Arc in France (1431) and of Thomas More in England (1535) are notorious illustrations of the difficulty in distinguishing religious from political differences. Indeed, it has been common, because of the experiences of the Middle Ages and of the Renaissance, to see the cause of political liberty as intimately related to the cause of religious liberty (and especially the liberty to do without religion).

The Enlightenment, beginning in the 17th century, attempted to purge Europe of the censorship that found political despotism allied with religious traditionalism. Alexis de Tocqueville was astonished to find in the United States, in the 1830s, that it was possible for ordinary men who stood for political freedom to be, and to remain, religiously devout. This was not the typical combination in the Europe of his day.

Even so, it should be recognized that the rigorous medieval theological–political regime against which moderns have rebelled did have at its core a principle that subjected the exercise of will (or sovereignty) to the test of wisdom. This principle, upon which the contemporary dedication to freedom of speech may ultimately depend, is reflected in Thomas Aquinas' insistence in *De veritate* (Q. 23), ". . . to say that justice depends simply upon the will is to

say that the divine will does not proceed according to the order of wisdom, and that is blasphemous."

THE 17TH AND 18TH CENTURIES

The struggle against censorship in the Anglo-American world in the 17th and 18th centuries took two principal forms. There was the effort to keep government from reviewing, before publication, any manuscript, and there was the effort to keep government from penalizing, after publication, any text that expressed forbidden sentiments. (There were throughout the Western world developments with respect to these matters similar to those in Great Britain and the United States, but they usually occurred later.)

The effort to eliminate "previous restraints" (also known as prior restraints) in Great Britain and in America had its roots in English constitutional experience. Previous restraint (or licensing) came to be regarded as an inheritance of Roman Catholic practices. And so, when the Anglican successor to the Roman Catholic Church was disestablished by the Puritans, it was something of a shock to John Milton to find Parliament reinstating licensing in 1643.

Milton's "Areopagitica" (1644) has remained the classic statement of the arguments against censorship, particularly in the form of previous restraint. Milton conceded that criminal prosecutions might, perhaps even should, follow upon the publication of certain writings. He insisted, however, that such works must not be suppressed before publication.

Milton's "Areopagitica"

Critical to Milton's position in support of freedom of the press is something that may not have been implicit in the traditional pre-Miltonian position against censorship—his confidence that truth, "in a free and open encounter," will overcome error. Related to this opinion is the assurance that it is a positive good for mankind to be exposed to error; only in this way may virtue be tested, strengthened, and made adequate to the trials of earthly life. Milton cannot praise "a fugitive and cloister'd virtue." This perspective seems to rest upon a Christian view of the world: truth may indeed win out in its encounter with error, if the struggle continues long enough and if divine aid is thrown into the balance, as Milton seems to assume it will be; an individual must not only act virtuously, but he must act virtuously because he has chosen to do so; he must be exposed to alternatives, as inevitably he will be, and he must choose rightly if he is to merit and secure eternal salvation.

A reliance upon due process of law (which Milton in effect calls for) is the vital concession that the community can be led to make to reason: it provides a safeguard that must be so well established in times of calm and reflection that it is held to firmly, as a tenet of a common political faith, when the community is almost beside itself with passion. And, Milton might add if he were to use modern terminology, due process provides the ground rules for that free and open encounter in which truth may indeed prevail over error.

Thus, it is against the polemical background provided by Milton's "Areopagitica" that the abandonment of prepublication censorship in England in 1695 could be properly seen as a great victory for liberty of the press in Anglo-American constitutional history. And so, in 1765–69, William Blackstone could say about the English common law with respect to liberty of the press in his *Commentaries on the Laws of England:*

Blackstone's *Commentaries*

The liberty of the press . . . consists in laying no *previous* restraints upon publications, and not in freedom from censure for criminal matter when published. Every freeman has an undoubted right to lay what sentiments he pleases before the public; to forbid this, is to destroy the freedom of the press: but if he publishes what is improper, mischievous, or illegal, he must take the consequence of his own temerity.

The next major step in the Anglo-American response to censorship problems may be seen in the First Amendment to the Constitution of the United States. That amendment, ratified in 1791, provides:

Congress shall make no law respecting an establishment of religion, or prohibiting the free exercise thereof; or abridging the

Freedom
of speech

freedom of speech, or of the press; or the right of the people peaceably to assemble and to petition the Government for a redress of grievances.

Similar provisions may be found in most of the state constitutions in the United States, although the connection between political and religious liberty is not always recognized to be as intimate as it is in the First Amendment.

Such a guarantee of freedom of the press as is found in U.S. constitutional documents has long been understood to foreclose the possibility of previous restraints, thereby confirming the definition of "liberty of the press" found in Blackstone's *Commentaries.* A few scholars and jurists have gone so far as to suggest that the First Amendment and the state constitutional provisions do no more than limit restraints prior to publication, but it is difficult to bring the "freedom of speech" language (often found in the same guarantees) within this suggestion, since there never had been (and, in the nature of things, could never easily be) previous restraint upon what might be spoken (as distinguished from what might be printed). Rather, as indicated above, "freedom of speech" is modelled upon the British parliamentary privilege, a privilege that should be generally available when a people becomes sovereign in the fashion of the American people. (In addition, the celebrated case of John Peter Zenger [1735] had already established for Americans the principle that truth was a defense in seditious libel prosecutions, thus going beyond Blackstone's position in still another respect.)

The traditional parliamentary privilege—which is still guaranteed in the United States to members of Congress and to state legislators—can be considered virtually absolute in the protection it provides legislators against being held accountable "in any other place" for what they utter in a legislative body. The question remains, of course, as to precisely what kinds of matters may be discussed freely, and without fear of sanction, by citizens entitled to such protection as is provided by the First Amendment.

The old-fashioned answer was that the kind of discussion primarily protected by the First Amendment is that of citizens engaged in investigating and assessing the public business. Such protected discussion may be found in art, in moral and scientific inquiry, and in advertising, as well as in obvious political discourse. Thus, whatever is suppressed because of political differences is likely, in the circumstances, to be "political." Another way of putting this is to say that the crime of seditious libel is not consistent with the First Amendment. Particularly influential spokesmen for this position in the 20th century have been Alexander Meiklejohn (1872–1964), Hugo L. Black (1886–1971), Harry Kalven, Jr. (1914–74), and Malcolm P. Sharp (1897–1980). It is a position epitomized by its questioning of the constitutionality of the Sedition Act enacted by Congress in 1798.

The Sedition Act made criminal the publication of "any false, scandalous and malicious writing . . . against the government of the United States, or either House of Congress . . . or the President . . . with intent to defame [them] or to bring them . . . into contempt or disrepute." This act, which was allowed to lapse after two years, has been generally repudiated by American jurists and scholars. The U.S. credo in these matters may well be found in Thomas Jefferson's First Inaugural Address (1801), in which he said, "If there be any among us who would wish to dissolve this Union or to change its republican form, let them stand undisturbed as monuments of the safety with which error of opinion may be tolerated where reason is left free to combat it."

The First Amendment guarantee of freedom of speech and of the press was anticipated, in effect, by the provision of the Constitution (drafted in 1787) that "Treason against the United States shall consist only in levying War against them, or in adhering to their Enemies, giving them Aid and Comfort." This, too, has made it difficult to prosecute citizens for their criticism of government, something that had been much easier to do under an expansive definition of treason. The First Amendment guarantee was anticipated as well by the assumption evident in the Declaration of Independence that a people is always entitled to examine and to assess the doings of its governments, all with a view to being able to replace any government deemed upon due consideration to be unsatisfactory.

There can be no doubt that the extensive freedom of Americans to discuss political matters can lead to serious abuses. But it is generally recognized that the abuses resulting from censorship of such discussion—whether in the form of previous restraints or in the form of postpublication sanctions—are apt to be even more serious for a community.

Perhaps not as generally recognized is that considerable self-restraint is required, especially on the part of intellectuals, if the best possible use is to be made of free discussion in the circumstances of a people. A call for such restraint (or self-censorship), as well as for both public enlightenment and respect for organized religion, may be seen in George Washington's Farewell Address (1796). Similarly, Lord Macaulay could say of the 19th-century British press, "Foreigners who dare not print a word reflecting on the government under which they live, are at a loss to understand how it happens that the freest press in Europe is the most prudish."

MODERN PRACTICES

The Soviet system.   The *Index,* which was abolished by the Roman Catholic Church in 1966, may be seen in another form in the Soviet Union, where there is a comprehensive system of supervision of manuscripts before publication. (Similar control, in varying degrees, is exercised in other countries with Marxist governments.) Such supervision, in the light of official Communist Party doctrines, is not limited to political discussions or to books and newspapers but seems to cover all kinds of subjects and all forms of publication, including broadcasts. This leads, in effect, to considerable self-censorship by authors seeking to be published in some form. Of course, the more "unreliable" authors are simply refused publication in the conventional places.

The comprehensive Soviet system has led to the development of a sophisticated mode of guarded expression in print, which is designed to conform with official proprieties even as signals are given to the more perceptive about impending political shifts. It has, as well, led to (or perhaps permitted the perpetuation of) such expedients as the transformation of the circus clown into a tolerated means for exhibiting and venting public exasperation with the regime. All in all, in such circumstances, the bearing of persecution on the art of writing can be seen.

There have been, in recent decades, periodic relaxations of control in the Soviet Union, but a pervasive and shameless control by the Communist Party oligarchy remains. A limited uncensored circulation is effected by privately copied manuscripts; a few authors have had their manuscripts published abroad. And then there are materials that are smuggled into the Soviet Union, as well as foreign radio broadcasts, which are "jammed" from time to time. But these exceptional modes provide uncensored information and discussion only to a very small number of Soviet citizens. The large body of citizens knows, by and large, only what the government has chosen to reveal, often being ignorant of critical conditions and developments in its own country (such as the serious illness of a Soviet leader) that are well known abroad.

This sort of control is justified as necessary for the protection of the state and the welfare of its citizenry. Some of the restrictions are designed to control information that is considered vital to national security; others are designed to keep citizens from being "misled," especially since a proper understanding of "dialectical materialism" is said to be necessary to determine what is relevant and what contributes to the health of the community and the well-being and moral soundness of citizens. Variations of the arguments used in the Soviet Union today may be found in medieval apologetics, in Confucian doctrines, in Plato's *Republic,* and in UNESCO proposals for "a new world information and communication order."

How seriously such arguments are to be taken depends, in part, on whose interest the rulers exercising this control truly serve. George Orwell, in his novel *Nineteen Eighty-four* (1949), displayed a ruling class that was evi-

Orwell's
*Nineteen
Eighty-four*

dently drawn in large part from his study of the practices of the ruling party in the Soviet Union. The rulers in *Nineteen Eighty-four,* when they speak most frankly, disavow serving any interest but their own, whatever they may say publicly about national security and national progress. Such ruthless self-centredness on the part of rulers fits the traditional definition of tyranny. (It is not necessary to be concerned here with whether or not such a completely self-centred tyranny, which must be rare, would be likely to withstand determined opposition by men and women willing to sacrifice themselves.)

The portrayal in *Nineteen Eighty-four* is particularly gripping because it suggests how extensive the modern control of ideas can be. (Developments with respect to computers and information banks subsequent to the publication of Orwell's novel make the prospects of comprehensive control seem even more ominous.) The ultimate in censorship may be seen, in the novel, in a technology and an ideology that permit government to edit not only what is being said today and tomorrow but also what is recorded or remembered to have been said yesterday. The Western reader of *Nineteen Eighty-four* is likely to be offended not only by its government's efforts to control political discussion but also by the official assumption that the individual has no standing worthy of serious consideration.

It is unlikely that any system of censorship in the world today, with the possible exception of that in the People's Republic of China, is as effective as that in the Soviet Union. But official secrecy, as well as tyranny, is something to which Russians have long been accustomed. (In the late 19th century, the Russians had perhaps the only extensive censorship system in the world.) It is instructive, therefore, to consider how censorship works today in countries with somewhat more experience in self-government.

Censorship under a military government. Particularly revealing in this respect was what happened in Greece between 1967 and 1974, when a conspiracy of junior army officers seized control of the government. The dependence of Greece upon foreign trade and tourism made it difficult to keep out the foreign press and foreign broadcasts. This meant, among other things, that the more educated citizens in the country were always fairly well informed about what was going on in the world at large. But information about domestic affairs (especially economic data) was hard to come by, since much of that kind of information depends in modern times (as in ancient China) upon official sources. (To cite other, perhaps better known examples, there is a chronic complaint about the unreliability of official Soviet statistics, and the strict censorship in Poland during the 1970s kept the Communist government there from becoming aware of how serious the country's economic problems were, leading to considerable domestic turmoil. Such regimes depend, in effect, upon free peoples to do their thinking for them about the most serious matters.)

The limits of government censorship in a country such as Greece, where the press (unlike the broadcast media) is not owned by the government, are in part determined by the fact that much of the business of daily life depends on fairly reliable newspaper operations. All kinds of information—about goods for sale, about schedules and timetables, about innumerable activities upon which an efficient daily life depends—must be published regularly and reliably in the press, whoever may be in power. This means that newspapers must not be unduly delayed in their appearance; it also means that if they are to continue to appear they must be profitable.

The censor who is too slow (that is, careful) in reviewing everything that is to appear in a forthcoming daily newspaper jams up the works. And if he is too restrictive in what he does permit, the paper is apt to become so dull that readers do not buy it. Either way, sales suffer and newspapers go out of business.

What happens in practice is that a rough accommodation develops between an editor and his censor. Each can make the duties of the other a constant aggravation. The accommodation worked out is rather like that which guards and inmates arrive at in their collaborative governance of a prison. One critical problem in maintaining indefinitely

Censorship in Greece, 1967–74

a system of censorship is, as Milton pointed out, that it is dull, unrewarding work for the typical censor—and so the quality of people drawn to it tends to deteriorate.

Of course, one way of avoiding much of the difficulty, expense, and inefficiency of a system of prepublication censorship is simply to allow each editor to publish as he chooses, subject to the risk of prosecution for whatever is published contrary to the standards laid down by the regime. But it is far from easy, even in a dictatorial regime, to prosecute effectively so long as some semblance of due process remains. It appears simpler for dictators to refuse to permit a particular newspaper report to be published than it is to explain in open court what was wrong with the report once published. Whether it is indeed simpler can be doubted, however, considering the mammoth effort required to supervise the many innocuous reports that make up the bulk of any newspaper.

It should be evident from these observations that "censorship" is used today in two senses. The more limited, perhaps more rigorous, sense refers to a system of prepublication control; the broader sense includes, in addition, sanctions visited upon a publisher after publication (whether or not the publication has previously been "approved"). Something analogous to prepublication censorship is often said, by contemporary psychologists, to operate in the human psyche to prevent the conscious awareness of any unacceptable desires harboured in the unconscious. Comparable suppression, as well as intimidation, may be seen in the political world, when prosecution and persecution for various kinds of associations and actions can render certain opinions virtually unthinkable.

Two meanings of "censorship"

Postpublication censorship does tend to be moderated to the extent that there is the rule of law in the community (including trials that are conducted more or less in public). The Greek military government of 1967–74 was repeatedly embarrassed by the trials it dared to conduct in public. The same could be said of the South African government since World War II, so long as an independent judiciary was trying sedition cases. (One result of this was that certain cases involving "national security" were removed, by act of the South African Parliament, from the ordinary jurisdiction of the courts. Or, to put this in terms familiar in Anglo-American law, nothing comparable to a habeas corpus hearing is permitted in South Africa today in certain categories of cases.) In the Soviet Union, on the other hand, the judicial proceeding in a political case seems, by and large, to be but another tool of government policy: in such circumstances, there may not be much to choose from between prior restraint and postpublication sanctions if an efficient allocation of resources is not a concern.

Censorship in the United States. *Freedom of the press.* One of the most dramatic attempts by the government of the United States to exercise prepublication restraint occurred in connection with the *Pentagon Papers* (1971), a "top secret" multivolume report on the Vietnam War that was surreptitiously supplied to various newspapers, which then began to publish it in installments. Each newspaper that managed to secure and thereupon to publish the report was enjoined in turn, at the request of the U.S. Department of Justice. The Supreme Court of the United States, after hearing arguments, lifted the injunctions and publication proceeded.

The Pentagon Papers

This case points up how difficult it is, in the United States today, to prevent publication, whatever recourse there may be to criminal sanctions or to damage suits after unauthorized or improper publication. Of course, it cannot be known whether the Supreme Court would have acted differently if the *Pentagon Papers* documents had been more current or if they had dealt with even more sensitive materials.

By the very nature of things, prepublication restraint is, in the United States, a rare occurrence. Thus, if each newspaper that began to publish the *Pentagon Papers* had published in one issue everything it had, that would have been the end of the previous-restraint case. And it should be obvious that that is the typical situation in the United States: the first the government usually knows about any publication is when the newspaper comes out—and by that time, of course, prepublication restraint is out of the question.

Thus, the U.S. government, in order to keep certain information out of the press, has to depend upon its ability to select those to whom sensitive information may be entrusted. Otherwise, the judgment of editors must be relied upon. There is nothing in the United States comparable to the Official Secrets Act and the "D" notice system in Great Britain, which, it seems, effectively restrain editors from publishing materials bearing certain restrictive designations. An attempt was made in 1983–84 by the U.S. government to require thousands of officials handling classified matter to pledge that they would submit any future writings for prepublication review by government censors. Opposition in Congress kept the new code from taking effect.

Private property and censorship

Contributing massively to the absence of censorship in any country is the existence there of considerable private property. Not only do personal resources provide a cushion against government unfriendliness, but they also provide independent access to the means of publication, if only in the form of a private printing with private circulation or of paid advertisements in the press. The attempts at censorship encountered in the United States today testify, in effect, to the importance of private property for freedom of the press. The instances of censorship that have been widely publicized generally have to do with public libraries, textbook selections, and government employment contracts. But in these instances, as with most of the repressive measures of the 1940s and 1950s, public funding, government authority, or a critical dependence upon public opinion—as in the case of the motion-picture and broadcast industries—is involved. Otherwise, there would be no effective way for either the government or public opinion to control what is published—certainly not when anyone with private means is determined to make his opinions known.

Parallel to the immunity provided by the institution of private property is that provided in the United States by academic freedom in colleges and universities. This freedom, which encourages scholars and teachers to traffic in unpopular truths, rests in part on the private property of tenured appointments. On the other hand, libel suits on behalf of another kind of private property—the interest everyone has in his reputation—are seen by some as a growing danger to freedom of the press. That is, concern has been expressed lest the protection provided by *New York Times Co.* v. *Sullivan* (1964) be eroded. In that case, the U.S. Supreme Court required that any public official who sues for damages because of an alleged falsehood prove that the falsehood had been issued with knowledge that it was false or in reckless disregard of whether it was false or not. The court was determined to protect the press from the prospects of large damage awards in libel cases that would intimidate it into drastic self-censorship. The court also saw itself as confirming the settled U.S. opinion condemning the Sedition Act of 1798.

A different kind of "protection" for the press, less welcome to journalists, was the decision by the U.S. government not to permit reporters to accompany the troops invading Grenada in 1983. Critical to the controversy on that occasion was a general concern that too much of the information necessary for adequate discussion of public affairs remains within the exclusive control of government. Thus, it is sometimes said, neither previous restraint nor postpublication restraint need be resorted to by a government able to shape public opinion simply by regulating the flow of vital information as it pleases. This, too, can be considered a form of censorship, the more insidious in that it is obviously sensible in some cases to restrict public access to information for the sake of legitimate defense, diplomatic and administrative efficiency, privacy interests, and professional confidential relations.

Still another form of censorship may take the form of the preferences government bodies exhibit through the financial and other support they distribute to artistic, scientific, and educational applicants. And yet it is generally recognized that such distribution can be helpful, perhaps even necessary, and that it has to be done on the basis of standards that must rely on the good faith judgment of public officials. Here, as elsewhere, an informed and vigilant citizenry may be the best guarantor of both quality and fairness.

Freedom of expression. Postpublication restraint was used in the courts, between 1948 and 1961, against leaders of the Communist Party in the United States. Even so, the indictments in those cases were couched in terms of a conspiracy to overthrow the government. That is, despite the unpopularity of the defendants and their political opinions in a time of considerable international tension, no U.S. government could rely merely on the fact that people found the opinions promulgated to be offensive. An effort had to be made to connect what the defendants were saying to what they (and others elsewhere) were likely to do.

Still, such prosecutions were confronted by the prohibition in the First Amendment that "Congress shall make no law . . . abridging the freedom of speech, or of the press." But the apparent absoluteness of that prohibition had long been subverted by the ill-conceived, yet all too influential, statement by Justice Oliver Wendell Holmes in *United States* v. *Schenck* (1919):

. . . the character of every act depends upon the circumstances in which it is done. The most stringent protection of free speech would not protect a man in falsely shouting fire in a theatre and causing a panic. [The] question in every case is whether the words used are used in such circumstances and are of such a nature as to create a clear and present danger that they will bring about the substantive evils that Congress has a right to prevent.

There does not seem to be much doubt that the man who deliberately causes a panic in a theatre should be dealt with firmly. But it is far from clear that this sensible conclusion has justified punishing men and women whose principal offense seems to have been that of raising fundamental (however ill-conceived) objections to the established political, economic, and social arrangements in the United States. Justice Holmes's constitutional flexibility in the Schenck case can be considered to have culminated in the later assurance by Chief Justice Fred M. Vinson in *Dennis* v. *United States* (1951), in which the convictions of a dozen Communist Party leaders were upheld:

Dennis v. United States

Nothing is more certain in modern society than the principle that there are no absolutes, that a name, a phrase, a standard has meaning only when associated with the considerations which gave birth to the nomenclature. . . . To those who would paralyze our government in the face of impending threats by encasing it in a semantic straitjacket we must reply that all concepts are relative.

This is hardly in the spirit of Milton's high confidence in the power of an enduring truth to prevail. Nor is it in the spirit of the Declaration of Independence, with its informed reliance upon natural rights, upon self-evident truths, and hence upon the right of revolution.

Be that as it may, it is unlikely that any of the prosecutions from the Schenck to the Dennis case and beyond for what was, in effect, sedition would succeed under present conditions. The sorts of things those defendants said are no longer considered dangerous by the community at large. Rather, the much more vexing question is whether any kind of speech is not entitled to First Amendment protection. That protection is now said to extend far beyond political discussion. Thus, advertising (or commercial speech) is said to be protected as is much (if not virtually all) obscenity, although reservations are heard about child pornography and about inducements to violence and the worst depravity. (Whether any particular utterance or action should be regulated has itself always been a political question open to free discussion.)

Much is made today of an asserted right of self-expression and of the related right to privacy. The arguments drawn upon in their support seem to be variations of those developed in John Stuart Mill's *On Liberty* (1859). Mill's arguments are invoked not only in opposition to government censorship but in opposition as well to those suppressive efforts by private organizations that are sometimes more effective than government can be in a liberal democracy. Particularly susceptible to the influence of private censors are the broadcasting media, especially since they are still subject in the United States to some government regulation. A different kind of private suppression has been usefully described in this fashion by Jamie Kalven: "Being badly edited is as close as most American writers ever come to being censored. It thus offers a vehicle for imagining the *experience* of censorship, for getting at what it *feels* like. My strongest impression is that the abuse of one's prose feels like an assault on one's mind." Similarly, Lord Radcliffe could speak of "the real licensors of thought today, the editors, the publishers, the producers, the controllers of radio and television."

Character and freedom

Lord Radcliffe could speak as well about "the apparent indifference of censors of all kinds to the depiction or portrayal of mindless violence and brutality, that witless rejection of civility that threatens to be the Black Death of the twentieth century." Thus, it is not usually noticed today that Mill recognized that a people has to be trained properly to make use of the considerable liberty he advocates. If, for example, a community should recognize that television is corrupting the young, distorting the political process, and generally playing havoc with education and the public character, is it really helpless to do anything about it? Would it be censorship to abolish altogether such a baleful influence? And if abolition of television should be considered censorship, may not that suggest that censorship is not altogether bad? What, in short, is the popular character presupposed for effective self-government, and how is that character properly to be developed and maintained?

Such questions reflect the fact that censorship and freedom of the press problems depend for their sensible resolution upon more general considerations of liberty, of the common good, and of the rights, virtues, and duties of citizens entrusted with self-government. Thus, Tocqueville could observe in *Democracy in America* (1835–40):

It cannot be repeated too often: nothing is more fertile in marvels than the art of being free, but nothing is harder than freedom's apprenticeship. The same is not true of despotism. Despotism often presents itself as the repairer of all the ills suffered, the support of just rights, defender of the oppressed, and founder of order. People are lulled to sleep by the temporary prosperity it engenders, and when they do wake up, they are wretched. But liberty is generally born in stormy weather, growing with difficulty amid civil discords, and only when it is already old does one see the blessings it has brought.

Among the blessings of liberty may be found the philosophical pursuits that have sometimes appeared so threatening to public order. Laurence Berns has reformulated the ancient dilemma posed by the trial of Socrates, "the greatest hero of freedom of thought"—a dilemma that exposes one of the roots of the perennial censorship controversy:

Is philosophy, the intransigent quest for truth (including the truth about politics and religion), inherently subversive? Does it necessarily undermine political society and conventional morality, or, on the contrary, is a good society impossible without freedom to philosophize?

BIBLIOGRAPHY.   In addition to the works of William Blackstone, Confucius, John Stuart Mill, John Milton, Plato, Alexis de Tocqueville, and Thomas Aquinas mentioned in the text, see GEORGE ANASTAPLO, *The Constitutionalist: Notes on the First Amendment* (1971), *Human Being and Citizen: Essays on Virtue, Freedom and the Common Good* (1975), his article on Greece in the 15th ed. of *Encyclopædia Britannica,* and his article on Confucian thought in *Great Ideas Today* (1984); LARRY ARNHART, *Aristotle on Political Reasoning* (1981); WALTER BERNS, *Freedom, Virtue and the First Amendment* (1957); REDMOND A. BURKE, *What Is the Index?* (1952); ZECHARIAH CHAFEE, *Free Speech in the United States* (1941); HARRY M. CLOR, *Obscenity and Public Morality* (1969), and (ed.), *The Mass Media and Modern Democracy* (1974), including an essay on the Pentagon Papers controversy and on the abolition of television; JOSEPH CROPSEY (ed.), *Ancients and Moderns* (1964), including essays by LAURENCE BERNS on Aristotle's *Poetics* and HILAIL GILDIN on John Stuart Mill's *On Liberty;* WILLIAM W. CROSSKEY, *Politics and the Constitution in the History of the United States* (1953, reissued 1978); LEO PAUL DeALVAREZ (ed.), *Abraham Lincoln, the Gettysburg Address, and American Constitutionalism* (1976); EDWARD DeGRAZIA, *Censorship Landmarks* (1969); MARTIN DEWHIRST and ROBERT FARRELL (eds.), *The Soviet Censorship* (1973); THOMAS I. EMERSON, *Political and Civil Rights in the United States,* 4th ed., 2 vol. (1976–79), a new ed. by NORMAN DORSEN, PAUL BENDER, and BURT NEUBORNE; GERALD GUNTHER (ed.), *Cases and Materials on Constitutional Law,* 10th ed. (1980); HARRY KALVEN, *The Negro and the First Amendment* (1965); STANLEY N. KATZ (ed.), *A Brief Narrative of the Case and Trial of John Peter Zenger,* 2nd ed. (1972); LEONARD W. LEVY, *Legacy of Suppression: Freedom of Speech and Press in Early American History* (1960); WILLIAM B. LOCKHART, Y. KAMISAR, and J.H. CHOPER (eds.), *Constitutional Law: Cases, Comments, Questions* (1980); HARVEY LOMAX (ed.), *A Contemporary Bibliography in Political Philosophy and in Other Areas* (1976); RALPH E. McCOY (ed.), *Freedom of the Press: An Annotated Bibliography* (1968; suppl., 1979); ROBERT MCDONALD, *Pillar and Tinderbox: The Greek Press and the Dictatorship* (1983); RICHARD MCKEON, ROBERT K. MERTON, and WALTER GELLHORN, *The Freedom to Read* (1957); ALEXANDER MEIKLEJOHN, *Political Freedom* (1960, reprinted 1979), MALCOLM P. SHARP, "Crosskey, Anastaplo and Meiklejohn on the United States Constitution," in *University of Chicago Law School Record* (Spring 1973); YVES R. SIMON, *The Philosophy of Democratic Government* (1951, reissued 1977); LEO STRAUSS, *Persecution and the Art of Writing* (1952, reprinted 1973), *Natural Right and History* (1953), and with JOSEPH CROPSEY (eds.), *History of Political Philosophy,* 2nd ed. (1972, reprinted 1981).

(GEORGE ANASTAPLO)

Human Rights

It is a common observation that human beings everywhere demand the realization of diverse values to ensure their individual and collective well-being. It also is a common observation that these demands are often painfully frustrated by social as well as natural forces, resulting in exploitation, oppression, persecution, and other forms of deprivation. Deeply rooted in these twin observations are the beginnings of what today are called "human rights" and the legal processes, national and international, associated with them.

This article is divided into the following sections:

Historical development

The expression "human rights" is relatively new, having come into everyday parlance only since World War II and the founding of the United Nations in 1945. It replaces the phrase "natural rights"—which fell into disfavour in part because the concept of natural law (to which it was intimately linked) had become a matter of great controversy, and the later phrase "the rights of Man," which was not universally understood to include the rights of women.

Most students of human rights trace the historical origins of the concept back to ancient Greece and Rome, where it was closely tied to the premodern natural law doctrines of Greek Stoicism (the school of philosophy founded by Zeno of Citium, which held that a universal working force pervades all creation and that human conduct therefore should be judged according to, and brought into harmony with, the law of nature). The classic example, drawn from the Greek literature, is that of Antigone, who, upon being reproached by Creon for defying his command not to bury her slain brother, defended her conduct by asserting that she acted in accordance with the immutable laws of the gods.

In part because Hellenistic Stoicism played a key role in its formation and spread, Roman law may similarly be seen to have allowed for the existence of a natural law and, with it, pursuant to the *jus gentium* ("law of nations"), certain universal rights that extended beyond the rights of citizenship. According to the Roman jurist Ulpian, for example, natural law was that which nature—not the state—assures to all human beings, Roman citizen or not.

It was not until after the Middle Ages, however, that natural law doctrines became closely associated with liberal political theories about natural rights. In Greco-Roman and medieval times, natural law doctrines taught mainly the duties, as distinguished from the rights, of "Man." Moreover, as evident in the writings of Aristotle and St. Thomas Aquinas, these doctrines recognized the legitimacy of slavery and serfdom and, in so doing, excluded perhaps the centralmost ideas of human rights as they are understood today—the ideas of freedom (or liberty) and equality.

For the idea of human (*i.e.*, natural) rights to take hold as a general social need and reality, it was necessary that basic changes in the beliefs and practices of society take place, changes of the sort that evolved from about the 13th century to the Peace of Westphalia (1648), during the Renaissance and the decline of feudalism. When resistance to religious intolerance and political–economic bondage began the long transition to liberal notions of freedom and equality, particularly in relation to the use and ownership of property, then were the foundations of what today are called human rights truly laid. During this period, reflecting the failure of rulers to meet their natural law obligations as well as the unprecedented commitment to individual expression and worldly experience that was characteristic of the Renaissance, the shift from natural law as duties to natural law as rights was made. The teachings of Aquinas (1224/25–1274) and Hugo Grotius (1583–1645) on the European continent, and the Magna Carta (1215), the Petition of Right of 1628, and the English Bill of Rights (1689) in England, were proof of this change. All testified to the increasingly popular view that human beings are endowed with eternal and inalienable rights, never renounced when humankind "contracted" to enter the social from the primitive state and never diminished by the claim of "the divine right of kings."

It was primarily for the 17th and 18th centuries, however, to elaborate upon this modernist conception of natural law as meaning or implying natural rights. The scientific and intellectual achievements of the 17th century—the discoveries of Galileo and Sir Isaac Newton, the materialism of Thomas Hobbes, the rationalism of René Descartes and Gottfried Wilhelm Leibniz, the pantheism of Benedict de Spinoza, the empiricism of Francis Bacon and John Locke—encouraged a belief in natural law and universal order; and during the 18th century, the so-called Age of Enlightenment, a growing confidence in human reason and in the perfectability of human affairs led to its more comprehensive expression. Particularly to be noted are the writings of the 17th-century English philosopher John Locke—arguably the most important natural law theorist of modern times—and the works of the 18th-century Philosophes centred mainly in Paris, including Montesquieu, Voltaire, and Jean-Jacques Rousseau. Locke argued in detail, mainly in writings associated with the Revolution of 1688 (the Glorious Revolution), that certain rights self-evidently pertain to individuals as human beings (because they existed in "the state of nature" before humankind entered civil society); that chief among them are the rights to life, liberty (freedom from arbitrary rule), and property; that, upon entering civil society (pursuant to a "social contract"), humankind surrendered to the state only the right to enforce these natural rights, not the rights themselves; and that the state's failure to secure these reserved natural rights (the state itself being under contract to safeguard the interests of its members) gives rise to a right to responsible, popular revolution. The Philosophes, building on Locke and others and embracing many and varied currents of thought with a common supreme faith in reason, vigorously attacked religious and scientific dogmatism, intolerance, censorship, and social–economic restraints. They sought to discover and act upon universally valid principles harmoniously governing nature, humanity, and society, including the theory of the inalienable "rights of Man" that became their fundamental ethical and social gospel.

All this liberal intellectual ferment had, not surprisingly, great influence on the Western world of the late 18th and early 19th centuries. Together with the practical example of England's Revolution of 1688 and the resulting Bill of Rights, it provided the rationale for the wave of revolutionary agitation that then swept the West, most notably in North America and France. Thomas Jefferson, who

(margin notes)

Influence
of the
Renaissance

Ideas of
Locke

Origins

had studied Locke and Montesquieu and who asserted that his countrymen were a "free people claiming their rights as derived from the laws of nature and not as the gift of their Chief Magistrate," gave poetic eloquence to the plain prose of the 17th century in the Declaration of Independence proclaimed by the 13 American Colonies on July 4, 1776: "We hold these truths to be self-evident, that all men are created equal, that they are endowed by their Creator with certain unalienable Rights, that among these are Life, Liberty and the Pursuit of Happiness." Similarly, the Marquis de Lafayette, who won the close friendship of George Washington and who shared the hardships of the American War of Independence, imitated the pronouncements of the English and American revolutions in the Declaration of the Rights of Man and of the Citizen of August 26, 1789. Insisting that "men are born and remain free and equal in rights," the declaration proclaims that "the aim of every political association is the preservation of the natural and imprescriptible rights of man," identifies these rights as "Liberty, Property, Safety and Resistance to Oppression," and defines "liberty" so as to include the right to free speech, freedom of association, religious freedom, and freedom from arbitrary arrest and confinement (as if anticipating the Bill of Rights added in 1791 to the Constitution of the United States of 1787).

In sum, the idea of human rights, called by another name, played a key role in the late 18th- and early 19th-century struggles against political absolutism. It was, indeed, the failure of rulers to respect the principles of freedom and equality, which had been central to natural law philosophy almost from the beginning, that was responsible for this development. In the words of Maurice Cranston, a leading student of human rights, " . . . absolutism prompted man to claim [human, or natural] rights precisely because it denied them."

The idea of human rights as natural rights was not without its detractors, however, even at this otherwise receptive time. In the first place, being frequently associated with religious orthodoxy, the doctrine of natural rights became less and less acceptable to philosophical and political liberals. Additionally, because they were conceived in essentially absolutist—"inalienable," "unalterable," "eternal"— terms, natural rights were found increasingly to come into conflict with one another. Most importantly, the doctrine of natural rights came under powerful philosophical and political attack from both the right and the left.

Burke, Hume, and Bentham

In England, for example, conservatives Edmund Burke and David Hume united with liberal Jeremy Bentham in condemning the doctrine, the former out of fear that public affirmation of natural rights would lead to social upheaval, the latter out of concern lest declarations and proclamations of natural rights substitute for effective legislation. In his *Reflections on the Revolution in France* (1790), Burke, a believer in natural law who nonetheless denied that the "rights of Man" could be derived from it, criticized the drafters of the Declaration of the Rights of Man and of the Citizen for proclaiming the "monstrous fiction" of human equality, which, he argued, serves but to inspire "false ideas and vain expectations in men destined to travel in the obscure walk of laborious life." Bentham, one of the founders of Utilitarianism and a nonbeliever, was no less scornful. "Rights," he wrote, "is the child of law; from real law come real rights; but from imaginary laws, from 'law of nature,' come imaginary rights. . . . Natural rights is simple nonsense; natural and imprescriptible rights (an American phrase), rhetorical nonsense, nonsense upon stilts." Hume agreed with Bentham; natural law and natural rights, he insisted, are unreal metaphysical phenomena.

This assault upon natural law and natural rights, thus begun during the late 18th century, both intensified and broadened during the 19th and early 20th centuries. John Stuart Mill, despite his vigorous defense of liberty, proclaimed that rights ultimately are founded on utility. The German jurist Friedrich Karl von Savigny, England's Sir Henry Maine, and other historicalists emphasized that rights are a function of cultural and environmental variables unique to particular communities. And the jurist John Austin and the philosopher Ludwig Wittgenstein in-

sisted, respectively, that the only law is "the command of the sovereign" (a phrase of Thomas Hobbes) and that the only truth is that which can be established by verifiable experience. By World War I, there were scarcely any theorists who would or could defend the "rights of Man" along the lines of natural law. Indeed, under the influence of 19th-century German Idealism and parallel expressions of rising European nationalism, there were some—the Marxists, for example—who, although not rejecting individual rights altogether, maintained that rights, from whatever source derived, belong to communities or whole societies and nations preeminently. Thus did F.H. Bradley, the British Idealist, write in 1894: "The rights of the individual are today not worth serious consideration. . . . The welfare of the community is the end and is the ultimate standard."

Yet, though the heyday of natural rights proved short, the idea of human rights nonetheless endured in one form or another. The abolition of slavery, factory legislation, popular education, trade unionism, the universal suffrage movement—these and other examples of 19th-century reformist impulse afford ample evidence that the idea was not to be extinguished even if its transempirical derivation had become a matter of general skepticism. But it was not until the rise and fall of Nazi Germany that the idea of rights—human rights—came truly into its own. The laws authorizing the dispossession and extermination of Jews and other minorities, the laws permitting arbitrary police search and seizure, the laws condoning imprisonment, torture, and execution without public trial—these and similar obscenities brought home the realization that law and morality, if they are to be deserving of the name, cannot be grounded in any purely Utilitarian, Idealist, or other consequentialist doctrine. Certain actions are wrong, no matter what; human beings are entitled to simple respect at least.

Today, the vast majority of legal scholars, philosophers, and moralists agree, irrespective of culture or civilization, that every human being is entitled, at least in theory, to some basic rights. Heir to the Protestant Reformation and to the English, American, French, Mexican, Russian, and Chinese revolutions, the last half of the 20th century has seen, in the words of human rights scholar Louis Henkin, "essentially universal acceptance of human rights in principle" such that "no government dares to dissent from the ideology of human rights today." Indeed, except for some essentially isolated 19-century demonstrations of international humanitarian concern to be noted below, the last half of the 20th century may fairly be said to mark the birth of the international as well as the universal recognition of human rights. In the treaty establishing the United Nations (UN), all members pledged themselves to take joint and separate action for the achievement of "universal respect for, and observance of, human rights and fundamental freedoms for all without distinction as to race, sex, language, or religion." In the Universal Declaration of Human Rights (1948), representatives from many diverse cultures endorsed the rights therein set forth "as a common standard of achievement for all peoples and all nations." And in 1976, the International Covenant on Economic, Social and Cultural Rights and the International Covenant on Civil and Political Rights, each approved by the UN General Assembly in 1966, entered into force and effect.

Human rights in the 20th century

Definition of human rights

To say that there is widespread acceptance of the principle of human rights on the domestic and international planes is not to say that there is complete agreement about the nature of such rights or their substantive scope—which is to say, their definition. Some of the most basic questions have yet to receive conclusive answers. Whether human rights are to be viewed as divine, moral, or legal entitlements; whether they are to be validated by intuition, custom, social contract theory, principles of distributive justice, or as prerequisites for happiness; whether they are to be understood as irrevocable or partially revocable; whether they are to be broad or limited in number and content—these and kindred issues are matters of ongoing debate and likely will remain so as long as there exist contending approaches to public order and scarcities among resources.

NATURE

Despite this lack of consensus, however, a number of widely accepted—and interrelated—postulates may be seen to assist, if not to complete, the task of defining human rights. Five in particular stand out, although it is to be noted that not even these are without controversy.

First, regardless of their ultimate origin or justification, human rights are understood to represent individual and group demands for the shaping and sharing of power, wealth, enlightenment, and other cherished values in community process, most fundamentally the value of respect and its constituent elements of reciprocal tolerance and mutual forebearance in the pursuit of all other values. Consequently, they imply claims against persons and institutions who impede realization and standards for judging the legitimacy of laws and traditions. At bottom, human rights limit state power.

Second, reflecting varying environmental circumstances, differing worldviews, and inescapable interdependencies within and between value processes, human rights refer to a wide continuum of value claims ranging from the most justiciable to the most aspirational. Human rights partake of both the legal and the moral orders, sometimes indistinguishably. They are expressive of both the "is" and the "ought" in human affairs.

Universal nature of human rights

Third, if a right is determined to be a human right it is quintessentially general or universal in character, in some sense equally possessed by all human beings everywhere, including in certain instances even the unborn. In stark contrast to "the divine right of kings" and other such conceptions of privilege, human rights extend, in theory, to every person on Earth without discriminations irrelevant to merit.

Fourth, most assertions of human rights—arguably not all—are qualified by the limitation that the rights of any particular individual or group in any particular instance are restricted as much as is necessary to secure the comparable rights of others and the aggregate common interest. Given this interdependency, human rights are sometimes designated prima facie rights, and it makes little or no sense to think or talk of them in absolutist terms.

Fifth and finally, human rights are commonly assumed to refer, in some vague sense, to "fundamental" as distinct from "nonessential" claims or "goods." In fact, some theorists go so far as to limit human rights to a single core right or two—for example, the right to life or the right to equal freedom of opportunity. The tendency, in short, is to de-emphasize or rule out "mere wants."

In several critical respects, however, this last postulate raises more questions than it answers. What does it mean to say that a right is fundamental? Does it entail some bare minimum only, or, more plausibly, does it admit to something greater? If the latter, how much greater and subject to what conditions, if any? In other words, however accurate, this last postulate is fraught with ambiguity about the content and legitimate scope of human rights and about the priorities, if any, among them. Except for the issue of the origin and justification of human rights, no cluster of preliminary human rights considerations is more controversial.

CONTENT

It cannot be disputed that, like all normative traditions, the human rights tradition is a product of its time. It necessarily reflects the processes of historical continuity and change that, at once and as a matter of cumulative experience, help to give it substance and form. Therefore, to understand better the debate over the content and legitimate scope of human rights and the priorities claimed among them, it is useful to note the dominant schools of thought and action that have informed the human rights tradition since the beginning of modern times.

Particularly helpful in this regard is the notion of "three generations of human rights" advanced by the French jurist Karel Vasak. Inspired by the three normative themes of the French Revolution, they are: the first generation of civil and political rights (*liberté*); the second generation of economic, social, and cultural rights (*égalité*); and the third generation of newly called solidarity rights (*fraternité*). Vasak's model is of course a simplified expression of an extremely complex historical record; it is not intended as a literal representation of life in which one generation gives birth to the next and then dies away.

The first generation.   The first generation of civil and political rights derives primarily from the 17th- and 18th-century reformist theories noted above, which are associated with the English, American, and French revolutions. Infused with the political philosophy of liberal individualism and the economic and social doctrine of laissez-faire, it conceives of human rights more in negative ("freedoms from") than positive ("rights to") terms; it favours the abstention rather than the intervention of government in the quest for human dignity, as epitomized by the statement attributed to H.L. Mencken that " . . . all government is, of course, against liberty." Belonging to this first generation, thus, are such claimed rights as are set forth in Articles 2–21 of the Universal Declaration of Human Rights, including freedom from racial and equivalent forms of discrimination; the right to life, liberty, and the security of the person; freedom from slavery or involuntary servitude; freedom from torture and from cruel, inhuman, or degrading treatment or punishment; freedom from arbitrary arrest, detention, or exile; the right to a fair and public trial; freedom from interference in privacy and correspondence; freedom of movement and residence; the right to asylum from persecution; freedom of thought, conscience, and religion; freedom of opinion and expression; freedom of peaceful assembly and association; and the right to participate in government, directly or through free elections. Also included is the right to own property and the right not to be deprived of one's property arbitrarily, each fundamental to the interests fought for in the American and French revolutions and to the rise of capitalism.

The "negative" rights

Of course, it would be error to assert that these and other first-generation rights correspond completely to the idea of "negative" as opposed to "positive" rights. The right to security of the person, to a fair and public trial, to asylum from persecution, and to free elections, for example, manifestly cannot be assured without some affirmative government action. What is constant in this first-generation conception, however, is the notion of liberty, a shield that safeguards the individual, alone and in association with others, against the abuse and misuse of political authority. This is the core value. Featured in almost every constitution of today's approximately 160 states, and dominating the majority of the international declarations and covenants adopted since World War II, this essentially Western liberal conception of human rights is sometimes romanticized as a triumph of Hobbesian–Lockean individualism over Hegelian statism.

The second generation.   The second generation of economic, social, and cultural rights finds its origins primarily in the socialist tradition that was foreshadowed among the Saint-Simonians of early 19th-century France and variously promoted by revolutionary struggles and welfare movements ever since. In large part, it is a response to the abuses and misuses of capitalist development and its underlying, essentially uncritical, conception of individual liberty that tolerated, even legitimated, the exploitation of working classes and colonial peoples. Historically, it is counterpoint to the first generation of civil and political rights, with human rights conceived more in positive ("rights to") than negative ("freedoms from") terms, requiring the intervention, not the abstention, of the state for the purpose of assuring equitable participation in the production and distribution of the values involved. Illustrative are the claimed rights set forth in Articles 22–27 of the Universal Declaration of Human Rights, such as the right to social security; the right to work and to protection against unemployment; the right to rest and leisure, including periodic holidays with pay; the right to a standard of living adequate for the health and well-being of self and family; the right to education; and the right

The "positive" rights

to the protection of one's scientific, literary, and artistic production.

Yet, in the same way that all the rights embraced by the first generation of civil and political rights cannot properly be designated "negative rights," so all the rights embraced by the second generation of economic, social, and cultural rights cannot properly be labeled "positive rights." The right to free choice of employment, the right to form and to join trade unions, and the right freely to participate in the cultural life of the community, for example, do not inherently require affirmative state action to ensure their enjoyment. Nevertheless, most of the second-generation rights do necessitate state intervention in the allocation of resources because they subsume demands more for material than for intangible values according to some criterion of distributive justice. Second-generation rights are, fundamentally, claims to social equality. Partly because of the comparatively late arrival of socialist–communist influence in the normative domain of international affairs, however, the internationalization of these rights has been somewhat slow in coming; but with the ascendancy of the Third World on the global stage, intent upon a "revolution of rising expectations," they have begun to come of age.

The third generation. Finally, the third generation of solidarity rights, while drawing upon, interlinking, and reconceptualizing value demands associated with the two earlier generations of rights, are best understood as a product, albeit one still in formation, of both the rise and the decline of the nation-state in the last half of the 20th century. Foreshadowed in Article 28 of the Universal Declaration of Human Rights, which proclaims that "everyone is entitled to a social and international order in which the rights set forth in this Declaration can be fully realized," it appears so far to embrace six claimed rights. Three of these reflect the emergence of Third World nationalism and its demand for a global redistribution of power, wealth, and other important values: the right to political, economic, social, and cultural self-determination; the right to economic and social development; and the right to participate in and benefit from "the common heritage of mankind" (shared Earth–space resources; scientific, technical, and other information and progress; and cultural traditions, sites, and monuments). The other three third-generation rights—the right to peace, the right to a healthy and balanced environment, and the right to humanitarian disaster relief—suggest the impotence or inefficiency of the nation-state in certain critical respects.

The "collective" rights

All six of these claimed rights tend to be posed as collective rights, requiring the concerted efforts of all social forces, to substantial degree on a planetary scale, and implying a quest for a possible utopia that projects the notion of holistic community interests. Each, however, manifests an individual as well as collective dimension. For example, while it may be said to be the collective right of all countries and peoples (especially developing countries and non-self-governing peoples) to secure a new international economic order that would eliminate obstacles to their economic and social development, so also may it be said to be the individual right of all persons to benefit from a developmental policy that is based on the satisfaction of material and nonmaterial human needs. Also, while the right to self-determination and the right to humanitarian assistance, for example, find expression on the legal as well as the moral plane, the majority of these solidarity rights tend to be more aspirational than justiciable in character, enjoying as yet an ambiguous jural status as international human rights norms.

Thus, at various stages of modern history—following the "bourgeois" revolutions of the 17th and 18th centuries, the socialist and Marxist revolutions of the early 20th century, and the anticolonialist revolutions that began immediately following World War II—the content of human rights has been broadly defined, not with any expectation that the rights associated with one generation would or should become outdated upon the ascendancy of another, but expansively or supplementally. Reflecting evolving perceptions of which values, at different times, stand most in need of encouragement and protection, the history of

the content of human rights also reflects humankind's recurring demands for continuity and stability.

LEGITIMACY AND PRIORITY

This is not to imply that each of these three generations of rights is equally acceptable to all or that they or their separate elements are greeted with equal urgency. First-generation proponents, for example, are inclined to exclude second- and third-generation rights from their definition of human rights altogether (or, at best, to label them as "derivative"). In part this is due to the complexities that inform the process of putting these rights into action. The suggestion of greater feasibility that attends first-generation rights because they stress the absence rather than the presence of government is somehow transformed into a prerequisite of a comprehensive definition of human rights, such that aspirational and vaguely asserted claims to entitlement are deemed not to be rights at all. The most forceful explanation, however, is more ideologically or politically motivated. Persuaded that egalitarian claims against the rich, particularly where collectively espoused, are unworkable without a severe decline in liberty and quality (in part because they involve state intervention for the redistribution of privately held resources), first-generation proponents, inspired by the natural law and laissez-faire traditions, are partial to the view that human rights are inherently independent of civil society and are individualistic.

Conversely, second- and third-generation defenders often look upon first-generation rights, at least as commonly practiced, as insufficiently attentive to material human needs and, indeed, as legitimating instruments in service to unjust domestic, transnational, and international social orders—hence constituting a "bourgeois illusion." Accordingly, while not placing first-generation rights outside their definition of human rights, they tend to assign such rights a low status and therefore treat them as long-term goals that will come to pass only with fundamental economic and social transformations to be realized progressively and fully consummated only sometime in the future.

In sum, different conceptions of rights, particularly emerging conceptions, contain the potential for challenging the legitimacy and supremacy not only of one another but, more importantly, of the political–social systems with which they are most intimately associated. As a consequence there is sharp disagreement about the legitimate scope of human rights and about the priorities that are claimed among them.

On final analysis, however, this liberty–equality and individualist–collectivist debate over the legitimacy and priorities of claimed human rights can be dangerously misleading. It is useful, certainly, insofar as it calls attention to the way in which notions of liberty and individualism can be, and have been, used to rationalize the abuses of capitalism; and it is useful, too, insofar as it highlights how notions of equality and collectivism can be, and have been, alibis for authoritarian governance. But in the end it risks obscuring at least three essential truths that must be taken into account if the contemporary worldwide human rights movement is to be objectively understood.

First, one-sided characterizations of legitimacy and priority are likely, over the long term, to undermine the political credibility of their proponents and the defensibility of their particularistic values. In an increasingly interdependent and interpenetrating global community, any human rights orientation that does not genuinely support the widest possible shaping and sharing of all values among all human beings is likely to provoke widespread skepticism. The last half of the 20th century is replete with examples.

Three essential truths

Second, such characterizations do not accurately mirror behavioral reality. In the real world, despite differences in cultural tradition and ideological style, there exists a rising and overriding insistence upon the equitable production and distribution of all basic values. U.S. Pres. Franklin D. Roosevelt's Four Freedoms (freedom of speech and expression, freedom of worship, freedom from want, and freedom from fear) is an early case in point. A more recent demonstration was the 1977 Law Day speech by then U.S. Secretary of State Cyrus R. Vance, in which he announced the U.S. government's resolve "to make the advancement of human rights a central part of our foreign policy" and defined human rights to include "the right to be free from governmental violation of the integrity of the person, . . . the right to the fulfillment of such vital needs as food, shelter, health care, and education, . . . [and] the right to enjoy civil and political liberties." Essentially individualistic societies tolerate, even promote, certain collectivist values; likewise, essentially communal societies tolerate, even promote, certain individualistic values. Ours is a more-or-less, not an either-or, world.

Finally, none of the international human rights instruments currently in force or proposed say anything whatsoever about the legitimacy or rank-ordering of the rights they address, save possibly in the case of rights that by international covenant are stipulated to be nonderogable and therefore, arguably, more fundamental than others (for example, freedom from arbitrary or unlawful deprivation of life, freedom from torture and from inhuman or degrading treatment and punishment, freedom from slavery, freedom from imprisonment for debt). There is disagreement, to be sure, among lawyers, moralists, and political scientists about the legitimacy and hierarchy of claimed rights when they treat the problem of implementation. For example, some insist on certain civil and political guarantees, whereas others defer initially to material and corporeal well-being. Such disagreements, however, partake of political agendas and have little if any conceptual utility. As the UN General Assembly has repeatedly confirmed, all human rights form an indivisible whole.

In short, the legitimacy of different human rights and the priorities claimed among them are a function of context. Because people in different parts of the world both assert and honour different human rights demands according to many different procedures and practices, these issues ultimately depend on time, place, setting, level of crisis, and other circumstance.

International human rights: prescription and enforcement

BEFORE WORLD WAR II

Ever since ancient times, but especially since the emergence of the modern state system, the Age of Discovery, and the accompanying spread of industrialization and European culture throughout the world, there has developed, for economic and other reasons, a unique set of customs and conventions relative to the humane treatment of foreigners. This evolving International Law of State Responsibility for Injuries to Aliens, as these customs and conventions came to be called, may be understood to represent the beginning of active concern for human rights on the international plane. The founding fathers of international law—particularly Francisco de Vitoria (1486?–1546), Hugo Grotius (1583–1645), and Emmerich de Vattel (1714–67)—were quick to observe that all persons, outlander as well as other, were entitled to certain natural rights; and they emphasized, consequently, the importance of according aliens fair treatment.

Except, however, for the occasional use of treaties to secure the protection of Christian minorities, as early illustrated by the Peace of Westphalia (1648), which concluded the Thirty Years' War and established the principle of equal rights for the Roman Catholic and Protestant religions in Germany, it was not until the start of the 19th century that active international concern for the rights of nationals began to make itself felt. Then, in the century and a half before World War II, several noteworthy, if essentially unconnected, efforts to encourage respect for nationals by international means began to shape what today is called the International Law of Human Rights (which for historical but no theoretically convincing reasons has tended to be treated separately from the International Law of State Responsibility for Injuries to Aliens).

Throughout the 19th and early 20th centuries, numerous military operations and diplomatic representations, not all of them with the purest of motives but done nonetheless in the name of "humanitarian intervention" (a customary international law doctrine), undertook to protect oppressed and persecuted minorities in the Ottoman Empire and in Syria, Crete, various Balkan countries, Romania, and Russia. Paralleling these actions, first at the Congress of Vienna (1814–15) and later between the two world wars, a series of treaties and international declarations sought the protection of certain racial, religious, and linguistic minorities in central and eastern Europe and in the Middle East. During the same period the movement to combat and suppress slavery and the slave trade found expression in treaties sooner or later involving the major commercial powers, beginning with the Treaty of Paris (1814) and culminating in the International Slavery Convention (1926).

In addition, toward the end of the 19th century and continuing well beyond World War II, the community of nations, inspired largely by persons associated with what is now the International Committee of the Red Cross, concluded a series of multilateral declarations and agreements designed to temper the conduct of hostilities, protect the victims of war, and otherwise elaborate the humanitarian law of war. At about the same time, first with two multilateral labour conventions concluded in 1906 and subsequently at the initiative of the International Labour Organisation (ILO; established in 1919), a reformist-minded international community embarked upon a variety of collaborative measures directed at the promotion of human rights. These included not only fields traditionally associated with labour law and relations (for example, industrial health, safety, and welfare; hours of work; annual paid holidays) but also—mainly after World War II—in respect of such core human rights concerns as forced labour, discrimination in employment and occupation, freedom of association for collective bargaining, and equal pay for equal work.

Finally, during the interwar period, the Covenant establishing the League of Nations (1919), while not formally recognizing "the rights of Man" and while failing to lay down a principle of racial nondiscrimination as requested by Japan (owing mainly to the resistance of Great Britain and the United States), nevertheless committed the League's members to several human rights goals: fair and humane working conditions for men, women, and children; the execution of agreements regarding traffic in women and children; the prevention and control of disease in matters of international concern; and the just treatment of native colonial peoples. Also, victorious powers who as "mandatories" were entrusted by the League with the tutelage of colonies formerly governed by Germany and Turkey accepted as "a sacred trust of civilization" responsibilities for the well-being and development of the inhabitants of those territories. (The arrangement was carried over into the UN trusteeship system and had serious repercussions more than a half century later in relation to the mandate entrusted to South Africa over the territory of South West Africa [now Namibia].)

As important as these pre-World War II human rights efforts were, however, it was not until after the War—and the Nazi atrocities accompanying it—that active concern for human rights on the international plane truly came of age. In the proceedings of the International Military Tribunal at Nürnberg in 1945–46, German high officials were tried not only for "crimes against peace" and "war crimes" but also for "crimes against humanity" committed against any civilian population even if in accordance with the laws of the country where perpetrated. While the tribunal, whose establishment and rulings subsequently were endorsed by the UN General Assembly, applied a cautious approach to allegations of "crimes against humanity," it nonetheless made the treatment by a state of its own citizens the subject of international criminal process.

HUMAN RIGHTS IN THE UNITED NATIONS

The Charter of the United Nations (1945) begins by reaffirming a "faith in fundamental human rights, in the dignity and worth of the human person, in the equal rights of men and women and of nations large and small." It states that the purposes of the United Nations are, among other things, "to develop friendly relations among nations based on respect for the principle of equal rights and self-determination of peoples . . . [and] to achieve international

International Law of State Responsibility for Injuries to Aliens

Human rights goals of the League of Nations

co-operation . . . in promoting and encouraging respect for human rights and for fundamental freedoms for all without distinction as to race, sex, language, or religion . . . ." And, in two key articles, all members "pledge themselves to take joint and separate action in cooperation with the Organization" for the achievement of these and related purposes. It is to be noted, however, that a proposal to ensure the protection as well as the promotion of human rights was explicitly rejected at the San Francisco Conference establishing the United Nations. Additionally, the Charter expressly provides that nothing in it "shall authorize the United Nations to intervene in matters which are essentially within the domestic jurisdiction of any state . . .," except upon a Security Council finding of a "threat to the peace, breach of the peace, or act of aggression." Moreover, although typical of major constitutive instruments, the Charter is conspicuously general and vague in its human rights clauses, among others.

Thus, not surprisingly, the reconciliation of the Charter's human rights provisions with the Charter's drafting history and its "domestic jurisdiction" clause has given rise to not a little legal and political controversy. Some authorities have argued that, in becoming parties to the Charter, states accept no more than a nebulous promotional obligation toward human rights and that, in any event, the United Nations has no standing to insist on human rights safeguards in member states. Others insist that the Charter's human rights provisions, being part of a legally binding treaty, clearly involve some element of legal obligation; that the "pledge" made by states upon becoming party to the Charter consequently represents more than a moral statement; and that the "domestic jurisdiction" clause does not apply because human rights, whatever isolation they may have "enjoyed" in the past, no longer can be considered matters "essentially within the domestic jurisdiction" of states.

When all is said and done, however, it is clear from the actual practice of the United Nations that the problem of resolving these opposing contentions has proved somewhat less formidable than the statements of governments and the opinions of scholars might lead one to assume. Neither the Charter's drafting history nor its "domestic jurisdiction" clause nor, indeed, its generality and vagueness in respect of human rights has prevented the United Nations—on the basis of individual petitions, statements from witnesses, state complaints, and reports from interested nongovernmental organizations—from investigating, discussing, and evaluating specific human rights situations. Nor have they prevented it from recommending or prescribing concrete action in relation to them, at least not in the case of "a consistent pattern of gross violations" of human rights, provided there has been a majority persuasive enough to force the action desired (as in the imposition by the Security Council in 1977 of a mandatory arms embargo against South Africa). Of course, governments usually are protective of their sovereignty (or domestic jurisdiction). Also, the UN organs responsible for the promotion of human rights suffer from most of the same disabilities that afflict the United Nations as a whole, in particular the absence of supranational authority and the presence of divisive power politics. Hence, it cannot be expected that UN actions in defense of human rights will be, normally, either swift or categorically effective. Nevertheless, assuming some political will, the legal obstacles to UN enforcement of human rights are not insurmountable.

UN Commission on Human Rights Primary responsibility for the promotion of human rights under the UN Charter rests in the General Assembly and, under its authority, in the Economic and Social Council and its subsidiary body, the Commission on Human Rights, an intergovernmental body that serves as the UN's central policy organ in the human rights field. Much of the commission's activity, initiated by subsidiary working groups, is investigatory, evaluative, and advisory in character, and the commission annually establishes a working group to consider and make recommendations concerning alleged "gross violations" of human rights referred to it by its Sub-Commission on Prevention of Discrimination and Protection of Minorities (on the basis of communications from individuals and groups, pursuant to Resolution 1503 [1970] of the UN Economic and Social Council, and sometimes on the basis of investigations by the subcommission or one of its working groups). Also, the commission has appointed special representatives and envoys to examine human rights situations on an ad hoc basis, who, in the course of preparing their reports, examine reliable information submitted in good faith, interview interested persons, or make on-site inspections with the cooperation of the government concerned.

In addition, the commission, together with other UN organs such as the International Labour Organisation (ILO), the UN Educational, Scientific and Cultural Organization (UNESCO), and the UN Commission on the Status of Women, drafts human rights standards and has prepared a number of international human rights instruments. Among the most important are the Universal Declaration of Human Rights (1948), the International Covenant on Civil and Political Rights (together with its Optional Protocol; 1976), and the International Covenant on Economic, Social and Cultural Rights (1976). Collectively known as the International Bill of Rights, these three instruments serve as touchstones for interpreting the human rights provisions of the UN Charter.

The Universal Declaration of Human Rights. The catalog of rights set out in the Universal Declaration of Human Rights, which was adopted without dissent by the General Assembly on December 10, 1948, is scarcely less than the sum of all the important traditional political and civil rights of national constitutions and legal systems, including equality before the law; protection against arbitrary arrest; the right to a fair trial; freedom from ex post facto criminal laws; the right to own property; freedom of thought, conscience, and religion; freedom of opinion and expression; and freedom of peaceful assembly and association. Also enumerated are such economic, social, and cultural rights as the right to work and to choose one's work freely, the right to equal pay for equal work, the right to form and join trade unions, the right to rest and leisure, the right to an adequate standard of living, and the right to education.

The Universal Declaration, it must be noted, is not a treaty. It was meant to proclaim "a common standard of achievement for all peoples and all nations" rather than enforceable legal obligations. Nevertheless, partly because of an 18-year delay between its adoption and the completion for signature and ratification of the two covenants, the Universal Declaration has acquired a status juridically more important than originally intended. It has been widely used, even by national courts, as a means of judging compliance with human rights obligations under the UN Charter.

The International Covenant on Civil and Political Rights and the Optional Protocol. The civil and political rights guaranteed by this covenant, which was opened for signature on December 19, 1966, and entered into force on March 23, 1976, incorporate almost all of those proclaimed in the Universal Declaration, including the right to nondiscrimination. Pursuant to the covenant, each state party undertakes to respect and to ensure to all individuals within its territory and subject to its jurisdiction the rights recognized in the covenant "without distinction of any kind, such as race, colour, sex, language, religion, political or other opinion, national or social origin, property, birth or other status." Some rights listed in the Universal Declaration, however, such as the right to own property and the right to asylum, are not included among the rights recognized in the covenant. Similarly, the covenant designates a number of rights that are not listed in the Universal Declaration, among them the right of all peoples to self-determination and the right of ethnic, religious, or linguistic minorities to enjoy their own culture, to profess and practice their own religion, and to use their own language. To the extent that the Universal Declaration and the covenant overlap, however, the latter is understood to explicate and help interpret the former.

In addition, the covenant calls for the establishment of a Human Rights Committee, an international organ of 18 persons elected by the parties to the covenant, serving in their individual expert capacity and charged to study reports submitted by the state parties on the measures they have adopted that give effect to the rights recognized in the covenant. As between the state parties that have expressly recognized the competence of the committee in this regard, the committee also may respond to allegations by one state party that another state party is not fulfilling its obligations under the covenant. If the committee is unable to resolve the problem, the matter is referred to an ad hoc conciliation commission, which eventually reports its findings on all questions of fact, plus its views on the possibilities of an amicable solution. State parties that become party to the Optional Protocol further recognize the competence of the Human Rights Committee similarly to consider and act upon communications from individuals claiming to be victims of covenant violations.

The International Covenant on Economic, Social and Cultural Rights. Just as the International Covenant on Civil and Political Rights elaborates upon most of the civil and political rights enumerated in the Universal Declaration of Human Rights, so the International Covenant on Economic, Social and Cultural Rights elaborates upon most of the economic, social, and cultural rights set forth in the Universal Declaration: the right to work; the right to just and favourable conditions of work; trade union rights; the right to social security; rights relating to the protection of the family; the right to an adequate standard of living; the right to health; the right to education; and rights relating to culture and science. Unlike its companion International Covenant on Civil and Political Rights, however, this covenant is not geared, with modest exception, to immediate implementation, the state parties having agreed only "to take steps" toward "achieving progressively the full realization of the rights recognized in the . . . Covenant," and then subject to "the maximum of [their] available resources." The covenant is essentially a "promotional convention," stipulating objectives more than standards and requiring implementation over time rather than all at once. One obligation is, however, subject to immediate application: the prohibition of discrimination in the enjoyment of the rights enumerated on grounds of race, colour, sex, language, religion, or political or other opinion; national or social origin; property; and birth or other status. Also, the international supervisory measures that apply to the covenant oblige the state parties to report to the UN Economic and Social Council on the steps they have adopted and the progress they have made in achieving the realization of the enumerated rights.

Other UN human rights conventions. The two above-mentioned covenants are by no means the only human rights treaties drafted and adopted under the auspices of the United Nations. Indeed, because there are far too many to detail even in abbreviated fashion, it must suffice simply to note that they address a broad range of concerns, including the prevention and punishment of the crime of genocide; the humane treatment of military and civilian personnel in time of war; the status of refugees; the protection and reduction of stateless persons; the abolition of slavery, forced labour, and discrimination in employment and occupation; the elimination of all forms of racial discrimination and the suppression and punishment of the crime of apartheid; the elimination of discrimination in education; the promotion of the political rights of women and the elimination of all forms of discrimination against women; and the promotion of equality of opportunity and treatment of migrant workers. (For particular agreements, see *Human Rights: A Compilation of International Instruments*, 3rd ed. [1978], published by the United Nations.) Many of these treaties are the work of the UN specialized agencies, particularly the International Labour Organization (ILO), and many also provide for supervisory and enforcement mechanisms—for example, the Committee on the Elimination of Racial Discrimination established under the International Convention on the Elimination of All Forms of Racial Discrimination of December 21, 1965.

UN human rights declarations. In addition to developing human rights standards and procedures through treaties, the UN General Assembly, impressed by the impact of the Universal Declaration of Human Rights, also has resorted to the proclamation of declarations as a means of promoting human rights. Adopted in the form of a resolution of the General Assembly, which technically is not binding on the member states in the sense of a treaty, a declaration, particularly when it enunciates principles of great and solemn importance, may nevertheless create within the international community strong expectations about authority and control. Perhaps the best known examples subsequent to the Universal Declaration, while not devoted exclusively to human rights considerations, are the Declaration on the Granting of Independence to Colonial Countries and Peoples (1960) and the Declaration on Principles of International Law Concerning Friendly Relations and Co-Operation Among States in Accordance with the Charter of the United Nations (1970).

HUMAN RIGHTS AND THE HELSINKI PROCESS

Post-World War II concern for human rights also has been evident at the global level outside the United Nations, most notably in the proceedings and aftermath of the Conference on Security and Cooperation in Europe, convened in Helsinki on July 3, 1973, and concluded there (after continuing deliberations in Geneva) on August 1, 1975. Attended by representatives of 35 governments that included the NATO countries, the Warsaw Pact nations, and 13 neutral and nonaligned European states, the conference had as its principal purpose a mutually satisfactory definition of peace and stability between East and West, previously made impossible by the period of the Cold War. In particular, the Soviet Union was concerned with achieving recognition of its western frontiers as established at the end of World War II.

There was little tangible, however, that the Western powers, with no realistic territorial claims of their own, could demand in return, and accordingly they pressed for certain concessions in respect of human rights and freedom of movement and information between East and West. Thus, at the outset of the Final Act adopted by the conference, in a Declaration of Principles Guiding Relations Between States, the participating governments solemnly declared "their determination to respect and put into practice," alongside other "guiding" principles, "respect [for] human rights and fundamental freedoms, including the freedom of thought, conscience, religion or belief" and "respect [for] the equal rights of peoples and their right to self-determination." It was hoped that this would mark the beginning of a liberalization of authoritarian regimes.

The Helsinki Final Act

From the earliest discussions, however, it was clear that the Helsinki Final Act was not intended as a legally binding instrument. "Determination to respect" and "put into practice" were deemed to express moral commitments only, the Declaration of Principles was said not to prescribe international law, and nowhere did the participants provide for enforcement machinery. On the other hand, the Declaration of Principles, including its human rights principles, always has been viewed as at least consistent with international law. Additionally, the fourth of four sections (commonly known as "baskets") of the Final Act provides for the holding of periodic review conferences in which the participating states are called upon "to continue the multilateral process initiated by the Conference." But most importantly, ever since their adoption, the Final Act's human rights provisions have served as important and widely accepted yardsticks for external scrutiny and appropriate recourse to perceived violations.

In sum, like the Universal Declaration of Human Rights and other declarations of the UN General Assembly, the Helsinki Final Act, though not a treaty, has created widespread expectations about proper human rights behaviour, and consequently it has inspired and facilitated the monitoring of human rights policy. Assuming some cordiality between East and West, the Helsinki Process may be said at least to hold out the potential for modestly beneficial results in the human rights arena.

REGIONAL DEVELOPMENTS

Action for the international promotion and protection of human rights has proceeded at the regional level in Europe, the Americas, Africa, and the Middle East. Only the first three of these regions, however, have gone so far as to create enforcement mechanisms within the framework of a human rights charter. The Permanent Arab Commission on Human Rights, founded by the Council of the League of Arab States in September 1968, but since then preoccupied by the rights of Arabs living in Israeli-occupied territories, has not brought a proposed Arab Convention on Human Rights to a successful conclusion and so far has tended to function more in terms of the promotion than the protection of human rights.

European human rights system. On November 4, 1950, the Council of Europe agreed to the European Convention for the Protection of Human Rights and Fundamental Freedoms, the substantive provisions of which are based on a draft of what is now the International Covenant on Civil and Political Rights. Together with its five additional protocols, this convention, which entered into force on September 3, 1953, represents the most advanced and successful international experiment in the field. A companion instrument, similar to the later International Covenant on Economic, Social and Cultural Rights, is the European Social Charter (1961), whose provisions are implemented through an elaborate system of control based on the sending of progress reports to, and the appraisal of these reports by, the various committees and organs of the Council of Europe. The instrumentalities created under the European convention are the European Commission of Human Rights and the European Court of Human Rights. The convention also makes use of the governmental organ of the Council of Europe, the Committee of Ministers.

The commission may receive from any state party to the convention any allegation of a breach of the convention by another state party. Also, provided its legal competence to do so has been formally recognized, the commission may receive petitions from any person, group of individuals, or nongovernmental organization claiming to be the victim of a violation of the convention. In such cases, the commission is charged to ascertain the facts and to place itself at the disposal of the parties to secure "a friendly settlement . . . on the basis of respect for Human Rights." If no such solution is reached, the commission is called upon to draw up a report, stating its opinion as to whether the facts disclose a breach, and to recommend action to the Committee of Ministers, including referral of the case to the European Court of Human Rights.

The jurisdiction of the court extends to cases referred to it by a state party whose national is alleged to be a victim of a violation, by a state party against whom a complaint has been lodged, and by any state party that may have referred the case to the commission. The court may not, however, receive a complaint by an individual applicant. Moreover, it may receive state complaints only if the defendant state has accepted its jurisdiction. This may be done ad hoc for a particular case or by a general declaration accepting the compulsory jurisdiction of the court. In either event, and in cases referred by the European commission as well, the judgment of the court is final. If a question is not or cannot be referred to the court, then the Committee of Ministers of the Council of Europe makes a final decision on human rights complaints.

The instrumentalities of the European convention have, over the years, developed a considerable body of case law on questions regulated by the convention; and the provisions of the convention are deemed, in some European states, part of domestic constitutional or statutory law. Where this is not the case, the state parties to the convention have taken other measures to make their domestic laws conform with their obligations under the convention.

Inter-American human rights system. In 1948, concurrent with its establishment of the Organization of American States (OAS), the Ninth Pan-American Conference adopted the American Declaration on the Rights and Duties of Man, an instrument similar to, but coming a full seven months before, the Universal Declaration of the United Nations and setting out the duties as well as the rights of the individual citizen (a throwback, perhaps, to Greco-Roman and medieval natural law theories). Subsequently, in 1959, a meeting of consultation of the American Ministers for Foreign Affairs created, within the framework of the OAS, the Inter-American Commission on Human Rights,

which has since undertaken important investigative activities concerning human rights in the Americas. Finally, in 1969, the Inter-American Specialized Conference on Human Rights, meeting in San José, Costa Rica, adopted the American Convention on Human Rights, which made the existing Inter-American Commission on Human Rights an organ for the convention's implementation and established the Inter-American Court of Human Rights, which sits in San José.

Both the substantive law and the procedural arrangements of the American convention, which entered into force in 1978, are strongly influenced by the UN covenants and the European convention, and they were drafted also with the European Social Charter in mind. Under the American convention, however, unlike its UN and European predecessors, the right of petition by individuals, groups of individuals, and nongovernmental organizations operates automatically. Under the UN system, the right of petition applies only when the state concerned has become a party to the Optional Protocol to the International Covenant on Civil and Political Rights, and under the European system a special declaration by the states concerned is required. On the other hand, again in contrast to the European system (but not the UN system), interstate complaints under the American convention operate only among states that have expressly agreed to such procedure.

African human rights system. In 1981, following numerous pleas by the UN Commission on Human Rights, interested states, nongovernmental organizations, and others dating as far back as 1961, the Eighteenth Assembly of Heads of State and Government of the Organization of African Unity (OAU), convening in Nairobi, Kenya, adopted the African Charter on Human and Peoples' Rights. The charter provides that it will become effective three months after ratification or adherence of a majority of the member states of the OAU, numbering 50 as of December 31, 1983. By the mid-1980s, the 26 ratifications or adherences needed had not been reached and the charter was, therefore, not yet in force.

Like its European and American counterparts, the African charter provides for the establishment of an African Commission on Human and Peoples' Rights, with both promotional and protective functions and with no restriction on who may file a complaint with the commission (signatory states, individuals, groups of individuals, and nongovernmental organizations, whether or not they are victims of the alleged violation). In contrast to the European and American procedures, however, concerned states are encouraged to reach a friendly settlement without formally involving the investigative or conciliatory mechanisms of the commission. Also, the African charter does not call for a human rights court. African customs and traditions, it is said, emphasize mediation, conciliation, and consensus rather than the adversarial and adjudicative procedures common to Western legal systems.

Four other distinctive features of the African charter are especially noteworthy. First, it provides for economic, social, and cultural rights as well as civil and political rights. In this respect it bears resemblance to the American convention, but is distinctive from the European convention. Next, in contrast to both the European and American conventions, it recognizes the rights of groups in addition to the family, women, and children. The aged and the infirm are accorded special protection also, and the right of peoples to self-determination is elaborated in the right to existence, equality, and nondomination. Third, it uniquely embraces two third-generation, or "solidarity," rights "as belonging to all peoples": the right to economic, social, and cultural development and the right to national and international peace and security. Finally, it is so far the only treaty instrument to detail individual duties as well as individual rights—to the family, society, the state, and the international African community.

INTERNATIONAL HUMAN RIGHTS IN DOMESTIC COURTS

Using domestic courts to clarify and safeguard international human rights is a new and still evolving approach to human rights advocacy. In addition to the inevitable interpretative problems of applying conventional and cus-

European Social Charter

The African Charter

tomary norms that are fashioned in multicultural settings, controversial theories about the interrelation of national and international law plus many procedural difficulties—carrying such labels as "standing," "act of State," and the "political questions doctrine"—burden the party anxious to invoke international human rights norms in the domestic context. To be sure, considerable progress has been made, as perhaps best evidenced in the far-reaching decision handed down by the U.S. Court of Appeals for the 2nd Circuit in 1980 in *Filartiga* v. *Pena-Irala*, in which the court held that the international prohibition of torture is unequivocally established in the law of nations and therefore to be honoured in U.S. courts. But as human rights scholar Richard Lillich has cautioned, ". . . in all likelihood the [national] judiciary will have to experience much more international human rights law consciousness-raising before [wholesale resistance to its domestic application] is rejected."

Conclusion

Whatever the current attitudes and policies of governments, the reality of popular demands for human rights, including both greater economic justice and greater political freedom, is beyond debate. A deepening and widening concern for the promotion and protection of human rights, hastened by the self-determinist impulse of a postcolonial era, is now unmistakably woven into the fabric of contemporary world affairs.

Substantially responsible for this progressive development has been, of course, the work of the United Nations, its allied agencies, and such regional organizations as the Council of Europe, the Organization of American States, and the Organization of African Unity. Also visibly helpful, however, particularly since the early 1970s, have been three other factors: the public advocacy of human rights as a key aspect of national foreign policies, made initially legitimate by the example of U.S. Pres. Jimmy Carter; the emergence and proliferation of activist nongovernmental human rights organizations such as Amnesty International (winner of the Nobel Prize for Peace for 1977), the International Commission of Jurists, and diverse church-affiliated groups; and a worldwide profusion of courses and materials devoted to the study of human rights both in formal and informal edutional settings. Indeed, in light of the weaknesses that presently inhere at the intergovernmental level of global and regional organization, it is likely that each of these factors will play an increasingly important role in the future. To be sure, formidable obstacles attend the endeavours of human rights policymakers, activists, and scholars. The implementation of international human rights law depends for the most part on the voluntary consent of nations; the mechanisms for the observance or enforcement of human rights are yet in their infancy. Still, it is certain that a palpable concern for the advancement of human rights is here to stay, out of necessity no less than out of idealism. As Nobel laureate and political dissident Andrey Sakharov once wrote from his internal exile in the Soviet Union:

"The ideology of human rights is probably the only one which can be combined with such diverse ideologies as communism, social democracy, religion, technocracy and those ideologies which may be described as national and indigenous. It can also serve as a foothold for those . . . who have tired of the abundance of ideologies, none of which have brought . . . simple human happiness. The defense of human rights is a clear path toward the unification of people in our turbulent world, and a path toward the relief of suffering."

BIBLIOGRAPHY

Documentary: UNITED NATIONS, *Human Rights: A Compilation of International Instruments,* 3rd ed. (1978), contains the texts of human rights treaties and other instruments established under the auspices of the United Nations. UNITED NATIONS, *Yearbook on Human Rights* (annual), documents national and international developments in the human rights field. See also JAMES AVERY JOYCE, *Human Rights: International Documents,* 3 vol. (1978); BURNS H. WESTON, RICHARD A. FALK, and ANTHONY A. D'AMATO (eds.), *Basic Documents in International Law and World Order* (1980); IAN BROWNLIE (comp.), *Basic Documents on Human Rights,* 2nd ed. (1981); RICHARD B. LILLICH (ed.), *International Human Rights Instruments: A Compilation of Treaties, Agreements, and Declarations of Especial Interest to the United States* (1983); and UNIFO, *International Human Rights Instruments of the United Nations* (1983).

General: Basic works on the subject include SIR HERSCH LAUTERPACHT, *International Law and Human Rights* (1950, reprinted 1973); JÓZSEF HÁLASZ (ed.), *Socialist Concept of Human Rights,* trans. from the Hungarian (1966); EGON SCHWELB, *Human Rights and the International Community: The Roots and Growth of the Universal Declaration of Human Rights* (1964); EVAN LUARD (ed.), *The International Protection of Human Rights* (1967); ASBJÖRN EIDE and AUGUST SCHOU (eds.), *International Protection of Human Rights: Proceedings of the Seventh Nobel Symposium, September 25–27, 1967* (1968); R. BILDER, "Rethinking International Human Rights: Some Basic Questions," *Wisconsin Law Review,* pp. 171–217, no. 1 (1969); JOHN CAREY, *UN Protection of Civil and Political Rights* (1970); VERNON VAN DYKE, *Human Rights, the United States, and World Community* (1970); MAURICE CRANSTON, *What Are Human Rights?* (1973); J. HUMPHREY, "The International Law of Human Rights in the Middle Twentieth Century," in MAARTEN BOS (ed.), *The Present State of International Law and Other Essays* (1973); MOSES MOSKOWITZ, *International Concern with Human Rights* (1974); MANOUCHEHR GANJI, *The Realization of Economic, Social, and Cultural Rights: Problems, Policies, Progress* (1975); RICHARD P. CLAUDE (ed.), *Comparative Human Rights* (1976); THOMAS BUERGENTHAL (ed.), *Human Rights, International Law, and the Helsinki Accord* (1977); FRANCISZEK PRZETACZNIK, "The Socialist Concept of Human Rights: Its Philosophical Background and Political Justification," *Belgian Review of International Law,* 13:239–278 (1977); FOUAD AJAMI, *Human Rights and World Order Politics* (1978); JAMES AVERY JOYCE, *The New Politics of Human Rights* (1979); B.G. RAMCHARAN (ed.), *Human Rights: Thirty Years After the Universal Declaration* (1979); MYRES S. MCDOUGAL, HAROLD D. LASSWELL, and LUNG-CHU CHEN, *Human Rights and World Public Order: The Basic Policies of an International Law of Human Dignity* (1980); RICHARD A. FALK, *Human Rights and State Sovereignty* (1981); LOUIS HENKIN (ed.), *The International Bill of Rights: The Covenant on Civil and Political Rights* (1981), and *The Rights of Man Today* (1978); S.P. MARKS, "Emerging Human Rights: A New Generation for the 1980s," *Rutgers Law Review,* 33:435–452 (Winter 1981); A.H. ROBERTSON, *Human Rights in the World: An Introduction to the Study of the International Protection of Human Rights,* 2nd ed. (1982); KAREL VASAK (ed.), *The International Dimension of Human Rights,* 2 vol., trans. from the French (1982); PAUL SIEGHART, *The International Law of Human Rights* (1983); and HURST HANNUM (ed.), *Guide to International Human Rights Practice* (1984).

Regional instruments and arrangements: J.E.S. FAWCETT, *The Application of the European Convention on Human Rights* (1969); S. MARKS, "La Commission permanente arabe des droits de l'homme," *Revue de droits de l'homme/Human Rights Journal,* 3:101–108 (1970); FREDE CASTBERG, *The European Convention on Human Rights,* trans. from the Norwegian (1974); COUNCIL OF EUROPE, *European Convention on Human Rights: Collected Texts* (1975); A.H. ROBERTSON, *Human Rights in Europe,* 2nd ed. (1977); THOMAS BUERGENTHAL and ROBERT E. NORRIS (eds.), *Human Rights: The Inter-American System* (1982–); R. GITTLEMAN, "The African Charter on Human and People's Rights: A Legal Analysis," *Virginia Journal of International Law,* 22:667–714 (1982); and U. UMOZURIKE, "The African Charter on Human and People's Rights," *American Journal of International Law,* 77:902–912 (October 1983).

Human rights journals: *Human Rights Law Journal* (quarterly); *Human Rights Quarterly* (formerly *Universal Human Rights*); *The Human Rights Review* (three times a year, 1976–81); *Revue des droits de l'homme/Human Rights Journal* (quarterly, 1968–79).

(BURNS H. WESTON)

Faraday

Michael Faraday, who became one of the greatest scientists of the 19th century, began his career as a chemist. He wrote a manual of practical chemistry that reveals his mastery of the technical aspects of his art, discovered a number of new organic compounds, among them benzene, and was the first to liquefy a "permanent" gas (*i.e.,* one that was believed to be incapable of liquefaction). His major contribution, however, was in the field of electricity and magnetism. He was the first to produce an electric current from a magnetic field, invented the first electric motor and dynamo, demonstrated the relation between electricity and chemical bonding, discovered the effect of magnetism on light, and discovered and named diamagnetism, the peculiar behaviour of certain substances in strong magnetic fields. He provided the experimental, and a good deal of the theoretical, foundation upon which James Clerk Maxwell erected classical electromagnetic field theory.

Early life. Michael Faraday was born on September 22, 1791, in the country village of Newington, Surrey, now a part of South London. His father was a blacksmith who had migrated from the north of England earlier in 1791 to look for work. His mother was a country woman of great calm and wisdom who supported her son emotionally through a difficult childhood. Faraday was one of four children, all of whom were hard put to get enough to eat, since their father was often ill and incapable of working steadily. Faraday later recalled being given one loaf of bread that had to last him for a week. The family belonged to a small Christian sect, called Sandemanians, that provided spiritual sustenance to Faraday throughout his life. It was the single most important influence upon him and strongly affected the way in which he approached and interpreted nature.

Faraday received only the rudiments of an education, learning to read, write, and cipher in a church Sunday school. At an early age he began to earn money by delivering newspapers for a book dealer and bookbinder, and at the age of 14 he was apprenticed to the man. Unlike the other apprentices, Faraday took the opportunity to read some of the books brought in for rebinding. The article on electricity in the third edition of the *Encyclopædia Britannica* particularly fascinated him. Using old bottles and lumber, he made a crude electrostatic generator and did simple experiments. He also built a weak voltaic pile with which he performed experiments in electrochemistry.

Faraday's great opportunity came when he was offered a ticket to attend chemical lectures by Sir Humphry Davy at the Royal Institution of Great Britain in London. Faraday went, sat absorbed with it all, recorded the lectures in his notes, and returned to bookbinding with the seemingly unrealizable hope of entering the temple of science. He sent a bound copy of his notes to Davy along with a letter asking for employment, but there was no opening. Davy did not forget, however, and when one of his laboratory assistants was dismissed for brawling, he sent around to Faraday's lodgings and offered him a job. Faraday began as Davy's laboratory assistant and learned chemistry at the elbow of one of the greatest practitioners of the day. It has been said, with some truth, that Faraday was Davy's greatest discovery.

When Faraday joined Davy in 1812, Davy was in the process of revolutionizing the chemistry of the day. Antoine-Laurent Lavoisier, the Frenchman generally credited with founding modern chemistry, had effected his rearrangement of chemical knowledge in the 1770s and 1780s by insisting upon a few simple principles. Among these was that oxygen was a unique element, in that it was the only supporter of combustion and was also the element that lay at the basis of all acids. Davy, after having discovered sodium and potassium by using a powerful current from

Studies with Sir Humphry Davy

a galvanic battery to decompose oxides of these elements, turned to the decomposition of muriatic (hydrochloric) acid, one of the strongest acids known. The products of the decomposition were hydrogen and a green gas that supported combustion and that, when combined with water, produced an acid. Davy concluded that this gas was an element, to which he gave the name chlorine, and that there was no oxygen whatsoever in muriatic acid. Acidity, therefore, was not the result of the presence of an acid-forming element but of some other condition. What else could that condition be but the physical form of the acid molecule itself? Davy suggested, then, that chemical properties were determined not by specific elements alone but also by the ways in which these elements were arranged in molecules. In arriving at this view he was influenced by an atomic theory that was also to have important consequences for Faraday's thought. This theory, proposed in the 18th century by the Dalmatian scientist Ruggero Giuseppe Boscovich, argued that atoms were mathematical points surrounded by alternating fields of attractive and repulsive forces. A true element comprised a single such point, and chemical elements were composed of a number of such points, about which the resultant force fields could be quite complicated. Molecules, in turn, were built up of these elements, and the chemical qualities of both elements and compounds were the results of the final patterns of force surrounding clumps of point atoms. One property of such atoms and molecules should be specifically noted: they can be placed under considerable strain, or tension, before the "bonds" holding them together are broken. These strains were to be central to Faraday's ideas about electricity.

Faraday's second apprenticeship, under Davy, came to an end in 1820. By then he had learned chemistry as thoroughly as anyone alive. He had also had ample opportunity to practice chemical analyses and laboratory techniques to the point of complete mastery, and he had developed his theoretical views to the point that they could guide him in his researches. There followed a series of discoveries that astonished the scientific world.

Faraday achieved his early renown as a chemist. His reputation as an analytical chemist led to his being called as an expert witness in some legal trials and to the building up of a sizable clientele whose fees helped to support the Royal Institution. In 1820 he produced the first known compounds of carbon and chlorine, C_2Cl_6 and C_2Cl_4. These compounds were produced by substituting chlorine for hydrogen in "olefiant gas" (ethylene), the first substitution reactions induced. (Such reactions later would serve to challenge the dominant theory of chemical combination proposed by Jöns Jacob Berzelius.) In 1825, as a result of research on illuminating gases, Faraday isolated and described benzene. In the 1820s he also conducted investigations of steel alloys, helping to lay the foundations for scientific metallurgy and metallography. While completing an assignment from the Royal Society of London to improve the quality of optical glass for telescopes, he produced a glass of very high refractive index that was to lead him, in 1845, to the discovery of diamagnetism. In 1821 he married Sarah Barnard, settled permanently in chambers at the Royal Institution, and began the long series of experimental researches on electricity and magnetism that was to revolutionize physics.

In 1820 Hans Christian Ørsted had announced the discovery that the flow of an electric current through a wire produced a magnetic field around the wire. In France, André-Marie Ampère showed that the magnetic force apparently was a circular one, producing in effect a cylinder of magnetism around the wire. No such circular force had ever before been observed, and Faraday was the first to understand what it implied. If a magnetic pole could be isolated, it ought to move constantly in a circle around a current-carrying wire. Faraday's ingenuity and laboratory skill enabled him to construct an apparatus that confirmed this conclusion. This device, which transformed electrical energy into mechanical energy, was the first electric motor.

This discovery led Faraday to contemplate the nature of electricity. Unlike his contemporaries, he was not convinced that electricity was a material fluid that flowed through wires like water through a pipe. Instead, he thought of it as a vibration or force that was somehow transmitted as the result of tensions created in the conductor. One of his first experiments after his discovery of electromagnetic rotation was to pass a ray of polarized light through a solution in which electrochemical decomposition was taking place in order to detect the intermolecular strains that he thought must be produced by the passage of an electric current. During the 1820s he kept coming back to this idea, but always without result.

In the spring of 1831 Faraday began to work with Charles (later Sir Charles) Wheatstone on the theory of sound, another vibrational phenomenon. He was particularly fascinated by the patterns (known as Chladni figures) formed in light powder spread on iron plates when these plates were thrown into vibration by a violin bow. Here was demonstrated the ability of a dynamic cause to create a static effect, something he was convinced happened in a current-carrying wire. He was even more impressed by the fact that such patterns could be induced in one plate by bowing another nearby. Such acoustic induction is apparently what lay behind his most famous experiment. On August 29, 1831, Faraday wound a thick iron ring on one side with insulated wire that was connected to a battery. He then wound the opposite side with wire connected to a galvanometer. What he expected was that a "wave" would be produced when the battery circuit was closed and that the wave would show up as a deflection of the galvanometer in the second circuit. He closed the primary circuit and, to his delight and satisfaction, saw the galvanometer needle jump. A current had been induced in the secondary coil by one in the primary. When he opened the circuit, however, he was astonished to see the galvanometer jump in the opposite direction. Somehow, turning off the current also created an induced current in the secondary circuit, equal and opposite to the original current. This phenomenon led Faraday to propose what he called the "electrotonic" state of particles in the wire, which he considered a state of tension. A current thus appeared to be the setting up of such a state of tension or the collapse of such a state. Although he could not find experimental evidence for the electrotonic state, he never entirely abandoned the concept, and it shaped most of his later work.

In the fall of 1831 Faraday attempted to determine just how an induced current was produced. His original experiment had involved a powerful electromagnet, created by the winding of the primary coil. He now tried to create a current by using a permanent magnet. He discovered that when a permanent magnet was moved in and out of a coil of wire a current was induced in the coil. Magnets, he knew, were surrounded by forces that could be made visible by the simple expedient of sprinkling iron filings on a card held over them. Faraday saw the "lines of force" thus revealed as lines of tension in the medium, namely air, surrounding the magnet, and he soon discovered the law determining the production of electric currents by magnets: the magnitude of the current was dependent upon the number of lines of force cut by the conductor in unit time. He immediately realized that a continuous current could be produced by rotating a copper disk between the poles of a powerful magnet and taking leads off the disk's rim and centre. The outside of the disk would cut more lines than would the inside, and there would thus be a continuous current produced in the circuit linking the rim to the centre. This was the first dynamo. It was also the direct ancestor of electric motors, for it was only necessary to reverse the situation, to feed an electric current to the disk, to make it rotate.

While Faraday was performing these experiments and presenting them to the scientific world, doubts were raised

about the identity of the different manifestations of electricity that had been studied. Were the electric "fluid" that apparently was released by electric eels and other electric fishes, that produced by a static electricity generator, that of the voltaic battery, and that of the new electromagnetic generator all the same? Or were they different fluids following different laws? Faraday was convinced that they were not fluids at all but forms of the same force, yet he recognized that this identity had never been satisfactorily shown by experiment. For this reason he began, in 1832, what promised to be a rather tedious attempt to prove that all electricities had precisely the same properties and caused precisely the same effects. The key effect was electrochemical decomposition. Voltaic and electromagnetic electricity posed no problems, but static electricity did. As Faraday delved deeper into the problem, he made two startling discoveries. First, electrical force did not, as had long been supposed, act at a distance upon chemical molecules to cause them to dissociate. It was the passage of electricity through a conducting liquid medium that caused the molecules to dissociate, even when the electricity merely discharged into the air and did not pass into a "pole" or "centre of action" in a voltaic cell. Second, the amount of the decomposition was found to be related in a simple manner to the amount of electricity that passed through the solution. These findings led Faraday to a new theory of electrochemistry. The electric force, he argued, threw the molecules of a solution into a state of tension (his electrotonic state). When the force was strong enough to distort the fields of forces that held the molecules together so as to permit the interaction of these fields with neighbouring particles, the tension was relieved by the migration of particles along the lines of tension, the different species of atoms migrating in opposite directions. The amount of electricity that passed, then, was clearly related to the chemical affinities of the substances in solution. These experiments led directly to Faraday's two laws of electrochemistry: (1) The amount of a substance deposited on each electrode of an electrolytic cell is directly proportional to the quantity of electricity passed through the cell. (2) The quantities of different elements deposited by a given amount of electricity are in the ratio of their chemical equivalent weights.

Faraday's work on electrochemistry provided him with an essential clue for the investigation of static electrical induction. Since the amount of electricity passed through the conducting medium of an electrolytic cell determined the amount of material deposited at the electrodes, why should not the amount of electricity induced in a nonconductor be dependent upon the material out of which it was made? In short, why should not every material have a specific inductive capacity? Every material does, and Faraday was the discoverer of this fact.

By 1839 Faraday was able to bring forth a new and general theory of electrical action. Electricity, whatever it was, caused tensions to be created in matter. When these tensions were rapidly relieved (i.e., when bodies could not take much strain before "snapping" back), then what occurred was a rapid repetition of a cyclical buildup, breakdown, and buildup of tension that, like a wave, was passed along the substance. Such substances were called conductors. In electrochemical processes the rate of buildup and breakdown of the strain was proportional to the chemical affinities of the substances involved, but again the current was not a material flow but a wave pattern of tensions and their relief. Insulators were simply materials whose particles could take an extraordinary amount of strain before they snapped. Electrostatic charge in an isolated insulator was simply a measure of this accumulated strain. Thus, all electrical action was the result of forced strains in bodies.

The strain on Faraday of eight years of sustained experimental and theoretical work was too much, and in 1839 he suffered a breakdown of his health. For the next six years he did little creative science. Not until 1845 was he able to pick up the thread of his researches and extend his theoretical views.

Later life. Since the very beginning of his scientific work, Faraday had believed in what he called the unity of the forces of nature. By this he meant that all the forces of nature were but manifestations of a single universal force and ought, therefore, to be convertible into one another. In 1846 he made public some of the speculations to which this view led him. A lecturer, scheduled to deliver one of the Friday evening discourses at the Royal Institution by which Faraday encouraged the popularization of science, panicked at the last minute and ran out, leaving Faraday with a packed lecture hall and no lecturer. On the spur of the moment, Faraday offered "Thoughts on Ray Vibrations." Specifically referring to point atoms and their infinite fields of force, he suggested that the lines of electric and magnetic force associated with these atoms might, in fact, serve as the medium by which light waves were propagated. Many years later, Maxwell was to build his electromagnetic field theory upon this speculation.

When Faraday returned to active research in 1845, it was to tackle again a problem that had obsessed him for years, that of his hypothetical electrotonic state. He was still convinced that it must exist and that he simply had not yet discovered the means for detecting it. Once again he tried to find signs of intermolecular strain in substances through which electrical lines of force passed, but again with no success. It was at this time that a young Scot, William Thomson (later Lord Kelvin), wrote Faraday that he had studied Faraday's papers on electricity and magnetism and that he, too, was convinced that some kind of strain must exist. He suggested that Faraday experiment with magnetic lines of force, since these could be produced at much greater strengths than could electrostatic ones.

Faraday took the suggestion, passed a beam of plane-polarized light through the optical glass of high refractive index that he had developed in the 1820s, and then turned on an electromagnet so that its lines of force ran parallel to the light ray. This time he was rewarded with success. The plane of polarization was rotated, indicating a strain in the molecules of the glass. But, once again, Faraday noted an unexpected result. When he changed the direction of the ray of light, the rotation remained in the same direction, a fact that Faraday correctly interpreted as meaning that the strain was not, after all, in the molecules of the glass but in the magnetic lines of force. The direction of rotation of the plane of polarization depended solely upon the polarity of the lines of force; the glass served merely to detect the effect.

This discovery confirmed Faraday's faith in the unity of forces, and he plunged onward, certain that all matter must exhibit some response to a magnetic field. To his surprise he found that this was in fact so, but in a peculiar way. Some substances, such as iron, nickel, cobalt, and oxygen, lined up in a magnetic field so that the long axes of their crystalline or molecular structures were parallel to the lines of force; others lined up perpendicular to the lines of force. Substances of the first class moved toward more intense magnetic fields; those of the second moved toward regions of less magnetic force. Faraday named the first group paramagnetics and the second diamagnetics. After further research he concluded that paramagnetics were bodies that conducted magnetic lines of force better than did the surrounding medium, whereas diamagnetics conducted them less well. By 1850 Faraday had evolved a radically new view of space and force. Space was not "nothing," the mere location of bodies and forces, but a medium capable of supporting the strains of electric and magnetic forces. The energies of the world were not localized in the particles from which these forces arose but rather were to be found in the space surrounding them. Thus was born field theory. As Maxwell later freely admitted, the basic ideas for his mathematical theory of electrical and magnetic fields came from Faraday; his contribution was to mathematize those ideas in the form of his classical field equations. Discovery of dia-magnetism

From about 1855, Faraday's mind began to fail. He still did occasional experiments, one of which involved attempting to find an electrical effect of raising a heavy weight, since he felt that gravity, like magnetism, must be convertible into some other force, most likely electrical. This time he was disappointed in his expectations, and the Royal Society refused to publish his negative results. More and more, Faraday began to sink into senility. Queen Victoria rewarded his lifetime of devotion to science by granting him the use of a house at Hampton Court and even offered him the honour of a knighthood. Faraday gratefully accepted the cottage but rejected the knighthood; he would, he said, remain plain Mr. Faraday to the end. He died on August 25, 1867, and was buried in Highgate Cemetery, London, leaving as his monument a new conception of physical reality.

(L. Pearce Williams)

Lavoisier

A French chemist and the father of modern chemistry, Antoine-Laurent Lavoisier was a brilliant experimenter and many-sided genius who was active in public affairs as well as in science. He developed a new theory of combustion that led to the overthrow of the phlogistic doctrine, which had dominated the course of chemistry for more than a century. His fundamental studies on oxidation demonstrated the role of oxygen in chemical processes and showed quantitatively the similarity between oxidation and respiration. He formulated the principle of the conservation of matter in chemical reactions. He clarified the distinction between elements and compounds and was instrumental in devising the modern system of chemical nomenclature. Lavoisier was one of the first scientific workers to introduce quantitative procedures into chemical investigations. His experimental ingenuity, exact methods, and cogent reasoning, no less than his discoveries, revolutionized chemistry. His name is indissolubly linked to the establishment of the foundations upon which modern science rests.

Lavoisier was born in Paris on August 26, 1743. His father, an *avocat au parlement* (parliamentary counsel), gave him an excellent education at the Collège Mazarin, where, along with a solid classical grounding in language, literature, and philosophy, he received the best available training in the sciences, including mathematics, astronomy, chemistry, and botany. Following his family's tradition, he pursued the study of law, and he received his license to practice in 1764. His inquiring mind, however, continually drew him to science. In 1766 he received a gold medal from the Academy of Sciences for an essay on the best means of lighting a large town. Among his early work were papers on the Aurora Borealis, on thunder, and on the composition of gypsum. Pursuing an early interest in rocks and minerals, he accompanied the geologist J.-E. Guettard on a long geological trip and assisted him in preparing his mineralogical atlas of France. In 1768, after presenting a paper on the analysis of water samples, Lavoisier was admitted to the academy as *adjoint-chimiste* (associate chemist). He passed through all the grades in the academic structure and was made director in 1785 and treasurer in 1791. Education and early work

Through his family, Lavoisier became independently wealthy in his early 20s. In 1771 he married Marie Paulze, who would later assist him in his work by illustrating his experiments, recording results, and translating scientific articles from English. In accordance with a common practice among the wealthy bourgeoisie at the time, his father bought him a title of nobility in 1772, and a few years later Lavoisier purchased the country estate of Fréchines, near Blois.

Scientific achievements. Lavoisier's name gained wide

recognition when, in 1770, he refuted the then prevalent belief that water is converted into earth by repeated distillation. By carefully weighing both the earthy residue and the distilling apparatus, he demonstrated that the solid matter came from the glass vessels and not from the water.

Study of combustion

Speculating on the nature of the traditional four elements—earth, water, air, and fire—Lavoisier began to investigate the role of air in combustion. On November 1, 1772, he deposited with the Academy of Sciences a note stating that sulfur and phosphorus when burned increased in weight because they absorbed "air," while the metallic lead formed when litharge was heated with charcoal weighed less than the original litharge because it had lost "air." The exact nature of the airs concerned in the processes he could not yet explain, and he proceeded to study the question extensively. In 1774 he published his first book, *Opuscules physiques et chimiques,* in which he presented the results of both his reading and his experimentation. That year Joseph Priestley prepared "dephlogisticated air" (oxygen) by heating "red precipitate of mercury." Lavoisier confirmed and extended Priestley's work. Perceiving that in combustion and the calcination of metals only a portion of a given volume of common air was used up, he concluded that the active agent was Priestley's new "air," which was absorbed by burning, and that "nonvital air," or azote (nitrogen), remained behind. He observed that birds lived longer in the new "eminently respirable air," as he described it, and he showed that this air combined with carbon to produce the "fixed air" (carbon dioxide) obtained by Joseph Black in 1754.

Recognition that the atmosphere is composed of different gases that take part in chemical reactions made it possible to identify the composition of many substances, particularly the acids. In a memoir presented to the academy in 1777, read in 1779 but not published until 1781, Lavoisier assigned to dephlogisticated air the name oxygen, or "acid producer," on the erroneous supposition that all acids were formed by its union with a simple, usually nonmetallic body. He explained combustion not as the result of the liberation of a hypothetical fire principle, phlogiston, but as the result of the combination of the burning substance with oxygen. On June 25, 1783, he announced to the academy that water was the product formed by the combination of hydrogen and oxygen; in this, however, he had been anticipated by the English chemist Henry Cavendish. As a member of a committee for finding ways to improve lighter-than-air flight with the newly invented balloons, he produced quantities of hydrogen, called "inflammable air," by decomposing water into its constituent gases. From his knowledge of the composition of water, Lavoisier was led to the beginnings of quantitative organic analysis. He burned alcohol and other combustible organic compounds in oxygen, and from the weight of water and carbon dioxide produced he calculated their composition.

Lavoisier published a brilliant attack on the phlogistic theory in 1786. Despite the opposition of Priestley and others, a growing number of scientists began to adopt his views. In 1787 a group of French chemists published the *Méthode de nomenclature chimique,* which classified and renamed the known elements and compounds. Reflecting Lavoisier's new discoveries and theories, the *Nomenclature* exerted a wide influence. Also influential was the revision in 1788 of Antoine-François de Fourcroy's popular *Élémens d'histoire naturelle et de chimie,* which was completely recast in terms of Lavoisier's views and according to the new chemical nomenclature. The following year Lavoisier and others established the *Annales de chimie,* a journal devoted to the new chemistry. Gradually the older approach based on the phlogistic theory lost adherents, and eventually Lavoisier's ideas were adopted universally.

The spread of Lavoisier's doctrines was greatly facilitated by the defined and logical form in which he presented them in his *Traité élémentaire de chimie* (1789). This classic book provided a concise exposition of his work and that of his followers and offered an introduction to the new approach to chemistry. In the prefatory "Discours préliminaire" Lavoisier set forth his views on the proper methods of scientific inquiry and scientific teaching, and he defended the new nomenclature. Those substances that could not be decomposed he termed *substances simples,* the elements out of which other matter was made. To a large extent the modern concept of an element, as against the ancient Greek idea, stems from Lavoisier. In the *Traité* he furnished a clear statement of his principle of the conservation of matter in chemical reactions. Nothing, he said, is created or destroyed; there are only alterations and modifications, and there is an equal quantity—an equation—of matter before and after the operation.

Other scientific work

In addition to his purely chemical work, Lavoisier, mostly in conjunction with the mathematician and astronomer Pierre-Simon Laplace, devoted considerable attention to physical problems, especially those connected with heat. The two carried out some of the earliest thermochemical investigations, devised an apparatus for measuring linear and cubical expansions, and employed a modification of Black's ice calorimeter in a series of determinations of specific heats. Regarding heat (*matière du feu*) as a peculiar kind of imponderable matter, Lavoisier held that the three states of aggregation—solid, liquid, and gas—were modes of matter, each depending on the amount of *matière du feu* with which the substances concerned were associated. He also worked at fermentation, respiration, and animal heat, looking upon the processes concerned as essentially chemical in nature. From measurements made in his pioneering biochemical experiments on animal heat and on the gases exchanged during respiration, he concluded that respiration was a type of oxidation reaction similar to the burning of carbon. A paper discovered many years after his death showed that he had anticipated later thinkers in explaining the cyclical process of animal and vegetable life.

Public service. Throughout Lavoisier's extraordinary career as a scientist, he carried on a simultaneous career as a public servant of remarkable versatility, contributing his talents in the areas of finance, economics, agriculture, education, and social welfare, among others. In 1768 he became an assistant in one of the revenue-collecting departments of the government, subsequently becoming a full titular member of the Ferme Générale, the main tax-collecting agency. The financial and organizational abilities he displayed as a farmer-general, along with his undoubted scientific and technical capacity, led in 1775 to his appointment as *régisseur des poudres* (a director of the gunpowder administration). With his customary energy he set about making improvements in the chaotic powder industry. He abolished the vexatious search for saltpetre in the cellars of private houses, increased the production of the salt, and improved the manufacture of gunpowder. The post enabled Lavoisier to move to the Arsenal of Paris, where he took up residence and equipped a superb laboratory. This establishment soon became a gathering place for the scientists and advanced thinkers of the day, and the dinners presided over by his wife became famous. After dinner the guests often would be escorted to the laboratory to witness or take part in a demonstration of some new experiment. Although an increasing number of public duties claimed Lavoisier's time, he regularly set aside one day a week for scientific investigations.

As his influence in the Academy of Sciences grew, so did his responsibilities. He was a member of numerous official committees to look into matters concerning the public. In 1781 the notorious Franz Anton Mesmer arrived in Paris, and Lavoisier (along with Benjamin Franklin) served on a committee to investigate his cures by "animal magnetism," pronouncing them a hoax. With another committee, he explored the hospitals and prisons of Paris and recommended remedies for their deplorable state. At Fréchines he started a model farm, where he demonstrated the advantages of scientific agriculture. In 1785 he was named to the government's committee on agriculture and as its secretary drew up reports and instructions on the cultivation of crops, promulgating various agricultural schemes. As a landowner in the province of Orléans, Lavoisier was chosen a member of the provincial assembly in 1787. There he devised measures for improving social and economic conditions in the area by such means as savings banks, insurance societies, canals, workhouses, and tax reforms. He advanced money without interest to the towns of Blois and Romorantin for the purchase of barley during the famine of 1788. He was associated with committees on hygiene, coinage, the casting of cannon, and public education. He was secretary and treasurer of the commission appointed in 1790 to secure uniformity of weights and measures throughout France, work that led to the establishment of the metric system.

A reformer and political liberal opposed to many aspects of the ancien régime, Lavoisier took an active role in the French Revolution. When the States General was reconvened in 1789, he became an alternate deputy and drew up the code of instructions for guidance of the deputies. He was elected to the commune of Paris and joined the moderate Society of 1789, a planning group. He became an administrator of the national treasury and published detailed analyses of the state of the nation's finances and its agriculture. But his membership in the unpopular Ferme Générale was alone sufficient to make him an object of suspicion to the authorities, and, despite his many services to the nation and his wide renown as a scientist, he came under increasingly severe attack from the more radical

pamphleteers. In 1787, at Lavoisier's suggestion, a wall had been erected around Paris to halt the flow of contraband into the city. The extremist revolutionary Jean-Paul Marat accused him of putting Paris in prison and of stopping the circulation of air. In 1791 the Ferme Générale was abolished, and Lavoisier was subsequently removed from his position in the gunpowder administration and forced to leave his home and laboratory in the Arsenal. In 1793 the Reign of Terror commenced, and, in spite of strenuous efforts by Lavoisier, the Academy of Sciences, along with the other learned societies, was suppressed. At the end of the year the Revolutionary Convention ordered the arrest of the former members of the Ferme Générale, and in May 1794 they were tried by the revolutionary tribunal. The trial lasted less than a day. Lavoisier and 27 others were condemned to death. That same afternoon, May 8, he and his companions, including his father-in-law, were guillotined at the Place de la Révolution (now Concorde). His body was thrown into a common grave.

(Denis Ian Duveen)

Lavoisier's fate in the Revolution

Planck

Max Planck made many contributions to theoretical physics, but his fame rests primarily on his role as originator of the quantum theory. This theory revolutionized our understanding of atomic and subatomic processes, just as Albert Einstein's theory of relativity revolutionized our understanding of space and time. Together they constitute the fundamental theories of 20th-century physics. Both have forced man to revise some of his most cherished philosophical beliefs, and both have led to industrial and military applications that affect every aspect of modern life.

Early life. Max Karl Ernst Ludwig Planck was born on April 23, 1858, in Kiel, Germany, the sixth child of a distinguished jurist and professor of law at the University of Kiel. The long family tradition of devotion to church and state, excellence in scholarship, incorruptibility, conservatism, idealism, reliability, and generosity became deeply ingrained in Planck's own life and work. When Planck was nine years old, his father received an appointment at the University of Munich, and Planck entered the city's renowned Maximilian Gymnasium, where a teacher, Hermann Müller, stimulated his interest in physics and mathematics. But Planck excelled in all subjects, and after graduation at age 17 he faced a difficult career decision. He ultimately chose physics over classical philology or music because he had dispassionately reached the conclusion that it was in physics that his greatest originality lay. Music, nonetheless, remained an integral part of his life. He possessed the gift of absolute pitch and was an excellent pianist who daily found serenity and delight at the keyboard, enjoying especially the works of Schubert and Brahms. He also loved the outdoors, taking long walks each day and hiking and climbing in the mountains on vacations, even in advanced old age.

Planck entered the University of Munich in the fall of 1874 but found little encouragement there from physics professor Philipp von Jolly. During his *Wanderjahr* (1877–78) at the University of Berlin, he was unimpressed by the lectures of Hermann von Helmholtz and Gustav Robert Kirchhoff, despite their eminence as research scientists. His intellectual capacities were, however, brought to a focus as the result of his independent study, especially of Rudolf Clausius' writings on thermodynamics. Returning to Munich, he received his doctoral degree in July 1879 (the year of Einstein's birth) at the unusually young age of 21. The following year he completed his *Habilitationsschrift* (qualifying dissertation) at Munich and became a *Privatdozent* (lecturer). In 1885, with the help of his father's professional connections, he was appointed *ausserordentlicher Professor* (associate professor) at the University

of Kiel. In 1889, after the death of Kirchhoff, Planck received an appointment to the University of Berlin, where he came to venerate Helmholtz as mentor and colleague. In 1892 he was promoted to *ordentlicher Professor* (full professor). He had only nine doctoral students altogether, but his Berlin lectures on all branches of theoretical physics went through many editions and exerted great influence. He remained in Berlin for the rest of his life.

Planck recalled that his "original decision to devote myself to science was a direct result of the discovery . . . that the laws of human reasoning coincide with the laws governing the sequences of the impressions we receive from the world about us; that, therefore, pure reasoning can enable man to gain an insight into the mechanism of the [world]. . . ." He deliberately decided, in other words, to become a theoretical physicist at a time when theoretical physics was not yet recognized as a discipline in its own right. But he went further: he concluded that the existence of physical laws presupposes that the "outside world is something independent from man, something absolute, and the quest for the laws which apply to this absolute appeared . . . as the most sublime scientific pursuit in life."

The first instance of an absolute in nature that impressed Planck deeply, even as a *Gymnasium* student, was the law of the conservation of energy, the first law of thermodynamics. Later, during his university years, he became equally convinced that the entropy law, the second law of thermodynamics, was also an absolute law of nature. The second law became the subject of his doctoral dissertation at Munich, and it lay at the core of the researches that led him to discover the quantum of action, now known as Planck's constant h, in 1900.

In 1859–60 Kirchhoff had defined a blackbody as an object that re-emits all of the radiant energy incident upon it; *i.e.*, it is a perfect emitter and absorber of radiation. There was, therefore, something absolute about blackbody radiation, and by the 1890s various experimental and theoretical attempts had been made to determine its spectral energy distribution—the curve displaying how much radiant energy is emitted at different frequencies for a given temperature of the blackbody. Planck was particularly attracted to the formula found in 1896 by his colleague Wilhelm Wien at the Physikalisch-Technische Reichsanstalt (PTR) in Berlin-Charlottenburg, and he subsequently made a series of attempts to derive "Wien's law" on the basis of the second law of thermodynamics. By October 1900, however, other colleagues at the PTR, the experimentalists Otto Richard Lummer, Ernst Pringsheim, Heinrich Rubens, and Ferdinand Kurlbaum, had found definite indications that Wien's law, while valid at high

Development of quantum theory

frequencies, broke down completely at low frequencies.

Planck learned of these results just before a meeting of the German Physical Society on October 19. He knew how the entropy of the radiation had to depend mathematically upon its energy in the high-frequency region if Wien's law held there. He also saw what this dependence had to be in the low-frequency region in order to reproduce the experimental results there. Planck guessed, therefore, that he should try to combine these two expressions in the simplest way possible, and to transform the result into a formula relating the energy of the radiation to its frequency.

Planck's formulation was hailed as indisputably correct. To Planck, however, it was simply a guess, a "lucky intuition." If it was to be taken seriously, it had to be derived somehow from first principles. That was the task to which Planck immediately directed his energies, and by December 14, 1900, he had succeeded—but at great cost. To achieve his goal, Planck found that he had to relinquish one of his own most cherished beliefs, that the second law of thermodynamics was an absolute law of nature. Instead he had to embrace Ludwig Boltzmann's interpretation, that the second law was a statistical law. In addition, Planck had to assume that the oscillators comprising the blackbody and re-emitting the radiant energy incident upon them could not absorb this energy continuously but only in discrete amounts, in quanta of energy; only by statistically distributing these quanta, each containing an amount of energy $h\nu$ proportional to its frequency, over all of the oscillators present in the blackbody could Planck derive the formula he had hit upon two months earlier. He adduced additional evidence for the importance of his formula by using it to evaluate the constant h (his value was 6.55×10^{-27} erg-second, close to the modern value), as well as the so-called Boltzmann constant (the fundamental constant in kinetic theory and statistical mechanics), Avogadro's number, and the charge of the electron. As time went on physicists recognized ever more clearly that—because Planck's constant was not zero but had a small but finite value—the microphysical world, the world of atomic dimensions, could not in principle be described by ordinary classical mechanics. A profound revolution in physical theory was in the making.

Planck's concept of energy quanta, in other words, conflicted fundamentally with all past physical theory. He was driven to introduce it strictly by the force of his logic; he was, as one historian put it, a reluctant revolutionary. Indeed, it was years before the far-reaching consequences of Planck's achievement were generally recognized, and in this Einstein played a central role. In 1905, independently of Planck's work, Einstein argued that under certain circumstances radiant energy itself seemed to consist of quanta (light quanta, later called photons), and in 1907 he showed the generality of the quantum hypothesis by using it to interpret the temperature dependence of the specific heats of solids. In 1909 he introduced the wave-particle duality into physics. In October 1911 he was among the group of prominent physicists who attended the first Solvay conference in Brussels. The discussions there stimulated Henri Poincaré to provide a mathematical proof that Planck's radiation law necessarily required the introduction of quanta—a proof that converted James (later Sir James) Jeans and others into supporters of the quantum theory. In 1913 Niels Bohr also contributed greatly to its establishment through his quantum theory of the hydrogen atom. Ironically, Planck himself was one of the last to struggle for a return to classical theory, a stance he later regarded not with regret but as a means by which he had thoroughly convinced himself of the necessity of the quantum theory. Opposition to Einstein's radical light quantum hypothesis of 1905 persisted until after the discovery of the Compton effect in 1922.

Einstein's role

Later life. Planck was 42 years old in 1900 when he made the famous discovery that in 1918 won him the Nobel Prize for Physics and that brought him many other honours. It is not surprising that he subsequently made no discoveries of comparable importance. Nevertheless, he continued to contribute at a high level to various branches of optics, thermodynamics and statistical mechanics, physical chemistry, and other fields. He was also the first prominent physicist to champion Einstein's special theory of relativity (1905). "The velocity of light is to the Theory of Relativity," Planck remarked, "as the elementary quantum of action is to the Quantum Theory; it is its absolute core." In 1914 Planck and the physical chemist Walther Hermann Nernst succeeded in bringing Einstein to Berlin, and after the war, in 1919, arrangements were made for Max von Laue, Planck's favourite student, to come to Berlin as well. When Planck retired in 1928, another prominent theoretical physicist, Erwin Schrödinger, the originator of wave mechanics, was chosen as his successor. For a time, therefore, Berlin shone brilliantly as a centre of theoretical physics—until darkness enveloped it in January 1933 with the ascent of Adolf Hitler to power.

In his later years, Planck devoted more and more of his writings to philosophical, aesthetic, and religious questions. Together with Einstein and Schrödinger, he remained adamantly opposed to the indeterministic, statistical worldview introduced by Bohr, Max Born, Werner Heisenberg, and others into physics after the advent of quantum mechanics in 1925–26. Such a view was not in harmony with Planck's deepest intuitions and beliefs. The physical universe, Planck argued, is an objective entity existing independently of man; the observer and the observed are not intimately coupled, as Bohr and his school would have it.

Worldview

Planck became permanent secretary of the mathematics and physics sections of the Prussian Academy of Sciences in 1912 and held that position until 1938; he was also president of the Kaiser Wilhelm Society (now the Max Planck Society) from 1930 to 1937. These offices and others placed Planck in a position of great authority, especially among German physicists; seldom were his decisions or advice questioned. His authority, however, stemmed fundamentally not from the official appointments he held but from his personal moral force. His fairness, integrity, and wisdom were beyond question. It was completely in character that Planck went directly to Hitler in an attempt to reverse Hitler's devastating racial policies, and that he chose to remain in Germany during the Nazi period to try to preserve what he could of German physics.

Planck was a man of indomitable will. Had he been less stoic, and had he had less philosophical and religious conviction, he could scarcely have withstood the tragedies that entered his life after age 50. In 1909, his first wife, Marie Merck, the daughter of a Munich banker, died after 22 years of happy marriage, leaving Planck with two sons and twin daughters. The elder son, Karl, was killed in action in 1916. The following year, Margarete, one of his daughters, died in childbirth, and in 1919 the same fate befell Emma, his other daughter. World War II brought further tragedy. Planck's house in Berlin was completely destroyed by bombs in 1944. Far worse, the younger son, Erwin, was implicated in the attempt made on Hitler's life on July 20, 1944, and in early 1945 he died a horrible death at the hands of the Gestapo. That merciless act destroyed Planck's will to live. At war's end, American officers took Planck and his second wife, Marga von Hoesslin, whom he had married in 1910 and by whom he had had one son, to Göttingen. There, on October 4, 1947, in his 89th year, he died. Death, in the words of James Franck, came to him "as a redemption."

(Roger H. Stuewer)

Bibliography: Recent Books

To supplement and update the bibliographies accompanying *Macropædia* articles, critical reviews of several recent books of interest and importance are presented here. Two books each address the fields of anthropology, economics, and history.

George Kennan finds in the alliance between France and Russia, formed in the 1890s, the seeds of World War I and the subsequent polarization of Europe. Elinor Langer's biography of Josephine Herbst is notable for its insights into the turbulent 1930s, including the world of Communist infiltration into Western governments.

Fernand Braudel looks at the rise and decline of "world economies" that successively dominated international trade and the economic milieu of their times. Charles Oxnard's book describes how anthropologists, aided by computer models, have changed the view of human evolution widely held since Darwin's day.

Stephen Kern focuses on a period immediately after Darwin and proposes that in less than four decades, from 1880 to 1918, the human understanding of the experience of time and space underwent basic changes that determined the unique character of the 20th century with all its technological marvels. Jane Jacobs sees the city-region as the vital force behind economic development—a role often overlooked by nation-states as they make decisions on economic policy.

The Fateful Alliance:
France, Russia, and the Coming of the First World War

By George Kennan. New York, Pantheon, 1984. 304 pages

Among contemporary diplomatic historians, few have been more persistently obsessed with the analogy between the causes and consequences of World War I and the present polarization in international relations than George Kennan. For him, also, the towering tragedy of that war is to be seen in its catastrophic consequences for Russia and the effects of Russia's collapse and revolution for Europe in general. Kennan the historian and Kennan the policy advocate are not easily distinguishable. In this book the chain of events leading up to the Great War (as World War I was once known) is presented as a paradigm that statecraft should not allow to recur. Power blocs are dangerous and bad.

The Fateful Alliance is the second volume in a Kennan trilogy that, when finished, will constitute the annals of European international relations from the last years of "Bismarckian Europe" (the 1880s) until the collapse, in wartime, of the Romanov dynasty and Russia's withdrawal from the war. This volume recounts the stages by which a strange alliance developed between tsarist Russia and republican France in the early 1890s, when Europe was enjoying general peace.

The Franco-Russian chapter of the prewar polarization of Europe into "two camps"—the Triple Alliance and the Triple Entente—is masterfully narrated. Yet it is also Kennan's curious purpose to portray the advent of this particular alliance as the principal source of the great tragedy that was to come.

To understand the specific events and decisions that precede great wars is not necessarily to demonstrate that, in the given context, other courses of action would have been safer, wiser, or better. *The Fateful Alliance* is a good

illustration of this. Kennan's account of the slow mating dance between a "radical" France and a "reactionary" Russia vividly illustrates how opposites pursuing their special interests in alliance can sometimes transform the contours of international politics. (Another such flip-flop was the Nazi-Soviet pact of 1939.) But the account is sparse on the matter of other options that might have been available to either or both parties.

In recounting the alliance's evolution, Kennan disapproves of what he observes. He plays favourites among the cast of characters, and he has his villains and fools. The wisest (to him) was Tsar Alexander III's foreign minister, Nikolay Giers, who was keenly, if impotently, alarmed at the fearsome implications of an ironclad political-military alliance with France. The chief Russian villain would appear to be Alexander himself. The tsar, as it turns out, seems to have been covertly entranced with the potential fruits of such an alliance—including the possible disintegration of imperial Germany.

It is worth noting that the French were the suitors in this romance, conniving in all sorts of clever Gallic ways to befriend the imperial court, where, in any event, they had many friends and fellow travelers. The products of this flirtation were the secret political-military agreements of 1893, which ultimately locked the two powers in alliance against Germany and its Triple Alliance.

It is perplexing to the reader at first why Kennan should single out this Franco-Russian rapprochement, among other developments before and after, as so uniquely portentous. In the particulars of Kennan's account, it is clear that these ideological opposites were not witlessly or foolishly blundering. Both parties knew full well what they were doing; they were both quite well informed on the correlation of forces in Europe at the time. They were realistic in judging their options. In neither government was there evidence of any serious opposition to the agreement.

What, then, brought them together? The entirely new element in European power politics after 1870 was imperial Germany, and it was with this German problem that European statecraft had to deal. After the Franco-Prussian War (1870–71), even Bismarck himself had realized the immensity of the problem, a product of his own successes. In his diplomacy, he sought to forestall a polarization of European politics that might consummate *Le cauchemar des coalitions*—the nightmare of anti-German coalitions—a traditional fear of Hohenzollern Prussia.

With this in mind, Bismarck fashioned the Three Emperor Alliance (*Dreikaiserbund*) to regulate relations between Germany, Austria, and Russia. When this was allowed to lapse, he replaced it with the Russo-German Reinsurance Treaty while simultaneously nurturing the Triple Alliance of Germany, Austria, and Italy. But Bismarck's epigonic successors, after his dismissal, fatally allowed the Russo-German Reinsurance Treaty to lapse in 1890, the year Kennan's story begins. Thus, in that year, Germany towered militarily over each of its diplomatically isolated neighbours, France and Russia. The fearsome rumours that England also would join the Triple Alliance proved false, but they spurred the Russians to seek a way out of their diplomatic isolation.

As this elegant book is both a history and a cautionary tale, the question arises: What options were open to Russia and France other than the quite logical and obvious one they chose? To this question, unfortunately, Kennan provides no clear answer, other than, characteristically, to deplore military solutions to political problems. For Russia, Kennan, with benefit of hindsight, sees the alliance as a catastrophe. In his words:

. . . [H]ow endlessly unfortunate, primarily for Russia but scarcely less for France and the remainder of Western Europe, turned out to be this involvement of Russia, through her ties to France, in the great Western European conflicts of the first years of this century.

This very personal compassion for the tragic fate of Russia is understandable in light of Kennan's earlier histories of the Russian Revolution, yet his judgment defies the climate of the times. Russia had been deeply involved in central and western European politics long before the events Kennan recounts here.

That Russia lay on the periphery of Europe did not mean it could indulge the luxury of isolation from events there, as the United States could at the time. Moreover, the imperial court at St. Petersburg was thoroughly permeated with European prejudices and preferences. The tsarina— no passive spectator to these events—was a Danish princess unlikely to entertain any affection for the Germans. The tsar himself was a cousin of the new German kaiser, whom he personally much disliked. The wife of his chief of staff (an official who played a crucial role in shaping the military entente) was French, the owner of a great chateau in the Dordogne. And so on. Insofar as it was politically effective, Russia was, and was regarded as, a normal if backward part of the European system and had been at least since the time of the empress Catherine the Great.

One is left with the impression that Kennan's personal solicitude for Russia's destiny prompts him to yearn for conditions that did not exist, in order to imagine that Russian history *might* have moved along a more pleasant path than the one leading to war, to revolution, and (in Edmund Wilson's famous phrase) "to the Finland Station."

This said, it also should be said that these explicit prejudices do not seriously flaw what is otherwise a superb work of diplomatic history. *The Fateful Alliance,* as narrative, is accomplished according to the highest standards of the profession. Its focus on personalities and their intricate relationships makes for fascinating reading, as does its subtle reconstruction of the atmosphere of late Victorian Europe.

It also has its lighter moments. In 1891, for instance, when the first glimmer of Franco-Russian détente appeared on the horizon, there was a serious ideological impediment: how could a very reactionary tsarist regime align itself with a very republican France, hotbed of revolutionary traditions? In the summer of 1891, when a French naval squadron made an unprecedented visit to Kronstadt (the naval base near St. Petersburg), a delicate protocol problem arose for the Russians. The "Marseillaise," the French national anthem, had to be rendered in salute. Yet to Russia the message of this anthem was scarcely less subversive than that of the "Internationale." The solution, Kennan recounts, was superbly tactful. As the republican squadron approached the reactionary base, the then famous Slavyanski Choir of St. Petersburg, massed on the deck of a Russian vessel, sang the "Marseillaise" as protocol required, but with Russian words composed for the occasion, which no Frenchman present was likely to understand. It is a pity that Kennan chose not to supply the text.

(PAUL SEABURY)

Josephine Herbst:
The Story She Could Never Tell

By Elinor Langer. Boston, Little, Brown, 1983. 384 pages

Above all, *Josephine Herbst,* by Elinor Langer, is a superb biography; it is controlled, handcrafted, and finely wrought. As though executing the successive stages of a sculpture,

Elinor Langer evokes different images of Josephine Herbst's life until, finally, we see her from diverse sides, facets clashing; despite the heroic efforts on the part of subject and biographer to bring them together, the disparate parts that make up Josephine Herbst are reassembled and yet remain unconstructed until the end. Highly regarded in the 1930s, Herbst knew all the literary lights of the day; she was close to the centre of literary activity in the U.S. and among the American expatriates scattered across Europe from Russia to Spain.

The biography places its emphasis on the mutual support and collective undermining of personal conflict, political struggle, and artistic expression within the person of Herbst. When Herbst herself integrated the personal and the political, her art cohered, and so her life seemed to her a seamless whole. Her novels, about herself, her friends, her families, her society, were based on the premise that individual behaviour was made sensible by its implications for social life. When she could not acknowledge and thus transmute her personal pain—as in, for example, her attitude toward loving women, or toward such political contradictions as that posed by Communism in practice—she could not achieve that integration. When a loved husband would not return, a beloved companion would not give of herself, and all action became mired in ambivalence and dependence, leaving nice theories of right relations sunk in self-pity, then her life fractured into the political and the personal, and Josephine Herbst could not complete her memoirs.

Her political vision was monochrome, her congenital radicalism so single-minded that she never wavered in her commitments. Only the world changed. "Do not look too hard for the 'origins' of her radicalism," Herbst's brother-in-law told her biographer, for "she simply *was* radical." The fact was demonstrably true. In a letter written almost 50 years after the Bolshevik Revolution of 1917, for which she maintained a lifelong enthusiasm, Herbst, following a declaration that "nothing so vital" as the Spanish Civil War of the 1930s would "ever come again," closed with a ringing affirmation: "I think it absolutely necessary, to continue on anytime available, the harassment and the protest. . . ." She meant "here" in the U.S., not "there" in the U.S.S.R. Aware of abuse in the Soviet Union, she would not admit as much in public because she thought that by doing so she would give aid and comfort to the real enemy at home.

Herbst railed against convention; she felt for the poor; she rejected existing institutions. In a letter to her parents she maintained that she believed in "revolution and the class war." The words were written in the 1920s. By the 1930s Herbst saw the Soviet Union, and hence, by imputation, the Communist Party of the United States, as the solution to all problems, for, as Langer writes in one of her many perceptive observations, Communism represented "the antithesis of the United States and its fulfillment simultaneously." At long last, Herbst believed, liberty might marry equality.

Herbst never joined the Communist Party, but she never criticized it either—not when it acquiesced in undermining the Republican cause in Spain, not during the purge trials, not on account of the Hitler-Stalin pact, not because of the horrors of the slave labour camps, not for any reason whatsoever. Herbst would not, Langer tells us, reject her past commitments. Langer mimics the words spoken during the U.S. House Committee on Un-American Activities hearings into allegations of Communist infiltration ("Are you now or have you ever been a card-carrying member . . ."), as she sometimes mirrors the style of her subject, when she declares that Herbst "was not now, nor would she ever be, a revisionist." Always in tune with the faintest stirrings of protest, Herbst was made happy, as happy as her impoverished personal life would allow, by the radicalism of the 1960s. In what might be regarded as her credo, she told friends to break an appointment with her in order to "go to the demonstration . . . whenever the people are in the streets, join them."

How can one account for her unregenerate opposition to established authority? Let us take our bearings from Langer, who became, by her own description, more than "distraught" when she found in Herbst's papers evidence linking Alger Hiss to Whittaker Chambers, evidence suggesting that Hiss may not always have been truthful. (Hiss, a former U.S. State Department official, was convicted of perjury in 1950 for testifying falsely that he had not passed government documents to a courier for a Communist espionage ring.) Langer commented afterward: "Why I cared so much about the innocence of Alger Hiss I could not have said exactly, but I did care. . . . If he had not been falsely accused, my entire interpretation of American history would be affected—and the interpretations of how many others, just like me?" Insofar as this interpretation of her reactions depended on an evaluation of the Soviet regime (for how else was one to assess responsibility for the arms race, security clearances, the entire panoply of the cold war?), the question *why* she cared was itself remarkable. Who needs Alger Hiss to pronounce judgment on the Gulag! The question made sense only if the Soviet Union did not matter but the United States did.

Herbst's love-hate affairs extended to her country. There are those who imagine America always as a cornucopia, forever rich, so that it is never wealth creation but always wealth distribution that matters. Herbst thought of her America as often repressive and always stable. Her love and her hate were both reserved for it: her hate for what it was, her love for what it might be. In America one was granted the luxury of condemning the institutions on which one was ultimately dependent for the right of protest. Both qualities, the love and the hate, had to be present and inseparable in order to ensure the survival of her radical vision. It was one that envisaged a life of purely voluntary association, without coercion, inequality, or, indeed, institutions. For if American democracy had been fragile, and in danger of succumbing to constant criticism, then going to the streets might have made things worse and not, as she always supposed, better.

What happened in the realm of social affairs when her vision of the "good life" was tried out? Josie Herbst and, indeed, as Langer suggests, others like her became confused. Knowing the answer, they did not dare to ask the question. The bulk of this engrossing book, which takes the reader into the centre of Herbst's personal despair, is, in fact, a chronicle of the abuse of a life without institutions. If in her experience no member of a couple could set the other free and yet remain committed, if the half-hollow words were invariably followed by wholly horrible deeds, how then could the ideal against which she measured American practices stand up to scrutiny? It could not and she did not expect it to. By keeping herself poor and America unworthy, she kept alive the most important legacy she had to leave—her radical constancy. The radical posture has sustained her memory in a way that it never could maintain her life. Josephine Herbst still has a lot to say about why people should "go to the demonstration," because the abuses of institutions still exist, but she has nothing at all to say about what they should do when they return home.

(AARON WILDAVSKY)

Civilization and Capitalism, 15th–18th Century
Volume 3: The Perspective of the World
By Fernand Braudel. New York, Harper & Row, 1984.
699 pages

This formidably large yet readable book is the third of three devoted by Fernand Braudel to the economic and social history of the world in the interval between the end of the Middle Ages and the beginning of the Industrial Revolution. The first volume, *The Structures of Everyday Life* (1982), concerned the basic stuff of human social existence—what people wore and ate, where and under what conditions they lived, and how such matters determined the development of regions, nations, and the world at large. In the second, *The Wheels of Commerce* (1983), the author turned to the commercial activities that connected these various human orders (shops, fairs, markets, and similar means of exchange) and in turn had a formative influence on them. Now, in the third and concluding volume of his study, Braudel takes up what he calls the world economy. More precisely, he takes up world economies, since over the period a number of them dominated the world in turn.

Not the whole world, of course. Braudel—the preeminent figure in the French school of history known as Annales, which treats of human affairs in structural rather than linear terms—acknowledges that vast areas of the world did not participate in any world economy at all. Yet in a sense the world economies discussed here do comprehend the world as we know it, since they are the parts that acquired a history, associated with names and events we recognize.

By world economies, Braudel means the arrangements whereby one place after another was able to accumulate and manipulate capital so as to dominate world trade in its time. Manipulation was as important as accumulation, for the domination was not simply a matter of great wealth. France was probably richer than England in the 18th century, but it never became the centre of a world economy, partly because it could never match the abilities and resources in the area of credit that gave England effective control of other nations' wealth. Similarly, Spain had all the gold and silver of America at its disposal, but it was the Genoese and later the Dutch who provided it with the credit it needed and, at least partly as a result, were able to create their own world economies.

In the West this position was achieved by cities such as Venice, Antwerp, Genoa, Amsterdam, and London and by nation-states such as Holland, England, and, later, the United States. In other parts of the globe, India, the Ottoman Empire, Russia, and China each dominated an economy that comprehended its world. Braudel does not pretend to know exactly what elements combined to create the various world economies that succeeded one another in the period with which he is concerned. Unlike political history, which is marked by formal, public pronouncements, economic developments are often hidden; they involve numerous private communications and can be "read" only by interpreting statistics and records that survive in haphazard fashion. Certainly one factor in the formation of a world economy—at least in the West—has been the capacity of a city or nation-state to operate trade routes. The dominant cities and states in successive world economies were all located on the sea. France, on the other hand, was a land power, and the unity it needed in order to contend with Holland or England could be supplied only by roads, which took a long time to build.

Another factor was the ability—or good fortune—that enabled one city or one nation to take charge of the local economies or regional arrangements of others and turn them to advantage. For without exception the world economies were built upon existing economies. There was (and is) in such economies a kind of imperialism, a power built on other powers that it did not create but subsumed. This involved a human activity quite as great as the political imperialism of the great powers, though its history is still largely untold.

A certain attitude, an ability to perceive the importance of economic power, has also been important. Before the middle of the 15th century we hear the doge of Venice warning his countrymen that if they elect a certain successor they will find themselves in a war that will impoverish them, whereas if they do otherwise they will become "the masters of the gold of Christendom." Thus, Braudel observes, the doge assumed that "Venetians of this time could understand that looking after one's ducats, dwellings and doublets was the road to true power; that it was possible to become 'masters of the gold of Christendom,' that is the entire European economy, by trade—and not by arms." And so they did, just as, many years later, the representatives of the British and Dutch East India companies realized that it was not necessary to conquer the East by arms or to occupy it militarily; sufficient to settle at the crucial places of production and the intersections of trade routes, "thus saving themselves the trouble of creating infrastructures, and leaving to local communities the task of transporting the goods to the ports, organizing and financing production and handling elementary exchange."

The implication that the object of each successive centre of the world economy was its own wealth and strength, and that this was achieved at the expense of other, subsidiary elements, is inescapable. In fact, it is the point. For capitalism, as Braudel uses the term—meaning the system of economic relationships that creates and operates world economies—is nothing if not self-serving, exploiting the component parts of the system for its own ends. Braudel distinguishes three areas in each world economy, the core, the periphery, and the semi-periphery, and argues that in every case the centre has enriched itself at the expense of the others. A case in point is South (and Central) America, which had an important place in the world economy of Europe but was ruthlessly stripped of its gold and silver while its inhabitants became slave labourers.

Capitalism for Braudel is thus not the "market economy" or the operation of "the free market." Rather, it is their antithesis, working to interfere in the market and skew its functioning to the advantage of the centre. Whereas for Marx monopoly was to be found only in the late stages of capitalism, for Braudel it is the essence of the institution, present from the beginning, and the object of its existence throughout. It is not the free market but an interference with the free market, an evasion of its "laws," a profiting from unequal competition.

Whether capitalism, on the whole, has been a good or a bad thing must be difficult to say, since Braudel does not say it. Such a question may be pointless with respect to any great world institution, or perhaps the answer is that good and bad are both present in such enterprises and inextricably mixed. However, capitalism is still very much alive, at least in half the world, where its operation is, if not global, certainly multinational and where, since the Industrial Revolution, it has added the means of production to its older methods of monopolistic control, marketing, distribution, and trade. So the question, if it can be asked intelligently, might be worth trying to answer.

Certainly the world economy—or successive world economies—have spread the world's wealth around, even if an inordinate portion of it landed at the centre. Venice helped bring the wealth of the East to Europe. First Antwerp and then Genoa served as conduits for Indian pepper and American silver. The Dutch brought the East Indies into the picture. The English did the same with India. But all this, besides being essentially parasitic, was accomplished at fearful cost—the despoliation of Byzantium, the ravaging of Mexico and South America, the exploitation of the East Indies, the transformation of the Indian subcontinent into an impoverished and dependent economic region.

Perhaps Braudel's own answer is implicit in his last chapter, where he asks not whether capitalism has been a good thing for the world but whether it can survive. There may be some doubt about its future, he acknowledges, especially in the face of the worldwide economic decline that seems to have begun in the early 1970s, but he thinks the result will be otherwise. "I may be quite wrong," he says, "but I do not have the impression that capitalism is likely to collapse of its own accord." That would require some great counterforce and he sees none—certainly not socialism, which has never triumphed except in violent circumstances. The danger that he perceives for capitalism comes from its own operation, which feeds on the smaller local activities of the market and could destroy them. A tendency for this to happen is always present, and when it does—as in the case of New York City, which lost the greater part of its small productive business a generation or so ago—the process is irreversible. What *must* survive, Braudel suggests, is this lower level of economic activity—the myriad operations of "the market" in communities all over the globe—on which capitalism rests and on which it must be able to draw for its multinational ends. For that lower level of activity is both the real source of wealth in the world and the source of innovation and ideas. Capitalism may spread and extend that wealth and those ideas, but it does not generate them.

So what is ominous, in Braudel's view, is not the threat of socialism but the tendency toward bigness and combination, often supported by the state. "There could be no more dangerous policy," he argues, than to encourage this process, which could well lead to a replacement of the monopoly of capital by a monopoly of the state; *i.e.,* socialism. Some way must be found that will "extend the area of the market" and at the same time put at its disposal "the economic advantages so far kept to itself by one dominant group in society." But that problem is not economic in nature; it is social and requires action not by capital but by the body politic.   (JOHN VAN DOREN)

The Order of Man:
A Biomathematical Anatomy of the Primates

By Charles Oxnard. New Haven, Yale University Press, 1984. 396 pages

More than a century after Darwin, evolution—the theory that any given species in the natural order is the product of changes in preexisting species—remains an unproved and perhaps unprovable hypothesis. At the same time, reason alone cannot deny it. It is unproved, and perhaps unprovable, because we have never seen it happen, and because the record of its having gone on, as indicated by fossil remains, is so fragmentary and uncertain that we cannot say what the steps in the progression were, at least as far as highly developed species such as humans are concerned. Yet we cannot reasonably doubt that some such process has taken place. We know of no living organism that has come into existence without parents, and we know that many species now present on the Earth, mammals among them, did not exist at an earlier time; therefore, they must have evolved from organisms that existed once. Creationists hold that each species was created by divine intervention, but that is a conclusion not of reason but of faith.

For Darwin himself, the question was why there are species at all—why not simply an infinite variety of individuals? Observation reveals that this is not the case, that types, or species, exist. Darwin, therefore, undertook to explain how this comes about. His theory was that every species has descended from previous generations through a process of natural selection in response to requirements of the environment, which encouraged that type to exist and discouraged others. The theory rested entirely on an inference; there was no way to re-create the process experimentally, nor is there now. For this reason, evolution must be regarded as a theory—though one that is supported by the fossil evidence, as well as by the findings of biogenetics and molecular chemistry.

For reasons that had little to do with science, the metaphor in which Darwin's century (and Darwin himself, though with some misgivings) conceived the theory was that of Progress. It was assumed that, for any given organism, a roughly linear descent had occurred from "lower" to "higher" forms, culminating in the existing types. Certainly such fossil evidence as there was, and what was known of the Earth's own evolution, tended to support such a metaphor (and still does). But this also created problems, chief among them being that so many steps in the progression, or links in the chain, were missing.

Nowhere was this lack more troublesome than in the case of man. Darwin speculated that man had descended from the apes, or some creature like them. But because the gap between man and the ape is very great, he assumed—as evolutionary theory has ever since—that one or more intervening species, now vanished, had once existed. Much effort has gone into the search for this "missing link"—or these missing links—but incontrovertible evidence of its (or their) existence has never been found. Not that this is really surprising. Given the long time span postulated for human evolution, the preservation of even a small fraction of the organic remains seems almost miraculous.

Still, it has always seemed important to discover such a link if at all possible, and over the years the subject has become rather more interesting and certainly more puzzling. For such remains as have turned up, especially in recent years, have not fit neatly into the theory of man's linear descent from some similar but more primitive creature. The effort to make them fit has only led to frequent redating of fossils, controversy as to what their dates really are, and doubt as to whether they are actually ancestral to man. So while we know much more about the whole matter than the scientists of an earlier day, we understand it no better and possibly not as well.

It is against this background that Charles Oxnard, a distinguished figure in the fields of evolutionary biology, anatomy, and anthropology, has written *The Order of Man: A Biomathematical Anatomy of the Primates.* Based on what he calls "the new revolution" in the study of human fossils, this work offers evidence for a different pattern—in some ways a different conception—of human evolution, with far-reaching implications concerning the ratio of culturally and biologically determined factors in the human makeup.

The pattern Oxnard describes is radiating rather than linear. It considers the fossil remains discovered in the past two decades, for example, by the Leakeys in Africa, as representing many lineages, not just one. And since these remains all indicate some of the attributes commonly thought of as human—bipedalism, tool-using and tool-making, communication, high intelligence, perhaps some measure of cultural development—the inference is that these attributes have appeared in other species besides *Homo sapiens.* They may not all have appeared together, and they may have been limited in some species. Nevertheless, this suggests that distinctively human characteristics came into being over an expanse of time much greater than the million or so years that the linear theory allows to distinctly human existence. Furthermore, the fossil remnants of such nearly human creatures as *Australopithecus* are so very old that the point at which they diverged from the great apes, supposing they did, must be older still, going back perhaps ten million years. This pushes back even further the time when the rudiments of human characteristics first appeared.

Oxnard bases these speculations not on new fossils he has dug up himself but on a complex series of measurements taken by computer methods and a sophisticated comparison of well-publicized finds made by others. He builds on the pioneering work in morphology of D'Arcy Thompson (whose classic *On Growth and Form* appeared in 1917) and of Solly Zuckerman (now Lord Zuckerman) at the University of Birmingham, England, where Oxnard trained before going to the University of Chicago and then to his current post at the University of Southern California. To this he adds a knowledge of molecular biology with respect to living species. The methods whereby the presumed physical and behavioural characteristics of long-extinct creatures are extrapolated from their remains are set forth in this book (which summarizes earlier works by the same author) in greater detail than the layman may like, though it must be said that Oxnard writes of even technical matters with clarity and grace. There are also ample diagrams and illustrations that allow the reader an adequate grasp of the main points of the argument.

The conclusions to which the volume leads have the advantage of encompassing recent fossil findings without attempting to cram them into a single linear pattern. They also fit standard biological theory a great deal better than the traditional idea of a linear progression toward *Homo sapiens,* with its assumption that this species appeared definitively at a given point in the past. Biologists know, or think they know, that life does not obey such theatrical rules. If a certain form of life is possible at all, it is likely to emerge wherever conditions permit, at more than one place and more than one time. This is consistent with what Oxnard's researches indicate: that "man" probably appeared many times over, during a very long period of time (perhaps millions of years) and in many places—not, for example, in just one cave in Africa.

The theory does not explain why so many of these humanoid species died out but, if it comes to that, we have difficulty saying why species of any sort have become extinct. Nor does it provide the "missing link." It says, rather, that "man" as we know him had many chances to establish himself, and the fact that he eventually did so is not the singular, all-but-miraculous event envisioned by earlier theorists. Rather, it was a gradual and perhaps discontinuous phenomenon such as the odds could favour. The reason we cannot find the missing link is that it never existed. Instead, there were many such links, in many cases existing simultaneously with "humans" before *Homo sapiens,* for reasons difficult to explain, was left alone. His distant cousins, such as the great apes and chimpanzees, may themselves be the survivors from among many now-extinct primate species.

But it is the psychosocial implications of this theory of human descent that are most interesting. For if man's distinctively human characteristics go back eight million or ten million years, then he has had much more time to develop as a distinct species than formerly was thought. What he is now amounts to the culmination of a very long process of "becoming," and his prior animal behaviour is so remote as to carry little weight.

Such a notion runs counter to the current beliefs of ethnologists and sociobiologists, who in recent years have emphasized the biological and primal elements in the human character as distinct from the psychocultural ones. But, as Oxnard observes, the idea "does not seem so extreme" when we consider the wide range of impulses that we share, to some extent, with other creatures. Aggression, for example, is a favourite connecting link for the sociobiological theorists, but *human* aggression is so much greater and has so many more applications than any aggressive behaviour observable in animals that it cannot fairly be laid to such a source. It makes much better sense when perceived as the product of a specifically human existence that for millions of years faced distinct difficulties requiring distinct psychic responses. So too with social mores. So too with, in Oxnard's words, "the enormous complexities of human creativity, from the making and using of simple tools and other implements, through the design of implements that are not only useful but pleasing to the eye and the touch, [to] the creations of those artists and scientists who have been among the geniuses of man."

Far better, it would seem, to suppose—as his evidence suggests—that the almost infinitely greater human ability is the product of long preparation. Far better to suppose that the evolution of the most complex of all species on Earth has occurred over a very long time, and that its achievements are a function, not of rudimentary powers shared with other primates, but of specifically human capacities that have been long in practice, however recently they have manifested themselves in sophisticated productions.

(JOHN VAN DOREN)

The Culture of Time and Space, 1880-1918

By Stephen Kern. Cambridge, Harvard University Press, 1983. 416 pages

In nearly every age throughout the history of the Western world, there has existed a sense of being different from ages that have gone before. Often the sense has been one of loss. The Athenians of Pericles' time, proud as they were of their great city, observed the disappearance of the simpler, heroic virtue they believed their people had possessed at the time when the Persian invasion was repulsed at Marathon and Thermopylae. In Rome, during the last days of the Republic, despair at the failure of republican rule was superseded by the confidence of the Augustan Age. Nevertheless, this new confidence did not fill the emotional void created by the decline of Hellenistic civilization; the apprehension of darkness and decay in human affairs, a conviction of the hopelessness of things, was countered only by Christianity. That in turn seemed in decline to the men of the 14th century, who felt the stirrings of the Renaissance before it had arrived. Subsequently, the 17th century was swept by revolutionary insights into scientific matters. A century later, however, Edward Gibbon stood upon the ruins of the Capitol at Rome and looked back across the trough

of superstition, as he regarded Christianity, to the distant mountain peak of the Classical Age, believing that the grandeur of that time had been recaptured during his own. Yet scarcely a century had passed before Matthew Arnold wrote sadly of the loss of faith suffered by the Victorian age, overwhelmed as it seemed to be by "the sick hurry and divided aims" of the times.

These are precedents, it might be argued, for the conviction prevalent in our own time that our situation, in its turn, is different from any that has gone before. So strong is this belief among us, and so pervasive, that we forget that it was common to ages gone by and that we are thus more akin to them than we suspect. On the other hand, there may be reason also to lay less emphasis on the underlying similarities and to examine instead the differences between our own time and past ages. It may be right to say that the very terms by which we define ourselves and the world in which we live have undergone a basic change, with the effect that we can hardly believe that we inhabit the same universe, let alone the same human order, as did our ancestors.

Such is the thesis of *The Culture of Time and Space, 1880-1918,* by Stephen Kern, associate professor of history at the University of Northern Illinois and author previously of *Anatomy and Destiny: A Cultural History of the Human Body.* Kern argues that a new understanding of time and space, two basic dimensions of all human experience, came about during the period 1880-1918, and that this development, along with the reshaping of human attitudes that occurred in consequence, is the one that has given the 20th century its unique character.

"From around 1880 to the outbreak of World War I," Kern writes, "a series of sweeping changes in technology and culture created distinctive new modes of thinking about and experiencing time and space. Technological innovations including the telephone, wireless telegraph, x-ray, cinema, bicycle, automobile, and airplane established the material foundation for this reorientation; independent cultural developments such as the stream-of-consciousness novel, psychoanalysis, Cubism, and the theory of relativity shaped consciousness directly. The result was a transformation of the dimensions of life and thought."

In a series of chapters Kern considers how the very nature of time, or at least our perception of it, was reordered by the institution of a standard clock time for the entire globe and the sense of connection that resulted. The sense of "public" time was evident when, through the workings of the telegraph, the whole world was witness to an event such as the sinking of the "Titanic" in 1912. At the same time, however, people began to recognize that there were many kinds of "private" time as well and that they were often at odds with the linear time we regard, or used to regard, as basic.

The underpinnings of many kinds of "private" time can be found in Einstein's theory of relativity (first presented in 1905), which recognized the importance of position relative to any moving object in the measure of its velocity and maintained that we can take the measure only in terms of our own reference system. Literature provided other demonstrations of the importance of the observer. Marcel Proust's long novel *À la recherche du temps perdu* (Eng. trans., *Remembrance of Things Past* [1913-27]) ranges widely back and forth over the lifetime of its narrator, although in chronological time the "action" of the novel takes place during a single evening. In James Joyce's *Ulysses* (1922), the novel's far-reaching implications for human morality are provided in the framework of an account of one day in the life of Leopold Bloom of Dublin.

The development of motion picture technology provided another medium that showed life as a kind of flux that could be both manipulated and recalled.

These two senses of time—one standard, public, and linear and the other heterogeneous, private, and recallable—both "arrived" in the period Kern discusses. The conflict between them transformed the sense of the past, the present, and the future that had hitherto prevailed. The change was seen not only in the time-altering technology of the age but in its art, philosophy, fiction, and plays, as well as in its physical and social sciences. For example, Proust, like the camera, sought both to recapture the past and to vary its rhythm and duration; cinema brought the capability of infinitely repeating the past; Sigmund Freud conceived the past as compressed in each human psyche, from which it could be elicited by analysis.

The sense of the present was altered, too, by the effects of the telephone and the telegraph, bringing instant and universal communication that transcended both time and space. Joyce was to experiment with "simultaneous" literature in *Finnegans Wake* (1939), while motion pictures juxtaposed different events upon a single screen. At the same time, Einstein was saying that, given the relativity of motion with respect to spatial and temporal coordinates, no determination of simultaneity in physics was strictly possible.

Similar contradictions complicated the sense of the future. While some effects of this seemed promising in terms of new technology and the hopes of social revolution that marked the age, others were threatening—for example, the implications of the law of entropy, discovered in the 1850s but only gradually having an effect upon human minds, and the discovery of atomic instability in the 1890s. The threatening aspects were explored in Brooks Adams's deeply pessimistic *The Law of Civilization and Decay* (1895), Spengler's prophetic *Decline of the West* (1918), and Thomas Mann's *The Magic Mountain* (1927), a novel begun before World War I, in which patients at a tuberculosis sanitarium, symbolizing the nations of Europe, wait helplessly upon their fate.

In the age of the bicycle, the automobile, the flickering motion picture, and the suddenly rapid, disjointed beat of popular music, all events seemed to occur with unprecedented speed. Speed itself became the objective of a new technology that was transforming the prewar "stabilized bourgeois world," as the writer Stefan Zweig described it, into something lacking both rules and security.

Kern devotes a further set of chapters to space and its component parts, defined as form, distance, and direction. "New ideas about the nature of space in this period," he writes, "challenged the popular notion that it was homogeneous and argued for its heterogeneity. Biologists explored the space perceptions of different animals, and sociologists the spatial perceptions of different cultures. Artists dismantled the uniform perspectival space that had governed painting since the Renaissance and reconstructed objects as seen from several perspectives. Novelists used multiple perspectives with the versatility of the new cinema. Nietzsche and José Ortega y Gasset developed a philosophy of 'perspectivism' which implied that there are as many different spaces as there are points of view. The most serious challenge to conventional space came from physical science itself, with the development in the early nineteenth century of non-Euclidean geometries."

New ideas about space generated conflicting responses and attitudes. Paul Cézanne's multiple perspectives were scorned; he could not sell his paintings until not long before the end of his life in 1906. The Cubism of Georges Braque and Pablo Picasso presented objects not only from multiple perspectives but from inside as well, so that the viewer was required to think of himself as moving around and within whatever the painting presented. With its juxtapositions, its fractured planes, its cacophony of forms, Cubism seemed, as Kern says, to have "cracked the mirror of art." In the words of Gertrude Stein, Cubism implied that "the framing of life, the need that a picture exist in its frame, remain in its frame, was over." The effect was unsettling. Equally so was the contemporaneous effect wrought on social life by the development of the camera and the telephone, the breakdown of social conventions and hierarchical orders, and the denial of privacy in the "open" architecture of Frank Lloyd Wright and in the beehive skyscrapers of the modern city.

In the same way, the sense of distance was affected. While the effect of the new technology was to contract distance, the sense of its importance grew. During the age there was evidence of growing concern with the size of things, especially the size of countries and empires, of colonies and stores of armaments. In all these spheres the major European governments—England, France, Germany, and Russia—competed and compared achievements. National boundaries were transcended by the telephone and the telegraph, by rail and air transport; but while nations were brought closer together, they were also made more wary of one another, more concerned for what they thought belonged to them. In Europe the result was the formation of competing interest groups that finally fought the war of 1914–18.

The climax came, Kern maintains, during the war itself or, more particularly, during the month of concentrated preparation for war between the assassination of Archduke Ferdinand of Austria at Sarajevo on June 28, 1914, and the outbreak of hostilities on August 1. During that period, elements of the new technology—telegraph, telephone, memorandums, press releases—combined to rush men and ministries, populations and countries, and finally Europe itself, into a war that seemed to arrive with the velocity of an express train. The world seemed hardly able to conceive of, let alone control, the newly transformed concepts of time, space, speed, and distance. Not surprisingly, the confusion that had characterized attitudes toward the new technology manifested itself again during this period. Countries mobilized for total war with unprecedented speed, while institutions created in less flexible frameworks stumbled and collapsed. Europe rushed to destruction in the manner of the "Titanic"—strong and confident, yet vulnerable and blind. The communications systems that brought awareness of the impending catastrophe nevertheless left nations helpless to prevent it.

The underlying effect of the war was to mount a further assault on the traditional understanding of both time and space. It caused history itself to be redefined, along with any sense of the future, and it shattered social, moral, and intellectual positions like the earth thrown up by shells in the trenches, where men knew neither direction nor location, and whole cities and the countryside around were ground to rubble. So destructive was the conflict that it became, Kern suggests, a "Cubist War." The landscape was fragmented and individuals became locked in a state of isolated consciousness, wholly disoriented, the inevitable fate of human beings in "no-man's-land."

Kern notes that one epitaph for the period was provided by Gertrude Stein. " 'Really,' she wrote, 'the composition of this war, 1914–18, was not the composition of all previous wars, the composition was not a composition in which there was one man in the center surrounded by a lot of other men but a composition that had neither a beginning nor an end, a composition of which one corner was as important as another corner, in fact the composition of cubism.' " The description seemed to her to accord with what she had observed earlier, after her first airplane flight, when she felt that she understood what her friend Picasso was trying to make clear to her and to the world—that, in her own words, again quoted by Kern, " 'the twentieth century is a century which sees the earth as no one has ever seen it, the earth has a splendor that it never has had, and as everything destroys itself in the twentieth century and nothing continues, so then the twentieth century has a splendor which is its own and Picasso is of this century, he has that strange quality of an earth that one has never seen and of things destroyed as they have never been destroyed.' "

(JOHN VAN DOREN)

Cities and the Wealth of Nations:
Principles of Economic Life

By Jane Jacobs. New York, Random House, 1984.
257 pages

For over 20 years, Jane Jacobs has shaped our thinking about cities. A generation of urban designers and planners was influenced by her classic reformulation of the relationship between local community vitality and physical design in *The Death and Life of Great American Cities.* From the community level, she moved to the city as a whole in *The Economy of Cities,* arguing that cities' long-term economic viability depended on their ability to continue to generate new activity by replacing imports with local production. Now she has expanded her view to yet a larger scale, taking on key issues of macroeconomics; namely, the causes of the economic rise and decline of regions and nations.

To this problem, Jacobs brings formidable strengths, notably an iconoclastic view of the world, a capacity to see both detail and generality in everyday reality, and an ability to write prose that is seductive in its clarity and coherence. Whole fields of research are dissected and encapsulated for the reader with impressive skill.

The central argument of the book remains true to the author's interest in the city and, in so doing, challenges conventional economics. As a rule, economists argue that the most important elements for study are those where key decisions are made: individuals or households for decisions about consumption; business firms for decisions about production; national governments for decisions about the factors affecting inflation, unemployment, and trade, especially the regulation of the money supply and trade with other nations. For Jacobs, this focus misses the core role of the city as the locus for economic development.

Cities that develop the capacity to replace imports with local production gain far more than additional jobs and income. Their economies grow more complex as profits and savings are reinvested in new lines of activity that generate both exports and additional import replacement. The cities' needs for food, labour, and materials in turn stimulate development in their hinterland regions, producing still more demand for goods and services. The result is a highly complex and diverse economy, continually developing new lines of activity as older ones decline or become subject to competition from other places seeking to replace their own imports or to generate exports.

In contrast to conventional economics, Jacobs argues that economic policy developed at the national level is pro-

foundly compromised by its need to reconcile the political and social demands of areas that are less stable, wealthy, or productive than import-replacing city-regions. Such areas may be supply regions that specialize in the production of one or more raw materials or products for distant city-regions without developing import-replacing cities of their own; transplant regions, in which industries have been relocated as branch plants; and city-regions in decline that are no longer able to sustain dynamic development. The first two of these may prosper temporarily, but they risk economic disaster if conditions in world markets change. The third type contains populations that typically have enjoyed prosperity and power and are faced with the loss of both. For valid social reasons, populations in all such regions exert pressure on national governments to reduce disparities or avert decline. Jacobs calls such actions, together with the transplantation of production, transactions of decline, since they drain capital from dynamic city-regions to areas where its economic impact is dissipated. She is pessimistic about the prospect of effective economic development occurring under such circumstances.

If the vital engine of economic development is the city-region, while decisions on economic policy are made at the national level in response to other issues—especially distribution of income—a fundamental conflict arises. Jacobs sees no escape from this dilemma. Her most unconventional, yet logical, solution is to advocate the dismantling of the nation-state itself in order to allow for local currencies and trade restrictions. This would make it possible for local economies to protect themselves during the critical years required to establish import-replacing production. Yet she is under no illusions about the political utopianism of such a proposal. She sees no realistic, specific solutions and advocates an open-ended policy of "drift," based on ecological ideas of system complexity, niche filling, and homeostasis. Her vision is of an economic order that is rich and diverse. Her expectation is that the processes of political and economic action make its conscious realization impossible.

Despite her lucid prose, Jacobs's argument is flawed. She ignores virtually all the work of the past two decades on how urban economies work. Although she sees and describes the world of her urban experience with great acuity, it is not complete. Her enthusiasm for the city and its multitude of small, interacting businesses does not come to terms with the existence of multinational conglomerates that control research and development as well as production. The increasing efficiency of communications and transportation supports her argument in part, but it also makes large-scale production and control more economical. Economic development is now occurring at both ends of the scale, and it is not clear that either will dominate in innovation.

In the end, Jacobs's attempt to encompass the totality of economic development fails because she, like the economists she criticizes, can see only part of the picture. Her vision differs from theirs, and it is attractive because it shows us what is best about the city—its autonomy, richness, vitality, and complexity. Her vision is humanistic, though she ignores the exploitation that has accompanied urban development. But before we accept it for those qualities, we need to look carefully at its adequacy for providing an understanding of economic reality. Economists should read this book to remind themselves of what they have forgotten. Others should enjoy it, but remain skeptical.

(MICHAEL B. TEITZ)

(Opposite page) Photograph; Setboun/Boccon–Gibod—Black Star

Chronology of Events of 1984

JANUARY

1 **Buhari to rule Nigeria.** Maj. Gen. Mohammed Buhari announced that he had taken over the government of Nigeria following the overthrow of Pres. Alhaji Shehu Shagari the previous day. After the successful bloodless coup, the constitution was suspended and all political parties were banned. Shagari, who had been reelected to a second four-year term in August 1983, was accused of leading the oil-rich nation to the brink of financial collapse.

Divestiture of AT&T takes effect. The American Telephone & Telegraph Co., which for decades had been a privately owned but government-regulated utility supplying virtually · all telephone service in the U.S., was formally broken up and reorganized along lines approved by a federal judge. By agreeing to sever all connections with its 22 Bell System subsidiaries, AT&T won approval for entry into the unregulated computer field. The former tightly knit national network of telephone companies would henceforth operate as seven independent regional organizations. AT&T would continue to provide long-distance telephone service and would retain ownership of Western Electric and Bell Laboratories.

Rebels destroy largest bridge in El Salvador. Leftist guerrillas destroyed the Cuscatlán Bridge in El Salvador after driving off several hundred government troops assigned to protect the area. The rebels also inflicted damage on a nearby hydroelectric plant situated on the Lempa River. Two days earlier another contingent of rebels overran and for 12 hours occupied the large military base at El Paraíso before withdrawing. The Cuscatlán Bridge, built in 1947, had special economic importance because it connected the eastern and western regions of the country.

Brunei becomes independent. Brunei, a self-ruling sultanate on the island of Borneo, became fully independent of Great Britain. The small nation, with a population of some 200,000, had been earning several billion dollars a year from its oil and natural gas reserves, giving it the highest per capita income in all of Asia. On January 7 Brunei joined the Association of Southeast Asian Nations (ASEAN), the first new member since the organization was founded in 1967.

3 **Syria frees captured U.S. pilot.** A U.S. Navy pilot, Lieut. Robert O. Goodman, Jr., was released by Syria after the Rev. Jesse Jackson made a personal appeal to Syrian Pres. Hafez al-Assad. The Syrian Foreign Ministry indicated that Syria was also responding to U.S. demands that the pilot be freed.

Goodman's plane had been downed on Dec. 4, 1983, during a bombing raid on Syrian positions east of Beirut, Lebanon. The U.S. air strike had been ordered after Syrian troops allegedly fired on two unarmed U.S. reconnaissance planes the previous day.

Riots in Tunisia quelled. Tunisian Pres. Habib Bourguiba declared a national state of emergency after riots occurred in Tunis, the capital, and several other cities. Calm was quickly restored after the government ordered the military into the streets and imposed an 11-hour curfew and a ban on all public gatherings. The anger of the demonstrators focused on a government-decreed 125% increase in the price of bread and grains. Because the 1983 Tunisian harvest had been poor, about half of the grain that the country needed had to be imported.

10 **Bignone arrested in Argentina.** Maj. Gen. Reynaldo Bignone, president of Argentina until he was replaced by Raúl Alfonsín on Dec. 10, 1983, was arrested and charged with abuse of authority, illegal detention, and covering up an illegal act. Accusations centred on the presumed murders of two Communist army recruits in 1976. Bignone was director of the War College, where the two men had been quartered up to the time of their sudden and unexplained disappearance.

Vatican and U.S. establish full diplomatic relations. The U.S. and the Vatican restored full diplomatic relations after an interruption of well over a century. Pres. Ronald Reagan acted over strong objections voiced by various Protestant,

Jewish, and civil liberties groups. The U.S. Congress in 1983 removed a legal obstacle to formal recognition by repealing an 1867 law that prohibited the establishment of a U.S. diplomatic mission at the Vatican. While the law was in effect, some U.S. presidents maintained unofficial ties with the Vatican through personal representatives who had no diplomatic status.

Denmark elects new Parliament. Danish Prime Minister Poul Schlüter, who came to power in September 1982 as head of a four-party minority coalition government, retained his post after national elections provided the coalition and its supporters with an absolute majority of one seat in the 179-seat Folketing (parliament). Schlüter's Conservative Party won 42 seats and its three coalition partners, the Liberal Democratic, Centre Democratic, and Christian People's parties, a total of 35. Because Schlüter could also depend on support from 10 Radical Liberals and 3 members representing Greenland and the Faeroe Islands, he in effect controlled a total of 90 seats. The previous Folketing had been dissolved in December 1983 after Schlüter's austerity budget was defeated by a vote of 93–77.

11 **Panel reports on Central America.** The National Bipartisan Commission on Central America, which had been constituted by President Reagan in July 1983, issued its official report. In general, the panel recommended long-term economic and military aid to the region and warned that the U.S.S.R. and Cuba, operating through Nicaragua, posed a serious threat to the area. The panel, however, disagreed with Reagan adminis-

MOSHE MILNER—SYGMA

West German Chancellor Helmut Kohl paid a visit to the Yad Vashem Holocaust memorial in Jerusalem during a six-day visit to Israel that began January 24.

Mass meetings and rallies erupted in Brazilian cities early in the year when the military government resisted a call for presidential elections by popular vote in transition to civilian rule. Crowds surged through São Paulo streets January 25, demanding direct elections.

C. EDINGER—GAMMA/LIAISON

tration policy when it recommended that continued aid to El Salvador be linked to progress in safeguarding human rights.

18 **Gromyko and Shultz meet in Sweden.** Soviet Foreign Minister Andrey Gromyko and U.S. Secretary of State George Shultz met during the course of an international arms-control conference in Stockholm. The private talks, widely viewed as the last immediate hope for lessening tensions between the world's two superpowers, produced no significant results. Although Gromyko had bitterly attacked U.S. policy during a conference speech earlier in the day, he appeared to respond positively to certain proposals Shultz and French Foreign Minister Claude Cheysson, speaking on behalf of NATO, had set forth as ways to reduce the risk of war in Europe. Gromyko, however, rejected other NATO proposals in favour of counterproposals drawn up by the Warsaw Pact nations.

19 **Islamic group welcomes back Egypt.** The Islamic Conference Organization, during a meeting in Casablanca, Morocco, voted to invite Egypt back into the organization. Egypt's membership had been suspended in 1979 after it signed the Camp David peace accords with Israel. An unstated condition for Egypt's reinstatement was reported to be a repudiation of the peace treaty. On January 30 Egypt publicly accepted the invitation.

U.S. lifts Polish sanctions. The U.S. government, noting a "general improvement in conditions" in Poland, announced it was lifting some of the sanctions it had imposed on the country after the imposition of martial law in December 1981. The news meant that Polish fishing fleets could once again operate off the coasts of California and Alaska and that a limited number of charter flights could be scheduled between Polish and U.S. cities. Poland's national airline, however, would still be denied landing rights at U.S. airports.

22 **King of Morocco urges calm.** King Hassan II of Morocco went on national television to reassure rioters that planned increases in the cost of bread, sugar, and cooking oil had been canceled. Indications of potentially serious unrest first became evident in the city of Marrakech when protesters took to the streets to denounce anticipated increases in fees for higher education. Complaints multiplied as discontent spread across the country, reaching heightened intensity in the northern coastal cities of Tetouan, Nador, and al-Hoceima. On January 25 the government said 29 persons had been killed and 114 injured during the turmoil. Unofficial estimates were considerably higher.

23 **Chinese premier returns home after North American visit.** Chinese Premier Zhao Ziyang (Chao Tzu-yang) departed Vancouver, B.C., after completing a 17-day visit to the U.S. and Canada. While in the U.S., Zhao signed a new accord on industrial cooperation and extended an earlier agreement on science and technology. On several occasions Zhao publicly affirmed that China, which hoped to work out a nuclear power agreement with the U.S., neither advocated nor encouraged nuclear proliferation. Zhao also pleaded for an expansion of trade. On January 17 Zhao addressed a joint session of the Canadian Parliament, the first leader of a Communist government ever to do so. During his visit he also awarded a contract to a Canadian company for the construction of ground stations that would permit China to receive satellite transmissions.

24 **Helmut Kohl visits Israel.** West German Chancellor Helmut Kohl began a six-day visit to Israel, during which he sought to reassure Prime Minister Yitzhak Shamir's government that whatever decisions were made on the sale of West German arms to Saudi Arabia, the legitimate concerns of Israel would be taken into consideration. Kohl noted, however, that his country shared with the U.S. and other Western democracies a sense of responsibility for maintaining peace in the Persian Gulf area. He pointed out that the U.S., Israel's staunchest ally, had committed itself to supply arms to Saudi Arabia in the hope that this would lessen the possibility of war in that part of the world.

25 **Thousands protest in Brazil.** At least 200,000 Brazilians held a peaceful demonstration in São Paulo, the country's largest city, to plead for greater democracy. The gathering, described as the largest such in the nation's history, was an attempt to persuade congressmen to support a constitutional amendment that would have presidential elections decided by popular vote rather than by members of the electoral college. Pres. João Baptista de Oliveira Figueiredo was said to favour the status quo because his fellow Social Democrats controlled the electoral college.

Relationship between Italy and the Vatican to be reformulated. The Italian Parliament received a revised version of the 1929 concordat that had defined relations between Vatican City State and Italy since the time of Mussolini. Premier Bettino Craxi remarked that "unsuitable and anachronistic" provisions of the old concordat would be eliminated in the new pact. Under terms of the new agreement, Vatican City would retain its status as an independent state headed by the pope, but Roman Catholicism would lose its status as the official state religion of Italy. Religious education in primary and secondary schools would be given to pupils only if requested by parents; in the past, exemptions from religious education had to be requested. Despite some 15 years of intermittent negotiations, some problems were still unresolved, including the tax status of certain church organizations.

Reagan addresses Congress. President Reagan, in his annual state of the union address, noted that the nation was well on its way to economic recovery even though not all Americans were sharing equally in the improvement. During his speech, which was delivered before a joint session of Congress, the president called on members of both parties to work together to reduce the mounting federal deficit. He also emphasized the urgent need for international arms control. Speaking directly to the Soviet people, Reagan remarked that a nuclear war cannot be won and must never be fought. He concluded: "If your government wants peace, there will be peace."

27 **Office of vice-president revived in the Philippines.** Philippine voters, given an opportunity to express their opinions on several constitutional amendments, overwhelmingly approved a referendum to restore the office of vice-president. No one, however, would fill that vacancy until after the next presidential election scheduled for 1987. Should Ferdinand E. Marcos, for any reason, cease to be president before that date, the speaker of the National Assembly would head the government for up to two months, the time limit established for new elections.

FEBRUARY

1 **Argentina restricts prosecution of military for past crimes.** Argentina's Senate voted 24–21 to limit the punishment of military personnel accused of killing and torturing civilians during the 1970s. The Chamber of Deputies was expected to follow suit. Pres. Raúl Alfonsín supported the measure on the grounds that severe retribution would likely destabilize the nation. Sen. Vicente Saadi, however, called the bill "a monstrosity . . . a disguised amnesty for 98% of the criminals who spilled blood." Though enlisted men would generally be exonerated if they simply followed orders, the verdicts and sentences of the military courts would be subject to civilian review.

2 **Lusinchi assumes presidency.** Jaime Lusinchi was sworn in as president of Venezuela and used his inaugural address to describe the nation as "a state out of control." The new chief executive assured international creditors that Venezuela, given sufficient time, would repay every dollar it had borrowed. But Lusinchi cautioned that decisions about rescheduling debts had to be made in the context of the nation's overall economic recovery.

3 **Zimbabwe to pressure rebels.** The Zimbabwe government announced that it was increasing its military strength in the province of Matabeleland where, it claimed, rebels trained and armed in South Africa were killing, raping, mutilating, and torturing civilians. Some church and human rights organizations had charged Prime Minister Robert Mugabe's troops with committing similar atrocities some months earlier during a military campaign against the region's Ndebele tribe. Joshua Nkomo, Mugabe's chief political rival, derived most of his support from the Ndebeles, but the government did not accuse him of fomenting the most recent turmoil.

5 **Lebanon's prime minister resigns.** Shafiq al-Wazzan, the prime minister of Lebanon, resigned together with his nine-member Cabinet. The three Muslim ministers had apparently yielded to pressure from fellow Muslims to dissociate themselves from the policies of Pres. Amin Gemayel, a Maronite Christian. Al-Wazzan and the remaining Christian ministers then also submitted their resignations. The U.S. immediately advised Gemayel to form a new government that included members of the opposition. The U.S. also announced that it would use air and naval power against antigovernment troops positioned near Beirut. The decision was seen as a warning to Syria and the Lebanese troops it supported to go no further in their attempt to overthrow Gemayel.

7 **Lebanese Army routed in West Beirut; U.S. troops to redeploy offshore.** Shi'ah and Druze Muslim militiamen captured West Beirut after an intense battle with government troops. The victors then proclaimed a cease-fire. According to one estimate, about 40% of the soldiers who had resisted the takeover later joined the militiamen or deserted from the military. President Reagan immediately condemned the "terrorism" in West Beirut and reaffirmed support for Pres. Amin Gemayel. He also announced that, in view of recent developments, the U.S. Marines stationed at the Beirut airport would be "redeployed" offshore. It seemed likely that France, Italy, and Great Britain would soon announce that their presence in Lebanon was no longer justified. The multinational peacekeeping force would then cease to exist.

9 **Yury Andropov dies in Moscow; Chernenko named successor.** Yury V. Andropov, general secretary of the Communist Party of the Soviet Union and official head of state as chairman of the Presidium of the Supreme Soviet, died in Moscow at the age of 69. He had held office less than 15 months and was only the sixth person to lead the nation since the Bolshevik Revolution of 1917. (The others were Lenin, Joseph Stalin, Nikita Khrushchev, and Leonid Brezhnev.) On February 13 Konstantin U. Chernenko, a 72-year-old bureaucrat, succeeded Andropov as head of the Communist Party. The next day Andropov was given a state funeral and buried in Red Square.

11 **Iran-Iraq war escalates.** The 40-month-old war between Iran and Iraq took on a new, ominous dimension when, for the first time, Iraq deliberately bombed nonmilitary targets. Iran immediately announced it would reply in kind. On February 16, after each side had attacked the other's cities, Iran launched a ground offensive in the direction of Basra. An estimated half-million soldiers were reported to be engaged in heavy fighting. On February 23, while Iran was claiming victories, Iraq announced that the drive had been blunted.

Nigerians accused of corruption. Nigeria's new military government announced that three former state governors had admitted amassing huge illegal fortunes during the presidency of Alhaji Shehu Shagari. Hundreds of others who had also been taken into custody faced similar charges. The government also called attention to several individuals who, it said, had fled the country after illegally appropriating millions of dollars before the coup of Dec. 31, 1983. Umaru Dikko, the former transport minister, was among the accused. After reaching England, he had maintained a high profile by repeatedly denouncing the new government in public interviews.

13 **Panama's president resigns.** Panamanian Pres. Ricardo de la Espriella, who had come to power in July 1982 following the resignation of Aristides Royo, startled the nation by resigning without explanation. Prominent members of his Cabinet also stepped down. Though de la Espriella was immediately replaced by Vice-Pres. Jorge Illueca, who had been serving as president of the United Nations General Assembly, the sudden turn of events necessitated a reevaluation of the presidential election slated for early May. It was to be the first in 16 years.

Texaco acquires Getty Oil Co. The U.S. Federal Trade Commission (FTC) gave its preliminary approval for Texaco, Inc., the nation's third-largest oil concern, to purchase the Getty Oil Co. Texaco then bought 56% of Getty's stock for $10.1 billion; it was the largest business merger in U.S. history. The FTC required Texaco, among other things, to sell several of its refineries and some 1,900 retail outlets in the Northeast.

Nicaragua sets election date. The government of Nicaragua announced that national elections to choose a president and constituent assembly would be held on November 4. The elections would be the first since the Sandinistas overthrew the regime of Pres. Anastasio Somoza Debayle in July 1979. Opposition leaders quickly went on record as saying that elections would be meaningless if campaigning

PATRICK DURAND—SIPA/SPECIAL FEATURES

U.S. Marines embarked from Beirut's Ouzi Beach when they were withdrawn February 26, four months after the disastrous truck-bomb attack on their Beirut headquarters that took a total of 243 lives.

was inhibited by gratuitous government restrictions.

22 **Violence continues in Punjab.** Violence again erupted in India's northern state of Punjab as Sikhs and Hindus continued to confront each other over basic religious, economic, and political issues. In the latest incident, Sikh militants reportedly killed about a dozen Hindus and wounded 30 others. Most of India's 13 million Sikhs live in Punjab, and efforts by the central government to contain the violence and mollify the Sikhs had been at best only marginally successful. Among other things, the Sikhs were demanding a change in the constitution, which failed to recognize a religious difference between Sikhs and Hindus, and greater political autonomy for Punjab, which is considered India's most prosperous state. Earlier demands for a Punjabi-speaking state had led to the separation of present Punjab from Hindi-speaking Haryana in 1966.

25 **Refugees flee Mozambique.** Officials in Zimbabwe announced that an estimated 100,000 Mozambican refugees had crossed the border into Zimbabwe during the past several months. Though many were close to starvation because of a severe drought in their homeland, most were also trying to escape the ravages of guerrilla warfare. The serious plight of the refugees was highlighted by health officials who pointed out that many of the new arrivals had such obvious symptoms of malnutrition as distended bellies and blindness. Cholera had also reached epidemic proportions. Zimbabwe itself faced an impending food shortage because it too had been hard hit by the drought.

26 **Hussein and Arafat meet in Jordan.** King Hussein of Jordan and Yasir Arafat, chairman of the Palestine Liberation Organization, resumed talks that both hoped would result in a joint policy for resolving the Arab-Israeli conflict. Egypt supported the discussions, but more extreme Arab groups did not. Arafat's position as official spokesman for the Palestinians had been seriously undermined when he was forced out of Lebanon after a stinging military defeat at the hands of PLO dissidents (backed by Syria) who fiercely opposed any compromise with Israel. Hussein had earlier indicated a willingness to speak on behalf of the Palestinians provided he received clear authorization to represent them in peace negotiations.

27 **Iraq threatens to hit oil tankers loading at Iranian terminal.** Iraq announced a blockade of Iran's main oil terminal at Kharg Island and said it would attack any tanker moving in that direction until Iran agreed to end the war. Iran had previously given notice that it would block the vital Strait of Hormuz connecting the Persian Gulf with the Gulf of Oman if its oil shipments were interdicted. Japan and Italy were among major industrialized nations that relied most heavily on Iranian oil. A report that Iraq had already attacked oil cargo ships berthed at Kharg Island could not be immediately verified.

29 **Trudeau announces resignation.** Canadian Prime Minister Pierre Trudeau announced his intention to resign as head of government and as leader of the Liberal Party as soon as a successor could be chosen at a national convention. Trudeau said he felt the time had come for "someone else to assume this challenge." After becoming prime minister in 1968, he held the reins of government until May 1979 when Joe Clark, leader of the Progressive Conservative Party, began his short nine-month tenure. Trudeau resumed the prime ministership when the Liberal Party was returned to power.

MARCH

2 **Hundreds killed in Nigeria.** Maj. Gen. Mohammed Buhari, the head of state of Nigeria, ordered troops to put an end to religious violence in the state of Gongola, where hundreds were being killed in the city of Yola. Traditionalist Muslims and members of the Maitatsine sect had fought fierce battles on several previous occasions. In 1980 some 4,000 people lost their lives, including Mohammadu Marwa Maitatsine, who had totally africanized the outlawed Islamic sect that bore his name.

Kenyan paper denies killings. The *Kenya Times,* a voice of the ruling Kenya African National Union party, denied charges lodged by a member of Parliament and several other officials that government forces had tortured and massacred many of the 5,000 Degodia tribesmen who had been rounded up in February. The central government's alleged antipathy toward the Degodia was said to stem from their ethnic ties to Somali guerrillas who had long fought for control of border territory claimed by both Kenya and Somalia.

4 **Iraq accused of using chemical weapons in Gulf war.** The speaker of Iran's Parliament claimed that some 400 Iranian soldiers had been killed the previous week by Iraqi chemical weapons. The next day a U.S. official said available evidence indicated that the Iraqis had used mustard gas, outlawed by the 1925 Geneva Protocol. Iraq denied the charge."

5 **Court sanctions Nativity scenes.** The U.S. Supreme Court, in a 5–4 vote, ruled that public financing of a Nativity scene did not of itself violate the doctrine of separation of church and state derived from the First Amendment to the Constitution. Chief Justice Warren E. Burger opined that a parallel could be found in masterpieces of religious art that are commonly exhibited in tax-supported museums. In the minds of the justices, however, the main point was that the crèche (like Santa Claus, Christmas trees, and Christmas carols) had become so much a part of traditional Christmas displays that government participation in promoting such manifestations posed no serious threat to the First Amendment.

Lebanon voids pact with Israel. The Lebanese government formally abrogated a 1983 agreement with Israel that called for the simultaneous withdrawal of Israeli, Syrian, and Palestinian troops from Lebanon but granted Israel a role in Lebanon's future. The latter concession so infuriated Arab leaders that Pres. Amin Gemayel concluded he had no alternative but to renounce the agreement if he hoped to bring Lebanon's warring factions together for talks of national reconciliation. When the conference of leaders of the major Lebanese factions got under way in Lausanne, Switz., on March 12, Gemayel pleaded for an end to the "nine years of insane and continuous war." The next day, after bitter wrangling, the conferees issued a joint call for an immediate cease-fire.

7 **Poles want crucifixes restored.** Polish students staged a sit-in at Stanislaw Staszic College in Mietne to demand that crucifixes removed from their classrooms in December 1983 be returned to their original places. Though protests at that time were largely ignored by authorities, the sit-in was apparently

On March 10 Colombian police seized a record $1.2 billion (estimated street value) of cocaine and cocaine base.
SMITH—GAMMA/LIAISON

viewed as more threatening because police were ordered to clear the campus and close the school. After the main council of the Roman Catholic episcopate met in Warsaw on March 13, Bishop Jan Mazur declared that the church was "not turning back" in its fight to have crucifixes displayed in classrooms. The next day Jozef Cardinal Glemp berated officials for being so insensitive to the religious feelings of Roman Catholics, who make up the vast majority of the population.

10 **Colombian drug centre raided.** Colombian police raided an isolated cocaine factory complex on the banks of the Yarí River and seized the largest and most valuable quantity of illegal drugs ever taken anywhere in a single operation. About 40 persons, including a U.S. pilot, were arrested after a gun battle with Communist guerrilla guards. The estimated street value of the 12,500 kg (27,500 lb) of cocaine and cocaine base was put at $1.2 billion.

12 **Jordanians go to polls.** For the first time in 17 years, Jordanians were allowed to vote for candidates in a national election. They cast ballots to select two Christians and six Muslims to fill vacancies in the 60-member House of Representatives. The election was, in addition, a historic event for women, who were permitted to vote for the first time.

Coal miners strike in U.K. Strike action by members of the National Union of Mineworkers closed down more than half of Britain's 174 collieries. The work stoppage was essentially a protest against the planned closing of mines and the consequent loss of thousands of jobs. Because no national vote was taken, many of the coal miners who did not strike accused union leaders of showing contempt for the will of the majority, who on three previous occasions during the past decade had voted nationwide not to strike.

Venezuela faces austerity. Venezuelan Pres. Jaime Lusinchi announced a series of austerity measures designed to revitalize the country's stagnant economy and facilitate renegotiation of the nation's $36 billion foreign debt. The financial crisis was due in great part to a drop in the price of oil, which normally accounted for more than 90% of Venezuela's foreign exchange earnings.

13 **EC ministers approve farm reforms.** The agricultural ministers of the European Communities (EC) finally reached agreement on a new multifaceted farm policy that they hoped would control the rising cost of farm subsidies. Among other things, the ministers lowered dairy production quotas, sanctioned fines against overproduction, and abolished border taxes and subsidies that had been at the heart of numerous complaints. A broader and more vexing problem facing the EC was Great Britain's demand that its share of the organization's budget be cut. On March 20 leaders of the EC concluded a two-day meeting in Brussels without resolving the divisive issue.

Britain's budget incorporates new tax structure. Nigel Lawson, Great Britain's chancellor of the Exchequer, presented the fiscal 1985 budget to the House of Commons. Major new features included a gradual decrease in corporation taxes; incentives for individuals to invest in stocks; a higher level of income before payment of personal income taxes; increased taxes on specified consumer goods; and an earlier collection of certain value-added taxes.

16 **Mozambique and South Africa sign historic peace pact.** Mozambique and South Africa signed a nonaggression treaty that obliged each nation to prevent its land, water, and airspace from being used in any way by "another state, government, foreign mil-

itary forces, organizations or individuals which plan or prepare to commit acts of violence, terrorism or aggression" against the other country. The prime minister of Swaziland (whose country is bounded by South Africa and Mozambique) was the only black African leader to accept an invitation to attend the signing ceremony. It was later revealed that Swaziland had secretly signed a similar treaty with South Africa in 1982.

17 **Ireland captures and extradites alleged terrorist.** Dominic "Mad Dog" McGlinchey, the 30-year-old chief of staff of the Irish National Liberation Army, was captured by police in County Clare after a 90-minute gun battle; in an unprecedented move, he was extradited the following day to British authorities in Northern Ireland to face charges of murder. On March 15 Irish Prime Minister Garret FitzGerald had reemphasized his government's position on such matters when he told a joint session of the U.S. Congress that Irish-Americans had a moral obligation to refuse to make "common cause, however speciously well-meaning, with people who advocate or condone the use of violence in Ireland for political ends."

20 **Soviet oil tanker hits mine off the coast of Nicaragua.** Five crewmen were reported injured when a Soviet oil tanker struck a mine outside Puerto Sandino, Nicaragua. The leader of the Nicaraguan Democratic Force, which operated from a base in Honduras and had U.S. backing, took responsibility for mining the area. The U.S.S.R. charged the U.S. with complicity and said it was guilty of "violating one of the fundamental principles of international law, the right of freedom of navigation." The Soviet Union also reserved the right to seek compensation for the damage done to the tanker and for the injuries sustained by the seamen. Several other ships had earlier hit mines planted in harbour areas by antigovernment guerrillas.

21 **Mitterrand visits United States.** President Reagan welcomed François Mitterrand to the U.S. with words of praise for the French president's courage and decisiveness in handling "international challenges that tested the character of Western leadership." Among other things, Mitterrand had sent French troops into Chad (its former colony) to limit the military operations of antigovernment forces. He had also actively encouraged the heads of other Western European countries to deploy U.S. nuclear missiles on their soil if no arms-control agreement was reached with the Soviet Union by the end of 1983. Mitterrand also urged the U.S. to allow Central American nations to find their own way to justice and democracy "without interference or manipulation."

22 **Yasuhiro Nakasone visits China.** Japanese Prime Minister Yasuhiro Nakasone arrived in China where he held talks with Deng Xiaoping (Teng Hsiao-p'ing), China's paramount leader, and other government officials. Nakasone formally notified his hosts that Japan would

Britain's National Coal Board's plans to close unprofitable mines precipitated a bitter and violent strike.
SUTTON—GAMMA/LIAISON

provide a $2.1 billion low-interest loan to China over the next seven years. The money, which was earmarked for major rail, port, and power projects, indicated that Japan and China had entered a new era of economic cooperation.

Israel to hold national elections. Israel's Knesset (parliament), after a stormy debate, voted to advance the date for national elections. It was a major defeat for Prime Minister Yitzhak Shamir, who headed a coalition government that could not reach agreement on what means should be taken to solve the country's crucial financial problems. On March 28 the politicians designated July 28 as election day.

24 **$22 million stolen in Italy.** Four armed men invaded a Brink's Securmark vault outside Rome and made off with nearly $22 million, most of it cash. It was the largest sum ever stolen at one time in Italy. An employee was forced to cooperate after his wife and child were taken hostage the previous night. The robbers left behind highly suspect evidence implicating the notorious Red Brigades.

25 **Salvadorans vote for president.** Neither José Napoleón Duarte of the centrist Christian Democratic Party nor Roberto d'Aubuisson of the far-right National Republican Alliance was able to secure 50% of the popular vote in the eight-candidate race for the presidency of El Salvador. The two front-runners, consequently, would face a runoff in four to six weeks. Though the voting was relatively undisturbed by guerrilla attacks, there was considerable confusion in some places where ballots and ballot boxes were in short supply and where voters had an inadequate understanding of the new voting regulations.

26 **President of Guinea dies.** Ahmed Sékou Touré, president of the western African republic of Guinea for 26 years, died during an emergency heart operation in Cleveland, Ohio. He had been the nation's only ruler since leading it to independence from France in 1958. Guinea's constitution required that a new leader be elected within 45 days.

31 **India yields to Sikh demand.** The Indian government bowed to at least one Sikh demand by announcing that the constitution would be amended to acknowledge Sikhism as a religion distinct from Hinduism. The document had treated Sikhism as a Hindu sect. The leader of the main Sikh political party then canceled the weekly public burnings of the constitution. Scores of people had been killed in recent weeks as militant Sikhs pushed their demands, including independence (or at least greater autonomy) for Punjab State.

Honduran officers ousted. Gen. Gustavo Álvarez Martínez, commander in chief of the Honduran armed forces and a staunch supporter of U.S. policies in Central America, was flown out of the country and into "permanent exile" just hours after he was forced to resign. The heads of the Army, Navy, and public security forces lost their commands at the same time. At a news conference in Costa Rica on April 3, Álvarez denied charges that he had been planning a coup or had embezzled government funds. His alleged meddling in government affairs and reputed failure to consult the supreme council of the military before making decisions had, it was said, created deep resentment.

APRIL

2 **Herzog ends visit to U.K.** Israeli Pres. Chaim Herzog ended a six-day visit to Great Britain. During a farewell lunch at Windsor Castle, he extended an invitation to Queen Elizabeth II to visit Israel as a "most honoured and welcome guest." The offer had significant political overtones because no member of the royal family had ever visited Israel. The queen, moreover, had just returned home from Jordan, the sixth Arab country she had visited during her reign.

3 **Guinea's military seizes power.** An unidentified spokesman for the armed forces in the west African nation of Guinea announced over the radio that the Army had taken over the government in a bloodless coup "in order to lay the foundations of a true democracy." The military immediately suspended the constitution, dissolved the ruling Guinean Democratic Party, imposed a nighttime curfew, and cut off all communications with the outside world. The following day the junta promised to encourage free enterprise and safeguard human rights. On April 5 Lansana Conté, a 39-year-old army colonel, became head of state. His denunciation of "racism" appeared to indicate that the Malinke tribe would no longer dominate politics as it had under the late Pres. Ahmed Sékou Touré.

4 **French labour union calls strike.** The Confédération Générale du Travail, the largest labour union organization in France, called a general strike that created widespread havoc, especially in the northeastern section of the country. The Communist-affiliated union, which generally supported Pres. François Mitterrand's Socialist government, felt compelled to fight plans for gradual cutbacks in steel, shipbuilding, and coal mining operations. Mitterrand assured workers that early retirement and retraining programs would be implemented for those who lost their jobs because of the cutbacks. He insisted that France had no alternative because the nation's future depended on modernization of its industries.

6 **Poles compromise on crucifixes.** The Polish government and the Roman Catholic Church revealed that a compromise had been reached on the display of crucifixes in government-operated schools and in certain other public places. Though full details of the agreement were not immediately known, the resolution of the crisis, which had created tension between the church and the government, meant that a church-directed foundation could now begin distributing money to private farmers. Western countries had pledged $2 billion over a period of five years for this purpose.

7 **Japan to increase U.S. imports.** After long and difficult negotiations, Japan agreed to increase its quotas for beef and citrus products imported from the U.S. Over the next four years total imports of high-grade U.S. beef would rise to 58,400 metric tons from the previous level of 30,800 metric tons. Citrus products during that same period would increase to 126,000 metric tons from 82,000 metric tons. Japanese farmers, who exercised considerable political power, had vigorously opposed opening up the market to more U.S. agricultural imports.

Cameroon coup fails. Paul Biya, president of the republic of Cameroon, reassured his radio audience that government troops had stifled a revolt by members of the Republican Guard, who were under the command of Col. Ibrahim Saleh. Intense fighting, however, reportedly continued in the capital city of Yaoundé for several more days. Other areas were not affected. There was a general assumption that Ahmadou Ahidjo, a Muslim who had

REZA—GAMMA/LIAISON

On April 5 Col. Lansana Conté (left) became leader of Guinea following a bloodless military coup.

ruled Cameroon for 22 years, was involved in the attempt to overthrow his Christian successor. Ahidjo was living in southern France under a sentence of death, which was imposed during his absence and later commuted to life imprisonment by his successor, for alleged involvement in a plot to overthrow Biya the previous summer.

French soldiers die in Chad. Nine French paratroopers were killed and seven others wounded in central Chad when an explosive device was apparently carelessly handled by one of the soldiers. Defense Minister Charles Hernu later reaffirmed France's determination to remain in Chad. Its stated mission was to train Chadian government forces, to assist the civilian population, and to deter Libyan-backed rebels from advancing farther south. France feared that a successful offensive could destabilize all of central Africa and perhaps the entire continent.

9 **Peru's prime minister resigns.** Peruvian Prime Minister Fernando Schwalb López Aldana resigned because he could not agree with Pres. Fernando Belaúnde Terry's plans to increase public spending. The International Monetary Fund had earlier advised Peru to make deep cuts in its budget deficit. On April 10 Sandro Mariátegui replaced Schwalb as prime minister and foreign minister. The new Cabinet included only members of Belaúnde's Acción Popular party.

10 **Congress repudiates U.S. role in mining Nicaraguan ports.** The U.S. Senate voted 84–12 in favour of a nonbinding resolution that condemned the U.S. role in mining Nicaraguan ports. At least eight ships from six nations had been damaged. Two days later the House of Representatives approved the same resolution 281–111. On April 5, one day after the U.S had vetoed a UN Security Council resolution condemning the U.S action, it was revealed that France had offered to help Nicaragua clear out the mines. Anger reached a high pitch on Capitol Hill when it became known that the Central Intelligence Agency (CIA) had trained the mine-laying Latin-American commandos and directed their operations from a U.S. ship lying offshore in international waters. The CIA had apparently not violated federal law, but in briefings to Congress references to the operation had been so casual and vague that few congressmen took notice of what was said.

Dock strike in India settled. The longest

strike in India's history was finally settled when government officials agreed to increase the wages of some 300,000 dock-workers by more than 20%. The strike, which began on March 16, tied up India's busiest ports and resulted in a daily loss of some $30 million. Confrontations with police were especially violent in Paradip, where 100 to 300 persons were reportedly killed.

U.S. repairs orbiting satellite. The crew of the U.S. space shuttle "Challenger," after a series of unsuccessful attempts, finally snared the Solar Maximum Mission satellite ("Solar Max") and hauled it into the space shuttle's cargo bay. The crew then replaced the attitude-control module that had become disabled in November 1980, about nine months after the satellite had been launched. On April 12 the robot arm of the space shuttle was used to place Solar Max in its proper orbit above the Earth, where it would continue to collect data on solar phenomena. The event marked the first time in history that major repairs had been made on a disabled satellite in space.

11 **Chernenko elected president.** Konstantin U. Chernenko, the 72-year-old general secretary of the Soviet Communist Party, was unanimously elected chairman of the Presidium of the Supreme Soviet. Though the post was largely ceremonial, it was equivalent to that of president and gave Chernenko the right to represent the U.S.S.R. in foreign affairs.

17 **British policewoman killed by gunfire from Libyan embassy.** A 25-year-old British policewoman was killed and ten antigovernment Libyan demonstrators were wounded by machine-gun fire that came from inside the Libyan People's Bureau (embassy) in London. In February revolutionary Libyan students had taken over the embassy from accredited diplomats. When British police sealed off the area, Libya responded by surrounding the British embassy in Tripoli. On April 22, after Britain had vainly asked to inspect the embassy for arms and explosives, Britain severed diplomatic relations with Libya and ordered its diplomatic staff out of the country. Five days later British and Libyan diplomatic personnel left their respective embassies under protective escorts.

Nigeria curbs press freedoms. The Nigerian government of Maj. Gen. Mohammed Buhari issued a decree that legalized the closing down of newspapers and radio and television stations that were judged to be detrimental to the nation's interests. The decree, which was made retroactive, also sanctioned the imprisonment of journalists who were deemed guilty of "inaccurate" reporting or of penning articles that were interpreted as ridiculing government officials.

19 **Judge decides "Amoco Cadiz" case.** Judge Frank J. McGarr of the U.S. District Court in Chicago ruled that the Standard Oil Co. (Indiana) and two of its subsidiaries bore total responsibility for damage incurred when the supertanker "Amoco Cadiz" ran aground and split in 1978; its entire cargo of 226,000 tons of crude oil was lost off the north coast of France. The oil befouled some 210 km (130 mi) of coastline and caused severe losses to many industries, notably fishing and tourism. McGarr announced that the money to be awarded plaintiffs in the case would be determined at a later date.

20 **London airport bomb injures 25.** A bomb that exploded in the baggage claim area of London's Heathrow Airport injured 25 persons, at least one seriously. It was not immediately known whether the bomb had been planted or had arrived in luggage aboard a recent flight. Airport police had been on special alert because of the crisis at the Libyan embassy, but no Libyan plane appeared to be involved because none had recently used Terminal 2, the scene of the attack.

West Germans oppose U.S. missiles. West Germans began a four-day series of demonstrations directed against the nuclear arms race and the deployment of U.S. missiles in Western Europe. About 20,000 persons formed a human chain that encircled the U.S. Army base in Mutlangen; police forcefully evicted a small group that had gotten inside the base. Another group in Munich formed a human chain around World War II debris. Organizers of the protest claimed that the police estimate of 200,000 was far below the actual number of participants.

Britain to leave Hong Kong in 1997. British Foreign Secretary Sir Geoffrey Howe announced that Great Britain would not exercise any administrative function in Hong Kong after its 99-year lease on the territory expired in 1997. Sir Geoffrey also said that his government and China were still discussing important issues affecting Hong Kong's future. Among other things, Britain hoped China would grant Hong Kong a high degree of autonomy so that its people could continue their present way of life.

26 **Karami named prime minister.** Lebanese Pres. Amin Gemayel appointed Rashid Karami prime minister in the hope that he could restore stability and unity to the war-ravaged nation. Karami called upon all contending factions to lay down their weapons and work together to save Lebanon. Karami, a Sunni Muslim who had already served as prime minister nine times between 1955 and 1976, was supported by Syria. He was, however, one of the few prominent Muslim political figures who had demonstrated his ability to work with influential members of the Christian community. His top priorities included formation of a Cabinet that represented all political and religious factions, revamping Lebanon's political system, and negotiating the withdrawal of Israeli troops from southern Lebanon.

27 **Swedes fined for illegal sales.** A U.S. federal judge fined Datasaab Contracting A.B., a Swedish electronics firm, $3.1 million for illegally exporting strategic U.S. radar equipment to the Soviet Union. The equipment substantially enhanced the ability of the U.S.S.R. to track manned bombers and coordinate air attacks against Western Europe and Central Asia. The company was found guilty of "treacherous conduct" for violating the terms of an export license it had been granted by the U.S. Department of Commerce in 1977.

28 **Israel detains bombing suspects.** Israeli security officials took into custody 20 persons suspected of participating in a foiled plot to blow up buses belonging to the Arab-owned Jerusalem-Klandia Bus Co. A spokesman said the government believed it had disrupted the operations of well-trained and dangerous anti-Arab Jewish terrorists, who may also have been responsible for bombing the cars of Arab mayors, attacking an Islamic school in Hebron, and carrying out other terrorist activities.

30 **Controls over Sudan tightened.** The state-controlled news agency in Sudan reported that Pres. Gaafar Nimeiry had assumed extraordinary powers following his declaration of a state of emergency the previous day. Nimeiry contended that drastic measures were necessary to protect the nation from its internal and external enemies. By presidential decree, authorities were given the right to search private homes, impose curfews and censorship, and control transportation.

Colombian minister assassinated. Rodrigo Lara Bonilla, Colombia's minister of justice, was assassinated in Bogotá by gunmen who may have been connected to illegal drug traffickers who had threatened to kill Lara if he continued his vigorous antidrug campaign. The minister's bodyguards, who were following in a jeep when the shooting occurred, overtook the motorcycle on which the gunmen were fleeing. One was shot and killed, the other captured.

MAY

1 **Reagan concludes China visit.** President Reagan ended a six-day visit to China that began in Beijing (Peking) on April 26 with a formal reception. The president delivered a major address the following day, but his remarks criticizing the Soviet Union and others extolling personal freedom, capitalism, and religious faith were omitted in the delayed telecast to the Chinese people. Similar remarks made the following day during an interview were likewise censored. During talks with China's top officials, Reagan explained his administration's policies toward Europe, the Middle East, Central America, and Taiwan. Both sides had earlier acknowledged that despite "fundamental differences in ideology and

Despite demonstrations such as this one urging a boycott of elections for the National Assembly on May 14, opponents of Philippine Pres. Ferdinand Marcos won more than 60 of 183 seats.

ANDY HERNANDEZ—GAMMA/LIAISON

institutions," cooperation in many areas was possible and mutually advantageous. During Reagan's visit China and the U.S. formalized agreements on scientific and cultural exchanges, economic cooperation, and the development of Chinese nuclear-power facilities.

2   **Pope visits Asia and Pacific area.** Pope John Paul II began one of his longest trips overseas, this one carrying him to Alaska (where he met President Reagan, who was returning to the U.S. from China), South Korea, Papua New Guinea, the Solomon Islands, and Thailand. The pope commemorated 200 years of Roman Catholicism in Korea with the canonization of 103 martyrs who died in the 19th century. During his stay the pontiff called for "a more humane society . . . where no one is a tool, no one left out, and no one downtrodden." In Papua New Guinea the pontiff celebrated mass in pidgin English before 180,000 tribesmen. After an eight-hour visit to Guadalcanal, John Paul flew to Thailand, a country more than 95% Buddhist.

6   **El Salvador holds runoff election.** Voters in El Salvador cast ballots in a runoff election that pitted José Napoleón Duarte, a member of the moderate Christian Democratic Party, against Roberto d'Aubuisson, leader of the extreme right-wing Nationalist Republican Alliance. It was the first presidential election in 50 years without military involvement. On May 11 the Central Election Council certified Duarte as the victor with 54% of the vote. D'Aubuisson and his supporters contended that the election was a farce because the U.S. Central Intelligence Agency had aided Duarte's campaign with money. On June 1 Duarte was sworn in as president.

Panamanians choose president. In Panama's first presidential election in 16 years, two of the seven candidates claimed victory because the vote was so close and the counting of the ballots was temporarily disrupted because of confusion. The front-runners were 83-year-old Arnulfo Arias Madrid and 45-year-old Nicolás Ardito Barletta. Arias Madrid,

whose previous three presidential terms were all terminated by coups, was head of the Partido Panamenista and represented a coalition of three political parties. Ardito Barletta, a former vice-president of the World Bank, represented the National Democratic Union, a six-party coalition. During the campaign there were charges that the National Defense Force would attempt to influence the election in Ardito Barletta's favour. On May 16 the election tribunal declared Ardito Barletta the winner.

Febres Cordero wins in Ecuador. Leon Febres Cordero Rivadeneira, leader of the conservative Social Christian Party, defeated Rodrigo Borja Cevallos, a member of the Democratic Left Party, in a runoff for the presidency of Ecuador. Febres Cordero was the candidate of the National Reconstruction Front, a six-party coalition representing centre-right and right-wing political views. Borja's philosophy was closer to that of outgoing Pres. Osvaldo Hurtado Larrea, whose austerity measures had led to strikes.

8   **Soldier kills Quebec legislators.** A 38-year-old Canadian Army corporal burst into the Quebec National Assembly, where he shot and killed 3 persons and wounded 13 others. He entered the assembly through a side door armed with a submachine gun, two handguns, and a hunting knife. After the shootings the corporal held the sergeant-at-arms hostage while the others fled. Four hours later he surrendered. On a prerecorded tape delivered to a radio station, the soldier said he wanted to destroy provincial government officials for "doing much wrong to the French language people of Quebec and Canada."

Gunmen attack Qaddafi barracks. At least 20 gunmen reportedly attacked a barracks on the outskirts of Tripoli in an attempt to assassinate Libyan leader Col. Muammar al-Qaddafi. The attackers, who were said to have been armed with rocket-propelled grenades and automatic weapons, were driven off by Libyan troops after several hours of fighting and, according to unconfirmed reports, were slain in a building where they had taken

cover. The first of several attempts to overthrow Qaddafi occurred in July 1970, less than a year after he seized power.

10   **World Court rules against U.S.** The International Court of Justice in The Hague ruled unanimously that the U.S. "should immediately cease and refrain from any action restricting, blocking or endangering access to or from Nicaraguan ports, and, in particular, the laying of mines." The U.S., which had terminated its activities in late March, accepted the court's preliminary ruling. At a later date the judges were expected to rule on Nicaragua's right to present its complaint before the court.

Denmark halts missile deployment. All 77 members of the parties in Prime Minister Poul Schlüter's coalition chose to abstain from voting when Denmark's Folketing (parliament) voted to halt payments to NATO for deployment of Pershing II and cruise missiles in Western Europe. The vote was 49 to 12. It appeared that the government was trying to avoid a confrontation with the Social Democrats during negotiations for a new four-year agreement on defense spending.

Haiti bans political activities. The interior minister of the Caribbean republic of Haiti issued a decree banning all political activities except those "of the president's party." All political pamphleteering was forbidden by a second decree. The announcements came just five days after Pres. Jean-Claude Duvalier reaffirmed his support for freedom of the press and respect for human rights.

12   **Bangladesh elections postponed.** Lieut. Gen. Hossain Mohammad Ershad, chief martial law administrator and president of Bangladesh, announced without explanation that the presidential and parliamentary elections scheduled for May 27 would be postponed until sometime in the winter.

13   **Talks on Namibia stalemated.** Kenneth Kaunda, president of Zambia and co-chairman of a meeting that brought together various factions fighting over the future of South West Africa/Namibia, announced that the three-day conference had concluded without agreement on even a final statement. Guerrillas of the South West Africa People's Organization and other groups had been fighting for 17 years to loosen South Africa's hold on the territory.

14   **Filipinos elect Assembly.** Filipinos who went to the polls to elect 183 members to the National Assembly gave opponents of Pres. Ferdinand Marcos unexpected victories, especially in metropolitan Manila. The success of the opposition was especially surprising because numerous voters followed the lead of Agapito Aquino, the brother of slain opposition leader Benigno Aquino, Jr., and boycotted the election. The government reported that, as of May 16, at least 91 persons had been killed in election-related violence. Complete election results still had not been announced more than two months after the balloting, but opposition candidates had captured 15 of the 21 seats at stake in metropolitan

Manila and, overall, at least 68 seats in the Assembly; independents won an additional 16 seats.

Mexican president visits U.S. Mexican Pres. Miguel de la Madrid Hurtado arrived in Washington, D.C., where he planned to discuss Mexico's financial problems, trade, tourism, high U.S. interest rates, Mexican workers in the U.S., and U.S. policy in Central America. President Reagan, in a televised address on May 9, had referred to the fighting in El Salvador as an attempt to destabilize the entire region. He remarked: "This Communist subversion poses the threat that 100 million people from Panama to the open border on our south could come under the control of pro-Soviet regimes." On May 16 de la Madrid, in a talk before the U.S. Congress, contended that the Central American conflict was the result of "economic deficiencies, political backwardness, and social injustice." He also warned against "the illusion of the effectiveness of force."

17 **OECD meets in Paris.** Ministers representing the 24 nations of the Organization for Economic Cooperation and Development (OECD) began their annual meeting in Paris. They agreed to take measures to reduce inflation, promote competition, liberalize trade, and inaugurate new trade negotiations through the General Agreement on Tariffs and Trade. They also concurred that more had to be done to alleviate the debts of third world nations and thus improve their prospects for economic growth and development.

19 **More die in Bombay riots.** At least 44 more persons were killed as fighting between Hindus and Muslims continued for a second day in and around Bombay, India. At least 20 of the fatalities occurred in the town of Bhiwandi when a house was set on fire. On May 21 army troops were ordered to restore order in Bombay. A reported 107 persons had lost their lives during the four days of rioting.

24 **Salvadorans found guilty in slaying of U.S. churchwomen.** A five-member jury found five former members of El Salvador's National Guard guilty of aggravated homicide, robbery, and aggravated destruction of property in the Dec. 2, 1980, murders of three U.S. nuns and one female lay assistant. The U.S. had brought great pressure to bear on the Salvadoran government to bring the guilty to trial and intensify its efforts to protect human rights. On June 18 each of the former guardsmen was sentenced to 30 years in prison, the maximum penalty allowed by law.

House votes emergency aid for El Salvador. The U.S. House of Representatives voted 267–154 to grant nearly $62 million in emergency military aid to El Salvador. Further funding for the Nicaraguan *contras* during the current fiscal year was voted down 241–177. A resolution explicitly barred the Central Intelligence Agency from using funds to support "directly or indirectly any military or paramilitary operations by any nation, government, organization, or individual in Nicaragua." On May 21 Salvadoran Pres. José Napoleón Duarte had asked Congress for aid without humiliating conditions.

27 **Egypt elects legislators.** Egyptians went to the polls to elect 448 members to the People's Assembly. Though Pres. Hosni Mubarak had promised the first free balloting since King Farouk was overthrown in 1952, there were scattered complaints of irregularities. Final tallies gave Mubarak's National Democratic Party 390 seats and 73% of the popular vote. The New Wafd Party won the remaining 58 seats with 15% of the vote, making it the largest parliamentary opposition Egypt had had since the 1952 revolution. The three other parties in contention all failed to qualify for representation in the Assembly because none received 8% of the vote.

Saudis get U.S. Stinger missiles. The U.S. government announced that it had decided to send Saudi Arabia 400 Stinger antiaircraft missiles and 200 launchers for use against possible Iranian air attacks on oil fields and other vital installations. The emergency shipment was in response to a Saudi request made some months earlier for 1,200 missiles and 400 launchers. Some 20 to 30 U.S. Army specialists would spend about ten days training the Saudis in handling the weapons.

28 **U.S. honours Vietnam war dead.** Eleven years after the end of the war in Vietnam, the only unidentified American military casualty was buried with full honours in the Tomb of the Unknown Soldier at Arlington National Cemetery near Washington, D.C. The serviceman, who was placed in a crypt near three others who lost their lives during World Wars I and II and the Korean War, was awarded the Medal of Honor, the nation's highest military decoration. President Reagan pledged that the government would continue its efforts to learn the fate of 2,447 servicemen and 42 civilians still listed as missing.

JUNE

1 **Shultz meets Nicaraguan leader.** U.S. Secretary of State George Shultz, after attending the inauguration of Salvadoran Pres. José Napoleón Duarte, flew to Nicaragua to speak directly with Daniel Ortega Saavedra, head of the ruling military junta. The U.S. said the visit, which Mexican Pres. Miguel de la Madrid had urged during his recent trip to the U.S., was part of the so-called Contadora peace process, not the start of bilateral negotiations. Shultz repeated U.S. demands that Nicaragua, among other things, cease supporting the rebels in El Salvador and dismiss its Soviet and Cuban military advisers. Nicaragua insisted that anything affecting its sovereignty or self-determination was not subject to negotiations.

U.K. jobless at postwar high. Great Britain's Department of Employment announced that the seasonally adjusted total of unemployed during May had reached its highest level since World War II. The more than three million jobless represented 12.7% of the work force. Officials were hard pressed to explain the statistics because the number of new jobs created in 1983 was estimated to be 150,000, some 20,000 more than the number of those who entered the work force.

6 **Indian troops attack Sikh shrine.** After a fierce day-long battle, Indian soldiers fought their way into the Golden Temple in Amritsar, the holiest Sikh shrine. The Indian government contended that extreme measures were necessary to end prolonged and mounting violence between Sikhs and Hindus in the state of Punjab. Conflicting reports indicated that between 450 and 1,200 persons had been killed, including Jarnail Singh Bhindranwale, the leader of the Sikh militants. He and other separatists had bitterly complained that Punjab was being economically exploited by the central government. Even though a Sikh general had led the attack, many Sikhs were outraged and took to the streets to protest.

RAPHAEL GAILLARDE—GAMMA/LIAISON

Armed Sikhs marched through the grounds of the Golden Temple in Amritsar, India, several days before the battle between Indian soldiers and Sikh separatists.

In addition some 1,200 Sikh soldiers were reported to have mutinied or deserted. Two days after the assault, Pres. Zail Singh, a Sikh, visited the temple and expressed surprise at the size and quality of the arsenal found there. The temple was reopened to worshipers on June 25.

7 **Democratic leaders meet in London.** The heads of the governments of Canada, France, Great Britain, Italy, Japan, West Germany, and the U.S. met in London for the tenth annual conference of the seven major industrialized democracies. Discussions extended to such topics as budget deficits, high interest rates, the huge debts of third world nations, the Iran-Iraq war, international terrorism, nuclear arms control, East–West relations, and the economic upturn that had taken hold in their respective countries.

12 **Supreme Court rules on job seniority.** In an important civil rights case, the U.S. Supreme Court ruled 6–3 that lower courts could not set aside bona fide seniority systems to preserve the jobs of minority workers who had been hired under affirmative action programs. The decision directly affected firemen in Memphis, Tenn., who had been laid off when a federal judge ordered the city to increase its percentage of black fire fighters.

Lebanese Cabinet wins approval. Lebanon's Parliament voted 53–15 to approve Prime Minister Rashid Karami's new "national unity" Cabinet, which represented the interests of all major political and religious factions. Despite efforts to bring the nation together, violence that had begun the previous day continued. More than 105 persons were reported killed and some 250 wounded during fighting between Muslim and Christian militiamen.

14 **Dutch postpone decision on missiles.** The Parliament of The Netherlands approved by a 79–71 vote the proposal made by the Cabinet on June 1 to postpone until Nov. 1, 1985, a decision on whether or not to deploy cruise missiles in that country. Though a few Christian Democrats failed to support the ruling coalition their party formed with the Liberals, the affirmative votes of a small group of Calvinists allayed fears that the government would have to call new elections.

Voters choose European Parliament. For the first time in five years, direct elections for the European Parliament got under way in Denmark, Great Britain, Ireland, and The Netherlands. Voters in Belgium, France, Greece, Italy, Luxembourg, and West Germany chose their representatives on June 17. Partly because the European Parliament was only an advisory body with no true legislative powers, voters generally seemed to have lost confidence in the organization's ability to unite Europe. In most countries the election appeared to be a referendum on the central government. In France, for example, there was strong support for Jean-Marie le Pen and his extreme right-wing National Front, which opposed socialism, and a dramatic rejection of Communist candidates.

Five Israeli dead came home in an exchange of prisoners and bodies between Israel and Syria on June 28.
SYGMA

Comecon holds summit in Moscow. The Council for Mutual Economic Assistance (Comecon), an organization of ten Communist nations (Bulgaria, Cuba, Czechoslovakia, East Germany, Hungary, Mongolia, Poland, Romania, U.S.S.R., Vietnam), concluded a three-day meeting in Moscow, its first full-scale summit in 13 years. Cuba, citing pressing security matters, was represented by a deputy. Yugoslavia, an associate member of Comecon, sent an observer. The delegates agreed to work more closely in planning their economies and to cooperate more fully in such areas as agriculture, metallurgy, machine production, and scientific and technological development.

16 **John Turner to succeed Trudeau.** During a convention in Ottawa, the Liberal Party chose 55-year-old John N. Turner to succeed Pierre Trudeau as party leader; Trudeau had earlier announced his decision to leave politics. With one brief interruption, he had been prime minister since 1968. As the new head of Canada's ruling party, Turner would automatically become prime minister. He officially assumed that office on June 30. Because Turner was no longer a member of Parliament, he was expected to run for a seat in the House of Commons from a riding (district) in British Columbia.

Uruguay arrests Wilson Ferreira. Wilson Ferreira Aldunate, a vociferous opponent of Uruguay's military government and chief spokesman of the Blanco Party, was arrested when the Argentine ferry on which he was traveling entered Uruguayan waters. An estimated 100,000 people were waiting to welcome Ferreira in Montevideo, despite a government prohibition against such gatherings. Ferreira had been banned from politics until 1999 and had been in exile for 11 years. Authorities reportedly questioned Ferreira and then charged him with aiding subversion, engaging in acts that could lead Uruguay into war, conspiring to violate the constitution, and attacking the morality of the armed forces. Members of the Blanco Party had indicated they would boycott the election scheduled for November if Ferreira was

not allowed to run. Ferreira's son and hundreds of other supporters were also taken into custody when navy ships intercepted the ferry.

18 **Sri Lanka president begins tour.** Sri Lankan Pres. Junius R. Jayawardene arrived in the U.S. to discuss international terrorism and the ethnic strife that raged between the Hindu Tamil minority in the northern region of Sri Lanka and the Buddhist Sinhalese. Some Tamils were demanding independence. While in London for talks with British Prime Minister Margaret Thatcher, Jayawardene charged that Tamils living in Britain were aiding fellow Tamils in Sri Lanka. During discussions in New Delhi, Jayawardene and Prime Minister Indira Gandhi could not reconcile their views on how much independence district councils in Sri Lanka should be accorded so that the Tamils would have a greater say in matters affecting their lives.

20 **Mitterrand visits U.S.S.R.** French Pres. François Mitterrand arrived in Moscow, where he held very frank talks with top officials. Though Pres. Konstantin U. Chernenko had warned that he would not discuss Soviet treatment of dissident Andrey Sakharov, Mitterrand insisted on bringing up the subject. He also criticized the U.S.S.R.'s continued military presence in Afghanistan and the occupation of Kampuchea by Soviet-backed Vietnamese troops. In addition, he defended NATO's deployment of nuclear missiles in Western Europe as a necessary response to Soviet SS-20 missiles. TASS, the Soviet news agency, reported that Chernenko, despite basic disagreements over France's foreign policies, was likely to accept the invitation he received to visit Paris.

21 **Latin Americans discuss debts.** Representatives of 11 Latin-American nations met in Colombia to discuss ways of alleviating the burden of their huge foreign debts, which were estimated to be in excess of $270 billion. Their concerns focused on high U.S. interest rates and protectionist policies that restricted Latin-American exports to developed countries. Several heads of government demanded substantial changes in the economic policies of lending nations in order to preserve democracy in Latin America and promote vital economic growth in the region.

24 **French protest school proposals.** An estimated one million people marched in Paris to protest a plan by the Socialist government of Pres. François Mitterrand to tighten state control over private schools. Thousands traveled to Paris to join the demonstration, which brought virtually all normal activities in the capital to a standstill. Among those opposing the government's plan were Jacques Chirac, the mayor of Paris, and former president Valéry Giscard d'Estaing. The controversial legislation, which was under consideration in the National Assembly, would provide government aid to private schools in proportion to the number of teachers who had obtained civil service status.

27 **Cuba releases U.S. prisoners.** The Rev. Jesse Jackson, a candidate for the Democratic presidential nomination, announced in Havana that Cuban Pres. Fidel Castro had agreed to release 22 American and 26 Cuban prisoners. Most of the Americans were being held on drug charges. Seven others, accused of hijacking, remained in prison. The releases were part of a larger plan to work for normalization of relations between the U.S. and Cuba and end the military conflicts in Central America. Castro also indicated a willingness to speed up discussions for the return to Cuba of hundreds of "undesirables" who had been deported along with refugees who entered the U.S. in 1980.

28 **Israel and Syria exchange prisoners.** Israel and Syria came together in the Golan Heights to exchange prisoners and turn over the bodies of soldiers who had died. The Red Cross supervised the procedure. Israel released 291 Syrian soldiers captured in Lebanon in 1982 and the bodies of 72 soldiers. In addition, 20 Golan Heights residents, arrested for resisting Israeli occupation,

were allowed to return home. Syria turned over the bodies of five Israeli soldiers and released three soldiers and three diplomats; the latter had been captured in Syrian-held territory in Lebanon.

Brazil debates new election rules. Brazilian Pres. João Baptista de Oliveira Figueiredo, facing what appeared to be insurmountable opposition, withdrew a proposed constitutional amendment calling for direct popular election of the president in 1988. Opponents hoped to win approval for a direct presidential election in November 1984, thereby abrogating the current legislation, which called for the election of a new president by the electoral college in January 1985.

29 **Five PLO factions reunite.** Five factions of the Palestine Liberation Organization (PLO) agreed to heal the split that had occurred in 1983 when rebels tried to oust Yasir Arafat as chairman. The talks, which took place in Yemen (Aden), involved Arafat's al-Fatah group and four Marxist-oriented guerrilla organizations known as the Democratic Alliance. The National Salvation Alliance, which had forced Arafat and his troops out

of Lebanon in December 1983, boycotted the meeting.

30 **Bolivian president kidnapped.** Bolivian Pres. Hernán Siles Zuazo was kidnapped at the presidential palace by some 60 police and army officers in what turned out to be an unsuccessful attempt to stage a coup. After Gen. Alfredo Villaroel, the commander in chief of the armed forces, announced that the military maintained unalterable support for the constitution, democracy, and the president, those involved in the plot apparently realized they had failed and sought sanctuary in the Venezuelan embassy. The president was rescued unharmed about ten hours after the kidnapping. The six civilians who had been paid to guard the president with grenades were granted safe passage to the Argentine embassy. On July 2 the government announced that about 100 persons had been arrested in connection with the affair, including Marcelo Galindo de Ugarte, a former Cabinet member who was said to have masterminded the coup attempt together with Col. Rolando Saravia Ortuño, who had gone into hiding.

JULY

1 **Sweden lifts price freeze.** Swedish Finance Minister Kjell-Olof Feldt announced that the government was prematurely lifting the price freeze that had been imposed on April 9 and was scheduled to last until the end of the year. The change was made possible, Feldt explained, because the nation had gotten the message that inflation had to be controlled. A major factor in the decision was an agreement between employers and union workers to observe the government's guidelines for wage increases.

3 **West Germans end long strike.** Metalworkers in the West German state of Hesse followed the lead of fellow union members in Baden-Württemberg and voted approval of a new work schedule that cut the workweek from 40 hours to an average 38.5 hours. The agreement also included a 3% increase in wages beginning July 1 and an additional 2% effective in April 1985, when the shortened workweek was due to begin. The union had originally demanded a 35-hour week with no cut in wages, partly in the hope that more of the unemployed would be hired. The 45-day strike, which was one of the costliest and longest in West Germany's history, affected about 450,000 workers.

4 **Lebanese Army occupies Beirut.** Some 9,000 soldiers forming reconstituted units of the Lebanese Army began taking over positions in Beirut that had been occupied in February by rival military factions. The deployment, which had been sanctioned by the new "unity" Cabinet and approved by the leader of the principal Christian militia and by two prominent Muslims commanding their own armed forces, was viewed as a significant step toward ending

the nine-year-old civil war. A few days earlier Druze Muslims had already begun pulling back their artillery from the capital. Prime Minister Rashid Karami, reflecting widespread jubilation in Beirut, declared that Lebanon was finally "on the road to salvation." On July 5 heavy machinery was used to begin removing wrecked cars and other debris that had formed the "green line" separating Christian East Beirut from Muslim West Beirut. Plans called for both Christian and Muslim soldiers to patrol the area. On July 11 the Cabinet appointed a special committee to work for the release of all soldiers still held captive.

Alfonsín dismisses top generals. Argentine Pres. Raúl Alfonsín asserted civilian control over the armed forces by forcing Gen. Jorge H. Arguindegui, army chief of staff, and Gen. Pedro Pablo Mansilla, commander of the 3rd Army Corps, into retirement. The next day he accepted the resignations of two other generals, both executives at a military industrial complex. The move, it was hoped, would lessen friction within the military high command, weaken resistance to cuts in the military budget, and facilitate investigations into violations of human rights that occurred while the military ran the country.

5 **Nigerian kidnapped in London.** Umaru Dikko, wanted in Nigeria on charges of illegally amassing millions of dollars while serving in the Cabinet of deposed president Alhaji Shehu Shagari, was found drugged but alive inside a crate at Stansted Airport outside London. Another man, who was conscious and carrying syringes and drugs, was also inside. Two other men, both unconscious, were found inside a second crate. Both crates had been labeled diplomatic baggage. On July 11 one Nigerian and three Israelis

were formally charged with kidnapping and drugging Dikko. On July 13 Britain ordered two Nigerian diplomats to leave the country. Nigeria's high commissioner was also notified that he would not be welcomed back in Britain.

Colombia rejects drug dealers' offer. Carlos Jiménez Gómez, the attorney general of Colombia, revealed that the government would not grant amnesty to leading drug dealers even if they abided by a promise to abandon their illegal activities. During a meeting in Panama with seven of Colombia's top drug dealers, Jiménez was asked to give guarantees that those trafficking in drugs would not be prosecuted or extradited to the U.S. In exchange, the drug dealers pledged to cease importing unrefined cocaine from Bolivia and Peru, stop exporting drugs to the U.S., dismantle their laboratories, disband their distribution network, pinpoint the locations of coca and marijuana crops, turn over property, and transfer overseas funds to Colombian banks to bolster the economy. The government believed drug dealers were responsible for the murder of the minister of justice in April and had intensified the already vigorous antidrug campaign that the minister had been waging.

Sikhs hijack Indian plane. Nine young Sikhs, later identified as followers of Jarnail Singh Bhindranwale, the militant Sikh leader who was killed when Indian troops attacked the Golden Temple in Amritsar on June 6, commandeered an Indian Airlines A-300 Airbus during a domestic flight to New Delhi. After threatening to blow up the plane, which carried 255 passengers and 9 crewmen, the hijackers released their hostages in Lahore, Pakistan, and surrendered to authorities. The hijackers had demanded $25 million from the Indian government for damage inflicted on the temple, the release of Sikhs who had been arrested, and the withdrawal of Indian troops from Punjab State.

7   U.S.S.R. and Egypt renew ties. The U.S.S.R. announced that it had chosen Aleksandr V. Belonogov as its ambassador to Egypt, the first to hold the post since 1981. On June 23, following discussions with the Soviet Union, Egypt had named Salah Bassiouni as its representative in Moscow. During an interview on July 28, Egyptian Prime Minister Kamal Hassan Ali made clear that his country's close relationship with the U.S. would not be adversely affected by the reestablishment of normal diplomatic ties with the Soviet Union.

14   Labour Party wins in New Zealand. In national elections New Zealand's Labour Party won 56 of the 95 seats in Parliament, thereby ending the nine-year-old tenure of Prime Minister Robert Muldoon and his conservative National Party. The National Party captured only 37 seats; the Social Credit Party took the remaining 2. As leader of the Labour Party since February 1983, David Lange, a 41-year-old lawyer who had never held a position in government, would succeed Muldoon. During the campaign Lange had taken a strong stand against nuclear weapons and had promised, if his party won the election, to renegotiate terms of the ANZUS alliance, a mutual security pact with Australia and the U.S. After meeting with U.S. Secretary of State George Shultz in Wellington on July 17, Lange announced that he would delay consideration of possible changes in New Zealand's military posture until after he had attacked the nation's economic problems. The U.S. promised to give Lange a "comfortable amount of time" to decide whether or not he would modify his resolve to ban U.S. nuclear warships from New Zealand ports.

16   Democratic Party opens convention. The Democratic Party opened its quadrennial national convention in San Francisco and on July 18 nominated Walter Mondale, vice-president during the administration of Pres. Jimmy Carter, as its presidential candidate. The following day the delegates approved Rep. Geraldine Ferraro of New York as Mondale's vice-presidential running mate. Ferraro was the first woman ever nominated by either Democrats or Republicans for so high a position. Though some characterized Mondale's choice of Ferraro as capitulation to pressure exerted by certain women's organizations, most saw it as a very positive development in U.S. politics.

17   French premier resigns. French Premier Pierre Mauroy, believing that "the time has come to change the government," submitted his resignation to Pres. François Mitterrand, who then named Laurent Fabius to the vacant post. At 37 the former minister of industry and research became the nation's youngest premier in more than a century. When Fabius offered the Communists four ministries in the new government, they

China's team parades at the opening of the summer Olympic Games in Los Angeles on July 28.

SIPA/SPECIAL FEATURES

refused and withdrew from the coalition they had formed with the ruling Socialists, who still held a sizable majority in the National Assembly. For months, with growing dissatisfaction, the Communists had tried in vain to persuade the government to take more forceful measures to solve the problem of unemployment.

21   Poland grants political amnesty. The Polish government announced that 652 political prisoners would be released within the next 30 days. Prisoners charged with high treason, espionage, or sabotage would not be freed, but thousands of lesser criminals would be set free or have their sentences shortened. Premier Wojciech Jaruzelski described the decision as a humanitarian act and an expression of the strength of the state, but he warned that he would not permit a return to anarchy. The amnesty, which had the approval of the Sejm (parliament), was announced on the eve of the 40th anniversary of Communist rule.

23   Israeli voters go to polls. Israeli voters were so evenly divided when they cast ballots for a new Knesset (parliament) that no one could foresee which of the two major political blocs would be able to form a new government. The Labour Alignment, headed by Shimon Peres, lost 3 seats, but the 44 it won placed it ahead of the ruling Likud bloc, led by Prime Minister Yitzhak Shamir; it lost 7 seats and wound up with a new total of 41. Preelection polls had indicated that Labour would win as many as 54 seats, so Likud supporters found reason to be elated. The remaining 35 Knesset seats went to 13 minor parties, 9 of which garnered less than 3% of the vote. Any party, however, winning 1% of the popular vote was guaranteed representation in the Knesset. The campaign was waged on such issues as Israel's runaway inflation and continuing economic crisis, the presence of Israeli troops in Lebanon, and the future of the West Bank, occupied by Israel.

The immediate political futures of both Labour and Likud appeared to depend on the outcome of negotiations with minor parties, for without their support neither major bloc could control a majority of 61 seats in the Knesset.

Indian Parliament opens. India's Parliament was thrown into turmoil during the first meeting of a scheduled five-week session when members of both houses walked out in anger. Leaders of 19 opposition parties earlier had been united in a resolve to fight Prime Minister Indira Gandhi's ouster of Farooq Abdullah as chief minister of the state of Jammu and Kashmir. When the matter was brought up in Parliament, the leaders of both houses refused to debate the issue. On July 12 a curfew had been imposed in the state capital of Srinagar to curb unruly crowds and prevent local supporters of the former minister from holding a planned demonstration the following day.

Spanish airline pilots end strike. Pilots employed by the government-operated Iberia Airlines of Spain ended the strike they had begun on June 19 to protest planned staff cuts. Both parties, anxious to end the conflict, had agreed to binding arbitration, but some pilots later charged that Juan Ignario Molto, the head of the government's official mediation board, had been biased when he rejected demands for 34 new pilot jobs and refused to recommend the reinstatement of ten pilots who were let go for alleged misconduct during the strike. Ignario Molto, however, approved a 3.5% increase in the pilots' 1984 salaries and no cuts in current staff levels.

25   Two Germanys ease curbs. West Germany approved private bank credits of about $330 million to East Germany, which reciprocated by easing its restrictions on travel and immigration to West Germany. East and West Germans would henceforth be allowed to spend more time in each others' countries, and West Germans would not be required to exchange as much money as before when they crossed the border. Other concessions included a relaxation of curbs on West German publications permitted in East Germany and the dismantling of automatic firing devices situated along the border.

26 Quebec's language bill impugned.
The Supreme Court of Canada ruled unanimously that certain provisions of Quebec's Charter of the French Language, popularly known as Bill 101, were unconstitutional because they were in conflict with Sec. 23 of the federal Charter of Rights and Freedoms. The national law guaranteed that children of Canadians educated in French or English anywhere in the country could receive a French or English education in any province where the number of students justified such schooling. Quebec's justice minister summed up his reaction during a news conference in Montreal, saying: "If you don't control language, the idea of cultural sovereignty no longer has any meaning."

Liberia restores political freedoms.
Gen. Samuel K. Doe, Liberia's head of state, lifted the four-year ban on political activities that had been imposed in 1980 when the military seized power. Doe also

announced that the *Observer* could resume publication. The daily had been closed down in February for remarks considered harmful to the government. On July 21 Doe had dissolved the People's Redemption Council and replaced it with a 57-member National Assembly that would exercise authority until constitutional rule could be restored through general elections toward the end of 1985. Liberia cherished the distinction of being the oldest republic on the African continent.

27 EC payment to Britain blocked.
The European Parliament voted 212–70 to block an initial payment of $600 million to Great Britain, even though the European Communities (EC) had decided in late June that rebates were due Britain for having had to bear an unfair share of the EC budget. An additional payment of $800 million was also approved along with future refunds on the value-added taxes Britain collects in the name of the EC. When Britain accepted the compromise settlement in June, the wrangling, which had gone on for several years, appeared to have ended. But the newly elected European Parliament voted to make the rebate contingent on finding a satisfactory solution to the EC's 1984 budget deficit. The move was calculated

to put pressure on Britain to reverse its veto of a supplementary budget that would have wiped out the deficit.

28 Olympic Games open in Los Angeles.
President Reagan formally opened the summer Olympic Games after some 7,800 athletes from a record 140 nations paraded into the Los Angeles Memorial Coliseum and took their places on the field. Nearly 100,-000 spectators—and millions of television viewers around the world—then watched a program of spectacular entertainment that lasted more than three hours. At one point the onlookers created a breathtaking effect when, on cue, they raised the large coloured cards that had been placed on their seats and created a sea of national flags. The Soviet Union, East Germany, Bulgaria, and a handful of other countries had refused to participate in the Games of the XXIII Olympiad of modern times. As always, there were many dramatic moments during the sports competitions as new champions were crowned and others, expected to win, fell short. U.S. athletes dominated the Games, winning a total of 174 medals including 83 golds. The Olympic torch was extinguished on August 12, and South Korea reconfirmed as the host nation for the 1988 Summer Olympics.

AUGUST

3 Civilians to run Uruguay.
The military government of Gen. Gregorio Conrado Álvarez Armelino reached agreement with opposition political parties to return Uruguay to civilian rule about three months after national elections on November 25. Once the new government was installed, the legislative assembly would work out an agreement with the military on what role it would play in the new government. The accord, however, would be subject to approval on Nov. 25, 1985, when voters would express their views in a plebiscite. Before negotiations with the Colorado Party, the Civic Union party, and the Broad Front got under way, the military had reinstated the political parties that constituted the Broad Front coalition, but its leader, recently released from prison, was forbidden to engage in politics. The Blanco Party refused to join the discussions because its leader, Wilson Ferreira Aldunate, had been arrested when he returned to Uruguay.

U.S. lifts more Polish sanctions. The U.S. responded to the political amnesty announced in Poland on July 21 by lifting more of the sanctions it had imposed on the country when leaders of Solidarity and its advisers were arrested by the military in December 1981. Planes of the Polish national airline would once again be allowed to land at U.S. airports, and scientific exchanges would be resumed. In addition, the U.S. promised that a "complete and reasonable implementation" of the amnesty would also pave the way for reconsideration of U.S. opposition to Poland's participation in the International Monetary Fund. Poland was anxious to have all U.S. sanctions lifted, including the ban on agricultural credits.

6 UN opens population conference.
The United Nations opened its International Conference on Population in Mexico City with representatives of 149 nations in attendance. The meeting, only the second such in ten years, was sidetracked by political issues raised in the context of population growth. The Soviet delegates wanted a resolution passed on arms control; the U.S. proposed an amendment supporting free economies; and Arabs sought condemnation of Israeli settlements in areas they occupied in the Middle East. The most openly contentious issue, however, was abortion, which the U.S. vehemently opposed as a means for controlling undesirable population growth. The U.S., in fact, had announced on June 17 that it would cut off aid to international population programs that practiced or advocated abortion. On the ninth and final day of the conference, the delegates issued a declaration of their chief concerns. They noted that although the rate of population growth worldwide had fallen from 2% a year to 1.7% during the past decade, 90% of future growth would occur in third world countries and create an even greater disparity between their standards of living and those of developed countries. The UN issued a call for more aid to expand family-planning programs in the third world.

9 Khomeini condemns mining of Red Sea.
Ayatollah Ruhollah Khomeini, the supreme authority in Iran, condemned those responsible for mining the Red Sea and rebuked his state radio for suggesting that Iran applauded such indiscriminate attacks on ships using the vital waterway. Suspicions

had focused on Libya and Iran as more and more ships reported being hit. On July 31, however, a group identifying itself as Islamic Jihad ("Holy War") claimed responsibility for laying 190 mines in the area to punish "imperialists" who had allegedly encouraged expansion of the Gulf war. On August 21 the Egyptian chief of staff pointed the finger of blame at the Libyan freighter "Ghat," which had spent two weeks in the Red Sea shortly before the first ship sustained damage. The mining created a significant hazard because the Red Sea and the Suez Canal together provided the only passage for ships traveling between the Mediterranean and the Indian Ocean. By late August France, Great Britain, Italy, the U.S., and the U.S.S.R. were conducting a systematic minesweeping operation in the area.

10 El Salvador to get more U.S. aid.
The U.S. Congress approved an additional $190 million in aid to El Salvador, $70 million of which was earmarked for the military. The House of Representatives had earlier rejected a limit of $40 million on military aid. Because the Senate had initially approved President Reagan's request for $117 million on military aid, the $70 million represented a compromise. The appropriations were part of a larger bill granting nearly $500 million in aid to countries in Central America. A few days later Great Britain was reported to have agreed to resume economic assistance to, and technological cooperation with, El Salvador. On August 28, partly in response to constant U.S. pressure, Pres. José Napoleón Duarte created a five-member commission to investigate five cases of political murder,

including the assassination of Archbishop Oscar Arnulfo Romero y Galdamez in 1980. In another incident, an estimated 74 villagers were massacred in Las Hojas in 1983 during an alleged military operation against rebels. No guerrilla activity had been reported in the area for several years. A Roman Catholic human-rights organization contended that as many as 50,000 people may have been killed during the four-and-a-half-year-old civil war. Most were said to have been noncombatants killed by the military.

China and Australia sign accord. Australia and China signed a broad statement of agreement in Canberra, Australia, to cooperate in all aspects of their respective iron and steel industries. The pact extended to exploration, mining, ore processing, exchanges of technology, and mutual investment in each other's industries. Among other things, the pact meant Australia would supply about half of the five million metric tons of iron ore needed to complete the first phase of the Baoshan steel mill situated north of Shanghai.

11 **Zimbabwe to get one-party rule.** Prime Minister Robert Mugabe's Zimbabwe African National Union-Patriotic Front party adopted a new party constitution that would turn Zimbabwe into a one-party, Marxist-oriented state "in the fullness of time and in accordance with the law and the Constitution." The constitution, approved before Britain formally relinquished control of the country in 1980, forbids major changes in the system of government before 1990 without the unanimous consent of Parliament; it also stipulates that multiparty rule continue until 1990. Zimbabwe was one of the few black African countries that still permitted minority parties to function. The Zimbabwe African People's Union, headed by Mugabe's longtime political rival Joshua Nkomo, held 20 of the 100 seats in Parliament; an additional 20 were reserved by law for whites. On August 12 Mugabe named the members of the new party Central Committee and the 15 members of a Politburo, which would be invested with supreme authority. Mugabe and his deputy were elected unopposed to the top posts in the Politburo.

Prime minister of Guyana retires. Ptolemy Reid, prime minister and first vice-president of the South American republic of Guyana, resigned his government posts for reasons of health. Reid, however, remained deputy leader of the ruling People's National Congress party and chairman of its central executive committee; he also became special adviser to Pres. Forbes Burnham. Desmond Hoyte assumed the duties of prime minister.

13 **Herzog warns against intolerance.** Israeli Pres. Chaim Herzog, speaking to the 120 members of the new Knesset (parliament), remarked: "The need of the nation at this time is tolerance. Tolerance must be stressed, raised to the heights of a value unparalleled in its importance and taught to the entire nation." The words had special significance because Rabbi Meir Kahane, who was elected to the Knesset as a member of the extremist Kach Party, had campaigned on a promise to expel all Arabs from Israel and the occupied territories. Some 2,000 protesters had earlier greeted Kahane outside the Knesset with cries of "Fascism will not return."

16 **Indian state minister dismissed.** Ram Lal, governor of the Indian state of Andhra Pradesh, dismissed Nandamuri T. Rama Rao as the state's chief minister on the grounds that Rama Rao no longer controlled a majority in the legislature. The news sparked immediate protests and united various opposition party politicians who charged that Prime Minister Indira Gandhi, who had appointed Lal, was systematically trying to eliminate state governments that opposed her. In recent months several chief ministers of other states had also been dismissed. Rama Rao's supporters charged Lal with "criminal assault on democracy." On August 23 the lower house of Parliament overwhelmingly endorsed an amendment permitting the central government to continue exercising direct control over the state of Punjab until October 1985. On August 29 S. D. Sharma replaced Ram Lal as governor of Andhra Pradesh, and on September 16 Rama Rao was reinstated as chief minister of the state.

John De Lorean acquitted. A federal jury in Los Angeles, after 29 hours of deliberation, found John Z. De Lorean innocent of all eight charges that had been brought against him for involvement in an alleged scheme to distribute 25 kg (55 lb) of cocaine. The prosecutor contended that the automaker, whose company was in receivership in Belfast, Northern Ireland, had entered "the dirty world of narcotics" because he had a driving need to succeed at any cost. The prosecution's chief witness was a convicted drug smuggler and self-confessed perjurer. The government also tried to bolster its case with videotapes, one of which showed De Lorean looking at a suitcase full of cocaine; he remarked it was better than gold. After the trial certain jurors said they believed the government was guilty of entrapment; i.e., going beyond legal limits when its agents lured De Lorean into making the drug deal. Other jurors simply felt the government had not proved its case.

20 **Violence in Sri Lanka continues.** According to government sources, violent clashes between Tamils and Sinhalese had claimed at least 95 lives in Sri Lanka during the previous several weeks. Unofficial estimates were substantially higher. The latest outbreak of violence began in the northern part of the country on August 4 when Tamil separatists killed two sailors who had reportedly been harassing local women. The Army, which was predominantly Sinhalese, then took several hundred male villagers into custody and set fire to more than 300 homes and shops. On August 11 as many as 19 persons may have been killed when a police station was blown up. The government blamed the incident on Tamil guerrillas, but the Tamil United Liberation Front party claimed that government forces had bombed the station because Tamil youth were being detained there. On August 14 the minister for national security announced that the government would replace or repair buildings that had been burned in Mannar on August 12 and pledged that any member of the security forces who was found guilty of such attacks would be severely punished. Sporadic violence, nonetheless, continued during the days that followed.

21 **Filipinos remember Aquino.** Nearly half a million Filipinos held rallies and marched in Manila to mark the first anniversary of the assassination of Benigno Aquino, Jr. When Aquino was shot to death just moments after he returned to the Philippines from the U.S., he was the most widely respected political opponent of Pres. Ferdinand Marcos. The Supreme Court had, in effect, sanctioned the demonstrations by dismissing government contentions that mass gatherings in Rizal Park and elsewhere would lead to violence.

Australia unveils 1984–85 budget. Paul Keating, treasurer of Australia, revealed details of the Labor government's fiscal budget for 1984–85, which began on July 1. The projected deficit was pegged at $A6.7 billion (U.S. $5.7 billion), a substantial improvement over the nearly $A8 billion deficit for fiscal year 1983–

COLES—SIPA/SPECIAL FEATURES

South Africa's new constitution created a legislative chamber of limited powers for Coloureds and one for Asians. Elections for representatives of both houses, held in August 1984, were sparsely attended.

84. Among other things, the new budget included a 17% decrease in income taxes for those earning less than $A240 a week and significant increases for those in upper-income brackets. Funds for export market development would be increased, but assistance to individual exporters would be curtailed. Tax incentives to encourage mining exploration would continue, and appropriations for education would rise 8%. The government would also increase by 13% its outlays for such programs as welfare benefits and housing.

22 **South Africans go to polls.** For the first time in South Africa's troubled history, people of mixed race (Coloureds) were allowed to elect the members of their own House of Representatives in the newly created tricameral Parliament. On August 28, Asians (mostly Indians) went to the polls to select those who would represent them through the House of Delegates. In both elections, the voter turnout was very low. Whites were guaranteed continued control of the government because their House of Assembly had veto power over both of the nonwhite legislatures. Blacks, who comprised more than 70% of the population, were excluded from the government. On September 5 Prime Minister P. W. Botha, who was unopposed, was chosen by the electoral college as South Africa's first executive president under the new system of government.

Republicans nominate Reagan-Bush. The Republican national convention, meeting in Dallas, Texas, departed from tradition when it simultaneously nominated President Reagan and Vice-Pres. George Bush as its standard-bearers in the November election. In his acceptance speech the following day, Reagan said he hoped to carry forward his administration's conservative policies during a second four-year term.

23 **Colombian rebels sign truce.** Two leftist guerrilla organizations, the Maoist Popular Liberation Army and the Workers' Self-Defense Force, signed truces with the government of Colombia. Both had received assurances that new efforts would be made to help

the poor and that abuses by the military would be halted. The government also pledged to undertake a national dialogue, with all political factions participating, to prepare an agenda of political, social, and economic reforms. A year-long truce with the Colombian Revolutionary Armed Forces (FARC), the largest of the left-wing rebel organizations, had already gone into effect in May. The latest truces, consequently, meant that only the National Liberation Army and a faction of FARC were prepared to carry on their military operations against the government.

Mongolian leader replaced. The Soviet press agency TASS revealed that, for reasons of health, Yumzhagiyen Tsedenbal, first secretary of the Mongolian People's Revolutionary Party and chairman of the Presidium of the Great People's Hural, had been relieved of both posts and replaced as first secretary by Zhambyn Batmunkh. Since 1974 Batmunkh had been chairman of the Council of Ministers, a post equivalent to that of premier. Batmunkh promised to maintain Mongolia's close relationship with the Soviet Union, which he described as the cornerstone of Mongolia's foreign policy.

Religion becomes issue in U.S. politics. During a speech delivered at an ecumenical prayer breakfast in Dallas, Texas, President Reagan remarked: "The truth is, politics and morality are inseparable, and as morality's foundation is religion, religion and politics are necessarily related." These and similar remarks kindled a national debate on the separation of church and state, a fundamental tenet of the U.S. Constitution. The often heated discussions, which persisted all through the presidential campaign, involved religious leaders as well as politicians. None challenged the Constitution, but many offered personal views of what separation of church and state meant in actual practice.

25 **Dangerous cargo sinks in North Sea.** The French freighter "Mont Louis" was rammed by a ferry in the North Sea and sank about 20 km (12 mi) off the coast of Belgium. Though no one was injured, the freighter's cargo of radioactive material, which was on its way to the Soviet Union, posed

a hazard of uncertain proportions. The crystallized uranium hexafluoride, which was enclosed in 30 steel canisters, was to have been enriched and then returned to make fuel for Western European nuclear power plants. By early October, divers had recovered all the cargo, though oil leaking from ruptured fuel tanks had caused concern during salvage operations.

28 **Peruvian general relieved of duties.** Gen. Adrian Huaman Centeno, head of Peru's antiterrorist forces, was dismissed by the military government after remarking that the activities of insurgents in the department of Ayacucho were attributable to government neglect and corruption. Huaman said the solution to the problems created by the Shining Path guerrillas "is not military and never has been." Before Huaman lost his command, there were accusations that some of his troops had abducted, tortured, and murdered suspected guerrillas. On August 23 a freshly dug mass grave was discovered in Ayacucho. Both the government and the guerrillas denied responsibility for the murders.

31 **Peres and Shamir to share power.** Israeli radio reported that Prime Minister Yitzhak Shamir, leader of the Likud bloc, and Shimon Peres, who headed the Labour Alignment, had agreed to form a national unity government and alternate as prime minister. After the July 23 national elections, neither had been able to persuade minor parties to support him in forming a 61-member majority in the Knesset (parliament). On September 5 Peres publicly confirmed the agreement and said he and Shamir would soon resolve their remaining differences. During the first half of the term, Peres would hold the post of prime minister with Shamir serving as his deputy and foreign minister. During the second 25 months, their roles would be reversed. After caucuses of each bloc had approved the arrangement, the Knesset formally sanctioned the unusual political alliance on September 14. The coalition of Labour and Likud would give the government 97 votes in the 120-seat Knesset until such time as the agreement proved unworkable.

SEPTEMBER

3 **Vatican criticizes liberation theology.** The Vatican released a 35-page document repudiating certain forms of liberation theology while acknowledging that it was a basically valid concept "centered on the biblical theme of liberation and freedom, and on the urgency of its practical realization." Though the Vatican asserted that "mankind will no longer passively submit to crushing poverty," it condemned the Marxist concept of violent class struggle as an unacceptable approach to attain social justice. The statement also noted that "atheism and the denial of the human person, his liberty and his rights, are at the core of the Marxist theory." It was the first time the Roman Catholic Church had directly addressed what it viewed as

a political radicalization of some of its priests and nuns, notably those working in Latin America and other third world countries. The Vatican also encouraged and praised those who respond generously and with an authentic evangelical spirit to the "preferential option for the poor."

Crisis averted in Thailand. Thailand's National Assembly averted a potentially serious national crisis by voting 371–76 to delay consideration of what role military officers might be allowed to play in government. The Assembly had already rejected a bill in 1983 that would have permitted military personnel to become members of the Cabinet. Gen. Arthit Kamlang-ek, supreme commander of the armed forces, supported a change in the constitution and was said to cherish hopes

of one day becoming prime minister. But he backed the Parliament's vote because he too feared that any immediate decision could have disastrous consequences.

4 **Liberals lose Canadian election.** In parliamentary elections in Canada, the Progressive Conservatives, under the leadership of 45-year-old Brian Mulroney, soundly defeated the ruling Liberal Party headed by Prime Minister John N. Turner. In capturing 211 of the 282 seats in the House of Commons, the Conservatives gained 111 seats and scored one of the greatest political victories in Canadian history. In the process they also won a plurality in every province. The Liberals, in their worst showing ever, won 40 seats, a net loss of 95. The New

Democratic Party took 30 seats and an independent from Quebec the only other vacancy. The Liberals had ruled Canada as a majority party for 16 years except for a nine-month period in 1979–80 when Joe Clark, a Progressive Conservative, replaced Pierre Trudeau as head of government. During a brief victory speech the day after the election, Mulroney remarked, "Our objective and our mandate is to create jobs and to get the economy of Canada moving again." He took the oath of office on September 17.

Chilean protesters slain. A two-day peaceful protest against the military regime of Gen. Augusto Pinochet Ugarte got under way in Chile despite fears that government disapproval might lead to violence. The demonstrations were organized by the Socialist Bloc, the Popular Democratic Movement, and Alianza Democrática. Fears of physical violence proved justified when police used dogs, clubs, water cannons, and firearms to disperse clusters of demonstrators, including 300 singing the national anthem in Santiago's main square. A French priest, shot while he sat at home, was among the nine reported killed. There were also reports of hundreds of arrests and scores of injuries. On September 11 Pinochet, in a speech marking the 11th anniversary of his rise to power, reaffirmed his intention to remain in office until elections were held in 1989.

Honecker puts off West German trip. Erich Honecker, general secretary of East Germany's Communist Party and chairman of the Council of State, canceled his planned visit to West Germany. It was widely believed that Honecker's decision not to visit Bonn at the end of the month was directly related to verbal attacks that began in the Soviet press after he indicated a willingness to improve relations with West Germany. Chancellor Helmut Kohl, speaking for West Germany, expressed optimism that Honecker's trip would eventually be rescheduled and that relations between the two Germanys would continue to improve. Five days later the leader of Communist Bulgaria, Todor Zhivkov, also announced that he would not be visiting West Germany as planned.

Car bomb explodes near Belfast. A car loaded with explosives was blown up in Newry, a town located about 53 km (33 mi) southwest of Belfast, Northern Ireland. No one was killed, but 71 persons were injured. The Provisional Irish Republican Army (IRA) took credit for the bombing. The incident was merely the latest in a long series of terrorist acts that had come to characterize the IRA's campaign to drive the British out of Northern Ireland and incorporate the territory into the Republic of Ireland. The Irish government had publicly condemned such IRA operations and had promised to cooperate with Northern Ireland to bring all terrorists to trial.

6 **Chun Doo Hwan visits Japan.** South Korean Pres. Chun Doo Hwan arrived in Tokyo for an official state visit. It was the first such visit since Korea gained independence from Japan in 1945. Japanese Prime Minister Yasuhiro Nakasone had initiated the new relationship by visiting South Korea in

Brian Mulroney's buoyant campaign led Canada's Progressive Conservative Party to the second greatest electoral gain ever, capturing 211 of the 282 seats in the House of Commons.
SAL DI MARCO—BLACK STAR

1983. During a banquet welcoming Chun, Emperor Hirohito touched upon a delicate subject when he expressed regrets over the "unfortunate past between us." He also acknowledged Japan's cultural debt to Korea. The next day Nakasone also spoke apologetically about the 35 years Japan had ruled Korea, saying, "The government and people of Japan feel a deep regret for this error and are determined to firmly warn ourselves for the future." Responding positively, Chun said his visit marked the beginning of a new era of partnership. His agenda included the acquisition of Japanese technology and a diminution of his country's huge trade imbalance with Japan. On September 8 Chun and Nakasone endorsed direct talks between the two Koreas even though Chun's past initiatives had failed. The possibility of admitting both Koreas to the UN was also discussed, but hopes appeared dim because North Korea had long insisted that such a step would permanently divide the country.

Typhoon devastates Philippines. Relief agencies in Manila reported that more than 1,300 persons had been killed by Typhoon Ike, which hit the southern Philippines on September 2. Hundreds of people were missing and uncounted thousands homeless. The typhoon, which packed winds up to 220 km/h (137 mph), was described by officials as the worst storm of the century.

7 **Mexico's debt rescheduled.** Mexico announced that, after six weeks of negotiations, its major creditor banks had agreed to reschedule debts amounting to $48.5 billion. One part of the settlement granted a postponement from 1990 to 1998 of the final payment on the principal. Under the new 14-year schedule, the principal payments were to rise each year, allowing the struggling Mexican economy to recover enough to meet its obligations. Also, while Mexico was to continue making huge interest payments on the debt, it did receive a more favourable interest rate that was expected to save the country about $350 million a year. The complex agreement still had to be approved by about 600 international banks before it became final.

Soviet chief of staff removed. The Soviet Union announced that Marshal Nikolay V. Ogarkov had been replaced

as chief of general staff by his deputy, Marshal Sergey F. Akhromeyev. Ogarkov had gained worldwide publicity when he appeared on television to give the official Soviet explanation of why one of its military jets had shot down a South Korean commercial airliner on Sept. 1, 1983. An apparent reluctance on the part of Soviet officials to explain the sudden change of command fueled speculation that Ogarkov had been dismissed because of serious disagreements with his superiors.

9 **Pope visits Canada.** Pope John Paul II began a 12-day visit to Canada that included stops in most of the nation's major cities. It was a historic event for Canada, which had never before played host to a reigning pope. John Paul, as expected, reiterated traditional Roman Catholic teachings on such things as divorce and abortion, but he also spoke of the need for toleration in Canada's pluralistic society, the rights of Eskimo and Indians, and the obligation of the rich to better the conditions of the poor.

10 **Ethiopia now a Communist nation.** Ethiopia officially became a Communist state with the establishment of the Workers' Party of Ethiopia as the only legal party. Lieut. Col. Mengistu Haile Mariam, head of state and chairman of the Provisional Military Administrative Council, would continue to rule the country as secretary general of the party. There was some uncertainty about the future status of the council, but seven of its members were named to the new 11-member Politburo; the other four were civilians. A Central Committee of 136 members was also created.

12 **Indonesian Muslims riot.** Some 1,500 Muslims went on a rampage in Tanjungpriok, the port of Indonesia's capital city of Jakarta, to protest the arrests of four members of their religious community. On September 10 the four had beaten a security guard when he entered their mosque to remove antigovernment posters. Gen. Benny Murdani, commander in chief of the armed forces, claimed three religious extremists had incited the crowd to riot by delivering inflammatory speeches in the mosque. It was not immediately clear how many were killed when the crowd attacked a police post and challenged police at other locations, but the list of fatalities included a family of three trapped in one of the many fires that had been set. The battle between Muslims and police was somewhat unusual inasmuch as the vast majority of Indonesia's 150 million people, including government officials, were adherents of Islam. It appeared, however, that religious extremists were concerned that Islam would eventually suffer if President Suharto succeeded in making all political and social groups accept the nondenominational *pancasila* ("five pillars") as the sole ideology of the nation. The five pillars are: belief in a supreme deity, humanitarianism, nationalism, democracy, and social justice.

Kim Dae Jung to return home. Kim Dae Jung, who had been convicted of sedition in South Korea and spent two and a half years in prison before being allowed to travel to the U.S., announced that he planned to return home toward the end of the year. He explained that he wanted "to participate in the people's struggle for the restoration of democracy and human rights." South Korea's justice minister warned that "necessary steps, according to the law" would be taken if Kim returned. Kim's 20-year sentence had been suspended in December 1982 so that he could receive medical treatment in the U.S.; a few months later he accepted a teaching post at Harvard University. As the nominee of the New Democratic Party in 1971, Kim ran for the presidency but lost to the incumbent, Park Chung Hee.

15 **Princess of Wales has second son.** A second child was born to the prince and princess of Wales in St. Mary's Hospital, Greater London. George Pinker, the obstetrician, had also delivered the couple's first son, Prince William, and seven other royal children. The newborn infant would be christened Henry Charles Albert David and known as Prince Harry.

18 **U.K. dockworkers end strike.** U.K. dockworkers ended a strike that had been called by union officials on August 24 to express support for striking coal miners who were involved in a long and bitter dispute with management. An earlier dock strike, called to protest against the use of nonunion labour, had recently been settled without major concessions to the workers. The latest work stoppage had not received enthusiastic support from rank-and-file union members as a whole or from other unions that were asked to support the cause.

20 **U.S. embassy in Lebanon bombed.** A car loaded with an estimated 175 kg (385 lb) of TNT was driven through a hail of bullets and around concrete barriers before being blown up in front of the U.S. embassy annex in East Beirut, Lebanon. It was the third car bomb attack on a U.S. compound in Beirut within 17 months. The explosion, which killed 14 people and demolished the front of the five-story building, was reportedly heard 15 km (10 mi) away. An anonymous caller claimed responsibility in the name of Islamic Jihad ("Holy War"). Little was known of this organization, and some experts believed the name was used by several independent terrorist groups to hide their true identities. On October 4 a U.S. official identified the dead driver of the car as a member of the Party of God, which was also linked to earlier attacks on U.S. installations in Lebanon and Kuwait.

22 **Manila police disrupt rally.** At least 2,000 soldiers and police in Manila moved in with nightsticks, tear gas, and water cannons to disperse about 3,000 demonstrators who had begun a 15-hour vigil near the presidential palace the previous night. The group was marking the 12th anniversary of the imposition of martial law, which had been lifted in 1981. Earlier in the day tens of thousands had gathered in downtown Manila to denounce the "U.S.-Marco dictatorship," abuses by the military, and economic conditions. On September 27 a second rally was held to protest against police brutality toward those who had attended the vigil. By the following day, 11 bodies had been found in various locations around Manila. All the victims, though still awaiting positive identification, were believed by opposition leaders to have participated in the second rally.

24 **Queen Elizabeth visits Canada.** Queen Elizabeth II arrived in New Brunswick to begin a 14-day tour of Canada. As official head of state, the queen was warmly received, even though Britain's legal ties to Canada had weakened considerably when Canada acquired its own constitution in 1982 and the right formally to establish its own laws. Before that time it was ruled under the terms of the British North America Act of 1867, which had been amended many times by the British Parliament at Canada's request.

25 **Argentina reaches accord with IMF.** After months of negotiations, Argentina reached a basic agreement with representatives of the International Monetary Fund (IMF) on how the two could best cooperate to manage Argentina's $45 billion foreign debt. The plan, which needed formal approval by top officials of the IMF and of creditor banks, would make it possible for Argentina to borrow urgently needed money and reschedule its current debts on more favourable terms. Argentina also hoped to reduce inflation, which was out of control, increase tax revenues, and take other measures to strengthen the nation's economy.

Jordan renews ties to Egypt. Jordan announced that it was restoring full diplomatic relations with Egypt. Even though Egypt had been invited in January to resume active participation in the Islamic Conference Organization, Jordan was the first Arab nation to move toward full reconciliation. Egypt had been ostracized from most of the Arab world for signing a peace treaty with Israel in 1979.

Pullout from Chad begins. By mutual agreement, France and Libya began withdrawing their troops from the central African republic of Chad. In 1983 France had gone to the defense of Pres. Hissen Habré, whose rule was being challenged by former president Goukouni Oueddei. Goukouni's forces had not posed a serious threat to the government until Libyan troops and weapons arrived in substantial numbers. On September 17 French Foreign Minister Claude Cheysson explained that no treaty had been signed with Libya and no guarantees had been exchanged. The withdrawal of troops was simply an understanding, he said, based on the simple principle that if "the Libyans stay, we stay; they go, we go; they return, we return." Once France had made it clear that it would react forcefully to any new offensive from the north, hostilities in Chad virtually ceased.

28 **Reagan and Gromyko confer.** President Reagan and Soviet Foreign Minister Andrey Gromyko held very "forceful and direct" discussions on the serious differences that divided their two countries. The most positive outcome of the long White House talks appeared to be Gromyko's willingness to continue discussions already begun with U.S. Secretary of State George Shultz. TASS, the Soviet news agency, reported that Gromyko had reaffirmed the Soviet Union's desire for a normalization of relations, but U.S. deeds, not words, would have to make that possible. Reagan reportedly urged that both superpowers give top priority to ending the arms race. In his speech to the UN General Assembly on September 27, Gromyko had blamed the U.S. for the stalemate but emphasized the need to resolve the impasse.

29 **Italy arrests Mafia suspects.** Some 2,000 Italian police, acting on information supplied by an Italian crime figure extradited from Brazil on July 15, began one of the largest roundups of alleged Mafia criminals in the nation's history. Warrants for scores of arrests had been issued after Tommaso Buscetta revealed or confirmed the identities and crimes of those taken into custody. Buscetta, a chief organizer of the illegal drug traffic between Sicily and the U.S., also gave police information on how the drug ring operated. Arrests of high-level organized-crime figures were also made in the U.S., which had recently signed a special extradition treaty with Italy.

Arms destined for IRA seized. Irish police, with the assistance of other security forces, intercepted a trawler carrying a large quantity of weapons believed destined for guerrillas belonging to the Provisional Irish Republican Army (IRA). Five persons aboard the ship were arrested and taken to Dublin's antiterrorist criminal court. Michael Noonan, Ireland's minister of justice, said it was quite clear that the New York-based Irish Northern Aid Committee (Noraid) had paid for the arms, "which kill people north and south of the Irish border." Martin Galvin, Noraid's publicity director, denied that the committee's funds were used "for any purpose other than for supporting the victims of British violence." The trawler's cargo included machine guns manufactured in the U.S., semiautomatic rifles from West Germany, and a collection of hand grenades, pistols, and ammunition. The arms seizure was called the largest in over a decade.

OCTOBER

2 **FBI agent called spy.** For the first time in history, an agent of the U.S. Federal Bureau of Investigation (FBI) was arrested and charged with espionage. Richard W. Miller, who had been with the bureau for 20 of his 47 years, was ordered held without bond in San Diego, Calif. During questioning he reportedly admitted turning over a 24-page classified document to Soviet agents. Authorities said it could give the U.S.S.R. "a detailed picture of FBI and U.S. intelligence activities, techniques, and requirements." A Soviet couple was also arrested and held without bond in Los Angeles. Because the woman had been interviewed many times before by the FBI, there were suspicions she may have been living the life of a double agent.

Soviets set space record. Three Soviet cosmonauts returned to Earth after spending 237 days in space, a new record for endurance. During this time, two other space teams rendezvoused with the crew aboard Salyut 7, an orbiting laboratory. Their long mission included six space walks, totaling 22 hours 50 minutes.

10 **U.K. miners union fined $250,000.** British Justice Sir Donald Nicholls imposed a tentative fine of $250,000 on the National Union of Mineworkers for contempt of court. On September 28 he had declared the seven-month-old miners' strike "unofficial" under the union's constitution and ruled that it could not, therefore, justify threats of disciplinary action against miners who had refused to strike. Though Nicholls gave the head of the union several days to weigh his options, the union leader quickly announced his intention to continue defying the court order. Nicholls also announced that if the fine was not paid within 14 days, he would consider seizing the union's assets. On October 30, after another series of inconclusive negotiations, Prime Minister Margaret Thatcher announced that her government would no longer discuss a settlement that differed significantly from the one reached the previous week with the mine deputies' union. An attempt the next day to reach an accord ended acrimoniously with the chairman of the National Coal Board and the head of the union blaming each other for the impasse.

12 **Thatcher target of bombing.** British Prime Minister Margaret Thatcher was the chief target of a bombing that occurred in the Grand Hotel in Brighton, where she and other members of the ruling Conservative Party were holding their annual conference. The explosives, which badly damaged the hotel and killed five persons, apparently had been planted many days earlier by members of the Irish Republican Army (IRA). British and Irish government officials believed the terrorist attack was an attempt not only to wipe out the upper echelon of the British government but to derail scheduled Anglo-Irish talks on Northern Ireland. The IRA had been trying for years to drive the British out of Northern Ireland and make the territory part of the Republic of Ireland.

15 **Duarte meets rebel leaders.** José Napoleón Duarte, president of El Salvador, traveled to the northern town of La Palma, where he held discussions with six rebel leaders for about five hours. No cease-fire was signed, but both sides agreed to form an eight-member commission to explore the possibilities of ending the five-year-old civil war. A representative of the Roman Catholic Church would moderate the discussions. When, during a speech at the UN on October 8, Duarte proposed peace talks, senior guerrilla leaders in Mexico City indicated their desire to participate. On October 5 government and rebel representatives independently confirmed that exchanges of prisoners had been taking place for several months.

17 **Britain cuts price of oil.** Britain created consternation in other oil-producing countries by lowering the official price of its North Sea oil by $1.35 a barrel. Norway had dropped the price of its oil by a reported $1.25 two days earlier, but the British decision was far more significant because it involved large-scale, long-term contracts. On October 18 Nigeria became the first member of the Organization of Petroleum Exporting Countries (OPEC) to follow suit; it unilaterally cut $2 from the price of a barrel of its oil. On October 22 the oil ministers of 6 of the 13 OPEC nations, together with oil representatives from Mexico and Egypt, began discussions in Geneva on what could be done to head off a threatening oil price war. The full-scale OPEC meeting that followed was only marginally successful. There was general agreement that OPEC's overall production should drop to 16 million bbl a day from the current ceiling of 17.5 million and that present price levels should be maintained, at least temporarily. Certain market analysts, however, were quick to point out that weak demand had already reduced OPEC's production to 16 million bbl per day.

CIA manual creates uproar. Edward P. Boland, Democratic chairman of the House Select Committee on Intelligence, revealed that his committee was investigating a controversial Central Intelligence Agency (CIA) manual that had been distributed to rebels fighting the Sandinista government in Nicaragua. One passage referred to the "neutralization" of carefully selected targets, such as court judges, police, and security officials. Many believed these words advocated, in euphemistic terms, political kidnappings and assassinations. On November 10 the White House announced that neither of two different groups investigating the manual had found any violation of law, although disciplinary action might be justified against those guilty of "lapses in judgment."

18 **Assad ends Moscow visit.** Syrian Pres. Hafez al-Assad ended a visit to the Soviet Union that had begun on October 15. Outside observers believed the visit emphasized, rather than resolved, basic differences between the two countries. Whereas Moscow continued to support Yasir Arafat, Damascus sought to dislodge him as chairman of the Palestine Liberation Organization (PLO). In a joint communiqué, mention was made of a "profound discussion" of the PLO and the need to preserve the unity of the organization. The Soviet Union and Syria were also supporting opposite sides in the Iran-Iraq war. There were, however, no differences of opinion when it came to condemning U.S. policies in the Middle East, most notably U.S. support of Israel.

19 **Polish priest kidnapped, then slain.** The Rev. Jerzy Popieluszko, an outspoken defender of the outlawed Polish labour union Solidarity, was kidnapped near Torun, a town on the Vistula River. On October 27 Poland's Interior Minister confirmed the nation's worst fears when he announced that a member of his agency had confessed to killing the 37-year-old priest. Police

JAMES NATCHWEY—BLACK STAR

Pres. José Napoleón Duarte of El Salvador met with six rebel leaders in the town of La Palma on October 15. Although a cease-fire agreement was not signed, further discussions on ending the civil war were planned.

frogmen recovered the body from a reservoir three days later. On October 31 an interior ministry official declared that three security officers would be charged with the murder. A postmortem examination indicated that Popieluszko had been tied up, gagged, and beaten before being dumped, probably unconscious but still alive, into the reservoir. On November 3 an estimated quarter of a million people attended Popieluszko's funeral at his parish church in Warsaw.

20 **China changes economic system.** The Central Committee of China's Communist Party officially approved economic reforms that would dramatically affect nearly every aspect of urban business. According to the new guidelines, many factory managers would be allowed to lease their facilities, then operate their businesses with unprecedented autonomy. They could hire and fire as they saw fit, set wages, award bonuses, select the products they chose to manufacture, and market their goods at a reasonable profit—all within certain limits. Direct competition for customers' dollars would generally determine which companies prospered and which failed. The government, however, would keep a close watch on inflation and retain ownership of the means of production, a basic premise of socialism. It would also retain control over such major industries as steel, coal, and transportation. In 1978 the notion of a centrally planned economy had been partially abandoned in rural areas to see what effect it would have on production. The program—which permitted pay incentives for increased productivity, the private cultivation and marketing of crops, and the raising of livestock for personal profit—proved highly successful. The new economic policies, China said, simply fulfilled "an urgent need to unclog the channels of circulation between town and country."

23 **Panel reports on Aquino killing.** The five-member panel investigating the August 1983 murder of Benigno Aquino, Jr., issued its long-awaited report. The group unanimously concluded that high-ranking military officers had plotted Aquino's murder. Top officials of the Philippine government had said a Communist agent had shot Aquino while he was being led off a plane by military escorts at Manila International Airport. Aquino had been Pres. Ferdinand Marcos's chief political opponent before being imprisoned on charges of sedition; he was prematurely released so he could undergo medical treatment in the U.S. Aquino died moments after he returned to Manila. The head of the investigating commission, Corazon Agrava, accused an air force general and six soldiers of the crime. The other four members of the panel contended in a separate statement that the evidence implicated 26 people, including Gen. Fabian C. Ver, the armed forces chief of staff and one of Marcos's closest associates. On October 24 Ver requested and received a leave of absence. A special civilian court would be asked to evaluate the reports and decide what indictments would be handed down.

Food shipments from the outside world finally began to pour into famine-plagued Ethiopia. Much of the food found its way to refugee camps such as this; critics charged, however, that some went to troops instead.

DAVID BURNETT—CONTACT

24 **Tensions mount in Chile.** The Chilean government imposed tough new restrictions on press coverage of demonstrations just one day after antigovernment forces carried out six bombings. The previous week a Communist group had taken responsibility for three blasts that blacked out Santiago for 24 hours. On October 26 a car bomb was exploded directly across the street from the main government building in the capital. Three days later the military government of Gen. Augusto Pinochet Ugarte sent 140 alleged dissidents into internal exile. The next day at least half of the country's work force supported a national strike. On November 10, with tensions still mounting, soldiers rounded up about 2,000 suspected dissidents; most were released after being questioned.

26 **Baby given baboon heart.** In a historic five-hour operation at the Loma Linda University Medical Center in California, a 12-day-old baby girl was given the heart of a baboon. "Baby Fae," whose identity was not revealed, had been born with hypoplastic left heart syndrome and would have died within a few days, doctors said, had she not received a transplanted heart. The operation raised a whole series of medical and ethical questions ranging from the propriety of the xenograft itself to the manner in which decisions were made before the unusual procedure was attempted. After several weeks of encouraging progress, Baby Fae died rather suddenly on November 15.

New suspects named in pope's shooting. Ilario Martella, an Italian judge, revealed in a newspaper interview that three Bulgarians and four Turks would be placed on trial for their alleged roles in plotting to assassinate Pope John Paul II in May 1981. Mehmet Ali Agca, who had already been convicted of shooting the pope in St. Peter's Square, had surprised authorities by declaring, long after he had begun serving his life sentence, that others had been deeply involved in the attempted assassination. During Agca's trial no serious attempt had been made to link anyone else to the crime, but a review

of the evidence appeared to indicate that Agca and another Turk had both fired, almost simultaneously, at the pope.

27 **World responds to Ethiopian famine.** Recently shot film footage of starving Ethiopians began providing international television audiences with graphic evidence of a famine so severe that experts believed hundreds of persons per day were dying from starvation. A spokesman for the U.S. Agency for International Development estimated that one-fifth of Ethiopia's 33 million people were in desperate need of food. Though various governments, relief agencies, and private individuals quickly responded to calls for aid, the immediate needs of the Ethiopian people were not the only concern. Those familiar with the recurring food crisis in Ethiopia and other parts of Africa firmly believed that a long-term solution was inextricably linked to agricultural education and more enlightened government policies.

28 **Nakasone retains post.** Japanese Prime Minister Yasuhiro Nakasone was reelected head of the ruling Liberal-Democratic Party (LDP) by senior members of his party. The victory meant that the 66-year-old veteran politician would become the first prime minister in more than a decade to head the Japanese government for more than one two-year term. Nakasone pledged to continue his pro-Western foreign policy and maintain tight control over government spending. When his new Cabinet was announced on October 31, the list contained the names of one woman, the first to hold such a post in 22 years, and of several members of Kakuei Tanaka's powerful LDP faction. Though Tanaka was appealing a bribery conviction, he remained one of the country's most influential politicians.

31 **Indira Gandhi assassinated.** Indian Prime Minister Indira Gandhi was shot and killed by two of her Sikh bodyguards as she walked toward her office inside the New

Delhi compound where she lived and worked. The assassination, which stunned the world and created a major political crisis in India, appeared to be an act of vengeance because Sikhs had sworn revenge after their most sacred shrine, the Golden Temple in Amritsar, was attacked by government troops on June 5. Rajiv Gandhi was hurriedly chosen to succeed his mother as prime minister. He urged the nation to remain calm, but the indignation of many Hindus could not be contained even by police. More than a thousand Sikhs were killed, many brutally, before the fury burned itself out. Hundreds of thousands of mourners converged on Teen Murti house, where Indira Gandhi lay in state. The vast crowd was so emotional that the police, at one point, had to clear the area to regain control of the situation. On November 3 Gandhi was cremated in a traditional Hindu ceremony attended by about a hundred foreign dignitaries.

Workers strike in Ecuador. More than half of Ecuador's one million workers participated in a 24-hour strike called by the leader of the United Labour Front. The union was protesting against the government's adoption of austerity measures that the International Monetary Fund had demanded as a condition for rescheduling Ecuador's $7 billion debt.

NOVEMBER

2   Angola ready to trim Cuban forces. A spokesman for the Reagan administration announced, after intense discussions with both Angola and South Africa, that Angola was prepared to reduce the number of Cuban troops in Angola and redeploy others away from its southern border if South Africa relinquished control of South West Africa. The UN recognized the former mandated territory as Namibia, with a right to independence. On November 16, after a two-day visit by a senior U.S. envoy, South Africa indicated that a peaceful resolution of the situation might be arranged during future talks with Angolan and U.S. representatives. South Africa had previously demanded the removal of all Cuban troops from the area before agreeing to discuss Namibia's future.

4   Sandinistas sweep election. In Nicaragua's first national election since the overthrow of Pres. Anastasio Somoza Debayle in July 1979, voters as expected chose Daniel Ortega Saavedra president with 63% of the popular vote. He had already headed the government as coordinator of a three-man junta. Members of the Sandinista National Liberation Front also won 61 of the 90 elected seats in the newly constituted National Assembly. Each of the six losing presidential candidates was also guaranteed a place in the 96-seat assembly. On December 4 the Council of State, a body of appointed deputies with limited powers, ceased to exist because its functions would be taken over by the new assembly after its inauguration in January 1985.

5   Blacks killed during South African protest. For the first time in South Africa's history, hundreds of thousands of black workers, students, and those simply opposed to the government's policy of apartheid joined in a strike. Officials reported that in various parts of the country, buses, trains, buildings, and homes were attacked with stones and homemade gasoline bombs. Before the turmoil subsided several days later, 24 blacks had been killed. On November 16 the government announced it had rounded up some 2,300 workers in a black township south of Johannesburg, the largest mass arrest in years. International awareness of the plight of blacks in South Africa had been sharpened in October with the news that Bishop Desmond Tutu had been awarded the Nobel Peace Prize. By the end of November antiapartheid protests, reminiscent of the antiwar demonstrations of the 1960s, were taking place all across the U.S.

6   Reagan wins reelection. Republican incumbent Ronald Reagan, running against Democratic candidate Walter Mondale for the presidency of the U.S., was retained in office with a record 525 electoral votes. He lost only Minnesota, Mondale's native state, and the District of Columbia, which together represented 13 electoral votes. In 1972 Richard Nixon also carried 49 states when he ran for reelection, but he amassed five fewer electoral votes than Reagan. Though the Republicans lost 2 seats in the Senate, they still held a 6-seat majority in the 100-seat chamber. The Republicans increased their representation in the House of Representatives by 14 seats, but their new total of 182 seats was far less than the 252 held by Democrats. One seat, in the 8th district of Indiana, remained in dispute. Reagan, at 73 the oldest candidate ever elected U.S. president, captured 59% of the popular vote and won the support of most major demographic blocs. Mondale was preferred by blacks, Hispanics, and Jewish men and by those with annual incomes under $12,500.

Chile placed under state of siege. Pres. Augusto Pinochet Ugarte declared a 90-day state of siege in Chile just one day after his Cabinet resigned. Though, under a previously declared state of emergency, he already possessed powers to censor the press and exile political dissidents, he contended that more sweeping authority was needed "to save democracy and liberty." On November 13 opposition to the new crackdown took the form of 16 separate bombings. The archbishop of Santiago was among those who openly denounced the new tactics of the military government. On November 15 military personnel and police rounded up several thousand men in a slum area of the capital. On November 28 a general strike called by a broad coalition of labour and political leaders was virtually nullified by military security forces. On December 7, in the fourth such operation in a month, security forces took some 5,000 persons into custody.

8   Israel discusses pullout from Lebanon. Israeli and Lebanese army officers met in the headquarters of the United Nations Interim Force in Lebanon to discuss conditions for the withdrawal of Israeli forces from southern Lebanon. Israel's main concern was the security of its northern border. On November 10 the talks were suspended because Israel had arrested 13 Shi'ah Muslims, but negotiations resumed on November 14 after 3 Shi'ahs were released. The next day Lebanon suggested that its Army take responsibility for patrolling southern Lebanon after Israel pulled out; it also demanded that Israel pay at least $8 billion in war reparations. Israeli officers responded that the Lebanese Army was incapable of carrying out the task and that reparations were not pertinent to the current discussions.

CLAUDE URRACA—SYGMA

Supporters of Sandinista leader Daniel Ortega Saavedra cheer him at a preelection rally. The Sandinistas won as expected, and Ortega was elected president.

11 **U.S. bishops discuss U.S. economy.** A committee of U.S. Roman Catholic bishops issued the first draft of a pastoral letter on the U.S. economy. It acknowledged that the U.S. economy had many positive aspects, but it pointed to hunger, loneliness, and racial discrimination as examples of ugly failures. The bishops said they believed "the level of inequality in income and wealth in our society and even more the inequality on the world scale today must be judged morally unacceptable." The bishops also called for de-emphasis on military programs and reemphasis on basic human needs. Several days before the pastoral was made public, a group of prominent Catholic laypersons took issue with the bishops' view of the economy. Their statement, written in great part by Michael Novak of the American Enterprise Institute, called free enterprise—not government efforts to redistribute wealth—the surest means of solving economic and social problems. The signatories included William E. Simon, a former secretary of the treasury, and Alexander Haig, a former secretary of state.

12 **Morocco quits OAU.** Morocco, a charter member of the Organization of African Unity (OAU), withdrew from the organization because it had seated delegates of the Saharan Arab Democratic Republic (SADR), Western Sahara's government-in-exile. The OAU had earlier recognized the force behind the SADR, the Popular Front for the Liberation of Saguia el Hamra and Río de Oro (Polisario Front) as legitimate representatives of the people of Western Sahara and acknowledged the right of the inhabitants to establish an independent nation. After Spain abandoned its colony (Spanish Sahara) in 1976, Morocco, Mauritania, and the Polisario Front all laid claim to the territory, but Mauritania eventually withdrew from the conflict.

16 **Qaddafi tricked by faked murder.** Libya announced that one of Col. Muammar al-Qaddafi's notorious suicide squads had assassinated Abdul Hamid Bakkush in Cairo on November 12. The next day Egypt revealed that Bakkush was still very much alive. After Egyptian authorities had learned of the plot against the former Libyan prime minister, they had persuaded Bakkush to pose as a murder victim splattered with blood. Photos of the faked assassination were then forwarded to the Libyan embassy in Malta, which had reportedly promised two British and two Maltese agents $250,000 to arrange the murder. After arriving in Cairo, they had unwittingly hired Egyptian undercover agents to help carry out the assassination. Under questioning, the men revealed how proof of the murder was to be transmitted to Libyan officials.

Libyan troops remain in Chad. Just one day after meeting Libyan leader Col. Muammar al-Qaddafi on the Greek island of Crete, French Pres. François Mitterrand admitted he had been hoodwinked into believing Qaddafi had honoured his September pledge to withdraw all Libyan troops from Chad, a former French colony in Africa. On November 10 both France and Libya had announced that

The news was good for U.S. Pres. Ronald Reagan and his wife, Nancy, on election night (November 6): he won a landslide victory over Democrat Walter Mondale.
AP/WIDE WORLD

they had completed the withdrawal of their respective military forces. In actual fact, it appeared that Libya had pulled out no more than 2,000 of the estimated 5,500 troops it had deployed in Chad. On December 7 French Foreign Minister Claude Cheysson, severely criticized for making France appear naive and foolish, was replaced by Roland Dumas.

19 **Explosion in Mexico kills hundreds.** A tremendous explosion near Tlalnepantla, a crowded suburb north of Mexico City, killed at least 452 persons and injured some 4,250 others. Hundreds were hospitalized, some in critical condition; countless others were still unaccounted for. Authorities believed that the series of devastating blasts was triggered by a truck that exploded in a San Juan Ixhuatepec gas storage plant. Balls of fire shot into the air and rained flaming debris on buildings and on homes where most people were still asleep. The chief of police of Mexico City estimated that 27 ha (66 ac) of the town had been virtually wiped out. Angry survivors blamed Pemex (the national oil monopoly Petróleos Mexicanos) for the disaster.

Polish tourists defect in Hamburg. West German officials were caught off guard when 192 Polish tourists left a cruise ship in Hamburg and sought political asylum in West Germany. Two days later Hans-Dietrich Genscher, West Germany's foreign minister, felt compelled to cancel a three-day visit to Warsaw just hours before his planned takeoff. The visit would also have involved him in other delicate situations, notably, how to react to pressure to lay a wreath at the grave of the Rev. Jerzy Popieluszko, who had been murdered by Polish officials on October 19, and another at the grave of a German soldier buried outside Warsaw. By November 24 a total of 428 Poles had defected after their ships had docked in West German ports.

22 **Talks on arms control to resume.** The U.S. and the Soviet Union announced that U.S. Sec-

retary of State George Shultz and Soviet Foreign Minister Andrey Gromyko would meet in Geneva on January 7 and 8 to draw up an agenda for future talks on limiting nuclear and outer space weapons. The announcement followed eight weeks of exchanges between President Reagan and Konstantin Chernenko, the leader of the Soviet Union. On November 16 Chernenko had publicly urged a return to the days of détente so that both nations could cooperate in solving some of the world's most pressing problems. Neither side, however, expected that agreement on arms control would come easily or quickly.

PLO meets in Jordan. Members of the Palestine National Council, the legislative voice of the Palestine Liberation Organization (PLO), met in Amman, Jordan, to discuss peace in the Middle East and the political future of Yasir Arafat. King Hussein supported the 55-year-old chairman of the PLO, but powerful opposition groups backed by Syria wanted a more radical Palestinian leader. They had, however, agreed during the summer to let the council decide Arafat's fate. The quorum gathered in Amman rejected Arafat's offer to resign and reconfirmed him as chairman. It was a significant political victory for Arafat. On December 6 Egypt urged the U.S. to reenter Middle East peace negotiations and persuade Israel to abandon its opposition to active PLO participation in peace talks.

23 **Four killed in Korean DMZ.** Three North Korean soldiers and one from South Korea were killed when a 22-year-old Soviet tourist suddenly sprinted toward the sector of Panmunjom controlled by South Korean and UN forces. Six other soldiers were wounded during the sudden exchange of gunfire in the demilitarized zone separating North and South Korea. The defector, who was not injured, later told U.S. authorities in Seoul that he had decided two years earlier "to go to the West" the first chance he got.

25 **Uruguay returns to civilian rule.** For the first time in 13 years, Uruguayans went to the polls to decide who would head their government. With virtually all the ballots counted, 48-year-old Julio María Sanguinetti of the Colorado Party emerged victorious with about 39% of the vote. Alberto Sáenz de Zumarán, candidate of the Blanco Party, was runner-up with about 33% of the ballots. In a significant show of national unity, he visited Sanguinetti in the early hours of the morning to concede defeat and offer his congratulations and support. The third major candidate, Juan José Crottogini, received about 21% of the vote. The demise of the 11-year-old military regime, headed since 1981 by Gen. Gregorio Conrado Álvarez Armelino, made Uruguay the eighth South American nation since 1980 to return to civilian rule.

Second man receives artificial heart. William J. Schroeder, a 52-year-old retired U.S. federal employee, became the second man in history to receive an artificial heart. Doctors at the Humana Heart Institute International in Louisville,

Ky., had to take Schroeder back into surgery shortly after the initial 6½-hour operation to stop excessive bleeding, but they expressed cautious optimism that the plastic and steel permanent prosthesis would function properly. After initially making remarkably rapid progress, on December 13 Schroeder suffered a stroke that did not appear to have been caused by his artificial heart. Cardiologists said that before his surgery Schroeder had been facing imminent death because his enlarged and badly diseased heart was fast approaching the stage of total failure.

26 **Iraq and U.S. restore diplomatic ties.** Iraq and the U.S. announced the restoration of full diplomatic relations. They had been severed in 1967 by Iraq and other Arab nations to protest against U.S. support for Israel in the Six-Day War. A U.S. State Department spokesman told reporters that improved relations with Iraq would not affect U.S. neutrality in the Iran-Iraq war.

29 **Treaty settles Beagle Channel dispute.** Chile and Argentina signed a treaty ending a bitter cen-tury-old dispute over control of the Beagle Channel at the southern tip of South America. The Vatican mediated a settlement that gave Chile sovereignty over the three disputed islands of Picton, Lennox, and Nueva and Argentina most of the strategically important waterway. The 124,000 sq km (48,000 sq mi) of water were also considered potentially rich in oil. The foreign minister of Chile called the treaty "a just, equitable, and honourable solution." Argentine voters had overwhelmingly approved the treaty on November 25.

DECEMBER

1 **Labor Party wins in Australia.** The Labor Party of Prime Minister Bob Hawke won Australia's parliamentary election, but the size of its victory was considerably smaller than expected. Because Hawke appeared to be personally well liked and because Australia's economy had grown impressively during his 21 months in office, Labor was expected to increase its parliamentary majority from a preelection total of 25 to perhaps 40 seats in the newly enlarged 148-seat House of Representatives. In the smaller 125-seat House, Labor had controlled 75 seats. Though it would command 82 in the new House, it would have a majority of only 16. Andrew Peacock, leader of the conservative opposition, hailed the results as a victory for his resurgent Liberal Party. Liberals had occupied 33 House seats before the election; in the new Parliament they would have 45. The National Party, which finished third, increased its representation from 17 seats to 21.

3 **Gas kills thousands in India.** A toxic gas that leaked from a Union Carbide insecticide plant in Bhopal, India, killed as many as 2,500 persons; many died in their sleep. About 200,000 others were affected, many possibly blinded for life. Doctors were uncertain how to treat the injured because they did not fully understand how methyl isocyanate, widely used in the manufacture of insecticides, attacks the eyes, internal organs, and skin with such devastating effect. They were also worried about medical problems that might manifest themselves sometime in the future. The incident at Bhopal was believed to be the worst industrial accident in history.

Grenada elects Herbert Blaize. In the first election in Grenada in eight years, and the first since the U.S.-led invasion of the island nation in October 1983, voters gave the New National Party (NNP) 14 of the 15 seats in Parliament. The next day Herbert A. Blaize, the 66-year-old leader of the NNP centrist coalition, was sworn in as prime minister. Blaize announced he would request that troops from neighbouring islands and the U.S. remain in Grenada until it was capable of handling its own security.

4 **Two slain on hijacked plane.** A Kuwaiti Airbus A-300 jetliner, after a stopover in the United Arab Emirates, was hijacked on its way to Pakistan by four Arabic-speaking gunmen. After forcing the pilot to fly to Iran, the terrorists threatened to blow up the aircraft at the Teheran airport unless Muslims held in Kuwait were released. The terror continued until shortly before midnight on December 9, when Iranian security forces stormed the plane and rescued the nine hostages still held captive. During the long ordeal, two U.S. government officials were shot and killed and other passengers severely beaten. The U.S. was especially critical of Iran's handling of the case and demanded that the terrorists be extradited to the U.S. to stand trial. Iran refused but said the men would be tried according to Iranian law.

Mikhail S. Gorbachev, widely believed to be the second most powerful politician in the Soviet Union, visited with British Prime Minister Margaret Thatcher during his trip to Great Britain in December.

7 **China questions rigid Marxism.** The author of an unsigned front-page article in China's official *People's Daily* said it was naive and foolish to think all of China's current economic problems could be solved by adhering slavishly to Marxist economic theories. Noting that Marx, Engels, and Lenin had lived in a different age, the author emphasized that knowledge of modern scientific and technological developments was needed to implement China's program of modernization. On December 10 the paper issued a "correction," criticizing the article for not stressing the continuing importance of Marxist principles. In a second article published on December 21, Marxism was called a guide to action, not a dogma to be worshiped. The writer remarked: "More than ever before, we cannot cut our feet to fit our shoes." China's new appraisal of Marxism implicitly justified the dramatic economic changes that had been introduced in rural areas in 1978 and extended to urban enterprises in 1984.

Bishop Tutu meets Reagan. Bishop Desmond Tutu, recipient of the 1984 Nobel Peace Prize, visited President Reagan in the White House to discuss U.S. policy toward South Africa. Though Tutu claimed that the plight of blacks in his native country was, in some respects, as bad as ever, Reagan firmly denied the black clergyman's contention that the U.S. was partially to blame because it had not exerted sufficient pressure on South Africa to change its policy of racial separation. Reagan, however, indicated a willingness to study all the suggestions Tutu had made during his visit. A spokesman later said that the administration's chief concern would be to explain U.S. policy more clearly and point out the positive results of the "quiet diplomacy" it had been pursuing.

Sri Lankan rebels continue attacks. Sri Lankan officials reported that more than 100 persons were killed when Tamil guerrillas attacked an army convoy about 295 km (185 mi) northwest of Colombo, the nation's capital. On December 1 nearly 150 were reported killed in similar attacks on two prison camps. Sri Lankan planes and boats were also engaged in a battle with eight boats suspected of carrying Tamil guerrillas from India; 60 persons were killed in that encounter. Four days later government soldiers took revenge for an attack on a military convoy by killing at least 85 persons; most were said to have been Tamil civilians. The Tamils, who were vastly outnumbered by Sri Lankan Sinhalese, had been demanding independence for their section of the country, which they called Eelam.

10 **Cuba agrees to take back emigrants.** The U.S. announced that Cuba had agreed in principle to take back about 2,500 "excludable" immigrants who had entered the U.S. in 1980. All had been classified as criminals or mentally ill; as such, they did not meet U.S. requirements for immigration. The U.S. promised it would resume normal processing of Cuban visa applications if the "excludables"—only a small segment of the 125,000 who had made the boat trip from the port of Mariel—were repatriated. Local officials in Florida expressed dismay that the federal government did not plan to provide special financial assistance to the state, which would probably have to absorb at least 20,000 additional Cubans a year for the indefinite future. A White House spokesman emphasized that the agreement with Cuba did not signal any change in U.S. policy toward that country.

11 **Italy continues anticrime campaign.** In Italy's continuing campaign against organized crime, police arrested about 100 suspects, mostly in the cities of Catania, Turin, and Milan. Among those arrested were several magistrates, state policemen, tax collectors, businessmen, and a prominent lawyer. More than 300 warrants had been issued, some for persons already serving time for other crimes. It was generally presumed that the police were acting on information supplied by Tommasi Buscetta, a self-confessed murderer who had turned informer; his brother had recently been murdered near Palermo, Sicily.

12 **Mauritania's leader ousted.** Lieut. Col. Mohamed Khouna Ould Haidalla, president of the Military Committee for National Salvation, which ruled Mauritania, was removed from power while on a visit to Burundi. The leader of the coup was Army Chief of Staff Lieut. Col. Maaouya Ould Sidi Ahmed Taya, who had served as premier until Haidalla assumed that responsibility in March 1984. Taya replaced Haidalla as head of the west African nation. The territory had been a French colony until 1960.

18 **Gorbachev visits London.** Mikhail S. Gorbachev, believed in the West to be the second most powerful politician in the Soviet Union, told members of the British House of Commons that the U.S.S.R. was prepared to negotiate a dramatic reduction in nuclear weapons with the U.S. He expressed special concern, however, about U.S. plans to develop what had been termed "Star Wars" technology. The goal of the program would be the deployment of highly sophisticated defensive weapons in outer space so that protected areas would be totally or relatively invulnerable to attack from nuclear missiles. The British press described the 53-year-old Gorbachev as strikingly more personable than other Soviet officials they had come to know.

Chinese Premier Zhao Ziyang and British Prime Minister Margaret Thatcher on December 19 signed an agreement formally returning Hong Kong to Chinese sovereignty in 1997.
SYNDICATION INTERNATIONAL/PHOTO TRENDS

19 **Pakistanis extend Zia's rule.** Pakistani voters approved a referendum that extended Pres. Mohammad Zia-ul-Haq's tenure an additional five years and sanctioned a proposal to place Pakistan under strict Islamic law. Attempts by Zia's political opponents to drum up support for a boycott of the election were undercut when the government decreed that anyone promoting a boycott would be subject to imprisonment for three years.

U.K. signs Hong Kong accord. British Prime Minister Margaret Thatcher and Chinese Premier Zhao Ziyang (Chao Tzu-yang) signed an agreement in Beijing (Peking) that guaranteed the return of Hong Kong to Chinese sovereignty on July 1, 1997. Britain's 99-year lease was due to expire at that time. China had earlier given assurances that Hong Kong's thriving capitalistic economy would be permitted to function for 50 years after the territory was incorporated into the People's Republic. Formal ratification of the treaty faced no serious opposition in either country.

23 **Terrorists bomb Italian train.** Twenty-nine people were killed and nearly 200 injured when bombs partially destroyed an Italian train as it sped through a 20-km (12 mi-)-long tunnel between Florence and Bologna. Most of the 700 passengers were holiday tourists. Police believed the destruction was caused by time bombs probably planted by right-wing terrorists with international connections.

24 **India elects Parliament.** Indian voters began casting ballots for a new Parliament, but 34 seats, notably those belonging to the states of Assam and Punjab, would not be filled until political upheaval in those regions abated. Unofficial results indicated that the Congress (I) party, headed by Prime Minister Rajiv Gandhi, had won 396 seats in the 542-seat lower house, the most lopsided victory in India's history. The results suggested that the Congress (I) party had received numerous sympathy votes following the assassination of Rajiv Gandhi's mother, Indira, on October 31.

25 **Vietnam attacks Kampuchean rebels.** The Vietnamese forces occupying Kampuchea launched an offensive against four Kampuchean rebel strongholds along the Thai border. According to unofficial reports, more than 60,000 civilians sought to escape the fierce tank and artillery fire by fleeing across the border. Thai authorities reported heavy casualties. The following day Vietnamese troops overran Rithisen, the rebels' largest camp. They next concentrated their attacks on Ampil, which was strongly fortified and was believed to be defended by about 5,000 anti-Communist guerrillas. The offensive appeared to be timed to weaken the rebels before the spring monsoon season arrived.

26 **Nakasone talks trade and defense.** Japanese Prime Minister Yasuhiro Nakasone told a group of U.S. reporters in Tokyo that he was not prepared to accept predetermined quotas of U.S. imports as a way to reduce the huge U.S. trade deficit with Japan. Such a solution, he believed, was unrealistic and inadvisable because, among other things, it relied on a managed economy rather than on free trade, which he supported. Nakasone also noted that Japan had increased its military budget by more than 6% annually for the past several years "for the sake of Japan, not for the sake of other countries." The prime minister was expected to discuss these same topics with President Reagan during their scheduled meeting in January 1985.

27 **Poland tries suspects in priest's murder.** Four Polish security police went on trial in Torun for the kidnapping and murder of the Rev. Jerzy Popieluszko in October. The government appeared to feel that some conciliatory or apologetic gesture was called for because a public trial in such circumstances was unprecedented in the Communist world. One defendant testified on opening day that he had been told that the abduction, even if it led to murder, had official approval. Three of the men, if convicted, faced possible execution; the fourth could receive a long prison sentence for abetting the crimes.

PEOPLE OF THE YEAR

Biographies

Akhromeyev, Sergey Fedorovich

On Sept. 6, 1984, the Soviet press agency TASS announced that Marshal Sergey Akhromeyev had replaced Marshal Nikolay Ogarkov as chief of general staff of the Soviet armed forces. Until his demotion Ogarkov, as the most senior of 15 deputy defense ministers, had been considered the most likely successor to Marshal Dmitry Ustinov (see OBITUARIES) as minister of defense. Possible reasons advanced for Ogarkov's surprise dismissal were that he was taking the blame for the fact that the Soviet policy of increasing deployment of SS-20 missiles targeted on Western Europe had provoked NATO counterdeployments, and that he had embarrassed both Ustinov and Konstantin Chernenko (q.v.), new general secretary of the Communist Party of the Soviet Union (CPSU), when in an interview in May he called upon the U.S.S.R. to compete more energetically with the U.S. in developing high-technology conventional weapons.

Marshal Akhromeyev was not expected to be as blunt as his predecessor. However, he did not, at least initially, command the same position as Ogarkov had done in the hierarchy of deputy defense ministers; it was noted that, when Ustinov was too ill to attend the annual military parade marking the anniversary of the Revolution on November 7, Akhromeyev was not selected to act as his deputy.

Born in 1923 into a peasant family, Akhromeyev joined the Red Army when he was 17 years old, on the eve of Germany's attack on the U.S.S.R. during World War II. By the end of the war he had reached the rank of major. Remaining in the Army he was placed in command of an infantry regiment, a division, and later an army. He completed a course at the Armour Military Academy in 1952 and later attended the Frunze General Staff Academy, from which he graduated in 1967. Without the experience of commanding any of the U.S.S.R.'s military districts (he became divisional chief of staff but not commander), he was appointed to the post of deputy chief of general staff in 1974. Five years later he won promotion to first deputy. In March 1983 he attained the rank of marshal. A Communist Party member since 1943, Akhromeyev was elected a member of the Central Committee of the CPSU in June 1983 and a deputy of the Supreme Soviet in March 1984.

(K. M. SMOGORZEWSKI)

Anderson, Sparky

When Sparky Anderson became manager of the Detroit Tigers early in the 1979 season, he said that if he did not win the World Series in five years he should be fired. Five years later, in 1984, the Tigers became the second major league team ever to lead their league throughout the season and win the World Series. "I never dreamed we'd have a team this good," Anderson said.

The Tigers won their first 9 games and 35 of their first 40. They finished the season 104–58, and Anderson was named the American League's manager of the year. The Tigers beat Kansas City in three straight games for the league championship and defeated San Diego in the World Series, four games to one.

Anderson was proud of proving he could build a winner from scratch. As the Cincinnati Reds' manager in 1970–78 he had a .596 winning percentage, averaged 96 victories a year, and finished in first or second place in eight of nine seasons, but he had inherited several future Hall of Famers. Anderson's Cincinnati teams won their division five times, four National League pennants, and two World Series, in 1975 and 1976. He was National League manager of the year in 1972 and 1975. With the Detroit victory in the World Series, Anderson became the first person to manage a world champion in each league.

When the Reds fired him, Anderson called it, "the worst thing in my baseball career." When the Tigers finished fifth, fourth, and fourth in his first three seasons in Detroit, there was suspicion that the Reds had made the right decision.

Anderson played only one major-league season, batting .218 for the last-place Philadelphia Phillies in 1959. Born Feb. 22, 1934, in Bridgewater, S.D., and raised in Los Angeles, he signed with the Los Angeles Dodgers immediately after high-school graduation in 1953. Except for his brief stint with the Phillies he was a minor-league infielder for ten seasons before he began managing in 1964. In 1955 a radio announcer nicknamed him for his scrappiness in arguing with umpires, and George Lee Anderson has been Sparky ever since.

His strength as a manager is not strategic maneuvering so much as his handling of people. Anderson uses whole 25-man teams, taking advantage of players' strengths and not expecting them to play beyond their limits. As his Cincinnati protégé, Pete Rose, said, "Sparky just tries to make it fun to go out and play."

(KEVIN M. LAMB)

Ardito Barletta Vallarina, Nicolás

On May 16, 1984, after ten days of challenges and accusations of fraud in the counting of the more than 600,000 ballots cast, Nicolás Ardito Barletta was declared president of Panama by 1,713 votes. The election was the country's first after 16 years of military rule; it had been agreed to during negotiations between the U.S. and Panama that led to the signing of the 1977 Panama Canal Treaty. Among negotiators for Panama had been Ardito Barletta, minister of planning and economic policy from 1973 to 1978, when he resigned as one of Gen. Omar Torrijos Herrera's trusted advisers to become World Bank vice-president for Latin America and the Caribbean.

Ardito Barletta was approached late in 1983 by friends in the Panamanian government about running for president. In February 1984 Ricardo de la Espriella unexpectedly resigned the office and was succeeded by the vice-president, Jorge Illueca, who did not enter the race. Ardito Barletta ran as the coalition candidate backed by the National Guard, and his candidacy had government support. In the election he defeated the 82-year-old three-time president (1940, 1949, and 1968) Arnulfo Arias Madrid, a Harvard-educated physician who had been ousted from office by a military coup each time he had served.

Ardito Barletta was born on Aug. 21, 1938, and grew up in Las Tablas, a town of 3,000. His great-grandparents had come from Italy and opened a grocery store; the family gradually expanded into farming and transportation. His father, however, chose another life. He entered politics and in 1940 was named mayor of Panama City by the then new president—his close friend, Arias.

The younger Ardito Barletta attended

North Carolina State University in Raleigh, where he earned a B.S. degree in agricultural engineering in 1959 and an M.S. two years later. He was a student at the University of Chicago between 1961 and 1966, when he returned to Panama to teach economics and advise government agencies. By 1971, when he returned to receive his Ph.D. in economics from the University of Chicago, he was recognized as one of Panama's brightest young economists.

In his October 11 inaugural address, preceded by a demonstration of 1,200 protesters that was quelled by the National Guard, Ardito Barletta pledged to repair the economy, fight corruption, and unite Panama's political parties. Calmly, he urged the military to "go back to the barracks." (SUSAN K. NELSON)

Assad, Hafez al-

Syria's hard-line, pro-Moscow Pres. Hafez al-Assad was one of the Arab world's longest surviving leaders, although ill health in early 1984 prompted speculation about the succession and the role of his brother Rifaat Assad, commander of the regime's praetorian guard. Assad was born in 1928 in Qardaha near Latakia into a peasant family of the Alawi sect. He joined the Ba'th Party in 1946 and, after a career as a student activist, enrolled in the military academy at Homs, graduating in 1955 as an air force pilot. Known to his friends as Abu Suleiman, Assad was posted to Cairo during the 1958–61 union between Egypt and Syria. On March 8, 1965, two years after the Ba'thists came to power, he was appointed commander in chief of the Air Force. He took part in the Feb. 23, 1966, overthrow of the Amin Hafez government, then, as defense minister, thwarted a countercoup seven months later. After the 1967 war with Israel, he headed the military wing of the Ba'th Party.

Following disputes within the party over Syrian intervention in Jordan, Assad took power in November 1970 and had his opponents arrested. He then embarked on a policy of widening contacts with other Arab countries, including Saudi Arabia. In 1971 he participated in a union with Egypt and Libya. Also in 1971, he was elected president of the republic by universal suffrage, and he was reelected for seven years in 1978. Despite his popularity with the electorate, Assad faced opposition from Sunni Muslim religious circles and from the left, which increased its pressure following the Syrian intervention in Lebanon that began in 1976. In 1983 Assad was forced to take harsh repressive measures, particularly against the extremist Muslim Brotherhood. His foreign policy, which led him to support Egypt's Pres. Anwar as-Sadat in the 1973 war against Israel, was based on a desire for a negotiated settlement of the Arab-Israeli conflict but also by a wish to see Syria achieve a dominant position in the Levant.

Assad was brought into the Camp David dialogue by U.S. Pres. Jimmy Carter, but he opposed the Camp David peace accords and in 1980 signed a 20-year friendship and cooperation treaty with the Soviet Union. In 1979 Assad had ambitions for a political union with Iraq, but the project ended with the discovery in mid-1979 of a coup attempt in Iraq in which Syria was alleged to be involved. The split deepened

after the Iran-Iraq war broke out in 1980, with Assad supporting Teheran and closing an overland Iraqi crude-oil pipeline to the Mediterranean. (JOHN WHELAN)

Bird, Larry Joe

After the Boston Celtics were eliminated from the 1983 championship play-offs of the National Basketball Association (NBA), Celtic forward Larry Bird promised, "I'm going to punish myself all summer and come back in better shape than ever so this doesn't happen again." People wondered how he could blame himself, 6 ft 9 in of work ethic wrapped in a basketball uniform.

But Bird got a key to the local high-school gym. He worked out long and late, and he made good on his promise. He was the most valuable player for the 1983–84 season, the second noncentre to win the award in 20 years. He also was named MVP for the play-offs, leading the

DAN HELMS—DUOMO

Celtics with 27.4 points per game and in 12 other categories, including assists, steals, defensive rebounds, and shooting percentage. Boston won the NBA championship in 1984, defeating the Los Angeles Lakers four games to three in the final round.

Bird is widely considered the best all-around professional basketball player despite substandard speed, jumping ability, and showmanship flair. He is an unusually good rebounder for his height and in 1983–84 ranked tenth in the NBA with 10.1 per game. He ranked seventh in scoring, averaging 24.2 points, mostly from outside the lane, with a step-back jump shot that compensates for his lack of jumping height. He led forwards with 6.6 assists per game and led all players with an .888 free-throw percentage. He was first team all-NBA for the fifth time in five seasons.

Bird almost did not play college basketball. He spent only 3½ weeks at Indiana University in 1975 before hitchhiking home and going to work as a garbage collector. The self-described "hick from French Lick" was homesick for the Indiana town where he was born Dec. 7, 1956. In the fall of 1976 he enrolled closer to French Lick, at Indiana State University in Terre Haute, where a street was named for him in 1984. With Bird playing there in 1976–79, Indiana State had a three-year

won–lost record of 81–13 and went 33–0 before losing the 1979 national championship game to Michigan State. In 1978–79 Bird was voted college player of the year.

His signing with Boston generated club-record ticket sales. The excitement was justified. The Celtics improved from 29–53 in 1978–79 to 61–21 in 1979–80, when Bird was rookie of the year. Boston then won the NBA championship the next season. (KEVIN M. LAMB)

Botha, P(ieter) W(illem)

In September 1984 P. W. Botha became South Africa's first executive president under a new constitution that marked a radical break with a British style of parliament. For the previous six years he had been the country's prime minister. He presented the new constitution as a major reform that, for the first time, introduced Coloureds (people of mixed race) and Asians into a tricameral Parliament but that still left the black majority to be represented separately through their ethnic homeland parliaments. Botha had tenaciously piloted the new constitution against strong opposition from ultraconservative elements in the Afrikaner community and was willing to risk dividing both his party and the Afrikaner *volk*. (Afrikaners in South Africa are whites of Dutch descent.) In a hard-fought referendum campaign to win endorsement for the constitution from the white electorate, he had urged Afrikaners "to come out of the *laager*" and to face the future. Rejecting the notion of the Afrikaners as a chosen race, he affirmed: "The God I believe in is big enough to be the God of others as well."

Botha was born in a village in the Orange Free State on Jan. 12, 1916. After college he became an organizer of the Cape Province National Party at the age of 20. Twelve years later he entered Parliament, with an established reputation as a shrewd party organizer. After holding several Cabinet posts, in 1966 he became defense minister and set about building up his power base. He became known as the spokesman for the Army, and under his leadership the South African Defence Force grew into what might be the strongest and best armed on the continent. He remained defense minister for two years after becoming prime minister in 1978. Although a strong believer in military power and in the use of force to defend the continuation of white rule over five-sixths of the country, Botha also came to recognize the importance of political change to try to win over the loyalty and cooperation of the country's black majority.

Botha sought in 1984 to win Western approval for his policies by making his first trip as head of government outside the continent, during which he visited the capitals of Western Europe. His main aim was to win acceptance of South Africa's role as the regional power in the subcontinent, but his mission was not spectacularly successful because of growing international hostility to South Africa's racial policies. While Western governments were willing to applaud his tentative attempts at reform, none felt he had yet gone far enough—a position also adopted by U.S. Pres. Ronald Reagan, to whom Botha had looked especially for support. (COLIN LEGUM)

Budd, Zola

Barefoot long-distance runner Zola Budd appeared ill-equipped for the situation in which she found herself throughout 1984: at the eye of a storm of controversy. At her track appearances in Britain she sought protection behind burly reporters of the *Daily Mail*, the newspaper that arranged her passage from her native South Africa, from the taunts of antiracist demonstrators who condemned the speed with which she, a white and celebrated South African, had been granted U.K. citizenship. After colliding with Mary Decker in the 3,000-m race at the 1984 Olympic Games at Los Angeles, leaving Decker sprawled at the side of the track, she finished the race seventh and visibly distraught, as the Los Angeles crowd roared its disapproval. Her hasty disqualification was later reversed, and the accident was generally regarded as an almost inevitable consequence of two front-runners who were both trying to dominate the race.

Yet this same apparently frail frame had accomplished truly remarkable running feats. In January the athletics world was electrified by the news that Budd had taken almost seven seconds off Decker's 5,000-m world record. Because of the sporting ban on South Africa, the time could not stand in the record books, and a confrontation with Decker, her childhood heroine, was impossible while she remained there. Asked about her own reasons for seeking British citizenship, which she was granted in March within two weeks of applying, Budd replied that she had run in solitude against the clock for too long. On the question of racial separation in South Africa she would not be drawn, maintaining that the system "began before I was born and will probably be resolved long after I die. In the meantime I want to run."

Budd was born in Bloemfontein, Orange Free State, on May 26, 1966. At 13 she broke her first national junior record and came within half a second of the 1,500-m senior record. Later she abandoned her studies in political science at the University of Orange Free State in order to concentrate on running. The strength of her ambition was called into question when she returned to South Africa after the Games to consider her future. If she chose to run again there, she would renounce her international career for good. She declined to do so, however, and instead returned to international competition when she won an 8-km road race in Switzerland at year's end. (LOUISE WATSON)

Buhari, Mohammed

When on the last day of 1983 the Nigerian Army once more took power, ousting the civilian government elected less than four months earlier, the soldier who emerged as the new head of state was a quiet man without the obvious forcefulness of character of his military predecessors in power. During his New Year's broadcast as head of state, Maj. Gen. Mohammed Buhari listed the many failings of former president Alhaji Shehu Shagari's regime—corruption, immorality and impropriety, forgery, fraud, embezzlement, and other crimes—and thereby set high standards for himself and his new government.

At 42 Buhari was a young man to head Africa's largest nation. A soft-spoken Fulani from Daura in the northern state of Kaduna, he was possessed of a deceptively gentle exterior, which, however, concealed a tough will. Although he was seemingly a shy, retiring man, it would be a mistake to imagine that he was not a leading force in the coup that brought him to power.

Born on Dec. 17, 1942, Buhari was a cadet at the Nigerian Military Training College and at the Mons Officers' Cadet School, Aldershot, England. He joined the Nigerian Army in 1962 and was commissioned in 1963. By 1975 he was a lieutenant colonel and was one of the movers in the coup that ousted Gen. Yakubu Gowon, head of the military government from 1966 to 1975. Buhari served as military governor of the former North Eastern State (at Maiduguri) in 1975, and he was briefly military governor of Borno State before he was appointed federal commissioner for petroleum resources by Lieut. Gen. Olusegun Obasanjo, who succeeded Brig. Murtala Mohammed after the latter's assassination. When this office joined the Nigerian National Oil Corporation to form the Nigerian National Petroleum Corporation in 1977, Buhari became chairman. At the same time, he was moved to the job of military secretary (Army) at Supreme Military Headquarters—the seat of the government. In 1979 he returned to full military duties and in 1980 was appointed general officer commanding, 4th Division; later he became general officer commanding, 1st Mechanized Division at Jos, Plateau State, where he remained until December 1983.

As head of state, facing formidable problems, Buhari maintained a low-key approach to his job. He might have a less forceful character than Mohammed or Obasanjo, but he was intelligent, able to grasp complex issues, and a firm disciplinarian known to stand on principle—all characteristics that should stand him in good stead. (GUY ARNOLD)

Bush, George Herbert

In August 1984, as the Republican national convention drew to a close, the only question some Republicans had was whether or not Vice-Pres. George Bush would be aggressive enough to meet the challenge posed by Rep. Geraldine A. Ferraro (*q.v.*), his lively Democratic opponent. Although he and his family had lived in Texas for 30 years, Bush was considered a genteel New Englander. Born on June 12, 1924, in Milton, Mass., son of an investment banker who was a Republican senator from Connecticut from 1962 to 1972, he grew up in affluent Greenwich, Conn., and attended exclusive private schools until 1942, when he saw active duty as a U.S. Navy pilot in World War II. After the war he attended Yale University, where he was a Phi Beta Kappa scholar and an athlete. In 1948, with a degree in economics, he moved to Texas, where he learned the oil business and formed his own offshore drilling equipment company.

Bush ran for the Senate in 1964 but lost. In 1966 and again in 1968 he was elected to the U.S. House of Representatives, where he supported several measures—including ending the draft—that his wealthy Republican constituents considered too liberal. He lost his second bid for the Senate in 1970, and over the next six years served as ambassador to the United Nations, chairman of the Republican National Committee, head of the first U.S. liaison office to Beijing (Peking), and director of the Central Intelligence Agency (CIA). In 1976 he resigned from the CIA to lay the groundwork for an unsuccessful 1980 attempt at the presidency. At that year's convention Ronald Reagan chose him as running mate to broaden the appeal of his conservative ticket. Throughout Reagan's first term Bush consistently supported the president, and he was rewarded with renomination as vice-president.

For the 1984 campaign Bush's press secretary, Peter Teeley, said in August: "We will be saying little about Mrs. Ferraro," and he predicted "a very hard-nosed and high-road campaign." In the next three months Bush again tirelessly proved his loyalty to Reagan and worked to shed his lingering "preppie" image.

On October 11 Bush met Ferraro in a televised debate between the vice-presidential candidates. The encounter produced no significant advantage for either advocate except when Ferraro was able to reproach Bush for patronizing her by a rather pompous offer to explain to her the intricacies of some aspects of foreign policy. His continuing demonstration of loyalty to Reagan and a conservative administration, however, won him more good marks for team play, points he could store against a run for the top job in 1988.

(SUSAN K. NELSON)

Carrington, Peter Alexander Rupert Carington, 6th Baron

Public service was the Carrington vocation. Peter Alexander Carington, the 6th baron, cared for no other way of life and eagerly abandoned the chairmanship of the General Electric Co. and other directorships to become secretary-general of NATO on June 25, 1984. As both a former secretary of state for defense and foreign secretary, he was amply qualified to take on that job at a crucial and difficult moment in the history of the 35-year-old alliance. Out of public office since his resignation as foreign secretary in 1982, Lord Carrington had continued to exercise some private influence with Prime Minister Margaret Thatcher, urging the importance of dialogue with the Soviet Union. He regarded that—the end of what he called "megaphone diplomacy"—as the necessary condition for the revival of public confidence in the NATO alliance.

Carrington's public life extended back over 3½ decades, during which he served under five Conservative prime ministers. Born June 6, 1919, he had a conventional aristocratic upbringing—Eton College, the Royal Military Academy (Sandhurst), and the Grenadier Guards. After service in World War II he became a junior minister under Winston Churchill. He entered Alexander Douglas-Home's Cabinet in 1963 and after the Conservatives' loss in the 1964 general election led the opposition in the House of Lords. With the Conservatives back in power in 1970, he became defense secretary and, in the last days of the Edward Heath government, energy secretary.

When the Thatcher government was formed in 1979, Carrington became foreign secretary. His charm and diplomatic skills, not least with the prime minister herself, enabled him to achieve a negotiated independence for Rhodesia (now Zimbabwe) and an end to the bloody civil war there. He then turned his attention to the Middle East and at the same time sought negotiated solutions to Britain's residual colonial problems, which included the Falkland Islands. While his back was turned in April 1982, the Argentines invaded the Falklands. Carrington resigned. His decision to do so was not just, as some said, a matter of honour; he had reached the conclusion that the war could not be waged with a foreign secretary who was in the House of Lords and under fire from sections of his own party and from the right-wing press.

(PETER JENKINS)

Castro, The Rev. Emilio

The World Council of Churches (WCC), the world's largest ecumenical organization, elected its first new general secretary in 12 years in July 1984. For its new leader the council chose Emilio Castro, a Uruguayan Evangelical Methodist known as a moderate proponent of many of the values of the "liberation theologians" but considered less strident than the man he replaced. Castro, 57, had already served 11 years as head of the WCC's Commission on World Mission and Evangelism and was known for trying to communicate with and reconcile those who felt alienated from the council without giving up his own beliefs. The fourth general secretary of the council, he was the first from the Southern Hemisphere.

Castro replaced Philip A. Potter, a West Indian who had led the ecumenical council to address the concerns of third world nations and frequently attacked the political and economic policies of the U.S. and the Western European nations, alienating many conservative Protestants in those countries. The new general secretary, who would take office for a five-year term Jan. 1, 1985, might be more diplomatic than his predecessor, but he insisted that he shared Potter's concerns.

The council had been accused in recent years of using a double standard in criticizing the Western powers and the Communist countries. In response, it was argued that Christians in the Communist countries would suffer if the council criticized their governments. Castro said that he would encourage reconsideration of that position and predicted that the issue would be a "hot potato" for some time. As an individual he criticized both Marxist materialism and Western capitalism.

Castro was born on May 2, 1927, in Montevideo, Uruguay, one of nine children in a Roman Catholic working class family. While still a growing boy he had a conversion experience that brought a new dimension to his faith, and he later gravitated into the Evangelical Methodist Church. After secondary school he went to Buenos Aires, Arg., to attend Union Theological Seminary there, and after graduation studied in Basel, Switz., with Karl Barth, still later pursuing a doctorate at the University of Lausanne. After working with his wife in several churches in Bolivia, he became pastor of Central Methodist Church in Montevideo.

Castro's election might help improve WCC relations with Roman Catholics and fundamentalist Protestants, for he had worked well with these groups despite

their recent alienation from the aims of the WCC leadership. He was also expected to improve communication between Orthodox Christians and the other Christian churches.

(DAVID A. OATES)

Chernenko, Konstantin Ustinovich

Outmaneuvered by Yury Andropov (see OBITUARIES) in the succession battle that followed the death of Leonid Brezhnev in November 1982, Konstantin Chernenko was successful in his second attempt. Four days after the death of Andropov on Feb. 9, 1984, Chernenko was elected general secretary of the Communist Party of the Soviet Union (CPSU) by a majority vote in the 12-member Politburo and a unanimous vote in the Central Committee (CC). His position was consolidated when he was appointed chairman of the Presidium of the Supreme Soviet (president) on April 11.

Chernenko had been singled out by Brezhnev to be his successor. To prepare him for his future role, Brezhnev insisted that Chernenko be present when prominent Communist leaders visited the U.S.S.R. and arranged that Chernenko accompany him on important trips abroad— to Helsinki, Fin., in 1975 and to Vienna in 1979. Nevertheless, his lack of experience in foreign affairs was judged to be a major reason for his defeat by Andropov in 1982. His eventual success was attributed in part to the fact that Andropov, in poor health for much of his short spell in office, had been unable to groom a successor.

Born into a peasant family on Sept. 24, 1911, in the village of Bolshaya Tes, Krasnoyarsk region, Siberia, Chernenko never knew his father, and his mother died when he was still a young boy. At the age of 12 he began working as a farm labourer, and at 15 he enlisted in the border troops of the Ministry of the Interior. He joined the Komsomol (Young Communist League) in 1926 and later (1929–30) served as head of the Komsomol propaganda department in his local district of Novoselkovo. A member of the Communist Party since 1931, he became a party official in Krasnoyarsk region in 1933 and regional secretary in 1941. After graduating from the Moscow school for higher party organizers in 1945, he was appointed first secretary in Penza.

Three years later, in what was to prove perhaps the most significant move of his career, Chernenko became head of the propaganda department in Moldavia. It was here that his relationship with Brezhnev was established. (Brezhnev served as first secretary of the party in Moldavia during the period 1950–52, and it was Chernenko who introduced him to the people of importance in the region.) Brezhnev was responsible for the developments that followed. In 1956 Chernenko was called to Moscow to take over the mass propaganda section in the CC; in 1960 he was made Brezhnev's chief aide, a position he retained until the latter's death; and in 1965 he was appointed head of the CC general department, which oversaw the CPSU's policy-making bodies.

Chernenko became a full member of the CC in 1971 and of the Politburo in 1978. He took over the post of CC secretary in charge of ideology after the death of Mikhail Suslov in February 1982. Described as the perfect bureaucrat, Chernenko reached the highest party office

without benefit of formal education or experience of state administration and despite the fact that he was apparently suffering from obstructive pulmonary emphysema, a condition that worsened as the year went on.

(K. M. SMOGORZEWSKI)

Clark, Michael

Within three years of his decision to turn independent dancer and choreographer, Michael Clark was acclaimed as the major talent in British "new dance." In 1983 he became choreographer-in-residence at Riverside Studios, a west London arts centre. There a program of his own work, performed by himself and three other dancers, premiered in the summer of 1984 and then toured widely.

Clark was born on June 1, 1962, in Aberdeen, Scotland, and trained for four years at London's Royal Ballet School before joining Ballet Rambert in 1979. The company's modern-dance repertory quickly drew attention to Clark as an outstanding and versatile artist, especially in unconventional works by Richard Alston, a leading young choreographer who devised further solos for Clark after the latter left the Rambert company in 1981. Clark's own early choreography was for Rambert workshop programs, and he participated in Britain's International Summer Course for Professional Choreographers and Composers in 1979, when it was directed by Glen Tetley, and in 1981, with Merce Cunningham and John Cage. On a visit to New York City Clark joined the U.S. dancer Karole Armitage and her company, touring with her there and in Europe; his first independent choreography, *Of a Feather, Flock* (1982), included her as a dancer.

Clark was described by the most experienced London critics as having "a mind and body at work that could be compared with Merce Cunningham's in his early years." The shock tactics of such works as *The New Puritans* (1983), involving provocative costumes, makeup, and punk rock music, gained him an unusual degree of media attention in areas removed from dance, but it also revealed a basis of assured dance technique that continued to reflect the benefits of his early training in classical ballet.

Concerning his most recent London appearances, *The Times* wrote that his audiences "were waiting to be outraged and were disconcerted to be offered an evening of exceptionally fine dancing." Combined with a development toward pure and more imaginative dance movement, Clark's achievement brought him commissions for new work to feature Rudolf Nureyev and others at the Paris Opéra in 1985, for the Scottish Ballet and London Festival Ballet, and with the U.S. filmmaker Charles Atlas in a co-production by WGBH-TV of Boston and Britain's Channel 4 network.

(NOËL GOODWIN)

Conté, Lansana

Col. Lansana Conté, head of the Military Committee for National Redress (CMRN) that assumed power in Guinea in April 1984, shortly after the death of Pres. Ahmed Sékou Touré (see OBITUARIES), was a typical product of the former French colonial army. Popular with the rank and file of the Guinean troops and with his fellow officers, he had the reputation of being discreet, courageous, and highly principled. Shortly after taking office he stated that the CMRN's basic task would be the restoration of human rights, which had ceased to exist in Guinea during Touré's long dictatorship.

In practice Conté found it no easy task to instill democratic ways into an administrative system that still bore overtones of the Touré regime. In December he took steps to increase his personal authority by taking over himself the posts of premier and defense minister. At the same time, he reshuffled the government, dropping nine members and bringing in five newcomers. He warned that further changes might be necessary in the interest of eliminating corruption and inefficiency.

Lansana Conté was born in 1934 at Coyah, some 30 km (18.6 mi) northeast of Conakry, the nation's capital. He was a member of the Susu ethnic group and a Muslim. He attended the military preparatory school at Buigerville, Ivory Coast, and the military college of Saint-Louis in Senegal, and in 1955 he enlisted in the French Army. In 1964, as a captain in the Guinean Army stationed on the island of Tamara in the Los Archipelago, he took part in the defense of Conakry during the attempted invasion from neighbouring Portuguese Guinea (now Guinea-Bissau) in November 1970.

As commander of the 5th Military Region, stationed at Boké, Conté fought with the Guinea-Bissau nationalists in 1973 during their struggle for independence from Portugal. After taking a technical course at Minsk in the Soviet Union, in 1974, he was in 1975 made deputy chief of staff of land forces, a post that he retained until Touré's death. In 1977 he headed the Guinean delegation at talks to settle a frontier dispute with Guinea-Bissau. Elected a deputy in 1980, he took part that year in the ruling Democratic Party of Guinea's official pilgrimage to Mecca.

(PHILIPPE DECRAENE)

Correa, Charles Mark

The Indian architect Charles Correa, recipient of the Royal Institute of British Architects Royal Gold Medal for 1984, was internationally noted for his concern with and devotion to the problems of housing in less developed countries. His major contribution had been to propound and realize a new philosophy for low-cost housing with unassuming projects for mass housing appropriate to the climate and social structure of third world nations, most notably India.

Combining the disciplines of architect, planner, teacher, and social philosopher, Correa's work took its inspiration from the challenges stimulated by the problems with which he dealt. His innovative designs made maximum use of open-to-sky spaces and low-rise, open-shaded structural form and were closely attuned to local conditions. Correa's central belief was that the solutions to low-cost housing lay not in form but in proper planning and land use and that government resources were best used in establishing the conditions in which people could create their own mass housing, given the materials and the planning expertise.

Correa was born in Hyderabad, India, on Sept. 1, 1930, and educated at St. Xavier's College, Bombay. He studied architecture at the University of Michigan and the Massachusetts Institute of Technology and began private practice in Bombay in 1958. In 1964 he and colleagues put forward proposals for the "restructuring" of Bombay to relieve that city's severe overcrowding. His solution, a twin city—New Bombay—across the harbour, sought to change the city's existing north–south linear structure to a circular multicentral one that would make maximum use of urban land and resources. In 1971 Correa was appointed chief architect for a new corporation established to design and develop New Bombay for two million people. In that capacity he created blocks of stepped housing with open areas, social outdoor spaces, multifunctional circulation, and open-shaded structures.

Although trained in the U.S. and much influenced by Le Corbusier, Correa used native solutions as his starting point, bearing in mind always predominant living patterns and shortages of resources. Energy conservation in warm climates dictated flexible spaces with little, if any, demarcation between internal and external areas. These requirements in turn determined architectural form and character. The box with a facade was, for Correa, a Western building form inappropriate to third world cultural, economic, and climatic circumstances. (SANDRA MILLIKIN)

Cruz, Joaquim Carvalho

More experienced athletes watched in awe as the 21-year-old Brazilian runner Joaquim Cruz set a blistering pace in every round of the 800-m event at the 1984 Olympic Games. With the three preliminary rounds and the final being run on consecutive days (August 3–6) in Los Angeles, most competitors were eager to conserve their strength. Cruz's stamina and courage proved more than equal to the task. He emerged victorious to win Brazil's first ever Olympic gold medal in a track event. Sadly, a throat infection prevented him from attempting to win a second in the 1,500 m later in the Games.

Born the son of a carpenter on March 12, 1963, in Brasília, Cruz grew up in Taguatinga, a poor suburb of Rio de Janeiro. As a retiring teenager he harboured an ambition to be a basketball player. It took all the faith of his coach, Luiz Alberto de Oliveira, to persuade him to persevere with running, an activity that he hated. His exceptional talent became apparent to the world in 1981; in that year he broke the 800-m junior world record with a time of 1 min 44.3 sec and beat the veteran Cuban Alberto Juantorena to represent the Americas in the event at the World Cup in Rome.

Nevertheless, Cruz's world-beating potential remained unrealized and largely unrecognized until 1984. Since 1983 he had been training quietly at the University of Oregon, where he moved after a short spell at Brigham Young University in Provo, Utah. He emerged from his sudden success eager to avoid the excessive zeal with which his native country greeted its sporting heroes. He would be happier, he suggested, "if my gold medal was honoured by building a track for athletes." It was a wish that sprang from need; previously, athletics had commanded virtually no interest in a country whose almost exclusive passion was soccer.

In the short post-Olympic season, Cruz toured the European athletics circuit in search of a world record. Improving with every outing, he ran his fastest 800 m in 1 min 41.77 sec on August 26 in Cologne, West Germany. His time was just 0.04 sec slower than the world record held by Britain's Sebastian Coe. Most commentators believed that the unassuming Brazilian would not be denied the prize much longer.

(LOUISE WATSON)

Cuomo, Mario

The 1984 Democratic national convention started off in rousing fashion when Gov. Mario Cuomo of New York gave his "tale of two cities" keynote address. His impassioned speech told of a nation divided into "the lucky and the left-out" and of the need for a new Democratic leadership to unify the "family of America" with renewed "common sense and compassion." Cuomo's eloquence and sense of purpose fueled speculation about his potentially bright political future.

Cuomo was born in the New York City borough of Queens on June 15, 1932, the son of an immigrant Italian grocer. In later years he often spoke of his father as his chief inspiration and role model for his personal and political life. As a youth he was a promising baseball centre fielder and played for a time on a Pittsburgh Pirates farm team. After receiving a B.A. (summa cum laude, 1953) and a law degree (1956) from St. John's University in New York City, Cuomo taught law at St. John's (1963–74) and maintained a legal practice in Brooklyn. His sharp negotiating skills in several controversial cases brought him widespread recognition and led to his entry into politics. He lost the nomination for lieutenant governor in 1966, but his campaign impressed Gov. Hugh Carey, who appointed him secretary of state. When Cuomo was defeated by Edward Koch in the New York City mayoral primary in 1977, Carey asked his old friend to join his reelection campaign in 1978 as lieutenant governor.

In 1982 Cuomo combined his outspoken support for liberal social policies with pragmatic hard work and a simple, conservative life-style and soundly defeated Mayor Koch in the primary and conservative Republican businessman Lewis Lehrman in the general election for governor. His traditional coalition of minorities and labour unions was difficult to hold together, but Cuomo brought vitality and dedication to the job and scored several early victories, including a compromise on the state budget and the passage of a controversial billion-dollar bond issue for highway repairs.

Cuomo drew national attention of a different kind in 1984 when he joined the growing controversy over legalized abortion. A devout Roman Catholic, he refused to condone abortion, saying he supported the church's antiabortion stand, but he refused just as vehemently to endorse the state's authority to ban it. In a speech at the University of Notre Dame in September, he stressed the need to separate personal moral beliefs from public policy in a pluralistic society.

(MELINDA SHEPHERD)

Delors, Jacques Lucien Jean

Jacques Delors was elected president of the European Communities (EC) Commission, the executive body of the EC, in July 1984 at the time of the change of government in France, and so he gave up his national post as minister of economy and finance that he had held since May 1981, when Francois Mitterrand became president. His new appointment was to take effect on Jan. 1, 1985.

For some time previously Delors had been a figure on the international scene, pleading for more aid for the less developed countries and for reform of the international monetary system. He left behind a strong imprint on the previous three years in French politics and was highly thought of in financial circles and at the Paris Bourse (stock exchange) because of his efforts to encourage savings. Above all, he had helped to restore confidence in the franc by sponsoring measures to control the country's trade deficit. A believer in dialogue, a former trade unionist, and the embodiment of nonsectarian policies, on leaving the government he took with him part of the positive image of the left.

Delors was born in Paris on July 20, 1925. After graduating in economics from the University of Paris, he joined the Banque de France, the French central bank, where he was a department head until 1962. He then served as head of the social affairs section of the Commissariat Général au Plan (the central economic planning commission) until 1969. In that year he became adviser to Pres. Georges Pompidou's premier, Jacques Chaban-Delmas, whose "new society" he helped to promote. After various other appointments, including an interlude as associate professor at the University of Paris-Dauphine, in 1976 Delors became the Socialist Party's national delegate for international economic relations. Elected to the European Parliament in 1979, he became chairman of its economic and monetary committee.

As minister of finance in the first government of Pierre Mauroy, Delors had sounded a warning note at the outset of Mitterrand's presidency. He ruffled the waters of the left by demanding a temporary halt to the rate of reform. After the first two devaluations of the franc and the thunderbolt of the freeze on prices and wages in 1982, the tone was set, and Delors came to stand for effort, severity, and austerity, especially with the third franc devaluation in March 1983. He finally won over President Mitterrand to his way of thinking, and the president in turn supported austerity measures. In May 1984 Delors presented the National Assembly with the prospect of a 1985 budget of a severity "without comparison to that of 1984."

(JEAN KNECHT)

Dickson, Brian

With the enactment in 1982 of the Charter of Rights and Freedoms, the Supreme Court of Canada (the country's highest court of appeal) entered a new era. The charter gave judges new authority to overturn laws and redress misconduct of police and public officials. The court, according to Chief Justice Brian Dickson, gained a "much more important function as an umpire between the state and the individual."

Dickson, an 11-year veteran of the court, was appointed chief justice in April 1984. His appointment rested solely in the hands of Prime Minister Pierre Elliott Trudeau but, once announced, it won almost unanimous approval from Canadian judges and lawyers. Admired for his sound and clearly drafted judgments, Dickson became known as a justice who was sensitive to the rights of individuals over the rights of institutions.

CHRIS SCHWARZ/EDMONTON JOURNAL

Born in Yorkton, Sask., on May 25, 1916, Robert George Brian Dickson received his university training at the University of Manitoba. He received an LL.B. from the Manitoba Law School in 1938. During World War II he served in the Royal Canadian Artillery. After the war Dickson became a successful lawyer in Winnipeg (1945–63) and a lecturer at the Manitoba Law School (1948–54). He then served as a judge of the Manitoba Court of Queen's Bench (1963–67) and of the Manitoba Court of Appeal (1967–73).

After his appointment to the Supreme Court of Canada in 1973, Dickson with great effort became fluent in French and acquainted himself with the legal system of Quebec. (The legal systems of Canada differed in that Quebec adopted the civil law system of continental Europe, while the rest of Canada adopted the common law [English] system.) Affable and courteous, Dickson soon became a popular jurist throughout the nation. In his judgments he maintained the primacy of existing provincial powers, siding regularly with the provinces against the federal government on questions of political jurisdiction.

The other eight justices on the Supreme Court are not bound by the opinion of the chief justice, but it was possible that Dickson might in time be able to build consensus around his opinions. If so, he could effectively dominate the decisions of the court, thereby putting his own stamp upon Canadian legal tradition.

(DIANE LOIS WAY)

Dikko, Alhaji Umaru

The spectacular but unsuccessful attempt by Nigerians to kidnap Umaru Dikko from Britain in a crate from Stansted Airport in July 1984 focused attention upon the former minister in the civilian government of deposed president Alhaji Shehu Shagari. Dikko was considered by many to be the Nigerian "most wanted" by the new regime to answer charges of corruption while in office. As a result of the attempted kidnapping, relations between Britain and Nigeria were temporarily brought to a low ebb. (*See* LAW: *International Law;* WORLD AFFAIRS [Africa South of the Sahara]: *Nigeria.*)

When the military, headed by Maj. Gen. Mohammed Buhari (*q.v.*), seized power again at the end of 1983, Dikko said he had "declared war" on the new regime. In Nigeria he was accused of setting aside $300 million (presumably of ill-gotten gains) to finance a mercenary-led expedition against the new government. The two chief charges against him were that he had received kickbacks while in office and that he had rigged the 1983 elections.

Dikko was born on Dec. 31, 1936, at Wamba, near Zaria, Kaduna State, northern Nigeria. In the late 1950s and early 1960s he lived in London, where he worked for the British Broadcasting Corporation's Hausa service. After the fall of Gen. Yakubu Gowon's regime in 1975, he was found guilty of corruption, but this did not prevent his political reappearance when the return to civilian rule took place in 1979. He was made minister of transport by Shagari, and because of his closeness to the president he became one of the most powerful politicians in the country. He was derided by his enemies for never having personally won an election. Dikko achieved the height of power as the manager of Shagari's 1983 election campaign, but by that time he had made many enemies and, it was said, was reappointed as minister of transport only because of Shagari's gratitude over the election result.

Dikko's return to power was seen by many as a denial of Shagari's claim that he would make an independent new start and root out corruption. Dikko was known as Shagari's "third ear," and it was rumoured that most important contracts required his approval. After the kidnapping attempt he appeared before the British High Court to answer questions concerning a $6 million rice shipment from the U.S. to Nigeria, for which payment had not been received.

(GUY ARNOLD)

Donald Duck

On June 9, 1984, the world-renowned animated film star Donald Duck celebrated, simultaneously, 50 years of life and fame. After being named an honorary Marine and then marching down Disneyland's Main Street U.S.A. in a ticker-tape rally and parade, Donald Duck proudly greeted several colleagues, including Daisy Duck, Goofy, Mickey and Minnie Mouse, and, perhaps most importantly, 79-year-old Clarence ("Ducky") Nash, whose high-pitched, squawky Donald voice had become familiar to millions over the past five decades.

Donald Duck's raucous and ornery personality was established during his 1934 debut in a Walt Disney short film entitled *The Wise Little Hen.* His stardom was assured one year later in a supporting, although persistent, fife-playing role in *The Band Concert,* starring Mickey Mouse. The determined and, indeed, stubborn personality of Mickey contrasted sharply with that

AP/WIDE WORLD

of the emotionally intemperate duck, who had been created by Art Babbit and Dick Huemer. Donald's solo debut followed in 1937 in *Donald's Ostrich.*

Meanwhile, Donald was also struggling to get his bearings in the arena of the comic strip. There stardom came a bit more slowly, with a first appearance in September 1934 but no major role until Sunday, Aug. 23, 1936, when, in the last panel of a "Silly Symphony" strip, the aggressive and mischievous little duck glared out at readers with a written promise of pranks to come. Drawn memorably by Al Taliaferro (although signed by Walt Disney), the irascible character was featured blasting a mosquito with a shotgun and, in so doing, inevitably destroying an entire wall of his house. The soon-daily comic strip serialized the gags of this popular prankster and his colleagues in mischief. The troublesome and often hilarious nephews—Huey, Louie, and Dewey—did not come onto the scene until Oct. 17, 1937.

Like many other Hollywood stars, Donald served his country during World War II, his most memorable contribution being the film *Der Fuehrer's Face,* which won an Academy Award in 1942. In April 1943 Donald, Daisy, and the nephews, drawn by cartoonist Carl Barks, appeared in their first comic book.

Although Donald rarely appears in new productions, he is, of course, always available for handshaking on America's coasts at Disneyland in California and Disney World in Florida. The 1984 "Walt Disney's World on Ice" show centred around his birthday celebration. He still delights a crowd and, indeed, has one of those ageless faces.   (BONNIE OBERMAN)

Duarte, José Napoleón

In his opening months as El Salvador's first democratically elected president in over half a century, José Napoleón Duarte seemed to need the skills of a physician as much as those of a statesman. In 1984 he took over a nation suffering from an internal hemorrhage—a nation dying from a civil war between the military and right-wing death squads and leftist insurgents. The five-year-old conflict had

destroyed the economy and killed an estimated 50,000 people.

As a first step toward restoring the nation's health, Duarte sought to curb the military. He appointed a Cabinet officer to assume control over the three internal security forces: the national guard, the national police, and the Treasury Military Police. Duarte also disbanded the Treasury police's intelligence unit, which allegedly had operated as a death squad.

He then directed his efforts toward dialogue with the left. In peace talks at La Palma, Chalatenango Province, on October 15, Duarte and guerrilla leaders agreed to form a joint commission that would seek to end the war. However, Duarte vowed to oppose expected rebel demands for a share of power, arguing that "power can only be given through a popular vote."

Duarte was born in San Salvador in 1925 and educated at the University of Notre Dame in the United States. Throughout his political career he promoted democracy as his ailing nation's only remedy. In 1960 he and some friends founded the Christian Democratic Party, which they hoped would win enough elections to reform the small wealthy group that held power and prevent a Communist-led revolt. The party became popular in San Salvador, where Duarte was elected mayor for three successive two-year terms during the 1960s. Duarte rewarded Salvadorans by providing them with basic services, such as street lighting, that they had never enjoyed before. In 1972 he ran for president against Col. Arturo Molina, but the military, fearing Duarte's penchant for reform, rigged the election. When Duarte later supported moderate officers opposed to the new regime, he was arrested, beaten, and exiled.

Returning to Salvadoran politics following the 1979 coup, Duarte became president of the civilian-military junta in December 1980. He presided over the beginnings of land reform and the partial nationalization of banks and export industries but was forced to resign as president in May 1982 following a shift of the balance of power to the right. Ultimate power remained with the extreme right until May 1984, when the nation's voters chose Duarte over Roberto d'Aubuisson, a right-wing extremist.   (MICHAEL AMEDEO)

Fabius, Laurent

"Do you know who best represents my way of thinking? Laurent Fabius," Pres. François Mitterrand once said. The president's choice of Fabius to succeed Pierre Mauroy as premier of the French government in July 1984 was, therefore, not surprising; but Fabius, speaking on television, was careful to emphasize the distinction between his policies and those of the president. Nonetheless, he certainly had the president's ear, the more so since he was, if not part of Mitterrand's family circle, at least one of his close friends. This was emphasized when Mitterrand entrusted to Fabius's wife, the sociologist Françoise Castro, the task of coordinating the work of the different think tanks and study groups associated with the Socialist majority.

Fabius, the son of an antique dealer who came from a family of Jewish converts to Roman Catholicism, was born Aug. 20, 1946, in Paris. He graduated from the

Institut des Sciences Politiques in Paris and then studied at the École Nationale d'Administration and the École Normale Supérieure—the classic education for highfliers in French public service and politics. A member of the Conseil d'État (1973–81), he was elected first deputy mayor of Grand-Quevilly in the Seine-Maritime in 1977 and then, in 1978 and 1981, deputy in the National Assembly for the département of Seine-Maritime.

Fabius's membership in the Socialist Party (PS) dated from 1974. He rapidly rose to become one of Mitterrand's most trusted economic advisers, as well as his principal private secretary when, as a member of the PS national secretariat from 1979, he became its press officer. He managed Mitterrand's presidential campaign in 1981 and was appointed minister-delegate for the budget in Mauroy's first government and then minister of industry and research in 1983. At the beginning of 1984 his responsibilities were elevated to those of a superminister for industrial restructuring, in which capacity he was given the job of saving the Lorraine steel industry.

After his appointment as premier, Fabius constantly appealed for Frenchmen to work together for the modernization of France. He appeared to be leaning in the direction of liberal Socialism. He was flexible in his attitudes, but even to his friends his personality was shrouded in an element of mystery.   (JEAN KNECHT)

Farrakhan, Louis

Louis Farrakhan burst upon the U.S. political stage in 1984 with a brand of raw, unbridled rhetoric that left millions of Americans startled, outraged, or simply baffled. The fortunes of Farrakhan and the Rev. Jesse Jackson (*q.v.*) were entwined by a history of distance from the political mainstream, suddenly supplanted by the heady conviction that a black man, Jackson, could make a credible run for the U.S. presidency. They had met more than a decade earlier but had gone on to establish power bases appealing to vastly different constituencies.

Farrakhan aroused consternation with his "death threat" (not meant literally, he said later) against a journalist (also a black) who had revealed Jackson's politically damaging ethnic slur against Jews as "Hymies." Farrakhan also referred to Hitler as "a very great man ... who rose Germany up from the ashes of defeat" (later half-recanted to "wickedly great"). His rhetoric employed the factually hazy but rivetingly apocalyptic vision that had been enormously effective in the creation by his mentor, Elijah Muhammad, of a multimillion-dollar business empire operated exclusively by and for blacks. Members of Muhammad's cult, the Nation of Islam, considered any reliance on "white devils" a pure path to betrayal.

Farrakhan, 51, born Louis Eugene Walcott, was raised in a Boston neighbourhood beset by tension as blacks replaced Jewish residents moving to the suburbs. He attended a racially integrated high school, winning high grades and attention as a track star and as a musician. A brief career as a calypso singer ended abruptly in 1955 with his conversion to the charismatic Elijah Muhammad's exotic vision of Islam.

He rose quickly in the Black Muslim movement, surviving its sometimes murderous internecine strife. When Elijah Muhammad died in 1975, Farrakhan was transferred from New York to Chicago headquarters but fell out with the founder's heirs, whom he considered weak and vacillating, though some of them were moving toward authentic Muslim doctrine. Three years later Farrakhan formed his own splinter-within-a-splinter sect, which in 1984 was said to have 5,000 to 10,000 formal adherents plus an unknown number of sympathizers.

In 1984 Farrakhan pledged a voter registration drive for Jackson and supplied his bodyguards, the "Fruit of Islam," for Jackson's early campaign appearances. But Farrakhan's continuing controversial statements, including a reference to the creation of the state of Israel as an "outlaw act" and a fund-seeking visit in June to Libya's Pres. Muammar al-Qaddafi, forced Jackson finally to repudiate at least the views for which Farrakhan had become notorious.   (JAMES L. YUENGER)

Febres Cordero, Léon

On Aug. 10, 1984, Léon Febres Cordero, representing the Social Christian Party (PSC), became president of Ecuador for a four-year term. He succeeded Pres. Osvaldo Hurtado Larrea in a peaceful transfer of power from one elected civilian government to another, following more than two decades of military dictatorships.

Febres Cordero was born in Guayaquil on March 9, 1931. After completing his studies in mechanical engineering at the Stevens Institute of Technology, Hoboken, N.J., and the Westinghouse Advanced School of Public Utility Engineering, Wilkinsburg, Pa., he returned to Ecuador to practice his profession in two large private companies and then to assume managerial positions in several industrial enterprises. In 1965 Febres Cordero started his political career as president of Guayaquil's Federation of Industry and also as president of the Association of Latin-American Industrialists. A member of the National Constituent Assembly of 1966, he then served as senator until 1970.

During the country's transition back to democracy in the late 1970s, Febres Cordero joined the PSC and was elected to Congress in 1979. In opposition, he became an outspoken critic of the reformist social programs of the Roldos and Hurtado administrations and assumed the leadership of the National Reconstruction Front at the next presidential election. After two rounds, Febres Cordero narrowly defeated his social democrat opponent, Rodrigo Borja, with 52% of the vote. The victory of his six-party conservative coalition largely represented the triumph of the populous coastal city of Guayaquil and its powerful businesses.

Febres Cordero stood for free market policies and believed that the country's recovery lay in bolstering private economic activity. His appeal, however, seemed to reflect Ecuador's tradition of personalist politics rather than popular support for conservative policies. Unlike his predecessor, Febres Cordero did not enjoy a congressional majority, and a dangerous political polarization was expected as some of his measures were put before Congress.

(ALEXANDER JOHNS CAMPBELL)

Ferraro, Geraldine Anne

The first woman to run for U.S. vice-president on a major party ticket, Geraldine Ferraro brought a heightened sense of dynamism and excitement and—for a brief time—optimism to the 1984 Democratic campaign.

Born in Newburgh, N.Y., on Aug. 26, 1935, she was the last child and only daughter of Italian-American parents. Her parents enjoyed modest economic success, but when Dominick Ferraro died in 1944, his widow, Antonetta, supported the family by crocheting beads on wedding dresses and evening gowns. When she married, Geraldine retained her maiden name to honour her mother, whose toil allowed Geraldine to receive a first-rate education at the Marymount School in Tarrytown and Marymount Manhattan College. After receiving a teaching degree at Hunter College, Geraldine Ferraro taught in the New York public schools and studied law at night at Fordham University. In the same week of 1960, she passed the New York state bar examination and married wealthy real estate investor John Zaccaro. For the next decade and a half she practiced law part-time while raising three children. In 1974 Ferraro became an assistant district attorney, heading a special bureau dealing with child abuse, sex crimes, and crimes against the elderly.

In 1978 Ferraro won election to Congress, representing New York's conservative 9th district. After easily winning reelection in 1980 and 1982, she gained a prominent position in the party as platform chair for the 1984 national convention. Walter Mondale's (q.v.) choice of Ferraro as his running mate was announced on July 12. Polls taken immediately afterward showed Mondale closing the sizable gap between himself and Pres. Ronald Reagan, but the euphoria was short-lived. During August Ferraro found herself on the defensive as questions regarding her own and her husband's finances became the focus of media coverage. No sooner did she seem to surmount that challenge with an extended and masterly press conference than she faced an onslaught of criticism regarding her position on abortion. As a devout Roman Catholic, Ferraro claimed personal opposition to abortion, but her pro-choice stance and backing of government-subsidized abortions for the poor made her the target of hecklers as well as Catholic clergymen.

Postelection analyses showed that Ferraro's presence on the ticket had failed to elicit the support Mondale had hoped for. Catholics, Italian-Americans, blue-collar workers, and—most surprisingly—women all voted more heavily for the Reagan-Bush ticket in 1984 than they had in 1980.

(JEROLD L. KELLMAN)

Finney, Albert

Albert Finney's return to the British stage in 1984 after a six-year absence was typical of the bluff working-class northerner, who made his first appearance on the London stage with the Birmingham Repertory Company in 1956 and left it in 1978 to go "for a stroll," as he put it. Ever since Kenneth Tynan at a Royal Academy of Dramatic Art (RADA) graduation performance in 1956 had pronounced the 20-year-

old Finney "a smouldering young Spencer Tracy," he had been climbing to the top rung of the ladder of fame but not without a few faltering steps and self-chosen interruptions.

Finney made his 1984 return at the Riverside Studios in London in the Jon Blair and Norman Fenton documentary *The Biko Inquest*, as actor-director-producer. This searing denunciation of South Africa's racial policies was the first venture of the newly formed United British Artists (UBA), in which Finney was joined by nine prominent writers, directors, and players to make "films and videos" and stage "plays." A revival by UBA at the Old Vic Theatre of John Arden's *Serjeant Musgrave's Dance,* with Finney as both actor and director, co-incided with his nomination for an Oscar for the role of the aging actor in the film of *The Dresser* and the Critics' Circle best actor award for his alcoholic British consul in John Huston's *Under the Volcano.*

Finney was born in Salford, near Manchester, on May 9, 1936. After graduating from RADA he went to the Birmingham Rep, to Stratford-on-Avon (in 1959), and finally to London's West End (*Billy Liar,* 1960), where he won international fame in John Osborne's *Luther.* He made his New York stage debut in 1963. Finney both acted and directed at London's Royal Court Theatre, where he served as assistant artistic director during 1972–75. His controversial *Hamlet* launched Peter Hall's first season at the newly opened National Theatre (1975), where he stayed for three years.

Finney's successful motion picture career began in 1960 with the hit *Saturday Night and Sunday Morning.* His best-known films included *Charlie Bubbles* (directed by himself), *Tom Jones, Murder on the Orient Express, Alpha Beta,* and *Annie.* He also appeared on television, where his most outstanding performance was as Pope John Paul II in 1983. Trying his hand at songwriting and horse breeding were only two other side interests of a many-sided character.   (OSSIA TRILLING)

Frayn, Michael

For Michael Frayn, 51-year-old playwright, novelist, philosopher, poet, translator, film scenarist, television writer and director, and former columnist, 1984 was an *annus mirabilis.* With *Noises Off, Benefactors, Number One,* and *Wild Honey* running simultaneously at four London theatres and his translation of *The Cherry Orchard* at Dublin's Abbey Theatre in the same year, he broke records previously held by Noël Coward and Christopher Fry. *Noises Off,* the prizewinning "best comedy of the year" of 1982, entered its fourth year in London and its third on Broadway, appeared on the playbills of five continents in over a dozen languages, and was slated for production at the Moscow Art Theatre. His much-praised fifth television travelogue, "Jerusalem," exposing the city's interreligious feuding, was followed by his first feature filmscript (*The Man of the Moment*), due to begin shooting in 1985. His second Chekhov translation (*Three Sisters*) was to be staged at the Manchester-based Royal Exchange Theatre in April 1985, and his third (*The Seagull*), commissioned for Nastassja Kinski and a London opening in 1985, was also announced.

Born Sept. 8, 1933, the son of a London salesman, Frayn was educated at Kingston Grammar School and at Emmanuel College, University of Cambridge, where he learned Russian and was editor of *Granta* magazine. He became a reporter (1957) and later columnist (1959–62) for *The Guardian* and then a columnist (1962–68) for *The Observer.* The author of a number of plays and documentaries for television, he was presenter of 40 of Independent Television's "What the Papers Say" programs. His five novels included the autobiographical, Hawthornden Prize-winning *The Russian Interpreter* (1966). He was also the author of a philosophical work, *Constructions* (1974), and of satirically revealing articles about Cuba (which inspired his play *Clouds*), Israel, Japan, Sweden, and the Soviet Union. The soft-spoken, highly articulate, libertarian philosophy-graduate, who began writing poetry at six years of age, emerged as one of Britain's most highly regarded literary figures.

(OSSIA TRILLING)

Gandhi, Rajiv

In a dramatic turn of events Rajiv Gandhi became prime minister of India after his mother, Indira Gandhi, was gunned down by Sikhs on her own personal bodyguard team on Oct. 31, 1984 (*see* OBITUARIES). The assassination, generally considered to be retribution for her June 1984 order for government troops to storm the Golden Temple in Amritsar, the Sikhs' most holy shrine, touched off a major political crisis as well as large-scale violence by Hindus, who randomly murdered more than 1,000 Sikhs.

As one of his first official acts as prime minister, Gandhi appealed for peace in a radio broadcast saying, "Nothing would

BALDEV—SYGMA

hurt the soul of our beloved Indira Gandhi more than the occurrence of violence in any part of the country." One day after the official 12-day mourning period, Gandhi was unanimously named (November 12) president of the Congress (I) party, and on the following day he called for parliamentary elections on December 24. Those elections returned him to power in a landslide dwarfing any experienced by his mother or his grandfather.

The first son of Feroze and Indira Gandhi, Rajiv was born on Aug. 20, 1944, but it was his younger brother, Sanjay, who was viewed as the heir apparent to the political dynasty that was founded by his grandfather, Jawaharlal Nehru (first prime minister of independent India), and maintained by his mother. Rajiv studied at Welham's School and the Doon School, Dehra Dun, and St. Columba's School, New Delhi, before studying engineering at the University of Cambridge. Though he did not earn a degree, he met his future wife, Sonia Maino, there and married her on Feb. 25, 1968. After obtaining a commercial pilot's license, Rajiv served as a pilot for Indian Airlines until he resigned in 1981. During the previous year Sanjay had been killed in an airplane crash, and Indira, anxious to groom a successor, persuaded a reluctant Rajiv to enter the political arena.

On June 15, 1981, Rajiv was elected to Parliament, and during the following two years he became more deeply involved in and apparently more enamoured of politics. In February 1983 Indira appointed Rajiv party secretary. Though some felt that perhaps he was too young and inexperienced to stand at the nation's helm, his firm and unruffled demeanour in the wake of the assassination earned him many admirers.

(KAREN JUSTIN)

Garneau, Marc

In July 1983 Marc Garneau answered an advertisement in a newspaper and thereby changed his life. He applied for a job as an astronaut. In December 1983 he was chosen from among 4,300 applicants to be one of six Canadians who would be trained to fly aboard the United States space shuttle. After an intensive eight-month training program, he became the first Canadian to be launched into space.

A payload specialist, Garneau was part of the seven-member crew aboard the U.S. space shuttle "Challenger" when it was launched from Cape Canaveral, Fla., on Oct. 5, 1984. During the eight-day mission he performed ten experiments involving space technology, space science, and the life sciences. He tested a computerized machine vision system designed to provide precise guidance information that would enable astronauts to approach, capture, and berth satellites in space. He also tested a sunphotometer, which was used to investigate the distribution of water vapour and gases in the Earth's atmosphere. He conducted experiments to investigate motion sickness in space and changes in sensory perception in space.

Born on Feb. 23, 1949, in Quebec City, Marc Garneau grew up in a military household, the son of a brigadier general. This may have influenced Garneau to join the Navy at the age of 16. He received a bachelor's degree in engineering physics from the Royal Military College in Kingston, Ont. (1970), and a doctorate in electrical engineering from the Imperial College of Science and Technology in London, England (1973).

During his career as a Canadian naval officer, Garneau served as a combat systems engineer (1974–76), an instructor in naval weapons systems at the Canadian Forces Fleet School in Halifax, Nova Scotia (1976–77), and a project engineer in

naval weapons systems (1977–80). From 1980 to 1983 he worked with the Naval Engineering Unit, where he was involved with testing ship-fitted equipment. In 1983 he was promoted to commander and transferred to Ottawa to become a design authority for all naval communications and electronic warfare equipment and systems. Garneau believed that it was this military experience in testing new equipment under field conditions that was the decisive factor in his becoming the first Canadian payload specialist.

(DIANE LOIS WAY)

Gibson, Mel

International film star Mel Gibson is a blend of Hollywood's best. His ingredients include the handsomeness of a Cary Grant, the cool innocence of a James Dean, and the silent expressiveness of a Clint Eastwood. Like the early Marlon Brando and Paul Newman, Gibson excels at portraying troubled young men—a mentally retarded labourer in *Tim,* a violent wanderer in *Mad Max,* and an unthinking mutineer in *The Bounty.* This ability to evoke the magic of the great stars has won Gibson admirers among audiences and film critics alike. In a review of the 1984 film *The Bounty,* the *Wall Street Journal* wrote that "when you put Mr. Gibson in front of a camera, heat does emerge; he crackles on screen with a presence that goes beyond good looks or acting ability."

Gibson first ignited audiences with his performance in *Mad Max* in 1979; two years later he turned on the heat again in the sequel, *The Road Warrior.* Both films, set in a barren and lawless future, feature Gibson as a man embittered by the murder of his family.

Gibson differs from other Hollywood greats in at least one respect: he speaks with an Australian accent. He was born in upstate New York in 1955, but he and his family immigrated to Sydney, Australia, 12 years later. After graduating from high school, Gibson considered becoming a journalist; however, his sister steered him into acting when she sent an application in his name to Australia's National Institute of Dramatic Art at the University of New South Wales. In 1977 he graduated from the institute and joined the State Theatre Company of South Australia, where he developed a passion for stage acting.

With his success in the Australian-made *Mad Max,* however, Gibson became identified with the screen rather than the stage. He received Australia's best actor award in 1980 and 1981 for his roles in the local films *Tim* and *Gallipoli.* The latter won good reviews abroad and established Gibson as a symbol of Australia's dynamic film industry. He enhanced his reputation with his role as a broadcast journalist in *The Year of Living Dangerously* (1982). In 1984 he completed his first U.S.-made feature, *The River.* Billed in advance as "a 1980s *Grapes of Wrath,*" the film would reveal whether Gibson possessed yet another attribute of Hollywood's best: the intelligent charm of Henry Fonda.

(MICHAEL AMEDEO)

Gorbachev, Mikhail Sergeyevich

During 1984 the apparently fragile state of health of Soviet Pres. Konstantin Chernenko (*q.v.*) gave rise to much speculation in the West as to who might eventually succeed him. The most likely contender was generally thought to be Mikhail Gorbachev, at 53 the youngest member of the Politburo—the policy-making body of the Communist Party of the Soviet Union (CPSU). Gorbachev's standing was boosted by his visit to the U.K. in December—his first major exposure to public view in a Western country since a visit to Canada in 1983.

In his capacity as chairman (from April 1984) of the Foreign Affairs Commission of the Supreme Soviet (parliament), Gorbachev led a 30-member parliamen-

tary delegation to London. He was entertained at Chequers (the country residence of British prime ministers) by Margaret Thatcher, who afterward said that she liked him and hoped to "do business" with him. Gorbachev described the encounter as "businesslike, constructive, and frank." The British popular press noted Gorbachev's affability and humour and also the charm of his elegant wife, Raisa. The outcome of the visit—cut short by the death in Moscow of Soviet Defense Minister Dmitry Ustinov (*see* OBITUARIES)—was favourably reported in the Soviet media.

Gorbachev was born on March 2, 1931, at Privolnoye, Stavropol territory, into a peasant family. He joined the Komsomol (Young Communist League) in 1946 and for four years worked as a combine harvester driver on a state farm. As a promising Komsomol member he was sent to Moscow University, where he graduated in law, and he then completed a correspondence course at the Stavropol Agricultural Institute. He joined the CPSU in 1952 and thereafter advanced steadily in the Stavropol city and territorial party organizations. In 1971 he was elected to the CPSU Central Committee (CC) and was appointed secretary for agriculture in 1978. In 1979 he became a candidate member of the Politburo and in 1980 a full member.

Gorbachev's rise to eminence owed much to the patronage of Mikhail Suslov (d. 1982), the leading party ideologue, and of Yury Andropov (*see* OBITUARIES). When Andropov succeeded Leonid Brezhnev as party leader he entrusted Gorbachev

with the task of reforming Soviet agriculture and also gave him responsibility for ideological questions.

(K. M. SMOGORZEWSKI)

Gordimer, Nadine

In 1984 a new book, *Something Out There: Stories by Nadine Gordimer,* was well received by critics, largely because of the title novella—a story about differing reactions among white persons in the area of Johannesburg, South Africa, to the destructive activities of a mysterious dark-coloured anthropoid. As the story progresses, the anthropoid becomes a symbol of different kinds of fear. Nadine Gordimer, a writer of fiction, is a white, English-speaking citizen of South Africa. Although she criticizes, often sharply, the white government's racial policies, that government no longer bans any of her writings.

Gordimer—whose father was a Lithuanian-born Jewish watchmaker and whose mother was an emigrant from England—was born in Springs, in the Transvaal, on Nov. 20, 1923. Disgusted from childhood with white society, she was rebellious and acquired a mediocre record in school. But from the age of nine she was a precocious writer. She started selling stories to adult periodicals in 1939. In 1948 she moved to Johannesburg, where she has continued to live.

Uys Krige, a South African writer, introduced Gordimer to a New York City literary agent in 1950. She then began contributing fiction and nonfiction to periodicals in the United States. From 1969 to 1971 she held several short-term academic appointments in the United States, and in 1975 she was visiting professor at Barnard College.

Many of Gordimer's stories are about the effects on personal character of the expectations of family and society. Some show whites being shaped by their advantages and blacks by their disadvantages. Some critics call Gordimer a great writer; others find her talent uneven. But none deny that she has offered artistic insight into her country's problems.

Something Out There is her ninth book of short stories, the others being *Face to Face* (1949), *The Soft Voice of the Serpent* (1952), *Six Feet of the Country* (1956), *Friday's Footprint* (1960), *Not for Publication* (1965), *Livingstone's Companions* (1971), *Selected Stories* (1976), and *A Soldier's Embrace* (1980). Her novels include *The Lying Days* (1953), *A World of Strangers* (1958), *Occasion for Loving* (1963), *The Late Bourgeois World* (1966), *Burger's Daughter* (1979), and *July's People* (1981). Most of her books have been published in the United States and Great Britain and must be imported into South Africa.

(CHARLES JOHNSON TAGGART)

Graham, Martha

One of America's greatest artists, Martha Graham turned 90 on May 11, 1984. After a dance career spanning 75 years, in which she was obsessed with change and evolution, the innovative and theatrical pioneer of modern dance still maintained a rigorous schedule, which in fact had changed little since she retired from dancing in 1970.

Graham was born in 1893 in Pittsburgh, Pa., and raised in Santa Barbara, Calif.

She began her dance training at age 16 in Los Angeles at Denishawn, the schools and dance company founded by Ruth St. Denis and Ted Shawn. A member of various dance companies until 1924, she then taught for two years at the Eastman School of Music in Rochester, N.Y. Her first appearance as an independent dancer-choreographer was in 1926, the year before she founded the Martha Graham School of Contemporary Dance.

Her dancers have been and still are instantly recognizable by the contraction-and-release technique pioneered by the lithe and sensuous Graham, whose goal in developing such sharp, stunning moves was to dramatize this most primitive aspect of human life. Her choreography moves with graphic sexual tension, and within this explosive atmosphere Graham rivets her interest on the actual movement, the shock effect, the drama created, for example, by a series of falls to the floor for which her dancers are famous. A Graham dancer keeps movement alive throughout the body, exemplified by the "spiral," a corkscrewlike movement flowing through a twisted torso. To create contrasts, however, Graham choreographs deliberately restrictive movements in order to achieve during a performance a quality of discovery for both dancers and audience.

Illnesses during the early 1970s and in May 1982 have been the only interruptions of Graham's activities. A driven artist who relies on less than six hours of sleep per night, the angular former dancer continues at age 90 to direct her company, which in 1984 presented two premieres, *Phaedra's Dream* and Graham's first treatment of Stravinsky's *The Rite of Spring*.

Graham has become one of the most famous choreographers and dancers in the world mainly because of her invention of a formalized dance vocabulary combined with a distinctive and rigorous training system. Thousands of students have passed through her school, including such well-known influential modern dance innovators as Merce Cunningham, Paul Taylor, and Alvin Ailey.

(BONNIE OBERMAN)

Gromyko, Andrey Andreyevich

Foreign Minister Andrey Gromyko's key role in the leadership of the U.S.S.R. was further emphasized in 1984 when he became the first Soviet leader to meet U.S. Pres. Ronald Reagan since the latter took office. During his visit to the U.S. in October, Gromyko delivered a stern condemnation of U.S. foreign policy when he addressed the UN General Assembly.

Gromyko had served under successive Soviet leaders Stalin, Khrushchev, Brezhnev, and Andropov (*see* OBITUARIES), and with each his role in both the government and the Communist Party of the Soviet Union (CPSU) increased. He became foreign minister in February 1957, a member of the CPSU Politburo in April 1973, and first deputy chairman of the Council of Ministers in March 1983. After his return from the U.S. in October 1984, Gromyko was awarded the Order of Lenin for the seventh time. Clearly, under the leadership of General Secretary Konstantin Chernenko (*q.v.*), his authority was continuing to grow, despite the fact that he had apparently supported Andropov against Chernenko in the succession battle that followed Brezhnev's death.

Gromyko was ambitious but wise enough not to identify himself entirely with any particular group at the top of the CPSU, and he had made few enemies. Although widely admired for his expertise, he was in the main merely the executor of a foreign policy formulated by the Politburo. Rarely advancing any new policies in public, he had served Stalin's post World War II cold war activities, Khrushchev's 1962 Cuban adventure, and Brezhnev's policy of détente. It was Khrushchev who once remarked, boorishly but to the point, "If I ask Gromyko to take his trousers off and sit on a block of ice, he will obey."

Born on July 18 (July 5, old style), 1909, at Starye Gromyki, Belorussia, Gromyko trained as an economist and was a member of the research staff of the Institute of Economics at the Soviet Academy of Sciences before 1939. In that year he was appointed to head the American division of the People's Commissariat of Foreign Affairs. He became Soviet ambassador to the U.S. in 1943. After a short spell as chief Soviet delegate to the UN, he was recalled to Moscow in 1946 to become deputy foreign minister. Apart from a year spent as ambassador to the U.K. (1952–53), he retained that post until 1957, when Khrushchev appointed him foreign minister in succession to Dmitry Shepilov.

(K. M. SMOGORZEWSKI)

Gross, Michael

West German swimmer Michael Gross collected four medals to become the most successful male swimmer in the 1984 Olympic Games in Los Angeles. His two gold medals, in the 100-m butterfly and the 200-m freestyle, were won in world record times—53.08 sec and 1 min 47.44 sec, respectively. He added a silver medal in the 4 x 200-m freestyle relay. By the second to last day of competition, Gross's appetite for victory had perhaps lost its edge, for the poolside competitors were astounded to see him finish second in the 200-m butterfly, the event for which he had been considered firmest favourite before the start of the Games.

Gross arrived at the Olympics with his credentials well established. At the European championships in Rome in August 1983, he set world records for the 200-m butterfly (1 min 57.05 sec) and the 200-m freestyle (1 min 47.87 sec), in the latter case beating his own record that he had taken earlier in the year from Rowdy Gaines of the U.S. Gross thus became the first male swimmer since Mark Spitz of the U.S. to hold world records in two different strokes at the same time.

Gross was born on June 17, 1964, in Frankfurt am Main, West Germany, where he continued to live and train, turning down offers to move to the U.S. Just before the Games he finished his education and enrolled for compulsory national service in the West German Army. His exceptional fitness assured that he would have excelled whether he had chosen swimming or almost any other sport, according to his coaches. The physical characteristic that brought him a particular advantage in the swimming pool, however, was his extraordinary arm span. Whereas most people have a span that is approximately equal to their height, Gross possessed a reach of 7 ft 5 in, a full 9 in longer than his height. For this reason he could swim a length of a pool in 29 strokes, an average of 5 strokes fewer than his competitors. The huge reach that allowed his progress through the water to appear so deceptively languid earned him the nickname "the albatross." The parallel could bear further scrutiny; the mystery that surrounded that giant seabird also attached to Gross through his renowned distaste for publicity.   (LOUISE WATSON)

Gushiken, Koji

It was one of the most exciting competitions of the 1984 Olympic Games in Los Angeles, watched on television by millions around the world. And when it had finished, Koji Gushiken of Japan had won the all-around medal in men's gymnastics by twenty-five thousandths of a point over American Peter Vidmar. In that instant Gushiken became a national hero, an athlete whose career up to that point had been marked by disappointments and injuries. After triumphing over Vidmar and Li Ning of China, the 27-year-old physical education teacher at Nippon College of Physical Education summed up his years of relentless training with the words, "I have persevered much for this moment."

Gushiken clinched the title—the most prestigious in gymnastics—by scoring 9.90 in the graceful, balletlike floor exercise, his last event of the evening. Vidmar and Li tried desperately to catch up on the parallel bars and high bar. As millions watched intently, Gushiken felt a surge of emotion and turned aside. "I did not watch," he said afterward; "the tears were starting to come and I was too overcome." Standing on the victory podium to receive his gold medal and listen to his country's national anthem, he could not help but think back on the ups and downs of his 16 years as a gymnast.

Born in Osaka on Nov. 12, 1956, Gushiken weighs a trim 58 kg (127.6 lb) and is 162 cm (5 ft 4 in) tall. He began gymnastics as a youth and suffered three serious injuries as his career progressed. In 1977, when he was a university student, torn ligaments in his left leg put him out of action for six months. After recovering he was sidelined with a broken ankle and a torn Achilles tendon. While convalescing he built up his upper body strength with weights and barbells. The will to excel finally paid off. He finished third all-around in the 1981 world championships in Moscow and second in the individual combined exercise at the world championships in Hungary in 1983.

Gushiken's greatest disappointment came in 1980 when Japan joined the U.S.-led boycott of the Summer Games in Moscow. He was in top form and had high hopes of winning the all-around title. When, four years later, he left for Los Angeles, his dream was to win two individual golds. The dream came true, for Gushiken also captured a gold medal by winning his specialty, the rings.   (JOHN RODERICK)

Hämäläinen, Marja-Liisa

The outstanding performer in the 1984 winter Olympic Games at Sarajevo, Yugos., when she won three gold medals and a bronze, Marja-Liisa Hämäläinen was undoubtedly the best woman Nordic skier that Finland had produced. Probably her most notable triumph at Sarajevo was in the stamina-sapping 20 km, when she defeated her great Soviet rival, Raisa Smetanina, by a narrow margin. Hämäläinen's three victories, added to that of a compatriot in the 90-m jump, equaled the most gold medals Finland had previously attained in a Winter Olympics, four at Chamonix, France, in 1924.

Hämäläinen was born in Simpele, Fin., on Sept. 10, 1955, and grew into a tall and slender blonde with a determination that matched her evident physical strength. With her father and brother also members of the Finnish national ski team, the family's enthusiasm for sports was a strong influence, and she also became a track athlete in the summer months when she was free from ski training. By profession Hämäläinen was a physiotherapist. She made her Olympic debut at the age of 20 in 1976 at Innsbruck, Austria, placing 22nd in the 10 km. Her first major success was as a member of the host country's winning relay team in the 1978 world Nordic championships at Lahti, Fin. In the 1980 Winter Games at Lake Placid, N.Y., she helped her country finish fifth in the 4 x 5-km relay and also placed 19th in the individual 5 km and 18th in the 10 km. These experiences paved the way for her to become something of a national heroine in a country renowned for its abiding preoccupation with sports.

In 1983 and 1984 she was for two consecutive seasons Finnish national champion at all three of the women's cross-country race distances—5 km, 10 km, and 20 km. During the same period, she won four Nordic World Cup events—over 5 km at Lahti and Reit im Winkl, West Germany, and in the 10-km contests at Anchorage, Alaska, and Labrador, Canada. During these tournaments she progressively developed the rhythmic style and form that earned gold medals in all three Olympic distances at Sarajevo and also a bronze in the team relay.   (HOWARD BASS)

Hamilton, Scott

In 1984, four years after he carried the United States flag in the opening ceremony of the 1980 Winter Olympics, Scott Hamilton carried it again in a victory lap around a Yugoslav ice rink. He had just won an Olympic gold medal in figure skating. He said that it represented the last 16 years of his life. When he ended his amateur career the next month, Hamilton had become the first figure skater since 1956 to win four consecutive world championships.

Hamilton was born Aug. 28, 1958, and was adopted six weeks later by Bowling Green (Ohio) State University professors Ernie and Dorothy Hamilton. Two years later he unaccountably stopped growing. In search of a favourable prognosis, his parents took him from doctor to doctor, one of whom gave him six months to live. He was eight when the staff at Boston Children's Hospital accurately determined that he had Shwachman's disease, a rare intestinal paralysis that impeded his absorption of nutrients from food.

He was teased by his bigger contemporaries. "Subconsciously, the whole experience made me want to succeed at something athletic," Hamilton said later. When he was nine, he tagged along with his older sister to the skating rink. The more time he spent at the rink, the more it appeared that the cool air was therapeutic. He started growing, although it was too late to reach normal size. Hamilton stopped at 5 ft 3 in and about 110 lb.

Hamilton's career was unspectacular until he dedicated it to his mother, who died in 1977, and was challenged by hearing from a judge in 1978 that he was too small ever to be successful. In 1980 he finished fifth in the Winter Olympics. During the next four years Hamilton developed a routine featuring more leaping and diving than swaying, more sport than ballet. He had an ear infection that affected his balance when he won the Olympic gold medal in 1984, the first for a U.S. male figure skater in 24 years. The performance was not up to his standards. He lost in a two-minute short program for the first time since 1982, and he apologized for not meeting the demands of his 4½-minute long program. He owed his victory to winning the compulsory figures for the first time in championship competition.

(KEVIN M. LAMB)

Hans Adam, Prince of Liechtenstein

In a ceremony in Vaduz, Liechtenstein, on Aug. 26, 1984, Francis Joseph II, reigning monarch of the 265-year-old principality, handed over the greater part of his executive authority to his eldest son and heir apparent, Prince Hans Adam. This transference of princely duties had been announced the previous July by the 78-year-old Francis Joseph, whose reign (since July 25, 1938) exceeded in length that of any other living monarch with the exception of Emperor Hirohito of Japan.

Prince Hans Adam (his name was that of Liechtenstein's first ruling prince) was born on Feb. 14, 1945. Together with his three brothers and sister he spent his early youth in the castle of Vaduz, but he was not isolated from everyday life among the principality's approximately 26,000 citizens; he attended primary school in the town and as a Boy Scout took part in camp life and other activities.

Like his father before him, Hans Adam underwent his secondary education at Vienna's celebrated Schotten Gymnasium (Scottish Academy) and at Zuoz in Switzerland, where he matriculated in the spring of 1965. After a period as a trainee assistant in a London bank, in the fall of 1965 he entered the Sankt Gallen (Switz.) School of Economics and Social Sciences, from which he was graduated in 1969. Two years previously, on July 30, 1967, he had married Countess Marie Kinsky von Wichinitz und Tettau. The couple had three sons and a daughter.

Prince Hans Adam took a keen interest in the principality's economic and financial problems and developments and in its relations with other nations. He was a firm believer in European unity, both economic and political. In 1972 his father entrusted him with the financial management of the princely estate, a task he performed with considerable success.

(K. M. SMOGORZEWSKI)

Hart, Gary Warren

In the opening days of the campaign for the Democratic presidential nomination in 1984, Gary Hart gained nationwide atten-

tion by finishing second to the favoured Walter Mondale in the Iowa caucuses on February 20 and first in the New Hampshire primary on February 28. Hart's program—which included an end to U.S. military involvement and aid in Central America, simpler weaponry, and changes in the laws governing income taxes, banks, pension funds, and pooling of technical research—had great appeal to those whom his staff called young urban professionals, or "yuppies." But his vague slogan, "the candidate with new ideas," led to the damaging accusation that he campaigned on form rather than substance.

Born Gary Warren Hartpence in Ottawa, Kan., on Nov. 28, 1936, he joined his parents and wife in changing their surname to

"Hart" in 1961. Apparently, "Hartpence" was a German name that had taken forms such as "Penz" and "Eberhartpence." He received a B.A. from Bethany Nazarene College in 1958, a B.D. from Yale Divinity School in 1961, and an LL.B. from Yale Law School in 1964. He became a lawyer for the U.S. Department of Justice in 1964, a special assistant to U.S. Secretary of the Interior Stewart Udall in 1966, and an instructor at the University of Colorado (Boulder) in 1967. He entered law practice in Denver in 1968.

Hart left law practice in 1970 to organize George McGovern's successful campaign to become the Democratic candidate for president in the 1972 election. After McGovern's defeat in the election, Hart resumed his law practice and wrote *Right from the Start* (1973), a book advocating a rethinking of liberal Democratic ideas.

In 1974, as candidate for U.S. senator from Colorado, Hart built a well-run organization and defeated better-known politicians in the Democratic primary and an incumbent Republican in the general election. As senator, he called for increased defense spending—but on simpler weaponry. He opposed liberal Democrats who advocated price controls on oil and gas, which his state produced. In 1979 he opposed federal loan guarantees to the troubled Chrysler Corp. But he joined liberals on environmental and human-service issues. In 1980 he was narrowly reelected.

In 1984 Hart proved to be the candidate whom Mondale had to beat. Short of money, Hart built organizations quickly in state after state. But Mondale pulled ahead and was in control when the Democratic national convention opened in July. When Mondale received a majority of the votes in the roll call, Hart successfully moved for his nomination by acclamation.

(CHARLES JOHNSON TAGGART)

Horne, Marilyn

Mezzo-soprano Marilyn Horne began 1984 by reaching three milestones in her illustrious career. Her autobiography, *Marilyn Horne: My Life,* had just been published; on January 16 she celebrated her 50th birthday; and three days later she sang the lead in George Frideric Handel's *Rinaldo* at the Metropolitan Opera, New York City. It was the first Handel opera ever performed at the Met and the culmination of more than nine years of effort by Horne. In 1975 she had appeared with the Houston (Texas) Grand Opera in a scaled-down version of *Rinaldo* that was tailored specifically for her coloratura skills. It took seven years before the opera received a more elaborate staging by the National Arts Centre of Canada. Horne's success at Festival Ottawa in 1982 finally gained *Rinaldo* enough recognition to take the Canadian production to the Met, celebrating its centennial season.

Rinaldo was the latest in a long series of triumphs for Horne. She was born in Bradford, Pa., and began singing as a child. In 1954, after studying at the University of Southern California, she dubbed the singing voice of Dorothy Dandridge in the motion picture *Carmen Jones* and made her opera debut with the Los Angeles Guild Opera in Bedrich Smetana's *The Bartered Bride.* She sang with the Gelsenkirchen City Opera Company in West Germany for several years before returning to the U.S. in 1960 in Alban Berg's *Wozzeck* with the San Francisco Opera. During this period she changed from a soprano to a mezzo. In 1961 she sang her first bel canto role in Vincenzo Bellini's *Beatrice di Tenda,* with Joan Sutherland, at Carnegie Hall. Horne made her long-awaited debut at the Met in 1970 in Bellini's *Norma.*

Although her exceptional vocal range and versatility drew applause in many traditional roles, it was in a succession of "trouser roles" (male characters intended to be sung by male castrati or by women), such as *Rinaldo,* that Horne staked her claim. While continuing her busy schedule of recitals, recordings, and traditional operas, Horne spent much of 1984 preparing yet another trouser role, in Handel's rarely performed *Orlando.*

(MELINDA SHEPHERD)

Hu Qili

Hu Qili (Hu Ch'i-li) became prominent in 1984 as one of the young Chinese leaders obviously being groomed to succeed such aging veterans as Deng Xiaoping (Teng Hsiao-p'ing) and Chen Yun (Ch'en Yun), whose roles in government were inevitably coming to an end. Hu strongly supported pragmatic reform policies designed to speed up China's modernization drive and was active in many important fields, including foreign affairs and the Communist Party rectification campaign.

Hu Qili was born in Youlin (Yulin) County, Shaanxi (Shensi) Province, in 1929 and educated at Beijing (Peking) University, one of China's top institutions. While a student at the university, he joined the Communist Youth League in 1948 and later became its secretary. As chairman of the Youth Federation, he led many delegations to foreign countries in the early and mid-1960s. Purged in 1967 as a "capitalist roader" by the radical faction, he reappeared in 1978 as vice-president of Qinghua (Ch'ing-hua) University. He served briefly as party secretary and mayor of Tianjin (Tientsin) in the early 1980s. In addition, he was elected to the powerful Secretariat of the party's Central Committee and appointed to the influential directorship of the office of the Central Committee in 1982.

Energetic, capable, resourceful, and relatively young, Hu was noted for his down-to-earth approaches to China's political and economic problems. He had a pleasant personality and an optimistic outlook and was publicly praised by Deng and others. Clearly he was destined to play a major role in Chinese affairs in the years ahead.
(WINSTON L. Y. YANG)

Hurd, Douglas Richard

There was some surprise when British Prime Minister Margaret Thatcher in her September 1984 Cabinet reshuffle picked Douglas Hurd to succeed James Prior as secretary of state for Northern Ireland. Not that there was ever much doubt that Hurd would eventually find his way to the Cabinet; he would have been there earlier in all probability had he not been so closely associated at an earlier stage of his political career with Edward Heath, whom Thatcher had deposed as leader of the Conservative Party in 1975. Hurd's career had been impeccable for an ambitious Conservative politician, but under the Thatcher regime the Heathites were out of favour. His ability won him junior positions, but after a time as minister of state at the Foreign and Commonwealth Office (1979–83), he was passed over for the Cabinet and moved sideways to the Home Office (1983–84).

Hurd was born in Marlborough, England, on March 8, 1930, the son and grandson of Conservative members of Parliament. A king's scholar at Eton, a scholar of Trinity College, University of Cambridge, and president of the Cambridge Union in 1952, he abandoned in 1966 a high-flying career in the diplomatic service—during which he served in Beijing (Peking)—for a backroom job in the Conservative Party. The Research Department, in those days a semidetached think tank, was a favourite stamping ground for up-and-coming Tories. It took Hurd only two years to come to the attention of Edward Heath, whose private secretary he became in 1968. In 1970 Heath became prime minister and Hurd his political secretary, a post he retained until the fall of the Heath government in 1974.

The unappealing job of secretary of state for Northern Ireland was one that guaranteed prominence, as well as danger, but almost certainly ruled out success. By a nice irony one of Hurd's political thrillers—the writing of which was his successful hobby—was set in Northern Ireland and called *Vote to Kill* (1975). No sooner had

he taken over the post than the Irish Republican Army staged its most spectacular mainland atrocity yet and nearly blew up the British Cabinet at the Grand Hotel, Brighton, where the Conservative Party conference was in progress.
(PETER JENKINS)

Inamori, Kazuo

Kazuo Inamori graduated from a third-rate university and began his career working for a third-rate ceramics company. Since that time he had violated most of the accepted rules of Japanese business, but he was rated Japan's most effective manager among top executives surveyed by a leading Japanese business magazine. The 52-year-old maverick won that accolade for the way he ran the Kyocera Corp. in Kyoto.

Inamori was both the founder and president of a thriving company that manufactured 70% of all ceramic packages used to house semiconductors. With a firm hold on that world market, he branched into solar power, copying machines, portable computers, and stereos. He was also looking forward to 1985, when the telecommunications industry was to become deregulated. Inamori then planned to assume the role of David and challenge the government Goliath, the Nippon Telegraph & Telephone Public Corp. The Kyocera name was well known in industrialized countries, and it had begun to attract wide attention in the third world because it was linked to plans to bring solar-powered electricity to remote village areas.

Kazuo Inamori was born in Kagoshima Prefecture on Jan. 30, 1932. He quit his first company job at the age of 27 and found a backer for a business venture that started with a handful of friends making ceramic components for television sets.

After specializing in ceramic packages for semiconductors, Inamori happily found himself in on the ground floor when the semiconductor business took off like a rocket in the U.S. Scenting big profits, he bought up a number of U.S. ceramic companies in 1976 and in 1979 acquired his first Japanese company, Cybernet Electronics. In 1983 he took over the Yashica camera company, which he retooled to manufacture printers. In fiscal year 1983 Kyocera's total sales exceeded $1 billion.

In a country that puts emphasis on graduation from the best schools, decisions reached by consensus, seniority, lifetime employment, and heavy dependence on bank borrowing, Inamori was, to say the least, different. He tended to make his own decisions and seek concurrence later, rewarded talent even in the young, did not hesitate to fire an employee who did not measure up to his tough standards, and avoided indebtedness. He had, however, one traditional Japanese trait: love of work. He urged his employees to eat, drink, and sleep work much the way artists and Olympic athletes do. "I don't believe in taking vacations for pleasure," he said. "I consider it happiness to work. I try to make my employees understand that philosophy." Slender, bespectacled, and looking younger than his years, Inamori was also a first-class showman. When the time came to advertise his solar products, he put solar-powered lights atop Mt. Fuji, Japan's most famous landmark.
(JOHN RODERICK)

Irons, Jeremy

In June 1984 Jeremy Irons earned the Tony award for best actor for his performance in Tom Stoppard's *The Real Thing.* The success that greeted his Broadway debut informed the actor's career to date with a pleasing symmetry, for it was in British theatre that his talent was first noted before he went on to achieve much greater fame on both sides of the Atlantic through his work in other media. His early stage career bore out his stated objective, which was to seek challenge and variety in his choice of parts. After serving his ap-

prenticeship at the Bristol Old Vic Theatre Company, Irons made his first London appearance in 1971 as John the Baptist in the musical *Godspell.* His subsequent roles ranged from Shakespearean (*The Taming of the Shrew*), through 18th-century comic (John O'Keefe's *Wild Oats*), to contemporary (Harold Pinter's *The Caretaker*). He also appeared in several television series, including "Love for Lydia" and "The Pallisers" during the 1970s.

It was ironic, therefore, that the two roles that brought Irons international acclaim also threatened to typecast him. He was first approached to play Sebastian Flyte in the television adaptation of Evelyn Waugh's *Brideshead Revisited,* but his single-minded pursuit of the part of Charles Ryder, which he felt would make greater demands on him, paid off. Then, before he had completed "Brideshead" and with only one previous film appearance, he was cast as Charles Smithson in the film of John Fowles's *The French Lieutenant's Woman* at the urging of Pinter, who wrote the screenplay. Both productions were first screened in 1981. In a conscious effort to shake off the image of emotionally stilted, upper-class Englishman that clung to both roles, he followed these successes with widely differing performances in the motion pictures *Moonlighting* (1982), *Betrayal* (1983), and *Swann in Love* (1984), convincing those who had doubted his ability to portray a full range of emotions.

Irons's background was not theatrical. Born on Sept. 19, 1948, in Cowes, Isle of Wight, England, Jeremy John Irons attended Sherborne public school in Dorset, gaining neither encouragement of acting talent nor adequate qualifications to study veterinary science, his first ambition. In 1965 he moved to London, where he did social work before beginning his acting career.   (LOUISE WATSON)

Jackson, The Rev. Jesse

An uncharacteristically contrite Jesse Jackson stood before the Democratic Party national convention in 1984 and said that if, in his "low moments," he had stumbled, "That was not my truest self." That was in July, after several months of a start-and-stop campaign by the first black man to make a serious bid for the U.S. presidency. It was a struggle marked by tub-thumping rhetoric, disorganization, dramatic visits to Syria (to bring home a black U.S. airman downed on a bombing mission over Lebanon) and to Cuba—and by the ultimately damaging "Hymie" affair.

After calling for the creation of a "Rainbow Coalition" of Americans of all colours to unite against the Reagan administration, Jackson was overheard calling Jews "Hymies" and New York City "Hymietown." The slur, and his failure for nearly two weeks to acknowledge it, virtually ruined his ability to appeal beyond black voters. The problem was aggravated by his refusal for many weeks to repudiate the leader of a radical Black Muslim sect, Louis Farrakhan (q.v.), who intensified public ire with a metaphorical death threat against the journalist who disclosed the "Hymie" remark and with scurrilous comments about Jews and Judaism.

Though Jackson won about 3.2 million votes during the Democratic primaries, his success was a patchwork affair. He led caucus votes in Virginia and South Carolina and won the Louisiana and District of Columbia primaries. He did well in New York City and Philadelphia but poorly in some other cities; for example, in Birmingham, Ala., and Detroit, black mayors delivered huge black pluralities for the Democratic front-runner, Walter Mondale.

The primary campaign generated a surge of black voter registration. It and the general election campaign reinforced Jackson's reputation as one of the nation's most eloquent public speakers; it also broke the taboo against a black running for president and heightened awareness of the growing importance of the black vote. But his gaffes helped restrict his appeal and prompted the widespread view that he was essentially a polarizer within the Democratic Party, and it left his future unclear.

Jackson was born Oct. 8, 1941, in Greenville, S.C. After studying at the University of Illinois he was graduated from North Carolina Agricultural and Technical College. He did some graduate study at Chicago Theological Seminary and was ordained a Baptist minister in 1968. In 1966 he helped found the Chicago branch of Operation Breadbasket and served as its director until 1971, when he founded People United to Save Humanity (Operation PUSH), in which he advocated black self-help.

After the election Jackson announced he was moving to his hometown of Greenville and loosening his ties to the Chicago-based Operation PUSH. He said that he would not seek political office but would concentrate on voter registration and expanding the "Rainbow Coalition."

(JAMES L. YUENGER)

Jackson, Michael

He sported a trademark rhinestone-studded glove on his right hand, and when the whispery-voiced pop superstar took centre stage during the 1984 Jacksons' "Victory Tour" to deliver his renditions of such songs as "Billie Jean," "Beat It," and "The Girl Is Mine," euphoric audiences were brought under the spell of the electrifying showmanship of Michael Jackson.

A talented singer, songwriter, and dancer, Michael Joseph Jackson was born on Aug. 29, 1958, in Gary, Ind., the seventh of nine children in a musical family. He was, from the age of five, a budding member of the Jackson Five (later the Jacksons) and was ultimately named leader of the vocal group by his older brothers.

In 1979, however, Jackson went solo and achieved unprecedented success; at the age of 25 he was already a multimillionaire. His album *Thriller* sold 38 million copies in 1984, thus becoming the biggest selling solo album of all time, and he garnered a record eight Grammy awards for his music (another solo record for a performer in a single year) in February 1984.

Probably the only bad note during the year was the igniting of his hair during the filming of a Pepsi commercial, when he sustained second- and third-degree burns on his scalp. He recovered quickly, however, and plans were put in motion to reunite the Jackson brothers for one final "Victory Tour" presumably to bolster the brothers' sagging career and to promote their new album *Victory*. The four-month, 13-city tour debuted in Kansas City, Mo., in July amid a spectacular array of special effects including green and red laser beams, bursts of smoke and light, and the master of fancy footwork, Michael Jackson, who wowed audiences with his moonwalks, Marcel Marceau mime walks, spins, kicks, glides, half turns, and flash-frame poses. Jackson also showcased the unbelievable range of his voice and delighted fans with the favourite "I'll Be There."

The magic of Michael Jackson, however, was guaranteed to endure; at year's end he was making preparations to take flight in Steven Spielberg's *Peter Pan*.

(KAREN JUSTIN)

Jenkins. The Right Rev. David Edward

When the then professor of theology at the University of Leeds was appointed bishop of Durham in March 1984, relatively few people had heard of him; by the end of the year the name of David Jenkins was known across the nation and beyond. At an early stage he announced his intention to speak out whenever opportunity afforded, and he began with a controversial TV program just two months after his nomination in which he questioned the traditional understanding of the Virgin Birth and the Resurrection. At his enthronement in September there was, as expected, more controversy, but (what was not expected) it was political, with the 59-year-old bishop commenting in his sermon on Britain's protracted coal strike and criticizing the government's social and economic policies.

Jenkins's critics fumed, and some tried to have him removed from office; it was even suggested that the lightning-ignited fire that struck York Minster on July 9 was a sign of God's displeasure at his consecration there. He was notable for engaging in dialogue with opponents, but he gave (as he asked) no quarter; a man who spoke didactically and logically, he was impatient with the sloppy thinker. His wife, Mollie—the couple had four grown children—maintained that he behaved as he did because he was deeply truthful and "very bad at dissembling."

Apart from his theology, critics thought Jenkins was unsuitable as a bishop because he had had almost no pastoral experience. Born Jan. 26, 1925, in London, he was educated at St. Dunstan's College, Catford, and at Queen's College, University of Oxford. During World War II he served in the Royal Artillery and was demobilized in 1945 with the rank of captain. For virtually the whole of his ministry since ordination in 1953 he had been in academic posts, in Birmingham, Oxford, Geneva, and Manchester, with visiting lectureships in Australia and the U.S. He was appointed professor at Leeds in 1979. There, he had a reputation as a sound academic, and he vigorously denied that he was a "liberal" theologian, just as he vehemently rejected accusations that his beliefs were unorthodox. Ironically, his book *Guide to the Debate About God* (1966) was regarded as a major contribution to clarifying the issues raised by John Robinson's *Honest to God*—the last time a bishop had provoked so much controversy.   (SUSAN YOUNG)

Kahane, Meir

On a platform calling for the expulsion of the 700,000 Arabs who are Israeli citizens as well as the 1.2 million Arabs of the occupied territories of the West Bank and Gaza, Brooklyn-born Rabbi Meir Kahane, founder of the Jewish Defense League in the U.S., was elected in July 1984 to the Israeli Knesset (parliament). Throughout his campaign the head of the tiny Kach Party promised the introduction of a bill to expel Arabs as his first act in the 120-member Knesset. Kahane's election resulted in widespread concern in Israel not only about the 52-year-old rabbi's inflammatory theories and espousal of racist violence but also about the feelings of the 25,000 people who elected him.

Kahane, born in Brooklyn, N.Y., on Aug. 1, 1932, first gained prominence in the late 1960s, when he founded the New York City-based, militaristic Jewish Defense League, through which he advocated his right to break any law he found inconsistent with traditional Judaic law handed down by God. In 1971 he moved to Israel, were he compiled a substantial arrest record. He established the small, extremist Kach Party, financed, according to Kahane, by U.S. sympathizers and populated by young Americans recruited by him. The party advocates a lowering of the Arab birthrate, desecration of Christian and Muslim holy sites, and vandalism of Arab neighbourhoods.

Both as the head of JDL and as an elected Knesset member, Kahane applauded terrorist activity and believed, perhaps ironically, that the reason to remove all Palestinians from Israeli territory is to save the

Jewish homeland from destructive rioting. Soon after his July election he marched through the Muslim quarter of Jerusalem's Old City calling for "Death to Arabs." A few days later he attempted to force his way inside the Dome of the Rock, one of the holiest shrines of Islam.

Criticism of Kahane at first came mainly from Israeli leftists, but later such mainstream politicians as the mayor of Jerusalem, the present and former prime ministers, and many Knesset colleagues dissociated themselves from him and his policies. Kahane maintained, however, that he had a great deal of tacit support, both in the Knesset and in the population in general.   (BONNIE OBERMAN)

Karajan, Herbert von

The controversy in which the celebrated Austrian conductor and opera producer Herbert von Karajan found himself in the early summer of 1984 was not his first. A musician whom many consider the greatest living conductor, Karajan had had a career dotted with both artistic and administrative disagreements and disputes.

The 76-year-old conductor of the Berlin Philharmonic Orchestra was born in Salzburg, Austria, on April 5, 1908. Karajan performed publicly as a pianist while still a young child. He studied music and piano at the Salzburg Mozarteum and in 1926 entered the Vienna Music Academy; he made his conducting debut with the academy's orchestra on Dec. 17, 1928. His meteoric rise began on March 2, 1929, with his leading of *Le nozze di Figaro* at the state theatre at Ulm, where he worked for the next five years. In 1934, at age 26, Karajan was appointed director/conductor of the Aachen Opera. Four years later he was appointed concurrently the conductor of the Berlin State Opera, where he established his base in 1941.

Through these years Karajan's fame grew rapidly. After World War II an affiliation with the Nazi Party was erased from his record, and he was appointed conductor of the Vienna Symphony Orchestra in 1948 and named its concert director for life in 1949. In 1955 he became principal conductor (for life) of the Berlin Philharmonic and, again concurrently, served as artistic director of the Vienna State Opera (1956–64) and at the Salzburg Festival (1956–60).

While acquiring this musical empire Karajan was simultaneously showing enormous interest in musical reproduction techniques and in attempting to alter traditional methods of opera production. Several disagreements over the latter brought about his resignation from the Vienna State Opera in 1964. Four years later he made his debut at the Metropolitan Opera in New York City. Karajan built his reputation on his self-assurance, his emotional attachment to faithfully executed performances, and his skillful arrangements. The 1984 dispute, which involved the hiring of a Karajan protégée clarinetist rejected by other orchestra members, was the latest in a series of struggles between the conductor and the Philharmonic players.

(BONNIE OBERMAN)

Karami, Rashid Abdul Hamid

Rashid Karami, who resumed a familiar role as prime minister of Lebanon in April 1984, was a veteran politician descended from a family of political and religious leaders of the Sunni Muslim community. He was born on Dec. 30, 1921, in the northern Lebanese village of Miriata. His father, Abdel Hamid Karami, was mufti of Tripoli, a member of Parliament, and, in 1945, prime minister. Rashid Karami, a graduate of Fu'ad University in Cairo, first entered politics in 1951 when he was elected a deputy for Tripoli. He became justice minister, joined the opposition, and then served in various Cabinets from August 1953 to July 1955. On Sept. 19, 1955, aged 33, he became Lebanon's youngest prime minister, but he opposed Pres. Camille Chamoun and espoused the anti-Western Nasserite views that were then fashionable, and six months later he resigned.

In 1958 Karami again became prime minister, appointed by Gen. Fuad Chehab, who succeeded Chamoun as president. With short breaks, Karami was prime minister until 1969, when he resigned after the bloody repression of a pro-Palestinian demonstration on April 23 of that year. In the 1970 presidential election the Chehabists lost to Suleiman Franjieh. In late 1974 Karami went into active opposition with Saeb Salam and Raymond Eddé. In 1975 President Franjieh, against his will, appointed Karami prime minister as the candidate of the Islamic leftist opposition; he was also minister of finance, defense, and information. In the civil war that followed, Karami collaborated with the Palestine Liberation Organization and with Kamal Jumblatt's National Movement.

In 1976 Karami supported the elevation to the presidency of Elias Sarkis, but his influence waned as the civil war intensified and the Syrians became involved. During the war Karami had proposed political reforms, but his moderate program remained a dead letter. In 1977 he declared that he would leave politics, but the following year he was reconciled with Franjieh. He maintained good relations with Syrian leaders in the years following the invasion of Beirut by the Israelis, and this proved to be the key to his return to power in 1984. Karami was a bachelor who spent most of his leisure time at Miriata and who enjoyed hunting. His backers called him "al Effendi," meaning "the Gentleman." Although he was fluent in English and French, he rarely spoke any language other than Arabic, in which he had a reputation for eloquence.   (JOHN WHELAN)

Kim Chong Il

Though North Korean Pres. Kim Il Sung had for a decade been grooming his son Kim Chong Il as his political heir, the campaign reached a climax in 1984. The promotion of pragmatic technocrats in January was seen briefly as a challenge to the authority of Kim Chong Il and his supporters, but the younger Kim's position as number two in North Korea was placed beyond doubt by a massive, nationwide propaganda campaign to mark his 42nd birthday on February 16. Said *Rodong Shinmun,* official newspaper of the Korean Workers' (Communist) Party (KWP): "Our party's revolutionary tradition has been generated through the Juche ['self-reliance'] Thought of the Great Leader [Kim Il Sung]. Therefore, the only way to develop the tradition is to continuously carry on the struggle to dye the whole society in the Thought as indicated by our Dear Guide Kim Chong Il."

Early in the year, according to South Korean intelligence sources, Kim Chong Il was named chairman of the KWP's powerful Military Commission, and in July North Korea's generals pledged to follow his "orders and directives." The succession was officially confirmed on August 6, when Radio Pyongyang for the first time referred to the younger Kim as "the sole successor to our Great Leader Kim Il Sung." During the year Kim Chong Il greatly stepped up the number of his public "inspirational tours" of the country. China had appeared to recognize his right of succession when it gave him a grand welcome during his trip to Beijing (Peking) in June 1983.

Kim Chong Il was born on Feb. 16, 1942, in Siberia's Maritime Province. His mother, Kim Chong Suk, was hailed as a revolutionary in her own right in North Korea. In 1945 Kim Chong Il was taken to northern Korea by his parents, but in June 1950, after the outbreak of the Korean War, he was removed to Manchuria for safety. He returned to Pyongyang two years later and finished secondary school there in August 1958. After graduating from the faculty of politics and economy at Kim Il Sung University in 1963, Kim Chong Il was sent to East Germany for training as a pilot.

The younger Kim's political career began in 1964 with his appointment to the KWP's organization and guidance bureau. In 1973 he became head of the party's propaganda department. In 1980 Kim Chong Il was appointed to a post in the KWP secretariat immediately behind his father, and two years later he gained a seat in the Supreme People's Assembly, North Korea's parliament.

(THOMAS HON WING POLIN)

Kirkpatrick, Jeane Jordan

When Jeane Kirkpatrick announced, shortly after election day in November 1984, her intention to resign as U.S. ambassador to the United Nations, the reason was widely assumed to be that her conservative admirers had failed in their campaign to make her secretary of state or national security adviser to Pres. Ronald Reagan. She said she wanted to return to teaching but let it be known that she would be willing to stay in the Reagan administration in a job of real consequence.

Her desire to step out of the UN was understandable after four years of constant combat with Soviet-bloc and third world delegates over using the organization as a sounding board for anti-U.S. (and anti-Israel) propaganda. The tough stands she took (always articulated pungently), had, she said, "substantially improved" the U.S. position despite the UN's "overblown, negative rhetoric."

Her route to power in the Reagan administration, and to the affections of the right wing, was unusual. Born on Nov. 19, 1926, in Duncan, Okla., the daughter of an oil wildcatter, she grew up in the Southwest and Midwest and attended Stephens College and Barnard College, where she received an A.B. degree in 1948. She earned an M.A. at Columbia University in 1950, studied in Paris, and won a Ph.D. in political science from Columbia in 1967 with

MARK REINSTEIN—PHOTOREPORTERS

a dissertation, subsequently published, on Juan Perón and Peronism. In the meantime she had taught political science and worked as a research analyst at the Department of State. In 1955, while she was a research associate at Georgetown University, she married Evron Kirkpatrick, a Minnesota political scientist who had managed Hubert Humphrey's first campaign for mayor of Minneapolis and who had just become executive director of the American Political Science Association.

Jeane Kirkpatrick returned to Georgetown as an associate professor in 1967, becoming a full professor in 1973 and Leavey professor of the foundations of American freedom in 1978. She had become a friend and admirer of Humphrey, and was embittered at what she saw as the destruction of his presidential campaign in 1968 by the left wing of the Democratic Party and by the party's capitulation to "antiwar, antigrowth, antibusiness, antilabor activists." While she maintained her party ties with like-minded Democrats, she found herself, with many of them, edging into the neoconservative camp. In 1977 she became a resident scholar at the American Enterprise Institute for Public Policy Research.

A 1980 magazine article in which she sharply criticized Pres. Jimmy Carter for allowing the growth of Soviet power caught Ronald Reagan's eye. He called her in to talk and, after considerable soul-searching, she campaigned for him. In 1981, after his election, Reagan appointed her to the UN job.   (JAMES L. YUENGER)

Lange, David Russell

Sworn in on July 26, 1984, David Lange, not yet 42, became New Zealand's youngest prime minister of the century. President of the Labour Party since February 1983, he had led it to victory in the July 14 election, ending the eight-year, three-term dominance of Sir Robert Muldoon's National Party administration. When Lange took over the party leadership from Sir Wallace ("Bill") Rowling, he expected to confront Muldoon's Nationals in Novem-

ber 1984. His moment came six months earlier when Muldoon gave the fragility of his majority in the House as reason for calling a snap election.

Lange was born in Auckland on Aug. 4, 1942, of German settler stock. His father was a doctor in the Auckland suburb of Otahuhu, and it was there that David learned something of the privation of others and absorbed the strong Methodist flavour of the home. He earned a law degree with ease at the University of Auckland and worked in London in the late 1960s. There he met his wife, Naomi, when both were active in the Methodist Church. They settled first in North Auckland, where Lange ran unsuccessfully as a Labour candidate for Parliament in 1976. He completed a master's law degree, settled into practice at Mangere, and gained nomination to a safe seat in a 1977 by-election, which he won. He was then a burly, witty people's lawyer with a family of three, a massive weight problem, continuing church involvement, and political supporters who were not satisfied with a party back bench. In 1979 he was elected deputy party leader, just missed election to the top spot in December 1980, and watched Labour narrowly defeated in 1981.

Lange underwent stomach bypass surgery for his weight problem and emerged as a stunningly groomed, better informed, less waspish challenger for the party leadership, which Rowling ceded to him. As head of New Zealand's fourth Labour government, he was compared to the third government's Norman Kirk for physical

CAMERA PRESS, LONDON

stature, charisma, and sense of the region; to the second government's Walter Nash for religious associations; and to the World War II government's Michael Savage for capacity to establish a new order of social services. Like all of them, he appeared to be threatened more by schisms in his own party than by his political opponents.
                                          (J. A. KELLEHER)

Le Pen, Jean-Marie

Jean-Marie le Pen and his National Front (NF), launched to the fore of the French political scene by the European parliamentary elections on June 17, 1984, unfurled anew the banner of the neofascist right at a time when all other French parties were

losing ground. Gaining 10.95% of the vote, much the same as that cast for the rapidly declining Communist Party, the NF capitalized on the exasperation of a substantial section of the French electorate toward the left.

The party's advance had already been indicated in the municipal elections in March 1983 and in the by-election in Dreux in September of that year. Its success at that time was due in part to its emphasis on two very popular themes: the struggles against any soft line on immigration and against insecurity. The NF made no secret of its xenophobia and added a racist odour to its neo-Poujadist slant.

The extent and significance of le Pen's following of more than two million French citizens was reflected in some outstanding successes in the 1984 balloting. With 19.4%, the NF overtook the Socialist and Communist parties in Bouches-du-Rhône, a traditional stronghold of the left; in Paris, which had for some time been shifting to the right, the party got more than 15% of the vote; and in Lyon it reached 17%.

Le Pen was born June 20, 1928, at La Trinité-sur-Mer in the département of Morbihan, the son of a fisherman. After a Jesuit schooling he graduated in law at the University of Paris. His political career began at the end of 1955. A volunteer in the parachute regiment, he had just returned from Indochina when he met Pierre Poujade, who needed associates to help lead his far right-wing movement of tradesmen and skilled workers. Le Pen, at the age of 27, was selected as a "Poujadist" candidate and in January 1956 was elected in Paris to become the youngest member of the National Assembly. A born activist, le Pen was not averse to a brawl at a public meeting and never missed an uproar in the Assembly. He reenlisted in Algeria and took part in military operations there in 1956 and 1957 before being expelled from Algiers because he was considered a liability by those who planned to establish an "Algérie française."

Le Pen was the director of a well-known phonograph record company and the heir of Hubert Lambert, a writer and former right-wing militant who had himself inherited the Lambert cement works. Leader of the NF since 1972 and still only 56, le Pen evidently had considerable ambitions for the 1986 legislative elections.
                                          (JEAN KNECHT)

Lloyd, Clive

When the West Indies cricket team trounced England by five tests to none in the summer of 1984, the defeat was the most one-sided ever suffered by England at home. Although Clive Lloyd's individual cricketing skills were eclipsed by those of the team's brightest stars, there was no doubt that his leadership was of vital importance. There was ample supporting evidence. When Lloyd first took over the captaincy, West Indies was languishing at the bottom of the league table of cricketing nations. Under his guidance it became unquestionably the strongest. During 1984 Lloyd announced his decision to end his long and distinguished career as captain early in 1985.

The son of a chauffeur, Clive Hubert Lloyd was born on Aug. 31, 1944, in Georgetown, British Guiana (now Guyana). After his father died when Lloyd was 14 years old, financial stringency dictated that he leave school and assume responsibility for supporting the family. The qualities of leadership were no doubt instilled early as a result. He worked as a clerk at Georgetown Hospital for six years before cricket became a full-time career.

After starting out with Demarara Cricket Club, Georgetown, in 1959, he made his debut for Guyana four years later. In the tradition of many West Indian cricketers, he moved to England to further his career. Lancashire County Cricket Club reaped the benefit; Lloyd joined the team in 1968, received his first cap the following year, and became captain in 1981. Always a brilliant fielder, he also became a prolific run scorer over the years, passing the 25,-000-run mark in first-class cricket in 1981. His bowling, too—he was a medium-paced seamer—was highly valued by his club.

Lloyd first joined the West Indies test side in 1966. He went on to become the longest serving player and captain in test-match history, leading the team from 1974, apart from a short break in 1978–79 when he joined Kerry Packer's World Series Cricket circuit. Lloyd's greatest influence, however, was on the nature of test cricket itself. He was instrumental in restructuring the West Indies team to include four, instead of the traditional two, fast bowlers to allow an uninterrupted pace attack on the batsmen. Ironically, the necessary depth of talent could be found among West Indians playing in English county cricket.   (LOUISE WATSON)

Lusinchi, Jaime

Venezuela's new president, Jaime Lusinchi, took office on Feb. 2, 1984, after winning 56.81% of the votes in the December 1983 presidential election. During his first year as president he had to contend with two major problems: revitalization of an ailing economy and elimination of corrupt practices that had flourished under previous administrations. Lusinchi was under intensive pressure from his Acción Democrática (AD) party as well as from the Confederation of Venezuelan Workers—the two legs of his successful campaign for the presidency—to improve the lot of his electorate or at least to protect it from the effects of the economic crisis and the radical changes in policy needed to stabilize a deteriorating situation. Lusinchi's prestige received a valuable boost in September when, on the eve of the annual meeting of the International Monetary Fund, he was able to announce a preliminary agreement with the country's chief bank creditors for the long-term rescheduling of the public sector's foreign debt.

As a first step in the fight against corruption, Lusinchi appointed a controller for the state body in charge of food importing and set up an inquiry to investigate executives who reportedly took bribes to authorize the purchase of 40,000 tons of black beans from Argentina. Officials at the Instituto de Obras Sanitas who violated the corporation's code were fired on the spot, and Lusinchi urged the business association Fédecameras to restrain its members who might try to benefit from corrupt practices. Show trials of officials in the Corporación Venezolana de Fomento and a court-martial of military chiefs over

arms purchases were held in order to discourage officeholders from participating in the pervasive bribery and corruption.

Jaime Lusinchi was born in 1924 in Clarines in the state of Anzoátegui. He studied medicine at the Central University of Venezuela. Politically active as a student, he joined AD on its foundation by Rómulo Betancourt in 1941. By November 1948 he was party deputy secretary, and after the military coup that month he was imprisoned and then expelled from the country. He went first to Argentina, then to Chile and the U.S., where he continued his medical training and qualified as a pediatrician. He returned to Venezuela in 1958 when the military dictatorship came to an end. After that he represented his state in the Congress and held various positions within the AD leadership.

(MICHAEL WOOLLER)

Lyubimov, Yury Petrovich

After enjoying a reputation for 20 years as the Soviet Union's leading and most controversial theatrical director, Yury Lyubimov encountered the "year of reckoning" in 1984. A lifetime devoted to promoting the art of the theatre, both as an actor and later as director, culminated in his removal from the management of the Moscow Theatre of Drama and Comedy on the Taganka (popularly known as "the Taganka") because of a prolonged stay in the West that began in 1983. This was followed by expulsion from the Communist Party, which he had joined in 1952 after serving in the Red Army throughout

World War II, and the loss of his Soviet citizenship, all within five months.

However, 1984 also had its consolations: the award, in London, of the *Standard* newspaper's prestigious best production prize for his first British production, his own adaptation of Dostoevsky's *Crime and Punishment* at the Lyric Theatre, Hammersmith, in the fall of 1983; his debut, directing the same play, at the Vienna Burgtheater; his much applauded debut (despite differences with some of his cast) at the Florence Maggio Musicale festival with Verdi's *Rigoletto;* and his acceptance of the artistic direction of the Paris Théâtre

de Bobineau. There were also countless invitations to stage drama or opera in Britain, West Germany, Sweden, Spain, Italy, Switzerland, and the U.S.

Born into a family of former serfs in Yaroslav Province on Sept. 30 (Sept. 17, old style), 1917, Lyubimov graduated from the Vakhtangov Theatre Studio in Moscow in 1939 and, after military service in World War II, returned as actor, director, and acting teacher at the Vakhtangov's Shchukin Drama School. With his 1963 acting class he staged Brecht's *The Good Woman of Setzuan,* whose cast formed the nucleus of the world-famous Taganka ensemble. He became its director in 1964. His fearless expression of his own artistic ideas, however, came into conflict with official opinion.

Anatoly Efros, himself dismissed from his own theatre in 1967 but later rehabilitated, was appointed to succeed Lyubimov but accepted the post only after protest, declaring Lyubimov to be the Soviet theatre's foremost directorial champion. Yury Trifonov (d. 1981), author of one of Lyubimov's greatest directorial successes (*The Exchange,* 1969), had praised Lyubimov's individuality and creative strength as that "of one who could not fit into another director's straitjacket."

(OSSIA TRILLING)

Machel, Samora Moisés

Mozambique's Pres. Samora Machel, an avowed Marxist who had had close ties to both the U.S.S.R. and China, surprised the world in March 1984 by entering into a security and economic treaty with South Africa known as the Nkomati accords. This sharp reversal of position was forced on him by the growing threat from the rebel Mozambique National Resistance (MNR), the periodic military attacks by South Africa, and severe economic troubles compounded by a savage drought. Not wishing to appear in the role of a defeated leader, he demonstratively appeared in full field marshal's uniform to sign the treaty with South Africa's Pres. P. W. Botha (*q.v.*) near Nkomati, a border town between their two countries.

Samora Moisès Machel was born at Xilembena in Gaza Province on Sept. 29, 1933. He began his schooling in a Protestant mission institution at the age of 9 and completed his education at 17 in a Roman Catholic mission school. Although he had reluctantly agreed to being baptized as a Catholic in order to be able to complete his early schooling, he refused to enter a seminary to continue with higher education. Instead, he took up nursing at a hospital in Lourenço Marques (now Maputo) and served as a nurse for ten years. He left the country in 1962 to join the clandestine Mozambique Liberation Front (Frelimo) and was sent for military training to Algeria. He took over responsibility for a sector of Frelimo's guerrilla operations in 1964 and quickly won prominence both as a commander and as a military organizer. He became Frelimo's leader in May 1970 and led his country to independence in June 1975.

Although an orthodox Marxist, once in office Machel proved himself to be a pragmatist. He accepted the necessity of maintaining formal but not close relations with South Africa, on which Mozambique was heavily dependent because of traditional economic and communications links. At the same time, he gave his support to the African National Congress (ANC) in its liberation struggle against South Africa. Then, though still firmly committed to their cause, he accepted as part of the Nkomati accords the need to prevent ANC guerrillas from using his territory. Although his colleagues in the African frontline nations did not approve of the ostentatious manner in which Machel signed the treaty with South Africa, they nevertheless gave him their backing in his decision to come to terms with Pretoria.   (COLIN LEGUM)

MacLaine, Shirley

Shirley MacLaine is a jill-of-all-trades and master of one—film acting. In 1984 audiences saw two of her most vivid portrayals: an endearing, elfish young woman in *The Trouble with Harry* and a demanding, domineering mother in *Terms of Endearment. The Trouble with Harry*, released in March after a 28-year absence from the screen, was MacLaine's film debut. *Terms of Endearment,* her most recent film, brought MacLaine the 1984 Academy Award for best actress. During the years between those works, MacLaine established herself as a versatile performer, winning praise for such roles as a prostitute in *Irma La Douce,* a suspected lesbian in *The Children's Hour,* and a former ballerina in *The Turning Point.*

In the late 1960s and early 1970s MacLaine took time off from films to play the real-life role of social and political activist. She helped register black voters in Mississippi, joined protests against the Vietnam war, and spoke out in favour of

equal rights for women. She became involved in presidential politics, campaigning for Robert Kennedy in 1968 and for George McGovern in 1972.

When her interest in politics waned during the mid-1970s, MacLaine immersed herself in mysticism. She later said that trance mediums and meditation had led her to discover other lives as a prostitute, her own daughter's daughter, and a male court jester under Louis XV of France.

MacLaine was born on April 24, 1934, in Richmond, Va. Her younger brother is actor Warren Beatty. She began practicing ballet as a toddler, and by age 12 she was accomplished enough to appear in ballets presented by the National Symphony Orchestra. When she grew too tall for ballet, she took her dancing shoes to Broadway, where she made summer appearances in the choruses of *Oklahoma!* and *Kiss Me, Kate.* In 1954, two years after graduating from high school, she became the understudy for the leading dancer in *The Pajama Game.* Life then imitated movie art: the leading dancer cracked her ankle, MacLaine performed in her place, and the audience burst into applause. Her biggest admirer that night proved to be Hollywood mogul Hal Wallis, who soon signed MacLaine to a long-term film contract.
             (MICHAEL AMEDEO)

Mahmood Iskandar ibni al-Marhum Sultan Ismail

In a ritual unique in the world, Malaysia's nine hereditary sultans met on Feb. 9, 1984, to elect one of their number to serve a five-year term as the country's eighth *yang di-pertuan agung* ("One Who Is Chief Among the Most Prominent"), or king. Their choice was the controversy-prone Sultan Mahmood Iskandar of Johore State. Sultan Mahmood, who was 52 on April 8, assumed the national throne on April 26, when the term of the outgoing king, Sultan Ahmad Shah of Pahang, expired.

The colourful, independent character of the new *agung* had been the subject of much discussion in Malaysian political circles. His clashes with the federal government on some issues helped prompt the administration of Prime Minister Datuk Seri Mahathir bin Mohamad to introduce in 1983 constitutional amendments—passed after a bitter struggle—designed to curb the *agung*'s power to veto Parliament-approved legislation. Mahmood's penchant for military uniforms and firearms, as well as a previous court conviction for homicide, also weighed on the minds of his countrymen.

Mahmood Iskandar was born in Johore Bahru in 1932, the eldest grandson of the powerful and very wealthy Sultan Ibrahim of Johore and the son of Tunku Ismail. After being educated by private tutors and at an English college in Johore Bahru, he continued his studies in Australia and Britain. It was in England that Mahmood met Josephine Trevorrow, a wealthy British textile manufacturer's daughter, whom he married in 1956. The couple returned to live in Johore Bahru, where Mahmood worked for the state government and treasury. Upon his grandfather's death in 1959, his father became sultan and Mahmood was made crown prince. In 1961, however, Sultan Ismail suddenly stripped Mahmood of his status as heir apparent, conferring it instead upon his younger brother. Court officials in Johore said the sultan had become increasingly unhappy about his eldest son's behaviour.

In 1972 Mahmood was charged with causing bodily injury to six people in three unrelated incidents and was fined by the High Court. On Oct. 15, 1976, Mahmood shot and killed a suspected smuggler. Six months later he was sentenced to half a year in jail, a fate he escaped only by

dint of a royal pardon from his father. The deathbed decision in 1981 by Sultan Ismail to pass his title back to Mahmood Iskandar sparked yet more controversy.
             (THOMAS HON WING POLIN)

Marino, Dan

In only his second season as a professional, Dan Marino thoroughly broke many National Football League records in 1984.

His 48 regular-season touchdown passes broke the NFL mark by 12. He set records with 5,084 passing yards, 362 completions, nine games of at least 300 passing yards, and four games of at least 400. In the 45–28 American Conference championship game, he set play-off records by passing for 421 yd and four touchdowns.

In his average game Marino completed 23 passes for 318 yd and three touchdowns. He carried the Miami Dolphins to a 14–2 record and the Super Bowl in spite of their ordinary defense and often invisible running attack and was voted the league's most valuable player.

"At some point, you have to come away with the feeling, this man is awesome," San Francisco coach Bill Walsh said before his team beat the Dolphins 38–16 in the Super Bowl. Before that Marino had passed for 8,170 yd and 77 touchdowns in 30 games. Miami's won–lost record in games he had started was 23–5.

But in the 1983 draft of college players, 5 quarterbacks and 26 players were claimed before Marino. His production had slipped as a senior, when his University of Pittsburgh team was 9–3 after 11–1 records the previous three seasons. After making the All-America team as a junior, when he finished fourth in voting for player of the year, Marino passed for only 17 touchdowns as a senior, compared with 37 the previous year, while his interceptions stayed at 23.

Daniel Constantine Marino, Jr., was born Sept. 15, 1961, in Pittsburgh. He unfailingly said that his hero and strongest influence was his father, a newspaper truck driver and patriarch of a devoutly Roman Catholic family of six.

Marino was a quick study as a professional, becoming the first rookie quarterback voted to start a Pro Bowl, although a knee injury kept him from playing. He was the first rookie since 1969 to lead a conference in passing. Despite his penchant for throwing deep, his interception percentage of .020 was a rookie record. Experts marveled over how quickly he threw the ball, cocking his arm only as far back as his ear. That release, plus his ability to find open receivers quickly and his willingness to challenge defensive backs, explained why he was sacked only 23 times during his first two seasons.   (KEVIN M. LAMB)

Maxwell, (Ian) Robert

Sixteen years after his first attempt to buy a national newspaper, Robert Maxwell fulfilled his long-held ambition in July 1984 when Reed International sold Mirror Group Newspapers (MGN) to Pergamon Press Ltd., of which Maxwell was founder and chairman. It was the most recent step in the rehabilitation of a man once described by a U.K. Department of Trade report as "not a person who can be relied upon to exercise stewardship of a publicly quoted company."

Born Jan Lodvik Hoch on June 10, 1923, in Slatina-Selo, Czech. (now U.S.S.R.), Maxwell completed only three years of formal education before joining first the resistance movement and later the British Army during World War II. He arrived in the U.K. in 1940. After two years spent in Berlin in the German section of the U.K. Foreign Office, he launched a business career so beset with extremes of success and failure that he came to be known as "the bouncing Czech."

In 1949 Maxwell founded Pergamon, the scientific and educational publishing concern that would ultimately provide the base for his enormous printing and publishing empire. First, however, an unsuccessful merger attempt between Pergamon and the U.S. Leasco Data Processing Equipment Corp. prompted a Department of Trade inquiry and caused Maxwell to lose the chairmanship in 1969 (he regained it in 1974). His political ambitions were dashed when, in 1970, he lost the seat he had held as Labour member of Parliament for Buckingham since 1964.

On taking control of MGN, Maxwell pledged that the *Daily Mirror* would fight for the return of a Labour government, but his brand of socialism did not preclude an uncompromising attitude toward the print-trade unions. Furthermore, the economic recession that had followed the arrival of a Conservative government facilitated his style of conducting business, which involved acquiring companies on the brink of insolvency and imposing rigorous modernization schemes. His most significant acquisition was that of the U.K.'s largest printing group, British Printing Corp. (renamed British Printing & Communication Corp. [BPCC]). After Maxwell became chief executive in 1981, BPCC's results showed a remarkable recovery. Asked how he found time to combine his two main interests, Maxwell remarked that "BPCC is a morning business, and the newspaper is an evening business." Somewhere in between he found time for numerous others, including chairing his local soccer club. (LOUISE WATSON)

M'Bow, Amadou Mahtar

As the international controversy about the United Nations Educational, Scientific and Cultural Organization's (UNESCO's) ideological orientation smoldered throughout 1984, the position of Amadou Mahtar M'Bow as the first African director general of that body was increasingly debated. Under M'Bow's decade-long stewardship, power alignments within UNESCO shifted to reflect more closely the interests of the many third world and Soviet-satellite nations that had become members in the 1960s and 1970s. Alienated and angry Western nations—whose governments contributed most of the agency's total budget—leveled charges of mismanagement, centralization of power, and Communist bias, to an important degree against M'Bow himself.

The academic and political career of the man at the centre of the UNESCO dispute was unified by a commitment to education as a means of reversing the effects of colonization and underdevelopment in his native Senegal and throughout black Africa. M'Bow was born to a devout Muslim farmer on March 20, 1921, in Dakar,

when Senegal was a French colony. During World War II he became the first black technical sergeant in the history of the French Air Force. After the war, he pursued degrees in history and geography at the University of Paris. By 1950 he had established himself as a Marxist student leader, becoming president of the Federation of Black African Students in France. Considered a threat to Senegal's government at a time when Senegal was an overseas territory of France, M'Bow was assigned to teach at a secondary school in isolated Rosso, Mauritania. His segregation ended in 1953 with his appointment as head in Senegal of a UNESCO-sponsored program in fundamental education.

After Senegal achieved independence in 1960, M'Bow served as minister of education under Pres. Léopold Senghor. During the late 1960s he was a member of the

BRIAN F. ALPERT—KEYSTONE

National Assembly and also held the post of minister of youth and culture.

In UNESCO M'Bow emerged as an outspoken critic of what he termed Eurocentrism. In the late 1960s he twice headed his country's delegations to UNESCO general conferences and was a member of the body's executive board, chairman of the group of African members, and head of the caucus of its 77 third world members. He was appointed in 1970 to the post of assistant director general for education by then director general René Maheu, whom he succeeded in 1974. His direct but conciliatory leadership style was affirmed by unanimous reelection in 1980, before Western dissatisfaction had reached disruptive proportions. By late 1984, however, his ability to mend cracks in UNESCO's foundations appeared tenuous at best; the U.S. withdrew from the organization, and the U.K. threatened to withdraw a year later.

(BRENDA E. BERMAN)

Meyer, Ray

Ray Meyer coached his first victory at DePaul University in 1942, a 42–16 win over Chicago Teachers College at the College Theatre, a 1,200-seat stucco building known as "The Barn." When he finished his career in 1984, 42 years and 1,078 games later, DePaul played at the Rosemont Horizon, a four-year-old suburban

arena seating 17,500. In the meantime, Meyer had made a national success story of the small Roman Catholic university on Chicago's North Side.

Meyer retired with a won–lost record of 724–354, the fifth largest number of victories by any coach at a major basketball college. He had 37 winning seasons and won at least 20 games in 12 of them, including the last seven. Meyer's seven-year record of 180–30 through 1984 was the best in the country. At 70, he passed the job on to one of his six children, 35-year-old Joey.

Raymond Joseph Meyer was born Dec. 18, 1913, in Chicago. His last-second basket won for St. Patrick's Academy the National Catholic High School championship in 1932. At the University of Notre Dame he played forward on the 1936 national championship team. After graduating he worked briefly as a social worker in Chicago and coached a girl's team. In 1940 he became an assistant to Notre Dame coach George Keogan, who recommended him two years later for DePaul's top job.

Inheriting a 10–12 team, Meyer coached his first DePaul squad to 19–5. His third team won the national championship, at that time decided in the National Invitation Tournament (NIT), in 1945. Meyer never won another national championship. His team finished fourth in the 1946 NIT and then went to 11 National Collegiate Athletic Association (NCAA) tournaments and five more NIT's after the latter became a consolation tournament. He nearly quit in the early 1970s, when he fought school administrators for a more competitive budget after an 8–17 record, his worst, in 1970–71. Meyer won. The school made him a full-time coach, relieving him of administrative duties, and hired his son Joey in 1973 as his first full-time assistant.

Two years later DePaul returned to the NCAA tournament for the first time in 11 years. In 1977–78 it ranked among the top 20 for the first time, when the Blue Demons went 27–3 and Meyer was national coach of the year. The next year DePaul finished third in the NCAA tournament, and Meyer became the fourth active coach ever elected to the Naismith Memorial Basketball Hall of Fame.

(KEVIN M. LAMB)

Mondale, Walter Frederick

After triumphing in an unexpectedly difficult fight for the Democratic Party's presidential nomination, Walter ("Fritz") Mondale was crushed in the Nov. 6, 1984, election by incumbent U.S. Pres. Ronald Reagan (*q.v.*). Garnering just 41% of the popular vote, Mondale won only his home state of Minnesota and the District of Columbia for a total of 13 electoral votes. His defeat—the Democrats' fourth in five presidential elections—sparked speculation that the Democrats had become the nation's minority party.

Although he was never a particularly charismatic figure, Mondale prior to 1984 had suffered few significant setbacks in his political career. That career began in Minnesota, where Mondale (the name was americanized by his great grandfather from the Norwegian Mundal) was born on Jan. 5, 1928, the son of an impoverished farmer and Methodist minister. In 1946 he enrolled in Macalester College in

St. Paul, and the following year he organized student volunteers who assisted Hubert Humphrey, Orville Freeman, and Karl Rolvaag in excluding leftists from the newly created Democratic-Farmer-Labor Party. After campaigning for Humphrey in the 1948 senatorial contest, Mondale went to Washington as executive secretary of Students for Democratic Action. He returned to Minnesota in 1950, earned his B.A. from the University of Minnesota, and, after two years in the Army, obtained his law degree from the University of Minnesota Law School. In 1958 Freeman, now the governor, appointed Mondale special assistant to the state attorney general and two years later named him to fill the unexpired term of the state attorney general.

When Humphrey resigned from his Senate seat to run for the vice-presidency in 1964, Mondale again was the beneficiary of an unexpired term, this time in the U.S. Senate, where he consistently earned a high rating (90% or better) from the liberal Americans for Democratic Action. Minnesotans returned him to the Senate in 1966 and 1972. In 1976 Mondale aggressively sought the second spot on the ticket with Jimmy Carter, and from 1977 to 1981 he was perhaps the most powerful vice-president in history. It was in those years, however, that he acquired the reputation for being closely tied to special-interest groups prominent in the Democratic Party. Out of office as of January 1981, Mondale immediately began his quest for the 1984 nomination. He seemed to have it secured, but setbacks at the hands of Colorado Sen. Gary Hart (q.v.) early in 1984 created a fierce primary fight before Mondale garnered enough delegates to claim the nomination. A lifelong crusader for equal opportunity, Mondale put his principles into action when he selected Geraldine Ferraro (q.v.) as his running mate. However, except for a brief period after the first Mondale-Reagan TV debate, during which the president appeared tired and confused, polls showed the Mondale-Ferraro ticket slipping further and further behind. As he saw the inevitable landslide taking shape, Mondale largely abandoned his cautious speeches and spoke eloquently in behalf of the activist, compassionate government he had always championed. Within 24 hours of his humiliating defeat, he retired from American electoral politics.

(JEROLD L. KELLMAN)

Mulroney, Brian

When Brian Mulroney was elected leader of the Progressive Conservative Party of Canada in 1983, he was seen as a man who could win a federal election for the party and also make gains for it in the province of Quebec, a Liberal Party stronghold. He fulfilled both those expectations in the Canadian federal election of Sept. 4, 1984. The Conservatives won a parliamentary majority by one of the largest margins of victory in Canadian history, 211 of the 282 seats in the House of Commons. Mulroney had chosen to run in the Quebec riding (electoral district) of Manicouagan, which included his hometown of Baie Comeau. During the campaign he presented himself to the people of Quebec as a native son who understood the special problems of that province. Mulroney won his seat along with 57 other Conservatives in Que-

bec. In the previous Parliament a Conservative had held only one of Quebec's 75 seats. Mulroney became Canada's 18th prime minister when he was sworn in on Sept. 17, 1984.

In the election campaign Mulroney put the Conservatives in the centre of the political spectrum. He promised efficiency in government management and an improvement in economic conditions. The Canadian public, weary of 16 years of almost uninterrupted Liberal Party rule, rewarded his efforts with a landslide vote in his favour.

TANNENBAUM—SYGMA

Born on March 20, 1939, in Baie Comeau, Martin Brian Mulroney received his B.A. degree from St. Francis Xavier University in Antigonish, Nova Scotia. While there, he came under the political influence of Robert Stanfield, then premier of Nova Scotia and later leader of the Progressive Conservative Party of Canada. Back in Quebec, Mulroney received a law degree from Laval University in Quebec City. Then, as a successful labour lawyer in Montreal, he polished his proficiency as a skillful negotiator and an adept conciliator. Both these qualities stood him in good stead in his political aspirations. Mulroney remained a member of the Conservative Party in Quebec, even though Quebec was a province where that party was all but invisible. In his 25 years as a Conservative in Quebec, he did not run for elected office but instead concentrated on gaining control of the provincial party apparatus and headed a subsidiary of a U.S. mining company. He was a candidate for the leadership of the national party in 1976 and 1983, winning the post in the latter year.

(DIANE LOIS WAY)

Nakadai, Tatsuya

The hallmark of Tatsuya Nakadai's acting was versatility. It reached its high mark in Akira Kurosawa's 1980 film Kagemusha, in which the actor played two roles, one of a powerful feudal lord, the other of his craven double. It was the ability to act nearly every kind of role convincingly that set him apart from most modern Japanese actors.

Born Motohisa Nakadai on Dec. 13, 1932, in Tokyo, Nakadai went to the

Haiyuza actors' school at the age of 20. He was 22 when he made his debut in films, a walk-on part in Kurosawa's Shichinin no Samurai (Seven Samurai). His first big part came two years later in Umetsugu Inoue's Hinotori (Fire Bird). In 1958 Nakadai gave a superb performance in Kon Ichikawa's Enjo (Conflagration), in which he portrayed a demented young monk who sets fire to a Kyoto temple. The film was taken from Yukio Mishima's novel Kinkakuji (The Temple of the Golden Pavilion; 1958). Nakadai's reputation was then firmly established in the three-part series (1959–61) called Ningen no Joken (The Human Condition), directed by Masaki Kobayashi.

Japan's renowned critic Tadao Sato noted that Nakadai exemplified the rare actor who is able to portray both strength and tenderness. These talents were particularly apparent in The Human Condition, when he played a man of sensitivity who refuses to maltreat Chinese prisoners in Manchuria during World War II. As a result, he is sent to the most dangerous war fronts and, after detention in a Soviet prisoner-of-war camp, escapes only to die in the snowy wastes. "In adverse situations this strong, samurai-like man remembers his beautiful wife and, by calling out her name, is able to endure his suffering," Sato wrote. "Nakadai's performance was a revolutionary transformation of the traditional Confucian dictum that a noble man does not love a woman."

In Kagemusha, winner of the 1980 Cannes International Film Festival Gold Palm, Nakadai played a thief who is saved from execution only because he is the exact double of a warlord facing death. The thief is forced to assume the role of his fallen lord and in time acquires the traits of a bona fide leader. Other Nakadai vehicles were Kobayashi's Seppuku (Harakiri; 1962), Kaidan (Kwaidan; 1964), and Joiuchi (Rebellion; 1967), as well as the Kurosawa films Yojimbo (1961), Tsubaki Sanjuro (1962), and Tengoku to Jigoku (High and Low; 1963).

(JOHN RODERICK)

Natta, Alessandro

Highly regarded within the Italian Communist Party (PCI) but little known to the public, Alessandro Natta was chosen to succeed Enrico Berlinguer (see OBITUARIES), a party leader of international stature, on June 26, 1984. The 66-year-old Natta followed a man who had guided the party for 12 years when he died at the age of 62. Inevitably, he was seen as a stopgap candidate who would allow the party to groom a younger man. Natta, however, took office in the best Communist tradition. He showed no complexes, rolled up his sleeves, and got on with the job.

Overshadowed by Berlinguer's reputation and the wave of national mourning that followed his death, Natta came to power with two notable advantages. Only ten days before his selection, the party had beaten the Christian Democrats for the first time in a national poll—the elections to the European Parliament. Second, the party united behind him: 227 votes for, none against, and 11 abstentions. A man who had seemed to be moving toward retirement was leader of the biggest Communist party in the West, with 1,650,000 members and 11.6 million votes in the European elections.

Natta was born on Jan. 7, 1918, in the northern Italian town of Imperia in Liguria. He was one of six children, and his parents ran a butcher's shop. His cleverness carried him to the Scuola Normale in Pisa, where he took a degree in literature. He became an active anti-Fascist during his university studies, which lasted from 1936 to 1941. While serving as an artillery officer in the Italian Army, he was wounded in a clash with the Germans in the Aegean theatre and imprisoned in Germany. He joined the PCI in 1945, became a town councillor, entered the national Parliament in 1948, and eventually led the party group in the Chamber of Deputies and edited its weekly magazine, *Rinascita*. At the time of his election to the leadership, he was serving as president of the party's disciplinary body, the Central Control Commission.

Natta's academic background was reflected in a touch of pedantry: a liking for Latin tags and exhaustive explanations. His affable, communicative manner was combined with a reputation for firmness within the party. Always a strong supporter of Berlinguer's policies, he inherited his predecessor's quest for a left-wing alternative government and his icy relations with the Socialists, who had chosen a different formula by serving in a coalition with the Christian Democrats.   (CAMPBELL PAGE)

Nimeiry, Gaafar Muhammad

Gen. Gaafar Nimeiry's 15th year as Sudan's head of state was possibly the most difficult of his career, and speculation grew as to how much longer he might stay in office. His decision to introduce the *shari-'ah* (Islamic) laws by simple decree was popular among many devout Muslims, especially in the rural areas, but it strongly offended non-Muslim southerners and secular Muslim northerners, as well as many orthodox Muslims who disapproved of the manner in which the laws were imposed. Many southerners were further upset by his decision to divide their region into three provinces in a way they claimed abrogated the Addis Ababa (Eth.) agreement of 1972 that had ended the long civil war.

In 1984 parts of the south (especially in the Upper Nile Province, the location of the country's newfound oil potential) were again in revolt. Foreign oil companies and other firms refused to continue to work because of the security risks. Nimeiry's long-standing personal foe, Libya's Col. Muammar al-Qaddafi, promised support to the military challenge to Nimeiry. His two major allies, Egypt and the U.S., showed concern about the trend of his policies at a time when the country's economy was already in deep trouble. Nimeiry's ill health was another source of concern.

Gaafar Nimeiry was born in Omdurman on Jan. 1, 1930. He studied in Koranic schools and was involved in student demonstrations from an early age. After three years in the Military College at Khartoum, he graduated as a lieutenant in 1952. Over the next 20 years he was continuously in trouble because of his associations with the clandestine Young Officers' Movement and his alleged involvement in several attempted coups. Finally, on May 25, 1969, he led a successful military coup

and became head of state as chairman of a Revolutionary Council. At first his regime was oriented to the Soviet bloc, but his policies changed after an abortive Communist coup in July 1971. He then entered into a close alliance with Egypt and the U.S. and resumed Sudan's traditional ties with Britain. He was elected president in a plebiscite in October 1971 and had his mandate renewed in 1977 and 1983. As a younger officer Nimeiry was not particularly known for his attachment to Islam, but he became increasingly drawn to Muslim fundamentalism in the late 1970s and risked plunging his country into a new period of turmoil by declaring Sudan to be an Islamic republic in 1983.

(COLIN LEGUM)

O'Connor, John Joseph

In 27 years as a U.S. naval chaplain, rising to the rank of rear admiral and chief of military chaplains, John J. O'Connor was largely remote from the doctrinal arguments swirling among Roman Catholics in the aftermath of the second Vatican Council. But during the 1984 presidential campaign, following his surprise appointment on January 31 as archbishop of New York, his blunt pronouncements rapidly made him a central and controversial figure.

"I don't see how a Catholic in good conscience can vote for a candidate who explicitly supports abortion," he said in June. That touched off an open battle with two prominent New York Democrats, Gov. Mario Cuomo and the vice-presidential candidate, Rep. Geraldine Ferraro (*qq.v.*), both of whom, as Catholics, had declared personal opposition to abortion but supported freedom of choice for others.

Then O'Connor enraged Jewish leaders by comparing abortion, "the killing of 4,000 babies a day in the United States, unborn babies, to the [Nazi] Holocaust." And he offended New York's homosexual community by fighting a city order that forbade agencies, *e.g.*, the church, having municipal contracts from discriminating against homosexuals in hiring.

In these and other comments the craggy-faced prelate bespoke a conservative church tradition reflected in the con-

victions of Pope John Paul II as well as in a broad strain of current U.S. political thought.

O'Connor was born on Jan. 15, 1920, in Philadelphia. He was ordained a priest in 1945 and entered the Chaplains Corps of the U.S. Navy in 1952. He saw service in both the Korean and Vietnam wars, advanced steadily in naval rank, and became senior chaplain at the U.S. Naval Academy. He rose in the hierarchy of the church as well, being named monsignor in 1966 and bishop in 1979. By then he was vicar general of the Military Vicariate.

Thus O'Connor's views were shaped in an overwhelmingly male society, both as a priest and in his naval career. He described the Vietnam war as a just war but wrote touchingly of his anguish at the sight of death. He took time out during those years to obtain advanced degrees in clinical psychology and political science, earning M.A.'s from St. Charles College and Catholic University of America and a Ph.D. at Georgetown University in 1970.

O'Connor was elevated to the New York post after a few months as bishop of Scranton, Pa. Late in 1984, echoing a pastoral letter by the nation's Catholic bishops, he said that his archdiocese would mount a "massive effort" to provide housing and food for the needy.   (JAMES L. YEUNGER)

Ozal, Turgut

Turgut Ozal became the 46th prime minister of Turkey after the victory of his recently formed Motherland Party in the general elections held Nov. 6, 1983, and took office on December 13. He came from a provincial, culturally conservative background, but this cultural conservatism was combined with political and economic liberalism. It was a combination often found among Turks born outside the secularized elite that ruled Turkey after the foundation of the republic in 1923.

Ozal was born in the eastern Turkish city of Malatya in 1927 and graduated as an electrical engineer from the Istanbul Technical University in 1950. Sent to the U.S. to specialize in engineering economics, he returned to join the small group of specialists put in charge of Turkey's rapid development program. As deputy director general of the Electrical Works Study Board, he drew up projects for a number of major hydroelectric installations. After the first military coup in 1960, Ozal helped found the new State Planning Organization (SPO) and also taught at the Middle East Technical University in Ankara. He worked on a number of major utility projects, including the Bosporus Bridge, and served as undersecretary of the SPO from 1967 to 1971.

Unlike the socialist planners who at first dominated the SPO, Ozal championed private enterprise within the national plan. In the 1970s, as the feud between right and left intensified, he found employment in the private sector. He sympathized with the National Salvation Party, of Islamic fundamentalist inspiration, but returned to the civil service under Suleyman Demirel, leader of the centrist Justice Party, in the latter's minority government late in 1979. As undersecretary to the prime minister and, once again, head of the SPO, Ozal devised and implemented a major program liberalizing the Turkish economy.

After the military takeover in September 1980, Ozal was made deputy prime minister in charge of the economy and given a free hand to push his program. He succeeded in slashing inflation, increasing exports, and restoring his country's creditworthiness, but he clashed with the ruling generals when his monetarist stance led to soaring interest rates and the bankruptcy of a major finance house. Resigning in 1982, he founded the Motherland Party the following year. Working within the framework established by the military but without their favour, he led the party to victory in the elections that inaugurated a return to civilian parliamentary rule.

(ANDREW MANGO)

Pastora Gómez, Edén

Nicaraguan guerrilla leader Edén Pastora Gómez was injured on May 30, 1984, in a bombing inside his encampment that killed seven people, including two journalists, and wounded 27 others. By the year's end the charismatic rebel had lost the leadership position of his rebel army.

In April Pastora and his troops in the Democratic Revolutionary Alliance (ARDE) had captured the Atlantic coast town of San Juan del Norte. Six days later Nicaraguan government forces regained control, and Pastora and his men melted back into the jungle. In June he was among rebel leaders tried in absentia; he was barred from any part in the November 4 election. By October the 47-year-old *contra* had been ejected as co-leader of ARDE, banned from his Costa Rican political base, and cut off from the U.S. aid sent to ARDE.

His problems stemmed from his refusal to ally with the larger, better outfitted rebel force along the Honduran border, the Nicaraguan Democratic Front (FDN). Pastora vowed not to consider such an alliance until the FDN purged itself of leaders who had been officers in the National Guard of deposed dictator Anastasio Somoza Debayle.

Pastora's obstinacy was rooted in his past. Born Jan. 22, 1937, in the northern Nicaraguan town of Dario, Edén was seven when his father was murdered by a Somoza guardsman in a dispute over land. Pastora did not forget. He was sent with the family's savings to Centro América high school in Granada, considered Nicaragua's best; he then studied medicine in Mexico. After three years he returned to Nicaragua as an anti-Somoza revolutionary.

His position remained unchallenged as mastermind and leader of the takeover of the National Palace on Aug. 22, 1978, an event Pastora—as Comandante Cero—was not expected to survive. Instead, the daring triumph galvanized Nicaragua and prepared the nation for the possibility that Somoza could be overthrown, as he was July 19, 1979; the raid had made Pastora a folk hero.

But on April 5, 1981, saying he was disenchanted with their increasing reliance on the Soviet Union and Cuba, Pastora left the Sandinistas and retreated into Costa Rica. Official government newspapers called him a "traitor." He began to amass troops into an army he named the Sandino Revolutionary Front, "the true Sandinistas," and led them into Nicaragua on sporadic raids. The Front was dissolved the next year to form ARDE. (SUSAN K. NELSON)

Peres, Shimon

When Shimon Peres presented his National Unity government to Pres. Chaim Herzog on Sept. 14, 1984, Israel's new prime minister also presented his country with both a personal and a constitutional innovation. Peres belonged to a generation and a breed that the great majority of Israelis did not know and did not fully understand. He had suffered from this incomprehension throughout his political life. Because he was not a populist politician like Levi Eshkol, Golda Meir, or Menachem Begin, he was suspect; because he was essentially a pragmatist his critics labeled him as unprincipled and ambitious. His close associates and those who had dealings with him, however, knew differently and trusted him as they would few others.

Peres was born on Aug. 1, 1923, in Vishneva, Poland, in a very small but intensely Zionist community of fewer than 200 Jewish families. In 1934 he followed his father to Palestine, where he underwent the customary Zionist youth training. He joined Haganah in 1947, then in 1948 went into the Navy Department of Israel's Ministry of Defense. There he came to the attention of Prime Minister David Ben-Gurion, who made him head of the department. In 1952 Ben-Gurion, who doubled as defense minister, appointed Peres as deputy director general of the Ministry of Defense with a brief to reorganize and modernize the Israel Defense Forces (IDF). Prior to this, Ben-Gurion had sent Peres to the U.S. as head of the Israeli defense mission there and for some intensive study at New York and Harvard universities. At the end of 1952 Peres became director general of the Ministry of Defense. The ministry and the IDF were ready when Israel drove Egypt from the Sinai Peninsula in 1956.

In 1959 Ben-Gurion appointed Peres deputy defense minister, a position he continued to hold under Ben-Gurion's successor, Levi Eshkol, until 1965. He then resigned to become secretary-general of the Rafi Party, formed by Ben-Gurion as a breakaway from the official Labour Party. Although not a member of the government, Peres was a principal architect of the national coalition that fought the Six-Day War in 1967. He rejoined the Labour Party in 1968 and became minister for the administered areas (the West Bank and Gaza) in the following year. In 1974 he was appointed defense minister under Yitzhak Rabin and, after Rabin's resignation in April 1977, acting prime minister. After the election of May 1977 brought Begin's Likud Party to power, he was leader of the opposition. (JON KIMCHE)

Reagan, Ronald Wilson

It was ironic that Ronald Reagan's landslide victory for president of the United States on Nov. 6, 1984, with 525 of 538 possible votes in the Electoral College, broke the record for total electoral votes that had been held since 1936 by Franklin D. Roosevelt. Roosevelt's riveting speeches had been a model for Reagan, a registered Democrat until 1962, and Reagan quoted him as well as Democratic presidents John F. Kennedy and Harry Truman in the campaign, despite his near-dismantling of many domestic programs envisioned by those men and their successors.

This use of historical figures was but one aspect of a campaign style that presented a kaleidoscope of "positive pictures" of an unflaggingly optimistic Reagan celebrating patriotism, opportunity, confidence, and hope. Under the banner of "Leadership That's Working," Reagan's speeches were simple messages that ignored issues such as the arms race, a massive federal debt, and unrest in Central America and avoided revealing any concrete plans for a second term. Instead, in his resonant, reassuring voice, the president told cheering audiences that the "U.S. was never meant to be a second-best nation" and that under him it had become a "giant, economically and militarily." His earnest, friendly persistence inspired national pride that had been dormant since the 1950s and that had long been déclassé in Democratic campaigns.

Reagan ran as both a "Mr. Nice Tough Guy" and an amiable Uncle Sam. His overwhelmingly white supporters—who ranged from schoolchildren to the elderly, from fundamentalist Christians to young urban professionals—echoed Reagan's view that Walter F. Mondale (q.v.), his Democratic opponent, was tied to "politics of the past."

When Reagan began to make regular campaign appearances, they were flawlessly managed by advance teams that ensured flattering lighting, good sound systems, an exact shade of blue for backdrops, and thousands of supporters and balloons. From his nomination in late August to the election, Reagan refused to answer questions from reporters on the road or to hold a news conference. But the people were listening to him and not to his opponent, even more so after Mondale announced his plan for a tax increase to offset deficits.

The only voting groups that did not support Reagan significantly were blacks, Jewish men, Hispanics, and those with incomes under $12,500.

Only twice, in televised debates with Mondale, did Reagan appear in territory outside his staff's protective control. In the first, on domestic policy, held October 7, Reagan faltered and looked pale. His commanding lead in the polls dropped, and his age, 73, first became an issue. In the second debate, on foreign policy, on October 21, he was asked about his age and deadpanned: "I will not make age an issue of this campaign. I am not going to exploit for political purposes my opponent's youth and political inexperience." He appeared more sure of himself in the second debate and recovered much of his earlier loss in the polls.

Born in Tampico, Ill., on Feb. 6, 1911, Reagan began a long career as a motion picture actor in 1937. He served as governor of California from 1967 to 1975 and was first elected president in 1980.

(SUSAN K. NELSON)

Retton, Mary Lou

Mary Lou Retton, the 16-year-old gymnast with size three shoes, vaulted over a padded horse and into a country's hearts in 1984 when she won the all-around gold medal in her sport at the Olympic Games in Los Angeles on August 30. Besides endearing herself to a nation, she shook up the gymnastics world, which had featured daintiness over athleticism.

Retton, at 4 ft 9 in and 94 lb, is unusually stocky for a gymnast, with strong legs catapulting her through routines that are powerful instead of delicate. On a typical vault she soars 14 ft. While other female gymnasts twist once with a single somersault, Retton is in the air long enough for a double twist and a 1¹/₂ back layout somersault.

She was born Jan. 24, 1968, in Fairmont, W.Va. Acrobatics classes at dancing school sparked her interest and she began attending gymnastics school at the age of seven. To prepare for the Olympics, Retton left home in early 1983 to train in Houston, Texas, with Bela Karolyi, who had defected from Romania two years earlier. Karolyi had coached 1976 Olympic sensation Nadia Comaneci.

Retton was still unknown among international gymnasts when she went to the 1983 American Cup as a substitute for an injured competitor. There she won gold medals in the vault, the floor exercises, and the all-around and tied for first on the uneven parallel bars, scoring 9.9 or better in six of eight events.

She was undefeated in the all-around through six international meets in 1984 and won the national 1984 all-around championship with perfect scores of 10 on the floor exercises and the vault. But six weeks before the Olympics, torn cartilage locked her right knee, and doctors expected her to miss the Games. Retton disagreed. She was in the gymnasium the day after her arthroscopic surgery.

No U.S. woman had ever before won an individual medal in Olympic gymnastics. Retton won four—a silver in the vault and bronzes in the uneven parallel bars and the floor exercises in addition to her gold in the all-around—and helped the U.S. women to a team silver medal as well.

(KEVIN M. LAMB)

Romanov, Grigory Vasilyevich

After Mikhail Gorbachev (q.v.), many Western Kremlinologists saw Grigory Romanov as the next most likely successor to Konstantin Chernenko (q.v.) as head of the Soviet leadership. A party boss in Leningrad from 1962, Romanov had become a candidate member of the Politburo in 1973 and a full member in 1976. After Yury Andropov (see OBITUARIES) succeeded Leonid Brezhnev in November 1982 as general secretary of the Communist Party of the Soviet Union (CPSU), Romanov in June 1983 became a secretary of the party's Central Committee (CC). Only Andropov, Chernenko, Gorbachev, and Romanov were both Politburo and CC members.

Although Romanov at 61 was one of the six Politburo members under the age of 70, he was a hard-liner in his attitude toward the West and so could be counted on to vote with those over 70, who formed the majority. This might give him an advantage over Gorbachev, generally believed to have a more flexible attitude. On the other hand, Romanov's personality might work against him; he had the reputation of being primitive, boorish, and arrogant.

Romanov emerged as a front-runner on Nov. 5, 1983, when he was chosen to make the keynote speech in celebration of the 66th anniversary of the "Great October Socialist Revolution." In a verbose oration that filled two pages of Pravda, he accused the West of unleashing a new cold war and proclaimed that "the imperialist circles will never establish their military supremacy over the U.S.S.R." In September 1984 Romanov was sent to Addis Ababa to represent the U.S.S.R. at the inauguration of the Workers' Party of Ethiopia. In his speech there he blamed the November 1983 collapse of the Geneva arms talks on the U.S. and accused Washington of aggravating world tensions. He promised Soviet military and other aid to the Ethiopian regime.

Romanov, the son of a peasant, was born on Feb. 7, 1923, at Zikhnovo, in the Borovichi district of Novgorod oblast (administrative region). He went to school in Leningrad and then became a student at the Shipbuilding Institute there. He graduated after serving in the Red Army during World War II and in 1946 started working as a designer in a shipyard. A member of the CPSU from 1944, in 1961 he was elected secretary of the Leningrad City Committee, and a year later Nikita Khrushchev made him secretary of the Leningrad region party organization.

(K. M. SMOGORZEWSKI)

Sakharov, Andrey Dmitriyevich

The health and whereabouts of exiled Soviet physicist and human rights activist Andrey Sakharov became a mystery in 1984. On May 2 the 63-year-old father of the Soviet Union's hydrogen bomb and a founder of the Committee for Human Rights started a hunger strike. Its purpose was to gain medical treatment abroad for his wife, 61-year-old pediatrician Yelena Bonner. A 17-day fast in 1981 by both Sakharovs had resulted in an exit visa for Bonner's daughter-in-law.

But 1984 was different. Western European leaders interceded on their behalf; Pope John Paul II called for prayers; the U.S. Congress passed a resolution favouring their emigration. By summer, however, sketchy, contradictory reports indicated that Sakharov had been moved from the couple's apartment in the industrial city of Gorky, possibly to a hospital for psychiatric "treatment." News was also meagre about Bonner. A Soviet-made videotape showed both appearing well, if seldom together. Reports late in the year indicated that Bonner had been sentenced to five years of internal exile for anti-Soviet slander.

Sakharov had written of Bonner's deteriorating heart condition as well as increasingly harsh Soviet treatment of her in "A Letter to My Scientific Colleagues," published March 1 in the New York Review of Books. The previous year, in a letter to a U.S. physicist, Sakharov expressed his views on the current nuclear arms buildup; although supportive of an eventual arms reduction, he wrote of the present need for "strategic parity" in order for the West to be able to bargain competitively with the Soviets.

Sakharov was born May 21, 1921, in Moscow. He graduated from Moscow State University in 1942 and went to work in a munitions factory. In 1953 his work and that of other Soviet scientists culminated in the detonation of the Soviet Union's first hydrogen bomb. Honours and luxuries were bestowed on him, but soon he began to speak out against additional tests in the atmosphere because of the radioactive fallout and long-term genetic damage they could cause. He was warned not to meddle in "political" decisions but continued his protests.

Hailed as a visionary and a man of peace abroad, Sakharov was reviled and demoted at home. After his first wife died in the late 1960s, he devoted himself to helping victims of Soviet injustices. In 1975 he won the Nobel Prize for Peace. Angry Soviet officials denied him a visa, and so Bonner read his speech and accepted his award in Norway. Undaunted, Sakharov continued to speak out. In 1980 his criticism of the Soviet invasion of Afghanistan resulted in exile to Gorky.

(SUSAN K. NELSON)

Santmyer, Helen Hooven

After more than 50 years of work on a 1,176-page novel about life in small-town Ohio, 89-year-old Helen Hooven Santmyer watched from her nursing home residence as her book was made a main selection of the Book-of-the-Month Club in 1984 and given a 150,000-copy first printing. The novel, entitled . . . And Ladies of the Club, was originally published by the Ohio State University Press in 1982 but sold only a few hundred copies. However, some persevering and well-connected fans directed the book toward a receptive literary agent and new publisher (Putnam), both of whom saw possibilities for success. Early in 1984, therefore, a novel written in longhand in a bookkeeper's ledger over a period of half a century was finally brought to the attention of the American public.

Helen Hooven Santmyer was born on Nov. 25, 1895, in Xenia, Ohio. She graduated from Wellesley (Mass.) College, worked in New York City as a secretary for the editor of Scribner's Magazine, received a bachelor of letters degree from the University of Oxford, and then in 1929 returned to Xenia. Two of her novels were published by Houghton Mifflin during the 1920s.

Santmyer was dean of women and head of the English department of Cedarville (Ohio) College from 1935 to 1953 and after that worked in Dayton, Ohio, as a reference librarian. In 1963 a book of her reminiscences, Ohio Town, was published.

. . . And Ladies of the Club was begun in the late 1920s as a contradiction to Sinclair Lewis's Main Street, a devastating 1920 satire of small-town America. Santmyer's book covers the years 1868–1932 and refers in its title to members of the local literary club. It is through the lives of these women that the social, political, and cultural changes of the Ohio town of Waynesboro are described and defended.

During the years between publication of Ohio Town and her first-time admission into a nursing home in 1976, Santmyer completed the work on her novel and submitted it in 11 boxes to her editor at Ohio State. She responded to the editor's requests to trim the manuscript by dictating the changes from her bed to an old friend who resided in a nearby room in Xenia's Hospitality Home East. Although Santmyer resided temporarily in the nursing home for seven years, she moved there permanently in April 1983, suffering from emphysema.

(BONNIE OBERMAN)

Sauvé, Jeanne

From the time she entered politics, Jeanne Sauvé demonstrated her leadership abilities. After her election to the Canadian House of Commons in 1972, she was appointed a member of the Cabinet as the minister of state in charge of science and technology. Thus she became the first Quebec woman to serve in the federal Cabinet. Eight years later the first order of business when Parliament convened on April 14, 1980, was the election of Jeanne Sauvé as the first woman speaker of the House. On Dec. 23, 1983, she was appointed the 23rd governor-general of Canada, the first woman to be so honoured.

As representative of Queen Elizabeth II in Canada, the governor-general was expected to open and close Parliament, sign proclamations and Cabinet orders, receive credentials of foreign ambassadors, and invest Canadian citizens with the Order of Canada. Illness forced Sauvé to postpone assumption of the position until May 1984, but she quickly made up for lost time. During the next six months she wel-

PAUL CHIASSON

comed the queen and Pope John Paul II to Canada, swore in two prime ministers, and opened a new Parliament.

The governor-general was born Jeanne Mathilde Benôit on April 26, 1922, in Prud'Homme, Sask.; however, she grew up in Ottawa. She attended the Université d'Ottawa before marrying Maurice Sauvé in Montreal on Sept. 24, 1948. The couple moved to London and then to Paris, where both studied at the University of Paris. Jeanne Sauvé received a diploma in French civilization in 1951. When they returned to Montreal in 1952, she began a career as a free-lance journalist and broadcaster. From 1952 to 1972 she worked as an interviewer and commentator for the Canadian Broadcasting Corporation French-language network and contributed articles to the *Montreal Star.*

Maurice Sauvé was a member of Parliament from 1962 to 1968. At his urging, Jeanne entered politics in 1972. She represented first the Montreal riding (electoral district) of Ahuntsic (1972–79) and then the Quebec riding of Laval-des-Rapides (1979–84). A member of the federal Cabinet from 1972 until elected speaker of the House in 1980, she served as minister of state in charge of science and technology

(1972–74), minister of the environment (1974–75), and minister of communications (1975–79). She then assumed the role of adviser to the secretary of state for external affairs (1978–80).

(DIANE LOIS WAY)

Scargill, Arthur

President of the National Union of Mineworkers (NUM) and the key figure in the miners' strike that was the leading issue in British domestic politics during 1984, Arthur Scargill was a rebel from an early age. He became a miner at Woolley, ten miles from his home village of Worsborough, on the outskirts of Barnsley, South Yorkshire, at the age of 15 in 1953. He was soon making trouble for both the union leadership and the management. He was recruited by the Communist Party's youth movement but at the end of the 1950s left and joined the Labour Party. The reasons for his defection seemingly had more to do with his own need for freedom of political action as a trade union militant than with revulsion against Stalinism or the repression in Hungary.

Scargill first became a national celebrity while he was still no more than a minor part-time union official. He had been active in local unofficial disputes in the Yorkshire coalfield in 1969 and 1970 and experimented with the flying pickets that were shortly to become famous. When the NUM called an official strike in 1972, he pressed for his tactics to be employed nationally against ports, power stations, and depots. NUM headquarters in London asked him to lead a picket of 200 miners against the Saltley Coke Depot in Birmingham. By the fifth day Scargill had mustered a force of 10,000. The police withdrew, and Scargill proclaimed "the greatest victory of the working class in my lifetime."

That year he worked his last shift at the colliery, and in 1973 he became the youngest person ever to be president of the Yorkshire miners. His organizational skills and presentational flair made him an effective champion. "We want jam today and jam tomorrow" was a typical Scargillism, indicating his attitude that nothing was too good for the miner. His reputation ensured his succession to the national presidency of the NUM when Joe Gormley stepped down in 1982.

Scargill moved the NUM headquarters from London to Sheffield and, impatient and bored with the Trades Union Congress, withdrew from its General Council. Two attempts to lead the NUM out on strike were voted down by the miners in pithead ballots, but in 1984, this time without a ballot, Scargill succeeded in launching a national work stoppage, although it was not observed in the Nottinghamshire coalfield and in some other localities. He hoped to achieve another Saltley, using the same sometimes violent mass picketing, but this time the forces of the state were better prepared.

(PETER JENKINS)

Senghor, Léopold Sédar

Léopold Sédar Senghor was received into the French Academy on March 29, 1984. His election to the company of the "40 immortals," on June 19, 1983, was among the supreme moments in a brilliant literary career which, at the same time, expressed a paradox of history. An exponent

of black consciousness and leader in the struggle against French colonialism, Senghor wrote in the language and the tradition of Baudelaire and Claudel. Underlying the life's work of this poet-statesman, for 20 years president of Senegal, was the urge to show Europe and Africa the riches that, as equals, they had to offer one another.

Born on Oct. 9, 1906, in the village of Joal, Senegal, the son of a merchant, Senghor was educated at mission school, then in a Catholic seminary. He won a scholarship to study in Paris, obtained the *licence-ès-lettres,* and wrote a thesis on Baudelaire while associating with the African writers of the *négritude* movement (notably Aimé Césaire) and the Americans of the Negro Renaissance. In 1935, the first African to pass the *agrégation,* he became a teacher. Taken prisoner in World War II, he was elected to the Constituent Assembly in 1945 and served as deputy from Senegal to the National Assembly until 1958. His first poems, *Chants d'ombre* (1945), celebrated the beauty of blackness and the "deep pulse of Africa." In *Hosties noires* (1948) he explored the fundamental unity of Africans and Europeans in the struggle against oppression, while *Éthiopiques* (1956) was set in a Senghorian symbolic universe with its roots in his village childhood, contrasted with the spiritual emptiness of urban Paris and New York City.

Appointed *ministre-conseiller* by Gen. Charles de Gaulle in 1958, Senghor led the Mali Federation (of Senegal and Soudan) and became president of Senegal when the federation was dissolved in 1960. As leader of his country and of the Union Progressiste Sénégalaise (later the Parti Socialiste

AGIP/PICTORIAL PARADE

Sénégalais), he was not without critics of his moderation or his Socialism. He continued to write and encouraged meetings of African writers. His collected poems appeared in 1977, and he received many honours for his literary work. He retired from the presidency in 1980. The symbolism of black and white, night and day, woman and man, and the need to reconcile these opposites, was the motive force of Senghor's poetry, as of his politics: "for how can one live, except in the Other . . . ?" he asked in a lyric for his French wife, Colette Hubert.

(ROBIN BUSS)

Seuss, Dr.

Theodor Seuss Geisel, popularly known by the pseudonym Dr. Seuss, celebrated his 80th birthday in March 1984 and his award of a Pulitzer Prize in April. He was acknowledged in the special citation by the Pulitzer committee for having contributed for nearly half a century to the education and reading enjoyment of countless American children.

Born March 2, 1904, in Springfield, Mass., Geisel attended the public schools there. In 1921 he entered Dartmouth College, where he was editor of a humour magazine that used many of his stories and illustrations. After graduation he began his career in 1927 as an advertising illustrator.

During the next ten years Geisel's cartoons appeared in such well-known magazines as *Life, Vanity Fair, Redbook,* and *The Saturday Evening Post.* His first children's book, *And to Think that I Saw It on Mulberry Street,* was published by Vanguard Press in 1937 after having been rejected by 27 other publishers. With it he began an extremely successful career of publishing children's books containing silly creatures and wonderful rhymes that would encourage literally millions of children throughout the world to like reading.

From 1943 to 1946 Geisel served in the U.S. Army Signal Corps and Information and Educational Division. He received the Legion of Merit for his educational films and in 1946 won his first Academy Award for the best documentary short subject, *Hitler Lives.* Two more Academy Awards followed in 1947 and 1951. In 1955, 30 years after his graduation, Dartmouth conferred upon him an honorary degree, citing his contributions to the world of children's books.

The year 1957 was a turning point for Geisel. *The Cat in the Hat,* published simultaneously by Random House and as a reading textbook by Houghton Mifflin, led to the formation within Random House of Beginner Books, of which Geisel became president. *How the Grinch Stole Christmas* was also published in 1957 and in 1971 won the Peabody Award for a television animated cartoon.

By the mid-1970s Geisel, as Dr. Seuss, had become universally known. His books had been translated into 17 languages, and more than 70 million copies had been sold. (By 1984 that number exceeded 100 million.) The 1984 Pulitzer Prize was the culmination of a career devoted to teaching children the joys of reading.

(BONNIE OBERMAN)

Severin, Giles Timothy

In 1984 Tim Severin, British writer, historian, and, above all, adventurer, undertook what he considered to be his most ambitious project to date—a reconstruction of the legendary voyage of Jason and the Argonauts in search of the Golden Fleece. The story of Jason describes his voyage from Iolcos (now Volos on the east coast of mainland Greece) to Colchis, at the extreme eastern end of the Black Sea (now in Georgia, U.S.S.R.). Severin's first task was to construct a replica of Jason's galley, the "Argo." The modern craft was built entirely of pine and used wooden pegs instead of nails to secure the planks. The modern-day Argonauts set off in May and

in 100 days successfully retraced the legendary route, by way of the Aegean Sea, the Dardanelles, the Sea of Marmara, the narrow and treacherous entrance to the Black Sea at the Bosporus, and the entire length of the Black Sea itself.

Severin's purpose was to test the factual basis of the legend by determining whether or not a 20-oar open galley could withstand the currents in the Bosporus and so penetrate the Black Sea. Previously, it had been assumed that ships built before the 5th or 6th century BC would not have been powerful enough to make the voyage. It was an area of research in which Severin had already made his mark.

Severin was born on Sept. 25, 1940, in Assam, India, and educated at the University of Oxford, where he studied geography and wrote a thesis on medieval Asian exploration. In his earliest expeditions he traced Marco Polo's journey on a motorcycle and explored the Mississippi River by canoe. His most celebrated adventure was to cross the Atlantic Ocean in a hand-stitched leather boat in 1977; the objective was to demonstrate the possibility that St. Brendan, the Irish monk, could have discovered America almost ten centuries before Columbus. In 1980–81 he reconstructed the fictional travels of Sindbad the Sailor from Oman to China. His accounts of *The Brendan Voyage* (1978) and *The Sindbad Voyage* (1982) were highly successful.

In re-creating Jason's voyage Severin fulfilled a long-held ambition, one for which he regarded his earlier exploits as preparations. His next scheme was to follow the wanderings of Odysseus as he returned home from Troy.   (LOUISE WATSON)

Sokolov, Sergey Leonidovich

After a flurry of mistaken speculation that Grigory V. Romanov (*q.v.*) would succeed Marshal Dmitry F. Ustinov (*see* OBITUARIES) as defense minister of the Soviet Union, Sergey Sokolov, first deputy minister of defense, was named to that sensitive post on Dec. 22, 1984. Regarded by members of the Politburo as probably the safest choice for the position, Sokolov, at the age of 73, was viewed as a tractable personality who would not disturb the delicate balance within the Communist Party leadership. His appointment also restored the tradition of naming a military man to the post, a custom that was broken in 1976 when Ustinov, a party technocrat, was appointed defense minister.

Sergey Leonidovich Sokolov was born on July 1, 1911, at Yevpatoriya, in the Crimea. The son of a white-collar worker, Sokolov briefly worked as a food packer before joining the Army in 1932. Two years later he became a member of the tank corps in the Far East, and in 1937 he joined the Communist Party.

During a 50-year military career Sokolov served in the Far East as commander of a special battalion of tank troops and in Europe as chief commander of the tank and mechanized troops of the 32nd Army. He survived Stalin's purges of the Red Army and steadily rose through the military ranks; his specialized training in tanks and mechanized armour at military academies, including the General Staff College, was regarded as an attractive asset to his career. In 1960 Sokolov was named chief

of the Moscow military district, and four years later he was made first deputy commander of the Leningrad military district. In 1965 he was made commander of the district, with the rank of colonel. As longtime deputy minister of defense (1967–84) Sokolov made at least 23 trips abroad, presumably to sell Soviet arms to the third world, and from 1979 he was believed to have overseen the Soviet offensive in Afghanistan.

Sokolov was not expected, as defense minister, to make any changes in Soviet military policy, but he was expected to lobby for increased military spending. The professional soldier was made a marshal of the Soviet Union in 1978.

(KAREN JUSTIN)

Swearingen, John Eldred, Jr.

On July 26, 1984, John Swearingen, a chemical engineer who had retired from the Standard Oil Co. of Indiana (Indiana Standard), was appointed—effective August 13—chairman of the board and chief executive officer of the Continental Illinois Corp. (CI), a major bank holding company. The appointment was without precedent in that it was made by William M. Isaac, chairman of the board of the Federal Deposit Insurance Corporation (FDIC).

On May 17 the FDIC had lent $1.5 billion to CI's key subsidiary, the Continental Illinois National Bank and Trust Co. of Chicago (CINB), which faced bankruptcy because for 90 days or more it had received no payments on $2.3 billion in outstanding loans—many of them bought from the defunct Penn Square Bank of Oklahoma City. Isaac also had guaranteed all of CINB's deposits—including amounts above the FDIC's official limit of $100,000.

By late July it was obvious that CINB was still in trouble. Isaac accepted the resignations of the officers and directors of CI and CINB and named Swearingen chairman of the board of CI. The FDIC offered to buy $4.5 billion of CINB's bad loans for $3.5 billion, with the bank taking a $1 billion loss, provided that CI stockholders would agree that their interest would be only 20% of CI. The FDIC would own the remaining 80%. In addition, the FDIC gave CINB another $1 billion. If collections on the loans should be less than $2.7 billion, the FDIC would get the rest of CI. On September 26 the stockholders approved, and Swearingen warned them that they might lose their 20%. Observers agreed, but most thought that Swearingen could save CI if anyone could.

Son of a blind man who was a successful school administrator, John Swearingen, Jr., was born in Columbia, S.C., on Sept. 7, 1918. After receiving a B.S. degree in chemical engineering from the University of South Carolina in 1938 and an M.S. from Carnegie Institute of Technology in 1939, he became a chemical engineer at Indiana Standard's laboratory in Whiting, Ind.

Indiana Standard, although incorporated in Indiana, has its headquarters in Chicago. Swearingen was transferred to that city to become the company's general manager of production in 1951. He became a director in 1952, vice-president in 1954, executive vice-president in 1956, and president in 1958. As president, chief executive officer from 1960, and chairman of the board from 1965, he promoted exploration and greatly increased Indiana Standard's control of its own crude oil. He also diversified the company into roadside restaurants and insurance, policies that proved highly beneficial during the shortages and embargoes of oil in the 1970s. He retired from Indiana Standard in September 1983.

(CHARLES JOHNSON TAGGART)

Takamiyama

The hour no great athlete likes to face arrived for Jesse Kuhaulua in May 1984. With tears in his eyes, he announced his retirement after 20 extraordinary years in the sumo ring. Retirement came just one month before his 40th birthday, which he had hoped to celebrate as an active *rikishi.* Kuhaulua's sadness was shared by millions of Japanese fans who knew him by his professional name of Takamiyama (High View Mountain) or, more affectionately, simply as Jesse. The 195-kg (429-lb) Takamiyama was one of the few non-Japanese to succeed in the sport of the ancient samurai, even though he never attained either of the two highest ranks. His popularity was partly due, some said, to the fact that his skills never quite matched those of the Japanese grand champions. Takamiyama captivated the Japanese not only by his unexpected successes in a purely Japanese spectacle but by his gravelly voice, his upturned eyebrows in victory, and his demonstrative unhappiness in defeat. All this contrasted with the impassivity of his fellow wrestlers. A man of wit and good humour, he appeared in playful roles on television, advertising everything from slumber suits to electronics.

Jesse Kuhaulua was born in Hawaii on June 16, 1944. He attended high school in Maui, where he took up sumo to strengthen his legs for football. In 1964 he went to Japan, a comparatively scrawny 115 kg (253 lb). During his career he set nearly every record for longevity, and in 1972 he became the first non-Japanese to win a 15-day tournament and the Emperor's Cup. On 12 occasions he defeated grand champions. Takamiyama married a Japanese and in 1980 became a Japanese citizen, a necessary qualification for running a stable of wrestlers in his retirement. His protégé, a barrel-shaped 20-year-old Hawaiian, was named Salevaa Atisone but wrestled as Konishiki. Jesse believed the 210-kg (462-lb) giant would become what he himself always wanted to be: a *yokozuna,* or grand champion. (JOHN RODERICK)

Tarkovsky, Andrey Arsenyevich

While in Milan, Italy, the celebrated Soviet film director Andrey Tarkovsky announced on July 10, 1984, his decision not to return to the U.S.S.R., thereby joining the growing group of outstanding Soviet artists and intellectuals in exile. Until the last moment he had intended simply to throw out a challenge to his country's authorities by demanding publicly whether they wanted him or not. In the end he decided that the answer was self-evident; artists of his individuality and independence did not suit current Soviet cultural policies.

Tarkovsky was born in Zavrazhe, Ivanora District, U.S.S.R., on April 4, 1932, the son of a famous Russian poet, Arseniy Tarkovsky. At the Moscow Cin-

ema Institute he studied under the veteran director Mikhail Romm. His first feature film, *Childhood of Ivan* (1962), won him an international reputation; the story of a young boy caught up in World War II, it had visual power and an epic manner that distinguished it sharply from the generality of Soviet patriotic subjects.

Tarkovsky first encountered official opposition with his next film, *Andrey Rublev,* an imaginative fresco of the life and times of the great medieval icon painter. The film was finished in 1967, but some years elapsed before it was given restricted showings. A spectacular adaptation of a science fiction fantasy, *Solaris* (1971), by the Polish author Stanislas Lem, was more favourably received, but both *The Mirror* (1974) and *Stalker* (1979) were criticized for "obscurity"—a damning fault according to the tenets of "socialist realism." Tarkovsky's films received awards at the Venice, San Francisco, Acapulco, and Cannes film festivals.

Tarkovsky was given permission to work abroad, and in Italy he made *Nostalgia* (1982). The title referred to the need and yearning for those national roots that Tarkovsky was soon to reject, in exasperation over the discrimination he had suffered from the Soviet cultural establishment, culminating in a refusal to permit his young son to join him abroad. After his defection Tarkovsky began production of a film in Sweden and directed *Boris Godunov* at London's Royal Opera House, Covent Garden—a new version of his much-praised production of the previous year. (DAVID ROBINSON)

Thompson, Daley

British decathlon competitor Daley Thompson appeared determined to vie not only for the title of best athlete of the 1984 Olympic Games but also for that of most controversial. After winning the gold medal in the decathlon, he was criticized for apparently failing to try to break the world record. The evidence against him was strong: his final tally of 8,797 points was just one point short of the record, and Thompson had run the final event, the 1,500 m, in a time almost 15 sec slower than his personal best. During his victory lap he wore a T-shirt bearing a message that made it clear that he, for one, agreed with suggestions that U.S. television coverage of the Games had been inexcusably chauvinistic. He also whistled while the U.K. national anthem was played during the medal ceremony, and he made what were perceived to be offensive remarks about Princess Anne during his postvictory press conference.

In other respects, too, Thompson departed from expected "British" behaviour. Off the track he was outspokenly confident about his own abilities. While competing he enjoyed a close rapport with the crowd, who responded to his uncomplicated displays of emotion at his own performances, whether good or bad. In Los Angeles the performances were, almost without exception, stunning. His times and distances for the ten events of the decathlon were: 100 m, 10.44 sec; long jump, 8.01 m; shot put, 15.72 m; high jump, 2.03 m; 400 m, 46.97 sec; 110-m hurdles, 14.34 sec; discus, 46.56 m; pole vault, 5 m; javelin, 65.24 m; and 1,500 m, 4 min 35 sec. What was more, his

battle with the world record holder, Jürgen Hingsen of West Germany, over the two days of the competition was among the most enthralling of the Games. By successfully defending the title he had won in Moscow four years earlier, Thompson became only the second man in history to win the decathlon at two Olympic Games,

equaling the achievement of Bob Mathias of the U.S. in 1948 and 1952.

Thompson was born in Notting Hill, west London, on July 30, 1958. His Nigerian father died when Daley was 12 years old, and his Scottish mother gave him the choice of finding a job or leaving home when she learned of his decision to become a decathlete. He left home, and within a year he was competing at the 1976 Olympic Games. (LOUISE WATSON)

Toivo Ja Toivo, Andimba

Andimba Toivo Ja Toivo was released from prison in March 1984 after 16 years, nearly all of which were spent on Robben Island, where South Africa confined many of its political prisoners. Despite his long incarceration Toivo, a pioneer in the struggle for the independence of South West Africa/Namibia, tried to resist being released until all the other Namibian political prisoners were freed with him; he was literally compelled to leave his prison cell. By then 59 and gray-bearded, Toivo at once announced his determination to resume his struggle for Namibian independence, but though he was the veteran leader of the South West Africa People's Organization (SWAPO) of Namibia, Toivo insisted that its younger president, Sam Nujoma, should continue as leader. Instead, Toivo was elected secretary-general. Despite his long years in prison he emerged a smiling, athletic figure, who greeted people with a beaming bear hug and showed no sign of being broken or embittered by his experience.

Toivo was born in an Ovambo village on Aug. 22, 1924, and received his early education in an Anglican school. After a rudimentary primary education he became a railway policeman and later enlisted in the South African Army, with which he saw service during World War II in North Africa. After demobilization he went to work in Cape Town, where in early 1950 he helped to form an organization to assist Ovambo contract workers in South Africa. In 1959 he helped to form the Ovambo People's Organization, the precursor to SWAPO.

When Toivo tried to smuggle a tape to the UN Trusteeship Council listing the grievances of Ovambo workers, he was arrested and placed under restriction in Ovamboland. In 1966 the authorities discovered a training camp for SWAPO guerrillas at Ongulumbashe in Ovamboland. Toivo and his associates were arrested and put on trial for treason two years later. He was sentenced to 20 years in prison. There he continued his defiance of South Africa, refusing to claim any of the privileges open to political prisoners. He spent some time studying for a degree through a correspondence course but was forced to give it up when sentenced to a period of solitary confinement. "Prison," he said, "is not a school; it is a university."

Toivo's release was considered an essential part of the U.S.-backed initiative aimed at bringing about Namibia's independence on terms acceptable to South Africa. It was hoped that under his moderating influence SWAPO would be drawn into the South African-supported Multi-Party Conference. Toivo quickly dispelled that illusion when he condemned the U.S. administration for its active support of South Africa in its "illegal and brutal" occupation of Namibia.

(COLIN LEGUM)

Trelford, Donald Gilchrist

In 1984 Donald Trelford survived a furious and public disagreement with the proprietor of *The Observer* to remain editor of Britain's longest running Sunday newspaper. The dispute followed the appearance in the April 15 edition of *The Observer* of Trelford's own account of alleged atrocities by government troops in Matabeleland, Zimbabwe. Accused by Roland ("Tiny") Rowland, chief executive of Lonrho Ltd., the newspaper's owner, of being "discourteous, disingenuous, and wrong," Trelford was equally outspoken in defending the truth of the article and his right to print it. In this he received the backing of the newspaper's journalists and its independent board of directors. After two weeks, during which Rowland threatened to sell *The Observer* to publisher Robert Maxwell (*q.v.*), the crisis subsided when Rowland reaffirmed his support for Trelford's editorship.

Trelford had forecast conflict in 1981 when *The Observer* was sold to Lonrho, an international conglomerate with extensive business dealings in Africa. He warned that Lonrho's best interests could not be served by affording editorial freedom to a newspaper that was not averse to criticizing governments in Africa and, indeed, closer to home. *The Observer*'s coverage of Africa was traditionally regarded as one of its strongest elements by those who shared its political stance.

Born on Nov. 9, 1937, in Coventry, England, Trelford attended school in Coventry and completed national service in the Royal Air Force before gaining a first-class degree in English at Selwyn College, University of Cambridge. After a short time on local papers, he became at 25 the youngest person ever to be editor of a national

newspaper (the *Nyasaland Times*). During his time there (1963–66), a period of great political change in southern Africa, he was also African correspondent for *The Observer, The Times,* and the British Broadcasting Corporation.

On returning to London in 1966, he joined the permanent staff of *The Observer* and advanced quickly to become deputy to owner-editor David Astor in 1969 and editor in 1976. He emerged as a skillful defender of the newspaper's editorial independence. In his first year as editor, he was instrumental in fending off a perceived threat when he rallied *Observer* journalists to oppose a proposed takeover bid by the Australian press magnate Rupert Murdoch. Later *The Observer*'s criticisms of Margaret Thatcher's government earned the disapproval of both Rowland and the previous owner, the Atlantic Richfield Co.

(LOUISE WATSON)

Turner, John

Although he had been out of political life since 1976, John Turner had always been viewed by Canadians as the logical successor to Prime Minister Pierre Trudeau. Thus it came as no surprise that on June 16, 1984, Turner was elected leader of the Liberal Party of Canada at the convention called to name a successor to the retiring Trudeau. Two weeks later Turner reached what he called his "crowning career achievement"; he was sworn in as Canada's 17th prime minister on June 30, 1984.

Turner soon called a federal election for Sept. 4, 1984, using for his campaign slogan, "Today we celebrate our future." His new preelection Cabinet, however, looked very much like Trudeau's old Cabinet, one that had become unpopular. Turner's campaign could not recover from some early blunders. He had always been pictured as an independent politician, yet he acceded to Trudeau's demands to place the latter's supporters in patronage positions, saying, "I had no option." Midway through the campaign, Turner put his political aspirations in the hands of Trudeau's former advisers. The Liberals lost the election, yielding control of even their old stronghold of Quebec. Turner, who won in the riding (electoral district) of Vancouver, Quadra, was the only Liberal candidate elected west of Winnipeg. As leader of the opposition in the House of Commons, he vowed that he would remain in politics and rebuild his party.

Born in Richmond, Surrey, England, on June 7, 1929, Turner went to Canada in 1932. After growing up in Ottawa, he attended the University of British Columbia, receiving a B.A. in political science in 1949. As a Rhodes scholar he attended the University of Oxford, earning a B.A. in jurisprudence in 1951 and a bachelor of civil law degree in 1952.

Returning to Canada, Turner practiced law in Montreal from 1953 until 1962 when he entered politics. He won the Montreal riding of St. Lawrence-St. George in the 1962 federal election. When his Montreal riding disappeared in redistricting, Turner won a seat for the riding of Ottawa-Carleton in 1968. During his parliamentary career he held several Cabinet positions: minister without portfolio (1965–67), registrar general (1967–68), minister of corpo-

rate and consumer affairs (1968), solicitor general (1968), and minister of justice and attorney general (1968–72). As minister of justice he initiated legal reform designed to make the administration of justice more equitable. Turner's last position in the Cabinet was minister of finance (1972–75).

(DIANE LOIS WAY)

Ueberroth, Peter V.

Having revived the Olympic movement, Peter Ueberroth moved on in 1984 to governing major league baseball. His year could be seen as the most eventful and satisfying a sports executive ever had, culminating when *Time* magazine named him "Man of the Year." And his name, meaning "over red" in German, was uncannily appropriate. The success of the 1984 summer Olympic Games stemmed from victories over red ink and the Red (Communist) boycott. Ueberroth managed a frugal and profitable Olympics that retained its lustre despite the absence of athletes from all but one Soviet-bloc country.

Ueberroth had turned a $5,000 investment into the country's second largest travel agency, First Travel Corp., with 200 offices and worth $10.1 million after 15 years. When the Los Angeles Olympic Organizing Committee (LAOOC) was looking for a tightfisted manager to be its president, an executive search firm pinpointed Ueberroth as its man. He accepted and took office April 1, 1979.

He took office only figuratively. The LAOOC office had been locked after a credit check that showed a $300,000 debt with no

assets. The Los Angeles Olympics would be the first backed by a national Olympic committee instead of a city. It followed Montreal's $1 billion debt and $1.5 billion expense in 1976 and Moscow's $9 billion expense in 1980, and it would have to come in under a $515 million budget. Ueberroth shepherded home a $215 million surplus by using existing facilities, commanding high television fees, appealing to corporate patriotism that generated money and services from big business, and appealing to personal patriotism in the recruitment of 72,000 volunteer workers.

Peter Victor Ueberroth was born Sept. 2, 1937, in Evanston, Ill. His mother died when he was four, and he moved often with his traveling-salesman father, who eventually settled in southern California. He attended San Jose State University on a water polo scholarship but said his favourite team sport was baseball.

The major league baseball owners elected Ueberroth unanimously March 3 to become commissioner from Oct. 1, 1984, through 1989. He was in office less than a week when umpires went on strike during the league championship series. He coaxed them back in time for the World Series.

(KEVIN M. LAMB)

Vieira, João Bernardo

Developments in Guinea-Bissau during 1984 reinforced Gen. João Bernardo Vieira's control over the former Portuguese territory, one of Africa's smallest nations. The removal from the post of premier in March of his former comrade-in-arms Victor Saudé Maria, whom he accused of having "exaggerated political ambitions," left him effectively head of government as well as chief of state.

Vieira, president of the Council of the Revolution since leading the November 1980 coup that overthrew former president Luis de Almeida Cabral, was born in Bissau in 1939. He received only local education and training as a chemist's assistant.

A pioneer of the African Party for the Independence of Guinea-Bissau and Cape Verde, he was sent to Conakry, Guinea, for military training. On his return, he built up a legendary reputation for skill and bravery as a guerrilla leader (under his nom de guerre, Nino) in the long war against the Portuguese. In 1961 he went on a guerrilla instruction course to China and later received further training in the U.S.S.R., Algeria, and Cuba. Military chief of Catió (1961–64) and of the southern front (1964–65), he developed tactics that were a key factor in defeating the Portuguese, who held him in high regard.

After Guinea-Bissau became independent in 1974, Vieira was appointed state commissioner for the armed forces and president of the National Assembly. Then, in 1978, when Premier Francisco Mendès was killed in an automobile accident, Vieira succeeded him. On Nov. 14, 1980, two days after the Assembly had adopted a new constitution that virtually denuded the office of premier of its powers, Vieira led the coup that overthrew Cabral. The coup was seen as a move by the blacks of the mainland to separate themselves from the mestizo-dominated Cape Verdians.

It took some time for Vieira to establish his position firmly; this was greatly helped after he released Cabral from prison in January 1982. In July of that year there was an abortive coup attempt against him, but by March 1983 he felt strong enough to set up a commission to examine plans to revise the constitution and electoral law. From the time he seized power, Vieira maintained a left-wing political approach.

(GUY ARNOLD)

Weizsäcker, Richard von

A respected centrist politician of the Christian Democratic Union (CDU), Richard von Weizsäcker was elected president of the Federal Republic of Germany on May 23, 1984. He succeeded Karl Carstens (also a Christian Democrat) and was the sixth chief of state since the founding of the federal republic in 1949.

As mayor of West Berlin since 1981, Weizsäcker had proved himself a firm administrator, but he also showed a tolerance toward minority groups and a gift for conciliation that helped restore a degree of tranquillity to the city after a particularly turbulent period. These qualities made him a natural choice for presidential candidate, and he was elected on the first ballot, receiving the votes not only of his own party and its coalition partner, the Free Democratic Party (FDP), but also those of many Social Democrats. In his address to the Bundestag at his swearing-in ceremony on July 1, he said that the Berlin Wall had failed in its objective of making people in both German states abandon their sense of unity. Instead, the wall had made these feelings stronger and more conspicuous.

Weizsäcker was born in Stuttgart on April 15, 1920, the son of a naval officer who became a senior diplomat, and brother of Carl Friedrich von Weizsäcker, the physicist and philosopher. Richard went to school in Basel, Copenhagen, Oslo, and Bern, cities to which his father was posted. After service as an infantry officer in World War II, he studied law and history at the Universities of Oxford, Grenoble, and Göttingen. A practicing lawyer from 1955, he was later an executive in the steel industry, a bank, and a chemical company. He joined the CDU in 1950.

A devout Protestant churchman, Weizsäcker was for many years president of the Evangelischer Kirchentag, the congress of the German Protestant church. He was elected to the Bundestag in 1969 and served on several policy drafting commissions. From 1979 until moving to Berlin he was deputy speaker of the Bundestag. For much of his political career he specialized in intra-German policy.

(NORMAN CROSSLAND)

Willis, Norman David

Within weeks of succeeding to the general secretaryship of Britain's Trades Union Congress (TUC) on Sept. 7, 1984, Norman Willis was seen by millions of television viewers struggling in vain to be heard at a mass meeting of miners in Port Talbot, South Wales. During his speech a noose was lowered in front of his face from the rafters of the meeting hall. His offense: he had, in the name of the trade union movement, condemned violence—never for him, he said, "the brick, the bolt or the petrol bomb."

No predecessor in his office—and he was the 17th incumbent—could have had quite such a baptism. The early retirement of Lionel Murray, who had been suffering from heart disease, opened the way to a deputy who had remained through ten years very much in the background. Born Jan. 21, 1933, in Hayes, Middlesex, Norman Willis left school at 16 to begin work as an errand boy at Transport House, headquarters of the Transport and General Workers' Union (TGWU). His family background was strongly trade union. He won a trade union scholarship to Ruskin College, University of Oxford, and subsequently took an honours degree at Oriel College. This cast him in the role of "intellectual" when he returned to Transport House to serve as personal assistant to TGWU General Secretary Frank Cousins and his successor, Jack Jones, through a period in which they successively dominated the trade union movement.

In 1974 Willis moved to the second highest job at TUC headquarters. Under Murray, however, it was not much of a job, and it became still less so in 1976 when two assistant secretaries were appointed with responsibilities in the key areas of economic policy and employment. Willis was left with administrative chores and played little part in the TUC's dealings with the government. However, he cultivated his contacts within the trade union movement, which were already extensive.

When Murray retired, Willis succeeded to a dismal scene. Murray's policy of "new realism," which in effect meant coming to terms with the Thatcher government, was in shreds, and the long and bitter coal miners' strike was in progress with no end to it in sight. The TUC had lost much of its previous influence and was split sharply politically between left and right. Willis's backroom skills and amiable manner were appropriate for holding things together through a time of troubles. Whether he would prove to have the vision and the leadership qualities for restoring the fortunes of the TUC remained to be seen.

(PETER JENKINS)

Wu Xueqian

In line with its economic open-door policy, China became increasingly active in foreign affairs during 1984, especially under the leadership of Foreign Minister Wu Xueqian (Wu Hsueh-ch'ien). Among other things, Wu achieved a diplomatic breakthrough in his successful negotiations with Britain for the return of Hong Kong to China in 1997. Since assuming office in 1982, Wu had traveled to over 40 countries and significantly improved China's relations with the two superpowers, the U.S. and the Soviet Union, without entering into an alliance with either.

Born in Shanghai in 1922, Wu was active in youth and student activities before and after he completed his education at Jinan (Tsinan) University in 1948. A close lieutenant of Communist Party General Secretary Hu Yaobang (Hu Yao-pang), then the leader of the Communist Youth League, Wu led many youth delegations to foreign countries in the 1950s as an official of the League's international liaison department. He was purged during the Cultural Revolution along with other leaders of the League, but he emerged in 1977 as deputy director of the international liaison department of the party's Central Committee and served briefly as deputy foreign minister before becoming foreign minister in November 1982.

Speaking few foreign languages and little known in the West before his appointment as foreign minister, Wu became an effective spokesman for China's foreign policies despite a lack of previous diplomatic experience. Amiable but firm on principles, he actively promoted China's image as a nonaligned nation to enhance its influence in the third world.

(WINSTON L. Y. YANG)

Nobel Prizes

The 1984 Nobel Prize winners included, as is often the case, some who had long enjoyed international reputations; others were scarcely known outside their own communities. The Prize for Peace went to Bishop Desmond Tutu, the general secretary of the South African Council of Churches, who had long fought to end by peaceful means his country's policy of apartheid (racial separation). Sir Richard Stone, a retired University of Cambridge professor, won the Prize for Economics for creating an accounting system for national economies. Jaroslav Seifert, a Czech poet little known outside his own country, was awarded the Nobel Prize for Literature. Three immunologists shared the Prize for Physiology or Medicine: César Milstein, who held both Argentine and British citizenship; Georges J. F. Köhler, a West German who did much of his research in England; and Niels K. Jerne, a British-born Dane. Carlo Rubbia of Italy and Simon van der Meer of The Netherlands shared the Prize for Physics for discovering three subatomic particles. The only American to receive a 1984 Nobel Prize was R. Bruce Merrifield of Rockefeller University, who was honoured for his work in chemistry. Each Nobel laureate received or shared the equivalent of about $190,000.

Prize for Peace

When the bells of the Chapel of the Good Shepherd at New York's General Theological Seminary began to peal on the morning of October 16, Bishop Desmond Tutu knew he had won the Peace Prize. Bishop Tutu was staying at the seminary as visiting professor of Anglican studies. At a press conference Tutu remarked that the award was not personal: "It is a corporate award. It belongs to all the black people of South Africa who have suffered, to all who have felt and lived with the evil of apartheid and are trying and striving for peace."

Desmond Mpilo Tutu was born in the Afrikaner town of Klerksdorp on Oct. 7, 1931. He carried with him clear memories of his youth, including seeing blacks rummaging through school garbage cans looking for food thrown away by white students. Denied the opportunity to study medicine, he became a teacher after graduating from one of South Africa's segregated colleges. At the age of 25 he began his studies for the ministry and was ordained in 1960. He studied in London and in 1975 was named the first black Anglican dean of Johannesburg. In 1978 he was appointed general secretary of the South African Council of Churches, a consistent opponent of apartheid.

The Nobel committee noted that the prize was a strong signal of support for the South African Council as well as its leader.

The committee said the award should be seen as "a renewed recognition of the courage and heroism shown by black South Africans in their ... peaceful ... struggle against apartheid." Although Tutu's crusade had led to severe scrutiny of the council and the repeated withdrawal of his passport, he had traveled abroad frequently to urge other governments to support the cause of South African blacks by exerting political and economic pressure to bring about change.

Tutu returned to South Africa after learning he had been awarded the Nobel Prize. The joyous welcome he and his wife received from singing and dancing supporters in Johannesburg was uninterrupted by the white authorities. Unlike the Communist government of Poland, which a year earlier had prevented Lech Walesa from personally receiving his award, South Africa permitted Tutu to get travel documents through normal channels to attend the December 10 awards ceremony in Oslo. On November 13 he was elected bishop of Johannesburg.

Prize for Economics

Simply put, Sir Richard Stone received the 1984 Nobel Memorial Prize in Economic Science for developing a uniform accounting system for measuring national incomes—the profits and wages of a country. The selection committee described Sir Richard as the person mainly responsible for creating an accounting system for nations that has been indispensable in monitoring their financial position, in tracking trends in national development, and in comparing one nation's economic workings with another's. Indeed, the system of elaborate double-entry bookkeeping, designed to show that expenditures by one sector of an economy provide income for another, had been adopted as an income reporting system by industrialized nations everywhere and was central to the work of such organizations as the United Nations, the International Monetary Fund, the World Bank, and the Organization for Economic Cooperation and Development.

John Richard Nicholas Stone was born Aug. 13, 1913, in London. He studied law for a short time at the University of Cambridge but then switched to economics. One of his mentors was the famed British economist John Maynard Keynes. Stone received his B.A. degree in 1935, then joined a London stock brokerage firm. While writing an economics newsletter, he gained his first awareness of the complicated workings of an economy. He proved so adept that at Keynes's request Stone became a top statistician for the British government. At the outset of World War II, Keynes and Stone wrote a paper entitled

"The National Income and Expenditure of the U.K. and How to Pay for the War." Stone continued to publish and at the urging of Keynes returned to Cambridge. His work in the 1950s built on Keynes's theory that a country's economic activity was determined by consumption, investment, and government spending. Stone found ways of measuring these elements and their interactions, eventually including such social factors as environmental pollution in his accounting equations. Critics pointed out that Sir Richard's system was not perfect. It might be inappropriate for comparisons of national welfare systems; it assumed that prices reflect a scarcity of goods and services, not applicable in Communist economies, where fixed-level prices do not relate to supply and demand; and recent analyses had not balanced reported trade deficits in some countries and surpluses in others. However, the Nobel committee found these disparities to be valuable in focusing attention on contemporary economic forces.

Sir Richard was knighted in 1978. He and his wife, Lady Giovanna, lived in Cambridge in an old house lined with books from floor to ceiling. The reputedly shy couple often read aloud together and delighted in the theatre. The economist loved nothing better than inviting an entire cast to his home after a performance.

Prize for Literature

The 1984 literature prize was awarded to a poet little known outside his native Czechoslovakia. Jaroslav Seifert, who enjoyed great respect among his countryfolk, finally achieved international acclaim at the age of 83. Seifert was cited by the Nobel committee for work that, "endowed with freshness, sensuality and rich inventiveness, provides a liberating image of the indomitable spirit and versatility of man. ... He is loved as dearly for the astonishing clarity, musicality and sensuality of his poems as for his unembellished but deeply felt identification with his country and its traditions."

Seifert was always concerned about politics, especially in Czechoslovakia. His early work, labeled proletarian, was filled with enthusiasm for the promise of the revolution in the Soviet Union. After a 1925 trip to the U.S.S.R., however, he became disenchanted with Communism and in 1929 turned to the Social Democratic Party. Some say his best work was done during the '20s and '30s, but his writings after the German invasion of Czechoslovakia in World War II also manifest intense distress. *Clothed in Light* (1940) was possibly his most popular work.

When the official Prague news agency CTK announced the Nobel award 3½ hours after Seifert had been chosen, it cited the poet's "positive attitude to man's struggle for social justice" and declared that his World War II works "were a great encouragement to the Czech nation." The network dispatch, however, enumerated Seifert's works only up to 1968, the year he condemned the Soviet invasion of Czechoslovakia and joined the national liberation movement that was crushed by invading troops.

After 1968 Seifert's works were available only underground or abroad in translation. Though the government had recently allowed republication of some of his poetry, which was difficult to obtain outside Czechoslovakia, two titles had been translated into English: *The Plague Monument,* published in 1980, and *The Casting of Bells,* published in 1983. Seifert's memoirs were published in Czech in Canada in 1981.

The first Czech to win the Literature Prize was born in Prague in 1901 into a working-class family. He published his first poem at age 19 and, after his schooling, supported himself as a journalist for many years before becoming a free-lance poet. The now ailing poet learned of his prize in Prague's Vinohrady Hospital. He was overjoyed at the news and seemed sincerely surprised. His wife of 56 years, Marie, who seemed more concerned about her husband's heart problems and diabetes, expressed regret that the prize had not come earlier in his life.

(BONNIE OBERMAN)

Prize for Chemistry

R. Bruce Merrifield of Rockefeller University in New York City was awarded the Nobel Prize for Chemistry for developing an efficient method for preparing the chainlike molecules of polypeptides and proteins from their basic constituents, the amino acids. All of the enzymes and many of the hormones present in the tissues of humans and other animals are members of these families of nitrogenous organic compounds. Merrifield devised his procedure—called solid-phase peptide synthesis, or SPPS—so that it could be automated, and commercial versions of his apparatus were in service all over the world. The principles of SPPS also had been extended to the preparation of substances not based on amino acids, such as polynucleotides, which play a vital role in studies of the structure of the nucleic acids.

The distinction between polypeptides and proteins is not sharp; their chemical structures are the same, but the molecules of proteins ordinarily are larger and commonly are folded and looped into complex three-dimensional shapes that are essential for their biological activities. The German chemist Emil Fischer (who won the Nobel Prize in 1902 for studies of sugars and purines) introduced the term polypeptide around 1899 for products he obtained by combining small numbers of amino acids. During the 20th century it was shown that all polypeptides and proteins are made up of various combinations of about 20 amino acids, strung together like the letters of different words.

In 1955 the U.S. biochemist Vincent du Vigneaud won the Nobel Prize for his research on the pituitary hormone oxytocin. In this project, which occupied several years, he had shown that the hormone is made up of eight amino acids; he found the order in which these components are arranged in the molecule; and, starting with the individual amino acids, he synthesized the compound. In 1958 the English biochemist Frederick Sanger won the first of his two Nobel Prizes for determining the pattern in which the 51 amino acids of the hormone insulin are joined together.

The method used by Merrifield's predecessors to synthesize a polypeptide from, say, 20 amino acids required 19 steps, each involving a chemical reaction between the amino group of one amino acid and the carboxyl (acid) group of another. Each reaction entailed several distinct procedures—measuring the proper amounts of the starting materials, dissolving them in a solvent, mixing the solutions, waiting for the reaction to proceed, separating the product from the solvent and any by-products and unconsumed starting materials, purifying the new compound, and verifying its identity. Many of these operations could be carried out easily and without loss of material, but others—notably, the purification of previously unknown substances—had to be painstakingly developed for each step. In most cases recovery of the desired pure product is not complete, and if only 3% is wasted at each stage, the 19-step synthesis will yield only 56% of the amount of the polypeptide that would have been obtained if no losses had occurred.

To streamline this cumbersome method, Merrifield used a solid substance with special properties. This material—analogous to a sponge that is permeated by water without being dissolved—is penetrated, but not dissolved, by organic liquids that dissolve amino acids. The solid also combines with the carboxyl group of an amino acid, leaving the amino group available for the next stage of the synthesis. To begin the preparation of a polypeptide, Merrifield treated the solid with a solution of the first amino acid of the chain. The ensuing reaction made the amino acid part of the solid, which was isolated and purified by simply filtering it and washing it with fresh solvent. The solid, which remained in the same vessel during the whole procedure, was immediately ready for treatment with a solution of the next amino acid. The same steps were repeated for each successive amino acid until the entire polypeptide chain was assembled. A final reaction detached the completed chain from its solid support.

Because every step could be carried out under the same conditions, varying only the amino acid to be used, the whole process could be performed by a machine programmed to dispense the proper volumes of solutions and solvents, mix them for the necessary time, filter, wash, and start again. The apparatus could be allowed to operate day and night without close attention.

Robert Bruce Merrifield was born on July 15, 1921, in Fort Worth, Texas. He was graduated from the University of California at Los Angeles in 1943 and received a Ph.D. in chemistry from the same institution in 1949. He then joined the Rockefeller Institute for Medical Research (now Rockefeller University) in New York City, becoming professor of biochemistry in 1966 and John D. Rockefeller, Jr., professor in 1983.

Merrifield proposed the idea of solid-phase peptide synthesis to his laboratory chief in 1959; within three years he had achieved substantial results. In 1964 he announced that his apparatus had produced a sample of the polypeptide bradykinin, composed of nine amino acids. A greater triumph was his synthesis of the enzyme ribonuclease, which consists of a chain of 124 amino acids.

Prize for Physics

The Prize for Physics was shared by two members of the staff of the European Organization for Nuclear Research (formerly the European Centre for Nuclear Research), or CERN, the headquarters and experimental laboratories of which are located near Geneva. Carlo Rubbia of Italy and Simon van der Meer of The Netherlands were cited by the Nobel committee for their leading roles in planning and executing the experiments, reported in 1983, that demonstrated the existence of the elementary particles called intermediate vector bosons. These massive, short-lived particles, designated W^+, W^-, and Z^0, are the carriers of the so-called weak force, which is involved in the radioactive decay of atomic nuclei and in the nuclear fusion processes that generate energy in the Sun and other stars.

The results obtained by Rubbia and van der Meer formed part of the principal pattern that had emerged in late 20th-century physics, namely, the search for a single explanation of all the diverse forces and particles that exist in nature. Since the early 1930s four apparently distinct interactions between bits of matter had been recognized—gravitation, electromagnetism, and the so-called weak and strong nuclear forces—but connections between them remained elusive for decade after decade. During the same period, increasingly powerful accelerators made it possible to detect and study scores of subatomic particles. Considerable progress was made in sorting these into families, but their sheer number implied that, if nature is indeed basically simple, there must be a deeper, undiscovered stratum of fundamental building blocks.

In 1979 the Nobel Prize was awarded to the three physicists who had been instrumental in devising a theory that electromagnetism and the weak force are different manifestations of a single kind of interaction. One of the experimental findings that influenced this Weinberg-Salam theory had been provided in 1973 by a research group at CERN directed by Rubbia. They had discovered neutral weak currents, which are interactions governed by the weak force in which no electrical charge is transferred between the affected particles. These interactions differed from any previously observed, but they are exact analogues of electromagnetic interactions, in which charged particles influence each other by exchanging neutral particles, the photons. In the unified electroweak theory, the photon—which has no mass—is one of a set of four carriers of force between particles; the other three, which had not been observed at the time the theory was formulated, are the intermediate vector bosons. The theory indicated that these particles, symbolized W^+, W^-, and Z^0, should have masses nearly 100 times that of the proton. Such massive particles could be expected to form only in processes releasing more energy than was available in any accelerator operating in the 1970s.

Rubbia realized, however, that the needed energy might be produced in head-on collisions of strongly accelerated protons and antiprotons. In such events, not only would the kinetic energy of the speeding particles be released, but so would that involved in the mutual annihilation of matter (the protons) and antimatter (the antiprotons). Rubbia proposed that the large proton synchrotron at CERN be modified so that colliding-beam experiments could be carried out. (The machine, an evacuated tube four miles in circumference and buried underground, had been constructed to accelerate a beam of protons to extremely high energy and direct it onto a stationary target.) Production and control of proton beams were well understood, but dense streams of antiprotons, all traveling at the same speed, had never been produced. Van der Meer responded to this challenge by inventing a mechanism that could measure the degree of nonuniformity in the antiproton beam at a point on the ring and trigger a device on the opposite side of the ring to modify the electromagnetic fields in such a way as to keep the particles from scattering out of the proper path and hitting the wall of the tube.

In 1983 experiments with the new device gave proof that the W and Z particles are indeed produced and have properties that agree with the theoretical predictions. Further analysis of the data from these experiments led Rubbia to conclude that in some decays of the W^+ particle, the first firm evidence of the existence of a new quark, called top, had been revealed. Discovery of this quark, the sixth member of its family, confirmed an earlier prediction that three pairs of these particles should exist. The quarks are the present candidates for the fundamental entities that make up the large collection of subatomic particles.

Rubbia was born on March 31, 1934, in Gorizia, Italy, and was educated at the Normal School of Pisa and the University of Pisa, receiving his doctorate from the latter in 1957. He stayed at Pisa as a member of the teaching staff for two years, then moved to Columbia University in New York City as a research fellow. He was appointed to the faculty of the University of Rome in 1960 and became a senior physicist on the staff of CERN in 1962. In 1970 he was appointed professor of physics at Harvard University and thereafter divided his time between Harvard and CERN.

Van der Meer was born on Nov. 24, 1925, in The Hague. He studied physical engineering at the Higher Technical School in Delft and thereafter joined the staff of the Philips Co., a Dutch electronics firm. In the physics laboratory at Philips the subject of his work was electron microscopy, a field for which the precise focusing of particle beams is crucial. He obtained a doctorate from the Delft University of Technology in 1956, then accepted a position at CERN, where he remained.

Prize for Physiology or Medicine

The Prize for Physiology or Medicine was divided among three immunologists: Niels Kai Jerne, who held joint British and Danish citizenship and was professor emeritus of the Basel (Switz.) Institute of Immunology; Georges J. F. Köhler, a West German who was leaving the Basel Institute to accept a co-directorship at the Max Planck Institute of Immune Biology at Freiburg, West Germany; and César Milstein, a citizen of both Argentina and Britain who was affiliated with the Medical Research Council in Cambridge, England. Jerne was regarded by other experts in his field as one of the principal architects of modern immunology. During his long career the results of his simple but definitive experiments led him to formulate three fruitful theories concerning the functioning of the immune system. The Nobel Prize announcement cited Milstein and Köhler for their discovery, announced in 1975, of a method for producing antibodies of unprecedented purity; their technique revolutionized many diagnostic and medical screening procedures and was expected to lead soon to therapeutic agents for the treatment of many intractable disorders.

The immune system is dispersed throughout most of the tissues of the body. It consists of cells called lymphocytes and protein molecules called antibodies. The lymphocytes, each of which secretes a single kind of antibody, are produced and processed in bone marrow, in the thymus, and in the spleen. These cells and antibodies are carried continuously through the body, reaching the tissues by way of the bloodstream and returning in the lymphatic fluid. The function of the antibodies is to attach themselves to cells or large molecules that originate outside the body of the individual in whom the antibodies have formed. Such foreign substances, which may range from the components of snake venom to a transplanted kidney, are called antigens.

An antibody combines with an antigen when a distinctively shaped site on the antibody molecule encounters a complementary site on the antigen, matching as do adjacent pieces of a jigsaw puzzle. To protect the body from the enormous diversity of possible antigens, the immune system maintains a corresponding variety of antibodies and automatically increases the supply of those that are called into play.

The first of Jerne's theories concerning the operation of the immune system dealt with the mechanisms by which it supplies antibodies appropriate to neutralize any kind of foreign matter, regardless of its structure. The second covered the steps that occur in the development of the system during the life of each individual. McFarlane Burnet and Peter Medawar won the Nobel Prize in 1960 for showing that the ability of antibodies to distinguish between components of their host and those of other individuals is not genetically determined but can be modified during the embryonic stage of prenatal life.

In 1974 Jerne proposed a third concept, called the network theory. In it he emphasized that the self-regulation of the immune system depends on a duality in the way lymphocytes and antibodies interact with antigens and with each other. Not only do these entities recognize and dispose of antigens, but they also possess features by which they themselves can be recognized and left unscathed.

The research of Milstein and Köhler solved a problem that had plagued immunologists for decades. To prepare substantial quantities of antibodies, previous scientists would inject an antigen into an animal, wait for antibodies to form, draw blood from the animal, and isolate the antibodies. The proteins obtained by this procedure almost never were pure, because typical antigens possess many recognizable sites, each of which leads to formation of a different antibody. Milstein and Köhler saw that if a way could be found to clone lymphocytes—to cause them to subdivide indefinitely in a culture medium—then the antibody molecules secreted by the resulting population would all be identical. Lymphocytes, however, are short-lived and cannot be cultivated satisfactorily, but Milstein and Köhler found that they could induce them to fuse with cells of a myeloma, a type of tumour that can be made to reproduce indefinitely. The hybrid cells indeed retained the two desired properties: like the lymphocytes, they secreted a single species of antibody molecules and, like the myeloma cells, they perpetuated themselves, providing potentially unlimited amounts of any desired antibody.

Jerne was born of Danish parents on Dec. 23, 1911, in London. He grew up in Denmark but attended the University of Leiden, Neth., receiving a bachelor's degree at the age of 16. He wrote that it then took him 12 years to decide on a profession. He was a researcher at the Danish State Serum Institute from 1943 to 1955 while studying medicine at the University of Copenhagen, which granted him a degree in 1951. He served as a chief medical officer for the World Health Organization from 1956 to 1962, then accepted research and teaching appointments in Switzerland, the U.S., and West Germany. After helping organize the Basel Institute of Immunology, he became its director from 1969 until 1980. He served a year at the Pasteur Institute in Paris before retiring.

Köhler was born in Munich on April 17, 1946. He attended the University of Freiburg, West Germany, receiving a doctorate in biology in 1974. He then joined Milstein at the Laboratory of Molecular Biology in Cambridge, where they discovered the method of preparing monoclonal antibodies. In 1976 Köhler joined the staff of the Basel Institute of Immunology; in 1984 he was appointed one of three directors of the Max Planck Institute of Immune Biology in Freiburg.

Milstein, who was born on Oct. 8, 1927, in Bahia Blanca, Arg., was educated at the Universities of Buenos Aires and Cambridge, receiving a doctorate from the latter in 1960. He had been a member of the staff of Argentina's National Institute of Microbiology since 1957 and retained that position until 1963, when he returned to England to join the Laboratory of Molecular Biology of the Medical Research Council in Cambridge. He was initially interested in the chemistry of enzymes but shifted his attention to antibodies when their structures were deciphered. He was a senior scientist at the laboratory when Köhler arrived as a postdoctoral fellow in 1974. Milstein was currently director of the division of protein and nucleic acid chemistry, having shared that position with Frederick Sanger until Sanger's retirement.   (JOHN V. KILLHEFFER)

Obituaries

Adams, Ansel (Easton), U.S. photographer (b. Feb. 20, 1902, San Francisco, Calif.—d. April 22, 1984, Monterey, Calif.), captured the majestic sweep of mountainous terrain and the natural American landscape in exquisite black-and-white photographs that were technical masterpieces of precision and sharp focus. Adams, who snapped his first photographs with a box Brownie camera during a 1916 visit to Yosemite Valley, trained as a concert pianist and began to photograph as an avocation in the style of pictorialism, which emphasized darkroom manipulation to produce a painting-like effect. When he met photographer Paul Strand in 1930, Adams was so impressed with Strand's "straight photography" that he adopted it as his own medium of expression. In 1931 Adams launched his professional career as a photographer, and in the following year his photographs were exhibited at the Smithsonian Institution in Washington, D.C. With such photographers

PHOTOREPORTERS

as Edward Weston and Imogen Cunningham, Adams in 1932 formed Group f.64, a loose association of progressive photographers who were exponents of straight photography. The group, though short lived, had a lasting influence and established photography as a distinct and legitimate art form. In 1935 Adams won international recognition when he published *Making a Photograph*, an instruction manual on photographic technique that was notable because it contained reproductions of his breathtaking prints. Adams, who steadfastly worked to increase public acceptance of photography as a fine art, directed (1940) the Pageant of Photography exhibition at the Golden Gate International Exposition in San Francisco, was co-founder (1940) of the world's first museum collection of photographs at the Museum of Modern Art in New York City, and in 1946 established the California School of Fine Arts in San Francisco, the first academic department to teach photography as a profession. From 1941 to 1942 Adams served as a photo-muralist for the U.S. Department of the Interior; the magnitude of his work prompted him to develop a "zone system" whereby the tone of each part of the scene could be predetermined. An ardent conservationist, who served as director of the Sierra Club from 1936 to 1973, Adams was three times a recipient of a Guggenheim fellowship, which enabled him to photograph national parks and monuments. A gifted teacher whose enthusiasm for his art never faltered, Adams imparted his wisdom and technique to gener-

ations of students. As the most widely exhibited and recognized photographer of his time, Adams was showered with awards and honours. In 1966 he was made a fellow of the American Academy of Arts and Sciences, and in 1980 he was the recipient of the U.S. Medal of Freedom. His photographs were published in more than 35 books and portfolios, including *Yosemite and the High Sierra* (1948), *My Camera in the National Parks* (1950), *This Is the American Earth* (1960), and *Ansel Adams: Images, 1923–1974* (1981).

Adams, Sir John Bertram, British engineer (b. May 24, 1920, Kingston upon Thames, England—d. March 3, 1984, Geneva, Switz.), was twice director general of the European Organization for Nuclear Research (CERN) at Geneva and was a leading figure in the assemblage of CERN's particle accelerators. He worked during World War II on radar development before moving to the U.K. Atomic Energy Research Establishment at Harwell, where in 1949 he made a major contribution to the creation of the 180-MeV cyclotron. Adams joined CERN in 1953, became director of its Proton Synchrotron Division the following year, and headed the team that built the high-energy accelerator inaugurated in 1959. In 1960 he was appointed CERN's director general but left shortly to return to Britain as director of the newly formed U.K. Atomic Energy Authority's (UKAEA's) Culham Laboratory. When it opened in 1965, Culham, as the site of the Joint European Torus (an experimental fusion device), became an internationally renowned centre for atomic research, and Adams, through his association with the Ministry of Technology and the UKAEA, became one of the British government's chief advisers on nuclear physics. He returned to CERN in 1969 to build the 450-GeV Super Proton Synchrotron and served as CERN's director general again from 1976 to 1980. A fellow of the Royal Society from 1963, Adams received the Faraday Medal of the Institution of Electrical Engineers in 1977 and was knighted in 1981.

Aiken, George David, U.S. senator (b. Aug. 20, 1892, Dummerston, Vt.—d. Nov. 19, 1984, Montpelier, Vt.), as the spirited Republican senator from Vermont (1941–75), spearheaded the food-stamp program, supported "liberal" farm policies such as crop price supports, and favoured rural electrification and the construction of the St. Lawrence Seaway, which opened the Great Lakes to deep-draft oceangoing vessels. A farmer who was an expert horticulturist and the writer of two scholarly tomes, *Pioneering with Fruits and Berries* and *Pioneering with Wildflowers,* Aiken gained a strong base of support from his nursery business before running for political office in 1930. He was first elected to the Vermont House of Representatives in 1930 and then served as lieutenant governor (1935–37) and governor (1937–41) of his home state. As a U.S. senator, Aiken became a Vermont institution with his longtime tenure, but he became better known to the nation for two straightforward remarks: in 1966 he told the Senate that the U.S. should simply declare victory and withdraw troops from Vietnam, and in 1973 he lambasted the Senate for its treatment of Pres. Richard Nixon by saying, "Impeach him or get off his back." Aiken, who earned a reputation for his candor, thrift (he spent $17.09 on his last campaign), and independence

of mind, was at the time of his retirement in 1975 the oldest senator, dean of the Senate, a member of the Agriculture Committee, and ranking Republican on the Foreign Relations Committee.

Aleixandre, Vicente, Spanish poet (b. April 26, 1898, Seville, Spain—d. Dec. 14, 1984, Madrid, Spain), winner of the Nobel Prize for Literature (1977), was almost unique among his generation of Spanish poets in that, largely because of ill-health, he remained in Spain throughout the Civil War and the years of Franco's rule but never compromised himself with the regime. Often described as a Surrealist (a label he rejected), he wrote vivid and colourful poetry deeply influenced by the works of Sigmund Freud and expressing, notably in *La destrucción o el amor* (1935; *Destruction or Love*), the primacy of procreative forces and a pantheistic philosophy of unity in man and universe. The son of a railway engineer, he lived in Malaga (1900–09) and in Madrid, where he studied law and business management. He taught commercial law (1920–22) and later worked for a railway company. He became ill with tuberculosis of the kidneys (1925) and during convalescence wrote his first poems. After the publication of *Ámbito* (1928; *Scope*), he became a friend of such contemporary poets as Federico García Lorca and Jorge Guillén. Under Franco, Aleixandre encouraged young writers of diverse schools and worked for the release of those imprisoned and a relaxation of censorship. In *En un vasto dominio* (1962; *In a Vast Dominion*) he faced and surmounted the problems of old age. English translations of some of his poems are to be found in the bilingual *Poems/Poemas* (1978) and *A Longing for the Light* (1979).

Alston, Walter Emmons, U.S. baseball manager (b. Dec. 1, 1911, Venice, Ohio—d. Oct. 1, 1984, Oxford, Ohio), as the low-keyed quiet man of baseball, was instrumental in sparking the Brooklyn (later Los Angeles) Dodgers professional baseball team to seven National League pennants and four World Series championships (1955, 1959, 1963, and 1965) during a 23-year career. Alston, who was dubbed "Smokey" in high school because of the speed of his fastball, later signed with the St. Louis Cardinals and played as a first baseman in the minor leagues for 12 years before striking out as a Cardinal in his only time at bat in the majors. In 1953 he was named manager of the Brooklyn Dodgers, and when the team moved to Los Angeles in 1958, the 1.9-m, 90-kg (6-ft 2-in, 200-lb) Alston continued to assert his easygoing managerial skills until his retirement in 1976. He was elected to the Baseball Hall of Fame in 1983.

Andropov, Yury Vladimirovich, Soviet head of state (b. June 15, 1914, Nagutskaya, Stavropol region, Russia—d. Feb. 9, 1984, Moscow, U.S.S.R.), was general secretary of the Communist Party of the Soviet Union (CPSU) from Nov. 12, 1982, and chairman of the Presidium of the Supreme Soviet (president) from June 16, 1983. He was the son of a railway employee probably of Armenian origin. In 1983 he joined the Komsomol (Young Communist League), worked for a time as a Volga boatman, and in 1936 graduated from the Inland Waterways Transport College at Rybinsk on the upper Volga. He joined the CPSU in 1939 and the following year was appointed first secretary of the

120

Komsomol organization in the Karelo-Finnish Autonomous Republic. By 1947 he had advanced to second secretary of the party Central Committee in Karelia.

The turning point in Andropov's career was his transfer in 1953 to Moscow, where he was assigned to "diplomatic work." A year later Nikita Khrushchev appointed him ambassador to Hungary, where he was instrumental in the suppression of the 1956 national uprising while supporting Janos Kadar as leader of the Hungarian Communists. Recalled to Moscow in 1957, he became head of the Central Committee's department supervising the Communist parties of "sister" republics. In May 1967 Leonid Brezhnev appointed Andropov head of the State Security Committee (KGB). A month later he was made candidate member and in April 1973 a full member of the Politburo. On April 22, 1982, Andropov was chosen to make the tra-

ditional speech commemorating Lenin's birth. He relinquished his post as head of the KGB, and on May 24 he was reelected to the Secretariat of the Central Committee. Two days after Brezhnev's death on Nov. 10, 1982, the Central Committee unanimously elected Andropov as general secretary. Almost immediately after his election Andropov started fighting corruption, which under Brezhnev had been on the increase. Andropov took some initiatives in foreign policy by adopting a conciliatory attitude toward China and by trying to create a division between Western Europe and the U.S. on trade and military issues. His only visit abroad as CPSU general secretary was to Prague in January 1983 for a meeting of the Political Consultative Committee of the Warsaw Treaty member states. At home he appealed for an efficient national economy through harder work and better social discipline, but with little result in the short duration of his leadership. After Aug. 18, 1983, he was not seen in public. The official medical conclusion was that he died from "interstitial nephritis, nephrosclerosis, secondary hypertension, and diabetes mellitus, complicated by a chronic kidney deficiency."

Antonov, Oleg Konstantinovich, Soviet aircraft designer (b. Feb. 7, [new style; Jan. 25, old style], 1906, Troitsa, near Moscow, Russia—d. April 4, 1984, Moscow, U.S.S.R.), after World War II designed a range of highly successful transport aircraft remarkable for their versatility. His inventions included the An-2 biplane, which with a minimum speed of 64 km/h (40 mph) could be used for civil or military passenger transport, communications, crop spraying, forestry patrol, and other purposes. Other Antonov designs were the An-10 turboprop passenger transport, the An-12 medium cargo transport, and the huge An-22 long-range transport. A graduate of the Leningrad M. I. Kalinin Polytechnic Institute, Antonov began his career designing gliders. In 1946 he was put in charge of experimental aircraft design and in 1962 was appointed designer general for the Soviet aircraft industry. Antonov joined the Communist Party of the Soviet Union in 1945 and was a deputy to the Supreme Soviet (parliament) during 1958–66. Among the

many distinctions he received were the State Prize (1952) and the Lenin Prize (1962).

Ariyoshi, Sawako, Japanese writer (b. Jan. 20, 1931, Wakayama, Japan—d. Aug. 30, 1984, Tokyo, Japan), carved a niche in Japanese literature with her short stories, murder mysteries, and historical novels that explored the culture, traditions, social structure, and domestic problems of classical and modern Japanese people; she was especially noted for examining sensitive social problems and became a national celebrity after she published *Kokotsu No Hito* (1972; *The Twilight Years,* 1984), a shocking exposé of the problems of the aged as viewed through the character of an 84-year-old man, Shigezo. The best-seller sold nearly 1.6 million copies within a year, and Ariyoshi donated the proceeds (minus the government's share) to nursing homes. Ariyoshi made her literary debut in 1956 with *Jiuta (Ballads),* a story about the conflicting values of a *jiuta* (a classical Japanese singing master) and his daughter. Her meticulously researched works enveloped the young, the elderly, the rich, the poor, and ordinary housewives as well as princesses and earned her a reputation as one of the country's most important and talented litterateurs. Though she often wrote on the problems facing women, she did not view herself as a feminist. Some of her other well-known works included *The River Ki,* a story that chronicled the lives of three generations of women from the turn of the century to the late 1950s; *Compound Pollution,* a novel about environmental pollution; *The Doctor's Wife,* the tale of Hanaoka Sheishu, the doctor who invented anesthetic for surgery, and his wife, who was relegated to his shadow; the historical *Diary of Princess Kazu;* the contemporary *Bad Woman;* and the murder mystery *The Curtain-Raising Bell Sounds Beautiful.* Her writings, which were translated into Chinese, Russian, Dutch, German, Portuguese, and English, made her an international figure in world literature. Ariyoshi was also an accomplished playwright and a gifted theatre director.

Arosemena Gómez, Otto, Ecuadoran politician (b. 1922?, Guayaquil, Ecuador—d. April 20, 1984, Salinas, Ecuador), was elected interim constitutional president of the country by the Constituent Assembly on Nov. 16, 1966, amid violent demonstrations, chiefly by left-wing students who had supported the candidacy of university lecturer Raúl Clemente Huerta. A lawyer by profession, Arosemena practiced law in Guayaquil before becoming a member of Parliament. As president of the country (1966–68), Arosemena criticized U.S. development aid as inadequate and demanded preferential treatment by the U.S. for Latin-American products. In October 1967, when U.S. Ambassador Wymberley Coerr criticized Ecuador's foreign policy in a speech, Arosemena declared Coerr persona non grata and gave him 48 hours to leave the country. A fiery politician, who served three months in prison for shooting a fellow lawmaker in the leg during a parliamentary debate, Arosemena returned to his seat after serving his sentence. His term was due to expire in August 1984 and he did not seek reelection.

Ashton-Warner, Sylvia, New Zealand teacher and writer (b. Dec. 17, 1908, Stratford, N.Z.—d. April 28, 1984, Tauranga, N.Z.), taught Maori and European children in rural areas of New Zealand and developed the Creative Capital Teaching Scheme, a system that sought to stifle destructiveness and encourage creativity through unconventional means. She outlined her teaching technique in her best-known work of nonfiction, *Teacher* (1963). Her experiences as a schoolteacher also formed the basis of her first novel, *Spinster* (1958), a best-seller that humorously described the antics of schoolchildren and chronicled the life of the schoolteacher who was "married" to 70 children. Though she never attended college, Ashton-Warner and her husband, headmaster Keith Henderson, taught in country schools for more than 20 years.

The educational theories she developed and the application of her methods to racially mixed classes, described in the passionate style of her books, were influential, especially in the U.S. After teaching for one year at the Aspen (Colo.) Community School Teaching Center, she published *Spearpoint: Teacher in America* (1972). Besides *Spinster,* which was later filmed as *Two Loves,* starring Shirley MacLaine, Ashton-Warner published four other novels and a fictionalized autobiography, *Myself* (1967).

Astor of Hever, Gavin Astor, 2ND BARON, British company director (b. June 1, 1918, Hever Castle, Edenbridge, Kent, England—d. June 28, 1984, Tarland, Aberdeenshire, Scotland), was chairman of the Times Publishing Co. Ltd. from 1959 to 1966. Though his father had bought *The Times* following the death of Lord Northcliffe in 1922 and ceded (1954) his shares in the newspaper to Gavin Astor, he continued to play a major role in running *The Times* as co-chief proprietor for the following decade. Gavin Astor, who was responsible for the family home at Hever Castle in Kent and *The Times,* found himself saddled with two large but costly assets. In 1966 he sold the majority holding in the newspaper to Lord Thomson of Fleet, retaining a 15% interest and continuing as life president. Educated at New College, Oxford, Astor served in the Army during World War II before being taken prisoner in 1944. After his release he worked in all departments of *The Times* as a preparation for the directorship, which he assumed in 1952. He was also, from 1959, chairman and then president of the Commonwealth Press Union, and he served as director of such companies as Electrolux Ltd. and the Monotype Corp. Ltd. He continued to maintain a close relationship with *The Times* until his death.

Atkinson, (Justin) Brooks, U.S. theatre critic (b. Nov. 28, 1894, Melrose, Mass.—d. Jan. 13, 1984, Huntsville, Ala.), was an extraordinary drama critic whose sagacious reviews for the *New York Times* (1925–60) probably exerted more critical influence on the stage than those of anyone else at that time. Atkinson, who was renowned for his evenhandedness, was reluctant ever to lambast a play or praise it too highly. His desire to become a journalist was a boyhood dream that materialized after he was graduated from Harvard University in 1917 and landed a job as a district reporter with the *Springfield* (Mass.) *Daily News.* In 1919 he moved to the *Boston Evening Transcript,* first as a police reporter and then as assistant drama critic to H. T. Parker. In 1922 he joined the *New York Times* as editor of the "Book Review" section and three years later became its drama critic. In this capacity Atkinson was regarded as an omnipotent reviewer whose candid observations could either make or break a Broadway play. His influence also extended to off-Broadway productions; by reporting the emergence of such talented newcomers as Geraldine Page, George C. Scott, and Jason Robards, Atkinson fostered the growth of this theatre. In 1942 Atkinson took a respite from his theatre chair to cover World War II and its aftermath for the *Times,* first in China and then in the Soviet Union. His scorching articles as the Moscow correspondent won him the 1947 Pulitzer Prize for foreign correspondence. His return to theatre criticism in 1946 was enthusiastically embraced by both readers and the theatre community, though Atkinson rarely socialized with the latter in order to maintain his objectivity. He announced his retirement as a theatre critic in 1959, and a Broadway theatre was named for him the following year. From 1960 to 1965 he was the author of a *Times* column, "Critic-at-Large," on any subject that struck his fancy. He formally retired in 1965. Besides his reviews, Atkinson wrote such books as *The Cingalese Prince; Broadway;* and *Henry Thoreau, Cosmic Yankee.*

Balasaraswathi, Indian dancer (b. 1919, Madras, India—d. Feb. 9, 1984, Madras), as a world-renowned classical dancer of the *bharata-natya,* one of the four classical Hindu dance dramas, was unequaled in the delicacy and intensity of feeling that she elicited during the *abhinaya* (mimed passages). Balasaraswathi, a ninth-generation descendant of musicians and dancers in South India, began her dance training at age four under the tutelage of Kandappa Pillai and later studied with Gauri Ammal, Chinayya Naidu, and Lakshmi Narayana Shastri. She made her debut at the age of seven and stunned dance masters with her expressiveness and rhythm. She likewise mesmerized audiences with her radiance and was especially gifted in evoking what some audiences felt was a spiritual experience. Besides touring Europe and the U.S., the legendary Balasaraswathi also taught dance at Wesleyan University (1962 and 1968), the University of California at Los Angeles (1968), the California Institute of the Arts (1972), and the Center for Asian Studies at the University of Washington in Seattle (1968 and 1973). Her spellbinding artistry was featured in a full-length documentary film, *Bala,* directed by Satyajit Ray in 1976.

Barzini, Luigi, Italian journalist (b. Dec. 21, 1908, Milan, Italy—d. March 30, 1984, Rome, Italy), gained an international reputation as an authority on the history, culture, and national character of his fellow countrymen with his witty and urbane book *The Italians* (1964). His father, also an influential journalist, founded the Italian-language newspaper *Corriere d'America* in the U.S., where Barzini studied at Columbia University, New York. As a roving London correspondent for the Milan *Corriere della Sera* from 1930, he covered the rise of Hitler, the inauguration of Franklin D. Roosevelt, and the Italian invasion of Ethiopia. In 1937 he was aboard the U.S. gunboat "Panay" when it was sunk by a Japanese aircraft during the war between Japan and China, and he helped rescue survivors. Though he had embraced Fascism as a youth, he later opposed it, and his hostility led in 1940 to his arrest on Mussolini's orders. After World War II, he founded the newspaper *Il Globo* in Rome and edited it until 1947. From 1958 until 1972 he was a Liberal Party deputy in the Italian Parliament. His publications included *Americans Are Alone in the World* (1953), *From Caesar to the Mafia* (1971), and *O America: When You and I were Young* (1977).

Basehart, Richard, U.S. actor (b. Aug. 31, 1914, Zanesville, Ohio—d. Sept. 17, 1984, Los Angeles, Calif.), was a versatile and seasoned performer on stage and screen before gaining popular appeal as Adm. Harriman Nelson on the television adventure series "Voyage to the Bottom of the Sea" (1964–68). Basehart's resonant voice first resounded through the theatre; he made his Broadway debut in 1938 and in 1945 won the New York Drama Critics Circle Award for his portrayal of the dying Scottish soldier in *The Hasty Heart.* He also appeared on stage in *Counter Attack, Land of Fame,* and *Othello.* In 1947 Basehart made his motion picture debut in *Cry Wolf* and compiled an impressive list of film credits; he portrayed a gangster in *He Walked by Night* (1948), a psychotic ledge jumper in *Fourteen Hours* (1951), a clown in *La Strada* (1954), and Ishmael in *Moby Dick* (1956). Basehart's most popular role, however, was on "Voyage to the Bottom of the Sea" as the commander of the "Seaview," an atomic-powered submarine that scoured the ocean bed for villains and monsters. Later in his career Basehart appeared in various commercials. He had narrated the closing ceremonies of the Summer Olympics on Aug. 12, 1984, several hours before suffering a series of strokes.

Basie, Count (WILLIAM BASIE), U.S. jazz pianist and bandleader (b. Aug. 21, 1904, Red Bank, N.J.—d. April 26, 1984, Hollywood, Fla.), was the legendary pianist and leader of one of the swingingest and tightest jazz bands in the country and a brilliant organizer who transformed swing from a solo effort to a group phenomenon

AP/WIDE WORLD

with an explosive orchestra that boasted star sidemen and vocalists. Though Basie originally wanted to become a drummer, he felt overshadowed by his contemporary Sonny Greer (later Duke Ellington's drummer) and instead studied in Harlem with the stride pianist Fats Waller (who had studied under James P. Johnson). Basie, a stride pianist himself, played in a flow of harmony until he adopted an individual subtle style that used time and space to devastating effect by utilizing great plains of silence dotted with exquisite melodic epigrams. He played as an accompanist for traveling vaudeville shows but in 1927 was stranded in Kansas City, Mo. In 1928 he joined Walter Page's Blue Devils, and when the band disbanded a year later he joined Bennie Moten's orchestra, a seminal Kansas City band. After Moten died in 1935, the band broke up and Basie formed a nine-piece band that played from the Reno Club in Kansas City. During one of the broadcasts from the club the announcer of an experimental radio program introduced Basie as the "Count," a moniker he carried throughout his life; one program was also heard by the jazz enthusiast John Hammond, who decided to promote Basie's band (expanded to 13 pieces) and as a result got them bookings in Chicago at the Grand Terrace and in New York at the Roseland Ballroom. In New York the band created a stir at the Famous Door on 52nd Street and recorded their first records for Decca, creating one smash hit after another, including "One O'Clock Jump" (Basie's theme song), "Swingin' the Blues," "Jumpin' at the Woodside," "Taxi War Dance," and "Tickle Toe." Basie's band was populated with such distinctive soloists as Lester Young, Herschel Evans, Buddy Tate, Harry Edison, and Dickie Wells. The songs they created were known as "head arrangements," fragments of improvised music put together spontaneously by the musicians in a process of trial and error. In 1950 the big-band era began to wane so Basie formed an octet, but in 1952 he organized a big band with a brassy new sound. They toured with Frank Sinatra and recorded such favourites as "April in Paris," "Li'l Darlin'," and "I Can't Stop Loving You." In 1976 Basie suffered a heart attack but within six months was back at the keyboard, though in later years he often rode on stage in a motorized wheelchair. During his lifetime, the master organizer received many honours. In 1982 a gala at Radio City Music Hall sponsored by the Black Music Association paid tribute to the innovative bandleader who changed the course of jazz history.

Bellonte, Maurice, French aviator (b. Oct. 25, 1896, Méru, Oise, France—d. Jan. 14, 1984, Paris, France), with Dieudonné Costes made the first nonstop flight from Paris to New York. The two, after meticulous preparations, left Paris on Sept. 1, 1930, and arrived in New York 37 hours later. The success of the journey was due largely to Bellonte's navigational skills. The flight, using advanced technical aids, ushered in an era in aviation that made transatlantic flying

commonplace. Bellonte served as a pilot during World War I and later was a pilot in Morocco. He joined the French Air Union, where he met Costes, and accompanied him on long-distance flights to China (a record 4,912 mi) and Hanoi in 1929. During World War II he served in the Resistance, and his awards included the Légion d'Honneur, the Croix de Guerre, and the Resistance and Aeronautical medals. He later served as inspector general of flight safety.

Bentley, Max, Canadian hockey player (b. March 1, 1920, Delisle, Sask.—d. Jan. 19, 1984, Saskatoon, Sask.), was the scourge of the National Hockey League while playing with the Chicago Black Hawks (1940–47), the Toronto Maple Leafs (1947–53), and the New York Rangers (1953–54) professional hockey teams. Bentley's slight frame belied his prowess on the ice. When he joined the Hawks as centre, he teamed up with his older brother Doug, a left wing on the team, and the two provided a powerful one-two scoring punch. During his career Bentley, who was nicknamed the "Dipsy Doodle Dandy of Delisle" because of his superb puck-handling ability, scored 245 goals and had 229 assists in 646 games. At the height of his career he was traded to the Maple Leafs and played on three Stanley Cup teams; he helped them capture Stanley Cups in 1947–48 and 1948–49. He ended his career with the Rangers after the 1953–54 season. He was inducted into the Hockey Hall of Fame in 1966.

Beny, Roloff, Canadian photographer (b. Jan. 7, 1924, Medicine Hat, Alta.—d. March 16, 1984, Rome, Italy), was an Abstract Expressionist painter before finding his niche as a photographer and using his lens to capture and preserve the beauty of past and present civilizations. Beny, who studied at the University of Toronto, Iowa State University, Columbia University in New York City, and New York University, took up residence in Rome in 1956. His preoccupation with sensual colours, beauty, and exotic places resulted in photographs that were meticulously arranged to create sumptuous books of extraordinary loveliness. His first volumes, which were devoted to Greece, included *A Time of Gods* (1962) and *Pleasure of Ruins* (1964), and were followed by *To Everything There Is a Season* (1967), a picture essay on Canada in honour of its centennial, and *Japan in Colour* (1967), which was awarded the gold medal for design at the annual Leipzig International Book Fair in East Germany. His books on Iran included *Persia: Bridge of Turquoise* (1975) and *Iran: Elements of Destiny* (1978).

Berlinguer, Enrico, Italian Communist leader (b. May 25, 1922, Sassari, Sardinia—d. June 11, 1984, Padua, Italy), served as secretary-general of the Italian Communist Party (PCI)—Western Europe's largest—from March 1972 and, as one of his country's most popular and respected political figures, was the leading proponent of Eurocommunism. The concept, which gained ground in 1968 after the Soviet invasion of Czechoslovakia, though still condemned by many Western Communists, involved a less doctrinaire party line and greater independence from Moscow (which implied, for Berlinguer, acceptance of Italy's NATO membership). Such concessions to the pluralistic democratic system would, Berlinguer hoped, help to achieve in Italy the "historic compromise" that he called for in 1973—a ruling coalition of Communists and Christian Democrats. Although this seemed a strong possibility after the 1976 election (in which the PCI took 34.4% of the votes against the Christian Democrats' 38.7%), it never happened, and in the 1979 and 1983 elections the PCI's share of votes declined. Berlinguer's family background was aristocratic and antifascist, his father being a socialist who became a deputy and later a senator. The young Berlinguer joined the PCI in 1943. The following year he was jailed for several months for taking part in demonstrations against the Fascist government. After World War II he was an organizer of

Communist youth in Milan and Rome, becoming a member of the PCI Central Committee in 1945 and of its executive in 1948. After holding various party posts in Rome and Sardinia, he became secretary for the Lazio region. In May 1968 he was elected to the Chamber of Deputies, and the following year he became deputy secretary to Luigi Longo, whom he succeeded as secretary-general in 1972.

Berman, Jakub, Polish politician (b. Dec. 24, 1901, Warsaw, Poland—d. April 10, 1984, Warsaw), was a Stalinist who wielded considerable power as *éminence grise* in the government of Boleslaw Bierut (1948–56), as a member of the Politburo of the Polish United Workers' (Communist) Party (PUWP) responsible for national security, ideology, and propaganda, and as deputy premier (1955–56). A former journalist and member of the small pre-World War II Communist Party, Berman spent the war years in the U.S.S.R. On his return to Poland he rapidly rose to a position of authority within the Communist Party as a firm adherent of Stalinism; he was believed responsible for the 1948 ouster of party Secretary-General Wladyslaw Gomulka (replaced by Bierut) and of other "deviationists" within the leadership. In the destalinization that followed Gomulka's return to power in 1956, Berman was expelled from the government and from the PUWP the following year. He was one of few Jews to attain a position of importance within the Polish leadership, and his activities in the Bierut period may have later fueled the anti-Jewish campaign launched by the Gomulka government in 1968.

Betjeman, Sir John, British poet (b. Aug. 28, 1906, Highgate, London, England—d. May 19, 1984, Trebetherick, Cornwall, England), was poet laureate from 1972 and one of the best-loved Englishmen of his time, as a poet, as an eccentric, as a television broadcaster, as an enthusiast for Victorian architecture, and as a gentle satirist of English life. His poetry, which gained huge public approval despite the scorn or indifference of highbrow critics, was written in regular verse with no concessions to modernism. He depicted English landscapes and characters with humour and nostalgia, though he could sometimes be insensitive. Though he was educated at Marlborough College and at the University of Oxford, he failed to earn a degree. Instead of taking over the family furniture business, he worked for the *Architectural Review* and later as a film critic and reviewer. During World War II he was with the Ministry of Information and served as press attaché at the British embassy, Dublin, acquiring a love of Ireland and its architecture. In *Ghastly Good Taste* (1933) he attacked orthodox views on architecture, and throughout his life he campaigned for threatened buildings, notably those of the unfashionable Victorian period. A High Anglican, he showed his extensive knowledge of English churches in *Collins Pocket Guide to English Parish Churches (1968),* which he edited, and in his television documentaries. Betjeman

also loved railroads, the suburbs, and other monuments to Victorian life. His first two volumes of poetry achieved little public success, but he attracted a wide readership with *Old Lights for New Chancels* (1940). He became a best-selling author with his prize-winning *Collected Poems* (1958) and his verse autobiography, *Summoned by Bells* (1960). Championed by some fellow poets, notably Philip Larkin, Betjeman began to achieve almost the status of the fashionably unfashionable, though some considered that his later work showed a decline. To the television public, he was instantly recognized as an archetypal English eccentric, a part that he played willingly. He was made a Commander of the Order of the British Empire in 1960, a Companion of Literature in 1968, and was knighted in 1969. A British Railways train was named for him shortly before his death.

Bhindranwale, Jarnail Singh, Indian Sikh priest (b. 1946, Rode, Faridkot District, Punjab, India—d. June 6, 1984, Amritsar, Punjab), was among hundreds of Sikh militants killed when Indian Army troops stormed the Golden Temple, the Sikhs' holiest shrine. He emerged in the 1980s as the most influential Sikh leader, spearheading a campaign for the establishment of a politically autonomous state ("Khalistan") in the Punjab, where over 50% of the population were Sikhs. On May 31, 1984, he announced that vast supplies of food and power usually supplied to the rest of India by the Punjab would be withheld. The government reacted swiftly, declared the Punjab a "restricted area," and besieged the Golden Temple. The son of a Punjabi Sikh leader, Jarnail Singh began his religious education at the age of five and remained a close disciple of his teacher, Sant (holy man, or priest) Kartar Singh Bhindranwale, who adopted him. After his mentor died in 1977, Bhindranwale assumed his title. A fanatical fundamentalist, Bhindranwale led (1980) an armed party against some Nirankaris (a group regarded by mainstream Sikhs as heretical) and was wanted by the police for deaths occurring in that and other incidents. Surrendering in September 1981, he was held for only three weeks; thereafter he directed an escalating campaign of civil sedition from the Golden Temple.

Bitsios, Dimitrios, Greek diplomat (b. 1915, Athens, Greece—d. Jan. 9, 1984, Athens), became foreign minister in 1974 in the government headed by Konstantinos Karamanlis that followed the fall of the military dictatorship and the restoration of democracy that year. A career diplomat from 1939, Bitsios headed departments of the Ministry of Foreign Affairs and was a delegate (1956–61) and permanent representative (1961–65 and 1967–72) to the UN. In 1966 he acted as political adviser to King Constantine. As foreign minister until 1977 he negotiated with U.S. Secretary of State Henry Kissinger on the establishment of a U.S.-Greek defense agreement, but this was not signed. Bitsios also wrote several books on foreign affairs and diplomacy.

Blackwell, Sir Basil Henry, British publisher (b. May 29, 1889, Oxford, England—d. April 9, 1984, Appleton, Oxfordshire, England), as the longtime chairman (1924–69) of B. H. Blackwell Ltd., the Oxford booksellers and publishers, combined business acumen with culture and a dedication to bookselling. The business, which developed from the bookshop opened by his grandfather in 1846, was moved to its premises in Broad Street by his father in 1879. Blackwell was educated at Merton College, Oxford, and worked for the Oxford University Press before joining his father in the family business in 1913 where he was responsible for extending its publishing activities. From 1921, in collaboration with Bernard Newdigate, he ran the Shakespeare Head Press, specializing in fine printing, and from 1922 as founder with Adrian Mott of Blackwell & Mott publishers, turned out works by Robert Graves, W. H. Auden, and Aldous Huxley. Blackwell was twice (1925 and 1926)

president of the International Association of Antiquarian Booksellers and twice (1934 and 1935) president of the Associated Booksellers of Great Britain and Ireland. He was also president of the Classical Association (1964–65) and of the English Association (1969–70). During the 1950s he was prominent in a campaign to abolish the practice of distorting prices at auction through rings of antiquarian booksellers. He was knighted in 1956.

Blin, Roger, French stage director (b. March 22, 1907, Neuilly-sur-Seine, France—d. Jan. 21, 1984, Paris, France), was an important figure in modern European theatre and won recognition for such avant-garde dramatists as Samuel Beckett and Jean Genet in the 1950s and '60s. He directed first productions of Beckett's *En attendant Godot (Waiting for Godot)* and *Fin de Partie (Endgame),* the former in Paris in 1953 after four years' struggle to find a theatre willing to accept it and the latter in London in 1958 after it had been refused by theatres in Paris. Blin also directed the premiere of Genet's *Les Nègres (The Blacks)* and *Les Paravents (The Screens)* in Paris in 1959 and 1966, respectively. He was closely associated with the actor and director Jean-Louis Barrault, under whom he studied mime, and with the playwrights Arthur Adamov and Antonin Artaud, whom he first met in 1928 and helped in 1935 to stage a controversial production of Percy Bysshe Shelley's *The Cenci.* Blin began his career as a film extra during the 1920s and he played mainly small parts in films until World War II. He made his directing debut in 1949. Blin's production of August Strindberg's *Ghost Sonata* was a failure in popular terms but it resulted in an association with Beckett, who determined that Blin should direct his work. He was awarded the Grand Prix National du Théâtre in 1976 and continued to work until the end of his life, his last production being Max Frisch's *Triptyque* at the Odéon in 1983.

Bloom, Ursula, British writer (b. Dec. 11, 1892, Chelmsford, Essex, England—d. Oct. 29, 1984, Nether Wallup, Hampshire, England), was the versatile author of more than 500 books on a wide variety of subjects. She wrote under the names of Lozania Prole, Sheila Burns, Mary Essex, and Rachel Harvey as well as under her own name. Bloom's works included romantic and historical novels, biographies, many books on her own life and her parents' lives, and volumes on domestic skills such as needlework and cooking. In her childhood her father, an eccentric clergyman, and her mother were divorced. Initially trained as a musician, Bloom supported her mother by playing the piano in a cinema. Later she began to work as a journalist, eventually becoming chief crime reporter for both the *Empire News* and the *Sunday Dispatch* while at the same time producing books on a production-line scale. Subjects she chose for biography included Judas Iscariot, Hitler's mistress Eva Braun, Queen Elizabeth I, and a number of more recent members of the British royal family. *Parson Extraordinary* (1963) was about her father, *Price Above Rubies* (1965) about her mother; a series of books with titles beginning *No Lady…* concerned her own experiences. Her last work appeared in 1976.

Blundell, Sir (Edward) Denis, New Zealand lawyer (b. May 29, 1907, Wellington, N.Z.—d. Sept. 24, 1984, Townsville, Queensland, Australia), served as governor-general of New Zealand from 1972 to 1977 after having served as New Zealand's high commissioner in London, where he tried to minimize the loss of trade between New Zealand and Britain when the latter finally joined the European Communities in 1973. Educated in New Zealand and at Trinity Hall, University of Cambridge, he was called to the bar at Gray's Inn in 1929 and in the same year joined a well-known legal firm in Wellington. Apart from the years of World War II, when he served with the 2nd New Zealand Division in Greece, Crete, the Middle East, and

Italy, he practiced in Wellington until 1968 and was president of the New Zealand Law Society (1962–68). He was knighted in 1967.

Bosanquet, Reginald, British television newscaster (b. Aug. 9, 1932—d. May 27, 1984, London, England), with his partner, Andrew Gardner, presented the Independent Television News (ITN) program "News at Ten" from 1967 to 1979 and made it one of the most popular current affairs programs on British television. His success was due to his informality, his engaging personality, and his sense of humour, all of which he conveyed while reading the news: he came to typify a style of television newscasting quite distinct from that pioneered on radio. Bosanquet, who was educated at New College, Oxford, joined ITN in 1955, working as a subeditor, then as a reporter in Africa and as a diplomatic correspondent. In 1959 he became a newscaster with "Dateline." A physical defect gave him his lopsided manner of speaking which endeared him to viewers; when he resigned in 1979 he was a national figure. His private life attracted attention: married three times, he made frequent appearances in the gossip columns. He was rector (1980–83) of the University of Glasgow and an active supporter of the World Wildlife Fund. His autobiography, *Let's Get Through Wednesday,* appeared in 1980.

Brassaï (GYULA HALASZ), Hungarian-born photographer (b. Sept. 9, 1899, Brasso, Hung. [now Brasov, Rom.]—d. July 8, 1984, Nice, France), used his camera to record life in the Paris streets, theatres, and bars in a bizarre parade of lovers, prostitutes, and eccentrics. He worked especially at night, relying mainly on existing light and avoiding the use of flash. His first book of photographs, *Paris de nuit* (1933), was a sensation, and some of his pictures, such as "La Belle de nuit," were frequently reproduced. After studying painting at Budapest and Berlin, he became Paris correspondent (1924) for various Hungarian newspapers. Under the influence of his friend André Kertesz, he took up photography in 1930. Brassaï received no formal training. His international fame was established and furthered by exhibitions at the Museum of Modern Art, New York City (1937 and 1968), at the Bibliothèque Nationale in Paris (1963), and in London (1979). From 1946 to 1965 he worked for the magazine *Harpers Bazaar,* and he provided the photographic backdrops for Jacques Prévert's ballet *Le Rendezvous.* During World War II Picasso encouraged Brassaï to return to drawing, and he published *Trente dessins* in 1946. His other books included *Séville en fête* (1954) and *Graffiti* (1960). In later publications, *Secret Paris of the Thirties* (1976; English translation 1978) and *Artists of My Life* (1982), the photographs were accompanied by extended captions.

Bratteli, Trygve Martin, Norwegian politician (b. Jan. 11, 1910, Nøtterøy, Norway—d. Nov. 20, 1984, Oslo, Norway), was chairman of Norway's Labour Party (1965–75) and prime minister (1971–72 and 1973–76). He was the son of a shoemaker and was educated at a public elementary school. Bratteli worked as a construction worker and on a whaling ship before joining the Labour Party and becoming editor (1934) of the Labour newspaper in Kirkenes. He was secretary (1934–40) and chairman (1945–46) of the party's youth section and edited its magazine. He remained in Norway after the German invasion (1940), joining the Resistance, but he was arrested in 1942 and spent the remainder of World War II in various concentration camps in Germany. After the war he became vice-chairman of the Labour Party (1945–65). He was elected to the Storting (parliament) in 1950 and under the premiership of Einar Gerhardsen served as minister of transport and communications (1960–64). Bratteli succeeded as party leader in 1965, forming a minority government in March 1971. An advocate of Norwegian accession to the European Communities (EC), he

resigned (October 1972) following the referendum by which EC membership was rejected. He returned to power a year later at the head of a coalition of the Labour and Socialist Alliance parties. He resigned as chairman of the Labour Party (1975) and as prime minister (January 1976). He wrote three books on politics, and his account (1981) of his concentration camp experiences became a best-seller.

Brautigan, Richard, U.S. novelist (b. Jan. 30, 1933, Tacoma, Wash.—death discovered Oct. 25, 1984, Bolinas, Calif.), enjoyed ephemeral success as a literary campus idol during the 1960s with such offbeat books as *Trout Fishing in America* (1967), *In Watermelon Sugar* (1964), and *A Confederate General from Big Sur* (1965), which blended comedy, satire, odd bits of information, and extended metaphors in a spontaneous style that was indicative of the hippie era. Brautigan's whimsical works were wildly optimistic and first gained favour in the literary underground. In later years U.S. critics viewed his novels as stale, though his popularity remained strong in France and Japan. Some of his other works included the novels, *Dreaming of Babylon: A Private Eye Novel, 1942* (1977) and *The Tokyo-Montana Express* (1980); a book of short stories, *Revenge of the Lawn: Stories 1962–70* (1971); and such verse as *Lay the Marble Tea: Twenty-Four Poems* (1959), *The Octopus Frontier* (1960), and *The Pill Versus the Springhill Mine Disaster (Poems 1957–1968).* Brautigan, apparently despondent over his loss of readership, took his own life.

Bricktop (ADA BEATRICE QUEEN VICTORIA LOUISE VIRGINIA SMITH), U.S.-born cabaret owner and entertainer (b. Aug. 14, 1894, Alderson, W.Va.—d. Jan. 31, 1984, New York, N.Y.), was the engaging proprietress of the ultrachic "Bricktop" café in Paris, which served as a favourite haunt for such prominent U.S. expatriate writers as Ernest Hemingway and F. Scott Fitzgerald. The light-skinned, red-haired singer was the daughter of black parents, though her mother was part Irish. The freckle-faced, cigar-smoking Bricktop launched her career in Harlem in the early 1920s but moved to Paris in 1924. She reigned as the legendary queen of café society there for two decades, and Cole Porter wrote a song, "Miss Otis Regrets," in her honour. Her protégés included such singers as Josephine Baker and Mabel Mercer and the jazz composer Duke Ellington. Bricktop was also credited with introducing the Black Bottom dance in Europe and with teaching it to the prince of Wales, later King Edward VIII. On one occasion she was compelled to eject John Steinbeck from her café for being "ungentlemanly," but the remorseful writer sent her a taxicab filled with roses to make amends. During the 1940s she ran a café in Mexico City, and in 1951 she opened a café in Rome. In 1961 Bricktop retired, saying, "I'm tired, honey, tired of staying up till dawn every day."

Brion, Marcel, French writer and historian (b. Nov. 21, 1895, Marseille, France—d. Oct. 23, 1984, Paris, France), was elected to the French Academy in 1964 on the strength of his reputation as a historian and literary critic. He specialized in the period of the Italian Renaissance and also wrote literary studies of Goethe and other figures of German Romanticism. Brion delved into art history with his book on Cézanne, published in 1975, and popular works on Pompeii and Herculaneum. He also published biographies and novels and was a noted contributor to the newspaper *Le Monde.* He was awarded the Croix de Guerre during World War I, then studied law and practiced for a time before becoming a full-time writer in 1925. He won a number of literary prizes, including the French Academy's Grand Prix de Littérature (1953) and the Prix Littéraire de Monaco (1956).

Brooke of Cumnor, Henry Brooke, BARON, British politician (b. April 9, 1903, Oxford, England—d. March 29, 1984, Mildenhall, Wiltshire, England), gained a reputation as a competent but sometimes inflexible minister while serving as home secretary from 1962 to 1964. He was educated at Balliol College, Oxford, and entered Parliament in 1938 as a Conservative. Brooke lost his seat in 1945 but was later adopted as candidate for Hampstead, returned to the House of Commons in 1950, and remained there until 1966, when he was made a life peer. Brooke's first ministerial appointment was in 1954, when he became financial secretary to the Treasury, and three years later he joined the Cabinet as minister of housing and local government. There he was responsible for carrying through his predecessor's Rent Bill which was strongly criticized as being biased against tenants and in favour of landlords. In 1961 Brooke assumed the newly created post of chief secretary to the Treasury and a year later became home secretary. A hard-liner, he was a controversial figure who had to face strong opposition in Parliament, where his debating skills were not always effective. His decision to deport Chief Anthony Enahoro to face a treason charge in Nigeria, and his attitude on immigration made him the target of attack by liberals. Defeated in the 1966 general election, he later took an active role in the House of Lords. He was made a privy councillor in 1955 and a Companion of Honour in 1964.

Brough, John, British orientalist (b. Aug. 31, 1917, Dundee, Scotland—d. Jan. 9, 1984, Bishop's Stortford, England), as professor of Sanskrit at the University of London (1948–67) and, from 1967, at Cambridge, was among the leading scholars of early Sanskrit literature and encouraged research in the field, both in the West and in India. His chief scholarly works were *The Early Brahmanical System of Gotra and Pravara* (1953) and *The Gandhari Dharmapada* (1962), while *Selections from Classical Sanskrit Literature* (1951) and *Poems from the Sanskrit* (1968) afforded the general reader an insight into the essential qualities of India's ancient literature.

Buendía Téllez Girón, Manuel, Mexican journalist (b. 1926?—d. May 30, 1984, Mexico City, Mexico), was an aggressive investigative reporter whose front-page newspaper column "Red Privada" ("Private Network"), which appeared in Mexico City's leading daily *Excélsior,* indicted corrupt politicians, exposed illegal practices, labour, and business, and attacked CIA involvement in Latin America. Buendía, a veteran journalist of 35 years, was the country's most influential and well-known political reporter; his column was syndicated in some 200 Mexican newspapers. He launched his newspaper career at *La Prensa* in 1948 and worked for several other dailies before joining *Excélsior* in 1978. Buendía's hard-hitting column often enraged those he investigated, and he received frequent threats on his life, which he acknowledged by carrying a pistol at all times. His most recent exposé had been aimed at corruption in the nation's oil industry and its powerful union. Buendía had also published three books: *The CIA in Mexico, Private Network*, and a university text on journalism. He was gunned down by an unknown assassin at point-blank range moments after he had left his office to deliver his final column, "Sick Society," a discussion about alcoholism and social deterioration. Buendía's stature as a journalist was so monumental that the president of Mexico, Miguel de la Madrid Hurtado, attended his wake, a rare tribute for a journalist.

Bunker, Ellsworth, U.S. diplomat (b. May 11, 1894, Yonkers, N.Y.—d. Sept. 27, 1984, Brattleboro, Vt.), was in the vanguard of delicate negotiations between The Netherlands and Indonesia, Saudi Arabia and Egypt, and Panama and the U.S. and headed the U.S. embassies in Argentina, India, and Italy but was best remembered as the unflappable U.S. ambassador to South Vietnam (1967–73) during the height of the war in Southeast Asia. Bunker, a Yale graduate, worked in his family's sugar business for some 35 years before he embarked in 1951 on a diplomatic career, during which he served under seven presidents. He was appointed ambassador to Argentina by Pres. Harry S. Truman and then was named ambassador to Italy in 1952. For the following three years he served as the first salaried president of the Red Cross. In 1956 he was appointed ambassador to India and Nepal; before he left India in 1961 he had helped distribute more than $5 billion in U.S. aid. In 1962 Bunker established a reputation as a troubleshooter when he mediated the dispute between The Netherlands and Indonesia over West New Guinea (now West Irian, Indon.). As a representative (1964–66) of the Organization of American States (OAS), he was a key member of a three-man OAS team sent to end factional fighting in the Dominican Republic that had begun after the assassination of dictator Rafael Trujillo in 1961. The imperturbable Bunker successfully helped install a provisional civilian president and was aptly dubbed "the Sly Fox" by the Dominicans. In diplomatic circles his calm and unruffled demeanour earned Bunker the nickname "the Refrigerator." When Pres. Lyndon B. Johnson named him ambassador to South Vietnam in 1967, he was assigned to use his influence to persuade South Vietnamese Pres. Nguyen Van Thieu to cooperate with U.S. efforts to negotiate peace with Hanoi. Though critics felt that Bunker was too protective of Thieu, who refused to compromise on the issue of negotiations with the Communists, Bunker was trusted implicitly by Presidents Johnson and Richard M. Nixon. At the end of Bunker's six-year tenure in Vietnam in 1973, including four years of "vietnamization," Bunker finally witnessed the withdrawal of U.S. troops. Many felt, though, that he had reached the pinnacle of his career when he negotiated the Panama Canal treaties; the first allowed for Panamanian control of the canal after the year 2000, and the second guaranteed the U.S. the right to defend the canal. Bunker permanently retired to his farm in Vermont in 1978 after both treaties were ratified.

Burton, Richard, British actor (b. Nov. 10, 1925, Pontrhydyfen, South Wales—d. Aug. 5, 1984, Geneva, Switz.), achieved early success as a stage actor with the Old Vic Company and was hailed as one of the finest Shakespearean actors of his generation. After his Hollywood film debut in 1952, he went on to play Antony opposite Elizabeth Taylor in the ill-fated epic *Cleopatra* (1963) and began a career of stardom and scandals. His first marriage ended in divorce, and his two marriages to Elizabeth Taylor (they were twice divorced) were an extravagant orgy of ostentation and overspending that delighted the world press. When they played together in Marlowe's *Doctor Faustus*, on stage and later on film, some felt that Burton himself had sold his soul for the trappings of stardom. However, the man and his career were rather more complex than a trite summary might suggest and,

whatever one's judgment of his private life, his achievement as an actor was considerable. Born Richard Jenkins, the 12th child of a miner, he made his stage debut in 1943 after he was coached by the man whose name he adopted. Burton's first major role was as Angelo in *Measure for Measure* while he was at the University of Oxford. After national service he made his first film, then appeared on the London stage in a series of plays by Christopher Fry. His extraordinary stage presence and his voice led to the Old Vic and Shakespeare, notably *Hamlet* and *Othello*. By the time of his departure for Hollywood, he was an undoubted star of the London theatre with an enthusiastic following. In 1960 he played King Arthur in *Camelot*, and he continued to appear on the New York stage, though his career was mainly in films; among the most outstanding of them were *Who's Afraid of Virginia Woolf?*, *The Night of the Iguana*, and *The Spy Who Came in from the Cold*. But by the 1970s Burton was suffering from a serious drinking problem; he admitted that the films he made during this period were second-rate and poorly played. He also admitted that acting came almost too easily to him, and he considered taking up a teaching fellowship at Oxford. His fifth marriage appeared to have brought some stability to his private life. His last film was *1984*; he played the interrogator O'Brien with an unusual restraint and intensity that showed he had lost none of his power and suggested that he might be less casual in the exploitation of his natural gifts.

Calvet, Joseph Étienne André, French violinist (b. Oct. 8, 1897, Valence-d'Agen, Tarnet-Garonne, France—d. May 4, 1984, Paris, France), founded the Calvet String Quartet in 1919 and was a noted interpreter of contemporary French music. His most celebrated recordings were of works by Fauré, Debussy, and Ravel, and he was also internationally acclaimed for his performances of Romantic music. From 1935 he taught at the Paris Conservatoire and after World War II founded a new quartet with young musicians. He was for many years president of the jury for the Marguerite Long-Jacques Thibaud competition.

Campbell, Clarence Sutherland, Canadian sports executive (b. July 9, 1905, Fleming, Sask.—d. June 24, 1984, Montreal, Que.), as the savvy president of the National Hockey League (NHL) from 1946 to 1977 (the longest reign in any professional sport) supervised the expansion of the league from 6 to 18 franchises, organized the players' pension fund, lengthened the schedule, and introduced the All-Star Game. Earlier, Campbell, a Rhodes scholar at Oxford, served as a lacrosse referee at the 1928 Olympics, and during World War II he commanded the 4th Canadian Armoured Division headquarters. After becoming president of the NHL, Campbell was involved in many disputes but was considered a fair arbitrator. However, in 1955, when he suspended Maurice Richard, the Montreal Canadiens' star, for the remainder of the season for bludgeoning a defenseman with his hockey stick and punching a linesman, riots erupted in Montreal. Without their star the team was quickly eliminated from the play-offs, and Campbell, refusing to back down on his disciplinary action, attended their next game and was kicked, punched, and pelted with garbage. Campbell, who was inducted into the Hockey Hall of Fame in 1966, retired as president of the NHL in 1977.

Capote, Truman (TRUMAN STRECKFUS PERSONS), U.S. novelist, short-story writer, and playwright (b. Sept. 30, 1924, New Orleans, La.—d. Aug. 25, 1984, Los Angeles, Calif.), as a scrupulous journalist and enfant terrible of American arts and letters enjoyed dual celebrity; he pioneered a new literary genre with his "nonfiction novel" (*In Cold Blood*) and, as a bibulous party-loving sybarite, entertained the rich and famous as well as television audiences with outrageous tales, recounted in a distinctively high-pitched Southern drawl. During his

childhood Capote was shuttled between aunts and cousins after his mother decided that she was temperamentally ill-suited to be a mother. A self-described "spiritual orphan" who spent his summers as a riverboat tap dancer and prize protégé to a fortune-teller, Capote drew on his experiences for many of his finely crafted stories. He abandoned formal education at age 17 and began working for *The New Yorker* magazine sorting and clipping cartoons. In 1945 he made a major literary coup with the haunting short story "Miriam," which he sold to *Mademoiselle* magazine; it won the O. Henry Memorial Award the following year, the first of four such awards he received. It was with his

first novel, though, *Other Voices, Other Rooms* (1948), a sensitive portrayal of a Southern boy's search for his father and his own identity, that he became famous at the age of 23. Capote, who strived for wealth and fame, was a master self-promoter; the dust jacket on his first novel, with a photograph of himself languishing on a sofa looking like a cherub in blond bangs and a checkered weskit, created almost a bigger sensation than the novel itself. The novel that established his reputation was *In Cold Blood*, a chilling nonfiction account of the two men who massacred a Kansas family. Capote spent six years interviewing the principals in the case, and critics were astonished by the long sections of dialogue that he recorded verbatim from memory. Some of Capote's other highly stylized works included *A Tree of Night* (1949), *The Grass Harp* (1951), *The Muses Are Heard* (1956), *Breakfast at Tiffany's* (1958; film version 1961), *Observations* (1959), and *Music for Chameleons* (1980). He was also co-author of the motion picture *Beat the Devil*, co-wrote the screenplay for *The Innocents*, and adapted some of his stories, including "A Christmas Memory" and "Thanksgiving Visitor," for television. In later years his dependence on drugs and alcohol stifled his productivity, and his long-awaited masterpiece *Answered Prayers* was unfinished at the time of his death.

Chan Sy, Kampuchean politician (b. 1932, Kompong Chhnang Province, Cambodia, French Indochina—d. December 1984, Moscow, U.S.S.R.), was premier of Kampuchea from February 1982 after having served as acting premier from December 1981, when his predecessor, Pen Sovan, was dismissed from office. Chan Sy, who joined the Khmer Viet Minh forces in 1950, left Cambodia (Kampuchea) in 1954 after the Geneva Conference of that year recognized Prince Norodom Sihanouk's government as the sole legitimate authority in independent Cambodia. A member of the Communist Party from 1960, Chan Sy was believed to have returned in 1970 after the coup that ousted Sihanouk and placed the pro-U.S. Lon Nol in power. Chan Sy, who was opposed to the ultranationalist Pol Pot, by whose partisans he was detained in 1973, next appeared on the scene in 1978, with the forces of the Kampuchean United Front for National Salvation that with Vietnamese support penetrated into eastern Cambodia in December of that year. After some months' military training in the U.S.S.R. in 1980 he was appointed deputy defense minister and the following year defense minister and vice-president of the Council of Ministers; the same year he also became a member of the Politburo of the People's Revolutionary (Communist) Party of Kampuchea. When Pen Sovan was replaced as party secretary-general by Heng Samrin, Chan Sy took over the premiership. Considered a steadfast adherent of Vietnam's Kampuchean policy, Chan Sy had made visits to Bulgaria and East Germany as well as to the U.S.S.R. In the National Assembly he represented his native province. Chan Sy's death in a Moscow hospital, where he was being treated for a cardiac ailment, was reported by the Vietnamese information agency on December 31. He was believed to have died some days earlier.

Chavan, Yeshwantrao Balvantrao, Indian politician (b. March 12, 1913, Satara, near Bombay, India—d. Nov. 25, 1984, New Delhi, India), held ministerial office for 15 years, serving successively under Prime Ministers Jawaharlal Nehru, Lal Shastri, and Indira Gandhi. He was minister of defense (1962–66), of home affairs (1966–70), of finance (1970–74), and of external affairs (1974–77). The son of a peasant, he was nevertheless educated at Rajaram College, Kolhapur, and at Poona University. For some years he practiced law at Karad. A determined nationalist, he favoured Communism and increasingly despised Mohandas Gandhi's policy of civil disobedience. Chavan became a guerrilla fighter in 1942 but was arrested and imprisoned in 1944. Elected to the Bombay Legislative Assembly (1946), he became the province's chief minister (1956) and was chief minister of the new state of Maharashtra (1960–62). When he was India's defense minister, his modernization of the Army and Air Force contributed to India's success in the 1965 and 1971 wars with Pakistan. Uneasy about the state of emergency declared by Indira Gandhi (1975), he nevertheless remained in her Cabinet, breaking with her only when, shortly before the election of 1977, he became leader of the official Congress parliamentary party. Chavan briefly served as deputy prime minister (1979), but he failed to form a government (July 1979) when invited to do so. He barely retained his seat in the 1980 election and further lost face by finally joining Indira Gandhi's Congress (I) party.

Chinamano, Josiah, Zimbabwean politician (b. Oct. 19, 1922, near Salisbury, Southern Rhodesia—d. Oct. 1, 1984, Harare, Zimbabwe), was vice-president and a leading member of Joshua Nkomo's opposition party, the Zimbabwe African People's Union (ZAPU). He had been active in the struggle to establish his country's independence as an African-ruled state and on his death was declared a national hero. Educated by missionaries, and at Fort Hare College in South Africa, he became a teacher and administrator in Southern Rhodesia. Increasingly involved in the struggle against white rule, Chinamano was first imprisoned in 1964 for political opposition and was frequently detained during succeeding years. When Rhodesia became the independent state of Zimbabwe in 1980, he was appointed minister of transport in Robert Mugabe's first Cabinet; he was dismissed with other ZAPU ministers two years later on alleged charges of plotting to overthrow the government. He remained a ZAPU member of Parliament.

Christensen, Lew, U.S. dancer, choreographer, and teacher (b. May 9, 1909, Brigham City, Utah—d. Oct. 9, 1984, Burlingame, Calif.), was a premier classical ballet dancer who mesmerized audiences with his performances. He was the first male ballet star in the U.S., creating in 1937 the title role in George Balanchine's *Apollo.* Christensen, together with his brothers, William (founder of Utah's Ballet West) and Harold (a one-time director of the San Francisco Ballet school), was responsible for ushering in

quality ballet in the western U.S. Christensen, who launched his career in the 1930s, danced with the American Ballet before serving as choreographer, ballet master, and soloist (1936–40) with Ballet Caravan and then as a soloist (1941–42) for Dance Players. In 1946 he joined the faculty of the School of American Ballet and became master of Ballet Society and later of the New York City Ballet. He left the latter post in 1952 to become director and principal choreographer of the San Francisco Ballet. As a choreographer he created such popular and diverse works as *Charade, Filling Station, Pocahontas, Jinx, Black Face, Con Amore,* a full-length production of *The Nutcracker,* and *Jest of Cards.* At the time of his death Christensen was co-director of the San Francisco Ballet.

Church, Frank Forrester, U.S. politician (b. July 25, 1924, Boise, Idaho—d. April 7, 1984, Bethesda, Md.), as a Democratic senator from Idaho from 1956 to 1980, served as one of the U.S. Senate's most persuasive and leading liberal voices and was best known as a champion of civil rights and environmental legislation and for his opposition to the Vietnam war. During World War II, Church interrupted his college education at Stanford University to serve as a military intelligence officer in Asia. After the war he returned to Stanford and was graduated in 1947. While pursuing a law degree at Harvard University he was afflicted with severe back pain and transferred to Stanford Law School in the hope that warmer weather would be kinder to his health. Though doctors subsequently discovered that he had cancer and gave him six months to live, Church recovered after surgery and radiation therapy and won a law degree in 1950. He then returned to his birthplace to practice law and made an unsuccessful bid for a seat in the Idaho legislature. In 1956 Church, a onetime Republican, ran for the U.S. Senate as a Democrat and defeated the Republican incumbent, Herman Welker. During his 24 years in office, Church sponsored legislation that supported civil rights, conservation, and social welfare (especially for the aged). He was equally active in foreign affairs, and in 1970 he co-sponsored the Church–Cooper amendment cutting off U.S. funding for the war in Cambodia, which was adopted that year. As chairman (1975) of the Senate Select Committee on Intelligence, Church gained a reputation as a dogged investigator of abuses by government agencies. He exposed widespread misconduct by the CIA and other intelligence agencies, which led to curbs of abuses. In 1976 Church waged an unsuccessful three-month campaign to secure the Democratic presidential nomination but the following year again exhibited his expertise in foreign affairs as a member of the Senate Foreign Relations Committee. He met and persuaded Cuban leader Fidel Castro to allow 84 U.S. citizens and their families to leave Cuba. In 1979 Church enthusiastically became chairman of the Foreign Relations Committee, but in the following year he was defeated in his bid for reelection.

Clark, Mark Wayne, general (ret.), U.S. Army (b. May 1, 1896, Madison Barracks, N.Y.—d. April 17, 1984, Charleston, S.C.), was a dynamic World War II commander whose greatest feat was as leader of the Allied forces during the hard-fought Italian campaign (1943–45) against the Axis powers, a grueling but successful 20-month-long battle from the toe to the top of the Italian boot. Clark, a graduate (1917) of the U.S. Military Academy at West Point, N.Y., was wounded while serving in France during World War I. In 1942 he rose to prominence as chief of staff of Army Ground Forces and then as deputy to Gen. Dwight D. Eisenhower. In the latter post he skillfully executed delicate assignments related to the Allied invasion of North Africa, including a daring mission to Algeria smuggled ashore from aboard a submarine to gain French support for the imminent invasion. In 1943 Clark, then 46 and the country's youngest three-star general, was chosen by Eisenhower to command the U.S. 5th Army,

which landed at Salerno, Italy, in September; later that month Clark secured the surrender of the Italian fleet and the government of Marshal Pietro Badoglio. In the following year, on June 4, his army captured Rome, the first enemy capital to fall. But his decision to concentrate on taking the city was criticized by some who felt that he could have annihilated the entire German Army had he pursued them. He was also held accountable for the controversial bombing of the historic abbey at Monte Cassino and for the ill-fated attempt to cross the Rapido River, where U.S. forces suffered more than 1,600 casualties. In December 1944 Clark was named commander of the 15th Army Group, and on May 2, 1945, the Germans surrendered to him in the north of Italy. He then was appointed Allied high commissioner in Austria before returning to the U.S. to command the 6th Army and then the Army Field Forces. In 1952 he became supreme commander of UN forces during the last year of the Korean War and held that post until the signing of an armistice in July 1953. Clark retired from the military the same year and from 1954 to 1965 served as president of the Citadel, a private military college in Charleston, S.C. His books included *Calculated Risk* (1950) and *From the Danube to the Yalu* (1954).

Coogan, Jackie (JOHN LESLIE COOGAN, JR.), U.S. actor (b. Oct. 26, 1914, Los Angeles, Calif.—d. March 1, 1984, Santa Monica, Calif.), as the first and greatest child star of silent motion pictures, endeared himself to audiences with his soulful eyes, cherubic face, and Buster Brown haircut. Coogan became the number one box-office attraction after co-starring with Charlie Chaplin in the classic film *The Kid* (1921), in which he combined comedy and pathos in his sensitive portrayal of an orphaned ragamuffin. Over the following ten years his films, including *Peck's Bad Boy* (1921), *Oliver Twist* (1922), *Little Robinson Crusoe* (1924), *Old Clothes* (1925), and two talkies, *Tom Sawyer* (1930) and *Huckleberry Finn* (1931), were unashamedly sentimental and exploited his role as the little tramp. He was also irresistible in *Daddy* (1923), *The Rag Man* (1924), and *Buttons* (1927). His star began to wane after he grew older, and Coogan, who had made millions, was shattered when shortly before his 21st birthday his father was killed in an automobile accident. Later, when his mother and stepfather denied him the money he had earned, Coogan sued—and lost a 1937 court battle to recover his earnings. Shortly thereafter the so-called Coogan Act was passed in California, protecting all child stars from similar circumstances by mandating that all juvenile earnings be deposited into court-administered trust funds. In 1937 Coogan became a stage actor and later was in constant demand as a character actor. Balding and obese in middle age, he became especially popular as the ghoulish Uncle Fester on the television program "The Addams Family" (1964–66). Coogan, who was married to Betty Grable, Flower Parry, and Anne McCormick, wedded his last wife,

Dorothea Lamphere, in 1951. Some of his last film appearances were in *John Goldfarb, Please Come Home* (1965) and *The Shakiest Gun in the West* (1968). He died two hours after having a heart attack.

Cooper, Tommy, British comedian (b. March 1922, Caerphilly, Wales—d. April 15, 1984, London, England), was a naturally funny man who was steeped in the tradition of the variety theatre and executed his most successful conjuring trick by reviving the spirit of music hall on television. Though he was a brilliant illusionist and a member of the Magic Circle, he built his act around tricks that went disastrously wrong, accompanied by a patter that from anyone else would have been humourless. Cooper discovered his comic talent while serving with the forces during World War II. He adopted the fez that was his trademark while stationed in North Africa and wore it perched on top of his 19-m (6-ft 3-in) frame. Though he appeared at the Windmill Theatre and the London Palladium before live audiences, he achieved his greatest success on television. When he collapsed on stage during a live television broadcast from Her Majesty's Theatre, the audience naturally assumed it was part of the act; however, Cooper died shortly afterward.

Cori, Carl Ferdinand, U.S. biochemist (b. Dec. 5, 1896, Prague, Czech.—d. Oct. 20, 1984, Cambridge, Mass.), with his wife, Gerty, determined how glycogen (animal starch) is catalytically converted, a discovery that led to a greater understanding of diabetes mellitus and earned them the 1947 Nobel Prize for Physiology or Medicine (a prize they shared with the Argentine physiologist Bernardo Houssay). Cori conducted his scientific training at the German University in Prague, where he met Gerty and where the two earned M.D.'s in 1920, the same year they married. After immigrating to the U.S. in 1922, the couple joined the Institute for the Study of Malignant Disease, Buffalo, N.Y., where he was a biochemist and she served as an assistant pathologist and as an assistant biochemist from 1922 to 1931. In 1931 they moved to the Washington University medical school, St. Louis, Mo., where they conducted their pioneering research. Cori served as professor of pharmacology and biochemistry and as chairman of the biochemistry department (from 1947). There, in 1936, they isolated from muscle tissue a previously unknown compound of the simple sugar glucose, glucose 1-phosphate (phosphate bound to a specific carbon atom on the glucose molecule). They found that this compound, also referred to as the Cori ester, represents the first step in the conversion of glycogen into glucose and also, because the reaction is reversible, in some cases the last step in the conversion of blood glucose to glycogen. In 1942 the Coris isolated and purified polysaccharide phosphorylase, the enzyme responsible for catalyzing the glycogen–Cori ester reaction. They used this enzyme to synthesize glycogen in a test tube. With this achievement they were able to formulate the "Cori cycle," in which they postulated that liver glycogen is converted to blood glucose that is then reconverted to glycogen in muscle tissue. The subsequent breakdown of the glycogen to lactic acid provides the energy used in muscle contraction. The lactic acid is used to reform glycogen in the liver to complete the cycle. The Coris then studied the ways in which hormones affect carbohydrate metabolism in animals. They determined that the hormone adrenaline (epinephrine) induces the formation of a type of phosphorylase enzyme that encourages the conversion of glycogen to glucose and also that the hormone insulin causes the removal of sugar from the blood by promoting the addition of phosphate to glucose. The latter discovery was essential to a better understanding of the disease diabetes mellitus. After the death of his wife in 1957, Cori did research on the physicochemical mode of action of enzymes involved in the breakdown of glycogen to lactic acid.

Cortázar, Julio, Argentine writer (b. Aug. 26, 1914, Brussels, Belgium—d. Feb. 12, 1984, Paris, France), was an important contemporary avant-garde Latin-American author whose works were characterized by subtle humour, originality, and a sinister sense of fantasy intertwined with themes that dealt with reincarnation and identity. His best-known novel, *Rayuela* (*Hopscotch,* 1966), which symbolized the abstract dance of humans and the mystical truth that the player perceives as he hops upon the last square of "heaven," was published in 1963. Cortázar grew up in Argentina and taught high school there (1935–45) until he became a translator for publishing houses. A political activist who supported the Cuban and Nicaraguan revolutions, Cortázar left Argentina in 1951 out of opposition to Pres. Juan Perón. Though he took up residence in France, he frequently participated in the demonstrations that were held every Thursday at the Argentine embassy in Paris. His early writings during the 1930s and '40s were composed under the pseudonym Julio Denis, but it was not until the 1960s that Cortázar's experimental works became widely hailed in the U.S. Besides *Rayuela,* he turned out numerous novels and short stories, most notably *Los premios* (1960; *The Winners,* 1965) and *El libro de Manuel* (1973; *A Manual for Manuel,* 1978). Cortázar, whose works reflected the influences of Edgar Allan Poe and Jorge Luis Borges, also published *Final del juego* (1956; *The End of the Game and Other Stories,* 1967), *Las armas secretas* (1959; *Blow-up and Other Stories,* 1968), and his final work, *Les autonautes de la cosmoroute* (1983). Though Cortázar became a French citizen in 1981, he never renounced his Argentine citizenship and returned briefly to the country shortly before the new civilian president, Raúl Alfonsín, was installed in December 1983.

Crankshaw, Edward, British writer (b. Jan. 3, 1909, Woodford, Essex, England—d. Nov. 30, 1984, Hawkhurst, Kent, England), was a specialist in the modern history of Russia and eastern and central Europe and served as Soviet correspondent for *The Observer* newspaper (1947–68). He was educated at Bishop's Stortford College and worked briefly on *The Times* before going to Vienna to teach English. During World War II he was posted to Military Intelligence because of his fluency in German but was later sent as a general staff officer attached to the British military mission in Moscow (1941–43). His experiences and what he learned of Russia, its history, and its people resulted in a number of original and perceptive studies, including *Russia and the Russians* (1947), *Russia by Daylight* (1951), *Russia Without Stalin* (1956), *Khrushchev's Russia* (1959), and *Khrushchev: A Biography* (1966). Crankshaw, who wrote his first studies of Vienna in 1938, returned to the subject of Austrian history with such brilliant and scholarly works as *The Fall of the House of Habsburg* (1963), *Maria Theresa* (1969), and *The Habsburgs* (1971). He was awarded Vienna's Ehrenkreuz für Wissenschaft und Kunst, first class (1964). He finally turned again to Russian themes, with a study of Tolstoy (1974) and *The Shadow of the Winter Palace: The Drift to Revolution 1825–1917* (1976). His last book, an anthology of his articles, *Putting Up with the Russians,* was published in 1984.

Crawford, Sir John Grenfell, Australian agricultural economist and administrator (b. April 4, 1910, Sydney, Australia—d. Oct. 28, 1984, Canberra, Australia), was the first vice-chancellor of the Australian National University (1968–73), its chancellor from 1976, and an adviser to the World Bank. Educated at Sydney and Harvard universities, he was a research fellow at Sydney (1933–35) and a part-time lecturer in agricultural economics (1934–41). He was economic adviser to the Rural Bank of New South Wales (1935–43) and in the latter half of World War II became director of the Bureau of Agricultural Economics in the Ministry of Postwar Reconstruction. Crawford was secretary to the Department of Commerce and Agriculture (1950–56) and to the Department of Trade (1956–60). A skilled international negotiator, he helped facilitate Australia's swift resumption of normal trade with Japan after the war. After resigning from the civil service in 1960, he served as director of the Research School of Pacific Studies at the Australian National University (1960–67). Crawford was a member of the World Bank's Economic Mission to India (1964–65) and served on many of the bank's committees.

Cronin, Joseph Edward ("JOE"), U.S. baseball player (b. Oct. 12, 1906, San Francisco, Calif.—d. Sept. 7, 1984, Osterville, Mass.), was the star shortstop and player-manager of the Washington Senators (1928–34) and Boston Red Sox (1934–47) professional baseball teams with a lifetime batting average of .301 and later presided as the easygoing president of the American League (1959–73). Cronin, a onetime bank clerk, began his 20-year professional baseball career with the Pittsburgh Pirates in 1926. In 1928 he was sold to the Washington Senators and became known for his outstanding clutch-hitting; he was named the American League's most valuable player in 1930, when he hit .346. He served as the Senators' manager from 1933 to 1934 before being sold to the Red Sox for $250,000 under a five-year, $50,000-a-year contract as player-manager. Though he took himself out of the regular lineup in 1942, he established an American League record in 1943 by belting five pitch-hit home runs. Cronin retired as an active player in 1945 when he broke a leg, but he continued to manage the club until 1947. He then served 11 years as a Red Sox executive before beginning his 14-year tenure as president of the American League. Cronin was elected to the Baseball Hall of Fame in 1956.

Culver, Roland Joseph, British actor (b. Aug. 31, 1900, London, England—d. Feb. 29, 1984, London), portrayed the impeccable English gentleman in more than 40 British plays and more than 50 British and U.S. films. He displayed a special flair for comedy and won his greatest stage success as Commander Rogers in Terence Rattigan's farce *French Without Tears* (1936). In the 1950s he gave distinguished performances in *Who Is Sylvia?* and *The Deep Blue Sea,* also by Rattigan. After leaving school he served during World War I as a pilot, then studied at the Royal Academy of Dramatic Art before spending several years in repertory theatre. After *French Without Tears* was filmed, he appeared in such motion pictures as *Night Train* (1939), *Spitfire* (1942), and the thriller *Dead of Night* (1945) and continued his stage career with such successes as *An Ideal Husband* (1943) and, in New York, *The Little Hut* (1953). In 1956 Culver appeared in his own play, *A River Breeze.* Although somewhat typecast as a character actor, his range extended from drama to comedy, and his later television performances, as "Uncle Vanya" and as the duke of Omnium on the serial "The Pallisers," exhibited the depth of his understated talent. His films during the postwar period included *Trio, Bonjour Tristesse, The Yellow Rolls-Royce,* and *Rockets Galore.* Culver published his memoirs, *Not Quite a Gentleman,* in 1979, and in 1980 he was made an officer of the Order of the British Empire.

Daly, Edward Joseph, U.S. airline executive (b. Nov. 20, 1922, Chicago, Ill.—d. Jan. 21, 1984, Orinda, Calif.), as the maverick founder (1950), chairman, and principal stockholder of World Airways, instituted the no-frills budget airfare in 1979, which featured one-way, cross-country tickets for $99.99. Daly, a self-styled "Wyatt Earp of the airline industry," parlayed the 1950 purchase of two war-surplus C-46 cargo planes into a highly profitable charter carrier service in the 1960s. Though he originally piloted the low-fare passenger service in the 1950s, the concept did not catch fire until the deregulation of the airline industry in 1978. When his no-frills fares touched off a price war among the major carriers, Daly lowered his fares even further in spite of World's plummeting revenues. His brainchild was near financial disaster in 1979 because of high fuel costs, competition, a strike, and a fleet of DC-10 jets that were temporarily grounded after the crash of an American Airlines DC-10 in Chicago. Under a $14 million debt-restructuring plan, World Airways was buoyed in 1982, and in 1983 the carrier showed a $12 million third-quarter profit. Daly also captured headlines in 1975 when, packing a pistol on his hip, he piloted an unauthorized airlift of orphans aboard the last U.S. plane out of Da Nang, South Vietnam.

Dart, Justin Whitlock, U.S. industrialist (b. Aug. 17, 1907, Evanston, Ill.—d. Jan. 26, 1984, Los Angeles, Calif.), was the perspicacious chairman of the executive committee of Dart & Kraft Inc., a food and consumer products conglomerate, and an outspoken member of Pres. Ronald Reagan's "kitchen cabinet," an advisory group of longtime friends. Shortly after graduating in 1929 from Northwestern University in Evanston, Dart married Ruth Walgreen, the daughter of the drugstore chain owner, and he joined Walgreens as a stock clerk. He rose to be president of the company in 1930 and in 1939 was named general manager; in the same year he and his wife were divorced. In 1941 Dart resigned from Walgreens to take command of the fledgling Rexall Drug Co. He soon turned Rexall into Dart Industries, a conglomerate whose subsidiaries manufactured Tupperware containers, Duracell batteries, and West Bend appliances. In 1977 Dart sold his interest in Rexall but kept his newer acquisitions, and in 1980 he formed an empire when he merged his company with Kraft Foods. Though he had been a close friend, supporter, and adviser to Reagan since the 1940s, Dart was adamant in his refusal to accept an administration position when Reagan became president. The crusty Dart quipped, "Ron has enough experience with Justin Dart to know that I don't want a damn thing from him." In spite of his protest Reagan named Dart to the board of directors of the Communications Satellite Corporation in 1982.

De Filippo, Eduardo, Italian actor and playwright (b. May 1900, Naples, Italy—d. Oct. 31, 1984, Rome, Italy), won widespread acclaim for his sensitive performances on stage and screen, was the prolific author of nearly 60 plays, and was also a director of drama and opera. By repute an illegitimate son of the Naples farce writer Eduardo Scarpetta, he was, in his teens, a member of Scarpetta's theatrical company. De Filippo and his two brothers founded their own Humorous Theatre in 1932, producing plays and later turning to film. His own plays were mostly set in Naples and often concerned the vagaries of family life, neatly portraying facets of class and background. They were widely translated and performed abroad, even in Moscow; in London some of his leading roles were played by Laurence Olivier. Among his most famous plays were *Naples Millionaire* (1945) and *Saturday, Sunday, Monday* (1959). In 1953 he became proprietor and director of the San Ferdinando Theatre in Naples. In later life he lectured on drama at the University of Rome; in 1981 he was honoured by appointment as senator for life.

Delmar, Kenny, U.S. radio personality (b. 1911, Boston, Mass.—d. July 14, 1984, Stamford, Conn.), was one of the best talents on the air during the golden age of radio during the 1930s and '40s and was probably best remembered as the blustery Senator Beauregard Claghorn, one of the stars of Allen's Alley on "The Fred Allen Show" (1946–49). Delmar's characterization of the ethnocentric Southern senator, who drank only from Dixie cups and refused to drive through the Lincoln Tunnel, was adapted from the mannerisms of a Texas cattle rancher who gave Delmar a ride when he was hitchhiking. The senator's favourite expression, "That's a joke, son," became one of the country's most

often mimicked phrases. The gifted impersonator touched off a nationwide panic in 1938 when, posing as the U.S. secretary of the interior and speaking in a voice that sounded like Pres. Franklin D. Roosevelt's, he announced that Martians were invading and destroying the Earth in the famous "War of the Worlds" radio broadcast presented by Orson Welles and "The Mercury Theatre on the Air." The simulated broadcast with its realistic news bulletins terrified hundreds of listeners who thought the reports were genuine. Delmar was also a regular on "The Danny Kaye Show," was host of the game show "Hollywood Jackpot" (1946), and the announcer on "The Jack Benny Program," "The RCA Victor Show," and "March of Time."

Dickinson, Thorold Barron, British film director (b. Nov. 16, 1903, Bristol, England—d. April 14, 1984, Woolton Hill, Berkshire, England), made significant contributions to British cinema with such films as *Gaslight* (1940) and *The Queen of Spades* (1949) and as a teacher at the Slade School of Fine Art, University of London. Educated at Keble College, Oxford, he worked as a stage manager in repertory theatre before joining Ealing Studios, first as an editor, then as director of *The High Command*. Shortly after making two documentaries on the Spanish Civil War in 1938, he directed *Gaslight,* a psychological thriller. During World War II he made films for the War Office and the Army Kinematograph Service. A dedicated professional craftsman, Dickinson never developed a marked individual style, though his best film, *The Queen of Spades,* was technically interesting. His later work included *Secret People* (1951) and an Israeli film, *Hill 24 Doesn't Answer* (1953–55). In 1960, after four years as head of film services for the UN in New York City, he created the film studies department at the Slade School where he served as professor from 1967 to 1971. He was also visiting professor of film studies at the University of Surrey (1975–77) and the author of *Soviet Cinema* (with Catherine de la Roche, 1948) and *A Discovery of Cinema* (1971). Dickinson, who was president (1958–66) of the International Federation of Film Societies, was made a Commander of the Order of the British Empire in 1973.

Dirac, Paul Adrien Maurice, British physicist (b. Aug. 8, 1902, Bristol, England—d. Oct. 20, 1984, Tallahassee, Fla.), was Lucasian professor of mathematics at the University of Cambridge from 1932 to 1969 and the creator of the complete theoretical formulation of quantum mechanics. He developed the work of Louis de Broglie, Werner Heisenberg, and Erwin Schrödinger by linking it to classical mechanical theory and advancing the theory of positrons, the basis of antimatter. Dirac published *The Principles of Quantum Mechanics* in 1930 and was awarded the Nobel Prize for Physics three years later. He was the son of a Swiss father and an English mother. He attended the University of Bristol, where he studied electrical engineering before conducting research in mathematics at St. John's College, Cambridge. A paper in 1925 made his first outstanding contribution to quantum theory. He was made a fellow of the Royal Society in 1930 and awarded the Royal Society's Royal Medal in 1939 and its Copley Medal in 1952. Dirac continued to refine quantum theory, but it was left largely to others to develop his later work on quantum electrodynamics. He became professor of physics at Florida State University in 1971 and was appointed to the Order of Merit in 1973.

Dors, Diana (DIANA FLUCK), British actress (b. Oct. 23, 1931, Swindon, England—d. May 4, 1984, Windsor, England), suffered in the long run from the publicity drive during the 1950s to make her a rival to Marilyn Monroe, becoming a celebrity before her acting talent had had time to mature and discover its own course. Throughout her career, from the film *Yield to the Night* (1956), in which she played a condemned murderess, to her stage role as Jocasta

in *Oedipus* (1974), she tried to escape from the "blond bombshell" image (later replaced by that of a bosomy, overweight matron) which overshadowed her comic gifts and sense of humour. She studied at the London Academy of Dramatic Art and made her screen debut at age 15 in *The Shop at Sly Corner* before signing a contract with the Rank Organisation. A later contract with RKO in Hollywood failed to develop her career, and in 1960 she sold her memoirs, suitably sensational, to a newspaper for £35,000. Most of her roles were predictable, and most of her films were second-rate thrillers. During the 1970s she appeared in a play, *Three Months Gone,* and a television series, "Queenie's Castle." After Dors declared bankruptcy in 1968, she married an actor, Alan Lake, her third husband, and she made headlines again in 1970 when Lake was imprisoned after a brawl. She later ran a newspaper advice column and, already suffering from cancer, appeared in a television slimmers' program. She faced her illness with courage and projected the personality that had been hidden behind a synthetic image. Her later memoirs, *For Adults Only,* lived up to its lurid title.

Eckstein, Otto, German-born economist (b. Aug. 1, 1927, Ulm, Germany—d. March 22, 1984, Boston, Mass.), was a leading proponent of using econometrics (the statistical and mathematical analysis of economic relationships) as a forecasting tool for government and business planning and was the co-founder of Data Resources, Inc., a leading economic forecasting company that served both private business and government. In 1938 Eckstein fled Germany with his parents and arrived in the U.S. the following year. While in his teens he had already decided to study economics and, after serving in the U.S. Army (1946–47), he earned a B.A. in economics at Princeton University in 1951. After receiving a Ph.D. from Harvard University in 1955, Eckstein joined the faculty there and imparted his views to generations of undergraduates, whom he was most fond of teaching. From 1964 to 1966 the staunch liberal served as a member of Pres. Lyndon B. Johnson's Council of Economic Advisers and helped formulate wage-price guidepost policies and some of the programs of the Great Society. After returning to Harvard he was recruited by Donald B. Marron (then president of Mitchell Hutchins, Inc., a small investment firm), and in 1968 the two founded Data Resources, which relied heavily on computers to analyze and forecast economic conditions. In 1979 Eckstein sold his booming business to McGraw-Hill and became a multimillionaire as a result of the transaction.

Edusei, Krobo, Ghanaian politician (b. 1915—d. Feb. 13, 1984), was a close associate of Kwame Nkrumah (independent Ghana's first prime minister and later president) and held various ministerial posts until Nkrumah's ouster in 1966. He belonged to a leading Ashanti family and worked in journalism before joining Nkrumah's Convention People's Party when it was founded in 1949. Imprisoned by the British authorities, he became the party propaganda secretary; then, when Ghana gained independence in 1957, Edusei was appointed minister of the interior. In 1962 Nkrumah dismissed him but later brought him back into the government as minister of agriculture. A scandal involving his wife's purchase of a £3,000 bed threatened his reputation. After the fall of Nkrumah, Edusei lost office and in 1968 was sentenced to 18 months' imprisonment. After his release he played some part in political affairs through the People's National Party until the fall of Pres. Hilla Limann in 1981 led to a further term of imprisonment. He was released shortly before his death.

Ehricke, Krafft A., German-born aeronautical engineer and physicist (b. March 24, 1917, Berlin, Germany—d. Dec. 11, 1984, La Jolla, Calif.), was a top-notch rocket specialist who during World War II served as a propulsion engineer in Germany's V-2 rocket program. Ehricke graduated from the Technical University of Berlin with a degree in aeronautical engineering; he also studied celestial mechanics and nuclear physics at the University of Berlin. In 1942 he began working at the secret Peenemünde rocket centre, where the V-2s, which devastated London in 1944, were developed and tested. In the U.S., Ehricke worked (1947–52) for the Army's missile program before joining the Convair division of the General Dynamics Corp. in San Diego, Calif. There he played a vital role in the design and development of such rockets as the Atlas (the nation's first intercontinental ballistic missile) and the Centaur (the first rocket to use liquid hydrogen as a propellant). A space enthusiast who envisioned flights to the Moon and planets and well-equipped space stations, Ehricke was also committed to what he termed the "extraterrestrial imperative" (man's obligation to expand the environmental and resource base beyond Earth in order to preserve life). Ehricke was chief scientific adviser to the space division of the Rockwell International Corp., builder of the manned Apollo spacecraft, and later the head of his own consulting concern, Space Global. In 1984 he was honoured with the Goddard Astronautics Award, given by the American Institute of Aeronautics and Astronautics.

Elliott, Michael Paul, British stage director (b. June 26, 1931, London, England—d. May 30, 1984, Manchester, England), played a major role in the creation of Manchester's Royal Exchange Theatre, which was immediately recognized as one of the country's leading repertory theatres. Elliott, whose name was particularly associated with the work of Henrik Ibsen, established his reputation in 1959 at the Lyric Theatre, Hammersmith, with a fine production of Ibsen's *Brand.* He was also recognized for his outstanding work in television. Educated at the University of Oxford, where he was responsible for his first amateur production, he joined BBC Television, where, over the course of his career, he directed more than 40 television productions, including many of the world theatre classics he had produced on stage. In 1961, at Stratford, he directed Vanessa Redgrave in *As You Like It* and was artistic director at London's Old Vic for the last season (1962–63) before the theatre became the home of the National Theatre Company in 1963. During the 1960s he worked on some notable productions for the Edinburgh Festival and the National Theatre, and he co-founded the 69 Theatre Company in Manchester (later the Royal Exchange Theatre Company), of which he was resident artistic director from 1973. Among its productions were *The Ordeal of Gilbert Pinfold, The Lady from the Sea,* and *The Family Reunion.* His television production of *King Lear,* with Laurence Olivier, won an Emmy award in 1983, and Elliott's final productions with the Royal Exchange included *The Dresser* (1980) and *Moby Dick* (1983). He was made an Officer of the Order of the British Empire in 1980.

Emmanuel, Pierre (NOËL JEAN MATHIEU), French poet (b. May 3, 1916, Gan, Basses-Pyrénées, France—d. Sept. 22, 1984, Paris, France), with the publication of *Tombeau d'Orphée* in 1941 became a leading poet of the resistance to German occupation of France during World War II. He also fought with the Resistance in the département of the Drôme. After the war Emmanuel was a prolific writer and sometimes a controversial figure; he resigned his seat in the French Academy over the election of Félicien Marceau, whose war record he had criticized. Emmanuel studied mathematics and philosophy and taught before meeting the poet Pierre-Jean Jouve. Their association profoundly influenced Emmanuel's work, and he developed a rhetorical style, treating Christian themes within a context of human suffering sharpened by his experience of Nazi brutality. The figure of Christ, like those of Orpheus and the German poet Hölderlin, haunts his

work. His works, including *Sodome* (1944), *Babel* (1951), *Jacob* (1970), and *Le Grand Oeuvre* (1984), drew on biblical themes and were, at the same time, a reflection on language. A Gaullist, he worked for French radio and was a visiting lecturer at several U.S. universities. His prose works included an autobiography, *Qui est cet homme?* (1948), and essays. Emmanuel was awarded the Grand Prix de Poésie of the French Academy in 1963, and he was a Chevalier of the Légion d'Honneur.

Fagerholm, Karl-August, Finnish politician (b. Dec. 31, 1901, Siuntio, Fin.—d. May 22, 1984, Helsinki, Fin.), as prime minister three times during 1948–58, faced strong opposition from the Communist Party and from the Soviet Union. Fagerholm was chairman (1920–23) of the barbers' union before becoming a Social Democratic member of Parliament in 1930 and served as minister for social affairs from 1937 to 1943. As leader of the Social Democrats, he was prime minister from 1948 to 1950, despite Communist opposition and accusations by the Soviet Union that he intended to undermine the Finnish-Soviet pact by taking Finland into NATO. During his second term, in 1956–57, he visited the Soviet Union, and relations appeared to have improved. After a period out of office he was reelected in August 1958 to head a coalition government against opposition from the Communists, who had become the largest party in Parliament. In December 1958 he was forced to resign after the recall of the Soviet ambassador. Fagerholm was a candidate for the presidency in 1956, but he was narrowly defeated by Urho Kaleva Kekkonen. He also served several times as speaker of Parliament.

Faiz, Faiz Ahmad, Pakistani poet (b. 1911, Sialkot, Punjab, India—d. Nov. 20, 1984, Lahore, Pakistan), was perhaps the most popular and gifted poet of postindependence Pakistan. Writing in Urdu, he was a notable master of the *ghazal,* a short lyric form, and wrote poignantly of adverse personal experiences, such as imprisonment. Educated at Government College, Lahore, he became a teacher, and during World War II he served in the Indian Army as a noncombatant, reaching the rank of lieutenant colonel. After the independence of Pakistan (1947) he became an editor and later editor in chief of the *Pakistan Times,* a Lahore English-language opposition newspaper. Accused, with various army officers, of plotting against the government of Liaquat Ali Khan, he was sentenced to seven years' imprisonment, serving nearly the full term. He was scarcely back with the *Pakistan Times* when, on the accession to power (1958) of Gen. Mohammad Ayub Khan, the paper was taken over by the government and its left-wing staff dismissed. During the presidency (1971–77) of Zulfikar Ali Bhutto, Faiz was commissioned to set up a National Council for the Arts. After Bhutto's fall he retired to Lahore but also edited a magazine entitled *Lotus,* published in Beirut. Almost a Communist in his political views, he sometimes acted as an unofficial intermediary with Moscow; he won the Lenin Peace Prize in 1962. His poetry was translated into English by V. G. Kiernan.

Ferencsik, Janos, Hungarian conductor (b. Jan. 18, 1907, Budapest, Hung.—d. June 12, 1984, Budapest), was musical director of the Budapest Opera and chief conductor of the Hungarian National Philharmonic Orchestra. As guest conductor he appeared frequently at the Salzburg and Vienna festivals and also conducted in London, Edinburgh, the U.S., Australia, and Japan. He studied at the Budapest National Conservatory before joining the State Opera in 1927. Ferencsik was musical assistant at Bayreuth in 1930–31, but for most of his career he remained deeply attached to his native country and its composers. His interpretations of Bartok and Kodaly were outstanding for their sobriety and attention to detail. Though Ferencsik was sometimes criticized for a lack of warmth, he was highly praised for his dedication to art.

Fixx, James Fuller, U.S. author (b. April 23, 1932, New York, N.Y.—d. July 20, 1984, Hardwick, Vt.), was a onetime 100-kg (220-lb), two-pack-a-day smoker who inspired a nation to take up jogging when he shed 60 lb (26 kg), became a marathon runner, and espoused the joys of physical fitness in his best-selling book *The Complete Book of Running* (1977). Fixx, a graduate of Oberlin (Ohio) College (1957), served as a magazine editor for *The Saturday Review, McCall's, Life,* and *Horizon* before launching his career as an author with *Games for the Superintelligent* (1972). Fixx had taken up jogging in 1967 to help rehabilitate a tendon pulled while playing tennis, and running became his avocation. His enthusiasm, coupled with his belief that running can increase life expectancy, reduce the risk of heart attack, and improve overall well-being, ensured the success of *The Complete Book of Running* and its sequel, *Jim Fixx's Second Book of Running* (1980), sales of which made him a millionaire. The guru of fitness, though, had a family history of heart disease; Fixx's father had been first stricken at 35 and had died at 43 of a massive heart attack. Ironically, Fixx, who ran 16 to 24 km (10 to 15 mi) per day, was found dead on a jogging path after experiencing a massive heart attack. Though some argued that genetics had prescribed his early death, others felt that had Fixx agreed to a medical exam his life might have been lengthened by a bypass operation, because an autopsy revealed two blocked coronary arteries. At the time of his death Fixx was completing *The Complete Book of Sports Performance,* which was to be published posthumously.

Foreman, Carl, U.S. screenwriter and producer (b. July 23, 1914, Chicago, Ill.—d. June 26, 1984, Beverly Hills, Calif.), wrote scripts for such blockbuster Hollywood motion pictures as *High Noon* (1952), *The Guns of Navarone* (1961), and *The Bridge on the River Kwai* (1957), the latter anonymously because he was blacklisted in 1951 after being labeled an "uncooperative witness" by the House Committee on Un-American Activities. Foreman, who dropped out of law school, worked variously as a newspaper reporter, fiction writer, play director, and even carnival barker before moving to Hollywood in 1938. There he was employed as a story analyst and as a film laboratory technician and began collaborating on low-budget Bowery Boys films. During World War II he served in the Army Signal Corps where he met director Frank Capra and helped make orientation and training films. In 1945 Foreman became a screenwriter for producer-director Stanley Kramer. He penned scenarios that dealt with social issues, including *Home of the Brave* (1949; about racism) and *The Men* (1950; about disabled veterans). In 1951, after he took what later became known as the "diminished Fifth" (he neither went to jail nor named names) before the House Committee on Un-American Activities, his career nose-dived. Though the State Department attempted to revoke his passport, Foreman won a legal battle to retain it and moved to London so he could produce for foreign filmmakers. Because he co-wrote the screenplay for *The Bridge on the River Kwai* under a pseudonym, he could not claim the Academy Award, and the author of the novel, Pierre Boulle, received the Oscar for the screenwriting.

Foucault, Michel Paul, French philosopher (b. Oct. 15, 1926, Poitiers, France—d. June 25, 1984, Paris, France), as professor of the history of systems of thought at the Collège de France from 1970, published the second and third volumes of his *Histoire de la Sexualité (History of Sexuality),* which confirmed his reputation as one of the leading figures in French intellectual life. Trained as a philosopher, in his work he abolished the boundaries between the histories of science, history, philosophy, and sociology. The son of a doctor, he taught at the University of Clermont-Ferrand between 1960 and 1968, as well as in West Germany and Sweden, then spent two years at the University of Paris-Vincennes. His first works studied the history of mental illness and its treatment. *Folie et Déraison: Histoire de la folie à l'age classique* (1961; *Madness and Civilization*) dealt with the classification of madness in the 17th century; similarly, in *Surveiller et punir* (1975; *Discipline and Punish*) he examined the origins of the modern penal system. Yet, as he said, all his works were concerned primarily with "the history of the present," and his readers, academics and nonacademics, in France and throughout the world, were left in no doubt that it was their own attitudes toward social minorities that were being questioned. Like his contemporaries Jacques Lacan and Louis Althusser, he went beyond the assertions of Marxism while retaining a lively social conscience. Quoting Nietzche ("Where will we find a history of love, of cupidity, envy, conscience, pity, and cruelty?"), he set out to study the history of sexuality in a post-Freudian world. The first volume, published in 1976, was criticized by some for what was seen as a lack of rigour.

Gallup, George Horace, U.S. pollster (b. Nov. 18, 1901, Jefferson, Iowa—d. July 26, 1984, Tschingel, Switz.), gauged the pulse of world public opinion for nearly 50 years as the pioneering inventor in 1935 of the Gallup Poll, a systematic sampling of public opinion that permanently influenced the conduct and the outcome of U.S. marketing and electioneering strategy. While earning a Ph.D. in journalism at the University of Iowa, Gallup, who was fascinated by statistics, devised a sampling technique that incorporated a diverse sampling of potential respondents. The poll featured a representative mixture that included all races and a proportionate number of rich and poor and

professionals and factory workers. He first implemented the poll for measuring reader interest in newspapers and advertisements. In 1936 Gallup extended his scope to politics and validated his techniques by predicting the reelection of Franklin D. Roosevelt (other polls, notably that conducted by the *Literary Digest* magazine, predicted a victory for Republican Alfred M. Landon). Thereafter Gallup's name became synonymous with the "straw vote," and his reputation survived his prediction that Thomas E. Dewey would beat Harry S. Truman in 1948. In that election, Gallup felt he had tabulated his results too early and decided that he would use the telephone to poll the public rather than continue sending return mail postcards. Gallup, who founded the American Institute of Public Opinion in 1935, also founded the British Institute of Public Opinion the following year, and thereafter more than 25 affiliates were formed in foreign countries. In 1958 he formed the Gallup Organization Inc., which encompassed a wide range of activities including market research. Earlier Gallup had taught journalism at the University of Iowa, Drake University (Des Moines, Iowa), and Northwestern University (Evanston, Ill.) and later founded Quill and Scroll, a high school journalism honour society.

Gandhi, Indira Priyadarshini, Indian politician (b. Nov. 19, 1917, Allahabad, India—d. Oct. 31, 1984, Delhi, India), served as prime minister of India (1966–77 and 1980 until her death) and seemed, from her long tenure of office, almost a fixed star in the international political firmament. The only child of Jawaharlal Nehru, first prime minister (1947–64) of independent India, Indira grew up in a family that was strongly nationalistic, and on more than one occasion her parents were imprisoned. She attended schools in India and Geneva before entering Somerville College, University of Oxford. She returned home without a degree, accompanied by Feroze Gandhi, a lower-middle-class Parsi, whom she married in 1942 against her father's wishes. Her first advance into active politics was in 1959 when she accepted the presidency of the Congress party. Almost at once Gandhi displayed her capacity for forceful if questionable action by manipulating the fall of a Communist government in the state of Kerala. Minister of information under Lal Bahadur Shastri, she was elected leader of the Congress party when he suddenly died in 1966; her election also made her prime minister, but politicians were mistaken when they believed she would prove malleable. In 1969 she showed ruthless acumen in acquiring the post of president of India for her own nominee, Varahagir Venkata Giri, but this action split the Congress. She nevertheless won a two-thirds majority when she called an early election in 1971. Thereafter success abroad (her decision to support the Bengalis against West Pakistan in 1971 and her incorporation of Sikkim in 1974) appeared to consolidate her position. Nevertheless, increasing economic difficulties aroused unrest, and in 1975 her personal credibility was threatened both by a judgment against her in the Allahabad High Court for misappropriation of funds and by her failure to carry an election in Gujarat on which she had staked her reputation. Using the time-honoured claim that national security was in jeopardy, she proclaimed a state of emergency in June, arrested some opposition leaders, imposed total press censorship, and governed by decree. During this period she implemented several unpopular policies, including large-scale sterilization as a form of birth control. Her Congress faction was roundly defeated in the 1977 elections, and both she and her son Sanjay, leader of the Congress Youth Wing, lost their seats in Parliament. During the succeeding government by the Janata Party (1977–80), she was twice briefly imprisoned (October 1977 and December 1978) on charges of abuse of funds and authority. The Janata government eventually collapsed through its own incompetence, and Indira Gandhi, who had already brilliantly contested and won by over 77,000 votes a by-election in the southern state of Karnataka in November 1978, led the Congress (I) to overwhelming victory in the election of 1980. She then faced a series of problems, the most serious of which proved to be the agitation for the establishment of an autonomous Sikh state in the Punjab. When the Sikhs threatened to withhold the Punjab's vast resources of food and energy from the rest of India, Gandhi ordered the Indian Army on June 6, 1984, to storm the Golden Temple at Amritsar, the Sikhs' holiest shrine, where the Sikh rebel leaders, including Sant Jarnail Singh Bhindranwale (*q.v.*), were gathered. The attack on the Golden Temple and the resulting casualties, variously reported as between 450 and 1,200 dead, apparently sealed Gandhi's fate. She was assassinated by Sikh bodyguards as she walked to her office inside a New Delhi compound.

Gaye, Marvin Pentz, Jr., U.S. singer (b. April 2, 1939, Washington, D.C.—d. April 1, 1984, Los Angeles, Calif.), was a mellow-voiced soul singer who became one of the leading stars of Motown Records during the 1960s and 1970s and an influential force in pop music with a string of hits that included "I Heard It Through the Grapevine," "Let's Get It On," and "Mercy Mercy Me (the Ecology)." Gaye, the son of a minister,

sang in the church choir before joining the U.S. Air Force. After his discharge he returned to Washington and formed the Marquees. He later went to Chicago to join the Moonglows, who sang backup to Harvey Fuqua. When Fuqua went to Detroit in 1960, Gaye moved also and the following year married Anna Gordy (sister of Motown president Berry Gordy, Jr.). Gaye acquired a Motown recording contract, and in 1962 he made a breakthrough with "Stubborn Kind of Fellow," which vaulted to the top of the charts. His career skyrocketed with such solo hits as "Can I Get a Witness?," "You're a Wonderful One," and "How Sweet It Is to Be Loved by You." He also made a successful series of duet recordings with Mary Wells ("Together"), Kim Weston ("It Takes Two"), and most notably with Tammi Terrell. The two produced "Ain't No Mountain High Enough," "Your Precious Love," "Ain't Nothing Like the Real Thing," and "You're All I Need to Get By." The three-year union ended tragically in 1970 when Terrell died at age 24 and Gaye disappeared from the music scene. He reemerged in 1971 and launched a new phase in his career by composing and producing *What's Going On,* a highly successful social protest album. Gaye's song lyrics, which reflected his concern about spiritual impoverishment, urban decay, and ecological problems, became sexually explicit with the release of "Let's Get It On" in 1973. During the mid-1970s, amid a bitter divorce and financial difficulties, his career plummeted, only to revive in 1982 with his Grammy award-winning hit, "Sexual Healing," which was featured on his best-selling album *Midnight Love.* Gaye, who had moved in with his parents, was apparently shot to death by his father after an argument over a missing insurance letter.

Gaynor, Janet (LAURA GAINOR), U.S. actress (b. Oct. 6, 1906, Philadelphia, Pa.—d. Sept. 14, 1984, Palm Springs, Calif.), starred as a diminutive red-headed waif in a series of motion pictures during the 1920s and 1930s and garnered the first Academy Award for best actress in 1929 for her winsome performances in such silent films as *Sunrise* (1927), *Seventh Heaven* (1927), and *Street Angel* (1928). Gaynor made a successful transition to the talkies and played the innocent opposite leading man Charles Farrell in a dozen romantic films including *Sunny Side Up* (1929), *High Society Blues* (1930), *Tess of the Storm Country* (1932), and *Change of Heart* (1934). During her halcyon days in Hollywood, Gaynor was also celebrated for her roles in *Daddy Long Legs* (1931), *State Fair* (1933), and *Carolina* (1934) and for creating the character of Esther Blodgett in the original version of *A Star Is Born* (1937). At the height of her career in 1939, she retired to marry her second husband, dress designer Gilbert Adrian. After his death in 1959, she wed producer Paul Gregory in 1964. Gaynor came out of retirement in 1957 to star with Pat Boone in *Bernardine,* her last screen appearance. In 1979 she starred in the Broadway musical *Harold and Maude.* In 1982 she suffered severe injuries when a van crashed

into the taxi in which she was riding. Gaynor never physically recovered from the accident, and her death was attributed to the cumulative effects of her injuries.

Gemayel, Pierre, Lebanese politician (b. Nov. 1, 1905, Bikfaya, Metn, Lebanon—d. Aug. 29, 1984, Beirut, Lebanon), was leader of the Phalange Party, which he founded in 1936, and a moderating force in the Lebanese Maronite Christian community. He studied to be a pharmacist and operated a chemist's shop before going to the Berlin Olympic Games in 1936 as captain of the Lebanese football (soccer) team. Impressed by the discipline of the Nazi movement, he founded the Phalange as a Lebanese nationalist party and fought for independence from France, although he avoided any cooperation with European Fascist movements. Gemayel joined the forces of Fouad Chehab against those of Camille Chamoun when a rebellion broke out in 1958, led by former prime minister Saeb Salaam. Gemayel was elected a deputy in 1960 and held various government posts. With the rise of the Palestinians as a force in Lebanese politics after 1967, the Phalange emerged as the leading supporter of the governmental structure of Lebanon as delineated under the National Pact of 1943. It was the Phalangist militia that started the 1975 civil war with a massacre of Palestinians. Even so, Gemayel was considered moderate in comparison with his son Bashir; he saved the Christian forces by his understanding with Syria and opposed Bashir's alliance with Israel.

Geoffrey-Lloyd, Geoffrey William Geoffrey-Lloyd, BARON, British politician (b. Jan. 17, 1902, Newbury, England—d. Sept. 12, 1984, London, England), as minister in charge of petroleum warfare (1940–45) devised the English Channel pipelines that supplied fuel for the Allied invasion forces in Europe. In 1940 he set up land and sea defenses against Hitler's projected invasion of Britain. He was responsible for the establishment of FIDO (Fog Investigation Dispersal Operations), a device of oil-burning braziers set alongside runways to facilitate all-weather flying, and of PLUTO (Pipeline Under the Ocean), which, with tankers, supplied fuel to the Allied forces after the D-Day landings in France in 1944. He was educated at Trinity College, University of Cambridge, and entered Parliament as a National Conservative in 1931, lost his seat in the 1945 Labour landslide, but sat again in the House of Commons, as a Conservative, from 1950 to 1974. Geoffrey-Lloyd was president of the Birmingham Conservative and Unionist Association (1946–76). As parliamentary undersecretary to the Home Office (1935–39), he was responsible for the successful development of air raid precautions, and as minister for fuel and power (1951–55) he made important changes in the mining industry and launched Britain's atomic energy program. As minister of education (1957–59), he stressed the importance of training in technology. Geoffrey-Lloyd was created a life peer in 1974.

Gobbi, Tito, Italian opera singer (b. Oct. 24, 1915, Bassano del Grappa, Italy—d. March 5, 1984, Rome, Italy), was a spellbinding operatic baritone who was considered one of the world's finest singing actors with vivid character portrayals that sometimes even overshadowed the quality of his singing voice. Gobbi studied in Rome and first appeared at the La Scala opera house, Milan, in 1942 as Belcore in *L'elisir d'amore,* but it was not until after World War II, with his performance at the 1952 Salzburg Festival, where he sang Mozart's *Don Giovanni,* that he achieved international renown. Gobbi excelled in works that tested his range of acting skills: he portrayed Iago in *Otello* and the title character in *Rigoletto* but was best known as the sinister Roman police chief Scarpia in Puccini's *Tosca,* a part he sang more than 800 times. In Chicago he made his debut as an opera director in Verdi's *Simon Boccanegra* (1965) and continued to direct and teach master classes, both in the U.S. and Europe, during the latter years of his life. Gobbi also appeared in several films and wrote an autobiography, *My Life* (1979).

Goodrich, Frances, U.S. playwright and screenwriter (b. 1891?, Belleville, N.J.—d. Jan. 29, 1984, New York, N.Y.), who together with her husband, Albert Hackett, wrote scores of films and plays but was best known for their play *The Diary of Anne Frank* (1955), a poignant World War II drama that chronicled the plight of a small group of Jews hiding from the Nazis in an Amsterdam garret. The play won both the Pulitzer Prize and the New York Drama Critics Circle Award as best American play that year. In 1959 the couple adapted the play into a motion picture. Though Goodrich's first aspiration was to be a theatrical actress (she made her debut in *Come Out of the Kitchen* in 1916), she began writing plays with Hackett in 1930. Their motion-picture credits included *Father of the Bride, Father's Little Dividend, Easter Parade, Lady in the Dark,* and *It's a Wonderful Life* (with Frank Capra).

Guillén, Jorge, Spanish poet and critic (b. Jan. 18, 1893, Valladolid, Spain—d. Feb. 6, 1984, Málaga, Spain), was one of the outstanding figures in the so-called Generation of 1927 that included Federico García Lorca and was considered by some to be the greatest Spanish poet of his time. His work, from his first volume, *Cántico* (1928), to *Final* (1981), had a remarkable unity of design, celebrating human spirituality but with an increasing pessimism as the poet was forced to confront the realities of his time. Guillén studied in Germany and Spain before taking a post at the University of Paris; he later taught in Germany, Italy, England, Latin America, and the U.S., where he lectured at Wellesley (Mass.) College and at Harvard. He was professor of Spanish literature in Seville from 1931 to 1939, leaving the country as a firm opponent of the Franco regime. His cycle of poems *Clamor* appeared during 1957–63, followed by *Homenaje* (1967) and *Y Otros Poemas* (1973). He was also a critic and translator, notably of the works of the French poet Paul Valéry. Guillén was awarded the first Cervantes Prize in 1976.

Guney, Yilmaz, Turkish film director (b. 1937, eastern Turkey—d. Sept. 9, 1984, Paris, France), achieved enormous popularity as an actor, then international acclaim as a director; his film *Yol* won the Palme d'or at the 1982 Cannes Film Festival. A controversial figure and a lifelong opponent of the Turkish regime, Guney was a Kurd who started his cinema career in 1958 after studying law and economics. Imprisoned in 1961 for writing a left-wing novel, he gained wide popularity from his release in 1963 until his retirement from acting in 1968. He turned to directing, was again imprisoned, and in 1974 was sentenced to 19 years' imprisonment for the murder of a judge. Protesting his innocence, he continued to direct through detailed shooting scripts from his cell; *Yol,* like *The Herd* and *The Enemy,* was directed in this way. Guney's films constituted a far-reaching analysis of Turkish society. In 1981 he escaped from an open prison, went to Switzerland, and then settled in France, where he was an active supporter of Kurdish causes. His last film, *The Wall,* described a revolt by children in a prison in Ankara. Less successful than *Yol,* it was criticized partly because of the use of child actors.

Haddad, Saad, Lebanese militia leader (b. 1935?—d. Jan. 14, 1984, Marj Vyun, Lebanon), led a militia group which, from 1978 to 1982, controlled the southern part of Lebanon with Israeli support. After 1982 and the Israeli invasion of Lebanon, this "Free Republic of Lebanon" declined in importance as Israel realized Haddad's inability to guarantee the area against attack from Palestinian guerrillas. Haddad, an officer in the Lebanese Army, formed his own militia force from Christian and Shi'ah Muslim troops after the collapse of the government in 1976. Israel considered him a useful ally against the Palestinians, and his militia group was responsible for helping to curb Palestinian guerrilla infiltration into northern Israel and serving as a network that informed Israel on activity in the area. On Sept. 16, 1982, a massacre of hundreds of Palestinian men, women, and children occurred at Sabra and Shatila refugee camps in West Beirut. Haddad's military force was implicated but was cleared of responsibility in 1983. The same year the Israelis wanted Haddad's militia integrated into the Lebanese Army, and, though the Lebanese government agreed, they would not allow Haddad to serve as the ranking commander in southern Lebanon. Haddad was reinstated to the Lebanese Army in January 1984, shortly before his death.

Harris, Sir Arthur Travers, British marshal of the Royal Air Force (b. April 13, 1892, Cheltenham, England—d. April 5, 1984, Goring-on-Thames, England), as commander in chief of Bomber Command from 1942 to 1945 earned the nickname "Bomber Harris" because he was identified with the policy of area bombing of German cities, which culminated in the destruction of Dresden in February 1945. After leaving school Harris worked as a prospector and farmer in Rhodesia, and during World War I he served with the 1st Rhodesia Regiment until 1915, when he joined the Royal Flying Corps. When the war ended, he became a squadron leader in the Royal Air Force (RAF). He was posted to India and Iraq, returning to the Middle East after commanding a bomber squadron in Britain. During this time he made important contributions to bombing theory, and from 1934 to 1937 he served at the Air Ministry in operations and intelligence, then as director of plans. In 1938 he headed the RAF mission in the U.S. and Canada before taking over as air officer commanding in Palestine and Transjordan (1938–39). With the outbreak of World War II, he was given command of a bomber squadron, then appointed head of the RAF delegation in Washington, D.C., before his appointment as commander in chief, Bomber Command, in February 1942. Three months later he launched the first 1,000-bomber raid on Cologne, giving a tremendous boost to British morale at a crucial stage in the war. But the effects on German morale were not as devastating as Harris had expected, and his almost obsessional commitment to area bombing resulted in his opposition to strategic bombing of French railways to prepare for the Normandy invasion; moreover, British losses were high. Eventually, with the European war won, Harris was made a scapegoat for a policy that had been generally accepted but that the public and its political leaders could now safely repudiate. "Bomber Harris" was blamed solely for the horrors of Dresden; and he was not honoured with other commanders in 1946. Harris was made a baronet in 1953 when he retired from his postwar job with the South African Marine Corporation.

Hellman, Lillian (Florence), U.S. playwright (b. June 20, 1905, New Orleans, La.—d. June 30, 1984, Martha's Vineyard, Mass.), was hailed as the grand dame of the American theatre and was perhaps the best craftsman of plays in the country with her cohesive dramas that featured convincing characters and precise dialogue set against a backdrop of evil and unscrupulous human behaviour. Hellman, courageous and principled, became a heroine in the U.S. when in 1952 she defied the House Committee on Un-American Activities by refusing to testify against her friends and flatly stating, "I cannot and will not cut my conscience to fit this year's fashions." She was even spirited as a child; at 14 she ran away from home and at 15 pawned a ring to purchase books. Hellman attended New York University (1922–24) and Columbia University (1924) before marrying writer Arthur Kober in 1925. During her marriage, which ended in divorce in 1932, she worked variously as a manuscript reader, theatrical play reader, and as a scenario reader in Hollywood. In 1934 she embarked on her own literary career as the author of the chilling *The Children's Hour*, a provocative story about the repercussions that take place when a malevolent child slanders two teachers as lesbians. Her earliest plays, pervaded with anger and bitterness, are nonetheless considered her finest works. She went on to write *The Little Foxes* (1939), a Southern saga of the greedy Hubbard family; *Watch on the Rhine* (1941), a thriller about Fascism; *Another*

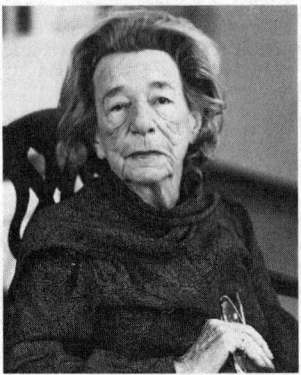

Part of the Forest (1946); and a Chekhovian drama, *The Autumn Garden* (1951). Hellman also translated and adapted Anouilh's *The Lark* (1955) and Voltaire's *Candide* (1957) before returning to drama with her last Broadway hit, *Toys in the Attic* (1960). Perhaps her most telling works were her three volumes of memoirs. *An Unfinished Woman* (1969) explored her tempestuous 30-year relationship with mystery writer Dashiell Hammett; *Pentimento* (1973) revealed a montage of personalities, especially the unforgettable Julia (the critically acclaimed 1977 motion picture *Julia*, with Jane Fonda portraying Hellman, was based on one chapter of the book); and *Scoundrel Time* (1976) was a scathing critique directed against her contemporaries who "named names" at the McCarthy witch-hunt trials. An activist who remained at the fore of politics to the end, Hellman championed civil rights and peace, called for the release of Soviet dissident prisoners, and sued in court to obtain the release of the Nixon White House tapes.

Herbert, (Alfred Francis) Xavier, Australian writer (b. May 15, 1901, Port Hedland, Western Australia—d. Nov. 10, 1984, Alice Springs, Australia), was a novelist whose most brilliant work was his first book, *Capricornia* (1938), a story set in the northern outback. Herbert was brought up among Aborigines and throughout his life remained passionately concerned with their ill-treatment by whites. The books that followed his first success, however, failed to please for a variety of reasons: in *Seven Emus* (1959) he irritated his readers with an eccentric form of punctuation; *Soldiers' Women* offended half his potential clientele with its thesis that without social restraint all women would be nymphomaniacs; *Poor Fellow, My Country*, although at 850,000 words the longest novel in the English language, was an ill-structured and somewhat unbalanced saga.

Heymanson, Sir (Sidney Henry) Randal, expatriate Australian journalist (b. April 18, 1903, Melbourne, Australia—d. Aug. 27, 1984, New York, N.Y.), as founder (1948) of the American Australian Association and chairman of its board from 1967, contributed notably to the strengthening of ties between the two countries. Educated at the University of Melbourne, he went to the University of London as a postgraduate student, subsequently lecturing there on political science and economics (1928–30). He was European correspondent for Australian Newspapers Service from 1928 to 1940. In the latter year he was sent to New York to open a North American bureau for the Herald and

Weekly Times Ltd., Australia's largest newspaper chain; he continued to run it until 1969. He was knighted in 1972.

Hill, Lister, U.S. senator (b. Dec. 29, 1894, Montgomery, Ala.—d. Dec. 20, 1984, Montgomery), as the longtime (1938–68) Democratic senator from Alabama, sponsored such social legislation as the act that created the Tennessee Valley Authority in 1933 and the 1946 Hill-Burton Hospital Act, which provided grants to build hospitals and medical centres in poor and rural areas. Hill, who entered the University of Alabama at age 16, earned a B.A. degree (1914) and law degree (1915) in only four years. In 1917, at 22, he was elected president of the Montgomery Board of Education, a position he held until his 1923 election to the U.S. House of Representatives. As a senator from 1938, Hill gained a reputation as a Southern orator with his slow, distinctive drawl; he sponsored such legislation as the Rural Telephone Act, the Rural Housing Act, the G.I. Bill of Rights for veterans of World War II and the Korean War, and Medicare and Social Security. In 1955, after becoming chairman of the Senate Labor and Public Welfare Committee and chairman of the Appropriations subcommittee in charge of financing the then Department of Health, Education, and Welfare, Hill was instrumental in securing passage of important education legislation. He retired from the Senate in 1968.

Himes, Chester Bomar, U.S. writer (b. July 29, 1909, Jefferson City, Mo.—d. Nov. 12, 1984, Moraira, Spain), wrote novels, short stories, and autobiographical works that were notable for their descriptive prose, but he was probably better known in Europe, especially France, for his violent detective yarns including *Cotton Comes to Harlem*, *The Crazy Kill*, and *The Heat's On*. Himes, who launched his writing career in prison while serving a 20-year sentence (he actually served 7) for armed robbery, devoted most of his writings to social protest and opposition to racism. His first novel, *If He Hollers Let Him Go* (1945), was followed by *Lonely Crusade* (1947), *The Third Generation* (1954), and *The Primitive* (1955). During the 1960s, after having lived in Mexico, France, and then Spain, Himes turned to crime novels and delighted readers with the adventures of such black detectives as Coffin Ed Johnson and Grave Digger Jones. Though his thrillers were written in English, they were originally published in France, and in 1957 he was awarded that country's Grand Prix de Littérature Policière. Himes also published two volumes of autobiography, *The Quality of Hurt* (1972) and *My Life of Absurdity* (1976). In 1970 *Cotton Comes to Harlem* was made into a successful motion picture, and in 1972 a sequel, *Come Back, Charleston Blue* (based on *The Heat's On*), was also filmed.

Hooker, Sir Stanley George, British aeronautical engineer (b. Sept. 30, 1907, Kent, England—d. May 24, 1984, Wotton-under-Edge, Gloucestershire, England), joined Rolls-Royce Ltd. in 1938 and was involved in many crucial developments in aircraft-engine design. He studied mathematics at Imperial College, University of London, and aeronautics as a research fellow at Brasenose College, Oxford. He worked in the Admiralty research department before joining Rolls-Royce, where he headed its research into superchargers. Hooker made a vital improvement in the Merlin engine used in the Spitfire fighter aircraft, raising its speed and height threshold significantly. After World War II Hooker moved to production and design of jet engines, but resigned in 1948 after the failure of the Avon engine. After he became chief engineer at the Bristol Aeroplane Co. Ltd. in 1951, Hooker developed the Olympus engine for the Vulcan bomber (predecessor of the Concorde engine) and the Pegasus engine, capable of horizontal and vertical thrust. The latter was used in the Kestrel aircraft and eventually led to the engine of the Harrier. He returned to Rolls-Royce when the company was merged with Bristol, but

retired in 1967. When Rolls-Royce collapsed in 1971 he was recalled and made group technical director and a director of the company to oversee the development and production of the RB-211 engine. He continued as technical adviser and consultant after his retirement in 1976. Hooker became a fellow of the Royal Society in 1962, was made a Commander of the Order of the British Empire in 1964, and was knighted in 1974. His autobiography, *Not Much of an Engineer*, was published in 1984.

Hoyt, Waite Charles ("Schoolboy"), U.S. baseball player (b. Sept. 9, 1899, Brooklyn, N.Y.—d. Aug. 25, 1984, Cincinnati, Ohio), as a powerful right-handed major league pitcher for 21 years (1918–38) recorded 237 victories, 182 losses, and an earned-run average of 3.59 but was best remembered as a New York Yankee who helped lead the famed "Murderers' Row" team of Babe Ruth and Lou Gehrig into the 1927 and 1928 World Series. In 1927 Hoyt led the American League with 22 victories and an earned-run average of 2.63. He won the first game of the World Series that year, which the Yankees won in four straight from the Pittsburgh Pirates. The following season Hoyt scored 24 victories and during the World Series beat the St. Louis Cardinals twice as the Yankees again swept the Series four straight. The "Schoolboy" was first signed by the New York Giants when he was only 15, but he spent three years in the minor leagues before joining the Boston Red Sox in 1919. It was as a Yankee, though, that he proved his mettle; in 1921 he tied a record set by Christy Mathewson in 1905 by pitching 27 World Series innings without allowing a run. In 1930 Hoyt was traded to the Detroit Tigers, and he later pitched for the Philadelphia Athletics, the Brooklyn Dodgers, the New York Giants, and the Pittsburgh Pirates. After his retirement as a player in 1938, Hoyt, a skilled raconteur, served as a broadcaster on radio and television for the Cincinnati Reds professional baseball team from 1942 until 1965. He was inducted into the Baseball Hall of Fame in 1969.

Hughes, Richard, Australian journalist (b. March 5, 1906, Melbourne, Australia—d. Jan. 4, 1984, Hong Kong), made his name as a foreign correspondent with scoops that included the first interview with the British spies Guy Burgess and Donald Maclean after their defection to the Soviet Union. He joined the *Melbourne Star* in 1935, went on to work for the *Sydney Daily Telegraph*, and in 1939 was posted to Tokyo where he developed an affection for Japan and a profound knowledge of the country. After serving in the U.S., and a period of illness, he reported the occupation of Japan during the immediate post-World War II years and later wrote notable reports from China for *The Sunday Times* of London. In 1956, in Moscow, he obtained his interviews with Burgess and Maclean. He later reported on East Asia for the Australian press and from 1972 wrote for *The Times* of London from Hong Kong where he was a well-known figure in the Foreign Correspondents' Club. Indeed, he so nearly typified the foreign correspondent that he was used as a character in books by Ian Fleming and John Le Carré. His own books included *Hong Kong: Borrowed Place, Borrowed Time* (1968) and *Foreign Devil* (1972). He was made Commander of the Order of the British Empire in 1980.

Hunter, Alberta, U.S. blues singer (b. April 1, 1895, Memphis, Tenn.—d. Oct. 17, 1984, New York, N.Y.), was a legendary cabaret star whose robust singing voice rang out in Chicago and New York City nightclubs during the 1920s and '30s but who gave up her career for two decades (1954–77) to serve as a nurse, then made a triumphant comeback in 1977 as a singer in New York City bistros. At the age of 11 the headstrong Hunter struck out on her own, singing for $5 a week in a Chicago honky-tonk. During her career she performed with such jazz greats as King Oliver, Louis Armstrong, Bricktop, Fats

Waller, and Eubie Blake and in 1921, with her release "How Long, Sweet Daddy, How Long," she became one of the first blues singers to make a recording. Two years later Hunter moved to New York City and began writing songs; her "Down-Hearted Blues" (1923) for Bessie Smith sold a million copies within months. On stage Hunter appeared in the all-black musical *How Come*, in the musical *Show Boat*, and in the 1939 play *Mamba's Daughter*. After the death of her mother in 1954, Hunter abandoned her singing career to serve as a scrub nurse for more than 20 years. When the hospital enforced a mandatory retirement at age 82 (thinking she was only 70), she resumed entertaining at the Cookery in Greenwich Village to enthusiastic audiences who joined her in snapping their fingers and clapping hands to the rhythm of her lively tunes. The feisty Hunter continued to delight audiences until shortly before her death.

Hurd, Peter, U.S. artist and illustrator (b. Feb. 22, 1904, Roswell, N.M.—d. July 9, 1984, Roswell), was an acclaimed regional painter who exhibited his deep affection for the Southwest with portraits of common folk against sere, light-drenched landscapes. His best-known work, "Portrait of José Herrera" (1938), established his reputation as a master painter using the egg tempera technique and was judged a public favourite at a 1952 exhibition. In 1921 Hurd entered the U.S. Military Academy at West Point, N.Y., but when he became interested in painting continued his studies at Haverford (Pa.) College. During the summer of 1924 he studied under N. C. Wyeth and then entered the Pennsylvania Academy of Fine Arts. In 1929 he married Wyeth's daughter Henriette (herself a painter), and the couple spent most of their lives at their ranch in San Patricio, N.M. The area served as an inspiration for Hurd, who reveled in drawing windmills, ranchhouses, cowboys, landscapes, tenant farmers, and fruit pickers. During World War II Hurd served as a war artist for *Life* magazine and in 1944 spent five months with the U.S. Air Transport Command in South America, Africa, India, Arabia, and Italy sketching a series of drawings. He was also noted for his fresco murals, which graced the walls at the U.S. Post Office at Big Spring, Texas, and at the former U.S. Post Office in Alamogordo, N.M. In 1964 he and his wife produced the *Time* magazine cover that proclaimed Pres. Lyndon B. Johnson "man of the year." In 1965 Hurd was commissioned to produce an official portrait of Johnson, but when the painting was completed Johnson rejected it as "the ugliest thing I ever saw." Nevertheless, the portrait is housed in the Smithsonian Institution's National Portrait Gallery in Washington, D.C. Hurd was also the illustrator of such books as *Last of the Mohicans* (1926) and *Great Stories of the Sea and Ships* (1933) and the author of *Art in America* (1963) and *Swallow* (1971).

Hutton, Ina Ray (ODESSA COWAN), U.S. bandleader (b. March 13, 1916, Chicago, Ill.—d. Feb. 19, 1984, Ventura, Calif.), was a curvaceous blond who became nationally known as the pioneering female bandleader of an all-woman orchestra, the Melodears, in 1935. Hutton, who sang and danced in such Broadway productions as *Clowns in Clover* and *Melody Revue* during the early 1930s, fronted the Melodears until 1940, when she became the leader of an all-male band and achieved even greater fame. She headed the band until 1947. During the early 1950s Hutton organized another all-female band that scored popular success on West Coast television. "The Ina Ray Hutton Show," a 30-minute musical variety show featuring only female guests, aired from July 4, 1956, to Aug. 31, 1956. Hutton retired from show business in the 1960s.

Huu, Tran Van, Vietnamese politician (b. 1896?, Vietnam—d. Jan. 17, 1984, Paris, France), was premier of Vietnam (1950–52) during a crucial stage in the French Indochina War (1946–54), which ended with the defeat of the French by the Viet Minh at Dien Bien Phu and the division of Vietnam into two military zones. Huu, a member of the wealthy landowning class and former governor of Cochinchina (southern Vietnam), was named premier by the French-appointed chief of state and former emperor Bao Dai in April 1950; he also held the portfolios of foreign affairs and defense. Huu pressed for greater independence for Vietnam while seeking more widely based Western aid in the struggle against the Communist Viet Minh. However, he was considered by many Vietnamese to be too representative of a narrow, French-influenced sector of society and failed to unite the country. In June 1952 he was replaced by Nguyen Van Tam and from 1955 lived in France.

Jacquot, Pierre, French army officer (b. June 16, 1902, Vrécourt, Vosges, France—d. June 29, 1984, Vrécourt), was a leader of the Resistance during World War II, was responsible for repatriating the French forces from Indochina in 1954, and was commander in chief of Allied Forces Central Europe from 1961 to 1963. He spent four years in the Foreign Legion, was trained in France and Belgium, and served with the intelligence service before the war. Jacquot also gained a reputation for his republican sympathies and, after being twice wounded before the fall of France, joined the Resistance in 1941. He was deputy to André Malraux as head of the maquis in the département of Corrèze, fighting the Das Reich division, and then organized the Alsace-Lorraine brigade. After the French defeat at Dien Bien Phu he was commissioner in Indochina, then, from 1956, French commander in chief in West Germany. Jacquot, who opposed the return to power of Gen. Charles de Gaulle in 1958, was made inspector general of the Army in 1959 before his appointment to NATO in 1961. He was the author of two books on military strategy.

Jaffe, Sam, U.S. actor (b. March 8, 1891, New York, N.Y.—d. March 24, 1984, Beverly Hills, Calif.), starred on Broadway and in such motion pictures as *Lost Horizon* (1937) and *Gunga Din* (1939) but was best remembered as the venerable, white-haired Dr. Zorba, thoughtful mentor of the scowling but brilliant neurosurgeon in the popular hospital drama "Ben Casey" (1961–66). As a boy, Jaffe sometimes performed with his mother in the then flourishing Yiddish theatre. His inquiring mind prompted him to major in engineering, and he served as a teacher and then as dean of mathematics at the Bronx Cultural Institute before he was again drawn to the theatre. Jaffe made his debut in 1915 with the Washington Square Players, and he appeared on Broadway in *The Jazz Singer* (1925) and *Grand Hotel* (1930) before making his motion-picture debut opposite Marlene Dietrich in *The Scarlet Empress* (1934). In 1937 he portrayed the high lama in *Lost Horizon* and two years later was hailed for his performance in the title role in *Gunga Din*. Besides the *Asphalt Jungle* (1950), which gained him an Academy Award nomination for best supporting actor, some of his film credits included: *Gentleman's Agreement, The Accused, I Can Get It for You Wholesale, The Day the Earth Stood Still,* and *Ben-Hur.* An accomplished pianist and composer, Jaffe was also fluent in six languages and was universally admired as the founder of the Equity Library Theatre, a showcase for budding actors and directors.

Jenkins, Gordon, U.S. arranger and composer (b. May 12, 1910, Webster Groves, Mo.—d. May 1, 1984, Malibu, Calif.), was a multitalented pop musician who excelled as an arranger, composer, conductor, and pianist noted for his one-finger solos but was probably best known for his 1945 composition "Manhattan Tower Suite," a four-section tribute to New York City. Jenkins left high school to play piano in a St. Louis speakeasy, but his first break came in the 1930s when bandleader Isham Jones hired him as a pianist and arranger. He later joined Woody Herman's band, and at the same time he was composing for Benny Goodman, Paul Whiteman, and Andre Kostelanetz. Jenkins wrote theme songs for Goodman ("Goodbye") and Herman ("Blue Prelude") and such other hits as "P.S., I Love You," "You Have Taken My Heart," "When a Woman Loves a Man," and "This Is All I Ask," which became a standard for singers. In 1937 he made his conducting debut in the Broadway musical *The Show Is On,* and in the following year he became musical director for NBC radio in California. Jenkins's shimmering arrangements showcased the performances of such stars as Judy Garland, Peggy Lee, and Frank Sinatra. In 1965 Jenkins won a Grammy award for his arrangement of Sinatra's "It Was a Very Good Year," and in 1973 he conducted Sinatra's television special.

John, Sir Caspar, British naval officer (b. March 22, 1903, London, England—d. July 11, 1984, Mousehole, Cornwall, England), was largely the creator (1938) of Britain's Fleet Air Arm (phased out in the late 1960s) and expanded it for use against the Japanese during World War II. An innovative and unconventional officer, he rose to hold the post of first sea lord (1960–64) and was posted admiral of the fleet (1962). A son of the painter Augustus John, he was educated at the Royal Naval College, Dartmouth, and trained (1925) as a naval pilot. By 1936 he was commander in the Naval Air Division at the Admiralty. During World War II he served in the Home and Mediterranean fleets; in 1943 he went to Washington, D.C., as head of the British Naval Air Service and assistant naval attaché (air). Postwar appointments included that of director of air organization and training. After commanding the 3rd Aircraft Carrier Squadron and Heavy Squadron (1951–52), he served ashore, becoming vice-chief of naval staff in 1958. In the early 1960s he persuaded Prime Minister Harold Macmillan to order a new generation of aircraft carriers, but the policy was reversed by Harold Wilson's government in 1967. Posted rear admiral in 1951, vice-admiral in 1954, and admiral in 1957, he was created a knight commander of the Order of the Bath in 1956.

Johnson, Uwe, German novelist (b. July 20, 1934, Cammin, Germany [now Kamien Pomorski, Poland]—d. March 12, 1984, Sheerness, England), established a new German postwar literature with novels that examined, in social and spiritual terms, the drama of the post-World War II division of Germany and the conflict between East and West. He studied in Rostock and Leipzig before working as a journalist and translator. In 1959, following the rejection on political grounds of *Mutmassungen über Jakob* (*Speculations About Jakob,* 1963), a brooding novel that described the death of a railway worker against the background of events in Hungary and Suez in 1956, he moved to West Germany, where the book was published and won the Formentor Prize. The contradictory views of East and West and the resulting conflicts were the themes of his novels *Das dritte Buch über Achim* (1961; *The Third Book About Achim,* 1967) and *Zwei Ansichten* (1965; *Two Views,* 1966), which established him as one of Germany's leading postwar writers. From 1975 he lived in England, teaching intermittently at Wayne State University, Detroit, and Harvard, while at the same time writing a cycle of novels, *Jahrestage* (*Anniversaries*), the last of which appeared in 1983. He was deeply depressed by the failure of Eastern European countries to achieve democratic forms of socialism, and he suffered in later years from alcoholism. His books were widely translated and admired, and his many awards included the Georg Büchner Prize (1971) and the Thomas Mann Prize (1978).

Johnston, (William) Denis, Irish dramatist, broadcaster, and scholar (b. July 18, 1901, Dublin, Ireland—d. Aug. 8, 1984, Dublin), achieved international fame with his second play, *The Moon in the Yellow River* (1931), which enjoyed long engagements in London and

New York. He also wrote a number of technically innovative and deeply characterized plays that recounted recent Irish history. Educated in Dublin and Edinburgh and at the University of Cambridge (England) and Harvard University, Johnston studied law but practiced it only briefly, becoming a producer at Dublin's Abbey and Gate theatres. He served as director of the latter from 1931 to 1936. He then worked in London for the British Broadcasting Corporation and served as a BBC war correspondent in the Middle East, North Africa, Yugoslavia, and Italy. He was program director for the BBC (1945–47) before holding a succession of academic posts in the U.S., notably at Smith College, Northampton, Mass., where he was head of the department of theatre and speech (1961–66). His plays included the subtle and complex *A Bride for the Unicorn* (1933), which won the critics' plaudits but lacked popular appeal, and *The Scythe and the Sunset* (1958). The book *Nine Rivers from Jordan* (1953) described his World War II experiences. Fascinated by the enigmas in the life of the Irish 18th-century author Jonathan Swift, he attempted to elucidate them in his play *A Dreamful of Dust* (1940) and a well-documented book, *In Search of Swift* (1959).

Kapitsa, Pyotr Leonidovich, Soviet physicist (b. July 8 [June 26, old style], 1894, Kronshtadt, near St. Petersburg [now Leningrad], Russia—d. April 8, 1984, Moscow, U.S.S.R.), shared the Nobel Prize for Physics in 1978 in recognition of his contributions to low-temperature physics, notably his research on the liquefaction of helium, during a career spanning some 60 years. Kapitsa studied at the Petrograd Polytechnic Institute and after graduation served as a lecturer there until 1921. In that year his professor, Abram Joffe, an eminent physicist, was instrumental in arranging Kapitsa's admittance to the Cavendish Laboratory in Cambridge, England, where he was befriended by Sir Ernest Rutherford and remained for almost 13 years. As director of magnetic research there from 1924, he designed apparatus that produced a magnetic field of 500,000 gauss—a strength not exceeded until 1956. Kapitsa was made a fellow of Trinity College, University of Oxford, in 1925 and four years later was elected to fellowship of the Royal Society—the first foreign scientist in 200 years to be so honoured. At Rutherford's instigation the Royal Society set up its Mond Laboratory for low-temperature and magnetic research, which Kapitsa directed (1930–34). There he designed apparatus that produced liquid helium more efficiently than had hitherto been possible. In 1934, however, his research at Cambridge ended; after spending a summer vacation in the U.S.S.R., he was refused permission to return to England. A year later he accepted the post of director of the Soviet Academy of Science's newly established S. I. Vavilov Institute of Physical Problems in Moscow. Rutherford agreed to the transfer of Kapitsa's apparatus from the Mond Laboratory to the Vavilov Institute, and Kapitsa continued his research into the properties of liquid helium, establishing in particular its "superfluidity," or virtual lack of resistance to flow. During World War II he designed equipment for the mass liquefaction of oxygen for use in the steel industry. In 1946 his moral convictions led him to refuse to work on nuclear weapons research, and as a result he was dismissed from his post. He remained under house arrest until after Stalin's death but was reinstated as head of the Vavilov Institute in 1955. He then worked on the application of low-temperature physics to the production of liquid rocket fuels for the Sputnik satellite program and more recently on the problems of controlled nuclear fusion.

Kastler, Alfred, French physicist (b. May 3, 1902, Guebwiller, Alsace, Germany—d. Jan. 7, 1984, Bandol, France), won the Nobel Prize for Physics in 1966 for his work on "optical pumping," a method of stimulating atoms in a particular substance so that they attain higher energy states. This allowed him to study the structure of the atoms and also, since the light energy used to stimulate the atoms was reemitted, marked an important step toward the creation of the maser and the laser. Kastler himself denied being the "father of the laser," for the development of which Charles Townes was awarded the Nobel Prize for Physics in 1964. Kastler's achievement was the discovery of a new method for studying atomic structures and in pointing the way toward various areas of further research. Perhaps his most lasting contribution to physics in France was as a teacher, from 1941 at the University of Paris and at the École Normale Supérieure and from 1968 as director of research at the Centre National de la Recherche Scientifique, where he trained a whole generation of physicists. He was also notable for his uncompromising stands on moral and political issues. Opposed to the Vietnam war, he was active from the 1950s in the antinuclear movement and played a significant part in the formulation of treaties to limit the spread of nuclear weapons, especially through the Pugwash Conferences. He condemned the attitudes of both the U.S. and the Soviet Union and was opposed to the French nuclear deterrent. He was elected a member of the Académie des Sciences in 1964.

Keating, Tom, British painter and picture restorer (b. March 1, 1917, London, England—d. Feb. 12, 1984, London), achieved notoriety in 1976 by admitting that he had "imitated" drawings by the 19th-century artist Samuel Palmer and claiming responsibility for more than 2,000 fakes of works by artists of various periods. He claimed that his paintings contained flaws easily detectable by expert analysis and that they had not been done for financial gain but to cause embarrassment to the art establishment. Charges of conspiracy and criminal deception brought against him were dropped in 1979 because of his ill health. Outside the art world, his trial caused amusement rather than panic, and after the publication of an autobiography, *The Fake's Progress* (1977; with Frank and Geraldine Norman), he enjoyed considerable fame. In 1982 he presented a television series in which he painted an "imitation" of work by a well-known painter, racily commenting on his predecessor's methods and the history of techniques. Another series, "Tom Keating on Impressionism," was shown shortly after his death. In 1983 a collection of his works fetched £72,000 at auction, though by that time the art experts had begun to hit back, alleging that he was not even a good faker. In a last ironic twist, the 205 paintings in his studio were auctioned after his death by Christie's for £274,610—some 25 times more than expected.

Khrushchev, Nina Petrovna, widow of former Soviet Communist Party first secretary Nikita Sergeyevich Khrushchev (b. 1900, Russia—d. Aug. 9, 1984, Moscow, U.S.S.R.), accompanied her husband on several state visits abroad, invariably charming her hosts. Married in 1924, she was Khrushchev's second wife (his first wife died in 1921). She had been a member of the Communist Party from 1920 but, like the wives of other Soviet politicians, she took no part in public life until it was suggested that she go with Khrushchev when he was invited to the U.S. by Pres. Dwight D. Eisenhower in 1959. Her poise and calm to some extent offset her husband's acerbity and occasional boorishness, both abroad and at home. After Khrushchev's fall from power (1964) the couple lived quietly outside Moscow. Khrushchev's death (1971) received little publicity in the U.S.S.R. and that of his widow even less, since her obituary notice followed usual Russian practice in listing her under her maiden name of Kukhartchuk and omitted that of her husband. She was said to have been buried beside Khrushchev in Moscow's Novodevichi cemetery.

King, The Rev. Martin Luther, Sr., U.S. clergyman and civil rights leader (b. Dec. 19, 1899, near Stockbridge, Ga.—d. Nov. 11, 1984, Atlanta, Ga.), was the influential pastor (1932–75) of the Ebenezer Baptist Church in Atlanta, one of the largest Baptist churches in the South, and the father of the Rev. Martin Luther King, Jr., the most prominent figure in the 1960s civil rights movement and winner of the 1964 Nobel Prize for Peace. King, who graduated from Morehouse College, Atlanta, in 1930, became a pioneer with his nonviolent preachings invoking racial equality, concern for the poor, and faith in God. In 1936 he led hundreds of blacks in a voting rights march on City Hall and, as a member of the National Association for the Advancement of Colored People Social Action Committee, played a leading role in a legal bat-

tle to equalize the salaries of black and white teachers in Atlanta. He also waged a battle to desegregate elevators in courthouses so that blacks could have access to voting registration. He later campaigned extensively for human rights and was believed instrumental in the 1976 election of Jimmy Carter to the presidency of the U.S. Though King's life was riddled with tragedy (his son Martin was assassinated in 1968; his only other son, A. D. Williams, drowned in 1969; and his wife, Alberta, was gunned down in 1974), "Daddy King" never became bitter in his efforts to promote civil rights.

Knopf, Alfred A., U.S. publisher (b. Sept. 12, 1892, New York, N.Y.—d. Aug. 11, 1984, Purchase, N.Y.), as the exacting founder in 1915 of the eminent publishing house that bears his name, enriched the cultural vistas of U.S. readers as the custodian of more than 5,000 titles, including works by such illustrious authors as Thomas Mann, T. S. Eliot, Willa Cather, and John Updike. Knopf, a 1912 graduate of Columbia University, New York City, established literary contacts there and then abroad while touring Europe. His wife, Blanche, was instrumental in helping him launch his publishing firm by introducing many South American and European authors. Knopf, whose publications were marked by a distinctive colophon, a

borzoi (Russian wolfhound), became known for the quality of the cosmopolitan works he published. His authors garnered 16 Nobel and 27 Pulitzer prizes. In 1966 his independent publishing concern became a subsidiary of Random House (itself owned by Radio Corp. of America), and in 1980 Random was acquired by S. I. Newhouse and Sons. A stickler who often bemoaned the increasing commercialism of the publishing industry, Knopf maintained strict control over the editorial content and commercial promotion of his books and paid special attention to the attractiveness of his publications. Knopf also served as the publisher from 1924 to 1934 of the *American Mercury*, an influential periodical founded by H. L. Mencken and George Jean Nathan in 1924. Knopf, who became chairman emeritus of his firm at the age of 80, later assumed the title of founding chairman. His contributions to the publishing industry were enumerated in 1965 by the Pulitzer Prize-winning writer John Hersey, who hailed Knopf as "the sworn enemy of hogwash, bunk, gas and rubbish, and a scourge of hypocrites and shoddyites."

Kodama, Yoshio, Japanese nationalist (b. Feb. 18, 1911, Fukushima Prefecture, Japan—d. Jan. 17, 1984, Tokyo, Japan), was an enigmatic ultrarightist whose powerful influence in Japanese politics remained shrouded by his skillful maneuvers until he was identified in 1976 as a central figure in the multimillion-dollar Lockheed Corp. bribery scandal. Kodama, who was an active member of the Patriotic Youth Corps, was sent to China during World War II to gather information and vital materials for Japan's imperial forces. While there he established the Kodama Agency and made a fortune by purchasing goods looted by Japanese troops. After the war he was imprisoned (1945–48) as a war criminal, though he never had a formal trial. When he returned to Japan, Kodama carried with him a vast amount of money, diamonds, and platinum. He later used his wealth to establish the Liberal Party (later the Liberal-Democratic Party) and served as a backstage power broker by helping key politicians gain high office. Kodama was instrumental in helping both Nobusuke Kishi and Kakuei Tanaka (who was also heavily involved in the Lockheed scandal) become prime ministers. In 1958 Kodama became a secret agent for Lockheed and used his influence to persuade politicians to purchase Lockheed jet fighters for Japan's Air Self-Defense Force. In February 1976 it was disclosed that Kodama had received $7 million from Lockheed for his services; in May Kodama was indicted for violating the foreign-exchange control law by receiving payments of 440 million yen in cash from Lockheed in 1973. He was also indicted on five other counts. Though the verdict on Kodama was due in 1982, it was suspended because he was too ill to appear in court.

Korner, Alexis, French-born blues musician and broadcaster (b. 1928, Paris, France—d. Jan. 1, 1984, London, England), was a pioneer in the post-World War II revival of traditional jazz and blues in Britain and one of the most accomplished white blues singers. During the early 1960s his band, Blues Incorporated, served as a stepping stone for such musicians as Paul Jones, Eric Clapton, and Mick Jagger. Charlie Watts and Brian Jones also played with his band, and the Rolling Stones virtually grew out of the Korner band at the Marquee Club, standing in for Blues Incorporated when Korner had another engagement. He came to England in 1940 and was educated at St. Paul's School where his interest in blues singing began to develop. He learned the guitar, which he played with two notable British jazz bands led by Ken Collyer and Chris Barber, and worked for record companies and for the BBC World Service. Later he established himself as a talented and witty writer and broadcaster. But he never achieved the popular success of some of those who started their careers at his Roundhouse Blues Club and the

Marquee. He remained an individualist, often playing in later years with the bass player Colin Hodgkinson.

Krasner, Lee (LENORE KRASSNER; MRS. JACKSON POLLOCK), U.S. painter (b. Oct. 27, 1908, Brooklyn, N.Y.—d. June 19, 1984, New York, N.Y.), made important contributions to the New York School of Abstract Expressionism but was overshadowed by the celebrity of her husband of 11 years, the renowned Abstract Expressionist painter Jackson Pollock (1912–56). Krasner, who decided to become an artist when she was 13, attended both the Women's Art School of Cooper Union (1926–29) and the National Academy of Design (1929–32) before she studied (1936–40) with Hans Hofmann, one of the most influential art teachers of the 20th century. When she met Pollock in 1936, her credentials were more impressive than his; but Pollock became the leading exponent of Abstract Expressionism with his radical "drip" paintings, and her successes became secondary. Nonetheless, she was an extremely gifted painter in her own right and used her mastery of draftsmanship and colour to produce paintings that were characterized by bold, outlined images. She was also one of the few women to express violence and force in her paintings. Her works, which included paintings, drawings, and collages, also evoked the influence of Matisse, Picasso, and Pollock, but it was not until 1965 that her accomplishments gained recognition, when a major retrospective exhibition at the Whitechapel Art Gallery in London showcased her powerful technique. Earlier in her career she produced a series of some 35 "Little Image" paintings (1946–49), small canvasses crowded with tiny images. She then moved on to collage paintings, but it was her large-scale canvasses produced in the 1960s, including "Charred Landscape" and "Another Storm," that won her renown. She reached the pinnacle of her career in 1983 when a retrospective of her works was launched and began a tour of U.S. museums.

Kroc, Ray Albert, U.S. entrepreneur (b. Oct. 5, 1902, Oak Park, Ill.—d. Jan. 14, 1984, La Jolla, Calif.), became a multimillionaire as the innovative founder in 1955 of the McDonald's hamburger empire and in 1974 became the outspoken owner of the San Diego Padres professional baseball team. Kroc, who never graduated from high school, was an enterprising

paper cup and milk shake machine salesman. When he discovered that a fast-food emporium in California was making 40 milk shakes at a time, Kroc became intrigued by its success. He purchased (1954) the franchise rights to the hamburger joint run by the McDonald brothers and parlayed his investment into the McDonald's fast-food empire that in 1984 boasted some 7,500 golden-arched restaurants in 32 countries. The first restaurant opened in Des Plaines, Ill., in 1955, featuring hamburgers for 15 cents, french fries for 10 cents, and milk shakes for 20 cents. A brilliant retailer, Kroc kept prices and operating costs low by hiring

part-time teenage help; yet he remained steadfast in the maintaining quality of the food and refused to use soybean filler in his hamburgers. By automating and standardizing operations, Kroc revolutionized the fast-food business and, despite heavy competition, his food chain remained the industry leader. Kroc's strategy included establishing his restaurants in rapidly growing suburban locations, where family visits to the local McDonald's became akin to a tribal ritual. Kroc also placed great importance on employing managers who were skilled in personal relations, and during the 1970s he emphasized company-owned outlets rather than franchises. Besides serving as president (1955–68), chairman (1968–77), and senior chairman (1977–84) of the McDonald's Corp., Kroc was the owner from 1974 to 1979 of the San Diego Padres baseball team, then a perennial loser, and once apologized over the public address system for the team's performance. When he gave up operating control of the team in 1979, the unflappable Kroc quipped, "There's a lot more future in hamburgers than in baseball." In 1982 McDonald's sales totaled $7.8 billion.

Lardner-Burke, Desmond William, South African-born Zimbabwean politician (b. Oct. 17, 1909, Kimberley, South Africa—d. Oct. 22, 1984, Harare, Zimbabwe), was a leading and notably reactionary member of Ian Smith's government during the period of illegal Rhodesian independence (1965–79). A wholehearted supporter of Smith's unilateral declaration of independence (UDI) and a firm believer in white superiority, as minister of justice, law, and order (1964–76) he rigorously suppressed all opposition, regarding African nationalist aspirations as subversive. Educated at St. Andrew's College, Grahamstown, he became a lawyer and moved to Southern Rhodesia, where he practiced at Bulawayo (1933–41) and later at Gwelo. He was a member of the legislative assembly in Salisbury (1948–53) and on its formation joined the white-elitist Rhodesian Front. He represented that party in the assembly from 1962 and began to press for independence from Britain. As minister of justice he punished infringements of decrees issued under the state of emergency introduced in 1966. He became minister of commerce and industry in 1976 but resigned from Smith's government in 1978. His book *Rhodesia: The Story of the Crisis* (1966) gave his account of UDI and of the events that preceded it.

Laskin, Bora, Canadian judge (b. Oct. 5, 1912, Fort William, Ont.—d. March 26, 1984, Ottawa, Ont.), presided over the Supreme Court of Canada as its chief justice from 1973 until his death and was hailed for his written opinions, which reflected his legal scholarship. Laskin earned a law degree from the University of Toronto and a graduate degree from Harvard Law School in 1937. He was made queen's counsel in 1956 and also taught law at Osgoode Hall Law School and the University of Toronto until 1965, when he was appointed to the Court of Appeal of Ontario. On March 23, 1970, Laskin became the first Jew named to the Supreme Court of Canada and, on Dec. 27, 1973, he was appointed chief justice by Prime Minister Pierre Elliott Trudeau. As chief justice, he wrote opinions that often dissented against the conservative opinions of his colleagues. In 1974 he wrote the unanimous opinion holding that Parliament could upgrade the position of the French language in the Canadian government, and in 1975 he was among the dissenting justices in a 6–3 decision to uphold a five-year-old law restricting abortion. The author of several books on land law and Canadian constitutional law, Laskin was unable to return to the bench in 1984 when he was hospitalized with pneumonia.

Lattimore, Richmond Alexander, U.S. poet and classical scholar (b. May 6, 1906, Baoding [Paoting], China—d. Feb. 26, 1984, Rosemont, Pa.), was the formidable poet of such works as *Ses-*

tina for a Far-Off Summer (1962), *The Stride of Time* (1966), and *Poems from Three Decades* (1972) but was also highly regarded for the poetic lyricism in his translations of Homer's *Iliad* and *Odyssey*. Lattimore, a graduate of Dartmouth College in Hanover, N.H., was a Rhodes scholar and studied the University of Oxford in 1929. He earned a Ph.D. from the University of Illinois in 1935, the same year he joined the faculty of Bryn Mawr (Pa.) College, where he taught the classics. His first volume of poetry, *Poems*, appeared in 1957, but it was as a translator of the Greek classics that he gained popularity. Lattimore's translations *The Iliad of Homer* (1951) and *The Odyssey of Homer* (1967) were masterpieces of contemporary English verse and became standard classroom textbooks. He also was hailed for such translations as *The Odes of Pindar* (1947), *Oresteia* (1953; by Aeschylus), *The Frogs of Aristophanes* (1962), *Iphigenia at Tauris* (1973; by Euripides), and *The Four Gospels and the Revelation* (1979). His poetic insights into the history, philosophy, and literature of Greece were uniquely his own. In 1984 the Academy of American Poets awarded Lattimore a $10,000 prize for his five volumes of original poetry.

Lawford, Peter, British-American actor (b. Sept. 7, 1923, London, England—d. Dec. 24, 1984, Los Angeles, Calif.), was a debonair leading man who capitalized on his boyish good looks, natural charm, and athletic build to star in a series of MGM romantic comedies during the late 1940s and early 1950s and was perhaps equally well known for his 12-year marriage (1954–66) to John F. Kennedy's sister Patricia. Lawford, who was privately educated by tutors in Britain, made his motion picture debut there at the age of eight in *Poor Old Bill* (1931). In his Hollywood debut in 1938, he portrayed a cockney lad in *Lord Jeff*, but it was not until he appeared in *Mrs. Miniver* (1942) that his career began to flourish. Some of his best known films included *A Yank at Eton* (1942), *The White Cliffs of Dover* (1944), *The Picture of Dorian Gray* (1945), *Son of Lassie* (1945), *Easter Parade* (1948), *Little Women* (1949), and *Ocean's Eleven* (1960). He also starred on such television shows as "Dear Phoebe" (1954–55), "The Thin Man" (1957–59), and "The Doris Day Show" (1971–72). Offscreen he was reputed to be a playboy and was a charter member of Frank Sinatra's "rat pack" gang. After the 1960s Lawford appeared mainly in character roles, but in later years his drug and alcohol addiction stifled his career. His last role was as a talent agent in the television movie "Malice in Wonderland," which was scheduled to be broadcast in 1985.

Lim Yew Hock, Singapore politician (b. 1914, Singapore—d. Nov. 30, 1984, Saudi Arabia), as chief minister of Singapore (1956–59) was leader of the all-party delegation that negotiated internal self-government for the then British crown colony. Educated at the Raffles Institution, to which he had won a scholarship, he became a trade union representative in a Singapore trade union legislative council. He became a minister (1955) under David Marshall, succeeding him as chief minister when Marshall resigned after having failed to win full independence from the British. Lim Yew Hock attended the Singapore constitutional conference at Lancaster House in London (1957), at which self-government was conceded. He suppressed Communist and anti-British movements in Singapore. In 1959 his Singapore People's Alliance was defeated at the polls by Lee Kuan Yew's People's Action Party. Lim Yew Hock retired from politics in 1963. Sent as high commissioner to Australia for the Federation of Malaysia (to which Singapore belonged, 1963–65), he was recalled in 1965 following a scandal. Subsequently a convert to Islam, he moved to Jidda and had associations with the World Islamic Development Bank.

Lindtberg, Leopold, Austrian-born theatre and film director (b. June 1, 1902, Vienna, Austria—d. April 18, 1984, Zürich, Switz.), served during the 1920s in Berlin as assistant to the famed theatrical producer and director Erwin Piscator, who was known for his ingenious Expressionistic staging techniques. But Lindtberg was driven out of Germany by the Nazis and from 1933 worked at the Schauspielhaus in Zürich, where he was responsible for the first production of Bertolt Brecht's *Mother Courage* (1941). He was also a noted director of opera and a pioneer in the Swiss film industry. Lindtberg studied literature and art at Vienna University, and though he considered a musical career, he eventually entered the theatre as an actor and later became a director. Lindtberg, who always acknowledged Piscator's influence on his work, became a Swiss citizen and during the post-World War II years directed in Austria and Israel as well as in Zürich. His first film was made in 1932 and was followed by some 20 others, including *The Last Chance* (1945) and *The Village* (1953), both of which won awards.

Lonergan, The Rev. Bernard Joseph Francis, Canadian theologian and philosopher (b. Dec. 17, 1904, Buckingham, Que.—d. Nov. 26, 1984, Pickering, Ont.), was a Jesuit and a leading proponent of one of the strongest theological movements in the Roman Catholic Church, transcendental Thomism (the application of the teachings of St. Thomas Aquinas in light of the method of philosophic analysis introduced by Immanuel Kant and its implications for restructuring modern culture). Lonergan, who entered the Society of Jesus in 1922, was especially noted for his championship of the Thomistic emphasis on intellectual inquiry. He sometimes found himself in conflict with the church over its emphasis on received doctrine because he believed, "We should have questions on everything, about everything." With such epistemological texts as *Insight: A Study of Human Understanding* (1957) and *Method in Theology* (1972), he sought to reshape and integrate theological inquiry with modern scientific advances. For many years he taught theology in Jesuit seminaries in Montreal and Toronto, was an expert consultant to the second Vatican Council (1962–65), and in later years conducted workshops at Boston College, where he served as visiting distinguished professor of theology from 1975 to 1983. Though he was regarded as one of the foremost thinkers of the 20th century, his works were considered difficult to interpret, and some of his contemporaries felt that the magnitude of his contributions would not fully be appreciated for several decades. At the time of his death he was working on a volume on economics.

Losey, Joseph, U.S.-born motion-picture director (b. Jan. 14, 1909, La Crosse, Wis.—d. June 22, 1984, London, England), was an uncompromising individualist and avowed leftist who was blacklisted and forced into exile in London after refusing to testify before the House Committee on Un-American Activities in 1951. Yet as an expatriate director, Losey achieved his greatest success. Losey, who studied medicine at Dartmouth College, Hanover, N.H., later earned (1930) an M.A. in English literature from Harvard University and wrote book and theatre reviews. He served as an assistant stage manager, then stage director, and in 1935 he traveled to Moscow as a reporter for *Variety* and attended classes conducted by Sergey Eisenstein, the foremost Soviet film director and theorist. During the 1930s and 1940s Losey directed productions for the stage, most notably Bertolt Brecht's *Galileo Galilei* (1947). Losey's first feature-length films, including *The Boy with Green Hair* (1948; about pacifism), *The Lawless* (1949; about racial intolerance), and *The Prowler* (1950; about police corruption), were powerful dramas with controversial social themes. In London he worked under pseudonyms until he attracted the attention of critics and audiences with a series of smash hits at the box office, including *The Damned* (1961), *King and Country* (1964), *Modesty Blaise* (1966), *Figures in a Landscape* (1970), *The Romantic Englishwoman* (1975),

and his outstanding collaborations with playwright Harold Pinter, including *The Servant* (1963), *Accident* (1967), and *The Go-Between*.

Lynch, Sir Phillip Reginald, Australian politician (b. July 27, 1933, Melbourne, Australia—d. June 19, 1984, Frankston, Australia), was deputy leader of the Liberal Party from 1973 to 1982, having served as a minister from 1966 to 1972 and as treasurer. He studied at Melbourne University before entering Parliament in 1966 and rapidly gained a reputation as one of his party's most effective politicians. Lynch was minister for the army (1968–69), for immigration (1969–71), and then for labour until the 1972 election, when the Liberals lost power to the Australian Labor Party (ALP). As deputy opposition leader he played an important role in defeating the ALP administration, and he became treasurer in 1975 but had to resign in 1977 because of his involvement in land deals. After serving (1975–82) as minister for industry and commerce, Lynch was obliged to resign because of ill health.

MacEntee, Sean, Irish politician (b. Aug. 22, 1889, Belfast, Ireland—d. Jan. 9, 1984, Dublin, Ireland), as *tanaiste* (deputy prime minister) of the Republic of Ireland (1959–65) under Sean Lemass, was the last survivor of the Irish politicians who had taken part in the Easter Rising of 1916. A Catholic, he was educated in Belfast and became a consulting electrical engineer and a registered patent agent. He served in the Irish Republican Army (1916–21) and was a member of the national executive committee of the Irish Volunteers (1917–21). Elected to the Dail for Sinn Fein in 1918, he was among those of his party who opposed the 1921 Anglo-Irish treaty. A founder member of the Fianna Fail party in 1927, he served in all of Eamon De Valera's governments, as minister for finance (1932–39 and 1951–54), for industry and commerce (1939–41), and for local government (1941–48). He was also minister for health (1957–59) and for social welfare (1958–61). Although of impeccable republican and revolutionary background, he argued that the unification of Ireland could be achieved only through winning the confidence of Ulster unionists. He published a volume of poetry in 1918 and *Episode at Easter* in 1966.

Machito (FRANK GRILLO), Cuban-American bandleader (b. Feb. 16, 1912, Tampa, Fla.—d. April 15, 1984, London, England), was instrumental in shaping modern jazz and helping to create salsa music (a special blend of Latin-American music that boasted elements of rhythm and blues, jazz, and rock) as the innovative leader of the Afro-Cubans, a dance band that included both black and Latin musicians. Machito (a nickname he was given at birth and then adopted when he formed his own big band) was a backup singer and maracas player in Cuba before he returned to the U.S. in 1937. He formed his band in 1943, and his brother-in-law, trumpeter Mario Bauza, orchestrated the progressive arrangements for the band, which performed at both Latin dance halls and jazz clubs with such bebop jazz artists as Dizzy Gillespie and Charlie Parker. The former adapted Machito's Afro-Cuban sound to small-group jazz, and in 1947 bandleader Stan Kenton used the rhythm section of the Afro-Cubans to create a song called "Machito." During the 1950s Machito and his band (the first dance band to sport a conga drum) showcased their jazz improvisations coupled with pulsing Latin rhythms at New York's Palladium ballroom. During the 1960s and '70s the Afro-Cubans toured extensively in the U.S., Europe, and the Far East.

Macleod, Joseph Todd Gordon, British author and broadcaster (b. April 24, 1903, Ealing, Middlesex, England—d. March 1984, Florence, Italy), became a familiar voice to millions of listeners as a newsreader and commentator on BBC radio during World War II and was also a distinguished poet and the author of four verse dramas. He studied at Balliol College, Oxford, and was called to the bar by the Inner Temple in 1928. He had already published a critical essay, *Beauty and the Beast* (1927), and in 1930 he attracted attention as a poet with *The Ecliptic*. Some of his later poetry on the Hebrides was published under the name Adam Drinan, including *Women of the Happy Island* (1944). Macleod dropped the pseudonym for his postwar poetry, the last volume of which was *An Old Olive Tree* (1971). In 1933 he became director of the Festival Theatre, Cambridge, writing plays for the repertory company, and was for a time the Labour Party candidate for Huntingdonshire. In 1938 he joined the BBC and, after leaving it in 1945, was managing director (1946–47) of the Scottish National Film Studios. Macleod also wrote books on theatrical history, including one in Italian and several on the Soviet theatre, and published an autobiography, *A Job at the BBC* (1947). He lived in Italy for the last 25 years of his life.

Magogo Sibilile Nantithi Ngangezinye kaDinuzulu kaSenzangakhona, Princess Constance, Zulu musicologist (b. 1900, Nongoma, Natal, South Africa—d. Nov. 21, 1984, Durban, South Africa), was a member of the Zulu royal house and the greatest living authority on Zulu music. She acquired from her grandmothers, wives of King Cetshwayo, knowledge of a repertoire developed from 18th-century traditions. A child of King Dinuzulu, she was left, on the early death of her mother, Queen Silomo, with the duty of caring for her two brothers, the future King Solomon Maphumuzana Nkayishana (reigned 1916–33) and Mshiyeni, who was regent (1933–48). At her brother's request she married (1923) Chief Mathole Buthelezi, as his tenth but principal wife, in order to quell a feud with his clan. Her son, Chief Gatsha Buthelezi of KwaZulu, became prominent as an upholder of black rights in South Africa. Although she knew no English and was a keen upholder of Zulu tradition, she was also a convinced member of the Anglican Church. Her theoretical knowledge of Zulu music was matched by her performing ability; her vocal range spanned three octaves, and she was skilled with the *ugubhu* musical bow. She advised on music for the film *Zulu* (1963) and on many broadcasts and recordings of Zulu music.

Malcuzynski, Karol, Polish journalist and broadcaster (b. June 20, 1922, Warsaw, Poland—d. June 13, 1984, Warsaw), was an independent-minded commentator on world affairs in the Polish media. He began his journalistic career covering the Nuremberg trials for *Robotnik*, a daily paper. From 1948 he was on the staff of the leading Communist paper, *Trybuna Ludu*, and in 1958 was appointed press attaché at the Polish embassy in London. After his return from London (1960) he joined the Polish television service as presenter (1961–76) of a current affairs program. In 1976 he was elected to the Sejm (parliament) as a nonparty member and sat on various parliamentary committees concerned with foreign affairs and cultural matters. Never a convinced Marxist, Malcuzynski welcomed the advent of the Solidarity movement. He was the author of several books, including one on the Nuremberg trials, and of numerous documentary film scripts and scenarios.

Malik, Adam, Indonesian statesman (b. July 22, 1917, Pematangsiantar, North Sumatra, Netherlands East Indies—d. Sept. 5, 1984, Bandung, Indon.), as a prominent and resilient figure in Indonesian politics was a nationalist political leader and later served as president (1971–72) of the UN General Assembly and as foreign minister (1966–77) and vice-president (1978–83) of his country. Malik, who was largely self-educated, was a militant nationalist who was jailed by the Dutch on several occasions in his quest for independence from their rule. In 1937 he founded the Indonesian news agency,

a press service for the insurgent movement. After independence in 1949 the agency became Indonesia's national press agency, and Malik served in various posts of the Sukarno government, notably as ambassador to the Soviet Union and Poland. Malik became increasingly disenchanted with Sukarno's autocratic rule and in the early 1960s developed a close association with General Suharto, who became president in 1965. The following year Malik was appointed foreign minister, and in this capacity he was instrumental in ending an armed confrontation with Malaysia, rejoining the UN (from which Sukarno had withdrawn in 1965), establishing in 1967 the Association of Southeast Asian Nations (ASEAN; an international organization formed by the governments of Indonesia, Malaysia, the Philippines, Singapore, and Thailand to promote economic, social, and cultural progress and to ensure the stability of the area), and obtaining a 30-year extension on the $3 billion debt to creditor nations that Sukarno had accumulated during his reign. A witty and eloquent diplomat, Malik was dubbed "Kantjil" (in Indonesian folktale the kantjil, a small and graceful deer, uses its agility and quick wit to escape dangerous situations) by those who recognized his shrewd political maneuvers. As president of the UN General Assembly, he presided over the admission of the People's Republic of China. He retired as a diplomat in 1977 and then served as Indonesia's vice-president from 1978 to 1983.

Manahan, Anna Anderson, claimed to be the Grand Duchess Anastasia b. 1901?—d. Feb. 12, 1984, Charlottesville, Va.), spent most of her lifetime trying to prove that she was Anastasia, the youngest daughter of Tsar Nicholas II, and the only survivor of the 1918 execution of the Russian imperial family. In her quest, Manahan claimed that she had eluded execution by hiding behind one of her three sisters. Her legal attempts to prove that she was the rightful heir to an $85 million dowry, presumably on deposit in the Bank of England, were ended in 1970 when a German court ruled it could not make a decision either for or against her and closed the case. Though she was the foremost of many pretenders, she was declared an imposter by Romanov relatives, and Russian historians discounted her genuineness by citing the fact that she did not speak Russian. In 1968 she moved to Charlottesville to marry historian John E. Manahan. Her life also became the subject of many books and a motion picture, *Anastasia*, starring Ingrid Bergman.

Marella, Paolo Cardinal, Italian prelate of the Roman Catholic Church (b. Jan. 25, 1895, Rome, Italy—d. Oct. 15, 1984, Rome), as apostolic delegate to Japan during World War II, visited Allied servicemen in prisoner-of-war camps. Later, as apostolic delegate to France, he had to apply the Vatican's restraining policy toward the worker priest movements. He was known as one of the more conservative-minded members of the Roman Curia. Educated at the Roman Seminary, Apollinaris, and at the Royal University in Rome, he was ordained priest in 1918. He became an official of the Sacred Congregation of Propaganda Fide in 1921 and in 1923 was sent as an auditor to the apostolic delegation in Washington, D.C., himself becoming apostolic delegate a year later. Consecrated bishop of the titular see of Doclea (1933), he served as apostolic delegate in Japan (1933–48), Australia, New Zealand, and Oceania (1943–53), and France (1953–59). He was created a cardinal in 1959 and was the first president (1964–73) of the Vatican's Secretariat for Relations with Non-Christians.

Mason, James Neville, British film actor (b. May 15, 1909, Huddersfield, England—d. July 27, 1984, Lausanne, Switz.), was featured in more than 100 films; he was a top box-office star in Britain in the late 1940s, and in Hollywood he was nominated for an Oscar for his role opposite Judy Garland in George Cukor's

remake of *A Star Is Born* (1954). He played antihero types and was featured as a sadist or a cad in such films as *The Man in Grey* (1943), *The Seventh Veil* (1945), and *Odd Man Out* (1947). As he grew older, he specialized in the roles of disappointed or psychologically flawed figures. He portrayed a drug addict in *Bigger than Life* (1956), Humbert Humbert in *Lolita* (1962), and a middle-aged suitor in *Georgy Girl* (1966). His last role was as the sadistic inventor of bizarre humiliations in the title role of Graham Greene's *Dr. Fischer of Geneva*, shown on British television after his death. Mason studied architecture at the University of Cambridge, but because of the Depression he could find no employment; he turned to his other interest, acting, and made his stage debut in *The Rascal* (1931). He was a member of the Old Vic company during its memorable 1933–34 season and was at the Gate Theatre, Dublin (1934–37). His film debut was in *Late Extra* (1935). Mason moved to Hollywood in 1946, where his numerous parts included Rommel in *The Desert Fox* (1951), Brutus in the film version of Shakespeare's *Julius Caesar* (1953), the martinet father in *Spring and Port Wine* (1969), and the old tutor in *Autobiography of a Princess* (1975). His own autobiography, *Before I Forget,* appeared in 1981. He had made his home in Lausanne for some years.

Mentschikoff, Soia, Russian-born legal scholar and educator (b. April 2, 1915, Moscow, Russia—d. June 18, 1984, Coral Gables, Fla.), was a formidable legal adversary who crushed opponents with indisputable logical arguments and shattered professional barriers by becoming the first woman to teach law at Harvard University (1947–49) and the University of Chicago (1951–74). While still a student at Columbia University Law School in New York City, Mentschikoff became research assistant to Karl Nickerson Llewellyn, who was chief drafter of the Uniform Commercial Code for the American Law Institute. The couple married in 1947, a decade after she graduated from Columbia, and after his death in 1962 she became drafter of the code. The aura that Mentschikoff maintained inspired both fear and admiration in her students; while she served (1974–82) as dean of the University of Miami School of Law, her students affectionately dubbed her "Czarina." She retired as dean in 1982 but continued to serve as a consultant, expert witness, and riveting public speaker.

Mercer, Mabel, British-born singer (b. Feb. 3, 1900, Burton-on-Trent, Staffordshire, England—d. April 20, 1984, Pittsfield, Mass.), was a gravelly voiced cabaret singer who for 70 years reigned supreme with heartfelt lyrical interpretations that made such songs as "Fly Me to the Moon" and "While We're Young" all-time favourites. Her singing, a unique blend of cadenced speech and vocalizing, inspired such singing stars as Leontyne Price, Billie Holiday, and Frank Sinatra, who dubbed her "the best music teacher in the world." When her husky contralto began to falter, Mercer compensated by becoming a master of inflection and phraseology. The daughter of a black American father and a white English mother whose family was in show business, Mercer became a dancer in the family music-hall act at age 14. After World War I she made her way to Paris and sang at Chez Florence, Le Grand Duke, and at Bricktop's, where she adopted an intimate style of singing while seated. After coming to the U.S. in 1938 (she became a U.S. citizen in 1952), she secured a long list of engagements at famous New York supper clubs where she rescued such songs as "Little Girl Blue" and "By Myself" from oblivion and gained a loyal following from both audiences and fellow singers. A grand actress who appeared at Carnegie Hall in 1977 and in London the same year after a 40-year absence, she went into a brief retirement in 1979 only to reappear in 1982 at the Kool Jazz Festival. In 1983 she was the recipient of the Presidential Medal of Freedom.

Merman, Ethel (ETHEL AGNES ZIMMERMAN), U.S. singer (b. Jan. 16, 1908?, New York, N.Y.—d. Feb. 15, 1984, New York), reigned as "queen of Broadway" for three decades (1930s–1950s) with a brassy verve and a clarion voice that belted out such hit songs as "There's No Business Like Show Business" and "Everything's Coming Up Roses." A one-time stenographer who was determined to become a singer, though she never had a voice lesson, Merman first appeared in vaudeville, notably with Jimmy Durante. In her Broadway debut in *Girl Crazy* (1930), Merman stopped the show by holding a high-C note for 16 bars during the second chorus of "I Got Rhythm." A musical comedy superstar who was dependable and self-assured, she dominated such Broadway shows as *Anything Goes* (1934), *Panama Hattie* (1940), *Annie Get Your Gun* (1946), and *Gypsy* (1959), which she and many others considered her best performance. Merman also starred in 14 motion pictures, including *We're Not Dressing, Alexander's Ragtime Band,* and *There's No Business Like Show Business,* and in such duplications of her Broadway triumphs as *Anything Goes* and *Call Me Madam.* In the latter the redoubtable Merman stole the show as the gum-chewing Mrs. Sally Adams with her renditions of "You're Just in Love," "The Hostess with the Mostes' on the Ball," and "Can You Use any Money Today?" The 16.8 m (5-ft 6-in) dynamo's effortless projection was best suited, however, to the Broadway stage, where she made famous such songs as "I Get a Kick out of You," "You're the Top," "Blow, Gabriel, Blow," "Friendship," "You Can't Get a Man with a Gun," and "Rose's Turn." The enduring star's biggest professional disappointment was the loss of the lead to Rosalind Russell in the film version of *Gypsy.* Merman retired from Broadway in 1970 after playing the title role in *Hello, Dolly!* but made her last major appearance in 1982 when she participated in a benefit concert at Carnegie Hall. The legendary first lady of musical comedy underwent surgery for a brain tumour in 1983 but never wavered from her credo, "Always give them the old fire, even when you feel like a squashed cake of ice."

Middleton, Ray(mond) Earl, Jr., U.S. actor (b. 1908, Chicago, Ill.—d. April 10, 1984, Panorama City, Calif.), was a vibrant baritone who enjoyed a 30-year career on Broadway as the leading man in such musicals as *Annie Get Your Gun* (1946), *Love Life* (1948), and *South Pacific* (1950). A graduate of the Juilliard School of Music, Middleton also sang with opera companies and was renowned for his versatility. On stage he also appeared in *Roberta* (1933), *Scandals* (1939), *Winged Victory* (1943), and *The Man of La Mancha* (1965). In Hollywood he won parts in such motion pictures as *Gangs of Chicago* (1940), *The Girl from Alaska* (1942), and *I Dream of Jeannie* (1952). He recently appeared on television in such programs as "M*A*S*H," "Two Close for Comfort," and "Knotts Landing."

Mili, Gjon, Albanian-born photographer (b. Nov. 28, 1904, Korce, Albania—d. Feb. 14, 1984, Stamford, Conn.), as an extremely versatile photographer for *Life* magazine for 45 years pioneered the use of stroboscopic photography (electronic flashes fixed repeatedly at high frequencies of hundreds of thousands of flashes per second) during the 1930s and visually captured the flow of movement of dancers, artists, and athletes. After immigrating to the U.S. in 1923, Mili studied electrical engineering at the Massachusetts Institute of Technology and conducted lighting research with the Westinghouse Lamp Co. until 1937. He spent his free time as an amateur photographer, but when high-speed electronic-flash units became available, he turned professional. After selling a photo of tennis player Bobby Riggs to *Life* magazine, he left Westinghouse and launched a lifelong association with *Life.* His stop-action photos, including "Picasso Drawing with Light" (1951) and "Carmen Jones" (1951), in-

fluenced two generations of photojournalists. After *Life* folded in 1972, Mili continued shooting pictures for special editions of the magazine, and when the new *Life* magazine appeared in 1978 he found a permanent showcase for his photographs. His innovative multiple-exposure prints appeared in such books as *Gjon Mili: Photographs and Recollections, Photographs of Picasso by Gjon Mili and Robert Capa,* and *The Magic of Opera.*

Miskine, Idriss, Chadian politician (b. March 15, 1948, N'Djamena, Chad [then part of French Equatorial Africa]—d. Jan. 7, 1984, N'Djamena), was Chad's foreign minister from October 1982 and a close ally of Pres. Hissen Habré. A Muslim and a member of the Hadjaral tribe, he had served under Pres. Félix Malloum as minister of transport, posts, and telecommunications before joining Habré's Armed Forces of the North (FAN) opposition movement in 1979. In June 1982 he helped in the recapture of N'Djamena, the country's capital, from Goukouni Oueddei's Transitional Government of National Union (GUNT). In 1983 Miskine was in command of government forces at the strategic northern town of Faya-Largeau against Goukouni's Libyan-backed troops, and he took a leading part in diplomatic moves against Libyan involvement in the conflict. By the end of 1983 he was negotiating in preparation for talks with the rebels to end the civil war, but he died shortly after his return from Addis Ababa, Eth., where he had been making the final arrangements for these talks. His death was viewed as a considerable personal and political blow to President Habré.

Mitchell, Clarence M., Jr., U.S. lobbyist (b. March 8, 1911, Baltimore, Md.—d. March 18, 1984, Baltimore), helped shape landmark civil rights legislation of the 1960s as an influential Washington lobbyist for the National Association for the Advancement of Colored People (NAACP) and the Leadership Conference on Civil Rights from 1950 to 1978. As a representative of the latter, he used his persuasive powers to gain passage of the Fair Housing Act of 1968. Mitchell earned a law degree from the Univer-

sity of Maryland Law School before becoming a prominent force in politics. He briefly worked as a journalist for the *Baltimore Afro-American* newspaper before becoming executive secretary of the Urban League in St. Paul, Minn., in 1937. He held a succession of government posts as a member of the Fair Employment Commission, the War Manpower Commission, and the War Production Board before joining the NAACP in 1945 as national labour secretary in the Washington office. From 1950 to 1978 he served as a successful lobbyist for the NAACP and attributed his many triumphs to working through existing laws to obtain civil rights legislation. Mitchell, known for his discipline, respect, and courtesy, also formed productive relationships with both Republican and Democratic legislators who admired his tenacity and sometimes referred to him as the "101st senator." He retired from the

NAACP in 1978 and resumed his legal practice in Baltimore.

Mohieddin, (Ahmad) Fuad, Egyptian politician (b. 1926—d. June 5, 1984, Cairo, Egypt), was prime minister from January 1982 and secretary-general of the ruling National Democratic Party, which was returned to power in the general election shortly before his death. A moderate social democrat, he had served loyally under three successive presidents. Mohieddin trained as a doctor at Cairo University and specialized in radiology. He was elected to the National Assembly in 1957. From 1968 to 1974 he was a governor of three provinces before taking ministerial office and later serving as deputy prime minister under Pres. Anwar as-Sadat. The 1984 election, while it brought an overwhelming victory for Mohieddin's party, which won 87% of the seats, was overshadowed by opposition claims of irregularities in the conduct of the poll.

Montagu, Ivor, British writer, film producer, and director (b. April 23, 1904, London, England—d. Nov. 5, 1984, Watford, England), was a leading British Communist before World War II and established a film career through his associations with Soviet filmmaker Sergey Eisenstein, U.S. director Alfred Hitchcock, and British producer Michael Balcon. From the late 1920s he was active in filmmaking, and for a time he was film critic for *The Observer* newspaper. He also contributed regularly to the Communist *Daily Worker.* In 1928 he helped to make an unsuccessful trio of film comedies written by H. G. Wells—*Bluebottles, The Daydream,* and *The Tonic.* Montagu served as co-director of *Wings over Everest* (1933) and producer of Hitchcock's *The Man Who Knew Too Much* (1934) and *The Thirty-nine Steps* (1935). He was adviser to the Soviet Film Agency (1941–45), and in 1948 he went to Ealing Studios as an associate producer.

Morecambe, Eric (JOHN ERIC BARTHOLOMEW), British comedian (b. May 14, 1926, Morecambe, Lancashire, England—d. May 28, 1984, Cheltenham, England), was the tall thin one, his partner, Ernie Wise, the short stubby one, in the most famous English comedy double act of all time. Not only were Eric and Ernie household names (and as immediately recognizable as under the more formal title, "Morecambe and Wise"), but their appeal was such that Prime Minister Harold Wilson, actress Dame Flora Robson, and conductor André Previn were among the many celebrities who were happy to appear on their television Christmas show. More astonishingly, they took the material of the music hall comedian, with its often appalling gags, puns, and catchphrases, and transferred it with success to the medium of television. Morecambe, who took his stage name from his birthplace, started his professional career at the age of 12 and met Ernest Wiseman during World War II; their first double act was at the Empire Theatre, Liverpool, in 1941. After the war they appeared in music hall, did a radio series, and in 1954 got their first television series, "Running Wild." It flopped, and their first real break came with the "Morecambe and Wise Show" in 1961. Morecambe was a born comedian, and the pair started by imitating Abbott and Costello, with Ernie as the comic and Eric as the "feed." With time, however, by what seemed to be a spontaneous process, the roles were reversed, Eric increasingly appealing for laughs to the audience over little Ernie's head. They moved from Independent Television (ITV) to the BBC, made three films (with only qualified success), and in 1978 went back to ITV. Ten years earlier Morecambe had had his first heart attack and in 1979 had open-heart surgery. From then on, exhaustion and ill health curtailed his activities. His last stage appearance, at Tewkesbury, preceded his death by only a few hours. Morecambe and Wise published a joint autobiography in 1973, and Morecambe's son Gary wrote a book, *Funny Man,* about him, but Morecambe's life could probably be glimpsed more adequately in his novel about an entertainer, *Mr. Lonely* (1981). Morecambe was created Officer of the Order of the British Empire in 1976.

Mujica Láinez, Manuel, Argentine novelist (b. Sept. 11, 1910, Buenos Aires, Arg.—d. April 21, 1984, Córdoba Province, Arg.), won the Argentine National Prize for Letters in 1957 with his novel *Invitados en el Paraíso* and gained an international reputation as the author of enigmatic works that combined history and fantasy. His novel *Bomarzo* (1962) was banned by the Argentine government, though widely translated and internationally successful as an opera, with music by Alberto Ginastera. Like most of his fiction, it was a baroque fantasy, written in an ironic and cultured style. His other novels included *Don Galaz de Buenos Aires* (1938), *Los ídolos* (1953), and *La casa* (1954). His more experimental later work, such as *El unicornio* (1965; Eng. trans. *The Wandering Unicorn,* 1983) and *De milagros y de melancolías* (1968), utilizes myth and allegory in a way reminiscent of the stories of Jorge Luis Borges. Mujica Láinez was also the author of two books of short stories, *Aquí viveron* (1949) and *Misteriosa Buenos Aires* (1951).

Nagano, Shigeo, Japanese industrialist (b. July 15, 1900, Matsue, Shimane Prefecture, Japan—d. May 4, 1984, Tokyo, Japan), was an energetic business tycoon who served (1969–84) as president of the Japan Chamber of Commerce and Industry (JCCI) and was so influential both in business and in politics that he was honoured as one of the "Four Heavenly Kings of the Business World." After graduating from Tokyo Imperial University in 1924, Nagano was persuaded by his mentor, Masao Shibusawa, to join Fuji Steelmaking Co., which was in the process of being rebuilt. By 1934 Fuji Steelmaking had merged with five other firms to form the Japan Iron & Steel Co., and Nagano became plant manager and director. During World War II he was assigned to the Japan Iron & Steel Control Corp., and he became president in 1944. When the Japan Iron & Steel Co. disbanded in 1950, Nagano became president of Fuji Iron & Steel Co., and he remained chief executive of the concern until 1970, when he engineered the merger of Fuji Iron & Steel with Yawata Iron & Steel to form Nippon Steel Corp., the country's largest steel company. Nagano then became chairman of Nippon and in 1973 honorary chairman. During his career he greatly contributed to Japan's economic development, and as president of the JCCI he promoted economic relations with foreign countries. Nagano, a mentor to politicians, used his influence in government to further his own visions; at the time of his death, his plan to construct a second canal in Panama and his goal to promote economic exchanges with the Soviet Union were on the formal semigovernmental agenda. The death of the cunning diplomat was viewed as an immediate blow to improvement in Japan-Soviet relations.

Naguib, Muhammad, Egyptian army officer (b. Feb. 20, 1901, Khartoum, Sudan—d. Aug. 28, 1984, Cairo, Egypt), was president and prime minister of Egypt in the first years after the 1952 revolution. Considered to favour a democratic, parliamentary government, he was ousted by Gamal Abdel Nasser in November 1954. Naguib held various military appointments before World War II and founded the *Magazine of the Egyptian Army*. Promoted to colonel, then brigadier, he fought in the war against Israel in 1948 and was wounded, having established a reputation as a patriotic and courageous officer. He was made major general in 1951 and by this time had been invited by Nasser to act as a figurehead for the Free Officers movement, which seized power in the coup of July 1952. He became commander in chief and, after the resignation of Ali Maher in September over land reform, prime minister. When the republic was declared in June 1953, he was made

president. He enjoyed wide popularity, but his attempts to curb the power of Nasser's Revolutionary Council led to a power struggle and his resignation in February 1954. He was reinstated as president, and for a time as prime minister, but was unable to rally opposition to the Army and, from Nov. 14, 1954, until his release by Pres. Anwar as-Sadat in 1970, was kept under house arrest. He played no further role in political affairs.

Neill, The Right Rev. Stephen Charles, British Anglican clergyman (b. Dec. 31, 1900, Edinburgh, Scotland—d. July 20, 1984, Oxford, England), served as bishop of Tinnevelly (Tirunelveli), India, from 1939 to 1945 and was a renowned missionary, lecturer, and writer. He was also a notable representative of the liberal evangelical tradition in the Church of England and made important contributions to the ecumenical movement. Neill took a leading role in negotiations that led to the establishment (1948) of the Church of South India, formed from the unions there of various Protestant denominations. He was associate general secretary of the World Council of Churches from 1948 to 1951 and a joint editor (1951–54) of *The History of the Ecumenical Movement, 1517–1948*. Between 1952 and 1972 he was involved, as general editor and later as director, with development of the Library of World Christian Books. A compelling speaker and prolific writer, he was a communicator rather than an original thinker. Among his best-known books were *Anglicanism* (1958) and *A History of Christian Missions* (1964). Educated at the University of Cambridge, he worked as a missionary in south India (1924–30) before becoming warden (1930–38) of Bishop's Theological College, Tirumaraiyur, and then bishop of Tinnevelly. It proved difficult for him to sustain administrative roles, and thereafter his service to Christianity was mainly as lecturer and author. He was professor of missions and ecumenical theology at the University of Hamburg, West Germany (1962–67), and held a chair at Nairobi, Kenya (1969–73). He wrote numerous books on Christian belief, character, society, and missions and on ecumenism; an adventure into exegesis was *The Interpretation of the New Testament* (1964), the text of his Bampton Lectures at Oxford. From 1979 he was assistant bishop in the diocese of Oxford.

Nemtchinova, Vera, Russian dancer and teacher (b. Aug. 26, 1899?, Moscow, Russia—d. July 22, 1984, New York, N.Y.), was a sensational classical and modern ballerina who starred with Serge Diaghilev's Ballets Russes from 1915 to 1926 but scored her greatest triumph in 1924 as the androgynous "Girl in Blue" in *Les Biches*. Her magnificent performance, wearing only a blue, stylized man's jacket over her leotard that accentuated her small waist and shapely legs, cast her as a new type of ballerina in the modern mold. In 1927 she helped organize the Nemtchinova-Dolin Ballet, which toured for a year in Europe. She exhibited her unique classical gifts as the prima ballerina from 1931 to 1935 with the Lithuanian State Ballet in Kaunas. She later appeared with the Ballet Russe de Monte Carlo, the Markova-Dolin Ballet, and in the U.S. with the Original Ballet Russe and Ballet Theatre. After she and her husband Anatole Oboukhov (a classical dancer and often her partner) settled in the U.S., she joined the faculty of New York's School of Ballet Arts in 1947 and in 1962 headed her own school of classical ballet, also in New York. Nemtchinova became one of the city's best-known teachers and worked until the day of her stroke on June 28, some two months before her 85th birthday.

Niemöller, (Friedrich Gustav Emil) Martin, German Protestant clergyman (b. Jan. 14, 1892, Lippstadt, Westphalia, Germany—d. March 6, 1984, Wiesbaden, West Germany), was an uncompromising theologian and pacifist who spent eight years (1937–45) in the Sachsenhausen and Dachau concentration camps because of his outspoken opposition to Adolf Hitler. Niemöller led the clerical opposition to Nazism after Hitler came to power in 1933 by agitating: "Not you, Herr Hitler, but God is my Führer." Though one of Hitler's last orders was that Niemöller and other leading prisoners should be executed, they were liberated by the Allies. After the war Niemöller became a passionate international advocate of disarmament and worked to rebuild the Protestant Church in Germany. The new (West) German regime accused him of sympathizing with Communism, and in 1959 Defense Minister Franz-Josef Strauss accused him of defam-

ing the armed forces. It was a surprising charge against a man who, having joined the German Navy in 1910, won the Iron Cross for his exploits as a submarine commander, recorded in his book *Vom U-boot zur Kanzel* (1934; *From U-boat to Pulpit,* 1939), and who, as a pastor of the Berlin parish of Dahlem during the 1930s, gained a reputation as a right-wing nationalist. After World War II he traveled widely, asserting the Germans' collective guilt for the war and propounding pacifism. In 1945 he was made head of the foreign relations department of the Evangelical Church in Germany, a post he held until 1956. He made frequent tours abroad, including a trip to the Soviet Union in 1952, and he favoured accepting Stalin's proposal for a disarmed but united Germany. He also called for nuclear disarmament and remained a controversial figure well into his 80s. Niemöller, who served as president of the World Council of Churches (1961–68), was the recipient of the Lenin Peace Prize in 1967.

O'Flaherty, Liam, Irish writer (b. Aug. 28, 1896, Inishmore, Aran Islands, Ireland—d. Sept. 7, 1984, Dublin, Ireland), penned riveting novels and short stories that combined brutal naturalism, psychological analysis, poetry, and biting satire with an underlying respect for the courage of his countrymen. His first novel, *Thy Neighbour's Wife* (1923), was followed by *The Black Soul* (1924) and *The Informer* (1925), a story about a dull-witted revolutionary who betrays his friend. The latter was adapted for the screen three times, most notably by John Ford in 1935. But O'Flaherty's most accomplished work was considered to be *Famine* (1937), which recounted the hardships created in a small farming community during the Irish famine of the 1840s. O'Flaherty was educated for the priesthood but gave up before ordination and won a scholarship to University College, Dublin. He formed a Republican corps (1913) but, "tired of waiting for the Revolution," left college and joined the Irish Guards, serving in France during World War I. He later traveled extensively throughout the world but returned in 1921 to Dublin, where as a self-proclaimed Communist he led a group who held the Rotunda building for several days. A committed Republican, he opposed the establishment of the Irish Free State and went to London in 1922, when he began his literary successes. O'Flaherty published more than 30 books, including such short stories as *Spring Sowing* (1923) and *The Mountain Tavern* (1929). A trip to the U.S.S.R.

AP/WIDE WORLD

resulted in his disillusioned *I Went to Russia* (1931). O'Flaherty spent World War II in the Americas but thereafter lived mainly in Dublin. He wrote two autobiographical volumes, *Two Years* (1930) and *Shame the Devil* (1934), and some poems and stories in Irish.

Osmany, Mohammad Ataul Ghani, Bangladesh army officer (b. 1919, Sylhet, Bengal—d. Feb. 16, 1984, London, England), was a follower of Sheikh Mujibur Rahman and commander in chief of the Bangladesh Army which campaigned against West Pakistan in 1971 for the independence of Bangladesh. Osmany served with the Indian Army during World War II, became a major at age 23, then joined the Pakistan Army after the partition of India in 1947. When the Awami League won the elections in East Pakistan in 1970, he took command of the Bangladesh guerrilla forces and after independence established the army of the new state. In 1973, after resigning from the Army and contesting the elections, he was appointed minister of defense but opposed plans for a one-party state. After Sheikh Mujibur's assassination in 1975, Osmany became defense adviser before forming the National People's Party. He ran twice unsuccessfully for the presidency. A firm believer in parliamentary rule, he quarreled with Army Chief of Staff (later president) Hossain Mohammad Ershad's plan to give a greater political role to the Army.

Owings, Nathaniel Alexander, U.S. architect and engineer (b. Feb. 5, 1903, Indianapolis, Ind.—d. June 13, 1984, Santa Fe, N.M.), as the protean co-founder in 1936 of the prestigious architectural firm of Skidmore and Owings (from 1939, Skidmore, Owings & Merrill) used his organizational expertise to preside over more than $3 billion in construction during a prolific 40-year career. Owings earned a B.S. degree from Cornell University, Ithaca, N.Y., and, together with Louis Skidmore, a top-notch designer, worked on the Chicago Century of Progress Exposition in 1933. The two formed their own company in 1936 and three years later hired engineer John Merrill as a partner. By using the group approach, the firm was able to tackle large-scale commissions, but the partnership's first big break came during World War II when they were hired by the U.S. government to build a secret town for 75,000 residents—Atom City, Oak Ridge, Tenn., headquarters of the U.S. atomic energy project. The firm's specialty, however, was skyscrapers. With the completion in 1952 of Lever House in New York City, which was built on only a portion of its site and ushered in an era of tall curtain-wall business buildings, Skidmore, Owings & Merrill became one of the foremost architectural firms in the nation. Owings, who made no claims to being a first-rate designer, nonetheless guided the firm through decades of prosperity. Some of the firm's other innovative commissions included the John Hancock Center, Chicago; the Crown Zellerbach Building, San Francisco; the Chase Manhattan Bank, New York City; and the Sears Tower, Chicago, which surpassed New

York City's World Trade Center as the world's tallest building. Owings also wrote two books, *The American Aesthetic* (1969) and *The Spaces in Between: An Architect's Journey* (1973), and was awarded the American Institute of Architects' Gold Medal in 1983.

Palewski, Gaston, French politician and diplomat (b. March 20, 1901, Paris, France—d. Sept. 3, 1984, Arnould, Essonne, France), was a close associate of Gen. Charles de Gaulle during World War II and served as minister of state, then president of the Constitutional Council until 1974. A man of considerable diplomatic skill and personal charm, he was seen at times as a subtle intriguer, a politician rather than a statesman. He studied at the École des Sciences Politiques and at the University of Oxford before joining the staff of Marshal L. H. G. Lyautey (1924–25), then of Paul Reynaud (1928–39). In 1940 he joined de Gaulle in London. As one of the few members of de Gaulle's staff with wide political experience, he became his chief political adviser and spokesman and persuaded Gen. Georges Catroux to leave Vichy and join the Free French. In 1947 he helped found the Rassemblement du Peuple Français, became a deputy of the National Assembly, and joined the government under Edgar Faure before going to Rome as ambassador in 1957. On his return in 1962 he was made minister of state for nuclear and space affairs. Vice-president of the Institut Charles de Gaulle, he was an art lover, a leading figure in the French campaigns for the preservation of treasures in Florence and Venice, and a member of the Académie des Beaux-Arts. He wrote an autobiography, *Hier et aujourd'hui* (1975), and *Le Miroir de Talleyrand* (1976).

Palmer, Leonard Robert, British philologist (b. June 5, 1906, Bristol, England—d. Aug. 26, 1984, Pitney, Somerset, England), was a classical scholar of international repute and a specialist in Greek and other early Mediterranean languages. But his interests were not confined to the archaic, and he took early note of the rise of structuralist theories in modern linguistics, later attacking the work of Noam Chomsky and his followers. He became well known to the general public after engaging in a controversy about the chronology of Minoan Crete; using philological evidence derived from the Linear B tablets and other inscriptions, he disputed many of the views put forward by the archaeologist Sir Arthur Evans. Educated in Wales, at Trinity College, University of Cambridge, and at Vienna University, Palmer lectured in classics at Manchester (1931–41) and then became a temporary civil servant engaged in World War II intelligence work. After the war he was professor of Greek at King's College, University of London (1945–52), and professor of comparative philology, University of Oxford (1952–71). His books included *Introduction to Modern Linguistics* (1936), *A Grammar of the Post-Ptolemaic Papyri* (1945), *Mycenaeans and Minoans* (1961), *The Penultimate Palace at Knossos* (1969), and *Studies in Aegean Chronology* (1984). His *Descriptive and Comparative Linguistics* (1972) was translated into Japanese as well as into several European languages.

Parrott, Sir Cecil Cuthbert, British diplomat and academic (b. Jan. 29, 1909, Plymouth, England—d. June 23, 1984, Abbeystead, Lancaster, England), was ambassador to Czechoslovakia from 1960 to 1966 and later professor (1971–76; afterward emeritus) of central and southeastern European studies at the University of Lancaster. In 1973 he published his full translation of Jaroslav Hasek's novel *The Good Soldier Schweik,* and this translation was recognized as the definitive English version of a masterpiece of European literature. Parrott studied at Peterhouse, Cambridge, and taught for three years before spending five years (1934–39) as tutor to Crown Prince Peter of Yugoslavia. He then joined the diplomatic service and served at the British legations in Oslo (1939–40) and

Stockholm (1940–45) before his first posting to Prague (1945–48). From 1954 to 1957 he was minister at the British embassy in Moscow; he then held an administrative post at the Foreign Office before returning to Prague as ambassador. After his retirement from the Foreign Service, Parrott went to Lancaster as professor (1966–71) of Russian and Soviet studies, but his main interest lay in Eastern European studies, and he made the Comenius Centre at the university a focus for Czechoslovak studies in Britain. His biography of Hasek, *The Bad Bohemian,* appeared in 1978 and a translation of stories by Hasek in 1981. He also wrote two volumes of autobiography, *The Tightrope* (1975) and *The Serpent and the Nightingale* (1977). He was knighted in 1964 and became a fellow of the Royal Society of Literature in 1979.

Paynter, (Thomas) William ("WILL"), British trade unionist (b. Dec. 6, 1903, Whitchurch, Cardiff, Wales—d. Dec. 11, 1984, Edgware, England), as general secretary (1959–68) of the National Union of Mineworkers (NUM) was responsible in the 1960s for negotiating a national wages structure that increased the NUM's unity and power in its strikes of the early 1970s. The son of a miner, he started as a pit boy at the age of 13, joining the South Wales Miners' Federation in 1918. Paynter took part in the General Strike (1926), joining the Communist Party soon afterward. He was elected check weighman at Cymmer colliery (1929), but his employers got him removed two years later. He was on the hunger marches of 1931, 1932, and 1936 and in 1937 went to Spain as political commissar of the British battalion in the International Brigade. He became a miners' agent for the Rhymney area (1939) and president (1951–59) of the South Wales miners. He resigned from the Communist Party on becoming (1969–72) a member of the Commission on Industrial Relations. Paynter was from 1972 a member of the Trades Union Congress and the Confederation of British Industry's Arbitration Panel. He published *British Trade Unions and the Problem of Change* (1970) and an autobiography, *My Generation* (1972).

Peccei, Aurelio, Italian business executive (b. July 4, 1908, Turin, Italy—d. March 14, 1984, Rome, Italy), founded in 1968 the Club of Rome, a group that originally included 25 intellectuals, which in 1972 published *The Limits to Growth,* a report that warned of impending environmental disaster unless population growth and industrial output were curbed. Peccei worked for the Fiat car company before World War II and was imprisoned by the Fascists. He later managed Fiat's subsidiary in Argentina from 1953 until 1957. He was then appointed head of Italconsult, a consultancy set up by the major Italian industrial companies, and from 1964 to 1967 served as managing director of Ing. C. Olivetti & Co. Peccei's interest in industrialization in the third world sparked projects in some 50 countries and led to the formation of an international investment group that channeled funds to Latin America. As president of the Club of Rome he limited membership to 100 and traveled widely, expounding his belief in the need for more just treatment of the less developed countries. He was the author of *The Chasm Ahead* (1969), *The Human Quality* (1976), and *One Hundred Pages for the Future* (1981).

Peckinpah, Sam (DAVID SAMUEL PECKINPAH), U.S. motion picture director (b. Feb. 21, 1925, Fresno, Calif.—d. Dec. 28, 1984, Inglewood, Calif.), was a temperamental, controversial, maverick filmmaker whose awesome accomplishments included the violent Western classics *Ride the High Country* (1962) and *The Wild Bunch* (1969), the monumental *Major Dundee* (1965), and the graphically violent *Straw Dogs* (1971). Peckinpah, who earned an M.A. in theatre arts from the University of Southern California, launched his career as a scriptwriter for television with such Westerns as "Gunsmoke," "The Rifleman," and "Broken Arrow." He made his debut as a film director with *The Deadly Companions* (1961), the first of 14 films notable for explicitly violent scenes of blood and gore. Some of his other films included *The Ballad of Cable Hogue* (1970), *Junior Bonner* (1972), and *The Killer Elite* (1975). His last motion picture, *The Osterman Weekend* (1983), was a box-office failure.

Peerce, Jan (JACOB PINCUS PERLEMUTH), U.S. opera singer (b. June 3, 1904, New York, N.Y.—d. Dec. 15, 1984, New York), as a silvery-voiced tenor with the Metropolitan Opera in New York City (1941–68) for nearly three decades, distinguished himself in Italian repertoire, especially in such roles as Alfredo in *La Traviata*, Rodolfo in *La Bohème*, Riccardo in *A Masked Ball*, and the duke in *Rigoletto*. Peerce, who made his singing debut at Radio City Music Hall in 1932, embarked on a career that spanned more than half a century. He made his debut at the Metropolitan Opera on Nov. 29, 1941, in a performance of *La Traviata* and became a sensation with his strong clear voice. Some felt that Peerce was able to maintain his singing voice for such a long time because he never forced it out of range. A master at producing perfect legatos, Peerce was hailed for his stylistic versatility, rhythmic elan, even scales, stage presence, and communicative ability. Some of his most memorable performances were in roles with the NBC Symphony under Arturo Toscanini; he was also featured on his own radio program, "Great Moments in Music," and made cameo appearances in such films as *Carnegie Hall, Tonight We Sing,* and *Goodbye, Columbus.* In 1971 Peerce made his Broadway debut as Tevye in *Fiddler on the Roof,* and the dynamic lyric tenor continued to perform until a stroke left him bedridden in 1982.

Penrose, Sir Roland Algernon, British painter and art collector (b. Oct. 14, 1900, London, England—d. April 23, 1984, Lewes, England), was a notable Surrealist painter but made his most significant contribution to British cultural life as founder of the Institute of Contemporary Arts (ICA) and as a powerful and informed advocate of modern European painting. Educated at Queen's College, Cambridge, he lived in Paris from 1922 to 1934 and, as well as developing his own style of painting, began a superb collection of modern works with special emphasis on Cubist and post-Cubist art. Penrose contributed significantly to the 1936 International Surrealist Exhibition in London, served with the Home Guard during World War II, and in 1947 founded the ICA. As chairman of the ICA until 1969 (then president) and as a trustee of the Tate Gallery (1959–66), he initiated and organized many of the most influential exhibitions of modern art in Britain, including highly successful exhibitions at the Tate: Picasso (1960), Ernst (1962), and Miró (1964). He also coordinated the ICA's two major exhibitions, "Forty Years of Modern Art" (1947) and "Forty Thousand Years of Modern Art" (1948–49), which helped to educate a wide public in the new idiom during the immediate postwar years. His friendship with Picasso provided material for an important study, *Picasso: His Life and Work* (1958). Other publications included *Miró* (1970), *Man Ray* (1975), and *Scrapbook, 1900–1981* (1981). Penrose was made a Commander of the Order of the British Empire in 1961 and was knighted in 1966.

Percival, Edgar Wikner, Australian aircraft designer and manufacturer (b. 1897, Albury, New South Wales, Australia—d. Jan. 21, 1984, London, England), founded Percival Aircraft Ltd. and repeatedly set records during the 1930s with his light aircraft, notably the Gull and the Mew Gull. A graduate of the University of Sydney, he was building gliders even before World War I. During the war he served with the Royal Flying Corps (later the Royal Air Force) and then as an Air Ministry test pilot. In 1923 he won the *Melbourne Herald* air race, and in 1929 Percival and the Hendy Aircraft Co. built a

plane that he flew in the 1930 King's Cup race. In 1932 he designed and built the three-seater Gull. Two years later Percival constructed the highly successful Mew Gull in which he won the Johnstone Memorial Trophy, the Oswald Watt Memorial Gold Medal, and the International Speed Trophy three times. In 1935 he made the first flight from Britain to Africa and back in a single day. By this time he had founded Percival Aircraft, of which he was chief designer and chief test pilot. He later formed Edgar Percival Aircraft Ltd. and continued into the 1950s to make successful designs for such purposes as crop-spraying.

Perkins, Carl Dewey, U.S. politician (b. Oct. 15, 1912, Hindman, Ky.—d. Aug. 3, 1984, Lexington, Ky.), as a liberal Democratic congressman from Kentucky (1949–84) championed the poor and needy by sponsoring such social legislation as federal aid to schools, college student assistance, child nutrition, coal mine safety, and aid to crippled children. Perkins, who was a rural lawyer and a member of the Kentucky General Assembly before being elected to Congress, succeeded Adam Clayton Powell, Jr., in 1967 as head of the powerful House Education and Labor Committee. Powell had been removed from office for alleged mismanagement of the committee staff and travel funds. Though some felt Perkins was perhaps too unsophisticated for the position because of his humble background, he demonstrated that he had one of the shrewdest political minds in the country. He steered Pres. Lyndon B. Johnson's antipoverty legislation through Congress in the 1960s, initiated the school lunch program, and secured a generous share of federal money for his 23-county district, one of the poorest in the nation. During the latter years of his tenure he bitterly opposed Pres. Ronald Reagan's attempts to cut back on social programs.

Petrillo, James Caesar, U.S. labour leader (b. March 16, 1892, Chicago, Ill.—d. Oct. 23, 1984, Chicago), as the autocratic president of the American Federation of Musicians from 1940 to 1958, engineered a musicians' strike in 1942 against record companies as a protest against not receiving royalty payments, even though Pres. Franklin D. Roosevelt urged him to relent, maintaining that music was essential to morale during World War II. The strike lasted 27 months, and the big record companies were forced to comply with Petrillo's demands. He established the Music Performance Trust Fund for royalty payments. Petrillo, a trumpeter who headed his own Chicago combo, was president of the Chicago Federation of Musicians for 40 years and built Local 10 into a one-man operation. In 1958, when members felt that a more temperate president was required for the American Federation of Musicians, Petrillo resigned but remained a consultant for the international union. During the 1960s he was active in promoting civil rights within the local unions.

Petrosian, Tigran Vartanovich, Soviet chess champion (b. June 17, 1929, Tbilisi, Georgia, U.S.S.R.—d. Aug. 13, 1984, Moscow, U.S.S.R.), as one of the greatest chess grand masters, was champion of the Soviet Union in 1959, 1961, 1969, and 1976, won the chess Olympics from 1958 to 1974, and reigned as world champion from 1963 to 1969. A shrewd positional-defensive player, he was particularly adept at crowding his opponents' pieces. Born of Armenian parents who died during World War II, Petrosian worked as a caretaker to support the rest of his family. He won the Georgian and Armenian chess championships shortly after the war and that of Moscow in 1951. A year later he qualified to participate in the world title matches and in 1962 at Curaçao was on points just ahead of other contenders, thus qualifying to challenge and defeat Mikhail Botvinnik (1963). He held his title against Boris Spassky in 1966 but lost to him in 1969. Although he continued to be featured in international competitions, Petrosian apparently lacked the

drive necessary to remain always first. In 1977 his match against Viktor Korchnoi at Florence, Italy, attracted much attention. Korchnoi had recently defected to the West, and Petrosian had joined with other Soviet chess champions in denouncing him. The contestants would neither shake hands nor speak to each other, Korchnoi, who won by a narrow margin, exhibiting bizarre paranoia. Petrosian published a book, *Chess and Philosophy,* in 1968.

Pidgeon, Walter, Canadian-born actor (b. Sept. 23, 1897, East St. John, New Brunswick—d. Sept. 25, 1984, Santa Monica, Calif.), was a stately gentleman who projected a solid, authoritative, and mature image that made him one of the best-loved motion picture stars during the 1940s, especially in the eight films in which he teamed up with Greer Garson, notably *Mrs. Miniver* (1942), *Madame Curie* (1943), and *Mrs. Parkington* (1944). Though Pidgeon made his motion-picture debut in the silent film *Mannequin* (1926), it was not until he had gained maturity, and was cast as a solid, pipe-smoking leading man, that he became a major box-office attraction. Some of his most inspiring roles included his portrayals of the village minister in *How Green Was My Valley* (1941), an English hunter who stalks Hitler in *Man Hunt* (1941), a veteran producer in *The Bad and the Beautiful* (1953), a scheming scientist in *Forbidden Planet* (1956), and a Senate majority leader in *Advise and Consent* (1962). Earlier in his career, Pidgeon starred on Broadway in musical comedy productions, but he was more successful in Hollywood, where his urbane wit coupled with Garson's charm made them one of the screen's most perfectly matched pairs. Pidgeon was nominated for an Academy Award for best actor for his performances in *Mrs. Miniver* and *Madame Curie,* but the Oscar eluded him. He also starred with Garson in *Blossoms in the Dust, Julia Misbehaves, That Forsythe Woman, The Miniver Story,* and *Scandal at Scourie.* Pidgeon, who made more than 100 films during his 47-year career, also appeared as the wily major in *Command Decision* (1948), the impresario Flo Ziegfeld in *Funny Girl* (1968), and an aging pickpocket in *Harry in Your Pocket* (1973), one of his last screen appearances. In his later years Pidgeon returned to the stage to appear with Jackie Gleason in *Take Me Along* and also made guest appearances on such television shows as "Dan August," "Ellery Queen," and "The Snoop Sisters."

Popieluszko, The Rev. Jerzy Aleksander, Polish Roman Catholic priest (b. Sept. 14, 1947, Okopy, near Bialystok, Poland—d. Oct. 20, 1984, Wloclawek, Poland), whose kidnapping and death at the hands of members of the Polish secret police scandalized the nation and severely shook the government of Gen. Wojciech Jaruzelski, was a supporter of the Solidarity movement from its inception in 1980. Popieluszko's main flock consisted of the workers at the Warsaw steelworks, and he was popular as a courageous defender of human dignity and rights. The son of a peasant, Popieluszko was educated at the Suchowola lyceum and in 1965 entered the Higher Seminary in Warsaw, where his studies were interrupted by his military service. He was ordained in 1972 by Stefan Cardinal Wyszynski. After administering successively two parishes near Warsaw, in 1978 he was transferred to the Zoliborz vicariate in the city. His "masses for the homeland," celebrated in his church of St. Stanislaw Kostka on the last Sunday of every month, regularly attracted thousands of the faithful. Popieluszko's condemnation of the failings of Communism also attracted the attention of the authorities, who threatened him with prosecution for slandering the state and poisoning public attitudes, but charges were not pressed following a general amnesty. When Popieluszko failed to return to his Warsaw home after a visit to Bydgoszcz, which he left by car on October 19, the government was faced with the possibility of widespread public protest. General Jaruzelski appointed Interior Minister Gen. Czeslaw Kiszczak to investigate the circumstances of Popieluszko's disappearance. In a television broadcast on October 27, Kiszczak revealed that three officers of his ministry—Capt. Grzegorz Piotrowski, Lieut. Waldemar Chmielewski, and Lieut. Leszek Pekala—had been arrested as organizers of Father Popieluszko's kidnapping. General Jaruzelski, assuming overall control of the Ministry of the Interior, suspended Col. Adam Pietruszka, head of the department to which the three kidnappers belonged; he also suspended Miroslaw Milewski, a member of the Politburo and a secretary of the Central Committee responsible for law and order. Further investigations revealed that Popieluszko had been beaten, trussed, and thrown into a reservoir at Wloclawek in the early morning of October 20. His body was discovered on October 30. The three kidnappers and their chief, Colonel Pietruszka, were brought to trial on December 27 on charges of murder.

Porter, Hal, Australian writer (b. Feb. 16, 1911, Melbourne, Victoria, Australia—d. Sept. 29, 1984, Ballarat, Victoria), produced impressive and successful novels, plays, short stories, and verse; perhaps his particular achievement was to imbue his work with all the sophistication and nuances of contemporary European writing without ever sacrificing its distinctive Australian character. His most acclaimed novel, *The Tilted Cross* (1961), was about the 19th-century convict-artist Thomas Griffiths Wainewright; in his play *The Professor* (1966) he skillfully explored the complexities of Australian-Japanese cultural relationships. Porter was probably best known for *The Watcher on the Cast-Iron Balcony* (1963), an autobiography chronicling his earlier years; the sequels, *The Paper Chase* (1966) and *The Extra* (1975), failed to match it. He was brought up in Bairnsdale, Victoria, and his first job was as a reporter for the Bairnsdale *Advertiser.* He was a schoolmaster during 1927–37 and 1941–49. After a year in Japan with the Australian Army Education Corps (1949–50), he became a producer at the Theatre Royal in Hobart, Tasmania (1951–52). Porter made his writing debut with a book of short stories in 1942, producing six more in this genre. Later works included a novel, *The Right Thing* (1971), and a volume of verse, *In an Australian Country Graveyard and Other Poems* (1974).

Powell, William Horatio, U.S. actor (b. July 29, 1892, Pittsburgh, Pa.—d. March 5, 1984, Palm Springs, Calif.), personified the suave, sophisticated gentleman with his pencil-thin mustache, urbane wit, resonant voice, and impeccable dress in nearly 100 motion pictures and achieved the pinnacle of his career as the martini-drinking, wisecracking detective Nick Charles in a series of six "Thin Man" films (1934–47). Powell appeared in more than 200 plays before making his silent motion-picture debut in 1922 as a villain in *Sherlock Holmes.* With the advent of sound, however, he became a master of sophisticated comedy with his gentlemanly demeanour and bantering humour, which was featured in such films as *My Man Godfrey* (1936), *The Great Ziegfeld* (1936), and *Life with Father* (1947). He began his screen career as a sleuth in 1929, playing Philo Vance in *The Canary Murder Case,* but his most unforgettable role as a detective was in the "Thin Man" films, in which Myrna Loy portrayed his wife, Nora. The two, who first appeared together in *Manhattan Melodrama* (1934), made such an ideal couple that they were teamed in the "Thin Man" series as a retired detective and a rich heiress. They were the ultimate in sophistication and wit (even owning an urbane wire-haired terrier named Asta), became models for dozens of aspiring Hollywood sleuths, and launched the madcap comedy vogue. Powell received three Academy Award nominations for best actor for his roles in *The Thin Man* (1934), *My Man Godfrey,* and *Life with Father.* After his last film role, as Doc in *Mr. Roberts* (1955), he retired to Palm Springs.

Priestley, J(ohn) B(oynton), English playwright and novelist (b. Sept. 13, 1894, Bradford, England—d. Aug. 14, 1984, Alveston, Warwickshire, England), as a prolific writer of rare versatility, reached the height of his fame in the 1930s and 1940s but was still producing a steady and diverse output well into the 1970s. In all, he produced over 100 books and plays, but he was most highly touted as a dramatist whose cleverly crafted plays often evoked the psychological phenomenon of déjà vu (the feeling that something presently happening has occurred before). Priestley first achieved widespread recognition with his second novel, *The Good Companions* (1929), which was later adapted for both stage and screen. From his skillful characterization of "ordinary" people and through his own forthright down-to-earth appearance and behaviour, he came to epitomize the archetypal Englishman. This role was strengthened by his enormously popular Sunday evening "Postscripts" (radio talks), given during the darkest days (1940) of World War II. Priestley was the son of a Baptist schoolmaster. He was educated in Bradford and then worked in a wool merchant's office while writing poetry and contributing to journals such as the *Bradford Pioneer* and *London Opinion.* He served in France throughout World War I and was wounded. After attending Trinity Hall, University of Cambridge, he worked in London as a publisher's reader and a free-lance journalist. After the novel *Angel Pavement* (1930), he attracted the most attention during the 1930s with such plays as *Dangerous Corner* (1932), *I Have Been Here Before* (1937), the farce *When We Are Married* (1938), and *Johnson over Jordan* (1939). *An Inspector Calls* (1946) showed his brilliant command of dramatic tension. Priestley's other works included *The English Comic Character* (1925), *English Journey* (1934), *Victoria's Heyday* (1972), and *The English* (1973). Besides a number of semiautobiographical novels, including *Margin Released* (1962), he published three volumes of autobiography: *Midnight in the Desert* (1937), *Rain upon Godshill* (1939), and *Instead of Trees* (1977). Priestley was a founder committee member of the Campaign for Nuclear Disarmament in the 1950s.

Rabinowitz, Louis Isaac, British-born rabbi (b. May 24, 1906, Edinburgh, Scotland—d. Aug. 8, 1984, Jerusalem, Israel), as chief rabbi in South Africa in charge of the Hebrew congregation of Johannesburg, the Transvaal, and the Orange Free State (1945–62), was a vigorous and persistent opponent of apartheid (racial separation). A notable scholar, he was deputy editor in chief of the *Encyclopaedia Judaica,* in charge of articles on the Talmud and on rabbinical literature. He later edited the *Judaica Yearbook.* While in South Africa he was professor of Hebrew at the University of the Witwatersrand. Educated in Yeshiva Etz Chaim in London and at the University of London, he served as rabbi in various London synagogues during the 1930s and in World War II as an army chaplain in the Middle East and in France. He was always strongly Zionist, early supporting Irgun Zvai Leumi, the Jewish extremist group in Palestine during the time of the British mandate (1920–48). Moving to Jerusalem on his retirement, he supported Israel's Herut Party, inheritor of Irgun's views, and as a member of it was elected to the Jerusalem municipal council, serving as deputy mayor (1976 and 1978). In 1962 he had been made emeritus chief rabbi of South Africa; in 1980 he became Worthy Citizen of Jerusalem.

Rahner, The Rev. Karl, German Roman Catholic theologian (b. March 5, 1904, Freiburg im Breisgau, Germany—d. March 31, 1984, Innsbruck, Austria), was a leading advocate within the Roman Catholic Church of Christian unity and of a pluralistic approach to theology. Rahner, who was accused by some in the Catholic hierarchy of an irresponsible attitude that threatened to undermine the faith, supported fellow theologians who were disciplined for their dissenting views. He was the author of numerous works, including his fundamental *Grundkurs des Glaubens* (1976; *Foundations of Christian Faith,* 1978), and was considered by many others to be the greatest Catholic theologian of his time. He joined the Society of Jesus (Jesuits) at the age of 18 and taught in Innsbruck until dismissed by the Nazis. After World War II he held chairs of philosophy in Munich and theology in Münster. In 1960, despite opposition from conservative theologians, Pope John XXIII appointed him an expert in the Second Vatican Council, where he played a vital role in the process of *aggiornamento,* helping Catholic thinking to adjust to developments in the modern world. In *Geist in Welt* (1939), Rahner examined the teachings of St. Thomas Aquinas in the light of contemporary ideas and concluded that if Aquinas had nothing to say on the central questions of modern philosophy, his theology was of no interest. This book defined the thrust of Rahner's work, always concerned with the relevance to mankind of Catholic theology. It was in the light of this that he criticized the church's devaluation of non-European cultures and appealed to it to become genuinely pluralistic in its thought.

Rauff, Walter Herman Julius, former German Waffen-SS officer (b. June 19, 1906, Kothen, Germany—d. May 14, 1984, Santiago, Chile), was one of the most important Nazi war criminals never brought to trial and was believed to have been responsible for the deaths of at least 97,000 Jews during World War II. Rauff, as a colonel in the Waffen-SS, designed the mobile gas chambers using exhaust fumes to kill Eastern European Jews; the number of his victims was estimated by some to have been as high as 250,000. At the end of the war he escaped justice, and in 1958 he went to live in Chile, where an appeal by the West German government for his extradition was rejected in 1963. However, both West Germany and Israel, as well as the Nazi hunters Simon Wiesenthal and Beate Klarsfeld, continued to campaign for his expulsion. In 1984, rejecting a further appeal, the Chilean foreign minister described his extradition as "inappropriate."

Rémy, Colonel (GILBERT RENAULT), French Resistance hero, writer, and politician (b. Aug. 6, 1904, Vannes, France—d. July 29, 1984, Guingamp, France), as head of an undercover agency in occupied France supplied British intelligence with invaluable information during World War II. After the liberation he served in Gen. Charles de Gaulle's provisional government (1944–46). Author of *Dix ans avec de Gaulle* (1971), he won the 1960 Prix du Quai des Orfèvres for a detective novel, *Le Monocle noir.* After studying law, he worked for the Banque de France before turning (1937) to the financing of films. Arriving in Britain in June 1940, he joined de Gaulle's Free French Forces and two months later returned secretly to France. By June 1942 the Germans had learned his identity; with his wife and five children he escaped to England, although his mother and other relations suffered the Gestapo's vengeance. Soon returning to France, he notified the British of German activities in Italy and North Africa as well as in France. He remained a member of the Gaullist Rassemblement du Peuple Français after 1946, organizing conferences and rallies, but eventually split with de Gaulle over issues that included Algeria. He was made a Commander of the Légion d'Honneur and an Officer of the Order of the British Empire and was awarded numerous military decorations.

Ridley, Arnold, British actor and dramatist (b. Jan. 7, 1896, Bath, England—d. March 12, 1984, London, England), wrote a classic comedy thriller, *The Ghost Train,* which opened in 1925 and ran for 655 performances, but he achieved even greater fame at the end of his career portraying Private Godfrey in the television series "Dad's Army." Ridley was educated at the University of Bristol, was wounded during World War I, and acted in repertory in Birmingham and Plymouth. *The Ghost Train*, his second play, was revived and made into a film and musical, and though he was the author of more than 30 other plays, he never duplicated his early success. Ridley abandoned acting during the 1930s to concentrate on writing and directing, served with the Army in World War II, and after the war played various parts on radio and television, notably in soap opera. He was over 70 when he joined the cast of "Dad's Army," and he appeared in the stage version of the series, which opened in 1975. His other plays included *Keepers of Youth* (1929), *Peril at End House* (adapted from Agatha Christie, 1940), and *Easy Money* (1947). He was made an Officer of the Order of the British Empire in 1982.

Robbins, Lionel Charles Robbins, BARON, British economist (b. Nov. 22, 1898, Sipson, Middlesex, England—d. May 15, 1984, London, England), was professor (1929–61) at the London School of Economics (LSE), chairman (1961–70) of the *Financial Times*, a director (1960–75) of *The Economist*, and a noted administrator in the arts and education. However, the achievement for which he would be best remembered was his chairmanship of the Robbins Committee. Its 1963 report paved the way for a major expansion of higher education in Britain and established the principle that such education should be available to everyone at the age of 18 who was qualified and willing to receive it. The son of strict Baptist parents, Robbins studied at the LSE and served as an artillery officer during World War I. During the 1920s he lectured at the LSE (1925–27) and at New College, Oxford (1924; 1927–29), before accepting the chair of economics at LSE. He resigned in 1961 to join the *Financial Times*, having previously left during World War II to become director of the economic section of the Offices of the War Cabinet. He returned to LSE as chairman of the Court of Governors in 1968 and continued to lecture there until he suffered a stroke in 1982. His many other activities included appointments with the Royal Academy, the Royal Opera House, the National Gallery, and the Tate Gallery, and he was the first chancellor (1968–78) of the University of Stirling. In *Higher Education Revisited* (1980) he reviewed some of the effects of the Robbins Report at a time, nearly 20 years later, when its principles and consequences were under question. He was the author of many books of economic analysis and theory and wrote *Autobiography of an Economist* (1971). Made a life peer in 1959, he played an active part in the House of Lords.

Robin, Leo, U.S. lyricist (b. April 6, 1900, Pittsburgh, Pa.—d. Dec. 29, 1984, Los Angeles, Calif.), was a prolific and Academy Award-winning songwriter who garnered the 1938 Oscar for best song for "Thanks for the Memory," from the motion picture *Big Broadcast of 1938*. The tune became comedian Bob Hope's theme song. Robin also wrote songs that became signatures of Maurice Chevalier ("Louise"), Jack Benny ("Love in Bloom"), and Eddie Cantor ("One Hour with You"). Robin, who attended the University of Pennsylvania Law School, first worked as a newspaper reporter and a publicist before moving to New York and collaborating with such noted songwriters as Ralph Rainger, Jerome Kern, Jules Styne, and Richard Whiting on a plethora of popular songs. Some of his hits included "Diamonds Are a Girl's Best Friend," "Beyond the Blue Horizon," "Blue Hawaii," and "My Ideal." He also served as librettist for such Broadway blockbusters as *Gentlemen Prefer Blondes* and *Hit the Deck* and wrote some 50 film scores, including those for *Little Miss Marker, Anything Goes,* and *Moon over Miami*. The excellence of his lyrics was so outstanding that he was nominated for an Academy Award nine times between 1934 and 1953.

Robson, Dame Flora McKenzie, British actress (b. March 28, 1902, South Shields, England—d. July 7, 1984, Brighton, England), was a versatile character actress who specialized in the role of the villainess, most notably as Lady Macbeth, the demonic Ellen Creed in *Ladies in Retirement* (1939), and the unhappy shoplifter in *Black Chiffon* (1949). Her diffidence, though, coupled with the roles she played—often those of unsympathetic, frustrated characters—prevented her from receiving the public acclaim that her superb professional skill and versatility merited. She first established her reputation in *Desire Under the Elms* (1931), *The Anatomist* (1932), and, notably, *All God's Chillun Got Wings* (1933). Her comic gifts were showcased in her portrayals of Mrs. Foresight in the Restoration comedy *Love for Love* and Gwendolen in *The Importance of Being Earnest* (Old Vic; 1933–34). An outstanding performance in one of her more usual roles was as the old lady in the television film of L. P. Hartley's *The Shrimp and the Anemone* (1977). Robson, who had won the Royal Academy of Dramatic Art's bronze medal, spent two seasons (1922–24) at the Oxford Playhouse under J. B. Fagan. Her dismissal as "not pretty enough" to play young female leads shattered her confidence, and for the next five years she worked as a factory welfare officer. Rescued for the theatre by Tyrone Guthrie, who had become director of the Festival Theatre, Cambridge, she performed successfully there in plays by Ibsen, Pirandello, Shakespeare, and Euripides. After the 1933–34 Old Vic season, the roles offered to her provided less scope, and she turned to films, making a hit as Queen Elizabeth I in *Fire over England* (1937). She then played a number of unrewarding roles in Hollywood before scoring such notable triumphs as *Captain Brassbound's Conversion* (1948), *Ghosts* (1958), and *The Aspern Papers* (1959). Her last London stage appearance was in 1969 in a revival of *The Old Ladies*. Robson was made a Dame of the Order of the British Empire in 1960.

Rock, John, U.S. obstetrician-gynecologist (b. March 24, 1890, Marlboro, Mass.—d. Dec. 4, 1984, Peterborough, N.H.), as a pioneer in the field of human reproduction, was an expert on fertility but captured world attention as the developer with Gregory Pincus and M. C. Chang of the first effective oral contraceptive in the 1950s. After several ill-fated business ventures, Rock entered Harvard University and then Harvard Medical School. His first research addressed the problem of infertility and in 1944, with Mirian F. Menkin, he achieved the first successful fertilization of a human ovum in vitro (literally, "in glass"; in a laboratory culture). He used his knowledge of infertility to aid him in the development of the Pill, which revolutionized sexual mores, population control, and the status of women after it was approved by the Food and Drug Administration in 1960. A devout Roman Catholic yet a leading supporter of population control, Rock found himself the centre of controversy within the church for his work on the Pill. In his 1963 book, *The Time Has Come: A Catholic Doctor's Proposals to End the Battle over Birth Control,* Rock called for a change in the church's stand against birth control and for new research into improved natural contraceptive methods that would be acceptable to all religious faiths and inexpensive enough for the poor. He steadfastly maintained that the Pill was a "natural" form of contraception because its ingredients, including estrogen and progesterone, were substances found in the body. After Pope Paul VI issued the 1968 encyclical that banned all forms of artificial contraception, Rock accused the pope of abdicating "responsibility for the ultimate welfare of all." During his longtime career Rock served as founding director (1926–56) of the Fertility and Endocrine Clinic at the Free Hospital for Women in Brookline, Mass., professor of gynecology for 30 years at Harvard Medical School, and director from 1956 of the Rock Reproductive Clinic, also in Brookline.

Ronning, Chester A., Canadian diplomat (b. Dec. 13, 1894, Fancheng (Fan-ch'eng), Hupeh [Hubei], China—d. Dec. 31, 1984, Camrose, Alta., Canada), embarked on a diplomatic career in 1945 after 25 years as a teacher in China and Canada and after having served in World War I with the RAF and in World War II with Royal Canadian Air Force intelligence (1942–45). Ronning, the son of missionaries who served in China, spent nearly 25 years in that country and was considered Canada's foremost expert on China. The energetic Ron-

ning served as counselor and chargé d'affaires of the Canadian embassy in China (1946–51), head of the American and Far Eastern Division in the Department of External Affairs (1951–53), ambassador to Norway and Iceland (1954–57), and high commissioner to India (1957–64). He retired from the diplomatic service in 1965 only to be called out of retirement the following year to promote peace talks between the U.S. and North Vietnam. With the permission of the U.S. State Department, he flew to Hanoi and had confidential talks with Premier Pham Van Dong to try to set up a framework for negotiating peace. Ronning reported that the premier would consider informal talks if the U.S. would stop all bombing. It was not until 1968, however, that Pres. Lyndon B. Johnson temporarily halted the bombing in most areas and the North Vietnamese agreed to negotiate. In 1971 Ronning was made a Companion of the Order of Canada, the country's highest honour.

Rotha, Paul, British documentary filmmaker (b. June 3, 1907, London, England—d. March 7, 1984, Wallingford, Oxfordshire, England), was a leading figure in the documentary film movement of the 1930s, generally seen as one of the most important achievements in British cinema. He studied at the Slade School of Fine Art and started work as a designer and graphic artist, while developing his enthusiasm for film. As an art critic for *The Connoisseur* magazine, he was also responsible for graphic design. Rotha wrote pioneering works of film criticism, including *The Film till Now* (1930), *Celluloid* (1931), and *Documentary Film* (1936). After delving into studio work he joined the Empire Marketing Board and directed *Contact, Rising Tide, Shipyard,* and *The Face of Britain,* combining exploration of the visual impact of film with social comment. Rotha later said that, like other members of the documentary movement, he started with an interest in film as an aesthetic medium and later discovered its political and sociological potential; unlike some, he remained a genuine radical while continuing to extend the aesthetic possibilities of film in such works as *World of Plenty* (1943), *Land of Promise* (1945), *The World Is Rich* (1947), and *World Without End* (1953). His last films of note were *The Life of Adolf Hitler* (1961) and *Silent Raid* (1962).

Ryle, Sir Martin, British radio astronomer (b. Sept. 27, 1918, Brighton, England—d. Oct. 14, 1984, Cambridge, England), was astronomer royal from 1972 to 1982 and in 1974 was awarded (jointly with Antony Hewish) the Nobel Prize for Physics for his pioneering work in radio astronomy. After earning a degree in physics at the University of Oxford in 1939, he was engaged during World War II in the development of radar. As a lecturer in physics at the University of Cambridge, he began to search for methods of studying radio waves from distant astronomical bodies, developing the technique of aperture synthesis using a combination of parabolic reflectors and analyzing the results by computer. At the Mullard Radio Astronomy Observatory, Cambridge, where he was director from 1957 to 1982, he was able to give a clear picture of the shape of radio galaxies and to continue his work in physics, using his observations in astronomy. His name was also associated with the model of the "evolving universe" that was gradually accepted by a majority of scientists, in opposition to the theory of "continuous creation." He was professor of radio astronomy at Cambridge from 1959 to 1982 and at the Mullard Observatory led an outstanding team of astronomers. Ryle became a supporter of nuclear disarmament—he was the author of *Towards the Nuclear Holocaust* (1981)—and a campaigner for the development of alternative sources of energy to replace both traditional and nuclear fuels. A foreign member of the Soviet Academy of Sciences and of the U.S. National Academy of Sciences, he was made a fellow of Trinity College, Cambridge, in 1949 and a fellow of the Royal Society in 1952 and was knighted in 1966.

Salan, Raoul Albin Louis, French army officer (b. June 10, 1899, Roquecourbe, Tarn, France—d. July 3, 1984, Paris, France), was one of four generals, opposed to Pres. Charles de Gaulle's policy of self-determination for Algeria, who led a military insurrection there in April 1961. The revolt collapsed after four days (April 22–26), and two of the ringleaders, Generals Maurice Challe and André Zeller, surrendered, while Salan and Gen. Edmond Jouhaud joined the Organisation de l'Armée Secrète (OAS). Under Salan's leadership the OAS, an organization of right-wing extremists dedicated to the concept of a "France from Dunkirk to Tamanrasset," conducted a ruthless campaign of terrorism and sabotage in France and Algeria. In April 1962, two months before Algeria gained its independence (July 3), Salan was arrested in Algiers. He was tried before a special tribunal and was found guilty of conspiring to assassinate de Gaulle; he was stripped of his military honours and sentenced to life imprisonment. In 1968 he was pardoned and released, and in 1982, under a general amnesty of all participants in the 1961 insurrection, he was reinstated as a general of the French Army. A graduate of the Saint-Cyr special military school, Salan was commissioned in 1919 and held the rank of major at the beginning of World War II. After France's capitulation he at first supported the Vichy regime, but then he joined de Gaulle's forces in French West Africa and as a divisional commander took part in the August 1944 invasion of southern France under Gen. Jean de Lattre de Tassigny. After the war he was sent to Indochina, where he was commander in chief (1950–53). In 1956 Salan was appointed commander in chief in Algeria and two years later backed—albeit ambiguously—the revolt by civilian and military supporters of the *Algérie française* movement that resulted in de Gaulle's return to power. The fact that Salan's occasional support for de Gaulle masked a deep-seated hostility emerged clearly in the volumes of memoirs, including *L'Algérie, de Gaulle et moi* (1974), which he published after his release from prison.

Schneider, Alan (ABRAM LEOPOLDOVICH SCHNEIDER), U.S. stage director (b. Dec. 12, 1917, Kharkov, Russia—d. May 3, 1984, London, England), was an avant-garde theatre director who was especially known for his U.S. productions of the plays of Nobel laureate Samuel Beckett, including *Waiting for Godot, Krapp's Last Tape, Happy Days,* and *Endgame.* After earning an M.A. in drama from Cornell University, Ithaca, N.Y., he taught speech and drama at the Catholic University of America,

Washington, D.C., for 11 years before making his Broadway debut as an actor in Maxwell Anderson's *Storm Operation* (1944). As a director Schneider pivoted from institutional to commercial theatre and won his first successes on Broadway with *The Remarkable Mr. Pennypacker* and *Anastasia.* He felt, however, that the turning point of his career came when he directed Beckett's *Waiting for Godot* in 1956 and learned to let a play speak for itself; this enlightenment became a hallmark of his distinguished career. A prolific and pioneering director of some of the most important productions in the U.S., Schneider also directed plays by Harold Pinter, Michael Weller, Bertolt Brecht, and Edward Albee. He won a 1962 Tony award for directing Albee's *Who's Afraid of Virginia Woolf?* Schneider's impressive list of U.S. premieres included *Dumbwaiter, Collection, Birthday Party, Moonchildren, Loose Ends, Entertaining Mr. Sloane,* and *Saved.* Schneider, who died of brain injuries after being struck by a motorcycle in London, was in the process of staging yet another first play by a new U.S. writer, James Duff's *War at Home.*

Schwartz, Arthur, U.S. composer (b. Nov. 25, 1900, New York, N.Y.—d. Sept. 3, 1984, Kintnersville, Pa.), teamed up with lyricist Howard Dietz in 1928 and instituted a new sophistication in Broadway songwriting during the 1930s with such smash hit songs as "Dancing in the Dark," "You and the Night and the Music," "Something to Remember You By," and "I Guess I'll Have to Change My Plan." A self-taught pianist, Schwartz practiced law from 1924 to 1928 until he was persuaded to pursue a musical career. In 1929 Schwartz and Dietz vaulted to stardom with their songs for *The Little Show.* Having established their reputation, the two forged ahead with such Broadway musicals as *The Band Wagon, Flying Colors, Revenge with Music,* and *Between the Devil.* After moving to Hollywood in 1938, Schwartz scored such motion pictures as *Navy Blues* (1941), *Thank Your Lucky Stars* (1943), *The Time, the Place and the Girl* (1946), and *You're Never Too Young* (1955) and produced the film musicals *Cover Girl* and *Night and Day.* He later became partners with Dietz again to write new songs for the motion picture *The Band Wagon,* including the show-business anthem "That's Entertainment," and the two later collaborated on the Broadway musicals *The Gay Life* (1961) and *Jennie* (1963).

Sharon, Arieh, Israeli architect and town planner (b. May 28, 1902, Jaroslaw, Poland—d. July 24, 1984, Paris, France), was director and chief architect of the National Planning Agency of Israel (1948–53) and president of the Israeli Association of Architects and Engineers (1965–71). Among his notable public buildings were the regional hospital at Beersheba and the Ichilov hospital and the Jewish Agency's headquarters at Tel Aviv. He also designed buildings for the Hebrew University of Jerusalem and the Weizmann Institute of Science at Rehovot. In 1973 Sharon contributed to a study for planned development of the Old City of Jerusalem (his recommendations were later ignored). Sharon won international recognition with his appointment as a member (1963–67) of the executive committee of the International Union of Architects and by his election as a fellow of the American Institute of Architects and as a member of the Royal Institute of British Architects. An early Jewish immigrant (1920) to Palestine, he studied architecture in Germany at Dessau and Berlin before returning to practice in Tel Aviv in 1932.

Shaw, Irwin, U.S. novelist (b. Feb. 27, 1913, Brooklyn, N.Y.—d. May 16, 1984, Davos, Switz.), was a master storyteller who achieved critical renown for his short stories, particularly those collected in *Sailor Off the Bremen and Other Stories* (1939), but was better known to the general public as the author of such bestselling novels as *The Young Lions* (1948), *Rich*

Man, Poor Man (1970), and *Beggarman, Thief* (1977). Shaw plied his trade while still attending Brooklyn College by writing plays for the college dramatic society and by composing dialogue for the "Andy Gump" and "Dick Tracy" radio shows. In 1936 he turned to drama with the antiwar play *Bury the Dead* and churned out such other plays as *Siege* (1937), *The Gentle People* (1939), *Quiet City* (1939), and *The Shy and the Lonely* (1941) before serving in World War II. Shaw's early fiction delved into the political, sociological, and historical issues of contemporary America, and when he published his first novel, *The Young Lions,* a story about two Americans and a German whose destinies cross on the battlefields, it was considered one of the most important novels to come out of World War II. His later novels, including *Rich Man, Poor Man, Evening in Byzantium, The Top of the Hill,* and *Bread upon the Waters,* were blockbuster commercial successes; they were often turned into movies or television miniseries but were panned by critics. Undaunted, Shaw quipped: "Tolstoy never repeated *War and Peace,* so why should I feel guilty?" At the time of his death, Shaw, who succumbed to a heart ailment, had 14 million copies of his hardcover and softcover books in print in some 25 languages.

Shchelokov, Nikolay Anisimovich, Soviet politician (b. Nov. 26, 1910, Almaznaya, Ukraine—d. Dec. 13, 1984, Moscow, U.S.S.R.), as a protégé of Leonid Brezhnev headed (1966–82) the U.S.S.R. Ministry of Public Order (from 1969 renamed the Ministry of the Interior) but was demoted and progressively disgraced under Yury Andropov (*q.v.*) and Konstantin Chernenko. His unannounced death and hasty funeral (December 15) gave rise to rumours that he had committed suicide because he was distressed at the possibility of a trial on corruption charges. The son of a miner, and himself a miner (1926–32) and engineer (1933–38), he joined the Communist Party of the Soviet Union (CPSU) in 1931. He became a local government and party worker in the Dnepropetrovsk region of the Ukraine (1938–41), served as a political officer in the Army (1941–46), and returned to Ukrainian local politics (1947–51). Through Brezhnev's influence he was transferred to Moldavia (1951), holding various political offices there. He was granted the rank of Soviet Army colonel-general (1967) and was advanced to full general (1976). Andropov, who as head of the Committee of State Security (KGB) had already been investigating corruption in Shchelokov's department, dismissed Shchelokov from office in December 1982 and removed him from membership of the CPSU Central Committee in June 1983. Under Chernenko he was stripped of military rank (November 1984).

Shehan, Lawrence Joseph Cardinal, U.S. prelate of the Roman Catholic Church (b. March 18, 1898, Baltimore, Md.—d. Aug. 26, 1984, Baltimore), as the eloquent archbishop of Baltimore (1961–74) desegregated Catholic schools (1962), advocated religious ecumenism, and took part in the civil rights movement by joining the Rev. Martin Luther King, Jr.'s 1963 March on Washington. Shehan, who studied for the priesthood at St. Mary's Seminary in Baltimore, was ordained in Rome in 1922. After serving (1923–41) as curate and then pastor of St. Patrick's Church, Washington, D.C., he was consecrated a bishop in 1945. The following year he moved to Baltimore, where he was auxiliary bishop for the archdiocese; he remained in that post until he served (1953–61) as bishop of the newly created diocese of Bridgeport, Conn. While he was there, 15 new parishes were created and 17 new churches were constructed. In 1961 he returned to Baltimore, where he presided as archbishop over the oldest Catholic see in North America. Shehan was elevated to cardinal in 1965, and the following year he was jeered when he testified in favour of open-housing legislation at a public hearing. An outspoken opponent of the war in

Vietnam, Shehan condemned it as "a scandal the Christian conscience can no longer endure." His longtime devotion to ecumenism resulted in his appointment by Pope Paul VI to the Vatican Secretariat for the Promotion of Christian Unity. Shehan, who encouraged democratic practices in the affairs of the archdiocese, often consulted priests and members of the laity in naming bishops. He retired in 1974.

Sholokhov, Mikhail Aleksandrovich, Soviet novelist (b. May 24, 1905, Veshenskaya, Rostov region, Russia—d. Feb. 21, 1984, Veshenskaya, U.S.S.R.), won the Nobel Prize for Literature in 1965 and was best known for his novels *Tikhiy Don* (4 vol., 1928–40) and *Podnyataya tselina* (1932–60). The first of these was translated into English in two parts as *And Quiet Flows the Don* (1934) and *The Don Flows Home to the Sea* (1940); the second was also translated in two parts as *Virgin Soil Upturned* (1935; published in the U.S. as *Seeds of Tomorrow*) and *Harvest on the Don* (1960). These books, chronicling the Don Cossacks' struggles against the Bolsheviks during the Civil War and their life under the postrevolutionary collectivization of their homeland, became international bestsellers. Of peasant stock, Sholokhov left school at 13 and served with the Red Army during the Civil War. After working two years in Moscow as a labourer, he returned to his native village. Meanwhile, he had begun to write and by the age of 21 had published three books, including *Donskie rasskazy* (1926; *Tales from the Don*, 1961). The publication of his major novels won for him the reputation of a foremost exponent of Socialist Realism, and his contributions to *Pravda* and other publications during World War II enhanced his standing with the Soviet leadership. He became a personal friend of Nikita Khrushchev, with whom he visited the U.S. in 1959, and was the recipient of numerous state prizes. Nevertheless, the high literary merit of the early Don novels, contrasted with Sholokhov's modest educational background and extreme youth during the period described in them, gave rise to controversy as to their true authorship. Doubts that had first surfaced as early as 1929 gained strength in the 1970s with the publication of a book by Aleksandr Solzhenitsyn suggesting that Sholokhov had made use of an unfinished manuscript left by an older Cossack writer and White Russian officer during the Civil War, Fyodor Kryukov. The fact that Sholokhov's later works never attained the same quality gave added credence to these doubts, which persisted but were never substantiated. A Communist Party member from 1932 and a member of the Supreme Soviet (parliament) from 1946, Sholokhov had little time for fellow writers who failed to toe the party line; his condemnation of Boris Pasternak contributed toward the latter's decision to refuse the 1958 Nobel Prize, and he denounced and ridiculed dissidents such as Andrey Sinyavsky, Yuly Daniel, and Solzhenitsyn.

Simpson, George Gaylord, U.S. paleontologist (b. June 16, 1902, Chicago, Ill.—d. Oct. 6, 1984, Tucson, Ariz.), established himself as a world-renowned expert on mammalian paleontology with his studies of continental migration of South American animals but was perhaps better known for his work on the modern biological theory of evolution and the philosophical implications of the acceptance of evolutionary theory as discussed in his most famous work, *The Meaning of Evolution* (1949). Simpson earned a Ph.D. from Yale University in 1926 and the following year began a 35-year association with the American Museum of Natural History, New York City, first as field assistant, then curator, and finally chairman of the museum's department of geology and paleontology. During his tenure he conducted numerous expeditions in search of fossils, including those to Patagonia (1930–31 and 1933–34) and Venezuela (1938–39) and an especially fruitful mission to Colorado (1953), where he discovered eight skulls of 38-cm (15-in)-tall creatures named dawn

horses, a species that had flourished some 50 million years earlier. His expeditions shed new light on fossil mammals, and he was with Louis and Mary Leakey at Fort Ternan in Kenya in 1961 when they unearthed the remains of a creature standing midway between the early apes and man. Simpson also served as professor of vertebrate paleontology at Columbia University until 1958, when he became professor of vertebrate paleontology at Harvard University, a post he held until 1970. He then served as professor at the University of Arizona until his retirement in 1982. During his prolific career Simpson published hundreds of scientific articles and such books as *Tempo and Mode in Evolution* (1944), *Major Features of Evolution* (1953), *The Principles of Animal Taxonomy* (1961), *Fossils and the History of Life* (1983), and *Discoverers of the Lost World* (1984).

Sinclair, Gordon Allan, Canadian broadcaster and journalist (b. June 3, 1900, Toronto, Ont.—d. May 17, 1984, Toronto), was a colourful personality who rose to national prominence and basked in the limelight as correspondent and travel writer (1922–43) for the *Toronto Star*, as an irreverent broadcaster on radio station CFRB in Toronto, and as a controversial panelist from 1957 on the television program "Front Page Challenge." Sinclair was permanently ejected from public school in 1915 and was fired from several jobs before he landed a job as a reporter with the *Star*. As a journalist during the Depression, he was assigned to travel with a group of hoboes from Canada to England. After he was recalled from the latter assignment he was sent in 1930 to Germany and Mexico; in 1931 he traveled to Spain, Morocco, and Algiers; and in 1932 he earned the distinction of becoming the first Canadian to circle the globe for his newspaper. During his journalistic career he made 23 foreign trips, circled the world four times, and chronicled his zany adventures in such books as *Footloose in India* (1932), *Cannibal Quest* (1933), and *Loose Among Devils* (1935). In 1943 the brash Sinclair launched a career in broadcasting and acquired a large following as the opinionated commentator of "news and comments" on CFRB. He took great delight in baiting his listeners by debunking the church, boasting about his wealth, and by poking fun at people he categorized as stuffed shirts. He even admitted that as a reporter he had been punched in the nose three times. Sinclair received the most mail of his career after his broadcast on June 5, 1973, when he scolded the world for being ungrateful to the Americans, "the most generous . . . people in all the Earth." Dubbing himself Canada's crankiest, oldest newsman, he also asserted that he had interviewed Hitler, the queen mother, Pope Pius XII, and Gandhi. His two volumes of memoirs, *Will the Real Gordon Sinclair Please Stand Up?* and *Will Gordon Sinclair Please Sit Down?*, were published, respectively, in 1966 and 1975.

Skeaping, Mary, British ballet dancer (b. Dec. 15, 1902, Woodford, Essex, England—d. Feb. 9, 1984, London, England), danced with Pavlova's company but achieved her greatest fame as a producer specializing in reconstructions of historical ballet styles. She studied under Francesca Zanfretta, Rudolph von Laban, Margaret Craske, and other notable teachers during her dancing career before teaching in South Africa and then joining Sadler's Wells as ballet mistress. As director of the Royal Swedish Ballet from 1953 to 1962, she produced historical reconstructions at the Drottningholm Theatre. This perfectly preserved 18th-century theatre, with the original stage machinery, was an ideal setting for her productions. Skeaping also worked on television productions of ballet, including the first live full-length ballet shown on BBC television, and made a series for Swedish television on dance styles. She wrote a history of 17th- and 18th-century Swedish ballet. She was made a Member of the Order of the British Empire in 1958 and was awarded the Order of Vasa (1961) and the Carina Ari Medal (1971).

Slipyj (Kobernyckyj-Dyckovskyj), Josyf Cardinal, head of the Ukrainian Catholic Uniate Church (b. Feb. 17, 1892, Zazdrist, Ukraine—d. Sept. 7, 1984, Rome, Italy), although effectively patriarch of his church, was never granted that title by the pope. Slipyj was ordained priest in 1917. After teaching theology for some years, in 1939 he was made titular archbishop of Serre and attached to the Lvov see. When the Uniate resident metropolitan-archbishop of Lvov, Andrej Szeptycki, died in 1944, Slipyj succeeded him. In July of that year Soviet forces occupied Lvov, and soon afterward Archbishop Slipyj and ten of his bishops were arrested and deported to Siberia. In 1946 the Ukrainian church, under pressure from the Soviet authorities, proclaimed its merger with the Russian Orthodox Church. As a result of an appeal by Pope John XXIII to Nikita Khrushchev, Archbishop Slipyj—then at a labour camp at Yeniseysk—was freed in 1963 on condition that he become a resident of the Vatican. Once there he assumed the role of spiritual head of all Uniate Ukrainians residing in the West and asked Pope Paul VI to name him patriarch. The pope, unwilling to offend Moscow, declined to do so, but in 1965 he created Slipyj a cardinal. In the course of his visits to Uniate communities in the West, he was awarded honorary degrees by Loyola University, Chicago, and the Catholic University of America, Washington, D.C. In the mid-1970s Slipyj began using the title patriarch. In 1975 a synod of Ukrainian bishops from Canada, Australia, France, West Germany, Great Britain, and the U.S. met in Rome and elected Archbishop Myroslav Ivan Lubachivskyj as coadjutor to Cardinal Slipyj with the right of succession.

Sokoine, Edward Moringe, Tanzanian politician (b. 1938, Monduli, Masai District, Tanganyika [now Tanzania]—d. April 12, 1984, near Morogoro, Tanzania), became prime minister in 1983 and was the heir apparent of Pres. Julius Nyerere, who had indicated that he would retire in 1985. A Masai, Sokoine was educated in Tanganyika and in West Germany before becoming a member of Parliament in 1965. He was appointed minister of state in 1970 and minister of defense (1972–77). He then served a term as prime minister, retiring because of ill health in 1980. He was replaced by Cleopa David Msuya, but in February 1983 Sokoine was recalled to take over from Msuya, reportedly because the country was on the verge of economic collapse. Sokoine instituted a campaign against black marketeering that led to widespread arrests. He died in an automobile accident after attending a parliamentary session in Dodoma, the country's future capital.

Souvanna Phouma, Prince, Laotian politician (b. Oct. 7, 1901, Luang Prabang, Laos—d. Jan. 10, 1984, Vientiane, Laos), was ambassador to France in 1958–59 and several times premier before the establishment of the People's Democratic Republic of Laos in December 1975. A moderate conservative and a nationalist, he tried to steer a centre course between the various factions within the country and the foreign powers directly or indirectly involved in the affairs of the region. But the shift of power in favour of his half brother Prince Souphanouvong, leader of the pro-Communist Pathet Lao, deprived him of his political base. Souvanna Phouma, a nephew of King Sisavang Vong, studied engineering in Vietnam and France and entered the public works service of French Indochina. He became premier and successfully negotiated the country's independence in 1953 but resigned in 1954. Souvanna Phouma was premier again from 1956 to 1958 and, after his return from the embassy in France, led the government for four months in 1960 before he had to flee to Cambodia. In 1961 and 1962 a series of meetings between Souphanouvong and Prince Boun Oum led eventually to the Geneva agreement of July 1962, which created a coalition government led by Souvanna Phouma. Attacked this time from the right, he

AGIP/PICTORIAL PARADE

came to lean more and more on the U.S., while the Pathet Lao stepped up its offensive. Corruption increased in Laos, as did U.S. and Thai influence. Souvanna Phouma led a final coalition from 1974, when his half brother returned to the capital, to 1975, when the Communists took over in Saigon. The Pathet Lao quickly established itself in Vientiane, and Souvanna Phouma was retired with the nominal title of government adviser.

Souvarine, Boris (BORIS SOUVART né BORIS LIFCHITZ), Russian-born French Communist (b. Nov. 6, 1895, Kiev, Ukraine, Russia—d. Nov. 1, 1984, Paris, France), used the pseudonym Souvarine after the intellectual revolutionary depicted in Émile Zola's novel *Germinal* and, as the last surviving original Comintern executive member, had been prominent in the foundation of the French Communist Party. He was also an early and notable opponent of Stalin. Of Jewish origin, he was taken to France at the age of 3 and at 14 began work as a jeweler. A socialist and pacifist, he opposed involvement in World War I although he served in the military from 1913 to 1915. Four years later he became a Bolshevik and founded, with Russian financing, the weekly *Bulletin Communiste*. Imprisoned with other activists following a strike in May 1920, he drafted the motion by which, at the Socialist Congress of Tours in December 1920, a party faction decided to join the Comintern and thus led to the establishment of the French Communist Party. Elected to the party's first steering committee, Souvarine went to Moscow to join the Comintern executive committee. He was expelled in 1924 for supporting Trotsky against Zinoviev in the power struggles that followed Lenin's death. Returning to France, he reestablished the *Bulletin Communiste* as an independent paper and founded the Marx-Lenin Circle. He broke with Trotsky in 1929, founding a group of Democratic Communists. Souvarine founded the periodicals *Critique sociale* (1931–34), *l'Observateur des Deux-Mondes* (1948), and *Contrat social* (1957–68) and contributed from its foundation (1959) to the anti-Soviet *Est et Ouest*. His severely critical 1935 biography of Stalin was revised in 1977.

Speidel, Hans, German army officer (b. Oct. 28, 1897, Metzingen, Württemberg, Germany—d. Nov. 28, 1984, Bad Honnef, West Germany), was a conspirator in the abortive 1944 army plot to assassinate Hitler. He later helped to build up West Germany's armed forces in the 1950s and was commander of Allied Forces Central Europe for NATO (1957–63). Speidel joined the German Army in 1914 and served on the Western Front during World War I before studying at Berlin, Tübingen, and Stuttgart universities. He was assistant to the German military attaché in Paris (1933–37) and, after holding other staff appointments, returned to France in 1940 as chief of staff, first to the German military governor of Paris (June–August) and then to the military governor of occupied France. Chief of staff to the Italian 8th Army fight-

ing on the Russian front (1942–spring 1944), he was then appointed chief of staff to Rommel's Army Group B in northern France and recruited Rommel for the anti-Hitler plot. Following its failure on July 20, 1944, the Gestapo interrogated Speidel for some weeks but failed to extract from him any admission of complicity. After the war he became a member of the history faculty of Tübingen University, but he was soon required to advise and represent the government on military matters; he was made commander in chief of the new West German armed forces in1955. He was president of the Foundation of Science and Politics (1964–78), and he published his memoirs in 1977.

Szabo, Laszlo Csekefalvi, Hungarian writer (b. Nov. 11, 1905, Budapest, Hung.—d. Sept. 27, 1984, Budapest), worked in the Hungarian Service of the British Broadcasting Corporation (BBC) from 1951 to 1972. He was a distinguished author, lecturer, and broadcaster who, although an émigré, eventually received recognition in his native country. Brought up in Kolozsvar, Hung. (now Cluj, Rom.), in Transylvania, he studied economic history at Budapest University and at the Sorbonne in Paris. He became literary director of the Hungarian State Broadcasting Corporation in 1935 and actively encouraged contemporary writers. Unwilling to cooperate after the German invasion of Hungary in March 1944, he resigned and, as a reward after liberation, he was appointed professor of art history at the Budapest Academy of Fine Arts. Szabo was not enamoured of the Soviet influence in his country and went to Rome on a scholarship in 1948. He remained in Italy until he was invited to London by the BBC in 1951, and he thereafter made that city his permanent home. He wrote several books of short stories and essays, the latter mainly on Hungarian and English literature. *Crossing at Dover* (1937) recorded his first visit to England; *Roman Music* (1940), his impressions of Italy. As well as a ten-volume critical edition of old Transylvanian prose writers (1942), he wrote on Byron, Keats, and Shelley (*Three Poets,* 1942) and a book of essays on Shakespeare, which was to be published posthumously.

Thill, Georges, French singer (b. Dec. 14, 1897, Paris, France—d. Oct. 16, 1984, Draguignan, Var, France), was the most famous French operatic tenor of the period between World Wars I and II. He appeared at the Paris Opera; at La Scala, Milan; at the Metropolitan Opera House, New York City; and in Vienna and Buenos Aires. He served in the French Air Force during World War I, studied at the Conservatoire, and made his debut at the Paris Opera in 1924. As its principal tenor for 16 years, he sang a wide repertory of French, Italian, and German opera, including Faust, Roméo, Samson, Tannhäuser, and Parsifal. His technique was outstanding, ranging from the tender and lyrical to the heroic, and he had an impressive stage presence. Thill made many recordings and appeared in Abel Gance's film *Louise.* In 1941 he left Paris for the Vichy zone of France but gave some concerts during the war years. In 1953 he made his debut at the Opéra-Comique. His last concert was at the Châtelet in 1956.

Thornton, Willie Mae ("BIG MAMA"), U.S. singer (b. Dec. 11, 1926, Montgomery, Ala.—d. July 25, 1984, Los Angeles, Calif.), was an aggressive, earthy blues singer who also played the drums and the harmonica and inspired such singers as Elvis Presley and Janis Joplin, who adopted her songs "Hound Dog" and "Ball and Chain." Thornton herself was influenced by such blues giants as Memphis Minnie, Junior Parker, Ma Rainey, and Bessie Smith. Thornton rose to stardom while touring with the Johnny Otis band when she shouted her biggest hit, "Hound Dog" (1953). In 1957 her popularity waned, so she began a series of engagements at San Francisco clubs. With the advent of the blues revival in the 1960s, Thornton's star shone brighter, especially after Joplin recorded

"Ball and Chain." During the 1970s and '80s Thornton appeared at major jazz festivals in the U.S. and Europe.

Tidyman, Ernest R., U.S. novelist and screenwriter (b. Jan. 1, 1928, Cleveland, Ohio—d. July 14, 1984, London, England), won an Academy Award in 1972 for his screenplay for the motion picture *The French Connection* (1971), only three years after embarking on a career as a screenwriter. Earlier, Tidyman, who was a high school dropout, spent 25 years as a journalist and was the author of such crime thrillers as *Big Bucks, Absolute Zero, The Billion Dollar Snatch, Line of Duty,* and *Table Stakes.* He also penned seven novels on which such films as *Shaft* (1971), *Shaft's Big Score* (1972), and *Shaft in Africa* (1973) were based and adapted the novels for the screen. Some of his other successful screenplays were *High Plains Drifter* (1973), *Report to the Commissioner* (1975), and *Street People* (1976). Tidyman's films for television included *The Guyana Tragedy—The Story of Jim Jones, To Kill a Cop,* and *Alcatraz: The Whole Shocking Story.*

Touré, Ahmed Sékou, president of Guinea (b. Jan. 9, 1922, Faranah, Guinea, French West Africa—d. March 26, 1984, Cleveland, Ohio), as the charismatic and eloquent president of the country since it gained independence from France in 1958, combined moderate foreign policies with ruthless repression of dissent at home. The son of a Muslim peasant family, he was expelled from technical school in Conakry for participating in a strike. While working for the government's postal and communication services, he advanced in the trade union movement, leading the Guinean branch of the Confédération Générale du Travail from 1948 and the Parti Démocratique de Guinée from 1952. By the time of his election as mayor of Conakry in 1955, he had a reputation as an outstanding orator of Marxist leanings. Elected as deputy to the French National Assembly in 1951 and 1954, he was barred from taking his seat there until 1956. His party won a landslide victory in Guinea's 1957 elections. The following year French Pres. Charles de Gaulle offered the French territories in sub-Saharan Africa a choice between partial autonomy within the French Community and complete independence. Declaring that "we prefer poverty in liberty to wealth in slavery," Touré was the only African leader to opt for independence. He sought aid from the Soviet Union but by 1961 was committed to nonalignment. The breach in relations with France, which was not healed until the mid-1970s, and greatly increased defense expenditure caused serious economic difficulties. Throughout Touré's rule plots and attempted coups d'état were cited as the reason for severe reprisals and a repressive internal regime. In 1970 he nearly fell to an attack by Portuguese and Guinean mercenaries from neighbouring Portuguese Guinea (now Guinea-Bissau): 92 people were executed for the attempt. After his adviser Diallo Telli (secretary-general of the Organization of African Unity [OAU], 1964–72) accused Touré of torturing political prisoners, Telli was eliminated, allegedly for involvement in a plot against the regime. But in international affairs Touré was an influential figure, especially in Africa, where he was slated to become chairman of the OAU at its May 1984 summit.

Trader Vic (VICTOR JULES BERGERON), U.S. restaurateur (b. 1903, San Francisco, Calif.—d. Oct. 11, 1984, Hillsborough, Calif.), was a colourful personality who in 1934 parlayed an Oakland, Calif., hamburger stand named Hinky Dink's into a $50 million-a-year restaurant empire. Trader Vic's, which boasted 21 establishments in six countries, specialized in a Polynesian-type cuisine and exotic cocktails, especially such famous rum concoctions as Missionary's Revenge and Mai Tai, which Bergeron invented. When he was six years old, Bergeron's left leg was amputated, but he never let his infirmity thwart his ambition. He was a frequent visitor to veterans' hospitals, where he bolstered the spirits of amputees, and was a self-made man who became a successful cookbook author, sculptor, painter, and jewelry maker. The flamboyant Bergeron opened his most famous dining spot in San Francisco in 1951, and the profits from this establishment alone led him to open luxury restaurants in Canada, Germany, Japan, England, and Singapore. He published his autobiography, *Frankly Speaking: Trader Vic's Own Story,* in 1973.

Truffaut, François, French film director (b. Feb. 6, 1932, Paris, France—d. Oct. 21, 1984, Neuilly, France), as a leading figure in the French *nouvelle vague* (New Wave) scored a triumph with his first feature film, *Les Quatre Cent Coups (The 400 Blows,* 1959), which became one of the most outstanding international successes of French cinema. The film fictionalized the events, but accurately conveyed the emotions, of Truffaut's own unhappy childhood and captured for him the prize for best director at the Cannes Film Festival. He was sent to live with his grandmother at an early age and became a cinema fanatic and a rebel whose

KATHERINE YOUNG

military service ended with desertion and a prison sentence. From 1953 he worked for the film department at the Ministry of Agriculture and then, thanks to the encouragement of critic André Bazin, wrote for the influential *Cahiers du Cinéma* condemning the mediocrity of contemporary French cinema and, like other New Wave figures, praising the Hollywood directors to whom he was to pay tribute in *Tirez sur le pianiste (Shoot the Piano Player,* 1960) and other films. It was his view that the director should be a film author —an *auteur*—with control over the entire creative process, including story line, dialogue, and the artistic style of the film as a whole. He continued to make short films before the success of *Les Quatre Cent Coups* and, two years later, of *Jules et Jim,* his other great success of the period. *Farenheit 451* (1966) received less critical acclaim, and until *La Nuit américaine (Day for Night,* 1972) won the Oscar for the best foreign film of 1973, his works received mixed reviews. Some of his films were certainly inferior, but they were always interesting; he was never afraid to experiment with new themes and styles, as in *L'Enfant sauvage (The Wild Child,* 1970), in which he himself appeared. He acted in other films, including Steven Spielberg's *Close Encounters of the Third Kind,* and wrote books, including a study of Alfred Hitchcock and *Les Films de ma vie* (1975). In 1979 he was honoured with a retrospective by the American Film Institute, and his last film, *Vivement, Dimanche (Lively, Sunday,* 1984), was hailed as one of his best since the early 1960s.

Tsarapkin, Semyon Konstantinovich, Soviet diplomat (b. June 4, 1906, Nilolayev, Ukraine—d. September 1984, Moscow, U.S.S.R.), was head of the Soviet Union's delegation at the Geneva disarmament talks held between 1961 and 1966. Educated at the Moscow Oriental

Institute, he worked in a smelting plant before being seconded for "advanced political training." He held posts in the Ministry of Foreign Affairs from 1937, acting successively as deputy head and head of the Second Eastern Department and then of the Far Eastern Department. From 1944 to 1947 he was head of the U.S. Department and as such attended the Dumbarton Oaks (1944) and San Francisco (1945) conferences that preceded the establishment of the UN. Minister at the Soviet embassy in Washington, D.C. (1947–49), he was deputy permanent representative to the UN Security Council (1949–54). He then returned to Moscow as head of the Foreign Office Division for International Organizations (1954–66). He was ambassador to West Germany (1966–71) and ambassador at large and a deputy foreign minister thereafter.

Tubb, Ernest Dale, U.S. country and western singer (b. Feb. 9, 1914, Crisp, Texas—d. Sept. 6, 1984, Nashville, Tenn.), was the pioneering "Texas Troubadour" who ushered in the "honky-tonk" sound with its forceful guitars and earthy lyrics and from 1943 was a regular member of Nashville's Grand Ole Opry. Tubb, who was almost 20 before he owned his own guitar, became friends in 1935 with Jimmie Rodgers's widow (she loaned Tubb Rodgers's guitar and arranged a recording session for him). Tubb's biggest hit, "I'm Walking the Floor over You," became his trademark and sold a million copies in 1941. During his career Tubb sold some 30 million records and recorded more than 250 songs, including such all-time favourites as "Waltz Across Texas," "Tomorrow Never Comes," "Goodnight, Irene," "Blue Christmas," and "I'm Bitin' My Fingernails and Thinking of You." The folksy Tubb always sported a cowboy hat and was known for his friendliness; he helped country music star Loretta Lynn launch her career by appearing in concerts and recording duets with her. The lanky baritone was inducted into the Country Music Hall of Fame in 1965.

Uemura, Naomi, Japanese mountain climber (b. Feb. 12, 1941, Hyogo Prefecture, Japan— presumed dead late February 1984, on Mt. McKinley, Alaska), was a fearless and daring adventurer who on Feb. 12, 1984, became the first solo climber to reach the 6,194-m (20,320-ft) summit of Mt. McKinley in winter. The 1.6-m (5-ft 4-in) tall Uemura initially took up mountain climbing to increase his self-confidence. In 1970 he became the first Japanese to reach the 8,848-m (29,028-ft) summit of Mt. Everest, the highest point on Earth. The intrepid adventurer compiled a stunning list of exploits: he had stood atop the highest peaks on six continents (all except Antarctica); he paddled a homemade raft some 6,500 km (4,000 mi) down the Amazon River; he made a solo trek across the Arctic wilderness from Greenland to Alaska; and in 1978 Uemura made history as the first person to trek by dogsled some 800 km (500 mi) from Ellesmere Island to the North Pole. His 57-day journey was fraught with danger, including pursuit by a polar bear and a night of terror stranded in the middle of a floe of ice. After his climb to the top of Mt. McKinley, Uemura began his descent during perilous weather and on February 13 lost radio contact. He was last spotted by a pilot on February 16 and was presumed dead after an eight-day search netted only his snowshoes, a diary, and the two poles he used to test the firmness of snow.

Ustinov, Dmitry Fedorovich, Soviet politician (b. Oct. 30, 1908, Samara [now Kuybyshev], Russia—d. Dec. 20, 1984, Moscow, U.S.S.R.), was minister of defense from 1976 and an influential member of the top Soviet leadership. An engineer by profession, he was largely responsible for expansion of the Soviet defense industry during and after World War II. The son of a worker, Ustinov graduated in 1934 from the Military Institute of Mechanics in Leningrad and worked first as a construction engineer, then as director of a Leningrad armament factory. When in June 1941 Germany attacked the Soviet Union, Stalin appointed Ustinov people's commissar of armaments, a position he kept under the titles of minister of armaments (1946–53) and minister of defense industries (1953–57). In that post he initiated the evacuation of the Soviet arms industry to beyond the Urals, out of the reach of the advancing German armies, and after the war he set the course by which the Soviet armed forces eventually

AP/WIDE WORLD

reached their current level. He was a full member of the Central Committee from 1952, and in 1957 Nikita Khrushchev made him a deputy premier, still with overall responsibility for the armaments industry. In 1963 he became both chairman of the Supreme Council of National Economy and first deputy premier. In 1965 he was elected a secretary of the Central Committee with responsibilities for the military, defense industry, and security organs, and he became a candidate member of the Politburo. As such, he worked closely with Yury Andropov, who in 1967 became head of the KGB. In April 1976, when Defense Minister Marshal Andrey Grechko died, Ustinov was appointed to replace him. At the same time, he was made a full member of the Politburo and marshal of the Soviet Union. During the 1970s Ustinov played an important behind-the-scenes role in Soviet-U.S. arms limitation negotiations and was present at the 1979 Vienna summit at which the second strategic arms limitation talks (SALT II) agreement was signed by Leonid Brezhnev and U.S. Pres. Jimmy Carter. On Brezhnev's death Ustinov was believed to have been the first to propose Andropov as his successor. Ustinov's last public appearance was on Sept. 27, 1984, when he presented the Order of Lenin to Andropov's successor, Konstantin Chernenko. He himself was twice awarded the Order of Lenin, was a Hero of the Soviet Union, and was a Hero of Socialist Labour.

Vaizey, John Ernest Vaizey, BARON, British economist, writer, and educator (b. Oct. 1, 1929, London, England—d. July 19, 1984, London), was professor of economics at Brunel University (1966–82) and head of the School of Social Sciences there (1973–81). From 1956 he had specialized in the economics of education and in a series of definitive books outlined the economic history of education in 20th-century Britain. His first work, *The Cost of Education* (1958), demonstrated the steady rise of per capita expenditure on education, even during the depression of the 1930s. Other influential books included *The Economics of Education* (1962), *Education in the Modern World* (1967), and *The Political Economy of Education* (1972). Educated at the University of Cambridge, he later held academic posts there and at the Universities of London and Oxford, as well as in Australia and the U.S. Outside his specialist field he produced a comment on recent world history in *The Squandered Peace* (1983), while *Scenes from Institutional Life* (1959) provided a devastating account of hospital life as he experienced it when suffering as a teenager from osteomyelitis. Created a life peer in 1976, he had been a lifelong supporter of the Labour Party, but in 1979 he resigned and joined the Conservatives.

Vasey, Sir Ernest Albert, British-born Kenyan financial consultant (b. Aug. 27, 1901—d. Jan. 10, 1984, Nairobi, Kenya), was minister of finance in the Kenyan Council of Ministers from 1952 to 1959. He emigrated to Kenya after serving on Shrewsbury Town Council. Vasey was twice mayor of Nairobi before entering the Legislative Council as member (1945–50) for Nairobi North, and in 1950 he was appointed member for health and local government. As minister for finance and development during the Mau Mau emergency he played an important role in ensuring increased funds for African development projects and in establishing relationships with international bodies for funding and aid. After his election to the Council of Ministers in 1958 was blocked by a boycott by African-elected members under the 1957 constitution, Vasey left for Tanganyika at the end of 1959 and served as finance minister in Julius Nyerere's government during 1960–62. From 1963 until his retirement in 1966 he was World Bank representative in Pakistan. During his retirement in Kenya he remained active in business and as a member of government committees. He was made a Knight Commander of the Order of the British Empire in 1959.

Vézelay, Paule (MARJORIE WATSON-WILLIAMS), British painter (b. May 14, 1892, Clifton, Bristol, England—d. March 20, 1984, London, England), turned from figurative painting in Post-Impressionist style to abstraction in the late 1920s. She worked both on canvas and in three-dimensional media to create abstract constructions. Vézelay studied in Bristol and at the London School of Art and worked as an illustrator and printmaker before joining the London Group in 1922. She visited Paris in 1920, took up residence there in 1926, and became a close friend of André Masson, Jean Arp, and other leading painters of the period. From 1934 she was a member of the group Abstraction-Création, but her career was interrupted by the outbreak of World War II. From 1939 she lived in England, largely forgotten by the public, but working steadily until the end of her life. Her work was seldom exhibited until a 1983 retrospective at the Tate Gallery, London, marked its rediscovery, and she was the subject of a television film made shortly before she died.

Von Zedtwitz, Waldemar, U.S. contract bridge player (b. 1896, Berlin, Germany—d. Oct. 5, 1984, Hawaii), captured 19 national contract bridge titles including the prestigious Vanderbilt Teams and Spingold Teams three times each, and became a towering figure in the sport as the reorganizer of the American Contract Bridge League, as a founder (1958) of the World Bridge Federation, and as a charter member of the National Laws Commission for which he helped revise the laws of the game. Von Zedtwitz was educated in Germany but in the 1920s he immigrated to the U.S. and became a citizen. In 1927 he won an auction bridge title and became a friend and favourite partner of Harold Vanderbilt, who invented the game of contract bridge. Von Zedtwitz later toured (1930) Europe with Ely Culbertson's team and was credited with inventing the forcing two-bid, the cornerstone of the Culbertson system. In 1948 Von Zedtwitz became president of the American Contract Bridge League and was instrumental in executing a major reorganization. In 1968 he retired from all official executive positions, but at the age of 74, despite failing eyesight, he reached the pinnacle of his career by winning, with Barbara Brier, the World Mixed Pairs Championship. He thus became the oldest person ever to win a world bridge title.

Wakhevitch, Georges, Russian-born stage and screen designer (b. Aug. 18, 1907, Odessa, Russia—d. Feb. 11, 1984, Paris, France), studied painting but found the most fruitful outlet for his talent in design for film, drama, and opera. His career was at its height during the years between director René Clair's first talking picture, *Sous les toits de Paris* (1930), and his last, *Les Fêtes galantes* (1965). Wakhevitch worked with most of the major French directors of that time, including Jean Renoir, Marcel Carné, Jacques Feyder, Jacques Becker, and Julien Duvivier. During the 1940s he collaborated with Jean Cocteau on the film *L'Éternel retour* and the stage ballet *Le Jeune homme et la mort.* Wakhevitch's versatility was striking, and his sets ranged from a full-scale reconstruction of the port of Anvers for a film by Yves Allegret to the bare simplicity of some of his stage work. He was particularly associated with the Paris Opéra and in later years established a highly successful collaboration with Peter Brook on his film *The Beggar's Opera* and later for the stage.

Wallace, Lila Bell Acheson, U.S. philanthropist (b. Dec. 25, 1889, Virden, Manitoba—d. May 8, 1984, Mt. Kisco, N.Y.), was the gracious and generous co-founder of *Reader's Digest,* a pocket-size monthly magazine that attained the largest circulation of any magazine in the world. As the daughter of a Presbyterian minister, she lived in various Midwestern towns while growing up. After graduating from the University of Oregon in 1917 she worked for the YWCA during World War I. In 1921 she married DeWitt Wallace, and the two launched the magazine the following year. Though she exerted little editorial control over the *Digest,* Wallace used $60 million of their fortune to endow various organizations. Her belief that "Beauty is medicine" prompted her to amass a multimillion dollar collection of modern art, mostly French Impressionism, and to donate millions to New York City's Metropolitan Museum of Art, which provided for the newly expanded Egyptian galleries. Her benevolence also contributed to the restoration of painter Claude Monet's house and magnificent gardens in Giverny, France;

DON HOGAN CHARLES

the construction of the World of Birds exhibition facilities at the Bronx Zoo; programs in music and drama at the Juilliard School of Music; the renovation of Boscobel House, an 18th-century Federal mansion near her home; and preservation of the ancient Egyptian temples at Abu Simbel, threatened with inundation by the Aswan High Dam. Her abiding interest in flowers and art was evidenced in the offices of *Reader's Digest,* where flower arrangements and oil paintings from her personal collection graced the tables and walls. Wallace, who served as co-chairman of the Reader's Digest Association, Inc., until 1973, assumed ownership of all of the company's voting stock after the death of her husband in 1981, and she remained director of the company until her death. In 1972 she was awarded the Presidential Medal of Freedom.

Waring, Fred(eric Malcolm), U.S. orchestra leader (b. June 9, 1900, Tyrone, Pa.—d. July 29, 1984, Danville, Pa.), as the dynamic founder

AP/WIDE WORLD

of the Pennsylvanians, a 55-member band and choral ensemble, "taught America to sing" and popularized choral music in the U.S. with more than six decades of road tours and radio, television, and motion-picture appearances. Waring, who was an engineering student at Pennsylvania State University, was rejected by the college glee club, so he formed his own band. Waring later withdrew from the university to pursue a career in music. He eventually added vocals and more instruments, and the Pennsylvanians emerged with the soft melodies and lush orchestrations that hence became their hallmark. His ensemble made the first electronic recording in 1925 and one of the first musical films, *Syncopation,* in 1929. On radio from 1933 to 1949 the Pennsylvanians attracted large audiences with their renditions of such hits as "Sleep," "Dream, Dream, Dream," and "I Love Music." On stage, the Pennsylvanians performed some 2,000 songs, 200 of which were composed by Waring. The group made their television debut in 1949 with an hour-long musical show, but with the advent of rock and roll their popularity began to wane. By 1976 the group was renamed the Young Pennsylvanians and consisted of only 20 members. Waring formally retired in 1980, and his death was expected to ensure the demise of the Pennsylvanians. The ingenious Waring was also the inventor of one of the first food processors, the Waring Blender, in 1937.

Weissmuller, Johnny (PETER JOHN WEISSMULLER), U.S. swimmer and actor (b. June 2, 1904, Windber, Pa.—d. Jan. 20, 1984, Acapulco, Mexico), captured five Olympic gold medals and set 67 world swimming records in the 1920s before he reigned as Tarzan of the Jungle in a series of glossy MGM motion pictures. Weissmuller grew up in Chicago and learned how to swim at around age nine in Lake Michigan and in public pools. His swimming prowess came to the attention of Bill Bachrach, the widely respected coach of the Illinois Athletic Club, when at age 15 Weissmuller outdistanced all rivals in impromptu races. For the next three years he underwent a strict training regimen in preparation for the Olympics. In the Olympic Games of 1924 he won three gold medals, for the 100-m and 400-m freestyle and the 800-m relay (he also won a bronze medal as a member of the U.S. water polo team); in the 1928 Olympic Games he garnered two more gold medals, for the 100-m freestyle and 800-m relay. A phenomenal freestyle swimmer, Weissmuller was, however, perhaps better known as the virile, vine-swinging Tarzan, protector of the jungle and of its animals and of the treetop home he shared with his wife, Jane, and son, Boy. The Tarzan series captured the imagination of audiences as they viewed the loincloth-clad Tarzan performing his classic chest-thumping call of the wild. Weissmuller starred as Tarzan from 1932 to 1948, then switched to the Jungle Jim series that lasted through the mid-1950s. "Jungle Jim" was also a

1955 television program. Besides his Jungle Jim and 12 Tarzan films, including *Tarzan the Ape Man* (1932), *Tarzan and His Mate* (1934), *Tarzan's Secret Treasure* (1941), and *Tarzan and the Amazons* (1945), he made cameo appearances in *Stage Door Canteen* (1943), *The Phynx* (1970), and *That's Entertainment Part Two* (1976). Weissmuller was married five times. In 1977 he suffered a series of strokes that left him an invalid for the remainder of his life.

Werner, Oskar (Oskar Josef Bschliessmayer), Austrian actor (b. Nov. 13, 1922, Vienna, Austria—d. Oct. 23, 1984, Marburg, West Germany), brought a boyish charm to his portrayal of the young German in François Truffaut's *Jules et Jim* (1961) and was nominated for an Oscar for his part in Stanley Kramer's *Ship of Fools* (1965). He joined the Vienna Burgtheater in 1941 and was well known as a stage actor by the time he made his first film in 1948. Werner went to Hollywood in the early 1950s to act in *Decision Before Dawn* (1951) and stayed there, with a contract to 20th Century-Fox for the next ten years. Later he worked primarily in Britain on such films as *The Spy Who Came in from the Cold, Fahrenheit 451* (1966), and *The Shoes of the Fisherman*. His other films included *Der Letzte Akt, Lola Montes* (1955), and *Voyage of the Damned* (1976). Werner also worked in the theatre and was involved with organizing film and drama festivals.

West, Jessamyn, U.S. novelist and short story writer (b. July 18, 1902, near North Vernon, Ind.—d. Feb. 23, 1984, Napa, Calif.), who, while bedridden with tuberculosis, penned the sensitive collection of short stories *The Friendly Persuasion* (1945), a best-selling book about a Quaker family living on the Indiana frontier during the Civil War. West, who also wrote the screenplay for the motion picture *Friendly Persuasion* (1956) starring Gary Cooper and Dorothy McGuire, published her first novel, *The Witch Diggers,* in 1951. After graduating from Whittier (Calif.) College in 1923, West was a schoolteacher before contracting tuberculosis. She was confined to a sanitarium for two years before being sent home, presumably to live out her last days. West's mother regaled her with tales of her Quaker ancestors' beginnings, and West used the stories for her inspiration. Though she also published such works as *Cress Delahanty* (1953), *Love, Death and the Ladies' Drill Team* (1955), *To See the Dream* (1957), and *Leafy Rivers* (1967), she was best remembered for *The Friendly Persuasion.*

Willson, Meredith, U.S. composer and lyricist (b. May 18, 1902, Mason City, Iowa—d. June 15, 1984, Santa Monica, Calif.), was a classical composer, a conductor, and a flutist with John Philip Sousa's band (1921–23) and the New York Philharmonic-Symphony Orchestra (1924–29) before turning to musical comedy and exhibiting his versatility as the composer, librettist, and lyricist of the smash-hit musical *The Music Man* (1957). The latter boasted such hit songs as "Seventy-Six Trombones," "Trouble in River City," "Till There Was You," and "Marian the Librarian" and became a landmark piece of Americana with its nostalgic view of life, love, and music in a small Midwestern town. Willson, who was often referred to as the quintessential "music man," directed as many as 17 musical radio programs per week from 1929 to 1932. After taking up residence in Hollywood in 1937 to direct NBC's musical activities, he wrote a symphony and composed "Nocturne" and "The Jervis Bay" for orchestra, the "O. O. McIntyre Suite" for piano, and "Song of Steel" for voice. Willson also helped Charlie Chaplin arrange and compose the score for *The Great Dictator* (1940) and wrote the score for *The Little Foxes* (1941). After serving as a major in the music division of the U.S. Armed Forces Radio Service during World War II, Willson returned to radio and began honing his skills as a wit and comedian, although critics were not amused by his homespun humour. In 1949 he became

the host of his own televised musical variety show, the "Meredith Willson Show," but it was for his musical comedies, including *The Music Man* and *The Unsinkable Molly Brown* (1960), and for his song "May the Good Lord Bless and Keep You" that he was renowned. Willson was also the composer of such popular songs as "You and I," "Two in Love," "Iowa," and "I See the Moon" and the author of three books: *And There I Stood With My Piccolo, Eggs I Have Laid,* and *Who Did What to Fedalia?*

Wilson, Jackie, U.S. singer (b. June 9, 1934, Detroit, Mich.—d. Jan. 21, 1984, Mount Holly, N.J.), had a remarkable singing range that, combined with his electric stage acrobatics, made him one of black America's most popular vocalists with a string of pop and soul hits that included "Lonely Teardrops," "Whispers," and "(Your Love Keeps Lifting Me) Higher and Higher." Though he was a Golden Gloves welterweight champion in his youth, Wilson was persuaded by his mother to abandon boxing. He adapted his fancy footwork in the ring to the stage when he became the lead singer for the Dominoes in 1953. His flamboyant interpretation of the song "St. Therese of the Roses" was instrumental in restoring the Dominoes to their previous popularity, but Wilson used his success to strike out as a solo artist in 1957. Wilson's first solo effort, "Reet Petite," was penned by the then struggling songwriter Berry Gordy, Jr. (later founder of Motown Records), and was followed by a string of hits, notably "Lonely Teardrops," "Talk that Talk," and "You Better Know It," all of which made him a star in nightclubs. In the 1960s he scored several other successes on the rhythm and blues charts with "Doggin' Around," "Night," "Whispers," and "Higher and Higher." During the 1970s Wilson became a member of Dick Clark's Good Ol' Rock'n'Roll revue and, while performing on stage in 1975, he collapsed following an apparent heart attack. The rhythm and blues pioneer remained semicomatose until his death.

Wilson, Peter Cecil, British art auctioneer (b. March 8, 1913, Gargrave, Yorkshire, England—d. June 3, 1984, Paris, France), as the visionary chairman of Sotheby's from 1958 to 1980, built the firm, which initially specialized largely in books and manuscripts, with a turnover of around £3 million in the mid-1950s, into a fine art auction house with an international reputation. Sotheby's opened branches throughout the world, boasted a turnover of some £235 million, and employed a staff of 1,900. Wilson's business acumen and determination prompted him to recognize the importance of the U.S. market. The firm's early expansion into the fine art field was bolstered by its acquisition in 1964 of the leading New York auction house, Parke Bernet. Wilson was educated at the University of Oxford and wrote for *The Connoisseur* before joining Sotheby's in 1936. By 1938 he was a partner and, on his return to the firm in 1946 after service with military intelligence during World War II, he took control of the department dealing in works of art. In 1954 he moved to the picture department and oversaw Sotheby's consultation on the sale of the collection of King Farouk of Egypt, though not as auctioneers. He also negotiated the sale of the Goldschmidt collection of Impressionist paintings, which was his first major triumph after he became chairman, with record prices including £220,000 for a Manet. The success of the auction was attributed to Wilson's flair for publicizing the event; this and his introduction of a variable rate of commission were among the innovations that helped Sotheby's to attract leading buyers and sellers. In 1965, after the takeover of Parke Bernet, he was first to use television satellite links between London and New York, extending this to five cities for a simultaneous auction in 1967. By 1978, when the Robert von Hirsch collection went for over £18 million, Sotheby's had outstripped its rivals, though Wilson's dominant position in the management of the firm left it dangerously

unbalanced on his retirement to the south of France in 1980.

Yadin, Yigael, Israeli Army officer, politician, and archaeologist (b. March 21, 1917, Jerusalem, Palestine—d. June 28, 1984, Israel), was chief of operations and acting commandant of the Israeli Army during the war with the Arab states in 1948 and deputy prime minister (1977–81), as leader of the Democratic Movement for Change (DMC), in the coalition that followed the Likud victory in the 1977 elections. But Yadin's most lasting fame was probably as an archaeologist; he was internationally renowned for his work on the Dead Sea Scrolls and then for the excavation of the fortress of Masada, where a small band of Jewish Zealots, besieged by a Roman army some 15,000 strong in AD 70–73, had committed suicide rather than surrender. Yadin joined the Haganah defense force in 1933, was effectively in command of the Israeli Army during the 1948 war, and was then made chief of staff. He resigned in 1952 over cuts in the defense budget and pursued an academic career, becoming professor of archaeology at the Hebrew University in 1963. Yadin secured some of the scrolls for Israel when they were sold and ex-

cavated a number of important sites, including Masada, which he described in *Masada: Herod's Fortress and the Zealots' Last Stand* (1966), one of his many books. After the 1973 Yom Kippur War he formed the DMC, which attracted a protest following from other political groups. In 1977 it won 15 of the 120 seats in the Knesset (parliament). He disagreed with Prime Minister Menachem Begin on Jewish settlement on the West Bank, and when eventually he joined Begin's government, this difference made the association a difficult one. His party lost ground and was eventually reduced to only three seats, so in 1981 Yadin did not stand for reelection.

Zakharov, Rostislav Vladimirovich, Soviet choreographer (b. Sept. 7, 1907, Astrakhan, Russia—d. January 1984), was head of the faculty of choreography at the Moscow State Institute of Theatre Arts and played a major role in the development of Soviet ballet during the 1930s and 1940s. He studied as a dancer and appeared with a ballet company in Kharkov before specializing in choreography, which he studied under Serge Radlov in Leningrad. Zakharov joined the Kirov Theatre in 1932 and four years later moved to Moscow, where he produced *The Prisoner of the Caucasus, Taras Bulba, Cinderella,* and *The Bronze Horseman* between 1938 and 1949. His work with the Bolshoi Ballet was greatly admired when the troupe visited Britain in 1956 and 1963. Zakharov particularly influenced the career of the ballerina Galina Ulanova, whose talent flowered under his direction, and he was also an outstanding choreographer of roles for male dancers. He was the author of books on choreography, twice awarded the Stalin Prize, and made a People's Artist of the Russian Soviet Federated Socialist Republic.

Agriculture and Food Supplies

Ample agricultural and food production in many parts of the world in 1984 contrasted with a continuing food crisis in Africa brought on by drought and civil and military conflicts. The tenth anniversary of the 1974 World Food Conference was an occasion for assessing substantial progress in, but also for acknowledging the persistent obstacles to, fulfilling its promise to end world hunger. It was also a year of preparation for dealing with surpluses generated by agricultural policies in both the European Communities (EC) and the U.S.

Production. World agricultural and food production increased about 4% in 1984, and per capita output rose about 2%, according to preliminary estimates of the U.S. Department of Agriculture's Economic Research Service. Developed-country agricultural output increased about 9%, largely because of the U.S. recovery from the severe 1983 drought and a bumper harvest in Western Europe. Among the centrally planned economies China maintained the large production gains made in 1983, and output was much improved in Eastern Europe; however, production fell in the Soviet Union.

In the less developed countries aggregate food production rose about 3%, and per capita output approximated the average rate of annual increase for the last decade of about 0.6%. Production declined in South Asia because of poor weather in Bangladesh, but all other regions made gains. Even in sub-Saharan Africa aggregate food production may have recovered a little from the depressed 1983 level, barely reversing the decline in per capita food production that had caused output per person to be below that in the mid-1970s.

Nevertheless, a large number of countries in sub-Saharan Africa were afflicted by dry weather during 1984, the second consecutive year of severe drought for many and the third for some. The director general of the UN Food and Agriculture Organization (FAO) in November termed the food situation of those countries tragic, saw little likelihood of improvement in the immediate future, and foresaw further deterioration during 1985. By the year's end the FAO had identified 21 countries facing exceptional food supply problems during 1984–85, 15 of which were experiencing severe difficulties before the poor 1984 harvests.

Food aid donors began new relief efforts, or intensified those already under way, in a difficult political atmosphere complicated by armed struggles in some countries and by hostile political relationships between some aid recipients and donors. In early December the FAO provisionally estimated food aid requirements of the 21 countries to be 5.2 million tons, about 1.8 million tons more than in 1984.

Conditions were most severe and widespread in eastern Africa. Ethiopia's main harvest late in the year was disastrous, down 80% from normal in some districts. People flooded into feeding camps, and thousands of deaths caused directly or indirectly by hunger were being reported. The Ethiopian government estimated that at least seven million people were at risk of starvation.

Relieving famine would be challenging enough in a country of Ethiopia's large size and rugged terrain, but the problem was compounded by civil warfare. Two of the districts worst affected by famine—Tigre and Eritrea—were ones in which armed separatists had been operating for many years. Ethiopia asked help to resettle half a million people, most living in contested areas. Some aid donors uncomfortable with the regime's Marxist character, including the U.S., were uneasy about the proposal's possible political motivation.

In Sudan the sorghum harvest was expected to be only

Table I. Selected Indexes of World Agricultural and Food Production
1976–78 average = 100

Region or country	Total agricultural production						Total food production						Per capita food production					
	1979	1980	1981	1982	1983	1984¹	1979	1980	1981	1982	1983	1984¹	1979	1980	1981	1982	1983	1984¹
Developed countries	107	105	109	110	102	111	107	105	109	111	103	112	106	103	106	107	99	106
United States	109	102	115	115	93	110	110	103	114	116	95	111	108	100	110	110	89	103
Canada	98	103	113	119	114	109	97	103	113	119	114	109	95	99	108	113	107	101
Western Europe	108	112	110	113	110	117	108	112	110	113	110	117	107	111	108	111	108	115
EC	109	113	112	114	111	117	109	113	112	114	111	117	108	112	111	113	109	115
Japan	101	90	92	94	94	100	101	91	92	95	95	100	100	88	89	91	90	95
Oceania	105	98	106	97	115	111	105	96	104	94	115	109	103	93	100	89	107	100
South Africa	102	107	120	107	93	101	101	106	121	107	92	100	96	99	110	95	79	84
Centrally planned economies	104	102	103	110	115	117	104	102	102	109	114	115	102	98	98	103	106	107
U.S.S.R.	98	95	92	98	102	101	97	95	91	97	103	101	95	92	88	93	98	95
Eastern Europe	103	97	101	104	103	109	103	97	101	104	102	109	101	95	99	101	99	105
China²	118	120	126	140	151	152	119	120	125	137	146	148	116	116	119	128	136	136
Less developed countries	104	107	112	113	115	119	104	107	112	113	116	119	99	99	102	100	100	101
East Asia³	107	109	116	118	122	124	106	109	117	119	123	125	102	102	107	106	108	108
Indonesia	110	120	132	128	137	140	109	120	132	130	138	141	104	111	120	115	120	120
South Korea	103	91	97	102	104	109	103	92	99	103	105	110	100	88	92	95	96	99
Malaysia	113	118	121	130	125	132	119	126	131	143	136	143	113	117	119	127	118	121
Philippines	104	108	114	112	112	110	104	108	113	111	111	109	98	100	102	97	95	92
Thailand	103	111	118	119	130	128	100	110	118	118	130	127	96	102	108	105	114	109
South Asia	100	103	110	108	120	120	99	102	110	108	122	121	95	96	101	96	107	103
Bangladesh	104	110	110	115	118	114	104	112	112	117	121	117	97	102	99	100	100	94
India	99	102	110	107	122	121	98	101	110	107	123	122	93	95	101	95	108	105
Pakistan	112	113	122	123	121	124	108	109	119	118	124	121	102	100	105	101	103	98
West Asia	102	103	103	109	110	114	103	104	104	111	110	114	97	96	93	96	93	94
Iran	99	88	86	85	88	88	100	89	86	86	89	88	93	81	76	73	74	71
Turkey	104	105	108	115	114	118	106	107	112	119	117	120	101	99	101	105	101	102
Sub-Saharan Africa⁴	105	108	111	112	108	114	106	108	112	113	108	113	100	99	100	98	91	92
Ethiopia	120	110	111	108	110	102	125	111	112	109	111	103	122	109	109	104	104	94
Nigeria	107	113	112	114	101	114	108	113	113	115	101	114	100	102	99	97	82	90
North Africa	105	110	105	116	110	116	104	109	104	117	111	117	98	100	92	101	93	95
Morocco	105	107	86	111	101	105	105	108	86	112	101	105	99	98	76	96	84	86
Egypt	107	111	112	114	116	118	105	109	111	115	118	121	99	99	98	99	99	99
Latin America	107	110	116	115	114	120	106	110	115	116	114	121	101	103	105	103	99	103
Argentina	110	99	108	116	111	118	111	100	112	118	114	121	107	95	104	108	103	107
Brazil	107	119	124	118	122	130	103	117	118	118	117	127	98	109	107	105	101	107
Colombia	114	120	121	121	119	121	114	120	121	120	122	122	109	113	111	110	106	105
Mexico	105	107	115	107	110	111	106	107	116	110	112	113	100	99	105	97	96	94
Venezuela	106	112	110	118	119	126	107	113	110	120	121	128	98	101	96	101	98	102
World	105	104	108	111	110	115	105	104	108	111	110	115	102	99	101	102	100	102

¹Preliminary. ²Represents about two-thirds of all field crops (includes all major field crops) but excludes livestock products. ³Excludes Japan. ⁴Excludes South Africa.
Source: USDA, Economic Research Service, International Economic Division, December 1984.

two-thirds and wheat less than half of the normal amounts. Sudan's foreign exchange reserves were very low, and in 1985 the country would have to rely upon food aid to meet its increased import requirements. Kenya's main harvest was estimated to be 40% smaller than in 1983. The threat of famine there was much less severe because of existing food aid commitments, the country's greater capacity to finance commercial imports, and a better developed logistical system for handling both the importation and internal distribution of food. Poor crops were also harvested in Burundi and Rwanda, and supplies remained low in Somalia and Tanzania.

In southern Africa the hardest hit countries were Angola, Botswana, Lesotho, Mozambique, Zambia, and Zimbabwe. Food supplies were considered by the FAO to be precarious in Mozambique, where struggles with insurgents hampered food distribution and seeds for 1985 crops were scarce.

Although harvests in the coastal countries of West Africa were much larger in 1984 because of rains that relieved the severe drought of 1983, many of the nations in the interior of West Africa once again faced serious problems. This was particularly true in the north, where harvests were likely to be smaller than the dismal 1983 crops. The prospects were worst in Chad, Mali, Mauritania, and Niger. Relief efforts were complicated by the need to move supplies through ports with limited handling capacity in neighbouring countries, some of which had been restricting transit of food, in order to reach the landlocked nations. (*See* WORLD AFFAIRS [Africa South of the Sahara]: *African Affairs:* Special Report.)

GRAINS. World wheat production in 1984–85 was expected to record another strong increase. EC wheat output was estimated to rise 25%, increasing pressure to boost exports. U.S. output rose but was still below previous highs, while the other leading exporting countries—Canada, Australia, and Argentina—all experienced significant declines.

The EC was said to have voluntarily limited its commercial exports of soft wheat and flour in 1983 and 1984 to offset advantages gained from its use of export subsidies. Because the strong U.S. dollar made products of that country expensive in terms of the currencies of importing nations, the EC was able to lower its export restitutions (subsidies) from about $40–$50 per ton to below $10. The restitution to EC exporters makes up for the difference between the EC's usually much higher internal prices and world trade prices.

Among importers Eastern Europe, China, and India recorded moderate gains in wheat output and were expected to increase consumption roughly in line with the increases. China had doubled its wheat production over the past decade and was the world's largest producer of wheat in 1983–84, exceeding both the U.S.S.R. and the U.S. Soviet wheat production fell for the second year in a row to an estimated 75 million tons, the lowest since 1975 and 45 million tons below the record 1978 crop. Its wheat output over the past four years had averaged only 80 million tons. Aggregate wheat production in the rest of the world might have increased slightly.

Chinese grain supplies were again so ample, thanks to good crops, that China was expected to export a million tons of corn. That and limited storage facilities appeared to influence China's failure, for the second straight year, to import the amount of wheat specified under the U.S.-China grain agreement. Two major U.S. grain trading organizations, the National Grain Trade Council and the Terminal Elevator Grain Merchants Association, voiced concern that new U.S. textile import regulations "will be paid for in reduced U.S. agricultural exports at the expense of American farmers." They claimed that China's past linkage of grain purchases to U.S. restrictions on textile imports might have cost as much as $500 million in lost sales in 1983–84. Previously, textile components produced

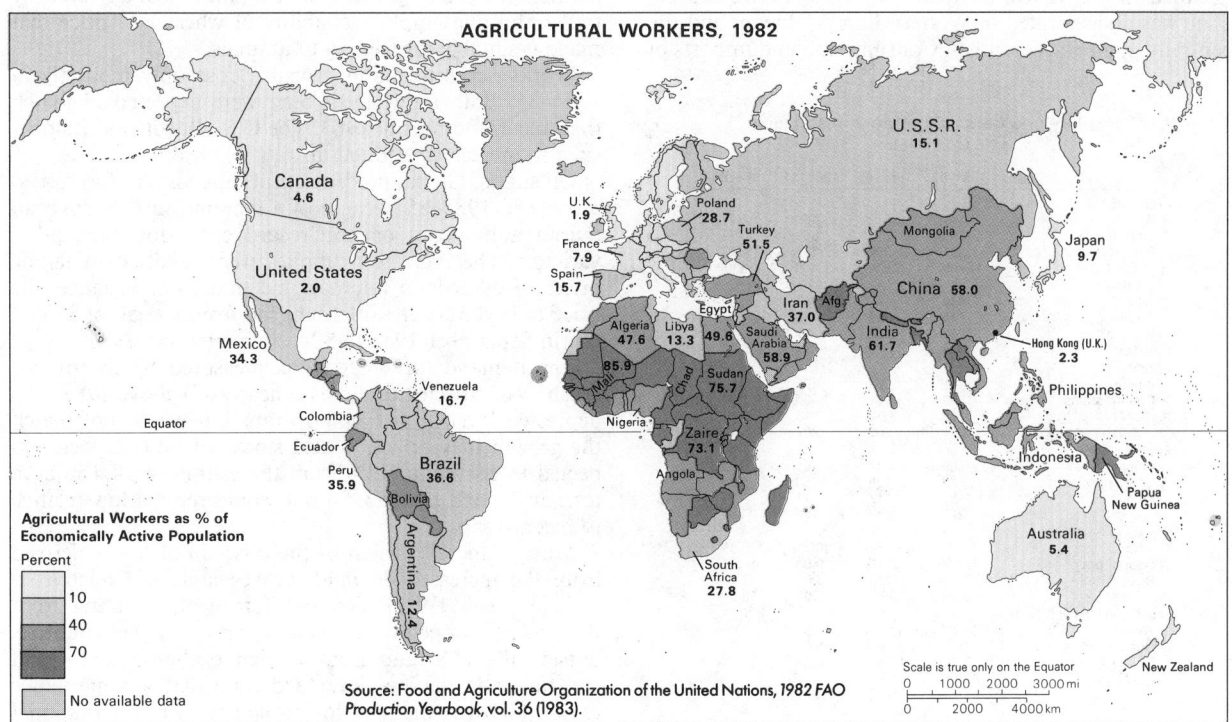

AGRICULTURAL WORKERS, 1982

Source: Food and Agriculture Organization of the United Nations, *1982 FAO Production Yearbook,* vol. 36 (1983).

The economically active population includes all workers producing goods and services: paid, unpaid, self-employed; seasonal, part-time, full-time; active or unemployed. Agricultural workers, as defined by the FAO, include owners of farms, paid agricultural workers, and unpaid workers on family farms. FAO data refer to commercial, subsistence, and mixed farming.

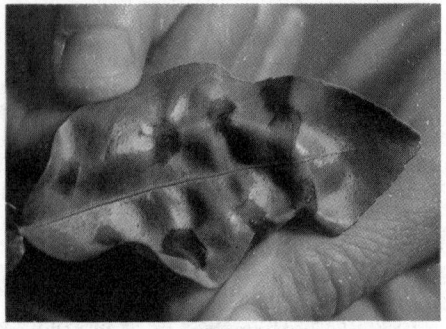

In the fall Florida's citrus industry was hit hard by citrus canker, a virulent disease that first appeared as spotted leaves (above) and quickly spread to destroy the tree. In an attempt to control the spread of the disease, state workers torched seedlings at several nurseries, including Ward's Nursery (left) in Avon Park.

PHOTOGRAPHS, DOUG CAVANAH/TAMPA TRIBUNE

in one country—as in China—that were sewn together in a second country were considered to be "substantially transformed" there and were thus counted against the second country's U.S. import quota. Now such products would be counted against the U.S. quota of the country that produced the original components, thus substantially reducing the exports of China. The U.S.-China grain agreement was scheduled to expire at the end of 1984, and its renewal was uncertain.

Soviet wheat imports were forecast to rise 25% to 26 million tons and to be almost entirely responsible for the modest increase forecast for world wheat trade in 1984–85. Gains in wheat exports by Australia and the U.S. were expected to be nearly matched by the EC, while Canada and Argentina would lose market shares.

Although the rate of growth in total world grain imports declined in the 1980s, compared with the 1970s, the decline was concentrated in Western Europe, Japan, and the centrally planned economies. Consumption and imports of

wheat and coarse grains in the other importing nations—mostly the less developed countries—at least matched the rates during the 1970s and possibly were accelerating.

World coarse grain production climbed sharply in 1984–85, based on recovery in U.S. output, which had been cut almost in half by drought and production control programs in 1983–84, and also on substantially larger crops in Western Europe and South Africa. The U.S.S.R. recorded the largest decline in production—the result of hot, dry weather—and was expected to cut its use of coarse grains. Nevertheless, a strong recovery in world utilization of coarse grains was expected, led by greater feed grain availability in the U.S. A strong increase in world trade in coarse grains was likely in 1984–85, led by the U.S. and Western Europe. The U.S. was expected to account for nearly all of the rise in world stocks of coarse grains. The demand for coarse grains was being inhibited, however, by the continuing ample availability of wheat at a price that made it suitable for feeding to animals.

World rice production probably rose only modestly in 1984–85. Both India and China were expected to match their record outputs of 1983. The U.S., Brazil, and Indonesia also increased production.

Oilseeds. Global production of oilseeds was forecast to recover in 1984–85 because of a rebound in U.S. soybean output and record or near-record crops for most other varieties. The increased supplies were reflected in falling prices of oilseeds in international trade. For instance, the price of soybeans at Rotterdam fell from a peak of $350 a ton in September 1983 to $245 in September 1984.

The demand for oilseeds, as measured by the oilseed crush, was expected to increase nearly 7% above 1983–84's depressed level of 141 million tons but would not match the growth in supplies. World stocks of oilseeds were expected to rise about 13% from the estimated 14.4 million tons at the end of 1983–84 but would remain low relative to recent years.

Most of the expansion of the oilseed crush was derived from the increased demand for vegetable oils relative to protein meals. Weak demand for meat, resulting from the slowness of economic recovery in developed countries outside the U.S. and from foreign exchange and credit constraints in the less developed countries, was the major reason for weak demand for protein meal in international trade. Consumption of nearly all of the major protein meals was expected to increase in 1984–85, but meal supplies were rising more rapidly as a result of greater crushing of

Table II. World Cereal Supply and Distribution
In 000,000 metric tons

	1981–82	1982–83	1983–84	1984–85[1]
Production				
Wheat	449	479	489	506
Coarse grains	769	779	689	789
Rice, milled	281	286	307	313
Total	1,499	1,544	1,485	1,608
Utilization				
Wheat	442	467	485	502
Coarse grains	740	753	759	772
Rice, milled	282	290	307	311
Total	1,464	1,510	1,551	1,585
Exports				
Wheat	101	99	103	106
Coarse grains	98	91	91	100
Rice, milled	12	12	13	12
Total	211	202	207	218
Ending stocks[2]				
Wheat	85	97	101	105
Coarse grains	112	138	68	86
Rice, milled	21	17	17	19
Total	219	252	186	210
Stocks as % of utilization				
Wheat	19.3%	20.7%	20.9%	20.8%
Coarse grains	15.2%	18.4%	9.0%	11.2%
Rice, milled	7.5%	5.9%	5.6%	6.1%
Total	15.0%	16.7%	12.0%	13.2%
Stocks held by U.S. in %				
Wheat	36.9%	42.5%	37.5%	35.9%
Coarse grains	60.7%	70.5%	46.2%	53.5%
Rice, milled	7.5%	13.4%	8.7%	11.1%
Total	46.3%	55.9%	39.2%	40.1%

[1] Forecast.
[2] Does not include estimates of total Chinese or Soviet stocks but is adjusted for estimated changes in Soviet stocks.
Source: USDA, Foreign Agricultural Service, November 1984.

Table III. World Production of Oilseeds and Products
In 000,000 metric tons

	1982–83	1983–84[1]	1984–85[2]
World oilseed production	178.8	166.4	184.9
Soybeans	93.3	81.9	90.2
Cottonseed	27.3	26.8	32.7
Peanuts	17.1	18.7	19.2
Sunflower seed	16.5	15.5	17.2
Rapeseed	14.8	14.3	15.9
Flaxseed	2.6	2.2	2.4
Copra	4.5	4.1	4.6
Palm kernels	1.8	2.0	2.1
Selected Northern Hemisphere crops			
U.S. soybeans	59.6	44.5	51.8
Chinese soybeans	9.0	9.8	10.0
U.S. sunflower seed	2.4	1.5	1.7
U.S.S.R. sunflower seed	5.3	5.0	5.1
U.S. cottonseed	4.3	2.8	4.8
U.S.S.R. cottonseed	5.0	4.6	5.0
Chinese cottonseed	7.2	9.3	11.0
Canadian rapeseed	2.2	2.6	3.1
Chinese rapeseed	5.7	4.3	4.0
Indian rapeseed	2.5	2.6	2.7
U.S. peanuts	1.6	1.5	2.0
Chinese peanuts	3.9	4.0	4.0
Indian peanuts	5.6	7.3	6.5
Selected Southern Hemisphere crops			
Argentine soybeans	4.0	6.2	6.0
Brazilian soybeans	14.8	15.4	15.7
Argentine sunflower seed	2.2	2.2	2.7
World production[3]			
Total fats and oils	57.3	56.4	59.4
Edible vegetable oils	42.3	41.3	44.4
Animal fats	13.2	13.2	13.0
Industrial and marine oils	1.8	1.9	1.9
High-protein meals[4]	95.9	91.6	97.1

[1] Preliminary.
[2] Forecast.
[3] Processing potential from crops in year indicated.
[4] Converted, based on product's protein content, to weight equivalent to soybeans of 44% protein content.
Source: USDA, Foreign Agricultural Service, November 1983 and November 1984.

Table IV. Livestock Numbers and Meat Production in Major Producing Countries[1]
In 000,000 head and 000,000 metric tons (carcass weight)

Region and country	1983	1984	1983	1984
	Cattle		Beef and veal	
World total	946.5	948.0	41.16	41.76
Canada	11.4	11.1	1.01	1.00
United States	114.0	112.1	10.75	10.76
Mexico	33.9	33.9	1.23	1.32
Argentina	58.3	58.4	2.44	2.52
Brazil	93.3	93.6	2.40	2.40
Uruguay	9.5	9.8	0.41	0.36
Western Europe	93.5	92.5	8.00	8.44
Eastern Europe	37.8	37.9	2.43	2.46
U.S.S.R.	119.4	121.0	7.00	7.20
Australia	21.8	22.5	1.39	1.27
India	248.7	249.7	0.30	0.30
	Hogs		Pork	
World total	705.9	700.2	50.81	50.81
Canada	10.4	10.4	0.85	0.86
United States	55.8	54.3	6.89	6.63
Mexico	15.8	15.0	1.20	1.15
Western Europe	105.0	102.5	12.17	12.23
U.S.S.R.	78.5	79.5	5.80	6.00
Japan	10.4	10.5	1.43	1.46
China	298.5	296.8	13.16	13.21
	Poultry		Poultry meat	
World total	...	...	23.35	23.85
United States	...	...	7.19	7.42
Brazil	...	...	1.58	1.49
EC	...	...	4.31	4.30
U.S.S.R.	...	...	2.60	2.70
Japan	...	...	1.27	1.33
	Sheep		Sheep, goat meat	
World total	667.7	670.7	4.53	4.60
			All meat	
Total	...	...	119.84	121.02

[1] Preliminary livestock numbers at year's end. Consists of 47 countries for beef and veal, 38 for pork, 42 for poultry meat, and 38 for sheep and goat meat; roughly the same coverage for animal numbers. Includes nearly all European producers, the most significant in the Western Hemisphere, and scattered coverage elsewhere.
Source: USDA, Foreign Agricultural Service, October 1984.

oilseeds to meet the demand for vegetable oils. Thus stocks of oilseed meals were likely to increase in 1984–85. The price of soybean meal (Rotterdam) fell steadily from the peak in recent years of $279 a ton in August 1983 to a low of $170–$180 in the fall of 1984, the lowest since 1977.

Although prices of edible vegetable oils were lower than in 1983–84, supplies remained relatively tight because of low carry-in oil stocks and the restraining influence of the weak demand for meals upon the crushing of oilseeds for oil. Thus vegetable oil prices were expected to remain above the levels of most recent years. Soybean oil prices at Rotterdam rose from a little under $400 a ton in the early months of 1983 to $914 per ton in May 1984 but fell to around $680–$695 a ton in the fall of 1984, partly because of competition from recovered Malaysian palm oil production. World output of palm oil had been growing around 8% annually since 1979, with Malaysia and Indonesia expanding production the most rapidly, Latin America only a little, and Africa hardly at all. As of 1984 palm oil accounted for about 14% of world consumption of vegetable and marine oils.

MEAT AND LIVESTOCK. Generally higher feed costs and weak demand for meat because of slow economic growth outside the U.S. were expected to cause growth in meat production in major producing countries to fall in 1984 below the 2% increase achieved in 1983. Most of the rise in 1984 output of beef and veal was accounted for by larger EC, Argentine, and Soviet production that offset declines in Oceania. U.S. beef and veal production probably about matched that in 1983, but cattle inventories fell. Soviet feed and forage supplies were nearly as ample as in 1983, and beef production continued to advance.

New incentives to the culling of EC dairy herds aimed at reducing milk production were largely responsible for a large increase in the slaughter of beef cattle that was likely to be maintained well into 1985. The resulting large EC purchases of meat for intervention stocks provided the stimulus for potentially much larger subsidized EC exports of beef to world markets. Traditional beef exporters, especially Australia and Argentina, were not pleased by the transformation of the EC from a major beef importer to probably the world's largest beef exporter in 1984.

A 10% decline in beef production in Oceania was accompanied by the beginning of a slow expansion in the region's cattle inventories. Strong wool prices relative to beef led some farmers to switch from cattle to sheep raising in Australia. Argentine cattle inventories continued to expand, but little immediate potential was seen for increased beef exports because domestic meat consumption was expanding more rapidly than production. In Brazil, however, both cattle inventories and beef exports were expanding.

World pork production was expected to be little changed from 1984. Lower U.S. and Eastern European output was about matched by gains in the U.S.S.R., Japan, and Canada. The sharp rise in feed prices in 1983 had led in the U.S. to increased culling of breeding hogs, but some rebuilding of hog inventories appeared under way.

World production of poultry meat continued to grow at about 2% annually in 1984. The U.S. was responsible for most of the increase, as its strong economic recovery and smaller supplies of pork and beef strengthened the demand for poultry. Poultry output was also expanding in the U.S.S.R.

High prices or short supplies of feed, together with weak demand for meat in many countries where the economic recovery had not spread rapidly, retarded poultry production. Brazil and France, major exporters of poultry meat to the previously rapidly growing Middle Eastern import markets, were facing reduced demand. Some major importers there, such as Saudi Arabia, were increasing their domestic output of poultry. Thailand joined Brazil as major competition to the U.S. in the Japanese poultry meat import market.

DAIRY PRODUCTS. World production of milk from cows was expected to decline in 1984, the first drop in many

Table V. World Production and Stocks of Dairy Products[1]

Region	Production of cow milk 1982	1983	1984[2]
	In 000,000 metric tons		
North America	76.8	78.4	76.5
United States	61.6	63.5	61.7
South America	19.1	19.0	18.9
Brazil	10.1	10.7	10.5
Western Europe	131.0	135.0	132.6
EC	108.2	111.8	109.2
France	27.4	27.9	27.6
West Germany	25.5	26.9	26.1
Italy	10.8	10.6	10.7
Netherlands, The	12.7	13.2	12.8
United Kingdom	16.7	17.3	16.1
Other Western Europe	22.8	23.2	23.4
Eastern Europe	39.6	41.6	42.6
Poland	15.3	16.1	16.8
U.S.S.R.	91.0	96.5	97.0
India	14.7	16.0	16.3
Australia/New Zealand[3]	12.2	12.6	13.7
Japan/South Africa	9.2	9.6	9.7
Total	393.6	408.6	407.3

Product/Region	Production 1983	1984[2]	Year-end stocks 1983	1984[2]
	In 000 metric tons			
Butter	6,826	6,712	1,450	1,691
EC	2,262	2,076	984	1,219
U.S.	589	520	227	181
Cheese	9,075	9,183	1,564	1,510
EC	3,602	3,752	598	611
U.S.	2,186	2,125	574	522
Nonfat dry milk	4,932	4,593	1,971	1,717
EC	2,485	2,153	935	731
U.S.	680	545	633	590

[1] Based on 38 major producing countries.
[2] Preliminary.
[3] Year ending June 30 for Australia and May 31 for New Zealand.
Source: USDA, Foreign Agricultural Service, December 1984.

years, as measures to control costly dairy surpluses in the EC and the U.S. offset sharp gains in output in Oceania. The resulting decreased availability of fluid milk for manufacture tended to reduce the output of dairy products. Nevertheless, continued large dairy surpluses in, and intense competition among, dairy-exporting countries resulted in a further downward slide in the prices of internationally traded dairy products and in an apparent breakdown of the International Dairy Agreement (IDA) under the General Agreement on Tariffs and Trade (GATT). World trade in dairy products expanded as the result of the lower prices and of the increased shipments of dairy products as food aid.

The EC's new five-year program designed to control milk production took hold rapidly and appeared to be resulting in the culling of one million more cows than normal

from the EC dairy herd for slaughter during April 1984 to March 1985. A substantial levy was charged on deliveries to dairies of fluid milk that exceeded the assigned quotas. The EC achieved a strong reduction in its stocks of nonfat dry milk (NFDM), partly because strong demand for cheese diverted milk away from the production of NFDM and also because of the continued heavy use of surplus liquid skim milk and NFDM for animal feed.

EC stocks of butter continued to grow rapidly despite an 8% decline in butter production in 1984. To reduce the surplus the EC again authorized the domestic distribution of 200,000 tons of "Christmas butter" at greatly reduced prices and the subsidized sale to the Soviet Union of an equal amount, effective November 1984, at $850 per ton. The minimum price permitted under the IDA was $1,200 per ton (f.o.b.).

The U.S. responded by withdrawing from the IDA on December 17; this would appear to give it a freer hand to dispose of its own, although much smaller, dairy surpluses on world markets. The U.S. milk diversion program, together with lower dairy support prices and higher feed prices, contributed to an estimated 3% reduction in the U.S. dairy herd during 1984. The scheduled end of the diversion program on March 31, 1985, could lead to some renewed growth in milk output, although further reductions in support payments were likely to be triggered in April and July 1985.

New Zealand's milk production and dairy herds both expanded in 1984 despite the existence of large stocks of butter and NFDM. The recent devaluation of the New Zealand dollar made that nation's dairy exports more competitive.

SUGAR. The International Sugar Agreement (ISA) that had governed world trade in sugar since 1977 expired at the end of 1984 after negotiators failed to agree upon a new pact with economic provisions. Instead, they created in July an "administrative" ISA whose activities were to be confined to consultative and statistical functions during 1985 and 1986. The major sugar-exporting countries could not agree on minimum market shares for individual exporters or on a basic regulatory mechanism. These countries included members of the ISA (Australia, Brazil, and Cuba) and the EC, a nonmember.

The negotiations were complicated by the competitive desires of exporting countries to rid themselves of large and costly sugar stocks. These large stocks had helped keep the

GRADZA—MAGNUM

This Chinese market operates on supply and demand. Farmers, once they have reached their state-set production quotas, are permitted to sell their products in "free markets." This approach was so successful, and resulted in such dramatic increases in agricultural production, that during 1984 the Chinese government moved toward similar arrangements in industry and commerce.

Table VI. World Production of Centrifugal (Freed from Liquid) Sugar

In 000,000 metric tons raw value

Region	1982–83	1983–84	1984–85[1]
North America	8.3	8.2	8.4
United States	5.1	4.8	4.9
Mexico	3.1	3.2	3.4
Caribbean	9.0	9.9	9.9
Cuba	7.2	8.2	8.2
Central America	1.7	1.7	1.8
South America	14.3	14.5	14.2
Argentina	1.6	1.6	1.5
Brazil	9.3	9.4	8.9
Europe	23.3	19.6	21.0
Western Europe	17.2	13.9	15.1
EC	14.7	11.6	12.8
France	4.8	3.9	4.4
West Germany	3.6	2.7	2.9
Eastern Europe	6.1	5.7	5.9
Poland	2.1	2.0	1.9
U.S.S.R.	7.4	8.7	7.8
Africa and Middle East	9.9	9.0	10.0
South Africa	2.3	1.5	2.4
Turkey	1.9	1.8	1.7
Asia	23.5	20.5	20.4
China	4.1	3.8	3.8
India	9.5	7.0	7.3
Indonesia	1.7	1.8	1.8
Philippines	2.5	2.4	1.9
Thailand	2.3	2.3	2.3
Oceania	4.0	3.4	4.0
Australia	3.5	3.2	3.6
Total	101.3	95.6	97.5

[1] Preliminary.
Source: USDA, Foreign Agricultural Service, November 1984.

ISA indicator price of freely traded sugar in world markets below the ISA floor since late 1981 and were to drive it down to about four cents a pound by the summer of 1984. That was below variable costs (those that fluctuate directly with changes in output) of even the most efficient producers, but it also overstated the impact upon the profitability of sugar production. In 1984 only about 20% of the world sugar trade was carried out in free markets. The remainder was exported at much higher prices under bilateral trade agreements or preferential arrangements.

World sugar production was again expected to increase in 1984–85 and to exceed consumption for the third time in four years. Of the major producers only Brazil reduced output, reacting to low world prices and stagnant domestic sugar consumption. World sugar stocks at the beginning of 1984–85 exceeded two-fifths of the total annual world sugar consumption.

Sugar consumption in the world's industrialized market economies was close to saturation in 1984, at 40–55 kg (88–121 lb) per person per year, and was tending to stagnate or decline. Consumption of high fructose corn syrup—now accounting for about one-third of all usage of caloric sweeteners—continued to rise rapidly, while low-calorie sugar substitutes such as aspartame were becoming more attractive to weight-conscious consumers.

Most of the growth in world sugar consumption was accounted for by less developed countries and the centrally planned economies, where per capita sugar consumption was much lower than in the developed world. However, consumption in those areas was constrained either by slow growth in income or by a shortage of foreign exchange with which to import sugar.

COFFEE. Rising export prices of coffee throughout the first half of 1984 triggered four increases of one million 60-kg (132-lb) bags each in the 1983–84 quota for member exporting countries of the International Coffee Agreement (ICA). The global quota stood at 60.2 million bags, compared with 55.5 million at the end of 1982–83. The rise in prices appeared to result from a forecast reduction in Brazilian and West African coffee output, the low quality of some coffee produced in those regions in 1983–84, and below-quota exports of coffee. Nevertheless, world produc-

tion of green coffee was expected to increase in 1984–85, and stocks were sufficient in most exporting countries to fulfill quotas. Although stocks were unevenly distributed, in total they were estimated to amount to at least 50% of annual coffee consumption at the beginning of 1984–85.

Both importing and exporting members of the ICA were concerned about the sale of coffee by ICA members to nonmember countries. Importing members of the ICA envied sales to nonmembers at prices about half those that were charged to members. Exporting members with burdensome coffee stocks or a pressing need to earn foreign exchange did not enjoy competition among themselves, often in the form of below-cost subsidized sales, that drove down the price of sales to nonmembers. Such sales supported increased coffee consumption in the Middle East, the U.S.S.R., and Eastern Europe. Major Latin-American coffee-exporting countries were exploring the possibility of establishing an adjustable floor price for sales to nonmembers. Some producers outside the region also appeared interested in the idea.

COCOA. World production of cocoa beans was expected to rise sharply in 1984–85, largely because of the recovery from a two-year drought by the Ivory Coast, which accounted for about one-fourth of world output. Production was also up in Brazil, the world's second largest producing country.

Grindings of cocoa beans in 1984 were estimated to exceed production for the second year in a row but to rise less than 1% above the 1,660,000 tons in 1983. Prices of cocoa beans exceeded the lower bound of the International Cocoa Agreement (ICCA) for the first time since July 1980. They climbed to about $1.19 per pound (New York futures, nearest three-month average) in May 1984, fell back

Table VII. World Green Coffee Production

In 000 60-kg bags

Region	1982–83	1983–84[1]	1984–85[2]
North America	18,082	15,344	16,679
Costa Rica	2,300	2,070	2,300
El Salvador	3,000	2,253	2,500
Guatemala	2,530	2,340	2,630
Honduras	1,800	1,550	1,600
Mexico	4,600	4,200	4,300
South America	35,439	47,185	44,035
Brazil	17,750	30,000	27,000
Colombia	13,300	13,000	12,800
Ecuador	1,800	1,380	1,500
Africa	20,912	18,417	20,847
Cameroon	2,100	1,350	2,000
Ethiopia	3,738	3,350	3,000
Ivory Coast	4,510	1,920	5,000
Kenya	1,534	2,123	1,100
Uganda	3,200	3,400	3,500
Zaire	1,354	1,480	1,550
Asia and Oceania	9,391	8,942	10,525
India	2,130	1,550	2,650
Indonesia	4,546	4,747	5,250
Total	83,824	89,888	92,086

[1] Preliminary.
[2] Forecast.
Source: USDA, Foreign Agricultural Service, 1984.

Table VIII. World Cocoa Bean Production

In 000 metric tons

Region	1982–83	1983–84	1984–85[1]
North and Central America	104	96	101
South America	461	415	489
Brazil	339	300	360
Ecuador	55	50	60
Africa	850	861	968
Cameroon	106	108	115
Ghana	178	158	185
Ivory Coast[2]	360	415	450
Nigeria[3]	156	125	160
Asia and Oceania	126	152	183
Malaysia	69	91	120
Total	1,542	1,524	1,741

[1] Forecast.
[2] Includes some cocoa marketed from Ghana.
[3] Includes cocoa marketed through Benin.
Source: USDA, Foreign Agricultural Service, October 1984.

to 97 cents in July, and rebounded to $1.04 in September. Prices had averaged 92 cents per pound in 1983.

The second of two negotiating conferences ended in November 1984 without an agreement on a new draft to replace the ICCA of 1980. A new feature of the 1984 discussions was an EC proposal to rely upon national stocking or stock withdrawal actions by cocoa producers—in addition to ICCA buffer stocks—rather than on export quotas to stabilize cocoa prices. The appropriate band within which cocoa prices should fluctuate also remained in question, with importing countries favouring a lower price bound than was in the current agreement.

In July the Cocoa Council extended the old agreement by one year to September 1985, including the $1.06-$1.46-per-pound price band. Members of the ICCA included 20 exporting and 23 importing countries but did not include the Ivory Coast (the world's largest exporter of cocoa beans) or the U.S. (the largest importer), which continued to oppose membership although both participated as observers at ICCA meetings. Another attempt to draft a new agreement was to be made after February 1985.

COTTON. Cotton production grew much more rapidly outside the U.S. in 1983 than was expected, offsetting the sharp decline in U.S. output. Total output in 1984 was expected to rise rapidly thanks to recovery in U.S. production and strong growth in Asian cotton harvests, most especially in China. Man-made fibre production in 1983 totaled 16.2 million tons, 53% of the total world fibre output, according to the Textile Economics Bureau, Inc. Man-made fibre output had declined to 14.1 million tons in 1982, accounting for 44% of all fibres.

Global use of cotton grew an estimated 1% in 1983–84 to 68.5 million bales (216 kg [480 lb] each) and was expected to accelerate in 1984–85, stimulated by stronger economic growth in many parts of the world. World trade in cotton in 1983–84, at 19.3 million bales, was little changed from the previous year, and only a modest increase was expected for 1984–85. End-of-season world cotton stocks hovered around 25 million bales but could increase sharply during 1984–85. International cotton prices continued to drift downward from their high of about 90.8 cents per pound in August 1983, reaching an average of 73.2 cents per pound in September 1984.

Food and Population. By 1984 a decade had passed since the World Food Conference and, although its goal of eliminating hunger had not been achieved, substantial progress had been made. Total world food production had risen an average of 2.2% annually since 1974, according to the FAO. The rate of growth in world population had slowed from about 1.9% annually to about 1.8%, but this still amounted to about 80 million additional people each

Argentine grain exports in 1984 brought that economically troubled nation significant reserves in foreign currencies—money that was targeted for the domestic economy rather than for payment of the country's huge foreign debt, the world's third largest.
H. VILLABOS—GAMMA/LIAISON

year. Per capita world food output had risen about 0.4% annually.

The approximately 3.3% annual growth in food production of the less developed countries (including China) was more than double that in the developed nations, but their faster population growth—2.1% annually—resulted in an increase in per capita output of about 0.5%. Some regions, including South America, East Asia, Southeast Asia, and China, achieved a higher figure. But per capita food production in sub-Saharan Africa—one of the few areas where the rate of population growth was still increasing—declined over the past decade.

The application of existing yield-increasing technologies and the development of new ones that were based on better understanding of biological processes were largely responsible for the gains in food production over the past decade. The expansion of cropland played a steadily declining role, averaging only about 0.2% annually in the 1980s. Only about one-half of the world's potentially arable land was being cultivated as of 1984, but the uneven distribution of potentially arable land among countries and the cost of developing it favoured the expansion of irrigation; increased use of fertilizers, chemicals, and machinery; improved management; and more intensive cultivation rather than an attempt to cultivate unused land. The gains in productivity, as measured by increased cereal yields, were greatest in the less developed countries of Asia, although the level achieved there was only half that in the developed nations. Progress in the less developed countries of Africa was only one-third that in Asia.

Preliminary estimates derived from the FAO's work on its fifth World Food Survey (to be completed in 1985) indicated that the less developed countries, as a group, increased dietary energy supplies (DES), as measured by the availability of calories per person per day, from an average of 2,140 in 1969–71 to 2,350 in 1979–81. Out of a group of 90 less developed countries previously studied in FAO's

Table IX. World Cotton Production
In 000,000 480-lb bales

Region	1982–83	1983–84	1984–85
Western Hemisphere	17.9	13.9	20.7
United States	12.0	7.8	13.3
Mexico	0.9	1.0	1.3
Brazil	3.0	2.5	3.0
Europe	0.8	0.8	1.1
U.S.S.R.	11.9	12.3	12.5
Africa	5.3	5.5	5.5
Egypt	2.1	1.9	1.8
Sudan	1.0	1.0	1.0
Asia and Oceania[1]	31.5	34.8	41.0
China	16.5	21.3	25.3
India	6.3	5.9	6.2
Pakistan	3.8	2.2	3.7
Turkey	2.2	2.4	2.6
Total	67.4	67.3	80.7

[1] Includes Middle East.
Source: USDA, Foreign Agricultural Service, November 1984.

Table X. Shipments of Food Aid in Cereals
In 000 metric ton grain equivalent

	Average 1979–80, 1981–82	1982–83	1983–84[1]	1984–85[1]
Australia	390	349	429	400
Canada	643	843	850	800
EC	1,355	1,571	1,628	1,580
By members	635	729	759	...
By organization	719	842	869	...
Japan	703	517	445	300
Sweden	104	87	89	80
United States	5,297	5,375	5,650	6,100
Others[2]	498	458	415	590
Total	8,990	9,200	9,506	9,850

[1] Partly estimated.
[2] Includes Argentina, Austria, China, Finland, India, Norway, OPEC Special Fund, Saudi Arabia, Spain, Switzerland, Turkey, and World Food Program, but not necessarily for all years.
Source: FAO, *Food Outlook,* December 1984.

Agriculture: Toward 2000, two-thirds showed improvement in DES.

Increased food imports were responsible for most of the increased per capita food availability in countries where significant gains were made, and they also prevented even further losses in countries where DES declined. Gross imports of food by the less developed countries, as a group, had almost doubled between 1969–71 and 1979–81 to 8% of total food supplies (caloric equivalent). As a result most of the less developed countries had to spend an increasing amount of their export earnings on food imports. Furthermore, debt servicing absorbed a substantial and increasing share of export earnings in those countries. These burdens raised questions about the ability of many of them to sustain such imports in the future.

Despite the fact that more people representing a larger proportion of the world's population were eating better in 1984 than at any other time in history, millions of people remained undernourished. The number might well have increased in absolute terms to roughly half a billion people, according to the FAO. Most were in Asia, but their numbers were growing most rapidly in Africa, where they represented a larger proportion of the population. Furthermore, a large proportion of them were young children, the nursing mothers of young children, the very old, and the unemployed. The success in increasing production of food and at the same time the persistence of hunger among these vulnerable groups led to a shift in emphasis from supply-increasing measures to those concerned with distribution and the creation of effective economic demand for food, especially through better employment opportunities, in the food-deficit countries.

The hard core of world hunger was represented in the FAO study of 90 countries by the 27 (total population of 363 million) that experienced declines in their DES between 1969–71 and 1979–81. Most were low-income countries, 15 of which were in Africa. Per capita food production (calorie weighted) in those nations declined by 1% annually over the period, a loss of about 230 cal per day. Food imports compensated for nearly one-third of the losses.

Food Security Arrangements. The attempts to negotiate a comprehensive international wheat agreement to coordinate national grain reserves foundered during the 1970s because of the divergent interests of the major exporting and importing countries, and by 1984 such efforts appeared to have been abandoned. Some movement was made internationally toward the establishment of regional reserves and the pre-positioning of food stocks as initiated by the U.S. in 1984. The International Monetary Fund created a compensatory financing facility in 1981 that was designed to ease the balance of payments problems of food-deficit countries growing out of temporary increases in imports of food caused by crop shortfalls and out of increases in the price of food imports. As of 1984 only five countries had made use of the facility. Its future was to be determined by a review to be completed by May 1985. Although the food-deficit countries continued to be vulnerable to the growing price instability of international grain markets, the adjustments from a food security point of view were less severe than had been anticipated in the early 1970s. The growing instability of international agricultural markets during the past decade reflected the effects of rigid agricultural policies in many countries, accompanied by protectionist trade policies designed to isolate domestic agricultural sectors from outside influences.

The combination of international organizations and ad hoc efforts by donor nations demonstrated the capability of successfully mobilizing emergency food assistance. The African food emergency indicated that the greatest potential for overtaxing that system derived more from man-made civil and military conflicts, which can complicate the relationship between donor and recipient, than from natural disasters. For instance, the World Food Program (WFP) approved 48 emergency operations in 1984 (as of November

AGIP/PICTORIAL PARADE

In the spring French farmers protested against Common Market agricultural price policies that aimed at reducing both subsidies and surpluses. The cow's sign reads "[Agriculture Minister Michel] Rocard has betrayed me."

During recent years of inflation and
high interest rates, economic pressures
continued for U.S. farmers, particularly
for those carrying large debt burdens for
the purchase of equipment, land, and
supplies. Farm failures were numerous,
making auctions of once highly profitable
farms, as at left in Iowa, commonplace in
the U.S. farm belt.
JEFF LOWENTHAL/NEWSWEEK

16), providing 511,750 tons of cereals and 63,450 tons of
other foods at a cost of $187 million. Of these emergencies,
33 were in Africa, 7 in Asia, 3 in the Middle East, and 5
in Latin America. About 56% of these resources were used
to help refugees, displaced persons, and victims of war and
civil disturbances. The remainder aided victims of natural
disasters.

The value of all food aid was about $3 billion in 1981,
roughly double that in 1974. Food aid in cereals, after declining to 5.8 million tons at the height of the 1970s food
crisis, had fluctuated between about 8.5 million and 9.9
million tons since 1975–76. The U.S., supplying almost
60% of all cereals aid in 1983–84, allocated most of it bilaterally. The Food Aid Convention under the International
Wheat Agreement—revised in 1980 and since extended to
June 1986—increased the minimum commitment of aid
donors from 4,250,000 tons of cereals annually to 7.6 million tons.

Contributions in 1984 to the International Emergency
Food Reserve (IEFR) administered by the WFP exceeded the
target of 500,000 tons by about 100,000 tons. The director
general of the FAO in November renewed his proposal
for increasing the target to two million tons, citing the
pressure of the African food emergency upon IEFR regular
resources. The large aid donors preferred to meet increases
in emergency needs by ad hoc contributions to the WFP or,
especially in the case of the U.S., by increased bilateral aid.

Foreign Aid. Official foreign assistance (excluding food
aid) to agriculture in less developed countries by governments and international institutions grew from about $4
billion at the time of the World Food Conference to about
$12.2 billion in 1981, a doubling of resources when ad-
justed for inflation. By 1980 agriculture was receiving about
25% of all such aid. The agricultural sectors in low-income
countries benefited increasingly from such assistance. The
multilateral agencies expanded the resources devoted to
food and agricultural development from 28% in 1973–
74 to about 40% in 1977–78, while national aid agencies
increased agriculture's share from 12 to 16 or 17%.

The total amount of official assistance leveled off in the
early 1980s and probably declined in 1983, in part because
of budgetary restraints in donor countries. The seventh replenishment of the International Development Association
(IDA)—the concessional lending arm of the World Bank—
was reduced to $9 billion for 1985–87. The sixth replen-

ishment of $12 billion was originally intended to cover the
1981–83 period but was "stretched out" to also include
1984. Thus funding availability had remained constant in
nominal terms at an annual average of $3 billion since
1978, although inflation had substantially reduced its real
value. The IDA in the early 1980s allocated 40% of its resources to agriculture, representing 20% of all concessional
assistance to agriculture.

The International Fund for Agricultural Development
(IFAD) grew out of the World Food Conference and was
established with initial resources of $1 billion for the 1978–
80 period, which were replenished with an additional $1.1
billion for 1981–83. The institution represented a coordinated effort by the industrialized nations and newly wealthy
petroleum-exporting countries to assist small farmers in
the least developed countries or in the least developed
sectors of more advanced developing nations. Project commitments had very nearly exhausted these resources by the
end of 1984.

The industrialized countries and petroleum-exporting
nations were unable to agree upon the second replenishment of IFAD. The latter wished to reduce their share (42%
of the 1981–83 replenishment), and Iran did not participate in recent meetings on the subject. The U.S. delayed
appropriating the $90 million balance of its contribution to
the first replenishment until late in 1984 as part of efforts
to limit budget expenditures.

The Consultative Group on International Agricultural
Research (CGIAR), together with the 13 international research centres that it supported, played an important role
in transforming agriculture in many less developed countries. Their success in creating high-yielding varieties of
rice, wheat, and corn was responsible for much of the
rapid increase in productivity and helped turn attention
to the possibilities of future gains from improved management and investment in irrigation facilities and water
control and in fertilizer production and distribution. The
multilateral agencies, governments, and foundations that
provided financing for the CGIAR system increased their
commitments from $20 million in 1972 to a projected
$182 million for 1984.

Agricultural and Trade Policies. After nearly a year of
debate the EC Council of Agricultural Ministers reached
agreement on several important agricultural issues. It introduced limitations on dairy production—an approach

In September a group of farmers met in Chicago at the Board of Trade to protest against low grain prices at a meeting with the directors of the futures exchange.
AP/WIDE WORLD

previously applied only to sugar—and reduced "intervention" (support) prices in nominal terms for a broad range of commodities for the first time. The latter action was still likely to result in a small overall increase in prices paid to most EC farmers in national currencies because of the operation of the complicated EC monetary system. Thus the EC showed little indication that it would soon effectively control surpluses in other agricultural sectors; the disposal of these surpluses had led to conflicts with its trading partners, particularly the U.S.

The rapid growth in costs of agricultural surplus disposal led to an EC budget crisis in 1983 that extended into 1984. It led to action by the EC heads of government to finance the growing expenditures for its common agricultural policy (CAP) by earmarking more of EC value-added taxes for agriculture. Such funding would not be available until 1986, however, and the proposed measures to control agricultural expenditures and supplementary budget expenditures still had to be approved by member nations. Thus more payments for the CAP would have to be delayed, and some budgetary reductions appeared inevitable.

Ironically, the appreciation of the U.S. dollar relative to EC currencies made the EC more solvent and reduced the pressures for reform of the CAP. U.S. commodities became more expensive in terms of foreign national currencies, thus making EC commodities more competitive, both domestically and in third-country markets. The resulting increased exports by the EC and narrowing of the gap between world and EC prices reduced the subsidies that the EC had to pay to its exporters. (*See* WORLD AFFAIRS [Western Europe]: *Western European Affairs:* Sidebar.)

In the U.S. discussions of agricultural policy turned to preparations for replacing existing basic farm legislation when the 1981 Agriculture and Food Act expired on Sept. 30, 1985. Policies that had supported farm prices at above market clearing levels, resulting in substantial government expenditures, were the target of many concerned with the federal government's prospective large budgetary deficits. The U.S. administration argued for pushing U.S. agriculture toward a more "market-oriented" approach that would move U.S. farm prices closer to world trade prices; such a policy would make U.S. agricultural exports more competitive.

Agricultural trade issues figured prominently in preparation work for a new round of multilateral negotiations under the GATT. No timetable was established, but talks could begin as early as 1986 if the major trading countries could agree on an agenda. In November 1982 the first GATT ministerial meeting held since 1972 had met in an atmosphere of increasingly hostile trade confrontations between major exporters, including the U.S., the EC, and Japan. The ministers agreed "to bring agriculture more fully into the multilateral trading system by improving the effectiveness of GATT rules . . . and to seek to improve terms of access to markets and to bring export competition under greater discipline." They established a Committee on Trade in Agriculture that was to examine "all measures affecting trade, market access, and competition and supply in agricultural products, including subsidies and other forms of assistance."

The committee presented its recommendations to the GATT contracting parties at the end of November 1984. The proposals represented a general plan of work for the committee in order for it to better define the agenda for future negotiations over agriculture. The committee recommended the preparation of a description of the measures that adversely affect agricultural trade and the periodic review of policies of GATT members that affect agricultural trade. The measures to be examined included export subsidies and other export aids such as subsidized credits, as well as import measures such as quantitative restrictions, agreements to voluntarily restrain exports, tariffs, and minimum price arrangements.   (RICHARD M. KENNEDY)

See also Gardening.

This article updates the *Macropædia* article The History of AGRICULTURE.

FISHERIES

There was little sign during 1984 that the world's fisheries had adjusted to the "200-mile regime." The 200-mi exclusive economic zone (EEZ), postulated in the Convention on the Law of the Sea in 1982, had first been generally accepted among coastal nations in 1977, but it had become apparent that more than seven years would be needed to bring order out of a fishing free-for-all that had led so many nations to claim the right to control their own fish stocks. However, at least one nation was giving the EEZ credit for improving the state of fish stocks. Norwegian Minister of Fisheries Thor Listau revealed in an interview that capelin stocks were now stable at a satisfactory level

Table XI. Whaling: 1982–83 Season (Antarctic); 1982 Season (Outside the Antarctic)
Number of whales caught

Area and country	Fin whale	Sei/ Bryde's whale	Hump-back whale	Minke whale	Sperm whale	Killer whale	Total	Percentage assigned under quota agreement[1]
Antarctic pelagic (open sea)								
Japan	—	—	—	3,224	—	—	3,224	45.59
U.S.S.R.	—	—	—	3,223	—	—	3,223	45.57
Brazil	—	—	—	—	—	—	—	8.84
Total	—	—	—	6,447	—	—	6,447	100.00
Outside the Antarctic								
Japan	—	482	—	324	439	8	1,253	
U.S.S.R.	—	—	—	—	—	—	165[2]	
Brazil	—	—	—	854	—	—	854	
Peru	—	251	—	—	—	—	251	
Iceland	194	71	—	212	87	6	570	
Spain	150	—	—	—	—	—	150	
Norway	—	—	—	1,963	—	—	1,963	
South Korea	—	—	—	898	—	3	901	
Others	11	—	—	209	—	—	220	
Total	355	804	—	4,460	526	17	6,327	

[1]Minke; Southern Hemisphere only.
[2]Represents gray whales; figure is included in both vertical and horizontal totals.
Source: The Committee for Whaling Statistics, *International Whaling Statistics*.

and that within three to four years the Atlantic-Scandinavian herring stock, virtually wiped out in the late 1960s, would once again support a good 40,000–50,000-metric ton fishery. Control over its EEZ had enabled Norway to stop herring fishing completely until stocks recovered.

The minister also reported on the outstanding success of the country's fish-farming program. Income from trout and salmon farming was expected to exceed 1 billion kroner in 1984, and breeding of cod, turbot, and flatfish also had proved successful. Meanwhile, scrapping subsidies and relocation schemes were being used to tailor the size of the fleet to the size of the fish stock. Such measures seemed to be setting the pattern for the 1980s. The European Communities (EC), now with a common fisheries policy to match the common agricultural policy, continued to work on a "grand plan" to share insufficient fish among a fleet that was admittedly about 50% over capacity.

Few big stern trawlers remained to Britain, West Germany, and France; displaced from their erstwhile hunting grounds in Iceland and the northwestern and northeastern Atlantic, those that had not found employment in offshore oil or been sold abroad had no alternative but the scrapyard. West Germany still had 14 big freezer trawlers, but German-caught fish now supplied only 14% of the home market. Nevertheless, Dutch owners continued to build even bigger stern trawlers around 96 m (315 ft) in length. The secret lay in their great refrigerated-hold capacity, which would enable them to double as refrigerated cargo ships, transporting or fishing as the market demanded. The

Netherlands also continued to build more powerful beam trawlers, although the secretary of state for fisheries went on record to say that the fleet was large enough. Dutch owners had difficulty disposing of secondhand vessels in order to pay for new ones, causing acute problems to at least one shipyard.

Accusations of quota jumping continued to be voiced in Europe, particularly by the law-abiding Scots, and the Danes' demand for a higher percentage of salable catch with their fish-meal landings also aroused Scottish ire. Fears over the effect of Spain's entry into the EC in 1986 were still widespread, despite reassuring articles in the press by Spanish politicians. In an interview with *World Fishing*, Spain's director of fisheries planning revealed that the Spanish fleet had shrunk by 4,300 units since 1982. Even so, its catching power was equal to that of the other EC partners put together, though not all of it was deployed in the northeastern Atlantic. The EC Commission proposed continued catch restrictions on Spain for six years after entry, until the EC fleet could be restricted to match EC fish stocks. On the Spanish side, it was pointed out that after Spain's entry the EC would represent the world's largest fishing group and fish market, with bargaining power that should mean more overseas fishing opportunities in exchange for EC consumer markets.

Spain was one of a number of countries to vote funds for the culture of fish and shellfish. Some $4 million a year for four years would be spent setting up aquaculture plants, with much of the juvenile fish and shellfish production released into the sea for restocking. This concept, which was also finding favour in France and West Germany, had long since been adopted by Japan and by the world's salmon fisheries.

Across the Atlantic, the massive injection of government capital into Canada's big but ailing fish industry had not worked the promised miracle. The newly formed Fishing Products International still had problems, associated with excessive stocks in a slow market and labour difficulties. It was expected that catches of herring and salmon would be poor and that shellfish markets would be affected by imported synthetic crabsticks and even scallop substitutes. An agreement was reached with the U.S.S.R. whereby the latter would be allowed to catch up to 100,000 metric tons annually within Canada's EEZ and would buy $12 million worth of Canadian fish. Exports of Canadian fish were generally higher and cod was plentiful, but the salmon fleet of 4,500 boats was too big, and $100 million was voted to cut it by half.

On the U.S. Pacific coast, Alaskan pollack was still riding high at an estimated 4.5 million tons, 300,000 tons more than in 1983. Another big trawler, the 60-m (200-ft) "Northern Glacier," left the Martinac yard to join the rush for pollack, much of which would end up as *surimi,* now being processed in the U.S. to satisfy a soaring demand for crabsticks and other synthetics. On the east coast, a $30 million plan was proposed to build a fish port at Brooklyn, N.Y., where vessels of up to 60 m could land their catches. Fish exports had risen 29% in 1983, though earnings were down. Not so healthy were the king crab fisheries of Alaska, dropping from a low 1983 catch of 7.7 million kg (17 million lb) to 4.5 million kg (10 million lb) in 1984; demand was also down, and the tanner crab had failed to take off. Tuna imports had doubled, but the U.S. tuna fleet was now half its 1981 level. San Diego (Calif.) cannery shutdowns had resulted in the loss of 5,000 jobs to canneries in Samoa and Puerto Rico.

Conscious of its need to increase fish production and to modernize its fishing industry, China sent delegations to

Table XII. World Fisheries, 1982[1]
In 000 metric tons

Country	Catch		Trade	
	Total	Freshwater	Imports	Exports
Japan	10,775.1	351.0	1,111.6	702.1
U.S.S.R.	9,956.7	993.0	44.1	338.6
China	4,926.7	1,574.5	...	94.0
United States	3,988.3	355.7	1,049.1	404.2
Chile	3,673.0	0.3	[2]	930.6
Peru	3,452.0	15.1	0.3	783.0
Norway	2,499.9	16.5	59.7	697.5
India	2,335.2	913.6	[2]	72.3
South Korea	2,281.3	59.2	...	21.6
Indonesia	2,020.0	510.3	83.5	80.2
Denmark	1,927.1	25.2	282.6	708.1
Thailand	1,920.0	170.0	45.8	395.6
Philippines	1,787.7	529.5	79.1	47.2
North Korea	1,550.0	85.0	81.0	339.5
Mexico	1,506.0	110.4	30.9	49.9
Canada	1,389.3	134.2	89.6	530.6
Spain	1,351.0	28.6	327.9	229.9
Vietnam	1,000.0	200.0	...	11.4
United Kingdom	910.1	2.4	787.5	275.7
Brazil	850.0	202.4	60.2	51.3
Iceland	788.7	0.4	1.3	361.4
France	764.5	2.3	509.0	158.4
Bangladesh	724.8	583.8	[2]	6.8
Malaysia	682.6	20.5	158.1	104.0
Ecuador	636.5	...	[2]	158.4
South Africa	624.3	0.8	38.4	43.9
Poland	604.9	27.3	71.3	100.2
Burma	584.4	153.6	[2]	2.1
Turkey	514.9	24.5	[2]	13.3
Nigeria	512.0	188.6	519.2	0.7
The Netherlands	505.5	4.9	409.5	489.9
Argentina	475.0	15.3	12.6	231.2
Italy	468.6	41.7	402.2	97.1
Morocco	361.7	1.4	[2]	107.7
Pakistan	337.3	68.2	0.2	19.5
West Germany	313.5	23.0	925.4	322.1
Sweden	259.0	12.8	207.0	126.8
Portugal	253.4	0.1	96.2	51.2
Faeroe Islands	248.7	0.9	5.8	91.7
East Germany	235.8	20.6	80.6	...
Romania	235.7	59.7	59.7	...
Tanzania	226.0	190.0	1.0	0.2
Ghana	224.0	43.9	5.9	...
Venezuela	213.4	21.8	27.6	0.5
Senegal	212.9	14.1	11.3	90.8
Other	5,665.3	...	...	...
World	76,772.8	9,390.8[3]	10,225.1[3]	10,597.4[3]

[1]Excludes whaling.
[2]Less than 100 metric tons.
[3]Includes unspecified amounts in Other category.
Source: United Nations Food and Agriculture Organization, *Yearbook of Fishery Statistics,* vol. 54 and 55.

A World Court decision awarding Canada a sizable portion of the rich fishing ground of Georges Bank, east of Cape Cod and south of Nova Scotia, may threaten Canadian fishermen with U.S. protectionist retaliation in the form of higher import duties.

JIM MERRITHEW—PICTURE GROUP

study the Western nations and their methods. To stimulate trade and exchange of information, a fisheries exhibition was organized in Guangzhou (Canton). China hoped to increase its current estimated annual fish production of 5,250,000 metric tons by 12%, with special emphasis on aquaculture. It acquired a new and well-equipped fisheries research vessel, the 56-m (184-ft) "Bei Dou," a gift from the Norwegian government. An agreement was reached with Uruguay to allow Chinese vessels to fish that country's waters. Japan remained the world's leading fishing nation in 1983, with a total production of 12 million metric tons. It was also the biggest importer of seafood, at 1,320,000 tons. Japanese exports of crabsticks had doubled in 1983 to 19,000 tons, 4,000 tons of which went to the U.S.; though other nations were planning to compete, 1984 seemed likely to be an equally good year. Japan's catch of Antarctic krill rose to 32,000 tons, but the Soviets remained the main exploiter of this rich reserve.

The Antarctic waters around the Falkland Islands were found to contain good quantities of squid, which was in ever greater demand. One British trawling company proposed using the Falklands as a base for foreign fishing vessels if the U.K. government would at last consent to claim a 200-mi EEZ around the islands. However, there were also fears that heavy fishing in the area would jeopardize the seal and whale population's food supply.

Developing fisheries were the subject of a much-heralded UN Food and Agriculture Organization conference in Rome. From it emerged a plan that embodied the lessons learned from the past 25 years' mistakes, most of which could be summed up as the application of "inappropriate technology" too fast and too soon. Some 800 delegates to the conference endorsed the program, but there seemed little chance that it would get financial backing. Rome was also the venue for a meeting of the world's fishery workers aimed at achieving international solidarity. The deaths of several people in The Netherlands were traced to imported prawns contaminated by Shigella, resulting in general tight-

ening up of hand-processing of shrimp and prawns in both The Netherlands and southeastern Africa. The incident underlined the need for efficient shrimp-peeling machines to handle the small European mud shrimp, a breakthrough that was always just around the corner.

Indian fisheries were still dominated by inshore and coastal operations despite attempts by the government to stimulate interest and investment in deep-sea operations. However, India's catch was now in the region of 2.5 million metric tons. Pakistan was also expanding its industry and had recorded a tenfold increase since independence in 1947. The outlook was also a little brighter in Chile and Peru, particularly the former, which in 1983 had moved to fourth place among fishing nations with 3,663,000 metric tons, 75% of it pilchards. Peru had denationalized the Pescaperu fish-meal operation. Production of fish meal was expected to reach 276,000 metric tons in 1984, and a small profit seemed likely. Mexico's troubled tuna and shrimp fisheries showed signs of mending the rift with the U.S., and very limited license concessions were made to the U.S. tuna fleet. There were rumours of Mexican-caught shrimp being smuggled into the U.S. to beat the embargo, imposed by the U.S. in 1980 in retaliation for Mexico's seizure of U.S. tuna boats fishing in Mexican waters.

Other developments included a 100-ton-a-day fish-meal plant in New Zealand to exploit the suddenly valuable orange roughy fish oil and a $5 million Malaysian deep-sea fish port project, with Japanese participation. Continued pressure for greater fuel economy spawned numerous fuel economizers, continued interest in sail, and much long-overdue soul-searching on the question of propulsion efficiency. Overall, it was again the year of the smaller boat, as costs soared and catches were increasingly restricted by regulations and quotas. Even so, the catching capacity of inshore boats was now many times that of equivalent craft of 25 years earlier.

The International Whaling Commission, meeting in Buenos Aires, Arg., in June, voted 22 to 7 to reduce the 1985 quota for Antarctic minke whales, to ban all hunting of sperm whales in the North Pacific from 1985, and to reduce the 1985 quotas for minke whales in the Northern Hemisphere. The earlier decision to ban all commercial whaling for five years beginning in 1986 was upheld. (See ENVIRONMENT.)   (H. S. NOEL)

This article updates the *Macropædia* article Commercial FISHING AND MARINE PRODUCTS.

FOOD PROCESSING

In the U.K. new legislation came into force in September 1984 covering both food and labeling. The Food Act 1984 consolidated legislation previously embodied in the Food and Drugs Act 1955 and a number of separate acts, all of which were revoked. The fact that this important new legislation took little account of modern technological advances drew criticism from the industry. The new Food Labelling Regulations 1984, which revoked all previous labeling regulations, also contained anomalies, particularly regarding low-calorie products, which in a health-conscious society were becoming ever more popular.

There were far-reaching technological implications in the agreement between the U.K. cereals and milling group, Ranks Hovis McDougall (RHM), and Imperial Chemical Industries to establish a jointly owned company, New Era Foods, to commercialize RHM's mycoprotein food ingredient, made by a fermentation process from wheat starch. Unlike other microbial protein products, the ingredient was intended as a direct human food and not as an animal feed ingredient.

On a lower financial level but also technologically significant was the purchase by private interests of Lensfield Products, a former subsidiary of the British company FMC (Meat) Ltd. Lensfield had developed a unique process of converting slaughterhouse bones into edible protein. From this protein the company made several ingredients used in meat products to improve nutritive value, texture, and cooking characteristics. The process was licensed to a Danish company, which was developing a combination of the bone derivatives with blood plasma to produce "reformed" meats identical in composition and nutritive value to natural meat.

In June the first North American factory of the Swedish Tetra Pak company was opened in Denton, Texas, the largest in the world for making aseptic cartons for liquid foods. Thus, after a slow start, the U.S. food industry was catching up with the rest of the world in the consumption of long-life milk products, desserts, fruit juices, and other liquid foods processed by the ultra-heat-treated (UHT) technique. Tetra Pak had sold more than 100 billion aseptic packages in its 80 world markets since it originated the technology in the 1950s.

Packaging Developments. Also from Sweden was a new type of composite container designed to replace the conventional tinplate or aluminum can. Made of a laminate of paperboard, plastic, and aluminum foil, the container was said to be cheaper and more economical than conventional packages for products like custard, snack foods, tea, coffee, and powdered milk. Called Cekacan, the container would be further developed and marketed by a consortium formed of the Swedish packaging group Åkerlund & Rausing, Europa Carton of West Germany, and Container Corp. of the U.S. A major advantage of the system was that packaging materials are delivered flat to the packaging line, where they are formed, filled, and sealed in-line automatically. The development highlighted two trends in food processing: international collaboration among companies to spread out huge development costs and the production of packaging in-line by continuous methods.

Further examples of the trend toward in-line packaging, in the beverages field, came from Nissei of Japan and Serac of France, the foremost companies specializing in the development and manufacture of equipment for the continuous automatic production of plastic containers. Both companies unveiled new advanced equipment that would enable beverage producers to make and fill their own plastic bottles, particularly the PET (polyethylene terephthalate) variety. In 1984 the volume of carbonated soft drinks in PET bottles in the U.K. reached 50% of the total. The same trend was seen in other developed countries, following the lead of the U.S., where PET bottles first began to be used in the mid-1970s and where this type of packaging was now dominant for carbonated soft drinks. PET bottles were also being used for cider and beer.

Labeling regulations, particularly in the European Communities, now required food packages to be marked with "sell by" dates and to carry coded information. Such information was printed automatically by machines mounted in the packaging lines, but some of these lines were now operating at such high speeds that conventional mechanical printers were unable to cope. To overcome this problem, ink-jet printers were developed that spray tiny droplets of ink in a pattern to reproduce the printed information; the pattern is formed under the influence of computer-controlled electrostatic fields, through which the spray of droplets is passed. Some of these printers were able to operate at speeds of more than 1,200 codes per minute and could be instantly programmed by console-mounted or remote microprocessor keyboards. The technique was applicable to irregular surfaces, and direct printing with edible inks on the soft surface of foods was possible.

When a container is internally pressurized, it is more rigid and therefore stronger than an unpressurized container. This enabled producers of carbonated beverages to use thinner-walled metal cans than other sectors of the food and drink industry. These lighter and cheaper cans were usually made by deep-drawing techniques and, since they had no side seam, they could carry all-round decoration for enhanced sales appeal. Reynolds Metals Co. of the U.S. developed a system in which a controlled amount of liquid nitrogen was injected into a product-filled can just before it was sealed. The liquid changed into gas and created internal pressure. When the can was opened the gas evaporated, leaving no trace. This technique produced internal pressure equal to that in cans of fully carbonated beverages, allowing still beverages and even foods to be packed in thin-walled containers.

Processing Technology. Glafascan Ltd. of the U.K. introduced a new model of its visual image analyzer for continuously measuring, by optical/electronic means, the ratio of lean to fat in raw meat. Meat passes on a continuously moving conveyor belt under a TV scanner; the scanner converts the picture image into a digital signal and sends the signal to a microprocessor, which calculates the lean-to-fat ratio. The information can be printed out or fed to processing machines, also under microprocessor control, so that the lean-to-fat content of the final product—a hamburger, for example—can be continuously monitored and controlled automatically. Such equipment was installed in a new Findus prepared-frozen-foods factory in Newcastle upon Tyne, England, probably the most modern of its kind

U.S. food producers courted "upscale" markets with new quality products. An example of the numerous gourmet frozen dinners is the "Le Menu" line introduced by Campbell Soup Co.

in the world. The factory made beefburgers and pizzas at the rate of 20,000 tons a year.

A Swiss manufacturer of meat-processing machinery, Hollymatic, developed a technique for overcoming the common problem of shrinkage in meat products when they are cooked. Called Jet-Flow, it was introduced at the Meatex exhibition in Birmingham, England, in April. Ground meat of the kind used to make burgers is light in texture and tender when it leaves the grinder because air is trapped among the meat granules, but all subsequent handling tends to drive the air out of the mix, toughening the meat in the process. Jet-Flow uses a special mold with a retractable segment that causes the meat entering the cavity to "jet" forward in a smooth unrestricted flow at twice the speed of a conventional system. The meat has little contact with the top and bottom plates of the mold and, as the meat flows into the cavity, fragmentation of the granules traps air in the mix, restoring the original texture. When the retractable segment closes, meat and air are trapped together. When the molded patty is released, it continues to expand because of the pressure of the air within it.

Information Technology. Information is the lifeblood of any industry, but it is effective only if it can be retrieved efficiently and rapidly. One of the world food industry's most efficient "information factories" was the Food Research Association (FRA), Leatherhead, England, which during the year made available a new data base for scientific and technical information (called FROSTI). This complemented its other data base (FOREGE, covering international food regulations), introduced in 1983.

During 1984 the FRA introduced a system whereby subscribers anywhere in the world, provided they had the necessary terminal and modem, could be connected to the data base computer at Leatherhead via the public telephone service and carry out a search at local call rates using a "package switching service." Any information in the FRA's data bases or data banks could be displayed on the subscriber's screen. This system allowed food processors anywhere to gain access to the latest information in the processing, packaging, scientific, technical, and legal fields in a matter of minutes and at very modest cost.

New Products. New products poured continuously from the development and marketing departments of food and drink companies. This was particularly true in the chilled and frozen foods sectors, where consumers seemed willing to pay a premium for convenience and quality. In the first four months of 1984, nearly 25% of the sales revenue of companies in these sectors in both the U.S. and Europe was accounted for by products that were not on the market in 1982.

"Health foods," a sector once thought to be restricted to faddists and cranks, continued to boom and gained respectability to the extent that major food companies were bringing out new products in the field. It was reported in September that a major British retail chain planned to devote a large proportion of its food shelves to a new range of "natural foods," including pure fruit juices, bottled spring water, cereals without salt or sugar, stone-ground whole-wheat flour, cookies without colouring or preservatives, decaffeinated coffee, herbal teas, and unrefined brown sugar.

A whole range of low-fat, low-calorie desserts, dairy products (including new low-fat cheeses), and beverages made their appearance. The availability of the new sweetener aspartame gave a boost to low-calorie products, particularly beverages, because of its superiority to saccharin in taste and the fact that it has no aftertaste. In Canada, where this sweetener had been available longer than in any other country, soft drinks sweetened with aspartame accounted for 30% of the total carbonated soft drink market.

Nonalcoholic and low-alcohol versions of beer, wine, and aperitifs continued to appear, despite sluggish acceptance by consumers. The promoters of these products believed—and market research bore them out—that the long-term prospects were good and that unrelenting antialcohol propaganda by medical and consumer lobbies, backed by increasingly severe drunk driving laws, would eventually have the same effect on alcohol consumption that the 30-year antismoking campaign had had on tobacco consumption. There was, for example, evidence to suggest that the efforts of MADD—Mothers Against Drunken Drivers—were having a significant effect on drinking habits in the U.S.

(ANTHONY WOOLLEN)

This article updates the *Macropædia* article FOOD PROCESSING. *See also* Environment; Health and Disease; Industrial Review: *Beverages; Textiles; Tobacco.*

Anthropology

The Miocene Epoch appeared frequently in the anthropological literature during 1984. Most investigators looked to this epoch, about 24 million to about 5.5 million years ago, as the time when the "last common ancestor of apes and humans" would be found. Hominoids radiated in Africa during the Early Miocene and throughout Eurasia in the Middle Miocene, and by the Late Miocene they may have been in tropical areas of Southeast Asia. Experts differed on the relationships and classification of the now considerable number of fossil specimens from this epoch. At least two groupings, Dryopiths (Early to Middle Miocene) and Ramapiths (Middle to Late Miocene), could be recognized.

Proconsul belongs to the early or Dryopith group. By 17.9 million years ago this earliest of the Miocene hominoids had already diversified into a number of species, and it was now recognized as a separate genus. More complete fossil finds during 1984 substantiated what some investigators previously had described as a "dental ape" with postcranial "monkey-like" features. *Proconsul* was a quadrupedal, probably tailless, tree-dwelling hominoid who walked with palms down like modern monkeys.

In the Ramapith group are a number of fossils from Africa, Asia, and Europe. One is *Sivapithecus,* which, thanks to two recent finds, was now known to have existed as early as 17 million years ago in Kenya and to have had a face with great similarities to that of the modern orangutan. The fact that the Ramapiths had thick, enameled teeth—a trait of *Homo sapiens* (modern man) and the orang but not of modern chimpanzees or gorillas—caused some debate among paleoanthropologists. There is much greater molecular similarity between *H. sapiens* and the chimp and gorilla than between *H. sapiens* and the orang, but a number of morphological traits are shared by humans and orangs and not by humans and the African apes. This is also true for growth rates in certain bones, similar gestation periods, lack of an estrous cycle, and other characteristics. Whether these similarities are attributable to relatedness or to parallel evolution was, of course, not known.

What did seem established was that *Sivapithecus* probably is not ancestral to either the chimp or the gorilla. Moreover, because *Sivapithecus* is so similar to *Ramapithecus,* considered since the 1960s as the probable first representative of the human line, there was doubt now that the latter is in the line to any of the hominids, including the australopithecines. This represented a significant change in thinking on the part of most paleoanthropologists. As more

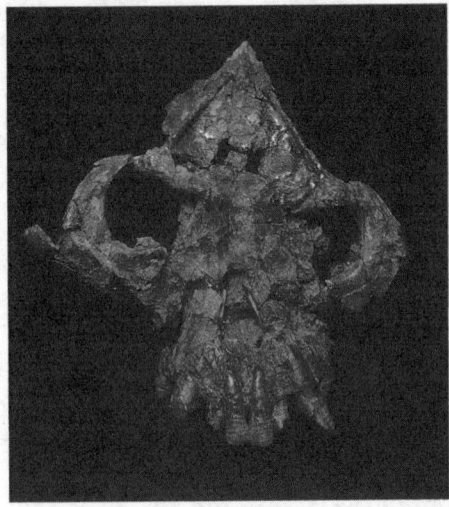 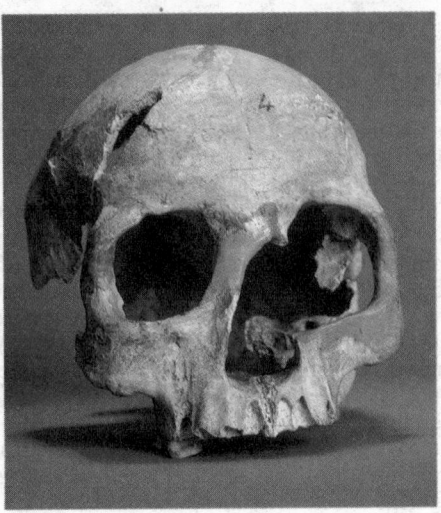

The specimen at far left is the most nearly complete skull yet found of *Sivapithecus* (lived 17 million to 8 million years ago). *Sivapithecus* is thought by some to be an ancestor of *Homo sapiens*, represented at near left by a Cro-Magnon skull found in France and dated between 13,000 and 20,000 years ago.

PHOTOGRAPHS, MARGO CRABTREE

fossils were found there was increasing recognition of the great radiation of diverse forms that occurred over very long periods of time. Bushy diagrams appeared to be more accurate than simple "trees" of relationship, though less satisfying in the quest to find the "last common ancestor."

The hominoid fossil abundance of the Miocene is not characteristic of the Pliocene, which began 5.5 million years ago with a gap of over 2 million years in the hominid fossil record. Recently reported was a femur from the middle Awash Valley of Ethiopia, which could date to 4 million years ago. Two other new finds of about this same date from Ethiopia were the Maka femur of a habitual biped, very similar to that of *Australopithecus afarensis,* and the Belohdelia cranial vault fragment, said to resemble that of a child found at Laetoli in Tanzania. Future research in the middle Awash Valley and in Kenya was expected to shed further light on this period, which may have been the time of the hominoid-hominid transition.

"Lucy," the 40% complete skeleton discovered at Hadar, Eth., continued to be discussed during 1984. While there was general agreement that "she" was bipedal, the question of whether it was the bipedalism of a modern hominid or that of a tree-climbing biped—or some gait in between— was researched and argued by functional anatomists. The specific issues were whether Lucy's legs were relatively too short to allow a fully bipedal striding gait and whether her curved hand and foot bones were indicative of a habitual arboreal habitat.

Australopithecus africanus and *A. robustus* seemed to be increasingly divorced from the ancestry to the later hominids—*Homo habilis, H. erectus,* and, thus, *H. sapiens.* One comparative study of the australopithecine face concluded that *A. africanus* was extremely specialized and thus not a candidate for ancestry in either the African ape or *Homo* lineage. That left rather a long gap between *A. afarensis* (c. 3 million years ago) and the earliest *H. habilis* (no earlier than 1.8 million), provided that *A. afarensis* could be considered generalized enough to qualify as a Pliocene ancestor of the *Homo* lineage. Regardless of these uncertainties, the australopithecines were a highly successful Pliocene group with a very extensive radiation. In 1984 the Sangiran fossil, *Meganthropus paleojavanicus,* was reported to have teeth similar to those of the australopithecines, reinforcing the speculation that these hominids ranged from southern Africa to Java.

For many years it had been tacitly assumed that two or more species of hominid tool user-makers could not coexist. However, continuing research at sites like Koobi Fora in Kenya provided evidence for the contemporaneous existence of two—and at times three—hominids, possibly all tool users. Whether they were hunters, scavengers, or both and whether they had real campsites or just stored their tools near animal kill sites was debated, but this did not detract from the fact of their coexistence. Perhaps the control of fire finally eliminated interhominid competition, but much research remained to be done on behavioural-lifeway differences between the proposed species.

Relatively little paleoanthropological research on the Pleistocene and Recent periods was reported during 1984. The Miocene and Pliocene had been centre stage for over two decades, ever since the Leakeys' dramatic discoveries at Olduvai Gorge in Tanzania. Reports on post-Pliocene hominids that did appear in the literature in late 1983 and 1984 included a further examination of the Petralona (Greece) skull, which may date to 400,000 years ago. Like a number of other hominids that, morphologically, are neither fully modern *H. sapiens* nor neanderthaloid, it was being placed in a taxonomically undefined category called Archaic *Homo sapiens.* Disagreement continued over whether these hominids are the ancestors of both the Neanderthals and modern humans.

What might be one of the oldest hominid sites in Europe was reported in 1984. The site, Velay, France, had not yielded any fossil hominid remains, although there was ample evidence of a Plio-Pleistocene fauna. Most remarkable was a 20-m (65-ft) wall built of basalt blocks. Dated between 1.3 million and 1,670,000 years ago, it was the oldest hominid structure in Europe. An early *H. sapiens* skull found by Mary Leakey in 1976 at the Ngaloba beds of Laetoli was dated at 120,000 ± 30,000 years BP (before present). The hominid occupation of the Laetoli beds thus spans over three and a half million years. A robust but otherwise modern *H. sapiens* was reported from Egypt. Known as the Nazlet Khater man, it was the oldest known modern human in Africa north of the Equator. Another candidate for the earliest North American human fell to modern dating techniques. The skeleton of Yuha man, excavated in 1971 in southern California, had originally been dated 19,000–23,000 BP, but direct radiocarbon determination by accelerator mass spectrometry indicated a date of only 4000 BP.

The "Ancestors" exhibit at the American Museum of Natural History in New York City was a bold effort to bring together, for the first time, all the original major hominoid and hominid fossils, though in the end many were represented by casts. Richard Leakey and a number ot other curators declined to lend their material for security reasons and because of its fragility. Some 40 fossils were exhibited, behind bulletproof glass, among them the australopithecines from South Africa. A resolution was introduced in the New York City Council to withdraw financial support from the museum as a protest against South Africa's apartheid (racial separation) policy, but it was defeated and the fossils remained on display.

(HERMANN K. BLEIBTREU)

See also Archaeology.

This article updates the *Macropædia* article HUMAN EVOLUTION.

Archaeology

Eastern Hemisphere. Only one reasonably spectacular archaeological discovery was reported for 1984. This was the announcement of the discovery on the southwestern coast of Turkey and initial clearance of the wreck of a merchant ship dating from the 14th century BC. As more of the cargo was retrieved by underwater archaeologists, much would be learned about ancient trading patterns in the eastern Mediterranean. Considerable publicity but not much substantive description attended the accidental exposure of the body of a pre-Roman man, evidently a sacrificial victim, in a peat bog in England. Perhaps a dozen such finds had already been made in Scandinavia. An article in the journal *Antiquity* presented substantial evidence that Heinrich Schliemann's claims regarding the circumstances of his finding "Priam's Treasure" at Troy in 1873 were grossly exaggerated. As has become almost a yearly event, Mt. Ararat in Turkey was climbed in search of Noah's Ark. Again no real evidence of the boat was found.

PLEISTOCENE PREHISTORY. For the very long early stages of human history, before the Ice Age ended, most archaeological activity focused on Africa and was predominantly concerned with human paleontology. A remarkable find by a member of Richard Leakey's fossil-hunting group occurred during the summer in northern Kenya. The almost

AP/WIDE WORLD

During the excavation of an ancient city in northern Afghanistan, which may have been founded by Alexander the Great, French archaeologists uncovered this stone spout fashioned after a comic mask.

complete skeletal remains of a male specimen of *Homo erectus,* directly ancestral to modern man, were discovered. Never before had so nearly complete a skeleton of such an early hominid been found. Analysis of the bones indicated that they were of a boy near 12 years of age who lived about 1.6 million years ago. Most surprisingly, the boy was estimated to have been 5 ft 4 in tall at his death and to have weighed as much as 150 lb, a size previously believed to have been attained only by a full-grown *Homo erectus.* The specimen also resembled modern man anatomically more closely than had been previously thought possible.

There was increasing evidence for the use of bone (as well as of chipped stone) tools from both Olduvai Gorge (Tanzania) and the Transvaal (South Africa) for as early as two million years ago. In China renewed excavations continued at Choukoutien (Chou-k'ou-tien) Locality 1 (the place where "Peking Man" was found), and large numbers of stone tools were recovered. For late Pleistocene times (about 15,000 years ago) excellent examples of groups of ovoid huts, each built of mammoth bones, were found at Mezhirich in the Dnepr River watershed in the Soviet Union. In the Enlène cave at Ariège, France, several excellent engravings of animals were found on fragments of a stone slab.

LATE PREHISTORIC EUROPE. A "mesolithic" (about 7000 BC) hunter-collector site at Hengistbury Head, Dorset, England, yielded evidence of the technology of Britain's earliest arrow makers. At Donegore Hill in northern Ireland the remains of the first Irish example of the typical "neolithic" causewayed (ditched enclosure) camp was excavated after it was located by means of an aerial survey. Near the Black Sea in the Soviet Union a domed burial chamber dated at about 2500 BC was found. The use of a dome at so early a time is remarkable.

MIDDLE EAST. In Egypt there was a considerable amount of routine activity (cleaning, copying, restoration), especially in the Luxor region, with archaeological teams from Canada, the United States, most Western European countries, Poland, Hungary, and Japan taking part. Five new tombs of officials of the time of Ramses II the Great (1304–1237 BC) were cleared at Sakkara. The first really exact detailed mapping of the pyramid field at Giza, done with the most up-to-date surveying instruments, was under way with support from the North American Research Center in Egypt. Archaeological activity in Yemen (San'a') continued to increase. Near San'a' (ancient Shibam), in tombs cut into a hillside, five well-preserved mummies from about 300 BC were found, an unusual find in the Eastern Hemisphere outside of Egypt.

Considerable activity took place in Israel during the year. Ofer Bar-Yosef of the Hebrew University was clearing an important early village site, Netiv Hagedud, north of Jericho. Even more remarkable was the yield of similar age (about 8000 BC) from a dry Negev cave. It consisted of much usually perishable material (textile fragments, basketry, rope, and wood), which gave archaeologists a more nearly complete idea of the full inventory of items originally used. Work also proceeded at a variety of sites of biblical importance, such as Lachish, Akko, Shiloh, Dor, and Tell el-Hesi, and on building remains in Jerusalem. Evidence of a primitive (perhaps not successful) iron smelter of the 13th century BC was found in southern Galilee. More work was done on the harbour at Caesarea, built by Herod the Great in 22–10 BC, and, nearby, detailed evidence of Mediterranean sea-level changes throughout the Holocene Epoch (the last 10,000 years) was obtained.

In Jordan work proceeded at 'Ain Ghazal, near Amman, where a cache of large clay figurines had been found in

1982. In Syria work at the important site of Ebla continued, the present focus being on comparatively late (about 1800 BC) levels rather than on those yielding the famous cuneiform tablets. As it had done earlier for the region behind a dam on the Euphrates River, the Syrian government made an international appeal for salvage teams to excavate sites that lay where a new flood pool would form behind a projected dam on the Khabur River. A share of the yield of artifacts would be available to the participants. In northern Iraq similar salvage work proceeded in the region behind a new dam on the Tigris River north of Mosul. Understandably, there was little archaeological activity in southern Iraq, where fighting with Iran continued.

Salvage archaeology also was under way in Turkey as the time for completion of two dams on the Euphrates River drew near. U.S., British, Dutch, French, West German, and Turkish archaeologists were involved. The joint prehistoric excavations of the Universities of Istanbul, Chicago, and Karlsruhe at the remarkable early village-farming community of Cayonu proceeded, emphasis being placed on the clearance of structures, clearly nondomestic in purpose, that were architecturally remarkable for so early a date (about 7500 BC). The important Italian excavations at Arslan Tepe, near Malatya, continued, as did the work of Turkish archaeologists at the Assyrian merchant colony of Kultepe and of West German archaeologists at the Hittite capital of Hattusa, at the site of modern Bogazkoy. The second season's work at Besiktepe, just southwest of Troy, was yielding important evidence for expanding knowledge of the Troy sequence. A new Swedish expedition was at work on Cyprus, recovering evidence of Egyptian, Levantine, and Greek contacts with the island about 1600–1200 BC.

THE GRECO-ROMAN WORLD. On Crete the British resumed work at the Minoan capital of Knossos, recovering possible evidence of child sacrifice. In France salvage excavations in an area to become a parking lot in the centre of Bordeaux yielded important remains of the city's past, from Gaulo-Roman through medieval times. In Britain a small bit of cloth from a Roman grave near Colchester was identified as Chinese silk. The analysis of rat bones in Roman remains in London indicated that the black rat (*Rattus rattus,* carrier of bubonic plague) had already reached England by about AD 250. At Coppergate, in Yorkshire, England, a 10th-century AD pit, rich in the finds of the Viking age, was cleared. (*See* Special Report.)

SOUTHERN AND EASTERN ASIA. In Pakistan a full-scale effort, with UNESCO support, proceeded to restore and protect the great Harappan city site of Mohenjo-daro. The site's architecture suffered from disintegration by saltwater. In India a marine archaeology unit found submerged site traces of late Harappan and post-Harappan date (about 1500 BC) off the country's east coast. A recent joint British-Indian effort analyzed evidence for the smelting of zinc. Until the 1700s much of Europe's zinc was imported from India. In Thailand a joint Thai-New Zealand team was examining the sites of early farmers. It appeared that the domestication of rice led eventually to the rise of city-states and to trade contacts with India and China.

In China two new assemblages of artifacts suggesting early-village settlements of the 7th–6th millennia BC were reported. One, P'ei-li-kang, showed evidence of pig-breeding millet farmers. The other assemblage, Ho-mu-tu, was found in the remains of a lakeside village; there, the researchers found traces of rice and of domesticated pigs and water buffalo. The many-chambered tomb of the second king of South Yueh (2nd century BC) was excavated near Canton.

(ROBERT J. BRAIDWOOD)

Western Hemisphere. A wide range of new developments took place in New World archaeology in 1984. Although trends often take several years to be defined after initial discoveries are made, 1984 was noteworthy for a series of new insights into the issues of man's first appearance in the New World, in both North and South America. Two discoveries in particular, one in the far north and one on the tip of South America, added significant new evidence concerning the continuing debate over when and in what form humans first inhabited the Americas.

A second major development during the year concerned the discovery of a Mayan site in Guatemala and an Inca site in Brazil, both undisturbed by the forces of development and destruction by looters. A third trend involved the continued discovery of significant new archaeological sites through ongoing salvage archaeology projects in both California and New York. Finally, in the realm of enhancing the speed and detail of recording as well as dramatically reducing the time that it takes archaeologists to gain control over their often massive amounts of data, 1984 could be characterized as the year of the microcomputer in archaeology, reflecting the recent availability of inexpensive yet powerful micros for both field and laboratory analysis.

NORTH AMERICA. Two discoveries in North America shed intriguing new light on the dates of man's first arrival and early lifeways on the continent, one in the far northern Yukon Territory of Canada and one in Texas. In the Yukon Richard Moran of the National Museum of Man in Ottawa discovered what he believed to be evidence of human presence in the New World dating to 72,000 years BP (before present). Excavations and surveys over the past 20 years had identified deeply buried layers by the Old Crow River. The field team found a mammoth's humerus bone that appeared freshly broken when first deposited and two bones of extinct bison, one with microscopic incisions that Moran and his colleague Pat Shipman of Johns Hopkins University interpreted with the aid of electron microscopy as having been made by human tools. If valid, these ancient indicators of human presence thousands of years before the currently accepted Pleistocene date of 10,000–12,000 years ago for man's first arrival in the New World would precipitate a new round of debates over current assumptions.

Although archaeologists had traditionally reserved arguments of human activity for finds with identifiable artifacts in direct association with extinct animal remains, new techniques were permitting observations based on more subtle clues, such as the above-cited cut marks. Although less controversial and much more recent than the Yukon discovery, possible bone alterations on a mammoth found by archaeologists excavating on a buried sandbar in southern Texas were believed to be suggestive of human activity. Two complete tusks and other body parts were found with multiple spiral bone fractures, suggesting that they had been hit and chopped at with some force soon after the animal died. The placement of the bones, the lack of evidence for turbulent water activity, and the broken and chipped bones themselves were being initially interpreted as traces of butchering activity by humans.

In addition to forcing archaeologists to revise earlier interpretations or at least question them, new excavations were also helping to fill gaps in the surviving written record of the historic period. Illustrating the often dramatic way in which such gaps can be augmented with unwritten material remains, a 75-member team of salvage archaeologists working at a construction site in Los Angeles discovered the "Lost Village of Encino," which they had been unable to pinpoint by means of surviving Spanish maps and

(continued on page 168)

Viking Age York Revisited

BY RICHARD HALL

Since its foundation by the advancing Roman 9th Legion in about AD 71, York has been the virtual "capital of the north" of England. Eboracum, enduring headquarters of Rome's northern British military command as well as a provincial capital and occasional imperial seat, eventually became Eoforwic, capital of the Anglian kingdom of Northumbria, a cross-channel trading centre with an archbishop's church and an internationally renowned monastic school. Although Eoforwic was not particularly large or densely populated, its wealth attracted the attention of the "great army" of Vikings that landed in East Anglia in AD 865. In 866 they marched to York and captured it, thus inaugurating nearly a century of Viking rule. This lasted until 954, when the reassertion of English power led to the expulsion of King Erik Bloodax. The loss of Scandinavian royal authority did not, however, result in the departure of all the descendants of Viking settlers. Up to the Norman Conquest and beyond, Jorvik, as it was now called, retained strong Scandinavian links.

York's Past Emerges. Until recently, the only archaeological clues to Jorvik were the Viking Age objects salvaged during 18th–20th-century building and road construction. This haphazard collection hinted at the amount of information buried below York, particularly in the vicinity of Ousegate, Coppergate, and Pavement, where most of the objects were found. In 1972, with the establishment of the York Archaeological Trust, a full-time rescue archaeology unit, it became possible, for the first time, to investigate this area properly. The undertaking began on a small scale, when the Trust contracted to excavate new vaults for Lloyds Bank at 6–8 Pavement.

The keyhole view of Viking Age York that emerged demonstrated the existence of up to 9 m (30 ft) of archaeological deposit in the area. Much of it was peaty, foul-smelling refuse from the Viking Age that held moisture like a sponge and therefore preserved organic objects such as wood, textiles, and leather, which rot to dust under normal, dry-soil conditions. This wider-than-usual range of surviving material was further augmented by the remains of domesticated and wild animals, plants, seeds, pollen, insects, and even microscopic eggs of various parasites. Upon analysis, all this presented a remarkably detailed picture of the past environment and climate and of the diet and health of the Anglo-Scandinavian population.

With this confirmation that there was an exceptional amount of light to be shed on a hitherto "dark age," the York Archaeological Trust eagerly grasped the opportunity, offered by a pending redevelopment in nearby Coppergate, to investigate four complete tenements. During more than

Richard Hall, deputy director of the York Archaeological Trust, directed the Coppergate excavations throughout and is now coordinating the research and publication of the discoveries. A fellow of the Society of Antiquaries and member of the Institute of Field Archaeologists, he is the author of Jorvik: Viking Age York *and* The Viking Dig.

five years of continuous excavation, between 1976 and 1981, the Trust was able to trace the history of 1,000 sq m (10,750 sq ft) in the heart of the area.

York's growth in the period after the Viking takeover was clearly demonstrated. After more than four centuries of abandonment during the Anglian era, the site was reoccupied in the period 850–900. Early in the 10th century the whole area was parceled out into long, narrow tenement strips, along lines that endured until the 19th century. The tenements were divided by fences made from woven twigs, and buildings made in a similar manner were erected at the Coppergate frontage, implying that Coppergate itself had been established.

The wattle buildings, which had no upper story, measured at least 8 × 4 m (26 × 13 ft) and served as both houses and workshops. Domestic debris included a wide range of animal bones and cereal and fruit remains, indicating a varied diet, largely garnered from estates in the Yorkshire countryside. A good food supply was a necessary corollary to the intestinal worms, growing up to 30 cm (11½ in) in length, with which all Jorvik's citizens were plagued.

Viking Skills. Apart from cooking, the most common domestic task was probably the making of clothing, from spinning and weaving to dyeing the cloth; for the first time, a wide variety of dye plants has been identified and correlated with traces of dye in the textile fragments. It was manufacturing, chiefly metalworking, however, that provided a livelihood for the occupants of early 10th-century Coppergate. Gold, silver, lead, copper, and iron were all worked, and production of cheap jewelry seems to have been one of these metalsmiths' stocks-in-trade.

YORK ARCHAEOLOGICAL TRUST; PHOTOGRAPH, MIKE S. DUFFY

Jorvik, the Viking Age predecessor of modern York in northern England, has been revealed by archaeologists, and excavated evidence is displayed on the site. This reconstructed house with model family is part of the exhibit.

More important, they were appointed as moneyers—royal agents responsible for striking the silver pennies that constituted the coinage of the realm. Their work was recognized through the discovery of lead trial pieces bearing the impressions of test strikings of dies and then of one complete die and a fractured die head, the first coin dies found anywhere in the Viking world.

The thatch-roofed wattle buildings that housed these activities were vulnerable to fire, storm, and decay and had to be replaced and repaired repeatedly. Finally, in the 970s, a remarkable series of sunken buildings was erected. Each building measured about 7.5 × 3.5 m (25 × 11½ ft), with floors cut as deep as 1.8 m (about 6 ft) below the surrounding ground surface. Two ranks of these structures were built at the street frontage. The ones in front probably were dwelling houses, while those in the rear served as workshops. Constructed of stout oak posts and planks, again probably with a thatch roof, they survived to a height of about 1.8 m in places, making them the best preserved Viking Age timber buildings in Britain and among the best anywhere.

At this time woodturners operated in one of the tenements, perhaps giving the street its Old Norse name—Coppergate, the street of the cup makers. An adjacent tenement was occupied by jewelers working amber and jet into beads, pendants, and rings. Among other important categories of objects found during the excavation is a group that demonstrates wide-ranging travel and trade contacts, extending from Scandinavia and northwestern Europe to the eastern Mediterranean, the Red Sea, and the Himalayas. Another group, which illustrates leisure activities, includes parts of several musical instruments, among them panpipes still in a playable condition.

Jorvik Re-created. Many of the half-million visitors to the excavation expressed the hope that the discoveries could be preserved and displayed at the site where they were found, a wish fulfilled in May 1984 when the Jorvik Viking Centre was inaugurated by the prince of Wales, a patron of the project since its inception. It was instantly popular, and within three months its visitors had exceeded 250,000. Here, in the hole created by the excavation, the visitor is transported back in time, riding a battery-driven car into a full-scale simulation of a part of Viking Age Coppergate, constructed wholly of modern materials and carefully based on the excavated evidence. The bustling street and buildings are peopled by figures whose conversations in Old Norse form part of a carefully researched sound montage. The smells of Jorvik are also re-created, an important element in any realistic simulation. The visitor then is transported into a re-creation of the excavation, where the timber building remains have been replaced on the spots where they were found, after preservative treatment in the conservation laboratory. The techniques of excavation and recording are also displayed. Leaving the time-car, the visitor walks through a replica of a conservation and environmental study laboratory to an Artifact Hall, where 500 of the excavated objects illustrate further aspects of life in Jorvik.

Using the most modern audiovisual display techniques, the Jorvik Viking Centre dramatizes the new understanding of Viking Age life made possible by the Coppergate excavation. It also highlights the urgent need to investigate similarly threatened development sites and demonstrates the range of methods and approaches used by late-20th-century archaeologists. The capacity crowds that have thronged the centre since its opening exemplify the wide public interest that currently exists in rescue archaeology and its results.

(continued from page 166
mission records alone. The 3,000-year-old village site, one of only three such finds in the last 30 years, appeared also to be the Gabrieleño Indian village that the Spanish explorer-priest Gaspar de Portola described on his 1769 expedition to California.

Similar rescue efforts demonstrated the survival of well-preserved colonial American remains sealed under the building basements in such unlikely places as New York City. Working throughout the winter of 1983–84, a team of 70 archaeologists under the direction of Joel Grossman used overhead stereo cameras, high-precision infrared computer transits, and microcomputers during their excavation to expose and record the original shoreline surfaces and building outlines of the Dutch West India Company (1650) in the Wall Street area of lower Manhattan. The more than 43,000 European and native artifacts recovered included a basket with a wooden game board and marbles buried in the former shore sand, yellow brick structures, buried wooden barrel cisterns, and the cobbled floor and walls of one of the first Dutch warehouses in New York. Partially filling a documentary gap in the surviving records, this rescue effort not only demonstrated the survival under 19th-century basements of well-preserved colonial remains but also showed that both lot lines and building locations had shifted and that the original land surface in New York City was some seven feet below the modern streets.

LATIN AMERICA. In Guatemala and Mexico it was rare for archaeologists to find undisturbed archaeological sites in general and unlooted tombs in particular. Looting activity aimed at supplying national and international art collections had either greatly disturbed or obliterated many Mayan centres, making it difficult or impossible for scientists to reconstruct their function, cultural affiliations, or place in time. Given the magnitude of this problem, it was all the more significant that researchers announced during the year the discovery of an undisturbed 1,500-year-old tomb of a nobleman at the site of Río Azul in northeastern Petén, Guatemala. In a joint Guatemalan-U.S. announcement the project sponsors, George E. Stewart of the National Geographic Society and Richard E. W. Adams of the Center for Archaeological Research, University of Texas at San Antonio, described the rare discovery as the first intact and properly excavated find in that area in 20 years. The tomb contained the body of an adult, 25 ceramic vessels, jade beads, and the unexpected presence of a pottery bottle with a screw-top cap. The concept of a threaded screw had been thought of as a characteristic of Old World culture, unknown to Western Hemisphere civilizations. Its discovery in undisputed association with a Mayan tomb dating to between AD 420 and 470 further weakened several long-standing assumptions concerning the nature and relative level of intellectual development in pre-Columbian America. The announcement coincided with the signing of a U.S.-Guatemalan treaty to stop or at least stem the flow of looted Guatemalan artifacts into the North American antiquities market.

In South America legends of lost Inca cities in the rugged interior of Brazil had circulated since the first European contact in the 16th century. During the year Brazilian archaeologist Aurelio Abreau of the São Paulo Archaeology Institute announced the discovery of a lost city of stone, high on a mountain plateau in the eastern state of Bahía. Known by its local name of Ingrejil, the site consisted of precision-cut stones fitted without mortar, with arches similar to the 15th-century architecture in the Inca city of Cuzco. If further study confirmed its Inca origins, this distant site, far beyond the Peruvian Andean homeland

A rare find by a University of Texas team, led by anthropologist Richard Adams, was this Mayan tomb that had never been looted by grave robbers. It is located at Río Azul in the remote jungle of Petén, in northeastern Guatemala. Highly sophisticated artifacts were found there, including a stone jar with a screw top.

WILBUR GARRETT © NATIONAL GEOGRAPHIC

of the Inca, would significantly expand the extent of the empire of those Indians. After seven years of survey and test excavations at the southern tip of Chile, Tom Dillehay of the University of Kentucky announced the discovery of an early man occupation or living site. Complete with structures, extinct animal remains, and unique tool and food remains, it could drastically alter the scientific understanding of man's earliest lifeways in the New World. Until this find most evidence of Paleo-Indian activities had been restricted to specialized tool-making or butchering sites often associated with distinctive "big game" fluted spear points. In contrast, at the 12,500–13,000-year-old site of Monte Verde, archaeologists found that the ancient inhabitants depended primarily on the sharp cutting edges of naturally occurring river cobbles. The living site revealed not a temporary workshop but 12 wishbone-shaped huts outlined with wooden foundations that appeared to have been covered by mastodon hide and with large clay-lined communal hearths outside their entrances. The footprint of a child eight to ten years of age was found impressed into the mud. The high level of preservation of the cold mud in the area yielded the remains of a variety of plant foods, including traces of potato. That plant foods played an important role in addition to meat was further demonstrated by the discovery of stone pestles and three crude wooden mortars with stakes placed around them to prevent shifting.   (JOEL W. GROSSMAN)

See also Anthropology.

Architecture

The 150th anniversary of the Royal Institute of British Architects (RIBA) was marked by an eight-month Festival of Architecture in Britain starting on April 30, 1984. The purpose of the festival was "to encourage a public awareness in the art of architecture and the built environment," and hundreds of events were held. It was the first nationwide festival of its kind and included exhibitions; an open house at RIBA's Portland Place, London, headquarters; lectures; films; jazz sessions; and a series of concerts in houses designed by Robert Adam. The open house included public participation events such as "The Demolition Show," which invited visitors to choose which famous London building they would most like to see demolished and then which modern structure might be put

on the site. The celebrations provided an opportunity to assess the achievements of architects and review the state of architecture. Unfortunately, many found both wanting. The general unpopularity of modern architecture among all except architects themselves was in marked contrast to the ever growing interest in historic buildings. (*See* ART EXHIBITIONS AND ART SALES.)

The backlash against the modern movement combined with the strength of the preservationists, whose argument was often that no matter how mediocre the old, modern replacement was bound to be worse, put mainstream architects very much on the defensive and made the festival more a forum for justifying and debating the state of architecture than for contented self-congratulation. The controversial nature of the debate was most publicly spotlighted by a speech made by the prince of Wales at the RIBA's Royal Gala evening at Hampton Court Palace on May 30. The prince took the opportunity to criticize modern architecture severely, singling out particularly the proposed "high tech" extension to the National Gallery of Art in Trafalgar Square by Ahrends Burton & Koralek (which in September was rejected as "inappropriate" by the secretary of state for the environment) and the Ludwig Mies van der Rohe-designed office tower for Mansion House Square in the City. While some attacked the prince for discourtesy in choosing the RIBA celebration as an opportunity to draw attention to the shortcomings of architecture, others felt that architects themselves had attracted criticism by their lack of apparent interest in the social effect of their schemes, and so were fair game.

Debate raged over the proposed Mies building as a public inquiry obtained evidence to help the planning authorities decide whether to allow the tower to be built. Nothing focused attention better on the current feeling for historicism than the essence of the two sides to the argument. Those opposed claimed that the plans were outdated, inappropriate, would require the demolition of buildings listed as historic landmarks, and would impose a wholly inappropriate structure on a sensitive London site. Experts were called to support contentions that the designs were not even by Mies. Those in favour of the scheme sometimes seemed most anxious that London should have a Mies building—rather like a museum collecting its first Picasso—unwittingly agreeing perhaps on the historicism of the design, which was new in the 1960s but now looked rather out of date, if not ordinary. The property developer,

The new High Museum of Art, with its steel panels clad in porcelain enamel, has proved a magnet for museum goers and tourists in Atlanta, Georgia. It was designed by Richard Meier & Partners and is called Meier's finest work.
EZRA STOLLER—ESTO

Peter Palumbo, had taken 14 years to acquire the whole of the site opposite the Mansion House. The designs for a 22-story office tower showed a building clad in bronze glass. A full set of working drawings had been signed by Mies two weeks before his death in 1969. Palumbo was able to muster the support of many of the leading British architects, including Norman Foster, James Stirling, and Richard Rogers.

Cultural and Educational Buildings. Museums, libraries, and cultural centres again exhibited some of the most noteworthy architectural ideas in 1984. Many were awarded in competition. An international contest in two phases was held to select a design for a new opera house for Paris, to be situated at the Place de la Bastille. More than 1,600 architects entered, and the designs of the 744 accepted were later put on public exhibition. An international jury selected six semifinalists, three of whom were chosen by Pres. François Mitterrand to produce detailed schemes. The winner, announced in November 1983, was Uruguayan-born Canadian architect Carlos Ott; his design featured a complex silhouette with a transparent curved facade fronting the Place de la Bastille through which a grand staircase would be visible. The overall silhouette was likened to a "giant mechanical piano." Accommodations would include a main hall to seat 2,800, a 1,000-seat hall, and a smaller rehearsal hall. Both the design and competition prompted debate on the function of opera and its cultural role in the musical life of Paris. The new opera house would surely represent an attempt to popularize opera and bring it to a wider Parisian audience.

Another international competition, this time for an Arctic Centre in Rovaniemi, Fin., called for two related museums devoted to Arctic geography and ecology and to the culture of the Lapps of Finland. The competition was open to architects of all countries bordering on the Arctic region and attracted 184 entries, including several from the U.S.S.R. Winners were the Danish team Søren Birch, Claus Bonderup, and Ellen Waade.

A new public library for San Juan Capistrano, Calif., designed by Michael Graves opened in December 1983 and was one of the most satisfactory small cultural buildings for some time. Graves's design was selected in a 1981 competition in which the requirements were for a one-story, 930-sq m (10,000-sq ft) community library that would harmonize with the Spanish heritage of San Juan Capistrano. Graves's design, in marked contrast to much new

southern California architecture, abstracted and reassembled the Spanish elements in a totally original manner, using traditional stucco walls and tile roofs. The town's old Mission provided, in the architect's words, "a sourcebook of images." The plan was of clearly defined separate spaces, likened to monks' cells around a cloister, in contrast to the easier-to-supervise centralized library plan. A separate children's area occupied its own wing, and stucco roof towers marked reading carrels. On the north side was a separate auditorium, and to the southwest were three lattice reading gazebos that would eventually be shaded by bougainvillea for outdoor reading. A profusion of towers supplied daylight, and the inside reading areas and book stacks were separated. The new library was popular with staff as well as readers, and attendance soared.

At Cornell University, Ithaca, N.Y., a new Performing Arts Center was being built in two phases. The first would include a 400–500-seat proscenium theatre, foyer, and dance studio, and the second would house a smaller flexible theatre space, studios, classrooms, and offices. The village-like ensemble on a hillside site would be tied together by an open-air loggia along the north elevation. Architects were James Stirling, Michael Wilford & Associates of London with Wank Adams Slavin Associates, New York City. Opening of the first phase was projected for early 1986.

A number of new museums were notable for their architectural qualities. In downtown Los Angeles the Museum of Contemporary Art, founded in 1980 as "a private museum with a public conscience," moved into the "Temporary Contemporary," an imaginative temporary headquarters consisting of two converted warehouses. Designed by Frank O. Gehry & Associates, it was to provide a home for the museum pending completion of a new $22 million building by architect Arata Isozaki.

The Temporary Contemporary opened in late 1983, and conversion costs were only just over $1 million. The project was a great success and was widely praised, attracting 10,000 members in the first two months. Gehry retained the industrial qualities of the interiors, using stark colour and new lighting to create spaces similar to those converted lofts used by many contemporary artists as studios. The two buildings were linked across a closed-off dead-end street with a canopy of steel and chain link creating a pedestrian plaza. The vast spaces were cleaned up and modified as required to meet earthquake, fire, and accessibility standards and given basic amenities. Some were sufficiently impressed with the results to suggest that the Temporary should become permanent. In all, Gehry's renovation provided 3,900 sq m (42,000 sq ft) of open exhibition space, 1,395 sq m (15,000 sq ft) of support areas, and 465 sq m (5,000 sq ft) of lobby, including bookstore and lounge.

In marked contrast was the elegant and formal High Museum of Art in Atlanta, Ga., by Richard Meier & Partners with its shimmering white porcelain panels and interior ramp. Definitely formal and postmodernist, it was described as Meier's finest work to date and a splendid monument to house a collection in the great museum tradition. The plan featured a skylit atrium surrounded by light-controlled galleries that permitted additional daylight by means of clerestories and side glazing. The general formal scheme was of a square rotated within a square. The main galleries were composed volumetrically of three cubes and a quarter cylinder, with a fourth cube, detached and rotated 45°, housing a separate auditorium. The primary circulation and design feature was a long ramp leading from street to curved reception lobby and inward into the central atrium, where it formed a double climbing ramp that provided vistas across the central space.

In Ottawa the Canadian government unveiled plans for two new museum buildings, one for the National Gallery of Canada and the other for the National Museum of Man. Architects for the National Gallery building were Moshe Safdie & Associates with the Parkin Partnership. Their design would provide 30,000 sq m (323,000 sq ft) of space to display Canada's largest collection of Canadian, U.S., and European art. The sandstone and glass design featured an entrance pavilion opening into a glazed ramp that led to a Great Hall, conceived as a modern glass reference to Canada's Parliamentary Library. The National Museum of Man, a 39,000-sq m (420,000-sq ft) structure to be located across the river at Hull, Que., featured an undulating masonry shell housing halls of varied heights in which contextual settings for collections of anthropology, history, and folk art could be created. Architects were Douglas Cardinal Limited with Tétreault, Parent, Languedoc & Associates.

The Dallas (Texas) Museum of Art, designed by Edward Larrabee Barnes & Associates, opened in January 1984. It embodied the latest in museum technology and design. (*See* MUSEUMS.)

Classical inspiration was clear in the design for the Hillel Center at Yale University by architects Roth and Moore. The new Jewish centre was designed to occupy a tight site only 11 × 29 m (35 × 95 ft), and the five-story structure of brick and stone with a slate roof featured a limestone base with conspicuous joints and a tall arched window rising

An international competition was used to chose the designer of a new opera house at the Place de la Bastille in Paris. The winning architect was Canadian Carlos Ott, shown here with his design in model form.

DE WILDENBERG—SYGMA

through the brick central area. The building would accommodate a library, dining room, chapel, cafe, and offices.

Public, Commercial, and Industrial Buildings. A significant number of speculative high-rise office and mixed-use towers were in the planning and construction stages in 1984. Their design variety illustrated the different modes of current design philosophy, ranging from the high-tech ultramodern to the neo-1920s and 1930s "moderne." In Minneapolis, Minn., the Norwest Center by Cesar Pelli would provide 185,000 sq m (2 million sq ft) of office and retail space on 66 floors. The structure, a stone base with a glass skin above, was to cost $150 million and be ready early in 1987. Kevin Roche John Dinkeloo & Associates were designers of a 30-story granite and glass-clad tower at 40 West 53rd Street, New York City. When completed in mid-1986, it was to house the American Craft Museum as well as offices and retail units.

The Wilshire/Midvale Tower in Los Angeles by Helmut Jahn was designed to provide 28 floors of office space at a cost of $50 million. The tower, to be completed by 1985, would be clad in granite, marble, limestone, and glass, traditional materials enjoying renewed favour. Metal panels and tinted glass over a polished granite base were materials chosen for the Merritt Tower, Baltimore, Md., by the Hillier Group; scheduled for completion in 1985, it would provide 29 floors of office and retail space. Morris Aubry Architects' design for One Nashville Place, Nashville, Tenn., was a hexagonal, sculpturelike structure of 23 stories to be clad in reflective glass.

I. M. Pei and Partners, Harry Weese and Associates, and WZMH Group were co-architects for Fountain Place in Dallas, a gigantic mixed-use complex comprising two pointed 60-story towers of glass that would provide 280,000 sq m (3 million sq ft) of space, including a luxury hotel and water garden. Harwood K. Smith & Partners of Dallas were architects for the Galleria in Metairie, La., a 149,000-sq m (1.6 million-sq ft) development of four turquoise-tinted glass-clad towers that included a 400-room hotel and a 156-unit apartment tower.

An aluminum and silver glass tower 35 stories high with a semicircular facade characterized the design by CRS Architects of Houston, Texas, for the Shenzhen Development Centre, Wu Free Zone, Shenzhen (Shen-chen) City in China. Offices, a conference centre, a hotel, and a health club would all be accommodated in the structure, which was scheduled for completion in the fall of 1986.

Other commercial projects on the drawing board in 1984 included the Crescent in Dallas, by Philip Johnson and John Burgee, a $1.6 million office, hotel, and retail complex characterized by slate mansard-roofed towers with limestone facades and wrought-iron roof balustrades. Associated architects were Shepherd & Boyd/USA. The scheme was described as "a celebration of art, history, and architecture."

An ambitious development proposal for Charles Square in Cambridge, Mass., was prepared by Cambridge Seven Associates for a 1.7-ha (4.2-ac) site adjoining the John F. Kennedy School of Government at Harvard Square. The multiple-building mixed-use complex of red brick and granite was designed to harmonize with the Harvard University buildings. Proposed were six separate interconnected structures with a landscaped courtyard, providing 86 condominium units and hotel, office, and retail space.

One of the most technologically advanced airports in the world, the King Khalid International Airport in Riyadh, Saudi Arabia, opened in late 1983. The vast flat desert site with almost no physical constraints allowed architects Hellmuth, Obata & Kassabaum with contractors Arabian

Bechtel Co. Ltd. to devise a system that would be dimensionally perfect in terms of circulation and convenience. There were five separate terminals, each based on an equilateral triangle (one a royal terminal with lavish decoration), allowing the shortest walk from curb to gate. Arched steel trusses formed a series of overlapping shells over the various terminals. A hexagonal mosque was centrally located in the complex, and the whole design was conceived in multiples of 30° and 60° angles—basic components of Muslim decorative motifs. The cost was $3.2 billion, and the projected traffic by the year 2000 was 15 million passengers a year.

A competition was held for a redesign of Copley Square in Boston, an important central space flanked by two of the city's greatest architectural set pieces—Trinity Church by H. H. Richardson and the Boston Public Library by McKim Mead and White. The winning design, chosen from 309 entries, was by Dean Abbott of the New York City firm Clarke & Rapuano. With its proposal to grass over 40% of the site, it would feature a blanket of greenery. Pushcarts and a farmer's market would, it was hoped, help draw visitors to the revitalized square.

Awards. The RIBA Gold Medal was awarded to Charles Correa (*see* BIOGRAPHIES), the foremost architect and planner in India. Correa was born in India but was trained as an architect at the University of Michigan and the Massachusetts Institute of Technology before returning to his native country. His most highly regarded building is the Mahatma Gandhi Memorial Museum in Ahmadabad, but he probably became best known for the design of low-cost housing for third world countries, especially New Bombay, a settlement of two million inhabitants across the harbour from the old city. A comparatively small number of entries resulted in only three other RIBA awards in the year of the 150th anniversary celebrations. These were the Yorkshire Bank headquarters in Leeds, England, by Abbey and Hanson, Rowe and Partners; Bishop Bateman Court at Trinity Hall, Cambridge, by Cambridge Design; and a doctors' surgery at Burnham Market, Norfolk, by Ian Steen of Cambridge.

The prestigious Pritzker Architecture Prize for 1984 was awarded to Richard Meier, praised for his "single-minded pursuit of new directions in contemporary architecture." The French Académie d'Architecture awarded its Gold Medal to Canadian architect Arthur Erickson.

American Institute of Architects Honor Awards went mostly to well-known designers with established reputations. New buildings predominated with only one award (for the R. J. Reynolds Tobacco Co. Building in Winston-Salem, N.C., by Croxton Collaborative and Hammill-Walker Associates) going to a renovation. There were 13 winners from 474 entries, and these included the Vietnam Veterans Memorial, Washington, D.C., by Cooper-Lecky Partnership and Maya Ying Lin; the Taft Residence, Cincinnati, Ohio, by Gwathmey Siegel & Associates; 333 Wacker Drive, Chicago, by Kohn Pedersen Fox Associates and Perkins & Will; the High Museum of Art, Atlanta (*see* above); Fragrant Hill Hotel, Beijing (Peking), by I. M. Pei & Partners; and Gordon Wu Hall, Princeton, N.J., by Venturi, Rauch & Scott Brown.

The deaths occurred during the year of Nathaniel Owings, a founding partner of Skidmore, Owings & Merrill; British architect Sir Frederick Gibberd; and Israeli architect Arieh Sharon. (*See* OBITUARIES.)   (SANDRA MILLIKIN)

See also Engineering Projects; Historic Preservation; Industrial Review.

This article updates the *Macropædia* article The History of Western ARCHITECTURE.

Art Exhibitions and Art Sales

In 1984, the year of the Los Angeles Olympics, that city also organized an Olympic Arts Festival during the summer months, which included a number of art exhibitions. There was no discernible thematic pattern to the various exhibitions planned as part of a cultural Olympics, but there was no doubt that many of them were highly successful. They ranged from the more traditional type of art exhibition to shows that aimed to extend the range of fine arts. One such was the major exhibition planned at the Museum of Contemporary Art in Los Angeles, entitled "The Automobile and Culture." Its goal was to examine the aesthetic properties of the automobile itself, something not always viewed as art. It included a look at the changing image of the car as demonstrated by more than 200 items—automobiles, paintings, sculptures, drawings, posters, and photographs dating from the early 1900s to the present day.

At the Los Angeles Memorial Coliseum, headquarters of many of the athletic events, a monumental sculpture by Robert Graham formed the gateway through which the Olympic torch was carried signaling the start of the Games. Graham's bronze sculpture incorporated large-scale figures of male and female athletes and was dedicated on June 1. At the ARCO Center for Visual Arts a corollary exhibition was mounted showing various studies for this major project, including preliminary maquettes and drawings. Also at the ARCO Center was an unusual exhibition entitled "Los Angeles and the Palm Tree: Image of a City." Drawing from works of art, advertisements, photographs, and even movie stills, it traced how more than 35,000 palm trees planted as preparation for the 1932 Los Angeles Olympics had affected the image and character of the city. A number of other exhibitions concentrated on the 1932 Olympics, including one at the Central Library showing archival documents and memorabilia and another at the County Museum of Natural History, which concentrated on the life-style of 1932.

A major exhibition on a more conventional note was mounted by the Los Angeles County Museum of Art. "A Day in the Country: Impressionism and the French Landscape" comprised 127 French Impressionist and Postimpressionist landscape paintings by most major artists of that period, including Monet, Pissarro, and Cézanne. Thirty-six of these were lent by the Louvre in Paris and would later be permanently installed at the new Paris museum, the Musée d'Orsay. Also part of the Olympic Arts Festival was a project whereby ten Los Angeles artists painted murals along the freeways throughout the city. A special show at the British Museum in London was devoted to the ancient Olympic Games and included scale models of ancient Olympia and antiquities drawn from the museum's own collection.

A number of important 1984 exhibitions concentrated on private collections rather than works of individual artists. One of the most splendid was the collection of modern paintings belonging to Baron Hans Thyssen-Bornemisza, shown at the Royal Academy in London in the autumn. The works, purchased in the last 20 years or so, formed one of the finest modern collections in private hands anywhere. As with all private collections, the personal taste of the collector and connoisseur was apparent, giving the collection and the exhibition a different slant from one prepared and selected by professional museum personnel.

Antoine Watteau was a household name among appreciators of painting at the turn of the 18th century and was then long overlooked. The first major international loan exhibition of his work opened in a triumphant show at the National Gallery of Art in Washington, D.C., in mid-1984 and was scheduled to go on to Paris and Berlin.

CHARLOTTENBURG PALACE, WEST BERLIN; PHOTOGRAPH, SCALA/ART RESOURCE

German Expressionist painters, particularly Ernst Kirchner and Karl Schmidt-Rottluff, were well represented. The earlier period of Impressionism was represented by a fine Degas and an excellent Cézanne, and there was an entire wall of Cubist pictures, with especially fine examples of Braque and Picasso. Later Expressionist artists, including Max Beckmann, and lesser known artists such as Karl Hubbuch were also represented in a collection that was particularly strong in figurative works of northern Europe. American pictures from the Thyssen-Bornemisza collection were on view at the Baltimore (Md.) Museum of Art in the autumn before starting a tour of seven U.S. cities.

An exhibition at the Manchester City Art Gallery in England in the summer, devoted to the works of François Boucher, was comprised largely of paintings, drawings, and prints from the Nationalmuseum, Stockholm, whose collection was formed by one of Boucher's principal patrons, Count Carl Tessin, who had been the Swedish ambassador to France. The exhibition was the first in England to be devoted to Boucher. Most of the works were decorative panels. There were no portraits, and only a few pieces of applied art supplemented the paintings. In Lausanne, Switz., a comprehensive exhibition of Impressionists drawn from private collections in French-speaking Switzerland was shown at the newly established Fondation de L'Hermitage. On show were works by local artists as well as examples by the better known Postimpressionists such as Cézanne and Bonnard.

"Beauty and Tranquility: The Eli Lilly Collection of Chinese Art" was the last of a series of centennial exhibitions held at the Indianapolis (Ind.) Museum of Art. Again, this was an exhibition based on a collection by one individual. The collection was founded after World War II by Eli Lilly, who had the museum in mind as an ultimate beneficiary. Some of the 167 works on display had never before been exhibited. The collection was remarkable, especially for one so recently formed, and was particularly rich in ceramics and early jade.

A number of architectural exhibitions were held in 1984. In London, as part of the celebrations of the 150th anniversary of the founding of the Royal Institute of British Architects (RIBA), the Barbican Art Gallery staged a fine display of architectural drawing. "Getting London in Perspective" examined the idea of the perspective technique in architectural drawing, ranging from the earliest examples to present-day methods using computer-aided skills. Drawings by such well-known artists and architects as Thomas

Sandby and Sir John Soane were included, as were works by many of the great 19th-century perspectivists. There were more than 200 line drawings, water colours, oils, and computer plans on display illustrating individual buildings, town planning schemes, and railway projects.

"The Art of the Architect," one of the closing events of the 1984 Festival of Architecture, was exhibited in the RIBA's headquarters and included approximately 130 original drawings from the institute's own collections. Its aim was to illustrate how architects have drawn in the past and the variety to be found in architectural drawings, ranging from the simplest of sketches to ambitious and pleasing perspectives showing the completed scheme either in reality or in imagination. Among the greatest masterpieces of the collection were works by Andrea Palladio, Inigo Jones, Robert Adam, and Sir Edwin Lutyens, including Lutyens's watercolour sketchbook for Gertrude Jekyll and many other models, books, manuscripts, and portraits. Twentieth-century designs included a model by Jørn Utzon of the Sydney (Australia) Opera House demonstrating its shell-like roof system.

"Design in America: the Cranbrook Vision 1925–1950," also devoted to architecture and design, was shown first at the Detroit Institute of Arts and later in the American wing of the Metropolitan Museum of Art, New York City. Cranbrook Academy of Art, near Detroit, which trained many artists and designers in the period 1925–50, is particularly well known for its own buildings, designed by the Finnish architect Eliel Saarinen. The exhibition would later travel to Helsinki, Fin., Paris, and London. An architectural exhibit at the Cooper-Hewitt Museum of Decorative Arts and Design, New York City, focused on the changes in skyscraper design in Manhattan that took place between World Wars I and II and, in particular, on the impact of a zoning law of 1916 that required skyscrapers to be set back. An exhibition entitled "Chicago and New York: More than a Century of Architectural Interaction" was shown at the Art Institute of Chicago and later traveled to Washington, D.C., Texas, and New York City. The relationship between the earliest designers of skyscrapers in Chicago and the famous Manhattan skyline was among the themes explored.

In Washington, D.C., the National Gallery of Art mounted several exhibitions on unusual themes. "Leonardo's Last Supper" was a three-part exhibition devoted to one famous work of art. The exhibition, which was also seen in Sydney, Toronto, and Amsterdam, was divided into three parts: the various preparatory drawings, lent by Queen Elizabeth II from her collection at Windsor Castle; works relating to the painting but by other artists; and a section devoted to the current work of restoration, including a full-scale "reconstruction" of the "Last Supper" made up from Polaroid photographs. This last was amazingly realistic. "The Folding Image: Screens by Western Artists of the 19th and 20th Centuries" was another unusual show at the National Gallery. It was the first to be devoted to modern Western screens and included 40 examples, most of which had never before been exhibited in public. Among them were a fine fivefold screen by the Swiss artist Paul Klee and a three-panel screen by Josef Hoffmann.

A number of important exhibitions were devoted to American themes. "American Folk Art: Expressions of a New Spirit," organized by the Museum of American Folk Art in New York City, was composed of items drawn from the museum's own collection. The exhibition was circulated by the American Federation of Arts and was seen in London at the Barbican Art Gallery and in late summer at the Minneapolis (Minn.) Institute of Arts. A larger exhibition devoted to the work of the painter William Merritt Chase, one of the leading American Impressionist artists, was shown at the Metropolitan Museum in New York. It was the first exhibition of Chase's work there since the large retrospective that followed his death in 1916. The Detroit Institute of Arts began its centennial celebrations with an exhibition entitled "Automobile and Culture! Detroit Style," which was to run until August 1986.

In The Netherlands a retrospective exhibition devoted to the work of Alphonse Mucha, known for his Art Nouveau posters, was shown in several places in 1984 and would finish its tour in Brussels in 1985. A major portion of the show was comprised of decorative panels, posters, and book illustrations by the artist, but there were also designs for decorative objects and architectural designs, including the facade and interior of the Art Nouveau jeweler George Fouquet's shop in the rue Royale, Paris.

A large and important exhibition devoted to Dutch 17th-century painting, "The Age of Vermeer and De Hooch—Masterpieces of 17th-Century Dutch Genre Painting," opened at the Royal Academy in London in September and continued through the autumn. The high point of the show was probably the four Vermeers and the opportunity to see them together. The exhibition, which consisted of 110 paintings carefully chosen from public and private collections throughout Europe and the U.S., included works by some artists rarely seen outside The Netherlands. The 17th-century paintings on view portrayed a world of rich, beautifully textured middle-class domestic interiors. The exhibition had previously been shown at the Philadelphia Museum of Art and at the Gemäldegalerie, West Berlin. "Danish Painting: The Golden Age," at the National Gallery, London, during September–November, comprised 80 paintings of the 1767–1858 period from Statens Museum for Kunst, Copenhagen. The exhibition was signally successful in revealing the many attractions of a school of European 19th-century painting previously little seen outside Denmark. Among the artists represented were C. W. Eckersberg (1783–1853), C Købke (1810–48), and C. Hansen (1804–80).

Also in London, the Tate Gallery held a number of important and well-attended exhibitions. "The Hard-Won Image" was devoted to figurative work by British artists as varied as William Coldstream, Francis Bacon, and David Hockney. In the spring the Tate held an exhibition devoted to the Pre-Raphaelites that showed those painters as a group or brotherhood, rather than as individuals. Although

there had been many shows in recent years devoted to members of the Pre-Raphaelite Brotherhood, this was the first to focus on the group itself. Many of the key paintings were assembled for this occasion from provincial and foreign galleries, as well as from the Tate's own collection. Three separate shows at the Tate were devoted to sculpture. "Sculptors and Modellers" concentrated on contemporary carved and modeled work. A second show consisted of two sculptors actually working at the gallery and producing works specifically for the exhibition. The third show, in the autumn, was entitled "Sculpture from the Body."

The Tate's major autumn show was devoted to the work of George Stubbs, the 18th-century English painter known particularly for his portraits of horses. The exhibition was dedicated to the U.S. collector Paul Mellon, who lent 13 canvases from his private collection, 14 canvases donated by him to the Yale Center for British Art, New Haven, Conn., and 27 drawings, also from the Yale bequest. A remarkable series of drawings of equine anatomy, done from dissections, were included, as were many of Stubbs's finest works such as "Whistlejacket," depicting a huge rearing stallion.

An exhibition hailed as the greatest assemblage of English Romanesque art ever brought together in the U.K. was shown at the Hayward Gallery in the spring and summer. About 800 pieces were gathered together, from major museums and private collections (including those of churches and private individuals) in Britain, Europe, and North America. The period covered was from 1066 to 1200, an era in which the arts of manuscript illumination and sculpture flourished, and the exhibition was rich in these fields. Many were surprised at how successfully works of this period could be displayed in the ultramodern ambience of the Hayward.

One of the high points of the winter in London was the exhibition entitled "The Genius of Venice, 1500–1600," held at the Royal Academy early in 1984. It provided a rare opportunity to see many important works side by side, including particularly fine examples by all the major Venetian artists of the 16th and 17th centuries, among them Titian and Veronese. There were, in all, about 140

A highlight of the Venice Biennale was a one-man show by Howard Hodgkin at the English pavilion. His small paintings, alive with colour and the deft articulation of intimate detail, include "Valentine," above.

paintings, 42 sculptures, 63 prints, and 84 drawings. The Titian portraits included one of John the Baptist from the Venice Accademia. Many of the objects on view were lent by remote or otherwise inaccessible private collections. Sebastiano's famous "Judgement of Solomon" from Kingston Lacy was on display to the public for the first time in many years.

An exhibition devoted to the works of Raoul Dufy, shown at the Hayward Gallery, included paintings, drawings, and murals, as well as tapestries, theatre designs, fabric designs, and ceramics, all chosen from the period from about 1911 to the 1930s. Dufy's love of music was indicated by various versions of his work entitled "Hommage à Mozart." In addition, there were many drawings depicting musicians and orchestras.

A number of noteworthy exhibitions were held in Australia. "The Moderns, Solomon R. Guggenheim Museum, New York; Peggy Guggenheim Collection, Venice" was the title of a show at the Art Gallery of New South Wales in Sydney. The exhibition made available to Australian art lovers many hitherto inaccessible works of major 20th-century artists in Europe and the U.S. Included were 80 works by 45 artists drawn from the Guggenheim collections in both New York and Venice. An exhibition of New Zealand art was shown at the Metropolitan Museum of Art in New York from the autumn until January 1985. "Te Maori: Maori Art from New Zealand Collections," organized by the American Federation of Arts with the cooperation of the New Zealand government, comprised objects from New Zealand museums, most of which were still owned by Maori tribes in that country. It was the first large-scale exhibit of Maori tribal artifacts to leave New Zealand. Most of the nearly 200 items on display were carved sacred objects enjoyable for their aesthetic appeal as well as for their symbolic and religious importance.

The Art Institute of Chicago showed an important exhibition of 91 works by the French Impressionist Edgar Degas, including sculpture, pastels, and drawings. An important exhibition entitled "Watteau: 1684–1721," at the National Gallery in Washington, marked the 300th anniversary of the birth of that French artist of the Rococo period. Included were some 40 paintings and 90 drawings.

A number of the finest examples of ancient Egyptian works of art were on show in Venice in the autumn. The works were unlikely ever again to be allowed to leave Cairo. In one of the greatest exhibitions in recent years, entitled "Treasures of the Pharoahs," 74 items ranging from the pre-Dynastic to the Greco-Roman era were on view at the Doge's Palace.   (SANDRA MILLIKIN)

ART SALES

Market Trends. The 1983–84 art market season saw exceptional prices for items of outstanding quality in nearly every field. The season started with West Germany paying £8,140,000 for a 12th-century illuminated manuscript of the Gospels commissioned by Henry the Lion, duke of Saxony, and ended with a mystery private purchaser bidding £7,370,000 for a J. M. W. Turner painting, "Seascape: Folkestone," which had belonged to the art historian Lord Clark. The highest auction price previously on record was $6.4 million for a Turner in 1980. The extraordinary prices at the top of the market, together with the strong dollar, meant that Christie's and Sotheby's announced, respectively, 53 and 47% increases in sterling turnover for the season. At the same time, the number of lots left unsold was the highest in many years.

An important shift in the motivation of middle-market buyers became apparent: art investment had yielded top

place to home decoration. This made for strong furniture prices, premium prices for usable silver such as candlesticks and wine labels, and a very strong market in decorative Chinese export porcelain. The strongest buying came from the U.S., from both private collectors and museums, with the purchasing power of the J. Paul Getty Museum causing considerable anxiety in Europe. The Getty repeatedly stressed its determination not to disrupt the market and was left far behind in the bidding for the £7,370,000 Turner. A 13th-century sienese panel painting of the Crucifixion, for which the museum had paid £1.8 million, was denied an export license from Britain and went to the Manchester City Art Gallery. (*See* MUSEUMS: *Sidebar.*)

U.S. financier A. Alfred Taubman became the legal proprietor of Sotheby's in October 1983 without making any revolutionary changes. However, the way very rich Americans descended on a selected handful of sales during the year, turning them into prestige social events and sending prices through the roof, may have reflected the new interest of Taubman and his friends. Outstanding single-collector dispersals of grand furnishings were most favoured, notably the contents of Mrs. Charles Wrightsman's Palm Beach, Fla., home, dispersed for $4,862,000 by Sotheby's in New York in May; the contents of Elveden Hall, Norfolk, dispersed on behalf of Lord Iveagh by Christie's, also in May, for £6 million (£2.5 million had been estimated); and the contents of Mrs. Florence J. Gould's villa in the South of France, dispersed by Sotheby's in Monaco for F 56,154,-700 in June.

Works of Art. The two top sales of the year were Christie's auction of 71 Old Master drawings from the duke of Devonshire's Chatsworth collection for £21.2 million in July and Sotheby's 109-lot sale of Impressionist and modern art in May, which made $39.3 million—a record total for any single auction. The duke of Devonshire had selected the drawings for the Christie's sale as a representative cross-section of the Chatsworth collection. They had first been offered to the British Museum at £5.5 million but turned down. A black chalk study of a man's head became the most expensive drawing ever sold at auction when it went for £3,564,000 to Mrs. J. Seward Johnson, widow of the U.S. pharmaceuticals millionaire. A sheet from the album of drawings compiled by Vasari, the 16th-century Florentine art historian, went to Ian Woodner, a U.S. collector, at £3,240,000.

Sotheby's Impressionist sale had been cleverly built around two major collections, 12 paintings from the estate of Mrs. Erna Wolf Dreyfuss and a collection of modern sculpture, mostly of monumental size, sent for sale by Mrs. J. Seward Johnson. Prices for the latter skyrocketed, with two separate Maillol bronzes reaching $1.1 million. A Dreyfuss Gauguin, "Mata Mua" of 1892, sold for $3,850,-000, a new auction record for the artist.

Post-World War II art, principally of the American school, moved up into a price range comparable with the best Impressionists. In November 1983 Mark Rothko's "Black, Maroons and White" sold for $1,815,000 to Shigeki Kameyama, a Tokyo businessman, at Sotheby's in New York. In May 1984 Alexander Calder's monumental sculpture "Grand Crinkly" sold for $852,500 at Sotheby's, and a Morris Louis scored $473,000 at Christie's. The market in 19th-century American painting continued strong. "The Trap Sprung" by William Sydney Mount made $880,000 in December 1983, and "A View of Boston" by Thomas Cole made $990,000 in June 1984. Agnew's, the London dealers, sold a portrait of Mrs. Thomas Gage by John Singleton Copley for over £1 million by inviting private tenders. Other outstanding picture prices included £972,-

000 for "The Plague at Athens" by Michiel Sweerts, a 17th-century Dutch artist, and £777,000 for "The Doncaster Gold Cup of 1838" by J. F. Herring, a new auction price record for a sporting painting.

The high prices paid for ornate antique silver by the London dealer Jacques Koopman was the outstanding feature of the year in the decorative arts market. He was helping to form a collection for Muhammad Mahdi at-Tajir, London ambassador of the United Arab Emirates and one of the richest men in the world. Virtually all the important silver that appeared at auction was bought by Koopman, and he set a new silver price record when he paid £484,000 with a partner for a silver shield designed by John Flaxman and made by the British royal goldsmiths in 1822. English furniture had a boom year with strong new interest from the U.S., especially in smart late 18th-century satinwood or inlaid furniture. A new interest in antique textiles was also gathering momentum, and turn-of-the-century decorative arts scored sensational prices.

Books. The book market had a buoyant season, with some very high prices paid for important books and manuscripts and a strong market in the middle range. Sotheby's, the traditional auction leaders, substantially increased the number of their specialist sales and began the practice of dividing libraries, whose contents would have been sold together in the past, among specialist auctions. This reflected Sotheby's new interest in marketing techniques. Business zeal also landed them with two much publicized problems: the Bolivian government, claiming ownership, won an injunction to stop the London sale of Che Guevara's Bolivian campaign diaries, valued at £200,000; and the New York state attorney general brought an action for fraud against Sotheby's for their representations concerning the ownership of about $2 million worth of Jewish books and manuscripts, which had disappeared from the Hochschule für die Wissenchaft des Judentum in Berlin in 1942 and reappeared in New York.

The most sensational price of the year was the £8,140,000 for the Henry the Lion Gospels (*see* above). Beside this, the aquisition by the British Museum from the duke of Rutland of a 13th-century Psalter written and illuminated in England at around £1.5 million seemed cheap. After long delays over the issuing of an export license, a copy of the 1297 version of Magna Carta was sold for $1.5 million by the Brudenell family of Deene Park, Northamptonshire, to H. Ross Perot, a Texas businessman, who placed it on loan to the National Archives in Washington, D.C. The sale of a copy of Shakespeare's first publication, the poem *Venus and Adonis,* for £129,600 was another landmark.

Musical manuscripts were again one of the strongest markets. Two movements of an unknown Haydn mass in D minor were sold for £151,200 at Christie's in March, and a manuscript of Mahler's First Symphony in D major (*The Titan*) made £143,000 at Sotheby's in May. A set of signatures of the signers of the Declaration of Independence went for $352,000, and an 1836 edition of Milton's poems annotated by Herman Melville sold for $110,000, as did the 390 17th-century manuscript pages of Thomas Traherne's *Commentaries of Heaven.* An autograph manuscript of Albert Einstein's 1929 article on his unified-field theory sold for $38,500, and Louis XVI's three-page draft of his speech to the States General in June 1789 went for £45,360. The return to popularity of colour plate books was signaled by Sotheby's London sale in February, when a first edition of Audubon's *Birds of America* made £1.1 million.

(GERALDINE NORMAN)

This article updates the *Macropædia* articles The History of Western PAINTING; The History of Western SCULPTURE.

Astronomy

Solar System. Although one normally thinks of astronomy as the study of objects beyond the Earth, the most novel astronomical "observation" of 1984 may well have been made by Earth itself 65 million years ago and only recently come to light. At that time the transition between the Cretaceous and Tertiary (C–T) geological periods occurred, and with it the extinction of many biological species, including the dinosaurs. In 1980 Luis W. and Walter Alvarez of the University of California at Berkeley and their collaborators suggested that the transition coincided with the impact of a large cometary or asteroidal body with the Earth. This conclusion was supported primarily by worldwide evidence for a layer of iridium present at the C–T boundary, an element rare on Earth but commonly found in abundance in meteorites. It was suggested that such an impact could have global atmospheric effects, leading ultimately to wholesale extinctions.

Late in 1983 two paleontologists at the University of Chicago, David M. Raup and J. John Sepkoski, presented evidence that over the past 250 million years several such mass extinctions accounted for the demise of more than 3,500 families of organism. Most astonishingly they reported that these extinctions came periodically, about every 26 million years. No geological explanation was forthcoming to account for such a long time scale or periodicity. Almost immediately and continuing throughout 1984, a host of astronomical explanations were offered.

One of the earliest suggestions, from Marc Davis and collaborators at Berkeley and independently from Daniel P. Whitmire of the University of Southwestern Louisiana and Albert A. Jackson IV of the Computer Sciences Corporation, Houston, Texas, was that the Sun has a dark (heretofore unseen) stellar companion, dubbed Nemesis and Death Star by the investigators and media. Such a star, moving about the Sun in a highly elliptical orbit and passing near it every 26 million years, could account for these events by the perturbations it would produce on the comets residing in the so-called Oort cloud, a halo of cometary bodies thought to surround the solar system far beyond the planet Pluto. Comets would then be sent crashing into the inner solar system, greatly increasing the chance that one or more would hit the Earth.

Alternatively, Michael R. Rampino and Richard B. Stothers of NASA's Goddard Institute for Space Studies in

Earth Perihelion and Aphelion, 1985

| Jan. 3 | Perihelion, 147,105,000 km (91,407,000 mi) from the Sun |
| July 5 | Aphelion, 152,097,000 km (94,508,000 mi) from the Sun |

Equinoxes and Solstices, 1985

March 20	Vernal equinox, 16:14[1]
June 21	Summer solstice, 10:44[1]
Sept. 23	Autumnal equinox, 02:07[1]
Dec. 21	Winter solstice, 22:08[1]

Eclipses, 1985

May 4	Moon, total (begins 17:20[1]), visible in Antarctica, Europe, Africa except W. Asia, U.S.S.R. except extreme NE, Australia, New Zealand, E S. America, the Indian Ocean, and the S Atlantic Ocean.
May 19	Sun, partial (begins 19:15[1]), visible in NE Asia, Japan, N of N. America, Iceland, extreme NW Europe, Arctic regions.
Oct. 28	Moon, total (begins 14:38[1]), visible in Europe, Asia, U.S.S.R., Africa, Australia, New Zealand, Greenland, Iceland, Antarctica, Arctic regions, the Arctic Ocean, the N Pacific Ocean, and the Indian Ocean.
Nov. 12	Sun, total (begins 12:09[1]), visible in Antarctica, and S of S. America.

[1]Universal time.
Source: *The Astronomical Almanac for the Year 1985* (1984).

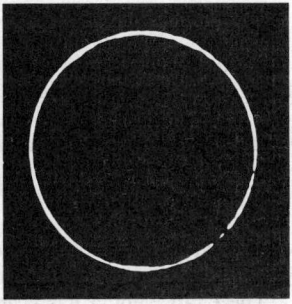

New York City, as well as J. M. Scalo and Roman Smoluchowski of the University of Texas, argued that the Oort cloud may be perturbed by the periodic motion of the Sun up and down through the plane of the Milky Way Galaxy and by motion in and out of its spiral arms.

By year's end both models had been examined and criticized on a number of grounds. The Nemesis hypothesis lacked direct observational confirmation of the star and faced serious theoretical challenges to its initial formation with the Sun and its long-term stability. The solar oscillation idea suffered from the apparent anticorrelation of the phase of the oscillation and of the extinctions. Both hypotheses remained intriguing, although speculative.

Two of the solar system's outer planets, Neptune and Uranus, also made headlines in 1984 following observations by Bradford A. Smith of the University of Arizona and Richard J. Terrile of the Jet Propulsion Laboratory, Pasadena, Calif. Although Neptune was discovered in 1846, its basic properties have been difficult to determine, owing primarily to its great distance from the Earth and to its cloud-covered surface. Taking a series of infrared photos of the planet over a six-day period and using computer enhancement to exaggerate the cloud features of the planet, the two researchers were able to determine its rotation period directly. They found it to be 17 hours 50 minutes and in a west-to-east direction like the Earth.

Unlike the Earth and Neptune, the planet Uranus has a spin axis lying in the plane of the ecliptic, the plane in which the planets orbit about the Sun. In 1977 rings were detected indirectly about the planet during observations of a star's passage behind it. During the year Smith and Terrile directly photographed the ring system. Using a highly light-sensitive charge-coupled device (CCD) attached to the 2.5-m telescope at Las Campanas Observatory in Chile, combined with computer image processing of the data, they were able to show the rings directly for the first time. The structures proved even more intriguing than had previously been thought, since they reflect only about 2% of the sunlight hitting them, making them much "blacker" than common carbon soot.

Stars. Following its launch in January 1983, the U.S.-Dutch-British Infrared Astronomical Satellite (IRAS) began a series of spectacular discoveries, most of which still remained to be analyzed at the end of 1984. Perhaps the most exciting initial report was of the possible discovery of a planetary system around the star Vega. The infrared observations suggested the presence of a disk or halo of solid material orbiting around and heated by the star and then reradiating in the infrared. Within a few months a second star, Fomalhaut, was found to have excess infrared emission, again a hint of the presence of orbiting solid material.

By mid-1984 ground-based observers, presumably spurred on by the IRAS discoveries, turned up infrared evidence for protoplanetary or planetary material around five more stars. A collaboration from Cornell University, Ithaca, N.Y., the University of California at Los Angeles (UCLA), and the University of Hawaii using the four-metre telescope at Kitt Peak, Arizona, and the infrared telescope on Mauna Kea, Hawaii, detected dusty material around the stars HL Tau and R Mon. A collaboration from the universities of Massachusetts, Wyoming, and Hawaii using the three-metre infrared facility on Mauna Kea did likewise for the stars Epsilon Eridani and Beta Pictoris, two nearby but fairly weak sources, as well as for the star Lynds 1551. In December astronomers from the University of Arizona and the National Optical Astronomy Observatories, Tucson, Ariz., reported ground-based infrared observations of a gaseous, planet-sized object, perhaps nine-tenths the size of Jupiter, in orbit around Van Biesbroeck 8, a faint star 21 light-years from the Earth.

At year's end a spectacular confirmation was made of the infrared observations. The star Beta Pictoris, having shown an infrared excess in scans in one direction across the object but not in the direction perpendicular to the first, was thus already suspected of possessing a disk of material. The team of Smith and Terrile turned their CCD system at Las Campanas to the star and produced a clear image of two protuberances, one on either side of the star. Though probably not planets, the lobes showed directly the disklike structure of what is probably a young (100 million-year-old) protoplanetary system.

Since the early 1900s scientists have employed a variety of techniques to detect cosmic rays with energies per particle as high as 10^{20} eV (electron volts). Until 1984, however, no observation had made a definite connection of these particles with their source or sources. During the year such an association seemed to have been made for the first time with the discovery of galactic sources of ultrahigh-energy (UHE) gamma rays, implying sources for particles with energies of at least 10^{17} eV.

The first and, as of late 1984, the only confirmed source of UHE gamma rays was the well-studied object Cygnus X-3. Discovered in 1967 as a variable X-ray source within our Galaxy, it was subsequently confirmed as a radio, infrared, X-ray, and gamma-ray source at energies as high as 10^{12} eV, displaying a 4.8-hour periodicity at all but radio wavelengths. This variation was attributed to the orbital period of a companion star, although no direct spectroscopic observations supported or refuted this conclusion.

During the year two groups independently reported detecting Cygnus X-3 at energies greater than 10^{16} eV, again modulated with the 4.8-hour period. M. Samorski and W. Stamm of the University of Kiel, West Germany, using the Kiel extensive air shower array, found a UHE luminosity 100 times greater than the Sun's total optical luminosity.

What made this result remarkable was both the high proton energies observed and their flux. The total luminosity of the source, some 10,000 times that of the Sun, implies that a few percent of its emission is being converted into UHE photons. Furthermore, since the photons must arise from accelerated particles that themselves do not radiate with 100% efficiency, the particles must have energies several times higher than their photons. This line of reasoning implies that the underlying fast-particle source is an incredibly powerful and efficient particle accelerator.

In the months following the discovery of UHE gamma rays from Cygnus X-3, two other well-known X-ray sources, Vela X-1 and Her X-1, were detected at UHE values. The combined observations suggested that many, if not all, galactic X-ray sources are also UHE gamma-ray sources.

The Crab Nebula has been called the Rosetta Stone of stellar astronomy. It is the remnant of a supernova that was witnessed in AD 1054 and that left behind an expanding shell of gas emitting radio waves and optical synchrotron radiation as well as a pulsar having a period of 33 milliseconds. This combination of attributes had been unique until 1984, when a group headed by Frederick D. Seward of the Harvard-Smithsonian Center for Astrophysics, Cambridge, Mass., reported the discovery of a pulsar outside the Milky Way and lying within one of its satellite galaxies, the Large Magellanic Cloud. Using X-ray data from the Einstein Observatory satellite, they discovered a pulsar with a 50-millisecond period. Like the Crab, it is imbedded in a young (1,000-year-old) supernova remnant. Carl Pennypacker of the Lawrence Berkeley Laboratory in California and John Middleditch of the Los Alamos (N.M.) National Laboratory also detected optical pulsations from the object, making it only the third pulsar seen at optical wavelengths to date and the first outside our Galaxy.

Galaxies. In extragalactic astronomy, as well as solar system astronomy, 1984 continued to be the year of IRAS. Though most of the infrared objects detected by that satellite lie within our own Galaxy, some IRAS sources proved to be external galaxies. One, called Arp 220, while peculiar in optical appearance, is an otherwise undistinguished, dim (14th-magnitude) galaxy at visible wavelengths. At infrared wavelengths, however, IRAS found it to be 100 times more luminous than a typical galaxy. Almost 99% of its emission is in the infrared. Only the quasars appear brighter at any wavelength. IRAS located two other such superluminous

infrared galaxies as well, leading theorists to speculate on the origin of such intense radiation. Suggestions ranged from a dust-enshrouded black hole that is accreting matter to a population of bright young stars embedded in dust left over from the star-formation process.

Our own Galaxy has such a dust-enshrouded nucleus, making optical observations of it difficult. Using the giant Very Large Array (VLA) radio telescope near Soccorro, N.M., three radio astronomers managed to penetrate the thick veil to reveal a spectacular filamentary structure there. Mark Morris of UCLA and Farhad Yusef-Zadeh and Don Chance of Columbia University found an arc of ionized gas forming a band of filamentary structures that stretched about 200 light-years above the plane of the Galaxy, each filament about ten light-years thick. Although the source of the structures was not known, they had the appearance of magnetic fields guiding ejected gas.

(KENNETH BRECHER)

See also Space Exploration.

This article updates the *Macropædia* articles GALAXIES; NEBULA; The PHYSICAL SCIENCES: *Astronomy and Astrophysics;* The SOLAR SYSTEM; STARS AND STAR CLUSTERS.

Botanical Gardens and Zoos

Botanical Gardens. Throughout the world there was increasing awareness that the needs of botanical science were changing and that many old concepts were no longer relevant. As the problems to be examined and solved were often common within a geographic area, regional cooperation and group support among botanical gardens was the logical step forward. In July 1984 a newly created European and Mediterranean Regional Group of the International Association of Botanic Gardens (IABG) held its inaugural meeting in Nancy, France. Over 60 delegates from 12 countries confirmed their institutions' commitment to the new regional body, examined common areas of interest, and decided on topics of immediate importance that should form the agenda for the next meeting, to be held in Durham, England, in 1985.

The American Association of Botanical Gardens and Arboreta, in many ways a model for such regional organizations, held its 1984 annual meeting at the Devonian Botanic Garden, University of Alberta, in June. The theme of the meeting was "Plants—the International Denominator," and formal sessions covered the role of botanical gardens in conservation of endangered species, research programs, plant breeding for colder climates, modern nursery practices, and plant introduction. A similar organization in the Soviet Union grouped 120 botanical gardens there, and it was hoped that these, as well as botanical gardens from other Eastern-bloc countries, would be represented at future meetings of the IABG European and Mediterranean Regional Group.

In recent years little had been known of botanical gardens in China, but a book published by the Science Press, Beijing (Peking), listed 11 new gardens and arboretums covering a total area of 1,500 ha (3,700 ac). The largest was Nanyue (Nan-yueh) Arboretum (540 ha; 1,300 ac) and the smallest, Shenyang (Shen-yang) Municipal Arboretum (4 ha; 10 ac). Currently, exchange of plant material with botanical institutes in China was limited, but there had been a significant number of exchange visits by scientific staff from Europe and North America during the last decade.

The first phase of a major new tropical greenhouse development at the Palmgarten in Frankfurt am Main, West

AP/WIDE WORLD

Scientists believe that this computer-enlarged photograph may show the beginnings of a new solar system around the star Beta Pictoris, some 293 trillion miles from the Sun. Analysis suggests that circumstellar matter seen in the upper left and lower right quadrants of the photograph is composed of the same materials that formed the planets of our solar system.

Octagonal pavilions of glass and a new greenhouse are features of the addition planned for New York City's Brooklyn Botanic Garden, shown here in an architect's model.

BROOKLYN BOTANIC GARDEN

Germany, was formally opened in May 1984. Covering an area of 2,500 sq m (27,000 sq ft), this structure was designed to accommodate a wide representation of tropical species including trees. Internal environmental control was achieved by a computer linked to a weather recording station, and the whole structure was double glazed to reduce heat loss during cold weather. Plantings included a mangrove swamp area and an important collection of Bromeliaceae transferred from the University of Heidelberg Botanic Garden.

A new botanical garden was established in Córdoba, Spain, as a joint venture between the university and the city council, with the latter providing considerable financial support. The garden, covering 5.5 ha (13.6 ac), would contain a representative collection of Iberian and, in particular, Andalusian flora and would feature conservation and educational themes. In Japan the Tsukuba Botanical Garden, attached to the National Science Museum, was formally opened; its research collections would display the particularly diverse vegetation of central Japan.

The Brooklyn (N.Y.) Botanic Garden and Arboretum began a $20 million conservatory complex that would include a new greenhouse and three pavilions. Completion of this development, as well as construction of a new education centre and renovation of the existing Palm House, was expected by 1986. Perhaps the most important building of its type in the world, the Palm House at the Royal Botanic Gardens, Kew, England, was to be completely renovated over the next two years. Built in 1848, the structure and, particularly, the glazing system were in urgent need of repair. Because the building was of considerable architectural importance, great care would be taken to ensure that restoration did not spoil the integrity of the original design.

(REGINALD IAN BEYER)

Zoos. Representatives of 27 countries attended the fourth World Conference on Breeding Endangered Species in Captivity, held Sept. 24–28, 1984, at Flevohof, Neth. Radical changes had taken place in the policies of zoos since the first conference was held in 1972. The "stamp-collection" approach was being superseded by an emphasis on more selective collections, with animals in more natural surroundings. Zoos were now increasingly concerned with the entire captive population of a species and with its genetic and demographic management, requiring cooperation between collections, both national and international. Even then the captive population was often small, and inbreeding could produce problems. Recent research at the National Zoological Park in Washington, D.C., showed

that, for 41 of 44 mammal species (of 21 families and 36 genera), mortality of inbred young was significantly higher than that of noninbred young.

A number of speakers at the conference, and at a parallel meeting of the Captive Breeding Specialist Group (a committee of the Species Survival Commission of the International Union for the Conservation of Nature), gave details of international and national cooperative management plans for particular species. Many of the plans were based on international studbooks, 60 of which were officially recognized in 1984, and on data from the U.S.-based International Species Inventory System (ISIS). A recent survey from ISIS showed that the great majority of wild animals currently held in zoos were captive-bred. While zoos strove to develop self-sustaining populations through captive breeding, this involved such problems as the cost of keeping surplus animals, the necessity and ethics of culling, and the difficulties of reintroduction in the wild when the original habitat had been destroyed.

Also raised at the conference was the whole question of the necessity and moral justification for keeping any wild animal in captivity, partly as a result of the appearance of a number of vociferous—and, indeed, militant—opposition groups, particularly in Britain and the U.S. It was important for zoos to present their own case objectively and clearly, and 1984 provided a number of achievements that could be cited in any argument. For example, there were now a number of reintroduction programs, based on captive-bred stock, that had reached the stage of release into the wild. In June ten golden lion tamarins were released into their native rain-forest habitat in the Poço das Antas Biological Reserve in Brazil. These animals, bred in a number of U.S. zoos, were sent to the Rio de Janeiro Primate Centre in late 1983 by the Smithsonian Institution's National Zoological Park in Washington, D.C. They stayed there for six months to adapt to local foods and climate before their release. In a similar well-planned and well-monitored scheme, the Arabian oryx was being reintroduced into reserves in Oman and Jordan.

There were some notable successes in artificial breeding that could enormously improve the breeding potential of individuals. In August 1983 five bongo embryos were collected nonsurgically from a single bongo in the Los Angeles Zoo and taken immediately to the Cincinnati (Ohio) Zoo, where they were transferred nonsurgically to four eland and one bongo. Pregnancy resulted in one eland and the bongo, and both gave birth in 1984 to normal bongo calves. In July 1983 in the London Zoo, an embryo from a Przewalski's horse was collected nonsurgically and transplanted into a domestic pony in Cambridge. In June 1984 the surrogate mother gave birth to a healthy, normal Przewalski horse foal. A female gaur born in the Buffalo (N.Y.) Zoo in March 1984 from a captive-bred mother had been sired by a male born in the Bronx (N.Y.) Zoo in 1981 as the result of an embryo transplant to a Holstein cow. This was an important step forward since it showed that an animal born from and raised by a surrogate mother could function normally and reproduce its own species.

(P. J. OLNEY)

See also Environment; Gardening.

Chemistry

Organic Chemistry. The crucial role that chemists would play in the imminent biotechnology revolution was highlighted by the announcement in October of the 1984 Nobel Prize for Chemistry. The award went to Bruce Merrifield of the Rockefeller University in New York City for work that transformed peptide chemistry. Peptides, short proteins made up of amino acids, had been difficult to make until Merrifield tried anchoring one end of the molecule to an insoluble resinous support and carrying out the chemistry at the free end. Over the past two decades this solid-state synthesis method had enabled such molecules as the enzyme ribonuclease to be made from its jigsaw of 124 amino acids. By the mid-1980s it was offering the means of constructing the peptides, proteins, and oligonucleotides necessary for important projects in biotechnology and genetic engineering.

Amino acids made headlines in Japan when researchers at the National Chemical Laboratory in Higashi, Japan, used a novel porous membrane to separate their right- and left-handed mirror-image forms, known as D and L isomers. This achievement also would aid developments in biotechnology because only L amino acids are found in living organisms and because L isomers are important in food and drug manufacture.

The synthesis of pure left- or right-handed products was the objective for work by Nobel laureate Herbert C. Brown and Bakthan Singaram of Purdue University, West Lafayette, Ind., who were attempting to introduce handedness, or chirality, into molecules to help in synthesizing analogues of naturally occurring compounds such as hormones, anticancer agents, and other drugs. Using the method of hydroboration, Brown produced a versatile borane derivative of *a*-pinene that would enable organic chemists to synthesize in pure D or L form virtually any compound that exists in both forms. In related work Kurt Mislow of Princeton University offered an exciting theoretical approach to understanding the way in which chemists could view chiral molecules. His clarifications resolved many confusing aspects of stereochemistry, the way in which atoms in a molecule are oriented in space.

While several important new reagents promised to simplify syntheses for organic chemists, the introduction of laboratory robots enabled a team at Purdue, led by Philip L. Fuchs, to optimize chemical reaction conditions for a synthesis, saving numerous manual operations. For 50 hours the microcomputer/robot system added chemicals, ran reactions, took samples, prepared them for analysis, recorded yields, and washed up afterward. In a year when the Chemical Abstract Service published its ten millionth abstract describing research work in chemistry, this innovation offered the daunting prospect of further accelerating chemical research and fueling the literature explosion.

Syntheses of note during the year included the fungal metabolite ±-quadrone, such complex sugars as lincosamine, and a new way to make morphine that promised easier syntheses of morphine analogues. The compound [7]circulene (1) and a molecule that acts like a jump rope (2) were among the interesting structures described in chemistry journals. Preparation of artificial coal by scientists at Argonne (Ill.) National Laboratory from naturally occurring clay and lignin would aid in understanding the way in which coal formed during geologic time.

Inorganic Chemistry. Less than two years after their probable discovery of element 109, scientists at the Heavy Ion Research Laboratory (GSI) in Darmstadt, West Germany, made element 108. This newest element filled another gap in the periodic table, a plan for classifying chemical elements developed by Dmitry I. Mendeleyev. The 150th anniversary of his birth was marked in February.

The synthesis of an unusual kind of inorganic catalyst during the year appeared to open the door to a new avenue of chemistry. Kenneth J. Klabunde and Yuzo Imizu of Kansas State University prepared a material from manganese and cobalt vapours cooled to liquid nitrogen temperatures ($-196°$ C, or $-320°$ F) with a solvent. Manganese, normally a poor catalyst, became activated by the cobalt, and the mixture of small clusters of metal atoms that formed was able to effect the hydrogenation of alkenes far better than either metal alone. In related work Lawrence Dubois and Ralph Nuzzo of AT&T Bell Laboratories deposited a metal vapour on alumina and silica supports and then passed a volatile organometallic compound over the surface. The resulting intermetallic compounds showed potentially useful electronic and catalytic properties.

Organometallic chemistry forged ahead with much emphasis on catalysis. Many organometallic cluster compounds, which have metal-atom clusters at the core of an organic shell, need carbon monoxide molecules in the framework to ensure stability, but at the expense of reactivity. Gregory Geoffroy, leading a team from Pennsylvania State University and the University of Delaware, made a rhodium cluster compound (3) with cycloocta-1,5-diene ligands instead of carbon monoxide. Preliminary work suggested that the material would be useful to the chemical industry. The record for the number of atoms in a mixed-metal cluster compound was pushed to 25 early in the year; the cluster (4) contained 13 gold and 12 silver atoms.

Reports of new molecules and novel types of bonding extended beyond the province of organometallic chemistry. A small molecule, C_3O, which only recently had been characterized in the laboratory, was detected in a dark interstellar cloud in the constellation Taurus by a team of U.S., Canadian, and Australian workers. On Earth confirmation of a triple-bonded link between phosphorus and nitrogen provided a rare opportunity to study bonding between elements of the first and second rows of the periodic table.

Physical Chemistry. Nuclear magnetic resonance (NMR) remained a newsworthy topic, partly because of interest in its use for the diagnostic imaging of the human body. For chemists NMR has long been an important tool for unraveling the structures of organic compounds. The technique makes use of the fact that the hydrogen atoms in such molecules spin like gyroscopes. This spinning creates a magnetic field. When placed in a larger magnetic field, the hydrogen nuclei line up with the field. Passing a radio wave through the sample causes them to tip out of balance. The energy emitted as they realign gives the chemist information relating to the identity, number, and location of other atoms in the vicinity.

Whereas samples consisting of single crystals provide sharply detailed NMR spectra, the molecular disorder in other kinds of solids had always resulted in smeared spectra until the emergence during the year of a technique called zero-field NMR. Developed by Alexander Pines and co-workers at the University of California at Berkeley, with Daniel P. Weitekamp at the University of Groningen in The Netherlands, the method involves a technique of magnetic field cycling combined with a data processing procedure called Fourier transformation. The net result is a simple spectrum that represents the nuclei spinning in the absence of a magnetic field. This innovation was expected to make a major contribution to understanding the structures of such materials as organic solids, polycrystalline semiconductors, and biological membranes.

Bonding theories underwent scrutiny when evidence accumulated for a new type of bond between carbon and hydrogen. In all organic compounds containing these two elements, strong, covalent bonds link them. With some elements other than carbon, however, hydrogen can form a type of weak bond called a hydrogen bond. Researcher Norman Sheppard at the University of East Anglia in the U.K. proposed that carbon, normally thought not to participate in hydrogen bonding, might be so involved as a result of his team's work on the way titanium dioxide catalyzes the polymerization of polyethylene. Infrared spectroscopy results suggested that, of the two CH bonds per carbon in polyethylene, one might be a hydrogen bond.

Conversion of solar energy using molecules that mimic photosynthesis sustained its high priority for research funding. One important development was the construction of a molecule comprising quinone, porphyrin, and β-carotene units by a team including workers from France and England and led by Thomas Moore of Arizona State University. Natural photosynthetic systems employ chlorophyll, a porphyrin, to trap light. Light stimulates electrons to pass through the photosynthetic membrane and aid various reactions to produce carbohydrates. A quinone-based unit in the natural system traps the electrons and ensures that the process is not reversible. Simulating the natural system, Moore's molecule used a porphyrin to trap the light, a quinone at one end of this molecule to trap the electron,

and a long β-carotene unit to hold the positive charge and keep the charges separated.

Analytical Chemistry. The barometer for this discipline, the annual Pittsburgh Conference and Exposition on Analytical Chemistry and Applied Spectroscopy, brought more than 24,600 visitors to Atlantic City, N.J., in March. In preceding years instrumentation companies had talked of computer systems that could log information on samples, assign identification numbers, generate lists of analyses, schedule experiments and tests, program instruments, store results, and produce reports. In 1984 many of those same companies actually exhibited such laboratory information-management systems and discussed the installations they had made. Though laboratory robots had been something of a curiosity a year earlier, manufacturers described systems that were improving productivity in industrial laboratories.

Of the range of new analytical instruments, special attention was given to ion chromatography, a form of liquid chromatography that can separate inorganic ions, and to the "hyphenated technique" of liquid chromatography-mass spectrometry (LC-MS). The key development in LC-MS was the thermospray, a new means of passing the sample fractions that had been separated by the chromatograph to the mass spectrometer, developed by Marvin L. Vestal of the University of Houston, Texas.

On the horizon were a number of devices that would complement the analyst's armory in the near future. They included a coated optical fibre that could detect tiny amounts of molecular hydrogen and, with other coatings, act as a sensor for a variety of chemicals. Designed for the U.S. Coast Guard by scientists at Argonne National Laboratory was a portable analyzer that could identify 12 gases and would help in dealing with chemical spill emergencies.

(GORDON WILKINSON)

See also Nobel Prizes.

This article updates the *Macropædia* articles Physical and Chemical ANALYSIS AND MEASUREMENT; CHEMICAL COMPOUNDS; CHEMICAL ELEMENTS; CHEMICAL REACTIONS; ENERGY CONVERSION; Principles, Methods, and Instruments of MEASUREMENT AND OBSERVATION; MOLECULES; The PHYSICAL SCIENCES: *Chemistry*.

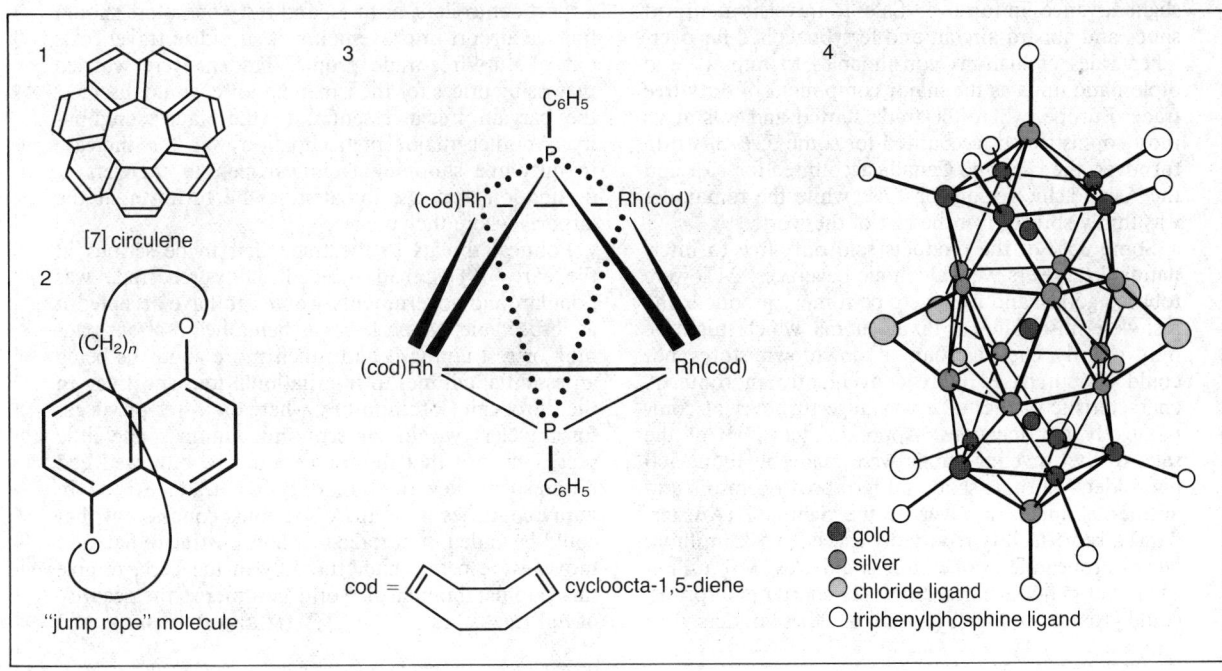

1 [7] circulene

2 (CH₂)ₙ "jump rope" molecule

3 cod = cycloocta-1,5-diene

4 gold
silver
chloride ligand
triphenylphosphine ligand

Consumer Affairs

There was no indication during 1984 of a decline in the consumer movement, although some had predicted that economic stagnation and the worldwide trend toward deregulation of industry would produce such a result. Particularly in the third world, there was increasing acceptance of consumer groups as representatives on national bodies. The establishment of consumer protection departments or councils by national governments (for example, in Botswana, India, and Argentina) was a significant development.

The year began with the celebration of the tenth anniversary of the Asia and Pacific Office of the International Organization of Consumer Unions (IOCU) and culminated in December in the IOCU's 11th World Congress in Bangkok, Thailand, which set the consumer movement's direction for the remainder of the decade. Confidence and international solidarity were also expressed in the second celebration on March 15 of World Consumer Rights Day.

Product safety, which had been emerging as a primary focus over the last few years, was established as the main program area of several international organizations. The IOCU expressed its long-term commitment to promoting consumer safety through its Consumer Interpol program, launched in 1981. Health issues, especially the marketing of drugs and the role of the pharmaceutical industry, became an even more prominent concern. A campaign against tranquilizers by a Brazilian consumer protection body, the Norwegian Consumer Council's program on patients' rights, and the exposure of the sales of harmful drug combinations ("*yachud* packages") by a small Thai consumer group were just three examples. Delegates to the

World Health Assembly in Geneva in May 1984 voted a hundred to one in favour of a resolution (opposed only by the U.S.) to convene a World Health Organization (WHO) meeting on drug marketing and information in 1985.

International Cooperation. The delineation between the consumer movement and environmental and similar groups became less sharp as they continued to work together in three major international networks: the International Baby Food Action Network (IBFAN), Health Action International (HAI), and Pesticide Action Network (PAN). The IOCU was a founder member of all three. At the World Health Assembly, HAI produced a combined video and exhibition called "Hard to Swallow," documenting irresponsible marketing practices and the wasted potential of modern drugs in the third world, as well as a series of five bulletins entitled "Health Now." IBFAN organized a major meeting on baby foods in Mexico City early in 1984. The seven-year boycott of Nestlé products was called off on October 4, since Nestlé had taken important steps toward maintaining the May 1981 WHO Code of Marketing of Breastmilk Substitutes. Other companies contravening the code then became the focus of attention. PAN held its first global symposium in February in Utrecht, Neth., where plans were worked out for a campaign against 12 pesticides, to be launched in June 1985. International cooperation was also evident at the UN Environment Program's annual governing council session in Nairobi, Kenya, in September, which adopted a global information scheme for all exports of banned and severely restricted harmful chemicals.

Perhaps the most significant step in the area of international cooperation on product safety was the release by the UN Secretariat on Dec. 30, 1983, of the new UN consolidated list of banned, withdrawn, severely restricted, and unapproved products. The list, containing 421 products

The Rise of Duty-free Trade

Every year the world's tourists and business travelers contribute to a branch of international trade worth some $5 billion. As of 1984, duty-free trade was creating new outlets, expanding existing ones, and showing slight advances in turnover. Sales to travelers at airport shops and aboard aircraft and ferryboats had far overtaken sales of high-tax consumables to military and diplomatic units as the major component of duty-free trade. Europe, where the trade started and was at its most sophisticated, accounted for some 53% of world turnover; the U.S. and Canada accounted for 13% and the Asia-Pacific region for 17%, while the remainder was thinly spread over the rest of the world.

Some 35% of the products sold duty-free to international travelers were alcoholic beverages, 24% were tobacco goods, and 21% were perfumery products; the rest were miscellaneous luxury items, which might be only slightly cheaper than at downtown stores but could be purchased more conveniently en route. A characteristic of the trade was huge turnover at comparatively few locations. Approximately 80% of the sales to the traveling public were made by about 500 big traders—airport shop and ferryboat operators and airlines. Annual turnover at the Schiphol (Amsterdam) airport facility reportedly exceeded $82 million; large European ferry operators could gross $40 million each; and major airlines, especially charter enterprises, could gross more than $10 million. These traders were

in the van of modern retailing, especially in their use of electronic recording to detail each transaction for customs supervision.

There was controversy over the extent to which airport controllers, airlines, and ferry operators should finance airport improvements or subsidize travel costs out of duty-free-trade profits. Traders were worried that rising prices for their merchandise would discredit the bargain image essential to the trade's credibility. Another major preoccupation was the increase in duty-free shopping facilities open to travelers at destination airports, threatening the turnover at the airports where they depart.

Political threats to the trade, felt to be serious in the early 1980s, had receded. Duty-free trade was popular, and governments seemed to have accepted it as respectable. Much less was being heard about banning or restraining it and much more about its being an essential adjunct to international tourism. Even in the European Communities, where duty-free privileges for travelers within an economic union made little sense, the risk that the trade would be outlawed had diminished. Nevertheless, duty-free trade existed in many countries by virtue of customs concessions that could be ended or curtailed by administrative fiat, and moves were being made, notably in the U.S., to give this popular branch of world commerce the security of full legal status.   (MICHAEL F. BARFORD) sold under 5,636 trade names, was distributed in 1984 to UN member governments.

Consumer protection had been on the UN agenda for years, and reports emanating from various UN bodies repeatedly confirmed that effective consumer protection was an essential part of social and economic development. *Draft Guidelines on Consumer Protection,* developed by the UN, outlined a basic set of principles designed to provide a minimum of protection to all the world's consumers. The guidelines received strong backing from the IOCU, but opposition forces succeeded in preventing a vote on the draft text at the annual plenary session of the UN Economic and Social Council in Geneva in July. The Consumer Policy Committee of the Organization for Economic Cooperation and Development (OECD) convened a special symposium on consumer policy and international trade in November in Paris, where the IOCU and the Bureau Européen des Unions de Consommateurs strongly opposed protectionistic measures that reduce competition.

Regional Developments. The European Communities (EC) Commission in Brussels organized a conference on product safety May 17–18, when it was proposed that member states should market lead-free gasoline (petrol) from 1986 and by 1989 at the latest. On June 5 the EC Council of Ministers adopted a proposal for a directive on misleading advertising. A 1984 IOCU study on television advertising across national frontiers focused on the situation in Europe, where plans for introducing direct broadcasting by satellite were most advanced.

In Latin America several governments, notably that of Argentina, expanded or intensified consumer protection efforts. New consumer groups appeared in Costa Rica, Uruguay, Peru, Suriname, and Ecuador. The IOCU, which was focusing its development work on Latin America, identified more than 40 consumer organizations and governmental bodies active in the region. In Africa, on the other hand, the consumer movement was still in its infancy in most countries. In the context of a fact-finding mission for HAI, an IOCU consultant visited seven countries and established contacts with groups and individuals interested in taking up consumer issues. Voluntary consumer groups existed in Sierra Leone, Kenya, Togo, Nigeria, Zimbabwe, Zambia, and Mauritius.

In Asia and the Pacific the maturing of the consumer movement was manifested in 1984 in celebrations of the 25th anniversary of the Australian Consumers' Association and the New Zealand Consumers' Institute and the tenth anniversary of consumer groups in several less developed countries in the region. Japanese consumer groups, which had been drawn into the world consumer movement following an international seminar organized by the IOCU in Japan in 1983, actively participated in a publicity campaign denouncing the establishment of a new Japanese company that specialized in the marketing and export of tobacco products to Southeast Asia.   (RUTH VERMEER)

In the U.S. the Senate Commerce Committee approved legislation requiring consumers to prove that a company was negligent in product liability cases, in addition to proving that the company's product caused harm. Under this legislation, only the first person to bring a product liability case would be able to win punitive damages. If enacted, the measure would preempt state product liability laws. The proposed bill would make it more difficult for consumers to win awards since, to prove negligence, a plaintiff would have to establish how the manufacturer made decisions about the product. Supporters of the legislation believed the number of claims brought against companies would be reduced and awards for consumers who won product

Competition among long-distance carriers: in Boston's Logan Airport terminal, pay phone customers have the choice of eight carriers at the touch of a button.
STEVE LISS

liability cases would be lower. Consumer groups were opposing the passage of the act.

By 1985 makers of processed foods would be required to disclose the sodium content of their products if the labels on the containers provided nutritional information. In addition, food companies would have to define the basis for such claims as "low-sodium." Excessive consumption of sodium (including sodium chloride, or common table salt) had been implicated in high blood pressure.

The Federal Reserve Board and the House of Representatives jointly proposed "truth in savings" legislation to standardize interest rate information in advertisements. The legislation was opposed by the American Association of Advertising Agencies. Sponsors of the measure argued that deregulation of the banking industry had made so many savings and investment plans available that consumers could not make valid comparisons. A survey conducted by Opinion Research indicated that consumers were not convinced that deregulation of the banking and telephone industries was good for them. More than half the respondents thought the public would pay more for banking services as a result of deregulation. About 60% thought the American Telephone and Telegraph Co. had benefited from divestiture, while only 14% saw advantages for the consumer.

The Federal Trade Commission (FTC) agreed to delete sections of a proposed rule that would have required used-car dealers to list a car's known defects on a window sticker. However, the rule did require the stickers to include the terms of the warranty, a suggestion that the consumer consult an independent mechanic, a statement as to whether the dealer was selling the car "as is," and a warning to get all promises in writing since spoken promises are difficult to enforce. The FTC's original used-car rule was vetoed by Congress in 1983, but it was revived when the Supreme Court held that congressional vetoes are unconstitutional.

By the end of 1984, 30 states had passed "lemon laws" giving the consumer recourse if a new car proved faulty.

These laws generally labeled a new car a "lemon" if it was repaired four times for the same type of problem or was in the repair shop for more than 30 days during the year of purchase. Most of the laws encouraged consumers to seek arbitration before suing. Proponents felt the lemon laws gave automobile manufacturers an incentive to make a better product. However, comparatively few automobiles had been returned under their provisions. In Connecticut, for example, 113,000 new cars were registered during the first 13 months the law was in force, but only 40 were returned.   (EDWARD MARK MAZZE)

See also Economic Affairs: *World Economy*; Industrial Review: *Advertising*.

Crime, Law Enforcement, and Penology

Violent Crime. TERRORISM. New additions were made during 1984 to the long and bloody list of terrorist assaults and assassinations. Heading the list were attacks on two prime ministers. On October 31 Indian Prime Minister Indira Gandhi was assassinated by two Sikh members of her bodyguard in reprisal for an Army assault earlier in the year on the Golden Temple at Amritsar. The temple, the holiest Sikh shrine, had been turned into an armed redoubt by Sikh extremists seeking independence. (*See* WORLD AFFAIRS [South Asia]: *India.*)

British Prime Minister Margaret Thatcher narrowly escaped death on October 12 when a bomb exploded in the Grand Hotel in Brighton, where she and other top-level members of the government were staying during the Conservative Party conference. Five persons, including a member of Parliament, died and 31 were wounded. The Irish Republican Army (IRA) claimed responsibility. (*See* WORLD AFFAIRS [Western Europe]: *United Kingdom.*) Earlier, on September 29, the Irish Navy seized a trawler containing a large cache of weapons destined for the IRA. The seizure, the largest in more than a decade, was thought to have been assisted by U.S spy satellite surveillance of vessels involved in the transatlantic shipment of weapons from IRA supporters in the U.S.

The political conflicts in the Middle East continued to spawn terrorist acts. On September 20 a suicide bomber in a van packed with explosives got within six metres (20 ft) of the U.S. embassy annex in East Beirut, Lebanon, before the vehicle blew up, killing at least 14 persons and injuring more than 60. This attack, like the suicide missions directed against U.S. and French installations in Beirut in 1983, was thought to be the work of a Muslim fundamentalist terrorist group, Islamic Jihad (Holy War). (*See* WORLD AFFAIRS [Middle East and North Africa]: *Middle Eastern Affairs:* Sidebar.)

State-sponsored terror, in particular, prompted the announcement in April of a new and more aggressive approach toward terrorism by the U.S., including possible preemptive strikes against suspected terrorist targets. On April 3 U.S. Pres. Ronald Reagan signed a secret security directive authorizing 26 federal intelligence and law enforcement agencies to put these plans into effect. The president also submitted to Congress a package of tough antiterrorist measures, among them a proposal to create a new crime of aiding terrorism. Critics of these measures claimed they were a threat to civil liberties.

In Israel, a nation with a long tradition of being tough on terrorism but dealing fairly with captured terrorists, controversy arose over a commando raid on April 13, which freed 34 hostages held captive by four Arab hijackers in a bus in the Gaza Strip. Israeli Army sources initially said the commandos killed two of the hijackers and one passenger during the rescue, while the remaining hijackers "died of their wounds" on the way to the hospital. This account was subsequently disputed by stories that first appeared in the American press. An official investigation of the incident concluded that the two hijackers captured alive died as a result of severe beatings inflicted by unnamed persons after the commandos stormed the bus. The results of the investigation shocked many Israelis, as did the arrest in late April of more than 20 persons accused of belonging to a Jewish underground terrorist network in the occupied West Bank. Those arrested were subsequently charged with involvement in a series of attacks, or planned attacks, on Palestinians, including the car bomb maiming of two West Bank mayors in 1980. (*See* WORLD AFFAIRS [Middle East and North Africa]: *Israel.*)

A dramatic siege of the Libyan people's bureau (embassy) in the heart of London began on April 17, when an unknown person in the embassy building fired a machine gun at a group of dissidents protesting against the regime of Col. Muammar al-Qaddafi. The shots killed a British policewoman and injured ten demonstrators. The siege ended after ten days with the breaking of diplomatic relations between Britain and Libya. Under international

(continued on page 187)

DEKEERLE—GAMMA/LIAISON

The Grand Hotel in Brighton, England, is shown after a terrorist bomb attack came within an ace of decimating the entire British Cabinet. Four floors at the front of the hotel collapsed, leaving four dead and over 30 injured. A fifth victim died a month later.

Crime, Law Enforcement, and Penology: Special Report

The Heroin
Epidemic Spreads

BY JEREMY LAURANCE

San Francisco in the middle sixties was a very special time and place to be . . . no matter which way I went I would come to a place where people were just as high and wild as I was . . . there was a fantastic universal sense that what we were doing was right . . . we were riding the crest of a high and beautiful wave." Thus Hunter S. Thompson, ferocious "gonzo journalist," in his 1971 book *Fear and Loathing in Las Vegas,* now a minor classic in the drug literature. California in the 1960s was the incubator of new styles of living, and psychedelic, mind-expanding drugs were a central element in an experiment that was soon being repeated around the world.

That picture has changed dramatically. The boom period of the '60s, which spawned the youth counterculture, flower power, and the injunction to "make love, not war," has given way to the gloomy, recession-hit '80s. Rising unemployment has led to a growing sense of cynicism, despair, and anger, especially among the young. "Consciousness expansion" has an outdated ring. "Multidrug abuse" is the new catchphrase: people take whatever comes to hand to blot out the pain and boredom of a life on the scrap heap. Every kind of drug has reached everywhere.

The Heroin Boom. According to UN reports, more people around the world are using addictive and illegal drugs than ever before, and the suppliers are increasingly allied with organized crime. Most of Western Europe is experiencing its worst heroin problems ever: 13,300 official addicts in West Germany, 20,000 in Italy (1982 figures). In Britain nearly 6,000 addicts were registered in 1983, an increase of more than 40% from the year before. But these figures vastly underrepresent the true number of addicts. In Britain, for instance, the total is thought to be around 50,000. The U.S. is estimated to have nearly half a million. The quantity of heroin seized by the authorities has risen too, from a world total of 2 metric tons in 1979 to 5.5 tons in 1981. This is only a fraction, perhaps one-tenth, of the total traded.

Though the use of every sort of drug has increased, attention has focused on heroin because of its powerful addictive properties. Most addicts prefer heroin, turning to other drugs only when it is in short supply. They want it for the "rush"—the sudden surge of euphoria—and for its analgesic properties. It is one of the most potent analgesics known. It kills physical and psychological pain, without affecting normal functioning—"the ideal drug for the recession," as one drug agency worker put it.

The availability of heroin in Europe has increased dramatically in recent years. For most of the '70s, Southeast Asia was the chief source. But at the end of the decade international events, chiefly the revolution in Iran, led to a surge in the flow of the drug. Middle-class Iranians escaping to Europe found in heroin a good way

Jeremy Laurance is health and social services correspondent for
New Society, *London, and has researched and written on recent developments relating to the drug problem.*

of exporting capital. Since 1981 the main source has been southwest Asia, especially the remote northwest frontier between Pakistan and Afghanistan. For the U.S., Mexico has been an important source.

Falling Price. A major reason for the recent boom in supply is that opium-growing countries in the third world have developed their own refining capacity for turning opium into heroin. Previously, opium was normally transported to the Mediterranean basin for refining. It takes ten kilograms of opium to make one kilogram of heroin (1 kg = 2.2 lb); this meant a series of transactions that pushed up the price and limited availability. According to a government-sponsored British researcher, Roger Lewis, one kilogram of heroin purchased in Pakistan in 1984 for £3,000 to £4,000 ($3,900–$5,200) might have cost £40,000 to £55,000 ($52,000–$71,500) if it had been obtained from laboratories in Marseille, France, or Palermo, Sicily, in 1980. As Lewis observes, it is obviously easier and cheaper for a free-lance trafficker to negotiate for a single kilogram near the Khyber Pass, where there is little or no threat of police intervention.

The boom in supply has led to a dramatic fall in the street price. In Britain a £5 ($6.50) bag of heroin would be enough for two people to have fun for an evening, about the same as an "evening's worth" of cannabis (marijuana, hashish, etc.). But cannabis is generally sold in larger quantities, so heroin can seem cheaper and is often easier to get. Almost every major British city has seen a rapid increase in availability, and the drug has spread to smaller towns and rural areas as well. The age of addicts has fallen with the price. In 1983 more than one in five newly registered addicts in Britain were under 21.

New Cult Drug. This spread has been helped by a breakdown in the taboo against heroin. This is linked to the fashionable use of cocaine, which grew sharply in the late '70s. Like cocaine, which is commonly "snorted"

DAVID KLINE—IMPACT FEATURES

Some of Pakistan's "bathtub laboratory" heroin producers can turn out nearly 140 kilograms (308 pounds) of pure heroin per week. For these operators there is no moral dilemma: "People want it and they pay well. . . . So I make it."

185

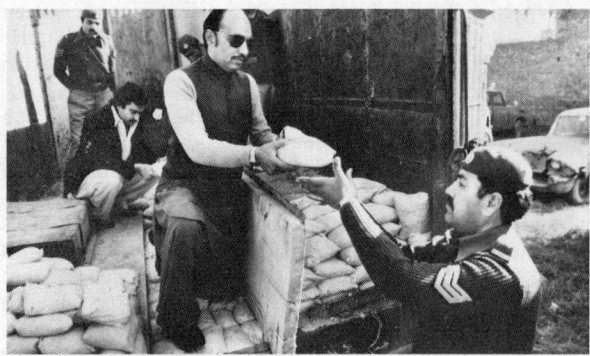

Drug agents in Peshawar, Pakistan, find a king's ransom in heroin hidden under the floor of a truck. For local deliveries the drug is hidden in baskets of produce carried by women and children.

(sniffed), heroin is a white powder suitable for snorting. It is increasingly being used in this way as a recreational drug at suburban parties, with the inevitable casualties. (It is widely—but mistakenly—believed to be less addictive when sniffed than when injected.) To some extent, heroin seems to have acquired the place in the drug subculture occupied by cannabis in the late '60s. Cannabis is now so widely accepted among the under-35s that the ritual of passing round an illicit joint at a party has lost its mystique. But heroin still has that quality of illicitness. It has become the cult drug of the '80s. The result has been a big increase in the number of addicts among the children of the richer middle classes.

However, the cheapness of heroin means it is just as likely to be used by unemployed teenagers in inner-city housing estates. There is no taboo against it because there is widespread ignorance of its dangers. It is just another white powder. Glue and "speed" (amphetamine sulfate) are sniffed, so why not heroin? In Britain, new wave music, from punk onward, contains a lot about heroin. Sid Vicious, of the hugely successful rock band the Sex Pistols, died of a much publicized heroin overdose.

Nature of the Problem. Can anything be done to control the epidemic? There is little agreement on an appropriate strategy. Much of the battle has been over what sort of problem it is: medical, social, or legal. Are drug abusers bad or sick? These very categories leave room for dissent. Most police activity, for instance, nets only minor offenders. Of the 23,000 caught in Britain in 1983, 87% were picked up for possession, most of them for possession of cannabis. If more police forces made a practice of cautioning these offenders rather than arresting

them, it would relieve the pressure on resources caused by the huge number of young people now using the drug and release manpower to concentrate on catching the bigger dealers. Paradoxically, some police activity may actually worsen the drug problem. Large seizures of cannabis increase its scarcity and push up its price, encouraging users to switch to the more easily smuggled, and increasingly cheap, heroin.

There is also considerable uncertainty over how to treat addicts. The outcome of treatment is unpredictable. People start taking drugs for different reasons and come off them in different ways. Having a supportive family and friends, a job, a lover may all be important. But so, too, may be knowing someone who died of an overdose, or being thrown into prison. Some drug workers argue that treatment has been overmedicalized. Drug abuse is essentially a social problem, they insist, with some medical problems attached.

Drug-taking is normal, not deviant behaviour. People in Western society consume vast quantities of alcohol, tobacco, tranquilizers, sleeping pills, painkillers, and so on to change the way they feel under the stresses of ordinary life. The addict is conspicuous only by his excessive and uncontrolled use of "hard" drugs. The growth in "excessive use" reflects the growing social stress caused by, for example, rising unemployment.

Valuable Cash Crop. Growth in use also reflects the growth in supply. Would it not be better to stop the drugs in their countries of origin? The trouble is the drug trade generates such enormous profits that some countries' economies depend on it. In the mid-'70s it was estimated that heroin was Mexico's most valuable commodity, accounting for 6% of its gross national product. In 1981 the hashish harvest in Lebanon was estimated at 10,000 metric tons; a report in *The Times* of London spoke of fields guarded by tanks. It has been estimated that 1,600 metric tons of opium were grown in Pakistan, Afghanistan, and Iran in 1979. In those countries the opium poppy is the only crop that is a consistent annual money-maker. The UN is offering economic incentives in an effort to tempt farmers in the region to grow other crops, but the incentives are not generous enough.

The drug problem is but one facet of the very much larger social and economic problems facing the West and its relations with the third world. Without substantial measures to deal with unemployment and social deprivation, which are unlikely to be forthcoming until all the Western economies pick up, there is no reason to suppose that the situation will improve. There is every likelihood that it will get worse.

As cannabis was the "cult drug" of the late '60s and early '70s, heroin was gaining widespread popularity as the new illicit drug of the '80s, resulting in an increase in users among the middle class. The availability and cheapness of the drug, however, meant it was just as likely to be used by the poor. Plainclothes officers apprehended these dealers during a crackdown on the heroin trade in New York City.

(continued from page 184)

law there seemed little else Britain could do, since foreign embassies remained immune from the jurisdiction of the host state. (*See* LAW: *International Law.*) On December 4 Arabic-speaking gunmen hijacked a Kuwaiti airliner and forced it to fly to Iran, where it remained for six days at the Teheran airport. Two American passengers were killed and others were terrorized before Iranian security forces stormed the plane. U.S. officials suggested that the hijackers were acting in collusion with the Iranian government, but Iran denied the allegation.

In September a commission appointed by the new civilian president of Argentina, Raúl Alfonsín, presented a chilling report of its nine-month investigation into the fate of the *desaparecidos* ("missing ones"); it concluded that at least 8,960 people had been killed by the armed forces in the late 1970s during the so-called dirty war against terrorists. (*See* WORLD AFFAIRS [Latin America and the Caribbean: South America]: *Argentina.*) In another Latin-American nation, Colombia, the minister of justice, Rodrigo Lara Bonilla, was assassinated in Bogotá on April 30. Lara's slaying was thought to be linked to his pursuit of drug traffickers operating at high levels of Colombian society. In the Philippines an official commission investigating the August 1983 assassination of opposition leader Benigno Aquino implicated high-ranking members of the military in the killing. (*See* WORLD AFFAIRS [Southeast Asia]: *Philippines.*)

MURDER AND OTHER VIOLENCE. In the U.S. the FBI's Crime Index figures for 1983 revealed a continuing decline of 7% in serious crime. According to the FBI, this was the first time the national crime rate had fallen for two consecutive years. Murder and robbery each fell 8%; aggravated assault dropped 2%; and forcible rape showed virtually no change. A report issued by the Justice Department's Bureau of Justice Statistics (BJS) showed that some 1.4 million fewer U.S. households experienced crime in 1983 than in 1982, a decrease that the BJS director, Steven R. Schlesinger, attributed to such factors as increased use of imprisonment, decline in the number of young adults in the crime-prone age groups, citizen crime-prevention programs, and higher arrest rates. U.S. police departments claimed that 46% of all violent crimes reported to them in 1983 were cleared. The clearance rate for the estimated 19,300 murders was 76%. More than half of these murders were perpetrated by relatives or other persons acquainted with the victim. Handguns were used in 44%.

The worst mass murder by a single killer in one day in U.S. history took place at a fast food restaurant in San Ysidro, Calif., on July 18. In what seemed to be a motiveless shooting spree, James Oliver Huberty killed 21 persons and injured 18 before he was slain by a police marksman. On May 8 in Quebec City, Denis Lortie, an army corporal, sprayed the hallways and main chamber of the Quebec National Assembly with machine-gun fire, killing 3 persons and wounding 13. Lortie subsequently surrendered to the legislature's sergeant at arms.

The apprehension of repetitive killers continued to present problems for a number of police forces. In Seattle, Wash., law enforcement authorities searched for clues to the identity of a murderer, dubbed the Green River Killer, who was believed responsible for the deaths of more than 20 young women since the summer of 1982. In April Christopher Bernard Wilder, a suspected fugitive serial killer and rapist on the FBI's Ten Most Wanted list, was finally stopped by police in Colebrook, N.H. Wilder, who had apparently gone on a wild killing spree, took his own life before he could be apprehended.

When the murderous rampage of James Oliver Huberty was ended—by a bullet from a police marksman—SWAT team members turned to help the wounded.
BARRY FITZSIMMONS/SAN DIEGO UNION

A year-long controversy over a gang rape in a tavern in New Bedford, Mass., ended in March with the conviction of four men on charges of aggravated rape and the acquittal of two other defendants. The trial, which attracted nationwide media attention, sparked concerns about the adverse publicity given to the ethnic origins of the accused, all of whom were Portuguese immigrants, and to the victim. Parents, teachers, and law enforcement officials across the U.S. and Canada were made increasingly aware of the frequency of sexual attacks on children, in most instances by offenders whom the child knew and trusted. In August a Canadian National Task Force on Child Abuse, after three years of study, concluded that "child sexual abuse is a largely hidden yet pervasive tragedy that has damaged the lives of tens of thousands of Canadian children and youths."

Another form of violent crime that prompted international concern was piracy. The worst acts of piracy were reported from the South China Sea, where pirates, most of them Thai fishermen, preyed on refugees from Vietnam. The UN High Commissioner for Refugees reported receiving information about almost 1,400 murders of boat people and 2,300 rapes since 1980. Despite two-year funding of a Thai antipiracy program by 11 Western nations, not a single pirate appeared to have been put behind bars.

Nonviolent Crime. POLITICAL CRIME. In Nigeria the new military government, which seized power late in 1983, began a crackdown on officials of the former civilian administration accused of corruption. Stiff prison terms were passed on nine former state governors. A bizarre attempt to smuggle Umaru Dikko (*see* BIOGRAPHIES), the transport minister in the last government, back to Nigeria to face corruption charges failed when customs officials at London's Stansted Airport found Dikko drugged and stuffed inside a crate bound for Lagos.

In the Soviet Union Yury Sokolov, former director of Moscow's best food store, Gastronom No. 1, was executed in July for gross corruption. Sokolov was alleged to have taken bribes while purveying scarce delicacies to high-ranking members of Moscow society. In September Anatoly Kolevatov, the former head of the Soviet circus, was sentenced to 13 years' imprisonment on corruption charges. Kolevatov, who was at the centre of a scandal linked to the family of the late Soviet leader Leonid Brezhnev, was believed to have been involved in a racket in which he demanded payment in diamonds for allowing artists to perform in the West. The wide publicity given these cases suggested that the new Soviet regime was continuing the crackdown on high-level corruption begun by the late Yury Andropov.

In early October U.S. Secretary of Labor Raymond Donovan and nine other people pleaded not guilty to charges of stealing more than $5 million from New York City on a subway construction contract awarded two years before Donovan joined President Reagan's administration. Donovan, who claimed the charges were politically motivated, was believed to be the first sitting Cabinet member in U.S. history to be indicted.

WHITE COLLAR CRIME AND THEFT. A U.S. Justice Department report released in February claimed that the increasing use of computer technology by financial institutions had created a new and fertile field for crime. Automated teller machines were said to be vulnerable to fraud, for example, when consumers wrote their personal identification numbers on their cards and the cards were later stolen. Electronic transfer of funds (EFT) by banks and corporations was growing at a rapid pace throughout the world, and the Justice Department warned that wire fraud committed by knowledgeable persons working inside the EFT system could produce massive illegal rewards.

In August a former *Wall Street Journal* reporter, his roommate, and a stockbroker were indicted on securities fraud charges in a scheme to trade stock with the help of inside tips about columns that had not yet appeared in the paper. The journalist, R. Foster Winans, was a writer for the *Journal*'s influential stock market column "Heard on the Street." It was alleged that Winans took $31,000 in payoffs in return for leaked information. The scheme was said to have netted $700,000. What began in 1983 as a claimed "journalistic coup of the century" ended in a courtroom in Hamburg, West Germany, in August as three persons were put on trial for fraud relating to production of the forged "Hitler Diaries." The trial of Konrad Kujau, the admitted forger, his companion Edith Lieblang, and a reporter, Gerd Heidemann, who negotiated the original purchase of the diaries by the magazine *Stern*, was expected to last several months. (*See* PUBLISHING.)

The U.S. Defense Department stepped up its war against waste, fraud, and abuse in its procurement program. Among the allegations of fraud was a claim by a former General Dynamics executive, Panagiotis Takis Veliotis, that the company had falsified many of the claims it presented to the U.S. Navy when requesting reimbursement for cost overruns. Veliotis, who had fled to his native Greece, was indicted in September 1983 on a charge of receiving $2.7 million in kickbacks on a General Dynamics project. In Britain police and senior managers of the government-owned Rolls-Royce marine engineering division reported in August that they were investigating the alleged theft and smuggling of millions of dollars worth of warship components. The suspected racket, believed to have begun in 1976, involved parts for engines used in destroyers owned by Iran and Argentina.

In February shipowners, bankers, insurers, and government officials met in Geneva to discuss methods of combating international shipping theft and fraud, estimated to cost the industry $1 billion a year. Offenses ranged from scuttling vessels to collect insurance to the theft of entire ships with their cargoes. Suggestions included a proposal to give all ships an international registration number and passport to identify them from slipway to scrapyard and the establishment of a satellite-monitored ship-tracking system that would reveal route deviations by crooked captains.

Law Enforcement. On October 2 the FBI arrested one of its own agents, together with a Soviet-born couple, on charges of conspiring to pass classified documents to the Soviet Union. The agent, identified as Richard Miller, was the first FBI member ever to be charged with espionage on behalf of a foreign government. Miller, a 20-year veteran with the FBI, was alleged to have sold secrets to Nikolay and Svetlana Ogorodnikov, both alleged to be officers in the KGB, the Soviet intelligence agency.

The Miller case came at a bad time for the FBI, already under fire for unorthodox "sting" operations like the one that ensnared carmaker John De Lorean. In August, after a much publicized 22-week trial, a Los Angeles jury found De Lorean not guilty of conspiring to sell $24 million worth of cocaine in an effort to bail out his bankrupt automobile company. The prosecution based its case on evidence gathered in an elaborate undercover operation in which federal agents had posed as drug dealers. Operations of this type were severely criticized by the U.S. House of Representatives Subcommittee on Civil and Constitutional Rights in a report released in May, and it seemed likely that Congress would seek to limit certain types of conduct in future undercover operations.

Despite such criticism, the FBI appeared to be making inroads into the upper echelons of criminal enterprises. In 1983, 113 members or associates of the 24 Mafia crime families in the U.S. were convicted after FBI arrests. More successful prosecutions of major members of the Mafia in the U.S., Canada, and Italy seemed likely as a result of disclosures by a Mafia chieftain, Tommaso Buscetta. Buscetta, whom Italian police claimed was the most important member of the Sicilian Mafia ever to break the traditional code of *omerta* ("silence"), had been a fugitive from both police and rival mobsters. In July he was extradited from Brazil to Italy on drug-trafficking charges. In late September, in what Italian Premier Bettino Craxi called a turning point in the fight against organized crime, Italian police began rounding up more than 300 suspected Mafia members as part of an investigation that had connections in both the

AP/WIDE WORLD

Mafia chieftain Tommaso Buscetta (centre) is led off an airliner in Rome after his extradition from Brazil. His subsequent confessions to Italian magistrates aided a major anti-Mafia operation in Italy, which subsequently spread to the United States.

U.S. and Canada. (*See* WORLD AFFAIRS [Western Europe]: *Italy*.) A report released in August by Criminal Intelligence Service Canada, a national organization of that country's police forces, claimed that motorcycle gangs had become as much of an organized crime threat to Canada as the traditional Mafia. The report said that the major gangs, like the Mafia, had amassed sufficient wealth from drug trafficking, prostitution, and theft to enable them to invest in legitimate businesses. Similar developments were reported in the U.S.

The U.S. Bureau of Justice Statistics reported in January that the cost of providing one round-the-clock, full-coverage police beat averaged about $153,000 per year. Of that total, almost 90% was devoted to personnel costs, with the remainder spent on patrol car maintenance. Costs of this magnitude helped explain reports from a number of less wealthy nations indicating that citizens there were receiving inadequate police protection, especially in poor neighbourhoods. In Brazil, for example, crime waves in Rio de Janeiro and São Paulo led to a number of reported lynchings of suspected criminals by irate citizens. In Indonesia government authorities appeared to condone the continuing activities of mysterious death squads, which were said to have executed up to 4,000 suspected criminals in 1983 alone. The squads were believed to obtain their recruits from the police and security forces.

(DUNCAN CHAPPELL)

Prisons and Penology. The trend from "treatment" to "punishment" of lawbreakers, evident in most Western countries from the mid-1970s, continued in 1984. Capital punishment still aroused the strongest feelings. In the U.S. more executions took place in 1984 than in the previous seven and a half years since the Supreme Court lifted its ban on the death penalty in 1976. A further rapid increase was predicted as some 1,300 condemned prisoners in 34 states began to exhaust the appeal process. In the U.K. a majority of police, prison officers, and the general public expressed support for hanging despite the decisive defeat of a bill restoring the death penalty in 1983. In May 1984 Japan finally declined Amnesty International's request to reconsider abolishing the death penalty. In France Jean-Marie le Pen (*see* BIOGRAPHIES), leader of the rightist National Front, called for its restoration.

Increasing judicial severity and rising crime rates led to the overcrowding and squalour in prisons reported from most countries. In the U.K. between 1972 and 1982, the average time spent in custody by untried and unsentenced prisoners doubled, the number of imprisoned fine defaulters doubled, and the number of convicted juveniles in Prison Department establishments trebled—this last after the replacement of Borstal training, with indeterminate sentences, by "youth custody" in May 1983. Home Secretary Leon Brittan announced the building of ten new prisons and the extension of parole to short-term prisoners—though the latter was coupled with a promise of restrictions on parole for very serious offenders, a measure thought likely to produce trouble in long-term prisons. Though crime rates in the U.S. were falling, the Department of Justice reported that the prison population had doubled in the last ten years. Among the causes was the introduction in many states of determinate sentencing, mandatory prison terms, sentencing guidelines, and other restrictions on the discretion of judges and parole boards. All but a few of the states were building new prisons, renovating or expanding existing prisons, or seeking legislative approval for capital improvements. In 38 states and the District of Columbia courts had ordered improvements in prison conditions or litigation on the subject was pending; at least 16 states

had adopted emergency release provisions. In France seven prisoners each cut off a fingertip and tried to send the flesh to the minister of justice in protest against prison conditions.

While hard-line thinking dominated, increasing interest was also shown in alternative responses to the crime problem. These included "neighbourhood watches" and similar projects for discouraging crime, "profits of crime" schemes to impoverish offenders instead of imprisoning them, and victim-support schemes to divert some of society's concern about crime from perpetrators to victims.

The rising public outcry in the U.S. against drunk driving and spouse abuse led to debate over whether imprisonment, at least for a short period, would deter (or cure) such behaviour or whether it would merely compound the overcrowding problem. Sentences of a few days in police cells for drunk driving offenses were passed by magistrates in Essex, England, at Christmas 1983, bringing praise from some quarters as a cheap and effective deterrent but criticism from others as a misuse of scarce police resources. Home Secretary Brittan undertook to clear police cells of all remanded prisoners by the end of 1983, but by February hundreds were in police cells again. Penal affairs proved a minefield for the home secretary in 1984. His proposal to introduce weekend imprisonment in the U.K. coincided with reports from The Netherlands that it had failed there and would be discontinued, and his decision to increase the number of detention centres employing the new, experimental "short, sharp shock" regime was preceded by leaked Home Office research evidence that inmates actually preferred the rigorous program to the idleness and boredom of ordinary detention centres.

Prison disturbances were fewer and less sensational than in some recent years, perhaps because of the authorities' growing skill at preventing or suppressing them. Prison officers in many countries were now trained in riot control, and in the U.S. robots were used in some prisons to guard cells. In the U.K., in January 1984, rioting prisoners at Peterhead Prison, near Aberdeen, caused £40,000 worth of damage before order was restored, and escapes from prisons rose by one-quarter. At Gartree Prison, Leicester-

An unfamiliar sight in Britain is an armed police officer. This officer is a member of the new Firearms Unit whose members are intensively trained as part of a new measure against terrorists.

shire, Michael Hickey, serving life for the murder of a Staffordshire newsboy in 1979, stayed on the prison roof for 91 days to protest his innocence. What was thought to be the first police investigation of prisoners' accusations against prison staff in Britain began in March after five inmates of Wandsworth Prison, London, alleged severe beating and kicking by seven prison officers. The Prison Department expressed concern over the growing practice of prisoners taking hostages, and there was also concern over the increasing use of drugs. A Home Office report published in September recommended procedural changes aimed at reducing the high incidence of suicides among prison populations.

Two British cases showed how difficult it could be to distinguish "bad" from "mad." Dennis Nilsen claimed at his trial in November 1983 to have killed 15 men. After hearing psychiatric evidence revealing *Alice in Wonderland*-like confusion about the relationship of "abnormality of mind" and "mental disorder," the jury rejected Nilsen's plea of diminished responsibility and convicted him of murder. At Peter Sutcliffe's trial in 1981 for the "Yorkshire Ripper" murders, psychiatrists gave evidence that he was insane, but the court rejected his plea of diminished responsibility, convicted him of 13 murders, and sentenced him to life imprisonment, recommending that he serve at least 30 years. In March 1984 prison and Broadmoor Hospital doctors diagnosed Sutcliffe as severely mentally ill, and he was moved from prison to a hospital.

Outside Europe and the English-speaking common-law countries, the penological climate remained generally harsher. When a general amnesty released some 40% of Polish prisoners in July 1984, there was a sudden wave of thefts, burglaries, and violence, quickly followed by public and media demands for a return to stricter police and judicial control. In August the Supreme Court of the U.S.S.R. approved the creation of "popular vigilante" groups to protect the interests of state and society from crime. The campaign against crime and corruption in China, in a departure from the Maoist policy of "reeducating" criminals, was reported to have resulted in over 5,000 executions. Immediately after a trial and a "public sentencing rally," offenders were paraded through the streets before being shot in the back of the neck. In Zimbabwe, by contrast, the High Court imposed long prison terms instead of the expected death sentences on six guerrillas convicted in August of machine-gunning Prime Minister Robert Mugabe's house in June 1982. Under the state of emergency declared in Sudan in April 1984, crimes such as possessing or consuming alcohol and "suspected intended adultery" became punishable by flogging, and theft by the surgical amputation of one or both hands. Many liberal Muslims as well as the 30% non-Muslim minority protested against this strict interpretation of the Qur'an, but Pres. Gaafar Nimeiry (*see* BIOGRAPHIES) remained convinced that it expressed God's will as well as deterring crime.   (C. R. M. DAVIES)

See also Law.

This article updates the *Macropædia* articles CRIME AND PUNISHMENT; POLICE.

Dance

North America. Emblematic of trends in U.S. dance in 1984, the ceremonies at the summer Olympic Games in Los Angeles featured choreographed spectacles, a tribute to George Balanchine, and break dancers in epidemic numbers. Both on tour and during the Olympic Arts Festival, Pina Bausch's Wuppertaler Tanztheater and the Japanese

Martha Graham's major new work in the season marking her 90th birthday was *The Rite of Spring,* set to Stravinsky's music. Terese Capucilli is shown here as the victim. Graham's 53-year-old masterpiece *Primitive Mysteries,* also performed in the 1984 season, drew better reviews.
MARTHA SWOPE

Butoh company Sankaijuku provoked controversy. Their bizarre theatricality and heavy tone struck some as profound, others as pretentious. Foreign attractions were many and diverse during the year, but no first-rank international classical ballet company visited the United States.

American Ballet Theatre's (ABT's) *Cinderella,* produced by Mikhail Baryshnikov with Peter Anastos as co-choreographer at a cost of $1 million, provided a box-office success coast to coast despite uneven choreography and Santo Loquasto's dreary decor. *Bach Partita,* Twyla Tharp's first work for ABT that was not made for Baryshnikov, was an artistic coup. Using principals and corps as egalitarian virtuosi, the work presaged a pushing forward of the neoclassical ballet idiom. Tharp's *Sinatra Suite,* a sweet and sour duet version of her company dance *Nine Sinatra Songs,* gave Baryshnikov's emotional depth and nuanced phrasing a perfect vehicle, with Elaine Kudo as his foil. Gelsey Kirkland, limpidly affecting in Antony Tudor's revived *The Leaves Are Fading,* bolted the company in midseason, leaving her future in doubt.

Baryshnikov agreed to stay on as artistic director of ABT for an unspecified period, without contract or pay. While the company made its first foreign tour in seven years (to Japan), he completed a Hollywood feature film. Royal Ballet principal choreographer Sir Kenneth MacMillan then joined Baryshnikov as part-time artistic associate, and John Taras left the New York City Ballet (NYCB) to serve as ABT associate director.

Twyla Tharp seemed to be everywhere in 1984. She danced with her company at the Brooklyn Academy of Music and on Broadway, choreographed the film *Amadeus,* and directed "Baryshnikov by Tharp" for public television. With Jerome Robbins at NYCB she co-choreographed the dense, witty *Brahms/Handel,* providing the most radical addition to the company repertory. Robbins's *Antique Epigraphs,* a benign view of sororal society, seemed an antidote to his early misogynist *The Cage.* His musicless *Moves* was also taken into the NYCB repertory. Peter Martins choreographed Bach suites for *Réjouissance,* featuring Suzanne Farrell. His romantic *A Schubertiad* inevitably paled alongside the season's landmark restoration of Balanchine's *Liebeslieder Walzer,* given a new setting by David Mitchell. After staging the Balanchine work, Karin von Aroldingen gave her last performance in it. New ballets by Bart Cook and Helgi Tomasson were introduced in Saratoga Springs, N.Y., and the company paid a first visit to Minneapolis, Minn. Jacques d'Amboise's name was retired from company rosters. (Peter Martins's retirement as a dancer was marked at the 1,000th performance of *The Nutcracker* on Dec. 6, 1983, in which Jerome Robbins made his debut as Drosselmeyer.)

The 50th anniversary of the School of American Ballet and of Balanchine's first U.S. ballet, *Serenade,* were commemorated in school and company performances. The first exhibition of Balanchine's television work was presented by the Museum of Broadcasting in New York. "Dance in America" produced "Balanchine," a two-part public TV tribute incorporating revelatory film of his early works.

There were important losses and shifts in regional ballet. Michael Smuin's resignation as artistic director of the San Francisco Ballet was announced and then denied by him, and he was rehired. Smuin also made news with his popular ballet *To the Beatles,* which featured break dancing. San Francisco Ballet founder Lew Christensen died unexpectedly, as did Boston Ballet founder E. Virginia Williams just before that company's commissioned premiere of Choo San Goh's first full-length ballet, *Romeo and Juliet.* Pres. Joel Garrick and artistic director Violette Verdy resigned in succession from the Boston company, leaving Bruce Wells temporarily in charge. Verdy rejoined the NYCB in a teaching capacity. Edward Villella sued the Eglevsky Ballet on the issue of whether he had resigned or been fired. And Ian Horvath, co-founder of the Cleveland (Ohio) Ballet, resigned.

New twists on tradition and popular culture abounded. In Houston, Texas, Ben Stevenson's *Lady in Waiting* brought vocalist Cleo Laine together with 40 singing dancers. Todd Bolender's space exploration ballet, *Voyager,* kept things up-to-date in Kansas City. The Dance Theatre of Harlem unveiled its Creole *Giselle,* set in the American South, to receptive critics in London and New York. The Joffrey Ballet was commissioned by the city of San Antonio, Texas, to create a ballet celebrating the city's history and diversity (*Jamboree,* by Gerald Arpino). Pacific Northwest Ballet's new production of *The Nutcracker,* with acclaimed designs by Maurice Sendak, proved too costly to bring east, but the company's programs for its Brooklyn Academy of Music debut included Lucinda Childs's first U.S. ballet commission, *Cascade.*

At the Joyce Theater in New York City, Christine Sarry and Natalia Makarova helped Eliot Feld celebrate the tenth anniversary of his company. Milwaukee (Wis.) Ballet mounted the first complete *La Sylphide* in the Midwest. Pennsylvania Ballet premiered ballets by Richard Tanner, Jean-Pierre Bonnefous, and Peter Martins in its new home at Philadelphia's Academy of Music. New York City was host to its first international ballet competition, with Igor Youskevitch as artistic director.

Modern dance titan Martha Graham (*see* BIOGRAPHIES) marked her 90th birthday in typically heroic fashion by choreographing Stravinsky's *The Rite of Spring,* a version unsparing in its sacrificial cruelty and frank sexuality. The National Endowment for the Arts awarded her $250,000 to preserve her works on film. Erick Hawkins celebrated his 50th year by dancing in his longest New York season to date. Alwin Nikolais's new works rekindled critical in-

terest. Merce Cunningham's *Pictures* and *Inlets II* further attested to a productive period in his career. Paul Taylor's creative binge continued with *Equinox* and . . . *Byzantium.*

The Alvin Ailey company became the first predominantly black troupe to play the Metropolitan Opera House (with Paris Opéra Ballet guest Patrick Dupond). Its City Center season offered premieres by Judith Jamison, Ailey, and Donald McKayle. The Met was turned into an ice palace for the John Curry Skating Company, which made a persuasive case for the art of ice dancing, with choreography by Curry, Laura Dean, Paul Taylor, Lar Lubovitch, Peter Martins, and Jean-Pierre Bonnefous.

Elders of the post-Cunningham generation showed unflagging vitality. David Gordon, commissioned to make new dances for ABT and the Dance Theatre of Harlem during the next season, premiered *Framework* with his own company, in which Power Boothe's picture frames collaborated in an intricate layering of movement, music, and dialogue. Kei Takei capped her 15th anniversary with a more than eight-hour marathon performance of her *Light* cycle, Parts 10–19. The Brooklyn Academy of Music's vanguard Next Wave Festival opened with the U.S. premiere of *The Games,* a sobering glimpse of the postnuclear future by Meredith Monk and Ping Chong, and closed with a revival of the Robert Wilson-Philip Glass magnum opera *Einstein on the Beach.* In between came new works by Remy Charlip, Bill T. Jones and Arnie Zane, Tim Miller, and Mark Morris. The 100th birthday of modern dance mentor and composer Louis Horst was observed with performances, lectures, and an exhibit. There were also exhibitions commemorating the 100th anniversaries of the deaths of the romantic ballerinas Fanny Elssler (at the Austrian Institute, New York City) and Marie Taglioni (at Harvard University).

The first annual "Bessie" Awards (named for educator Bessie Schönberg), sponsored by Dance Theater Workshop, honoured 28 innovative independent artists and companies. The American Dance Festival paid tribute on its 50th anniversary to Hanya Holm (a $25,000 Samuel H. Scripps Award), conferred a series of "golden" anniversary commissions, presented the first International Modern Dance Festival in Durham, N.C., and then took the festival to Japan. Other major awards went to Harold, Lew, and William Christensen (Capezio) and Lincoln Kirstein (Pres-

During the summer of 1984 break dancing exploded out of the ghetto and into the mainstream of American culture. These youngsters are "breaking" in Minneapolis/Saint Paul, Minnesota.

idential Medal of Freedom). Tap dancer Howard ("Sandman") Sims was named National Heritage Fellow.

Along with regional dance pioneers Christensen and Williams, the dance world lost Bentley Stone (co-choreographer with Ruth Page of *Frankie and Johnny*), dancer-teacher Vera Nemchinova (*see* OBITUARIES), and Broadway performer Avon Long.

In Canada the Toronto International Festival, the largest music and dance festival in Canadian history, commissioned a new production of John Cranko's *Onegin* by the National Ballet of Canada, in which rising ballerina Sabine Allemann attracted notice. Les Grands Ballets Canadiens revived Fernand Nault's *Tommy* and introduced James Kudelka's *Alliances.* Annette av Paul announced her retirement. The Royal Winnipeg Ballet brought Peter Wright's *Giselle* to the Brooklyn Academy of Music, where wraithlike Evelyn Hart was compared to Gelsey Kirkland. Ballet Eddy Toussaint celebrated its tenth anniversary with an homage to jazz ballet teacher Eva Von Genscy. Initiating a lively cultural exchange, Montreal's Danséchange took eight American independent choreographers to Montreal and nine Canadians to New York.

(SALI ANN KRIEGSMAN)

Europe. Faced with the increasing innovations of modern dance, Britain's Royal Ballet added six new works to the repertory of its two companies, more than for some years past. All were by present or former company dancers, of whom David Bintley and Michael Corder enjoyed burgeoning reputations as choreographers, while Jennifer Jackson and Ashley Page were debutants of much promise. There were celebratory performances for the 80th birthday of Sir Frederick Ashton, the company's founder-choreographer, but no new work.

Another former Royal Ballet dancer, Michael Clark (*see* BIOGRAPHIES), became an acknowledged leader of British modern dance. As resident choreographer at Riverside Studios, a west London arts centre, he formed his first independent group with three other dancers (all with classical ballet backgrounds). Their venture drew unprecedented media attention as well as new and younger audiences. Previously Clark had verged on the grotesque in reacting against his classical training, but a single new work, *Do You Me? I Did,* evidenced a more imaginative direction.

London Contemporary Dance Theatre and Ballet Rambert (a modern-dance company despite its name) had led the vanguard of contemporary dance in Britain since the mid-1960s, and both continued to present new works by such established choreographers as Richard Alston, Christo-

pher Bruce, Robert Cohan, and Siobhan Davies. Among the flourishing small groups, Janet Smith and Dancers toured the Far East; The Kosh, a popular group of more gymnastic style, visited West Berlin; and the innovative Extemporary Dance Company went to Brussels (as did the Michael Clark dancers). In contrast the classical Northern Ballet Theatre, based at Manchester, acquired the first Chinese choreography for a British company in Chiang Ching's *Fu,* a dramatic dance allegory of power hunger and its consequences, with music and design also by Chinese artists.

The regular pattern of intercontinental exchanges in dance brought European tours by several U.S. companies, including those of Alvin Ailey, Merce Cunningham, Martha Graham (which was due to undertake a six-week residency in Florence, Italy, with a view to setting up a new modern dance centre there), Lar Lubovitch, and Paul Taylor, and the Dance Theatre of Harlem. The National Ballet of Cuba, under founder-director Alicia Alonso (still performing ballerina roles at 62), visited Britain, the U.S.S.R., France, and Italy.

From the U.S.S.R. the so-called Moscow Classical Ballet, previously unseen in the West, gave seasons at Paris and London. It drew large audiences on its name and the presence of the Bolshoi Ballet's Ekaterina Maximova as guest ballerina but offered more reward in the standard of dancing than in choreographic content. In Tbilisi, Georgian S.S.R., George Gershwin's *Porgy and Bess* opera was produced as a ballet, with choreography by company director Mikhail Lavrovsky, who also obtained *Serenade* as the first Balanchine ballet staged by a Soviet company.

The Leningrad Kirov Ballet was a major success in Vienna. That city also had become the scene of a leading biennial festival of classical and contemporary dance on an international scale; Tanz '84 featured 82 performances in six weeks. The city's "Kaiser Franz tourist image" was later reportedly erased by two modern dance works: Bernd Bienert's *Alpenglühn,* a feminist quest accompanied by electroacoustic and folk music, and a satirical fantasy, *Wien, Wien, du bist allein,* by Liz King and her two-year-old Vienna Dance Theatre.

In Czechoslovakia the enterprising Prague Chamber Ballet, formed in 1975 by Pavel Smok to develop a new classical repertory, obtained its first national subsidy. A comparable company was formed in Athens as Nausikaa Dance Theatre by Aimé de Lignière. He was formerly with the Royal Ballet of Flanders, in Belgium, where the Ballet Contemporain de Bruxelles, directed by Normando Tor-

Maurice Béjart's Ballet of the 20th Century opened a new full-length work at the Palais des Congrès in Paris in February. The new ballet is *Messe pour le temps futur* ("Mass for a Future Time"), based on a text by Dom Helder Camara, archbishop of Recife, Brazil.

res, inaugurated the city's historic Grand Place as a new location for an open-air international forum of dance.

Celebratory programs marked the 25th anniversaries of the Ballet of the Twentieth Century, first formed in Brussels by Maurice Béjart, and of the Netherlands Dance Theatre, directed by the Czechoslovak-born Jiri Kylian. Both companies pioneered a style of European contemporary dance largely independent of U.S. influences, in which elements of classical ballet technique were significantly blended. Both had attracted a second generation of young audiences to supplement those now grown older but still faithful.

The Béjart ballet continued to promote dance as a popular spectacle, often in large spaces such as sports arenas, and with a bias toward featuring men dancers more prominently than women. New works in 1984 ranged from *Messe pour le temps futur,* associating philosophical concepts with traditional Oriental and other third world music, to a danced version of Mozart's *The Magic Flute* (using a tape recording).

Kylian also borrowed from opera to choreograph Maurice Ravel's *L'Enfant et les sortilèges* as a pantomime fantasy and created his own 25th ballet for the Netherlands company in *Lullaby,* to the Alban Berg violin concerto. He brought forward a new choreographer, Spanish company dancer Nacho Duato, whose two works, *Jardi Tancat* and *Danza y Rito,* reportedly signaled an exceptional talent. The first of these later won the premier prize at the international choreographic competition in Cologne, West Germany.

West German dance interest remained centred on the Stuttgart Ballet, under the continuing direction of the Brazilian-born Marcia Haydée, and on the Hamburg Ballet, where the U.S.-born John Neumeier added to his cycle of Mahler-based "symphonic" ballets with *Gustav Mahler's Sixth Symphony,* of which there were contrary opinions as to its success. In modern dance the Wuppertaler Tanztheater, directed by Pina Bausch, continued to arouse enthusiasm and controversy at home (and in its New York debut) for its innovative style of relating dance movement to a form of theatre drama.

From the Komische Oper in East Berlin the ballet company took Tom Schilling's unconventional version of *Swan Lake* to the Edinburgh Festival. It restored Tchaikovsky's music to the original (pre-Petipa) sequence and presented the story in terms of a *Hamlet*-like psychological tragedy, but it lacked sufficient strength of choreography. The Paris Opéra Ballet took to Edinburgh a triple bill on commedia dell'arte themes from the more adventurous repertory encouraged by Rudolf Nureyev during his first season as artistic director, which also included a "Soirée Stockhausen" at the Opéra-Comique in Paris.

French Minister of Culture Jack Lang announced increased dance funding and the setting up of "national choreographic centres" in 12 provincial cities as well as state dance colleges at Nanterre and Marseille. Prizewinners in an international choreographic competition at Bagnolet were enabled to show their works in London, drawing the comment from *The Times* that they looked as if trained dancers were no longer needed to perform them. The Ballet du Nord, formed and directed by the Cuban-born Alfonso Catá at Roubaix, consolidated its reputation and began touring abroad in Tunisia, later in Egypt and Jordan.

Multiple changes in artistic directors brought the Danish-born Peter Schaufuss his first such appointment at London Festival Ballet, while Egon Madsen, another Dane, left Frankfurt, West Germany, for the Swedish Royal Ballet, and the Royal Ballet of Flanders appointed the Soviet expatriate Valery Panov. Ronald Hynd, a London free-lance choreographer, returned to the Bavarian Staatsoper Ballet, Munich, where he had been director from 1970 to 1973. Adel Orosz was appointed to the Hungarian National Ballet, Doris Laine to the National Ballet of Finland, and the New York-born William Forsythe to the Frankfurt Opera Ballet.

The deaths occurred during the year of Serge Lido, a Russian-French photographer of international fame who specialized in ballet; Mary Skeaping (*see* OBITUARIES), British dancer and teacher, former member of the Anna Pavlova company, ballet-mistress of Sadler's Wells Ballet, and director of the Swedish Royal Ballet (1953–62), noted for her productions of 19th-century and earlier classics; and the Soviet choreographer Rostislav Vladimirovich Zakharov (*see* OBITUARIES), twice Stalin Prize winner and one of the first to apply the Stanislavsky dramatic method to ballet. (NOËL GOODWIN)

See also Music; Theatre.

This article updates the *Macropædia* article The History of Western DANCE.

LOS ANGELES OLYMPIC COMMITTEE

Japan's avant-garde Butoh dance group, Sankaijuku, took North American audiences by storm during its summer and fall 1984 tour of the U.S. and Canada.

Disasters of 1984

The loss of life and property from disasters in 1984 included the following:

Aviation

January 2, Al Qatranah, Jordan. A military transport plane carrying 13 persons crashed because of a "technical fault"; all aboard were killed.

January 10, Sofia, Bulg. A TU-134 Bulgarian airliner crashed while attempting to land in Sofia after traveling from East Berlin; all 50 persons aboard were killed.

February 28, Near Zaragoza, Spain. A U.S. Air Force C-130 Hercules transport plane crashed in the snow-covered Sierra del Moncayo during dense fog shortly after the pilot had radioed that he would attempt an emergency landing because of inclement weather; all 17 Americans and a Spanish officer on board were killed.

March 23, Near P'ohang, South Korea. A U.S. Marine Corps helicopter, participating in joint military maneuvers, crashed into a mountain; all 29 U.S. and South Korean servicemen were killed.

May 8, Ezbet Beni Salama, Egypt. An Egyptian jet crashed in the desert; 19 persons on the ground as well as the two crewmen were killed.

June 28, Brazil. A twin-engine turboprop airplane slammed into a mountainside during a rainstorm some 160 km (100 mi) north of Rio de Janeiro; all 16 persons aboard were killed.

August 5, Near Dhaka Airport, Bangladesh. A Fokker F-27 passenger airplane crashed while attempting to land in a rainstorm; all 49 persons aboard were killed in the country's worst air disaster since independence in 1971.

August 19, Near Uttoxeter, England. A twin-engine Varsity aircraft slammed into power lines and crashed after developing engine trouble; 11 of the 14 persons aboard were killed.

August 24, San Luis Obispo, Calif. A Wings West Beechcraft C-99 commuter airplane carrying 15 persons and a single-engine Rockwell Commander airplane carrying a flight instructor and a student collided in midair and scattered fiery wreckage over an 8.1-ha (20-ac) radius; all 17 persons were killed in the crash.

September 18, Quito, Ecuador. A DC-8 cargo plane slammed into a telephone pole, exploded, and scattered burning debris over a two-block radius; 60 persons were killed, 56 of them on the ground, and 75 persons were injured in the crash.

October 19, Omsk, U.S.S.R. A Soviet jetliner slammed into a fuel truck on the airport runway; all 150 persons aboard were reportedly killed.

November 23, Near Castres, France. Two French transport planes crashed in midair and 13 crewmen and passengers were killed; 7 others were missing and presumed dead.

December 6, Jacksonville, Fla. A Provincetown-Boston Airline plane crashed in a wooded area, minutes after takeoff, when its tail broke away in flight; all 13 persons aboard were killed.

December 22, Eastern Nepal. A Royal Nepal Airlines plane crashed and 15 of the 23 persons aboard were killed.

Fires and Explosions

January 14, Pusan, South Korea. An early-morning hotel fire, possibly ignited by an overheated kerosene stove kept in the hotel's fourth-floor sauna, swept through the building and trapped patrons in their rooms; 37 persons were killed and at least 76 others were injured.

February 25, Cubatão, Brazil. A blaze followed by an explosion occurred in the shantytown of Vila Socó after a ruptured gasoline pipeline leaked fuel in ditches surrounding the shantytown; a month-long investigation confirmed that as many as 500 persons (though only 86 bodies were found) were incinerated.

March 24, Mandalay, Burma. A huge fire rampaged through the country's second largest city and razed some 2,700 buildings, leaving more than 23,000 people homeless; the blaze, started by a spark that ignited a pile of coconut husk fibre in a cushion-maker's house, killed ten persons.

March 27, Jamnagar, India. At an air force base four training bombs exploded as they were being loaded into a truck for recharging; the blast incinerated the truck as well as a building at the base, claimed the lives of 12 persons, and injured 25 others.

May 11, Jackson Township, N.J. A fast-burning fire at the eight-trailer Haunted Castle at Six Flags Great Adventure park claimed the lives of eight teenagers; the blaze started when a youth lit a cigarette lighter to find his way, and the flame accidentally ignited a large piece of foam-rubber pad.

Mid-May, Severomorsk, U.S.S.R. A huge explosion at a naval ammunition depot triggered a chain reaction of other explosions and fires; at least 200 to 300 persons were believed dead, including firefighters and ordnance technicians who were killed when ammunition they were defusing in an attempt to prevent more fires exploded in their faces.

May 23, Lancaster, England. A gas explosion in an underground water-treatment plant claimed the lives of at least 13 persons.

May 28, Taipei, Taiwan. A fire that started in the second-floor restaurant of a 14-story hotel claimed the lives of 19 persons and injured 53 others; the blaze, apparently caused by a short circuit resulting from a leaking roof, was confined to the second floor, but many patrons on upper floors succumbed to the noxious fumes coming from burning nylon carpeting.

July 4, Beverly, Mass. An 80-year-old wood-and-brick rooming house that catered to transients, former mental patients, and alcoholics was deliberately set afire by an arsonist; 14 of the 36 occupants died in the fast-burning fire, and 7 others were admitted to area hospitals.

July 22, Near Pilgrim's Rest, South Africa. A bolt of lightning struck a hut and set it afire; 13 girls attending a tribal initiation school were killed in the blazing hut, and 27 of the 58 others who escaped were treated for multiple burns.

July 23, Romeoville, Ill. A massive explosion at a Union Oil Co. refinery claimed the lives of 17 persons and caused more than $100 million in damages; the blast occurred apparently because of a mechanical failure in a 16.8-m (55-ft) tower holding propane.

August 2, Madras, India. A bomb concealed in a piece of luggage exploded in a passenger lounge at the Madras International Airport; 23 persons were killed and 24 others were wounded in the blast.

August 16, Off the coast of Brazil. A blaze erupted on an offshore oil platform when gases released during drilling caught fire; 16 persons were injured in the inferno, and 40 others escaped the fire in a rescue boat only to drown when the craft capsized in heavy seas.

October 18, Paterson, N.J. A fire, started by a disgruntled resident of the Alexander Hamilton Hotel, swept through the first floor of the structure and sent noxious fumes throughout the building; 13 persons died of smoke inhalation

On June 8 a tornado destroyed the small Wisconsin town of Barneveld, killing 9 people and injuring 150. The tornado was one of 49 spawned by a major storm system.

and 57 others were injured, 4 of them critically.

October 23, Baguio, Phil. A fire, possibly touched off by a broken light bulb, swept through the luxurious Pine Hotel following ceremonies commemorating the 40th anniversary of Gen. Douglas MacArthur's return to the Philippines; 17 persons were killed, 9 of them from a U.S. American Legion group.

October 29, Near Jakarta, Indon. A fire triggered a series of ammunition explosions at the headquarters of the Indonesian Marine Corps; at least 25 persons were killed and more than 100 others were injured.

November 1, Manila, Phil. An early-morning fire swept through the seventh floor of the Ambassador Hotel; 10 persons were killed and 20 others were treated at nearby hospitals.

Early November, Medenec, Czech. A fire in a home for the disabled killed 26 residents and injured 2 others.

November 19, Tlalnepantla, Mexico. A gas truck apparently exploded in a storage area for liquefied gas and touched off about a dozen explosions that sent balls of fire shooting into the air and masses of debris showering down on a 20-block area; the death toll was placed at 452, and some 4,250 persons were seriously injured in the inferno.

December 2, Tbilisi, U.S.S.R. A gas explosion, caused by a natural gas leak, devastated a nine-story apartment building; at least 100 persons were reportedly killed.

December 13, Punjab Province, Pakistan. A natural gas pipeline explosion occurred when pressure built up in the pipeline; 16 persons were killed in the blast and 11 others were injured.

Marine

January 22, Off Tawitawi Island, Phil. A ferry capsized in high seas en route to Sibutu Island, near Sabah, Malaysia; some 96 persons, mostly women and children, were feared drowned.

January 24, The English Channel. The "Radiant Med" freighter capsized and sank when gale-force winds and 9-m (30-ft) waves pummeled the vessel; at least 16 seamen drowned.

March 3, Lake Kwania, Uganda. A boat carrying wedding guests capsized; 11 persons drowned.

May 6, Near Cox's Bazar, Bangladesh. A ferry capsized and 22 persons reportedly drowned; 8 others were missing and feared dead.

June 3, Atlantic Ocean. The "Marques," a 36-m (117-ft) British square-rigged ship, capsized and was abandoned by its 28 crew members and passengers when it was assaulted by a killer squall during a race from Bermuda to Halifax, Nova Scotia; 18 persons were missing, one body was recovered, and 9 survivors were rescued by ships and helicopters that searched the turbulent North Atlantic.

Early June, Off the coast of Indonesia. A passenger ferry sprang a leak and sank in the north Java Sea; 24 persons were missing and presumed drowned.

July 7, Near Huntsville, Ala. A triple-decked riverboat carrying 18 persons from SCI, the largest aerospace business in the city, capsized on the Tennessee River when it was buffeted by a "tornadic wind shear"; 11 aboard drowned in the mishap.

July 19, Off the western coast of India. A 50-boat fleet of fishing trawlers apparently sank during monsoon rains; at least 400 fishermen were missing and presumed dead.

August 13, Off the coast of Sabah, Malaysia. A ferry carrying some 200 Indonesian timber workers capsized; only 6 of those aboard were rescued by fishermen.

September 24, Off the coast of Nossi-Be, Madagascar. An overloaded launch carrying at least 80 passengers, some 45 more persons than the craft was designed to hold, sank in heavy seas; at least 31 persons drowned.

Late September, Rapti River, Nepal. An overcrowded wooden boat capsized in the swollen Rapti River; nearly 100 passengers were feared drowned.

October 2, Hamburg, West Germany. The "Martina," a chartered ferry that was carrying 40 persons on a birthday cruise, sank after colliding with tugboat "Therese"; 19 persons were feared dead in the rain-swept Hamburg harbour.

October 28, Off the coast of Marinduque Island, Phil. A ferry sank during a fierce tropical storm, and more than 100 persons were missing and presumed drowned.

Mining

January 18, Near Takada, Fukuoka Prefecture, Kyushu, Japan. A fire in the Miike coal mine trapped 96 miners who were working in the shaft some 213 m (700 ft) under the Ariake Sea; 83 workers were killed when carbon monoxide filled the shaft. Thirteen others were rescued.

April 21, Eastern Yugoslavia. A methane gas explosion in the Strmosten pit, 250 m (820 ft) underground at the Resavica coal mine, killed at least 33 miners and injured 14 others.

June 20, Near Taipei, Taiwan. An explosion in a coal mine occurred when a coal trolley tripped over a cable, causing a spark that ignited gas in the tunnel; 74 miners were known dead and 26 others were trapped and feared dead because of poisonous gas in the tunnel.

July 10, Northern Taiwan. A fire in a coal mine, caused by a short circuit in a compressor, trapped 125 miners deep inside a tunnel; 101 miners were killed, 2 were missing, and 22 others were rescued in the country's worst mining disaster to date.

Early November, Hebei Province, China. Extensive coal mine flooding led to the deaths of at least ten persons.

December 5, Near Taipei, Taiwan. A coal mine explosion claimed the lives of 93 miners who were trapped underground at the time of the blast; one miner, who was rescued four days after the accident, maintained that he had survived by resorting to cannibalism.

December 19, Wilberg, Utah. A fire, one mile inside a coal mine, claimed the lives of 27 miners; the blaze apparently started when flames erupted from a coal-conveyor belt while the miners were trying to break a one-day production record.

Miscellaneous

February, Northeast Ghana. An outbreak of meningitis killed 103 persons and afflicted 1,500 others.

February–June, India. A dysentery epidemic rampaged through four Indian states; at least 3,290 persons were known dead, nearly 3,000 of them in West Bengal State.

Early May–Mid May, Feira de Santana, Brazil. A fast-spreading virus, with an unknown cause, claimed the lives of 252 children in two weeks.

May, Bangladesh. Dysentery and an assortment of intestinal diseases claimed the lives of 950 persons, most of them children.

May 4, Cairo, Egypt. A four-story house collapsed and 25 persons were killed in the rubble; 26 others were injured.

May 7, Near Allahabad, India. An overhead power line became entangled in bicycles that were perched on top of an overcrowded bus, resulting in a surge of electricity that electrocuted 35 of the 75 passengers aboard the bus.

July 30, Bangkok, Thailand. At least 19 persons were trampled to death and some 40 others were injured at an annual charity giveaway when more than 2,000 persons surged to receive bags of rice and money.

August 17, Cairo, Egypt. A five-story building housing 90 persons collapsed only one day after an inspector had deemed that the structure needed only slight repairs; 10 persons were killed.

Late August, Wakefield, England. A salmonella outbreak at a mental hospital killed 26 persons who were poisoned by spoiled beef; two weeks later 16 others were still suffering from symptoms associated with food poisoning.

October 1, Tamil Nadu, India. A wall in a motion picture theatre collapsed and crushed 14 persons to death.

November 7, Munnar, India. A rope bridge collapsed over a swollen stream in the southern state of Kerala when some 150 children crowded onto it to watch a helicopter land; rescue workers, whose efforts were hampered by mud, feared that at least 125 children were dead.

November 9, Tanta, Egypt. A decrepit five-story apartment building collapsed; 12 residents were killed and 17 others were injured.

December 2, Bhopal, India. A cloud of deadly methyl isocyanate gas leaked from the Union Carbide Corp.'s pesticide plant when a valve in an underground storage tank broke under rising pressure; some 200,000 people over 65 sq km (25 sq mi) were affected by the poison, as many as 2,500 persons were believed killed, and as many as 100,000 survivors were in danger of blindness, sterility, kidney and liver damage, tuberculosis, and brain damage as a result of exposure to the lethal gas.

Natural

January 12–16, Northern Europe. Severe snowstorms coupled with gale-force winds pum-

Near Tlalnepantla, a suburb of Mexico City, repeated explosions in a storage area for liquefied gas on November 19 killed at least 452 persons and gravely injured some 4,250.
CLASON-PRESS—GAMMA/LIAISON

An express train crowded with commuters and tourists derailed July 30 near Polmont, Scotland, possibly as a result of striking a cow on the tracks. The death toll was 13 and 44 were injured.

AP/WIDE WORLD

meled Britain, Scotland, Scandinavia, and parts of France and Germany; at least 22 deaths were attributed to the five-day onslaught in Britain alone.

January 30–31, Swaziland. A hurricane battered the country for two days; at least 13 persons were killed.

January 31–February 2, Mozambique, South Africa, Swaziland. Killer cyclone Domoina lashed southern Africa for three days with the heaviest rains in 25 years; severe flooding killed at least 124 persons and left thousands of others homeless.

February 4, United States. Arctic cold and blowing snow invaded the country from Canada, immobilizing much of the Plains states; at least 33 persons were known dead, including 23 in Minnesota and North Dakota.

February 7, Western Europe. Severe storms pummeled Western Europe with snow, gales, and heavy rain; 13 persons were killed as a result of the blizzardlike weather, including 8 crew members who drowned when their ship sank in the English Channel.

Early–Mid February, Java, Indonesia. Two weeks of severe monsoon rains precipitated flooding that killed 26 persons and affected about 300,000 others.

February 28, Midwestern and Eastern U.S. A deadly winter storm crippled cities from St. Louis, Mo., to Detroit to Buffalo, N.Y., where drifting snow caused major highways to be blocked and forced airports to close. Schools, offices, and factories in many of the major cities closed for two days; at least 29 deaths were attributed to the storm.

March 9, Eastern U.S. A powerful winter storm that blew in from Canada was dubbed the "Alberta Clipper" and blasted the Northeast with up to a foot of snow, making roads impassable; there were 23 storm-related deaths.

March 14, New England, U.S. The worst March snowstorm of the century dumped from 30 to 90 cm (1 to 3 ft) of snow from eastern New York to Maine; at least 11 deaths were blamed on the storm.

March 19–23, Western U.S. Winter storms precipitated a heavy snowstorm in the Rocky Mountains and caused severe thunderstorms accompanied by hail in Texas and Oklahoma; 27 deaths were attributed to the week-long onslaught.

March 20, Gazli, U.S.S.R. An earthquake,

measuring 9 on the 12-point Soviet scale, rocked the natural-gas-producing town of Gazli; buildings were destroyed, 100 persons were injured, and some casualties were assumed owing to the magnitude of the quake.

March 28, South Carolina and North Carolina. A string of tornadoes cut a 480-km (300-mi) swath of destruction across the two states, engendering one of the worst natural disasters in the century; hardest hit were Newberry, Winnsboro, and Bennettsville, S.C., where a shopping centre was flattened, and Red Springs, N.C. More than 70 persons were killed, 51 of them in North Carolina, and property damage was estimated in the billions of dollars.

April 12, Mahajanga, Madagascar. A cyclone packing winds of 241 km/h (150 mph) wrecked 80% of the port city and killed at least 15 persons; 30 others were seriously injured.

April 21, Water Valley, Mississippi. Torna-

does, spawned by severe thunderstorms, ravaged northern Mississippi on the eve of Easter Sunday; tornadoes were sighted in 15 different locations in the northern part of the state, but hardest hit was Water Valley, where 7 persons lost their lives. Another 5 persons were killed in Philipp, and the statewide death toll was 15.

April 26, Morris, Okla. A deadly tornado flattened more than half the homes and businesses in the town and claimed the lives of 11 persons; tornadoes elsewhere in the state killed 3 others and injured 100.

May 6–9, Southern U.S. Severe thunderstorms complicated by tornadoes caused widespread flooding in Appalachia and the states of Kentucky, Louisiana, Tennessee, Ohio, Maryland, and West Virginia; at least 14 persons were killed and some 6,000 others were left homeless.

May 13–16, Bangladesh and India. A four-day downpour precipitated floods and landslides in Bangladesh and northeastern India; at least 136 persons were known dead and 100 others were injured.

May 27, Dongchuan (Tung-ch'uan) City, Yunnan (Yun-nan) Province, China. Torrential rains triggered a landslide that buried buildings including a supply and marketing cooperative, a bank, and a post office; at least 100 persons were killed and 50 others were injured.

May 27, Tulsa, Okla. An overnight downpour of up to a foot of rain flooded more than 2,100 homes and left thousands homeless; at least 12 persons died when their cars were swept off roads by rising water.

Late May, Rio Grande do Sul, Brazil. Widespread flooding left nearly 10,000 persons homeless and was blamed for the deaths of 17 persons.

Late May, Sri Lanka. Heavy rains triggered landslides in the south and in eastern Kalutara District; 42 persons died and some 3,000 families were affected.

Late May–Early June, Northeastern United States. A slowly moving rainstorm dumped 23 cm (9.2 in) of rain, precipitating widespread flooding; 18 deaths were attributed to the storm and thousands were left homeless.

Early June, Northeastern India. Heavy rain caused severe flooding that claimed the lives of at least 38 persons.

June, Bangladesh and India. Monsoon floods ravaged the two countries and left tens of thousands of people homeless; some 200 persons were believed dead in the month-long downpour.

June 3, Taipei, Taiwan. Eight solid hours of

SANDRO TUCCI—GAMMA/LIAISON

A leaking storage tank at a pesticide plant in Bhopal, India, produced a lethal cloud of methyl isocyanate gas on December 2. As many as 2,500 persons were killed, and some 100,000 survivors faced long-term illnesses as a result of exposure to the gas.

torrential rain, the heaviest in 11 years, caused landslides and severe flooding; 25 persons were killed.

June 8, Barneveld, Wis. A killer storm spawned 49 tornadoes that swept through the Plains and upper Middle West, where a total of 16 persons were killed; hardest hit was Barneveld, where 9 people were killed and 150 were injured, 57 of them seriously. The small town was completely demolished by a twister that flattened 90 homes and 30 businesses or public buildings.

June 9–10, Central U.S.S.R. Deadly tornadoes packing hurricane-force winds ravaged the towns of Ivanovo, Gorky, Kalinin, Kostroma, and Yaroslavl; the raging winds uprooted trees, smashed brick houses, and destroyed factories. Hundreds were feared dead.

Late June, Ambon, Indon. Week-long landslides, triggered by heavy rains, claimed the lives of 11 persons on the island; 11 others were missing.

June 29, Kumamoto, Japan. A landslide, caused by heavy rains, buried 14 persons; rescuers were conducting a search for others still missing.

July 4–7, South Korea. Torrential rains triggered extensive flooding that washed away bridges and roads, closed schools, and isolated villages; at least 14 persons were known dead, 23 others were missing, and more than 1,800 persons were left homeless.

Mid-July, Recife, Brazil. Five days of torrential rains precipitated floods and mudslides that left at least 13 persons dead and 1,000 others homeless in and around the city.

August 31–September 3, Seoul, South Korea. The city was inundated with 33 cm (13 in) of rain, which caused severe flooding; 81 persons were known dead and 36 others were missing and feared dead; property damage was estimated at more than $7 million.

September 2–3, Philippines. Raging Typhoon Ike roared through seven major islands in two days and left an estimated 1,120,000 people homeless; the storm, the fiercest to hit the country in the century, was responsible for more than 1,300 deaths.

September 6, Off the coast of Beihai (Pei-hai), China. Typhoon Ike unleashed hurricane-force winds that battered the coast of Guangxi Zhuang (Kwangsi Chuang) Autonomous Region and left 13 persons missing at sea after their fishing boats were demolished; factories and houses collapsed in Beihai, Qinzhou (Ch'in-chou), and Fangcheng (Fang-ch'eng).

Mid-September, Nepal. A severe downpour precipitated floods and mudslides that killed more than 150 persons.

September 16–17, Cape Verde. A violent storm battered the drought-stricken archipelago, left 31 persons dead, and caused heavy damage.

October, Central Vietnam. Severe flooding caused by heavy rains killed 33 persons and left more than 38,000 families homeless.

October 9, Maravilha, Brazil. A tornado rampaged through a farming community and touched down on every building in town; at least ten persons were killed and hundreds of others were injured.

Early November, Central Philippines. Deadly Typhoon Agnes roared through the country with winds reaching 298 km/h (185 mph); at least 300 persons were killed, some 100,000 families were left homeless, and property damage was estimated at $40 million.

November, Colombia. Relentless rain caused the worst flooding in a decade; at least 40 persons were known dead.

November 24, Europe. Raging storms packing hurricane-force winds that ripped roofs off houses, flooded roads, and blocked highways with fallen trees led to the deaths of at least 14 persons in England, West Germany, The Netherlands, France, and Belgium.

December 31, Assam, India. A severe earthquake measuring 6 on the Richter scale caused heavy damage to high-voltage power and telephone lines and to hundreds of adobe and thatched huts; at least 20 persons were killed.

A fire one mile inside a Wilberg, Utah, coal mine killed 27 miners in mid-December.

AP/WIDE WORLD

Railroads

February 10, Bahadurgarh, India. A passenger shuttle train rammed into the rear of a stationary train, the Punjab Mail express, knocking three cars of the Punjab Mail off the tracks and killing 43 persons on that train; at the time of the accident the Punjab Mail was just leaving the station when for an unknown reason someone pulled the emergency stop cord.

February 29, Near Halle, East Germany. A collision between a local and an express train in heavy fog resulted in the deaths of 11 persons; 46 others were injured.

June 18, Angola. A passenger train that was barreling down the tracks crashed some 255 km (160 mi) southeast of Luanda; the accident, which claimed 50 lives, occurred apparently because the engineer was drunk.

July 14, Divaca, Yugos. A freight train crashed into the rear of a holiday 14-car express train carrying 1,500 passengers, causing the last three cars of the express train to derail; 36 persons, most of them in the last car of the express, died in the accident.

July 30, Near Polmont, Scotland. Three cars of a crowded six-car express train derailed; 13 persons were killed and 44 others were injured in the accident. Officials reported that the mangled remains of a cow or bull were found on the tracks, but they refused to speculate whether or not the animal had caused the derailment.

October 31, San Justo, Brazil. A train crashed into a commuter bus at a suburban railroad crossing and 43 persons were killed; though railroad officials maintained that the bus had circumvented the railroad gates, the bus company insisted that the gates had been raised.

November 22, Bombay, India. A packed rush-hour commuter train derailed when a coupling between the front coach and the following cars apparently snapped; 25 persons were killed when the train slammed through fencing along the rail line, and 100 others were injured.

December 23, Near Florence, Italy. A time bomb, apparently planted by terrorists aboard a train packed with holiday travelers, exploded when the train was in a tunnel; 29 persons were killed and nearly 200 others were injured.

Traffic

January 5, Near Butwal, Nepal. A minibus skidded off the road; 15 persons were killed.

January 30, Near Rupnagar (formerly Ropar), Punjab, India. A school bus filled with children and workers smashed through the railings of a bridge and plunged into a deep canal after swerving to avoid a bicyclist; approximately 80 persons were feared dead.

April 29, Eastern Uganda. A truck, filled with mourners who were returning from a funeral, overturned on a bridge; 29 persons were killed.

June 9, Near La Grita, Venezuela. A bus loaded with students from the Jáuregui Military Academy crashed into the guardrail of a bridge, rolled over, and then caught fire; 33 cadets died in the crash and ensuing blaze.

June 25, Bukoba, Tanzania. A bus crashed into a tree; 33 persons were killed and 74 were injured.

July 8, Orissa, India. A truck loaded with miners who were returning home after a festival skidded off the road and overturned; 18 persons were killed and 86 others were injured, 13 of them seriously.

September 1, Damagun, Nigeria. A bus and an oil tanker collided, and at least 40 persons were feared dead in the accident.

September 5, Near Shillong, India. A state-owned bus plunged into a deep gorge after the driver lost control of the vehicle while rounding a sharp bend in a mountain road; at least 21 persons were killed and 24 others were seriously injured.

September 7, Corum, Turkey. A farm tractor-trailer plunged off a cliff; 16 persons were killed and 19 others were injured.

September 23, Near Badrinath, India. A bus carrying Hindu pilgrims returning from a mountaintop temple skidded off a winding highway and plunged into a gorge in the Himalayan foothills; 34 persons were killed and 11 others were injured.

October 24, Central Brazil. A driver lost control of a bus and the vehicle overturned; at least 11 persons were killed.

October 26, Near Bujumbura, Burundi. A bus toppled off the road into a ravine; 43 of the 61 persons aboard were killed, and the other 18 passengers were seriously injured.

November 25, Ilgaz, Turkey. A bus carrying two newly married couples and their reception guests slammed into a truck in dense fog that limited visibility; all 4 newlyweds were killed, as were 27 other persons.

Earth Sciences

GEOLOGY AND GEOCHEMISTRY

During 1984 developments in the earth sciences, including the prospect of significant budgetary increases, held promises of rapid advances in the future. In the U.S. federal funding agencies reviewed the five research areas that had been identified in 1983 by the joint Committee on Science, Engineering, and Public Policy as those in which significant dividends could be expected from incremental investment: (1) seismic investigations of the continental crust, (2) continental scientific drilling, (3) physical and chemical investigations of geological materials, (4) establishment of a global digital seismic array, and (5) satellite geodesy.

The first area was already represented by Cocorp (Consortium for Continental Reflection Profiling), which had discovered many deep geological features since its inception in the mid-1970s. Two new university corporations were formed in 1984 to represent the second and fourth areas. DOSECC, Inc. (Deep Observation and Sampling of the Earth's Continental Crust), would plan and manage a program of scientific continental drilling with expected funding from the National Science Foundation. IRIS (Incorporated Research Institutions for Seismology) worked out a ten-year plan to establish new seismographic arrays for delineating the large-scale three-dimensional structure of the continental crust and underlying mantle. The fifth area, concerned with determining the size, shape, and gravity field of the Earth and the locations of its features, was represented by programs of the National Aeronautics and Space Administration (NASA). The third area so far lacked national organization.

Scientists submitted a detailed proposal for the first deep drill hole in the U.S. The program provided for two wells at a southern Appalachian site, a shallow, 2,440-m (8,000-ft) hole to penetrate the Brevard Fault and a deep, 10,670-m (35,000-ft) well into a zone that was believed to represent a basal thrust of regional extent beneath the crystalline rocks of the Piedmont Region. In addition to calibrating previous Cocorp studies of the region and testing geological and geophysical models, the drill holes would provide new data obtainable by no other means, including fluid and energy-flux measurements and in situ measurement of rock strengths and stress fields.

The third research area identified above includes the geochemical study of trace elements and isotope tracers in mantle rocks and mantle-derived magmas, which continued to yield data with controversial interpretations. The conventional interpretation of the mantle in terms of two rock reservoirs, with a layer of peridotite depleted in basaltic components overlying undepleted peridotite and with each layer convecting independently of the other, was challenged strongly in 1984 by two alternative interpretations. In one, the reservoirs consist of two mantle layers of different composition (peridotite above eclogite); in the other, mantlewide convection transports large, irregular masses having chemical characteristics different from the host mantle.

During the year a study of the decay products of radioactive isotopes contained in garnet inclusions in South African diamonds placed the age of the diamonds at more than 3,000,000,000 years and indicated the complexity of mantle events. The discovery suggested a scenario in which the formation of komatiite 3,500,000,000 years ago depleted the mantle source in basaltic components. The mantle was then enriched in incompatible elements before

the diamond encapsulated the garnet 3,200,000,000 years ago. The diamonds were finally brought to the surface in a kimberlite eruption 90 million years ago. The geochemical approach to the delineation of mantle reservoirs and the chronology of metasomatic events (changes in chemical composition) complements the geophysical approach to mantle convection.

The proposed global digital seismic array promised to yield the most fundamental data to date for understanding the geology and the geochemistry of the crust. Research groups at Harvard University and the California Institute of Technology published results of the use of surface waves to map the seismic-wave velocity and anisotropy of the upper mantle in three dimensions on a global basis, much the way computed tomography reconstructs two- and three-dimensional images from series of X-rays. Robert W. Clayton of Caltech obtained similar tomographic data for the whole mantle using inversion techniques for body waves. These results began to reveal, for the first time, the shape of mantle convection, which is the driving force for the lithospheric plates that make up the Earth's crust as well as the deep-seated component of most geological processes.

Geologists continued to be intrigued by questions concerning past collisions of extraterrestrial bodies with the Earth. Have major impacts occurred with regularity? Are they sufficiently energetic to cause wholesale extinctions of life forms? Do periodicities or cycles exist in the fossil record of extinctions and in the record of impacts? Does the fossil record match the impact record? The discussions that these questions provoked drew on evidence from paleontology, geology, geochemistry, and planetary sciences and carried philosophical implications for the doctrines of uniformitarianism and catastrophism.

Most species of animals and plants that have existed on the Earth are now extinct. There is much evidence that mass extinctions occurred during relatively short periods of special stress and that one of these happened toward the end of the Cretaceous Period, about 65 million years ago. The recent discovery of unusually high concentrations of iridium and other trace elements in clay marking the boundary of the Cretaceous and Tertiary periods was claimed to be evidence for extraterrestrial material. It was proposed that the explosion associated with the high-velocity impact of a comet or large meteorite disrupted the Earth's climate and ecosystems sufficiently to cause mass extinctions and to distribute the iridium across the Earth's surface. During the year Bruce F. Bohor and colleagues of the U.S. Geological Survey reported that quartz grains in the Cretaceous-Tertiary boundary clay layer in Montana had features typical of shock metamorphism, which they considered to be compelling evidence for a high-velocity impact on the Earth.

The scope of the discussion was broadened by a report from David M. Raup and J. John Sepkoski, Jr., of the University of Chicago, whose detailed statistical analysis of a mass of data produced evidence that mass extinctions occurred at intervals of roughly 26 million years. They argued that Earth processes do not operate with such regularity, and they therefore favoured extraterrestrial causes. Walter Alvarez and Richard A. Muller of the University of California at Berkeley reported that most large impact craters caused by meteorites or comets have occurred on Earth in a 28.4 million-year cycle, corresponding remarkably with the periodicity of mass extinctions. They claimed this correspondence to be powerful evidence that mass extinctions were caused by major impacts. Other investigators proposed that the extraterrestrial causes might be related to the orbital period of an unseen stellar companion of the

Sun that periodically perturbs the orbits of the comets and initiates a shower of impacts on the Earth, or to the time required for the solar system to oscillate about the plane of the Galaxy, which was estimated to be 30 million–36 million years (*see* ASTRONOMY).

Anthony Hallam of the University of Birmingham, England, considered these speculations to be premature, pointing out that the 26 million-year cyclicity found by Raup and Sepkoski would be much less evident had they used one of the other two geological time scales available, instead of the Harland time scale, which they had adopted. He also noted large errors in dating for many of the boundaries between rock strata.

Speculations about the gas composition of comets would be replaced by direct measurements if plans of the European Space Agency were successful. The agency intended to send a spacecraft, called Giotto, to intersect the route of Halley's Comet as it passed within reasonable distance of the Earth between November 1985 and March 1986, whereupon two mass spectrometers would analyze the gases evolving from the comet's icy head. Some scientists, however, expressed their concern that Giotto's rather delicate instruments might not survive the bombardment by particles expected in the harsh environment of the comet's plasma region.

Instruments using laser technology and techniques of radio astronomy had been in position long enough by 1984 that, for the first time, the measurement of rates of movement of drifting continents could be made directly. The measured rates proved to be consistent with rates deduced indirectly from magnetic anomalies studied in the ocean basins. Northern and southern California, which ride on separate lithospheric plates, were found to be approaching each other at 6.6 cm (2.6 in) per year.

(PETER JOHN WYLLIE)

GEOPHYSICS

Seismic activity during 1984 included very few strong earthquakes and no shocks greater than magnitude 8. On February 17 an earthquake in the Hindu Kush region of Pakistan and Afghanistan killed 4 and injured 13. Between April 22 and May 13 four shocks across southern and central Italy and one in the Adriatic Sea resulted in a total of 10 deaths and more than 170 injuries.

Several smaller earthquakes detected between late 1983 and late 1984 were notable because they were either large or rare for the regions in which they occurred. On Oct. 7, 1983, a shock recorded in the Adirondack Mountains of New York near Blue Mountain Lake had a magnitude of 5.2 and was the largest in the state since 1944. An earthquake in Belgium on Nov. 8, 1983, caused 2 deaths, injured 26, damaged hundreds of buildings in Liège and vicinity, and was felt in four countries. At magnitude 4.7 it was the largest in eastern Belgium since 1938. On April 23, 1984, an earthquake of magnitude 4.1, centred in Lancaster County, Pa., was felt from western Connecticut to northern Virginia but caused no damage.

Although no major volcanic eruptions took place during the year, several volcanoes remained quite active. On the island of Hawaii Mt. Kilauea, which had begun erupting in January 1983, experienced more than 25 eruptive episodes through August 1984. Each episode lasted two to four days and typically began with an abrupt increase in harmonic tremors, an indication that lava was welling to the surface. Very quickly thereafter lava flowed and lava fountains spouted. The fountains frequently reached heights of 250–300 m (820–985 ft), sending lava several kilometres down the mountain. After two or three days such activity stopped

A powerful earthquake, measuring 6.9 on the Richter scale, struck Japan's Nagano Prefecture in September. A landslide swept away homes on hillsides in the village of Otaki.
ASAHI—SHINBUN

abruptly, and the lava tended to flow back into the vents and fissures. Usually the summit deflated throughout the active phase, but when relative quiet returned, it began reinflating for the next sequence. Lava flow was greatest during the 18th major phase of this eruption sequence, on April 18–21, 1984. The flow extended 14 km (8.7 mi) down the slope, destroying three houses and stopping a kilometre from the sea.

In August 1983 seismic activity increased markedly around the Rabaul Caldera on the island of New Britain in the Pacific Ocean. From a total of more than 5,000 recorded tremors in October 1983, the monthly frequency increased steadily to a peak of 13,794 identifiable events in April 1984, after which it decreased at about the same rate at which it had grown. As a result of this activity, a stage-2 alert, a warning that an eruption may occur within weeks or months, was issued in November 1983 to the 70,000 residents within 15 km (9.3 mi) of the caldera centre, which included 25,000 living in the city of Rabaul, located in the northern section of the caldera. Locations of the hypocenters ranged from the surface to 3 km (1.9 mi) below ground and were centred on Mt. Tavurvur, a small postcaldera volcanic cone. Although some fissures appeared, no eruption ensued.

Geothermal energy systems based on hot-water and steam wells were under development throughout the world for both electric power generation and heating. In addition to direct steam-generating systems in use or planned, binary systems, which transfer heat from near-boiling water to a fluid having a lower boiling point, were under construction in the U.S. in the Heber Valley and the Salton Sea geothermal fields in southern California and in Long Valley in east-central California.

Working to exploit another source of geothermal energy, hot dry rock, scientists from the Los Alamos (N.M.)

National Laboratory built the world's deepest and hottest hot-dry-rock thermal reservoir. First a pair of wells was drilled to a depth of 4,270 m (14,000 ft) on the flank of an extinct volcano in the Jemez Mountains of New Mexico. Then cold water was pumped down one hole under high pressure, producing a reservoir of fractured granite at a temperature of about 260° C (500° F). Although this system was developed as a research project, its initial operation, during which cold water was injected down one well and through the reservoir and then collected at the second wellhead as steam, generated 35 MW thermal.

The research vessel "Glomar Challenger" made its final voyages to close the 15-year Deep Sea Drilling Project (DSDP). Leg 92 traversed the South Pacific from Papeete, Tahiti, to Balboa, Panama, with the objective of studying past hydrothermal activity along oceanic ridges by sampling sediment-covered areas for evidence of disturbance by currents. Two hydrothermal pulses were identified, one having occurred between 5 million and 8 million years ago and the other between 21 million and 25 million years ago. In addition, the overall pattern of fluctuation suggested a two million-year cycle in hydrothermal activity in the region. Legs 93 and 95 studied the New Jersey Transect in the North Atlantic. On Leg 93 six holes were drilled at sites ranging from the abyssal plain to the edge of the continental shelf.

The objective of Leg 94 was to obtain hydraulic piston cores across the climatically sensitive middle and high latitudes of the North Atlantic, from 37° to 53° N. Samples were taken from sites northeast of the Azores, in King's Trough, and on the Feni and Gardar drifts. These sites are in a region of major interaction between warm ocean surface water and cold continental air masses. Previous coring and seismic profiling had shown that this region had been subjected to greater glacial-interglacial temperature oscillation than any other oceanic area. Seismic profiles had revealed anomalously thickened sediments in the form of waves tens of metres high and kilometres from crest to crest, seemingly formed by bottom circulation. Two such waves were sampled on Leg 94, but no primary structures could be identified as having been formed by bottom currents.

During Leg 96, which concluded the DSDP, nine sites were occupied on the Mississippi Fan in the Gulf of Mexico and the adjacent Orca and Pigmy basins.

(RUTLAGE J. BRAZEE)

HYDROLOGY

Representatives of the 30 member countries of UNESCO's Intergovernmental Council of the International Hydrological Program (IHP) met in Paris in March 1984 to review the status of IHP II projects begun between 1981 and 1983 and to prepare for implementing IHP III (1984–89). Observers representing 39 political entities and 13 international organizations also attended. IHP II had dealt successfully through rapporteurs and working groups with a number of topics in the fields of scientific hydrology, education, public information, and water-resource management infrastructure; more than a score of international symposia and workshops had taken place in connection with these projects. The Intergovernmental Council approved the detailed Program and Plan of IHP III titled *Hydrology and the Scientific Bases for the Rational Management of Water Resources for Economic and Social Development*. The program specified a number of study projects within 18 general themes, emphasizing not only the scientific aspects but also the educational effort in transferring knowledge, techniques, and skills.

In October the presidents of Brazil and Paraguay inaugurated the generation of electricity at Itaipú Dam on the Paraná River, which forms part of the boundary between the two countries. The project, which would eventually generate 12,600 MW, was the world's largest hydroelectric dam. In November Brazil brought on line another large hydroelectric dam, with a generating capacity of 8,000 MW, located on the Tocantins River in the northern part of the country.

The African drought worsened during 1984. Drought conditions and consequent catastrophic food shortages persisted across the sub-Saharan Sahel belt of several countries and spread to an increasing number of nations in central and southern Africa. More than 30 countries were affected and 24 of these severely stricken. Somalia's government issued an emergency decree allowing the importation of water trucks and tankers to help alleviate drought conditions. (*See* WORLD AFFAIRS [Africa South of the Sahara]: *African Affairs*: Special Report.)

Streamflow remained normal or above normal in most of the U.S. during the year. The combined flow of the three largest rivers that drain more than half of the conterminous U.S.—the Mississippi, St. Lawrence, and Columbia—was 21% above the long-term average but 3% less than in 1983. Annual streamflow was well above average in 15 states and

SANDRO TUCCI—GAMMA/LIAISON

Mayon volcano in the Philippines, located about 320 kilometres (200 miles) south of Manila, erupted early in September, threatening a village a few miles from the crater; its population was evacuated safely. In 1814 a massive eruption of Mayon brought death to 1,200 people.

parts of 24 states although well below average in Hawaii and in most of Texas. During May extensive flooding occurred in the Rocky Mountains and the Pacific Northwest as a result of rapid snowmelt. Persistent rains over the eastern central part of the country during May caused widespread floods. Flooding was especially severe in Tulsa, Okla., where damages were estimated at $150 million. In September Hurricane Diana brought heavy localized rain and severe flooding to the North Carolina coast. On July 1 the Great Salt Lake in Utah stood at 4,209.25 ft (1,283 m) above sea level, the highest level since 1873, as a result of intense rainfall and rapid snowmelt.

Contrary to a common perception, the U.S. was not running out of water. Nevertheless, according to a summary of conditions in 50 states, a wide variety of problems limited the available supply. The *National Water Summary 1983—Hydrologic Events and Issues,* prepared by the U.S. Geological Survey, described current hydrologic conditions and reviewed the major hydrologic issues facing the U.S. The issues included water availability, water quality, hydrologic hazards, and management. Problems most frequently voiced in the 50 states were declining groundwater levels, acid precipitation, groundwater contamination, flooding, land subsidence, erosion and sedimentation, and dam failure. Competition for freshwater was increasing, and water availability was of particular concern in the western states.

Between 1950 and 1980 water use in the U.S. increased from 1,200 to 2,000 gal per day per person. In recent years the rate of surface-water reservoir construction slowed considerably while at the same time groundwater use increased. There was also growing recognition that the best reservoir sites had been put to use and that new reservoir development would likely be less cost-effective than it had been in the past. Water-level declines due to withdrawal of large volumes of groundwater were major concerns in the High Plains region (Kansas, Colorado, New Mexico, Oklahoma, and Texas), southern Arizona, and parts of California. Several large regions experienced water-level or artesian-water-level declines in excess of 12.2 m (40 ft). Such declines, although necessary to induce water to flow to points of withdrawal, increased pumping costs and decreased well yields. Contamination of groundwater and surface water was a growing problem. Sources of contamination included sewage-treatment plants, industrial plants, runoff from coal mines, urban and agricultural runoff, feedlots, landfills, and saline water.

A recent report of the U.S. Environmental Protection Agency (EPA) listed groundwater contamination as a major environmental issue of the 1980s. The report, *Ground Water Protection Strategy,* described the nature and extent of groundwater contamination, state and federal programs for groundwater protection, and the EPA's strategy to protect groundwater. The EPA designated six aquifers as sole or principal sources of drinking water. They underlie Tucson, Ariz.; Kings and Queens counties, N.Y.; Upper Rockaway River Basin, N.J.; Ridgewood, N.J.; Nantucket Island, Mass.; and Block Island, R.I. The designation required that all federally funded projects in the vicinity of such a sole-source aquifer be evaluated to determine their potential for groundwater pollution or depletion.

(JOHN E. MOORE)

METEOROLOGY

Weather had its devastating effects on various parts of the world in 1984. In the U.S. the winter of 1983–84 started with the coldest December in 53 years—a sharp contrast to the "El Niño winter" of 1982–83, which had been one of the warmest on record. The December freeze took 425 lives nationwide, while in early February a blizzard in North Dakota and Minnesota killed another 23 people. A winter storm on February 24–28 blanketed the central Midwest through New England with 25–50 cm (10–20 in) of snow and was blamed for at least 29 deaths. The heaviest March snowfalls since 1888 brought transportation and business in many northeastern cities to a halt.

Tornadoes and severe thunderstorms plagued much of the U.S. during the year. The death toll of 124 was the highest since 1974. The most devastating outbreak occurred during the late afternoon and evening of March 28, when 23 violent tornadoes swept through North and South Carolina killing 57 people, injuring 1,300, and leaving 3,000 homeless. Record snowpacks in the western U.S. mountains, saturated soils east of the Rockies, and torrential rainstorms elsewhere resulted in severe floods throughout the country.

The 1982 and 1983 hurricane seasons were the calmest in more than a half century, and it looked as if the 1984 season would follow suit. But on August 29 the first tropical storm formed and was followed by Bertha and Cesar two days later. In a little over a month the U.S. National Hurricane Center tracked ten named storms in the Atlantic and Gulf of Mexico, three of which became hurricanes. Two storms affected the continental U.S. Although Hurricane Diana initially built up strength offshore with winds of

RAVELL CALL

Freshwater melt from the enormous mountain snowpack of the 1983–84 winter flowed into Utah's Great Salt Lake, raising the water level to its highest in more than 100 years.

Tornadoes devastated rural sections of North and South Carolina in late March but skipped major cities. Here Pete and Sally Outlaw sit on what remains of their home in McColl, South Carolina.

TIM WRIGHT—GAMMA/LIAISON

217 km/hr (135 mph), when it went inland at Cape Fear, S.C., winds diminished and precautionary measures kept the death toll to three indirect fatalities. Damages from Hurricane Diana were estimated at $60 million. Another tropical storm, Isidore, hugged the coastline from Florida northward, bringing much rain and some local flooding to the East Coast.

Flooding in Bangladesh and northern India in May left 136 dead and 1½ million people homeless. More floods in Bangladesh in June and July killed another 200 and affected 30 million people. Flooding and landslides from heavy rains at the end of August killed 130 people in South Korea.

A persistent drought in southern Africa cut food production in half. While tropical storm Domoina brought some relief with heavy rains to Mozambique, South Africa, and Swaziland, it caused flooding that resulted in 139 deaths. Kenya suffered the worst drought in more than 40 years, and people in the African Sahel region faced the likelihood of another year of food and water shortages. (*See* WORLD AFFAIRS [Africa South of the Sahara]: *African Affairs:* Special Report.)

Several harsh winter storms struck northern Europe in January, killing 49 in England and Ireland. Winds of 160 km/hr (100 mph) were recorded in Great Britain, and 48 cm (19 in) of snow fell in Scotland and northern England. In February a winter storm caused major flooding in northern and western West Germany.

Much of the loss of life, the costly damage (an average of $20 billion annually in the U.S. alone), and the great disruption of economic activity due to the weather is caused by weather phenomena occurring over a small geographic area (2–2,000 km) and over a short time period (within 24 hours). These mesoscale, or stormscale, phenomena

include the tornado, the downburst, violent squall lines and thunderstorms, flash floods, and local heavy snowfalls. They also include freezing rain, dense fog, and conditions leading to episodes of extreme local pollution.

In recent years research and operational meteorologists have launched a major drive to reduce the losses and ameliorate the economic and social effects of stormscale weather. Steady increases in basic scientific knowledge have been paced by technological gains in the capability to detect, measure, communicate, integrate, display, and disseminate vast amounts of weather information, and together these advances have formed the basis for a revolution in stormscale meteorology. Foremost among technological achievements has been the well-developed and research-tested operational Doppler radar. In 1984 a program to provide the U.S. with a new generation of these instruments was well under way by the departments of Commerce, Transportation, and Defense. The new equipment would provide critical information on interior storm circulations and permit radar operators to better detect tornadoes in the earliest stages of development, as well as downbursts that threaten aircraft safety during landing and takeoff. It would also provide estimated rates of precipitation, leading to improved forecasts of flash floods.

(RICHARD E. HALLGREN)

This article updates the *Macropædia* article CLIMATE AND WEATHER.

OCEANOGRAPHY

The term El Niño refers to an anomalous, irregular warming of the sea surface in the eastern tropical Pacific Ocean near the coasts of Peru and Ecuador. During 1982–83 this warming was the most intense ever recorded, extending well westward of the date line in the Pacific. The first sign of it was a weakening of the trade winds, which usually blow from east to west in a band several thousand kilometres wide encompassing the Equator and adjacent regions. At the height of El Niño, the trades vanished altogether over much of the tropical Pacific, and the weather there changed drastically.

Although El Niño showed signs of ending in the tropical Pacific by midsummer of 1983, its effects continued to be felt in California coastal waters through much of 1984. Changes in the global wind field associated with the phenomenon were so great that they measurably changed the Earth's rate of rotation about its axis. El Niño prompted organization of an international project to study year-to-year variability of the tropical ocean and the global atmosphere. Concurrently oceanographers began to plan a world ocean circulation experiment.

The first sign of the 1982–83 El Niño along the southern California coast was the appearance of unusually warm water (by about 1.1° C, or 2° F) in October 1982. By the beginning of 1983 this warming had spread north of the Canadian border. In the spring of 1983 the usual abundance of nutrients and zooplankton offshore was absent even though nutrient levels near shore had not changed greatly. By August 1983, however, nutrient levels near shore had also fallen. Zooplankton counts offshore were among the lowest ever taken. By June 1984 offshore conditions appeared to be returning to normal; the thick layer of warm, arid El Niño water was giving way to a thinner, nutrient-rich surface layer. But as late as September the sea-surface temperature off San Diego was still above the seasonal normal. Thus, although the tropical El Niño ended in mid-1983, the California El Niño appeared to have lingered almost a year longer.

At the height of El Niño, in January 1983, the perturbation of global winds caused the Earth to take about five ten-thousandths of a second longer to complete one rotation about its axis than it usually does in January. It had been known for several years that the seasonal change of global winds alters the Earth's rate of rotation—owing to the fact that the rotations of the solid Earth and its atmosphere are coupled and share a total angular momentum that must be conserved. In January, when winds in the Northern Hemisphere blow most strongly from the west, the atmosphere rotates faster; in compensation a day lasts about a thousandth of a second longer than it does in July, when Northern Hemisphere winds are more gentle. During the El Niño the tropical trade winds (which normally blow from the east and oppose atmospheric rotation) were much reduced or even absent, thus allowing a further increase in the atmospheric rotation rate and making the day longer than usual.

The 1982–83 El Niño catalyzed an already existing interest in predicting such events into an international research program called TOGA. The acronym derives from the two physical systems, the tropical ocean and the global atmosphere, whose interaction is believed to govern much of climate change. One of the greatest handicaps scientists faced in trying to detect the onset of an El Niño was the lack of a precise global picture of the normal seasonal variation of these two systems. TOGA's first aim was to fill in the details of this picture, which subsequently should reveal much about the way events in one part of the system influence events elsewhere and thus about the way that the anomalous events initiating an El Niño influence distant regions.

Because it can store so much heat, the ocean is thought to be an important influence on global climate. Small changes in ocean temperature or in the global distribution of ocean temperature may be accompanied by significant changes in the transport of heat between tropics and high latitudes. Consequently TOGA had an oceanic as well as an atmospheric component. In addition to their involvement with TOGA, oceanographers would be carrying out a simultaneous World Ocean Circulation Experiment (WOCE).

Although traditional shipborne studies were to be an important part of WOCE and TOGA, new methods of observing ocean circulation would be needed if the uptake, transport, and release of heat by the oceans were to be understood. A satellite orbiting the Earth and measuring the distance from satellite to sea surface to within a few centimetres by timing the passage of radar pulses from satellite to sea surface and back again could supplement conventional shipborne measurements of deep-ocean conditions and provide much improved estimates of ocean circulation. If the travel times of sound waves transmitted through the water across major ocean basins were carefully measured for five or ten years, small but observable changes in travel time might reveal basinwide changes of ocean temperature and consequently of ocean heat storage—changes too small to be detected with present-day measurement techniques but yet large enough to influence global climate.

Planning for both TOGA and WOCE occupied a great deal of research effort during 1984. Their execution would constitute a major part of oceanographic research during the next decade.   (MYRL C. HENDERSHOTT)

See also Disasters; Energy; Life Sciences; Mining and Metallurgy; Space Exploration; Sports and Games: *Spelunking.*

This article updates the *Macropædia* articles ATMOSPHERE; The EARTH; EARTHQUAKES; The EARTH SCIENCES; GEOCHRONOLOGY; Principles, Methods, and Instruments of MEASUREMENT AND OBSERVATION; OCEANS; PLATE TECTONICS; RIVERS; VOLCANISM.

Economic Affairs

The recovery in the world economy that began in 1983 gained further momentum during 1984. Thus growth for the year in the member countries of the Organization for Economic Cooperation and Development (OECD) was estimated at 4.5–5% as against an advance of some 2.5% in 1983. As in 1983, the fastest growth was achieved by non-European member countries. The star performer was the United States, where gross domestic product (GDP) was heading for a gain of 6.5%, as compared with 3.7% in the previous year. Japan, too, did very well with an increase of about 5%. Western European growth rates were generally more modest; overall the advance was about 2.5%, with the figure fluctuating from 1.4% in France to 2.5% in West Germany. All European countries did better than in 1983 except the U.K., where the 1983 growth rate of 2.9% fell back in 1984 to 2%. This setback was largely the result of a protracted strike by British coal miners, which paralyzed two-thirds of the coal industry's capacity for most of 1984.

Contrary to some hopes, the strengthening of the recovery did not lead to a marked fall in the high level of unemployment nor, contrary to widespread fears, was it accompanied by a significant acceleration in inflation. Toward the end of 1983 the total number of unemployed stood at 31.8 million in the OECD area, compared with 32.8 million at the start of the year. This gave rise to expectations that as the recovery accelerated during 1984 there would be a further significant decrease. However, at the end of 1984 the overall number out of work was calculated at 31.5 million, representing virtually no improvement from the position at the start of the year. The reasons varied from country to country, but in general terms it seemed that a significant part of the extra output was generated by an improvement in labour productivity rather than by an increase in employment. Unemployment showed a sizable decrease in the U.S. but increased markedly in Western Europe.

Consumer price inflation in the OECD area was estimated at just over 5% for 1984, broadly the same as in the previ-

Table I. Real Gross Domestic Products of Selected OECD Countries

% change, seasonally adjusted at annual rates

Country	Average 1972–82	1979	1980	1981	1982	1983	1984*
United States†	2.2	2.4	−0.3	2.3	−1.7	3.4	6.0
Japan†	4.3	5.1	4.9	4.0	3.0	3.0	4.8
West Germany†	2.0	4.1	1.9	0.2	−1.1	1.3	3.0
France†	2.7	3.3	1.1	0.2	1.7	0.7	1.3
United Kingdom†	1.4	1.6	−2.0	−2.0	1.2	3.1	2.5
Canada†	2.8	3.2	0.5	3.8	−4.8	3.0	4.5
Italy†	2.6	4.9	3.9	−0.2	−0.3	−1.2	2.3
Total major countries†	2.5	3.2	1.1	1.8	−0.3	2.6	4.5
Australia	2.6	4.2	1.5	4.1	0.1	1.2	6.0
New Zealand	1.5	0.9	−0.1	4.0	−0.7	1.7	1.5
Austria	2.6	4.8	3.2	0	1.1	1.9	2.0
Belgium	2.3	2.4	3.0	−1.8	−0.1	0.5	1.5
Denmark	1.9	3.7	−1.1	0.1	3.1	2.5	2.8
Finland	3.1	7.6	6.0	1.3	1.3	3.0	4.5
Greece	3.1	3.7	1.6	−0.4	0	0.3	1.8
Ireland	3.6	2.5	2.8	1.1	1.4	1.0	1.5
Netherlands, The	1.9	2.1	0.9	−1.2	−1.4	1.0	1.5
Norway	3.7	5.1	3.9	0.8	−0.6	3.2	2.0
Spain	2.6	0.2	1.5	0.3	1.1	2.3	2.0
Sweden	1.6	4.3	1.9	−0.6	−0.1	2.3	3.3
Switzerland	0.5	2.5	4.6	1.9	−2.0	−0.1	2.8
Total OECD countries	2.4	3.1	1.2	1.6	−0.2	2.4	4.5

*OECD projection.
†GNP.
Sources: Adapted from OECD, *Economic Outlook*, July 1984; National Institute of Economic Review; EIU Estimates.

ous year. The rates varied widely from country to country, with the lowest increases (2–3%) achieved by Japan and West Germany, while France, Italy, and a number of smaller European countries were facing inflation rates of 7–11%. In most cases, however, the actual figures represented a decrease from the previous year's performance and could, therefore, be regarded as mildly encouraging. Apart from a fairly slow rise in wages because of the high levels of unemployment, the fight against inflation was also assisted by the trend of commodity prices. Thus, in the wake of a 13% fall in average oil prices in 1983, there was a further reduction of 3% in 1984. World prices of minerals and metals were also estimated to have dropped on average by 6% and, while food prices recorded an increase, it was thought to have been marginally below the gain of 7% in 1983.

In the larger economies of the OECD area, approximately half of the total growth in GDP resulted from increases in private consumption. This compared poorly with 1983, when higher private consumption expenditure provided as much as 79% of the overall GDP gain, and indicated that the 1983 consumer boom had lost considerable momentum. This was because by 1984 the level of personal savings was relatively low and could not provide the same stimulus to spending that it had in 1983. In sharp contrast, however, private investment activities became considerably more buoyant in 1984.

In 1983 private investment contributed little or nothing to economic growth but, because of a good increase in company profits, an improvement in business confidence, and relatively low interest rates in most countries, such investments showed a sharp advance almost everywhere and acted as a major stimulus to economic growth in 1984. Exports were also a major source of strength, accounting for as much as 30% of total gross national product (GNP) growth, compared with less than 5% in the previous year. Public spending, however, provided little, if any, stimulus, as several governments made further efforts to reduce expenditures and budget deficits.

The above circumstances were true of all principal OECD countries with the exception of West Germany, where public expenditure was thought to have risen faster than in 1983. Private investment expenditure rose particularly fast (approximately 13%) in the U.S., but there were good

gains in most other OECD countries except Canada, where the signs pointed to a modest decrease. The situation with regard to consumer spending varied widely; while the U.S. and Italy did better than in the preceding year, Japan and West Germany were largely unchanged, and in the U.K. and France growth was well below that of 1983. Exports in all principal countries, with the possible exception of Italy, grew faster than in 1983. All in all, it was estimated that during 1984 the volume of world trade rose by 7–8%, compared with a gain of only 2% in the previous year. The growth in manufactured goods trade was particularly rapid (8.5%), while the increase in trade in oil lagged behind at only 5%.

The world currency markets were dominated by the sustained, and generally unexpected, strength of the U.S. dollar. Its effective exchange rate was 118 at the end of 1983, but by late October 1984 it had risen 10% to 129. There was considerable discussion (and disagreement) as to why the dollar performed so well, although one important reason was the relatively high level of interest rates in the U.S. This was largely the result of generally restrictive monetary policy followed by the U.S. government, a policy that was pursued to a greater or lesser degree by all other developed economies. There was a widespread tendency to reduce the target growth rates of key monetary aggregates, although most European governments were inclined to prevent a significant rise in interest rates for fear of weakening the recovery.

On the whole, fiscal policies were also strict. There was a sustained desire to reduce the level and proportion of deficit financing everywhere, which ruled out any significant increases in public expenditure and injections of demand into the economy. At the end of 1984 it seemed that most countries were able to achieve a reduction in public deficits, although it was clear that progress was not as pronounced as had been hoped for at the start of the year.

NATIONAL ECONOMIC POLICIES

Developed Market Economies. UNITED STATES. What at first appeared to be the second leg of a spectacular economic upswing ran out of steam halfway through 1984, and the recovery stalled. Although the rapid pace of economic activity during the first half of the year was unsustainable, the sharp drop in the rate of economic growth was much steeper than the economic policymakers had anticipated and led to a major shift in monetary policy in November.

The strong surge in activity that occurred during the closing months of 1983 gathered pace in the new year, enabling the GNP to expand by an astounding annual rate of 10.1% in the first quarter. This was followed by a more sedate 7.1% in the next quarter. A slowdown in the second half was widely predicted, but the actual figures for third-quarter GNP growth, even before they were revised down to 1.9%, rang the alarm bells. It was not only the lowest quarterly growth rate since 1982 but, more ominously, most economic indicators were signaling that there would be no upturn in the final quarter of 1984. The economy appeared to be teetering on the brink of a recession, having swung from boom to bust conditions in one quarter. On the basis of OECD figures in late December, the GNP registered a gain of 6.75% in 1984, compared with 3.2% growth in 1983. While this was an excellent outcome on its own, the likely future course of the economy gave rise to some anxiety.

The main contributors to economic growth in the first half of the year were stockbuilding, personal consumption, private residential investment, and federal government expenditure. As the economic recovery cycle matured, a

Table II. Percentage Changes in Consumer Prices in Selected OECD Countries

% changes in consumer prices in

Country	1979	1980	1981	1982	1983	1984*
United States	11.3	13.5	10.4	6.1	3.2	4.2
Japan	3.6	8.0	4.9	2.7	1.9	2.3
West Germany	4.1	5.5	5.9	5.3	3.3	2.1
France	10.8	13.6	13.4	11.8	9.6	6.9
United Kingdom	13.4	18.0	11.9	8.6	5.1	5.0
Italy	14.8	21.2	19.5	16.6	14.5	8.6
Canada	9.2	10.2	12.5	10.8	5.9	3.4
Austria	3.7	6.4	6.8	5.4	3.3	5.6
Belgium	4.5	6.6	7.6	8.7	7.7	5.3
Denmark	9.6	12.3	11.7	10.1	7.3	6.2
Finland	7.5	11.6	12.0	9.3	8.1	6.6
Greece	19.0	24.9	24.5	21.0	20.5	18.9
Iceland	44.1	57.5	51.6	49.1	86.7	18.1
Ireland	13.3	18.2	20.4	17.1	10.4	7.9
Luxembourg	4.5	6.3	8.1	9.4	8.6	3.9
Netherlands, The	4.2	6.5	6.7	5.9	2.8	2.8
Norway	4.8	10.9	13.6	11.3	8.4	6.1
Portugal	23.9	16.6	20.0	22.4	25.6	27.1
Spain	15.7	15.5	14.6	14.4	12.1	11.3
Sweden	7.2	13.7	12.1	8.6	9.0	7.7
Switzerland	3.6	4.0	6.5	5.6	3.0	2.7
Turkey	63.5	94.3	37.6	32.7	29.2	65.4
Australia	9.1	10.2	9.7	11.2	10.2	3.9
New Zealand	13.8	17.1	15.4	16.1	7.4	7.9
Total OECD countries	9.8	12.8	10.5	7.8	5.3	5.0

*Twelve-month rate of change (not directly comparable with annual changes).
Sources: OECD *Economic Outlook*, July 1984; OECD *Main Economic Indicators*.

In June the leaders of the seven major industrial democracies met in London for discussions concerning world economic issues. In attendance were (left to right) Gaston Thorn, president of the European Communities' Executive Commission; Prime Minister Yasuhiro Nakasone of Japan; Prime Minister Pierre Trudeau of Canada; Pres. Ronald Reagan of the U.S.; Prime Minister Margaret Thatcher of the U.K. (standing at podium); Pres. François Mitterrand of France; Chancellor Helmut Kohl of West Germany; and Premier Bettino Craxi of Italy.

J. L. ATLAN—SYGMA

number of unsatisfactory features appeared. Industrial production, which earlier in the year was held back by the surge in imports, reached a plateau in the summer and went into a decline in September. However, even at that level the index stood at seven percentage points above the previous year's level. What was worrisome, however, was a sharp decline in durable goods orders in September and October. In line with the rapid real income growth, personal consumption expanded a healthy annualized rate of 6% during the first half of 1984. As the pace of employment gains and real growth in wages slowed down, so did personal consumption. In October it declined for the first time since the recovery got under way in 1982. An early casualty of this trend was the volume of retail sales, which softened in the spring and leveled out early in the summer. Other unfavourable economic statistics available in the closing months of the year related to the decline in housing starts (down 9% from 1983) and lower after-tax corporate profits (down 7%).

The slowdown in economic activity seemed to have been hastened by two structural imbalances in the economy, the huge federal deficit and the rising trade deficit. The large-scale funding of the federal deficit coupled with the borrowing needs of the private sector kept interest rates at a very high level throughout most of the year (one of the highest levels in real terms in the postwar period). This in turn attracted foreign funds and strengthened the external value of the dollar, leading to an upsurge in imports. Thus a growing gap appeared between growth in demand and growth in output. Under such conditions a slowdown in demand appeared to have had an amplified effect on the level of economic activity.

Thanks to the extraordinary buoyancy of the economy during the first half of the year, further progress was made in reducing unemployment. Most of the gains took place in the opening months of the year, when the unemployment rate fell to 7.8%, compared with 8.5% at the end of 1983. Although the rate of job generation in April, at 400,000, was in excess of the monthly average in the first quarter, as the recovery matured it drew more and more people into the job market; therefore, it became difficult to achieve further reductions in the unemployment rate. The rate leveled out at about 7.4% and, given the weakness of the economy in the closing months, a slight deterioration was likely as the number of new entrants exceeded the number of new jobs created. In spite of this slowdown, the U.S. economy had achieved a 3% reduction in its unemployment rate since 1982, while the unemployment rate in European economies showed no sign of falling.

Contrary to the fears of the financial markets that the robust strength of the economy would stoke up inflationary flames, consumer price inflation remained low at about 3.25% with minor monthly variations. The reasons for this good performance lay mainly in the moderation in business costs brought about by corporate cost-cutting programs, moderation in wage increases, and, above all, the strength of the dollar. Significantly, the differential between the rises in consumer prices and producer prices was of the order of 2%, enabling producers to restore depleted profit margins without adding significantly to the inflationary forces.

With an exceptionally strong currency and a booming domestic market, it was not surprising that the U.S. trade deficit rose sharply. The astonishing quarterly growth rates in imports during the closing quarter of 1983 were outstripped by an explosive 47.1% increase (at an annualized rate) in the first quarter of 1984. Although it moderated significantly in the following two quarters, for 1984 as a whole a growth of 24% in imports was likely to have occurred. Exports, by contrast, were estimated to have expanded by only 4% through 1984. Consequently, the

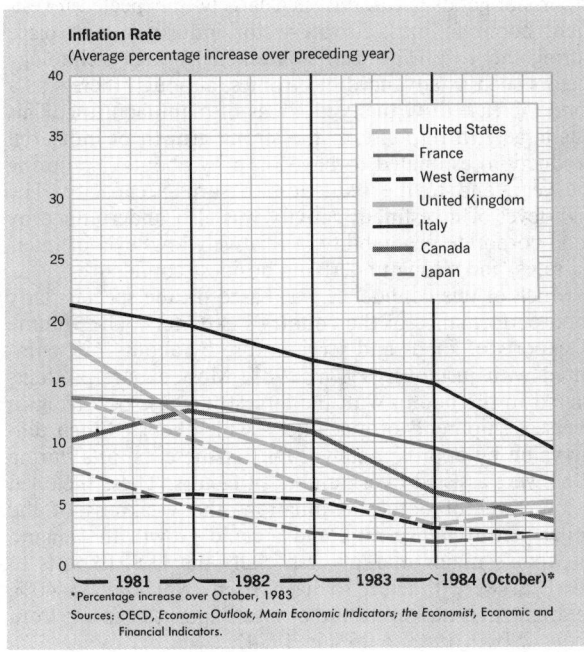

Inflation Rate
(Average percentage increase over preceding year)

- United States
- France
- West Germany
- United Kingdom
- Italy
- Canada
- Japan

1981   1982   1983   1984 (October)*
*Percentage increase over October, 1983
Sources: OECD, Economic Outlook, Main Economic Indicators; the Economist, Economic and Financial Indicators.

trade deficit was expected to widen to $130 billion. This already enormous deficit led to a marked deterioration in the current account deficit. During the first half of the year it widened to nearly $44 billion (from $35.5 billion for 1983 as a whole), and full-year expectations were for over $100 billion. The massive current account payments gap was largely plugged by capital inflows from overseas, lured by the high interest rates and the strength of the dollar. The counterpart of the enormous trade deficit was that the U.S. economy acted as a locomotive to help pull the other OECD countries out of the recession.

The tenor of fiscal policy remained basically expansionary despite a modest reduction in the federal budget deficit to $176 billion during the fiscal year 1984 (ended September 30). The previous year's deficit was $196 billion. The improvement in the budgetary deficit was due to the faster-than-expected growth in the economy, which boosted government revenue while holding down spending. Many of the benefits of higher economic growth were offset, however, by higher interest payments on the national debt. The administration's budget proposals introduced in February for fiscal 1985 (beginning in October 1984) envisioned annual federal deficits of about $200 billion for the next five years. In contrast with previous years, the budget made no bold proposals for cutting taxes or changing spending patterns. However, in the face of strong opposition in Congress, U.S. Pres. Ronald Reagan proposed a compromise to cut the deficit over the next three years by $150 billion. The effect of this in the short term was negligible and in the longer term doubtful, as it was subject to an unusually high degree of uncertainty. As the extent of the economic slowdown dawned on the administration in October, leading to forecasts of higher deficits in the current fiscal year, it was faced with an acute dilemma. Budget cutting at a time when the economy was on the brink of a recession would further slow down the economy. The path projected by the administration was to achieve deficit cuts through rapid economic growth. Therefore, it had little choice but to nurse the deficit to support the economy.

In keeping with its policy of "leaning against the wind," which resulted in cautious tightening in the second half of 1983, in February 1984 the Federal Reserve Board (Fed) announced its targets for the monetary growth ranges. They were slightly lower than in the previous year and indicated the Fed's determination not to accommodate readily the government's borrowing requirements. During the first half of the year the rapid growth in GNP was accompanied by a big boost in the monetary aggregates (M1 and M2), leading to a 1.5% jump in interest rates to 12.5%. Fearing that a further rise in interest rates could weaken the domestic financial system and lead to greater debt problems in Latin America, and also concerned about a possible overheating of the economy, the Fed judged that higher interest rates would be inappropriate. To contain the monetary growth it engineered a monetary freeze by sharply restricting the growth of bank reserves. This had the desired effect, and M1 (the short-term money aggregates) at the beginning of September was not different from the position at the end of May. In the next two months the monetary aggregates grew nearer the lower end of the target range, reflecting the slowdown in the economy. To boost the flagging economy a gradual relaxation in policy was introduced at the beginning of September. This encouraged a drop of two percentage points in short-term interest rates but was insufficient to reverse the trend of slow money growth.

In November the Fed announced a cut in its discount rate from 9 to 8½%, signaling a further relaxation in

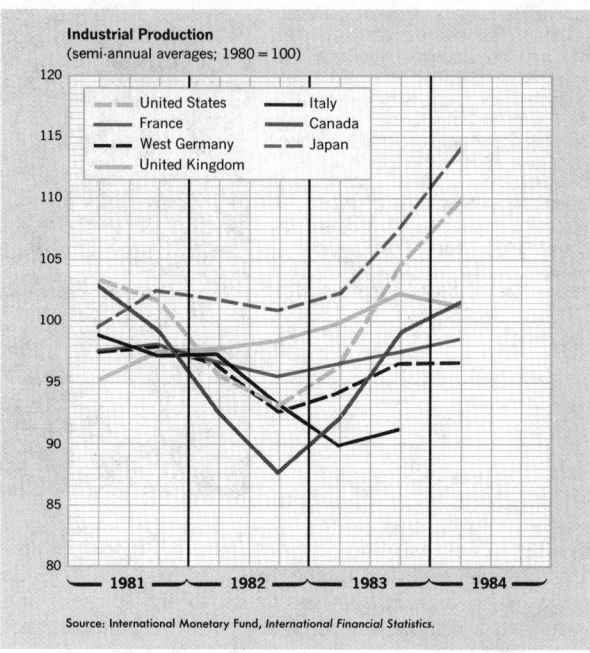

Industrial Production
(semi-annual averages; 1980 = 100)

Legend: United States, France, West Germany, United Kingdom, Italy, Canada, Japan

Source: International Monetary Fund, *International Financial Statistics.*

its policy. The statement accompanying the move made it clear that, given the stable inflationary conditions, the Fed's strategy had shifted from preventing the resurgence of inflation to preventing the economy from slipping into a recession. Responding to the Fed's move, the money markets further reduced interest rates in late November and early December, paving the way for greater liquidity and, it was hoped, more buoyancy.

JAPAN. The year 1984 was a good one for the Japanese economy. Despite the absence of any significant stimulatory action by the government, gross national product rose by more than 5%. This represented a marked improvement over the previous year's gain of 3.7% and topped the official growth target, set at the beginning of the year, by about one percentage point. All major sectors of the economy recorded an increase, but the greatest stimulus came from private plant and equipment investments and exports of goods and services. A largely unexpected investment boom in most private-sector industries took place during the year. The lead was taken by high-technology sectors such as advanced electronics, although there was a good increase in virtually all areas of manufacturing. This was largely in response to the strong growth of industrial production, estimated to have risen by about 11% during the year, and to the reduction in surplus capacity. The high level of investment activity was also underpinned by good corporate profitability, a relatively low level of interest rates, and strong underlying business confidence.

Much of this confidence was based on the spectacularly good performance of the country's exporters. The volume of exports of goods and services rose by about 16%, compared with just over 9% in 1983. Most export products shared in the boom, with the largest increase occurring in overseas shipments of machinery, which boosted their dollar value by approximately 20%. Japanese exports during 1984 were assisted by a number of factors. These included a low level of domestic inflation, the weakness of the dollar/yen exchange rate, and a rapid growth in demand in Japan's major markets, especially the U.S. Exports to the U.S. were thought to have risen by about 35–40%, enlarging that nation's share of total Japanese exports from about 29% in 1983 to 35% in 1984.

**Table III. Standardized Unemployment Rates
in Selected OECD Countries**

% of total labour force, seasonally adjusted

Country	1979	1980	1981	1982	1983	1984*
Canada	7.4	7.5	7.5	10.9	11.8	11.3
United States	5.7	7.0	7.5	9.5	9.5	7.7
Japan	2.1	2.0	2.2	2.4	2.6	2.7
Australia	6.2	6.0	5.7	7.1	9.9	9.0
France	5.9	6.3	7.3	8.0	8.0	8.6
West Germany	3.2	3.0	4.4	6.1	8.0	8.1
Italy	7.5	7.4	8.3	8.9	9.7	10.4
Sweden	2.1	2.0	2.5	3.1	3.5	3.3
United Kingdom	5.6	7.0	10.7	12.5	13.1	13.2

*Partially estimated.
Source: OECD *Main Economic Indicators*.

While the strong performance of the country's exports provided an invaluable stimulus to GNP growth, it also made the strains in Tokyo's economic relations with other countries more acute. Although imports also rose faster than in the previous year, the balance of trade with most larger trading partners moved further into Japan's favour. Overall, the current account of the balance of payments was expected to yield a surplus of some $33 billion, representing an increase of nearly 50% over the previous year. Not surprisingly, therefore, the U.S. and most European countries became increasingly critical of the apparent lack of restraint by Japanese exporters and the perceived reluctance of the Tokyo authorities to dismantle the nation's remaining import controls.

Faced with a growing chorus of overseas dissatisfaction and threats of retaliatory trade protectionism, the government unveiled a package of import liberalization measures in April. These included tariff cuts on more than 70 items, including wine, wool, and paper products, which were of particular importance to the U.S. New quotas were also established for imports of beef and citrus products, and further steps were taken to make it easier for government agencies to buy abroad. At the same time, the Ministry of Finance announced measures to liberalize capital flows in and out of the country, under pressure from the U.S. government.

Of the other principal areas of demand, consumer expenditure was heading for a relatively modest increase of some 3%, not substantially different from the gain chalked up in 1983. The main reason for this was the compara-

tively slow rise in real incomes, a result of the relatively small wage awards recorded in both 1983 and 1984 (4 and 4.3%). In the public sector, demand was even weaker. At the end of the year it was expected that public investment would show a volume decrease of some 3% and that public consumption would grow by only 1.5%. Both figures compared poorly with the previous year's achievements and reflected the government's policy not to provide any fiscal stimulus to the economy. Thus the budget for the 1984–85 fiscal year provided for an increase in expenditure of only 0.5% in nominal terms, the smallest increase in 31 years and a real decrease when inflation was taken into account. This rather austere approach was not the result of fears that a more generous spending program might lead to an overheated economy but instead was forced by the necessity of reducing the already high level of deficit financing. In 1983 some 26.5% of public expenditure was covered by deficit financing bonds, and the aim was to reduce this figure to 25% in 1984–85.

By contrast, monetary policy was fairly relaxed throughout the year. After sustained pressure by the business community, the Bank of Japan's discount rate was dropped by 0.5% to 5% in October 1983 and, although the authorities resisted demands for a further reduction in 1984, the money supply was allowed to grow at a rapid rate in order to accommodate the funding needs of a rapidly expanding economy. One result of this policy was a marked differential between Japanese and U.S. interest rates. Despite the improvement in the balance of payments, this had the effect of weakening the external value of the yen. Thus the year started off with a yen/dollar exchange rate of 224.7 yen per dollar (average for first quarter 1984), but by the beginning of December the figure stood at 247 yen to a dollar.

Despite the rapid economic growth, inflation remained under control and at a lower level than in most other industrial countries. The index of retail prices recorded a rise of only some 3%, while the index of wholesale prices showed hardly any movement. Unemployment during the year increased marginally but, at 2.79% of the labour force in July, it remained extremely low by international standards.

UNITED KINGDOM. During 1984 the United Kingdom economy slowed down significantly in comparison with the previous year. On the basis of partial figures it was estimated that 1984 would achieve no more than a gain of 2%

AP/WIDE WORLD

This mid-September activity at the World Money Centre of London's National Westminster Bank reflected the losses sustained by the pound sterling throughout the year. Its weakness was most pronounced against the U.S. dollar, but there was also some deterioration against other major currencies.

Japan's Ministry of Finance took steps to liberalize the flow of capital into and out of the country—under pressure from the U.S. government. One result was heightened activity among traders at Tokyo currency exchanges (above).

CHARLES STEINER—PICTURE GROUP

in GDP, representing a drop of about one-third from the increase of 2.9% chalked up in 1983. This was contrary to the experience of most other major developed countries and was entirely due to a partial strike in the mining industry that paralyzed two-thirds of the country's coal-producing capacity for some nine months of the year. The effect of the strike, which was accompanied by widespread and violent picketing, was to depress the level of industrial production and to slow down the rise in earnings, personal disposable incomes, and expenditures by private consumers. Industrial output, which went up by 3.2% in 1983, fell by some 1%. Apart from coal, however, most other areas of industry recorded a satisfactory increase; manufacturing output as a whole was thought to have risen by some 2%, compared with 2.5% in the preceding year.

Average earnings rose by just under 7%, as against 8.5% during 1983. The principal reason for the slowdown was the miners' strike, but another contributory factor was the unexpected ability of both public and private employers to maintain the level of wage settlements at generally the same level as in 1983. In consequence, personal disposable incomes rose relatively slowly, and this, together with a cyclical weakening in demand for consumer durables, resulted in gains of only 2% in spending on private consumption, compared with a rise of 4.2% during the previous year. Another comparatively sluggish sector of demand was government current expenditure. Owing largely to efforts by the authorities to control the public-sector borrowing requirement, this rose by only about 1%, as against an increase of 2.6% in 1983.

In contrast to 1983 both fixed investment and exports did rather well. Private fixed investment was supported by improving corporate profitability and a steady improvement in medium-term business confidence. There was also a good recovery in private house building, partly supported by the easy availability of mortgages. Against this, however, had to be set a modest decline in public-sector investment resulting from efforts to control government spending. Nevertheless, the overall total still revealed a welcome rise of 7.5–8%, compared with an increase of 4.5% during the previous year.

Exports, which performed poorly in 1983, also staged a significant recovery. Boosted by the sustained strength of overseas economic growth, a further increase in labour productivity, and a spectacular deterioration in the external value of sterling, the volume of overseas shipments rose rapidly, if somewhat erratically, during the year. By early December it seemed that for the year as a whole exports would increase by about 5%, compared with a gain of only 1% in 1983. The volume of imports, however, was also expected to rise relatively fast, by about 7%, partly because the miners' strike resulted in large overseas purchases of oil and coal and partly because the investment boom led

to strong demand for overseas machinery and equipment. This, together with the weakness of sterling, had an adverse effect on the balance of payments; as the year drew to a close, it was expected that the previous year's surplus in the current account would be wiped out and even turned into a small deficit.

During 1984 the authorities maintained the fiscal and monetary stance pursued in the previous two years. The three principal objectives remained to control public expenditure, to guard against the reemergence of domestic inflationary pressures, and, at the same time, to accommodate the recovery begun in the previous year. In practical terms this did not allow any significant relaxation of fiscal policy or injection of demand.

Thus, although the chancellor of the Exchequer introduced some concessions in direct personal and corporate taxation as part of his spring budget, there were compensating increases in some indirect taxes, changes in the timing of value-added tax payments on imports, and reductions in some business tax allowances. The overall effect, therefore, was broadly neutral, and there was renewed commitment to the aim of reducing the level of the public-sector borrowing requirement as a percentage of gross domestic product.

Monetary strategy was also stable, with a target range for the growth of the money supply of 4–8%. The actual figures stayed within the range for the most part, with growth averaging about 6.5%, broadly the same as in the previous year. The level of interest rates, however, rose somewhat. This was not the result of official policy; in fact, government strategy was to prevent any significant upward movement in rates for fear of weakening the modest tempo of economic recovery. Instead it was the consequence of U.S. developments. Although the downward trend that occurred in most of 1983 continued in the first few months of 1984, by the second quarter high U.S. interest rates had forced an upward movement that continued to July. This brought the average of the London clearing banks base rate to 12%, compared with 9.5% one year earlier. From July onward there was some downward movement, and by early December the rate was down to 9.5%. Partly because of high U.S. interest rates, weak oil prices, and the concern over the miners' strike, sterling lost considerable ground during 1984. Its weakness was most pronounced against the U.S. dollar, with the average value for the first three quarters of the year falling to $1.38, compared with $1.52 in 1983. There was also some deterioration against other major currencies; the effective exchange rate, as calculated by the International Monetary Fund (IMF), declined to 81.2 in the third quarter, as against 88.4 in the same period of the previous year.

Despite the weakness of sterling, inflation remained well under control. The index of retail prices rose by only 5.1%

during the first nine months, only 0.5 of a percentage point faster than in 1983. Certainly, as the year drew to a close, there were no signs of any acceleration; in fact, there was some evidence that the figure for the year as a whole would be marginally below the 5% mark. As in 1983, however, the one big disappointment was the level of unemployment. Toward the end of 1983 there were some signs that the underlying trend was changing and that the number of people out of work would decline in 1984. However, unemployment started to rise early in 1984 and remained on a steady upward curve throughout, with the result that late in the year 3.1 million workers, or 12.9% of the labour force, were unemployed, compared with 12.4% at the start of the year.

WEST GERMANY. Following a 1.3% growth in GNP during 1983, which somewhat unusually was led by consumer demand, 1984 got off to a good start, and the economy appeared to be on course for a 3 to 3.25% growth. More encouragingly, the more usual engines of growth, namely, exports and investment, appeared to have taken over from consumer demand. But in May a seven-week strike by metalworkers disrupted the economy, leading to a significant slowdown. The GNP, having risen by nearly 5% in the first quarter, declined by 1.5% in the second. However, after the strike was over, the economy quickly regained its stride, and an annual growth of 2.5% was likely to have been achieved.

Reflecting the restrictive economic policies in force, growth in consumer demand slowed down. During the first half of the year retail sales (by value) rose 3.3% from the corresponding period of the previous year. No significant change in this trend was expected for the remainder of the year. Private consumption in total was not expected to grow by more than 1% during 1984. Among other demand components, investment, particularly construction and spending on plant and equipment, was buoyant. Growth of 5 and 3%, respectively, was confidently forecast for those sectors based on the actual results during the first nine months of the year.

Export growth was by far the most vibrant sector during 1984. Thanks to the high value of the dollar, accompanied by a sharp economic upswing in the U.S., exports to that nation rose by 47% during the first six months. Exports to other European Communities (EC) countries rose nearly 12% during the same period. Judging by the strong recovery after the disruption caused by the strike, exports in total were likely to have expanded by nearly 10% for the year as a whole, increasing West Germany's share of world exports to over 11%. Imports also rose strongly, in particular during the metalworkers' dispute, and thus eroded the trade surplus. Indications were that the full-year trade surplus during 1984 could be well under DM 40 billion, compared with the 1983 surplus of DM 42 billion. Similarly the current account of the balance of payments was likely to have registered a smaller surplus than the previous year's DM 10 billion because of a larger deficit on invisible transactions (those not reflected in statistics of foreign trade, such as tourism).

By far the most impressive economic achievement during 1984 was the reduction in the inflation rate to 2%, the lowest level since 1969. The improvement came from an enviably low base and against a background of a weak mark against the U.S. dollar. A rise of 8–10% in unit labour costs (annualized) following the settlement of the metalworkers' dispute was another obstacle easily cleared. West Germany's unemployment rate of about 9.3% of the work force was not too bad by international standards. However, it was a source of concern to the economic policymakers that the recovery was not accompanied by a sharp increase in employment as in the U.S. On the contrary, a steady small increase in joblessness raised the average number of unemployed from 2.2 million in 1983 (9.1% of the work force) to 2.3 million in 1984. Since the real growth rate during the remainder of the current economic cycle was unlikely to accelerate significantly, no early improvement in the unemployment rate was foreseen.

Encouraged by its success in 1982 and 1983 in reducing public spending and borrowing below the planned levels, the government aimed for more of the same during fiscal 1984. The objective of the 1984 budget was a federal deficit of DM 33.5 million and an overall deficit (including federal, regional, and local governments) of DM 50 million. Based on incomplete data for the final quarter, it appeared that the federal deficit would be under DM 30 million (1.7% of GNP) and the overall public-sector deficit under DM 50 million (2.8% of GNP). Judging by the remarks of the OECD that the budget in 1984 would have been in structural surplus, the question arose as to whether fiscal policy was too tight. The West German government did not share doubts, however, and the draft estimates for the 1985 federal budget showed that a further tightening of fiscal policy was in the offing.

The monetary targets set by the Bundesbank for 1984, a growth in money stock of between 4 and 6%, signaled the authorities' intention to tolerate no upsurge in inflationary impulses. As it turned out, however, the central bank did not encounter any need to restrain monetary growth. In fact, despite the industrial dispute in the summer, through-

In June Donald Regan, U.S. treasury secretary (left), and Argentine Finance Minister Bernardo Grinspun met in Washington to discuss Argentina's huge foreign debt.

out most of the year the money stock expanded at the lower end of the range. Although the discount rate was raised by a symbolic 0.5% in June, this was done to counter the strength of the dollar and had little impact on money market rates.

As the pace of economic activity quickened after the summer, it increasingly appeared that money growth would contract in real terms unless it could be stimulated to expand at the upper end of the range. At a time when the engine of growth was expected to switch once more to domestic demand, it worried economic observers that both strands of economic policy should be firmly stuck in a contractionary mode in real terms.

FRANCE. Following the introduction of the austerity measures in March 1983, the economy was widely predicted to slump with little or no growth prospects during the following year. However, a deep recession did not materialize, and the GDP registered a 0.9% gain during 1983. The modest buoyancy in economic activity in evidence during the closing quarter was carried into 1984. However, unlike the previous six months, stimulus to growth was not provided by consumer spending or by export demand but by a buildup of stocks. Given this underlying weakness in two major demand components, it was not surprising that economic activity slowed down in the spring and summer. Incomplete data for the final quarter pointed to a hesitant recovery, supporting government forecasts of an overall 1.4% growth in GDP for 1984 as a whole.

As the year unfolded, consumer confidence eroded along with real wages and job prospects. This led to stagnation in private consumption. Retail sales, for example, declined by 9% during the first ten months of 1984 and, apart from a seasonal recovery in the final months, no real upturn was expected. Industrial production mirrored closely the weak demand and the general sluggishness of the economy. After experiencing an encouraging rise early in the year, it slowed down. The production of automobiles and consumer durables suffered most, while output of machinery and equipment was reasonably buoyant, reflecting the improving business climate and recovery in corporate profitability. Overall, industrial output was not expected to be more than 1% higher than in 1983.

The stabilization measures adopted by the government since late 1982 in response to inflation and balance of payments crises (in part caused by the 1981–82 expansionary policies) continued to bear fruit during 1984. Thanks to the relatively faster economic growth rates enjoyed by its major trading partners, France showed a steady, if unspectacular, growth in exports, while import growth was held back by sluggish consumer demand. As a result the trade deficit, which had fallen to F 43.5 billion in 1983 from the previous year's record of F 93.3 billion, was on target to come down to F 19 billion in 1984. A similar reduction in the balance of payments was also expected, reducing the deficit to F 25 billion, compared with the 1982 record of F 79.3 billion.

Encouraging progress was also made on the inflation front. The annual inflation rate was reduced to 7% by the end of October 1984, compared with 9.3% at the beginning of the year. An effective prices and incomes policy succeeded in moderating the pace of wage increases, which exerted a downward pressure on inflationary forces, as did steady import prices. However, even at the 7% level France's inflation rate was above those in West Germany, the U.S., and the U.K. and also above the government's medium-term target of under 5%.

Employment in France as in other developed countries was a casualty of restrictive anti-inflationary policies.

Unlike some of its neighbours, France was able to keep unemployment below the two million mark until 1984 by shielding its nationalized industries from the full effects of the international recession. This policy was relaxed in 1983, thereby accelerating the closing of obsolete and excess production facilities. As a result the numbers out of work rose rapidly to more than 2.5 million at the end of October, compared with 2 million at the beginning of the year. This worsening trend was expected to continue well into 1985 and bring the unemployment rate up to the EC average of about 10%.

In line with the stabilization measures adopted in 1982, fiscal policy remained reasonably tight. The previous year's target of limiting the budget deficit to 3% of GDP was reaffirmed in 1984. However, in spite of an F 11 billion cutback on capital expenditure halfway through the year in order to compensate for the unforeseen and rapidly rising costs of industrial restructuring and unemployment, the budget deficit exceeded the target by about F 11 billion, or 0.3% of GDP. The 1985 budget proposals unveiled in September represented a shift in the thinking of the economic policymakers. Emulating the U.S. and the U.K. with cuts in direct taxation, the Socialist administration joined those who believed that the resulting improvement on the supply side would more than compensate for any cuts in demand. The 1985 budget proposed to cut the tax burden around F 45 billion (equal to 1% of GDP), to be paid for by higher indirect taxation and a reduction in government spending. The overall budget deficit was planned at F 140 billion or 3% of GDP, unchanged from the 1984 target.

Monetary policy was in harmony with the restrictive fiscal stance. The money growth targets were reduced to a 5.5–6.5% band (1983 actual 10.5%). Because this meant a tight ceiling on bank credit, coupled with a high public-sector borrowing requirement and high interest rates in the U.S., nominal interest rates remained unchanged. Given a slight improvement in the inflation rate, this meant that real interest rates rose during the year and exerted a greater pressure than was probably intended.

Less Developed Countries. The pace of economic development among the less developed countries continued to lag behind the gently accelerating level of economic activity in the industrialized nations. The less developed countries were constrained by sluggish demand for their exports, stagnant commodity prices, high interest rates, and limited foreign exchange earnings. Coupled with a legacy of high indebtedness and untamed inflationary expectations, many of those countries had to follow restrictive economic policies that held back growth rates.

OUTPUT. According to World Bank estimates, during 1983 (the latest year available) the rate of economic growth in all of the less developed countries, taken as a group, was 2.3%, a marginal increase over 1982. This meant that for the fourth year in a row the actual growth rate achieved was less than the medium-term average (1973–79) of 5.2%. However, given the spreading and strengthening growth conditions in the industrialized countries during 1984, it was expected that this would lead to a mild export-led recovery. A modest improvement in the balance of payments positions of the less developed countries, augmented by an easier trend in interest rates, was also anticipated. Although it seemed certain that the economies of many less developed countries would end 1984 in better shape than in 1983, overall growth rates were unlikely to approach those of the industrialized countries or their own medium-term average.

In spite of some recovery during 1983, economic perfor-

China benefited from economic reforms, one result of which was enough economic freedom to allow successful individuals to buy such luxuries as private automobiles. A chicken farmer became the first Chinese peasant to own a private car—a $4,650 Toyota.

UPI/BETTMANN

mance was patchy in the less developed world. Low-income countries in Asia with a dominant agricultural sector experienced good growth rates. China and India benefited from reforms and favourable weather conditions. On the other hand, low-income African countries suffered a decline in economic growth despite higher export prices available. This was in part due to an export failure caused by drought and by political problems.

Declining oil prices were a boon to middle-income oil-importing countries, but with the exception of those countries in East Asia, their growth rates lagged. The World Bank attributed the progress of the countries in East Asia

to their pursuance of economic policies that favoured the operation of free market mechanisms, realistic relative prices, export incentives, and support for the agricultural sector. The economies of other middle-income countries stagnated or declined during 1983. Latin America fared worst with a steep decline in GDP. Chronic balance of payments problems coupled with high interest rates forced restrictive economic policies aimed at holding back domestic demand and curtailing imports.

Oil-exporting middle-income countries fared badly as a result of the drop in oil prices. A reduction in their export earnings together with the high international interest rates increased their debt service burden and reduced the availability of international finance. Faced with these threats to economic stability, many of them had to curtail imports, defer investment projects, and reduce domestic demand. Because of such policies their GDP's declined.

CONSUMER PRICES. In contrast to the developed nations, inflation among the less developed countries did not follow a downward trend. The IMF attributed this to the accommodating fiscal policies pursued in particular by the non-oil less developed countries. During 1983 the inflation rate in the less developed world averaged more than 35%, compared with 27% in 1982. Once again the average figure was unduly distorted by the poor performance of a few large countries. Encouragingly, the median annual rate of inflation was unchanged at about 10%. The lowest inflation rate was in Asia for the second year in a row. The IMF attributed this to timely adjustment programs aimed at fiscal and monetary restrictions, correction of price distortions, and trade liberalization. By contrast the highest inflation rates occurred in non-oil Middle Eastern countries such as Israel and in Latin America, where Argentina, Brazil, and Mexico were notable examples. Many major oil-exporting countries experienced stable inflationary conditions, thanks to restrictive government policies necessitated by weakening oil exports and economic activity. However, a few countries in that group posted very high inflationary figures.

According to IMF sources many less developed countries were committed to policies designed to reduce inflationary pressures. Since such policies in the short term often lead to higher prices, an improvement in inflation before the

Table IV. Changes in Output in the Less Developed Countries, 1979–83
In %

| Area | Annual average 1967–76 | Change from preceding year | | | | |
		1979	1980	1981	1982	1983
All less developed countries*	5.7	5.2	2.5	2.4	2.1	2.3
Oil-exporting countries†	7.0	3.7	−2.0	−4.0	−4.3	−1.1
Non-oil less developed countries						
Weighted average	5.6	5.1	5.0	2.8	1.3	1.6
Median	5.0	4.8	3.7	3.3	2.0	1.7
Africa‡	4.8	2.5	2.2	3.0	1.8	1.2
Asia‡	5.0	4.7	5.4	5.1	4.5	6.5
Europe‡	5.5	3.9	1.5	2.3	2.4	0.6
Middle East‡	5.6	4.3	6.8	5.4	3.4	4.2
Western Hemisphere	6.6	6.7	6.1	0.2	−1.6	−2.3

*Median.
†Arithmetic average.
‡Weighted average.
  Source: Adapted from IMF, *Annual Report 1984*; World Bank, *Annual Report 1984*.

Table V. Changes in Consumer Prices in the Less Developed Countries, 1979–83
In %

| Area | Annual average 1967–76 | Change from preceding year | | | | |
		1979	1980	1981	1982	1983
Oil-exporting countries*	n/a	10.9	13.2	13.2	8.1	11.4
Non-oil less developed countries*†	15.9	24.8	32.0	31.3	32.9	44.1
Africa	10.3	22.5	23.3	28.2	18.3	19.5
Asia†	10.3	6.7	12.5	10.5	5.9	5.9
Europe	9.0	25.9	37.9	24.0	23.5	23.3
Middle East	9.6	25.9	42.2	34.0	36.1	40.3
Western Hemisphere	27.5	50.1	58.6	65.3	78.4	122.7

*Weighted average.
†Excluding China.
  Source: Adapted from IMF, *Annual Report 1984*.

Table VI. Balances of Payments on Current Account, 1979–83

In $000,000,000

Area	1979	1980	1981	1982	1983
Industrial countries	−5.1	−38.1	4.8	3.2	2.8
Less developed countries					
Oil-exporting countries	62.5	111.0	53.4	−12.0	−16.2
Non-oil less developed					
countries	−62.0	−87.7	−109.1	−82.2	−56.4
Africa	−9.9	−12.9	−14.0	−12.5	−10.8
Asia	−16.9	−25.4	−23.2	−14.6	−10.7
Europe	−10.1	−12.7	−10.4	−6.9	−5.5
Middle East	−7.2	−7.1	−11.5	−9.3	−12.0
Western Hemisphere	−21.4	−33.1	−45.5	−38.8	−18.5
Total	−4.6	−14.8	−50.9	−91.0	−69.8

Source: Adapted from IMF, *Annual Report 1984.*

end of 1984 was not likely. Nevertheless, a slight decline in their budgetary deficits as a percentage of GDP and a deceleration in domestic credit expansion were in evidence— both favourable signs.

TRADE AND CURRENT ACCOUNT POSITION. Thanks to economic recovery in the industrialized countries, the volume of world trade expanded strongly in 1983 and 1984. This enabled the less developed countries to increase their exports in volume terms. Exports to the U.S. from the less developed countries rose by no less than 20% in dollar terms. Equally encouragingly, non-oil commodity prices rose by 20% in dollar terms during the 18 months to May 1984. In turn, the terms of trade of the oil-importing less developed countries improved by 2% during 1983, having fallen by 20% in the previous five years. Not surprisingly, the erosion in oil prices resulted in a deterioration in the terms of trade for the oil-exporting countries.

A major improvement in the current account deficits of the non-oil less developed countries was also much in evidence during 1983. The deficit, which stood at $82 billion in 1982 (having declined from a peak of $109 billion in 1981), fell to $56 billion in 1983. In contrast to the previous year's improvement, the gains of 1983 were achieved with only a marginal further cutback in the volume of imports. A further reduction in the deficit was expected during 1984, reflecting the buoyant economic conditions in the U.S.

The major oil-exporting countries during 1983 succeeded in arresting the rapid decline in their current account balances that had taken place during the previous three years. From a peak of a $111 billion surplus in 1980, the balance slumped to a deficit of $12 billion in 1982, reflecting a sharp decline in demand for oil because of the worldwide recession and oil-conservation measures adopted by the industrialized countries. Such a massive swing in their fortunes forced the oil exporters to adopt restrictive economic policies. By 1983 these policies had begun to have the desired effect, and their current account deficit worsened only marginally to $16 billion. No significant improvement during 1984 was likely in spite of the gathering pace of economic activity in the U.S. and in other industrialized

nations. This was mainly due to the continuation of the conservation measures and the high value of the dollar (in which crude oil was priced). The latter increased the local currency cost of gasoline in most developed countries and held back demand.

Because most of the current account deficit of the less developed countries after 1980 was financed by private loans, outstanding medium- and long-term loans rapidly climbed to $538 billion in 1982. This coincided with falling export earnings and high interest rates, and so the ability of some of the largest borrowers—in particular Mexico, Brazil, and Argentina—to service their debts was brought into question. This situation eventually led to an effective freeze on new commercial loans. To avoid a default by a major country, which would have triggered a banking crisis in the West, the banks, together with the international financial institutions, mounted coordinated efforts to stave off the danger.

The main feature of the package that they put together was "debt restructuring" and "rescheduling" accompanied by limited new lending to enable the debtor countries to meet their obligations. During 1983 the number of countries that had their debts rescheduled rose to a record level of 16 (6 in 1982), while 17 countries had their debts restructured. Although these short-term measures provided a valuable breathing space for the less developed countries, the availability of external finance remained very tight. This had the effect of depressing levels of economic activity and making longer term adjustments more difficult to achieve. This task was also bedeviled by increased protectionist tendencies among the developed nations. Without easy access to the expanding economies of the developed world, the less developed countries faced an uphill struggle to resume renewed growth and sustained improvement in trade balances.

Centrally Planned Economies. In 1984, for the first time since 1969, a meeting of top party and government leaders from the ten member states of the Council for Mutual Economic Assistance (Comecon) took place in Moscow on June 12–14. The session concluded with two documents being adopted. One was devoted to economic cooperation within Comecon and the other to the world situation and political problems.

The summit meeting had been expected since February 1981, when the then Soviet leader Leonid Brezhnev recommended that it should take place "in the near future." Later it became obvious that the delay was caused not only by the deaths of Brezhnev and then of his successor, Yury Andropov, but also by the considerable conflicts of interests of the member countries. The mere fact that the summit meeting was finally held might be regarded as a political success for all nations concerned.

One of the main tasks of the Moscow summit was to agree on means of further economic integration for the member countries. The so called "Complex program" for integration through closer coordination of economic plans

Table VII. Output of Basic Industrial Products in Eastern Europe, 1983

In 000 metric tons unless otherwise stated

Country	Anthracite (hard coal)	Lignite (brown coal)	Natural gas (000,000 cu m)	Crude petroleum	Electric power (000,000 kw-hr)	Steel	Sulfuric acid	Cement
Bulgaria	240	32,124	...	...	42,876	2,820	8,604.0	5,640
Czechoslovakia	26,916	102,408	32,016	96	75,972	15,024	1,244.4	10,500
East Germany	...	227,968	...	...	104,928	7,224	926.4	11,784
Hungary	2,832	22,392	246,000	2,004	25,704	3,612	606.0	4,248
Poland	191,064	42,528	192,780	252	125,880	16,236	2,786.4	16,164
Romania	8,004	30,396	1,680,000	12,000	69,996	...	...	...
U.S.S.R.	486,768	154,764	19,880,256	618,000	1,395,996	152,496	24,696.0	127,992

In June the Council for Mutual Economic Assistance (Comecon) held its first full-scale summit meeting since 1969 in Moscow. All ten Comecon member states were present, each with its delegation of top party and government leaders.
TASS/GAMMA

and policies had been agreed to in 1971, but its implementation was slow and inefficient.

At the 1984 summit meeting top party and government leaders agreed on a long-term strategy based on four major initiatives: closer coordination of economic and policy planning; joint 15–20-year scientific and technical programs to cover, in particular, electronics, atomic energy, automation, and space technology; direct cooperation between industrial enterprises and the establishment of multilateral industrial firms; and joint solutions to major problems of mutual interest. The most significant agreement appeared to be that dealing with direct contacts between factories of member countries. Such contacts could accelerate the introduction of advanced technology to various enterprises, which could be especially advantageous to the U.S.S.R.

Table VIII. Soviet Trade with Eastern European Countries
In 000,000 rubles, current prices

Country	Exports			Imports		
	1981	1982	1983	1981	1982	1983
Bulgaria	4,374.5	4,884.6	5,510.8	3,696.9	4,288.1	5,053.3
Czechoslovakia	4,382.3	5,047.5	5,871.6	4,104.8	4,731.9	5,420.4
East Germany	5,526.1	6,419.6	6,797.8	5,154.6	5,776.2	6,595.7
Hungary	3,306.7	3,707.2	4,058.0	3,300.4	3,746.4	4,007.0
Poland	4,931.3	4,812.9	5,274.3	3,220.8	4,097.0	4,786.7
Romania	1,779.1	1,423.6	1,639.6	1,673.1	1,683.4	1,665.3

Source: U.S.S.R. Foreign Trade Statistics/Moscow.

Table IX. Soviet Crude Petroleum and Products Supplied to Eastern Europe
In 000 rubles

Country	1981	1982	1983
Bulgaria	1,310,920	1,546,132	1,784,757
Czechoslovakia	1,617,945	2,067,504	2,433,526
East Germany	1,744,515	2,414,248	2,749,140
Hungary	913,503	1,120,233	1,156,962
Poland	1,613,405	1,889,191	2,185,268
Romania	523,641	66,314	185,201

Source: U.S.S.R. Foreign Trade Statistics/Moscow.

Currently, the Soviet Union played a major part within Comecon as the supplier of fuels, energy, and raw materials. These supplies were paid for by other member countries by means of deliveries of industrial equipment. These were often obsolete items of low technical standard and inferior quality. Better products were usually reserved for export to Western markets in order to earn hard currency. The proposed direct links at factory level could result in the production of advanced technology that would be utilized in the internal Comecon market.

There were obstacles that would have to be resolved if such a program were to succeed. Basically, problems arose from the existence of strong central controls and the bureaucratic maze that was firmly entrenched in the Communist countries' economies. Similar ideas had been suggested before, as long as 20 years earlier, by the then Soviet premier Alexey Kosygin. Another problem, inherent in Comecon, was caused by the differing economies of the member countries. The U.S.S.R. was a superpower; East Germany, Czechoslovakia, Hungary, Poland, Romania, and Bulgaria were industrialized nations; and Cuba, Mongolia, and Vietnam were less developed countries. All those countries had different economic priorities and interests, and this created tensions and occasional clashes among them. The less developed countries frequently demanded an increase of economic aid to stimulate their industrial development, while the industrialized nations had considerable interest in trading with the West. Most of these countries had large debts that would have to be paid off in hard currency. The repayment of these debts would allow them to obtain new credits from the West with which to purchase advanced technology and consumer goods.

In the political and economic climate of 1984, the prospects for closer cooperation with the West were limited, and it became apparent that many of the European members of Comecon had decided to gear their economies toward closer links with the U.S.S.R. Bulgaria and Czechoslovakia adopted a deliberate policy of tying their economic development even more closely to the U.S.S.R. than in previous years. Romania and Poland were forced by their economic situations to reduce their trade with the West and had to increase their reliance on the Soviet Union and trade with other Comecon countries. East Germany and Hungary retained the most economic links with the West, but again the political climate was not conducive to any significant expansion.

Pres. Fidel Castro of Cuba was the only top-level national leader who did not attend the Moscow summit meeting. He was represented by Vice-Pres. Carlos Rafael Rodríguez. Castro's absence was explained by the "tense and complex" situation in Central America. Cuba, however, was host for the regular 39th session of Comecon. This took place in Havana on October 29–31. Castro made the opening speech, but the Comecon Executive Committee report was presented by Rodríguez. He condemned the "discriminatory political policy" and the embargo and trade bans imposed by the industrialized countries of the West. In spite of this, the national income produced by the Comecon countries as a whole rose in 1983 by 3.8% over 1982. At the same time, overall foreign trade of the Comecon member countries increased by 8% at current prices. Trade among Comecon members developed at a faster pace, however, rising 11% in 1983.

The Moscow meeting noted the successful development of mutually beneficial cooperation between Comecon and Yugoslavia and the maintenance of cooperation with Finland, Iraq, and Mexico. In addition, an agreement on cooperation between Comecon and Nicaragua came into effect in February 1984.

At the Havana conference Soviet Premier Nikolay Tikhonov said that the volume of the U.S.S.R.'s trade with the Comecon countries would be in excess of 71 billion rubles in 1984, an increase of 56% over 1980. Tikhonov confirmed that the U.S.S.R. would continue to deliver oil and various raw materials to the countries and to increase its exports of natural gas and electricity. He said that an agreement had been signed on participation by Comecon member countries in the construction of the Krivoy Rog uranium combine. Tikhonov also discussed the need for increased collaboration on production and stated that a number of Soviet enterprises were in the process of arranging direct cooperation with enterprises in Poland and East Germany. A Soviet-Czechoslovak association for industrial robots equipment was also being organized.

Bulgarian Premier Grisha Filipov asserted that the policy of the U.S. and its NATO allies was aimed at achieving military superiority in the world and that this was having a negative effect on the development of international economic relations. Czechoslovak Premier Lubomir Strougal, speaking about the economic situation of his country, said that the main positive aspect was the renewal of economic growth. He gave his support to the new forms of cooperation among the socialist countries. Istvan Sarlos, the Hungarian deputy premier, said that his country intended to strengthen the unity of the Comecon nations but also regarded the international division of labour as essential. He added that Hungary would continue in its efforts to streamline the system of economic management.

Polish Deputy Premier Zbigniew Messner said that the orientation of the Polish economy toward closer relations with the Comecon countries, and especially with the U.S.S.R., was a "permanent and irreversible direction of the strategy of Poland's social and economic development." He said that the coordinated plans should give more attention to technological progress in microelectronics and provide for increased mechanization and equipment for

The Organization of Petroleum Exporting Countries opened its 70th regular conference in Vienna early in July. The meeting was presided over by Libya's secretary of oil, Kamel Hassan Maghur (above), who opened the conference with criticism of the United Kingdom and Norway for producing too much oil.
AP/WIDE WORLD

the nuclear power industry. Messner also emphasized that Poland's limited material means, as well as the growing cost of capital expenditure in the mining and raw materials industries, made it impossible for the nation to maintain its present level of mineral extraction. Participation of interested countries in raw materials investments in Poland and in the building of new coal mines in the Lublin basin would be necessary if Poland was to maintain exports to Comecon countries.

Romanian Premier Constantin Dascalescu said that a long-term collaboration program should provide the Comecon countries with the necessary supplies of energy, fuels, and raw materials. He stressed the need for intensified effort and more measures to develop industrial specialization and cooperation in production.

Castro, who delivered the summing-up speech on the first day of the Havana conference, drew delegates' attention to problems facing less developed countries. He said that all the member states of Comecon had modestly but enthusiastically helped Angola, Mozambique, Tanzania, Ethiopia, Guinea-Bissau, the Congo, the Saharan Arab Democratic Republic, Yemen (Aden), Kampuchea, Laos, Guyana, and Nicaragua. He emphasized the advance of socialism as a sociopolitical system.

But, as had happened so often before, neither the Moscow summit nor the Havana conference produced any significant results. The general tendency toward increasing trade and other forms of economic cooperation within Comecon became more apparent. At the same time, however, several member states, especially Hungary, emphasized the need to expand trade with the West, and all member states, including the Soviet Union, expressed a general desire to maintain active trade relations with Western industrialized countries.

INTERNATIONAL TRADE
In 1984 there was a resurgence of world trade the likes of which had not been seen since 1976. As with any such resurgence, it was fueled by economic growth in the major industrialized economies, particularly in the U.S. Canada and Japan were able to boost their exports to the U.S., and this in turn enabled them to increase their imports. Western Europe did not experience such exhilarating economic expansion, and import growth there was below the 7.5% achieved for overall world trade. The non-oil less developed countries were able to expand their exports, particularly their manufactured goods to the U.S. and Japan. Oil exporters faced increased demand, too, as a result of both stronger economic activity and a rebuilding of inventories. The overall result was that the trade balance of the OECD countries slipped an additional $24 billion into deficit, the OPEC (Organization of Petroleum Exporting Countries) nations were able to improve their trade balance by some $10 billion, and the non-oil less developed countries boosted their trade accounts by about $12 billion. Other non-OECD countries (mainly Comecon) accounted for the remainder.

Among the industrialized countries the picture was that of a massive further fall into deficit by the U.S., offset partially by general improvement in the trade balances of most other countries. The major exception was the U.K., which continued to drift further into the red. Otherwise, industrial economies were able to take advantage of the trade boom, particularly as the gradual strengthening of the dollar made life very difficult for U.S. exporters. Japan was the main beneficiary, moving into even more substantial surplus, while there were modest gains for West Germany and Canada. France and Italy both remained in deficit but were able to maintain a reduction in those shortfalls. The minor industrialized countries were able to improve their trade positions substantially as import demand from the major economies grew by over 9%. Overall, trade balances of the seven major economies (U.S., Canada, U.K., France, West Germany, Italy, and Japan) came to a deficit of $39 billion, compared with a $6 billion deficit in 1983; in contrast, the other OECD countries improved their combined trade deficit from $14 billion to $5 billion in 1984. Thus for the OECD as a whole, the trade deficit rose from $20 billion to $44 billion.

All of that rise, and more, could be explained by the headlong plunge of the U.S. into deeper deficit. From a $61 billion deficit in 1983, which at that time seemed impossible to sustain without a crash in the value of the dollar, the trade deficit widened to a previously unthinkable $130 billion. Despite this, the dollar's value continued to hold steady on the world exchanges, and this only exacerbated the problem. Import prices rose scarcely at all in dollar terms, whereas desperate U.S. exporters were squeezed out of world markets by an inability to remain competitive in the face of such a rise in the real exchange rate. During the first half of 1984, import volumes were 30% above those for the first half of 1983, but there was a tailing off in the second half of the year. The factors pushing up imports in the first half—rebuilding of inventories and an upsurge in consumer spending—petered out in the second half, and there was some relief late in the year from a temporary fall in the dollar. Overall, though, imports rose a staggering 24% in 1984, while exports were indeed fortunate to achieve even a 5% growth. Although the U.S. could always rely on a substantial surplus on invisibles, the current account balance was plunged further into the red, to the tune of $90 billion.

Japan was able to take advantage of the increased export opportunities offered by the U.S. market and was able to increase annual volume by 12%. On the domestic front, consumer spending did not expand rapidly, but there was a renewal of private investment in plant and equipment. The overall effect on domestic demand was favourable, and industrial production was considerably above the level of 1983. Because the Japanese import most of their raw materials and a large proportion of their semimanufactured components, the result of the rise in production was an increased demand for imports; the volume of imports rose 9% over 1983. The trade surplus widened further, therefore, to $43 billion, from $31.7 billion in 1983, while the current account surplus moved up to $31 billion, an increase of $10 billion over the previous year. Significantly, this rise did not lead to any noticeable increase in demands to restrain further Japanese inroads into Western markets. With most economies enjoying a minor boom in demand and with a major one in the U.S., where unemployment fell rapidly, the political pressures to do something about the Japanese were less intense.

West German exporters were not able to benefit as much from the upsurge in world trade, even though the U.S. was West Germany's second largest export market, after France. There were two reasons for this. First, the West German companies remained heavily dependent on the European market, where trade growth was much less impressive. Second, the seven-week strike by metalworkers had severe effects on the production and export of many goods, especially those of the automotive industries. Nevertheless, export demand was a major factor in boosting economic activity in 1984, along with substantial increases in fixed investment, especially in the construction industry. Consumer demand was much weaker, and this damped down demand for imports. The metalworkers' strike had little negative effect on import trade, however, and indeed may have boosted it because West Germany required substitutes for unavailable domestically produced goods. Therefore, import growth rose 6%. This helped to keep down the improvement in the trade surplus, which at the year's end totaled just under $24 billion. Offsetting this was the substantial West German deficit on invisibles, so

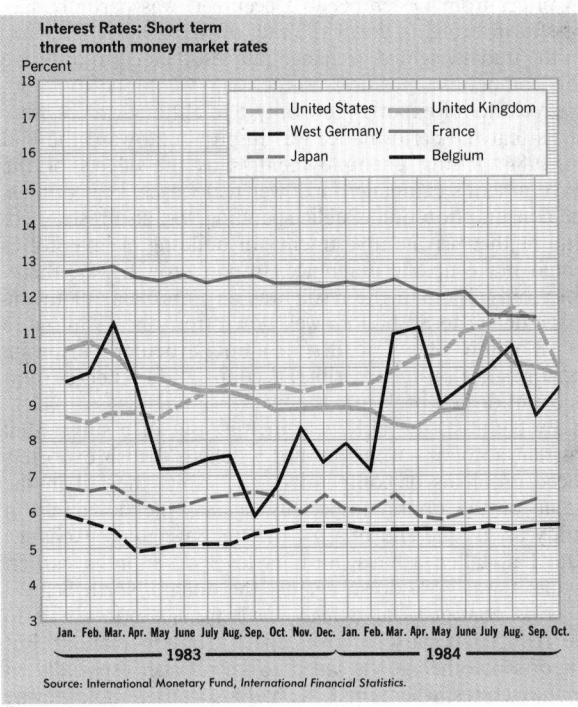

Interest Rates: Short term
three month money market rates
Percent

- - - - United States   - - - - United Kingdom
––––– West Germany   ––––– France
- - - - Japan   –––– Belgium

Jan. Feb. Mar. Apr. May June July Aug. Sep. Oct. Nov. Dec. Jan. Feb. Mar. Apr. May June July Aug. Sep. Oct.
––––––– 1983 –––––––   ––––––– 1984 –––––––

Source: International Monetary Fund, *International Financial Statistics.*

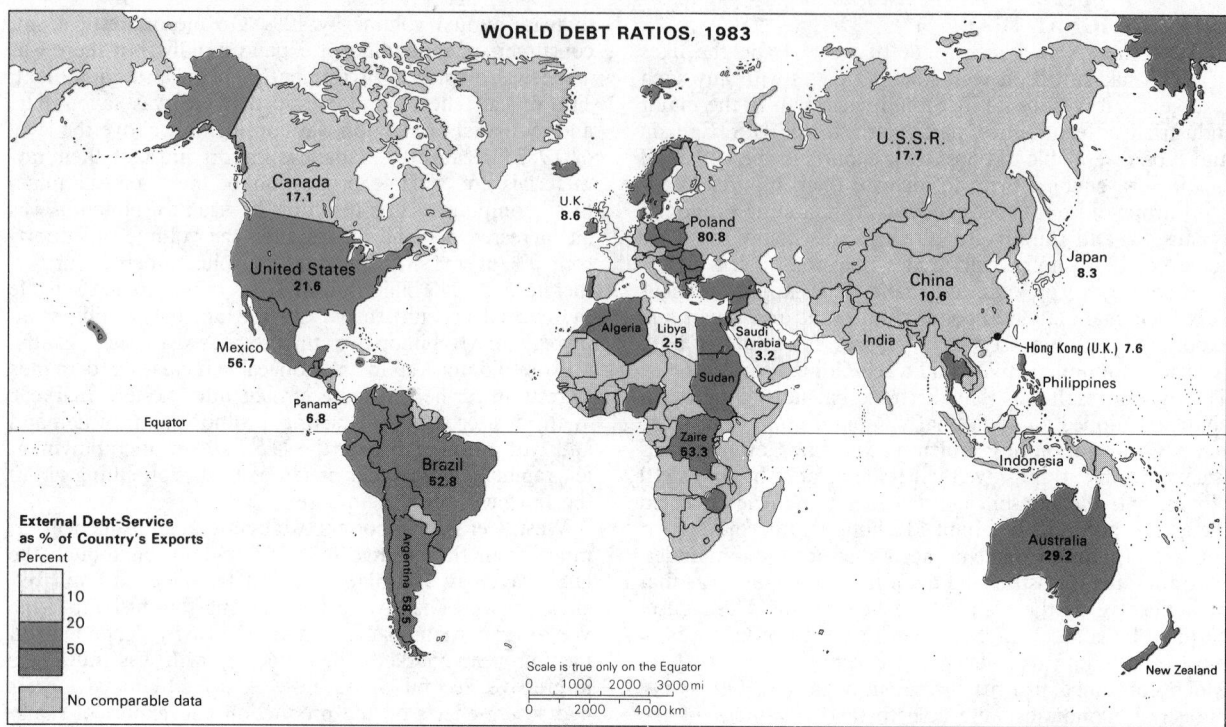

WORLD DEBT RATIOS, 1983

External Debt-Service
as % of Country's Exports
Percent

10
20
50

No comparable data

Scale is true only on the Equator
0   1000   2000   3000 mi
0   2000   4000 km

Economic analysts use various indicators in determining creditworthiness of a country. One of these is debt-service ratio. Traditionally, analysts worried when a country had to spend more than one-fifth of its annual export earnings making payments on its medium- and long-term external debt. Today, many countries have debt-service ratios much higher than 20%. In Latin America such ratios are especially high.

ORIGINAL DATA FROM MORGAN INTERNATIONAL DATA, OCTOBER 1984, COPYRIGHT 1984 BY MORGAN GUARANTY TRUST COMPANY. USED BY PERMISSION.

that the current account surplus moved up only slightly to $5 billion.

Export growth in France was distinctly unimpressive, again partly because of the French dependence on the European market. But poor competitiveness was also a problem, and French exporters found it difficult to obtain markets in OPEC and less developed countries, where previously they had been successful. The government's efforts to secure lower wage increases, with a target of 5% increases in prices from December to December, was partially successful in bringing down the rate of inflation. A 3% drop in the trade-weighted exchange rate also helped to improve the competitive position as the year went on. Even so, the volume of exports grew only 5%, although there were signs that the performance was improving toward the end of 1984. Rising unemployment, plus the effects of the government's campaign for lower real wages, kept domestic consumption dull. Public spending was also restrained, and neither private investment nor building of inventories could make up the difference. Import growth was, therefore, only 3%, and the result was an improvement in the trade deficit to $3 billion, well down from the 1983 figure of $8 billion. Therefore, despite a not particularly inspiring performance on the invisibles account, the French current account drifted back into the black.

By contrast, the U.K. was drifting out of a substantial current account surplus toward a deficit. British exporters faced problems of competitiveness despite the fall in the value of the pound (especially against the dollar) from midyear. By the end of 1984 the trade-weighted exchange rate had fallen 10% against its level 12 months earlier, while it was 15% down against the dollar. North Sea oil exports continued at a high level, though prices had to be reduced because of overcapacity in the market. But exports of other goods failed to keep pace, especially in manufactures, where the U.K. had lost considerable leeway

in the last few years. Nevertheless, exports did grow by 7%, just below the world average, though oil exports rose substantially more than that. Import growth at 8% was above the world average, despite the fact that the boom that began in 1983 was starting to fizzle. Even allowing for the effects of the miners' strike, which it was estimated took one percentage point off GDP growth, there was little vigour in the economy. But the uncompetitiveness of domestic producers, allied to the fact that in some areas domestic capacity had been severely reduced by the effects of the 1980–81 recession, allowed imports to benefit from what little growth there was. Therefore, the trade balance ended up $3 billion in the red; the current account was only marginally in the red, but this was a poor result after the more than $6 billion surplus achieved in 1983.

Italy achieved a small surplus in its current account balance in 1984. The expansion of West German and French markets, though not rapid, was sufficiently strong to help Italian exports grow by 5% in volume. But imports also expanded, by about 4.5% in volume. This expansion was surprising because domestic demand was generally very depressed. High interest rates constrained investment, and the public sector was also held back by the need to reduce public-sector deficits. Anti-inflation measures and in particular the limitation of the *scala mobile,* a means of partially protecting Italian workers against inflation, were restraining influences on private consumption and thus on import demand. Inventories were at low levels, however, and it seemed likely that much of the import growth resulted from the need to rebuild those inventories to more satisfactory levels.

It was happy days for Canadians in 1984. With their giant neighbour to the south snapping up imports as fast as Canada could dispatch them, there was no difficulty in achieving substantial growth in exports. After a rapid expansion at the end of 1983 and the beginning of 1984, export volumes remained fairly steady throughout the rest of the year. This was sufficient to give a $13\frac{1}{2}$% increase for the year. A similar situation occurred with imports; after a jump in the first part of 1984, the level declined slightly but, nevertheless, a 12% increase was achieved. Thus the Canadian trade surplus improved from $15 billion in 1983 to $18 billion in 1984, with the substantial invisibles deficit resulting in a current account surplus of $13 billion.

Other industrialized countries generally achieved improved trade and current account balances. Most of the smaller European economies were able to achieve substantial increases in exports. Ireland was particularly active, with an 11% gain. With import volumes held down because of depressed domestic demand, there was a trade surplus for most of the year. Other star performers were Spain and Portugal, where high export volume growth was achieved together with low import growth in the face of deficient domestic demand. That helped to improve trade balances for both countries, though Spain remained in substantial deficit. Australia's booming economy created a rise in imports but was also able to take advantage of the general increase in world trade to boost exports. Norway, on the other hand, achieved substantial import growth despite a not particularly buoyant economy; it appeared to be suffering from problems similar to those of the U.K.

With the industrialized countries experiencing a miniboom, the demand for raw materials and semimanufactures from the non-oil less developed countries rose substantially. While this in turn enabled them to increase their imports of manufactures from the industrialized countries, they were nevertheless able in general to improve their trade balances. From an estimated $29 billion trade deficit in 1983, their combined deficit improved to only $17 billion in 1984. Of this total, the newly industrializing non-oil less developed countries (especially Taiwan, South Korea, and Singapore) were able to boost their exports by 10% and to

improve their combined trade surplus from $1 billion to $6 billion in 1984. The other non-oil less developed countries were able to increase exports only by about 7%, and this left them with a combined trade deficit of $23 billion in 1984. Among the impressive performers was Brazil, which achieved an $11 billion trade surplus through increased exports of such staples as coffee and soybeans and also of manufactured goods such as steel. The improvement in the trade balances of the less developed countries caused their overall current account deficit to fall from $43 billion to $34 billion, though those figures are subject to more than normal uncertainty.

The OPEC countries also improved their trade balances as the demand for oil rose with increased economic activity and a need to rebuild depleted inventories. Despite keen competition in the market for oil, thanks to the effects of non-OPEC producers such as the U.K., Norway, Mexico, and Egypt, the production limits of 17.5 million bbl per day fixed by OPEC were regularly exceeded during 1984 and for the whole of the year were estimated to have exceeded 18 million bbl per day. Although the oil market was weak, with some market prices reduced during the year, the boost to OPEC revenues from this increased production was likely to have increased their combined trade surplus to $55 billion in 1984. The OPEC countries had a massive deficit on invisibles, however, and it was likely that they had a combined current account deficit of $8 billion in 1984, well down from the $19 billion deficit of 1983.

INTERNATIONAL EXCHANGE AND PAYMENTS

When the world economy is booming, international economic problems seem less bothersome. The crisis of third world debt that erupted in 1982 subsided in 1984, thanks to two years of major debt rescheduling by the commercial banks working with the IMF, together with an upsurge in world trade. Less developed countries that had rescheduled their debt found their economies restrained by the need to comply with IMF targets. However, with improved trade results, the financial needs of many less developed nations diminished. But many funds thus freed were diverted to the U.S., where the record current account deficit resulted in an inordinate need for foreign funding.

The external financing needs of the U.S. dwarfed the requirements of any other country or group of countries in the rest of the world. Despite a massive current account deficit, the U.S. managed to maintain its stock of foreign exchange reserves over the year and even showed an increase. Because of the dollar's continuing high value, investment in other countries seemed particularly cheap to U.S. companies and individuals, and the outflow of direct and portfolio investment was at record levels. In order to balance the books, therefore, the U.S. economy had to borrow at unprecedented rates from the rest of the world.

It was able to do this only because it continued to offer high interest rates, in real terms at least. The real interest rate on government long-term debt, for example, was invariably 2% higher than in the other major economies. When it is remembered that many of the latter had to keep nominal interest rates higher than they would have liked, in order to forestall a further slide of their currency against the dollar, the drawing power of the U.S. interest rates becomes particularly apparent.

That drawing power manifested itself in a continuing upward movement in the value of the dollar. Although it rose only slightly against the Japanese yen, it made significant headway against all other major currencies and was about 8% up in trade-weighted terms by the end of the year. Therefore, investors were presented with a high-re-

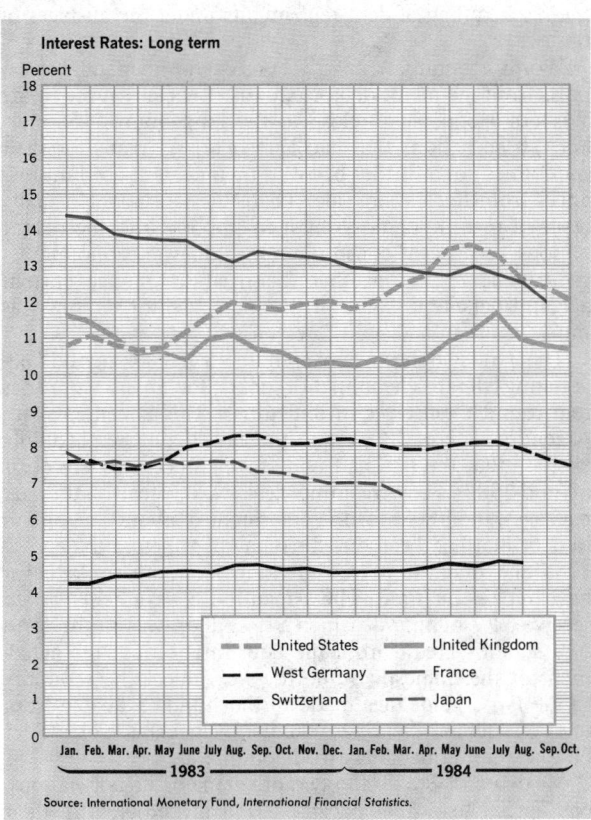

Interest Rates: Long term

Percent

United States
West Germany
Switzerland
United Kingdom
France
Japan

Jan. Feb. Mar. Apr. May June July Aug. Sep. Oct. Nov. Dec. Jan. Feb. Mar. Apr. May June July Aug. Sep. Oct.
1983   1984

Source: International Monetary Fund, *International Financial Statistics.*

turn investment with the prospect of currency gains in an economy that was politically stable and in which economic recovery was more widespread and faster than elsewhere. Not surprisingly, investors took up the U.S. offerings; one of the visible results was the continuing strength of the stock market on Wall Street.

The problem with the successful financing of the U.S. requirements was that as 1984 progressed it was generally believed that the situation could not last much longer, but it was impossible to know when the crunch would come. During the year it became clear that the government deficit was getting out of control, and shortly after President Reagan's reelection it was estimated that it could reach

$200 billion in fiscal 1985. But the president had promised to raise taxes only as a last resort and not to reduce the scope of the expensive Social Security system. Thus he had to either reduce other public spending or continue with a large deficit. That would mean keeping interest rates at a high level in order to attract both the internal and foreign financing required to fund that deficit. High interest rates would be likely to dampen the economic recovery in Europe and elsewhere, since those economies would either have to match U.S. rates or face a further decline in their currencies against the dollar.

But high interest rates will attract foreign capital only as long as confidence exists in the economy. There were signs during the latter half of 1984 that that confidence was beginning to diminish. No one doubted the ability of the U.S. to repay its foreign liabilities, especially given its high level of gold reserves. But a temporary loss of confidence in U.S. economic management could lead to a serious run on the dollar. It was believed that a substantial proportion of the money flowing into the U.S. was speculative in nature and would be withdrawn once it appeared that the dollar was on the wane. The magnitude of the inflows of foreign capital was such that if their level were to fall by 10%, the foreign exchange reserves of the U.S. would be rapidly depleted.

The world financial markets were, therefore, extremely jittery toward the end of 1984, reflecting fears that the economic difficulties facing the newly reelected president would precipitate a dollar decline. No one wanted to be last out of a declining dollar, but then none wanted to be first out either. The same fears had been prevalent during 1983—"it can't go on like this, the dollar's got to give"— but it went from strength to strength in 1984. That strength of the dollar, and the high level of interest rates, could have spelled disaster for the major debtor nations in the less developed world in 1984. That they did not was due to two main factors: the strength of the world recovery and the rescheduling of debt repayments under the auspices of the IMF.

World economic recovery boosted the demand for exports from the major debtor nations, especially those in the Western Hemisphere, close to the burgeoning U.S. market. Those nations that had agreed to IMF plans for their economies got a further boost of their current account balances from the import side. There the IMF targets usually resulted in little or no growth in imports into the debtor nations because of constraints on domestic economic activity. The result was that the need to finance current account deficits in some of the major debtor nations was much less than had been foreseen.

The IMF had been active in the 1983–84 period, negotiating the rescheduling of debts for many countries that found themselves in difficulties. The agreement with Argentina late in 1984 was the last major rescheduling exercise that the IMF had undertaken since the debt crisis of mid-1982. The Argentine deal was typical of the IMF packages; it allowed for the deferment of about $13 billion in debt that had been due for repayment before the end of 1985 and that the weak Argentine economy could never have repaid on time. The Argentine government was to receive $1.7 billion, of which $1.4 billion was in the form of a standby credit, from the IMF. In addition, the agreement of the domestic authorities to subject the economy to the IMF's guidelines made further funds available from the commercial banking system. Fresh loans worth $4.2 billion were immediately forthcoming.

Mexico and Brazil, the two other major debtor nations, had agreed to similar packages, and the progress in their

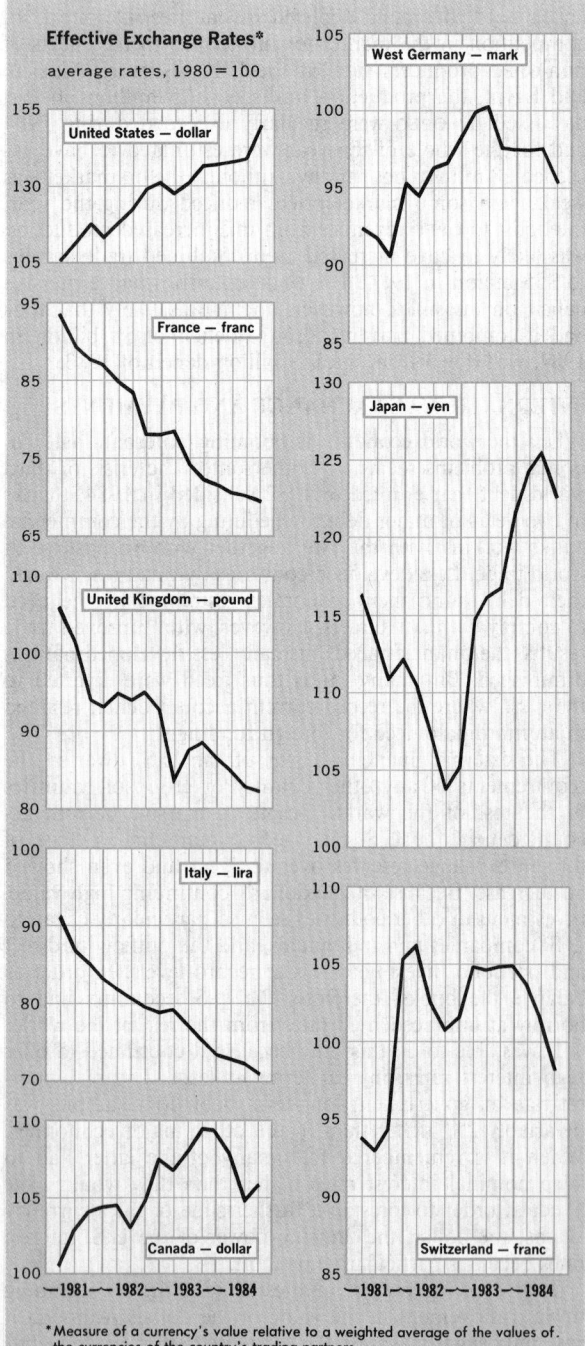

Effective Exchange Rates*

average rates, 1980 = 100

United States — dollar

France — franc

United Kingdom — pound

Italy — lira

Canada — dollar

West Germany — mark

Japan — yen

Switzerland — franc

—1981—1982—1983—1984

*Measure of a currency's value relative to a weighted average of the values of the currencies of the country's trading partners.

Source: International Monetary Fund, *International Financial Statistics*.

economic position was marked. Brazil's current account moved closer to overall balance during the year, while Mexico's external balance improved. Those two countries, together with Argentina, had threatened the stability of the world financial system in 1982, but the IMF had managed to steady the situation.

The IMF began in 1984 to turn to the next stage of its global economic effort, which was to extend through 1985 and beyond. This would seek to provide stability through balanced economic growth in the major debtor nations, to be accompanied by more favourable loan terms and conditions for the less developed countries from the commercial banks. Several factors had made attainment of that objective difficult and were expected to continue to do so. First, the continuing high level of U.S. interest rates effectively determined the Eurodollar interest rate on which most commercial bank lending to less developed countries was based. The high level in 1984 was not as much of a problem as it could have been, because of the reduced need for borrowing and the rescheduling arrangements for the major debtors. Eurodollar rates fell by 2–3% during the year, and this also eased the burden. However, an upturn in U.S. interest rates would lead to increased financing costs that could wipe out the gains from rescheduling.

A second factor that made the IMF's objective difficult to attain was that the economic upturn in 1983–84 was not accompanied by as much investment in the less developed countries as might have been expected. Partly that reflected the financial problems of the less developed nations, but it also mirrored the concern of multinational corporations about restrictions on free trade in key markets such as Europe and the U.S. Investors in the less developed nations usually look for markets in those economies, but high unemployment had led to restraints there in previous years, and there was concern that a downturn in the world economy would lead to a resurgence of those restrictions. Thus, while the U.S. continued to invest heavily abroad, there was a greater emphasis on doing so in the industrialized countries, or in selected less developed countries, especially in the Far East. European and Japanese multinationals were even more wary.

The upshot was a smaller contribution to total capital financing from direct investment in the less developed countries, leading to a need for capital from other sources. What was even more significant, however, was that this investment would normally be expected to generate the export revenues needed to pay off existing debts. The future ability of the less developed nations to finance their debt service could thus have been impaired.

A third factor was that the citizens of many of the major less developed countries also had little confidence in their own economies. Outflows of private capital from those countries were not as significant as they had been in 1982, but, nevertheless, they represented a drain on the resources of the less developed countries for two reasons. One was that the initial transfer of capital caused a need for external inflows (usually bank lending) to balance the overall payments account. The other was that the returns on the exported capital (and much of this was estimated to be in land and other property) were not repatriated to the domestic economy, where they could have further boosted the external account, but were retained in the U.S. or some other appropriate haven.

A fourth factor, which was not so important in 1984 but could emerge again in future years, was that the commercial banks in the U.S. and to a certain extent elsewhere were still jittery about the quality of their loan portfolios. In 1984 the crash of the Continental Illinois National Bank

showed that it was not just bad foreign debts that could bring down a major bank. This caution manifested itself in an increase in Eurobond lending in 1984. Eurobonds tend to be used only by extremely good risk borrowers and in recent years increased their share of total international bank lending from less than 10% of new lending in 1981 to 40–50% in 1984. Greater prudence by the banking and financial community, while necessary and reasonable, could lead to financing problems for some less developed countries and cause the start of another period of instability.

The international financial system could look back on 1984 as a year in which positive progress was made in resolving some of the problems that stemmed from the oil price crises of the 1970s and that surfaced in the 1980s. But many potential pitfalls remained as the IMF tried to lead the way through the rest of the decade.   (EIU)

This article updates the *Macropædia* articles BANKS AND BANKING; ECONOMIC GROWTH AND PLANNING; GOVERNMENT FINANCE; INTERNATIONAL TRADE.

STOCK EXCHANGES

Most of the world's major stock markets scored gains in 1984. Despite sluggish economic growth, relatively high unemployment, exchange-rate disturbances, and unsettling political developments, 13 of the 18 major stock price indexes were higher at the end of 1984 than at the end of 1983. (*See* TABLE X.) In countries where economic activity and stock market prices followed divergent patterns, equity prices were generally anticipating that the world economy would continue to recover from the 1981–82 recession. Economic weakness, however, was prevalent throughout the industrialized world and stemmed mainly from restrictive monetary policies, excessive debt structures, and retrenching by private lending institutions.

The pace of economic recovery in the Western industrial world was very uneven in 1984. The transition from an inflationary environment to one of disinflation was reflected in widespread price weakness in world commodity markets, which put downward pressure on overall price levels and lessened inflationary expectations. Although periods of commodity price weakness had their usual negative impact on inflation rates, the nominal level of interest rates generally did not decline as fast as inflation, with the result that the real rate of interest remained stubbornly high. Moreover, some economies benefited more than others from disinflationary trends. For example, the strong performance of the U.S. and Japan was aided by lower oil prices. In contrast, Europe and most of the third world countries that pay for oil in U.S. dollars actually experienced higher oil prices, because the surging value of the U.S. dollar meant that they had to buy slightly cheaper oil with much more costly currency. Similarly, high interest rates had a disproportionately negative effect on many third world countries as relatively more of their export earnings had to be diverted away from their domestic economies to pay the interest on their foreign debt. On the other hand, imports into the U.S. increased sharply in 1984, thereby providing an element of strength in an otherwise weak recovery of world trade, as well as enabling some international debt problems to become more manageable.

As the year came to a close, the trends of most stock markets throughout the world seemed predicated on the assumption that international economic recovery could generate its own upward momentum without triggering higher inflation. Yet the age of the current economic cycle suggested that this economic expansion was in its final stage, and many large and small nations faced the need to develop policies that would increase production, reduce inefficiencies that hampered productivity and investment, limit government spending, and reduce unemployment. Moreover, high real interest rates threatened to aggravate the debt problems of third world countries and limit prospects for a prolonged period of economic stability.

In short, the road to sustained worldwide prosperity was paved with obstacles. The success of the Western industrialized world in adjusting to a slower, more consistent growth pattern that would not reignite inflation but would gradually cut unemployment and avoid erecting new barriers to international trade would likely determine the overall direction of equity markets in 1985.   (ROBERT H. TRIGG)

United States. The stock market disappointed investors in the U.S. in 1984. The Dow Jones Industrial Average achieved its high for the year on January 6, when it closed at 1,286.64, before falling to a low of 1,086.57 on July 24. After a brief rally on a record volume of trading in August, the index drifted until December, when there was a modest upturn. Securities prices ended 1984 not far from the levels at the beginning of the year. The Dow Jones Industrial Average, the market's most closely watched barometer, ended 1984 at 1,211.57, down 3.74% for the year.

Investor expectations were bullish at the beginning of the year because of strong economic growth, but concerns about potential high interest rates and resurgent inflation caused investors to be nervous about the stock market. Earnings disappointments triggered massive sell-offs. On a single day in July, ITT Corp. lost nearly one-third of its market value after directors unexpectedly cut the dividend. The increased market share of pension funds and other pools of money, accounting for an estimated 65% of New York Stock Exchange (NYSE) volume, added to the volatility of share prices.

Major corporations such as Chrysler and Bethlehem Steel sold huge amounts of stocks in their pension funds in order to buy bonds and lock in generous yields. According to one estimate, individuals alone sold nearly $124 billion more than they bought in stocks in 1984. This record amount of net selling contrasted with a $39.4 billion net in 1983. Some $90 billion worth of shares, 4.5% of the total market value of all corporate stocks, were taken off the market owing to mergers and acquisitions and to repurchases by corporations of their own stocks. Salomon Brothers Inc. was the leading manager of underwritten public securities offerings in 1984 with a total of $21.2 billion in 186 offerings.

Despite ongoing uncertainties about the price of oil, the strength of the dollar, the size of the federal government deficit, and international debt strains, inflation was moderate with an increase in the consumer price index of 3.7%. The prime interest rate began 1984 at a level of 11% and rose to 11.5% on March 20, 12% on April 6, 12.5% on May 9, and a peak of 13% on June 26. It declined to 12.75% on September 28, 12.5% on October 17, 12% on October 29, 11.75% on November 8, and 11.25% on November 27. By the end of the year it was 10.75%. This pronounced decline affected yields on most fixed-income securities.

Volume on the NYSE rose 7% in 1984 with turnover of 23,071,031,447 shares, compared with 21,589,576,997 in 1983. There were 1,185 issues that declined and 1,109 that advanced in 1984. On an earnings-per-share basis the industries with the best performances were automotive, up 331%; general machinery, up 290%; containers, up 148%; and building materials, up 141%. The worst performers were savings and loan institutions, down 41%; real estate, down 33%; nonbank financial institutions, down 24%; and oil service and supply, down 14%. The most actively traded issues on the NYSE were AT&T, 415.4 million

shares; IBM, 287.4 million; Exxon, 232.2 million; General Motors, 191.6 million; and Ford Motor, 189.2. Bond volume was down 8% at $6,982,291,000 from the 1983 figure of $7,572,315,000. Turnover on the American Stock Exchange (Amex) fell 25.7%, from 2,081,270,000 to 1,545,-010,000, the biggest year-to-year drop since 1974. Wang Laboratories, Inc., was the most actively traded stock on the Amex with a turnover of 85.4 million shares. Bond sales totaled $371,990,000, down 6% from the $395,190,-000 posted in 1983.

Table X. Selected Major World Stock Price Indexes*

Country	1984 range† High	1984 range† Low	Year-end close 1983	Year-end close 1984	Percent change
Australia	788	546	775	726	− 6
Austria	59	53	56	59	+ 5
Belgium	165	135	136	158	+16
Denmark	225	162	214	167	−22
France	183	156	165	181	+10
West Germany	1,108	918	1,033	1,108	+ 7
Hong Kong	1,207	746	875	1,200	+37
Italy	230	192	191	230	+20
Japan	11,577	9,703	9,894	11,543	+17
Mexico	1,280	819	840	1,158	+38
Netherlands, The	147	119	129	145	+12
Norway	297	222	222	287	+29
Singapore	1,072	785	1,002	813	−19
South Africa	1,105	854	966	935	− 3
Spain	155	102	100	141	+41
Sweden	1,595	1,303	1,445	1,354	− 6
Switzerland	389	355	384	386	+ 1
United Kingdom	952	755	776	952	+23

*Index numbers are rounded and limited to countries for which at least 11 months' data were available on a weekly basis.
†Based on daily closing price.
Sources: *The Economist, Financial Times, Barron's, The New York Times.*

Table XI. U.S. Stock Market Prices

Month	Railroads (6 stocks) 1984	Railroads (6 stocks) 1983	Industrials (400 stocks) 1984	Industrials (400 stocks) 1983	Public utilities (40 stocks) 1984	Public utilities (40 stocks) 1983	Composite (500 stocks) 1984	Composite (500 stocks) 1983
January	112.90	90.26	187.50	162.02	68.50	61.89	166.39	144.27
February	102.29	91.73	177.14	165.15	66.25	61.52	157.25	146.80
March	103.41	95.45	177.85	170.33	65.25	62.13	157.44	151.88
April	103.58	100.90	178.57	176.78	64.34	62.95	157.60	157.71
May	100.93	109.37	177.60	184.10	64.94	64.88	156.55	164.10
June	94.36	110.91	174.20	187.42	64.90	64.14	153.12	166.39
July	90.53	113.04	171.70	188.32	64.66	65.06	151.08	166.96
August	100.83	112.03	186.86	183.16	68.11	64.85	164.42	162.42
September	103.03	121.86	188.10	188.61	69.71	66.00	166.11	167.16
October	...	120.37	...	189.00	...	69.10	...	167.65
November	...	119.43	...	185.86	...	68.95	...	165.23
December	...	116.19	...	185.18	...	66.95	...	164.36

Sources: U.S. Department of Commerce, *Survey of Current Business;* Board of Governors of the Federal Reserve System, *Federal Reserve Bulletin.* Prices are Standard & Poor's monthly averages of daily closing prices, with 1941–43 = 10.

Table XII. U.S. Government Long-Term Bond Yields

Month	Yield (%) 1984	Yield (%) 1983	Month	Yield (%) 1984	Yield (%) 1983
January	11.29	10.37	July	12.82	11.10
February	11.44	10.60	August	12.23	11.42
March	11.90	10.34	September	11.97	11.26
April	12.17	10.19	October	...	11.21
May	12.89	10.21	November	...	11.32
June	13.00	10.64	December	...	11.44

Source: U.S. Department of Commerce, *Survey of Current Business.* Yields are for U.S. Treasury bonds that are taxable and due or callable in ten years or more.

Table XIII. U.S. Corporate Bond Yields

Month	Yield (%) 1984	Yield (%) 1983	Month	Yield (%) 1984	Yield (%) 1983
January	12.20	11.79	July	13.44	12.15
February	12.08	12.01	August	12.87	12.51
March	12.57	11.73	September	12.66	12.37
April	12.81	11.51	October	...	12.25
May	13.28	11.46	November	...	12.41
June	13.55	11.74	December	...	12.57

Source: U.S. Department of Commerce, *Survey of Current Business.* Yields are based on Moody's Aaa domestic corporate bond index.

The National Association of Securities Dealers Automated Quotations system (Nasdaq) reported turnover volume of 15,158,819,587 shares, a decline of 5% from the year-earlier figure of 15,908,574,451. This was the first year-to-year decline since 1974.

Mutual funds turned in a disappointing performance in 1984. Most failed to do as well as the Standard & Poor's Composite Index of 500 stocks. Equity income funds, those that invest heavily in blue-chip stocks paying large cash dividends, rose an average of 9.71% in 1984, according to Lipper Analytical Securities Corp. They were surpassed only by fixed-income funds, which averaged a 10.91% gain. The poorest performers were gold-oriented funds, down 27.9%.

The Standard & Poor's Index began the year at 166.39 and declined irregularly to 151.08 in July, rose sharply in August to 164.42, and then drifted within a narrow range of that figure to the end of the year. (See Table XI.) On December 31 the index closed at 167.24, up 0.59% for 1984. The 400 stocks represented in the Standard & Poor's Industrial Average began the year at 187.50, fell to 177.14 in February, and declined irregularly to a low of 171.70 in July. The August rally carried the average up to 186.86, and its peak was achieved in September. At the year's end it closed at 186.36, up 0.47% for the year. Public utilities traded within a more narrow price range, although the pattern of decline in the first half of the year followed by substantial recovery in the second prevailed. Railroad stocks declined from 112.90 in January 1984 to 90.53 in July before recovering to 100.83 in August and 103.03 in September.

Yields on U.S. government long-term bonds (Table XII) were higher in 1984 than in 1983. After starting the year at 11.29% in January, they climbed to 13% in June before slipping to 12.82% in July and 11.97% in September. Yields of the highest grade corporate bonds were also above 1983 levels, opening at 12.20%, peaking in June at 13.55%, and dipping to 12.66% in September. (See Table XIII.) Prices of stocks and bonds moved closer to equilibrium as the price-earnings ratio of the Standard & Poor's 500 declined to about 10 from 13 in 1983.

The futures and options markets expanded in 1984 with the Standard & Poor's 100 stock index option, traded on the Chicago Board Options Exchange, trading 64.3 million contracts, up 500% from the 10.6 million contracts in 1983. On the Amex, option trading rose 2.5% to a record 38.9 million contracts. The Chicago Mercantile Exchange and the Singapore International Monetary Exchange launched a project to trade commodity futures jointly.

The stock markets underwent significant structural changes in 1984 as competition for securities listings by the various exchanges heated up. New product development, longer operating hours, and changes in listing standards were common strategies. Trading linkages to boost volume and liquidity were established between the Boston and Montreal stock exchanges, allowing traders in Montreal to place orders in Canadian stocks listed in Boston. The Amex and the Toronto Stock Exchange worked on a pilot plan to link their trading floors electronically. The NYSE and the London Stock Exchange explored joint ventures in securities trading and reporting of market data. The National Association of Securities Dealers began an automated stock-order execution system designed to find customers the best available price speedily and handle trades of 500 shares or fewer automatically. New financial products proliferated because of the merger and acquisition boom, deregulation, and internationalization of markets. The subordinated exchangeable variable-rate note was particularly popular. It provided a borrower with greater financing flexibility at better rates than long-term bonds.

The Securities and Exchange Commission (SEC) initiated its Electronic Data Gathering, Analysis and Retrieval system pilot project, "Edgar," whereby publicly held companies were to file financial reports and register securities electronically. More than 250 companies volunteered for the project. The SEC also launched a project for 24-hour worldwide stock trading. A possible merger of the NYSE and the Pacific Stock Exchange, which would expand trading hours substantially, was being negotiated at year's end.

Canada. Investors in Canadian stocks had a disappointing year in 1984. The Toronto Stock Exchange's broadly based 300 composite index ended 1984 at 2,400.33, down 6.7% from 1983. Volume declined 13% to 2,120,000,000 shares, while value fell 17.1% to $26,680,000,000. Bell Canada Enterprises Ltd., the most widely held stock, led the Toronto Stock Exchange's most active list for 1984, trading 47.5 million shares and closing at $33.50, up $2. The Montreal Stock Exchange boosted its activity with a 26.5% rise in share-trading activity, to 400.9 million shares, and a value increase of 37.8% to $7,010,000,000 as a result of generous provincial tax concessions and aggressive marketing. The Vancouver Stock Exchange suffered a major scandal on October 19 with the precipitous collapse in the value of nine listed companies during the last hour of trading. In response, the exchange raised trading eligibility standards and imposed tighter controls on promoters.

The backbone of Canadian stock markets—mining, for-

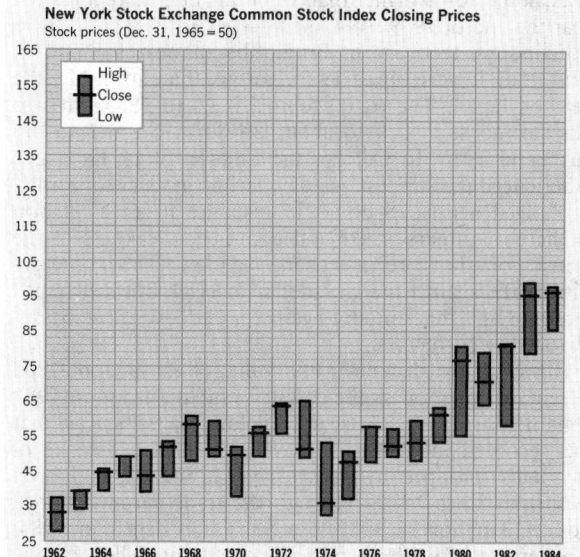

New York Stock Exchange Common Stock Index Closing Prices
Stock prices (Dec. 31, 1965 = 50)

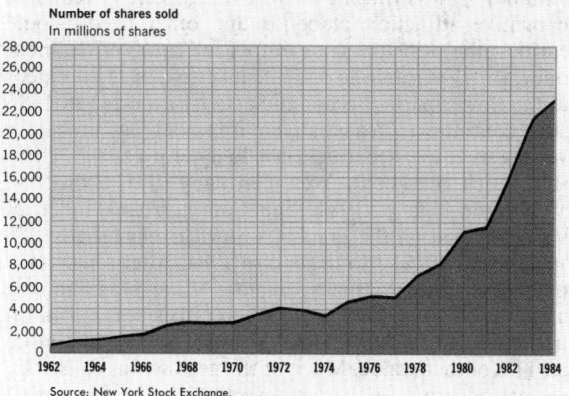

Number of shares sold
In millions of shares

Source: New York Stock Exchange.

est products, and oils—were the victims of a continuing worldwide slump in commodity prices. On the Toronto Stock Exchange gold-mining stocks declined 29.8%, other mining stocks 22.5%, forest products 7.6%, and oil stocks 14.2%. Interest rates were unstable in 1984. The prime rate moved up from 11 to 13.5% in the first half of the year but then dropped back to 11.25% by the year's end. Bellwether bonds such as the Canada 10.25%/2004, yielding 11.61%, and Bell 12.65%/2003 (AAA) at 12.22% were below their levels of a year earlier.

In a major move to encourage local investment, the Quebec Stock Savings Plan allowed investors to deduct from taxable income purchases of new stock issues in Quebec-based companies. For smaller companies the deduction was 150% of the purchase price. The provincial government also provided subsidies to cover costs of initial public offerings by private corporations.

(IRVING PFEFFER)

Western Europe. Stock markets in the four leading Western European countries—the United Kingdom, West Germany, France, and Italy—were uniformly strong during 1984. In other European stock markets, higher prices prevailed in Spain, Norway, Belgium, The Netherlands, Austria, and Switzerland. On the bearish side were Denmark and Sweden.

In the U.K. the *Financial Times* index of 30 industrial issues traded on the London Stock Exchange rose for the fifth year in a row. From the end of 1983 to the end of 1984, stock prices on average increased 23%. The *Financial Times* industrial price index ended 1984 at an all-time peak, some 134% higher than when the bull market started near the end of 1979.

Economic recovery in Britain began near the end of 1981, but it was much less vigorous than in either the U.S. or Japan. The (GDP) topped 2.9% in 1983 but was expected to slip back to about 2% for 1984 and to dip further in 1985. In October the London Stock Exchange experienced the steepest one-day decline in its history when it plunged nearly 28 points in response to an escalation of the coal miners' strike and continued weakness of the British pound in foreign-exchange markets. The pound declined 20% against the U.S. dollar in 1984, but it dropped less than half that amount against a trade-weighted basket of 16 other currencies.

However, the decline in the value of the pound failed to reignite inflation as the country's inflation rate in 1984 remained at about 5%, sharply below the 22% peak that was recorded in 1980. Moreover, the U.K.'s balance of payments, propped by sales of North Sea oil, had been in surplus since 1980, although the trade surplus slipped from $13 billion in 1981 to a $3 billion deficit in 1984. The strength in equity prices was also propelled by the continuing downswing in interest rates, thereby reducing the relative attraction of bonds and other fixed-income securities, the principal competitors for equity-investment money. As 1984 came to a close, investors were confident that the slower pace of economic activity expected in 1985 would continue to foster an environment favourable to investing in equity securities on a long-term basis.

The stock market in West Germany also recorded a new all-time high in 1984. The Commerzbank index of 60 issues traded on the Frankfurt Stock Exchange rose 7% from the end of 1983 to the end of 1984. After a relatively modest rise during January, average share prices moved steadily lower until early May, when prices began to drop much faster. From May 8 until July 25 equities lost more than 11% of their value. Much of the decline was caused by investor concern over the metalworkers' strike that threat-

ened to have nationwide effects throughout the economy. While the strike proved to be one of the longest and most costly in West German history, it had no appreciable adverse effects on West German exports. The strongest U.S. dollar against the Deutsche Mark in more than a decade made West German goods relatively cheap in international markets, particularly against U.S. counterparts. This gave the West German economy, which exported almost a third of its production, a much-needed boost. Once investors became aware that the country's still fragile economic recovery would not be halted, stock prices turned upward. In December, after an advance that proceeded virtually without pause from late July, the Commerzbank index broke the 1,100 level for the first time. The rally added more than 20% to equity values and was reinforced by the government's 1985 budget announcement that price stability would be the number one priority despite the nation's 9% unemployment rate. News that the government had approved lower income taxes in two stages beginning in 1986 and that it would resist pressures to raise interest rates even though the Deutsche Mark was relatively weak in foreign-exchange markets also helped the strong performance in stock prices.

In France the stock market finished 1984 with an overall gain of 10%. The index of share prices on the Paris Bourse reached its high for the year on October 26, and its low was established on January 3. The bullish tone in the market that had been generated the previous year by Pres. François Mitterrand's program to encourage government austerity and promote capital investment carried into 1984. By the end of January stock prices were up nearly 9%. Labour unrest, however, threatened to undermine the economic recovery program, and persistent weakness in the French franc in foreign-exchange markets raised doubts that the country's international trade accounts, which had been

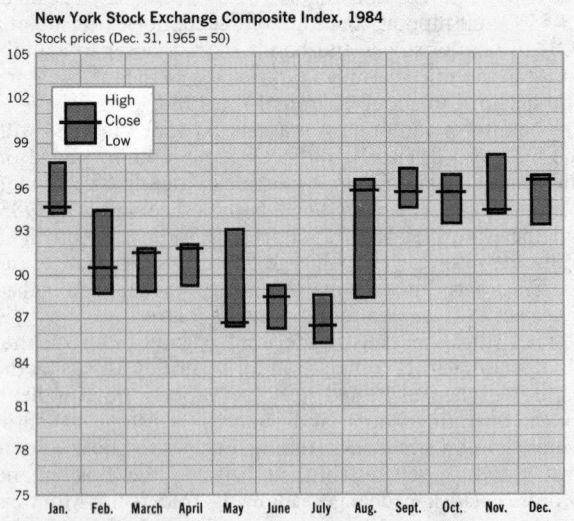

New York Stock Exchange Composite Index, 1984
Stock prices (Dec. 31, 1965 = 50)

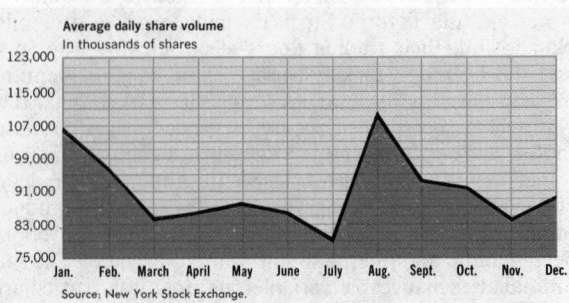

Average daily share volume
In thousands of shares

Source: New York Stock Exchange.

Specially decorated for the occasion, this trading post at the London Stock Exchange handled shares of British Telecom for the first time as the denationalized company was sold publicly.
GEORGES DEKEERLE—GAMMA/LIAISON

plagued by deficits, could be balanced without further austerity measures. By the middle of March nearly the entire gain in stock prices since January had been wiped out.

However, the ensuing recovery added 12% to equity values over the next eight weeks before profit taking ended the rally. During the decline that followed, stock prices actually dipped below the March lows. The nearly 13% drop from mid-March to the end of July was triggered mainly by news that industrial production had dropped in July and by reports that government spending was continuing to outpace the nominal increase in the nation's output of goods and services. However, stock prices began to rally in August and ended the year in a strong uptrend. At the close of 1984 stock prices were nearly 16% higher than at the end of July.

The strong stock market in Italy also reflected hopes that the slowdown in worldwide inflation and gradually declining interest rates eventually would produce sustained economic growth and a substantially lower unemployment rate. The index of share prices on the Milan Stock Exchange in 1984 followed a pattern generally similar to that in the U.K. but with somewhat less volatility. The upswing initiated in mid-June, which topped out on August 28, added 9% to equity values. Stock prices drifted slightly lower over the next seven weeks before staging a rally that carried the index above its August peak. As worldwide interest rates eased in the fall of 1984, economic forecasts called for Italy's output of goods and services to jump 3% the following year while, at the same time, planned limitations on public spending would reduce the nation's budget deficit and curb wage increases.. Despite uncertainty over whether the country would accept the economic and financial discipline necessary to produce long-term price stability, stock prices closed 1984 at their best levels, up 20% for the year as a whole although nearly 25% below the record highs set in 1981.

In Spain the price index of shares traded on the Madrid Stock Exchange finished 1984 with the largest average gain (41%) among the major world stock price indexes. Moreover, this stellar performance followed a 16% increase in 1983. The Spanish government's austerity program, designed to increase factory output, curb wages, and reduce government spending, showed some signs of success. Economic growth in 1984 was expected to be about 3%, up from 2.2% the previous year, while inflation fell to 8.5% from over 12%.

Higher stock prices also prevailed in Norway and Belgium. From the end of 1983 to the end of 1984, equity values increased 29 and 16%, respectively. The trend in equity prices in Norway seemed to be heavily influenced by the country's surging oil revenue, the government's plans to channel surplus cash into the private sector to finance plant and equipment modernization, and a wave of mergers and acquisitions by cash-rich Norwegian companies.

The disparity between lacklustre economic activity and a strong stock market was evident in The Netherlands. Real economic growth was nominal in both 1983 and 1984, and the unemployment rate was the highest among Western industrialized countries. Nevertheless, the price index of industrial shares traded on the Amsterdam Stock Exchange jumped 12% in 1984. Contributing to the wave of bullish sentiment was evidence that Dutch industry had become more competitive as a result of the strong U.S. dollar and the government's success in reducing public-sector pay and social benefits for 1984 by 3%. In both Austria and Switzerland the seesaw movement of stock prices resulted in moderate net increases in the leading stock indexes. On the Vienna Stock Exchange prices were 5% above the 1983 close, while the price index of issues traded on the Zürich Stock Exchange ended 1984 up 1%.

The stock markets in Denmark and Sweden both experienced lower prices on an annual basis for the first time since 1979. Average share prices on the Copenhagen Stock Exchange peaked on January 20 and finished 1984 some 22% lower than at the end of 1983. The bull market came to an end after the national election in which the ruling coalition marginally increased its total number of seats, and investors began to doubt whether the balance of payments and public-sector gains would continue. In Sweden the index of share prices traded on the Stockholm Stock Exchange fell 6% in 1984. Stock prices began to erode in late March when it became apparent that the Swedish government would be unable to maintain its wage-restraint program. Moreover, to counter the inflationary effects of relatively high wage settlements, the government reinstated price controls and tightened monetary policy.

Other Countries. Stock prices in Japan rose 17% in 1984, continuing the bull market that began near the end of 1977. The Nikkei Dow Jones average of leading industrial shares reached its 1984 high on December 4 and its low on July 23. Widespread expectations of relatively strong growth in economic activity, a record trade surplus, and the relative strength of the Japanese yen against the U.S. dollar fueled the advance.

In Mexico the stock market enjoyed the second largest increase among the major indexes listed in Table X. The

Bolsa Stock Exchange's 38% gain in 1984 was achieved against a background of renewed real growth in the Mexican economy and strong trade surpluses, along with the realization that the burden of financing the country's enormous foreign debt would continue to suppress economic growth and job creation.

The Hong Kong stock market was also a star performer in 1984. The index of 33 stocks traded on the Hong Kong Stock Exchange gained 37% after having risen 12% in 1983. The vigorous upswing was spurred by the announcement of details of a proposed agreement between the British and Chinese governments ending concern over the eventual form of the British colony's political and economic system after 1997, when the British lease on Hong Kong would expire and China would gain sovereignty.

The influence of lower prices for raw materials, especially oil and precious metals, was particularly apparent in Australia. With world economic activity at relatively low levels, the demand for Australia's vast natural resources and mineral wealth was somewhat less than robust. As a result, the All Ordinaries index of the Sydney Stock Exchange finished 1984 with a loss of 6%.

Singapore's stock market failed to reflect equity price trends prevailing in Hong Kong and Japan. The *Singapore Straits Times* index of industrial share prices slipped 19% in 1984, with most of the decline taking place after prices set a record high of 1,072 on February 8. The market was depressed by investors' concern over the effects of speculation in the real-estate property market and over the lack of economic recovery in Singapore's two major industries, oil refining and ship repair.

In South Africa the 1984 stock market started with a bang and ended with a whimper. The industrial share price index of shares traded on the Johannesburg Stock Exchange reached a record high on March 26 but ended the year down 3%. Rising social unrest and declining gold prices hampered economic recovery. Rumours that the U.S. was on the verge of implementing economic sanctions against the country as a protest against its apartheid (racial separation) policies also clouded the prospects for future economic growth.

Commodity Markets. The year 1984 was one of generally lower prices in international commodity markets. *The Economist*'s commodity index, which measures spot prices in U.S. dollars for 29 internationally traded foodstuffs,

nonfood agricultural products, and metals, plunged some 16% from the end of 1983 to the end of 1984. Major factors included a relatively sluggish economic recovery in Europe, record high real interest rates, the prolonged strength in the U.S. dollar's foreign-exchange rate, lower oil prices, and continuing disinflation.

Sharply lower prices prevailed in the two major sectors of *The Economist*'s index of dollar commodity prices. The average 1984 price levels of both foodstuffs and industrial raw materials were down 15% each. Within the industrial materials component both metals and nonfood agricultural products were also off about 15%.

Plunging crude oil prices—on both the world spot and futures markets—in reaction to price cuts, ample supplies, and slack demand had a major unsettling effect on virtually all commodities markets. The spot market value of the most widely traded North Sea crude fell to $26.70 per barrel at the end of 1984 from $29.40 per barrel a year earlier, a drop of 9%. That put downward price pressure on other crudes, including Arab light and Libyan Es Sider, and had a bearish influence on futures markets in other commodities. Since lower oil prices were generally viewed as a harbinger of a further slowing of U.S. inflation, falling oil quotations tended to depress non-U.S. currency futures and precious metals; this, in turn, led to selling in soybeans, coffee, cocoa, and other futures markets as well.

In international currency markets the U.S. dollar in 1984 set an 11½-year high against the West German Deutsche Mark, a seven-year high against the Swiss franc, a two-year high against the Japanese yen, and a record high against the French franc; the British pound registered a record low of $1.16275. The dollar appreciated 19% against the Swiss franc, 16% against both the Deutsche Mark and French franc, and 9% against the yen. The dollar's strength was bolstered by the prospects of continued low inflation in the U.S., which made the real rate of return on dollar-denominated investments, with their relatively high interest rates, even more attractive.

The strength of the U.S. dollar in foreign-exchange markets was also a major factor in depressing prices of industrial raw materials and soft commodities. The spot prices of copper, aluminum, silver, and zinc all were significantly lower at the end of 1984 than a year earlier. The disinflationary pressures in the world economy forced industrial commodity users to cut consumption or switch to alternative materials rather than pass along higher raw-material costs in the form of higher prices. In soft commodities the prices of both soybeans and cocoa fell more than 20%, while coffee slipped 10% and wheat 6%. Demand for U.S. commodities tended to drop as the dollar's growing strength raised the dollar-denominated cost of U.S. goods sold outside the country. In addition, relatively high interest rates reduced the incentive of commodity users to hold inventories.

The price of gold, an inflation bellwether, fell to its lowest level since July 1982. At the end of 1983 gold closed in the London market at $381.50 an ounce. At the outset of 1984 the price of gold moved higher and in early March traded over $405. After declining to the $370 level by early May, it drifted higher over the next several months but failed to break $400. During the subsequent decline gold reached its lowest price of the year on the final day of 1984 at $309, for a net loss of 19% for the year as a whole. With continued strength of the U.S. recovery and strong indications that dollar inflation remained under control, there was no pressing need to hold gold as a hedge against a depreciating U.S. currency.   (ROBERT H. TRIGG)

This article updates the *Macropædia* article MARKETS.

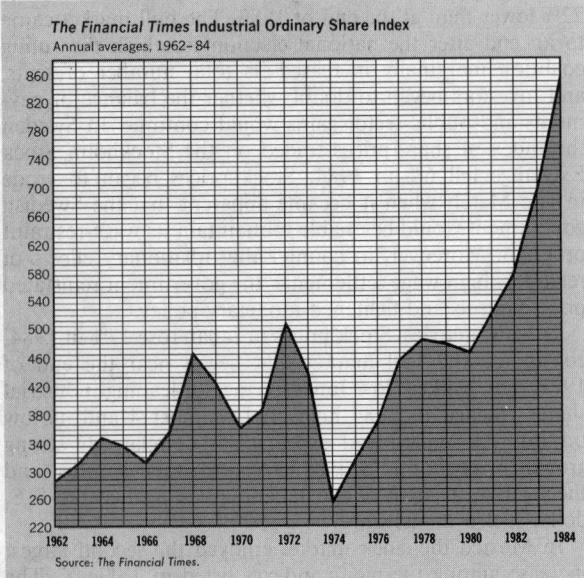

The Financial Times Industrial Ordinary Share Index
Annual averages, 1962–84

Source: The Financial Times.

Education

The plight of unemployed school-leavers continued to be a central concern of governments in the industrialized countries throughout 1984. Youth training programs were reinforced, partly in order to equip young people with useful skills but also—according to the criteria, mainly—to provide *le parking,* as the French put it, for the unemployed. In England this led to sharp differences between the 104 local education authorities and the government ministries, notably the Department of Employment. It seemed to the local authorities that the Department of Employment was taking over more and more functions of the localities through the Manpower Services Commission. Attempts to insist on technical and vocational training were particularly resented, although in practice this seemed to be one of the few ways of attracting finance from the central government.

These difficulties aside, it was becoming increasingly obvious that the old systems of training for industry, such as apprenticeship, were in decline. By 1984 the number of apprenticeships in England had fallen from about 100,000 four years earlier to 40,000. In Australia Peter Kramel, a leading educator and vice-chancellor of the Australian National University, proposed scrapping the apprenticeship system altogether and replacing it with a training program that would cover up to 300,000 trainees. The Belgian government took the draconian decision to raise the school-leaving age from 14 to 18 in stages, to reduce the unemployment rate. In France the Socialist government planned to offer job training to all school-leavers under 21. The program was announced by the new premier, Laurent Fabius, who estimated the cost at some £250 million. In West Germany, where more than 200,000 school-leavers failed to find training places in 1984, the federal education minister, Dorothee Wilms, declared that she intended to retain the so-called dual system, under which training places were found in private industry but training was provided by vocational educational establishments (the *Berufsschulen*). Apprenticeships in West Germany had declined by some 7%, despite the enormously increased demand. The European Communities (EC) published *Policies for Transition,* the findings of a series of experimental youth-training projects that it had financed since 1976. The report recommended that the principle of active learning be applied

in schools, particularly for those who had rejected education. Work in Clydebank, Scotland, showed how much the young felt they had gained from work experience programs where they were treated like adults. Other important areas of concern were counseling and guidance, assessment, and staff development. Finally, the report argued that community involvement and a coordinated approach were essential if young people were to be helped.

Education for girls was under scrutiny in a number of countries. In Australia a report written by a ten-member, all-woman working party, set up by the Commonwealth Schools Commission, argued that the phasing out of single-sex schools might be one of the reasons why initiatives to counter sexism in schools and improve career prospects for girls had failed. Many girls feared being unsuccessful in the mixed and highly competitive environment of a coeducational school. In Denmark a controversial report claimed that girls were less suited than boys to occupations involving computers, which were said to be "innately masculine." Only 12% of engineering students were, in fact, women. Male-female differences, the report contended, were rooted in childhood and could not easily be eradicated in school.

The World Bank report for 1984 underlined the poor progress of women's education in the less developed countries. It estimated that two-thirds of the world's illiterates were women. Illiteracy continued to be an intractable problem in many third world countries. The Nigerian government announced a "war against illiteracy," and Nicaragua reported spectacular progress following a four-year nationwide literacy improvement campaign. There remained, however, the familiar difficulty of maintaining literacy at a functional level.

There was evidence in more sophisticated countries of a swing in emphasis toward parental participation in schooling. Even in relatively conservative Austria, the Ministry of Education announced that every school should have a parents' association and declared its intention to amend the School Education Act to give parents specific rights. The U.K. minister of education, Sir Keith Joseph, announced plans to make parents a majority on school governing bodies. This was not well received by the local authorities and teachers' unions, and even the parents' associations appeared dubious.

Corporal punishment emerged as an issue in those EC countries that had not abolished it following the finding of the European Court that parents should have the right

Sherleen Sisney, of Louisville, Ky., received a golden apple—after being chosen as 1984 National Teacher of the Year—from Pres. Ronald Reagan during the awards program at the White House on April 9. The event is sponsored by the Encyclopædia Britannica Companies, *Good Housekeeping* magazine, and the Council of Chief State School Officers.

Sixty seconds of controversial silence: Prayer? Meditation? Alabama says it is legal in public schools. Whatever it is, these third-grade students in a New Jersey school are practicing it.

JAMES POZARIK/TIME MAGAZINE

to prevent corporal punishment from being administered to their children. In Ireland the cane had been banned abruptly in February 1982, but a survey in Dublin by the Irish National Teachers' Organisation showed that 49% of teachers thought discipline had suffered as a result. In England a sizable number of local authorities did not ban the cane on the grounds that the matter should be left to the schools' discretion. It was expected that a number of court battles would result.

Primary and Secondary Education. Confrontations between church and state had not been a major feature of educational politics for several years, but they reemerged in several countries in 1984—most notably in France, where opposition from the Roman Catholic Church led to the scrapping of an education bill affecting church schools, and the education minister was forced to resign. Over a million people marched on the Place de la Bastille in June to protest against the bill. The government had proposed the establishment of a single, nonreligious state educational system. This would have meant giving civil servant status to staff in private (*i.e.*, church) schools and the appointment of watchdog bodies to oversee the schools. Neither measure survived church and parental opposition. Nonetheless, it was decided that private schools would be subject to the same budgetary limitations as those in the state sector and would no longer be able to take on new staff when they wished. Moreover, head teachers would no longer be allowed a free hand in the choice of staff but would have to consult local education authorities.

In Italy there were signs of dissent between church and state over financial support for church schools, though the issue was not as important there as in France. The Italian constitution appeared to be ambiguous on the subject. The Roman Catholic orders in Italy ran some 25% of the *scuole matrone* (for very young children) and 5% of the elementary, middle, and secondary schools. A serious dispute broke out between the Maltese government and the Roman Catholic Church over the church's 72 schools, serving about one-third of the school population, when the government indicated that the church should not charge fees. (*See* WORLD AFFAIRS [Western Europe]: *Malta.*) In

Australia, much to the annoyance of the Australian Teachers' Federation, the government decided to increase the subsidy to private schools. This went counter to the Labor Party's campaign promises, but it was well received by the Roman Catholic authorities and was seen as a prudent political expedient.

The relationship between religion and the schools received considerable attention in the U.S., where interpretation of the constitutionally mandated "wall of separation" between church and state became an issue in the presidential campaign. Pres. Ronald Reagan advocated a constitutional amendment that would permit organized prayer in the public schools, although even religious leaders were divided on the subject. Meanwhile, the constitutionality of an Alabama law allowing a period of silent prayer or meditation in public school classes awaited determination by the Supreme Court. Also in the Supreme Court was a Grand Rapids, Mich., plan to send enrichment and remedial teachers into parochial schools. The Reagan administration failed in its efforts to obtain tuition tax credits for parents of children in private (mainly parochial) schools, but Congress did pass a law permitting religious groups to hold gatherings on school property before and after school hours if other groups were allowed to do so. Closings of Roman Catholic schools in the U.S. stabilized; just 31 closed in 1983, according to a 1984 report. Lay teachers made up three-fourths of the staff teaching the 2,970,000 parochial-school students, a reversal of the ratio in the 1960s.

Concern about standards was evident in a number of countries. In Spain a national survey found that only 30% of six- to seven-year-olds could list the days of the week and only 40% knew how to make simple measurements. Nonetheless, the survey report went on to argue that "standards were too demanding." In Australia a national survey published in August claimed to demonstrate neglect of the educational needs of immigrants and aboriginals. In West Germany the heads of training for the Daimler-Benz automotive firm and Hamburg's Commerzbank complained that skills in writing were deplorably low. Inevitably, the teachers were blamed, together with the recent emphasis on oral work in schools and the excessive use of multiple-choice questions in examinations.

In England and Wales, where curriculum had traditionally been left to the teachers, the national inspectorate began issuing guidelines called *Curriculum Matters,* setting forth the standards that children should achieve at different ages. In January, in a major speech at a conference in Sheffield (it became known as the Sheffield speech), Sir Keith Joseph announced his commitment to "criterion referenced testing" in secondary schools. There would be recognized standards that children would be expected to achieve, and Sir Keith called for 90% of secondary-school children to be brought to the minimum standard or above. (*See* Sidebar.) He later announced that the two national examinations, the General Certificate of Education and the Certificate of Secondary Education, would be merged.

Despite the rash of critical reports on U.S. schools published in 1983, a 1984 Gallup Poll indicated that the confidence of Americans in their schools was the highest in a decade. Of those polled, 42% gave their local schools an "A" or "B" rating, and an increasing number said they would be willing to pay more in school taxes. Public confidence in schools had been eroding steadily since the mid-1970s. Although the poll also showed that Americans had increased confidence in teachers, the movement to require competency tests for prospective teachers gained momentum. Fourteen states now required such tests. Less was heard about competency testing of students, however, as scores on the Scholastic Aptitude Test (used as a basis for college entrance) appeared to have stabilized after several years of decline. Some improvement was also apparent in achievement test scores of elementary-school pupils. Beginning in 1985, the National Assessment of Educational Progress planned to test some 90,000 elementary and secondary students in computer literacy. About 95% of U.S. schools now had computers, and some 2,000 robots were in use in the nation's high schools.

As U.S. schools opened in the fall of 1984, costs increased despite some small declines in enrollment at the elementary and college levels. (The number of high school students rose slightly.) The total cost of U.S. education was $240 billion, with public elementary and secondary schools accounting for $134.5 billion, public collegiate institutions for $63 billion, private kindergarten-through-12th-grade schools for $10 billion, and private colleges and universities for $32.5 billion. Of this, 40% came from state governments, 24% from local governments, 8% from the federal government, and the rest from a variety of sources, including tuition, fees, endowments, and gifts. One-fourth of all Americans were involved in schooling as either students or staff. At the start of the 1984–85 academic year, the number of teachers in the U.S. totaled 3.1 million and the number of administrators and instructional staff, 300,-000. An estimated 255,000 students and 15,000 teachers were involved in teachers' strikes, representing a decline from the previous year.

On the 30th anniversary of the U.S. Supreme Court's decision in *Brown* v. *Board of Education of Topeka,* which outlawed racial segregation in the public schools, one-third of black and Hispanic students were in schools where a majority of the students belonged to minority groups;

in 1968 the proportion had been two-thirds. About 400 school districts were operating under court-ordered desegregation plans, and 4% were under court-ordered busing plans. Holding to its position that busing is not a desirable remedy for segregation, the Reagan administration continued to support magnet schools, where special programs were designed to attract children of all races, as an alternative. The administration also took the position that courts should not continue to supervise schools once desegregation had been effected; even if resegregation occurred, the courts should not intervene unless the Constitution was violated.

The greatest single change in primary schooling in Europe took place in the Soviet Union, where, from September 1, all six-year-olds were entitled to attend school. Formerly, the age for starting school had been seven. It was expected that the effect on enrollment would be gradual, with an extra 1.2 million children in 1984, rising to 4 million within a few years. In accordance with an election pledge, the new Labour government in New Zealand was committed to smaller classes in the first three years of primary school. Even though the number of five- to eight-year-olds was falling, an additional 2,500 teachers would be needed. In the U.S. the Bureau of Labor Statistics warned that 500,000 more kindergarten and elementary-school teachers would be needed by 1995 and that shortages would also exist in such fields as math, science, vocational education, and remedial education. The current upturn in the birthrate would mean more pupils, and fewer students were being attracted to the teaching profession.

The old complaint that secondary education was not sufficiently oriented to work in the real world continued to be heard in a number of countries, in both East and West. In China, for example, it was announced that half of the

English for Seven-Year-Olds

In 1984 England's Department of Education and Science began for the first time to specify the standards that schools might reasonably be expected to achieve in the various subjects of the curriculum. The first set of criteria, published in September, applied to "English from five to 16." The booklet said that at the age of seven, for example, most children should be able to:

Listening. Listen to simple instructions and carry them out accurately; comprehend the main ideas in simple items of information or explanation given orally; listen actively, so as to be able to ask questions, make comments, and respond in other relevant ways to what they have heard; maintain their listening attention for a reasonable length of time when their interest is engaged; follow an uncomplicated plot in a story and recall the main events; listen responsively to the language and the patterns of sound and rhythm of rhymes and poems.

Speaking. In all oral activities, speak sufficiently clearly and audibly to be understood; narrate simple experiences and series of events; explain what they are doing when involved in a task; when taking part in a group task, discuss it constructively with the other children; express their feelings to known adults and to other children; ask relevant questions; describe what they have observed; converse confidently in social situations; speak in role in dramatic play; use gesture

and movement in association with the voice when effective communication demands it.

Reading. Read and understand labels, simple notices, and written instructions; read with understanding simple stories, rhymes, and passages of information, to themselves and aloud; know the alphabet, and apply their knowledge of alphabetical order when consulting simple dictionaries and other reference books; have sufficient fluency and motivation to become engrossed in books because of the interest and enjoyment they derive from them; use books as sources of information to support aspects of their work in the classroom.

Writing. Write legibly; write about personal experiences in prose and in poetry; associate their writing with pictures, graphs, plans, and diagrams; record simple investigations and other practical experiences accurately, and comment on the results; write simple stories of reasonable coherence; write informal letters to relatives and friends; set down directions and instructions when there is a clear purpose for doing so; write descriptions in which the salient features are conveyed clearly; use a sufficiently wide vocabulary for the purposes of their writing; use a sufficient variety of sentence structures to express not only sequence (" ... and ... then," etc.) but other relationships between events, experiences, and ideas (" ... when ... because ... if," etc.); use full stops and capital letters appropriately.

Over one million French citizens marched on the Place de la Bastille in June to protest against the government's plan to establish a single, nonreligious state educational system.

W. KAREL—SYGMA

senior secondary schools (ages 15–18) were to be converted to vocational schools. This caused some resentment, since the Chinese have traditionally held a literary education in the highest esteem. There was also a serious shortage of vocational teachers, and it was announced that several training colleges for technical teachers were being opened. The U.S. Congress passed a five-year vocational-education bill aimed at modernizing the country's vocational-education programs, which in many cases were still teaching outdated skills, and increasing coordination with private industry. The appointment of Jean-Pierre Chevènement to succeed Alain Savary as France's minister of education marked a shift in policy toward gearing education to industry and turning out more technicians and engineers. Savary's priority had been to create a more democratic educational system.

An important research report on early education, *Young Children Learning: Talking and Thinking at Home and at School* by Barbara Tizard and Martin Hughes, appeared in England in September. It strongly challenged a number of time-honoured assumptions made by nursery- and primary-school teachers. The authors argued that there had been a professional takeover of education for children under five, although the home was, in fact, a more important learning environment than the school. All children, whether middle or working class, were learning far more at home than in nursery schools. Even more surprising was the claim that working-class children do not underachieve at school because of any language deficit at home; their poor command of language at school is more likely to be the fault of their teachers. The authors refuted Jean Piaget, the Swiss psychologist who had claimed that children of four are not capable of thinking logically or seeing the world from any viewpoint other than their own. Observations of children's talk at home and school showed them

to be powerful and determined thinkers. The Piagetian theory had led schools and play groups to underestimate children's interests and abilities.

Probably the most significant report on secondary schooling was produced by David Hargreaves and a supporting committee for the Inner London Education Authority. Entitled *Improving Secondary Schools,* it was a careful and practical inquiry into what London schools were achieving and how much underachievers could be helped. Hargreaves stressed the need to bring in truants and insist on homework since, in effect, failure to do homework consistently over a five-year period deprived a child of a whole year of schooling. The committee saw no reason to doubt the alarming conclusions of a Leicester University research study, which showed that one-third of primary-school graduates did worse on tests at the end of their first year of secondary school than they had at the end of primary school.

While many school systems attempted to cope with large and underachieving ethnic groups, Turkey faced almost the opposite problem—reassimilating the children of returning *Gästarbeiter* ("guest workers") who had grown up in West Germany. Summer schools were set up for this purpose, but they seemed to be having limited success. A controversial proposal advanced in Turkey was to extend the teaching of Arabic, chiefly because links with Arab countries were increasing. It was resisted by many teachers who feared that, in the secular Turkish state, many teachers of Arabic would use the Qur'an as a medium of instruction.

Higher Education. In South Africa widespread unrest spilled over into the universities. (*See* WORLD AFFAIRS [Africa South of the Sahara]: *South Africa.*) The entire student body at the University of Transkei was expelled in September for refusing to end a lecture boycott, and the University of the Western Cape and the University of the North (Lebowa) were also affected. Farther north, in Zimbabwe, Prime Minister Robert Mugabe was host to talks on higher education involving 11 countries of eastern and southern Africa. The participants explored a number of topics, including the exchange of academics. The talks led to formation of the Association of Eastern and Southern African Universities. The so-called Harare Declaration establishing the association was signed by universities in Botswana, Ethiopia, Uganda, Lesotho, Somalia, Swaziland, Tanzania, Malawi, Mauritius, Kenya, Zambia, Mozambique, and Zimbabwe. Sudan was also a member, and Madagascar, Comoros, Seychelles, and South West Africa/Namibia were eligible for membership once they acquired universities.

Australia was one of the few countries to increase funding for higher education, the first such increase in seven years. Sen. Susan Ryan, the minister of education and youth affairs, announced a plan to fund 50,000 new higher education places by 1990, though it appeared that only 4,000 of these would exist by 1987. There would also be 1,600 new jobs for academics—about half the number urged by the Commonwealth Tertiary Education Commission. In China the need for highly qualified manpower led to the spread of evening and spare-time schools. Some 140 evening universities were reported with approximately 150,000 students, most of whom undertook to study 12 hours a week. Uneasy compromise was the order of the day in Poland. The independent trade union Solidarity, now driven underground, claimed in August that the university reforms it had won had been largely whittled away since 1981. Martial law had reduced the effect of reforms, and

(continued on page 230)

Theatre in Education

BY IOLA LLOYD SMITH

Theatre in Education (TIE) is the culmination of theatre's long history as a learning medium. Since its creation in Coventry, England, in 1965, actors have visited schools to perform educational plays with the children. This method works, for children prefer to learn by doing rather than by hearsay. Today, professional TIE companies are working throughout Britain. They receive financial support from the Arts Council and from local education authorities and offer a free service to the schools.

Making History Live. The secret of TIE's success is very simple. It uses the power and magic of theatre to make learning fun. When presented as a play, history is not just a list of boring facts—it is real people living in credible situations. By participating with the actors, children gain firsthand experience of how people used to live. For example, a Cardiff company taught local history by TIE to junior school students, aged seven to nine. The Industrial Revolution was made meaningful to these children, for they were able to observe and join in with the actors and so experience the problems faced by 19th-century workers. The production gave a total picture of events, depicting how geography, economics, and social history are interrelated. Such topics tend to be isolated from one another in the curriculum, but TIE encourages children to examine issues from the widest possible viewpoint.

TIE performances always require audience participation. This takes the form of physical movement in productions for small children, while adolescents' plays demand a deeper intellectual and emotional involvement. For this reason, many plays for the 16-plus age group portray topical social issues, thereby helping to prepare young people for their adult roles in the community. Gwent Theatre's *Inner City Limits* was a mature investigation of street violence and social unrest. Set in Toxteth, Liverpool, during the riots of 1981, it illustrated the futility of violence. The lead role was a disillusioned youngster, a teenage victim of the social ills of unemployment, poor housing, and urban decay. Yielding to peer-group pressure, he had originally joined the rioters, but eventually he came to realize that "Violence is not the answer. It's an agent of destruction, not of change."

Such plays complement the teacher's work because they help young people understand the world they live in. Another performance of this type is *Example,* a portrait of Derek Bentley's unjust execution in 1953 for a crime he never committed. This production, like most TIE plays, was accompanied by a teacher's workpack, or kit. Nottingham Playhouse's workpack was created for use in English and drama lessons, and it looked outward from the Bentley case to investigate related issues such as

Iola Lloyd Smith is a freelance journalist and former press officer for BBC Wales. Her articles have appeared in a number of publications, including The Sunday Times, *the* Financial Times, *and* The Guardian.

the ethics of capital punishment. Follow-up work is an integral part of TIE, and teachers are expected to continue the project when the actors have left. The ensuing work ranges from class discussion groups to art, drama, and creative writing. To encourage even greater creativity, some companies have organized playwriting competitions for young people.

A Wide Appeal. Actors participating in TIE have to be very flexible. They must devise productions for all age and ability groups, so their work extends from in-depth analysis of social problems with 18-year-olds to teaching math to the very young. Theatre can make numbers entertaining, as Welsh infants discovered when *Snap, Crackle, and Pop* came to school. The actors played measuring games with the children, introduced them to the shapes of various objects, and taught capacity by pouring orange juice into various sized tumblers.

The mentally handicapped also benefit from TIE. Working with actors increases their confidence and social skills. In *The Lost Aquanaut*, children went in search of an explorer believed trapped beneath the sea. To compensate for the children's short concentration spans, the actors devised a fast-moving plot involving communication with "undersea creatures" to encourage speech development and crossing an obstacle course to stimulate coordination. As follow-up to the play, a group of mentally handicapped children composed "sea music" on the school's percussion instruments.

Language development is also encouraged in mainstream schools. TIE is a successful method of teaching both foreign languages to English-speaking children and English as a second language to ethnic minorities. Leeds Playhouse's *Friends and Neighbours* introduced English culture to young Asians by illustrating some of the housing and neighbourhood problems faced by multicultural inner-city communities.

GWENT THEATRE

Students watch, engrossed, as the Gwent Theatre presents its educational, dramatic investigation of street violence and social unrest, *Inner City Limits.* The message is clear: violence is not the answer.

Reaching Tomorrow's Adults. Essentially, TIE is a means of talking to children on a level they can understand about some of the problems they will face as the adults of tomorrow. Pollution is an obvious issue, so Coventry's Belgrade Theatre devised *Drink the Mercury* to expose the dangers of discharging industrial waste into the sea. In the play, the mercury discharge contaminated the fish and subsequently poisoned the villagers. Although the play was set in Japan, the children realized that the threat of such an industrial disaster is equally applicable to Britain. Health education is another area in which some companies work. Thus Chameleon Theatre of Southampton presented a biology-based play that pinpointed the dangers of alcoholism, and the South Glamorgan Health Authority supported a junior school project that stressed the importance of dental hygiene.

In secondary schools emphasis is placed on careers teaching. This topic is well suited to TIE—actors can introduce young people to the situations they will encounter in the world of work. This was the objective of Torch Theatre's *Factory*. Unlike most TIE productions, *Factory* was staged in a theatre. Accuracy demanded that the entire building be converted into an assembly line. Job descriptions and account sheets were provided for the teenagers, who were divided into worker and management groups. Labour-management relations were experienced firsthand; the workers objected to producing a cardboard cutout doll in the basement while management held committee meetings in the comparative luxury of the director's office. But the teenage managers realized that it was not all sweetness and light at the top—the factory was almost bankrupt. Conflict with the workers was inevitable, and the solution was left entirely to the youngsters. Some were anxious to negotiate, but others refused. This play was deliberately open-ended.

Social Communication. TIE encourages pupils to develop a social conscience. Theatre is a medium of social communication and is therefore the perfect vehicle for this kind of learning. Social learning and environmental education were combined in the Torch Theatre junior play *Never Laugh at Live Dragons*, staged to celebrate the International Year of the Child (1979). The topic was chosen because "Dragons represent the fears, hopes, and expectations of people all over the world." The production was devised by children. The company corresponded with schools worldwide requesting contributions, and they received an overwhelming response. Paintings, stories, and even a model of a dragon's head were submitted and exhibited during the production run. The actors fashioned the material into a script that included mythical dragons, the legend of St. George, and Chinese dragon rain charms. On a literal level, the play was an entertaining story colourfully presented, but figuratively it said much more: dragons don't live only in fairy tales; hunger, war, neglect, and disease still exist. In a play such as this, TIE tells universal truths.

The dramatist Bertolt Brecht believed that "audiences should be made to think." TIE certainly lives up to that maxim. It encourages young people to develop a critical, questioning outlook. But it delves deeper, for as well as emphasizing the academic learning commonly found in formal curricula, TIE develops emotional and sensory learning. The educational theme and the power of theatre work together to create a memorable, dynamic experience. As Cardiff's TIE company observes, "To live successfully in the modern world individuals require a range of skills far beyond the '3 Rs.' We're all thinking and feeling beings needing an education that caters for both."

(continued from page 228)

three university rectors had had their elections overruled. The "bonus points" system was also the subject of much contention. Under this system, students with a worker or peasant background were given bonus marks toward examination results. Evidently, some Communist Party meetings had condemned the practice on the grounds that there was only one society in a socialist state.

In Europe the story was one of rising demand for higher education and cutbacks in the institutions set up to provide it, resulting in intractable problems of reconciling quantity and quality. Italy provided an example. Since 1968, when admission to Italy's universities was liberalized, the upper-secondary-school diploma had given access to any university faculty. As a result, the student population had doubled over 15 years, from 550,000 to 1.1 million—all without any real change in the structure of the institutions. A number of institutions, however, had followed the example of Milan's Luigi Bocconi Commercial University, which used a system of programmed admission. In West Germany 1,270,000 students were registered in universities in 1983–84, 38% of whom were women and 5.5% of whom came from overseas. This enrollment was about 6% higher than in the previous year, although probably only a quarter of the registered students were attending classes full-time. However, the proportion of school-leavers qualified for university entrance continued to increase, to just under 30%.

Moves to reduce the length of the courses in West German universities were not conspicuously successful. In Denmark, however, a firm decision was made to cut the M.A. degree course from six years to five. To qualify teachers for posts in upper secondary schools, the Danes introduced a two-year course followed by three years of advanced instruction. In The Netherlands the Dutch Open University (modeled on the British example) attracted 14,000 potential students aged from 26 to 40, 10,000 more than had been anticipated.

Two U.S. Supreme Court decisions in 1984 affected institutions of higher education. In a case involving Grove City (Pa.) College, the court held that the federal law prohibiting sex discrimination in schools and colleges receiving federal money applies only to the program or department where discrimination has been found, not to the entire institution. In adopting a narrow reading of Title IX of the Education Amendments of 1972, the court upheld the position taken by the administration. Grove City had not been accused of sex discrimination, but it had refused to file an "assurance of compliance" on the grounds that federal aid to its students did not make it a recipient under the law. The court did rule that such indirect aid was sufficient to set the law in motion. The court also ruled that young men who receive federal financial assistance must offer proof of draft registration. Some colleges had objected to being placed in the position of helping to enforce federal law.

A survey by the American Council on Education found that U.S. college students were focusing more and more on financial rewards as the aim of their education. College graduates in 1984 found increased job opportunities but lower starting pay. Prospects were brightest for graduates in technical fields such as electrical engineering and computer science. Holders of bachelor's degrees in electrical engineering could command salaries averaging around $26,000, while graduates in other fields started as low as $12,000. College tuition in the U.S. rose by an average of 8%. Even with this increase and a decline in the pool of potential college freshmen, many institutions experienced a surge of applications as the economy improved.

Magnet schools, intended to attract students beyond their own neighbourhoods, are advocated by the U.S. government as an alternative to desegregation by forced busing. This magnet school in Venice, California, offers computer courses to its young students.

BEN MARTIN/TIME MAGAZINE

Despite the interest among students in "learning to earn," a report on U.S. schools and colleges issued by the federal Department of Education strongly recommended that all students be required to take more liberal arts courses. Other recommendations in the report, *Involvement in Learning: Realizing the Potential of American Higher Education,* included reducing the number of part-time professors and assigning the best instructors to teach incoming students. Although the report deplored the 50% dropout rate for college undergraduates and urged efforts to improve test scores, Secretary of Education Terrel Bell, in introducing it, expressed the opinion that the nation's institutions of higher learning were in better condition than its elementary and secondary schools.

The continuing expansion of post-secondary education provided one of the threads running through discussions at the eighth assembly of the Conference of Rectors, Presidents, and Vice-Chancellors of the European Universities, held in Athens in September. Most university teachers agreed that in the 1990s, with more adults in the student population, universities would need to transform their teaching styles and curricula. The situation was perhaps best articulated by Jean Celeyrette, president of the University of Lille III in France. He identified two groups of students—the 18-year-olds, who saw higher education as a job apprenticeship, and adult students with experience of professional life, for whom the university offered intellectual recuperation. The first group wanted vocational courses and needed a well-structured curriculum; the latter wanted a more general humanistic course.

(JOEL L. BURDIN; TUDOR DAVID)

See also Libraries; Motion Pictures.

This article updates the *Macropædia* articles History of EDUCATION; TEACHING.

Energy

In 1984, for the second year in a row, the behaviour of the international oil markets favoured consumers. Although the demand for oil products in the United States increased as the result of the nation's strong economic recovery from the recession, economic growth elsewhere in the world continued to be feeble. Consequently, oil prices tended to remain weak throughout the year.

This weakness persisted despite events in the Persian Gulf. Other than the Iranian seizure of an Iraqi oil field on the border between the two combatants, the general stalemate in their war continued. In January, however, Iraq threatened to attack any vessel attempting to take on a cargo of oil at Kharg Island, Iran's main oil port. That threat was carried out, and attacks continued throughout the year. By the year's end dozens of ships had been targets and several had been sunk. Iran responded with a few ineffectual attacks on tankers calling at Arabian ports and with threats of its own to close the Strait of Hormuz, at the entrance to the Persian Gulf, to all shipping.

As the attacks continued into the summer, there was some nervousness in oil markets but no panic. The excess of production over consumption earlier in the year had resulted in the accumulation of large stocks of crude oil and oil products throughout the world. The market was dealt a heavy shock in July, however, when Saudi Arabia purchased ten Boeing 747 airplanes and paid for them with 46 million bbl of oil. The release of so much oil on an already weak market brought the market close to collapse, a situation that was barely averted through production restraint by members of the Organization of Petroleum Exporting Countries (OPEC) and cooperation in maintaining prices from non-OPEC producers such as the United Kingdom.

A second crisis hit the international oil market in late October. Saudi Arabia increased the ratio of heavy crude oil to light crude oil in the "mix" of oil its purchasers were required to take. The effect of this was to reduce the price of Saudi oil. Norway followed by reducing the price of its North Sea oil. Because this Norwegian oil is virtually the same as that produced in the British sector of the North Sea, the United Kingdom promptly followed suit and reduced the price of its oil by $1.35 per barrel. The chain reaction continued with a $2 reduction by Nigeria, whose crude petroleum competed with North Sea oil.

The prospect of a price war and market collapse prompted an emergency meeting of OPEC. At the meeting the members decided to hold the line on OPEC posted prices by reducing total OPEC production quotas by 1.5 million bbl a day, to 16 million bbl. In December OPEC agreed to restructure its pricing mechanism in light of the growing demand for heavier crude oils, with the adjustments to be reviewed before the end of January 1985, but Algeria and Nigeria declined to endorse the accord. Nigeria also threatened to break ranks over an arrangement for auditing members' prices and production.

During the first half of the year the oil industry in the United States experienced a convulsion of acquisitions by the major companies. In rapid succession, Texaco Inc.

acquired Getty Oil Co., Standard Oil Co. of California (renamed Chevron) acquired Gulf Oil Co., and Mobil Corp. acquired Superior Oil Co. These acquisitions were among the largest in history. (Marathon Oil, previously acquired by U.S. Steel Corp., bought up the United States subsidiary of Canada's Husky Oil, Ltd., in a smaller but still substantial transaction.)

The most disappointing dry hole of all time was recorded during the year. In January it was confirmed that a well drilled on the Mukluk Prospect in the Beaufort Sea, 105 km (65 mi) northwest of the giant Prudhoe Bay oil field on the Alaskan coast, had found nothing. The companies involved in the exploration had been so confident of another giant discovery that they had spent $140 million in constructing an artificial island and in drilling the well. Results in the Canadian portion of the Beaufort Sea were more encouraging. A discovery off the Mackenzie River delta, 75 km (47 mi) north of Tuktoyaktuk, N.W.T., gave promise of the first commercial field offshore in the Canadian Arctic. The Persian Gulf region continued to add to its already huge reserves. Two discoveries in Kuwait boosted that country's reserves by an amount equal to the total reserves of the U.S. Colombia also boasted discovery of a giant oil field in the Llanos basin in the northeastern part of that country.

Among other events concerning oil, the Canadian Supreme Court upheld the federal government's ownership of the giant Hibernian oil field located in the North Atlantic some 240 km (150 mi) east of St. John's, Newfoundland. The decision, which resolved a dispute between Newfoundland and the Canadian federal government, cleared the way for development of the field, which had been discovered in 1980. The change in Canada's government as a result of the September national election further increased the likelihood of prompt development. In Australia the decision by the federal government in September to allow crude oil exports brought that country into the ranks of oil-exporting nations. The oil was to come from the Fortescue field in the Bass Strait, between the state of Victoria and Tasmania.

With respect to natural gas, the U.S. Federal Energy Regulatory Commission decided, in a landmark ruling issued in July, that "take-or-pay" provisions in natural gas purchase contracts were unenforceable. Under such provisions gas pipelines were required to pay producers for gas even if they could not take the gas because there was no demand for it. At almost the same time, the Canadian government relaxed its price controls on natural gas exports. The previous minimum price of $4.04 per thousand cubic feet was reduced to $3.10. The move was welcomed by Canadian producers, who had been unable to match domestic U.S. prices and were consequently exporting less than half the quantity permitted by their government.

This action by Canada put pressure on Mexico to follow suit in pricing its gas exports to the United States. In October, after the level of exports had fallen to the minimum contract quantity, only 60% of that authorized, the Mexican government decided to suspend the exports rather than reduce prices.

A project to produce methane (natural gas) by drilling wells into coal seams began commercial production in September. The gas was produced from seams 790 m (2,600 ft) below the surface in the Black Warrior Basin, northeast of Tuscaloosa, Ala. Methane occurs in almost all coal and because of its explosive quality constitutes a serious danger in underground coal mining. Wells are frequently drilled to drain off the gas in order to lessen the danger of explosion, but this was the first to exploit the methane in coal for commercial purposes without any associated coal mining.

On New Year's Day 1984 France began receiving natural gas via pipeline from the Soviet Union. The Soviet government implied that the gas was coming from fields in western Siberia via a 4,500-km (2,800-mi) pipeline, but Western experts doubted that the huge pipeline project could have been completed in the less than two years since it was begun. In any event, the gas arrived in the midst of a general oversupply situation in western Europe, and future needs for Soviet gas were cast in doubt by additions to reserves in the North Sea. The giant Troll field in the Norwegian sector, discovered in 1980, was declared commercial, with more than 1.5 trillion cu m (55 trillion cu ft) of reserves. The British announced the first significant gas discovery west of the Shetland Islands. Reserves in The Netherlands' Groningen gas field, second largest in the world at the time of its discovery in 1959, were found to be 25% larger than originally estimated.

Natural gas also made the news in the Far East. The first

PAUL CONKLIN

These windmills are some of the thousands that have been constructed in California's Altamont Pass by companies involved in the commercial exploitation of wind-generated electric power. The location, in the hills east of San Francisco, is unsuitable for homes because of its strong and frequent winds.

This nuclear power station at Lingen, West Germany, is one of 11 under construction in that country. Here steel containers for the plant's 1,300-megawatt pressurized water reactor are being erected. The plant, begun in 1982, was expected to be operating in 1988.

CAMERA PRESS/PHOTO TRENDS

discovery of either oil or gas as a result of activity in the South China Sea was announced in August. A commercial find was made 100 km (65 mi) southwest of Hainan Island.

The major event in coal was a strike in the United Kingdom. (*See* WORLD AFFAIRS [Western Europe]: *United Kingdom.*) A strike of coal miners in the United States was barely averted. Settlement on a new contract was reached at the end of September, on the day that the old contract expired. This was the first time in 20 years that the expiration of a labour contract in the coal industry was unaccompanied by a strike. Reflecting in part the accumulation of stocks in anticipation of a strike, U.S. coal production during the week before the contract expired set an all-time record of 18.4 million metric tons.

Also in the United States, plans for a pipeline to carry pulverized coal suspended in water from Wyoming to Texas were abandoned when its sponsors failed to obtain congressional legislation granting the right of eminent domain to such pipelines. A contract was signed for the export of 800,000 tons per year of Alaskan coal to be shipped from Seward to South Korea, with deliveries to begin in 1985; this would be the first use of Alaskan coal outside the state. A historic development in U.S. coal imports was recorded with the first importation of coal from Colombia, for use in power plants in Florida.

The Soviet Union announced the discovery of a giant deposit of anthracite in Yakutiya, in eastern Siberia, claimed to be larger than any Siberian deposit previously found. Reserves were estimated at more than 3,000,000,-000 metric tons.

The nuclear power industry in the U.S. continued to decline with the cancellation of six nuclear units, totaling 6,780 MW of capacity, that were planned or under construction. Four of the cancellations were by the Tennessee Valley Authority. Another, involving the Zimmer plant in southern Ohio, was accompanied by the unprecedented decision to convert the plant to coal despite the fact that it was 97% complete.

In a national referendum in Switzerland in September, voters defeated (55 to 45%) two strongly antinuclear initiatives. Among other things, the measures would have prohibited the construction of any new nuclear power plant or replacement of an existing plant, the construction of

fuel processing or reprocessing plants, or the construction of any power plant larger than 35 MW. (Nuclear power plants supplied about 30% of total electricity demand in Switzerland in 1984.)

Unruly weather caused problems for electric systems in the U.S. and the U.K. In March a severe storm ravaged the east coast of the U.S. from the Carolinas to New England, knocking out service to more than one million customers. A rare earthquake in the British Isles damaged electrical equipment in Wales, causing blackouts for 5,000 customers.

In Africa Zaire began operation of the world's longest high-voltage, direct-current transmission line, extending for 1,700 km (1,050 mi) between the provinces of Inga and Shaba. Next door, South Africa entered the nuclear age with the inauguration of a nuclear power station at Koeberg, on the Atlantic coast north of Cape Town.

In the field of nonconventional energy, a milestone was reached in July when a plant near Beulah, N.D., began the first commercial production of synthetic "natural" gas from coal. Two months earlier another synthetic gas project had begun operation in the Mojave Desert near Daggett, Calif. The project was designed to test the use of synthetic gas for power generation. The gas fuels a gas turbine, and the heat from the turbine is used to make steam to drive a second turbine.

Also in the Mojave Desert a solar "power tower," after two years of testing, began generating electricity for the local power grid. The plant consists of a 10-MW boiler atop a tower on which the Sun's rays are kept focused by 1,818 computer-directed mirrors. The U.K. also inaugurated a solar power plant, a 30-kw experimental facility with 34,-560 solar cells feeding power into the local grid. In Israel commercial power production began from a 5-MW "solar pond" facility. The plant uses water from the bottom of the Dead Sea and is based on the principle that, in a pond of standing salt water, heat from the Sun's rays is trapped in the saltier, heavier water at the bottom.

A contract was signed between Mexico and southern California electric utilities whereby Mexico would supply 110 MW of power from its geothermal field at Cerro Prieto, 32 km (20 mi) north of Mexicali. The field was the third largest in the world. (BRUCE C. NETSCHERT)

COAL

In 1984—as in other recent years—expert assessment indicated bright long-term prospects for coal, though the immediate outlook was blighted by the weak and uncertain recovery from recession. Analysis by the UN Economic Commission for Europe (ECE) revealed that gross energy consumption in Western Europe and North America continued to decline in 1983, owing to the weakness of the recovery in Europe. With strong U.S. growth in general output during that year (3.4%), the energy decline in the U.S. was slight (−0.4%). The centrally planned economies grew at 3.4% for Eastern Europe and 4% for the U.S.S.R., with energy consumption rising at roughly parallel rates.

A marked difference between the capitalist and socialist economies developed in regard to the substitution of coal for oil. The percentage share of solid fuels in gross energy consumption rose slightly in Western Europe from 23.3% in 1973 to 24.3% in 1982, and in North America from 19.5% in 1973 to 25.4% in 1983. But in Eastern Europe there was a decline from 71% in 1970 to 60.2% in 1982, and in the U.S.S.R. from 44.2% to 31% over the same period.

These various changes corresponded to a small increase of 0.5% over 1982 in world production of hard coal at 2,934,000,000 metric tons in 1983 (all absolute figures given below are in metric tons). China became the world's largest producer with 687,630,000 tons, or 23.4% of the total, followed by the former leading producer, the U.S. (22.5%), and the U.S.S.R. (19%). Poland held its strong position with 191,-092,000 tons (6.5%). Ten countries combined yielded 93.1% of the world's hard coal. In addition to those already named, they were South Africa, India, the U.K. (where a strike severely reduced output in 1984), Australia, West Germany, and Canada. (The share of the various world regions in producing hard coal is shown in the accompanying table.)

Although Latin America had a relatively low output, it grew considerably—by 14.6%—from 1982, the main contributors being Brazil and Chile. Other noteworthy relative increases, although on small absolute figures, took place in the Philippines

(70.3%), Zimbabwe (24.1%), and Tanzania (150%). Australia's output increased 14.8% to 111 million tons, and it was the world's second largest exporter after the U.S. Poland, in second position for many years before its internal political troubles, was third. The largest coal importer continued to be Japan, though on a slightly reduced scale compared with the previous year.

There was an increase of 1.8% in world production of brown coal, which reached 1,081,000,000 tons in 1983. East Germany was again the largest producer, with more than one-quarter of world output, followed by the U.S.S.R. and West Germany.

TRADE. Both the quantity and the proportion of hard coal traded internationally fell, as did both U.S. and ECE exports. Bucking the general trend, however, exports from Australia, Canada, Poland, and the U.S.S.R. rose. Overall there was a further decline in coal prices—that for coking coal dropped by almost one-quarter between the end of 1981 and the end of 1983—and a relatively small increase in stocks. The Chase Manhattan Bank, in its world coal trade forecasts, expected at least some increases in trade in 1984. It estimated that while U.S. exports might decline, those of the other major exporters would increase.

RESEARCH. The International Energy Agency (IEA) Coal Research division published its *Concise Guide to World Coalfields* in 1983. Based on the concept of "accessible coal" in "significant coalfields," it provided a realistic evaluation of future availability of coal supplies. In addition, IEA Coal Research greatly expanded its computerized Coal Data Base, with an allied Coal Research Projects Database. Responding to widespread anxieties about environmental effects, it published work on flue gas desulfurization (FGD). As of 1984 FGD was the only technology capable of routinely reducing sulfur in emissions and readily capable of being fitted to existing installations (retrofitted). The study discussed performance, regeneration, retrofitting, and environmental and legal constraints.

In regard to converting oil-fired boilers to coal, an important obstacle found by IEA Coal Research was the uncertainty of industrialists about government intentions

Share of World Regions in Hard Coal Production
Percentage of global production

Region	1982	1983
Europe (excluding U.S.S.R.)	17.0	16.6
U.S.S.R.	19.0	19.0
North America	25.4	23.7
Latin America	0.7	0.8
Asia	29.4	30.9
Africa	5.1	5.2
Oceania	3.4	3.8
Total	100.0	100.0

Source: UN Economic Commission for Europe, *The Coal Situation in the ECE Region in 1983 and Its Prospects* (August 1984).

concerning natural gas and pricing. Analyses of experiences in Denmark, The Netherlands, the U.K., and the U.S. were published in a report dealing with retrofitting of various types of oil boilers, costs of new technologies such as fluidized bed boilers, and environmental control costs.

Public pressure on authorities and industry to protect the environment continued in all industrial countries, and the European Communities (EC) Council of Ministers adopted a "framework directive" to combat air pollution. The most important pollutants affected were expected to be sulfur compounds and oxides of nitrogen. The U.K. Central Electricity Generating Board (CEGB)—though disputing that coal burning was a main cause of pollution and damage—announced four major projects for research and development to reduce nitrogen oxide and sulfur dioxide emissions from coal-fired power stations.

FORECASTING. At the beginning of 1984 the World Energy Conference (WEC) published reports on world energy prospects that had been prepared for its New Delhi, India, conference during the previous year. An important theme was that the easing of energy supply problems should not lead to complacency about the ease of maintaining adequate supplies in the forthcoming decades: "The present climate of ease must not delay the implementation of policies in the fields of the rational use of resources and oil substitution." The WEC accepted UN projections of total world population reaching 6,000,000,000 by 2000 and 7,700,000,000 by 2020. As possible types of world development it considered two scenarios suggested by the Organization

PHIL MATT/THE NEW YORK TIMES

Modern coal-burning power plants require modern control centres. This one governs a new plant in Somerset, New York, which burns 5,000 tons of coal per day to generate electric power. The plant was completed ahead of schedule and under budget.

for Economic Cooperation and Development with the indicative titles of "normative-cooperative" and "increasing world tensions." Under the former, world gross national product (GNP) would grow at an annual rate of 3.6% by 2000, then at 2.9% by 2020; the latter would put GNP growth at 2.6% by 2000 and 2% by 2020.

Population, economic, and energy demand growth rates were all scaled down compared with earlier estimates. Yet even the new lower figures would call for adjustments by consumers accustomed to the convenience of oil fuels if they were to switch to coal. For the world tensions scenario, coal consumption was multiplied 2.5 times between 1978 and 2020 from 1.78 to 4.4 GTOE (gigaton oil equivalent; 1 GTOE = 44 x 10^{18} joules = 1.5 gigatons of solid mineral fuels). Oil consumption was little altered, but simultaneous large increases were postulated in gas, hydroelectric, nuclear, "new energies," wood, and waste consumption.

As of 1984 oil accounted for 39% of world demand and its reserves for 13% of proven nonrenewable resources; coal provided only 25% of current demand but accounted for 70% of proven reserves. WEC estimated that by 2020 there would be 460 GTOE of proven reserves of coal, while 120 to 140 GTOE would have been extracted; however, oil and gas might be exhausted and nuclear sources precarious without the use of fast breeder reactors. The WEC urged greater efficiency in using energy, large increases in production and transport capacity, notably for coal, and greater attention to the needs of the third world.

(ISRAEL BERKOVITCH)

ELECTRICITY

As the most flexible and universally usable source of energy, electricity was the focus of a significant part of the activity that goes under the general heading of conservation. The developed countries, which had operated on the basis that providence, under whatever name it was worshiped, would always provide, learned otherwise from the oil providers, and by 1984 many nations had "use of energy" programs; a notable example was France with its Agence Française pour la Maîtrise de l'Énergie. There was also a strong incentive for collaboration between countries, and in 1984 the U.K. and the U.S. signed an agreement to share knowledge gained.

Although conservation in the most general sense could not be · considered as anything but advantageous, it had to be considered critically; obviously any saving in the cost of generation had to be greater than the cost of installing and maintaining the conservation system. In 1984 this concern was being given considerable thought by academic economists.

An aspect of conservation in its general meaning of preserving the environment was the phenomenon of "acid rain," caused by the production of gases such as sulfur dioxide and nitrogen oxides that form acids and fall in rain, killing fishes in lakes as well as destroying vegetation. Acid-making gases had been produced naturally for thousands of years, but it was the localized predominance of man-made gases, largely but not entirely in the effluent from thermal power stations, that in recent years had aroused protests. In

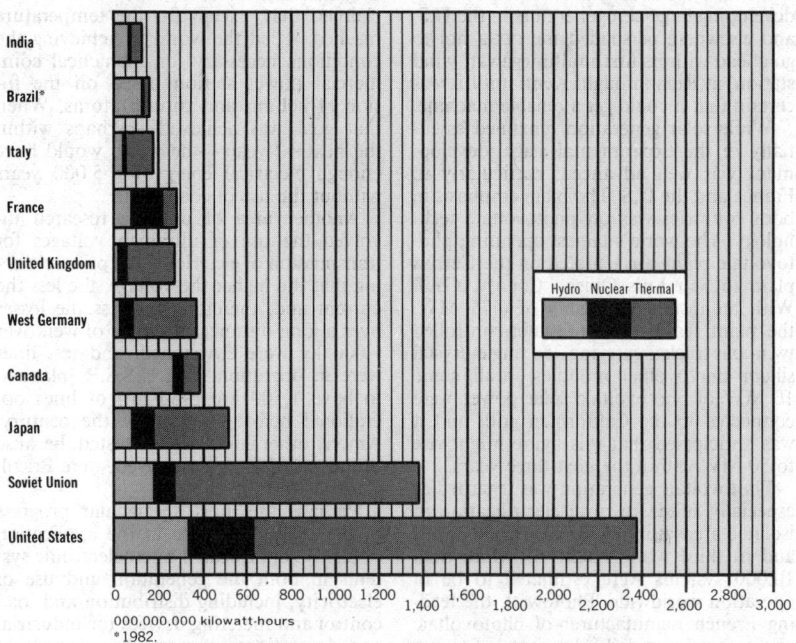

Electrical Power Production of Selected Countries, 1983
By source

Hydro Nuclear Thermal

000,000,000 kilowatt-hours
* 1982.

Sources: U.S. Department of Energy, 1983 *International Energy Annual;*
United Nations, *Monthly Bulletin of Statistics.*

West Germany about 20% of the country's coal-fired power stations were being shut down, while the remaining 80% were being fitted with apparatus to remove sulfur compounds from the effluent. In the U.K. the approach was more cautious, and research into the complex chemistry and biology of inland waters and forests was still in progress. (*See* ENVIRONMENT.)

Leaving aside such politically controversial environmental considerations, the fact remained that coal was still on the whole the preferred fuel for the generation of electricity. The U.S., for example, had been called the Persian Gulf of coal because of its huge reserves, enough to last for 300 years. The U.K. had enormous reserves as well. In countries with suitable topography, water power was an important means of electricity generation; such nations included Austria, Norway, Sweden, Canada, and Brazil. The U.S.S.R. also had considerable water power harnessed for electricity. In all countries not so blessed, however, uranium, used to generate nuclear energy, was second to coal. In this type of electricity generation, France was in the lead in 1984, with some 55% of electricity generated coming from the nuclear network of the state utility, Électricité de France; in 1984 the utility comprised 38 operational plants with a total capacity of 30,600 MW. In the U.K. nuclear generation accounted for some 16% of total production, and in the U.S., despite recent setbacks suffered by the nuclear power industry, it accounted for more than 13%.

In January six member countries of the European Communities—Belgium, France, Italy, The Netherlands, the U.K., and West Germany—signed an agreement to cooperate in the development of a plutonium-fueled fast breeder reactor for

commercial power generation. France and the U.K. were the two countries with the most advanced research programs in this field, and in February Électricité de France and the CEGB signed a separate cooperation agreement. The French utility was planning to increase its already considerable exports of electricity (13,000,000,000 kw-hr in 1983), with a 1990 target of 20,-000,000,000 kw-hr. In addition, France's two-way cross-Channel link with Britain, allowing the flow of current to be reversed to meet peak loads in either country, was being constructed during 1984.

The use of renewable—and free—sources of energy for generating electricity was still being extensively researched. The Sun and the wind were the most promising of such energy sources; tides and waves were not now front-runners despite the great amount of research on such projects as the proposed Severn barrage in the U.K. However, British research in this field would be the basis for the world's first wave-power generating plant; this was to be built by the Norwegian Department of Energy, in cooperation with private industry, off Norway's west coast near Bergen and was scheduled for completion by the end of 1985.

In the U.S. a considerable number of "wind farms" were working successfully, notably at the Altamont Pass in California, where more than 2,000 microprocessor-controlled windmills had been erected in the past two years and an additional 550 were to be installed in 1984–85. In 1983 wind power provided 31 million kw-hr of electricity to the Pacific Gas & Electric utility, enough for the needs of about 5,000 homes and representing a saving of nearly 52,000 bbl of oil.

In the U.K. a Department of Energy research program on wind power was assessing British-built wind turbines. As part of the program à three-megawatt-capacity aerogenerator was approved for erection in the Orkney Islands. However, troubles in developing large aerogenerators in the U.S. and elsewhere persuaded the CEGB not to go ahead with its first multimegawatt wind station, at Richborough, Kent, until it was certain that it could get a reliable machine.

While solar generation remained essentially in the experimental stage, development was well advanced, particularly in France and the U.S. The main emphasis in both countries was on photovoltaic technology. The world's largest operating photovoltaic plant was situated on the Carrisa plain in San Luis Obispo County, Calif. With an installed capacity of 6.75 MW, the plant featured a computer-controlled twin-axis tracker carrying 256 single-crystal silicon photovoltaic modules. In all, some 10 MW of photovoltaic solar power were connected to the Californian grid, and it was anticipated that this figure might rise to 50 MW within the next three years.

Photovoltaic generation was regarded as especially suited to rural electrification in isolated areas not linked to electricity grids and in third world countries. More than 10,000 systems were estimated to be in operation worldwide. Photowatt, the leading French manufacturer of photovoltaic equipment, provided solar-powered television sets to African countries as well as supply systems for small villages. In Saudi Arabia a U.S. system was supplying a rural community of 7,000 inhabitants with power for lighting, television, water pumping, and irrigation. From 1975 to 1983 solar electricity costs fell from about $30 a watt to about $6–$7 a watt. The development of less expensive polycrystalline silicon was expected to reduce the cost still further, perhaps to $4 a watt by 1986 and $2.50 a watt by 1990.

There was further progress during the year in research that might well lead in the future to important developments in the generation and application of electrical energy. The huge Joint European Torus experiment on nuclear fusion at Culham, England, began operations, and it was claimed that, except for the temperature reached, it led the world in achieving the conditions necessary for a practical commercial power station based on the fusion of helium and tritium atoms. When that goal was achieved—perhaps within the next 40 years—the world would have enough electrical energy for 5,000 years without the use of coal or oil.

Another area of ongoing research involved the use of ultrahigh voltages for transmission of electricity, the principle being that the higher the voltage, the less the current and, therefore, the less the losses over a long distance. Voltages of well over 1,000 kv were envisioned, and test lines were in operation. The U.S.S.R. planned to have 1,500 km (930 mi) of lines operational before the end of the century. Among other countries interested, because of the vast distances involved, were Brazil, Canada, and the U.S.

Perhaps the most spectacular progress of the year took place in the application of highly sophisticated microelectronic systems in both the generation and use of electricity, including distribution and load control and metering devices for industrial and domestic consumers. An example of the latter was the Credit and Load Management Unit (Calmu) undergoing trials in some areas of the U.K.   (C. L. BOLTZ)

NATURAL GAS

World proven reserves of natural gas rose to an estimated 90,325,000,000,000 cu m (90,325 billion cu m or bcm) as of Jan. 1, 1984, compared with 88,054 bcm a year earlier. The U.S.S.R. continued to have by far the largest reserves of any country, with 36,000 bcm, 40% of the world total, followed by Iran with 11,380 bcm and the U.S. with 5,645 bcm. While U.S. reserves fell during 1983, some major gas-producing

countries recorded significant additions to their resources, including the U.S.S.R., Norway, and The Netherlands.

During 1984 the first major gas finds offshore from China and South Africa were reported. Both discoveries could open up previously untapped areas for further exploration. The South African discovery was the first significant oil or gas field to be found in a drilling program that had lasted nearly 20 years. Norway cut its estimate of recoverable reserves in the giant Troll field from 1,600 bcm to 1,287 bcm after the first year's drilling on East Troll. With Norway's proven gas reserves estimated at 2,039 bcm, Troll nevertheless remained a very significant field for that country.

World commercial production of gas in 1983 totaled 1,548 bcm, little different from the two preceding years. The U.S.S.R. clearly overtook the U.S. as the world's largest gas producer. Soviet gas production rose from 502 bcm in 1982 to 536 bcm in 1983, while U.S. production fell markedly, from 503 to 450 bcm. Other producers were still far behind, led by The Netherlands with 73 bcm, Canada with 71 bcm, and Romania and the U.K. with 40 bcm each. The U.S.S.R. was also the leading gas consumer, using 479 bcm, and exporter, sending 59 bcm by pipeline to Eastern and Western Europe. (The U.S.S.R. also imported 2 bcm from Afghanistan.) Other countries that recorded major increases in gas production included Algeria, which increased production by one-third to 36 bcm in order to expand its exports; The Netherlands; China; Australia; and Indonesia. The amount of gas flared fell to 106 bcm, equivalent to 6% of world gross gas production. The Middle East, with only 2.5% of world commercial gas production, accounted for 45% of all flaring, because the region had inadequate facilities to handle all the gas produced in association with oil.

Perhaps the biggest gas development to become operational in 1984 was Australia's North West Shelf project. The first gas from the offshore North Rankin field arrived in Perth through a 1,500-km (930-mi) pipeline in August. Proven recoverable reserves in the North West Shelf area amounted to 852 bcm. Initially, they would supply Western Australia, but in the second phase of the project up to six million metric tons a year of liquefied natural gas (LNG) would be exported to Japan, with deliveries starting in 1989.

In Europe an increased quantity of gas became available in 1984. Soviet gas deliveries under the fourth contract with Austria began in July. In May Italy finally signed a contract to buy gas from the new Siberian pipeline; instead of the 8 bcm a year foreseen in the 1981 agreement with the U.S.S.R., Italy would now take just over 4 bcm a year during the 1980s and 6 bcm a year in the 1990s, in addition to some 7 bcm a year under previous contracts. It was believed that Italy achieved lower prices in this contract than had been the case in earlier Soviet deals for supplies to West Germany and France. West Germany's major gas importer, Ruhrgas, also obtained a price reduction in the first contract for supplies from the Urengoi field in Siberia. The Ruhrgas contract envisioned supplies reaching 10.5 bcm a year by 1990, with an extra 0.65 bcm a year for West Berlin. The U.S.S.R. also agreed to supply

THE NEW YORK TIMES

In California utilities companies are increasingly looking to alternative energy sources for electric power. This photovoltaic generating facility converts solar energy to electricity.

gas to Turkey and announced plans for a major new pipeline to carry Siberian gas to its Eastern European allies.

With an abundance of gas available, Western Europe was becoming a buyers' market. The Netherlands was forced to offer Belgium a short-term price concession in order to keep out Soviet gas. Libya cut the price of its LNG deliveries to Italy and Spain, but Spain was in dispute with Algeria because it had not taken the quantities of LNG they had agreed on. France was seeking a price cut from the U.S.S.R. and achieved a 10% reduction in the quantities it was contracted to take from Algeria. Algeria agreed to double the capacity of its section of the trans-Mediterranean pipeline that supplied Italy, so that it could carry 12 bcm a year, and was negotiating to supply Yugoslavia as well.

Elsewhere in the world Malaysia agreed to supply Singapore with gas and began negotiations on exporting LNG to South Korea. Qatar agreed on plans to develop its massive North Dome field, initially for local use but with an eye to eventually selling LNG to Japan, when markets were less glutted. A Japanese consortium was trying to arrange for the development of the Soviet gas fields on Sakhalin Island, which could provide Japan with LNG. After years of delay Canada's troubled Western LNG project, designed to supply LNG to Japan, suffered another setback when the company managing the project withdrew. An unusual use for gas reported during the year was the conversion of a Canadian ferry, the "Queen of Alberni," which would be the world's first passenger ship to run on natural gas.

(RICHARD J. CASSIDY)

A section of the pipeline that would bring natural gas from the Urengoi field in Siberia was laid across a river in the Soviet Union with the help of East German workers.
CAMERA PRESS/PHOTO TRENDS

PETROLEUM

In 1984 OPEC was again in the limelight as it defended its marker price of $29 per barrel and a production ceiling of 17.5 million bbl a day agreed upon by the organization's members in March 1983. More spectacular, but less interruptive of oil supplies than many had anticipated, was the heightening of hostilities between Iran and Iraq to include Gulf shipping. The damage caused was relatively minor in relation to the tonnage of oil being transported through the Strait of Hormuz.

This situation once more caused problems for the unity of OPEC members as political and economic problems had to be resolved. OPEC had withstood the financial strains and dropping demand for its oil in the face of price discounting and the exceeding of production quotas by some members, a weakening of the spot market, continuing disputes over differentials, and, in October, price reductions by Norway, the U.K., and Nigeria. OPEC preserved a general consensus at its meeting in July and retained it in Geneva at the end of October, when a reduction in its production quota by 1.5 million bbl a day was agreed on in order to sustain price levels. In December, however, Nigeria and Algeria refused to accept a plan allowing for the temporary readjustment of price differentials. Demand for oil increased marginally, but its fluctuations throughout the year created uncertainty in the markets. One of the problems for OPEC was a reduction in the year in oil revenues of 21%, down to $160 billion from the peak of $279 billion

in 1980. The 12% upturn in OPEC production by mid-1984 was a relief. In the same period U.S. oil imports also rose.

The apparent surplus of oil production caused a drop in the number of drilling rigs in operation in the U.S., from a 1981 peak of 5,636 to 2,510 in 1983. At the end of 1983 a Soviet drill at Kolskiye on the Kola Peninsula penetrated to 12,000 m (39,600 ft), the deepest hole ever drilled. Drilling in some promising areas, such as offshore China and the Beaufort Sea, remained inconclusive. Oil, however, was struck for the first time in Jordan early in 1984, and much encouragement was given to onshore developments in the U.K. by recent discoveries. The difficulty and cost of exploration was reflected in recent oil company mergers in the U.S. The most notable, between Gulf Oil Co. and Standard Oil Co. of California, was attractive because of a matching of respective assets in production and marketing.

RESERVES. During the last decade or so the absolute level of world recoverable "published proved" reserves had fallen by some 5% overall. The total at the end of 1983, 677,700,000,000 bbl, was a minor increase of 300 million bbl over the 677,-400,000,000 bbl at the end of 1982. Western Hemisphere reserves increased slightly to 18.4% of the world total, 124,100,000,-000 bbl, at the end of 1983, with 12.1% in Latin America. Middle Eastern reserves also increased, to 54.5% of the world total, from 369,000,000,000 bbl in 1982 to 369,700,000,000 bbl in 1983. African reserves decreased slightly to 56,900,000,000

bbl, 8.4% of the world total, whereas those for Western Europe increased slightly, to 23,700,000,000 bbl, 3.5% of the world total. The Soviet Union's share of world reserves remained at 9.3%, 63,000,000,000 bbl, but China's was marginally lower at 2.8%, 19,100,000,000 bbl. The U.S. share declined 5.1% to 34,500,000,000 bbl, compared with 36,900,000,000 bbl in 1982. OPEC held 66.1%, 448,300,000,000 bbl.

PRODUCTION. World oil production fell by 1% in 1983 in comparison with 1982. The Middle East registered the greatest regional fall, 9.4%, from 13,250,000 bbl a day to 12,005,000 bbl a day. The share of the major producer, Saudi Arabia, with 9.4% of the world total and under half of the regional share of 21.4%, fell by 20.7%, from 6,695,000 to 5,330,000 bbl a day. The Middle East share fell below those of the U.S.S.R., 22.4%, 12,520,000 bbl a day, and the U.S., 15.6%, 8,655,000 bbl a day.

Among individual Middle Eastern countries there were increases in Kuwait (1.6%; 715,000 bbl a day) and Oman (17.5%, 380,-000 bbl a day) but decreases in Abu Dhabi (10.4%; 795,000 bbl a day) and Qatar (9%; 310,000 bbl a day). Iran raised its production by 5% (compared with 49.4% in 1982) to 2,530,000 bbl a day, a total world share of 4.6%. Iraq's production fell slightly and, at 1,005,000 bbl a day, was 1.8% of the world total.

Indonesian production, 2.3% of the world total, fell by 2.7% to 1,315,000 bbl a day, but Australasia's increased by 10% to 460,000 bbl a day. African production as a whole decreased slightly to 4,765,000 bbl a day with declines in Algeria (6%, to 980,000 bbl a day) and Nigeria (3.4%, to 1,245,000 bbl a day) but increases in Gabon (3.3%, to 160,000 bbl a day) and Egypt (9.8%, to 775,000 bbl a day). In Western Europe British production increased by 11.1% to 2,360,000 bbl a day, 4.2% of the world total and accounting for two-thirds of the regional share of 3,485,-000 bbl a day. Also in Western Europe, output was up in Denmark (28.4%), Italy (27.5%), and Norway (24.7%).

Production in Latin America dropped by 2.1% to 6,430,000 bbl a day, but there were wide variations. Brazil, Colombia, and Ecuador were up by, respectively, 21.1% (to 335,000 bbl a day), 6% (155,000 bbl), and 12.1% (235,000 bbl), but production in Mexico, Trinidad, and Venezuela registered falls of, respectively, 1.8% (to 2,950,-000 bbl a day), 9.9% (160,000 bbl), and 5.7% (1,850,000 bbl). Total North American production was steady at 11,745,000 bbl a day, compared with 11,685,000 bbl in 1982. Output in China rose by 4.2% to 2,135,000 bbl a day, 3.8% of the world total. Soviet production was constant, 12,-520,000 bbl a day against 12,430,000 bbl in 1982. World production, excluding the U.S.S.R., Eastern Europe, and China, was down by 1.8% to 41,335,000 bbl a day. For members of OPEC, which produced 32.5%

of the world total, there was an 8.1% decline to 18,275,000 bbl a day.

CONSUMPTION. World oil consumption, which had peaked in 1979 at 64,115,000 bbl a day, averaged 57.9 million bbl a day in 1983, a drop of 1.1% from 1982. The decline occurred mostly in the industrial countries as a result of the economic recession, which particularly affected fuel oil sales. The less developed countries in general increased their consumption of all petroleum products. The fall in consumption was greatest in Western Europe, 3.1%, for a world total share of 20.9% at 12,190,-000 bbl a day. Only Switzerland (9.4%) and Turkey (1.5%) showed increases. Belgium and Ireland had the greatest declines, 9.2% each. West Germany remained the biggest consumer with 3.9% of the world total at 2,320,000 bbl a day. Consumption in North America was down by 1.5% at 16,125,000 bbl a day, 27.5% of the world total; Canada's consumption fell by 8.8% to 1,420,000 bbl a day. The U.S. remained the largest consumer, with 25.1% of the world total, 14,705,000 bbl a day.

Consumption declined in Latin America by 2.5%, 7.8% of the world total at 4,555,000 bbl a day. Increases were registered in the Middle East, 2.8%, for a world share of 3.2% at 1,805,000 bbl a day; in Africa, 1.1% (2.9% of the world total at

1,670,000 bbl a day); in South Asia, 1.8% (1.7%; 955,000 bbl); and in Southeast Asia, 0.8% (4.1%; 2,290,000 bbl). Consumption in Japan, the third largest consumer, fell by 1% to 4,360,000 bbl a day, 7.4% of the world total. China's consumption, 3% of the world share, rose by 2.7% to 1,705,000 bbl a day. The U.S.S.R., the second largest consumer, with 16.1% of the world total, had a minor increase of 0.4% to 9,115,000 bbl a day.

REFINING. Overall world refining capacity fell again in 1983, by 3.7% to 76,065,-000 bbl a day, the lowest total since 1977. Most of the loss occurred in the industrial countries. Western European capacity, 22% of the world total, fell by 7.3% to 16,715,000 bbl a day. Individual declines within the region included France (13.7% to 2,370,000 bbl a day), Italy (11.4% to 3.1 million bbl), West Germany (9.5% to 2,280,000 bbl), and Spain (6.8% to 1,440,-000 bbl).

Soviet refining capacity, at 12 million bbl a day, 15.8% of the world total, rose by 2.1%. Canadian capacity fell by 10.4% to 2,025,000 bbl a day and that of the U.S. by 5.9% to 15,865,000 bbl. Venezuelan capacity declined 9.9% to 1,225,000 bbl. The rest of the world varied. In the Middle East as a whole, capacity was almost unaltered, down 0.1% to 3,560,000 bbl a day, 4.7% of the world share, but Kuwait rose 8.3%. Africa was down 0.6% to 2,340,000 bbl a day, but South Asia was up 2.3% to 1,020,000 bbl a day. The capacity of the U.S.S.R., Eastern Europe, and China together rose by 1.8%, half of the previous five-year average increase, to 16,830,000 bbl a day, 22.2% of the world total. Japanese capacity was reduced by 9.6% to 4,975,000 bbl a day, 6.5% of the world total. Indonesia, however, lifted its capacity by 48.1%, 1% of the world total. Refinery throughputs declined as a whole by 1.5% in 1983, to 54,850,000 bbl a day.

TANKERS. The decline in the size of the world tanker fleet from its 1977 peak of 332.5 million tons deadweight (dw) continued, and in 1983 tonnage fell by 6.8% to 283.2 million tons dw, the lowest total since 1974. Tanker ownership was divided among independents (57.7%), oil companies (35.1%), and governments (7.2%). In regard to flag ownership, Liberia ranked first with 76.4 million tons dw (27%); it was followed by Japan, with 26.3 million tons dw (9.3%); Norway, 18.9 million tons dw (6.7%); Greece, 21.1 million tons dw (7.4%); the U.S., 16.5 million tons dw (5.8%); the U.K., 15.3 million tons dw (5.4%); and Panama, 15 million tons dw (5.3%).

Tankers between 205,000 and 285,000 tons dw constituted 36.9% of the world tanker fleet by size, followed by 17.1% for those of 65,000 to 125,000 tons dw. Supertankers of 285,000 tons dw and over totaled 45.9 million tons dw, 16.2% of the world total. Some 24,355,000 bbl a day of oil were transported in tankers, down by 4.7% from 1982. Of that total Western Europe imported 35.6% and the U.S., 20.5%.

(R. W. FERRIER)

See also Engineering Projects; Industrial Review; Mining and Metallurgy; Transportation.

This article updates the *Macropædia* articles ENERGY CONVERSION; FOSSIL FUELS.

When this concrete base for a drilling platform was completed, it was towed from Stavanger, Norway, to a fjord 80 kilometres (50 miles) away, where the deck section was to be mounted atop the base. The 275-metre (902-foot)-high ensemble was then to be towed into drilling position in Mobil Oil's Statfjord field in the North Sea.

Engineering Projects

Bridges. In Canada construction started early in 1984 on a four-lane, high-level crossing over one channel of the Fraser River in Vancouver, B.C. Reaching from the eastern shore of the river to Annacis Island, it would be the world's longest-span stayed-girder bridge, with a main span of 465 m (1 m = 3.3 ft). A low-level bridge was to cross the other channel.

Both steel and concrete designs for the high-level bridge were submitted for bids. The steel bid was substantially below that of concrete. The bridge was expected to take three years to build and would provide a clearance of 56 m over the shipping lanes, the twin-legged towers being both placed on dry land. The composite steel and concrete deck would be carried by a deep plate girder situated along each outer edge of the deck, and the girders would be given added support by 23 cables extending from each leg of the towers; the cables would be protected from corrosion by heavy plastic covers. To reduce wind loading and eliminate the risk of oscillation, the leading edges of the deck were to be streamlined; wind-tunnel tests showed the structure to be aerodynamically stable.

The Hooghly Bridge in India, with a main span of 457 m, was similar in design to that described above, though it would carry six traffic lanes. Arguments over details of the design had held up construction (begun in 1972), but fabrication of the steel had begun, and India could, for a short period, hold the record for the world's longest-span stayed-girder bridge.

Design for a second bridge across the Bosporus was begun during 1984. The Turkish government insisted that it wanted the same design as for the successful first bridge, which, with six traffic lanes, carried more than six million vehicles annually; consequently, Turkey awarded the design contract to the London firm of Freeman Fox & Partners, which designed the first bridge. The second bridge was to have a main span of 1,100 m, compared with 1,075 m for the first. Apart from the Humber Bridge in England, whose main span of 1,410 m was the longest in the world, the two Bosporus bridges would have the longest spans outside the U.S.

In Japan work proceeded on the Honshu-Shikoku bridge links, where the most northerly crossing included the massive six-lane Akashi Kaikyo suspension bridge for both road and rail. Previously the main span had been designed to be 1,700 m with both towers sited in very deep water with fast currents. By increasing the span to 2,000 m, the engineers could place the towers in shallower water, easing construction problems. To achieve such a span engineers might have to adopt a new deck form since the traditional U.S. truss would be too heavy and the British trapezoidal box might not be aerodynamically stable. A solution might be found by employing the concept of a perforated bridge deck of shallow, streamlined box units, one for each traffic lane, separated by gratings that act as air vents. Wind-tunnel experiments in Britain and Italy suggested that spans of that type well in excess of 2,000 m were feasible. A perforated deck had been proposed for the Messina crossing between Italy and Sicily, where a single span of 3,300 m would be required, and for fixed links such as those across the English Channel and the Strait of Gibraltar, for which spans of 2,000 m were envisioned.

Cost of maintenance and renovation of existing bridges continued to be a frightening problem for engineers and the authorities. In the U.S. the cost of bridge renovations that were needed to cope with expected increases in traffic

This bridge is scheduled for completion in December 1985 and will replace the drawbridge that presently spans Biscayne Bay in Florida. It will be 26 metres (84 feet) high at its highest point to accommodate the boats that leave the bay's many harbours.
PAUL CONKLIN

volumes and loads, and to replace low-grade concrete used in bridge substructures in the early 1960s, was put at $30 billion–$40 billion. Salt used to counter icing was now recognized as a prime cause of corrosion of bridge decks. Checks by one British local authority showed that salt concentrations ten times greater than required had been applied, with consequent damage to structures. Efforts were also being made to improve the design of expansion joints in order to reduce penetration by the salt to the pier tops and substructure. Similarly, improved waterproof membranes for bridge decks were being sought to prevent the salt from reaching steel reinforcement and reducing bond strengths in concrete decks. Alternatively, steelwork at vulnerable points might be protected by a plastic sheath, but this could not easily be done for the reinforcement in concrete decks. Efforts were also being made to evaluate the bond strengths of new materials that could be injected into cracks to repair defective concrete. Strengthening of some existing concrete bridges might be achieved by bonding steel plates onto the concrete if current trials proved successful.   (DAVID FISHER)

Buildings. The large-scale use of teflon-coated woven fibreglass fabric as a roof membrane, pioneered on a large scale at Saudi Arabia's Jidda airport, was being used on other projects during 1984, including Basildon town centre in the U.K. and an international stadium south of Riyadh in Saudi Arabia. The stadium was designed to seat 67,000 and would have a multipeak tent type of roof of the fabric, shaped by steel cables. A ring of 24 60-m-high tube-sectioned masts was to support the roof, and a 134-m-diameter ring cable would bound an open section above the playing areas. The sophisticated electrical system would have its own power plant, and services would include electronic scoreboards, television and radio facilities, and a complex security system with electronic locks and visual monitoring. Also under construction during 1984 was a new gymnasium in Taiwan having a 131-m-diameter roof formed of composite steel and concrete. The roof, in the shape of a 2-m-deep, two-layer geodesic dome with a rise of 17.4 m, was being constructed on a mound of earth at ground level. The whole 4,700-metric ton assembly, including a concrete inner ring beam, was to be lifted 30 m to its permanent support on V-shaped columns using

24 330-ton prestressing jacks. At the top was an outer ring beam, and the gap between the two was to be filled with concrete; then the outer beam would be posttensioned, and cross connections would be installed.

A notable large-span structure completed in the U.K. in 1984 was Liverpool's Festival Hall. This had a three-pinned cylindrical roof 78 m long by some 60 m clear span. The ends were semicircular in plan and had spherical roof surfaces. The overall structure consisted of a series of closely spaced braced arched frames over the central cylindrical section and a single layer of curved radial beams over the end parts. The central area was clad in translucent polycarbonate sheeting and the end parts with profiled aluminum sheet.

A number of prestigious tall buildings were completed or under construction during 1984. The award-winning 174-m-high 780 Third Avenue in New York City was the first diagonally braced tube structure built with concrete. Only 21 m wide, its 8:1 height-to-width ratio made it one of the world's most slender buildings. Construction was well under way on the giant Raffles City Complex in Singapore. This would be one of the tallest and largest single developments in Asia. It comprised a 72-story hotel tower, a 42-story office tower, a 28-story twin-core hotel block, and a 7-story podium, three stories being underground. Meanwhile, in Hong Kong work continued on the new 175-m-high headquarters building for the Hong Kong & Shanghai Banking Corp.; eight massive steel masts were linked by bold bridgelike trusses at four levels from which the floors were hung. Innovative preassembled modules, fully fitted out with services, were being used. The centrepiece of the building was a 52-m-high atrium that formed the main banking hall.

The reuse of old buildings by refurbishment or by completely rebuilding the interiors while maintaining historic facades was increasingly practiced in Europe. In this way a 19th-century factory at Rouen-Darnetal in France was transformed into the Normandy School of Architecture. The factory was 163 m long and had a total floor area of 1,200 sq m on four levels. Because the existing internal structure and foundations were too insubstantial for the additional loading, a complete new concrete-framed structure was installed within the existing shell. Where possible, parts of the original structure were retained. Another example,

of a different type, was the conversion of the massive structure of a former cement plant in Barcelona, Spain, into an architect's office. Here there was a triple contrast between the old, gnarled exposed concrete surface of silos, the grass and trees on the flat roofs, and the glimpses of new and precise fenestration and colonnades. The resulting appearance was both monastic and reminiscent of Roman ruins.

(GEOFFREY M. PINFOLD)

Dams. The big event in dam construction during 1984 was China's decision to proceed with a feasibility study to construct the Three Gorge Dam project on the Chang Jiang (Yangtze River). This giant project, consisting of an 11 million-cu m concrete gravity dam, 165 m high and 1,924 m long, was initially planned in the early 1940s by John Savage of the U.S. Bureau of Reclamation. The plan was revived following China's successful experience in constructing the Gezhouba (Ke-chou-pa) Dam, 40 km (25 mi) downstream from the Three Gorge site. The State Planning Commission assembled 12,000 engineers, designers, technicians, and supporting staff. More than 35,000 workers were employed on the construction of the Gezhouba Dam, and they were expected to provide the experienced workers that would be needed for the Three Gorge project. The Chinese planned an all-China team to do the designing and construction, drawing upon international consultants when necessary. The cost of the project was estimated at more than $7 billion.

Other nations also were planning large-scale projects. Brazil was planning a 17,000-MW hydroelectric scheme on the Xingu River, the cost of which was estimated to be $15 billion. Pakistan was planning the Kalabagh Dam on the Indus River. It would have a 12,000,000,000-cu m reservoir and a power plant that eventually would supply 3,000 MW. The estimated cost was $3 billion. Spain outlined a program of construction for 56 dams to be built in the next decade and started the Alanghe and Los Molinos dams to provide municipal water and irrigation.

Bhutan, one of the poorest countries of the world, completed its 40-m-high Chukha Dam, located high in the Himalayas on the Wanghu River, with a 336-MW power plant. The power would mainly go to India until use could be found for it in Bhutan.

Dam technology was also moving forward. Additional

roller-compacted concrete, or "rollcrete," dams were being planned, using modifications of concrete mix and different facing systems to provide for steeper slopes with higher tensile strength. Rollcrete dams held promise for improved economy of construction.

The Soviets were planning to build the 275-m-high Kambaratinskaya Dam by exploding the banks of the Naryn River. The blast was expected to deposit 100 million cu m of rock in the riverbed to form the dam. The dam was located in a remote area where such technology could be employed without serious environmental objections. This method could save much construction time and cost.

In Brazil the impact of filling the Tucurui reservoir called for 86 teams of men with boats and helicopters to evacuate people and animals from the area to keep them from drowning on isolated islands soon to be submerged. Approximately 18,000 people were affected. The major problem was that the local population consisted mainly of Indians, who were unable to read and were thus unaware of the danger of remaining in the area.

Failure at the uncompleted Carsington Dam in England, prior to filling, brought dam safety issues to the forefront again. Approximately one-third of the upstream face of the 1,250-m-long, 35-m-high earth-fill dam slid away. Design weakness was blamed for the accident, and it later became apparent that the entire dam would have to be rebuilt.

Safety conferences concentrated on establishing a definition of an "unsafe dam." The consensus was that a dam was unsafe if (1) it could not pass half of the probable maximum flood without overtopping; (2) overtopping would cause failure of the dam; and (3) failure would cause loss of life downstream. Of the 68,000 dams in the U.S., 8,800 were inspected and 2,900 were evaluated as unsafe. As part of the dam safety program, studies were being made to determine the route of a flood after a dam failure. Predetermining the areas affected by a hypothetical dam breach

Major World Dams Under Construction in 1984[1]

Name of dam	River	Country	Type[2]	Height (m)	Length of crest (m)	Volume content (000 cu m)	Gross reservoir capacity (000 cu m)
Altinkaya	Kizilirmak	Turkey	E,R	195	604	2,600	5,763,000
Ataturk	Euphrates	Turkey	E,R	184	746	85,000	48,700,000
Bath County, Upper	Back Creek	U.S.	E,R	143	731	18,000	43,790
Boruca	Terraba	Costa Rica	E,R	267	700	43,000	14,960,000
Bureya	Bureya	U.S.S.R.	G	139	810	3,561	20,900,000
Casa de Piedra	Rio Colorado	Argentina	E	25	11,000	16,000	3,600,000
Chapeton	Paraná	Argentina	E,G	34	6,554	37,910	53,750,000
Colbun	Maule	Chile	E	116	530	15,000	1,490,000
Dabaklamm	Dorferbach	Austria	A	220	332	1,000	235,000
Dongjiang	Laishui	China	A	157	438	940	8,120,000
Dorna	Lerez	Spain	G	151	163	68	27,500
El Cajon	Humuya	Honduras	A	226	382	1,480	5,650,000
El M'Jara	Ouergha	Morocco	E	87	1,600	25,000	4,000,000
Gallito Ciego	Jequetepeque	Peru	E,R	112	750	15,000	400,000
Grand Maison	Eau d'Olle	France	E,R	160	550	12,500	140,000
Guavio	Orinoco	Colombia	E,R	243	390	17,755	1,020,000
Guri (Raúl Leoni)	Caroni	Venezuela	E,R,G	162	11,409	77,971	138,000,000
Hrusov-Dunakiliti	Dunaj	Czechoslovakia	E,G	29	31,500	18,340	199,000
Ilha Grande	Paraná	Brazil	E,G	29	7,060	11,573	30,000,000
Itaparica	São Francisco	Brazil	E,R	105	4,150	16,530	10,700,000
Karakaya	Euphrates	Turkey	A	173	462	2,000	9,580,000
Kenyir	Trengganu	Malaysia	E,R	150	800	16,500	13,600,000
Khudoni	Inguri	U.S.S.R.	A	201	545	1,475	365,000
Kishau	Tons	India	E,R	253	360	18,400	2,400,000
Kouilou	Kouilou	Congo	A	137	345	390	35,000,000
Lhakwar	Yamuna	India	G	192	440	2,000	580,000
Lower Tunguska	Lower Tunguska	U.S.S.R.	E,G	200	6,200	23,000	45,000,000
Lower Usuma	Usuma	Nigeria	E	49	1,350	93,000	100,000
Maqarin	Yarmuk	Jordan	E,R	164	700	21,000	486,000
Menzelet	Ceyhan	Turkey	E,R	151	425	8,000	19,500,000
Naramata	Naramata	Japan	E,R	158	520	12,300	90,000
Oosterschelde	Vense Gat Oosterschelde	The Netherlands	E,G	50	9,000	50,000	2,780,000
Porto Primavera	Paraná	Brazil	E,G	38	11,385	8,441	18,500,000
Ray Roberts (Aubrey)	Trinity	U.S.	E	43	4,561	15,475	986,000
Revelstoke	Columbia	Canada	E,R,G	153	1,620	13,000	5,180,000
Rogun	Vakhsh	U.S.S.R.	E	335	660	75,500	13,300,000
Rocandor	Uruguay	Brazil/Argentina	E,R	78	1,600	6,500	33,580,000
Salvajina	Cauca	Colombia	E,R	160	360	3,500	904,000
San Rouge	Agno	Philippines	E	210	1,130	43,150	990,000
São Felix	Tocantins	Brazil	E,R	160	1,950	34,000	55,200,000
Sardar Sarovar	Narmada	India	G	155	1,210	6,100	9,600,000
Tehri	Bhagirathi	India	E,R	261	570	22,750	3,539,000
Thein	Ravi	India	E,R	160	565	16,187	3,280,000
Tres Irmaos	Tiete	Brazil	E,G	67	3,700	15,000	3,450,000
Upper Wainganga	Wainganga	India	E	43	181	6,290	50,700,000
Warna	Warna	India	E,G	91	1,580	15,310	964,000
Yacyreta-Apipe	Paraná	Paraguay/Argentina	E,G	41	72,000	81,000	21,000,000
Zillergründl	Ziller	Austria	A	186	506	1,355	90,000
Major World Dams Completed in 1983 and 1984[1]							
Amaluza (Daniel Palacios)	Paute	Ecuador	A,G	167	420	1,200	120,000
Baishan	Songhuajiang	China	G	150	670	1,630	6,215,000
Canales	Genil	Spain	E,R	158	340	1,217	71,000
Gura Apelor Retezat	Riul Mare	Romania	E,R	168	450	9,020	225,000
Inguri	Inguri	U.S.S.R.	A	272	680	3,960	1,100,000
Itaipu	Paraná	Brazil/Paraguay	E,R,G	196	7,900	29,200	29,000,000
La Grande No. 4	La Grande	Canada	E,R	125	3,780	16,800	19,530,000
Longyangxia	Huang He	China	G	172	342	1,750	24,700,000
Los Leones	Los Leones	Chile	E	179	510	9,200	106,000
Mazar	Mazar	Ecuador	G	175	400	1,600	500,000
Mosul	Tigris	Iraq	E	131	3,500	23,000	12,500,000
Nurek	Vakhsh	U.S.S.R.	E	300	704	58,000	10,500,000
Oymapinar	Manavgat	Turkey	A	185	360	560	300,000
Ozkoy	Gediz	Turkey	E,R	180	420	11,251	940,000
Sterkfontein	Nuwe Jaar Spruit	South Africa	E	93	3,060	19,800	2,656,000
Thomson	Thomson	Australia	E,R	164	1,180	13,300	1,175,000
Tokuyama	Ibi	Japan	E,R	161	420	15,000	660,000
Tucurui	Tocantins	Brazil	E,G	93	10,677	64,300	43,000,000
Yacambu	Yacambu	Venezuela	E,R	158	107	3,000	427,000

[1] Having a height exceeding 150 m (492 ft); or having a volume content exceeding 15 million cu m (19.6 million cu yd); or forming a reservoir exceeding 14,000 × 10⁶ cu m of capacity (12 million ac = ft).
[2] Type of dam: E = earth; R = rockfill; A = arch; G = gravity.

(T. W. MERMEL)

was needed so that warnings could be sent only to those areas threatened, thereby avoiding widespread panic.

Statistics produced by the review of the recent World Register of Dams revealed that on a worldwide basis more than 1,000 dams were being built per year during the 1950–77 period and that the rate of construction fell to 680 dams per year in 1978–82. Of these dams, 83% were constructed of earth and rock fill, and 17% were gravity, arch, and buttress dams in which concrete was used.

(T. W. MERMEL)

Roads. A slowly recovering world economy held construction of new highways to a minimum in most nations, while road agencies tested innovative ways to maintain and rehabilitate existing highway networks. Delegates from 86 countries attending the tenth International Road Federation World Meeting in Rio de Janeiro, Brazil, pledged to support efforts to obtain increased financing for new roads, particularly in third world countries.

In the United States 96% of the 68,382-km (1 km = 0.62 mi) Interstate System was open to traffic at the end of 1984. Several U.S. states, including Wisconsin, Pennsylvania, Illinois, Texas, and South Carolina, were considering conversion of Interstate highways to toll facilities in order to overcome the shortage of conventional financing. The city of Atlanta, Ga., completely rebuilt its 194-km freeway system while maintaining traffic.

In Latin America three toll highways connecting major cities in Ecuador were planned, with a total length of 114 km. Chile's North-South Highway, 3,118 km in length, was being completely reconstructed. In Paraguay the repaving of the Tacuara–Santa Rosa Highway was expected to stimulate the economy, while in the Boayaca and Antander departments of Colombia 660 km of farm-to-market roads were being built at a cost of $64 million. Mexico allocated $836 million toward maintenance of its 41,500-km federal road network in 1984.

In Asia work began on the first superhighway in China. The $250 million 150-km road was to connect Beijing (Peking) with Tianjin (Tientsin) and the harbour of Xingang (Hsin-kang). The Jakarta Intra-Urban Toll Road System, under construction in Indonesia's capital city, was designed to reduce massive traffic congestion. The Hong Kong Island Eastern Corridor, a highway built almost entirely on reclaimed land and elevated structures, was opened in June 1984. The Bangkok Expressway System neared completion, and Thailand was also planning two toll highways linking Sawan with Pathum Thani and Saraburi with Nakhon Ratchasima, for a total of 430 km. Japan's growing toll road system reached 3,936 km.

In Australia the last link of the Auburn–Paramatta Freeway, west of Sydney, was under construction. Also, builders completed a 245-km road linking Australia's major tourist attraction of Ayers Rock with the highway from Adelaide to Alice Springs.

In the Middle East plans for a 1,600-km highway linking Kuwait, Saudi Arabia, Qatar, the United Arab Emirates, and Oman were approved by the six-nation Gulf Cooperation Council. A four-lane highway bypassing the city of Cairo was to be built at an estimated cost of $500 million, while Jordan announced a program to construct or upgrade 2,240 km of roads. In Iraq construction was almost complete on the main highway leading to the Jordanian border, and work was in progress on the 104-km highway from Ramailah to Safwan on the border with Kuwait.

The first toll road in South Africa's Transvaal was opened in 1984, and work on a second toll road, between Springs and Krugersdorp, began. Construction of Niger's segment of the Trans-Sahara Highway began in 1984, covering the 428-km section from Zinder to Agadez. A segment of the Trans-West African Highway in Ghana was begun in 1984, between Daboase and Takoradi, at a cost of $17 million.

In January a major 13-km segment of the $1,275,000,-000 M-25 motorway encircling London was opened to traffic. The British government reversed its earlier decision to permit contractors to build privately financed highways to be repaid through tolls and royalty payments. West Germany began upgrading its expressway system, beginning with the ring road around Cologne. France's largest road project was the A86 ring road around Paris, with a total projected cost of $213 million. Of the total 80 km, 35 were in service at the end of 1984. (HUGH M. GILLESPIE)

Tunnels. The building of urban subway and mass transit systems continued to provide a major source of opportunity for tunneling contractors while at the same time offering one of the best long-term investments that any city or country could make. As Hong Kong's mass transit Island Line neared completion, Singapore began letting contracts for its own new system and provided continuity of work for many Southeast Asian contractors and engineers. A considerable amount of tunnel work was associated with hydroelectric power generation; China purchased two 10.75-m-diameter Robbins tunnel-boring machines (TBM's) from the Chicago municipal authorities for use in the ten kilometres of hard-rock tunnels connecting the Basuo Dam to the Pearl River basin as part of the Tianshengqiao (T'iensheng-ch'iao) hydroelectric project. In southeast Turkey the $450 million Ataturk project, one of the world's largest hydroelectric and irrigation schemes, got under way; work commenced on 26.4 km of water-diversion tunnels through rock, using the latest equipment for drill and blast excavation.

The city of Cairo started a massive rehabilitation of its 60-year-old sewerage and wastewater system. The overall cost of the project in the master plan, which was conceived by a consortium of U.S., British, and Egyptian consulting engineers, amounted to $2,577,000,000. The initial stages, involving works on the east bank side of Cairo, called for slurry shield tunneling machines to be used for driving tunnels through the Nile deposit sands and silts that underlie much of the city centre. Contracts for these were awarded, and as a result the possibility of an interesting competition arose. For the first time the slurry-shield technologies of West Germany and Japan could be competing, on equal terms, on connecting sections of tunnel.

The West German-built Hydroshield, at 10.64-m diameter said to be the world's largest, completed its section of Rome's Aurelia Tunnel for the Italian State Railway. The 1.2 km of twin-track tunnel were connected into Camerone Station after a successful but somewhat lengthy period of construction. Also from West Germany, the giant Wirth hydraulic shaft borer completed a 166.5-m-deep shaft for the Ruhr coal mines. This 5.8-m-diameter, 21.5-m-long machine bored vertically downward, keeping its cutterhead immersed in bentonite slurry, and pumped its excavation spoil hydraulically to the surface. Another novel machine developed in West Germany successfully carried out its unique task at Hamburg. The 75-year-old Elbe River Tunnel was threatened by dredging and riverbed erosion. Using a combined oil-rig-type platform and compressed-air working chamber, engineers placed a 60-cm-thick reinforced concrete slab of approximately 2,200 cu m along the roof of the twin tunnel. This famous and still useful tunnel was thus preserved.

Reports from Sweden indicated that the U.S.S.R. might have used clean fission nuclear charges to excavate natural gas storage caverns in the salt beds of the Caucasus Mountains in Astrakhan. The method was pioneered in the U.S. some years earlier under the title "Project Plowshare," but it was abandoned in the face of political and environmental objections. During the year details were released by the U.S. government of an air force field trial to test the feasibility of a "deep basing egress system." In essence it involved a 3.82-m-diameter, 1,800-hp Robbins vertical TBM that bored its way up to the surface from an impregnable bunker sited deep in a Nevada mountain. The smooth bore produced by the Robbins TBM could act as a launch tube for ballistic missiles that would be held in reserve for retaliatory strikes against an aggressor long after the initial conflict. (GEOFFREY J. NOBLETT)

This article updates the *Macropædia* articles BUILDING CONSTRUCTION; PUBLIC WORKS.

Environment

During 1984 environmental issues were discussed mainly by professional scientists and at the intergovernmental level, while the voluntary movement remained comparatively quiet. The debates were dominated by the issue of acid rain, and several European governments announced their intention to reduce emissions of sulfur dioxide from factories and power stations within their territories. The British, however, continued to question the relationship between sulfur dioxide emissions and acid deposition. In Europe the pressure to reduce atmospheric pollution came mainly from West Germany and may have been due to the continued rise in influence of the environmentalist Green Party.

In Britain acid rain was not the only issue of public concern. An accidental discharge of radioactive waste from the British Nuclear Fuels Ltd. (BNFL) Sellafield installation in November 1983 contaminated 24 km (15 mi) of Cumbrian beaches and led eventually to prosecution of the company. Controversy surrounding this incident was intensified by allegations that the incidence of leukemia among children living in villages close to Sellafield was much higher than the national average.

Reports of several studies confirmed the view of many atmospheric scientists that the consequences of climatic modification resulting from the release of carbon dioxide—the "greenhouse effect"—might be very grave. Other studies of the world climate confirmed that the Northern Hemisphere was growing warmer in ways consistent with the "greenhouse effect" calculations. Despite the UN plan to halt the spread of deserts, many millions of hectares of farmland continued to be lost each year. In September the Worldwatch Institute reported that, mainly as a result of bad farming practices, the amount of cultivable land per person in the world as a whole might be reduced by one-third by the end of the century.

An industrial accident of catastrophic proportions occurred on December 3, when toxic gas leaking from an insecticide plant in Bhopal, India, killed as many as 2,500 persons and affected thousands of others. (See *Toxic Chemical Wastes,* below.)

INTERNATIONAL COOPERATION

Acid Rain. The main environmental issue of the year was discussed at the economic summit of Western leaders held in London on June 9. The final communiqué included an announcement of a worldwide study of the problem. Earlier, on March 21, environmental and health ministers from Austria, Canada, Denmark, West Germany, Finland, France, The Netherlands, Norway, Sweden, and Switzerland signed an agreement in Ottawa committing them to reduce sulfur dioxide emissions by 30% over ten years. Each had already adopted the 30% target and some, such as Canada and France, had set a goal of lowering emissions to half their 1980 levels.

Acid rain was the main topic at a three-day conference held in Munich, West Germany, June 25–27, which was attended by delegates from 31 countries and representatives from several international agencies. An important outcome was the decision by the U.S. and the U.S.S.R. to renew their lapsed 1972 agreement on environmental research.

PETER B. KAPLAN/LIFE MAGAZINE © 1984 TIME INC.

Tracer balloons, like this one aloft over Sudbury, Ontario, one of North America's most smoke-polluted areas, indicate wind currents while planes and ground stations monitor tracer gas released from the offending smokestacks.

Thirteen nations, for the first time including Belgium, Luxembourg, and Liechtenstein but excluding Britain and the U.S., pledged to reduce their industrial emissions of sulfur dioxide by 30% by 1993. The U.S.S.R., East Germany, and Bulgaria pledged more modestly to reduce, by the same proportion and date, the amount of sulfur dioxide emitted by their installations and transported to other countries. Martin Holdgate, of the British Department of the Environment, said more information was needed on the true cause of acid rain, since sulfur dioxide emissions in Europe had fallen by 37% between 1970 and 1983. Agreeing on the need for more research, William Ruckelshaus, director of the U.S. Environmental Protection Agency (EPA), said the U.S. had spent $93 million on acid rain research since 1980. The conference called for a reduction in emissions of nitrogen oxides from cars and stationary installations, more rational use of energy, more research and international cooperation, more consultation on methods of sampling and analysis, increased use of less polluting technologies, and continuation of the European program for monitoring air pollutants.

On September 24, at the general assembly of the Federation of Nature and National Parks, held in Derbyshire, England, the 70 delegates from 13 countries were told that acid rain might be causing human deaths. Hans Bibelriether of the Bavarian National Park (West Germany) reported deaths of babies from throat infections in areas of severe air pollution. (See *National Developments,* below.)

UN Environment Program. UNEP's annual report, *The State of the Environment 1983,* published in March, identified as of immediate concern the disposal of hazardous wastes, acid rain, and the environmental implications of growing plant crops for energy production.

On April 13 representatives of countries bordering the Mediterranean met under UNEP auspices in Athens to consider the progress of the Mediterranean Action Plan, a nine-year monitoring program that they had commissioned. They decided to take no action on the recommendation that they should adopt quality criteria with respect to heavy-metal contamination of seafood and the microbiological quality of shellfish and bathing beaches. UNEP had found nearly one-quarter of all Mediterranean beaches to be unsafe for bathing. However, mercury, the most serious heavy metal pollutant, was found to be less hazardous than had been supposed. A separate UN survey, discussed by scientists at a UNEP workshop in Siena, Italy, in September, found that 98% of the mercury that enters the Mediterranean is released by volcanic vents, principally Mt. Etna, and is accompanied by selenium, which binds to the same sites in the human body as mercury but without toxic effects.

In May a special session of UNEP proposed a new 20-year plan of action, costing $90 billion, to combat the spread of deserts. Delegates were told that about 21 million ha (1 ha = 2.47 ac) of farmland were being lost each year, seriously affecting 135 million people, yet only 25% of the budget allocated to the original 1977 plan had been donated and, of that, only 20% had been spent in the field, most of it ineffectively. In July UNEP called on governments to tighten controls on the export of hazardous chemicals, especially to the third world. A notification plan was proposed under which exporting countries would have to supply information to importers, including details of their own restrictions or bans on use of the substance being moved.

UN Population Conference. Delegates from 132 countries attended the second UN International Conference on Population, held in Mexico City in August. There was general agreement that world population was no longer increasing so rapidly as to constitute a crisis, although some countries continued to have difficulty balancing their rates of population growth and economic development. The latest estimates suggested that world population would

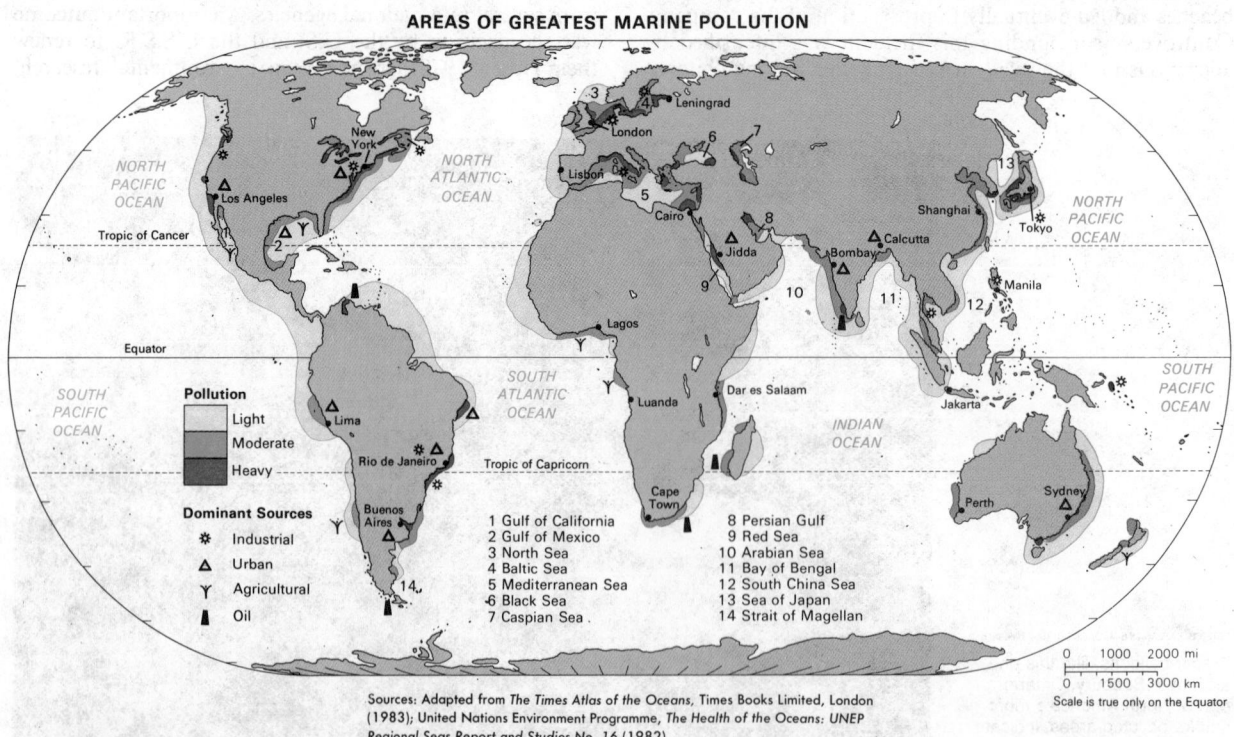

AREAS OF GREATEST MARINE POLLUTION

Pollution
Light
Moderate
Heavy

Dominant Sources
✳ Industrial
△ Urban
Y Agricultural
▮ Oil

1 Gulf of California
2 Gulf of Mexico
3 North Sea
4 Baltic Sea
5 Mediterranean Sea
6 Black Sea
7 Caspian Sea

8 Persian Gulf
9 Red Sea
10 Arabian Sea
11 Bay of Bengal
12 South China Sea
13 Sea of Japan
14 Strait of Magellan

Scale is true only on the Equator

Sources: Adapted from *The Times Atlas of the Oceans*, Times Books Limited, London (1983); United Nations Environment Programme, *The Health of the Oceans; UNEP Regional Seas Report and Studies* No. 16 (1982).

Urban pollution, particularly significant along the northern Mediterranean coast, consists of treated and untreated sewage and solid waste. Industrial pollutants include chemicals, wood pulp, and mining wastes. Agriculture generates pesticides, chemical fertilizers, and highly saline irrigation wastewater.

stabilize at around 10,000,000,000 people during the 21st century. The UN defended its support and funding for population policies that some delegates held to be coercive, in particular those pursued in China. The most controversial issues were abortion and sterilization. Speaking for the U.S., James L. Buckley said his country would contribute financially only to programs that did not include abortion and were not coercive. U.S. funds had been denied for abortion since 1974, but the new policy would deny them to all organizations performing or promoting abortion, regardless of whether the money was to be used specifically for that purpose. The U.S. position was widely condemned by other delegates.

European Communities. Estimating the cost to the EC of air pollution by sulfur dioxide and nitrogen oxides at $1.4 billion to $4.2 billion a year (allowing only $20 million of that for damage to human health and taking no account of damage to historic monuments), the EC Commission proposed measures in January that would cost about $370 million a year for 25 years. These would impose controls on large industrial installations, reducing total emissions of sulfur dioxide by 60%, nitrogen oxides by 40%, and dust by 40%. The principle of monitoring gaseous emissions at their sources and imposing limits was agreed to on March 2 by the EC environment ministers, but because of a compromise demanded by Britain, which opposed fixed limits, the measures could take effect only with the unanimous agreement of the Council of Ministers.

On June 28 the environment ministers agreed that by January 1989 lead-free petrol (gasoline) must be on sale throughout the Community, that all cars had to be able to run on it by 1991, and that leaded petrol would not be sold anywhere in the Community by the end of the century.

Council of Europe. The fourth European Ministerial Conference on the Environment, held at Vouliagmeni, Greece, April 25–27, was attended by delegates from 21 member states and Finland. The theme was "coastal areas, river banks and lake shores; their planning and management in compatibility with the ecological balance," and the emphasis was on European intergovernmental cooperation. A set of guidelines, prepared by Greece, was endorsed and commended to governments and to the Committee of Ministers of the Council of Europe. The guidelines sought to reconcile economic development with environmental protection and suggested that environmental protection might enhance economic development.

NATIONAL DEVELOPMENTS

Acid Rain. The British government remained doubtful of the efficacy of remedying the effects of acid rain by reducing British emissions of sulfur dioxide. In a briefing document prepared for a meeting held in London in December 1983, the Department of the Environment accepted that acid deposition contributed to the acidification of lakes and streams in sensitive areas but said there was little evidence that long-range transport of pollutants had damaged forests. On Jan. 9, 1984, a report from the Warren Spring Laboratory pointed out that sulfur dioxide emissions had decreased since 1970 in Britain, West and East Germany, Norway, and Sweden, while emissions of nitrogen oxides increased until 1980. A few days later the U.K. Review Group on Acid Rain agreed with this but announced its finding that rainfall over the whole of Britain was unnaturally acid, in places as acid as that in Scandinavia.

The Department of the Environment told the House of Commons Select Committee on the Environment on June 11 that damage to European forests was believed to be due mainly to ozone produced photochemically from nitrogen oxides. It was supported in this by the results of research commissioned by the Department of Energy, which found that damage did not correlate well with sulfur dioxide concentration once dry deposition was omitted from the calculation. At altitudes of more than 600 m (1,968 ft), where most damage occurred, ozone concentrations were often high over long periods; however, it was not known how ozone caused damage. The House of Lords Select Committee on the EC issued a report, *Air Pollution,* in July, which was strongly critical of the EC recommendations. (See *International Cooperation,* above.)

In August the Watt Committee on Energy Report No. 14, *Acid Rain,* emphasized the role of nitrogen oxides and hydrocarbon emissions that produce ozone photochemically. On August 6 two reports in the *Coal and Energy Quarterly* published by the National Coal Board threw further doubt on the importance of sulfur dioxide, pointing out that damage to silver fir trees was observed in England in 1858, before modern power stations or petrol engines were built; that British conifer forests showed none of the symptoms reported from West Germany other than those that had been known for many years; and that rye grass, grown experimentally in filtered air enriched with sulfur dioxide, suffered none of the damage that resulted when it was grown outside in air with the same concentration of sulfur dioxide.

The scientific picture was still unclear, however. On September 27, for example, David Fowler of the Institute of Terrestrial Ecology told an international conference organized by the Scottish Wildlife Trust at the University of Edinburgh that a 25% reduction in sulfur dioxide emissions between 1978 and 1982 had halved the incidence of acid rain in rural Scotland. The Commons committee published its report, *Acid Rain,* on September 6. It called for a 30% reduction in sulfur dioxide emissions by 1990, to be achieved entirely by modification of power stations.

More than one-third of West German forests had been damaged by acid rain, according to a national survey discussed by a committee of the Bundestag (federal parliament) on Oct. 24, 1983. In Bavaria and the Black Forest, nearly half the trees were said to be damaged. In January Federal Interior Minister Friedrich Zimmermann told the Bundestag that federally funded research into the problem was costing DM 56 million a year, with various Länder funding their own research. New limits on emissions from power stations announced in 1983 would reduce sulfur dioxide emissions from 3.5 million metric tons to 550,000 tons. In June 1984 the Bundestag voted almost unanimously against a plan proposed by Zimmermann to start up a coal-fired power station at Buschhaus, near Helmstedt, Lower Saxony, without filters to reduce sulfur dioxide emissions. A compromise was accepted by the Bundestag, however, and the Cabinet approved the start-up on August 1. The power station was to be fitted with filters as quickly as possible, would burn only low-sulfur coal, and an older power station nearby would be closed when the Buschhaus station opened. Environmentalists objected that no provision was made for checking sulfur dioxide emissions and that the station might revert to burning high-sulfur coal.

In The Netherlands, in May, Environment Minister Pieter Winsemius released a plan to reduce industrial sulfur dioxide emissions by 70%, nitrogen oxide emissions from motor vehicles by 30%, and ammonia released from agricultural fertilizers by 50% by the end of the century. It had been reported by the State Forestry Service in January that acid rain was slightly affecting virtually every conifer plantation in the country. In France the government announced in May that it wished to halve sulfur dioxide emissions before 1990. A report commissioned by the Czechoslovak government in 1980, partially reprinted in the Austrian newspaper *Die Press* in October 1984, stated that more than 400,000 ha of Czechoslovakia's forests were affected by acid rain and that more than one-quarter of them might be irreversibly damaged by the year 2000. In January the International Union for Conservation of Nature and Natural Resources reported evidence of acid rain damage to the East Transvaal Highveld in South Africa, downwind from Witwatersrand and Johannesburg.

In August 1984 New York became the first state to legislate on acid rain. By the end of the year scientists were to identify the areas of the state most at risk and determine the levels of sulfur deposition those sites could tolerate. Rules governing industrial burning of coal and oil were to be produced by 1986 and would come into force two years later.

The "Greenhouse Effect." The U.S. administration rejected the recommendations of an EPA report published in October 1983 calling for the prohibition of carbon dioxide emission, the injection of sulfur dioxide into the stratosphere to induce climatic cooling, and large-scale afforestation. The report said these measures were needed to counter a rise in temperature caused by the increasing atmospheric concentration of carbon dioxide. It warned that the average world temperature might rise 2° C (3.6° F) by 2040 and 5° C (9° F) by the end of the 21st century. A report on the same subject by the National Academy of Sciences, also published in October 1983, was only slightly less alarming. Its model of energy use predicted smaller carbon dioxide emissions and a temperature rise of between 1.5° and 4.5° C (2.7° and 8.1° F) by the year 2100.

The National Science Foundation reported in January 1984 on studies into ways of countering the threat that it had commissioned from engineers at the Massachusetts Institute of Technology and Stanford University. The recommendations were based largely on increasing the efficiency of energy use and promised to reduce carbon dioxide emission substantially. In March two British scientists, Philip Jones and Mick Kelly, of the Climatic Research Unit at the University of East Anglia, reported evidence that the Northern Hemisphere was warming. Their data, they said, were consistent with a "greenhouse effect" induced by carbon dioxide.

Freshwater Pollution. *The Nitrogen Cycle of the United Kingdom,* a report sponsored and published on January 24 by the Royal Society, said that nitrate levels in drinking water in the U.K. had exceeded recommended safety limits and that in 12 rivers for which data were available levels had risen between 50 and 400% over a 20-year period. The problem was especially acute in the southeast and the Midlands, and by the mid-1990s average concentrations in the Thames could reach the World Health Organization's recommended limit of 11.3 parts per million, with maximum concentrations markedly higher. In January a leakage of phenol into the River Dee from a factory owned by Ferro (GB) contaminated the water supply serving two million people in Clwyd, Wales, many of whom reported symptoms of poisoning. On July 25 Part II of the Control of Pollution Act 1974 came into force. It covered all estuaries and coastal waters and some underground waters and required greater public disclosure of discharges and of actions by water authorities.

Late in September the North Rhine-Westphalia water authority in West Germany published a report stating that the condition of the Rhine River had improved during 1983. The oxygen content had increased, and heavy metals no longer threatened to contaminate drinking water. Chlo-

ride and hydrochloric acid continued to cause concern, however, and the river was still rated as between "massively" and "critically" polluted. In the U.S.S.R., Lake Ladoga, near Leningrad, was reported in January as being seriously polluted by the Priozyorsk pulp mill.

Land Conservation. Austria revived plans, dating from the 1950s, to build a dam and hydroelectric plant on the Danube, in the 8,000-ha Hainburg Forest, the largest primeval riverine forest in Europe. The dam, which would divert water into a walled canal, would destroy 800 ha of forest and prevent the annual spring flooding of the remainder. The Danube Power Corporation said the hydroelectric plant would allow some fossil-fueled power stations to be closed, thus reducing acid rain pollution, but environmentalists feared that if the river ceased to flow through, and be purified by, the forest, the groundwater on which Vienna depends for its water might be polluted. A petition opposing the dam obtained 150,000 signatures. The proposal was supported, however, by some 40,000 construction workers, who marched through Vienna on May 17. The project was later put off.

According to a discussion document prepared by Derek Ratcliffe, chief scientist at the Nature Conservancy Council, and released in January, only "pathetic remnants" of Britain's countryside would be left unless destruction was halted. He said that, since 1949, 95% of old hay meadows had been destroyed and almost half the remainder damaged; 80% of chalk downlands had been plowed; at least 30% of old broadleaved woodland had been felled; and 90% of the countryside had no statutory protection. At the end of February the Department of the Environment published its *Survey of Derelict Land,* showing that although 17,000 ha of land were reclaimed between 1974 and 1982, the total area of derelict land in Britain increased during that period from 43,273 to 45,683 ha. On March 14 the Department of the Environment and the Ministry of Agriculture, Fisheries, and Food agreed on a plan to prevent the further conversion of marsh grazing land in the Norfolk Broads.

The "Danube Circle," an unofficial Hungarian environmental group, started seeking Austrian support in September for its opposition to a joint Hungarian-Czechoslovak plan to divert most of the water of the Danube through a canal to a power station at Gabcikovo, Czech. The plan would involve building a dam at Nagymoros and flooding the most scenic stretch of the river. The scheme was first agreed on in 1977, but work stopped on the Hungarian side in 1981, allegedly for lack of funds. In the autumn of 1983 a new agreement was signed, and the completion date was advanced from 1990 to 1994, this time with an offer of Austrian financial help in return for a power supply. This, said the Circle, was impractical since the river was at its lowest in winter when power demand was highest, and the scheme was intended only to supply peak demand. The main objection, however, was based on fears of contaminating the groundwater that supplied eight million people in northern Hungary and on loss of wildlife.

Early in June details began to emerge of the damage caused over two years by extensive forest fires that had raged through remote parts of Kalimantan, Indonesia. West German experts said half the trees there had been destroyed, 3.6 million ha of rain forest was gone, and in some places fires had burned intermittently for a year. Slash-and-burn peasant farmers were blamed.

Radioactive Wastes. A television documentary program, "Windscale, the Nuclear Laundry," made by Yorkshire TV and shown on Nov. 1, 1983, claimed that children in several villages near the Sellafield (formerly Windscale) processing plant in Cumbria showed a markedly higher

In December a toxic-gas leak at a Union Carbide pesticide plant in Bhopal, India, caused hundreds of the town's residents to die immediately, and thousands more died in the days that followed from injuries suffered during the leak. Because of the great number of fatalities, mass burials and cremations were necessary.

SANDRO TUCCI—GAMMA/LIAISON

incidence of leukemia than the national average. The next day the secretary of state for the environment, Patrick Jenkin, ordered an inquiry, headed by Sir Douglas Black, former president of the Royal College of Physicians. The Black report, *Investigation of the Possible Increased Incidence of Cancer in West Cumbria,* published on July 23, 1984, found that, although the incidence of leukemia was high, it was not unique and could not be linked conclusively with Sellafield discharges.

In November 1983 radioactively contaminated waste became mixed with waste water at the Sellafield plant, and some was accidentally released into the sea, where it contaminated seaweed and other solid matter that was washed ashore. Eventually, 24 km of beaches were contaminated and closed to the public until the end of July 1984. As the cleaning operation proceeded, more contaminated material was washed ashore, possibly from other routine releases of waste. The incident led to a police investigation, and on October 4 the company was committed for trial, charged with five offenses under the Radioactive Substances Act 1960 and the Nuclear Installations Act 1965. In October 1983 BNFL had promised to reduce discharges of plutonium and americium, and in June 1984 it launched a study aimed at virtually eliminating all its radioactive discharges into the sea. The company's annual report on discharges, issued in September, showed a fall from 96,171 curies in 1982 to 67,570 curies in 1983, including an estimated 1,600 curies released in the November accident.

On August 25 the French cargo ship "Mont Louis," owned by the Compagnie Générale Maritime, collided with the West German car ferry "Olau Britannia" and sank 18 km (11 mi) from the Belgian coast near Ostend. No one was injured, but the "Mont Louis" was carrying 225 metric tons of uranium hexafluoride in 30 containers bound for enrichment in the U.S.S.R. Salvage was hampered by bad weather, and the ship released 400 tons of fuel oil, contaminating the Belgian coast. None of the containers leaked any of its contents, however, and the last one was recovered on October 4.

Late in 1983 more than 100 Mexican workers received high doses of radiation when three maintenance workers at a medical clinic in Ciudad Juárez loaded a radiotherapy machine onto a Ford truck and took it to a scrapyard. A lead shield broke, releasing 7,200 pellets of cobalt-60, which contaminated the steel. Subsequently, part of the steel was used to make bars for reinforced concrete, while the remainder was sent to a mill in St. Louis, Mo., to be made into legs for restaurant tables. The movement of the steel was stopped on Jan. 25, 1984, and by mid-February U.S. authorities had located all but about 6% of the affected table legs. Some of the bars had been used in buildings, and in Arizona they were ordered removed from a private home, a state prison, and a medical centre.

Toxic Chemical Wastes. On the night of December 3, some 45 metric tons of methyl isocyanate escaped from a pesticide plant in Bhopal, India, owned by the Indian subsidiary of Union Carbide Corp., a U.S.-based multinational. The highly toxic gas spread over the poor residential neighbourhood surrounding the factory, killing many of the inhabitants immediately and creating a panic as others attempted to flee. By mid-December the official death count had passed 1,300, but since many of the bodies were buried or cremated en masse for fear of epidemics, the exact toll might never be known; estimates ran as high as 2,500. An estimated 100,000 others were affected, and a massive relief operation was undertaken.

Both the Indian government and the company began investigations into the accident, but when Warren Anderson and Keshub Mahindra, the chairmen of Union Carbide and of its Indian subsidiary, arrived in Bhopal, they were arrested; Anderson was later allowed to return to the U.S. The stocks of methyl isocyanate remaining in the plant were neutralized in a carefully monitored operation between December 16 and 23. Despite its excellent safety record, a similar pesticide plant owned by Union Carbide in Institute, W.Va., was closed by the company pending the investigation at Bhopal. Meanwhile, suits for damages running into the billions were filed in the U.S. on behalf of the victims, although the jurisdiction of U.S. courts in the matter was unclear. In a press conference, Anderson insisted that Union Carbide was in good financial condition and had no intention of declaring bankruptcy, as Manville Corp. had done when faced with huge lawsuits over damages allegedly caused (over a much longer term) by asbestos. The disaster raised disturbing questions concerning the siting of factories processing dangerous materials, safety precautions taken by multinational corporations, regulations governing safety and mandating indigenous work and supervisory forces in third world nations, and the fragility of modern industrial society generally.

Following a television program and an article in *Der Spiegel* magazine alleging birth defects downwind of a Hamburg factory making the insecticide lindane, regulations were passed by the city government requiring the removal of waste contaminated by dioxins from sites at Zersetzer and Georgswerder. The orders were upheld by a court on June 18, and on June 20 the owners of the factory, C. H. Böhringer Sohn, said they could not comply and the factory would close. In West Berlin fears of dioxin poisoning from 7,000 metric tons of heating oil that had been mixed illegally with 25 tons of used oil contaminated with chlorine and sulfur compounds led to calls for the establishment of a police force for environmental protection.

Early in July traces of chlorinated dioxin were found in soil samples near the Re-Chem International waste disposal plant at Bonnybridge, Scotland, which specialized in the incineration of polychlorinated biphenyls, and on August 1 other samples were found to contain heavy metals. Unexpected illness and deaths were reported among farm livestock in the area. The evidence was controversial, but on September 17 the company announced that the Bonnybridge plant would close on October 19 for financial reasons.

In January the EPA announced plans to spend up to $250 million over four years to investigate hundreds of waste-disposal sites in the U.S., especially those believed to contain dioxins. Later in the year the House of Representatives voted $10.2 billion for the second five years of the "superfund" program for cleaning up waste-disposal sites, on condition that the EPA accelerate its study of sites, starting with 150 new locations each year. At least 19,000 potentially dangerous sites were known, but in four years only six had been cleaned. On November 9 Pres. Ronald Reagan signed a bill tightening federal standards for toxic waste disposal and mandating compliance by small companies that were previously exempt. In the same month Ruckelshaus announced his resignation as EPA head and Lee M. Thomas, deputy director for solid waste and emergency responses, was named to succeed him. Ruckelshaus was credited with restoring credibility to the agency, which had been demoralized by scandals involving mismanagement and alleged sweetheart deals with dumpers.

In Japan fears were expressed about dangers of mercury contamination from used alkaline-manganese and "button" batteries in urban waste dumps. Japan was producing nearly 3,000,000,000 such batteries a year, containing some 70 metric tons of mercury. Consumer groups called for the batteries to be separated from other waste for disposal.

Asbestos. On August 1 new regulations came into force in the U.K. requiring the licensing of all employers who wished their workers to handle asbestos. New exposure limits were set at 0.2 fibres per millilitre of air for brown asbestos and 0.5 fibres per millilitre for white.

In May it was reported that the EPA was planning to recommend a ban on asbestos in a wide range of building materials, totaling about half of all U.S. asbestos consumption. A total ban on asbestos in ten years was envisioned, provided substitutes had been developed. The Occupational Safety and Health Administration was said to be planning a reduction in the permitted exposure to asbestos at work to 0.2 or 0.5 fibres per millilitre of air during any eight-hour period.

Lead. In July the EPA proposed a 91% reduction in the amount of lead permitted in gasoline, leading to a total ban by the 1990s, when cars that could not use unleaded fuel would have been scrapped. Following a November 1983 agreement between the West German government and car manufacturers, the Cabinet decided in September 1984 that, from Jan. 1, 1989, all new motor vehicles would have to be fitted with catalytic converters to reduce exhaust emissions. Cars with an engine capacity larger than two litres would have to meet the requirement a year earlier.

Pesticides. On May 10 the U.K. minister of agriculture, fisheries and food, Michael Jopling, told the House of Commons that the voluntary arrangements governing the use of pesticides would be given statutory force as soon as practicable. On August 6 it was reported that the ministry had drafted a law fixing limits for pesticide residues in food for human consumption and giving ministers powers to set limits for other farm products. The sale and use of DDT was banned from October 1. In West Germany the government banned the use of paraquat in August.

Nuclear Protest. Following the accidental discharge from the Sellafield plant (*see* above), divers belonging to the Greenpeace environmental protest group tried to locate and block the mouth of the discharge pipe. Poor visibility defeated the attempt, but on Nov. 22, 1983, BNFL obtained a court injunction to halt the Greenpeace action (which Greenpeace obeyed) and sought sequestration of all U.K. Greenpeace funds. Greenpeace filed a counterclaim over contamination of its crew, divers, and equipment, then broke the injunction. The organization was fined £50,000 on December 1 for contempt of court, reduced on Jan. 13, 1984, to £36,000 plus £4,000 costs.

In Japan the attempt by local citizens to close down a nuclear power station in Fukushima Prefecture, about 240 km (150 mi) northwest of Tokyo, failed when the lawsuit they had been pursuing for more than nine years was dismissed by a Tokyo court. The plaintiffs maintained that permission for the station had been improperly given because of irregularities in safety screening. In June 1,800 riot police were called in to control a demonstration at a public hearing into a license application for a nuclear power station in Saga Prefecture. In April nearly 3,000 West German demonstrators used burning straw bales to block roads at Guelden, near the Gorleben site of a proposed nuclear fuel-reprocessing plant. More than 20 demonstrators were arrested.

"Green" Politics. In Switzerland the Ecologist Party won two seats in the national Parliament at the October 1983 general election. A national referendum on nuclear power was held on Sept. 22–23, 1984, following controversy over the planned construction of new power stations at Kaiseraugst near Basel and Verbois near Geneva. Both aroused strong local opposition, and violent protests halted work at Kaiseraugst. However, the referendum produced a 55% majority in favour of nuclear power.

The West German Green Party had its greatest success of the year in the June elections to the European Parliament, when it secured seven seats and thus replaced the Free Democrats as the third largest political grouping in the West German delegation. Earlier in June the Greens in Hesse had cooperated with the Social Democrats (SPD) in a so-called red-green alliance that formed a majority in the state assembly. The Greens performed well in elections in two other Länder. In Baden-Württemberg on March 25 they increased their share of the vote from the 5.3% polled in 1980 to 8% and their seats in the state assembly from six to nine. In local elections in North Rhine-Westphalia on September 30, they won 9.2% of the overall vote, again surpassing the Free Democrats.

Notwithstanding their success, the Greens suffered from some internal disagreements, mainly over the rotation of Bundestag seats. Their members were expected to resign halfway through the session and be replaced by others. Former Bundeswehr general Gert Bastian resigned from the Green faction in the Bundestag on February 9 and continued to sit as an independent. On April 5 Waltraud Schoppe, Antje Vollmer, and Annemarie Borgmann were elected to lead the faction, replacing Petra Kelly, Marie-Luise Beck-Oberdorf, and Otto Schily. Bastian and Kelly opposed the idea of rotation, and Schily favoured an alliance with the Social Democrats, which was opposed by more fundamentalist Green Party members. At a meeting held March 3–4, it was agreed that Green members of the European Parliament would be rotated. There was some hostility to the EC in general as being out of sympathy with the Greens' environmentalist and antinuclear aims.

(MICHAEL ALLABY)

WILDLIFE CONSERVATION

In December 1983 it was reported that 50 critically endangered golden-headed lion tamarins (*Leontopithecus chrysomelas*) had been smuggled out of Brazil into Belgium. Little could be done, since Belgium's ratification of the Convention on International Trade in Endangered Species of Wild Fauna and Flora (CITES) did not become effective until Jan. 1, 1984. Jeremy Mallinson, writing in *Oryx* (April 1984), warned that all three species of lion tamarin could be extinct by 1990 unless dramatic changes occurred to prevent inroads into their last remnants of habitat in Brazil. In June ten zoo-born golden lion tamarins (*L. rosalia*) were released into Brazil's 5,000-ha Poço das Antas Biological Reserve.

An EC directive banning importation of harp and hooded seal pup skins into EC countries came into effect on Oct. 1, 1983, and would remain valid for two years. As a result of the ban, Norway's major sealskin-processing company closed its fur-dressing factory, and it was estimated that the 1984 Canadian seal hunt was reduced to one-third of the 1983 level and to one-tenth the level of previous years.

Many other government bans came into effect. Sudan banned all exports of unworked ivory from January 1; Malaysia banned the export of crab-eating macaques (*Macaca fascicularis*) to the U.S., where they were used for weapon research, from June 15; South West Africa/Namibia banned the capture and export of wild birds; Tanzania stopped trade in the masked lovebird (*Agapornis personata*) and the commercial export of cheetah and leopard skins; and China banned frog catching in Beijing (Peking) and the sale of frogs and tadpoles for chicken food.

In the U.S. some 40 people involved in illegal international trade in protected birds of prey were arrested in June as the result of a three-year undercover operation. The birds included gyrfalcons (*Falco rusticolus*), prized by falconers as the "bird of kings." Despite a ban on imports of rhino horn by Yemen (San'a'), more than 50% of the rhino horn on the world market in 1984 was still being exported to that country. Indiscriminate shooting of migratory birds continued in Greece, in defiance of the EC directive on the conservation of wild birds. An encouraging development occurred on Dec. 1, 1983, when the Bonn Convention on the Conservation of Migratory Species of Wild Animals came into effect.

At the 36th meeting of the International Whaling Commission, held in Buenos Aires, Arg., in June, all commercial catch quotas except two were reduced. Of special importance was the reduction in quotas for minke whales in the Southern Hemisphere by nearly 40%, from 6,655 in 1983–84 to 4,224 in 1984–85, because of scientific advice that there were far fewer minke whales than previously believed. Japan, Brazil, and the U.S.S.R. objected to the reductions.

In November the U.S. and Japan reached an agreement whereby Japan undertook to end all whaling by 1988 and the U.S. agreed not to impose sanctions against Japan if it continued to catch sperm whales after the IWC-mandated moratorium on such whaling took effect in 1985. Environmental groups strongly objected to the arrangement.

A MacGillivray's petrel (*Bulweria macgillivrayi*), a species last seen 129 years earlier, was rediscovered in May by Dick Watling, a British naturalist, when a bird crashed on his head. Two more herds of captive-bred white or Arabian oryx were released into the wild, 31 into the Shaumari Reserve in Jordan in October 1983 and 8 into Oman in April 1984. The herd released in Oman in 1982 numbered 13 and was completely established. This was the first time an animal that had become extinct in the wild had been successfully reintroduced. New Zealand's program to restore the Chatham Island black robin (*Petroica traversi*) resulted in an increase from 9 to 20 birds in the 1983–84 breeding season and the establishment of a second population, on South East Island. The species had numbered only five individuals, on Little Mangere Island, in 1980. The program involved transferring robin eggs to nests where they were hatched and fostered by Chatham Island tits, leaving the robins to lay and hatch second clutches.

In Mauritius a pair of captive-bred pink pigeons (*Nesoenas mayeri*) was released as a first step toward increasing the wild population of 15–20 birds. A decision was made to take the eight remaining wild echo parakeets (*Psittacula echo*) into captivity for breeding. Efforts to increase the number of whooping cranes in the U.S. continued; at the end of 1983 a record 107 were living in the wild. Also in the U.S., the California condor (*Gymnogyps californianus*) recovery program, which had received a boost in 1983 with the addition of seven birds to the captive flock (bringing the total to nine), suffered a setback when two wild condors died: one in November 1983 from cyanide poisoning and the other, in March 1984, apparently from

AP/WIDE WORLD

A nonsurgical embryo transplant between different species resulted in the birth of a bongo to an eland. Both are species of African antelope.

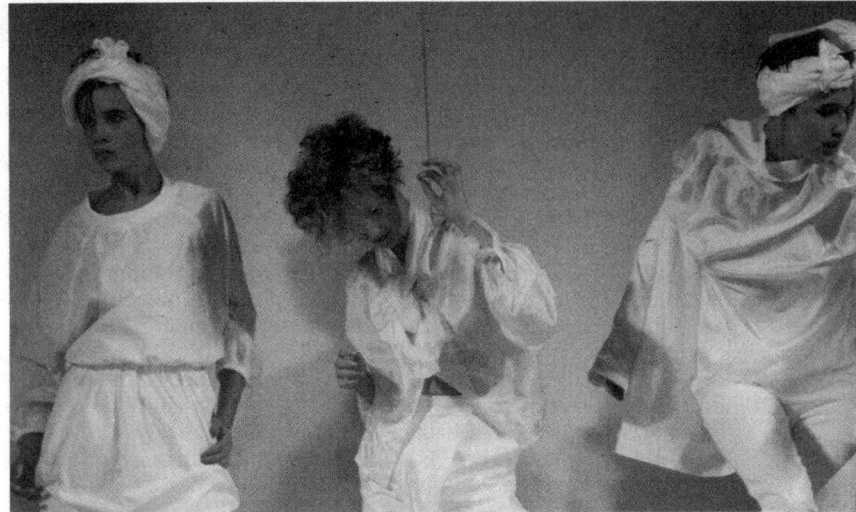

The garish fashion influence of the punks (above) lost its driving force, and fuller, softer lines characterized new fashions. An all-black winter look gave way to all white for summer, shown at left in silks and cottons.

(LEFT) LYNNE FRANKS LIMITED; (ABOVE) GIBSON/SPOONER—GAMMA/LIAISON

lead poisoning. The black-footed ferret (*Mustela nigripes*) survey in Wyoming found 128 animals, compared with 88 in 1983, but extensive searches had revealed none outside the Meeteetse region where they were rediscovered in 1981.

In 1983 the future had looked bleak for China's 300 giant pandas, threatened with starvation following the mass flowering and dieback of bamboo. Only 20 pandas were found dead in the winter of 1983–84, however, and not all had died of starvation. Some bamboo species had remained available, and the pandas had ranged farther in search of food than had been predicted. In northern Quebec, in what the Audubon Society described as "a major environmental catastrophe," thousands of caribou drowned while attempting to cross two rivers during their annual migration. Native leaders blamed the Hydro-Quebec utility for permitting an excessive flow of water over a dam, but this was denied by the utility and by provincial officials.

"Firsts" in captive breeding during the year included: the Madagascar angulated tortoise (*Geochelone yniphora*), which was nearing extinction in the wild; yellow-spotted sideneck turtles (*Podocnemis unifilis*), an endangered South American species; bongo (*Boocercus euryceros*) twins from embryo transplants into an eland (*Taurotragus oryx*) and a bongo in the U.S.; and a Przewalski horse born to a domestic horse in the U.K. as a result of an embryo transfer.

The Kerala state government in India announced in April that it intended to abandon the Silent Valley hydroelectric project. The area, home of the endangered lion-tailed macaque (*Macaca silenus*), would be included in the Silent Valley National Park. In Malaysia conservationists were urging the government to stop the Bakun hydroelectric project in Sarawak, which would flood 300 sq km (116 sq mi) of land and destroy much wildlife. A dam on the Tonantins River, 400 km (250 mi) south of Belem in Brazil, would eventually flood 3,000 sq km (1,160 sq mi), much of it virgin forest. Both the Brazilian authorities and the company responsible for the hydroelectric project were aware of the possible huge loss of animal life, and a veterinarian was appointed to minimize it. Little was likely to be achieved, however, for even if the animals were captured there were no satisfactory sites for their release.

(JACQUI M. MORRIS)

See also Agriculture and Food Supplies; Botanical Gardens and Zoos; Energy; Historic Preservation; Life Sciences; Transportation.

This article updates the *Macropædia* article CONSERVATION OF NATURAL RESOURCES.

Fashion and Dress

Individuality was the watchword in fashion throughout 1984. The message was "Shake it all up and produce your own look." Wiser advice would have been "Take your pick but beware of pitfalls." However, the temptation was great, and exaggerations were plentiful.

During the fall of 1983 and the early months of 1984, women, by adopting the all-black look, presented an image of grief and despair. Mourners after some great disaster? Influence of the depiction of atomic devastation in the TV movie "The Day After"? Black it was from head to foot in big, loose shapes, with dolman sleeves and around-the-body wrapping borrowed from the Japanese, clasped in by big bold belts. Trousers were cropped, and shoes, also black, had low heels and pointed toes.

Another look, popular with students, was borrowed from the men's wardrobe without alteration or fitting. The big tweed overcoat, rounded at the top, with huge collar and wide lapels, was worn over gray flannel trousers full and baggy to the point of being clownesque—oversize, overfull, overlong, and overtough. The tough, mannish look also appeared in sleek black leather in the form of a loose blouson and matching skirt that could be tight and above the knees or full and below the calf. Even ponchos appeared oversize, with big patch pockets and low hemlines.

In contrast to this avant-garde trend, which was always better when taken in fragments and not as a whole, was the well-mannered, well-tailored, more sophisticated interpretation of mannish fashion with a military influence. This was the style of the London Sloane Rangers and of those taking their lead from Diana, princess of Wales. In Paris, where the well-bred young working women were known as the BCBG or "Bon Chic Bon Genre," favoured items included the traditional trench coat, the loden coat, the soft-crowned tweed hat with turned-down brim, and the plain wool or cashmere fringed scarf in bright colours, replacing the previous winter's large shawl. Providing the "preppy" look were the tartan pleated skirt, the Oxford shirt with necktie, and the twin sweater set, preferably in cashmere. Even the long-forsaken string of pearls was back. On the streets of American cities a common sight was the young working woman conservatively "dressed for success" except for expensive running shoes—usually exchanged for conventional footwear when she reached her office.

The deep batwing armhole prevailing in sweaters brought

them to hipbone level. Many featured squares and circles in the best Art Deco tradition of the 1920s. The plain models had a wide, boat-shaped, collarless neckline that later on in the season was stretched to bare one shoulder. Except for the fancier cowboy or Midwest style, ankle-high bootees, laced, buttoned, or hooked over the instep and with pointed toes and low, stumpy heels, were important for the winter look. At the approach of spring they were exchanged for pumps with single or double straps crossing the instep on the diagonal, thus retaining the covered look. Almost invariably, these were in crimson red.

The spring silhouette was shaped like a triangle, broad at the top and tapered from hips to hemline. Hemlines continued to waver, with the mini finding adherents among the young. For those who could not make up their minds on skirt lengths, the answer was pants. These were now cropped to well above the ankle, bringing them more or less to the level of the lengthened skirt, which was full and often divided. Pants kept their baggy winter aspect, with gathers and pleats under a more or less wide waistband. On the street they were often worn with cropped tweed jackets. The die-hard, second-skin type still had a vast number of followers, however, particularly when warm weather brought out white cotton. Jodhpurs made a brief appearance. Jeans were out of the fashion picture except for very casual wear.

After the all-black winter look came the all-white summer look, giving city streets a prolonged-weekend appearance. In this holiday-in-town category was the full, bias-cut, below-the-calf skirt, worn with a loose top, often in a very open knit and featuring an off-the-shoulder effect in a stretched bateau line or a low vee at the back. It was white for mannish and tailored shirts, for ample, dolman-sleeved blouses, pants, shorts, clipped jackets or boleros, miniskirts, and dresses. White was also the favourite colour for accessories, along with a warm shade of camel brown shown in high-heeled, open sandals, handbags, and belts.

In keeping with this cleaned-up look were the jogging clothes—not just improvised getups but specially designed outfits. They had blousing tops, and the matching pants could be either snug-fitting, with zip fastening molding the leg to knee level, or ample and held up by suspenders.

On London's King's Road the punks had lost their stamina. They no longer surprised or even seemed odd. Though the outside world had sometimes harboured the spiky multicoloured hairdo, with standing centre cockscomb and short flattened sides, punks had lost their driving force. They just survived in a world that had moved on, like any other tourist attraction.

In midsummer sparks from the Olympic torch reached the sportswear market, which was quick to pick up the athletic look. Swimsuits, cut in one piece, were covered with Olympic slogans, spelling out Los Angeles in huge letters down the front or featuring the five Olympic rings on a stars and stripes background. Circular cutouts as large as portholes gave extra freedom to plain jersey sheath dresses, and jersey was also the choice for hooded blousons and jumpsuits. Boxers' white terry cloth wraps, with shoulder padding and deep pockets, were thrown over short, beaded evening dresses just as casually as over one-piece swimsuits. The flared skating dress in plain jersey was decked out with pearls and gold chains. Padded fencing suits, judoka costumes, runners' and jumpers' shorts and trunks, all inspired sportswear manufacturers and found their way to the fashion world. The Olympic rings appeared as dangling earrings or as metal clasps on belts.

After many years of garments labeled as fun clothes and intended to amuse, it was suddenly discovered that clothes could also be meant to please and even to charm. This trend was particularly noticeable in evening clothes, which were closely fitted and draped on one hip. When two deep flounces gave a swing to the skirt, the sources of inspiration that came to mind were the numerous film and stage versions of *Carmen* shown during the year. Tops were generally black, with a boat-shaped neckline and long sleeves, or they might be worn with elbow-length gloves. The flounced skirt, like the top in paper-weight taffeta, was in very bright colours. In a longer version, with a single flounce emphasizing the wrap effect, the skirt became very narrow to just above the ankle and unwrapped only slightly for walking. A more casual evening look was suggested by the coatdress with satin lapels, knee length and beltless.

Jewelry made a forceful comeback. Earrings, totally out for many seasons except for the gold or diamond pinpricks for pierced ears, became a must from morning till night. They grew in size and sparkle as the day declined and dripped with diamonds like chandeliers at night. For day wear, chunks of metal, plain or inserted with coloured stones, attracted attention. Big hoops of colour, or plain white ones, dangled from the ears. Bracelets, too, returned after a similar blackout period, worn in twos or threes alongside the wristwatch.

Among the tender pastels along Charm Alley, the palest of hydrangea pink was selected for angora knitwear and for silk lingerie. Makeup trends followed the mood of clothes. With the Olympic look and the new boyish hairdo went fresh colours and a healthy complexion, heightened as if by sea air. For the lips, there was a choice of pink hinting of amethyst or a bright, pungent vermilion. Porcelain shades in pink and mauve went with the hydrangea pink. For a special occasion, yellow on the eyelids was remarkable and light-catching.   (THELMA SWEETINBURGH)

Men's Fashions. Leisure clothes generally and sports clothes in particular were the principal influences on men's fashion in 1984. They also helped to revive a sense of dressing for the occasion by men in Australia, America, and throughout Europe. Whole new lines of clothes specially designed for leisure wear were introduced at the menswear trade fairs in Amsterdam; Copenhagen; Cologne, West Germany; Florence, Italy; Helsinki, Fin.; Paris; and London. Trade fairs in the U.S. and Australia confirmed the trend to more comfortable clothes in natural fabrics, cottons and linens for summer outfits and wool for the winter.

The "layered" look lasted throughout the year. For spring and summer the layers consisted of a cellular cotton vest worn under a longer-than-usual sports shirt, which in turn was worn under a shorter-than-usual jacket or blazer. Tailored shorts, shorter and smarter, were in cotton or linen and sometimes formed part of a lighter weight two-piece summer suit. Except for business occasions and evening dress, shirttails were worn outside the pants.

The fashion for wearing two, three, or even more garments over one another continued into the autumn and winter seasons, with wool or cotton shirts worn under boldly patterned knitwear and sports jackets or blazers—plus, on really cold days, an overcoat. The raincoat reemerged as a transparent, ankle-length garment.

Younger men turned to close-cropped hairstyles and adorned themselves with jewelry. T-shirts bearing either a slogan or a motif, or sometimes both, continued to be popular. Businessmen continued to choose conservatively styled suits but in lighter weight fabrics, with discreet but colourful patterns. Active sports clothes, tennis shirts and shorts, cablestitch cricket sweaters, club-striped blazers, the riding man's hacking jacket and jodhpurs—even football and rugby shirts—all provided fashion inspiration for designers of clothes for not-so-active spectators.

At the 30th Cologne International Men's Fashion Week, a panel of designers discussed "Fashions for the 1990s." In the panel's view, casual clothes that could be worn by either sex would disappear, and there would be a return to more standard dressing and a strong redefinition of gender roles. (STANLEY H. COSTIN)

See also Industrial Review: *Furs.*

This article updates the *Macropædia* article DRESS AND ADORNMENT.

Gardening

Gardening continued to be an important contributor to the U.S. economy in 1984. It was estimated that eight million American families spent $1.2 billion on lawn and garden supplies and services. A survey conducted by *Better Homes and Gardens* magazine underscored the importance of the garden centre/nursery industry as the main source of supply. It also indicated that the use of home gardening services, particularly lawn care, was rising.

Spring was still the prime planting season for U.S. gardeners, according to a survey conducted by the American Association of Nurserymen. Nearly two-thirds of retail garden centres and nurseries purchased more plants for the 1984 spring season than they had the previous year, and even higher spring sales were expected in 1985, but these same nurseries kept a lower inventory for fall. The industry spurred promotion of its "Fall Is for Planting" theme, designed to encourage more home gardeners to take advantage of good autumn weather. Environmental consciousness had created a modest change in the use of garden supplies. There was a slight reduction in homeowners' applications of herbicides and pesticides, along with an increased awareness of the value of native plant materials. On the whole, gardeners were becoming better educated and demanding a greater variety of better-quality plants. This trend encouraged the growth of small "mom-and-pop" nursery operations propagating select and unusual varieties.

The interior plant industry was also experiencing rapid growth as more and more shopping malls and office buildings were being constructed with inner spaces that needed not only professional design and installation of foliage and flowering plants but also continuing professional care. The increasing demand for interior landscaping plants also nurtured the tissue-culture industry, which utilized sterile laboratory conditions to clone plants.

The tomato remained the home gardener's favourite vegetable, according to a survey conducted by the Gallup Organization for Gardens for All, the National Association for Gardening, but the amount of broccoli being raised had increased nearly two and a half times; it was estimated that home gardeners raised about 25,000 tons of broccoli a year. Gardening continued to be Americans' number one outdoor leisure activity, and eight out of ten households surveyed engaged in at least one form of gardening, either outdoor or indoor. Enthusiasm for gardening cut across all income groups, though the emphasis on vegetables as opposed to flowers tended to rise inversely with income. Sixteen percent of vegetable gardeners and 22% of flower gardeners had incomes over $40,000; 35% of vegetable and 35% of flower gardeners were in the $20,000–$40,000 range; 33% of vegetable and 28% of flower gardeners made $10,000–$20,000; and 16% of vegetable and 14% of flower gardeners had incomes under $10,000.

In Europe the International Garden Festival was held for the first time in Britain, on a derelict dockside site in Liverpool. Despite a very short period for construction, the festival was judged to have been a success, attracting 3.3 million visitors during the six months it was open. There were more than 20 "international gardens," the highest number of international participants at such an exhibition to date.

Visiting gardens remained a popular pursuit in Britain, further stimulated by the English Tourist Board's special promotion in 1984. There was, at last, some recognition by the British government that gardens are worthy of state expenditure. The Historic Buildings and Ancient Monuments Commission planned to compile a preliminary register of "important" gardens, the first step toward assessing the need for grants toward restoration. Other European countries such as The Netherlands, France, and Denmark already had such lists.

As in the U.S., the gardening industry was flourishing in Britain. At an autumn trade exhibition, the value of the garden and leisure industry was estimated to be approaching £1,000 million at retail prices. Newly raised or introduced plants seemed to be gaining acceptance by gardeners much more quickly than in earlier years. A new technique for raising and transplanting seedlings of certain flower and vegetable crops, widely used commercially, was spreading on a smaller scale to production for amateurs of certain bedding plants such as begonia, impatiens, and sweet peppers. The young plants (known as "speedlings") are raised in small modules of peat, which are sent, tightly packed, by mail, for immediate transplanting. The advantage is that the period of germination, which is often difficult for amateurs, is left to the specialists, and growers can get the number of plants they want.

The awards for seed-raised plants in Europe, under the Fleuroselect organization, went to a dwarf, double-flowered, yellow *Rudbeckia* called Goldilocks, raised by Hursts (of England), and to the *Gazania* Ministar Tangerine, raised by Benary (of Switzerland). Both received bronze medals. The main awards by the Royal National Rose Society went to Anisley Dickson, a pink floribunda raised by Dickson in Northern Ireland; Grouse, a ground-cover rose raised by Kordes in West Germany; and, for scent, Perdita, raised by David Austin in England.

(JOAN LEE FAUST; ELSPETH NAPIER)

See also Agriculture and Food Supplies; Environment; Life Sciences.

Health and Disease

General Developments. Leading the medical news in 1984 was the announcement by researchers in the United States and in France that they had identified a type of human cancer virus that apparently causes AIDS, or acquired immune deficiency syndrome. Robert Gallo and associates at the U.S. National Cancer Institute announced their finding in April, identifying the virus as human T-cell lymphotropic virus, type III, or HTLV-III. At the Institut Pasteur in Paris a French team identified what seemed to be the same or a quite similar virus, which they designated LAV, or lymphadenopathy-associated virus.

AIDS, originally thought to be an infection confined to homosexual men, was first identified in 1981. By late 1984 more than 6,600 cases had been reported in the U.S. Death within two years of diagnosis remained the rule.

The discovery of the viral cause of the disease raised hopes for the ultimate production of an anti-AIDS vaccine

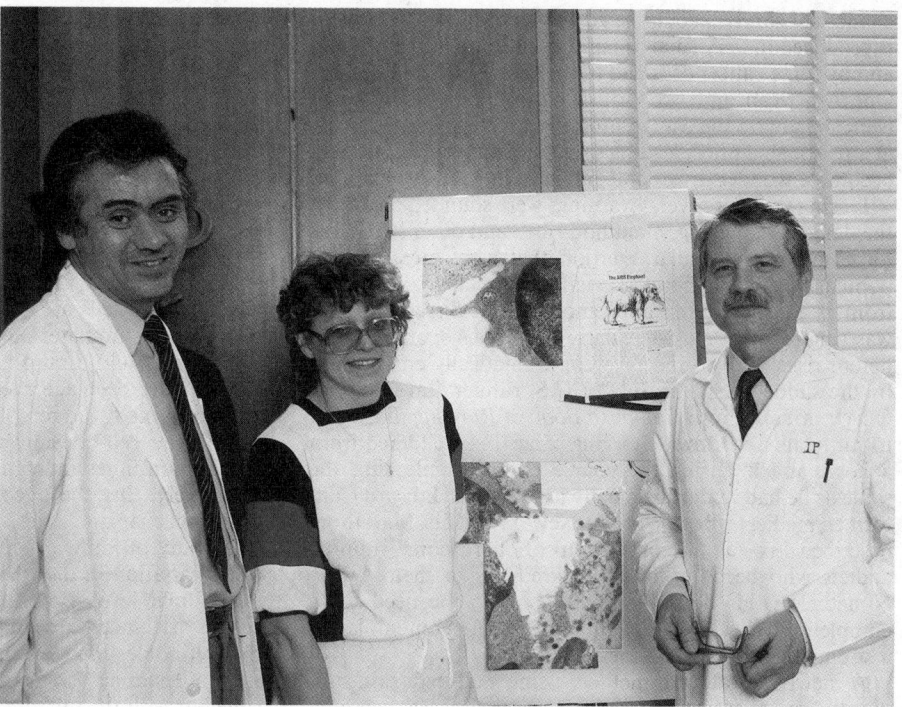

A major development in the search for a cure for AIDS (acquired immune deficiency syndrome) was the identification by French scientists of a virus they called LAV (lymphadenopathy-associated virus) that apparently causes AIDS. The French team worked at the Institut Pasteur in Paris and were, from left to right, Jean-Claude Chermann, François Barre Simoussi, and Luc Montagnier.
MICHEL PHILIPPOT—SYGMA

for those at greatest risk and, possibly, a preparation of antibodies that could be used to treat established cases. In the meantime, the first priority was the development of a method to determine if a given sample of blood contained the virus. Such a test would enable blood bank officials to screen donor blood and thereby avoid using AIDS-contaminated blood for transfusions.

Also capturing headlines during 1984 were two controversial applications of organ transplant technology. In the first case, doctors at Loma Linda (Calif.) University Medical Center performed an animal-to-human transplant on a two-week-old infant born with a fatal heart defect. The malformed heart of the tiny patient, who was known only as "Baby Fae," was replaced with the healthy heart of a young baboon. Controversy over the highly experimental nature of the procedure—the first of its kind—and its questionable therapeutic value to the patient continued long after her death on November 15, 20 days after the surgery.

On November 25, at Humana Hospital Audubon in Louisville, Ky., William J. Schroeder, 52, of Jasper, Ind., became the second human to receive a total artificial heart implant. The surgery was performed by William C. De-Vries, who pioneered the procedure in 1982. Barney Clark, DeVries's first patient, had died of multiple systems failures 112 days after receiving his mechanical heart. Schroeder's initially remarkable recovery was marred by a series of strokes. At year's end, however, Schroeder's physicians remained optimistic about his prospects for a satisfactory recovery.

The National Heart, Lung and Blood Institute published the results of a ten-year study designed to see if lowering cholesterol could prevent heart disease. The institute recruited some 4,000 middle-aged men with blood cholesterol levels in the upper 5% range for U.S. males. Half of the men were given a placebo and followed a diet designed to reduce their cholesterol level by a few percentage points. The other half received a cholesterol-lowering drug, cholestyramine, and followed the same low-cholesterol diet. Men in the drug-treated group showed reductions of about 13.4% in blood cholesterol levels and a 24% decrease in

deaths from heart attack and coronary artery disease. In December an expert panel convened by the U.S. National Institutes of Health recommended that specific dietary measures be adopted by all Americans to reduce their blood cholesterol levels.

In March the *New England Journal of Medicine* carried a report of the first tests on a natural protein—tissue-type plasminogen activator (t-PA)—capable of dissolving the clots that precipitate heart attacks. Philip Ludbrook, professor of medicine at Washington University, St. Louis, Mo., said that if heart attack victims could be treated with t-PA within seven hours of the onset of chest pains, their

IRA WYMAN—SYGMA

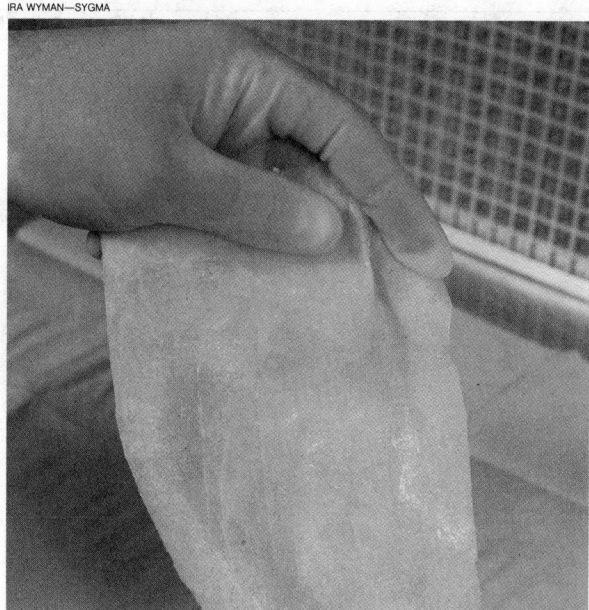

A technique that used sheets of skin grown in laboratory cultures from undamaged skin cells to treat burn victims was applied successfully in the treatment of five- and six-year-old brothers burned over 97% of their bodies.

chances of survival could be greatly improved. The protein is produced in very small quantities in some human tissues and by some cancer cells and is, therefore, extremely costly. One American and two British biotechnology companies were already on the way to producing the agent in quantity at a reasonable price, leading to predictions that t-PA could become a wonder drug comparable in impact to penicillin.

During the year several warnings were sounded regarding the dangers of jogging, marathon runs, and other strenuous forms of cardiovascular exertion that were increasing in popularity and claiming as victims participants suffering from established, often undiagnosed heart disease. Squash was singled out as a particularly hazardous sport. The inherent risks of overexertion were dramatically emphasized by the sudden death in July of U.S. runner Jim Fixx (*see* OBITUARIES), whose *Complete Book of Running* did much to stimulate a worldwide jogging craze. Fixx, 52, died from a heart attack during the course of a ten-mile run, the same as he had undertaken daily for 17 years. Edward Colt, former medical director of the New York City Marathon, described Fixx as one of a group of "hard core" running addicts who become "brutal taskmasters to themselves." Nonetheless, his death drew attention to the need for a complete physical examination for anyone contemplating a strenuous program of fitness training.

A newly developed method using cultured skin implants—or "test-tube" skin—for burn victims was reported to be clinically successful in 1984. The first patients to receive the innovative treatment, two boys with severe burns over 97% of their bodies, were treated at the Shriners Burn Institute in Boston. The technique involved removing small patches of skin from unburned areas of the victims' bodies; these patches, separated into individual skin cells, reproduced themselves in laboratory cultures, producing sizable pieces of new skin. Within 12 weeks researchers had obtained more than half a square yard of skin for each boy. The new skin, placed on the burned areas of the boys' bodies, was not rejected. The Boston physicians said they knew of no other patients with comparable burns who had survived.

Research into the cellular molecular events that give rise to cancers maintained its recent promise and momentum. In February M. D. Waterfield and his team at the Imperial Cancer Research Fund laboratories in London, together with scientists from Rehovot, Israel, and Genentech, Inc., in San Francisco, published new findings about the nature of cancer-causing genes, or oncogenes. They reported that a virus that causes leukemia in chickens contains an oncogene whose structure is almost identical to that of a receptor on human cell surfaces that responds to the so-called epidermal growth factor (EGF). EGF is normally produced when certain cells are required to divide for tissue growth or repair; it stimulates the appropriate receptors to activate cell division and disappears when the necessary cell duplications have been achieved. The implication is that, in the absence of EGF, the receptor-mimicking oncogene "switches on" the cell-division mechanism, so that uncalled-for growth continues indefinitely and a cancer results, or, alternatively, that the oncogene somehow jams the normal on-off mechanism.

A study of known hereditary cancers suggested still another variation in the role of genes in growth regulation at the cellular level. Bruce Ponder and colleagues at the Institute of Cancer Research in Surrey, England, concluded that retinoblastoma, a tumour of the eye that tends to run in families, may be associated not with an inherited oncogene but with the inherited absence of a gene that normally switches off abnormal growth. This finding suggested that other kinds of tumours might also be linked to the lack of a specific growth-regulating gene.

Developments in in vitro fertilization and embryo transfer also gained momentum in 1984. In January Carl Wood of Melbourne, Australia, announced the birth of the first child developed from a donor egg. The mother was infertile as a result of premature menopause. The egg was fertilized in vitro by her husband's sperm and then implanted in her womb. A healthy baby had been born to the couple in November 1983.

A few weeks later a California woman, under the care

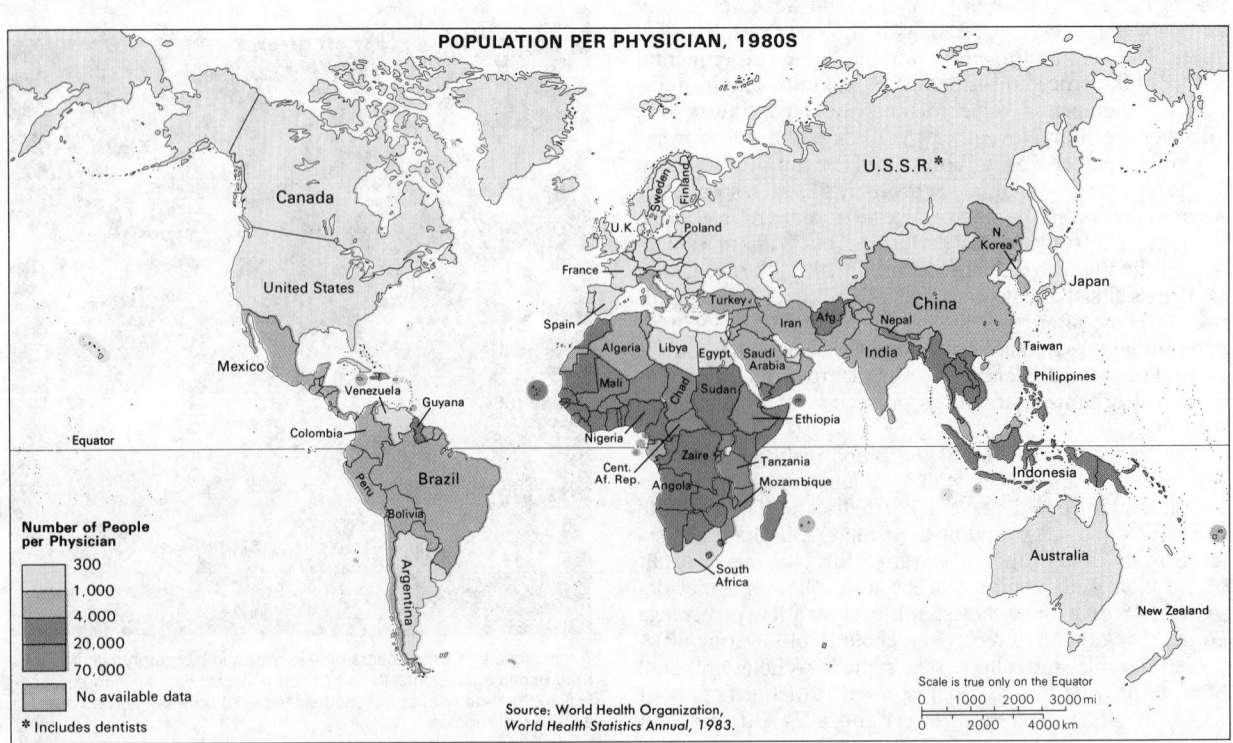

POPULATION PER PHYSICIAN, 1980S

Number of People per Physician

300
1,000
4,000
20,000
70,000
No available data

* Includes dentists

Source: World Health Organization,
World Health Statistics Annual, 1983.

Scale is true only on the Equator
0   1000   2000   3000 mi
0   2000   4000 km

of John Buster of the Harbor-UCLA Center at Torrance, gave birth to a child conceived by artificial insemination with her husband's sperm in the womb of a surrogate. The microscopic embryo was flushed from the donor's womb and transferred to that of the recipient without surgical intervention.

Wood received credit for another "first" in March when one of his patients gave birth to an infant developed from a frozen embryo. The embryo was one of six recovered in an earlier procedure and frozen in liquid nitrogen at −196° C (−321° F) for eight weeks. Three of the six were subsequently thawed and transferred to the mother's womb. One became implanted, resulting in the birth of a healthy baby girl. A number of women in Australia, Britain, and elsewhere became pregnant by this technique during the course of the year.

Robert Edwards of Cambridge, a pioneer in the "test-tube" baby technique, told a Helsinki, Fin., conference in May that he expected the thousandth such baby would be born by the end of 1984. A number of multiple test-tube births, including quads and triplets, were recorded during the year. Such births resulted from the implantation of several embryos in a single procedure in order to increase the chances of a successful pregnancy.

The British Medical Association issued a report in March claiming that brain-scan studies had provided direct evidence showing "beyond doubt that permanent brain damage still commonly occurs in men who box, whether professionally, or as amateurs," and that an outstanding feature of the brains of dead boxers is the "massive number" of altered brain cells. The revelation a few weeks later that Muhammad Ali, the former world heavyweight champion, was showing signs of a brain disorder almost certainly resulting from his career in the ring lent dramatic force to boxing abolitionists' case, seeming to contradict the claim that skilled professionals, fighting under controlled conditions, avoid the damage suffered by amateur sluggers. (*See* SPORTS AND GAMES: *Boxing:* Sidebar.)

International Aspects. In April the World Health Organization (WHO) launched a campaign to convince governments that cancer is a growing problem in third world countries, where the disease now claims more victims than in the developed nations. WHO hoped shortly to produce an inexpensive vaccine (a costly version was already available) to protect against infection by the hepatitis-B virus. This type of hepatitis causes a majority of the liver cancers that are responsible for a quarter of a million deaths every year. The organization also resolved to discourage the escalating promotion of cigarette smoking in the third world, to discourage tobacco chewing and encourage early diagnosis of the oral cancers that the habit causes, and to encourage the triennial screening of women for cervical cancer, particularly in Latin America, where the disease now most commonly occurs.

Despite ongoing efforts, malaria remained a major problem in the third world, with insecticide-resistant mosquitoes and drug-resistant malarial parasites continuing to thwart earlier hopes of eradicating the disease. In Brazil, for example, there was a 70% rise in the number of cases reported during the first three months of 1984 compared with the same period in 1983. However, work continued toward the goal of producing an antimalarial vaccine.

The other side of the fertility question—unchecked population growth—was examined at the International Conference on Population, sponsored by the United Nations and held in Mexico City in August. Delegates from 149 countries agreed to spend more money on developing new methods of birth control and on improving the safety and

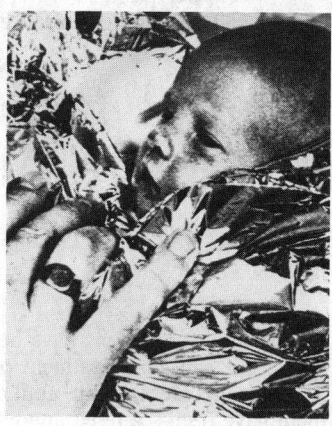

This infant was the world's first born from a frozen embryo. It was fertilized in vitro, frozen, and later implanted in its mother's uterus.
AP/WIDE WORLD

efficacy of existing techniques. The program, estimated to cost $4 billion in the coming year alone, was intended to curb the continuing rapid increase in world population, which was expected to reach 6,100,000,000 by the turn of the century. The final agreement was greeted with relief, particularly because U.S. Pres. Ronald Reagan had earlier threatened to withdraw his country's support from nations and agencies that countenanced abortion as a method of family planning. A month earlier Pope John Paul II had reiterated the Roman Catholic Church's total opposition to artificial contraception, and the Vatican refused to support the conference resolution.

Regulation and Legal Matters. Perhaps the greatest public concern over the social aspect of medical matters during 1984 was aroused by the legal, ethical, and practical problems created by interferences with the natural processes of reproduction. Since the birth of Louise Brown, the world's first test-tube baby, in 1978, extensions and variations of the original technique had developed at such a pace that society and the law now faced unique situations for which no protocols existed.

One of the most highly publicized controversies of 1984 surrounded the fate of two frozen embryos whose wealthy "parents" had been killed in an aircraft accident in 1983. The dead woman's eggs had been fertilized by sperm from an anonymous donor. Relatives of the deceased couple objected to suggestions that the "orphaned" embryos be reared to maturity in a surrogate womb in order to claim their inheritance.

Surrogate motherhood, whereby a fertile woman is made pregnant by artificial insemination, using the sperm of the husband of a sterile woman, was even more controversial, although several agencies undertaking to arrange such a service were active during the year. In Australia a woman who had agreed to act as a surrogate mother refused to give up the child, and her right so to do seemed to be protected by the New South Wales Artificial Conception Act, which denied the donor of sperm to be used for artificial insemination any claim to paternity. However, no provisions of this legislation dealt specifically with the problems surrounding surrogacy. This incident and the "orphaned" embryo affair well illustrated the manner in which even the most current legislation lagged behind advances in reproductive technology.

The most throughgoing investigation into the problems surrounding "human fertilization and embryology" was taking place in Britain, where, in July 1984 an official committee chaired by Dame Mary Warnock presented a comprehensive report on the ethical and legal issues. The Warnock committee report recommended that a statutory

(continued on page 258)

Mental Patients in the Community

BY JOHN A. TALBOTT, M.D., AND BOB GROVE

Mental institutions have been the traditional site for the care and treatment of the severely and chronically mentally ill until relatively recently. While there have been scattered attempts to provide community treatment, going back to that in Geel, Belgium, in the 13th century, no widespread movement in this direction occurred until the mid-20th century.

The Case in the United States. In 1955 the census in state mental hospitals in the United States reached its peak of 560,000 after almost two centuries of steady increase; currently it has fallen to about 120,000. The reasons for this dramatic decline in the state hospital population are several: first, the introduction into these facilities of effective antipsychotic medications that, while not "curing" schizophrenia and other serious illnesses, did permit the calming of their crippling symptoms such as hallucinations, delusions, and intense anxiety; second, the influence of a philosophy that held that treatment in the community, which was closer to home, job, and family, was better, cheaper, and more humane; third, the pressure from civil libertarians to end involuntary commitment to hospitals, to permit patients to refuse treatment, and to seek to have patients receive treatment in the "least restrictive environment"; and fourth, the economic forces set into motion by the federal government's enactment of Medicare, Medicaid, and Supplemental Security Income legislation, which enabled states to shift part of the burden of funding of the severely and chronically mentally ill from almost 100%-state-tax-levy money for state hospital care to largely federal auspices for community care.

The massive shift in the locus of care of the severely and chronically mentally ill is commonly referred to as deinstitutionalization. Unfortunately, this shift was not the result of a carefully planned or well-implemented policy. Indeed, in September 1984 the American Psychiatric Association, in its first comprehensive report on deinstitutionalization, termed the movement "a major societal tragedy" and called for "a revamping of the mental health system." The problems that have ensued have arisen because, while the concept was sound, it had never been fully tested, and the elements in the community that were necessary for its success were not in place. Technically, then, while the patients were shifted ("depopulation"), the resources were not ("deinstitutionalization"). Lacking is a "system" of community care that provides all the services patients had formerly received in institutions. There have not been enough housing settings, job opportunities, rehabilitation services, or professionals trained to deliver high-quality care. Nor has there been a continuum of care facilities

John A. Talbott, M.D., is Professor of Psychiatry at Cornell University Medical College and Associate Medical Director of the Payne Whitney Psychiatric Clinic in New York City. He is President of the American Psychiatric Association.
Bob Grove is Projects Officer of the Richmond Fellowship for Mental Welfare and Rehabilitation, London.

within communities (from halfway houses, to supervised residences, to group homes, to independent apartments) to meet the varying needs of former patients. Moreover, descriptions of effective programs of community care are few and thus have not provided appropriate "models."

Further, since deinstitutionalization not only moved people from institutional to community settings but attempted to block the flow of new patients into the public system, thousands of new or young chronically mentally ill persons, who have never been admitted to a hospital, have also been affected. Those blocked from coming in have found their way into the streets in unprecedented numbers (25–50% of the estimated 250,000 to 3 million homeless have serious mental illness other than alcoholism and drug abuse). In addition, a substantial number of this new group of chronically mentally ill persons have been incarcerated in the criminal justice system.

Only recently have sophisticated methods been developed for assessing how former mental institution inmates are faring. Thus we now know that: (1) the chronically mentally ill are readmitted to hospitals three times as often as before deinstitutionalization began; (2) only one-third of those living in the community are without symptoms of mental illness; (3) with each hospitalization, only 30–50% return to work, and 70% of those go to less-skilled jobs than they held before; (4) only a quarter have "normal family lives" although some 65% return to live with families; and (5) only 50% continue to take medications prescribed for them, and fewer—about 25%—remain in aftercare programs following discharge. The last factor is of special importance since medication and psychotherapy are the two treatment elements that prevent or forestall readmission to a hospital or exacerbation of an illness.

At present there are in the U.S. a number of well-designed and well-researched community care programs, all of which have been compared with conventional mental hospital care. They include psychosocial rehabilitation programs, such as the Fountain House in New York City, which provides job training, housing, and social rehabilitation, as well as access to medical and psychiatric care; home care programs, such as one carried out in Louisville, Ky., that utilizes visiting nurses to provide medications and counseling for patients and their families about everyday problems; arrangements such as one in San Francisco, called Soteria House, in which former patients share housing with young, nonprofessional live-in peers, and a comprehensive alternative to hospital care in Madison, Wis., that provides all the services a patient would receive in a hospital, but in community settings. When all these community programs are looked at together and compared with traditional hospital treatment and follow-up care, several conclusions emerge. The patients do at least as well and often (especially regarding symptoms) do better than those hospitalized. They prefer community care to institutional treatment. And the programs, patient for patient, are slightly less expensive than institutional treatment plus customary follow-up.

However, despite the widespread acceptance of their effectiveness and efficiency, there is no area of the United States that has achieved implementation of a fully integrated system of community care. The reasons for this are many: negative attitudes of professionals, elected officials, and ordinary citizens; legal and regulatory barriers; structural and administrative obstacles to an organized system; the lack of an integrated community support and care program; insufficiently trained personnel; economic incentives that reward institutional rather than community care, treatment of disease rather than its prevention, and treatment of acute rather than chronic illnesses; and a lack of governmental responsibility, with designated division of labour between federal, state, and local authorities.

The United Kingdom. The move toward care in the community in the United Kingdom also began in the mid-1950s, when dissatisfaction with the large mental hospitals coincided with the general use of psychotropic medication to control psychotic disorders. As in the U.S., the effects of the new drugs enabled the doctors responsible for the care of the mentally disordered to unlock the doors of the wards and to move out of the hospital patients whose more florid symptoms had subsided. A number of hospitals changed from a mostly custodial approach toward a therapeutic one, and with this the recognition grew of the relationship between the behaviour of the mentally disordered and their environment.

Following the 1959 Mental Health Act, which reflected the changes in treatment and attitude toward mental illness, a series of reports in the early 1960s put forward specific plans for the closure of large hospitals and the development of alternative services. Since that time progress has been halting and uneven. The depopulation of large hospitals—the inpatient population halved between 1954 and 1978—was not accompanied by development of community-based residential and day-support schemes. In 1975 a White Paper, *Better Services for the Mentally Ill,* acknowledged this and predicted that it would take more than a generation of committed action to provide minimally acceptable services.

In the last decade the restructuring of the National Health Service has resulted in firm closure dates for the large hospitals and the development of community-based psychiatric services in which psychiatric nurses and social workers operate in multidisciplinary teams to enable people with mental disability to remain in or return to the community. Health authorities and local authorities have been required to set up Joint Care Planning Teams to coordinate local services, and also to work with Joint Consultative Councils, where voluntary organizations and other groups are represented. It is the policy of the present government that funds released by the closure of the large hospitals should be redirected, with the help of small amounts of "pump-priming" money, toward community-based services. It is also intended that the care of the chronically disordered should be shifted increasingly toward the voluntary and private sectors. These changes are planned to occur over the next decade.

In the U.K. the voluntary sector has always acted as provider of community-based services for the mentally disordered. Since World War II, however, a small number of organizations have acted as pressure groups representing the interests of the mentally ill and pressing for innovation in mental health care. The National Association for Mental Health (MIND), founded in 1946, working through local mental health associations, promotes public awareness and facilitates the establishment of housing, day facilities, workshops, and support groups. Throughout the U.K. the Richmond Fellowship runs a wide range of hostels and other facilities, based on "therapeutic community" principles, and has also led in community care and staff training in a number of other countries including Australia, New Zealand, and the U.S. The U.K. is in many ways further advanced in providing community care for the mentally ill than most other countries in Western Europe, and debates about the rights and needs of emotionally and mentally disturbed people have received widespread public attention. Nonetheless, the stigma and fear associated with mental illness still prevail and prevent those who have been mentally ill from receiving equal treatment in housing and employment; the same factors also handicap organizations that exist to establish community-based services. In addition, the concentration of scant resources on the chronically ill has prejudiced the claims of younger people who could, with short-term help, avoid long-term malaise or even suicide. Obviously chronically sick people need help, but assistance for them to the exclusion of younger people with potential to live a healthy life is shortsighted.

The Italian Experience. In contrast to the U.K. and the U.S., where mental hospital populations declined from the mid-1950s, Italy's hospital population declined very little before 1968. In the late 1960s a group of Italian psychiatrists led by Franco Basaglia implemented major changes in mental health care in the cities of Gorizia and Trieste and established a pressure group that changed the balance of power in Italian psychiatry. Psychiatrists strove to empty the asylums and set up programs in the community to support and house the former inmates. In 1978 a law was passed mandating the closure of the large mental hospitals throughout Italy and requiring community-based services to be established to replace their functions. However, the provision of hospital alternatives was less than fully successful, and many severely disturbed people have been left to roam the streets without homes or support; recent public reaction has been such that one of the first promises of the new premier, Bettino Craxi, elected in 1983, was that he would reopen the asylums. Such a step would be gravely disappointing to those who see community care as the way forward; the controversy, however, does highlight the need for good advance planning, proper financing, and intensive public education. (*See* HEALTH AND DISEASE: *Mental Health.*)

Australia. An initiative by the Commonwealth government has moved toward the closure of some Australian asylums. Prior to 1970 developments in the treatment of psychiatric disorder had followed much the same pattern as in the U.S. and the U.K. A rising tide of concern regarding community care found formal expression in 1973 through studies and programs instituted by the Department of Health. In that year the minister of health announced a Cabinet decision to assist the states with their programs on community mental health, with the intention of reducing dependence on institutional care.

The Mental Health and Related Services Assistance Law in October 1973 established a wide range of government-financed projects providing residential and day care for a number of disadvantaged groups including the mentally ill. A change of government in 1975, however, brought a shift in policy toward the states' bearing full responsibility for the costs of programs. Provision is now uneven, depending on the priorities of the state governments, and, as in the U.K., there is insufficient public sympathy for the plight of the mentally ill. The conviction in many countries is growing that, while the mentally ill and others with long-term handicaps or disabilities should be firmly integrated into local communities, they should not be wholly dependent on the exigencies of local government finances for essential services. Moreover, the right to live in residential areas and have access to services according to need should have legal underpinning.

Community treatment of the mentally ill is an approach that has been tested in several countries. Persons treated in the community fare well if they receive high-quality, ongoing care. The challenge for the future is to implement existing knowledge and to allot resources to make such care widely available.

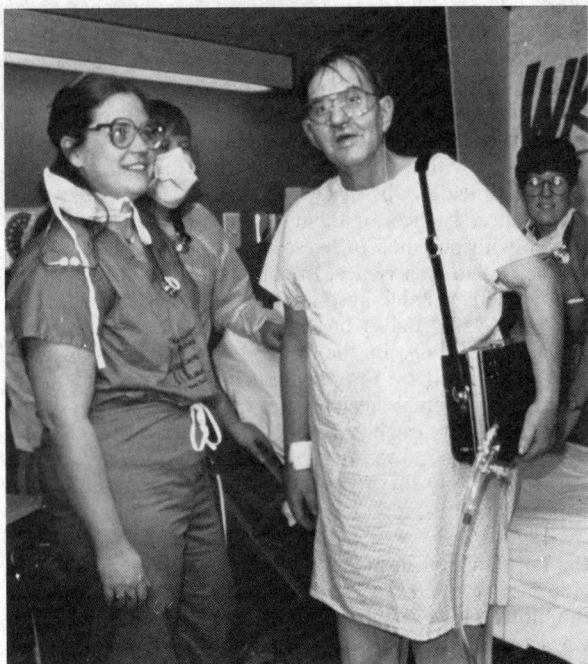

William Schroeder, the second person to undergo surgery to replace his heart with a mechanical pump, is able to move more freely for short periods of time with the aid of a battery-powered driver.

WILLIAM STRODE, HUMANA—BLACK STAR

(continued from page 255)
authority be established to license and regulate specified infertility services and areas of scientific or medical research involving human genetic material. The report advised that experiments on embryos more than 14 days old be illegal, that no embryo used for research be implanted in a human womb, and that no human embryo be implanted in the womb of another animal. Surrogate motherhood would become illegal. As might be expected, the proposed restrictions on embryo research and surrogacy came in for particular criticism from scientists involved in these fields.

Legal issues related to cancer were centred largely around several claims that man-made radiation had caused an abnormal incidence of the disease in some localities or groups. In Britain an official report, published in July, offered a "qualified reassurance" to the residents of Cumbria, following the revelation on a television program that the incidence of childhood leukemia in an area surrounding a nuclear reprocessing plant at Sellafield was ten times the national average. However, the public and many experts remained unconvinced that the subsequent government inquiry had effectively refuted the claim that leakage of radioactive material from the plant was responsible for this "cluster" of the disease.

There were also claims that the above-ground testing of atomic weapons had caused cancers in some residents of the state of Utah and in servicemen and aboriginals in Australia. In January Carl Johnson, a Denver physician, published a report in the *Journal of the American Medical Association* claiming that of 4,000 Mormons who were resident in Utah between 1951 and 1962, 288 had various forms of cancer diagnosed between 1967 and 1975—109 more cases than would be expected. In May a U.S. federal judge awarded $2,660,000 to the families of nine cancer victims in the region, holding that the 1951–62 atmospheric weapons tests at the Nevada test site had been responsible and that the government had failed to give warning of the dangers of fallout and the need for protection. Another

1,000 plaintiffs, suing on behalf of 375 cancer victims, awaited resolution of their cases. In October a Royal Commission in Australia began an intensive nine-month investigation into charges that inadequate precautions surrounding British bomb tests during the 1950s and '60s had resulted in cancers and other ill effects of radiation among veterans who took part and among aboriginal inhabitants of the regions involved.

The 1979 class action suit filed by Vietnam veterans against the makers of Agent Orange was settled in 1984 in one of the largest single settlements in the history of class action law. In May, only hours before jury selection was to have begun, seven chemical companies that manufactured dioxin—a toxic chemical contained in Agent Orange—agreed to pay the veterans $180 million. About 15,000 veterans and their families were included in the class action, and hundreds of thousands of Americans could be eligible under the terms of the settlement. Despite the resolution of the legal claim, the scientific issue of whether dioxin caused any serious health problems among the veterans remained a subject of debate. The judge cast doubt on the plaintiffs' case and refused to award typical high fees to their attorneys who brought the action.

In another major health-related legal settlement, Merrel Dow Pharmaceuticals, manufacturer of the drug Bendectin (called Debendox in Britain), agreed to pay $120 million to settle claims that the drug had caused birth defects. Bendectin had been the only drug approved by the U.S. Food and Drug Administration (FDA) for the treatment of morning sickness in pregnancy. Merrell Dow ceased manufacture of the drug in 1983, citing the pressures of litigation rather than any evidence that the drug was harmful.

In November 1983 a U.S. federal jury had awarded damages to a Columbus, Ga., man who alleged that his mother had died from taking the subsequently banned antiarthritis drug Oraflex (known as Opren in Britain), manufactured by Eli Lilly and Co. Some 400 U.S. claimants had been awarded compensation by the end of 1984, but the fate of more than 600 British potential litigants remained in doubt, the U.S. courts having refused to hear their cases in that country. Eli Lilly said that out-of-court settlements might be considered on an individual basis.

The artificial sweetener aspartame continued to be attacked by U.S. consumer groups in 1984. The lobbying group Common Cause asked Congress to investigate FDA approval of aspartame. The group questioned the additive's effects on behaviour and challenged tests that supposedly cleared the substance of charges that it produced brain tumours and genetic defects.

Medical Economics. Australia launched a national health insurance scheme at the beginning of February, with all taxpayers having an extra 1% added to their bills to pay for the plan. Under the new system, 85% of medical costs would be refunded by the federal government. Pensioners and very low earners would get free health care. Most Australians were expected to take out additional private health insurance to pay for facilities and services not covered by the scheme.

Britain's National Health Service was ordered to implement stringent economies by the government, notably by "privatizing" certain services such as cleaning and catering. Also, "general managers" were to be appointed, with wide-ranging executive powers, to take over many of the controlling functions at present exercised by multiprofessional management teams and local and regional committees. The spending cuts were expected to increase medical unemployment. In June the British Medical Association claimed that 2,000 doctors were out of work—a situation that had never arisen before. The profession called for restrictions on the entry and employment of doctors from the Commonwealth and elsewhere and for a limit to be placed on the period in which those admitted for postgraduate experience and training could stay.

(DONALD W. GOULD; GINA KOLATA)

MENTAL HEALTH

Controversy surrounded efforts aimed at reducing the numbers of the mentally ill confined to hospitals and asylums. A meeting of experts in Trieste, Italy, convened by the World Health Organization, expressed disappointment at the slow rate at which the transfer of patients into the outside world was being achieved.

In Italy some 10,000 Italian mental patients were at large, lacking proper care, who would have been in mental hospitals but for a law enacted in 1978 that prohibited admissions or readmissions to asylums after 1982 on the grounds that long-term hospitalization does more harm than good. Instead, the mentally disabled were to be cared for by short-term treatment in small psychiatric wards attached to general hospitals, by a network of outpatient clinics, by health workers, and in day-care centres. In Verona, where there was an active program of community support, the scheme was working well, the number of patients requiring hospital treatment having fallen by 34% since 1978, while the number of short-term admissions had increased. No outpatients were destitute, and accident and suicide rates among the mentally disabled were low. However, in much of the rest of the country the necessary facilities were still lacking, largely because of opposition from psychiatrists, said to regard the new law as a threat to their authority, and from the families of patients because of added responsibilities; there was talk of repeal of the act.

Meanwhile, France was considering introducing legislation on the Italian style, Switzerland was making a scheme work well with generous funding, and Tanzania had halved the number of beds in psychiatric hospitals and given village health workers the task of caring for the mentally as well as the physically ill. But in Britain, Canada, and the United States similar moves to reduce the mental hospital populations were criticized by many of the professionals involved who regarded the releases taking place as too hasty, since stringent economies in health spending meant that adequate alternative care within the community was not being made available. (*See* Special Report.)

The deleterious effects of unemployment on mental health were made clear by several British studies during the course of the year. In February a paper in the *British Journal of Clinical Psychology* described a survey of 954 unemployed working-class men from different parts of the country. A quarter of the men questioned revealed that, in addition to anxiety and depression, they could not manage tasks requiring concentration, quick thinking, and decision making as well as they had been able to while still working, and the longer the period of unemployment suffered, the more marked the slowing down of thought processes became. Figures published in the British magazine *New Society* in January showed that more than half of all men who attempt suicide are unemployed and that those unemployed for more than a year are 19 times more likely to try to kill themselves. The results of a three-year study of over 1,000 young people aged 16 to 25 who had visited the London Central YMCA were published in September. Among those with no recent experience of unemployment, 17% had suffered episodes of depression so profound that they had considered taking their own lives, but the suicidal proportion among the short-term and long-term unem-

ployed rose sharply to 24 and 26%, respectively. In the same month, a report drawn up for the British government's Office of Populations Censuses and Surveys showed that unemployed men are more than twice as likely to commit (as opposed to attempting) suicide and are 80% more likely to have a fatal accident.

A London conference on marriage and health was told that divorce poses a major health hazard but that the problem "has been completely ignored by medicine, government, and society." Jack Dominian, a psychiatrist and director of the Marriage Research Centre at London's Central Middlesex Hospital, told the conference that more people in Britain were affected by broken marriages than by unemployment and that 29% of separated and divorced men and women suffered minor psychiatric illnesses and depression. He claimed that marital disharmony and breakdown was a key factor in between 60 and 83% of suicide attempts. Britain's Royal College of General Practitioners provided family doctors with a new set of codes for noting broken engagements and marriages, bankruptcies, job losses, and bereavements on their patients' records so that the effect of important "life events" on subsequent mental and physical health could be monitored.

At the end of 1983 a psychiatric patient successfully sued a New York doctor for prescribing a phenothiazine—one of the major antipsychotic tranquilizers—on the grounds that such drugs are known to cause a pattern of severe neurological side effects characterized by involuntary motor movements and twitching of the face and tongue, known as tardive dyskinesia, and the courts in Massachusetts decreed that the victims of serious psychoses cannot be given antipsychotic drugs against their will. These court cases reflected the continuing public concern over the widespread long-term use of these agents by many psychiatrists, particularly as a routine means for managing wards full of potentially difficult patients in long-stay hospitals.

(DONALD W. GOULD)

This article updates the *Macropædia* article MENTAL DISORDERS and Their Treatment.

DENTISTRY

The most important step forward in the prevention of tooth decay since the discovery of fluoride's benefits was the use of pit and fissure sealants. A major study conducted by the Medical College of Georgia School of Dentistry, involving 382 Augusta, Ga., schoolchildren, provided conclusive evidence that sealants—plastic coating applied to the biting and chewing surfaces of children's molars—are nearly 100% effective in preventing decay as long as they remain bonded to the tooth surfaces.

Injuries to the mouth and jaws of athletes were a matter of growing concern in sports medicine. For protection against hazards such as airborne hockey pucks and elbows to the chin, athletes need more than lightning reflexes. According to the American Dental Association, athletic mouth guards prevented more than 200,000 dental sports injuries each year. The devices not only lower the incidence and severity of injuries to the teeth and mouth during athletic training and competition; they act as a buffer against concussions, jaw fractures, and neck injuries as well. Before the U.S. National Alliance Football Rules Committee made mouth guards mandatory in 1962, 50% of all injuries among high school players occurred in or around the mouth. That figure had dropped to fewer than 0.5%.

A synthetic material that replaces portions of the jaw in the mouth promised to help overcome denture slippage, one of the commonest drawbacks of dentures. The substance, hydroxylapatite, had been used successfully in some 20,000 patients and had proved superior to other procedures for building new bone in the mouth.

In the mouth, teeth are embedded in the bony structure referred to as the alveolar ridge, which is part of the lower and upper jaws. Dentures sit on the alveolar ridge after the natural teeth are removed. When the natural teeth are gone, however, the alveolar bone erodes, eventually leaving little or no bone on which to anchor dentures. As a result, dentures tend to slide, glide, and slip in the mouth. Under conventional procedures, dentists remove a piece of hip bone, which is then reimplanted in the patient's jaw. However, reimplanted bone tends to erode owing to the pressure of supporting the denture. In addition, the reimplantation surgery causes discomfort and is often poorly tolerated by older patients. According to John N. Kent, of the Louisiana State University Dental School, the new bone implants have the potential for helping two million to three million people who wear dentures.

Oral pathologists had suspected for some time that people who smoke and drink heavily might have a greater chance of getting cancer in certain areas of the mouth than do persons who indulge in only one of these habits. A study conducted by researchers at the University of Iowa College of Dentistry found that alcohol enhances the uptake of tobacco carcinogens by the sensitive floor-of-the-mouth tissues, where most oral cancer lesions develop.

(LOU JOSEPH)

VETERINARY MEDICINE

An important new international honour, the King Baudouin of the Belgians International Development Prize, was awarded to British veterinarian Walter Plowright in Brussels on Nov. 21, 1984. The prize, worth BF 4 million, is for a substantial contribution toward third world development. Plowright played a leading role in the development of a highly successful vaccine against rinderpest (cattle plague), a veterinary disease that was and could still be a major economic scourge in Africa, the Near East, and India. The vaccine utilized a live virus rendered nonvirulent, which was stable in most field conditions. The manufacturing process employed tissue culture techniques that enabled the vaccine to be produced cheaply and in large quantities. One dose produced lasting immunity without inducing any adverse side effects. Similar techniques were employed by

Plowright and his colleagues at the East African Veterinary Research Organisation in Kenya to produce a range of vaccines with profoundly beneficial potential against other major and minor diseases of food animals in the tropics.

Ultrasonic scanning, a technique widely used in hospitals, was being adapted for veterinary use as a safe and practical method of diagnosing animal pregnancies. Scientists working at the Agricultural Research and Advisory Centre, New South Wales, Australia, and at the Hill Farming Research Organization, Scotland, used portable ultrasound equipment for on-farm diagnoses. The ability to identify pregnant animals and the number of fetuses they are carrying has important implications; it would enable pregnant sheep to be given appropriate quantities of food in order to optimize birth weights of offspring and increase the chances of survival of entire litters. A further benefit is that ewe mortality could be lessened by reducing the incidence of metabolic disorders.

Minute amounts of copper in grazing land for sheep and cattle are known to be essential to the growth of the animals. In some areas these traces of copper are in short supply. However, in attempting to provide adequate copper supplementation, there is a significant risk of toxicity. Two new gradual-release formulations were devised to overcome the problem of safe, long-term administration of copper supplements to grazing herds. Similar slow-release supplementation formulations could be applied to other essential elements such as cobalt, iodine, and selenium, deficiencies of which may be encountered in livestock farming.

(EDWARD BODEN)

See also Life Sciences; Nobel Prizes; Populations and Population Movements; Social Security and Welfare Services.

This article updates the *Macropædia* articles DISEASE; MEDICINE.

Historic Preservation

As of November 1984, 84 countries had ratified or accepted the International Convention Concerning the Protection of the World Cultural and Natural Heritage. New adherents in 1984 were Mexico, the U.K., Yemen (San'a'), Zambia, Qatar, and New Zealand. The convention's World Heritage Committee held its eighth session in Buenos Aires, Arg.,

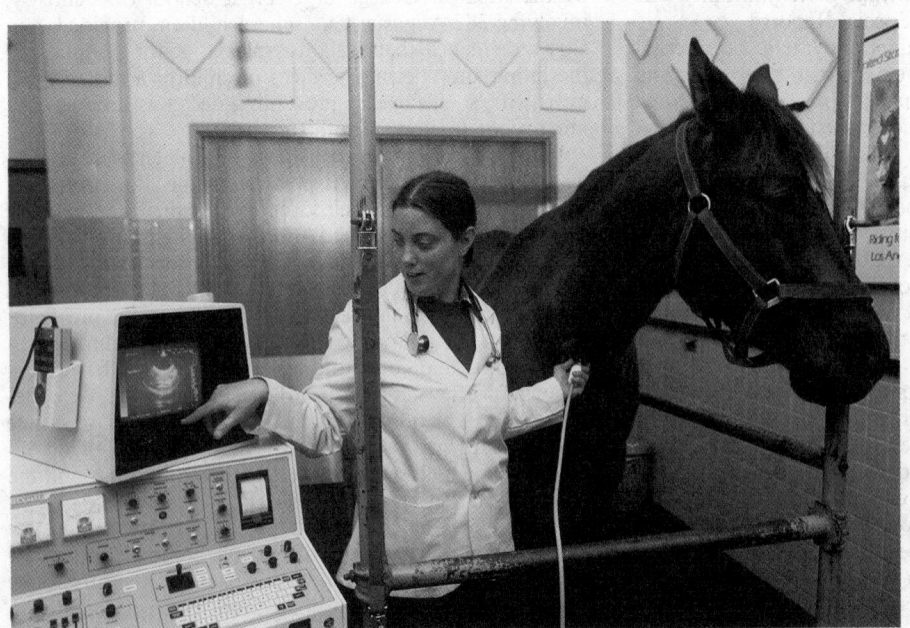

Ultrasound scanning, a technique with a variety of applications widely used in hospitals, was being adapted for veterinary use by a number of research groups in 1984. One such group was located at the New Bolton Center, a rural campus of the University of Pennsylvania's School of Veterinary Medicine. Here Virginia Reef uses ultrasound to check Bucky's pacemaker, which was inserted with the help of ultrasound monitoring. Bucky—a show horse—was the first horse given a pacemaker; the device corrected his severe arrhythmia, a condition that caused lapses of up to ten seconds between heartbeats.

during October–November 1984. After careful evaluation of national recommendations, 23 properties were added to the World Heritage List, bringing the total to 186 sites in 51 countries. Among additions to the list were the ruins of the Jesuit missions for the Guaraní Indians (17th and early 18th centuries), northeastern Argentina; the historic port, fortress, and colonial complex of Cartagena de Indias (16th to early 19th century), Colombia; the castles of Augustusburg and Falkenlust (both 18th century), Brühl, West Germany; the Sun Temple (13th century), Konarak, India; 7th- to 9th-century monuments at Mahabalipuram, India; the archaeological site of Anjar (8th-century Umayyad city), Lebanon; the archaeological site of Baalbek (Hellenistic and Roman periods), Lebanon; the archaeological site of Byblos (approximately 2800 BC through the Roman period), Lebanon; the archaeological site of Tyre (2750 BC through the Roman period), Lebanon; architectural works of Antonio Gaudí (Güell Park, 1900–1920s; Palacio Güell, 1886–90; Casa Milá, 1906–19), Barcelona, Spain; Burgos Cathedral (13th–16th century), Spain; the Mosque of Córdoba (8th–16th century), Spain; the Alhambra (13th–17th century) and Generalife (14th century), Granada, Spain; El Escorial Palace and Monastery (primarily 1561–84), near Madrid, Spain; the Statue of Liberty (1871–86), New York City; and Vatican City (primarily 9th–17th century).

Australia ratified the Convention for the Protection of Cultural Property in the Event of Armed Conflict, thus becoming the 72nd contracting member state. The convention, adopted at The Hague, Neth., on May 14, 1954, by an international conference of states convened by UNESCO, contains provisions for the safeguarding of movable or immovable property of great importance to the cultural heritage of peoples, irrespective of its origin or ownership, and makes respect for such property obligatory.

Based on agreements with the governments of Yemen (San'a'; North Yemen) and Yemen (Aden; South Yemen), two international campaigns to safeguard the cultural heritage were launched by the director general of UNESCO in December 1984. The campaign in North Yemen was to restore and preserve the historic city of San'a'. Its world-famous multistoried structures date, in general, from the Islamic period, but their sophisticated construction, high standards of comfort, aesthetic appeal, and subtle adaptation to the local climate indicate a long and continuous building tradition. The campaign in South Yemen was for the conservation of the monuments and sites of historic, cultural, and natural value in the river valley of the Wadi Hadhramaut and, in particular, the architectural heritage of the city of Shibam. In ancient times Hadhramaut was famous for frankincense and myrrh and as a gathering point for the incense trade. Although less widely known, the multistoried structures of the old walled city of Shibam are as significant historically and aesthetically as those of San'a'. Both projects involved large-scale programs of integrated regional development.

The International Council on Monuments and Sites (ICOMOS) published the second "Analytical Index: A Selection of Technical Literature on the Conservation of Historic Monuments" as part of its October 1984 Newsletter. Although brief and in a formative stage, this series, available from the UNESCO-ICOMOS Documentation Centre in Paris, would be an important reference for all concerned with historic preservation.

One of the most innovative and successful national programs to encourage the preservation of historic structures was initiated in the U.S. in 1976. Since then the Internal Revenue Service income-tax code had contained incentives

Scaffolding shrouds the Statue of Liberty on her perch above New York Harbor while a $30 million repair job proceeds, funded almost entirely by private donations. The restoration was scheduled to be finished in time for a gala harbour celebration on July 4, 1986.
BRIAN F. ALPERT—KEYSTONE

to encourage capital investment in income-producing historic buildings and to stimulate the revitalization of historic neighbourhoods. Over 11,000 projects had been certified, among them the Art Deco Chrysler Building (1929–30) in New York City and Union Station (1896) in St. Louis, Mo. Construction and rehabilitation costs from 1976 to 1984 exceeded $7 billion.

The attraction of Britain's historic buildings and sites for tourists was evident from figures published by the British Tourist Authority. Among the most popular were Windsor Castle and its precincts (2.8 million visitors in the first half of 1984); the Tower of London (2,182,000); the Royal Botanic Gardens, Kew (1,057,900); Edinburgh Castle (818,100); and Stonehenge (604,700). In some cases the numbers of visitors posed a problem for those responsible for conservation. Some sections of the 2,000-year-old, 117-km (73-mi)-long Hadrian's Wall, built by the Romans to keep the Picts at bay, were being eroded by the passage of approximately 150,000 visitors a year. Plans to prevent further damage were under consideration during the year.

The fragility of much of the world's architectural heritage was dramatically highlighted on July 9, when York Minster in England, Europe's largest Gothic cathedral, was struck by lightning and the roof of its 13th-century south transept was destroyed by fire. Restoration would take two to four years, at an estimated cost of £1 million.

(JOHN POPPELIERS)

See also Architecture; Environment; Museums.

Human Rights

The denials of human rights given most attention in the news media and by well-known human rights organizations, such as Amnesty International, are those that directly affect individuals, such as imprisonment, torture, and execution. It must not be forgotten, however, that human rights as defined in the Universal Declaration of Human Rights include a much broader range of political and civil rights, as well as economic and social rights. In 1984 hundreds of thousands remained in prison for their beliefs, and millions lived in fear. Torture was still common in at least a third of the world's countries, while less than a third enjoyed political and civil liberties. Yet the continued expansion and improvement of rights in the democracies, a democratic trend in Latin America, and greater openness in much of the Communist world offered hope.

The Developed Democracies. Comparatively speaking, the condition of human rights in this group of countries was far superior to that elsewhere. However, since the free news media were largely concerned with this world, much of the reporting on human rights highlighted failures of the Western democracies to live up to the highest standards. By definition, political rights are guaranteed in these countries, as are such civil liberties as freedom of the press and the right to a fair trial. Serious lapses occurred just beyond the edge of the democratic world, however. Thus monopolization of the airwaves by the government continued during the year in Malta, and the exclusion of a number of leaders from the political process, the arrests and trials of others, and repression of the large Kurdish minority continued to characterize Turkey.

The most poignant human rights problem within the developed democracies stemmed from the continued violence in Northern Ireland, resulting in suspension of the usual guarantees of civil society. A much more widespread problem for the democracies was the treatment of aliens, or discrimination against people not of the majority community. These might be people from former colonies, "guest workers," or illegal immigrants. Thus Koreans were discriminated against in Japan, Algerians in France, Mexicans and many others in the U.S. In an ever more interdependent world, the question of the right to residence and ultimately to citizenship of people from other countries was certain to remain contentious, since it pitted the international human rights of individuals against the rights of groups to protect their own interests and even to preserve their own identities.

The strongest human rights accusations against the U.S. related to its foreign policy and, in particular, to the use of force. U.S. efforts in Central America, especially its support of the *contras* in Nicaragua, continued to be widely criticized because of the immediate effect on human lives and the long-term exacerbation of regional conflict.

The Communist World. Although the Communist world was no longer homogeneous, the adherence of Communist states to Marxist-Leninist principles led to denial of a number of basic human rights. In what could be called the fanatic hermit states, such as North Korea and Albania, there were no human rights in the internationally recognized sense. Little information was available on their internal situation, and what did emerge suggested harsh and arbitrary rule.

By comparison, "traditional" Communist states like the Soviet Union and its imitators were open societies. It was known in the West that there were thousands of prisoners of conscience in the U.S.S.R. and that, with very few ex-

A South African policeman pursues a university student who hid in a bus during a Johannesburg demonstration against a new constitution enfranchising Coloureds and Asians but not blacks.
DAVID BARRIT—GAMMA/LIAISON

ceptions, all who did not follow the party line were jailed or expelled. The treatment of Andrey Sakharov (*see* BIOGRAPHIES) and his wife, sick and in internal exile, proved to be a major human rights cause during the year. Among other states in this category, thousands were still being held in "reeducation camps" in Vietnam and Laos. Within Romania the least signs of opposition were suppressed, despite the independent international stance of the country's rulers. Although many political prisoners were released during the year in Cuba, large numbers continued to be held, and rights to freedom of expression were systematically denied. The other major human rights violations of states in this group concerned foreign invasion or occupation. The Soviet presence in Afghanistan represented a massive denial of the right to self-determination and was accompanied by atrocities against civilians. The Vietnamese occupation of Kampuchea might also be considered a human rights violation, although the possibility that the Vietnamese were preventing the return of the genocidal Pol Pot regime mitigated criticism.

A third group of Communist states offered more hope. The leaders of states such as Hungary and China looked to the West for economic and other forms of support, and the resulting political and cultural "opening" led to a considerable decline in the repression of individuals. At the same time, the leaders were wedded to Communist political institutions, and the opening could be closed at any time. Most states in this group still had a large number of prisoners of conscience—particularly Yugoslavia and China. Nearly all prisoners of conscience in Poland were released during the year, and there were evidences of relatively free thinking, at least in educated circles, in Poland, Hungary, Czechoslovakia, and even East Germany. Bulgaria seemed to be edging closer to this group.

The Non-Communist Third World. Third world states ranged from democracies with very few human rights violations, such as Costa Rica and Venezuela, to severely repressive states such as Haiti and Burma. In many ways India, the "world's largest democracy," provided a mirror of third world problems because its difficulties were better publicized than those of its neighbours. During 1984 hundreds of Sikhs were killed by the Indian Army and thousands were jailed following demonstrations meant to bring down the government. (*See* WORLD AFFAIRS (South Asia): *India.*) There were also reports of hundreds of thousands of poor young people living as bonded servants and of frequent "dowry killings" of wives. The police continued to be accused of unnecessary brutality. Yet through it all the Indian people were vigorously represented by those they had elected in free and well-contested elections, and problems were reported at length in the free press.

It was a good year for democracy in Latin America. Argentina's new president moved vigorously to reestablish the rule of law. An attempted coup against a struggling democratic regime was turned back in Bolivia. Successful democratic transfers of power occurred in Venezuela and Ecuador. Brazil edged closer to democracy, and Uruguay, despite continued repressions, opened its political process to a major segment of the opposition. Peru's embattled democracy hung on against a vicious rural terrorism, though it employed methods that were, in turn, condemned for their cruelty. Colombia's conservative president managed to move his guerrilla opponents toward integration in the political system. In Central America democratic elections in Guatemala and El Salvador were steps forward. Murders of civilians in El Salvador declined during the year, though they still represented a major concern. Civilian supremacy moved closer to reality in Honduras. When Nicaragua held elections in November, many hoped that the military-Marxist rulers would recognize the political and civil rights of their people more fully, but their antidemocratic ideology, a civil war, and the inability of the opposition to reach an acceptable compromise made this unlikely.

The state of human rights in Africa, on the other hand, was dismal. South Africa's problems were the best known (*see* WORLD AFFAIRS (Africa South of the Sahara): *South Africa*), but denials of human rights were even more severe in much of the rest of the continent. Malawi allowed no breath of criticism to go unpunished, and tens of thousands perished in Uganda at the hands of undisciplined rebel and government forces. A similarly uncontrolled army seemed to be in charge in Ghana, although the death rate was much lower. By formally establishing a Communist party and a one-party state, Ethiopia continued to march toward

the seemingly paradoxical ends of anarchy and Marxism-Leninism. Sudan's decision to enforce Islamic law helped turn its southern non-Muslims back into guerrillas.

Israel remained the only functioning democracy in the Middle East, though its treatment of Arab rights in the occupied territories and Lebanon represented a continuing problem. States such as Syria, Iraq, and Saudi Arabia showed little respect for any internationally accepted human rights. Political leaders were generally self-selected or selected by tiny elites, and rights to public expression were nonexistent. Through a partly free electoral process and the liberalization of discussion, Egypt demonstrated new concern for political rights, an opening mirrored in part in a Jordanian election. Iran was a mixed phenomenon. Elections and parliamentary processes showed considerable acceptance of democratic norms, and there was real discussion and opposition within theologically prescribed limits. On the other hand, those not theologically acceptable, such as Communists and Baha'is, were crushed mercilessly.

Farther east, Malaysia and Thailand allowed some political choice and expression of opinion, but Sri Lanka's democracy had been largely destroyed by the inability of the government to accommodate political opponents. Indonesia's "guided democracy" permitted only a minimum of dissent. In the Philippines the military was implicated in the murder of a political opposition leader, and in many rural areas the cruelty of the military forces had led to a resurgence of Communism. Yet the government's efforts at compromise had managed to reduce tension in Muslim areas, and the 1984 legislative elections allowed more genuine opposition than was common in the region.

(RAYMOND DUNCAN GASTIL)

See also Race Relations.

This article updates the *Macropædia* article HUMAN RIGHTS.

Industrial Review

Manufacturing activity in the Western world recovered from its decline in 1982 and rose by about 4% in 1983. Output in the advanced countries increased by more than

Table I. Index Numbers of Production, Employment, and Productivity in Manufacturing Industries
1975=100

Area	Relative importance[1] 1975	Relative importance[1] 1983	Production 1982	Production 1983	Employment 1982	Employment 1983	Productivity[2] 1982	Productivity[2] 1983
World[3]	1,000	1,000	121	126	...	...	...	...
Industrial countries	868	841	118	122	...	...	...	...
Less industrialized countries	132	159	142	152	...	...	...	...
North America[4]	315	315	116	125	...	...	...	...
Canada	27	24	104	111	93	...	112	...
United States	288	291	118	127	102	101	116	126
Latin America[5]	74	78	127	131	...	...	...	...
Brazil	27	23	129	107	...	...	...	...
Argentina	15	10	76	83	...	...	...	...
Mexico	12	13	146	133	151	138	97	96
Asia[6]	159	198	147	155	...	...	...	...
India	11	13	140	145	124	...	113	...
Japan	109	126	140	145	101	101	139	144
South Korea	...	...	256	297	...	...	...	...
Europe[7]	416	376	112	113	...	...	...	...
Austria	8	8	121	122	93	89	130	137
Belgium	14	10	113	116	...	...	...	...
Denmark	6	6	122	127	94	93	130	137

Area	Relative importance[1] 1975	Relative importance[1] 1983	Production 1982	Production 1983	Employment 1982	Employment 1983	Productivity[2] 1982	Productivity[2] 1983
Finland	6	7	131	135	101	99	130	136
France	80	71	111	112	92	90	121	124
West Germany	115	105	114	115	95	91	120	126
Greece	3	3	121	121	135	134	90	90
Ireland	1	1	141	151	111	104	127	145
Italy	43	40	125	118	100	...	125	...
Netherlands, The	16	14	114	114	82	78	139	146
Norway	6	5	97	96	97	86	100	112
Portugal	4	5	151	152	...	...	...	...
Spain	24	22	109	...	77	74	142	...
Sweden	17	14	95	101	80	77	119	131
Switzerland	13	11	107	107	93	89	115	120
United Kingdom	50	38	94	96	76	72	124	133
Yugoslavia	11	13	145	147	134	...	108	...
Rest of the world[8]	36	33	...	...	...	...	...	...
Oceania	18	15	101	101	...	...	...	...
South Africa	7	8	132	...	...	...	...	...
Centrally planned economies[9]	...	...	139	144	...	...	...	...

[1] The 1975 weights are those applied by the UN Statistical Office; those for 1983 were estimated on the basis of the changes in manufacturing output since 1975 in the various countries.
[2] This is 100 times the production index divided by the employment index, giving a rough indication of changes in output per person employed.
[3] Excluding Albania, Bulgaria, China, Czechoslovakia, East Germany, Hungary, Mongolia, North Korea, Poland, Romania, the U.S.S.R., and Vietnam.
[4] Canada and the United States.
[5] South and Central America (including Mexico) and the Caribbean islands.
[6] Asian Middle East and East and Southeast Asia, including Japan.
[7] Excluding Albania, Bulgaria, Czechoslovakia, East Germany, Hungary, Poland, Romania, and the U.S.S.R.
[8] Africa and Oceania.
[9] These are not included in the above world total and consist of the European countries listed in note 7 above.

Table II. Pattern of Output, 1980–83
Percent change from previous year

	World[1]				Developed countries				Less developed countries				Centrally planned economies[2]			
	1980	1981	1982	1983	1980	1981	1982	1983	1980	1981	1982	1983	1980	1981	1982	1983
All manufacturing	0	0.6	−4	4	−1	0.3	−4	3	7	−1	4	6	5	2	3	4
Heavy industries	−0.2	0.5	−4	4	−1	0.7	−5	4	6	−1	4	7	5	3	4	4
Base metals	−5	−1	−11	3	−6	−1	−14	2	4	−1	5	6	1	0.2	0.3	3
Metal products	1	1	−4	3	0.6	2	−4	3	6	−5	2	7	6	4	4	5
Building materials, etc.	0.2	−3	−5	3	−1	−3	−7	3	7	0.5	2	5	2	2	3	5
Chemicals	−1	0.6	−2	6	−3	0.5	−4	6	7	1	6	7	4	2	3	1
Light industries	0	0.1	−1	4	−1	−0.5	−2	3	5	3	3	6	4	−0.3	1	3
Food, drink, tobacco	3	2	1	3	1	2	−0.3	1	7	4	6	7	0.6	1	3	5
Textiles	−0.6	−2	−3	3	−2	−3	−5	2	2	−1	0.4	4	2	−0.3	−1	0.4
Clothing, footwear	−3	−1	−3	2	−5	−3	−4	0.6	4	8	3	7	5	3	0.5	0.7
Wood products	−3	−4	−3	5	−4	−5	−6	6	5	−4	3	14	3	1	3	3
Paper, printing	2	0.5	−0.6	5	1	0.2	−1	5	5	4	5	5	3	2	3	4

[1] Excluding centrally planned economies.   [2] Excluding China.
Source: UN, *Monthly Bulletin of Statistics.*

3%, and more rapidly in less industrialized areas. In the centrally planned economies the progress was similar to that in the West.

These overall changes concealed wide variations. Output in North America rose rapidly, at a rate of about 7%; the increase was slower in Japan and not more than marginal in Western Europe; in Italy production fell appreciably, and only some of the smaller producers (such as Belgium, Denmark, Finland, Ireland, and Sweden) achieved any noteworthy growth. This pattern of industrial production reflected the exceptional economic boom in the U.S. and the relative stagnation in Europe. Similar fluctuations characterized the less industrialized world as well; output in Brazil and Mexico declined in contrast to progress in Argentina, steady growth in India, and continued explosive increases in South Korea.

During the first half of 1984 the rapid growth in the

Table III. Annual Average Rates of Growth of Manufacturing Output, 1968–83
Percent

Area	1968–73	1973–79	1979–81	1982	1983
World[1]: market economies	6.0	2.1	1.6	−3.2	3.9
Industrial countries	5.7	1.5	1.4	−4.4	3.4
Less industrialized countries	8.7	5.9	3.2	4.0	6.5
Centrally planned economies[1]	8.8	7.5	3.7	3.0	3.9

[1] For definition *see* Table I.
Source: UN, *Monthly Bulletin of Statistics.*

Table IV. Output per Hour Worked in Manufacturing
1975 = 100

Country	1978	1979	1980	1981	1982	1983
France	121	129	131	132	137	142
West Germany	113	118	116	120	122	129
Italy	111	122	127	130	131	130
Japan	124	132	137	137	137	141
U.K.	108	109	108	112	116	123
U.S.	109	112	115	119	122	128

Source: National Institute, *Economic Review.*

Table V. Manufacturing Production in the U.S.S.R. and Eastern Europe[1]
1975 = 100

Country	1980	1981	1982	1983
Bulgaria[2]	134	140	147	152
Czechoslovakia	126	129	131	135
East Germany[2]	127	133	137	143
Hungary	118	122	124	125
Poland	126	111	108	115
U.S.S.R.	126	130	134	140

[1] Romania not available.
[2] All industries.
Source: UN, *Monthly Bulletin of Statistics.*

United States continued, but it showed signs of slowing down in the second half of the year. Progress was considerably slower in Western Europe, but there was an advance in Japan. Two years of 3–4% growth in the advanced industrialized countries represented a marked change from the slow progress in 1973–81 and the recession in 1982, even though the rate remained well below that of the years prior to 1973.

The most important feature of industrial development in 1983 and in recent years in general was the growth of the microelectronics industry. Microelectronics had radically changed the whole range of telecommunications and information technology; its wide application resulted in novel forms of production control in industry, the construction and dissemination of industrial robots, and the computerized automation of many processes in manufacturing, commerce, and banking. Many new consumer products based on microelectronics, including computers designed for home and personal use, were also successfully brought onto the market.

Apart from electronics, chemicals and paper and wood products led the 1983 growth in the developed countries, though livelier investment activity helped the recovery of the metal and building materials industries, too. The consumer industries were less vigorous. This contrasted with the experience of the centrally planned countries and less industrialized areas, where the food and allied industries were among those growing at the highest rate.

Labour productivity in manufacturing improved significantly, but also at different speeds. The highest rates of change in output per hour worked in manufacturing were reached in West Germany, the U.K., and the U.S., where productivity rose from 5 to 6%; the rise was less in Japan and France (3–4%), and productivity fell slightly in the Italian manufacturing industry.

Industrial unemployment started to decline in 1983—and continued to do so in 1984—in the U.S., but it remained at historically high levels in most European countries, tending generally further upward though at a much lower rate than in previous years. Only a very few countries, such as Japan and Switzerland, succeeded in avoiding unemployment on a massive scale.

Manufacturing output continued its uninterrupted growth in the U.S.S.R. Polish industry started recovering after 1982, when it reached its lowest recent level in the midst of that country's political troubles. Progress in Hungary was slow, while in the other Eastern European countries—East Germany, Bulgaria, and Czechoslovakia, in that order—the rate of growth varied between 3 and 4.6%.

(G. F. RAY)

ADVERTISING

The U.S. Federal Communications Commission (FCC) voted to increase the maximum number of AM and FM radio and television stations that could be owned by a company or individual from 7 of each to 12 and to remove nearly all ownership restrictions by 1990. The FCC argued that deregulation would improve the quality of programming and increase competition for advertising dollars. The new rule was scheduled to go into effect by April 1985, but it was being challenged by Congress and in the courts. The FCC also removed its restrictions requiring commercial television stations to broadcast a certain amount of news and local programming as well as its limits on the number of commercials for each show.

The price of advertising on telecasts of U.S. college football games dropped by 50% at two major television networks—from $60,000 for a 30-second spot in 1983 to $30,000 in 1984—because of uncertain ratings and the increased number of games that could be televised. As the result of an antitrust ruling by the U.S. Supreme Court, the networks were now allowed to negotiate directly with individual schools and conferences for broadcasting rights rather than negotiating through the National Collegiate Athletic Association, which had regulated college football broadcasts for 33 years. The ruling also opened the market for syndication and cable distribution of college football games. Meanwhile, a sharp drop in the TV ratings for professional football threatened its position as the premier vehicle for advertising aimed at men.

ABC invested more than $500 million in telecasting the Olympics. Ratings for the Winter Games were disappointing, but more than 40% of television viewers during August had their sets tuned to the Summer Games at Los Angeles. ABC earned more than $435 million in revenues for its 180 hours of summer Olympic coverage, about double the amount it normally earned for the same time spots. The Olympics had 30 official sponsors, 57 licensees, and more than 60 suppliers. Companies such as AT&T, McDonald's, and Champion International spent $4 million to $15 million each to become sponsors and promotion for advertising and promotion.

China Central TV, the national network of China, signed a barter agreement with CBS to purchase 64 hours of programming. Under the terms of the agreement, CBS would be responsible for finding advertisers willing to spend $300,000 to get their names before China Central TV's audience of some 630 million viewers. The two networks would share advertising revenues. The CBS package was expected to run about once a week during prime time hours.

Colourful billboards advertising the products of such companies as Exxon, Kodak, and Coca-Cola appeared in many cities in China in 1984. (See WORLD AFFAIRS [East Asia]: *China.*) China had opened its borders to advertising agencies in 1978, and by 1983 expenditures for advertising of foreign goods totaled about $17 million. More than half the advertisements in China were placed by Japanese companies and handled by Dentsu, Inc., Japan's—and the world's—largest advertising agency.

Advertising Age's June 1984 International Survey found 21 agencies billing more than $100 million to foreign clients; 18 were based in the U.S. They ranged from McCann-Erickson Worldwide, with $1,360,000,000 of non-U.S. billings accounting for 68% of its total billings to Kenyon & Eckhardt ($103 million and 26.3%). Three European firms were on the list. Saatchi & Saatchi Compton Worldwide, of London, ranked fifth, with $938.8 million in non-English billing (54.9% of its total). Eurocom Group and Publicis-Intermarco-Farner, both of Paris, ranked 16th and 18th.

Each year *Advertising Age* publishes a list of the 100 leading advertisers in the U.S. for the previous year. In 1983 these advertisers accounted for $18.9 billion in expenditures, compared with $17.1 billion in 1982, an increase of 10.5%. The top five national advertisers were Procter & Gamble, Sears, Beatrice, General Motors, and R. J. Reynolds Industries.

A study by researchers at the University of Southern California found that the average cost of a television commercial in the U.S. in 1983 was $197,000. The survey covered advertising for 62 of the top 200 brands. Companies spent nearly $1 million per brand in 1983 on commercials that were never shown on the air. The cost of rejected material represented 35% of total television commercial development costs. Almost one-quarter of finished television commercials were rejected at a cost of about $135,000 each.

The battle of the hamburgers went international in 1984 as McDonald's Corp., Burger King Corp., and Wendy's International matched advertisements in Europe, the Pacific, and other markets where the hamburger chains had outlets. Burger King spent $2.1 million on advertising in West Germany and planned to spend similar amounts in ten other European countries, Asia, and Australia. McDonald's and Wendy's became involved in a controver-

sial comparative advertising campaign in Australia.

Pharmaceutical companies in the U.S. started to mount advertising campaigns promoting public awareness of certain diseases and advertising prescription drugs directly to consumers. Previously, they had marketed their products exclusively to doctors. The first advertisements were aimed at getting high-risk patients to their doctors. Responding to these campaigns, the Food and Drug Administration (FDA) prepared guidelines for such advertisements. The American Medical Association favoured consumer advertisements directed toward disease prevention but opposed messages focusing on treatment.

The U.K. lifted restrictions preventing lawyers, doctors, architects, and accountants from advertising. Most other countries already allowed professional firms to promote their services in the media. British firms would be able to advertise their rates and services in newspapers, magazines, and on radio but would be prohibited from advertising on television. In addition, comparative advertising would not be permitted.   (EDWARD MARK MAZZE)

AEROSPACE

In 1984 the U.S. recovery from recession began to improve the fortunes of the international air transport industry. Nevertheless, improved trade failed to generate proportional increases in revenue and profits as deregulation and overcompetition continued to cast shadows. The International Air Transport Association estimated that at least $50 billion would be needed over the next decade to replace obsolete or environmentally unacceptable equipment, equivalent to $5 billion a year or, in terms of new equipment, to 50 Boeing 747s or 150 Boeing 767s.

To raise funds without having to take on large debt obligations, operators were turning to what U.S. industry called "creative financing," mainly through lease ar-

The Ligue du Droit des Femmes (League for the Rights of Women) published this ad in three French newspapers in order to call attention to advertising that is demeaning to women. The ad was timed to coincide with a debate that opened in the National Assembly on a law that would increase restrictions on discrimination against women.

On March 12 an agreement formalizing national support for the construction of the Airbus A320, a 150-seat commercial aircraft, was signed by the governments of France, West Germany, Britain, and Spain. The aircraft was scheduled to be ready for service in 1988 and would enable Airbus Industrie to compete with Boeing and McDonnell Douglas.
CAMERA PRESS/PHOTO TRENDS

rangements, the issue of new stock, and the purchase of used aircraft. Banks in any case had become cautious about extending credit to all but a few carriers, having been badly burned by the collapse of Braniff and its overambitious expansion plans a year or so earlier. (In fact, Braniff began operating again in March after a 22-month lapse of service.) "Creative financing" was shown to work by the staggeringly large order of American Airlines, announced in March, for no fewer than 67 McDonnell Douglas MD-82 transports, with options on an additional 100. The initial order was estimated to be worth approximately $1,350,000,000 and, with options, could exceed $3.3 billion. MD-82 was the designation of what was previously known as the DC-9 Super 80, a 150-seat revision of the long-serving, widely selling DC-9 family. Together with an order from Federal Express for six DC-10s that relaunched the commercial version of that Douglas wide-body trijet, the MD-82 activity put McDonnell Douglas firmly back into the air transport business after a period of uncertainty. A West Coast company, Lockheed, was, however, clearly pleased to be out of this field. Having ended production of the L-1011 TriStar in 1983 and cut its losses, Lockheed recorded its profit for 1983 as the highest in its history. The L-1011 remained the company's only passenger airliner, although it was talking about entering the 150-seat market.

Meanwhile, Boeing, the world's top airliner firm, continued to do well as it recouped its heavy investment on new aircraft and product improvement. During the year the company rolled out its 100th Boeing 767 200-seat transport. The 767 had only two engines rather than the four of the 707 it replaced, and Boeing was devoting much effort to convincing the U.S. Federal Aviation Administration that the 767 was safe enough for extended overwater operation. Existing U.S. rules required two-engine passenger-carrying aircraft to remain within 60 minutes of flying time from the nearest suitable airfield when operating over water. In Europe the rule stipulated 90 minutes, but even so it was too restrictive to permit direct North At-

lantic operation for the 767. Europe also wished to see long-range versions of its Airbus A300 certificated for unrestricted operation.

In February Boeing flew the 737-300 version of the 737, its popular small twin-engine jet. The 737-300 and MD-80 family together made up what had come to be called the derivative transport market; they represented an attempt to ease the capital burden of acquiring new equipment by substantially upgrading earlier designs in order to satisfy the requirement for economical 150-seat aircraft. The principal measure was the fitting of new, quiet, low-fuel-consumption high-bypass engines.

While the two major derivative airliners were selling well (the MD-80 had more than 450 and the 737-300 more than 150 orders by November), their sponsors were clearly concerned about competition that would be provided by the launch, long awaited, of the Airbus A320 to meet the important 150-seat market. After several years of deliberation, an agreement formalizing national support for the Airbus was signed by the governments of France, West Germany, Britain, and Spain on March 12 to build the world's first "new" 150-seater, with a choice of European or U.S. engines and entry into service in 1988. Boeing, which for several years had pooh-poohed prospects for an aircraft in this category, immediately dusted off plans for its own design, called the 7-7. Not all U.S. industry was antagonistic toward the A320, however, notably the engine and equipment sectors, which stood to gain handsomely from those airlines that specified U.S. systems.

The Anglo-French Concorde supersonic transport, which began service with British Airways (BA) and Air France eight years earlier, started a BA service to Miami, Fla., in March. Despite a severely limited route structure, the U.K. aircraft had at least been making money via extensive chartering; perhaps because of this, the British government finally withdrew its financial support from the project. In agreement with British Airways, the government in August sold it the eighth Concorde (which had been mothballed) together with £9.3

million worth of spare parts and equipment. During the same month, the Soviet airline Aeroflot announced that the U.S.S.R.'s supersonic transport, the Tu-144, had finally been withdrawn from service. The high cost of operation was cited as the main reason, along with engine and aerodynamic inefficiency.

Perhaps the most important development in military aviation was the threat being posed by a new generation of Soviet combat aircraft. U.S. intelligence predicted that the U.S.S.R. would field two new fighters during 1984 to complement the MiG-31 Foxhound interceptor, deployment of which began in 1983. The two newcomers were the MiG-29 Fulcrum and the Su-27 Flanker. The first was equivalent in size and performance to the General Dynamics F-16 so-called lightweight fighter, and the second approximated in a similar way the larger McDonnell Douglas F-15 Eagle. All were said to have advanced radar and weapons systems and, because of their eventually likely numerical superiority, were creating a grave worry for the U.S. Department of Defense. The latter was accordingly putting greater urgency into upgrading its current inventory of combat types, including the now 30-year-old B-52, and launching the new Advanced Tactical Fighter (ATF) to complement and eventually replace the F-15.

Another Soviet craft, the swing-wing Blackjack bomber, was due to enter service in 1986 and would have a better range and weapon load than the similar U.S. Rockwell B-1B. The original B-1, planned as a B-52 replacement in 1970, was canceled by Pres. Jimmy Carter in 1977 but reinstated by Pres. Ronald Reagan in 1981 as the B-1B. The first of 100 production aircraft was rolled out in early September, a few days after one of the four original B-1A's, taken out of storage to hasten development, crashed during trials. Loss of this aircraft, however, was not expected to delay the program.   (MICHAEL WILSON)

AUTOMOBILES

The recession may not have ended for the world automobile industry in 1983, but car output was substantially higher than in 1981 or 1982. Production of commercial vehicles also showed a marked upturn. All major producing nations except for Australia achieved higher automobile output in 1983. In commercial vehicles the picture was more mixed, with rises in output for the U.S., Japan, France, Italy, Spain, and Canada but declines for West Germany, the United Kingdom, Sweden, Australia, and the U.S.S.R. World car output at 29,494,000 units was up from 26,441,000 in 1982 but below the record 30,885,000 of 1978. Commercial vehicle output at 9,948,000 units was up from 9,290,000 in 1982 but again contrasted with the 1978 peak of 10,962,000.

For the fourth consecutive year Japan was the nation in which the most cars were manufactured, although the United States narrowed the gap compared with 1982. Japan's preeminent position in commercial vehicle production, heavily dependent on many units in the lightest weight sector, was unchallenged.

Through the first half of 1984 the world picture changed substantially. The U.S. overtook Japan in car output with 4,217,-

000 units against Japan's 3,163,000, both figures being higher than in the first half of 1983. Italy, Spain, and Australia also increased production, but output fell in France, West Germany, and the United Kingdom. Car sales for the half year were higher in the U.S., Japan, Italy, Australia, and the U.K. but lower in France, West Germany, and Spain.

Europe. Higher output of cars and generally stable or increased sales in Europe (the U.K. posted a record 1,790,000 new car sales in 1983) were not the full story. Because of excess production capacity there were small, if any, real profits for virtually all large European manufacturers. Substantial discounting in showrooms across the continent, especially in the U.K., contributed to the generally higher sales figures in 1983 and through the first half of 1984. Such profits as were recorded (or in other cases reduced losses) reflected improvements in productivity more than they did increased sales.

For France the handwriting had been on the wall for many years. Only in late 1983 and into 1984 did that country face the fact that its industry was heavily overmanned in comparison with other nations. Britain, in the early 1980s, had shed labour as part of its drive to become competitive. By 1984 France was moving in the same direction but with greater labour unrest as an accompaniment. France's dominant Regie Renault also found itself losing ground as its aging model range lost favour in both home and export markets. The new Supercinq, "25," and Espace models were expected to recover some of the lost ground in late 1984 and beyond. The Peugeot-Citroën-Talbot group struck a winner with the small "205" model launched in 1983.

West Germany began 1984 in a buoyant mood with expectations of record output, home sales, and exports. However, the call of the powerful metalworkers union for a 35-hour workweek erupted into strike action beginning on May 14. This dispute, involving approximately 450,000 workers, became the worst strike in West German industrial history, lasting nearly seven weeks and causing the loss of more than

360,000 cars. The impact was felt throughout the nation's industry.

The Italian industry continued to enjoy growth into 1984 with the dominant Fiat empire recording profits, a rising share of its home market, and good export performance. The award-winning Uno model was responsible for much of this, but it was by no means a one-model success story.

In Britain fortunes were mixed. The major success story was the revitalization of Jaguar, sales of which soared from a low of 13,400 worldwide in 1980 to 28,000 in 1983 and more than 30,000 in 1984. The company was denationalized in mid-1984, separating completely from the state-controlled BL group. Rolls-Royce and specialist sports/luxury makers Lotus and Aston Martin Lagonda also enjoyed new health and increased production, boosted particularly by sales gains in North America. For Austin Rover production fell back slightly despite the introduction of the new Maestro model in 1983 and the Montego in 1984. Ford and, to a much lesser extent, Vauxhall (the General Motors [GM] subsidiary) continued to invest in Britain and promised the U.K. government that they would increase output there.

United States. The U.S. automobile industry's recovery from four years of sharp profit declines entered its second successive year in 1984. So dramatic was the second year of the recovery that by the end of the first nine months, the automotive Big Three—GM, Ford Motor Co., and Chrysler Corp.—had posted earnings totaling a combined $7.6 billion. That compared with the combined $6.3 billion the trio had earned for all of 1983, which was then an industry record.

The impressive profits were the result, in part, of a 22% increase in new car sales in the 1984 model year ended September 30, to 7.9 million cars from the 6.5 million sold in the 1983 model year. Though sales rose 1.4 million units in one year, they still trailed the all-time industry record of 10 million sold in 1973.

The fact that earnings skyrocketed even though unit sales numbers were far from record levels indicated the other reason that the industry was so financially healthy—

cost-cutting measures begun during the 1979–82 recession.

Industry executives were pleased by the unit sales and profit increases, but the industry-wide euphoria was short-lived when the automakers announced executive bonuses. During a year in which Detroit eventually would face new contract negotiations with the United Automobile Workers union (UAW), it was announced that General Motors chairman Roger Smith received a $625,000 salary plus an $865,000 bonus for 1983 and that Ford chairman Philip Caldwell got $520,534 in salary and $900,000 in bonus pay. The bonus of Chrysler chairman Lee Iacocca was not revealed. Under provisions of Chrysler's federally guaranteed loans with the government, bonuses were not paid. Stockholders had to approve resumption of bonuses at the annual shareholders meeting in June. They did, but the amounts were not to be disclosed until the next meeting in 1985.

W. Paul Tippett, chairman of American Motors Corp., was not awarded a bonus because his company failed to report a profit for 1983. Late in 1984 Tippett was named senior adviser of North American operations for AMC's partner Renault. José Dedeurwaerder, AMC president, was given Tippett's position as chief executive officer.

The bonuses touched off a stir among UAW members because workers had made concessions at GM and Ford during the recession. Eventually the UAW failed to reach new contract terms with GM before the September 14 deadline and went on a one-week selective strike. (See LABOUR-MANAGEMENT RELATIONS.) Chrysler escaped labour problems because its contract with the UAW extended to 1985. Chrysler also kept its stockholders (many of them union workers) happy by announcing that it would resume paying quarterly dividends. In the first quarter of 1984 Chrysler declared a 15-cent-per-share common-stock dividend. Chrysler had not paid a dividend since the second quarter of 1979, when the payout was 10 cents a share.

While labour and management wrestled with each other, consumers grappled over the cars they were building. Shortages of cars were prevalent almost all year, especially the larger mid-size, full-size, and luxury models as well as sporty performance cars, products that all carried high price tags and high profits.

Although Detroit was working overtime to build big cars to meet demand, the best-selling car in the market in the 1984 model year was the subcompact Chevrolet Cavalier. It bumped the subcompact Ford Escort from the sales leadership the latter had enjoyed in the 1983 model year. The top ten sales leaders in the 1984 model year were Cavalier (371,836), Escort (339,209), Oldsmobile Cutlass Supreme (334,060), Chevrolet Celebrity (307,777), Chevrolet Impala/Caprice (264,625), Oldsmobile Delta 88 (259,937), Honda Accord (256,489), Ford Tempo (255,727), Oldsmobile Ciera (252,669), and Buick Century (208,745). The Honda total included 119,336 cars built at its new plant in Marysville, Ohio.

During the 1984 model year GM sold 4,663,776 cars, compared with 3,876,006 in 1983, a 20% increase; Ford sold 1,906,806 versus 1,481,382 in 1983 for a 29% increase; Chrysler sold 946,575, compared

In Great Britain, sales worldwide of Jaguar automobiles soared after reaching an all-time low in 1980. The company was denationalized in mid-1984, and the initial stock offering sold out immediately.

with 819,209 in 1983, a 16% increase; American Motors sold 201,275 against 183,005 in 1983 for a 9% gain; and Volkswagen sold 86,600, compared with 83,223 in 1983, a 4% increase. Honda's 119,336 Accords sold in the U.S. in 1984 compared with 32,398 sold a year earlier when production was just getting under way.

Imported cars accounted for record sales of 2.4 million units in 1984, bringing combined domestic/import totals to 10.3 million units versus a combined 8.8 million in 1983. The combined sales of 10.3 million was the highest since 1979, when sales of 8.6 million domestic cars and 2.2 million imports added up to 10.8 million. The record remained 11.8 million in 1973—10 million domestics and 1.8 million imports. In the 1984 model year imports accounted for a 23.5% share of total sales, down from their 26.5% share in 1983 and from their record high of 27.8% in 1982.

Japanese automakers, in their fourth year of what was to have been a three-year agreement to limit voluntarily the shipment of cars into the U.S., also faced shortages of vehicles throughout the year. The quotas had been raised to 1,850,000 cars to be shipped into the U.S. during the fiscal year started April 1, 1984, up from 1,680,000 the previous fiscal year.

Though some new models were delayed, the U.S. Environmental Protection Agency went ahead with its listing of the most fuel-efficient cars on the road for the 1985 model year. The two-passenger Honda Civic captured the title as the highest mileage entry for the second consecutive year. The Civic was rated at 49 miles per gallon (mpg) for city driving and 54 mpg for highway driving. Honda's mileage title also marked the second successive year that the crown had been won by a gasoline-engine-powered car. In 1983, when the Civic took first place, it deposed the diesel-engine-powered Volkswagen Rabbit, which had held the title for six years. The Chevrolet Chevette and Ford Escort both finished in the EPA's top five. Both cars were powered by diesel engines obtained from Japanese sources—Chevette's from Isuzu and Escort's from Mazda Motor Corp.

When the EPA rankings were announced in the fall, it marked the first change in the procedure since the agency began its annual listing in 1974. Responding to consumer criticism that the mileage ratings were unrealistically high, the EPA calculated both city and highway mileage and then subtracted 10% from the city and 22% from the highway figure in arriving at the numbers posted on new car window stickers.

The 1985 model year also marked the end of the escalating Corporate Average Fuel Economy (CAFE) standard on new cars. Starting in the 1978 model year, CAFE laws required each automaker to obtain a prescribed mileage minimum from its fleet of cars sold. In 1978 CAFE started at 18 mpg, moving up gradually to 27.5 mpg for 1985. Both GM and Ford had failed to meet CAFE for 1983 and 1984, and both said that they expected to miss again for 1985. Penalties of $5 for every one-tenth mile per gallon under the average were to be levied against an offending automaker for each car sold in the model year, but a provision of the law allowed the automak-

ers to apply credits from prior years when they exceeded CAFE toward those years in which they missed. An automaker, however, could borrow back from only three successive prior years; therefore, GM and Ford could run out of borrowing power in 1986. Chrysler had exceeded CAFE every year since 1978, and for 1985 its CAFE estimate was 27.7 mpg.

The U.S. auto industry continued to focus on new cars during 1984. In the fall American Motors rolled out a new convertible version of the Renault Alliance; Ford brought out a luxury compact imported from Ford of Europe called the Merkur; Chrysler started building a new pair of compact, front-wheel-drive models called H-bodies that had the names Dodge Lancer and Chrysler LeBaron GTS; Chrysler also brought out a new full-size, front-wheel-drive model called the Plymouth Caravelle. Caravelle a year earlier had been the Chrysler E-Class car. At GM a trio of new compact, front-wheel-drive N-body cars appeared called the Pontiac Grand Am, Buick Somerset Regal, and Oldsmobile Calais.

Except for the eventual appearance later of the Chevrolet Astro minivan, GM had little new to offer in 1985. But the automaker announced major plans for 1986, when it would replace the last of its large, rear-drive cars with smaller, front-wheel-drive versions. Cars to be replaced were the Buick LeSabre, Oldsmobile Delta 88, Buick Riviera, Oldsmobile Toronado, Cadillac Eldorado, and Cadillac Seville.

Major changes among imports for 1985 were a totally restyled Maxima from Nissan that was converted from rear to front drive and a total remake of the Toyota Cressida, which remained a rear-drive car. Honda added a four-wheel-drive Civic. Mercedes did not add new cars but announced a price freeze on all autos at 1984 levels. Volkswagen began producing a replacement for the Rabbit in the U.S. called the Golf.

Nissan announced that it would join Volkswagen, Honda, and Toyota (in partnership with GM) in producing cars in the U.S. The Japanese firm said that it would begin building its subcompact Sentra model in the U.S. at its Smyrna, Tenn., truck plant in April 1985.

The GM/Toyota joint-venture subcompact went into production in December. The car was called Nova, resurrecting a name last used at Chevrolet in 1979. GM announced that in addition to the small Toyota car, its strategy for the next few years would be to import small automobiles from Japan and South Korea to sell through its Chevrolet and Pontiac dealer network. In 1984 Chevrolet dealers on the West Coast of the U.S. began selling the Chevrolet Sprint, a car built by Suzuki of Japan. On the East Coast Chevrolet dealers began selling a car built by Isuzu of Japan called the Chevrolet Spectrum.

Japan. New car sales in October 1984 totaled 325,480, 0.2% down compared with the same month of 1983. It marked the fourth month in a row that new car sales had been lower than in the corresponding month of 1983. Sales were sluggish late in 1984, partly owing to the fact that the biennial Tokyo automobile show was not being held and, consequently, few new

models appeared. The prospect for 1985 was somewhat more encouraging, taking into account the fact that the economy continued to be strong and consumers were beginning to spend more.

In September it was announced that in fiscal 1983 (ended March 1984) gasoline consumption per unit reached an all-time low in Japan of 964 litres. This represented a reduction of 235 litres in ten years.

The remarkable technological advances of the modern car were seen during the year in many new production and "concept" cars from Japan and Europe. Multivalve engines, new materials such as ceramics, and much wider application of microchip technology to engine management were either in production or promised for the next-generation vehicles. Turbocharging of both gasoline and diesel engines was becoming commonplace. Both West Germany and Japan were also bringing four-wheel-drive capability into both high-performance and everyday cars, led by Audi, Toyota, Subaru, and Porsche.

(JAMES L. MATEJA; JOHN R. WEINTHAL)

BEVERAGES

Beer. World beer production in 1983 totaled an estimated 968.5 million hectolitres (hl; 1 hl = 26.4 U.S. gal), approximately the same as in 1982. Production in Europe was boosted by a good summer, with an average increase per country of 0.4%. Output in the U.S., which produced almost one-quarter of the world total, remained stable, but almost all other brewing nations in the Americas suffered downturns, notably Mexico and Colombia. The top five brewing nations—the U.S., West Germany, the U.S.S.R., the U.K., and Japan—together brewed more than 51% of the world's beer. Output grew fastest in 1983 in the Far East, with notable increases in production in Japan (4.2%), the Philippines (13%), and South Korea (18%). Estimates for China indicated that production there in 1983 grew at a modest pace, less than 2% over that in 1982. In early 1984 it was announced that a Hong Kong-Macao consortium, cooperating with Stella Artois in Belgium, planned to spend $6.4 million on a brewery and bottling plant in China's Zhuhai (Chu-hai) economic zone.

The winter of 1983–84 proved kind to barley crops in Europe, and with good yields and plentiful supplies available from Australia and Canada, it was likely that spring-sown barley would be cut back. France increased its exports of barley malt by more than 12%, and the U.S.S.R. proved a major new purchaser of malt from both France and the U.K. The U.S.S.R. also established itself as a major hop producer, with 11,775 ha (29,084 ac) under cultivation, as compared with 19,785 ha (48,868 ac) in West Germany and 15,050 ha (37,173 ac) in the U.S.

Two international brewing deals involving famous beer brand names were consolidated during the year. The U.S. brewing giant Anheuser-Busch granted a license to British brewers Watney Mann & Truman to produce Budweiser beer in the U.K. In Europe the British company Allied Breweries entered into agreement with Technika, the Bulgarian licensing authority, to have Skol lager brewed under license by Bulgarsko Pivo, the state brewing organization.

(MICHAEL D. RIPLEY)

Budweiser beer, long a favourite in the U.S., sought its place in the British market after production was licensed to U.K. brewers.

ANHEUSER-BUSCH INTERNATIONAL, INC.

Spirits. The spirits market at last showed some encouraging signs of growth, with exports of Scotch whisky earning £738,-413,000 in the first ten months of 1984. Although this represented an increase of just 1% over the same period in 1983, it was, nevertheless, an indication that the industry was emerging from some years of recession-influenced decline. Worldwide, the most encouraging performance came from cocktails and low-strength liqueurs like Bailey's Irish Cream and Grand Metropolitan's Malibu, indicative of a growing preference for light and versatile drinks. Malibu was now available in about 80 markets, while Bailey's dominated the cream liqueur markets in the U.S. and U.K. Having achieved success in the U.S. market, the Japanese whisky firm Suntory launched its Midori melon liqueur in the U.K. De Kuyper produced a banana-flavoured drink called Daktari, and Bacardi intro-duced Bezique, a citrus-flavoured drink, into a Scottish test market.

In Japan the traditional white spirit, shochu, outsold whisky for the first time, registering a 30% increase to move into second place behind sake. Nevertheless, whisky sales in Japan rose by 5%. In the U.K. whisky accounted for 48.5% of all spirit sales. This represented a 2% drop since 1977, accounted for entirely by the increase in vodka's share from 10.3 to 12.5% over the same period.

While the U.K. had been following the U.S. trend to lighter spirits, dark rum had been making its first tentative moves into the U.S. The market was dominated by Bacardi, with sales of its white rum and Bacardi Gold totaling two million cases a year. Importers of traditional dark and amber rums to the U.S. were emphasizing a premium image and price, and sales were already said to be matching Canada's 600,000 cases. West Germany was the largest European market for rum with 4.8 million cases, although this represented an 8% decrease from 1982.

(ANTONY C. WARNER)

Wine. Indications were that 1984 would prove to be a poor year for viticulture. Production in many of the leading wine-producing countries was lower than in the previous year, and quality was generally mediocre.

Within the European Communities (EC), whose members produced 169 million hl in 1983, production in 1984 was estimated at 150 million hl. Italian production, the largest, was estimated at 72 million hl, compared with a final figure of 82.9 million hl for 1983; France's fell from 68.8 million hl to an estimated 62 million hl; West Germany's declined from 13 million hl to 10 million hl; and output in Greece and Luxembourg remained steady at around 5 million hl and 150,000 hl, respectively.

Among the Italian regions, Emilia-Romagna and Apulia registered declines of 15–20%, Veneto 20%, Trentino-Alto Adige 30%, and Sicily 20%. In France the Bor-deaux harvest of around 2.7 million hl was the lowest in several years, and production in the Burgundy and Loire regions was also reduced. The Champagne harvest was estimated at 1.5 million hl and that of Alsace at 750,000 hl. Elsewhere in Europe, including the Eastern-bloc countries, harvests were also generally lower.

While the fall in EC production would help alleviate marketing problems arising from accumulating stocks, the impending EC membership of Spain and Portugal, both considerable producers, posed new problems. Provisional agreement on ways of matching future production to demand was reached at the EC summit meeting in Dublin in December. Also a matter of concern was recent U.S. legislation that might result in protectionist measures against EC wine exports.

U.S. wine production fell sharply from the record 19.5 million hl of the 1982–83 season to an estimated 14.8 million hl in 1983–84, the lowest in six years, because of bad weather. In South America harvests were also lower; Argentina's production fell by some 4 million hl to 21 million hl. Chilean output, however, was boosted by harvests from recently planted vineyards. In Australia there was a marked increase in wine consumption at the expense of beer. Wine sales boomed in the U.K.

(MARIE-JOSE DESHAYES-CREUILLY)

Soft Drinks. The soft-drink industry experienced steady growth in the United States during 1984. Much of the expansion resulted from a strong upward trend in sales of diet soft drinks. Aspartame, trade named NutraSweet, a high-potency artificial sweetener approved for soft-drink use in the U.S. in 1983, contributed to the dramatic boost in the diet market.

Also during the year several new products were introduced by soft-drink companies. Each one was designed to appeal to specific consumer interests.

The introduction of aspartame in the U.S. and the number of new products were related. Aspartame was an impor-

Table VI. Estimated Consumption of Beer in Selected Countries

In litres[1] per capita

Country	1981	1982	1983
West Germany	146.9	147.9	148.3
Czechoslovakia	140.1	146.3	147.8
East Germany	140.7	147.0	...
Luxembourg	123.0	124.0	138.6
Denmark	125.13	128.59	133.97
Belgium	124.3	132.7	128.0
Australia[2]	132.2	128.9	123.7
Ireland	116.4	115.0	121.0
New Zealand	121.8	121.1	114.1
United Kingdom	111.4	109.5	110.5
Austria	104.8	108.5	109.4
United States	93.3	92.0	92.0
Hungary	89.2	89.7	89.0
Netherlands, The	89.47	81.96	87.53
Canada[3]	84.4	86.48	83.49
Venezuela	83.9	75.3	...
Switzerland	70.2	71.9	70.3
Bulgaria	57.8	59.5	61.2
Spain	55.2	56.9	58.4
Finland	57.24	55.96	57.37
Romania	50.0	50.0	...
Norway	44.81	47.07	45.32
Colombia	45.0	50.0	54.0
Yugoslavia	45.0	45.0	...
Sweden	45.0	46.6	44.7

[1] One litre = 1.0567 U.S. quart = 0.8799 imperial quart.
[2] Years ending June 30.
[3] Years ending March 31.

Table VII. Estimated Consumption of Potable Distilled Spirits in Selected Countries

In litres[1] of 100% pure spirit per capita

Country	1981	1982	1983
Luxembourg	9.5	8.25	8.0
East Germany	4.8	4.8	...
Hungary	4.97	4.76	4.8
Poland	4.3	4.2	4.1
Czechoslovakia	3.6	3.56	3.4
U.S.S.R.	3.3	3.3	3.3
Canada[2]	3.51	3.43	3.15
Bulgaria	3.17	3.05	3.04
Spain	3.0	3.0	3.0
Peru	3.0	3.0	...
United States	3.04	2.93	2.86
Finland	2.76	2.82	2.83
Netherlands, The	2.52	2.57	2.63
West Germany	2.84	2.53	2.46
Cyprus	2.1	2.1	2.3
Sweden	2.48	2.45	2.25
Belgium	2.13	2.04	2.17
Switzerland	2.11	2.2	2.16
Iceland	2.23	2.12	2.1
France[3]	2.0	2.0	2.0
Yugoslavia	2.0	2.0	...
Romania	2.0	2.0	...
Japan	1.84	1.97	2.0
New Zealand	2.0	2.0	1.69
United Kingdom	1.68	1.58	1.63

[1] One litre = 1.0567 U.S. quart = 0.8799 imperial quart.
[2] Years ending March 31.
[3] Including aperitifs.

Table VIII. Estimated Consumption of Wine in Selected Countries

In litres[1] per capita

Country	1981	1982	1983
Italy	92.9	91.4	91.4
Portugal	71.7	78.4	90.0
France	89.0	88.0	85.0
Argentina	73.2	73.8	71.1
Spain	59.0	57.0	57.0
Luxembourg	42.0	48.3	53.6
Switzerland	48.2	49.3	48.3
Greece	44.9	44.0	45.0
Chile	43.7	54.7	39.1
Austria[2]	35.1	35.3	37.4
Hungary	29.7	31.8	33.0
Yugoslavia	26.9	28.2	...
Romania	28.9	28.0	...
West Germany	24.7	24.8	26.5
Uruguay	25.0	25.0	...
Bulgaria	25.2	24.8	22.6
Belgium	21.0	21.7	21.7
Australia[2]	18.2	19.1	19.7
Denmark	16.09	17.35	18.86
Netherlands, The	12.95	14.15	13.87
Czechoslovakia	16.0	14.6	13.5
U.S.S.R.	12.8	12.9	12.9
New Zealand[2]	14.5	13.2	12.8
Cyprus	10.8	11.8	11.8
Sweden	9.72	10.43	10.8

[1] One litre = 1.0567 U.S. quart = 0.8799 imperial quart.
[2] Years ending June 30.

Source: Produktschap voor Gedistilleerde Dranken, *Hoeveel alcoholhoudende dranken worden er in de wereld gedronken?*

tant motivation behind the development of new low-calorie products and reformulations of traditional ones. Diet soft drinks also grew in international markets such as Japan, where previously there had been little interest. Technical advances resulted in significant changes in regular (nondiet) soft-drink formulations. Modern technology produced new high-quality corn sweeteners that were available at reasonable cost.

Soft drinks containing fruit juice constituted one of the most significant new product areas for the industry in 1984. Whereas soft drinks containing up to 4% fruit juice had existed for some time, new beverages introduced in 1984 contained up to 10% fruit juice. This development placed soft drinks in more direct competition with noncarbonated juice drinks and with the so-called natural soft drinks, which were garnering a new group of health-conscious consumers. Many bottlers of carbonated beverages also diversified into noncarbonated fruit drinks. Aseptic packaging, including the Swedish Tetra Pak (Brik Pak in the U.S.) and the West German plastic bottles of Rommelag Kunstsoff-Maschinen, played an important part in this development.

The same increased consumer interest in food ingredients prompted the further development of two soft-drink categories based on the exclusion of a particular ingredient. The caffeine-free and sodium-free soft drinks that were introduced in 1983 found a niche among consumers. Caffeine-free soft drinks were introduced by every major company and quickly carved out a respectable market share.

(DWIGHT C. REED)

BUILDING AND CONSTRUCTION

In 1984 the U.S. construction industry experienced a continuation of the recovery that had started at the beginning of 1983. The recovery was stimulated by large dollar outlays for both private and public construction. In the private sector residential construction continued to be a major contributor, while in the public sector the main impetus came from substantially higher outlays for highways and streets.

On an annual rate basis, the monthly value of new construction put in place in June 1984 was $310,631,000,000, based on figures released by the Department of Commerce, and it was expected that outlays for the entire year would be at a record level of $305 billion. Even after adjustments were made for inflation, it appeared that outlays in 1984 would be greater than in the peak year of 1978. Thus the four-year decline in the industry that began in 1979 had been reversed in both 1983 and 1984.

The Department of Commerce composite construction cost index stood at 158.6 (1977 = 100) in June 1984, compared with 157.1 for 1983. The rate of inflation in 1984 was low according to all the indexes of producer prices of materials used in building construction.

The average effective commitment interest rate for 25-year conventional mortgages (75% loan-to-price ratio) was 13.15% in June 1984, compared with an average rate of 13.3% in 1983. The average monthly rates had moved down throughout 1983 but edged back up in 1984. The median

price of a new house sold in the U.S. in September 1984 was $80,000, but it appeared that the median price for the entire year would be slightly lower. The median price in 1983 was $75,300. The average price of a new house sold in September 1984 was $100,000. This was higher than in most of the other months, and it seemed likely that the average for the entire year would be $96,500. The average price in 1983 was $89,800.

The other members of the Organization for Economic Cooperation and Development revealed clear responses to changes in the U.S. economy in 1983 and 1984. In Canada long-term interest rates, though slightly higher than in the U.S., showed a similar pattern of change. The gross national product (GNP) was expected to rise about 4% in 1984 and 2% in 1985. The increase in 1984 was due mainly to exports to the U.S. and consumer spending. Urban housing starts in 1984 were running 15% below the 1983 level, and this was one of the major factors contributing to the expectation of a lower level of economic growth in 1985.

Western Europe also responded favourably to improved economic conditions in the U.S. In Great Britain the economy expanded in 1983 because of an increase in fixed investments, attributable mainly to an increase in home building stimulated by lower interest rates. Private housing investment rose 22.9% in 1983 and was expected to increase 15.2% in 1984. Public housing investment rose only 2.4% in 1983, however, and the forecast was for a rise of 3% in 1984. Private fixed investment, up only 2% in 1983, was expected to increase 11.4% in 1984. The outlook for 1985 was for a sharp decline in both public and private housing. In France the economy was sluggish during 1983 and the first half of 1984, but the prospects for 1985 were improved.

The West German recovery of 1983 continued in the first quarter of 1984, supported by a high level of fixed investment, but the forecast was for a decline in investment and construction in 1985 due to rising interest rates. The recovery in Italy also continued into 1984, and the expected increase in investment should have a favourable effect on all types of construction. In Japan industrial production was increasing rapidly in 1984, fueled by a high level of exports and an increase in private investment in plant and equipment. Private house building, however, was recovering very slowly.

(CARTER C. OSTERBIND)

CERAMICS

After decades of research and development, automotive ceramics finally appeared poised for significant production. Japan took an initial step by introducing silicon nitride glow plugs and precombustion chambers made by Kyocera Corp. into Isuzu diesel engines. The first large-volume application, however, was expected to be in turbochargers, which were in increasing demand as a means to achieve improved fuel efficiency and power output from small, light engines. Mitsubishi Heavy Industries in Japan used sintered silicon nitride hot-side turbine rotors in the turbochargers it produced for some 1985 cars. Ishikawajima-Harima Heavy Indus-

tries Ltd. was expected to follow in 1986 with a turbocharger using sintered silicon nitride for both hot-side and cold-side rotors, an approach that might eliminate ceramic-metal joining problems. Other applications, including ceramic parts and ceramic coatings for most high-temperature surfaces of diesel engines, appeared increasingly likely.

Economic improvements contributed significantly to U.S. ceramic industry sales in 1983. Glass companies, the largest sector of the U.S. ceramic industry, with annual sales exceeding $16 billion, benefited particularly from increased automobile and home sales. Sales of flat glass rose from 16 to 23% of all glass sales in 1983, while the percentages of container and technical glass sales fell slightly. Annual porcelain enamel sales, about $4 billion, also benefited from the improved housing market and consumer spending; appliances accounted for over 90% of those sales. Whiteware producers, particularly manufacturers of bathroom fixtures and wall and floor tile, gained for the same reasons and had total sales of about $2.2 billion.

Advanced ceramics, with sales of almost $4 billion, represent a variety of high-technology products, many of them new and rapidly growing. Most advanced ceramic sales, 65%, were capacitors, ferromagnetic and piezoelectric devices, and ceramic substrates and microelectronic chip packages for the electrical and electronic industries. About 21% were sales of automotive spark plugs. The remaining 14% included high-temperature structural and wear- and corrosion-resistant products, bioceramics, cutting tools, and fibre optics.

Fibre-optics sales continued to grow rapidly, mainly for telephone system applications, but many fibre-optic producers were also preparing to produce cables designed for computer data transmission. The combined fibre-optic market in the United States alone was predicted to grow from $700 million in 1984 to $1.6 billion in 1987 and $3 billion by 1990.

While fibre optics and high-temperature engine components were emerging areas of advanced ceramics in Japan, electroceramics was a relatively mature field in which sales were already growing rapidly. Open-market sales of insulating substrates and integrated circuit (IC) packages for the microelectronics industry, about $1 billion annually throughout the world, were dominated in 1983 by Japanese companies. Kyoto Ceramic Co. alone, including its U.S. subsidiary Kyocera, controlled about 60% of this open international market. Few U.S. companies were competing in the open market; many large U.S. microelectronics producers either made their own substrates and IC packages or bought them from captive U.S. subcontractors. The value of those U.S. products was not included in the above sales figures.

Japan also dominated rapidly growing areas of piezoelectric ceramics, with a 90% share of worldwide sales of lead zirconate titanate for FM radio and TV applications and for filters used to control radiofrequency and electromagnetic interference. U.S.-Japanese competition was still intense, however, in the relatively new and rapidly growing area of multilayer ceramic (MLC) chip capacitors. These are made by building up alternating, very thin ceramic

Ceramic automobile engines, like this one on display at Tokyo's Seibu department store, have been developed experimentally in Japan. The first large-volume application of ceramics to automobiles, however, was expected to be in turbochargers.
KAKU KURITA/THE NEW YORK TIMES

dielectric and conductive metal layers on a substrate to achieve required electrical capacitance values. The assembly is then cut up into individual small MLC chip capacitors, which are then fired to achieve their final properties. In 1984 such chip capacitors were beginning to replace tantalum capacitors in the electronics industry, but their real potential appeared to be in their compatibility with surface mounting technology that was expected to dominate future developments in microelectronics and integrated circuitry. (In surface mounting technology, components are mounted to contacting pads on the surface of a circuit board, with no pins running through the thickness of the board. Interconnections are made by means of holes and leads formed within the board itself.)

(NORMAN M. TALLAN)

CHEMICALS

The strong resurgence of the U.S. economy that started during 1983 after the deep recession of 1981–82 generated a corresponding rebound in chemical industries throughout the world. Figures compiled by the European Council of Chemical Manufacturers' Federation (CEFIC) showed that sales of chemical companies in industrialized non-Communist countries (the U.S., Western Europe, Japan, and Australia) rose 5% in 1983 to $463,444,000,000, up from $443,186,000,000 in 1982. The addition of substantial sales from other American countries, such as Canada, Mexico, and Brazil, put total world chemicals sales in 1983 at well over $500 billion.

U.S. shipments of chemicals, as reported by the Department of Commerce, increased 10%, from $172,803,000,000 in 1982 to $190,230,000,000 in 1983. The recovery gathered momentum in 1984. During the first half of the year, shipments amounted to $108,092,000,000, 16% higher than in the first half of 1983.

Increased physical output, rather than higher prices, was responsible for the higher sales volume in the U.S. Actual production of chemicals, as measured by the Federal Reserve Board's production index, rose 10%, from an average of 196.1 in 1982 (1967 = 100) to 215 in 1983. Prices,

according to the Department of Labor's index of producer prices, remained essentially constant, increasing from 292.3 in 1982 (1967 = 100) to 293 in 1983.

The trend in production for U.S. chemicals continued through the first six months of 1984, although prices moved higher. The seasonally adjusted Federal Reserve Board production index for chemicals increased to 227.9 in May and 232.2 (preliminary) in June. The Department of Labor's producer price index increased each month during the period and reached 302.6 in June.

One of the dark clouds for the U.S. chemical industry was a deterioration of its position on exports. In large part because of the strength of the dollar relative to the currencies of the U.S.'s major trading partners, the chemical trade balance fell sharply. In 1983 chemical exports from the U.S. dropped 1% to $19,750,800,000 from $19,890,500,000 in 1982, while imports rose 14% to $10,779,400,000 from $9,493,-500,000 in 1982. As a result, net chemical exports fell 14% from $10,397,000,000 in 1982 to $8,971,400,000 in 1983. Moreover, during the first half of 1984 exports rose 13% to $10,987,100,000, but imports soared 25% to $6,753,000,000. Therefore, net chemical exports for the U.S. during the first six months of 1984 amounted to $4,234,100,000.

More important for future trade was the spectre of large quantities of low-cost chemical commodities produced by countries with cheap, abundant hydrocarbon raw materials. At the November 1984 meeting of the Chemical Manufacturers Association in Houston, Texas, Richard Heckert, vice-chairman of the board and chief operating officer of E. I. du Pont de Nemours, said that his firm had determined that 174 petrochemical plants—excluding any in the U.S. and Western Europe but including Canada—would be added to the worldwide total by 1988, increasing world petrochemical capacity by at least one-third.

Japan's chemical industry, the second largest in the non-Communist world, started to pick up during the summer of 1983. For the full year sales of chemicals (excluding fibres) climbed sharply, according to CEFIC. Despite the strong dollar,

Japan's chemical dollar sales rose 9% to $80,604,000,000. Output increased 6% as the index of chemical production rose to 108.8 (1980 = 100) in 1983 from 102.5 in 1982. Chemical prices declined 2%; the chemical price index, 96.9 in 1982, was 95 in 1983.

Japan was struggling with a negative balance of trade in chemicals, an unusual situation for that country. It did manage to cut its deficit, however. Exports in 1983 increased 10% to $6,984,000,000, and imports increased only 6% to $7,210,000,000. Thus the country's net chemical imports were reduced from $438 million in 1982 to $226 million in 1983. In the first half of 1984 chemical exports soared more than 24% to $4.1 billion, bringing them just about into balance with chemical imports.

Among the steps taken by Japan to solve its chemical problems was a plan to cut production capacity for ethylene, a key petrochemical feedstock, by 36% to four million metric tons per year. Also agreed upon was a plan to reduce capacity for major polymers by March 1985. Demand for chemicals continued to rise in 1984, and the plans to cut capacity were moving ahead. By the beginning of February the country's 17 major producers of polyvinyl chloride, a major polymer, had cut capacity to 1.5 million metric tons per year, just slightly above 1983 demand of 1.4 million metric tons per year.

West Germany's chemical industry also sprang back in 1983, and the recovery continued in 1984. CEFIC reported that sales in Deutsche Marks rose 8%, but the changes in currency valuations made the 1983 increase more modest when measured in dollars. Sales in 1983 totaled $49,742,000,-000, 3% higher than in 1982. Production in 1983 was 7% higher than in 1982; the production index of 103.4 (1980 = 100) in 1983 compared with a figure of 96.4 in 1982. Prices remained relatively stable; the 1982 price index of 113.7 rose to only 113.9 in 1983.

Traditionally, West Germany's chemical makers depend on exports to take up a significant share of their output, and in 1983 the country continued to improve its chemical trade balance. CEFIC reported that exports increased 5% in 1983 to $24,-040,000,000 (48% of the country's chemical sales). Imports, meanwhile, rose only 4% to $13,601,000,000. The favourable balance of trade, therefore, went up 6% to $10,439,000,000.

In the first quarter of 1984 the Association of the German Chemical Industry estimated that sales were up 15% over the first quarter of 1983. Profits were expected to be even better. West German chemical executives did not expect to maintain that pace for the full year, but for the first six months of 1984 the big three West German chemical companies—Hoechst, BASF, and Bayer—reported sales increases ranging from 14 to 18.4% and earnings boosts ranging from 73 to 105%.

The U.K. and France increased chemical sales in their own national currencies during 1983, but their sales were lower in dollars, according to CEFIC. In the U.K. chemical sales declined 4% to $27,162,-000,000, while in France they were off 2% to $30,559,000,000.

CEFIC reported that the U.K. and France continued to post favourable trade balances in chemicals in 1983. The U.K.'s net chemical exports, however, dropped 19% to $2,745,000,000, while France increased its net chemical exports 24% to $2,595,-000,000. During 1984 the chemical industries in both countries were prospering as they benefited from the same healthful business climate that was aiding their global counterparts.   (DONALD P. BURKE)

ELECTRICAL

With a 1983 turnover of $1.2 billion, Bharat Heavy Electricals of India became the 12th largest manufacturer of electrical power equipment in the world. Another example of the rapid growth of the electrical equipment manufacturing industry in less developed countries came from South Korea. There, Hyundai Corp. expanded from automobiles into diesel generating sets, transformers, 36-kv switchgear, electric motors, and hydroelectric turbines. Hyundai had grown from a small garage business in 1943 to a corporation with a turnover of $10,876,000,000 in 1983.

Developments in those and other countries were causing the old, established electrical firms in the industrialized nations to reassess their market strategy. In a message to share owners, General Electric Co. (GE) referred to "the accelerated technological and market change in an era of slower worldwide growth and greatly intensified competition." The company reported that its long-term strategy was to focus on a number of businesses in three distinct areas: high technology, services, and core businesses. A major focus in the high-technology area was factory automation, a market that was expected to reach $300 billion by 1990. Services included construction and nuclear power, and the core businesses involved major appliances, lighting, turbines, and transportation equipment. Between 1981 and 1985 GE was expected to have spent $2.5 billion in renewing, restructuring, and reconceptualizing these businesses.

In 1983 GE's sales totaled $26,797,000,-000, yielding net earnings of $2,024,000,-000 ($1,817,000,000 in 1982). The other major U.S. electrical firm, Westinghouse Electric Corp., had sales of $9,532,000,-000 in 1983 and an operating profit of $477.9 million ($523.8 million in 1982). In a continuation of the restructuring of its business portfolio, Westinghouse in 1983 completed the sale of its lamp operations and acquired several companies, including Unimation, Inc., the leading robot manufacturer. With the distribution transformer industry in the U.S. working at only 40% of capacity, Westinghouse closed one of its transformer plants, at Greenville, Pa., permanently and shut down another, at Sharon, Pa., for six months beginning in September 1984.

In contrast, business commentators in Britain believed that General Electric Co. Ltd. (GEC) of the U.K. had lost its sense of direction. Pretax profits of £670.5 million on a turnover of £5,600 million in 1983–84 were virtually the same as in the previous year. Critics said that the company was not giving its core electrical businesses as much financial backing as it might. GEC had a "cash mountain" of £1,500 million and had recently been spending outside the electrical field, having, for example, bought a stake in a large whisky com-

pany in 1984. Refuting these criticisms, the company pointed to a £42 million increase in pretax profits from its electronic systems and components division, indicating a strengthening of the firm in high-technology growth areas.

Siemens AG of West Germany began a research and investment program costing DM 1 billion. It included the automation of production systems, a market in which the company expected growth to exceed 15% per annum. Siemens was the sixth largest electrical company in the world, with a 1983 turnover of DM 39.5 billion and profits of DM 802 million. Another West German company, AEG-Telefunken AG, was back on course after weathering a difficult spell. In 1982 the company operated at a loss and in 1983 returned a small profit after its creditors agreed to write off DM 1.8 billion of the DM 3 billion that they were owed. In 1984 the company broke even without any outside assistance and planned to build new factories in West Berlin for power electronics and railway systems.

Despite a worldwide downturn in power-plant sales, Toshiba Corp. of Japan increased its exports of heavy electrical equipment by 3% in 1983. The company's total sales rose 13% to 2,707,000,-000,000 yen and profits were 59 billion yen. In 1984 the company planned to spend 140.8 billion yen on research and development, 18% more than in 1983 and 57% above 1982. In 1983 Toshiba led the international consortium that installed the world's largest air-cooled hydroelectric generator at Venezuela's Guri power station.

The French heavy electrical giant Creusot-Loire went into receivership at the end of June 1984. The nationalized French banks wanted a large say in the operation of not only the company but also its sister electrical firms Jeumont-Schneider and Merlin Gerin. The parent company, Schneider SA, regarded these moves with suspicion, fearing that the French gov-

ernment wanted to nationalize the whole group. As no buyer was found for the whole company, Creusot-Loire's rail interests were acquired by Jeumont-Schneider, and Framatome bid for its turbine and nuclear activities.   (T. C. J. COGLE)

FURNITURE

Retail sales of home furniture in the U.S. in 1984 showed a 12.7% improvement over 1983, with a dollar volume of $22,111,-000,000. Pent-up consumer demand after the recession, moderate increases in residential construction, and a healthy economy accounted for the gain. Real growth (adjusted for inflation) was 10.6%. Furniture manufacturers' shipments rose to a value of $12,924,000,000. The first and fourth quarters accounted for the bulk of the increase.

On Jan. 1, 1984, the National Association of Furniture Manufacturers and the Southern Furniture Manufacturers Association merged to become the American Furniture Manufacturers Association (AFMA), with a membership representing 66% of U.S. residential furniture production. According to the AFMA, manufacturers' shipments of wood bedroom, dining room, and occasional furniture rose 14.1% in 1984 to $6,392,000,000, upholstered furniture shipments increased by 12.1% to $4,323,-000,000, and metal and other furniture totaled $2,202,000,000, up 9.2%. The AFMA Econometric Forecast predicted somewhat lower totals for 1985.

The shape of the U.S. retail market continued to change. In the larger markets at least, full-service furniture stores were giving way to chains like Levitz and Wickes, which could dominate a region with special promotions and heavy advertising, and specialty stores selling a single class of product, such as dinettes or outdoor furniture. Other growing trends were warehouse stores that offered most lines but charged extra for services and catalog (mail-order) sales.

According to a study by the U.S. In-

CITY, CHICAGO

Memphis, a Milan-based furniture group, and its founder, Ettore Sottsass, have put that Italian city at the forefront of avant-garde furniture design with unconventional shapes and colours.

A GoBot changes from a car into a robot with a few easy moves. GoBots, originated in Japan as Robo Machines, and other similar toys that turn into such things as motorcycles, trucks, and jet fighters were extremely popular in 1984.

ANTONIO SUAREZ/TIME MAGAZINE

ternational Trade Commission, imports of furniture to the U.S. had doubled between 1979 and 1984 and now accounted for 8% of the market. Encouraged by the high U.S. dollar, the Scandinavian countries, France, Italy, and Spain intensified their efforts to gain a larger share of the U.S. market, the world's largest. However, Taiwan was the largest exporter to the U.S., with $206 million worth of furniture in 1983, more than twice the value of furniture shipped by any other country.

Early American and 18th-century furniture styles continued to be the mainstay of the U.S. trade. The newest trend was Eurostyle, based on European, especially Italian, designs featuring bright-coloured upholstery on low-slung frames, marble-top tables, and chairs and occasional tables in lacquered finishes. Many of these designs were being copied by contemporary-minded U.S. manufacturers. The Memphis look, created by Ettore Sottsass and a group of his fellow Italian designers in 1983, influenced the avant-garde market. The furniture was witty, with poster-coloured lacquers and unconventional shapes, more art than functional furniture. The Milanese influence was expected to shape contemporary furniture trends for several years to come. The other major design story was Neoclassic, with such elements as columns, imitation marble pedestal bases, and ebonized trim.

Innovations included the sofabed with full box spring mattress replacing conventional foam. The incliner sofa, incorporating an action-chair mechanism at one or both ends, became popular after failing to catch on when it was introduced five years earlie·. Following a dozen years of controversy between the U.S. Consumer Product Safety Commission and the upholstered furniture industry over a proposed regulation requiring all upholstered furniture to be made cigarette burnproof, Congress passed a law naming an interagency and furniture industry panel to make a binding recommendation within 30 months.

(ROBERT A. SPELMAN)

FURS

U.S. retailers of furs enjoyed excellent business in 1984, and at year's end they appeared to be headed for another sales record, approaching $1.5 billion. This was the 13th consecutive year of sales growth, despite two economic recessions. The principal reason was fashion and the involvement of leading designers. This, plus the

rapid westernization of Japanese dressing habits, also explained the exploding fur business in Japan, where sales had multiplied more than tenfold in the past decade, reaching nearly 300 billion yen (more than $1.2 billion) in 1984. To a lesser extent, retail fur sales also improved in such important markets as West Germany and Italy, where economic problems, compounded by the strong U.S. dollar, had impeded sales of most luxury items for at least three years.

The New York manufacturing market, considered the most important in the international trade, was hobbled by a three-month strike. The situation not only hastened the industry's natural attrition but also encouraged retailers to rely more heavily on imports, mainly from the Far East and Canada. U.S. fur apparel imports were increasing at a 50% rate, and it appeared they would account for approximately half the nation's retail sales in 1984. One result was the loss by South Korean manufacturers of duty-free status under the Generalized System of Preferences granted to products from less developed areas.

Prices of ranched mink increased about 10% during the year. International mink production rose slightly and at year's end appeared to be approaching an all-time record of 28 million pelts that would be traded internationally in 1985. An important addition to this scene was China, which in less than a decade had built its mink production to about three million pelts. China scheduled its first mink auction for February 1985 in Hong Kong.

Production of wild furs decreased in the U.S., the chief source, mostly because of weather extremes. Another factor was the strong dollar, which curbed European buying and depressed prices. Antifur activities appeared to increase in 1984, most noticeably in Europe, where thousands of mink and foxes were cut loose from pens on farms. (Almost all returned voluntarily at feeding time.) In the U.S. antifur activities were mainly confined to legislative efforts aimed at banning use of steel leghold traps, though little progress was made in this direction.

(SANDY PARKER)

GAMES AND TOYS

In 1984 there was a marked decline internationally in the sale of electronic toys and a return to popularity, welcome to many long-established manufacturers, of traditional items. Dolls and their accessories and plush toys were in greater de-

mand by girls, particularly the successful "Cabbage Patch Kids" of Coleco Industries Inc., which made headlines when they were in short supply late in 1983. The Cabbage Patch phenomenon continued in the U.S. throughout 1984 and extended to many international markets. Retailers in the U.K. were reported to have sold many of the dolls to U.S. tourists anxious not to disappoint children at home at Christmastime. More than six million Cabbage Patch dolls were shipped by Far East producers to Coleco. Traditional board games also experienced good sales during the year.

Popular with boys in many countries during the year were robot figures that could be transformed into vehicles. The original metal die-cast models, called Robo Machines, were designed and manufactured by the Japanese company Bandai. When introduced to the U.S. and Europe and named GoBots, they achieved remarkable success, and demand quickly outran supply. In the U.K. orders placed by retailers in the autumn could not be executed until 1985, and Tonka Toys, the U.S. manufacturer, reported that it had received more than $100 million worth of orders since January. The success of the concept prompted a rival manufacturer, Hasbro Industries, to produce similar toys called Transformer figures, which were widely advertised and in much demand.

ERC Statistics International Ltd., one of the largest independent research agencies in Europe, in a research paper published in July, estimated that worldwide toy exports had reached $4.6 billion and that 72% of that amount originated in the Far East. Hong Kong, Taiwan, South Korea, and Japan together accounted for 93% of Far East toy exports, and two-thirds of the total was shared by Hong Kong and Japan.

The effect of the growth of the Far East toy industries was being keenly felt by European manufacturers. Import penetration in France increased from 39% of total sales in 1978 to 55% in 1983. In the U.K. the proportion rose from 35 to 57%, and even in West Germany, a traditional toymaking country, 50% of the toys sold were now imported. In the U.S. toy imports represented 27% of sales, and 68% of that total was attributed to the Far East. The highest degrees of penetration by toys of Far Eastern manufacture were achieved in Australasia, where they represented 80% of toy imports, and in the countries of the Middle East, where the total was 75%. The Hong Kong Trade Development Council said that 54% of all toys made in the colony went to the U.S. Britain, Hong Kong's second largest customer, took 7%.

Character merchandise was becoming a major feature of toy manufacture, particularly in the U.S., where licensed items represented 28% of total sales. This was three times the level in Europe, where the U.K., sharing a common language with the U.S., was a fertile ground for product lines based on U.S. films and television series. Even so, U.S. concepts formed a lower proportion of character merchandise items sold in the U.K. than in most European countries. This was because indigenous British characters such as Postman Pat, Danger Mouse, the Mr. Men, Paddington Bear, and Roland Rat were more plentiful in Britain than elsewhere in Europe. In the U.S. a trend emerged in the licensing industry that resulted in the characters of leading toymakers finding their way into homes on such products as clothing, giftware, linen, and books. Tonka's GoBots, Hasbro's My Little Pony and G.I. Joe, Mattel Corp.'s Barbie and Masters of the Universe, and Coleco's Cabbage Patch were just a few of the well-known names that were licensed to manufacturers in other consumer goods fields.

Hasbro Industries, considered by many to be the fastest growing firm in the U.S. toy industry, announced in midyear that it had acquired the Milton Bradley Group in a transaction valued at $360 million. Hasbro expected that the combined operation of the two companies would rival in volume that of Mattel, the largest toy manufacturer in the U.S. In the U.K. Britains Ltd., a private company founded in 1860, was acquired by Dobson Park Industries, a publicly owned company whose subsidiary, Petite International, manufactured toy typewriters. Britains was the originator in the 1890s of hollow cast-metal toy soldiers. In recent years they had abandoned lead as a material in favour of plastics and had achieved worldwide success with models of farm animals and equipment.

Toys-R-Us, the U.S. company that claimed to be the world's largest toy specialty retail chain, announced the establishment of a company in the U.K. It was expected that a number of the company's supermarket-style toy stores would begin to operate in Britain in 1985. The company had already expanded into Canada, Singapore, and Kuwait.

(THEODORE V. THOMAS)

GEMSTONES

The feared downturn in the gemstone and jewelry market did not materialize in 1984, but merchants did little more than hold their own. The 1983 Christmas period had passed off quite well in most countries, but trade then settled back to the previously depressed levels. As always, sales of classic stones held up, and the major salesrooms reported remarkably good results.

De Beers continued to regulate the diamond sights (viewings by prospective buyers) with a firmer hand than in more favourable times. It was rumoured that some of the sightholders had their privileges terminated, but this reflected the state of the market more than any infringement of rules by those concerned. Large stones continued to command their own prices. The year brought no overt threats

by any major producing country to go it alone in marketing. Soviet diamonds, after disappearing from the market for a time, reappeared with the customary price fluctuations.

Coloured stones began to move again, although very slowly. The demand for tanzanite and tsavolite gained in strength following reports that mining in Tanzania had resumed. The classic stones still fetched high prices, and some success was reported in the detection of altered colour in members of the corundum group (ruby and the variously coloured sapphires). Ruby from Burma continued to appear sporadically, no doubt as the result of smuggling. Sri Lanka's disturbed political situation affected its trade to some extent.

Attempts at synthesizing opal were still being made, even though many synthetic and imitation opals were already established on the market. A number of synthetic rubies were still in the experimental stage. The U.S. Kashan and Ramaura rubies, both now on the market, could be identified by trained gemmologists. No developments in synthetic emeralds or diamond simulants occurred during the year.

Demand for the rarer stones (which are usually too soft or otherwise unsuitable for ornamental wear) picked up, and several institutions began to buy for scientific and educational collections. The private collector also reappeared as a force in the market. Sales of gemstone rough were limited only by shortages of most of the finer materials. The growth of cutting at mining centres made it more difficult for the lapidary to get the type of material he wanted at a reasonable price.

(MICHAEL O'DONOGHUE)

GLASS

The year brought a number of developments in the glass industry, with investment in new products and technology. In the technological field, King, Taudevin, and Gregson of the U.K. developed a process whereby asbestos could be rendered

harmless by mixing it with additives such as glass at a temperature exceeding 900°C (1,652° F); a new company, VITRIFIX, was formed to promote the process. British Rail was replacing steel gantries in East Anglia with resin-coated composites based on glass fibre. E. I. du Pont de Nemours produced a combination of polyester reinforced with glass and elastomer that could be used as a substitute for metal in certain components of cars, sports equipment, and household appliances. The Frauenhofer Institute in Würzburg, West Germany, was now able to make layers of glass as thin as one-thousandth of a millimetre for use in electronics and as contact lenses. Sumitomo of Japan was starting production of optical fibres in North Carolina, and the U.K. General Electric Co. Ltd. doubled its fibre output.

The packaging industry showed signs of recovery, and there was considerable investment in new equipment. United Glass Containers converted one of its furnaces at Harlow to green glass, the only one in continuous operation in the south of England. Rockware Glass refurbished its Knottingley plant, investing in furnaces and modern high-technology support equipment, while in its Wheatley plant it installed a furnace with microprocessor-controlled instrumentation. Canning Town Glass opened a high-technology furnace at Queenborough. A new furnace also came into production at Verrerie Ouvrière d'Albi, France. The British Glass Manufacturers' Federation continued its support of home delivery of milk and also started an advertising campaign to support glass packaging.

There was continued U.S. investment in flat glass. Guardian Industries obtained a 48% share in Spain's Vidrieriás de Llodio with the aim of financing a new float-glass plant, and Monsanto was investing several million dollars in Belgium to increase production capacity of interlayer film for laminated glass, used in the automotive and building trades. Pilkington Brothers Ltd. of the U.K., whose acquisition of a

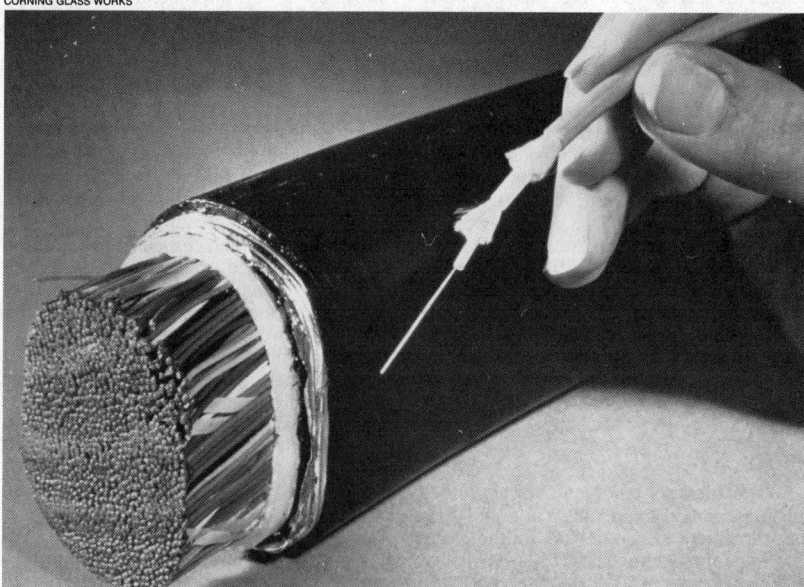

CORNING GLASS WORKS

Fibre optics is a field with immense potential in communications. This single glass optical fibre (right) can carry over 1,000 phone messages simultaneously, as compared with the standard copper cable (left), which contains 256 pairs of wires and has the same carrying capacity.

30% share in Libbey-Owens-Ford was subject to a U.S. Federal Trade Commission ruling that it first dispose of its remaining interests in Canada and freeze its Mexican involvement, reached an agreement with Rio Tinto to buy the latter's Tunnel Building Products subsidiary.

Vegla of West Germany, which was modernizing its production, planned to replace the float-glass installation at Cologne-Porz, the first one built in West Germany. Tanzania's first glass factory, at Mbagalla, was due to start production at the end of 1984. As regards new products, AFG of Tennessee introduced a new technique of making float glass in mini-sized plants, ideal for the smaller market, and the Glass Bossuyt Co. presented its multicoloured toughened glass at the Batibouw Exhibition in Belgium.

The quantity of recycled glass continued to increase, totaling 2,527,000 metric tons in member countries of the EC. A French system of waste-glass collection that avoided breakage made it possible to place more used bottles back on the market.

(ALISON FREED)

INSURANCE

Tightening markets and increasing prices for private insurance were the rule in many parts of the world during 1984. Global insurance premiums were in excess of $500 billion in a very competitive environment. Although some life insurance costs decreased, prices for other insurance and reinsurance rose with increasing momentum throughout the year. Most noticeable were higher premiums for liability, health, motor vehicle, ocean marine, and aviation coverages.

Worldwide insurance premium volume had expanded at an average annual rate of approximately 10% during the past decade. North America and Europe accounted for four-fifths of total premiums. The U.S. led individual countries with 45%; Japan had 15%, followed by West Germany, the U.K., and France. Insurance development varied greatly among countries according to the level of industrialization and amount of disposable income. Switzerland and the U.S. had per capita annual premiums of about $1,000, while 16 other countries had between $300 and $700 and about 50 had $100 or less.

The focus by U.S. insurers on international insurance sharpened in 1984 with the purchase of the American Foreign Insurance Association by Cigna Corp. Cigna now challenged American International Group, the leader with $2.5 billion in foreign premium volume. Other U.S. companies, though much smaller, were also competing internationally with large foreign-based insurers, such as the General Accident, Royal, and Zurich. In the global reinsurance market, excluding Lloyd's of London, the top professional reinsurers writing reinsurance only were Munich Re (West Germany), Swiss Re (Switz.), and General Re (U.S.).

In the U.K. premium income of British insurance companies rose by 23% in long-term (principally life) insurance and by 10% in general (nonlife) insurance. Premiums totaled almost £24,000 million. Automobile insurance was unprofitable, and fire and crime losses were at record heights. There were catastrophic fire losses in several warehouses, with one at an industrial estate in northwest London causing damages estimated as high as £200 million. Lloyd's of London continued to attract more individuals to underwriting memberships. The number increased by 8% to nearly 24,000, despite some evidence of unfair treatment by agents in the past. The members of one large syndicate obtained refunds of £38 million for misappropriated funds. Lloyd's accounts published in 1984, which under the three-year system relate to 1981, showed overall profits of £152 million on premiums of $3.3 billion. A major income-tax-law change in March terminated the century-old U.K. practice that permitted deductability of some individual life insurance premiums.

In the U.S. the Life Insurance Marketing and Research Association predicted that sales of new life insurance would rise by 12–14% in 1984 to $8 billion, compared with average annual new business growth of 4–6% in the 1960s and 7–9% in the 1970s. Sales of investment-oriented contracts such as "universal life" now included one-fourth of new ordinary life policy premiums. The trend toward broadened financial services for clients progressed, with a number of the larger insurance, investment, real estate, and other organizations combining through mergers or other affiliations. Insurers and agents split on proposed legislation that would permit banks to diversify into insurance. A bill that would reduce restrictions of the Bank Holding Company Act was defeated, but similar legislative proposals were anticipated in 1985. Three-fourths of the larger banks indicated that they had formal plans for entering the insurance business.

U.S. property and liability insurance experienced one of its worst years ever, with underwriting losses of $10 billion reported by midyear. Although annual projected premiums increased nearly 7%, the anticipated combined loss and expense ratio was more than 115, up from 112 in 1983. The poor results were partially attributed to heavy windstorm losses early in the year. Many analysts suggested that this might be the bottom of the underwriting cycle, with underwriting losses leveling out and record premium growth of 8–11% in 1985.

Considerable controversy arose within the industry regarding the new comprehensive general liability forms of the Insurance Services Office (ISO). The proposed basic policies, unless endorsed to provide broader coverage, would be on a "claim-made" basis, include an occurrence-aggregate limit, and exclude most pollution liability. The ISO reported that simplified "plain-language" auto and homeowner policies had been approved in almost all states. Among the more spectacular insurance losses in 1984, almost $300 million was paid for communications satellites unsuccessfully deployed in February and June. (See SPACE EXPLORATION.) Asbestos-related litigation continued to make headlines, as three major insurers announced a $315 million settlement with Manville Corp. Changes in Medicare and health insurance benefits implemented tighter controls on hospital payments in order to combat escalating medical costs. Insurance laws or rulings were passed in several states prohibiting use of sex as a factor in insurance pricing. (DAVID L. BICKELHAUPT)

IRON AND STEEL

World steel activity took a turn for the better toward the end of 1983. Output for the year reached approximately 660 million metric tons, more than 2% higher than the very depressed level of 1982. However, this modest improvement meant that steel demand remained substantially below the levels attained in the early 1970s, and that it was not universal among steel-producing countries. While 1983 U.S. production rose 12% above the exceptionally low figure for 1982 and production in many less developed countries also showed some advance, Japan and most EC countries experienced reductions. Overall improvement continued and broadened in 1984, and world steel output for the year might well exceed 700 million tons, although it was not expected to approach the world record level of 747 million tons in 1979. Moreover, as 1984 progressed, there was growing evidence of a slackening in the steel recovery of Western countries.

The mild upturn in total world demand for steel, together with continuing efforts in traditional Western steel-producing countries to eliminate obsolete production facilities and in some cases to make appreciable net reductions in capacity, was far from resolving the long-term problem of structural excess capacity worldwide. Furthermore, the exceptional strength of the U.S. dollar (in which much trade in steel on the world market was conducted) increased the value to exporters, in terms of their respective national currencies, of their sales on the world market, thus reducing pressures on them to raise the price in dollars. It also greatly increased the attraction of the U.S. market to imports and was, therefore, an important factor in the continuing pressure on U.S. authorities to provide increased protection for the domestic steel industry through invocation of various clauses of the U.S. Trade Act.

The U.S.-EC arrangement of October 1982 limiting, by export licensing, imports from the EC into the U.S. of many general steel products continued to operate tolerably well from the point of view of both parties. It was to run until the end of 1985, subject to consultations during that year to review the possibility of extending and modifying the arrangement. In contrast, protracted discussions between EC and U.S. authorities on compensation of the EC for import restrictions on certain special steel products, imposed in 1983 under the import relief clauses of the Trade Act, ultimately ended in disagreement and exercise by the EC of its rights under the General Agreement on Tariffs and Trade to impose corresponding restrictions on U.S. exports to the EC (in practice, of nonsteel products).

Much wider in its potential effect was a general import relief case brought by Bethlehem Steel Corp. and the United Steelworkers of America under Sec. 201 of the Trade Act early in 1984 against imports of steel from all sources. The various stages of these proceedings culminated in a U.S. presidential decision announced on Sept. 18, 1984. This remitted to the U.S. trade representative the negotiation of voluntary restraint arrangements with main supplying countries, with the general objective of reducing the total import share of the U.S.

Thin-slab casting could revolutionize U.S. production of steel sheet. National Steel Corp., one of the smaller U.S. steelmakers, has tested a process for making steel sheet so thin it need not be rolled.

J. KEVIN FITZSIMONS/BUSINESS WEEK

market to 18.5% from some 24% at the time of the decision. Discussions in this context with a number of countries began during the fall, and in late November the U.S authorities announced formal unilat-eral restriction of imports of tubes and pipes from the EC to a level equivalent to 5.9% of the U.S. market under the 1984 Trade and Tariff Act. This had the effect of immediately halting all further imports of those products from the EC for the rest of 1984.

The EC continued to develop its program for long- and short-term steel crisis measures. A key element was the restructuring of the industry and the reduction of its capacity, associated with the steel State Aids Code of August 1981. According to the code, the release of national public aid directly to steel companies was conditional on the industry's achieving net capacity cuts totaling 26.7 million metric tons (from a 1980 base figure) of hot rolled steel production in the EC as a whole, and also on the acceptance by the European Commission that the restructuring plans of aided firms were likely to lead to financial viability by 1986.

The short-term market support measures, intended as interim devices pending rebalancing of the fundamental supply position in the EC through the restructuring of production facilities, were extended to the end of 1985. These included quota restrictions on production of main steel products and their delivery in the EC market and, since January 1984, statutory minimum prices for hot and cold rolled strip and sheet, plates, and heavy sections. Breaches of either the quotas or minimum prices were subject to financial penalties. In late October 1984 the EC Council of Ministers agreed that the European Commission should negotiate voluntary restraint arrangements with the governments of the countries that were the principal exporters of steel to the EC. The tonnages to which exporting countries would be asked to commit themselves would be somewhat higher than in 1984 to reflect the improvement of demand in the EC.

Table IX. World Production of Crude Steel
In 000 metric tons

Country	1979	1980	1981	1982	1983	1984 Year to date	No. of months	Percent change 1984/83
World	746,680	716,210	707,660	644,870	662,710			
U.S.S.R.	149,090	147,930	148,520	147,150	152,000*	65,000	5	+2.0
U.S.	123,690	101,460	109,590	67,640	75,620	65,190	9	+17.5
Japan	111,750	111,400	101,680	99,550	97,170	78,670	9	+10.1
West Germany	40,040	43,840	41,610	35,880	35,730	29,650	9	+11.8
China	34,490	37,120	35,600	37,020	39,930	17,920	5	+8.5
Italy	24,250	26,500	24,780	24,010	21,670	17,990	9	+13.4
France	23,360	23,180	21,260	18,400	17,610	14,060	9	+10.6
United Kingdom	21,460	11,280	15,570	13,710	14,990	11,380	9	+1.1
Poland	19,220	19,490	15,720	14,800	16,400*	8,330	6	+2.5
Canada	16,050	15,900	14,810	11,870	12,830	11,130	9	+19.3
Czechoslovakia	14,820	14,930	15,270	15,030	15,100*	5,180	4	+2.0
Brazil	13,890	15,310	13,230	13,000	14,660	13,700	9	+29.4
Belgium	13,540	12,420	12,380	9,990	10,160	8,420	9	+13.0
Romania	12,910	13,180	13,030	13,060	13,500*	†		
Spain	12,250	12,640	12,900	13,150	12,730	9,960	9	+4.5
India	10,130	9,510	10,780	11,000	10,310	7,890*	9	+2.3*
South Africa	8,880	9,070	9,010	8,200	7,000	5,570*	9	+9.2*
Australia	8,120	7,590	7,640	6,370	5,610	4,650	9	+13.7
South Korea	7,610	8,560	10,750	11,760	11,920	9,700	9	+12.0
East Germany	7,020	7,310	7,470	7,170	7,500*	3,090	5	+1.0
Mexico	7,020	7,160	7,660	7,060	6,920	5,600*	9	+11.6*
Netherlands, The	5,810	5,270	5,470	4,350	4,480	4,280	9	+30.5
North Korea*	5,400	5,800	5,500	5,800	5,900	†		
Luxembourg	4,950	4,620	3,790	3,510	3,290	2,950	9	+24.3
Austria	4,920	4,620	4,660	4,260	4,410	3,650	9	+12.0
Sweden	4,730	4,240	3,770	3,900	4,210	3,350	9	+13.7
Hungary	3,910	3,770	3,650	3,700	3,800*	1,550	5	−2.5
Yugoslavia	3,540	3,630	3,980	3,840	4,140	2,790*	9	−11.3*
Argentina	3,200	2,690	2,530	2,910	2,940	1,950	9	−11.4
Taiwan	3,190	3,420	3,160	4,150	5,020	3,940*	9	+7.1*
Bulgaria	2,480	2,570	2,480	2,590	2,800*	1,160	5	−3.7
Finland	2,460	2,510	2,430	2,410	2,420	1,940	9	+10.3
Turkey	2,400	2,540	2,430	2,840	3,800	3,130	9	+21.7
Venezuela	1,480	1,980	2,030	2,280	2,320	2,010*	9	+20.6*
Iran	1,430	1,200*	1,200*	1,200*	1,200*	†		
Switzerland	890	930	930	840	850*	†		
Greece	810	870	910	910	860	580	8	+3.6
Egypt	800	800	900	950	950*	†		

*Estimated.   †1984 figures not yet available.
Sources: International Iron and Steel Institute; United Nations.

Table X. World Production of Pig Iron
In 000 metric tons

Country	1979	1980	1981	1982	1983
World	527,420	506,480	495,570	450,320	453,510
U.S.S.R.	108,300	107,280	107,770	106,720	110,000*
Japan	83,830	87,040	80,050	77,660	72,940
U.S.	78,930	62,340	66,740	39,280	44,210
China	36,730	38,020	34,170	35,540	37,500*
West Germany	35,180	33,870	31,880	27,620	26,600
France	18,960	18,680	16,960	14,720	13,500
United Kingdom	12,760	6,260	9,470	8,330	9,480
Brazil	11,590	12,690	10,760	10,800	10,720
Italy	11,330	12,150	12,260	11,540	10,310
Poland	10,970	11,380	8,870	8,110	9,300*
Canada	10,910	10,890	9,740	8,000	8,570
Belgium	10,860	9,990	9,810	7,830	8,030
Czechoslovakia	9,530	9,820	9,900	9,530	9,450*
Romania	8,880	9,100	8,860	8,640	8,950*
India	8,770	8,510	9,470	9,640	9,160
Australia	7,760	6,980	6,740	5,950	5,060
South Africa	7,020	7,200	7,370	6,760	5,220
Spain	6,450	6,370	6,560	5,990	5,430
South Korea	5,060	5,580	7,930	8,440	8,020
North Korea	5,000	5,400	5,000	5,250	5,300*
Netherlands, The	4,810	4,330	4,600	3,620	3,750
Luxembourg	3,800	3,570	2,890	2,590	2,320
Austria	3,700	3,490	3,480	3,120	3,320
Mexico	3,490	3,640	3,770	3,590	3,540
Sweden	2,910	2,380	1,770	1,780	2,010
Hungary	2,390	2,210	2,210	2,200	2,000*
East Germany	2,380	2,450	2,420	2,140	2,200*
Yugoslavia	2,370	2,440	2,820	2,700	2,840
Turkey	2,300	2,140	2,050	2,170	2,720
Finland	2,040	2,020	1,970	1,940	1,900
Taiwan	1,760	1,720	1,610	2,700	3,420
Bulgaria	1,450	1,540	1,520	1,560	1,650*
Argentina	1,110	1,040	920	1,020	910
Norway	650	620	570	480	570
Chile	610	650	600	450	540
Venezuela	510	500	420	210	170

*Estimated.
Source: International Iron and Steel Institute.

A recent small but significant development on the world steel scene was the appearance for the first time in Japan of steel imports from less developed countries, mainly Far Eastern. Although at around two million metric tons a year they represented only a very small share of the Japanese market in 1983, it seemed certain that the role in steel of several less developed countries would continue to grow.

(TREVOR J. MACDONALD)

MACHINERY AND MACHINE TOOLS

In 1983 worldwide machine-tool production was valued at $19.4 billion. The world's leading producer was Japan with production worth an estimated $3.5 billion. Second was West Germany with production worth $3.2 billion, followed in order by the U.S.S.R. ($3 billion), the U.S. ($2.1 billion), and Italy ($1 billion).

The most prominent exporter of machine tools was West Germany with exports estimated at $1.9 billion, followed by Japan with $1.3 billion. The major machine-tool consuming nation in 1983 was reported to have been the U.S.S.R. with consumption worth $4 billion. (Consumption is defined as domestic production plus imports minus exports.) Second was the U.S. ($2.7 billion), followed by Japan ($2.5 billion).

The percentage of the U.S. machine-tool market served by foreign suppliers continued to rise in 1983, reaching approximately 33%. Annualized data for the early months of 1984 indicated that the figure for the year might exceed 40%. For certain types of machine tools the import penetration was substantially higher. For numerically controlled (NC) lathes, for example, imports were expected to account for about two-thirds of U.S. consumption, and for machining centres, about three-fourths. (Numerically controlled machines are those that use stored numerical data to control machine functions; machining centres are multipurpose NC machines having automatic tool-changing capabilities.)

In 1983 the U.S. was continuing to feel the effects of a global economic slowdown. As a consequence, shipments of machine tools to both domestic and foreign purchasers were low for the second straight year. Shipments totaled $1.8 billion, with $1.6 billion going to customers in the U.S. The level of total shipments was off approximately 65% from the record high of $5.1 billion set in 1981. The backlog of unfilled orders also declined markedly, to $1 billion from a 1980 high of $5.5 billion. Figures for 1984, however, indicated that the backlog for the year would climb toward $2 billion.

In Japan machine-tool production in 1983 declined 10% from 1982. In monetary value, 60% of Japan's production in 1983 involved products that were numerically controlled, compared with 54% in 1982. NC drilling machines experienced an astonishing growth of 230% from the previous year. In 1983 machining centres accounted for 34% of all NC machines produced, while lathes totaled 27%. The major foreign suppliers of machine tools to Japan in 1983 were, in order of importance, West Germany, the U.S., and Switzerland.

West German production of machine tools continued the decline that had begun after 1980, when production totaled $5.4 billion. In 1983 it totaled $3.7 billion. As with other countries, the bulk of the production, about 70%, was in the metal-cutting area. West German exports were primarily grinding, polishing, and honing machines. Milling and boring machines were the major imports. West German exports of metal-cutting machines in 1983 were primarily to the U.S.S.R. and France.

(JOHN B. DEAM)

MICROELECTRONICS

The microelectronics industry in 1984 continued to be one of very high growth combined with increasing technical complexities. The total output of the industry exceeded $20 billion annually, and its impact on the medical, computer, communications, military, and other industries was increasing. Innovation continued at a rapid pace. Prominent in the area of memory storage were the new 256-kilobit (K) dynamic random-access memories (RAM's) and the 64K static RAM's. (One kilobit equals 1,024 bits, a bit being the smallest unit of usable data. A 256K memory can store the equivalent of about 80 double-spaced typewritten pages of text. Memory in static RAM's retains its contents even when the main current is turned off; this is not the case with memory in dynamic RAM's.) Most of the progress was coming from Japan, and by 1984 the number of patents in memory designs in Japan exceeded those in the U.S. Japan also became the manufacturing leader in memories, with 60% of the total annual output. The complexity of memories continued to increase, and at the same time there was a reduction in the cost to three millicents per bit for dynamic RAM's.

The trend toward more powerful central processing units, combined with the decreasing cost of memories, peripheral equipment, and software, was adding tremendous processing capabilities to personal computers at comparatively low prices. The personal computer of 1985 that would be selling for under $5,000 had the processing capability of a $1 million mainframe machine in 1965 and a $250,000 minicomputer in 1975.

One of the most significant changes in the microelectronics industry was the rapid development of semicustom very large-scale-integration (VLSI) devices. This product category includes gate arrays and standard cells. Gate arrays are geometric patterns of gates that are implemented by three or four transistors. (A gate is a device that transmits a signal when specified input conditions are met.) To complete the design the gates are interconnected with a metal pattern. In standard cells gates are connected to form building blocks that are used to complete designs for very large-scale integrated circuits (VLSIC's). Sales growth of these semicustom products was in excess of 100% in 1983–84 but this was expected to slow to 40% by the late 1980's.

The driving force in the semicustom area was the application of powerful computer tools to the design process. The traditional design of a complex VLSIC was done by means of manual layout. With the development of powerful computer tools from Stanford University and the University of California, combined with the low cost of computer power, the design process was becoming highly automated and was being modified to fit the software tools. The result was the development of gate arrays with counts of 10,000 gates and standard cells with counts of 20,000 gates. High-complexity gate arrays could be made available to customers in 8 weeks and standard cells in 16 weeks, compared with up to two years for the conventional manual process. (HANDEL H. JONES)

NUCLEAR INDUSTRY

Nuclear power in 1984 maintained a significant cost advantage over coal and other forms of energy, according to a survey by the Nuclear Energy Agency of the OECD. This economic advantage would hold, the report said, even if capital costs for nuclear energy increased by 50%, if nuclear fuel costs became two or three times higher, or if nuclear stations operated at below 50% load factor.

In 1983 (excluding the Soviet bloc) 17 reactors of more than 150 MW entered commercial service. At the beginning of 1984, 238 such units were in service, with a total installed capacity of 174,817.2 MW.

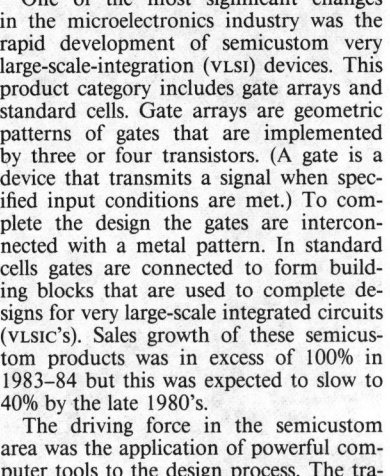

A contrast-enhancement coating applied during the fabrication of semiconductor wafers makes possible the production of microchips with ultrasmall circuits. The wafer at right is coated. The process was developed at General Electric's Research and Development Center in Schenectady, New York.

Shoreham nuclear power plant located on New York's Long Island was one of many nuclear facilities plagued by opposition from surrounding communities, endless delays, and escalating costs. In 1984 construction was nearly a decade behind schedule, and the total cost would be around $4 billion, as compared with the original estimate of $241 million.

BILL PIERCE/TIME MAGAZINE

These included 122 pressurized light-water reactors (PWR's), 61 boiling water reactors (BWR's), 18 pressurized heavy-water reactors (PHWR's), and 26 Magnox reactors. Analysis of performance to the end of 1983 put a Japanese PWR at the head of the list, followed by a Canadian PHWR, a West German BWR, and another Canadian PHWR.

International Atomic Energy Agency figures for 1983 revealed that France produced 48.3% of all its electricity by nuclear power, the highest proportion for any country. French nuclear plants produced a total of 137 million megawatt-hours (MWh), second only to the United States, which produced 310 million MWh.

European collaboration on the development of commercial fast breeder reactors was to take place under a new agreement signed between Britain's Central Electricity Generating Board (CEGB) and Electricité de France (EDF). A memorandum of understanding was also signed by the governments of Belgium, France, West Germany, Great Britain, and Italy.

In the U.S. the Office of Technology Assessment, which advises Congress on technological issues, published a plan for the revitalization of the U.S. nuclear-power industry. This plan called for improvements in the management and regulation of nuclear power and for the standardization of light-water reactors, based on the advanced safety concepts being designed by Westinghouse Electric Corp. and General Electric Co. If these steps were not enough to restore public confidence, the report said, then gas-cooled and heavy-water designs as established in other countries should be investigated.

The top of the crippled Three Mile Island-2 reactor pressure vessel was finally raised in July, producing lower radiation levels in the reactor building than had been anticipated. The U.S. Nuclear Regulatory Commission postponed once more the approval for restarting the Three Mile Island-1 reactor, which had been expected during the summer.

A spill from the waste-handling plant at Sellafield in the United Kingdom was the subject of inquiries by both the operator, British Nuclear Fuels, and the Department of the Environment. Although the discharged materials contained less radioactivity than the maximum level permitted, they did not disperse as they were intended to do. British Nuclear Fuels immediately introduced new control systems to prevent the recurrence of a similar sequence of events. (*See* ENVIRONMENT.)

The public inquiry on the proposed CEGB Sizewell-B station, Britain's first PWR, became that nation's longest inquiry, reaching 24 months by the end of 1984. The other nuclear power operator in Britain, the South of Scotland Electricity Board, made a case to the inquiry for continuing with the advanced gas-cooled reactor (AGR) program. The AGR's that were operating, including units commissioned recently, were producing high-performance figures as compared with PWR's.

One of the main new international nuclear market prospects was the Turkish program, but no orders were placed during the year. Continuing problems over the financing of the projects protracted the negotiations. In Egypt bids for a two-unit PWR station at ad-Dabah were under consideration by the Egyptian Nuclear Power Plants Authority and its consultants, Motor Columbus.

The largest reactor to be commissioned in the world to date, the 1,500-MW Ignalinsk-1 unit, reached full power in the Soviet Union. A second unit was under construction, and two more were planned to begin operation in the 1990s. Problems with the nuclear reactor factory, Atommash, continued. In addition to the delays already experienced in 1983, it was reported that several of the buildings at the plant were suffering from substantial subsidence.

The rupture of a pressure tube in the Pickering unit 2 reactor in Canada in 1983 led to investigations at the operating plant and at Canadian laboratories to determine the significance of the event for other units. It was found that only early Candu reactor designs, such as Pickering units 1 and 2, were at risk. The pressure tubes had suffered local cooling due to a slight sagging of the tube that produced contact with the surrounding tube. The investigation found that the particular alloy used in the early designs could become brittle under such conditions, but the different alloy used in later designs would not suffer the same embrittlement. The designer, Atomic Energy of Canada Ltd., had intended that the pressure tubes be replaceable to extend the reactor's design life. Therefore, Ontario Hydro, the operator of the two units affected, decided to replace all the tubes in the two reactors, and the work on them began during the year. Other units were to be checked during forthcoming routine maintenance periods to prevent the sagging problem.

With the world's first commercial nuclear power plants reaching (and exceeding) the end of their design lives, a number of countries began to let contracts for decommissioning. The U.S. Department of Energy appointed General Electric Co. to oversee the dismantling of the Shippingport 60-MW light-water reactor. The project involved the removal of radioactive materials and equipment to make the site suitable for unrestricted use. The Niederaichbach 100-MW gas-cooled heavy-water reactor in West Germany, due to be dismantled and the site returned to a "green field," would be one of the first commercial reactors in the world to be completely removed.

After a long period of inactivity in the home market, the nuclear industry's hopes for revival in Italy were boosted by the industry minister's announcement that equipment orders for two sites in the north of the country would be placed by the end of the year. A national referendum in Switzerland to decide whether to continue with the country's nuclear-power program resulted in a cautious "yes." However, the opposition to commissioning the next Swiss reactor, at Kaiseraugst, was likely to continue unabated.

Demonstrations, both intentional and inadvertent, of the safety of the transportation of nuclear materials received considerable attention in the media. In England the CEGB held a demonstration test in which a fuel flask was dropped from a height of 9 m (29½ ft) onto one corner of its lid, the most vulnerable point, without breaking the seal. An even more dramatic (some said "theatrical") demonstration, in which a flask was fixed solidly in the path of a 140-ton locomotive hauling three 33-ton railcars, was also conducted. The flask was struck, again on the most vulnerable corner, at 160 km/h (100 mph) and was not broken by the impact. Such tests were dismissed as publicity stunts by antinuclear groups.   (RICHARD A. KNOX)

PAINTS AND VARNISHES

In 1984 the fortunes of the paint industry again followed the movement of the various national economies. As industrial activity quickened in the U.S., paint manufacturers reported volume gains of some 20%. Strong export growth helped the Dutch and British industries to score good advances in volume and value. French paint makers, however, saw volume fall by about 4%, although value increased 8%, and the Portuguese industry suffered a contraction of 9%. Denmark showed higher growth in volume (9.5%) than in value (9.3%), while Sweden combined a volume loss of 0.6% with a 16% gain in value.

The Japanese industry reported modest volume growth of about 2%. In Thailand the 60 licensed manufacturers experienced an 8% increase by volume, while one of Malaysia's 37 paint makers developed the first nondrip gloss paint for tropical use. China was reported to have some 1,200 paint factories, many of them operating on a profit incentive basis. Paint consumption in Egypt exceeded local manufacture, and rapid expansion was planned. In sub-Saharan Africa, Nigeria had the largest paint industry but was handicapped by difficulties in importing raw materials.

Economic pressures in Europe led to several mergers and acquisitions. The most interesting case was probably the battle for the largest independent paint company in the U.K., Donald Macpherson. An opening bid by the Becker chemical group of Sweden provoked a counterbid from the British company Yule Catto. After further leapfrogging, the state-backed Finnish group, Kemira, eventually won control for its Tikkurilan paint subsidiary. Becker, however, returned to the U.K. scene by buying 75% of the important Goodlass Wall company from the Cookson Industries group. Another change of control involved the Valentine group, producing paints in several parts of Europe. After protracted negotiations, Britain's Imperial Chemical Industries acquired control of most of the continental businesses. Valentine U.K., however, was bought by

the West German giant BASF (Bayerische Anilin-und-Soda Fabrik) through its British subsidiary Glasurit Beck.

Technical change in paint formulations accelerated, often under political or environmental pressure. The West German industry responded to concern over air pollution by pledging a voluntary reduction of 25% in its use of organic solvents over five years. The U.K. industry announced an early end to the use of lead driers in decorative paints.   (LIONEL BILEFIELD)

PHARMACEUTICALS

In much of the Western world, the prospects for generic drug manufacturers improved measurably in 1984 as the result of efforts to reduce costs to consumers and to government-funded medical assistance programs. In Ireland generic drug manufacturers walked out of the main pharmaceutical manufacturers' association to form their own group. In Britain so-called parallel imports (importation back into the country of brand-name drugs from cheaper markets overseas) undercut the profits of British brand-name drug manufacturers. The most significant advance for generic competition, however, came in the U.S., where passage of the Waxman-Hatch Abbreviated New Drug Application/Patent Restoration Act opened the door to the introduction of generic versions of about 125 brand-name drugs approved by the FDA since 1962. Previously, generic versions of such drugs had been treated as new drugs by the FDA. The agency began a reorganization to speed the approval process, and it was expected that less expensive versions of familiar brand-name drugs would begin arriving in U.S. drugstores by early 1985.

The Waxman-Hatch bill was a trade-off. The generic part of the industry would benefit from the speedup in the approval procedure, which could result in the appearance of generic (and cheaper) versions of perhaps 30 of the 200 most-prescribed drugs and a probable tripling of generic drug sales in the U.S. during the next five years. At the same time, the brand-name manufacturers (as represented by the Pharmaceutical Manufacturers Association) were conceded a longer patent term for drugs whose introduction was delayed by the regulatory process. Brand-name drug man-

ufacturers would receive up to five years of restored patent life and certain other exclusive marketing rights once a drug was approved.

In addition, PMA members were granted ten years of exclusive marketing for 50 drugs approved during the "transition period" (from January 1982 to the time the bill was enacted), regardless of patent status. This provision had been fought for by a "dissident" element of the PMA after a majority of member companies were prepared to accept a tougher version of the bill, and the struggle cost the jobs of three top PMA officers.

In other developments, a Greek government pricing policy, announced after a two-and-a-half-year price freeze, touched off an exodus of pharmaceutical firms from that country. India's continued insistence that multinational firms be majority-owned by Indian nationals hindered new drug-company investment there and probably contributed to a shortage of some leading drugs. In Mexico a presidential decree was designed to control prices and reduce imports. The multinational companies quickly began litigation to fight the measure. Despite lower court injunctions (on the basis that the decree was "unconstitutional"), the government forged ahead with its plans.   (DONALD A. DAVIS)

PLASTICS

The plastics industry worldwide started 1984 on a note of optimism. These hopes were well justified in the U.S. where, following a 15% growth in demand for plastics products in 1983 over 1982, a similar order of expansion was maintained, with the processing sector working at near to maximum capacity. In Europe the industry's performance was modest but reasonable, if less ebullient than in North America. However, as far as the large-tonnage "commodity" thermoplastics were concerned, a note of renewed uncertainty became apparent late in 1984.

There were several reasons for this. In the first place, it was generally conceded that measures taken to reduce gross overcapacity for these materials (which together account for some 75% of total plastics production) had been inadequate. From the peak year of 1979 to 1984, consumption

AVTEK CORPORATION

First flight for plastic plane: the Avtek 400 is a new airplane designed for business use, and its airframe is nearly all made of lightweight, high-strength composites—*i.e.*, plastics.

of the two major materials—low-density polyethylene (LDPE) and polyvinyl chloride (PVC)—actually declined. This was particularly serious in the case of LDPE, because the first Saudi Arabian plants making this material came on stream punctually toward the end of 1984. Their output of cheaper material, based on abundant local supplies of gas, was expected to affect the European market in 1985.

The slackening of efforts to rationalize the European industry after 1982 appeared to have been due to the impression of a false dawn created by some recovery in the following two years—to which rebuilding of run-down stocks certainly contributed. Especially in France and Italy, it also reflected the tendency for the state to take over distressed firms rather than subject them to the discipline of the market. Even in Japan, where the Ministry of Trade and Industry insisted on tough rationalization—about one-third of petrochemical capacity was closed down—there remained intense concern about foreign competition, both at home and in Japan's main export markets in Southeast Asia.

The situation was better in the case of the more specialized engineering plastics, whose high added value was seen as offering altogether brighter prospects for the industry than competition in low-cost commodity materials. In this sector the fruits of intensive research, mainly in the U.S., began to be available during 1984 in the form of supertough and other improved grades of such established plastics as nylon, acetal, and thermoplastic polyester—further extending their ability to replace metals in many components. World consumption of engineering plastics now exceeded one million metric tons, some 40% of which was in Europe. Du Pont expected the annual increase to average 8%, creating a four million-ton-a-year market by the end of the century. This could be compared with the existing global demand for commodity materials of 30 million tons or so.

The modified engineering plastics typified a strong continuing trend in polymer research toward blends, alloys, and composites. Such materials were far more sophisticated in their processing characteristics than earlier, relatively simple plastics that behaved predictably. Their development was one factor that began to have a profound effect on molders and other converters serving major end-use sectors such as the automotive, electronics, domestic and business appliance, telecommunications, and other high-technology industries.

Processors began to realize that, to survive in this field, they needed to develop new skills in polymer technology and component and tool design through increased emphasis on computer-aided techniques, finite element analysis, and similar methods. Plastics processing was a natural area for near-total automation, and microelectronics was entering more and more into all aspects of the business. In Japan robot-controlled factories had become an actuality.   (ROBIN C. PENFOLD)

PRINTING

Leaders of the world's printing and publishing industries, gathered in Venice, Italy, in 1984, concluded that the threat of the "new media" had been vastly overestimated. Print, the 400 delegates agreed,

had an excellent future on its own and in partnership with electronic media. Nevertheless, the structure of the industry was changing. In Britain Robert Maxwell (see BIOGRAPHIES), head of Pergamon Press, British Printing & Communications Corp., and the country's largest cable TV system, added the Daily Mirror to his holdings and formed a transatlantic prepress partnership. Centralized prepress facilities would handle publishers' material, and the smaller process houses would be unable to compete in capital investment. The first such centres were now in existence in Britain, the U.S., Japan, and Singapore.

At the Los Angeles Olympics, a portable colour picture scanner-transmitter, provided by Sci-Tex of Israel, was used to transmit pictures by satellite to newspapers around the world. A graphic-arts quality electronic colour preproof system from Dr.-Ing Rudolf Hell in West Germany found ready users, despite its $400,000 price tag. In phototypesetting, new CRTronic 300 and Autologic APS-5 systems brought new levels of performance at budget prices. A New York typesetting shop developed a talking proofreader. The unit read typeset copy and had a 10,000-word vocabulary for spelling out words. Financial printers established links among world business centres with the aim of providing instant printing for stock issues and the like without having to transport film across the oceans. Donnelley Satellite Systems was set up to provide satellite page-transmission services around the globe. The first links, mainly for international newspapers and newsmagazines, were established between the U.S., Britain, Singapore, and other centres.

In Singapore a print and publishing giant was formed by the merger of Times Publishing and Chinese newspaper interests. Late, but not too late, U.S. rotogravure catalog and magazine printers wholeheartedly adopted offset-gravure conversion techniques, already established in Europe and Japan. Japan became an important customer for new rotogravure presses from Albert. In web offset, eight-page presses again came to the fore. The first ten-unit machine from Harris Graphics was due to be installed. Two West German-based manufacturers, Miller-Nohab and M.A.N.-Roland, introduced new models.

For the first time, large-circulation newspapers outside the U.S. began to place substantial press orders, the largest from the Daily Telegraph in Britain, for Rockwell-Goss Headliner offset presses. The Uniman system became a best-seller, with the largest of these presses ever made going to Thai Rath in Bangkok, Thailand. China started making Western printing equipment under license.   (W. PINCUS JASPERT)

RUBBER

A year of record sales by many automobile manufacturers paced the rubber industry in the United States to its best showing during the 1980s. The U.S. tire industry shipped nearly 193 million automobile tires in 1984, the highest number since the record 210 million in 1978. Of that 1984 total, 51.3 million were sold as original equipment and 141.5 million were sold on the replacement market. Radials accounted for 78% of the tires sold. Truck tire shipments totaled 40 million units.

The tire industry operated at over 90% of capacity for the year, and many companies added radial-manufacturing capacity by operating plants seven days a week.

The strong U.S. dollar encouraged a flood of tire imports, as 21% of the total U.S. replacement market was supplied by imports. Increased imports from South Korea led the U.S. tire manufacturers to file an antidumping case with the U.S. government's International Trade Commission.

The strong performance by the automobile manufacturers was also felt in other areas of the U.S. rubber industry. The hose market, a substantial portion of which was used for automobiles, totaled $1,050,000,-000 in 1984, and the v-belt market reached $502 million. Flat belting sales totaled $276 million.

Suppliers to the U.S. rubber industry also enjoyed a good year, as the nation's total rubber consumption increased more than 13% over 1983. Consumption of natural rubber increased 21% to 775,000 metric tons, and synthetic rubber consumption rose 10% to almost two million metric tons. Styrene butadiene rubber, the "tire rubber," was the most consumed of the synthetics, but longer wearing radial tires and small automobiles slowed its growth. The fastest growing synthetic was ethylene propylene diene because of its widespread use in single-ply roofing for commercial buildings. More than 51 million sq m (550 million sq ft) of this roofing was sold in 1984, amounting to $275 million.

In Europe in 1984 gains by rubber product manufacturers over the previous year were modest owing to industry restructuring and cost-cutting moves. The strong U.S. dollar prompted many product manufacturers and suppliers to step up export activities to the U.S. Dunlop Holdings, a British firm, reported that its main profit centre was now in the U.S. High inflation remained a problem in many of the European countries.

While European companies were looking to the U.S. for increased sales, several U.S. firms managed to increase their European business. Monsanto Co. opened a thermoplastic rubber plant in England, and E. I. du Pont de Nemours started up a chlorosulfinated polyethylene elastomer facility in Northern Ireland. Phillips Petroleum Co. purchased a carbon black operation in The Netherlands and France.

In the U.S. Witco Chemical Corp. bought another carbon black manufacturer, Continental Carbon Co., but the U.S. government stopped a proposed acquisition of Ashland Chemical Co.'s carbon black operations by Sid Richardson Carbon Co. The International Trade Commission also denied trade protection for the domestic footwear industry, where imports had captured over 70% of the market. More than 30 footwear factories closed during 1984 in the U.S.

A large proportion of the shoe imports originated from the Pacific rim countries led by South Korea and Taiwan, and this area was also increasing its manufacturing of such other rubber products as tires and inner tubes. The southeastern Pacific region is the main area for growing natural rubber, and many countries there, particularly Malaysia, were stepping up efforts to control production of goods made of that commodity. Malaysia, the largest natural rubber producer, encouraged foreign investments and joint ventures in different rubber-manufacturing operations.

Malaysia also passed a law requiring domestic ownership of at least half of any operation, which prompted Uniroyal, Inc., to sell its rubber plantations in the country. The Malaysian Rubber Research and Development Board announced that there would be a new grading scheme for Standard Malaysian Rubber (SMR), the first change since 1965. It would eliminate the old standard ribbed smoked sheet rubber because of its technical inferiority. After Malaysia, the other top natural-rubber-producing countries were Indonesia, Thailand, China, India, and Sri Lanka.

Pricing of natural rubber suffered in 1984, dropping to the lowest level in two years. Prices for SMR 20 began the year at 52 cents per pound and closed the year at 42 cents. The low prices worried industry observers because it was believed that they might force a switch by the growers to more lucrative crops.

Worldwide consumption of both natural and synthetic rubber increased in 1983, natural reaching almost 4 million metric tons and synthetic amounting to approximately 8,260,000 metric tons. Consumption of both continued to increase during the first half of 1984, with natural rubber accounting for 2.1 million metric tons and synthetic for 4.5 million metric tons. U.S. consumption of natural rubber in 1983 was 665,000 metric tons, the highest level since 1979, followed by Japan with 504,-000 metric tons and China with 405,000 metric tons. The EC countries consumed 633,000 metric tons, and Eastern Europe accounted for 405,000 metric tons. In synthetics, the Japanese consumed 851,000 metric tons and the EC and Eastern Europe 1.3 million and 2.4 million, respectively.   (DONALD SMITH)

SHIPBUILDING

Despite the advice of the major shipowners, government agencies, and leading international banks, so many new orders were placed for ships that once again there would soon be too much capacity in relation to demand. For the world shipbuilding industries the volume of orders placed made virtually no difference in a bad situation. The bulk of the orders for new vessels continued to go to Far Eastern shipyards, which by 1984 had more than 17% of the world order book, up from 2.5% six years earlier. Japan remained the world shipbuilding leader but with strong

competition from South Korea, where attractive credit terms were available.

At mid-1984 the tonnage of new ships on order totaled 58,566,897 tons deadweight (dw), compared with nearly 63 million tons dw in 1983, a fact that underlined the lack of confidence in any meaningful upturn in the shipping market in the immediate future. Bulk carriers led the list of orders with a total of 37,345,364 tons dw, followed by tankers at 12,802,489 tons dw, dry cargo ships (not bulk carriers) at 4,849,726 tons dw, and containerships with just over 3.5 million tons dw.

The distribution of the new ship orders among the world's shipyards was similar to that in 1983, with Japan leading the list at 26.3 million tons dw, followed by South Korea with 10 million tons dw—figures that showed that South Korean yards were no longer capturing so many orders at the expense of those in Japan. Brazil remained in third place with just over 3.1 million tons dw, almost the same as in the previous year, and Poland was again in fourth position with 2,130,000 tons dw.

Figures for China's shipyards revealed that country's successful efforts to expand its shipbuilding output and at the same time earn valuable foreign currency. China was in fifth position in the table with 1.6 million tons dw, just ahead of Spain, where new building orders totaled 1.5 million tons dw. Tenth in the tonnage-on-order list was the U.S.S.R. with 1.2 million tons dw. Next came the U.K. with 513,-000 tons dw and the U.S. with 470,000 tons dw. The U.S. registered a slight improvement; apart from valuable U.S. Navy orders, there were also a few merchant ship orders as well as several important repair and conversion contracts. In the U.K. the heavy losses in the state-owned British Shipbuilders (which involved several shipyards) led the government to try to sell some of its yards to private ownership.

The most unusual feature of the world shipbuilding order book was the remarkable list of cruise liners under construction for U.S., British, Dutch, Swedish, and Finnish ownership; several of these vessels were in the 40,000- to 45,000-tons-dw category. U.S. shipbuilders became more competitive in regard to price, and Tacoma Boatbuilding Co. won an order for a $100 million, 800-passenger vessel for the Gulf Pacific Cruise Line. There were two major reasons for the increase in orders for cruise ships, one being the steady expansion of the market and the other the tightening up of safety regulations for passenger vessels,

which resulted in older vessels' becoming unsuitable.

The first merchant ship contract placed in the U.S. in two years came from the Exxon Shipping Co. and was for two very large crude carriers, each of 209,000 tons dw and worth a total of $250 million. The yard that won the order was the National Steel and Shipbuilding Co.

Two factors reduced the gloom in the world shipbuilding industry. First, the level of ship scrapping was maintained at about 20 million tons dw, mostly tankers but some 5% bulk carriers. Second, there was an all-around effort among the Western European countries to reduce shipbuilding subsidies—although Italy and France increased theirs. In Portugal the giant Lisnave shipyard complex came under threat of closing, and in Spain dramatic reductions were made in the shipbuilding labour force. Inexpensive new ships attracted certain shipowners, who bought them and put them into lay-up until the market should rise slightly; at that time they would immediately be placed in service, forcing the market down again.   (W. D. EWART)

TELECOMMUNICATIONS

Advances in telecommunications in 1984 were limited, in the main, to technical improvements rather than breakthroughs. Much of the activity centred around national and international legislative and judicial bodies and standards organizations, which decided who should perform which telecommunications chores with what technologies.

In the U.S. the deregulated and broken-up AT&T, in its first year of operation, met both successes and failures. On the plus side, at least for the short term, AT&T's strong telecommunications engineering and science skills were unaffected by the breakup, although some layoffs and early retirements were carried out to streamline company operations. On the minus side, some of the firm's much-heralded major projects failed to get off the ground. For example, one of the first versions of its nationwide value-added network was sent back to the drawing board. Such a network would allow disparate computers from different manufacturers to communicate with each other over every transmission medium from copper-based twisted wire pairs to glass-based fibre optics. AT&T would ensure that all the appropriate data conversions were made.

Deregulation, at least in its early stages, appeared to be a mixed blessing. The first result of the Jan. 1, 1984, AT&T breakup for the U.S. home telephone consumer was higher prices. Meanwhile, many of the firms offering competing services, ranging from plain-old-telephone service (POTS) to a host of sophisticated communications services for both voice and data, were making less than a handsome profit, and some were showing a loss. A number of these firms had rushed into the field with less than adequate technological and marketing expertise and without a large financial cushion.

Some firms that had found niches in the telecommunications business long before deregulation were also taking their lumps, in part because of the number of new players on the scene. For example, Satellite Business Systems, an IBM-backed firm that

The newest luxury cruise ship of the Holland America Line, the "M. S. Noordam," was christened in 1984 at Le Havre, France.

provided Earth-satellite-based voice and data communications to businesses, found itself scrambling to maintain its market share.

Meanwhile, despite the mixed results in the U.S., there were signs that deregulation fever might spread worldwide. Japan and England, both major telecommunications-dependent nations, began looking into ways to change their monolithic telecommunications industries. The goal was to increase competition and stimulate new products and services.

Direct-broadcast-satellite (DBS) television service did not fare well in either the U.S. or Europe. Hailed as a technique to bring the benefits of television to remote areas, DBS failed to attract customers, and several efforts were put on hold or stopped altogther. Similarly, services bringing text and picture information to the home or office television screen (known collectively as teletex or videotex) continued to seek a market. The chief problem was convincing potential consumers that the service provided something they needed and could not get otherwise. Specialized applications for specific businesses (*e.g.,* tanker locations for the oil industry) were a notable exception.

On the other hand, cellular telephony—telephones in automobiles—showed every sign of being a success. In this case, the technology met the real need of busy people to keep in touch while traveling or stuck in traffic. There was, however, one cloud on the industry's horizon—the imminent appearance of miniature, inexpensive, wireless pocket telephones that could be carried anywhere.

Local networks used to link computers in a building or on a campus continued to make their mark. Some industry observers believed they were pulling ahead of private branch exchanges (PBX's) in the race to become the method of choice in computer communications. However, the multimegabits-per-second-data-rate local networks were unsuitable for voice transmissions, leaving that task to the PBX's, which could also handle data transmissions up to 64 or so kilobits per second. Anxious to cover all its bases, IBM bought part of Rolm, a major PBX manufacturer.

The Geneva-based International Organization for Standardization made considerable progress during the year in formalizing international acceptance of a series of protocols—software rules that would ensure successful communication among computers in both local and international telecommunications networks. At the same time, the increased flow of data that would result worried some officials, especially in Europe, where distances between borders are short. There were fears that blurred distinctions between public- and private-sector information, control and taxation problems, and other issues arising from the free flow of data across frontiers would create problems faster than they could be solved. Legislation regulating such data flows was passed in a number of countries.

(HARVEY J. HINDIN)

TEXTILES

There were further signs in 1984 of general recovery in the world's textile industry. However, there was a huge decline in the long-lasting fashion for denim, and denim manufacturers supplying the jeans makers found themselves with far too much capacity for the market. The textile trade was not sure what would replace denim as a "fashion fabric."

Capacity for building textile machines, worldwide, was far in excess of needs, and most manufacturers were operating below capacity. Companies with something new to offer in terms of technology or production rates were experiencing good business, but otherwise there was evidence of continuing contraction.

The complaints by technologically advanced countries of "cheap imports from low-labour-cost countries" were being reversed. As automation increased, the quality of products improved, but a strong infrastructure was needed to provide technical maintenance and ensure that the equipment was kept running round the clock. The complexities of an automatic system of spinning or high-speed air-jet weaving were far beyond the financial reach of less developed countries, which also lacked the requisite support services. Just how far the pendulum would swing back toward the technically advanced textile manufacturers had yet to be seen, but clearly there was a movement in that direction. (PETER LENNOX-KERR)

Wool. World production in the 1983–84 season (ended June 1984) totaled 1,637,-000 metric tons clean, 0.5% higher than in 1982–83. A rise of 2% was forecast for 1984–85, most of it in Australia and New Zealand. Prices were maintained in 1984 only with significant support from the Australian Wool Corporation (AWC). The overall floor price was left unchanged for 1984–85, and the level of support declined in the latter half of the 1983–84 season. Support was again needed as the main selling season began in August, however, and the AWC stockpile increased in the third and fourth quarters of the year. Floor-price purchases were mainly of 22–26-micron wools carrying above-average fault. Demand for finer merino wool was ahead of supply, forcing prices up throughout the year. Crossbreds were generally in steady demand, and there was little recourse to floor-price purchases.

Continued currency volatility had a disturbing influence on prices. Weakness in the South African rand resulted in better clearances there than in Australia. South America's close connection with the U.S. dollar reduced that area's recent importance as a wool supplier in the latter half of the year.

World usage of wool showed a rising trend, according to estimates issued by the U.K. Commonwealth Secretariat. The latest figures available, for the fourth quarter of 1983, showed an increase of between 8 and 9% compared with a year earlier. However, the Secretariat's figures also showed that wool was tending to lose ground to man-made fibres within the industry.

(H. M. F. MALLETT)

Cotton. Drought in many cotton-growing areas of Africa and in the U.S. reduced crops in the 1983–84 season, bringing expectations of higher prices. In a number of countries—France, Belgium, The Netherlands, the U.K., South Korea, Japan, and Australia—less cotton was being spun into yarn. In the U.K. there was a fall from 51 million kg (112 million lb) of cotton yarn spun in 1982 to 49.9 million kg (110 million lb) in 1983. In the same period the volume of imports of yarns and threads rose from 36.6 million to 46.8 million kg (80.7 million to 103 million lb). There were signs that this trend would continue despite attempts to control the flood of imports from low-cost production areas through international agreements such as the Multi-Fibre Arrangement. The impli-

Airborne public telephones became a reality in 1984 with Airfone Inc.'s service installed on six airlines and scheduled for three others. The ability to make calls in flight was an instant hit with passengers.

cation was that there was still a substantial market for poorer quality and cheaper goods, perhaps a reflection of growing levels of unemployment in developed countries and a consequent reduction in spending power.

Western textile producers, as well as machine builders, were becoming increasingly conscious of a growing threat from China. Cotton yarn production in China rose from 1,872,000 metric tons in 1970 to 3,170,000 tons in 1981, and there was an 8.2% increase between 1980 and 1981. Cotton fabric production rose similarly, from 7,500,000,000 m (8,200,000,000 yd) in 1970 to 14,270,000,000 m (15,600,000,000 yd) in 1981. Currently China processed about one-quarter of the world's cotton, and its share continued to grow.

(PETER LENNOX-KERR)

Silk. The International Silk Association reported total world production of raw silk for 1982 as 1,432,400 bales of 60 kg (approximately 130 lb) each and demand as 867,300 bales. China was the largest producer with 396,200 bales; Japan was second and the U.S.S.R. third. Japan was the biggest single consumer (322,600 bales). The scene continued to be overshadowed by Japan's government-held stock of raw silk, which by the end of 1983 amounted to 174,588 bales, or ten months' production. Japan declared its intention to solve the problem without disturbing the world market and adopted China's policy of promoting silk in Europe.

China, still the major exporter of silk, noted an improvement in demand, although actual supply was down as a result of adverse weather. Supply and demand were approximately in balance, and prices of raw silk were increased slightly. A phenomenon in 1983 was the accelerating demand for types of waste silk and spun silk yarn, which China was unable to satisfy. Prices increased rapidly, doubling over 12 months for some qualities. Possible reasons were the increasing efficiency of Chinese raw-silk production, resulting in a decline in the amount of waste; a growing demand in the West for such relatively new items as knitted silk underwear and silk hand-knitting yarn; and a demand by spinners of other fibres for silk for blending.

The Indian silk industry, based to a considerable extent on tussah (wild silk), continued to grow. The improving efficiency of the Karnataca silk exchange enabled the reelers to obtain better prices for their silk and encouraged production.

(ANTHONY H. GADDUM)

Man-Made Fibres. A slow shift in man-made-fibre technology and production was under way. In Britain, the U.S., and Japan there were still signs of excess capacity in commodity fibres such as polyester, acrylic, and nylon. The major French fibre producer was switching from acrylic production to a nonwoven spunbonded fabric based on polyester. This material was gaining rapidly in such areas as geotextiles, used to stabilize soil and improve construction of roads, dams, reservoirs, and similar projects.

From its inception, viscose rayon has been manufactured by converting cellulose into a solution that is extruded through a spinneret into a sulfuric acid bath; there the material coagulates into a gel and is subjected to drawing and washing until it

eventually emerges as a cellulosic fibre or filament. Using a process under development in Britain and the U.S., the cellulose would be converted into a "dope" made with a solvent. This could then be extruded downward through a chamber in which hot air circulates upward and evaporates the solvent (later to be recovered), thus creating fibres. This was the technique currently used for acetate, another cellulosic. The process might shorten viscose rayon fibre production by some 80–90% and should be far more economic, possibly enabling viscose rayon to stage a comeback.

Production of synthetic fibres appeared to be increasing in the third world. Libya was shortly to start making its own nylon and polyester fibres, and there were plans to produce polyester in Kenya and Tanzania. (PETER LENNOX-KERR)

TOBACCO

After a hesitant 1983, world cigarette sales rose gently in 1984 to a new peak of about 4,600,000,000,000. Third world gains more than made up for losses in advanced countries, where steep tax rises provided the bite to match the antismokers' bark. In the trendsetting U.S., low-tar cigarettes lost ground again as smokers, equating mildness with insipidity, drifted back to brands of more robust flavour.

The 5,950,000,000 kg (13,118,000,000 lb) of leaf that the world's tobacco farmers grew in 1984 exceeded demand. This signaled future stock-disposal problems for the U.S., Greece, Turkey, and India.

In advanced countries of North America, Europe, and Asia, computer-aided automation of tobacco factories was turning what had been a labour-intensive industry into a thinly staffed one. Installation of elaborate closed-loop equipment was imminent; this would be able to monitor and adjust the smoking performance of cigarettes, one by one, as they were being made at 8,000 or more per minute. The purpose was to ensure that each cigarette actually had the tar and nicotine content that a rising number of governments required pack inscriptions to declare.

Every unit of the previously little-coordinated industry of China, by a wide margin the world's largest tobacco-growing and cigarette-consuming nation, began to be absorbed into an all-powerful state monopoly. China's 145 factories, setting out on a vast modernization and refurbishment program, made about 22% of the world's cigarettes in 1984, when its farmers grew 24% of the world's tobacco. Only a small amount of Chinese tobacco moved in world trade in 1984, but other leaf-exporting countries were worried that China could wreck the world supply-demand equilibrium if it diverted only a fraction of its huge production into international markets.

Retailers and wholesalers dealing only with tobacco goods were becoming fewer in many developed countries and might be almost extinct by the late 1990s. Large-scale traders in general merchandise, such as supermarkets selling tobacco products for sideline profit, were capturing their trade. Only in monopoly countries (such as Japan, France, Italy, and Spain), where retailers were fewer and monopolies could demand specialization, was retail fidelity to tobacco commerce assured. Leading

cigarette brands would always find retail outlets, but numerous makers of minor brands, pipe tobaccos, cigars, and snuffs feared that their products might not in the future be able to reach their relatively small markets for lack of adequate distribution links between factories and smokers. Pipe makers shared this anxiety.

(MICHAEL F. BARFORD)

TOURISM

World tourism expanded steadily during 1984 following the rather hesitant and uneven recovery initiated in 1983. Travel demand had begun to level off in 1980. Although the recession had not stopped holiday-taking as such, the majority of travelers had shown greater caution in expenditures, had traveled shorter distances, and had chosen less expensive accommodations. Now, as tourism prospered once more, World Tourism Organization (WTO) preliminary estimates for 1984 revealed a 2.1% growth in international movements of persons for holiday, business, and family reasons to 300 million, while dollar receipts were valued at $100 billion, for a 3.9% increase. As in 1983, the available indications were that domestic travel grew more rapidly than international travel in 1984.

In West Germany, the world's biggest spender on international travel, tour bookings were slow early in 1984 under the influence of a metalworkers' strike, but by July there was a veritable boom in travel, with Greece, Israel, Morocco, Spain, Tunisia, and Yugoslavia among the most popular destinations. Overall, West Germans took 2–3% more foreign trips than in 1983. The world's second biggest spender on international travel was the U.S. An exceptionally strong dollar boosted U.S. travelers' spending power abroad, and as inflation rates declined households shifted expenditures to travel following two years of heavy disbursements on appliances and automobiles. Forecasts were for at least a 3% gain in overseas travel involving more than 10.5 million U.S. citizens. Of this total, 5.5 million visited Europe (10% more than in 1983) and about 2 million visited Japan. Domestically, 107 million Americans took summer vacations in 1984, about the same as 1983, but the number of trips for all purposes rose by 3%. More foreign visitors entered Canada, especially from the U.S. and West Germany, and there was a rebound in domestic tourism.

The benefits of the drastic peso devaluation were felt by Mexican tourism. There, domestic travel declined, while international arrivals by air rose by 15%. Caribbean tourism got off to a good start in early 1984; 7.6 million stopover arrivals were expected for the full year, a 3% rise over 1983. Destinations such as Aruba, Cayman Islands, Dominica, and Martinique all reported hotel registrations up by more than 10%. Travel in South America continued to be subdued in 1984 under the cloud of lingering economic problems at home and currency weaknesses against the U.S. dollar.

In Europe, Spain headed for a record 42 million visitors and $7.5 billion in receipts. This represented 4% more arrivals than in 1983, while hotel registrations increased 10%. Factors behind this success were a prolongation of the vacation season, an increase in the length of stay, and more upmarket arrivals. Among other European countries Austria showed a 2% increase in arrivals, France nearly 4%, Greece 11%, Turkey 16%, and Yugoslavia over 25%. The trend toward later holiday bookings by Europeans led in some countries—such as the U.K.—to a price war among tour operators.

In Asia, Hong Kong continued to be one of the most successful destinations, with a 13% boost in arrivals and a 10% increase in receipts. China, too, continued to expand its facilities for tourism. Hong Kong's hotels also found themselves in demand as hosts for a relatively new but growing clientele—incentive groups—as more companies decided that vacations were an ideal carrot to spur their employees on to better performance. Thailand showed signs of recovery from the slight decline registered in 1983; a major promotion was planned to attract visitors from Australia, with a new resort being developed in Hua Hin. In Bangkok, however, occupancies continued to sag. Both Japan and New Zealand recorded positive growth.

In Africa overnight stays by tourists in Morocco increased 5%, and Senegal had a 6% growth in hotel registrations. However, the continent still seemed some way from making substantial inroads in the international market as its share of world tourism marked time at 2%. Political and social factors and the continuance of the Gulf war undermined attempts of Middle Eastern countries to stage a tourism revival.

The U.S. Travel and Tourism Administration's new in-flight survey of overseas visitors to the U.S. revealed that they were prosperous and middle-aged. Average family income was a substantial $42,270, while the average age of adults was 39 years. California, New York City, and Florida were the main destinations. Average trip length was 25 nights, and the average ex-

The 1984 Louisiana World Exposition opened in New Orleans in May. The event was plagued by financial problems and poor attendance, which was far below expected levels.
AP/WIDE WORLD

penditure was $1,100. In 1983 the nearly $14 billion spent by U.S. travelers in foreign countries was distributed as follows: Mexico, $3,576,000,000; Canada $2,160,-000,000; Europe and the Mediterranean, $4,412,000,000 (of which the U.K. had $1,061,000,000); and Caribbean and Central America, $1,519,000,000.

Industry indicators confirmed the improved performance of world tourism in 1984. Airline traffic continued to boom; the 20 members of the Association of European Airlines reported a record summer season. Hotels showed signs of recovery; indications for 1984 were for increased occupancy, with revenues per room 5–10% above 1983 levels. (PETER SHACKLEFORD)

WOOD PRODUCTS

Rising demand from the home-building and furniture-manufacturing industries was widely predicted to stimulate worldwide growth in the wood products industry through 1984. In the U.S. particularly, the industry felt that it had seen the end of the recession. The 60% gain in housing starts for 1983 increased further early in 1984, with January and February bringing the projected annual rate to 2.2 million units, the highest since the construction boom of 1978. Good growth continued during the year but slowed as mortgage interest rates topped 14%; construction contracts fell in September to their lowest level of the year. Continuing the upward trend from mid-1983, demand for pulp and paper improved.

In September the U.S. Senate passed a bill enabling timber companies to avoid paying more than $1 billion for timber they had contracted to buy at prices far above current market rates. Softwood lumber producers and trade associations lobbied the administration to discuss a voluntary softwood restraint or quota with Canada. While these political moves were being made, the timber industry looked at ways of developing markets for low-grade hardwoods; there was increasing emphasis on the transfer of new ideas from research

to promote better wood use, from the mill to the final wood product.

In Europe there were no dramatic increases in softwood demand. Some improvement, however, took place in the panel- and particle-board industries. Toward midyear the growing strength of the U.S. dollar and the much-improved U.S. economy persuaded North American lumber producers to concentrate on domestic markets; their European customers were finding U.S. timber prices high and having difficulties in finding markets for their products. Perhaps worst hit was Belgium, but the French wood products industry also declined as housing starts continued their six-year downward trend. Elsewhere the situation was patchy. The timber trade in Italy, for example, picked up at midyear.

Increased effort was put into raising forest productivity; genetic improvements to yield higher quality seeds were given more attention. EC experts called for better firefighting resources. The cost of one hectare (2.47 ac) of forest destroyed was estimated by the French authorities at about $8 million. In the U.K. in 1983, 1,600 ha had been destroyed, and the Mediterranean region lost 145,000 ha. The proposal also called for better protection against acid rain, a particular problem for West Germany and central Europe.

A development affecting the wood products industry worldwide was the formation of the International Tropical Timber Organization in October. The agreement to establish ITTO, for planning global supply and distribution of the timber, was signed by 88 producing and consuming countries. Asian countries supplied more than three-quarters of the tropical timber in world trade during 1984, and exports were up, especially to the U.S. Japanese wood products producers faced difficulties as the country was forced to buy finished goods from nations that previously supplied logs to its now-ailing plywood industry. Hardest hit of Asian wood products industries was perhaps that of the Philippines, where worker unrest and government cutbacks compounded a deteriorating export market. China continued its emergence as a growing market for wood products, and further implementation of its 1979 Forestry Act stimulated domestic output. In Africa and South America efforts in reforestation were intensified. Worldwide, the use of satellites for mapping and computers for making forest inventories helped aid the better development of wood resources.

(GORDON WILKINSON)

See also Agriculture and Food Supplies; Consumer Affairs; Economic Affairs; Energy; Information Processing and Information Systems; Labour-Management Relations; Mining and Metallurgy; Photography; Television and Radio; Transportation.

This article updates the *Macropædia* articles BEVERAGE PRODUCTION; ELECTRONICS; ENERGY CONVERSION; FORESTRY AND WOOD PRODUCTION; FURS, LEATHERS, AND HIDES; INDUSTRIAL GLASS AND CERAMICS; Chemical Process INDUSTRIES; Extraction and Processing INDUSTRIES; Manufacturing INDUSTRIES; Textile INDUSTRIES; INSURANCE; MARKETING AND MERCHANDISING; PRINTING, TYPOGRAPHY, AND PHOTOENGRAVING; TELECOMMUNICATIONS SYSTEMS; TOOLS.

Table XI. Major Tourism Earners and Spenders in 1983	
Major spenders	**Expenditure**
West Germany	$15,035,000
United States	13,944,000
United Kingdom	6,096,000
Japan	4,431,000
France	4,282,000
Canada	3,888,000
Netherlands, The	3,242,000
Austria	2,869,000
Switzerland	2,300,000
Belgium/Luxembourg	2,096,000
Italy	1,822,000
Sweden	1,607,000
Norway	1,580,000
Australia	1,250,000
Denmark	1,211,000
Spain	896,000
Major earners	**Receipts**
United States	11,187,000
Italy	9,033,000
Spain	6,897,000
France	7,228,000
United Kingdom	5,526,000
Austria	5,491,000
West Germany	5,462,000
Switzerland	3,152,000
Canada	2,570,000
Belgium/Luxembourg	1,711,000
Netherlands, The	1,431,000
Denmark	1,307,000
Greece	1,174,000
Sweden	1,057,000
Australia	991,000
Yugoslavia	929,000
Portugal	833,000

Source: World Tourism Organization, Madrid.

Information Processing and Information Systems

The information-processing industry grew steadily and strongly throughout 1984, with all industry sectors from semiconductors to personal computers to large-scale systems scoring impressive gains. The hearty appetite of U.S. businesses for greater information-processing resources resulted in record sales for virtually every major U.S. computer maker. So strong was the demand for semiconductors—the tiny chips that process and store computer information—that such chip makers as Intel Corp. held orders for the entire year's worth of output in January. But in the home, or personal, computer market, cutthroat price competition led to dwindling profits and a growing number of bankruptcy filings by microcomputer firms. Even industry giant IBM Corp. stumbled upon entering the home computer market, as the public proved unwilling to pay premium prices for the PCjr, the home computer that IBM made available in large quantities for the first time in 1984.

Industry Developments. A personal computer market shakeout, which had begun in 1983, continued in 1984, a year when computer makers experienced the odd combination of record sales and sliding profits. Some personal computer makers, such as Victor Technologies, Inc., and Gavilan Computer Corp., sought protection from their creditors in federal bankruptcy court, while others found themselves having to slash retail prices drastically to keep pace with the price cutting of industry leaders. Radio Shack, for example, dropped the price of its popular TRS-80 personal computer from $2,000 to $1,300, while IBM chopped nearly 25% off the prices of its line of personal computers. Nonetheless, sales of personal computers to business users alone were expected to top $10 billion during the year.

Despite the growing number of business failures in the personal computer arena, there was one significant new competitor added in 1984, American Telephone and Telegraph Corp. (AT&T). Throughout the year AT&T announced several new computer products, including a line of powerful minicomputers, that placed the company in an increasingly formidable competitive position vis-à-vis such industry leaders as IBM and Digital Equipment Corp. Many industry analysts believed that a competitive struggle between AT&T and IBM for computer industry dominance loomed in the decade of the 1980s.

With a stated goal of growing from a $40 billion-per-year company in 1983 to a $100 billion firm by 1990, IBM made several bold moves in 1984 in an attempt to become the computer leader in every market segment. Most notably, IBM bought Rolm Corp., maker of data communications equipment, for $1.3 billion. The acquisition, IBM's first in 22 years, was intended to give the company a strong market presence in an area (communications) in which it had been relatively weak. The move was also seen as giving IBM a good opportunity to expand its role in the burgeoning office automation market, where Rolm's voice and data communications equipment, known as private branch exchanges or PBX's, had been successful.

IBM also made a bold thrust into the microcomputer software market, announcing a series of software products. Until 1983 IBM had been content to let other developers supply software. On the high end of the product scale, sales of IBM mainframes, or large-scale computers, as well as sales of mainframe data-storage devices (disk drives) reached record levels as the company continued to capture an increasing share of total mainframe sales.

On the international front the European Economic Community (EEC) ended its four-year investigation of alleged antitrust activities by IBM. As part of the agreement with the EEC, IBM said that it would make voluntary alterations in its marketing practices in Europe. But IBM's concessions in ending the dispute fell far short of what the EEC had originally attempted to impose on the firm, and industry observers felt that IBM emerged from the investigation as unscathed as it had in 1982 when the U.S. government ended a 13-year antitrust suit against the company.

Japanese computer makers, which had experienced only limited success selling to the U.S. market, tried new tactics in 1984 to increase U.S. sales. Fujitsu Ltd. raised its stake to 49% in California-based Amdahl Corp., one of only two major U.S. suppliers of IBM-compatible mainframe computers. Fujitsu began selling some of its machines, including a high-speed supercomputer, under the Amdahl label. Hitachi Ltd., another leading Japanese computer maker, began supplying all the IBM-compatible mainframes sold by California-based National Advanced Systems Corp., the other major U.S. supplier of that equipment. National Advanced Systems suspended all U.S. manufacture of mainframes in favour of selling the Japanese machines.

Fujitsu remained Japan's largest computer maker for the year to March 1984, continuing to outperform IBM Japan Ltd. Sales for the year for Fujitsu totaled 661.3 billion yen, while those for IBM Japan amounted to 612.2 billion yen. They were followed by NEC Corp. (520.3 billion yen), Hitachi (443 billion yen), and Toshiba Corp. (183 billion yen). The Japanese computer makers increased their exports during the year by 20–70%, depending on the particular firm.

While the Japanese domestic market for personal computers was not as explosive as that of the U.S., demand expanded in 1984 for both business and private uses. The most successful product was the eight-bit MSX machine, designed chiefly to run video game and educational software packages based on a standard set by Microsoft and other U.S. firms.

Throughout the year the U.S. government found itself embroiled in several controversies related to the mass computerization of American society. Several groups, including 9 to 5, the National Association of Working Women, presented evidence that they claimed showed that working on computer video-display terminals (VDT's) caused potentially harmful side effects, especially to pregnant women. But other groups, including computer industry trade organizations, joined the American College of Obstetricians and Gynecologists in presenting evidence to the contrary and urged the U.S. Congress not to press for legislation regulating terminal use. Nonetheless, an increasing number of pregnant VDT operators began asking for, and often receiving, temporary reassignments.

In the U.S. the steadily growing incidence of "hacking," breaking into sensitive computer files, prompted Congress to approve overwhelmingly a computer crime bill, as many states had done previously. Congressional action came after hackers in 1984 accessed credit files of the Information Services Division of TRW Inc., as well as unclassified files of the National Aeronautics and Space Administration. The crime bill made it a federal offense to enter government computers illegally but left it to the states to punish those caught breaking into private-sector computer files. The House of Representatives also approved a bill making it a federal crime to gain access to medical records illegally, a year after hackers accessed medical records of cancer

The U.S. Customs Service stepped up efforts in 1984 to halt the illegal flow of high technology from the United States to Communist nations. This computer equipment, bound for the Soviet Union, was seized in West Germany in late 1983.

DEPARTMENT OF DEFENSE; PHOTOGRAPH, ED BOSANKO

patients at the Memorial Sloan-Kettering Cancer Center in New York City.

Technology. A series of developments both in the U.S. and in Japan focused attention on artificial intelligence, the ability of a computer system to "think" and make humanlike decisions rather than simply doing what it is programmed to do. Japan approached the midpoint of its fifth-generation computer project, the object of which was to develop commercially available, large-scale computer systems that could, among other things, program themselves. In the U.S. several computer makers, including IBM and Digital Equipment Corp., introduced powerful desktop computers for under $20,000, computers powerful enough to run the highly sophisticated and complex software programs that characterize artificial intelligence.

That amount of computer power was made possible in great measure by the widespread commercial use for the first time of 256-kilobit memory chips. (One kilobit equals 1,024 bits, a bit to a computer being the smallest increment of usable data.) These chips, with the ability to store four times the information of their predecessor 64-kilobit chips, made it possible to load rudimentary artificial intelligence programs into desktop computers. Rapidly emerging commercial applications of artificial intelligence included natural language processing (the ability of a computer to understand and follow simple English-language commands such as "get the payroll file" instead of a complex machine code) and economic forecasting.

A laboratory of the government-run Nippon Telegraph & Telephone Public Corp. in Japan developed a high-speed, silicon-based random-access computer memory chip. The one-kilobit chip attained an access time of 0.85 nanosecond, three to four times faster than that of comparable memories currently used in supercomputers.

AT&T's Unix emerged in 1984 as a strong favourite to become the computing community's operating system of the future. (An operating system is the software, or programming instructions, that tells all other software loaded onto the computer exactly how to operate.) The most attractive feature of Unix was its portability, which allowed it to operate on a broad range of computers from small personal models to mainframes, whereas other operating systems typically were machine-specific.

Fujitsu Ltd. announced in February that it had developed a high-performance operating system for its large-scale computers and started delivery to major users. The new system, called OSIV/F4MSP E20, had 128 times more capac-

ity for processing information than conventional equivalents. Hitachi hoped to unveil its operating system for large computers by the end of 1984.

The rapid proliferation of microcomputers throughout the corporate environment spurred development of communications software that enabled microcomputers to "talk" to larger computers and swap data. These so-called micro-mainframe links were among the most popular new software products of 1984. Major vendors rushed products to market that would allow microcomputer users to access information stored in mainframe memory files.

But while the march of computer technology generally went along briskly in 1984, there was one notable technical failure. California-based Trilogy Ltd., which tried to change the face of computer technology with a radical semiconductor design to be used in computers many times more powerful than current large-scale machines, canceled plans to produce both the semiconductor and the computers the company was to build around them. Trilogy had raised more than $250 million in venture capital and other private funding but never produced a single item for sale.

(WILLIAM E. LABERIS)

This article updates the *Macropædia* article INFORMATION PROCESSING AND INFORMATION SYSTEMS.

Labour-Management Relations

There was little uniformity in labour-management relations developments in 1984. The most notable trend was the contraction of some industries. When this was set against a background of heavy and, in some countries, still rising unemployment, it was a frequent cause of dispute as to the number of jobs lost and as to what help should be given to displaced workers.

United Kingdom. Industrial relations in Britain were especially troubled. In particular, the year was dominated by a strike in the coal industry, arguably the biggest dispute in the U.K. since the General Strike of 1926. In early March apprehension about the intentions of the National Coal Board (NCB) as to the future size of the industry (it had been announced that 20 pits were likely to be closed and that 20,000 workers would probably lose their jobs) led the National Union of Mineworkers (NUM)—the union covering the vast majority of workers in the industry—to support strike action against the NCB's plans in several coalfields. Later, the union—though without taking a full vote of its members—declared a national strike. Workers in several areas, however, did not agree with the union's action, and about one-third of the miners remained at work.

In the months that followed, the union's position remained adamantly that no pit should be closed, however uneconomic, unless the coal was exhausted or unsafe to mine. The NCB, for its part, held that it must be free to close pits that were not commercially viable. The possibilities of resolving the dispute were not helped by the intransigence of the miners' leader, Arthur Scargill (*see* BIOGRAPHIES), who was widely viewed as seeing the strike not only as a move against pit closings but also as a means of striking a blow against the policies of the Conservative Party government. Though somewhat less dogmatic, NCB chairman Ian MacGregor maintained the firm conviction that the mines had to be operated as nearly as possible in accord with normal commercial principles.

The dispute was accompanied by the deployment of thousands of "flying pickets" to prevent miners who wished to work from entering the pits despite the 1980 Employment Act, which forbids action by strikers away from their places of work. There were some ugly cases of attacks on working miners. Police were used to prevent violence but were themselves frequently involved in violent confrontations. Delivery of coal by sea to steel mills was met by the refusal of dockworkers to handle it and twice led to widespread dock strikes.

As the end of the year neared, prospects for an agreed resolution of the dispute seemed remote. There was some drift back to work, but it was not substantial. Meanwhile, the NUM became increasingly embroiled in a number of legal actions, and sequestrators were appointed to try to secure payment of an unpaid fine (most of the union's funds had been transferred out of the country).

In January the British government announced that in view of the special nature of the intelligence-gathering work carried out at the Government Communications Headquarters (GCHQ) at Cheltenham, the government was withdrawing the right of staff employed there to be members of independent trade unions. Monetary compensation of £1,000 was offered for the loss of the right, and the staff members were afforded the opportunity of joining an approved staff association of workers. The government's action aroused deep anger in trade union circles, and a day of protest was called by the civil service unions and supported by the Trades Union Congress (TUC). The unions also took their protest to the courts.

Lionel ("Len") Murray retired in September as general secretary of the TUC after 11 years in the post. He was succeeded by Norman Willis (see BIOGRAPHIES), formerly deputy general secretary, whose earlier working life before coming to the TUC had been spent in the Transport and General Workers' Union (TGWU). Ron Todd, an official of the union with a background in the automobile industry, was elected to succeed Moss Evans as general secretary of the TGWU, Britain's biggest union.

The Trade Union Act of 1984 received the royal assent in July. It placed three main duties on unions; namely, for executive committee members to be elected directly by members in secret ballot, for strike action to be preceded by a secret ballot if legal immunity from civil court action were to be retained, and for decisions to operate a political fund to be reviewed at least every ten years. The provisions were being introduced by stages. The first major test of the strike ballot provision came in November, when a strike at the Austin Rover division of the BL automobile company collapsed after the company had brought legal actions against a number of unions on the grounds that no secret ballot had been held prior to the strike.

United States and Canada. Despite the country's high economic growth and substantial increase in employment, U.S. labour unions in 1984 remained generally more concerned with job security than with higher pay. The major negotiations of the year, in the automobile and coal mining industries, resulted in relatively modest wage increases. Prior to the contract, six days of selective strikes against General Motors Corp. by the United Automobile Union (UAW) had idled about 100,000 workers. Subsequently, the company's Canadian workers rejected the terms accepted by workers in the U.S., but after a strike a modified agreement was reached. The Canadian automobile workers made it known that in the future they wanted a greater degree of independence from the Detroit headquarters of the union. The Chrysler Corp. elected Owen Bieber, the new president of the UAW, to its board. (A former UAW president, Douglas Fraser, now retired, had been elected to the board in 1980.) Unusually for U.S. union practice, a

Canadian, Lynn Williams, was elected to head the important United Steelworkers of America.

A practice that generated some controversy during the year was a move by certain employers to introduce two-tier bargaining. Under this arrangement new workers could be engaged on terms considerably less favourable than those applicable to existing employees already covered by a union contract. Negotiations between the U.S. Postal Service and unions representing most of the nation's postal workers broke down in July over this issue. A federal fact-finding panel was organized to study the dispute, with binding arbitration to follow.

A U.S. Supreme Court ruling in February found that a bankruptcy court might free a company from its contracts with unions without requiring proof that the contracts threatened the company's survival; it was necessary only to demonstrate that the contracts were a financial burden. The court added that a company might abrogate a collective agreement as soon as it filed for bankruptcy without waiting for the decision of a bankruptcy judge. The court's ruling seemed likely to have an appreciable impact on collective bargaining practice, but its effect was reversed by legislation enacted by the U.S. Congress later in the year.

Continental Western Europe. Labour-management relations in France were often uneasy during the year, notably in those parts of industry that were contracting. The major automobile companies and the metals firm of Creusot-Loire were particularly in the news in this respect. After the Communist Party ministers left the government in July, there were signs that the pro-Communist Confédération Générale du Travail (CGT), the largest French trade union organization, would adopt increasingly militant policies.

In an interesting initiative, the Conseil National du Patronat Français (CNPF) announced, on the basis of a specially commissioned survey, that employers could create 471,000 new jobs over the next three years if administrative constraints on companies were eased. Subsequently there was a series of wide-ranging central national framework negotiations concerning increased flexibility in the labour market. The final stages, just before Christmas, envisaged

(continued on page 290)

Owen Bieber (left) was elected to the board of directors of the Chrysler Corp. after becoming president of the United Automobile Workers (UAW). Bieber is shown here with a UAW vice-president, Steve Yokich, during negotiations with Ford.

Unions in Trouble

BY JEROLD L. KELLMAN

Big labour was in big trouble in 1984. Observers disagreed as to how organized labour had reached what was clearly a nadir of its power to win economic benefits through collective bargaining and social-welfare benefits through the legislative process. But few challenged the assertion that unions were faring poorly and had little prospect of improving their fortunes markedly in the near future.

Union supporters in the U.S. tended to identify a number of villains—primarily multinational corporations, union-busting law firms, the National Labor Relations Board, the U.S. Supreme Court, and, especially, the Reagan administration—acting in intentional or unintentional concert to reverse nearly 50 years of labour progress. Union opponents, on the other hand, tended to see the roots of labour's woes in decades of greed, during which often-corrupt union leaders had forced industry into a noncompetitive status with their demands for huge increases in wages and benefits. Eventually, according to this view, labour brought about its own demise as companies were forced to lay off workers, close plants, seek cheaper means of production elsewhere in the world, turn increasingly to robots rather than workers, and/or halt the steady rise in pay.

In essence, the positions of union supporters and opponents had changed little since the 1930s. The roles of innocent victim (exploited worker or vulnerable corporation) and greedy perpetrator (robber baron or union boss) in the labour-management drama had remained unaltered over time. But the drama itself might be outdated. Less partisan analysts of labour's current plight tended to see unions as creatures of an industrial age struggling to adapt themselves to a postindustrial era in which workers increasingly performed service rather than manufacturing functions and wanted to share in the corporate decision-making process.

Facts and Figures. The numbers painted a portrait of unions in peril. In 1984 fewer than 20% of U.S. nonfarm workers belonged to unions, down from a peak of about 35% following World War II. During Pres. Ronald Reagan's first term, membership in the AFL-CIO declined from 14.9 million to 13.7 million, with most of the loss occurring in the "Rust Bowl" industries, especially steel and automaking. In this period, for example, the active membership of the United Steelworkers dropped 25%, from one million to 750,000. Had it not been for the sizable growth in public-sector unions (state and local government employees), total union membership would have fallen even further.

Lane Kirkland, president of the AFL-CIO, attributed much of the membership loss to the "Reagan recession."

Jerold L. Kellman is president of the publishing company Gabriel House, Inc. His books include The First One Hundred Years *and* A Writer's Guide to Chicago-Area Publishers.

Clearly, many laid-off workers stopped paying union dues, and unions could not organize the unemployed who wanted but could not obtain jobs in traditionally unionized industries. But the decline went beyond swings in the economic cycle. The industrial production jobs lost in 1981 and 1982—and the union memberships that went with them—did not reappear in equal numbers when economic recovery took hold in 1983 and 1984.

As union membership declined, so did union clout at the bargaining table. During the first half of 1984, contract settlements produced average annual wage increases for unionized workers of 2.8%, less than half of what unions had been able to achieve three years earlier. In fact, there was evidence that wages of nonunion workers were increasing at a faster rate than those of unionized workers. The results of representation elections suggested that workers were questioning the value of union membership. In 1970 unions won more than 50% of such elections; by 1982 their success rate had fallen below 44%.

In Britain union membership has tended upward or downward with the fortunes of the Labour Party, resembling a plateau in times of closely matched Labour-Conservative strength. After holding between 11 million and 12 million in the early 1970s, it climbed to more than 13.2 million in 1979, during the Labour government of James Callaghan. The nationwide labour unrest of that year ushered in the Thatcher government, and with it came the beginnings of sharp membership decline. Both trends, of course—political strength and union membership—reflect broad public sentiment, which in the Thatcher era was running strongly against the unions, and especially against the avowedly radical Marxist leaders furthest to the left in Britain's generally socialist trade union movement.

In the U.S. unions grew into a potent force in American society by organizing industrial workers (mostly men) in the Northeast and Midwest. To survive in the 1980s, unions knew they must organize high-tech and other white-collar workers (in many instances women) who increasingly lived in the South and Southwest. It was not an impossible task. The Teamsters, battered by deregulation of their industry as well as recession, had successfully recruited airline, government, and health care workers into their ranks. It was, however, an exceedingly difficult task. The Sun Belt states lacked a history of pro-union sentiment, and women—who now constituted more than half the work force—were entering the job market at a time when employers were not as ruthlessly exploitative as the old industrial bosses, whose iron-fisted practices gave rise to the union movement in the first place. In the minds of many white-collar workers, unions seemed at best irrelevant and at worst antithetical to their interests.

Labour Under Assault. While many union leaders recognized that the transition from an industrial to a postindustrial economy was responsible for much of their trouble, they also saw far more easily identifiable enemies. According to most unions (the Teamsters in the U.S. being the notable exception), Ronald Reagan and Margaret Thatcher had conducted an antilabour vendetta from the time they assumed office.

Unionists cited many factors: the U.S. recession of 1981–82, which created a huge pool of potential strikebreakers among the unemployed; President Reagan's refusal to formulate an industrial policy that would protect basic industries—and hence thousands of jobs—from foreign competition; a pro-Reagan National Labor Relations Board that made it easier for companies to shift production to nonunion facilities and had a record backlog of more than 1,400 untried cases involving union grievances; a conservative Supreme Court that, in February 1984, gave broad discretion to economically troubled companies wishing to cancel labour contracts *before* an actual bankruptcy petition was approved; the U.S. government's firing of 11,000 striking air-traffic controllers in 1981; the failure to enforce rigorously federal health and safety standards in the workplace; the gutting of the "safety net" of social legislation that labour had worked for decades to establish; the decision of Britain's National Coal Board to close about 20 unprofitable mines and lay off more than 10% of the country's coal miners. In the minds of most unionists, all these added up to a declaration of war on organized labour by conservative, pro-business administrations in the U.S. and Great Britain.

Encouraged by government's antiunion stance, business leaders adopted strategies designed to blunt labour's effectiveness. One involved the hiring of so-called union-busting law firms that specialized in blocking organizing drives. The bankruptcy laws—even the threat of filing a bankruptcy petition—were also viewed as weapons that could be used to break union contracts or, at the very least, could be held over labour's head at the bargaining table. The repercussions of the Continental Airlines bankruptcy in 1983, which resulted in sharp wage cutbacks and longer working hours for unionized employees, were felt throughout U.S. industry.

Labour on the Attack. In October 1983, before the first of the U.S. presidential primaries, the AFL-CIO decided to throw its considerable political weight behind Democrat Walter Mondale. The union saw the election of 1984 as so crucial to its future that, for the first time in its existence, it endorsed a candidate before the primaries were held. Not only did the AFL-CIO want to do everything in its power to defeat Reagan, it also wanted to reestablish itself as the preeminent power among the competing constituencies within the Democratic Party.

The union spent nearly $5 million on Mondale's behalf during the primaries, and it launched a massive campaign to register voters for the fall election. To be successful, union political strategists calculated, they would have to deliver 65% of the union-household vote, some ten million votes in all. In 1980 Reagan had won nearly 45% of the union rank and file, an accomplishment union leaders vowed not to let happen again. It did happen, however, as Reagan scored a resounding victory in the November election, again winning approximately 45% of the union-household vote. Adding insult to injury, Mondale was forced to spend much of the campaign refuting the charge that he was the creature of "special interests," including, most prominently, labour unions. With even their ability to deliver their own membership in question, and overt union support becoming more a minus than a plus, the unions faced a serious reassessment of their political strategy.

Meanwhile, outside the political arena, other strategies were being considered by the union leadership. Stressing that the very suffering they had undergone had given new life to the U.S. union movement, leaders vowed to launch massive organizing drives to boost membership. By their own admission, organizing had become a low priority during the good times prior to 1981. But the depleted membership rolls and empty dues coffers made organizing more of a concern than it had been in nearly five decades.

At least a few union leaders were also considering a new strategy of attack called the corporate campaign. Devised by Ray Rogers, head of a consulting firm that aided unions, the corporate campaign was designed to build a broad-based coalition that would bring political and economic pressure to bear against a company's corporate backers in an effort to alter management attitudes. In its most notable success to date, Rogers's corporate campaign forced the J. P. Stevens Co., which had resisted unionization for 17 years, to recognize and bargain with the Amalgamated Clothing and Textile Workers Union in 1980. In the course of the Stevens campaign, for example, threats by unions and religious organizations to withdraw their pension funds from management of the Manufacturers Hanover Trust Co. led to the resignation of the chairman of Stevens from Hanover's board of directors, and the chairman of Avon Products, Inc., quit the Stevens board after a number of women's groups threatened to boycott Avon products. Rogers's message was that workers have other weapons besides the strike. Their savings accounts, insurance policies, pension investments, stock proxies, purchasing power, and votes can all be pitted against the creditors and other parties that influence a company's management.

The Pact Is Prologue. For the most part, however, unions were seeking a less adversarial role vis-à-vis management. While taking a public stance of "no more concessions"—such as those given in contract negotiations with Chrysler and, to a lesser extent, with other automakers in the early 1980s—union leaders privately conceded that the days of winning big wage increases were over. The emphasis now was on job security and—in the case of a few companies—winning labour representation on corporate boards of directors.

In September 1984 General Motors and the United Auto Workers signed a pact (ratified by the membership in October) that, in the minds of many analysts, set the tone for labour negotiations in the foreseeable future. The three-year agreement included a very modest wage increase of 2.25% for the first year and lump-sum payments of 2.25% for the second and third years; the lump-sum payments, however, were not really wage increases in that they would not be taken into consideration when figuring wage-based company benefits.

At a time when the corporation was announcing record profits and huge executive bonuses, GM insisted that it needed to hold down labour costs in order to remain competitive with foreign carmakers. The UAW, under Pres. Owen Bieber, countered with proposals aimed at job security. Eventually—after a one-week strike had idled more than 100,000 workers at 17 GM plants—the two sides worked out a settlement that included a GM commitment to spend $1 billion over six years to retrain workers whose jobs were eliminated by technological gains, plant consolidations, and shifting of purchasing and production to other countries ("outsourcing"). Affected workers would continue to receive the same wages and benefits during their tenure in the "job bank."

The GM-UAW pact involved many other provisions, of course, but it was this swap of moderate wage demands for job security that led many to call it the new standard for labour-management contracts. Indeed, Ford quickly followed in GM's footsteps with a similar, albeit more modest, job-security program in its pact with the UAW. Interestingly, however, GM workers in Canada went on strike rather than accept the provisions ratified by their U.S. counterparts. The Canadian UAW workers had been far less plagued by layoffs and, consequently, were less concerned about job security. As their strike idled 20,000 GM workers in the U.S., the Canadians were insisting on a wage hike higher than 2.25%, and they got it.

(continued from page 287)

asking the government to soften certain administrative and fiscal provisions and also covered the introduction of technological change, the duration and flexibility of working time, dismissal procedures, the operation of representative bodies within enterprises, fixed-term contracts of employment, and part-time work. However, an agreement on this basis was rejected after reference back by union negotiators.

In West Germany, which had previously enjoyed generally peaceful industrial relations, determined campaigns by the metal and the printing and paper labour unions to secure a 35-hour workweek led to major strikes in both industries. The metal strike lasted nearly seven weeks, and at its height some 450,000 workers were affected, directly or indirectly. The dispute was settled, on the basis of a reduction to a workweek of $38\frac{1}{2}$ hours from April 1, 1985; the $38\frac{1}{2}$ hour provision would not be terminable before Sept. 30, 1986. The hours could be varied, subject to certain limits, by negotiation within an enterprise or operating unit in order to suit production requirements, on the condition that the average of $38\frac{1}{2}$ hours be maintained. The settlement also provided modest wage increases.

In the printing industry, industrial action lasted even longer than in metals. The dispute was finally settled on the basis of a $38\frac{1}{2}$ hour week beginning April 1, 1985, the agreement not to be terminated before March 31, 1987.

Spain again experienced numerous strikes during the year. Negotiations were difficult, and when a nationwide two-year agreement was reached on October 9, only one of the two major union organizations signed. The wage increases agreed upon were not excessive, though the agreement provided for them to be revised should inflation rise above the government's forecasts. The agreement contained a number of provisions concerning social security, employment, and training, including the setting up of a tripartite employment solidarity fund.

In Sweden the traditionally centralized bargaining system for manual workers in private industry gave way to regional bargaining. There was some criticism of the friction in individual negotiations, which also often resulted in rather costly agreements. Talks were held to consider a new framework for future negotiation procedures.

South Africa. The black workers' National Union of Mineworkers took a vote and struck in September. The workers wanted an average 25% pay increase, while the employers offered 14%. It was the first legal strike by the union, following the government's new industrial relations legislation. The strike was quickly settled on the basis of an offer of improved holiday payment, increasing the value of the overall package to about 16.3%.   (R. O. CLARKE)

The views expressed in this article are the author's and should not be attributed to any organization with which he may be connected.

See also Economic Affairs: *World Economy*; Industrial Review.

This article updates the *Macropædia* article WORK AND EMPLOYMENT.

Law

Court Decisions. In 1984 the various judicial tribunals throughout the world handed down a number of significant decisions, many of which involved, unusually, the application of international law principles.

DECISIONS OF INTERNATIONAL SIGNIFICANCE. In a case that attracted considerable attention in the U.S. and was debated by Pres. Ronald Reagan and Walter Mondale during the presidential election campaign, Nicaragua filed an application with the International Court of Justice (ICJ) alleging that the U.S. had violated its sovereignty by using military force against it, in violation of the UN Charter and the treaty establishing the Organization of American States. The U.S. refused to accept, for the time being, the jurisdiction of the ICJ regarding this matter. It was this act of declination that surprised many observers and caused the ensuing political debate. (See *International Law,* below.)

Equally surprising had been Libya's agreement to allow the ICJ to decide its disputes with Tunisia and Malta over delimitation of the continental shelf, cases that were still before the court in 1984. These cases involved billions of dollars in oil revenues, and procedural squabbles indicated the importance that all parties attached to the final rulings. Thus, for example, in the case of Libya and Tunisia, the court, for the first time in its history, was asked by both parties to construe its 1982 judgment, though once before one party had asked for such an interpretation.

In addition, for the first time, one party asked the court to revise its judgment. Meanwhile, in the case of Libya and Malta, the procedure was clouded by an attempted intervention by Italy, which claimed that any decision regarding the establishment of the continental shelf for Malta and Libya would affect it. Apparently both Malta and Libya rejected this offer of intervention, and the court finally ruled that Italy was not entitled to intervene.

The House of Lords, the highest court in the U.K., construed the State Immunity Act 1978 in the case of *Alcom Ltd.* v. *Republic of Colombia.* This act had drawn international attention because it reflected local concern that "diplomatic immunity" had been abused. Since Great Britain is one of the strongest advocates of the concept of full immunity for diplomats, the Alcom Case was viewed with particular interest. The 1978 act allows a creditor to use normal collection procedures, including garnishment and attachment, against an embassy for commercial debts incurred in the normal course of its operations. Thus, for example, under this law a foreign embassy could not evade the obligation to pay for food provided by local merchants on the grounds of diplomatic immunity. In the Alcom Case, a lower court had allowed the general bank account of Colombia to be garnished without requiring the creditor to prove that the debt was a commercial— as contrasted with a sovereign—one. The House of Lords held that the garnishment could not be upheld without such proof.

In a case of considerable "cold-war" significance, the International Civil Aviation Organization, a quasi-judicial body, finally handed down its long-awaited decision on Korean Air Lines flight 007, shot down in 1983 by a Soviet

Elizabeth Hishon was denied a partnership after seven years as an associate in the Atlanta law firm of King & Spalding. Her right to bring suit on the grounds of sex discrimination was upheld by the U.S. Supreme Court.

U.S. Gen. William Westmoreland brought a $120 million libel suit against CBS television, charging that its documentary on the Vietnam war had held him up to "scorn, contempt, and ridicule." The documentary implied, among other things, that Westmoreland, then commander of U.S. forces in Vietnam, had conspired with other top military officials to deceive policymakers in Washington and the public about enemy strength. He is shown here flanked by his attorneys.

AP/WIDE WORLD

jet fighter when it strayed into Soviet airspace. In a resolution put forward by the U.S. and opposed vigorously by the U.S.S.R., the tribunal decided to accept its staff report to the effect that Soviet officials did not try hard enough to identify the South Korean passenger airliner before attacking it and that there was no evidence the plane was on a spying mission.

In *Regan* v. *Wald,* the U.S. Supreme Court held that congressional resolutions prohibiting Americans from engaging in any transactions with Cuba, "direct or indirect," justified a ban issued by the executive department on U.S. citizens' traveling to Cuba. The majority opinion stated that "Cuba, with the political, economic, and military backing of the Soviet Union, has provided widespread support for armed violence and terrorism in the Western Hemisphere. Cuba also maintains close to 40,000 troops in various countries in Africa and the Middle East in support of objectives inimical to United States foreign policy interests." In view of these considerations, preventing Cuba from earning hard currency through American tourism justified a limitation on the generally recognized right of Americans to travel freely. Four of nine justices dissented, largely on the grounds that the due process clause of the U.S. Constitution protects the rights of Americans to travel anywhere in the world.

RIGHT TO COUNSEL. The U.S. Supreme Court and the European Court of Human Rights both handed down significant opinions regarding the right of indigents to counsel. In *Goddi* v. *Italy,* the European Court of Human Rights held that an accused had not been properly represented on appeal, as was his right under Art. 6(3) of the European Convention for the Protection of Human Rights and Fundamental Freedoms. The accused was absent from the appellate hearing on his conviction because he was imprisoned for an unrelated offense. He had not been notified of the appellate hearing, though a lawyer who had formerly represented him, but no longer was retained, did receive a notice. The appellate court appointed an attorney to represent him but did not give the attorney a proper opportunity to prepare by examining the file or consulting the accused. Under these circumstances, the appellate court was judged to have operated in contravention of the convention when it ruled that the accused's sentence should be increased.

In *Van der Mussele* v. *Belgium,* a Belgian lawyer contended that his nonvoluntary assignment to defend an indigent, with no possibility of a fee, amounted to "forced or compulsory labour" in violation of the convention. This point had been made privately by many European advocates, but the European Court of Human Rights ruled against the position.

The U.S. Supreme Court held in *U.S.* v. *Cronic* that the fact that assigned counsel was given only 25 days to prepare to defend an accused against criminal charges involving a complicated check-kiting scheme, and that counsel was young and inexperienced in criminal matters, did not necessarily mean the accused was not properly represented. The test, said the court, is not whether adequate representation inferentially seems to be absent under the circumstances but whether the actual trial reveals inadequacies in this regard.

DOUBLE JEOPARDY. In *Goddi* v. *Italy,* the European Court of Human Rights, while ruling that the accused was not properly represented by counsel, held that a sentence could be increased on appeal where proper procedures had been observed. The U.S. Supreme Court came to an opposite conclusion in *Arizona* v. *Rumsey.* It held, in effect, that a sentence may never be increased after it has been imposed. The case involved a situation in which an accused was found guilty and sentenced to life imprisonment. The conviction was reversed on appeal, and the case remanded for a new trial. On the remand, the accused was again convicted but this time was sentenced to death. The court said this sentence violated a constitutional prohibition against "double jeopardy."

SEX. France's highest court, the Cour de Cassation, held in the case of *S.* v. *Procureur Général près la Cour d'Appel de Nancy* that a surgical operation resulting in a change of sex did not entitle the person on whom it was performed to make appropriate changes in his or her birth certificate or to change a forename. The court pointed out that the public interest in the identity of a person is greater in this case than the right of the individual to make public changes in that identity.

In an opinion without a name, the Spanish Constitutional Court decided that an unborn fetus is not a human being for purposes of some criminal laws. Specifically, it ruled that a woman who had an abortion abroad had committed no crime. The case reversed a celebrated decision of the Supreme Court of Spain that the woman, by acquiescing in a foreign abortion, had committed a crime against "another Spaniard," presumably the unborn child.

The U.S. Supreme Court in *Equal Employment Opportunity Commission* v. *Shell Oil Co.* laid down important guidelines for determining the validity of statistical evidence in ascertaining whether or not an employer is guilty of sex or racial discrimination in hiring, in contravention of the Civil Rights Act of 1964. Shell was accused of such discrimination but denied the charge. The Equal Employment Opportunity Commission produced limited evidence of specific cases of discrimination and sought to prove the larger case by the use of statistical evidence. In this connection, it sought to subpoena information from Shell. Shell moved to quash the subpoena on the grounds that it could not be requested until a prima facie showing of discrimination had been established. The court disagreed, holding that Shell must turn over the information in question.

The court took the position that statistical evidence is important in establishing racial and sexual discrimination. Implicitly, it seemed to endorse the debated assertion that nondiscriminatory employment practices ultimately will produce a work force with a composition approximating that of the available labour force, whereas discriminatory practices will result in a work force in which women and minorities are underrepresented. Thus employers must reveal evidence to proper authorities as to the racial and sexual mix of their employees, even where no prior evidence has been produced indicating that the employer has been guilty of discrimination. In the principal cases against the employer, however, the commissioner must not rely on statistical evidence where more particular evidence is available.

RELIGIOUS FREEDOM. An important decision regarding "religious freedom" was handed down by the U.S. Supreme Court in *Lynch* v. *Donnelly.* For about 40 years the city of Pawtucket, R.I., had erected a Christmas display in a public park situated in the central shopping area. The display included, among other things, a Christmas tree, a Santa Claus house, and a Nativity scene. An action was brought to enjoin the inclusion of the Nativity scene on the grounds that the use of public funds to erect it violated the establishment clause of the First Amendment to the Constitution. This clause prohibits state or federal governments from establishing any religion and requires them to keep church and state separate.

The Supreme Court held that the city of Pawtucket had not violated this constitutional provision. It stated that the Constitution does not mandate a "wall" of separation between church and state but rather mandates accommodation of all religions and forbids hostility toward any. In short, said the court, it is incorrect to take an absolutist approach to the establishment clause and invalidate mechanically all government conduct that gives special recognition to religion in general or even one faith in particular. Rather, the court must scrutinize challenged conduct on a case-by-case basis to determine whether, in reality, it establishes a religion or religious faith or tends to do so.

(WILLIAM D. HAWKLAND)

International Law. The pressures on international law increased during 1984 as the loosening of state inhibitions noted in previous years continued. This appeared particularly in a growing disrespect for state boundaries and for the sanctity of diplomatic premises and representatives. In the U.S. commentators on the right wing began openly to question the validity of legal rules in international inter-

course, and U.S. Ambassador to the UN Jeane J. Kirkpatrick, in distinguishing between "forces used to conquer and victimize and forces used to liberate," came close to reviving the doctrine of the "just war." At the same time, and in contrast, there was a surge in international adjudication.

DIPLOMATIC IMMUNITY. Diplomatic law suffered many blows throughout the year. Nigeria threatened to search all diplomatic bags during a 12-day banknote change in April and May, but several ambassadors, after protesting, ceased all movement of bags so as to maintain the principle of diplomatic immunity. Kuwait began to X-ray diplomatic bags early in the year, claiming that this did not constitute "searching." Several ambassadors protested, and the U.K. stopped sending bags altogether, although the majority of embassies accepted the practice, later adopted also by Iraq.

The question of diplomatic bags, which often were not bags but huge crates or containers, was prominent in one of the two diplomatic causes célèbres in England during the year. In July two such crates, addressed to the Ministry of External Affairs in Lagos, were stopped and opened at Stansted Airport just as they were about to be loaded onto a Nigerian Airways flight. They were found to contain a heavily sedated Nigerian exile, former transport minister Alhaji Umaru Dikko (*see* BIOGRAPHIES), and a well-known Israeli anesthesiologist, plus two other Israelis. Their loading was being supervised by a Nigerian diplomat, but because there were no official diplomatic seals on the crates, immunity was not claimed. The Nigerian government refused to waive the immunity of its London diplomats to allow them to be questioned, but evidence appeared to implicate some of them. Two Nigerian diplomats were expelled, and the high commissioner was advised not to return to his post in London. In retaliation, Nigeria expelled two British diplomats, and the U.K. high commissioner was advised to leave.

An even more blatant misuse of diplomatic status occurred in April when, during a peaceful demonstration, a submachine gun was fired from the Libyan People's Bureau (embassy) in London, killing a woman police officer on crowd-control duty and wounding 11 others. Diplomatic immunity of the premises was respected until diplomatic relations between Libya and the U.K. were broken off. Police then broke into and searched the premises in the presence of a representative of the Saudi Arabian embassy. The two prime suspects both possessed diplomatic status and left Britain with the other members of the embassy.

Diplomatic immunity was upheld by the House of Lords in *Alcom Ltd.* v. *Republic of Colombia.* (See *Court Decisions,* above.) The French Supreme Court, in *Iran* v. *Commisariat à l'Énergie Atomique,* upheld the exemption of a foreign state from execution procedure except when the goods seized were part of a commercial activity governed by private law. Diplomatic asylum was an issue in Prague, Czech., where East Germans wishing to emigrate took refuge in the West German embassy, and in Durban, where South African leaders of the Natal Indian Congress sought refuge in the British consulate against detention without trial. These and other incidents led to widespread proposals to review the 1961 Vienna Convention on diplomatic relations.

INTERNATIONAL ADJUDICATION. The caseload of the ICJ was the largest in 30 years, with six cases pending or decided: (1) Canada/U.S. (maritime boundary in the Gulf of Maine—judgment delivered October 12); (2) Libya/Malta (continental shelf) and (3) Tunisia/Libya (revision and interpretation of 1982 continental shelf judgment; see *Court Decisions,* above); (4) Nicaragua/U.S. (military and paramilitary activities in and against Nicaragua) and intervention application by El Salvador; (5) Burkina Faso (Upper Volta)/Mali (boundary); (6) *Yakimetz* v. *UN Secretary-General* (review of award by UN administrative tribunal).

Procedural issues arose in the Nicaraguan case since, in order to forestall judicial proceedings, the U.S. hastily made a supplementary declaration on April 6 excluding from its acceptance of the compulsory jurisdiction of the ICJ "disputes with any Central American state or arising out of or related to events in Central America," this proviso to take effect immediately and to apply for two years. On April 9 Nicaragua filed its action and requested interim protective measures, which the U.S. resisted on two main grounds of lack of jurisdiction: (1) Nicaragua's acceptance of compulsory jurisdiction in 1929 had never been officially communicated to the League of Nations; and (2) the U.S. declaration of April 6 effectively excluded from the present case the U.S. acceptance of compulsory jurisdiction in 1946. The ICJ, nevertheless, issued the requested interim order on May 10, declaring itself "provisionally" competent, and on November 26 it agreed to hear the case. (*See* WORLD AFFAIRS: *United Nations.*)

Nils Mangård, a Swedish member of the U.S.-Iran Claims Tribunal, was physically attacked in September by two of the Iranian judges in the corridors of the Peace Palace in The Hague, Neth., because he gave rulings in favour of the U.S. The Swedish president of the tribunal canceled all meetings for two weeks to let tempers cool. Earlier, in April, the tribunal had decided by a 6–3 majority that it had jurisdiction over claims by dual U.S.-Iranian nationals if the claimant's dominant and effective nationality during the relevant period was U.S. The three Iranian dissenting judges then made a joint statement accusing the majority of bad faith and attacking "the so-called neutral arbitrators" as unbalanced. A decision the previous December had given awards of $7,140,000 and $2,860,000 to an American parent company and subsidiary, respectively, in respect of their loss of shares in the Iran America International Insurance Co. when it was nationalized (*American International Group, Inc.* v. *Iran*). That same month the U.S. Court of Appeals for the 9th circuit denied jurisdiction in an action for damages brought against Iran by Americans held hostage in the U.S. embassy in Teheran in 1979–81 and their families on grounds of sovereign immunity (*McKeel* v. *Iran*), and in March 1984 the Court of Appeals for the District of Columbia did the same (*Persinger* v. *Iran*).

Nationalization by the Ethiopian government was attacked before the U.S. Court of Appeals for the 6th circuit, where the act of state principle was held not to apply because of the 1953 Treaty of Amity between Ethiopia and the U.S., and so the case was permitted to continue (*Kalamazoo Spice Extraction Co.* v. *PMGSE*). On the other hand, jurisdiction was denied on sovereign immunity grounds in *Banque Campafina* v. *Banco de Guatemala;* and in *Jackson* v. *China* a default judgment against China in relation to bearer bonds issued in 1911 was set aside because the question of sovereign immunity required adversarial argument.

Two new international tribunals began activity. In January the Court of Justice of the Cartagena Agreement (Andean Pact) was formally inaugurated, and the Judicial Tribunal of the Organization of Arab Petroleum Exporting Countries (OAPEC) began hearing preliminary objections in its first case (*Iraq* v. *Syria*), concerning Syria's closing of the transit pipeline carrying crude oil to the Mediterranean.

SOVEREIGNTY AND BOUNDARY DISPUTES. The Beagle

Improvised minesweeper clears Nicaraguan harbours after mining by antigovernment *contras*, with the help of the U.S. CIA. In November the International Court of Justice accepted Nicaragua's suit demanding a halt to U.S. support of antigovernment activities despite the U.S. administration's assertion that the court did not have jurisdiction in this case.

MEISELAS—MAGNUM

Channel dispute was finally settled, with sovereignty over the three islands of Picton, Lennox, and Nueva and up to 12 mi of adjacent territorial waters going to Chile, but with Argentina retaining control of a 30- to 40-mi exclusive economic zone in the Atlantic. A treaty between the U.K. and China was signed in December whereby, when the lease of the New Territories ran out in 1997, the whole colony of Hong Kong would be retroceded to China to be administered for at least 50 years under a constitution that retained its existing liberal economic regime.

In August Libya and Morocco signed a treaty of union which, however, would not affect either state's sovereignty. Settlement of Guatemala's claim to Belize was slightly facilitated by an unpublished agreement between Guatemala and the U.K. to reopen consular relations. China and India agreed on the negotiating terms for discussing the demarcation of their border. Proposals were made to adjust the maritime boundary between Sweden and Finland, altering the sovereignty of some islets, and a treaty was signed in November on the seabed and fishery boundary between Sweden and Denmark. Costa Rica and Nicaragua agreed in May to set up a commission to supervise their border. In the same month, West Germany and The Netherlands concluded a treaty on environmental cooperation in the Ems Estuary and the Dollart Basin after six years of negotiation. Discussions continued between Norway and the U.S.S.R. on the continental shelf boundary in the Barents Sea.

Breaches of sovereignty and border incursions increased. The most dramatic were connected with submarines. The covert breaches of Swedish territorial waters by foreign submarines noticed in previous years continued. A report by the Swedish Navy documented 25 confirmed occasions in 1983, and a later report noted 10 between March and September 1984. In February a major incursion was reported in the sensitive Karlskrona area; the unsuccessful search for the intruder lasted some six weeks. In November seabed tracks of foreign minisubmarines, similar to those found in 1983 on the Swedish seabed in Hårsfjorden, were found in Japanese waters just off Hokkaido. The U.S. aircraft carrier "Kitty Hawk" collided in the Sea of Japan with a Soviet submarine that had been shadowing it for four days. In September a submerged Soviet submarine illegally passing through the Strait of Gibraltar collided with a Soviet merchant vessel.

Technical violations of Swedish sovereignty occurred when French warships began exercises inside Swedish waters, instead of steaming full line ahead as is correct for warships using the right of innocent passage. The failure of a U.S. warship to notify its passage, as required by international law, was connected with the U.S. refusal to recognize Sweden's extension of its territorial waters from 3 to 12 mi. Soviet border-patrol boats operated by the State Security Committee (KGB) several times crossed the Swedish sea border off Gotland. Among other infringements of maritime sovereignty, the most blatant was the planting by U.S. agents of mines in the principal Nicaraguan harbours and their approaches.

Swedish airspace was violated by a Soviet attack plane and Norwegian airspace by a Swedish fighter plane, in both cases while on maneuvers. Soviet bombers violated Japanese airspace over the Tsushima Strait twice during November. South Africa bombed Lubango deep inside Angola. U.S. planes regularly flew in Nicaraguan airspace, and Nicaraguan planes bombed the Costa Rican border hamlet of San Isidro. Air attacks in the Persian Gulf as part of the Iraq-Iran war led Saudi Arabia to proclaim a new "defensive air perimeter" in international airspace as a form of "contiguous zone."

(NEVILLE MARCH HUNNINGS)

See also Crime, Law Enforcement, and Penology; World Affairs: *United Nations.*

This article updates the *Macropædia* articles CONSTITUTIONAL LAW; INTERNATIONAL LAW.

Libraries

During 1984 there was further deterioration in the financing of libraries worldwide, with some exceptions. Since the change of government in France, for instance, libraries there had received considerably more attention, and new policies in information and library services were initiated. Consideration was being given to the development of outreach services, including those for the aged, the mentally and physically handicapped, and for ethnic minorities.

There was also a resurgence of interest in libraries in China, where a building of 240,000 sq m (2.6 million sq ft) being constructed for the National Library was one of the key national development projects. A number of university library buildings were also in the process of construction. The China Society of Library Science was established, and in May the Secretariat of the Communist Party Central Committee set up an Administrative Bureau of Library Affairs, with corresponding bureaus in each of the provinces. In Malaysia a new university was being established in the northern part of the country, and plans were under way for a new library building there. Malaysian libraries were also concerned with the development of information services, and a consultant, under the auspices of UNESCO, was assisting in developing policy. A UNESCO team involved in identifying needs for possible World Bank funding was active in Indonesia and was to report in due course on the development of library services.

A matter of concern in many countries was the separation of library and information services. In Africa, for instance, UNESCO, in cooperation with the International Development Research Centre (Ottawa), was supporting the development of two schools of information science, one in Addis Ababa, Eth., and one in Ibadan, Nigeria; the latter would be quite separate from the department of library studies at the University of Ibadan. In many Commonwealth countries the public libraries had been developed on the basis of British library practice in the 1960s, while there was a trend in the corresponding private sectors toward information- rather than library-oriented services. In Britain the division was apparent in the stand taken by the Library Association in favour of providing information services free to clients, as opposed to the commercial valuation placed on information by the private sector.

The division between public- and private-sector institutions had existed for many years in industrialized countries and was institutionalized at the international level with the existence of the International Federation for Documentation and the International Federation of Library Associations. In the current conditions of world recession, the differences, which had appeared to be diminishing, now seemed to be sharpening. The main reason for this state of affairs in industrialized countries was that more and more information was available through electronic sources—by computer and telecommunications. Hence libraries were under attack in the sense that fewer resources were being allocated to them when alternative sources of information seemed more easily accessible.

In some regions lack of hard currency continued to be a major problem. In Nigeria—and West Africa generally—little money was available for the purchase of new books and journal subscriptions, with the result that formerly well-maintained collections were deteriorating rapidly. One of the principal antidotes to a complete lack of book imports into some of the less developed Commonwealth countries was the British Council, which celebrated its 50th anniversary in 1984. Librarians of British Council libraries in many countries had made considerable contributions to cultural development and library practice.

(P. HAVARD-WILLIAMS)

In the U.S. the Library of Congress moved forward on new projects to help libraries answer the staggering question of how to handle growing, aging collections. Visitors to its automation lab could inspect a prototype "jukebox" occupying 1.4 sq m (15 sq ft) of space and capable of storing one million pages of text in digital form. The jukebox held 100 optical discs; readers at remote terminals could select the page of text desired, and the jukebox "played" it with a laser beam and transmitted it electronically. Storage capacity was expected to double in the later stages of the pilot program. On June 15 the Library opened to the public another application of compact disc storage: selected historic visual materials stored on analogue videodiscs and displayed on a video screen through a computer program. Both projects offered hope for storing immense amounts of text and graphic information indefinitely while providing widespread access to it. To help save valuable original materials from deterioration, the Library cleared the way for a mass deacidification program in a special facility, where some 500,000 volumes a year would be treated. Papermaking processes used from the early 19th century left

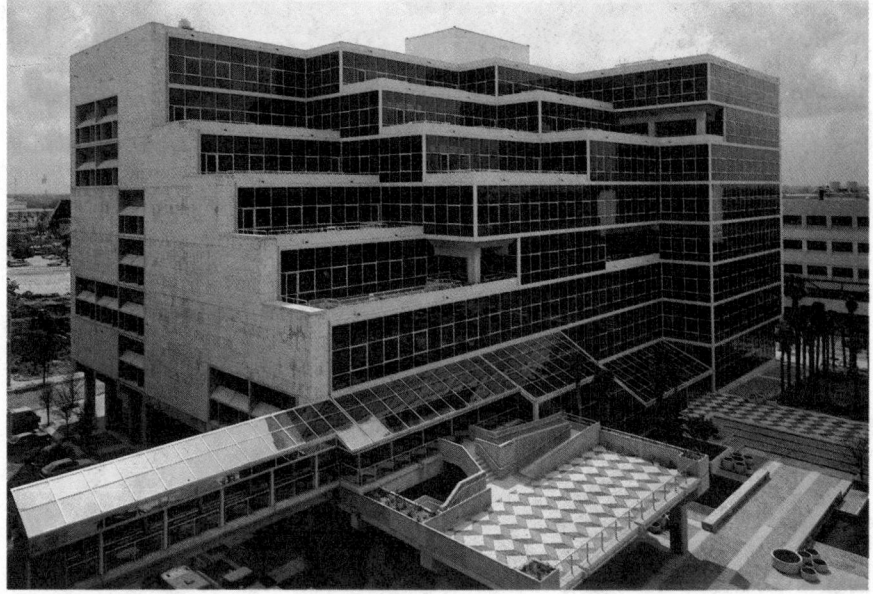

This new main library in Fort Lauderdale, Florida, was dedicated in April. It serves the county library system as well as three academic institutions. It contains some 256,000 square feet in its eight floors.

BROWARD COUNTY MAIN LIBRARY, FORT LAUDERDALE, FLORIDA

an acidic residue that eventually causes the paper to disintegrate, putting vast amounts of current library holdings at risk.

Researchers despairing of a "national bibliographic network" that would allow searches through thousands of libraries from a single terminal could take heart from a "linked systems project" begun in the fall. Three major systems, with on-line files of millions of titles, attacked the technological barriers to intercommunication. Cooperating were the Library of Congress, Research Libraries Group, and Washington Library Network. Pres. Ronald Reagan recommended termination of the 28-year-old Library Services and Construction Act, the major federal aid program for libraries, but Congress voted in October to extend it to 1989. Congress also added direct funding for services to Indian tribes and library literacy activities, among other new initiatives.

Recent statistics released during 1984 showed total U.S. public library circulation at 1,070,000,000. The nation's academic libraries held more than 1,200,000,000 items. Libraries of all types spent $127 million for on-line data-base use. New library school graduates earned a median salary of $16,994, while the average top-of-the-range salary for library directors was $37,563.   (ARTHUR PLOTNIK)

This article updates the *Macropædia* article LIBRARIES AND LIBRARY SCIENCE.

Life Sciences

ZOOLOGY

During 1984, findings from geographic regions around the world revealed the prevalence of complex biological phenomena on a global scale and gave insight into several classical issues in zoology. Advances were made in understanding the ecology and behaviour of animals in general through careful observations of particular species; such empirical contributions were essential in supporting, refuting, or modifying current theories. Evolutionary questions were addressed in a variety of ways, and a combination of structural, biochemical, and fossil evidence was used to reinterpret the phylogenetic relationship between apes and human beings. Changes in the biological status of several endangered species were noted throughout the world.

Research on an African mammal, a South American snail, and a North American bird added to an appreciation of the complexity of natural selection and associated evolutionary phenomena. Jennifer U. M. Jarvis of the University of Cape Town, South Africa, in collaboration with Richard D. Alexander of the University of Michigan and Paul W. Sherman of the University of California at Berkeley, discovered that the naked mole rat, a burrowing rodent of northeastern Africa, has a social structure that is strikingly different from those of other mammals. Naked mole rats live in underground colonies and possess a cooperative social system similar to that of the social insects. Each colony has one female that functions as a queen, producing all of the young. The duty of fertilization often is assumed by only one male in the colony, while the remaining males and females function as workers in the subterranean tunnels. According to the investigators the naked mole rat was the only mammal known in which most members forgo competitive reproduction among individuals in favour of a social system that benefits the whole reproductive unit.

Another finding further complicated the conventional concept that each individual of a species promotes its own genetic material foremost by direct mating with the opposite sex. Warton Monteiro, José Maria G. Almeida, Jr., and Braulio S. Dias of the University of Brazil studied a freshwater snail that is capable of functioning as either a male or a female on different occasions. By means of a series of genetic experiments they documented that male snails of this species sometimes passed on viable sperm—and thus genetic material—other than their own. These males had previously mated as females and still retained foreign sperm in their reproductive tracts. When they later mated as males, the foreign sperm, which had become mixed with their own, gave rise to offspring whose fathers had never mated with their mothers.

In a study of cliff swallows in Nebraska, Charles R. Brown of Princeton University discovered the most extensive case of brood parasitism ever reported within a species of birds. Although many species of birds are known to lay their eggs in the nests of other species and rely on foster parents to rear their young, the cliff swallows, which live in dense nesting colonies, practice parasitism of this type on each other. Apparently, the phenomenon is so widespread

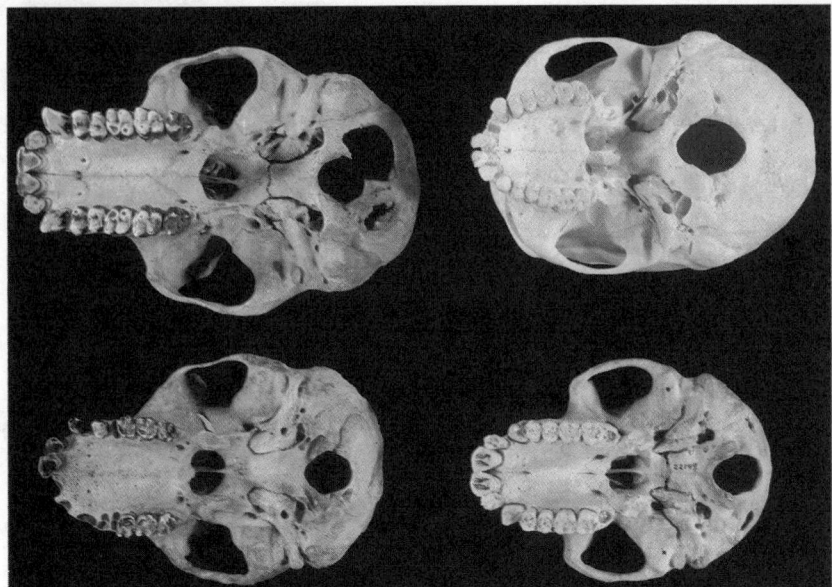

Comparison of teeth and palates of these skulls (seen from below) supported Jeffrey H. Schwartz's theory that humans are more closely related to orangutans than to African apes. Clockwise from lower right: human, orangutan, chimpanzee, gorilla.

J. H. SCHWARTZ, UNIVERSITY OF PITTSBURGH; PHOTOGRAPH, S. DALEY

among cliff swallows that a parasitic egg layer, who may also tend a nest of her own, can fall prey to the same guile from another female in the colony.

A series of separate experiments involving embryo implantation during the year held promise for the continued survival of certain genetic stocks and endangered species and provided insight into embryological and cytogenetic processes. Independent research teams—Carole B. Fehilly, S. M. Willadsen, and Elizabeth M. Tucker at the Agricultural Research Council's Institute of Animal Physiology in Cambridge, England, and Sabine Meinecke-Tillmann and B. Meinecke at Justus Liebig University in Giessen, West Germany—successfully developed interspecific crosses between sheep and goats. Both sets of investigators produced sheep-goat chimeras by micromanipulating and combining components of the blastocyst stage of embryonic development and transplanting the mixed embryo to the female of one of the species. These were the first clearly successful efforts to bring goat-sheep fetuses to term, although numerous attempts had been made earlier to hybridize the two species.

The first primate to be born following implantation of the fetus in another species was a macaque that was carried to term in the womb of a rhesus monkey, a closely related species, at the University of Texas Health Science Center at San Antonio. The embryo was conceived in the laboratory from sperm and egg of the parent macaques, a species native to Southeast Asia, and several days later was implanted into its rhesus surrogate mother. Likewise, a horse at the Louisville (Ky.) Zoo received a zebra embryo transplant and successfully gave birth, whereas at the Cincinnati (Ohio) Zoo a common African antelope gave birth to an implanted bongo, a rare species of antelope that ranges from West Africa to Kenya. The last experiment was reportedly the first successful embryo transplant between different genera. These feats, plus several more involving other species, emphasized the potential for embryonic manipulation in propagating rare and endangered species in a manner not previously possible.

Rare, endangered, and newly discovered species continued to occupy the research interests of scientists worldwide. In Japan and the U.S., the Japanese crested ibis and dusky seaside sparrow, respectively, were thought close to extinction. The ibis had some chance for survival since a few

individuals were known to exist in China, but the last four known survivors of the sparrow were all males. The dusky seaside sparrow would be the first North American bird to become extinct since passage in the U.S. of the 1973 Endangered Species Act. The snail darter, once an endangered fish species known from a single waterway in Tennessee, was discovered in several other stream systems, and consequently its status was officially changed to "threatened" during the year.

Although emphasis and attention often focused on waning or recovering species, zoological discoveries by Roy W. McDiarmid of the U.S. Fish and Wildlife Service and an international team of scientists led to an awareness of species that had not even been known to exist. In an exploratory biological survey of the Guiana Highlands in South America, the investigators initiated a study to examine the flora and fauna of the most isolated and inaccessible portion in Venezuela. During the first year of study, a variety of species apparently new to science, including plants, insects, amphibians, and reptiles, were found at the study site. While revealing that unexplored areas still exist on Earth, the research also should provide solutions to many biogeographic and evolutionary problems related to the origin and relationships of animal species.

The first finding of a magnetically sensitive material in a species of migratory bird known to respond to the Earth's magnetic field was reported by Robert C. Beason and Joan E. Nichols of the State University College of Arts and Sciences, Geneseo, N.Y. The bobolink migrates between Canada and Argentina, farther than most other species of North American birds. The investigators used behavioural experiments to demonstrate the bobolink's ability to detect and use the geomagnetic field during migratory orientation. Birds were then examined for magnetically sensitive materials. Iron oxide deposits were found concentrated in the nasal region and around the olfactory nerves adjacent to nerve fibres. These deposits were presumed to respond to magnetic fields in some way the birds can detect.

After reviewing morphological, biochemical, and fossil data, Jeffrey H. Schwartz of the University of Pittsburgh, Pa., proposed that the closest living relatives of human beings are the orangutans of Borneo and Sarawak rather than the traditionally accepted gorillas and chimpanzees of Africa. The proposed phylogenetic relationship was based partly on a suite of traits shared by humans and orangutans but absent in the other great apes. The traits include thick molar enamel, the ability to grow long hair, and a propensity for copulation throughout the female menstrual cycle rather than at restricted times of the month. Mitochondrial DNA analyses of the hominoids also provided evidence that humans and orangutans are more closely related to each other than to gorillas, chimpanzees, or gibbons. In addition, it was suggested that the fossil hominoid *Sivapithecus* (or *Ramapithecus*), already relegated to a position of close relationship with orangutans, may also be broadly related to the fossil hominid *Australopithecus* and modern man.

Lower on the phylogenetic scale, meaningful fossil finds were made in Africa. M. Mahboubi of the University of Oran, Alg., and colleagues reported the earliest known fossil record of a proboscidean, the group that includes elephants and mammoths. The material from the early Eocene Epoch (about 50 million years ago) in Algeria emphasized the antiquity of the evolution of the order Proboscidea on the African continent. The first fossil records of marsupials in Africa were also discovered. The remains were taken from the Eocene in Algeria by Mahboubi and colleagues and from the Oligocene Epoch (between 38 million and 26 million years ago) in Egypt by T. M. Bown of the U.S. Geological Survey and E. L. Simons of the Duke University Primate Center, Durham, N.C. The findings led investigators to conclude that marsupials entered Africa from Europe, where fossils had been found previously, but became extinct before they could disperse extensively on the African continent.   (J. WHITFIELD GIBBONS)

Entomology. The 17th International Congress of Entomology, attended by more than 2,000 representatives of 77 countries, was held in Hamburg, West Germany, in August 1984. Of the recent advances reported, some of the most notable concerned the neuroendocrine functions of insects and allied arthropods.

Radical changes were proposed to the "classical" concept of the insect brain, a structure typically composed of three bilaterally paired lobes, which have been said to correspond to the ganglia (concentrations of nerve cells) of three ancestral body segments that had fused to form the preoral parts of the head. Of the paired lobes, the protocerebrum had been associated with an "optic" segment, the deutocerebrum with an "antennal" segment, and the tritocerebrum with a further preoral ("labral") segment.

N. J. Strausfeld of the European Molecular Biology Laboratory, Heidelberg, West Germany, and co-workers, using a technique of tracing individual nerve cells by impregnating them through a cut end with a "backfill" of cobalt salt, showed that nerve cells linking the optic lobes with the brain in fact go to the deutocerebrum, which properly should be considered the most anterior analogue of segmental ganglia. The deutocerebrum was found to possess glomerular clusters of dendrites (branching extensions of nerve cells) that receive sensory inputs from the antennae, head hairs, and certain sensilla (simple sense organs) in the mouthparts as well as other clusters that control movements of the antennae.

In contrast, the protocerebrum appeared to be a nonsegmental, unique cephalic development having higher integrative and neuroendocrine functions. In confirmation of this view, Joseph Larsen of the University of Illinois and others described blind cave beetles that have no optic lobes yet particularly large protocerebral centres. Meanwhile, J. Chardonneret of the University of Dijon, France, offered evidence of a "tetrocerebrum," closely associated with the tritocerebral lobes, which in a sense restored the concept of a three-segmented origin of the preoral head and brain.

Mark Brown and Arden Lea of the University of Georgia found an analogue of the vertebrate enteropancreatic system in the mosquito midgut, an apparently simple, tubular structure that functions as stomach and intestine. They described scattered, flask-shaped endocrine cells that send thin extensions to surrounding digestive cells and secrete peptides (small proteins) immunologically similar to pancreatic hormones.

Glenn Wiggins of the Royal Ontario Museum told a symposium on systematics that only a fraction of insect and arachnid species, which vastly outnumber all other living animals combined, had yet been described. But because they permeate terrestrial biological systems, progress in identifying them—and the roles they play—was crucial to the management of renewable natural resources and to the maintenance of the long-term ecological stability of the world, now threatened as never before by the effect of the human species.

Ophrys orchids mimic the females of certain bees in both appearance and smell and are pollinated during attempts of the male bee to copulate with the lip of the flower. Hannes Paulus and Claudia Gack of Albert-Ludwig University, Freiburg, West Germany, found that the males soon learn to ignore any one group of flowers, but because no two blooms are exactly alike in appearance or bouquet, the bees continue to visit new flowers and thus ensure cross-pollination.

Males of a coccinellid (ladybird) beetle, *Illeis galbula,* seek out and guard the pupae of females for as long as five days before emergence, a behaviour unique among insects, according to Aola Richards of the University of New South Wales in Australia. Fierce fighting between the guard male and other males often follows emergence, with the guard having a 70% chance of winning and copulating with the female. Copulation lasts about 90 minutes, which is long enough for the female to become nonreceptive to other males thereafter, although midcopulation takeovers may occur.

Another example of male aggression among beetles was reported by K. Peschke of Bayerische-Julius-Maximilians

These *Ophrys* orchids mimic the females of certain bees in appearance and smell, thus encouraging males of the species to attempt mating and so pollinate the plant.

University, Würzburg, West Germany. The staphylinid (rove beetle) *Aleochara curtula,* when responding to the sex pheromone of the female, can ward off attacks by other males by producing small quantities of the female scent himself. This strategy, however, makes the male less attractive to the female, and a trade-off between avoidance of competition and reduced acceptance in courtship determines the amount of female pheromone produced by the male.

Although insects are known to inhabit an extraordinarily wide range of terrestrial habitats, one of the most extreme was reported by Shiro Kohshima of Kyoto (Japan) University. A newly discovered chironomid midge (a species of *Diamesa*) was found feeding on blue-green algae and bacteria in the undersnow meltwater of Himalayan glacier ice. The adults had reduced antennae and wings, and females made Sun-compass upstream migrations by walking on the snow surface, counteracting downstream flow of eggs and larvae.

H. Sittertz-Bhatkar of CSAT, Tabasco, Mexico, and associates reported an unexpected entomological consequence of the eruption of the volcano El Chichón in Mexico in 1982. The fine alkaline ash, composed mostly of silica and aluminum oxide, abraded the integument (outer covering) of insects in the region, causing severe water loss. Penetration of intersegmental membranes and ingestion of ash during cleaning also may have contributed to the death of a large number of hard- and soft-bodied insects. Honeybees appeared particularly susceptible.   (PETER W. MILES)

This article updates the *Macropædia* article INSECTS.

Ornithology. That all crows originated from an Australian songbird that colonized Asia 35 million years ago was just one conclusion of an ambitious reclassification of the world's birds, using the methods of molecular biology. Charles Sibley and Jon Ahlquist of Yale University had spent the past nine years comparing genetic material, DNA, from about 1,000 bird species (more than 10% of the world's total). The work revealed many evolutionary relationships that had been confused or concealed by traditional taxonomy based on physical structure and behaviour. The intent of the project was to measure the true "genetic distance" between species and thence to draw an evolutionary tree showing when they diverged from common ancestors. The anatomical and behavioural characters used by traditional taxonomists are often misleading, because unrelated species living in similar environments may develop similar features.

Sibley and Ahlquist showed that most Australian songbirds have a common ancestry, like the marsupials. That relationship was not previously recognized because they share no distinctive feature like the marsupial pouch, so taxonomists often placed Australian birds in the corresponding European families. In fact, Australian nuthatches, warblers, flycatchers, thrushes, and wrens are related to each other rather than to their European look-alikes. The DNA studies also indicated that a few groups of birds now found elsewhere in the world, such as the crows, originated in Australia.

The Yale biologists used a tool called DNA–DNA hybridization. They heated DNA, extracted from the birds' cells, to separate its two intertwined strands. Single strands from two different species were then induced to recombine to give a hybrid double strand. Differences between the sequences of the nucelotide building blocks in the different strands weakened the bond between them. Consequently, when heated, the hybrid molecule dissociated at a lower temperature than pure double-stranded DNA from either species. Sibley and Ahlquist used that temperature difference to measure the genetic distance between the two

A burrowing owl, an inhabitant of California, stands guard outside its nest, a former ground squirrel burrow. When threatened, it produces a hissing sound like the rattle of a rattlesnake—which often occupies similar quarters.

S. L. CRAIG—BRUCE COLEMAN, INC.

species, which could be translated approximately into the span of time in which the genetic material of the two species had gone their separate evolutionary ways after diverging from a common ancestor. The Yale work, it was said, "represents the most ambitious and fundamental effort to date to revolutionize taxonomy by using methods of molecular biology." When the calibration between temperatures of dissociation and absolute dates becomes more confident, Sibley and Ahlquist might provide the first evolutionary tree with dated branching points for all existing families of an entire class of vertebrates, the birds.

An Arctic tern, a swallow-shaped seabird, that was banded in England was found less than four months later in Australia, 17,500 km (10,800 mi) away. Arctic terns are full migrants; *i.e.,* all the birds travel south in the fall. In certain other species only some move out. European blackbirds, for example, are among these "partial migrants." When the days grow shorter, some blackbirds in southern Germany move to southern France, Spain, or North Africa, whereas others face the winter in their regular breeding grounds. Herbert Biebach of West Germany's Max Planck Institute for Behavioural Physiology in Seewiesen investigated how the stay-at-homes survive and the advantages and disadvantages of their choice. Biebach found that the birds had to deal with two threats: cold and a low food supply. Experiments in a climate-controlled chamber showed that the birds cope with cold and declining fat reserves by reducing their energy demand, particularly by lowering their body temperature at night from a normal 41° C (106° F) to 39° C (102° F). In addition, they improve their insulation by fluffing up their feathers until at extremely cold temperatures they become downy balls. Fluffing increases the thickness, and thus the effectiveness, of the insulation, and it reduces the ratio of surface area to volume as the birds become more spherical in shape. Furthermore, the feathery ball provides shelter for the poorly insulated beak, head, and legs.

Taken together, these conservation measures allow European blackbirds to survive at −30° C (−22° F) and below and to maintain normal working temperature during the day as long as they can find enough food to keep up adequate fat reserves. "The critical factor for the birds," reported Biebach, "is less the conservation of heat than the production of heat, which has to be about five times as high at −30° than at +20°. Or, to put it another way: The real threat is not freezing, but starving." Despite the costs, nonmigration has its benefits, at least in mild winters. Stay-at-homes stake out their territories before the migrators return and thus get the advantage in mating and nesting. On the other hand, migrators come out on top after severe winters. This two-option life-style, with its division of risk, raises the species' chances of survival.

In California, burrowing owls nest and roost in ground squirrel burrows, a refuge frequently used by rattlesnakes. When threatened, burrowing owls produce a vocal hiss very similar to a rattlesnake's rattle. It may be that the similarity is coincidental; that it is due to convergent evolution, *i.e.*, the particular sound happens to be best for both animals; or that natural selection has caused owls to copy rattlesnakes as a form of protective mimicry. Experiments suggested that the last explanation was true—that burrowing owls hiss like rattlesnakes to deter would-be intruders.

(JEFFERY BOSWALL)

This articles updates the *Macropædia* article BIRDS.

MARINE BIOLOGY

A five-year cruise program in tropical and subtropical Pacific waters clearly indicated the existence of assemblages of mesopelagic fish (fish living at oceanic mid-depths) associated with large circular currents called gyres, with subgroups of fish often restricted to specific gyres. The kinds of fish found in gyres showed low productivity and differed markedly from high-productivity assemblages along the Equator. A voyage from Fiji to the Bay of Biscay revealed considerable regional differences in the distribution of neuston, minute organisms living at the very surface of the ocean. Permanent neuston were most numerous in open tropical waters, whereas temporary neuston consisting of juveniles and migrants from deeper plankton occurred in upwelling and coastal areas.

A question relating to commercially exploitable Antarctic krill (*Euphausia superba*) concerned the whereabouts of their developmental stages. From measured sinking rates of newly shed eggs, it was predicted that they should hatch at a depth of 850 m (2,800 ft). The mesopelagic zone of the ocean (200–1,000 m, or 650–3,300 ft) is often characterized as being food-poor, but observations from a new one-person submersible off California repeatedly encountered very dense aggregations of copepod crustaceans (as high as 26 million per cubic metre). The copepods, being eaten by sea smelt (*Leuroglossus*), were quiescent and probably in diapause (enforced dormancy), associated with times of no upwelling and food scarcity in surface waters.

Benthic (bottom-living) consumers of zooplankton may feed on open-water plankton, but evidence was growing for their dependency on the larvae or adults of benthic invertebrates; this proved to be the case for tropical reef corals and for New England temperate-water soft corals and anemones. The behaviour of feather stars, stalkless crinoid invertebrates that feed by trapping plankton in their feathery arms, was recorded by time-lapse photography on Australia's Great Barrier Reef over one month in 1983; their postures were seen to change according to current but not to light. Studies off Hong Kong demonstrated a high diversity of species in a subtropical locality having marked seasonal and salinity changes. These and other studies questioned the stability-time hypothesis, which states that species diversify most in environmentally stable habitats of the deep ocean and shallow tropical seas and least in

unstable habitats such as estuaries. Most food webs that have been constructed for coastal sea-grass systems, which are often nursery grounds for commercially fished crustaceans, have stressed the importance of fish predators but not birds. Australian studies showed intense predation of shrimps by wading birds such as spoonbills.

On Nova Scotia coasts there are two forms of eelgrass (*Zostera marina*), a subtidal perennial form and an annual form in shallower water. Study of the life history of the annual form revealed its adaptations in combating the effects of winter ice: it has small investment in below-ground parts and high reproductive effort, and it overwinters as seeds. Settlement and attachment of the planktonic larvae of Pacific red abalone (*Haliotis rufescens*) are normally induced by contact with molecules deriving from crustose red algae. The algal metabolite mimics the action of gamma-aminobutyric acid (GABA). Other potent inducers of settlement were found in blue-green algae, the large-scale culture of which may permit development of techniques to induce settlement of mollusks of importance in fisheries. Many marine coelenterates and mollusks possess symbiotic photosynthetic dinoflagellates called zooxanthellae. Continuity of the symbiosis is ensured by parental transfer of zooanthellae to offspring, either by random contact or by chemical attraction between symbiont and host. Yet another possible method of transfer was recently demonstrated whereby zooxanthellae were eaten by an "intermediate host" (under experimental conditions, *Artemia,* or brine shrimp), which was itself consumed by the final host.

The Antarctic limpet *Nacella concinna* was shown to form unique "stacks" of up to eight males and females at times of spawning, presumably to increase the chances of successful fertilization. New data over the years 1843–1982 from mission records in Samoa permitted a more detailed description than hitherto of the annual spawning of palolo worms. These segmented marine worms exhibit unique breeding behaviour by breaking in half, whereupon their tail sections swim to the surface to release eggs and sperm. According to the records, they spawn between October 8 and November 23, within a day or two of the third quarter of the Moon. Spawning occurs once or twice during the six-week period, depending on the relative timing of lunar and solar cycles, which coincide on the 19-year Metonic cy-

JEFF SIMON—BRUCE COLEMAN, INC.

Shortly after hatching, this sea turtle will head out to sea. The females may return to nest some 15 to 30 years later, guided perhaps—as new research indicates—by olfactory imprinting that allows them to recognize home waters.

cle. Semilunar reproduction of the intertidal midge *Clunio* was shown to be cued by combined cycles of temperature and light in addition to tidal agitation and moonlight. Similar cues were implicated in a newly described semilunar cycle of growth of otoliths (mineral crystals making up part of a balance organ of the ear) in the flounder *Platichthys stellatus*.

Following similar studies on coral reef fishes, a temperate-water fish species *Coryphopterus* on the U.S. Pacific coast was shown to defend territory during both reproductive and nonreproductive periods. Territoriality and social dominance ranks impose a well-defined social structure.

Antifouling treatments often involve toxic paints, gases, electric currents, and ultrasonic waves, many of which may cause other deleterious effects. A more benign method, successfully tested on barnacles, involved the use of low-frequency (30-Hz) sound. As barnacle cyprid larvae explore for suitable settlement sites, they temporarily attach by means of the antennules. Studies in the U.K. showed that this attachment is not by suction but by the secretion of a proteinaceous adhesive substance by the antennules. "Footprints" of this material might possibly serve as the chemical stimulus mediating gregarious settlement among barnacles. (ERNEST NAYLOR)

This article updates the *Macropædia* articles CRUSTACEANS; FISHES; MOLLUSKS; etc.

BOTANY

It has been recognized for some time that plants can be immunized against diseases caused by viruses, bacteria, and fungi. Within the past several years numerous studies have indicated that plants can also be induced to resist insect attack and that such resistances are systemically mediated. Although several systemic wound signals in plants have been identified and studied, virtually nothing is known about the events that occur at the cellular or molecular levels.

It recently was shown that four hours after wounding (crushing with a hemostat) the lower leaves of potato and tomato plants, the yields of protoplast—the contents of the cell exclusive of the cell wall—from unwounded upper leaves dropped 25% below yields from leaves of uninjured plants (controls); eight to ten hours after wounding, the yields dropped to less than half those of the controls. Protoplast yields were decreased even further after multiple woundings, and a striking decrease in protoplast yields from unwounded leaves also occurred when the lower leaves were injured (chewed) by tobacco hornworms. These dramatic decreases were ascribed to protoplast lysis (dissolution), which could possibly be occasioned by a systemic signal, released by wounding, that weakens the cytoplasmic membrane holding the cell contents together. By eliciting changes in the properties of plant cells, the signal could play a role in mobilizing the defenses of the plant against insect attack.

Calcium is known to regulate many biochemical processes in animal cells. It does so by first binding to and activating the protein calmodulin, an apparently ubiquitous molecule in eukaryotic cells (cells containing a membrane-bound nucleus). Calmodulin then activates an enzyme, a protein kinase, that phosphorylates (adds phosphate groups to) other enzymes or proteins. Although calcium has been thought to play a role in various physiological processes in plants—*e.g.,* geotropism (orientation to gravity), abscission (leaf fall), and cyclosis (streaming of cellular protoplasm)—its mode of action has not been elucidated. In a study conducted during the year it was shown that the phosphorylation of several soluble and membrane-bound proteins isolated from the coleoptiles (leaf sheaths) of maize (Indian corn) was markedly increased in the presence of calcium, whereas the presence of a calmodulin inhibitor, chlorpromazine, resulted in a pronounced reduction in calcium-promoted phosphorylation. Thus, in the experimental system, protein phosphorylation was modulated by calcium and calmodulin, suggesting that calcium may regulate certain physiological processes in maize, and indeed in all plants, in the same way.

Maize (*Zea mays* subspecies *mays*), the most important cereal crop of the Western Hemisphere, consists of a single stalk supporting a terminal tassel or male inflorescence (a flower-bearing system of branches) and several ears or female inflorescences that, following fertilization, bear many rows of soft, exposed kernels.

For the past century a controversy has existed among botanists as to the origin of maize. Some have argued that modern maize arose from a now extinct wild maize, whereas others have contended that its progenitor was the wild grass teosinte and that the ear of maize evolved from the female inflorescence of teosinte.

The several-stalked teosinte, like maize, bears separate male and female inflorescences. The male inflorescences resemble those of maize and occur at the tips of the stalks. The female inflorescences, however, unlike those of maize, bear at maturity only two rows of kernels enclosed in hard fruit cases. The striking differences between the female inflorescences of teosinte and of maize have made it difficult to accept the female inflorescence of teosinte as the progenitor of the maize ear.

During the year a new theory emerged for the origin of the maize ear. According to the catastrophic sexual transmutation theory, enunciated by Hugh H. Iltis of the University of Wisconsin at Madison, the maize ear arose when, as a consequence of hormonal changes triggered by abnormal environmental conditions or viral or fungal infection, a branch of the teosinte tassel suddenly became feminized. Thereafter, selection brought about by agricultural cultivation played a major role in the evolution of maize. Although Iltis felt that sexual transmutation can probably be induced under controlled laboratory conditions, until such could be demonstrated, the ancestry of corn appeared destined to remain shrouded in mystery and controversy. (LIVIJA KENT)

MOLECULAR BIOLOGY

Cell-to-Cell Communication and Cancer. A giant step in the evolution of higher life was that from single, free-living cells to multicellular organisms, for it opened the way to development of the incredibly rich variety of living things that now inhabit virtually the entire surface of the Earth. Whereas free-living cells need only interact with their environment, the component cells of an animal or plant need to interact with each other. The free-living cell is a generalist independently concerned with, and able to accomplish, only those actions that further its own survival, growth, and multiplication. In contrast, the cells of an animal or plant are specialists, each type performing distinct functions so that the aggregate may survive, grow, and multiply. This specialization implies both communication among the constituent cells and rigid controls upon their metabolism, multiplication, and other functions.

New information about the means by which cells communicate and influence each other's actions has grown at a dizzying pace. There have been two broad fronts in this spectacular advance. One deals with the chemical messengers that carry the signals and the other with the receptors on cells that bind the messenger molecules and then intitate the chain of events that constitutes the appropriate response. An examination of a single action of the hormone epinephrine will make these generalizations more concrete.

When an animal faces an emergency calling for flight or for fight, the brain signals the adrenal glands, which respond by releasing epinephrine. This molecule is carried by the bloodstream to the liver, where it binds to specific receptor proteins on the outer surface of the liver cells. Occupancy of these receptors by epinephrine causes them to combine, via a coupling protein, with the membrane-associated enzyme adenylcyclase. This enzyme then catalyzes the production of 3,5-cyclic adenylic acid, abbreviated CAMP, on the inside surface of the cell membrane. The CAMP diffuses to and activates another enzyme called a protein kinase, which catalyzes the phosphorylation (addition of phosphate groups to) and consequent activation of still another enzyme called phosphorylase kinase. This enzyme in turn catalyzes the phosphorylation and activation of the enzyme that finally breaks down glycogen to glucose in the liver cell, so that glucose will be available to fuel the muscle cells that must carry out the flight or fight orders.

Why are there so many steps in the cascade of events between the binding of epinephrine to the cell-surface receptor and the release of glucose from the cell? One reason is that the amplification provided by the catalytic nature of each step is multiplied by that of each other step, resulting in an enormous overall amplification. Thus, for each epinephrine molecule bound, many millions of glucose molecules will be released.

Early attempts to apply the methods of microbiology to the study of mammalian cells revealed that such cells, unlike independent bacteria, would not grow in chemically defined media but depended upon the presence of very complex biological fluids, such as blood serum. Attempts were made, almost from the outset, to discover the chemical messengers in blood serum that were responsible for stimulating the growth of mammalian cells in culture. Success in this endeavour was slow in coming for several reasons, but years of dedicated efforts aided by fortunate happenstances finally led to the isolation and characterization of a number of growth factors.

All of the growth factors studied as of 1984 have proved to be polypeptides, *i.e.,* short protein molecules made up of amino acids linked together by peptide bonds, and all are effective at very low concentrations. One growth factor isolated from blood serum is released into the serum by blood platelets and is therefore called platelet derived growth factor, or PDGF. It is a chain of approximately 120 amino acids that stimulates cell growth and division. It is effective at the level of 0.001 microgram (0.03 trillionths of an ounce) per millilitre.

Cells that have been transformed into cancer cells show unrestrained growth and a markedly diminished need for the growth factors provided by blood serum. This observation raised the possibility that transformed cells might produce their own growth factors. In fact, cells transformed by the virus SV40 do produce at least one peptide growth factor. This reasoning in turn suggests that overproduction of such growth factors, or a change in the number of responsiveness of the receptors, may be an important cause of cancer.

Viruses that cause cells to become cancerous do so by introducing specific genes, called oncogenes, into the cells. Recently it was shown that the polypeptide coded for by the viral oncogene $p28^{v-sis}$ is nearly identical to PDGF. Other oncogenes are known to code for enzymes that catalyze the phosphorylation of proteins at a particular amino acid

called tyrosine. These enzymes are called tyrosine protein kinases. It cannot be a coincidence that the receptors for peptide growth factors that have been isolated to date possess tyrosine protein kinase activity. Both peptide growth factors and their receptors are thus clearly implicated in the etiology of cancer.

If cell-to-cell communication is mediated by chemical messengers, such as the peptide growth factors, many such factors should exist and should exhibit specificity for different target cells. By late 1984 nearly three dozen peptide growth factors had been identified, and some of their names reflect the specificity with which they act. Epidermal growth factor, endothelial-cell growth factor, and nerve growth factor are examples of this nomenclature. Occasionally the same growth factor has been isolated from different sources and on the basis of different physiological effects. Human urine, for example, contains a substance that inhibits gastric acid secretion. It was named urogastrone and, when isolated, proved to be identical to epidermal growth factor.

In a few cases growth factors have been discovered because of effects caused in the living animal, rather than effects on cells in culture. For example, investigators found that injecting extracts of mouse submaxillary gland into newborn mice, which like kittens are born with their eyelids sealed shut, hastens the opening of the eyelids and the eruption of teeth. Isolation of the active component of the submaxillary glands yielded the epidermal growth factor. Again, transplantation of a type of cancerous tissue into a chick embryo was seen to stimulate nerve growth; the submaxillary glands of male mice were found to be a rich source of this nerve growth factor, which was then isolated. Subsequently, tiny amounts of nerve growth factor, added to the culture medium, stimulated rapid growth of nerve cells in culture.

Peptide growth factors might well play a crucial role in the developing animal. During development of the nervous system, for example, nerves grow out from the central nervous system to the tissues to be innervated. Specific nerves must grow to and connect with specific target tissues, be they endocrine glands, muscles, or eyes. What guides the growth of the nerve fibres to the target tissues? The response of nerve cells in culture to nerve growth factor provides a clue: nerve fibres grow up a concentration gradient of nerve growth factor. From this observation it is possible to imagine target tissues secreting specific nerve growth factors whose concentration gradients attract the ingrowth of nerves from particular parts of the developing central nervous system.

Receptors, which bind peptide growth factors with great specificity and affinity, are found on the surface of responsive cells. The isolation of some of them is an accomplishment at least as impressive as the isolation of the growth factors themselves. The receptors isolated thus far are all intrinsic membrane glycoproteins (proteins combined with sugar molecules) that exhibit a tyrosine protein kinase activity. As already noted above, phosphorylation of enzymes through the action of protein kinase is one way to modify their catalytic activity. It appears likely that peptide growth factors, in binding to their cell surface receptors, activate the tyrosine protein kinase activity associated with those receptors. This event, in turn, leads to phosphorylation of, and modification of, the activities of other enzymes, which ultimately control the metabolism and growth of the cell.

Studies of peptide growth factors and of their receptors have opened a new window on the complexity of the events that control the growth, division, and differentiation of cells. It seems reasonable that further research will lead to an understanding of why some animals can regrow lost appendages and why certain cells escape from normal controls on their growth and become cancerous.

(IRWIN FRIDOVICH)

Are All Enzymes Proteins? The metabolism of any living cell depends upon thousands of concurrent chemical reactions, each of which must proceed easily and at a carefully controlled rate. Yet the vast majority of these reactions would not occur to any measurable degree were it not for the presence of catalysts to accelerate them, without the catalysts being consumed in the process. Moreover, these catalysts are specific, each accelerating a single reaction, and they are subject to control by the actions of activators or inhibitors or by certain chemical modifications so that the reactions catalyzed can be modulated to meet the changing needs of the cell as it goes through growth and differentiation and adapts to changing environmental conditions.

The catalysts that meet these specifications are called enzymes and, until recently, all that had been purified and studied had proved to be proteins. Indeed, for the past 50 years the statement "All enzymes are proteins" has been one of the basic tenets of biochemistry. Proteins are made by joining amino acids end-to-end in linear arrays, which can then fold into compact, almost globular, structures. The properties of the completed protein depend upon the sequence of amino acids in the linear chain, much as the meaning of a word depends upon the sequence of letters in it.

As many as 20 different amino acids are used in proteins, and most chains are usually between 100 and 1,000 amino acids long. This set of choices obviously allows for a tremendous variety of protein structures; *e.g.*, given 20 different amino acids one can construct 20^{100} different sequences that are 100 amino acids long. Biochemists have long felt that only proteins could provide the chemical diversity needed by enzymes.

Nevertheless, work during the past few years suggests that there are exceptions and, in particular, that some enzymes may be composed of ribonucleic acid (RNA). Like proteins, RNA is made up by joining building blocks—in this case, nucleotides—into linear arrays. Also like proteins, the properties of the final molecule depend upon the linear sequence of the building blocks and upon the chain length. Although RNA comprises only four different kinds of nucleotides and thus offers fewer possibilities for diversity than proteins, 4^{100} different sequences for an RNA molecule only 100 nucleotides long is still a very large number.

In the early 1980s Thomas Cech and his colleagues at the University of Colorado were investigating how a ciliated protozoan, *Tetrahymena,* makes its 26S ribosomal RNA (rRNA). This particular RNA is found in a subcellular organelle called the ribosome, and it functions in the biosynthesis of proteins. The 26S rRNA of *Tetrahymena* is a chain containing about 2,800 nucleotides, but it is first made in the cell as a precursor molecule about 3,200 nucleotides in length.

The 400 extra nucleotides of the precursor are found linked together near the centre of the molecule. Such chains are often found in large RNA molecules and are called intervening sequences, or introns. Conversion of the precursor to the mature RNA involves clipping out the intervening sequence and rejoining the ends of the remaining sequences. This process, referred to as RNA splicing, must be carried out with such precision that only the intervening sequence is removed.

The investigators anticipated that the cell used at least two different kinds of enzymes to accomplish the splicing reaction: one or more to recognize and cut the intervening sequence out of the RNA molecule and another to rejoin, or ligate, the two remaining pieces. But in late 1982 Cech and his colleagues found to their surprise that the precursor molecule, dissolved in a suitable salt solution and in the presence of a specific nucleotide, was converted to the mature form in the absence of enzymes. In essence, it spliced itself. Apparently the precursor molecule folded so as to facilitate the spontaneous removal of the intervening sequence and the rejoining of cut ends.

Can this self-splicing precursor of 26S rRNA be considered an enzyme? Certainly it performed functions on itself that would otherwise have required enzymes. Unlike the catalytic enzymes, however, it acted only once because during the process of self-splicing it altered its own structure so that it could not again facilitate the same process. Because it exhibits only some of the properties of enzymes, the self-splicing rRNA has been called a ribozyme.

A little more than a year after this discovery, Sidney Altman at Yale University, Norman Pace at the National Jewish Hospital in Denver, Colo., and their associates reported finding RNA that does behave like an enzyme. They were studying transfer RNA's in the common bacteria *Escherichia coli* and *Bacillus subtilis.* Transfer RNA's (tRNA's) are small molecules, only 75 nucleotides long, that are essential for protein biosynthesis, serving to carry amino acids to the growing end of the protein strand. They are first synthesized as precursor molecules with extra nucleotides at both ends. Their conversion into the mature tRNA form requires removal of these nucleotides, and a number of enzymes have been shown to cause this trimming reaction.

One of these enzymes, ribonuclease P, cleaves off the supernumerary nucleotides at one end of the precursor tRNA. When finally purified, it was found to be made up of both a protein subunit and an RNA subunit. Prior experience with enzymes made it reasonable to assume that the catalytic activity resided in the protein subunit, but careful study demonstrated that catalysis was the function of the RNA subunit.

Observation of catalytic RNA in ribonuclease P was expected to spur the search for other cases. Promising candidates include peptidyl transferase, which catalyzes the formation of the peptide bond at the growing end of a protein strand during its biosynthesis; it contains both RNA and protein subunits. The 1,4-*a*-glucan branching enzyme, which is essential in the synthesis of certain branched polysaccharides, is likewise a protein-RNA complex.

The finding that RNA can exert catalytic action also casts a new light on the early stages of biological evolution. In present-day organisms, DNA directs the synthesis of RNA, which directs the synthesis of proteins. In turn, some of these proteins are the very enzymes needed to catalyze the replication and repair of DNA. A beautiful self-perpetuating circular process, this system is also a classic chicken-and-egg problem for scientists trying to understand its origin. Which came first, nucleic acids or protein, and how did it all get started? The existence of DNA or RNA possessing intrinsic enzymic activity could eventually provide a way out of this conceptual impasse.

(ROBERT E. WEBSTER)

See also Earth Sciences; Environment.

This article updates the *Macropædia* articles Animal Behaviour; Biochemical Components of Organisms; The Biological Sciences; Cancer; Ecosystems; Endocrine Systems; The Principles of Genetics and Heredity; Biological Growth and Development; Organs and Organ Systems; Reproduction and Reproductive Systems.

Literature

The 1984 Nobel Prize for Literature was awarded to Jaroslav Seifert, an 83-year-old poet from Czechoslovakia. (*See* No-bel Prizes; *Eastern European Literature,* below.) This sur-prised the literary world of London, where other candidates for the prize had been predicted as the winner. The British Broadcasting Corporation, for instance, had prepared ra-dio programs in honour of the Nigerian playwright Wole Soyinka (for his 50th birthday) and the British novelist Graham Greene (for his 80th). However, Seifert was not un-known, and his success was especially welcomed by the *Lon-don Magazine,* which had published a book of Seifert's verse under the notably British title *Umbrella from Piccadilly.*

In France the Prix Goncourt was awarded to the 70-year-old Marguerite Duras, best known as a playwright. Born in French Indochina, Duras had long been concerned with relationships between Europeans and Asians. This was apparent in her film *Hiroshima mon amour* (1959). Her prizewinning novel, *L'Amant,* offered a similar theme, with its account of a love affair between a French girl (poor, but privileged in the colonial world) and a Chinese man (wealthy, but a member of the subject race) in the Indochina of the 1920s.

African book fairs were held in Nigeria and Zimbabwe, with intense discussion both of education and of commer-cial problems—low incomes, the poor infrastructure, and the lack of foreign exchange. The Nigerian gathering, the Ife Book Fair, almost coincided with the "New Writing in Africa" conference in London, also in November. The result was that the London conference, at the Common-wealth Institute, was not dominated by West Africans but offered scope to East Africans, notably Ngugi wa Thiong'o of Kenya.

A remarkable festival for Arab writers was held in war-torn Iraq. The Festival of Poetry and Youth brought many authoritative Arab poets to Baghdad, some of them eager to support the secular state of Iraq against the Muslim fundamentalists of Iran, others concerned with inspecting and examining conditions in Iraq and reporting back to their own peoples—in Egypt or Bahrain, Mauritania or Saudi Arabia. Pres. Saddam Hussein at-Takriti of Iraq wel-comed the poets, asking: "How can a nation at war hold a festival of poetry? In Baghdad we have the singing-birds, while in Tehran the ravens croak."

AP/WIDE WORLD

Jaroslav Seifert

ENGLISH

United Kingdom. Political tension and conflicting dogmas affected literary production in the U.K. in two ways: there was a spirit of helpless anger in much imaginative work, and there was also a desire to play safe, to promote what was known to be "accessible" and popular. "Accessibility" became even more of a vogue word. The government's apparent reverence for market forces alarmed many read-ers and writers. The threat to impose new taxes on books and journals was especially disturbing; it seemed that in the world of literature, as well as the spheres of education, theatre, and productive industry, "uneconomic" had be-come the new word for bad and "profitable" the new word for good.

However, one of the government's most ardent literary supporters, Paul Johnson, praised the book industry for "taking advantage of the depression" to increase profits. Publishers (he wrote in the *Spectator*) had "taken advantage of the depression to trim staffs, introduce labour-saving machinery, eliminate much trade-union nonsense . . . and, above all, adopt modern, scientifically-based methods of doing business." He was pleased to see that British pub-lishers had turned out 38,980 new books in 1983, up from 24,654 in 1972, and that fiction, good or bad, represented almost 50% of the total. There were, however, far fewer new books about science produced by this scientifically based industry, and there was a comparable drop in the sale of poetry—"not surprisingly," commented Johnson, "since the great majority of poets write verse which people cannot be bothered to puzzle out."

Other writers found the economic climate less cheering. Marina Warner complained in *The Sunday Times* that the literary department of the Arts Council had had its government grant almost cut in half, on the grounds that literature was "sustained by a large and profitable com-mercial publishing industry." She held that this was like claiming that opera need not be subsidized because there was a large and profitable popular music industry, and she asserted that London publishers were always inducing writers to produce worthless but profitable "potted histo-ries and captions to Victorian family albums." The book industry, however, expressed self-assurance in its judgment of literary merit. The Book Marketing Council set up a committee to nominate "the 12 best novels of our time." The result of their deliberations enraged the prolific and well-read novelist Anthony Burgess, who speedily brought out a critical book listing the best 99 English-language novels since 1939. Burgess's successful study, *Ninety-Nine Novels: The Best in. English Since 1939—A Personal Choice,* led readers and writers to consider the idea that a "personal choice" might be better than a committee choice when literary prizes were being offered.

A new committee was formed to award the valuable new Betty Trask Prize for young authors "on the strength of a romantic novel (or other novel of a traditional rather than experimental nature)." One of the committee mem-bers, Margaret Forster, admitted that they could not agree what the late Miss Trask, the donor of the prize money, had meant by her stipulations. They began to use the word "trasky" to mean "readable, accessible, and moving," without foul language, and with nothing that was "sexually explicit." They also discovered that Miss Trask, herself a romantic novelist, had been a severe critic of the book industry.

Fiction. The committee that presented the Booker McConnell Prize for fiction was described by Salman Rushdie, a former prizewinner, as a group of Killjoyces and Anti-Prousts. The chairman, Richard Cobb, had announced that he had not read the works of James Joyce or Marcel Proust and that he did not want the prize to go to any novelist resembling those experimental writers. He would prefer the prizewinner to be a novel of appeal, an accessible, perhaps "trasky" novel. There were six novels on the final Booker list, and five of them were quietly competent stories about "the literary world."

The winner, *Hotel du Lac* by art historian Anita Brookner, was a story about a romantic novelist bruised by her unhappy life and by the selfishness of her fellow guests in a dismal Swiss hotel. Penelope Lively's *According to Mark* told of a literary man writing a biography of another literary man and falling in love with his subject's granddaughter. From India came Anita Desai's *In Custody,* concerning an accident-prone teacher of literature and his efforts to interview a wild old Urdu poet; this was an original and surprising book, about men rather comically honouring and congratulating one another while treating ambitious women dismissively. The witty scholar David Lodge offered in *Small World* a comedy about teachers of literature attending academic conferences. Julian Barnes, with *Flaubert's Parrot,* presented a provoking account of Gustave Flaubert's career as observed by a dull and incompetent literary biographer who unwittingly reveals the sorrows of his own life.

The only one of the six Booker contenders to keep the literary world out of his novel was J. G. Ballard, with *Empire of the Sun.* Best known for his ambitious science fiction, Ballard based his new novel on his experiences as a small boy imprisoned by the Japanese in Shanghai during World War II. He was criticized both for being too autobiographical and for allegedly distorting history, but he excited genuine interest outside the narrow literary world. Though Ballard did not win the Booker Prize, he received *The Guardian*'s fiction award.

The most defiant novel of the year was Kingsley Amis's *Stanley and the Women.* It won no prizes and could not find a U.S. publisher because it was held to be antifeminist. It concerned an apparently ordinary London businessman whose son had gone mad; his unhappiness was exacerbated by the behaviour of his wife, his ex-wife, and (worst of all) his son's female psychiatrist. The father's distrust of women was encouraged by a male psychiatrist and expressed in woundingly neat, cruelly sexist observations of women's behaviour. The book was chosen by several male writers as the novel of the year, with defiant comments. "Courageous (or audacious)," wrote Anthony Burgess. "Far too dangerous for the Booker prize," wrote Bernard Levin. "No wonder the Yanks won't publish it," wrote John Osborne.

A spirit of nervous anger was apparent in other novelists. William Golding, the 1983 Nobel Prize winner, wrote *The Paper Men,* a savagely sportive book about a much-honoured English novelist behaving brutally to a U.S. scholar studying his work. Kingsley Amis's son, Martin Amis, produced an unpleasant story called *Money* about a disgusting English film director in the U.S. being punished for his sins—but many readers enjoyed the younger Amis's command of language. More "accessible" was another splenet : novel, *Thinks,* by the versatile and prolific Keith Water-house. A genial, humorous journalist with a regular column in a popular newspaper, Waterhouse was already known for writing semicomic novels of frightening bitterness. The principal character in *Thinks* was a fairly disgusting executive in commercial radio on his way to a premature death, and his story was told entirely through his brutal and childish thoughts, like balloons in a cartoon strip, without quoting his more polite conversation.

Muriel Spark offered in *The Only Problem* the story of a man studying the Book of Job, meditating on God and human suffering in deliberate isolation but disturbed by silly people—his selfish wife and her terrorist friends, the police, and the press—until he began to feel like Job himself. This remarkable blend of religious thought and heartless-seeming sexual comedy was highly praised by Graham Greene. Anthony Burgess's three-part story, *Enderby's Dark Lady,* had similar characteristics but was more lighthearted. The main story was about the poet Enderby trying to produce a musical about Shakespeare in the U.S., but it was preceded by a brilliant historical yarn and followed by an eerie science fiction tale, both written about Shakespeare by the talented but ridiculous Enderby.

A more controversial but funny comedy about an Englishman in the U.S. was *Stars and Bars* by William Boyd, the tale of a shy Briton attempting to adapt to American customs and finding freedom, at last, through the anarchy of New York City and a Deep South menaced by gangsters. Beryl Bainbridge surprised admirers of her modern comedies with *Watson's Apology,* an almost historical novel

JERRY BAUER
Anita Brookner

about a Victorian middle-class murder. With *Morning Star* the prolific Simon Raven, having completed his addictive "Alms for Oblivion" novel series, made a good start on a new series with the biblical title "The First-Born of Egypt"; this series would concern the children of the characters in the former series, decadent and sinful Conservative gentlemen circling around their old Cambridge college.

Mr. Noon, a previously unpublished (and unfinished) autobiographical novel by D. H. Lawrence, was quietly welcomed. The death of the novelist, playwright, and essayist J. B. Priestley (*see* OBITUARIES) was quietly regretted; his books and plays were still so frequently read and performed that his long, productive life scarcely seemed at an end.

LETTERS, LIVES. Feelings of sorrow at the death of poet and critic Sir William Empson (*see* OBITUARIES) were tempered by reading his new book, *Using Biography,* which dealt combatively with such writers as Dryden, Fielding, Marvell, and Yeats. Provocative as ever, Empson's posthumous book annoyed younger, more conservative critics—for instance, the novelist and critic A. N. Wilson, who declared that the new book proved Empson to have been "a nasty and shallow old man." Wilson himself produced a biography of the poet, novelist, and essayist Hilaire Belloc. John Gross remarked: "Hilaire Belloc was an unpleasant man and at first sight A. N. Wilson might seem well suited to be his biographer. . . . Mr. Wilson, as readers of his novels will know, is something of a specialist when it comes to writing about squalid behaviour. . . . "

There were respectable biographies of such writers as Thomas Carlyle, Joseph Conrad, Edmund Gosse, Arthur

Ransome, and Leslie Stephen, but perhaps most attention was paid to Peter Ackroyd's achievement in publishing *T. S. Eliot*—without the support of the Eliot estate. The book began: "I am forbidden by the Eliot estate to quote from Eliot's published work, except for purposes of fair comment in a critical context, or to quote from Eliot's unpublished work or correspondence." Though this explanation was not crystal clear, readers gathered that Eliot's widow did not want Ackroyd's book to be regarded as an "authorized" biography.

Two remarkable new books blended biography and autobiography with information about nations remote from British experience. Graham Greene celebrated his 80th birthday with *Getting to Know the General: The Story of an Involvement,* an account of his friendly relationship with Omar Torrijos Herrera, the brigadier general of Panama's National Guard and the country's "strongman" for 13 years. The book added to the respect in which Greene was held for his understanding of foreign politics. Comparable with it was V. S. Naipaul's *Finding the Centre,* linking the author's early life in Trinidad with a recent visit to the Ivory Coast. Naipaul's two essays made use of the author's sense of self-exile and his severe observation of third world countries to provoke thought about the modern marriage of ancient magical ritual and new technology in the governments of the "underdeveloped" or "developing" world.

POETRY. The death of John Betjeman (*see* OBITUARIES) dismayed the British. Partly through television, he had become the most popular and "accessible" poet laureate ever appointed. Kingsley Amis wrote: "He leaves a great gap in the national life and sadness in many hearts, including those of thousands who never met him." He was consistent in the near-Victorian style with which he discussed modern life and its relationship with the past, often in a melancholy spirit, often with a mocking wit, often in a mood of celebration. No other poet was eager to succeed Betjeman as poet laureate; his was a difficult act to follow. Most readers wanted the more retiring Philip Larkin. He had produced at least one poem, "Cut Grass," worthy of musical setting and at least one occasional poem suitable for a laureate, his celebration of the new Humber Bridge. But as the laureate's crown drew nearer, Larkin's poetic output shrank. The eventual choice of Ted Hughes was unexpected and controversial—"like appointing a grim young crow to replace a cuddly old teddy bear," as Philip Howard wrote in *The Times*—although Hughes, at 54, was scarcely a youngster. His harsh depictions of the life-death struggle in the animal world seemed to many far removed from the celebration of royal and national events required of the poet laureate. Nevertheless, Hughes was highly esteemed and his reputation had grown steadily since his first collection, *The Hawk in the Rain* (1957).

In the meantime, Peter Levi became professor of poetry at the University of Oxford, defeating James Fenton, Frank Prince, Gavin Ewart, and the spirited Duncan McCann. Among the younger poets, Blake Morrison's *Dark Glasses* dealt with the idea of being a spy, with particular reference to the policeman who spied on Coleridge during his revolutionary period. Craig Raine and Andrew Motion took control of the poetry published by the firms Faber & Faber and Chatto & Windus, and both published poetry books of their own; Motion's was titled *Dangerous Play* and Raine's, *Rich* (almost echoing *Money,* the novel by his friend Martin Amis). The ever growing number of poetry presses and magazines outside London was noted by Mick Imlah in the *Times Literary Supplement,* and he added new evidence for the theory that more people in Britain wrote poetry than read it.   (D. A. N. JONES)

United States. FICTION. A notable feature of 1984 was fiction from major writers in minor forms. Examples included Saul Bellow's first collection of short stories since *Mosby's Memoirs* in 1968, a murder mystery from Norman Mailer, and a satirical gothic tale from John Updike. Most of the stories in *Him with His Foot in His Mouth* were vintage Bellow, exhibiting the rueful humour, the compassion, the cerebral play, the richly detailed Chicago settings, and the brilliant style that characterize his best fiction. Norman Mailer's *Tough Guys Don't Dance* was far less ambitious than his last venture into genre fiction, 1983's massive historical novel *Ancient Evenings,* but was not much more successful in dealing with the demands of its form. Despite an effectively moody setting and a great deal of violence, the book suffered from weak characterization and a byzantine, unconvincing solution. *The Witches of Eastwick,* John Updike's first novel since the widely praised *Rabbit Is Rich* in 1981, was a deft, ironic account of satanism let loose in a small Rhode Island town in the late 1960s that satirized, among other things, the feminism of that period.

Novels about Lincoln by Gore Vidal and King David by Joseph Heller revealed interesting contrasts in their treatment of cultural icons and in their response to the requirements of historical fiction. In *Lincoln* Vidal added an impressively researched fourth novel to the historical cycle that includes *Burr, 1876,* and *Washington, D.C.* Confining itself to the period of Lincoln's presidency, Vidal's portrait was predictably a long way from Carl Sandburg's hagiography but was also, despite a few bits of debunking, a long way from caricature. Minutely observing Lincoln through the eyes of some of his closest associates, the book skillfully showed their growing awareness of a complex nature that combined cunning and vision, patience and ruthlessness. *God Knows,* Heller's first novel since *Good as Gold* in 1979, was an eloquent, extravagant, blackly comic monologue in which David in old age reflects on the story of his life, which he, with the arrogance and astuteness of a great artist, asserts is "the best in the Bible." Historical research was less in evidence in Heller's novel than was persistent, farcical anachronism; thus David claims to have authored, not only the Psalms, but the *B-Minor Mass,* Mozart's *Requiem,* and Handel's *Messiah.* But his earthy, eccentric voice was as brilliant a creation as Vidal's meticulously documented Lincoln.

In his first novel since *A Good School* in 1978, Richard Yates remained sturdily in the realistic mainstream. Taking place between the end of World War II and the 1970s, *Young Hearts Crying* showed lives ravaged by an obsession not so much with the arts as with being an artist. The tragic impact of the same period on a West Virginia family was the subject of perhaps the most enthusiastically praised fiction of 1984, *Machine Dreams,* a first novel by Jayne Anne Phillips, who enhanced the reputation as one of the most gifted writers of her generation that was established in 1979 with her collection of short stories, *Black Tickets.* A minutely remembered, unreclaimable past was also brilliantly evoked in *At the Border,* a first novel by Robert Hemenway, whose fine collection of short stories, *The Girl Who Sang with the Beatles,* appeared in 1970.

Comic novels were not notably abundant during the year, but there were funny books from Alison Lurie and T. Coraghessan Boyle and an irritating one from Erica Jong. Lurie's seventh novel, *Foreign Affairs,* was a witty, beautifully constructed story of the ironically contrasting fortunes of two pairs of lovers—one graceful and the other awkward—that was somewhat marred by the intrusive presence of its author. The presence of its author totally overwhelmed Erica Jong's *Parachutes and Kisses,* her third novel to feature the heroine of her best-selling *Fear of Flying,* Isadora Wing, now turned 40 and more determinedly, if less amusingly, Rabelaisian than ever. Boyle's new novel exhibited the comic and narrative resourcefulness of his earlier books, *The Descent of Man* and *Water Music. Budding Prospects,* a wildly ironic fable about a failure who comes to terms with himself by failing spectacularly once again, this time in the dope business, showed Boyle a master of comic strategies, from gross slapstick to cerebral fantasy.

In her shrewd, skillful fourth novel, *Democracy,* Joan Didion employed her customary precise dialogue and enigmatic imagery to provide what she styled "fitful glimpses" of an affair and its aftermath, against a background of affluence and politics in various Pacific capitals. *Pitch Dark,* Renata Adler's first novel since *Speedboat* in 1976, was a lively but formless monologue by a woman trying to come to terms with a long-term but unsatisfying love affair. Employing the device made famous by Mary McCarthy in her novel *The Group,* Alice Adams's *Superior Women,* a study of the varying fortunes of five Radcliffe graduates, was well crafted but thin.

Continuing a recent trend in American literature, regional literature was strongly represented during 1984. Probably the most celebrated literary debut of the year was Padgett Powell's first novel, *Edisto.* It describes the richly comic impressions of Simons Manigault, an impossibly precocious 12-year-old who is coming of age in the New South; Powell demonstrated a shrewdness in observation and an eccentric inventiveness in the use of language that more than compensated for the implausibility of his narrator. An equally vivid but more credible young narrator was created by Ivan Doig in his beautifully crafted second novel, *English Creek.* Doig, whose brilliant, bittersweet memoir of growing up in Montana in the 1930s, *This House of Sky,* was nominated for a National Book Award in 1978, returned to that time and place in a lovingly detailed recollection of a memorable summer in the life of 14-year-old Jick McCaskill. The first book of fiction by Janet Kauffman marked the appearance of another impressive new regionalist. The 12 stories collected in *Places in the World a Woman Could Walk* exhibited a tough-minded compassion and lyrical realism in their depictions of rural life.

One of the most highly visible publishing phenomena of 1984 was the Elderly Novelist. Both the oldest and most ballyhooed of these was 88-year-old Helen Hooven Santmyer (*see* Biographies), author of the best-selling . . . *And Ladies of the Club,* a massive re-creation of small-town life in Ohio between 1868 and 1932. Originally conceived by its author as an answer to the satire of Sinclair Lewis's *Main Street,* Santmyer's novel (which took her 50 years to complete) combined soap-opera situations and an encyclopedic account of the details of daily life in its celebration of middle-class values. A more impressive, if less publicized, debut was that of 73-year-old Harriet Doerr, whose first novel, *Stones for Ibarra,* was a quiet, poetically rendered story of the experiences of an American couple living in a remote village in Mexico.

Among the year's best popular fiction was *The Businessman* by Thomas Disch, one of the most interesting science fiction writers to appear during the last two decades. Disch's novel was a funny, nasty piece of gothic slapstick that, among other things, casts the late John Berryman in the role of a reluctant, bibulous Virgil conducting a tour of the next world. From veteran science fiction writer Robert Heinlein, author of the cult classic *Stranger in a*

Saul Bellow

John Updike

Strange Land, came an interesting reworking of a biblical tale. *Job: A Comedy of Justice* employed an ingenious series of parallel universes to show a hero afflicted not with the loss of kin and goods but the loss of identity itself. Louis L'Amour, prolific author of best-selling Westerns, deserted his familiar genre in *The Walking Drum,* a generally successful novel set in 12th-century Europe that was as meticulously researched as his re-creations of frontier life. Irving Wallace's *The Miracle* combined his familiar best-selling formula of careful research and potboiling style in an interesting soap opera that takes place at the Shrine of the Blessed Virgin at Lourdes.

History, Biography, and Belles Lettres. In *The March of Folly: From Troy to Vietnam,* Pulitzer Prize-winning historian Barbara Tuchman examined "the pursuit of policy contrary to self-interest." Tuchman presented four cases in which, she asserted, such folly led to disaster: the Trojan Horse, the intransigence of the medieval popes in dealing with Protestant reformers and that of the ministers of George III in dealing with the American colonists, and U.S. involvement in Southeast Asia. Although Tuchman's book contained passages of brilliant narrative and polemic, it was weakened by the dissimilarity of her historical examples and the superficiality of her treatment. *Changes in the Land,* the first book by 30-year-old Yale historian William Cronon, won the 1984 Francis Parkman Prize. Subtitled *Indians, Colonists, and the Ecology of New England,* Cronon's book was a vivid, persuasive study of the environmental impact of successive groups of inhabitants in shaping the landscape of New England. *Andrew Jackson and the Course of American Democracy, 1833–1845* by Robert V. Remini completed the author's fine three-volume life of that president. Covering Jackson's second administration and active later years, Remini's biography was scholarly but frankly partisan, written in part, as the author acknowledged in his introduction, to counter the "general assault on Jackson and his works" in recent years. The second and final volume of another large-scale effort at rehabilitation, Stephen E. Ambrose's *Eisenhower,* dealt with the years from his first election as president until his death in 1969. Historian and political columnist Garry Wills brilliantly examined Washington's role as America's drabbest political icon. *Cincinnatus: George Washington and the Enlightenment* took a fresh look at "the way educated artists and propagandists shaped a deliberately didactic image of the nation's first great leader."

Studs Terkel added another outstanding oral history to the series that includes *Hard Times, Working,* and *Division Street: America.* His ironically titled *"The Good War": An Oral History of World War II* was a fascinating and often moving collection of interviews with an extraordinary variety of people, from one of the physicists who worked on the atomic bomb to one of the Andrews Sisters singing group. *The Nightmare Years: 1930–1940*, the second volume of *20th Century Journey: A Memoir of a Life and the Times* by celebrated foreign correspondent William L. Shirer, was a lively, opinionated account of his adventures as a reporter covering the rise of Hitler's Third Reich.

Alfred Kazin's *An American Procession* was a series of brilliant portraits of a number of major writers during what he considers the "crucial century" of American literature, the period between 1830 and 1930. Beginning with the oracular figure of Emerson and concluding with the modernism of John Dos Passos and F. Scott Fitzgerald, Kazin selected those writers he believed were the most significant contributors to the creation of a characteristically American literary voice. Emerson, the seminal literary figure whom Kazin, borrowing from Whitman, places at the head of "the American procession," was also the subject of an interesting, unconventional biography by John McAleer, whose *Ralph Waldo Emerson: Days of Encounter* abandoned strict chronology in favour of brief, vivid episodes. *Walt Whitman: The Making of an American Poet*, by the late Paul Zweig, was an admirably complete account of Whitman's development as a poet that was highlighted by splendid readings of some major poems. *Frost: A Literary Life Reconsidered*, a sympathetic biography by William H. Pritchard, was a partially successful effort to adjust the savagely harsh image of the poet created by Lawrance Thompson's official three-volume life.

Two excellent but very different studies of controversial anthropologist Margaret Mead appeared during the year. *With a Daughter's Eye* was a personal memoir of Mead and her husband, anthropologist Gregory Bateson, by their child, Mary Catherine Bateson. Jane Howard's *Margaret Mead* was an exhaustive record of Mead's life that collected accounts from some 300 informants. Another brilliant memoir of a famous parent was *Home Before Dark*, Susan Cheever's candid but loving portrait of her father, the late John Cheever, that discusses his struggles with alcoholism and homosexuality.

Harvard University Press had the first best-seller in its 71-year history in a slim memoir of her early life by Southern writer Eudora Welty. Originating in a series of three lectures given at Harvard in April 1983, *One Writer's Beginnings* beautifully evoked what Welty styled her "sheltered life" in Jackson, Miss., and how her early fiction grew out of it.

POETRY. Both *People Live Here*, Louis Simpson's selection of his poems written over the last 24 years, and a new collection, *The Best Hour of the Night*, amply demonstrated his versatility and growth as a poet. There was a bulky collection of the poems of the late Richard Hugo, who died in 1982, which included 22 new poems. *Making Certain It Goes On* exhibited both the sameness of much of Hugo's poetry and the strength of his last work. The poems in John Ashbery's new book, *A Wave*, were typically subtle and teasing, containing some of his best work since the Pulitzer Prize-winning *Self-Portrait in a Convex Mirror* in 1975. The year's choice for the Yale Series of Younger Poets, awarded annually to a first book of poetry, was *The Evolution of the Flightless Bird* by Richard Kenney.

(FITZGERALD HIGGINS)

Canada. For many authors 1984 was a year of significant changes in direction. One of the more radical departures, for example, was Matt Cohen's abandonment of southern Ontario for the vicious vicissitudes of 14th-century Spain. In *The Spanish Doctor*, a Jewish medical man finds the times difficult ones in which to survive, let alone prosper.

Timothy Findley made an even longer leap from the wars of the 20th-century to the disasters of prehistory in *Not Wanted on the Voyage*, his lyrically haunting evocation of Noah's trials during the Flood. In *Berlin Solstice*, Sylvia Fraser enters a country more tantalizingly and insanely bleak than any she had described before as she encounters the Germany of the Third Reich. Josef Skvorecky travels in the opposite direction in time and space, finally succeeding in crossing with and from the Old World to the New in his *The Engineer of Human Souls*—an experience that engenders a state of mind akin to a jazz fugue in which improvisation continuously re-creates reality. A sharp contrast in both content and style is Alexander Dewdney's *The Planiverse*, in which a computer scientist and his class encounter the life and mores of a two-dimensional planet.

Other writers remained in or returned to more familiar territory, among them Pauline Gedge in *The Twelfth Transforming*, a charming retelling of the story of the pharaoh Akhenaten. Audrey Thomas was equally at home in her *Intertidal Life*. Richard B. Wright's gentle satire *Tourists* explores that most traumatic of cultural shocks, being trapped with one's fellow tourists in an insufficiently foreign country. David Watmough returns with a former hero, Davey Bryant, in *Fury*. *Among Friends* is L. R. Wright's delicately compelling tale of three women struggling to make sense of their lives.

Short fiction is an endemic art form in Canada, and many new collections were on view. Included were Norman Levine's vintage collection *Champagne Barn* and Robin Skelton's first public venture into fiction, *The Man Who Sang in His Sleep*. In *The Elizabeth Stories*, Isabel Huggan uses the device of a series of interconnected stories to illuminate the coming of age of a large and unlovely girl in a small Ontario town. *In the Meantime*, Elizabeth Smart's latest, presents prose and poetry previously unpublished or long out of print. Andreas Schroeder coined the term micronovel for his *Toccata in "D,"* in which a boy's Canadian life and German heritage are cleverly counterpointed. Timothy Findley's *Dinner Along the Amazon*, set in a world where happiness always happens yesterday, transmutes an almost unbearable anguish into an endurable beauty. For baseball aficionados, W. P. Kinsella was back at home plate with *The Thrill of the Grass*, and for science fiction buffs, Spider Robinson's *Melancholy Elephants* included 14 sorties into the author's incredible imagination. In her first book of short stories, *The Promise*, Wanda Campbell conveys the struggle of women caught between the cultures of immigrant settlers and of the indigenous, and indigent, Indians and Métis.

Among poets, Ralph Gustafson led the way with three books ranging from the spontaneous (*Impromptus*) to the classical (*Manipulations on Greek Themes*) and beyond (*Directives of Autumn*). Raymond Souster's *Collected Poems: Volume 5* contained many old favourites, while his *Jubilee of Death* honoured the Canadian troops who fought at Dieppe. Penny Kemp produced *Animus* and *Binding Twine*. In *Piling Blood*, Al Purdy rampages from the early days of the planet to Winnipeg and small-town strip joints, laughing all the way, but in *Morning and It's Summer* he reflects more serenely on his themes.

Mary di Michele produced *Necessary Sugar*, and Roo Borson tells how it was *The Whole Night, Coming Home*—experiences in which she could have used the companionship of *The Bedside Book of Nightmares* by Suniti Namjoshi. An even more detached and ironic viewpoint is expressed in Margaret Atwood's tenth collection, *Interlunar*, which turns on the symbol of the invisible moon between the old and the new. Equally lunatic in her own idiosyncratic style is Catherine Ahearn's *Luna-Verse: Love Poems.* Dorothy Livesay celebrated her 75th year and love of life in *Feeling the Worlds,* while in *The Granny Poems* by sean o huigan, a 92-year-old woman reminisces about herself and her 52 descendants. James Reaney's *Imprecations* is an amused and amusing study of swearing. In *The Terracotta Army,* Gary Geddes tells how the first emperor of China ordered 8,000 clay men and horses to accompany him in the afterlife. David Helwig won the CBC's annual poetry competition with *Catchpenny Poems.* Collected works included the posthumously published *Collected Poems of Miriam Mandel,* winner of the 1973 governor-general's award for poetry, and *The Collected Poems of Sir Charles G. D. Roberts,* sometimes called the father of Canadian poetry. (ELIZABETH WOODS)

Josef Skvorecky　　　　Jean Genet

FRENCH

France. The major literary prizes for 1984 were well deserved and reflected some significant features of contemporary literature. This was not always the case. The Goncourt and the Renaudot went to women, something that had not happened with the Goncourt since 1979, despite the important contribution of women writers to the novel in France, especially over the past two decades. Marguerite Duras's *L'Amant,* though it was the work of one of the most individual voices in modern fiction, was characteristic in that it was an autobiographical novel exploiting the borderline between fiction and reality. It told of the author's adolescence in Indochina and her love affair with a Chinese, leaving the reader to assess from personal experience how much we all fictionalize the past. The Renaudot winner, Annie Ernaux, also returned to her childhood in her novel *La Place,* though in the very different setting of a working-class family. It was a year for looking back and for reassessments.

The bicentenary of the death of Diderot provided the occasion for seminars and studies of this attractive figure of the Enlightenment, but since it was sandwiched between Stendhal (b. 1783) and Hugo (d. 1885), the anniversary was slightly overshadowed. Jean-Paul Sartre continued to attract attention and was one of the literary personalities remembered by Françoise Sagan in *Avec mon meilleur souvenir.* There was also a reassessment of the work of the novelist Roger Vailland, who died in 1965, with the publication of his journalistic writings and the memoirs of Elisabeth Vailland, *Drôle de vie,* recalling the life of a man who was both a political militant and a libertine.

Reviewing intellectual life since World War II, Jean-Paul Aron mounted a sustained attack on *Les Modernes,* while Michel Baglin (*Les Maux du poème*) considered the paradox of many poets and few readers. Gaston Gallimard, whose publishing house had played such a central role in the literature of the century, was the subject of a biography by Pierre Assouline. Former premier Raymond Barre published *Réflexion, pour demain,* and Edgar Faure and Michel Debré, two other political figures from earlier times, published volumes of memoirs. The Socialist regime of François Mitterrand was assessed in his biography by Catherine Nay (*Le Noir et le rouge*), and education, one of his major headaches during the year, was the subject of Hervé Hamon and Patrick Rotman's *Tant qu'il y aura des Profs.*

The historical novel seemed to be declining in popularity, though *Néropolis* by Hubert Monteilhet, portraying the conflict of Christians and Jews in the 1st century AD, aroused interest, partly because of the accusation that it was anti-Semitic. The most interesting recent excursions into the genre had, in any case, involved experimentation; this was taken to the limit by Pierre Guyotat, whose *Le Livre,* a historical fiction in reverse, was written without punctuation in a dialect that made it almost impenetrable, though the essays in *Vivre* helped to explain Guyotat's intentions, as well as exploring his preoccupation with erotic and pornographic themes. The continuing fashion for *le rétro,* evidenced in the popular albums of adult cartoon strips, could hardly be counted as history since it looked back to a past within living memory. Like Duras and Ernaux, several novelists evoked the world of their youth, notably Michel Déon (*Je vous écris d'Italie*) and Bernard-Henri Lévy, whose *Le Diable en tête* won the Prix Médicis. Claude Mauriac, in *Zabé,* cast doubt on the accuracy of his narrator's memory while leaving none about his nostalgia for Parisian low life in the 1930s and 1940s.

Despite considerable dissimilarities of theme and treatment, these novels shared a common need to establish a strong sense of period and, in most cases, of place. The past and abroad represented more easily encompassed realities than the here and now, though Morgan Sportes, in *La Dérive des continents,* scrambled chronology and topography in his semi- (or pseudo-) autobiographical account of a journalist's experiment with hallucinogenic mushrooms in Mexico. Bertrand Visage won the Prix Femina for *Tous Les Soleils,* 12 interlinked stories set in Sicily that turned out in the end to be a single, cleverly constructed novel. Augustin Gomez-Arcos returned to his native Spain for a satirical and savage analysis of the fascist mentality, *Un Oiseau brûlé vif.*

The complex structure of Angelo Rinaldi's *Les Jardins du consulat,* the sociological analysis of Guy Croussy's *Le Sphinx,* the ironic fantasies of Gilles Charpentier's *Les Manuscrits de la marmotte,* and the chronology of Jacques Almira's *Terrass Hôtel* made some demands on their readers. The same was true of Christiane Rochefort's *Le Monde est comme deux chevaux,* a deliberate attempt at breaking new ground. Other well-established writers who published new works during the year included Jean Cayrol (*Qui suis-je?*), Muriel Cerf (*Une Pâle Beauté*), Michel del Castillo (*La Gloire de Dina*), André Stil (*Le Petit Boxeur*), and Didier Martin (*L'Amour dérangé*). Henri Troyat completed his biography of Anton Chekhov and, late in 1983, Jean Genet, one of the most controversial figures in post-World War II literature, achieved an unusual degree of respectability for a former convict with the award of the Grand Prix National des Lettres. The Swiss poet Philippe Jaccottet brought his notebooks up to 1979 with *La Semaison* and published *À travers un verger,* three short prose texts that gave an insight into the mind of an individualistic writer more concerned with the effort to capture the lasting truths of nature than with recounting the incidents of his life. It made a change.

The second and third volume of Michel Foucault's *Histoire de la sexualité* appeared shortly before the death, in June, of this major figure in French intellectual life. Others who died during the year included Henri Michaux, the historians Marcel Brion and Philippe Ariès, and the poet Pierre Emmanuel. (*See* OBITUARIES.) The Senegalese poet and statesman Léopold Sédar Senghor (*see* BIOGRAPHIES) was received into the French Academy following his election in 1983.   (ROBIN BUSS)

Canada. In late 1983 Francine Noël published a first novel, *Maryse,* which not only was a success in the bookstores but was praised among critics as well. The novel tells the story of Maryse, a young woman who, carried away by the repercussions in Quebec of the cultural revolution that took place in France in May 1968, goes to live with a group of friends making the difficult apprenticeship to liberty and to first loves. One after another, the episodes remind the reader of a generation of youth who, wanting to translate imagination into power, threw themselves into the newest and most marginal of experiences. Although not innovative in matters of style and language, Noël provides the detail that gives the story fullness and holds the reader's attention.

Danielle Dubé received the Prix Robert Cliche in 1984 for her novel *Les Olives noirs.* In it she tells of a young Québécois couple, Pierre and Christiane, who set themselves up on the Côte d'Azur and, with their friend François, experience the events of October 1970 and the end of the Franco regime in Spain. Their theoretical discussions about politics and love give rise to contradictions and expose the deep-seated motivations of individuals. The content is interesting, although the form is not original. Since the publication of *La Guerre, yes sir!* and *Céleste Bicyclette,* no one had doubted the talents of Roch Carrier, but in *De l'amour dans la ferraille* the author makes his talents even more evident with a masterful text in which his love of life, his sense of humour, and his unbridled imagination flow in waves. In more than 500 pages, Carrier tells of two adolescents whose adventures range from the saintly to the sexual.

Also worthy of note was the appearance of *La Détresse et l'enchantement* by the late Gabrielle Roy. The incomplete autobiographical narrative, which was undertaken in the 1970s, recalls the childhood and youth of the author. The work shows the careful attention to detail that characterized Roy's writing.   (ROBERT SAINT-AMOUR)

GERMAN

Literature that mingled realism and fantasy was a prominent feature of 1984. It was illustrated in what many considered the two outstanding novels of the year, Botho Strauss's *Der junge Mann* and Adolf Muschg's *Das Licht und der Schlüssel.* The former developed the romantic themes of illusion and reality, notably in relation to the theatre, in a series of loosely connected stories, some of them modern *märchen,* in which the conventions of space and time were splendidly disregarded. Muschg was reflecting more on the nature of art in his "novel of the education of a vampire"; the contemporary Dracula's nocturnal mission was at once therapeutic bloodletting and the telling of tales. Appropriately enough, the Romantic author E. T. A. Hoffmann was born again in Peter Henisch's entertaining *Hoffmanns Erzählungen.* Literature as therapy was also a theme of Ingomar von Kieseritzky's satire *Obsession,* in which the narrator finds that writing, not the sex clinic, enables him to get over an unhappy love affair. The artistic

millieu was the setting for Thomas Bernhard's *Holzfällen,* which succeeded in blurring the distinction between art and reality to the extent that its author was sued by an Austrian composer who believed himself slandered in the novel.

Underlying all these works was a topic that preoccupied many writers, the search for identity. In Alban Nikolai Herbst's *Die Verwirrung des Gemüts,* a complex montage of narrative, newspaper cuttings, and reflections, three facets of this search appear in the form of narrator, protagonist, and the persona the latter invents for himself. Volker Elis Pilgrim's *Die Elternaustreibung* portrayed the breakup of a homosexual marriage; its narrator realizes that his failure to be authentic is due to the subconscious domination of his character by his parents. The conflict of the generations was a subsidiary theme of both these novels—others treated that of the sexes. In Gisela Elsner's grotesque satire of marital relations, *Die Zähmung,* the psychologically weaker male takes on not merely the conventional social attributes of the dominant female but also her physical features. Markus Werner described a comparable constellation in *Zündels Abgang,* in which the male attempt to break away ends in silence in a psychiatric ward.

The impersonal, inhospitable modern city—the appropriate setting for Herbst's novel—was exploited by other writers, notably Matthias Zschokke, whose *Prinz Hans* mediated the urban scene through the mind of a simple-witted foreigner. Paris was the setting for Eva Hiller's *Berührungsverluste;* the title, "fear of contact," might serve for much contemporary fiction. F. C. Delius's *Adenauerplatz* was more directly aggressive, contrasting West Germany's wealth with the poverty of the third world as a Latin-American nightwatchman makes his rounds in a West German city. The rise of the "Greens" was reflected in Peter Hartling's *Das Windrad,* in which the owner of a printing plant sells his business, abandons his family, and joins the ecology movement. The reality of the "good life" in the countryside was more convincingly if elegiacally portrayed by the Swiss author Silvio Blatter. His ironically entitled *Kein schöner Land* portrayed the rape of the countryside by a complacent establishment, from which the only escape seemed to be emigration.

The Nazi past, discernible in many of these novels, was the specific setting of others. Erich Loest's *Die Mäuse des Doktor Ley* used fantasy in his tale of the man who was the double of Hitler's notorious labour minister. Both Fritz J. Raddatz (*Kuhauge*) and Andreas Okopenko (*Kindernazi*) described, in semiautobiographical fashion, childhood in Germany and Austria, respectively, during the Third Reich. Stefan Heym's *Schwarzenberg* used a little-known incident from the end of World War II to sketch a utopian picture of what might have been had the U.S. and the Soviet Union not intervened. Jörg Fauser's *Rohstoff* took its material from the 1960s student movement, looking back in disillusionment at the drugs and sex scene into which it degenerated. Hans Christoph Buch's *Die Hochzeit von Port-au-Prince,* part historical novel, part documentation, part fantasy, was a highly topical portrayal of external interference in the Caribbean between the 18th and 20th centuries.

From East Germany, Erwin Strittmatter's *Der Laden* was a story of village life in the 1920s told by an omniscient, often ironic narrator. Jürgen Lehmann's *Hochzeitsbilder* described contemporary village life: increased prosperity did not necessarily lead to a more dignified or humane society, and the gulf between the generations was as strong as ever. Renate Apitz's *Hexenzeit* continued a mode set the previous year by Irmtraud Morgner; stages in the life of the principal characters were played out against the mythological background of the Norns, and the motif of witchcraft was related to feminism. Potentially the most important East German novel of the year, Günter de Bruyn's *Neue Herrlichkeit,* was withdrawn from publication at the last moment, probably because of its depiction of opportunism in high places.

Significant new collections of poetry appeared from, among others, Ernst Günther Bleisch (*Zeit ohne Uhr*), Erich Fried (*Es ist was es ist*), Sarah Kirsch (*Katzenleben*), and, posthumously, Rainer Brambach (*Auch im April*).

(J. H. REID)

SCANDINAVIAN

Denmark. Serious thrillers were a feature of recent Danish literature. Leif Davidsen's *Uhellige alliancer* was a tightly knit novel set in the Basque region of Spain, revealing unfortunate links with the fascist past. Klaus Rifbjerg's *En omvej til klostret* (1983) had cultural rather than political overtones in its account of nightmare experiences in Rome. Willy August Linnemann's *Hinsides horisonten* was in a related category, combining a murder with social satire and the questions of guilt and happiness. There were elements of the thriller in Martha Christensen's *Den midterste dag,* an examination of human relationships resulting when a couple gives hospitality to the husband's younger brother, despite his criminal record.

A complete contrast was Dorrit Willumsen's long novel based on the life of Madame Tussaud, *Marie.* It could be placed within the framework of women's literature in its presentation of Marie as a determined and confident artist, despite the social odds against her, but it also reflected the artist's need to renounce and to accept loneliness.

Knud B. Thomsen's *Borgmesteren i Monteporco* combined comic sense with a tragic dimension. The fascist mayor of an Italian village during World War II fears the arrival of the Allies yet dislikes the Germans. This was a serious analysis of a man for whom any outcome was likely to be defeat. Benny Andersen's short stories, *Over skulderen* (1983), also varied between tragedy and comedy, revealing the barriers between people and seeking to discover how they arise. Some affinity of themes, if not of style, was to be seen in Grethe Heltberg's *Vækst,* showing that happiness is not always where it might be expected. Grethe Heltberg struck a more personal note in the reflective *Født for rædsel eller for roser,* in which age and death are central themes, while in *Om kager, jomfruer og verdens gang* she was at her best as a highly conscious stylist.

The young poet Bo Green Jensen continued his seven-volume analysis of the ways of civilization in *Mondo sinistro* (1983) and *Undergangstestamentet,* ranging from abstract, allusive, almost surrealist visions to a deceptive simplicity. Simplicity was present in Klaus Rifbjerg's *Det svævende træ,* which was partly a homage to the ordinary. In *84 digte* Henrik Nordbrandt was more critical of modern European life. William Heinesen published his collected poems, *Samlede digte.* The 1983 Danish Academy Prize was awarded to Jess Ørnsbo.   (W. GLYN JONES)

Norway. Strained economic conditions forced Norwegian publishers to reduce their book lists considerably. Modern man, shaped by the dishonest manipulations of the mass media and the systematic lies of the establishment, formed the theme of Jan Kjærstad's *Homo Falsus eller det perfekte mord,* where humour, sophisticated style, and technique combined to produce an outstanding novel. The decadent charm of the Oslo bourgeoisie of the 1980s was amusingly and maliciously portrayed in Ebba Haslund's novel *Døgnfluens lengsel.* Karsten Alnæs's well-written and

Vera Henriksen

Sven Delblanc

humorous novel *Kom kjærlighet* told how a young student's break with his bourgeois family background and his attempt to find a place within a left-wing political milieu were reconciled in his love affair with and subsequent marriage to his widowed aunt, 19 years his senior. Marital conflict and human beings stretched to the point of violence were dealt with in Tore Tveit's collection of short stories, *Hemmeligheter.*

Johannes Heggland's epic tetralogy, *Brødet frå havet,* centred round the life of the thrice-widowed Anna Gyria in a 19th-century fishing/farming community in western Norway, was brought to a splendid close with *Ljosken frå paradis.* Vera Henriksen's historical novel *Spydet,* a continuation of *Odins ravner,* captured with profound insight the atmosphere of the 10th-century world of the sagas. In her second novel, *Det stumme rommet,* Herbjørg Wassmo confirmed an outstanding talent in her description of the troubled life in a small northern Norwegian community of an illegitimate girl, the product of her mother's affair with a German soldier. Jahn Otto Johansen's *Det hendte også her* was a documentary devoted to the fate of Jews in Norway, nearly half of whom were exterminated by the Germans. Knut Hamsun's son Tore Hamsun provided an unusual novel, *Mannen fra havet,* describing the experiences of a 20th-century man mysteriously transported back in time to the Germany of about 1890. Tore Stubberud's *Et værelse i natten* was a semidocumentary attempt to explain the long unproductive period following Trygve Gulbranssen's trilogy *Beyond Sing the Woods,* which took the world by storm in the 1930s.

Cosmic awareness and the appreciation of spiritual values were well expressed in Hans Børli's collection of poems *Frosne tranebær. 20 Contemporary Norwegian Poets* was a bilingual anthology edited by Terje Johanssen. Novels in which Knut Hamsun gave expression to his disillusionment were comprehensively analyzed by Atle Kittang in *Luft, vind, ingenting.*   (TORBJØRN STØVERUD)

Sweden. In *Kanaans land,* Sven Delblanc reached volume three of his fictionalized but basically authentic family saga, with his settler-parents reaching their promised land of Canada in the 1920s and surviving droughts and the depression before giving up and returning home. Even more directly autobiographical was Jan Myrdal's *En annan värld,* chilling recollections of accompanying his celebrated parents, Nobel Prize winners Gunnar and Alva Myrdal, to the U.S. in 1938 (they took their then 55-year-old son to court over the first part, *Barndom,* published in 1982).

Delblanc and Myrdal were established masters of narration; at the other end of the biographical spectrum were two first novels showing promise, Fredrik Ekelund's *Stuv*

Malmö, kom! and Mare Kandre's *I ett annat land.* Ekelund rebelled against his middle-class background and worked as a dockhand in Malmö for seven years, learning from the university of life and making friends across class barriers; Kandre presented lyrical fragments showing a youngster's process of self-discovery. A purely fictional re-creation of two young people's lives was found in *Kungariket Atlas* by Heidi von Born, whose specialty is the subtle presentation of psychosocial reality. Here she provided an uncomfortably convincing picture of a shabby environment in a precisely located Stockholm district.

The year's most ingenious novel was P. C. Jersild's *Den femtionde frälsaren.* Jersild is adept at the picaresque mode, here set in late 18th-century Venice and presented as a memoir by a man who gets involved with a direct descendant of a son (!) of Jesus of Nazareth. The virtuoso narration entertains while the reader seeks its allegorical implications. Torgny Lindgren took the material for *Bat-Seba* straight from the Bible; in writing of King David's beloved in a diction at once direct and poetic, he succeeded in investing the story with universality, without plagiarizing Pär Lagerkvist, Sweden's Nobel laureate in the genre. Erik Beckman's *Katt och sten* was purportedly a free rendition of themes from Genesis, but it was an open question how many readers actually understood his elliptical and idiosyncratic prose.

Three prestigious poets published collections: Lars Gustafsson (*Fåglarna*), Kjell Espmark (*Den hemliga måltiden*), and Göran Printz Påhlson (*Säg minns du skeppet Refanut?*). Göran Palm published *Sverige en vintersaga,* a satirical blank verse account of the state of Sweden past and present.   (KARIN PETHERICK)

ITALIAN

Italian literature during the year registered a definite shift toward introspection, a contraction of all horizons to the sphere of the individual, and usually private, self as the only safe area of inquiry. This was taken to imply growing misgivings about radicalism and, indeed, about literature's ability to do anything more than offer consolation. Thus, with *Palomar,* Italo Calvino brought an astronomer's telescope to bear on details of the Earth's landscapes and human culture, experiences, and speculations. His quest yielded no answer, except perhaps the feeling that every attempt to understand and modify oneself and one's own environment is foredoomed. Ferdinando Camon described his *Storia di Sirjo* as a "parable for the new generation." In simple didactic form, it tells how a typical middle-class youth experiences, in turn, political protest, terrorism, imprisonment, drugs, love, and finally "inner revolution"—

JERRY BAUER
Italo Calvino

i.e., self-discovery through group analysis. As a work of fiction it lacked imagination, while as sociological inquiry it seemed far too general and simplistic. More effective, thanks to its exacting style, was Carmelo Samonà's *Il custode,* where the ostensible victim of a kidnapping, confined in spatial and temporal isolation, without memories or plans, tries to understand himself and to communicate with his phantom jailers.

Psychological themes and stylistic refinement also characterized the work of three distinguished women novelists. Francesca Duranti, in *La casa sul lago della luna,* tells of a translator who, having found a little-known novel by an Austrian writer, translates it and achieves the acclaim and fortune he had long been seeking. In the process, however, he is mesmerized by the ambiguity between what is real and what is imaginary and lets himself die. Ambiguity was central to much of Francesca Sanvitale's *L'uomo del parco,* a gloomy novel, focused on four stages of the narrator's life, where the real and imaginary merge to produce often surreal effects. Gina Lagorio's *Tosca dei gatti* deals with a lonely woman who lives and dies for her cats. Tosca's cats make up an intensely human microcosm that is observed with great sensitivity and freshness. Unfortunately, the author felt compelled to build around her delicate story a rather dull and contrived framework in which a writer observes Tosca. The story was a success, but the story about the story was unconvincing.

Two novels, while still introspective, were in a different stylistic register. Dario Bellezza's *Turbamento* was a kind of coded delirium that initially impressed with its exuberant desire to transgress literary language but soon became slack, mannered, and self-indulgent. By contrast, Aldo Busi's first novel, *Seminario sulla gioventú,* while written in uninhibited language, seemed more skillfully wrought and achieved a higher degree of freshness and authenticity. The book is the long and complex diary of a young homosexual's intellectual and spiritual development. Particularly captivating was Mario Tobino's *La ladra,* a little novel showing that friendship between different social classes is hurtful and ultimately, perhaps, impossible. Giovanni Arpino's *La sposa segreta* is an amusing sort of American-style comedy in which a woman tries to find a wife for her computer-mad son. Alberto Moravia's *La cosa,* a book of short stories, is principally about sex and its aberrations but perhaps about literature too, as the only way out of the tedium of life. Giovanni Mariotti's *Butroto. Un'avventura di Uc de la Bacalaria* tells the delightful and sharply satirical story of a typical journalist in search, for the sake of a scoop, of an imaginary country where nothing ever happens.

Two major poetic works were Giovanni Giudici's *Lume dei tuoi misteri* and Attilio Bertolucci's *La camera da letto.* Though both are narrative in structure and register, Giudici seemed to proceed by lyrical flashes, while Bertolucci developed a more colloquial and relaxed style.

In the field of the essay, *Cari figli del 2053* by Vittorio Buttafava, a reportage of the evils of our time, is addressed to the children of today as an act of faith in the future of mankind. Perhaps most successful in this category was *L'amicizia* by Francesco Alberoni, who managed to handle his subject—friendship through the ages—straightforwardly while giving the impression of systematic thought and originality.   (LINO PERTILE)

SPANISH

Spain. Since 1973 Julián Ríos, known only to ardent followers of Spain's literary vanguard, had been composing Book I of his projected five-part *Larva* cycle: *Babel de una noche de San Juan.* When this "carnovelesque microchaosm" appeared in late 1983, a few bewildered critics pronounced its 600 neo-Joycean pages unreadable. Loosely focused on the London wanderings of two characters, *Larva* is a cross-indexed, self-annotating text of multilingual word orgies, complete with drawings, a photo album, and a fold-out map of Kensington-Chelsea, where the book's fragmented action takes place. Readers sympathetic to Ríos's baroque humour and tumultuous style discovered in *Larva* (I) an instant postmodern classic, without doubt the most disturbingly original Spanish prose of the century.

More conventional was Miguel Delibes's epistolary novel *Cartas de amor de un sexagenario voluptuoso* (1983), which recorded the pathetic postal romance of a retired journalist attracted by a widow's ad in a lonely hearts magazine. Gonzalo Torrente Ballester filtered a lyrical memoir through poetry and myth in *Dafne y ensueños;* later in 1984 his *Quizá nos lleve el viento al infinito,* an allegory on the nature of personal identity, blended elements of science fiction and the spy novel. Much of the year's best fiction combined social or psychological themes with the basic formulas of the detective story: Juan Marsé's *Ronda del Guinardó,* Rosa Montero's best-seller *Te trataré como a una reina,* and Francisco González Ledesma's *Crónica sentimental en rojo,* winner of the Planeta Prize, all explored violent lives in Barcelona. In *Otoño indio,* Alfonso Grosso chose the University of Iowa as the setting—and professors as the prey—to re-create the myth of the Midwest American hero; and Manuel Vázquez Montalbán resurrected his popular detective hero, Pepe Carvalho, whose assignment in *La rosa de Alejandría* was to solve the mystery of his own authenticity. In other directions, Jesús Fernández Santos won high praise for the sober yet haunted realism of *Los jinetes del alba,* a love story set in pre-Civil War León, and Luis Goytisolo's complex analytical novel, *Estela del fuego que se aleja,* revealed the processes of memory and literary invention by which fiction animates and explains, rather than merely reflects, the world of real experience.

At the end of 1983 Francisco Ayala won the National Prize for narrative with the second volume of his memoir, *Recuerdos y olvidos: El exilio,* while the poetry award went to Claudio Rodríguez for his four books of verse (1953–76), collectively entitled *Desde mis poemas.* Luis Rosales's book of new poems, *Oigo el silencio universal del miedo,* was exceptional in a year that saw many poets consolidating previously published work in major new collections.

The poet Vicente Aleixandre, winner of the 1977 Nobel Prize for Literature, died in December (*see* OBITUARIES).

(ROGER L. UTT)

Latin America. The deaths of writer Julio Cortázar and critic Angel Rama (late 1983) were untimely events in a year in which several of Latin America's most renowned figures were silent. The most important exceptions were Mario Vargas Llosa, Gustavo Álvarez Gardeazábal, Isaac Goldemberg, and Reynaldo Arenas.

Vargas Llosa's *Contra viento y marea* (late 1983) is a volume of essays and journalistic writing that originally appeared between 1962 and 1982. The literary essays include substantial commentary on two of Vargas Llosa's adolescent heroes, Sartre and Camus. His often cited essays "Literature and Fire" and those on the vocation of the writer in Peru are included. The trajectory of the political essays ranges from Vargas Llosa's unequivocal support of the Cuban revolution in the early 1960s to his criticism of all authoritarian regimes by the 1970s.

Works published by the three major novelists mentioned each involved a special situation. In *Pepe Botellas,* Álvarez Gardeazábal, a Colombian writer, presents a Cuban setting and portrays the life of a Cuban exile in Colombia; his collage of historical and fictional texts is an acute analysis of power politics in Latin America. Arenas, a Cuban writing in exile in the U.S., published a novel in English titled *El Central* (translated by Anthony Kerrigan). A unique combination of poetry and prose, it relates the story of an adolescent conscripted by the government and assigned to brutal labour in a Cuban sugar mill. The third special case is the Peruvian Goldemberg, who resides in New York; his *Tiempo al tiempo,* published in the U.S. in the original Spanish, is a novel of daring narrative techniques dealing with Jewish history and culture in Lima.

María Luisa Puga, Rafael Gaona, and Alejandro Sandoval published the principal novels of the year in Mexico. The most impressive, Puga's *Pánico o peligro,* is about the life and personal relationships of a woman in Mexico City. The central conflict is between commitment and just words, and the central theme is the difference between experience felt and experience expressed in language. Gaona's short novel *Cada quien para su santo* narrates a period from childhood to womanhood in the life of a lesbian who belongs to the capital's working class. The basic conflict in this work is between communion and alienation. The poet Sandoval's *La justa fatiga,* a family novel set in the provinces, incorporates social protest by presenting the circumstances of railroad workers.

The end of military rule in Argentina resulted in the publication of novels on a wide range of themes, but with emphasis on testimonial fiction dealing with the repressive events of the 1970s. Enrique Medina, Pedro Orgambide, Mempo Giardinelli, and Luisa Valenzuela were among the most important writers to publish novels. Medina's *Con el trapo en la boca* (late 1983) novelizes the social and spiritual disintegration of Argentina. Set in Buenos Aires, it deals with a working-class woman who rebels against a male-dominated society. In addition, Medina published a best-selling historical novel dealing with the period of the 19th-century dictator Juan Manuel de Rosas, *Una sombra donde sueña Camila O'Gorman.* Orgambide also wrote a historical novel, *El arrabal del mundo.* Giardinelli, writing in exile, published a short novel set in the Chaco region of Argentina, *Luna caliente* (late 1983).

Despite the end of 11 years of military rule in Uruguay, the majority of the established writers continued to work abroad. Enrique Estrázulas published his third novel, *Ladrón de música,* in Spain. One of the most noteworthy novels to appear in Montevideo was Salvador Puig's *Lugar a dudas.* Mario Benedetti's poems *Geografías* dealt with exile. The poet Eduardo Espina, winner of the Premio Municipal, published a volume of poems in Mexico, *Valores personales.*

Political instability in Central America limited the publication and distribution of literature. The Guatemalan Roberto Quezada won a national novel contest with *Ardillas enjauladas,* a social protest novel similar to Miguel Asturias's *El Señor Presidente.* Hugo Lindo of El Salvador created a novel in the science fiction vein, *Yo soy la memoria* (late 1983). *One Day of Life* (late 1983) appeared as the English translation of *Un día en la vida* (1980) by El Salvador's Manlio Argueta.

In addition to Álvarez Gardeazábal, several of Colombia's major novelists published works. Plinio Apuleyo Mendoza's *La llana y el hielo,* which features characters who are living writers, is a novel dealing with power. One of Colombia's most accomplished woman writers, Fanny Buitrago, published her fourth novel, *Los amores de Afrodita.* Luis Fayad's *Los parientes de Ester* (previously published in Spain) was a best-seller in Colombia during mid-1984.

(RAYMOND L. WILLIAMS)

PORTUGUESE

Portugal. The search for new ideas and modes of expression continued to be the main pursuit of contemporary Portuguese writers of fiction. In *Amadeo,* a narrative centred on the life and work of a distinguished modernist painter, Amadeo de Souza-Cardoso, Mário Cláudio seized moments and images of great emotional intensity, retrieved in the colours and shapes of paintings, in old papers, and in the draft of a secret biography that comes unexpectedly into his hands. These elliptic sketches, set in the old family house, have an eerie quality that anticipates the early death of the artist when the village is struck by an epidemic in 1918. Gradually the pieces of the jigsaw puzzle combine to form different patterns of meaning that challenge the conventional biography and reveal the ambiguities of writing and human experience. The contradictory demands of art and life emerge in their extreme complexity, posing disturbing questions to the reader of this haunting book.

The old house was also the place of memory in Vergílio Ferreira's novel *Para sempre.* The aging narrator revisits the empty rooms, touches unused objects, and by linking minor events reenacts the story of his love for his dead wife. In the flow of his reminiscences other characters appear, but they are all seen as projections of the narrator's inner solitude. This was a theme familiar to Ferreira, but here the narrator's individual tragedy, in spite of some diffuse tirades against society, attains a poignant cogency not found in any of his previous novels.

The publication of *Poesia 1961–1981* by Gastão Cruz was probably the principal literary event of the year. One of the most interesting poets of his generation, Cruz collected in this volume the poems of two decades that he believed had stood the test of time. Characteristic of his poetic diction was a freedom of rhythm and word association that ebbed and flowed with the consistent integrity of a musical composition. Death and frustration were current motives in a poetry that relied on concrete imagery and used the body as a metaphor to express the anguish of a diseased world.   (L. S. REBELO)

Brazil. During 1984 three major Brazilian literary figures died: the highly respected dramatist Jorge Andrade ("A moratória"); the poet Pedro Nava, who earlier in the year had published the sixth volume of his memoirs; and one of Brazil's true popular novelists, José Mauro de Vasconellos (*Meu pé de laranja lima, Rosinha, minha canoa*). *Leia Livros,* the major national publication dedicated to current books, temporarily ceased publication but was resurrected with the title *Novo Leia Livros.*

Interest in theatre, screen, and television dominated the cultural scene. A successful production of Luís Alberto de Abreu's view of contemporary São Paulo life appeared: "Sai de frente que atrás vai gente." Also of note was a portrait of the early years (1953–71) of the Arena Theatre of São Paulo by Sábato Magaldi. Gomes Dias's "O Bem Amado" (Brazil's version of the "Dallas" television series) returned to the small screen after its cancellation caused a public outcry. The distinguished semiotician and poet Décio Pignitari analyzed the status of Brazilian television in his *O óbvio e o misterioso.* Sílvio Tendler's film *Jango,* about former president João Goulart, and Nelson Pereira dos Santos's *Memórias do cárcere,* based on the autobiography of the novelist Graciliano Ramos, were successes in Brazil and abroad.

João Cabral de Melo Neto's *O Auto do Frade* is a symbolic, poetic biography of the martyred Brazilian hero, which probes the question of the abuse of power. The poetry of Carlos Pena Filho (1929–61), a contemporary of the Modernists, was "recovered" and published by Edilberto

Coutinho. *Quizumba,* a collection of poems by Roberto Piva, aims to stretch understanding of the term poetry to its limits. A curious critical survey of the theme of desire in Brazilian poetry was prepared by Affonso Romano de Sant'Anna, and Geraldo Carneiro published an equally curious biography of the late Vinícius de Moraes. Orides Fontela's collection of poetry, *Alba,* was considered the most important revelation of the year.

Rubem Fonseca's novel *A grande arte,* which centres on the skill of murdering with one blow of a knife, was a prizewinning best-seller. Similarly, Dalton Trevisan's *Meu querido assassino* reflected on the country's high crime rate. New fiction by *gaúchos,* writers of southern Brazil, included works by Moacir Scliar, who once again returned to his Jewish roots, and by Tânia Faillace, Lya Luft, and Antônio Carlos Resende. Adélia Prado wrote a fictional, feminist spiritual memoir, and Oswaldo França Júnior and Silviano Santiago also published new fiction. Lygia Chiappini M. Leite, analyzing the role of literature in the educational process in Brazil, suggested the need for "democratization" of the texts.   (IRWIN STERN)

RUSSIAN

Soviet Literature. Much of Soviet literature published during 1984 was marked by fervent appeals for peace, détente, and greater trust and mutual understanding between nations. Yevgeny Yevtushenko's impassioned antiwar poem *Mum and the Neutron Bomb* was nominated for the 1984 State Prize of the U.S.S.R. I. Shklyarevsky's poem *The Word for Peace,* urging the people of the world to stop the arms race, abandon fratricidal wars, and save the planet from a nuclear holocaust, also caught the public imagination. The antiwar theme was echoed in new poetry by Andrey Voznesensky, David Samoilov, Robert Rozhdestvensky, Yury Levitansky, Yevgeny Vinokurov, Vladimir Sokolov, and many poets of the younger generation.

A number of the year's novels had political themes, among them Aleksandr Prokhanov's *The Africanist,* M. Domogatskikh's *To the South of the Benkhai River* (Book 2), and Yuly Semyonov's *The Press Centre: Anatomy of Political Crime.* The circumstances pertaining to the conclusion of the 1918 Treaty of Brest-Litovsk between Soviet Russia and Germany were the subject of the historical novel *Petrograd-Brest* by Belorussian writer Ivan Shamyakin.

Critics noted the antifascist, antiwar ethos in new works about the Great Patriotic War (World War II). These included Boris Vasiliev's novel *I Recollect the War,* Yelena Rzhevskaya's novella *Voroshen Heat,* Vyacheslav Kondratev's short stories, and S. Aleksevich's documentary book *War Is Not for Women,* dedicated to women's heroism on the World War II battlefields. New insights into the plight of the Soviet people in wartime were provided by Daniil Granin, Albert Likhanov, Vladimir Yeremenko, Oleg Smirnov, and other prose writers. The foreign policy context and remembrance of the Great Patriotic War were also strong in Anatoly Ananyev's novel *Years Without War,* in which he reflected on the destiny of his country in a panoramic survey of the entire postwar world.

Philosophical, ethical, and psychological quest was the common note in new works by a group of authors now in their 40s. Common to Vaclav Mikhalsky's novel *Secret Graces,* Vladimir Makanin's *Where the Earth Was Merging with the Hills,* and Anatoly Kurchatkin's *The Running Star,* among others, was a Chekhovian spirit of deep psychological penetration. A refreshing note in modern poetry was introduced by Igor Zhdanov, A. Yeremenko, A. Parshchikov, Aleksandr Tkachenko, and some other poets of the younger generation. Its intrinsic features were a complex poetic form, metaphor, and irony. Praiseworthy trends were also discernible in Soviet literary criticism, as evidenced in new books and reviews by Lev Anninsky, Vladimir Gusev, Igor Zolotussky, V. Kamyanov, and others.

The death occurred in February of the novelist Mikhail A. Sholokhov (*see* OBITUARIES), author of the four-volume *And Quiet Flows the Don*. (SERGEY CHUPRININ)

Yevgeny Yevtushenko   Aleksandr Solzhenitsyn

Expatriate Russian Literature. Except for translations and reprints, 1984 was a somewhat lean year in regard to Russian books published abroad. The new titles that did appear included an important work, *Fevralskaya revoliutsia* ("The February Revolution") by George Katkov—the first title in the "Contemporary History" series started by the exiled Russian author Aleksandr Solzhenitsyn. A new title was added to "Our Past," another series put out by the same publishing house, YMCA Publishers in Paris. This was *Chetyre treti nashey zhizni* ("Three-quarters of Our Life"), a book of memoirs by Nina Krivosheina. Solzhenitsyn himself continued his chronological series of works on Soviet history with two large volumes of *Oktiabr 1916* ("October 1916"), also published by YMCA, in which he took up the narrative where his *August 1914* had left off. An authoritative biography of Solzhenitsyn by the British author Michael Scammell was published by Norton in New York.

Nomenklatura, Mikhail Voslensky's "anatomy of the Soviet ruling class," was published by Overseas Publications Interchange in London. (An English translation was brought out by Bodley Head, with an introduction by the Yugoslav dissident Milovan Djilas.) It was the most thorough and informed exposé to date of the Soviet "new class," its mentality and its life-style. The author, a historian and previously a senior researcher at the Soviet Academy of Sciences, had been an interpreter at the Nuremberg trials after World War II and then served on the Allied Control Commission in Germany. Voslensky immigrated to the West in 1972 and taught at West German and Austrian universities.

Two Russian books that were published in translation in a number of countries were the late Vasily Grossman's *Life and Fate* and *Krasnaya ploshchad* ("Red Square"), a political thriller by F. Neznansky and E. Topol, originally published in Russian by Possev in Frankfurt am Main, West Germany.

In the Soviet Union the writer Valery Marchenko died in a Perm labour camp at the age of 37. The poet Valentin Sokolov, who had spent 34 years in labour camps and prison hospitals, died in the Chernyakhovsk special psychiatric hospital. The Ukrainian poet Mykola Horbal was rearrested two days before completing his five-year term

of imprisonment. Charged with "circulating anti-Soviet slander" in private conversations, he faced up to three additional years in prison. (GEORGE THEINER)

EASTERN EUROPEAN LITERATURE

For the third time in five years a writer from the Communist part of Europe won the Nobel Prize for Literature. In awarding the 1984 prize to the greatest living Czech poet, Jaroslav Seifert, the Nobel committee in Stockholm described his poetry as fresh, sensual, and richly inventive, providing "a liberating image of the indomitable spirit of man." (*See* NOBEL PRIZES.)

Unlike the two previous Eastern European laureates—Czeslaw Milosz (1980) of Poland, who lived in the U.S., and Elias Canetti (1981) of Bulgaria, who resided in England—Seifert had remained in Prague, both during the Nazi occupation (1939–45) and following the Communist takeover of 1948. He had gone unpublished in the 1950s and again in the 1970s as a result of his brave and uncompromising stand against repression and censorship. Reviled in 1969, when after the Soviet occupation he refused to bring the Czechoslovak Writers' Union, of which he was president, to heel, and then neglected by the authorities until his 80th birthday in 1981, Seifert then received official acclaim as a great Czech poet. English translations of his most recent collections of verse, *Morovy sloup* (*The Plague Column*) and *Destnik z Piccadilly* (*Umbrella from Piccadilly*) had been published in London in recent years.

A samizdat (literary underground) edition of George Orwell's *1984,* as well as copies of the book printed by an exile publisher in Cologne, West Germany, circulated in Czechoslovakia. The introduction, by Milan Simecka, compared the fate of the novel's hero with his own experience of life under Communism. An extract from Simecka's text was read by the British dramatist Harold Pinter at an event devoted to *1984* and organized by the Royal Shakespeare Company together with *Index on Censorship* at London's Barbican Theatre on January 18. Samuel Beckett's play *Catastrophe*—dedicated to the Czech playwright Vaclav Havel during his recent imprisonment—and Havel's *Chyba* ("Mistake") were given their first British performances on the same occasion, while actor Derek Jacobi read a chapter from Tadeusz Konwicki's *A Minor Apocalypse*—a book banned by the Polish authorities but published in the Polish *Zapis* samizdat quarterly and subsequently in translation throughout the world.

The Polish amnesty of July 1984 led to the release of a large number of political detainees, including the writers Jan Jozef Lipski, Marek Nowakowski, and Adam Michnik. The last named, a historian and leading Polish dissident, had to be removed from prison by force, as he refused to recognize the right of Gen. Wojciech Jaruzelski's regime to imprison those who opposed it by peaceful means. Rigorous censorship remained in force, but as in previous years it was obviated by numerous samizdat publications produced in Poland as well as by those printed abroad and smuggled into the country. The latter included the first translation into Polish of a work by the Russian philosopher Lev Shestov, *Apoteoza nieosczywitosci* ("Apotheosis of the Nonobvious"); published by Kontra in London, it was immediately reprinted by a clandestine publisher in Poland. Kontra also brought out a posthumous book by its founder, Szymon Szechter, *W sobote u Minki i inne bajki* ("Saturday with Minka, and Other Tales"), and the Polish original of *Nie kocha sie pomnikow* (*Monuments Are Not Loved*), the author's life story written in collaboration with Nina Karsov, who took over the running of Kontra after Szechter's death.

The collected poems of Slavko Milhalic, a leading Croatian poet, were published by the *Greenfield Review* (Greenfield Center, N.Y.) under the title *Atlantis*. Another Yugoslav, the popular Serbian author Dragoslav Mihailovic, scored a great success with his novel *Cizmani* ("Boot Wearers"), brought out by the Prosveta publishing house in Belgrade.

Several interesting volumes by Hungarian writers, both living in Hungary and in exile, appeared. They included the first collection of plays by the well-known poet Sandor Weores, *Szinjatekok;* a new collection of verse by Istvan Vas, *Raerunk* ("No Hurry"); and Gyozo Hatar's short novel, *Pepito es Pepita* ("Pepito and Pepita"). Written as long ago as 1956, Hatar's novel first appeared in a French translation seven years later but only in 1984 became available in the original Hungarian, thanks to Aurora publishers in London. The author's style, wrote George Gomori in his review in *World Literature Today,* had Sternean qualities that "clearly set Hatar apart from his more traditional contemporaries in Hungarian literature."

Writing in the same U.S. journal, Marguerite Dorian pointed to a phenomenon that was strikingly demonstrated in the Western reaction to Jaroslav Seifert's Nobel award. Reviewing the English edition of selected verse by a leading Romanian poet, Nichita Stanescu *(Ask the Circle to Forgive You),* published by Globe in New York, she discussed the translation of poetry from "a minor culture and language" into a major one and pointed out that, while there were many translations of German, French, and Russian writers, "contemporary Czech, Bulgarian or Romanian poetry continues to remain virtually unknown to Western readers." (GEORGE THEINER)

JEWISH

Hebrew. Three topics dominated the Israeli literary scene during 1984: protest literature on the war and occupation in Lebanon; the figure of the poet Natan Alterman (1910–70); and a growing interest in Arab-oriented writing. Among the several books of protest poetry was a collection edited by Hanan Haver and Moshe Ron. The works on Alterman included Boaz Arpali's study of *Simhat Aniyim, Bein haNisgav Veha'ironi* by Ruth Kartun-Blum, essays on his political poetry edited by Dan Laor, and an index to names mentioned in *haTur haShevi'i* by Sonia Rosenberg. Israeli-Arab literature was featured in a special issue of *Moznayim,* and Arab life was highlighted in Shimon Balas's *haHoref haAharon* and in *Aravi Tov,* written by Yoram Kaniuk under the Arabic pseudonym "Yusuf Sharara."

Notable novelistic works were Y. Ben-Ner's *Protocol,* Hanoch Bartov's *Be'emtsa haRoman,* Y. Auerbach-Orpaz's *haElem,* Benjamin Tammuz's *Pundako shel Yirmiyahu,* Amalia Kahana-Carmon's *Lema'la Bemontifer,* and David Grossman's *Hiyukh haGedi.* Short-story collections were published by Yoram Kaniuk, Aharon Appelfeld, A. Dorit, and Mikhal Govrin. The posthumous novel *Sof Davar* by Ya'akov Shabtai also appeared.

Meir Wieseltier, winner of the Elite Prize, published a retrospective collection of his poetry written between 1959 and 1972. Similar collections by Itamar Yaoz-Kest, A. Hillel, and Ezra Zussman appeared, as well as volumes of new works by Gavriela Elisha, Mikhal Senunit, Arye Sivan, T. Carmi, Yehoshua Tan-Pi, Shin Shalom, and Natan Yonatan, who was awarded the Brenner Prize. First collections were published by Ilan Sheinfeld and Anat Levit. The last book by Zelda (Mishkofsky), *Shenivdela Mikol Merhak,* appeared after her death. Amir Gilboa, one of Israel's most beloved poets, died on Sept. 2, 1984.

Interesting works of criticism included Yosef Oren's his-

torical study of Israeli literature, Y. Bacon's analysis of Hayyim Nahman Bialik's prosody, and S. Werses's work on Bialik's prose and essays. Other noteworthy publications included a collection of Tel Aviv stories, *Deyokna shel Ir,* in honour of the city's 75th anniversary, a compilation of humour and satire by G. Kressel, and reissues of several early poetic works by Uri Zvi Greenberg. The academic journal *Hasifrut* celebrated its 15th anniversary and the start of a new series. (WARREN BARGAD)

Yiddish. A diverse body of Yiddish poetry was produced during the year. *Between Now and Never* showed Leyzer Aykhenrand's considerable imaginative power in reflecting on the fateful position of European Jewry during the '40s. The same theme found trenchant expression in Yitskhok Burshteyn-Finer's sensitive volume of poems, *Together.* Rokhl Kramf displayed remarkable mastery of poetic diction and raised provocative metaphysical questions in her fourth collection, *Down in the Heights.* Khaym Plotkin achieved a stark simplicity and directness in his volume of concentrated verse, *With Open Eyes.* A highlight of the year was M. M. Shaffir's finely honed *Under the Canopy of Stars,* fraught with allusive vocabulary and lighthearted humour. A bizarre visionary, Shloyme Shvarts, unfolded a curious canvas of persons and places in his sixth collection, *Autumnal Fire.*

Two novelists in Israel and two in Romania sketched painful vignettes of contemporary Jewry caught up in communal catastrophe. From Israel came Yoysef Erlikh's novel *The Rich Poor Man,* an exploration into the psychology of a newcomer to that country as he adjusts to his new life. Meir Yelin tells of Jewish life and Gentile heroism in the ghetto of Kaunas, Lithuania, in *Barefoot on the Snow. Encounters . . . encounters* by Khaym Goldenshteyn deals with Romania during World War II. In his novel *The Travels of Benyumin IV,* Iso Schapira describes his cultural and political involvement in France, Germany, Romania, and Spain during the '20s and '30s.

Critic Leyzer Podriatshik exhibited a special interest in Soviet Yiddish letters in his collection of analytical essays, *Chats with Others and with Myself.* A distinguished reference work, Leonard S. Klein's four-volume *Encyclopedia of World Literature in the Twentieth Century,* provides considerable new material about recent Yiddish authors.

Poems and plays written in the Warsaw Ghetto during 1940–43 by Yitskhok Katsenelson, a Hebrew-Yiddish writer who perished in the Holocaust, were assembled and edited by Yekhiel Szejntuch in *Yiddish Ghetto Writings.* Arguably the most significant accomplishment by Soviet scholars in the area of Jewish studies was the publication of *A Russian-Yiddish Dictionary,* consisting of 40,000 Russian words, an essay on the origin and development of the Yiddish language, and a précis of Yiddish grammar. *Bridges,* a journal publishing translations of Yiddish writers into Hebrew and vice versa, made its appearance in Israel. (THOMAS E. BIRD; ELIAS SCHULMAN)

CHINESE

China. The so-called Anti-Spiritual Pollution Campaign against liberal intellectuals, writers, and artists launched in 1983 finally came to an end in early 1984 as a result of their strong resistance and unfavourable reactions from abroad. Certain Western ideas and views on art and literature were no longer condemned. In fact, there appeared to be a renewed interest in Western artistic and literary forms. The Communist authorities, however, still stressed that artistic and literary creations should serve the people and socialism and should educate and guide people to believe in socialism and the Communist leadership.

For the first time, a play revealing inside stories about the press, *Thursday's Page Four of Our Paper* by Wang Chenggang (Wang Ch'eng-kang), was presented to a Chinese audience. Exposing the dark side of Chinese journalism as well as the efforts of devoted journalists, it became an instant hit on the Chinese stage for its realistic portrayals of characters with human weaknesses as well as strengths. Another play, *Pot, Bowl, Dipper, and Pan Symphony,* an adaptation by Pang Jiangming (P'ang Chiang-ming) of a popular novelette by Jiang Zilong (Chiang Tzu-lung), also became an instant success for its interesting themes, humorous language, and truthful presentation of social and personal conflicts.

While a few poets continued to create personal and purely lyric poetry, it was such fiction writers as Zhang Kangkang (Chang K'ang-k'ang) who attracted the most attention for their vivid descriptions of the sufferings and agonies of Chinese youth.

Taiwan. In 1984 Taiwan witnessed the rise of the conservative faction of the ruling Nationalist Party at the expense of the liberals. As a result, Taiwan veered sharply to the right and adopted a more rigid policy toward art and literature.

The most visible literary achievement in 1984 was reflected in the highly successful adaptations, on both stage and screen, of a number of stories and novels by such noted writers as Pai Hsien-yung and Huang Ch'un-ming. Most became both artistic and commercial successes. Wang Chen-ho's novel *Rose, Rose, I Love You* exposed the evils associated with U.S. soldiers who came to Taiwan for rest and recreation during the Vietnam war in the late 1960s. Criticized by some for its explicit sexual descriptions, it became a best-seller and was widely praised by critics for its truthful presentation of human behaviour.

(WINSTON L. Y. YANG)

JAPANESE

Probably the most publicized literary event of the year in Japan was the 47th International PEN Congress in early April. It was 17 years since a PEN Congress had been held in Tokyo, and the contrast between the two meetings was dramatic. The first was notable for a naive aspiration toward international literary contacts on the part of Japanese writers, and most of the speeches concerned Western influence on Japanese literature. At the 47th Congress more serious attention was paid to Japanese literature, and there were speeches concerned with European, American, and even Chinese responses to Japanese authors. Considerable publicity was given to a "political" aspect of the congress, at least in the Japanese newspapers. The executive of the Japan PEN chose "The Nuclear Situation and Literature" as the general theme for the congress, despite the opposition of conservative members, who feared it would be utilized by leftists for political propaganda. On the whole, however, the tone of the speeches and discussions was reasonable and restrained.

The Tanizaki Prize was given to the two novelists Senji Kuroi and Yuichi Takai. Kuroi's *Gregarious* and Takai's *The Sky of This Country* made an interesting pair, since both dealt with the urban setting but in different periods. *Gregarious* was concerned with the involved relationship between four families living in a Tokyo neighbourhood. The pace of the narration was rather slow, and nothing spectacular happened in the story, but the oppressive texture of daily life in overcrowded Tokyo was cleverly conveyed. By contrast, *The Sky of This Country* dealt with Tokyo in the last phase of the Pacific War (World War II). The stress of the war years was the main theme of the novel,

Senji Kuroi
KYODO NEWS SERVICE

and the minute details of daily life of that gloomy period were evoked with uncanny accuracy, but Takai's style was objective and restrained, and the atmosphere was almost serene. In contrast with Kuroi and Takai, Kenji Nakagami could be called a champion of Japanese Vitalism, with a style that was exceptionally vigorous and dynamic. His *The Wings of the Sun-Goddess* concerned the picaresque pilgrimage of a curious group of old women, and his *Tales of Kumano* was a lively combination of personal episodes and evocations of mythical motifs.

Tsutomu Minakami's *Ryokan* and Miyoji Ueda's *This Life, This World* were remarkable achievements in literary biography. Ryokan was a hermit-priest of the later Edo period, whose saintly, naive behaviour and delicate poetic sensibility were described by Minakami with insight and sympathy. Ueda's book consisted of four portraits of religious personalities of various periods, and his fusion of sensitive poetic analysis with personal meditation proved quite effective. (SHOICHI SAEKI)

See also Art Exhibitions and Art Sales: *Art Sales;* Libraries; Nobel Prizes; Publishing.

This article updates the *Macropædia* article The History of Western LITERATURE and articles on the literatures of the various languages.

Mathematics

The most important mathematical event of 1984 was the surprising solution by Louis de Branges of Purdue University, West Lafayette, Ind., of a famous old conjecture in the field of complex analysis. Many mathematicians believed that a solution would require significant new mathematical tools; some thought that the conjecture was false. Yet by employing old results in clever new ways, de Branges accomplished what many believed to be impossible.

The problem that de Branges solved was proposed in 1916 by the German mathematician Ludwig Bieberbach while he was studying the coefficients of power series—polynomials having an infinite number of terms—that represent what are called analytic functions of a complex variable. These functions form the central core of much of modern analysis and mathematical physics and have innumerable applications in engineering.

Analytic functions are very smooth: they have neither sharp corners nor abrupt changes. Bieberbach explored the limits beyond which analytic functions could not go. His conjecture, in essence, sets limits on the growth of the coefficients of analytic functions, thereby describing inherent limits on their curvature.

Analytic functions act on complex numbers, numbers of

the form $a + bi$, in which i signifies the imaginary square root of -1. Complex numbers arise commonly as solutions to quadratic equations, given by the famous quadratic formula of high school algebra. Like ordinary real numbers, complex numbers can be added and subtracted, multiplied and divided. Unlike real numbers, however, they cannot be represented on a number line. Because each complex number includes two ordinary numbers, the a and the b, it takes a two-dimensional plane to represent the geometry of complex numbers.

Complex numbers are traditionally denoted by the letter z. The magnitude (or absolute value) of a complex number, denoted by $|z|$, represents its distance from the origin (the complex number 0). Polynomials in complex numbers work just like ordinary polynomials; so do power series, which look like infinite polynomials. For example, the expression $3z^3 + 2z + 7$ is a polynomial in the complex variable z, whereas the expression $z^2 + 2z^3 + 3z^4 + \ldots$ is a power series that represents an analytic function.

An analytic function establishes a relationship between the complex number z and the function's value, say w, at z; this relationship is usually expressed by the shorthand notation $w = f(z)$. If the numbers z are selected from a certain region in the plane of complex numbers, their "image points"—the numbers w—form a new region, usually with a shape different from the original. In this way the analytic function is said to map the original region to the new one, as if the old region were a city and the new region a street map for the city. The most commonly mapped region is the unit disk, the circular disk having a radius of one unit and centred at the origin. The behaviour of an analytic function on the unit disk provides a total picture of its behaviour on the entire plane, the only difference being a matter of scale.

The nicest analytic functions are those in which two different points on the original region are never mapped to the same point. They are called univalent functions, since each value comes from just one original point. Bieberbach's conjecture is just this: every univalent analytic function $z + a_2z^2 + a_3z^3 + \ldots$ (normalized as $a_0 = 0$, $a_1 = 1$) defined on the unit disk has the property that the magnitude of the coefficient a of the nth term in its power series can be no larger than n. In symbols, $|a_n| \leq n$.

Bieberbach proved this conjecture only for the coefficients of the first and second terms. It took more than 60 years for others to verify it for the coefficients of the third, fourth, fifth, and sixth terms; proving it for all coefficients simultaneously seemed quite beyond reach. Recently, using a different approach, the Soviet mathematician I. M. Milin of the University of Leningrad proved that the coefficient of the nth term of such functions is never more than 1.24 times n. Others reduced this factor to 1.07. De Branges proved an even stronger conjecture of Milin, from which the Bieberbach conjecture follows as a direct consequence.

De Branges had worked on this particular problem for more than seven years, most recently reducing the issue to a certain inequality that he began testing by computer to determine if it could possibly be true. Then, fortuitously, he discovered that the inequality had been proved in 1976 by Richard Askey of the University of Wisconsin and George Gasper of Northwestern University, Evanston, Ill.

Pulling together all the pieces, de Branges produced a 350-page manuscript containing the proof. Subsequently, Milin and his Soviet colleagues verified the proof and reduced its essence to about 15 pages.

(LYNN ARTHUR STEEN)

This article updates the *Macropædia* articles ANALYSIS (in Mathematics) and The History of MATHEMATICS.

Military Affairs

In the field of military affairs 1984 was a surprisingly static year. The conflicts and developments that occurred were continuations of existing ones. But the U.S. presidential election focused attention on Pres. Ronald Reagan's defense policy during his first term. The basic policies he had established seemed likely to be continued in his second term. Election rhetoric had obscured the president's success in rebuilding a bipartisan consensus in support of his reestablishment of the traditional postwar foreign and defense policy of containing the Soviet Union.

In 1980 President Reagan inherited diminished U.S. defense forces and budgets plus a widespread belief that the U.S. had become incapable of using force to protect its vital interests. The combination of those two factors had made the Soviets, their Cuban and Vietnamese allies, and other nations more willing to use force to further their interests. The Reagan administration had thus sought to rebuild both U.S. military capabilities and the will to use them. Under Secretary of Defense Caspar Weinberger the decline in the defense budget as a percentage of gross domestic product (GDP) was reversed. From a post-1950 low of 5% it rose to 6.5% in 1982 and was headed for some 8% in the late 1980s. Inflation had made this relatively modest burden, which was lower than the pre-Vietnam war average of 10% of GDP, large in monetary terms. For fiscal 1985 it was nearly $300 billion (actually $292.9 billion) of a 1983 gross domestic product of $3,264,800,000,000. The first Reagan administration's defense budgets, after congressional reductions, had increased by only 7% in real terms. As a share of the federal budget, defense was rising from about 24 to 33% from 1980 to 1988.

The bulk of the budget allocations (85%) went to general-purpose forces (GPF), with strategic, intermediate, and theatre nuclear forces (S/INF, TNF) accounting for only 15%. The administration's S/INF modernization programs had been controversial but were approved except for the MX Peacekeeper intercontinental ballistic missile (ICBM). What candidate Reagan in 1980 had called the window of vulnerability of the U.S. (the nation's vulnerability to a Soviet first strike) was still open but was beginning to close. TNF modernization was also under way.

Quantitatively, U.S. GPF were not much larger in personnel and equipment. Qualitatively, however, they were far more effective. In 1980 a large proportion of the GPF had been paper forces with inadequate personnel and obsolete or inoperative equipment. In 1984 personnel quality was the highest in the history of the all-volunteer force (AVF), and equipment was being modernized.

The Reagan administration did not publicly announce an overall strategic concept for the use of these forces. Implicitly, it was to rely on U.S. nuclear weapons to deter major Soviet attacks on areas of vital interest, such as Western Europe, and on a combination of U.S. GPF and allied forces to deter or defeat limited attacks by the Soviets or other powers in other areas, such as Latin America. Within the Western alliance the U.S. would concentrate, for geographic and technical reasons, on providing the nuclear deterrent and also mobile air and naval forces for deployment to threatened areas but would supply only limited numbers of ground forces. The allies of the U.S. would provide the bulk of the local ground and air plus some naval forces.

During President Reagan's first term the use of U.S. forces had been very limited but enough to reestablish U.S. credibility. The U.S. Navy had shot down two threatening

Libyan jets in 1981. The U.S. along with the Organization of Eastern Caribbean States, had liberated Grenada in 1983. U.S. military casualties had also been limited, totaling fewer than 1,000, mostly incurred by the U.S. peacekeeping force in Lebanon. The Soviets and their allies had refrained from using their forces to expand the areas under their control except, unsuccessfully through 1984, in Central America.

Critics complained that the U.S. military buildup was excessive and unaffordable. The criticism that the Reagan administration was too willing to use military force confused its rhetoric with reality. Its belligerent talk had been accompanied by carefully controlled and limited action. Critics of particular weapons systems made some valid points, especially concerning overpricing and quality. But on balance, the first Reagan administration's defense policy had been relatively successful. U.S. budgets and forces were being rebuilt after a decade of neglect.

UNITED STATES

U.S. armed forces in 1984 totaled 2,135,900 personnel (198,000 women). Retention rates were the highest since the introduction of the AVF.

Modernization of the U.S. S/INF continued. The aging B-52 force of the Strategic Air Command (SAC) was reduced to 151 B-52G's and 90 B-52H's (first deployed in 1959 and 1962, respectively). Of the B-52G's, 90 were being converted to carry 12 AGM-86B air-launched cruise missiles (ALCM) each. SAC also had 56 FB-111A medium-range nuclear bombers.

The first production model of 100 B-1B strategic bombers was completed ahead of schedule and under cost. The first squadron was scheduled to become operational in 1985. The B-1B was designed to fly at very low levels and defeat enemy radar by a combination of technologies that minimized its radar and infrared visibility. Initially, it was to function as a penetrating bomber and later as an ALCM

carrier. Its long range and large weapons load also would make it usable in regional conflicts, supplementing the 61 B-52G's that were retained in a conventional role.

The advanced technology (stealth) bomber continued under development in 1984. Because it utilized radically new technologies, its cost, performance, and development time were uncertain.

With the B-52 force near the end of its useful life, the B-1B would fill an important gap. The success of the B-1B program was marred by the tragic crash of one of four B-1A test aircraft, which killed Rockwell's chief test pilot, Tommie Douglas Benefield.

The vulnerability of the U.S. land-based fixed-silo ICBM force remained a major problem. By the end of 1984 the Soviets were able to destroy 90–95% of it in a first strike. As of 1984 the effective U.S. ICBM force was 1,000 Minuteman II and Minuteman III missiles and silos, but without the reload capabilities that the Soviets had. Only the 550 Minuteman III's were modernized missiles carrying multiple independently targeted reentry vehicles (MIRV). The 450 Minuteman II's were nearly 20 years old. The 37 obsolete Titan II missiles were being retired.

After intense political debate, production of the first of 100 new MX Peacekeeper ICBM seemed likely but by no means certain to be authorized. Deployment was to be in existing Minuteman silos, which could not survive a Soviet attack. Development of the small (weighing about 11,350 kg [25,000 lb]) single-warhead Midgetman ICBM was continuing. Deployment modes being considered included a land-mobile version carried in armoured vehicles.

The ballistic missile nuclear submarine (SSBN) force rose to 35 carrying 592 submarine-launched ballistic missiles (SLBM). Four new Ohio-class SSBN each carried 24 Trident I/C-4s, which were to be replaced by the Trident II/D-5 SLBM in 1988–89. Older SSBN comprised 12 Franklin-class (192 Trident I/C-4s) and 19 Lafayette-class (304 Poseidon C-3s).

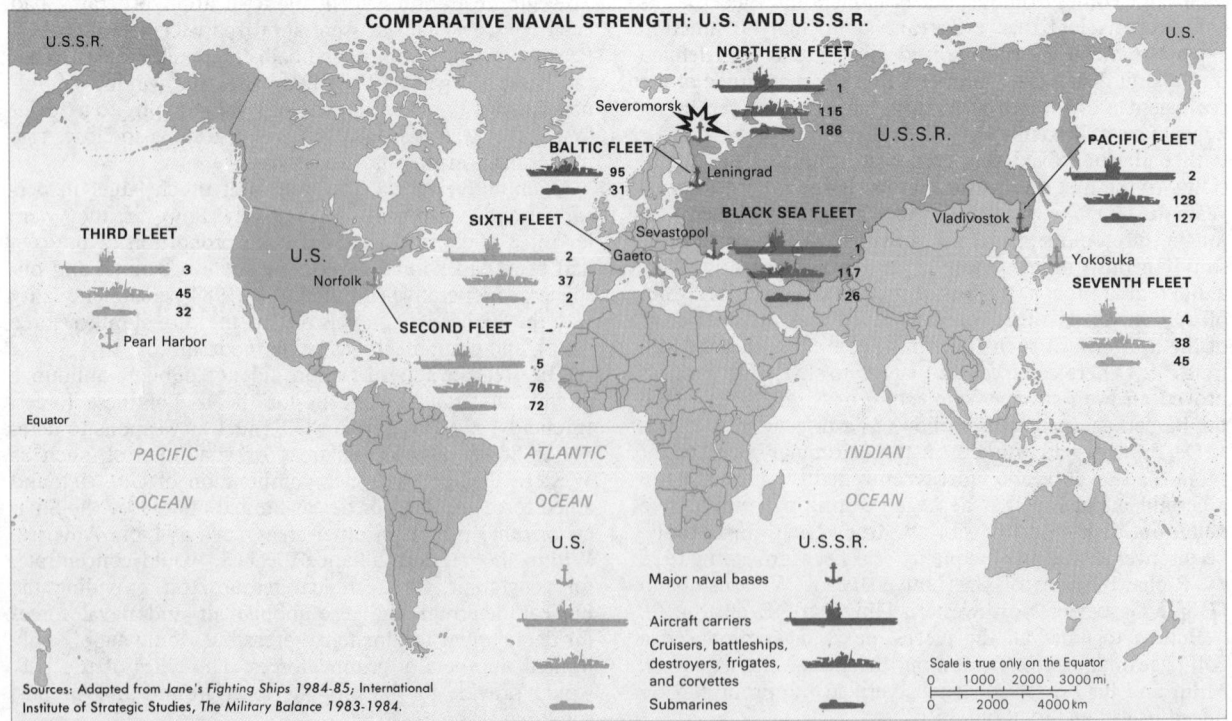

Deployment of major naval vessels of the Soviet Union and the United States (best estimates of 1983 for the U.S. and 1984 for the U.S.S.R., excluding reserves, inactive vessels, and ships under construction). Severomorsk (headquarters of the Soviet Northern Fleet) was the site of a series of explosions in May that did extensive damage.

Deployment of submarine-launched nuclear cruise missiles began, with four nuclear cruise-missile submarines so equipped. A total of 700 BGM-109A Tomahawk sea-launched cruise missiles (SLCM) was planned. An additional 2,300 conventionally armed Tomahawk SLCM were being deployed so that each vessel would carry a mix of nuclear and conventionally armed missiles. Dispersing the nuclear SLCM would enhance their survivability.

The North American Aerospace Defense Command remained minimal, with only 90 F-15 Eagle and 38 Canadian CF-188 (F-18) Hornet interceptors. To balance the Soviets' antisatellite (Asat) system, the U.S. was developing and testing an Asat system carried by F-15 Eagles. In a television address on March 23, 1983, President Reagan proposed a space-based defensive system that became popularly known as the "Star Wars" defense. (*See* Special Report.)

The U.S. Navy continued building toward a 600-ship navy, with 206 major surface combatants, 91 nuclear attack submarines (SSN), and personnel totaling 564,800. These provided 13 carrier battle groups (to rise to 15), each with an attack wing of 70–95 aircraft plus escorting surface vessels and SSN. The modern (post-1955) aircraft carrier fleet of 11 comprised 4 nuclear and 7 conventionally powered carriers. Modern aircraft included 240 F-14A Tomcat interceptors, 120 A-6E Intruders, and 25 F-18A Hornet strike planes and electronic warfare/airborne electronic warning aircraft. A second recommissioned World War II battleship, the "Iowa," joined the "New Jersey"; both were equipped with Tomahawk surface-to-surface missiles. The 9 nuclear and 19 conventionally powered guided weapons (GW) cruisers included two new Ticonderoga-class ships with the Aegis fleet air defense missile/radar system. Other major surface combatants included 37 GW and 31 gun/antisubmarine warfare (ASW) Spruance-class destroyers, plus 41 GW and 53 gun frigates.

The Marine Corps with 196,600 personnel formed, with the Navy, the main U.S. power-projection force. It was organized in three divisions, each with its integral air wing. Modern aircraft included 48 F-18 Hornet interceptor/strike aircraft, 50 A-6E Intruder strike aircraft, and 45 AV-8A/C Harrier vertical/short takeoff and landing (V/STOL) interceptor strike aircraft. The 61 amphibious warfare ships carrying the Corps included 5 Tarawa and 7 Iwo Jima helicopter/Harrier carriers.

The 594,500-strong Air Force had some 3,700 combat aircraft. Modern types included 384 F-15 Eagle interceptors, 456 F-16 Fighting Falcon fighter-bombers, and 34 E-3A/8 Sentry airborne warning and control systems. Among older types were 570 F-4 Phantom fighter-bombers/reconnaissance, 230 F-111A/D/E/F medium bombers, and 288 A-10A Thunderbolt ground-support aircraft.

The Army, with 780,800 personnel, formed 16 divisions (18,500 men each): 4 armoured, 6 mechanized, 3 infantry, 1 light infantry, 1 air assault, and 1 airborne. Armour included 1,483 M-1 Abrams tanks and 1,100 M-2/3 Bradley mechanized infantry combat vehicles (MICV), both new, plus some 9,000 M-60A1, M-60A2, and M-60A3 Patton tanks and 12,300 M-113 armoured personnel carriers (APC). New missile systems included 63 multiple-launch rocket systems and 60 Patriot surface-to-air missiles (SAM). The Army manned the two new INF systems, the Pershing II intermediate-range ballistic missile (IRBM; range 1,800 km [800 mi]) and the BGM-109A Tomahawk ground-launched cruise missile (GLCM; range 2,500 km [1,100 mi]). A total of 48 Pershing II's and 64 GLCM were operational.

(continued on page 322)

Table I. U.S./NATO–Soviet Strategic and Intermediate Nuclear Force Balance, July 1984

Weapons systems	Range (km)	Payload¹ (000 lb)	Warheads, yield²	CEP³	Speed (Mach)	Number deployed
UNITED STATES Strategic Forces						
Intercontinental ballistic missiles (ICBM)						1,000
Titan II	15,000	8.3	1×9 mt	1,300	...	37–0⁴
Minuteman II	11,300	1.6	1×1–2 mt	370	...	450
Minuteman III Mod 1	14,800	1.5	3×170 kt	280	...	250
Mod 2	12,900	2.4	3×335 kt	220	...	300
Submarine-launched ballistic missiles (SLBM; in 36 nuclear submarines)						520
Poseidon C-3	4,600	3.3	10×50 kt or 14×50 kt	450	...	304
Trident I/C-4	7,400	3.0	8×100 kt	450	...	288
Manned bombers and air-launched cruise missiles (ALCM)						
B-52G	12,000	70	...	...	0.95	151
B-52H	16,000	70	...	...	0.95	90
FB-111A	4,700	37.5	...	...	2.5	56
AGM-86B ALCM	2,400		200 kt	...	0.7	1,008
U.S./NATO Intermediate Nuclear Forces⁵ (Total: 702 weapons, 342 delivery systems)						
Intermediate-range ballistic missiles (IRBM)						
U.S. Pershing II	1,800	...	5–50+ kt	45		48
Manned bombers and ground-launched cruise missiles (GLCM)						
U.S. F-111 E/F	4,700	28	3		2.5	230⁶
Tomahawk	2,250	0.2	200 kt	100	0.7	64
BRITAIN (Strategic Nuclear Forces only)⁷						
Submarine-launched ballistic missiles (SLBM; in 4 nuclear submarines)						
Polaris A-3	4,600	1	3–6×200 kt	900		64
Strike aircraft						
Buccaneer	3,700	12	2	...	0.95	25⁴
Tornado	2,800	16	2	...	0.95	80
FRANCE (Strategic and INF)⁷						
Submarine-launched ballistic missiles (SLBM; in 5 nuclear submarines)						
MSBS M-20	3,000		1×1 mt			80
Intermediate-range ballistic missiles (IRBM)						
SSBS S-3	3,500	...	1×1 mt			18
Strike aircraft						
Mirage IVA	3,200	16	1×60 kt	...	2.2	28
Mirage IIIE	2,400	19	2×15 kt	...	1.8	30
Super Etendard	1,500	2	2×15 kt	...	1.0	36
SOVIET UNION Strategic Forces						
Intercontinental ballistic missiles (ICBM)						c. 1,700+
SS-11 Mod 1	10,500	2	1×1 mt	1,400	...	} 520
Mod 3	8,800	2.5	3×100–300 kt	1,100	...	
SS-13 Savage	10,000	1	750 kt	2,000	...	60
SS-16	9–10,000	...	3×150 kt	...	...	200⁸
SS-17 Mod 1	10,000	6	4×750 kt	450	...	} 150
Mod 2	11,000	3.6	6 mt	450	...	
Mod 3	10,000		4×20 kt	...		
SS-18 Mod 1	12,000	16.5	20 mt	450	...	
Mod 2	11,000	16.7	8×900 kt	450	...	} 308
Mod 3	10,500	16	20 mt	350	...	
Mod 4	11,000	16.7	10×500 kt	300	...	
SS-19 Mod 2	10,000	7.5	5 mt	300	...	} 360
Mod 3	10,000	8	6×550 kt	300	...	
Submarine-launched ballistic missiles (in 65 nuclear plus 14 diesel submarines)						c. 1,000
SS-N-5 Serb	1,400	...	1×1–2 mt	2,800	...	45
SS-N-6 Mod 1,2	3,000	1.5	1×1 mt	900	...	368
Mod 3	3,000	1.5	2×200 kt	1,400	...	
SS-N-8 Mod 1	7,800	1.5	1×1 mt	1,300	...	292
Mod 2	9,100	8	1×800 kt	900	...	
SS-N-17	3,900	2.5	1×1 mt	1,500	...	12
SS-N-18 Mod 1	6,500	5	3×200 kt	1,400	...	224
Mod 2	8,000	...	1×450 kt	600	...	
Mod 3	6,500	...	7×200 kt	600	...	
SS-N-20	8,300	...	9–12×200 kt	...	...	40
Manned bombers						c. 380
Tu-95 Bear B/C	12,800	40	3–5	...	0.78	100
Mya-4 Bison	11,200	20	4	...	0.87	43
Tu-26 Backfire B	8,000	17.5	4	...	2.5	235
Soviet INF (Total: c. 4,823 warheads, c. 1,423 delivery systems)						
Variable/intermediate/medium-range ballistic missiles (V/I/MRBM)⁹						
SS-4 Sandal	2,000	3	1×1 mt	2,300		223
SS-20 Mod 1	5,000	1.2	1×1.5 mt			
Mod 2	5,000	...	3×150 kt	c. 400		c. 1,200
Mod 3	7,400	...	1×50 kt			...
Medium/short-range ballistic missiles and sea-launched cruise missiles¹⁰						
SS-22 MRBM	1,000	...	1×500 kt	300		c. 100
SS-N-12 G/SLCM	1,000	...	1×350 kt	2.2		c. 100
Manned bombers¹¹						745
Tu-16 Badger	4,800	20	2	...	0.8	410
Tu-22 Blinder	4,000	12	2	...	1.5	160

¹ Payload refers to a missile's throw weight or a bomber's weapons load.
² For MIRV and MRV the figure to the left of the multiplication sign gives the number of warheads and the figure to the right is the yield per warhead. For bombers, weapons per bomber are given.
³ Circular Error Probable: the radius (in metres) of a circle within which at least half of the missile warheads aimed at a specific target will fall.
⁴ Obsolete systems being withdrawn; excluded from number deployed
⁵ INF systems are missiles with ranges or aircraft with unrefueled combat radii of 1,000 km or more; combat radii are about one-third or less of the range.
⁶ Total deployed worldwide, including FB-111A; 150 is the inventory normally based in Europe within striking range of Europe.
⁷ British nuclear forces are under national control, but may be assigned to NATO. French nuclear forces are controlled and targeted independently of NATO.
⁸ Mobile SS-16 ICBM reported deployed, based on SS-20 V/IRBM.
⁹ Total deployed against both NATO and China theatres; two-thirds are thought to be deployed against NATO. Three missiles per launcher.
¹⁰ Although not classified as Soviet INF, Soviet M/SRBM and G/SLCM could hit targets in Western Europe and are therefore shown for illustrative purposes.
¹¹ Total deployed worldwide. Of these, about half are allocated to Soviet Naval Aviation (some 190 Tu-16, 35 Tu-22, and 100 Tu-26). Two-thirds of the remaining strike bombers and ASM carriers are considered deployed against NATO. Tu-26 Backfire is now counted as strategic.

Sources: International Institute for Strategic Studies, *The Military Balance 1984–1985*; and *Aviation Week and Space Technology*. Figures for Soviet forces, especially INF, can only be estimates.

Star Wars: President Reagan's Strategic Defense Initiative

BY ROBIN RANGER

The single most important strategic question to be answered during the second term of U.S. Pres. Ronald Reagan was whether the U.S. would build a strategic defense system against potential nuclear attacks from the Soviet Union. If the U.S. did so, it would reverse the 20-year-old doctrine of mutual and assured destruction (MAD).

This doctrine led the U.S. to dismantle its strategic defensive forces and concentrate on strategic offensive forces. The MAD theory maintained that if these offensive forces were guaranteed to inflict unacceptable damage on the Soviet Union after the most effective possible Soviet attack on them, then deterrence would be assured. Since the Soviets had the same capability of guaranteeing retaliation, deterrence would be mutual and assured.

President Reagan's March 23, 1983, nationwide television address proposed the construction of a U.S. strategic defensive system, replacing MAD with the doctrine of mutual and assured survival (MAS). Because parts of this system would be space-based, the speech was quickly dubbed "Star Wars." It was controversial and confusing because the president's rhetoric exaggerated the extent of the initial changes. Reagan held out a vision of an impenetrable defensive shield over the U.S. that would render nuclear weapons "impotent and obsolete." In fact, what he subsequently proposed, in March 1984, was a five-year research and development program for strategic defenses to cost $26 billion.

This program raised three questions. First, at the doctrinal level, was the shift from MAD to MAS desirable? Second, at the technical level, could a strategic defensive system be built that would be effective and affordable? Third, what would be the implications for arms control of the U.S.'s building such a system?

The answers to these questions differed sharply depending on whether they were given by those for or against the strategic defensive system. Those in favour included the president; his chief scientific adviser, George Keyworth II; and Secretary of Defense Caspar Weinberger. Those opposed included McGeorge Bundy, a former national security adviser; George F. Kennan, a former ambassador to the Soviet Union; Robert S. McNamara, a former secretary of defense; and Gerard Smith, a former U.S. ambassador to the strategic arms limitations talks. As the "Star Wars" debate heated up, it became apparent that the real answers lay between these two extremes.

The Doctrinal Debate. At the doctrinal level proponents of MAD argued that it was a statement of the unalterable technical facts of nuclear deterrence. No defensive system

Robin Ranger is associate professor, Defense and Strategic Studies Program, School of International Relations, at the University of Southern California.

could provide complete protection from a large-scale nuclear attack. Even a very small percentage of the 50,000 weapons in the superpowers' nuclear stockpiles would be enough to cause unacceptable damage. Any attempt by the U.S. to build strategic defenses would thus be futile. It could also be destabilizing because it would force the Soviets to increase their offensive forces and could lead them to develop defensive systems of their own. The result would be a less stable balance of nuclear deterrence at much higher costs. Moreover, MAD provided the doctrinal foundation for strategic arms control by limiting the size of strategic offensive forces needed to assure deterrence.

Proponents of MAS argued that MAD was immoral in principle. It held the populations of both superpowers hostage to a Soviet decision to attack the U.S. or to a limited nuclear conflict arising out of accident or miscalculation. While the U.S. government was committed not to strike first, they argued, the Soviets were not, and the Soviet people had no control over the actions of their government. In practice, MAD was being rendered technologically obsolete by improvements in accuracy that were making strategic offensive forces vulnerable to attack and also by improvements in defensive systems. The Soviets were ahead of the U.S. doctrinally with their recognition of these realities and their rejection of MAD.

On balance, the doctrinal debate came out in favour of a move away from a pure MAD doctrine to one favouring a balance between offensive and defensive forces. Although this indicated a move toward MAS, it would be a long time before the balance of deterrence would be based on MAS, if indeed it ever would be. But there was a clear case in principle for having some strategic defenses if this was technically feasible, as it now was. How large such defenses should be was a question to be answered pragmatically on the basis of cost and effectiveness.

Even limited strategic defenses could stabilize the balance of deterrence by making the theoretical chances for a successful attack appear much less attractive to a potential attacker in two ways. First, Soviet planning for an attack on U.S. strategic nuclear forces would have to assume, as a matter of prudence, that attacking Soviet forces would function at the lower end of their performance spectrum while the defending U.S. forces would function at the higher end of theirs. Such planning would drive up Soviet requirements for the offensive forces needed to mount a successful strategic attack, making this less attractive. Second, a whole new range of uncertainties about the interaction of attacking Soviet forces with defending U.S. forces would make calculations of the chances of a successful Soviet strategic attack even more problematic.

These doctrinal considerations were particularly important because the size and characteristics of Soviet strategic forces were such that they had a major first-strike capability against the U.S., at least in theory, which the U.S. could not match. Such a Soviet capability could, unless offset by the U.S., create instability during major international crises. It seemed preferable for the U.S. to prevent this by building defensive rather than offensive strategic forces. These could also offer some much-needed protection to the U.S. population in the event of a very limited attack, by the Soviets or other nuclear powers, caused by accident or miscalculation.

As of 1984 the U.S. had no protection at all against most forms of nuclear attack. The only exception was the North American Aerospace Defense Command operated by the U.S. and Canada. It was very small and of limited effectiveness against Soviet bombers.

The Technical Issues. In regard to technical issues, two questions appeared. First, could a defense system be effective enough to make it worth deploying? Second, could the costs of such a system be brought low enough to make deployment possible on a scale large enough to be effective?

Two expert panels, the Defensive Technologies Study Team, headed by James C. Fletcher, and the Future Security Strategy Study, led by Fred S. Hoffman, were set up after the "Star Wars" speech to assess the technical and policy implications of a U.S. ballistic missile defense (BMD) system. Their reports led the administration to conclude that a BMD system was both technically feasible and affordable over the long term—10 to 20 years. The technologies had so matured that a unified research and development effort would soon be productive. Accordingly, the administration established a central office to coordinate the Strategic Defense Initiative (SDI) under Lieut. Gen. James Abrahamson. It adopted a building-block approach to the construction of a BMD system. This broke the total construction of a BMD system down into its components and established a BMD research, development, and deployment program. Initially, BMD technology would offer a moderately effective defense only of hard military targets, such as U.S. ICBM silos, plus a limited defense of the population. Later, this could be upgraded. Neither military nor civilian targets could be protected against an all-out Soviet attack, but this was unlikely because all-out retaliation by the U.S. would ensue. What was necessary was a defense against more limited attacks that would make them so ineffective as to deter them.

On technical grounds such a defense seems feasible because of the new possibilities of what became known as a layered, preferential defense. The principle is that attacking missiles should be intercepted in each of the four phases of their flight: boost (from launch to booster burnout); early midcourse (deployment of warheads and decoys); late midcourse (from deployment to reentry into the atmosphere); and terminal (from reentry to detonation). Interception in the first and fourth phases would be partly inside the atmosphere (endoatmospheric) and partly outside (exoatmospheric). The cumulative effects of a four-tier layered defense are surprisingly large even if each tier is only moderately effective. For example, if each tier could destroy only half the attacking force, the cumulative effect would be to destroy 94% of the attack. Even more would be destroyed if the later layers of the defense could concentrate on the surviving attacking force, with a shoot–look–shoot-again capability.

The preferential defense concept compounds the attacker's problems by concentrating defense forces around some, rather than all, of the targets being attacked. For example, the U.S. might decide to defend only half of its force of 1,000 ICBM's but constantly change the status of each ICBM between defended and nondefended. A potential Soviet attacker would therefore have to plan to attack each U.S. ICBM as if it were defended, a much harder task.

The potential components of a layered defense system are many. They include laser battle stations in space and directed energy weapons, thereby giving rise to the nickname "Star Wars." But they also include air-based platforms and ground-based missiles. The sensors to detect attacks could be based on the ground, in the air, or in space, as could the information systems to process the data gathered. Sensors could be radar, optical, and infrared (heat detecting). The attacking missiles and warheads would be destroyed mainly by nonnuclear kill (NNK)

mechanisms, although some very small nuclear weapons might also be used.

A dramatic demonstration of the new defensive technologies occurred in 1984. The U.S. Army Ballistic Missile Defense Command successfully intercepted a dummy warhead launched by a Minuteman ICBM after it had traveled 1,600 km (1,000 mi) in space and destroyed it with an NNK in the form of a large metal umbrella spread out by the intercepting vehicle.

Critics claimed that a BMD system was too complex to be effective because it would have to work perfectly the first time it was used. The technical demands on a BMD system would certainly be formidable, but this did not mean they would be insurmountable. Overall, the SDI approach made technical sense by investigating pragmatically what a BMD system could and could not do. Moreover, neither research nor deployment of such a system would be funded by a skeptical Senate and House of Representatives unless they were convinced of its merits.

Arms Control Issues. The issues centring on arms control were the most controversial because they involved conflicting predictions about the future. Opponents of SDI argued that, in principle, it would militarize space. It would also undermine the 1974 Protocol to the Anti-Ballistic Missile (ABM) Treaty of 1972 banning more than one ABM site for each superpower—the last major surviving arms control agreement. Without the treaty's limits on defensive systems it would be much more difficult, probably impossible, to achieve limits on strategic offensive nuclear forces. The SDI would also make it impossible to obtain an agreement that would prevent the deployment of effective antisatellite systems.

Proponents of SDI argued that the choice was not so simple. In principle, space has already been militarized. Both superpowers relied on their space satellites for a wide range of military functions and for the verification of arms control agreements. The Soviets had deployed an operational antisatellite system for over a decade, necessitating a countervailing U.S. deployment. The Soviets had also deployed an ABM system far exceeding the treaty limits and were building the items needed to deploy a nationwide ABM system for the late 1980s. They were completing a massive ABM radar and battle-management system at Krasnoyarsk. Since the Soviets had never complied with the ABM treaty, the SDI could hardly undermine it. Moreover, the SDI did not deter the Soviets from agreeing to the Jan. 7, 1985, meeting between U.S. Secretary of State George Shultz and U.S.S.R. Foreign Minister Andrey Gromyko to launch the umbrella arms control talks covering offensive and defensive weapons, both nuclear and conventional.

President Reagan's SDI was thus a historic turning point in the evolution of U.S. strategic nuclear doctrine and forces. It reestablished the doctrinal case for defensive as well as offensive forces. It recognized the new technological realities making effective strategic defenses possible over the next 20 years. It reaffirmed the need for the U.S. to maximize deterrence of a potential Soviet attack. It also provided for defense if deterrence failed. Constructive criticism from within the U.S. and from its NATO allies in Europe would ensure that resources would be allocated to the SDI only when they would produce effective defense. It would also guarantee that the U.S. would continue to seek effective arms control agreements. In the long run a balance of nuclear deterrence between superpowers with defensive as well as offensive forces promised the best hope of preserving a situation in which no nuclear weapons would ever be used.

(continued from page 319)

The U.S. forces abroad (total personnel) remained concentrated in Europe (about 350,000) and the Pacific (some 139,000, including 40,000 in South Korea). There were also about 20,000 in the Caribbean/Latin America.

U.S.S.R.

The Soviet military machine remained the most powerful in the world. Personnel totaled 5.1 million (including 1.5 million command and general support personnel), plus 1.1 million paramilitary security forces. Defense spending remained high at 13–14% of gross national product (GNP), about $267 billion. The surprise September replacement of Marshal Nikolay Ogarkov by his deputy, Marshal Sergey Akhromeyev (*see* BIOGRAPHIES), as chief of staff remained unexplained.

The Strategic Rocket Forces had 415,000 troops and continued to increase their superiority over U.S. and NATO S/INF in missile and warhead numbers plus warhead yields and accuracy. As of 1984 the Soviets had a first-strike capability that the U.S. would not have during the rest of the 20th century. The figures shown in Table I underestimate the Soviet advantage because the U.S.S.R. also deployed 1,000–3,000 reload missiles for their ICBM, IRBM, and SLBM launchers. New systems being tested and deployed included two ICBM, the PL-4 SS-X-24 and PL-5 SS-X-25 (both mobile); five long-range cruise missiles, three similar to the U.S. Tomahawk, the SS-NX-21 SLCM, the SSC-X-4 GLCM, and the AS-X-15 ALCM (all in the 3,000-km [1,400-mi] range), plus two much larger long-range G/SLCM; and the SS-NX-23 SLBM. The two new Typhoon-class SSBN, each carrying 20 SS-N-20 MIRV'ed SLBM, were the world's largest, displacing 23,000 tons.

The strategic bomber force comprised the new Blackjack A, larger than the U.S.'s B-1B; 100 older Bear B/C's plus resumed production of the Bear H as an ALCM launcher; and 130 Tu-26 Backfire B's. Additional medium-range bombers included 125 Tu-22 Blinder A/B's and 220 obsolete Tu-16 Badgers.

Soviet strategic defensive forces were also large. The Soviet National Air Defense Troops (Voyska-PVO) formed a separate service with some 370,000 personnel, 4,000 interceptors, and 9,600 SAM launchers at 1,000 fixed sites. The latest SAM, the SA-X-12, had a tactical antiballistic missile (ABM) capability. Soviet upgrading of the ABM system around Moscow, plus the construction of other ABM radars, would enable the U.S.S.R. to field a nationwide ABM system.

The 1.8 million-strong Army was organized into 50 tank, 136 motor rifle (mechanized), 15 artillery, and 7 airborne divisions (7,000–14,000 men each). Equipment remained at much higher levels than for the U.S., its NATO allies, and China. It included 51,000 tanks (the modern types comprising 7,700 T-72/80 and 8,000 T-64, plus 35,000 older T-54/-55/-62); 70,000 armoured fighting vehicles; and 34,-000 artillery pieces, including new self-propelled 203-mm, 152-mm and 122-mm guns.

Deployment of the Soviet Army forces was roughly two-thirds against NATO-Europe and one-third against China. There were three theatre commands, plus a central strategic reserve military district with 16 divisions. The Western theatre command controlled 30 Soviet divisions (16 tank, 14 motor rifle) and 45 non-Soviet divisions in Central and Eastern Europe, plus 65 divisions (23 tank, 37 motor rifle, 5 airborne) in the European U.S.S.R. The Southern theatre command controlled 30 divisions, mainly motor rifle, including some 115,000 troops occupying Afghanistan. Despite their illegal use of chemical and bi-

The Northrop F-20 Tigershark tactical fighter excelled in computer-aided bomb-drop tests at Edwards Air Force Base in California. All drops met or exceeded goals; one bomb struck within two feet of the centre of the target.
AUTHENTICATED NEWS INTERNATIONAL

ological weapons and scorched-earth tactics, Soviet forces, after five years, had still failed to establish control over the Afghanistan countryside. Soviet casualties were estimated at 15,000–20,000, and morale problems were severe. The Far Eastern theatre controlled 52 divisions (7 tank, 45 motor rifle). Large overseas deployments were in Syria (7,000), Vietnam (7,000), and Cuba (4,600), with smaller ones of 500–2,500 troops each in Algeria, Angola, Ethiopia, Iraq, Laos, Libya, Yemen (Aden), and Yemen (San'a').

The 400,000-strong Air Force had some 3,260 combat aircraft and 2,300 helicopters. The two new fighters, the MiG-29 Fulcrum and the Su-27 Flanker, also had ground attack capabilities, especially the former. Of the 4,000 fighters possessed by the Voyska-PVO and the Air Force, modern types included 50 MiG-31 Foxhound A's, 380 MiG-25 Foxbat A/E's, and 2,100 MiG-23 Flogger B/G's. Of the 2,600 fighter-bombers, modern types included 730 MiG-27 Flogger D/J's, 850 Su-17 Fitter D/H's, 630 Su-24 Fencer A/C's, and 75 Su-25 Frogfoot ground-attack aircraft. Reconnaissance aircraft totaled 620, including 170 MiG-25 B/D's. Operations using the 4,100 helicopters were increasingly important, especially those using heavily armed attack and assault helicopters such as the Mi-24 Hind E and Mi-8 Hip E, as well as the Mi-8 Hip C and Mi-17 Hip H. These air assets, together with those of the air defense force, were being reorganized into the air forces of the military districts under the theatre of military operations. This provided for greater flexibility in concentrating air forces for offensive and defensive operations as required.

The Navy (490,000 personnel), combining defensive, offensive, and power-projection capabilities, had 293 major surface combatants and 211 attack and 67 cruise-missile submarines, both nuclear and conventional. A nuclear-powered attack cruiser was being built to carry fixed-wing interceptor strike aircraft, supplementing the limited V/STOL fighter and helicopter capabilities of the four Kiev-class carriers and two Moskva-class cruisers. A second Kirov-class nuclear-powered GW battle cruiser and a second Slava-class GW cruiser were added to the 8 GW and 17 GW ASW cruisers. The 45 GW destroyers included 3 new Sovremennyys and 4 new Udaloys. Of the 49 nuclear cruise-missile submarines, 2 were of the new Oscar class.

The main deployment of the Soviet Navy was in the Northern Fleet based in the Kola Peninsula (180 submarines and 80 major surface combatants) and the Pacific Fleet (133 submarines and 88 major surface combatants). The Naval Air Force had 839 combat aircraft, including 105 Tu-26 Backfire B's. The Soviet Navy's continued operational difficulties were dramatized by the explosion of much of the Northern Fleet's conventional ammunition depot at Severomorsk in May.

WARSAW PACT

The Soviet cancellation of East German leader Erich Honecker's planned visit to West Germany dramatized the growing gap between Soviet interests in Eastern Europe and those of its Warsaw Pact allies. So also did the continuing strong support in Poland for the illegal Solidarity trade union movement. There were thus increasing political uncertainties in the Eastern bloc about the degree of non-Soviet Warsaw Pact support for a putative Soviet invasion of NATO-Europe. Soviet forces included 20 divisions in East Germany, 2 in Poland, and 4 in Hungary. Poland had the largest forces of the Eastern European nations, totaling 323,000 personnel and including a 210,000-strong Army with 3,450 T-54/-55/-72 main battle tanks and a 91,000-strong Air Force with 675 combat aircraft (400 MiG-21/U/-23 interceptors). Czechoslovakia's 207,-000-strong forces, the second largest, comprised an Army of 148,000 with 3,500 T-54/-55/-72 tanks and an Air Force of 59,000 with 439 combat aircraft (252 MiG-21/-21U/-23 interceptors).

East Germany's armed forces totaled 172,000, mainly an Army of 120,000 with 1,500 T-54/-55/-72 tanks (plus 1,600 in storage) and an Air Force of 38,000 with 360 combat aircraft, including 300 MiG-21F/MF/PF/U-23 interceptors. Hungary's armed forces, with 105,000 personnel, comprised an Army of 84,000 with about 1,200 T-54/-55/-72 tanks and an Air Force of 21,000 with 145 MiG-21/-23 interceptors. All four countries allocated much lower proportions of their GNP's to defense than did the U.S.S.R.; 1982 figures were 6.5% for East Germany, 5.2% for Czechoslovakia, about 4% for Poland, and 2.4% for Hungary.

NATO

By 1984 NATO had survived the four-year crisis caused by its 1979 decision to deploy 572 new INF (108 Pershing II IRBM and 464 GLCM). These partly balanced the much larger Soviet deployment of SS-20 IRBM, totaling 396 launchers each with one missile plus two reloads for a total of 3,564 warheads (each missile had an average of three warheads). NATO's INF modernization program had been opposed by a massive Soviet propaganda campaign, accompanied by popular protest movements across Western Europe. As a result the NATO-Europe governments had pressured the U.S. to negotiate an arms control agreement that would limit both sides' intermediate nuclear forces. Negotiations started in 1981 but were broken off by the Soviets in 1983. NATO, therefore, began deploying INF in 1983 as scheduled in three countries: the U.K., Italy, and West Germany. Belgium and The Netherlands were sched-

uled for future deployment, but Belgium was deferring its decision on whether to do so until early 1985, and The Netherlands would not make a final determination until the following November.

In one sense NATO had won a major victory. It had begun to implement its 1979 decision despite Soviet and domestic opposition and without experiencing any of the terrible unspecified adverse actions threatened by the Soviets. But, in another sense, the crisis suggested serious weaknesses in the alliance. It had experienced great difficulties in agreeing to a militarily inadequate response to a major increase in Soviet INF. NATO's INF balance sheet was thus a mixed one. Deployment would continue until 1988.

Two further problems facing NATO were the sharing of the defense burden and emerging conventional weapons technologies, dubbed E.T. The 1978 Long Term Defense Program had committed all alliance members to a 3% annual real (after-inflation) increase in defense spending. But as of 1984 only three major military powers had met this goal: the U.S., U.K., and France, plus Canada. In 1983 West Germany's spending remained constant in real terms, while that of Belgium, Denmark, and The Netherlands decreased. As a proportion of GDP the U.S. was spending 50–300% more than its allies, and there was increasing U.S. pressure to correct this imbalance.

The introduction of E.T. exacerbated these difficulties. Most of the new conventional weapons were manufactured by the U.S. and so would have to be bought by NATO-Europe. They made possible NATO's adoption of a new follow-on forces attack doctrine for larger, deeper conventional air counterattacks against Soviet/Warsaw Pact invaders, but such counterattacks conflicted with the doctrine of forward defense favoured by West Germany.

UNITED KINGDOM

Defense expenditure for 1983–84 was $23,844,000,000 (5.3% of GDP in 1982). The all-volunteer forces were efficient but relatively small and short of modern equipment. The Army of 161,500 had 70 new Challenger and 900 Chieftain main battle tanks plus 2,338 MICV/APC. The Royal Air Force (RAF) had 93,000 personnel and about 620 combat aircraft. About 80 of the new Tornado GR-1 multirole combat aircraft were being deployed in fighter, ground-attack, and reconnaissance models, replacing 72 Phantom fighters. Other modern aircraft included 36 Harrier GR-3/T-4 V/STOL, 48 Jaguar GR-1 ground-attack fighters, 24 Jaguar GR-1 reconnaissance, and 28 Nimrod MR-1/-1A/-2 maritime reconnaissance aircraft. The Royal Navy was the third largest in the world with 71,300 personnel. It had 28 attack submarines (13 nuclear) and 56 major surface combatants including 3 ASW carriers with Sea Harriers, 12 GW destroyers, and 42 general-purpose frigates. Royal Marine personnel totaled 7,600.

The major overseas deployment was the British Army of the Rhine with 56,800 Army and 10,200 RAF personnel. An additional 4,000 personnel manned the Falkland Islands base. Modernization of Britain's national nuclear forces (NNF) continued with the construction of SSBN carrying U.S. Trident II SLBM with U.K. nuclear warheads.

FRANCE

Defense spending in 1984 by France's Socialist Pres. François Mitterrand was estimated at $16,817,000,000; in 1982 it represented 4.2% of GDP. Modernization of France's NNF continued, with five SSBN operational, one being refitted, and one under construction. Replacement of the M-20 SLBM with the M-4 had been delayed, but development of the Hades IRBM—designed to replace the 18 S-3 IRBM—

Table II. Approximate Strengths of Regular Armed Forces of the World

Country	Military personnel in 000s			Warships[1]			Jet aircraft[3]		Tanks[4]	Defense expenditure as % of GNP[6]
	Army	Navy	Air Force	Aircraft carriers/ cruisers	Submarines[2]	Detroyers/ frigates	Bombers and fighter-bombers	Fighters/ reconnaissance		
I. NATO										
Belgium	65.1	4.6	21.0	—	—	4 FFG	90 FB	39, 18 R	330	3.4
Canada[5]	13.0	5.5	15.3	—	3	4 DDG, 16 FF	24 FB	80 F	114	2.1
Denmark	18.1	5.9	7.4	—	5	5 FFG, 5 FF	60 FB	16,16 R	208	2.4
France[7]	304.5	67.7	99.1	2 CV, 1 CVH, 1 CG	17, 6 SSBN	19 DDG, 25 FFG	28 B, 261 FB	165, 45 R, 42 MR	1,102	4.2
Germany, West	335.6	36.2	106.0	—	24	7 DDG, 5 FFG, 6 FF, 6 DD	406 FB	60, 87 R, 19 MR	4,227	4.1
Greece	135.0	19.5	23.5	—	10	14 DD, 2 FFG, 5 FF	153 FB	113, 19 R, 16 MR	1,781	7.0
Italy	260.0	44.5	70.6	1 CVH, 2 CAH	10	4 DDG, 11 FFG, 4 FF, 1 DD	153 FB	113, 29 R, 14 MR	1,770	2.6
Luxembourg	0.7	—	—	—	—	—	—	—	—	1.2
Netherlands, The	64.7	16.8	16.8	—	6	2 DDG, 16 FFG	90 FB	36, 18 R, 17 MR	925	3.3
Norway	19.5	7.5	9.5	—	14	5 FFG	72 FB	7 MR	100	3.0
Portugal	39.0	15.4	9.5	—	3	17 FF	70 FB	4 R	48	3.4
Spain	240.0	57.0	33.0	1 CVH	8	11 DD, 11 FFG, 33 FF	33 FB	114, 9 R, 6 MR	760	2.5
Turkey	500.0	46.0	56.0	—	14	13 DD, 2 FF	280 FB	32, 35 R	3,532	5.2
United Kingdom	161.5	71.3[8]	93.0	3 CVH	15, 13 SSN, 4 SSBN	11 DDG, 42 FFG	194 FB	96, 27 R, 28 MR	900	5.3
United States	781.0	761.6[8]	594.5	2 BBG, 4 CVN, 13 CV, 9 CGN, 19 CG, 5 LHA, 7 LPH, 14 LPD, 23 LSD/T	91 SSN, 35 SSBN, 4 SSGN,	37 DDG, 31 DD, 41 FFG, 53 FF	300 SB, 230 B, 2,200 FB	922, 190 R, 328 MR/ASW	12,023	6.5
II. WARSAW PACT										
Bulgaria	105.0	8.5	34.0	—	2	2 FFG	72 FB	80, 36 R	1,860	2.9
Czechoslovakia	148.0	—	59.0	—	—	—	152 FB	252, 37 R	3,500	5.2
Germany, East	120.0	14.0	38.0	—	—	2 FFG	47 FB	300, 12 R	1,500	6.5
Hungary	84.0	—	21.0	—	—	—	—	145	1,230	2.4
Poland	210.0	22.5	91.0	—	3	1 DDG	220 FB	430, 55 R, 10 MR	3,430	4.0
Romania	150.0	7.5	32.0	—	—	—	70 FB	224, 18 R	1,380	1.6
U.S.S.R.	3,340.0	490.0[8]	1,285.0[9]	3 CV, 2 CVH, 2 CGN, 26 CG, 8 CA	136, 65 SSN, 65 SSBN, 14 SSB, 49 SSGN, 18 SSG	45 DDG, 23 DD, 32 FFG, 152 FF	378 SB, 570 B, 2,720 FB	4,200, 900 R, 135 MR	51,000	13–14
III. OTHER EUROPEAN										
Albania	30.0	3.0	7.2	—	3	—	—	100	100	...
Austria	45.3	—	4.7	—	—	—	34 FB	—	170	1.3
Finland	30.9	2.7	3.0	—	—	—	—	51	—	1.8
Ireland	12.2	0.9	0.8	—	—	—	—	—	—	2.0
Sweden[10]	47.0/800.0	9.6	9.0	—	12	2 DD	115 FB	216, 54 R	770	3.6
Switzerland[10]	20.0/1,100.0	—	3.0/45.0	—	—	—	177 FB	103, 16 R	860	2.1
Yugoslavia	191.0	12.0	38.0	—	7	2 FFG	200 FB	150, 35 R	—	5.2
IV. MIDDLE EAST AND MEDITERRANEAN; SUB-SAHARAN AFRICA; LATIN AMERICA[11]										
Algeria	110.0	8.0	12.0	—	—	2 FF	138 FB	113, 4 R	700	1.9
Egypt	315.0	33.0	113.0	—	12	5 DD, 3 FF	216 FB	235, 38 R	1,750	8.6
Iran[12]	250.0	20.0	35.0	—	—	3 DD, 4 FFG	85 FB	14 R	1,000	14.2
Iraq[12]	600.0	4.5	38.0	—	—	—	17 B, 192 FB	264	4,820	...
Israel[10]	104.0/600.0	9.0/10.0	28.0/37.0	—	3	—	526 FB	28 R	3,600	35.7
Jordan	68.0	0.3	8.0	—	—	—	46 FB	35	550	12.1
Kuwait	10.0	0.5	2.0	—	—	—	30 FB	20	240	5.7
Lebanon[13]	19.0	0.3	1.0	—	—	—	—	3	—	...
Libya[14]	58.0	6.5	8.5	—	6	1 FFG	9 B, 204 FB	285, 7 R	2,800	...
Morocco	125.0	6.0	13.0	—	—	—	42 FB	—	120	9.0
Oman	16.5	2.0	3.0	—	—	—	40 FB	—	18	23.8
Qatar	5.0	0.7	0.3	—	—	—	—	8	24	...
Saudi Arabia	35.0	2.5	14.5	—	—	—	65 FB	80	450	17.7
Sudan	53.0	2.0	3.0	—	—	—	34 FB	—	73	3.7
Syria	190.0	2.5	120.0	—	—	2 FF	213 FB	290	4,100	13.4
Tunisia	30.0	2.6	2.5	—	—	1 FF	—	—	52	3.0
United Arab Emirates	40.0	1.5	1.0	—	—	—	3 FB	30	118	9.8
Yemen, North	35.0	0.6	1.5	—	—	—	—	65	664	16.4
Yemen, South	24.0	1.0	2.5	—	—	—	67 FB	36	450	...
Angola[15]	40.0	1.5	1.5	—	—	—	63 FB	—	445	...
Ethiopia[16]	300.0	2.5	3.5	—	—	—	150 FB	—	1,120	...

continued. Medium-range and tactical nuclear forces were also being increased.

Military personnel totaled 471,000, 304,500 of whom were in the Army. There were 1,100 AMX-30 and 165 new AMX-30B2 main battle tanks, 835 AMX-10P/PC/VOA MICV, and about 3,000 APC. These were organized in six armoured, two light armoured, and two motor rifle divisions, plus a Rapid Action Force for overseas intervention of one parachute, one air portable marine, one light armoured, and one alpine division. The Air Force of 99,150 personnel had 492 combat aircraft, the newer models including 120 Mirage F-1C and 14 Mirage 2000C interceptors plus 30 Mirage 5F and 120 Jaguar A ground-attack fighters. The 67,700-strong Navy's 48 major surface combatants included 2 light and 1 helicopter carrier, 19 destroyers, and 26 frigates; the Navy also had 17 attack submarines (2 SSN).

Approximately 24,000 personnel from all services were deployed overseas, with an additional 48,500 in West Germany. There was a withdrawal of French forces from southern Chad during 1984 as Libyan forces withdrew to the north—though not out of Chad as promised.

WEST GERMANY

West Germany's defense budget totaled $17,396,000,000 in 1984 and represented 4.1% of GDP in 1982. Standing armed forces totaled 495,000, more than half volunteers, rising to 1,250,000 on mobilization, plus 20,000 paramilitary forces. The 335,600-strong Army totaled 12 divisions organized in 5,000-man brigades, of which 66 were tank, 62 armoured infantry, 33 armoured artillery, 9 parachute, and 4 mountain. Armour included 800 new Leopard 2 and 2,437 Leopard 1 main battle tanks, plus about 2,546 MICV and 3,655 APC. Artillery, antiaircraft guns and missiles,

	Military personnel in 000s			Warships[1]			Jet aircraft[3]			Defense expenditure as % of GNP[6]
Country	Army	Navy	Air Force	Aircraft carriers/cruisers	Submarines[2]	Destroyers/frigates	Bombers and fighter-bombers	Fighters/reconnaissance	Tanks[4]	
Kenya	13.0	0.65	—	—	—	—	12 FB	—	76	...
Madagascar	20.0	0.65	0.5	—	—	—	12 FB	—	—	...
Mozambique[17]	14.0	0.7	1.0	—	—	—	35 FB	—	300	...
Nigeria	120.0	4.0	9.0	—	—	1 FFG	42 FB	—	65	...
Somalia	60.0	0.5	2.0	—	—	—	17 FB	39	—	...
South Africa[10]	67.4/404.5	6.0	10.0	—	3	—	12 B, 32 FB	40, 25 MR	250	...
Tanzania	38.5	0.85	1.0	—	—	—	—	11	30	...
Zaire	22.0	1.5	2.5	—	—	—	—	7	—	...
Zimbabwe	40.0	—	1.0	—	—	—	5 B, 14 FB	—	20	...
Argentina	100.0	36.0[8]	17.0	1 CV	3	7 DDG	8 B, 170 FB	20 R 5 MR	255	...
Brazil	183.0	46.0[8]	45.0	1 CV	7	10 DD, 6 FFG	38 FB	14, 28 MR	75	...
Chile	53.0	28.0	15.0	1 CA	3	3 DDG, 2 DD, 2 FFG	48 FB	11, 8 MR	171	...
Colombia	57.0	8.5	4.2	—	2	2 DD, 3 FFG	25 FB	—	—	1.1
Cuba	125.0	12.0	16.0	—	3	—	51 FB	200	850	9.7
El Salvador	39.0	0.3	2.3	—	—	—	29 FB	—	—	...
Mexico	344.5	20.0[8]	5.5	—	—	3 DD, 4 FF	—	12 F, 14 MR	—	3.9
Nicaragua	60.0	0.2	1.5	—	—	—	...	...	63	...
Peru	75.0	20.5	40.0	2 CA	9	10 DD, 2 FFG	15 B, 47 FB	2 MR	300	8.2
Venezuela	27.5	12.0	4.8	—	3	6 FFG, 2 FF	20 B, 16 FB	46	75	1.7
V. FAR EAST AND OCEANIA[11]										
Afghanistan[18]	40.0	—	6.0	—	—	—	135 FB	—	450	...
Australia	32.8	17.0	22.7	—	6	3 DDG, 10 FFG	24 FB	58, 16 MR	103	3.2
Bangladesh	73.0	5.3	3.0	—	—	3 FF	16 FB	10	50	1.6
Burma	163.0	10.0	7.5	—	—	—	—	—	25	3.5
China	3,160.0	350.0[8]	490.0	—	100, 2 SSN, 1 SSBN	14 DDG, 17 FFG, 5 FF	620 B, 500 FB	4,600, 130 R	11,000	4.2
India	960.0	47.0	113.0	1 CV	8	3 DDG, 10 FFG	50 B, 276 FB	445, 25 R, 13 MR	2,900	3.3
Indonesia	210.0	42.8[8]	29.0	—	2	9 FF	34 FB	16	—	3.3
Japan	155.0	44.0	46.0	—	14	26 DDG, 6 DD, 16 FF	50 FB	250, 16 R, 71 MR	830	1.0
Korea, North	700.0	33.5	51.0	—	21	4 FF	70 B, 410 FB	260	2,500	10.2
Korea, South	540.0	49.0[8]	32.6	—	—	11 DD, 7 FF	330 FB	72	1,200	6.0
Laos	50.0	1.7	2.0	—	—	—	—	20	30	...
Malaysia	100.5	11.0	13.0	—	—	2 FFG	19 FB	3 MR	—	8.2
Mongolia	33.0	—	3.5	—	—	—	—	12	130	...
New Zealand	5.6	2.8	4.4	—	—	4 FFG	12 FB	5 MR	—	2.0
Pakistan	450.0	11.0	17.6	—	6	8 DDG	119 FB	170, 10 R, 3 MR	1,421	7.1
Philippines	60.0	28.0[8]	16.8	—	—	7 FF	24 FB	22	—	2.3
Singapore	45.0	4.5	6.0	—	—	—	68 FB	8 R	—	...
Taiwan	369.0[8]	38.0	77.0	—	2	22 DD, 9 FF	377 FB	19, 8 R, 29 MR	309	7.8
Thailand	160.0	32.2	43.1	—	—	6 FF	14 FB	39, 7 R, 10 MR	150	5.0
Vietnam	1,000	12.0[8]	15.0	—	—	3 FF	110 FB	180	1,900	...

Note: Data exclude paramilitary, security, and irregular forces. Naval data exclude vessels of less than 100 tons standard displacement. Figures are for July 1984.

[1]Aircraft carrier (CV); aircraft carrier, nuclear (CVN); helicopter carrier (CVH); general purpose amphibious assault ship (LHA); amphibious transport dock (LPD); amphibious assault ship (helicopter) (LPH); dock/tank landing ship (LSD/T); battleship (BBG); heavy cruiser (CA); guided missile cruiser (CG); guided missile cruiser, nuclear (CGN); helicopter cruiser (CAH); destroyer (DD); guided missile destroyer (DDG); frigate (FF); guided missile frigate (FFG); N denotes nuclear powered.
[2]Nuclear powered attack submarine (SSN); ballistic missile submarine (SSB); guided (cruise) missile submarine (SSG); coastal (C); N denotes nuclear powered.
[3]Bombers (B), fighter-bombers (FB), strategic bombers (SB), reconnaissance fighters (R); maritime reconnaissance (MR) data include jet combat aircraft from all services including naval and air defense. MR also includes propeller drive ASW and ECM aircraft; data exclude light strike/counter-insurgency (COIN) aircraft.
[4]Main battle tanks (MBT), medium and heavy, 31 tons and over.
[5]Of Canada's total military personnel, approximately 49,000 are not identified by service.
[6]Figures for NATO members are for GDP.
[7]French forces were withdrawn from NATO command structure in 1966, but France remains a member of NATO.
[8]Includes marines.
[9]Figure includes the Strategic Rocket Forces (375,000) and the Air Defense Force (550,000), both separate services.
[10]Second figure is fully mobilized strength.
[11]Sections IV and V list only those states with significant military forces.
[12]Losses in Iran-Iraq war made remaining force estimates uncertain.
[13]Figures approximate, given Lebanon's civil war and division.
[14]Some advanced Libyan aircraft are maintained and manned by Soviet/Warsaw Pact crews.
[15]Plus 19,000 Cubans and 500 East Germans serving with Angolan forces.
[16]Ethiopia also has 3,000 Cuban plus other Soviet bloc troops and a 150,000-strong People's Militia.
[17]Plus Cuban, Warsaw Pact, and Chinese advisers and technicians.
[18]Figures approximate, given Soviet occupation of Afghanistan. Excludes about 115,000 Soviet occupation troops.

Sources: International Institute for Strategic Studies, 23 Tavistock Street, London, *The Military Balance 1984–1985, Strategic Survey 1983–84.*

and antitank guns and guided weapons were also deployed in large numbers.

The Air Force had 106,000 personnel with 486 combat aircraft. These included 60 new Tornados, 53 older F-4 Phantoms, and 90 obsolete F-104G ground-attack fighters, plus 60 F-4F interceptors and 60 RF-4E reconnaissance planes. The 36,200-strong Navy was designed for coastal warfare in the Baltic, with 38 fast-attack craft equipped with guided missiles plus 7 GW destroyers, 5 GW frigates, and 24 coastal submarines. The naval air arm consisted of 123 combat aircraft, including 47 Tornados and 30 F/TF-104G attack planes.

ARMS CONTROL AND DISARMAMENT

President Reagan's first term ended without any arms control agreements having been reached with the Soviet Union. This and the Reagan administration's allegations of Soviet violations of the letter and spirit of previous agreements combined to produce a major debate on U.S. arms control policy. The Reagan administration and its supporters argued that it was the Soviets who were responsible for the failure of the arms control process. According to this point of view, the Soviets had always rejected proposals for agreements that would be balanced, effective, and verifiable, insisting instead on ones that mainly would limit forces, either directly or indirectly. Violations by the Soviets of their legal and political obligations under the few arms control agreements that had been reached were detailed for the first time in President Reagan's January report and in the later study by the General Advisory Committee on Arms Control and Disarmament.

Critics claimed that the intransigence of the Reagan administration had prevented agreements from being reached. Overall, the arms control record since the 1963 Limited

Test Ban Treaty suggested that both the administration and its critics were correct in arguing that the traditional arms control process had been a relative failure. Such agreements as had been negotiated had imposed few effective limits on the nuclear and conventional forces of the U.S. and U.S.S.R. or other nations. Hopes that limited agreements would be followed by more far-reaching ones had proved illusory. Several agreements remained unratified, notably the 1979 SALT II treaty (expiring on Dec. 31, 1985) and the 1974 Threshold Test Ban Treaty. The strategic arms reduction talks and negotiations on reducing INF had been broken off by the Soviet Union in 1983. Those on mutual and balanced force reductions between NATO and the Warsaw Pact remained deadlocked. Soviet use of chemical and biological weapons in violation of the 1925 Geneva Protocol and the 1972 Biological Weapons Convention continued.

The future prospects for arms control thus seemed dim, particularly for limits on weapons. The U.S. had agreed to discuss this subject with the Soviets as part of broader negotiations on nuclear weapons, but the latter insisted that the talks focus on space weapons.

MIDDLE EAST

The Middle East remained the most militarily unstable area in the world. Its sharp divisions on economic, political, racial, and religious issues were reflected in the high relative levels of defense spending and large military forces of the major regional powers. The Iran-Iraq war entered its fifth year with no end in sight. Lebanon remained divided. Israel's 1982 intervention had started the expulsion from Lebanon of the Palestine Liberation Organization, which was later completed by Syria to ensure its unchallenged control over Lebanon north of the Awali River. South of the river, Israel continued an increasingly costly and unpopular occupation. The symbolic international peacekeeping force of U.S., Italian, French, and British troops was withdrawn after suffering casualties from terrorist bombings. These continued with the September suicide bombing of the U.S. embassy annex in East Beirut.

Syria's Pres. Hafez al-Assad emerged as a regional strongman with massive Soviet replacement of lost equipment. Syrian armed forces personnel totaled 362,500, with an Army of 240,000 forming four armoured and four mechanized divisions. Equipment included 1,100 new T-72 and 1,200 T-62, plus 1,800 older T-54/-55, main battle tanks and 2,000 BMP/BTR-series MICV/APC.

The separate Air Defense Command had 50,000 personnel manning 102 batteries with Soviet SA-2/-3/-5/-6 surface-to-air missiles. The 70,000-strong Air Force had some 503 combat aircraft. Losses in Lebanon in 1982 made the Air Force's effective strength uncertain, but it included 50 MiG-25 Foxbat A, 40 MiG-23 Flogger E, and 200 MiG-21 PF/MF interceptors, plus 70 MiG-23 Flogger F and 40 Su-20 fighter-bombers. Defense spending, at $3,210,000,-000 in 1984, was 13.4% of GNP in 1982.

Israel remained the region's strongest military power, especially in quality. Its defense spending burden was increasingly difficult to support; even with massive U.S. aid, reaching $1,350,000,000 in 1984, defense consumed 35.7% of GNP in 1982. Inflation was running 400% per year. From a population of only 4.2 million, Israel raised a standing armed force of 141,000 that would rise to 500,000 on mobilization. The Army of 104,000 formed 11 armoured divisions and 33 armoured and 10 mechanized infantry brigades. There were some 3,600 main battle tanks, including 250 new Israeli-built Merkava I/II's and 1,210 M-60s, plus 4,000 MICV/APC. The 28,000-strong Air Force had

555 combat aircraft, including 40 U.S. F/TF-15 Eagles, 75 U.S. F-16A/B Falcons, and 150 Israeli Kfir C1/C2/C7 interceptor/fighter-bombers.

Egypt's armed forces totaled 460,000, with defense spending, at $3,715,000,000 in 1984–85, representing 8.6% of GNP in 1982. The nation's conversion from Soviet to Western equipment was continuing, only one-third of the Soviet equipment being effective. The Army of 315,000 had 350 U.S. M-60A3 and 500 effective Soviet T-54/-55/-62 main battle tanks. The 27,000-strong Air Force's effective aircraft comprised 33 F-4E Phantoms and 53 Mirage 5SDE2 fighter-bombers, plus 34 F-16A and 54 Mirage 5SDE1 interceptors. Jordan's small but effective Army (68,000 personnel) had 750 main battle tanks, and the Air Force (8,000) had 46 F-5E/F and 35 Mirage F/1C/E fighter-bombers.

The Iran-Iraq war continued as a World War I-type conflict of attrition between entrenched infantry supported by artillery and limited quantities of armour. Casualties were heavy in both lives and equipment, causing the figures in Table II to be very rough estimates. Iraq initiated air strikes on oil tankers in the Persian Gulf to limit Iranian earnings from oil exports that were used to buy military supplies. The very small strike forces available to Iran and Iraq limited damage to shipping to tolerable levels, avoiding a spread of the conflict.

Libya continued to exacerbate the regional conflicts. It stalled its withdrawal from northern Chad, and Egyptian sources identified it as the source of mines in the Red Sea. The Libyan forces remained large, totaling 73,000 personnel with 2,800 main battle tanks and 535 combat aircraft.

SOUTH, EAST, AND SOUTHEAST ASIA

The October 31 assassination of India's Prime Minister Indira Gandhi dramatized the potential for conflict in the Indian subcontinent. Its communities were sharply divided along religious, racial, and economic lines, and political boundaries cut across communal ones. The Soviet Union was attempting to emphasize these divisions, hoping that the fragmentation of India and its neighbours into smaller states would increase Soviet influence there. Despite this, India, whose two regional rivals, China and Pakistan, were anti-Soviet, aligned itself with the U.S.S.R., especially as an arms supplier. Since the U.S. supported both China and, especially, Pakistan, India generally adopted an anti-U.S. position.

This might be modified in the future, but probably not by much. The continued Soviet occupation of Afghanistan and increased border incidents with Pakistan made Soviet military strikes into the Baluchistan area of Pakistan more likely. This necessitated increased U.S. military aid to Pakistan, also intended to dissuade Pres. Mohammad Zia-ul-Haq from publicizing the nuclear weapons capability Pakistan was believed very close to achieving.

Despite this U.S. aid, Pakistan's armed forces totaled only 478,600 personnel, mainly an Army of 450,000 with 1,420 main battle tanks (mostly Type-59). The Air Force of 17,600 had 314 combat aircraft, including 6 F-16 Falcon and 50 Mirage 5PA3 fighter-bombers. The defense budget in 1983–84 was $1,873,000,000; in 1982 it was 7.1% of GNP.

India's armed forces totaled some 1,120,000 personnel, including many Sikhs. Most remained loyal to the government despite Prime Minister Gandhi's military assault on their major shrine, the Golden Temple at Amritsar, and the mob violence directed at Sikhs after her assassination by two Sikh security guards. The 960,000-strong Army had 2,900 main battle tanks, including 300 new T-72s. The Air

The U.S. Navy recommissioned the World War II battleship USS "Iowa," shown here testing her 16-inch guns in the Gulf of Mexico during naval acceptance tests.

AP/WIDE WORLD

Force of 113,000 had 920 combat aircraft, including 72 MiG-23 Flogger H and 50 Jaguar GR-1 fighter-bombers, plus 400 MiG-21 and 45 MiG-23 Flogger B interceptors. Defense spending, $6,326,000,000 in 1984–85, was 3.3% of GNP in 1982.

China's forces remained strong in manpower (4 million) but weak in modern equipment. Defense spending was estimated at 4.2% of GNP. China's nuclear stockpile was small, with limited numbers of comparatively old, vulnerable delivery systems. These included about 6 ICBM (DF-4/-5), 60 DF-3 IRBM, and 50 DF-2 medium-range ballistic missiles, along with 120 H-6 medium bombers. One Xia-class SSBN with 12 CSS-NX-3 SLBM (modified DF-3s) was operational. The Army (3,160,000 personnel) had only 11,450 main battle tanks (mostly T-59/-69), while the 490,000-strong Air Force's 5,300 combat aircraft were modifications of old Soviet models.

In Southeast Asia the largest active military power was Vietnam, with armed forces, mostly Army, totaling 1,227,-000. The Army had about 2,000 main battle tanks. The 15,000-strong Air Force had 290 combat aircraft. Deployment of occupation forces abroad included 160,000 in Kampuchea and 40,000 in Laos. Evidence of illegal Vietnamese use of Soviet-supplied chemical and biological weapons, especially against the Hmong people of Laos, continued to mount.

Although North Korea's forces were larger than South Korea's, they remained inadequate for the purpose of full control. The balance was 784,500 personnel, 2,675 main battle tanks, 1,000 APC, and 740 combat aircraft (mostly older types) for the North, versus 622,000 personnel, 1,200 main battle tanks, 850 APC, and 440 combat aircraft (mostly modern types) for the South.

Despite U.S. pressure, Japan refused to spend more than 1% of GNP on defense; its 1984 total was $12,488,000,000. Japan's armed forces personnel totaled 245,000, including an Army of 155,000 with 1,000 main battle tanks. The Air Force and Navy had 46,000 and 44,000 personnel, respectively. Equipment included 50 Japanese-made F-1 fighter-bombers, 40 F-15J/JD Eagle and 110 F-4EJ Phantom fighter-bombers, 32 destroyers (23 GW), 18 frigates, and 14 submarines. Taiwan's armed forces, totaling 484,000, continued to provide a credible defense against China. The Army, with 330,000 personnel, had 309 main battle tanks, and the 77,000-strong Air Force had 547 combat aircraft, including 256 F-5E/F fighter-bombers. Defense spending in 1984 was $3,574,000,000; in 1982 it represented 7.8% of GNP.

AFRICA SOUTH OF THE SAHARA

The major conflicts in sub-Saharan Africa remained those between South Africa and Angola and between the white and nonwhite populations of South Africa. South Africa continued to be the dominant military power in the region, with armed forces totaling 83,400, rising to 404,500 on mobilization. Equipment included 250 main battle tanks, 1,200 Ratel MICV, and 304 combat aircraft. These were extremely effective forces with considerable combat experience. Defense spending, estimated at $2,940,000,000 for 1984–85, was 3.8% of GNP in 1982.

South Africa's conflict with Mozambique was settled during the year by negotiation, leaving that with Angola. The latter's armed forces, of poor quality, totaled 43,000, plus 19,000 Cubans and 700 Soviet advisers. South Africa and Angola were both trying to ensure the presence of a friendly government in South West Africa/Namibia when and if that territory became independent. At the same time, South Africa was supporting the National Union for the Total Independence of Angola (UNITA), which was trying to overthrow the Angolan government. The resulting conflicts were mostly low-level guerrilla operations but occasionally involved division-sized units (15,000 troops). A cease-fire agreement between South Africa and Angola failed to end guerrilla activity.

LATIN AMERICA

The November crisis over the possible Soviet shipment of MiG-21 fighter-bombers to Nicaragua demonstrated the vulnerability of Latin America to the forces of instability, both internal and external. Depressed economic and social conditions encouraged revolutionary movements, and the increased Soviet willingness to aid such movements directly and indirectly, with Cuban forces, was a new and destabilizing factor. Latin America's armed forces were primarily internal-security infantry troops with little equipment. They were poorly paid and often poorly led. They were also small relative to the size and population of their countries, as shown in Table II.

Because of the low levels of these armed forces, Soviet aid was able to build Cuba into a major regional military power, with armed forces totaling 153,000, including significant overseas deployments in Angola (19,000), Ethiopia (3,000), Libya (3,000), and Nicaragua (3,000). These forces were well trained and effectively led, with Soviet and Warsaw Pact personnel in key positions, establishing an influence out of proportion to their size. Hence the U.S. and Central American concern over the rapid expansion of Nicaragua's armed forces to a total of 61,800 in a population of nearly 3.2 million. In 1984 Nicaragua received Soviet armour, armed helicopters, antiaircraft guns, and missiles. While the Sandinista government claimed that this aid was needed to defeat U.S.-supported antigovernment guerrillas, it would also increase Nicaragua's ability to intervene in its neighbours' affairs.

Nicaragua was already intervening in El Salvador, where the democratically elected government of Pres. José Napoleón Duarte was facing approximately 10,000 rebel guerrillas aided by Nicaraguan and Cuban forces and with Soviet-supplied weapons. Against these President Duarte had armed forces totaling 41,650, mostly Army. With U.S. economic and military assistance, his government seemed to be winning popular support, while the Army was gaining ground against the rebels. Nevertheless, the situation remained highly unstable and potentially dangerous.

(ROBIN RANGER)

See also Space Exploration.

This article updates the *Macropædia* article The Technology of WAR.

Mining and Metallurgy

Mining activity worldwide during 1983 and 1984 was influenced by the realization that much of the ground lost by base metals during the early 1980s would be regained only slowly, if at all. However, in regard to light metals, gold, coal, and gemstones, both short- and medium-term prospects remained good as long as efficiency in planning and operations remained high and attention to marketing and technological development remained aggressive. For commodities representing environmental or health hazards for which substitution was possible (such as lead, asbestos, or mercury), both production and prospects continued to decline.

Mining Magazine's annual survey of mining activity worldwide (covering 29 major metals and nonmetals in the Western world) indicated a world total of about 1,200 mines handling more than 150,000 tons of ore annually. It estimated an additional 6,000 to 7,000 smaller mines, although 90% of the output was concentrated in the large operations.

Exploration. By the December 9 deadline for signing the UN Convention on the Law of the Sea, 159 countries (though not the U.S., U.K., or West Germany) had signed; by year's end, 14 had ratified it. Of those that signed, four—India, the U.S.S.R., France, and Japan—had applied for "pioneer" status, which would confer exclusive exploration and mining rights in seabed areas beyond national exclusive economic zones (EEZ's). Many countries had already begun or extended activity in their EEZ's, both to assess the economic potential of the zones and to protect their sovereignty within them.

On land the strongest area of activity was gold prospecting. New deposits were identified at such localities as Pickle Lake, Ontario; Yatani, Japan; Kelantan Estate, Malaysia; Wagga Wagga, New South Wales, Australia; Higginsville, Griffin's Find, and Bardac in Western Australia; and Gebeit and Jebel Negeim in Sudan. These and dozens of other finds were a mixture of both entirely new prospects and new discoveries at existing sites. With the price of gold ranging from $300 to $400 per ounce, not all the deposits would be economically exploitable, but many analysts believed that those price levels in 1984 were largely the result of a strong U.S. dollar and that higher prices would eventually follow. The government of Yemen (Aden) concluded an agreement for gold prospecting by U.S.S.R. scientists and engineers in the Hadhramaut.

Mine Operations. Among the most visible issues associated with mine operations during the year were job security and transitional arrangements for workers at mines that were closing, safety, and environmental/waste problems. Both North America and Western Europe had experienced mine closings in recent years. In Belgium the prospective closing of the Winterslag coal mine brought about a one-day (October 31) demonstration by Limburg miners; the same-day response of the mine owners was a promise of continuation of activity at present levels until at least 1988. Far less successful was the bitter coal miners' strike in the United Kingdom, which began in March in Yorkshire and was punctuated by violence throughout the remainder of the year. Large portions of the British public were alienated by the behaviour of members of the National Union of Mineworkers, and the strike's substantive issues (originally a combination of wage demands, an overtime ban, and labour suspicions about the fairness of the National Coal Board) remained unresolved at the year's end. (*See* WORLD AFFAIRS [Western Europe]: *United Kingdom.*)

The decline of base metals prices during the past several years resulted in many mine closings in the U.S. This was particularly true in the copper industry, where 25 mines closed, representing three-quarters of all copper-mine closings worldwide. Similar displacements (though on a smaller scale) took place in Malaysia, where about 40% of the work force in tin mining had been lost since 1980.

Safety. Several events during the year confirmed the position of mining as among the most dangerous occupations in the world. A February inquest into the September 1983 deaths of 68 men in a coal mine explosion at Hlobane in South Africa assigned responsibility to the mine owners, who had failed to ensure ventilation adequate to prevent the accumulation of the methane gas that caused the explosion. South Africa's 140,000 coal miners were employed by an industry that had, according to a former director of the British Health and Safety Executive, a safety record six times worse than the industry in the U.K.

Two coal mine disasters in Taiwan in a period of weeks during June and July brought regulatory action, but too late. The first disaster, at Hai-shan, took 74 lives; it led to safety inspections of 40 coal mines but not of the Mei-shan mine, where 103 miners died less than a month later. After the second accident all 124 coal mines in the country closed temporarily. Even this, however, had no useful effect, as double cave-ins at the Hai-shan mine on December 5 took an additional 93 lives before the year's end.

A fire on January 18 at the Ariake coal mine (Omuta, Japan) took the lives of 83 miners at a facility that had been known for its computerized safety equipment. A police investigation concluded that failure by company officials to notify and evacuate miners promptly contributed to the fatalities. Responsibility had not been established at the year's end for the December 19 fire at the Wilberg (Utah) coal mine where 27 workers died, although excessive use of machinery in an attempt to set a one-day production record was cited as a possible cause.

Business and Markets. The intimate web of relationships connecting mining activity with national economic development, government policy, and finance presented planners in all those areas with a particularly knotty set of problems. Bolivia, for example, which traditionally depended upon export earnings from tin and other base and precious metals (tin typically comprising about two-thirds of the total), was discovering in 1984 the consequences of its past complacency, both in terms of loss of markets for tin and of failure to develop alternate products and strategies to that main product. Low international market prices for tin had led the sixth International Tin Agreement to limit exports by members after 1982 in order to raise prices. Low exports and continued low prices produced major shortfalls in earnings that Bolivia was not in a position to meet by substituting other products. Comibol (Corporación Minera de Bolivia), the nationalized properties of the Patino, Aramayo, and Hochschild families after 1952, had since its creation become increasingly bureaucratized and politicized—to the extent that by late 1983 worker demands for participation were met by surrendering control of the board to the worker representatives. By 1984 Comibol had begun to take up the problems inherent in its current predicament and had begun active exploration for gold in the northeast.

Weakened international prices also affected much larger economies, but these often had the option of substituting resources. The U.S.S.R., for example, had sold some 200 to 300 metric tons of gold annually during 1982–83 to finance grain and other external account transactions. Reduced gold prices then obliged the Soviet Union to seek those foreign currencies by sales of diamonds at as much as 10 to 15% below market prices.

If there was a success story in metals markets during the year, it was probably the light and minor metals, which staged several successive advances on the London Metal Exchange. These included antimony (recovering along with the auto industry), bismuth, cadmium, and cobalt.

Technology. Technological advances continued to take place in mining and metallurgical engineering. The Battelle Memorial Institute's Columbus (Ohio) laboratories were conducting a 26-month study to advance knowledge of biotechnology for applications in mining, chief of which was probably bioleaching (separation of ore metals from gangue by biological action). One process announced in some detail by P. M. Mineral Leaching Technologies, Inc., was a process utilizing a bacterium (*Thiobacillus ferrooxidans*) to extract gold from pyrite (iron sulfide) crystals by oxidizing the crystals, thereby creating a sulfuric acid solution in which the gold dissolves. In addition to providing a replacement for the high-pressure, high-temperature techniques currently needed to accomplish the same task, the process has the benefit of converting the arsenic and antimony that may be present into far less toxic compounds.

Although many biological technologies were perceived as being too slow and too inefficient in their uptake of the desired metal, their low output of pollutants and their low energy requirements should continue to interest potential users.

A symposium at the Institution of Mining and Metallurgy in London early in the year highlighted both specific applications of computers to mining problems and the range of problems to which the techniques might have application. Some of these applications included modeling of ore bodies, both for resource estimation and for actual mine operations; process control applications, such as those in an ore-processing plant requiring frequent monitoring; and statistical applications in marketing and estimating costs.

Eriez Magnetics of Erie, Pa., demonstrated a working model of a superconducting magnetic separator that it believed had immediate application in a wide range of situations, such as the removal of ferrous impurities from kaolin clays or impure coals. The design's low power consumption and very fast on/off cycles were particularly attractive.

Production. The United Nations overall indexes of mining production for 1983 and the first two quarters of 1984 (*see* Table) indicated few strong trends since 1980. The 40% drop in oil production and simultaneous 60% gain in coal output were the most significant, and the similarity of experience in metals among all kinds of national economies was also striking.

According to data compiled by the U.S. Bureau of Mines, of a group of 69 mineral commodities for which information was reasonably complete and could be released (for a number of smaller commodities production data could not be published for proprietary reasons), output in 1983 rose for 33, fell for 34, and remained unchanged for 2. Among the metals, losers outnumbered gainers by 23 to 12. The gainers included aluminum, gold, silver, zinc, chromium, and the platinum-group metals. The losers, however, included some of the most important metals: lead, nickel, tin, and copper. Among the nonmetals, gainers outnumbered losers 21 to 11. Gainers included some major commodities indicative of activity in agriculture, industry, and construction: rock phosphate, industrial diamonds, and cement.

The United States mining sector, with an estimated mine value of $21,207,000,000, registered an 8% improvement as compared with the 22% decline of the previous year.

Indexes of Production, Mining and Mineral Commodities

(1980 = 100)

	1979	1980	1981	1982	1983	1984 I	1984 II
Mining (total)							
World[1]	102.1	100.0	97.7	90.5	89.0	83.1	...
Centrally planned economies[2]	97.9	100.0	99.4	102.3	104.1	107.0	106.1
Developed market economies[3]	96.5	100.0	103.3	98.8	97.5	104.4	98.8
Less developed market economies[4]	106.8	100.0	93.5	82.5	80.2	63.8	...
Coal							
World[1]	96.7	100.0	100.6	102.2	102.0	106.2	...
Centrally planned economies[2]	99.0	100.0	98.4	102.5	104.3	108.5	105.4
Developed market economies[3]	95.1	100.0	101.2	101.1	98.2	100.4	91.4
Less developed market economies[4]	94.0	100.0	116.3	115.0	128.8	161.4	...
Petroleum							
World[1]	104.0	100.0	96.4	87.0	85.3	75.6	...
Centrally planned economies[2]	97.0	100.0	102.1	104.5	106.5	109.6	109.2
Developed market economies[3]	94.6	100.0	105.9	101.5	99.8	110.9	101.5
Less developed market economies[4]	108.6	100.0	91.8	79.4	77.6	57.8	...
Metals							
World[1]	98.1	100.0	100.5	94.1	90.2	92.0	...
Centrally planned economies[2]	91.5	100.0	88.7	89.9	92.9	95.8	96.5
Developed market economies[3]	102.4	100.0	100.1	90.6	91.5	95.7	99.6
Less developed market economies[4]	95.0	100.0	102.2	97.6	88.8	88.3	...
Manufacturing (total)	99.7	100.0	100.5	98.5	102.3	107.9	...

[1] Excluding Albania, China, North Korea, Vietnam.
[2] Bulgaria, Czechoslovakia, East Germany, Hungary, Poland, Romania, U.S.S.R.
[3] North America, Europe (except centrally planned), Australia, Israel, Japan, New Zealand, South Africa.
[4] Caribbean, Central and South America, Africa (except South Africa), Asian Middle East, East and Southeast Asia (except Israel and Japan).
Source: UN, *Monthly Bulletin of Statistics* (November 1984).

The processed value of this mine output was approximately $218 billion in 1983, also about an 8% improvement over 1982. The mine value of metals in 1983 was approximately $5,669,000,000, a 2.3% gain over 1982 but still 37% below 1981 production levels. Nonmetals showed almost a 10% gain over 1982, reaching a value of $15,538,000,000, but as with the metals they failed to regain output values of 1981.

Among the metals a notable performance was recorded by gold, which attained an output of 1,957,379 troy ounces, a level not exceeded since 1953. This was attributed to activity by small producers and by-product activity by large producers of base metals whose principal product was beset by low prices. Other metals showed only moderate reactions to market forces; however, some of the major metals had experienced severe losses in 1982.

Among the nonmetals a very strong 11% production gain was recorded in 1983 by cement, reflecting the fortunes of the construction industry. For the same reason, clay and gypsum recorded similar 14 and 16% gains over 1982, as did aggregates for concrete, sand, and gravel, together recording a 12% gain. Exceptional declines of 27 and 17%, respectively, were recorded by potash and salt. The most significant loss, however, was the 61% decline in barite, consumed largely by the slumping petroleum drilling industry.

Aluminum. World production of bauxite, the principal ore of aluminum, was estimated to have fallen about 4.6% during 1983, totaling about 71 million metric tons. The leading producer continued to be Australia, at an estimated 23 million tons (off about 2.5% from 1982), followed by Guinea with an estimated 9 million tons (about 19% below its 1982 output) and Jamaica with about 7.4 million tons, a decrease of 10% from 1982. Output of alumina (aluminum oxide, the concentrated intermediate stage in the production of aluminum metal) was estimated to have fallen by about 7%, to slightly more than 29 million tons, about 25% of which was produced by Australia. World production of aluminum metal increased for the first time since 1980. For the most part the modest recovery of the economies of the major industrialized nations in the second half of 1983 resulted in an increased utilization of already available stock and refining capacity. Total output of aluminum equaled about 14.9 million tons, a slight increase of 2% over 1982. U.S. production stabilized after experiencing a significant decline in output in 1982. Its 3.4 million tons represented 24% of world production. The U.S.S.R. produced an estimated 2.2 million tons, Canada 1.2 million tons, and West Germany and Norway both about 800,000 tons. Output in Australia increased by 25% over 1982 to 524,000 tons, whereas Japanese production continued to decline severely (1,203,000 tons in 1980; 282,000 tons in 1983). India replaced Haiti as a member of the 11-country International Bauxite Association.

Antimony. Reduced demand for antimony after 1977 in the automotive and construction industries was reflected in the continued decline of production levels in 1983. The total output of ore declined 10% from 1982 to 48,400 metric tons, with most of the main cutbacks occurring in Bolivia and South Africa, the major Western producers. Bolivia and South Africa, at 10,500 and 6,300 tons, respectively, were both down about 30% from 1982. Output in China and the U.S.S.R., the second and third producers at 10,000 and 9,000 tons, respectively, remained virtually unchanged from 1982. A long-anticipated improvement in demand by the battery manufacturing industry during the second half of 1983 led Western producers to rethink production levels for 1984.

Cement. World production of cement during 1983 increased by 3.8% over 1982 levels, reflecting an expansion in construction activity in both developed and less developed countries. Except for the 20% increase in output for the United States, the world's increased production was distributed fairly evenly among the other leading producers. Total output of cement was about 925 million metric tons, of which the U.S.S.R. (the leading producer), with approximately 127 million metric tons, accounted for about 14% of the world total. China was second with 96 million metric tons, followed by Japan with 86 million metric tons. Stimulated by a resurgence of construction activity, the cement industry in the U.S. increased output from 64 million metric tons in 1982 to 70 million metric tons in 1983.

Chromium. World mine production of chromite, the principal ore of chromium, was estimated by the U.S. Bureau of Mines to have risen by 2.7% during 1983 to a total of about 11.2 million metric tons. The U.S.S.R., which in recent years had overtaken South Africa as the world's leading producer, produced an estimated 3.8 million metric tons. It was followed by South Africa at about 2.4 million metric tons, Albania with 1.5 million metric tons, and Brazil with 1 million metric tons. Producing at only 55% of capacity, the Rand Mines and Transvaal Consolidated Land in South Africa (producing 1,039,000 metric tons) remained the largest individual producer of chromite in the world.

Copper. World mined copper output fell during 1983 to an estimated 7,960,000 metric tons, a decline of about 1% from the previous year. Chile remained the leading copper producer in the world with an output of 1,250,000 tons (about a 1.2% increase over 1982) in spite of a low demand for the metal. The U.S. followed with 1,050,000 tons, nearly 8% below its 1982 production level. Other major producers included the U.S.S.R., with an estimated 1 million tons, Canada 625,000 tons, Zambia 580,000 tons, and Zaire about 490,000 tons. Blister copper production (smelter output) increased slightly from the previous year. More than half of the world's output came from four countries: the U.S.S.R., which led with 1.2 million tons, followed by Japan, Chile, and the U.S., producing about 1 million tons each. World output of refined copper increased by about 144,000 tons (about 2%) to approximately 9.7 million tons. Canada's output increased by nearly 40% (a rebound from major strikes in 1982) to an estimated 464,000 tons. However, there was a nearly 6% decline in the U.S., to 1,581,000 tons. A significant increase (30%) in Zaire's output to 227,000 tons and two new Asian producers, Oman and the Philippines, contributed to the increase in copper production worldwide.

Gold. Mine production of gold rose in 1983, gaining about 3.6% and reaching an estimated total of 1,385 metric tons. South Africa's long-time dominance of the world market continued in 1983, its output of 680 tons representing nearly 50% of world production. Estimates placed the U.S.S.R. second at about 20% of world production, although it experienced a 4.2% decline from 1982. Canada's production of 71 tons, about 9% more than in 1982 (and 5% of the world total), largely the result of expansion of existing mines, enabled it to become the world's third most important producer. Brazil ranked fourth (replacing the U.S. at 50 tons, with China trailing behind it) with an output of 51 tons, about a 47% increase over 1982. Production of alluvial gold in most Latin-American countries increased in 1983 with the major currency devaluations increasing domestic gold prices to record levels, while total production from the region amounted to 134 tons, about 10% of the world total. Production in the Philippines, at 33 tons, was mainly from alluvial mining, and the by-product copper producers continued to suffer from the effects of the depressed base metal markets. The rate of increase in Australian production slowed somewhat in 1983, reaching 32 tons. The Horseshoe Lights mine resumed operations in 1983, having been forced to close in 1982. The six companies that controlled eight contiguous mining operations in the Orange Free State of South Africa were planning a merger to create the biggest gold-mining complex in the world.

Iron. World production of iron ore fell by about 4.5% in 1983 to approximately 750 million metric tons. The U.S.S.R., producing nearly 35% of the world total, led in output with 245 million tons, followed by Brazil with 92 million tons, a 7% decrease, and Australia with 80 million tons, also a slight decline from the previous year. China increased its production by about 1.5% to 72 million tons as the fourth largest producer, while India remained fifth with 39 million tons. The United States at 38.6 million tons, an increase of about 7% over 1982, surpassed Canada, whose production totaled 32.4 million tons. The slight increase in demand was not substantial enough to offset the worst two-year slump suffered by the steel industry since the depression of the 1930s. The continued decline in trade, though not as marked as in 1982, nevertheless affected all producers, especially South Africa, India, Canada, Liberia, Chile, and Peru. World production of pig iron decreased by 3.3% to an estimated 440 million tons. The top three producing nations were: the U.S.S.R. at about 107 million tons, a small decrease from 1982, and Japan at 73 million tons and the United States at 44 million tons, both with slight increases in production.

Lead. World mine output of lead totaled about 3,350,000 metric tons in 1983, down by some 3% from 1982. Countries with market economies accounted for 74% of the total. Australia produced 478,000 tons, thus surpassing the United States (458,000 tons) as the largest producer. Other major mining countries included Canada with 259,000 tons, Peru with 213,000 tons, and Mexico with 167,000 tons. Output of refined metal in the non-Communist world, including production from secondary recovery, totaled approximately 3,940,000 tons. The main producer was the United States with some 1,006,000 tons, down slightly from 1,032,000 tons in 1982. Reported consumption of lead in the U.S. increased by about 5% during the year, though controls limiting industrial and automotive applications continued in effect.

Magnesium. World production of magnesium in 1983 was estimated to have dropped about 5.1% from the previous year, to a total of approximately 260,000 metric tons. About 38.4% of this figure, or 100,000 metric tons, was produced (mostly from brines) in the U.S.; this represented a 13% decline from 1982. The U.S.S.R. was thought to be the second leading producer with about 81,000 metric tons (principally from magnesite ore), an increase of about 3.8% from 1982. Norway was the third leading producer with its 36,000 metric tons representing a 3.7% increase over 1982.

Manganese. World mine production of manganese ore, at about 22 million metric tons, was estimated to have fallen about 4.3% from 1982. The Soviet Union's 10.2 million metric tons accounted for more than two-fifths of total production in 1983. South Africa, the second leading producer of manganese, slowed ore production to 3 million metric tons in 1983. Production in Brazil remained static at about 1.4 million metric tons.

Mercury. World mine production of mercury in 1983 totaled about 192,000 34.5-kg (76-lb) flasks, remaining roughly equivalent to the 1982 output of 192,160 flasks. The U.S.S.R. remained the world's largest producer, with an estimated output in 1983 of 64,000 flasks, compared with 57,000 flasks in 1982. It was followed by Spain, producing about 48,000 flasks, the United States with 25,000 flasks, and China with about 20,000 flasks. Two other major producers, Algeria and Mexico, produced 11,000 and 6,000 flasks, respectively.

Molybdenum. World mine production of molybdenum, at about 54,400 metric tons (a decline of 40% from 1982 levels), was the lowest since 1965. The United States, whose output decreased by nearly two-thirds to about 13,600 metric tons, was replaced by Chile, with about 14,500 metric tons, as the world's leading producer. Other main producers included the U.S.S.R., with 11,300 metric tons, and Canada, suffering a more than 35% fall in output during 1983, with 10,500 metric tons. Large inventories at the beginning of 1983 and decreased demand during the year forced many producers to cut back production far below capacity. Mine closings that characterized North American operations in 1982 continued into 1983.

Nickel. World mine production of nickel rose an estimated 14.1% in 1983, totaling 693,000 metric tons. The West's economic recovery, particularly in capital-goods sectors such as engineering and electrical businesses, helped account for the increase. The U.S.S.R. remained the world's largest producer with an output of 204,000 tons, an increase of 20% over 1982. Canada, the second largest producer, mined 122,000 tons in 1983, up 38% from the previous year. Occupying third place, Australia increased output 20% to 99,000 tons. In the United States production plummeted 87% to only 440 tons, largely because of the prolonged shutdown of the Hanna Mining Co.'s nickel operation in Riddle, Ore.

Phosphate Rock. In 1983 world production of phosphate rock increased 8.2% to 134,321,000 metric tons. The output of the U.S., the world's largest producer, rose 8.5% to 41,890,000 tons. In the U.S.S.R. production amounted to 27.7 million tons, up 1.8% from the previous year. Morocco, the third largest producer, registered a gain of 13.2% to 20,106,000 tons. In China, the world's only other significant producer, output increased 6.6% to 12.5 million tons. Most phosphate rock went into the making of fertilizers, for which there was an increased demand during the worldwide economic recovery of 1983.

Platinum-Group Metals. World production of the platinum-group metals (platinum, iridium, palladium, osmium, rhodium, and ruthenium) rose in 1983 by 1.5% to about 6.6 million troy ounces. The U.S.S.R. produced more than half of the world total with approximately 3.6 million troy ounces, followed by South Africa with about 2.6 million troy ounces. Canadian production declined by 30% from the previous year, while U.S. output remained the same as in 1982 at about 8,000 troy ounces.

Silver. World silver production increased in 1983 to an estimated 394 million troy ounces, up by 4% from 1982. Mexico regained its supremacy as the major producer, followed by Peru and the U.S.S.R. Estimated figures for the top three producing countries were: Mexico 57 million troy ounces, an increase of approximately 15%; Peru 55.2 million troy ounces, up about 4%; and the U.S.S.R. 50.7 million troy ounces, up about 1%. Other leading producers included the U.S. with 43.1 million troy ounces, Canada with 39.2 million troy ounces, and Australia with 33.5 million troy ounces. In Mexico and Peru the rehabilitation and reactivation of old mines contributed to the upswing in production. Higher silver prices stimulated silver production worldwide, with the most dramatic increase in Mexico, where production topped a record set in 1945. Production figures in the U.S. also reached a record high, up 7% from 1982.

Tin. Mine production of tin in market economy countries was about 172,900 metric tons in 1983, down by more than 9% from 1982. The major producing nations were Malaysia with about 41,500 tons, down about 20% from 1982, Indonesia at 27,000 tons, Bolivia at 25,800 tons, Thailand at 20,600 tons, and Brazil at 13,300 tons. The U.S.S.R. and China accounted about equally for almost all the production (variously placed in the range of 30,000 to 60,000 tons) in the centrally planned economy countries. Western smelter production of tin also fell about 9% to 163,000 tons. The leading producers were Malaysia with 53,000 tons, Indonesia with 28,600 tons, and Thailand with 19,400 tons. The Association of Tin Producing Countries was launched in August 1983 with the main purpose of promoting research and development so as to boost declining tin consumption, mainly in the manufacture of solder for the electronics industry and tinplate for beverage cans. The International Tin Council continued its price-support measures through imposing export controls and maintaining buffer stocks, although the efforts may have been diluted by increased production in nonmember countries and by smuggling within Southeast Asia.

Titanium. World production of titanium sponge metal declined by about 12% during 1983 to a total of 65,770 metric tons. The drop reflected a lower demand for the metal by the weakened commercial aircraft industry. The U.S.S.R. was the leading sponge producer for which data were available, with about 40,000 metric tons. U.S. production was estimated at 11,800 metric tons. Australia continued to lead in ilmenite and rutile production; output of ilmenite in Australia accounted for about one-third of the world total.

Tungsten. World mine production of tungsten declined by about 17% during 1983 to a total of 37,350 metric tons. China was believed to be the chief producer at about 10,000 tons. The U.S.S.R., at 9,000 tons, was followed in order by Bolivia, Australia, South Korea, Austria, Portugal, and the U.S., all of which produced between 1,100 and 3,000 tons each.

Zinc. According to data from the U.S. Bureau of Mines, mine output of zinc rose by about 2.5% during 1983, reaching a total of approximately 6,160,000 metric tons. Canadian output of 971,000 metric tons represented a small gain of about 0.5% over 1982. Other important producers included Australia, at 670,000 tons showing a total gain over 1982 of about 6.5%; Peru 576,000 tons, up 2.1%; Mexico 257,000 tons, up 11%; and the U.S., 280,000 tons, down about 6.7%. Metal production rose by about 6.8% in response to increased demand; Mexico registered the highest increase, about 51,000 tons or 40% over 1982, as a result of the completion of a new refinery at San Luis Potosí. In the U.S. mine and metal production were down 20,000 and 9,000 tons, respectively, because of mine closings and the continued closure of the Corpus Christi zinc refinery in Texas.   (WILLIAM A. CLEVELAND)

Metallurgy. With the increasing performance requirements of advanced aerospace systems, the mechanical properties of conventionally produced ingot metallurgy materials were being pushed to their limit. In an effort to improve properties such as stiffness and high-temperature strength and stability, metallurgists developed a metal matrix composite system in which two basically dissimilar materials are combined to arrive at a product whose final properties are superior to the individual constituents. A metal matrix composite is typically produced by combining a metal that has good strength and ductility with fibres that have low ductility but are very strong, stiff, and stable at elevated temperatures. Generally the fibres are three to four times stronger than the metal matrix and, because most of the fibre systems are ceramic materials, they are stable to much higher temperatures than metals.

The most critical factor in the successful development of a metal matrix composite is the strength of the interfacial bond between the metal and the fibre. Because there are four ways of producing a metal matrix composite, a number of methods are available to improve the bond. The first two use a blending process. In one case a powder having the composition of the matrix produced by rapid solidification is mixed with fibre. The mixture is consolidated under pressure at a temperature slightly above the melting point of the metal. During the consolidation process the alloy elements in the partially liquid metal react with the surface of the fibre and form a bond. In the second blending process the fibres are added directly to the liquid metal. Once a homogeneous distribution of fibres is achieved, the metal and fibres are cooled to room temperature. The blending process results in a microstructure containing randomly oriented fibres. The resulting billets from these two processes are then extruded, forged, or rolled into a product shape. During fabrication the fibres tend to become aligned in the direction of working and are fractured. The reduction in the length of the fibres decreases their effectiveness as strengthening or stiffening agents.

The third method of producing a composite is to use a casting procedure in which the liquid metal is drawn up by a vacuum into a container packed with fibres. The fourth method involves the roll bonding of fibres between thin sheets of metal. The last two techniques result in a composite with aligned fibres and, therefore, highly directional properties. In some applications strength in a particular direction is required, and in those cases an aligned microstructure is imperative. Consequently, the application will dictate which of the processing schemes is required.

Ion implantation gained in popularity as an alternative to conventional surface treatments, for example, for improving the wear resistance of steel and tungsten carbide tooling. This process does not involve plating, bonding, or otherwise adding a surface to a surface. There is no dimensional change or coating that can peel off or delaminate with time. Rather, in ion implantation the surface is bombarded with highly accelerated ions. These ions are forced into the surface. The type of ion to be used is dictated by the desired application. For example, if wear resistance is required, nitrogen is used; the nitrogen introduced by the bombarding process reacts with iron in the matrix to produce a uniform distribution of hard nitride particles. The presence of these hard particles reduces wear.

(THOMAS H. B. SANDERS, JR.)

See also Earth Sciences; Energy; Industrial Review: *Iron and Steel.*

Motion Pictures

English-Speaking Cinema. UNITED STATES. Both the box-office successes of 1984 and Hollywood's run-of-the-mill production testified to the falling age level of the economically dominant majority of the cinema audience. The big hits of the year—Steven Spielberg's *Indiana Jones and the Temple of Doom,* Ivan Reitman's *Ghostbusters,* Joe Dante's *Gremlins,* John Avildsen's *The Karate Kid,* and Leonard Nimoy's *Star Trek III: The Search for Spock*—were all adventure fantasies of obvious, undemanding attraction for younger teenage audiences. Another substantial box-office winner, Albert Magnoli's *Purple Rain,* an effective vehicle for a current pop idol, Prince, also clearly addressed similar age groups.

Current fashions in dance and music for the young produced a whole crop of pop musical films, including Herbert Ross's *Footloose,* Joel Selberg's *Breakin',* Stan Latham's *Beat Street,* and Marcelo Epstein's *Body Rock.* Walter Hill's *Streets of Fire* extended the pop musical form to a vision of a future world of urban violence.

This young and presumably impressionable audience was also being exposed to a new genre of films produced by the revived cold war atmosphere. The most alarming of these was John Milius's *Red Dawn,* which imagined an invasion of the U.S. by a combined force of Soviets and Cubans (murderers and rapists to a man) and the formation of a guerrilla resistance by high-school students. By comparison, Paul Mazursky's *Moscow on the Hudson,* about a Soviet defector's experiences in the U.S., was a much more sober view of the ideological confrontation of East and West.

Other artists preferred to contemplate America's past. The second film directed by the actor Richard Benjamin, *Racing with the Moon,* was a study, beautifully staged and played, of two young men spending their last days in a small town before going to war in 1942. Robert Benton's *Places in the Heart* was a loving tribute to his own Texas hometown in the 1930s, while Barry Levinson's *The Natural,* from Bernard Malamud's novel, was an epic fantasy set in the world of professional baseball in the 1930s. In *A Soldier's Story* Norman Jewison dealt with racial tensions at a U.S. Army base in Louisiana during World War II.

Individualists made their contributions to the year's films. John Cassavetes's *Love Streams,* starring Cassavetes and his wife, Gena Rowlands, was a characteristic intimate character study of a neurotic, erratic pair of siblings. Robert Altman continued his strategy of filming stage plays with the solo performance of Philip Baker Hall in Donald Freed and Arnold Stone's *Secret Honour,* a fictional representation of a paranoid Richard Nixon making one last tape in an effort to clear his name. Paul Bartel applied his black and eccentric comic vision to the world of journalism in *Not for Publication.*

Woody Allen, the outstanding master of U.S. film comedy, played the title role in his own *Broadway Danny Rose,* a loving tribute to the people on the outer fringes of popular show business. Notable new directors who made their mark during the year were Marisa Silver (daughter of the director Joan Micklin Silver), whose *Old Enough* was a sharply observed study of the friendship of two New York schoolgirls from markedly different social strata, and Christopher Cain with *The Stone Boy,* a touching study of the emotional tensions in a middle-class family after the death of a son.

The distinguished Soviet director Andrey Konchalovsky directed the U.S. production *Maria's Lovers,* a portentous and overblown fable about a man returning from World War II a victim of psychosomatic impotence. Other foreign directors permanently settled and working in Hollywood were Milos Forman of Czechoslovakia, who made a popular adaptation of Peter Shaffer's play about Mozart, *Amadeus,* and Louis Malle of France, whose *Crackers* adapted Mario Monicalli's 1958 success, *I Soliti Ignoti,* as a slight "caper" comedy.

As had been the case in recent years, many films were released during the Christmas holiday season. Among the most notable in the drama category were David Lean's *A Passage to India* (Lean's first movie in 14 years), Roland Joffé's *The Killing Fields,* Alan Parker's *Birdy,* and Francis Ford Coppola's *The Cotton Club.* The science fiction genre was well represented by David Lynch's *Dune,* Peter Hymas's *2010* (a sequel to the popular *2001: A Space Odyssey*), and John Carpenter's *Starman.* Comedies included Blake Edwards's *Micki and Maude,* Garry Marshall's *The Flamingo Kid,* and Martin Brest's *Beverly Hills Cop.*

At the annual awards ceremony of the Academy of Motion Picture Arts and Sciences in Hollywood in April, *Terms of Endearment,* a sentimental melodrama directed by James L. Brooks, received the awards for best picture, best actress (Shirley MacLaine; *see* BIOGRAPHIES), best supporting actor (Jack Nicholson), best director, and best screenplay adaptation (from a novel by Larry McMurtry). The best actor award went to Robert Duvall for his performance in *Tender Mercies,* which also took the Oscar for best original screenplay. Best supporting actress was Linda Hunt, who played a man in *The Year of Living Dangerously.* Ingmar Bergman's *Fanny and Alexander* was judged the best foreign-language film and also received the awards for cinematography, art direction, and costume design. *The Right Stuff,* which dramatized the achievements of the first U.S. astronauts, took Oscars for film editing, original score, sound, and sound effects editing.

GREAT BRITAIN. The conviction that British cinema was on the eve of a great renaissance faded somewhat as production money became more difficult to obtain, new government legislation removed beneficial tax concessions, and the National Film Finance Corporation was disbanded. The period of optimism had produced no clear sense of purpose, policy, or direction. Many of the new directors seemed obsessed with nostalgia for schooldays during the war and in the postwar era (Zelda Barron's *Secret Places,* Barbara Rennie's *Sacred Hearts,* Gavin Millar's *Secrets,* and most of Goldcrest Productions' "First Love" series). Sometimes, though, nostalgia produced richer and tougher films. Thus Malcolm Mowbray made his feature film debut with *A Private Function,* a black comedy from a script by Alan Bennett and set in the days of postwar austerity, while James Scott's *Every Picture Tells a Story* was a loving portrayal of the poverty-stricken early years of the director's father, the painter James Scott.

Among the established new generation of British directors, Bill Forsyth made a characteristic eccentric comedy, *Comfort and Joy,* relating the adventures of a local radio disc jockey among the ice cream mafiosi of Glasgow. Richard Eyre's *Laughterhouse,* an eccentric miniature

Steven Spielberg's hit movie *Indiana Jones and the Temple of Doom,* starring Harrison Ford in the title role, assaulted audiences' senses from beginning to end. The movie was the long-awaited successor to *Raiders of the Lost Ark,* and both movies were patterned after the classic action movie and Saturday serial.

British epic about a stubborn farmer who decides to walk his Christmas geese to London, shared the 1984 Venice Festival prize for the best film made for television.

Following *Another Time, Another Place,* Michael Radford directed a new adaptation of George Orwell's *1984.* Sober and intelligent, the film, in its concern to re-create Orwell's vision strictly in the style and terms of the 1940s, emphasized the realism of the original work—rather a description of the real terror of the Stalinist East than a prediction of the future.

Of older established directors, Stephen Frears—mostly known for his television films—made a stylish thriller, *The Hit,* while James Ivory adapted Henry James's *The Bostonians,* finely shot in U.S. locations and with a prestigious cast led by Vanessa Redgrave and Christopher Reeve. Two debuts seemed auspicious: after a career in theatre and television, Roland Joffé directed an ambitious study of the Cambodian tragedy, *The Killing Fields;* and Werner Grusch, without fanfare, made the excellent *White Elephant,* the story of a brash young British executive who arrives in Ghana intent on setting up business there, only to find that the local culture is too powerful for him.

Although U.S. financed, Hugh Hudson's *Greystoke: The Legend of Tarzan, Lord of the Apes* was nominally British in origin. Its great cost and ambitions were largely nullified owing to extensive cutting after the director failed to deliver a film of the previously agreed-upon length.

IRELAND. Ireland's effort to establish a true indigenous cinema produced a number of original works. Pat O'Connor's *Cal* followed well-established precedents in depicting the tragedy of a young man caught up in sectarian fighting. Pat Murphy's *Anne Devlin* dramatized the life of a famous 19th-century patriot. Cathal Black's *Pigs* was a vividly realized Dublin *Lower Depths,* while Sean O'Mordha's *Samuel Becket, Silence to Silence* offered an affectionate portrait of the Irish-born writer and recluse.

WALES. The year saw the unprecedented production of two Welsh-language films, Stephen Bayly's *. . . And Pigs Might Fly,* about the impact of two Japanese businessmen on the life and society of a depressed village, and Karl Francis's *The Happy Alcoholic,* a feeling study of a man's descent into (far from happy) alcoholism.

AUSTRALIA. Without contributing any major works to the international scene, Australian filmmakers continued to demonstrate a great range of subject and treatment, from Gil Brealey's moving story of the rehabilitation of a severely handicapped young person, *Annie's Coming Out,* to an ambitious re-creation of industrial wars of the 1930s, *Strikebound,* in which the very young Richard Lowenstein made his debut as a director; from Paul Cox's lacerating

depiction of the breakup of a marriage, *My First Wife,* to Russell Mulcahy's effective horror film about the depredations of a giant marauding feral pig, *Razorback.*

NEW ZEALAND. New directors of talent continued to emerge. Vincent Ward's *Vigil*—seductive in its fine visual qualities, even if its scenario, about a young girl's painful discoveries of the adult world, was not wholly realized—represented New Zealand at the Cannes Film Festival. Bruce Morrison's *Constance* portrayed a beautiful Auckland schoolteacher who tries disastrously to live up to Hollywood ideals of femininity. Michael Firth's *Heart of the Stag* was a drama of violent family relationships, set in the remote outback.

PAPUA NEW GUINEA. Chris Owen's very lively drama *Tukuna,* about a village boy disoriented by the Western influences that invade his country, marked Papua New Guinea's emergence as a film-producing centre.

CANADA. A few films stood out among the generality of English-language production, which was mostly dedicated to low-budget thrillers, horror pictures, and television drama. Alexis Kanner's *Kings and Desperate Men* was an imaginative political thriller about a radical teacher who takes over a television station at gunpoint. In *Unfinished Business* director Don Owen followed the later fortunes of characters he had first shown 20 years earlier in *Nobody Waved Goodbye.* Allan King returned to documentary with an original experiment in *Who's in Charge.* Setting up a meeting of 20 unemployed people but providing no chairman for them, King gave a practical demonstration of the workings and shortcomings of anarchy.

Western Europe. FRANCE. The most ambitious production of the year, Alain Corneau's early-century colonial epic, *Fort Saganne,* had only limited success with the public. The major box-office triumph of the year proved to be Ettore Scola's *Le Bal,* based on a stage musical that used a dance hall to epitomize the history of modern France. Another major commercial success was one of France's large output of thrillers, Claude Berri's *Tchao Pantin.*

Three directors of the New Wave generation were active during the year. Alain Resnais's *L'Amour à mort* was a sombre yet stylish religiophilosophical reflection upon love and death; Eric Rohmer's *Les Nuits de la pleine lune* was a seductive fable about present-day love and loneliness, in the manner of Alfred de Musset, and Jacques Rivette's *L'Amour part terre* was a characteristic caprice about two young women who find themselves guests in the home of an eccentric and mysterious playwright. In *Un Dimanche à la campagne* a director of a younger generation, Bertrand Tavernier, adapted a bittersweet period novel by a classic writer of the French cinema, Pierre Bost.

Foreign directors scored significant successes. Soviet Georgian director Otar Yoseliani created a delightful fantasy, *Les Favoris de la Lune,* an almost wordless quadrille of Parisian life in which incidents are linked by certain valuable objects that are passed from hand to hand as symbols of acquisition and greed. Volker Schlöndorff adapted Marcel Proust with *Un Amour de Swann,* starring Jeremy Irons (*see* BIOGRAPHIES) in the title role. The result was opulent, unimaginative, but hugely successful. The great cameraman Nestor Almendros made his directorial debut in association with Orlando Jiménez Leál in *Improper Conduct,* a fierce attack on the Castro regime's persecution of homosexuals in Cuba.

ITALY. Alongside a large output of local comedies, works of note were few. Outstanding was *Kaos,* an epic story cycle based on Luigi Pirandello's Sicilian stories, directed by the brothers Vittorio and Paolo Taviani. Francesco Rosi's *Carmen* was a lengthy, naturalistically staged, and musically conscientious screen version of Bizet's opera. A small and unpretentious work, Pupi Avati's *Noi Tre,* related with great elegance, humour, and intelligent speculation an incident from the life of the boy Mozart.

WEST GERMANY. The outstanding achievement of the year was *Heimat,* Edgar Reitz's 16-hour family epic of 60 years of German life. Originally produced for a television audience, this extraordinarily sustained film, which raised the soap opera to an art form, later proved capable of appealing to a worldwide theatrical audience. Another ambitious commercial work was Wolfgang Petersen's adventure fantasy *The Neverending Story.* Werner Herzog took his unit to Australia to film the English-language, *Wo die grünen Ameisen träumen.* While the film purported to show the confrontation between ancient aboriginal culture and modern industrial development, the "ethnography" was largely of the director's own invention.

SCANDINAVIA. Now permanently reconciled to his native Sweden after some years of exile, Ingmar Bergman directed a small-scale conversation piece, *After the Rehearsal,* entirely set on the stage of a theatre, where an actress talks to her director about her life and memories. Apart from this the most notable Swedish films of the year were two documentaries, Agneta Elers-Jarleman's *Beyond Sorrow, Beyond Pain,* about the director's valiant efforts to rehabilitate her former lover, almost hopelessly wrecked as a result of an automobile accident; and Stefan Jarl's ecological warning, *Nature's Revenge.*

SPAIN. The outstanding success of the year, and Spain's Cannes Festival entry, was Mario Camus's *Los Santos Innocentes,* a richly detailed rural drama that incidentally offered a severe criticism of social inequalities, which, it was intimated, still persisted in Spain. A film of more direct political protest, Pedro Costa Muste's *El Caso Almería,* reconstructed a recent case in which three Civil Guards were accused of torturing and murdering suspected Basque terrorists.

GREECE. Greece's most prestigious filmmaker, Theo Angelopoulos, completed *Journey to Cythera,* a long and self-consciously artistic film about the return from the U.S.S.R. of an old revolutionary. The second feature film by Tonia Marketaki, *A Time for Love,* a love story set among workers in Corfu early in the century, clearly established her as one of the most important directors currently working in Greece.

Eastern Europe. U.S.S.R. Two veteran Soviet directors demonstrated remarkable durability. At 81 Yuli Raizman directed *A Time of Wishes,* a shrewd and human portrait of a woman unfulfilled by her lot in socialist society. The 78-year-old Sergey Gerasimov not only directed *Lev Tol-*

stoy but also played the main role; the film, however, was somewhat pedestrian. Younger directors produced considerably fresher work than had been seen for some time in the Soviet Union. Alexander Mitta made a vivacious fairy-tale fantasy, *A Tale of Wanderings,* in cooperation with Czechoslovakia and Romania. Yury Chulyukin's *I Don't Want to Grow Up* was a singularly human story of a child unfairly pushed by his parents' honourable ambitions for his betterment. Director Andrey Tarkovsky (*see* BIOGRAPHIES) went into exile in July.

POLAND. Despite the setbacks to Polish cinema during the years of martial law, some works of imagination and energy emerged. Juliusz Machulski's *Sex Mission,* masquerading as a farcical science-fiction story about a future world without males, succeeded in presenting vivid metaphors for every kind of political tyranny. Krzysztof Zanussi's *The Year of the Quiet Sun,* unusually sentimental for that director, presented, through its story of a Polish woman who falls in love with a U.S. soldier immediately after World War II, a fierce condemnation of the waste and injustice of war.

HUNGARY. The most notable releases of 1984 were two films that had been held back by censorship. Marta Meszaros's *Diary for My Children,* completed two years earlier, was a remarkable autobiographical reminiscence of the adolescence of a girl brought up in Stalinist U.S.S.R. and her return to postwar Hungary. Gyula Gazdag's *The Resolution,* held up for a decade, was an equally remarkable documentary exposing the machinations of a local Communist Party organization to influence the dismissal of the chairman of a farming collective.

CZECHOSLOVAKIA. Of the leading figures from the flowering of Czech cinema before 1968, the only two who had remained to work in the country, Jiri Menzel and Vera Chytylova, both directed black but politically innocuous comedies. Menzel's *Snowdrop Celebration,* a dark-edged comedy of rural life, was adapted from stories by Bohumil Hrabal, a key writer for the pre-1968 filmmakers. Chytylova's *The Very Late Afternoon of a Faun* was about the amorous pursuits of an aged Don Juan.

YUGOSLAVIA. Political satire continued to prove a fruitful field in the Yugoslav film. Predrag Antonijevic made his debut with *Nothing but Praise for the Dead,* a sharp satire set in the era of the "Cult of Personality," while Goran

Sir David Lean's cinematic version of E. M. Forster's *A Passage to India* was generally rated a must-see for its pageantry, cinematography, and acting.

Paskalievic's *The Illusory Summer of '68* was an ironic comedy about the effects upon Yugoslavia of Alexander Dubcek's frustrated efforts to establish "Communism with a human face" in Czechoslovakia.

Latin America. CUBA. After the vigour of the first revolutionary years, the Cuban cinema seemed to have passed into a doldrum period, characterized by insignificant melodramas. The best film of the year was Tomás Gutiérrez Alea's *Hasta cierto punto,* a critique of Latin-American machismo that acknowledged a persistent clash between revolutionary ideals and individual aspiration.

BRAZIL. A more liberal climate made possible sharp critical views of recent history. The outstanding film of the year was Nelson Pereira Dos Santos's *Memorias do Carcere,* adapted from Graciliano Ramos's novel about prison experiences in Brazil in the mid-1930s but discovering pertinent modern analogies. *Verde Anos* looked at the years of political repression from the point of view of the very young, contemporaries of the directors, Carlos Gerbase and Giba Assis Brasil. José Batista de Andrade's *A Proxima Vitima* was a drama about a television journalist's battle to expose social abuses.

ARGENTINA. In Argentina, too, a more liberal atmosphere resulted in critical review of the recent past. Hector Olivera's *No habrá más penas ni olvidó (Funny, Dirty Little War)* was a vivid tragicomedy about a local civil war in the late years of Peronism. Bebe Kamin's *Los Chicos de la guerra* followed the unhappy fortunes of three Argentine boys from their birth in the totalitarian era of the early 1960s to the tragic farce of the Falkland Islands/Islas Malvinas war. Maria Luisa Bemberg, the country's first major woman director, succeeded in filming a historical story—about a woman of the 19th century who fell in love with a priest—that had previously been forbidden by censorship.

Asia. JAPAN. The biggest commercial success of 1984 was Koreyoshi Kurahara's spectacular *Antarctica,* the story of the first Japanese Antarctic expedition, in 1958, though the film's attractions seemed to lie as much in the sentimental appeal of the expedition's dogs as in the heroism of the venture itself. Historical reconstruction also characterized Keisuke Kinoshita's sentimental but moving *Children of Nagasaki,* a film adaptation of long-banned writings by Takashi Nagui, a physician who witnessed the nuclear holocaust. The compulsion to succeed as a factor of contemporary Japanese life came under satirical attack in Yoshimitsu Morita's *Family Game,* the story of how a teacher hired to coach the youngest child of aspiring middle-class parents brings absurdist chaos to the family.

HONG KONG. Routine entertainment fare continued to proliferate. Tsui Hark's crime comedy *Aces Go Places* represented a superior example of innumerable comedies, and Jackie Chan's ambitious period adventure *Project A* stood out among the martial arts films that remained a staple production genre. More ambitious undertakings were Allen Fong's *Ah Ying,* the story of a poor girl who defies social odds to win a place in drama school, and Ann Hui's *Love in a Fallen City,* which skillfully re-created the historic atmosphere of Hong Kong in the 1940s as a background for its sentimental story.

TAIWAN. Taiwanese filmmakers showed a special penchant for shameless tearjerkers in the style of Yu Kang Ping's *Papa Can You Hear Me Sing?* However, King Hu, the Hong Kong master of historical reconstruction, made a comedy costume spectacular, *The World's Best Men,* while Hun Hsiao-hsien's *The Boys from Fengkuei* was a lively and sympathetic picture of the adventures and relationships of a group of dispossessed youngsters.

SOUTH KOREA. Two filmmakers of merit emerged: Lim Kwon Taok with a story about a young teacher's experiences in an isolated and closely knit village, *Village in the Mist;* and Lee Doo Yong with *The Wheel,* a costume film recalling Kenji Mizoguchi's classic *Chikamatsu Monogatari* in its story of a subjugated woman of the Yi dynasty who runs away with her lover.

NORTH KOREA. The most ambitious North Korean film of the year was a co-production with Czechoslovakia. Directed by Choe Un Hui, *The Emissary Who Did Not Return* was designed as a national epic, set at the time of the 1907 Hague Peace Conference.

CHINA. Chinese filmmakers continued to reexamine abuses of the period of the Cultural Revolution; thus Wu Tianming's (Wu T'ien-ming's) *Uncharted River* feelingly traced the sufferings of three men employed as loggers in Hunan, while Zhao Zhunzhong's (Chao Chun-chung's) *Girls' Dormitory* treated, with greater sentimentality, the effects of the revolution among young women university students. Socialist morality stories continued as a staple product; for example, Xie Tieli's (Hsieh T'ieh-li's) *Bao and His Son* related the sorrows of an old man whose son falls in with rich, lazy, and antisocial people.

INDIA. India's greatest living filmmaker, Satyajit Ray, was interrupted in the production of *The Home and the World* by severe illness, but the film, completed by his son, was shown at the Cannes Film Festival. Adapted from a novel by Rabindranath Tagore and set in 1905, the period of resistance to Lord Curzon's "divide-and-rule" policy, it described a wife's awakening to political awareness. Ray's Bengali contemporary, Mrinal Sen, wrote and directed *The Ruins,* an elegiac story set in a crumbling rural mansion occupied by an ailing old woman and her lonely daughter.

The gifted younger generation of directors was very active during the year. Shyam Benegal made an ambitious documentary biography of *Pandit Nehru;* Girish Karnad's *Utsav (Festival of Love),* based on a classic Sanskrit play, set out "to revive the two qualities which ancient Indian literature had, but which we seem to have lost in the course of the last 1,000 years—sensuousness and humour"; the avant-gardist Mani Kaui's *Dhrupad* was a celebration of India through its music; Ghoutam Ghosh's *The Crossing,* an indictment of the hardships still forced on India's Untouchables, represented the country at the Venice Film Festival. *The Mirage,* a low-budget film describing the breakup of a family under stress, marked a notable debut for Nirad N. Mohapatra. (DAVID ROBINSON)

Nontheatrical Motion Pictures. At the American Film Festival in New York City, the "best of festival" Emily Award went to *The Miracle of Life,* one of the "Nova" series of science documentaries, directed by Bo G. Erikson and Carl O. Lofman. James L. Limbacher, noted film librarian and historian, lauded cinematographer Lennart Nilsson, who filmed the "marvels of conception . . . showing the interior of the human male and female reproduction organs."

At Asolo, Italy, the 12th International Festival of Films on Art and Biographies of Artists awarded first prize to a U.S. government film by the Smithsonian Institution, *American Film Palaces.* The Scientific and Technical Festival at Katowice, Poland, awarded first prize in its secondary-school category to Encyclopædia Britannica Educational Corp.'s *The Rock Cycle.* A University of Southern California student, W. O. Garrett, took the grand prize at the Malta Amateur Festival for his film *The De Luxe,* a sensitive story of an unwed mother of two.

(THOMAS W. HOPE)

See also Photography; Television and Radio.

This article updates the *Macropædia* article MOTION PICTURES.

Museums

The British Museum was again in the news in 1984, as demands that the Elgin Marbles be returned to Greece continued. More controversial was the sale of drawings from the famous collection of Old Master drawings belonging to the duke of Devonshire at Chatsworth House in Derbyshire, the majority to foreign collections. (*See* Sidebar.)

Facilities and Administration. One of the major events in the museum world in 1984 was the reopening of the Museum of Modern Art in New York City after its rebuilding and expansion, which had taken several years. The museum was founded in the 1930s, with the intention of its becoming "the greatest museum of modern art in the world." The new galleries doubled the exhibition space, and although painting and sculpture still occupied the larger spaces in the new museum, more exhibition area was now devoted to the various applied arts, including printing, architecture, graphic and industrial design, and film and photography. Money for the new development of the museum was raised by selling the air rights to a developer who built an apartment tower above the museum itself. The new galleries housed some 800 works, including much of the sculpture collection. Also in New York City a new museum, the Center for African Art, opened.

The new Dallas (Texas) Museum of Art opened in 1984, the centrepiece of that city's downtown arts district. The

BERNARD GOTFRYD/NEWSWEEK

New York City's Museum of Modern Art emerged from its four-year metamorphosis in shining glass during 1984. Its new west wing occupies the first 6 floors of a 44-story building built on MOMA's air rights; the upper levels are residential.

The English architect James Stirling designed the New State Gallery in Stuttgart, West Germany, which opened in March. Called witty and monumental by critics, its design draws as much attention from tourists as the collections it houses.
THE NEW STATE GALLERY STUTTGART/AUTHENTICATED NEWS INTERNATIONAL

building, by Edward Larrabee Barnes & Associates, was praised for its compatibility with its environment. Preservation and access were important considerations, and the new Dallas museum was said to be particularly successful in welding those two sometimes conflicting requirements.

In Stockbridge, Mass., where Norman Rockwell lived for 25 years, the residents voted to permit construction of a $3.3 million park and gallery devoted to his works. In California the Rifkind Center for German Expressionist Studies—largest in the world with 5,000 prints and 4,000 volumes—opened at the Los Angeles County Museum of Art, while the J. Paul Getty Museum in Malibu pursued its plans to build a large art centre in Los Angeles. (*See* Sidebar.) The newly opened Museum of Art in Fort Wayne, Ind., was funded with $4 million from private sources. In Ottawa the National Gallery of Canada began construction of its first permanent building, an $80 million structure featuring extensive use of natural light.

The International Museum of Photography, formerly located in the George Eastman House in Rochester, N.Y., planned to move to the National Museum of American History of the Smithsonian Institution in Washington, D.C., and was to be renamed the National Center for the Study of Photography. Its collection included 600,000 photographs and negatives.

In January French Minister for Culture Jack Lang announced plans for enlargement of the highly successful Centre National d'Art et de Culture Georges Pompidou (the Beaubourg) in Paris. Also in France the first museum to be devoted to wallpaper opened at Rixheim, near Mulhouse, in splendid 18th-century buildings that were formerly the factory of the wallpaper manufacturer Zuber. Zuber gave the museum more than 130,000 wallpaper patterns, forming a complete record of its output from 1790 to the present. The Scottish National Gallery of Modern Art opened in its permanent home in Edinburgh in mid-August. Its opening show, devoted to 20th-century artists, was entitled "Creation: Modern Art and Nature." In Toledo, Spain, a new museum attached to the Toledo Cathedral was devoted to the cathedral's collection of sculpture and decorative arts. Works by El Greco, Bellini, and Caravaggio were among those shown.

New Acquisitions. The William S. Glazier Collection of illuminated manuscripts, said to be one of the best privately owned such collections in the U.S., was given to the Pierpont Morgan Library in New York City. The gift was

"The Getty Factor": Impact on the Art World

In 1953 oil multimillionaire J. Paul Getty opened a museum at his ranch in Malibu, Calif. Over the years his gifts to the museum continued, with several well-publicized million-dollar purchases in the early 1970s.

Getty died in 1976 and left the bulk of his personal assets to the museum. In April 1982 the J. Paul Getty Museum received the proceeds from the estate, $1.5 billion. Then, early in 1984, Getty Oil was sold to Texaco, enriching the J. Paul Getty Trust to a staggering $2.2 billion. The trust, established as a separate entity, is a private operating foundation and must dispose of 4.25% of its assets annually to avoid taxation. Accordingly, it announced that it planned to spend $90 million per year exclusively in the area of the visual arts.

What impact this sum will have on the art market is hard to measure. The Getty Trust repeatedly denied that it intended a wild buying spree, and for at least the first few years much of the operating budget will be spent on building a vast art complex in West Los Angeles. Also, for some years governments throughout the world have devoted considerable attention to keeping "masterpiece" quality works in private hands from being exported. This has had a considerable impact on the Getty's buying.

However, despite the trust's considerable efforts not to affect the market, there is indeed what the British press calls the "Getty factor." For example, during the year the duke of Devonshire decided to sell 71 Old Master drawings. He first offered the group to the British Museum for £5.5 million ($7.7 million). The museum countered with £5.25 million, but no agreement was reached. The duke then took the drawings to Christie's auction house, where, to no one's real surprise, they fetched £21.2 million. Most went to foreign collections, and seven were bought by the Getty for £6.35 million. The sale stirred up a great controversy, and export licenses were temporarily withheld while British interests sought to keep the drawings in the country.

The Getty's wealth is not the only factor. Most of the works it has gone after have been of very high quality, works that would always have brought premium prices. Nevertheless, the Getty has already had a significant effect on the art world. Henceforward, all museums and collectors in fields in which the Getty is interested must plan their purchases carefully. (WILLIAM P. MILLER, JR.)

hailed by the director as the most important addition to that department of the library since the days of J. Pierpont Morgan and his son in the early 1900s.

Also in New York the Metropolitan Museum of Art acquired a major collection of paintings and drawings by the Swiss artist Paul Klee, donated by Heinz Berggruen, The museum announced that it hoped to show the entire collection in 1986–87. A portrait by Thomas Gainsborough, "The Countess of Sussex and Her Daughter," was acquired by the Toledo (Ohio) Museum of Art for its newly reinstalled English Gallery.

The Los Angeles Museum of Contemporary Art pur-

chased a group of 80 post-World War II paintings and sculptures—Pop and Abstract Expressionist—from the Milanese collector Count Giuseppe Panza di Biumo for $11 million. The Getty Museum purchased 18,000 photographs from nine private collections for about $20 million, the largest such acquisition in the history of photography.

Another fine English portrait was acquired by the National Portrait Gallery in London. William Hogarth's portrait of William Jones of about 1740 was virtually unknown, having been exhibited only once (at the Royal Academy in 1882). This three-quarter-length picture was one of Hogarth's finest early portraits. The National Gallery in London purchased its first work by French Revolutionary artist J.-L. David, a portrait of 1795 depicting Jacobus Blauw. (JOSHUA B. KIND; SANDRA MILLIKIN)

See also Anthropology; Art Exhibitions and Art Sales.

This article updates the Macropædia article MUSEUMS.

Music

Classical. A year of consolidation rather than exciting achievement, 1984 was marked by celebration of one of music's sadder anniversaries. Fifty years earlier, between February and June 1934, three of Britain's greatest composers, Sir Edward Elgar, Gustav Holst, and Frederick Delius, had died. Almost everywhere retrospectives of their works appeared, such as Jerrold Northrop Moore's definitive, if occasionally confusing, study of Elgar and a further edition of Delius's correspondence. Even in France (where Delius lived for over 30 years but was, and continued to be, strenuously ignored) room was found in concert and radio programs for his music. Yehudi Menuhin returned to Paris to play, for the first time in half a century in that city, Elgar's *Violin Concerto,* while France Musique, the nation's state-controlled music channel, broadcast a series under the generic title "Londres, 1934."

SYMPHONIC MUSIC. Few if any significant premieres took place during 1984. The most notable exception was the world premiere (under the direction of Sir Colin Davis), at one of the closing programs of the Boston Symphony Orchestra's 1983–84 season, of Sir Michael Tippett's essentially pacifist oratorio *The Mask of Time.* Primarily concerned with the kind of cosmic and human preoccupations familiar from Polish composer Krzysztof Penderecki's earlier *Kosmogonia, The Mask of Time,* Tippett's most extended score in years, was received enthusiastically by most listeners, both in the U.S. and at its subsequent U.K. premiere (as part of the 1984 Henry Wood Promenade Concerts), when the conductor was Toronto Symphony Orchestra conductor in chief Andrew Davis.

On the orchestral front the most interesting development in the U.S. was the appointment of European-born Christoph von Dohnanyi as music director of the Cleveland (Ohio) Orchestra. A musician of classic pedigree (his grandfather was the composer, pianist, and teacher Erno von Dohnanyi), he had enjoyed a burgeoning reputation with the Vienna Philharmonic. Consequently, interest in his forthcoming tenure at Cleveland ran high, although doubts were voiced about the leisurely, somewhat bland readings of the mainstream classics that had appeared so far. An orchestra once renowned (in George Szell's day) as one of North America's most brilliantly lucid was, it was felt, in danger of losing a degree of character.

Elsewhere in the U.S. the German-born Günther Herbig was appointed principal conductor of the Detroit Symphony Orchestra in succession to Antal Dorati; the Dutchman Edo de Waart renewed his connection with the San

Francisco Symphony; and the young British conductor Simon Rattle (principal of the U.K.'s City of Birmingham Symphony) continued to make beautiful music with a clearly enthusiastic Los Angeles Philharmonic at the orchestra's Chandler Pavilion. Meanwhile, the Philadelphia Orchestra marked its move to the city's Memorial Hall in Fairmount Park with a full-scale restoration of the hall that included the installation of 1,260 acoustic tiles. Riccardo Muti, while remaining director of the Philadelphia, was to become musical director of La Scala, Milan, in 1986.

One of the year's happier events was a whistle-stop visit to various European capitals by Swiss-born Charles Dutoit and a much-improved Montreal Symphony. Never, it was concluded, had playing of such quality been heard from a Canadian orchestra, a judgment confirmed by London-Decca's decision to issue it a long-term recording contract.

In Vienna Claudio Abbado continued his work with the city's Philharmonic (Leonard Bernstein and James Levine were other welcome visitors), despite performances of the European classics that, as so often when La Scala's music director was in charge, seemed just a little too sleepy and overcosseted for their own good. Another popular guest in the Austrian capital (and at Salzburg) was the magisterial Herbert von Karajan (*see* Biographies), his relationship with the Philharmonic prospering afresh as his relationship with the rival Berlin Philharmonic became more strained.

In the U.K., where the London Symphony Orchestra celebrated its 80th anniversary, the 1984 Proms season at the capital's Royal Albert Hall wended its way through an unusually hot, dry summer. A particular (if unexpected) high spot occurred on the penultimate night, when ailing maestro Lovro von Matacic was obliged to cancel at the last moment and Stanislav Skrowaczewski (currently in charge of the U.K.'s Manchester Hallé Orchestra) stepped in to direct what proved a thoroughly exciting Beethoven *Choral Symphony.*

In Scotland Sir Alexander Gibson handed over artistic control of the Scottish National Orchestra to the Finnish-born Neeme Jarvi, best known for an enterprising series of phonograph albums with Sweden's neglected Göteborg Symphony. In France 1984 marked the 50th anniversary of the founding of the ORTF (Office de Radiodiffusion et Télévision Française) Orchestra.

OPERA. The three biggest sensations of the operatic year carried, alas, more copy for the gossip columnists than interest for opera buffs. Despite a handful of brilliantly successful productions (such as the 1983–84 run of Puccini's *Turandot*), it was announced that Lorin Maazel's contract

as music director of the Vienna State Opera would not be renewed when it expired in 1985. The general message to his successor, Claudio Abbado, seemed to be one of "Good luck—you'll need it."

Further sensations attended West Germany's prestigious all-Wagner Bayreuth Festival, where, in a season of generally undistinguished productions, the new Sir Peter Hall-Sir Georg Solti *Ring* tetralogy continued to founder as last-minute cast changes once again disrupted conductor Solti's "dream team" and also upset a series of major recording plans. Even worse trouble bedeviled Soviet director Yury Lyubimov's (*see* Biographies) strenuously avant-garde Florence Festival production of Verdi's *Rigoletto.* Two conductors withdrew at rehearsal stage (one of them the rising star Giuseppe Sinopoli), along with the lead baritone Piero Cappuccilli, while soprano Edita Gruberova declared herself dismayed in the extreme ("it's not art") and audiences erupted with regularity in a frenzy of booing.

Altogether happier, if not unbrushed by controversy, the premiere at the Opéra de Paris (Palais Garnier) of Olivier Messiaen's hugely sprawling *Saint François d'Assise* was nothing if not spectacular, a forest of characteristically Messiaenesque orchestral pyrotechnics underpinning stage work and vocal lines of often startling beauty. Conductor Seiji Ozawa was considered to have scored a particular success. Also new to the Paris Opéra were productions of Chabrier's *The Star*, Dargomizhsky's *The Stone Guest*, Gluck's *Alceste*, Henze's *The English Cat*, the original version (courtesy Florence Opera) of Puccini's *Madame Butterfly*, and Verdi's *Jerusalem* and *Macbeth*, while soprano Julia Migenes-Johnson, fresh from the success of the film *Bizet's Carmen*, directed by Francesco Rosi, won further laurels with a number of appearances.

A noteworthy feature of the U.S. operatic scene was the variety of high-quality concert opera performances staged in a number of cities. Concert opera made possible the presentation of some less widely performed works for which the cost of full theatrical production might be too great, with the participation of singers free perhaps for only a single performance. Examples were the Chicago Symphony's *Moses and Aaron* (conductor, Solti) and *Wozzeck* (conductor, Abbado) in Chicago and the Philadelphia Orchestra's *Macbeth* (conductor, Muti) in Philadelphia and at Carnegie Hall, New York City. Carnegie Hall had its own opera-in-concert series (artistic director, Matthew Epstein) comprising three opéras comiques, Offenbach's *La Périchole*, Ambroise Thomas's *Mignon*, and Massenet's *Chérubin*, all with Frederica von Stade.

(LEFT) SOTHEBY PARKE BERNET. (BELOW) CULVER PICTURES

Richard Strauss composed the song "Malven" in 1948 for the soprano Maria Jeritza. They appear together below. At left is the autograph score, inscribed, "To my beloved Maria, this last rose." Discovered after Jeritza's death in 1982, the manuscript was auctioned in December by Sotheby's.

New York City's Metropolitan Opera concluded its celebratory centennial season with a lengthy gala evening devoted to its traditional involvement with ballet and other attractions not strictly operatic. Among those taking part were Yves Montand, Lillian Gish, Alvin Ailey, Dame Margot Fonteyn, Alexandra Danilova, Erik Bruhn, Alicia Alonso, Antoinette Sibley, and Rudolf Nureyev.

In the U.K. the Glyndebourne Festival Opera celebrated its half century in pleasantly intimate style, while the Royal Opera House, Covent Garden, and the English National Opera (with ex-Chicago Symphony artistic administrator Peter Jonas as managing director) competed for London's operagoers. The English National (as usual) scored on points for initiative with Britten's *The Turn of the Screw* and *Gloriana,* Dvorak's *Rusalka,* Janacek's *Fate* and *The Makropoulos Affair,* Prokofiev's *War and Peace,* Richard Strauss's *Arabella,* Tchaikovsky's *Mazeppa,* Verdi's *The Sicilian Vespers,* Wagner's *The Flying Dutchman,* and the Kurt Weill-Bertolt Brecht *Mahaganny Songs.*

ALBUMS. Since early 1983 a hectic rear-guard action had been under way from a vociferous and influential group of audiophiles displeased with perceived flaws in the revolutionary Dutch-Japanese-developed Digital Audio Disc (DAD), also called compact disc (CD). As 1984 drew to a close, a few lone voices were still heard proclaiming the alleged virtues of the older analog technology (among them Doug Sax, president of the highly regarded Sheffield Lab company). Analog, it was argued, was more faithful than digital to the original sound. But in the mass market, upon which the success or failure of the new sound source depended, CD was pronounced a success, the most optimistic industry estimates now suggesting that the demise of the traditional vinyl LP disc could be as little as five years away. Major advantages of CD were considered to be the complete absence of background and surface noises and its greatly improved dynamic range.

Among major recording companies only Angel-EMI and the now moribund RCA were dragging their feet, the former still relying on CD pressings supplied by its Japanese associate, Toshiba. Certain producers, however, were still edgy, Columbia-CBS and the U.K.-based Nimbus showing a marked reluctance to offer review materials to certain of the more critical hi-fi journals. An underlying reason was the continued fragility of the recession-troubled marketplace; published figures showed, for example, that sales of the seminal *Gramophone* magazine had slumped from 74,198 copies monthly for the period January–June 1972 to 58,673 copies monthly for 1983 and that the average page count had declined by one-third. However, economic indicators were pointing upward at the year's end.

Important album releases of the year included first-ever recordings of Auber's *Fra Diavolo,* Chabrier's *The Star,* Debussy's *The Fall of the House of Usher,* and Poulenc's *Seven Responses for Tenebrae* (all French EMI); Marc-Antoine Charpentier's *Medée* (French Harmonia Mundi); Elgar's *The Black Knight* (Angel-EMI); a newly edited Mozart *Requiem* (L'Oiseau-Lyre); Penderecki's *Te Deum* and *Lacrimosa* (Angel-EMI); and Schubert's recently discovered (and reconstructed) Tenth Symphony (Ricercar).

Also of interest were new recordings of the complete Beethoven lieder (featuring baritone Dietrich Fischer-Dieskau) and Ravel *mélodies* (both Angel-EMI); Britten's *The Turn of the Screw* (Philips) and *War Requiem* (Angel-EMI); Janacek's *Jenufa* (London-Decca); a CD-only Karajan-Mahler Ninth Symphony (DGG); and two complete CD Wagner *Ring* cycles (from, respectively, Eurodisc and London-Decca, the latter reissuing the classic 1960s Solti-Vienna Philharmonic recordings).

A new production at the Paris Opéra was *Jerusalem,* one of the operas of Verdi's youth, under the direction of the Italian conductor Donato Renzetti. Cecilia Gasdia sang the role of Hélène, and Veriano Luchetti sang Gaston.
KEYSTONE

Losses to the world of music in 1984 included conductor Janos Ferencsik, baritone Tito Gobbi, tenor Georges Thill, violinist Joseph Calvet, and scholar-conductor Imogen Holst. (*See* OBITUARIES). (NICK HARPER)

Jazz. Though 1984 was a year marked by an uncommon number of deaths of jazz musicians, there were no signs of diminished vigour in the music. Festivals continued to proliferate, notably in Europe, and U.S. artists toured widely despite the continued strength of the dollar. Nightclubs and concerts flourished, notably in New York City. In the record market reissues of vintage jazz, in particular from the 1950s, were dominant, but much new music was released as well, almost all by small companies. A notable exception was Columbia Records' continued support of Wynton Marsalis, giving the brilliant young New Orleans-born trumpeter a high degree of visibility. Marsalis became the first artist to win both jazz and classical Grammy awards, as best instrumental soloist, and he performed in both roles on the Grammy telecast. Ever suspicious of success, much of the jazz press responded by subjecting Marsalis's new jazz album, which features him with a large ensemble including strings, to criticism. His new classical LP, however, was warmly received.

The astonishing Austrian-born gypsy guitarist Bireli Lagrene, at 17 Marsalis's junior by five years, made his U.S. debut at New York's Kool Jazz Festival in a tribute to Django Reinhardt and was hailed as that great virtuoso's heir. The festival also paid homage to two living giants of jazz: multitalented Benny Carter, who in his 77th year continued to create remarkable music as an alto saxophonist, trumpeter, composer, and arranger; and trendsetting tenor saxophonist Illinois Jacquet. The timeliness of such tributes was underscored by the festival's Count Basie night. Planned as a pre-80th birthday party, it instead became a memorial. The veteran bandleader and pianist, long in failing health but determined to carry on to the end, died on April 26 (*see* OBITUARIES).

Basie's funeral service, held at Harlem's famous Abyssinian Baptist Church, was a remarkable ingathering of the jazz community the likes of which might not be seen again. The shortest and most poignant of the eulogies was delivered by Basie's taciturn guitarist, Freddie Green. "I was with him for 46 years," he said. "What am I going to do now?" His question was answered when Basie's adopted son, Aaron Woodward, announced that the band would be kept alive. Among the mourners were four associates who would also die before the year was out: veteran booking agent Willard Alexander, who represented Basie for more than 30 years and was instrumental in launching Benny Goodman's band; manager and record producer Teddy Reig, Basie's right-hand man for decades; and two distinguished alumni of the band, trombonist Vic Dickenson and reedman-arranger-composer Budd Johnson.

Other veterans of the big-band era who died in 1984 were the still active pioneer of Afro-Cuban jazz, Machito (*see* OBITUARIES), former leaders Claude Hopkins and Ina Ray Hutton (*see* OBITUARIES), trombonist-singer Trummy Young, bassist Gene Ramey, and master drummer Shelly Manne. Further deaths included three famous blues singers representing different generations and styles: Alberta Hunter (*see* OBITUARIES), a contemporary of Bessie Smith; Willie Mae ("Big Mama") Thornton (*see* OBITUARIES), rooted in country blues; and Esther Phillips, as "Little Esther" a star of rhythm and blues at 14.

In late 1983 Artie Shaw, once Benny Goodman's chief rival and retired from music since 1955, announced the formation of a big band under his musical direction, to be fronted by clarinetist Dick Johnson. When the band made its formal debut in December 1983 at the reopening of Glen Island Casino (once one of the swing era's most famous venues for bands), it was conducted by the 74-year-old Shaw himself. His personal aura and voluble commentary tended to overshadow Johnson's able re-creations of classic Shavian solos. Shaw said that he wanted the band to sound as if there had been an Artie Shaw Orchestra during the intervening 30 years and commissioned a good deal of new music; however, it seemed routine and rather pallid compared with the best vintage material.

One of the year's most interesting records was an all-star tribute to Thelonious Monk, *That's the Way I Feel Now,* which brought together the talents of not only such established jazz artists as Gil Evans, Elvin Jones, Johnny Griffin, Barry Harris, Steve Lacy, Randy Weston, and Charlie Rouse but also prominent figures from fusion (Carla Bley), rhythm and blues (Dr. John), and, perhaps most significantly, rock (Todd Rundgren, Peter Frampton, Joe Jackson, Chris Spedding, and the group Was [Not Was]). All approached Monk's challenging compositions with respect, and on balance the two-record set was a considerable artistic achievement. Another ecumenical event involving Monk was the active support of the Beethoven Society of Washington, D.C., in fund-raising efforts to establish a performing arts centre in Monk's memory in his birthplace, Rocky Mount, N.C.

Festival appearances in New York, Chicago, and Europe and the release of an excellent record brought to international attention an unusual eight-piece group from New Orleans, The Dirty Dozen Brass Band. Made up of jazzmen of the younger generation, it featured music rooted in the time-honoured marching-band tradition of New Orleans, one of the parent styles of jazz, and retained its unique zest. But its approach to repertory was eclectic, blending the traditional with pieces by Charlie Parker and Thelonious Monk and original works reflecting even more recent influences. The music sometimes brought to mind the neotraditional ventures of modernists David Murray, Arthur Blythe, and Henry Threadgill, but above all it was yet another instance of the bridging of stylistic and generational gaps in jazz and of the intriguing revitalization of New Orleans as a seedbed of new voices in the music.

(DAN M. MORGENSTERN)

Popular. There is nothing the pop music industry likes more than a dash of hysteria and success stories that verge on the fantastic, and in 1984 there were massive and bizarre success stories on both sides of the Atlantic. In the U.S. the phenomenon was called Michael Jackson (*see* BIOGRAPHIES), and in Britain it was Frankie Goes to Hollywood. Both provided high-class dance music; both relied on distinguished producers; and both were heavily promoted through the use of expensive and elaborate videos. (*See* Sidebar.) Beyond that, they seemed to have nothing in common at all. America's star was religious, something of a mysterious recluse, had the Peter Pan image of the eternal child, and was a sensational live performer. By contrast, the British stars traded in sexual outrage (at least at the start of their career), came from an ordinary working-class background in Liverpool (the Beatles' hometown), and by the end of 1984 had yet to give live performances in their homeland, although they did tour the U.S.

Michael Jackson's success was all the more remarkable because he brought out no new solo album during the year. His album *Thriller* was, in fact, released in 1982, but it kept selling and selling and by the end of 1984 had sold over 45 million copies worldwide and was still among the best-sellers in many countries. This made it by far the biggest success in pop music history, and so the expectations were that Michael Jackson would mount some spectacular live shows as a follow-up. He did give a Victory Tour, but instead of going out solo he was reunited with his brothers, with whom he had previously worked in the Jackson Five. Michael was not yet a teenager when the Jacksons had their first number one hit together, "I Want You Back," in 1970, and at the start of the 1984 tour he was still only 25. The Jackson's Victory Tour started in Kansas City, Mo., on July 6 and was expected to become by far the largest grossing U.S. tour of the year. There was no disappointment with the shows or with Michael's peformance, but the joint Jackson album *Victory* in no way matched *Thriller.*

In Britain, meanwhile, the Frankie Goes to Hollywood group made an equally remarkable impact, yet all they did was release two singles and one double album. The band was signed to a new, highly adventurous label, ZTT. Its first Frankie single, "Relax," was released at the end of October 1983 and became a massive best-seller in Britain after being widely banned for its suggestive lyrics. It remained on the best-seller list for over eight months, and the follow-up "Two Tribes" went straight to number one in Britain, as did the band's debut album, *Welcome to the PleasureDome.* All were elaborately produced, and British fans would have to wait until 1985 to see if their heroes could perform so well live.

While those two acts dominated the year, pop styles in both the U.S. and Britain continued to diversify. In the U.S. the newly successful rock stars tended to be entertainers like Prince (the most successful new black performer of the year with his best-selling album *Purple Rain*) and the flamboyant Cyndi Lauper with *She's So Unusual* or traditional-style rock journeymen like Huey Lewis and the News, whose *Sports* was one of the year's best-sellers, and the Cars with *Heartbeat City.* Bruce Springsteen was among the most successful live performers of the year and released a strong new album, *Born in the U.S.A.* The heavy-metal sound was also popular, as exemplified by Van Halen's *1984.*

Apart from Prince, other successful black American performers of the year included the veteran Tina Turner, who returned to the best-sellers with her album *Private Dancer* and singles like "What's Love Got to Do with It," Lionel

Music Videos

The origins of music videos, filmed versions of popular songs, sometimes are traced to the "soundies" of the 1930s, short films made by such jazz musicians as Duke Ellington. And certainly dance sequences from later films bear resemblances to music videos. But it is generally agreed that rock videos, the first of the modern music videos, have their origins in the 1960s movies of the Beatles. Sequences such as "Can't Buy Me Love" from *A Hard Day's Night* are, in fact, sometimes shown as videos.

The first modern music videos were made in the late 1970s, and they soon became a staple of British and U.S. television. By the early 1980s MTV, a U.S. cable channel with 24-hour programming of videos, had been established, and local stations and the national networks offered video programs. The 1st Annual MTV Video Music Awards were presented in 1984. A recent development is the video bar, with "video jockeys" or "veejays" programming the mix of film clips. Video jukeboxes and collections of videos for the home cassette player are available.

By 1984 videos included virtually all forms of popular music, but it was rock that established the music video as a distinctive form. The best of the rock videos project all of the music's energy and irreverence. They are short (usually about three minutes, the length of the typical record cut) and commonly have razzle-dazzle, lightning-quick editing, often juxtaposing psychedelic and surrealistic images. Like the music itself, they frequently seem designed to shock. But even rock videos can be thoughtful and romantic, and this is perhaps the prevailing style in videos of country and other forms of music.

The two basic types of music videos are "performance" (tapes of performers) and "concept" videos (basically a sequence of images and actions, sometimes in the form of a narrative to dramatize or comment on the lyrics). Rock videos frequently mix the two, cutting back and forth from one to the other. Performance videos tend to predominate in types of music other than rock.

Music videos began as a promotional device to sell rock recordings (they are credited with creating such stars as Cyndi Lauper and Duran Duran). But, like many other commercial endeavours, they have taken on a life of their own.   (ROBERT RAUCH)

Richie with *Can't Slow Down,* and the Pointer Sisters with *Break Out,* while Chaka Khan scored on both sides of the Atlantic with "I Feel for You." It was a year for style, not experiment, in American music, but a handful of bands did try to break away from the commercial and the predictable, often by taking inspiration from 1960s styles. The Dream Syndicate and R.E.M. pointed the way that new U.S. music could develop.

Meanwhile, the second "British invasion" of the U.S.

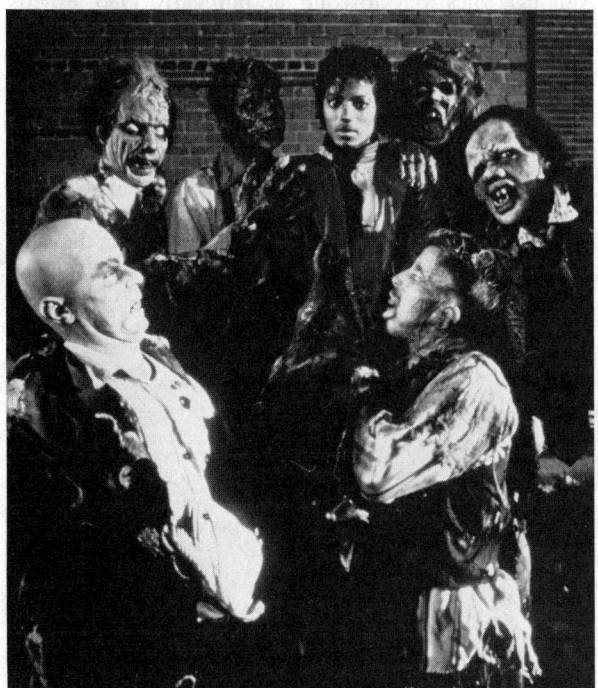

VESTRON VIDEO

Michael Jackson with a company of ghouls in the rock music video *Thriller.* The star's explosive performances won him an unprecedented eight Grammy awards. (For more on videos, *see* the Sidebar, above.)

continued, with white, stylish bands mixing a little English eccentricity with music that was most often influenced by American soul styles. Boy George and Culture Club remained popular, releasing a new album, *Waking Up with the House on Fire,* and touring the U.S. Other white English soul boys like Duran Duran and Wham! also succeeded in the U.S., as did the new wave of British guitar bands, such as U2 (actually from Dublin) and Big Country (from Scotland).

In Britain itself those same bands continued to be popular. Both the new soulful stylists like Wham! (a duo who exuded a clean-cut charm reminiscent of crooners from the 1950s) and the new guitar bands like Big Country ended the year playing in large stadiums as well as concert halls. But the main political event in Britain during the year, the miners' strike, with its implications for the growing division between north and south, also influenced the pop scene. While British pop had been largely nonpolitical since the punk and "2-tone" era of the late 1970s, there now emerged a new brand of protest singer, as demonstrated by performers like the Redskins and soloist Billy Bragg. At the end of the year a number of Britain's top performers, including Boy George, Sting from the Police, Wham!, and members of Duran Duran, joined together to record "Do They Know It's Christmas?" about the famine in Ethiopia. All proceeds from the record, which went immediately to the top of the charts, were donated to famine relief.

From outside the two major markets, Britain and the U.S., there were attempts to popularize Soca, the music of the East Caribbean, and there was also continuing interest in African music. King Sunny Adé and his African Beats again toured Britain and the U.S. with considerable success, but Nigeria's second best known performer, Fela Kuti, was arrested on currency charges as he was leaving Nigeria for a major U.S. tour. There were accusations that his arrest was motivated by the controversial political nature of his songs.   (ROBIN DENSELOW)

See also Dance; Motion Pictures; Television and Radio; Theatre.

This article updates the *Macropædia* article The History of Western MUSIC.

Philately and Numismatics

Stamps. The market for rare stamps and postal history items continued to improve in 1984, with buyers tending to be interested collectors rather than speculators. The lower end of the market was less active. A less happy development was the emergence of packaged thematic collections of stamps inscribed "Leaders of the World." Most of them were issued by small Pacific and Caribbean islands whose philatelic affairs were handled by advisers in the U.K. Railway locomotives and racing cars were featured in the designs, which had no association with the issuing islands.

The National Postal Museum in London held the first of 30 auctions planned to dispose of registration sheets of stamps and other material of philatelic interest surplus to requirements of the Post Office and the museum. The initial sale in April realized a disappointing £76,731 (£170,000 had been projected), and legal difficulties caused the postponement of further sales. The Cecil Neild collection of Falkland Islands, bequeathed to Clare College, Cambridge, realized £105,800 (Harmer's, London). A remarkable accumulation of over 1,000 letters dated between 1569 and 1601 and addressed to the brothers Corsini, merchant bankers of Florentine origin trading in Lombard Street, London, was sold in September by Christie's/Robson Lowe for £53,720. The year's largest single-country auction was the sale of the Harold W. Fisher collection of Great Britain for £352,560 (Phillips, London). The unique Swedish 1855 three-skilling-banco error of colour (yellow instead of green) was sold for £265,000 (David Feldman, Zürich, Switz.).

Esselte, the Swedish conglomerate that controlled Stanley Gibbons through Letraset, sold Gibbons to a management consortium backed by Barclays Bank. In March the company applied to the Stock Exchange for its shares to be dealt on the unlisted securities market, but permission was refused on the grounds that the company chairman, Clive H. Feigenbaum, was not acceptable to the Quotations Committee. Feigenbaum resigned and sold his interest to Ionian Securities, which required him to repurchase at full book value (£455,000) stamp stock Feigenbaum had exchanged for the shares that had given him control. In September Gibbons sold its stake in Frimärkshuset AB of Stockholm to the remaining (Swedish) shareholders.

In June the congress of the British Philatelic Federation (BPF) was held in the Isle of Man for the first time. Four new signatories to the Roll of Distinguished Philatelists were Anton Jerger (the first Austrian national to sign the Roll), Renato Mondolfo (Italy), Leon V. Rapkin (Great Britain), and Robert G. Stone (U.S.). The BPF Congress medal was awarded to R. Geraint Jones of Colwyn Bay,

North Wales. Two leading British philatelic journals ceased publication in June: *Stamp Collecting* (founded in 1913) and *Philatelic Magazine* (founded in 1911).

An important meeting in Madrid in April brought together representatives of the Fédération Internationale de Philatélie (FIP), the International Federation of Stamp Dealers' Associations, and Ascat, the international group of stamp catalog editors and publishers, with observers from the Universal Postal Union. Steps were taken to unify action over the spate of unnecessary issues of stamps and other matters of common interest. The major FIP-sponsored international exhibitions were held in Madrid in April–May, Sydney, Australia, in September, and Seoul, South Korea, in October. (KENNETH F. CHAPMAN)

Coins and Paper Money. Throughout 1984 U.S. officials studied ways to protect the "greenback" from would-be counterfeiters using improved colour copying machines. Possible changes included the use of three-dimensional optical devices, light background colours, or security threads on bills of all denominations. Experts said such enhancements would make the world's best-known currency almost impossible to duplicate on the new generation of copiers. If the secretary of the treasury endorsed a specific recommendation during 1985, revamped bills would begin circulating by the following year. Research indicated that by 1987 as many as 2,000 sophisticated colour copiers would be in use in the U.S. and that 21% of the people with access to such machines would attempt to duplicate paper money. Officials promised that the basic designs currently on U.S. bills would be maintained. Meanwhile, the U.S. Supreme Court voted 5–4 to uphold a law prohibiting publishers from printing pictures of U.S. currency unless the pictures were in black and white and in sizes significantly smaller or larger than the original bill.

The U.S. Mint continued to sell commemorative coins during 1984 to help finance the Los Angeles Olympic Games. The government offered two types of silver dollars and a $10 gold coin, each depicting an Olympic scene. Although sales were to continue into early 1985, experts predicted that the U.S. Mint would dispose of just 10% of the 52 million coins it was permitted to make under federal law. Assuming the projection was on target, the U.S. and Los Angeles Olympic committees would receive about $65 million from the coin program. Also in 1984, the Mint resumed selling to collectors sets of uncirculated coins made in Philadelphia and Denver. The so-called mint sets were last issued in 1981.

In the U.K. the Royal Mint stopped producing the halfpenny in March on the grounds that it cost more to make than it was worth. The government planned to demonitize the coin, ending its more than seven centuries of service as legal tender. Starting in 1985, British coinage would feature

COURTESY, BRITISH ROYAL MINT

A monarch matures: Raphael Maklouf's portrait of Queen Elizabeth II was to adorn circulating coins of the United Kingdom beginning in 1985. It would replace the earlier portrait (far left) on coins circulated from 1968 to 1984.

a new portrait of Queen Elizabeth II that more accurately reflected the appearance of the 58-year-old monarch. The likeness would be just the third of Queen Elizabeth on circulating coins since her reign began in 1952 and the first change since 1968. Some other British Commonwealth nations were expected to place the same portrait on their coinage after the U.K. introduced it.

Many countries issued new types of coins and currency in 1984, especially nations with high inflation. For example, Mexico began the process of replacing its coinage with new pieces, to be denominated from 1 to 200 pesos. The Bank of Israel introduced into circulation a new note worth 10,000 shekels; just three years earlier, 100 shekels had been the country's highest-denomination bill. The rare-coin market continued its slow recovery from the recession-induced slump of the early 1980s. Numismatic keepsakes managed a 7.4% price gain in the 12 months ended June 1, according to a Wall Street securities company—good enough for third place on a list of 14 investment vehicles.

Many U.S. collectors searched their pocket change for 1983-dated Lincoln cents with distinct double lettering on the tails side. A malformed die produced at least 5,000 such cents. Prices for the error coins fluctuated with reports of new finds, but some dealers paid $60 or more for an uncirculated specimen. (ROGER BOYE)

This article updates the *Macropædia* article COINS AND COINAGE.

Photography

In 1984 the most striking technological developments in conventional, silver-image photography were evidenced by a marked improvement in colour films. Electronic imaging made strong advances; video cameras in several formats became a mass consumer item, while prototype magnetic-disk still cameras were shown to be practical for special applications. Culturally, the world lost several important photographers, and some photography museums experienced major changes.

Photo Equipment. Improvements in colour-film technology resulted in an unprecedented number of new colour negative and transparency films being brought to market by film manufacturers around the world, including Kodak, Fuji, Agfa, 3M, and Konica (Konishiroku). Moderate-speed (ISO 50–200) and high-speed (ISO 400) films provided finer grain, greater sharpness, and improved colour rendition. Ultrahigh-speed films (ISO 800–1600) raised the upper limits of colour-film sensitivity with remarkably little loss in image quality.

To help boost sluggish disc camera sales, Kodak introduced an improved third-generation Disc film that used the T-grain technology first introduced in Kodacolor VR 1000 in 1982. The company also brought forth a new premium-quality black-and-white printing paper, Kodak Elite. Available in three contrast grades and a range of sizes, this fibre-base paper provided an unusually wide tonal range from rich blacks to brilliant whites.

For 35-mm camera design it was a year of refinements and modest improvements rather than startling novelty. A number of new single-lens-reflex (SLR) cameras incorporated a "multiprogram" approach to exposure automation, in which the user was given a choice of programmed modes. In each case the camera selected an appropriate combination of aperture and shutter speed but would favour either depth-of-field or action-stopping ability depending on the program chosen.

The Ricoh XR-P, for example, offered three programmed sequences. With a normal daylight scene having an exposure value (EV) of 12 and ISO 100 film, if the user chose the normal "P" program, the camera selected 1/125 second at $f/5.6$, a good general-purpose compromise. If maximum depth-of-field was particularly important, say for a close-up of flowers, choosing the "PD" (depth) mode would result in an exposure of 1/40 second at $f/9.5$. If the user wanted a fast shutter speed to stop action or to permit use of a hand-held telephoto lens, choosing the "PA" (action) mode would yield 1/300 second at $f/3.7$. Thus some degree of creative control was fused with the reliability of automated exposure. The XR-P also offered other, more familiar exposure modes including aperture-priority automatic exposure, two types of automatic flash exposure, and manual.

Similarly, the sophisticated Canon T50 included three programmed sequences among its total of eight modes and a switch-operated choice between two kinds of through-the-lens exposure metering: full-field averaging and spot. Three programs also were provided in the Contax 159MM in addition to aperture-priority automatic exposure and manual.

AP/WIDE WORLD

Photography lost a great name with the death in 1984 of Ansel Adams (*see* OBITUARIES), famed for his representations of nature and the environment. Characteristic is this "Winterstorm, Yosemite National Park."

Tony Suau of the *Denver Post* won the 1984 Pulitzer Prize for feature photography for work including photos of mass starvation in Ethiopia and "Lost but Not Forgotten," the poignant photo at left showing a widow grieving at her husband's grave marker.

ANTHONY SUAU—AP/WIDE WORLD

The outpouring of new "auto-everything" 35-mm compact cameras, so evident the previous year, continued at an extraordinary rate as manufacturers vied to find a novel feature that would differentiate theirs from the rest. Beginning with the Pentax Super Sport and soon followed by the Minolta Freedom I and II and others, 35-mm compacts began to be provided with sensors for DX-coded film. The DX system, introduced by Kodak the previous year and subsequently adopted by most major film makers, comprised a mechanical and electronic coding of 35-mm film and cassettes that provided information to properly equipped cameras and photofinishing machines. The immediate benefit to the user of a compatible camera was a correct, automatically set ISO rating.

Although only one DX-compatible 35-mm SLR, the Konica TC-X, was introduced during the year, the expected appearance of many other models in 1985 would soon make the DX system virtually universal for all 35-mm cameras, compact and SLR alike.

Video cameras made big strides into the market once dominated by conventional 8-mm movie equipment. Kodak introduced and brought to market its Matsushita-built version of a video camcorder (combination video camera and recorder) using the new compact 8-mm videotape format, the details for which were standardized by the world's leading film, camera, tape, and electronics companies in 1984.

Other firms that announced 8-mm video camcorders during the year included General Electric, Polaroid, and Fuji. In response to the challenge of the 8-mm videotape format, new camcorders and compact video cameras based on conventional half-inch VHS and Beta formats were introduced. The JVC Videomovie GR-C1U camcorder was a well-designed all-in-one unit that used 20-minute VHS-C (for compact) cassettes. The trend in separate video cameras, which required attachment to a recorder, was toward compact, lightweight, simple-to-operate models.

Although only in the prototype stage, filmless, magnetic-disk still cameras demonstrated their practicality for special applications. During the 1984 Summer Olympics in Los Angeles, Canon used an electronic colour still camera (part of its Still Video System D413) to record events and transmit the images within 24 minutes via telephone to Tokyo, where newspapers reproduced them in colour. The Canon device employed a new 400,000-pixel charge-coupled-device sensor jointly developed by Canon, Inc., of Japan and Texas Instruments of the U.S., and the images were recorded on a "video floppy" disk less than 50 mm (2 in) wide, which held as many as 50 pictures.

At the annual Photokina trade fair in Cologne, West Germany, Panasonic privately demonstrated working models of a prototype electronic still camera, and Copal showed, but did not demonstrate, a prototype of its Video Floppy Camera CV-1. Production models of these and other electronic still cameras were expected to be available within a year or two for specialized professional applications in journalistic, forensic, medical, industrial, and research photography.

Cultural Trends. The world's photographic community lost a number of its distinguished practitioners during the year, including Ansel Adams, Gjon Mili, Brassai (*see* OBITUARIES), and Garry Winogrand.

Adams, at 82 the most famous photographer in the U.S., was also widely known for his environmentalist activities and as a teacher, originator of the zone system, and promoter of photography as a fine art. Mili, 79, combined technical expertise in electronics with a creative photographer's eye to become a pioneer of ultrahigh-speed electronic flash. Brassai (Gyula Halasz) left his native Hungary before World War II for Paris, where he made his home thereafter. His most famous work was his reportage of Parisian nightlife. Garry Winogrand, 56, began as a photojournalist but later developed a personal style as a street photographer that established him as one of the most influential photographers of his generation.

Among major exhibitions during the year was an impressive retrospective of Irving Penn's lifework at New York City's newly renovated Museum of Modern Art. At Photokina the main cultural attraction was a series of exhibitions centred on the theme of "The Printed Photograph," while the Museum Gruber showed a choice selection from its L. Fritz Gruber collection.

The photographic art world was astonished when the J. Paul Getty Museum in Malibu, Calif., announced its acquisition of two of the world's most important private collections of photographs, those of Samuel Wagstaff, Jr., and Arnold Crane, plus several smaller but choice collections in the U.S. and Europe. Virtually overnight the museum's newly created department of photography had established itself as one of world importance.

In Great Britain the 60-year-old Kodak Museum at Harrow was transferred to the recently opened National

Museum of Photography, Film, and Television in Bradford, Yorkshire. Citing financial reasons and lack of storage space, the trustees of the International Museum of Photography at George Eastman House, Rochester, N.Y., announced that the museum's entire collection of photographs, films, and equipment would be transferred to the Smithsonian Institution in Washington, D.C., while Eastman House would be maintained primarily as a monument to the founder of the Eastman Kodak Co. A strong countermovement to keep the collection in Rochester, however, prevented a final decision on the move by year's end.

The 1984 Hasselblad Award for photography, given by the Hasselblad Foundation in Göteborg, Sweden, went to 82-year-old Mexican photographer Mañuel Álvarez Bravo. In Japan a photo documentary on "Bahr" and "Sahara" by Kazuyoshi Nomachi received the third Ken Domon prize. Nomachi, although a relatively young photographer, had been taking pictures in North Africa since 1977. Frenchman Jacques-Henri Lartigue received the 1984 Cultural Prize of the German Photographic Society in Cologne, and in the U.S., Gilles Peress received the W. Eugene Smith Memorial Grant for Humanistic Photography.

The 1984 Pulitzer Prize for spot news photography was awarded to Stan Grossfeld of the *Boston Globe* for a photograph of frightened Palestinian children being loaded aboard an evacuation bus in Tripoli. The Pulitzer feature photography award went to Tony Suau of the *Denver Post* for his coverage of starvation in Ethiopia. At the 1984 Pictures of the Year awards, co-sponsored by the National Press Photographers Association and the University of Missouri School of Journalism, Steve Ringman of the *San Francisco Chronicle* was named Newspaper Photographer of the Year, and James Nachtwey of Black Star was named Magazine Photographer of the Year.

(ARTHUR GOLDSMITH)

See also Motion Pictures.

This article updates the *Macropædia* article PHOTOGRAPHY.

Physics

Particle Physics. The excitement in 1983 caused by the discovery of the W+, W−, and Z0 particles at the European Laboratory for Particle Physics (CERN) in Geneva continued into 1984. These three particles, called intermediate vector bosons or weakons, carry the weak interaction between pairs of interacting subatomic particles. The weak interaction, in turn, governs many nuclear decay processes and is one of three forces important in nuclear and particle physics. Continued experiments with proton-antiproton colliding beams at CERN produced more of these elusive and very short-lived particles, allowing more precise values to be ascribed to their physical properties and in particular their masses.

In 1984 the intermediate vector bosons themselves became instrumental in the discovery of what could be the long-anticipated sixth, or top, quark. Quarks are the constituents of such particles as protons, neutrons, and pi mesons. Together with the electron and its relatives, collectively called leptons, quarks are the basic building blocks of matter. The familiar world of matter is made up of two kinds of lepton—the electron and the electron neutrino—and two kinds of quarks—the up and down quarks. Other quarks and leptons are known from high-energy studies, and the most widely accepted theory to account for them postulates that they exist in pairs. The up and down quarks form a pair, as do two experimentally observed quarks, the strange and charmed quarks. When evidence mounted in

the late 1970s for a fifth quark, dubbed the bottom quark, finding its mate became essential for the current theory to remain intact.

Previous searches for the top quark had been carried out on PETRA, a colliding-beam machine at DESY (German Electron Synchrotron) in Hamburg, West Germany, using electrons and their antimatter counterparts, positrons, at a total collision energy of about 40 GeV (billion electron volts). Although unsuccessful, they allowed scientists to put a lower limit of about 20 GeV on the mass of the top quark, since it would have materialized as one component of a two-quark (a top quark and a top antiquark) particle with a total mass of 40 GeV or less. During the year, however, a careful search through records of the decays of the newly discovered W particles at CERN yielded six events that appeared to indicate the existence of the top quark.

It had been predicted that the charged intermediate vector bosons, the W+ and W−, with masses of 81 GeV, sometimes decay into a top and bottom quark. The top quark then decays further into a charged lepton (either positive or negative, depending on the charge of the W), a neutrino, and another bottom quark. Finally the two bottom quarks decay into two tightly bunched groups, or jets, of other particles. In all six events at CERN the total energy of final products—the lepton, neutrino, and two jets—was found to be of the order of 80 GeV, leading researchers to infer that a W was the starting particle. The sum of the energies of the lepton, neutrino, and the less energetic of the two jets was 40 GeV on the average. Since these three entities are the expected products of the top quark, 40 GeV becomes a very rough estimate of its mass.

Controversy remained over the accuracy of measurement of the masses of the particle jets, since this was the first time that these masses had been used in such a "definitive" observation of a new particle. The total energy (hence, mass) of the jet was obtained by calorimetry (measurement of generated heat) and then attributed to a fictitious single particle replacing the jet. A satisfactory resolution was needed in the near future because colliding-beam machines of higher energy than that used at CERN (270 GeV per particle), which in 1984 were at the planning stage, would require accurate measurement of jets for analysis of the events.

Nevertheless, expectations were high that the top quark indeed had been observed, that it had a mass in the range of 30–50 GeV, and that it would provide a final confirmation of the standard theory of the elementary particles. Further study of the properties of the top and bottom quarks could help explain why six different varieties exist when only two, the up and down quarks, seem necessary to construct the universe.

Low-Temperature Physics. The light isotope of helium, 3He, which has two protons and one neutron in its nucleus, continued providing physicists with surprises. At temperatures just short of absolute zero, of the order of a few thousandths of a degree Kelvin (K), it forms a series of three superfluid phases known as A, A1, and B. These phases exist in the liquid state of 3He, and their superfluid properties—for example, no resistance to flow (zero viscosity)—are direct manifestations of the quantum behaviour that dominates at low temperatures.

Until the past year the first two phases had attracted the most interest since they are anisotropic; that is, their physical properties are different in different directions in the liquid. Phase B was rather neglected since it seemed to be isotropic. It now appeared, however, that 3He-B is unique in that it displays a property known as particle-hole asymmetry, which reveals itself in a range of anomalous effects. In particular, a very high absorption of ultrasound observed in ^{3}He-B can be understood in terms of the superfluid's acting like a giant molecule in a coordinate space that takes into account momentum (mass times velocity) and position. Such results added to the picture of the superfluid state as Cooper pairs of helium atoms (analogous to the specialized pairings of electrons responsible for superconductivity) whose cooperative behaviour extends over distances that are large compared with the actual spacing of the atoms themselves.

More surprising was the discovery by a Finnish-Soviet collaboration that ^{3}He-B displays magnetic properties. The group rotated the liquid in a cylindrical cryostat and monitored its response in a magnetic field. As the temperature of the liquid was lowered to a critical value, a spontaneous magnetization appeared suddenly and concurrently with a change in the structure of the vortex being induced by the rotation. The researchers believed that the magnetization originated in a ferromagnetic core that formed in the centre of the vortex. It had been pointed out previously that the interior of neutron stars—gravitationally collapsed stars whose interior electrons and nuclear protons have been squeezed together to form neutrons—can be considered a neutron superfluid and that, as the fluid rotates, it will also acquire vortices that have ferromagnetic cores. Thus one of the major goals of physicists, to provide fundamental explanations that encompass a wide range of phenomena and materials, appeared well vindicated by this achievement.

The possible coexistence of magnetism and superconductivity, once thought to be completely incompatible, has been a fruitful area of research for some years. The results obtained thus far have allowed insight into the origins of both phenomena. The compound erbium rhodium boride, $ErRh_4B_4$, has been known for some time to be a "reentrant" superconductor, reverting to ferromagnetic, nonsuperconducting behaviour at 0.9 K, well below the critical temperature of 8.7 K at which it first becomes superconducting. Within the few tenths of a degree Kelvin through which the compound passes in transition from superconductivity to ferromagnetism—between 1.5 and 0.9 K—both phenomena seem to exist simultaneously. Investigators speculated that the erbium atoms form a crystal lattice largely independent of the other elements in the compound, allowing it to provide the compound's magnetic activity without interference from the Cooper-paired electrons of rhodium and boron, which provide the superconductivity. Thus, in this case, the electrons taking part in superconductivity do not seem to be the same ones producing the reappearing ferromagnetism.

During the year interest focused on two other exotic materials, the uranium-beryllium alloy UBe_{13} and a cerium-copper-silicon compound, $CeCu_2Si_2$, both of which are paramagnetic (weakly magnetic) at high temperatures and behave as if they were heading toward a true ferromagnetic state as the temperature is lowered. Unexpectedly, however, both pass into the superconducting state just below 1 K. Furthermore, the electrons that are involved in the superconductivity are apparently the same ones that form the magnetic system; they vacillate between superconducting and magnetic states at the transition point of the compounds.

These electrons were believed to originate from inner shells in the uranium and cerium atoms (rather than from the population of ordinary conduction electrons) and so experience a certain drag or impeded mobility from interactions with other inner-shell electrons. Consequently, they act as if they had extremely high masses—more than one thousand times the mass of a free electron. The coupling

of these "heavy electrons" into Cooper pairs produces a new, unusual form of superconducting behaviour. From early indications, this superconducting state is compatible with high magnetic fields. If it can be created at temperatures of a few degrees Kelvin, it may form the basis for tremendously improved superconducting magnets.

(S. B. PALMER)

See also Nobel Prizes.

This article updates the *Macropædia* articles ELECTRICITY AND MAGNETISM; PHYSICAL PRINCIPLES AND CONCEPTS; The PHYSICAL SCIENCES: *Physics;* SUBATOMIC PARTICLES.

Populations and Population Movements

DEMOGRAPHY

The rate of growth of the world's population declined for the first time in human history, according to the "State of World Population 1984" report of the UN Fund for Population Activities. During the preceding decade the rate had dropped from 2 to 1.7%. Despite this decline and its long-range implications, population numbers continued their inexorable increase. The International Demographic Center of the U.S. Census Bureau reported that the Earth's population, estimated at 4,766,323,000 at mid-1984, would reach 6,168,683,960 by the year 2000. A number of public and private organizations reported that the "population explosion" had not ended. The *World Development Report 1984* of the World Bank stated that the world's population could grow to 10,000,000,000 by 2050, with the greatest increases in the poorer countries. The Population Reference Bureau pointed out that population had doubled since the end of World War II and estimated that it would double again in 40 years. The UN Population Division's new world estimates projected a rise from the current 4,700,000,000 to 6,100,000,000 by 2000 and 8,200,000,000 in 2025.

At the UN International Conference on Population, held in Mexico City in August 1984, 149 delegations reviewed the progress made since the first conference adopted the World Population Plan of Action in 1974. Governments were urged to give priority to programs integrating population and social and economic development, to reduce

World's 25 Most Populous Urban Areas[1]

Rank	City and Country	City proper Population	Year	Metropolitan area Population	Year
1	Tokyo, Japan	8,389,800	1984 estimate	29,002,000	1981 estimate
2	New York City, U.S.	7,086,100	1982 estimate	17,451,300	1982 estimate
3	Mexico City, Mexico	8,831,100	1981 estimate	16,248,500	1981 estimate
4	Osaka, Japan	2,631,100	1984 estimate	16,224,000	1983 estimate
5	São Paulo, Brazil	8,726,600	1981 estimate	13,042,400	1981 estimate
6	London, U.K.	6,754,500	1983 estimate	12,231,200	1983 estimate
7	Cairo, Egypt	5,881,000	1983 estimate	12,001,000	1983 estimate
8	Los Angeles, U.S.	3,022,200	1982 estimate	11,930,000	1982 estimate
9	Shanghai, China	6,320,872	1982 census[2]	11,885,000	1983 estimate
10	Rhine-Ruhr, W.Ger.		[3]	10,984,000	1982 estimate
11	Buenos Aires, Arg.	2,910,000	1983 estimate	9,677,200	1981 estimate
12	Seoul, South Korea		[4]	9,204,300	1983 estimate
13	Beijing, China	5,597,972	1982 census[2]	9,179,700	1983 estimate
14	Calcutta, India	3,291,655	1981 census	9,165,650	1981 census[2]
15	Rio de Janeiro, Brazil	5,090,700	1980 census	9,014,274	1980 census
16	Paris, France	2,176,243	1982 census	8,706,963	1982 census
17	Moscow, U.S.S.R.	8,202,000	1983 estimate	8,396,000	1983 estimate
18	Bombay, India		[4]	8,227,332	1981 census[2]
19	Chicago, U.S.	2,997,200	1982 estimate	7,974,500	1982 estimate
20	Nagoya, Japan	2,108,400	1984 estimate	7,968,000	1981 estimate
21	Tianjin, China	5,142,565	1982 census[2]	7,790,200	1983 estimate
22	Jakarta, Indonesia		[4]	6,556,000	1981 estimate
23	Chongqing, China	2,673,200	1983 estimate	6,511,100	1983 estimate
24	Manila, Philippines	1,725,500	1983 estimate	6,406,300	1983 estimate
25	Tehran, Iran		[4]	5,734,200	1982 estimate

[1]Ranked by population of metropolitan area.
[2]Preliminary figures.
[3]An industrial conurbation within which no single central city is identified.
[4]City proper not identified by reporting countries.

The Reagan administration threatened to withdraw U.S. aid to international population programs—like this family-planning clinic in Senegal—that practiced or advocated abortion as a means of birth control.
BERYL GOLDBERG/THE NEW YORK TIMES

mortality levels and improve life expectancy, and to gather the full range of vital statistics and improve civil registration systems.

Birth Statistics. An estimated 3,614,000 births occurred in the U.S. in 1983, 2% less than in 1982. The birthrate was 15.5 live births per 1,000 population, a decline of 3% from the previous year, and the fertility rate fell by 4%, to 65.4 births per 1,000 women aged 15–44. The National Center for Health Statistics attributed the drop in part to the declining number of women in the younger childbearing ages. The trend continued into 1984. For the 12-month period ended in June, there were 2% fewer births than in the same period a year earlier.

Detailed data for 1981 show that, while there was a slight increase in the number of births from 1980, other measures of fertility declined. The birthrate and fertility rate were lower, and birthrates by age of mother fell among mothers aged 15–34 and 40–45 and increased slightly among mothers aged 35–39. The total fertility rate, the estimated number of births to 1,000 women during their childbearing years, was 1,815 children in 1981, 14% below the generational replacement level of 2,110 children. The total fertility rate for white women was 18% below replacement and for black women, 4% above replacement. There were 686,605 births to unmarried mothers in 1981, a 3% increase over 1980. The racial differential in nonmarital birthrates had declined. The rate for black women was seven times the rate for white women in 1975, but by 1981 it had fallen to four times. In 1981 about one in ten white births and half of all black births were to unmarried mothers. Because of the large influx of Asian immigrants in the preceding 20 years, there was a marked increase in births to Asian mothers.

According to the Population Reference Bureau, recent estimates of world crude birthrates ranged from an average of 16 births per 1,000 population for more developed countries to 32 for less developed countries. Africa had the highest regional rates; in Nigeria the birthrate was 49. The overall birthrate in Latin America was 31 and in Asia, 29. North America and Europe had the lowest regional birthrates, 15 and 14, respectively, although Japan, with a birthrate of 13, was at the same level as the northern and western European countries. Total fertility rates had declined worldwide. In 1960 this rate was estimated at 6 lifetime children per woman in the less developed countries; recent estimates put that figure at 4.4. High rates were noted for Kenya (8) and Libya (7.2) in Africa and for Jordan and Syria (7.3), Oman (7.1), and Iraq and Bangladesh (7) in Asia. The European countries averaged the lowest rates (1.8), with Denmark and West Germany on the bottom with 1.4.

Death Statistics. The provisional count of deaths in the U.S. in 1983 was 2,010,000, about 1% more than in 1982. The estimated death rate was the same for both years: 8.6 per 1,000 population.

The leading causes of death in 1983 were:

Cause of death	Estimated rate per 100,000 population
1. Diseases of the heart	327.6
2. Malignant neoplasms	188.3
3. Cerebrovascular diseases	66.8
4. Accidents and adverse effects	39.0
5. Chronic obstructive pulmonary diseases	28.4
6. Pneumonia and influenza	22.9
7. Diabetes mellitus	15.2
8. Suicide	12.4
9. Chronic liver disease and cirrhosis	11.9
10. Atherosclerosis	11.1
11. Homicide and legal intervention	8.2
12. Conditions of the perinatal period	8.1
13. Nephritis, nephrotic syndrome, and nephrosis	7.9
14. Septicemia	5.7
15. Congenital anomalies	5.5

Heart disease, cancer, and stroke accounted for over two-thirds of all deaths (67.8%) in 1983.

World death rates averaged 11 per 1,000 population. Declines in mortality usually offset any fertility declines, so natural increase remained at relatively high levels in most less developed countries. For example, in western Africa a death rate of 18 and a birthrate of 49 resulted in a natural increase of 31 persons per 1,000 population, or a 3.1% population increase. At such a rate the population could double in 23 years. In contrast, for northwestern Europe the estimated death rate was 11 and the birthrate 13, resulting in an annual increase of 0.2%. These countries would take over 400 years to double their populations.

Infant and Maternal Mortality. The infant mortality rate in the U.S. in 1983 was the lowest ever recorded: 10.9 deaths of infants under one year per 1,000 live births. The 3% decline from 1982 was related to a drop of 4% in the death rate for infants under 28 days. The decline continued into the first half of 1984. Detailed data for 1981 show that the infant mortality rate for blacks was almost twice as high as that for whites, 20 as compared with 10.5. While rates for both groups had fallen, the differential had remained the same since the mid-1960s.

Rates of infant mortality continued to fall in the more developed countries, to a level of 19 deaths per 1,000 live births, but they remained high in the less developed countries, averaging 94 per 1,000 live births. The rate was estimated to be 150 or more in several countries of Africa (Benin, The Gambia, Guinea, Liberia, Mali, Sierra Leone, Burkina Faso [formerly Upper Volta], Malawi, and Angola) and Asia (Afghanistan, Kampuchea, East Timor

[Indonesia], and Yemen [San'a']). Rates were lowest in northern and western Europe (Finland 6.5; Sweden 6.8) and Japan (6.6).

Maternal mortality declined throughout the world between 1972 and 1981, according to the UN, but remained high in many countries. For less developed regions relatively low rates were reported for Egypt (82.3 maternal deaths per 100,000 live births) and Uruguay (55.9). Lowest rates were reported for Norway (2), Northern Ireland (3.7), and Denmark (3.8), while Guadaloupe, Iceland, and Luxembourg had no maternal deaths. In the U.S. the trend had been downward since 1950; in 1983 there were 290 deaths, and the rate was 8 deaths per 100,000 live births. Detailed data for 1981 show that black women were three times as likely as white women to die of causes related to pregnancy.

Life Expectancy. The expectation of life at birth reached a record high in the U.S. in 1983, 74.7 years for the total population. For white persons it was 75.2 years and for all nonwhites, 71.3 years. Black life expectancy was 69.6 years. Women, on average, were expected to outlive men: average life expectancy was 71.6 years for white males, 65.2 for black males, 78.8 for white females, and 73.8 for black females.

Worldwide, life expectancy was estimated at around 61 years, with the more developed countries averaging 73 years and the less developed, 58 years. The UN reported that the expectation of life at birth was highest for the women of Iceland, 79.7 years. For men the longest expectancy, 73.8 years, was found in Japan.

Marriage and Divorce Statistics. The number of marriages in the U.S. declined in 1983 for the first time since 1975. According to provisional reports, there were 2,444,000 marriages in 1983, down 2% from 1982. The marriage rate also fell, from 10.8 to 10.5 per 1,000 population. Final data for 1981 reveal that the trend toward later age at marriage was continuing. The median ages of bride and groom at first marriage were 22 and 23.9, respectively, compared with 20.6 for brides and 22.5 for grooms in 1970. About 45% of all marriages in 1981 were remarriages of one or both partners.

The number of divorces in the U.S. declined in 1983 for the second consecutive year, to 1,179,000. The divorce rate was 5 per 1,000 population, lower than it had been since 1977. According to final figures for 1981, the median duration of marriages ending in divorce was 7 years, compared with 6.8 years for 1980. An estimated 1,180,000 children were involved in divorce or annulment in 1981, and more than 5 million children, or 9% of all children under 18, were living with a currently divorced parent.

The latest UN *Demographic Yearbook* (1982) included marriage and divorce statistics from a number of countries. The highest marriage rates for men (number of marriages per 1,000 marriageable men) were found in Egypt (120.9), Iraq (111.6), Bulgaria (87.6), and Romania (86.1), while the highest for women were in Iraq (134.6), Libya (101.9), and Egypt (98.9). The U.S., Canada, and Poland had similar rates (about 61). For adult women wishing to marry, the best prospects were in Greenland, where nearly six out of every ten men were available to marry, followed by the Cook Islands, Martinique, and Sri Lanka. For men the largest percentage of women available for marriage were to be found in Réunion, Martinique, Greenland, and Guadeloupe. The highest annual divorce rates (number of divorces per 1,000 married couples) were reported for Réunion (32.5) and the U.S. (22.8). The lowest rates were found in Cyprus (0.9), Sri Lanka (1), Mauritius (1.2), and Costa Rica (1.3).

Censuses and Surveys. The UN Statistical Office reported that planning for the 1990 round of censuses was already under way. The UN was engaged, with the World Bank, in a National Household Survey Capability program, designed to aid countries in developing survey expertise.

The World Fertility Survey report on Tunisia revealed that country's relatively low birthrate for Africa (33). One reason was the rising age at marriage. Legal minimums of 17 years for women and 21 for men were established by law in 1964. The mean age at first marriage for women was 24 years, very high for a less developed country. The total fertility rate dropped from 7.1 children per woman in 1966 to 5.2 in 1981. The World Fertility Survey report for Egypt also showed declines in fertility, from 7 children per woman in the 1960s to 5.3 in the late 1970s. More country reports from the World Fertility Survey would be forthcoming in 1985.   (ANDERS S. LUNDE)

See also World Data.

INTERNATIONAL MIGRATION

Immigration policies of the developed, richer countries in 1983–84 continued to be organized around the themes of control and repatriation. Continued high unemployment in those countries and increasing levels of activity by right-wing parties created an anti-immigrant, restrictionist framework within which governmental policies were structured.

In France, for example, Jean-Marie le Pen's (*see* BIOGRAPHIES) extremist National Front party, much of whose support derived from its anti-immigration campaign, made gains in a series of local elections in 1983–84 and won ten seats in the 1984 elections to the European Parliament. Reacting to this, on October 10 the Socialist government of Pres. François Mitterrand announced new measures to control immigration, including sending an extra 1,000 immigration officers to key entry points. Other measures seen as worrying by human rights organizations and immigrant communities included the decision to end the automatic right of entry for immigrants' families, who would now have to apply from their countries of origin. Permission would be dependent on proof that the relative in France had a stable job and possessed sufficient money.

British immigration controls continued to be challenged on the basis that they were racially based and discriminatory. The home secretary's April decision to grant British citizenship within ten days of application to the white South African athlete Zola Budd (*see* BIOGRAPHIES) was seen as proof of those charges. At the same time, deportations continued despite appeals from members of Parliament, local governments, and immigrant and community organizations. In 1983, 2,242 immigrants were served with deportation orders, 374 were "removed," and an additional 176 departed "voluntarily." The number of immigrants from the New Commonwealth (nonwhite Commonwealth) and Pakistan fell to a new low of 27,550, according to Home Office statistics.

In September 1984 the European Court of Human Rights began hearing cases brought against the British government's 1983 immigration rules, which denied to women settled in Britain, but not to British citizens, the right to bring in foreign fiancés and husbands. The rules allowed women who were British citizens to bring in fiancés and husbands provided the primary purpose of the marriage was not the man's entry into Britain, with the onus of proof on the couple. More than half of all such applications were being refused.

Australian immigration policy continued "to emphasize family reunion, refugees, and to a lesser extent skilled labour and business migration," in the words of the minister for immigration and ethnic affairs, S. J. West. The number of migrants visaed under family categories rose from just over 18,000 in 1982–83 to 36,739 in 1983–84 (of a total of 62,350), and the 1984–85 target was 42,000 (of an overall target of 72,000). West's statement reflected the political controversy raging in Australia over the racial origins of new immigrants; a Gallup Poll published on Aug. 27, 1984, indicated that 60% of Australians disapproved of the decreasing number of immigrants from the U.K. and continental Europe as compared with Asia. On numerous occasions West took pains to deny that the government was discriminating in favour of Asians.

In the U.S. the political controversy surrounding immigration from Mexico and Central America continued. It was estimated by immigration authorities and the Ford Foundation that more than 500,000 displaced Central Americans—the majority from El Salvador—were in the U.S. illegally. The U.S. government consistently refused to accord political refugee status to Salvadorans, Hondurans, and Guatemalans because, it was alleged by critics, granting such status would cast doubt on the bona fides of U.S.-supported regimes. In the face of widespread evidence of the operation of death squads in those countries and of the fate awaiting returned refugees—more than 1,000 a month were being deported from Los Angeles alone— a movement to offer them sanctuary developed among church people. In April the Chicago Religious Task Force on Central America reported that there were 110 sanctuary churches in 60 cities around the country.

Congress adjourned in October without completing action on the Simpson-Mazzoli bill, which proposed the most far-reaching changes in U.S. immigration law in two decades. The main opposition to the bill centred on its clauses imposing penalties on employers who knowingly hired illegal immigrants and those setting a quota under which farmers could bring in seasonal farm workers. The labour unions opposed the latter on the grounds that such labour would undercut U.S. farm workers' wages. The former was opposed by employers' organizations and, most strenuously, by Hispanic organizations, which argued that such a provision would lead to widespread discrimination by employers who would simply refuse to hire any Hispanics. (LOUIS KUSHNICK)

REFUGEES

There were no spectacular changes in the worldwide refugee situation during 1984, but the need for massive international assistance for the large concentrations of refugees in regions such as the Horn of Africa and Pakistan remained as pressing as ever. UN High Commissioner for Refugees Poul Hartling, opening the annual session of his 41-nation executive committee in October, urged governments to take more active steps toward alleviating the problems faced by refugees. The occasion was marked by the award of the 1984 Nansen Medal to Capt. Lewis Hiller, captain of the U.S. merchant ship "Rose City," and members of his crew, who rescued 85 Vietnamese refugees, including 30 children, in September 1983 when their boat foundered in a storm. Distress calls from "boat people" in the South China Sea were often ignored by passing ships, despite the existence of a program whereby shipowners were compensated for expenses incurred when their vessels changed course to rescue refugees.

The voluntary repatriation of Ethiopians from Djibouti, begun in September 1983, continued, and the special program offering assistance to returnees was extended through 1984. Some 200,000 Ugandans also repatriated voluntarily from Zaire, and Guineans began returning to their country after a change of government in April. Political turbulence in many African countries was exacerbated by the continuing drought, and there were significant new influxes of refugees into the Central African Republic, Ethiopia, Somalia, Swaziland, Sudan, Zaire, Zambia, and Zimbabwe. A major event concerning African refugees was the convening in Geneva in July of the second International Conference on Assistance to Refugees in Africa (ICARA II), which UNHCR sponsored along with the UN and the Organization of African Unity. The three-day meeting examined refugee needs and the related developmental and infrastructural requirements of host countries. Donor countries announced pledges of $18.5 million toward UNHCR's Africa programs. A steering committee of the sponsors continued to follow developments.

In Pakistan, where three million or so Afghan refugees with their livestock were creating considerable environmental problems, the World Bank was participating in a $20 million pilot project designed to provide employment for both refugees and the local population in such sectors as

JIM MORIN/MIAMI HERALD

When the U.S. House of Representatives passed the Simpson-Mazzoli immigration bill—by a slender margin in June—expressions of relief and dismay greeted the action. The bill, which was stalled in conference committee as the session ended, would have granted amnesty to illegal immigrants long resident in the U.S. but placed sanctions on employers who hired new illegal immigrants. One cartoonist cast the Congress as King Canute holding back the waves of immigrants.

Voluntary repatriation of Ethiopian refugees under the auspices of the United Nations High Commissioner for Refugees continued in 1984. This woman is a returnee at a reception centre in Ethiopia.

UNHCR, PHOTOGRAPH, L. GUBB

forestry, water resources management, and road improvement. UNHCR's assistance program in Pakistan totaled $85 million in 1983 and remained its largest in any country.

Indochinese refugees seeking asylum elsewhere in the Southeast Asian region, as well as those leaving the region for resettlement overseas, continued to decline in numbers. Between Jan. 1 and Sept. 30, 1984, a total of 31,547 refugees arrived by boat or overland while 49,-877 departed, leaving 160,987 in UNHCR camps. Some 240,000 Kampucheans located in settlements along the Thai-Kampuchean border were receiving assistance from other agencies. The number of refugees from the region resettled with UNHCR assistance since 1976 rose to 945,-540. In addition, 276,000 were locally resettled in China, while 2,396 Laotian refugees returned to their country under a UNHCR-coordinated program of voluntary repatriation. The special program for assistance to Kampuchea also continued. By Sept. 30, 1984, 67,680 refugees had left under UNHCR's Orderly Departure Program. Pirate attacks on "boat people" continued, and a $3.7 million antipiracy campaign, funded by 12 nations and conducted mainly by Thailand, was renewed in June.

In Central America rising political tensions and economic deterioration in the region continued both to provoke new refugee flows and to hamper attempts to integrate existing groups locally. From April to September 1984 the number of refugees in Central America and Mexico increased by about 5,000—mostly from Nicaragua—to a total of over 340,000. In Belize, Costa Rica, Panama, and Nicaragua local integration programs for both urban and rural refugee groups continued, although mounting polit-

ical tensions and economic difficulties made implementation of such projects increasingly difficult. In Honduras and Mexico plans to relocate Salvadoran and Guatemalan refugees away from the border areas in rural settlements had to be revised, and sizable numbers of refugees remained dependent on UNHCR for relief assistance.

In Europe the growing influx of refugees from Soviet-bloc countries into Austria was a matter of concern for the Austrian government. Their numbers (5,368 in 1983) had risen by 46% during the year ended October 1984, while fewer refugees were being granted asylum in third countries, notably Australia, South Africa, and the U.S.

(UNHCR)

This article updates the *Macropædia* article POPULATION.

Publishing

Although the effects of the recession continued to be felt in varying degrees, 1984 was a year of considerable activity in the publishing industry, marked by mergers, takeovers, and the launching of new enterprises. For book publishers in the West an issue of continuing importance was copyright. In France the highly respected newspaper *Le Monde* ended its 40th year facing the threat of bankruptcy, while in Britain *The Times* (in its 199th year) and its stablemate *The Sunday Times* together achieved their first profitable year since their 1981 acquisition by Rupert Murdoch. Meanwhile, a new press baron, Robert Maxwell (*see* BIOGRAPHIES), made his entry into Fleet Street (*see* below).

In its annual *World Press Freedom Review,* the International Press Institute referred to free speech as a "dying right." The French and British governments reacted with extreme sensitivity to leaks of information to the press, and in Britain demands for "freedom of information" legislation were rejected. In the U.S. legislation aimed at restricting the scope of the Freedom of Information Act failed to win congressional approval. Elsewhere, Mauritius, Nigeria, Pakistan, Singapore, Sri Lanka, and Yugoslavia were among the countries where press freedom was severely limited during the year.

With the impending withdrawal from UNESCO of the U.S. and possibly of the U.K. and other countries, little was heard during 1984 of the "new world information order" sponsored by that organization.

Newspapers. For Britain's national newspapers it was the year of the Reuters share flotation and of Robert Maxwell's arrival, at last, as a newspaper proprietor. Reuters, famous as the first international news agency, was to be Fleet Street's crock of gold. A financial crisis at the end of the 1930s had led to a rescue, aimed at keeping the firm independent and British-owned, that put the greater part of the shares into the control of the main national newspaper proprietors, some provincial newspaper publishers, and a scattering of individuals. The shares were to be held in trust and could not be traded. But as the cost of international newsgathering soared and profitability dropped, the Reuters executive management in the early 1970s put the agency into the vanguard of what was to prove immensely profitable new territory, the electronic dissemination of commercial information. For its nominal owners, a public flotation of shares in this leading company in a rich and fashionable sector would unlock many millions of pounds—perhaps, it was speculated in 1983, as much as £1,000 million. By 1984 expectations were more realistic, and the perceived need to preserve the company's independence forced an agreement among the Fleet Street owners to limit the proportion of shares they would sell.

Even so, the flotation was enthusiastically received; some obscure individuals and a handful of Reuters executives found themselves millionaires, and the bigger publishers had windfalls approaching £100 million for investment elsewhere.

The rest of 1984, however, belonged to Robert Maxwell. A prominent figure in publishing and other fields for 20 years, he had never realized his ambition of acquiring a national newspaper. When, in April, he bid for *The Observer* in the wake of a disagreement between its effective owner, the tycoon Roland ("Tiny") Rowland, and the editor, Donald Trelford (*see* BIOGRAPHIES), the event was generally seen as a ritual replay of his earlier tries, and so it proved. Within weeks, however, Maxwell had made a swift and successful £13.4 million bid that gave him ownership of three national newspapers: the *Daily Mirror* (its 4.5 million sales second only to the Murdoch-owned *Sun*) and its sisters the *Sunday Mirror* and the *Sunday People*. Ownership of the Mirror Group Newspapers had passed to the Reed International paper and commercial empire, but in 1983 Reed decided to demerge the newspapers. A new chairman, Clive Thornton, was brought in to devise a scheme that would float the Mirror group while retaining the position of the *Daily Mirror* as the only mass-circulation daily with a left-of-centre political stance. This tricky task was approaching fruition when the Reed board, virtually overnight, sold out to Maxwell. Thornton never returned to his desk.

Maxwell lost no time in putting his personal stamp on the *Daily Mirror,* with initiatives ranging from an effort to mediate in the miners' strike to personal delivery of a planeload of food to the starving Ethiopians. But his most immediate effect on the competition was to raise the stakes in the continuing bingo war by promising a top prize of no less than £1 million, promptly matched by the rival Murdoch and Express groups. The bingo craze had already spread to *The Times.* At the end of June the once-austere "Thunderer" launched Portfolio, based on the ups and downs of Stock Exchange prices, with relatively modest prizes of £2,000 a day and £20,000 on Saturdays. The game boosted *The Times*'s static circulation by around 85,000 in a week, to above 460,000, but by mid-autumn it had gone no higher, and as the paper's bicentenary year approached, it was still handing out case prizes. *The Times*'s rivals did not seem to suffer. The *Daily Telegraph*'s circulation slipped only slightly, while *The Guardian* by November was approaching the half-million mark. The main compet-itive changes came in the Sunday sector, with a successful relaunch of the Murdoch-owned *News of the World* in tabloid format, adding about half a million copies at the expense of its main rivals.

In West Germany newspapers were disrupted by 13 weeks of selective strikes by the print union, IG Druck und Papier, in pursuit of its demand for a cut in the workweek. The dispute ended in July with a new agreement that coupled a 38½-hour week with the possibility of local deals on flexible hours. In France, as the fortunes of the Paris daily *Libération* continued to climb, *Le Monde* endured a new crisis. With its sales declining and cumulative losses approaching $10 million, its editor in chief, André Laurens, resigned after the journalists, who held constitutional power, refused to accept his rescue plan for the paper. The French government's controversial press bill aimed at limiting the concentration of newspaper ownership was approved by the National Assembly in September, but Premier Laurent Fabius stated that it would not take effect before the 1986 legislative elections.

In Sweden *Stockholms Tidningen,* the capital's only Social Democratic newspaper, announced its bankruptcy in August, after the ruling Social Democrats and the trade unions had refused further funding. In Italy closure of the neofascist daily *Il Secolo d'Italia* marked the financial crisis facing all the party-backed dailies, including the Communist *L'Unità.* Ownership of the respected independent *Corriere della Sera,* in court receivership for two years following the Banco Ambrosiano collapse, was taken up by a consortium that included the state-owned Mediobanca, Fiat, and Pirelli.

Observers detected a new campaigning spirit among leading Soviet newspapers, with the aim of exposing bureaucratic corruption. In China a leading article in the *People's Daily* actually announced that Marxism-Leninism could not answer contemporary problems—a line that, however, was swiftly disassociated from the leadership's view.

(PETER FIDDICK)

In an era when the spread of electronic media was said to have eroded public appetite for the printed word, U.S. newspapers in 1984 continued to prosper. Total circulation reached an all-time high of 62,644,603, according to the 1984 *Editor & Publisher International Yearbook,* representing a gain of 0.25% over 1983, and the Newspaper Advertising Bureau reported a rise in advertising volume to $21.2 billion, 16% above 1983's record level. The number of daily newspapers dropped by ten, to 1,701, reflecting

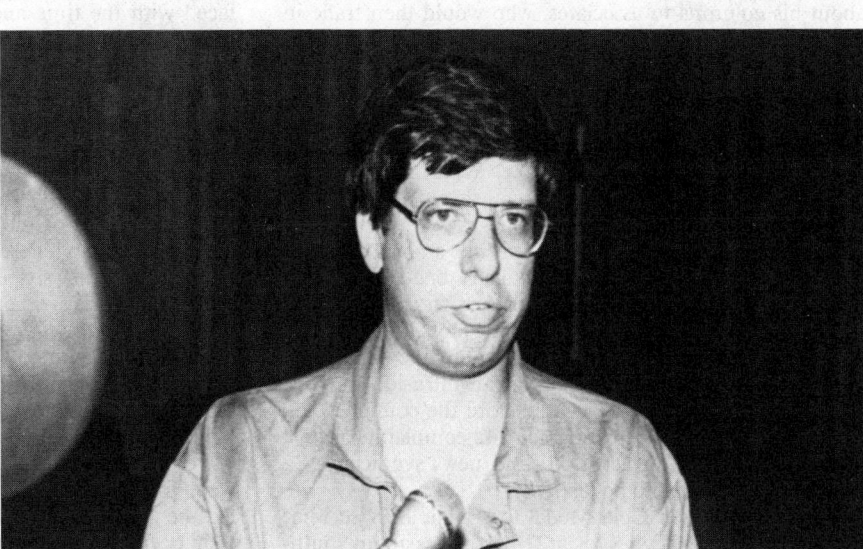

Editorial writer Richard Hargraves was jailed when he refused to reveal his sources for an editorial that led to a libel suit. He was released two days later after two of the sources came forward.

the merger of ten into ten others, while eight new dailies were launched and eight old ones folded. The long-term shift away from afternoon publication continued, with the number of "PM's" dropping from 1,310 to 1,284 and afternoon circulation from 29,313,090 to 28,802,461. At the same time, the number of morning newspapers rose from 434 to 436 and morning circulation from 33,174,087 to 33,842,142. The number of "all-day" newspapers fell from 33 to 29. Sunday newspapers continued to proliferate, from 768 to 772, and Sunday circulation increased from 56,260,764 to 56,747,436.

Unlike many countries, the U.S. remained a nation of local newspapers. Only a handful of dailies attempted to circulate nationally. Perhaps the most dramatic news on the national-newspaper scene in 1984 was the disclosure by the Audit Bureau of Circulation (ABC) of its first report on readership for *USA Today,* a daily launched by the Gannett chain in 1982 and sold in dozens of U.S. cities. According to the ABC, *USA Today* was selling an average of 1.1 million copies a day, making it the nation's third-largest daily, after the *Wall Street Journal* (2 million) and the *New York Daily News* (1.4 million). Nonetheless, *USA Today* was reported to have lost an estimated $100 million in 1984, believed to be the biggest deficit ever sustained by a U.S. daily.

The U.S. Supreme Court handed the press its first major libel victory in more than a decade. In a 6–3 decision the court upheld an appeals court verdict overturning an award against the magazine *Consumer Reports,* which had given a negative review to loudspeakers manufactured by the Bose Corp. The court ruled that *Consumer Reports* had not shown "actual malice," meaning that it did not print a statement knowing it to be false or did not show reckless disregard for the truth. The decision was of major importance for newspapers, which routinely print evaluations of a wide range of items.

After angering newspaper editors by refusing to allow press coverage of the 1983 U.S. invasion of Grenada, the Defense Department agreed to form a permanent "pool" of media representatives that would supply future invasion reports for the press at large. Initially, the "pool" included only broadcast, magazine, and wire service representatives, but after loud protests from newspaper editors, the Pentagon agreed to accommodate newspaper representation. Another troubling government action involved R. Foster Winans, a *Wall Street Journal* columnist who was fired by the paper after admitting that he had leaked information about his columns to associates, who would then trade in stocks likely to be affected by his articles. Winans and his alleged collaborators were later indicted by federal authorities on 61 counts of fraud and conspiracy, resting on an unusual, and to many journalists disturbing, theory that the reporter had a "duty" to disclose his financial interest in the stocks about which he wrote. While many editors would have acknowledged that Winans's conduct was unethical, few agreed that it was also illegal.

The major casualty of the year was not a newspaper but the National News Council, an industry body established in 1973 as a voluntary forum for discussing complaints of unfairness and inaccuracy against the press. The council had won the trust of many newspapers, but a few—notably the *New York Times*—considered it an intrusion into the editorial process. In the 11 years before the council voted to end its operations, it investigated 242 complaints against newspapers, television networks, and news syndicates, 82 of which were found to be justified.

The 1984 Pulitzer Gold Medal for Public Service went to the *Los Angeles Times* for a 27-part series about south-ern California's Latino population. The award for national reporting was given to John Noble Wilford of the *New York Times* for reporting on a variety of scientific topics. Karen Elliot House of the *Wall Street Journal* received the international reporting prize for a series of interviews with Jordan's King Hussein. The award for editorial writing went to Albert Scardino of the *Georgia Gazette,* a Savannah weekly with a circulation of only 3,000. Vermont Royster, editor emeritus and a columnist for the *Wall Street Journal,* was cited for his commentary, while Paul Goldberger, senior architecture critic of the *New York Times,* received the prize for criticism. Local reporting awards went to *Newsday,* a suburban daily published on New York's Long Island, for coverage of the legal battle involving "Baby Jane Doe," an infant born with severe physical defects, and to the *Boston Globe* for a series on local race relations.

(DONALD MORRISON)

Magazines. The British magazine market continued in a lively vein. The giant International Publishing Corporation (IPC) group (owned by Reed International), having survived a long dispute with its journalists with the loss of only one title, continued its policy of decentralization. Three titles, including the relatively new young women's monthly *Options,* went with a former IPC publisher to his new company, Carlton. The sociological weekly *New Society* was put up for sale and became a stablemate of the independent left-wing political weekly *New Statesman.*

The trend for mass-circulation women's weeklies was to slide, while smaller, glossy, and very expensive titles like *Vogue* and *World of Interiors,* continued to grow. Audrey Slaughter, an established editor, launched the monthly *Working Woman* (with backing from the U.S. magazine of that title), aimed at executive and management women and aspirants. At the other end of the scale, the biweekly *Just Seventeen,* launched by East Midlands Allied Press in 1983, passed the quarter-million mark and announced weekly publication for 1985.

In West Germany the trial resulting from the 1983 "Hitler diaries" fraud perpetrated on *Stern* magazine began in August and continued through year's end. West Germany's other leading newsmagazine, *Der Spiegel,* brought an action in the British High Court against Sir James Goldsmith, the food tycoon and former publisher of the quickly defunct *Now!* magazine. In 1981 *Now!* had reported Goldsmith's claim that a 1962 campaign by *Der Spiegel* exposing West German military malpractices had been "orchestrated by the KGB." *Der Spiegel* sought to repudiate the claim but, faced with the time and resources Goldsmith was putting into the case, settled for a public statement that he had not intended to imply that Soviet intelligence controlled it. Goldsmith nevertheless followed up with full-page newspaper advertisements claiming "a victory for the West."

One of the most famous black magazines in South Africa, *Drum,* passed into Afrikaner ownership when its white founder, Jim Bailey, sold it and his City Press to Nasionale Pers, publishers of the National Party organ *Die Burger.* The staff, led by Percy Qoboza, formerly editor of the banned black newspaper *The World,* was given assurances of freedom of expression. In Budapest the English-language *New Hungarian Quarterly,* a surprising flower of the post-1956 Kadar regime, which had brought many Hungarian writers and other cultural figures to Western notice, celebrated its quarter-centenary.   (PETER FIDDICK)

U.S. magazine revenues were up in 1984 and, on a wave of optimism, an unusual number of new periodicals were founded. Computer and special interest magazines led the group. The most spectacular magazine story of the year occurred when nude shots of Vanessa Williams, the

The elegant image of *The New Yorker* magazine became something of a dartboard for criticism when one of its writers acknowledged that he had repeatedly modified facts, scenes, and actual statements in the interest of improving the point of a story.

M.G. LORD/NEWSDAY

reigning Miss America, were published in *Penthouse*. The furor caused the first black Miss America to give up her crown. Despite criticism, *Penthouse* reported record sales. Other controversies went to court. Supreme Court decisions against *Hustler* and the *National Enquirer* expanded the right of a plaintiff to sue in any state or community where a magazine is widely distributed, rather than being limited to the place where it is published. Some publishers thought the decisions would open the floodgates to an increased number of libel actions. *The New Yorker*'s standards for accuracy received a setback when a veteran writer, Alastair Reid, admitted he had concocted anecdotes and quotes to make his points. Reid, who admitted only five such instances since 1959, said he no longer used such modifications. Commented *The New Yorker* editor William Shawn: "He made a journalistic mistake . . . it was done for literary reasons."

Although a shakeout of the 600 or so computer magazines seemed likely, even more such titles appeared during the year, among them *Computers in Education, Macworld, Online Data Access, TI Professional Computing, Computers in Banking, Personal Software Magazine, Software Author,* and *Technology Network*. The Audit Bureau of Circulation reported that in late 1983 *Compute* had recorded a circulation gain of almost 250%; *Personal Computing* had risen 106% and *Popular Computing*, 67.4%. The leading personal computer magazines in 1984 included *Computer and Electronics* (550,000 circulation), *Personal Computing* (460,000), *Byte* (420,000), *Popular Computing* (310,000), and *Compute* (270,000).

Magazines are quick to follow—if not always to lead— entertainment and social trends. Three new examples were *Trivia Quest,* a monthly featuring 720 questions and answers in 12 categories; *Walking World,* aimed at promoting walking (not jogging or running) as a sport; and *Video Movies,* which reviewed videotapes and discs available for rent. *FMR*, "the most beautiful magazine in the world," with a devotion to the fine arts and a $6 cover price, made a major advertising splash as the most "refined" title of the year. Fairchild launched a companion to its highly successful women's magazine, *W,* a flashy news tabloid featuring stories on fashion and celebrities. Fittingly called

M, the new twin magazine was directed at the upscale men's market, particularly the rich middle-aged man.

While revenues for most magazines increased in 1984, the spectre emerged of cost increases to come. One expert believed magazine publishing costs would rise 34% from 1983 to 1986, with paper accounting for the largest increase, followed by wages, circulation expenses, and postage. Meanwhile, the conservative political-economic weekly *U.S. News & World Report* was sold for $182.5 million in cash to Mortimer Zuckerman, the real estate magnate who had rescued *Atlantic*. Zuckerman promised to improve the coverage of the magazine, one of the most widely read in the U.S. with 2.2 million circulation.

The year's prestigious National Magazine Awards went to ten national magazines. Those hailed for general excellence and design were *The New Yorker, Seventeen, Vanity Fair, The New Republic, New York Magazine, Esquire, House and Garden* (2 awards), *Outside, National Geographic,* and *The American Lawyer.*

The biggest single fund-raiser for a magazine in 1984 was held at the Metropolitan Museum of Art in New York City. The famous joined forces to donate money to *Index on Censorship,* which reported on repression throughout the world and since 1972 had championed the cause of thousands of jailed dissidents. Supported by individuals and such groups as the Ford Foundation and the Arts Council of Great Britain, the journal also drew attention to writers who could not be published in their own countries.

(WILLIAM A. KATZ)

Books. After the previous year's encouraging upturn in business, 1984 did not bring the breakthrough that some U.K. publishers had hoped for. Recovery overseas was aided by the continued weakness of the pound sterling against the U.S. dollar, and the added price competitiveness that this provided pushed up export turnover by about 15% in real terms. The best overseas book markets were Europe, the Middle East, the Far East, Australia, and North America. Africa, South Asia, and Central and South America remained problem areas characterized by low institutional investment, low levels of foreign exchange for book and raw materials imports, an increasing number of trading restrictions in the form of import duties and quotas, and an ever growing burden of outstanding debts and suspended trading accounts.

In the U.K. government spending cutbacks applied extreme pressure on textbook orders. The 1983 boom in computer book sales also seemed to have evaporated, paralleling the U.S. experience. There were strong suspicions during the year that the government intended to boost taxation income by imposing a value-added tax on books. A major campaign to oppose this move was immediately launched by publishers and received strong support from booksellers, authors, librarians, and educators. Lightening an otherwise rather gloomy year was the growing industry promotional pressure via the Book Marketing Council and the enormous and developing public interest in the Booker-McConnell Prize.

Copyright was again a dominant issue during the year. The amended Indian Copyright Act of 1983 had introduced compulsory reprint legislation in line with the Paris texts of 1971, and both the British and U.S. publishing industries had anxiously awaited developments. In August 1984 further amendments to the act spelled out in detail Indian government intentions; 1985 could well turn out to be one of the most crucial years in recent publishing history as publishers around the world feel the impact of compulsory local licensing and discover whether the Indian book industry and government could prevent local editions from spilling out into world markets. India also passed very severe new antipiracy measures. These were largely the result of the impact of video piracy on the powerful Indian film industry, but literary copyrights would also share the better protection. Elsewhere, tough new antipiracy legislation was expected in Nigeria and Ghana, while Singapore, South Korea, and China announced their intention to redraft copyright legislation in order to provide better and more effective copyright protection.

The Frankfurt Book Fair—always a useful barometer of world trading conditions—moved into new quarters in 1984 following an extensive rebuilding program aimed at relieving recent pressure on exhibitor space. Once again attendance was up from previous years with approximately 6,000 publishers attending and with British publishers as usual the largest foreign contingent. The overall verdict was good, if not overwhelming, business and continued— if cautious—optimism for 1985.   (ANTHONY A. READ)

George Orwell, no doubt, would have been pleased. In the year made notorious by his classic *1984,* Orwell (1903–50) achieved new renown when the novel became a U.S. best-seller once again. The renewed success of Orwell's novel of one man's rebellion against a totalitarian state provided some small assurance that the worst of his predictions had not yet come to pass.

That was not the only good news for U.S. publishers. The broad economic recovery that had begun to be felt by publishers in mid-1983 continued throughout that year and into 1984. When final figures for 1983 were compiled by the Association of American Publishers (AAP), the tally showed an industry total of $8.6 billion in sales, for an increase of 9.5% over sales in 1982. Almost every category of publishing enjoyed substantial increases in 1983, with trade or general books up 17%, religious books up 16%, subscription reference book sales improving nearly 12%, and professional, technical, and business books also up by almost 12% in dollar sales. Early estimates in 1984 showed a continuation of the strong sales pattern established during the last half of 1983, while sales trend indicators in the summer showed adult hardcovers improving at a 20% pace over 1983, children's paperbacks up an astonishing 69%, and more modest gains in the adult paperback field. At the end of the first half of 1984, overall book sales had risen nearly 9% over the comparable period of 1983 on a 5% increase in units.

Perhaps reflecting the health of publishing, there was also a return in 1984 of one of the industry's most controversial topics of years past—the corporate takeover. In contrast to earlier years, however, 1984's publishing acquisitions were often made by other publishers rather than large outside corporations. The first of these was the purchase of Scribner Book Co. and its subsidiaries Atheneum and the 138-year-old Charles Scribner's Sons by Macmillan Inc., another well-established name in U.S. publishing, for approximately $15 million in Macmillan's common stock.

A long-running battle in the torrid paperback romance market, an extremely lucrative sector of mass-market publishing, came to an end of sorts when Harlequin, the Canadian-based leader in the field, bought the arch-rival Silhouette line from Simon & Schuster Inc. for $10 million plus a variable amount based on future earnings. Later in the year the sizable Random House empire (itself owned by Newhouse Communications, a large media conglomerate) expanded with the acquisition of Times Books, the book-publishing division of the New York Times Co. Another takeover with certain repercussions was the $295 million purchase of Waldenbooks, the nation's largest chain of bookstores with 862 outlets, by K Mart Corp., the nation's

Two of the oldest and most prestigious U.S. publishing companies merged when Macmillan (founded 1869) purchased Scribner Book Companies, which included Charles Scribner's Sons (founded 1846). The famous Scribner's bookstore on Manhattan's Fifth Avenue was sold to Rizzoli International Bookstores.

CARL MYDANS/TIME MAGAZINE

second largest retailer. The publishing and bookselling industry was waiting to see if K Mart's discounting strategies would be implemented by Waldenbooks, a change that would radically affect bookselling in the U.S.

In contrast to the generally favourable economic news, some of the bloom had come off publishing's most prized rose of a year before—computer books and book-related computer software. What seemed like a booming market only a few months earlier had plunged into a disaster zone for the unlucky, with too many books by too many publishers. Early in 1984 there were nearly 5,000 computer-related titles in print, with an additional 2,000 scheduled for publication during 1984. The result was a glut of unsold books that were being returned to publishers.

There was also a cautionary mood among paperback publishers, who a decade earlier had seen sizable advances paid for best-selling hardcover books turn into expensive mistakes. While there were several auctions of note during the year, fewer reprinters seemed to be getting involved. That was certainly the case with novelist Arthur Hailey, whose *Strong Medicine,* along with eight earlier novels including best-sellers *Airport* and *Hotel,* was sold for a little more than $2 million to Dell Books, the only bidder. Few paperback publishers were willing to take a chance on one of the year's most news-making books, . . . *And Ladies of the Club,* a novel by Helen Hooven Santmyer (*see* BIOGRAPHIES) that ran well over 1,000 pages and that attracted national media attention because of the author's advanced age. Paperback rights were sold for $396,000, but uncertainty over how such a lengthy book could be published in a paperback format limited the bidding.

Other newsmaking books of the year included a spate of titles that raised the issue of standards of accuracy in book publishing and the publisher's responsibility for substantiation. The first of these was C. David Heymann's *Poor Little Rich Girl,* a biography of Barbara Hutton that was recalled by Random House when several key points of fact were called into question. Although Random House dropped the book, it was reedited and later published by

Lyle Stuart. A biography of Francis Cardinal Spellman to be published by Times Books had to be revised when allegations of the religious leader's homosexuality could not be sufficiently substantiated. Another book offering a controversial theory about the Roman Catholic Church also raised questions of substantiation. *In God's Name* by David A. Yallop became an international best-seller for the allegations it made about the death of Pope John Paul I, who the author claimed was murdered on the orders of members of the Vatican hierarchy. In a particularly ironic case, Random House delayed publication of a book about morality entitled *Telling Right from Wrong* when it was discovered that a letter praising the book had been forged by the book's author.

On the First Amendment front it was a generally good year for the book world. Several states that had enacted obscenity legislation were forced to overturn those laws. In Texas a law requiring that biblical creationism be taught along with evolutionary theory was dropped. The federal government backed away from a plan requiring advance review of any writing by former government employees prior to publication. However, a bill restricting the use of children in pornography was signed into law.

Finally, there was little encouragement in a major national survey of U.S. reading habits completed by the Book Industry Study Group. The study showed that, while there were eight million more readers in 1983 than in 1978, there was a decline in readers among those under 21 years old as well as those over 65. The survey also showed that readers in the U.S. spent an average of 11.7 hours per week on books, magazines, and newspapers, compared with more than 16 hours per week spent watching television.

(KENNETH C. DAVIS)

See also Literature.

This article updates the *Macropædia* article PUBLISHING.

Race Relations

Racial violence and support for racist and neofascist political parties and organizations continued to increase during 1984, while living conditions for people of colour in the U.S. and Western Europe deteriorated still further. At the same time, there was an increasing level of political activism among black, Hispanic, and immigrant communities.

Great Britain. Evidence of structural racism, lack of police protection for the black population in the face of increasing levels of racial violence, and a continuing deterioration of relations between the police and the black community continued to dominate race relations in Britain during 1984. In May the Policy Studies Institute (PSI) published *Black and White Britain,* its third comprehensive survey of the position of black people in Britain. The researchers had expected to find a reduction in the level of inequality since their 1967 and 1974 reports. "Instead we found a complex jumble of old and new inequalities." According to the report, "racialism and direct racial discrimination continue to have a powerful impact on the lives of black people," and the position of black people in Britain of the 1980s "remains largely, geographically and economically, that allocated to them as immigrant workers in the 1950s and 1960s."

In the area of employment, it was shown that black people were more likely to be unemployed and to remain unemployed for longer periods than whites, and that black workers in employment were more likely to receive lower pay and to be in lower status jobs. A Department of Employment study published in June provided the most

Memphis firefighters were the subject of a U.S. Supreme Court decision that lower courts could not set aside bona fide seniority systems to preserve affirmative-action programs.

LEAPTROTT/THE COMMERCIAL APPEAL

up-to-date unemployment rates: West Indian men, 20.6%; West Indian women, 14.5%; Asian men, 16.9%; Asian women, 17.9%; white men, 9.7%; white women, 8.7%. Rising levels of joblessness among black youth and increased discrimination in hiring in both the private and public sectors were uncovered. Both the Commission for Racial Equality and the School of Advanced Urban Studies, University of Bristol, found patterns of exclusion of black youngsters from employer-based youth training schemes— those most likely to lead to permanent employment. On the other hand, as the result of an equal opportunity campaign by the Greater London Council, the number of black firemen in the London Fire Brigade rose from 6 in 1981 to 63 in 1984. The government's record in this area was described as "halfhearted" in the annual report of the London Association of Community Relations Councils, published in September, and the Leicester Child Poverty Action Group claimed that the Home Office and the Department of Health and Social Security "united to lay down administrative and procedural measures which effectively discriminate against black people."

The year was marked by reports of racial violence directed against Britain's black population. The PSI report estimated that the Home Office's 1981 calculation that Asians were 50 times, and West Indians 36 times, more likely than whites to be the victims of a racial attack was a gross underestimate. According to the PSI, the statistics were ten times worse when incidents not reported to the police were included.

Continental Western Europe. Neofascist political successes leading to racial violence and right-wing, anti-immigrant policies by elected governments increased during the year. In France the National Front led by Jean-Marie le Pen (*see* BIOGRAPHIES) gained 11% of the vote and won ten seats in the election to the European Parliament. Its campaign, fundamentally based on anti-immigrant policies, received considerable support from the press, which linked immigrants with crime, violence, drugs, lowered educational standards, and poor housing. This legitimated racism was accompanied by a growing incidence of racial attacks throughout France.

In January violence erupted at the Peugeot-owned Talbot automobile factory at Poissy, where white nonstrikers attacked black strikers; the black workers were protesting against the company's plans for reducing the work force, under which 80% of those laid off were black. In April the government announced a program to give financial assistance to unemployed immigrants to return to their countries of origin. This repatriation policy had previously been condemned by the Socialists. In November Jacques Chirac, the Gaullist leader, in launching his party's new policy documents, moved to the right to capture the ground occupied by Le Pen's openly racist National Front. Chirac linked the effect of abortion on France's low birthrate with the threat of large-scale black immigration. "In 30 years' time there will be four times as many men in the South of the Mediterranean [*i.e.*, North Africa] as in the north. It will then be impossible to stop the men of the south moving northward if we do not boost the birthrate."

West Germany also experienced an escalation of racial violence and the growth of neo-Nazi groups. In September the Social Democratic Party reported that it had details of 158 neo-Nazi and other extremist right-wing groups that were currently active in the country. These included the Zyklon B group in West Berlin, the Belsen Scene in Düsseldorf, the Ku Klux Klan in Mainz, and the Committee for the Extermination of Aliens (*i.e.*, Turkish *Gastarbeiter* or "guest workers") in Munich. In Austria a survey published by Hilde Weiss of the University of Vienna suggested that one-quarter of the population was strongly anti-Semitic; only 15% of those questioned claimed to have no such prejudice.

South Africa. Prime Minister P. W. Botha's (*see* BIOGRAPHIES) 1983 success in gaining white support for his new constitution—which gave some recognition to Indians and Coloureds but excluded the country's majority black population—led in 1984 to a revival of militant black opposition, an escalation of police violence, and the use of Defence Force troops to try to control the black African townships. Furthermore, 70% of Coloured voters and 80% of Indian voters boycotted the August elections to the new three-chamber Parliament. In an unsuccessful attempt to silence the United Democratic Front (UDF), which had affiliations of more than 600 organizations with a combined membership of more than three million people, the government arrested its leaders in August. The action was condemned by the South African Roman Catholic bishops' conference, which felt "compelled to express our deep dismay at the action taken by the South African government in detaining the UDF leaders." The bishops further declared that the elections "are a poor substitute for a genuine democratic evolution in South Africa."

Black protests, including school boycotts and stay-away campaigns by black workers, were widespread. By November it was estimated that the resulting death toll had risen to about 155, and a civil liberties group estimated that over 1,000 opponents of apartheid (racial separation) had been detained. On October 5 the law and order minister, Louis Le Grange, reported that for the period August 1 to September 20, 65 of the 80 people who died had been killed by the police. Government officials were unwilling to say how many of the people killed after September 20 had been killed by the police. (*See* WORLD AFFAIRS [Africa South of the Sahara]: *South Africa.*)

One of the crucial issues agitating African youths was "Bantu education," which was underfinanced and grossly inferior to that provided for whites. In 1983 more than 50% of black matriculation pupils failed to gain even a secondary school-leaving certificate (the equivalent of a high school diploma in the U.S.), representing a 2.5% increase over the 1982 failure rate. Fewer than 10% obtained a university entrance pass.

United States. Relations between the Reagan administration and the black community continued to deteriorate during the year. In January the U.S. Commission on Civil Rights—which, as reconstituted late in 1983, closely reflected the administration's views—reversed an earlier position and deplored the use of quotas to correct the effects of discrimination. Over one-third of all blacks in the U.S. lived in poverty, as defined by the government, and the gap between black and white unemployment levels continued to widen. The National Urban League, using its "Hidden Unemployment Index," estimated that 33% of blacks overall and 70% of black teenagers were either unemployed or in partial employment at levels of pay below the poverty line. As a result, blacks were disproportionately affected by the administration's cuts in programs designed to assist the poor.

In 1984 black Americans focused on political mobilization to put their needs on the political agenda. Much of the impetus came from the campaign of civil rights leader Jesse Jackson (*see* BIOGRAPHIES) for the Democratic presidential nomination. Jackson, the first black to be generally considered a serious candidate for the presidency, stressed voter registration and, partly as a result of his efforts, more than 183,000 black people registered between January 1983 and April 1984 in the five Southern states alone. Jackson also insisted that he was not "the black candidate" but aimed to form a Rainbow Coalition that would include, especially, Hispanics, women, and other victims of discrimination. The Rainbow Coalition strategy was partially successful. Jackson's vote in the Democratic primaries was greater than the proportion of blacks in the population, and he won 34% of the Puerto Rican vote in New York and 20% of the Latino vote in California, but it was not enough to provide the delegate strength needed for nomination at the Democratic convention. Nevertheless, the Jackson candidacy marked an important step in the empowerment of blacks in mainstream politics. In the general election in November, estimated that 91% of black voters cast their ballots for Walter Mondale, the Democratic candidate. Hispanic support for Mondale was also marked, with an estimated 69% voting for him. (*See* WORLD AFFAIRS [North America]: *United States:* Special Report.)

(LOUIS KUSHNICK)

See also Human Rights.

J. GUICHARD—SYGMA

In France a dispute erupted at a Peugeot automobile factory between striking workers threatened with dismissal—mostly immigrants—and workers still holding jobs—mostly Frenchmen.

Religion

The words "religion" and "politics" were yoked in news stories throughout 1984 in all parts of the world. The most dramatic clash took place in India, which was torn apart by religious strife when Prime Minister Indira Gandhi was fatally shot October 31 by her own Sikh bodyguards. Apparently the assassination was an act of revenge triggered by the Army's June attack on the Golden Temple in Amritsar, the holiest shrine of the Sikh faith, which had been turned into an armed fortress by Sikh extremists. After the assassination, deadly street battles broke out between Hindus and Sikhs. (See *Hinduism,* below.) Just a few days earlier, an Italian judge indicted three Bulgarians and five Turks in the 1981 assassination attempt on Pope John Paul II. The judge said the attack was part of an "international plot" to kill the pontiff. In such a year, it was not surprising that Anglican bishop Desmond Tutu (*see* NOBEL PRIZES), a symbol of the clash between church and state over apartheid (racial separation) in South Africa, was awarded the Nobel Peace Prize. The black leader, director of the South African Council of Churches when the award was announced, was subsequently chosen as bishop of Johannesburg.

To an uncommon degree, religion was a major issue in the U.S. presidential campaign. Pres. Ronald Reagan (*see* BIOGRAPHIES), formally announcing his intention to run for reelection, prefigured one aspect of his campaign when, as a supporter of prayer in the public schools, he promised to help "find room in our schools for God." On the Democratic side, the three finalists in the presidential primaries were former vice-president Walter F. Mondale, the son of a Methodist minister; Sen. Gary Hart of Colorado, a former divinity school student; and Jesse Jackson, a black Baptist minister. (*See* BIOGRAPHIES.) The primary campaign reached its most acrimonious level after the *Washington Post* reported that Jackson, in a private conversation, had described New York Jews as "Hymies" and New York City as "Hymietown." Fuel was added to the fire when Louis Farrakhan (*see* BIOGRAPHIES), a Jackson supporter and head of the Nation of Islam, in a radio address warned Milton Coleman, the black *Post* reporter who broke the story, that "one day soon we will punish you with death." Subsequent remarks by Farrakhan about Jews were widely reported, and black-Jewish relations, increasingly tense in recent years, reached a new low when Jackson balked at demands that he repudiate Farrakhan's support. A conciliatory speech by Jackson at the Democratic convention eased but did not completely heal the rift.

With the "New Christian Right" forming an important segment of Reagan's constituency, the religious factor loomed even larger at the Republican convention in Dallas, Texas. Before the convention, Sen. Paul Laxalt of Nevada, head of Reagan's campaign, sent a letter to fundamentalist ministers reminding them that "President Reagan had been faithful in his support of issues of concern to Christian citizens." Then, at a prayer breakfast near the convention site, Reagan asserted that "religion and politics are necessarily related" and went on to accuse opponents of public-school prayer of being "intolerant of religion." In a benediction at the convention, Jerry Falwell, fundamentalist leader of Moral Majority, referred to Reagan and Vice-Pres. George Bush as "God's instruments in rebuilding America." Such incidents prompted a growing debate on the relationship of church and state in the U.S. and moved Mondale, the Democratic presidential nominee, to devote a major address to the subject before a Jewish forum. "The Queen of England, where state religion is established, is called defender of the faith," he said. "But the President of the United States is the defender of the Constitution, which defends all faiths." Meanwhile, Rep. Geraldine Ferraro, the Democratic candidate for vice-president, had suggested that Reagan could not be a good Christian because his policies were so cruel to the poor.

Although the policy of the nation's Roman Catholic bishops was not to support any candidate or party, Archbishop John J. O'Connor of New York (*see* BIOGRAPHIES) generated a storm of controversy when he said he did not see "how a Catholic in good conscience can vote for a candidate who explicitly supports abortion." His remarks drew immediate rejoinders from two prominent lay Catholics, Representative Ferraro and New York Gov. Mario Cuomo (*see* BIOGRAPHIES). In a lecture on "Religious Belief and Public Morality," Cuomo told a University of Notre Dame audience that the abortion issue should not be "the exclusive litmus test of Catholic loyalty." (See *Roman Catholic Church,* below.) In deeds as well as words, religious leaders played a significant role in the campaign. Led by Jackson, black churches served as voter registration centres that were expected to swell the ranks of Democratic voters. Counterbalancing this effort was a well-organized drive by the New Christian Right to register Protestant fundamentalists, most of whom were expected to vote Republican.

To avoid further entanglement in election-year politics, the U.S. Roman Catholic bishops waited until after the November election to make public the first draft of a 50,000-word pastoral letter, "Catholic Social Teaching and the U.S. Economy." After hearing testimony from 125 theologians, economists, business and labour leaders, and government officials from both liberal and conservative administrations, the bishops credited the American economic system for "an encouraging record of performance" but also charged that the record was flawed by "massive and ugly failures." The prelates pointed to such "failures" as a "morally unjustified" unemployment rate, a "woefully inadequate" welfare system, unacceptable levels of inequity in income, and excessive military spending. To correct these shortcomings, the bishops' draft called for job-creation programs, tax reforms, the retraining of displaced workers, and the reduction of third world debt.

Meanwhile, church-state issues generated debate and action in all three branches of government. Congress debated a measure requiring schools to allow silent prayer in the classroom, but it approved (and the president signed) a controversial bill allowing religious groups the same access as nonreligious groups to public-school facilities before and after school hours. Supporters argued that the "equal access" bill fulfilled constitutional guarantees of free speech. Opponents contended that it breached the "wall of separation" between church and state and warned that the measure could force schools to provide space for radical political groups and religious cults.

The establishment of full diplomatic ties between the U.S. and the Vatican, once an issue that sharply divided the nation, was achieved by the Reagan administration without intense opposition. In September, however, Americans United for Separation of Church and State filed a lawsuit challenging the legality of the exchange of diplomats. On the administrative level, U.S. delegates to the International Conference on Population in Mexico City were instructed to uphold a policy opposing the use of U.S. government funds for abortions overseas.

Other church-state issues were hammered out in the courts. By a 5–4 vote, the U.S. Supreme Court ruled that a city may include a Christian Nativity scene as part of a city-owned Christmas display. The American Civil Liberties Union, with the National Council of the Churches of Christ in the U.S.A. (NCC) and the American Jewish Committee, had brought suit against Pawtucket, R.I., arguing that the display discriminated against non-Christians and violated the constitutional ban against government establishment of religion. (*See* LAW.) At a time when numerous American churches were providing sanctuary for political refugees from Central America, an all-Hispanic jury in Brownsville, Texas, returned a guilty verdict against a religious lay worker who had transported three illegal aliens. The defendant, Stacy Lynn Merkt, told the court she feared the refugees would be killed or tortured if they were returned to El Salvador. After exhausting his legal remedies, Sun Myung Moon, the Korean-born founder of the Unification Church, began serving an 18-month prison sentence for failing to pay personal taxes on $162,000 in interest earned from a church bank account.

Skirmishing between governmental and religious authorities was a worldwide phenomenon. In France some one million protesters walked through the streets of Paris to demonstrate their opposition to a government proposal that would have given the state new powers to regulate France's mostly Catholic private schools. In Poland the government precipitated "the war of the crosses" by ordering the removal of crucifixes from public schools. The conflict was resolved when the government announced that crucifixes could be hung in dormitories and school libraries but not in lecture halls. Civil unrest erupted again in October when Jerzy Popieluszko (*see* OBITUARIES), a popular priest and supporter of the banned Solidarity labour movement, was killed by government agents. (*See* WORLD AFFAIRS [Eastern Europe]: *Poland.*) The Soviet government turned down a request from Pope John Paul II for permission to visit Lithuania, a Soviet republic with a predominantly Catholic population. The Lutheran World Federation, at its international gathering in Budapest, Hung., suspended from membership two white churches in southern Africa for failing to reject unequivocally the South African government's policy of apartheid. (See *Lutheran Communion,* below.) A long-standing dispute between U.S. and Salvadoran officials ended when Salvadoran judges convicted five former National Guard members accused of killing four U.S. churchwomen in 1980. Leaders of the Baha'i faith continued to accuse the Islamic government in Iran of carrying out a policy of genocide against that nation's Baha'i minority.

In Italy some lingering church-state tensions were eased when the Vatican and the Italian government signed a historic concordat that ended Roman Catholicism's status as the established religion of the country. Under the new pact, Rome ceased to be a "sacred city," but Italy would continue to recognize the Vatican City State as an independent and sovereign state in the middle of Rome. Most observers said the concordat was made possible when the Vatican agreed to pay $240 million to creditors of the Banco Ambrosiano, which collapsed in 1982. This settled a conflict that began when it was learned that Roberto Calvi, the bank's president at the time of its collapse, used to his advantage "letters of patronage" from Archbishop Paul C. Marcinkus, president of the Institute for Religious Works, popularly known as the Vatican bank.

Pope John Paul proved again in 1984 that he was not a "prisoner of the Vatican." In May he made a "pilgrimage" to Asia, highlighted by rites celebrating the 200th anniversary of Roman Catholicism in Korea. In part, his visit was a recognition of the surging growth of Christianity in South Korea. In June he spent six days in Switzerland, where

U.S. Pres. Ronald Reagan designated William A. Wilson, here presenting his credentials to Pope John Paul II, as the first 20th-century U.S. ambassador to the Vatican. Groups concerned with the separation of church and state promptly filed a lawsuit.
AP/WIDE WORLD

one of his major stops was the Geneva headquarters of the World Council of Churches (WCC). There he joined Philip Potter, the WCC's outgoing general secretary, in leading an ecumenical prayer service. The papal plane next took him to Canada for a 12-day, coast-to-coast trip. In October he was in the Dominican Republic for ceremonies marking the 500th anniversary of the first European voyages to the Western Hemisphere.

The pope had business to take care of at home, as well. Getting his own house in order, he made several key changes at the top level of the Curia. Recognizing the importance of Africa in the future of Catholicism, the pontiff named Bernardin Cardinal Gantin of Benin as prefect of the Congregation for Bishops. After the changes, 16 of the 22 top positions in the Curia were held by non-Italians.

The theological conservatism of John Paul's regime expressed itself in several ways. Especially active during the year was Joseph Cardinal Ratzinger, the scholarly German theologian who headed the Sacred Congregation for the Doctrine of the Faith. In the spring the Congregation ordered the removal of imprimaturs from two books widely used in U.S. churches: *Sexual Morality* by Philip S. Keane and *Christ Among Us,* an adult catechism by Anthony Wilhelm. Subsequently, Ratzinger's office issued a long-awaited critique of "liberation theology," the attempt, especially in Latin America, to translate the Christian doctrine of salvation into terms of social and political liberation. The 35-page document criticized "certain forms of liberation theology" that "uncritically borrow" Marxist thought. (See *Roman Catholic Church,* below.)

On the ecumenical scene, a changing of the guard took place at the WCC in Geneva and the NCC in New York City. Named to succeed Potter at the WCC was Emilio Castro (*see* BIOGRAPHIES), a Methodist minister from Uruguay, who had played a major role in developing a Protestant form of liberation theology. At the NCC, Claire Randall was succeeded as general secretary by Arie R. Brouwer, who formerly headed the Reformed Church of America.

Conservative Judaism entered a new stage in its history when the Jewish Theological Seminary in New York City admitted women for the first time as candidates for ordination to the rabbinate. (ROY LARSON)

PROTESTANT CHURCHES

Anglican Communion. Two events in July 1984 dominated the Anglican year: the sixth meeting of the Anglican Consultative Council (ACC) in Nigeria and the blaze at York Minster, which destroyed part of the medieval roof.

There were some fears that the ACC meeting might have to be abandoned because of the diplomatic row between Britain and Nigeria caused by the kidnapping of Nigeria's former transport minister, Umaru Dikko (*see* BIOGRAPHIES). The meeting went ahead as planned, however, with 60 delegates from 31 provinces tackling a wide range of topics. There was a general feeling that the meeting had achieved a better balance than its predecessors between doctrinal matters and mission, unity and social justice. Thus, for example, the council called on member churches to renew their commitment to evangelism, but it also called for talks with the World Muslim Federation over the increasing tensions experienced by Christians in Islamic countries. Delegates deplored the consecration earlier in the year, by bishops in Australia, of a presiding bishop for the breakaway Church of England in South Africa without any prior reference to the ACC.

The fire at York Minster was thought to have been caused by an unusual lightning strike. Although the damage would cost millions of pounds and take many years to repair, none of the treasures within the building was seriously harmed. The great rose window was cracked but could be completely restored. Many people saw the lightning as a sign of God's judgment on the Church of England for admitting David Jenkins (*see* BIOGRAPHIES) to its bench of bishops. Just three days before he had been consecrated bishop of Durham in the minster, despite his expressed doubts about the traditional understanding of such central tenets as the Virgin Birth.

In August the new Anglican-Roman Catholic International Commission (ARCIC II) met in Durham and made "substantial progress" toward agreement on the doctrine of salvation. Also in August, the Anglican-Orthodox Joint Doctrinal Commission met near Dublin and announced new agreements, despite major unresolved difficulties caused by the ordination of women in some Anglican provinces. Despite the possible ecumenical implications, on November 30 the General Synod voted to permit the ordination of women as priests. This, however, was only the first step in a long process that would include, among other things, submission of the proposal to Parliament.

Stephen Neill, a noted ecumenical theologian and prolific author, died in July (*see* OBITUARIES). (SUSAN YOUNG)

Baptist Churches. Even as Polish Baptists were jubilantly reporting to the Baptist World Alliance that 200 persons had been baptized in 1983 and 40 in the first quarter of 1984, many Baptists in the U.S. were reacting to their own perceived threats. In Kansas City, Mo., Southern Baptists in convention session routed the moderate forces. The 14 million-member denomination elected as president Charles Stanley, pastor of the First Baptist Church in Atlanta, Ga., and a former director of Moral Majority. Measured by the usual criteria,

When lightning caused a fire that gravely damaged the medieval roof of York Minster in July, many Britons read it as an act of divine displeasure over the recent consecration there of Canon David Jenkins as bishop of Durham. Jenkins had suggested that the Virgin Birth of Christ and the Resurrection—essential elements of the Christian faith—might be more symbolic than literal and that one could be a good Christian without holding such beliefs.
PICK—SYGMA

Stanley had not been overly "supportive" of the Southern Baptist Convention (SBC), but his prominence in the ultraconservative movement apparently was more significant to the messengers (delegates) than bureaucratic credentials.

Also reflecting the conservative mood was a resolution to bar the ordination of women, even though some 250 women were already ordained in the SBC. In his defense of the resolution, Carl Henry, noted evangelical theologian and sometime editor of the conservative magazine *Christianity Today,* stated, "Scriptures teach that women are not in public worship to assume a role of authority over men lest confusion reign in the local church."

Baylor University in Waco, Texas, a Southern Baptist-supported school, was again in the headlines for alleged heresies. This time the dispute centred around the employment of a Mormon on the faculty of the language department. Many Baptists, especially of the conservative group, would hold that Mormons are a non-Christian cult. Such conservatism did not go unchallenged, however. A group of church members from SBC churches in Louisville, Ky., formed their own resolution regarding the ordination of women, quoting Gal. 3:28, in which the Apostle Paul insists that the sexes are equal in Christ.

The SBC meetings reflected the resurgence of other U.S. Baptists, mostly independent of denominational affiliation, who aligned themselves on the "pro-moral" side in the election campaign. Baptists, particularly independent Baptists, had traditionally stressed personal conversion and had not concerned themselves publicly with social and political issues, insisting, from their origins, on the "wall of separation" between church and state. In 1984 they emerged as a major political force. (See *Introduction,* above.) In a more direct political involvement, Baptist minister Jesse Jackson (*see* BIOGRAPHIES) ran in the Democratic presidential primary, with black churches forming an important segment of his power base.

(NORMAN R. DE PUY)

Christian Church (Disciples of Christ). A panel appointed by the general minister and president of the church declared

its own "nuclear pacifism" after a study and called on church members to consider carefully the responsibilities of the church in peacemaking. The study was designed to spur the congregationally governed Disciples, numbering 1.1 million in the U.S. and Canada, to enter the national debate on the nuclear threat.

The Disciples celebrated 50 years of cooperative fund-raising to support their world work and a century of missionary involvement in Asia. Churches around the world claiming origins in the American frontier movements of Alexander Campbell and Barton W. Stone, at their quadrennial world convention in Jamaica, elected Lindsay A. Jacobs of New Zealand convention president.

A group of some 600 Christians, mostly of Pentecostal backgrounds, who had banded together as the Christian Association (Disciples of Christ) in Guatemala, asked for and received a relationship to North American Disciples. The church's General Board urged Congress to approve a redress of grievances of Japanese-Americans interned as security risks during World War II. The Disciples had taken a similar position in 1942, despite the war hysteria of the day.

(ROBERT LOUIS FRIEDLY)

Churches of Christ. Combating hunger throughout the world was a major emphasis of the churches of Christ in 1984. The 3,000-member Richland Hills Church in Fort Worth, Texas, collected some $750,-000 for relief efforts in southern Africa. Manna International, a hunger-relief program in Redwood City, Calif., worked primarily with young people in weekend fasts simulating real world situations. Manna's West Coast Day of Prayer and Fasting netted $75,000 for Ethiopia. Over $2 million was raised by the Ferry Road Church in West Monroe, La., for an emergency relief effort in Ghana. Following a relief program in Poland two years earlier, the church there had grown from 600 to 2,000.

Ira North, minister for the 5,000-member Madison (Tenn.) Church and teacher of the televised "Amazing Grace Bible Class," and Jimmy Lovell, founder of the World Bible School, died in 1984. David Davenport was named sixth president of Pepperdine University in Los Angeles. Twenty-seven churches across the U.S. each baptized a hundred persons or more; the church in Boston led with over 400. Good growth was reported among churches in Papua New Guinea, and an effective campaign was held in San José, Costa Rica.

(M. NORVEL YOUNG)

Church of Christ, Scientist. Initiating a two-year worldwide series of workshops on Christian healing, the church reaffirmed its century-long commitment to exploring the practical contemporary implications of biblical healing. At the church's annual meeting in Boston in early June 1984, church officials noted the awakening interest in biblical healing among other Christian denominations as a promising "sign of the times."

The *Christian Science Monitor* celebrated its 75th anniversary at the close of 1983 and launched a weekly news and feature radio program, "Monitoradio," in January 1984. The hour-long series was being broadcast over more than 100 stations in the U.S. Fully completed in May, the nondenominational Bible exhibit at the church's Boston headquarters had been visited by more than 66,000 people since its initial opening in 1982.

Zadie Hatfield of Hingham, Mass., succeeded James K. ("Kay") Kyser of Chapel Hill, N.C., as president of the Mother Church. Hatfield had served as a trustee of the Christian Science Publishing Society before devoting her full time to the healing ministry. (NATHAN A. TALBOT)

Church of Jesus Christ of Latter-day Saints. In April Russell M. Nelson, a prominent heart surgeon, and Dallin H. Oaks, a Utah Supreme Court justice and former president of Brigham Young University, filled vacancies in the Council of the Twelve Apostles. New general presidencies of the women's Relief Society and Young Women were installed. Six leaders were appointed to serve for three to five years in the First Quorum of the Seventy, the first time General Authorities had been appointed for a limited period. In June members of the First Quorum of the Seventy were appointed to constitute presidencies for each of the church's 13 major geographic areas throughout the world. Thus, while much administration of the 5.6 million-member church had been decentralized, supervision by general church leaders was enhanced. Traditional stake (diocese) conferences were combined to provide increased contact with church leaders while decreasing their travel.

To facilitate coordination of independent genealogical research, a family registry was established. The church's Genealogical Department released a software package developed for management of genealogical information using home computers. The Museum of Church History and Art, in downtown Salt Lake City, Utah, was dedicated in April. A temple was dedicated in Mexico City in December 1983, and the first of a series of small temples of standardized architecture was dedicated at Boise, Idaho, in May 1984. Additional temples were opened in Dallas; Sydney, Australia; Manila; and Taipei, Taiwan.

Church officials joined with Roman Catholic, Jewish, and Protestant leaders in deploring antidenominational propaganda and religious intolerance.

(LEONARD J. ARRINGTON)

Jehovah's Witnesses. The corporate publishing agency of Jehovah's Witnesses, the Watch Tower Bible and Tract Society, was granted a charter in the Court of Common Pleas of Allegheny County, Pa., in 1884. To observe the centennial of this event, crowds of Jehovah's Witnesses gathered in Three Rivers Stadium in Pittsburgh on Oct. 6, 1984, to hear talks by Watch Tower officials. Visitors came from more than 40 countries. The program was transmitted to some 34 Assembly Halls of Jehovah's Witnesses throughout the U.S. and Canada, bringing the listening audience to more than 100,000.

To date, the society had printed more than 40 million copies of a modern speech Bible, the *New World Translation of the Holy Scriptures.* During the summer a revised "Reference" edition of this Bible was released, containing extensive marginal references, footnotes, an index of Bible words, and an appendix.

The steady growth of Jehovah's Witnesses during the past century was noted at the 117 "Kingdom Increase" district conventions held in the U.S. during 1984 and attended by 1,159,898 persons. The "Kingdom Increase" theme was developed at conventions in more than 200 lands, scheduled through the end of 1984 and in early 1985. (FREDERICK W. FRANZ)

Lutheran Communion. Representatives of most of the world's 70 million Lutherans met in Budapest, July 22–Aug. 5, 1984, for the seventh assembly of the Geneva-based Lutheran World Federation (LWF). It was the first such gathering in Eastern Europe. Delegates chose Presiding Bishop Zoltan Kalday of the host Lutheran Church in Hungary as LWF president until the next assembly, in the early 1990s. He succeeded Diocesan Bishop Josiah Kibira of the Evangelical Lutheran Church in Tanzania. Notwithstanding some criticism of Kalday's leadership style during his quarter century as head of his denomination, and suggestions by some that his church was too friendly with Hungary's Communist government, Kalday was elected on the second ballot, with 173 votes to 124 for Bodil Sølling, associate general secretary of the Danish Lutheran relief and development agency and the first woman to run for the post.

Southern Africa and ecumenism were among the major agenda items, which included discussions and reports on 13 issues, among them the role of women, racism, peace, youth, worship, and communications. The assembly voted (222–23, 29 abstentions) to suspend the membership of two small, white southern African denominations on the grounds that in practice they do not oppose apartheid and are not moving toward unity with the great majority of the region's Lutherans, who are black. In approving a "statement on the self-understanding and task" of the LWF, the assembly defined it as an "expression and instrument" of a worldwide "Lutheran communion" and located it in the "one ecumenical movement" in cooperation with other Christian world communions and the WCC. In the wake of some assembly criticism about the small number of women in LWF leadership positions, the new LWF executive committee, at its meeting after the assembly, chose the first LWF female vice-president in history (the

LWF has five vice-presidents) and named women to chair three of the four LWF commissions. It also decided to have a special meeting in February 1985 to name a successor to retiring LWF General Secretary Carl Mau.

Plans to bring together two-thirds of Canadian and U.S. Lutherans in new denominations in each country (in 1986 and 1988, respectively) moved forward. The Churches of Norway and Sweden continued to loosen their ties to the state. The synod of the Evangelical Church of Finland failed to achieve the three-quarters majority necessary to approve ordination of female pastors and thus continued to be the largest Lutheran denomination without them. (THOMAS HARTLEY DORRIS)

Methodist Churches. The Bicentennial Conference of the United Methodist Church held in Baltimore, Md., in May 1984 celebrated the formation of the Methodist Episcopal Church at the "Christmas Conference" held in that city 200 years earlier. Bishop William R. Cannon, delivering the episcopal address, strongly denounced militarism. The conference approved a "missional priority" in local ethnic-minority congregations for the next four years and endorsed a budget of $25 million to support new congregations and build new churches. The total budget was set at $350 million, with the largest single item, $159 million, for world service programs.

The subject debated at the greatest length was homosexuality. Members decided to retain the wording in the Book of Discipline which states that "homosexuals are persons of sacred worth" but added that "since the practice of homosexuality is incompatible with Christian teaching, self-avowed practicing homosexuals are not to be accepted as candidates, ordained as ministers, or appointed to serve in the United Methodist Church."

During 1984 the British Methodist Church published *Hymns and Songs,* replacing the 50-year-old Methodist hymnbook. The Baltimore conference followed this lead by appointing a committee to produce a hymnbook for the United Methodist Church. Requests for the use of inclusive and nonsexist language were considered, together with a more general report on the avoidance of sexist, racist, and ageist language throughout the worship and liturgy of the church.

Statements on social principles were strengthened and basic freedoms reaffirmed. A commitment was made to work for freedom for all people, along with a dedication to peace and the rule of justice and law. Concern was expressed for the rights of minority groups, the need to protect the Earth's resources, the unequal distribution of wealth, and the needs of the homeless and hungry. Pressure to adopt a tougher line on abortion was resisted.

In Britain the bicentennial was celebrated by a service during which a marker was erected at Pill, near Bristol, where the first preachers ordained by John Wesley sailed for America in 1784. Plans for the 15th World Methodist Council (WMC) and Conference, to be held in Nairobi, Kenya, in July 1986, were approved at a meeting of the WMC Executive Committee in Frankfurt am Main, West Germany. The WMC Evangelism Committee staged an old-fashioned "World Camp Meeting" at Ocean Grove, N.J. A Methodist minister, Emilio Castro (*see* BIOGRAPHIES) of Uruguay, was chosen as general secretary of the WCC with effect from Jan. 1, 1985.

(PETER H. BOLT)

Pentecostal Churches. The Church of God in Christ was the largest American Pentecostal denomination, according to the *Yearbook of American and Canadian Churches, 1984.* The predominantly black church, which began in 1895, grew to 3,709,661 members in 1983 from the 425,000 reported in 1965. Second largest was the largely white Assemblies of God (1,879,182 adherents in 1983).

In 1984 both the Assemblies of God and the Church of God (Cleveland, Tenn.) announced the beginning of satellite television networks to serve their local churches. The International Church of the Foursquare Gospel announced publication of a "complete" textbook of systematic pentecostal theology. "Toward a pentecostal/charismatic theology" was the theme of the annual meeting of the Society for Pentecostal Studies, held in November.

The Open Bible Standard Churches, Inc., reported that its world mission program had expanded from 12 countries in 1970 to 25 in 1983, while the Elim Fellowship began mission work in Canada. The Assemblies of God led the U.S. in organizing new churches in 1983, with 343 new congregations. The Pentecostal Holiness Church reported 52 new churches during the year.

In August 1984, 10,000 persons attended the second National Conference on the Holy Spirit in Springfield, Mo., sponsored by the Assemblies of God. In the same month the Pentecostal Fellowship of North America met in Cleveland, Tenn., where speakers emphasized the theme "Pentecostal Worship." The Church of God (Cleveland, Tenn.) reelected E. C. Thomas as general overseer for another two years.

(VINSON SYNAN)

Reformed, Presbyterian, and Congregational Churches. The decision taken by the World Alliance of Reformed Churches (WARC) at the General Council in Ottawa (August 1982), to suspend from the privileges of membership two South African churches because of their support of apartheid, was followed in July 1984 by a decision of a similar nature by the Lutheran World Federation. (See *Lutheran Communion,* above.) Thus the two main streams deriving from the 16th-century Reformation agreed not only in condemning apartheid but also in disciplining members who supported it.

Within the framework of the long-term study program "Called to Witness to the Gospel Today," launched by the Ottawa General Council, two major consultations were held in 1984. One, in Cairo, was held in connection with the annual meeting of WARC's Executive Committee. The other, in Monterrey, Mexico, was organized by the Latin-American Association of Reformed and Presbyterian Churches (AIPRAL).

Jan. 1, 1984, marked the 500th anniversary of the birth of Huldrych Zwingli, the Swiss reformer whose theological heritage largely contributed to shaping the subsequent Reformed and Presbyterian family of churches. Centennial celebrations commemorating the founding of their churches were held by Presbyterians in South Korea and in Indonesia. The Reformed Church of France was preparing a commemoration of the "Revocation of the Edict of Nantes" (1685), which caused the emigration of hundreds of thousands of Huguenots.

In the field of ecumenical debate, most Reformed, Presbyterian, and Congregational churches were studying the so-called Lima Papers on "Baptism, Eucharist, and Ministry." Reactions seemed to express satisfaction that such a paper was possible and, at the same time, reservations because traditional Reformed tenets all too often seemed subsumed under "Catholic" formulations. Two reports, *God's Reign and Our Unity* (the report of the Anglican-Reformed International Commission) and *Baptists and Reformed in Dialogue,* were published. Exploratory encounters were held by representatives of the WARC with representatives of the Disciples of Christ and of the Mennonite World Conference.

Some churches, especially in the Northern Hemisphere, were debating the question of homosexuality; in view of the strong biblical condemnation of homosexuality, this opened up a wider debate on the understanding of the authority of the Bible. The attribution of gender to God came under discussion when the Church of Scotland's General Assembly considered a study group's report entitled *The Motherhood of God.* (ALDO COMBA)

Religious Society of Friends. Calls for prophetic leadership among Quakers characterized the triennial gathering of Friends United Meeting (one of the three main groupings in the U.S.) in Los Angeles. In his Johnson lecture at this event, William Rogers of Guilford College, Greensboro, N.C., emphasized the necessity, for those who would serve the world's needs, of returning constantly to the source of spiritual power.

A similar need felt by Friends in Britain led London Yearly Meeting to choose the theme of rededication. The controversial decision taken in 1983 to withhold part of the income tax of some employees at Friends House, London, in support of their conscientious objection to paying for defense, led to legal action being taken by the Inland Revenue against the clerk and assistant clerk of Meeting for Sufferings (the employing body and the executive committee of British Friends).

Philadelphia Yearly Meeting, at the centre of the large grouping of "liberal" East Coast American Friends, decided to undertake a membership drive, conscious that its numbers had fallen by 25% since 1960. The work of the American Friends Service Committee was concentrated on Central America. Many Friends meetings supported the sanctuary movement, housing Salvadoran and other refugees from the region. (DAVID FIRTH)

Salvation Army. There was an expansion of Salvation Army work during 1984. The movement continued to grow rapidly in South Korea and East Africa, and in Brazil the Army's operations extended into the northeast. The first Salvation Army Congress in Portugal was held under the leadership of Army officers who had pioneered the work there 12 years earlier. In the U.S. the Army's emergency services were mobilized when tornadoes struck several southern states and during flooding in Florida and New Jersey.

Salvation Army leaders from 85 countries assembled in West Berlin for a ten-day conference under the direction of the international leader, Gen. Jarl Wahlström. Through the good offices of the bishop of the Evangelical Church in East Berlin, all conference delegates were able to cross into East Germany in full uniform as religious leaders.

In Great Britain the Salvation Army Social Services celebrated the centenary of its residential social work program. A service of thanksgiving was held in St. Paul's Cathedral, London. On April 1 Commissioner Francy Cachelin (great-grandson of Gen. William Booth, the Army's founder) was appointed leader of the Army's evangelical forces in Britain. (ROB GARRAD)

Seventh-day Adventist Church. The denomination's goal of adding 1,000 new members a day for 1,000 consecutive days appeared well within reach as 1984 ended. Additions were running 8% above statistical projections, and total membership topped 4.4 million. The "1,000 days" would end in mid-1985, when the church was to hold its world conference in New Orleans, La.

The church's 50-year-old radio program, "The Voice of Prophecy," moved ahead with its plan to add new stations on the Satellite Radio Network, bringing the number of stations carrying the broadcast to 363 in the U.S. and Canada. Plans also were implemented to place a 100-kw shortwave station on Guam, which was expected to reach 2,000,000,000 people. The two evangelistic monthly magazines *Signs of the Times* and *These Times* were merged. The new journal, with a circulation of nearly 500,000, retained the name *Signs of the Times.*

In September Adventist Historic Properties, an organization based in Battle Creek, Mich., purchased the home, barn, and 10 ha (25 ac) of land in Low Hampton, N.Y., formerly owned by William Miller. Miller stirred the country 150 years ago with his announcement that the Second Advent of Christ would take place in 1844. The Seventh-day Adventist Church grew out of the Millerite awakening. More than 6,000 delegates attended a Pan-American Youth Congress in Mexico City, Dec. 18–22, 1984. The theme of the congress was "Sow Love in All the World."

The transplantation of a baboon heart into an infant known as Baby Fae, the first such operation in the U.S., was performed in October at the Loma Linda (Calif.) University Medical Center, an Adventist institution. (*See* HEALTH AND DISEASE.)

During the year further efforts were made to recover approximately $20 million of church funds, loaned over 15 years to a California real estate developer who went bankrupt in 1981. In 1984 insurance companies paid more than $4 million to the church. It was expected that additional moneys would come from the sale of assets of the bankrupt estate.

(KENNETH H. WOOD)

Unitarian (Universalist) Churches. Culminating a three-year, denomination-wide participatory process, the 23rd General Assembly of the Unitarian Universalist Association (UUA), meeting in Columbus, Ohio, June 25–30, 1984, gave initial approval to a new statement of "Principles and Purposes." The statement reflects the pluralism of the movement and its roots in—but now extending beyond—Judaism and Christianity.

The General Assembly drew 1,300 delegates and friends from the U.S. and Canada. A resolution affirming the practice of Unitarian-Universalist clergy performing homosexual union (marriage) services was the first such statement by a mainstream denomination. The UUA reported 50% more settled women ministers in its churches than any other denomination, and the number of nonwhite religious leaders and seminary students had tripled since 1982. Contributions through the Annual Program Fund had increased in each of the last five years.

The 56th annual General Assembly of Unitarian and Free Christian Churches (Great Britain and Ireland) met in Brighton, England, April 13–16. Government authorities were urged to provide proper housing for homeless and low-income families, and greater support was asked for the training of Welsh clergy at Memorial College.

The 23rd annual meeting of the Canadian Unitarian Council was held May 17–19 at Banff, Alta. Three "theme workshops" dealt with the personal challenge of social action, spirituality, and religious education. The largest delegation of North American Unitarian Universalists in history attended the 25th triennial conference of the International Association for Religious Freedom, held July 26–August 1 in Tokyo. The 3,200-member Church of the Larger Fellowship observed 40 years of tying together isolated Unitarian Universalists by mail.   (JOHN NICHOLLS BOOTH)

The United Church of Canada. At the 30th (biennial) General Council meeting of Canada's largest Protestant denomination, held at Morden, Man., in August 1984, the 371 commissioners (delegates) faced a workload of 95 resolutions and 145 petitions. Expected to arouse the most debate was a report on "Sexual Orientation and Eligibility for the Order of Ministry." Its principal conclusion was "that in and of itself sexual orientation should not be a factor determining membership in the order of ministry of The United Church of Canada." Council voted to leave the decision with congregations, presbyteries, and conferences as these courts are quite capable of ruling on the fitness of candidates for ordination. At the same time, Council asked the church, through its divisions (offices), to continue the development of an educational program that would enable church members to "study homosexuality in the context of human sexuality, and to continue working toward a comprehensive statement concerning responsible sexual lifestyles for all members. . . ." The resolution also recommended encounter and dialogue with gay and lesbian persons.

Robert F. Smith, minister of Shaughnessy Heights United Church, Vancouver, B.C., was elected moderator, succeeding W. Clarke MacDonald. In other business, Council resolved to appeal to the government of Mexico on behalf of refugees from Guatemala living in camps there and to keep an open door to refugees from Central America. The Canadian government was asked to "strongly and publicly con-

demn all military intervention in Central America," especially that of the U.S. Another resolution expressed similar abhorrence of the Soviet invasion of Afghanistan. Several resolutions focused on apartheid in South Africa. On peace and disarmament, Canada was asked to become a nuclear-weapon-free zone and to "present a resolution to the UN declaring possession of nuclear weapons, as well as their use, to be a crime against humanity. . . ."

(NORMAN K. VALE)

United Church of Christ. In concert with several other Protestant denominations in the U.S., the United Church of Christ (UCC) was studying and shaping a response to several major theological documents, including the report of the third round of dialogues between Lutheran and Reformed churches and a document on "Baptism, Eucharist and Ministry" from the WCC. At a November meeting of the Consultation on Church Union, the UCC joined the other seven member denominations in endorsing a statement of theological consensus. The statement, designed as a basis for eventual merger, would be sent back to the churches for consideration.

On Feb. 1, 1984, C. Shelby Rooks, for ten years president of Chicago Theological Seminary, became executive vice-president of the United Church Board for Homeland Ministries, succeeding Howard E. Spragg. Many UCC people gathered in Greensboro, N.C., to express thanksgiving for the fruitful ministry and devoted leadership of J. Taylor Stanley, one of the church's key leaders for nearly 50 years, who died on Dec. 9, 1983.

Members of the Pacific Island Asian-American Ministries, a special interest group recognized by the church's General Synod, celebrated its tenth anniversary by gathering for worship and planning in Hawaii in early July. Also held in July were the second National Meeting of Women, in Milwaukee, Wis., and the second National Youth Event, at the University of Illinois in Champaign-Urbana. The comprehensive Amendments to the Constitution and By Laws concerning definitions and understanding of the church's ministry were declared in force by virtue of favourable votes of a majority of the church's conferences.

The UCC continued to work for peace and the slowing of the arms race, fairness to all in U.S. immigration policies, human rights in the U.S. and throughout the world, the defeat of apartheid in South Africa, and a reduction of violence everywhere.

(AVERY D. POST)

ROMAN CATHOLIC CHURCH

The year 1984 could be described as one of consolidation for the Roman Catholic Church. There were no notable new initiatives, and Vatican control was reasserted over movements that had appeared to be slipping out of control. The mood was summed up in Pope John Paul's visit to French Canada in September. Though the facts of Quebec's "quiet revolution" were admitted (sharp decline in religious practice, loss of the church's institutional power), John Paul called for "courage" in resisting the effects of secularization.

One effect of this tough-minded policy was an outright attack on "liberation theology." It began with the leaked publication

in March of an article by Joseph Cardinal Ratzinger, prefect of the Sacred Congregation for the Doctrine of the Faith, which warned that certain theologians were subject to Marxist influences. Three names were mentioned: Hugo Assmann, Gustavo Gutiérrez, and Jon Sobrino SJ.

On September 3 an Instruction (officially dated August 6) was published by the same Congregation. Although it recognized the legitimacy of the commitment to social justice, it deplored the use of "Marxist analysis." No names were mentioned, but Ratzinger explained that this was to prevent unnamed theologians from feeling that they were not concerned. One theologian who was very much involved was the Brazilian Franciscan Leonardo Boff, who was summoned to Rome for a "colloquy" on September 7. He emerged smiling, partly because he was aided by Paulo Cardinal Arns and Aloisio Cardinal Lorscheider, both also Franciscans, who by their presence refuted the suggestion that a gap was opening up between the Brazilian hierarchy and a so-called popular church welling up from the "base communities," which were an essential element of the pastoral policy of the Brazilian bishops.

Three priests who were ministers in the left-wing Nicaraguan government were urged to resign because holding ministerial office was incompatible with the new code of canon law. Fernando Cardenal SJ, his poet brother Ernesto, and Foreign Minister Miguel d'Escoto alleged that Nicaragua was in an emergency situation in which exceptions could be allowed, but the pope made it quite clear that he wanted them out of office. In December Fernando Cardenal was expelled by the Jesuit order.

Similar toughness was shown toward the U.S. bishops. The establishment of diplomatic relations between the U.S. and the Vatican was opposed by some conservative Protestants as a breach of separation of church and state, but liberal Catholics objected even more strongly, believing that the administration would henceforth have a greater hold over U.S. Catholics. Many of the latter regretted that, especially in Central America, the policies of the U.S. and the Vatican seemed to be strikingly convergent.

The Democrat's choice of Geraldine Ferraro as the party's vice-presidential candidate reanimated this debate. As a Catholic she was criticized by some bishops because she distinguished between her "personal" views on abortion (she opposed it) and her judgment as a legislator in a pluralist society (she was prepared to tolerate it). New York Gov. Mario Cuomo was implicitly attacked by the new archbishop of New York, John J. O'Connor (see BIOGRAPHIES), on the same grounds. Though this was probably not the intention, the effect was to lend support to the Republican cause. The cautious distinction between religion and politics that had marked John F. Kennedy's campaign was no longer observed. (See Introduction, above.)

A similar display of Catholic muscle could be noticed elsewhere. French Catholics held a series of massive demonstrations against the Mitterrand government's proposals to integrate Catholic schools into the state system, to such good effect that the plan was dropped in September. In Poland the primate, Jozef Cardinal Glemp, though

Friar Leonardo Boff of Brazil, a leading advocate of "liberation theology," was summoned to the Vatican for questioning about his controversial views.

AP/WIDE WORLD

accused by some of excessive submissiveness to the state, defended the right of the church to place crucifixes in public schools and pleaded for the release of political prisoners. The murder of the popular priest Jerzy Popieluszko brought an outpouring of public outrage, but the situation was somewhat defused when, on instructions from top government officials, government agents were arrested and charged with the crime. (*See* WORLD AFFAIRS [Eastern Europe]: *Poland.*)

The most important ecumenical event was Pope John Paul's visit to the WCC in Geneva on June 12. The pope contrasted the Roman Catholic view of unity centred in the papacy with the more federal view of the WCC. "That is our Catholic conscience," he said bluntly, "and fidelity to Christ forbids us to give it up." (See *Introduction,* above.)

In July Pope John Paul began a new series of lectures on the immorality of birth control, shocking some by his contention that "natural" methods could be just as immoral as "artificial" methods. The Vatican defended this position at the UN International Conference on Population at Mexico City in August and was unexpectedly delighted to find that the U.S. supported its opposition to funding pro-abortion programs.

Two deaths made 1984 the end of an era. Karl Rahner (*see* OBITUARIES), probably the most influential Catholic theologian of the last three decades, died on March 30. His last act was to support liberation theologian Gutiérrez. The death of Josyf Cardinal Slipyj (*see* OBITUARIES) at 92 on September 7 meant that the leadership of the Ukrainian Catholic Church passed into the hands of Metropolitan Myroslav Lubachivski of Philadelphia. (*See* WORLD AFFAIRS [Western Europe]: *Vatican City State.*)   (PETER HEBBLETHWAITE)

THE ORTHODOX CHURCH

Signs of external cordiality and unity were numerous in the life of the worldwide Orthodox Church. These included a visit by Archbishop Seraphim of Athens to the patriarch of Serbia in Belgrade, Yugos. (October–November 1983), a visit by Patriarch Pimen of Moscow to Romania (October

1983), and the reception of Metropolitan Dorotheos of Prague at the ecumenical patriarchate in Istanbul (May 1984). This last visit indicated that nonrecognition by the ecumenical patriarch of an autocephalus (independent) church established by Moscow (as is the case for Czechoslovakia) does not prevent cordial and sacramental relations. The future pan-Orthodox "Great Council," still in preparation, would be called on to solve pending administrative problems, but meanwhile the status quo remained peaceful.

Even more significant, in view of the international situation, was the visit of the head of the Orthodox Church in Poland, Metropolitan Basil of Warsaw, to the U.S. as guest of the Orthodox Church in America. A heavy legacy of hostility between Roman Catholics and Orthodox had made it difficult for the sizable Orthodox minority in Poland to participate fully in the movement of religious and national enthusiasm associated with the independent trade union Solidarity. However, the Orthodox did not want to be identified as supporters of the "big brother" to the East and liked to think that they, too—and not just the Roman Catholics—had friends in America.

Official Orthodox unity also manifested itself at the level of ecumenical relations. Meetings of the Orthodox-Anglican Consultation (Odessa, U.S.S.R., Sept. 13–19, 1983, and Dublin, August 1984) and the Orthodox-Roman Catholic Dialogue (Crete, May 30–June 8, 1984) took place as scheduled, although the latter disappointed some observers by failing to produce an agreed statement.

Behind appearances of official normality, several signs indicated that the struggle for survival of Orthodox communities in Eastern Europe had become more difficult. In Yugoslavia the Kosovo region was the scene of violent clashes between a growing Albanian Muslim population and Christian Serbs. The purported passivity of the government provoked protests by the Orthodox hierarchy.

In the Soviet Union an interesting debate was taking place in the official press about the forthcoming millennium of Christianity in Rus (1988). Marxist ideologists proposed to ignore the date because of its obvious religious significance, but others favoured recognizing it as a "cultural" and "national" event. The Orthodox Patriarchate of Moscow was preparing celebrations, with the obvious hope of attracting public attention to the country's Christian history. Meanwhile, it actively participated in government-sponsored peace propaganda. Especially in remote areas, however, antireligious repression was quite active. Three Orthodox priests were known to have received prison terms for distributing religious literature, and an active bishop, Nikon of Perm, was retired without explanation.   (JOHN MEYENDORFF)

EASTERN NON-CHALCEDONIAN CHURCHES

This group of ancient Eastern Churches—the Armenian, Coptic (or Egyptian-Christian), Ethiopian, Syrian Jacobite, and Catholicosate of the East (Malabar, India)—were dominated by concerns connected with the Middle East situation. At

the end of the year the Egyptian government announced that Patriarch Shenuda III of the Copts would be released from confinement in time to conduct a Christmas service early in January. He had been banished to the monastery of Amba-Bishoi by Pres. Anwar as-Sadat, for fear of communal clashes between Muslims and Christians. During the year he had received visitors from western religious groups, including a team sent by the NCC, and had been given the opportunity to exercise some of his administrative duties.

The Syrian Jacobite patriarch paid a visit to Pope John Paul II. During the visit an announcement was made concerning some possibilities for sacramental sharing by the faithful of the two churches.

(JOHN MEYENDORFF)

JUDAISM

The future of Judaism and the Jewish people has always been a preoccupation among Jewish thinkers from the time of Abraham, who worried about the future because he had no heir, to the present day. Especially among American Jews, concern about the future arises, in particular, because of the low Jewish birthrate and the high rate of marriage between Jews and unconverted gentiles. A number of substantial efforts to address these questions came to the fore in 1983–84. A conference on Jewish Population Growth, held in New York in November 1983, debated how to encourage Jews to have, and raise, more children. Robert Gordis, a theologian, exhorted Jewish community institutions "to place the population problem at the head of their priority lists."

Efforts to encourage young Jews to choose Jewish mates, including Jewish dating services, programs for singles in synagogues, and youth organizations, also attracted attention. A still more important initiative derived from outreach to the children of intermarried couples. In this regard, the Reform movement had taken an important step by declaring the child of a Jewish parent, whether mother or father, to be Jewish. Prior to this decision, status as a Jew descended only from the mother. The decision, thus far, had found acceptance only within the Reform movement.

A more broadly shared consensus involved the importance of efforts to win new believers to Judaism, whether or not marriage was an issue. Once again the Reform movement took the lead, but the Reform and more traditional wings of Judaism found it difficult to work together. In Denver, Colo., a joint six-year effort by Orthodox, Reform, Conservative, and Reconstructionist rabbis to instruct potential converts collapsed in 1983. The Reform and Reconstructionist movements continued to favour conversion, which was seen as a way of dealing with the problem of assimilation, but Conservative and Orthodox rabbis viewed the process with skepticism.

Three perennial issues resurfaced. One was an ongoing debate on the importance of the destruction of European Jewry in World War II (the Holocaust) for the formation of Judaism today. Rabbi Gustav Buchdahl, speaking at a Holocaust memorial service on April 9, 1984, stated, "We have been in the shadow of death for forty years. . . . It is high time that we were brought back from that . . . guilt-ridden insanity." Buchdahl urged Jews to learn from the normal and healthy life of the Jews who were murdered rather than placing emphasis solely on their tragic deaths.

A second issue was the character of Jewish leadership. Arthur A. Cohen, distinguished theologian and novelist, stated, "To know what is Jewish, Jewish leaders must be more than born Jews and wealthy." He pointed out that the Jewish moral agenda will not be exhausted even when the State of Israel is secure: "Unless there is a trying of the Jewish conscience within the Jewish community, Jews will become not only a trying people but a boring one."

A third issue addressed the relationship between Jews of the Diaspora and those of the State of Israel. Israelis saw American Jews as more secure and influential than American Jews saw themselves. Polls conducted in the U.S. and in the State of Israel revealed that Israelis were less concerned about anti-Semitism than American Jews, and American Jews were less worried about their own assimilation than Israelis. Israelis regarded American Jews as living in "exile," but American Jews did not take that view.

Despite the diverse sources of tension and conflict, there was a discernible trend toward renewed encounter between Orthodox Judaism and the non-Orthodox world. Jack Nusan Porter, writing in the Boston *Jewish Advocate* (June 16, 1983), claimed that a dialogue had begun. Interviewing Orthodox Jewish leaders in Boston, as well as philanthropic community leaders, he found that the Jewish community was more willing than in the past to help finance Orthodox institutions. The Orthodox for their part were less estranged from the community at large than had been the case for a generation. Porter observed, "There is no monolithic Orthodox Jewish voice. Orthodox Jews want to be involved in the community as individuals."

(JACOB NEUSNER)

BUDDHISM

In the spring of 1984, Buddhists, both Tibetan Buddhists and others, commemorated the 25th anniversary of the Dalai Lama's flight from Tibet, an event that in one sense foreshadowed the current struggle of Buddhist communities in some other Asian countries. China's takeover of Tibet, which had enjoyed relative autonomy for centuries under a form of Buddhist theocracy, produced a tragic diaspora of many of the Dalai Lama's followers. The Beijing (Peking) regime's claim to success in modernizing Tibet was countered by Tibetans who accused the Chinese of destroying Buddhist institutions on a massive scale, violating human rights, and "eliminating" one million Buddhist political prisoners. Equally heartbreaking was the situation in Indochina, where continued hostilities between Vietnam and Kampuchea had all but destroyed the historic legacy of Buddhism.

In China the regime recognized a degree of religious freedom and even allowed party cadres to assist at such cultural rites as weddings and funerals in order "to identify with the masses." In Japan Buddhist-based new religions continued to compete with older Buddhist schools in cultural and peace activities, although the older schools still dominated Buddhist scholarship.

The most sacred shrine of the Sikh religion, the Golden Temple at Amritsar, India, was the site of a fierce battle between Indian government troops and Sikh militants. The incident helped fuel widespread anger among Sikhs and may have set in motion the assassination of Prime Minister Indira Gandhi by two Sikhs in October.
AP/WIDE WORLD

Meanwhile, Buddhism fared well in the West. Scholarly conferences on the 13th-century Zen master Dogen and on "Paradigm Shifts in Buddhism and Christianity" were held in Los Angeles and Hawaii, respectively, and a conference on Christian and Buddhist meditation was held in Boulder, Colo. Buddhists were engaged in such ambitious translation projects as the Nyingma edition of the Tibetan Canon and the Chinese Tripitaka. It was discovered in 1983 that the interior of a small Kamakura statue of the Bodhisattva Jizo (Kshitigarbha) in the Museum of East Asian Art at Cologne, West Germany, contained over 6,000 votive slips from adherents, including highly influential political leaders, as well as several Chinese and Sanskrit manuscripts, a priceless Lotus scripture printed in Southern Sung China, and two Buddha figures.

The 14th general conference of the World Fellowship of Buddhists, which was to have been held in Jakarta, Indon., in the winter, was shifted to Sri Lanka and postponed to the summer of 1984. Shoson Miyamoto, founding president of the Japanese Association of Indian and Buddhist Studies, and the Venerable Jinarthana, secretary-general of the Maha Bodhi Society in India, died late in 1983.

(JOSEPH M. KITAGAWA)

HINDUISM

For Hinduism the year's events were dominated by the bitter strife between Sikh militants and the Indian government, culminating in the Indian Army's June 6 attack on the most sacred shrine of Sikhism, the Golden Temple in Amritsar, and the assassination of Indian Prime Minister Indira Gandhi on October 31 by two of her Sikh bodyguards. The death of the prime minister was followed by days of fierce Hindu-Sikh riots in which some 1,000 Sikhs were killed. (*See* WORLD AFFAIRS [South Asia]: *India*.) Although political issues were prominent, the strife had a religious basis. Since its founding in the 15th century, Sikhism has always had a problematical relationship with Hinduism. Hindus and Indian politicians have generally regarded Sikhism as a sect of Hinduism, while a zealous group of Sikhs, the Akalis, have sought to purge Sikhism of any elements of Hindu ritual and belief and have resisted further absorption. The actions of the central government were seen by Sikh militants as an attempt by Hindus to subjugate Sikhism totally.

Tensions between Hindus and Muslims in India exploded into some of the worst communal riots since independence. Riots in Bhiwandi and Bombay in May and June left more than 300 people dead. The conflict was initiated by a speech by the head of a Hindu organization (the Shiv Sena) attacking Islam and Indian Muslims. Although less bloody (15 dead), riots in Hyderabad in July underscored further the uneasy relationship between the majority Hindu and minority Muslim communities. A continuing irritant was the conversion of Harijans (Hindu outcastes) to Islam, occasioned in part by the desire of Harijans to escape Hindu caste discrimination. In 1984 conversions of whole Harijan villages took place, especially throughout southern India. In a report to the prime minister in January, a militant Hindu group, the International Aryan League, again blamed oil-rich Islamic countries for instigating these conversions by offering money. In an effort to counteract such conversions and retain India's identity as a Hindu country, a national campaign was launched in September by a group comprising a dozen Hindu organizations, including the Shiv Sena. Legal bans at the central government level on conversions, the use of foreign funds for missionary activities by non-Hindus, and cow slaughter were among its stated objectives.

Two important archaeological finds in India were reported. In the jungles of Madhya Pradesh hundreds of exquisite stone images dating from the 4th to the 11th century AD were found at the site of an as yet unexcavated temple dedicated to the goddess Hinglaj. In Himachal Pradesh nine more settlements were discovered belonging to the Harappan culture, which predated the Vedic period and is believed to have influenced the development of popular sectarian Hinduism.

Outside India, the International Association for Krishna Consciousness (Hare Krishna) reported great increases in membership and activities in France. Followers of Bhagwan Shree Rajneesh reported significant gains in West Germany and the U.S. In Oregon the Rajneesh Humanity Trust announced in August that the organization's three-year-old town of Rajneeshpuram was providing refuge to homeless persons from the U.S. and abroad.

(H. PATRICK SULLIVAN)

ISLAM

Violence affected much of the Muslim world in 1984. In Lebanon the terrorist group identifying itself as the Islamic Jihad ("Holy War") claimed responsibility for acts ranging from the assassination of the president of the American University in Beirut in January to the suicide bombing of the U.S. embassy in East Beirut in September. Little was known about this group except that it expressed anti-U.S. sentiments. Allegations were made that it represented Shi'ah extremists, encouraged by Iran. (*See* WORLD AFFAIRS [Middle East and North Africa]: *Middle Eastern Affairs:* Sidebar.)

The civil war in Lebanon continued, as did the war between Iran and Iraq. Muslims were directly involved in bloody riots in Bombay, India, in May. A fragile peace continued in Assam, scene of serious troubles the year before. In Lahore, Pakistan, riots between differing Islamic groups erupted in May at the principal mosque. Nigeria suffered hundreds of deaths when activists, identified as Muslim fundamentalists, attacked in Yola in late February and early March. Alleged fundamentalist attacks were also suppressed in other Muslim lands, including Malaysia.

The fourth meeting of the Islamic Conference Organization, representing all Muslim countries except Egypt, Afghanistan, and Iran, was held in Casablanca, Morocco, in January. Its agenda centred on political af-

fairs, especially the Arab-Israeli situation. Egyptian membership had been suspended because of the Camp David agreements with Israel, but Egypt was invited to return after negotiations and did so in April. Within Egypt, tensions between Muslims and the Christian Copts eased. Egyptian university students appeared much less subject to fundamentalist agitation than in earlier years. A lengthy trial was held of alleged Muslim extremists accused of attempting to overthrow the government.

In Pakistan attempts were made to suppress the Ahmadiyah sect, a group formed in the 19th century and considered heterodox. Efforts at implementing Muslim religious law continued with the announcement in June that, beginning in 1985, interest would not be paid on bank accounts. In Sudan Pres. Gaafar Nimeiry (*see* BIOGRAPHIES) also continued the implementation of Islamic law, but resistance was strong in the south and a state of emergency was declared in April. Turkey continued to move toward a more conservative social stance—for example, regarding proper women's dress—as interest in Islamic practices increased.

In China more Islamic activities were allowed by the government, and official photographs were distributed showing many worshipers in mosques. Islam continued to spread in the U.S., where a centre was developed in New Mexico. It was estimated that some 70,000 foreign students in the U.S. were Muslims, and a study indicated that, despite differences in attitudes among them, they sought to develop their own personal understandings and Islamic interests. (*See* Special Report.)

(REUBEN W. SMITH)

WORLD CHURCH MEMBERSHIP

Reckoning religious adherence is a precarious exercise. Where minorities are persecuted, dissimulation and deception become survival tactics. Different religions and even different Christian churches vary in their theories and methods of counting and reporting. Some simply depend on government population statistics. For others, "numbering the people" is forbidden.

Some count only adult males and heads of families; some count all adults; others count adults, children, servants, and retainers. Some count contributors; others estimate communicants or constituents.

Different procedures are followed even within the same religion. Quite reliable statistics are available on the mission fields and for renewal movements in Islam, Buddhism, Hinduism, and Christianity. Where a religion has been established for centuries (*e.g.*, Christianity in Europe, Hinduism in India), whole national populations may be counted as adherents, a practice that has become highly problematical with the decline of religious observance and the rise of antireligious ideologies. Although Albania is the only officially atheist state, the 20th century has produced a number of governments hostile to all traditional religions. It is difficult to get satisfactory estimates for the populations they control.

The traditional listing of religions, used by scholars since the comparative study of religions became an academic discipline, makes no provision for several religions or faiths now numerous and/or influential; *e.g.*, Baha'i, Ch'ondokyo, Umbanda, the Unification Church, the religions of the Sikhs and Jains (usually—and erroneously—subsumed under "Hinduism"). Taoism and Confucianism are now so blended in many areas that it is becoming common practice to refer to "Chinese folk-religion." Finally, each year brings reports of major movements of populations, reflected, for example, in the striking increase of Eastern religions in the religious statistics of western and northern Europe.

The reader is advised to reflect carefully upon the statistics reported and to refer to articles discussing the different countries and religions when pursuing the subject in depth.   (FRANKLIN H. LITTELL)

This article updates the *Macropædia* articles The Buddha and BUDDHISM; CHRISTIANITY; EASTERN ORTHODOXY; HINDUISM; Muhammad and the Religion of ISLAM; JUDAISM; PROTESTANTISM; The Study and Classification of RELIGIONS; ROMAN CATHOLICISM; and *Micropædia* entries on the various denominations.

Estimated Membership of the Principal Religions of the World

Religions	North America[1]	South America	Europe[2]	Asia[3]	Africa	Oceania[4]	World
Total Christian	260,924,600	197,642,000	334,467,100	103,740,700	147,400,400	18,781,100	1,062,955,900
Roman Catholic	142,433,400	186,660,800	178,000,400	57,300,100	57,950,100	5,230,600	627,575,400
Eastern Orthodox	5,650,600	351,200	45,100,000	2,340,000	8,800,200[5]	390,100	62,632,100
Protestant[6]	112,840,600	10,630,000	111,366,700	44,100,600	80,650,100[7]	13,160,400	372,748,400
Jewish	7,610,700	738,600	4,110,200	4,290,700	229,400	73,900	17,053,500
Muslim[8]	1,580,900	405,100	20,200,600	378,100,100	153,220,400	87,000	553,594,100
Zoroastrian	2,700	2,600	14,000	228,200	1,100	1,000	249,600
Shinto[9]	45,000	—	—	32,000,000	—	—	32,045,000
Taoist	32,000	13,000	13,500	20,000,000	800	2,900	20,062,200
Confucian	99,000	58,000	440,000	157,500,000	2,000	18,000	158,117,000
Buddhist[10]	330,000	240,000	240,000	248,770,100	15,000	23,700	249,618,800
Hindu[11]	310,000	635,000	440,000	458,600,000	850,000	325,000	461,160,000
Totals	270,934,900	199,734,300	359,925,400	1,403,229,800	301,719,100	19,312,600	2,554,856,100
Population[12]	395,365,000	262,963,000	766,325,000	2,777,385,000	536,589,000	24,458,000	4,763,085,000

[1] Includes Central America and the West Indies.

[2] Includes the U.S.S.R. and other countries with established Marxist ideology where continuing religious adherence is difficult to estimate.

[3] Includes areas in which persons have traditionally enrolled in several religions, as well as China with a Marxist establishment.

[4] Includes Australia and New Zealand as well as islands of the South Pacific.

[5] Includes Coptic Christians, of restricted status in Egypt and precariously situated under the Marxist junta in Ethiopia.

[6] Protestant statistics vary widely in style of reckoning affiliation. See accompanying article on "World Church Membership."

[7] Includes a great proliferation of new churches, sects, and cults among African Christians.

[8] The chief base of Islam is still ethnic, although missionary work is now carried on in Europe and America. In countries where Islam is established, minority religions are frequently persecuted and accurate statistics are rare.

[9] A Japanese ethnic religion, Shinto declined rapidly after the Japanese emperor surrendered his claim to divinity (1947); a revival of cultic emphasis in recent years has had chiefly literary significance. Shinto does not survive well outside Japan.

[10] Buddhism has produced several renewal movements in the last century that have gained adherents in Europe and America. Although persecuted in Tibet and sometimes elsewhere in Asia, it has shown greater staying power than other religions of the East. It also transplants better.

[11] Hinduism's strength in India has been enhanced by its connection with the national movement, a phenomenon also observable in the world of Islam. Modern Hinduism has developed several renewal movements that have won some adherents in areas outside traditional Hindu territory.

[12] United Nations, Department of International Economic and Social Affairs; data refer to midyear 1984.

(FRANKLIN H. LITTELL)

Muslims Next Door

*New neighbours, formerly unnoticed,
now attract attention in the U.S.*

BY MARTIN E. MARTY

Muslims, the world's second largest religious group, are perhaps its most newsworthy. Though lacking a single front-page leader to match Roman Catholicism's pope, they do not lack impact on international affairs. Their religion, Islam, which means "submission" to Allah, fires the war between Iran and Iraq and inspires Afghan tribes that resist the Soviet Union. Islam was at the heart of the Iranian revolution that put the Ayatollah Ruhollah Khomeini in the headlines and kept him there. Muslims want to go their separate way in the Philippines, while India and Pakistan see recurrent flare-ups of strife between Muslims and Hindus. The politics of oil and Islamdom's strategic place between the Soviet bloc and Western nations ensure that the mix of religion and power will keep Muslims in the news.

New Neighbours. Elsewhere in this volume, the number of Muslims around the world is estimated at 553,594,100, with fewer than two million in the United States. Religious statistics are impossible to assemble with accuracy, however. It is often said that one-seventh of the world was Muslim at mid-century and that every fifth human is now somehow a part of the Islamic peoples, so rapid is growth through high birthrates and aggressive missionary work.

While informed Americans are aware of Islam far away, they are only beginning to recognize the Muslims next door. Most representatives of Islamic groups insist that there are at least two million and some claim up to five million Muslims in the United States. To provide a sense of scale, this means that there are more Muslims in the U.S. than there are Greek Orthodox or (largely northern) American Baptists or Disciples of Christ. Muslims are approaching the Episcopalians in numbers and by many reckonings are half as numerous as the Jewish population. Yet they have gone largely unnoticed.

The newsworthiness of the controversial Minister Louis Farrakhan (*see* BIOGRAPHIES), head of the tiny but very visible Nation of Islam, deflected notice from the quieter Muslim next door. Farrakhan, on centre stage for his support of presidential candidate Jesse Jackson and his denunciation of Jews and Israel, claimed the mantle of Elijah Muhammad's Nation of Islam, which numbered between 150,000 and 200,000 at the time of the leader's death in 1975. Elijah's son Warith Muhammad, first imam of the American Muslim Mission, has taken the rest of his father's movement toward orthodoxy and, he hopes, toward a time when Islam will achieve status as the largest American faith after Christianity. Orthodox Muslims reject all claims of the Farrakhan-led Nation of

Islam, but he carries the Muslim name into the headlines.

Discriminating non-Muslim citizens are finding good reasons for understanding Muslims. These include everything from neighbourliness and learning how to deal with professionals, like the many physicians who come from Islamic backgrounds, to enlarging American pluralism and strategic necessity. Many American Muslims admit that opposition to Israel motivates their political activities, while the time-honoured desire to win converts impels them to be heard, from campus to suburb to ghetto.

A Growing Presence. Islam, like Christianity, is divided into sects, beginning with the larger Sunni and the smaller Shi'ah, the latter best known because of Khomeini's adherence to it. In America it is denominationalized; there are a Muslim Mosque, an Islamic centre, and an Islamic Society, each of which claims many local attachments. These and other groups are organized in over 300 cities.

Islam has been present in America since colonial times, "Moors" having been among the early exploration parties. Not until late in the 19th century was this faith institutionalized, however, under the leadership of a onetime U.S. consul in Manila, Mohammed Alexander Russell Webb, who converted in 1888 and by 1893 was representing Islam at the famed World's Parliament of Religions in Chicago. Muslim numbers grew as 20th-century immigrants came from Lebanon, Syria, India, and elsewhere. Soon there were centres in Michigan City, Ind., and Toledo, Ohio. Cedar Rapids, Iowa, had a small

STEVE MILLER/THE NEW YORK TIMES

A Muslim student from Pakistan, seated on a prayer rug in her room at a Pennsylvania college, reads her Qur'an. Some 75,000 Muslims from abroad were studying at U.S. colleges and universities.

Martin E. Marty is Fairfax M. Cone distinguished service professor of history of modern Christianity at the University of Chicago and associate editor of The Christian Century.

Inflammatory statements by Muslim leader Louis Farrakhan (speaking at left) led some to encourage Jesse Jackson to disavow his support during Jackson's bid for the Democratic presidential nomination. Farrakhan led the Nation of Islam, originally founded by Elijah Muhammad. The latter's son Warith Muhammad (above) headed the American Muslim Mission, which adhered to more orthodox Muslim beliefs and practices.

(LEFT) JACQUES CHENET/NEWSWEEK; (RIGHT) BRENT JONES

mosque in the 1930s. But few paid attention to these quiet if exotic gatherings of respectable citizens.

The strategic power of Muslim nations in the politics of oil, the brain drain of physicians and other professionals from such nations to the U.S., and the activities of agents of firms and governments based in Islamdom, together with the presence of Muslim students at American universities, began to force non-Muslims to take note of these orthodox followers of the Qur'an, the revelation of Allah through the Prophet Muhammad. Washington, for diplomatic and religious reasons alike, has taken note. The major Islamic Center was completed in that city in 1956. The nation's capital also has been the scene of Black Muslim eruptions. In 1984 Islam made news there when the Smithsonian Institution began to entertain plans for an Islamic art and cultural centre on the Mall. Congress stepped back from its support of this at least partly religious element in a $75 million museum of Near Eastern, Asian, and African art currently under construction, partly because of uncertainty about whether to accept a $5 million Saudi Arabian gift. There was also concern about potential demands by other faiths to be represented, along with nervousness about security.

Learning to Get Along. Something of the veil shrouding the Muslim presence was drawn back by the press in 1984, notably in Colin Campbell's article "Moslem Students in U.S. Rediscovering Islam" in the May 13 *New York Times.* Campbell tracked the 75,000 foreign Muslim students in the United States and found them to be increasingly self-conscious. Some adopted the "fundamentalist" outlook that Americans associated with Khomeini and militant Islamic parties everywhere. Most spoke up for the dismantling of Israel. Almost all were "staggered," according to Harvard professor Lisa Anderson, by the freedom enjoyed in the United States, but many were puzzled over the government's support of overseas regimes that they regarded as authoritarian. Because Islamic students from various countries tended to make common cause, Hartford Seminary professor Yvonne L. Haddad claimed, "The United States is the womb where Islamic consciousness is being created."

Ibrahim Saddiq of the Islamic Society of North America in Plainfield, Ind., argues that these Muslim students— and the many other followers of Islam who live in America—do want to be "interactive" with American society. They do not seek the theocratic style—in which Allah rules—that Islam normally favours but that would in any case be denied in the United States. They sound very traditionally American in their support of family ties and personal moral integrity. In their local communities an imam normally leads them in prayer and worship, and there also may be an emir who administers these loosely related outcroppings of Islam.

Christian America takes note of these neighbours who follow the practices of their faith. They are growing accustomed to the sight of people at ritual prayer five times a day. Airlines provide menus that conform to Islamic law, and large firms recognize Muslim holidays, just as many prisons have done where Black Muslims have been a motivating force.

The Christian leadership takes more and more note, usually in a tolerant if still nervous way, for it is hard to eradicate totally the habits inherited from 1,400 years of conflict with this third "people of the book," who share elements of the Bible and memories with Jews and Christians. A widely syndicated article in the Christian press by Harold Vogelaar, a Protestant missionary teacher in Cairo, gave advice. "Be accepting of your partner as a Muslim. Treat a Muslim with respect. Grant the sincerity of that faith. . . . Be aware of the stereotypes: backward, sensual, rich, war-like, untrustworthy, dirty. Name them off to yourself and then bury them. . . . Avoid an argument. . . . Ask honest questions. . . . Expect to be challenged."

All such attitudes seem in place, given the urgent need to understand Islam internationally. Headlines necessarily stress conflict—to the point where it may be hard to realize that behind all the news of warfare there is a fully orbed religion that meets many human needs. The Muslims next door, in white and black communities alike, are making their presence felt. Vogelaar's advice seems sound: "Expect to be challenged."

Social Security and Welfare Services

An event of great significance in the field of social security was the publication in 1984 by the International Labour Organization (ILO) of a report entitled *Into the Twenty-first Century: The Development of Social Security*. The report was the result of two years' work by a group of ten independent experts commissioned by the director general of the ILO to examine arguments concerning the current role of social security in industrialized countries and the scope for its future development. The group was chaired by Pierre Laroque (France) and had as its reporter Brian Abel-Smith (U.K.).

As the report stressed, social security was currently under attack from opposite camps. On the one hand, it was accused of aggravating the economic crisis by reducing savings, undermining the incentive to work, and so on; on the other, it was blamed for failing to solve the problem of poverty, for discriminating against women, and for not treating equally those with similar needs. The report found that the first accusation was unjustified. Regarding the shortcomings of social security, a number of important recommendations were made. A long-term aim should be to ensure that the minimum benefits paid to those not at work would provide a level of living amounting to at least half the average net disposable income per capita, with appropriate adjustments for families of different composition. There should be a national minimum wage of at least this amount, and it was also recommended that by the year 2000 a national minimum income should be guaranteed for all residents, whether or not they had previously been in employment, subject to a means test.

While making these proposals concerning a minimum income, the report stressed that this should be an addition to and not a substitute for existing social security programs. The idea of replacing universal systems by selective means-tested schemes was emphatically rejected, since this would lead to poor services for poor people and to the polarization of society into those with good company benefits and those provided for under stigmatized means-tested programs.

Questions concerning women figured prominently in the report, which stated that it is a denial of a basic human right to treat women less (or more) favourably than men solely by reason of their sex. Thus unequal pension ages for men and women should be abandoned, discrimination in coverage and benefits under occupational pension schemes abolished, and dependents' and survivors' benefits made the same for both sexes. Unemployment or disability benefits payable to a man or to a single woman should not be denied to a married woman, and parental benefits should be payable to either the mother or the father.

Presumably inspired by recent U.S. legislation, the report criticized compulsory retirement, which it regarded as justifiable only if the employer could prove that a worker was no longer able to do any work that could be offered. The report recommended that employees and the self-employed should have the right to reduce their weekly working time and receive a partial pension during the transition to full retirement, as was already the case in Sweden.

On the all-important question of social security financing, the report recognized that the immediate "crisis" had been caused, above all, by low economic growth and heavy unemployment. An underlying assumption of the report was that the future would see substantially higher levels of employment and a resumption of growth, though not at the rates of the 1950s and 1960s. It was argued that the idea of using private plans to replace social security would do nothing to solve the problem of tax resistance, since it made little difference to the worker-taxpayer whether money was withheld by the state or by the employer. Indeed, privatization could make things worse, given the higher administrative costs and full funding requirements of private schemes. As for tax concessions granted to private pension plans, the report recommended that these be strictly limited and eventually abolished.

It remained to be seen whether the Abel-Smith report would achieve a place in the history books alongside the 1942 Beveridge Report, which laid the foundations of the "welfare state," but there were some interesting parallels. Both reports were conceived in difficult times and heralded a brighter future.

National Developments in Social Security. Recent developments did not give much cause for complacency. An important package of cost-cutting measures came into force in West Germany at the beginning of 1984. Taking advantage of the slowdown of inflation, the government introduced a new method of adjusting benefits; pensions were increased in 1984 in line with the rise in wages in 1983 rather than the average of the years 1980–82, as would have been the case under the previous procedure. The eligibility conditions for disability pensions were tightened so as to prevent claims from people (women, in particular) who had not been economically active in at least three out of the last five years. Lower unemployment benefits were introduced for beneficiaries without dependent children, and extended maternity pay was reduced from DM 750 to DM 510 a month. The lump-sum settlement for recipients of a widow's or widower's pension who remarried was reduced from five times to twice the annual pension.

Cuts in The Netherlands in 1984 were substantial and represented the first stage in the government's controversial long-term plans for social security. Maximum unemployment and disability insurance benefits were lowered from 80% of previous earnings to 77.6% in January 1984 and to 75.2% in July. The declared intention of the government was to press ahead with its cost-cutting program, in particular by tightening the conditions for receiving disability benefits and ultimately by treating the disabled in the same way as the unemployed. If the government were to achieve this objective, disabled people would have their benefits progressively reduced to a flat-rate social minimum.

During the year social security figured prominently in public discussion in the U.K., where the government launched a series of reviews of the major benefits. The review teams, which were chaired by ministers, would not publish their findings; rather, they would prepare internal reports for the secretary of state, who would then publish a Green Paper (consultative document). The government's intentions were unclear, but the narrow terms of reference of the reviews and, especially, the exclusion of any proposals that would involve increased expenditure were indicative.

Improvements in social security took place in some parts of the world. Algeria, for instance, started to implement a comprehensive reform at the beginning of 1984 which unified the benefits, administration, and financing of all the separate schemes that had previously provided for different categories of workers. As a result, employees and self-employed persons, including those working in agriculture, were now covered by the same legislation. Apart from the improved benefits going to certain categories of workers as a result of standardization, the reform increased

Few major social-welfare programs in the U.S. avoided major budget cuts by the Reagan administration. One of them was the Head Start program for early childhood education. Acclaimed by educators, Head Start was in its 19th year. Here youngsters in the program enjoy an annual party in New York City's Central Park.

WILLIAM SAURO/THE NEW YORK TIMES

the pension accumulation rate to 2.5% of earnings for each year of service; previously the rate had been 1.3% for wage earners and 2% plus child supplements for civil servants. The maximum net pension might not exceed 80% of net earnings, except when retirement was deferred beyond the normal pension age (60 for men, 55 for women). Disability pensions, previously payable to workers whose earning capacity was reduced by at least two-thirds, were now available to those whose earning capacity was reduced by half.

Greece introduced a new unemployment benefit plan in response to the rising level of unemployment. The scheme was aimed particularly at school-leavers who, if they remained on the unemployment register for more than 12 months, would qualify, for the first time, to receive benefits for up to six months. For workers who had already been in employment, the plan provided a three-month extension of benefits and a reduction in the duration of employment required to qualify. On the other hand, refusal of a job offered by the employment office would now lead to two years' disqualification from benefits.

An interesting change in the way social security was administered took place in Hungary. For more than 30 years the system had been the responsibility of the trade unions, and in the 1950s it constituted their major function. From July 1984 this responsibility was passed to an autonomous body nominated by the government and including representatives of unions, employers, cooperatives, and other interests. Benefit provisions remained unchanged, but as the economic reform in Hungary gathered momentum, it seemed likely that social policy would play a more important role than in the past.   (ROGER A. BEATTIE)

Social Security was a leading issue in the 1984 U.S. election, as the presidential candidates vied with one another in pledging not to tamper with the system. In the first televised presidential debate and in his speeches, Democrat Walter F. Mondale tried to portray Pres. Ronald Reagan as an insensitive budget-cutter who had a "secret plan" to trim Social Security benefits and who wanted to cut or had cut other social programs. Although the president and his aides had talked of changes earlier in the year, Reagan promised in the debate that he would never reduce

Social Security benefits for "the people that are now getting them." After additional prodding by Democrats, the president broadened the pledge to include future retirees. The president's claim that his budget cuts had not hurt the poor was disputed by two nonpartisan reports. The Congressional Research Service found that cuts in cash welfare payments included in the administration's 1981 program had pushed more than half a million people into poverty, and a Congressional Budget Office study showed that families with incomes below $10,000 a year lost $23 billion in after-tax income and benefits over three years.

Congress ended a three-year dispute over Social Security disability payments by enacting legislation that would make it more difficult to cut off benefits. The conflict stemmed from a 1980 congressional mandate requiring a nationwide review of the disability rolls. Between March 1981 and April 1984 some 1.2 million cases were reviewed, and 491,300 people—about 19% of the workers in the $17.5 billion program—were ruled ineligible for benefits because they were no longer considered severely disabled. About half of that group had their benefits reinstated upon appeal, and after "horror stories" began to appear in the media, the three-year crackdown was suspended in April 1984. The new legislation provided, among other things, that once a person was placed on the disability rolls, the Social Security Administration, in most cases, would have to prove that the beneficiary's medical condition had improved before it could cut off benefits.

In an effort to halt soaring increases in Medicare costs, Congress set limits on the fees physicians could charge elderly persons covered by the program. Under the new guidelines, incentives would be offered to encourage doctors to accept "assignment" of Medicare claims—meaning that they would charge only the amount that Medicare concluded was "reasonable" for a particular service. In addition, the fees that all doctors could charge Medicare patients were frozen at the second quarter 1984 level until Sept. 30, 1985. The possibility of even sharper cutbacks in Medicare became a campaign issue. Officials had estimated that the program would need nearly $200 billion in added revenues to survive through 1995.

As a result of 1975 legislation tying Social Security payments to the inflation rate, benefits in 1985 would automatically increase 3.5% for the 37 million Social Security recipients and 4 million aged, blind, and disabled persons receiving Supplemental Security Income. The rise in Social Security would provide $15 a month more (to $449) for the average retired worker living alone and $26 more (to $776 a month) for the average elderly couple. To pay for the increases, the wage base for Social Security payroll taxes would go up in 1985 from $37,800 to $39,600. The tax rate already had been scheduled to rise from 6.7 to 7.05%, so the maximum payroll tax for an individual in 1985 would be $2,791.80, compared with $2,532.60 in 1984. The tax rate for self-employed persons would rise from 11.3 to 11.8%.

Congress extended for two years the Head Start program, which provides educational, health, nutrition, and other social services to disadvantaged preschool children. Head Start was one of the few major antipoverty programs that had not been cut back sharply by the Reagan administration. In other congressional action, $20 million a year in fiscal 1985–86 was authorized for block grants to help states set up child-care programs in school facilities and support efforts to disseminate information about the availability of care for children, the elderly, and the handicapped. Child care became a major national issue in 1984 following reports that children had been sexually abused in day-care centres in California and New York. Congress also authorized $2,140,000,000 in fiscal 1985 and $2,280,-000,000 in fiscal 1986 for low-income energy assistance. The allocation formula was revised to base state allocations on total energy expenditures by low-income households, including both heating and cooling costs. However, no state would receive less in 1985 than in 1984, and states were protected against sharp reductions in fiscal 1986. A federal grant program for family planning and adolescent family-life projects to aid pregnant teenagers was reauthorized for one year. No change was made in the policy that permitted, but did not require, federally funded family planning services to notify parents of teenagers seeking contraceptives. The Reagan administration had sought to require notification.

A Census Bureau survey found that 66 million people in some 36 million households—nearly 30% of the U.S. population—received cash or noncash benefits during the third quarter of 1983. By far the largest program was Social Security, many of whose recipients also benefited from other programs. About 42 million Americans, or one out of every six, received benefits under federal programs based on need (such as food stamps, welfare, Medicaid, subsidized housing). These means-based benefits went to some 13% of white households, 42% of black households, and 33% of Spanish-origin households. (DAVID M. MAZIE)

See also Education; Health and Disease; Industrial Review: *Insurance.*

This article updates the *Macropædia* article SOCIAL WELFARE.

Space Exploration

The continuing success of the space shuttle and U.S. Pres. Ronald Reagan's endorsement of a manned space station brought new hope in 1984 to the U.S. National Aeronautics and Space Administration (NASA). In the autumn Italy announced that it would establish a national space agency to operate all Italian space activities and represent the country in international space programs. On May 9, 1984, the European Space Agency (ESA) celebrated 20 years of

First Buck Rogers did it in comic strips of the 1930s. Now U.S. astronauts do it (as Bruce McCandless at top). "It" is maneuvering in space with jet-powered backpacks. Ray guns? Not yet. But remember where—and when—you saw the maneuvering first.

(TOP) AP/WIDE WORLD. (BOTTOM) FROM "THE COLLECTED WORKS OF BUCK ROGERS IN THE 25TH CENTURY", COURTESY, CHELSEA HOUSE PUBLISHING, NEW YORK

cooperation in space at the European Space Research and Technology Centre in The Netherlands. Later, in June, experimenters from ESA and NASA met in Italy to discuss results from scientific experiments; the group also discussed ESA participation in future NASA space stations. Generally, it was concluded that ESA would need at least a year and a half to define its role in a cooperative venture in a space station.

Progress toward the commercialization of space took place in 1984 when 3M Corp. submitted to NASA a multimillion-dollar plan for the use of the space shuttle in developing its new products. It called for as many as 72 missions through 1995. NASA also began discussions with the Chrysler Corp., Ford Motor Co., and General Motors Corp. to determine whether those companies would be interested in placing experiments aboard the space shuttle. NASA established policy concerning two requirements when "a significant government contribution" is requested by private industry for cooperative agreements: "First, the private sector must have significant capital at risk, and second, there must be significant potential benefits for the nation." Clearly reflecting the political and economic philosophy of the Reagan administration, the agency added, "If the private sector is willing to make the necessary investment, the project's success should be determined by the marketplace and creativity of the entrepreneur rather than the government's opinion of its viability."

Manned Flight. As 1983 ended, activity by both the U.S. and U.S.S.R. increased, in the former case aboard the space shuttle and in the latter aboard the Salyut space station. Despite President Reagan's endorsement during the year of a manned space station for the U.S., the Office of Management and Budget and the congressional Office of Technology Assessment opposed the plan. In addition, several prominent scientists were less than enthusiastic about the space station, preferring unmanned space probes instead.

On Feb. 8, 1984, a new crew for Salyut 7 was launched from the Soviet space centre at Tyuratam, Kazakh S.S.R., on Soyuz T-10. The cosmonauts included Leonid Kizim, Vladimir Solovyev, and Oleg Atkov. Docking with the Salyut took place on February 9. The new crew quickly settled in and began a series of scientific experiments that included metal plating by means of a special vaporizer, biomedical studies in weightlessness, and photographic and visual observations of the Earth.

On April 3 a new crew was launched from Tyuratam in Soyuz T-11. It consisted of Yury Malyshev and Gennady Strekalov, both Soviet cosmonauts, and Rakesh Sharma from India. The new members assisted in the ongoing experiments. Sharma was involved with an Indian-developed device for measuring the movement and output of the heart in a specified time, and he also performed yoga exercises to see if they could assist in offsetting the effects of weightlessness on the human body. Malyshev, Strekalov, and Sharma returned to the Earth on April 11 in Soyuz T-10.

On July 17 Vladimir Dzhanibekov, Igor Volk, and Svetlana Savitskaya, the first woman to walk in space, were launched to Salyut 7 in Soyuz T-12. They joined in the ongoing experiments and then returned to the Earth on July 29.

Kizim, Solovyev, and Atkov returned to the Earth in Soyuz T-11 on October 2 after spending a record 237 days in space. In addition to their experiments aboard Salyut, the crew spent more than 19 hours performing five extravehicular space walks to maintain and repair the space station.

The U.S. space shuttle orbiter "Challenger" was launched from the Kennedy Space Center at Cape Canaveral, Fla., on February 3. Its primary mission was to place two communications satellites into orbit and to evaluate the manned maneuvering unit (MMU). The crew consisted of Vance Brand, Ronald McNair, Bruce McCandless II, Robert Stewart, and Robert Gibson. Stewart and McCandless successfully checked out the MMU's, which were to be used on the succeeding mission.

Attempts to launch the Westar 6 and Palapa B-2 satellites at first appeared successful because they left the "Challenger's" cargo bay as planned. However, the solid-propellant orbital transfer motors on both satellites failed. Thus neither reached its desired orbit. Plans were made by NASA and insurance underwriters almost immediately to retrieve the satellites and return them to the Earth on a subsequent mission. The "Challenger" returned to the Earth on February 11 at the Kennedy Space Center.

On April 6 "Challenger" lifted off from Kennedy with the mission of retrieving and repairing the Solar Maximum Mission (Solar Max) satellite. Its crew was made up of Robert Crippen, Richard Scobee, Terry Hart, George Nelson, and James van Hoften. Despite some difficulties, the repair was made, and the solar satellite was returned to orbit. The crew also launched the Long Duration Exposure Facility, which carried 57 experiments and was to remain in orbit for ten months before being brought back to the Earth in a subsequent shuttle mission. The "Challenger"

returned to the Earth on April 13, landing at Edwards Air Force Base in California.

The "Discovery" shuttle orbiter was launched for the first time from the Kennedy Space Center on August 30 after a two-month delay caused by malfunctions. Aboard were astronauts Henry Hartsfield, Jr., Michael Coats, Steven Hawley, Richard Mullane, Charles Walker (a civilian employee of McDonnell Douglas Corp.), and Judith Resnik. Its mission was to place Satellite Business Systems, Telstar, and Leasat communications satellites into orbit. All three were launched without incident. A 31-m (102-ft) solar-power array was also tested and worked well. However, an unusual occurrence marred the mission, although it was not a serious threat to the crew. Wastewater that was dumped overboard froze into an icicle about 45 cm (18 in) long. It was removed by astronaut Hartsfield using the "Discovery's" remote manipulator arm. The "Discovery" landed at Edwards Air Force Base on September 5, as planned.

"Challenger" returned to space on October 5 after being launched from the Kennedy Space Center. Its crew, the largest launched to date in the space shuttle, consisted of five men and, for the first time, two women. They were Robert Crippen, Jon McBride, David Leestma, Paul Scully-Power, Sally Ride (making her second flight), and Kathryn Sullivan, who became the first U.S. woman to make a space walk. Also included was the first Canadian astronaut, Marc Garneau (*see* BIOGRAPHIES). The mission of the flight was to deploy the Earth Radiation Budget

AP/WIDE WORLD

First woman to walk in space was Soviet cosmonaut Svetlana Savitskaya, shown here emerging from her Soyuz space capsule upon landing on Earth July 29. She also was the first woman to make two trips into space.

Satellite to study the exchange of energy between the Earth and Sun. Other activities included operation by Garneau of a Canadian experiment package. "Challenger" returned to the Earth on October 13, landing at the Kennedy Space Center.

"Discovery" was launched from Kennedy on November 8 with a crew consisting of Frederick Hauck, David Walker, Dale Gardner, Joseph Allen, and Anna Fisher. After deploying two communications satellites, the crew maneuvered "Discovery" to about 10 m (35 ft) from the Palapa B-2 satellite that had gone into a useless orbit after being launched from "Challenger" in February. Allen and Gardner then went into space and, with the aid of "Discovery's" mechanical arm, brought the satellite back to the orbiter and stowed it in the cargo bay. Later they repeated the procedure with Westar 6, which also had misfired after being launched from "Challenger." "Discovery" landed at the Kennedy Space Center on November 16. The two retrieved satellites were to be repaired and sold for relaunching.

Launch Vehicles. As 1984 began, expendable, commercially marketed space launch vehicles for unmanned satellites continued to be developed. Space Services, Inc., continued work on its Conestoga II solid-propellant launch vehicles for small payloads. Starstruck, Inc., launched its first prototype Dolphin on August 3 over the Pacific Ocean. It was a partial success. Transpace Carriers, Inc., received the right to market and launch the Delta vehicle manufactured by McDonnell Douglas. Several large firms planned to market their long-proved and used launch vehicles. Martin Marietta Corp. encouraged the use of its Titan for launch of U.S. Air Force satellites, as did General Dynamics Corp. with its Atlas Centaur. Both companies would be in competition with the space shuttle and ESA's Ariane.

On August 4 Ariane III made its first voyage into space from the launch site at Kourou, French Guiana. In establishing itself as a potent competitor to the space shuttle, the French-developed launch vehicle put into orbit the ECS 2 and Telecom 1A satellites. As 1984 continued, the French space agency, Centre National d'Études Spatiales, further developed its studies of the Ariane 5P. This vehicle would have two large solid-propellant strap-on boosters, as did the U.S. Titan 34D.

China also announced its entry into the marketplace as a launcher of unmanned satellites. On September 21, with the signing of a formal technology exchange agreement with the U.S., China announced its intention of entering into competition with U.S. and ESA—and, presumably, with Soviet—launch services. Its new launch vehicle was to be capable of placing 400 kg (900 lb) into geostationary orbit (an orbit in which a satellite remains over the same location on the Earth at all times).

In the Soviet Union development continued on two new expendable space boosters. The larger of the two was expected to have an orbital capability of 150,000 kg (330,-000 lb) and the other could place in orbit about 5,000 kg (33,000 lb).

Japan also continued planning for its heavy-lift space launch vehicle. The H-2 was designed to have an orbital capability of 1,500 kg (3,300 lb). The vehicle would meet Japan's needs in the 1990s.

Unmanned Satellites. During 1983 and 1984 scientists involved in the Infrared Astronomical Satellite, launched in January 1983, released some of the data gathered by the spacecraft. A joint project of the U.S., U.K., and The Netherlands, the satellite revealed what might be a planetary system around the star Vega. It also detected vast new dust clouds that could help explain the formation of the Solar System and discovered five new comets near the Earth.

On January 24 ESA sent commands to GEOS 2 to boost it out of its geostationary orbit, thereby making room for another satellite in an already crowded orbit. Plans were made to do the same thing to its OTS 2 satellite. GEOS 2 was reactivated for an additional year at the request of West Germany and Switzerland.

In the Soviet Union scientists revealed some of the data obtained by its Astron satellite, which was in a highly eccentric orbit. The satellite made observations in the infrared and ultraviolet (UV) ranges of the spectrum. One of the scientists on the project said, "A number of qualitative new data have been obtained; in particular, an excess of UV radiation which is possibly connected with an increase in the activity of galaxies."

In midyear Brazil announced that it would begin launching its own satellites in the 1990s. Brazilian technicians were being trained by a Canadian aerospace company. The first two satellites were to be environmental sensors and would be launched in 1989 and 1990. Components of the satellites were scheduled to be test-flown aboard the space shuttle in 1987 with a Brazilian astronaut aboard.

In August Intelsat marked its 20th year of successful service. Over the years the organization had created a global communications satellite network that provided service to 170 nations. Comsat, the U.S. prototype of the organization, was established in 1962 under the Communications Satellite Act.

AGIP/PICTORIAL PARADE

An Ariane launch vehicle of the European Space Agency (ESA) lifts off March 4 from the ESA base at Kourou, French Guiana, to place in orbit a new telecommunications satellite in the Intelsat 5 series.

Major Satellites and Space Probes Launched Oct. 1, 1983–Sept. 30, 1984

Name/country/ launch vehicle/ scientific designation	Launch date, lifetime*	Physical characteristics				Experiments	Orbital elements			
		Weight in kg†	Shape	Diameter in m†	Length or height in m†		Perigee in km†	Apogee in km†	Period (min)	Inclination to Equator (degrees)
Meteor 2 (10)/U.S.S.R./ A I/1983-109A	10/28/83	2,750 (6,063)	cylinder with two panels	1.5 (4.92)	5 (16.4)	Weather satellite	780 (485)	901 (560)	101.0	81.2
Molniya 1 (59)/U.S.S.R./ A IIe/1983-114A	11/23/83	1,800 (3,968)	cylinder with cone and six solar panels	1.6 (5.25)	5 (16.4)	Communications satellite	465 (289)	39,150 (24,327)	702.0	62.8
STS 9 ("Columbia")/U.S./ Space Shuttle/1983-116A	11/28/83 12/8/83	2,035,976 (4,488,559)	delta with two solid boosters and external tank	24 (78.7)	37 (121.4)	Conduct experiments aboard Spacelab	242 (150)	254 (158)	89.5	57.0
Molniya 3 (22)/U.S.S.R./ A IIe/1983-123A	12/21/83	2,000 (4,409)	cylinder with cone and six solar panels	1.6 (5.25)	4.2 (13.78)	Communications satellite	736 (457)	40,635 (25,249)	736.0	62.8
China 14/China/CZ III/ 1984-008A	1/29/84	‡	‡	‡	‡	Probable test of new propulsion system	461 (286)	6,586 (4,092)	163.4	36.1
STS 41-B ("Challenger")/U.S./ Space Shuttle/1984-011A	2/3/84 2/11/84	2,036,592 (4,489,917)	delta with two solid boosters and external tank	24 (78.7)	37 (121.4)	Launched two communications satellites that failed to reach desired orbits	277 (172)	286 (178)	90.1	28.5
Soyuz T-10/U.S.S.R./A II/ 1984-014A	2/8/84 4/11/84	7,000 (15,432)	sphere and cone with two solar panels	2.2 (7.22)	7.5 (24.61)	Ferried crew to Salyut 7 space station	226 (140)	274 (170)	84.9	51.6
Ohzora/Japan/N II/ 1984-015A	2/14/84	180 (397)	cube with four solar panels	‡	‡	Middle atmospheric measurements	354 (220)	865 (537)	96.9	74.6
Raduga 14/U.S.S.R./D Ie/ 1984-016A	2/15/84	2,000 (4,409)	cylinder with two solar panels	2 (6.6)	5 (16.4)	Communications satellite	‡	‡	1,440.0	1.3
Landsat 5/U.S./Delta/ 1984-021A	3/1/84	2,087 (4,601)	cube with one solar panel	2 (6.6)	6 (19.7)	Earth resources satellite	683 (424)	698 (434)	98.6	98.3
Uosat 2/U.K./Delta/ 1984-021B	3/1/84	50 (110)	cube	0.3 (0.98)	0.8 (2.62)	Scientific satellite	683 (424)	696 (432)	98.5	98.6
Ekran 12/U.S.S.R./D Ie/ 1984-028A	3/16/84	2,000 (4,409)	cylinder with two solar panels	2 (6.6)	5 (16.4)	Television broadcast satellite	‡	‡	‡	‡
Molniya 1 (60)/U.S.S.R./ A IIe/1984-029A	3/16/84	1,800 (3,968)	cylinder with cone and six solar panels	1.6 (5.25)	5 (16.4)	Communications satellite	646 (401)	40,579 (25,215)	717.9	62.9
Soyuz T-11/U.S.S.R./A II/ 1984-032A	4/3/84 10/2/84	7,000 (15,432)	sphere and cone with two solar panels	2.2 (7.22)	7.5 (24.61)	Ferried crew to Salyut 7 space station	200 (124)	240 (149)	88.6	1.3
STS 41-C ("Challenger")/U.S./ Space Shuttle/1984-034A	4/6/84 4/13/84	2,040,000 (4,497,430)	delta with two solid boosters and external tank	24 (78.7)	37 (121.4)	Retrieval and repair of Solar Maximum Satellite; launching of Long Duration Exposure Facility satellite	473 (294)	483 (300)	94.2	28.5
LDEF 1/U.S./Space Shuttle/1984-034B	4/7/84	9,700 (21,385)	twelve-sided open-grid structure	4.27 (14.01)	9.14 (29.99)	Scientific experiments; to be retrieved from orbit after ten months in space	473 (294)	483 (300)	94.2	28.5
China 15/China/CZ III/ 1984-035A	4/8/84	900 (1,984)	‡	‡	‡	Communications satellite	35,735 (22,205)	35,835 (22,267)	1,436.1	0.9
Spacenet 1/U.S./Ariane I/ 1984-049A	5/22/84	1,195 (2,635)	cube with two solar panels	‡	‡	Communications satellite	‡	‡	1,440.0	‡
Navstar/U.S./Atlas F/ 1984-059A	6/13/84	771 (1,700)	polygon with two solar panels	5.33 (17.49)	‡	Navigation satellite	20,017 (12,438)	20,345 (12,642)	718.0	62.5
Meteor 2 (11)/U.S.S.R./ A I/1984-072A	7/5/84	2,750 (6,063)	cylinder with two solar panels	1.5 (4.92)	5 (16.4)	Weather satellite	954 (593)	974 (605)	104.0	81.5
Soyuz T-12/U.S.S.R./A II/ 1984-073A	7/17/84 7/29/84	7,000 (15,432)	sphere and cone with two solar panels	2.2 (7.22)	7.5 (24.61)	Ferried crew to Salyut 7 space station	203 (126)	248 (154)	88.8	51.6
GMS 3/Japan/N II/ 1984-080A	8/2/84	‡	cylinder	‡	‡	Weather satellite	‡	‡	1,440.0	‡
ECS 2/ESA/Ariane III/ 1984-081A	8/4/84	1,175 (2,590)	cube with two solar panels	2.2 (7.22)	2.4 (7.87)	Communications satellite	‡	‡	1,440.0	‡
Telecom 1A/France/ Ariane III/1984-081B	8/4/84	1,185 (2,612)	octagon with two solar panels	2.18 (7.15)	3.01 (9.88)	Communications satellite	‡	‡	1,440.0	‡
Molniya 1/U.S.S.R./ A IIe/1984-089A	8/24/84	1,800 (3,968)	cylinder with cone and six solar panels	1.6 (5.25)	5 (16.4)	Communications satellite	467 (290)	40,877 (25,400)	737.0	62.8
STS 41-D ("Discovery")/U.S./ Space Shuttle/1984-093A	8/30/84 9/5/84	2,041,748 (4,501,284)	delta with two solid boosters and external tank	24 (78.7)	37 (121.4)	Place three satellites in orbit and test solar array	298 (185)	301 (187)	90.5	28.5
SBS 4/U.S./Space Shuttle/ 1984-093B	8/30/84	580 (1,279)	cylinder	2 (6.6)	6 (19.7)	Business communications satellite	‡	‡	‡	‡
Leasat/U.S./Space Shuttle/ 1984-093C	8/31/84	7,940 (17,505)	cylinder	4.26 (13.98)	6 (19.7)	Communications satellite	‡	‡	‡	‡
Telstar 3C/U.S./Space Shuttle/ 1984-093D	9/1/84	‡	cylinder	‡	‡	Communications satellite	‡	‡	‡	‡
China 16/China/‡/ 1984-098A	9/12/84 9/29/84	‡	‡	‡	‡	‡	174 (108)	389 (242)	90.2	67.9

* All dates are in universal time (UT).   † English units in parentheses: weight in pounds, dimensions in feet, apogee and perigee in statute miles.   ‡ Not available.

(MITCHELL R. SHARPE)

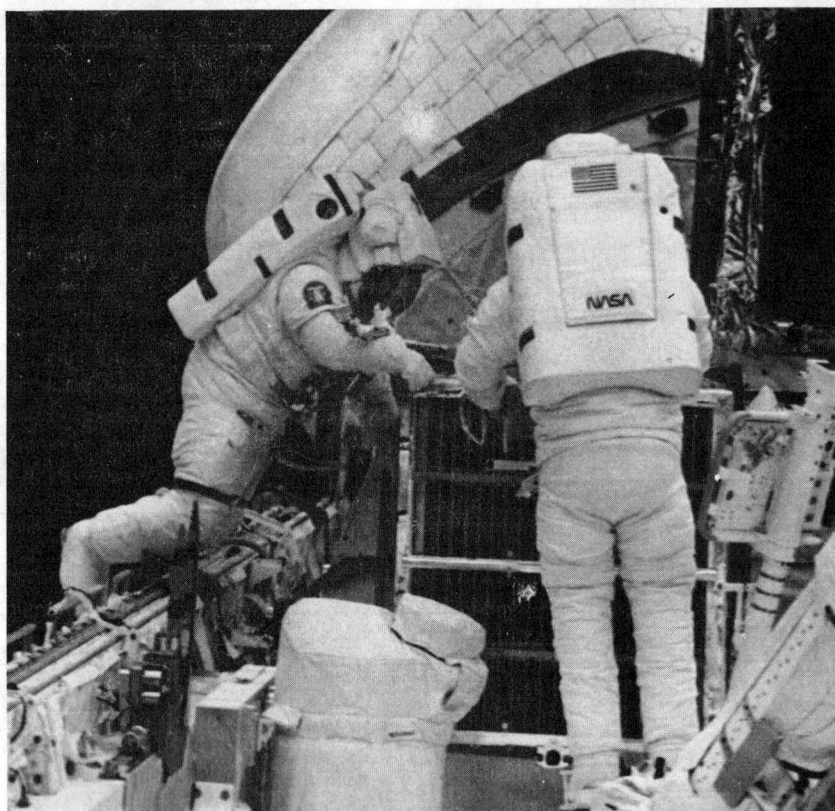

Astronauts on the space shuttle "Challenger's" April flight dubbed themselves the Ace Satellite Repair Co., in token of their mission: to retrieve, repair, and reinsert in orbit the malfunctioning satellite Solar Max. Despite repeated problems they succeeded. Here George Nelson (left) and James van Hoften work to remove the satellite's ailing main electronic box.
AP/WIDE WORLD

Probes. NASA's fiscal 1985 budget request included funding for a Mars probe to be launched in August 1990. The orbiter would provide data on the climate and surface chemistry of the planet. Using information from the Viking mission, scientists believed that they could determine when water produced the planet's deep canyons, where it went, and perhaps whether it could have sustained some form of life on Mars.

NASA also made plans to reorient the Pioneer probe that was in orbit about Venus so that it could view Halley's Comet in early 1986. It would be a major observation by the U.S. because it would be able to study the comet when it was at perihelion (closest to the Sun). The probe, launched in 1978, would employ its ultraviolet spectrometer to study the gases and dust emanating from the comet. The observation was expected to last between six and eight weeks in February and March 1986. In mid-April the Pioneer made a practice maneuver to observe Comet Encke.

In January the Soviet Union revealed several details of how modifications were made to the basic Venera Venus probes to adapt the Venera 15 and 16 for radar mapping of the planet. Changes included larger propellant tanks, a large area of solar cells, and a larger diameter for the pencil-beam antenna's reflector. A special airtight compartment was provided for the side-looking radar and other instruments.

In February scientists at the NASA Ames Research Center in California presented new evidence for gigantic, active volcanoes on Venus. Data were presented to support the hypothesis that major eruptions, many times greater than any on the Earth during the past 100 years, occur every five to ten years. Other data on lightning in the planet's dense clouds also suggested the presence of volcanic activity, especially in the regions of Beta Regio and Atla Regio, both recent volcanic sites.

During the same month, NASA announced that the Galileo probe that was to enter the atmosphere of Jupiter was complete and in final testing before its launch in May 1986 for a landing in August 1988. In addition to the atmospheric probe, an orbiter would circle Jupiter for an estimated 20 months, taking as many as 50,000 high-resolution pictures. Construction of the Giotto probe of Halley's Comet continued in Europe during the year. It was anticipated that the finished spacecraft would be delivered to ESA in February 1985. Launch aboard the Ariane was scheduled between July 7 and 15, 1985, with an anticipated encounter on the night of March 13–14, 1986.

ESA had to delay its International Solar Polar Mission probe because of changes in the U.S. space shuttle program. The launch date was now expected to be in May 1986. U.S. participation in the international project was limited to providing the space shuttle as a launch vehicle and tracking facility. On June 13 the U.S. probe Pioneer 10 marked its first year in interplanetary space. The probe left the Solar System after having been launched in 1972. It overcame potential destructive obstacles when it passed through the asteroid belt on its way to outer space.

(MITCHELL R. SHARPE)

See also Astronomy; Earth Sciences; Industrial Review: *Aerospace; Telecommunications;* Military Affairs; Television and Radio.

This article updates the *Macropædia* article EXPLORATION: *Space Exploration.*

Sports and Games

AERIAL SPORTS

Joe Kittinger, a 56-year-old retired U.S. Air Force colonel, became the Charles Lindbergh of ballooning in 1984 with the first solo flight across the Atlantic, traveling a distance of 5,690 km (3,535 mi) from Caribou, Maine, to the

Italian Riviera in just under 84 hours. His feat eclipsed the transatlantic distance record of 5,001 km (3,107 mi) set by Ben Abruzzo, Larry Newman, and Maxie Anderson in their first manned balloon crossing of the Atlantic in 1978, though those three retained the transatlantic duration record of 137 hours, 5 minutes, and 50 seconds.

Kittinger, a former combat pilot who was decorated for gallantry in Vietnam and spent a year as a prisoner of war, made the crossing in a ten-story helium-filled balloon named "Rosie O'Grady's," taking off from Maine in the early hours of September 14 and landing in trees near the Italian Mediterranean shore on the afternoon of September 18. He broke an ankle falling ten feet from the balloon's open fibreglass gondola. Of six balloonists who previously had attempted to make solo crossings of the Atlantic, all failed and two died.

In other balloon achievements John Petrehn of the U.S. flew his Barnes Firefly in January 1984 from Huron, S.D., to Middletown, Ill., to set a world distance record for subclass AX-7 hot-air balloons of 851.3 km (529.02 mi) and a duration record of 24 hours, 11 minutes, and 54 seconds. On June 19 Josef Starkbaum of Austria set a subclass AX-7 altitude record of 12,375 m (40,600 ft).

In the 17th World Parachuting Championships for Style and Accuracy, held August 27–September 9 at Vichy, France, Sergey Skovropat of the U.S.S.R. led a strong Soviet team by taking first place in men's individual accuracy with a score of three centimetres (the measure of landing distance from a target disk measuring five centimetres in diameter). Dirk Boidin of Belgium lost a tiebreaker to finish second with a three-centimetre score, and Silvio Di Tecco of Italy was third with four centimetres.

In men's individual style Nikolay Ushmaev of the U.S.S.R. placed first with a score of 28.84 sec; Gerd Harzbecker of East Germany was second with 29.04; and

Ronald Eilenstein of East Germany was third with 29.45. The men's overall individual competition was won by Eilenstein with a score of 7 points, while Jean Dermine of France finished second with 12 and Viacheslav Valunas of the U.S.S.R. was third with 14. Men's team accuracy results were: U.S.S.R. first, 32 cm; Yugoslavia second, 35 cm; Austria third, 36 cm. The U.S.S.R. won the men's team overall with 3 points, the U.S. placing second with 10 and East Germany third with 20.

In the women's individual accuracy competition Yu Mei of China finished first with a score of five centimetres. Elena Subocheva of the U.S.S.R. followed with seven centimetres, while third was taken by He Xiaohong of China with eight centimetres. Barbara Harzbecker of East Germany won the women's individual style competition with 30.28 sec. Helen Bennett of the U.S. was second with 30.38 sec, and Elena Burkova of the U.S.S.R. finished third with 30.73 sec. Harzbecker also triumphed in the women's individual overall competition with 7 points. Cheryl Stearns of the U.S. was second with 10, and Li Rongrong of China placed third with 15.

Women's team accuracy was won by the U.S.S.R. with 33 cm, second going to China with 41 cm and third to East Germany with 42 cm. In women's team overall competition the U.S.S.R. was again first, with 4 points. East Germany was second with 8 and China third with 11.

The world record for largest free-fall formation, 72 jumpers, was nearly beaten on April 21 at De Land, Fla., when a U.S. team managed to assemble a formation of 90 skydivers for 2.7 seconds. Though the feat was photographed for verification, it failed to achieve the three-second duration required for world records in that category. On June 22 over Muskogee, Okla., a U.S. team set an eight-canopy speed formation record of 51.67 sec.

Though there was no championship international soaring competition during the year, a number of the world's best sailplane pilots gathered to compete at the Flying M Ranch in Nevada in late July. Frederico Blatter of Switzerland won the open class prize; Hans Peter Ublacker of Austria took the 15-m contest; and Erwin Sommer of West Germany triumphed in the standard class. Also of West Germany, Ingo Andresen took the sports class, and Walter Binder was the winning pilot in the double-seater contest.

On July 25 Sommer, with Andresen as passenger, claimed a new world record of 162 km/h (100.68 mph) for multiplace glider speed around a 100-km (60-mi) triangular course. The next day the same team flew the same distance at 177.2 km/h (110.1 mph).

The U.S. (Schweizer) 1-26 championships, a sentimental favourite among glider pilots, were held at Hobbs, N.M., July 5–14. The winner was Harry Baldwin with 4,653 points, followed by David Mockler with 4,542 and Charles Shaw with 4,442.

The Fédération Aéronautique Internationale, world governing body for sport aviation, confirmed the Dec. 20, 1983, world record glider claim of West Germany's Hans Werner Grosse for a speed of 159.6 km/h (99.2 mph) over a 500-km (300-mi) course in an ASW 22 at Alice Springs, Australia. Also confirmed was West German pilot Erwin Muller's and passenger Karl Senne's Dec. 16, 1983, record claim for a multiplace glider out-and-return distance of 1,052.7 km (654.1 mi), set in a Janus C at Bonsprings, Australia.

A world record speed of 35.7 km/h (22.2 mph) for man-powered airplanes over a triangular course of 1,500 m (0.9 mi) was set by Holger Rochelt of West Germany at Neubiberg, West Germany, on August 8.

(MICHAEL D. KILIAN)

PHILIPPE LEDRU—SYGMA

Woodcutters carried Joe Kittinger, a retired U.S. Air Force colonel, to a rescue helicopter when he broke an ankle crash-landing his balloon near Savona, Italy—after making the first solo transatlantic balloon flight in September.

ARCHERY

Darrell Pace of Hamilton, Ohio, won the men's gold medal and Seo Hyang Soon of South Korea the women's championship in the Olympic Games, the most important archery competition of 1984. In the world field archery championships, the winners were Gert Bjerendal of Sweden in men's freestyle (sights on the bow), Lisa Buscombe of Canada in women's freestyle, Lars Welen of Sweden in men's bare bow (no sights on the bow), and Giuseppina Meini of Italy in women's bare bow.

The Olympic competition took place August 8–11 in Long Beach, Calif., with a record entry of 109 archers from 35 nations. Each competitor shot two rounds of 144 arrows per round. A men's round consisted of 36 shots each from 30, 50, 70, and 90 m; a women's round was 36 shots each from 30, 50, 60, and 70 m.

While the boycott of Soviet-bloc nations kept away a strong group of Soviet women, the men's competition was not significantly affected. The favourites were the 27-year-old Pace and 30-year-old Rick McKinney of Glendale, Ariz., rivals for a decade. Pace scored 2,616 points, breaking the Olympic record of 2,571 that he had set in 1976 while winning the gold medal. He defeated McKinney by 52 points, a huge margin. McKinney won the silver medal by one point over Hiroshi Yamamoto of Japan by putting his last shot into the centre 10 ring.

In the women's competition, Seo, barely 17 years old and a national team member only four months, upset Li Lingjuan of China 2,568 to 2,559. Kim Jin Ho of South Korea, the world champion, took the bronze medal with 2,555. Had Li scored a bulls-eye on one target instead of missing it completely, she would have won the gold medal.

The world field championships, in which there was competition in both freestyle and barebow, were held August 20–25 in Hyvinkää, Fin. Each archer shot 28 targets a day for two days, with four arrows per target. The distances varied from 10 to 80 m. The closest struggle was in men's freestyle, where Bjerendal and McKinney tied for first at 963. Bjerendal won the title on the tie-breaking rule because he hit more field-round targets than McKinney, 111 to 110.

Pace won the United States Olympic trials June 4–9 and the U.S. men's championship July 17–20, both in Oxford, Ohio. Ruth Rowe of McLean, Va., was the women's winner in both competitions.   (FRANK LITSKY)

AUTOMOBILE RACING

Grand Prix Racing. The rules governing international Formula One motor racing remained unchanged during 1984, but at last the turbocharged 1½-litre racing engines, developing upward of 600 hp, became supreme, and the day of the older 3-litre Ford-Cosworth V-8 power unit, nonturbocharged, was clearly over. Races were run as before on a fuel-limit basis, but cars tended to run without stopping to refuel, so that very quick stops at the replenishment pits became less of a factor.

The drivers' world championship remained open until the last Grand Prix at the Estoril Autodrome in Portugal, when Niki Lauda (Austria), in second place, gained enough points to win for the McLaren team, using Porsche-TAG V-6 engines. During the season Ken Tyrrell was banned for infringement of the rules of Formula One racing, and by early in the year the McLarens had proved superior and had clinched the manufacturers' world championship.

The season opened in Brazil with Alain Prost (France) winning in Rio de Janeiro in a McLaren MP4 from Keke Rosberg (Finland) in a Williams; Elio De Angelis (Italy) finished third in a Lotus 95T. In the South African Grand

Prix at Kyalami, Lauda won for McLaren, with his teammate Prost following him home; third place went to Derek Warwick (U.K.) driving a Renault RE50.

At Zolder in the Belgian Grand Prix, victory went to the Ferrari of Michele Alboreto (Italy), with Warwick's Renault second. René Arnoux of France in a Ferrari placed third. At Imola the San Marino Grand Prix was won by Prost from Arnoux; De Angelis finished third a lap behind in a Lotus-Renault. Lauda was in winning form again in the French Grand Prix at Dijon in May, with Patrick Tambay (France) second for Renault and Nigel Mansell of the U.K. third in a Lotus-Renault.

Heavy rain did its best to ruin the Monaco street race, and there was much comment when it was stopped for that reason before the full distance had been driven. Prost was in the lead, with Ayrton Senna of Brazil closing on him; third place went to Stefan Bellof of West Germany in a Tyrrell; the severe conditions were reflected in a fastest lap of only 104.283 km/h, by Senna (1 km = 0.62 mi).

The scene then moved to Canada, where the race in Montreal was won by Nelson Piquet of Brazil in a Brabham BT 53 (fastest lap 178.858 km/h), with Lauda second and Prost third. The Detroit Grand Prix followed, and Piquet drove in world-champion form to his second straight victory. An impressive performance by Martin Brundle (U.K.) achieved second place for Tyrrell, with De Angelis finishing third. The U.S. Grand Prix then took place for the first time in Dallas, Texas, over a 3.9-km circuit, the slowest in current Grand Prix racing. Rosberg won for the Williams team, with Arnoux second and De Angelis third.

The competition then returned to Europe, where the British Grand Prix over the Brands Hatch course was won by Lauda from Warwick; Senna's Toleman finished third. McLaren supremacy was demonstrated in the German Grand Prix at the Hockenheimring. The McLaren-TAG's of Prost and Lauda came in first and second. Third place was taken by Warwick's Renault. The Austrian Grand Prix had the benefit of the splendid Österreichring for its setting. Lauda won from Piquet, with Alboreto's Ferrari third. The Dutch Grand Prix at Zandvoort was dominated by the McLaren-Porsche cars, Prost winning from Lauda, with Mansell's Lotus-Renault third. The Italian Grand Prix at Monza in September was won by Lauda, with Alboreto's Ferrari second and Riccardo Patrese of Italy third in an Alfa Romeo 184T. No U.S. Grand Prix was held in the east in 1984, and the next contest was at the new Nürburgring circuit as an extra race called the European Grand Prix. There, Prost continued the McLaren supremacy with a victory over Alboreto's Ferrari, while Piquet gained third for Ecclestone's Brabham-BMW team. An intense season closed with a good race in the Portuguese Grand Prix over the new Estoril Autodrome. Lauda started from far behind but worked his way with great skill and coolness into second place at the end of the 298.2-km circuit, losing to his teammate Prost but gaining enough points to become the 1984 world champion. (For table of Formula One winners during the year, see *Sporting Record,* below.)

Rallies and Other Races. Long-distance endurance races were again dominated by Porsche, but there was interest in seeing what difference Jaguar would make—it was little—with its return to this class of racing, particularly at Le Mans, France. A Porsche-March 83G won the Daytona (Fla.) 24-hour race from a Porsche 935 and a Jaguar XJR-5. At Monza the 1,000-km race went to the Ickx/Mass Rothmans-Porsche 956, but the result was marred by disqualifications and bickering. The Silverstone 1,000 km was a victory for the same combination, from two other Porsche 956s. If there was proof needed of Porsche

Niki Lauda of Austria won the Formula One Grand Prix of Italy at Monza in this McLaren-Tag-Porsche on September 9.
AP/WIDE WORLD

superiority in this competition, it came at Le Mans, with Porsche 956s in the first seven places of the famous 24-hour marathon. Both Jaguars retired, one with oil-pump failure and the other in a crash. In the ADAC German 1,000-km race, Porsche 956s finished first and second, and a Lancia-Martini took third place; in the equivalent race at Brands Hatch, England, six Porsches finished ahead of a Lancia-Martini. The world endurance championship of manufacturers was secured by Porsche at Spa, where those cars took the first eight places in the 1,000-km contest, ahead of a Tiga-Ford. The Tourist Trophy Race at Silverstone was a victory for a BMW Csi, from a Jaguar XJS and two more BMW's. The world championship round finished at Fiji, where Porsches finished in the first five places.

In rallying, four-wheel-drive cars were becoming essential to good finishes and, not unexpectedly, the Audi-Quattro won the world rally championship for manufacturers. Ari Vatanen of Finland, driving a Peugeot-built four-wheel-drive, rear-engined 205 Turbo 16, won Finland's 1,000 Lakes Rally and also the Lombard RAC Rally. Audi-Quattro won the Monte Carlo Rally, but Lancia Rallys were in the three places behind the Quattros in Cyprus, with a Renault 5 Turbo fifth. In the Kenya Safari

AP/WIDE WORLD

Rick Mears flashes the victory sign after winning the Indianapolis 500 with a record-setting average speed of 163.612 mph (263.301 km/h).

Rally a Toyota Celica won from an Open Manta 400 and a Quattro. Two Quattros led the Acropolis Rally over two Lancia Rallys, and Audi also won the Scottish and the New Zealand Sanyo rallies. In Cyprus an Audi-Quattro won from an Opel and a Sunbeam-Lotus. Audi's driver, Stig Blomqvist of Sweden, was the 1984 world rally champion driver.   (WILLIAM C. BODDY)

U.S. Racing. Rick Mears won the world's premier automobile race, the Indianapolis 500, with a record-setting average speed of 163.612 mph (263.301 km/h). The race was worth $2,795,399 to the 33 competitors, and Mears, later injured at a Championship Auto Racing Team (CART) race in Canada, won $434,061 of that purse. The winner's Penske Pennzoil Z-7 March Cosworth led 119 of the 200 laps, as only 18 of the 33 drivers finished. The race time of 3 hours 3 minutes 21.66 seconds was 44 seconds faster than that set in 1972 by Mark Donahue. Mears won by two laps over Colombia's Roberto Guerrero (March Cosworth). Al Unser, Sr., finished third, Al Holbert fourth, Michael Andretti fifth, and A. J. Foyt sixth.

Former world champion Mario Andretti was one of the early leaders at Indianapolis, but his Lola broke down. However, he won the CART season crown, including a victory in the inaugural Meadowlands Grand Prix, which, because of its location a few miles from midtown New York City, had the potential to become one of the world's major events. Andretti won a record $913,307 for the season.

The CART competition continued to expand to road courses. Race victories were spread among a number of drivers, with third-place Bobby Rahal and fifth-place Danny Sullivan among the new double victors. Mears placed fourth overall.

In National Association for Stock Car Auto Racing (NASCAR) competition, the ascendancy of the Ford Thunderbirds early in the season caused the General Motors divisions to work overtime to catch up. However, Cale Yarborough drove a Chevrolet to victory in the Daytona 500—richest U.S. stock car race—and also won at the Pocono 500 in Long Pond, Pa. Richard Petty, driving a Pontiac Grand Prix, won the Daytona Firecracker 400 for an incredible 200th major victory, far ahead of anyone else.

The NASCAR championship was not decided until the final race of the season at Riverside, Calif., when Terry Labonte and his Chevrolet finished third to gain the crown.

Chevrolet's Harry Gant placed second, and Bill Elliott in a Thunderbird was third.

The International Motor Sports Association (IMSA), which sanctions the most important road races in the U.S., saw Randy Lanier in his March 83G Chevrolet win the prototype class of the Camel GT Series and a $60,000 bonus. But in the 24 Hours of Daytona, Sarel Van der Merwe of South Africa, driving a March 83G Porsche Turbo, upset the defending Porsche 935 Turbos to gain the victory before the largest crowd ever to see that race. Later in the season the Porsche 962 driven by Al Holbert and Derek Bell of the U.K. reeled off a string of victories, but it was too late to overcome Lanier.

The Sports Car Club of America (SCCA) kept the once redoubtable Can-Am Series for prototypes alive yet another year, and Michael Roe of Ireland in a VDS Chevrolet won six races. The Trans Am series was dominated by Ford as Tom Gloy, Gregg Pickett, and Willy T. Ribbs in Capris were the leaders. Gloy won the title. In SCCA pro rallying, under a new format in 1984, the old antagonists New Zealander Rod Millen in his unique four-wheel-drive Mazda RX-7 and John Buffum in an Audi-Quattro fought for the title. Buffum won. Meanwhile, two contests of racing greats occurred. In the Mazda InterAmerican Challenge, contested in identical RX-7 GSL-SE sports cars and limited to drivers from the Western Hemisphere, Ribbs outdueled Michael Andretti, Emerson Fittipaldi, and Tom Sneva to win first place. The International Race of Champions, contested in specially prepared Chevrolet Camaros, was won by Cale Yarborough of NASCAR.   (ROBERT J. FENDELL)

BADMINTON

The year 1984 was one of change for badminton. Not only did the form of play to determine the world team championships change dramatically, but the titleholders of both the Uber and Thomas cups also changed.

For the first time in the history of the International Badminton Federation, the world team championships for both the women (Uber Cup) and the men (Thomas Cup) took place in the same year and at the same place, Kuala Lumpur, Malaysia. Defending champions were Japan (Uber Cup) and China (Thomas Cup). In Uber Cup competition the once-mighty women from Japan looked like shadows of their former selves. China dominated the tournament entirely, followed by England and South Korea. South Korea lost to China in the semifinals 5–0, and England lost to China in the finals 5–0.

Play for the Thomas Cup saw a strong Indonesian team best the Chinese 3–2. In the first match Luan Jin of China defeated Liem Swie King of Indonesia 7–15, 15–11, 15–10. The second match resulted in a victory for Hastomo Arbi of Indonesia over Han Jian of China by scores of 14–17, 15–6, 15–8. In the third singles match Yang Yang of China triumphed over Icuk Sugiarto of Indonesia 15–9, 15–10. The fourth match was a doubles contest in which Indonesia evened the score when Chritian Hadinata and Hastomo Arbi defeated the Chinese team of He Shangguan and Jian Guoliang 18–13, 15–10. With the score now tied at two apiece and one match left to play, Liem Swie King and Kartono Hariatmanto of Indonesia rose to the occasion and defeated the Chinese pair of Sun Zhian and Tian Bingyi 18–14, 15–12 to gain the Thomas Cup.

(C. R. ELI)

BASEBALL

For the seventh time in as many years, the 1984 major-league baseball season ended with a new world champion. Also, on October 1 Peter V. Ueberroth (*see* BIOGRA-

PHIES) succeeded Bowie Kuhn as commissioner. The sport enjoyed another successful season, although attendance decreased in both leagues, perhaps because division races during the final weeks lacked drama.

World Series. The Detroit Tigers, clearly the best team during the 162-game regular season, also dominated the World Series. They defeated the San Diego Padres, four games to one, to capture their first title since 1968.

In the Series opener at San Diego's Jack Murphy Stadium on October 9, Detroit ace right-hander Jack Morris pitched a complete game, and Larry Herndon clubbed a two-run home run in the fifth inning to propel the American League champions to a 3–2 victory over the Padres. One night later San Diego's veteran utility player Kurt Bevacqua hit a three-run homer to lift the National League champions to a 5–3 conquest over the Tigers.

Having achieved a desirable split of two games at their opponents' stadium, the Tigers then swept the Padres out of the Series with three consecutive victories in Detroit. On October 12 the Tigers prevailed 5–2 after being issued 11 bases on balls by Padres' pitchers, who in so doing tied a Series record. Both teams combined to leave 24 runners on base, also a Series mark. Marty Castillo, Detroit third baseman, hit a two-run homer.

On October 13 Alan Trammell, the outstanding Tiger shortstop, authored a pair of two-run homers as the American League champions won 4–2 behind another complete-game performance by Morris, who yielded just five hits. Then on the gray and dreary late afternoon of October 14, the Tigers defeated the Padres 8–4 to clinch the World Series. Kirk Gibson hit two home runs and batted in five runs, though the winning run was batted in by Rusty Kuntz, who lifted a soft sacrifice pop fly to second baseman Alan Wiggins on which Gibson scored from third.

Trammell, an excellent fielder who had worked on his hitting during the last few years, had 9 hits in 20 at bats for five games and was named most valuable player for

Relief pitcher Willie Hernández (left, with arm in air) and catcher Lance Parrish (right) celebrate after the Detroit Tigers beat the San Diego Padres 8–4 to win the World Series.

In April Pete Rose of the Montreal Expos made his 4,000th career hit, the second player in the history of baseball to reach that number. The all-time record was still held by Ty Cobb with 4,191 career hits.

AP/WIDE WORLD

the Series. Meanwhile, San Diego's starting pitchers had a difficult time. They lasted only 10⅓ innings (of a possible 42) and surrendered 16 earned runs to compile an unenviable 13.94 earned run average. Tiger batters hit a lusty .455 against San Diego starters, though the Padre relievers excelled. Tiger manager Sparky Anderson (*see* BIOGRAPHIES) became the first manager to win World Series in both leagues.

Detroit's title underscored the changing nature of baseball from year to year. Since the New York Yankees repeated as World Series champions in 1978, subsequent winners had been the Pittsburgh Pirates, Philadelphia Phillies, Los Angeles Dodgers, St. Louis Cardinals, and Baltimore Orioles. Moreover, the last three baseball seasons had produced 12 different division champions, the maximum number possible.

Play-offs. The Tigers defeated the Kansas City Royals, champions of the American League West, three games to none to win the pennant. The Tigers used strong pitching by Morris and left-handed reliever Willie Hernández plus three home runs to trounce the Royals 8–1 at Kansas City on October 2. On October 3 Johnny Grubb hit a two-run double in the 11th inning to give the Tigers a 5–3 conquest. On October 5, at Detroit, Milt Wilcox hurled two-hit ball for eight innings, and Hernández then saved a 1–0 victory.

The National League play-off series was more theatrical. The upstart Chicago Cubs smashed five home runs in their own Wrigley Field and humbled the Padres 13–0 on October 2. The next day the Cubs prevailed 4–2 to gain a 2–0 advantage in the best-of-five series. Only one team, the 1982 Milwaukee Brewers, had rebounded from such a deficit to achieve a pennant, but the Padres were not disturbed by the odds, or history.

On October 4, at San Diego, Ed Whitson worked eight strong innings, and the Padres won 7–1. Two days later

Steve Garvey stroked a dramatic two-run homer in the ninth inning to give the Padres a 7–5 decision. Garvey had three other hits and a total of five runs batted in (RBI's).

On October 7 the Cubs jumped to a 3–0 lead and had their best pitcher, Rick Sutcliffe, on the mound. However, the Padres capitalized on Chicago misplays and combined several important hits to complete their comeback with a 6–3 triumph. The pennant was the first for San Diego, an expansion franchise formed in 1968.

Regular Season. The Tigers were a rare wire-to-wire winner in the American League East, considered baseball's most competitive division. They won their first 9 games and soared to a 35–5 record, eventually winning the division by 15 games. Sparky Anderson ascribed the performance to exceptional talent, fine attitude, and the off-season acquisition of Hernández from the Philadelphia Phillies.

The Kansas City Royals were surprise champions of the American League West, where the Chicago White Sox had won by 20 games in 1983. But the Royals played solidly during the second half of the season and won the division by three games over the California Angels and Minnesota Twins.

The San Diego Padres were bolstered by veteran relief pitcher Rich ("Goose") Gossage and, under manager Dick Williams, gained the National League West championship by 12 games over the Atlanta Braves and Houston Astros. The Padres had played better than .500 baseball in only one previous season and had never finished higher than fourth place.

The Cubs, who had been a distant fifth in 1983, won the National League East by 6½ games over the New York Mets. With several timely trades, general manager Dallas Green virtually remade Chicago from a disaster in spring training to the first Cub team to win a championship since 1945. Among the newcomers who contributed were outfielders Gary Matthews and Bob Dernier, formerly in Philadelphia, and Sutcliffe, who was obtained from the Cleveland Indians in mid-June.

In the 51st major league All-Star Game, the National League defeated the American 3–1 at San Francisco on July 10. Pitching was the outstanding feature of the contest, especially in the fourth and fifth innings when Fernando Valenzuela and Dwight Gooden each struck out three American League players in a row to set a new All-Star Game record.

Don Mattingly waited until the final game of the season to edge New York Yankee teammate Dave Winfield for the American League batting title. Mattingly finished at .343.

Final Major League Standings, 1984

AMERICAN LEAGUE East Division					NATIONAL LEAGUE East Division				
Club	W.	L.	Pct.	G.B.	Club	W.	L.	Pct.	G.B.
Detroit	104	58	.642		Chicago	96	65	.596	
Toronto	89	73	.549	15	New York	90	72	.556	6½
New York	87	75	.537	17	St. Louis	84	78	.519	12½
Boston	86	76	.531	18	Philadelphia	81	81	.500	15½
Baltimore	85	77	.525	19	Montreal	78	83	.484	18
Cleveland	75	87	.463	29	Pittsburgh	75	87	.463	21½
Milwaukee	67	94	.416	36½					

West Division					West Division				
Club	W.	L.	Pct.	G.B.	Club	W.	L.	Pct.	G.B.
Kansas City	84	78	.519		San Diego	92	70	.568	
California	81	81	.500	3	Atlanta	80	82	.494	12
Minnesota	81	81	.500	3	Houston	80	82	.494	12
Oakland	77	85	.475	10	Los Angeles	79	83	.488	13
Chicago	74	88	.457	10	Cincinnati	70	92	.432	22
Seattle	74	88	.457	10	San Francisco	66	96	.407	26
Texas	69	92	.429	14½					

Chicago Cubs (left to right) Ron Cey, Rick Sutcliffe, Jody Davis, Ryne Sandberg, and Leon Durham celebrate after the Cubs clinched the National League East title. The Cubs beat the Pittsburgh Pirates 4–1 to win their first championship since 1945.

AP/WIDE WORLD

Tony Armas slugged 43 homers for the Boston Red Sox to lead the league in that department. He also won the RBI title with 123, one more than teammate Jim Rice. Mike Boddicker (20–11) of the Baltimore Orioles was the only American League pitcher to win 20 games. The Kansas City Royal's Dan Quisenberry paced relief pitchers with 44 saves.

Tony Gwynn of San Diego captured the National League batting crown with a .351 average, 30 points better than Pittsburgh's Lee Lacy. Dale Murphy of the Atlanta Braves and Mike Schmidt of the Philadelphia Phillies tied for home run honours with 36, while Schmidt tied Gary Carter of the Montreal Expos for most RBI's, 106. Joaquín Andújar of the St. Louis Cardinals led the league in victories with 20, and teammate Bruce Sutter had 45 saves.

Mike Witt of the California Angels pitched the 12th perfect game in major league history on September 30, when he beat the Texas Rangers 1–0. On April 21 David Palmer of the Montreal Expos pitched five perfect innings against St. Louis, but the game was halted by rain. Morris hurled the only other no-hitter during the 1984 season, defeating the White Sox on April 7.

Postseason honours in the American League were dominated by Willie Hernández, who was voted most valuable player and also winner of the Cy Young award for best pitcher. Sparky Anderson was named manager of the year, and first baseman Alvin Davis of the Seattle Mariners was rookie of the year. In the National League, the Chicago Cubs won three of the four awards. Second baseman Ryne Sandberg was most valuable player, Rick Sutcliffe was the Cy Young winner, and Jim Frey was manager of the year. Nineteen-year-old Dwight Gooden of the New York Mets was voted rookie of the year, the youngest ever.

(ROBERT WILLIAM VERDI)

Latin America. The Licey Tigers from the Dominican Republic were the only 1982–83 Caribbean champions to win a title again in the 1983–84 winter season. In Venezuela the Zulia Eagles gained their first national pennant in 15 years behind the solid pitching of Luis Leal and the batting of Terry Francona. A team from Los Mochis, Sinaloa, the Cane-Cutters, led by third baseman Aurelio Rodríguez, was the surprising winner of Mexico's Pacific League. In Puerto Rico the Mayagüez Indians had to fend off a strong challenge from the Ponce Lions (1981–82 champions) before securing the island's professional baseball title.

Those four league champions met in February in San Juan, P.R., to play the Caribbean Series. The Zulia Eagles emerged victorious, winning their first Caribbean title ever, even though they were defeated by the second-place Los Mochis Cane-Cutters in the final game of the Series. The Licey Tigers and the Mayagüez Indians tied for last place with only one victory each. The result was an obvious disappointment to the heavily favoured Mayagüez team.

Outside of the official winter Caribbean circuit, the Aguila Brewers from Barranquilla won the pennant of Colombia's Professional Baseball League. During the summer, the Yucatán Lions became the champions of the AAA Mexican Baseball League by defeating the Ciudad Juárez Indians (1982 winners) in the final series. In Mexico's National Baseball League the Zacatecas Gophers won the title in a hard-fought championship series against the Unión Laguna Falcons.

(SERGIO SARMIENTO)

Japan. The Hiroshima Toyo Carp of the Central League, down 3–1 in the best-of-seven Japan Series, rallied to defeat the Hankyu Braves of Nishinomiya four games to three. It was their third championship and their first in four years. The victory was the first for a Central League team since the Yomiuri Giants of Tokyo won in 1981. Throughout the Series the Carp pitchers effectively held down the powerful batters of the Braves. Especially outstanding was Kazuo Yamane, who hurled the first three games. Among the Carp batters outfielder Kiyoyuki Nagashima, who was voted the most valuable player, clubbed three homers and batted in ten runs.

In the Central League the Carp won their fourth pennant after a lapse of four years. It was a triumph for pitchers and batters, young members and veterans, and also for manager Takeshi Koba. Although the Carp suffered some injuries during the season, they displayed the consistent power needed to win the championship. During the middle of the season the Carp had a batting slump but, led by outfielder Koji Yamamoto and infielders Sachio Kinugasa and Takehiko Kobayakawa (the most valuable rookie), the team recovered and shook off the challenge by the Chunichi Dragons of Nagoya.

Toshio Shinozuka of the Giants won the Central League batting title with .334. Masaru Uno of the Dragons and Masayuki Kakefu of the Hanshin Tigers of Osaka shared the home run title with 37 each. Kinugasa captured the RBI championship with a record 102. Kazuhiko Endo of the Taiyo Whales of Yokohama pitched the most victories with 17. The most valuable player award was won by Kinugasa, who, along with his RBI record, batted .329 and hit 31 home runs.

In the Pacific League the Braves captured their tenth pennant and their first since 1978. During the first half of the season the leading pitcher and batter of the Braves were both absent because of injury, but the young players of the team kept it in the lead. The Braves clinched the championship by a margin of 8½ games after leading the league from May 19 on. Manager Toshiharu Ueda demonstrated particular skill in his handling of young pitchers. Among the batters worthy of special mention was Greg ("Boomer") Wells of the Braves, who won the batting championship with .355, the home run title with 37, and the RBI championship with 130. He was the first non-Japanese player to win this triple crown. Yutaro Imai of the Braves topped the Pacific League pitchers with a record of 21–9, the second time that he had won that title. The most valuable player award was won by Wells.   (RYUSAKU HASEGAWA)

BASKETBALL

United States. PROFESSIONAL. In a year of transition for the National Basketball Association (NBA), one of its oldest and best traditions wrote a new chapter. The Boston Celtics won their 15th NBA championship in a bitter, bruising seven-game final play-off with the Los Angeles Lakers.

That was a fitting finish to the era of Arnold ("Red") Auerbach, the fiery coach and general manager who taught the Celtics how to win. Auerbach, 67, stepped down after the 1983–84 season, though he retained the title of club president and planned to be a consultant.

The record book is ample proof that Auerbach was a giant in his profession. He coached the Celtics to nine NBA titles between 1956 and 1966. Auerbach had an unbroken string of eight straight championships, a feat unprecedented in major-league sports, when he gave up coaching to concentrate on the general manager's post. In that spot his genius continued to produce championship banners for the Boston Garden rafters. The Celtics added a half-dozen more, including the 1983–84 season's courageous comeback against the Lakers.

When the 1983–84 Celtics had a problem on the court, they put in a hurry-up call for Larry Bird (*see* BIOGRAPHIES), a 6-ft 8-in forward with an incredible blend of talent and desire. In his fifth professional season, Bird be-

Kareem Abdul-Jabbar of the Los Angeles Lakers blocks a shot attempted by Larry Bird of the Boston Celtics. The action occurred in the first quarter of the NBA championship final on June 12.
AP/WIDE WORLD

came the dominant player in the game, driving the Celtics to a title and himself to most valuable player honours.

Bird averaged 27.4 points and 14 rebounds in the final play-off. It was a true championship series, because Boston (62–20) and Los Angeles (54–28) had the NBA's best records during the 82-game season.

Sparked by Earvin ("Magic") Johnson and Kareem Abdul-Jabbar, who had broken Wilt Chamberlain's career scoring record of 31,419 points on April 5, the confident Lakers split the first two games of the final showdown in Boston, then destroyed the Celtics 137–104 in Los Angeles to take the series lead. Bird then proved to be the Celtics' saviour. Telling his teammates they had played "like a bunch of sissies" in game three, Bird lit the fuse that sent the Celtics back home with a 2–2 deadlock in the best-of-seven set. They regained control by intimidating the Lakers and shutting off their fast break.

When the Celtics won the fifth game 121–103 in a Boston Garden steambath of heat and humidity, the die was cast. The Lakers forced it to the limit, then fell 111–102 in the decisive seventh game on June 12, the latest that an NBA season had ever ended.

It was an upbeat finish for a campaign that had started with the NBA referees locked out and temporarily replaced after threatening to strike. The dispute was not settled until Dec. 9, 1983.

In November 1983 Commissioner Lawrence F. O'Brien startled the basketball world by announcing that he would step down after nine years on the job. He turned the reins over to his assistant, David J. Stern, at the all-star game in Denver on January 29. Stern faced an immediate crisis when the San Diego Clippers defied the NBA by moving to Los Angeles, in direct competition with the Lakers. Calling it a "flagrant disregard of NBA procedure," the new commissioner filed a $25 million damage suit, seeking to revoke the Clippers' franchise. Pending a decision by the courts, the Clippers were allowed to play their home games in the Los Angeles Sports Arena.

NBA Final Standings, 1983–84

EASTERN CONFERENCE Atlantic Division			WESTERN CONFERENCE Midwest Division		
Team	Won	Lost	Team	Won	Lost
Boston	62	20	Utah	45	37
Philadelphia	52	30	Dallas	43	39
New York	47	35	Denver	38	44
New Jersey	45	37	Kansas City	38	44
Washington	35	47	San Antonio	37	45
			Houston	29	53

Central Division			Pacific Division		
Team	Won	Lost	Team	Won	Lost
Milwaukee	50	32	Los Angeles	54	28
Detroit	49	33	Portland	48	34
Atlanta	40	42	Seattle	42	40
Cleveland	28	54	Phoenix	41	41
Chicago	27	55	Golden State	37	45
Indiana	26	56	San Diego	30	52

Despite the so-called salary cap taking effect for all 23 teams in 1984–85, payrolls continued to escalate. The first 1984 draft choice, Akeem Olajuwon, gained a six-year contract worth about $7.3 million from the Houston Rockets, and Olympic Games hero Michael Jordan, first pick of the Chicago Bulls, signed a seven-year $6 million deal.

The highest-scoring game in NBA history was played Dec. 13, 1983, in Denver. The Detroit Pistons needed three overtimes to outlast the Denver Nuggets 186–184.

COLLEGE. Georgetown and Patrick Ewing had known the taste of frustration in 1982, but the victory banquet was theirs in 1984. The Hoyas finally made it to the top in college basketball with an 84–75 triumph over the University of Houston. The first National Collegiate Athletic Association (NCAA) tournament championship for the Washington, D.C., school erased the sting of a last-minute loss to North Carolina in the 1982 tourney final.

That was true for 7-ft centre Ewing and his coach and mentor, John Thompson, but doubly so for Fred Brown, the only senior on the Georgetown roster. Brown's careless pass had been the fatal turnover against North Carolina, but there was no repetition of that error in 1984.

The emotion on the Houston side of the Seattle Kingdome was frustration, a familiar one for the Cougars. This was their second straight loss in the NCAA final and the fifth time that coach Guy Lewis had fallen short after taking his team to the final four.

Disappointment was not confined to the coach and fans. Akeem Olajuwon, the All-American 7-ft centre from Nigeria, betrayed his emotion by criticizing teammates after the loss. Olajuwon eventually decided not to make a third try for the elusive NCAA crown, skipping his senior year to become an instantly rich professional rookie.

The pregame ballyhoo about a battle of the titans between Ewing and Olajuwon failed to materialize. Neither man was a decisive factor, with Olajuwon shackled by early foul trouble that limited him to 15 points and 9 rebounds, well under his career averages. Ewing also had subpar totals, ten points and nine rebounds, but the Hoyas used their spread offense and deep bench to take control. Two freshman substitutes, Reggie Williams and Michael Graham, racked up 11 of the winners' 15 second-half field goals, keeping Houston at bay.

The Cougars came within three points of the lead midway through the last half but got no closer. Ewing applied the crusher, working inside for a short-range basket to put Georgetown ahead 68–60 with only five minutes left in the game.

Strong defense was the key to the Hoyas' 34–3 season and national title. They routed Kentucky 53–40 in the semifinal. In the other semifinal Houston barely escaped elimination, edging Virginia 49–47 in overtime.

The curtain came down on the 42-year coaching career of Ray Meyer (see BIOGRAPHIES) at De Paul, leaving him with a brilliant 722–354 record. The last defeat was a heartbreaker, Wake Forest knocking the Blue Demons out with a 73–71 overtime comeback in the NCAA tournament.

Responding to pressure from schools anxious to share the prestige, the NCAA boosted its 1985 tournament field from 53 to 64 teams. That was expected to present still more problems for the National Invitation Tournament (NIT) in the crucial area of luring an attractive field of contestants. The 1984 NIT championship was won easily by Michigan, 83–63, over Notre Dame.

In women's basketball the University of Southern California charged to the NCAA title by defeating Tennessee 72–61. Twins Pam and Paula McGee scored 17 points each for the Women of Troy, while All-American Cheryl

Miller added 16. Behind the 18-point contributions of Mary Ostrowski and Tanya Haave, Tennessee clung to the lead until the closing minutes.

A major change for 1985 was to result in women's teams using a smaller basketball. It would measure 28 to 29½ in (70 to 73.75 cm) in circumference, weigh 18 to 20 oz (0.5 to 0.56 kg), and have narrow ⅛-inch (0.3-cm) seams.

(ROBERT G. LOGAN)

World Amateur. The U.S. regained the Olympic men's basketball title in Los Angeles, defeating Spain 96–65 in the final. Yugoslavia, the reigning champion, had been eliminated 74–61 by Spain in the semifinal and eventually took the bronze medal. Canada placed fourth and Italy fifth, followed by Uruguay, Australia, West Germany, Brazil, China, France, and Egypt.

The absence of the Soviet Union, which had won the European men's Olympic qualification tournament, was clearly felt, and the absence was even more significant in the women's competition; the Soviet team had been undefeated in Olympic, world, and European women's championships for more than 20 years. However, none of the other teams taking part in the Olympics could compete with the U.S. women, who won the gold medal with ease, beating South Korea 85–55 in the final. China defeated Canada 63–57 for the bronze medal. (China had won the women's Olympic qualification tournament, held

ADAM STOLTMAN—DUOMO

Cheryl Miller (No. 9) jumps for the U.S. women's basketball team in its defeat of Yugoslavia in the summer Olympic Games. The tall Miller (6 feet 3 inches), daughter of a former college star, has been called the best women's basketball player in the world.

in Havana, whereas South Korea had finished sixth. South Korea, however, gained a surprise 69–56 win over China in Los Angeles.)

The European men's Olympic qualification tournament, held in France, was dominated by the Soviets, who were undefeated. Their closest match was 104–91 against Great Britain, the surprise team of the tournament. Spain took second place, with France and West Germany narrowly defeating Great Britain to capture the other two places in Los Angeles.

Brazil won the Pan-America tournament, followed by Uruguay and Canada. The African championship, which also provided Olympic qualification, was played in Alexandria, Egypt, and was won by the host country, which beat Angola 94–68 in the final. Senegal finished third. In the Asian championships, held in Hong Kong, China defeated Japan 95–71 to take the title, with South Korea third. In the junior men's world championship final, played in Majorca, Spain, in August 1983, the U.S. triumphed over the Soviet Union 82–78.

The 17th Inter-Continental Cup competition for champion clubs was held in Buenos Aires, Arg., in October 1983 and was won by Obras Santarias, of the host city. Cantu, Italy, placed second, and in third was Penarol of Montevideo, Uruguay.

The 1983–84 European Champions' Cup for men was won by Virtus Roma, which defeated FC Barcelona 79–73 in the final. Madrid won the European Cup-Winners' Cup, beating Olimpia Milan 82–81 in the final. The other men's European cup competition, the Korac Cup, was won by the French club Orthez, which defeated the Yugoslav team Red Star Belgrade in the final for the third successive year. The women's European Champions Cup final was played in Budapest, Hung., between Levski Spartak of Sofia, Bulg., and AS Vincenza, the defending champions, of Italy. The Bulgarian team triumphed 82–77.

The World Congress of the Fédération Internationale de Basketball Amateur (FIBA) was held in Munich, West Germany, in June 1984. The congress approved several modifications to the rules of the game, to come into effect as of the 1984–85 season. The most notable was the introduction of a three-point basket for shots taken from behind a semicircular line marked 6.25 m (20.5 ft) from the basket. At the congress five new member countries were admitted to FIBA for a total membership of 161 nations.

(MELVIN D. WELCH)

BILLIARD GAMES

Billiards. The 39th world three-cushion billiard championship was conducted in Krefeld, West Germany, on April 27–29, 1984. The international 12-man field consisted of defending champion Raymond Ceulemans and Ludo Dielis of Belgium, Nobuaki Kobayashi and Yoshio Yoshihara of Japan, Dieter Müller and Gunter Siebert of West Germany, Adolfo Suárez of Peru, Allen Gilbert and George Ashby of the United States, Rini van Bracht of The Netherlands, Luis Doyharzabal of Argentina, and Egidio Vierat of France. Coming into the tournament, the averages of these national champions ranged from 0.976 for 1961 world champion Suárez to 1.426 for Kobayashi and 1.460 for Ceulemans. In a change of format the usual round-robin play was replaced by three flights of four contestants each, reducing the number of contests from 66 to 26 and the days required from six to three.

In the opening rounds van Bracht quickly defeated Ashby 60–26 in 38 innings. In the meeting between Kobayashi and Vierat the former established his superiority with a 60–24 win in 36 innings. Ceulemans, coming off a major

victory, surprised spectators with a lacklustre but winning performance, defeating Suárez 60–45 in 56 innings. The fourth contestant to move to the semifinals was Dielis, who had wins over Siebert (60–42 in 59 innings) and Yoshihara (60–36 in 30 innings).

In the first match of the semifinals Kobayashi's aggressive attack against Ceulemans brought him victory by 60–42 in 42 innings. The match between Dielis and van Bracht seesawed to an anxious conclusion when the latter surged 25 points to 59, one short of victory. Given a second chance, Dielis came back to win 60–59. In the match for third and fourth place, Ceulemans defeated van Bracht 60–47 in 38 innings, by far his best game in the tournament. In the title match both Kobayashi and Dielis started cautiously and were 46–42 at 28 innings. From that point Dielis's game faltered in the face of his opponent's skillful safeties, and Kobayashi finally triumphed 60–49 with a tournament average of 1.388.

Pocket Billiards. With the lure of cash prizes and all-expense-paid vacations to Italy, the Billiard Congress of America (BCA) found itself host to 900 men and women contestants in Fort Worth, Texas, May 24–28. The attractions were the eighth U.S. national eight-ball championships and the sixth All-American eight-ball team championships.

For the national eight-ball events 112 men and 64 women were entered. Initially, the men were divided into 16 flights; the winners then moved on to double-elimination matches, which produced four finalists: Ralph Cortez of Fort Worth; Charlie Shootman of Colorado Springs, Colo.; Louie Lemke of St. Paul, Minn.; and Ernie Layman of Newfoundland. In the "races to seven" to determine the championship, Cortez edged out Layman in a 7–6 match. Cortez then took on Shootman and had him down 5–2 before the latter, a perennial champion or finalist at BCA events, turned the tables to win 7–6. The contest was now between Lemke, who had not lost a match in three days of play, and Shootman, who had lost to him earlier. In the all-but-picture-perfect test that ensued, only four shots missed their mark in 12 games. Lemke broke first and ran out. Shootman broke and ran out. Lemke broke and ran out. Shootman broke and ran down to the eight-ball but missed it, allowing Lemke to run out and take a 3–1 lead. Shootman then broke and ran out. Lemke broke and scratched, and Shootman ran out. Lemke broke again and ran out. Shootman broke, but no balls dropped, again allowing Lemke to run out and take a 5–3 lead. Shootman broke but scratched, and for the third time Lemke came through, to go ahead 6–3. Shootman broke and ran out to make it 6–4. Lemke broke but missed a rail shot, allowing Shootman to catch up to 6–5. A worried Lemke then broke again, choosing to hit the second ball in the rack in order to increase his chances of dropping a ball. It worked. Carefully clearing the table to the cheers of the spectators, he won the title.

In the women's division of the U.S. national tournament, the winners of eight flights made it to the semifinals. Then, in double-elimination "races to five," Joyce Darling and Ann Smith tied for seventh and eighth place, while Cindi White and Laura Smith took fifth and sixth. The four finalists included former champion Belinda Campos-Beardon from Austin, Texas; Fran Crawford of Anaheim, Calif.; Linda Hoffman of Arlington, Texas; and Janene Hague from Hastings, Minn. Fourth place was decided when Crawford lost to Hague. Hague and Hoffman then played for the right to challenge unbeaten Campos-Beardon for the championship. With the contest tied at four games each, Hague appeared to be a certain winner of the fifth game when she ran down to the eight-ball and had a short, straight shot to take the match. She missed. Hoffman did not, and she took the opportunity to run out and advance to the finals. In the championship match Hoffman elected to change her game style, having been defeated earlier 5–0 by Campos-Beardon. Breaking with a soft shot, she hoped to minimize her adversary's opportunity for open shots. After four games the score was 2–2, but Campos-Beardon then drew away to win the title 5–3.

For the All-American events 64 men's and 59 women's teams entered. The winner for the first time was the Green Acres men's team from Fort Worth, which consisted of co-captains Jack Roach and Robbie Carlock, Ralph Cortez, Phil Martin, Jackie Reagor, Bill Ferguson, Don Montgomery, and Jack Felan. The runner-up team was Silver Saddle from Pueblo, Colo. In third and fourth places, respectively, were the 1983 champions, Mike's Lounge of Pittsburgh, Pa., and the All Stars of Colorado Springs. In the women's division first and second places went to North Star Tavern of Sacramento, Calif., and the Corner Pockets of Colorado Springs.

As part of a recent trend in pocket billiards, a number of commercially sponsored tournaments continued to grow rapidly. Typical of them was the Lite Beer World Series of Tavern Pool. In its third annual competition the tourney attracted almost 50,000 entrants to its qualifying rounds and brought 1,395 finalists to Las Vegas, Nev., in June. An astounding 742 players showed up for the women's amateur eight-ball contest, in which Robin Hansen-Bell, a 28-year-old mother of five, gained her first major victory. Mike Shaver of Weston, W.Va., beat out 281 other contestants to win the men's amateur eight-ball tournament. In the professional nine-ball division Dallas West of Rockford, Ill., held off 96 other players to win the $25,000 first prize.   (ROBERT E. GOODWIN)

Snooker. Steve Davis of England retained the world professional snooker title in May when he defeated fellow Londoner Jimmy White in a thrilling final by a score of 18 frames to 16. Davis's supremacy in the sport was reaffirmed when he went on to retain the Jameson International Masters title in October and to defeat defending champion Alex Higgins of Northern Ireland in the final of the U.K. professional championships in December. White won the Benson and Hedges Masters in January and partnered Higgins to victory in the world professional doubles championships in December, when the pair defeated Willie Thorne of England and Cliff Thorburn of Canada by 10 frames to 2 in the final.   (LOUISE WATSON)

BOWLING

World Tenpins. The first-ever International Amateur Bowling Invitation tournament, held in Las Vegas, Nev., concurrently with the Olympic Games, was a showcase for a sport with Olympic ambitions. The finals were televised live and seen by an estimated two million viewers. The 48 bowlers from 15 nations who had been invited to compete included the best amateur bowlers of all continents. In the final play-offs Paeng Nepomuceno of the Philippines defeated Jack Jurek of the U.S. 227–181 in the men's division; in the women's division the winner was Mary Mohacsi from Livonia, Mich., and the runner-up Jette Hansen of Denmark. Nepomuceno had twice won the Bowling World Cup.

The tenth Fédération Internationale des Quilleurs world tenpin amateur championships were held in Caracas, Venezuela, during Oct. 21–30, 1983. Sweden dominated the championships with five gold, three silver, and three bronze medals. The U.S. won its only gold medal when in the very last match and game Tony Cariello of Chicago captured the men's masters title after a duel with Mats Karlsson of Sweden, 225–196. Twenty-eight tournament records were broken. The winners were: men's division: singles (six games), Armando Marino (Colombia) 1,357; doubles (six games), Great Britain and Australia, co-champions, each 2,515; trios (six games), Sweden 3,899; teams of five (six games), Finland 6,365; all-events (24 games), Karlsson 5,242; Masters, Cariello 225. Women's division: singles (six games), Lena Sulkanen (Sweden) 1,293; doubles (six games), Denmark 2,409; trios (six games), West Germany 3,532; teams of five (six games), Sweden 5,866; all-events (24 games), Bong Coo (Phil.) 4,806; Masters, Sulkanen 213.

The most important annual singles event, the Bowling World Cup, was bowled in Mexico City in 1983. Australia's Jeanette Baker captured her second straight victory, while Chu Yu-tien won Taiwan's first major tenpin crown in the men's division.   (YRJÖ SARAHETE)

U.S. Tenpins. "I just came here to have a good time, do the best I could and visit some of my old friends," said Earl Anthony. "I never expected to win another major event." The quotation is from an acceptance speech by Anthony, of Dublin, Calif., who had just received a check for $40,-600—professional bowling's largest prize in 1984—after he won the American Bowling Congress's (ABC's) Masters tournament in Reno, Nev.

In the fall of 1983 Anthony, then 45, announced that he was retiring from Professional Bowlers Association (PBA) competition, where he had been the dominant bowler for more than a decade. In 1984 he would enter only the Masters, said Anthony, who led the PBA in earnings with $135,605 in 1983.

In the Masters tournament Anthony went undefeated in seven matches to earn the number one seed in the televised final round. Anthony then downed Gil Sliker of Washington, N.J., by a score of 191–175 in the championship game.

Seven men, each of whom had won two PBA tournaments during 1984, appeared to be the chief contenders to succeed Anthony, the 1983 honouree, as bowler of the year. They were Marshall Holman, Mark Roth, Pete Weber, Wayne Webb, George Pappas, Rickie Sajek, and Gary Skidmore.

In the Queens tournament at Niagara Falls, N.Y., co-sponsored by Avon and the Women's International Bowling Congress (WIBC), a Japanese entrant was the winner for the third time in four years. Kazue Inahashi, a 33-year-old professional bowler from Tokyo, finished with eight strikes in the title game to defeat Aleta Sill of Cocoa, Fla., 248–222. Inahashi's prize was $25,850.

Japanese bowlers also won two of the four major championships in the WIBC tournament, which attracted 45,664 entrants. Inahashi contributed 657 as All Japan won the Division I team event with 3,019. Shinobu Saitoh of Tokyo, who scored 660 for All Japan, captured the all-events title with a nine-game total score of 1,922. Other Division I winners included: singles, Frieda Gates, North Syracuse, N.Y., 712; doubles, Bea Hoffman and Sue Reese, Novato, Calif., 1,292.

Bob Goike of Detroit set a record in the all-events competition with a score of 2,142 in the ABC tournament in Reno. Goike scored 672 in the team event, 710 in doubles, and 760 in singles. Bob Antczak of Chicago and Neal Young of Louisville, Ky., each rolled 764 to tie for the ABC singles title. The Minnesota Loons, from St. Paul, Minn., shot 3,228 to win the team event. In doubles Chris Cobus and John Megna of Milwaukee, Wis., won with 1,383.

(JOHN J. ARCHIBALD)

BOXING

During the era between 1964 and 1979 Muhammad Ali (U.S.) dominated the world heavyweight boxing scene; he was succeeded by Larry Holmes (U.S.), whose five-year grip on the title ended with his relinquishment of it in 1983. Since that time no heavyweight had dominated the World Boxing Council (WBC) or World Boxing Association (WBA) heavyweight championship. Holmes had defended his WBC crown 17 times. On relinquishing it, he was immediately recognized as champion by the newly formed International Boxing Federation (IBF), which, despite its self-styled title, was not recognized internationally. The vacant WBC championship was taken over by Tim Witherspoon (U.S.) after he outpointed Greg Page (U.S.), but a few months later Pinklon Thomas (U.S.) took the title from Witherspoon. Page won the WBA heavyweight title from Gerrie Coetzee (South Africa). Holmes boxed only once in 1984, stopping James ("Bonecrusher") Smith in 12 rounds owing to a cut eye. Ali, retired since 1981, received more publicity than any active heavyweight, though, sadly, this was because he entered a hospital for tests on suspected brain damage. (See Sidebar.)

Carlos de León (P.R.) retained the WBC cruiserweight title, defeating Anthony Davis (U.S.) and Bashiru Ali (Nigeria). WBA cruiserweight champion Osvaldo Ocasio (P.R.) lost his crown to Piet Crous (South Africa), who outpointed him. Michael Spinks (U.S.) remained WBC and WBA light-heavyweight champion, outpointing Eddie Davis (U.S.). Marvin Hagler (U.S.) remained the world's best middleweight for both the WBC and WBA, stopping Juan Domingo Roldán (Arg.) in ten rounds and Mustafa Hamsho (Syrian-born U.S. citizen) in three, but the WBC ceased to recognize him as champion because he agreed to fight Hamsho over 15 rounds—a distance accepted by the WBA—and not over the 12 rounds insisted on by the WBC. However, the WBC reinstated him in December. Thomas Hearns (U.S.) retained the WBC junior-middleweight crown with a points win over Luigi Minchillo (Italy) and knockout victories against Roberto Durán (Panama) and Fred Hutchings (U.S.). The WBA title, left vacant when Durán relinquished it, was won by Mike McCallum (Jamaica) when he outpointed Sean Mannion (U.S.).

The anticipated boost to the welterweight division by the return to the ring of Sugar Ray Leonard (U.S.), the former undisputed world champion who had been retired two years following surgery for a detached retina, did not take place. Leonard duly made his comeback in a nontitle contest against Kevin Howard (U.S.), having insisted that thumbless boxing gloves be used. Though Leonard stopped Howard in nine rounds, he announced his permanent retirement at the end of the fight. Milton McCrory (U.S.) and Don Curry (U.S.), who had shared Leonard's title after he had retired the first time, carried on. McCrory retained the WBC crown, beating Milton Guest (U.S.) and Gilles Elbilia (France), each in six rounds. Curry kept the WBA version, outpointing Marlon Starling (U.S.) and stopping Elio Díaz (Venezuela) and Nino La Rocca (Italy).

Bruce Curry (U.S.), brother of the WBA welterweight champion, lost the WBC junior-welterweight title in a surprising defeat when he was stopped in ten rounds by Bill Costello (U.S.). Costello then defeated Ron Shields and Saoul Mamby, both from the U.S. The WBA junior-welterweight championship went to Johnny Bumphus (U.S.), who outpointed Lorenzo García (Arg.) for the vacant crown; Bumphus, however, lost the title in his first defense when Gene Hatcher (U.S.) knocked him out in the 11th round.

After two successful defenses of his WBC lightweight title against Roberto Elizondo (U.S.) and Howard Davis (U.S.), Edwin Rosario (P.R.) suffered a four-round defeat against José Luis Ramírez (Mexico). A new WBA lightweight champion was also crowned when Livingstone Bramble (U.S.) beat Ray ("Boom Boom") Mancini (U.S.). After Hector ("Macho") Camacho (U.S.) gave up the WBC junior-lightweight title, it was taken over by Julio César Chavez (Mexico), who stopped Mario Martínez (Mexico) in eight rounds. The WBA championship also changed hands when Rocky Lockridge (U.S.) knocked out Roger Mayweather (U.S.) in the first round. Lockridge kept the title, stopping Moon Tae Jin (South Korea) in 11 rounds at Anchorage, Alaska, the first world boxing championship ever staged there. Wilfredo Gómez (P.R.) captured the WBC featherweight title from Juan Laporte (P.R.) and then lost it to Azumah Nelson (Ghana), while Eusebio Pedroza

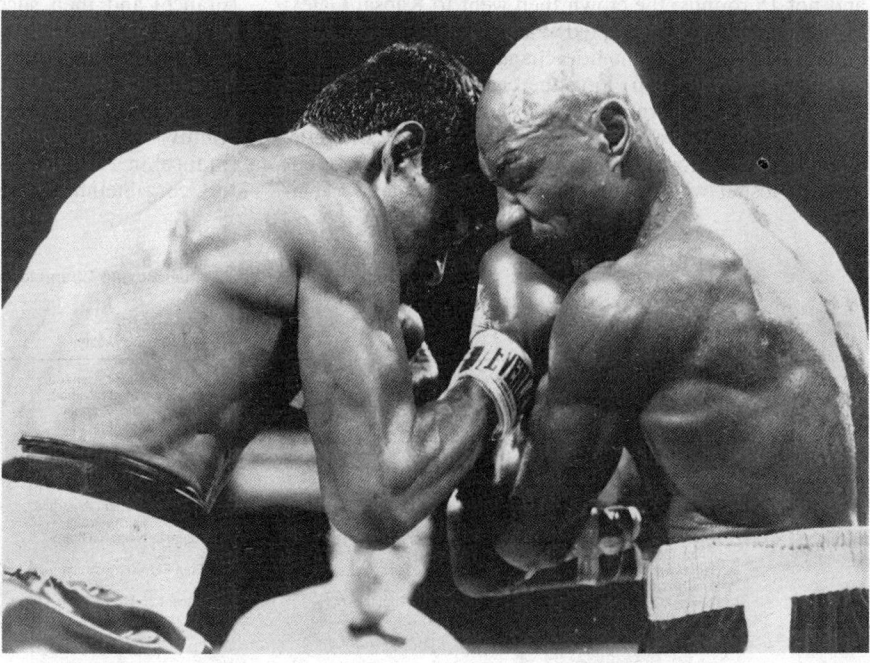

Marvin Hagler (right), here in a close exchange with Mustafa Hamsho, prevailed with a knockout in the third round of their October fight in New York City's Madison Square Garden to retain the middleweight championship.

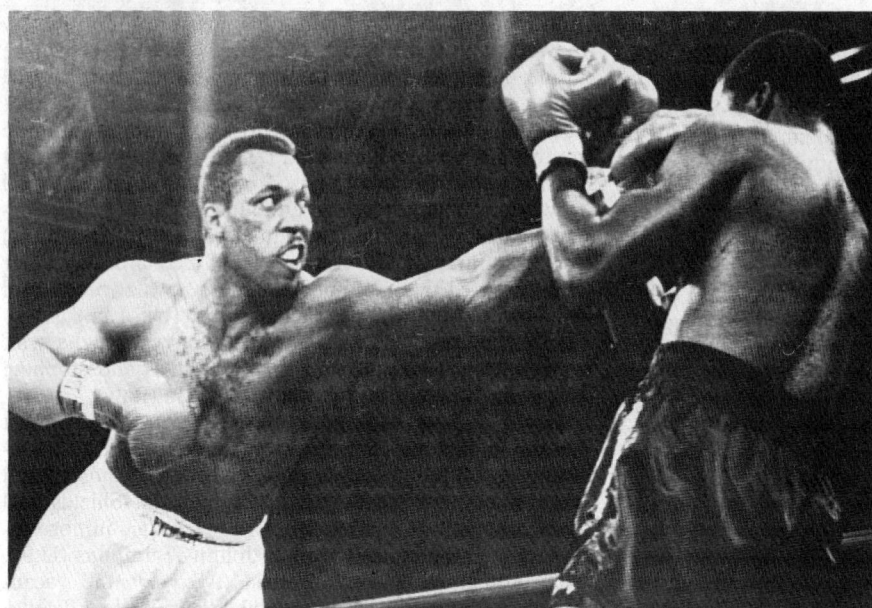

Pinklon Thomas (left) took the World Boxing Council heavyweight title from Tim Witherspoon by decision in this match at Las Vegas, Nevada, in August.

AP/WIDE WORLD

(Panama) retained the WBA version for the 18th time, outpointing Angel Mayor (Venezuela).

The junior-featherweight championship changed hands in both sections. Juan Meza (Mexico) caused one of the big upsets of the year when he won the WBC crown by knocking out Jaime Garza (U.S.) in the first round. It was Garza's first defeat after 40 successive wins. The WBA title passed from Leonardo Cruz (Dominican Republic) to Loris Stecca (Italy) and then on to Victor Callejas (P.R.), who knocked out Stecca in eight rounds. Albert Davila (U.S.) held on to the WBC bantamweight championship, stopping Enrique Sánchez (Dominican Republic) in 11 rounds, while the WBA title went to Richie Sandoval (U.S.), who beat Jeff Chandler (U.S.) and Edgar Román (Venezuela).

The superflyweight division should have had one undisputed champion when WBA champion Jiro Watanabe (Japan) outpointed Payao Poontarat (Thailand), the WBC titleholder, over 12 rounds, but the WBA stripped Watanabe of the title because he had agreed to fight over 12 and not 15 rounds; the crown then went to Kaosai Galexi (Thailand). The WBC accepted Watanabe as its new champion. The WBC flyweight title changed hands four times. Koji Kobayashi (Japan) took the crown from Frank Cedeno (Phil.) in two rounds but lost it to Gabriel Bernal (Mexico), also in two rounds. Bernal retained the title, knocking out Antoine Montero (France) in 11 rounds, but he then lost it when outpointed by Sot Chitalada (Thai-

land). Santos Laciar (Arg.) retained the WBA championship by outpointing Juan Herrera (Mexico). Chang Jung Koo (South Korea) continued as WBC junior-flyweight king, beating Chitalada and Katsuo Tokashiti (Japan), while the WBA title was won by Francisco Quiroz (Dominican Republic) with a ninth-round knockout against Lupe Madera (Mexico). Quiroz then retained his crown by knocking out Victor Sierra (Panama) in two rounds.

In Europe Steffen Tangstad (Norway) ended the three-year reign of Lucien Rodriguez (France) in the Frenchman's seventh defense of his European heavyweight title. The fight took place in Copenhagen, professional boxing having been banned in Norway. At light heavyweight, Rudi Koopmans (Neth.) defended that championship for the tenth time and was forced to retire in eight rounds against Richard Caramanolis (France). In his next contest, however, the Frenchman was knocked out in six rounds by Alex Blanchard (Neth.). Tony Sibson (England) won the middleweight championship from Louis Acaries (France) and then successfully defended it against Mark Kaylor (England), thereby taking over the Commonwealth and British titles from Kaylor. Sibson then relinquished the British title. Herol Graham (England) relinquished the junior-middleweight crown, and the vacant title went to Jimmy Cable (England). Cable then stopped Said Skouma (France) in 11 rounds but lost the championship on points to Georg Steinherr (West Germany). After the European

European, Commonwealth, and British Boxing Champions
as of Dec. 31, 1984

Division	Europe	Commonwealth	Britain
Heavyweight	Steffen Tangstad, Norway	Trevor Berbick, Canada	Dave Peace, Wales
Cruiserweight	...	Chisanda Mutti, Zambia	...
Light heavyweight	Alex Blanchard, Neth.	Lottie Mwale, Zambia	Dennis Andries, England
Middleweight	Tony Sibson, England	Tony Sibson, England	Vacant
Junior middleweight	Georg Steinherr, West Germany	Ken Salisbury, Australia	Jimmy Cable, England
Welterweight	Gianfranco Rosi, Italy	Sylvester Mittee, England	Lloyd Honeyghan, England
Junior welterweight	Patrizio Oliva, Italy	Billy Famous, Nigeria	Terry Marsh, England
Lightweight	René Weller, West Germany	Graeme Brooke, Australia	George Feeney, England
Junior lightweight	Pat Cowdell, England	Lester Ellis, Australia	...
Featherweight	Barry McGuigan, N.Ire.	Azumah Nelson, Ghana	Barry McGuigan, N.Ire.
Junior featherweight	...	...	...
Bantamweight	Ciro De Leva, Italy	Paul Ferreri, Australia	John Feeney, England
Superflyweight	...	...	...
Flyweight	Charlie Magri, England	Vacant	Hugh Russell, N.Ire.
Junior flyweight	...	...	...

Boxing Union had stripped Gilles Elbilia (France) of the welterweight title, it was taken over by Gianfranco Rosi (Italy), who outpointed Perico Fernández (Spain). Patrizio Oliva (Italy) and René Weller (West Germany) retained the junior-welterweight and lightweight championships, respectively. The junior-lightweight crown passed from Alfredo Raininger (Italy) to Jean-Marc Renard (Belgium) and then on to Pat Cowdell (England). Barry McGuigan (Northern Ireland) retained the featherweight crown. Walter Giorgetti (Italy) retired following a brain scan, and the bantamweight championship was then won by Ciro De Leva (Italy) when he outpointed John Feeney (England). Charlie Magri (England) won the flyweight title, knocking out Franco Cherchi (Italy) in one round.

Stewart Lithgo (England) won the first-ever Commonwealth cruiserweight championship, stopping Steve Aczel (Australia) in 11 rounds, but he then lost the title to Chisanda Mutti (Zambia). Ken Salisbury (Australia) won the junior-middleweight title, outpointing Nelson Bosso (Zimbabwe). Sylvester Mittee (England) captured the vacant welterweight crown, stopping Fighting Romanus (Nigeria). Graeme Brook (Australia) won the lightweight

championship, outscoring Claude Noel (Trinidad). John Sichula (Zambia) gained the junior-lightweight title by knocking out Langton Tinago (Zimbabwe) in five rounds, but he then lost it on points to Lester Ellis (Australia).

In the U.K. four new champions were crowned. Dennis Andries (England) outpointed light-heavyweight champion Tom Collins (England). Jimmy Cable (England) won the vacant junior-middleweight title, outpointing Nick Wilshire (England)). Terry Marsh (England) relieved Clinton McKenzie (England) of the junior-welterweight crown. Hugh Russell (Northern Ireland), the former bantamweight champion, outpointed Kelvin Smart (Wales) to become flyweight champion and then successfully defended his crown by stopping Danny Flynn (Scotland) in eight rounds.

Olympic Games. The U.S. won 9 of a total of 12 gold medals at Los Angeles. Final results: super heavyweight, Tyrell Biggs (U.S.) outpointed Francesco Damiani (Italy); heavyweight, Henry Tillman (U.S.) outpointed Willie Dewit (Canada); light heavyweight, Anton Josipovic (Yugos.) walkover; middleweight, Shin Joon Sup (South Korea) outpointed Virgil Hill (U.S.); light middleweight,

---

Boxing: The Risk of Injury

A motion calling for a campaign to influence public opinion to ultimately ban boxing, both professional and amateur, was passed by a clear majority at the British Medical Association's (BMA's) annual meeting at Manchester, England, in July 1984. And in December the American Medical Association (AMA), meeting at Honolulu, overwhelmingly adopted a similar resolution. BMA secretary John Harvard predicted that a ban in the United Kingdom might well be achieved in five to ten years. In March the BMA's Board of Science had published a report condemning the sport since it had been proved that it could cause ocular and brain damage. The BMA claimed that since the end of World War II at least 340 boxers throughout the world had died from injuries sustained in the ring, while hundreds more had been blinded, had had their sight seriously impaired, or had suffered permanent brain damage. Britain's Amateur Boxing Association and the armed services had cooperated in giving evidence, but the BMA regretted that the British Boxing Board of Control (BBBC), in charge of professional boxing in the U.K., had not. The BBBC stated that its suggestion for an independent inquiry, on the grounds that the BMA report would of necessity be biased, had been ignored. The BBBC's chief medical officer, Adrian Whiteson, did not deny the risks but said there were even more risks in other sports. He claimed that Britain led the world with such safety precautions as brain scans and intensive eye examinations and that 70 brain scans on active boxers had revealed no damage.

Several countries had previously reported on the risks of brain and eye damage to boxers. In 1982, following several fatalities around the world, important antiboxing reports were issued by the the AMA, the World Medical Association, the Australian Medical Association, the Swedish government, and the Swedish Society of Medical Sciences. The American body's influential *Journal* called for a ban in 1983. Professional boxing was banned in Sweden in 1969 and in Norway in 1982. The World Boxing Council, the European

Boxing Union, and the BBBC, following fatalities in 1983, reduced championship fights from 15 rounds to 12, but the World Boxing Association continued to hold 15-round championship contests. In some U.S. bouts thumbless gloves were introduced in 1984 in an attempt to cut down eye damage.

Not all doctors supported the campaign against boxing. Some pointed out the serious injuries that occur in other sports, such as rugby, football, automobile racing, and steeplechasing, but the doctors who wanted to see boxing banned stated that while injuries in other sports are accidental, in boxing blows are deliberately aimed at the head to render an opponent senseless. At the 1984 Olympic Games compulsory headguards were used by boxers for the first time, and ringside physicians were empowered to override the referee if they believed the contest had been allowed to continue too long. The BMA, however, stressed that headguards are no protection against brain injury.

(FRANK BUTLER)

BEN SHARAV/THE RING

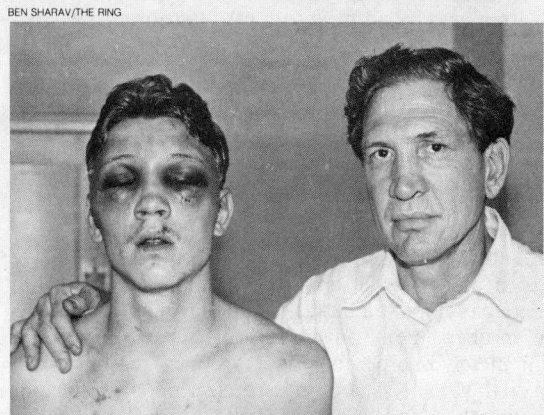

Billy Collins, Jr. (left, with his father), the day after his last fight in June 1983 against an opponent from whose gloves half the padding had been removed. He sank into depression, took to drinking, and died in a one-car accident in March 1984.

Frank Tate (U.S.) outpointed Shawn O'Sullivan (Canada); welterweight, Mark Breland (U.S.) outpointed An Young Su (South Korea); light welterweight, Jerry Page (U.S.) outpointed Dhawee Umponmaha (Thailand); lightweight, Pernell Whitaker (U.S.) stopped Luis F. Ortiz (P.R.); featherweight, Meldrick Taylor (U.S.) outpointed Peter Konyegwachie (Nigeria); bantamweight, Maurizio Stecca (Italy) outpointed Hector López (Mexico); flyweight, Steve McCrory (U.S.) outpointed Redzep Redzepovski (Yugos.); light flyweight, Paul Gonzales (U.S.) walkover.

(FRANK BUTLER)

CHESS

The most important events of 1984 in chess were the world championship matches. An indication as to the likely challengers of Anatoly Karpov (U.S.S.R.) for the men's world championship and Maya Chiburdanidze (U.S.S.R.) for the women's title came in the official international rating lists issued in January. Garry Kasparov (U.S.S.R.) was ranked first on the men's list with 2,710 points, just ahead of Karpov, who had 2,700. They were followed by Viktor Korchnoi (Switz.) and Ljubomir Ljubojevic (Yugos.) 2,635, Ulf Andersson (Sweden) and Rafael Vaganian (U.S.S.R.) 2,630, Lajos Portisch (Hung.) 2,625, Robert Hübner (West Germany) and Mikhail Tal (U.S.S.R.) 2,620, and Lev Polugaevsky (U.S.S.R.) and Boris Spassky (U.S.S.R.) 2,615. Pia Cramling (Sweden) was a new leader in the women's division with 2,405 points. She was followed by Chiburdanidze with 2,385, Nana Alexandria (U.S.S.R.) 2,370, Nona Gaprindashvili (U.S.S.R.) 2,330, and Elena Ahmilovskaya (U.S.S.R.) 2,300.

The opening rounds of the matches to determine who would challenge Karpov took place in London late in 1983. At the end of this competition Kasparov and former world champion Vassily Smyslov, both of the U.S.S.R., had qualified to play one another for the right to challenge Karpov. The contest took place in Vilnius, Lithuanian S.S.R., in April, and Kasparov won decisively.

There was a long interval before the final match between Karpov and Kasparov started in Moscow, during which both players prepared for the contest along with their selected seconds and chosen analysts. It was apparent that both challenger and champion were in top form, Karpov having won first prize at the Phillips and Drew tournament in London in April with 9 points out of 13 and Kasparov having made his way through determined top-flight opposition to gain the challenge round. Although it was clear that Karpov was by no means an easy target, most experts thought that the younger man was likely to win in a contest that would produce much fine chess.

On November 18 in Moscow, with Yugoslav grandmaster Svetozar Gligoric acting as chief arbiter, one of the longest and dreariest of world championship matches in the history of chess began. It soon became obvious that something was very wrong with Kasparov's play, which was weak in precisely those areas where he had previously excelled. If there was an opportunity for attack, he never took it; if there was an opportunity for a feeble and ill-considered attempt at attack, he took that. Thus, for an example, in one game he advanced his KN pawn in front of his king merely in order to weaken his own king's position. In the sixth game Kasparov missed clear opportunities for a winning attack and eventually drew; in the 16th game he missed several opportunities to draw and eventually lost. Thus Karpov soon was leading 5–0 with a large number of drawn games.

The astonishing nature of the match became apparent when Karpov, instead of going in for the kill against a

demoralized opponent, was content to sit back and agree on draws without the slightest attempt to gain the initiative. Remarkably, the world champion gained his 5–0 lead without producing a single decent attacking game. The only piece of good play he provided was the result of some excellent adjournment analysis on the part of his fine group of seconds and analysts. At the end of the year, after having played a record 36 games, Karpov led 5–1 and needed only one more victory to retain his world title for three more years.

In the women's world championship tournament Chiburdanidze retained her title by defeating Irina Levitina, also of the Soviet Union, by a score of 8½ points to 5½. The match took place in Volgograd in the U.S.S.R.

The Chess Olympiad, previously scheduled for the autumn in Thessaloniki, Greece, was rescheduled to start on November 18. The Soviet team, which was competing without either Karpov or Kasparov, was reckoned to be not quite as formidable as usual. However, Aleksandr Beljavsky, Rafael Vaganian, Lev Polugaevsky, Vladimir Tukmakov, Artur Yusupov, and Andrey Sokolov proved easily sufficient to retain the team world championship with 41 points out of a maximum of 66. The United Kingdom finished second with 37 points, followed by the U.S. with 35, Hungary with 34½, Romania with 33, and West Germany and France with 32½. A total of 88 teams entered the tournament.

Soviet supremacy was just as marked in the women's team competition, where, out of a possible total of 42 points, the U.S.S.R. scored 32. Bulgaria finished second with 27½, followed by Romania 27, West Germany and China 26, and Hungary 25.

In other competition during the year, the fourth all-grandmaster Bugojne (Yugos.) International Tournament was won by Jan Timman of The Netherlands. Two immigrants to the U.S. from the Soviet Union, Roman Dzindzichashvili and Sergey Kudrin, shared first place in the U.S. Open competition. The U.S. women's title was won by Diane Savareide of Santa Monica, Calif., and the U.S. men's championship went to Lev Alburt of New York City. The world correspondence championship was won by Victor Palciauskas of Fullerton, Calif.

(HARRY GOLOMBEK)

CONTRACT BRIDGE

The seventh World Team Olympiad was held at Seattle, Wash., in 1984. The withdrawal of the majority of Communist countries from the Los Angeles Olympic Games affected Eastern European bridge entries, and Poland's entry was not announced until shortly before the tournament.

Phillips and Drew Tournament

Scotch Game

White Jan Timman	Black Anatoly Karpov	White Jan Timman	Black Anatoly Karpov
1 e4	e5	2 Nf3	Nc6
3 d4	exd4	4 Nxd4	Nf6
5 Nxc6	bxc6	6 e5	Qe7
7 Qe2	Nd5	8 c4	Ba6
9 Qe4 (a)	Nb6	10 Nd2	0-0-0
11 c5	Bxf1	12 cxb6	Ba6
13 bxa7	Kb7	14 Nb3	f6
15 f4	fxe5	16 fxe5	Re8
17 Bf4	Qh4 ch	18 g3	Qh5
19 Rc1	Ka8	20 h4	d5
21 Qe3	g5	22 Bxg5	Bb4 ch
23 Kf2	Rhf8 ch	24 Kg2	Rxe5
25 Qxe5	Qf3 ch	26 Kh2	Qf2 ch
27 resigns (b)			

(a) A better move would have been 9 b3.
(b) Because of 27 Kh3 Bc8 ch, 28 g4 Rf3 ch followed by mate.

Fifty-five countries competed in the Open Olympic series, in which two pools of 27 teams completed round robins and four teams from each pool qualified for the quarterfinal stage. The eight qualifiers were: Pool A—Poland, Denmark, Austria, France; Pool B—Indonesia, U.S., Italy, Pakistan. In the Women's Olympiad all 23 teams met in a round robin that was dominated throughout by the young Netherlands team, with the U.S., France, and Great Britain as the other three semifinalists.

In the Open the 1983 Bermuda Bowl finalists, the United States and Italy, were both eliminated in the quarterfinal stage, the U.S. by Austria and Italy by Denmark. France, the defending Olympic champion, overpowered Indonesia, and Poland beat Pakistan. The semifinals in both the Open and Women's Olympiads used the same boards, which made for interesting comparisons. In the Open series France defeated Denmark after a dramatic struggle 164–149, and Poland came from behind to beat Austria 147–143. In the Women's Olympiad semifinals Great Britain triumphed over The Netherlands 188–56 (including 17 round-robin points), and the U.S. triumphed over France 138–107.

France was soon out of contention in the 96-board Open final. At the halfway stage the Polish team led 149–38, and the final score in Poland's victory was 236–156. The new Olympic champions, one of the youngest teams in the event, included Krzysztof Martens and Tomasz Przybora, Piotr Gawrys and Henryk Wolny, and Piotr Tuszynski and Jacek Romanski, all world champions for the first time; their nonplaying captain, Marian Frenkiel, gained his second world title. The second-place French team included Paul Chemla, Michel Perron, Henri Szwarc, Hervé Mouiel, Fivo Paladino, and Félix Covo. Nonplaying captain for France was Pierre Schemeil.

In the 64-board final of the Women's Olympiad, the U.S. defending champions, with a round-robin carryover of 22½ points, beat Great Britain 109½–99. Members of the U.S. team were Jacqui Mitchell, Gail Moss, Carol Sanders, Betty Ann Kennedy, Kathy Wei, and Judi Radin; nonplaying captain was James Zimmerman. The British women silver medalists included Sally Horton, Sandra Landy, Nicola Smith (née Gardener), Pat Davies, Gillian Scott-Jones, and Sarah Scarborough; their nonplaying captain was Hugh Kelsey.   (HAROLD FRANKLIN)

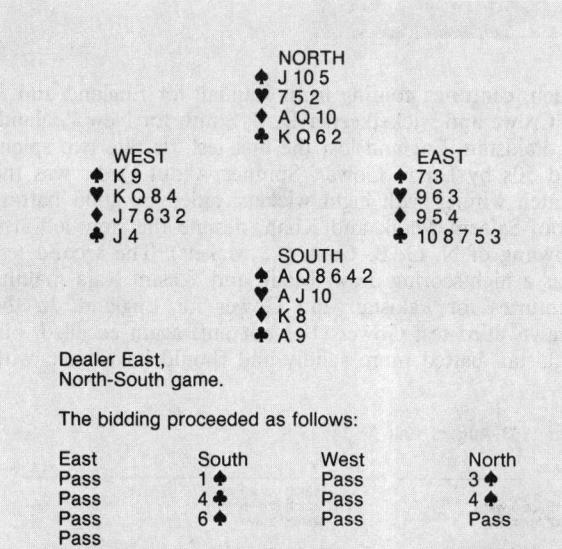

NORTH
♠ J 10 5
♥ 7 5 2
♦ A Q 10
♣ K Q 6 2

WEST
♠ K 9
♥ K Q 8 4
♦ J 7 6 3 2
♣ J 4

EAST
♠ 7 3
♥ 9 6 3
♦ 9 5 4
♣ 10 8 7 5 3

SOUTH
♠ A Q 8 6 4 2
♥ A J 10
♦ K 8
♣ A 9

Dealer East,
North-South game.

The bidding proceeded as follows:

East	South	West	North
Pass	1 ♠	Pass	3 ♠
Pass	4 ♣	Pass	4 ♠
Pass	6 ♠	Pass	Pass
Pass			

In the Open final the contract at both tables was six spades. The U.S. women reached the same contract, while the British women achieved the inferior contract of six no trump. At all four tables West led the king of hearts, and the six no trump contract was doomed. The French declarer in the Open won the first heart and immediately played three rounds of clubs, the third being ruffed by West. West then cashed a heart, and declarer later took a losing spade finesse to go down two. For the U.S. women Gail Moss showed a better technique when she cashed three diamonds before tackling clubs (with only five diamonds against six clubs, this was clearly a better line). West, Sandra Landy, ruffed the third club; by that time she was able to count declarer as 6–3–2–2 and knew that her last six cards were trumps. If she led a heart, declarer would be obliged to ruff and with no entry in dummy would be obliged to lay down the ace of spades. Landy offered her a losing option by leading a diamond, which declarer ruffed in dummy with the jack and underruffed in hand. She reflected at length before finding the right answer and declining the "Greek gift." She played the ace and dropped the king.

At the fourth table Tomasz Przybora for Poland showed the best technique. He saw at once that if three clubs and three diamonds stood up, he had no problem. He saw also that if the third club was trumped, he would have no entry to dummy to take a spade finesse. At trick 2, therefore, he led a spade to the ace. This gave him the extra chance of dropping the blank king in the West hand and would also have won if West had held a singleton trump and two clubs or two diamonds.

CRICKET

The 1983–84 international cricket season was dominated by West Indies, which, under the captaincy of Clive Lloyd (*see* BIOGRAPHIES), triumphed over India, Australia, and England and never came close to losing a match. In contrast, England lost in New Zealand and Pakistan, was trounced at home by West Indies, and had the worst of a draw with Sri Lanka at Lord's. Australia at home beat a weak Pakistan but lost heavily in the Caribbean. New Zealand followed its triumph over England by winning in Sri Lanka, and India and Pakistan played three draws. The Asian Cup, played at Sharjah in the United Arab Emirates, was won by India, with Sri Lanka second and Pakistan third.

A three-match series between India and Pakistan, under the captaincy of Kapil Dev and Zaheer Abbas, respectively, ended in a draw. It was remarkable for bad weather, an innings of 201 by A. D. Gaekwad for India, and the success of slow bowlers, of whom Pakistan's Mohammed Nazir was the most successful.

India was overwhelmed by West Indies, which won two matches by an innings. Only sturdy batting by Sunil Gavaskar and Dilip Vengsarkar enabled India to save three games. The pace of Malcolm Marshall and Michael Holding was decisive for West Indies, supported by superb batting by C. G. Greenidge, Vivian Richards, and Lloyd. Gavaskar passed Sir Donald Bradman's record of 29 test centuries.

Australia, under K. J. Hughes, beat Pakistan 2–0, largely thanks to its four fast bowlers, Dennis Lillee, G. F. Lawson, C. G. Rackemann, and R. N. Hogg. G. N. Yallop scored a remarkable 268 and A. R. Border, Greg Chappell, Hughes, W. B. Phillips, and K. C. Wessels also made centuries. The leading Pakistan batsmen were Mohsin Khan, Qasim Umar, and Javed Miandad, all of whom made centuries. The fifth test, won by ten wickets, marked the end of test cricket for three of Australia's greatest, Chappell, Lillee, and Rodney Marsh, who retired in a blaze of glory. Chappell made 182 and thereby became the highest scorer in Australian test cricket, eclipsing the great Bradman. Lillee took four wickets in each innings, and Marsh held five catches in the second innings.

England, under Bob Willis, toured New Zealand, under Geoff Howarth, and Pakistan, under Abbas, and was humiliated by New Zealand by an innings and 132 runs in

West Indies dominated the 1983–84 international cricket season. West Indies batsman D. L. Haynes stands poised during play in the third test of the series in England. England was beaten in the series 5–0.

PRESS ASSOCIATION, LONDON

the second test. England had begun well in the first test, thanks to centuries by Ian Botham and D. W. Randall and good bowling by Botham (5 for 59), but New Zealand saved the game with a sterling partnership by M. D. Crowe (100) and J. V. Coney (174 not out). In the second test England was bowled out for 82 and 93, the first time in any test that it had failed to make a hundred in either innings. The pitch (area on the playing field between the wickets) was in bad condition, but New Zealand made 307 on it, Richard Hadlee following a fine 99 by taking eight wickets. The third test was a high-scoring draw on a bland

pitch, centuries coming from Randall for England and J. J. Crowe and wicketkeeper D. S. Smith for New Zealand. In Pakistan, England lost the first test, despite two splendid 50s by David Gower. Spinner Abdul Qadir was the match winner with eight wickets, aided by good batting from Saleem Malik and Khan, despite the slow left-arm bowling of N. G. B. Cook (11 wickets). The second test was a high-scoring draw, Malik and Wasim Raja making centuries for Pakistan and Gower for England. In the drawn third test Gower (173 not out) again excelled, but Pakistan batted more solidly and should have won, with

Test Series Results, September 1983–August 1984

Test	Host country and its scores		Visiting country and its scores		Result
1st	India	275 and 176 for 0 wkt	Pakistan	288	Match drawn
2nd	India	374	Pakistan	337 and 18 for 0 wkt	Match drawn
3rd	India	245 and 268 for 8 wkt dec	Pakistan	322 and 42 for 1 wkt	Match drawn
1st	India	207 and 164	West Indies	454	West Indies won by an innings and 83 runs
2nd	India	464 and 233	West Indies	384 and 120 for 2 wkt	Match drawn
3rd	India	241 and 103	West Indies	281 and 201	West Indies won by 138 runs
4th	India	463 and 173 for 5 wkt dec	West Indies	393 and 104 for 4 wkt	Match drawn
5th	India	241 and 90	West Indies	377	West Indies won by an innings and 46 runs
6th	India	451 for 8 wkt dec	West Indies	313 and 64 for 1 wkt	Match drawn
1st	Australia	436 for 9 wkt dec	Pakistan	129 and 298	Australia won by an innings and 9 runs
2nd	Australia	509 for 7 wkt dec	Pakistan	156 and 82 for 3 wkt	Match drawn
3rd	Australia	465 and 317 for 7 wkt	Pakistan	624	Match drawn
4th	Australia	555	Pakistan	470 and 238 for 7 wkt	Match drawn
5th	Australia	454 for 6 wkt dec and 35 for 0 wkt	Pakistan	278 and 210	Australia won by 10 wkt
1st	New Zealand	219 and 537	England	463 and 69 for 0 wkt	Match drawn
2nd	New Zealand	307	England	82 and 93	New Zealand won by an innings and 132 runs
3rd	New Zealand	496 for 9 wkt dec and 18 for 0 wkt	England	439	Match drawn
1st	Pakistan	277 and 66 for 7 wkt	England	182 and 159	Pakistan won by 3 wkt
2nd	Pakistan	449 for 8 wkt dec and 137 for 4 wkt	England	546 for 8 wkt dec	Match drawn
3rd	Pakistan	343 and 217 for 6 wkt	England	241 and 344 for 9 wkt dec	Match drawn
1st	West Indies	230 and 250 for 0 wkt	Australia	279 and 273 for 9 wkt dec	Match drawn
2nd	West Indies	468 for 8 wkt dec	Australia	255 and 299 for 9 wkt	Match drawn
3rd	West Indies	509 and 21 for 0 wkt	Australia	429 and 97	West Indies won by 10 wkt
4th	West Indies	498	Australia	262 and 200	West Indies won by an innings and 36 runs
5th	West Indies	305 and 55 for 0 wkt	Australia	199 and 160	West Indies won by 10 wkt
1st	Sri Lanka	215 and 97	New Zealand	276 and 201 for 8 wkt dec	New Zealand won by 165 runs
2nd	Sri Lanka	174 and 289 for 9 wkt dec	New Zealand	198 and 123 for 4 wkt	Match drawn
3rd	Sri Lanka	258 and 142	New Zealand	459	New Zealand won by an innings and 61 runs
1st	England	191 and 235	West Indies	606	West Indies won by an innings and 180 runs
2nd	England	286 and 300 for 9 wkt dec	West Indies	245 and 344 for 1 wkt	West Indies won by 9 wkt
3rd	England	270 and 150	West Indies	302 and 131 for 2 wkt	West Indies won by 8 wkt
4th	England	280 and 154	West Indies	500	West Indies won by an innings and 64 runs
5th	England	162 and 202	West Indies	190 and 346	West Indies won by 172 runs
1st	England	370	Sri Lanka	491 for 7 wkt dec and 294 for 7 wkt dec	Match drawn

Khan's fine century and an all-round performance from Sarfraz Nawaz.

West Indies defeated Australia in the Caribbean 3–0 through the fast bowling of Joel Garner, Marshall, and Holding, supported by high-class batting in which six batsmen made centuries. The giant Garner bowled the most overs and took 31 wickets, and the leading batsmen, D. L. Haynes, Greenidge, and Richards, were joined by two new centurions, Richie Richardson and wicketkeeper P. J. Dujon. Australia's Border scored more runs (521) than any West Indian, including 98 and 100 not out in the second test.

The fast bowling of Hadlee (23 wickets) was the decisive factor in a 2–0 win for New Zealand in a three-match series against Sri Lanka, captained by Duleep Mendis. E. J. Chatfield and S. L. Boock each took five wickets in an innings. John Reid was the only New Zealand centurion, though Howarth made two 60s in the first test. Medium-paced bowler Vinodhan John took 16 wickets for Sri Lanka, and Roy Dias made a good century in the second test.

England was overwhelmed at home 5–0 by West Indies. Two of the tests were won by an innings and the others by wide margins. Again the executioners were fast bowlers Garner, Marshall, and Holding. R. A. Harper, a tall off-spinning all-rounder, offered invaluable contrast. Seven centuries were scored, two each by Greenidge and H. A. Gomes and one each by Richards, Dujon, and Haynes. In reply, England could offer little, despite three successive centuries by A. J. Lamb and one by Graeme Fowler. The captain, Gower, in his first big test at home, could find no form with the bat, and Botham was an erratic genius with the bat and an expensive liability with the ball, though he had one great performance at Lord's in his old style, taking eight for 103 in an innings and making 30 and 81.

The English season ended with a first test at Lord's for Sri Lanka, which achieved a comfortable draw and appeared to be much the better side. Sidath Wettimuny made 190 in his first Lord's test, and the captain, Mendis, 111 and 94. The Sri Lankans showed up England's mediocre and unimaginative performance. Only Lamb, with his fourth century in six tests, was in their class.

Essex retained the English county championship after an exciting tussle with Nottinghamshire, which failed by only three runs to win the final match. In the one-day competitions Middlesex beat Kent in the NatWest Trophy; Lancashire defeated Warwickshire in the Benson and Hedges Cup; and Essex won the John Player Special League. Hadlee (Notts and New Zealand) became the first player since 1967 to achieve the double of 1,000 runs and 100 wickets in a season, and J. K. Lever (Essex) also took over 100 wickets. M. W. Gatting (Middlesex) headed the first-class averages, and he and G. A. Gooch (Essex), D. Amiss and A. Kallicharran (both Warwickshire), and R. Robinson (Nottinghamshire) all scored more than 2,000 runs.

In Australia, Western Australia won the Sheffield Shield. In South Africa, Transvaal won the Currie Cup, and in West Indies, Barbados won the Shell Shield. In New Zealand, Canterbury won the Shell Trophy. In India, Karnataka won the Irani Cup, North Zone retained the Duleep Trophy, and Bombay won the Ranji Trophy. In Pakistan, National Bank won the Qaid-i-Azam Trophy, and Karachi Blues won the Patron's Trophy.   (REX ALSTON)

CYCLING

Advances in cycling technology made 1984 a year of records and prompted the sport's governing bodies to consider the introduction of limitations on bicycle design. The most revolutionary step was the appearance of solid-disk rear wheels, made of carbon fibre to reduce turbulence. Italian rider Francesco Moser used them in Mexico City when he covered 51.151 km in one hour to break the 12-year-old world record set by Eddy Merckx of Belgium by 1.72 km.

U.S. riders won nine cycling medals at the Olympic Games in Los Angeles. Connie Carpenter-Phinney, who had competed at the 1972 Olympic Games as a speed skater, won the women's road race, and Alexi Grewal took the men's road race title. Other U.S. successes took place on the track, where Steve Hegg in the individual 4,000-m pursuit and Mark Gorski in the sprint broke Olympic outdoor records with times of 4 min 35.57 sec and 10.49 sec, respectively. (For table of Olympic winners see *Track and Field Sports*: Special Report, below.)

The absence from the Olympics of the powerful Eastern European nations affected the results in Los Angeles. At the Friendship Games in Moscow, held for those countries that had boycotted the Olympics, Ginguatas Umaras (U.S.S.R.) set an indoor world best of 4 min 33.63 sec for the 4,000-m pursuit, the U.S.S.R. set a new world record (4 min 14.26 sec) for the 4,000-m team pursuit, and Lutz Hesslich of East Germany recorded the fastest-ever flying-start 200-m time of 10.021 sec.

In professional road racing Laurent Fignon of France won the Tour de France for the second successive year and denied compatriot Bernard Hinault a record-equaling fifth victory in a duel that held the nation's attention for almost a month. Greg Lemond of the U.S. finished third, and Scotland's Robert Millar was fourth as well as winning the mountains award. The first-ever Tour de France for

1984 Cycling Champions*

Event	Winner	Country
WORLD AMATEUR CHAMPIONS—TRACK		
Men		
Tandem sprint	J. Greil, F. Webber	West Germany
50-km motor paced	J. de Nijs	The Netherlands
Women		
Sprint	C. Paraskevin	U.S.
Individual pursuit	R. Twigg	U.S.
WORLD PROFESSIONAL CHAMPIONS—TRACK		
Sprint	K. Nakano	Japan
Individual pursuit	H.-H. Oersted	Denmark
50-km points	U. Freuler	Switzerland
One-hour motor paced	H. Schütz	West Germany
Keirin	R. Dill-Bundi	Switzerland
WORLD PROFESSIONAL CHAMPION—ROAD		
Individual road race	C. Criquelion	Belgium
WORLD CHAMPIONS—CYCLO-CROSS		
Amateur	R. Simunek	Czechoslovakia
Professional	R. Liboton	Belgium
MAJOR PROFESSIONAL ROAD-RACE WINNERS		
Tour de France	L. Fignon	France
Tour of Italy	F. Moser	Italy
Tour of Spain	E. Caritoux	France
Paris–Nice	S. Kelly	Ireland
Milan–San Remo	F. Moser	Italy
Tour of Flanders	J. Lammerts	The Netherlands
Paris–Roubaix	S. Kelly	Ireland
Flèche Wallonne	K. Andersen	Denmark
Liège-Bastogne-Liège	S. Kelly	Ireland
Bordeaux–Paris	H. Linard	France
Dauphiné-Libéré	M. Ramirez	Colombia
G.P. de Midi Libre	D. Garde	France
Tour of Switzerland	U. Zimmermann	Switzerland
Circuit Het Volk	E. Planckaert	Belgium
Amstel Gold	J. Hanegraaf	The Netherlands
G.P. de Frankfurt	P. Anderson	Australia
Paris–Brussels	E. Vanderaerden	Belgium
G.P. des Nations time trial	B. Hinault	France
Dunkirk 4-day	B. Hinault	France
Tirenno Adriatico	T. Prim	Sweden
Ghent–Wevelgem	G. Bontempi	Italy
Tour of Romandie	S. Roche	Ireland
Tour de l'Avenir	C. Mottet	France
Tour of Britain	O. Czougeda	U.S.S.R.
Berlin–Prague–Warsaw†	S. Soukhoroutchenkov	U.S.S.R.

*Events contested in the Olympic Games not included in world championships program.
†Amateur.

At the Olympic Games in Los Angeles, U.S. cyclist Alexi Grewal (right) sprinted past Steve Bauer of Canada to win the men's road race title.

PAUL KENNEDY—LONG PHOTOGRAPHY, INC.

women, which was held in conjunction with the men's event but over shorter distances, was won by Marianne Martin of the U.S.

The 1984 world championships, excluding Olympic events, took place in Barcelona, Spain. The track program was held on a new outdoor 250-m velodrome. Hans-Henrik Oersted of Denmark established a world best of 5 min 44.36 sec as he won the individual 5,000-m pursuit, and Koichi Nakano of Japan gained a record eighth successive victory in the sprint. Urs Freuler of Switzerland won the professional points race for a fourth consecutive year. The

U.S. retained both women's track titles: Connie Paraskevin completed a hat trick of sprint golds, and Rebecca Twigg regained the 3,000-m pursuit title she had won previously in 1982. Unheralded Claude Criquelion of Belgium won the professional road race, and Steve Bauer of Canada added a bronze medal to his Olympic silver.

(JOHN R. WILKINSON)

FENCING

Something new was added to the international fencing scene in August 1984 when China's 23-year-old Luan Jujie captured the women's foil gold medal at the Olympic Games. The victory was the first ever scored by a Chinese fencer in either world championship or Olympic competition.

Luan's success marked the attainment of a level sought since 1974, when China entered world championship competition in fencing for the first time. Competing at Long Beach's Civic Center in California before an enthusiastic crowd, she impressed onlookers with her intelligent and patient style that helped her score repeated touches with her sudden, single lunges.

Otherwise, Europeans, as in past years, dominated the competition with Italy, France, and West Germany sharing the remainder of the gold medals. The Italians finished first in three of the events, while the French and West Germans each gained golds in two.

Mauro Numa of Italy helped the Italians to two of their first places by capturing the men's individual foil tournament and then pacing his countrymen to victory in the five-man team foil event. Matthias Behr of West Germany placed second to Numa in the individual foil, with Italy's Stefano Cerioni gaining third place. West Germany finished second in team foil, and France was third.

The Italians' other gold medal was gained in team sabre, France placing second and Romania third. In individual sabre top honours went to France's Jean-François Lamour. He was followed by Marco Marin of Italy and Peter Westbrook of the United States in that order.

West Germany gained its gold medals in the remaining two team events, women's foil and men's épée. Second in women's team foil was Romania, followed by France and

AP/WIDE WORLD

In a brilliant final bout of fencing, Mauro Numa (right) of Italy bested Matthias Behr of West Germany to win the men's individual foil competition at the Olympic Games in August. Behr won the silver medal.

Italy. In team épée France finished second ahead of Italy, China, and the United States. In individual épée France made a powerful showing, sandwiching a first place by Philippe Boisse and a third by Philippe Riboud around a second place finish by Sweden's Bjorne Vaggo.

The women's team foil tournament—the foil is the only weapon with which women compete—was decided in less than two hours. The triumph marked the first time that West Germany's women had won the event since it was first introduced to the Olympic Games in 1960. West Germany was led by Cornelia Hanisch and Christiane Weber, both of whom won three of their four contests against the Romanians. (MICHAEL STRAUSS)

FIELD HOCKEY

At the Olympic Games held in Los Angeles in July–August 1984, Pakistan defeated West Germany 2–1 in overtime to win the gold medal. The silver medal was won by West Germany and the bronze by Great Britain, which beat Australia 3–2 in the play-off for third and fourth places. India, winner of the gold medal in the 1980 Olympic Games, placed fifth, followed by The Netherlands, New Zealand, Spain, Kenya, Canada, Malaysia, and the U.S. Two months later West Germany turned the tables on Pakistan with a 4–2 victory in Brussels at a special international match arranged by the Fédération Internationale de Hockey (FIH).

In December 1983 Australia won the ten-nations tournament in Hong Kong with a 3–1 victory over Pakistan in the final. India defeated Great Britain 3–0 in the play-off for third and fourth places. Canada finished fifth, followed by Malaysia, South Korea, Japan, Hong Kong, and China. In a four-nation round-robin tournament at West Berlin in April–May 1984, Australia again placed first, with India second, West Germany third, and The Netherlands fourth. Earlier, India tied Pakistan 2–2 in a special international match in New Delhi.

Indoors, England won the home countries championship in Edinburgh, defeating Scotland 6–4 early in January. In the following month England gained the silver medal in the European championship at the same place. West Germany won the gold medal and The Netherlands the bronze. Scotland finished fourth, followed by France fifth and Italy sixth.

In women's hockey The Netherlands won the gold medal in the Olympic Games round-robin tournament for six nations, followed by West Germany with the silver and the U.S. with the bronze. There was a tie for third place between the U.S. and Australia, and the medal winner was decided on a penalty stroke competition. Canada finished fifth and New Zealand sixth.

The U.S. won a four-nation tournament at Melbourne in March, followed in order by Canada, Australia, and New Zealand. At West Berlin in April The Netherlands finished first, followed by Great Britain, West Germany, and the U.S. in a round-robin tournament. England lost the home countries title 1–0 to Ireland after holding it for four successive years. (SYDNEY E. FRISKIN)

FOOTBALL

Association Football (Soccer). There was an encouraging swing to more exciting and attractive soccer during 1984, with the emphasis on winning rather than avoiding defeat. It was particularly apparent in the European championship (for nations) held in France during June, when the four semifinalists, France, Spain, Portugal, and Denmark, all had scoring as first priority. The trend was also seen in South America.

Off-field hooliganism by fans continued in 1984, as did illegal payments and bribes that afflicted several countries, including Belgium, Hungary, and Yugoslavia. In Belgium eight Standard Liège players were questioned by the police after Eric Gerets, former captain of Standard, admitted paying Waterschei players to lose a crucial match that gave Standard the title in 1982. Gerets, a player with AC Milan during 1984, was suspended by the Italian club and later by the Belgian Football Association, as were several of the others involved.

EUROPEAN CHAMPIONSHIP. France, the host country, won the 1984 European championship, defeating Spain with goals by Michel Platini and Bruno Bellone in the final in Paris on June 27. Platini, the French captain who played in Italy with Juventus, broke the deadlock 11 minutes into the second half and in so doing epitomized the attacking flair that was the hallmark of the competition. His first goal came when he curled a free kick around the line of defending players; the goalkeeper, Luis Arconada, dived to his left to catch the ball but then let it squeeze out from beneath his body and over the line. Buoyed by this gift, the French attack battered away at the Spanish goal, producing some fine saves from Arconada and timely tackles. During the last 15 minutes Spain surged forward, but in the last minute a quick break by the French, instigated by Jean Tigana, allowed Bellone to dash through and chip the ball over the keeper into the net.

The championships had been split into two groups of four nations for the preliminary rounds, and in Group One both France and Denmark managed to score five in a match. Scoring in the other group was not so prolific as Spain and Portugal triumphed to join France and

Table I. Association Football National Champions

Nation	League winners	Cup winners
Albania	Labinoti	17 Nendori
Argentina	Ferrocarril Oeste	
Austria	Austria Vienna	Rapid Vienna
Belgium	Beveren	AA Ghent
Bolivia	Bolívar	
Brazil	Fluminense	
Bulgaria	Levski Spartak	Levski Spartak
Chile	Colo Colo	
Colombia	América	
Cyprus	Omonia	Apoel
Czechoslovakia	Sparta Prague	Dukla Prague
Denmark	Lyngby	Lyngby
Dominican Rep.	La Vega	
Ecuador	Nacional	
England	Liverpool	Everton
Finland	Ilves Tampere	Kuuysi Lahti
France	Bordeaux	Metz
Germany, East	Dynamo Berlin	Dynamo Dresden
Germany, West	Stuttgart	Bayern Munich
Greece	Panathinaikos	Panathinaikos
Guatemala	Aurora	
Honduras	Vida de la Ceiba	
Hungary	Honved	Siofok Baygasz
Iceland	Akranes	Al Akranes
Ireland	Shamrock Rovers	University Coll., Dublin
Italy	Juventus	Roma
Luxembourg	Avenir Beggen	Avenir Beggen
Malta	Valleta City	Hamrun Spartans
Mexico	América	
Netherlands, The	Feyenoord	Feyenoord
Northern Ireland	Linfield	Ballymena
Norway	Vålerengen	Moss
Paraguay	Olimpia	
Peru	Sporting Cristal	
Poland	Lech Poznan	Lech Poznan
Portugal	Benfica	Porto
Romania	Dinamo Bucharest	Dinamo Bucharest
Scotland	Aberdeen	Aberdeen
Spain	Athletico Bilbao	Athletico Bilbao
Sweden	IFK Göteborg	IFK Göteborg
Switzerland	Grasshoppers Zürich	Servette
Turkey	Trabzonspor	Trabzonspor
U.S.S.R.	Dniepr	Dynamo Moscow
U.S.	Chicago Sting	
Uruguay	Central Español	
Wales	—	Wales
Venezuela	Universidad de los Andes	
Yugoslavia	Red Star	Hajduk Split

France defeated Spain for the European association football (soccer) championship. The French captain, Michel Platini, booted in one of the winning goals past Spanish goalkeeper Luis Arconada, who dived on the ball but let it squeeze out from under him.
KEYSTONE

Denmark in the semifinals. France beat Portugal 3–2 in overtime in a semifinal of quality in Marseille on June 23. Defender Jean-François Domergue put the French into the lead in the first half from a well-worked free kick, and Platini kept Manuel Bento leaping and diving to contain the score. Then with a quarter of the game to go, Rui Jordão headed home to tie the score for Portugal. In the first part of the 30-minute overtime, Jordão volleyed home. The French rose to the occasion, however, as Domergue tied the match, and Platini scored the winning goal in the final seconds. Spain and Denmark also played an overtime match in their semifinal in Lyon the following day. Thanks mainly to the superb efforts of goalkeepers Arconada and Denmark's Ole Qvist, neither team could manage a goal during the extra period. So it went to a penalty shoot-out, which Spain won 5–4.

EUROPEAN CHAMPIONS' CUP. Liverpool, the English champion, regained the premier club trophy in Europe by defeating Roma, the Italian representatives, 4–2 in a penalty shoot-out before nearly 70,000 spectators in Rome on May 30. The game had ended in a 1–1 tie, and the two teams had battled through overtime without adding to the scores. Phil Neal scored after 14 minutes for Liverpool after goalkeeper Franco Tancredi dropped a cross. Subsequently, Roma improved, and Bruce Grobbelaar was forced to make some fine saves before being beaten three minutes from the halftime break by Roberto Pruzzo. Fear of losing seemed to dominate the second-half play, but in the closing stages Liverpool tested Tancredi, and Roma, with Bruno Conti as the mainspring, evoked some good Grobbelaar saves. The drama continued to the shoot-out with Steve Nicol—playing as a substitute—directing the first spot kick over the bar. The other four Liverpool kickers were on the mark, but Roma's World Cup players Conti and Francesco Graziani both shot over the bar to allow Graeme Souness, the Liverpool captain, to collect the trophy.

EUROPEAN CUP-WINNERS' CUP. Juventus of Italy took the Cup-Winners' Cup on May 16 in Basel, Switz., before a capacity crowd of 60,000. The Italians turned in a steely performance to edge Porto of Portugal 2–1. With a host of World Cup stars, Juventus was expected to run roughshod over Porto, but the Portuguese club fought hard. Juventus went ahead with a shot from Beniamino Vignola after 12 minutes. Much of the fine Juventus midfield work stemmed from the promptings of the team's Polish international player Zbigniew Boniek, and Porto had to keep the ball from reaching him. Porto swung back into the game after a half hour when Stefano Tacconi in the Juventus goal seemed to be a little slow in going for a shot from A. Sousa that tied the score. But Juventus persevered, and the nimble Boniek reached a chip from Vignola and touched the ball into the net. Porto again rallied and twice drew fine reflex saves from Tacconi. During the second half Juventus boldly went out to extend its lead but wasted opportunities and eventually decided instead to protect its advantage; Claudio Gentile was switched to mark the lively Fernando Gomes, and even though Porto made its permitted two substitutions, bringing on Irish striker Micky Walsh and midfield man José Costa to boost its attack, it was unable to alter the destiny of the trophy.

OLYMPIC GAMES. The football tournament at the 1984 Olympics in Los Angeles was initially divided into four groups: Group A—Chile, France, Norway, Qatar; Group B—Cameroon, Canada, Iraq, Yugoslavia; Group C—Brazil, Morocco, Saudi Arabia, West Germany; and Group D—Costa Rica, Egypt, Italy, the U.S. From each group the top two went on to the quarterfinals, with the following results: Italy 1, Chile 0; France 2, Egypt 0; Brazil 1, Canada 1 (Brazil won on a penalty shoot-out 4–2); Yugoslavia 5, West Germany 2. In the semifinals France beat Yugoslavia 4–2, and Brazil defeated Italy 2–1. France then beat Brazil in the final 2–0 to become the Olympic champion. The attendance at the final, 101,799, was a U.S. record for soccer. Unusually, countries were permitted to field their national professional teams.

NORTH AMERICAN SOCCER LEAGUE. The problems of the North American Soccer League (NASL) increased rather than abated during the year, and at the end of the season in

October 1984 the component clubs had dwindled to five: Cosmos (New York), Minnesota, Tampa Bay, Toronto, and Vancouver. The rest were disbanded, merged, or went into the indoor league. The Chicago Sting defeated the Toronto Blizzard to become Soccer Bowl champions by winning the first two legs of a three-leg final; the Sting then left the NASL and moved indoors. The two Sting-Blizzard games highlighted the major problem, lack of attendance. On October 1 in Chicago a mere 8,352 fans paid to see the game—a poor return from a city with a catchment area of some eight million people. In that match the Blizzard took the lead after 15 minutes when Bruce Wilson, the captain, drilled the ball between the legs of goalkeeper Victor Nogueira into the net. In the second half the Sting moved more purposefully and tied the score with a header from Pato Margetic. Then, with less than five minutes remaining, Manny Rojas slotted in the winner for Chicago.

The return match in the Varsity stadium at Toronto two days later attracted double the number of fans, who generated an enthusiasm often missing from NASL games. Yet for all their enthusiasm the Canadian supporters had to endure Chicago's taking a 2–0 lead with goals by Mark Simanton (17 minutes) and Margetic (68 minutes). After the second goal the Blizzard sent in John Paskin, who quickly reduced the lead to 2–1, and two minutes later Roberto Bettega tied the score. Margetic staged a late show by scoring the winning goal with eight minutes left.

(TREVOR WILLIAMSON)

LATIN AMERICA. After several years of disappointment an Argentine team finally won a major world-class trophy in 1984. The Club Atlético Independiente of Avellaneda, a town just outside Buenos Aires, defeated Great Britain's Liverpool in Tokyo on December 9 to win the Inter-Continental Cup, the unofficial world championship for professional clubs. Earlier in the season Independiente outplayed Grêmio of Porto Alegre, Brazil, to win the Libertadores de América Cup; Grêmio had won this South American championship and the Inter-Continental Cup in 1983. Independiente's international accomplishments, though, were of little help in the hard-fought Argentine football league; Ferrocarril Oeste of Buenos Aires won the national title.

Grêmio did not fare any better within Brazil; the team was defeated by Vasco da Gama of Rio de Janeiro in the national semifinals. In the Brazilian championship series Vasco da Gama played another team from Rio de Janeiro, Fluminense. The traditional rivalry between the two was heightened by the fact that Fluminense was led by the outgoing head coach of Brazil's national team, Carlos Alberto Pereira, while Vasco was managed by the new national coach, Eduardo Antunes ("Edú"). Fluminense and Pereira were the winners in the confrontation.

A star-studded América, from Mexico City, was clearly the best team in Mexico's football league. In Uruguay Peñarol, a team that had dominated the national football scene for years, was unable to repeat its overpowering performances of 1982 and 1983, and so Central Español was able to become the surprise winner of the league championship. In Paraguay, Colombia, and Bolivia, though, Olimpia of Asunción, América of Cali, and Bolívar of La Paz repeated their triumphs of 1983.

Colo Colo of Santiago won the Chilean football title, while Nacional of Quito was the champion in Ecuador. Sporting Cristal of Lima took the Peruvian league, and Universidad de los Andes de Mérida became the Venezuelan champion. In Central America Aurora won in Guatemala and Vida de la Ceiba in Honduras. La Vega gained the national title in the Dominican Republic.

(SERGIO SARMIENTO)

Rugby. RUGBY UNION. The 1983–84 period was one of unusual achievements, the most notable of which was perhaps Scotland's feat of defeating all the other countries in the Five Nations Tournament in one season. This was the first time that such a grand slam had been achieved since 1925. The Five Nations Tournament indeed had an exciting climax, with Scotland and France, each of which had defeated everybody else, meeting on the last day of the tournament at Murrayfield, Edinburgh, for the championship and the grand slam. Scotland, captained by Jim Aitken and coached by Jim Telfer, eventually won the match 21–12. France finished second, with Wales third, England fourth, and Ireland last. Ireland lost all four of its matches, and England's only victory was over Ireland.

During the period leading up to the Five Nations Tournament—before Christmas 1983—England fared better than the other countries. Having beaten the touring Canadians 27–0 at Twickenham in October, England went on to defeat the All Blacks of New Zealand 15–9 on the same field in November. The All Blacks were on an eight-match tour of Scotland and England, during the course of which they drew 25–25 with Scotland at Murrayfield in the only other international match of the tour. In the same period, the Japanese held Wales to a score of 29–24 at Cardiff on their five-match tour of the U.K., and Wales was defeated 24–6 by Romania in Bucharest. In May 1984, the Romanians beat Scotland, also in Bucharest, 28–22.

AP/WIDE WORLD

In the third quarter of this game against the New Orleans Saints on October 7, Walter Payton of the Chicago Bears set a new career record for rushing (12,317 yards), surpassing by 5 yards that of Jim Brown, formerly of the Cleveland Browns, to become the top runner in the history of pro football.

Brigham Young University won the unofficial national collegiate football championship with a 13–0 record. The championship was clinched in the Holiday Bowl against Michigan. Robbie Bosco (holding ball), Brigham Young's quarterback, returned to finish the game after suffering injuries earlier in play. He made a 13-yard pass to Kelly Smith (21) in the end zone for the winning touchdown.
RAVELL CALL

In May and June England went on a seven-match tour of South Africa, winning four games, drawing one, and losing two. The two that were lost were the two test matches of the tour, the scores being 33–15 at Port Elizabeth and 35–9 at Ellis Park, Johannesburg. In the two tests South Africa's Springboks scored nine tries to England's none. Danie Gerber, a forceful centre three-quarter back, scored three tries in the Ellis Park Test and one at Port Elizabeth.

The All Blacks were especially busy in June, July, and August, playing five tests during that time, two against France in New Zealand and three against the Wallabies in Australia. For their eight-match tour of New Zealand the French were without their long-standing captain, Jean-Pierre Rives, the leadership being taken over by Philippe Dintrans, the hooker. The French won all six of the provincial games, playing handsome, open rugby, but the All Blacks got the better of them in the tests, winning 10–9 at Christchurch and 31–18 at Auckland.

It came as something of a surprise, therefore, when the All Blacks were defeated 16–9 in their first test match against the Wallabies at Sydney. The second test, at Brisbane, resulted in a win for the All Blacks by 19–15, and then in the deciding contest, at Sydney, the All Blacks scored a narrow victory of 25–24.

RUGBY LEAGUE. The Southern Hemisphere countries again showed their strength when Great Britain toured Australia and New Zealand in mid-1984. The British team failed to win any of the six tests that they played in those two countries. Australia defeated Great Britain 25–8 in Sydney, 18–6 in Brisbane, and 20–7 in Sydney again. On the New Zealand section of the tour, Great Britain was beaten 12–0 at Auckland, 28–12 at Christchurch, and 32–16 at Auckland. On the way home, however, Great Britain managed to defeat Papua New Guinea 38–20 at Port Moresby. Earlier in the year Great Britain had won both the customary tests against France, the scores having been 12–0 at Avignon and 10–0 at Headingley.

(DAVID FROST)

U.S. Football. PROFESSIONAL. Led by the passing and running of quarterback Joe Montana, the San Francisco 49ers won the championship of the National Football League (NFL) by defeating the Miami Dolphins 38–16 in the Super Bowl on Jan. 20, 1985, at Stanford, Calif. Mon-

tana, voted the game's most valuable player, threw for three touchdowns and ran for one. His 331 yd passing set a Super Bowl record, as did San Francisco's total of 537 yd gained and 31 first downs. Miami quarterback Dan Marino (see BIOGRAPHIES) was rushed throughout the day by the effective 49er defense but set a Super Bowl record of 29 passes completed (one for a touchdown) out of 50 attempts.

San Francisco, the first NFL team to win 15 games in a regular season, won the Western Division of the NFC by allowing the league's fewest points and scoring the second most. The 49ers' offense also ranked third in rushing yards, fourth in passing yards, and second in total yards behind conference-leading passer Montana. Kicker Ray Wersching led NFL scorers with 131 points.

Table II. NFL Final Standings and Play-offs, 1984							
AMERICAN CONFERENCE				NATIONAL CONFERENCE			
	W	L	T		W	L	T
Eastern Division				**Eastern Division**			
*Miami	14	2	0	*Washington	11	5	0
New England	9	7	0	*New York Giants	9	7	0
New York Jets	7	9	0	Dallas	9	7	0
Indianapolis	4	12	0	St. Louis	9	7	0
Buffalo	2	14	0	Philadelphia	6	9	1
Central Division				**Central Division**			
*Pittsburgh	9	7	0	*Chicago	10	6	0
Cincinnati	8	8	0	Green Bay	8	8	0
Cleveland	5	11	0	Tampa Bay	6	10	0
Houston	3	13	0	Detroit	4	11	1
				Minnesota	3	13	0
Western Division				**Western Division**			
*Denver	13	3	0	*San Francisco	15	1	0
*Seattle	12	4	0	*Los Angeles Rams	10	6	0
*Los Angeles Raiders	11	5	0	New Orleans	7	9	0
Kansas City	8	8	0	Atlanta	4	12	0
San Diego	7	9	0				

*Qualified for play-offs.

Play-offs	
Wild-card round	**American finals**
Seattle 13, Los Angeles Raiders 7	Miami 45, Pittsburgh 28
New York Giants 16, Los Angeles Rams 14	
American semifinals	**National finals**
Miami 31, Seattle 10	San Francisco 23, Chicago 0
Pittsburgh 24, Denver 17	
National semifinals	**Super Bowl**
Chicago 23, Washington 19	San Francisco 38, Miami 16
San Francisco 21, New York Giants 10	

Marino set five NFL passing records with 48 touchdowns, 362 completions, 5,084 yd gained, nine 300-yd games, and four 400-yd games. Marino's 108.9 passer rating led the league. The Dolphins, with a won-lost record of 14–2, led the NFL with 433.5 total yards and 313.6 net passing yards per game and became the first team with two pass receivers to gain 1,300 yd in a season, Mark Clayton and Mark Duper. Clayton's 18 touchdown catches set a league record, and he tied the Los Angeles Raiders' Marcus Allen for the NFL's most touchdowns.

Few important offensive records survived the season, although league scoring dropped 1.3 points per game to 42.4, the second highest since the 1970 merger with the American Football League. Eric Dickerson of the Los Angeles Rams set single-season records with 2,105 rushing yards, 2,244 total yards from scrimmage, and 12 games with at least 100 yd gained rushing. James Wilder of the Tampa Bay Buccaneers had a record 407 rushing attempts. Art Monk of the Washington Redskins set a record with 106 pass catches.

Walter Payton of the Chicago Bears broke Jim Brown's career rushing record by 997 yd, finishing the season with 13,309. Payton, who had 1,648 yd rushing in his tenth season, also set career records with 63 100-yd games, 3,047 rushing attempts, three 2,000-yd seasons in total yards from scrimmage, and 17,294 combined yards on runs, passes and kick returns. Charlie Joiner of the San Diego Chargers broke the career receiving record with 657 catches.

Chicago and the New York Giants were the only play-off teams that had not been in the ten-team tournament the previous season. Chicago won the NFC Central Division, Washington won the NFC Eastern Division, and the Rams and the Giants were NFC wild-card teams. In the AFC Miami won the Eastern Division, the Pittsburgh Steelers won the Central Division, and the Denver Broncos won the Western Division; the wild-card teams were the Raiders and the Seattle Seahawks.

In the wild-card round of the play-offs, Seattle defeated the defending champion Raiders 13–7, and the Giants beat the Rams 16–13. The American Conference semifinals resulted in a 31–10 victory by Miami over Seattle

and a 24–17 upset triumph by Pittsburgh over Denver. In the National Conference semifinal round, San Francisco defeated the Giants 21–10, and Chicago triumphed over Washington 23–19. Miami qualified for the Super Bowl by defeating Pittsburgh 45–28 in the American Conference finals, as did San Francisco with a 23–0 victory over Chicago in the National Conference title game.

Chicago set an NFL record with 72 quarterback sacks, including 17½ by NFC leader Richard Dent. Mark Gastineau of the New York Jets led the NFL with 22. Chicago's offense led the league with the fourth highest rushing yards in NFL history, an average of 185.3 per game. Chicago's defense allowed the fewest total yards (241.4) and rushing yards (86.1) per game and finished just 2.1 yd behind New Orleans' league-low 153.3 passing yards allowed per game.

Seattle's defense led the league with 38 interceptions, 25 fumble recoveries, and a turnover differential of plus-24. Seattle safety Ken Easley's ten interceptions were the most by one player. Seattle coach Chuck Knox was NFL coach of the year, because the Seahawks overcame an injury to 1983 conference rushing leader Curt Warner in their first game. The Seahawks' defense and kicking teams scored nine touchdowns on returns. Denver, which finished one game ahead of Seattle at 13–3, was similarly opportunistic with eight touchdowns on returns and a plus-21 turnover differential.

Other league leaders were Roy Green of the St. Louis Cardinals, whose 1,555 yd on 78 pass receptions was third highest in NFL history; Tony Eason of the New England Patriots, who threw only eight interceptions and had the highest touchdown-interception ratio with 23 touchdown passes; the Atlanta Falcons' Steve Bartkowski, with a .673 pass-completion percentage; the Kansas City Chiefs' Jim Arnold, with a 44.9-yd gross punting average; Miami's Reggie Roby, with a 38.1-yd net punting average; the Cincinnati Bengals' Mike Martin, with a 15.7-yd punt return average; the Jets' Bobby Humphery, with a 30.7-yd kickoff return average; and the Seahawks' Norm Johnson, with an .833 field-goal percentage. The NFL had its highest league-wide field-goal percentage, .719.

The NFL's biggest problems off the field were the moving

AP/WIDE WORLD

The San Francisco 49ers beat the Miami Dolphins 38–16 to win the National Football League championship in the Super Bowl on Jan. 20, 1985. San Francisco running back Carl Monroe (32) dives over Miami Dolphins defenders to score a touchdown in the first quarter.

of franchises and the two-year-old United States Football League (USFL), which bid player salaries up and signed almost one-third of the top 100 rookies. The Colts moved to Indianapolis after 31 seasons in Baltimore. NFL owners said that antitrust laws made them powerless to stop similar shifts as franchise owners in Philadelphia, New Orleans, and St. Louis indicated that they might want to move.

The Philadelphia Stars defeated the Arizona Wranglers 23–3 in Tampa, Fla., on July 15 for the USFL championship. The Stars then merged with Pittsburgh and moved to Baltimore as the financially troubled league trimmed down from 18 teams to 14. Philadelphia and Arizona allowed the fewest points in the league (12.5 and 15.8 per game, respectively), and the Houston Gamblers scored the most. In yardage, Houston gained the greatest total, and Arizona allowed the least. Philadelphia's 16–2 regular-season record was the league's best. League-leading USFL players included most valuable player Jim Kelly of Houston, with 44 touchdown passes and 5,219 yd passing; league-leading passer Chuck Fusina of Philadelphia, with a .649 completion percentage; Birmingham's Joe Cribbs with 1,467 yd rushing; Houston's Richard Johnson with 115 catches and 1,455 yd receiving; Houston's Toni Fritsch with 130 points; and New Jersey's Herschel Walker and Tampa Bay's Gary Anderson with 21 touchdowns.

COLLEGE. Brigham Young University won the unofficial national collegiate football championship in 1984. Its 13–0 record was only the second in the history of the National Collegiate Athletic Association's (NCAA's) Division 1-A, which encompassed the biggest schools. Brigham Young's championship, clinched in a 24–17 victory over Michigan in the Holiday Bowl on December 21, was controversial because the Cougars' Western Athletic Conference was not considered among the country's best. But no other Division 1-A team was undefeated. Second-ranked Washington (11–1) was the only team with just one blemish on its record, and third-ranked Florida (9–1–1) was the only other team with fewer than two defeats. With a 24-game winning streak, Brigham Young became the fifth team in a row to win its first national championship.

Another unlikely champion was Doug Flutie of fifth-ranked Boston College (10–2), a 5-ft 9¾-in quarterback who became the first passer in 13 years to win the Heisman Trophy, awarded to the country's best college player. Boston College, which had gone 0–11 in 1978, finished 31–11–1 for Flutie's four seasons and won its first bowl game in 44 years, 45–28 over Southwest Conference champion Houston in the Cotton Bowl, Jan. 1, 1985. Flutie shattered career records for passing yardage and total offense, and he captured hearts across the country when he threw the ball 64 yd into a gusting wind on November 23 for a 48-yd touchdown on the last play of a 47–45 victory over Miami.

Flutie was leading passer with 152.9 rating points, followed closely by Brigham Young's Robbie Bosco with 151.8 and Miami's Bernie Kosar with 148.7. Boston College also edged Brigham Young in scoring, 36.7 points per game to 36, but Bosco outgained Flutie in total offense, 327.7 yd per game to 327.5. Brigham Young beat runner-up Boston College in yards per game, 486.5 to 483.4, and had 346.2 passing yards per game for its seventh passing title in nine seasons. Army led the country with 345.3 yd rushing per game.

Keith Byars, of Big Ten winner Ohio State, led the country with 1,655 yd rushing, 144 points, and 2,284 all-purpose yards. But Ohio State (9–3) lost the Rose Bowl 20–17 to Pacific Ten winner Southern California, giving the Pac Ten its first overall lead in the bowl series, 20–19.

Washington led the country defensively by allowing five yards per play and intercepting 27 passes. The Huskies also had a nation-high turnover differential of plus-28 and won the Orange Bowl 28–17 over Oklahoma (9–2–1), the Big Eight champion. Fourth-ranked Nebraska, a 28–10 Sugar Bowl winner over 8–3–1 Louisiana State, allowed the fewest points and yards per game (9.5 and 203.3). UCLA (9–3) won the Fiesta, the other New Year's Day bowl game, 39–37 over Miami (8–5).

Other top defenses for the season were Texas Tech against the pass (114.8 yd per game) and Oklahoma against the run (68.8 yd per game). Virginia Tech's defense ranked third in total yards and second in scoring and against the run, led by Outland Trophy winner Bruce Smith at defensive tackle. Texas defensive tackle Tony Degrate won the other prize for the country's top lineman, the Lombardi Award.

Florida won the Southeast Conference but was banned from bowl games because of recruiting violations. Other conference winners were Maryland in the Atlantic Coast, Toledo in the Mid-American, Nevada-Las Vegas in the Pacific Coast, Alcorn State in the Southwestern, Montana State in the Big Sky, Eastern Kentucky in the Ohio Valley, Boston University and Rhode Island in the Yankee, and Pennsylvania in the Ivy League.

Mississippi Valley State, a small school from the NCAA's Division 1-AA, kept scoreboards blinking with 60.9 points, 640.1 total yards, and 496.8 passing yards per game. In Division 1-AA play-offs Montana State improved from 1–10 to 12–2 and beat Louisiana Tech 19–6 for the championship. Other national championships for smaller schools went to Troy (Ala.) State in Division II, which defeated North Dakota State 18–17, and in Division III to Augustana (Ill.), which beat previously undefeated Central (Iowa) 21–12 and extended its unbeaten streak to 24 games. The National Association for Intercollegiate Athletics (NAIA) championship game ended in a 19–19 tie between Carson-Newman (Tenn.) and Central Arkansas, and Linfield (Ore.) defeated Northwestern (Iowa) 33–22 for the NAIA Division II crown.

Canadian Football. The Winnipeg Blue Bombers scored 27 points in the second quarter to beat the Hamilton Tiger-Cats 47–17 in the Grey Cup game for the Canadian Football League championship on November 18 at Edmonton, Alta. It was Winnipeg's first Grey Cup appearance since 1965 and first championship since 1962.

Defensive plays set up the scoring outburst, which overcame a 17–3 deficit. David Shaw's 34-yd interception return set up one touchdown. Stan Mikawos scored the next one with a 22-yd return of a fumble forced by one of Tyrone Jones's four quarterback sacks. Winnipeg quarterback Tom Clements, who played with painfully bruised ribs, was voted the game's most outstanding player after completing 20 of 29 passes for 281 yd and two touchdowns. Sean Kehoe, who ran 12 times for 89 yd, was the outstanding Canadian player.

Neither finalist had finished first in its division. Hamilton had a 6–9–1 regular-season record but upset 9–6–1 Toronto in the Eastern Division championship game. Winnipeg, after an 11–4–1 regular season, defeated 12–3–1 British Columbia for the Western Division title.

Winnipeg won individual honours when running back Willard Reaves was named the league's most outstanding player and centre John Bonk the top offensive lineman. British Columbia linebacker James Parker was voted the top defensive player, Montreal running back Dwaine Wilson the top rookie, and Montreal tight end Nick Aragki the outstanding Canadian player.   (KEVIN M. LAMB)

GOLF

Not for some years had there been such public approval of the four winners of golf's major championships as in 1984. There was as much rejoicing early in the season when Ben Crenshaw, so often a crown prince but one seemingly destined never to be king, at last won the Masters as there was later when Lee Trevino took the U.S. Professional Golfers' Association (PGA) championship. Sportsmanship and good humour were two of the outstanding qualities as Frank ("Fuzzy") Zoeller collected his first U.S. Open championship, and the exciting talent of Severiano Ballesteros of Spain again caught the imagination when he won the British Open for a second time.

It was widely feared that the 32-year-old Crenshaw, an enthusiastic golf historian and one almost in awe of its great traditions, might never win the major championship he had craved for so long. He came to Augusta, Ga., in April with his expectations lifted only by a high finish the week before in the Greensboro (N.C.) tournament. Twice already a runner-up in the Masters, he had often put an unnecessary burden on his shoulders with a poor first round. But on this occasion there seemed to be a new resolve about him, particularly after he shot a 67 in the first round to lead the field. An old driver he had found in his travels may have lost him distance, but it did bring him accuracy, which had frequently been the weakest part of his game. Although he was quickly overhauled in the second round by Mark Lye, who began 69, 66, Crenshaw held his ground and after the rain-delayed third round stood two strokes behind Tom Kite and one behind Lye. The anxiety that comes with never having won a major championship undermined Kite as Crenshaw suddenly went from strength to strength. Often an inspired putter, Crenshaw could do no wrong on Augusta's swift and undulating greens and with a final round of 68 for a total of 277, 11 strokes under par, beat Tom Watson by two strokes.

In the U.S. Open at Winged Foot Golf Club near New York City, Crenshaw began with an 80 and failed to qualify for the last two rounds. Hale Irwin set the pace for three rounds with two 68s and then a 69. Meanwhile, both Greg Norman of Australia and Zoeller had advanced to within a single stroke of the leader. In the riveting fourth round Irwin quickly faded, Zoeller took command, and Norman finished strongly with a cluster of single-putt holes that very nearly won him the championship. Instead he and Zoeller tied with 276, 14 under par. Zoeller won the play-off the following day with a 67 to Norman's 75.

Zoeller's victory was immensely popular. On the last hole of regulation play Norman missed the green with his second shot, his ball coming to rest in a grandstand from where he was allowed to drop it clear without penalty. He then pitched onto the green and holed a very long putt for a four. All this was watched by Zoeller as he waited to play his own second shot to the green. However, he thought Norman's putt was for a birdie three rather than a par four, and with a broad grin he produced a white towel which he waved in mock surrender. When the two came to the 18th green in the play-off round, it was Norman who produced the white towel.

A British Open championship at St. Andrews, Scotland, the home of golf, is always a special occasion, and the victory by Ballesteros, who finished two strokes ahead of Watson and Bernhard Langer of West Germany, was no exception. For two days the dominating figure in the tournament was a little-known Australian, Ian Baker-Finch. It was his first British Open, but with rounds of 68 and 66 he established an unlikely three-stroke lead over Ballesteros, Trevino, and Nick Faldo, who was ultimately to be

Ben Crenshaw won the U.S. Masters golf championship at Georgia's Augusta National Golf Club on April 15. His score of 277 was 11 under par. He defeated Tom Watson by two strokes. It was his first major tournament victory.
AP/WIDE WORLD

the leading British player for the second consecutive year. However, a strong move was soon made by Watson, who was not only seeking a third successive British Open victory but also trying to equal Harry Vardon's long-standing record of six championships. After three rounds Watson had caught Baker-Finch and was two ahead of Ballesteros and Langer.

It quickly became evident that the destiny of the title lay between Ballesteros and Watson, the lead changing hands more than once until they came to the last few holes tied. Much depended on how each played the 17th, the legendary Road Hole that had caused many players much trouble throughout the week. Ballesteros, playing the hole first, got his first par four of the championship and then followed it with a birdie three on the 18th for a final round of 69 and a four-round total of 276. It was too much for Watson. After what appeared to be a perfect drive on the 17th, he inexplicably overhit the green with his second shot up against a stone wall and took a five. Since Ballesteros had by then sunk his putt on the 18th hole for a birdie, Watson needed an eagle two on that hole to tie, which proved to be beyond him. The Spaniard collected a first prize of £55,000, prize money having been increased by 10% by the Royal and Ancient in midchampionship as record crowds of more than 187,000 came to watch the week's play.

It had been ten years since Trevino had last won a major championship, and at the age of 44, plagued as he was by a bad back and pressed as he was by the increasing demands of being a television commentator, it was suspected that he was well into the dusk of a splendid and colourful career. But at the Shoal Creek golf course in Birmingham, Ala., he shed the years as dismissively as he shrugged aside aching muscles with some of the best golf of his life. With rounds of 69, 68, 67, and 69, he became the first man to win the PGA tournament without once scoring in the 70s. The longer the championship went on, the stronger Trevino became as he shook off the challenges of Lanny Wadkins and Gary Player of South Africa, who shared second place four strokes behind. With Player approaching his 49th birthday—and still good enough to score 63 on his second round—it was an encouraging week for those over 40.

As usual it was the U.S. players who dominated the major championships, and it was another of their number, Fred Couples, who won the Tournament Players' Championship, which some would regard as the fifth most important event of the year. A strong young man, Couples established himself with a second round of 64 at the Tournament Players' Club at Ponte Vedra, Fla., and then proceeded to hang on to beat Trevino by a stroke. His total of 277, 11 under par, was fine golf on one of an increasing number of courses owned by the U.S. PGA tour and featuring what had become known as "stadium" golf with natural terracing for spectators beside the fairways and greens.

There were claims that the Suntory match-play championship at Wentworth in England should demand world status, particularly now that it had celebrated its 21st anniversary. It was won for the third time in four years by Ballesteros when he defeated Langer, his main rival in Europe, by two and one in the 36-hole final. Not since 1978 had a U.S. player, Bill Rogers, won the title, and the disinclination of major U.S. golfers to compete could rebound on the U.S. if they wished to continue winning the Ryder Cup.

The Americans did give match-play golf a tentative revival in the first U.S. tournament of the year, the Tucson (Ariz.) Open. It was won by Tom Watson, who went on to become the leading money winner for the fifth time in eight years with $476,260. He was at the top of the list for practically the entire year, though he was briefly threatened toward the end by another Watson—Denis, a South African. In three years Denis Watson had never finished higher than 74th on the U.S. circuit until near the end of the 1984 season, when he won three tournaments in quick succession. One of them was the richest tournament on the PGA tour, the Panasonic Las Vegas Invitational, with prize money totaling $1,122,500.

Jack Nicklaus continued to limit his schedule but still revealed his mastery when he won the Memorial tournament on the course he designed, Muirfield Village, in Ohio. There was also a promising debut on the U.S. tour by Norman, who won two tournaments and was twice beaten in play-offs for others. Faldo also recorded a rare British

victory in the U.S. when he won the Sea Pines Heritage Classic at Hilton Head Island, S.C.

Prize money on the European circuit continued to increase, and for the second time in four years Langer was the leading money winner with a record £139,000. He won four tournaments—the French, Irish, Dutch, and Spanish championships. At Sunningdale, England, Gordon Brand, Jr., won the Panasonic-sponsored European Open, scoring a ten-under-par 270, three strokes ahead of Ballesteros and Neol Ratcliffe of Australia, who tied for second place.

The U.S. Ladies Professional Golf Association (LPGA) tour continued to grow with annual prize money surpassing $8 million. The leading money winner was Betsy King with $263,815. The prime prize, however, went to Hollis Stacy when she won the U.S. Women's Open for the third time, by a stroke from Rose Jones.

After a short interval the British Women's Open championship was revived in grand style under the sponsorship of the Japanese firm Hitachi Ltd., and it was appropriately won by a Japanese player, Ayako Okamoto, in a commanding manner. In often wild and windy weather on a tough course at Woburn in Bedfordshire, England, she was the only player to break par for the tournament, scoring 289 for the four rounds and winning by 11 strokes. As with two tournaments in Japan, the British event was part of the U.S. LPGA tour, but the U.S. players got no nearer to gaining the title than did the British. Second place was shared by Betsy King (U.S.) and Dale Reid (U.K.).

The high prize money in the British Women's Open, $200,000, enabled Reid to overtake Katrina Douglas, who had dominated the European circuit for most of the season, at the top of the European money list, though for consistency week in and week out it was Douglas who took the honours. This was gratifying to Douglas. She had turned professional early in the season after being omitted from the British Curtis Cup team, which was due to meet—and was defeated by—the U.S. at Muirfield in Scotland. It was, nevertheless, a close match, only a point separating the two teams over the two days; one putt that was missed by Penny Grice on the 18th green made all the difference.

AP/WIDE WORLD

Hollis Stacy kisses the trophy she received after winning the U.S. Women's Open at the Salem Country Club, Peabody, Massachusetts, in July.

Surprisingly, for a match on Scottish soil, there was not one Scot on the British team, although one of those left out, Gilliam Stewart, later won, as an amateur, a professional tournament at the Belfry, near Birmingham, England.

If amateur golf was in apparent decline, it was because of the rush of young players to turn professional at the earliest opportunity. The amateur circuit had, therefore, become a sort of training ground for the future. Notably, in the U.K., José-Maria Olazabal of Spain, who had won the Boys' championship in 1983, now triumphed at senior level, beating Colin Montgomerie of the U.K. in the final at Formby, Lancashire. Scott Verplank defeated Sam Randolph in match play at Oak Tree Golf Club in Edmond, Okla., to win the U.S. amateur title.

(MICHAEL E. J. WILLIAMS)

GYMNASTICS

The United States ranked first in both men's and women's gymnastics at the 1984 Olympic Games in Los Angeles. It was the first time since 1904 that the U.S. men had been accorded top team honours; the women had never had an individual all-around gold medalist. The men's team, led by three-time Olympian Bart Conner, won the team gold medal over the reigning world champions from China. Mary Lou Retton (*see* BIOGRAPHIES) became the first U.S. woman to win the all-around, defeating Ecaterina Szabo of Romania by 0.050 point. The nonparticipation of the U.S.S.R. affected both the men's and women's competitions; the nonparticipation of East Germany slightly affected the women's events.

The exercises were performed with more "risk, originality, and virtuosity" (official interpretation by the International Gymnastic Federation) than in any previous international competition. Although more perfect scores of ten were awarded by the judges' panel, this was no indication that the judges were becoming more lenient. The routines of the gymnasts merited the higher scores.

The U.S. victory in the men's team event over China was unexpected, yet earned. The U.S. won by scoring higher in the compulsory exercises. The victory of Romania over the U.S. in the women's competition was expected. Retton's victory over Szabo in the women's all-around was a major upset, resulting from two tens for Retton in the vault and floor exercises, compared with a single ten on the balance beam and 9.95 in floor exercises for Szabo. Szabo was best in the individual events, placing first in the vault, the floor exercise, and the balance beam (shared with teammate Simona Pauca). First place in the uneven parallel bars was shared by Julianne McNamara (U.S.) and Ma Yanhong (China).

The top three men in the all-around competition were within 0.125 point of one another. The winner was Koji Gushiken of Japan (*see* BIOGRAPHIES), followed by Peter Vidmar (U.S.) and Li Ning (China). In the individual events Li won the floor exercise, shared the side horse (pommel horse) with Vidmar, and tied with Gushiken on the rings. Conner won the parallel bars, Lou Yun of China the long horse vault, and Shinji Morisue of Japan the horizontal bar.

Rhythmic gymnastics was introduced as an individual all-around event for women in which gymnasts exhibit with hoops, balls, streamers, and Indian clubs. The absence of Bulgaria and the U.S.S.R. affected the final results. Lori Fung of Canada won an unexpected victory over Doina Staiculescu of Romania 57.950 to 57.900 (out of a possible 60). Regina Weber (West Germany) won the bronze medal. (CHARLES ROBERT PAUL, JR.)

See also *Track and Field Sports:* Special Report, below.

Koji Gushiken of Japan won the gold medal for the men's individual all-around gymnastics competition at the Olympic Games in Los Angeles in August. He defeated Peter Vidmar of the U.S. by 0.025 point.
ROBERT HAGEDOHM—LONG PHOTOGRAPHY, INC.

HANDBALL

Naty Alvarado of Los Angeles won his sixth United States Handball Association (USHA) national open singles title by defeating John Sabo of Summit, N.J., 21–7, 21–9 at the Merritt/Security Court Club in Baltimore, Md. In the USHA's open doubles competition, Alvarado and Vern Roberts of Tucson, Ariz., defeated Dennis Haynes and Jaime Paredes of Los Angeles 21–14, 21–17 for the title. In masters play for men 40 and over, Pat Kirby of Tucson triumphed over Neal Manning, also of Tucson, 21–12, 21–13. Rosemary Bellini of New York City defeated Diane Harmon of Long Beach, Calif., 21–17, 21–12 for the women's singles title. In women's doubles Allison Roberts and Gloria Motal of Cincinnati, Ohio, defeated Bellini and Harmon 21–14, 21–7.

In three-wall action at Toledo, Ohio, in September, Alvarado defeated Roberts 21–15, 21–9 for the U.S. singles title. Alvarado and Roberts won the doubles by defeating Ken Ginty of New York City and Sabo 15–21, 21–6, 11–1. In masters play for men 40 and over, Tom Natale of Tucson defeated Ken Crespi of Detroit 21–19, 21–5, while George Miller and Jay Dillon of Toledo triumphed over Manning and Terry Nolan of Tucson 21–20, 21–6 for the doubles championship. Ed Novak of Warren, Mich., defeated George Jackson of New York City 21–8, 21–5 for the golden masters title for men 50 and over. Ed Beirne and Floyd Olson of Chicago beat Jackson and Sonny Schaefer of New York City in the doubles 21–19, 21–5. In action for men 60 and over, Max Lasskow and Henry Saftcheck of New York City defeated Jerry Breen and Tony Bertoni of Detroit 21–7, 21–0. Bellini gained the women's open singles title with a 21–4, 21–17 victory over Roberts. It was Bellini's third straight national championship.

(TERRY CHARLES MUCK)

HORSE RACING

Thoroughbred Racing and Steeplechasing. UNITED STATES AND CANADA. In an effort to generate more interest in horse racing in the United States, Thoroughbred racing in 1984 inaugurated the Breeders' Cup, a one-day, late-season extravaganza of seven stakes worth $1 million to $3 million apiece. The $10 million outlay had been provided by approximately 9,500 owners and breeders throughout the world but primarily from the U.S. The Breeders' Cup organization previously had distributed another $10 million to racetracks throughout the U.S. to increase the value of numerous races.

The seven Breeders' Cup races were held at Hollywood Park in California before a crowd of 64,254 and in 1985 were scheduled to take place at Aqueduct Race Track in New York City. In addition to their rich purses, the stakes were a strong factor in determining most of the year's Eclipse Awards. Winners of these prizes, in voting conducted by the National Turf Writers Association, *Daily Racing Form,* and the Thoroughbred Racing Associations, included: two-year-old colt, Chief's Crown; two-year-old filly, Outstandingly; three-year-old colt, Swale; three-year-old filly, Life's Magic; older male horse, Slew o' Gold; older filly or mare, Princess Rooney; male turf horse, John Henry; female turf horse, Royal Heroine; sprinter, Eillo; and steeplechaser, Flatterer, which had won the previous year.

The 1984 prize was the sixth Eclipse Award earned by the nine-year-old gelding John Henry. He and Slew o' Gold, champion three-year-old colt of 1983, were the chief contenders for 1984 horse of the year honours, won in 1983 by All Along.

Other Eclipse Award winners were: jockey, Pat Day; apprentice jockey, Wesley Ward; trainer, Jack Van Berg; owner, John Franks, for the second consecutive time; and breeder, Claiborne Farm. C. V. Whitney was voted a special Eclipse Award for his years of distinguished service to racing. The awards for Day and Van Berg were their first. Day won 400 races to earn his third consecutive races-won title. Van Berg led the trainers with 258 victories, the eighth time he had done so. Ward, 16, won 335 races. His mounts earned $5,188,642, a record for a first-year rider.

Two Eclipse winners died shortly after triumphing in stakes that clinched championships for them. Swale, which had won the Florida and Kentucky Derbies, succumbed to a mysterious internal disorder eight days after capturing the Belmont Stakes. Eillo succumbed to a severe colic attack a few weeks after taking the Breeders' Cup Sprint at six furlongs. The four-year-old son of Mr. Prospector had won eight of ten starts, including five stakes.

Besides Swale, John Henry was the only other Eclipse Award victor that did not compete in a Breeders' Cup race. A leg injury made him inactive. By winning the Kentucky Derby and the Belmont Stakes, Swale captured two of the three events that make up the Triple Crown for three-year-olds. The third race, the Preakness Stakes, was won by Gate Dancer.

Prior to winning the Breeders' Cup Juvenile at one mile, Chief's Crown had accounted for four other stakes: the Saratoga Special, Hopeful, Cowdin, and Norfolk. Outstandingly finished second by half a length behind Fran's Valentine in the Breeders' Cup Juvenile Fillies, also at one mile, but was moved up to first when her rival was disqualified and placed tenth because of a flagrant foul at the top of the straightaway. Outstandingly subsequently won the $1 million Hollywood Starlet to earn Eclipse honours.

Finishing second to the older champion, Princess Rooney, in the Breeders' Cup Distaff at 1¼ mi was enough to gain for Life's Magic the title in the three-year-old filly division. Life's Magic earlier had won the Mother Goose, Monmouth Oaks, Alabama, and Beldame. Princess Rooney's other major successes took place in the Vanity and Spinster.

Slew o' Gold carried a five-for-five season's record into the Breeders' Cup Classic at 1¼ mi but faltered to finish a close third to Wild Again and Gate Dancer. It was a roughly run race during the final furlong, with Slew o' Gold squeezed between Wild Again on the inside and Gate Dancer on the outside. Gate Dancer subsequently was penalized for crowding and exchanged placings with Slew o' Gold. A son of 1977 Triple Crown winner Seattle Slew, Slew o' Gold won the Woodward Stakes, Marlboro Cup, and Jockey Club Gold Cup to earn a $1 million bonus.

Royal Heroine won three other stakes besides the Breeders' Cup Mile on the turf, in which she defeated male rivals. She finished second to John Henry in the Budweiser-Arlington Million. John Henry finished first in six of nine starts, increasing his earnings to a record $6,597,947. His major victories, along with the Budweiser-Arlington Million, were in the Hollywood Invitational, Sunset, and Turf Classic.

Sam-Son Farm's champion two-year-old colt Dauphin Fabuleux was voted Canada's horse of the year. Sam-Son Farm also raced the champion three-year-old filly Classy 'n Smart, winner of the Canadian Oaks. In the Triple Crown events for three-year-olds, Key to the Moon won the Queen's Plate; Val Dansant, the Prince of Wales; and Bounding Away, a filly, the Breeders' Stakes.

(JOSEPH C. AGRELLA)

EUROPE AND AUSTRALIA. Two performances stood out during the 1984 European flat-racing season, those of El Gran Señor in the Two Thousand Guineas, at Newmarket, England, on May 5 and of Teenoso in the King George VI and Queen Elizabeth Diamond Stakes, at Ascot, England, on July 28. Both colts beat strong fields in commanding style. Sagace was just as impressive in the Prix de l'Arc de Triomphe, at Longchamp in Paris on October 7, but conditions were very much in his favour and against many of his rivals.

The older horses, in general, provided excellent sport throughout the year, but the autumn brought disappointment, with few two-year-old colts emerging as obvious prospects for the 1985 classics. However, at least three fillies, the French-trained Triptych and the Irish pair Alydar's Best and Park Appeal, ensured plenty of interest in the future. Park Appeal was unbeaten in four races, including the Moyglare Stud Stakes and the Tattersalls Cheveley Park Stakes, and Alydar's Best in two, the Silken Glider Stakes in Ireland and France's most important juvenile event, the Grand Critérium. Although trained in different countries, Triptych, which won the Prix Marcel Boussac by four lengths, and Alydar's Best were both owned by Alan Clore. David O'Brien, trainer of Alydar's Best, announced an ambitious plan for the horse, the principal objective being victory in the 1985 Epsom Derby. O'Brien won that race for the first time in 1984, when Secreto wore down El Gran Señor, which was trained by his father, Vincent. Secreto forced his nose in front to win by a short head.

El Gran Señor raced just once more, taking the Joe McGrath Irish Sweeps Derby by one length from Rainbow Quest. But he was only half the horse at the Derby distance that he had been over one mile at Newmarket, where he won the General Accident Two Thousand Guineas by 2½ lengths from Chief Singer, with Lear Fan and Rainbow Quest a further four lengths and three lengths behind. Chief Singer went on to win the St. James's Palace Stakes, the Norcros July Cup, in which he beat the two next best sprinters in Europe (Never So Bold and Committed), and the Swettenham Stud Sussex Stakes. Lear Fan did not reappear for 14 weeks and then ran away with the Prix Jacques le Marois at Deauville, France, beating the subse-

On June 17 Swale, the three-year-old offspring of Triple Crown winner Seattle Slew, died after completing a morning gallop at Belmont Park in New York. His death came just eight days after his victory in the 116th running of the Belmont and six weeks after his winning of the 110th Kentucky Derby.

JEBB HARRIS—GAMMA/LIAISON

quent Dubai Champion Stakes winner, Palace Music, by four lengths.

Rainbow Quest, in addition to his second place in the Irish Derby, was an easy winner of the Great Voltigeur Stakes and also ran third behind Darshaan and the Irish 2,000 Guineas winner, Sadler's Wells, in the Prix du Jockey-Club. Darshaan gained his fifth consecutive victory there and appeared to have a strong claim as the best distance-running three-year-old in Europe. Then, however, Darshaan failed completely, in company with four other French challengers, in the King George VI and Queen Elizabeth Diamond Stakes. The 1983 Epsom Derby victor, Teenoso, which had won the Grand Prix de Saint-Cloud at the start of July, finished first 2½ lengths in front of Sadler's Wells.

JACQUELIN DUVOISIN/SPORTS ILLUSTRATED

The sloppy track at Belmont Park did not stop five-year-old Fit to Fight from winning the $341,000 Brooklyn Handicap by 12½ lengths. The race gave him a sweep of the three-race Belmont Series known as the Handicap Triple Crown.

Sadler's Wells, which performed with great courage throughout the season and won the Eclipse Stakes, gained a fitting further reward when he won the first running of the Phoenix Champion Stakes from the French colt Seattle Song at Phoenix Park on September 8. This race offered easily the richest prize ever contested in Ireland.

Teenoso should have reappeared in the Trusthouse Forte Prix de l'Arc de Triomphe, but a leg injury forced his withdrawal two days before the race. It was run on very sticky going, which few of the contestants enjoyed. The lightly raced Sagace, which had missed much of the season because of injury, handled it best and won by an easy two lengths from the best three-year-old filly in Europe, Northern Trick; the 1983 Arc winner, All Along, was six lengths back in third place. With the exception of the Arc, prize money for major events in France compared unfavourably with that in Britain, where, after some years of resistance to the idea, a decline in the Levy Board's contribution to prizes forced the Jockey Club to allow commercial sponsorship of the classics, a policy that both the Irish and French had adopted long ago.

Provideo was a long way from being a champion, but no account of the year would be complete without a mention of this two-year-old colt, which ran 24 times for 16 wins, 6 seconds, and 1 third in Britain and one unplaced outing at the end of the year in California. He equaled the British record for the number of wins scored by a juvenile, set by The Bard in 1885.

Freddy Head won his sixth jockeys' championship in France, while Steve Cauthen, who had gone to Britain in 1979, captured his first. Cauthen's 130 winners was the lowest total achieved by any champion since 1967 but was sufficient to make him the first U.S. jockey to gain the title since Danny Maher in 1913. When he won the St. Leger brilliantly on Commanche Run, Lester Piggott rode his 28th classic winner, breaking Frank Buckle's (1766–1832) record.

A six-year-old Irish mare, Dawn Run, was the star of the European jumping season, winning the Wessel Cable Champion Hurdle in Ireland, the Waterford Crystal Champion Hurdle in England, and the Grande Course de Haies d'Auteuil in France. Burrough Hill Lad won the Cheltenham Gold Cup and the 1984 King George VI steeplechase. He was trained by Jenny Pitman, whose 1983 Grand National winner, Corbière, again ran well in

Harness racing records continued to topple. The Standardbred stallion Trenton (above), then a three-year-old, in 1982 paced the fastest mile for all ages at 1 minute 51³/₅ seconds. In 1984 Colt Fortysix took over as the fastest race-winning pacer, trotting a mile in 1 minute 50³/₅ seconds.

ALVIN CUMMINS, SHANNONDALE FARM, LEXINGTON, KY

that race to finish a close third behind Hallo Dandy and Greasepaint. Special Cargo won the Whitbread Gold Cup. John Francome was champion jump jockey in Britain for the sixth time and also set a new record for jumping victories in May, when he rode his 1,036th winner.

Strawberry Road, the 1982–83 horse of the year in Australia, showed that he was a match for the best in the world with a victory in the Grosser Preis von Baden in West Germany and creditable performances in other important races in France and the U.S. Emancipation, a mare that won 19 times in a 28-race career, was his successor as horse of the year. Black Knight won Australia's richest race, the Melbourne Cup, from the favourite, Bounty Hawk, which had won the 1983–84 season Victoria Derby and Channel 7 Australian Derby.

Strawberry Road and Bounty Hawk represented Australia in the Japan Cup at Tokyo on November 25 but could finish no better than seventh and eighth behind Katsuragi Ace, the first locally trained winner in four runnings of this invitational event. The British representative, Bedtime, finished 1¹/₂ lengths back in second, inches in front of the year's Japanese Triple Crown winner, Symboli Rudolf.   (ROBERT W. CARTER)

Harness Racing. So great was the speed improvement in harness racing by 1984 that Niatross no longer held any race records and relied on his time trial of 1 min 49¹/₅ sec to keep his name among the world's records. In the United States, Colt Fortysix, a three-year-old pacer, became the fastest race-winning harness horse of all time with a Grand Circuit victory in 1 min 50³/₅ sec on a mile track. He also won the $336,717 Little Brown Jug in 1 min 55 sec. However, Niatross's first crop of two-year-old offspring dominated their age group, his son Nihilator winning the $2 million Woodrow Wilson pace in 1 min 52⁴/₅ sec. The Tyler B. colt Dragon's Lair won the two-year-old Breeders' Crown, defeating Nihilator in 1 min 54¹/₅ sec on the ⁵/₈th-mi track. The pacing Triple Crown was split three ways as Troublemaker won the Messenger Stakes and On the Road Again the Cane Pace after Colt Fortysix had won the Little Brown Jug. Cornstalk, with a 1-min 53⁴/₅-sec mile at the Illinois State Fairgrounds in Springfield, became the world's fastest race-winning three-year-old trotter (tied the next day at the same track by the three-year-old filly Fancy Crown), and Historic Freight won the $1,219,000 Ham-

bletonian with a 1-min 57³/₅-sec heat and 1-min 59³/₅-sec final at the Meadowlands in New Jersey. The Roosevelt International Trot was won by Lutin d'Isigny, and this European visitor also won the Challenge Cup.

In Australia Gammalite won the Inter-Dominion Grand Final, and Sir Castleton won the Trotters' Grand Final. Ten-year-old Double Agent won the Miracle Mile in Sydney, while in Melbourne Wooffer Karamea defeated the previously unbeaten Pride of Hilary in the $35,000 Galaxy Grand Slam for two-year-olds. Karamea Duplicity became the top money-winning harness mare in Australia with earnings of more than $200,000 by the end of her four-year-old season. Australia's one-mile record holder, Popular Alm, after being out of racing for nearly a year with a cracked bone, returned in October to beat a top-class field of handicap pacers at Moonee Valley.

Enterprise won the $180,000 Auckland Cup in New Zealand, while Roydon Glen took the New Zealand Derby at Christchurch. The $125,000 New Zealand Cup was won by Camelot from Our Mana and Dillon Dale, while Dillon Dale captured the Benson and Hedges Free for All and Sir Castleton took the Trotters' Free for All. In Paris Lurabo won the Prix d'Amérique with a time of 2 min 3.9 sec for the 2,600 m on a wet track.   (NOEL SIMPSON)

ICE HOCKEY

North America. The Edmonton Oilers and their leader, Wayne Gretzky, finally realized their potential in the 1983–84 season, defeating the New York Islanders to claim the National Hockey League's Stanley Cup. The Islanders had been hoping to equal the Montreal Canadiens' record of five consecutive Stanley Cups by beating the Oilers, as they had in a four-game sweep the previous year. But the fleet Oilers stopped the Islanders this time in a 4–1 series. Long termed "the team of the future," the Oilers finally matured, while the Islanders seemed to age just past their prime and were caught in the transition between new players and old. The final game began with a two-goal burst by Gretzky and ended with two quick goals by Pat LaFontaine for a 5–2 victory in Edmonton's home rink.

UPI/BETTMANN

Wayne Gretzky of the Edmonton Oilers holds the Stanley Cup overhead exultantly after the Oilers defeated the New York Islanders 5–2 in the final game of the series to win the National Hockey League championship.

On the way to the championship, Oiler centre Mark Messier won the Conn Smythe Trophy as the most valuable player in the play-offs. Gretzky, meanwhile, added several more records to his impressive file, even topping one of his own marks. He won the Art Ross Trophy as the league's top scorer for the fourth consecutive year, equaling a record set by Gordie Howe and Phil Esposito. He scored 87 goals and had 118 assists for 205 points. His closest competitor for the trophy had 126 points.

Gretzky, in his fifth NHL season at the age of 23, won the regular-season award for most valuable player, the Hart Trophy. He thus became the first player in NHL history to win the trophy for five consecutive years. Gretzky's scoring drive was hampered by his absence from six games due to a shoulder injury (his team lost all six games without him), but he set a mark for the highest assists-per-game average in the regular season with 1.59 and broke his own record for the highest points-per-game average with 2.77. He also won one of the NHL's newer trophies honouring the player with the best "plus-minus" record; that is, the number of times a player is on the ice for his team's goals minus the number of times he is on the ice for opponents' goals. Gretzky's plus-minus figure was an astounding plus 76.

Other trophy winners included Tom Barrasso of the Buffalo Sabres, voted best goaltender (Vezina Trophy) by the league's general managers. He also won the Calder Trophy as rookie of the year, only the third goaltender to win both trophies in one year. Mike Bossy of the New York Islanders won the Lady Byng Trophy for most gentlemanly player, as he had done the previous season. Rod Langway of the vastly improved Washington Capitals was voted the Norris Trophy for the second year in a row as best defenseman. His teammate Doug Jarvis won the Selke Trophy for best defensive forward, and the Capitals' Pat Riggin and Al Jensen won the Jennings Trophy as the best goaltending team. The Masterton Trophy for sportsmanship and dedication to hockey went to veteran Brad Park, who was playing his first year with the Detroit Red Wings after a long career with Boston and New York.

The league's number one choice in the amateur draft was Mario Lemieux, a centre with Laval in the Quebec Major Junior Hockey League. He was chosen by the Pittsburgh Penguins after compiling an incredible scoring record of 133 goals and 149 assists in 70 games for his junior team in the 1983–84 season. Critics were hailing him as the next Wayne Gretzky.

The year was one of significant managerial changes, with two former top players jumping into the role of general manager of their former teams. They were Rogie Vachon, a former goaltender for the Los Angeles Kings, and Bobby Clarke, the centre who had been the soul of the Philadelphia Flyers during their best years. Vachon hired Pat Quinn to begin the 1984–85 season as coach. Clarke put Mike Keenan in charge of the Philadelphia players. In other coaching changes Dan Maloney took over the Toronto Maple Leafs, Bob Berry moved from Montreal to Pittsburgh, Doug Carpenter became coach of the New Jersey Devils, and Bill LaForge took over Vancouver. Meanwhile, Al Arbour, longtime coach of the New York Islanders, decided to remain in that capacity for at least another season.

In the American Hockey League the Maine Mariners, a New Jersey Devils affiliate, defeated the Rochester Americans, a Buffalo Sabres farm club, four games to one for that league's championship. In the Central Hockey League's last championship before the league folded, the Tulsa Oilers emerged as champions, defeating the two-time defending champions, the Indianapolis Checkers, four games to zero.

The Tulsa team, a farm club of the New York Rangers, lost its rink about two-thirds of the way through the season. Renamed the "Central Hockey League" Oilers, they then played the remainder of their season on the road.

A sad note for the hockey community was the death on June 24 of former league president Clarence S. Campbell (see OBITUARIES). He had served as president for 31 years, retiring in 1977 after guiding the league through a series of expansions that saw it grow from a 6-team operation to the current 21.   (ROBIN CATHY HERMAN)

European and International. Because of the 1984 Olympic Winter Games, it was considered impractical to stage a separate 1984 world championship. In addition, the two tournaments could not be concurrent, as in the past, because the world championship was not open to professionals.

The International Olympic Committee's revised definition of an amateur simply as one who had not played in the National Hockey League of North America was regarded by most as unsatisfactory, if not ludicrous, a judgment that was illustrated by the presence of Richard Cunningham on the Austrian Olympic team. There was no provision in the rules for those who had played in any other professional league, and Cunningham was a classic example. He was eligible to compete in the Olympics even though he had

Table I. NHL Final Standings, 1984

	Won	Lost	Tied	Goals	Goals against	Points
Prince of Wales Conference						
PATRICK DIVISION						
New York Islanders	50	26	4	357	269	104
*Washington	48	27	5	308	226	101
*Philadelphia	44	26	10	350	290	98
New York Rangers	42	29	9	314	304	93
New Jersey	17	56	7	231	350	41
Pittsburgh	16	58	6	254	390	38
ADAMS DIVISION						
*Boston	49	25	6	336	261	104
*Buffalo	48	25	7	315	257	103
*Quebec	42	28	10	360	278	94
*Montreal	35	40	5	286	295	75
Hartford	28	42	10	288	320	66
Clarence Campbell Conference						
NORRIS DIVISION						
*Minnesota	39	31	10	345	344	88
*St. Louis	32	41	7	293	316	71
*Detroit	31	42	7	298	323	69
*Chicago	30	42	8	277	311	68
Toronto	26	45	9	303	387	61
SMYTHE DIVISION						
Edmonton	57	18	5	446	314	119
*Calgary	34	32	14	311	314	82
*Vancouver	32	39	9	306	328	73
*Winnipeg	31	38	11	340	374	73
Los Angeles	23	44	13	309	376	59

*Clinched playoff berth.

Table II. 1984 Winter Olympic Ice Hockey Tournament

	Won	Lost	Tied	Goals	Goals against	Points
GROUP A						
U.S.S.R.	5	0	0	42	5	10
Sweden	3	1	1	34	15	7
West Germany	3	1	1	27	17	7
Poland	1	4	0	16	37	2
Italy	1	4	0	15	31	2
Yugoslavia	1	4	0	8	37	2
GROUP B						
Czechoslovakia	5	0	0	38	7	10
Canada	4	1	0	24	10	8
Finland	2	2	1	27	19	5
United States	1	2	2	16	17	4
Austria	1	4	0	13	37	2
Norway	0	4	1	15	43	1
MEDAL ROUND						
U.S.S.R.	3	0	0	16	1	6
Czechoslovakia	2	1	0	6	2	4
Sweden	1	2	0	3	12	2
Canada	0	3	0	0	10	0

Soviet ice hockey players congratulated goaltender Vladislav Tretyak after their victory over Czechoslovakia to win the gold medal at the Olympic Winter Games in Sarajevo, Yugoslavia, in February.
AP/WIDE WORLD

played in more than 300 league games in the now-defunct World Hockey Association. For more than five years, while playing for the Toronto Toros during the 1970s, Cunningham was reputed to have been paid more than $100,000 a season. How he could be eligible to compete in the Winter Olympics when another player would be expelled for having played in just one NHL match, for a pittance, defied logical explanation.

In the Olympic Winter Games at Sarajevo, Yugos. (see *Winter Sports:* Special Report, below), the Soviet Union won the championship with eight straight victories. Czechoslovakia finished second, and Sweden was third. The top scorers (including assists) were Erich Kühnackl of West Germany and Raimo Summanen of Finland, each with 14, but the highest goal scorers were Nikolay Drozdetskiy of the U.S.S.R. and Peter Gradin from Sweden, with 10 and 8, respectively. The most successful goaltenders were Vladislav Tretyak of the U.S.S.R. and Jaromir Schindel of Czechoslovakia.

The Thayer Tutt Trophy was contested in Grenoble, France, during March 20–29 between eight national teams not competing in the Olympics. East Germany was the victor, winning its most crucial game 5–1 against second-place Switzerland, which finished only one point behind. Romania placed third. The Netherlands, the only team to take

a point from East Germany, finished fourth, followed by Hungary, Japan, France, and China in that order. The annual Izvestia Tournament, contested during Dec. 16–21, 1983, was won by the host nation. Czechoslovakia placed second and Sweden third.

A rare opportunity to compare the world's best national teams, when largely at full strength and including both professionals and amateurs, occurred in the Canada Cup tournament held in Canada September 1–19. Competing nations included Canada, Czechoslovakia, Sweden, the U.S., the U.S.S.R., and West Germany. The winner was Canada, which defeated Sweden by two straight victories in a best-of-three final, winning the first 5–2 and the second 6–5.

In the second game the Canadians scored four goals in the opening seven minutes before the Swedes scored at all. After West Germany and Czechoslovakia had been eliminated in the initial round, Sweden beat the U.S. 9–2 in the first sudden-death semifinal. In the other semifinal Canada defeated the Soviets 3–2, the match going into 13 minutes of overtime. The All-Star team selected from the series included Vladimir Myshkin (U.S.S.R.) in the goal, Rod Langway (U.S.) and Paul Coffey (Canada) on defense, and forwards Sergey Maharov (U.S.S.R.) and Wayne Gretzky and John Tonelli (both Canada).

Great Britain had its most progressive season for more than 20 years through the formation of a new Heineken League. It embraced 38 teams in four divisions, the premier division comprising the nine leading clubs in England and Scotland. The Dundee Rockets became British champions for a third successive year; the tournament semifinals and final were the first ice hockey matches to be played at Wembley Stadium for ten years.

The eighth world junior (under 21) championship, contested in Norrköping, Sweden, from Dec. 25, 1983, to Jan. 3, 1984, was recaptured by the U.S.S.R., which had won in each of the first four years of the series. Finland placed second and Czechoslovakia finished third after a 6–4 victory over fourth-place Canada, the defending champion. The other Group A contestants were Sweden, Switzerland, the U.S., and West Germany; 14 other nations participated in groups B and C, held in France and Italy, respectively.

(HOWARD BASS)

LACROSSE

Men. In 1984 men's lacrosse was featured in the Olympic Games with exhibition contests between the U.S., Australia, Canada, and England. In addition there were a California team and the Iroquois team, composed mostly of North American Indians.

In U.S. competition Johns Hopkins was the champion university, and the South beat the North 11–8. Hobart College won the Third Division championship, defeating Long Island University 15–10 in the final match. The outstanding players for the year were Tim Nelson (attack) from Syracuse University, Del Dressel (midfield) from Johns Hopkins University, Tom Haus (defense) from the University of North Carolina, and Larry Quinn (goalkeeper) from Johns Hopkins. The coaching award went to Tony Seaman of the University of Pennsylvania.

In Australia, Western Australia won the championship of the states. The champion club in Victoria was Surrey Park, while Glenelg won in South Australia and East Freemantle in Western Australia. The "fairest and best" players were: for the interstate championship S. Ellis; in Victoria J. Vazzoler; in South Australia M. Weir; and in Western Australia J. Gower.

In Canada Peterborough, Ont., was the intermediate

champion; the Founder's Trophy went to Point Edward, Ont.; the President's Cup to Orangeville, Ont.; and the Minto Cup (juniors) to Whitby, Ont. The McConaghy Cup was awarded to Joe Nieuwendyk as outstanding Minto player.

In England Cheadle won the Iroquois Cup, beating Kenton. Cheadle also won the North of England Senior Flags and was the First Division League champion. Paul Short was named best player of the series. Cheshire won the county championship at both senior and junior levels. Kenton won the South of England Senior Flags.

(CHARLES DENNIS COPPOCK)

Women. With long-term preparation for the 1986 world tournament in view, the U.S. team that toured the U.K. in September 1984 was a young and relatively inexperienced one. Nonetheless, the team showed great skill, teamwork, and fitness in its convincing wins over the five territories and the Combined Universities. It also defeated England Reserves 9–6, Wales 13–1, and Scotland 8–2 but lost the test series against England. These last three thrilling matches opened with a narrow victory (9–8) for England, won with last-minute scoring; the U.S. replied with determined confident lacrosse to win the second test 8–6. The deciding test at the Oval, London, was another close contest, won by England 8–6. Canada also visited Britain in the fall of 1984, losing 11–4 to Wales and 11–2 to Scotland, but defeating Young England 8–6.

In British domestic competition the South and England dominated. Middlesex again won the All-England Counties Tournament, beating its old rival Surrey 5–2 in the final. South Reserves won the Territorial Reserves Tournament, with the Midlands as runner-up. South struggled in the territorial championship, losing to the West but defeating the other territories and winning the title on goal difference. The All-England Clubs and Colleges Tournament took place in the absence of the titleholder, Bedford College of Higher Education, on tour in the U.S., and was won by St. Mary's College, Twickenham, which beat I. M. Marsh 5–0 in a one-sided final. In the home internationals England defeated England Reserves 9–4 and crushed Wales 15–3 but had to work for a 6–2 victory over Scotland.

(MARGARET-LOUISE O'KEEFFE)

LAWN BOWLS

The fifth men's world championships, staged at Aberdeen, Scotland, dwarfed other events in 1984. The winners and runners-up in the four events were: singles, Peter Belliss (New Zealand) beat Willie Wood (Scotland); pairs, George Adrain (Scottish substitute) and Skippy Arculli (U.S.) defeated David Bryant and Tony Allcock (England); triples, Stan Espie, Sammy Allen, and Jim Baker (Ireland) beat Brian Rattray, Doug Lambert, and Jim Boyle (Scotland); fours, George Turley, Julian Haines, John Bell, and Allcock (England) triumphed over Rowan Brassey, Jim Scott, Morgan Moffat, and Phil Skoglund (New Zealand). Overall, Scotland collected the most points and so became the first country to retain the W. M. Leonard Trophy. Adrain, a Scottish international player, was omitted from his country's world championships team and agreed to be a standby substitute ready to fill a vacancy caused by illness for any country, and so in the pairs he took the place of Jim Candalet of the U.S. and with Arculli won the championship. The second most important event during the year was Granada Television's £25,000 "Superbowl." The first prize of £10,000 was won by Bryant. At Worthing, Sussex, Wynne Richards (Mid-Surrey) won the English national singles championship, Len Haynes and Ollie Jones (Lenham, Kent) the pairs, Pip and Len Branfield and Gordan

James (Clevedon, Somerset) the triples, and Chris Price, Laurence and Peter Pull, and Russell Morgan (Boscombe Cliff) the fours. John Bell (Wigton) won the British Isles singles.

(C. M. JONES)

MARTIAL ARTS

Judo. Yasuhiro Yamashita finally captured an Olympic gold medal in judo by winning the open-weights event during the Los Angeles Summer Olympics. It was the only major judo medal the 26-year-old Tokai University judo coach had never had an opportunity to win. His Olympic triumph confirmed his reputation as the undisputed world judo champion. Three other Japanese *judoka* also captured gold medals in Los Angeles: Hitoshi Saito, a heavyweight; Shinji Hosokawa, an extra-lightweight; and Yoshiyuki Matsuoka, a featherweight. Two South Koreans also took home gold medals: Ha Huyoung Zoo, a half-heavyweight; and Ahn Byeong Keun, a lightweight. The two remaining gold medals went to Frank Wieneke of West Germany, who won the half-middleweight event, and Peter Seisenbacher, an Austrian, who captured the middleweight event. Yamashita also won the All-Japan Championships for an unprecedented eighth straight year. In April, he decisioned Saito in the final of the world's only major judo tournament without weight classes. At the third Women's World Championship in Vienna in November, the European grip on women's judo was broken when Kaori Yamaguchi (Japan) won the featherweight title, Ann-Marie Burns (U.S.) took the lightweight gold, and Natasha Hernández (Venezuela) won the middleweight title. But it was Ingrid Berghmans (Belgium) who dominated the meet by winning both the open and 72-kg events. Karen Briggs (U.K.) won the bantamweight gold.

Karate. Great Britain was the pretournament favourite at the seventh World Karate Championships, held in mid-October at Maastricht, Neth. Some 500 *karateka* from

Douglas Vieira of Brazil (right) seems to have Korea's Ha Huyoung Zoo discomfited during Olympic judo action. Ha recovered, however, to best Vieira and win the gold medal in the half-heavyweight class.

48 countries came together to vie for top honours. Britain won the team title and three individual events in the WUKO (World Union of Karate-do Organizations)-sponsored tournament. Jim Collins of Scotland won the 70-kg class, Peter McKay took the 80-kg crown, and Jerome Atkinson won the over-80-kg title. Other winners in the men's events included Toon Stelling of The Netherlands in the 75-kg class, Ramon Malave of Sweden in the 65-kg category, and Dieter Betzien of West Germany in the 60-kg class. Emanuel Pinda of France won the open class championship. In the women's events, Sophie Berger of France won the 53-kg class, Tomoko Kinishi of Japan the 60-kg competition, and Guusje van Mourik of The Netherlands the over-60-kg title. The World Cup tournament was staged in Budapest, Hung., March 25–April 1, with *karateka* from 40 countries competing. Japan won three *kumite* (fighting) gold medals: Hideo Yamamoto in the 75–80-kg class, Seiji Nishimura in the 65–70-kg category, and Yuichi Suzuki in the 60–65-kg class. In other events, Agostino of Italy won the 55–60-kg event and Angelo Spataro of Belgium the 70–75-kg category. Hiroko Moriya of Japan won the women's *kata* (prescribed forms) title; in the women's *kumite* competition, Venezuela, France, and The Netherlands each produced a gold-medal winner. During the first competition for the International Karate Champions Cup held April 3–4 in Belgrade, Yugos., Masaaki Yokomichi of Japan won first place over Dianuba Guazzaroni of Italy and Nenad Batocanin of Yugoslavia, who was disqualified. Forty *karateka* from Japan, the U.S., Italy, and other European countries competed. In the three karate events at Japan's National Athletic Meet October 13–15 in Nara Prefecture, Teruhiro Motohashi won the heavyweight title 3–1 with three *jodan-zuki* (upper straight punches). Mitsuhiko Yabe captured the middleweight class 3–0, and Kazushige Masuzaki took the lightweight title 3–2, both winning with *jodan-zuki*. The team title went to Fukuoka Prefecture over Nara Prefecture 2–1. In the All-Japan Shotokan Championships sponsored by the Japan Karate Association (JKA), Hideo Yamamoto added the individual *kumite* title to the gold medals he had won the previous year at the JKA World Championships in Cairo and at the spring World Cup competition in Budapest. Mikio Yahara took first place in the *kata* competition.

Kendo. Four policemen dominated the 1984 All-Japan Kendo Championships at Tokyo's Nippon Budokan in November. Tetsuo Harada of Kyoto defeated Hayato Kajiya of Saitama Prefecture with two *men* (helmet) strikes. Two other policemen tied for third place. The two finalists had been first-round losers in the National Police Champi-

onships on June 1, when Hide Iwahori emerged the winner. In the All-Japan Women's Kendo Championships on May 3 in Osaka, Satomi Fukunoue of Tokyo won the title with *kote* (forearm) and *do* (side) strikes. The national men's prefecture team championship, also held in Osaka, was won by Miyagi, which defeated Tochigi 4–1 in the final. In the European Kendo Championships in May, Jean Lopicollo (France) beat Eberhard Riemann (West Germany) 2–1 for the individual title, while France edged Italy 3–2 for first place in the team competition. During the kendo tournament held in Aichi Prefecture on March 25, Keiyu Murayama defeated Kuniyoshi Okusono.

(ANDREW M. ADAMS)

MOTORBOATING

Unlimited hydroplanes made headlines during 1984 American Power Boat Association (APBA) racing with the reintroduction of turbine engines to competition. Turbine power had been used before by one team, but not until 1984 did others try it. Three teams ran the "whoosh machines" with moderate success and with great promise for the future.

In 1984, for the first time in recent years, the "triple crown" events of unlimited hydroplane racing—the APBA Gold Cup, world championship, and national high point title—were won by three different teams. Lee ("Chip") Hanauer of Seattle, Wash., and the turbine-powered "Atlas Van Lines" won the APBA Gold Cup in Tri-Cities, Wash., taking home the prestigious trophy for the third consecutive year. In a surprise victory Steve Reynolds of Kirkland, Wash., drove the "Miss Tosti Asti" to the world championship in Houston, Texas, also with the help of turbine power. But Jim Kropfeld of Cincinnati, Ohio, and his conventionally powered "Miss Budweiser" held their own against the turbines during the season, winning six out of ten races to claim the national high point title. Hanauer and "Atlas Van Lines" made history in the sponsor's hometown of Evansville, Ind., where Hanauer blasted out a record-setting lap of 226.717 km/h (140.818 mph).

APBA's Offshore racing division had a notable season, expanding its reach to all four U.S. coasts. With a race added to the previous year's ten-race circuit, Offshore competition drew entries from across the U.S., dashing its reputation as an East Coast sport.

George Morales of Miami, Fla., successfully defended his title of Offshore world champion in Class I at the season-ending championship race in Key West, Fla. Morales, driving the 50-ft (15-m) "MerCruiser Special," won the title on points after victories in two of the three preliminary events. Other Offshore class world champions

Three 240-horsepower Mercury outboard engines powered this 8-metre (32-foot) Scorpion hull made and piloted by Julio de-Varona as he set a new outboard record for the Miami to New York City 2,024-kilometre (1,257-mile) course.

for 1984 included Ben Kramer of Hollywood, Fla., in Class II, Italy's Amelio Riganti in Class III, Justo Jay of Miami in Class IV, Pete Aitkin of Westport, Conn., in Class V, and Jeff Kalibat of Island Park, N.Y., in Class VI.

In the competition for consistency Al Copeland of Metairie, La., took top honours, winning the Offshore national high point title in his Class I "superboat," "Popeye's/ Diet Coke." Copeland also achieved a record time for Class I, 209.946 km/h (130.401 mph). But it was Mike Drury of New Orleans, La., in his Class II boat "Innovation" who really shook the record books. His time of 211.042 km/h (131.088 mph) bettered the previous class record by nearly 18 km/h (11 mph).   (HILARY R. SPITTLE)

MOTORCYCLING

Freddie Spencer of the U.S., riding a Honda, was considered a near certainty to become the 500-cc motorcycle road-race world champion for 1984, as he had in 1983. He was defeated, however, by fellow countryman Eddie Lawson (Yamaha). In the sidecar class the Dutch pair Egbert Streuer and Bernard Schnieders outdrove the highly rated Swiss Rolf Biland and Kurt Waltisperg (LCR-Yamaha), who managed no better than fourth in the final listing.

A first-time world champion, in the March–September 12-meeting series, was Christian Sarron (France; Yamaha), who rode with great consistency to win the 250-cc title. The other class winners were Stefan Dörflinger (Switz.; Zündapp), 80 cc; and 13-time world champion Angel Nieto (Spain; Garelli), 125 cc. Still regarded by many as the high point in U.K. sport, the June Tourist Trophy races on the Isle of Man produced record speeds in several events, most notably a lap at 190.75 km/h (118.48 mph) by Joey Dunlop (Honda) of Ulster during the Senior race. Dunlop later became the Formula One world champion on a Honda.

World motocross winners were André Malherbe (Belgium; Honda), 500 cc; Heinz Kinigadner (Austria; KTM), 250 cc; and M. Rinaldi (Italy; Suzuki), 125 cc. In the Motocross des Nations, held in Finland in September, a U.S. team took the 500-cc world team championship for the fourth time.

World trials champion, for the third consecutive time, was Eddy Lejeune (Belgium; Honda). In the International Six Days Enduro, based at Assen during the first week of October, the home Dutch team (Honda) won the premier, Trophy, contest. The Vase competition was won by East Germany. Erik Gundersen (Denmark; GM) finished the year as world speedway champion.   (CYRIL J. AYTON)

MOUNTAINEERING

The onslaught on the highest mountains continued in 1983–84. Available statistics for the Himalayas and Karakoram indicated that 45 expeditions were in Nepal after the 1983 monsoon, 21 of them successful in their climb, but many fatalities occurred. Six climbers died within a week (October 8–13). During the 1983–84 winter there were 11 expeditions in the field, 8 of which were successful; of the five mountains over 7,500 m (25,000 ft) attempted, two were climbed. In the 1984 premonsoon period, 33 expeditions were in Nepal, 16 of them successful.

In the Indian sectors of the Himalayas, there were 57 Indian and 83 foreign expeditions (20 of which went to Nun Kun alone) in early 1984. In Pakistan, in 1983, 44 expeditions from 14 countries attempted 24 peaks. The 5,800-m (19,000-ft) peaks were attempted by 25 expeditions. Of individual peaks, K2 was attempted by 3 parties, none successfully; Broad Peak (now known as Falchan Kangri) by 6 expeditions, 3 successfully; and Nanga Parbat by 11 expeditions.

This intense activity triggered responses from the various governments. In Nepal the royalties to be paid by expeditions were increased; those for Mt. Everest, for example, were raised from NRs 15,000 to NRs 25,000 and for the other 8,000-m (26,200-ft) peaks, from NRs 14,000 to NRs 18,000. The Nepalese authorities now required expeditions to pay for the services of a liaison officer and three other men at base camp, at larger salaries; charges for porters and insurance were increased, and expeditions applying to climb were required to complete all formalities within four months. The Nepalese Ministry of Tourism also renamed 34 peaks; thus Jannu became Kumbkhakarna, Tent Peak became Kirat Chuli, and Wedge Peak became Ramthan Chang.

The Indian Mountaineering Federation published a list of peaks open to mountaineers. At the same time, the local authorities in highly frequented areas became increasingly worried by litter problems. After the monsoon in 1984, a Royal Nepalese Police cleanup expedition set off for Everest, but it was not clear how far their activities would extend. In Garhwal partial bans and limits on access and farming were unsuccessful in protecting local flora and fauna in the Sanctuary and Rishi Ganga, and a complete ban on access to these areas for any purpose was imposed.

Noteworthy ascents were that of Broad Peak North (the highest previously virgin peak in the Karakoram), Kangchenjunga solo by P. Beghin (the fifth 8,000-m peak to be climbed solo, after Nanga Parbat, Everest, Dhaulagiri I, and Makalu), and traverses of Gasherbrum I and II and of the three main peaks of Kangchenjunga.

(JOHN NEILL)

POLO

Once again the highlight of the international polo season was the International Polo Day at the Guards Polo Club in England. In the competition for the Coronation Cup, England I (Alan Kent, Julian Hipwood, Lord Charles Beresford, and H. Hipwood) was defeated by the Rest of the World (C. Forsyth, C. Gracida, Silvio Novaes, and Owen Rinehart). England II (J. Lucas, W. P. Churchward, J. Horswell, and the prince of Wales) also lost, against Spain (V. Prado, I. Domecq, P. Domecq, and R. Echevarrieta). In the World Cup, held in the U.S., the same Anadariya combination that won in 1983 was again successful (J. Hipwood, H. Hipwood, C. Gracida, and M. Gracida). The most prestigious New Zealand tournament, the Savile Cup, was won by Wanstead, which came back strongly against Hololio Farms to snatch victory by 7 goals to 6.

In England the British Open championship was won convincingly by Southfield (D. Yeoman, A. Kent, Owen Rinehart, D. Jamison) with a resounding 9–2 victory over the BB's Polo Team (Christian Heppe, H. Hipwood, Stuart Mackenzie, I. Hunt). Southfield also won the Warwickshire Cup, defeating Cowdray Park 6–5. The BB's Polo Team narrowly lost the Queen's Cup 10–9 against Foxcote, and they were runners-up yet again in the Royal Windsor Cup against Windsor Park. However, success finally came their way with victories in the County Cup against Windsor Park and in the European Polo Academy championship against Maidensgrove.   (COLIN J. CROSS)

RACKETS

Back injury prevented John Prenn from defending his world title against challenger William Boone in 1984, but he retained the Canadian title, beating David McLernon 3–1 in Montreal; he lost the final of the U.S. Open in New York to Boone 3–0. Boone won the British amateur singles title when he beat Mark Nicholls 3–0 in the final. He

Heather McKay (right) bested Lynn Adams in the Ektelon National racquetball competition, an event sanctioned by the Women's Professional Racquetball Association. The match, played in Anaheim, California, was worth $7,000 to McKay.

MILO MUSLIN

crushed Randall Crawley to win the Celestion invitation singles and repeated that victory in the final of the British Open. In doubles Boone and Crawley retained their British Open title by defeating Prenn and James Male, the first ambidextrous player to reach a major final, in four straight games, but they were taken the full seven games before beating Prenn and Charles Hue Williams in the final of the British amateur championship. Shannon Hazell (Wellington) won the British professional title, beating Norwood Cripps (Eton) 3–0.   (ROY MCKELVIE)

RACQUETBALL

For the first time in five years there was a repeat U.S. national champion in men's professional racquetball. Mike Yellen of Southfield, Mich., became the first player since Marty Hogan of San Diego, Calif., to accomplish back-to-back championships. Yellen gained his top ranking on the strength of his exceptional victory in the DP Leach National championships. There he and Hogan met in the finals, each knowing that the winner of the match would win not only the tournament but also the year-end top ranking. In what was described as "a dazzling display of racquetball," Yellen and Hogan battled through a 3¼-hour marathon before Yellen captured the title 6–11, 11–1, 10–11, 11–8, 11–6.

An unfortunate sidelight to the race for top honours was the absence of Bret Harnett of Las Vegas, Nev., winner of the equally prestigious Ektelon National championships a month earlier. Had Harnett been able to reach the finals match at the DP tournament, he would have claimed the crown captured by Yellen. However, a hand injury forced him to miss the tournament and forfeit any chance at the top ranking.

In women's play Heather McKay from Toronto, Ont., won her third Women's Professional Racquetball Association (WPRA) championship in five years. In the finals she defeated Lynn Adams of Costa Mesa, Calif., 21–17, 21–16, 18–21, 11–21, 15–10.

International competition came to the fore during 1984 as racquetball continued its efforts to become a legitimate, international sport. At the world games in Sacramento, Calif., the U.S. captured the title, largely because of its undefeated women's team. Canada's Ross Harvey won the men's open division.   (CHARLES S. LEVE)

REAL TENNIS

Christopher Ronaldson (Hampton Court) was defeated in March 1984 for the first time since early 1981, losing the final of the Scottish Open to Lachlan Deuchar of Australia. Ronaldson also was beaten by Wayne Davies of Australia 6–4, 6–1, 4–6, 6–2 in the final of the World invitation singles at Sea Court, Hayling Island, England. Despite these setbacks, Ronaldson retained his British Open, British professional, and U.S. Open titles and added the French Open and U.S. professional championships to his successes. In the British Open Ronaldson beat Deuchar 6–5, 6–3, 6–5; he then repeated his victory over the Australian in the French Open and the British professional championships. In the U.S. Open and U.S. professional championships, he beat another Australian, Barry Toates, a professional, at Newport, R.I.

Ronaldson also won the two major doubles events, the British Open with an amateur, Michael Dean, and the World tournament with Toates. Alan Lovell retained his amateur singles title, beating Dean, with whom he then paired to take the doubles. Katrina Allen won the Ladies championship, defeating Lesley Ronaldson, wife of the world champion, 3–6, 6–2, 6–1.   (ROY MCKELVIE)

RIVER SPORTS

In the flat-water races at the 1984 Olympic Games at Los Angeles, New Zealand won the most gold medals (four), while Canada and Sweden tied for the most medals overall (six). Greg ("Buck") Barton of Michigan won the bronze medal in the men's flat-water 1,000-m single kayak race, the first Olympic canoe and kayak medal for the U.S. since 1972. (For tabulated results of the Olympic competition, see *Track and Field Sports:* Special Report, below.)

The U.S. national flat-water championships took place August 22–25 at Lake Placid, N.Y. Olympic medalist Barton won all three men's single kayak races. Cathy Hearn won the women's single kayak events.

The U.S national championships in white-water slalom were held August 3–5 near Tariffville, Conn. Mike McCormick won the men's kayaking, Wendy Stone the women's kayaking, and David Hearn the men's single canoe race. At the U.S national championships in wild-water racing (downriver white-water), held April 21–22 on the Peshtigo River in Wisconsin, John Fishburn of Montana won his third consecutive national title. Fishburn placed eighth at the pre-world championships, held June 9–10 at Garmisch, West Germany. The first-place finisher was Joerg Winfried of West Germany.

At the U.S national marathon championships, held June 9 and 10 on Saranac Lake in New York, Fletcher Anderson of Colorado finished first in the men's single kayak race. Theresa Haught of Virginia was first in the women's race.

The third marathon world cup took place in August at Carrick on Shannon in Ireland. Rod Kinch of the U.K. was first in the men's single kayak race, and Ann Plant of the U.K. was the winner in the women's. The other first-place finishers were from the U.K., Ireland, and Denmark. The top U.S. competitors were Kay Edwards and Ann Hopkinson, who finished fourth in the women's double kayak race.   (ERIC LEAPER)

RODEO

The Professional Rodeo Cowboys Association (PRCA) enjoyed another record-breaking season in 1984, with 635 rodeos across North America and $13,776,848 in prize money. During the year's finale, the National Finals Rodeo (NFR) in Oklahoma City in December, the season's top 15 in each event competed for more than $900,000 in prize money. Oklahoma City had played host to the NFR for 20 years, but less than a week after the 1984 contest, the PRCA board of directors voted to accept an offer from Las Vegas, Nev., to move the rodeo to that city in 1985. The offer included guaranteed prize money of $1.5 million.

Dee Pickett of Caldwell, Idaho, won the all-around cowboy title for 1984 with total winnings of $122,618. The total included $30,648 in NFR earnings in calf roping and team roping. He and partner Mike Beers of Rufus, Ore., were also named team roping world champions with $57,557 each in the event.

Defending all-around champ Roy Cooper of Durant, Okla., was runner-up in 1984 but won his sixth world calf roping championship with $89,703. One big surprise during the year was Don Gay, who won a record eighth bull riding championship. Gay, 31, of Mesquite, Texas, had retired at the end of 1982 because of overwhelming muscle damage incurred from riding more than a thousand bulls during his career. He recuperated for a year, then returned to win the 1984 title with earnings of $77,327.

Other PRCA world champions included Brad Gjermundson of Marshall, N.D., $78,150 in saddle bronc riding; Larry Peabody of Three Forks, Mont., $78,741 in bareback riding; John W. Jones of Morro Bay, Calif., $63,863 in steer wrestling; Guy Allen of Lovington, N.M., $41,289 in steer roping; and 14-year-old Charmayne James of Clayton, N.M., $53,500 in Women's Professional Rodeo Association (WPRA) barrel racing.

Elsewhere in rodeo, Mel Coleman of Pierceland, Sask., was named all-around champion in the Canadian Professional Rodeo Association with $26,284 in earnings. And Jan Howell of Tishomingo, Okla., took the WPRA all-around at the All-Women's Rodeo Finals in Fort Worth, Texas, with $4,150. Dan Dailey of Wauchula, Fla., had been the perennial all-around champion in the International Professional Rodeo Association (IPRA), taking five all-around crowns with around $50,000 in earnings each year. But the IPRA changed formats, naming champions based largely on the outcome of the International Finals Rodeo held each January in Tulsa, Okla. Dailey lost the 1983 world title to Mike Fletcher of Clarksville, Texas, but won the national all-around for 1983 and again in 1984, with top winnings of $43,751. The 1984 world IPRA titles were to be decided again at the International Finals in January and February 1985.

All-around champions in the National Intercollegiate Rodeo Association included Nancy Rea of Southern Arkansas University and John Opie of Blue Mountain Community College. The Youth National Finals Rodeo continued to gain in popularity; it featured the top contestants from youth rodeo associations around the country, including high school and Little Britches. The rodeo was held in Fort Worth in November; while no all-around champion was named, individual event winners—and every contestant—shared in nearly $70,000 worth of merchandise, awards, and college scholarships. It was possible that the contest would move to Oklahoma City in 1985, replacing the NFR.   (RANDALL E. WITTE)

ROWING

The U.S. and Canada made a significant impact on world rowing in 1984 by winning medals in all but one of the 14 Olympic events. However, East Germany continued its overall supremacy in world-class events in spite of being among the nations absent from the Olympics.

World rowing was almost at full strength for the pre-Olympic regatta in Lucerne, Switz., where the East Germans won 6 of the 14 Olympic-class events. Their suc-

Oxford (foreground) won the 130th University Boat Race against Cambridge by 3¾ lengths after a 24-hour delay caused by damage to Cambridge's boat during a practice start.
PRESS ASSOCIATION, LONDON

cesses included the men's double and quadruple sculls and four of the women's classes. This performance, coupled with their domination of the world junior championships, indicated clearly that East German crews and scullers were probably the fastest in 17 of the 32 world-class events.

In the men's events at the Olympic Games, held on Lake Casitas near Los Angeles, the U.S. won the gold medal in double sculls, three silver medals, and a bronze. Canada triumphed in the eights—as it had done at Lucerne—and also took two bronze medals. Six nations shared the other men's titles. Great Britain won a gold medal in coxed fours for the first time; West Germany took the quadruple sculls; Finland and Italy repeated their Lucerne wins in single sculls and coxed pairs; Romania won the coxless pairs; and in the coxless fours the U.S.—winner in Lucerne—finished second to New Zealand. New Zealand also won a bronze medal in coxed fours, while Australia collected a silver in the quadruple sculls and a bronze in the eights.

The long-awaited confrontation in single sculls between Pertti Karppinen of Finland and Peter Kolbe of West Germany (who had each won twice against the other in world and Olympic sculls finals) fulfilled all expectations. Kolbe led by half a length at 500 m and held his position until Karppinen challenged at 1,500 m. Karppinen needed another 400 m to gain a slight lead, but Kolbe remained close until he faltered in the last few strokes, allowing Karppinen to win by 1.95 sec.

The tightest finish took place in the eights. The Canadians led from the first stroke, with Australia lying one-third of a length behind at the halfway mark. Over the last 500 m the U.S. overhauled Australia but just failed to catch Canada by 0.42 sec. In quadruple sculls Australia finished 0.43 sec behind West Germany, while the U.S. had a 1.32-sec margin over Belgium in double sculls. After leading Britain by 1.55 sec beyond halfway in the coxed fours, the U.S. was cut back to a lead of less than half a second at 1,500 m. Then the British went ahead 250 m from the finish to win by 1.64 sec.

The women's events were dominated by Romania with five gold medals. The U.S. won in the eights, as it had also done at Lucerne. The U.S. and Canada each won silver medals in two events to finish second and third, respectively, in the medal table. (For tabulated results of the Olympic competition, see *Track and Field Sports:* Special Report, below.)

The Windglider sailboards were included in the Olympic Games for the first time in 1984. The event was won by Stephan van den Berg of The Netherlands.

PAUL KENNEDY—LONG PHOTOGRAPHY, INC.

The world junior championships, held in Jönköping, Sweden, were dominated by East Germany with wins in all but 3 of the 14 events. Among the major surprises was East Germany's loss to France by inches in the eights in a breathtaking finish. The French also won two silver medals and a bronze.

In competition in England the only overseas winners at the Henley Royal Regatta were Brown University of Providence, R.I., in the Ladies Plate (eights) and the Bagsvaerd Roklub and Kolding Roklub of Denmark in the Double Sculls Cup. Oxford won the 130th University Boat Race by 3¾ lengths in record time, after an unprecedented 24-hour postponement because Cambridge had crushed its bows against a moored barge during a practice start. Cambridge's lead in the series was cut to 68–61.

(KEITH OSBORNE)

SAILING

In the 1984 Olympic Games yachting competition held at Long Beach, Calif., a sailboard was included, increasing the sailing events to seven classes. In the Finn class (single-handed dinghy) an outsider, Russell Coutts (New Zealand), outstripped the favourites to win the gold medal. John Bertrand (U.S.) and Terry Neilson (Canada) put up a good fight and won the silver and bronze medals, respectively. The Flying Dutchman class was dominated by the U.S. and Canadian teams, skippered by Jonathan McKee (gold) and Terry McLaughlin (silver), respectively. This pair consistently showed greater boat speed, particularly to windward; after a tight battle Great Britain's Jo Richards took the bronze medal with a second place in the last race.

The Tornado class was won comfortably by Rex Sellers (New Zealand), who found that extra bit of speed to put together a magnificent series, beating Randy Smyth of the U.S. The defending world champion, Chris Cairns (Australia), took the bronze medal. In the 470 class the unheralded Spaniards Luis Doreste and Roberto Molina quietly amassed a stunning points lead in the first five races to win the gold. The favoured U.S. boat, skippered by Steve Benjamin, was disqualified in the fifth race for a premature start and finished second, ahead of the French team skippered by Thierry Peponnet. The only female helmsman in the Olympics, Great Britain's Cathy Foster, won the last race, Britain's only win in any class.

In the Soling class Robbie Haines (U.S.) had won the gold medal by the end of the sixth race, but competition for the silver and bronze went to the last race, when they were won by Torben Grael (Brazil) and Hans Fogh (Canada), respectively. The Star class, the oldest in the Olympics, had five different winners in the first five races. In the last race there was a four-boat battle for the gold medal between Bill Buchan (U.S.), Giorgio Gorla (Italy), Joachim Griese (West Germany), and Kent Carlson (Sweden). The alert Buchan, spotting a wind shift, went past Gorla to take the winning gun and with it the gold medal; Griese won the silver and Gorla the bronze.

The Windglider sailboards, in the Olympics for the first time, had some close races. Preregatta favourite Stephan van den Berg from The Netherlands sailed a steady conservative series and won the gold medal comfortably. Randall Steele of the U.S. and New Zealand's Bruce Kendall took the silver and bronze medals. Thus the U.S. team won a medal in every class, including three golds; New Zealand

World Class Boat Champions

Class	Winner	Class	Winner
Cadet	Mariano Parado (Argentina)	International Canoe	Steve Clark (United States)
Contender	Barry Watson (Australia)	International 14	Will Henderson (United Kingdom)
Enterprise	Alan Gillard (United Kingdom)	Hornet	Peter Bennett (United Kingdom)
Europe	Joachim Hellmich (West Germany)	J24	Dave Curtis (United States)
Flying Dutchman	Jonathan McKee (United States)	OK	Glen Collins (Australia)
Flying Fifteen	Graham Lillingston (United Kingdom)	Solo	Geoff Carveth (United Kingdom)
Fireball	Gary Smith (Australia)	Star	Giorgio Gorla (Italy)
505	Deane Blatchford (Australia)	Topper	Ian Fryett (United Kingdom)
5.5 Metre	François Homberger (Switzerland)	Tornado	Chris Cairns (Australia)
470	David Barnes (New Zealand)	Youth Laser	Stuart Childerley (United Kingdom)
H Boat	Morten Nielsen (Denmark)	Youth Laser II	Stefan Segar (Switzerland)

won two gold medals and a bronze to finish second, ahead of third-place Canada with one silver and two bronzes.

The Atlantic was the target of the big yachts and multihulls. First Patrick Moran (France) with a crew of three in "Jet Services" made the voyage of 4,800 km (3,000 mi) from Sandy Hook, N.Y., to Cornwall's Lizard Peninsula in 8 days 16 hours 33 minutes, reducing Marc Pajot's 1981 record by $17\frac{1}{2}$ hours. Then in the *Observer*/Europe 1 single-handed transatlantic race from Plymouth, England, to Newport, R.I., Yvon Fauconnier (France) in "Umupro Jardin V" won in 16 days 6 hours 25 minutes after receiving a 16-hour allowance for rescuing fellow competitor Philippe Jeantot from his capsized boat "Crédit Agricole." The speeds and light rigs of these huge single-handers were, however, beginning to cause concern; both "Jet Services" and "33 Export" hit submerged objects at high speeds and suffered severe damage.

The final transatlantic event (4,800 km) was from Quebec to Saint-Mâlo, Brittany. The size limit was a massive 85 ft but the boats were fully crewed. After nine days, Loic Caradac and his team in "Royale II" crossed the line just over 15 minutes ahead of Pierre Follenfant's team in "Charente Maritime II." (ADRIAN JARDINE)

SHOOTING

Marksmen from 17 nations participated in the 1984 Olympic Games at Los Angeles. The United States and China each won six medals, while Great Britain won four, Italy three, and France two. The Grand American trapshooting tournament was held at Vandalia, Ohio, and the U.S. rifle and pistol championships took place at Camp Perry, Ohio.

Trap and Skeet. Three competitors at the Olympic Games broke 192 clay pigeons out of a possible 200. In the shoot-off, Luciano Giovannetti of Italy missed only one target of 25 to win the gold medal. Francisco Boza of Peru missed two to gain second place, while Dan Carlisle of the U.S. missed three to take third. High overall winner at the 1984 Grand American trapshooting tournament was Leo Harrison III with a score of 983 out of a possible 1,000. Ray Stafford was second with 982, and Kay Ohye finished third with 977. The women's championship was won by Lou Ann Munson, who scored 947.

Matt Dryke of the U.S. won the gold medal for skeet at Los Angeles by tying the Olympic record of 198 out of a possible 200. Ole Rasmussen of Denmark and Luca Rossi of Italy both scored 196. Rasmussen then broke two more targets in the shoot-off to take the silver medal and leave Rossi the bronze.

Rifles. The standard rifle, three-position event at the Olympics was won by Wu Xiaoxuan of China with 581 out of a possible 600. Ulrike Holmer of West Germany and Wanda Jewell of the U.S. each fired 578. In the shoot-off Holmer took the silver medal by two points. The English match, fired from the prone position, was won by Ed Etzel of the U.S. with 599 out of 600. Michel Bury of France and Michael Sullivan of Great Britain tied for second with 596. Bury then bested Sullivan by two points to break the tie. The small-bore free-rifle match was won by Malcolm Cooper of Great Britain with 1,173. Daniel Nipkow of Switzerland placed second with 1,163, and Alister Allan of Great Britain was third with 1,162.

The gold medal for the moving target event at the Olympics was won by Li Yuwei of China with a score of 587. Helmut Bellingrodt of Colombia took the silver with 584, while Huang Shiping of China took the bronze with 581. Philippe Heberle of France won the Olympic men's air rifle match with 589. The silver medal was taken by Andreas Kronthaler of Austria and the bronze by Barry Dagger of Great Britain. Pat Spurgin of the U.S. took the gold medal in the women's air rifle match with a score of 393. Edith Gufler of Italy was second with 391, while Wu Xiaoxuan of China was third with 389.

At Camp Perry, Ron West of Zanesville, Ohio, won the U.S. small-bore rifle championship with 6,398–536X, one point short of the national record. Marsha Beasley of Arlington, Va., won the women's championship with 6,392–495X. Gary Stephens of Columbus, Ga., was high junior with 6,386–495X. The U.S. high-power rifle championship went to Pat McCann of Staunton, Ill., for his record score of 2,377–119X. Norma McCullough was the women's high-power rifle champion with 2,346–99X.

Handguns. In the small-bore sport pistol event at the 1984 Olympics, Linda Thom of Canada and Ruby Fox of the U.S. posted scores of 585. A one-point lead in the shoot-off gave Thom the gold medal. Patricia Dench of Australia finished third with 583. The free pistol competition at the Olympics was won by Xu Haifeng of China with 566. Ragnar Skanaker of Sweden took the silver medal with 565 and Wang Yifu of China the bronze with 564. Takeo Kamachi of Japan won the gold medal in the rapid-fire pistol event with a score of 595. The silver medal went to Corneliu Ion of Romania for his 593 and the bronze to Rauno Bies of Finland with 591.

The 1984 U.S. national pistol championship was won by James Laguna with a score of 2,640–137X. Cheerie Shaw was the women's champion with 2,529–70X.

(ROBERT N. SEARS)

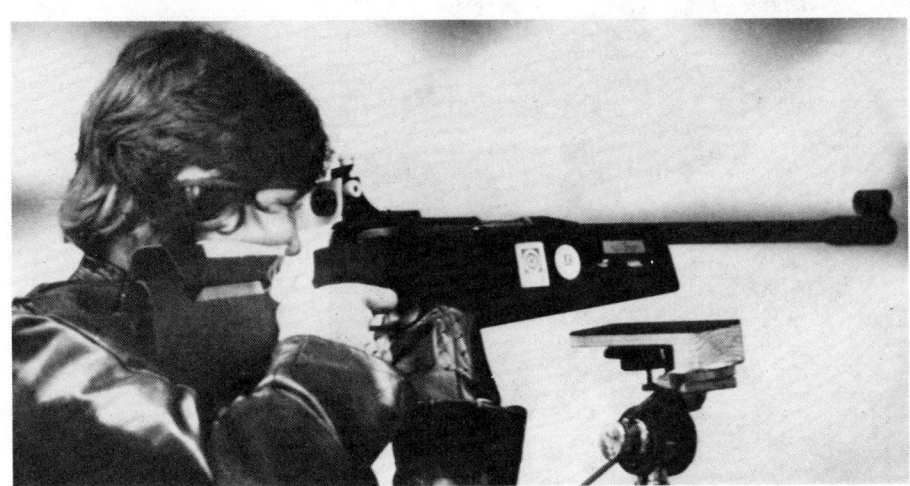

Pat Spurgin of Billings, Montana, won a gold medal in the women's air rifle competition at the Olympic Games in Los Angeles.

Joe Fargis of Petersburg, Virginia, representing the United States, rides Touch of Class to a gold medal in the individual jumping competition at the Summer Olympic Games in Los Angeles.

TARDY/PERRIN—GAMMA/LIAISON

SHOW JUMPING

The U.S. won two team gold medals in equestrian events at the 1984 Olympic Games at Los Angeles in August. In the three-day event the victorious U.S. team (186 penalty points) consisted of Mike Plumb on Blue Stone, Torrance Fleischmann on Finvarra, Bruce Davidson on J. J. Babu, and Karen Stives, who won the individual silver medal, on Ben Arthur.

The British team (189.2 penalty points) won the silver medals; it comprised Virginia Holgate, who won the individual bronze, on Priceless, Diana Clapham on Windjammer, Lucinda Green on Regal Realm, and Ian Stark on Oxford Blue. Third was West Germany (234). The individual gold medal was won by Mark Todd on Charisma for New Zealand.

The U.S. won the show-jumping team gold medals from Great Britain and West Germany with only 12 faults, an Olympic record. The U.S. team included Melanie Smith on Calypso, Joe Fargis on Touch of Class, Conrad Homfeld on Abdullah, and Leslie Burr on Albany. Great Britain (36.75 faults), represented by Michael Whitaker on Overton Amanda, John Whitaker on Ryan's Son, Steven Smith on Shining Example, and Tim Grubb on Linky, won the silver medals, and West Germany (39.25 faults) took the bronze. The U.S. also won the individual gold medal with Fargis and the individual silver with Homfeld, the bronze going to Heidi Robbiani on Jessica V for Switzerland. West Germany, led by individual champion Reiner Klimke on Ahlerich, won the team gold medals in dressage from Switzerland and Sweden.

(PAMELA MACGREGOR-MORRIS)

SPELUNKING

During 1984 both the longest and the deepest caves in the world were extended. In Kentucky the 78.4-km (48.7-mi) Roppel Cave was connected with the Mammoth Cave–Flint Ridge combined system, and this, together with some small discoveries in the same caves, resulted in a total underground length of 473.68 km (294.33 mi). Steady exploration and mapping in the world's second longest cave, the Swiss Hölloch, brought it to 147.11 km (91.41 mi). In the U.S.S.R. the known length of the Optimisticheskaya cave increased a little, to 147 km (91.34 mi). Relatively small extensions in Jewel Cave (S.D.) to 110 km (68.35 mi) and in Ozyornaya (U.S.S.R.) to 107.6 km (66.86 mi) maintained them in fourth and fifth places, respectively. The attainment of seventh place by the Sieben Hengste system in Switzerland (65 km; 40.39 mi) resulted from the

JERRY WOOLDRIDGE

Cobweb Cave was discovered in May 1984 by members of a British expedition that spent two months in Borneo.

discovery at a depth of 625 m (2,051 ft) of a connection with the F1 system.

The Gouffre Jean Bernard (Haute-Savoie, France), already the world's deepest cave, increased in overall depth to 1,535 m (5,036 ft) when explorers joined the two systems B21 and B22. Unconfirmed reports from the U.S.S.R. indicated that Snezhnaya was explored to 1,402 m (4,600 ft), making it the second deepest known. In the French Gouffre Berger, Patrick Penez dived to a depth of 50 m (164 ft) below the surface of the last sump, bringing the total depth to 1,248 m (4,094 ft) and making it the fifth deepest.

Cave divers made several successive advances in the Australian Cocklebiddy Cave, which consists almost entirely of level roomy passages filled with water beneath the Nullarbor Plain. First Ron Allum and several others, in a series of dives totaling 15 hours, extended the previous final "sump" (which included some air spaces) from 2 km (1.24 mi) to 2.65 km (1.65 mi) and reached the 500-m (1,640-ft) Toad Hall. Then divers from the Spéléo Club de Paris, led by Francis le Guen, penetrated 1.46 km (0.91 mi) into another sump beyond Toad Hall, spending 39 hours under water in all and finally being stopped by passages too narrow for their air tanks. A few weeks later the Australian divers were able to pass the French limit by using smaller tanks, but these held only enough air to allow the Australians to get 240 m (787 ft) farther, making the overall length of the cave 7.05 km (4.38 mi), 6.24 km (3.88 mi) of it submerged. Although the overall submerged length of Cocklebiddy Cave constituted a world record, the length of its longest individual sump was less than the 2,337 m (7,667 ft) already explored upstream from Friedman Sink at Manatee Springs, Fla. Sheck Exley and other divers had explored this to a point where it was blocked by boulders. In contrast, Cocklebiddy was still open at the farthest point reached. Jochen Hasenmayer passed his own previous world record for deep diving in a cave by reaching 200 m (656 ft), breathing an oxygen-helium mixture, in the Fontaine de Vaucluse (France). Cameras lowered to 243 m (797 ft) showed that the passage still continued downward at that point. (T. R. SHAW)

SQUASH RACKETS

All the major men's titles in 1984 were won by a young Pakistani, Jahangir Khan (born December 1963). He thus continued his uninterrupted string of victories begun in April 1981. In October 1983 he won the International Squash Rackets Federation (ISRF) world individual title in New Zealand, defeating his countryman Qamar Zaman in the final. Khan, Zaman, and Maqsood Ahmad won the ISRF world team title, beating England (Hidayat Jahan, Gawain Briars, and Philip Kenyon) in the final. Khan then traveled to England where he triumphed over Zaman in the final of the ICI Perspex World Masters. In December he took the World Open crown, beating surprise Australian finalist Chris Dittmar.

In the spring of 1984 Khan won the French Open, besting Dean Williams (Australia) in the final, and the British Open for the third time by beating Zaman. Both events utilized a blue-floored, transparent court, together with white and yellow balls. The British Open, at the Wembley Conference Centre, London, was notable for an audience at the final match of 2,603—a world record. Ken Hiscoe (Australia) won the British Open veterans title for the second time, but Kevin Parker (Australia) in the Open vintage and Jonah Barrington (Ireland) in the over 35s won their divisions for the first time. England regained the European men's team title by defeating defending champion Sweden

In the world of squash in 1984 two Pakistani players led the rest: Jahangir Khan (foreground) and Qamar Zaman. Khan continued his unbeaten record by defeating Zaman to win the British Open.
DUNCAN HOLDSWORTH—CAMERA PRESS/PHOTO TRENDS

in the 1984 final, and in May Khan won the North American Open hardball squash title.

In the women's world individual championships held in Perth, Australia, in late 1983, Vicki Cardwell (Australia) won the individual title, beating Rhonda Thorne (Australia) in the final. In the team event Australia defeated England in the final. In the British Open Susan Devoy of New Zealand captured the title, triumphing over Lisa Opie of England in the final. England's women again won the European team championship.

On the junior scene, Robin Friday (Australia) won the 1983 world women's junior championship, beating Helen Paradieser (Australia) in the final. In Calgary, Alta., Chris Robertson of Australia won the 1984 world men's junior championship by defeating David Lloyd (England) in the final. In the team final Australia defeated England.

(ANDREW SHELLEY)

SURFING

The 1984 world amateur championships of the International Surfing Association (ISA) were held at Oceanside, Calif., in fair-to-good surf conditions, with 250 contestants representing 14 nations. Scott Farnsworth of the U.S. became the new world amateur champion as the U.S captured the first four places in the men's open. In the women's division Janice Aragon of the U.S. won the title. Making it a clean sweep, the U.S. scored 702 in team points, with Australia second with 670 and Hawaii third with 347. The ISA scheduled the next world championship for 1986 in Great Britain.

The Association of Surfing Professionals, headed by Ian Cairns of Australia, refused to sanction Hawaii's Triple Crown competition, and so the top 16 surfers did not compete there. The winter of 1983–84 was, therefore, the first time that the giant waves on the north shore of Oahu did not decide the fate of the money competitors. Hawaii's Michael Ho won the Triple Crown with a spectacular finish in the World Cup, easily winning it and also taking second place behind Dane Kealoha of Hawaii in the other two events, the Pipeline Masters and the Duke Kahanamoku Surfing Classic. (JACK C. FLANAGAN)

SWIMMING

For the first time since 1932, the summer Olympic Games in 1984 returned to the United States. As was the case in 1980, the Games failed to produce the major aquatic competition that always had been an Olympic highlight. Joining the Soviet Union in a boycott, "questioning the security of their athletes" but generally conceded to be in retaliation for the U.S.-led boycott of the 1980 Games in Moscow, were teams from East Germany and 12 other Soviet-bloc nations.

As a result of the boycott, U.S. swimmers dominated the Olympic competition. Male swimmers won 9 of 15 events and the women 11 of 14, the largest number ever by the U.S. The U.S. finished first and second in nine events and won all five relays.

For the year 19 world records were set by men, 11 at the Olympic Games. Five world records were set by women, all by swimmers from East Germany beginning with Kristin Otto on May 23 in the 200-m freestyle. Her time of 1 min 57.75 sec lowered by almost 0.5 sec the record of 1 min 58.23 sec set by Cynthia Woodhead of the U.S. in 1979. The remaining four women's records were set in Moscow at the Friendship Games held in August.

For the first time ever in the Olympics, there was a tie for first in the women's 100-m freestyle, the U.S. pair of Nancy Hogshead and Carrie Steinseifer sharing a gold medal with times of 55.92 sec. The individual swimming star of the Olympics was Michael Gross (*see* BIOGRAPHIES) of West Germany. On July 29 he was timed in 1 min 47.44 sec in the 200-m freestyle to erase his seven-week-old mark of 1 min 47.55 sec set in the West German championships on June 8. The following day Gross won the 100-m butterfly with a time of 53.08 sec, lowering the previous world record of 53.38 set at the U.S. Olympic trials on June 26 by Pablo Morales. On August 3 it took a world record by Australia's Jon Sieben in the 200-m butterfly to defeat Gross. Sieben's time of 1 min 57.04 sec sliced 0.01 sec off the West German's world record. Swimming the final 200 m of the 4 x 200-m freestyle relay, Gross just missed beating the anchorman for the winning U.S. team, which set a world record of 7 min 15.69 sec. The U.S. quartet of Mike Heath, David Larson, Jeff Float, and Bruce Hayes lowered the world record of 7 min 18.87 sec set by the U.S. team of Geoff Gaberino, Larson, Hayes, and Rich Saeger in the preliminary competition.

In other Olympic events a world record was set on July 29 in the 100-m breaststroke by Steve Lundquist of Jonesboro, Ga. His time of 1 min 1.65 sec erased the one-month-old mark of 1 min 2.13 sec set by John Moffet in the U.S. Olympic trials. Injury destroyed Moffet's hopes of winning the gold medal in the Olympics. On August 2 Victor Davis of Canada lowered his 200-m breaststroke world time of 2 min 14.58 sec, set at the Canadian Olympic trials on June 19, by more than a second to 2 min 13.34 sec. On July 30 Alex Baumann of Canada laid claim to being the world's greatest swimmer, setting a world record in the 400-m individual medley with a time of 4 min 17.41 sec to erase his previous world mark of 4 min 17.53 sec established at the Canadian trials. Five days later Baumann won his second Olympic gold medal in world record time for the 200-m individual medley. His time of 2 min 1.42 sec bettered the mark of 2 min 2.25 sec that he had set in 1982.

On August 2 at the Olympics the U.S. quartet of Chris Cavanaugh, Heath, Matt Biondi, and Rowdy Gaines was timed in 3 min 19.03 sec set for the 4 x 100-m freestyle relay, bettering the old mark of 3 min 19.26 sec set by a U.S. team in 1982. On the final day of Olympic swim-

ming, August 4, the U.S. team of Rick Carey, Lundquist, Morales, and Gaines took almost 1 sec off its 1983 world record of 3 min 40.42 sec with a time of 3 min 39.30 sec for the 4 x 100-m medley relay.

The 1984 Friendship Games for the nations that boycotted the Olympics, produced five world swimming records. East Germany dominated the women's events, winning 11 of 14 while the Soviets won the other 3. The Soviet men dominated their events, winning ten gold medals to East German's five in the 15 events. The East German women set four world records. On August 21 the team of Otto, Karen Konig, Heike Friedrich, and Birgit Meineke was timed in 3 min 42.41 sec for the 4 x 100-m freestyle relay. The previous record of 3 min 42.71 sec had also been set by East Germany in the same pool in 1980. On August 23 Silvia Gerasch was timed in 1 min 8.29 sec for the 100-m breaststroke, lowering the previous record of 1 min 8.51 sec set in 1983 by East Germany's Ute Geweniger. Three days later the quartet of Ina Kleber, Gerasch, Ines Geissler, and Meineke was timed in 4 min 3.69 sec in the 4 x 100-m medley relay, lowering the previous record of 4 min 5.79 sec set in 1983 by East Germany. Kleber, the backstroke swimmer leading off the relay, was timed in 1 min 0.59 sec to erase the old mark of 1 min 0.86 sec set by Rica Reinisch of East Germany in 1980. On August 21 Sergey Zabolotnov of the Soviet Union lowered the men's 200-m backstroke world record to 1 min 58.41 sec.

A comparison of times achieved at the Olympics and the Friendship Games showed that the women's times in Moscow surpassed the gold and silver medal Olympic times on 19 occasions and the men did so 10 times. If the ten nations in the Friendship Games had competed in the Olympics, the U.S. total of 21 gold medals would have been reduced to 11. (For table of world swimming records set during the year, see *Sporting Record,* below.)

Diving. At the Olympics, Greg Louganis of Mission Viejo, Calif., became the first man in 56 years, and the third ever, to win gold medals in the platform and the springboard events in the same Olympic Games. His U.S. teammate Bruce Kimball of Ann Arbor, Mich., moved past two Chinese divers into second place in the platform competition. With a final total of 710.91 points, Louganis

Duet synchronized swimming was a new event at the 1984 summer Olympic Games, and the event was won by the U.S. team of Tracie Ruiz (left) of Bothell, Washington, and Candy Costie of Seattle, Washington.

became the first man to reach a score of 700 in platform diving. He achieved a perfect 10 and 9s and 9.5s on his final dive, a reverse 3½ somersault, the most difficult dive a person can attempt from the 10-m board. Kimball's second-place total was 643.50. Earlier in the Olympic program Louganis had routed his competition in the 3-m springboard, scoring 754.41 points to 662.31 for Tan Liangde of China. Ron Merriott, Rockford, Ill., finished a close third with 661.32.

In the women's 10-m platform China won its first aquatic gold medal, as Zhou Jihong improved her third-place performance in the 1982 world championships. Zhou scored 435.51 and never trailed Michele Mitchell of Mission Viejo, who scored 431.19 for the silver medal. Wendy Wyland of Mission Viejo won the bronze medal. In the 3-m springboard Sylvie Bernier of Canada, who had finished third in the 1983 Pan American Games, surprised the heavily favoured U.S. divers, winning the gold medal with 530.70 points. She was followed by Kelly McCormick of Long Beach, Calif., with 527.46. McCormick's mother, Pat, had won both the springboard and platform events in the 1952 and 1956 Olympics. Chris Seufert of Ambler, Pa., won the bronze medal.

Two weeks after the Olympics, Louganis added another milestone to his amazing career. On August 21–25 at Santa Clara, Calif., he won the 1-m and 3-m springboard events and the 10-m platform at the U.S. outdoor diving championships, giving him 29 national diving titles in seven years of competition.

Synchronized Swimming. For the first time, synchronized swimming was added to the Olympic program. Swimmers from ten countries entered the event. Tracie Ruiz of Bothell, Wash., received a perfect score of 10 from one judge on her way to the gold medal in the solo competition. Carolyn Waldo of Canada and Miwako Motoyoshi of Japan won the silver and bronze medals, respectively. The solo event was not added until May 30, when the International Olympic Committee announced that it was willing to add the event at that late date because it would not increase the number of participants, all of the competitors already having entered the duet event.

Ruiz and Candy Costie won the duet championship for the U.S. with 195.584 points. The Canadian pair, Sharon Hambrook and Kelly Kryczka, won the silver medal, falling short by 1.35 points of upsetting the U.S. swimmers. The bronze medalists were Saeko Kimura and Motoyoshi of Japan. (For table of results of the Olympic Games, see *Track and Field Sports:* Special Report, below.)

(ALBERT SCHOENFIELD)

TABLE TENNIS

Featuring 16 of the top male competitors in table tennis, the fifth World Cup tournament took place in Kuala Lumpur, Malaysia, in early September 1984. Jiang Jialiang of China was the winner, followed in order by Kim Wan of South Korea, Ulf Bengtsson of Sweden, Kiyoshi Saito of Japan, and Jan-Ove Waldner of Sweden. As a result of his triumph, Jiang moved up from fifth to second in the world rankings, behind Cai Zhenhua of China.

Earlier in the year, in April, the European championships were held in Moscow. In men's team competition France was the winner, with Poland finishing second, Sweden third, Czechoslovakia fourth, and Yugoslavia fifth. The women's team title was won by the Soviet Union, ahead of Yugoslavia, Hungary, The Netherlands, and Sweden in that order. In the five-set men's singles final Bengtsson defeated Andrzej Grubba of Poland 21–16, 15–21, 21–12, 14–21, and 21–19. The women's individual championship

was won by Valentina Popova of the Soviet Union. In the final she defeated teammate Fliura Bulatova 15–21, 21–15, 21–17, 21–16. Victorious in the men's doubles were Zoran Kalinic and Dragutin Surbek of Yugoslavia, who won over Sweden's Erik Lindh and Waldner. The Soviet pair of Popova and Narine Antonian triumphed in the women's doubles over Branka Batinic and Gordana Perkucin of Yugoslavia. Jacques Secretin of France joined Popova to win the mixed doubles from Jindrich Pansky and Marie Hrachova of Czechoslovakia.

The Mediterranean championships took place at Messina in Sicily during September 1983. In the men's team competition Turkey was the winner, followed in order by Italy, Yugoslavia, France, and Greece. The women's team title was won by Yugoslavia, with France placing second, Italy third, Greece fourth, and Turkey fifth. Other nations competing in the tournament were Egypt, Tunisia, Libya, Malta, and Cyprus. In the men's singles Massimo Costantini of Italy won the crown over fellow Italian Giovanni Bisi. Gordana Perkucin of Yugoslavia was the women's champion, with Marina Cergol of Italy placing second. The Italian team of Pero and Silveri triumphed in the men's doubles over fellow countrymen Costantini and Bisi. Yugoslavia's Cepic and Perkucin won the women's doubles over Zampini and Danda of Italy. Bisi and Cergol paired to win the mixed doubles title for Italy over Guilbert and Saunet of France.   (ARTHUR KINGSLEY VINT)

1984 World Rankings

MEN	WOMEN
1. Cai Zhenhua (China)	1. Cao Yanhua (China)
2. Jiang Jialiang (China)	2. Dai Lili (China)
3. Xie Saike (China)	3. Tong Ling (China)
4. Jan-Ove Waldner (Sweden)	4. Yang Young Ja (South Korea)
5. Wang Huiyuan (China)	5. Jiao Zhimin (China)
6. Mikael Appelgren (Sweden)	6. Qi Baoxiang (China)
7. Andrzej Grubba (Poland)	7. Ni Xialiang (China)
8. Kiyoshi Saito (Japan)	8. Valentina Popova (Soviet Union)
9. Ulf Bengtsson (Sweden)	9. Marie Hrachova (Czechoslovakia)
10. Fan Changmao (China)	10. Fumiko Shinpo (Japan)

TENNIS

The most successful tennis player of either sex in 1984 was Martina Navratilova of the United States, and when she won both singles and doubles in the French Open championships in Paris in June, she earned not only $117,640 as normal prize money but $1 million for the "Grand Slam." This was given by the International Tennis Federation (ITF) for becoming singles champion of Australia, France, Wimbledon (England), and the U.S. within 12 months. Navratilova was the third woman to achieve the feat and the first player to be rewarded for it financially. Later in the year she retained her singles and doubles titles at Wimbledon and in the U.S. Open. At the end of the latter tournament in September, her current year's earnings, measured only in prize money, totaled $2,025,256. It brought her career earnings over a ten-year period to a record $8,429,835.

Administratively, tennis reverted to undivided control. The dispute between the commercial World Championship Tennis (WCT) organization based in Dallas, Texas, and the other organizations was resolved. WCT withdrew its lawsuit against the Men's International Professional Council, the Association of Tennis Professionals, and the ITF and agreed to stage its events within the framework of the Grand Prix circuit.

Tennis was a demonstration sport in the Olympic Games in Los Angeles. Full Olympic status was secured for the 1988 games in Seoul, South Korea. At Los Angeles national associations nominated players who were under 21.

All played as amateurs. The men's singles was won by Stefan Edberg (Sweden) and the women's by Steffi Graf (West Germany), aged only 15.

Record crowds attended the major tournaments in 1984. The Wimbledon championships, held in 13 sessions, drew 391,673. At Flushing Meadow, N.Y., the U.S. Open attracted 391,814 spectators for its 23 sessions.

Men's Competition. The ITF named John McEnroe (U.S.) as "world champion" for his performance in 1983. The junior world championship title was given to Edberg. McEnroe in 1984 was again the outstanding player, in singles and, with Peter Fleming (U.S.), in doubles. Ivan Lendl (Czech.) gave McEnroe close competition, but Jimmy Connors (U.S.) did less well than in the past.

The Volvo Grand Prix winner for 1983 was Mats Wilander (Sweden). He ended the season with a strong victory in the 1983 Australian championships at Melbourne. He showed unexpected grass court skill and beat McEnroe in the semifinal 4–6, 6–3, 6–4, 6–3. In the final he defeated Lendl 6–1, 6–4, 6–4. Later in the season Wilander's performance was marred by injury.

The Grand Prix Volvo Masters' championship at Madison Square Garden, New York City, in January was won by McEnroe. He beat Wilander 6–2, 6–4 in the semifinal and Lendl by 6–3, 6–4, 6–4 in an impeccable final performance. McEnroe also won the WCT finals in Dallas in May, again defeating Lendl 6–2, 4–6, 6–3, 6–7, 7–6.

The West German championship singles in Hamburg went to Juan Aguilera (Spain). The Italian title in Rome was won by Andrés Gómez (Ecuador), the 1982 victor. The French championship, staged in Paris in May and June, was a turning point for Lendl. He achieved his first success in a Grand Slam event after being a losing finalist four times. He won the semifinal 6–3, 6–3, 7–5 against Wilander and the final from McEnroe 3–6, 2–6, 6–4, 7–5, 7–5. It was the longest singles final in 50 years.

McEnroe won the Wimbledon singles in July for the third time in five years. He beat unseeded Pat Cash (Australia) 6–3, 7–6, 6–4 in the semifinal. In the other semifinal Connors beat Lendl 6–7, 6–3, 7–5, 6–1. Then, in the most one-sided Wimbledon final since 1938, McEnroe beat Connors 6–1, 6–1, 6–2. McEnroe also won the U.S. Open singles, for the fourth time in six years. In his most difficult match he beat Connors 6–4, 4–6, 7–5, 4–6, 6–3 in the semifinal. In the final he avenged his French defeat against Lendl 6–3, 6–4, 6–1. The losing semifinalist to Lendl was Cash, a quarterfinal winner against Wilander. The appearance of Cash in the last four of the singles in

both Wimbledon and U.S. events signaled a tennis revival in Australia. Cash was the ITF world junior champion in 1981.

The outstanding doubles pair was McEnroe and Peter Fleming. They won the Grand Prix Masters' tournament for the sixth successive time and the Wimbledon title for the fourth time in six years. McEnroe became the first player to retain both men's singles and doubles Wimbledon titles since Don Budge (U.S.) in 1938.

Mark Edmondson (Australia) and Paul McNamee (Australia) won the 1983 Australian Open, where Fleming and McEnroe lost in the third round. The West German championship went to Edberg and Anders Jarryd (Sweden), and the same pair beat Fleming and McEnroe in the U.S. Open semifinal, where the final was won by John Fitzgerald (Australia) and Thomas Smid (Czech.). The French doubles competition was won by Henri Leconte (France) and Yannick Noah (France), the first home pair to do so since 1946.

A record 63 nations took part in the Davis Cup. In the first round of the World Group, comprising 16 nations, Italy beat Great Britain 3–2 indoors at Telford, Salop, and subsequently in a play-off at Eastbourne, Yugoslavia beat Britain 4–1. Great Britain was thus relegated to the zone rounds for 1985 despite improved form by John Lloyd, the leading British player, who reached the last eight of the singles in the U.S. championship.

Other relegated nations were Romania, Denmark, and New Zealand. Promoted nations were the U.S.S.R. and Spain, respective winners of the two European zones. The U.S.S.R. beat Israel in the Zone "A" final in Donetsk, while Spain defeated Hungary in Budapest in the Zone "B" final. Chile, winner of the American Zone final against Brazil in Santiago, and Japan, winner against Pakistan in Rawalpindi, also earned promotion.

The U.S. (McEnroe, Connors, Fleming) and Sweden (Wilander, Henrik Sundström, Jarryd, Joakim Nyström, Edberg) reached the World Group final without danger. Sweden beat Ecuador 4–1, Paraguay 4–1, and Czechoslovakia 5–0. A win by Sundström against Lendl initiated the unexpectedly wide superiority over Czechoslovakia. The U.S. won 5–0 in Bucharest against Romania and 5–0 against Argentina in Atlanta, Ga.

Defending champion Australia lost the trophy when beaten decisively by the U.S. in the semifinal at Portland, Ore. It was the 40th meeting between them and the 23rd victory for the U.S. McEnroe beat Cash in the first singles, Connors defeated Fitzgerald in the second, and Fleming

Martina Navratilova (far left) won the United Jersey Bank Tennis Classic in Mahwah, New Jersey. She also won singles and doubles in the French Open and the "Grand Slam" by winning singles championships in Australia, France, Wimbledon, and the U.S. in 12 months. At left, John McEnroe beat Ivan Lendl in the U.S. Open men's singles finals. It was his fourth U.S. Open men's singles championship.

and McEnroe beat Edmondson and McNamee in the doubles without losing a set. The U.S. thus advanced to the championship round for the 54th time. Sweden, runners-up to Australia in 1983 and winners against Czechoslovakia in 1975, played in the finals for the third time only. In one of the major upsets of recent years Sweden defeated the U.S. 4–1. Sweden won the first two singles matches, as Wilander beat Connors 6–1, 6–3, 6–3, and Sundström defeated McEnroe 13–11, 6–4, 6–3. The Swedes then clinched the Cup when their doubles team of Edberg and Jarryd triumphed over McEnroe and Fleming 7–5, 5–7, 6–2, 7–5. The only win for the U.S. was McEnroe's 6–3, 5–7, 6–3 victory over Wilander.

Women's Competition. The dominance of Navratilova invited comparison with players of other eras, Maureen Connolly (U.S.) of the 1950s and Helen Wills Moody (U.S.) and Suzanne Lenglen (France), who flourished before World War II. At the age of 27 (she was born in Prague on Oct. 10, 1956) Navratilova appeared to have reached her peak. She won the French championship for the second time, Wimbledon for the fifth, and U.S. for the second.

In December 1983 Navratilova won the Australian title in Melbourne 6–2, 7–6 against Kathy Jordan (U.S.). In January 1984 Hana Mandlikova (Czech.) beat Navratilova 7–6, 3–6, 6–4 to deny what would have been a 55th consecutive singles victory. Subsequently, Navratilova's singles record was unmarred, and by October she had won 65 singles matches in succession.

In winning the French championship in Paris in June, Navratilova beat Mandlikova 3–6, 6–2, 6–2 in the semifinal, her only concession of a set. In the final she beat Chris Evert Lloyd (U.S.) 6–3, 6–1. At Wimbledon she lost no set in the singles, winning her quarterfinal match 6–3, 6–2 against Manuela Maleeva (Bulg.), her semifinal 6–3, 6–4 over Jordan, and the final 7–6, 6–2 from Evert Lloyd. In the U.S. Open she beat Wendy Turnbull (Australia) 6–4, 6–1 in the semifinal and Evert Lloyd 4–6, 6–4, 6–4 in the final.

Evert Lloyd, beaten by Navratilova in the three major singles finals, was second only to her Czech-born rival but failed to win one of the major titles for the first time since 1973. Maleeva (born Feb. 14, 1967) was a precocious challenger at the top level and the first Bulgarian to do so well. She won the Italian championship, held in Perugia in May, by beating Evert Lloyd 6–3, 6–3 in the final. Later in the summer she won the U.S. Clay Court singles in Indianapolis, Ind.

Navratilova and Pam Shriver (U.S.) were as dominant in doubles as was Navratilova in singles. The Grand Slam titles fell to them as a matter of course, and Navratilova set a record when she retained both singles and doubles championships at both Wimbledon and the U.S. Open.

There was a marked decline in the quality and quantity of performance by two players of note, Tracy Austin (U.S.) and Andrea Jaegar (U.S.). Their former precocious successes, with Austin becoming U.S. champion at the age of 16 and Jaeger a Wimbledon quarterfinalist at 15, caused many to wonder whether they had burned out their talent too early.

Czechoslovakia (Mandlikova, Helena Sukova, Iva Budarova, Marcella Skuherska) retained the Federation Cup, held in São Paulo, Brazil, in July. Bulgaria (Manuela and Katarina Maleeva) beat Great Britain (Jo Durie, Anne Hobbs, Amanda Brown) in the first round but later lost to Yugoslavia, which was beaten by Czechoslovakia in the semifinal. Australia (Turnbull, Anne Minter, Elizabeth Sayers) beat the U.S. (Kathy Jordan, Kathy Horvath, Anne Smith) 2–1 in the semifinal. In the final Czechoslovakia

beat Australia 2–1 when Mandlikova and Sukova beat Sayers and Turnbull in the doubles 6–2, 6–2.

The U.S. (Evert Lloyd, Barbara Potter, Alycia Moulton, Sharon Walsh) beat Great Britain (Durie, Hobbs, Brown, Annabel Croft, Virginia Wade) 5–2 at the Royal Albert Hall, London, to win the Wightman Cup for the 46th time in 56 contests. Evert Lloyd set a new record by winning all 24 sets in 12 singles matches.   (LANCE TINGAY)

TRACK AND FIELD SPORTS

Victim of a major boycott for the third consecutive time, the Olympic Games nevertheless highlighted the 1984 track and field season. The eight days of track and field activity in Los Angeles, August 3–11, produced keen competition among athletes of the 94 participating nations. Attendance at 15 morning and evening sessions totaled a record 1,129,465 people. Missing from the Games were the Soviet Union and several other nations within the Soviet sphere of influence, including Eastern European athletics powers East Germany, Poland, and Czechoslovakia. In 1980, when the Olympics were held in Moscow, the United States, West Germany, Canada, and 33 less strong nations boycotted. Most of the 1984 boycotters competed in the Friendship Games held in Prague, Czech., August 16–18 and in Moscow, August 17–18.

Men's International Competition. Carl Lewis of the United States was, as expected, the foremost figure in track and field competition at Los Angeles. He won three individual events and anchored a winning relay team, exactly duplicating the 1936 success of U.S. athlete Jesse Owens. Lewis first won the 100 m in 9.99 sec, the fourth fastest time for the distance at low altitude. He then long jumped 8.54 m (28 ft ¼ in) and next won the 200 m in 19.80 sec, an Olympic record and third fastest of all time. The 23-year-old finished off his busy week by running a swift finishing leg in the 4 x 100-m relay. With teammates Sam Graddy, who had finished second in the 100, Ron Brown, and Calvin Smith leading the way, Lewis finished to achieve a world record 37.83 sec for the quartet. The record, the only one in track and field, came a year and a day after Lewis, Smith, Emmit King, and Willie Gault had run a record 37.86 sec in the world championships.

No other man won more than one individual race in the Olympics, but Sebastian Coe of the United Kingdom won a first and a second. The world record holder in the mile in the 1980 Olympics. He finished second to Joaquim Cruz of Brazil (see BIOGRAPHIES) in the 800 m, 1 min 43.64 sec to Cruz's meet record of 1 min 43.00 sec, and then was a strong winner in the 1,500 m with an Olympic record 3 min 32.53 sec. Coe's 800-m time also was under the Olympic mark, and he was the only man to better two Olympic records.

Six more Olympic marks were established, the most impressive being the 8,797 points scored in the decathlon by Daley Thompson (see BIOGRAPHIES) of the United Kingdom. He fell just one point short of equaling the world record. Thompson and Coe were the only athletes, men or women, to successfully defend Olympic titles won in 1980, and Coe became the first man to win successive 1,500-m titles.

Olympic records also fell to Said Aouita of Morocco in the 5,000 m, Roger Kingdom of the U.S. in the 110-m hurdles, Ernesto Canto of Mexico in the 20-km walk, and Raúl Gonzáles of Mexico in the 50-km walk. Aouita's 13 min 5.59 sec was the third best ever, while Kingdom became the fourth swiftest hurdler ever with his 13.20-sec clocking. Canto was timed in 1 hour 23 min 13 sec and Gonzáles in 3 hours 47 min 26 sec. Running the 4 x 400-m relay in 2 min 57.91 sec, the second fastest time ever, were Sunder Nix, Ray Armstead, Alonzo Babers, and Antonio McKay (U.S.). It was the second gold medal for Babers, victor in the 400 m in 44.27 sec, just 0.01 sec slower than the low-altitude world best.

Edwin Moses of the U.S., winner of the 400-m hurdles in 1976 but unable to run in 1980 because of the boycott, ran 47.75 sec for his second Olympic gold medal and his 90th consecutive victory. Also impressive were Julius Korir of Kenya, surprise champion in the steeplechase in 8 min 11.80 sec, a time bettered by only four men; Alberto Cova of Italy, whose 10,000-m time was a slowish 27 min 47.54 sec but who confirmed his dominance of the event; and Carlos Lopes of Portugal, at 37 years the oldest winner, capturing the marathon in 2 hours, 9 min, 21 sec, an Olympic best.

In non-Olympic competition eight men established 11 world records, the busiest being Sergey Bubka of the Soviet Union. The 1983 world champion broke the world pole vault record four times in 1984, the best performance of 5.94 m (19 ft. 5¾ in) taking place on August 31 at Rome. Second place in that meet was Thierry Vigneron of France, who vaulted 5.91 m (19 ft 4¾ in) for his fourth world record only to lose it quickly to Bubka.

Aside from the world record in the 4 x 100-m relay that was set in the Olympics, there were no new world marks set on the track during the year at less than 10,000 m. At that distance Fernando Mamede of Portugal ran 27 min 13.81 sec. The only other track mark was in the infrequently contested 20,000-m walk, in which Canto lowered the world standard to 1 hr 18 min 39.9 sec.

Three new world marks on the field and one in the decathlon, contested on both the track and the field, completed the year's record-breaking activity. Zhu Jianhua of China moved his own high jump record up to 2.39 m (7 ft 10 in), while Yury Syedikh of the Soviet Union regained the hammer throw record, which he last set in 1980, with a toss of 86.34 m (283 ft 3 in). Equally prodigious was the 104.80-m (343-ft 10-in) javelin throw of East Germany's Uwe Hohn. The decathlon record was the third world mark in three years for Jurgen Hingsen of West Germany, who racked up a tally of 8,798 points.

Women's International Competition. Twenty-two world records were established by 18 women and two relay teams during the year, but only half of them were set in the more frequently contested Olympic events. Only one of the records in Olympic events came from outside the Eastern European bloc of nations. Whereas the Olympic Games felt the absence of men primarily in the field events, especially in the throws, competitors from the boycotting nations almost certainly would have dominated the women's portion of the Games.

The only non-Eastern European woman to set a world record in an Olympic track and field event was Evelyn Ashford of the U.S. She earned a world mark, her second, with 10.76 sec in the 100 m, an especially noteworthy achievement because it was made at low altitude. Her 10.79 sec of 1983 had been accomplished at 1,831 m (6,007 ft), where less-dense air contributes to faster sprint times.

Only four records were set after the Olympics. The Friendship Games produced one when Irina Meszynski of East Germany threw the discus 73.36 m (240 ft 8 in). She lost her record nine days later when Zdenka Silhava of Czechoslovakia reached 74.56 m (244 ft 7 in).

Three women and one national team continued to set new records. East Germany's Marita Koch equaled her own mark of 21.71 sec at 200 m and anchored the national team in the 4 x 400-m relay with a world-record time of 3 min 15.92 sec. It was her 13th entry in the world record list. Tamara Bykova of the Soviet Union high jumped 2.05 m (6 ft 8¾ in), her third world mark in two years, but lost the record to Lyudmila Andonova of Bulgaria, who cleared 2.07 m (6 ft 9½ in). Tatyana Kazankina of the U.S.S.R. gained her fifth and sixth world records when she ran 2,000 m in 5 min 28.72 sec and 3,000 m in 8 min 22.62 sec.

The U.S.S.R. provided two more new record holders. Margarita Ponomaryeva took the 400-m hurdle mark under 54 sec when she clocked 53.58 sec, and Natalya Lisovskaya put the shot 22.53 m (73 ft 11 in).

East Germany continued to dominate the heptathlon, an event in which Ramona Neubert had set three world records. In 1984 a new champion was crowned, Sabine Paetz, with 6,867 points.

World records were set in seven events not contested in the Olympics. The one-mile record was lowered to 4 min

(LEFT) AP/WIDE WORLD; (RIGHT) PERRIN/TARDY—GAMMA/LIAISON

The 90th consecutive victory in the 400-metre hurdles for Edwin Moses (far left) of the U.S. team won him his second Olympic gold medal at the Summer Games in Los Angeles. (Left) Carl Lewis, here winning the 100-metre dash, won three other gold medals at the Summer Olympics, reinforcing his bid for the mantle of Jesse Owens.

The eagerly awaited 3,000-metre duel between top contenders Mary Decker and Zola Budd in the summer Olympic Games ended with Decker lying in pain on the infield after she and Budd bumped twice during the race. Budd regained her balance but, upset by the incident, finished a poor seventh.

AP/WIDE WORLD

15.8 sec by Natalya Artyemova of the U.S.S.R. At 2,000 m Zola Budd (*see* BIOGRAPHIES), who gained British citizenship by emigrating from South Africa, ran 5 min 33.15 sec, and Mary Decker of the U.S. was timed in 5 min 32.7 sec. Both records were surpassed by Kazankina's later mark.

In both the long distance events, the 5,000 and 10,000 m, there were new world records. Ingrid Kristiansen of Norway ran the 5,000 in 14 min 58.89 sec, while the Soviets' Olga Bondarenko covered the 10,000 in 31 min 13.78 sec.

The Soviet Union national team ran the 4 x 800-m relay in a world-record 7 min 50.1 sec, and four records were established in walking races that had recently been added to the list of officially recognized events. The 5,000-m walk mark was improved three times, twice by Sue Cook of Australia. Her times were 22 min 6.34 sec and 22 min 4.42 sec, but Yan Hong of China ended the year as record holder with a mark of 21 min 40.2 sec. Olga Krishtop of the Soviet Union walked 10,000 m in a record time of 44 min 56.10 sec.

With the Soviet bloc boycotting the Olympic Games, the United States had its best Olympics ever in women's track and field, winning 7 of 17 events. The U.S. produced the individual star of the Games in Valerie Brisco-Hooks, who won three gold medals. Brisco-Hooks had not been considered a top Olympic prospect at the beginning of the year, but she progressed strongly in the late spring. In the Olympics she won the 200 m in 21.81 sec and the 400 m in 48.83 sec and was on the victorious 4 x 400-m relay squad, which ran 3 min 18.29 sec. All three times were Olympic records. Rivaling Brisco-Hooks for attention was Joan Benoit of the U.S., who won the highly publicized first Olympic marathon ever held for women. (See *Marathon Running and Cross Country,* below.)

Bringing back memories to longtime Olympic fans was Ulrike Meyfarth of West Germany. When she was 16, she captured the 1972 Olympic high jump title in her home country of West Germany. At Los Angeles she regained the championship, leaping 2.02 m (6 ft 7½ in). Joining Meyfarth as an Olympic record breaker in a field event was Tessa Sanderson of the United Kingdom with a throw of 69.56 m (228 ft 2 in) in the javelin.

Ashford bettered the Olympic 100-m mark with a time of 10.97 sec and then won another gold as a member of the 4 x 100-m relay team. Two gold medals also went to Chandra Cheeseborough, who was on both winning relay teams. She also finished second in the 400 m.

U.S. Competition. While no U.S. male established a world record in 1984, the men did launch a steady attack on national records. Johnny Gray alone earned four U.S.

marks in the 800 m, running 1 min 43.74 sec before placing third in the Olympics and 1 min 43.28 sec twice and 1 min 42.96 once after the Games.

Mike Tully was equally busy, raising the U.S. pole vault mark three times to a best of 5.82 m (19 ft 1 in). Earl Bell interrupted that stream of records when he cleared 5.80 m (19 ft ¼ in) to become the first U.S. athlete to vault over 19 ft. Other national bests were achieved by shot putter Brian Oldfield, 22.19 m (72 ft 9¾ in), high jumper Dwight Stones, 2.34 m (7 ft 8 in), and hammer thrower Bill Green, 76.52 m (251 ft).

In addition to the 200-m and 400-m records by Brisco-Hooks, new women's marks were set in three events. Judi Brown ran the 400-m hurdles in 54.99 and then 54.93 sec; the discus was thrown 65.20 m (213 ft 11 in) by Leslie Deniz; and the heptathlon record was raised to 6,611 and then 6,714 points by Jane Frederick.

In indoor team competition Arkansas won the men's National Collegiate Athletic Association (NCAA) tournament, and Nebraska took the women's. The Athletic Congress (TAC) champions were Bud Light (men) and Atoms (women). No team score was kept in the European championships, where Vigneron set an indoor vault mark of 5.85 m (19 ft 2¼ in). Outdoors the NCAA was won by Oregon (men) and Florida State (women). Bud Light won the TAC title for men, while Puma and Energizer took the women's meet.

Marathon Running and Cross Country. As with other track and field competition, the high point of the 1984 marathon season was reached during the Olympic Games. In the first women's Olympic marathon, Benoit, holder of the best time in the marathon for a woman, won in 2 hr 24 min 52 sec, the third fastest time ever and the fastest in a race for women only. Well after Benoit had completed her run, the race provided one of the Games' moments of high drama when Gabriela Andersen-Schiess of Switzerland staggered toward the finish line, obviously in agony. Carlos Lopes of Portugal, one of the prerace favourites, won the men's race in 2 hr 9 min 21 sec.

The fastest and most significant non-Olympic race was the Chicago marathon. The surprise winner was Steve Jones of the United Kingdom with a world's best time of 2 hr 8 min 5 sec. Lopes finished second, and Rob de Castella of Australia, who had been favoured to win the Olympics, was third.

The international cross-country championships were held in the U.S. for the first time, at East Rutherford, N.J., on March 25. The winner was the 37-year-old Lopes, who had also won in 1976. Maricica Puica of Romania, Olympic

(continued on page 425)

The 1984 Summer Olympic Games

BY DON PIERSON

Overcoming skepticism and fear, the 1984 Olympic Games reminded the world of the optimism and cheer inherent in them. They reminded us of exactly why we put up with them. As usual, the athletes did the reminding, tapping the politicians and organizers and cynics on the shoulder to make way for the real Games.

When the events of the XXIII Olympiad began, paranoia was replaced by people. Instead of worrying about runaway capitalism, smog, crowds, ticket prices, traffic, heat, security, and faraway venues, the people traded Olympic pins. They did it with such passion that pin trading became one of the most notable features of the Los Angeles Games.

More people (nearly six million) bought more tickets for more money ($151 million) to see more athletes (7,800) from more countries (140) than in any other Olympic Games. This despite the boycott by the Soviet Union, joined by 14 other countries allied with it (Afghanistan, Angola, Bulgaria, Cuba, Czechoslovakia, East Germany, Ethiopia, Hungary, Laos, Mongolia, North Korea, Poland, South Yemen, and Vietnam). The Soviets, however, might have known better than anyone else that the Olympics are not a party easily spoiled. They threw one in Moscow in 1980, and U.S. politicians kept U.S. athletes away. That boycott included 62 nations, but 81 others took part. World records were set, gold medals were won, and the Games went on.

The 1984 Games were incomplete but not hollow. No Olympic Games have included every country. The people who come rarely pity themselves; they pity only the people who do not. The Soviet presence would have added drama, excitement, and competition, but the U.S. was unable to allay Soviet fears of conspiracies to subvert their athletes and of possible violence. Uncertainty was a price they would not pay. The question is whether the Soviet absence subtracted from those intangibles that never fail to elevate the Olympics.

These Games exceeded expectations. Although they could have accomplished that simply by avoiding catastrophe, they provided much more.

Controversy and Achievement. It was not an Olympics without controversy. Reality could never measure up to the euphoria of a stunning opening ceremony produced by Hollywood. Silver medalists in Greco-Roman wrestling from Sweden and in the men's 10,000-m run from Finland were disqualified for drug abuse. Egypt and Italy fought on the soccer field. Boxing officials turned their sport into a farce. It was too hot for ideal marathons.

The memories that linger, however, are of the speed of Carl Lewis and Valerie Brisco-Hooks, not those of doping and traffic control. The anxiety over auto congestion was overwhelmed by the tiny figure of Joan Benoit alone

---

Donald C. Pierson, a sportswriter at the Chicago Tribune, is the author of several sports books including Renaldo Nehemiah: The Bionic Hurdler and The Trojans: Southern California Football.

on the freeway, running away with the first women's marathon. The shining smile of gymnast Mary Lou Retton (see BIOGRAPHIES) cut through every layer of smog.

The inconvenience of security precautions paled before the drama of Mary Decker's fall after she and Zola Budd (see BIOGRAPHIES) bumped in the 3,000 m, the heartbreak of Budd as she ran on gamely but no longer with the will to win, the agony of Swiss marathoner Gabriela Andersen-Schiess as she staggered into the stadium, unconscious of everything but the need to reach the finish line. We remember the grace of hurdler Edwin Moses, not the greed of commercialism; the thrill of the torch relay, not the bill. We were moved by the sportsmanship of boxer Evander Holyfield, disqualified on a technicality after a fight he had clearly won, and by his embarrassed opponent, Yugoslavia's Anton Josipovic, inviting him onto the victory stand, transcending the incompetence of officials.

It is the majesty of diver Greg Louganis, the dominance of British athletes Sebastian Coe and Daley Thompson (see BIOGRAPHIES), the skill of the Chinese women's volleyball team, the miracle of the U.S. men gymnasts, the determination of U.S. cyclists, the surprise of two Moroccan track gold medalists, the power of the U.S. basketball teams, the perfection of synchronized swimmers that stick in the mind.

The spirit of participation was captured by New Zealand archer Neroli Fairhall, believed to be the first paraplegic to take part in an Olympics. She competed from a wheelchair, pointing out, "There's nothing in the rules that says you can't sit down." And does anyone remember how much it cost for a ticket to see Greco-Roman heavyweight wrestler Jeff Blatnick, who had overcome cancer, fall to his knees and weep after winning a gold medal?

Organization and Finance. For Peter Ueberroth (see BIOGRAPHIES), president of the Los Angeles Olympic Organizing Committee (LAOOC), the memories start with the thousands of volunteers in southern California who worked for nothing and saw nothing, yet wanted to be a part of it because it was something. The efficiency and geniality of most of the volunteers contrasted with the mood of Los Angeles in 1978, when 73% of the electorate voted against paying for the Games. The result was an Olympics that for once provided hope instead of despair for future competitions.

Money was the root of the hope. Montreal citizens are still paying $559.6 million of the $1 billion debt left by that city's 1976 Games. Moscow spent an estimated $9 billion for the 1980 Olympics. But in 1984 Los Angeles operated on a no-frills budget of $525 million and turned a profit of $150 million. Los Angeles Mayor Tom Bradley and a group of businessmen had persuaded a reluctant International Olympic Committee (IOC) to absolve government from financial responsibility for the Games. It was an unprecedented idea accepted mainly because the IOC had few alternatives. Although the LAOOC insisted that no public funds were spent on the Games, city officials later estimated that federal, state, and local governments spent approximately $100 million for security.

The profit was so staggering that it left sponsors, spectators, and the media wondering why prices were set so high. The LAOOC announced that $50 million of the profit would go to the U.S. Olympic Committee, $50 million would fund a youth sports program in southern California, $25 million would go to 38 amateur sports federations, and $25 million would be held in reserve to cover the closing costs for the committee.

ABC Television paid $225 million for exclusive TV rights to the Games. When the Soviets announced their

Mary Lou Retton (left photo), U.S. gymnast from West Virginia, won the gold medal in the women's all-around in the Summer Olympics over the pre-Games favourite, Ecaterina Szabo of Romania. Retton had undergone knee surgery only six weeks earlier. At right, Daley Thompson of the United Kingdom takes the high jump in Summer Olympic decathlon competition at Los Angeles. He scored a total of 8,797 points and became the second man to win the demanding event twice.

(LEFT) DAVID KENNERLY—GAMMA/LIAISON; (RIGHT) AP/WIDE WORLD

boycott, ABC reserved the right to renegotiate the price downward. But when subsequent ratings showed that more than 2,000,000,000 people had watched worldwide, ABC paid in full. The large audience was attributed partly to the success of U.S. athletes.

Greece protested the selling of the Olympic torch for $3,000 a kilometre to whoever wanted to run with it. The response in the U.S. was to stand in line to pay or just to watch as the torch crisscrossed the country.

Organizers were able to use existing facilities in southern California, including the Coliseum that had served the 1932 Olympic Games. For the traditional Olympic village, they used the campuses of local universities. Where new facilities were required, organizers convinced sponsors to build them. McDonald's Corp. built a swimming and diving stadium. The Southland Corp. constructed a cycling velodrome, and Atlantic Richfield Co. built the Coliseum track and seven other tracks for training.

The organizing committee limited the number of sponsors to 30, plus another 50 official licensees or suppliers. This was far more exclusive than the 381 official products of the 1980 Winter Games in Lake Placid, N.Y., and the price reflected the exclusivity. However, corporate ingenuity was not restricted. Fuji Photo Film of Japan paid $9 million to be a sponsor, leaving Kodak in the dark. Kodak quickly saw the light, became the official film of the U.S. track and field team, set up an unofficial headquarters across the street from Fuji, and gave away free film to official photographers.

With venues scattered 240 km (150 mi) apart, there were visions of logistical nightmares. Instead, businesses were encouraged to stagger working hours and motorists to carpool. The system worked well enough to move other cities to study it.

Effects of the Boycott. The Soviet-led boycott affected competition in most sports but not in every event. Track and field, for instance, suffered in women's events more than in men's and in throwing events more than in jumping and running.

Coe and Thompson were two winners who could truly argue that their medals were not tainted. They were the only two track and field champions who repeated their triumphs of 1980. Thus, Coe beat half the world in the 1,500-m run in 1980 and the other half in 1984. Thompson did the same in the decathlon. Evelyn Ashford of the U.S. won the gold medal in the women's 100-m dash, then settled the rivalry with her East German nemesis, Marlies Gohr, by traveling to Europe to beat her in world record time.

The nine U.S. boxing gold medals were won in the absence of five world champions from Cuba. Women's gymnastics was buoyed by the presence of Romania, the only Eastern-bloc country to attend. Women's swimming is dominated by the absent East Germany. Women's basketball missed the Soviets more than did men's basketball. Weight lifting, wrestling, cycling, canoeing, rowing, modern pentathlon, soccer, fencing, and team handball were affected more than were archery, equestrianism, field hockey, yachting, shooting, and judo.

U.S. athletes were so dominant that IOC president Juan Antonio Samaranch of Spain complained to ABC about biased television coverage. But other countries were able to pick up a raw feed of video coverage from ABC and attach their own commentary. Concern about growing professionalism among competitors did not keep crowds from greeting an athlete such as the highly paid Moses with genuine affection. The usual outcry for amateurism seemed to be quietly dying along with the concept.

Hope for the Games in Seoul, South Korea, in 1988 was bolstered by bids for 1992 from Barcelona, Spain; Amsterdam; Paris; and Brisbane, Australia. There was interest from Athens for 1996 and from China for 2000. The Olympics seemed alive again.

This article updates the *Macropædia* article OLYMPIC GAMES.

Olympic Champions, 1984 Summer Games, Los Angeles

Team Sports

	Men	Women
Basketball	United States	United States
Football	France	—
Handball	Yugoslavia	Yugoslavia
Hockey, Field	Pakistan	Netherlands
Volleyball	United States	China
Water Polo	Yugoslavia	—

Archery

Men's round	D. Pace (U.S.)	2,616 pt
Women's round	Seo Hyang Soon (S.Kor.)	2,568 pt

Boxing

Lt. flyweight	P. Gonzales (U.S.)	Welterweight	M. Breland (U.S.)
Flyweight	S. McCrory (U.S.)	Lt. middleweight	F. Tate (U.S.)
Bantamweight	M. Stecca (Italy)	Middleweight	Shin Joon Sup (S.Kor.)
Featherweight	M. Taylor (U.S.)	Lt. Heavyweight	A. Josipovic (Yugos.)
Lightweight	P. Whitaker (U.S.)	Heavyweight	H. Tillman (U.S.)
Lt. welterweight	J. Page (U.S.)	Superheavyweight	T. Biggs (U.S.)

Canoeing

500-m Canadian singles	L. Cain (Canada)	1 min 57.01 sec
500-m Canadian pairs	Yugoslavia	1 min 43.67 sec
1,000-m Canadian singles	U. Eicke (W.Ger.)	4 min 06.32 sec
1,000-m Canadian pairs	Romania	3 min 40.60 sec
500-m kayak singles (men)	I. Ferguson (N.Z.)	1 min 47.84 sec
500-m kayak singles (women)	A. Andersson (Sweden)	1 min 58.72 sec
500-m kayak pairs (men)	New Zealand	1 min 34.21 sec
500-m kayak pairs (women)	Sweden	1 min 45.25 sec
1,000-m kayak singles	A. Thompson (N.Z.)	3 min 45.73 sec
1,000-m kayak pairs	Canada	3 min 24.22 sec
500-m kayak fours (women)	Romania	1 min 38.34 sec
1,000-m kayak fours	New Zealand	3 min 02.28 sec

Cycling

Points race	R. Ilegems (Belgium)	37 pt
Match sprint	M. Gorski (U.S.)	10.49 sec (best 200 m)
1,000-m time trial	F. Schmidtke (W.Ger.)	1 min 06.10 sec
4,000-m indiv. pursuit	S. Hegg (U.S.)	4 min 39.35 sec
4,000-m team pursuit	Australia	4 min 25.99 sec
100-km team time trial	Italy	1 hr 58 min 28 sec
Indiv. road race (men)	A. Grewal (U.S.)	4 hr 59 min 57 sec
Indiv. road race (women)	C. Carpenter-Phinney (U.S.)	2 hr 11 min 14 sec

Equestrian Sports

	Individual	Team
Dressage	R. Klimke (W.Ger.) on Ahlerich	West Germany
3-day event	M. Todd (N.Z.) on Charisma	United States
Jumping	J. Fargis (U.S.) on Touch of Class	United States

Fencing

	Individual	Team
Foil	M. Numa (Italy)	Italy
Epee	P. Boisse (France)	West Germany
Sabre	J.-F. Lamour (France)	Italy
Women's foil	L. Jujie (China)	West Germany

Gymnastics

	Men	Women
Team championship	United States	Romania
Individual all-around	Koji Gushiken (Japan)	M. L. Retton (U.S.)
Parallel bars	B. Conner (U.S.)	
Uneven parallel bars	—	J. McNamara (U.S.) and Ma Yanhong (China) (tie)
Horizontal bar	Shinji Morisue (Japan)	
Horse vault	Lou Yun (China)	E. Szabo (Rom.)
Side horse	Li Ning (China) and P. Vidmar (U.S.) (tie)	—
Balance beam		E. Szabo (Rom.) and S. Pauca (Rom.) (tie)
Rings	Li Ning (China) and Koji Gushiken (Japan) (tie)	—
Floor exercise	Li Ning (China)	E. Szabo (Rom.)
Rhythmic competition	—	L. Fung (Canada)

Judo

60-kg class	Shinji Hosokawa (Japan)	86-kg class	P. Seisenbacher (Austria)
65-kg class	Yoshiyuki Matsuoka (Japan)	95-kg class	Ha Hyoung Zoo (S.Kor.)
71-kg class	Ahn Byeong Keun (S.Kor.)	95-kg+ class	Hitoshi Saito (Japan)
78-kg class	F. Wieneke (W.Ger.)	Open class	Yasuhiro Yamashita (Japan)

Modern Pentathlon

Individual—D. Masala (Italy) 5,469 pt   Team—Italy 16,060 pt

Rowing

Men (2,000-m course)

Single sculls	P. Karppinen (Finland)	7 min 00.24 sec
Double sculls	United States	6 min 36.87 sec
Quadruple sculls	West Germany	5 min 57.55 sec
Pairs without coxswain	Romania	6 min 45.39 sec
Pairs with coxswain	Italy	7 min 05.99 sec
Fours without coxswain	New Zealand	6 min 03.48 sec
Fours with coxswain	Great Britain	6 min 18.64 sec
Eights with coxswain	Canada	5 min 41.32 sec

Women (1,000-m course)

Single sculls	V. Racila (Rom.)	3 min 40.68 sec
Double sculls	Romania	3 min 26.75 sec
Quadruple sculls with coxswain	Romania	3 min 14.11 sec
Pairs without coxswain	Romania	3 min 32.60 sec
Fours with coxswain	Romania	3 min 19.30 sec
Eights with coxswain	United States	2 min 59.80 sec

Shooting

Free pistol	Xu Haifeng (China)	566 pt
Rapid-fire pistol	Takeo Kamachi (Japan)	595 pt
Sport pistol (women)	L. Thom (Canada)	585 pt††
Running game target	Li Yuwei (China)	587 pt
Small-bore rifle, 3-position (men)	M. Cooper (Gt.Brit.)	1,173 pt‡
Small-bore rifle, 3-position (women)	Wu Xiaoxuan (China)	581 pt†
Small-bore rifle, prone	E. Etzel (U.S.)	599 pt§
Air rifle (men)	P. Heberle (France)	589 pt†
Air rifle (women)	P. Spurgin (U.S.)	393 pt††
Skeet shooting (open)	M. Dryke (U.S.)	198 pt§
Trapshooting (open)	L. Giovannetti (Italy)	192 pt

*World record. †Olympic record. ‡Equals world record. §Equals Olympic record.

Swimming and Diving

Men

100-m freestyle	R. Gaines (U.S.)	49.80 sec†
200-m freestyle	M. Gross (W.Ger.)	1 min 47.44 sec*
400-m freestyle	G. DiCarlo (U.S.)	3 min 51.23 sec†
1,500-m freestyle	M. O'Brien (U.S.)	15 min 05.20 sec
100-m backstroke	R. Carey (U.S.)	55.79 sec
200-m backstroke	R. Carey (U.S.)	2 min 00.23 sec
100-m breaststroke	S. Lundquist (U.S.)	1 min 01.65 sec*
200-m breaststroke	V. Davis (Canada)	2 min 13.34 sec*
100-m butterfly	M. Gross (W.Ger.)	53.08 sec*
200-m butterfly	J. Sieben (Australia)	1 min 57.04 sec*
200-m individual medley	A. Baumann (Canada)	2 min 01.42 sec*
400-m individual medley	A. Baumann (Canada)	4 min 17.41 sec*
4 × 100-m medley relay	United States	3 min 39.30 sec*
4 × 100-m freestyle relay	United States	3 min 19.03 sec*
4 × 200-m freestyle relay	United States	7 min 15.69 sec*
Springboard diving	G. Louganis (U.S.)	754.41 pt
Platform diving	G. Louganis (U.S.)	710.91 pt

Women

100-m freestyle	C. Steinseifer (U.S.) and N. Hogshead (U.S.) (tie)	55.92 sec
200-m freestyle	M. Wayte (U.S.)	1 min 59.23 sec
400-m freestyle	T. Cohen (U.S.)	4 min 07.10 sec†
800-m freestyle	T. Cohen (U.S.)	8 min 24.95 sec†
100-m backstroke	T. Andrews (U.S.)	1 min 02.55 sec
200-m backstroke	J. DeRover (Neth.)	2 min 12.38 sec
100-m breaststroke	P. Van Staveren (Neth.)	1 min 09.88 sec†
200-m breaststroke	A. Ottenbrite (Canada)	2 min 30.38 sec
100-m butterfly	M. T. Meagher (U.S.)	59.26 sec
200-m butterfly	M. T. Meagher (U.S.)	2 min 06.90 sec†
200-m individual medley	T. Caulkins (U.S.)	2 min 12.64 sec
400-m individual medley	T. Caulkins (U.S.)	4 min 39.24 sec
4 × 100-m medley relay	United States	4 min 08.34 sec
4 × 100-m freestyle relay	United States	3 min 43.43 sec
Synchronized swimming (solo)	T. Ruiz (U.S.)	198.467 pt
Synchronized swimming (duet)	T. Ruiz and C. Costie (U.S.)	195.584 pt
Springboard diving	S. Bernier (Canada)	530.70 pt
Platform diving	Zhou Jihong (China)	435.51 pt

Track and Field

Men

100-m dash	C. Lewis (U.S.)	9.99 sec
200-m dash	C. Lewis (U.S.)	19.80 sec†
400-m dash	A. Babers (U.S.)	44.27 sec
800-m run	J. Cruz (Brazil)	1 min 43.00 sec†
1,500-m run	S. Coe (Gt.Brit.)	3 min 32.53 sec†
5,000-m run	S. Aouita (Morocco)	13 min 05.59 sec†
10,000-m run	A. Cova (Italy)	27 min 47.54 sec
Marathon	C. Lopes (Portugal)	2 hr 09 min 21 sec
110-m hurdles	R. Kingdom (U.S.)	13.20 sec†
400-m hurdles	E. Moses (U.S.)	47.75 sec
3,000-m steeplechase	J. Korir (Kenya)	8 min 11.80 sec
4 × 100-m relay	United States	37.83 sec*
4 × 400-m relay	United States	2 min 57.91 sec
20-km walk	E. Canto (Mexico)	1 hr 23 min 13 sec
50-km walk	R. Gonzales (Mexico)	3 hr 47 min 26 sec
High jump	D. Moegenburg (W.Ger.)	2.35 m
Long jump	C. Lewis (U.S.)	8.54 m
Pole vault	P. Quinon (France)	5.75 m
Triple jump	A. Joyner (U.S.)	17.26 m
Shot put	A. Andrei (Italy)	21.26 m
Discus	R. Danneberg (W.Ger.)	66.60 m
Hammer throw	J. Tiainen (Finland)	78.08 m
Javelin	A. Haerkoenen (Finland)	86.76 m
Decathlon	D. Thompson (Gt.Brit.)	8,797 pt††

Women

100-m dash	E. Ashford (U.S.)	10.97 sec†
200-m dash	V. Brisco-Hooks (U.S.)	21.81 sec†
400-m dash	V. Brisco-Hooks (U.S.)	48.83 sec†
800-m run	D. Melinte (Rom.)	1 min 57.60 sec
1,500-m run	G. Dorio (Italy)	4 min 03.25 sec
3,000-m run	M. Puica (Rom.)	8 min 35.96 sec†
Marathon	J. Benoit (U.S.)	2 hr 24 min 52 sec
100-m hurdles	B. Fitzgerald-Brown (U.S.)	12.84 sec
400-m hurdles	Nawal El Moutawakel (Morocco)	54.61 sec†
4 × 100-m relay	United States	41.65 sec
4 × 400-m relay	United States	3 min 18.29 sec†
High jump	U. Meyfarth (W.Ger.)	2.02 m†
Long jump	A. Stanciu (Rom.)	6.96 m
Shot put	C. Losch (W.Ger.)	20.48 m
Discus	R. Stalman (Neth.)	65.36 m
Javelin	T. Sanderson (Gt.Brit.)	69.56 m†
Heptathlon	G. Nunn (Australia)	6,390 pt

Weight Lifting

Flyweight	Zeng Guoqiang (China)	235.0 kg
Bantamweight	Wu Shude (China)	267.5 kg
Featherweight	Chen Weiqiang (China)	282.5 kg
Lightweight	Yao Jingyuan (China)	320.0 kg
Middleweight	K.-H. Radschinsky (W.Ger.)	340.0 kg
Light heavyweight	P. Becheru (Rom.)	355.0 kg
Middle heavyweight	N. Vlad (Rom.)	392.5 kg†
(First) Heavyweight	R. Milser (W.Ger.)	385.0 kg
(Second) Heavyweight	N. Oberburger (Italy)	390.0 kg
Superheavyweight	D. Lukim (Australia)	412.5 kg

Wrestling

	Freestyle	Greco-Roman
Light flyweight	R. Weaver (U.S.)	V. Maenza (Italy)
Flyweight	S. Trstena (Yugos.)	Atsuji Miyahara (Japan)
Bantamweight	Hideaki Tomiyama (Japan)	P. Passarelli (W.Ger.)
Featherweight	R. Lewis (U.S.)	Kim Weon Kee (S.Kor.)
Lightweight	You In Tak (S.Kor.)	V. Lisjak (Yugos.)
Welterweight	D. Schultz (U.S.)	J. Salomaki (Finland)
Middleweight	M. Schultz (U.S.)	I. Draica (Rom.)
Light heavyweight	E. Banach (U.S.)	S. Fraser (U.S.)
Heavyweight	L. Banach (U.S.)	V. Andrei (Rom.)
Superheavyweight	B. Baumgartner (U.S.)	J. Blatnick (U.S.)

Yachting

Windglider	S. Van Den Berg (Neth.)	Tornado class	New Zealand
Finn class	R. Coutts (N.Z.)	Star class	United States
470 class	Spain	Soling class	United States
	Flying Dutchman class	United States	

*World record. †Olympic record. ‡Equals world record. §Equals Olympic record.

(continued from page 421)

3,000-m champion, won the women's race. Ethiopia won its fourth consecutive men's team title, while the United States won the team competition and finished second in the men's.

The Athletic Congress championship runs were won by Pat Porter, taking the men's title for the third straight time, and Cathy Branta, who five days earlier had earned the NCAA gold medal. Ed Eyestone won the NCAA men's race, and the team championships went to Arkansas for the men and Wisconsin for the women. (For table of world track and field records set during the year, see *Sporting Record,* below. For table of results of the summer Olympic Games, *see* Special Report.)   (BERT NELSON)

VOLLEYBALL

The highlight of 1984 in volleyball was the competition at the Olympic Games in Los Angeles. The United States captured the men's gold medal, with Brazil finishing second and Italy third. For women China was first, followed in order by the U.S. and Japan. The gold and silver medals for the U.S. were the first ever won by that nation in Olympic or world competition. The previous best for a U.S. team was a third place by the women at the 1982 world championships.

The ten nations originally scheduled to compete in the Olympics for the men included Argentina, Brazil, Bulgaria, Canada, Cuba, Egypt, Japan, Poland, the U.S., and the Soviet Union, the 1980 Olympic champions. For the women's competition the originally qualified teams were the 1980 Olympic champion Soviet Union, China, Japan, East Germany, Brazil, Cuba, Peru, and the U.S. In late May when the Soviet Union and its allies withdrew from the Olympics, substitute teams were selected from the order of

AP/WIDE WORLD

The U.S. men's volleyball team won the gold medal at the Olympic Games in Los Angeles. In the gold medal match the U.S. defeated Brazil in three quick games. Italy took the bronze medal.

finish at the final qualification played in Barcelona, Spain. For the men they were South Korea for the Soviet Union, Italy for Poland, China for Cuba, and Tunisia for Bulgaria. For the women the substitute teams were South Korea for the Soviet Union, West Germany for East Germany, and Canada for Cuba.

The women's competition at the Olympics probably was not greatly affected by the boycott. China, Japan, and the U.S., the eventual winners, were the pretournament favourites for medals. Although the Soviets and Cubans would have provided interesting competition and might have upset a favoured team, the top medals certainly would have been distributed among the pretournament favourites. In the finals China took the first game against the U.S. 16–14 after watching its 14–9 lead evaporate. China then exploited the psychological advantage resulting from its first win to capture the second game by a convincing 15–3 margin and followed with a routine victory of 15–9 in the third game. For the bronze medal Japan dispatched Peru 3–1. South Korea, West Germany, Brazil, and Canada finished fifth through eighth, in that order.

On the men's side the boycott definitely affected the final Olympic standings. Since 1977 the Soviet Union had won every major international title of significance, and it certainly would have won a medal in the 1984 Games. However, it might not have been a gold. Both Brazil and the U.S. had defeated the Soviets in recent encounters, and the U.S. just prior to the boycott had defeated the Soviets four straight times in the U.S.S.R. The Cubans also might have earned a medal at the Games.

In the men's gold medal match the U.S. crushed Brazil in three quick games, 15–6, 15–6, and 15–7. It was a remarkable triumph for the U.S., which had placed 13th at the 1982 world championships. Italy defeated Canada 3–1 for the bronze medal. Finishing in fifth through tenth places were South Korea, Argentina, Japan, China, Tunisia, and Egypt.   (ALBERT M. MONACO, JR.)

WATER POLO

Although the United States did not participate in the water polo competition in the 1976 and 1980 Olympic Games, it was co-favoured, along with the Soviet Union, to win the gold medal in the 1984 Olympics. The U.S.S.R. had won in 1980 and was the defending world champion, but the U.S. team had almost beaten the Soviets in the Tungsram Cup, the most important tournament prior to the Olympics.

However, owing to the boycott of the Olympics by the U.S.S.R. and many of its allies, the Soviet Union and two other top finishers from the 1982 world championships (second-place Hungary and fifth-place Cuba) did not participate in the 1984 Games. The U.S. thus became the favourite, with the major challenge expected to come from West Germany. The game between the two countries proved to be exciting. The West Germans missed an easy opportunity to score in the last seconds, allowing the U.S. to win 8–7.

Only the Yugoslavians then stood between the U.S. squad and the gold medal. When the two teams met, both were undefeated and untied. The U.S. jumped out to a 5–2 advantage midway through the third quarter. However, the Yugoslavians scored three unanswered goals to tie the game at 5–5 with three minutes remaining. Neither team was able to score again, and the tie gave the Yugoslavians the gold medal because they had a better goal difference in the previous games. The U.S. finished second, followed by West Germany, Spain, Australia, and The Netherlands.

(WILLIAM ENSIGN FRADY)

WATER SKIING

Sammy Duvall of Orlando, Fla., continued his string of overall victories against the world's best water skiers by adding championships in the U.S. National Open, the Masters, and the Pan American to the overall triumph he scored in the 1983 world tournament in Sweden. Individual honours in the U.S. National Open went to Bob LaPoint of Lake Tahoe, Calif., in slalom with 58 buoys; Cory Pickos of Eagle Lake, Fla., in tricks with 9,840 points; and Mike Morgan of Lake Wales, Fla., in jumping with a top leap of 55.7 m (184 ft).

Andy Mapple of Great Britain won the Masters slalom title with 62 buoys. Pickos again dominated tricks with 9,940 points, 60 points off the world record he had set earlier in the year. Mike Hazelwood of Great Britain was best of the Masters jumpers with a leap of 56.6 m (187 ft).

Duvall scored the best jump of the Pan American meet, 57.3 m (189 ft), in taking overall honours. The slalom title went to Lucky Lowe of Winter Haven, Fla., with a top run of 62 buoys, while Pickos again trounced the trickers with a record-tying 10,000 points.

In women's competition international overall honours were split between Ana María Carrasco of Venezuela and Deena Brush of West Sacramento, Calif. Carrasco took the 1984 Masters overall crown for the first time, and then Brush turned the tables on the Venezuelan in the Pan American. Brush also won the U.S. national overall title, with victories in slalom (61¼ buoys) and jumping (39.9 m [131 ft]). Fourteen-year-old twins, Tawn and Britt Larsen of Madison, Wis., tied for first in open women's tricks with identical runs of 7,740 points. Britt gained the gold medal when her sister elected not to enter the runoff.

Camille Duvall, Sammy's sister, won the Masters slalom with a run of 57½ buoys. Karin Roberge of Orlando upset Carrasco in tricks with 5,990 points, while Sue Lipplegoes of Australia beat the women jumpers with a top leap of 42.1 m (139 ft). Brush won the slalom (58 buoys) and jumping (40 m [135 ft]) in the Pan American. Carrasco took the gold in tricks with a new world record run of 8,350 points, but she was 41 points behind Brush in the overall scoring.   (THOMAS C. HARDMAN)

WEIGHT LIFTING

China, competing in its first Olympic Games, won gold medals in four of the ten weight classes. West Germany and Romania each won golds in two classes, while Italy and Australia won the remaining two. The six top countries

(the U.S.S.R., Bulgaria, Czechoslovakia, East Germany, Hungary, and Poland) from the 1983 world championships did not participate. The only medalist taking part in the Games out of 30 from the 1983 world championships, Gelu Radu (Rom.), won the silver medal in the 60-kg (132-lb) class. Eight of the lifters who had ranked immediately below the 1983 world champions won Olympic medals. They included gold medalists Wu Shude of China in the 56-kg (123.2-lb) class and Yao Jingyuan of China in the 67.5-kg (148.5-lb) class. Three others won silver medals, and three won bronze.

The outstanding lifter at the Olympics was Nicu Vlad of Romania in the 90-kg (198-lb) class. He set Olympic records in both individual lifts (the snatch and the clean and jerk) as well as in his total lift of 392.5 kg (863.5 lb). His total lift exceeded the winning total lifts in the next two higher weight classes. Other gold medalists included Noberto Oberburger of Italy in the 110-kg (242-lb) class; Dinko Lukim of Australia, whose total lift of 412.5 kg (907.5 lb) in the super heavyweight (over 242-lb) class set an Olympic record; Zeng Guoqiang of China in the 52-kg (114.4-lb) class; Chen Weiqiang of China in the 60-kg (132-lb) class; Karl-Heinz Radschinsky of West Germany in the 75-kg (165-lb) class; Petre Becheru of Romania in the 82.5-kg (181.5-lb) class; and Rolf Misler of West Germany in the 100-kg (220-lb) class.   (CHARLES ROBERT PAUL, JR.)

WINTER SPORTS

The continuing expansion of interest in sports on snow and ice was enhanced in 1984 by the extensive worldwide television coverage of the winter Olympic Games (*see* Special Report). World Cup skiing and international figure skating attracted considerably increased numbers of spectators, and the star appeal of such events was perhaps largely responsible for the greater participation in them at the recreational level on every continent.

Skiing. Rapidly expanding facilities for skiing on plastic slopes and with roller skis on grass enabled more people to practice technique between snow seasons and in areas with little or no snow at all. This was notably effective in Spain, the U.K., and South Africa. Meanwhile, extra snow was made more readily accessible above ski resorts through the addition of various means of mechanical ascent to higher altitudes, thereby widening the choice of terrain and lengthening the season for many skiers. Equipment became more sophisticated, with fierce rivalry among manufacturers.

ALPINE RACING. The 18th annual Alpine World Cup

West Germany's Karl-Heinz Radschinsky won the summer Olympic Games gold medal in weight lifting in the middleweight division at Los Angeles with a weight of 150 kilograms (330 pounds) in the snatch and 190 kilograms (418 pounds) in the jerk.

series covered 37 men's and 34 women's events spanning four months at 33 sites in 12 countries in Europe and North America. It proved a triumph for Switzerland, Pirmin Zurbriggen capturing the men's cup, Erika Hess regaining the women's, and the national team outpointing second-place Austria to retain the concurrently decided Nations Alpine Cup. It was the first time that the Swiss had gained all three prizes in the same season.

Zurbriggen achieved his title without topping the standings in any single event, although he finished a close second in the giant slalom. Once more, Ingemar Stenmark, the veteran Swedish slalom specialist, had to be content with second overall place for men after declining to compete in the downhill. He won the giant slalom for a seventh time and placed second in the slalom. Overall third was Marc Girardelli of Luxembourg, and the top downhill racer was yet another Swiss, Urs Räber.

Hess, the 1982 women's winner, finished narrowly ahead of her long-standing rival, Hanni Wenzel of Liechtenstein, who had won in 1978 and 1980. Tamara McKinney, the U.S. title defender, finished third. Hess was leading scorer in the giant slalom, McKinney in the slalom, and Maria Walliser of Switzerland in the downhill.

The presence of Stenmark and Wenzel, who were each barred from the Olympics as "extreme professionals," along with a great number of performers from the major nations, emphasized the high general competitive standard of the World Cup races. The Cup competition was widely regarded as the sport's main test of consistent ability.

Georg Ager of Austria retained the men's international professional tour title, followed by Jarle Halsnes of Norway and Hans Hinterseer of Austria. Norway's Toril Forlund won the women's professional title for a fifth time, the last four in succession. Jocelyne Perrilat of France was runner-up, with Christina Grassl from Sweden third.

NORDIC EVENTS. The fifth Nordic World Cup series, for cross-country racing, spanned four months with eight men's and eight women's meetings in ten countries. The men's title was won by Gunde Svan of Sweden. His compatriot Thomas Wassberg finished second, ahead of Harri Kirvesniemi from Finland. The women's crown was retained by Marja-Liisa Hämäläinen (see BIOGRAPHIES) of Finland, with Raisa Smetanina of the Soviet Union second and Inger-Helen Nybratten third for Norway.

The first World Cup in Nordic combination, combining cross-country and jumping and contested at eight events in as many countries, was gained by Tom Sandberg of Norway. Uwe Dotzauer from East Germany placed second, and Geir Andersen of Norway was third.

The Nordic World Cup jump title, decided at 17 hills in 11 countries, went to an East German, Jens Weissflog. He deposed the defending champion, Matti Nykänen of Finland, who was runner-up; Pavel Ploc of Czechoslovakia was third. The jumping team world championship, on the rebuilt Titlis jumping hill at Engleberg, Switz., on February 26, was a victory for the Finns, with a foursome comprising Nykänen, Jari Puikkonen, Pentti Kokkonen, and Markku Pusenius. The East Germans placed second, and the Czechoslovaks were an unexpected third. The world ski-jump distance record was beaten twice in 24 hours by Nykänen, whose best leap covered 185 m at Oberstdorf, West Germany, on March 17.

In the world biathlon championships, combining cross-country skiing with rifle shooting, at Ruhpolding, West Germany, on January 15–22, Peter Angerer of the host country won both individual events. In the 10 km he defeated Terje Krokstad of Norway by 2.1 sec, with Frank-Peter Rötsch third for East Germany. In the 20

km Angerer had a 38.3-sec margin of victory over Tapio Piipponen of Finland, while Rolf Storsveen of Norway finished third. The team relay was won by East Germany, with the West Germans and Norwegians second and third. The Biathlon World Cup series, ending at Holmenkollen, Norway, was won by Rötsch, ahead of Angerer and Erik Kvalfoss of Norway.

OTHER EVENTS. In an international speed-skiing contest at Les Arcs, France, on April 20, a new world record women's speed of 200.780 km/h (124.759 mph) was set by Melissa Dimino of the U.S. The progress of freestyle skiing marked time a little, with main competitions restricted to North America. It was hoped that an international circuit involving Europe would be resumed in subsequent seasons.

Ice Skating. A spate of new rinks on a worldwide scale brought the sport geographically within range of many who had previously been denied the opportunity to participate in it. The standard of instruction rose particularly in Asia, where many Japanese and Chinese skaters were seen to be approaching high levels of achievement. There was a boom in ice dancing, while indoor short-track racing flourished more than before in countries without outdoor speed circuits.

FIGURE SKATING. The 74th world championships, held in Ottawa on March 19–24, were contested by 115 skaters from 21 nations. Capacity crowds of 10,000 attended the finals at the Civic Centre. Two of the four titles changed hands. Katarina Witt captured the undefended women's crown. The East German Olympic gold medalist led in every stage of the event, with Anna Kondrashova, the Soviet runner-up, trailing well behind. Elaine Zayak of the U.S., the 1982 champion, took the bronze. The outstanding jumper in the contest was Midori Ito, a 14-year-old Japanese schoolgirl, whose final sixth place was due to relatively weak compulsory figures.

A notable host-nation triumph was accomplished by Paul Martini and Barbara Underhill, who became the first Canadian world pairs champions since Otto and Maria Jelinek in 1962. The powerful Martini used the 13-in height difference between the two to telling advantage in overhead lifts and a throw triple salchow. Oleg Vasiliev and Elena Valova, the defeated Soviet title defenders who had won the Olympic gold medal only a month earlier, finished second. The bronze medal was won by Tassilo Thierbach and Sabine Baess, the East German victors in 1982.

Scott Hamilton (see BIOGRAPHIES) of the U.S. comfortably clinched the men's title for the fourth successive year. Although outpointed in the free skating by Brian Orser, the Canadian runner-up, Hamilton had established a gap in the compulsory figures that was mathematically too wide to close. Aleksandr Fadeev of the U.S.S.R. finished third. Orser and the fourth-place finisher, Jozef Sabovcik of Czechoslovakia, each landed the still-rare triple axel jump.

Christopher Dean and Jayne Torvill won their fourth straight ice dance title for Britain, ending their amateur championship career on the highest possible note, riveting attention and stirring emotions with their innovative free-dance interpretation of Ravel's *Bolero*. For technical merit, four of the nine judges awarded scores of six and the others 5.9. Then, for artistic presentation, as in the Winter Olympics, an unbroken row of nine maximum sixes flashed across the scoreboard. Before this, Torvill and Dean had collected seven sixes in the three compulsory dances, the first such scores ever to be awarded in that segment of the competition, and their "Spanish Caprice" set-pattern paso doble gained another perfect row for presentation. Their tally of sixes during this championship was thus an

(continued on page 430)

The Olympic Winter Games

BY HOWARD BASS

The XIV Olympic Winter Games, held at Sarajevo, Yugos., during Feb. 7–19, 1984, were contested by a record entry of 49 nations—12 more than the previous best—represented by 1,590 competitors (1,181 men and 409 women). The number of events was increased to 39 by the introduction of the women's 20-km cross-country competition in Nordic skiing. Eleven nations shared the gold medals, East Germany gaining nine; the U.S.S.R. six; the U.S., Finland, and Sweden four each; Norway three; Switzerland, Canada, West Germany, and Italy two apiece; and Great Britain one.

On Mt. Bjelasnica, Bill Johnson became the first U.S. skier to win the Olympic downhill. Peter Müller of Switzerland was runner-up. Another Swiss skier, Max Julen, won the giant slalom on a rugged, quickly rutting course, with Jure Franko, the host nation's most successful competitor at the Games, placing second, and Andreas Wenzel (Liechtenstein), the 1980 silver medalist, finishing third. Adding to their nation's most triumphant Olympic year in alpine skiing, the U.S. twins Phil and Steve Mahre won gold and silver medals, respectively, in the slalom, when the first run claimed 21 victims and the second 13 more.

After leading when the race was abandoned because of impossible conditions the previous day, Michela Figini, 17, from Switzerland, became the youngest-ever Olympic gold medalist in alpine skiing by winning the women's downhill on Mt. Jahorina with a two-run aggregate only 0.05 sec faster than her compatriot Maria Walliser. Figini was a month younger than another Swiss, Marie-Theres Nadig, had been when she took the downhill and giant slalom at Sapporo, Japan, 12 years earlier. Debbie Armstrong, who had never before won an international race, won the giant slalom for the U.S., ahead of her more experienced compatriot Christin Cooper, with third-place Perrine Pelen of France preventing Tamara McKinney from completing a U.S. clean sweep. Italy's Paoletta Magoni, also without a previous international victory, achieved another upset by winning the slalom in poor visibility, with Pelen runner-up. Notable absentees from the alpine skiing were Sweden's Ingemar Stenmark and Hanni Wenzel of Liechtenstein, each slalom and giant slalom winner in 1980 but banned from competition in 1984 as "outright professionals."

In the Nordic cross-country skiing on Mt. Igman, Thomas Wassberg beat fellow Swede Gunde Svan in the grueling 50 km, with Aki Karvonen of Finland third. Nikolay Zimyatov of the U.S.S.R. retained the 30-km title that he had won in 1980 but this time in more difficult gale-force winds. He had more than a minute to spare over his compatriot Aleksandr Zavyalov. The third-placed

Svan said that he had been "neither physically nor psychologically prepared for such weather," but in calmer conditions he won the 15 km from Karvonen. As anchor man in the winning Swedish relay team, Svan achieved a final medal tally of two golds, a silver, and a bronze.

Marja-Liisa Hämäläinen (see BIOGRAPHIES) of Finland was the outstanding woman Nordic skier, winning all three cross-country events and adding a bronze for her part in the team relay, which was won by Norway. In the 5 km she proved too strong for Berit Aunli of Norway. The Soviet veteran Raisa Smetanina was denied first place by a narrow margin in the first women's 20-km event, and she also finished second in the 10 km.

Matti Nykänen of Finland won the spectacular 90-m jump on Mt. Igman, taking an unassailable lead with a breathtaking first leap of 119.1 m; runner-up was Jens Weissflog of East Germany, who had earlier outleaped second-place Nykänen on the adjacent 70-m tower. Tom Sandberg of Norway won the separate Nordic combination event, with the two best jumps and second place in the 15-km cross-country portion, to outpoint Jouko Karjalainen of Finland.

Peter Angerer, the West German ski-shooter, took the 20-km biathlon comfortably from Frank-Peter Rötsch of East Germany, but the third-place Norwegian, Erik Kvalfoss, turned the tables on runner-up Angerer in the 10-km event. The Soviet team won the biathlon relay from Norway.

Wolfgang Hoppe and his East German crews dominated the bobsledding on Mt. Trebevic, with four-man and two-man victories confirming superiority over his compatriot Bernhard Lehmann, who finished second in both events. On the same track Paul Hildgartner of Italy convincingly won the men's luge toboggan singles, holding off a late challenge from the Soviet runner-up, Sergey Danilin. Hildgartner had been Olympic silver medalist in the event in 1980 and winner of the doubles in 1972. The two-seater luge race was won by Hans Stangassinger and Franz Wembacher of West Germany, followed by Evgeny Beloousov and Aleksandr Belyakov of the Soviet Union. Steffi Martin led an East German clean sweep in the women's singles, with Bettina Schmidt and Ute Weiss finishing second and third.

The Zetra ice arena, near the city centre, drew capacity crowds of 8,500 to see the figure skating, climaxed by well-nigh faultless performances by Britain's Torvill and Dean—the masterly Jayne Torvill and Christopher Dean—in gaining the ice dance title. They collected a record 19 maximum six marks on the way, including an unbroken row from the nine judges for their free-dance presentation. Andrey Bukin and Natalia Bestemianova from the Soviet Union finished a distant second.

Scott Hamilton (see BIOGRAPHIES) won the men's title for the U.S., his all-round capability proving too good for Canadian runner-up Brian Orser, whose top-scoring free skating was not enough to overhaul the lead that Hamilton had established in the compulsory figures. The women's finish was a cliff-hanger between Katarina Witt of East Germany and Rosalynn Sumners of the U.S., the nine judges dividing 5–4 in Witt's favour. The pairs title went to Oleg Vasiliev and Elena Valova from the U.S.S.R., who withstood strong pressure from the U.S. runners-up, brother and sister Peter and Kitty Carruthers.

On the adjacent outdoor speed-skating circuit, Gaétan Boucher from Canada gained two gold medals, in the 1,500-m and 1,000-m events, outpacing Sergey Khlebnikov, the Soviet runner-up each time. Boucher also finished third in the 500-m sprint, won by Sergey Fokichev of the

---

Howard Bass, winter sports correspondent for several newspapers, is the author of many books on the subject, including The Magic of Skiing, International Encyclopaedia of Winter Sports, *and* Let's Go Skating.

At left, the vaunted British team of Jayne Torvill and Christopher Dean, as expected, won the Olympic gold medal in ice dancing at Sarajevo, Yugoslavia. At right, Phil Mahre (U.S.) won the men's slalom. Above, Bill Johnson (U.S.) won the men's downhill ski race, the first gold medal taken in that contest by an American.

(LEFT AND ABOVE) AP/WIDE WORLD; (RIGHT) TARDY/PERRIN—GAMMA/LIAISON

U.S.S.R., with Japan's Yoshihiro Kitazawa second. When the 5,000 m was won by Tomas Gustafson of Sweden, the Soviet runner-up, Igor Malkov, swore to avenge his 0.02-sec defeat. He kept his word and after 25 grueling laps in the 10,000 m beat Gustafson by 0.05 sec.

Karin Enke of East Germany became queen of the speed track with a medal tally of two golds and two silvers in the four women's events, setting a new world record when winning the 1,500 m and taking the 1,000 m with equal conviction; Andrea Schöne of East Germany was second in each race. Another East German, Christa Rothenburger, defeated Enke in the 500-m sprint, as did Schöne in the 3,000 m.

The Soviet ice hockey team, though perhaps not so invincible as many had believed, recaptured the title after seven straight victories (*see also* ICE HOCKEY). Their last win, by 2–0, was crucial against the Czechoslovak runners-up, who also had not previously lost. The Soviets thus equaled Canada's record of six Olympic titles. Sweden gained the bronze medal after a 2–0 victory over Canada, which finished fourth.

This article updates the *Macropædia* article OLYMPIC GAMES.

Olympic Champions, 1984 Winter Games, Sarajevo

Alpine Skiing		
Men		
Downhill	B. Johnson (U.S.)	1 min 45.59 sec
Slalom	P. Mahre (U.S.)	1 min 39.41 sec
Giant slalom	M. Julen (Switzerland)	2 min 41.18 sec
Women		
Downhill	M. Figini (Switzerland)	1 min 13.36 sec
Slalom	P. Magoni (Italy)	1 min 36.47 sec
Giant slalom	D. Armstrong (U.S.)	2 min 20.98 sec
Nordic Skiing		
Men		
15-km cross-country	G. Svan (Sweden)	41 min 25.6 sec
30-km cross-country	N. Zimyatov (U.S.S.R.)	1 hr 28 min 56.3 sec
50-km cross-country	T. Wassberg (Sweden)	2 hr 15 min 55.8 sec
40-km ski relay	Sweden	1 hr 55 min 6.3 sec
70-m ski jump	J. Weissflog (East Germany)	215.2 pt
90-m ski jump	M. Nykänen (Finland)	231.2 pt
Nordic combined	T. Sandberg (Norway)	422.595 pt
Women		
5-km cross-country	M.-L. Hämäläinen (Finland)	17 min 4.0 sec
10-km cross-country	M.-L. Hämäläinen (Finland)	31 min 44.2 sec
20-km cross-country	M.-L. Hämäläinen (Finland)	1 hr 1 min 45.0 sec
20-km ski relay	Norway	1 hr 6 min 49.7 sec
Biathlon		
10 km	E. Kvalfoss (Norway)	30 min 53.8 sec
20 km	P. Angerer (West Germany)	1 hr 11 min 52.7 sec
30-km relay	U.S.S.R.	1 hr 38 min 51.7 sec

'Olympic record. †World record.

Figure Skating		
Men	S. Hamilton (U.S.)	3.4 pt
Women	K. Witt (East Germany)	3.2 pt
Pairs	E. Valova and O.Vasiliev (U.S.S.R.)	1.4 pt
Ice dancing	J. Torvill and C. Dean (U.K.)	2.0 pt
Speed Skating		
Men		
500 m	S. Fokichev (U.S.S.R.)	38.19 sec
1,000 m	G. Boucher (Canada)	1 min 15.80 sec
1,500 m	G. Boucher (Canada)	1 min 58.36 sec
5,000 m	T. Gustafson (Sweden)	7 min 12.28 sec
10,000 m	I. Malkov (U.S.S.R.)	14 min 39.90 sec
Women		
500 m	C. Rothenburger (East Germany)	41.02 sec'
1,000 m	K. Enke (East Germany)	1 min 21.61 sec'
1,500 m	K. Enke (East Germany)	2 min 3.42 sec†
3,000 m	A. Schöne (East Germany)	4 min 24.79 sec
Ice Hockey		
Winning team	U.S.S.R. (beat Czechoslovakia 2–0 in final)	
Bobsledding		
Two man	East Germany	3 min 25.56 sec
Four man	East Germany	3 min 20.22 sec
Tobogganing (Luge)		
Men (single)	P. Hildgartner (Italy)	3 min 4.258 sec
Men (double)	H. Stangassinger and F. Wembacher (West Germany)	1 min 23.620 sec
Women (single)	S. Martin (East Germany)	2 min 46.570 sec

(continued from page 427)
unprecedented 29. Soviet runners-up for a third time were Andrey Bukin and Natalia Bestemianova, with third place gained by Michael Seibert and Judy Blumberg of the U.S.

SPEED SKATING. Oleg Bozhiev captured the men's world championship for the U.S.S.R. in Göteborg, Sweden, on February 25–26. Andreas Ehrig of East Germany placed second and Hilbert van der Duim, the Dutch 1982 winner, finished third. In the individual events Bozhiev won the 1,500 m and van der Duim the 500 m; Geir Karlstad of Norway and Michael Hadschieff from Austria took the 5,000 m and 10,000 m, respectively.

Karin Enke of East Germany, the previous year's runner-up, became a convincing new women's champion at Deventer, Neth., on January 28–29. Her East German compatriots Andrea Schöne, the defending champion, and Gabi Schönbrunn finished second and third, respectively. Enke won three of the four distances, Schöne finishing first in the 5,000 m.

In the separate world sprint championships, at Trondheim, Norway, on March 3–4, Gaetan Boucher of Canada gained the men's title, ahead of Sergey Khlebnikov of the U.S.S.R. and Kai Arne Engelstad of Norway. The women's title was retained by Enke, followed by two Soviet racers, Valentina Lalenkova and Natalia Shive.

Six new world records—three men's and three women's—were all established on March 23–24 at Medeo, U.S.S.R. Bozhiev lowered the 1,500-m mark to 1 min 53.26 sec. Another Soviet skater, Viktor Shasherin, covered the 5,000 m in 6 min 49.15 sec, and his compatriot Igor Malkov clocked the 10,000 m in 14 min 21.51 sec. All three new women's times were set by Schöne: the 1,500 m in 2 min 3.34 sec, the 3,000 m in 4 min 20.91 sec, and the 5,000 m in 7 min 34.52 sec.

In the fourth world short-track (indoor) championships, at Peterborough, England, on April 5–7, Guy Daigneault of Canada regained the men's title he had won in 1982, followed by Tatsuyoshi Ishihara of Japan and Michel Daigneault, the champion's younger brother. Mariko Kinoshita of Japan became the new women's champion, ahead of Sylvie Daigle, the Canadian title defender, with third place tied between another Canadian, Nathalie Lambert, and Bonnie Blair of the U.S. A general Japanese upsurge was evident in the indoor sport, in which up to eight at a time race against each other, in contrast to pairs competing against the clock outdoors.

Bobsledding. Notable achievements before the Olympics occurred in the World Cup events at Cervinia, Italy, in January, when both two-man and four-man honours went to Detlef Richter's East German crews. There was an agitated controversy later in the month concerning the appearance of the Soviet Union's revolutionary rocket-shaped sleds, with which they took first and third places, driven by Janis Kipurs and Sintis Egmanis, respectively, in the two-man event of the European championships at Igls, Austria. Richter's second place prevented a clean sweep by the fast-starting Soviets, whose other crew finished fourth.

Following a scramble by many nations to copy the new Soviet sled, Klaus Kotter, president of the Fédération Internationale de Bobsleigh et de Tobogganning (FIBT), announced that in the future there would be just one uniform bob design. The FIBT feared that the sport otherwise could become as obsessed with design as Formula One automobile racing and thus detract from riders' technical skills.

The Soviet four-man sled failed to win jury approval at Igls, and the Soviets were told to lower the back and increase the width between the push handles to conform with the regulations. The Soviet racers were later disqual-

Rosalynn Sumners of Edmonds, Washington, won the U.S Figure Skating Championship at Salt Lake City. Here she is performing her long routine. The national championship win was her third.
FOCUS ON SPORTS

ified when their sleds were found to be overweight. The Swiss sled steered by Silvio Giobellina took the European four-man title, with Richter again finishing second and another Swiss sled, driven by Ekkehard Fasser, third.

Tobogganing. Luge tobogganing, still practiced mainly in central Europe, gained added prominence because of the Sarajevo Winter Olympics, where the Trebevic course was used for both luge and bobsledding. However, the non-Europeans proved to be far less experienced because the sport had not gained nearly such a firm foothold in North America or Asia.

The most successful lugers were the veteran Italian Paul Hildgartner and the East German Steffi Martin, who gained the men's and women's world titles, decided concurrently with those of the Olympics. Hans Stangassinger and Franz Wembacher of West Germany, prominent as partners for eight seasons, won the doubles event.

The customary dominance of Swiss riders on the Cresta Run for skeleton toboggans at St. Moritz, Switz., was challenged by James Sunley, who became the first Englishman to break the course record in its 99-year existence only to see it further lowered the same day, February 19, to 51.75 sec by Franco Gansser of Switzerland. En route to his record, Gansser also set a new mark of 41.99 sec for the shorter distance from the Junction intermediate station.

The 75th Grand National was won on February 11 by Gansser, with Sunley runner-up and Christian Nater of Switzerland third. The other course classic, the 61st Curzon Cup, was also taken by Gansser. His compatriot Nico Baracch placed second, and Sunley was third.

Curling. Norway won the 26th men's world championship for the Air Canada Silver Broom at Duluth, Minn., on April 1–8. Defeating Switzerland 8–5 in the final, Norway achieved its second title, its first having been won in 1979. Eigil Ramsfjell, the skip, had also been on the previous winning team. His foursome was completed by Sjur Loen, who had first appeared in the championships in 1974 at the age of 15, Gunnar Meland, and Bo Bakke. The Swiss skip, Peter Attinger, had also lost to Norway in the 1979 championship final.

Defending champion Canada, skipped by Mike Reilly, was eliminated in the semifinal, losing 9–8 to Switzerland in an extra end. Norway edged Per Lindeman's Sweden rink 5–3 in the other semifinal, which had been tied 3–3 after nine ends before Norway scored two in the tenth. The six other contestants included the U.S., West Germany, Scotland, Austria, Italy, and Denmark.

Connie Laliberte with her Winnipeg rink won the sixth women's world championship for Canada with a resounding 10–0 victory in the final over Switzerland, the defending champions, at Perth, Scotland, on March 25–April 1. Canada had previously won in 1980. Aided by sisters Jan Arnotte and Corinne Peters and newcomer Chris More, Laliberte cruised comfortably through the round-robin section before ousting Norway 8–6 in the semifinal stage. In the other semifinal the Swiss, skipped by Brigitte Kienast, beat West Germany 8–7.

The U.S. captured the tenth men's world junior championship at Cornwall, Ont., on March 11–18 with a hard-fought 7–6 success over Switzerland in the final. The victors, comprising Al Edwards (skip), Mark Larson, Dewey Basley, and Kurt Disher, defeated Scotland, the early favourites, 4–1 in the semifinal; the Swiss had a bye for that round. The U.S. previously had won in 1979.

Japan, with 6,000 registered curlers—there had been none five years earlier—became the first Pacific nation to join the World Curling Federation and expressed a hope to participate in the world championships of 1986. Curling was added to the program of the 1988 Winter Olympics in Calgary, Alta., but only as a demonstration sport, as it had been at the Games of 1924, 1932, and 1964.

(HOWARD BASS)

See also *Ice Hockey*, above.

WRESTLING

Wrestling. The top wrestling event in the world in 1984 was the Olympic Games, held in July and August in and near Los Angeles. Although team champions are not crowned in the Olympics in wrestling, the United States would have won the freestyle with seven gold medals and two silver medals out of the ten weight classes. The team scores were United States 52, Japan 37, South Korea 26, and Canada 15. Romania won the Greco-Roman championship with 31 points, followed by the United States with 26, Sweden 21, and Yugoslavia 20. The Soviet Union and its allies boycotted the Games.

In the freestyle competition Robert Weaver of the U.S. was the winner in the 48-kg (105.5-lb) class, and Saban Trstena of Yugoslavia triumphed at 52 kg (114.5 lb). Other winners for the U.S. included Randy Lewis at 62 kg (136.5 lb), David Schultz at 74 kg (163 lb), his brother Mark Schultz at 82 kg (180.5 lb), Ed Banach at 90 kg (198 lb), his brother Lou Banach at 100 kg (220 lb), and Bruce Baumgartner at 100+ kg. Hideaki Tomiyama of Japan was the champion in the 57-kg (125.5-lb) class, and You In Tak of South Korea won at 68 kg (149.5 lb).

No single country was dominant in Greco-Roman wrestling. Romania had two champions, Ion Draica at 82 kg and Vasile Andrei at 100 kg, as did the U.S. with Steven Fraser at 90 kg and Jeff Blatnick at 100+ kg. The other winners were Vincenzo Maenza of Italy (48 kg), Atsuji Miyahara of Japan (52 kg), Pasquale Passarelli of West

Germany (57 kg), Kim Weon Kee of South Korea (62 kg), Vlado Lisjak of Yugoslavia (68 kg), and Jouko Salomaki of Finland (74 kg).

A dramatic moment occurred at the conclusion of the 100+-kg event in the Greco-Roman division. After winning the gold medal Jeff Blatnick of the U.S. dropped to his knees in the middle of the mat, tears streaming down his face. He had won a bout against cancer (Hodgkin's disease) a year before the Olympics.

The indomitable University of Iowa won its seventh straight National Collegiate Athletic Association wrestling championship. Iowa scored 123.75 points, followed by Oklahoma State University with 98 points and Pennsylvania State University with 70.5 points. (MARVIN G. HESS)

Sumo. Although there were no major promotions in sumo in Japan, an important development during the year was the widely publicized retirement of 39-year-old Hawaiian-born sumo wrestler Takamiyama (*see* BIOGRAPHIES) in May after a brilliant 20-year career. Also noteworthy were the spectacular rises of Samoan-American Konishiki and 6-ft 6-in Japanese Kitao in the last two of the six annual 15-day tournaments. *Ozeki* (champion) Wakashimazu won two tourney championships, and the three *yokozuna* (grand champions)—Chiyonofuji, Kitanoumi, and Takanosato—each won one; in an upset the other championship went to low-ranked Tagaryu.

Takamiyama not only was the first foreign *rikishi* (sumo wrestler) in history to win an official sumo tournament, in July 1972, but also set several all-time records, including 12 victories over *yokozuna*. In a sort of Hawaiian changing of the guard, Konishiki (born in Hawaii of Samoan parents) sent shock waves through the sumo world when he went on a four-day rampage and defeated many competitors during the Aki *basho* (Autumn tournament) in September.

The year began with *yokozuna* Takanosato winning the *yusho* (tourney title) of the Hatsu *basho* (New Year's tournament) in January with a strong 13–2 record. In March his stablemate, *ozeki* Wakashimazu, won his first tourney championship in the Haru *basho* (Spring tournament) in Osaka with a nearly perfect 14–1 record. In the May Natsu *basho*, *yokozuna* Kitanoumi, who had collapsed in January with a disappointing 8–7 record, surprised sumo experts by overpowering all opposition to chalk up a perfect 15–0 record and gain his 24th *yusho*. The Nagoya *basho* in July was also won with a perfect 15–0 record as *ozeki* Wakashimazu captured his second championship in three tournaments.

The Aki *basho* (Autumn tournament) in September turned out to be the most surprising tournament in years. Not only did an ordinary *maegashira* named Tagaryu, ranked near the bottom of the Makunouchi Division in the number 12 position (out of 14 *maegashira* ranks on each of the east and west sides), steal the *yusho* from the top contenders with an amazing 13–2 record, but Konishiki turned the sumo world topsy-turvy with his awesome victories over four of the most powerful *rikishi* in sumo—*yokozuna* Chiyonofuji and Takanosato, *ozeki* Wakashimazu, and *sekiwake* (junior champion) Onokuni—to finish as runner-up with an outstanding 12–3 record. In the final tournament of the year, the Kyushu *basho* in Fukuoka in November, Chiyonofuji was in top shape and dominated the action by achieving a 14–1 record for his first title of the year and tenth championship of his career. Kitao upset one *yokozuna*, three *ozeki*, and a *sekiwake* in the first week and was hailed as a future *yokozuna*.

(ANDREW M. ADAMS)

This article updates the *Macropædia* article Major Team and Individual SPORTS and *Micropædia* entries on the various sports.

SPORTING RECORD

The following information updates the *Micropaedia* article SPORTING RECORD. For results of the summer Olympic Games, see *Track and Field Sports:* Special Report, above. For results of the winter Olympic Games, see *Winter Sports:* Special Report, above. *See also* sections on individual sports within the article SPORTS AND GAMES.

Aerial Sports, 1984
Lighter-than-air craft (balloons) distance solo record: Joe W. Kittinger (U.S.) in "Rosie O'Grady's," 3,535 mi (5,656 km) from Caribou, Maine, to Savona, Italy, Sept. 14–18

Automobile Racing, 1984
Formula One Grand Prix Race Results:

Race	Driver	Car	Average speed
Brazilian	A. Prost	McLaren MP4	179.511 km/h
South African	N. Lauda	McLaren MP4	206.587 km/h
Belgian	M. Alboreto	Ferrari 126C4	185.430 km/h
San Marino	A. Prost	McLaren MP4	187.254 km/h
French	N. Lauda	McLaren MP4	202.023 km/h
Monaco	A. Prost	McLaren MP4	100.775 km/h
Canadian	N. Piquet	Brabham BT53	174.185 km/h
Detroit	N. Piquet	Brabham BT53	131.499 km/h
U.S. (Dallas)	K. Rosberg	Williams FW09	129.219 km/h
British	N. Lauda	McLaren MP4	200.212 km/h
German	A. Prost	McLaren MP4	211.803 km/h
Austrian	N. Lauda	McLaren MP4	223.876 km/h
Dutch	A. Prost	McLaren MP4	186.050 km/h
Italian	N. Lauda	McLaren MP4	220.514 km/h
European	A. Prost	McLaren MP4	191.751 km/h
Portuguese	A. Prost	McLaren MP4	180.540 km/h

World Drivers' Championship: Lauda, 72 pt; Prost, 71½ pt; De Angelis, 31½ pt
Constructors' World Championship: McLaren-Porsche/TAG, 143½ pt; Ferrari, 56½ pt; Lotus-Renault, 44½ pt
U.S. Auto Club (USAC), Indianapolis 500: R. Mears, with an average speed of 163.612 mph (263.415 km/h)
FIA International Rally Championship for Makes:
Le Mans 24-hour Grand Prix d'Endurance: Pescarolo and Ludwig in a Porsche
Monte-Carlo Rally: Rohel and Geistdorfer in an Audi Quattro
East African Safari Rally: Bjorn and Waldegard in a Toyota Celica

Badminton, 1984
Women's International Championship (Uber Cup): China
Men's International Championship (Thomas Cup): Indonesia

Baseball, 1984
Hall of Fame inductees: Rick Ferrell, Pee Wee Reese, Harmon Killebrew, Luis Aparicio, Don Drysdale
New Record for Career Strikeouts: 3,874 set by Nolan Ryan (1966–   )
Tied Record for Single Season Saves: 45 by Bruce Sutter
World Series Results: Detroit (AL) 4 games, San Diego (NL) 1 game

Basketball, 1984
World Amateur Champions (Olympic Champions in 1984): men: United States; women: United States
National Collegiate Athletic Assn. (NCAA):
Division I: men: Georgetown; women: Southern California
Division II: men: Central Missouri State
National Invitational Tournament (NIT): Michigan
Amateur Athletic Union of the U.S. (AAU): Las Vegas Paul-Son Dice
National Basketball Assn. (NBA) professional champions: Boston Celtics

Bowling, 1984
American Bowling Congress (ABC): All-events Champion: R. Goike (2,142); Singles Champions (Regular Division): R. Antczak and N. Young (tied at 764)

Boxing
Champions as of Dec. 31, 1984:

	World Boxing Council (WBC)	World Boxing Assn. (WBA)
Heavyweight	P. Thomas (U.S.)	G. Page (U.S.)
Cruiserweight	C. de León (Puerto Rico)	P. Crous (S.Africa)
Lt. heavyweight	M. Spinks (U.S.)	M. Spinks (U.S.)
Middleweight	M. Hagler (U.S.)	M. Hagler (U.S.)
Jr. middleweight	T. Hearns (U.S.)	M. McCallum (Jamaica)
Welterweight	M. McCrory (U.S.)	D. Curry (U.S.)
Jr. welterweight	B. Costello (U.S.)	G. Hatcher (U.S.)
Lightweight	J. L. Ramírez (Mexico)	L. Bramble (U.S.)
Jr. lightweight	J. C. Chavez (Mexico)	R. Lockridge (U.S.)
Featherweight	A. Nelson (Ghana)	E. Pedroza (Panama)
Jr. featherweight	J. Meza (Mexico)	V. Callejas (Puerto Rico)
Bantamweight	A. Dávila (U.S.)	R. Sandoval (U.S.)
Super flyweight	J. Watanabe (Japan)	K. Galexi (Thailand)
Flyweight	S. Chitalada (Thailand)	S. Laciar (Argentina)
Jr. flyweight	Chang Jung Koo (S.Korea)	F. Quiroz (Dominican Republic)

Chess, 1984
Women's World Champion: M. Chiburdanidze, U.S.S.R.

Cricket
Test Cricket, 1877–Aug. 29, 1984, All-time Standings*:

	Eng.	Aust.	S.Af.	W.Ind.	N.Z.	India	Pak.	Sri L.
England	...	83/72	46/38	21/34	30/27	27/31	13/23	1/1
Australia	95/72	...	29/13	26/15†	8/5	20/11	11/9	1/0
South Africa	18/38	11/13	...	‡	19/6	‡	‡	‡
West Indies	30/34	16/15†	‡	...	5/9	22/27	7/8	‡
New Zealand	3/27	2/5	2/6	3/9	...	4/11	1/12	4/1
India	8/31	8/11	‡	5/27	10/11	...	4/23	1/0
Pakistan	3/23	8/9	‡	4/8	8/12	6/23	...	2/1
Sri Lanka	0/1	‡	‡	‡	0/1	‡	0/1	...

*Reading across, the first figure is the all-time number of wins and the second the number of drawn matches against a given opponent. The number of losses to any opponent can be ascertained by reading downward. †Including one tie. ‡No matches.

Dog Racing, 1984
American Greyhound Derby won by Dutch Bahama (owner: Herb Koerner), covering ³/₈ mi in 37.75 sec

Football, 1984
Association Football Major Tournaments:
Inter-Continental Cup won by Independiente of Argentina
European Champions' Club Cup won by Liverpool of England
European Cup-Winners' Cup won by Juventus of Italy
UEFA Cup won by Tottenham of England
Libertadores de América Cup (South American Champions' Cup) won by Independiente of Argentina
European Championship won by France
U.S. Professional National Football League (NFL) Results:
National Conference Championship: San Francisco 23, Chicago 0
American Conference Championship: Miami 48, Pittsburgh 28
Super Bowl XIX: San Francisco 38, Miami 16
U.S. College Football Champions:
National Champion: Brigham Young
Best total offense: Brigham Young, averaging 486.5 yd per game
Best rushing offense: Army, averaging 345.3 yd per game
Best passing offense: Brigham Young, averaging 346.2 yd per game
Best scoring average: Boston College, averaging 36.7 pt per game
Best total defense: Nebraska, averaging 203.3 yd per game
Best rushing defense: Oklahoma, averaging 68.8 yd per game
Best passing defense: Texas Tech, averaging 114.8 yd per game
Best scoring defense: Nebraska, averaging 9.5 pt per game
Canadian Football League Professional Championship (Grey Cup): Winnipeg Blue Bombers 47, Hamilton Tiger-Cats 17

Rugby Union International Matches, 1871–Dec. 15, 1984*:

	Eng.	Scot.	Ire.	Wales	Brit. Isles†	S.Af.	N.Z.	Aust.	France
England	...	47/16	54/8	35/12	...	2/1	3/0	4/0	32/6
Scotland	37/16	...	47/4	37/2	...	3/0	0/2	6/0	26/2
Ireland	34/8	43/4	...	28/5	...	1/1	0/1	6/0	25/4
Wales	42/12	49/2	53/5	...	...	0/1	3/0	7/0	36/3
British Isles†	...	...	...	...	...	14/6	5/3	12/0	...
South Africa	6/1	5/0	8/1	6/1	20/6	...	19/2	21/0	11/4
New Zealand	10/0	10/2	8/1	8/0	24/3	13/2	...	54/4	16/0
Australia	7/0	4/0	4/0	4/0	2/0	7/0	19/4	...	4/1
France	21/6	26/2	28/4	18/3	...	3/4	4/0	8/1	...

*Reading across, the first figure is the all-time number of wins and the second the number of drawn matches against a given opponent. The number of losses to any opponent can be ascertained by reading downward.   †The British Isles ("British Lions") is a combined team from England, Ireland, Scotland, and Wales.

Rugby League Test Matches, 1908–July 28, 1984*:

	Great Britain	Australia	New Zealand	France
Great Britain	...	49/4	5/2	7/2
Australia	43/4	...	33/0	22/3
New Zealand	23/2	19/0	...	11/3
France†	12/2	12/3	11/3	...

*Reading across, the first figure is the all-time number of wins and the second the number of drawn matches against a given opponent. The number of losses to any opponent can be ascertained by reading downward.   †France was accorded Test status and began playing in this series of matches in 1954.

Golf, 1984
Major Tournament Winners:

	men	women
U.S. Open	F. Zoeller (U.S.)	H. Stacy (U.S.)
U.S. Amateur	S. Verplank (U.S.)	D. Richard (U.S.)
U.K. Open	S. Ballesteros (Spain)	A. Okamoto (Japan)
U.K. Amateur	J. Olazabal (Spain)	J. Rosenthal (U.S.)
U.S. PGA	L. Trevino (U.S.)	...
Masters	B. Crenshaw (U.S.)	...
Eisenhower Trophy (Hong Kong)	Japan (T. Sakata, K. Kato, N. Kimura, K. Oei)	...
Curtis Cup (Muirfield, Scot.)	...	United States 9½, Great Britain and Ireland 8½
World Cup (Rome)	Spain (J. Cañizares, J. Rivero)	...

PGA leading money winner: T. Watson ($476,260)

Horse Racing, 1984

Trotting World Record (1-mi track):
  Cornstalk, Aug. 15, 1984, at Springfield, Ill. (1 min 53⁴/₅ sec)
  Fancy Crown, Aug. 16, 1984, at Springfield, Ill. (tied record)

Pacing World Record (1-mi track):
  Colt Fortysix, Aug. 16, 1984, at Springfield, Ill. (1 min 50³/₅ sec, slightly slower than the time-trial record of 1 min 49¹/₅ sec set by Niatross in 1980)

Major Thoroughbred Race Winners:

Country	Race	Winner	Jockey	Owner
United States	American Derby	At the Threshold	P. Day	W. C. Partee
	(dead heat)	High Alexander	G. Gallitano	No Limit Farm
	Arkansas Derby	Althea	P. Valenzuela	D. Aykroyd, H. Alexander, H. Groves
	Arlington Classic	At the Threshold	P. Day	W. C. Partee
	Arlington Handicap	Who's For Dinner	M. Venezia	Tartan Stable
	Arlington-Washington Futurity	Spend a Buck	C. Hussey	Hunter Farm
	Belmont	Swale	L. Pincay, Jr.	Claiborne Farm
	Blue Grass	Taylor's Special	P. Day	W. F. Lucas
	Breeders' Cup Juvenile	Chief's Crown	D. MacBeth	Star Crown Stable
	Breeders' Cup Juvenile Fillies	Outstandingly	W. Guerra	Harbor View Farm
	Breeders' Cup Sprint	Eillo	C. Perret	Crown Stable
	Breeders' Cup Mile	Royal Heroine	F. Toro	R. E. Sangster
	Breeders' Cup Distaff	Princess Rooney	E. Delahoussaye	Mrs. P. J. Tucker
	Breeders' Cup Turf	Lashkari	Y. Saint-Martin	The Aga Khan
	Breeders' Cup Classic	Wild Again	P. Day	Black Chip Stable
	Brooklyn	Fit to Fight	J. Bailey	Rokeby Stable
	Budweiser-Arlington Million	John Henry	C. McCarron	Dotsam Stable
	Coaching Club American Oaks	Class Play	J. Cruguet	P. M. Brant
	Delaware	Adored	L. Pincay, Jr.	Mrs. E. D. Jacobs
	Flamingo	Time For a Change	J. Bailey	O. M. Phipps
	Florida Derby	Swale	L. Pincay, Jr.	Claiborne Farm
	Futurity	Spectacular Love	L. Pincay, Jr.	D. Green
	Gulfstream Park	Mat Boy	J. Valdivieso	Noroma Stable
	Hialeah Turf Cup	Nijinsky's Secret	J. Velez, Jr.	Mrs. J. McDougald
	Hollywood Derby	Procida	C. Asmussen	S. Niarchos
	(2 divisions)	Foscarini	D. McHargue	J. Carlisle, J. Sheridan
	Hollywood Futurity	Stephan's Odyssey	E. Maple	H. de Kwiatkowski
	Hollywood Gold Cup	Desert Wine	E. Delahoussaye	Cardiff Stud Farm, T90 Ranch
	Hollywood Turf Cup	Alphabatim	C. McCarron	Stonechurch Farm
	Jockey Club Gold Cup	Slew o' Gold	A. Cordero, Jr.	Equusequity Stable
	Kentucky Derby	Swale	L. Pincay, Jr.	Claiborne Farm
	Kentucky Oaks	Lucky Lucky Lucky	A. Cordero, Jr.	L. Combs II, Equusequity Stable
	Man o' War	Majesty's Prince	V. Bracciale	J. D. Marsh
	Marlboro Cup Invitational	Slew o' Gold	A. Cordero, Jr.	Equusequity Stable
	Meadowlands Cup	Wild Again	R. Migliore	Black Chip Stable
	Metropolitan	Fit to Fight	J. Bailey	Rokeby Stable
	Monmouth	Believe the Queen	D. Miller, Jr.	Bohemia Stable
	Preakness	Gate Dancer	A. Cordero, Jr.	K. Opstein
	Rothmans International	Majesty's Prince	L. Pincay, Jr.	J. D. Marsh
	Santa Anita Derby	Mighty Adversary	E. Delahoussaye	Mr. and Mrs. F. Yoder
	Santa Anita	Interco	P. Valenzuela	D. I. Sofro
	Suburban	Fit to Fight	J. Bailey	Rokeby Stable
	Travers	Carr de Naskra	L. Pincay, Jr.	V. K. Payson
	Turf Classic	John Henry	C. McCarron	Dotsam Stable
	Washington, D.C., International	Seattle Song	C. Asmussen	S. Niarchos
	Widener	Mat Boy	J. Valdivieso	Noroma Stable
	Wood Memorial	Leroy S.	J. Cruguet	J. A. Nerud
	Woodward	Slew o' Gold	A. Cordero, Jr.	Equusequity Stable
England	One Thousand Guineas	Pebbles	P. Robinson	M. Lemos
	Two Thousand Guineas	El Gran Señor	P. Eddery	R. Sangster
	Derby	Secreto	C. Roche	L. Miglietti
	Oaks	Circus Plume	L. Piggott	Sir R. McAlpine
	St. Leger	Commanche Run	L. Piggott	I. Allan
	Coronation Cup	Time Charter	S. Cauthen	R. Barnett
	Ascot Gold Cup	Gildoran	S. Cauthen	R. Sangster
	Coral Eclipse Stakes	Sadler's Wells	P. Eddery	R. Sangster
	King George VI and Queen Elizabeth Diamond Stakes	Teenoso	L. Piggott	E. Moller
	Sussex Stakes	Chief Singer	R. Cochrane	J. Smith
	Benson & Hedges Gold Cup	Cormorant Wood	S. Cauthen	R. J. McAlpine
	Dubai Champion Stakes	Palace Music	Y. Saint-Martin	N. B. Hunt
France	Poule d'Essai des Poulains	Siberian Express	A. Gilbert	M. Fustok
	Poule d'Essai des Pouliches	Masarika	Y. Saint-Martin	The Aga Khan
	Prix du Jockey Club	Darshaan	Y. Saint-Martin	The Aga Khan
	Prix de Diane Hermès	Northern Trick	C. Asmussen	S. Niarchos
	Prix Royal-Oak	Agent Double	F. Head	J. Wertheimer
	Prix Ganay	Romildo	C. Asmussen	G. Oldham
	Prix Lupin	Dahar	A. Lequeux	B. McNall
	Grand Prix de Paris	At Talaq	A. Murray	Hamdan al-Maktoum
	Grand Prix de Saint-Cloud	Teenoso	L. Piggott	E. Moller
	Prix Vermeille	Northern Trick	C. Asmussen	S. Niarchos
	Prix de l'Arc de Triomphe	Sagace	Y. Saint-Martin	D. Wildenstein
	Grand Critérium	Alydar's Best	C. Roche	A. Clore
Ireland	Irish 2,000 Guineas	Sadler's Wells	G. McGrath	R. Sangster
	Irish 1,000 Guineas	Katies	P. Robinson	T. Ramsden
	Irish Sweeps Derby	El Gran Señor	P. Eddery	R. Sangster
	Irish Oaks	Princess Pati	P. Shanahan	Mrs. J. Mullion
	Irish St. Leger	Opale	D. McHargue	Snailwell Stud
	Phoenix Champion Stakes	Sadler's Wells	P. Eddery	R. Sangster
Italy	Derby Italiano	Welnor	L. Piggott	Scuderia Concarena
	Gran Premio del Jockey Club	Gold and Ivory	S. Cauthen	P. Mellon
West Germany	Deutsches Derby	Lagunas	G. Bockskai	Gestüt Fährhof
	Grosser Preis von Baden	Strawberry Road	B. Thomson	R. Stehr
	Grosser Preis von Berlin	Abary	G. Bockskai	Gestüt Fährhof
	Preis von Europa	Gold and Ivory	S. Cauthen	P. Mellon

Karin Enke of East Germany won the women's overall speed-skating title at Deventer, Neth., in January.
TANJUG PRESS AGENCY/AUTHENTICATED NEWS INTERNATIONAL

Ice Hockey, 1984
National Hockey League Champion (Stanley Cup): Edmonton Oilers

Lawn Bowls, 1984
Singles: New Zealand (P. Bellis)
Pairs: Scotland-United States (G. Adrain, S. Arculli)
Triples: Ireland (S. Espie, S. Allen, J. Baker)
Fours: England (G. Turley, J. Haines, J. Bell, A. Allcock)
Team: Scotland

Motorcycling, 1984
World Road Race Champion: E. Lawson (U.S.) on a 500-cc Yamaha
Tourist Trophy: R. McElnea (U.S.) on a Suzuki; 115.61 mph (186.06 km/h)
Speedway (Track) Champion: E. Gundersen (Denmark)

Rowing, 1984
Diamond Challenge Sculls: C. L. Baillieu (Leander Club)
Grand Challenge Cup: Leander and London R.C. (6 min 22 sec)
University Boat Race: Oxford defeated Cambridge, setting a new record of 16 min 45 sec for the 4-mi 374-yd (6,755-m) course; Cambridge now has 68 wins, Oxford 61, and one dead heat

Shooting, 1984
World Record (1,173 pt) equalled by M. Cooper (U.K.) in the small-bore free rifle—3 × 40 shots at 50 m

Show Jumping, 1984
Grand Prix of New York: won by N. Skelton (U.K.) on Apollo

Skiing
World Cup:
  Alpine Events: *men:* P. Zurbriggen (Switz.); *women:* E. Hess (Switz.)
  Nordic Events: *men:* G. Svan (Sweden); *women:* M.-L. Hämälainen (Finland)
  Nordic Jumping: *indiv.:* J. Weissflog (E.Ger.); *team:* Finland
  Nordic Combined: T. Sandberg (Norway)
  Biathlon: F.-P. Rotsch (E.Ger.)
World Distance Jumping Record: M. Nykänen (Finland), 607 ft (185 m)
Women's Speed Skiing: M. Dimino (U.S.), 124.759 mph (200.780 km/h), March 30 at Les Arcs, France

Squash Rackets, 1984
Men's World Championship: J. Khan (Pakistan)

Surfing, 1984
World Amateur Championships: *men:* S. Farnsworth (U.S.); *women:* J. Aragon (U.S.)

Swimming, 1984
World Swimming Records Set—Men:

200-m freestyle	M. Gross (W.Ger.)	1 min 47.55 sec
	M. Gross (W.Ger.)	1 min 47.44 sec
200-m backstroke	R. Carey (U.S.)	1 min 58.86 sec
	S. Zabolotnov (U.S.S.R.)	1 min 58.41 sec
100-m breaststroke	J. Moffet (U.S.)	1 min 02.13 sec
	S. Lundquist (U.S.)	1 min 01.65 sec
200-m breaststroke	V. Davis (Canada)	2 min 14.58 sec
	V. Davis (Canada)	2 min 13.34 sec
100-m butterfly	P. Morales (U.S.)	53.38 sec
	M. Gross (W.Ger.)	53.08 sec
200-m butterfly	J. Sieben (Australia)	1 min 57.04 sec
200-m indiv. medley	A. Baumann (Canada)	2 min 01.42 sec
400-m indiv. medley	J.-P. Berndt (E.Ger.)	4 min 19.61 sec
	A. Baumann (Canada)	4 min 17.53 sec
	A. Baumann (Canada)	4 min 17.41 sec
4 × 100-m medley relay	United States (R. Carey, S. Lundquist, P. Morales, R. Gaines)	3 min 39.30 sec
4 × 100-m freestyle relay	United States (C. Cavanaugh, M. Heath, M. Biondi, R. Gaines)	3 min 19.03 sec

4 × 200-m freestyle relay	United States (G. Gaberino, D. Larson, B. Hayes, R. Saeger)	7 min 18.87 sec
	United States (M. Heath, D. Larson, J. Float, B. Hayes)	7 min 15.69 sec

World Swimming Records Set—Women:

200-m freestyle	K. Otto (E.Ger.)	1 min 57.75 sec
100-m breaststroke	S. Gerasch (E.Ger.)	1 min 08.29 sec
100-m backstroke	I. Kleber (E.Ger.)	1 min 00.59 sec
4 × 100-m freestyle relay	East Germany (K. Otto, K. Konig, H. Friedrich, B. Meineke)	3 min 42.41 sec
4 × 100-m medley relay	East Germany (I. Kleber, S. Gerasch, I. Geissler, B. Meineke)	4 min 03.69 sec

Tennis, 1984
Davis Cup: Sweden
Wightman Cup: United States
French Open: *men:* I. Lendl (Czech.); *women:* M. Navratilova (U.S.)
Wimbledon: *men:* J. McEnroe (U.S.); *women:* M. Navratilova (U.S.)
U.S. Open: *men:* J. McEnroe (U.S.); *women:* M. Navratilova (U.S.)
Australian Open: *men:* M. Wilander (Sweden); *women:* C. Evert Lloyd (U.S.)

Track and Field, 1984
World Outdoor Records Set—Men:

10,000 m	F. Mamede (Portugal)	27 min 13.81 sec
4 × 100-m relay	United States,	37.83 sec
20,000-m walk	E. Canto (Mexico)	1 hr 18 min 39.9 sec
High jump	Zhu Jianhua (China)	2.39 m (7 ft 10 in)
Pole vault	S. Bubka (U.S.S.R.)	5.85 m (19 ft 2¼ in)
	S. Bubka (U.S.S.R.)	5.88 m (19 ft 3½ in)
	S. Bubka (U.S.S.R.)	5.90 m (19 ft 4¼ in)
	T. Vigneron (France)	5.91 m (19 ft 4¾ in)
	S. Bubka (U.S.S.R.)	5.94 m (19 ft 5¾ in)
Hammer throw	Y. Syedikh (U.S.S.R.)	86.34 m (283 ft 3 in)
Javelin throw	U. Hohn (E.Ger.)	104.80 m (343 ft 10 in)
Decathlon	J. Hingsen (W.Ger.)	8,798 points

World Outdoor Records Set—Women:

100 m	E. Ashford (U.S.)	10.76 sec
200 m	M. Koch (E.Ger.)	21.71 sec (equals record)
1 mile	N. Artyemova (U.S.S.R.)	4 min 15.8 sec
2,000 m	Z. Budd (U.K.)	5 min 33.15 sec
	M. Decker (U.S.)	5 min 32.7 sec
	T. Kazankina (U.S.S.R.)	5 min 28.72 sec
3,000 m	T. Kazankina (U.S.S.R.)	8 min 22.62 sec
5,000 m	I. Kristiansen (Norway)	14 min 58.89 sec
10,000 m	O. Bondarenko (U.S.S.R.)	31 min 13.78 sec
5,000-m walk	S. Cook (Australia)	22 min 6.34 sec
	S. Cook (Australia)	22 min 4.42 sec
	Yan Hong (China)	21 min 40.2 sec
10,000-m walk	O. Krishtop (U.S.S.R.)	44 min 56.10 sec
400-m hurdles	M. Ponomaryeva (U.S.S.R.)	53.98 sec
4 × 400-m relay	East Germany	3 min 15.92 sec
4 × 800-m relay	U.S.S.R.	7 min 50.17 sec
High jump	T. Bykova (U.S.S.R.)	2.05 m (6 ft 8¾ in)
	L. Andonova (Bulgaria)	2.07 m (6 ft 9½ in)
Shot put	N. Lisovskaya (U.S.S.R.)	22.53 m (73 ft 11 in)
Discus throw	I. Meszynski (E.Ger.)	73.36 m (240 ft 8 in)
	Z. Silhava (Czech.)	74.56 m (244 ft 7 in)
Heptathlon	S. Paetz (E.Ger.)	6,867 points

Winter Sports, 1984
Bobsledding:
  World Cup: *two-man:* East Germany; *four-man:* East Germany
Curling Champions: *men:* Norwegian Team (at Duluth, Minn.); *women:* Canadian Team (at Perth, Scotland)
Luge:
  Singles: *men:* P. Hildgartner (Italy); *women:* S. Martin (E.Ger.)
  Doubles: H. Stangassinger and F. Wembacher (W.Ger.)
Figure Skating Champions:
  Indiv.: *men:* S. Hamilton (U.S.)
         women: K. Witt (E.Ger.)
  Pairs: P. Martini and B. Underhill (Canada)
  Ice Dancing: C. Dean and J. Torvill (U.K.)
Speed Skating Champions:
  Overall: *men:* O. Bozhiev (U.S.S.R.); *women:* K. Enke (E.Ger.)
  500-m: *men:* H. van der Duim (Neth.); *women:* K. Enke (E.Ger.)
  1,500-m: *men:* O. Bozhiev (U.S.S.R.); *women:* K. Enke (E.Ger.)
  5,000-m: *men:* G. Karlslad (Norway); *women:* A. Schöne (E.Ger.)
  10,000-m: *men:* M. Hadschieff (Austria); *women:* K. Enke (E.Ger.)
  Sprint: *men:* G. Boucher (Canada); *women:* K. Enke (E.Ger.)
Speed Skating Records Set:
  1,500-m: *men:* O. Bozhiev (U.S.S.R.) 1 min 53.26 sec
          women: A. Schöne (E.Ger.) 2 min 3.34 sec
  3,000-m: *women:* A. Schöne (E.Ger.) 4 min 20.91 sec
  5,000-m: *men:* V. Shasherin (U.S.S.R.) 6 min 49.15 sec
          women: A. Schöne (E.Ger.) 7 min 34.52 sec
  10,000-m: *men:* I. Malkov (U.S.S.R.) 14 min 21.51 sec

Yachting, 1984
Bermuda Race: won by F. Curren, Jr., in the 48-ft sloop "Pamir"

Television and Radio

No major country lacked some form of radio and television service in 1984. Approximately 865 million radio sets were in use throughout the world, including about 478.7 million, or 55%, in the United States. Television sets numbered about 448 million, of which approximately 174 million, or 39%, were in the U.S. The Soviet Union, with 75 million, or 17%, ranked second, and Japan was third with 29.3 million, or 6.5%, according to estimates published in the 1984 *Broadcasting/Cablecasting Yearbook.* Other *Broadcasting* estimates of television sets included West Germany, 21.5 million; United Kingdom, 18.6 million; France, 16.5 million; Brazil, 15.2 million; Italy, 13.5 million; Canada, 12.4 million; Spain, 9.7 million; China, 9.5 million; Poland, 8 million; Mexico, 7.5 million; Argentina, 5.9 million; East Germany, 5.8 million; Australia, 5.5 million; The Netherlands, 4.3 million; Czechoslovakia, 4.1 million; Yugoslavia, 3.9 million; Egypt, 3.8 million; Turkey, 3.6 million; Saudi Arabia, 3.5 million; and Sweden, 3.2 million.

Approximately 8,200 television stations were on the air or under construction throughout the world. About 2,200 were in the Far East, 2,110 in Western Europe, 1,490 in the U.S., 920 in Eastern Europe, 180 in South America, 105 in Mexico, 100 in Canada, and 50 in Africa. There were about 17,500 radio stations, most of which used the amplitude-modulation (AM) system of transmission, although the proportion of frequency-modulation (FM) stations was growing. In the U.S. there were about 10,340 radio stations, of which 5,415, or 52%, were FM.

Organization of Services. In the U.S. Pres. Ronald Reagan's policy of deregulation continued to remove restrictions from both broadcasters and cable operators. The Federal Communications Commission (FCC) in July relaxed its rules in order to allow any one entity to own or control as many as 12 AM, 12 FM, and 12 television stations; in the past, 7 stations in each service had been the upper limit. The new rule was widely criticized—in Congress and elsewhere—insofar as it applied to television, and the FCC agreed to postpone the TV change at least until April 1, 1985. Later in the year the FCC amended the so-called 12-12-12 rule so that as of April 2, 1985, an entity would be permitted to own 12 TV stations as long as those stations did not operate in markets collectively containing more than 25% of the nation's homes. The FCC also initiated a proceeding to consider whether it could and should relax or eliminate the so-called fairness doctrine, which required stations to present all sides of controversial public issues if they presented any side.

In another proceeding, following up on proposals it had issued in 1983, the commission deregulated commercial television along lines already used in deregulating radio, eliminating its guidelines as to the amount of time devoted to commercials and other nonentertainment programming and dropping its requirement that broadcasters formally confer with community leaders about local needs that should be addressed in programming. The broadcasters, however, would be required to place in their public inspection files, on a quarterly basis, a list of at least five to ten issues to which the station had given particular attention in its programming over the preceding three months and would have to indicate how each issue had been treated.

Cable television continued to expand. The A. C. Nielsen Co., the leading measurer of national television audiences, estimated that in July the number of cable-equipped U.S. households was 36,105,500, or 42.9% of all U.S. TV homes, a gain of 9.6% or 3,175,360 cable homes in 12 months.

At the summer Olympic Games in Los Angeles, broadcasting and print journalists jammed the allocated sections of the Coliseum. In all about 10,000 reporters and sound or camera technicians attended.
ROSS—WEST LIGHT/WOODFIN CAMP & ASSOCIATES

Broadcasting identified 26 basic cable networks, capable of reaching from 300,000 to 31.8 million homes each, plus nine major pay-cable services, of which the largest were as follows (with estimates of their subscribers as of May 31, 1984): Home Box Office (HBO), 13.5 million; Showtime, 5.4 million; the Movie Channel, 3.1 million; Cinemax, 2.7 million; the Disney Channel, 1 million; and the Playboy Channel, 684,000.

Cable continued to experience growing pains, however. Some of the large multiple system operators found that in order to win franchises from major cities, they had sometimes promised to provide substantially more services than they could in fact afford. As a result operators building systems throughout the U.S. were in many cases pleading with officials for relief and seeking to renegotiate franchise terms, often in an atmosphere of acrimony. But there was also some good news for the cable operators. A unanimous U.S. Supreme Court in June handed down a decision that substantially loosened city and state authority over cable, affirming the FCC's authority instead. This was a major win for cable operators, who for years had been at odds with the National League of Cities (NLC) and the U.S. Conference of Mayors (USCM) over state and municipal regulations that the cable industry considered excessive and unjust. In the end the NLC, USCM, and the National Cable Television Association compromised their differences and lent their support to congressional legislation to establish a national cable policy.

The prospects for direct broadcast satellite (DBS) operations, relaying programming via satellites in space directly into homes equipped with special antennas, or "dishes," lost some of its glamour in 1984. U.S. Satellite Communications Inc., which had launched DBS operations in 1983 with five channels of programming beamed to a 33-county area around Indianapolis, Ind., found subscriber growth was taking place more slowly than expected. After a $40 million stock offering was unsuccessful, the company made a tentative agreement in September to merge with Satellite Television Corp. (STC), a subsidiary of Communications Satellite Corp. (Comsat). STC had been having troubles of its own; it was unwilling to commence DBS operations without partners, and its chief prospects for partnership, CBS and Paramount Pictures, had backed down.

Television's biggest growth area in 1984 centred on videocassette recorders (VCR's), the devices that could record broadcast TV programs and play them back later, or could play movies or other programming on prerecorded cassettes that were rented or bought. In 1981, six years after the Sony Corp. had introduced the first VCR models (Betamax), it was estimated that 4% of U.S. TV households were equipped with VCR's. The real growth began in 1983, and by mid-1984 it was estimated that 13% of U.S. homes had VCR's. A study by the A. C. Nielsen Co. revealed that 74% of the programs recorded in the home were network programs, predominantly soap operas or others with continuing story lines, including miniseries.

In the U.K. both the BBC and Independent Television (ITV) had a relatively quiet year. For the BBC the major problem was the dual one of its declining share of the audience and its request for an increase in the license fee. The corporation replaced the managing director of its TV services, Aubrey Singer, and brought in a former ITV executive, Michael Grade, to run BBC 1. In October it proposed that the annual license fee be raised from £46 to £60–£70. The controversy over the higher fee was fueled by outside proposals that the BBC (either on its radio services or on TV) should sell a limited amount of advertising. Saatchi & Saatchi, a leading agency, argued that one minute of TV advertising a day could cover all of the BBC's increased costs until 1990. These views found favour with the government, although the prospect of BBC advertising was so controversial that few people expected it to be allowed without some additional years of debate. In November the government reduced funding for the BBC's external services by £1 million a year.

For ITV the most notable events were two strikes at Thames Television, the largest ITV company. The first resulted in a blackout of the company's programs, which led the company's executives, during the second strike, to operate the studio and output equipment themselves. TV-am, the ITV breakfast-time company, which had suffered upheavals of staffing, finance, and programs, began to settle down and gain audiences and income. Channel 4 consolidated its impressive performance with more innovative and attractive programs. In radio the year was marked by the emergence of several pirate stations; in October the Independent Broadcasting Authority deregulated its licensed stations so they could compete more effectively.

In Spain a statute published in January approved the principle of a national "third" TV channel, and each autonomous region was encouraged to apply for a license. Private companies were not permitted. In Portugal a national poll showed that 71% of the population wanted a third channel and that they preferred private, commercial broadcasting over an extension of the state monopoly.

Throughout Europe cable television grew more slowly than expected. Most countries passed enabling legislation and licensed system operators, but the number of households subscribing both to existing services and to the "new" pay-TV services remained disappointingly low.

While the broadcasters were reassured by cable's slow growth, they were perplexed and unsettled by the plans for satellite broadcasting. Each of the leading systems, based

on the aerospace industries of the U.K., France, and West Germany, respectively, were postponed amid continuing doubts of DBS's desirability and viability. The launch in May of Japan's first DBS, Yuri-2A, did not augur well for the new technology. Two of its three transponders failed, and the satellite was unable to provide an operational service. Meanwhile, several new TV services began to extend their coverage by using midpower satellites to distribute TV to cable systems.

In Italy the ten-year saga of private television reached a climax when Silvio Berlusconi purchased a dominant position in his rival's major private channels and, almost simultaneously, the government allowed the private TV companies to provide national networks. Previously the companies had been nominally restricted to local programs. As a result Italy's two public national channels were now in competition with three private national channels. In addition, the regional RAI-3 was in competition with a larger number of regional and local private stations.

In India the government met its target of opening a new transmitter every week in order to extend TV coverage to thousands of remote villages. It aimed to reach 70% of the country by the end of the year, partly by terrestrial coverage and partly with the Insat satellite system. The Australian government held a succession of inquiries into the Aussat satellite system. The Australian Broadcasting Tribunal suggested that a major inquiry into the commercial networks be held before decisions were made about Aussat, scheduled to be launched in 1985–86 and likely to carry only Australian Broadcasting Corporation services. In New Zealand the government approved a third channel to be run by a new private company.

Programming. Action-adventure dramas were on the increase, and situation comedies were somewhat fewer in the prime-time television schedules that the U.S. networks offered for the 1984–85 season. Action-adventure series increased by about 10% from the 1983–84 schedule's total, reaching 35, while the number of situation comedies dropped by about 8%, to 22. Some of the situation comedy deficit was made up by such so-called "reality" comedies as "People Do the Craziest Things" and "Foul-Ups, Bleeps & Blunders." In total, the three major networks introduced 21 new series. CBS, winner of the prime-time ratings race in 1983–84, brought in five new series totaling 3½ hours; ABC, second in 1983–84, introduced eight new series adding

Television network and newspaper exit-polling techniques used to forecast election results while some polls were still open were highly controversial.

up to 7 hours; and NBC, third again, introduced nine new series totaling 7½ hours.

To accommodate the new entries the networks had, of course, to cancel an equal number of hours of established programming. For the most part their decisions to cancel were based on audience ratings, with the least successful programs usually the first to go. NBC included among its castoffs all survivors of the nine new series it had introduced a year earlier. ABC dropped ten series, including some that had been among the ratings leaders for several years but had begun to slip, such as "Happy Days" (on the air for 11 years), "Fantasy Island" (5 years), and "Hart to Hart" (4 years). CBS's dropouts were mostly relatively new series. The schedule for 1984–85 contained only 5 of the 22 new series the networks had introduced one year earlier. They were "Hardcastle and McCormick, " "Hotel," and "Webster" on ABC and "Scarecrow and Mrs. King" and "AfterMASH" on CBS.

From the start of the season on September 24 through November 25, "The Cosby Show," a new NBC comedy, averaged a 21.7 rating in the Nielsen measurements, ranking sixth among regular series. The only other new entries among the top 40 series were CBS's "Murder, She Wrote," which ranked 15th, and NBC's "Highway to Heaven," which was 26th. The top ten series in the ratings for that period were, in order, "Dallas," "Dynasty," "NBC Monday Night Movie," "The A-Team," "60 Minutes," "The Cosby Show," "Simon & Simon," "Falcon Crest," "Magnum, P.I.," and "Hotel."

The new season's lineup of nonseries programming continued the trend toward increasing reliance on made-for-television movies. Major motion-picture production companies normally released their theatrical movies for exhibition on pay cable about six months before releasing them for network broadcast; by the time such movies reached the networks, especially those that had been successful at the box office, they had been widely seen, and their network audiences were far smaller than would have been the case a few years earlier, when cable was in fewer homes. Estimates published in *Broadcasting* in March 1984 indicated that during the first five months of the 1983–84 season, the networks had carried more than twice as many made-for-television movies (76) as first-run theatrical films (35). More significantly, perhaps, the average rating for the made-for-TV movies was 19 (19% of U.S. television homes had watched), 23% higher than the average for the theatrical movies.

In cable television the major programming services were using more and more material, that they had produced themselves or had produced for them. Even the broadly based pay services that relied chiefly on theatrical movies, such as HBO, Showtime, Cinemax, and the Movie Channel, were underwriting new dramatic, comedy, and children's series; miniseries; made-for-TV movies; and specials. An especially popular format was music video programs. (*See* MUSIC: *Sidebar.*) More sports programming was also offered on cable.

News remained a television staple, with the presidential and congressional elections providing the news story of the year. The commercial networks broke with tradition at the Democratic and Republican presidential nominating conventions; for the first time, all three rejected so-called gavel-to-gavel coverage of all floor activities, electing to provide "selective" coverage instead. Politicians did not like the change, but apparently many viewers did, although the audience ratings for extended political coverage were, as always, much lower than for conventional television entertainment programs.

In the 36th annual Emmy awards, the Academy of Television Arts and Sciences named "Hill Street Blues" the outstanding drama series for the fourth consecutive year and again chose "Cheers" as the outstanding comedy series. "He Makes Me Feel like Dancin' " won the Emmy for children's programming; "The Sixth Annual Kennedy Center Honors: A Celebration of the Performing Arts" won for variety, music, or comedy programs; "Something About Amelia" for drama special; "Concealed Enemies" for limited series; "Placido Domingo Celebrates Seville" for classical program in the performing arts; "Garfield on the Town" for animated program; "America Remembers John F. Kennedy" for informational special; and "A Walk Through the 20th Century with Bill Moyers" for informational series.

Emmies for lead actor and actress in a dramatic series went to Tom Selleck of "Magnum, P.I." and Tyne Daly of "Cagney & Lacey." John Ritter of "Three's Company" and Jane Curtin of "Kate & Allie" won for lead actor and actress in a comedy series, and Laurence Olivier of "Laurence Olivier's 'King Lear' " and Jane Fonda of "The Dollmaker" won for lead actor and actress in limited series or special. Cloris Leachman of "Screen Actors Guild 50th Anniversary Celebration" won for individual performance on a variety or music program. Supporting actor and actress awards were presented to Bruce Weitz and Alfre Woodard, both of "Hill Street Blues," in the drama series category; to Art Carney of "Terrible Joe Moran" and Roxana Zal of "Something About Amelia" for limited series or specials; and to Pat Harrington, Jr., of "One Day at a Time" and Rhea Perlman of "Cheers" in the comedy series category. Producer David Wolper was voted unprecedented "special recognition" by the academy's board of governors for his production of the opening and closing ceremonies of the summer Olympic Games at Los Angeles.

In the 11th annual Emmy awards for daytime programming, top honours went to "General Hospital" as the outstanding drama series, "$25,000 Pyramid" in the game show category, "Woman to Woman" in the talk/ service classification, "Merv Griffin Show" for outstanding variety series, and "Captain Kangaroo" and "Smurfs" for outstanding children's entertainment.

The popularity of sports on television continued and, if anything, intensified. A U.S. Supreme Court ruling in June voided college football contracts that the National Collegiate Athletic Association (NCAA) had awarded ABC and CBS, terminating more than 30 years of NCAA control over TV coverage of its members' football teams. The upshot was far more television coverage of far more college teams.

Broadcasting estimated that TV and radio networks and stations and cable operators would pay $501.4 million for college and professional football TV rights in 1984. The estimate was 6.5% below the $536.6 million figure for 1983 but, unlike the 1983 total, did not count the many local deals resulting from the Supreme Court decision. *Broadcasting* also estimated that broadcasters and cable operators paid $268 million, an increase of more than 75%, for rights to broadcast major league baseball in 1984. The big television sports event of the year was the Summer Olympics in Los Angeles. ABC, which had paid $225 million for the TV rights, averaged a 23.5 rating and 45 share of audience for the 16 nights of coverage.

In radio, music and news remained the staples, with individual stations specializing in formats ranging from country and rock to classical music, news, and information combinations and all-news operations. *Broadcasting*'s annual analysis of programming on the ten highest rated radio stations in the top 50 U.S. markets found that adult contemporary, or currently popular, music had taken over first place in popularity. Among all U.S. stations, however, country music was the most popular full-time format.

The Public Broadcasting Service (PBS) network introduced a fall lineup for 1984–85 that officials described as offering viewers "more choice and a wider range than PBS has ever had." Highlights included "Wonderworks," a new 26-part family entertainment series dealing with "rites of passage" that young people experience while growing up; "Heritage: Civilization and the Jews," an $11 million, nine-part epic filmed in 19 countries, chronicling more than 3,000 years of history of the Jewish people; and "The Constitution: That Delicate Balance," a 13-part series in which experts dealt with constitutional issues.

Facing competition from new cable systems and satellite launches, Western European state-run and private service broadcasters set about a reappraisal of their expenditure and revenue for years ahead. Many broadcasters, appreciating the need for economizing on production costs, set about joint co-production enterprises more in the spirit of relieving accountants' anxiety than of fruitful creative partnerships. The viewing public certainly became more aware of this trend in 1984—and often reacted unfavourably to it.

Perhaps the consistently highest quality in any particular type of program during the year was in documentaries—usually the cheapest program category to produce. This was borne out both by the results from those festivals having several entry categories and by comparative viewing in different countries. The winner in the documentary category at the Prix Italia Festival was the bleak "Nuclear Holocaust" from Japan's NHK. At the International Emmy awards, the documentary prize went to Britain's Channel 4 for "The Heart of the Dragon" series, which offered an insight into life in China.

British program makers, usually remarkably successful at the major television festivals, were exceptionally so in 1984. The BBC won the Critics' Prize at the Prix Italia Festival with "An Englishman Abroad," Central Television won the Prix Italia for drama with "Made in Britain," and London Weekend Television took the RAI Prize for Music

(also awarded during the Prix Italia Festival) with "Ralph Vaughan Williams—a Symphonic Portrait." In the International Emmy awards the drama prize went to Granada Television's "The Jewel in the Crown," a 14-part series set in the days of Britain's fading power in India. Channel 4 won the performing arts category for its production of "The Tragedy of Carmen" directed by Peter Brook. The award for popular arts went to a situation comedy series produced by Thames Television, "Fresh Fields," a lighthearted look at the continuing need for the emancipation of women in their spouses' eyes. Thames Television also won the children's category Emmy for a delightful version of Kenneth Grahame's classic story "The Wind in the Willows."

France's Antenne 2 also paid tribute to composer Georges Bizet with its version of *Carmen,* which won the Prix Italia for music. The RAI documentary and drama prizes were both won by Swedish Television's channels, SV2 winning the documentary prize with "The Miracle of Life" and SV1 the drama with "Duel in Midwinter." In the former the production team used startling fibre-optic photographic technology to take the viewer on an internal tour of the human reproductive system.

Many broadcasters, while producing programs of very high quality, also needed to attract viewers repeatedly and cheaply with productions that were relaxing to watch or perhaps provided quick and harmless excitement. Thus during the year there was an increase in the output of game shows in many countries. In Italy the harsh competition between the state broadcaster RAI and the private commercial stations yielded more game shows and other domestically produced variety and light entertainment programs.

In France the broadcasting of feature films began in November with an over-the-air subscription service, Canal Plus, much to the anxiety of French filmmakers and cinema owners. Since an undue proportion of the ordinary French broadcasting channels' airtime was taken up with "talking head" programs, Canal Plus might well prove popular.   (PAUL A. BARRETT; RUFUS W. CRATER;
JOHN HOWKINS; LAWRENCE B. TAISHOFF)

NBC's "The Cosby Show" presents a lesson in economics for Bill Cosby's TV son, Theodore (right), who claimed good grades were unimportant.

A 14-part British television series, "The Jewel in the Crown," dramatized the last years of Great Britain's rule in India. Two members of the huge cast were Susan Woodridge (foreground), who portrayed a young Englishwoman, and Art Malik as her Indian lover. The conflicts that resulted from their relationship provided a major theme of this intricate saga.

GRANADA TELEVISION, U.K.

Amateur Radio. The number of amateur ("ham") radio operators continued to increase. In the U.S. the total reached 421,732 in 1983, the latest year for which figures were available from the American Radio Relay League, the leading organization of ham operators. This total represented a 3.8% increase from 406,417 a year earlier. Throughout the world licensed amateur radio operators numbered approximately 1.4 million.

Ham operators provided vital communications services in emergency or other conditions when normal links were down. In the spring of 1984, for example, amateur operators were at the heart of a rescue mission that saved a Norwegian fishing vessel stranded 565 km (350 mi) off the coast of Florida for three days.

(RUFUS W. CRATER; LAWRENCE B. TAISHOFF)

See also Industrial Review: *Advertising; Telecommunications; Motion Pictures; Music.*

This article updates the *Macropædia* article BROADCASTING.

Theatre

The running battles between central and local government and between the Arts Council of Great Britain (ACGB) and its clients were highlighted by the October publication of the U.K. Policy Studies Institute's (PSI's) survey (*Funding the Arts in Europe*). The survey reported on the 1983 Munich (West Germany) congress of the Council of Europe on public funding; it deplored the absence of long-term planning in Britain, compared with other member nations, and stressed the need for increasing funding. The increase in the ACGB grant from just under £102 million to £105 million announced by U.K. Arts Minister Lord Gowrie in December was attacked by ACGB Chairman Sir William Rees-Mogg as being well below inflation and harmful to the well-being of the arts in general, besides jeopardizing the very existence of many theatrical enterprises.

The PSI report showed that there was increased spending on the arts in France, for example, where protection of the "national heritage" was as much a matter of civic pride as of wise husbandry. It remained to be seen what effect the withdrawal of the U.S. and possibly eventually Britain and other countries from UNESCO, which financed the International Theatre Institute, would have on the theatre as a whole.

Great Britain and Ireland. The ACGB's John Whiting Award was won by the Egyptian-born playwright Karim Alrawi. The ACGB also started a Trust for Special Funds and distributed grants to writers and others engaged in theatrical production. However, because of a lack of funding most of its large- and medium-scale drama tours would have to be curtailed or abandoned, according to ACGB Secretary-General Luke Rittner.

The National Theatre (NT) was among the most outspoken critics of the government decisions. The new policy of its director, Sir Peter Hall, which involved dividing its activities among five distinct companies under separate directors, would be at risk if funding remained at current levels. The exceptional burden of having to pay £2 million a year merely to keep the building open was acknowledged to be a crippling one. The NT broke even during the year to March 1984, but the figures to March 1985 were expected to bring a deficit of £200,000.

Despite Hall's concerns 1984 was a fruitful year. The adaptation by Michael Frayn (*see* BIOGRAPHIES) of Chekhov's first play, entitled *Wild Honey,* won several awards, including those given by the Society of West End Theatre, which were renamed the Laurence Olivier Awards (LO). The LO award for best actor in a revival went to Ian McKellen, who also won the *Plays and Players* (*P&P*) best actor award as Platonov, the play's protagonist; both LO and *P&P* awards for the best design went to John Gunter; and Christopher Morahan won not only the same two awards for the best direction but a third director award made by *Drama Magazine* (*DM*). Roger Lloyd Pack was given the *DM* supporting role award for his portrayal of Osip in *Wild Honey* and of Victor in Harold Pinter's one-acter *One for the Road.* Morahan shared his *DM* award for best director with Peter Gill, who won for his staging of Sam Shepard's *Fool for Love* and Thomas Otway's *Venice Preserv'd.* Alison Chitty won the *DM* designer's award for the Otway production. Memorable performances at the NT included Frances de la Tour as George Bernard Shaw's *Saint Joan,* Michael Pennington in the lead role of Mark Rozovsky's *Strider—the Story of a Horse,* Hywel Bennett in *She Stoops to Conquer,* and Ian McKellen in the title

Starlight Express was one of the most popular, and one of the most critically disdained, of London's entries in the new theatre season. Here Jeffrey Daniel rollerskates and sings.
DONALD COOPER/TIME MAGAZINE

role of Hall's partly modern-dress, hence politically updated, production of *Coriolanus.*

The Royal Shakespeare Company (RSC) had to make do with only two awards, the first being the *DM* prize for best supporting actress to Zoe Wanamaker for her moving rendering of Katrin in Howard Davies's eye-catching version of Bertold Brecht's *Mother Courage and Her Children,* at the Barbican. Other fine performances there were her Adriana in *Comedy of Errors* (director: Adrian Noble), Emrys James's Malvolio in *Twelfth Night,* Daniel Massey's Duke in *Measure for Measure* (director: Noble), and Antony Sher's *Richard III,* seen only at Stratford. For his Richard, Sher shared a *DM* best actor award with Brian Cox's detective inspector in Ron Hutchinson's drama of Irish terrorism, *Rat in the Skull,* at the Royal Court and his Ned Darrell in *Strange Interlude.* Cox also won the LO award for his performance in the Irish play.

At the RSC's Pit Theatre three new plays of special merit were *Softcops,* a study of crime by Caryl Churchill; *Red Star,* a Pirandellian drama in a Soviet setting by Charles Wood; and Ron Daniels's production of Stephen Poliakoff's partly autobiographical *Breaking the Silence.* Other new plays in the subsidized sector were, at the Royal Court, Michael Hastings's *Tom and Viv,* a part-documentary about T. S. Eliot; G. F. Newman's *An Honourable Trade,* about corruption among politicians; and *Minor Complications,* by Elizabeth Bond, about Anglo-Indian attitudes.

At Hampstead Kenneth MacMillan made his London directing debut with Tennessee Williams's *Kingdom of Earth,* later followed by the world premiere of a U.S. play about the Vietnam war's aftermath, *War at Home* by James Duff, and Howard Brenton's *Bloody Poetry,* with Byron and Shelley as the main roles. Other imports from the U.S. were Howard Fast's *Thirty Pieces of Silver;* Eugene O'Neill's *Strange Interlude,* with Edward Petherbridge in the LO prizewinning supporting role of Charles Marsden and Glenda Jackson winning both the *DM* and *P&P* awards as Nina Leeds; *On Your Toes* (the *DM* best musical production), which won for Natalia Makarova the LO award for best actress in a musical and for Tim Flavin the *P&P* promising newcomer prize; and Larry Shue's *The Nerd,* starring Rowan Atkinson. The LO best actress in a new play award went to Thuli Dumakude in the title role of the South African antiapartheid *Poppie Nongena* at the Riverside, where Lindsay Anderson's production of *Playboy of the Western World,* Virginia Woolf's forgotten

one-acter *Freshwater,* and the antiapartheid *Biko Inquest,* with Albert Finney (*see* BIOGRAPHIES) playing and directing, were also seen.

The Old Vic's subscription policy earned the management 65% capacity audiences in its first year of operation. Outstanding were the Johannesburg Market Theatre's *Saturday Night at the Palace* and Glenda Jackson in Racine's *Phedra.* The Greenwich staged the historical parable play, *Two Planks and a Passion* by Anthony Minghella, *P&P* winner of the most promising playwright award for his *A Little like Drowning* at Hampstead. Under Ian Albery's aegis the Warehouse offered a triple bill of Samuel Beckett plays and a season of Edinburgh Fringe successes that included the Hull Truck Theatre's LO prizewinning comedy of the year, John Godber's *Up 'n' Under.*

Awards in the private sector ranged from Michael Frayn's drama of marital trouble, *Benefactors* (LO and *P&P* best play), to Marcia Warren (LO for best supporting actress) in *Stepping Out,* Clive Mantle (*P&P* for the most promising newcomer) in *Of Mice and Men* at the Mermaid Theatre, Maureen Lipman (LO best comedy performance) in *See How They Run,* and Vanessa Redgrave (LO best actress in a revival) as Miss Tina in *The Aspern Papers.* The LO musical of the year went to *42nd Street.* Other awards, besides that to Makarova, went to Paul Clarkson, who won the LO award for best actor in a musical for his performance in Melvyn Bragg's *The Hired Man,* and to Ned Sherrin, winner of the LO award for outstanding achievement in musicals for the concept of *The Ratepayers' Iolanthe,* in which the Greater London Council spokesman Ken Livingstone and the prime minister met in a head-on clash. Andrew Lloyd-Webber's *Starlight Express,* though without an award, followed his successes of *Cats* and *Evita* with solid bookings for months to come, while he himself brought Sue Townsend's musical, *The Secret Diary of Adrian Mole,* into town.

The Field Day Theatre Company's double bill in Belfast, with *The Riot Act* by Tom Paulin (director: Stephen Rea), inspired by *Antigone,* and *High Time* by Derek Mahon, inspired by Molière's *The School for Husbands,* was followed by the RSC's touring production of *The Winter's Tale* and *The Crucible* (later seen in London) at the Belfast Festival. Also performed at the Belfast Festival was Stewart Parker's *Northern Star,* about the northern Irish patriot Henry Joy McCracken. The Dublin Festival, however, had to be dropped because of a lack of cash, leaving artistic director

Michael Colgan free for his work as manager at Dublin's Gate Theatre, where Joan O'Hara won the Harvey's of Bristol best actress award and Nigel Boyd and Jo Vanek the costume and set design awards for *A Woman of No Importance*. Other Harvey awards went to Tom Murphy for the Abbey's 1983 production of *The Gigli Concert* and to Godfrey Quigley for his part in that play. The best director was Patrick Mahon for *The Great Hunger* at the Peacock. Other awards went to Fidelma O'Dowda in *Trafford Tanzi*, to Ray McBride in *The Wood of the Whispering*, and to the 80-year-old critic of the *Evening Herald*, John Finegan. Ray McAnally, director of *The Glass Menagerie* at the Abbey, was slated to succeed Joe Dowling as artistic director.

France, Italy, Spain, Low Countries. Outstanding at the Comédie Française were Tristan l'Hermite's *The Death of Seneca* (1644) and *Bérénice* (director: Klaus Michael Gruber), as was also Ludmila Mikaël's *Bérénice and Célimène*. At Jean-Louis Barrault's theatre in Paris his productions of *Angelo, Tyrant of Padua* by Hugo, *Business Is Business* by Mirbeau, and Beckett's *Company*, starring Pierre Dux, winner of the Plaisir du Théâtre award, were noteworthy. Featured at the Odéon were Giorgio Strehler's masterly productions of *The Tempest*, which won him the French critics' award for best production (1983), *Minna von Barnhelm* (both with the Milan Piccolo company), and Corneille's *The Illusion*. Other French critics' awards went to Marilu Marini (best actress) in Copi's *The Seated Woman;* Luc Bondy for his production of *Undiscovered Country*, in which Michel Piccoli won the best actor award; and Bernard Bloch and Jean-Pierre Wenzel for the best new play (*Vaterland*). The French critics' Revelation award was shared by Monique Lepeu as Gertrude Stein in her own play and Marianne Épin in *Le Pain dur*. Jérôme Savary won the Dominique Prize (founded by the late critic Léon Dominque) for his production of *Cyrano de Bergerac*, while the Society of Authors' award was shared by Samuel Beckett and Françoise Dorin.

Noteworthy new plays included Loleh Bellon's *Such Tender Bonds*, Rémo Forlani's *Grandpa*, Nina Companeez's *The Hour Glass*, and Janine Worms's *Hunting Dragons;* revivals included plays by Guitry, Roussin, Ionesco, Archard, Bourdet, Anouilh, and Billetdoux (*Chin-Chin*, staged by Peter Brook, with his wife, Natasha, and Marcello Mastroianni). Among imports were *To Damascus* with Michel Bouquet, *Right You Are, if You Think So* with Robert Hirsch, *Gone with the Wind* with Daniel Olbryschski, *The*

Persians (director: Sylvia Montfort), and *Duet for One* with Anne Duperey.

Highlights of the Italian season were Racine's *Phèdre* (director: Luca Ronconi); Luigi Squarzina's production of *Orestes;* Emilio Isgro's production in dialect of *The Choephoroe*, updated to modern Sicily; Vittorio Gassman's *Macbeth;* Gabriele Lavia's *Hamlet*, with Rossella Falk as Gertrude; Sergio Reggi's *Shylock;* Raf Vallone in Franz Jung's *Nostalgia* at the Milan Piccolo (director: Klaus Michael Gruber); and Corrado Augias's *Honest Iago*, starring Eros Pagni. Fernando de Rojas's *La Celestina* and Lope de Vega's *The Knight from Olmedo* in Madrid and Luis Pasqual's striking productions of *As You Like It*, in Catalan, and of *The Lights of Bohemia*, in Spanish (which opened at the Paris *Théâtre de l'Europe* in Barcelona), were outstanding. There were, once again, two plays by Paul Willems in Brussels, while Jan Fabre's *The Power of Theatrical Follies*, a Belgian-Dutch co-production, was seen at the Holland, Nancy, and Venice festivals.

Switzerland, West and East Germany, Austria. Jerzy Jarocki staged Babel's *Sunset* and Jiri Menzel Goldoni's *The Coffee House* at the Zürich Schauspielhaus. The novelty in Basel was a staged version of O'Casey's autobiography as *Vivas to Those Who Have Failed*. West German awards by the *Theater Heute Magazin* (*THM*) went to Klaus Pohl's *The Old Country* (first seen at Vienna's Burg Theater), Franz Xaver Kroetz's *Fear and Hope in the German Federal Republic*, and Peter Stein's *Three Sisters* at the Berlin Schaubühne, where George Tabori also directed Hungarian exile Istvan Eorsi's *The Interrogation*. The Andreas Gryphius Prize was awarded to Hans Sahl, the New York-based German-Jewish playwright.

Other highlights in West Germany included John Hopkins's sensational *Losing Time* (director: Peter Zadek) in Hamburg, Zadek's scandalous version of Joshua Sobol's *Ghetto* (first seen in Haifa) in Berlin, Tovstonogov's production of an Ostrovsky at the Schiller, and the world premiere of Kurt Barsch's *Checkpoint Charlie* at the Schlosspark. Vienna offered *Poor Cyrano!* by Kohout at the Akademie and Yury Lyubimov's (*see* BIOGRAPHIES) *Crime and Punishment* at the Burgtheater, while Edward Albee staged two of his own plays at the English Theatre. Jutta Hoffman won the *THM* award in *Yerma* (director: Zadek) at the Munich Chamber Theatre, which also received a special *THM* award for its record of outstanding performances. The directing debuts of Axel Richter and Horst Sagert at the Berliner Ensemble were notable, as were Dieter Mann's

MARTHA SWOPE

Tom Stoppard's play *The Real Thing*, a success in London, went to Broadway accompanied by general acclaim. Here Glenn Close (Annie) and Jeremy Irons (Henry) discuss plays and cricket.

Sunday in the Park with George was Stephen Sondheim's new musical comedy, based on the life of the Neo-Impressionist painter Georges Seurat and focusing on his masterwork, "Sunday Afternoon on the Island of La Grande Jatte." It won the Drama Critics Award.
MARTHA SWOPE

Lopakhin, his first role since taking over the artistic management of the Deutsches Theater, and Thomas Langhoff's prizewinning production of *Ghosts* at the Deutsches.

Eastern Europe, Scandinavia, Israel. Saltykov-Shchedrin's *Messrs Golovlevy* brought Innokenti Smoktunovsky back to the Moscow Art Theatre. Yevgeny Lazarev moved from the Mayakovsky in Moscow, where he staged Boris Gorbatov's musical *The Law of Winter,* to take over the Malaya Bronnaya from Anatoly Efros. Two versions of Rozewicz's new *The Trap,* first performed in Oslo, were staged in Poland by Jerzy Grzegorzewski and Kazimierz Braun. Kazimierz Dejmek won the state prize for Wyspianski's *The Wedding* at the Polski. In Bulgaria new plays by Haitov, Yordan Radichkov, and Stanislav Stratiev (whose *Roman Baths* was seen at the Nancy Theatre of the Nations Festival) were featured at the seventh Quinquennial Sofia Theatre Review. In Romania new works by Gabor Andor, Eugen Barbu, Paul Everac, Iosif Naghu, and Tudov Popescu were presented in Bucharest.

The 400th anniversary of Peter Bornemisza was marked by a musicalized version of his *Hungarian Electra* at the Castle Theatre in Budapest, where Sandor Weores's *The Two-Headed Beast* and plays by Endre Veszi, Gyorgy Spiro, Laszlo Gyurko, and Tibor Gyurkovics were also seen. The highlight of the Novi Sad Festival was *The Double Bottom* by Goran Stefanovski and of the Belgrade season, Vida Ognjenovic's dramatization of Dragoslav Mihailovic's *When the Gourds Flowered.*

Ludvig Holberg's 300th anniversary was celebrated, both in Norway and in Denmark, with numerous revivals, foremost among them *Erasmus Montanus* in Oslo and Copenhagen. Ingmar Bergman's return to Sweden after his self-imposed exile was marked by a production of *King Lear* at the "Dramaten," which also presented the world premiere of Mrozek's *Summer Day.* Three notable events in Helsinki were Ralf Långbacka's version of Henrik Tikkanen's war novel *The Last Hero* at the City, Eugen Terttula's production of *Mannerheim in Poland* at the National, and Jack Witikka's presentation of Bo Carpelan's tragicomedy of prewar Finland, *Christmas Eve,* at the Swedish theatres.

In Israel Peter James's production of *Joseph and the Amazing Technicolour Dreamcoat* and Hanoch Levine's

new play, *The Suitcase Packers* (also seen at Nancy), were staged at the Cameri. Attention also was focused on a drug-problem drama at the Habimah and on Leonard Schach's production of *Not Now Darling* and Shimon Zimmer's musical *The Married Woman* at the Neve Zedek.

(OSSIA TRILLING)

United States. Broadway has long been known as the "Fabulous Invalid." The epithet is a gleeful, even joyous paean to the New York commercial theatre's seemingly everlasting ability to rally despite regular predictions of its imminent demise. However, 1984 was a sobering year in this respect, for it struck fear into the hearts of Broadway's hardiest champions. As depressing as statistics had been over the years, none had been more discouraging than the unused theatres of the early '80s, and gloomier still was the artistic quality of what actually was produced.

What was wrong with Broadway was a crisis of confidence compounded by economic conditions that made independent producing all but impossible. According to the official count, 28 productions opened in Broadway theatres during the year. Many of these were only technically "Broadway" productions, for the count included repertory productions at the nonprofit Circle in the Square Theatre (Clifford Odets's *Awake and Sing,* Noël Coward's *Design for Living*) as well as small shows mounted in little theatres in the Broadway district (A. R. Gurney's *The Golden Age,* for example). Were Broadway's year limited to commercial presentations in full-size theatres, it would have to be considered almost nonexistent.

This sorry state of affairs was indicated by the season's hits and prizewinners as much as by its failures. For example, the theatre's own prizes, the Tony award and the Drama Critics Circle Award, were both given to Tom Stoppard's *The Real Thing,* a perfectly clever play though hardly one to warrant deep respect. It won four other Tony awards, including best actor (Jeremy Irons [see BIOGRAPHIES]) and best actress (Glenn Close). However, a more likely candidate was David Mamet's *Glengarry Glen Ross,* which won the year's Pulitzer Prize for drama. This was an original, funny, and savage indictment of morality in American business, a theme that had been Mamet's concern in such earlier works as *American Buffalo. Glengarry Glen Ross* is named for a real-estate development that a group of lame-brained salesmen are peddling for the sake of cheesy incentive awards. They are prepared, indeed willing and eager, to destroy their customers and even each other for the sake of those awards, and their employer puts them up to it from beneath the anonymous moral umbrella of business-is-business.

Bleakly funny, energized by rhythms of scatological dialogue that Mamet raises to poetry, *Glengarry Glen Ross* is a modern counterpart to Arthur Miller's *Death of a Salesman,* which, coincidentally, was successfully revived during the year. Although the 1949 drama holds up as a masterwork of 20th-century theatre, the success of the revival was doubtless due to the presence of Dustin Hoffman as Willy Loman. His first stage appearance in 20 years confirmed Hoffman's original reputation as a powerful actor of classical technique. His movie fame served to bring new audiences to the theatre, providing a service far greater than the mere presentation of a great play.

There was little else to cheer the serious playgoer on the Broadway of 1984. A new David Rabe play, *Hurlyburly,* did well enough to move up from an outlying theatre, but its success on Broadway was less attributable to quality than to such well-known names as director Mike Nichols and stars Sigourney Weaver, Christopher Walken, and William Hurt. Other new plays, having no movie actors to rescue them, closed quickly, among them Arthur Kopit's *End of the World,* the Italian import *Accidental Death of an Anarchist* by Dario Fo, and *Play Memory* by the Canadian Joanna Glass.

Few funny plays were produced. Broadway had become too expensive for comedies, and those that were mounted during the year hardly seemed worth the effort. One was a success, the British farce *Noises Off* by Michael Frayn, which revealed both onstage and backstage action of a jaded cast performing in a seedy touring production of an English comedy.

Musicals, ultimately, will set a season's tone on Broadway, and there the news was most dire of all. *La Cage Aux Folles* won the year's Tony award, but that prize is based on the Broadway season, which runs from September to September. *La Cage* opened in 1983. The prestige musical of 1984 was Stephen Sondheim's *Sunday in the Park with George,* and it won the Drama Critics Award. Based on the life of the French Neo-Impressionist painter Georges Seurat, the show examines the creation of his masterpiece "Sunday Afternoon on the Island of La Grande Jatte." This was a novel notion for a musical, and of course anything that Sondheim does is of importance. The result, however, was interesting rather than satisfying and by no means a successful work. Among the few other musicals produced, *The Rink* had Liza Minnelli, but audiences were not happy to see her playing a supporting and unglamorous role. A musical version of William Saroyan's *The Human Comedy* was more cantata than theatre. There simply were no other new musicals, and a pair of revivals (*Oliver* and Rudolf Friml's operetta *The Three Musketeers*) failed outright.

The final measure of 1984 on Broadway was in one sense the most depressing and yet in another the most heartening development of the year; a pair of productions by Britain's Royal Shakespeare Company—*Cyrano de Bergerac* and *Much Ado About Nothing*—both starring the brilliant actor Derek Jacobi, became the "hot tickets" of the year. While these were not products of the American commercial stage, they did show that a youthful and enthusiastic audience existed for quality theatre, even with ticket prices at $45. Further substantiating this, the plays shown off-Broadway were solid and popular. They ranged from comedy (Wendy Wasserstein's *Isn't It Romantic?*) to

drama (Lanford Wilson's *Balm in Gilead*) and musicals (a revival of Sondheim's *Pacific Overtures*).

The institutional theatres in New York and throughout the U.S.—the "regional" or "repertory" theatres—seemed finally to have adjusted to the "Reaganomics" of minimal government subsidies. Lowering their budgets and finding new sources of help, mainly from corporations, they sought freshness in programming. For example, Joseph Papp's New York Shakespeare Festival presented stripped-down and sassy versions of such operas as Donizetti's *Don Pasquale,* retitled *Non Pasquale,* and a *La Bohème* that starred rock star Linda Ronstadt (none too secure in the upper ranges). In Connecticut the Hartford Stage Company mounted a fresh version of Arthur Schnitzler's rarely produced *Anatol,* while the Yale Repertory Theatre staged August Wilson's new play, *Ma Rainey's Black Bottom* (subsequently transferred to Broadway).

Canada. The year in Canada was, as always, dominated by the Stratford (Shakespearean) Festival, which remained the most prestigious classical theatre on the North American continent. After many years of presenting ever fewer plays by Shakespeare in the main theatre, artistic director John Hirsch rebounded with four of them on the big Festival Theatre stage. A certain commercialism might have been read into the choice of such favourites as *A Midsummer Night's Dream, Romeo and Juliet,* and *The Merchant of Venice;* the fourth play was *Love's Labour's Lost.* The Festival seemed similarly conscious of the box office in the choice of programming for its intimate Avon Theatre: a Gilbert and Sullivan festival including *Iolanthe, The Gondoliers,* and *The Mikado,* Tennessee Williams's *A Streetcar Named Desire,* and Terence Rattigan's *Separate Tables.*

At the Shaw Festival at Niagara-on-the-Lake there was similarly popular programming: Shaw's *Androcles and the Lion* and *The Devil's Disciple;* Coward's *Private Lives* and *The Vortex;* and, of all things, a revival of the Jerome Kern musical comedy *Roberta.* Thus in Canada, where it is reasonable to infer that subsidy sources were particularly dry in 1984, the need to appeal to the largest possible audiences was recognized.

(MARTIN GOTTFRIED)

See also Dance; Music.

Transportation

The most sensitive indicators of the health of the transportation industry in 1984 were growth rates in air travel and motor vehicle production and the amount of unused shipping capacity. Variations in these factors reflected the year's moderate economic recovery. A centennial review of the automobile industry suggested that the automobile would continue to be the most ubiquitous form of mechanized transport beyond the end of the century. Growth in civil aviation was accompanied by a new price skirmish over the North Atlantic route, but deregulation had little effect on air fares within Europe. At the luxury end of the travel market, the £125 million, 44,000-ton cruise ship "Royal Princess" was launched. At the other extreme, a lack of serviceable trucks was partly responsible for the many thousands of deaths from starvation in Ethiopia.

(DAVID BAYLISS)

AVIATION

At the close of 1984 the airline industry appeared to be emerging from the depression of recent years. According to estimates prepared by the International Air Transport Association (IATA), its members—which included most major international airlines—ended the year with an operating profit of almost $3 billion on international scheduled services and a net profit before taxes of about $1 billion. Operating revenue was $40 billion.

This result was better than previously forecast and the best in more than seven years; in 1983 the IATA members' operating profit on all services was $1.4 billion—2% of revenue—and the net result was a break-even. In each of the three preceding years there had been both an operating loss and a net loss. The results, however, remained inadequate for the financing of future aircraft fleets. The IATA estimated that member airlines would need to invest from $150 billion to $200 billion (at 1984 prices and exchange rates) in aircraft, equipment, and fixed assets. No great improvement in the financial situation was foreseen during the next two years.

Unit cost (per available metric ton-kilometre) on IATA international scheduled services fell from 40.3 cents in 1980 to about 37.1 cents in 1983 and an estimated 37.3 cents in 1984. The cost of fuel per available ton-kilometre in 1983 was 9.51 cents, 9.7% less than in the previous year. Although fuel costs had stabilized, many non-U.S. carriers failed to benefit because of the strength of the U.S. dollar, the currency in which fuel prices were fixed. Fuel constituted about one-quarter of airlines' operating costs.

World traffic in 1983 totaled 145,520,000,000 ton-km (1 km = 0.62 mi), according to preliminary figures from the International Civil Aviation Organization (ICAO), an increase of 5.7% over 1982 and the greatest rate of increase recorded since 1979. Of total traffic, 95% was accounted for by scheduled services and 47% by international scheduled services. The passenger traffic of IATA members

UPI/BETTMANN

Air Florida announced July 3 that it had filed for bankruptcy and was suspending operations at once—leaving passengers holding tickets for Air Florida flights that day at a loss as to where to turn for transportation. This was the scene at the airlines counter at Miami International Airport.

increased by approximately 9% in 1984, according to preliminary estimates. The fastest growth rate—around 15%—was recorded in the freight sector, but freight, traditionally priced at marginal "fill-up" rates, did little to improve yield (rate of revenue per ton-kilometre). Passenger traffic growth on routes between the Middle East and Far East remained particularly strong in 1983, with an increase of 17%. On North- and mid-Pacific routes growth was 9%. There was a decline in traffic on some other routes, and markets in Africa and Latin America were depressed.

In the U.S., whose air transport industry accounted for some 38% of the world total, traffic growth in the first nine months of 1984 was patchy, and profitability remained elusive. Passenger traffic on the 11 major airlines, at 307,-975,000,000 passenger-km, was 3.4% above the first nine months of 1983, but the load factor (the percentage of available seats occupied by paying passengers) sagged from 61.8 to 60.2%. However, the 14 fastest growing national carriers raised their passenger traffic by 29.1% to 41,226,-000,000 passenger-km in the same period. The overall increase in the U.S. scheduled industry for the period was 7.3%. Instability in the wake of the 1978 deregulation was still apparent in the U.S. industry. Some new carriers continued to experience meteoric growth—notably People Express, which carried 6.5 million passengers in the first nine months of 1984 and was growing at around 150% a year. (A new cut-rate challenger on the North Atlantic route was the U.K.-based Virgin Atlantic.) Meanwhile, Air Florida filed under Chapter 11 of the federal bankruptcy laws and was merged with Midway, while the reconstituted Braniff was forced to lease out aircraft and crews to other airlines. Pan American reported continuing losses. Marking the final step in deregulation, the Civil Aeronautics Board, which had regulated airline fares and schedules, was ceremonially "closed forever" at year's end.

In Europe a measure of air-service liberalization was agreed on in June between the British and Dutch governments, giving airlines the possibility of opening new services and charging fares with approval only from the country of origin. Other European countries showed little sign of following suit. The British government's plans for the future development of civil aviation in the U.K. were outlined in a White Paper, *Airline Competition Policy,* published in October. The first service under a European Communities directive permitting new routes between provincial airports was opened between Billund, Den., and Southend, England, by Maersk Air on Nov. 29, 1984. Potentially far-reaching moves toward airline deregulation were taken in Canada, but the outlook was uncertain because of the change of government in September.

There were 20 scheduled-service accidents and 805 passenger fatalities in 1983, according to ICAO preliminary figures. The accident rate of 0.08 per 100 million passenger-km had been fairly stable for ten years.

(DAVID WOOLLEY)

SHIPPING AND PORTS

There was a slight improvement in world trade in 1984, particularly as regards the movement of bulk cargoes such as iron ore, grain, and coal, but hope of a real upswing was crushed by an influx of new bulk-carrier tonnage. The world tanker market remained flat; that it became no worse was due to maintenance of a relatively high rate of scrapping of 10- to 15-year-old vessels, many of them very large crude carriers. The tonnage of vessels sold for scrap did not reach the 1983 level, but it exceeded 20 million tons deadweight (dw), still a high figure.

Idle tonnage at the end of September totaled 65,890,000

tons dw, a distinct improvement over the 100 million tons dw of a year earlier. The actual number of ships in lay-up was 1,435, including 335 tankers totaling 50,140,000 tons dw, 16% of the world tanker tonnage. The average size of the 1,100 dry-cargo ships in lay-up was much smaller than the tankers; they totaled 15,750,000 tons dw, or 4% of the world dry-cargo tonnage. Among the major maritime nations, Denmark had the most ships in lay-up, representing 26% of its fleet, followed by France (20%), Greece (18%), Italy (16%), Liberia (15%), the U.K. (14%), and the U.S. (13%).

There was another small decline in the total tonnage of the world merchant fleet, from 422.6 million gross registered tons (grt) to 419 million grt. The largest national fleet was again that of Liberia, 62,050,000 grt, followed by Japan with 40,360,000 grt. The U.K. fleet recorded one of the greatest reductions, from 19,120,000 to 15,870,000 grt.

The world shipping recession significantly reduced the volume of traffic moving through the Panama Canal, and average daily transits dropped to around 30, compared with the usual 36–38. Traffic through the Suez Canal fell slightly as a result of the Gulf war. The level of throughput of cargo at the world's major ports reflected the slight upswing in the economies of the countries concerned. Handling facilities for bulk cargoes such as coal, iron ore, grain, and sugar were improved at several major ports including Hamburg, West Germany, Rotterdam, Neth., and Le Havre, France. The Chinese government passed a decree giving priority to port development. The first stage involved the upgrading of 50 deep-sea berths at 17 major ports, where a current annual capacity of 78 million metric tons would be increased by over 15%. (W. D. EWART)

FREIGHT AND PIPELINES

The limited improvement in the level of economic activity led to an increase in freight movement, although it was not sufficient to solve the problems of the industry entirely. Air freight grew in volume and variety, with 37 courier services in the U.K. alone and lifts of 130 metric tons between New York and Amsterdam. A herd of 164 cattle was carried in a single jumbo jet from Canada to Scotland.

The really heavy loads were carried by the railways. There was growth in the 8,000- to 12,000-metric-ton heavy-train sector, as well as increasing interest in the "megatrain" class as a way of increasing productivity. A 31,000-ton coal train formed of 375 cars and measuring 5.5 km in length operating between Chardzhou and Tashauz in the Turkmen S.S.R. probably set a record as the heaviest train ever. New freight railways opened in China between Beijing (Peking) and Qin-huang-dao (Ch'in-huang-tao), in Iraq between Baghdad and Basra, and in Canada at Tumbler Ridge, B.C.

Intermodal freight continued to grow faster than freight traffic generally. Over 10% of rail traffic in North America was made up of piggyback and container movements, and high growth rates in containerization were also reported in South America and the Indian subcontinent. Road haulage continued to rely on a growing proportion of heavy trucks. In the U.S. an interstate heavy-truck network was defined in an effort to overcome problems caused by interstate variations in permitted weights.

Pipeline construction rates were highest in the U.S., the U.S.S.R., Canada, and the Middle East. Oil and gas lines in the U.S. totaled 700,000 km and in the U.S.S.R., some 250,000 km. Major lines recently opened included a 1,500-km gas line connecting Dampier to Perth in Western Australia and a 2,500-km crude-oil line between Kholmogorskaya and Klin in the U.S.S.R. The relatively flat oil

This 1.1-metre pipe was readied to carry natural gas from the Soviet Union to West Germany. The scene is near Vilseck in the region of Oberpfalz, near Nuremburg, West Germany.
HORST SCHAFER—PHOTO TRENDS

and gas market, along with growing environmental concern, meant that a number of major projects were being critically reviewed.

ROADS AND TRAFFIC

The gasoline-powered automobile would reach its 100th year in 1985 and seemed set to survive well into the next century. There were over 350 million passenger cars on the world's roads, one for every 13 people, and annual production amounted to about 30 million units. Coping with this traffic put a growing strain on roads, and the necessity of maintaining and rebuilding existing roads, especially where traffic densities were high, was leading to some important innovations. In New York City pavements were being quickly and successfully repaired using glass-fibre webbing and bitumen, and in Washington, D.C., the Woodrow Wilson Memorial Bridge was completely redecked while remaining open to traffic.

Substantial road-building activity continued in most countries. A start was made on construction of China's first motorway (expressway), between Beijing and Tianjin (Tientsin), and in Hong Kong the first section of the spectacular Eastern Corridor highway was opened. The M-25 motorway around London was three-quarters complete, and the A86 ring road around Paris was half finished. The U.S. Interstate System now covered 66,000 km and was 96% complete. Major projects under way included a new route linking Venezuela and Ecuador across Colombia, a new road linking Bassein and Manywa in Burma, and upgrading of the north–south road in Pakistan.

Vehicle fuel economy continued to improve, with the U.S. car fleet produced in 1984 required by law to average 27 miles per gallon (about 9 litres per 100 km), compared with 14.2 mpg in 1973. Tests in Sweden showed that high-quality road surfacings could reduce fuel consumption by as much as one-third. In Brazil the market share of alcohol-fueled new cars reached 70%, while in Malaysia taxis, trucks, and tractors were run successfully on diesel fuel made from palm oil. With 200,000 people killed annually in traffic accidents, road safety was an important public issue. The wearing of seat belts by drivers and front-seat passengers was now compulsory in 35 countries. In the U.S., with by far the highest traffic death toll, the first mandatory-seat-belt law, in New York State, went into effect.

INTERCITY RAIL

Major railway development projects were reported in 43 countries, with 16,000 km of railway under construction and 15,000 km in the planning stage. The U.S.S.R. headed the list with 3,500 km under construction. The Baikal-to-Amur railway, one of the biggest railway projects of the century, was opened; completion of its 3,145 km involved the construction of 200 bridges. The Soviet railways now totaled 145,000 km of track and carried traffic amounting to 350,000,000,000 passenger-km and 3,700,-000,000,000 metric ton-km a year.

In France the travel time between Paris and Lyon was cut to two hours, and the new Train à Grande Vitesse (TGV) fast service westward from Paris—the TGV-Atlantique—was authorized at a cost of F 13 billion. In the U.S. travel time between New York City and Washington, D.C., was reduced to 2 hours 50 minutes, and the Metroliner reached maximum speeds of 190 km/h on the run from New York City to Boston. Major electrification projects recently completed included the lines from Angers to Le Mans (France), Pogromnoye to Pugachevsk (U.S.S.R.), and Koindong to Monpochin (North Korea). Over half of North Korea's railways were now electrified. With the completion of work on five trunk lines, 7,000 km out of China's 60,000-km network would be electrified by 1990. The first section of the Zimbabwe railways to be electrified was completed in 1984.

Interest in providing high-speed passenger services in heavily traveled corridors between 200 and 600 km long continued to mount, with eight corridors under study in the U.S. alone. A recent development in rail passenger services was the running of direct trains between major international airports and some of the remoter cities in their catchment areas. In England direct rail services operated between Gatwick Airport near London and Manchester some 300 km away, while in Switzerland Geneva was connected by direct services to several cities in eastern France.

URBAN MASS TRANSIT

The extension of metro (subway) networks continued, with approximately 15 km a month being added to the world's systems. New metro systems were under construction in some 20 cities, including Shanghai, Singapore, Pusan (South Korea), Medellín and Bogotá (Colombia), Lagos (Nigeria), Bangkok (Thailand), and Warsaw and Lodz (Poland). After 12 years in the building, the Calcutta (India) subway was opened. During the year the Kharkov (U.S.S.R.) metro was switched to automated train operation.

Interest in light urban railways and tramways continued to grow, and there were now over 300 systems operating worldwide, over half of them in Eastern-bloc countries. New systems were opened in Manila and Buffalo, N.Y., and work was proceeding on systems in Vancouver, B.C., Portland, Ore., the California cities of San Jose, Santa Clara, and Sacramento, Tunis, Hong Kong, Toronto, and in London's dock area. The magnetically supported and propelled (maglev) people-mover system at the Birmingham (England) International Airport/National Exhibition Centre went into service. At the world's longest maglev test track, in Emsland, West Germany, a test vehicle exceeded 200 km/h. Also in West Germany, a light monorail went into operation at Dortmund University, and in Japan the Kabura monorail in Kita-Kyushu was also operational. Railbus technology was expanding slowly. A British system was demonstrated in Malaysia, Thailand, Denmark, and Greece; a Japanese system was being built at Tarumi; and a Hungarian vehicle was under development for suburban and rural operation.

Diesel and petrol (gasoline) buses and electric trolley buses continued to dominate mass transit in most cities. There was innovation both through the use of microelectronics in controlling, maintaining, and planning conventional technology and in motive systems, with diesel/electric hybrids running in the U.S., the U.K., South Africa, and Japan.   (DAVID BAYLISS)

See also Energy; Engineering Projects; Environment; Industrial Review: *Aerospace; Automobiles.*

This article updates the *Macropædia* article TRANSPORTATION.

Magnetic repulsion levitates this experimental Japanese high-speed vehicle 0.4 inch above the track, and propulsion, by means of a linear motor system, moves it forward at extremely high speeds. It is silent and is intended for passenger service to and from Tokyo's International Airport at Narita.

World Affairs

The year 1984 was rung in on an ominous note—and for more than its literary associations. Not for a long time had there been so much tension between the superpowers. Some alarmist observers went further and invoked parallels with that other *annus horribilis,* 1914. Following the deployment of the first land-based cruise missiles in Western Europe at the end of 1983, the Soviet Union withdrew from arms-control talks. If someone had been nursing illusions about the possibility of improved relations with the U.S. administration (the late Soviet leader Yury Andropov stated), there was no longer room for such wishful thinking. The tenor of the Soviet media recalled the cold war. The boycott of the Olympic Games in Los Angeles was another manifestation of Soviet anger.

Such anger was understandable in view of the NATO decision to carry out, albeit with several years' delay, the decision to match the Soviet arms buildup in Europe. For many years the Soviet Union had invested a considerable percentage of its gross national product in a military buildup; it must have seemed intolerable to be deprived of the fruits of that investment. But Soviet anger was not directed only against U.S. Pres. Ronald Reagan and his advisers. It was equally directed against Western Europe, including some governments that had tried hard to meet Soviet concerns halfway. It was directed against China and Japan, which could hardly be held responsible for the deployment of Euromissiles. During the first half of 1984 the Soviet Union became committed to a policy of virtual self-isolation—a puzzle to friends and foes alike, for such a strategy certainly did not serve its best interests. Perhaps it was connected with the interregnum in Moscow. Andropov died on Feb. 9, 1984, and Konstantin Chernenko, his successor, lacked experience in foreign policy and was reported to be in indifferent health. A few hard-line speeches apart, he did not seem to take a very active part in the conduct of politics. Speculation about yet another succession was soon under way. If there had been a sense of lack of direction in the Kremlin since the Brezhnev period ended, such feelings became even stronger.

The mood in Moscow was in contrast to the new buoyancy felt in Washington. The major problems besetting U.S. foreign policy had by no means gone away: unrest in Central America continued; there were setbacks in the Middle East; and looming in the background was that major time bomb, the international debt problem and growing U.S. dependence on foreign investment. Yet, on the credit side, there was a new moderation in U.S. foreign policy—much in contrast to the rhetorical excesses of 1982–83— and a general feeling that America had at last overcome the Vietnam trauma, that its economic, political, and military position in the world had improved, that the country, in short, was itself again. This new self-confidence explained in large part the reelection of President Reagan in November.

America's optimism was not shared in equal measure by the countries of Western Europe. They could not show the same economic progress, and they had much less success in coping with unemployment. Furthermore, the inability to transform the European Community into an effective foreign policy factor narrowly circumscribed Europe's role on the world scene. Still, there was more stability in Europe than the pessimists had predicted only a few years earlier. Despite the economic and social tensions, antidemocratic forces made no substantial progress. The new rapprochement between West and East Germany was certainly an

World Affairs: Contents

For your convenience this article groups the countries of the world by the geopolitical regions to which they belong. Certain related topics, such as United Nations, Dependent States, and various regional affairs articles (*e.g.*, Middle Eastern Affairs), are also included. The complete list of these topics appears below in alphabetical order, each indicating the page where it may be found. Articles on the various countries update the *Macropædia* articles of the same name except where otherwise noted.

encouraging development, though the Soviet Union could be trusted to take care that this new entente should not become too cordial (Erich Honecker had to cancel his visit to Bonn). But the very fact that a conflict no longer existed in the centre of Europe, regarded until recently as the flashpoint in the East-West conflict—that, on the contrary, the two Germanys were actively striving for a minidétente—was a reassuring new factor in world politics.

Even the most sanguine optimists had not assumed that 1984 would see peace in the Middle East. No solutions were in sight to conflicts that had lasted for years, decades, or even generations. The war between Iraq and Iran continued, though on a more limited level than before. There was no fighting between Israel and its Arab neighbours, and the Palestine Liberation Organization did not recover from the blows it had suffered in Lebanon. Israel, with a new government of "national unity," indicated willingness to withdraw its troops from Lebanon. Egypt continued to mend fences with some of its neighbours, and Libya entered into a close alliance with Morocco. All things considered, 1984 was, by Middle Eastern standards, almost peaceful.

Developments in other parts of the globe showed conflicting trends. Democratization in Argentina and Brazil and the apparent willingness of the warring factions in El Salvador to put an end to the civil war were encouraging signs. The continued repression in Afghanistan, the internal and external tensions in India (of which the murder of Prime Minister Indira Gandhi was but one manifestation), Pakistan, Sri Lanka, and Bangladesh contained the seeds of dangerous conflagrations.

Measured by perfectionist standards, 1984 was an unsatisfactory year. Most of the conflicts and tensions persisted, and no progress was made on the road to a safer world. Yet absolute yardsticks are of little use in world affairs. Compared with the apocalyptic noises that had ushered in the year, 1984 proved to be relatively uneventful. If, during the first half of the year, Soviet spokesmen expressed their firm conviction that a dialogue with warmongers and revanchists was pointless, contacts between the two superpowers were, in fact, renewed during the second half, and so were Soviet talks with China and Japan. Prospects for limited strategic and political agreements appeared better at the end of the year than at its beginning. It was probably too early to speak about a thaw, but the political barometer had certainly risen by several points. The main problems confronting the West, the Soviet bloc, and the third world alike seemed to be economic rather than political in character. To put it differently, the political tensions, however dangerous, appeared to be controllable at least in the short term. There was no such certainty with regard to the economic difficulties, internally and among the nations.

(WALTER LAQUEUR)

This article updates the *Macropædia* article 20th-Century INTERNATIONAL RELATIONS.

UNITED NATIONS

Issuing his third successive pessimistic annual report on the UN's work, UN Secretary-General Javier Pérez de Cuéllar observed on Sept. 9, 1984, that the once "majestic vision" of the international organization had been "clouded by the differences of the major powers." Member states had made little progress toward disarming, controlling the arms race, or reducing the world's fears of nuclear confrontation and international violence. They had also sidestepped the UN in using force themselves and in acting independently. "Great-power tension" had harmed the UN, according to Pérez de Cuéllar; disputes between Security Council members had even made it impossible at times "to take any peacekeeping action at all," and these frustrations had led the general public to conclude erroneously that something was "wrong with the United Nations and with the concept of internationalism." The secretary-general's thesis was more than borne out by the year's events.

South Africa. The Security Council met January 4–5 to consider Angola's urgent complaint that South African forces were continuing an advance into Angolan territory that had begun on Dec. 23, 1983. South Africa insisted that it had no desire to control a "single centimetre" of Angola but it was determined to protect the people of South West Africa/Namibia from "terrorist attacks" launched by the South West Africa People's Organization (SWAPO) from Angola and with Angolan support. Despite South Africa's arguments, the Security Council, on January 6, strongly condemned the military action as a threat to international peace and security. With the U.S. and the U.K. abstaining, the Council voted to demand that South Africa halt all acts of aggression against Angola and withdraw unconditionally from its territory. It also said that South Africa should compensate Angola for damages. The secretary-general reported on January 10 that South Africa had rejected the resolution.

Later, South Africa agreed to a 30-day disengagement of its forces starting January 31, but basic problems remained unresolved. Both the U.S. and South Africa insisted, as a precondition for a settlement, that 30,000 Cuban troops supporting the Angolan government withdraw; Angola maintained that it needed Cuban help to protect itself against South Africa; and the UN majority argued that the presence of Cuban troops in Angola should not prevent South Africa from granting Namibia its independence. In November Angola proposed that UN forces gradually replace the Cubans over the next three years. South Africa wanted the Cubans to leave in 12 weeks.

During the year various UN organs pressed South Africa to abandon apartheid (racial separation). On August 17 the Security Council, by a vote of 13–0, condemned South Africa's new constitution, declaring it, and the elections planned in connection with it, null and void. The constitution created two new chambers in the country's Parliament, one for people of mixed race (Coloureds) and one for South Africans of Asian origin, but made no provision for the black majority.

On September 28 the General Assembly, by a vote of 133–0, also condemned the new constitution and it called on the Security Council to do what it could to avert the greater tensions in southern Africa that the new document might cause. The U.S. and the U.K. abstained in both the Council and Assembly votes, explaining that, although they opposed apartheid, they found some of the resolution's language unacceptable.

Famine. Besides being concerned with Africa's political problems, the UN was preoccupied with famine conditions there. On November 3 the Assembly unanimously approved a UN report stating that 150 million people were facing hunger and malnutrition in Chad, Ethiopia, Mozambique, and elsewhere. Delegates suggested that the root causes of Africa's economic and social ills lay in the international economic environment, a decline in commodity prices, increasing debt service payments, a lack of incentives for farmers and other producers, natural calamities, and structural problems in many African economies. On November 6 the secretary-general named Kurt Jansson (Finland), a retired UN official, as assistant secretary-general for emergency operations in Ethiopia, and in December he established an Office for Emergency Operations in

Africa to coordinate all organizations and agencies concerned with the famine problem.

Central America. The Security Council met on February 3 to hear a Nicaraguan complaint that "Somozist and mercenary counter-revolutionary forces trained and financed by the . . . United States" were increasingly subjecting it to acts of aggression. In early April the Council considered Nicaragua's complaints that the U.S. had mined its harbours and was otherwise escalating aggression against it, but on April 4 the U.S. vetoed a resolution calling for such actions to end immediately. The U.S. characterized the resolution as unbalanced because it expressed no concern for attacks that Nicaragua allegedly was mounting against neighbouring El Salvador, Honduras, and Costa Rica.

On April 6 the U.S. informed the UN that it was temporarily modifying its acceptance of the compulsory jurisdiction of the International Court of Justice and would not be a party to any case involving Central America for the next two years. Nonetheless, on April 9 Nicaragua complained to the court that the U.S. was using military force against it and intervening in its internal affairs. On November 26 the court voted 14–1—Judge Stephen M. Schwebel, an American, dissenting—to reject the U.S. contention that it did not have jurisdiction in the case, and it ruled 11–5 that the U.S. could not unilaterally alter the terms under which it had originally accepted the court's jurisdiction in 1945. It reaffirmed preliminary orders issued on May 10 asking the U.S. to refrain from taking any action against Nicaraguan ports and, in particular, not to lay mines there. (*See* LAW.)

Falkland Islands/Islas Malvinas. During its 1982 war with Argentina, the U.K. established an "exclusion zone" banning foreign ships and aircraft from approaching closer than 200 mi to the Falkland Islands/Islas Malvinas. On February 1 Pres. Raúl Alfonsín of Argentina asked the U.K. to lift its restrictions and agree to a UN role in peacekeeping on the islands. Britain rejected both requests, saying that no role existed for the UN in protecting the islands and that, although Britain did not intend to maintain the zone indefinitely, it would not be rushed into lifting it. In July the two countries started to talk in Bern, Switz., but the talks ended indecisively. On November 1 the General Assembly approved (89–9–54) a resolution asking Britain and Argentina to resume negotiations.

Afghanistan. In August the UN sponsored a week of indirect talks in Geneva between the Afghan and Pakistani governments on the political future of Afghanistan. On November 15 the General Assembly demanded (119–20–14) for the fifth successive year that the U.S.S.R. withdraw its estimated 100,000 troops from that country.

Korea. On March 7 the International Civil Aviation Organization (ICAO), by a secret vote of 20–2–9, condemned the Soviet Union for shooting down a Korean Air Lines jet on Sept. 1, 1983, killing all 269 people aboard. The report found no evidence to sustain the Soviet charge that the airliner was on an intelligence-gathering mission. On May 10 ICAO's 152 member states unanimously approved a new rule providing that governments may require civilian aircraft illegally flying in their airspace to land and may set "severe penalties" for such violations but may not use military force against them. This amendment to an existing treaty would have to be ratified by 102 members before it took effect.

North Korean troops and soldiers of the UN Command in Korea exchanged gunfire at the truce village of Panmunjom on November 24. Three North Korean soldiers and one South Korean were killed, and a U.S. soldier serving with the UN forces was wounded. The incident, the most serious to occur between the two Koreas in eight years, began when a Soviet tour guide defected across the Joint Security Area.

Arab-Israeli Relations. On January 17 the secretary-general pressed 42 leaders attending an Islamic summit conference in Casablanca, Morocco, to work toward an international conference on the Arab-Israeli conflict. King Hussein of Jordan echoed the suggestion on November 22, when he called on Palestinians to seek a UN conference to negotiate for the return of Israeli-occupied territories under the terms of Security Council Resolution 242 (1967). However, the Palestine Liberation Organization (PLO) only partially endorsed the king's suggestion and continued to ignore the resolution because it did not mention a Palestinian state and required Arab recognition of Israel.

The Israeli-occupied territories were the subject of letters to UN organs in January, when Arabs complained that the Israeli Knesset (parliament) was threatening to impose laws aimed at annexing the land and discriminating against the Palestinian people. In response, the Security Council on January 26 reminded all concerned that the Geneva Convention on the Protection of Civilians in Wartime applied to both the West Bank and the Gaza Strip and forbade fundamental changes in established legal regimes.

On April 2 Israel stated that 52 civilians had been wounded in an attack in Jerusalem and that a "PLO terrorist faction" had claimed responsibility. Israel reserved its right to seek out and severely punish those responsible "for these inhuman acts of wanton bloodshed." The secretary-general expressed shock at the news of the attack, which again highlighted the urgent need to resume the search for a just and lasting Middle East settlement.

Lebanon. In an effort to fill the vacuum being created as the members of the multinational force (Britain, France, Italy, and the U.S.) withdrew from Beirut, France asked the Security Council on February 15 to consider establishing a UN military presence in the Lebanese capital. The Security Council voted on the French resolution on February 29, but it was not adopted because of the Soviet Union's negative vote. The U.S.S.R. objected that the resolution failed to demand that "foreign [*i.e.,* U.S. and French] warships" withdraw from the Lebanese coast and did not bar artillery fire, aerial bombardment, or any other interference in Lebanese affairs.

Arabs complained to the Security Council on May 21 that on May 15 Israel used 1,500 troops at the Ein El-Hilweh refugee camp near Sidon (southern Lebanon) to demolish three houses and to cause death and destruction. Between August 29 and September 6, the Security Council met several times to discuss Israeli practices in southern Lebanon. The Lebanese accused Israel of "inhumane, fascist" policies, while the Israelis said they had to curb increasing attacks by Shi'ah guerrillas against Israeli forces and had for that reason restricted access from the rest of the country. Lebanon sponsored a resolution asking Israel to respect the rights of civilians in the region and to ease restrictions on the movement of people and goods. The U.S. vetoed it on September 6, however, calling it one-sided because it did not address problems in parts of Lebanon controlled by Palestinians and by Syrian troops.

Talks aimed at arranging for 12,000 Israeli troops to withdraw from Lebanese territory occupied in 1982 began on November 8 at the headquarters of the UN Interim Force in Lebanon (UNIFIL) in Naqura. After one session, however, Lebanon suspended them because Israel had detained four Shi'ahs it suspected of taking part in guerrilla operations. Talks resumed after UN mediation secured the

(continued on page 452)

UNESCO, 1984

BY PAUL SEABURY

At the end of 1984, the United States withdrew from membership in the United Nations Educational, Scientific and Cultural Organization. A few weeks earlier, Britain announced its intention to withdraw in late 1985. These moves climaxed a decade of growing concern among Western democracies over the combative political uses being made of the organization by the Soviet Union, its allies, and militant Arab and third world states. It also reflected concern over reports of internal mismanagement of UNESCO under its director general, Amadou-Mahtar M'Bow (*see* BIOGRAPHIES).

UNESCO's Changing Face. Formed in 1945, immediately after World War II, UNESCO in its early years revived League of Nations intellectual and scientific exchanges deemed to foster greater international cooperation and understanding. It was then composed chiefly of Western European nations, plus the United States and Canada. During the postwar Stalinist period, the Soviet Union and its satellites refused to participate—abstentions that accentuated the organization's democratic characteristics. The locating of UNESCO's headquarters in Paris reinforced the European character of the organization, though substantial U.S. contributions to personnel and budget also meant that UNESCO gained from strong, positive U.S. commitments to its educational and scientific resources. One early role of UNESCO was to foster projects aimed at cultural reconciliation between European nations, after generations of hatred and two catastrophic wars. But the organization's scientific and educational work soon spread across the globe, encompassing literacy programs, cross-cultural cooperation, the preservation and restoration of archaeological treasures, and collaborative scientific undertakings.

During the 1960s and 1970s, UNESCO's membership expanded drastically. The Soviet Union, its satellites, and other Communist-oriented states joined, but the expansion was accelerated chiefly by the admission of scores of recently decolonized nations of Asia, Africa, and the Caribbean. The founding states thus became a small minority of UNESCO's members, even as their financial contributions continued to account for the larger part of its resources. (The U.S. contribution in 1984, for instance, was 25% of the total budget.)

This new composition profoundly altered the ideological correlation of forces in UNESCO, as in other international organizations. Most of the new members, aside from the Soviet bloc, were underdeveloped; most also were either authoritarian or totalitarian in their internal political organization. Many were represented at UNESCO by intellectuals hostile to Western cultural values and resentful over legacies of what they regarded as Western imperialism. Nearly all of them regarded education, science, and culture as matters to be superintended by state planners.

Paul Seabury is professor of political science at the University of California at Berkeley. His books include The Rise and Decline of the Cold War *and* The Wilhelmstrasse.

Western Disenchantment. UNESCO's crisis comprised a complex admixture of political and administrative problems. In 1984, when the organization permitted staff members of the General Accounting Office (an arm of the U.S. Congress) to inspect its books, massive misallocations of funds and other abuses were discovered. In 1983 a poll of UNESCO staffers showed deep internal demoralization, as many experienced civil servants and competent scholars were supplanted by left-wing Africans, radical Arabs, and pro-Soviet third world personnel. When officers of the KGB (the Soviet state security organization) masked as UNESCO employees were expelled from France by the French government, they remained on the payroll "on extraordinary leave." (UNESCO projects in war-torn Afghanistan, it was found, were virtually controlled by Soviet officials and sympathizers.)

Internal administrative matters were not the chief cause of concern to Western member states, however. During the 1970s the organization was transformed into a sounding board for selective radical third world causes, including relentless attacks on such member states as Chile, Israel, and South Africa. Radical third world movements, even some "nonaligned" states, and the Soviet Union sought to use UNESCO as a means to endorse—and thus legitimate—state controls on the free flow of information and ideas. Western news media were attacked as agencies of imperialism, and attempts were made to establish universal standards for the licensing and control of journalists. In pursuit of a "new international economic order," many UNESCO member states sought to gain the organization's endorsement for state control of private-sector enterprises. Such projects aroused fears among Western observers that UNESCO had transgressed permissible limits of state control in free societies.

Work from Within or Walk Out? The U.S. announcement spurred debate among other Western governments and among private organizations in the West as to the organization's future. Had UNESCO become hopelessly politicized by this turn of events? Should the democracies choose to work for reform from within, or should they follow the U.S. lead in getting out? Could UNESCO's original basic principles be better served outside this flawed organization than within it? Would the withdrawal of the democracies mean abandoning the field to states hostile to Western values? Over and above such questions

AP/WIDE WORLD

Just as UNESCO was about to undergo an investigation spearheaded by the U.S. for alleged financial and administrative inefficiency, a highly suspicious fire heavily damaged its Paris headquarters.

lay the larger implications of this debate, for other universal-membership organizations, such as the General Assembly itself, were similarly flawed.

In late 1984 one West German observer, himself critical of UNESCO, wrote: "In a world rent by dissension there are not too many instruments of worldwide . . . cooperation to counteract what often appears to be unsolvable . . . conflicts. . . . If peace is to be more than a state of non-war, then cooperation . . . in science, education and the arts is vitally important." But this classic liberal argument begged the question as to whether UNESCO had itself become a theatre of conflict, simply mirroring the struggles going on outside its halls. Some reformers hoped that member states, fearful of crippling financial losses if Western contributions were withdrawn, might lay aside their ideological biases and agree once again to concentrate on programs that reflected true cultural cooperation, rather than on causes that accentuated global and regional conflicts. As 1984 ended, the outcome of the crisis remained in doubt.

UNESCO's Problems—Louder and Larger, But Not New

William Benton, publisher and chairman of Encyclopædia Britannica from 1943 until his death 30 years later, served as U.S. representative to the Executive Board of UNESCO under Presidents John Kennedy, Lyndon Johnson, and (briefly) Richard Nixon. He had been a member of the U.S. delegation to the London conference in 1945 that founded the organization and chairman of the U.S. delegation to its first general conference in Paris in 1946. He believed devoutly in its stated objectives, and his enthusiasm for the organization was so great as to be almost boosterish. Even so and even then, as only a handful of his associates knew, he was greatly disturbed at indications of usurpation by the director general of decision-making powers of the member states, the wasteful size and rigidity of the bureaucracy, and the readiness of the Secretariat to be a sounding board for Soviet propaganda. Following are excerpts, never before published, of some of his unclassified correspondence about the clay feet of the UN agency whose mission he loved. (EDITOR)

● Of the "clout" of the director general, then René Maheu, Amadou Mahtar M'Bow's predecessor: "A tough and cynical French intellectual. He has come up the hard way and fully appreciates the potential power of his position—which is considerable." (Benton to President Kennedy, Oct. 28, 1963)

● Of expressing displeasure at UNESCO's management: "If we want to indicate to Maheu that we are far from thrilled with his leadership, and deeply concerned about our relationships with him, one way to do so is to see that President Johnson pays no attention to him or to UNESCO when he comes to Paris. And then to make very clear to Maheu why this is so." (Benton to Robert H. B. Wade, U.S. permanent representative to UNESCO, March 12, 1965)

● Of the dangers of UNESCO's spreading itself too thin: "My point is that UNESCO can't do *everything*, or a little bit of everything. Its leaders should work out a list of priorities, and instead of allocating a small portion of the UNESCO budget to each of an infinite variety of activities, they should concentrate UNESCO funds and energies in the fields where UNESCO has the greatest chance of making its greatest impact— and soon." (Benton's September 1946 speech to the first meeting of the U.S. National Commission for UNESCO; quoted back to Benton by Wade, Dec. 23, 1965, as it had become evident to both that this sound recommendation had been ignored)

● Of wasted manpower in the UNESCO bureaucracy: "I asked him [Maheu] about Al Roseman's recommendation that there were fifty people on the UNESCO staff who are getting about $10,000 a year [about $40,000 in 1984 dollars], on the average, but who ought to be retired. (Al said that most of them were French.) Maheu agreed, but he said he could not do it. . . .

● Of the director general's ability to manipulate the votes he needs: "He [Maheu] knows how to get the votes at any time from unimportant people. The education ministers who are here, except from Africa, are insignificant. Maheu controls them. He can always control them. He likes to show off and demonstrate that he can pile up the 74 votes against the group which controls 85% of the budget. . . .

"But I have always suggested that it's no great trick to be a popular director general with the countries to which you are giving away money." (Benton to Richard Aherne, a foreign service officer, Nov. 9, 1964)

● Of Soviet propaganda: "What has struck me in the debate on the peaceful coexistence and colonialism and all the other Russian slogans in the period I have been serving on the Executive Board . . . is Maheu's supineness in the face of the Russian propaganda. He buys the developing countries with money. He buys the Soviets with rhetoric. The Soviets know that rhetoric is more important than the money. . . .

"The United States has constantly been on the defensive. We have had few offensive possibilities until last Friday morning's announcement of our decision to pledge nothing to the Special Fund at the meeting of the pledging committee. I told Mr. Maheu in May of 1963 that we had this as a weapon. He laughed at me and even scoffed at me at the idea that we would use it. I didn't think we would use it myself. . . ." (*Ibid.*)

● Of the shift of control from the member states to the director general: ". . . There is no doubt at all that in UNESCO . . . there has been a shift in the exercise of control away from the governing bodies and toward the Permanent Secretariat. . . . It is my judgment that budgets cannot continuously be set up without any regard whatsoever to the willingness of the contributors to put up the money." (Benton to Wade, Nov. 19, 1963)

● Of the director general and commitments: "Yes, Maheu does not stay bought. He does indeed 'wiggle out of commitments.'" (Benton to Wade, Sept. 27, 1966)

Maheu retired, then died, in 1973. He was succeeded by M'Bow, who took up where the "tough, cynical French intellectual" left off.

The International Court of Justice at The Hague voted unanimously on November 26 to accept Nicaragua's suit demanding a halt to U.S. support for military activities against Nicaragua's Sandinista government.
UPI/BETTMANN

(continued from page 449)
release of three of the men on November 14 and were expected to continue for months.

Iran-Iraq. At a press conference at UN headquarters on January 4, Iran's representative displayed samples of what he alleged was evidence of Iraq's having used chemical weapons against his country in the war that began in 1980. After spending six days in Iran, a team of UN specialists (Australian, Spanish, Swedish, and Swiss) reported on March 26 that they had found substantial evidence that "chemical weapons in the form of aerial bombs" containing mustard gas and nerve agents had been used in the areas they inspected. On March 30 the Security Council strongly condemned the use of chemical weapons and called on the belligerents to observe strictly the 1925 Geneva Protocol forbidding states to use poison gas and bacteriologic methods of warfare.

Other Developments. Citing the exchange of ambassadors on April 17 between the self-proclaimed Turkish Republic of North Cyprus and Turkey, the Security Council voted 13–1–1 on May 11 to condemn "secessionary actions" on Cyprus. UN officials attempted throughout the year to mediate the dispute between the government of Cyprus and the Turkish Cypriot community, while the UN Force in Cyprus continued to maintain the status quo.

Membership in the UN rose to 159 with the admission on September 18 of Brunei, a former British protectorate. By December 9, the deadline for states to sign the UN Convention on the Law of the Sea, the number of signatories was 159, and 14 states had ratified it.

At the end of the year the U.S. withdrew from UNESCO in accordance with the notice it had given on Dec. 28, 1983, when it alleged that UNESCO had unnecessarily politicized its work, was antagonistic toward free societies, and was unnecessarily expanding its budget. On November 22 the U.K. gave notice of withdrawal for similar reasons. Singapore followed suit in December but cited its "limited resources" as the reason. (*See* Special Report.)

(RICHARD N. SWIFT)
This article updates the *Macropædia* article UNITED NATIONS.

COMMONWEALTH OF NATIONS

The year 1984 proved a restless one for the Commonwealth in the aftermath of the conflict over the Falkland Islands/Islas Malvinas between the U.K. and Argentina in 1982, the invasion of Grenada in 1983, and the Nigerian coup on the last day of 1983. Brunei, a self-governing sultanate in treaty relationship with the U.K., achieved independence at midnight on Dec. 31, 1983, bringing the Commonwealth membership to a total of 49 countries. Brunei had participated in the Commonwealth under special arrangements since February 1981.

Many members of the Commonwealth suffered a common vulnerability, and this prompted the November 1983 Goa Declaration. It called for a collective security mechanism that would be able, without the need for neocolonialism or intervention, to deter aggression against small nations. A 14-member committee was set up in July to study the special needs of countries whose independence rested on common consent rather than self-defense—in particular those small island states where the development of offshore exclusive economic zones brought new wealth but also the danger of exploitation by larger neighbours.

Practical steps to achieve regional collaboration were indicated by the increased activity of U.K. forces in Nauru, Tuvalu, Tonga, and Vanuatu, small countries that would require rapid aid if attacked. New Zealand developed its rapid deployment force, intended both to assist after natural disasters and to act as a regional peace force for those islands that looked to New Zealand as leader of the Polynesian world. A regional Commonwealth heads of government meeting (CHOGM) took place in Papua New Guinea in August. The 18 countries present included the newest, Brunei, and special members Nauru, the Maldives, and Tuvalu, which did not attend the full biennial CHOGM. At the meeting Australia showed concern about deteriorating relations between Papua New Guinea and Indonesia over their shared land border.

At the same time, unrest within Commonwealth member countries was, if anything, on the increase. The Turkish-Cypriot unilateral declaration of independence in November 1983 had further divided Cyprus's Greek and Turkish communities. Sri Lanka's Tamil population stepped up agitation for a separate Tamil state following the riots between Tamils and Sinhalese in 1983. Canadian Indians called for increased self-determination for their lands, particularly in the Northwest Territories.

The Commonwealth took more than 13% of U.K. exports and accounted for over 30% of U.K. non-oil overseas investment, while 73% of the U.K.'s bilateral aid went to the Commonwealth. Public and private aid and development outflows from the U.K. to less developed countries during 1983 totaled £3,776 million. Private outflows totaled £2,581 million, including £55 million in voluntary aid. Of the £1,170 million worth of public aid, over £693 million was bilateral and £26 million went to the U.K. dependencies, which continued to exercise a priority claim. The largest proportion of aid went to the poorest countries, with the aim of developing indigenous skills and supporting renewable resources. India, Kenya, Tanzania, and Sri Lanka received the highest allocations. The Commonwealth Fund for Technical Cooperation (CFTC) increased its funding to £23 million in 1984–85, compared with £20 million in 1983–84. Out of a total investment of £755 million, the Commonwealth Development Corporation (CDC) initiated new projects worth £100 million in 1983 in such countries as Vanuatu, Zimbabwe, and Uganda. The CDC was involved in some 42 joint ventures with British companies.

(MOLLY MORTIMER)

Political Parties

The following table is a general world guide to political parties. All countries that were independent on Dec. 31, 1984, are included; there are a number for which no analysis of political activities can be given. Parties are included in most instances only if represented in parliaments (in the lower house in bicameral legislatures); the figures in the last column indicate the number of seats obtained in the last general election (figures in parentheses are those of the penultimate one). The date of the most recent election follows the name of the country.

The code letters in the affiliation column show the relative political positions of the parties within each country; there is, therefore, no entry in this column for single-party states. There are obvious difficulties involved in labeling parties within the political spectrum of a given country. The key chosen is as follows: F-fascist; ER-extreme right; R-right; CR-centre right; C-centre; L-non-Marxist left; SD-social democratic; S-socialist; EL-extreme left; and K-Communist.

The percentages in the column "Voting strength" indicate proportions of the valid votes cast for the respective parties, or the number of registered voters who went to the polls in single-party states.

Political Parties

Country and name of party	Affili-ation	Voting strength (%)	Parlia-mentary represen-tation
Afghanistan			
Pro-Soviet Government since April 27, 1978			
Albania (November 1982)			
Albanian Labour (Communist)	—	99.9	250 (250)
Algeria (March 1982)			
National Liberation Front	—	99.9	281 (261)
Angola (August 1980)			
Movimento Popular de Libertação de Angola (MPLA)	—		203
Antigua and Barbuda (April 1984)			
Antigua Labour Party	C	...	16 (13)
Progressive Labour Movement	L	...	0 (3)
Independents	—	...	1 (1)
Argentina (October 1983)			
Movimiento Justicialista Nacional (Peronist)	CR	40.0	111
Unión Cívica Radical	C	51.0	129
Partido Intransigente	L	2.3	3
Others	—	6.7	11
Australia (December 1984)			
National	R	...	21 (17)
Liberal	C	...	45 (33)
Labor	L	...	82 (75)
Austria (April 1983)			
Freiheitliche Partei Österreichs	R	5.0	12 (11)
Österreichische Volkspartei	C	43.2	81 (77)
Sozialistische Partei Österreichs	SD	47.8	90 (95)
Others	—	4.0	0 (0)
Bahamas, The (June 1982)			
Progressive Liberal Party	CR	53	32 (30)
Free National Movement	L	43	8 (2)
Others	—	...	3
Bahrain			
Emirate, no parties	—	—	—
Bangladesh			
On March 24, 1983, Gen. Hossain Ershad seized power from the civilian government	—	—	—
Barbados (June 1981)			
Democratic Labour	C	47.1	10 (7)
Barbados Labour	L	52.2	17 (17)
Belgium (November 1981)			
Vlaams Blok	ER	...	1 (1)
Volksunie	R	...	20 (14)
Front Démocratique Francophone/ Rassemblement Wallon	R	...	8 (15)
Parti Libéral {Flemish	CR	...	28 (22)
{Wallon	CR	...	24 (15)
Parti Social-Chrétien {Flemish	C	...	43 (57)
{Wallon	C	...	18 (25)
Parti Socialiste Belge {Flemish	SD	...	26 (26)
{Wallon	SD	...	35 (32)
Parti Communiste	K	...	2 (4)
Others	—	...	7 (1)
Belize (December 1984)			
United Democratic Party	R	...	21 (5)
People's United Party	C	...	7 (13)
Benin (November 1979)			
People's Revolutionary Party	—	—	336
Bhutan			
A monarchy without parties	—	—	—
Bolivia (June 1980)			
Movimiento Nacionalista Revolucionario	R	20.1	44 (43)
Unidad Democrática y Popular	C	38.7	57 (37)
Acción Democrática Nacionalista	L	15.0	...

Country and name of party	Affili-ation	Voting strength (%)	Parlia-mentary represen-tation
Five other parties	—		
Botswana (September 1984)			
Botswana Democratic Party	C	...	29 (29)
Botswana People's Party	L	...	1 (1)
Botswana National Front	EL	...	4 (2)
Brazil (November 1982)			
Movimento Democrático Brasileiro	CR	44.1	200
Partido Democrático Social	C	39.4	234
Partido Trabalhista Democrático	S	6.7	24
Partido Trabalhista Brasileiro	S	5.5	13
Partido dos Trabalhadores	EL	4.3	8
Brunei			
Legislative Council	—		33
Bulgaria (June 1981)			
Fatherland Front			
Bulgarian Communist Party }			271
Bulgarian Agrarian Union }	—	99.9	99 400 (400)
No party affiliation }			30
Burkina Faso			
National Revolutionary Council since August 1983	—	—	—
Burma (October 1981)			
Burma Socialist Program Party	—	99.0	464 (464)
Burundi (October 1974)			
Tutsi ethnic minority government	—	—	—
Cameroon (May 1983)			
Cameroonian National Union	—	99.3	120 (120)
Canada (September 1984)			
Progressive Conservative	CR	50.0	211 (103)
Liberal	C	28.0	40 (147)
New Democratic	L	19.0	30 (32)
Others	—	...	1 (0)
Cape Verde (December 1980)			
African Party for the Independence of Guinea-Bissau and Cape Verde	—	93.0	
Central African Republic			
Military Committee of National Recovery took power on Sept. 1, 1981	—	—	—
Chad			
Military government since 1975	—	—	—
Chile			
Military junta since Sept. 11, 1973	—	—	—
China, People's Republic of (February 1978)			
Communist (Kungchantang) National People's Congress	—	...	3,500
Colombia (March 1982)			
Partido Conservador	R	...	84 (86)
Partido Liberal	C	...	114 (109)
Unión Nacional de Oposición	L	...	1 (4)
Comoros (March 1982)			
Federal Assembly	—		38
Congo (July 1979)			
Parti Congolais du Travail	—		115
Costa Rica (February 1982)			
Partido de Liberación Nacional	R	55	33 (25)
Partido Cristiano Democrático	C	30	18 (27)
Three left-wing parties	L	15	6 (5)
Cuba (December 1981)			
Partido Comunista Cubano	—	99.0	499 (481)
Cyprus			
Greek Zone: (May 1981):			
Democratic Rally	R	31.89	12

Country and name of party	Affili-ation	Voting strength (%)	Parlia-mentary represen-tation
Democratic Party	CR	19.50	8
Socialist Party (EDEK)	S	8.17	3
Communist Party (AKEL)	K	32.79	12
Turkish Zone (June 1981):			
National Unity Party	—	42.6	18 (30)
Socialist Salvation Party	—	28.6	13 (6)
Republican Turkish Party	—	15.1	6 (2)
Democratic People's Party	—	8.1	2 (0)
Turkish Union Party	—	5.5	1 (0)
Czechoslovakia (June 1981)			
National Front	—	99.5	200 (200)
Denmark (January 1984)			
Conservative	R	23.4	42 (26)
Liberal Democratic (Venstre)	CR	12.1	22 (21)
Christian People's	CR	2.7	5 (4)
Progress	C	3.6	6 (16)
Radical Liberal (Radikale Venstre)	C	5.5	10 (9)
Centre Democrats	C	4.6	8 (15)
Social Democrats	SD	31.6	56 (59)
Socialist People's	EL	11.5	21 (20)
Left Socialists	EL	2.7	5 (5)
Others	—	...	0 (0)
Faeroe Islands and Greenland	—		4 (4)
Djibouti (May 1982)			
One-party state: National Assembly	—		65
Dominica (July 1980)			
Freedom Party	C	...	17 (3)
Labour Party	L	...	2 (16)
Independents	—	...	2 (2)
Dominican Republic (May 1982)			
Partido Reformista	R	37.0	... (42)
Partido Revolucionario	L	48.4	... (49)
Others	—		
Ecuador (January 1984)			
Popular Democracy	R		4
Democratic Party	CR		5
National Reconstruction Front			
{ Social Christian Party			9 }
{ Radical Liberal Party			4 }
{ Conservative Party	CR	...	2 } 16
{ National Revolutionary Party			1 }
{ Others			0 }
Concentration of Popular Forces	C		7
Democratic Left (Izquierda Democrática)	L		25
Democratic Popular Movement	EL		3
Left Broad Front	EL		2
Others	—		9
Egypt (May 1984)			
New Wafd Party	R	15.12	57
National Democratic Party	CR	72.99	391
Socialist Labour Party	L	7.07	0
National Progressive Unionist Party	L	4.17	0
Others	—		0
El Salvador (March 1982)			
Alianza Republicana Nacionalista	R	29	19
Partido de Conciliación Nacional	CR	13	14
Partido Acción Democrática	C	18	3
Partido Cristiano Democrático	C	40	24
Equatorial Guinea (August 1983)			
National Assembly	—	...	41
Ethiopia			
Military government since 1974	—	—	—
Fiji (July 1982)			
Alliance Party (mainly Fijian)	—	...	28 (36)
National Federation (mainly Indian)	—	...	22 (15)
Others	—	...	2 (1)
Finland (March 1983)			
National Coalition Party (Conservative)	R	22.1	44 (47)

Political Parties

Country and name of party	Affiliation	Voting strength (%)	Parliamentary representation
Swedish People's Centre (including former Liberal) Party	R	4.6	11 (10)
Christian League	C	17.6	38 (40)
Rural Party	C	3.0	3 (9)
Social Democratic	C	9.7	17 (7)
People's Democratic League (Communist)	SD	26.7	57 (52)
Green Party	K	14.0	27 (35)
Others	—	1.5	2 —
	—	...	1 (0)
France (June 1981)			
Centre-Right:			
Gaullists (Rassemblement pour la République)	R	...	83 (148)
Giscardians (Union pour la Démocratie Française)	CR	...	64 (137)
Other	—	...	11 (6)
Union of Left:			
Parti Radical	L	...	14 (10)
Parti Socialiste	SD	...	269 (103)
Parti Communiste	K	...	44 (86)
Others	—	...	6 (1)
Gabon (February 1973)			
Parti Démocratique Gabonais	—	...	70
Gambia, The (April 1982)			
People's Progressive Party	C	61.7	27 (28)
Three other parties	—	...	8 (7)
German Democratic Republic (June 1981)			
National Front (Sozialistische Einheitspartei and others)	—	99.2	500 (500)
Germany, Federal Republic of (March 1983)			
Christlich-Demokratische Union	} R	38.2	{ 191 (174)
Christlich-Soziale Union		10.6	{ 53 (52)
Freie Demokratische Partei	C	6.9	34 (53)
Sozialdemokratische Partei Deutschlands	SD	38.2	193 (218)
The Green (Ecology) Party	—	5.6	27 (0)
Others	—	0.4	0 (0)
Ghana			
Military dictatorship since Dec. 31, 1981	—	—	—
Greece (October 1981)			
Progressive Party	R	1.7	0 (5)
New Democracy Party	CR	35.9	115 (172)
Panhellenic Socialist Movement (Pasok)	SD	48.1	172 (93)
Greek Communist Party	K	10.9	13 (11)
Others	—	2.3	0 (19)
Grenada (December 1984)			
New National Party	C	...	14
Grenada United Labour Party	R	...	1
Others	—	...	0
Guatemala (July 1984)			
National Liberation Movement	R	13.2	21
Revolutionary Party	CR	7.2	10
Christian Democrats	C	17.2	22
National Union of the Centre	C	14.5	22
Five other parties	—	...	13
Guinea			
Military Committee for National Redress in power since April 1984	—	—	—
Guinea-Bissau			
Governed by the Council of the Revolution since Nov. 14, 1980	—	—	—
Guyana (December 1980)			
People's National Congress	—	...	(37)
People's Progressive Party	—	...	(14)
Others	—	...	(2)
Haiti (February 1984)			
Conseil National d'Action Jean-Claudiste	—	...	59
Honduras (November 1981)			
Partido Nacional	R	42.0	34 (33)
Partido Liberal	CR	54.0	44 (35)
Partido de Innovación y Unidad	C	2.5	3 (3)
Partido Demócrata Cristiano	C	1.5	1 (0)
Hungary (June 1980)			
Patriotic People's Front	—	97.6	352 (352)
Iceland			
Independence (Conservative)	R	38.7	23 (21)
Progressive (Farmers' Party)	C	19.0	14 (17)
Social Democratic	SD	11.7	6 (10)
Social Democratic Alliance	EL	7.3	4 —
People's Alliance	K	17.3	10 (11)
Feminists	—	5.5	3 —
India (December 1984, figures incomplete			
Congress (I)	C	...	395 (351)
Communist Party of India (Marxist)	K	...	22 (35)
Communist Party (pro-Soviet)	K	...	6 (10)

Country and name of party	Affiliation	Voting strength (%)	Parliamentary representation
Other opposition parties and independents	—	...	121
Indonesia (May 1982)			
Golkar (Functional Groups)	—	64.3	342
United Development Party	—	27.8	94
Indonesian Democratic Party (merger of five nationalist and Christian parties)	—	7.9	24
Iran (May 1984)			
Islamic Republican Party	R	...	251
Iraq			
Military and B'ath Party governments since 1958	—	...	...
Ireland (November 1982)			
Fianna Fail (Sons of Destiny)	C	...	75 (81)
Fine Gael (United Ireland)	C	...	70 (63)
Irish Labour Party	L	...	16 (15)
Others	—	...	5 (7)
Israel (July 1984)			
Tehiya	ER	4.0	5 (3)
Kach	ER	1.2	1 —
Likud { Herut / Liberal	R	31.9	41 (48)
National Religious	CR	3.5	4 (6)
Agudat Israel	C	1.7	2 (4)
Yahad	C	2.2	3 —
Ometz	C	1.2	1 —
Labour Alignment { Labour / Mapam	SD	34.9	44 (47)
Civil Rights	SD	2.4	3 (1)
Shinui	SD	2.6	3 (2)
Progressive List for Peace	EL	1.8	2 —
Hadash	K	3.4	4 (4)
Others	—	...	7 (5)
Italy (June 1983)			
Movimento Sociale Italiano	F	6.8	42 (30)
Partito Liberale Italiano	CR	2.9	16 (9)
Democrazia Cristiana	C	32.9	225 (262)
Partito Repubblicano Italiano	C	5.1	29 (16)
Partito Social-Democratico Italiano	L	4.1	23 (20)
Partito Socialista Italiano	SD	11.4	73 (62)
Partito Radicale	EL	2.2	11 (18)
Partito Comunista Italiano	K	29.2	198 (201)
Südtiroler Volkspartei	—	0.5	3 (4)
Others	—	4.2	10 (8)
Ivory Coast (October 1980)			
Parti Démocratique de la Côte d'Ivoire	—	99.9	100
Jamaica (December 1983)			
Jamaica Labour Party	L	...	60 (51)
People's National Party	SD	(Boycotted)	(9)
Japan (December 1983)			
Liberal-Democratic	R	...	250 (284)
Komeito (Clean Government)	CR	...	58 (33)
Democratic-Socialist	SD	...	38 (32)
Socialist	S	...	112 (107)
Communist	K	...	26 (29)
Others	—	...	27 (26)
Jordan			
Royal government, no parties	—	—	60
Kampuchea (May 1981)			
Kampuchean United Front for National Salvation (Vietnamese-backed)	—	99.0	117
Kenya (September 1983)			
Kenya African National Union	—	48.0	158
Kiribati (January 1983)			
House of Assembly, no formal parties	—	...	35
Korea, North (February 1982)			
Korean Workers' (Communist) Party	—	100.0	615 (579)
Korea, South (March 1981)			
Korean National	CR	...	25
Democratic Justice	C	...	151
Democratic Korea	L	...	81
Democratic Socialist	S	...	2
Others	—	...	17
Kuwait (February 1981)			
Princely government with elected Parliament, no parties	—	—	30
Laos, People's Democratic Republic of			
Lao People's Revolutionary Party	—	...	...
Lebanon (April 1972)			
Maronites (Roman Catholics)	—	...	30
Sunni Muslims	—	...	20
Shi'ah Muslims	—	...	19
Greek Orthodox	—	...	11
Druzes (Muslim sect)	—	...	6
Melchites (Greek Catholics)	—	...	6
Armenian Orthodox	—	...	4
Other Christian	—	...	2
Armenian Catholics	—	...	1

Country and name of party	Affiliation	Voting strength (%)	Parliamentary representation
Lesotho			
Constitution suspended Jan. 30, 1970	—	—	—
Liberia			
People's Redemption Council since April 1980	—	—	—
Libya			
Military government since Sept. 1, 1969	—	—	—
Liechtenstein (February 1982)			
Vaterländische Union	CR	53.5	8 (8)
Fortschrittliche Bürgerpartei	C	46.5	7 (7)
Luxembourg (June 1984)			
Parti Chrétien Social	CR	...	25 (24)
Parti Libéral	C	...	14 (15)
Parti Ouvrier Socialiste	SD	...	21 (14)
Parti Communiste	K	...	2 (2)
Ecologists	—	...	2 (0)
Others	—	...	0 (4)
Madagascar (August 1983)			
Advance Guard of the Malagasy Revolution (Arema)	C	64.8	117 (112)
Madagascar Independence Congress	L	8.8	9 (16)
Movement for Proletarian Power	L	11.1	3 —
People's Party for National Unity	L	10.6	6 (7)
Madagascar National Independence Movement (Monima)	L	3.7	2 —
Malawi (June 1983)			
Malawi Congress Party	—	...	101 (87)
Malaysia (April 1982)			
National Front (Barisan Nasional)			
United Malays National Organization		70 }	
Malaysian Chinese Association		24	
Malaysian Indian Congress		4 } 133 (131)	
Gerakan		5	
Sabah and Sarawak		30 }	
Opposition Parties			
Democratic Action Party		9 }	
Partai Islam Malaysia		5 } 21 (23)	
Independents		7 }	
Maldives (February 1975)			
Presidential rule since 1975	—	—	—
Mali			
Military government since Nov. 19, 1968	—	—	—
Malta (December 1981)			
Nationalist Party	R	...	31 (31)
Labour Party	SD	...	34 (34)
Mauritania			
Military government since April 25, 1981	—	—	—
Mauritius (August 1983)			
Independence (Labour) Party	}		(2)
Parti Mauricien Social-Démocrate	} C	... } 41	(2)
Mouvement Socialiste Mauricien	}		—
Mouvement Militant Mauricien	L	...	19 (42)
Parti Socialiste Mauricien	—	—	— (18)
Organisation du Peuple Rodriguais	—	...	2 (2)
Mexico (July 1982)			
Partido Revolucionario Institucional	CR	...	296 (296)
Partido Demócrata Mexicano	CR	... }	
Partido Acción Nacional	C	... }	
Partido Auténtico de la Revolución		}	
Partido Socialista de los Trabajadores	L	} 104 (104)	
Partido Popular Socialista	S	}	
Partido Comunista Mexicano	K	... }	
Monaco (January 1978)			
Union Nationale et Démocratique	—	...	18 (17)
Mongolia (June 1981)			
Mongolian People's Revolutionary Party	—	99.9	354 (354)
Morocco (September 1984)			
Union Constitutionelle	CR	...	83 —
Rassemblement National des Indépendants	CR	...	61 (141)
Mouvement Populaire	CR	...	47 (44)
Istiqlal (Independence)	C	...	41 (49)
Union Socialiste des Forces Populaires	L	...	36 (16)
Others	—	...	38 (14)
Mozambique (December 1977)			
Frente da Libertação do Moçambique (Frelimo)	—	...	210
Nauru (December 1983)			
Independents	—	...	18
Nepal (May 1981)			
140-member Parliament, 122 elected and 28 appointed by the king; no parties	—	—	—
Netherlands, The (September 1982)			
Christian Democratic Appeal	CR	29.3	45 (48)

Political Parties

Country and name of party	Affiliation	Voting strength (%)	Parliamentary representation
Liberals (VVD)	C	23.0	36 (26)
Democrats 1966	C	4.3	6 (17)
Labour (PVDA)	SD	30.4	47 (44)
Others	—	13.0	16 (15)
New Zealand (July 1984)			
New Zealand Party	CR	12.0	0 —
National (Conservative)	CR	36.0	37 (47)
Social Credit	C	8.0	2 (2)
Labour Party	L	43.0	56 (43)
Others	—		0 (0)
Nicaragua (November 1984)			
Democratic Conservative Party	CR	14.0	14
Independent Liberal Party	C	9.6	9
Popular Social Christian Party	L	5.6	6
Sandinista National Liberation Front	L	66.8	61
Socialist Party of Nicaragua	EL	1.4	2
Communist Party of Nicaragua	K	1.5	2
Marxist-Leninist Popular Action Movement	K	1.0	2
Niger			
Military government since April 1974	—		—
Nigeria			
Military government since December 1983	—		—
Norway (September 1981)			
Høyre (Conservative)	R	...	54 (41)
Kristelig Folkeparti	CR	...	15 (22)
Senterpartiet (Agrarian)	C	...	10 (12)
Venstre (Liberal)	C	...	2 (2)
Party of Progress	C	...	4 (0)
Arbeiderpartiet (Labour)	SD	...	66 (76)
Sosialistisk Venstreparti (Socialist Left)	S	...	4 (2)
Oman			
Independent sultanate, no parties	—		—
Pakistan			
Military government since July 5, 1977	—		—
Panama			
Since July 1982 a civilian president under "indirect" military supervision	—	—	—
Papua New Guinea (June 1982)			
Pangu Party	—	34	50 (39)
United Party	—	7.2	9 (38)
People's Progress Party	—	10	14 (18)
National Party	—	10	13 (3)
Independents	—	20.9	4
Paraguay (February 1983)			
Partido Colorado (A. Stroessner)	R	90.0	40
Opposition parties	—	10.0	20
Peru (May 1980)			
Acción Popular			98
Alianza Popular Revolucionaria Americana	—		58
Popular Christian Party	—	...	10
Philippines			
Martial law lifted Jan. 17, 1981	—		—
Poland (March 1980)			
Front of National Unity			
Communists		261	
Peasants	} —99.0	113	460 (460)
Democrats		37	
Non-party		49	
Portugal (April 1983)			
Democratic and Social Centre	R	12.4	30 (46)
Social Democratic Party	CR	27.0	75 (82)
Socialist Party	SD	36.3	101 (66)
United People's Alliance	K	18.2	44 (41)
Qatar			
Independent emirate, no parties	—		—
Romania (March 1980)			
Social Democracy and Unity Front	—	98.5	369 (349)
Rwanda (December 1983)			
National Revolutionary Development Movement	—	...	70
Saint Christopher and Nevis (June 1984)			
People's Action Movement	CR	...	6 (3)
Nevis Reformation Party	CR	...	3 (2)
Labour Party	L	...	2 (4)
Saint Lucia (May 1982)			
United Workers' Party	C	...	14 (5)
St. Lucia Labour Party	S	...	2 (12)
Progressive Labour Party	EL	...	1 (0)
Saint Vincent and the Grenadines (July 1984)			
St. Vincent Labour Party	CR	41.4	4 (11)
New Democratic Party	C	51.4	9 (2)
United People's Movement	L	3.2	0 (0)
Others	—		0 (0)

Country and name of party	Affiliation	Voting strength (%)	Parliamentary representation
San Marino (May 1983)			
Communist coalition			
Partito Comunista			15 (16)
Partito Social Democratico		...	9 (9)
Partito Socialista Unitario			8 (8)
Christian Democrats		...	26 (26)
São Tomé and Príncipe (1975)			
Movimento Libertação	—	—	—
Saudi Arabia			
Royal government, no parties	—		—
Senegal (February 1983)			
Parti Socialiste	CR	79.9	111 (83)
Parti Démocratique Sénégalais	L	14.0	8 (17)
Rassemblement National Démocratique	EL	2.6	1 —
Ligue Démocratique	K	1.1	0 —
Seychelles (August 1983)			
People's Progressive Front	—	59.3	23
Sierra Leone (June 1978)			
All People's Congress	CR	...	85 (70)
Singapore (December 1984)			
People's Action Party	CR	64.38	77 (75)
Workers' Party	L	12.79	1 (0)
Democratic Party	—	3.7	1 (0)
Solomon Islands (October 1984)			
National Democratic Party	L		1
United Party	—		13
People's Alliance Party	—		12
Solomone Ano Sagufenua	—	...	4
Independents	—		7
Somalia (December 1984)			
Somalian Revolutionary Socialist Party	—	99.86	171 (171)
South Africa (April 1981)			
Herstigte Nasionale Partij	ER	13.8	0 (0)
National Conservative Party	R	...	0 —
National Party	R	56.1	131 (134)
South Africa Party	CR	—	(3)
New Republic Party	C	7.7	8 (10)
Progressive Federal Party	L	19.1	26 (17)
Spain (October 1982)			
Alianza Popular	R	25.35	105 (9)
Unión Centro-Democrático	C	7.26	11 (168)
Partido Socialista Obrero Español	SD	46.07	201 (121)
Partido Comunista Español	K	3.87	5 (23)
Catalan nationalists	—	3.73	12 (8)
Basque nationalists	—	1.91	8 (7)
Herri Batasuna (Basque radicals)	—	0.97	2 (3)
Others	—		6 (14)
Sri Lanka (July 1977)			
United National Party	R	...	140 (19)
Freedom Party	C	...	8 (91)
Tamil United Liberation Front	C	...	18 (12)
Communists and others	—	...	2 (44)
Sudan (December 1981)			
Sudanese Social Union	—	...	151
Suriname			
National Military Council since 1980	—		—
Swaziland			
Royal government, no parties	—		—
Sweden (September 1982)			
Conservative	R	23.6	86 (73)
Centre	CR	15.6	56 (64)
Liberal	C	5.9	21 (38)
Social Democrats	SD	45.9	166 (154)
Communists	K	5.5	20 (20)
Switzerland (October 1983)			
Christian Democrats (Conservative)	R	...	42 (44)
Republican Movement	R	...	0 (1)
National Campaign	R	...	5 (2)
Evangelical People's	R	...	3 (3)
Swiss People's (ex-Middle Class)	CR	...	23 (23)
Radical Democrats	C	...	54 (51)
League of Independents	C	...	8 (8)
Liberal Democrats	L	...	8 (8)
Social Democrats	SD	...	47 (51)
Progressive Organization (Socialists)	EL	...	3 (3)
Communist Party	K	...	1 (3)
Environmentalist Party	—	...	3 (3)
Others	—	...	3 (3)
Syria (November 1981)			
National Progressive Front	—	...	195 (159)
Others	—	...	0 (36)
Taiwan (Republic of China)			
Nationalist (Kuomintang)	—	...	773
Tanzania (October 1980)			
Tanganyika African National Union	C	...	111 (218)
Zanzibar Afro-Shirazi (nominated)	L	...	40 (52)
Thailand (April 1983)			

Country and name of party	Affiliation	Voting strength (%)	Parliamentary representation
Prachakorn Thai	ER	...	36
Chart Thai (Thai Nation)	R	...	73
Social Action Party	C	...	92
Democratic Party	C	...	56
Siam Democratic Party		...	18
National Democratic Party		...	15
Independents	—		24
Four other parties	—		10
Togo (December 1979)			
Rassemblement du Peuple Togolais	—	96.0	67
Tonga (May 1981)			
Legislative Assembly (partially elected)	—		21
Trinidad and Tobago (November 1981)			
People's National Movement	C	...	26 (24)
Organization for National Reconstruction	—		0 —
National Alliance:			
United Labour Front	L	...	8 (10)
Democratic Action Congress	EL	...	2 (2)
Tunisia (November 1981)			
National Front (led by the Parti Socialiste Destourien)	—	94.6	136 (121)
Turkey (November 1983)			
Nationalist Democracy Party	R	23.0	71
Motherland Party	CR	45.0	212
Populist Party	C	30.0	117
Tuvalu (September 1981)			
No political parties	—		...
Uganda (December 1980)			
Uganda People's Congress Party	—		68
Democratic Party	—		48
Union of Soviet Socialist Republic (November 1984)			
Communist Party of the Soviet Union	—	99.99	1,500 (1,500)
United Arab Emirates			
Federal government of seven emirates	—		—
United Kingdom (June 1983)			
Conservative	R	42.4	397 (339)
Alliance			
Liberal	C	} 25.4	17 (11)
Social Democratic	C		6 —
Labour	L	27.6	209 (268)
Communist	K		0 (0)
Scottish National Party		1.1	2 (2)
Plaid Cymru (Welsh Nationalists)	—	0.4	2 (2)
Ulster Unionists (three groups)	—	...	15 (10)
Social Democratic and Labour Party	—	...	1 (1)
Sinn Fein (Northern Ireland)	—		1 —
United States (November 1984)			
Republican	CR	...	183 (166)
Democratic	C	...	252 (267)
Uruguay (November 1984)			
Colorado Party (Conservative)	R	38.6	40
Unión Cívica	CR	2.3	2
National (Blanco) Party	C	32.9	36
Frento Amplio (Broad Front)	L	20.4	
Vanuatu (New Hebrides) (Nov. 1983)			
Vanuaaku Pati	C	...	24 (26)
Others	—	...	15 (13)
Venezuela (December 1983)			
COPEI (Social Christians)	CR	28.31	... (88)
Acción Democrática	L	44.25	118 (88)
Movimiento al Socialismo	SD	...	(11)
Partido Comunista Venezolano	K	...	(7)
Others	—	...	(7)
Vietnam, Socialist Republic of (April 1981)			
Communist Party	—	...	...
Yemen, People's Democratic Republic of			
National Liberation Front	—	—	—
Yemen Arab Republic			
Military government since 1974	—		—
Yugoslavia (May 1982)			
Communist-controlled Federal Chamber	—		220 (220)
Zaire (October 1977)			
Legislative Council of the Mouvement Populaire de la Révolution	—	...	268
Zambia (October 1983)			
United National Independence Party	—	67.0	125
Zimbabwe (February–March 1980)			
Zimbabwe African National Union	—	63.0	57 —
Zimbabwe African People's Union	—	24.0	20
United African National Council	—	8.0	9
Rhodesian Front (Europeans)	—		20

(K. M. SMOGORZEWSKI)

Africa South of the Sahara

AFRICAN AFFAIRS

Africa's worst drought in history, affecting 44% of the entire continent, entered its fourth year in 1984; it compounded the effects of the troubled world economic situation and the policy failures suffered by many African governments. Consequently, the continent's preoccupation was with economic problems even more than security. Nevertheless, security concerns remained acute in a number of countries and threatened regional stability in southern Africa and the Horn of Africa. Recognition of these dangers, together with the impact of the economic crises, led to a number of surprising and possibly significant treaties being concluded.

Organization of African Unity. Shaken by the internal crises of 1982 and 1983, the Organization of African Unity (OAU) was in no shape to undertake any new initiatives under the chairmanship of Ethiopia's Lieut. Col. Mengistu Haile Mariam. Crippled by financial difficulties, it grappled without success in trying to resolve the three most serious conflicts involving its own members—the conflict over the Western Sahara, which pitted Morocco against Algeria, Mauritania, and a majority of the remainder of OAU members; the civil war in Chad, which found Libya lined up against virtually all of Chad's neighbours, who supported France's military intervention on the side of Pres. Hissen Habré; and the conflicts in southern Africa over South West Africa/Namibia's independence and the challenge by armed liberation movements to the South African regime.

The OAU was scheduled to hold its 20th annual summit in Conakry, Guinea, in midyear, but following the military takeover there the meeting was delayed until mid-November and was held instead at the OAU headquarters in Addis Ababa, Eth. By then the problems in both Chad and the Western Sahara had apparently eased, not because of OAU initiatives but because of a sudden change of political direction by Col. Muammar al-Qaddafi of Libya. He reached an agreement with France for the withdrawal of both Libyan and French troops from Chad (which the French honoured though the Libyans did not) and, by making peace with his long-standing adversary King Hassan II of Morocco, he helped to ease the conflict over the Western Sahara, since Libya had been a prominent supporter of the Saharan Arab Democratic Republic (SADR), Western Sahara's government-in-exile. However, the OAU pressed for a referendum on self-determination among the Saharans. Then, when the SADR occupied its seat for the first time at the November summit, Morocco left the OAU in protest, becoming the first country to do so. Zaire was the only country to withdraw its delegation in support of Morocco. Tanzania's Pres. Julius Nyerere was reelected OAU chairman for 1984–85.

Southern Africa. Two surprising developments held out the promise of reducing violence in the region. The first occurred in February when South Africa and Angola signed a cease-fire agreement in Lusaka, Zambia. South Africa agreed to withdraw all its forces from southern Angola by March 31, while Angola undertook to curb the guerrilla activities of the Namibian South West Africa People's Organization (SWAPO). The agreement was seen as an essential prelude to concluding a cease-fire between South Africa and SWAPO, implementing the UN Security Council's Resolution 435 on Namibian independence, and securing the withdrawal of Cuban combat troops from Angola. However, progress was slower than expected. South Africa had not withdrawn all its forces by the end of the year, its stated reason being that the Angolans had not curbed SWAPO

South Africa's Prime Minister P. W. Botha listens as Mozambique Pres. Samora Machel hails a historic nonaggression pact between the two countries. The pact marked a major breakthrough in South Africa's relations with neighbouring black states.
SYGMA

effectively. Nevertheless, negotiations among all the parties to the Namibian conflict continued throughout the year and made sufficient progress to encourage the view that agreement on Namibian independence and on the withdrawal of Cuban troops from Angola would be achieved in 1985.

Even more surprising was the signing of the Nkomati accord between South Africa and Mozambique in March. The accord went far beyond a cease-fire and was presented by both sides as a peace treaty. Each nation undertook to deny the use of its territory for attacks against the other. Mozambique for its part would withdraw facilities for guerrilla operations by the African National Congress (ANC), while South Africa would end transborder military attacks and suspend its support for the rebel Mozambique National Resistance. The accord also provided for economic and technical cooperation, with Marxist Mozambique expressing a strong desire to establish improved trade and aid terms with its neighbour. The agreement between Pres. Samora Machel (*see* BIOGRAPHIES) and South Africa's leader, P. W. Botha (*see* BIOGRAPHIES), was signed near the banks of the Nkomati River at the border between the two countries.

Although the other African frontline states (Tanzania, Angola, Zambia, Zimbabwe, and Botswana) supported Machel's decision, Zimbabwe, Botswana, and Lesotho strongly resisted South Africa's efforts to involve them in similar treaties. It was revealed that South Africa and Swaziland had signed a secret treaty in 1982 that went beyond the Nkomati accord in that it provided for joint security operations against the ANC and other armed guerrillas.

Horn of Africa. The existence of a pro-Soviet regime in Ethiopia added to the complexities in the Horn. Somalia, which had expelled the Soviets in 1977, complained that Ethiopian Army units, supported by Cubans, were crossing its border in support of opposition elements seeking to overthrow the Somali regime. Meanwhile, rebel Ethiopian movements in the Ethiopian regions of Eritrea, Tigre, Wallo, and Sidamo accused the Soviets and Cubans of military involvement in the campaigns to suppress them.

(continued on page 459)

Africa's Hungry Millions

BY COLIN LEGUM

By the end of 1983 an estimated 150 million inhabitants of sub-Saharan Africa were faced with food shortages so severe that they bordered on famine conditions. Two out of every five Africans in 24 countries were affected. Among the worst-hit countries were Chad, Ghana, Mali, Ethiopia, Mozambique, Somalia, and Senegal, whose combined shortages were estimated at more than one million metric tons of cereal grains over and above pledged international food aid.

The immediate cause of this critical situation was the most prolonged drought in recent history; it affected 44% of the total land area of the continent and accentuated the rate of desertification to 70,000 sq km (27,000 sq mi) a year. The outlook remained forbidding. Reporting in July 1984, the UN Food and Agriculture Organization (FAO) estimated that the next harvest in the famine-stricken countries would be below 14 million metric tons of cereal grains, almost one-quarter less than had been produced only two years earlier. By 1983 production of these crops had already slumped by 35% below the average in the previous five years. According to the UN Economic Commission for Africa (ECA), a sum of $8.8 billion per year over a five-year period would be needed to boost food production, improve agriculture generally, and develop the transportation, communications, and industry needed for sustained growth.

Underlying Causes. Drought—which normally runs a seven year cycle in the areas bordering the Sahara and in parts of eastern and southern Africa—is only one of a number of factors responsible for the continent's parlous food situation. Insects have severely damaged crops in the cassava belt from Senegal to Mozambique, while in many parts of Africa outbreaks of rinderpest (an acute infectious disease affecting cattle) are taking a heavy toll. Bushfires have scorched West Africa, and war and civil strife have disrupted farming in many areas. Some of the affected countries are landlocked, and existing transportation and communications facilities in those nations are inadequate.

Other major contributory reasons for this agricultural crisis have been an actual decline in the amount of food grown in all but six sub-Saharan countries (Kenya, Malawi, Swaziland, Cameroon, Ivory Coast, and Rwanda); the rapid growth of population; shortages of essential inputs for agricultural development (fertilizers, insecticides, rural transport, and fuel) owing to foreign exchange shortages, partly due in turn to the impact of higher oil prices on the world market since 1975; the rapid rate of urbanization; the failure to diversify; and bureaucratic and financial constraints, which, in many cases, were the result of misconceived government policies that encouraged industrial growth at the expense of agriculture.

In the early 1960s—the first decade after independence from colonial rule—farm output in 39 black African countries rose by 2–3% a year, which kept pace with the population increase but not with the rising purchasing power of the growing urban population; however, in the 1970s farm output grew by only 2.3% a year, half as fast as population growth. This imbalance between the growth of food production and population grew even wider in the first years of the 1980s.

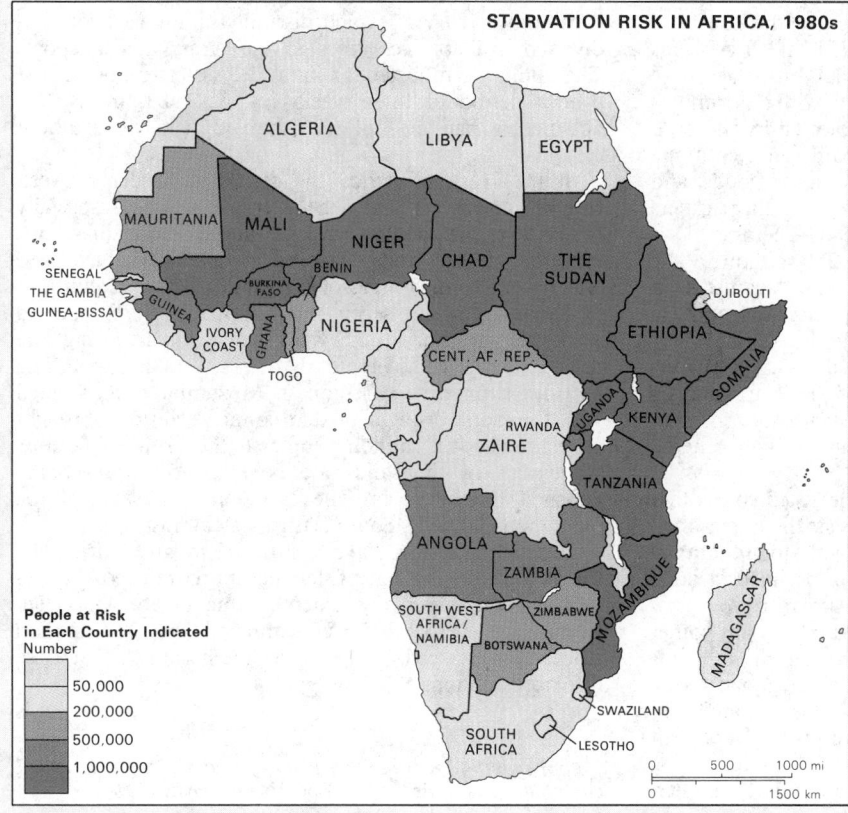

STARVATION RISK IN AFRICA, 1980s

People at Risk in Each Country Indicated
Number
50,000
200,000
500,000
1,000,000

0   500   1000 mi
0   1500 km

Millions of people in Africa have been facing starvation in recent years, and the situation continues to worsen. Worst hit are the countries of the Sahel and eastern Africa. Among the causes are prolonged severe droughts in already marginal areas, a continuing population explosion, political instability in many countries, and development policies of central governments that favour the industrial sector over the agricultural.

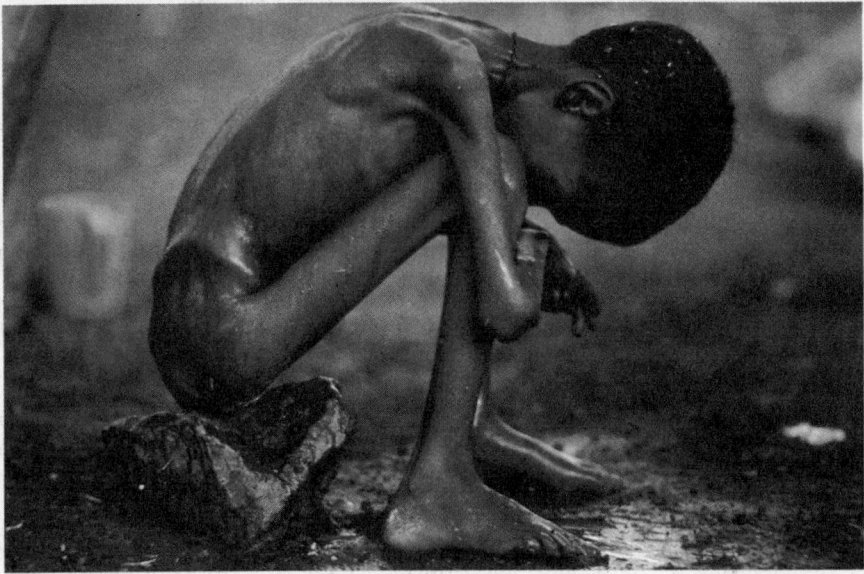

This starving Ethiopian girl waits at a relief camp for orphans for food and water and hope that probably will not reach her in time to matter.
DAVID BURNETT—CONTACT

Population in the continent has been growing at a rate of 2.9% since 1960 and reached 439 million in 1980. In a few countries, such as Kenya and Zimbabwe, the rate has been over 3% a year. Based on current growth figures, the ECA calculated that the population will have more than doubled to 1,100,000,000 by the year 2008. The ECA also reported that Africans, per capita, had almost 12% less home-grown food in 1980 than a decade earlier, imported food having trebled during that time. The commission predicted that unless food production were to increase commensurately with the rise of population, the requirements for food imports would rise by 4% a year over the next 25 years. Also, by the end of that period Africa, the least industrialized of all the continents, would need to import 90% of all its capital goods.

Economic Factors. The rapid exodus to the towns of people from the countryside—where 75% of all Africans still live—has left fewer people on the land to grow more food for the exploding urban population. This trend is thought likely to increase if, as was projected by the ECA, incomes of the farmers in the next two decades continue to decline in comparison with the cost of goods and services. But in the urban areas to which the farmers are going, 77 million Africans are already unemployed—a figure that is predicted to increase to 250 million by the end of the century. The ECA warned that "against such a background of misery and social injustice, the political situation [in Africa] would inevitably be difficult." A similarly grim warning was given to the U.S. Congress by the economist Eliot Berg, author of the World Bank's study on *Accelerated Development in Sub-Saharan Africa;* he described Africa's economic crisis as "severe, general, and worsening."

Apart from the agricultural crisis, he listed four other causes accounting for this situation. First, there is a crisis of stagnant or declining production with total national output (gross domestic product) having declined steadily since the 1960s; the economy of the African region grew more slowly in the 1970s than did that of any other developing region—only half as fast as South Asia, for example. Second, a crisis exists in internal and external economic balances; with budgets tightly squeezed and non-salary expenditures cut to the bone, routine government functions have been severely impaired by an increasing shortage of funds to operate and maintain public facilities.

Third, the continent's share of world trade in most of its commodities has declined, especially in agricultural export crops. In the 1960s this share increased by 2%; in the 1970s it fell by 2%. Finally, there is an institutional crisis; for example, weak government decision-making capacities have resulted in expenditure allocations that have frequently been out of line with expressed national priorities, while financial and administrative controls have also often been weak.

The Refugees. Military and civil conflicts have contributed in a number of countries to the disruption of agriculture and the displacement of rural populations. The most severely affected areas were Chad, the Horn of Africa, and southern Africa. The impact of drought on Chad, which borders on the Sahara, was aggravated by the continuing civil war, which disrupted administration and diverted available resources to the Army and weapons. The country's minister for natural disasters reported that over a period of three weeks in late 1983, more than 500 people had died of starvation in just two southern districts.

In the Horn of Africa the disturbed border between Ethiopia and Somalia and the internal conflicts—especially in Eritrea and Tigre—have produced more than two million refugees and displaced people who have fled either from conflict areas or in search of food. Conditions in Ethiopia, where seven million people were reported to be facing starvation, were worse than during the disastrous drought of the early 1970s. In southern Africa the long-simmering rebellion in Mozambique, combined with the worst drought in that country's history, brought an estimated 4.5 million people to the brink of famine, while tens of thousands are believed to have actually perished from hunger. The situation in several of the black homelands in South Africa was almost as grim.

Drought and war have combined to give Africa the unenviable distinction of having more refugees—about four million—than any other continent. The UN High Commissioner for Refugees estimated that $55 million would be needed in 1984 to meet the basic needs of these displaced millions.

Colin Legum is a noted authority on African affairs and a regular contributor to the Britannica Book of the Year.

(continued from page 456)

Sudan accused Ethiopia, as well as Libya, of giving support to the rebel Sudan National Liberation Movement in southern Sudan, which was opposed to Pres. Gaafar Nimeiry (*see* BIOGRAPHIES). Egypt, which had close political and military ties with Sudan, showed increasing concern about the security and economic problems faced by its ally.

Coups and Inter-African Affairs. Two successful coups occurred in Africa during 1984. The military took over Guinea in April following the death of the veteran pan-Africanist Pres. Ahmed Sékou Touré (*see* OBITUARIES), and in Mauritania in December Lieut. Col. Mohamed Khouna Ould Haidalla was ousted as president in the latest of that country's palace revolutions. In Nigeria, where a military coup ousted the newly reelected civilian government of Pres. Alhaji Shehu Shagari at the end of 1983, former party leaders and officials were put on trial for corruption. The regime of Capt. Thomas Sankara changed Upper Volta's name to Burkina Faso and embarked on radical domestic and foreign policies.

Lengthy negotiations over the dissolution of the former East African Community, which had consisted of Kenya, Tanzania, and Uganda, were finally completed with agreement on the apportionment of assets. Kenya accepted the largest liability, and Uganda emerged as the major beneficiary. The ending of the dispute brought a new spirit of cooperation marked by agreements to continue a number of technical and scientific services on a joint basis.

Attempts were made to create a new momentum in the affairs of the flagging 16-nation Economic Community of West African States. The most hopeful new development was an agreement in principle among some of its leading members to create a regional military and security system. The Undugu states, a new grouping of politically moderate nations (Egypt, Sudan, Uganda, Zaire, the Central African Republic, and Rwanda), apparently hoped to influence political developments on key African issues.

Political Systems. The most significant constitutional change during the year was the completion of Ethiopia's conversion into a structured Communist state with the launch of the Workers' Party of Ethiopia (WPE) in September. Unlike other professedly Marxist-Leninist nations in Africa, Ethiopia had been carefully building up the WPE with the active cooperation of Soviet-bloc nations over the previous seven years, during which time thousands of vanguard Marxist cadres had been trained. It presented perhaps the boldest Communist experiment so far witnessed in Africa.

In September South Africa ceased to have a parliamentary system based on the British model. Instead, it adopted a republican constitution with a strong executive president who presided over a tricameral Parliament that consisted of elected representatives from the white, Coloured (mixed race), and Asian populations; blacks remained unrepresented. The new system broke with tradition by including nonwhites in the central parliamentary system for the first time.

Elections were held on the basis of a multiparty democratic system in a number of countries, including Botswana, where the ruling Botswana Democratic Party, led by Pres. Quett Masire, was returned with an overwhelming majority in Parliament. Prime Minister Chief Leabua Jonathan promised a return to multiparty elections in Lesotho after a lapse of almost ten years.

External Relations. The U.S. was increasingly isolated in its attempt to keep up the diplomatic momentum for an agreement on Namibian independence and, in consequence, to secure the departure of Cuban troops from Angola. The other four members of the Western contact group (Britain, France, Canada, and West Germany) refused to accept the U.S.'s insistence on linking the Cuban issue with Namibian independence, and indeed France formally withdrew from the group. In collaboration with Zambia the U.S. administration succeeded in helping to negotiate the Angolan–South African cease-fire agreement, and it also played a part in forging the Nkomati accord, this time in association with Portugal, which was playing an increasingly active role in southern Africa.

The British government found itself trapped in two angry controversies over developments not of its own making. First, relations with Nigeria were seriously disturbed when Britain's security forces frustrated a plan to abduct from the U.K. a former Nigerian minister, Umaru Dikko (*see* BIOGRAPHIES), who was wanted to stand trial in Nigeria on major charges of corruption. Second, a serious row developed with South Africa in September over Britain's decision not to evict six black and Indian antiapartheid campaigners who had taken refuge in the British consulate in Durban. Three of the six left the consulate in October and the remainder in December, after detention orders on all six had been lifted. Five of the six were subsequently arrested and charged with treason.

The Soviet bloc strengthened its alliance with Ethiopia. However, two countries with which the U.S.S.R. had treaties of friendship—Angola and Mozambique—felt themselves compelled by economic and security considerations to turn increasingly to the West for aid and trade and, more upsetting to Moscow, to enter into agreements with South Africa.

Economic and Social Affairs. Famine threatened millions of Africans, particularly in the southern, eastern, and Sahelian regions of the continent. (*See* Special Report.) In Ethiopia alone some six million people faced death from starvation. Chad and Mozambique were among the other countries that were most severely affected. The drought impacted seriously on the economies of almost half of the continent's 51 countries and contributed to further reductions in food production, already well below domestic needs. While the average population growth had been about 3% annually, food production had increased by less than 2% per year since 1960, even before the onset of the latest drought catastrophe. Overall, the continent was expected to register a decline in gross domestic production for 1984, having gained only 0.2% in 1983. Its share in world trade continued to decline, growing in volume by only 1.8% and in value by 3.3% a year over the previous 20 years.

(COLIN LEGUM)

See also *Dependent States*, below.

ANGOLA

A people's republic, Angola is located on the Atlantic coast in southwestern Africa. The small exclave of Cabinda is separated from Angola by a strip of Congo. Area: 1,246,700 sq km (481,350 sq mi). Pop. (1984 est.): 7,324,000. Cap.: Luanda. Monetary unit: kwanza, with (Oct. 29, 1984) a free rate of 30.82 kwanzas to U.S. $1 (37.20 kwanzas = £1 sterling). President in 1984, José Eduardo dos Santos.

The opening weeks of 1984 were dominated by the powerful military offensive launched by South Africa on the southern districts of Angola in December 1983. The campaign had been intended to preempt an expected attack on South Africa by forces from the South West Africa People's Organization (SWAPO). Attempts to reach a cease-fire and to secure the withdrawal of South African troops at first foundered on the conflicting demands made by the two governments. Angola called for the unconditional implementation by mid-March of a scheme leading to independence for South West Africa/Namibia, in line with UN proposals. South Africa insisted on the prior withdrawal of Cuban troops from Angola.

After the UN Security Council passed a unanimous resolution calling for the unconditional withdrawal of South African troops, they began to pull out in mid-January. By the end of the first week in February, an unofficial cease-fire was in operation in southern Angola and northern Namibia. A week later Angolan officials met representatives of South Africa and the U.S. in Lusaka, Zambia, to discuss a permanent cease-fire on Angola's southern border. The outcome was an agreement whereby South Africa was to withdraw all its troops from southern Angola, while Angola undertook to ensure that no Cuban or SWAPO forces would be allowed to occupy the vacated areas. It was also suggested that Angola had received an assurance that political moves in Namibia need not await the total withdrawal of the Cubans. This was of particular importance because the Angolan Army still relied heavily on the Cuban military presence as a protection against the rebel forces of the National Union for the Total Independence of Angola (UNITA).

In March Pres. José Eduardo dos Santos, accompanied by his ministers of defense and agriculture, visited Cuba. Together with Pres. Fidel Castro, they drew up an agreement for the gradual withdrawal of Cuban troops from Angola, provided South Africa went forward with the plan for Namibian independence. The agreement, accompanied by a vigorous denunciation of South Africa's apartheid policy, did little to improve Angola's relations with South Africa. In November the Angolan government conceded that the two issues should be linked together, though the timing of a Cuban withdrawal remained to be decided. Both sides made serious efforts to fulfill the provisions of the cease-fire agreement. Angolan troops even clashed with SWAPO fighters in an endeavour to prevent them from moving into the forbidden zone. These developments pleased neither the U.S.S.R. nor some of Angola's African allies. In July Pres. Julius Nyerere of Tanzania warned the members of the Southern African Development Coordination Conference against cooperating with Pretoria for short-term economic ends lest this should seem to condone South Africa's apartheid policy.

In the meantime Jonas Savimbi, leader of UNITA, repeatedly called for peace and a government of national unity and demanded the right to take part in any negotiations concerning Namibia. He threatened to concentrate his attacks on Angola's cities if these concessions were not forthcoming. An assault against Sumbe, a coastal town 256 km (160 mi) south of Luanda, in March was an indication that Savimbi was not making idle threats. Throughout the year further UNITA attacks disrupted the country, and in July a petroleum pipeline in the Cabinda exclave was cut by explosives. In an effort to force the U.K. government to deal directly with UNITA, Savimbi held 16 Britons and a Portuguese hostage for 11 weeks from February until May.

Continuing drought, coupled with the high cost of war, led to a further decline in the country's economy. Agriculture suffered particularly, with the result that Angola, formerly self-sufficient in food production, remained a major food importer. Income from petroleum suffered as a result of continuing low prices, while all attempts to increase the output of other raw materials fell far short of their targets.

(KENNETH INGHAM)

This article updates the *Macropædia* article SOUTHERN AFRICA: *Angola*.

BENIN

The republic of Benin is on the southern coast of West Africa, on the Gulf of Guinea. Area: 112,600 sq km (43,-475 sq mi). Pop. (1984 est.): 3,856,000. Cap.: Porto-Novo. Monetary unit: CFA franc, with (Oct. 29, 1984) a par value of CFAF 50 to the French franc and a free rate of CFAF 470.60 to U.S. $1 (CFAF 568 = £1 sterling). President in 1984, Brig. Gen. Mathieu Kerekou.

Pres. Mathieu Kerekou was reelected unopposed on July 31, 1984, by 189 of the 190 commissioners (members) of the Revolutionary National Assembly who voted. Earlier in the year, on February 18, the Assembly had extended the presidential mandate and that of the legislature from three to five years; at the same time, the number of commissioners was reduced from 336 to 196. On August 4 President Kerekou announced the composition of the new National Executive Council, which comprised 15 ministers as against 22 previously. The president remained minister of defense, and Frederic Affo, formerly ambassador to Cuba, became minister of foreign affairs and cooperation.

Political prisoners released under an amnesty announced on August 1 included former army colonel Alphonse Alley, head of state in 1967–68. In 1973 Alley had been condemned to 20 years' imprisonment for plotting to overthrow the military government established by Kerekou following his October 1972 coup.   (PHILIPPE DECRAENE)

This article updates the *Macropædia* article WESTERN AFRICA: *Benin*.

BOTSWANA

A landlocked republic of southern Africa, Botswana is a member of the Commonwealth. Area: 581,987 sq km (224,-706 sq mi). Pop. (1984 est.): 1,032,000. Cap.: Gaborone. Monetary unit: pula, with (Oct. 29, 1984) a free rate of 1.47 pula to U.S. $1 (1.78 pula = £1 sterling). President in 1984, Quett Masire.

In Botswana's fifth democratic election, held in early September 1984, the ruling Botswana Democratic Party (BDP) swept back to power. The BDP won 29 of the 34 directly elected seats, the Botswana National Front 4, and the Botswana People's Party 1. The government's biggest loss was the defeat of Archie Mogwe, the foreign minister.

Pres. Quett Masire used the occasion of his first official visit to the U.S., in May, to publicize the fact that South Africa was exerting considerable pressure on his government to sign a mutual nonaggression pact, following the earlier agreement reached between South Africa and Mozambique. He stressed that his government had never allowed subversive activity against the South African regime to be carried out from Botswana.

The government's approach to the economy was characterized by caution. Diamond production had improved in 1983, and the continuing drought meant that beef sales had been especially high as farmers destocked. The pula was devalued by just over 5% in July 1984. Eight international firms were invited to submit feasibility studies for a 1,000-km (600-mi) railway line to link the Botswana system with that of South West Africa/Namibia.   (GUY ARNOLD)

This article updates the *Macropædia* article SOUTHERN AFRICA: *Botswana*.

BURKINA FASO

Burkina Faso (formerly Upper Volta) is a landlocked republic of West Africa. Area: 274,200 sq km (105,900 sq mi). Pop. (1984 est.): 6,733,000. Cap.: Ouagadougou. Monetary unit: CFA franc, with (Oct. 29, 1984) a par value of CFAF 50 to the French franc and a free rate of CFAF 470.60 to U.S. $1 (CFAF 568 = £1 sterling). Head of state in 1984, Capt. Thomas Sankara.

The National Revolutionary Council (CNR) headed by Capt. Thomas Sankara celebrated its first year in power on Aug. 4, 1984, and at that time changed the country's name from Upper Volta to Burkina Faso ("country of honest men"). The year began with a series of trials of members of previous regimes accused of corruption and embezzlement. Maj. Gen. Sangoulé Lamizana, head of state from 1966 to 1980, was acquitted on January 5, but subsequent trials of other former leaders resulted in a number of convictions and prison sentences of varying severity. Col. Saye Zerbo, head of state during 1980–82, was sentenced to 15 years in prison, with 7 years suspended, and ordered to reimburse the nation CFAF 61 million.

Opposition to the regime was manifested in a teachers' strike in March. The discovery on May 27 of a planned coup attempt, allegedly with foreign backing, was followed by the execution on June 11 of seven of those implicated. On August 19 Sankara dissolved the government and on September 1 appointed a new one that excluded members of the Marxist Patriotic League of Development (LIPAD), a constituent body of the CNR. During October, 11 LIPAD members were arrested, but 8 were later released.

The orientation of the new government seemed to favour a rapprochement with France, whose African policy Sankara previously had criticized. In September Sankara visited Cuba and in November China, where he obtained a loan of CFAF 1 billion.　　　(PHILIPPE DECRAENE)

This article updates the *Macropædia* article WESTERN AFRICA: *Burkina Faso.*

BURUNDI

Burundi is a landlocked republic of central Africa. Area: 27,834 sq km (10,747 sq mi). Pop. (1984 est.): 4,691,000. Cap.: Bujumbura. Monetary unit: Burundi franc, with (Oct. 29, 1984) a free rate of FBu 105 to U.S. $1 (FBu 127 = £1 sterling). President in 1984, Col. Jean-Baptiste Bagaza.

In June 1984 Burundi was host for the seventh summit of the Great Lakes Economic Community, consisting of Burundi, Rwanda, and Zaire. The summit called for increased economic ties among the member countries, an objective that would require the liberalization of each country's individual trading policies. In fact, most of Burundi's economic efforts were directed toward ensuring that development kept pace with population growth.

Burundi remained heavily dependent upon foreign aid, particularly from the International Development Association, Belgium, France, West Germany, and the Organization of Petroleum Exporting Countries. Burundi was a focal point within Africa for West German aid, much of which was concentrated upon the provision of better water supplies. In July West German Minister for Economic Cooperation Jürgen Warnke visited the country.

On December 11–12 Pres. François Mitterrand of France and 17 African heads of state met in Bujumbura for the 11th Franco-African summit. The meeting was dominated by the situation in Chad, where Libya had apparently failed to match the French withdrawal of troops. (See *Chad,* below.)

Col. Jean-Baptiste Bagaza, the only candidate of the only legal party, was returned for a second term as president on August 31 with 99.6% of the vote.　　　(GUY ARNOLD)

This article updates the *Macropædia* article CENTRAL AFRICA: *Burundi.*

CAMEROON

A republic of western central Africa, Cameroon lies on the Gulf of Guinea. Area: 465,458 sq km (179,714 sq mi). Pop. (1984 est.): 9,412,000. Cap.: Yaoundé. Monetary unit: CFA franc, with (Oct. 29, 1984) a par value of CFAF 50 to the French franc and a free rate of CFAF 470.60 to U.S. $1 (CFAF 568 = £1 sterling). President in 1984, Paul Biya; prime minister to January 25, Luc Ayang.

Pres. Paul Biya, who on Jan. 14, 1984, was elected unopposed to his first full five-year term with 99.98% of the votes cast, was faced less than three months later by a mutiny of disaffected members of the presidential guard. The mutiny, which began on April 6, was put down by

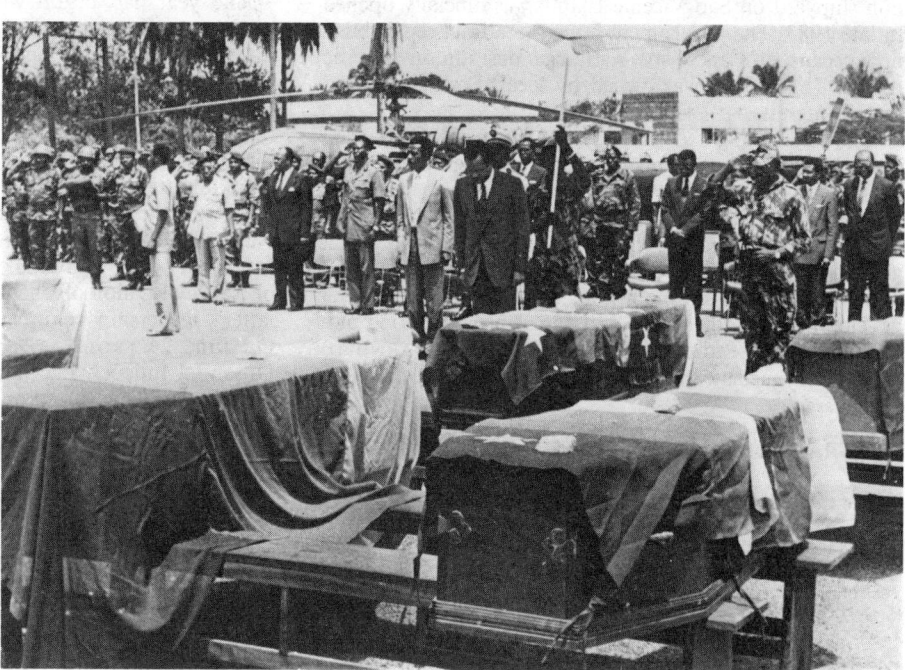

Pres. Paul Biya (centre, wearing dark suit and white shirt) of Cameroon pays his respects to some of those who died fighting a revolt that was staged by disaffected members of the presidential guard.

forces loyal to the president after several days of heavy fighting. Officially, the death toll was put at 70, but unofficial estimates ranged from 500 to 6,000. More than 1,000 mutineers were arrested and, in the first of a series of trials, 35 were condemned to death on April 30 and executed the next day. In July Amnesty International disclosed reports of 120 executions since the mutiny. A state of emergency in Yaoundé and the surrounding region, decreed to last six months, took effect from April 18.

Sweeping changes in the composition of the executive bodies of the Cameroonian National Union (the sole political party) on May 24 and of the government on July 7 brought more of President Biya's closest supporters to the forefront. An opposition movement calling itself the Cameroon Liberation Front claimed responsibility for the destruction of a Cameroon Airlines Boeing 737 at Douala airport on August 30. First reports were of more than 100 killed, but the government, attributing the incident to a fuel leak on the aircraft, said that it had caused only three deaths.   (PHILIPPE DECRAENE)

This article updates the *Macropædia* article WESTERN AFRICA: *Cameroon.*

CAPE VERDE

The republic of Cape Verde occupies an island group in the Atlantic Ocean about 620 km (385 mi) off the west coast of Africa. Area: 4,033 sq km (1,557 sq mi). Pop. (1984 est.): 308,000. Cap.: Praia. Monetary unit: Cape Verde escudo, with (Oct. 29, 1984) a free rate of 80.13 escudos to U.S. $1 (96.71 escudos = £1 sterling). President in 1984, Aristide Pereira; premier, Pedro Pires.

During 1984 Cape Verde was the site of several important meetings on Namibia. South African, Angolan, and U.S. officials met there in January, and the first publicly admitted direct negotiations between South Africa and the South West Africa People's Organization took place there in July. Cape Verde and Guinea-Bissau both expressed support for their fellow Portuguese-speaking countries, Angola and Mozambique, in the accords they reached with South Africa during the year. (See *African Affairs,* above.)

The country's largest economic project, the $37.5 million shipyard on São Vicente Island, was officially opened in late 1983. The government hoped to attract repair business because of Cape Verde's strategic position on Atlantic routes. The project was owned by local, Portuguese, and Dutch interests.

Since the drought of the early 1970s, Cape Verde had been economically dependent to a large extent upon repatriated earnings from its citizens overseas; there were, for example, 350,000 Cape Verdians in the U.S. The government also relied heavily on foreign aid. During the year a general cooperation agreement was signed with Portugal, and France agreed to fund fishing, irrigation, and industrial developments. Both France and Japan provided food aid. In July Premier Pedro Pires visited Cuba. (GUY ARNOLD)

This article updates the *Macropædia* article WESTERN AFRICA: *Cape Verde.*

CENTRAL AFRICAN REPUBLIC

The Central African Republic is a landlocked state in central Africa. Area: 622,436 sq km (240,324 sq mi). Pop. (1984 est.): 2,585,000. Cap.: Bangui. Monetary unit: CFA franc, with (Oct. 29, 1984) a par value of CFAF 50 to the French franc and a free rate of CFAF 470.60 to U.S. $1 (CFAF 568 = £1 sterling). Head of state and chairman of the Military Committee of National Recovery in 1984, Gen. André Kolingba.

Gen. André Kolingba undertook a radical reshuffle of his government on Jan. 23, 1984. Nine ministers were dropped, including the minister of finance, Gen. Sylvestre Bangui, and six new ones were appointed. General Kolingba retained the defense portfolio.

The country's severe economic difficulties were aggravated by the influx of more than 10,000 refugees from southern Chad. In the capital political tension continued, and students at the University of Bangui went on strike in January. Opposition leader Abel Goumba, released from detention under an amnesty in August 1983, was rearrested with other leading politicians on Jan. 27, 1984, and was held under house arrest until the end of the year. Central Africans in France set up an organization there in April dedicated to restoration of the constitution that had been suspended by the military regime.

French military bases in the Central African Republic provided an essential link in the supply line for France's operations in neighbouring Chad, and in November the French contingent in the country was supplemented by troops withdrawing from Chad. In October three Central African youths and several French soldiers were injured when the youths tried to break into a French army camp at Bangui.   (PHILIPPE DECRAENE)

This article updates the *Macropædia* article CENTRAL AFRICA: *Central African Republic.*

CHAD

Chad is a landlocked republic of central Africa. Area: 1,284,-000 sq km (495,755 sq mi). Pop. (1984 est.): 4,880,000. Cap.: N'Djamena. Monetary unit: CFA franc, with (Oct. 29, 1984) a par value of CFAF 50 to the French franc and a free rate of CFAF 470.60 to U.S. $1 (CFAF 568 = £1 sterling). President in 1984, Hissen Habré.

On Sept. 17, 1984, following intense diplomatic activity, France and Libya agreed on the mutual withdrawal of their forces from Chad. Late in the year, however, it appeared that Libya had not fulfilled its part of the bargain. Chad was among the African countries suffering most severely from the prolonged drought. (See *African Affairs,* above.)

The year had begun with talks sponsored by the Organization of African Unity (OAU) aimed at reconciling the warring Chadian factions. Postponed from December 1983, the talks opened in Addis Ababa, Eth., on Jan. 9, 1984, but collapsed after four days; Pres. Hissen Habré had refused to attend them for reasons of protocol involving the status accorded his rival for power, former president Goukouni Oueddei.

During the year the political structure of both Habré's National Liberation Front-Armed Forces of the North (FROLINAT-FAN) and Goukouni's transitional Government of National Union of Chad (GUNT) underwent changes, the latter's leadership being weakened by internal dissension. On June 24 FROLINAT-FAN was replaced by a National Union for Independence and the Revolution (UNIR), under Habré's presidency, and on August 7 six of the constituent factions of GUNT set up a National Liberation Council. Habré reshuffled his government on July 24. The post of foreign minister, vacant since the death of Idriss Miskine (*see* OBITUARIES) in January, went to Gouara Lassou.

The Franco-Libyan evacuation, including that of Zairian troops supporting Habré, was reported completed by November 9. However, reports from U.S. sources later in the month indicated that Libyan troops remained in the northern part of the country. Libya denied the accusation. The apparent failure of the peace initiative caused severe

French paratroopers arrived in Chad's capital city, N'Djamena, on their way out of the country in compliance with a Franco-Libyan accord for withdrawal of their forces.
AP/WIDE WORLD

embarrassment to France, which declined to send troops back into Chad.   (PHILIPPE DECRAENE)

This article updates the *Macropædia* article WESTERN AFRICA: *Chad*.

COMOROS

The republic of Comoros is an island state in the Indian Ocean off the east coast of Africa. Area: 1,862 sq km (719 sq mi), excluding the island of Mayotte, which continued to be a de facto dependency of France. Pop. (1984 est., excluding Mayotte): 387,500. Cap.: Moroni. Monetary unit, Comorian franc, with (Oct. 29, 1984) a par value of CF 50 to the French franc and a free rate of CF 470.60 to U.S. $1 (CF 568 = £1 sterling). President in 1984, Ahmed Abdallah; premier to December 31, Ali Mroudjae.

Pres. Ahmed Abdallah was reelected unopposed for a new six-year term on Sept. 30, 1984, by 99% of the voters. On December 31 he assumed the functions of head of government when the Federal Assembly approved a constitutional amendment abolishing the post of premier.

President Abdallah rejected the possibility of France's continuing the special status as a de facto French dependency that it had extended to the island of Mayotte for a five-year period from 1979. He continued to campaign for Mayotte's reintegration into Comoros and announced his intention of revising the constitution to facilitate this move. France had previously stated that the views of the inhabitants of Mayotte would be sought in a referendum that was to have been held before the end of 1984 but was subsequently deferred.

Mohammed Ahmed, who had been Abdallah's co-president during May–October 1978, died on Jan. 27, 1984, aged 70. Ahmed had helped Abdallah plan the May 1978 coup. Australian courts convicted three alleged mercenaries arrested in 1983 on charges of plotting to overthrow the Comoran government.   (PHILIPPE DECRAENE)

This article updates the *Macropædia* article INDIAN OCEAN ISLANDS: *Comoros*.

CONGO

A people's republic, Congo is in central Africa on the Atlantic Ocean. Area: 342,000 sq km (132,047 sq mi). Pop. (1984 est.): 1,745,000. Cap.: Brazzaville. Monetary unit: CFA franc, with (Oct. 29, 1984) a par value of CFAF 50 to the French franc and a free rate of CFAF 470.60 to U.S. $1 (CFAF 568 = £1 sterling). President in 1984, Col. Denis Sassou-Nguesso; premiers, Col. Louis Sylvain Ngoma and, from August 7, Ange-Édouard Poungui.

At the third congress of the ruling Congolese Labour Party (PCT), held on July 27–31, 1984, Col. Denis Sassou-Nguesso was unanimously reelected president of the republic and of the PCT Central Committee. A constitutional reform adopted by the congress made the president also virtually the head of government, while the importance of the premier's role was reduced. Jean-Pierre Thystère Tchicaya, responsible for ideology and education and previously the PCT's second most influential figure, was removed from the Central Committee and replaced by Ambroise Noumazalaye (premier in 1966–68).

Early in August Ange-Édouard Poungui, the director general of the Congolese Commercial Bank and financial adviser to the president, replaced Col. Louis Sylvain Ngoma as premier. The composition of the new government, with the president responsible for defense and security, was announced on August 11. In a further constitutional change, achieved by presidential statute on August 23, a Constitutional Council was formed under the presidency of former premier Ngoma. The new body assumed certain functions of the Supreme Court concerning political matters.

In November Colonel Sassou-Nguesso announced that former president Joachim Yhombi-Opango had been released from detention. General Yhombi-Opango, president during the period 1977–79, had been imprisoned in March 1979 when Sassou-Nguesso came to power.

(PHILIPPE DECRAENE)

This article updates the *Macropædia* article CENTRAL AFRICA: *Congo*.

DJIBOUTI

The republic of Djibouti is in the Horn of northeastern Africa on the Gulf of Aden. Area: 23,200 sq km (8,900 sq mi). Pop. (1984 est., excluding refugees): 335,000. Cap.: Djibouti. Monetary unit: Djibouti franc, with (Oct. 29, 1984) a free rate of DF 174 to U.S. $1 (DF 210 = £1 sterling). President in 1984, Hassan Gouled Aptidon; premier, Barkat Gourad Hamadou.

During 1984 the regime of Pres. Hassan Gouled Aptidon drew renewed criticism from Amnesty International for its violations of human rights, particularly those of the Afar community. In November it was reported that nine Afars imprisoned since August 1983 had been released; they had been held on charges relating to the intertribal violence that had followed Djibouti's independence from France in 1977.

Djibouti attained some international prominence as a result of minesweeping operations by the U.S., British, and French navies in the Red Sea and the Gulf of Suez during the summer; the French Navy conducted operations from its permanent base at Djibouti. In August President Gouled visited Paris for discussions with Pres. François Mitterrand on this topic. In March Gouled received Ethiopia's head of state, Lieut. Col. Mengistu Haile Mariam. Construction of the highway to Berbera in Somalia began in October.

Djibouti was among the African countries severely affected by drought and received $215,000 in emergency assistance from the European Communities in April. Otherwise France remained the leading source of aid.

(PHILIPPE DECRAENE)

This article updates the *Macropædia* article EASTERN AFRICA: *Djibouti*.

EQUATORIAL GUINEA

The republic of Equatorial Guinea consists of Río Muni, on the Atlantic coast of West Africa, and the offshore islands of Bioko and Annobon. Area: 28,051 sq km (10,831 sq mi). Pop. (1983 prelim.): 304,000. Cap.: Malabo. Monetary unit: ekwele (plural: bipkwele), with (Oct. 29, 1984) a par value of 2 bipkwele to the Spanish peseta and a free rate of 344.16 bipkwele to U.S. $1 (415.40 bipkwele = £1 sterling). President of the Supreme Military Council in 1984, Lieut. Col. Teodoro Obiang Nguema Mbasogo; premier, Capt. Cristino Seriche Bioko.

Difficult relations with Spain continued for most of 1984 following Equatorial Guinea's decision in 1983 to join the Central African Customs and Economic Union (UDEAC) and the Central Bank of West African States. Spain reduced its aid in the fields of education, health, and defense, while a spokesman for the Spanish Ministry of Foreign Affairs described Equatorial Guinea's decision to join the CFA franc zone from Jan. 1, 1985, as "the best thing that could have happened," an ambiguous statement in light of the mistrust that developed between the two countries. As Spain pointed out, Equatorial Guinea soon discovered that the UDEAC authorities demanded conditions similar to those Madrid had insisted upon before supplying support for the country's currency.

In December 1983 Pres. Teodoro Obiang Nguema led a delegation on a visit to Morocco, which had offered financial assistance in the form of loans. Moroccan military personnel were training Equatorial Guinea's forces, and Moroccans supplied the president's personal bodyguard.

Significant gas deposits were discovered 36 km (22.5 mi) off the coast of Malabo Island, though their development potential remained to be determined. Perhaps to signify an end to bickering, Spain presented President Obiang Nguema with a 28-seat aircraft. In August the president went on an official visit to China. (GUY ARNOLD)

This article updates the *Macropædia* article WESTERN AFRICA: *Equatorial Guinea*.

ETHIOPIA

The socialist state of Ethiopia is in the Horn of northeastern Africa, on the Red Sea. Area: 1,223,600 sq km (472,400 sq mi). Pop. (1984 est.): 34 million. Cap.: Addis Ababa. Monetary unit: birr, with (Oct. 29, 1984) a par value of 2.07 birr to U.S. $1 (free rate of 2.44 birr = £1 sterling). Head of state and chairman of the Provisional Military Administrative Council in 1984, Lieut. Col. Mengistu Haile Mariam.

September 1984 marked the tenth anniversary of the overthrow of Emperor Haile Selassie's government in Ethiopia and, more significantly, the culmination of preparations by the Commission for Organizing the Party of the Working People of Ethiopia (COPWE) for the establishment of the Workers' Party of Ethiopia (WPE). The party was officially established on the final day of the founding congress, which took place September 6–10 in Addis Ababa. At the same time, COPWE was dissolved. With only a few exceptions, elections to the WPE Central Committee and Politburo produced virtually the same hierarchy that had existed in COPWE, with Lieut. Col. Mengistu Haile Mariam as

secretary-general and the majority of members drawn from the Provisional Military Administrative Council (PMAC). However, the secretaries appointed to the 11-member Politburo included four civilians. The PMAC was to remain in existence until the WPE produced the constitution of the People's Democratic Republic of Ethiopia.

The founding congress was attended by a significant number of African heads of state and representatives from socialist countries. Notably absent was Pres. Fidel Castro of Cuba, who had maintained strong relations with Ethiopia since 1974. The U.S.S.R. was represented by Grigory Romanov (*see* BIOGRAPHIES), a powerful member of the Soviet Politburo. Mengistu presented a report that, while including a political review, focused chiefly on the problems of economic development. The congress also considered and approved a ten-year (1984–94) plan for economic and social development. The plan aimed at a significant annual growth rate of 6.5% and was designed to double gross domestic product by 1994. Its stated general objective was to improve the material and cultural well-being of the population, with particular emphasis on food production, clothing, shelter, health, and access to water. However, it also demanded a very high rate of domestic savings to finance modernization of the economy, and it relied to a significant extent on external assistance.

Mengistu emphasized the need to increase food production and to create a reserve of grain to offset the continuing drought conditions. A plan to organize half of agricultural workers into cooperative units, with the aim of increasing output by using more advanced technology, was approved. The continuing famine ravaging many regions of Ethiopia was brought dramatically to Western attention when films showing conditions in the drought-stricken areas were shown on television in the U.K., the U.S., and elsewhere. Contributions of food were pledged by governments and private sources, though much of the food had to be shipped by slow sea voyage, and distribution was made more difficult by poor transportation facilities and secessionist activity in some of the hardest-hit regions. It was estimated that 300,000 persons may have died since the beginning of the year. (See *African Affairs:* Special Report, above.)

Considerable improvements to rural infrastructure were projected, including nearly 1,000 tractor and combine-harvester hiring stations. Road transport capacity was expected to increase by 100%. (The 295-km [183-mi] road linking the towns of Waldey in Wallo [Welo] Province and Wereta in Gondar Province was completed in December 1983; constructed as a joint venture between the governments of Ethiopia and China, it was the only east-west road running across the central highlands.) The need to make the best use of natural resources was underlined by the allocation to all sectors of over 1 billion birr for research and development, as well as a large program for mineral surveys.

The processes of modernization and development received considerable impetus. As a result, there was some basis for confidence that during the course of the ten-year plan, local industry would be able to supply larger quantities of equipment and reduce foreign-exchange outlay on industrial and consumer goods, as well as initiate the export of manufactured goods. Major industrial investment completed, or about to become operational, totaled well over 1 billion birr. Among the projects under construction were a spare-parts and hand-tools factory, established, with Italian assistance, at a cost of 176 million birr, and a water-pumps and pipes manufacturing unit, set up with assistance from North Korea. Technical aid and assistance were also being supplied by the U.S.S.R., Poland, Cuba, Japan, Czechoslovakia, Hungary, and East and West Ger-

Hundreds of workers marched through Ethiopia's capital, Addis Ababa, in September during the grand celebration of the tenth anniversary of that country's Marxist revolution. After the pomp and circumstance, the government turned to the distribution of welcome gifts of food supplies for drought- and famine-afflicted millions.

AP/WIDE WORLD

many. Mengistu paid an unannounced visit to Moscow in December.

The government's concerted military offensive against the secessionist forces in Eritrea and Tigre appeared to have had little success. Fighting occurred in both these areas, as well as in the Ogaden, despite the efforts of the Ethiopia and Somalia to negotiate a peace settlement there. There were signs that the various guerrilla groups were joining forces. In March the Eritrean People's Liberation Front (EPLF) reached an agreement to work with another Eritrean nationalist group. Meanwhile, the Tigre People's Liberation Front, which already had links with the EPLF, agreed to cooperate with the Western Somali Liberation Front, which was fighting in the Ogaden. One of the aims of the agreement was to bring together all the guerrilla movements opposed to the Mengistu regime. In January over one million youths registered for the national military service announced in May 1983, and some were immediately sent for military training.

This article updates the *Macropædia* article EASTERN AFRICA: *Ethiopia.*

GABON

Gabon is a republic of central Africa, on the Atlantic Ocean. Area: 267,667 sq km (103,347 sq mi). Pop.: in 1984 estimates varied from 564,000 to 1,682,000. Cap.: Libreville. Monetary unit: CFA franc, with (Oct. 29, 1984) a par value of CFAF 50 to the French franc and a free rate of CFAF 470.60 to U.S. $1 (CFAF 568 = £1 sterling). President in 1984, Omar Bongo; premier, Léon Mébiame.

Good relations between Gabon and France were restored in 1984. The previous year's differences, partly caused by the publication in France of a book that criticized Pres. Omar Bongo's regime and his private life, were glossed over, aided by visits to Libreville by French Premier Pierre Mauroy March 31–April 2 and by French Defense Minister Charles Hernu in May. The reconciliation, sealed by a three-day state visit to Paris by President Bongo in October, emphasized Gabon's economic reliance on France.

Besides being its main trading partner, France supplied some 80% of the foreign preferential aid received by

Gabon; French technical assistants in the country in 1984 numbered more than 600. There was also close military cooperation between the two countries; France maintained a permanent detachment of 600 troops in Libreville under a 1960 defense agreement. The Hernu visit in May coincided with the sale to Gabon of six French Mirage V fighter-bombers.

On the domestic front there was little change; in a government reshuffle in March four new ministries were created, but the leading posts remained in the same hands. In August Gabon and Mauritius agreed to establish diplomatic relations.   (PHILIPPE DECRAENE)

This article updates the *Macropædia* article CENTRAL AFRICA: *Gabon.*

GAMBIA, THE

A republic and member of the Commonwealth, The Gambia extends from the Atlantic Ocean along the lower Gambia River in West Africa; it is surrounded by Senegal, with which it has formed an administrative union called Senegambia. Area: 10,690 sq km (4,127 sq mi). Pop. (1983 prelim.): 695,900. Cap.: Banjul. Monetary unit: dalasi, with (Oct. 29, 1984) a free rate of 4.14 dalasis to U.S. $1 (5 dalasis = £1 sterling). President in 1984, Sir Dawda Jawara.

During 1984 discussions between The Gambia and Senegal concentrated on the economic and monetary aspects of the Senegambian confederation, the merger between the two countries that was slowly taking shape. A meeting was held in Dakar, Senegal, in August to discuss the precise nature of the proposed free-trade zone.

With drought again affecting agriculture, The Gambia continued to receive food aid. The Islamic Development Bank made a grant of $300,000 and a loan of $1 million. An outbreak of army worms was reported to be affecting all cereal-growing areas.

In April the International Monetary Fund provided a standby loan of $13.4 million. External grants and loans remained the main source of development finance. The most important development project was the building of a bridge and barrage across the Gambia River some 125 km (80 mi) upstream from its estuary.

In April an additional 24 people were sentenced to death in connection with the attempted coup of 1981. The Court of Appeal had upheld most of the 39 death sentences announced previously, but no executions had actually taken place.   (GUY ARNOLD)

This article updates the *Macropædia* article WESTERN AFRICA: *The Gambia.*

GHANA

A republic of West Africa and member of the Commonwealth, Ghana lies on the Gulf of Guinea. Area: 238,533 sq km (92,098 sq mi). Pop. (1984): 12,205,576. Cap.: Accra. Monetary unit: cedi, with (Oct. 29, 1984) a free rate of 38.69 cedis to U.S. $1 (46.70 cedis = £1 sterling). Chairman of the Provisional National Defense Council in 1984, Jerry John Rawlings.

The chairman of the Provisional National Defense Council, Jerry John Rawlings, warned that 1984 would be a hard year as Ghana continued to suffer the effects of severe drought. Further devaluations of the cedi were announced in March (14%), September (9.09%), and December (25%), following the 91% devaluation of October 1983. The economy remained heavily dependent on international aid. The International Development Association (IDA) provided credits worth $93 million, while aid and technical assistance were supplied by a number of countries, including both the U.S. and the U.S.S.R. In September the International Monetary Fund agreed to a standby arrangement worth $183 million.

Prospects for petroleum development were more encouraging. The 21-year-old Tema refinery was to be rehabilitated with financing provided by the European Investment Bank and the IDA, while Canadian aid was to be used to drill two offshore oil wells. The government invited international oil companies to bid for exploration and production licenses covering 70% of the country's offshore waters.

In June Ghana reopened its borders with Togo and Ivory Coast, closed since September 1982 in an effort to prevent smuggling. Rawlings visited neighbouring Burkina Faso (Upper Volta) in February.   (GUY ARNOLD)

This article updates the *Macropædia* article WESTERN AFRICA: *Ghana.*

GUINEA

The republic of Guinea is located in West Africa, on the Atlantic Ocean. Area: 245,790 sq km (94,900 sq mi). Pop. (1984 est.): 5,297.000. Cap.: Conakry. Monetary unit: syli, with (Oct. 29, 1984) a free rate of 24.80 sylis to U.S. $1 (29.93 sylis = £1 sterling). President in 1984, Ahmed Sékou Touré until March 26; premier until April 3 and interim head of state from March 27 to April 3, Louis Lansana Beavogui; head of the Military Committee for National Redress from April 3, president from April 5, and premier from December 18, Col. Lansana Conté; premier from April 5 to December 18, Col. Diara Traoré.

Flown to the U.S. after suffering a heart attack, Pres. Ahmed Sékou Touré (*see* OBITUARIES) died in a hospital in Cleveland, Ohio, on March 26, 1984. His body was returned to Guinea for a state funeral on March 30 that was attended by many African heads of state and other foreign dignitaries. In accordance with the constitution, Premier Louis Lansana Beavogui took over as interim head of state on March 27.

The following week, on April 3, the regime was toppled in a bloodless military coup led by Col. Lansana Conté (*see* BIOGRAPHIES) as head of a Military Committee for National Redress (CMRN), which replaced the former ruling Democratic Party of Guinea (PDG). A government comprising 25 army officers and eight civilians (including one woman, as minister for social affairs) was appointed, with Col. Diara Traoré as premier. The downfall of the 26-year-old dictatorship was greeted with rejoicing by Guineans at home and in exile. It was followed by a variety of liberalization measures and by the arrest of PDG leaders, who were brought to trial in November. Beavogui, who was among those arrested, died in a hospital in August. In a reshuffle of the government on December 18, Conté took over the posts of premier and defense minister and Traoré became minister of education.

Normalization of relations with France proceeded rapidly. Premier Traoré was received by Pres. François Mitterrand in Paris in June and in July, and France extended a F 30 million credit to Guinea. Traoré also visited the U.K. in July.   (PHILIPPE DECRAENE)

This article updates the *Macropædia* article WESTERN AFRICA: *Guinea.*

In the aftermath of a bloodless military coup that followed the death of Pres. Ahmed Sékou Touré in March, demonstrators defaced posters with the likeness of Touré. The downfall of the 26-year-old dictatorship was greeted with rejoicing.

GUINEA-BISSAU

A republic of West Africa, Guinea-Bissau lies on the Atlantic Ocean. Area: 36,125 sq km (13,948 sq mi). Pop. (1984 est.): 842,000. Cap.: Bissau. Monetary unit: peso, with (Oct. 29, 1984) a free rate of 84.44 pesos to U.S. $1 (101.92 pesos = £1 sterling). President of the Council of the Revolution to May 14, 1984, and chairman of the Council of State from May 16, João Bernardo Vieira; premier to March 10, Victor Saúde Maria.

During 1984 Pres. João Bernardo Vieira (*see* BIOGRAPHIES) consolidated his position in Guinea-Bissau by carrying out a series of purges within the Cabinet and the ruling African Party for the Independence of Guinea-Bissau and Cape Verde (PAIGC). Most significant was the dismissal in March of Premier Victor Saúde Maria, distrusted because of his right-wing tendencies and accused of plotting to stage a coup. Two other ministers suspected of collusion were sacked in May.

The thrust of other political developments was to legitimize the 1980 coup that had brought Vieira to power. On March 31 elections were held to eight regional councils, which in turn elected 150 deputies to the revived National Assembly. The Assembly was convened in May as the mandate of the Council of the Revolution expired. A new constitution reaffirmed the power of the PAIGC to define state policy and provided for a Council of State whose chairman would automatically be head of state. The Assembly unanimously elected Vieira to the post. In July he announced his new government, in which the post of premier was abolished.

A meeting of donor countries and organizations agreed to find 75% of the $171 million required to finance a four-year development plan. Portugal's promise of aid signaled better relations with its ex-colony.   (GUY ARNOLD)

This article updates the *Macropædia* article WESTERN AFRICA: *Guinea-Bissau.*

IVORY COAST

A republic of West Africa, the Ivory Coast lies on the Gulf of Guinea. Area: 320,763 sq km (123,847 sq mi). Pop. (1984 est.): 9,561,000. Cap.: Abidjan. Monetary unit: CFA franc, with (Oct. 29, 1984) a par value of CFAF 50 to the French franc and a free rate of CFAF 470.60 to U.S. $1 (CFAF 568 = £1 sterling). President in 1984, Félix Houphouët-Boigny.

The problem of the eventual succession to Pres. Félix Houphouët-Boigny and the repercussions of the world economic recession were matters of growing concern in Ivory Coast during 1984. The president's 79th birthday was celebrated on October 18, but public rumour attributed even greater age to him, and certainly the responsibilities he had borne for a quarter of a century had left their mark. A muted opposition to his rule had begun to emerge. In September Defense Minister Jean Konan Banny, after referring in a television broadcast to the circulation of tracts criticizing the ruling Democratic Party of the Ivory Coast and the president, countered the criticism by listing the achievements of Houphouët-Boigny's presidency.

At the party congress in March the emphasis was on austerity in all branches of the economy. During the year Ivory Coast negotiated the rescheduling of an external debt estimated to exceed $7 billion. France, the principal source of foreign aid and technical assistance, was to reduce the number of its technicians in Ivory Coast by half, from 4,000 to 2,000, by 1985; this would represent an annual saving of F 200 million for Ivory Coast. Doubts about the eventual size of the 1984–85 season's cocoa crop were a disturbing factor in international cocoa trading during the year, since Ivory Coast was the world's largest producer.

The economic decline was reflected in the growing incidence of street crime, often linked with drug addiction. In July the government announced the formation of an "antigang brigade."   (PHILIPPE DECRAENE)

This article updates the *Macropædia* article WESTERN AFRICA: *Ivory Coast.*

KENYA

A republic and member of the Commonwealth, Kenya is in eastern Africa, on the Indian Ocean. Area: 580,367 sq km (224,081 sq mi), including 11,230 sq km of inland water. Pop. (1984 est.): 19,633,000. Cap.: Nairobi. Monetary unit: Kenya shilling, with (Oct. 29, 1984) a free rate of K Sh 15.22 to U.S. $1 (K Sh 18.38 = £1 sterling). President in 1984, Daniel arap Moi.

What was claimed to have been the worst drought in Kenya in a century finally broke in October 1984 when heavy rains fell in inland districts. The failure of the spring rains had led to an appeal to Western nations in June for supplies of corn (maize), wheat, and powdered milk. In September a campaign was launched to limit consumption of water. The break in the drought encouraged farmers to plant quick-maturing crops, but even if this proved successful, the country would still have to rely heavily on imported grain for several months. In the meantime, more than a million people received famine relief food. Speaking at a rally in Kisumu in July, Minister of Labour Robert Ouko claimed that the food shortages were due at least in part to hoarding by senior government officials.

Faced with these adverse conditions, the national food program, which aimed to achieve self-sufficiency by 1990, made little progress. Fluctuating prices for export crops led to uncertainty in the economy, though the sharp increase in the price offered for tea, coupled with a rising demand, aroused hopes that tea production might be stepped up appreciably despite demands from India and Sri Lanka that export quotas be introduced.

As a result of its close political and economic ties with the West, Kenya continued to receive $100 million a year in aid from the U.S., and it was hoped that the signing of the Arusha (Tanzania) agreement in November 1983 would lead to improved trade relations with Uganda and Tanzania. The agreement provided for the disposal of the assets of the East African Community, which had broken up in 1977, and was followed immediately by the reopening of the border between Kenya and Tanzania. In March flights by Kenyan and Tanzanian airlines between Nairobi and Dar es Salaam were resumed. The two countries also agreed to accept joint responsibility for the outstanding debts of the Community because the third member, Uganda, had received the smallest share of its assets; the net cost of the debts to Kenya and Tanzania was $150 million. The 1967 treaty that had brought the Community into existence was finally abrogated by the three countries in May.

A judicial inquiry into allegations that Charles Njonjo, former minister of constitutional affairs, had been involved in a plot to seize the presidency continued until August, but there was no clear indication of its eventual outcome. In September Njonjo was expelled from the ruling Kenya African National Union along with 14 others.

In December 1983 Pres. Daniel arap Moi pardoned 7,000 prisoners, all of them minor criminals, to mark the 20th anniversary of independence. In March, however, air force Pvt. Hezekiah Ochuka and air force Sgt. Pancras

During what was claimed to be the worst drought in Kenya in a century, many people were forced to travel miles from their homes to find water. In October rains came at last to the inland districts.
AP/WIDE WORLD

Okumu were found guilty of leading the attempted coup of 1982 and were sentenced to death. A month later air force Pvt. Robert Odhiambo became the 14th man to receive the death sentence in connection with the attempted coup. None of the sentences had been carried out by year's end, however, and two had been quashed by the High Court.

Throughout 1983 there had been disturbances on the northeastern border arising from disputes over grazing grounds between two tribes of nomadic Somali. The Kenyan government ordered the parties to surrender the arms that they had acquired illegally, and when one group failed to respond, its members were rounded up by government troops. Local representatives claimed that in February 1984 some 300 of those detained had died as a result of starvation, thirst, and ill treatment. The government rejected the accusation but admitted that 50 or so people had been killed while resisting troops or trying to escape.

President Moi reassured church leaders in September that freedom of speech in the pulpit would be protected. Radio Kenya had announced that there would be no further religious broadcasts because priests had used them to attack government policies. (KENNETH INGHAM)

This article updates the *Macropædia* article EASTERN AFRICA: *Kenya*.

LESOTHO

A constitutional monarchy of southern Africa and member of the Commonwealth, Lesotho forms a landlocked enclave within South Africa. Area: 30,355 sq km (11,720 sq mi). Pop. (1984 est.): 1,474,000. Cap.: Maseru. Monetary unit: loti (plural: maloti), at par with the South African rand, with (Oct. 29, 1984) a free rate of 1.79 maloti to U.S. $1 (2.16 maloti = £1 sterling). King, Moshoeshoe II; prime minister in 1984, Chief Leabua Jonathan.

A new political grouping opposed to the leadership of Chief Leabua Jonathan emerged in Lesotho during 1984. The United Democratic Alliance, later renamed the Basotho Democratic Alliance, was reportedly formed with the encouragement and support of South Africa. South African Foreign Minister R. F. (Pik) Botha was present at the meeting in Pretoria in January when six key dissidents founded the Alliance. Phoka Chaolane was its chairman, and another prominent member of the group was Charles Molapo, former minister of information who had resigned in June 1983. The Alliance announced that if it gained power in Lesotho it would ban Communism from the country. In August Prime Minister Jonathan accused Pretoria of offering him bribes to sign a nonaggression pact similar to the one concluded between South Africa and Mozambique earlier in the year.

The economy remained sluggish. In February the government introduced a standstill budget, the most important feature of which was a new sales tax designed to make Lesotho less dependent on revenues from the South African Customs Union. Inflation reached record levels, while debt servicing, at 144 million maloti, was the largest item of recurrent expenditure. The country suffered from drought for the third successive year. (GUY ARNOLD)

This article updates the *Macropædia* article SOUTHERN AFRICA: *Lesotho*.

LIBERIA

The republic of Liberia is located in West Africa, on the Atlantic Ocean. Area: 99,067 sq km (38,250 sq mi). Pop. (1984 est.): 2,601,000. Cap.: Monrovia. Monetary unit: Liberian dollar, at par with the U.S. dollar, with a free rate (Oct. 29, 1984) of L$1.21 to £1 sterling. Head of state in 1984, Gen. Samuel K. Doe.

The year 1984 was a deeply troubled one for Liberia. Events included the uncovering of conspiracies to overthrow the government, an increase in the number of political prisoners, a treason trial, and frequent firings of ministers by the head of state, Gen. Samuel K. Doe. In April, 13 people were sentenced to death for their involvement in a plot to seize power. At the same time, Doe granted a pardon to the alleged leader of the conspirators, Brig. Gen. Thomas Quiwonkpa, who had fled the country.

In July, in keeping with the promise to return the country to civilian rule in 1985, the People's Redemption Council was dissolved, the ban on political parties lifted, and an interim National Assembly appointed. Doe announced that he would be a candidate in the 1985 presidential elections.

However, mounting tensions and repression accompanied these moves. Another alleged coup plot caused Doe to cut short a visit to Europe in mid-August. A series of political arrests followed. The University of Liberia was closed, and a student demonstration in August was brutally dispersed by troops; according to one report, there were 50 deaths. Minister of Information G. V. Kromah was dismissed in September for saying that the Liberian people would not accept dictatorship. Ten persons arrested in connection with the plot were freed in October.

The condition of the economy remained poor throughout the year. (GUY ARNOLD)

This article updates the *Macropædia* article WESTERN AFRICA: *Liberia*.

MADAGASCAR

The republic of Madagascar occupies the island of the same name and minor adjacent islands in the Indian Ocean off the southeast coast of Africa. Area: 587,051 sq km (226,662 sq mi). Pop. (1984 est.): 9.6 million. Cap.: Antananarivo. Monetary unit: Malagasy franc, with (Oct. 29, 1984) a free rate of FMG 630.99 to U.S. $1 (FMG 761.60 = £1 sterling). President in 1984, Didier Ratsiraka; premier, Lieut. Col. Désiré Rakotoarijaona.

Twice during 1984 Antananarivo was the scene of civil violence. On September 5, following a broadcast announcement that the practice of martial arts was to be banned, as many as 2,000 kung fu enthusiasts set fire to a building formerly occupied by the Ministry of Youth and Sport and also attacked the city's police headquarters. The police opened fire, but no casualties were reported. According to Radio Madagascar the ban was imposed following "acts of provocation and aggression by amateurs of the martial arts which have recently disturbed public order and security in the capital and its surroundings." In December there was more serious violence when, ignoring the ban, a gang of kung fu enthusiasts attacked premises occupied by a rival gang of youths, resulting in more than 50 deaths.

Madagascar was hit by natural disaster in April when Cyclone Kamisey caused many deaths in the north of the island and rendered thousands homeless. Much of the town of Antsiranana was destroyed. The Soviet Union supplied food and other aid valued at $3 million, and aid was also provided by Japan, France, the U.S., and the U.K.

The economy was badly affected by declining production and exports of the nation's main crops—coffee, cloves, and vanilla, and the balance of payments deficit widened significantly during the first quarter of the year. The International Monetary Fund, which in April had granted a one-year standby credit of $34.9 million, made available an additional credit of $14.9 million in June. Also in June the government announced a three-year plan for agricultural development.

The Indian Ocean Commission, consisting of Madagascar, Mauritius, and Seychelles, with the Comoros and the French dependency of Réunion as observers, met in Antananarivo in July. In October there were moves to revive traditional economic ties between Madagascar and Réunion. (PHILIPPE DECRAENE)

This article updates the *Macropædia* article INDIAN OCEAN ISLANDS: *Madagascar*.

MALAWI

A republic and member of the Commonwealth, Malawi is a landlocked state in eastern Africa. Area: 118,484 sq km (45,747 sq mi). Pop. (1984 est.): 6,839,000. Cap.: Lilongwe. Monetary unit: kwacha, with (Oct. 29, 1984) a free rate of 1.53 kwacha to U.S. $1 (1.85 kwacha = £1 sterling). President in 1984, Hastings Kamuzu Banda.

At the beginning of April 1984, Pres. Hastings Kamuzu Banda dissolved his Cabinet. He brought in two new ministers, created a new community services portfolio, and retained several posts himself. He gave no explanation for his action. In June, after a vigorous campaign by Amnesty International, the Church of Scotland, and a number of other bodies, President Banda commuted to life imprisonment the death sentences passed in 1983 on Orton Chirwa, an opposition leader and former minister of justice, and his wife.

It was decided in January that the kwacha should be pegged to a group of currencies comprising those of seven of Malawi's leading trading partners (the U.S., the U.K., South Africa, West Germany, Japan, France, and The Netherlands) instead of to the International Monetary Fund's Special Drawing Right. At a conference of aid donors in February, the minister of finance announced that over $100 million was required, in addition to more than $300 million already raised, to assist with development projects in 1984 and 1985. There was a particular need to restore external communications, which had been damaged by saboteurs. (KENNETH INGHAM)

This article updates the *Macropædia* article SOUTHERN AFRICA: *Malawi*.

MALI

Mali is a landlocked republic of West Africa. Area: 1,240,-192 sq km (478,841 sq mi). Pop. (1984 est.): 7,720,000. Cap.: Bamako. Monetary unit: CFA franc, with (Oct. 29, 1984) a par value of CFAF 50 to the French franc and a free rate of CFAF 470.60 to U.S. $1 (CFAF 568 = £1 sterling). President in 1984, Gen. Moussa Traoré.

Negotiations between Mali and Burkina Faso (formerly Upper Volta) over their common frontier entered a new phase on March 12, 1984, when delegations from the two countries met to discuss demarcation, cross-border traffic, and related problems. Meanwhile, the dispute was being considered by the International Court of Justice at The Hague, Neth. Mali's other frontier dispute, with Algeria, appeared to have been settled when on April 26 demarcation of the border was completed in accordance with the agreement reached in May 1983. Other developments in foreign relations included the signing in Bamako in May of an agreement with the U.S.S.R. on cultural and scientific cooperation. In September Pres. Moussa Traoré visited Mauritania for talks with Pres. Mohamed Khouna Ould Haidalla and Algeria's Pres. Chadli Bendjedid; the recently announced union of Morocco and Libya was believed to have been the main topic of discussion.

The frontier dispute with Burkina Faso had previously caused it to block Mali's reentry into the West African Monetary Union. However, with settlement of the dispute in sight, Burkina Faso withdrew its objections, and on February 17 Mali signed the readmission agreement. The membership entailed substitution of the CFA franc for the Mali franc (CFAF 1 = MF 2) as of June 1.

Traoré sacked five ministers when he formed a new government in December. (PHILIPPE DECRAENE)

This article updates the *Macropædia* article WESTERN AFRICA: *Mali*.

MAURITANIA

The republic of Mauritania is on the Atlantic coast of West Africa. Area: 1,030,700 sq km (398,000 sq mi). Pop. (1984 est.): 1,823,000. Cap.: Nouakchott. Monetary unit: ouguiya, with (Oct. 29, 1984) a free rate of 66.62 ouguiya to U.S. $1 (80.41 ouguiya = £1 sterling). Presidents of the Military Committee for National Salvation in 1984, Lieut. Col. Mohamed Khouna Ould Haidalla and, from December 12, Lieut. Col. Maaouya Ould Sidi Ahmed Taya; premiers, Lieutenant Colonel Taya until March 8, Lieutenant Colonel Haidalla until December 12, and, from December 12, Lieutenant Colonel Taya.

On Dec. 12, 1984, while Mauritania's head of state, Lieut. Col. Mohamed Khouna Ould Haidalla, was attending the Franco-African summit in Bujumbura, Burundi, former premier Lieut. Col. Maaouya Ould Sidi Ahmed Taya seized power in Nouakchott in a bloodless coup. Taya had been premier and defense minister from 1981 until a major ministerial reshuffle on March 8, 1984, when Haidalla replaced him in both functions and he reverted to his earlier post as army chief of staff. Haidalla returned home in December and was arrested.

This new palace revolution, the latest of several since the Military Committee for National Salvation came to power in 1978, reflected conditions of increasing political and economic instability. The government changes in March resulted from opposition within the regime to Haidalla's recognition on February 27 of the Saharan Arab Democratic Republic (SADR), Western Sahara's government-in-exile. Those opposed feared that the move would bring Mauritania into direct conflict with Morocco, still engaged in military action against the Popular Front for the Liberation of Saguia el Hamra and Río de Oro (Polisario Front), the Algerian-backed movement behind the SADR.

The regime's military priorities weighed heavily on the country's chronically weak economy, already hard hit by drought conditions. Domestic food production was estimated at only about 5% of requirements. (See *African Affairs:* Special Report, above.)   (PHILIPPE DECRAENE)

This article updates the *Macropædia* article WESTERN AFRICA: *Mauritania.*

MAURITIUS

The parliamentary state of Mauritius, a member of the Commonwealth, occupies an island in the Indian Ocean about 800 km (500 mi) east of Madagascar and includes the island dependencies of Rodrigues, Agalega, and Cargados Carajos Shoals. Area: 2,040 sq km (787.5 sq mi). Pop. (1984 est.): 1,018,000. Cap.: Port Louis. Monetary unit: Mauritian rupee, with (Oct. 29, 1984) a free rate of Mau Rs 15.07 to U.S. $1 (Mau Rs 18.18 = £1 sterling). Queen, Elizabeth II; governor-general in 1984, Sir Dayendranath Burrenchobay; prime minister, Aneerood Jugnauth.

Mauritius experienced further political divisions and increasing economic difficulties during 1984. The government coalition of the Mauritius Socialist Movement (MSM), the Labour Party, and the Social Democratic Party, which had won general elections in 1983, fell apart in February 1984 when the Labour Party decided to leave, apparently in response to pressure on it to merge with the MSM. The decision was not supported by all the Labour deputies. A week later Prime Minister Aneerood Jugnauth dismissed Labour Party leader Sir Satcam Boolell from his Cabinet post of minister of economic planning and development. He was replaced by Beergoonath Ghurburrun, leader of a group of Labour Party deputies who had elected to continue supporting the government.

As a result of discussions with the International Monetary Fund (IMF), the government increased the price of rice, flour, and sugar in March. The move was aimed at releasing the unused portion of a standby credit agreed on with the IMF in 1983. The government resisted pressure to devalue the currency, which would have pushed the price of staples even higher.

A major dispute developed between the government and the press over a proposal that all newspapers should lodge a deposit of Mau Rs 250,000 as security against libel claims that might be brought against them. The scheme, which was seen as an attack on press freedom since it would have forced at least some of the island's smaller newspapers out of business, was dropped in July, just before it was due to come into effect.   (GUY ARNOLD)

This article updates the *Macropædia* article INDIAN OCEAN ISLANDS: *Mauritius.*

MOZAMBIQUE

The people's republic of Mozambique is located in eastern Africa, on the Indian Ocean. Area: 799,400 sq km (308,650 sq mi). Pop. (1984 est.): 13,216,000. Cap.: Maputo. Monetary unit: metical, with (Oct. 29, 1984) a free rate of 43.73 meticals to U.S. $1 (52.78 meticals = £1 sterling). President in 1984, Samora Machel.

The catastrophic drought that affected many parts of Africa brought famine and heavy loss of life to Mozambique. The acute food shortage meant that foreign exchange had to be diverted to pay for emergency food imports, and the production of export crops—cashew nuts, sugar, and cotton—was also seriously affected. In February more than 100 people were killed, thousands were made homeless, and many more lost their crops as a result of flooding in the wake of a cyclone that swept over southeastern Africa.

After preliminary talks in January and a conference in February, an important series of agreements with South Africa was signed on March 16 near the Nkomati River, on the border between the two countries. The fundamental agreement concerned security. The two countries entered into a nonaggression pact under which each agreed to ensure that its territory would not be used as a base from which guerrilla attacks could be launched on the other. In effect, the African National Congress (ANC) would no longer be able to rely on Mozambique for covert assistance in its campaign against the South African government. Similarly, the Mozambique National Resistance (MNR) would no longer be trained and supplied by South Africa. The MNR had repeatedly disrupted transport, terrorized considerable areas of the country, and sabotaged power supplies.

The ANC condemned the treaty, and leaders of a number of African countries, notably Pres. Julius Nyerere of Tanzania, were critical of its objectives. For a bankrupt Mozambique, however, it meant the prospect of economic cooperation with South Africa and the hope that in areas terrorized by the MNR and ravaged by famine peace might be restored.

After lengthy discussions, Mozambique, South Africa, and Portugal signed a further agreement in Cape Town, South Africa, in May. South Africa agreed to pay an increased tariff for electricity supplied from the Cabora Bassa hydroelectric dam and to share responsibility with Mozambique for the security of the dam and of electricity supplies. The hope was that Portugal might quickly pay off the remainder of the loans incurred for the construction of the dam, and Mozambique could then enjoy the profits of the enterprise.

Not all the supporters of Pres. Samora Machel *(see* BIOGRAPHIES) approved of the rapprochement with South Africa. In June Machel dismissed three ministers, two of them, Lieut. Gen. Armando Guebuza and Maj. Gen. Mariano Matsinhe, dedicated Marxists. The activities of the guerrillas did not decline markedly, but South African Foreign Minister R. F. (Pik) Botha visited Maputo at the end of June bringing assurances of his government's intention to fulfill its obligations under the Nkomati accord. In July Machel visited China to seek increased aid. He met Chinese Premier Zhao Ziyang (Chao Tzu-yang), and the two signed an agreement for further economic and technical cooperation. China gave its support to the Nkomati accord, as did North Korea, which Machel also visited.

In August a further agreement was signed with South Africa aimed at redevelopment of the harbour and related services in Maputo. Then, on October 3, the government and MNR leaders met in Pretoria and gave their assent to a joint declaration on a cessation of armed conflict.

They asked South Africa to monitor the cease-fire and to assist in reconstructing the economy, and a tripartite commission was created to oversee implementation of the agreement. Doubts remained about the sincerity of South Africa's commitment. South Africa insisted, however, that it was making every attempt to prevent further guerrilla activity in Mozambique.   (KENNETH INGHAM)

This article updates the *Macropædia* article SOUTHERN AFRICA: *Mozambique*.

NIGER

Niger is a landlocked republic of West Africa. Area: 1,189,-000 sq km (459,100 sq mi). Pop. (1984 est.): 6,277,600. Cap.: Niamey. Monetary unit: CFA franc, with (Oct. 29, 1984) a par value of CFAF 50 to the French franc and a free rate of CFAF 470.60 to U.S. $1 (CFAF 568 = £1 sterling). Chief of state and president of the Supreme Military Council in 1984, Brig. Gen. Seyni Kountché; premier, Ahmid Algabid.

In February the last 14 of the several hundred students arrested the previous May during a strike at the University of Niamey and other educational establishments were released. On April 14, the eve of the tenth anniversary of his becoming president of Niger, Seyni Kountché announced the release of his predecessor as head of state, Hamani Diori, and of Djibo Bakary, former secretary-general of a now-banned political party. Diori had been president of Niger from its independence from France in 1960 until ousted by the 1974 coup. He had been detained since that time, and Bakary since 1975; both had been under house arrest since 1980. Some 40 other detainees implicated in a coup attempt in March 1976 were also released. Meanwhile, the report of a commission of inquiry into the October 1983 coup attempt was awaited.

In May Kountché visited Beijing (Peking), where he was promised a loan of CFAF 2 billion toward completion of the Niamey sports stadium. In November, with French backing, Niger was able to negotiate a rescheduling over ten years of its foreign debt, estimated at CFAF 25 billion in 1984.   (PHILIPPE DECRAENE)

This article updates the *Macropædia* article WESTERN AFRICA: *Niger*.

NIGERIA

A republic and member of the Commonwealth, Nigeria is located in West Africa, on the Gulf of Guinea. Area: 923,-768 sq km (356,669 sq mi.) Pop. (1984 est.): 94,502,000. Cap.: Lagos. Monetary unit: naira, with (Oct. 29, 1984) a free rate of 0.88 naira to U.S. $1 (1.06 naira = £1 sterling). Chairman of the Supreme Military Council in 1984, Maj. Gen. Mohammed Buhari.

The new military government in Nigeria faced two major problems during 1984: the need to establish its own credibility and the continuing economic depression. The return of a military government in a coup on the last day of 1983 was generally welcomed by Nigerians. There was widespread relief that a corrupt and inefficient government had been removed with little bloodshed. The biggest failure of the administration of former president Alhaji Shehu Shagari concerned its handling of the economy. How well the new government of Maj. Gen. Mohammed Buhari (*see* BIOGRAPHIES) dealt with this question would be the touchstone of its success.

The leaders of the coup established a 19-member Supreme Military Council (SMC), with Buhari as its chairman, head of state, and commander in chief of the armed forces. The SMC on January 18 appointed a Federal Executive Council (Cabinet), which included 11 civilian and 7 military members. It soon became clear that the military was not contemplating a quick return to civilian control.

The government's most urgent concern was to tackle the international debt. At the beginning of 1984 Nigeria's short-term debts stood at an estimated $5 billion, although figures varied. The International Monetary Fund (IMF) continued to insist that Nigeria devalue its currency, but the suggestion was resisted in Lagos. Instead the government completed an informal arrangement with its principal trade creditors that involved restructuring $2 billion worth of short-term debts and allowed Nigeria to sidestep the IMF.

In a well-planned exercise carried out in April and May, the government closed the borders and changed the currency. The move, designed to render worthless any currency that was held abroad and to stop smuggling, was largely successful. An austerity budget cut capital spending by 40% and current spending by 17%, compared with the 1983 figures. These measures were introduced against a background of 100% inflation, a wage freeze, and high prices for staple goods. As though to emphasize these problems, for the third successive year Lagos was rated the most expensive city in the world for business people. Also during April several thousand illegal immigrants from neighbouring nations were rounded up and deported.

The decline in economic fortunes was illustrated by

Maj. Gen. Mohammed Buhari (standing at right in car), the chairman of Nigeria's Supreme Military Council, reviews the troops during Army Day celebrations in the capital city of Lagos. Following the coup, which took place on the last day of 1983, the new government under Buhari had to deal with many problems, including Nigeria's large international debt.

the massive drop in imports from Nigeria's major trading partners. In 1983 imports from West Germany had fallen to one-quarter of their 1982 level, while those from Denmark, Japan, and the U.S. had been almost halved. One source of slight relief was provided when the Organization of Petroleum Exporting Countries (OPEC) agreed to allow Nigeria to increase its petroleum export quota from 1.3 million bbl a day to 1,450,000 bbl a day for the month of September. In October Nigeria cut the price of its principal grades of petroleum by $2 per barrel, thereby becoming the first member of OPEC to defy openly the official price structure set in 1983. The Oil Ministry declared its intention to maintain the higher petroleum quota for the forseeable future.

The government established tribunals to try some 475 former ministers and senior government officials who had been arrested after the coup and were awaiting trial on charges of "economic sabotage, corruption, and unjust enrichment." Yet almost at once Nigeria apparently dropped its demand for the return of exiled millionaires from the U.K. and the U.S. Then in July there was a spectacular attempt to kidnap the former transport minister, Umaru Dikko (*see* BIOGRAPHIES), who was abducted in London and later released from a crate that was apparently about to be flown to Nigeria. Recriminations passed between Nigeria and the U.K., yet neither government wanted to see relations seriously endangered, and the affair was passed over relatively quickly. In October some 250 of those detained on corruption charges were released, though others received sentences of as much as 21 years in prison.

In November a spokesman for the Nigerian government denied that there was any truth in a British newspaper report claiming that 42 people had been executed for plotting to assassinate members of the military leadership in October. (GUY ARNOLD)

This article updates the *Macropædia* article WESTERN AFRICA: *Nigeria.*

RWANDA

> The landlocked republic of Rwanda is situated in central Africa. Area: 26,338 sq km (10,169 sq mi). Pop. (1984 est.): 5.8 million. Cap.: Kigali. Monetary unit: Rwanda franc, with (Oct. 29, 1984) a free rate of RF 122.27 to U.S. $1 (RF 147.68 = £1 sterling). President in 1984, Maj. Gen. Juvénal Habyarimana.

Following elections to Rwanda's National Assembly in December 1983, in which all candidates represented the ruling National Revolutionary Development Movement, Pres. Juvénal Habyarimana reshuffled his Cabinet in January 1984. Five ministers lost their posts and several ministries were combined. In the same month, Habyarimana pardoned 2,500 prisoners.

It was a quiet year politically, enabling Rwanda to concentrate on development issues. A substantial European Communities program was designed to improve food production. The International Development Association offered a loan of $9 million to improve the Ntaruka power station and the country's power transmission network. Rwanda and Zaire were to cooperate in a project to obtain methane gas from Lake Kivu.

President Habyarimana's official visit to West Germany in March–April was returned later in the year by the West German minister for economic cooperation, Jürgen Warnke. Rwanda was receiving substantial assistance from West Germany. Aid amounting to DM 470 million of a promised total of DM 532 million had already been disbursed.

In an effort to protect its reserves of foreign currency, the Bank of Rwanda imposed restrictions on nonessential imports in March. (GUY ARNOLD)

This article updates the *Macropædia* article CENTRAL AFRICA: *Rwanda.*

SÃO TOMÉ AND PRÍNCIPE

> The republic of São Tomé and Príncipe comprises two main islands and several smaller islets that straddle the Equator in the Gulf of Guinea, off the west coast of Africa. Area: 964 sq km (372 sq mi). Pop. (1984 est.): 100,000. Cap.: São Tomé. Monetary unit: dobra, with (Oct. 29, 1984) a free rate of 45.46 dobras to U.S. $1 (54.87 dobras = £1 sterling). President in 1984, Manuel Pinto da Costa.

In January 1984 the UN Food and Agriculture Organization (FAO) published a report in which São Tomé and Príncipe was listed among 24 African countries facing the likelihood of major hunger or starvation conditions as a result of crop failures. The 1984 harvest was expected to be a poor one for the third consecutive year. The situation was aggravated by the fact that the tiny country made little impact on the international scene and so experienced difficulty in attracting overseas aid.

Portugal and its former African colonies began a process of mending fences. At a meeting in August the five Portuguese-speaking countries—São Tomé and Príncipe, Cape Verde, Guinea-Bissau, Angola, and Mozambique—announced that they intended to introduce a common currency that would be linked to the Portuguese escudo.

Joaquim Rafael Branco, the subject of controversy in 1983 when he had criticized the Portuguese government for the inadequacy of its aid, was removed from his post of minister of education, culture, and information during a Cabinet reshuffle. (GUY ARNOLD)

This article updates the *Macropædia* article CENTRAL AFRICA: *São Tomé and Príncipe.*

SENEGAL

> The republic of Senegal is located in West Africa, on the Atlantic Ocean; it surrounds the country of The Gambia, with which it has formed an administrative union called Senegambia. Area: 196,722 sq km (75,955 sq mi). Pop. (1984 est.): 6,352,000. Cap.: Dakar. Monetary unit: CFA franc, with (Oct. 29, 1984) a par value of CFAF 50 to the French franc and a free rate of CFAF 470.60 to U.S. $1 (CFAF 568 = £1 sterling). President in 1984, Abdou Diouf.

The year was marked by changes in the top echelons of the ruling Socialist Party (PS) and by splits within the party. On April 11 former premier Habib Thiam resigned from the presidency of the National Assembly and was succeeded by Daouda Sow. On October 9 Pres. Abdou Diouf dismissed Foreign Minister Moustapha Niasse and appointed Ibrahima Fall to replace him. Niasse's dismissal followed violent confrontations between rival factions of the PS in Casamance and Sine-Saloum provinces, resulting in at least four deaths. Municipal elections on November 25, boycotted by Abdoulaye Wade's Senegalese Democratic Party and 11 other opposition parties, resulted in a 96.35% vote for the PS. Casamance Province, the scene of separatist violence in 1983, was split into two administrative regions. In March and April, 119 of the 265 separatist demonstrators held in detention were provisionally released.

Senegal was among the African countries seriously affected by drought. In July it was host to a conference on desertification at which 22 countries were represented. During a visit to Dakar in January, France's Premier Pierre

Mauroy announced that French food aid for the year would be doubled to 10,000 metric tons of cereals. France also agreed to provide budgetary aid totaling F 200 million for 1984–85. In March Senegal reached agreement on the rescheduling of half its total foreign debt of $1,370,000,-000. A new standby arrangement with the International Monetary Fund was reached in principle in December.

Léopold Sédar Senghor (*see* BIOGRAPHIES), president of Senegal from its independence in 1960 until 1980, was admitted to the French Academy in March 1984, the first African to be so honoured.   (PHILIPPE DECRAENE)

This article updates the *Macropædia* article WESTERN AFRICA: *Senegal*.

SEYCHELLES

A republic and member of the Commonwealth, the Seychelles consists of about 100 islands in the Indian Ocean, 1,450 km (900 mi) from the east coast of Africa. Area: 453 sq km (175 sq mi). Pop. (1984 est.): 64,700. Cap.: Victoria. Monetary unit: Seychelles rupee, with (Oct. 29, 1984) a free rate of SR 7.15 to U.S. $1 (SR 8.63 = £1 sterling). President in 1984, France-Albert René.

In presidential elections held in Seychelles on June 17, 1984, Pres. France-Albert René, the sole candidate, was returned for a second five-year term when he received 92.6% of the votes cast. Five ministers—Joseph Belmont, Ogilvy Berlouis, Jacques Hodoul, Esmé Jumeau, and James Michel—were reappointed to their posts in the Council of Ministers (Cabinet), which had been dissolved in anticipation of the elections. The sixth, Maxime Ferrari, had asked to be relieved of the foreign affairs and economic planning portfolios, and his duties were assumed by René.

The most encouraging economic development was a sharp upturn in tourism following two poor years for the industry. Earnings from fishing licenses and port dues, another important economic indicator, also increased, but otherwise the economy remained sluggish.

Seychelles received substantial aid during the year, including grants from both the U.S. and the U.S.S.R. The African Development Bank agreed to provide a loan worth SR 58 million for the fisheries industry, and an agreement was reached with the European Communities allowing EC vessels to fish in the Seychelles' exclusive economic zone. Shridath Ramphal, secretary-general of the Commonwealth, visited the country to open the new central bank.   (GUY ARNOLD)

This article updates the *Macropædia* article INDIAN OCEAN ISLANDS: *Seychelles*.

SIERRA LEONE

A republic of West Africa and member of the Commonwealth, Sierra Leone lies on the Atlantic Ocean. Area: 71,740 sq km (27,699 sq mi). Pop. (1984 est.): 3,805,000. Cap.: Freetown. Monetary unit: leone, with (Oct. 29, 1984) a free rate of 2.49 leones to U.S. $1 (3 leones = £1 sterling). President in 1984, Siaka Stevens.

In January 1984 at least three people died in Freetown when student protests about food and fuel shortages turned violent. The unrest coincided with a convention of the ruling All People's Congress (APC), at which Pres. Siaka Stevens set up a commission to investigate the troubles. Two-thirds of approximately 100 prisoners detained after disturbances on the Liberian border in November 1983 were released in July.

The APC convention reelected President Stevens as party secretary-general. Stevens carried out minor reshuffles in his Cabinet in May and again in September, when the most important change was the moving of Abdulai Conteh from the Foreign Affairs Ministry to replace Salia Jusu-Sheriff as finance minister.

Despite a poor economic performance and continuing foreign-exchange difficulties, the overall economic picture as presented in the June budget showed a slight improvement over 1983. The collection of customs revenue had become more efficient, and private capital inflows had increased, although the improvement was matched by higher capital outflows to cover the country's debts. Higher production figures were achieved for bauxite, rutile, iron ore, and gold. In August the government announced several measures designed to curb smuggling.   (GUY ARNOLD)

This article updates the *Macropædia* article WESTERN AFRICA: *Sierra Leone*.

SOMALIA

A republic in the Horn of northeastern Africa, the Somali Democratic Republic, or Somalia, lies on the Gulf of Aden and the Indian Ocean. Area: 637,000 sq km (246,000 sq mi). Pop. (1984 est.): 5,505,000. Cap.: Mogadishu. Monetary unit: Somali shilling, with (Oct. 29, 1984) a free rate of 17.03 Somali shillings to U.S. $1 (20.56 Somali shillings = £1 sterling). President in 1984, Maj. Gen. Muhammad Siyad Barrah.

During 1984 Pres. Muhammad Siyad Barrah's government battled to retain political control and to maintain the precarious economic recovery in the face of political unrest and worsening climatic conditions. Somalia was one of the countries most vulnerable to the drought conditions that were affecting huge areas of Africa. (See *African Affairs: Special Report*, above.) The autumn 1983 rains had been poor, and at the end of the year the Cabinet had attempted to relieve the resulting food shortages by introducing a measure that allowed farmers to sell their produce on the open market rather than through the state agency. It also permitted private persons to import foodstuffs and other essentials on favourable terms for a three-month stopgap period. However, the 1984 rains again proved disappointing, and by the end of the year Somalia was in need of special food relief.

The situation was aggravated by the presence of an estimated 700,000 refugees who had fled to Somalia during the 1977–78 Ogaden war with Ethiopia. Their fate remained undecided, though initiatives were being taken to provide land for those who wished to settle permanently in Somalia. During 1984 their numbers were swelled still further by people fleeing conflict and famine in Ethiopia.

On June 1 President Barrah announced a Cabinet reshuffle in which six ministers were dismissed and others were given new posts. The move followed earlier dismissals and redeployment of personnel in the Army and the ruling Somali Socialist Revolutionary Party.

Since 1981 the International Monetary Fund (IMF) had afforded the country $105 million worth of credits. In April 1984 the Cabinet rejected IMF terms for a renewed $183 million extended credit facility, which included cutbacks in state industries and defense and further devaluation of the currency. However, negotiations were renewed in September, the Somali shilling was devalued by nearly 50%, and the credit facility was secured.

The position on the Ethiopian frontier had remained at a stalemate since Ethiopian troops backing Somali rebel groups had invaded in 1982, only to dig in barely 20 km (12.4 mi) from the border. There were several violent episodes during 1984, notably in January when six

Ethiopian MiG jet fighters bombed the town of Borama and nearby villages in the northern sector. Forty people were killed and more than 80 injured, many of them pupils at the local school.

The country continued to be troubled by internal rebellion, much of it fueled by the conviction of groups based in the north of the country that they were discriminated against by a government that drew its support from the centre and south. On November 24 dissident sympathizers hijacked a Somali Airlines jet and forced it to land at Addis Ababa, Eth. The hijackers demanded the release of 7 young people under sentence of death for subversion and of 14 prominent political figures, including Ismail Ali Abokor, former vice-president, who was arrested in 1982 on treason charges. However, after a three-day siege the hijackers surrendered without their demands' having been met, though they received asylum in Ethiopia. In December the Somali National Movement rebel group claimed that the government had executed 28 people in retaliation for a guerrilla offensive. (VIRGINIA R. LULING)

This article updates the *Macropædia* article EASTERN AFRICA: *Somalia.*

SOUTH AFRICA

The Republic

South Africa occupies the southern tip of Africa, with the Atlantic Ocean to the west and the Indian Ocean to the east. It partially surrounds the four former black states of Bophuthatswana, Ciskei, Transkei, and Venda (whose independence is not recognized by the international community). Area: 1,123,226 sq km (433,680 sq mi). Pop. (1984 est.): 26,749,000. (Area and population figures exclude the four former black states.) Executive cap., Pretoria; judicial cap., Bloemfontein; legislative cap., Cape Town. Monetary unit: rand, with (Oct. 29, 1984) a free rate of R 1.79 to U.S. $1 (R 2.16 = £1 sterling). State president to Sept. 14, 1984, Marais Viljoen; prime minister and, from September 14, executive state president, Pieter Willem Botha.

DOMESTIC AFFAIRS. The new constitutional order embodied in the controversial Constitution Act of 1983 and endorsed by a two-thirds majority of South Africa's white electorate came into operation on Sept. 4, 1984. By that date the restructured Parliament made up of three separate chambers—a white House of Assembly (in effect the existing 178-member legislature), a Coloured House of Representatives (85), and an Asian House of Delegates (45)—had taken shape after bitterly contested elections against a background of widespread and at times violent controversy. Those who regarded the new system as an entrenchment of apartheid (racial separation) and condemned the omission of the majority black population from the constitution called for a boycott, with the result that there was a low turnout in the August polls. About 20% of the Coloured (mixed descent) and 18% of the Asian (mainly Indian) populations voted. The Labour Party led by Allan Hendrickse won nearly all the seats in the House of Representatives, and the National People's Party under Amichand Rajbansi gained a narrow majority over the official opposition party, Solidarity, in the House of Delegates.

Meeting for the first time in joint session, representatives of the majority parties in the three houses unanimously elected Prime Minister P. W. Botha (*see* BIOGRAPHIES) as the executive state president with wide-ranging constitutional powers, including those of prime minister. Botha appointed an 18-member Cabinet, with both Hendrickse and Rajbansi as ministers without portfolio, to handle "general affairs" (foreign policy, defense, and finance) and three five-member councils to deal with "own affairs"

(including education, housing, local government, and the arts) in each chamber. A network of joint standing committees was created to reach consensus on draft legislation dealing with "general affairs" and borderline cases before submission of the legislation to Parliament. Failing such consensus, the final say would rest with the president or, at his discretion, with the reconstituted 60-member President's Council of whites, Coloureds, and Asians, in which the ruling National Party (NP) held a majority.

The local government affairs of urban blacks were recognized as being among the urgent issues facing the special Cabinet committee appointed to consider the political future of the black population within the new framework. The wider issue was defined by Botha at the opening of the first session of the new Parliament. "We realize," he said, "that the constitution does not provide for the diversity which marks the South African population. Democratic political participation must also be further extended among our black compatriots in order to meet the demands of justice." The belief still prevailed, however, that the political future of blacks was tied to that of their ancestral "homelands." This was rejected by organizations such as the United Democratic Front and other bodies that could claim to be the voice of the black population.

Together with various grievances of a local nature, the immediate black reaction to the new constitution played a part in the wave of unrest and open defiance of the law that swept through densely populated black residential areas in the Vaal Triangle (notably in the townships of Sharpeville, Evaton, and Sebokeng), Soweto, sections of the Orange Free State goldfields, and the Eastern Cape. Erupting in the wake of the disturbances during the Coloured and Asian election campaigns, the township disorders were accompanied by large-scale school boycotts and violent demonstrations. An estimated 100 people died during the protests, and many more were injured and arrested. The police took drastic action in attempting to restore law and order. Finally, after nearly two months of unrest, a massive force of 7,000 police and Defence Force troops mounted an operation in the main trouble centres of Sebokeng and Sharpeville on October 23. It ended with hundreds of arrests and summary trials, mostly on minor charges. While conceding that the lawlessness had to be stopped, critics inside and outside South Africa considered that the use of the military to quell civil unrest was unjustified.

Despite continued raids and thousands more arrests, rioting continued to be reported in parts of the Transvaal and the Eastern Cape. In several black townships public gatherings and the funeral processions of reputed victims of police action were frequently banned, followed by arrests when the bans were defied. While some long-standing banning and detention orders were lifted, overall there was a marked increase in the number of detentions without trial.

The minister of education and training, Gerrit Viljoen, announced various improvements in the educational facilities for black pupils as well as in the channels of communication between the authorities and black students, parents, and teachers. Viljoen also held out the prospect of a new national department that would embrace all education, including that of blacks, a development hitherto rejected by the government. While these moves were generally welcomed, they were still regarded by many South Africans as basically cosmetic.

The right-wing Conservative Party gave further proof of the support it enjoyed in rural areas of northern Transvaal in by-election victories over the NP. In predominantly English-speaking Natal, on the other hand, there were signs of a swing to the NP. At its Natal congress, the official

In August a large-scale boycott was staged during the first elections since South Africa's establishment of a tricameral Parliament, which included separate houses for the white, Coloured, and Asian populations. The boycott was called to protest against the continuing denial of rights for blacks and subordination of the Coloureds and Asians under the new constitution.

DAVID BARRIT—GAMMA/LIAISON

opposition, the Progressive Federal Party, decided to open its membership to persons of all races in disregard of the 1968 Act prohibiting mixed political parties. In September the new Citizenship Amendment Act came into effect, granting automatic citizenship to immigrants between 15 and 25 years of age with a minimum of five years' residence and requiring the males to register immediately for compulsory military service.

A notable event was the awarding of the 1984 Nobel Peace Prize to Bishop Desmond Tutu (*see* NOBEL PRIZES), secretary-general of the South African Council of Churches, in October. Coming in the midst of the turbulence in the black townships, the award was seen by many at home and abroad as evidence of international sympathy for the cause of peaceful change with which Tutu was identified. The following month Tutu was elected Anglican bishop of Johannesburg. He was the first black churchman to hold the post, the second most important in the country's Anglican hierarchy.

FOREIGN RELATIONS. After intensive negotiations, South Africa and Mozambique reached an agreement aimed at ending the armed conflict that had punctuated their relations since Mozambique became independent. The Nkomati accord, signed by Botha and Pres. Samora Machel (*see* BIOGRAPHIES) on March 16, committed each country to cooperate in putting an end to the use of its territory for acts of aggression and incitement against the other. (It was later revealed that a similar agreement had been reached between South Africa and Swaziland two years earlier, but Botswana and Lesotho had declined Pretoria's overtures.) The accord meant, in practice, that Mozambique would prevent such bodies as the African National Congress (ANC) from operating across the border against South Africa and that the latter would stop lending aid to the Mozambique National Resistance (MNR) insurgency movement. In a separate pact, South Africa undertook to assist in protecting the Cabora Bassa dam, which had been put out of action repeatedly by the MNR. The Nkomati accord provided a much-needed stimulus to Mozambique's harassed economy and opened up new opportunities to South African and international business interests and investment. As time passed, ANC bases in Mozambique were dismantled and many of the guerrillas moved into Swaziland, where they were rounded up and either jailed or deported to other African countries. MNR guerrilla opera-

tions continued, however, and Pretoria and Maputo began cease-fire negotiations with the insurgents.

The major problem that remained in South Africa's relations with its neighbours was the situation in Angola, closely related as it was to the future of South West Africa/Namibia. The position was complicated by three factors: the virtual state of civil war in Angola; the frequent incursions by the South West Africa People's Organization (SWAPO) from Angola into Namibia; and the military actions by the South African Defence Force against SWAPO bases deep in Angola. Following negotiations between Pretoria, Luanda, and a delegation from the U.S., an agreement was signed in Lusaka, Zambia, under which South Africa and Angola pledged to end the undeclared state of war that existed between them. It called for a phased withdrawal of South African troops from southern Angola and for Angola to keep SWAPO out of the evacuated area, with a joint monitoring commission to supervise the operations. In the ensuing months South Africa's withdrawal was halted 60 km (40 mi) north of the Namibian border on the plea that SWAPO was still operating in the area. Angola accused South Africa of stalling and also of continuing to support rebels opposed to Angola's Marxist government. In an unexpected development, the co-founder of SWAPO, Andimba Toivo Ja Toivo (*see* BIOGRAPHIES), was released from prison by the South African authorities in March.

Pressures were maintained at the UN for the implementation of Resolution 435 on Namibian independence. At its September session, the General Assembly adopted a resolution (the U.S. and U.K. abstaining) condemning the new constitution, primarily because it excluded the black population. A similar but more strongly worded resolution was passed by the Security Council, with the U.S. abstaining. South Africa warned that it might cease its peace initiatives in southern Africa if these condemnations continued.

Relations with the U.K. deteriorated markedly after six antiapartheid campaigners took refuge in the British consulate in Durban and the British refused to evict them. South Africa retaliated by refusing to return four South Africans to the U.K., where they faced charges for selling arms to South Africa in defiance of a UN embargo. Three of the "Durban six" left the consulate in October and were immediately detained. The others left in December after detention orders on all six were lifted, but five of the six were subsequently arrested on treason charges.

In midyear Botha made a round of official visits to eight Western European capitals, where he exchanged views on South African and world affairs with his counterparts.

THE ECONOMY. In presenting the 1984–85 budget, Finance Minister Owen Horwood stressed that, notwithstanding its inherent economic strength, South Africa continued to be faced with a situation calling for sacrifices from every section of the population. The budget provided for total estimated expenditure of R 25 billion, almost 12% more than in the previous year, in the framework of an economy that demanded, besides a sounder balance of payments, a lowering of the inflation rate, then running at 11–12%. The general sales tax was raised from 7 to 10 cents, and a number of foodstuffs were exempted from the tax for the first time. This was followed immediately by a number of price increases.

Later in the year a government commission was appointed to examine the whole tax system. In June Horwood resigned and was succeeded by Barend du Plessis, who was pledged to a policy of strict budgetary control. Cuts to the tune of R 650 million were announced, including a token R 108 million in the defense budget of R 3,755,000,000, which was still 21% above the previous year's total and was exceeded only by the education budget.

A progressive decline in the gold price, which fell below $340 an ounce, affected the economy as a whole. It was accompanied by a depreciation in the exchange value of the rand. The weaker rand stimulated exports and put a brake on imports, with the result that by the end of the third quarter the balance of trade, which had been running at a deficit for some time, showed a surplus of R 355 million.

The climate of economic instability was reflected in increased unemployment and industrial unrest and by a marked upward trend in the number of insolvencies. On the other hand, investors and industrialists were reported to be showing a more active interest in the government's decentralization scheme, which offered incentives for the establishment of industries in underdeveloped rural areas, particularly in or near the black homelands.

Bophuthatswana

The republic of Bophuthatswana consists of six discontinuous, landlocked geographic units, entirely surrounded by South Africa except for one unit that borders Botswana on the northwest. Area: 40,000 sq km (15,444 sq mi). Pop. (1984 est.): 1,417,000. Cap.: Mmabatho. Monetary unit: South African rand. President in 1984, Lucas Mangope.

The economy and communications loomed large in the affairs of Bophuthatswana during 1984. In common with other former homelands, it received support from South Africa in the form of direct aid, supplemented by various agreements on taxation, customs duties, and monetary policy derived from the original independence settlement. In 1983–84 nearly 43% of the state budget was financed from these sources. An agreement concluded with the Development Bank of Southern Africa involved a contribution of R 85 million toward existing projects and a further loan for future projects. Several industrial areas near the South African border secured a housing loan of $50 million from a South African-headed banking group. An international airport was built at Mmabatho, and there were plans for an international airline.

Proposals for the partial rectification of Bophuthatswana's fragmented borders by an exchange of land with South Africa were turned down by the government, which undertook to draw up its own plan.

Ciskei

Bordering the Indian Ocean in the south, Ciskei is surrounded on land by South Africa. Area: 5,386 sq km (2,080 sq mi). Pop. (1984 est.): 709,000. Cap.: Bisho. Monetary unit: South African rand. President in 1984, Lennox Sebe.

While South Africa contributed materially toward Ciskei's annual budget, differences between the two governments came to the surface. The government of Pres. Lennox Sebe complained of interference in the internal affairs of Ciskei, and South Africa criticized Ciskei's alleged extravagance. Examples cited were the decision to construct an international airport near Bisho and the training of pilots in Israel when there was no commercial airline. Conciliatory moves were made on both sides, particularly on the part of Sebe, who reversed his previous opposition to South Africa's concept of a southern African confederation.

Sustained efforts to attract foreign investment led to the announcement of plans for the establishment of a number of new factories and the extension of existing ones, creating some 9,000 new job openings. In the meantime, Ciskei faced high unemployment and sporadic labour unrest.

Transkei

Bordering the Indian Ocean and surrounded on land by South Africa, Transkei comprises three discontinuous geographic units, two of which are landlocked and one of which borders Lesotho. Area: 43,553 sq km (16,816 sq mi). Pop. (1984 est.): 2,517,000. Cap.: Umtata. Monetary unit: South African rand. President in 1984, Kaiser Daliwonga Matanzima; prime minister, George Matanzima.

Through its official Development Corporation, Transkei was in the forefront of the program launched by the South African-sponsored Decentralization Board to encourage the establishment of labour-intensive industries in economically underdeveloped areas by means of financial inducements. Since early 1983 the corporation had succeeded in attracting investment capital for more than 30 new industries. While this doubled the productive potential of Transkeian industry, it was considered disappointing in terms of the effort spent on the operation. For that and other reasons, a public inquiry was ordered into the corporation's workings.

In 1983–84 Transkei received more than R 400 million from South Africa. In the face of criticism, the government forged ahead with plans for an international airport and a deep-sea harbour.

Venda

The landlocked republic of Venda is located in extreme northeastern South Africa. Area: 6,198 sq km (2,393 sq mi). Pop. (1984 est.): 396,000. Cap.: Thohoyandou. Monetary unit: South Africa rand. President in 1984, Patrick Mphephu.

Venda's first parliamentary election since independence was won by the ruling Venda National Party, led by Patrick Mphephu, with a majority of 40 seats against 4 held by the Venda Independent Party. The opposition leader, Gilbert Bakane, claimed that the results had been manipulated and demanded that the returns be invalidated.

Like other former self-governing homelands, Venda benefited in 1983–84 from grants-in-aid and other payments from South Africa amounting, in all, to R 114 million, about 70% of its budget. (LOUIS HOTZ)

See also *Dependent States,* below.

SUDAN

A republic of North Africa, the Sudan has a coastline on the Red Sea. Area: 2,503,890 sq km (966,757 sq mi). Pop. (1984 est.): 21,160,000. Cap.: Khartoum. Monetary unit: Sudanese pound, with (Oct. 29, 1984) a par value of LSd 1.30 to U.S. $1 (free rate of LSd 1.53 = £1 sterling). President and prime minister in 1984, Gen. Gaafar Nimeiry.

Opposition to the government of Pres. Gaafar Nimeiry (*see* BIOGRAPHIES) spread from the south to the north of Sudan during 1984. Non-Muslim rebels in the south, resentful over the division of their region into three provinces and angered by the imposition of Shari'ah (Islamic law) in 1983, formed themselves into the Sudan National Liberation Movement and harassed military units in the area. Some southern troops joined the rebels when they learned they were to be moved to the north and replaced by Muslims.

The severity and fundamentalist nature of the Islamic law enforced by the government also began to arouse opposition in the north. There was rioting at the University of Khartoum in February, and in March 2,000 doctors went on strike to protest conditions in the medical service. Despite the arrest of 70 leaders, the strike continued until the government made concessions. On April 29 Nimeiry declared a state of emergency and gave the Army and police authority to enter houses and to censor mail. Breaches of the emergency laws resulted in the creation of special courts to mete out summary justice against offenders. Six senior members were removed from the Cabinet in May, and there was a further Cabinet reshuffle in December.

Egypt, usually a staunch ally, showed its strong disapproval of the severity of the punishments inflicted by the emergency courts. Though the state of emergency was suspended in September, the U.S., which regarded Sudan as a bastion against the spread of Communism in northern Africa, was also worried. The World Bank and International Monetary Fund were baffled by the confusion caused by the islamization of the economy in September.

Both Sudan and Egypt accused Libya of responsibility for an air raid on Omdurman on March 16. Libya responded by claiming that the attack had been perpetrated by dissident Sudanese.   (KENNETH INGHAM).

SWAZILAND

Swaziland is a landlocked monarchy of southern Africa and a member of the Commonwealth. Area: 17,364 sq km (6,704 sq mi). Pop. (1984 est.): 598,000. Cap.: Mbabane. Monetary unit: lilangeni (plural: emalangeni), at par with the South African rand, with (Oct. 29, 1984) a free rate of 1.79 emalangeni to U.S. $1 (2.16 emalangeni = £1 sterling). Regent in 1984, Queen Ntombi; prime minister, Prince Bhekimpi Dlamini.

In March 1984, after the signing of a nonaggression pact between Mozambique and South Africa, it was revealed that Swaziland had reached a similar agreement with South Africa in February 1982. The accord committed each country to curb any terrorist activity on its soil that might threaten the other. The Swazi authorities had since cracked down on members of the African National Congress, banned by the Pretoria regime. In December the two countries agreed to exchange permanent trade representatives, who would have full diplomatic immunity.

There was evidence that the power struggle prompted by the death of King Sobhuza II in August 1982 continued. Prince Sozisa Dlamini was removed as deputy head of state in September after being accused of planning to lead a military coup in June. Also in June, Finance Minister Sishayi Nxumalo and Foreign Minister Richard Dlamini were dismissed, along with the chiefs of the armed forces and the police. The Liqoqo, Swaziland's Supreme Council of State, claimed the four had been plotting to seize power from the regent, Queen Ntombi.

The economy was suffering from the effects of drought and a disastrous cyclone at a time of world recession. The budget's main targets were to control government spending and provide incentives for investment and job creation.

(GUY ARNOLD)

This article updates the *Macropædia* article SOUTHERN AFRICA: *Swaziland*.

TANZANIA

The republic of Tanzania, a member of the Commonwealth, consists of Tanganyika, on the east coast of Africa, and Zanzibar, just off the coast in the Indian Ocean, which includes Zanzibar Island, Pemba Island, and small islets. Area: 945,050 sq km (364,886 sq mi). Pop. (1984 est.): 19,993,000. Seat of government, Dar es Salaam; capital designate, Dodoma. Monetary unit: Tanzania shilling, with (Oct. 29, 1984) a free rate of T Sh 17.92 to U.S. $1 (T Sh 21.62 = £1 sterling). President in 1984, Julius Nyerere; prime ministers, Edward Moringe Sokoine to April 12 and, from April 24, Salim Ahmed Salim.

In May 1984 Tanzania, Kenya, and Uganda signed an agreement distributing the assets and liabilities of the former East African Community, whose collapse in 1977 had led to the closing of the border between Kenya and Tanzania. Those two countries accepted responsibility for most of the outstanding debts and agreed to pay compensation to Uganda. Following the reopening of the border in November 1983, negotiations to encourage tourist traffic between Kenya and Tanzania took place in January.

While relations with Kenya improved, those between the mainland and Zanzibar deteriorated. Protests in Zanzibar came to a head in January when Aboud Jumbe, president of Zanzibar and vice-president of Tanzania, resigned. During the previous 12 months there had been growing criticism of Zanzibar's subordination to the mainland, particularly in economic matters. Jumbe was succeeded as interim president of Zanzibar by Ali Hassan Mwinyi, who, as the only candidate, was elected president in April. Internal security was tightened from the moment of Jumbe's resignation, and his leading supporters were transferred from important posts in the administration. Bashir Abssah Kway-Swanzi, the attorney general of Zanzibar, and his predecessor, Wolfango Dourado, were arrested, and other senior ministers were forced to resign. Dourado argued that Zanzibar should be treated as an equal partner in a federation rather than as a subordinate member of a union, and he faced the possibility of being charged with treason.

Pres. Julius Nyerere was forced to reduce and reshuffle his Cabinet after the death of Prime Minister Edward Moringe Sokoine (*see* OBITUARIES) in a car accident in April. Sokoine, who had been regarded as a likely successor to Nyerere as president, had been recalled to office in 1983 after retiring in 1980 for reasons of health. He was succeeded by Salim Ahmed Salim, a career diplomat, who moved from the Foreign Affairs Ministry. In September details of a plan to stage a coup in early 1983 emerged when a magistrate's court heard initial proceedings against 14 soldiers and 5 civilians accused of involvement.

The seriousness of the economic situation was reflected in the continuing decline in per capita income and in the government's decision in June to devalue the currency by 26%. The decision, taken as a result of considerable pressure from the International Monetary Fund, aroused resentment in Zanzibar because the island's leaders were not consulted. A new departure in a country dedicated to socialism was indicated in July when Abdulrehman Mohamed Babu, former minister of economic affairs, was reported in the government-owned *Daily News* to have said that capitalism would do the country good. This unofficial comment was echoed a month later by the new prime minister. Speaking in Mwanza in August, Salim urged regional commissioners and party leaders to encourage private investment in agriculture in order to bolster the country's flagging food supply.　　　(KENNETH INGHAM)

This article updates the *Macropædia* article EASTERN AFRICA: *Tanzania.*

TOGO

A republic of West Africa, Togo is situated on the Bight of Benin. Area: 56,785 sq km (21,925 sq mi). Pop. (1984 est.): 2,947,000. Cap.: Lomé. Monetary unit: CFA franc, with (Oct. 29, 1984) a par value of CFAF 50 to the French franc and a free rate of CFAF 470.60 to U.S. $1 (CFAF 568 = £1 sterling). President in 1984, Gen. Gnassingbe Eyadema.

Pres. Gnassingbe Eyadema reshuffled his government on Sept. 13, 1984. Atsu Koffi Amega, formerly Togo's ambassador to the UN, became foreign minister, replacing Anani Kuma Akakpo Ahianyo; Komla Alipui succeeded Tete Tevi-Benissan as minister of economy and finance; Koffi Djondo became minister of state enterprises; Koffi Edoh, minister of technical education and professional training; and Ayaovi Adodo, minister of planning and industry.

The seventh summit meeting of the Economic Community of West African States (ECOWAS) took place in Lomé in November. In his opening address, President Eyadema spoke of the grave economic difficulties faced by ECOWAS members as a result of the world economic recession and the severe drought affecting many areas of the region. Togo's own drifting economy was badly affected by the depressed world market for phosphates, its principal export. The country was burdened with an external debt of around $1 billion, or about $360 per inhabitant, as compared with an average annual per capita income of $380.

(PHILIPPE DECRAENE)

This article updates the *Macropædia* article WESTERN AFRICA: *Togo.*

UGANDA

A landlocked republic and member of the Commonwealth, Uganda is located in eastern Africa. Area: 241,139 sq km (93,104 sq mi), including 44,081 sq km of inland water. Pop. (1984 est.): 14,206,000. Cap.: Kampala. Monetary unit: Uganda shilling, with (Oct. 29, 1984) a free rate for traditional exports, essential imports, and official loans of U Sh 479.30 to U.S. $1 (U Sh 578.50 = £1 sterling) and with (Dec. 31.1983) a free rate for other transactions of U Sh 290 to U.S. $1 (U Sh 420.10 = £1 sterling). President in 1984, Milton Obote; prime minister, Erifasi Otema Allimadi.

Pres. Milton Obote, in his role as minister of finance, announced in June 1984 that Uganda had achieved a balance of payments surplus for the first time in more than ten years. There had also been a growth rate in the economy of 5% for the previous two years. On the strength of the improvement the government was able to merge the two-tier foreign exchange rate that had been introduced two years earlier at the insistence of the International Monetary Fund. (Under the two-tier system the free rate for traditional exports, essential imports, and official loans was U Sh 479 to $1. For all other transactions it was U Sh 290

to $1.) A considerable increase in tea production was also reassuring, as was the U.K.'s offer of more than $11 million in aid at the end of January. Nevertheless, problems remained after the disastrous years of former president Idi Amin's rule and the war that overthrew him.

The main obstacle to recovery continued to be the threat to security in the region to the north and west of Kampala from armed guerrillas opposed to Obote's government. Their most spectacular success in 1984 was an attack on a military barracks at Masindi, 224 km (140 mi) northwest of the capital, in February. Damage to a power station in August caused a five-day blackout in and around Kampala. In January a British accountant and three Swiss engineers were killed by gunmen in two separate incidents, and in May a French Roman Catholic priest was shot and killed.

In an attempt to curb guerrilla activities the Army carried out numerous sweeps through areas where the rebels were thought to be hiding. Civilians frequently suffered during these military operations, and the troops were accused of indiscriminate cruelty. The government admitted that troops had been responsible for setting fire to houses and stealing property, as well as killing a number of people at a theological college and seminary near Kampala in May while pursuing guerrillas. A Commonwealth military training team completed two years in Uganda in March and was replaced by a British team. In August the government suspended military ties with the U.S. after the U.S. ambassador, among others, was outspokenly critical of the country's human rights record.

According to some reports, denied by the government, thousands of people were killed in the clashes between troops and guerrillas in the centre of the country. Many more thousands were rendered homeless. Elsewhere, more normal conditions prevailed, though in April many people fled for security to the northeastern town of Soroti when threatened by cattle raiders from Karamoja, a region that had suffered heavily at the hands of Amin's troops when they withdrew in 1979 and, since then, from drought.

President Obote made a number of attempts to demonstrate that his policy was one of reconciliation. In January he appointed a committee to recommend action concerning several thousand applications from Asians and others for the restoration of businesses and property that they had lost under Amin's regime. In July 700 prisoners were released, and an appeal was made to exiles to return home. Strong criticism of the government was permitted in the National Assembly. The opposition Democratic Party felt considerably encouraged by its participation in a two-day conference and rally of Christian Democrats from Europe, Asia, and Latin America, which took place in Kampala in October.　　　(KENNETH INGHAM)

This article updates the *Macropædia* article EASTERN AFRICA: *Uganda.*

ZAIRE

The republic of Zaire is located in central Africa with a short coastline on the Atlantic Ocean. Area: 2,344,885 sq km (905,365 sq mi). Pop. (1984 est.): 32,084,000. Cap.: Kinshasa. Monetary unit: zaire, with (Oct. 29, 1984) a free rate of 38.46 zaires to U.S. $1 (46.42 zaires = £1 sterling). President in 1984, Mobutu Sese Seko; prime minister, Kengo wa Dondo.

After dismissing two of his ministers in early February 1984, Pres. Mobutu Sese Seko of Zaire promoted his eldest son, Nyiwa Mobutu, to the position of secretary for foreign affairs, the second most important post in the Cabinet. In March it was announced that Mobutu, who had already served two seven-year terms as president, would be the sole candidate in presidential elections scheduled for November since no other candidacy had been declared. The elections were brought forward to July, and Mobutu received 99.16% of the votes cast.

On March 27 bomb explosions in Kinshasa killed two people and injured five others. Responsibility was claimed by two opposition groups, but the publication of their communiqué in Brussels angered the Belgian government, which announced that it was unacceptable for opposition groups to use Brussels as a base for operations against Zaire. It was reported in June that several people, most of them members of the Mouvement National Congolais-Lumumba, had been arrested in connection with the explosions. In November French troops helped the Army quell an uprising in the town of Moba, Shaba Province, in which more than a hundred people died. The Mobutu regime claimed that antigovernment rebels mounted the attack and accused the governments of Belgium and Tanzania of involvement. Opposition sources in Belgium, including exiled former prime minister Nguza Karl-I-Bond, suggested that an army mutiny was the origin of the troubles.

Portugal's Pres. António Ramalho Eanes visited Zaire in March and discussed technological aid. When Eanes expressed approval of the negotiations between Angola, Mozambique, and South Africa, Mobutu stressed that the importance of the struggles being waged by the South West Africa People's Organization and the African National Congress against the regime in South Africa must not be overlooked. His response was surprising in view of the fact that his government had provided logistical support to antigovernment forces in Angola.

In April Mobutu visited Paris, where he had talks with French Pres. François Mitterrand as well as with representatives of French business interests, and was promised further French aid. During his visit 200 students from Zaire were arrested and questioned by French police after they had attempted to demonstrate against violations of human rights in Zaire. The government announced that Zaire had given sanctuary to more than half a million refugees, mainly from Angola and Uganda, providing an indication of the peace and stability prevailing in the country. Nevertheless, a Belgian Socialist deputy who was due to travel to Kinshasa with a delegation from the European Parliament in March was refused a visa after she requested a meeting with the minister of the interior to discuss human rights.

In July President Mobutu visited Belgium at the invitation of King Baudouin I to try to improve relations between the two countries. On the official front the visit was a success. The Belgian government seemed ready to increase its loan to Zaire, to increase the credit made available by the National Bank, and to revive the mechanisms for guaranteeing investments. In addition, arrangements were made for a team of Belgian businessmen to visit Zaire to investigate ways of increasing cooperation. The response from unofficial quarters was less friendly. The Zaire Committee on Human Rights claimed the president's visit gave the impression that Belgium approved of a situation in which human rights were being undermined, an accusation Mobutu denied.

At its weekly meeting on August 24 the executive committee considered a progress report, covering the first quarter of the year, on the implementation of the International Monetary Fund (IMF) adjustment program adopted in September 1983. A clear improvement over the corresponding period of 1983 was noted. Domestic prices were continuing to stabilize, and the depreciation of the currency had moderated since the devaluation of the previous September. There were signs that the rate of inflation—76% in 1983—would fall to 50% by the end of 1984, and IMF experts in the Bank of Zaire were anxious to ensure that the estimated budget deficit was not exceeded. Although the government was working hard to fulfill the IMF program, there was some feeling that the economic pressures on the country were unduly severe. In particular, it was thought that the percentage of the budget earmarked for debt servicing was too high, and it was hoped that there might be some rescheduling of the debt in 1985.

At the end of May the International Development Association made a grant of $26 million to Zaire to rehabilitate its railway system, which was essential for transporting minerals and agricultural products. The intention was to improve the country's capacity for track maintenance as well as to replace and repair locomotives and railroad cars. Earlier in the month agreement was reached over the rescheduling of $360 million of the debt owed by the government to the U.S.

Throughout the year there were problems with Zambia because of border incidents involving smuggling of emeralds and corn (maize). An invitation by the Zambian government to the U.S. to mediate in the dispute early in the year produced no results, and in August the problem flared up again. Zambia deported more than 2,000 people accused of smuggling, and Zaire retaliated by rounding up and allegedly ill-treating a number of Zambians, some of whom subsequently fled the country. Several meetings took place between officials of the two countries in an attempt to calm the situation.   (KENNETH INGHAM)

This article updates the *Macropædia* article CENTRAL AFRICA: *Zaire*.

ZAMBIA

A landlocked republic and member of the Commonwealth, Zambia is in eastern Africa. Area: 752,614 sq km (290,586 sq mi). Pop. (1984 est.): 6,443,000. Cap.: Lusaka. Monetary unit: kwacha, with (Oct. 29, 1984) a free rate of 1.99 kwacha to U.S. $1 (2.40 kwacha = £1 sterling). President in 1984, Kenneth Kaunda; prime minister, Nalumino Mundia.

Zambia's budget, presented in January 1984, painted a gloomy picture. It predicted that a slight growth in gross domestic product would be offset by a marked increase in the population. Another factor militating against recovery was the prolonged drought, which again severely reduced the corn (maize) crop. Nevertheless, the International Monetary Fund and the World Bank were satisfied that Zambia was adhering to the conditions they had laid down for dealing with the country's problems. In May a meeting of international financiers in Paris pledged further aid and acknowledged the need to reschedule the government's debts. In an attempt to lower the trade deficit, a minimum duty of 10% was imposed on all imported goods from October 1.

Pres. Kenneth Kaunda in February played a prominent role in the formulation of an agreement between South Africa and Angola that, it was hoped, would accelerate moves to achieve independence for Namibia/South West Africa. Three months later Kaunda co-chaired a conference on Namibia in Lusaka that brought together representatives of the South West Africa People's Organization and the South African government. However, the talks ended in deadlock. To mark the 20th anniversary of independence in October, Kaunda released 239 people from prison and detention.   (KENNETH INGHAM)

This article updates the *Macropædia* article SOUTHERN AFRICA: *Zambia*.

ZIMBABWE

A republic and member of the Commonwealth, Zimbabwe is a landlocked state in eastern Africa. Area: 390,759 sq km (150,873 sq mi). Pop. (1984 est.): 8,060,000. Cap.: Harare. Monetary unit: Zimbabwe dollar, with (Oct. 29, 1984) a free rate of Z$1.43 to U.S. $1 (Z$1.72 = £1 sterling). President in 1984, the Rev. Canaan Banana; prime minister, Robert Mugabe.

Like many other countries in tropical Africa, Zimbabwe suffered during 1984 from a third successive year of drought. However, the anticipated disaster was mitigated by an unexpected late rain that saved corn (maize) crops from destruction, and by the use of improved agricultural materials and methods. Less corn was planted in favour of crops better able to survive drought, such as soybeans, cotton, sorghum, and tobacco (one of the main foreign currency earners). Although the corn crop was the biggest since independence (1980), the country had to import about 25% of its corn requirement, also for the first time since independence. Production from the small plots of peasant farmers, stimulated by price increases for early delivery, increased sharply, and large-scale white farmers produced yields exceeded only in the U.S.

Toward the end of March Minister of Finance Bernard Chidzero announced strict measures to reduce the drain on currency. The remittance of all income abroad was banned for at least a year except for pensions and approved expatriate salaries. The measure affected all foreign investors. Particularly badly hit were former residents who had left the country with only the limited sums they were permitted to take by the government and who relied upon income from property and investments that they had been forced to leave behind.

The budget introduced by Chidzero in July also reflected the weakness of the economy. Seventeen government departments had their incomes reduced, and a number of new taxes were introduced, including a drought relief surcharge of 10% on the basic tax on all companies and a 5% surcharge on individuals. Yet only a few weeks later the need to bolster internal security resulted in the expenditure of $35 million on armoured cars bought from Brazil.

Prime Minister Robert Mugabe began the year by slimming down his Cabinet. The most significant individual change was the transfer of Herbert Ushewokunze from the Home Affairs Ministry, where he had been criticized for his use of emergency powers, to the Ministry of Transportation. He was succeeded as minister of home affairs by Simbi Mubako, who in early February imposed a dusk-to-dawn curfew over a 2,500-sq mi area of southern Matabeleland and ordered a large number of troops into the district to suppress the growing antigovernment guerrilla activity. Mubako claimed that his measures had an immediate salutary effect, but Joshua Nkomo, leader of the opposition Zimbabwe African People's Union (ZAPU), accused the security forces of committing atrocities against civilians suspected of supporting the guerrillas. Roman Catholic Church leaders also protested against the way in which the Army prevented food supplies from reaching the area in the hope of crushing opposition. The restriction upon the movement of food supplies was lifted in March, but not before considerable numbers of people were threatened with starvation. Mugabe visited southern Matabeleland in April and commented that he was happy with the work of the security forces. He criticized church leaders, claiming that they had become agents of Nkomo. The curfew was eased on April 9 as a result, it was said, of U.S. intervention, and it was finally lifted in August.

A ban was imposed on opposition party meetings in the centre of the country in June and extended shortly afterward to Mashonaland West. The aim of the ban was to deny comfort and support to bandits. It formed part of a more general attack on Nkomo's party, but it also indicated to observers that insurgency had already begun to spread beyond the borders of Matabeleland. Violence also broke out at the opening of Parliament later in the month after members of the opposition parties booed the arrival of Pres. Canaan Banana and Mugabe. On July 24 Parliament voted for another six-month extension of the state of emergency, which had been in force since 1965.

In February Mugabe announced that, if the majority of people wanted it, Zimbabwe would have one-party rule after the elections due to be held before February 1985. He criticized strongly the existing constitution, which, until 1990, required a unanimous vote in Parliament before any major constitutional change could be introduced. Strong opposition to Mugabe's proposal was voiced by Nkomo and by Ian Smith on behalf of the Republican Front (renamed the Conservative Alliance later in the year). Nevertheless, Mugabe took every opportunity to impress his view on public opinion, and it formed the main theme at the congress of the ruling Patriotic Front party, the Zimbabwe African National Union (ZANU [PF]), in August. Congress responded enthusiastically and urged the adoption of Marxist-Leninist principles, though it was announced that the proposed constitutional changes would not be implemented immediately.

In the hope of demonstrating the wholehearted nature of the victory he anticipated in the forthcoming elections, Mugabe ordered the unconditional release in September of Bishop Abel Muzorewa, former prime minister, who had been detained without trial since November 1983. The bishop, it was promised, would be free to lead his United African National Council in the elections. In early October the government also lifted the ban imposed in June on ZAPU meetings in the centre of the country. At the same time, the government threatened to reimpose restraints if either party encouraged violence.

In October ZAPU held its own congress, the first in ten years. Although the leadership had been greatly reduced, Nkomo expressed pleasure at the large attendance of party supporters. While calling for an undefined united front, he rejected the idea of a one-party state resulting from any agreement with Mugabe's government. He also delivered a vigorous attack on the government's failure to revive the economy, on the conduct of the antiguerrilla campaign in Matabeleland, and on state corruption. He was reelected president of ZAPU, while Joseph Msipa was elected vice-president in place of Josiah Chinamano (see OBITUARIES), who died on October 1.

Following the assassination of a ZANU (PF) senator, Moven Ndlovu, in the southern border town of Beitbridge on November 9, all the members of the rural council of the district—three whites, together with six black ZAPU supporters— were served with 30-day detention notices after they had fled from riots that broke out in the town at the instigation of ZANU (PF) supporters. Mugabe reacted strongly and dismissed the two remaining members of ZAPU from his Cabinet. One of them, Cephas Msipa, had been elected ZAPU secretary-general the previous month. The time had come, Mugabe said, for ZAPU to be declared an enemy of the people. Two days later three senior ZAPU officials were detained under emergency laws. Later in the month Jini Ntuta, a ZAPU member of Parliament and staunch supporter of Nkomo, was shot dead on his farm in Matabeleland.

The exodus of white settlers from Zimbabwe was said to have continued at a high level. More than 19,000 left the country in 1983, reducing the white population to about 100,000, compared with its peak of 270,000 in the 1960s. Insecurity and endemic violence were the main reasons given for the departure of the whites. Support for Ian Smith's Republican Front also declined, and by May 1984 the Front held only 7 of the 20 seats reserved for whites in Parliament. The main reason given for the decline was that the party had not detached itself from old assumptions and attitudes.

In July Mugabe paid a five-day visit to London, where he took part in a seminar organized by the Commonwealth Institute to discuss the progress made by the nine countries involved in the Southern African Development Coordination Conference. Later in the month Bulgarian Premier Grisha Filipov visited Zimbabwe, and Mugabe took the opportunity to express his country's continuing appreciation of the help given by Bulgaria during Zimbabwe's struggle for independence.   (KENNETH INGHAM)

This article updates the *Macropædia* article SOUTHERN AFRICA: *Zimbabwe.*

Middle East and North Africa

MIDDLE EASTERN AND NORTH AFRICAN AFFAIRS

The Gulf war between Iran and Iraq, which entered its fifth year in September 1984, dominated Middle Eastern affairs, pushing to one side the issues of Arab-Israeli relations and the future of the Palestinians. Syrian and Israeli forces remained in Lebanon, although by the end of the year the new governments in Lebanon and Israel had resumed discussions aimed at bringing about an Israeli withdrawal. A rapprochement between Egypt and the other Arab nations was facilitated by Jordan's decision to resume diplomatic relations, severed when the peace treaty between Egypt and Israel was signed in 1979.

The Gulf War. The year brought little prospect of an end to the conflict between Iran and Iraq. Iranian land offensives in March and again in October were only minor ones, and the promised final push to end the land war did

AP/WIDE WORLD

Pres. Ahmed Sékou Touré of Guinea headed a delegation from the Islamic Conference Organization that invited Egypt to rejoin the ICO. Egypt's Pres. Hosni Mubarak took the microphone to tell reporters he accepted.

not materialize. During the autumn campaign there were heavy casualties as Iran recaptured some 50 sq km (19.3 sq mi) of land taken by Iraq in 1980. Conflict in the air escalated to include attacks on international shipping in the Gulf as Iraq tried to deter tankers from approaching Iranian oil ports and Iran took retaliatory action.

In March conservative Arab states agreed to a watered-down version of an Iraqi plan to persuade major industrialized countries to stop dealing with Iran. The agreement was reached at an emergency meeting of Arab League foreign affairs ministers in Baghdad, Iraq, on March 14. However, Iran's main trading partners—Italy, Japan, the U.K., and file Germany—failed to react positively to the suggestion. Iraqi Foreign Affairs Minister Tariq Aziz said that Western countries were "prolonging the war" by continuing to buy oil from Iran and threatened that tanker attacks might be increased to bring Iran "to its senses."

The Iraqi position was expected to be helped by the resumption of diplomatic relations with the U.S., severed in 1967. After Aziz visited Washington at the end of November for talks with Pres. Ronald Reagan and Secretary of State George Shultz, the Iraqi interests section at the Indian embassy in Washington was closed and replaced by a full embassy. Baghdad maintained that a resumption of full relations had been contemplated for some time, but the announcement had been held back to avoid showing any sign of weakness in light of Iraq's setbacks in the Gulf war.

The possibility that Iran might attack the oil fields of the region—the most important issue for those not directly involved in the conflict—appeared less likely after the shooting down of at least one and possibly two Iranian warplanes by Saudi Arabian jet fighters on June 5. It was the first time Saudi Arabia had clashed directly with the forces of revolutionary Iran since September 1980. The incident also revealed that, despite Iranian propaganda, the revolutionary government in Teheran was unable, or unwilling, to escalate the tit-for-tat war against international shipping in the Gulf. This raised hopes among member countries of the Gulf Cooperation Council (GCC) and their allies that Iran had been checked on both land and sea and that a decisive Iranian victory was now a much more distant possibility. In July the newly elected president of the Islamic Conference Organization (ICO), Pres. Dawda Jawara of The Gambia, announced that he would launch a fresh initiative to end the war, but little hope was held out for its success.

Gulf Cooperation Council. The fifth summit meeting of the GCC (Saudi Arabia, Bahrain, Kuwait, Oman, the United Arab Emirates, and Qatar) took place in November in Kuwait. Defense and security matters headed the agenda. The GCC called on the warring parties in the Gulf war to begin a dialogue and urged international organizations to begin mediation attempts. Concern about the Gulf war and the possibility that it might spread to the Arabian Peninsula also prompted the GCC to improve its own defense capabilities with a coordinated defense program. It was announced that the GCC had established a joint defense force to react quickly to attack from outside the region, although the force was reported to be a temporary measure.

The GCC had made impressive progress toward economic integration since its inception in 1981 but, though a free-trade area had been created, variations in practice still existed. Member states remained strongly nationalistic on this and other matters of policy, including those of East-West relations and investment. Relations between the GCC and the European Communities (EC) were badly strained during 1984 as serious differences arose over the access of Gulf petrochemicals to European markets. The issue came to a head after the EC decided in June to impose a 13.5% tariff on imports of Saudi Arabian methanol. A meeting between top Gulf and EC officials took place in Bahrain on November 7–8, but no agreement was announced. Since the General Agreement on Tariffs and Trade precluded a unilateral lowering of tariffs, the only way to allow more Saudi Arabian methanol into European markets would be to increase duty-free quotas and ceilings under the Generalized System of Preferences.

The collapse of financial surpluses in the economies of GCC member states was imposing severe restraints on their ability to implement some prestigious joint projects. Among the development plans to be dropped was one to build a large refinery at Salalah in southern Oman, which would have provided a safe haven for tankers. The GCC continued to study proposals for an oil export pipeline linking Kuwait and the Indian Ocean coast, but plans for a GCC railway and a joint electricity grid now seemed only distant possibilities.

The Arab World and Arab-Israeli Relations. A major development during 1984 was the growing stature of King Hussein of Jordan in Middle Eastern affairs. On June 17 Hussein offered Jordanian military help to Iraq and the other Gulf states to confront any possible threat from Iran. Jordan took a major step toward reintegrating Egypt into the Arab fold by its decision in September to restore diplomatic relations, severed as a result of the bilateral Egypt-Israeli peace agreement. Speaking on July 11, after talks with Pres. François Mitterrand of France, Pres. Hosni Mubarak of Egypt echoed Jordanian thinking by giving his support to the idea of an international conference on the Arab-Israeli conflict. Syria, which insisted that such a conference should be held under UN auspices, accused France of trying to promote a separate peace agreement between Jordan and Israel. On June 13, after completing a tour of five Middle Eastern countries, UN Secretary-General Javier Pérez de Cuéllar reported that there had been strong

backing for a conference in Cairo, Beirut, Damascus, and Amman. However, the idea had been totally rejected by the Israelis, who insisted on direct negotiations with individual Arab countries.

On September 25, shortly after taking office, Israel's Prime Minister Shimon Peres (see BIOGRAPHIES) said that his new government of national unity had not yet examined the Middle Eastern peace plan proposed by U.S. President Reagan in 1982. The plan had been rejected out of hand by former prime minister Menachem Begin's Likud government. On November 8 the Israeli government and the new Lebanese government led by Prime Minister Rashid Karami (see BIOGRAPHIES) began talks aimed at bringing about a withdrawal of Israeli forces from southern Lebanon. Although the talks went ahead with the agreement of Syria's Pres. Hafez al-Assad (see BIOGRAPHIES), Damascus made it clear in advance that it rejected Israel's plans to deploy the Israeli-backed Lebanese militia force in a buffer zone along the border.

Addressing the Palestine National Council (PNC) at its meeting in Amman on November 23, King Hussein proposed "peace in exchange for territories," specifying that Israel return all areas occupied in 1967, including East Jerusalem. His solution was opposed by both the main Israeli political parties, who maintained that a withdrawal from the entire West Bank would make Israel's borders indefensible. The PNC meeting also heard Hussein call for an international conference that would, in effect, provide a forum for direct negotiations between Israel and the Arabs. However, two senior members of the Palestine Liberation Organization (PLO) expressed reservations. The PNC meeting was marked by acrimony between Yasir Arafat's supporters in the PLO and a breakaway faction of his own al-Fatah group. Led by Said Musa, the opposition comprised the strongly pro-Syrian Popular Front for the Liberation of Palestine-General Command, Saiqa, and the Popular Struggle Front. Caught in the middle was the bloc led by the Popular Front for the Liberation of Palestine

Islamic Jihad

Since 1982 a new movement has emerged in the Middle East, a region already well used to terrorism. Islamic Jihad, or "Islamic Holy War," has quickly earned a reputation as the most mysterious of terrorist groups. In 1983–84 it claimed responsibility for four attacks on U.S. diplomatic and military installations that killed more than 315 people. It also boasted of an assassination in Spain, the kidnapping of three Americans and a Saudi diplomat in Lebanon, and the mining of the Red Sea. Yet the group remained invisible except for anonymous telephone calls to international wire services in which a male voice, speaking classical Arabic to cover any accent, began with the words: "In the name of God, the compassionate, the merciful."

There were doubts that Islamic Jihad, as a proper organization, actually existed. No names or location had been publicly identified. It was widely believed that "Islamic Jihad" was a convenient cover name for a host of fundamentalist movements and cells throughout the Middle East. The little hard evidence available indicated that the operatives were extreme religious fundamentalists of the Shi'ah faith, with links to Iran, the only major Middle East state with a Shi'ah-dominated government. Some experts believed

there might be a tiny elite representing different Shi'ah groups that carried out acts in the name of Islamic Jihad. These groups included Jundallah ("Soldiers of God"), Dawa ("The Call"), Islamic Amal ("Islamic Hope"), and Hizbollah ("Party of God"). All of Islamic Jihad's targets have been Western or moderate, usually pro-Western Muslim nations.

The emergence of Islamic Jihad should be understood in the context of the rising tide of fundamentalism in the Muslim world, although most fundamentalists were not thought to be extremists. The particular radicalism among some Shi'ah might also be linked to their minority status within Islam. The rise of Ayatollah Ruhollah Khomeini in Iran served as a spark for movements elsewhere. In Teheran there were several hard-line Shi'ah mullahs from the Arab world who, intelligence sources claimed, operated as "religious guides" to Shi'ah recruits training to become "volunteers for martyrdom" for the groups thought to be used by Islamic Jihad. After Iran, Shi'ah fundamentalists were strongest in Lebanon, but they reportedly also had cells in Iraq, Kuwait, Bahrain, and Saudi Arabia, as well as informal links with Sunni fundamentalists in North Africa.   (ROBIN B. WRIGHT)

The Iran-Iraq war escalated as both sides attacked foreign tankers in the Persian Gulf. Iraqi missiles struck the Saudi Arabian tanker "Al Ahood" and rendered it unsalvageable.
SIPA/SPECIAL FEATURES

and the Democratic Front for the Liberation of Palestine. This bloc had been anxious to avoid an open split in the PLO but had been constrained by the fact that it was based in Damascus and was thus vulnerable to Syrian pressure.

Yasir Arafat resumed talks with King Hussein during a visit to Amman on May 2, when the two leaders called on Arab states to help free the occupied lands. Arafat denied Kuwaiti press reports that the PLO wanted to move its headquarters from Tunisia to Egypt.

U.S. Policy. Some limited hopes that the U.S. might embark on a fresh initiative toward achieving peace in the Middle East arose following President Reagan's reelection in November. Arab leaders had always argued that the U.S. provided the vital ingredient for a settlement with Israel over the occupied territories, and they judged that Reagan would have more time for the Middle East during his second term. Although there was no immediate evidence of enthusiasm in the White House for reviving the stalled 1982 peace initiative, the U.S. was expected to encourage the emergence of a centrist bloc in the Arab world that would include Egypt, Iraq, Jordan, Saudi Arabia and its GCC allies, and the pro-Arafat group in the PLO. In the months before the election the White House had become increasingly cautious about appearing to favour the Arab cause. When Kuwait, a pro-Western GCC state, asked for a supply of Stinger antiaircraft missiles, the request was rejected in June and the Kuwaiti government was forced to seek advanced weapons from the U.S.S.R.

On May 15 Saudi Foreign Minister Prince Saud al-Faisal warned that Israel would depart from its present policies only if the U.S. changed its stance toward its closest friend in the Middle East. In an interview with the *Christian Science Monitor,* Prince Saud said the U.S. had to stop hoping for a fundamental change in the Arab attitude toward land seized by Israel in the 1967 war. He also complained about efforts in the U.S. Congress to have the U.S. embassy in Israel moved from Tel Aviv to Jerusalem. Evidently not reassured by President Reagan's indication that he would veto such a proposal, Prince Saud warned that Saudi Arabia would break off diplomatic relations with the U.S. if its embassy was moved.

North Africa. At least 15 international freighters were damaged, in most cases only slightly, by a series of blasts thought to have been caused by mines in the Suez Canal, the Gulf of Suez, and the southern Red Sea in July and August. Egypt was forced to seek technical assistance from Western countries to identify the source of the explosions. A multinational force of minesweepers found only

one mine of recent make—later identified to be of Soviet manufacture. The Islamic Jihad ("Holy War") organization claimed responsibility. (*See* Sidebar.) For its part, the Egyptian government at first hinted at Iranian and Libyan involvement but later laid the blame squarely on Libya.

Relations between Libya and Egypt were at a low ebb even before the mining incident. Later there were semi-official reports that President Mubarak had refused to meet a Libyan envoy who was offering $5 billion to Egypt if it cooled relations with Israel. The report went on to say that Libyan leader Muammar al-Qaddafi had been involved in authorizing the mining of the Red Sea. Tripoli was in trouble again over an incident involving an alleged assassination attempt on a prominent Libyan exile in Cairo. (See *Libya,* below.) The Egyptians claimed to have uncovered Libyan assassination plots aimed at several world leaders.

The agreement signed between Morocco and Libya at Oujda, Morocco, in August, with its promise of a union between the two countries, threatened to upset the political balance in northwest Africa. Algeria, Tunisia, and Mauritania all criticized the agreement as likely to impede the search for a wider union in the Maghrib. A brief military skirmish between Algerian and Moroccan troops in June, later described as "a mistake," hinted at the state of tension existing between the two countries.

The rapprochement between Morocco and Libya represented a major setback to U.S. attempts to isolate Qaddafi, since Morocco was one of the U.S.'s principal allies in Africa. The French showed concern because of the potentially unsettling effect of such a union on the other states in the region, but France also hoped that it might open the way for better relations between France and Libya.

(JOHN WHELAN)

ALGERIA

Algeria is a republic of North Africa on the Mediterranean Sea. Area: 2,381,741 sq km (919,595 sq mi). Pop. (1984 est.): 20,841,000. Cap.: Algiers. Monetary unit: dinar, with (Oct. 29, 1984) a free rate of 5.11 dinars to U.S. $1 (6.17 dinars = £1 sterling). President in 1984, Col. Chadli Bendjedid; premiers, Mohamed Ben Ahmed Abdelghani and, from January 22, Abdelhamid Brahimi.

For Algeria 1984 was a year of relative disappointment. Hopes of unity among North African states had been encouraged by the treaty agreed on between Algeria and Tunisia and adhered to by Mauritania in 1983. These hopes were dashed, however, by news of the Moroccan-Libyan treaty of unity signed in mid-August 1984. The new treaty was clearly designed to supplant the earlier one and was also designed, by Morocco at least, to exclude any negotiated settlement over the Western Sahara issue.

Disappointment turned to fury at the start of September when Pres. François Mitterrand of France visited Morocco. The Algerian government considered that the visit gave effective approval to the treaty, since it coincided with a referendum on the proposal, and that it ran directly counter to previous trends in French policy, which had been to foster equality in contacts in North Africa. Mitterrand went to Algiers on October 19 in an attempt, not entirely successful, to resolve the tension.

Economic progress during the year was not as great as anticipated. Forecasts of a current-account and balance of payments surplus proved overoptimistic; at the end of the year the balance of payments was more or less even, while the current account was in deficit. Major reasons were the loss of petroleum and gas export sales and the high level of debt repayment. Petroleum production continued to be depressed, while sales of gas were severely affected by the fact that Algeria's price was generally considered too high. The growing problems in the economy were highlighted during the fifth congress of the National Liberation Front in December 1983, when it was agreed that agriculture should have absolute priority in development. This concern was reflected in the new 1985–89 development plan, approved by the Cabinet on July 2.

Other domestic developments underlined the essentially conservative nature of Pres. Chadli Bendjedid's administration. The president was reelected unopposed on January 12, and on January 22 he appointed a new Cabinet in which Abdelhamid Brahimi took over as premier. In the same month a large number of arrests decimated the ranks of fundamentalists, Marxists, and feminists, although they, together with a number of Berber prisoners, were released during an unexpected amnesty in May. Other fundamentalists, however, were tried in early September in connection with the unrest of 1982. Fundamentalism was apparently still considered the major threat to domestic calm. An attempt was made to appease popular opinion in September when a family legal code clearly inspired by Islam was introduced.

The conservatism apparent in domestic affairs was not generally reflected in foreign affairs, where a distinct hardening of attitude could be identified. There was evidence of renewed interest in Eastern Europe, with visits by Bendjedid to Hungary and Czechoslovakia in March and increased economic relations with Yugoslavia and the U.S.S.R.

(GEORGE JOFFÉ)

This article updates the *Macropædia* article NORTH AFRICA: *Algeria*.

BAHRAIN

The monarchy (emirate) of Bahrain consists of a group of islands in the Persian Gulf between the Qatar Peninsula and Saudi Arabia. Area: 668 sq km (258 sq mi). Pop. (1984 est.): 409,000. Cap.: Manama. Monetary unit: dinar, with (Oct. 29, 1984) a free rate of 0.38 dinar to U.S. $1 (0.46 dinar = £1 sterling). Emir in 1984, Isa ibn Sulman al-Khalifah; prime minister, Khalifah ibn Sulman al-Khalifah.

The escalation of the Iran-Iraq war to include attacks on shipping in Gulf waters close to Bahrain had little effect on the business life or political stability of the island during 1984. A good indicator of international confidence was the rise in assets of the 77 offshore banking units to $62.4 billion by the end of June. However, declining oil revenue—production stood at around 40,000 bbl a day—deepened Bahrain's dependence on neighbouring Saudi Arabia and its allies in the Gulf Cooperation Council (GCC). Emir Sheikh Isa ibn Sulman al-Khalifah announced in June that a desalination plant would be paid for by King Fahd of Saudi Arabia, while the GCC was to provide up to $1 billion to bolster air defenses.

A visit to the U.K. by the emir in April served to strengthen Bahrain's connection with its closest European ally. British companies had earned steady business in the country, although during recent years they had been on the sidelines of most industrial projects. The Dutch-built causeway linking Bahrain with Saudi Arabia, scheduled to open on National Day in December 1985, was the most spectacular infrastructure scheme in progress; it was expected to lead to a boom in tourism from the mainland, though expatriates predicted that it might also result in restrictions being introduced to bring Bahrain closer in line with the Islamic life-style prevailing on the mainland. During 1984 bids were tendered for the first phase of the Gulf University, a project financed by the GCC.

(JOHN WHELAN)

This article updates the *Macropædia* article ARABIA: *Bahrain*.

CYPRUS

An island republic and member of the Commonwealth, Cyprus is in the eastern Mediterranean Sea. Area: 9,251 sq km (3,572 sq mi). Pop. (1984 est.): 657,000. Area and population figures include the Turkish Cypriot state that has occupied the northern third of the island since 1974, though its existence is not internationally recognized. Official population estimates may not take into account the recent and reportedly extensive Turkish immigration and Greek emigration. Cap.: Nicosia. Monetary unit: Cyprus pound, with (Oct. 29, 1984) a free rate of £C 0.62 to U.S. $1 (£C 0.75 = £1 sterling). President in 1984, Spyros Kyprianou.

The year marked the tenth anniversary of the Turkish invasion in 1974. Since then Cyprus had been divided, with Turkish Cypriots controlling the northern 37% of the island. The year started gloomily after the previous November's declaration of an independent state in the north, recognized only by Turkey, but it ended on a note of optimism after a series of UN-sponsored talks led to plans for a meeting between Pres. Spyros Kyprianou and Turkish Cypriot leader Rauf Denktash in mid-January 1985.

Denktash got peace moves under way with a New Year's package of proposals, which, however, was promptly rejected by the Greek Cypriots. Kyprianou countered with his own proposals, also promptly rejected. Political strains on the Greek side became apparent when the powerful Communist AKEL Party, allied to the centre-right Democratic Party of Kyprianou, attacked the president for dragging his feet on talks with the Turks. Denktash produced another shock in April, when Turkey and northern Cyprus exchanged ambassadors. Kyprianou went to the UN Security Council, where he secured Resolution 550, the toughest condemnation of Turkish policy ever produced by that body.

The UN launched a new initiative in August, with both sides sending representatives to Vienna. The Turkish Cypriots offered to return the deserted city of Famagusta and freeze moves to consolidate independence, while the Greek Cypriots promised to make great efforts to draft an acceptable federal framework. Kyprianou and Denktash then went to New York for indirect talks with UN Secretary-General Javier Pérez de Cuéllar. Substantial progress was made, with Denktash offering major concessions on territory and dropping demands for a rotating presidency. The Greek Cypriots produced a promising package for a federal legislature giving Turkish Cypriots 50% of the seats in an upper chamber and 30% in the lower. On that note, the two men decided they were close enough to agree to a summit meeting.

The economy remained healthy, despite warnings from experts that the island was living above its means. Inflation fell slightly to 4%, and unemployment hovered around 3%. A rise in the 1984 trade deficit was countered by growth in tourist income and a flourishing invisible trade in shipping, insurance, and banking, so the balance of payments surplus was expected to be around £C 25 million. In the Turkish Cypriot north, however, the economic outlook was bleak. Per capita income was one-third of the $5,000 annual average in the south, and inflation topped 50%.

In December the UN Security Council unanimously renewed the mandate of its peacekeeping force in Cyprus for another six months.   (THOMAS O'DWYER)

EGYPT

A republic of North Africa, Egypt has coastlines on the Mediterranean and Red seas. Area: 997,667 sq km (385,201 sq mi). Pop. (1984 est.): 47,120,000. Cap.: Cairo. Monetary unit: Egyptian pound, with (Oct. 29, 1984) an official rate of LE 0.83 to U.S. $1 (free rate of LE 1.01 = £1 sterling) and a special transactions rate of LE 1.20 to U.S. $1 (LE 1.45 = £1 sterling). President in 1984, Hosni Mubarak; prime ministers, Ahmad Fuad Mohieddin until June 5 and, from July 17, Kamal Hassan Ali.

Foreign Relations. The restoration of Egypt to the Arab fold, after five years in the wilderness following the 1978 Camp David accords and subsequent peace treaty signed in 1979 with Israel, began with Jordan's decision, announced on Sept. 25, 1984, that diplomatic relations between the two nations should be resumed. Pres. Hosni Mubarak immediately paid an official visit to Amman, and King Hussein visited Cairo in December. Jordan's move was greeted with hostility by Libya and Syria. In the Gulf states little official comment was made except by Oman, where a Foreign Ministry spokesman applauded the initiative.

Jordan's lead was likely to be followed in 1985 by other Arab countries including Iraq, which had started receiving military aid from Egypt before the death of Pres. Anwar as-Sadat in 1981. A visit to Egypt in 1983 by Yasir Arafat, chairman of the Palestine Liberation Organization (PLO), and his reception there by President Mubarak ensured that the PLO would not officially condemn Jordan.

Jordan reestablished economic links with Egypt in December 1983, and in January 1984 the leaders of Islamic countries invited Egypt to rejoin the Islamic Conference Organization (ICO). Although this development fell short of Egypt's ultimate aim—to rejoin the Arab League, which it had once dominated—it was achieved without having to denounce the treaty with Israel, though the treaty had been attacked at successive ICO summit meetings.

The moves to reintegrate Egypt into the mainstream of Arab politics came against a background of frigidity in dealings with Israel. The second anniversary of the Israeli withdrawal from the Sinai on April 25 was marked by fresh signs of deterioration in relations between the two countries. Minister of State for Foreign Affairs Boutros Boutros Ghali described the treaty with Israel as "frozen." His remark followed a quarrel about Egypt's decision to cut diplomatic links with Costa Rica and El Salvador because they had moved their embassies in Israel from Tel Aviv to Jerusalem. Despite this stand, however, it was clear that the Mubarak government was maintaining dialogue with Israel. On Dec. 29, 1983, Deputy Foreign Affairs Minister Shafie Abdel-Hamid met with Israeli Prime Minister Yitzhak Shamir in Jerusalem and Tel Aviv to explain Egypt's reception of the PLO chairman the previous week. Ghali indicated that Egypt was ready to reopen talks with Israel about Palestinian independence provided that Jordan and the Palestinians were involved.

Relations with Libya continued at a low ebb because of suspicions that Libya was involved in laying mines in the Red Sea during the summer. Although anxious to play down the threat to ships passing through the Suez Canal, the government blamed the Libyans. The unpredictability of the Libyan government was demonstrated in an offer made by the Libyans in March to reopen their border with Egypt, which had been closed since 1977, if Egypt would reciprocate. Only days later, on March 20, Presi-

UPI/BETTMANN

U.S. Navy minesweeping helicopters were among those of several nations deployed in the Red Sea and the Gulf of Suez at Egypt's request to clear mines, which some believed had been covertly sown by Libya. Here an RH-53D helicopter tows a magnetic minesweeping sled in an earlier exercise.

dent Mubarak issued a warning to Libya not to interfere in the internal affairs of Sudan, with which Egypt had signed a defense pact in 1976. This followed alleged Libyan involvement in a bombing incident at Omdurman, near Khartoum, on March 16. In November Egypt claimed Libyan agents had attempted to assassinate an anti-Qaddafi Libyan living in Egypt. (See *Libya,* below.)

On the international front the Mubarak administration took action to improve relations with the U.S.S.R., whose last ambassador had been expelled by Sadat in September 1981. As a result of the government's decision to resume ties with Moscow, the Soviets named Aleksandr Belonogov as their ambassador in July, while Egypt reciprocated by naming Salah Basyuni, who took up his post as ambassador on August 24. The Soviet Union also offered to increase economic aid to Egypt. The value of bilateral trade in 1983 was just over $600 million, a total that the Soviets hoped to boost to more than $700 million in 1984–85. Relations with Bulgaria also appeared to be warming. President Mubarak's predominantly pro-Western stance, however, seemed unlikely to change.

In the years since Camp David, the U.S. had poured billions of dollars into Egypt to balance its aid to Israel. Between 1978 and September 1983, the U.S. Congress had authorized nearly $9.5 billion in economic and military aid to Egypt, compared with a total over the previous 32 years of slightly more than $4 billion. In November 1983 Congress approved $2,325,000,000 for 1984–85, while in February 1984 U.S. Pres. Ronald Reagan requested a total of $2,170,000,000 for 1985–86. The package for 1985–86 was, however, considered too low by Cairo. On February 5 the economy and foreign trade minister, Mustapha Kamal as-Said, visited Washington to ask for more. Egypt wanted its existing military debt, amounting to some $3.6 billion, to be written off, but U.S. officials faced election-year pressure from the Israeli lobby to prevent such a move.

Domestic Affairs. At home a general election on May 27 resulted in a victory for President Mubarak's National Democratic Party, which won 390 seats in the 448-member National Assembly. The opposition New Wafd Party took 58 seats to give Egypt its biggest parliamentary opposition since the 1952 revolution—though it was a right-wing opposition to a conservative ruling party. Allegations of ballot rigging were made by the left-wing Unionist Progressive Party, which polled 4.1% of the vote. In total, 43.14% of the 12.3 million registered voters went to the polls. Turnout was low (20%) in urban areas but higher (60%) in rural districts. Despite the complaints, the elections were considered to be the fairest since 1952. The New Wafd's leadership, under the veteran Fuad Serageddin, was predominantly middle class. The party's resurgence allowed its electoral ally, the banned Muslim Brotherhood, headed by Omar Talmassani, to gain two seats. As the governing party remained committed to a mixed economy, the New Wafd was thought likely to oppose the details rather than the principles of government policy.

The death of Prime Minister Ahmad Fuad Mohieddin (*see* OBITUARIES) on June 5, coming so soon after the election, gave impetus to plans for a Cabinet reshuffle. On July 17 acting prime minister Kamal Hassan Ali, foreign minister in the previous government, was confirmed in the post of prime minister. The appointment upstaged Defense Minister Muhammad Abdel-Halim abu Ghazala, who was generally considered to be Egypt's second most powerful figure. The Foreign Ministry was given to former UN ambassador Esmat Abdel-Megid, who was called out of retirement. The most significant demotion was that of Hassan Abou-Basha, whose move to local government and

popular development from the Interior Ministry was said to be the result of the allegations of vote rigging. The changes left Ghali as the longest serving member of the government and gave Planning Minister Ahmad al-Ganzouri the key position in economic planning in the absence of an overall economic overlord. On August 29 President Mubarak led mourners at the funeral of Egypt's first president, Muhammad Neguib (*see* OBITUARIES).

The Economy. The new government faced a brighter economic picture than that inherited by Mubarak from the Sadat era. The current account deficit had narrowed from more than $2 billion in 1981–82 to approximately $1 billion for the fiscal year 1983–84, while the balance of payments was in surplus. An important support for the economy was the earnings repatriated by three million Egyptians working in the Persian Gulf states. Their remittances, totaling as much as $3.5 billion in 1983–84, were boosted by the strong dollar and by the streamlining of the Egyptian exchange rate.

Petroleum revenue, which reached a peak of $3 billion in 1981–82, was adversely affected by lower world prices, though production was steady at 840,000 bbl a day in 1983–84. Reserves were estimated at 4,850,000,000 bbl. The oil industry forecast that 17 exploration agreements would be signed by 12 oil companies during fiscal 1984–85, with a commitment to spend a total of $645 million in order to search for new deposits in the Gulf of Suez, the Western and Eastern deserts, and the northern Sinai.

The most reliable of Egypt's foreign-exchange earners contined to be the Suez Canal, with transit dues set to top $1 billion for the first time in 1984–85. Tourism also increased because of the relaxation in foreign-exchange transaction rules. Non-oil exports held steady, and a good cotton harvest was anticipated. On the deficit side, however, food imports continued to drain Egypt's foreign-exchange reserves: with one million more mouths to feed every ten months, the food subsidy bill canceled out oil revenue. Subsidies for energy cost Egypt $3.5 billion a year.

During its first weeks in power, the new Cabinet appeared to offer little that was new in response to the country's economic problems. Ministers promised increased efficiency in the public sector. There was some evidence of this in regard to energy; a large-scale expansion of refining capacity was under way, the aim of which was to achieve national self-sufficiency by 1988. Abdel-Hadi Muhammad Kandil, newly appointed to the post of petroleum and mineral wealth minister, announced an energy conservation program aimed at 200 factories that was to be carried out with World Bank aid. Some reports suggested that Mubarak would use his election victory to gain support for a series of price reforms, a move persistently urged by the World Bank and the International Monetary Fund. But the low voter turnout appeared to convince the government that the time was not ripe for implementing austerity measures.

(JOHN WHELAN)

IRAN

The Islamic republic of Iran is in southwestern Asia on the Caspian and Arabian seas and the Persian Gulf. Area: 1,648,000 sq km (636,000 sq mi). Pop. (1984 est.): 43,088,000. Cap.: Teheran. Monetary unit: rial, with (Oct. 29, 1984) a free rate of 93.21 rials to U.S. $1 (112.50 rials = £1 sterling). Supreme *faqih* (spiritual leader) in 1984, Ayatollah Ruhollah Khomeini; president, Sayyed Ali Khamenei; prime minister, Mir Hossein Moussavi.

The effects of the Gulf war dominated Iran during 1984. Initiatives in the conflict were lost by the Iranian side as its financial, economic, and military strength diminished relative to that of Iraq. Symbolic of Iranian frustrations, a major offensive begun at midnight on February 15 that was declared a "final push" to end the war made slow and expensive progress. The main thrust of the attack in the south-central sector was repulsed. The only important gain was made in the south, where a separate amphibious incursion breached Iraqi lines and took the Majnoon oil field.

It was strongly believed that the Iranian authorities would follow up their spring offensive with a new and overwhelming drive westward in late spring or summer. Large numbers of troops were mobilized, reputedly as many as 400,000, in preparation for the assault. However, the summer passed with only minor skirmishing in the land war and, when a new offensive was launched in October, it was small in scale and confined to a limited area of the central sector. Iranian abandonment of mass human-wave battle tactics during 1984 was brought about by increasing Iraqi abilities to counter their effects.

Iraqi supremacy in the air war became apparent during the early months of 1984. In April the Iraqis intensified their blockade of Iranian oil terminals and commercial ports, using French-supplied Super Étendard aircraft armed with Exocet missiles. Iran attempted to retaliate against Iraqi air attacks on oil tankers serving Kharg Island by striking at ships moving to or from Arab nations' ports in the Persian Gulf. The tanker war rose to dangerous levels in May and early June as Iraqi raids and Iranian replies threatened to throw the region into chaos and end oil exports from the Gulf. Arab nations of the Gulf reacted strongly, and Saudi Arabian aircraft shot down one and possibly two Iranian fighter planes in June, signaling clearly that the international community would act against Iran to ensure freedom of navigation. The situation was exacerbated for Iran by its deteriorating ability to risk its tiny number of functioning military aircraft against a stronger enemy. Iraqi air attacks on Kharg Island and on the tankers disrupted but did not halt Iranian oil exports.

Mediation efforts were of no avail as the Iranian leadership held fast to its war aims of unseating Iraqi Pres. Saddam Hussein, regaining all Iranian territories, and exacting war reparations. The only area on which agreement was reached between the two sides was on June 12, when attacks on civilian targets were stopped after discussions under UN auspices.

In foreign affairs Iran became more isolated during the year. Only Syria remained firmly by Iran's side, signing a joint letter of understanding that ensured Iranian oil supplies to Syria on generous terms in return for the closing of the Iraqi oil export pipeline through Syria. Other Arab nations, especially those in the Gulf, closed ranks against Iran through the Gulf Cooperation Council and began to offer serious resistance to Iranian pressures. Most significantly, the U.S.S.R., goaded by Iranian attacks on the pro-Soviet Tudeh Party, moved solidly behind Iraq in the war by providing new weaponry, spare parts, and financial credits. The U.S., while remaining officially neutral, closely supported Saudi Arabia with electronic early warning and missile systems and reestablished diplomatic relations with Iraq, a further sign that U.S. and Soviet policies toward the war coincided. In December four Arabic-speaking terrorists hijacked a Kuwaiti airliner to Teheran, where some witnesses said they secured new weapons. They held hostages for six days, executing two Americans among them. Reacting to world opinion, Iranian troops overpowered the hijackers, whom Iran promised to try.

Domestic politics were quiet. The regime maintained a strong if heavy-handed control of the population. Follow-

ing advice from the country's leader, Ayatollah Ruhollah Khomeini, domestic issues such as land reform and trade were settled in favour of the private sector, suggesting a slight swing away from the more radical aspects of the revolution. Elections for the Islamic Assembly were held in February, resulting in the return of mainly clerical members.

(KEITH S. MCLACHLAN)

IRAQ

A republic of southwestern Asia, Iraq has a short coastline on the Persian Gulf. Area: 438,317 sq km (169,235 sq mi). Pop. (1984 est.): 15 million. Cap.: Baghdad. Monetary unit: dinar, with (Oct. 29, 1984) a par value of 0.31 dinar to U.S. $1 (free rate of 0.38 dinar = £1 sterling). President in 1984, Saddam Hussein at-Takriti.

The escalation of the Gulf war between Iran and Iraq during 1984 to include attacks on oil tankers in international waters and assaults on the Iranian oil terminal at Kharg Island produced new difficulties for the Iraqi regime. The war entered its fifth year on September 22 with land hostilities at a stalemate; however, the possibility of an Iranian breakthrough, though widely discounted, could not be excluded. Attacks on international shipping began in February, intensified on March 26, when Iraq used its French-supplied Exocet missiles to attack two non-Iranian vessels, and continued throughout the year. Iraq warned that any vessel venturing within a 50-mi radius of Kharg Island risked attack, while Iran responded by striking at tankers in waters south of this "exclusion zone."

President Saddam Hussein at-Takriti appeared to be moving toward a closer relationship with the U.S.S.R. During a visit to Moscow on April 24–26, First Deputy Premier Taha Yassin Ramadan signed two cooperation agreements dealing with an expansion of trade and increased ties in the oil and energy sectors. Similar protocols concluded earlier allowed for Soviet help in building nuclear power stations and developing an oil field. A joint Iraqi-Soviet statement issued on April 25 attacked the U.S. for trying to intervene in the Gulf under the pretext of guaranteeing freedom of navigation.

F. LOCHON—GAMMA/LIAISON

As the Iran-Iraq war continued, Iran suffered huge losses during major offensives that took place in late February and early March. Iran's death toll was particularly high as a result of the use of human assault waves. Many of the Iranian dead and captured were as young as nine or ten.

Paradoxically, the accords with Moscow took place against a background of improved relations with the United States. U.S. Vice-Pres. George Bush stated in April that an Iranian victory in the Gulf war would pose an unprecedented threat to the region. Speaking to the *Los Angeles Times* in May, Hussein said that the administration's condemnation of Iraq for its alleged use of chemical weapons in the war was his major complaint against the U.S. He also accused the U.S. of discussing with Israel the possibility of bombing chemical plants in Iraq. In November, however, the two countries agreed to resume full diplomatic relations, severed since the 1967 Arab-Israeli war. The U.S. State Department said the move would not affect U.S. neutrality in the Gulf war.

Foreign Affairs Minister Tariq Aziz made it clear that better relations with the U.S.S.R. did not imply any reconciliation between his government and the Iraqi Communist Party, which he described as displaying a "negative attitude." In May Aziz announced that he hoped for further progress in talks with the Patriotic Union of Kurdistan (PUK), which was seeking greater autonomy from the central government for Iraq's Kurdish minority. A cease-fire in the northeast of Iraq was reported in May. Discussions with the PUK, whose leader was Jalal Talabani, were reported to be continuing in a positive atmosphere. They were believed to centre on Kurdish demands for participation in the central government.

On January 3 the National Assembly approved the 1984 budget, which gave priority to defense, war-related projects, education, and social welfare. Though no detailed figures were released, the budget was to be modeled closely on that of 1983, implying that tight import controls would be maintained. Government statements were clearly designed to encourage the private sector to play a greater role in economic development.

The difficulties posed by the war to the export of crude oil continued to dog the economy, forcing the government to seek major rescheduling agreements for its debts to foreign contractors. In late September, however, a consortium led by the Italian company Saipem started work on a new crude-oil pipeline that was to run from Zubair in southern Iraq through Saudi Arabia and link up with the existing Saudi Arabian export pipeline, Petroline. Work was to be finished by May 1985, and the Iraqi section of the line was to be operated by a Saudi Arabian concern. The move was thought likely to delay for at least a year any development of the proposed export pipeline to Jordan's Red Sea port of Aqaba. On May 3 Hussein told the Kuwaiti press that the U.S.S.R. had tried to convince Syria to reopen the export pipeline to the Mediterranean port of Banias, which had been shut down in 1982.

Although the Arab Gulf states were helping to finance Iraq's war effort, a difficult year lay ahead. The payment of debts rescheduled by European governments in 1983 was to fall due in 1985. The government tried to maintain an appearance of normality by regularly inviting foreign companies to discuss design or construction contracts.

(JOHN WHELAN)

ISRAEL

A republic of southwestern Asia, Israel is situated on the Mediterranean Sea. Area: 20,700 sq km (7,992 sq mi), not including territory occupied in the June 1967 war. Pop. (1984 est.): 4,179,000. Cap.: Jerusalem. Monetary unit: shekel, with (Oct. 29, 1984) a free rate of 502.10 shekels to U.S. $1 (606 shekels = £1 sterling). President in 1984, Chaim Herzog; prime ministers, Yitzhak Shamir and, from September 14, Shimon Peres.

After 36 years of restless statehood, Israel found 1984 a year with a difference. The political giants of the past—the founding fathers and mothers of the state—had become little more than fading political memories and in many cases not even respected ones. A new generation of leaders had taken over and, far more significantly, a new and different nation was taking shape. For the first time in Israel's modern history since the heady days of 1948, domestic politics and interests overshadowed national security in the discussion of foreign policy (though less so in its application). Especially in light of the country's continuing economic difficulties, domestic politics coloured all comment by politicians and media alike.

Domestic Affairs. The first six months of 1984 were marked by a mood of national divisiveness and uncertainty such as the country had not experienced since 1950, in the immediate aftermath of the war of independence. In 1950 the initiative to overcome the problems facing the nation had come from the political leadership. In 1984 it came from the people. The year saw the beginning of a popular or populist change in the attitude of the Israeli citizen to government and the governing institutions, whose word had hitherto been unquestioned. The change peaked in the aftermath of the seemingly deadlocked general election in July, and it was given voice by Pres. Chaim Herzog. Although he might have overstepped the constitutional niceties of his office when he called for the formation of a national unity government in light of the evenly balanced outcome of the national vote, nevertheless he reflected a profound public mood and the popular yearning for good, clean, nonpartisan, and open government.

For more than 30 years Israel had been the victim—and, at times, the beneficiary—of secret government. It was a condition imposed not so much by the choice of the leaders as by the legacy of British mandatory rule. This was compounded by the electoral system dictated by the UN as a condition of Israeli independence. It was designed to prevent hasty decision making and, by protecting the veto of small minority groups, to encourage consensus decisions, ordinarily impossible to achieve. The polarization of Israeli society was further emphasized by the rapid politicization of professional appointments in government service. The practice of the previous Likud government of Prime Minister Menachem Begin was followed by his successor, Yitzhak Shamir: members of "the family," the intimate associates of Begin during his underground days, and their nominees enjoyed a priority claim to government posts usually reserved for professional diplomats and civil servants.

The first weeks of 1984 made grievous inroads into the credibility of both the government and the opposition. On February 7, after a delay of almost two years, the government authorized the release of the Karp Report, a substantive document prepared by Deputy Attorney General Yehudit Karp, together with an impressive panel drawn from the legal profession and the police. It had looked into charges of ineffective law enforcement on the West Bank by the Israeli police and Army in cases where Jewish settlers were the alleged perpetrators of offenses. After investigating a considerable number of cases, the panel concluded that there had been deliberate laxness in the application of the law to Jewish settlers. At the other end of the political spectrum, the Labour Party was rocked by the suicide of Yaacov Levinson, one of the most powerful and influential men in the party, a leading banker, industrial promoter, and financial adviser to the Labour leadership. He had been under investigation for allegedly improper transactions, which he firmly denied. His suicide followed

Eventual partners in a government of national unity, Shimon Peres (right foreground) shakes hands with Prime Minister Yitzhak Shamir as they met August 1 to negotiate an arrangement. Peres's Labour Party narrowly bested Shamir's Likud bloc in the July elections, but neither was able to organize a governing coalition. In the final power-sharing agreement, Peres was to be prime minister and Shamir deputy prime minister and foreign minister until midterm, when they would switch jobs.

MILNER—SYGMA

what his family described as hounding by the media.

There were major personality clashes in all parties, and the government's narrow parliamentary majority looked ever more uncertain. On March 22 it required only a few personal defections from the governing Likud coalition to produce a government defeat in the Knesset (parliament) and a call for early elections (passed by 61 votes to 58). Labour was the first to resolve the leadership problem. Yitzhak Navon, the popular and respected former president, returned home and announced that he would run for a Knesset seat on the Labour list. Some thought he would make a more attractive leader than Shimon Peres (*see* BIOGRAPHIES), who had narrowly lost the two previous elections, but Labour chose to retain Peres. The old rivalry between Peres and former prime minister Yitzhak Rabin was also settled when Rabin was promised the Defense Ministry if Labour won. The Likud coalition was still beset by internal differences, however. Shamir's authority was challenged by Deputy Prime Minister David Levy and by former defense minister Ariel Sharon.

With the opinion polls predicting a runaway success for the Alignment (comprising the Labour Party and Mapam, a much smaller party), the outcome had been seen as a foregone conclusion before the country voted on July 23. In the event, however, it was extremely close. The final result gave the Alignment 44 seats and 35% of the vote, while Likud won 41 seats and 32% of the vote. The election brought the first representation in the Knesset for Kach, led by Rabbi Meir Kahane (*see* BIOGRAPHIES), a party advocating forcible expulsion of Palestinians from Israel and the Israeli-occupied territories. (For tabulated results, see *Political Parties,* above.)

At first it seemed impossible to produce a viable government from the election result, since it was clear that neither Peres nor Shamir could command enough support to form a coalition government. It was Herzog's shrewd understanding of the public mood that broke the deadlock. Even though party bureaucracies were inclined to resist his call for a government of national unity, they had to give way to the unmistakable swell of popular opinion. An agreement was signed under which Peres was to hold the post of prime minister and Shamir that of foreign affairs minister for the first half of the parliamentary term, at which point they were to exchange portfolios. The government's inner Cabinet was made up of ten ministers, four from Labour, one from Yahad, and five from Likud. In addition to Peres and Shamir, it included Navon, Rabin, Levy, and Sharon. The national unity government won

a motion of confidence in the Knesset on September 13. In December Shas, a small religious party, resigned from the government after the religious affairs portfolio had been awarded to the leader of the National Religious Party rather than to the leader of Shas.

Foreign Affairs. The Likud government faced a succession of daunting problems in the early months of 1984. As the year began, Shamir found himself dealing with the implications of the unexpected meeting in Cairo between Egypt's Pres. Hosni Mubarak and Yasir Arafat, chairman of the Palestine Liberation Organization, at the end of 1983. Shamir viewed the meeting as "a severe blow to the peace process" that Egypt and Israel had set in motion, with U.S. help, at Camp David in 1978. However, the U.S. welcomed the encounter, and Shamir considered this harmful to the cause of peace.

At the same time, the Lebanese imbroglio was becoming increasingly obscure. On January 10 Lebanese Pres. Amin Gemayel announced that the Lebanese Army was about to deploy south of Beirut on the coastal road to the Awali River positions occupied by the Israelis, as a first step toward taking over the Israeli positions in southern Lebanon. Twelve months later President Gemayel was still making the same pronouncement, and the Lebanese Army still had not moved south out of Beirut. Similarly, Shamir announced on January 11 that an early Israeli pullback from south Lebanon was "a possibility," but Israel wanted the Lebanese government to carry out the terms of the agreement with Israel signed on May 17, 1983. However, by the time Shamir spoke it was no secret that the agreement had been aborted following Syrian intervention. To make an Israeli withdrawal conditional on Lebanese acceptance of the agreement was to rule out withdrawal in the foreseeable future.

The death on January 14 of Maj. Saad Haddad (*see* OBITUARIES), commander of the independent militia that controlled much of southern Lebanon, added a complicating factor. Although Haddad had been criticized for his close association with Israel and for allowing Israel to equip and train his small force, nevertheless he had played a significant role in maintaining peace on the frontier between Israel and Lebanon and in creating a nonsectarian force composed of Maronite Christians, Shi'ah Muslims, and Druze from local villages. Israel wanted him replaced by an officer who had the approval of the Beirut authorities, but this proved impossible in view of the Syrian veto over all major policy decisions by the Lebanese government. His successor was Maj. Gen. Antoine Lahad, an experienced

Maronite Christian officer.

On January 2 Shamir firmly rejected a proposal by the opposition Labour Party that the UN peacekeeping force in Lebanon (UNIFIL) be deployed in some areas to be evacuated by the Israel Defense Forces, in order to prevent Palestinian guerrillas from reestablishing themselves in the south and threatening Israeli villages in northern Galilee. Before the end of the year, however, the establishment of UNIFIL in southern Lebanon had become a major plank in the policy of the new unity government.

On February 15 President Gemayel agreed to an eight-point plan presented by a Saudi mediator, which stipulated cancellation of the May 17 agreement with Israel and seven other decisions linked to Israeli and Syrian withdrawal from Lebanon. By the end of the year the only item in the Saudi Arabian plan that had been implemented was cancellation of the agreement. However, by that time Israel and Lebanon were again engaged in negotiations designed to ensure Israel's security on its northern border as a prelude to total Israeli withdrawal from Lebanon. The talks, which were on a purely military level, were held at the border post of Nakoura under UN auspices. After six weeks, during which they had made no noticeable progress, the talks were adjourned on December 20 until 1985.

As the year drew to an end, there was a new mood in foreign affairs. Relations with the U.S. were encouragingly good, and the personal friendship between Peres and Pres. François Mitterrand rekindled the almost dying flame of friendship with France. Despite all its problems, Israel was again moving more positively among the nations. Much of its strength and increasing influence in many countries, especially in Africa and in Southeast Asia, could be attributed to Shamir's pragmatic direction of foreign affairs.

(JON KIMCHE)

JORDAN

A constitutional monarchy, Jordan is located in southwestern Asia and has a short coastline on the Gulf of Aqaba. Area: 94,946 sq km (36,659 sq mi), including about 5,440 sq km occupied by Israel in the June 1967 war. Pop. (1984 est.; including Israeli-occupied West Bank): 3,360,000. Cap.: Amman. Monetary unit: dinar, with (Oct. 29, 1984) a free rate of 0.40 dinar to U.S. $1 (0.49 dinar = £1 sterling). King, Hussein I; prime ministers in 1984, Mudar Badran and, from January 10, Ahmad Abdel Obeidat.

The decision of King Hussein of Jordan to restore diplomatic relations with Egypt, announced on Sept. 25, 1984, was seen as an important step on the path to restoring Egypt to the Arab fold. Groundwork for the decision had been laid by a trade protocol that had been signed with Egypt in December 1983, covering cooperation in trade, employment, and banking. Jordan thus joined Oman, Sudan, and Somalia, the only Arab countries not to sever relations with Egypt after the Camp David accords with Israel were signed in 1978. The new link was considered a danger to Jordan's improving relations with Syria, which had been poor since the outbreak of the Gulf war in 1980. Egyptian Pres. Hosni Mubarak and King Hussein exchanged state visits before the end of the year, Mubarak going to Amman in October and Hussein to Cairo in December.

In a speech to Parliament on January 16, Hussein set forth the dimensions of his Middle East policy. While appearing to acknowledge the Palestine Liberation Organization (PLO) as the sole legitimate representative of the Palestinian people, he also strongly defended Jordan's action of April 1950 in unilaterally annexing the West Bank

of the Jordan River. Hussein was reiterating the view that in the event of an Israeli withdrawal from the West Bank, the only future for the area would be a return to Jordanian suzerainty. In February Hussein and PLO chairman Yasir Arafat resumed their efforts to find a common solution to the problem of the future of the Palestinians. Speaking before the Palestine Liberation Council in Amman in November, the king proposed an international conference, with PLO participation, to work toward a regional settlement.

In January King Hussein summoned Jordan's National Assembly. There had been no elections to the Assembly since 1967, when Israel occupied the West Bank, and in 1974 it had been dissolved in recognition of the PLO's claim to represent the West Bank. Since then it had met only once, in 1976. When Parliament reconvened on Jan. 9, 1984, representatives from the occupied West Bank took their places alongside those from the East Bank. They voted for a formula to fill the empty seats in the 60-member National Assembly and then agreed to hold new elections. The following day Hussein announced a reshuffled Cabinet in which the Palestinians had a stronger voice. The new prime minister was Ahmad Abdel Obeidat, who was also defense minister. A woman, Leila Sharaf, was appointed information minister, while Taher al-Masri, a West Bank Palestinian, became foreign affairs minister. The first by-elections to the Assembly since 1967, and the first in which women could vote, took place on March 12. Six Muslims, three of them fundamentalists, and two Christians were elected to the vacant East Bank seats.

Following the U.S. decision in March not to supply Jordan with Stinger antiaircraft missiles, military cooperation talks took place with the U.S.S.R. and France. Press reports in September suggested that the Soviets had offered to supply military hardware in exchange for a rapprochement between Jordan and Syria. On September 16, after a meeting with Obeidat, France's Defense Minister Charles Hernu announced the establishment of a Franco-Jordanian committee to study Jordan's military requirements.

An overall balance of payments surplus of 15.4 million dinars ($41.3 million) was recorded in 1983 despite a significant rise in the trade deficit during the year. Expatriate remittances rose by 15% to the equivalent of $1.1 billion. Labour Ministry figures suggested that 320,000 Jordanians were working abroad, many of them in the Gulf states. On Jan. 2, 1984, Prime Minister Mudar Badran announced that petroleum had been discovered in "good quantities," though no precise information was released. The discovery was believed to have been made in the Azraq desert, east of Amman. Most of Jordan's petroleum needs were currently met by imports from its close ally, Iraq, and from Saudi Arabia.

Relations with Libya were severed on February 22 in retaliation for an attack on the Jordanian embassy in Tripoli on February 18. Ties had already been strained by Libya's suspicion that Hussein was taking on the mantle of spokesman for the Palestinians following his move to recall Parliament.

(JOHN WHELAN)

KUWAIT

A constitutional monarchy (emirate), Kuwait is in the northeastern Arabian Peninsula, on the Persian Gulf. Area: 17,818 sq km (6,879 sq mi). Pop. (1984 est.): 1,715,000. Cap.: Kuwait City. Monetary unit: dinar, with (Oct. 29, 1984) a free rate of 0.30 dinar to U.S. $1 (0.36 dinar = £1 sterling). Emir, Sheikh Jabir al-Ahmad al-Jabir as-Sabah; prime minister in 1984, Crown Prince Sheikh Saad al-Abdullah as-Salim as-Sabah.

On Aug. 15, 1984, Kuwait concluded an arms-purchase agreement with the U.S.S.R. by which the Soviets were to supply surface-to-surface and surface-to-air missiles to the emirate. Kuwait was the only member of the Gulf Cooperation Council (GCC) to maintain diplomatic relations with Moscow. The contract followed the U.S.'s refusal earlier in the year to sell shoulder-fired Stinger antiaircraft missiles to Kuwait, although the U.S. was to proceed with its plans to assist in the training of pilots.

In March six people, of whom five were from Iraq and the other was a Lebanese Christian, were sentenced to death for their part in a series of bomb attacks in Kuwait City in December 1983. One person from Kuwait was among seven others who received sentences of life imprisonment. The bombers attacked several targets, including the French and U.S. embassies. The explosion at the U.S. embassy, which caused extensive damage and claimed four lives, represented the worst single act of terrorism in Kuwait since independence in 1961. The bombings appeared to have commanded very little popular support.

In early December a Kuwaiti airliner was hijacked by four Arabic-speaking terrorists and taken to Iran, where it remained on the tarmac at Teheran airport for six days before being stormed by Iranian security forces. Two U.S. citizens on board the plane were killed by the hijackers, and other passengers were brutalized before the episode ended. Although Iran did not officially announce the hijackers' demands, they were apparently seeking the release of the Kuwaiti prisoners convicted in connection with the 1983 bombings.

Significant new discoveries of petroleum made during 1984 added between 23 billion and 33 billion bbl to Kuwait's known reserves, which at the end of 1983 totaled 67 billion bbl. Among the members of the Organization of Petroleum Exporting Countries, only Saudi Arabia had greater reserves. Should the new discoveries be confirmed, Kuwait's oil supplies would last for more than 230 years at current rates of production. As a response to the Gulf war between Iran and Iraq, the Kuwait Petroleum Corporation was stockpiling petroleum at the European operations of Gulf Oil, over which it had direct control.

Planning Minister Abdel Rahman Abdullah al-Awadi announced in July that a draft five-year economic development program had been approved by a Cabinet committee. However, final details would have to be coordinated with the plans of other GCC member nations.

(JOHN WHELAN)

This article updates the *Macropædia* article ARABIA: *Kuwait.*

LEBANON

A republic of southwestern Asia, Lebanon is situated on the Mediterranean Sea. Area: 10,230 sq km (3,950 sq mi). Pop. (1984 est.): 3.1 million. (The population of Lebanon, including about 500,000 Palestinian refugees, is thought to have declined since the outbreak of civil war in 1974, but reliable figures are not available.) Cap.: Beirut. Monetary unit: Lebanese pound, with (Oct. 29, 1984) a free rate of LL 8 to U.S. $1 (LL 9.65 = £1 sterling). President in 1984, Amin Gemayel; prime ministers, Shafiq al-Wazzan and, from April 30, Rashid Karami.

The new government headed by Prime Minister Rashid Karami (*see* BIOGRAPHIES) took office on April 30, 1984. For the first time since 1975, the administration included leaders of all the main political tendencies in Lebanon. The participation of Shi'ah Muslim leader Nabih Berri was assured by his appointment as minister of state for southern Lebanon and for reconstruction. Druze leader Walid Jumblatt accepted the public works, transport, and tourism portfolio. The finance minister was another veteran, former president Camille Chamoun, while the leader of the Christian Phalange Party, Pierre Gemayel (*see* OBITUARIES), also became a Cabinet minister before he died on August 29. Relationships among the members of the Cabinet were often less than harmonious. The Cabinet's decision to revive the peace process and to begin deliberations on political reforms was preceded by inflammatory statements from Jumblatt in which he labeled Pres. Amin Gemayel a "fascist" and a "butcher."

Violence continued unabated. Fighting broke out on August 26 on the Green Line in Beirut between rival militias and the Army. On the same day, the prime minister announced a cease-fire in Tripoli, where a week before 100 people had been killed in sectarian fighting. Other outbreaks included the storming of the Saudi Arabian consulate and U.K. embassy by Shi'ah militants on August 24 and the Israeli attack on August 28 on a Palestinian detention centre on the Beirut–Damascus road, in which 100 people were killed or wounded. These incidents were followed by the September 20 bombing of the U.S. embassy annex in Beirut. In early September a car-bomb explosion aimed at Education and Labour Minister Selim al-Hoss appeared to break the etiquette of the nine-year-old civil war—that direct attacks on politicians were to be avoided.

The political crisis that led to the new government's taking office began on February 5, when the Cabinet led by Prime Minister Shafiq al-Wazzan resigned. On February 7

AP/WIDE WORLD

The Cabinet of Lebanon's new government under Prime Minister Rashid Karami met in June. At the head of the table is Pres. Amin Gemayel; at left are the Druze leader Walid Jumblatt (front) and Prime Minister Karami (to Jumblatt's left); at right front facing Jumblatt and Karami is Shi'ah Muslim leader Nabih Berri.

U.S. Pres. Ronald Reagan announced that most of the U.S. Marines in Beirut were to be redeployed to offshore ships, and the following day the British contingent of the multinational peacekeeping force pulled out as well. Italy then announced plans to withdraw, and finally France followed suit in March. Fighting enveloped Beirut on February 2 when Druze forces pounded Christian East Beirut from the hills to the southeast. The same day, the Lebanese Army and Phalange Party forces hit at the Shi'ah suburbs of southern Beirut. The use of the Army in such a partisan manner led to the government's collapse.

These events appeared to leave Lebanon a partitioned country. The dividing lines between the warring factions had never been so clearly defined. The only area in dispute by midyear was a thin slice of coastal territory south of Beirut, held by Muslim insurgents at the end of the 1975-76 civil war but infiltrated by Phalangist forces after the 1982 Israeli invasion.

By late October some political progress had been made by the new government. The Chamber of Deputies (parliament) elected Hussain al-Hussaini as its new speaker in succession to Kamel al-Asaad, who had been in office for 12 years. The election of a Muslim speaker was followed by demands from Berri and Jumblatt that political reform be put at the top of the Cabinet's agenda. They wanted equal parliamentary representation for Muslims and Christians, rather than the existing 6 to 5 balance in favour of the latter.

In October the Cabinet approved an austerity budget for 1985 in which proposed total expenditure, at LL 10.8 billion, showed little change from 1984. Muslim ministers opposed high spending on defense and, led by Berri, they succeeded in securing an aid allocation for the Israeli-occupied south of the country. The government's main economic problem was said to be its inability to collect customs duties because of the proliferation of illegal ports. Nevertheless, on July 9 Beirut airport resumed operations after a five-month hiatus. As part of a security plan agreed to at the end of June, Beirut port was also reopened.

On September 18 an agreement was announced for the establishment of a 40-member committee to draft a constitution that would introduce power sharing among the various communities. Political leaders also agreed that, apart from constitutional reform, the biggest problem confronting Lebanon was reconstruction. In June Muhammad Atallah, head of the Council for Development and Reconstruction, estimated the cost of a ten-year reconstruction plan for public amenities at more than $17 billion.

On his return from Jidda on July 29, Karami announced that Saudi Arabia had promised "substantial sums" for reconstruction work, though he stressed that, on the whole, Lebanon had fared badly with Arab aid pledges. A report published by the Foreign Affairs Ministry in August claimed that since 1980 Arab aid had reached $385 million, only 19% of the total committed for the 1980–84 period. The largest sums had come from Saudi Arabia, the United Arab Emirates, and Kuwait, though virtually no aid had been received since the end of 1981.

With economic ills mounting, the Banque du Liban announced new currency regulations in early October in an attempt to halt the drastic slide in the value of the Lebanese pound. Commercial banks had to reduce their foreign-currency holdings from a maximum 50% of capital to 15%. The new measures were a response to attacks by speculators on the pound, which had previously been regarded as a stable currency despite the political unrest.

In August talks began in Baghdad about a new agreement on imports of Iraqi petroleum for the refinery at Tripoli.

The refinery, closed as a result of damage sustained during fighting among Palestinian factions in late 1983, reopened on August 10. Petroleum was being transported from Iraq by pipeline and tanker via Turkey. Lebanese officials were seeking a commitment from Iraq to buy Lebanese products in return for the oil.

Maj. Saad Haddad (see OBITUARIES), commander of the Israeli-backed Christian militia that controlled the south of the country, died on January 14.   (JOHN WHELAN)

See also *Middle Eastern Affairs,* above.

LIBYA

A socialist country of North Africa, Libya lies on the Mediterranean Sea. Area: 1,749,000 sq km (675,000 sq mi). Pop. (1984 est.): 3,648,000. Cap.: Tripoli. Monetary unit: Libyan dinar, with (Oct. 29, 1984) a free rate of 0.30 dinar to U.S. $1 (0.36 dinar = £1 sterling). Chief of state in 1984, Col. Muammar al-Qaddafi; secretaries-general of the General People's Committee (premiers), Jadallah Azzuz at-Talhi and, from February 16, Muhammad az-Zaruq Rajab.

Libya's economy suffered throughout 1984 because of low world demand for crude oil and refined products. Revenues were estimated at under $15 billion, far short of the amount necessary to sustain the pace of economic development of the 1970s. Though the progressive strengthening of the U.S. dollar, in which oil was traded, somewhat mitigated the effects, the options of Libya's leader Col. Muammar al-Qaddafi at home and overseas were nevertheless severely constrained by the low revenues.

Despite the poor short-term economic prospects, the government decided to go ahead with an ambitious project to construct a pipeline to bring nonreplenishable water 900 km (560 mi) to the coast from Kufrah and Tazerbo in the southeast. The pipeline was the first phase of a project that would cost an estimated $11 billion–$20 billion.

A British woman police constable was killed by a bullet fired from the Libyan People's Bureau (embassy) in St. James's Square, London, while anti-Qaddafi demonstrations were taking place outside the building on April 17. For the next ten days the bureau was under siege until its occupants were allowed to leave the country, escaping detention in Britain under the conventions of diplomatic immunity. A later inquiry revealed that Libya had authorized the bureau staff to fire on demonstrators; a coded message to that effect had been picked up by French intelligence, though there had been no time to pass on details to the British authorities. The killing of policewoman Yvonne Fletcher was not part of a planned Libyan reprisal, but it provided a focus for growing resentment in Britain against elements of the Libyan community. In March a series of bomb attacks apparently perpetrated by pro-Qaddafi Libyans hit newsstands carrying anti-Qaddafi journals and the homes of antiregime Libyans in London and Manchester.

Diplomatic relations between Libya and Britain were severed during the siege. Four Libyans arrested in connection with the London bombings were clearly of importance to the Libyan leadership because six British citizens were arrested in Libya in May and used to bargain for the release of the detained Libyans. Two were set free on September 2 after a group of British members of Parliament had visited Tripoli to seek their release, and in December Qaddafi promised to recommend the release of the others early in 1985. In August a wealthy Libyan businessman, Ali al-Giahour, was mysteriously assassinated while awaiting trial in connection with the London bombings.

Internal opposition to Qaddafi was galvanized by the

After being sentenced to 1–15 years in prison for taking part in food riots, these Moroccan students began a hunger strike. By early September, when this photograph was made, the strike was in its second month and three had died.

HASKI LIBERATION—GAMMA/LIAISON

events in Britain. On May 8 the National Front for the Salvation of Libya, a Sudan-based opposition group inspired by the Muslim Brotherhood, managed a sensational series of shootings in Tripoli. These violent events were significant because Libya's society was not a violent one, and the scale of the conflict reflected a deep-seated and committed opposition. Swift reprisals took place. Throughout July suspected opponents of the government were tried in summary courts convened by local "popular committees," and those found guilty were hanged.

Elsewhere, Qaddafi was diligent in repairing broken fences. The rapprochement between Jordan and Egypt was roundly denounced in September, but by then Libya's own relations with Morocco had been cemented by an agreement establishing a "union of states" between the two countries. September also saw the beginnings of the withdrawal of French and Libyan troops from Chad. However, by mid-November most of the Libyan troops apparently remained while France—to the acute political embarrassment of Pres. François Mitterrand—withdrew completely. Pres. Hissen Habré of Chad had been understandably skeptical about Libya's intentions. Libya and Greece signed a $1 billion economic cooperation agreement in September, during a visit to Libya by Prime Minister Andreas Papandreou, and in December Qaddafi met with Spanish Premier Felipe González in Majorca.

In November relations between Libya and Egypt deteriorated further when four men were arrested in Cairo and charged with plotting to assassinate Abdul Hamid Bakkush, a Libyan political foe of Qaddafi, on orders from Libya. In an elaborate ruse, Egyptian officials used faked photographs of an apparently shot and bleeding Bakkush to trick Libya into announcing, mistakenly, that the assassination had been carried out.   (J. A. ALLAN)

This article updates the *Macropædia* article NORTH AFRICA: *Libya*.

MOROCCO

A constitutional monarchy of North Africa, Morocco has coastlines on the Atlantic Ocean and the Mediterranean Sea. Area: 458,730 sq km (177,117 sq mi). Pop. (1984 est.): 21,495,200. (Area and population figures refer to Morocco as constituted prior to the purported division of Western

Sahara between Morocco and Mauritania and the subsequent Moroccan occupation of the Mauritanian zone in 1979.) Cap.: Rabat. Monetary unit: dirham, with (Oct. 29, 1984) a free rate of 9.32 dirhams to U.S. $1 (11.25 dirhams = £1 sterling). King: Hassan II; prime minister in 1984, Mohammad Karim Lamrani.

Throughout 1984 Morocco continued to be preoccupied by its relationships with other nations in North Africa. The year opened with serious riots in various towns throughout the country; demonstrations in Marrakech in the first week of January were followed by violent riots in Nador and Al-Hoceima. When the troubles died down at the end of January, more than 100 people were dead and 1,500 in prison. The government accused fundamentalists and left-wingers of fomenting the troubles. Of 61 Islamic fundamentalists put on trial in Casablanca, 13 were sentenced to death for plotting the overthrow of King Hassan II.

In reality the riots were caused by an increasingly difficult economic situation. The government had tried to stimulate investment by reducing its subsidies on consumer products and energy prices. These factors, together with various local irritations, created the conditions for the riots. As a result the government recast its 1984 budget, restoring subsidies worth 1.5 billion dirhams.

Further problems faced the government in regard to the Western Sahara. Morocco intensified its military hold over the region by extending the defensive wall that already surrounded the major towns of Laayoune, Smara, and Bou Craa to include Haouza, temporary capital of the Popular Front for the Liberation of Saguia el Hamra and Rio de Oro (Polisario Front). The Polisario Front began a major campaign against the Moroccan occupation in June. After Dakhla was attacked in July, Morocco warned Mauritania, which had recognized the Saharan Arab Democratic Republic (SADR) government-in-exile in February, that it would respond to any attack from Mauritanian territory. Morocco left the Organization of African Unity in November over the OAU's seating of the SADR.

Partly, no doubt, in response to the Saharan situation, Morocco proposed a treaty of unity to Libya in July. The treaty was signed at the Moroccan border town of Oujda on August 13 and was overwhelmingly approved in a referendum at the end of the month. The treaty enraged Algeria, which saw it as an attack on its own proposals for North African unity and as an attempt by Morocco to avoid diplomatic isolation because of its stance on the Sahara.

In mid-September Morocco held national elections, one year after the previous parliamentary session had ended. The delay was caused by the king's apparent desire for a settlement of the Western Sahara issue before elections took place. The results confirmed the dominance of centrist parties, although the traditional nationalist party, Istiqlal, fared rather badly, while the major left-wing party, the National Union of Popular Forces, did surprisingly well. (For tabulated results, see *Political Parties*, above.

(GEORGE JOFFÉ)

This article updates the *Macropædia* article NORTH AFRICA: *Morocco*.

OMAN

The sultanate of Oman occupies the southeastern part of the Arabian Peninsula, facing the Persian Gulf, the Gulf of Oman, and the Arabian Sea. A small part of the country lies to the north and is separated from the rest of Oman by the United Arab Emirates. Area: 300,000 sq km (120,000 sq mi). Pop.: in 1984 estimates ranged from 1 million to

1.5 million; no census has ever been taken. Cap.: Muscat. Monetary unit: rial Omani, with (Oct. 29, 1984) a free rate of 0.34 rial to U.S. $1 (free rate of 0.42 rial = £1 sterling). Sultan and prime minister in 1984, Qabus ibn Sa'id.

During 1984 an increase in Oman's petroleum production and its strategic position outside the Gulf war zone led to a surge of confidence in Sultan Qabus ibn Sa'id's regime. Oman's known petroleum reserves stood at 4,000,000,000 bbl, a figure that was rising by about 300 million bbl a year as exploration continued.

In October the sultanate was reported to be in the final stages of negotiating the purchase of Tornado multirole jets from the U.K. Sultan Qabus took a keen interest in the security of the Gulf region. The issue figured high on the agenda when Saudi Arabia's defense and aviation minister, Prince Sultan ibn Abdel-Aziz, made a three-day visit in July. Through the Gulf Cooperation Council (GCC), Oman was to receive $1.8 billion for defense spending over 12 years. The visit of U.S. Vice-Pres. George Bush on May 18–20 served to emphasize the close political links between Oman and the U.S., evidenced by Oman's support for the Camp David peace accords between Egypt and Israel and a military agreement that allowed the U.S. access to Oman in times of emergency.

In January Sultan Qabus replaced Commerce and Industry Minister Muhammad Zubair with Salim Abdullah al-Ghazali, previously secretary to the Cabinet. Ahmad Sowaidan al-Baluchi became minister of posts, telegraph, and telephones. "Omanization" of the economy accelerated in 1984 as more government contracts were awarded to local companies. A local institution took over 14 branches of the British Bank of the Middle East, which had done business in the sultanate for 36 years and remained the country's largest foreign bank. (JOHN WHELAN)

This article updates the *Macropædia* article ARABIA: *Oman.*

QATAR

A monarchy (emirate) on the Arabian Peninsula, Qatar occupies a desert peninsula on the west coast of the Persian Gulf. Area: 11,400 sq km (4,400 sq mi). Pop. (1984 est.): 276,000. Cap.: Doha. Monetary unit: riyal, with (Oct. 29, 1984) a free rate of 3.65 riyals to U.S. $1 (4.40 riyals = £1 sterling). Emir and prime minister in 1984, Sheikh Khalifah ibn Hamad ath-Thani.

Emir Sheikh Khalifah ibn Hamad ath-Thani of Qatar undertook a tour of four Asian countries in April 1984. In India he signed a five-year economic and technical agreement that called for joint ventures and other collaboration between the two countries, and in South Korea he signed a technical and staff-exchange agreement. Other economic and trade understandings were reached with Pakistan and Japan. During his visit to India the emir suggested establishing a committee of nonaligned countries to help settle the Iran-Iraq war. The conflict had moved closer to Qatar with the attacks on petroleum tankers in Gulf waters.

Qatar's ambitious project to extract liquefied natural gas from the North Field, designed to provide Qatar with income after oil revenues had dwindled in importance, progressed a step further during the year. On June 25 a tripartite agreement on the development was signed by the Qatar General Petroleum Corporation, British Petroleum, and Compagnie Française des Pétroles-Total.

On several occasions during the year Qatar appeared to breach its petroleum production quota of 300,000 bbl a day set by the Organization of Petroleum Exporting Countries. Sources within the oil industry suggested that the government was also discounting oil prices in order to bring in vitally needed revenue. Stringency measures introduced by the government at the end of 1982 had resulted in an exodus of many surplus expatriate workers from the country. However, foreign-assets holdings, which amounted to $15 billion, had not been seriously undermined by the fall in oil revenues. (JOHN WHELAN)

This article updates the *Macropædia* article ARABIA: *Qatar.*

SAUDI ARABIA

The kingdom of Saudi Arabia occupies four-fifths of the Arabian Peninsula, with coastlines on the Red Sea and the Persian Gulf. Area: 2,240,000 sq km (865,000 sq mi). Pop (1984 est.): 10,841,000. Cap.: Riyadh. Monetary unit: riyal, with (Oct. 29, 1984) a free rate of 3.53 riyals to U.S. $1 (4.26 riyals = £1 sterling). King and prime minister in 1984, Fahd.

During 1984 Saudi Arabia reacted decisively to the threat posed to the stability of the Gulf by the escalation of the conflict between Iran and Iraq. On June 5 Saudi Arabia scored an important military and propaganda victory when its F-15 advanced interceptor jet fighters shot down at least one, and possibly a second, Iranian F-4 Phantom aircraft in Saudi Arabian airspace. (A Saudi spokesman claimed that only one fighter had been brought down, but according to U.S. sources two Iranian aircraft had been destroyed.) Teheran confirmed on June 7 that one Phantom had been shot down, but it claimed that the incident had happened over international waters. The Saudi Arabian chargé d'affaires was handed a protest note by the Iranians, but they stopped short of mentioning reprisals, saying only that Iran would respond severely to any similar incidents.

The Saudi action demonstrated that the Iranian threat to shipping and oil installations on the western littoral of the Gulf could be countered, although not without the help of intelligence provided by U.S.-supplied airborne warning and control system (AWACS) surveillance aircraft. The U.S. decision to supply the Saudi Arabians with a KC-10 airborne tanker gave them the capability of keeping their

ROBERT AZZI—WOODFIN CAMP & ASSOCIATES

In late May the U.S. sent 400 Stinger antiaircraft missiles to Saudi Arabia. The missiles were to be used in Saudi Arabia's effort to establish a protected zone for shipping along the western coast of the Persian Gulf.

strike force in the air over the protected zone. The U.S. also offered to supply naval protection to vessels serving Arab ports on the Gulf.

Saudi Arabia's moves to strengthen its defenses would be greatly enhanced by the announcement, expected in January 1985, of the winner of the $3 billion–$4 billion contract for the command, control, and communications system for the AWACS aircraft. An important element in the contract was to be its inclusion of an offset program. Under Saudi Arabian government policy, the firm that bid successfully for the contract would be obliged to reinvest about one-third of the total value of the contract in high-technology industries in Saudi Arabia.

Saudi Arabia remained the tenth largest importer of goods in the world, although in 1983 the total value of its imports dropped by 2.8%, compared with the previous year's figure, to 135.4 billion riyals ($38 billion). In 1983 the kingdom's single most important supplier was the U.S., which provided almost 20% of total imports. Although no official export figures were released, it was known that exports continued to be made up almost exclusively of hydrocarbons, despite the fact that a number of downstream industries had been established, particularly in the petrochemicals sector. By November Saudi Arabia's oil production had been cut to less than 4 million bbl a day to support the drive by the Organization of Petroleum Exporting Countries (OPEC) to stabilize oil prices. At its autumn meeting in Geneva, OPEC agreed on a ceiling of just under 4.4 million bbl a day for the kingdom. Earlier, on August 20, King Fahd, in an unusual move for him, made a statement in which he pointed out that Saudi Arabia's oil production had been cut to 4.1 million bbl a day because of pressure on OPEC by the industrialized countries. King Fahd told a meeting of Saudi Arabian students that, if OPEC remained "steadfast and firm," the problems caused by the current excess in worldwide petroleum-production capacity could be solved.

There were signs that the kingdom could expect an increasingly tough reception for its non-oil exports from the industrialized countries. In June the European Communities (EC) slapped a 13.5% tariff on Saudi Arabian methanol at the request of The Netherlands. In an angry response, on August 20 the industry and electricity minister, Abdel-Aziz az-Zamil, described the tariff as "unjustified" and maintained that the EC quota for Saudi Arabian methanol was "inadequate." The minister went on to say that the EC had promised not to impose tariffs on other products, but the EC later denied the suggestion. Hopes of reaching an agreement rested on talks at the institutional level between the EC and the Gulf Cooperation Council (GCC). Saudi Arabia, which opened its second export methanol plant in the industrial city of Jubail in August, was already by far the most significant exporter to the EC. Clearly, the kingdom was likely to suffer most among GCC member states from a continuation of the dispute.

In an unusual move that shook the petroleum markets, in midyear Saudi Arabia increased its production temporarily in order to pay for four Boeing wide-bodied commercial airliners that had been supplied to Saudia, the national airline. The airline was to be shifted to the private sector, according to the published outline of the fourth five-year (1985–90) development plan, although details of the proposal, and of the plan itself, would not be available before 1985. It was thought conceivable that Saudi Arabia would place greater emphasis on barter agreements when negotiating sales of petroleum during the upcoming plan period.

In a statement on October 17 the finance and national economy minister, Sheikh Muhammad Ali Abalkhail, denied widespread reports that the government was illegally withholding payments from contractors in a bid to improve its cash flow. Abalkhail alleged that some companies had been making incorrect claims about delayed payments in order to persuade their banks to defer loan repayments or provide new credits. A firm of London brokers, Rowe & Pitman, claimed on November 16 that $20 billion had been lent by foreign bankers to various Saudi Arabian companies, many of which were encountering problems in making repayments because of a collapse in construction tender prices. The brokers maintained that Saudi Arabia faced a budget deficit of $10 billion in the current (1984–85) fiscal year, while oil production had fallen 60% since 1981.

Aramco, the state national oil company, had revenues of $16.4 billion during the first half of 1984, 3.6% below the corresponding period of 1983. A similar performance during the second half of the year would result in the lowest full-year earnings since 1978. Aramco accounted for more than 95% of Saudi Arabia's total oil revenue. Aramco was expected to operate a proposed crude-oil export pipeline from Iraq to Saudi Arabia that would enable the Baghdad government to gain access to Saudi Arabian export terminals.

The belt-tightening measures practiced by the government were accompanied in 1984 by a growing emphasis on local participation in government tenders. A circular from the Finance Ministry on August 6 redefined the policy that had come to be known as the "30% rule," under which a foreign company working on a government contract was obliged to subcontract 30% of the value of the work to Saudi Arabian firms. It was made clear, much to the disappointment of Western interests, that joint ventures between Saudi Arabian and foreign partners did not enjoy the same status as companies that were 100% locally owned. The difficulties facing joint-venture concerns were illustrated in September when the U.S.-Saudi contractor Carlson al-Saudia collapsed, leaving an entire expatriate work force to be repatriated by the Saudi government.

In a government change, Ghazi Abdel-Rahman al-Gosaibi, a distinguished technocrat and well-known Arabic poet, was replaced as health minister by Faisal Abdel-Aziz al-Hegelan. Gosaibi was said to have had differences of opinion with members of the royal family over the awarding of public contracts. He was later appointed ambassador to Bahrain, where the new causeway, providing a road link between Bahrain and Saudi Arabia, was to be opened in 1985.

The opening of the prestigious King Khalid international airport at Riyadh in November 1983 resulted in an immediate increase in passenger traffic to the capital, which had previously been served with international flights only by the national carrier. At the same time, senior Saudi Arabian businessmen believed that there were unlikely to be any new projects on a similarly large scale. The outline of the fourth five-year plan stressed social objectives rather than infrastructure targets. The employment of Saudi Arabian women was touched on as an issue, though the outline made it clear that women would enter the productive sector only insofar as their employment was consistent with the principles of Islam. Nursing and teaching were two occupations in which women already worked. Some technocrats believed that women would also be able to find employment in the computer industry.

The kingdom aimed to achieve greater self-sufficiency in defense industries. In Brazil on October 9, the defense and aviation minister, Prince Sultan ibn Abdel-Aziz, and

Brazil's Foreign Affairs Minister Ramiro Elysio Saraiva Guerreiro signed an agreement for cooperation in weapons manufacture and technology exchange. Prince Sultan announced in August that the kingdom had already achieved self-sufficiency in some light weapons and handguns. Earlier in the year, during a visit to the U.K. in February, Crown Prince Abdullah ibn Abdel-Aziz, the deputy prime minister, was shown new British military equipment, including the Challenger tank and the Rapier surface-to-air missile system, although there were no reports of an order being placed.　　　　　　　　　　(JOHN WHELAN)

This article updates the *Macropædia* article ARABIA: *Saudi Arabia*.

SYRIA

> A republic of southwestern Asia, Syria is on the Mediterranean Sea. Area: 185,180 sq km (71,498 sq mi). Pop. (1984 est.): 9,934,000. Cap.: Damascus. Monetary unit: Syrian pound, with (Oct. 29, 1984) a par value of LS 3.93 to U.S. $1 (free rate of LS 4.71 = £1 sterling). President in 1984, Gen. Hafez al-Assad; premier, Abdul Rauf al-Kasm.

Pressure mounted in 1984 on Pres. Hafez al-Assad (*see* BIOGRAPHIES) to reduce Syria's military obligations in Lebanon, both by withdrawing troops and by cutting off aid to various factions. The military confrontation with Israel in 1982 had cost more than $1 billion, and during 1984 military commitments in Lebanon cost Syria $250,-000 a day. On July 26 President Assad agreed to back the second stage of Lebanon's peace plan, after a meeting with Lebanese Prime Minister Rashid Karami.

President Assad's health—he was suffering from a heart ailment—continued to cause concern in Damascus at the beginning of the year. The president met several foreign visitors, including the U.S. civil rights leader and presidential aspirant Jesse Jackson (*see* BIOGRAPHIES), who successfully arranged for the release of a captured U.S. airman. However, with the president working a reduced day, tensions mounted within the ruling elite. Tanks and infantry units took to the streets of the capital on February 27. The move was apparently aimed at underlining the authority of the president's controversial younger brother, Rifaat al-Assad, commander of the defense brigade that had acted as President Assad's guard since he came to power in 1970. Rival commanders then placed their own forces on alert, but the crisis was defused by an all-night session of the Ba'th Party's regional command on February 29–March 1. President Assad reasserted his authority by ordering the principal armed units to return to their barracks.

The Cabinet resigned on March 6 to clear the way for a restructuring of the government. Premier Abdul Rauf al-Kasm was immediately asked to remain. as head of the new Cabinet. Rifaat al-Assad was one of three new vice-presidents who were appointed on March 11. In late May he paid a visit to Moscow, accompanied by two army officers who earlier had deployed troops in opposition to his own. The visit was said to indicate a relaxing of tension. In an interview in early July, Defense Minister Mustafa Tlas claimed that Rifaat al-Assad's defense brigades had been disbanded and integrated into the regular Army. In September he was reported to be living temporarily in Switzerland, and it seemed clear that the president had asked or ordered his brother to remain abroad. He returned to Syria in late November without incident.

In his own first visit abroad since his illness began in November 1983, President Assad went to Libya on August 23 for talks with Libyan leader Col. Muammar al-Qaddafi and to Algeria two days later. In October Assad received an envoy from King Hassan II of Morocco, who delivered an invitation for Syria to attend an Arab summit. In the same month he also undertook his first visit to the U.S.S.R. since 1982.

The oil and natural resources minister, Ghazi ad-Drubi, confirmed in October that reserves of light crude petroleum had been found in the northeastern Deir az-Zor region. He reported that one deep well had been discovered, although press reports later suggested that the find would yield only 7,000 bbl a day. Dependence on Iran for crude oil had become a feature of the budget, since output from Syria's wells amounted to only 173,000 bbl a day in 1983. To reinforce its relationship with Iran, evidenced by its support for that country in its war with Iraq, the government signed a trade and economic agreement with Iran in Damascus on February 19. The outstanding feature of the 1984 budget was its heavy allocation for defense spending, which absorbed $3.2 billion, 20% more than in 1983. Though providing for a deficit of $638 million, the budget continued the trend of cutting subsidies, a measure that had often caused unrest in Arab states.

Indicating improved relations with Jordan, a Jordanian economic team arrived in Damascus on July 30. In September a trade agreement was signed covering Jordan's purchase of agricultural products. Syrian officials continued to grumble privately about the fact that promises of Arab aid remained unfulfilled.　　　　　(JOHN WHELAN)

TUNISIA

> A republic of North Africa, Tunisia lies on the Mediterranean Sea. Area: 154,530 sq km (52,644 sq mi). Pop. (1984 census): 6,966,173. Cap.: Tunis. Monetary unit: dinar, with (Oct. 29, 1984) a free rate of 0.83 dinar to U.S. $1 (1 dinar = £1 sterling). President in 1984, Habib Bourguiba; prime minister, Mohammed Mzali.

During early 1984 Tunisia's ruling Parti Socialiste Destourien (PSD) faced the most serious social unrest since the nation achieved independence from France in 1956. The rioting that began late in 1983 in southern areas, following the government's announcement that the price of bread

LAURENT SOLA—GAMMA/LIAISON

When the price of bread was doubled in Tunisia in January, rioters took to the streets. When the disturbances reached the capital, Tunis, the cumulative effect of bloodshed and disorder led to a price retreat.

was to be doubled in 1984, spread to the capital in the first week of January. A state of emergency was declared on January 3, and three days later Pres. Habib Bourguiba rescinded the price increase. An official commission of inquiry into the riots reported in April that 89 persons had been killed and 938—including 348 police—wounded.

Blame for allowing the riots to develop fell on Interior Minister Driss Guiga, whom Bourguiba dismissed from office and excluded from the PSD Political Bureau. Guiga, who took refuge in the U.K., was later accused of high treason and on June 16 was sentenced in his absence to ten years of hard labour. Meanwhile, several hundred rioters were brought to trial, some of whom received prison sentences ranging from 5 to 30 years.

Despite the riots Prime Minister Mohammed Mzali, who remained Bourguiba's most likely successor, continued to press for liberalization; but in August Mohammed Saya, formerly believed to be out of sympathy with Mzali's policies, was recalled as ambassador to Rome and reappointed minister for supply by Bourguiba. Further ministerial changes were made in October, when Ridha Ben Ali, who had headed the commission of inquiry into the riots, became minister of justice.

Opposition to the government continued from within the labour unions and among the staff and students of the University of Tunis; during the second half of the year there was a buildup of strike action, culminating in a general strike on November 26 at the phosphate mining centre of Metlaoui. In a conciliatory gesture toward Islamic fundamentalists, Bourguiba marked his 81st birthday in August by ordering the release of 17 of their leaders imprisoned since September 1981.

In January Tunisia blamed Libya for damage by saboteurs to the oil pipeline running from Algeria into Tunisia. In May, following Libyan accusations of Tunisian complicity in a foiled attack on Libyan leader Col. Muammar al-Qaddafi, Tunisia withdrew its ambassador in Tripoli. In June, however, Tunisian frontier guards seized by Libya were released, and in July a joint security commission was set up to discuss differences between the two countries. A series of agreements, including accords on trade and cooperation in sports, were signed on December 30.

Tunisia's economic difficulties were compounded by the effects of the bread riots. U.S. Pres. Ronald Reagan sent his ambassador at large, Gen. Vernon Walters, to Tunis on January 11 to offer aid, and in February France agreed to supply "immediate support" to a total value of F 560 million.   (PHILIPPE DECRAENE)

This article updates the *Macropædia* article NORTH AFRICA: *Tunisia*.

TURKEY

A republic of Asia Minor and southeastern Europe, Turkey has coastlines on the Aegean, Black, and Mediterranean seas. Area: 779,452 sq km (300,948 sq mi), including 23,698 sq km in Europe. Pop. (1984 est.): 48,591,000. Cap.: Ankara. Monetary unit: Turkish lira, with (Oct. 29, 1984) a free rate of 416.51 liras to U.S. $1 (502.73 liras = £1 sterling). President in 1984, Gen. Kenan Evren; prime minister, Turgut Ozal.

Local elections held on March 25, 1984, strengthened the authority of the government formed by Turgut Ozal (*see* BIOGRAPHIES), leader of the Motherland Party (MP) and winner of the November 1983 general elections that brought an end to three years of military rule in Turkey. The MP's share of the poll dropped only slightly, from 45 to 41.5%. However, on the left the Populist Party fell from

30 to 9%, while 23% of the vote went to the Social Democratic Party, which had not been allowed to compete in the general elections. The MP won the majority of provincial and local councils, including those of the main cities.

The results of the local elections did not halt protests by human rights activists inside and outside Turkey. Martial law remained in force in some parts of the country, arrests and trials of alleged terrorists and other subversives continued, and the number of executions since the 1980 military takeover reached 27. More than 1,200 leading Turkish intellectuals presented a petition to Pres. Kenan Evren calling for liberalization of the regime. Proceedings were started against the organizers of the petition. The leaders of the banned Confederation of Revolutionary Trade Unions were freed pending the conclusion of their trial, but the leaders of the Turkish Peace Association remained in prison, although a retrial was ordered. The European Communities failed to unblock aid allocated to Turkey but subsequently frozen to protest military rule.

Kurdish nationalism again posed a major threat. Terrorists said to be members of the Kurdish Workers Party (PKK) were operating from territory in northern Iraq controlled by the Barzani faction of the Kurdish Democratic Party. When a security operation was launched in the southeastern part of the country, Iraq allowed the Turkish Army to penetrate its territory in pursuit of the terrorists but Iran refused to cooperate. This aggravated Turkey's difficulty in remaining neutral in the Iran-Iraq war.

Ozal visited both Iran and Iraq, as well as Pakistan and Libya, while Evren went to Saudi Arabia and to the Islamic Conference Organization summit in Casablanca, Morocco. Soviet Premier Nikolay Tikhonov visited Ankara in December. Meanwhile, Turkey's relations with several Western countries remained troubled. Armenian terrorism aimed at Turks living abroad continued, claiming one victim in Iran and another in Austria. Turkey took exception to references by U.S. congressmen and French officials to the killing of Armenians in Turkey during World War I. Relations with the U.S. were also soured both by cuts in U.S. aid, which nevertheless remained considerable, and by attempts to link some of the aid to the resettlement of Greeks in the Turkish-occupied tourist town of Famagusta, Cyprus. Ozal's tenure of office had opened with gestures of goodwill toward Greece, but the exchange of ambassadors between Turkey and the self-styled Turkish Republic of Northern Cyprus, as well as incidents in the Aegean Sea, rekindled tension. In March Greece threatened to withdraw its ambassador from Ankara, and in October it closed one air corridor in the Aegean during NATO exercises.

Regulations governing foreign trade and currency exchange were liberalized in January. Exports increased faster than imports, and inflation, which had fallen to around 30% in 1983, exceeded 40%. The slide in the value of Turkish currency continued, with a 50% loss of value against the U.S. dollar in one year. In October Ozal lost two of his lieutenants, Minister of Finance Vural Arikan and Minister of the Interior Ali Tanriyar, following an open disagreement in Parliament.   (ANDREW MANGO)

This article updates the *Macropædia* article TURKEY AND ANCIENT ANATOLIA.

UNITED ARAB EMIRATES

Consisting of Abu Dhabi, Ajman, Dubai, Fujairah, Ras al-Khaimah, Sharjah, and Umm al-Qaiwain, the United Arab Emirates is a federation of seven largely autonomous emirates located on the eastern Arabian Peninsula. Area: 77,700 sq km (30,000 sq mi). Pop.: (1984 est.): 1,290,000. Cap.:

Abu Dhabi. Monetary unit: dirham, with (Oct. 29, 1984) a free rate of 3.64 dirhams to U.S. $1 (4.39 dirhams = £1 sterling). President in 1984, Sheikh Zaid ibn Sultan an-Nahayan; prime minister, Sheikh Rashid ibn Said al-Maktum.

During 1984 the economy of the United Arab Emirates (U.A.E.) began to suffer from the effects of the Gulf war between Iran and Iraq. On October 31 the Organization of Petroleum Exporting Countries (OPEC) cut the U.A.E.'s petroleum production quota from 1.1 million bbl a day to 950,000 for 1985. The reduction would put further strain on the economy. Before the OPEC meeting, the U.A.E. had appeared to favour reductions in price rather than production as a means of dealing with the fall in demand.

The federal government budgeted for a deficit of $1.5 billion in 1984, although it was thought possible that the actual total, when it was announced in 1985, would be smaller. Within the budget of Abu Dhabi, as distinct from the federal budget, the foreign aid provision was a likely casualty. In the past, foreign aid had accounted for more than 13% of the emirate's oil revenues.

The U.A.E.'s trade with Iran provoked criticism from Iraq. During the year two trade attachés were posted to the Iranian embassy in Abu Dhabi, one of Iran's few full diplomatic missions in the Arab Gulf countries. The relationship with Iran was not without incident, however. In June an Iranian patrol boat arrested a Sharjah-based survey ship near the island of Abu Musa. The island, claimed by Sharjah, had been seized by Iranian forces in 1971, on the eve of the U.A.E.'s independence.   (JOHN WHELAN)

This article updates the *Macropædia* article ARABIA: *United Arab Emirates.*

YEMEN, PEOPLE'S DEMOCRATIC REPUBLIC OF

The People's Democratic Republic of Yemen (Yemen [Aden]; South Yemen) is located in the southern coastal region of the Arabian Peninsula, on the Gulf of Aden and the Arabian Sea. Area: 336,870 sq km (130,066 sq mi). Pop. (1984 est.): 2,147,000. Cap.: Aden. Monetary unit: dinar, with (Oct. 29, 1984) a par value of 0.34 dinar to U.S. $1 (free rate of 0.41 dinar = £1 sterling). Chairman of the Presidium of the Supreme People's Council and prime minister in 1984, Ali Nasir Muhammad Husani.

Pres. Ali Nasir Muhammad Husani's visit to Moscow from Sept. 29 to Oct. 8, 1984, strengthened relations between South Yemen and the U.S.S.R. His government supported the Soviet boycott of the Los Angeles Olympic Games, and he had come under intense pressure from within the ruling Yemen Socialist Party to adopt a more pro-Soviet stance and to temper his enthusiasm for unification with Yemen (San'a'; North Yemen).

South Yemen's chronic trade deficit improved slightly in 1983, but a huge gap remained between the value of exports at $30 million and imports at $756 million. In 1983 almost one-quarter of trade was with Communist countries. Nevertheless, South Yemen remained open, at least nominally, to foreign investment from Western countries, although few offers were forthcoming. Representatives of more than three dozen international petroleum companies attended a presentation by South Yemen in London on March 29. However, they were disappointed to learn that the most promising concession—in the Shabwah area bordering North Yemen—was already being developed under contract to the government by the Soviet Union.

(JOHN WHELAN)

This article updates the *Macropædia* article ARABIA: *People's Democratic Republic of Yemen.*

YEMEN ARAB REPUBLIC

The Yemen Arab Republic (Yemen [San'a']; North Yemen) is situated in the southwestern coastal region of the Arabian Peninsula, on the Red Sea. Area: 200,000 sq km (77,200 sq mi). Pop. (1984 est.): 5,902.000. Cap.: San'a'. Monetary unit, rial, with (Oct. 29, 1984) a par value of 5.41 rials to U.S. $1 (free rate of 6.93 rials = £1 sterling). President in 1984, Col. Ali Abdullah Saleh; premier, Abdel Aziz Abdel Ghani.

North Yemen signed a 20-year friendship and cooperation treaty with the U.S.S.R. on Oct. 9, 1984, in Moscow. Pres. Ali Abdullah Saleh, whose government also concluded a comprehensive trade and aid agreement with the European Communities, was believed to be interested in obtaining economic aid from the Soviets. North Yemen was already heavily dependent on Soviet weapons.

Smuggling across the border with Saudi Arabia provoked a clash between Yemeni border guards and Saudi security forces in January. San'a' had sought to open two customs checkpoints, which Riyadh regarded as a territorial encroachment. In November a group of Yemenis seized a Saudi Arabian passenger airliner and flew it to Teheran, Iran, where the hijackers were arrested.

Prime Minister Abdel Aziz Abdel Ghani's government continued to place heavy reliance on aid from Arab and multilateral lending agencies. A $75 million contract was awarded to a Turkish company for construction of a new dam at Marib. The Yemen Oil and Mineral Corporation confirmed in July that oil had been discovered in the al-Jawf basin. The deposits were small by Gulf standards but could prove vital to the economy, in view of the chronic balance of payments deficit.   (JOHN WHELAN)

This article updates the *Macropædia* article ARABIA: *Yemen Arab Republic.*

East Asia

CHINA

The People's Republic of China is situated in eastern Asia, with coastlines on the Yellow Sea and the East and South China seas. Area: 9,572,900 sq km (3,696,100 sq mi), including Tibet and excluding Taiwan. (See *Taiwan*, below.) Pop. (1984 est., excluding Taiwan): 1,032,244,000. Cap.: Beijing (Peking). Monetary unit: yuan, with (Oct. 29, 1984) a market rate of 2.64 yuan to U.S. $1 (3.19 yuan = £1 sterling). General secretary of the Chinese Communist Party in 1984, Hu Yaobang (Hu Yao-pang); president, Li Xiannian (Li Hsien-nien); premier, Zhao Ziyang (Chao Tzu-yang).

China marked the 35th anniversary of the establishment of Communist rule on the mainland with bold new departures in economic and political reform. In an unprecedented attempt to loosen the grip of the central planning apparatus on the management of the national economy, the Chinese Communist Party (CCP) announced a major effort to increase the role of market forces in stimulating urban economic development. China's reformist leadership, effectively headed by elder statesman Deng Xiaoping (Teng Hsiao-p'ing), also reinforced its policy of promoting younger, more technically skilled officials into positions of responsibility. In foreign policy China achieved important successes with the United States but did not garner comparable breakthroughs in relations with the Soviet Union. China also concluded a historic agreement with Great Britain that would return Hong Kong to Chinese sovereignty in 1997.

Domestic Affairs. Chinese internal politics were dominated by the impending succession to the 80-year-old Deng Xiaoping and assuring the continuity of Deng's policies. Despite his advancing years Deng remained actively involved in the political process. Along with his close allies in the party and state structures (Hu Yaobang [Hu Yao-pang] and Zhao Ziyang [Chao Tzu-yang]), Deng sought to sustain and advance the process of political reform. This entailed further efforts to root out those provincial and local officials who continued to resist Deng's dismantling of the political legacy of Mao Zedong (Mao Tse-tung), who led the CCP for more than 40 years until his death in 1976.

Deng's continuing involvement in the political process reflected the importance of further institutionalizing his policies while he remained physically vigorous. Even as Deng pressed the case for political reform, however, he encouraged other senior colleagues in the party and Army to relinquish their posts to much younger leaders. But there also appeared to be scattered resistance to some of his reformist policies. Renewed calls for the eradication of Cultural Revolution factionalism indicated that pockets of opposition still existed, even if they did not produce a major challenge to Deng's overall program.

Deng also curtailed a campaign against "spiritual pollution" during the spring, easing concerns among China's intellectuals and scientists that they might yet again be the target of attack for their professional expertise and independent opinions. He insisted that it was possible to build a "socialist material civilization" faithful to the ideological tenets propounded by China's reformist leadership.

However, the party rectification campaign launched in late 1983 to evaluate the political loyalty of the CCP's 40 million members remained at a preliminary stage. In late November the party Central Committee announced that the scope of those efforts would be much wider in 1985, including written assessments of the credentials of all party members. This plan was expected to lead to the expulsion of those members implicated in China's radical upheavals of the 1960s and 1970s, as well as those found guilty of corruption.

To accelerate the process of political change, the CCP Central Committee also announced a national conference of party delegates, to be held in September 1985, when new members would be added to this high-level leadership body. Younger officials who had made a particular contribution to the Chinese modernization effort were to be singled out for promotion, thereby enabling Deng to advance successor generations committed to maintaining economic and political reform.

In addition, Deng sought to repair relations with the defense establishment. Some senior commanders had expressed reservations about China's recent departures from Maoist political and economic orthodoxy and had tried to restrict the scope of political reform. Like their long-entrenched peers in the party, numerous military leaders resented Deng's efforts to reduce their power and privileges. The military had not fared particularly well under the budgetary restrictions imposed in recent years, and it was also being urged to increase significantly its production of goods for civilian consumption, thereby further curtailing the production of defense hardware.

To counteract possible disgruntlement within the military high command, Deng and his colleagues significantly heightened attention to the long-deferred goal of military modernization. Increased Chinese purchases of sophisticated technology from abroad (some with potential military applications) and selective acquisitions of defense equipment from the West underscored the leadership commitment to gradually enhancing China's military capabilities. Equally important, there was increased emphasis upon military professionalism. The National Day celebrations on October 1 featured China's first military parade in a quarter of a century, with Deng personally reviewing the troops. Weapons systems on display included land- and sea-based missiles from China's small but growing nuclear arsenal as well as a broad range of conventional equipment.

The Economy. China's senior leaders undertook dramatic steps to improve the prospects for meeting the national goal of quadrupling agricultural and industrial output between 1980 and 2000. In a series of extraordinary decisions taken by the CCP Central Committee at a plenary session held in late October, the ruling party hierarchy announced a major shift away from central planning in the urban economy and toward a hybrid model of economic development that combined such planning with a free market system.

The reforms were intended to emulate the highly successful changes in agricultural policy first introduced in the late 1970s. Under this rural responsibility system, China's farmers could retain profits from production that exceeded quotas specified by the state. This policy led to a major upturn in China's agricultural economy and to huge increases in the annual incomes of many families in the rural areas.

The new reform package marked a fundamental break with the Soviet-style planning system introduced in China during the 1950s. Chinese economic planners had long sought to reconcile the encouragement of initiative in the large state-owned enterprises that comprised the core of China's industrial system with the centralized control

China's new flexibility in economic terms is highlighted by the growing presence of advertising. Billboards that once were covered with political slogans now advertise numerous products and services.

required by a planned socialist economy. The new policy conceded the failure to achieve such a balance. The decisions presaged unprecedented autonomy for these enterprises, which would now be permitted to retain a larger share of their profits after making their tax payments to the state. Other reforms were to include provisions for wage increases and material incentives for workers; increased encouragement for small-scale private enterprise in the cities (especially in the service sector); additional remuneration for Chinese intellectuals, scientists, and technical personnel; enhanced authority for Chinese plant managers; and a gradual easing of price controls on many Chinese industrial products, although controls would remain in effect for vital industrial commodities.

Chinese officials conceded that the process of urban reform would be far more difficult to implement than were the agricultural reforms, and that it would take at least five years to introduce the new policies. But by 1984 Chinese factory managers had already been granted much greater latitude both in their plant operations and in seeking markets for their products. Major increases in the production of consumer items and various light industrial goods were already in evidence, with China's industrial growth rate for 1984 estimated at 12% over that of 1983.

China also undertook major efforts to expand the role of foreign investment in the modernization effort. Since 1979 China had attracted more than $8 billion in such funds. During April it was announced that 14 coastal cities would be permitted to establish special economic zones like those created five years earlier in four locations in Guangdong (Kwangtung) and Fujian (Fukien) provinces. These zones provided favourable tax incentives for foreign investors who assisted in the development of new factories producing goods for export, and they had already proved extremely successful. China also sought to attract additional foreign investment in joint ventures, repeatedly stressing that the country had made a fundamental decision to expand its economic ties with the outside world.

The upgrading of backward plant technology in China's industrial enterprises was very high on the list of economic priorities, with advanced foreign technology playing a particularly important role in this effort. In November the State Economic Commission announced plans to allocate more than $20 billion for the acquisition of imported technology and equipment during the 1985–87 period; an additional $15 billion was earmarked for the purchase of domestic technology for various factories and enterprises. Local governments would also be granted more authority than in the past to make those investment decisions. As a result of these new plans, China would soon spend the bulk of its substantial foreign exchange reserves, which had grown by more than $15 billion during the past four years.

These steps reflected internal deliberations over China's seventh five-year plan, scheduled to begin in 1986. Most of the targets for the sixth five-year plan had already been met or exceeded, but major infrastructural investments would be needed to sustain the rapid economic growth achieved in recent years. Senior economic planners announced that the priorities in the 1986–90 period would be diversification in agricultural products, upgrading existing industrial enterprises rather than building new ones, increasing the availability of raw materials for economic construction, launching a major expansion of energy resources (especially coal), and improving China's antiquated and overburdened transportation system. Leading officials (including Premier Zhao) also acknowledged the imperative need for reform in China's irrational pricing system, particularly for energy and raw materials.

Foreign Affairs. China furthered its efforts of recent years to expand ties with the West and with Japan, to diminish tensions with the Soviet Union, and to foster a political and security environment conducive to the nation's development goals. Notable achievements were scored in the first and third areas, but the outlook for Sino-Soviet relations and Sino-Vietnamese relations remained far more clouded.

Relations between China and the U.S. continued the marked improvement evident in 1983. A series of senior leadership visits—by Premier Zhao to the U.S. in January, by U.S. Pres. Ronald Reagan to China in April, and by the Chinese minister of national defense, Zhang Aiping (Chang Ai-p'ing), to the U.S. in June—underscored the mutually reinforcing interests of the two nations. Despite continued Sino-U.S. differences over Taiwan and over U.S. policies toward the third world, both sides voiced a clear desire to expand the scope of their economic, political, and technological ties. The high-level leadership visits did not result in immediate breakthroughs, but they set the stage for an expansion of Sino-U.S. relations in numerous areas.

Among those areas, U.S. technological and economic assistance ranked highest on the Chinese list of priorities. Following intensive negotiations, a U.S.-Chinese accord on peaceful nuclear cooperation was initialed during President Reagan's visit. This agreement created the prospect of sales of U.S. nuclear power equipment to China. However, subsequent allegations of Chinese assistance to a covert Pakistani nuclear weapons effort and U.S. urgings that China offer more binding assurances on its opposition to nuclear proliferation put ratification of the pact in jeopardy. A visit to the U.S. by the Chinese minister of foreign trade resulted in a new accord on technical and industrial collaboration and was expected to lead to increased U.S. assistance for Chinese energy development and China's electronics industry. U.S. sales of high technology to China rose sharply, although Chinese officials complained that the United States still remained overly restrictive in its export controls. Despite such complaints a series of reciprocal visits between Chinese and U.S. defense officials presaged a more direct U.S. role in upgrading the technological capabilities of the Chinese armed forces.

Sino-Japanese ties also experienced consolidation and expansion. Japanese Prime Minister Yasuhiro Nakasone visited China in March, reciprocating General Secretary Hu's visit to Japan the previous November. The two sides affirmed their long-term interest in amicable relations and established a joint committee to study the prospects for collaboration into the 21st century. In conjunction with the U.S., China and Japan also discussed means for reducing tensions between North and South Korea. Japan's position as China's leading trading partner was reinforced by Tokyo's role in the development of China's economy and the rebuilding of its industrial infrastructure. Sino-Japanese trade was expected to surpass $11 billion for 1984, nearly double the volume of trade between China and the U.S. Despite these successes Japan declined Chinese requests to participate far more extensively in the exploitation of China's untapped natural resources.

The outlook for Sino-Soviet relations appeared far less certain. Although both China and the U.S.S.R. continued to profess interest in improved ties, it proved far more difficult to achieve that goal than to assert it. The Chinese and Soviet vice-foreign ministers exchanged visits to one another's capitals in the spring and fall, continuing a consultation process initiated in late 1982. In addition, Foreign Ministers Wu Xueqian (Wu Hsueh-ch'ien; see BIOGRAPHIES) and Andrey Gromyko held joint talks during

The changes in China's economic structure, with unprecedented relaxation of the rigid system of central planning and economic control, were approved by the Central Committee in late October. Shown are, from left, Chen Yun (Ch'en Yun), Premier Zhao Ziyang, Deng Xiaoping, and Hu Yaobang, general secretary of the Communist Party.
NEW CHINA/SOVFOTO

the UN General Assembly session in October, the first contacts at such a high level since China joined the United Nations in 1971.

But such discussions made little substantive headway. China continued to insist that there could be no fundamental improvement in Sino-Soviet relations without concrete actions by Moscow to remove what Beijing (Peking) deemed the three major obstacles to closer ties: the Soviet military presence along China's northern borders (including 135 SS-20 missiles) and in the Mongolian People's Republic; the Soviet occupation of Afghanistan; and Soviet support for the Vietnamese occupation of Kampuchea. The U.S.S.R. not only refused to acknowledge the legitimacy of those preconditions but also increased sharply its military presence and activities in all those areas.

The Chinese seemed particularly concerned about the buildup of Soviet naval and air power in Vietnam. In November 1983 the U.S.S.R. stationed TU-16 medium-range bombers in Vietnam, the only such aircraft deployed outside Soviet borders. In April units from the Soviet Pacific Fleet staged joint amphibious maneuvers with Vietnam in the Gulf of Tonkin. Under such circumstances China insisted that it would continue to oppose the expansion of Soviet military power, even as Beijing acknowledged that it remained better to talk with Moscow than not to talk.

However, a sharp escalation in Sino-Vietnamese border tensions in April and Soviet displeasure over the results of President Reagan's visit to China led Moscow to abruptly postpone the impending visit of Soviet First Deputy Premier Ivan Arkhipov to Beijing. Arkhipov (who had served as the senior Soviet adviser in China during the 1950s) finally made his long-awaited trip in December. The two sides signed accords on economic and technical cooperation, scientific and technological exchange, and the establishment of a joint committee to oversee Sino-Soviet economic relations. Plans were also announced for a long-term trade agreement, to be signed in 1985. Although Sino-Soviet trade continued to register significant gains, slightly surpassing $1 billion for 1984, this figure was small in comparison with China's trade and technological relations with the West.

China's most significant diplomatic accomplishment during 1984 was the signing on December 19 of a Sino-British accord over the future of the British crown colony of Hong Kong. This vibrant capitalist enclave along China's southeastern coast was home to nearly 5.5 million people, more than 98% of whom were ethnically Chinese; many of them had previously fled China's Communist system. Under the agreement, sovereignty over Hong Kong and other nearby territories would revert to China in 1997, the date when Britain's lease on Hong Kong was to expire. However, the Chinese government pledged to permit Hong Kong a high degree of autonomy, including the maintenance of its present capitalist system, for 50 years after the reversion to Chinese sovereignty and continuation of its status as a free port. China also agreed that all present rights and freedoms enjoyed by the Hong Kong population would be retained after 1997. The explicitness of these commitments appeared to reassure Hong Kong's anxious citizens about their future prospects after the transfer of sovereignty.

China's increasing emergence on the international scene was also much in evidence at the summer Olympic Games in Los Angeles, the first occasion of China's full participation in the modern Games. Along with Romania and Yugoslavia, China was one of three Communist nations to defy the Soviet-led boycott of the Olympics. The Chinese team garnered a total of 32 medals, including 15 gold medals. As further testimony to its ambitious goals in international athletics, China was named the host country for the 1990 Asian Games and hinted that it would make a bid to be host to the Summer Olympics in 2000.

(JONATHAN D. POLLACK)

JAPAN

A constitutional monarchy in the northwestern Pacific Ocean, Japan comprises an archipelago with four major islands (Hokkaido, Honshu, Kyushu, and Shikoku), the Ryukyus (including Okinawa), and minor adjacent islands. Area: 377,727 sq km (145,841 sq mi). Pop. (1984 est.): 120,160,000. Cap.: Tokyo. Monetary unit: yen, with (Oct. 29, 1984) a free rate of 246.4 yen to U.S. $1 (297.4 yen = £1 sterling). Emperor, Hirohito; prime minister in 1984, Yasuhiro Nakasone.

Domestic Affairs. In the general election for the (lower) House of Representatives, held Dec. 18, 1983, the governing Liberal-Democratic Party (LDP) had returned only 250 official candidates, 6 short of a majority of the 511-seat chamber. The following week the LDP secured nine more seats by admitting successful conservatives to the party. Shortly thereafter the LDP engineered a pact with the New Liberal Club (NLC), which provided eight additional seats, thus ensuring a majority capable of controlling chairs and pluralities in key committees. The NLC had split off from the LDP seven years earlier over the issue of political corruption.

When the 101st session of the Diet convened on February 6, party strength was: LDP 259; Japan Socialist Party (JSP) 112; Clean Government Party (Komeito) 58; Democratic Socialist Party (DSP) 38; Japan Communist Party (JCP) 26; NLC 8; Social Democratic Federation (Shaminren) 3; independents 7. After the June 1983 election for the upper house, the LDP continued to hold a majority of 137 of the 252 seats in the House of Councillors. In April Chairman Yoshikatsu Takeiri of the Komeito announced that his party was forming a committee to look into coalition with the LDP.

At the opening of the Diet in February, Prime Minister Yasuhiro Nakasone concentrated on domestic affairs, out-

American political cartoonist Ranan R. Lurie's creation, Taro-san, a character similar to the U.S. Uncle Sam and the British John Bull, was unveiled officially in Tokyo in August 1983. The character was adopted by cartoonists around the world as a symbol of Japan.

lining the need for administrative, fiscal, and educational reforms. He soon encountered severe opposition, however, centring on the government's "negative growth ceiling" for budgetary requests for fiscal 1985. By June 15 opposition parties had been coaxed out of a four-week Diet stalemate, and in the period before August 8 the Nakasone administration recorded impressive legislative accomplishments. For example, on July 2 Masaharu Gotoda became the first director general of the new Management and Cooperation Agency, which merged the old Administrative Management Agency and most of the bureaus in the Office of the Prime Minister. By July 20 the lower house had passed a draft revision of the health insurance law, cutting salaried workers' benefits by 10%. It also voted to create an advisory body that would be responsible to the prime minister and would draft proposals for educational reform. The lower house considered bills to privatize two state-run enterprises, the Japan Tobacco and Salt monopoly and Nippon Telegraph and Telephone (NTT). All these bills, except for the NTT reorganization, passed both houses.

On September 25 Prime Minister Nakasone announced his wish to be reelected to a second term as president of the LDP. He stressed the importance of completing his priority projects of administrative, fiscal, and educational reform. Earlier, in June, former foreign minister Kiichi Miyazawa in effect signaled his desire to run for the LDP presidency by proposing an expansionist economic program designed to double Japan's assets by the end of fiscal 1995. Miyazawa, by urging lower interest rates and other measures to stimulate investment and growth, thus publicly opposed Nakasone's austerity program. Other potential candidates included Toshio Komoto, director general of the Economic

Planning Agency (EPA), and Foreign Minister Shintaro Abe. In preprimary maneuvers, former prime minister Kakuei Tanaka's powerful faction supported Nakasone. Although Tanaka had been found guilty of bribery in the Lockheed aircraft procurement case and was not technically a member of the LDP, he nevertheless controlled the largest faction within the party. Other faction leaders were highly critical of Nakasone for relying on Tanaka's support, but on October 29 opposition within the party dissolved. On October 30 Nakasone was reelected president of the party by a plenary caucus of the LDP members of the Diet and was thus assured of continuing as prime minister. On October 31 he appointed his new Cabinet, in which, as expected, three recent rivals, Abe, Noboru Takeshita, and Komoto, appeared as foreign minister, finance minister, and state minister, respectively.

In August the EPA announced that Japan's gross national product (GNP) for fiscal year 1983 (ended March 1984) totaled 278,216,300,000,000 yen ($1,159,300,000,000) in nominal terms. The inflation-adjusted growth rate for fiscal 1984 was projected at 4.1%. Private research institutions predicted rates varying from 5 to 5.4% for the year ending March 1985. In June 1984 the unemployment rate, however, reached a record high seasonally adjusted rate of 2.81%. Consumer prices actually declined in June to an index of 111.8 (1980 = 100).

Deliberations on the fiscal 1984 budget began in the lower house on February 13, but passage was hampered by legislative deadlock. On April 10 the budget was finally approved by the upper house, the first time implementation had been delayed until mid-April. The general account budget totaled 50,627,200,000,000 yen, to be financed by 34,596,000,000,000 yen in tax revenues, 3,351,000,000,-000 yen in nontax revenues, and 12,680,000,000,000 in debt. The Finance Ministry announced that the budget was the most austere in 29 years, showing an increase in expenditures of only 0.5% over fiscal 1983. Expenditures for defense, however, increased by 6.88%, though defense spending still remained below the politically established 1% of GNP. Yielding to pressure from the LDP, in July the government approved a record 7% increase in defense outlays for the 1985 fiscal year.

In its 1984 White Paper released September 14, the Japan Defense Agency (JDA) stressed that the nation's defense effort was still "inadequate." The Soviet military buildup in northeast Asia continued to pose a "potential threat," the JDA announced, but it admitted that Western efforts had "significantly improved" the East-West military balance. The DSP agreed that the government's call for an increase in defense was "appropriate"; the JSP argued that the Nakasone administration was following "a dangerous policy course"; and the JCP contended that the administration supported the U.S. policy of deterrence, thereby allowing Japan to become a potential target of nuclear attack.

Marking the 39th anniversary to the moment (11:02 AM) of the second nuclear strike, on August 9 some 22,-000 persons offered silent prayers at the Peace Park in Nagasaki for the 70,000 killed and the equal number still suffering from aftereffects of the bomb. At the ceremony Prime Minister Nakasone called for an end to the "vicious circle of nuclear arms proliferation."

On September 5 the 25-member Ad Hoc Advisory Council on Education Reform held its first meeting in Toyko. The panel, which was to study reform of the college entrance examination system, was charged by the prime minister to reexamine the U.S.-pattern, four-tiered structure of general education. Its opinion on school violence, rife at the lower secondary level, was also sought. The council was headed by a triumvirate consisting of Michio Okamoto, former president of Kyoto University, Tadao Ishikawa, rector of Keio University, and Sohei Nakayama, a senior business leader.

Foreign Affairs. After the seven-nation summit conference of Western industrial democracies, held in London in early June, Prime Minister Nakasone offered an optimistic assessment of the highly politicized meeting. He cited as a major accomplishment the leaders' agreement to expand dialogue and explore areas of cooperation with the U.S.S.R. The biggest disappointment was the failure to obtain a commitment toward beginning a new round of trade liberalization talks.

Certainly relations with the U.S. in 1984 were dominated by trade problems. High-level discussions had begun in November 1983, when U.S. Pres. Ronald Reagan visited Tokyo. The thorny issue of continuing Japan's voluntary restraints on automobile exports was settled at that time (in favour of the U.S.), but negotiations involving tariff reductions, imports of beef and citrus products, purchases of satellite equipment, and liberalization of financial markets were postponed. On April 8, in Washington, Agriculture Minister Shinjiro Yamamura and U.S. Trade Representative William Brock reached a compromise whereby Japan would increase its beef imports by 6,900 metric tons per year until the volume reached 58,400 tons in fiscal 1987. Over the same period, Japan's imports of oranges would increase by 11,000 metric tons per year to 126,000 metric tons. Japan's Central Union of Agricultural Cooperatives (Zenchu) denounced the agreement and demanded price support for Japanese mandarin oranges. Nonetheless, on August 14 in Washington, Japan's Ambassador Yoshio Okawara and Brock exchanged notes putting the agreement into effect.

U.S. Vice-Pres. George Bush was in Tokyo May 8–10, when he pressed Japanese officials to take prompt action on financial liberalization. Finally, in a report released simultaneously in Tokyo and Washington on May 29, Japan pledged to deregulate interest rates gradually, to ease restrictions on Euroyen transactions, and to permit foreign financial institutions to enter the trust banking business in Japan. U.S. banks in particular had their eyes on the growing volume of Japanese pension funds. Meanwhile, Japanese officials and businessmen were unanimous in deploring the decision made by the U.S. International Trade Commission on July 11 to impose quotas and tariffs on steel imports. They cautiously expressed concern over the support of local-content legislation for automobiles in the U.S. Democratic Party platform and the perceived protectionist stance taken by the party's presidential nominee, Walter Mondale.

Relations with the U.S.S.R. remained chilly. On August 31, in a meeting in Moscow with a former foreign minister, Yoshio Sakurauchi, Soviet Foreign Minister Andrey Gromyko denounced Nakasone's foreign policy and flatly rejected Japan's claims to four Soviet-occupied islands in the southern Kuriles. On June 26 the Soviet government notified Japan of its intention to terminate the existing fishing agreement governing the open seas and waters near the U.S.S.R. Nonetheless, late in October Prime Minister Nakasone welcomed a Soviet delegation headed by Dinmukhamed Kunayev, a member of the Politburo, who visited Tokyo to discuss Japanese-Soviet relations.

Prime Minister Nakasone was in Beijing (Peking) March 23–25, visiting Premier Zhao Ziyang (Chao Tzu-yang), Communist Party General Secretary Hu Yaobang (Hu Yao-pang), and elder statesman Deng Xiaoping (Teng

Hsiao-p'ing). Both sides expressed concern over the continued growth of Soviet military power in East Asia and expressed their common desire to reduce tensions in the Korean Peninsula. On July 9, in the first visit to Japan by a Chinese defense minister, Zhang Aiping (Chang Ai-p'ing) told his Japanese counterpart, JDA director Yoko Kurihara, that the U.S.-Japan security treaty was "necessary to strengthen Japanese defense capability."

In July Foreign Minister Abe was in Seoul, arranging with his counterpart, Lee Won Kyung, for the "historic visit" to Japan by the president of South Korea, Chun Doo Hwan. In January 1983 Nakasone had made the first official visit to Korea by a Japanese prime minister in 37 years, and President Chun's return visit, which took place September 6–8, was the first visit to Tokyo by a Korean head of state since the end of the Japanese occupation. He was received by Emperor Hirohito, who referred to Japan's colonial rule of Korea between 1910 and 1945 as their "unfortunate past." Chun and Nakasone agreed that unification of North and South Korea should be attained only by direct talks between the two parties. Among opposition parties, the Komeito and the DSP were generally supportive of the rapprochement with South Korea, while the JSP and the JCP sharply criticized Chun's visit as a further step toward a military alliance between the two countries. Yoshihiro Inayama, chairman of the powerful Japan Federation of Economic Organizations (Keidanren), commented that the visit was "opportune" and pledged cooperation among businessmen. Noboru Goto, president of the Japan Chamber of Commerce and Industry, said that the sensitive issue of technology transfer between Japan and South Korea should be handled by the private sectors on a case-by-case basis.

In Jakarta, Indon., July 12–13, at a ministerial meeting of the Association of Southeast Asian Nations (ASEAN), Foreign Minister Abe unveiled a three-point Japanese plan toward peace in Kampuchea: (1) Japan would support peacekeeping forces in the area after a phased Vietnamese withdrawal; (2) democratic nations would dispatch personnel to supervise elections in an independent Kampuchea; and (3) Japan would provide economic cooperation and

Emperor Hirohito of Japan (right) received South Korea's Pres. Chun Doo Hwan and his wife during their September visit. On this first visit by a Korean head of state since 1945, the emperor referred to Japan's colonial rule of Korea as their "unfortunate past."

technical assistance for reconstruction in the Indochinese countries. In the period April 30–May 6, Prime Minister Nakasone visited Pakistan and India. The purposes of the trip were to demonstrate that Japan, as a member of the Western alliance, had abandoned past timidity in foreign affairs and sought an active political role and to lend added weight to Japan's voice at the London summit. At the same time, Japan recognized India's importance as current chairman of the conference of nonaligned nations and Pakistan's influential place among Islamic powers.

Alarmed by the dangerous escalation of the war in the Persian Gulf, Japan launched diplomatic activities to restrain both Iran and Iraq. Prime Minister Nakasone and Foreign Minister Abe asked an Arab delegation—generally pro-Iraqi in orientation—for cooperation when the group visited Tokyo in late May. Late in September, at the UN General Assembly in New York City, Foreign Minister Abe met with his counterparts from the U.S.S.R., the U.S., and China. In his major speech before the Assembly, Abe urged a ban on chemical weapons (allegedly used by Iraq) and protection for commercial ships in the Persian Gulf, steps that would help bring about "a just and honourable solution" to the Iran-Iraq war. He added that Japan supported the South Korean proposal for the simultaneous entry of North and South Korea into the UN "as a step in the eventual unification process."   (ARDATH W. BURKS)

KOREA

A country of northeastern Asia, bordered by the Sea of Japan, the Korea Strait, and the Yellow Sea, Korea is divided into two parts roughly at the 38th parallel.

On Oct. 9, 1983, a powerful bomb planted by North Korean commandos at the Martyr's Mausoleum in Rangoon, Burma, exploded, killing 17 visiting South Korean government officials. The shadow of that traumatic event continued to affect relations between Seoul (South Korea) and Pyongyang (North Korea) in 1984. Possibly stung by international outrage and condemnation of the "Rangoon massacre," the Communist administration of North Korea launched three conciliatory initiatives during the year.

In January Pyongyang publicly proposed tripartite talks between itself, the U.S., and South Korea on reunification of the divided peninsula. The overture was notable in that it marked the first time Pyongyang seemed ready to accept the South Korean government on an equal footing in a formal conclave. Seoul, however, quickly spurned the proposal. The North's second overture came in April, when one of its leading sports officials proposed to his southern counterpart that the two sides meet to discuss the formation of a united Korean team for the upcoming Olympic Games to be held in Los Angeles. Seoul agreed, and sports officials from the two governments met at the village of Panmunjom in the demilitarized zone (DMZ) on April 9 to examine the issue. The talks quickly broke down, however, as the southern delegate demanded an apology for the Rangoon bombing, and the northern delegate walked out in protest.

In September Pyongyang made its third offer, which brought a more promising response. After severe floods devastated large parts of South Korea, the North offered $12 million in relief. Each side had in the past made similar offers in time of natural calamity; on each occasion the gestures had been summarily spurned as propaganda. This time, however, Seoul accepted. This was followed by a South Korean initiative leading to talks on trade and development, which opened in a cordial atmosphere at Panmunjom on November 15. On November 24, however,

there was another setback when a Soviet defector ran to the UN side of the DMZ; shots were exchanged, and one South Korean and three North Korean soldiers were killed. Three days later North Korea postponed further economic talks, although both sides expressed hope that the meetings would be rescheduled in the near future.

Republic of Korea (South Korea)

Area: 98,992 sq km (38,221 sq mi). Pop. (1984 est.): 40,-578,000. Cap.: Seoul. Monetary unit: won, with (Oct. 29, 1984) a free rate of 824.81 won to U.S. $1 (995.55 won = £1 sterling). President in 1984, Chun Doo Hwan; prime minister, Chin Iee Chong.

In South Korea domestic politics were dominated by the continuing efforts of Pres. Chun Doo Hwan to foster conciliation with opponents to his rule. The trend, begun in 1983, had encountered a temporary setback as security considerations came to the fore again after the Rangoon bombing. By December 1983, however, Chun had felt sufficiently confident to announce two major amnesties covering more than 400 political offenders, ranging from politicians and priests to academics and university students. In February 1984 Chun restored civil rights to 202 opposition politicians, and six months later he granted a special pardon to 1,730 persons who had violated national-security and criminal laws. Though violent student demonstrations erupted in April at major universities and there were clashes between students and police, President Chun generally made good his promise to keep police and security agents away from the campuses. Another upsurge of student violence occurred in the fall.

With an eye to the general elections expected to be called in February 1985, South Korea's major opposition groups announced in June the formation of a broad coalition called the Consultative Committee for Promotion of Democracy. A year in the making, the alliance was co-chaired by two leading oppositionists, Kim Dae Jung and Kim Young Sam. It was decided to drop previous tactics of confrontation in favour of a cautious dialogue with Chun, who had declared repeatedly that he would step down when his seven-year term expired in 1988. In September Kim Dae Jung announced that he planned to end two years of exile in the U.S. and return home in January 1985 to work for democracy in his country.

The diplomatic event of the year was undoubtedly Chun's successful state visit to Japan in September, the first ever by a modern Korean head of state to that country. Japanese Prime Minister Yasuhiro Nakasone's journey to South Korea in January 1983, the first to Korea by a Japanese leader in almost four decades, had broken the ground. Chun's return visit symbolized a new era of cordiality between Seoul and Tokyo, which had annexed Korea early in the century and ruled it harshly as a colony for 35 years. The highlight of Chun's visit was the much-anticipated, though indirect, apology by Emperor Hirohito for that bitter historical chapter. Little of substance, however, was achieved by the visit. Differences that remained between the two countries included the issues of Seoul's trade deficit and the transfer of Japanese high technology. Japan promised to push hard for the admission of both Korean regimes into the UN, a development that Seoul desired.

The U.S. during the year reaffirmed its military commitment to the security of South Korea. After a visit by U.S. Secretary of Defense Caspar Weinberger in May, the U.S announced that it would improve the terms of its military sales to Seoul and boost the size of its 40,000-strong force in South Korea by 2,500 in 1985.

The general thaw in relations between Seoul and China continued, though in pursuing that course the two nations risked the displeasure of their friends in Taiwan and North Korea, respectively. In August Seoul redressed the balance somewhat when it released six people convicted of hijacking a Chinese plane who were wanted by China and sent them, instead, to Taiwan.

Perhaps the most important visitor to South Korea during the year was Pope John Paul II, whose five-day tour in May gave the country's 1.7 million-strong Roman Catholic Church a substantial boost in prestige. It also benefited President Chun, as the long-standing friction between church and state was eased by the goodwill that the visit generated. Before a million onlookers in Seoul's capacious Yoido Plaza, the pontiff canonized 103 martyrs in the largest such ceremony in 700 years and the first to be celebrated outside the Vatican.

The economy continued its remarkable comeback from the disastrous year of 1980, when political unrest, global recession, and bad harvests had combined to produce a negative growth rate of 5.2%. Building on an impressive 1983 growth of 9.3%, the highest in the world, the national economy continued to surge ahead, with an increase in exports leading the way. Gross national product was expected to expand by a rate similar to that of the previous year, and inflation was projected to remain relatively low. Economists predicted an annual average growth rate of 7.5% during the current five-year plan, which was to end in 1986. To finance such dynamic advances, however, the country had to borrow heavily. At $43 billion, the foreign debt was the fourth largest in the world.

Democratic People's Republic of Korea (North Korea)

Area: 121,929 sq km (47,077 sq mi). Pop. (1984 est.): 19,630,000. Cap.: Pyongyang. Monetary unit: won, with (Oct. 29, 1984) a nominal exchange rate of 1.30 won to U.S. $1 (1.57 won = £1 sterling). General secretary of the Central Committee of the Workers' (Communist) Party of Korea and president in 1984, Marshal Kim Il Sung; chairmen of the Council of Ministers (premiers), Li Jong Ok and, from January 27, Kang Song San.

In North Korea the year began with a reshuffle in the top ranks of the government. After a meeting of the Supreme People's Assembly (parliament), it was announced that Premier Li Jong Ok would be replaced by his deputy Kang Song San. Other technocrats were promoted to senior jobs in the government. Kim Chong Il (*see* BIOGRAPHIES) continued to consolidate his position as second in command and political successor to his father, Pres. Kim Il Sung. Seoul intelligence sources reported early in 1984 that the younger Kim had been made chairman of the powerful Military Commission of the Workers' Party, a post that would enable him to wield substantial influence over the armed forces. In August Kim Chong Il's ascent was officially confirmed when Radio Pyongyang referred to him, for the first time, as "the sole successor to our great leader Kim Il Sung."

The field of foreign affairs was marked by important contacts between President Kim and top leaders of North Korea's two principal supporters, China and the U.S.S.R. Kim demonstrated once more his skill at extracting equal measures of aid and backing from the rival Communist powers. He was host to Hu Yaobang (Hu Yao-pang), general secretary of the Chinese Communist Party, in Pyong-yang shortly before making his first trip to the U.S.S.R. in 17 years in late May. Hu pledged China's support for Pyongyang's proposal to hold reunification talks between the two Korean governments and the U.S. And in Moscow, though he irked his hosts by failing to tilt their way in the Sino-Soviet dispute, Kim managed to secure promises of increased military and economic assistance.

Reversing a long-standing policy of self-reliant isolationism, in January the government called for improved economic and technical ties with all nations that respected its "sovereignty," including capitalist countries with which it had no diplomatic relations. The motivation, according to analysts, was an attempt to give the lethargic economy a major shot in the arm, as China's recent "open-door" policy had done.

The trend gathered momentum in September when the Supreme People's Assembly passed a joint-venture law that would permit the country to attract foreign investment and to develop trade with capitalist countries. The government was apparently seeking foreign capital to help in establishing an export industry through which it could earn much-needed hard currency for development.

(THOMAS HON WING POLIN)

In September North Korean trucks delivered flood relief supplies to South Korea, the first aid to pass between the two countries since the peninsula was divided.

MONGOLIA

> A landlocked people's republic of eastern Asia, Mongolia occupies the geographic area known as Outer Mongolia. Area: 1,566,500 sq km (604,800 sq mi). Pop. (1984 est.): 1,860,000. Cap.: Ulan Bator. Monetary unit: tugrik, with (Oct. 29, 1984) a nominal exchange rate of 3.78 tugriks to U.S. $1 (4.56 tugriks = £1 sterling). First secretaries of the Mongolian People's Revolutionary (Communist) Party in 1984, Yumzhagiyen Tsedenbal and, from August 23, Zhambyn Batmunkh; chairman of the Presidium of the Great People's Hural (chief of state) to August 23, Tsedenbal; chairman of the Council of Ministers (premier), Batmunkh.

On Aug. 23, 1984, Yumzhagiyen Tsedenbal, first secretary of the Mongolian People's Revolutionary (Communist) Party and chairman of the Presidium of the Great People's Hural (council), was unexpectedly relieved of both these positions and replaced as first secretary by Zhambyn Batmunkh, who had been chairman of the Council of Ministers (premier) since 1974. The new appointment was agreed on unanimously by an extraordinary plenary session of the party's Central Committee. As Tsedenbal also ceased to be a member of the party's Politburo, the plenary session elected Tserendashiyen Namsray as a full member to fill the vacancy.

Demchigiyen Molomjamts, the secretary of the Central Committee, informed the plenary session that "Comrade Tsedenbal had to be replaced because of his poor health." The move followed three years of party purges by the increasingly autocratic Tsedenbal, who was known for his unyielding pro-Soviet stance. Batmunkh was not expected to soften allegiance to Moscow, but there was speculation that his selection might signal a touch of flexibility.

In June Stefan Olszowski, the Polish foreign minister, spent a few days in Ulan Bator discussing international affairs with his Mongolian counterpart, Mangalyn Dugersuren. He was received by Batmunkh, who seemingly had already taken over many of Tsedenbal's functions. In October Batmunkh visited Moscow. (K. M. SMOGORZEWSKI)

TAIWAN

> Taiwan, which consists of the island of Taiwan (Formosa) and surrounding islands off the coast of China, is the seat of the Republic of China (Nationalist China). Area: 36,002 sq km (13,900 sq mi), including the island of Taiwan and its 77 outlying islands, 14 in the Taiwan group and 63 in the Pescadores group. Pop. (1984 est.): 18,735,000. (Area and population figures exclude the Quemoy and Matsu groups, which are administered as an occupied part of Fujian [Fukien] Province.) Cap.: Taipei. Monetary unit: new Taiwan dollar, with (Oct. 29, 1984) a free rate of NT$39.13 to U.S. $1 (NT$47.23 = £1 sterling). President in 1984, Chiang Ching-kuo; presidents of the Executive Yuan (premiers), Sun Yun-suan and, from May 20, Yu Kuo-hwa.

The leadership of Taiwan in 1984 reinforced its effort to remain politically and economically viable in the face of renewed pressures to conciliate with the Communist government on the Chinese mainland. The island continued its extraordinary record of economic growth, having recovered fully from the slump evident in the early 1980s. In an attempt to ensure a smooth political transition from the older generation of mainlanders who had long dominated Taiwan's politics, a Taiwan-born technocrat (Lee Teng-hui) was selected as vice-president and the presumptive successor to the 74-year-old Chiang Ching-kuo.

The principal underpinnings of Taiwan's ability to resist formal association with the People's Republic of China (PRC) were the island's economic prosperity and political stability and its close if unofficial ties with the United States. Taiwan's economy continued to register remarkable gains in 1984. Economic growth for the year surpassed 10%, outstripping earlier projections of 7.5% and with virtually no inflation. Growth was fueled principally by an extraordinary foreign trade performance. Two-way trade for the year was expected to easily exceed $50 billion, and per capita income surpassed $3,000, a level achieved by few less developed countries. Total trade with the United States for the year was expected to surpass $21 billion, propelling Taiwan to fifth place among the U.S.'s trading partners. But the imbalance in this trade favoured Taiwan by approximately $10 billion, leading to renewed pressures from the U.S. for Taiwan to reduce import duties and increase its purchases of American products. Taiwan's economy was becoming increasingly diversified as the island's highly skilled labour force turned its energies toward utilization of more advanced production technologies. Exports of electronics products surpassed sales of textiles by an increasingly wide margin.

The island's economic growth also facilitated an increasing political maturation as younger generations of leaders began to exert more influence on Taiwan's political directions. The selection of 61-year-old Lee Teng-hui as vice-president best typified the growing Taiwanization of the island's politics. Although the selection of mainlander Yu Kuo-hwa to succeed the ailing Sun Yun-suan as premier was intended to counterbalance Lee's appointment, the long-term trends favoured the native Taiwanese, who in 1984 comprised 85% of the island's population.

Taiwan continued to be unresponsive to overtures from the PRC. Chinese leader Deng Xiaoping (Teng Hsiao-p'ing) argued that the formula of "one China, two systems" used for resolving the future of Hong Kong was equally applicable to Taiwan, with both Deng and Chinese Premier Zhao Ziyang (Chao Tzu-yang) renewing their past assurances that Taiwan could retain its capitalist economic and social system after reunification with the mainland. Taiwan's leaders rejected these appeals, however, and insisted that no negotiations were possible with the Communist government. But these disclaimers did not preclude a lively indirect trade and unofficial contacts between scholars, scientists, and athletes.

Despite such contacts, Taiwan's leaders reiterated that maintaining the island's defense preparedness was among their uppermost priorities. An agreement in August 1982 between the U.S. and China had led to a gradual reduction in U.S. military sales to Taiwan. As a result of those cutbacks, increasing efforts were under way by Taiwan to design and produce its own weaponry. In March a domestically produced jet trainer developed by Taiwan's aviation industry was flight-tested for the first time.

(JONATHAN D. POLLACK)

South Asia

AFGHANISTAN

> Afghanistan is a landlocked people's republic in central Asia. Area: 652,225 sq km (251,825 sq mi). Pop. (1984 est.): 17,650,000 (though estimates vary, by 1984 the exodus to Pakistan and Iran accounted for approximately 4.5 million). Cap.: Kabul. Monetary unit: afghani, with (Oct. 29, 1984) a free rate of 82.02 afghanis to U.S. $1 (99 afghanis = £1 sterling). President of the Revolutionary Council in 1984, Babrak Karmal; prime minister, Sultan Ali Keshtmand.

Muslim insurgency against the Soviet-backed government of Afghanistan increased sharply during 1984. Afghanistan

A classic ambush was conducted in April by Afghan rebels against a Soviet convoy. The Afghans cut off the trucks with antitank rocket blasts in front of and behind the enemy column and then devastated the convoy with machine-gun fire.

CHRIS GREGORY—GAMMA/LIAISON

continued to be dependent on the U.S.S.R. for military aid, food supplies, fuel, and even medical treatment for its leaders. Afghanistan's relations with the West remained strained, and its relations with Asian nations, with the exception of India, showed no visible improvement. After five years of Soviet military presence, the nation was slowly but steadily becoming a satellite of Moscow.

On January 2 the U.S.S.R. rejected a UN resolution demanding the withdrawal of foreign troops from Afghanistan. The resolution, which did not name the U.S.S.R. directly, had been co-sponsored by 44 countries and adopted in the General Assembly the previous November. The most important diplomatic development of the year took place in Geneva, where talks were held in late August under UN auspices. Afghan Foreign Minister Shah Mohammad Dost and his Pakistani counterpart, Sahabzada Yaqub Khan, did not meet face to face but held negotiations through the UN special representative for Afghanistan, Diego Cordovez. Cordovez visited Teheran, Kabul, and Islamabad during April for preparatory discussions. Nothing concrete emerged from the August talks, however; UN officials refused to comment, except to say privately that another round of discussions would be held later, possibly in 1985. The three main items under discussion were international guarantees of Afghanistan's security, the return to Afghanistan of the approximately 4.5 million refugees from Pakistan and Iran, and withdrawal of more than 100,000 Soviet troops from Afghanistan.

The Geneva talks were held under the shadow of Pakistani claims in July and August that air and artillery attacks on Pakistan from Afghanistan had killed some 100 people. The allegation was promptly denied by Kabul, but Pakistan-based foreign journalists taken on a tour of the affected areas confirmed the attacks. The affair heated up when the U.S. State Department issued a statement on August 24 "deploring the attacks on Pakistan." On August 31 a bomb exploded outside the international airport at

Kabul, killing 13 people and wounding 207. Pres. Babrak Karmal accused Pakistan of masterminding the incident.

On January 1 new draft laws were proclaimed under which all Afghan youths over 18 years of age were to be conscripted into the Army. The move was seen as part of a desperate attempt to check the depletion of the Army, which had fallen to 30,000–40,000 personnel from 80,000–90,000 before the Soviet invasion. President Karmal led his country's delegation to the funeral of Soviet Pres. Yury Andropov in Moscow in February. Karmal was again in Moscow from July 9 to August 3 for "medical treatment."

News of confrontations between insurgents and Soviet-aided Afghan troops came from various districts, with conflicting reports about successes. Heavy fighting was reported from Qandahar City, Afghanistan's second largest city, on January 10. According to some sources, over 100 troops were killed in the operation, but the city remained under insurgent control. The Afghan media denied these reports. On February 1 Kabul radio claimed successes against the insurgents, reporting that 600 "bandits"—the official term for insurgents—had been killed during January.

The battle for control of the strategic Panjsher Valley near Kabul continued. The government launched major offensives in April and again in July, claiming on each occasion that it had cleared the valley of rebels, though the claim was disputed by Western diplomats and by subsequent events. Independent reports put casualties among Soviet and Afghan troops during the July 18–24 offensive at 2,000, with the insurgents and valley residents suffering equally.

In November Western diplomats said the Soviets were sending Afghan children to the Soviet Union for ten years of indoctrination. However, there was no independent confirmation of the report.   (DILIP GANGULY)

BANGLADESH

A republic and member of the Commonwealth, Bangladesh is in the northeastern part of the Indian subcontinent, on the Bay of Bengal. Area: 143,998 sq km (55,598 sq mi). Pop. (1984 est.): 97,488,000. Cap.: Dhaka. Monetary unit: taka, with (Oct. 29, 1984) a free rate of 25.35 taka to U.S. $1 (30.60 taka = £1 sterling). President in 1984, Lieut. Gen. Hossain Mohammad Ershad; prime minister from March 30, Ataur Rahman Khan.

Political opposition to Lieut. Gen. Hossain Mohammad Ershad increased during 1984 as Bangladesh's major opposition grouping, the 22-party Movement for the Restoration of Democracy (MRD), stepped up its national campaign calling for an end to his military rule. Ershad's election schedule, announced late in 1983, proposed that presidential elections take place on May 24, 1984, and parliamentary elections on November 25. In response, the MRD demanded that elections for Parliament be held first, that a caretaker government be appointed before polling day, that the ban on political activity be lifted, and that political prisoners be freed.

In a move to bolster his image before he attended the Islamic summit conference in Morocco in January, Ershad announced that he had received a favourable response to his plans from the opposition. However, 100 political leaders replied that they had rejected his invitation to hold talks on Bangladesh's future. The first call by the MRD for a national strike on January 4 evoked a lukewarm response. Nevertheless, the opposition parties emerged as clear victors in municipal elections in February. Violent clashes in a number of towns followed announcement of the results, and the government was forced to close the University of Dhaka.

Attempting, unsuccessfully, to avert a second general strike scheduled for March 1, Ershad proposed new plans to hold presidential and parliamentary elections jointly on May 27 and to allow political activity from March 26. The revised dates did not meet with the approval of the opposition, who walked out of negotiations on April 10. Ershad later conceded another major demand; elections to Parliament would take place ahead of presidential elections, with the former set for December 8. At the same time, it was announced that the elections would be held under conditions of martial law. Opposition demands for a caretaker government were rejected. Renewing its calls for the immediate lifting of martial law, the MRD launched week-long protests on July 26 and again on September 17. There was also an unprecedented 26-day strike by 5,000 journalists and associated staff, which ended on August 7. On October 27 Ershad postponed the elections indefinitely "in consideration of the prevailing situation."

General Ershad's political actions during the year were interpreted as attempts to gain popular support in preparation for polling day. In March he appointed four new civilian ministers, all members of the Army-sponsored Jana Dal (People's Party), and released a number of former government ministers from prison. On March 29 he appointed as his prime minister Ataur Rahman Khan, leader of the Jatiya Dal (National League) and an 11-party opposition grouping. The Cabinet was enlarged by three further appointments from the Jana Dal in June. On August 1 Ershad ordered the closing of martial-law courts.

Bangladesh's links with China grew stronger during the year. Beijing (Peking) emerged as one of its major military suppliers, and trade between the two countries reached an annual total of some $30 million. Relations with the U.S.S.R. became strained following the expulsion of 14 Soviet diplomats and officials in December 1983 and January 1984. Various unsolved problems continued to trouble relations with India, including disputes over India's attempts to construct a fence along their common border. King Jigme Singye Wangchuk of Bhutan visited Bangladesh in February. Ershad, who visited Iraq in September, severed diplomatic links with Liberia because of that country's decision to reestablish relations with Israel.

During the year severe monsoon floods caused over 1,000 deaths, damaged almost 600,000 homes, and destroyed an estimated 1.7 million metric tons of agricultural crops. Gen. Mohammad Ataul Ghani Osmany, commander of the Bangladeshi liberation army in the 1971 fight for independence from Pakistan, died in February (*see* OBITUARIES).   (DILIP GANGULY)

BHUTAN

The monarchy of Bhutan is a landlocked state situated in the eastern Himalayas between China and India. Area: 40,000 sq km (15,440 sq mi). Pop. (1984 est.): 1,417,000. Official cap., Thimphu; administrative cap., Paro. Monetary unit: ngultrum, at par with the Indian rupee (which is also in use), with (Oct. 29, 1984) a free rate of 12.10 ngultrums to U.S. $1 (14.60 ngultrums = £1 sterling). Druk gyalpo (king) in 1984, Jigme Singye Wangchuk.

Two decades of planned development appeared to be transforming the economy of landlocked Bhutan from an isolated barter system into a transitional market economy, with particular stress being placed on developing trade contacts with other countries. Consequently, the number of donor countries who were willing to assist the kingdom

increased during 1984. A new five-year trade agreement signed with India in December 1983 preserved the existing free-trade arrangement with India but allowed Bhutan greater freedom to conduct trade with third countries.

Bhutan took a bold step by agreeing to hold talks on the demarcation of its boundary with China. A Bhutanese delegation spent four days in Beijing (Peking) in April to discuss the issue. King Jigme Singye Wangchuk, on a four-day visit to India in January, reiterated his policy of special relations with New Delhi. He also visited Dhaka in February and signed trade and cultural agreements with Bangladesh.

Bhutan took part in the Olympic Games for the first time, sending a six-member team of archers—archery being the national sport. In a further opening to the outside world, during 1985 permission was to be granted to international expeditions to attempt several of Bhutan's previously unclimbed Himalayan peaks.   (DILIP GANGULY)

This article updates the *Micropædia* article BHUTAN.

INDIA

A federal republic of southern Asia and member of the Commonwealth, India is situated on a peninsula extending into the Indian Ocean with the Arabian Sea to the west and the Bay of Bengal to the east. Area: 3,064,063 sq km (1,183,041 sq mi), excluding the Indian-occupied portion of Jammu and Kashmir. Pop. (1984 est.): 726 million. Cap.: New Delhi. Monetary unit: rupee, with (Oct. 29, 1984) a free rate of Rs 12.10 to U.S. $1 (Rs 14.60 = £1 sterling). President in 1984, Zail Singh; prime ministers, Indira Gandhi and, from October 31, Rajiv Gandhi.

Domestic Affairs. The assassination of Prime Minister Indira Gandhi (*see* OBITUARIES), the widespread riots that broke out in its wake, and the deaths of as many as 2,500 people in an industrial accident in Bhopal made 1984 a nightmare year in India. Indira Gandhi was shot on the morning of October 31 by two security guards in her home in New Delhi. The shock convulsed the nation and the world. The claim by extremist Sikhs that they had avenged her decision to send the Army into the Golden Temple in Amritsar, Punjab, in June led to anti-Sikh riots in various parts of India. More than one thousand lives were lost, and hundreds of shops, houses, and vehicles were looted or burned. The worst disorders took place in the capital.

On the evening of October 31 Rajiv Gandhi (*see* BIOGRAPHIES), Indira Gandhi's 40-year-old son, was sworn in as prime minister. He appealed for calm and ordered stern action against rioters. The situation was brought under control in three days. The government also announced that the murder would be investigated by a commission headed by a judge of the Supreme Court. The Congress (I) party, which had a two-thirds majority in Parliament, unanimously elected Rajiv Gandhi as its leader on November 2. Rajiv Gandhi reappointed all but three members of the old Council of Ministers (Cabinet). In a broadcast on November 12 he outlined a policy of continuation and innovation. The following day it was announced that elections to the Lok Sabha (lower house of Parliament) were to take place on December 24 and 27, except in Assam and Punjab, where no date was set.

The elections resulted in an overwhelming victory for Rajiv Gandhi and the Congress (I). With ballots still being counted at year's end, Congress (I) had already won 395 of the 508 seats contested in the election (of 542 in the Lok Sabha), the biggest margin of any government since India became independent. Rajiv Gandhi was sworn in on December 31, together with his new 39-member Council

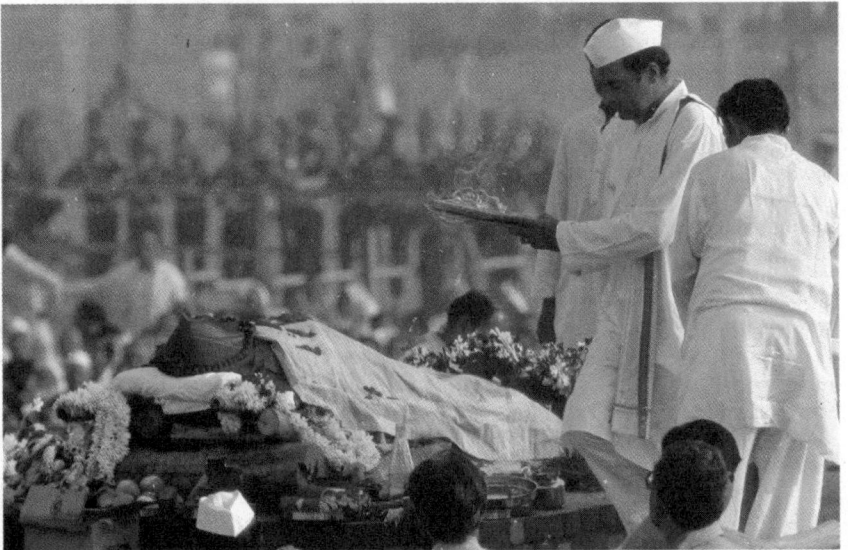

India's Prime Minister Rajiv Gandhi prepares to ignite the funeral pyre of his mother on the banks of the Jumna River in New Delhi. The late prime minister Indira Gandhi was slain by Sikh members of her bodyguard.

BOCCAN GIBOD/SETBOUN—BLACK STAR

of Ministers. In forming the new Cabinet, he dismissed more than half of the former ministers, including Prahab Mukherjee, finance minister since 1981, who was succeeded by former commerce minister V. P. Singh. Rajiv Gandhi kept the foreign affairs portfolio, while former planning minister Shankarrao Chavan became home affairs minister, and P. V. Narasimha Rao was moved from home affairs to defense.

In the early months of 1984 violence in Punjab mounted steadily. The Akali Dal, which was agitating for an autonomous Sikh state, broke off talks after an anti-Sikh outburst in neighbouring Haryana state in February, and although behind-the-scenes negotiations continued, they produced no results. Meanwhile, extremist groups acknowledging the leadership of Jarnail Singh Bhindranwale (*see* OBITUARIES) escalated their activities, and the number of

India's Sikh Community

Guru Nanak (1469–1539), the founder of the Sikh faith, was a social and religious reformer in 15th-century India. Nanak rejected the idolatry of Hinduism, challenged the authority of the caste system, and preached monotheism. He instituted a congregational mode of worship where his disciples, or Sikhs, met as equals and meditated on his teachings. Nanak did not, however, refute the essential Hindu beliefs of karma and rebirth, and the Sikhs remained within the larger Hindu framework. Nanak was succeeded by nine gurus who propagated his gospel until the death of the tenth guru, Gobind Singh, in 1708. Ram Das, the fourth guru, established a pilgrimage centre for the Sikhs by founding the holy city of Amritsar, where his successor, Arjun, later built a Sikh temple, Harmandir, also known as the Golden Temple. Amritsar became the religious capital of Sikhism.

By the 17th century the Sikhs were facing religious persecution by their Muslim rulers. Responding to this challenge, Gobind Singh founded a militant brotherhood of Sikhs known as the Khalsa, or "pure." Baptism into the brotherhood was a martial pledge in the cause of righteousness and changed the male convert's surname to Singh, or "lion." Five visible symbols were also adopted, including the wearing of uncut hair and a small dagger to show solidarity. All Sikhs did not accept the Khalsa baptism, however. It was also common for one member of a Hindu family to embrace the Khalsa. For 400 years the Sikh and Hindu communities remained interlinked and overlapping.

With the 20th century came the devolution of power to Indians by the British imperial authorities. The establishment of elected provincial legislative bodies brought the beginnings of communal political competition. As part of a much larger Hindu community, Sikh leadership was of little consequence, but as a distinct minority group they had a platform from which to fight. Among Sikhs, seats in the legislative bodies and recruitment into the civil service and the Army were restricted to the Khalsa. In the 1920s rising Sikh consciousness brought them into conflict with the government over control of Sikh temples. The agitation culminated with the passage, in 1925, of a Sikh shrines act establishing the Shiromani Gurdwara Prabandhak Committee (SGPC), an elected committee for the management of all Sikh shrines. The act also effectively defined a Sikh as a member of the Khalsa and consequently had profound implications for the development of a separate Sikh identity.

The SGPC rapidly became both an arena and a base for Sikh political action. Its agitational wing, the Akali Dal, became the major Sikh political organization. From the outset, the SGPC and the Akali Dal drew upon symbols of a separate Sikh identity in the articulation of demands for political or economic advantage for the Sikhs. On India's independence, in 1947, the Akali Dal demanded the establishment of a separate Sikh state. In the 1960s the SGPC and the Akali Dal were the base for agitation for a Sikh-dominated state that resulted in the division of the present Punjab from Hindi-speaking Haryana. Recently, Sikh aspirations found expression in a campaign for greater autonomy and in a demand for the creation of an independent Sikh nation of the Khalsa—Khalistan.

(RAJIV A. KAPUR)

murders, assaults, and bank robberies increased sharply. The extremists also collected arms in the Golden Temple in Amritsar, the Sikhs' holiest place of worship.

On June 2 Indira Gandhi reiterated the government's desire to come to a negotiated settlement, but she also announced that the Army was to go to the aid of civilian powers in Punjab. On the night of June 5 units of the Army entered the premises of the Golden Temple, where they encountered heavy fire. The resistance ended in the early hours of June 7. The bodies of Bhindranwale and several other extremist leaders were found in the temple. A day earlier a number of Akali Dal leaders had been removed from the temple and taken into custody. An official White Paper on the action, published on July 10, put the civilian and terrorist casualties at 554 killed and 121 injured and army casualties at 92 killed and 287 injured.

Although the government maintained that the action was aimed not against Sikhs or their religion but at preventing the misuse of religious places for antinational activities, there was considerable anger among Sikhs. Sikh cadets deserted their posts in several army centres. Pres. Zail Singh and union Cabinet minister Sardar Buta Singh, both Sikhs, were described by the high priests of the Golden Temple as *tankhaiya* (renegades to the faith). Several Sikh organizations abroad reiterated their support for the creation of Khalistan, an independent Sikh state. (*See* Sidebar.)

Sikh extremist activities continued after the Golden Temple action. In July an Indian Airlines plane with 264 persons on board was hijacked during a flight from Srinagar, Jammu and Kashmir, and taken to Lahore, where the hijackers gave themselves up to the Pakistani government.

In August another domestic flight with 93 persons on board was hijacked. The hijackers were arrested in Dubai, United Arab Emirates, and later returned to India. On September 25 Indira Gandhi announced that the Army would be withdrawn from the Golden Temple. Zail Singh revisited the temple on September 27 after the priests rescinded their ban on him.

The tragedy at Bhopal, the capital of Madhya Pradesh, began in the early hours of December 3, when methyl isocyanate, a deadly gas used in the manufacture of pesticides, escaped from a tank at a plant owned by the Indian subsidiary of the U.S. firm Union Carbide Corp. The gas drifted over the densely populated area around the plant, where many of the residents died in their sleep, while others, fleeing the gas cloud, overwhelmed the local medical facilities. The death toll was estimated as high as 2,500, making it the worst industrial accident in history. Since the very young and the very old were particularly susceptible, a disproportionate number of the victims were children. In addition, large numbers of people were suffering such aftereffects as eye irritation and respiratory problems; doctors reported that the recovery rate was encouraging, but the long-term effects of exposure were not known. Investigations by both the Indian government and the company were begun. (*See* ENVIRONMENT.)

Throughout the year opposition parties were busy with efforts to forge a united front in expectation of snap parliamentary elections. In October the Dalit Mazdoor Kisan Party was formed under the leadership of Charan Singh, prime minister between July 1979 and January 1980. This new grouping of the Lok Dal, the Democratic Socialist

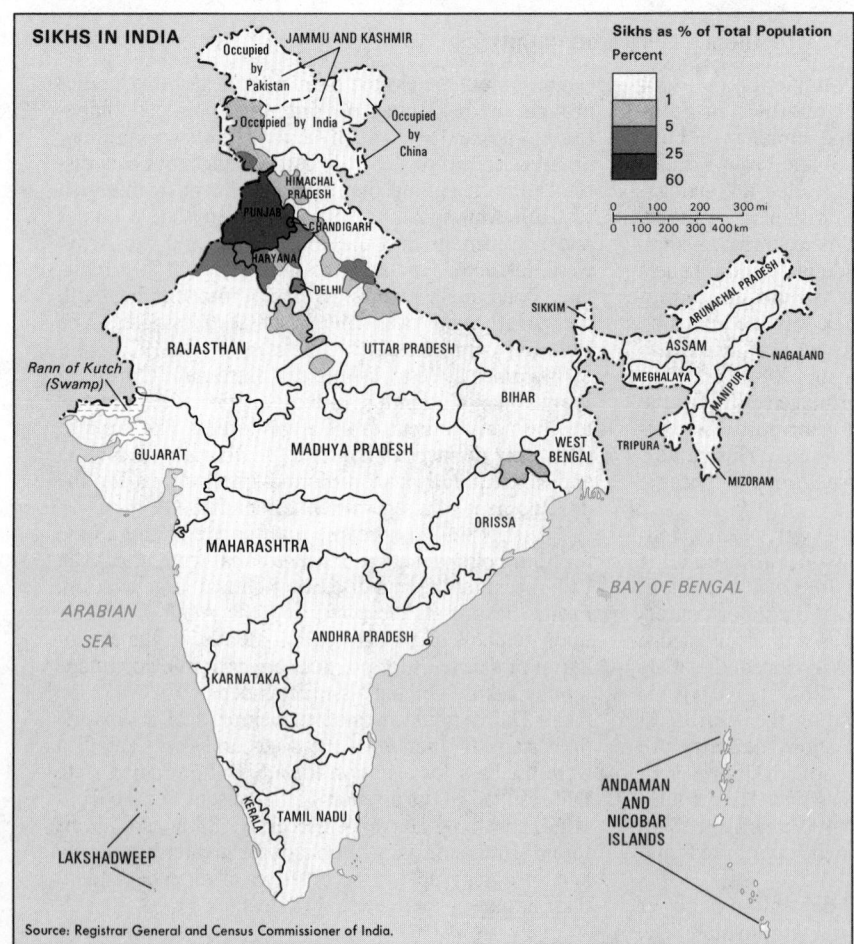

The Sikhs make up only about 2% of India's total population. The state of Punjab, in which they are a majority, helps India achieve self-sufficiency in food grain. Sikh separatist demands from the government of India include the right to establish their own agricultural price policies, complete control of flowing-water resources, the exclusive use of Chandigarh, a union territory/city that serves as the capital of both Punjab and Haryana, and total independence from India for the areas having a Sikh majority. This would include the state of Punjab and parts of adjoining Haryana State.

Source: Registrar General and Census Commissioner of India.

Party, and the Rashtriya Congress signaled a break between the Lok Dal and the Bharatiya Janata Party.

There were changes of government in Sikkim, Jammu and Kashmir, and Andhra Pradesh. In May the governor of Sikkim dismissed the chief minister, Nar Bahadur Bhandari, and the state was brought under president's rule. In July, following a split in the National Conference in Jammu and Kashmir, the state governor demanded and secured the resignation of Farooq Abdullah on the grounds that he had lost his majority. Abdullah's brother-in-law, G. M. Shah, formed a government and won a vote of confidence in the state assembly on July 31. In August several members of the ruling Telugu Desam Party in Andhra Pradesh broke away, and their leader, N. Bhaskara Rao, was sworn in as chief minister on August 16 after the governor dismissed N. T. Rama Rao and his Cabinet. Rama Rao maintained that he commanded a majority, and when Bhaskara Rao did not comply with a directive that he should prove his majority on the floor of the state assembly, he was dismissed, and Rama Rao was reinstated as chief minister on September 16. On the completion of the five-year term of the vice-president, G. M. Hidayatullah, Defense Minister R. Venkataraman was elected to that office in August. Several amendments to the constitution were adopted. One was to enable Punjab to remain under president's rule beyond the period of one year.

Hindu-Muslim riots broke out in Bhiwandi, Bombay, and Hyderabad. An explosion caused extensive damage to Madras airport in August. Responsibility for the assassination on November 27 of Percy Norris, the U.K. deputy high commissioner in Bombay, was claimed by the Revolutionary Organization of Socialist Muslims. Squadron leader Rakesh Sharma became the first Indian in space when he took part in a Soviet space mission in April.

The Economy. Grain production reached an all-time high of 154 million metric tons. Agricultural output as a whole was 10% above the previous year, and industrial performance showed a growth of 7.5%. Domestic production of crude oil reached a level of 30 million metric tons, compared with 10.5 million metric tons five years earlier. The rate of inflation was in the range of 6–7%. Foreign reserves rose to a level of Rs 63,450,000,000, and the government decided to forgo the third tranche of 1.1 billion Special Drawing Rights from the International Monetary Fund. In June the Aid-India Consortium pledged assistance of $4 billion for 1984–85. It was announced in November that India would not press its application for a $2 billion loan from the Asian Development Bank.

The union government budget provided for total expenditure of Rs 425,360,000,000 with a deficit of Rs 17,620,000,000. Some 60% of proposed expenditure was earmarked for development activities and 16% for defense. The budget simplified the tax system, particularly direct taxation. The approach paper for the seventh five-year (1985–90) plan was adopted by the National Development Council in July. It defined the major objectives as food, work, and productivity and envisaged an outlay of Rs 1,800,000,000,000.

Foreign Affairs. Relations with Pakistan remained uneasy because of the feeling that it was giving sanctuary, help, and training to Sikh secessionists. Publicly, however, both sides reaffirmed their desire for cooperation. Visa restrictions were introduced for the visits of all foreigners. Efforts to bring about a reconciliation between Tamils and the government in Sri Lanka and between Iran and Iraq did not yield much in the way of results, but discussions with China made some headway.

Important visitors in India during the year included the king of Bhutan, the emir of Qatar, the presidents of Yugoslavia and Sri Lanka, the vice-president of the U.S., and the prime ministers of Czechoslovakia, Finland, Japan, and Vanuatu. The only foreign visits undertaken by Indira Gandhi during the year were to Libya and Tunisia and, earlier, to Moscow for the funeral of Soviet Pres. Yury Andropov. The cremation of Indira Gandhi on November 3 was attended by representatives of 114 nations.

(H. Y. SHARADA PRASAD)

MALDIVES

A republic and member of the Commonwealth in the Indian Ocean, the Maldives consists of about 2,000 small islands southwest of the southern tip of India. Area: 298 sq km (115 sq mi). Pop. (1984 est.): 173,200. Cap.: Male. Monetary unit: rufiyaa, with (Oct. 29, 1984) a free rate of 7.57 rufiyaa to U.S. $1 (9.13 rufiyaa = £1 sterling). President in 1984, Maumoon Abdul Gayoom.

During 1984 the group of tiny islands that comprises the Maldives continued its struggle to make an entrance into a wider world. Tourism represented the means to accomplish this aim, and the industry was now the most promising aspect of the country's economy, accounting for a higher proportion of national income than fishing.

Pres. Maumoon Abdul Gayoom visited London in June to give the opening address at a Commonwealth conference on the problems facing small states. The Maldives, which had joined the Commonwealth only in 1982, had benefited substantially from membership. Scholarships had been made available to its students, and a survey of the country's industrial possibilities and training needs had been carried out.

In July the Maldives acted as host to a meeting of seven foreign ministers who met in Male to discuss the development of a new regional association, the Committee for South Asian Regional Cooperation. The committee had been set up by India, Bangladesh, Pakistan, Bhutan, Sri Lanka, Nepal, and the Maldives during a meeting in New Delhi, India, in August 1983. The association had launched an integrated program of action that was to be concerned with such practical matters as joint commerce, technical exchanges, transport, and sport.   (GUY ARNOLD)

This article updates the *Macropædia* article INDIAN OCEAN ISLANDS: *Maldives*.

NEPAL

A constitutional monarchy, Nepal is a landlocked country in the Himalayas between India and the Tibetan Autonomous Region of China. Area: 147,181 sq km (56,827 sq mi). Pop. (1984 est.): 16,178,000. Cap.: Kathmandu. Monetary unit: Nepalese rupee, with (Oct. 29, 1984) a free rate of NRs 16.12 to U.S. $1 (NRs 19.46 = £1 sterling). King, Birendra Bir Bikram Shah Deva; prime minister in 1984, Lokendra Bahadur Chand.

Possibly the most important event in Nepal in 1984 was the five-day visit by Chinese Pres. Li Xiannian (Li Hsien-nien) in March, the first visit by a Chinese head of state to Kathmandu since the two countries established diplomatic relations in 1955. China gave Nepal extensive help in constructing highways, hydroelectric projects, and modern textile and paper mills. Beijing (Peking) fully supported Nepal's proposal to declare itself a zone of peace. Nepal also dispatched its first official trade delegation to Tibet, while in September Tibet agreed to admit tourists from Nepal. This would help Nepal to attract more foreign visitors, already an important source of income.

At home the government tightened control over the registration and publication of newspapers. The regulations, announced on February 7, prohibited the publication of any material that might affect Nepal's relations with friendly countries or disparage any religion or class of Nepalese society. Resident foreign correspondents were restricted to Kathmandu and its immediate surrounding areas.

Prime Minister Lokendra Bahadur Chand reshuffled his Cabinet in April and again in September in attempts to win support from critical factions within the legislature. The government unveiled a NRs 9.8 billion ($613 million) budget for 1984–85.   (DILIP GANGULY)

PAKISTAN

A federal republic, Pakistan is in the northwestern part of the Indian subcontinent, on the Arabian Sea. Area: 796,095 sq km (307,374 sq mi), excluding the Pakistani-controlled section of Jammu and Kashmir. Pop. (1984 est., excluding some 2.8 million Afghan refugees): 91,019,000. Cap.: Islamabad. Monetary unit: Pakistan rupee, with (Oct. 29, 1984) a free rate of PRs 14.42 to U.S. $1 (PRs 17.40 = £1 sterling). President in 1984, Gen. Mohammad Zia-ul-Haq.

During 1984 Pakistan's military government remained firmly entrenched. Pres. Mohammad Zia-ul-Haq had promised to lift martial law by early 1985 after instituting an Islamic political system. He revealed the main outlines of his project: it was to involve establishing an Islamic-style assembly in which there would be no opposition; the prime minister would be appointed by the president, who would have more power than at present. Zia announced that at an "appropriate time" he would reveal details of the election date and the constitution, as well as the role of the Army and the political parties, which had been banned since 1979.

AP/WIDE WORLD

Pakistan blamed the Afghan government for bomb attacks on Pakistani border towns during the late summer directed against Afghan rebels and sympathizers taking refuge across the mountainous border. Nearly three million Afghan refugees were in Pakistan in 1984.

His political opponents felt that, rather than transferring power to freely elected representatives of the people, the aim of the president was to transform the dictatorship into a less military regime with the backing of Islamic fundamentalists. Opposition leaders pointed out that in 1977 and 1979 Zia had promised to organize a national vote and had failed to do so on both occasions. The Movement for the Restoration of Democracy (MRD), a grouping of opposition parties, rejected the program entirely and demanded a return to the 1973 parliamentary constitution. However, the MRD failed to make any visible impact on the people; an uneasy alliance, it grouped politicians who had been in violent opposition to one another prior to the 1977 coup d'état that had brought Zia to power.

During the year General Zia announced a series of measures to strengthen Islamic fundamentalism. On August 21 the first presidential order introducing Islamic punishments was promulgated. In March birth control was discouraged in Pakistan, a country with one of the highest birthrates in the world, when the government-appointed Council of Islamic Ideology reported that contraception was forbidden by Islamic tradition in all but a few exceptional circumstances. In a nationwide referendum on December 19, a reported 98% of those voting endorsed Zia's islamization policies. Zia had said previously that a favourable vote would be interpreted as a mandate for him to remain in office five more years.

Zia faced problems in Sind Province, where students clashed with police in October while protesting against the government. Five students were killed, according to the government, though the opposition put the toll at 17. There were reports of demonstrations in 20 towns.

On August 21 a special military court formally charged 98 people, including two sons of the executed former prime minister Zulfikar Ali Bhutto, with conspiring to overthrow the government. They were accused of being members of the foreign-based Al Zulfikar organization, which had hijacked a Pakistani airplane in March 1981. In January General Zia allowed Benazir Bhutto, daughter of the late prime minister, to join her mother in London. Bhutto had been under house arrest for more than two years.

On June 11 the government presented a $7.2 billion budget designed to satisfy consumers and bolster national defense. The modernization of the Army remained a priority, absorbing one-third of the budget, while overall military spending increased by 15% over the previous year. The economy grew by 4.5% in 1983, against an expected growth of 6.5%. The rate of inflation was estimated to be running at just under 10% for fiscal 1983–84.

Following a series of bomb blasts in the offices of Afghan resistance organizations in Pakistan, the government ordered the organizations on July 30 to shift their offices from border towns to the countryside. In 1984 there were some 2,850,000 Afghan refugees in Pakistan. Another problem was the sudden increase in drug trafficking on Pakistani soil. The drug inflow swelled the number of addicts in the country in 1984 to 300,000; two years earlier the official figure had been fewer than 100. In May two Frenchmen became the first Western addicts to die in Pakistan.

General Zia's relations with the U.S., China, and Japan remained cordial, while those with India and the U.S.S.R. remained uneasy. Visitors to Islamabad during the year included Japanese Prime Minister Yasuhiro Nakasone Chinese Pres. Li Xiannian (Li Hsien-nien) and Premier Zhao Ziyang (Chao Tzu-yang), U.S. Vice-Pres. George Bush, Malaysian Prime Minister Mahathir bin Mohamad, Romanian Pres. Nicolae Ceausescu, and Turkish Prime Minister Turgut Ozal.   (DILIP GANGULY)

SRI LANKA

A republic and member of the Commonwealth, Sri Lanka occupies an island in the Indian Ocean off the southeast coast of peninsular India. Area: 65,610 sq km (25,332 sq mi). Pop. (1984 est.): 15,756,000. Cap., Colombo; capital designate, Sri Jayawardenapura. Monetary unit: Sri Lanka rupee, with (Oct. 29, 1984) a free rate of SL Rs 25.81 to U.S. $1 (SL Rs 31.15 = £1 sterling). President in 1984, Junius Richard Jayawardene; prime minister, Ranasinghe Premadasa.

Renewed violence in 1984 shattered hopes of an early return to normality after the riots between the majority Sinhalese and the minority Tamil populations that shook Sri Lanka during 1983. There were violent clashes between troops and Tamil separatists in the Tamil-dominated northern region of the island in late March–early April, in August, and in late November–early December. Government sources stated that more than 400 people died during the unrest as Tamils continued their campaign for an independent Tamil state. Pres. Junius Jayawardene's efforts to resolve the ethnic divisions around the conference table met with little success. Leaders of the Tamil United Liberation Front either refused to join in negotiations or rejected as inadequate the government's proposals to devolve power to the regions. The other parties strongly resisted the idea of any major devolution of power.

A new Ministry of National Defense, headed by Lalith Athulathmudali, was created in March to counter the threat from Tamil separatists. Soon afterward the government issued one of its toughest statements in condemnation of India's alleged involvement in the Tamil campaign. There were allegations in Parliament that India, traditional home of the Tamil people, was helping to train guerrillas. In April the government cracked down by setting up naval patrols in the Palk Strait, which separates the two countries. The Indian government reported in August that as many as 40,000 Tamil refugees had crossed from Sri Lanka to India since the previous year's troubles.

President Jayawardene visited China and South Korea during the year, as well as the U.S. and the U.K., where he explained his government's stand on the Tamil question. Former members of the U.K. Special Air Service were assisting in the training of police commando units, which were to replace the Army in troubled areas. The government was also reportedly receiving advice on antiterrorist measures from Israel.   (DILIP GANGULY)

Southeast Asia

SOUTHEAST ASIAN AFFAIRS

In 1984 the six-year-old struggle for Kampuchea remained at the nexus of Southeast Asian politics and diplomacy. What seemed a promising initiative in the early part of the year eventually fizzled. By year's end neither Vietnam, which stationed some 170,000 troops in Kampuchea, nor the Association of Southeast Asian Nations (ASEAN), the driving force behind an international effort to have those forces withdrawn, had budged noticeably from its position. Indeed, fortified by growing support for its cause, at the UN ASEAN stiffened its stand against Vietnam, the strongest military power in Southeast Asia. Kampuchea was also the focal point of great-power involvement in the region: China, the U.S., the Soviet Union, and Japan all took an active interest in the struggle. Economically, Communist Indochina continued to lag, but ASEAN had a banner year in growth terms.

The year began with ASEAN's admission, on January 7, of newly independent Brunei (the other members: Indonesia, Malaysia, the Philippines, Thailand, and Singapore), the first expansion of the grouping since its founding in 1967. The next month a new effort at breaking the Kampuchea deadlock was signaled by the visit to Hanoi of Indonesia's powerful armed forces commander, Gen. Benny Murdani. Coming the week after a visit by Indonesian Foreign Minister Mochtar Kusumaatmadja to the Soviet Union, Vietnam's chief backer, Murdani's excursion marked the first time in four years that a senior ASEAN official had been to Hanoi. The general was quoted by Vietnam's official news agency as saying that there would "never be a conflict between our two countries" and that Hanoi was not a threat to Southeast Asia—a direct contradiction of the long-standing position of other ASEAN members such as Thailand and Singapore.

Though Murdani's remarks raised eyebrows in ASEAN capitals, there was a general willingness to see if a more conciliatory attitude toward Vietnam could produce results on Kampuchea. "Jakarta has long been the ASEAN member best disposed to Hanoi," explained one Thai Foreign Ministry official. "If anyone in the association is well-placed to reach the Vietnamese, it's the Indonesians." Hopes were raised further when a seminar of leading Vietnamese and Indonesian scholars in Hanoi had a thorough and friendly exchange of views on Kampuchea. The hopes were dashed in March, however, after a much-anticipated trip by Vietnamese Foreign Minister Nguyen Co Thach to Jakarta and Bangkok. Indonesian President Suharto urged his guest to consider ASEAN's proposal for a phased withdrawal of Vietnamese troops, together with the notion of an international force to keep the peace while Kampuchean elections were organized. Thach flatly rejected Suharto's offer, arguing that such an arrangement would do little to assuage his country's fear of "the Chinese threat." Instead, he said that the key issue was the "elimination" of Khmer Rouge military chief Pol Pot and his "followers and associates." Suharto was noncommittal, but Thach's proposal was quickly dismissed by some ASEAN members and by the two non-Communist partners in the Democratic Kampuchea resistance coalition, who closed ranks anew with the Khmer Rouge. In Bangkok Thach beat an embarrassed retreat and cut short his stay as important meetings failed to materialize. (See *Kampuchea,* below.)

The Jakarta setback seemed to change Indonesian thinking about Vietnam and its intentions in Kampuchea. Foreign Minister Mochtar condemned Thach for spurning "a sincere appeal coming from the highest level." Less than two weeks later, at the end of March, Vietnamese forces attacked Khmer resistance camps near the Thai-Kampuchean border. Shortly afterward, Vietnamese soldiers clashed with Thai troops, as well as with Chinese forces on the Sino-Vietnamese frontier. A special meeting of ASEAN foreign ministers in May criticized Hanoi's armed assaults on "civilian encampments" and its formal rejection of ASEAN's peace proposals. Vietnam, for its part, condemned a visit to China by Thailand's supreme military commander, Gen. Arthit Kamlang-ek. At their annual conference in July, ASEAN's foreign ministers issued a scathing communiqué chastising Hanoi for its continuing "aggression" in Kampuchea and its intransigence over efforts to resolve the conflict. Vietnam launched another major offensive against the resistance groups in December.

With tensions flaring anew, concern was expressed about Moscow's continued upgrading of the U.S.-built Cam Ranh Bay naval base in Vietnam—and not only by ASEAN. A paper published by U.S. military analyst Patrick Garrity as-

Vietnam's "protection" of Kampucheans from the murderous Pol Pot regime drove many of them to refuge in neighbouring Thailand; here some of those refugees wait in line for water in a Thai camp.

AP/WIDE WORLD

serted that Vietnam was now home to 5,000–8,000 Soviet advisers. Besides providing training and technical guidance to the Vietnamese armed forces, they operated radar at Cam Ranh and other military installations in Vietnam. Other experts believed the Soviet technicians ran a monitoring station at Da Nang designed to eavesdrop on Chinese radio broadcasts. Some reports suggested that the site was a key communications link with Soviet submarines in the southwest Pacific. Apart from provisioning Soviet warships traveling between the Baltic Sea and Siberia, Cam Ranh was being increasingly used by the Soviets as a centre for aerial reconnaissance missions covering all Southeast Asia.

Such developments led some ASEAN states to turn to the U.S. for help in strengthening their own armed forces. For much of the year, the Thai government was negotiating for the purchase of sophisticated F-16 jet fighters, a proposal that gained the backing of Pres. Ronald Reagan. Similar planes were sought by Singapore, which had ordered four airborne warning and control systems (AWACS) aircraft and ground-support units estimated to cost nearly $1 billion. Decisions by Australia and New Zealand to keep military units in Malaysia and Singapore, respectively, for the next decade and beyond were generally welcomed in ASEAN. Even so, the association's leaders remained wary of being drawn into big-power conflicts.

ASEAN's relations with the region's other big power, Japan, were centred on trade problems, although Tokyo did make an ill-fated attempt to mediate in the Kampuchea dispute. (See *Vietnam*, below.) Growing trade gaps in Japan's favour led to charges by Southeast Asians of "economic colonialism" and fears of a drift into dependence. ASEAN leaders were particularly disturbed because raw materials still comprised the bulk of their exports to Japan, and they claimed that the Japanese market was virtually closed to their manufactures and agricultural and fisheries products. Japanese investors in Southeast Asia were also chided for their reluctance to transfer technology or expertise to the local countries.

Another problem facing Southeast Asia was narcotics. For the second year in a row, the notorious Golden Triangle (the tri-border area of Thailand, Burma, and Laos) produced a bumper opium crop. "This year we expect 500 to 700 tons to be harvested," said one Western narcotics agent. Estimates by experts indicated that Thailand would produce 30 to 50 tons, Laos about 100 tons, and

warlord-infested northern Burma the rest. Much of the opium was refined into heroin in secret laboratories in Burma, then smuggled into Thailand for shipment to the region and beyond. Golden Triangle opium was especially important in 1984 as political and military turbulence reduced the supply from the Golden Crescent region of Iran, Afghanistan, and Pakistan.

The resettlement of Indochinese refugees remained a major headache for ASEAN governments. Though new arrivals of "boat people" were down to 2,000 a month, resettlement in third countries had slowed to a trickle. Since 1981 the number of boat people in first-asylum nations awaiting resettlement had remained stable at 40,000, more than half of them in the ASEAN states. ASEAN countries were refusing temporary asylum to new arrivals; refugees were being treated more harshly to deter others from leaving Vietnam; and there was a growing reluctance to pick up boat people on the high seas.

ASEAN's dynamic economies sprinted out of the residual effects of global recession. With the exception of the politically troubled Philippines, member countries recorded gross national product growth rates between 6 and 10%. As a composite unit, the stock exchanges of Singapore and Malaysia, 70% of whose shares were co-listed, became Asia's leading equity exchange after Japan in terms of capitalization. However, major difficulties remained in the area of economic cooperation among ASEAN countries. Seventeen years after the association's founding, frustrations were growing—especially in the private sector—over the slow pace of progress. A scheme of preferential trading arrangements (PTA) had been drawn up in 1977 to promote intra-ASEAN commerce through tariff concessions of 20 to 25%, but by 1984, PTA covered only 2% of total trade within ASEAN. With intra-ASEAN trade accounting for just 15% of the grouping's overall commerce, pressure was intensified to make the PTA system work more effectively. Industrial cooperation was also cited as an area in need of improvement.   (THOMAS HON WING POLIN)

BRUNEI

The sultanate of Brunei is located on the northern coast of the island of Borneo, on the South China Sea. Area: 5,765 sq km (2,226 sq mi). Pop. (1984 est.): 216,000. Cap.: Bandar Seri Begawan. Monetary unit: Brunei dollar, with (Oct. 29, 1984) a free rate of Br$2.15 to U.S. $1 (Br$2.59 = £1 sterling). Sultan and prime minister in 1984, Sir Muda Hassanal Bolkiah Mu'izzadin Waddaulah.

After 96 years as a British protectorate, the tiny sultanate of Brunei became fully independent on Jan. 1, 1984. Celebrations held on February 23 (officially designated Independence Day) were attended by the prince of Wales and other foreign dignitaries. The following day the new state became the 159th member of the UN; on January 7 it had become the sixth member of the Association of Southeast Asian Nations. One of Asia's wealthiest nations, oil-rich Brunei remained an absolute monarchy. Although Sultan Sir Muda Hassanal Bolkiah introduced a Cabinet system of government, his family dominated the top positions. The sultan was prime minister, finance minister, and home affairs minister. His father was defense minister, and his two younger brothers held the portfolios of foreign affairs and youth, culture, and sports.

Exports of oil and natural gas provided 98% of Brunei's revenues and allowed the government to institute a welfare state. With reserves expected to last well into the next century, economic diversification was proceeding slowly. A potential social problem centred on Brunei's estimated

The sultan of Brunei, Sir Muda Hassanal Bolkiah (left), took his seat at the head of his newly independent country's delegation at the United Nations in September.

NEAL BOENZI/THE NEW YORK TIMES

55,000 ethnic Chinese residents, who had traditionally dominated commerce and formed the labour pool for the oil and gas industries. Only one-tenth of them held citizenship, and in late 1984 signs were emerging that the authorities might be trying to ease them out in favour of the majority Malays. (THOMAS HON WING POLIN)

This article updates the *Macropædia* article EAST INDIES: *Brunei*.

BURMA

Burma is a republic of Southeast Asia with coastlines on the Bay of Bengal and the Andaman Sea. Area: 676,577 sq km (261,228 sq mi). Pop. (1983): 35,313,905. Cap.: Rangoon. Monetary unit: kyat, with (Oct. 29, 1984) a free rate of 9.03 kyats to U.S. $1 (10.90 kyats = £1 sterling). Chairman of the State Council in 1984, U San Yu; prime minister, U Maung Maung Kha.

In 1984 Burmese troops were involved in what was described as the biggest counterinsurgency operation since ethnic insurgent groups took up arms against Rangoon 35 years earlier. Government troops adopted a new tactic in their January–March offensive by cracking down on smuggling operations, the sole source of income for the separatist groups, who included the Burmese Communists, Kachin, Shan, Lahu, Karenni (Kayah), and Karen. A government statement issued on April 15 claimed that during the previous year troops had killed nearly 2,500 rebels and captured some 650 in clashes that included 16 "major battles" in the border areas. The Army had suffered 528 dead and 1,370 wounded. The government also announced the surrender of 1,342 rebels. The offensive sparked a refugee exodus. According to reports from Bangkok, Thailand, over 10,000 civilians fled to Thailand during the first three months of 1984.

During Pres. U San Yu's ten-day visit to Japan in early July, Tokyo pledged credits worth 46 billion yen to Burma. Australia and China also agreed to provide financial assistance. Sino-Burmese relations remained close and cordial, despite the fact that China continued to give material and moral support to the outlawed Burmese Communist Party. China maintained party-to-party relations with the Communist Party rather than with the ruling Burma Socialist Program Party.

The government announced that during the 1984–85 fiscal year it would invest some $30 million in the search for mineral deposits—gold, diamonds, and petroleum—in an effort to end Burma's dependence on agriculture and forestry. (DILIP GANGULY)

INDONESIA

A republic of Southeast Asia, Indonesia consists of the major islands of Sumatra, Java, Kalimantan (Indonesian Borneo), Celebes, and Irian Jaya (West New Guinea) and approximately 3,000 smaller islands and islets. Area: 1,919,443 sq km (741,101 sq mi). Pop. (1984 est.): 160,275,000. (Area and population figures include former Portuguese Timor.) Cap.: Jakarta. Monetary unit: rupiah, with (Oct. 29, 1984) a free rate of 1,061.67 rupiah to U.S. $1 (1,281.43 rupiah = £1 sterling). President in 1984, Suharto.

During 1984 Indonesia's public-affairs calendar was dominated by the continuing effort of the government to impose the state ideology, *pancasila* (the five principles: belief in a supreme deity, humanitarianism, nationalism, democracy, and social justice), on all political, social, and religious organizations. Officials said that such a move would greatly help consolidate national unity in such a geographically far-flung and ethnically diverse country as Indonesia. Opponents of the scheme, however, feared that it was an attempt by government authorities to extend their control over all elements in society. Well-informed analysts thought that the plan was, above all, aimed at controlling a perceived rise in Islamic fundamentalism, which might threaten the secular state.

The government won a victory in December 1983 when the Nahdatul Ulama, the most influential Islamic grouping, accepted *pancasila* as its sole guiding principle. This gain was consolidated in 1984 when the United Development Party (PPP), the country's largest Islam-based political coalition, followed suit. But the cost was considerable; there was bitter and divisive bickering over the issue among major factions within the PPP. One result of the party's resolution was a dent in its credibility, especially among fundamentalist Muslims. During the following month tensions boiled over. Islamic radicals denounced the authorities for suppressing their religion and called for a jihad ("holy war") to be waged until "the last drop of blood" had been shed. In defiance of official warnings a march took place in Jakarta's impoverished port area of Tanjungpriok. It drew military fire and resulted in at least 20 deaths and more than 100 arrests.

A series of vigilante-style killings that had begun in early 1983 continued to be a source of controversy at the beginning of the year. The executions, usually carried out at night by means of a handgun, were almost always of young male criminals. The number of victims had climbed to more than 4,000 by 1984, according to some estimates. Lawyers and human rights advocates expressed deep concern, but the average Indonesian seemed to welcome the killings as an effective deterrent against violent crime, which had risen notably in recent years. Though the military and security forces denied having a role, it was widely believed that the slayings were the work of soldiers and policemen who had lost patience with the increasing boldness of criminals and the slowness of the courts in implementing justice. After a spate of adverse international publicity early in the year, the killings began to taper off.

Indonesia experienced problems with its neighbours Papua New Guinea and Australia. A crackdown in January on secessionist rebels in the easternmost province of Irian Jaya brought protests from Papua New Guinea, which borders the province, and for several months strained the delicate relations between the two countries. A new border agreement signed October 29 did not entirely mend the rift. The difficulty in relations with Australia stemmed from the ruling Australian Labor Party's demand that the Australian government refuse to recognize Indonesia's 1976 annex-

Indonesia's President Suharto (left) and Palestine Liberation Organization Chairman Yasir Arafat embrace. The PLO leader visited Indonesia in July for talks on the Iran-Iraq war and other Middle East developments.

ation of East Timor, a former Portuguese colony. Amid a storm of debate and recrimination, Australian Prime Minister Bob Hawke and Foreign Minister Bill Hayden managed to have the demand watered down at their party's federal conference in July, narrowly averting a serious crisis in relations between the two nations.

According to a report released by the World Bank in May, the Indonesian economy fared better than expected, growing by a rate of 4.5% in 1983, as compared with virtually zero growth in 1982. The World Bank warned, however, that caution and restraint were still needed in planning. President Suharto announced Indonesia's fourth five-year (1984–89) plan, in which total budget expenditure for fiscal 1984–85 was set at 20,600,000,000,000 rupiah, an increase of 24.1% over the previous year. Expenditure on development was to grow by 12.6%, and state subsidies on domestic oil prices were cut for the third successive year. President Suharto set the annual growth target for the new five-year plan at 5%. Economists judged that this might be difficult to attain, however, given local and global economic conditions as well as the nation's heavy dependence on income from oil and natural gas.

(THOMAS HON WING POLIN)

This article updates the *Macropædia* article EAST INDIES: *Indonesia.*

KAMPUCHEA

A republic of Southeast Asia, Kampuchea occupies the southwestern part of the Indochinese Peninsula, on the Gulf of Thailand. Area: 181,035 sq km (69,898 sq mi). Pop. (1984 est.): 6,118,000. Cap.: Phnom Penh. Monetary unit: riel. Secretary-general of the People's Revolutionary (Communist) Party of Kampuchea and president of the Council of State in 1984, Heng Samrin; president of the Council of Ministers (premier) to late December, Chan Sy.

Events in Kampuchea in 1984 continued to be dominated by the struggle at home and by foreign powers to settle the country's political fate. Diplomatic initiatives by China and Vietnam early in the year ultimately amounted to little. On the battlefields of Kampuchea, significant gains were made by the guerrilla forces of the Democratic Kampuchea (DK) resistance coalition against Vietnam's occupying troops,

estimated at 160,000, and the army of its client regime in Phnom Penh under Pres. Heng Samrin.

The year began with the three DK partners—the (Communist) Khmer Rouge, the (anti-Communist) Khmer People's National Liberation Front (KPNLF) under former premier Son Sann, and the Armée Nationale Sihanoukist (ANS) under Prince Norodom Sihanouk, president of the government-in-exile—patching up their quarrels of 1983 under the mediation of Beijing (Peking). China, chief backer of the Khmer Rouge, promised to step up the flow of arms and aid to the coalition's two less powerful, non-Communist factions.

In an effort to shore up his country's position in Kampuchea, Vietnamese Foreign Minister Nguyen Co Thach went on a tour of Indonesia, Australia, and Thailand in March. However, his attempt to pry the Khmer Rouge loose from the DK alliance by focusing on the murderous record of Khmer Communist leader Pol Pot during the period 1975–79 seemed to backfire. The two non-Communist partners in the resistance unequivocally proclaimed their desire to see the Khmer Rouge remain in the coalition.

As diplomatic efforts to settle the Kampuchean conflict sputtered, the action switched to the military front. Beginning in mid-January, DK guerrillas, spearheaded by the Khmer Rouge, launched a series of major attacks on Vietnamese-held towns and military positions in Kampuchea. Equipped with new mortars and other heavy infantry weapons from China, the Communist forces hit Hanoi's troops harder than at any other time during the five years of fighting. The guerrillas kept up the pressure for two months, undermining Hanoi's standing claim that the resistance was little more than a minor irritant in military terms.

In late March Vietnam decided to hit back in strength. Before the onset of monsoon rains made operations difficult for armoured forces, Vietnamese troops assaulted a number of Khmer Rouge and KPNLF strongholds at the Thai-Kampuchean border. Superior firepower enabled the attackers to overrun some of the guerrilla bases, but a determined, ultimately successful stand by the KPNLF at Ampil scored further propaganda points against Hanoi. Vietnam's

Son Sann, former premier of Kampuchea and leader of the Khmer People's National Liberation Front, greets followers. Significant gains were made during the year by the guerrilla resistance to Vietnam's occupying troops.

attacks also brought hostile responses from Thailand and China. Claiming that Vietnamese soldiers trespassed into Thai territory during one of their operations, Thai forces counterattacked and reportedly killed 70 of Hanoi's troops.

Unwilling to commit more of their own men, the Vietnamese in 1984 concentrated on strengthening Pres. Heng Samrin's army. However, the attempt to "Khmerize" the war was hampered by inadequate training and lack of motivation. Defections to resistance ranks were not uncommon. The DK coalition, meanwhile, faced its own problems. Alarmed by the steady growth in strength and stature of its non-Communist partners, the Khmer Rouge began to mount occasional attacks on their forces in the second half of the year. With the advent of the dry season, Vietnamese forces launched a major offensive against resistance camps near the Thai border late in December.

Famine loomed once again. Drought and typhoons in 1983 had damaged substantial portions of the country's crops, and the UN Food and Agriculture Organization projected early in 1984 that Kampuchea might face severe food shortages from the third quarter on. For the first time, the Heng Samrin administration conducted a survey of private enterprises with the aim of introducing taxes. With the help of Soviet technical advisers, work progressed on construction of a 100-channel satellite communications station in Phnom Penh and expansion of the deep-sea port at Kompong Som.

Chan Sy (see OBITUARIES), premier since February 1982, died in late December.   (THOMAS HON WING POLIN)

This article updates the *Macropædia* article Mainland SOUTH-EAST ASIA: *Kampuchea*.

LAOS

A landlocked people's republic, Laos is in the northern part of the Indochinese Peninsula. Area: 236,800 sq km (91,400 sq mi). Pop. (1984 est.): 4,097,000. Cap.: Vientiane. Monetary unit: kip, with (Oct. 29, 1984) a free rate of 35.07 kip to U.S. $1 (42.33 kip = £1 sterling). President in 1984, Prince Souphanouvong; premier, Kaysone Phomvihan.

The major political event of 1984 in Laos was the convening in January of the fifth session of the third plenum of the Lao People's Revolutionary (Communist) Party (LPRP). During the conclave, criticism was leveled at virtually all ranks of the leadership. Presided over by Kaysone Phomvihan, who was party leader as well as premier, the plenum noted that directives had not been implemented to the full, that the development of production was slow, and that the culture, education, and health sectors were suffering. It also called for improvements in the training of cadres and the use of foreign aid. Other priorities announced were the strengthening of national defense and public security, increased agricultural production, and the promotion of collectivization.

A leading political figure passed from the scene: Prince Souvanna Phouma (see OBITUARIES), who had been premier of Laos during the period 1962–75, died in Vientiane on January 10. His son, Prince Mangkra, in exile in Paris, said he feared that his father's death had removed a moderating influence in Laotian affairs.

A border dispute erupted between Laos and Thailand in March when Laotian troops moved into an area where three villages were claimed by Bangkok. After armed clashes between the two sides, the Thai Army reclaimed the villages in June, apparently without bloodshed. However, a war of words soon broke out. Vientiane linked the incident with its allegations that Thailand was lending assistance to Khmer resistance forces opposing the government in

Kampuchea, to which Laos was allied. Vietnam joined the fray, accusing Bangkok of colluding with China to oppress the Indochinese states. Hanoi also renewed its charges that Beijing (Peking) was training Laotian refugees in Chinese territory and sending them back into Laos to undermine the Vientiane regime. In May the semiofficial Thai News Agency reported that right-wing Laotian rebels had ambushed and killed 40 Vietnamese and Laotian government troops in the province of Saravan in southern Laos.

Reducing the economy's traditional reliance on Thailand was a subject that continued to engage Vientiane's leaders and their allies. Experts from the U.S.S.R. and Eastern Europe were increasingly active in Laos, building roads and other infrastructure projects. Vientiane revealed that the Soviets were to construct a 400-km (250-mi) oil pipeline that would connect the country with the Vietnamese coastal city of Vinh. The general aim of these ventures was to build a Laotian economy more closely linked with Communist Vietnam and Kampuchea. In an attempt to increase its control over private firms, the import-export business, and illicit trade across the Thai frontier, the government issued an instruction on the registration of enterprises and the collection of taxes from the private sector.

(THOMAS HON WING POLIN)

This article updates the *Macropædia* article Mainland SOUTH-EAST ASIA: *Laos*.

MALAYSIA

A federal constitutional monarchy of Southeast Asia and member of the Commonwealth, Malaysia consists of the former Federation of Malaya at the southern end of the Malay Peninsula (excluding Singapore) and Sabah and Sarawak on the northern part of the island of Borneo. Area: 329,747 sq km (127,316 sq mi). Pop. (1984 est.): 14,704,000. Cap.: Kuala Lumpur. Monetary unit: ringgit, with (Oct. 29, 1984) a free rate of 2.39 ringgits to U.S. $1 (2.88 ringgits = £1 sterling). Supreme heads of state in 1984, with the title of *yang di-pertuan agung,* Tuanku Sultan Haji Ahmad Shah al-Musta'in Billah ibni al-Marhum Sultan Abu Bakar Ri'ayatuddin al-Mu'adzam Shah and, from April 26, Tuanku Mahmood Iskandar ibni al-Marhum Sultan Ismail; prime minister, Datuk Seri Mahathir bin Mohamad.

The political life of Malaysia was unusually eventful during 1984. On Dec. 15, 1983, a five-month-long constitutional crisis was resolved when the acting king, Sultan Tuanku Jaafar, agreed to sign a bill that took away the monarch's power of veto over legislation passed by Parliament. The move ended a period of tension during which mass demonstrations and counterdemonstrations over the issue were held by supporters of the government and of Malaysia's nine hereditary sultans, who every five years selected one from among their own ranks to be *yang di-pertuan agung* (king). The settlement paved the way for the smooth accession to the federal throne of Sultan Mahmood Iskandar (see BIOGRAPHIES) of Johore State in April 1984, succeeding Sultan Ahmad Shah of Pahang.

Hardly had the constitutional debate been resolved when another crisis flared up within the Malaysian Chinese Association (MCA), the second largest political party and a key partner in the ruling National Front coalition. Angered by the attempts of Tan Koon Swan, the party vice-president, to challenge him for his job, MCA Pres. Neo Yee Pan expelled Tan and 13 of his associates in March. Tan fought back, successfully convening in May an extraordinary general meeting of party delegates, which reinstated him. The decision, however, was condemned by Neo as illegal and invalid, and the dispute went to the courts. Meanwhile, the struggle within the MCA was troubling top officials of its National Front partner, the dominant United Malays National Organization (UMNO). By late in the year the signs were that Neo and Tan would settle their differences out of court in order to end the debilitating paralysis of the party.

Within UMNO itself, Prime Minister Mahathir bin Mohamad was returned unchallenged as party president in UMNO's triennial election on May 25. However, a fierce battle for the deputy presidency erupted between the incumbent, Deputy Prime Minister Musa bin Hitam, and Finance Minister Tengku Razaleigh Hamzah. Musa, who was supported by Mahathir, won the election by a clear margin. Indeed, the results of voting for other senior UMNO posts showed an impressive consolidation of support for the three-year-old administration of Mahathir and Musa. Two months later Mahathir reshuffled his Cabinet, moving Razaleigh to the less prestigious trade and industry portfolio and giving the finance job to leading entrepreneur Daim Zainuddin. Ghazali bin Shafie was replaced as foreign affairs minister and dropped from the Cabinet.

The government faced a burgeoning challenge from Muslim fundamentalists in the northern states of Kedah, Kelantan, Perlis, and Trengganu. Extremists in the opposition Partai Islam (PAS) called for an Iranian-style revolution that would install an Islamic government in Kuala Lumpur. In August the authorities announced a ban on the party's *ceremahs* ("closed-door meetings"), which was promptly denounced by its leaders. Said a senior PAS official: "As an Islamic party, we will continue to find loopholes in this man-made law and continue to spread the word of Allah." That prompted Mahathir to issue his strongest warning yet on the fundamentalists; Malaysians, he said in September, must be "cautious and wary of people who blatantly use democracy to bring about a system to end democracy." Before long, government sources were circulating reports of a PAS "hit squad" formed to assassinate top UMNO leaders.

In the wake of the global recession of 1981–82, Malaysia's economic planners displayed a mood of caution. Government indebtedness had more than doubled since 1980, and Deputy Prime Minister Musa said that, despite the continued enthusiasm of bankers to lend, Malaysia would have to scale down its borrowings. Presenting a midterm review of the fourth five-year (1981–85) plan in March, Mahathir reported that national growth had averaged 6.2% a year in 1981–83, against a previous projection of 7.6%.

The public sector of the economy was to be trimmed by selling off public enterprises to private business.

(THOMAS HON WING POLIN)

This article updates the *Macropædia* article Mainland SOUTHEAST ASIA: *Malaysia.*

PHILIPPINES

Situated in the western Pacific Ocean off the southeast coast of Asia, the republic of the Philippines consists of an archipelago of about 7,100 islands. Area: 300,000 sq km (115,800 sq mi). Pop. (1984 est.): 53,618,000. Cap.: Manila. Monetary unit: peso, with (Oct. 29, 1984) a free rate of 19.14 pesos to U.S. $1 (23.10 pesos = £1 sterling). President in 1984, Ferdinand E. Marcos; prime minister, Cesar Virata.

Elections on May 14, 1984, for 183 National Assembly seats revealed "an undercurrent of discontent," according to Pres. Ferdinand Marcos. Opponents of his New Society Movement, who had 13 seats in the old assembly, won more than 60, including 15 of 21 in metropolitan Manila. The campaign was marked by widespread violence; returns were suspiciously slow in coming in from many areas, and critics of Marcos charged that fraud kept the opposition from winning a majority of seats.

On June 30 the new assembly began a parliamentary system of government, although Marcos retained the power to rule by decree. He named a new Cabinet with few changes. Cesar Virata remained prime minister, and Marcos's wife, Imelda, was reappointed minister of human settlements despite not having been a candidate in the elections.

On January 27 voters overwhelmingly approved four constitutional amendments, but voting in the referendum was light, in part because of an opposition boycott. One amendment reestablished the office of vice-president beginning in 1987. The vice-president would replace the 15-member executive committee that currently would succeed the president and call new elections in case of his death or incapacity. Although reportedly having health problems, Marcos said that he intended to seek reelection in 1987.

The referendum was opposed by a massive demonstration in Manila, the largest since the funeral of opposition leader Benigno S. Aquino, Jr., who was murdered on Aug. 21, 1983. It was led by his younger brother, Agapito, who became a key figure among opposition elements ranging from conservatives to the pro-Communist left. Other large

In October Corazon Agrava (writing in photo at left) submitted to Pres. Ferdinand E. Marcos the report of the probe into the murder in 1983 of exiled opposition leader Benigno Aquino. Her colleagues on the commission issued a separate report that implicated Gen. Fabian C. Ver (below) intimately in the conspiracy. Agrava did not name Ver, the armed forces chief of staff, in her report as having had any role in the assassination.

(LEFT) AP/WIDE WORLD; (RIGHT) OWEN FRANKEN/SGYMA

demonstrations followed throughout the year, some of them violent, demanding a return to democracy. In late December, 12 opposition leaders signed a declaration of unity in opposition to Marcos.

An independent commission appointed by Marcos to investigate the death of Aquino made its findings public in October. The majority of the commission concluded that a military conspiracy led by armed forces Chief of Staff Fabian C. Ver was responsible for the assassination. Ver subsequently took a leave of absence from his post. Commission chairman Corazon Agrava did not indict Ver but did assert military complicity. Opposition leaders criticized the commission for not naming President Marcos chief instigator of the plot.

Economic problems that were intensified but not caused by the political repercussions of Aquino's slaying plagued the country during 1984. The inflation rate, which had been about 10% at the time of his death, was unofficially estimated at between 40 and 50% a year later. The unemployment rate was rising to 25%, and gross national product declined by about 4%. The income gap between rich and poor continued to widen. The government devalued the peso by 22.2% on June 6, and it took other steps intended to improve the economy. However, foreign investors were reluctant to put money into such an uncertain political situation. On December 23 it was announced that the Philippines had reached agreement with Western creditor nations on a major restructuring of its foreign debt.

The Communist New People's Army continued to widen its guerrilla war. Marcos said that it had 6,800 armed insurgents by mid-1984, but a U.S. Defense Department official estimated that 10,000 guerrillas plus sympathizers influenced 20% of the country's villages. The official said in September that the guerrillas had "probably doubled their activities over the past year." Meanwhile, a Philippine military commander claimed on June 1 that the separatist struggle of Muslims for a "Moro homeland" in the southern islands was virtually over.

(HENRY S. BRADSHER)

SINGAPORE

Singapore, a republic of Southeast Asia and member of the Commonwealth, occupies a group of islands, the largest of which is Singapore, at the southern extremity of the Malay Peninsula. Area: 618 sq km (239 sq mi). Pop. (1984 est.): 2,529,000. Monetary unit: Singapore dollar, with (Oct. 29, 1984) a free rate of S$2.15 to U.S. $1 (S$2.59 = £1 sterling). President in 1984, Chengara Veetil Devan Nair; prime minister, Lee Kuan Yew.

For much of 1984 the political arena in Singapore was dominated by preparations for general elections on December 22 and the quickening of "self-renewal" within the ruling People's Action Party (PAP). The last of the old guard of government ministers, some of whom had served in the Cabinet for more than two decades, resigned from the PAP's central executive committee during its conference on September 30. The elections resulted in a sweeping victory for the PAP, which gained 77 of the 79 seats in Parliament, many of which were uncontested. At the same time, however, there was a significant drop (over 10%) in the PAP's share of the total vote.

Attracting the most attention among a crop of new PAP election candidates was Brig. Gen. Lee Hsien Loong, eldest son of the prime minister and, until his retirement from the post in September, chief of staff of the Singapore Armed Forces. The younger Lee won his seat with a convincing majority. His sudden emergence on the political scene, accompanied by strong hints from his father that he was destined for high office, inevitably raised charges of nepotism. These were firmly denied by the prime minister and other top government officials.

The election campaign focused on major social issues that sparked considerable controversy. One was the government's attempt to persuade university-educated women to marry and have more than one child. Prime Minister Lee had previously expressed concern that genetic dilution of Singapore's talent pool might result if educated citizens did not reproduce enough. Under an incentive program announced during the year, offspring of mothers with university degrees were to be given priority admission to elite schools, while poor and less-educated women were offered a housing grant of S$10,000 if they chose to undergo sterilization after their first or second child.

The economic recovery picked up steam. For the first half of 1984 gross domestic product registered an impressive 9.7% growth, while productivity improved by 7.9%, one of the highest growth rates in the world. Inflation, though still low by global standards, increased from 1.2% in 1983 to 2.9% for the first half of 1984. The Singapore International Monetary Exchange, Asia's first financial futures market, opened officially in September. Linked by a mutual offset system to the Chicago Mercantile Exchange, it doubled to 12 the number of hours available to global monetary dealers. (THOMAS HON WING POLIN)

This article updates the *Macropædia* article Mainland SOUTHEAST ASIA: *Singapore.*

THAILAND

Thailand is a constitutional monarchy in Southeast Asia, on the Andaman Sea and the Gulf of Thailand. Area: 513,115 sq km (198,115 sq mi). Pop (1984 est.): 50,832,000. Cap.: Bangkok. Monetary unit: baht, with (Oct. 29, 1984) a free rate of 22.95 baht to U.S. $1 (27.70 baht = £1 sterling). King, Bhumibol Adulyadej; prime minister in 1984, Gen. Prem Tinsulanond.

In 1984 simmering tensions between Thailand's powerful military establishment and the government flared into a crisis. The episode began in early August when a group of young military officers dismissed for involvement in an abortive coup in 1981 made peace with Gen. Arthit Kamlang-ek, supreme commander of the armed forces and long regarded as a potential prime minister. Within days hundreds of military officers had petitioned Prime Minister Prem Tinsulanond to approve a two-year extension of Arthit's tenure as supreme commander. (He was due to reach the official retirement age in 1985.) Rumours of a deepening schism between the military and the government spread as Army-backed MP's tried to reintroduce a bill, narrowly defeated in 1983, that would amend the constitution to allow actively serving military officers to take top posts in the civil administration. The move, together with the revelation that Prem was suffering from a heart condition, created an atmosphere of crisis. Tensions cooled, however, when on August 26, Prem's 64th birthday, Arthit led a delegation of several hundred military and police officers to the prime minister's residence to pledge loyalty to the government. Shortly afterward, Arthit advised MP's to postpone debate on the amendment, which they did.

Prem's pivotal position as the only leader acceptable to all the kingdom's major political forces was underscored during his 12-day absence for a medical checkup in the U.S. A day after his departure in mid-September, Army infighting surfaced dramatically when two leading "Young Turks" were arrested by senior military officers. Though they were released the following day, the episode prompted accusations of a frame-up. After frenetic consultations with Arthit and King Bhumibol, another crisis was averted when public apologies were offered all around. Meanwhile, U.S. doctors gave Prem a clean bill of health, though anxieties were stirred anew when he entered a hospital with a pulmonary ailment only days after his return.

The authorities continued to make significant progress in their fight against Communist insurgency. In December 1983 more than 5,000 members and supporters of the outlawed Communist Party of Thailand (CPT) surrendered to Arthit in a ceremony that was broadcast nationwide. More did so during 1984. The government in return granted them an amnesty in accordance with its standing policy. On July 3 security forces scored their single biggest success against the Communist leadership by arresting 16 CPT members in Bangkok. Thailand also made headway in its efforts to strengthen its military defense. During a visit to Washington, D.C., in April, Prem secured the support of U.S. Pres. Ronald Reagan for Bangkok's attempts to purchase F-16A jet fighters from the U.S.

The government became increasingly impatient about the slow progress being made in resettling Indochinese refugees on its territory, who over the years numbered more than 300,000. The government warned the UN High Commissioner for Refugees that if the process was not speeded up, it would consider transferring refugees to "austere" camps on the border with Kampuchea.

After a year of artificially inflated growth in 1983, the economy was steered along a course of greater restraint. The national budget for fiscal 1985, unveiled in June, reinforced the austerity policy and included a record deficit of 35 billion baht. The government's decision in November to devalue the baht by 17.3% was opposed by, among others, General Arthit, who criticized the move for the effect it would have on the purchase of U.S. weapons and aircraft.

(THOMAS HON WING POLIN)

This article updates the *Macropædia* article Mainland SOUTHEAST ASIA: *Thailand*.

VIETNAM

The people's republic of Vietnam occupies the eastern part of the Indochinese Peninsula in Southeast Asia and is bounded on the south and east by the South China Sea. Area: 329,465 sq km (127,207 sq mi). Pop. (1984 est.): 58,280,000. Cap.: Hanoi. Monetary unit: dong, with (Oct. 29, 1984) a free rate of 10.42 dong to U.S. $1 (12.58 dong = £1 sterling). Secretary-general of the Communist Party in 1984, Le Duan; chairman of the National Assembly, Nguyen Huu Tho; chairman of the State Council (president), Truong Chinh; chairman of the Council of Ministers (premier), Pham Van Dong.

The political scene in Vietnam was relatively stable throughout 1984, with the top leadership still dominated by the "old-guard" revolutionaries, in particular the troika of Communist Party Secretary-General Le Duan, Premier Pham Van Dong, and Pres. Truong Chinh. The principal issue in national affairs was economic reform. The liberalizing measures introduced in 1979 included production incentives for peasants and workers and more decentralization in economic planning. The measures had succeeded in improving production substantially, but they came under fire from orthodox-minded ideologues within the leadership. Foreign affairs was again dominated by the repercussions of Vietnam's military occupation of Kampuchea.

A hint of the intensifying debate over economic reform surfaced at the fifth plenum of the Communist Party in December 1983, when Le Duan frankly acknowledged that there had been "differing views" on the question of economic administration. Though they had proved to be effective, the reforms had also fostered a thriving black market, chaotic price rises, and corruption. Le Duan stressed that these tendencies should be checked, but he made it clear that the liberal policies would continue.

The hand of the reformers appeared to be strengthened at the sixth plenum, held in July 1984. The plenum called for two sets of guidelines. The first urged greater decentralization, the closing of state enterprises with substandard productivity, freedom for successful managers to hire and fire as they saw fit, and autonomy for individual operators to raise loans, even from foreign sources. At the same time, the plenum criticized private enterprise, reemphasized the importance of state-run ventures, advocated higher wages for state employees and soldiers, and demanded increased collectivization. The second set of directives was believed to be aimed in particular at the southern half of the country, where three-quarters of the land was still privately owned. During the year senior officials in Hanoi called for broader economic relations with the outside world, including capitalist countries. Le Duan's sudden visit to India in September—one of his rare trips abroad—was seen as an effort to begin the process.

In December the government claimed to have uncovered a plan to carry out a coup in 1985. Death sentences were passed on 5 people who were among 21 found guilty of treason and espionage. During the trial China was accused of funding the plot, which was allegedly backed by Thailand and the U.S.

The results of the economic reforms had been most visible in the countryside, where a record grain harvest of 17 million metric tons in 1983 capped three years of steady improvement. Production began well in 1984, but adverse weather, including two devastating typhoons, threatened to reduce the final tally. Though food production actually grew faster than the population during the period 1980–83, a national demographic conference in October warned that Vietnam's population had passed the 60 million mark and was expanding by 1.3 million, or 2.1%, a year. To avoid having to find an extra 400,000 metric tons of food annually, the government was aiming for a drastic cut in the population growth rate to 1.7%.

Even as they predicted better times by the 1990s, officials were admitting that the national economy was in dire straits. The official unemployment figure of one million did not include the vast number of underemployed. The inflation rate had been running at 50–60% during the previous few years, and the dong was being sold on the black market at up to 17 times the official rate of 11 dong to the U.S. dollar. According to the International Monetary Fund, Vietnam's foreign debt had risen to more than $6 billion, an increase of over 50% compared with the 1980 figure. The balance of payments deficit was expected to grow from around $800 million in 1982 to $1 billion in 1984. Even grant aid from the U.S.S.R. and its Eastern-bloc allies had been declining substantially.

As a partial remedy, Vietnam was fostering a greater measure of economic cooperation with its Indochinese neighbours and satellites, Laos and Kampuchea. Since the first meeting between the heads of government of the three countries in February 1983, there had been calls for them to supplement their already close military, political, and ideological ties with better economic relations. The chairmen of their respective state planning commissions met together for the first time in February 1984 in Ho Chi Minh City. The three governments agreed to coordinate

In July Vietnam turned over to the U.S. the remains of eight American soldiers listed as missing in action during the Vietnam war.
AP/WIDE WORLD

their five-year plans from 1986, when the current plans of Vietnam and Laos were to be completed and Kampuchea's first plan was scheduled to begin.

The major elements in Vietnam's foreign relations changed little during 1984. The U.S.S.R., which was supplying military and other aid worth about $1 billion a year, remained by far Hanoi's most important ally. The Soviets continued their militarization and modernization of the U.S.-built naval base at Cam Ranh, a move that disturbed neighbouring countries ranging from the members of the Association of Southeast Asian Nations (ASEAN) to China. Hanoi's diplomatic efforts to split ASEAN's membership on the contentious issue of Vietnamese troops in Kampuchea did not get far; the non-Communist Southeast Asian bloc remained united on the issue.

The chilly state of Hanoi-Beijing (Peking) relations did not improve either. In March–April Vietnamese troops pursued Khmer resistance guerrillas over the border into Thailand and triggered serious military clashes on the Sino-Vietnamese border. In October Japan opened ministerial-level talks with Hanoi for the first time since Vietnam's invasion of Kampuchea in December 1978. However, Hanoi unceremoniously rejected Tokyo's offer of massive aid for the reconstruction of Indochina in return for withdrawal from Kampuchea. Though they extended subtle peace feelers toward the U.S., the Vietnamese were apparently unable to give satisfaction on the two issues the U.S. regarded as the main obstacles in the way of a normalization of ties: the Vietnamese presence in Kampuchea and the question of U.S. servicemen missing in Indochina since the U.S.-Vietnam war. (THOMAS HON WING POLIN)

This article updates the *Macropædia* article Mainland SOUTHEAST ASIA: *Vietnam*.

Western Europe

WESTERN EUROPEAN AFFAIRS

A renewed impetus to increase commercial and political cooperation between Western European countries became evident during 1984. At the same time, however, there was also a series of grave internal crises within the ten-nation European Communities (EC; the European Economic Community [EEC], the European Coal and Steel Community [ECSC], and Euratom). Faced with a continuing world economic recession and mass unemployment

as well as new uncertainties about Europe's role in the confrontation between the nuclear superpowers, Western European governments strove to find a new definition of their common interests and goals.

Most of the headlines during the year were provided by a succession of internal conflicts over the future shape of the EC budget and some of its key spending policies. At various times during the year there were even fears that the bonds holding the EC together might be sundered because of disagreements over those issues. During the French presidency of the EC Council in the first half of the year, the French government made strenuous efforts to further the cause of Western European unity. By the end of the year, however, although some of the most explosive short-term issues had been resolved, major question marks remained over the future of the Community and its planned expansion to include Portugal and Spain by 1986.

A desire by the core countries of the EC to step up cooperation on common defense and security policies was reflected in plans to relaunch the Western European Union (WEU) as a forum for such cooperation. Part of the impetus behind the revival of the WEU was the belief among Western European countries that some of the assumptions underlying the NATO alliance between the U.S. and Western European countries might be changing. In addition, there was the desire to see European NATO states play a stronger and more united role in dialogue with the U.S. about the future of East-West relations.

Uncertainties about the future pattern of relations between the U.S. and Western Europe in regard to military security were compounded by continuing world economic difficulties. During the year there were episodic tensions across the Atlantic over trade policy, but more especially over the U.S. administration's massive federal budget deficit and the resultant high interest rates. As the year drew to a close, there was growing concern in Western Europe that, despite the economic recovery in the U.S., Europe remained gripped by recession.

Despite the differences in political character among Western European governments, there was a remarkable consensus in terms of internal economic policies. During 1984 the Socialist governments in France, Portugal, Spain, and, to some extent, Sweden fell into line with the firm monetary and deflationary orthodoxy of the dominant right-of-centre governments in Western Europe.

However, the strains that the economic recession had

imposed on national government finances had the effect of exacerbating internal EC relations. An EC summit meeting held in Brussels in March failed to resolve the related issues of reform of the EC budget, reform of the EC's common agricultural policy (CAP), and distribution of the burden of financing that budget among EC member nations. The British government, in particular, insisted that it would not permit any general increase in EC budget revenue unless CAP spending was brought under strict control. (*See* Sidebar.) In addition the British government wanted a long-term agreement reducing and limiting its net contributions to the Community's budget.

Political friction generated by this complex of interrelated disputes was aggravated early in 1984 when it was confirmed that the EC budget would be heavily overspent during the year. The EC Commission in Brussels proposed that emergency loan funds be raised from the member states, but the proposal served only to complicate the effort to reach agreement over the U.K. budget rebate. Yet another difficulty was created by the involvement of the European Parliament. On a number of occasions during the year it voted not to endorse the agreement to award a rebate to the U.K. on its 1984 budget contribution.

Against this inauspicious background an EC summit was held at Fontainebleau, France, in June. There the leaders of the ten nations agreed on a formula granting the U.K. long-term rebates on its budget payments, on measures to curb the future growth in farm spending, and on a staggered increase in the payments to the EC of percentages of national value-added taxes. There was general relief at the measure of agreement that these accords represented. Nevertheless, doubts remained about the willingness of member governments to implement the tough, politically unpopular measures that would be required in order to put into practice the resolution on agricultural reform.

At a summit meeting of the European Communities, British Prime Minister Margaret Thatcher gave her approval to an accord that settled Britain's long-standing protest over its contributions to the Communities' budget.
LIPCHITZ—AP/WIDE WORLD

French Pres. François Mitterrand's call for a new treaty on European unity met with a lukewarm reception. Although his plea received some verbal support, few other member governments seemed prepared to take concrete steps that would result in a transfer of national sovereignty to the EC. As one way forward, the French envisioned restricting the use of the power of veto in the EC Council of Ministers, allowing more decisions to be made by majority

Western Europe's Common Agricultural Policy

With an annual budget of more than $16 billion, and with its butter and grain "mountains" and its wine and milk "lakes," the European Communities' (EC's) common agricultural policy (CAP) is probably the best known facet of that organization. The CAP represents one of the few genuine common policies that integrates the economies of the ten member nations of the EC, but its extravagance and waste have led to bitter and growing criticism.

The six founding member countries of the EC signed the Treaty of Rome that inaugurated the Common Market in 1957, but it was not until 1960 that the basic principles of the CAP were formulated. The fundamental objective of the CAP was a laudable one: to ensure reasonable self-sufficiency in foodstuffs for the peoples of the EC, given growing world uncertainties over food supplies, and to guarantee a reasonable income to Europe's politically powerful farming communities. The chosen means was to be a system of prices fixed annually by EC agriculture ministers and paid to farmers without specific regard for the state of market demand.

At one level the CAP has been remarkably successful over the past 10 to 15 years. Output and farm incomes have risen sharply, and this has helped lift traditionally economically depressed rural regions of the EC closer to average levels of prosperity. On the other hand, output has surged far past any level that could be justified by the demand for food or by the need to maintain prudent surplus supplies. Production of milk, wine, and some cereals and meats rocketed under the stimulus of high, guaranteed prices during the late 1970s and early 1980s. This resulted in the so-called food mountains and lakes—the reserves held by the EC authorities as a result of having to buy up excess production not needed by European consumers. The cost of financing these surplus stockpiles has been a rapidly growing element in the burgeoning CAP budget, as has been the cost of trying to export surplus food through the use of export subsidies to match now generally lower world food prices.

There has been growing recognition in recent years that the CAP is in urgent need of reform. Apart from any other factor, CAP spending has been taking the lion's share of the total annual EC budget. During 1984, as a climax to highly complex and politically difficult EC budget reform negotiations, the member nations did agree to impose some limits on future farm price guarantees. However, the proposed price curbs and output tax levies seemed insufficient to reduce the overall level of farm spending without triggering social unrest in politically key farming communities in France and the Benelux countries.

(JOHN PALMER)

vote. The suggestion did not meet with the approval of other members.

Progress on implementing the Fontainebleau accord continued at a fitful pace during the second half of the year. The enthusiastic commitment of the Irish government, which succeeded to the presidency of the EC Council on July 1, succeeded in making some progress at the Dublin summit in December. EC leaders reached agreement on measures to curb the already chronic wine surplus, an essential step toward enlargement of the Community in view of the additional wine-producing capacity that Spain and Portugal would provide. There was also a qualified acceptance of the proposal that the EC should work toward closer political cooperation. However, Greek Prime Minister Andreas Papandreou threatened that Greece would veto the enlargement process if the Community failed to provide generous development aid for Greek farmers.

The second direct elections to the European Parliament took place in June. The average turnout of voters in the ten EC countries was disappointing; at 57%, it was 5% lower than the figure in the previous elections, held in June 1979. Overall the results showed a slight swing to the left. The Socialist group was confirmed as the largest transnational faction in the Strasbourg assembly. Other notable features of the results were gains by the ultraright-wing National Front, lead by Jean-Marie le Pen (*see* BIOGRAPHIES), in France and by the militant antinuclear Green parties in West Germany, Belgium, and The Netherlands.

It became clear that the new European Parliament would remain as insistent as its predecessor that the views of its elected members should be accorded far greater importance by EC decision makers. The assembly elected Pierre Pflimlin, veteran politician and former French premier, as its new president. The move seemed likely to ensure that Strasbourg, rather than Brussels, would remain the main site of the European Parliament's meetings. In July Jacques Delors (*see* BIOGRAPHIES), former French finance minister, was appointed president of the EC Commission. He was to succeed Gaston Thorn at the start of 1985. The appointment of Delors was generally welcomed, but there was widespread disappointment over the relatively undistinguished appointments made by member nations to fill other vacancies for EC commissioners.

In September the governments of EC member countries announced the adoption of a package of far-reaching measures setting Community-wide norms and standards for industrial products. At the same time, the Commission announced a compromise settlement of a four-year dispute with the U.S. computer giant, IBM, over Commission charges that IBM had abused its position to undermine its Western European competitors. The autumn also saw the revival of trade frictions with the U.S., mainly over U.S. proposals to impose new curbs on imports of European specialty steels. Furthermore, Western European governments were concerned about the size of Japan's trade surplus and the unrelenting loss of international competitiveness being suffered by Europe's key industrial sectors.

During October the EC was bitterly criticized by its African, Caribbean, and Pacific (ACP) partners in the Lomé Convention. The less developed countries accused the EC of betraying its promises to increase economic aid and to improve access to European markets for their exports. Nevertheless, in November the 64 ACP countries and the EC reached agreement to renew the trade, aid, and development agreement for an additional five years from February 1985. This third agreement under the Lomé Convention was worth 7.4 billion European currency units. On the other hand, the EC governments encountered some criticism in Washington for their decision in September to increase economic aid to Central American nations. EC foreign ministers also endorsed proposals for a peace settlement in El Salvador that mirrored the approach of the Latin-American Contadora Group.

Those Western European governments that were interested in pursuing greater cooperation in security matters regarded NATO as an inappropriate forum for discussion because it was a U.S.-led organization. On the other hand, the Danish, Greek, and Irish governments objected to the EC's being used for the development of defense policies that might compromise their own independence or neutralist policies. There remained the option of reviving the WEU, a body that grouped Belgium, France, Italy, Luxembourg, The Netherlands, the U.K. and West Germany, and that aimed to promote collective self-defense as well as economic and social collaboration. The WEU, formed in 1954, had languished in recent years. Meetings of the WEU took place in November after the participating governments stressed their determination not to tolerate any split with the U.S. that might threaten the unity of NATO.

In spite of a growing consensus on security and East-West issues, Western European governments disagreed on foreign-policy issues on a number of occasions during the year. There was some apprehension, notably in France and Italy, about the increasing emphasis being placed by the West German government on its ultimate objective of German reunification. There were also differences in approach between the Socialist governments in France and Greece, on the one hand, and other EC governments over policies toward less developed countries and, to some extent, toward the crises in the Middle East and southern Africa. In April the remaining nonagricultural trade barriers between the EC countries and the members of the other Western European trade bloc, the European Free Trade Association, were finally removed.   (JOHN PALMER)

See also Economic Affairs; Military Affairs.

ANDORRA

A landlocked independent co-principality of Europe, Andorra is in the Pyrennes Mountains between Spain and France. Area: 468 sq km (181 sq mi). Pop. (1984 est.): 40,-000. Cap.: Andorra la Vella. Monetary units: French franc and Spanish peseta. Co-princes: the president of the French Republic and the bishop of Urgel, Spain, represented by their *veguers* (provosts) and *batlles* (prosecutors). An elected Council General of 28 members elects the first syndic, in 1984 Francesc Cerqueda Pascuet; chief executives, Oscar Ribas-Reig and, from May 21, Josep Pintat-Solans.

On Dec. 12, 1983, Andorrans elected a new 28-seat Council General (parliament), in which Conservatives predominated. During the first four months of 1984 Oscar Ribas-Reig, the chief executive, tried to push through the Council General a law introducing an income tax, a measure deemed necessary to balance the principality's budget. However, as many of Andorra's inhabitants refused to pay taxes, the government was forced to abandon the project.

On April 30 Ribas-Reig and his government resigned, and on May 21 the Council General elected Josep Pintat-Solans to replace him. The new head of government, a 59-year-old importer and tobacco manufacturer, had represented the commune of Sant-Juli-de-Loria since 1982. He was the sole candidate for office and obtained 26 votes, with two councillors abstaining. Pintat-Solans's main task would be to find means to cover the budget deficit, amounting to 840 million pesetas.   (K. M. SMOGORZEWSKI)

This article updates the *Micropædia* article ANDORRA.

AUSTRIA

The republic of Austria is a landlocked state of central Europe. Area: 83,855 sq km (32,376 sq mi). Pop. (1984 est.): 7,579,000. Cap.: Vienna. Monetary unit: schilling, with (Oct. 29, 1984) a free rate of 21.54 schillings to U.S. $1 (26 schillings = £1 sterling). President in 1984, Rudolf Kirchschläger; chancellor, Fred Sinowatz.

The loss of the Socialist Party of Austria's (SPÖ's) overall parliamentary majority in April 1983 and the end of Bruno Kreisky's long tenure as chancellor and party leader ushered in a difficult time for the party. Initially, the decision over whether to go into opposition or to govern in coalition with the Freedom Party of Austria (FPÖ) gave rise to lively discussion among the SPÖ rank and file. Discussion became heated when the coalition set up under SPÖ chairman Fred Sinowatz introduced an austerity package aimed at reducing the 1985 budget deficit. Heavy increases in taxes and duties, including value-added tax, rail fares, and postal charges, took effect from January 1984, resulting in a reduction of real incomes. The tax on savings account interest imposed at the same time reduced savings and favoured the flight of capital abroad.

Thanks to a massive injection of public funds designed to preserve existing employment and create new jobs, the unemployment rate remained below the average for countries within the Organization for Economic Cooperation and Development. Jobs in the state-owned industries were especially under threat, however, owing to a combination of recession and structural problems. During 1981–83 losses of these concerns amounted to some 15 billion schillings. Marketing difficulties and modernization led to part-time working and layoffs. Another grave problem was youth unemployment, and a program of "national action" to combat it was approved unanimously by Parliament. In October 1983 the tenth national congress of the Austrian Federation of Labour had committed itself to the gradual introduction of a 35-hour workweek. Plans to lower the pensionable age and extend vacation time were contested by the opposition.

Environmental problems were the subject of heated controversy that frequently cut across party lines. Austria, surrounded by industrial countries and a crossroads for international traffic and commerce, suffered pollution of its forests, lakes, and farmland caused by its neighbours' industrial activity as well as its own. The government's energy policy aroused public anger, and there was vigorous opposition to the building of new power stations. A national referendum was initiated against one planned at Hainburg on the Danube and the project was later shelved. Meanwhile, the fate of the Zwentendorf nuclear power station, completed in 1978 but still nonoperational, remained in doubt.

The state of the economy and differences among the SPÖ leadership over alleged tax evasion by former finance minister and vice-chancellor Hannes Androsch were probably the main reasons for the Socialists' losses in provincial elections and opinion polls during 1984. In September Chancellor Sinowatz undertook an extensive reshuffle of his Cabinet in which the ministries of finance, foreign affairs, family affairs, transport, and education changed hands. The changes indicated a shift toward greater pragmatism in government policy. Economic prospects seemed reasonably favourable; forecasts for 1984 and 1985 estimated growth at 2% and 2.7–3%, respectively, unemployment at 4.6% and 4.4–4.5%, and inflation at 5.5% and 4–4.3%.

The controversial conference centre in Vienna's "UN City" was completed with financial aid from Arab countries. In August Austria became involved in the East-West war of words following U.S. allegations, later shown to be unfounded, that U.S. technological equipment was passing through Austria to the Soviet Union, where it was being put to military use. Relations with Italy (Premier Bettino Craxi visited Austria in February, the first such visit in more than a century) were strained by demonstrations in Innsbruck in September for the reunification of South Tirol (Italy's Bolzano Province) with Austria.

The first state visit by an Austrian president to the U.S. occurred during February–March, when Pres. Rudolf Kirchschläger took part in an extensive program of ceremonies, including visits to New York City, Chicago, and San Francisco, as well as Washington, D.C.

(ELFRIEDE DIRNBACHER)

AP/WIDE WORLD

A car bomb exploded in front of the Turkish embassy in Vienna in June. The bomb, which may have been operated by remote control, killed an embassy employee who was driving the car at the time of the explosion.

BELGIUM

A constitutional monarchy, the Benelux country of Belgium is situated on the North Sea coast of northwestern Europe. Area: 30,519 sq km (11,783 sq mi). Pop. (1984 est.): 9,872,000. Cap.: Brussels. Monetary unit: Belgian franc, with (Oct. 29, 1984) a free commercial rate of BF 62.47 to U.S. $1 (BF 75.40 = £1 sterling) and a free financial rate of BF 61.81 to U.S. $1 (BF 74.61 = £1 sterling). King, Baudouin I; prime minister in 1984, Wilfried Martens.

Putting Belgium's finances on an even keel remained an elusive objective for the Social Christian-Liberal government throughout 1984. The public debt stood at BF 4,250,000,000,000 by the end of the year, while interest payments alone represented nearly one-quarter of all expenditure in the 1985 election-year budget. Special powers that had allowed the government to take measures without referring to Parliament lapsed on March 31, but the majority of Belgians approved of the so-called recovery laws; these further restricted the system of automatic wage indexation and rescinded or limited a series of tax deductions, bringing the burden of taxation to 47% of gross national product. Most of the larger cities also introduced severe austerity measures. Brussels was to lose one-fifth of its public employees by 1988 while raising taxes by 45% and reducing capital expenditure by one-third.

Parliament approved the immigration bill introduced the previous year by Jean Gol, minister of justice and institutional reform. It favoured the integration of foreign workers but also imposed restrictions on their residence in certain communes. It was also agreed that a bonus should be offered to unemployed immigrants from outside the European Communities who were willing to return to their country of origin. Unemployment remained above 500,000 throughout the year. Trade unions urged the introduction of a 35-hour week to redistribute available work. One plan suggested a shorter workweek combined with fuller use of equipment and machines through more weekend and shift work. Some of these ideas were gradually put into practice by industry. During negotiations with trade unions on a new central agreement, the Federation of Belgian Enterprises promised to create some 100,000 part-time jobs over the next three years in exchange for greater flexibility in employment relations.

Belgium and Luxembourg reached a cooperation agreement concerning the Belgian state-controlled steel concern Cockerill-Sambre, Arbed of Luxembourg, and Sidmar, owned jointly by the two governments. This prompted the Belgian government to assume responsibility for Cockerill-Sambre debts amounting to BF 51 billion. Responsibility for future losses in the so-called national industrial sectors of coal and steel was imposed on the two regions concerned, Wallonia and Flanders. An agreement to convert the Cockerill-Sambre debt into capital was concluded with private financial institutions, which agreed to finance future needs to a total of BF 27 billion.

Much of the persistent tension between the French and Dutch language communities centred around José Happart and his refusal to speak Dutch, even though he had been appointed mayor of Voeren (Fourons), officially situated in Dutch-speaking Flanders. His appointment was annulled by the Limburg standing body of the provincial council, but he remained in office pending his appeal to the High Court of Laws. On June 17 he was elected to the European Parliament with a big personal vote on the list of the Walloon Socialists. This caused friction with the party's Flemish counterpart, which did not want Happart to sit in the socialist group in the European Parliament. The two socialist parties also clashed over the installation of cruise missiles at the Florennes air force base; the Flemish Socialists flatly refused to agree to their presence on Belgian territory. In November the Cabinet decided to delay its decision on the matter until early 1985. Dissatisfaction with the 1980 reform of state structures was repeatedly expressed. A parliamentary study group was created to suggest possible improvements.

In August the French cargo ship "Mont Louis" sank in the English Channel off Ostend after colliding with a cross-Channel ferry. Salvage operations, completed in October, attracted considerable attention when French authorities revealed that the cargo had consisted of containers of nuclear waste. (JAN R. ENGELS)

This article updates the *Macropædia* article The Low Countries: *Belgium.*

DENMARK

A constitutional monarchy of north central Europe, Denmark lies between the North and Baltic seas. Area: 43,080 sq km (16,633 sq mi), excluding the Faeroe Islands and Greenland. Pop. (1984 est.): 5,109,000. Cap.: Copenhagen. Monetary unit: krone, with (Oct. 29, 1984) a free rate of 11.06 kroner to U.S. $1 (13.35 kroner = £1 sterling). Queen, Margrethe II; prime minister in 1984, Poul Schlüter.

The year began with a general election on Jan. 10, 1984, generally regarded as superfluous, since its results changed little in the Danish Folketing (parliament). The main government party, the Conservatives, made some gains, while the opposition Social Democrats lost a little support, though they remained the largest single party. The government coalition parties, the Conservative, Liberal Democratic (Venstre), Centre Democratic, and Christian People's parties, increased their total to 77 of the 179 seats in the chamber. Given that they could count on the support of ten Radical Liberals and three of the deputies elected by Greenland and the Faeroe Islands, they could now expect to command an absolute majority of one. (For tabulated results, see *Political Parties,* above.)

The Social Democrats were expected to exert some influence over government policy in the areas of foreign relations and defense policy. However, a certain lack of trust had developed between the government and the Social Democrats for two main reasons. First, the Social Democrats had voted against the budget in December 1983, thus defeating the government and precipitating the general election. Hitherto, voting against the budget had been considered unthinkable for a "responsible" party, in or out of office. Second, the Social Democrats threatened the broad unity on defense matters that had existed since Denmark first joined NATO in 1949. At their party congress in the fall of 1984, they passed a resolution calling for the banning of nuclear weapons from Denmark during times of peace, crisis, and war. Foreign Minister Uffe Ellemann-Jensen claimed that Danish security policy lost credibility as a result.

After the election, the budget was approved with little alteration by the Folketing, with the Social Democrats abstaining. The government's economic policies began to show dramatic results. Severe austerity measures succeeded in reducing the budget deficit, while the balance of payments deficit, though it did not fall, resulted mainly from imports of raw materials and machinery for industry. There was a net increase of some 10,000 jobs, and the number of employed workers was higher than ever before. It could be said that those with jobs were better off than they had been when the government came to power two years earlier.

At the opening of the new parliamentary session in October, Prime Minister Poul Schlüter stressed the positive aspects of the economic situation. Others, however, maintained that the results had been achieved in spite of—and not because of—government policy. Former prime minister Anker Jørgensen, leader of the Social Democrats, suggested that the economy had been assisted by external factors and accused the government of ignoring the problems of the unemployed and old-age pensioners and the declining standards of health- and child-care service.

The government still faced considerable budget and balance of payments deficits. The national debt was calculated at the equivalent of 80,000 kroner per capita. Furthermore, for some years there had been pressure to reform the country's overcomplicated tax laws in an effort to close the loopholes that allowed "legal" tax evasion.

The government was also involved in a wrangle with the municipal councils. Because the government had imposed an austerity policy on the municipalities without lowering taxes, the councils had accumulated considerable amounts of money. When the central government suggested that these funds should be used to offset the national budget deficit, the idea was strongly resisted by the councils, who regarded it as an attack on their democratic freedom.

Denmark's petroleum production had increased considerably in recent years, and in September its first North Sea gas field went on stream. It was predicted that within two years Denmark might be supplying almost 40% of its energy needs from indigenous sources.

(STENER AARSDAL)

FINLAND

The republic of Finland is in northern Europe, on the Gulf of Bothnia and the Gulf of Finland. Area: 338,145 sq km (135,559 sq mi). Pop. (1984 est.): 4,854,000. Cap.: Helsinki. Monetary unit: markka, with (Oct. 29, 1984) a free rate of 6.37 markkaa to U.S. $1 (7.68 markkaa = £1 sterling). President in 1984, Mauno Koivisto; prime minister, Kalevi Sorsa.

For Finland 1984 was a year devoid of major incident, appearing to vindicate those who advocated the special relationship with the U.S.S.R. and social consensus in a domestic setting. On April 26 Pres. Mauno Koivisto became one of the first foreign leaders to visit the U.S.S.R. after the funeral of Soviet Pres. Yury Andropov, and observers noted that his successor, Konstantin Chernenko, invited Koivisto before any of the Warsaw Pact leaders. In September the Social Democratic prime minister, Kalevi Sorsa, paid an official visit to the U.S.S.R., attending the signing of a 28 billion ruble ($33 billion) accord for 1986–90 that would consolidate the large Soviet share in Finland's foreign trade and speed the extension of a pipeline bringing Soviet natural gas into Finland.

Some sensitive observers detected ambivalences in the Soviet tone toward Finland, but on the whole there was nothing to suggest anything but delight on the part of the U.S.S.R. at having at least one reliable country along its frontiers. It seemed unlikely that Moscow would take exception to the visit to Finland in October of East German leader Erich Honecker, since it had been arranged before Honecker fell into some disfavour with the Soviets. Finland echoed Soviet enthusiasm for a tenth anniversary jubilee of the Helsinki Final Act in 1985 and expressed concern about a new generation of U.S. medium-range missiles to be deployed in the Norwegian Sea.

The Western component in neutral Finland's balancing act was most apparent from Koivisto's official visit to the U.K. in November and a boom in exports to market economies. The forest industries were the first to benefit from the economic upturn, closely followed by metals and engineering. By fall unemployment had dropped to 4.5% from an average of 6.1% in 1983, while the commonest prediction was for 4% growth in the economy in both 1984 and 1985. A threatened general strike was averted, thanks to a last-minute pay formula submitted by industrialist Matti Pekkanen on March 4, which allowed the centre-left government's anti-inflationary guidelines to be upheld. However, several small professional unions staged strikes fueled by disenchantment over the long-term erosion of pay differentials. A doctor's stoppage that gradually spread nationwide and local actions by teachers caused considerable inconvenience.

The Communist Party's 20th congress in May failed to heal the division between a nationalist, reformist majority and a pro-Moscow, hard-line minority. The majority effectively snubbed Moscow by replacing Jouko Kajanoja with Arvo Aalto as chairman. It also swept the minority off the Central Committee and Politburo, apparently making a formal split into two parties unavoidable.

Finland came under unusual scrutiny from Amnesty International. For the first time, the human rights organization listed a prisoner of conscience in a Finnish jail—Pertti Haaparanta, a university lecturer and conscientious objector, who was later pardoned. In August Amnesty named six Soviet fugitives who had been repatriated by Finland against their will between 1974 and 1982. Having consistently denied such a practice, senior Finnish officials now issued their own figures, all below those of Amnesty. In June the Finnish organizers of an international physicians' conference on preventing nuclear war, conscious of a large Soviet presence, refused to let the stepdaughter of Andrey Sakharov (see BIOGRAPHIES) plead on her parents' behalf.

An episode on January 3 provided insight into Finland's delicate position. President Koivisto told a newspaper that a Norwegian journalist who had written a book about Finland "cannot engage himself in our affairs in the way he does." The implication of this and of Koivisto's criticisms of the Finnish press was that no foreigner should attempt to evaluate the situation in Finland and that the "free" debate that allegedly distinguished Koivisto's term from that of Urho Kekkonen, who preceded him, was a chimera.

(DONALD FIELDS)

FRANCE

A republic of western Europe, France includes the island of Corsica in the Mediterranean Sea and has coastlines on the English Channel, the Mediterranean, and the Atlantic Ocean. Area: 544,000 sq km (210,000 sq mi). Pop. (1984 est.): 54,879,000. Cap.: Paris. Monetary unit: franc, with (Oct. 29, 1984) a free rate of F 9.41 to U.S. $1 (F 11.36 = £1 sterling). President in 1984, François Mitterrand; premiers, Pierre Mauroy and, from July 17, Laurent Fabius.

Domestic Affairs. The main event of 1984 in France was Pres. François Mitterrand's choice of a new government in July that excluded Communist Party (PC) ministers, thus confirming the breakup of the Union of the Left. The strategy of the second part of the president's seven-year term was indicated by his decision to replace Pierre Mauroy as premier with Laurent Fabius (see BIOGRAPHIES). In fact, the change meant a reversal of the government's economic and social policies, as well as a revision of dogmatic Socialism and a cautious return to a form of liberalism.

Mitterrand began the year by promising a continuation

of the effort toward national recovery. He concentrated above all on explaining his economic policies, which were designed to maintain a course marked by austerity and industrial modernization; either France would prove capable of withstanding international competition or it would head toward decline. In political circles it was felt that the president had adopted a new tone that at last seemed to accord with the reality of the situation. However, the prospect of continued austerity was not acceptable to public opinion, which showed its disapproval in various ways.

The left suffered a serious defeat in the elections for the European Parliament on June 17, when the government majority parties were easily outstripped by the opposition. With only 11.2% of the vote, the PC continued to decline; this was the lowest percentage for the PC since 1928, when it had obtained 11%. The Socialist Party (PS) won 20.8%, the first time since 1973 that it had achieved less than 21%. The opposition Rassemblement pour la République (RPR) and the Union pour la Démocratie Française (UDF) together received 43%. Apart from the failure of the left, which had been anticipated since the municipal elections of 1983, the elections were remarkable for the considerable rise in support for the far-right National Front led by Jean-Marie le Pen (*see* BIOGRAPHIES), which won almost 11%. The extent of Le Pen's success was a surprise and as much of an embarrassment to the opposition as to the left. The National Front sent ten delegates to the Parliament, the same number as the Communists, while the united opposition list had 41 members elected and the PS 20.

A week after this snub to the government, and in the same challenging spirit, Paris witnessed the largest demonstration organized there since the city was liberated from the Nazis in World War II. This time the issue was freedom of education, specifically, a proposal to merge private (mainly Roman Catholic) schools with the public-school system. The march, which took place without incident, brought together between one million and two million participants from every part of France. It was preceded by several major demonstrations in Bordeaux, Lyon, Rennes, Lille, and Paris, all in support of private Catholic education.

Mitterrand produced his first startling piece of news in early July with the announcement of a referendum bill on the extension of the system of referenda to cover matters concerned with civil liberties. As a proposed revision of the constitution, however, it had to be passed in the same wording by both the National Assembly and the Senate. The opposition, holding a majority in the Senate, decisively rejected the proposed referendum. In addition, the bill on private education was abandoned because of the strong public opposition, and Parliament was to discuss a new measure.

Mitterrand's second shock was the formation of a new government. On July 17, after the president accepted Mauroy's resignation, Laurent Fabius, who had been minister of industry and research since March 1983, was appointed premier. The new Cabinet was composed of Fabius (PS), premier; Gaston Defferre (PS), minister of state, planning and development; Pierre Bérégovoy (PS), economy, finance, and budget; Robert Badinter (PS), justice; Claude Cheysson (PS), foreign affairs; Charles Hernu (PS), defense; Pierre Joxe (PS), interior and decentralization; Michel Rochard (PS), agriculture; Edith Cresson (PS), industrial redeployment and foreign trade; Jean-Pierre Chevènement (PS), education; Georgina Dufoix (PS), social affairs and national solidarity; Paul Quilès (PS), town planning, housing, and transport; Michel Crépeau (Left Radicals [MRG]), trade, crafts, and tourism; Roland Dumas (PS), European affairs and government spokesman; Michel Delebarre (PS),

labour, employment, and training; Huguette Bouchardeau (United Socialist Party [PSU]), environment; Hubert Curien (PS), research and technology.

At the age of 37, Fabius was the youngest premier in the last three republics. A number of leading figures left the Cabinet without controversy, including Education Minister Alain Savary, author of the aborted bill for the reform of private education, who resigned, and Jacques Delors (*see* BIOGRAPHIES), minister of economy, finance, and budget, who was elected president of the Executive Commission of the European Communities (EC). However, the most striking feature of the new government was the PC's abandonment of the four posts, two of them ministerial, which it had held in the previous Cabinet. The break had been decided by the Central Committee of the PC when it was unable to obtain the guarantees it had demanded in the social and economic fields. Shortly afterward, PC leader Georges Marchais confirmed that his party no longer belonged to the government majority. The four new arrivals in the government were Joxe, leader of the Socialist group in the National Assembly; Chevènement, former minister for research and industry; Delebarre, former director of Mauroy's private office; and Curien, president of the council of the European Space Agency.

On July 24 Fabius obtained a vote of confidence from the Assembly by 279 votes to 157, with 46 abstentions. For the first time since the left's coming to power in 1981, the Communist *députés* abstained on a vote of confidence. Fabius described modernization of the economy and a "bringing together" of the people as the guidelines for his policy. In fact, the grand strategy of the second part of the seven-year presidential term was emerging. It aimed to restore the government's weakened credibility and to regain the support of public opinion. It had to achieve a consensus, at least in foreign policy and on the issues of civil liberties, security, and the condition of the elderly.

In a limited government reshuffle announced in December, Dumas took over as foreign affairs minister in succession to Cheysson, who left the post to become an EC commissioner. Minister of Culture Jack Lang was reinstated in the Cabinet. By the end of the year, not only Mitterrand but also the opposition leaders Jacques Chirac, former president Valéry Giscard d'Estaing (who was returned to the National Assembly in a by-election in September), and former premier Raymond Barre saw a marked fall in their popularity. Public opinion failed to react to parliamentary events such as the appeasement on the issue of private schools, the debate on the budget for 1985, or the possibility that, after the parliamentary elections in 1986, a left-wing president might have to govern with a right-wing parliamentary majority; people were more concerned about inflation and unemployment. In

In a July reorganization of the French government President François Mitterrand replaced Premier Pierre Mauroy (left) with Laurent Fabius, 37, youngest French premier in over 100 years.

In mid-February truck drivers blockaded roads throughout France in a protest that encompassed many grievances. The nationwide traffic jam ended when the government agreed to hold talks on the truckers' demands.

ALAIN NOGUES—SYGMA

the last resort, the government's ability to deal with those two black spots in the economy would form the basis for judging President Mitterrand's Socialist experiment.

The most serious problem was without doubt the unemployment crisis. Premier Mauroy earlier maintained that unemployment was the price that had to be paid for the austerity policies, which the government had no intention of abandoning. The number of unemployed reached 2,360,000 by the end of October and seemed likely to rise to 2.5 million by the end of the year. There had been some improvement in the rate of inflation, since the rise in prices for September was only 0.5%, in line with the prediction of 6.7% for the whole of 1984. However, price rises in France over the 12 months to August reached 7.4%, as against 1.7% in West Germany, 1.9% in Japan, 3.7% in Canada, 4.2% in the U.S., and 5% in the U.K. Among the major industrialized countries, only Italy, at 10.6%, fared worse. There was an improvement in foreign trade, with surpluses in the balance of payments in August and September, reducing the deficit since the start of the year to some F 20 billion. However, the original forecast had allowed for a deficit of only F 10 billion, and it was clear that the struggle to reduce it had to continue. Finally, after several years of large deficits, the Department of Social Security had a surplus of F 13 billion.

In the wake of successive government-imposed price rises on bread, telephone charges, transport, rents, and gasoline (which wiped out the slight reduction in taxes), employees, encouraged by their trade unions, organized marches and strikes during the year to protect their wages and jobs. There were strike actions among transport workers, civil servants, coal miners, dockyard workers, and customs officials; unrest and disruption among farmers in Brittany; and marches to Paris by steelworkers from Lorraine. The country was also shaken by the slowdown in the automobile industry. Layoffs were announced in turn by Talbot, Peugeot, and Citroën. Renault was considering eliminating 7,000 jobs, but in October the company put forward a revolutionary new industrial plan to retrain employees whose jobs were threatened. Job losses following the collapse of Creusot-Loire, the country's leading mechanical engineering firm, threatened to cause problems.

Foreign Affairs. On June 6–7 ceremonies were held to commemorate the 40th anniversary of the Allied landings in Normandy that preceded the liberation of France at the end of World War II. The ceremonies were attended by President Mitterrand, Queen Elizabeth II of the U.K., Queen Beatrix of The Netherlands, King Olav V of Norway, King Baudouin I of Belgium, Grand Duke Jean of Luxembourg, U.S. Pres. Ronald Reagan, and Canadian Prime Minister Pierre Trudeau.

For much of the year Mitterrand's foreign-policy decisions were received at home with a degree of acceptance that provided some compensation for the poor response to his internal policies. The disengagement of French troops from Lebanon was greeted with general approval by all political parties. By the end of March the last French soldiers in the multinational peacekeeping force had left Lebanon. In November Mitterrand's visit to Syria—the first visit by a French head of state since Syria became independent—indicated that the French withdrawal from Lebanon had facilitated an improvement in relations between the two countries. During the year Mitterrand also visited Jordan and Egypt to discuss the Iran-Iraq war.

At the end of March Mitterrand spent a week in the U.S., where he held talks with President Reagan and appealed for a dialogue with Moscow during an address to the U.S. Congress. As a logical next step, Mitterrand went to Moscow in June to investigate the possibility of a renewal of the dialogue between East and West. During his visit he showed courage that was recognized in France and abroad, notably in solemnly stating his feelings on the case of the Soviet dissident Andrey Sakharov (*see* BIOGRAPHIES), in internal exile in Gorky, and repeating his disapproval of Soviet actions in Afghanistan and Poland. In October Moscow agreed to the release of the French journalist Jacques Abouchar, who had been captured by Soviet troops and sentenced to 18 years' imprisonment for entering Afghanistan without a visa. The surprise move was credited by some to the firm line Mitterrand had taken with the Soviet authorities.

However, the most undeniable success was achieved by Mitterrand during his six-month presidency of the EC Council of Ministers. At the end of June its summit in Fontainebleau reached agreement on the British contribution to the EC budget after five years of bitter bargaining. The agreement allowed for an increase in the financial resources of the EC and the entry of Spain and Portugal in 1986. At their 43rd summit in June, France and West Germany agreed to renew military cooperation on a large scale.

Mitterrand's visit to the U.K., October 23–26, commemorated the 80th anniversary of the Franco-British Entente Cordiale. He took the opportunity to reiterate his appeal to the U.S. and the U.S.S.R. to resume negotiations on strategic arms reductions, and he urged the U.K. to play an increased part in the development of European unity. A bizarre incident threatened to mar his otherwise successful state visit. During a security check by British police at the residence of the French ambassador, a small amount of explosive material was discovered. British police accused the French of deliberately hiding the explosives in order to test British security operations, whereas the French claimed that the security forces of both countries had agreed in advance to conduct a test.

In mid-September France and Libya agreed to evacuate their troops from Chad, where they had been supporting opposite sides in the civil war. At first the agreement was received with the same general approval that had greeted the earlier disengagement from Lebanon. (The presence of 3,300 French troops in Chad was costing some F 1 million a day.) However, after France completed its withdrawal in early November, U.S. and French intelligence reports revealed that Libya had failed to honour its side of the bargain. Mitterrand's meeting with Libyan leader Col. Muammar al-Qaddafi in Greece on November 15 took place amid mounting criticism, at home and abroad, of France's handling of the affair. He failed to secure a Libyan withdrawal. Not only did the affair pose a threat to the credibility of France's policies in Africa, it also damaged France's relations with the U.S. In France's view, the U.S. had threatened the success of the peace initiative by publicizing its reports that Libyan troops remained in Chad. The U.S., on the other hand, considered that France had fallen into a Libyan trap.

There was concern in Algeria, as well, about the new direction of French policy in North Africa. Mitterrand's visit to Morocco in August–September, coinciding as it did with the Moroccan referendum on its treaty of union with Libya, appeared to confer France's approval on the treaty. Mitterrand journeyed to Algiers in October in an effort to dispel the anxieties of the Algerian government.

(JEAN KNECHT)

See also *Dependent States,* below.

GERMANY, FEDERAL REPUBLIC OF

The Federal Republic of Germany (West Germany) is in central Europe, on the North and Baltic seas. Area: 248,687 sq km (96,019 sq mi). Pop. (1984 est., including West Berlin, which is an enclave within East Germany): 61,313,400. Provisional cap.: Bonn. Monetary unit: Deutsche Mark, with (Oct. 29, 1984) a free rate of DM 3.06 to U.S. $1 (DM 3.70 = £1 sterling). Presidents in 1984, Karl Carstens and, from July 1, Richard von Weizsäcker; chancellor, Helmut Kohl.

Politicians of all the established parties in West Germany sank in public esteem during 1984 as more light was thrown on the so-called Flick affair, a scandal that centred on payments made to the parties by the giant Flick industrial concern over many years. The affair led to the resignations of a senior minister and of the speaker of the Bundestag (parliament). It aggravated the increasing problems faced at home and abroad by the centre-right coalition government of the Christian Democratic Union (CDU), its Bavarian wing, the Christian Social Union (CSU), and the Free Democratic Party (FDP). The nonchalant style of leadership practiced by federal Chancellor Helmut Kohl came under attack.

Domestic Affairs. Public prosecutors, who showed a commendable measure of independence and determination in their investigations, alleged that the Flick group had paid out DM 25 million ($6.9 million) in attempts to buy influence in Bonn. The biggest private concern in West Germany, Flick employed more than 42,000 people worldwide and controlled a myriad of firms, including Krauss-Maffei (producers of the Leopard II tank), Dynamit Nobel (makers of chemicals and explosives), a paper company, and producers of baths, pipes, and concrete. It also had large interests in insurance, in the carmakers Daimler-Benz, and in the U.S. chemicals company W. R. Grace.

The most eminent victim of the affair was Count Otto Lambsdorff, the minister of economics, who resigned in June when he was formally charged with corruption, a charge he strongly denied. He was alleged to have waived tax liability on Flick's sale of Daimler-Benz shares in return for donations to FDP funds. In October Rainer Barzel resigned as speaker (president) of the Bundestag after failing to persuade an all-party inquiry of his innocence. He was alleged to have received payments from Flick for resigning as CDU leader in favour of Helmut Kohl in 1973. Barzel, who contested the chancellorship in the 1972 fed-

eral election, did not dispute that he had received the money in question but maintained that it was a payment for his professional advice to Flick in his capacity as a lawyer. Lambsdorff was replaced as economics minister by Martin Bangemann, another member of the FDP and a former member of the European Parliament. Barzel was succeeded in November by Philipp Jenninger (CDU), one of Kohl's closest aides and a specialist on relations with East Germany.

Chancellor Kohl himself appeared before the parliamentary investigation in November to answer claims that he had received payments from Flick for party funds. The chancellor was closely questioned for seven hours. He insisted that he had committed no offense and that there was nothing wrong with industry's making properly documented gifts to party funds. However, the public prosecutor rejected his suggestion that the tax authorities had long known about these practices and had turned a blind eye. Willy Brandt, the chairman of the Social Democratic Party (SPD), and Hans-Dietrich Genscher, the foreign minister and FDP leader, gave evidence about contributions made to their respective parties. Another witness was Franz-Josef Strauss, premier of the Bavarian state assembly and chairman of the CSU, whose party was also a Flick beneficiary.

Hans-Jochen Vogel, the parliamentary leader of the SPD, suggested that, although it would be exaggerated to speak of a national crisis, there was indeed a crisis of confidence in the establishment. Kohl's coalition, all three members of which were affected by the Flick affair, lost ground during the year. The Green Party, the only group untainted by the scandal, gained support.

The repercussions of the affair were seen as one reason for the low turnout—barely 60%—in municipal elections held in Baden-Württemberg in October. The Green Party tripled its share of the vote to around 7%, while all the other parties lost ground. In local elections held in North Rhine-Westphalia in September the Greens polled 9.2%, making them the third force in West Germany's most populous state. The Christian Democrats' share of the vote fell from 46.3% in 1979 to 42.1%. The Social Democrats, who controlled the state government in this SPD bastion, suffered slight losses but emerged as the strongest party overall, winning 42.5%, compared with 44.9% five years earlier. The Free Democrats did poorly, polling an average of less than 5% and so failing to win any seats in many of the 420 city and town councils that were contested.

The only state election held during the year took place in Baden-Württemberg in March. The Greens achieved third place with 8% of the vote (compared with 5.3% in the previous election), while the FDP received 7.2% (8.3%), the SPD 32.4% (32.5%), and the CDU 51.9% (53.4%). The Christian Democrats were reasonably satisfied to have maintained their overall majority, but the loss of support for the FDP raised doubts in many Christian Democrat minds about the stability of the Liberals as national partners. Elections to the European Parliament on June 17 again proved a triumph for the Green Party, which beat the FDP to gain third place behind the CDU-CSU coalition and the SPD. The CDU-CSU coalition won 41 seats, the SPD 33, and the Green Party 7. By receiving 8.2% of the vote, the Green Party for the first time passed the minimum 5% of the vote required to send representatives to the Parliament. Support for the FDP, in contrast, fell from 6% in 1979 to 4.8% in 1984, leaving the party without representation.

On May 23 Richard von Weizsäcker (*see* BIOGRAPHIES) of the CDU was elected federal president in succession to Karl Carstens, who had held the office since 1979. An electoral college made up of the members of the Bundestag, together with delegates from the state assemblies and West Berlin, elected Weizsäcker by 832 votes to 68 for the only other candidate, Luise Rinser of the Green Party. During the year Genscher announced his decision to relinquish the leadership of the FDP in 1985. In April Petra Kelly, Marie-Luise Beck-Oberdorf, and Otto Schily were replaced as parliamentary leaders of the Green Party by Antje Vollmer, Waltraud Schoppe, and Annemarie Borgmann.

The year started badly for the government. In January it was reported that the country's senior officer at NATO headquarters, Gen. Günter Kiessling, had been suspended from duty in December 1983 on suspicion that he had frequented bars used by homosexuals and therefore represented a security risk. Kiessling denied the allegations. After several weeks, during which increasingly uncertain evidence was produced and publicly aired, he was reinstated, though he then decided to take early retirement. The affair shook the reputation of Defense Minister Manfred Wörner (CDU), who had ordered the general's suspension and had shown an unsure hand in dealing with the case.

Business expansion suffered a severe setback in the first half of the year, largely as a result of strikes in the metalworking and printing industries. The disputes concerned the unions' demands for the introduction of a 35-hour week. Eventually, a compromise was reached whereby the workweek would be shortened to 38.5 hours from April 1, 1985. The disputes were the longest and most bitter in the two industries since World War II, and the settlement opened the door to a shorter workweek in all industrial sectors. The strike of metalworkers was particularly damaging, not only because its effect was far-reaching (it involved members of West Germany's biggest union, IG Metall), but also because it seriously disrupted the car-manufacturing industry and related sectors. The unions argued that a shorter workweek would create new jobs. On the other hand, the employers maintained that the best way to reduce unemployment, which remained at well over two million, was to spread part-time work and settle for more modest pay increases.

A move by Friedrich Zimmermann, the right-wing CSU interior minister, to tighten the immigration rules still further was defeated in the Cabinet, mainly because of opposition from the Free Democrats. Zimmermann wanted to reduce the maximum age at which foreign children could join parents living in West Germany from 16 to 6. However, he told the Bundestag in September that foreign children would continue to be admitted up to the age of 16 only if their parents made efforts to send them to German schools. The proposed curbs were principally aimed at West Germany's Turkish population, which accounted for more than 1.5 million of the country's 4.5 million foreign residents.

An alarming government report showed that half of the country's forests were damaged or dying as a result of acid rain. The damage was increasing at a faster rate than expected and included the destruction of deciduous trees, which had previously remained relatively unscathed. More than 97% of the fir trees in the industrial state of North Rhine-Westphalia and about 86% of those in Bavaria were diseased. Zimmermann said the main cause of the damage seemed to be sulfur dioxide and nitric oxide and their compounds. (*See* ENVIRONMENT.)

The government decided to extend the period of national service from 15 to 18 months in order to keep the Bundeswehr, the armed forces, at full strength as the effects of the falling birthrate began to tell. Legislation was being prepared, and it was intended that the first group of servicemen to be affected would be called up in 1989. Defense Minister Wörner's plans provided for a peacetime Bundeswehr strength in the 1990s of 456,000 men, plus 15,000 reservists. This would keep the total only slightly below the current 495,000. Without the introduction of longer national service, it would fall to 290,000.

Foreign Affairs. The policy of the Kohl government toward the Soviet Union and its allies contrasted sharply with that of the SPD administration of former chancellor Helmut Schmidt. Whereas Schmidt saw himself as an "interpreter" of East-West relations, practicing a considerable degree of independence, Kohl declared that direct contact between the U.S. and the Soviet Union could not be replaced by talks between the medium-sized and small countries that were members of the two alliances. West Germany, said Kohl, had a fundamental interest in continuing a dialogue with all the Warsaw Pact countries. Despite a hardening of positions on some central questions, the chancellor believed that the Soviet Union was not looking for direct confrontation with the West; indeed, in certain areas—wherever this approach was in its immediate interest, as in the economic and environmental sectors—the Soviet government appeared willing to make use of existing contacts and was at pains that they should not be broken off.

The arrival of new U.S. intermediate-range nuclear missiles—the first of which were installed in December 1983 with considerably less domestic fuss than had been expected—caused a deterioration of relations between Bonn and Moscow. For the first time in many years, West Germany was subjected to a barrage of hostile Soviet propaganda. It was accused of revanchism and of seeking to regain the eastern territories, now in the U.S.S.R. and Poland, that it lost after World War II. It was notable, however, that relations between East and West Germany remained reasonably good despite the colder East-West climate. (*See* Eastern Europe: *German Democratic Republic, below.*) Kohl claimed that his government was the object of unjustified attacks from the Soviet Union and some other Warsaw Pact countries. He said he would stand firm in the face of political slander and would continue to seek better relations with the Soviets.

Pressure from Moscow led to the abrupt cancellation in September of visits to West Germany by East German leader Erich Honecker and Bulgarian leader Todor Zhivkov. Pres. Nicolae Ceausescu of Romania, however, went ahead with his visit to Bonn in October. His talks centred on ways of restarting negotiations on medium-range

AP/WIDE WORLD

West Germany's economics minister, Otto Lambsdorff, facing indictment in a bribery scandal involving a West German industrial concern, resigned his post late in June.

At Freiensteinau, West Germany, peace movement members knelt in the path of a West German Army armoured car on NATO maneuvers. Soldiers later pulled the demonstrators away, and the vehicle and its crew went on with their mission.
AP/WIDE WORLD

missiles, disarmament, and trade. He also discussed the situation of ethnic Germans in Romania, whose difficulties in securing permission to emigrate had been a matter of concern in Bonn. The visit was the first by a Warsaw Pact leader to a NATO country since the breakdown of the Soviet-U.S. talks on intermediate-range nuclear missiles in Geneva in 1983. While stressing that his country's independence was not affected by its membership in the Warsaw Pact or the Soviet-bloc Council for Mutual Economic Assistance, Ceausescu echoed the Soviet line that there had to be a freeze on missile deployment in Europe before arms talks could be resumed. In November a proposed visit by Foreign Minister Genscher to Poland was canceled at the last minute, because the West Germans claimed that Warsaw had placed "unacceptable conditions" on the trip. The cancellation of the visit, which would have been the first by a NATO foreign minister since the Polish regime lifted martial law, provoked further accusations of West German revanchism from Soviet-bloc countries.

After months of tough bargaining with Washington, West Germany agreed in September to a significant increase in its payments toward NATO's infrastructure program. It was to pay some DM 5.8 billion over six years as its share of the program to improve air bases, ports, fuel pipelines, equipment, and munitions storage. The German contribution, accounting for 26.5% of the total, was considerably more than Bonn originally had been prepared to pay. Even so, it was still below the amount demanded by senior NATO officers, who had the support of the U.S. administration. Earlier, Kohl and Genscher spoke of the need to make a greater contribution to NATO's defense program, and West Germany was as worried as other Western European countries about moves by U.S. senators to force a reduction in the number of U.S. troops in Europe if the Europeans did not raise their share of the costs. The Defense Ministry hoped that the acrimonious quarrel with Washington was now settled.

Ignoring the misgivings of the U.S., West Germany unilaterally extended its North Sea territorial waters south and west of Helgoland to improve surveillance of maritime traffic in the congested waters of the German Bight.

The U.S. strongly opposed the extension on the grounds that it would set a precedent for East Germany and other Communist countries in the Baltic and thus hinder NATO surveillance of the maritime activities of the U.S.S.R. and other Eastern-bloc nations. The area around Helgoland was one of the busiest sea-lanes in the world, and the number of near collisions and potential environmental disasters there had been growing.

In July Kohl visited China, West Germany's third largest trading partner. Trade and economic relations were the main themes of his talks, and an agreement was reached for the assembly of Volkswagen cars in China. In November President Weizsäcker paid a five-day official visit to France, where he was told by Pres. François Mitterrand that their two countries should serve as the driving forces behind the construction of a stronger Europe, with a view to opening up the East-West dialogue.

(NORMAN CROSSLAND)

This article updates the *Macropædia* article GERMANY: *Federal Republic of Germany.*

GREECE

The republic of Greece occupies the southern part of the Balkan Peninsula and several adjoining island groups in southeastern Europe, in and between the Ionian and Aegean seas. Area: 131,957 sq km (50,949 sq mi). Pop. (1984 est.): 9,984,000. Cap.: Athens. Monetary unit: drachma, with (Oct. 29, 1984) a free rate of 125.60 drachmas to U.S. $1 (151.60 drachmas = £1 sterling). President in 1984, Konstantinos Karamanlis; prime minister, Andreas Papandreou.

The most significant political event of 1984 in Greece was the first party congress of the ruling Panhellenic Socialist Movement (Pasok) in Athens in May. It was important not simply because it came a full ten years after Pasok was founded, or for confirming Prime Minister Andreas Papandreou as its leader by democratic process, but because it revealed that the party base was far more radical than its leadership had portrayed it to be. The standing ovation given to "General" Markos Vafiadis, leader of the Communist-dominated insurgents who had tried to seize power in Greece after World War II, reflected the frustrations of generations of Greek leftists who had been relegated to second-class citizenship for almost four decades by an intolerant right wing.

This graphic redefinition of Pasok's ideology affected elections to the European Parliament, which took place on June 17. Dominated as it was by national issues, the campaign resulted in a polarization between Pasok and the conservative opposition, the New Democracy Party, that all but wiped out support for the small parties. Compared with the 1981 general election, Pasok's share of the vote was reduced from 48 to 41%, while New Democracy's rose from 36 to 38%. The pro-Moscow Greek Communist Party (KKE) made modest gains.

Pasok maintained support in the countryside, where the substantial cash advantages from Greece's membership in the European Communities were felt. However, a downward trend in the cities, already apparent in elections to professional associations and student unions, was no doubt prompted by the government's inability to check inflation, curb unemployment, and end the recession. The decline in the quality of life in the cities aggravated the trend. Papandreou tried to react to these setbacks through frequent Cabinet reshuffles, but his failure to adjust policies led to confusion and undermined business confidence.

That the loss of centrist support for the Socialist government was not more pronounced was probably due to New Democracy's inability to offer a credible alternative. At the end of August New Democracy's ailing leader, Evangelos Averoff, resigned. The party's parliamentary group met on September 1 and, by a surprising 70 to 41 vote, elected as its leader Konstantinos Mitsotakis, a Cretan liberal. Mitsotakis had been Papandreou's main adversary in his father's Centre Union party 20 years earlier. His election triggered a fierce personal attack from the prime minister that, if anything, served to rally New Democracy behind the new leader. Papandreou came under strong pressure to call a surprise election a year early, in the autumn of 1984, to catch his rival unprepared, but the prime minister decided against taking the risk.

In international relations there was little change in the desultory pattern that had become the government's hallmark. While paying lip service to a "proud and independent" foreign policy, the administration bowed with remarkable pragmatism to the constraints imposed by a growing dependence on Western arms, money, and sympathy to confront what the Greeks saw as a military threat from Turkey. Papandreou paid an official visit to Libya but, at the same time, his government sought discreetly to improve relations with Israel. He visited Poland to praise the regime there, but at home he endorsed an old commitment to allow NATO surveillance aircraft to use bases in Greece.

The idea of creating a nuclear-free zone in the Balkans was promoted during a meeting of experts in Athens, though Turkey maintained its opposition to the proposal. A significant development in the Balkans was the opening of a dialogue with Albania to secure greater respect for the human rights of the Greek ethnic minority in that country. In exchange, Papandreou indicated that he was ready to renounce Greece's territorial claim on North Epirus (southern Albania) and agreed to end the formal state of war that existed between the two countries under a 44-year-old Greek law.

Greece continued to boycott and harass NATO exercises in the Aegean Sea because, by not including the Greek island of Lemnos in its maneuvers, the alliance was in effect bowing to Turkey's claims that the island could not be militarized. Relations with Turkey had been frozen since the Turkish Cypriot community in Cyprus proclaimed its independence, with Ankara's encouragement, in November 1983. The lack of progress on the Cyprus problem, despite astute efforts by the UN, discouraged Greece from responding to repeated peace overtures from the new Turkish government.

The Papandreou government continued to advertise its support for pro-Soviet positions on East-West relations, the deployment of missiles in Europe, and disarmament. This helped it to secure the cooperation of the KKE in keeping the lid on the smoldering labour front. However, there were increasing signs that the U.S. government was losing patience with some of Papandreou's rhetoric, though this was muted during the U.S. election campaign in view of the powerful Greek-American vote. U.S. resentment was triggered by the expulsion of a Central Intelligence Agency agent from Greece for his involvement in an illegal house search in Athens in April. The Americans claimed that Greek authorities had been uncooperative in a plan to trap an Arab suspected of trying to plant suitcase bombs aboard Western airliners. When the Greeks set the man free, the

AP/WIDE WORLD

In July Greek workers at U.S. military bases in Greece went on strike. After 27 days the workers went back to their jobs. The settlement increased the number of salary raises allowed over an entire span of employment.

U.S. administration revealed how sensitive it had become on matters of international terrorism by suspending the sale of second-hand jet fighters to Greece.

On March 28 Kenneth Whitty, deputy representative of the British Council, and his secretary were killed in a daytime attack in central Athens, and on April 3 a U.S. Air Force sergeant narrowly escaped death when he was fired on as he drove to Athens airport. No arrests were made for either terrorist attack. (MARIO MODIANO)

ICELAND

Iceland is an island republic in the North Atlantic Ocean, near the Arctic Circle. Area: 103,000 sq km (39,769 sq mi). Pop. (1984 est.): 240,000. Cap.: Reykjavik. Monetary unit: króna, with (Oct. 29, 1984) a free rate of 33.90 krónur to U.S. $1 (40.92 krónur = £1 sterling). President in 1984, Vigdís Finnbogadóttir; prime minister, Steingrímur Hermannsson.

Developments in Iceland during 1984 were strongly influenced by economic measures taken the previous year to reduce the rate of inflation. In May 1983 the automatic link between wages and prices was cut, thus eliminating one of the main forces behind the inflationary spiral. Inflation quickly subsided from an annual rate of 130% in early 1983 to 25–30% at the beginning of 1984 and to 13–15% later in the year, by far the lowest in more than a decade. At the same time, there was a sharp reduction in real gross national product, which declined by 6% in 1983.

Real wages fell sharply by an average of some 18% between 1983 and 1984 because prices continued their upward course, albeit at a slower rate, for some time after wages ceased to be adjusted to prices. Discontent was brewing in the trade unions as a result. The public employees' union was the first to present its demands, calling a strike on October 4 that lasted 27 days. The strike was bitter, with both sides equally determined to win. The government wanted to avert another wage explosion and a renewed inflationary surge, while the union wanted to restore the lost purchasing power of its members' salaries. In the end the government gave in and agreed to a 21% increase, to be spread over a period of 14 months until the end of 1985. Other unions secured similar increases, and hopes of bringing the inflation rate below 10% were dashed. In November the government devalued the króna by 12% in an attempt to protect the competitiveness of its exports in the wake of rises.

These developments took place against a background of the country's main economic problem: declining fish stocks. The decline had come about partly as a result of overfishing and partly because the temperature of the sea around Iceland had fallen slightly since 1981, making reproduction of certain whitefish (cod and haddock, for example) more difficult. Overfishing also meant that it had become more difficult for fish to reach reproductive age. Efforts had been made to limit catches, but in 1984 tougher measures were introduced. The fishing fleet was issued boat-by-boat quotas for catches of cod and other whitefish for the year, and the overall catch of whitefish was reduced from 580,000 metric tons in 1983 to 512,000 metric tons in 1984.

Because of the problems of the fishing industry, Iceland's export earnings were not growing in line with the demand for imports. The government had to hold down overall demand in the economy and hence domestic output. Real gross national product declined by some 1–1.5% in 1984, the third year in succession when total production had fallen.

The right-of-centre coalition of the Independence Party and the Progressive Party, which came into office in May 1983, concentrated on reducing inflation and promoting a market economy, following several years of considerable state intervention. Efforts were made to halt the growth of the government sector, to return some government enterprises to the private sector, to bring interest rates into line with prevailing market forces (previously they had been below market rates), and to liberalize foreign-exchange transactions. The coalition partners enjoyed good support in the public-opinion polls during the first part of the year, but their rating slipped considerably at the time of the strike and in its aftermath.

In the autumn the government concluded negotiations with Alusuisse, the Swiss owner of an aluminum smelter in Iceland, for a large increase in the price of electric power sold to the concern from domestic power stations. The low price that Alusuisse had paid for its electricity had been a source of poor relations between the company and the government for some time. Pres. Vigdís Finnbogadóttir ran unopposed for a second four-year term and was reinaugurated on August 1. Iceland's first woman president, she remained highly popular. In April she paid a four-day state visit to Finland. In February Iceland experienced the first armed robbery in its history when a shop's receipts worth $63,000 were taken at gunpoint on the way to the bank. The robbers were caught two days later.

(BJÖRN MATTHÍASSON)

IRELAND

The Republic of Ireland, separated from Great Britain by the North Channel, the Irish Sea, and St. George's Channel, shares its island with Northern Ireland to the northeast. Area: 70,285 sq km (27,137 sq mi). Pop. (1984 est.): 3,575,000. Cap.: Dublin. Monetary unit: Irish pound (punt), with (Oct. 29, 1984) a free rate of Ir£1 to U.S. $1 (Ir£1.20 = £1 sterling). President in 1984, Patrick J. Hillery; prime minister, Garret FitzGerald.

The government of the Republic of Ireland faced two major tasks during 1984. The first was to produce an effective range of options for Northern Ireland, as the meetings of the New Ireland Forum came to an end. The second was to resolve the country's mounting economic difficulties. Both were tackled with considerable energy and resourcefulness, though in neither case was the outcome entirely satisfactory.

The New Ireland Forum had been sitting since May 1983. It had successfully brought together the three main political parties in the republic, the coalition partners Fine Gael and Labour and the opposition Fianna Fail, and the main Catholic nationalist party in Northern Ireland, the Social Democratic and Labour Party. The forum was not attended by any other political groupings from Northern Ireland. Though its deliberations during the early months of 1984 were punctuated by internal disagreements and rumours of incompatibility, the four parties reached agreement and on May 2 published a report putting forward three options for debate about Northern Ireland.

The first was the expected proposal for a united Ireland. The second was a suggestion that there should be a form of joint authority over the North, with Britain and the Republic of Ireland acting as joint guarantors for the unionist and nationalist populations, respectively. The third was for a federal or confederal arrangement, with both the Republic of Ireland and Northern Ireland having their own parliaments but at the same time subscribing to a third, joint assembly with responsibility for such matters

On a sentimental journey to the home of his forebears, U.S. Pres. Ronald Reagan visited Ireland in early June and addressed a joint session of Parliament at Leinster House in Dublin.
AP/WIDE WORLD

as security, relations within the European Communities, and defense.

However, on the very day the report was published, the consensus that it appeared to represent began to fall apart. Charles Haughey, leader of Fianna Fail, declared that his party favoured only the first option, that of a united Ireland, thus casting a shadow over the publication of the report and inviting its rejection by unionists in the North and the more hard-line politicians in Britain, Northern Ireland, and the republic. Nevertheless, the debate that followed produced positive reactions on all sides and led to further reports from both the Official Unionist and Democratic Unionist parties in Northern Ireland. The initiative also established a framework for discussion between the British and Irish governments. When Prime Minister Garret FitzGerald expressed outrage at the Provisional Irish Republican Army's attempt on the lives of the British Cabinet members in October, it was suggested that one effect of the Brighton bomb attack might be to bring London and Dublin closer together. However, at a news conference following a two-day meeting between FitzGerald and British Prime Minister Margaret Thatcher in November, Thatcher brusquely dismissed all three of the forum's proposals on Northern Ireland as unacceptable.

There was evidence of a hardening of attitude in Dublin toward the security problems in the North. In March the Supreme Court ruled that Dominic McGlinchey should be extradited to Northern Ireland, where he was accused of involvement in terrorist offenses. McGlinchey, described as the most wanted man in Ireland, was suspected of being the leader of the Irish National Liberation Army. He had absconded during proceedings to extradite him in 1982. After being recaptured on March 17, he was immediately handed over to the authorities in the North, thus becoming the first person to be extradited for alleged terrorist offenses from the republic to Northern Ireland.

The move took place against a background of general acceptance that certain alleged offenses were so grave that they could not be justified by being described as "political," a defense that had been used successfully in the Irish courts in the past. The spread of terrorism into the republic itself was evidenced by several violent encounters. One of the worst occurred in December 1983 during the rescue of Don Tidey, a supermarket executive kidnapped by the Provisional IRA, when a soldier and a policeman were killed.

The unequal partnership within the government coalition between the main party, Fine Gael, and the Labour Party came under increasing stress as a result of the troubled economy. Unemployment rose steadily during 1984, reaching a record 220,000 in the middle of the year. The two parties had agreed on an economic program that involved considerable spending cuts and reflected a determination to bring public expenditure and borrowing under control. The objective was to phase out the current budget deficit during the lifetime of the coalition partnership. While the prospects for achieving this aim dwindled during the latter half of the year, further plans for tackling the country's economic woes were constructed and endorsed by the partnership and revealed in October. The strategy, entitled "Building on Reality," combined further reductions in government spending with selective efforts at reflation and job creation. It was agreed to against the background of a steady increase in the unpopularity of the government. Yet the evidence of numerous opinion polls had a cementing effect on the partnership, which saw no option other than to continue economic stringency in the hope that falling inflation and greater competitiveness would bring about a recovery.

U.S. Pres. Ronald Reagan—whose own election-year policies were regarded as being responsible for at least some of the monetary and fiscal problems on the Irish side of the Atlantic—visited the republic in June in search of his roots in Ballyporeen, the village in County Tipperary from which an ancestor of his had emigrated to the U.S. in the mid-19th century. In spite of massive security, Reagan and his wife, Nancy, endeared themselves to the Irish people in what was regarded as a faultless public relations exercise, mainly designed for home consumption.

The year was marked by the deaths of the Irish writer Liam O'Flaherty and of Sean MacEntee, who had been the last surviving member of the first Fianna Fail government (*see* OBITUARIES). It was the centenary year of the Gaelic Athletic Association, celebrations of which were extensive and noisy.   (MAVIS ARNOLD)

See also *United Kingdom*, below.

ITALY

A republic of southern Europe, Italy occupies the Apennine Peninsula, Sicily, Sardinia, and a number of smaller islands in the Mediterranean Sea. Area: 301,278 sq km (116,324 sq mi). Pop. (1984 est.): 56,799,000. Cap.: Rome. Monetary unit: lira, with (Oct. 29, 1984) a free rate of 1,900.41 lire to U.S. \$1 (2,293.80 lire = £1 sterling). President in 1984, Alessandro Pertini; premier, Bettino Craxi.

Italy's coalition government of Christian Democrats, Socialists, Republicans, Social Democrats, and Liberals survived opposition pressure and an unusual number of internal disputes during 1984. Voters gave an important appraisal of party performances in elections for the European Parliament and in local elections. The death of the Communist Party leader, Enrico Berlinguer (*see* OBITUARIES), was mourned across party boundaries. The government fought hard to improve economic prospects by cutting wage indexation and tackling the problem of tax evasion by the self-employed. The power of organized crime and the state's efforts to suppress it kept alive the sensitive issue of moral standards in public life.

Domestic Affairs. Pres. Alessandro Pertini's New Year's message expressed sympathy for antinuclear demonstrators and refused to distinguish between U.S. and Soviet responsibility for the nuclear arms race. The political criticism that greeted his speech did nothing to diminish his general popularity. Pertini, at 88, was reportedly eager to stand for another five-year term in 1985.

In February the government, led by Socialist Premier Bettino Craxi, boldly decided to impose cuts in wage indexation by decree, despite its failure to win agreement from the largest of the three trade union confederations, the mainly Communist CGIL (Confederazione Generale Italiana del Lavoro). The CGIL began a campaign against the measure. A demonstration in Rome on March 26, variously estimated as attracting between 500,000 and a million marchers, was described by Berlinguer as the biggest in the history of the republic. In Parliament the Communists managed to prevent the decree from being ratified by the constitutional deadline in mid-April. The government then issued a further decree, though some members of the coalition were unhappy over the worsening relations between the government and opposition and the split in the trade union movement.

The Socialist Party congress in Verona reelected Craxi as party leader by acclamation on May 14. It was an endorsement of his decisive style of leadership. On February 29 Ciriaco De Mita was reelected leader of the country's biggest party, the Christian Democrats, despite disappointing results in the 1983 general elections. Enrico Berlinguer, leader of the Communist Party for 12 years, was taken ill on June 7 while campaigning in Padua for the elections to the European Parliament and died four days later. President Pertini symbolized the nation's grief at the loss of an honest, dedicated man by flying to Berlinguer's bedside and bringing his body back to Rome on the presidential plane. The funeral on June 13 was attended by leading figures in national life and by an estimated crowd of one million. On June 26 the Communists chose their new leader, Alessandro Natta (*see* BIOGRAPHIES), a senior figure in the party who had worked closely with Berlinguer and supported his policies.

Berlinguer's death was thought to have influenced voting in the European elections, which took place on June 17. For the first time the Communists headed a national poll with 33.3% of the vote, compared with the Christian Democrats' 33%. The Christian Democrats were more than satisfied, however, since they gained almost the same share of the vote as in the 1983 general elections. Many commentators had concluded that their disappointing performance then heralded a period of sharp and irreversible decline. The Socialists had the most reason to be saddened. The party providing the current premier might have expected to receive an electoral bonus, but the Socialists won only 11.2% of the vote, slightly less than in 1983. Elections in 88 municipalities and one region, Sardinia, a week later gave more encouragement to the Christian Democrats. In Sardinia they stayed in first place, ahead of the Communists.

Craxi had promised a thorough review of the coalition's problems and prospects once the European elections were over. The parliamentary committee investigating the secret Masonic lodge P2 had already indicated in a preliminary report that it regarded the membership lists in the possession of the authorities as sound. Its final report on July 3 endorsed that view and embarrassed the government because Pietro Longo, budget minister and leader of the Social Democrats, appeared in the lists, although he had always denied membership. A crisis was averted when, on July 12, he quietly stepped down from his govern-

Italian Communists, long a turbulent factor in national elections and frequent victors in local ones, led in a national poll for the first time in the election to select delegates to the European Parliament. Ugo Vetere, mayor of Rome, savours the victory at a rally in Piazza Navona.

ment post, though he remained leader of his party. In the improved climate, the coalition completed its review successfully, though the Christian Democrats believed Craxi's leadership would come under scrutiny again in mid-1985, when most municipal, provincial, and regional elections were due.

In early January Giuseppe Fava, a journalist who had written extensively about the Mafia, was shot dead in Catania, Sicily. In reviewing recent statistics, judges agreed that organized crime in the form of the Sicilian Mafia, the Neapolitan Camorra, and the Calabrian N'Drangheta had spread throughout Italy, and that the profits from the drug trade had made crime international. Rivalry between two branches of the Camorra brought violence to a Naples suburb in late August when criminals opened fire on the street, killing eight people and wounding five. On September 25 the Sicilian financier Michele Sindona, already serving a 25-year sentence in the U.S., was sent back to Italy under a new arrangement for temporary extradition. Sindona faced trial for fraud and conspiracy to murder. When the trial was over, he was to be returned to the U.S. On October 5 Foreign Minister Giulio Andreotti barely survived an opposition motion calling for him to resign because of his allegedly questionable relationship with Sindona.

In the autumn magistrates and police launched one of their biggest assaults against the Mafia by issuing 366 warrants based on information given by Tommaso Buscetta, the first Mafia chief to break the organization's code of silence before the law. U.S. and Italian authorities cooperated closely in following up the leads provided by Buscetta. The Mafia apparently reasserted itself by murdering eight men in Palermo on October 18.

Terrorism returned to the streets of Rome when the director general of the multinational force of observers in Sinai, the U.S. diplomat Leamon Hunt, was shot dead outside his house in February. The Italian Red Brigades claimed responsibility. On October 19 a Rome judge ordered the arrest of Gen. Pietro Musumeci, a former deputy head of Sismi, the military secret service, and three other officers. The charges included embezzlement, conspiracy, and illegal possession of arms and explosives. The arrests followed a report by a parliamentary committee overseeing the work of the secret services, which had accused Sismi of serious irregularities at the time when the general was a serving officer. Sismi's role in negotiating with the Camorra and the Red Brigades for the release of a kidnapped Christian Democrat politician in 1981 was heavily criticized. In November seven Lebanese were arrested near Rome, foiling what Italian authorities believed was a plot to blow up the U.S. embassy. Documents the men were carrying indicated that they may have belonged to the shadowy terrorist group known as Islamic Jihad ("Holy War").

Italy and the Vatican signed a new concordat on February 18. It replaced Mussolini's 1929 concordat and recognized that Roman Catholicism was not the official religion of Italy. School instruction in the Catholic religion would be optional. In May the Institute for Religious Works (IOR), the Vatican bank, took part in the final settlement arranged by the liquidators of the failed Banco Ambrosiano group, which had been run by the late Roberto Calvi. The Vatican, hard hit by its involvement with Calvi, agreed to contribute some $240 million. It was stressed that IOR was making the payment in recognition of a moral involvement but not culpability. A report on the 1981 assassination attempt on Pope John Paul II, submitted to Italian authorities by Judge Ilario Martella in November, implicated Bulgarian officials in a conspiracy to kill the pope and asserted that a second gunman, besides Mehmet Ali Agca, was involved.

Foreign Affairs. The Italian contingent in the multinational peacekeeping force in Lebanon was warmly welcomed when it returned to Italy in late February. It had won a reputation for competence and good relations with the local population. In late August three Italian minesweepers and a support ship joined U.S., British, French, and Soviet vessels clearing mines from the Gulf of Suez. There was a brief but sharp row with West Germany in September after Andreotti stated that there were two Germanys and two there should remain. Bonn objected strongly to his rejection of West Germany's commitment to the idea of eventual reunification.

Despite the efforts of the antinuclear movement, the siting of cruise missiles in Sicily never became a burning issue, and the government had no difficulty in maintaining its commitment to NATO. Andreotti was the first of three Western foreign ministers to meet Soviet Foreign Minister Andrey Gromyko in Moscow in April, but he failed to break any new ground in East-West relations. Toward the end of the year the premier began a series of meetings with other Western European leaders as he prepared for Italy's six-month presidency of the European Communities' Council of Ministers from Jan. 1, 1985.

The Economy. In his annual report at the end of May, Carlo Ciampi, governor of the Bank of Italy, said that the high level of public spending was the economy's most serious problem. Exports were increasing, but inflation was not falling fast enough and the unemployment rate stood at 12%. The government, in preparing its budget for 1985, aimed to bring inflation down to 7% from an expected 10% in 1984. It also wanted to hold public spending at the same level in real terms and to reduce the public-sector deficit. Trade unionists, as victims of the government's cuts in wage indexation earlier in the year, fully supported the finance minister's plan for new methods of assessment designed to end tax evasion by the self-employed.

(CAMPBELL PAGE)

LIECHTENSTEIN

A landlocked constitutional monarchy of central Europe, Liechtenstein is united with Switzerland by a customs and monetary union. Area: 160 sq km (62 sq mi). Pop. (1984 est.): 27,000. Cap.: Vaduz. Monetary unit: Swiss franc, with (Oct. 29, 1984) a free rate of SwF 2.52 to U.S. $1 (SwF 3.04 = £1 sterling). Sovereign prince, Francis Joseph II; deputy head of state from Aug. 26, 1984, Prince Hans Adam; chief of government, Hans Brunhart.

On July 1, 1984, the electors of Liechtenstein approved a new law extending the right to vote to women. The motion was passed by a narrow margin of 2,370 votes to 2,251. On two previous occasions, in 1971 and 1973, the proposal had been rejected by the all-male electorate. In recent years external sources had exerted a certain amount of pressure on the principality to change its laws; in 1978 Liechtenstein had been admitted to the Council of Europe on condition that it broaden the franchise.

Francis Joseph II, ruling prince of Liechtenstein for 46 years, stepped down on August 26 and handed over the bulk of his executive authority to his eldest son and heir, Crown Prince Hans Adam (*see* BIOGRAPHIES). It was reported that one of Prince Hans Adam's objectives was to propose Liechtenstein for membership in the UN.

The economy remained relatively untouched by the recent recession. Unemployment was virtually unheard of, and the inflation rate continued to be low.

(K. M. SMOGORZEWSKI)

This article updates the *Micropædia* article LIECHTENSTEIN.

LUXEMBOURG

The Benelux country of Luxembourg is a landlocked constitutional monarchy in western Europe. Area: 2,586 sq km (999 sq mi). Pop. (1984 est.): 366,000. Cap.: Luxembourg. Monetary unit: Luxembourg franc, at par with the Belgian franc, with (Oct. 29, 1984) a free rate of LF 61.81 to U.S. $1 (LF 74.60 = £1 sterling). Grand duke, Jean; prime ministers in 1984, Pierre Werner and, from July 20, Jacques Santer.

The general election held on June 17, 1984, brought to an end the centre-right coalition of Social Christians and Liberals that had ruled Luxembourg for three decades. The greatest gains were made, unexpectedly, by the Socialists, who increased their share of seats by 7 to 21. The Ecologists entered the Chamber of Deputies for the first time, winning two seats. (For full results, see *Political Parties,* above.) Though the traditional coalition parties still held a majority of 39 in the 64-seat Chamber, Grand Duke Jean considered that the Socialists had won enough support to be given the opportunity to take part in government.

After several weeks of bargaining, the Social Christians and Socialists reached an understanding, and the new government was sworn in on July 20. The Cabinet comprised five Social Christians and four Socialists. Social Christian Jacques Santer became prime minister, replacing Pierre Werner, who retired. Jacques Poos, leader of the Socialists, was deputy prime minister and foreign minister.

The swing to the left was thought to have resulted in part from a rise in unemployment to 2%, an unusually high figure for Luxembourg, coupled with a decline in the steel industry. Grand Duke Jean visited the U.S. in November.

(K. M. SMOGORZEWSKI)

This article updates the *Macropædia* article The Low Countries: *Luxembourg.*

MALTA

The republic of Malta, a member of the Commonwealth, comprises the islands of Malta, Gozo, and Comino in the Mediterranean Sea between Sicily and Tunisia. Area: 320 sq km (124 sq mi). Pop. (1984 est.): 332,200. Cap.: Valletta. Monetary unit: Maltese lira (formerly Maltese pound), with (Oct. 29, 1984) a free rate of Lm 0.46 to U.S. $1 (Lm 0.55 = £1 sterling). President in 1984, Agatha Barbara; prime ministers, Dom Mintoff and, from December 22, Carmelo Mifsud Bonnici.

Dom Mintoff, prime minister of Malta since 1971, resigned on Dec. 22, 1984, and turned over the reins of government to his chosen successor, Carmelo Mifsud Bonnici, senior deputy prime minister. Mintoff, 68, had reportedly been considering retiring for some months but had delayed doing so until the crisis over the future of Malta's church schools had eased. Mifsud Bonnici, 51, was a lawyer who had served as minister of education since September 1983.

In April a new law enabled the government to deny a license to secondary schools not providing free education and to take them over and run them at the expense of the owner, which in most cases was the Roman Catholic Church. Eight church schools were denied a license. Negotiations between the Vatican and the Maltese government failed to ease the growing tension, and in September the church kept all its 72 schools closed. The disruption spread after the teachers' union, calling for better working conditions, issued a work-to-rule directive to its members in state schools. When the government locked out those following the directive, the union called a strike that lasted for seven weeks and was marked by a number of violent incidents. In November striking teachers returned to work, and a modus vivendi was reached between the church and government for the current scholastic year, allowing all schools to reopen. Meanwhile, the law enacted in October 1983 to nationalize certain church property was annulled as unconstitutional.

There were a number of bomb incidents during the year. Malta and Libya signed a treaty of friendship covering political, economic, and military cooperation during a visit by Libyan leader Col. Muammar al-Qaddafi to Valletta in November. Mintoff's four-day trip to the U.S.S.R. in December confirmed the importance of Malta's role in Soviet strategy in the Mediterranean. (ALBERT GANADO)

MONACO

A sovereign principality on the northern Mediterranean coast, Monaco is bounded on land by the French département of Alpes-Maritimes. Area: 1.90 sq km (0.73 sq mi). Pop. (1984 est.): 28,000. Monetary unit: French franc, with (Oct. 29, 1984) a free rate of F 9.41 to U.S. $1 (F 11.36 = £1 sterling). Chief of state, Prince Rainier III; minister of state in 1984, Jean Herly.

Pres. François Mitterrand of France paid an official visit to Monaco on Jan. 19–20, 1984. It was the seventh visit to the principality by a French head of state, the last having been by Charles de Gaulle in October 1960. On the occasion of Mitterrand's visit, Jean-Charles Rey, president of the National Council (parliament), described Monaco as being a "discrete, modest, but faithful ally of France." During the visit agreement was reached on the demarcation of Monaco's territorial waters and on restrictions to overflying of the principality. In August the prince of Wales visited Monaco.

Prince Rainier's elder daughter, Princess Caroline, who had married Stefano Casiraghi in December 1983, gave birth to a son in June 1984. The child was baptized Andrea Albert. (K. M. SMOGORZEWSKI)

This article updates the *Micropædia* article MONACO.

NETHERLANDS, THE

A constitutional monarchy of northwestern Europe, The Netherlands, a Benelux country, is on the North Sea. Area: 41,509 sq km (16,027 sq mi). Pop. (1984 est.): 14,437,400. Cap., Amsterdam; seat of government, The Hague. Monetary unit: guilder, with (Oct. 29, 1984) a free rate of 3.45 guilders to U.S. $1 (4.16 guilders = £1 sterling). Queen, Beatrix; prime minister in 1984, Ruud Lubbers.

During 1984 political debate in The Netherlands centred on the issues of nuclear weapons and the level of social benefits. The nuclear-weapons debate reached a climax in June when the government of Prime Minister Ruud Lubbers clarified its position after a long period of consultation and negotiation. The government decided that it was prepared in principle to accept the stationing of 48 U.S. medium-range cruise missiles in The Netherlands, but that the final decision would be delayed until Nov. 1, 1985. If the Soviet government had not frozen its deployment of SS-20 missiles by 1988, some of the cruise missiles would then be stationed; the number would depend on the progress of East-West arms-control negotiations.

According to Lubbers, the government's objective was to create the possibility of influencing disarmament negotiations by pressing the Soviets to show willingness to restrict missile deployment. However, the decision could also be interpreted as a clever attempt to reconcile the wishes of the Christian Democratic Appeal (CDA) and the Liberal

Party (VVD), the two government parties. The VVD, which favoured deployment, concluded that the government had in fact decided to accept the missiles, since it was inconceivable that the U.S.S.R. would be influenced by the feelings of a small country like The Netherlands. On the other hand, the CDA, which was divided on the issue, was satisfied that the government had given priority to a policy of arms control. In a parliamentary debate on June 14, the proposal was accepted by 79 votes to 71. Seven CDA members refused to accept the motion, and the government secured a majority only with the support of the small right-wing parties.

In an effort to reduce the budget deficit, the minister of social affairs and employment, Jan de Koning, announced cuts in social benefits that came into effect in July. The outline of budget measures contained in the queen's speech, delivered to Parliament by Queen Beatrix on September 18, suggested that the purchasing power of those on lower incomes would not be reduced. When pressed on the question by Joop den Uyl, parliamentary leader of the Socialist Party (PVDA), however, Lubbers was forced to admit that such an interpretation was incorrect.

The government appeared optimistic about economic prospects in the short term. However, the trade unions were concerned about the threat to lower-income groups, while employers objected that the government had not done enough to bring about economic recovery. In Parliament the budget proposals were opposed by the PVDA, which predicted that they would divide society into "haves" and "have-nots."

From March to October a parliamentary committee conducted an inquiry into relations between the government and the Rijn-Schelde-Verolme (RSV) industrial concern, which had gone bankrupt despite receiving substantial financial support from the government. Mismanagement, particularly with regard to a pipeline project in Algeria and a coal-mining venture in the U.S., had resulted in huge losses. The inquiry revealed that the government had not kept Parliament fully informed, and that the government itself had not known the full extent of the problems RSV faced.

Pres. François Mitterrand of France paid an official visit to The Netherlands on February 6–7. The decline of the French language in the Dutch educational system and the political tensions threatening the European Communities were discussed. One indication of the worsening social climate in The Netherlands was the rise of the semifascist Centrum Party, which began to make a showing in some local elections.   (DICK BOONSTRA)

See also *Dependent States,* below.

This article updates the *Macropædia* article The Low Coun-tries: *The Netherlands.*

NORWAY

A constitutional monarchy of northern Europe, Norway occupies the western part of the Scandinavian Peninsula, with coastlines on the Skagerrak, the North Sea, the Norwegian Sea, and the Arctic Ocean. Area: 323,895 sq km (125,057 sq mi), excluding the Svalbard Archipelago and Jan Mayen Island. Pop. (1984 est.): 4,140,600. Cap.: Oslo. Monetary unit: krone, with (Oct. 29, 1984) a free rate of 8.88 kroner to U.S. $1 (10.72 kroner = £1 sterling). King, Olav V; prime minister in 1983, Kåre Isaachsen Willoch.

The year 1984 opened dramatically, with one of the biggest espionage scandals in Norway's recent history. In January Arne Treholt, a Foreign Ministry official and former junior Cabinet minister, was arrested while preparing to leave Oslo with secret documents allegedly intended for his contacts in the Soviet State Security Committee (KGB). It subsequently emerged that he had also earned "consultancy" fees for information given to the Iraqi government. Months passed without a date being set for Treholt's trial. In early October an Oslo newspaper, *Dagbladet,* published a letter, reportedly smuggled from his prison cell, in which he claimed that he had been "framed" by the FBI.

Because of Treholt's close connections with the opposition Labour Party, particularly some of its leading left-wing personalities, it seemed likely at first that the incident would damage Labour and benefit the ruling centre-right coalition of the Conservative, Christian People's, and Centre parties. Some observers thought it might even affect the outcome of parliamentary elections due in September 1985. Later, however, the Treholt debate faded, and the economy again became the dominant political issue.

Norway benefited in a number of ways from the strong U.S. dollar. Export earnings and tax revenues from offshore oil and gas were far higher than forecast, partly because output from the Anglo-Norwegian Statfjord field exceeded expectations but also because, with petroleum prices fixed in dollars, the krone price was higher than ever before. The strong dollar also boosted earnings from more traditional exports such as shipping services, paper and pulp, light metals, ferroalloys, and fish. Coupled with a 5 billion kroner fall in imports of goods and services for the oil sector, the high exports gave a record balance of payments surplus of 14.9 billion kroner for the first six months of 1984. This compared with a 16.3 billion kroner surplus for all of 1983, itself a record year. Industrial output rose slightly, as did the total number of people in employment. Nevertheless, registered unemployment remained high, by Norwegian standards, at just over 4% of the labour force. Young people and women were hardest hit.

The government of Prime Minister Kåre Willoch had been criticized for the tight rein on public spending that it had maintained since taking office in 1981. Although this policy had helped to slow the inflation rate to 6.5% in 1984, from 13.6% in 1981, it had not created new jobs. Moreover, it had affected education, health services, and care of the elderly. In its budget proposals for 1985, drawn up with an eye to the forthcoming elections, the government went some way toward meeting these criticisms. The draft budget provided for marked increases in expenditure in order to stimulate growth and for cuts in both personal and corporate taxation. Much of the extra money was earmarked for the social services, regional development, local government (including health services), education, and development aid. As in previous years, spending on defense rose steeply, by 1.4 billion kroner to 14.3 billion kroner.

A key issue during the year was the fate of a £20 billion gas-sales agreement with the U.K. covering the export of gas from the Sleipner group of fields on the Norwegian shelf. Norway needed to begin this development quickly in order to maintain offshore construction activity and to prevent a steep fall in petroleum production and revenues in the 1990s. A provisional deal signed in February between Statoil, the state petroleum company, and the British Gas Corporation (BGC) laid the technical and economic foundation for an integrated development project. However, the U.K. government insisted on revising the agreement, apparently believing that BGC had overestimated Britain's gas needs in the early 1990s, when Sleipner was expected to come on stream. Negotiations dragged on throughout the year, and in August Statoil warned that the 1990 start-up date had been pushed back to 1991.   (FAY GJESTER)

See also *Dependent States,* below.

PORTUGAL

A republic of southwestern Europe, metropolitan Portugal is on the Atlantic coast of the Iberian Peninsula, which it shares with Spain. Area: 91,985 sq km (35,516 sq mi), including the Azores and Madeira island groups/archipelagoes in the Atlantic. Pop. (1984 est.): 10,198,000. Cap.: Lisbon. Monetary unit: escudo, with (Oct. 29, 1984) a free rate of 163.38 escudos to U.S. $1 (197.20 escudos = £1 sterling). President in 1984, Gen. António dos Santos Ramalho Eanes; premier, Mário Soares.

Portugal's coalition government comprising the Socialist Party (PSP) and the Social Democratic Party (PSD), which had come to power in June 1983, survived a crisis in March 1984 when the PSD congress voted to remain in the coalition. Deputy Premier Carlos Mota Pinto, president of the PSD, won endorsement for his policy of continuing the alliance when his motion secured 55% of the vote. The leader of the opposing faction was João Bosco Mota Amaral, president of the Azores regional assembly, who received the backing of former premier Francisco Pinto Balsemão. However, elements within the PSD continued to express opposition to the alliance with the PSP, and Mota Pinto's control over the party was tenuous, since his supporters did not command an overall majority on the PSD national council. Marcelo Revelo de Sousa, leader of a small but influential right-wing faction on the council, was one of the most vocal opponents of the alliance.

At the same congress, Mota Pinto successfully introduced statutory amendments that effectively curbed the power of the party secretary-general. In June the holder of that post, António Capucho, resigned from the Cabinet, where he had held the quality of life portfolio.

A further crisis developed in June when Mota Pinto himself threatened to resign and withdraw the PSD from the coalition because of disagreements over economic policies. At the same time, Premier Mário Soares (PSP) faced mounting pressure from the far left over rising prices. Soares reacted by challenging his critics to propose an alternative policy and introducing a motion of confidence in the Assembly on June 7; the result gave him the endorsement he needed. He followed up this success by broadcasting a speech to the nation in which he reminded the people of his election promise to tackle the serious budget and current-account deficits by means of austerity measures.

The split in the coalition was caused by long delays in implementing promised economic reforms. Austerity measures introduced at the end of 1983 had brought a return of international banking confidence, but they also affected the country's lower-paid workers. The second stage of the government's financial recovery program was designed, among other things, to mitigate the effects of austerity. It also aimed to introduce revised guidelines for banking and insurance, as well as various fiscal reforms, including a value-added tax. Also, in anticipation of Portugal's accession to the European Communities (EC), scheduled for 1986, the government was seeking to restructure regional planning in order to take full advantage of EC funds. One of its most important aims was to reorganize several large public-sector concerns whose failures had proved a drain on national resources; the need to conduct a thorough review of their finances had seriously delayed the entire program. Finally, in July, the program was presented for discussion to the Council for Social Coordination, a newly established body made up of representatives from government, industry, and the trade unions.

It was revealed that Lieut. Col. Otelo Saraiva de Carvalho, a key figure in Portugal's 1974 revolution who had run second to Pres. António dos Santos Ramalho Eanes in the 1976 presidential election, had been arrested, along with over 40 others, during the period June 19-20. The security crackdown was directed against suspected members of an urban guerrilla group known as the Popular Forces of April 25 (FP-25), which had come to prominence in 1980 and had claimed responsibility for several terrorist murders, acts of industrial sabotage, and bank robberies. Many of those arrested were members of the extreme left-wing Forces of Popular Unity, a political group (of which Carvalho was a founder member) not previously linked with the terrorist acts. In October Carvalho was formally charged with founding, promoting, and directing the FP-25 terrorist organization. The FP-25 claimed credit for a grenade explosion at the U.S. embassy in Lisbon on November 25, which caused some property damage.

A new and tougher internal security and civil protection bill was put before the Assembly just as the June arrests took place. The bill proposed to grant police the powers to carry out house searches, intercept mail, and tap telephone conversations without obtaining a warrant in advance in cases where suspected terrorism was involved. The Assembly was also considering a proposal to set up an intelligence agency to combat international and domestic terrorism—no such organization had existed since the revolution. The government bill was a response to a number of international terrorist incidents, including the 1983 assassination of a Palestine Liberation Organization official at a Socialist International meeting and the assault by Armenians on the Turkish embassy in Lisbon.

In mid-October it was announced that Portugal's 1984 budget deficit would exceed original forecasts by 73 billion escudos, or 41.5%. The deficit was swelled by the need to provide extra funds for the money-losing public sector and because a forecast transfer to the budget of Banco de Portugal profits worth 45 billion escudos could not take place. The widening of the budget deficit meant that Portugal would not be able to meet the deficit target set out in its 1984 letter of intent to the International Monetary Fund, and a revised figure was agreed on. Gross domestic product was expected to fall by 1.5% in 1984, after declining by 0.1% in 1983. Growth was expected to pick up by 1985 as private consumption increased.

In October Minister of Finance Ernani Lopes signed an agreement in Luxembourg whereby the EC undertook to use its best efforts to ensure that Portugal became a member of the Community by Jan. 1, 1986. Negotiations on

AP/WIDE WORLD

Portuguese Premier Mário Soares (right) embraces Bolivian Vice-Pres. Jaime Paz Zamora as the latter learns during a Lisbon visit that his president, Hernán Siles Zuazo, has been kidnapped by a military faction in La Paz, Bolivia.

enlarging the EC with the addition of Spain and Portugal had stalled during the summer in the face of disagreements among existing members about the terms of accession.

Portugal was visited by U.K. Prime Minister Margaret Thatcher in April and by South Africa's prime minister, P. W. Botha, in May.　　　　　　　　　(MICHAEL WOOLLER)

See also *Dependent States*, below.

SAN MARINO

The republic of San Marino is a landlocked enclave in northeastern Italy. Area: 61 sq km (24 sq mi). Pop. (1984 est.): 22,800. Cap.: San Marino. Monetary unit: Italian lira, with (Oct. 29, 1984) a free rate of 1,900.41 lire to U.S. $1 (2,293.80 lire = £1 sterling). The republic is governed by two *capitani regenti,* or co-regents, appointed every six months by a popularly elected Grand and General Council. Executive power rests with the Congress of State, composed of the co-regents, three secretaries of state (for foreign and political affairs, internal affairs, and economic affairs), and seven ministers. In 1984 the secretaries of state were, respectively, Giordano Bruno Refi, Alvaro Selva, and Emilio della Balda.

The left-wing coalition of Communists, Socialists, and United Socialists, which had retained power in the 1983 general elections, continued to govern San Marino throughout 1984. The co-regents Renzo Renzi, a Communist, and Germano de Biagi, a Socialist, were succeeded at the end of their six-month term of office in April by Gloriana Ranocchini, a Communist, and Giorgo Crescentini, a Socialist.

A law promulgated in 1928 had denied the women of San Marino the right to retain their nationality, and hence their right to vote, work, and own or inherit property, if they chose to marry outside the republic. A proposal to change this law, proclaimed by the republic's judiciary in 1982 and rejected in a referendum the following year, was finally instated on March 27, 1984.

The Socialist secretary of state for foreign and political affairs, Giordano Bruno Refi, attended the Stockholm Conference on Confidence- and Security-Building Measures and Disarmament in Europe, which began its first session on January 17.

During the year the republic issued a series of coins depicting nine scientists whose discoveries represented vital contributions to the advancement of civilization.

　　　　　　　　　　　　　(K. M. SMOGORZEWSKI)

This article updates the *Micropædia* article SAN MARINO.

SPAIN

A constitutional monarchy of southwestern Europe with coastlines on the Bay of Biscay, the Atlantic Ocean, and the Mediterranean Sea, Spain shares the Iberian Peninsula with Portugal; it includes the Balearic and Canary island groups, in the Mediterranean and the Atlantic, respectively. Area: 504,750 sq km (194,885 sq mi). Pop. (1984 est.): 38,-430,000. Cap.: Madrid. Monetary unit: peseta, with (Oct. 29, 1984) a free rate of 171.71 pesetas to U.S. $1 (207.25 pesetas = £1 sterling). King, Juan Carlos I; premier in 1984, Felipe González Márquez.

The regional election campaign in Spain's Basque Country in February 1984 was violent from the outset. On February 23 Enrique Casas Vila, a senator and Basque Socialist Party candidate, was murdered. Responsibility was initially claimed by an extreme faction of the Euzkadi ta Azkatasuna (ETA; Basque Homeland and Liberty), but ETA later denied being involved, and the killing was claimed by another group. A general strike throughout the Basque Country on February 24 was timed to coincide with the senator's funeral, attended by Premier Felipe González Márquez, a close friend of the murdered man. In elections to the regional parliament held two days later, the ruling Basque Nationalist Party won 32 of the 75 seats, and the Basque Socialist Party strongly increased its showing by winning 19 seats. Herri Batasuna (United People), a political arm of ETA, held its 11 seats but announced that it would continue to boycott the Basque parliament. In December José Antonio Ardanza became premier of the regional government, succeeding Carlos Garaicoetxea, who resigned.

Responsibility for the murder of five ETA members between December 1983 and February 1984 was claimed by the Antiterrorist Liberation Groups (GAL), a new group that was apparently carrying out retaliatory killings. Herri Batasuna accused the ruling Partido Socialista Obrero Español (PSOE; Spanish Socialist Workers Party) of arming the GAL, though informed speculation at the time suggested that the GAL assassins were in the pay of disenchanted Basque business people or drug dealers. In October a radical change in French policy was indicated by the extradition to Spain of five ETA members to stand trial on terrorist charges, and during 1984 France exiled a number of other active ETA members. Partly as a result of this increased pressure on ETA, over 100 guerrillas took advantage of the Spanish government's offer allowing them to be rehabilitated into society after standing trial. Despite these successes, acts of

UPI/BETTMANN

In November over one million people jammed Madrid's largest boulevard to protest against the government's attempts to curtail the role of the Roman Catholic Church in schools.

violence in the Basque Country continued.

Regional elections in Catalonia in April confirmed the ascendancy of the ruling centre-right Convergencia i Unio (CIU), which won 72 of the 135 seats. The victory endorsed the CIU's appeal for the fullest possible transfer of powers from Madrid to Catalan jurisdiction. Although support for the Socialists increased to 41, they were the principal losers since the final result rejected their campaign call for closer links and cooperation with the central government. In May long-dormant charges were brought by the attorney general against Jordi Pujol, president of the Catalan regional parliament, and 24 others, all former executives of the failed Banca Catalana. The charges involved embezzlement and falsification of bank documents between 1974 and 1982, when the bank collapsed.

The central government's plans to modernize the iron and steel and shipbuilding industries encountered heavy resistance from unions, but plans for light industry and textiles moved forward more smoothly. The unemployment rate reached 18.6% in November, the highest in Europe. After protracted negotiations among the government, trade unions, and employers' organizations, a two-year pact was signed in October limiting wage rises to 5.5–7.5% in 1985 and 4.5–6.5% in 1986. The government was to extend welfare entitlements to a greater percentage of the unemployed, while the employers secured a reduction in social security contributions and additional tax incentives.

In his state of the nation speech in October, Premier González claimed that the transfer of power to regional governments was a principal achievement of his administration, and he stressed the need for a spirit of cooperation. The major surprise in his speech was the announcement that the promised referendum on Spain's membership in NATO would take place by February 1986. (The González government had suspended Spain's membership after it came to power in December 1982.) In his reply, Manuel Fraga Iribarne, leader of the opposition and of the Alianza Popular, was deeply critical of the speech and of the government's record on unemployment, inflation, and security matters. Following the debate, the opposition alleged that during the 1982 election the PSOE had been partly funded by the West German Social Democratic Party and the Flick holding concern, whose payments to West German politicians were already a subject of great controversy there. (See *Germany, Federal Republic of,* above.) Fraga himself admitted receiving electoral contributions from the West German Christian Democratic Union.

The issue of Spain's proposed accession to the European Communities (EC) by January 1986 loomed large as crucial deadlines in the accession timetable were passed. The EC's failure to offer comprehensive plans on some of the more controversial topics provoked accusations from the Spanish that the EC was not negotiating in good faith. However, there was a breakthrough at the EC summit in Dublin in December, when an agreement on wine production was reached.

Relations with Portugal were strained throughout the year by almost constant poaching in that country's waters by Spain's fishing fleet. There were also confrontations between EC fishery-protection vessels and the Spanish fleet, as well as an increase in the number of fishing incidents between Spain and its North African neighbours. The government held talks with the U.K. on fully reopening Spain's border with Gibraltar, in accordance with the 1980 Lisbon Declaration. In November Spain agreed to reopen the border by February 1985, and the U.K., while insisting that it would honour the wishes of the Gibraltarians in any future negotiations, agreed to discuss the issue of the U.K.'s sovereignty over Gibraltar.

King Juan Carlos I's visit to Moscow in May illustrated the new mood of reconciliation between Spain and the U.S.S.R. González was strongly criticized at home for his unannounced meeting with Libyan leader Col. Muammar al-Qaddafi in Majorca on December 19. Qaddafi denied allegations that he was helping to fund the ETA and assured González that the new rapprochement between Libya and Morocco would not harm Spanish interests in North Africa.   (MICHAEL WOOLLER)

SWEDEN

A constitutional monarchy of northern Europe, Sweden occupies the eastern side of the Scandinavian Peninsula, with coastlines on the North and Baltic seas and the Gulf of Bothnia. Area: 486,661 sq km (187,901 sq mi). Pop. (1984 est.): 8,341,000. Cap.: Stockholm. Monetary unit: krona, with (Oct. 29, 1984) a free rate of 8.72 kronor to U.S. $1 (10.52 kronor = £1 sterling). King, Carl XVI Gustaf; prime minister in 1984, Olof Palme.

Against a background of increasing tension between the two superpowers, Sweden during 1984 became one of the few places where the U.S. and the Soviet Union were still talking with one another about disarmament. The Stockholm peace conference—the Conference on Confidence- and Security-Building Measures and Disarmament in Europe—opened in an appropriately chilly January. It was attended by 35 foreign ministers, including U.S. Secretary of State George Shultz and Soviet Foreign Minister Andrey Gromyko (*see* BIOGRAPHIES). Prime Minister Olof Palme referred to it as "a symbol of hope." The conference itself was deadlocked for most of the year on procedural matters, flaring briefly to life now and again when one superpower denounced the other's policies. Nonetheless, it constituted a meeting place between West and East, with plenty of time remaining before a final resolution had to be submitted to the Conference on Security and Cooperation in Europe in November 1986.

Sweden's own foreign affairs were once again dominated by alleged violations of its territory, this time by both submarines and aircraft. Once again there were searches for unidentified foreign submarines in Swedish territorial waters. The longest and costliest to date was concentrated off the southern naval base of Karlskrona and ended inconclusively in April. The high point of the search came on March 4, when the Swedish Navy claimed that frogmen who were presumably trying to escape from a trapped midget submarine had attempted to come ashore on an island but had been driven back by submachine-gun fire. At the close of the bizarre proceedings, however, the Navy was able to produce very little evidence that unidentified foreign submarines had in fact penetrated Swedish defenses.

While no nation was named as the aggressor, the search did little to improve relations with the Soviet Union, which had been at a low ebb since 1981, when a Soviet Whisky-class submarine carrying nuclear weapons actually ran aground near Karlskrona. This and various other submarine incidents led to protests from Sweden and increasing irritation in Moscow. At first Palme's government continued its attempts to "normalize" relations with the Soviet Union, and he was attacked by opposition leaders for failing to convey sufficient concern over the incidents to the Soviets. Palme placed great emphasis on the fact that Gromyko, during his visit to Stockholm in January, denied that Soviet submarines had repeatedly entered Sweden's territorial waters.

However, a further controversy in August produced new

protests to the Kremlin. On this occasion concern was prompted by the alleged intrusion of a Soviet jet fighter into Swedish airspace over the island of Gotland in the Baltic Sea on August 9. The intruder reportedly remained in Swedish airspace for nearly five minutes and came within 2 km (1.3 mi) of a Swedish commercial airliner during that time. Palme delivered a fighting speech to the Social Democratic Party's congress in September in which he reaffirmed Sweden's policy of neutrality and threatened to sink foreign submarines violating Swedish waters. "We do not give way on questions concerning our national sovereignty and international law," he said.

In June Premier Zhao Ziyang (Chao Tzu-yang) of China visited Sweden during a tour of six Western European countries. Premier Zhao called for the development of closer economic cooperation between China and Sweden.

In October the government introduced a number of tax increases with the aim of cutting domestic consumption in order to avoid a surge in imports in 1985. The increases affected the prices of alcohol, cigarettes, gasoline, electricity, and charter air travel. The move was expected to push up the rate of inflation slightly to about 7% by the end of the year. Overall, however, Sweden's economic situation continued to show a steady improvement. This augured well for Palme's Social Democratic Party, which faced general elections in 1985.   (CHRIS MOSEY)

SWITZERLAND

A landlocked federal republic in west central Europe, Switzerland consists of a confederation of 26 cantons (six of which are demi-cantons). Area: 41,293 sq km (15,943 sq mi). Pop. (1984 est.): 6,435,800. Cap.: Bern. Monetary unit: Swiss franc, with (Oct. 29, 1984) a free rate of Sw F 2.52 to U.S. $1 (Sw F 3.04 = £1 sterling). President in 1984, Leon Schlumpf.

The major political issue in Switzerland at the beginning of 1984 was the threat by the Social Democratic Party to withdraw its representative from the federal government in retaliation for Parliament's failure to elect the party's candidate, Lilian Uchtenhagen, to the seven-member federal Council (Cabinet) in December 1983. Party membership throughout the country was divided on the issue, however, and by mid-February, after much heated public and private discussion, the Social Democratic executive decided, in the interest of "realistic moderation," to remain in the government. A situation that might have deteriorated into a government crisis was therefore avoided.

As if to prove that Parliament's decision not to elect Uchtenhagen had not been due in any way to the fact that she was a woman, a few months later another woman, Elisabeth Kopp, a centre-right Radical Democrat, became the first to be elected to the federal Council when she replaced Rudolf Friedrich, of the same party, who resigned unexpectedly for reasons of health. Kopp took over the Department of Justice and Police, previously headed by Friedrich. One of her tasks would be the delicate one of formulating and implementing policies on political refugees and requests for asylum. In December Parliament elected Kurt Furgler, a Christian Democrat, to serve as president for 1985 in succession to Leon Schlumpf. Furgler was to assume the office for the third time.

On February 26 a referendum was held on a popular initiative, sponsored mainly by left-wing groups, that called for a form of civilian service in place of military service for conscientious objectors. The proposal was defeated by 1,360,960 votes to 770,891 on a 52.2% turnout. Although the number of conscientious objectors had increased only

For the first time, a woman was elected to the Bundesrat, the seven-member governing Council of Switzerland. She was Elisabeth Kopp, shown here being sworn in in the capital city of Bern.

AP/WIDE WORLD

slightly during recent years, the issue remained on the agenda and awaited a new, more precisely formulated proposal. On May 20 an initiative sponsored by the Social Democratic Party to combat the abuse of banking secrecy and power was defeated by all the cantons and 73% of the voters in a national plebiscite.

In March the National Council (lower chamber of parliament) voted by 112 votes to 78 in favour of Switzerland's ultimate adherence to the UN, on the condition that it received a formal guarantee of its continued "permanent and armed neutrality." At the end of the year the Council of States (upper chamber of parliament) also voted in favour by 24 votes to 16. The issue cut across party lines. A referendum on the proposal, required by the constitution before it could be adopted, was not expected to take place before 1986. Meanwhile, nearly all opinion polls taken since 1980 suggested that the Swiss people were opposed to joining the UN. The dilemma facing the Swiss was intensified by the lively debate over the future of UNESCO, one of the UN specialized agencies. (See *United Nations:* Special Report, above.) Switzerland had been a member of UNESCO since shortly after its foundation, and the Swiss government let it be known that it was unlikely to follow the decision of the U.S. and the U.K. to withdraw from the organization, favouring instead continued cooperation in an attempt to bring about reform from within. Nevertheless, the criticism leveled at the agency seemed unlikely to engender enthusiasm for membership in the UN itself.

Switzerland's desire for a formal guarantee of its permanent and armed neutrality required that it maintain a credible display of defensive military strength. In 1984 military expenditure once again all but equaled the amount spent on the highly developed system of social benefits, while all other budget items trailed behind at a considerable distance. The 1985 federal budget deficit was estimated at Sw F 22.6 billion.

During 1984 all major economic indicators revealed a moderate improvement, which was expected to continue in 1985. The important watch-making industry again experienced difficulties in the face of international competition, especially from Japan. However, it regained some ground thanks to various innovations, including mass production of a cheap but sturdy "swatch."   (MELANIE STAERK)

UNITED KINGDOM

A constitutional monarchy in northwestern Europe and member of the Commonwealth, the United Kingdom comprises the island of Great Britain (England, Scotland, and

Wales) and Northern Ireland, together with many small islands. Area: 244,100 sq km (94,248 sq mi), including 3,218
sq km of inland water but excluding the crown dependencies
of the Channel Islands and Isle of Man. Pop. (1984 est.):
56,236,000. Cap.: London. Monetary unit: pound sterling,
with (Oct. 29, 1984) a free rate of £0.83 to U.S.$1 (U.S.
$1.21 = £1 sterling). Queen, Elizabeth II; prime minister in
1984, Margaret Thatcher.

A single event dominated 1984 in the U.K.: the strike by
members of the National Union of Mineworkers (NUM),
which began on March 6 and which continued as the year
ended. This dominance was maintained in spite of other
events that enabled 1984 to live up to its chilling reputation, although not exactly in the manner George Orwell
had imagined. On April 17 a burst of automatic gunfire
ripped across the shady quiet of St. James's Square, London, during a demonstration against the Libyan regime,
and a young policewoman, Yvonne Fletcher, fell dead.
The shots had been fired from the first-floor window of
the Libyan People's Bureau (embassy). The building was
under siege for ten days before its occupants were allowed
to return, under the conventions of diplomatic immunity,
to Libya. On October 12 a bomb planted by the Irish Republican Army (IRA) sliced from top to bottom the elegant
Grand Hotel in Brighton, where Prime Minister Margaret
Thatcher and members of her Cabinet were staying for the
annual Conservative Party conference. Thatcher narrowly
escaped with her life. Five people were killed, and others
were seriously maimed and injured, including Secretary
of State for Trade and Industry Norman Tebbit. These
disparate acts of terrorism contributed powerfully to the
atmosphere of violence that characterized the year.

Domestic Affairs. Violence became a common feature of
the miners' strike, bringing to an end Britain's reputation
as a good-tempered country with a talent for conducting
disputes in peaceable fashion. Great passions were aroused
for several reasons. At the root of the dispute was the
issue of jobs, since the strike was taking place against a
background of persistent and, indeed, still rising unemployment, which as the year began achieved a new record
of 3.2 million. Later in the year the number of long-term
unemployed—people out of work for a year or longer—
rose above one million for the first time.

From the beginning the strike bitterly divided the miners'
union. The first industrial action took place in Yorkshire
and Scotland, where strikes were called on the authority of
the area executives of the NUM to protest against proposed
pit closures. When on March 6 the National Coal Board
(NCB) chairman, Ian MacGregor, reaffirmed the NCB plan
for accelerated streamlining of the coal industry, the NUM
national executive endorsed the strikes in Yorkshire and
Scotland and, without holding a national ballot of NUM
members, offered official approval to any other area that
would join the action. Despite the fact that several area
ballots showed a majority against striking, the strike soon
spread to about three-quarters of the industry.

Violence on the picket lines multiplied and escalated,
and the weapons began to include not only bricks and iron
bars but also rivet guns and fire bombs. Arthur Scargill
(*see* BIOGRAPHIES), president of the NUM, refused again
and again to condemn it, blaming only the "state violence"
of the police. Whoever was responsible for the violence,
the police certainly contributed to the scale of the confrontations. Often faced with several thousand pickets who
had gathered to prevent small handfuls of men from reporting to work, police forces mustered similar or superior
numbers. Television viewers became accustomed to the
spectacle of mounted police in cavalry charges and police

on foot beating shields with truncheons as they advanced.
According to the opinion polls, however, a majority of
the British public formed squarely behind the forces of
authority.

Ostensibly the dispute was about the economics of the
coal industry, which was consuming an annual subsidy
that had grown to £1.3 billion. On March 6 the NCB put
forward a plan for reducing output by about 4%, which
would have entailed closing 20–25 pits with the loss of
20,000 jobs. What was really at issue, however, was the
clash between the NCB's insistence that it had to have the
right to manage the industry and Scargill's insistence that
no pit could be closed on economic grounds. Negotiations
between the NCB and the NUM served only to highlight
the intransigence of both MacGregor and Scargill and to
illustrate that this fundamental and substantive difference
was immune from procedural solution.

From the government's point of view, the NCB could
not afford to lose the dispute since the government's own
authority was on the line. The miners' strike of 1974 had
quickly led to power cuts and obliged the government to
place industry on a three-day week. In 1984 preparations
had been made, and substantial stocks of coal were available. Supplies continued to enter the country from abroad,
mostly through the smaller ports. The fact that this was
possible indicated that support for the miners among members of other trade unions was lukewarm. Two attempts
to call a dock strike in sympathy with the miners both
petered out for want of rank-and-file support.

There had been rumours that by about November coal
stocks would run short, obliging the government to attempt to move coal from strike-bound power stations.
Troops might have been necessary for the task, and the
temperature of the dispute would undoubtedly have been
raised. The government believed that Scargill was looking
forward to that moment as one that would at last bring
the wider Labour movement into the struggle. However, it
was not to be. By early autumn the government was finally
confident that the electricity supply could be maintained
until at least March 1985.

The Labour movement—the Trades Union Congress
(TUC) and the Labour Party—faced an extremely tricky
situation. The left wing of both the Labour Party and the
trade-union movement immediately espoused the miners'
cause. However, Labour Party leaders and the majority of
union leaders calculated that Scargill was likely to lose.
Moreover, few of them desired to see his tactics prevail.
On the other hand, a rout of the miners by the Thatcher
government would be a cataclysmic event for the whole
Labour movement. Labour leaders judged that the best
outcome would be a qualified victory for the miners themselves at the expense both of Thatcher's—or, strictly speaking, the NCB's—closure plan and of Scargill's opposition to
all closures on economic grounds. To this end, attempts to
promote compromise were made by a number of prominent people in the Labour movement, including Norman
Willis (*see* BIOGRAPHIES), the new general secretary of the
TUC, but all were in vain.

The strike brought an abrupt end to Neil Kinnock's
honeymoon period as leader of the Labour Party. Elected
to succeed Michael Foot at the Labour Party conference
in October 1983, Kinnock faced the task of broadening
the party's appeal to the electorate without reopening and
aggravating the ideological divides within it. The miners'
dispute made this task immeasurably more difficult. During its first few weeks Kinnock was accused of ambivalence
on the issue of whether or not the miners should vote nationally in support of a walkout before being ordered out

on strike. Later he was accused of inadequately condemning the violence on the picket lines.

Nor were the miners Kinnock's only difficulty. The balance between left and right within the party was at best uneasy. In midsummer Kinnock mounted a bid to amend the constitutional procedures by which Labour members of Parliament were subject to reselection by their local constituency parties during the lifetime of each Parliament. It was proposed that voting should be conducted on a one-person, one-vote system (although only on an optional basis) instead of at restricted party meetings. At the Labour Party conference in Blackpool in October, Kinnock saw his proposal defeated, a humiliating experience at the end of his first year in office. An alliance of trade-union traditionalists, fearful that a precedent would be set in favour of ballots, and of the left wing, jealously guarding its control over many local parties, conspired against the reform.

The other opposition to the government—the electoral Alliance of the Social Democratic Party (SDP) and the Liberal Party—appeared to have neither gained nor lost support as a result of the miners' dispute, in spite of the unambiguous support of the SDP leader, David Owen, for the state against Scargill. In elections to the European Parliament on June 14, the Alliance failed to win a single seat. Yet on the same day, it scored a remarkable victory in a by-election at Portsmouth South, overthrowing a large Conservative majority. Nevertheless, the outcome of the European polls, and of the local council elections on May 3, suggested that while the Alliance could score by-election surprises, as the Liberal Party had done on its own many times in the past, it was no nearer to becoming an alternative force capable of winning power, or even a large number of seats, in general elections.

The political map therefore appeared to have changed little since the previous year's general elections. Labour had make a modest recovery, largely at the expense of the Alliance, while the Conservative vote had scarcely slipped at all. It was a remarkable state of affairs, and one that had a direct bearing on the conduct of the government. In normal circumstances the governing party would expect to be suffering a decline in popularity a year into its second term of office. Moreover, the government had become accident-prone—one example was the widely criticized effort to ban workers at Government Communications Headquarters from belonging to a union. Thus it was difficult to understand why the government's standing continued to be so high. After March one explanation was the so-called

Scargill factor; the public appeared to be rallying behind the government against the threat from Scargill and the miners, just as it had done during the war against Argentina over the Falkland Islands/Islas Malvinas in 1982. However, another and more permanent explanation was that the opposition was cripplingly split. The result was what a leading Conservative member of Parliament described as an "electoral dictatorship."

Indeed, in the House of Commons some of the most effective opposition during the year came from the government's own side. Revolts were mounted against the government's proposal to cancel elections to the Greater London Council and six metropolitan county councils pending the proposed abolition by April 1986 of that tier of local government. Eventually the proposal to cancel the elections was defeated in the House of Lords, and the government agreed to a compromise that allowed the elected councillors an extra unelected term of office. Disquiet was also expressed in both houses about the government's plans to limit the local rates (property taxes) that could be levied by a number of local authorities that had been singled out as high spenders. To some Conservatives the move smacked of a centralization foreign to the traditions of their party. Later there were substantial backbench revolts against a proposal to cut the foreign aid budget, clumsily announced by the Treasury while the nation was being appalled by reports of the famine in Ethiopia, and against a proposal by Secretary of State for Education Sir Keith Joseph to increase the financial contribution of parents for the support of university students. The size and the force of the latter rebellion caused the government to retreat with some rapidity and a good deal of indignity.

In September Thatcher revealed a small-scale reshuffle of her Cabinet in which the most important appointment was that of Douglas Hurd (*see* BIOGRAPHIES) to replace James Prior, who resigned as secretary of state for Northern Ireland. Other new members of the Cabinet were Minister for the Arts Lord Gowrie and David Young, former chairman of the Manpower Services Commission, who was appointed minister without portfolio.

Prince Henry Charles Albert David (known as Prince Harry), second child of the prince and princess of Wales and third in succession to the throne, was born on September 15. In July the country experienced an earthquake that was thought to have been the worst since 1884. With its epicentre in northwestern Wales, the quake measured 5.5 on the Richter scale.

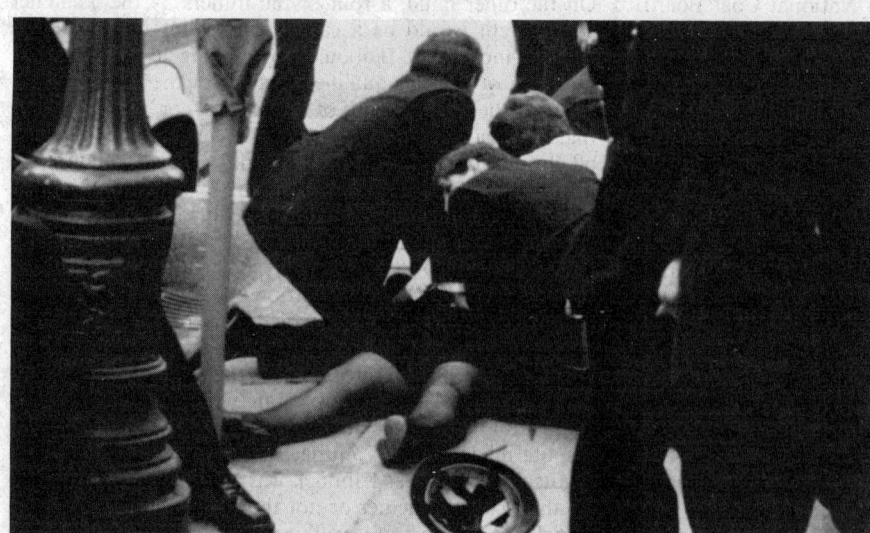

AP/WIDE WORLD

On April 17 during a demonstration against Libyan chief of state Col. Muammar al-Qaddafi in front of the Libyan embassy in London, machine-gun fire from within the embassy wounded ten exiled Libyan demonstrators and killed a British policewoman. The shootings started a ten-day diplomatic standoff, which ended when the two countries allowed the peaceful evacuation of their diplomatic staffs. Britain severed diplomatic ties with Libya.

The Economy. Chancellor of the Exchequer Nigel Lawson scored a success with his budget in March. Its major provision was a further reduction in direct taxation. The cut was chiefly financed by increases in indirect taxation. Important reforms were also made in the structure of business taxation. His budget, the chancellor declared boldly, was designed to "set the government's course for this Parliament." By the autumn, however, when the new political season opened, the pound had plummeted against the U.S. dollar from over $1.40 at the beginning of the year to below $1.20, while unemployment surged upward alarmingly to reach almost 3.3 million, over 13% of the registered work force, in September.

It was the increase in unemployment that caused the most worry, partly because the miners' strike was contributing to the impression that Britain was becoming more sharply divided into "two nations," one affluent, one poor; one employed, one massively unemployed; one southern, the other northern. The archbishop of Canterbury, Robert Runcie, gave an interview to *The Times* on October 8 in which he queried the objectives of the government's economic policies and warned that Britain was becoming a society marred by "growing poverty and despair and a sense of powerlessness." A chorus of churchmen, including the newly consecrated bishop of Durham, David Jenkins (*see* BIOGRAPHIES), spoke up in similar vein, to the great irritation of Conservative Party leaders who were accustomed to the old idea that the Church of England was "the Conservative Party at prayer."

The government, however, remained unmoved by these moral strictures. Lawson held firmly to his belief that there was no solution to unemployment within the power of government other than to promote the market forces that would eventually reduce it. He announced his annual round of spending cuts in November, after what was said to have been an unusually bitter haggle between the Treasury and the spending departments, and held out the prospect of more tax cuts in his spring 1985 budget.

Foreign Affairs. For the first half of the year, the conduct of foreign affairs was dominated yet again by the long-running dispute over Britain's contribution to the budget of the European Communities (EC). At Fontainebleau, France, in June, however, with the elections to the European Parliament safely completed, a compromise was reached. Thatcher agreed to an arrangement that granted the U.K. a considerably smaller rebate on its budget contributions than she had been demanding but one that eliminated the need for a tiresome and wounding annual haggle. In exchange she consented to an overall increase in the EC budget. The deal gave hope that the U.K.'s relations with its EC partners could in the future be conducted on an amicable, routine, and constructive basis. The U.K. was "in Europe" at last, said some; others among its long-exasperated continental partners remained doubtful.

The U.K. government broke off diplomatic relations with Libya during the siege of the Libyan People's Bureau in April. Diplomatic relations with Nigeria were also severely strained after British police in July foiled a kidnap attempt on Umaru Dikko (*see* BIOGRAPHIES), a former minister in Nigeria's deposed civilian government who was living in London. In other spheres of foreign affairs there was evidence of a less strident tone on the part of Thatcher's government and, perhaps most notably, on the part of Thatcher herself. Her visit to Hungary in February was her first to a Soviet-bloc nation since taking office in 1979. In December she journeyed to China to sign the agreement reached earlier in the year between the U.K. and Chinese governments on the future of Hong Kong after the U.K.'s

Arthur Scargill, the militant head of Britain's National Union of Mineworkers, suffered injuries during a strike that involved an increasingly violent series of confrontations with police.
PETER ARKEL/SPOONER—GAMMA/LIAISON

lease on the territory expired in 1997. There was progress, too, toward a negotiated settlement of the dispute with Spain over the future of Gibraltar. The visit by Mikhail Gorbachev (*see* BIOGRAPHIES), an influential member of the Soviet Politburo, in December was the first to the U.K. by a top Soviet leader in 17 years. Within days of her talks with Gorbachev, Thatcher was in the U.S. to reassure Pres. Ronald Reagan that her government remained committed to the U.S. approach to arms-control negotiations.

Northern Ireland. Closer to home, as always, was the Irish question. During most of the year there was hope, chiefly in Dublin, that the mid-November summit meeting between Thatcher and Irish Prime Minister Garret FitzGerald would achieve, if not a breakthrough, at least some kind of progress toward bringing a new political dimension to the seemingly intractable problem of the future of Northern Ireland. The expectation derived from a number of factors, including FitzGerald's willingness to go a long way toward qualifying the republic's nationalist claims upon Northern Ireland, the ever present need for greater cooperation in security matters between the U.K. and Ireland in their common struggle against terrorism, and the deterioration of political life in Northern Ireland.

In May the Forum for a New Ireland, a study group of nationalists from Northern Ireland and the republic, produced a report offering three options for Northern Ireland's future that, although initially given a cool reception in London, were recognized to be at least moderate in spirit and cogent in intent. (See *Ireland,* above.) The private discussions between Thatcher and FitzGerald in November were said to have gone well, but at her press conference after the meeting, Thatcher brushed aside each of the options advanced by the New Ireland Forum report, along with the main thrust of its analysis of the problem, in terms that caused great offense and disillusion in Ireland. Thus, at the end of 1984, as at the end of all previous years in the recent past, the Irish question was no nearer to solution.

(PETER JENKINS)

See also *Commonwealth of Nations,* above; *Dependent States,* below.

VATICAN CITY STATE

> The independent sovereignty of Vatican City State is surrounded by but is not part of Rome. As a state with territorial limits, it is properly distinguished from the Holy See, which constitutes the worldwide administrative and legislative body for the Roman Catholic Church. Area: 44 ha (108.8 ac). Pop. (1982 est.): 736. As sovereign pontiff, John Paul II is the chief of state. Vatican City is administered by a pontifical commission of five cardinals headed by the secretary of state, in 1984 Agostino Cardinal Casaroli.

Important developments in the Vatican's relations with the outside world during 1984 were the establishment of full diplomatic relations with the United States in January and the signing of a new concordat with Italy in February, replacing the previous one of 1929. (*See* RELIGION: *Introduction.*) Underlining the Vatican's influence in world affairs was the successful outcome in November of its arbitration in the Beagle Channel dispute between Argentina and Chile.

In a reshuffle within the Curia in April, Agostino Cardinal Casaroli remained secretary of state but received a special mandate as representative of the pope in the latter's capacity as temporal head of state. Sebastiano Cardinal Baggio became president of the Commission of Cardinals for the Vatican City State, relieving Casaroli of some of his routine administrative functions. Baggio was replaced as prefect of the Sacred Congregation for the Bishops by Bernardin Cardinal Gantin of Benin, the first African prelate to occupy this important post. Remaining pro-president of the Commission of Cardinals was Archbishop Paul Marcinkus, controversial head of the Institute for Religious Works (the Vatican bank), which in June paid $240 million to creditors of the failed Banco Ambrosiano, in whose transactions it had been involved. (*See* RELIGION: *Introduction.*)

Among visitors to the Vatican were Pres. Alessandro Pertini of Italy and U.S. Vice-Pres. George Bush. The visit in September by Msgr. Liudas Povilonis of Lithuania was allowed by the Soviets following their earlier refusal to au-

Pres. Alessandro Pertini of Italy paid the first official visit to the Vatican by an Italian head of state in 12 years. A new concordat between Italy and the Vatican was signed in February.

thorize an intended visit to Lithuania by Pope John Paul II.

(MAX BERGERRE)

See also Religion: *Roman Catholic Church.*

This article updates the *Micropædia* article VATICAN CITY STATE.

Eastern Europe and the U.S.S.R.

EASTERN EUROPEAN AFFAIRS

During 1984 Eastern European politics were dominated by a number of trends, some more visible than others. Most obvious was the complex issue of how the states of Eastern Europe should arrange their relations with the West at a time when the Soviet Union viewed the West with growing disfavour. This discrepancy raised several underlying issues concerning the extent to which Eastern European states were free to pursue their own interests, how far these could diverge from the Soviet definition of the interest of the Soviet alliance system as a whole, and how far Moscow was willing to go in sacrificing Eastern European interests to the pursuit of its own designs. The divergence was demonstrated most strikingly by the ups and downs of relations between East and West Germany and the forced postponement of the long-heralded visit by the East German leader, Erich Honecker, to Bonn. (See *German Democratic Republic,* below.)

The essence of the problem was that, from the Soviet perspective, East-West relations had deteriorated badly after the successive crises in Afghanistan and Poland and NATO's deployment of intermediate-range nuclear missiles in Europe, despite vociferous Soviet objections. In the Soviet view, this should have resulted in a de facto freeze on all East-West contacts. Several of the Eastern European states took a different line for their own reasons, some of them economic, some political. Indeed, it was evident by the summer of 1984 that the Eastern European states concerned—East Germany, Hungary, Romania, and, more stealthily, Bulgaria—were signaling that they could not afford to cut themselves off from the West. The first three of these states had serious debt repayment problems, which they could meet only by relying on Western goodwill. All of them, having been exposed to the whole complex range of Western technology and culture during the 1970s, concluded that they could not accept isolation.

The determination of these states to maintain tolerable relations with the West—meaning, primarily, West Germany—was such that by the spring of 1984 a kind of tacit, informal association had come to emerge in support of what came to be called "minidétente." Thus, early in the year, the Hungarians strongly stated the right of every socialist state to determine its own interests and maintained that conflicts of interest between socialist states were a perfectly normal development. When the Hungarians found themselves under attack from the pro-Soviet Czechoslovak party, the East Germans signaled their clear backing for the Hungarian argument. In much the same way, Honecker ostentatiously visited Romania in August 1984 as a way of making public East Germany's support for Romania's commitment to maintaining good relations with the West. On the other hand, the close Soviet allies felt they had no option but to line up with the U.S.S.R. when Moscow decreed that the Olympic Games in Los Angeles should be boycotted. Only the Romanians attended.

Much of the confusion in Eastern Europe over the limits of autonomy in foreign policy had their ultimate origins in the confusion reigning in the Kremlin. During Yury Andropov's first few months in power—up to the middle of 1983—the outlines of a tighter Soviet-bloc strategy toward the West could be discerned. Several high-level Soviet statements at this time, including declarations by Andropov and his eventual successor, Konstantin Chernenko, stressed the importance of integration among the Warsaw Pact countries. After Andropov fell ill, however, a discernible drift in Soviet policy-making set in.

Under Chernenko, this absence of clarity persisted, as the Soviet Politburo turned out to be internally divided. Thus both hard and softer voices were heard, and the Eastern Europeans evidently concluded that they could and should stress their own national interests. One result was that the various Soviet-Eastern European conferences could achieve little in the way of policy coordination. Warsaw Pact foreign ministers, for example, met (as they customarily do) every six months, but they issued rather bland communiqués, implying a degree of disagreement. Overall, the year in bloc affairs was marked by a measure of disunity, a sense of drift and of the transitional nature of the Soviet leadership, during which the Eastern Europeans sought to carve out as much autonomy for themselves as they could manage. Only the diehard pro-Soviet Czechoslovak leadership remained untouched. The Polish leadership was too weak domestically and too dependent on Soviet goodwill internationally to play a very active role.

While these issues tended to preoccupy public attention in Eastern Europe, certain observable social trends were causing increased concern. In every Eastern European country, to a greater or lesser extent, there were indications of social malaise. Alcoholism, divorce, suicide, industrial diseases, high pollution levels, the spread of economic crime, and drug abuse all appeared to be on the rise. It was difficult to determine what was cause and what was effect, but many analysts argued that the loss of broader individual and collective horizons and a sense of aimlessness produced by the far-reaching system of state control could be regarded as contributory factors.

The figures were certainly alarming. It was unofficially reported from Hungary (total population 10.7 million) that, at any given time, something on the order of 100,000 young people were sniffing glue. In Poland at least 40,000 drug addicts were known in Warsaw alone. The consumption of alcohol was on the rise throughout the area; in Czechoslovakia (population 15.5 million), 170,000 persons were designated as alcoholics. In Poland the Ministry of Health warned of the spread of food poisoning because of low standards of hygiene in food handling. The deterioration of the environment was widely admitted, as was the inability of the authorities to introduce costly remedial measures. Thus, in Poland, the proportion of surface water classified as unfit for even industrial or agricultural use had risen to 48% by 1980 and was still rising. All the Eastern European countries were notorious for high emission levels of sulfur dioxide, the principal cause of acid rain. There were also widespread complaints of dangerously high concentrations of nitrogenous compounds in vegetables and of various metals in livestock. Although direct cause and effect could not be demonstrated, this did imply a correlation with a fall in life expectancy and a rise in infant mortality. (GEORGE SCHÖPFLIN)

See also Economic Affairs; Military Affairs.

ALBANIA

A people's republic in the western Balkan Peninsula of southeastern Europe, Albania is situated on the Adriatic Sea. Area: 28,748 sq km (11,100 sq mi). Pop. (1984 est.): 2,906,000. Cap.: Tiranë. Monetary unit: lek, with (Oct. 29, 1984) a free rate of 8.33 leks to U.S. $1 (10.05 leks = £1

sterling). First secretary of the Albanian (Communist) Party of Labour in 1984, Enver Hoxha; chairman of the Presidium of the People's Assembly (president), Ramiz Alia; chairman of the Council of Ministers (premier), Adil Carcani.

Albania continued to be one of the most politically isolated countries in the world during 1984. Its leader, Enver Hoxha, retreated into the background, apparently to complete his memoirs, while Ramiz Alia, a Politburo member and chairman of the Presidium of the People's Assembly, ran day-to-day affairs of state.

In May two Albanian Foreign Ministry officials visited West Germany, and Franz-Josef Strauss, premier of the Bavarian state assembly, spent a "short holiday" in Albania in August. No diplomatic relations existed between the two countries. In the past Albania had demanded substantial war reparations from West Germany as a condition of establishing relations, but it now seemed possible that investment by West German companies in Albanian industrial projects might be considered acceptable.

Talks between Greece and Albania began in Athens in May. Greece dropped its territorial claims on southern Albania but insisted that Albania guarantee to respect the religious and human rights of its Greek minority (numbering 400,000 according to some estimates, though the Albanian government put the figure at 28,000). Since Albania was officially an atheist state, the government denied the existence of the Greek Orthodox faith among its population.

(K. M. SMOGORZEWSKI)

BULGARIA

The People's Republic of Bulgaria is on the eastern Balkan Peninsula of southeastern Europe, along the Black Sea. Area: 110,912 sq km (42,823 sq mi). Pop. (1984 est.): 8,969,-000. Cap.: Sofia. Monetary unit: lev, with (Oct. 29, 1984) a free rate of 1.08 leva to U.S. $1 (1.31 leva = £1 sterling). General secretary of the Bulgarian Communist Party and chairman of the State Council (president) in 1984, Todor Zhivkov; chairman of the Council of Ministers (premier), Grisha Filipov.

Changes in the makeup of the Bulgarian government, including new appointments to the Politburo, announced on Jan. 3, 1984, were apparently motivated by a need to strengthen the management of the economy.

Celebrations of the 40th anniversary of Bulgaria's "popular revolution," held September 9, were attended by delegations from all Soviet-bloc countries. The Soviet delegation was headed by Politburo member Mikhail Gorbachev (*see* BIOGRAPHIES), who praised the Bulgarian leadership's efforts to develop good-neighbourly relations among all Balkan countries and "to make the Balkan peninsula a zone of peace free from nuclear weapons." Bulgarian Communist Party General Secretary Todor Zhivkov proclaimed in his report that over the past 45 years Bulgaria had changed from a purely agricultural land into an industrial-agricultural one; industrial production in 1983 was 84 times greater than in 1939.

Ten days before the anniversary celebrations, on August 30, bombs exploded at Varna airport, at Plovdiv railway station, and at other locations, reportedly causing several deaths. Zhivkov was en route between Varna and Plovdiv on the same day; strict security measures were immediately put into effect in Sofia. In April Zhivkov, perhaps the U.S.S.R.'s most stalwart ally, was cordially received in Poland, and on May 31 he met Soviet Pres. Konstantin Chernenko in Moscow. Soviet pressure was seen as the reason for postponement of his planned visit to West Germany in September.

In continued efforts to dissociate itself from the May 1981 attempt on the life of Pope John Paul II, Bulgaria published an appeal (dated March 18) addressed to the pope by Patriarch Maksim, head of the Bulgarian Orthodox Church. He called for the release of Sergey Antonov, a Bulgarian airline official held in custody in Italy since November 1982 after he was identified as an accomplice by the would-be assassin, Mehmet Ali Agca. The pope replied on April 20 that neither he nor the Italian government could influence the decision of the investigating magistrate.

(K. M. SMOGORZEWSKI)

CZECHOSLOVAKIA

The federal socialist republic of Czechoslovakia is a landlocked state of central Europe. Area: 127,889 sq km (49,378 sq mi). Pop. (1984 est.): 15.5 million. Cap.: Prague. Monetary unit: koruna, with (Oct. 29, 1984) a commercial rate of 6.67 koruny to U.S. $1 (8.05 koruny = £1 sterling). General secretary of the Communist Party of Czechoslovakia and president in 1984, Gustav Husak; federal premier, Lubomir Strougal.

The year 1984 brought little cheer to Czechoslovakia. Although the economy had performed rather better in 1983 than in 1982, the general atmosphere was one of stagnation. No significant initiatives, whether economic, political, or social, were launched during the year. The economic figures for 1983 were moderate, showing a 2.2% growth of net material product, but they fell far short of the 1981–85 plan targets. Indeed, the target figure for 1981–83 was an increase of 8.1–9%, whereas the actual growth figure for this period was 1.8%. What was more, even the improved 1983 figure was purchased at the cost of higher energy inputs and advancing ecological damage.

What was regarded as one of the most significant contributions to the understanding of Czechoslovakia's economic dilemma came not from official sources but from a 15-page discussion document issued by Charter 77, the opposition group that continued to exist despite intermittent government harassment. It was written by Vladimir Kadlec, one-time rector of the Prague School of Economics and minister of education until 1968, when he had been purged from office. Kadlec argued that the official statistics were less favourable than they appeared and, in particular, that the continued throttling of investment was likely to have deleterious consequences for the economy throughout the 1980s. The rejuvenation of capital stock was falling behind, and the cost of new investment was rising alarmingly. Kadlec also noted the decreasing ability of Czechoslovak products to compete in world markets, so that, despite

the high level of industrialization, Czechoslovakia's export profile resembled that of a third world country, relying ever more heavily on raw materials rather than on manufactured goods. The amount of unsalable goods being produced was alarming. So was the cost of industry, which was particularly energy and materials intensive.

As in previous years, there was evidence that economic analysts, and even some members of the political elite, had an inkling of what was going wrong and why. The ailing federal premier, Lubomir Strougal, noted in a speech to the National Assembly in March that demand for consumer goods outstripped supply, that the rate of innovation remained low, and that the productivity of both labour and capital was unsatisfactory. Despite the persuasiveness of the diagnosis, there was no sign of the political will needed to effect meaningful reforms.

The stagnation was also reflected in continuing complaints about the state and quality of the Communist Party of Czechoslovakia (CPC) membership. In particular, there was evidence of unease in senior party circles because the older generation of activists—those around 50 years of age and over, whose commitment to the party was regarded as sufficient to make them reliable—was not being replaced by a similar cadre of younger people. There was constant criticism that too many new recruits to the party were not taking their membership duties sufficiently seriously, that too many were passive, and that too many fell by the wayside before the end of their two years' probation. Despite the fact that the CPC was supposedly a workers' party, comparatively few blue-collar workers were joining, and only 31% of members were active manual workers. At the same time, it was recognized that the shortage of technologically qualified members was an obstacle to the formulation and supervision of the sophisticated policy of economic management that the country's technological complexity demanded.

None of these factors deterred the hard-line wing of the CPC from launching an international ideological offensive. On March 30 the party daily newspaper, *Rude Pravo,* published a harshly worded article strongly criticizing ideological deviations in Communist countries that were placing national interests above those of internationalism. No country was named, but Hungary, Romania, and East Germany were understood to be the targets, because these countries were attempting to maintain good relations with the West at a time when the U.S.S.R. was increasingly retreating into its shell. The campaign sputtered on during the spring and early summer. It appeared that the U.S.S.R., while not fully accepting every aspect of the Czechoslovak position, was giving it some backing, not

A new plant for the production of cyclohexanone was built in eastern Czechoslovakia. Cyclohexanone is the most common organic precursor of caprolactam, which is used in the production of polyamide fibres (nylon). The plant—the largest of its kind in Europe—is capable of producing some 80,000 tons of cyclohexanone a year.

least because it was convenient for Moscow to have Prague making hard-line statements from which it could always dissociate itself.

The principal domestic target of Czechoslovak hard-liners remained religion. A letter written in August 1983, in which the writer had protested to the authorities about the treatment of religious believers, had been attributed to Frantisek Cardinal Tomasek, archbishop of Prague. It developed that, in fact, it had been written by someone else, and that it might have been leaked deliberately by the authorities in order to embarrass the cardinal. There was some truth, however, in the letter's description of the repression of organized religious life. The authorities clearly interpreted any sign of religious belief as tantamount to an intolerable political affront. The strength of religion was an indication of the ineffectiveness of Communist propaganda, notably among members of the younger generation. The authorities may have been especially concerned about the discontent—much of it expressed through religious channels—that greeted the decision to deploy intermediate-range nuclear missiles on Czechoslovak soil.

Charter 77 also associated itself with protests over the missile question and issued a document demanding an open debate on the issue. Other Charter documents were devoted to the problem of political prisoners, to internal developments within the group, to international questions, and to the peace movement. On August 21, the anniversary of the Soviet-led invasion of Czechoslovakia in 1968, the group called for the withdrawal of Soviet forces and for Czechoslovakia's right to self-determination to be respected. (GEORGE SCHÖPFLIN)

GERMAN DEMOCRATIC REPUBLIC

A people's republic, the German Democratic Republic (East Germany) is in central Europe on the Baltic Sea. Area: 108,333 sq km (41,827 sq mi). Pop. (1984 est.): 16,702,-000. Cap.: East Berlin. Monetary unit: Mark of Deutsche Demokratische Republik, with (Oct. 29, 1984) a free rate of M 3.06 to U.S. $1 (M 3.70 = £1 sterling). General secretary of the Socialist Unity (Communist) Party and chairman of the Council of State (president) in 1984, Erich Honecker; chairman of the Council of Ministers (premier), Willi Stoph.

After months of uncertainty, the proposed visit by the East German leader Erich Honecker to West Germany was called off in September 1984. It was canceled under pressure from the U.S.S.R., which had been conducting a propaganda campaign against Bonn in light of the deployment of new U.S. intermediate-range nuclear missiles on West German territory. (The first Pershing II missiles were deployed in West Germany in December 1983.) However, Honecker had shown that he wished to protect relations with West Germany from the cooler East-West climate, not least for economic reasons. Honecker stated that the time was not ripe for the visit, since it was obvious that East German expectations would not be met. This was taken as a reference to his previous demands that West Germany should recognize a separate East German citizenship and that the diplomatic missions in Bonn and East Berlin should be upgraded to the status of full embassies. The West German minister for intra-German relations, Heinrich Windelen, said that he would have been prepared to discuss these matters, but West German Chancellor Helmut Kohl maintained that nothing could come from such discussions.

Soviet Foreign Minister Andrey Gromyko attended the celebrations of the 35th anniversary of the founding of the German Democratic Republic in East Berlin in September.

The occasion was used by Honecker to proclaim his country's loyalty to Moscow and to wipe out any trace of the strain in relations caused by the public disagreement over East German policy toward the West during the preceding months. Writing in the Soviet newspaper *Pravda,* Honecker stressed that East and West Germany could never be united and that there could be no concessions on the question of the independence of each from the other in foreign and domestic affairs. He criticized assertions by West German politicians that the German question remained open and made no mention of the role intra-German relations could play in strengthening European security. Gromyko was seen as the main architect of the Soviet campaign against closer relations between East and West Germany. East Germany agreed, however, to expand its relations with the U.S. after Foreign Minister Oskar Fischer and U.S. Secretary of State George Shultz met for discussions in New York City. Further consultations were to take place through diplomatic channels.

Unofficial peace groups were weaker than they had been in 1983, and their interest shifted away from nuclear issues to environmental concerns. The church estimated that the unofficial groups had no more than 2,000 members. Their links with Western peace movements were gradually cut off, and they were disillusioned by the lack of effectiveness of Western militants, despite their greater room for maneuver. Yet by turning to environmental issues the unofficial groups failed to make peace with the authorities, because their action was interpreted as a new expression of dissent, approaching high treason in its seriousness. Church leaders were primarily concerned with three objectives that they believed would benefit a much broader group of citizens. They wanted a less rigid approach to ideology in schools, fairer treatment of conscientious objectors, and greater emphasis on pastoral work. Pacifists were faced with prison sentences, and those who opted for national service without arms frequently found that they were refused admission to universities afterward.

The government remained acutely aware that it had not yet fully succeeded in establishing its legitimacy in the eyes of many of its citizens. East Germany was fully accepted as a sovereign state, with most countries extending diplomatic recognition. Furthermore, it was one of the world's ten leading industrial states and was generally believed to possess the best military force, after that of the U.S.S.R., in the Warsaw Pact. Nevertheless, many East Germans remained unsure about the status of their country. Honecker turned to Martin Luther, Frederick the Great, and even Otto von Bismarck as well as Schiller, Goethe, and Wagner in an effort to create a sense of separate nationhood.

With more than 30,000 East Germans allowed to immigrate to West Germany in the first nine months of the year, the total 1984 figure seemed likely to become the highest since the Berlin Wall was built in 1961. Only 11,000 had left for the West in 1983. Many would-be refugees sought asylum in West German embassies of other Soviet-bloc countries, causing considerable embarrassment to the West German government. After protracted negotiations, most were returned home to apply for exit visas in the normal way, the East German authorities having promised that there would be no recrimination. The view in Bonn was that the legal method of leaving the country worked and that to give in to the refugees on a large scale would jeopardize the arrangement. Moreover, the East Germans kept their promise to remove the automatic shooting devices installed along the border between East and West Germany.

In October Honecker visited Finland, his first trip to a non-Communist country after calling off his visit to West

Germany. Scheduled interviews with the media in Helsinki were canceled, apparently to spare him questions about the Kremlin's role in his decision not to go to Bonn.

(NORMAN CROSSLAND)

This article updates the *Macropædia* article GERMANY: *German Democratic Republic.*

HUNGARY

A people's republic, Hungary is a landlocked state in central Europe. Area: 93,036 sq km (35,921 sq mi). Pop. (1984 est.): 10,679,000. Cap.: Budapest. Monetary unit: forint, with (Oct. 29, 1984) a free rate of 50.35 forints to U.S. $1 (60.77 forints = £1 sterling). First secretary of the Hungarian Socialist Workers' (Communist) Party in 1984, Janos Kadar; chairman of the Presidential Council (chief of state), Pal Losonczi; president of the Council of Ministers (premier), Gyorgy Lazar.

First Secretary Janos Kadar of the Hungarian Socialist Workers' (Communist) Party was the only Communist leader outside the U.S.S.R. who appeared to have a close personal relationship with Soviet Pres. Yury Andropov, whom he had referred to as an "old acquaintance." It was not surprising, therefore, that the foreign offices of Western countries decided that Kadar was the obvious go-between in reviving a sensible dialogue between West and East. During the second half of 1983 Budapest had become a centre of unusual diplomatic activity. There were more visits to the capital during 1984, both before and after the death of Andropov on February 9 and his replacement by Konstantin Chernenko.

British Prime Minister Margaret Thatcher visited Budapest on February 2–4, her first official journey to a Soviet-bloc country since taking office. She was followed in April by Bettino Craxi, premier of Italy, and in June by West German Chancellor Helmut Kohl. The aim of these leaders of NATO countries was to try to keep open lines of communication between East and West. They returned home, however, convinced that the results of their conversations with Kadar had not been dramatic. On October 15–16 Kadar became the first Soviet-bloc leader to be received by French Pres. François Mitterrand in Paris.

Visitors from the U.S.S.R. included Soviet Foreign Minister Andrey Gromyko, who arrived on April 17 to hold discussions with Kadar, Premier Gyorgy Lazar, and Foreign Minister Peter Varkonyi. After their meeting they issued a joint communiqué pointing out that, if the U.S. and its allies were prepared to return to the situation as it had been prior to the deployment of new intermediate nuclear forces in Europe in December 1983, then a turn away from confrontation and toward a policy of détente and cooperation would be possible. On June 13 Kadar was received by Chernenko in Moscow. A joint communique stipulated that the two leaders had been in full agreement in their appraisal of the international situation.

Kadar journeyed to Moscow as head of the Hungarian delegation to the 38th session of the Council for Mutual Economic Assistance (Comecon), at which party leaders and premiers of the ten member countries were present. The long document signed at the end of the summit meeting on June 14 was mainly a political manifesto supporting Soviet policies, with only a few clauses mentioning the need for mutual help. After the meeting, Mihaly Sumai, deputy chairman of the Hungarian Research Institute for World Economy, told a conference of Hungarian party officials that Comecon had made slow progress during its 35 years of existence in developing constructive programs. It was vital for Hungary, he went on, to develop its relations with Comecon "more intelligently, more flexibly, and with increasing regard to the advantages and disadvantages of all parties concerned."

Though relatively the most prosperous member of the socialist camp, Hungary had to find more than $700 million to service its external debts during 1984. Peter Veress, minister for foreign trade, declared at the end of April that the foreign currency would be raised mainly from the sale of meat and other agricultural products abroad. In connection with its efforts to boost exports, the government announced that from July 12 some domestic retail prices would be increased by 10–30% as part of a continuing policy of reducing state subsidies on all but the most basic items.

It was announced on May 24 that the World Bank was granting Hungary a $90 million loan to increase its production of crude petroleum and natural gas. Experts predicted that it might be possible to double Hungary's crude petroleum output, which in 1983 had amounted to 2,004,000 metric tons. The effect of this would be to reduce petroleum imports by almost one-quarter.

(K. M. SMOGORZEWSKI)

POLAND

A people's republic of eastern Europe, Poland is on the Baltic Sea. Area: 312,683 sq km (120,727 sq mi). Pop. (1984 est.): 37 million. Cap.: Warsaw. Monetary unit: zloty, with (Oct. 29, 1984) a free rate of 125.49 zlotys to U.S. $1 (151.47 zlotys = £1 sterling). First secretary of the Polish United Workers' (Communist) Party and chairman of the Council of Ministers (premier) in 1984, Gen. Wojciech Jaruzelski; chairman of the Council of State (chief of state), Henryk Jablonski.

During 1984 Poland began to emerge from the diplomatic isolation imposed by the U.S. and its European allies following the proclamation of martial law by Gen. Wojciech Jaruzelski's regime in December 1981. Within days of the imposition of martial law, the U.S. had announced economic sanctions that included halting exports of agricultural and dairy products to Poland, withdrawing most-favoured-nation status from Polish imports to the U.S., refusing to support Poland's application to join the International Monetary Fund (IMF), suspending the operation of Poland's airline on U.S. territory, and withdrawing Poland's fishing privileges in U.S. waters. U.S. Pres. Ronald Reagan had stated that the sanctions would remain in effect until martial law was lifted, supporters of the Solidarnosc (Solidarity) trade-union movement were freed from imprisonment, and a dialogue between the government and the people of Poland was reopened.

Following the lifting of martial law in July 1983 and the granting of an amnesty to Solidarity supporters in July 1984, the U.S. administration ended the two last-mentioned sanctions, though the other, more economically damaging measures remained in place. The administration also announced that it would consider withdrawing its opposition to Poland's application for IMF membership if the amnesty for political prisoners was judged to be fully implemented.

General Jaruzelski had protested vociferously against the U.S. action in unilaterally breaking economic agreements between the two countries and alleged U.S. interference in Poland's domestic affairs. The Polish Institute of International Affairs had been instructed in 1983 to prepare a report on U.S.-Polish relations during the 1980–83 period. The work, which appeared in April 1984, alleged that the loss to Poland resulting from the economic sanctions to-

Mourners framed with flowers a portrait of the Rev. Jerzy Popieluszko, an eloquent pro-Solidarity priest, after his murder in late October by a trio of ostensibly off-duty state security police.
LASKI—BLACK STAR

taled $12.5 billion. It also asserted that President Reagan's strategy had a long-term aim of undermining the stability of Poland and hence the central European region.

Another, purely diplomatic "sanction"—that Western statesmen and high-ranking diplomats should avoid contact with Warsaw—lapsed during the year. For 33 months after the imposition of martial law, only the leaders of Communist countries made the journey to Poland. However, international respectability was restored in October when Austrian Foreign Minister Leopold Graz went to Warsaw. He was followed by Greek Prime Minister Andreas Papandreou and Malcolm Rifkind, Britain's undersecretary of state for foreign and Commonwealth affairs. However, West German Foreign Minister Hans-Dietrich Genscher's visit, scheduled for November, was canceled at the last minute.

Jaruzelski flew to Moscow on May 4 to receive the Order of Lenin from Soviet Pres. Konstantin Chernenko. On the same day, the two leaders signed a 15-year agreement on economic, scientific, and technical cooperation which stressed the need to work together to reduce dependence on the West and to restore Poland's position as a prominent trading partner of the U.S.S.R. Poland had slipped from second to fourth place over the previous four years. During the visit Chernenko deprecated what he termed U.S. attempts to "bleed Poland white" and expressed the wish of Soviets to see the Polish United Workers' (Communist) Party quickly restored to full strength.

Support for Solidarity among the people of Poland remained strong. At a May Day parade in Warsaw, Jaruzelski claimed in his speech that the future belonged to socialism,

while in the streets of the capital and many other cities riot squads used truncheons, tear gas, and water cannons to disperse thousands of workers who were demonstrating in support of the outlawed trade union.

The amnesty offered to political opponents of the government in 1983 had met little success. Minister of Justice Lech Pomeracki therefore prepared a bill that offered a new and more generous amnesty. It was submitted to the Sejm (parliament) on July 20 and passed into law the following day, when it was approved by 365 votes to 4, with 6 abstentions. Among those released from prison were 11 leaders of Solidarity and the Workers' Defense Committee (KOR), including Jacek Kuron, Adam Michnik, Henryk Wujec, and Zbigniew Romaszewski. The trial of these four KOR leaders, who were charged with conspiring to overthrow the state, had been suspended on July 18 in anticipation of the amnesty. When Jaruzelski declared the amnesty on July 21, the 40th anniversary of the People's Republic of Poland, he maintained that the socialist system in Poland had now regained enough strength to permit the promulgation of an amnesty that was "more than a humanitarian gesture." The move apparently went against the wishes of the Soviets.

Pomeracki revealed on September 20 that 1,569 had been freed to that date, including 630 political prisoners. The amnesty covered those convicted of and awaiting trial for antistate offenses, as well as those serving short sentences for minor criminal offenses. The results were welcomed by Jozef Cardinal Glemp, the Roman Catholic primate of Poland, and by Solidarity founder Lech Walesa. Two Solidarity leaders, Wladyslaw Frasyniuk and Jozef Pinior, were rearrested at the end of August after holding meetings with those who had continued Solidarity's operations underground after the union was banned.

In an effort to regulate relations between church and state, Jaruzelski wished to conclude a concordat with the Vatican, but Cardinal Glemp insisted that such a step would have to be preceded by a law defining the legal foundation of the church. On September 11 the Soviet newspaper *Izvestiya* published an article accusing the Warsaw government of "weakness" in its dealings with anti-Soviet provocateurs, naming among them the Roman Catholic priest Jerzy Popieluszko (*see* OBITUARIES). On October 30 Popieluszko's body was found at the bottom of a reservoir, 11 days after he had been kidnapped by three officers of the security police who reportedly confessed to the murder. A crowd estimated at 200,000 gathered in Warsaw for the funeral. An unprecedented public trial of the three officers charged with the murder and a fourth charged with abetting the crime opened on December 27. The first defendant to testify claimed he had been assured that the plot had high official approval.   (K. M. SMOGORZEWSKI)

ROMANIA

A socialist republic on the Balkan Peninsula in southeastern Europe, Romania has a coastline on the Black Sea. Area: 237,500 sq km (91,700 sq mi). Pop. (1984 est.): 22,794,000. Cap.: Bucharest. Monetary unit: leu, with (Oct. 29, 1984) an official rate of 5.15 lei to U.S. $1 (free rate of 6.22 lei = £1 sterling). General secretary of the Romanian Communist Party, president of the republic, and president of the State Council in 1984, Nicolae Ceausescu; chairman of the Council of Ministers (premier), Constantin Dascalescu.

On May 26, 1984, Pres. Nicolae Ceausescu of Romania opened the Danube-Black Sea canal, a huge project that had taken 11 years to complete. The amount of earth excavated was reportedly greater than that involved in the building of either the Suez or Panama Canal. If West Germany completed the final section of the Rhine-Main-Danube canal, the two together would provide a direct link between the North and Black seas.

At the 13th congress of the Romanian Communist Party (RCP), held in Bucharest November 19–22, Ceausescu was reelected general secretary and elections to renew the 23-member Executive Political Committee and the 10-member Secretariat took place. In his keynote address to the congress, Ceausescu defended the ambitious industrialization program that had created much of the foreign debt and taken up a large part of the national income during the 1970s. He claimed that the resulting industrial base had allowed Romania to overcome the hardships stemming from the world economic recession. The congress approved a five-year (1986–90) plan as well as guidelines for growth up to the year 2000. The five-year plan envisaged average annual growth of 7.6–8.3% and set detailed production targets for industry. An improvement in external finances, due in large measure to a reduction in imports from Western nations, enabled Romania in March to cancel the final installment of a standby credit agreed to with the International Monetary Fund in 1981.

Ceausescu continued to mark out a foreign policy for Romania that was increasingly independent of the U.S.S.R. In January Soviet Foreign Minister Andrey Gromyko visited Bucharest and invited Ceausescu to Moscow to discuss the problems of unity and cooperation among Communist parties. There were suggestions from some sources that Romania might raise objections to the renewal of the Warsaw Pact treaty due to take place in 1985. Romania had criticized increases in the Warsaw Pact defense budget because of the burden being placed on the country's economy. Gromyko's visit was preceded by an article in the Romanian press that repeated the call to the U.S.S.R. and the U.S. to halt further deployment of intermediate-range nuclear missiles and to resume disarmament negotiations. During Gromyko's visit it was announced that Moscow had agreed to supply 1.5 million metric tons of crude oil to Romania at the same favourable price enjoyed by other member countries of the Council for Mutual Economic Assistance. Romania again stepped out of line when it attended the Olympic Games in Los Angeles in July–August, the only Soviet-bloc country to do so.

On August 23 a military parade was held in Bucharest to mark the 40th anniversary of the overthrow of Marshal Ion Antonescu's pro-German dictatorship, which ended Romania's allegiance to Nazi Germany and signaled its entry into World War II on the Allied side. Speaking at a joint session of the Central Committee of the RCP and the National Assembly, Ceausescu described the events of 1944 as "a national liberation organized and led by the RCP in alliance with other political forces and the Army." This was the latest in a series of official pronouncements in which the role of the RCP in those events had been upgraded, while the role of the Soviet Army was effectively eliminated. The August parade was attended by 158 delegates from 112 countries, including several heads of state. The Soviet representative was Vitaly Vorotnikov, a relatively junior member of the Politburo.

Ceausescu's visit to West Germany in October was the first by a Warsaw Pact leader to a NATO country since the breakdown of the Geneva arms-limitation talks in November 1983. The visit was cut short in advance by two days, ostensibly because West German Foreign Minister Hans-Dietrich Genscher was to meet the Romanian delegation on its arrival, rather than Chancellor Helmut Kohl.

(K. M. SMOGORZEWSKI)

UNION OF SOVIET SOCIALIST REPUBLICS

The Union of Soviet Socialist Republics is a federal state covering parts of eastern Europe and northern Asia. Area: 22,402,200 sq km (8,649,500 sq mi). Pop (1984 est.): 273.4 million. Cap.: Moscow. Monetary unit: ruble, with (Oct. 29, 1984) a free rate of 0.87 ruble to U.S. $1 (1.05 rubles = £1 sterling). General secretary of the Communist Party of the Soviet Union and chairman of the Presidium of the Supreme Soviet (president) to Feb. 9, 1984, Yury V. Andropov; general secretary from February 9 and president from April 11, Konstantin U. Chernenko; chairman of the Council of Ministers (premier), Nikolay A. Tikhonov.

Domestic Affairs. When Yury Andropov (*see* OBITUARIES) died in February 1984, he was succeeded as general secretary of the Communist Party of the Soviet Union (CPSU) by Konstantin Chernenko (*see* BIOGRAPHIES). The latter became the first person over 70 to become CPSU leader and the first politician to acquire the highest party office after failing in a previous bid. In November 1982 Andropov had been powerful enough to push aside Chernenko to become general secretary after the death of Leonid Brezhnev, despite the fact that Chernenko had clearly enjoyed the support of Brezhnev. Had Brezhnev lived a little longer than he did, it would have been unlikely that Andropov could have succeeded him, since it was revealed at the latter's death that he had required the services of a dialysis machine to treat a kidney ailment since February 1983, six months before he disappeared from public view. At the same time, had Andropov survived for a short time longer, then Chernenko's health might have ruled him out of the succession. His speech at Andropov's funeral was poorly delivered, and his shortness of breath became evident every time he had to deliver a speech. It was widely believed that he was suffering from emphysema.

Given the level of international tension, not to speak of the sluggish domestic economy, the Soviet Union needed crisp, decisive leadership. Since the late 1970s, however, the country had been led by men who were not fully fit. Clearly the interests of the CPSU Politburo, which acted as the electoral college in choosing the CPSU general secretary, and those of the nation did not coincide. By some accounts Chernenko had failed to become Brezhnev's successor in November 1982 by the narrowest of margins. Andropov's strongest supporters were Foreign Minister Andrey Gromyko (*see* BIOGRAPHIES), Defense Minister Marshal Dmitry Ustinov (*see* OBITUARIES), and Politburo members Mikhail Gorbachev and Grigory Romanov (*see* BIOGRAPHIES). Under Andropov all four became more influential, and Romanov acquired a coveted secretaryship of the Central Committee (CC) of the CPSU in June 1983.

When it came to electing a successor to Andropov, Chernenko was in a strong position. During the time that Andropov had been incapacitated, Chernenko was apparently regarded as deputy general secretary, and he chaired Politburo meetings. The other two strong contenders for the position were Gorbachev and Romanov. Romanov was too inexperienced and a newcomer to the Moscow party scene, having moved from Leningrad to assume his CC secretaryship. Gorbachev, on the other hand, was being groomed by Andropov as his successor and was traveling abroad to gain experience in foreign affairs. He was prevented from succeeding Andropov primarily by his age. At 53 he was the youngest man in the Politburo and, if given the top position, might well have remained there for at least 20 years, long enough to obliterate the leadership aspirations of the older generation of Politburo members. Consequently, the older generation moved to retain power.

French Pres. François Mitterrand (right) called on Soviet Pres. Konstantin Chernenko (left) in June with a plea for Andrey Sakharov that brought gasps from their audience but no action by the Kremlin. Chernenko also rebuffed the prospect of talks with U.S. Pres. Ronald Reagan but modified his stand after the U.S. elections.
TASS/SOVFOTO

In order to move from party to national leader, Chernenko needed to acquire a leading state office. Since 1964 it had not been possible to hold the posts of CPSU general secretary and chairman of the Council of Ministers (premier) simultaneously. Andropov had been chairman of the Defense Council and chairman of the Presidium of the Supreme Soviet (president), and within two months of his death Chernenko had been appointed to both those offices. Chernenko thus became the third party leader in succession to fill those positions, indicating that it was now apparently established practice for the party leader to do so. However, it quickly became evident that Chernenko's new offices conferred authority but only a limited amount of real power. A ruling triumvirate emerged consisting of Chernenko, Ustinov, and Gromyko, the latter also first deputy premier.

Some tension was evident in relations between the CPSU and the military during the year. Chief of General Staff Marshal Nikolay Ogarkov was summarily dismissed in September and replaced by his deputy, Marshal Sergey Akhromeyev (see BIOGRAPHIES). The main reasons for the Politburo's decision to demote Ogarkov appeared to be his handling of the press conference called to justify the shooting down of the South Korean airliner by Soviet jet fighters in September 1983 and an interview with him that was published in the armed forces newspaper, *Krasnaya Zvezda,* on May 9, 1984.

The May interview was frank in revealing that Ogarkov was at odds with other leading military figures. He viewed the continuing buildup of nuclear weapons as pointless, given that no country could achieve a first-strike capability. The fact that some conventional weapons had become as destructive as nuclear weapons altered completely the manner in which the initial stages of a conflict would be fought. U.S. research into high technology, especially its applications in space, had profound implications for the methods and forms of armed struggle and even for the military power of the state. Ogarkov appeared to be stating that there were two schools of thought about military doctrine, the conservative and the radical, and that he belonged to the latter group. The radical school favoured a greater role for high technology and a rethinking of tactics in favour of flexibility and mobility. Ogarkov was critical of the inertia of the military-industrial establishment. However, the conservative school, based on the traditional use of tanks and artillery, emerged victorious.

The 40th anniversary of the victory over Germany in World War II was to be celebrated with great pomp in 1985. The importance with which the occasion was re-

garded by the CPSU and the government served two purposes: to upgrade the standing of the military and military preparedness, and to emphasize the fact that the U.S.S.R. was capable of defeating any challenge to its sovereignty.

Ogarkov did not sink without a trace. The information that he had been appointed to the post of commander in chief of the Western theatre of operations was not published in the Soviet press but was supplied to Western correspondents by Romanov during a visit to Helsinki in October. Ogarkov then appeared in East Berlin for discussions with East German leader Erich Honecker and Gen. Heinz Hoffmann, the East German minister of national defense. Their meeting was given prominence in East Germany, but it was not mentioned in the Soviet media. When Ustinov failed to appear at the parade commemorating the 67th anniversary of the Bolshevik Revolution on November 7, the main speech was delivered by Marshal Sergey Sokolov (see BIOGRAPHIES), first deputy minister of defense, although precedent suggested that Akhromeyev should have deputized for Ustinov. Solokov, aged 73, was named to succeed Ustinov after the latter's death on December 20. Chernenko did not attend Ustinov's funeral, possibly because of the bitterly cold weather.

The KGB state security force increased its standing during the year. In May it was announced that the highest rank in the KGB was henceforth to be that of generalissimo, a title conferred only on Stalin since the Revolution. Gen. Viktor Chebrikov, the KGB chairman, did not advance to this rank, but he acquired the right to wear a marshal's star.

The campaign against corruption continued, and two senior foreign trade officials were executed for taking large bribes. In Belorussia a thorough shakeup of the police and judicial organs was ordered after it was revealed that four murders had been blamed on innocent people from whom confessions had been extracted by torture. Three others were later sentenced to death for the murders.

More stringent laws were adopted to restrict further the access of Soviet citizens to Westerners. It became a crime to pass on "information which constituted a professional secret" to foreigners. Since the term professional secret could cover a wide range of information, the new law afforded the police far-reaching powers. Citizens who invited a foreigner to stay at their homes without reporting the fact to the authorities became liable to a fine of 50 rubles. New fences topped with barbed wire were erected around foreigners' residential compounds in Moscow.

In June the newspaper *Pravda* gave prominence to the burden borne by women. It was claimed that the average woman working in the home walked 15–20 km (9.3–12.4

Stately rituals laid the late Soviet leader Yury Andropov to rest (in a cemetery outside the Kremlin) upon his death in February. Here the senior members of the Politburo stand beside his bier. From left (front row): Grigory Romanov, Mikhail Solomentsev, Mikhail Gorbachev, Viktor Grishin, Dmitry Ustinov, Nikolay Tikhonov, Konstantin Chernenko.
GAMMA/LIAISON

mi) daily to carry out some 50 different operations, only 15% of which were mechanized. Shopping, usually performed by women, had become a tiring chore, with the amount of time spent standing in line having risen from 30,000,000,000 to 37,000,000,000 hours annually over the previous decade. The figures implied that the time spent shopping had increased by 25%, while the population had grown by 10% over the decade. More than 500 hours a year were spent on the activity by the average shopper.

Alcoholism remained the main social problem. Official statistics revealed that the consumption of alcohol had reached an annual per capita level of 4.2 litres (11.1 gal), placing the U.S.S.R. near the top in a comparison of consumption in different countries. These figures were based only on state-produced alcohol and omitted the home brew, *samogon*, consumption of which was estimated to be high. An article in *Pravda* reached the pessimistic conclusion that little could be done to halt the spread of alcoholism among the population.

Very few Armenians and Soviet Germans were permitted to leave the U.S.S.R. during 1984, while Jewish emigration was well below a thousand for the year. The decline illustrated the Kremlin's radical change of course in its emigration policy. It no longer believed that its foreign-policy objectives were furthered by issuing a large number of exit visas. Indeed, Soviet Jews were warned to stop demonstrating because their protests harmed the image of the U.S.S.R. abroad. The Anti-Zionist Committee, founded in April 1983, became more and more active in emigration affairs. A press conference in May was largely devoted to opposing emigration. It was made clear that a major task of the committee was to "defend" Soviet Jews against those who were attempting to induce them to emigrate. Chernenko's attitude toward anti-Semitism remained the same as Brezhnev's: it was a "nationalistic aberration" that was "alien to socialism." Chernenko also followed Brezhnev in equating Zionism with anti-Semitism. However, an article published in *Pravda* in May linked Zionism with fascism, a sentiment that had previously appeared in the Soviet media but never before so strongly and at such length in the party's official organ. By implying that a Zionist "fifth column" existed in every country where Zionists were to be found, the article made the assumption that the primary loyalty of Zionists in the U.S.S.R. and other socialist countries was to Israel.

Estonia was much in the news during the latter part of the year. A *Pravda* editorial in August laid bare the failings of the local party and claimed that not all leading cadres regarded participation in ideological work as their responsibility. Some leading officials were guilty of "personal immodesty, conceit, and misuse of office." Nationalism was rife, and citizens had to be convinced that being part of the U.S.S.R. guaranteed a bright future for the republic. A high-ranking official in the Komsomol (Young Communist League) and his wife defected while on an official visit to Finland in August. Since Finland refused to grant political asylum to Soviet citizens, the couple took the ferry to Stockholm, where they were granted asylum by the Swedish authorities. They claimed that the increasing "russification" of their homeland had forced them to leave, and they hoped that international pressure would oblige the Soviet authorities to allow them to be joined by their baby daughter. In November another Komsomol official from Estonia asked for political asylum in Sweden after taking the same route.

The election of Boris K. Pugo, Latvia's former KGB chief, as first secretary of the CPSU in that republic underlined the importance being attached to matters of law and order (the province of the KGB as well as international security). In Lithuania an official Academy of Sciences survey estimated that 27% of those aged 18 and over were religious believers—although the Roman Catholic Church put the figure much higher. In Georgia three members of the National Liberation Organization of Georgia received relatively light sentences in February, though T. Chikhladze, a Georgian Orthodox priest, was sentenced to death in August for "banditry and hijacking." Mustafa Dzhemilev was sentenced for the sixth time in February for campaigning for the right of Crimean Tatars to return to their ancestral homeland.

An increase in atheist propaganda was evident in 1984. In October a *Pravda* editorial complained that not enough was being done to combat religion. Special concern was expressed about Lithuania, Armenia, and the Muslim Central Asian republics. It was evident that Islam was increasingly influential. An official publication put the number of believers in the U.S.S.R. at 9–10% of the adult population. A Leningrad propagandist made the point that, whereas young people could enter a church free of charge, they had to pay to go into the city's Museum of Atheism.

The Economy. The growth in industrial output was targeted at 3.4% for 1984, and during the first nine months of the year it exceeded 4.1%. The rise in labour productivity was put at 3.7%. Although production of petroleum and coal marginally exceeded planned levels, quantitatively the amounts were lower than in 1983. The output of margarine, vegetable oil, citrus fruit, watches, dishes, refrigerators, and freezers fell below that envisioned in the plan.

Transport remained a bottleneck. It was estimated that at any one time one-third of the nation's trucks were out of service. With 88% of the nation's fuel and minerals coming from Siberia and the far east of the U.S.S.R., the pressure on the railways had increased. The Baikal-Amur railway was officially completed in October.

A candid article by an Estonian scientist that appeared in the government newspaper *Izvestiya* in June illustrated the difficulties facing the campaign to step up innovation in Soviet industry. He stated that there was "still no economic mechanism regulating the relationship between science and production." Until this happened it would be "difficult to speak of major changes in the rates of development of scientific-technical progress" in the economy in general, though the criticism did not apply to the defense sector. A new five-year computer plan was unveiled involving the U.S.S.R. and seven other member countries of the Council for Mutual Economic Assistance (Comecon). Among the goals was the construction of a fifth-generation computer.

If the performance of industry gave some grounds for satisfaction, that of agriculture caused nothing but anguish. Western specialists estimated the harvest at about 170 million metric tons, a total that would require the U.S.S.R. to import 45 million–50 million metric tons of grain during 1984–85. At a CC meeting convened in October to review the situation, it was decided to increase the amount of irrigated and drained land over the years 1985–2000 by about 12 million ha (29.6 million ac). During the last 20 years $134 billion had been spent on irrigation and drainage, though as a means of solving the country's food problem, the policy had met with little success, given the fact that

land fell out of use as quickly as new land was added to the arable area. Many organizations involved in irrigation and drainage had a poor reputation for technical efficiency. Chernenko conceded that the problem of supplying many cities with foodstuffs, and meat in particular, remained acute. Gorbachev, the CC secretary for agriculture, might have been expected to launch the new plan, but he remained silent, indicating perhaps that he was no longer responsible for the rural sector. The minister of agriculture and the minister of water economy were sharply criticized in the main speech by Premier Nikolay Tikhonov.

An article that appeared in *Pravda* in May gave pause for thought. The author stated that over the last 30–40 years the black-earth belt—the "breadbasket" of the country—had lost one-third of its humus (the organic portion of soil) and that the layer of fertile soil had been reduced in depth by 10–15 cm (4–6 in).

Foreign Affairs. The policy of détente was declared officially dead by Leonid Zamyatin, CC secretary for international affairs, on Soviet television on May 26. In September the Soviet news agency TASS reported that relations between the superpowers had fallen to the "lowest level in their entire history" and that the fault lay with U.S. Pres. Ronald Reagan, who believed that arms negotiations could be conducted only from a position of strength. In a major speech on November 6 Gromyko made the point that it was "totally absurd" for the U.S. to believe that the route to disarmament lay through an unprecedented arms race. However, Gromyko's visit to Washington and the UN in September was the first signal that the U.S.S.R. was preparing to resume arms talks. After Reagan's reelection an agreement was reached that Gromyko and U.S. Secretary of State George Shultz would meet in Geneva in January 1985 to pave the way for wider talks. The Soviet demand that NATO withdraw its Pershing II and cruise nuclear missiles from Western Europe as a precondition of the talks was quietly dropped.

In May the U.S.S.R. announced its decision to withdraw from the summer Olympic Games in Los Angeles. The Soviets accused the U.S. of using the Games as an occasion to encourage anti-Soviet hysteria. The boycott was later joined by other Communist countries including those of Eastern Europe, with the exception of Romania and Yugoslavia. The Soviets criticized the choice of Seoul, South Korea, as the venue for the 1988 Summer Games.

The Soviets made little progress in Afghanistan, though their tactics became a little clearer. They sought to occupy the towns and drive the population opposed to them from the countryside. Relations with China barely improved, despite considerable Soviet efforts to bring the two countries closer together. After being canceled abruptly by the Soviets earlier in the year, the visit to Beijing (Peking) of First Deputy Premier Ivan Arkhipov took place in December, when accords on cooperation in trade and science were signed. The Chinese foreign minister's meeting with Gromyko at the UN in September was the first at that level for two years. Relations with Japan went from bad to worse as the Japanese announced that they were developing a new tank, a new antisubmarine helicopter, and a new radar system as part of a defense buildup. The U.S.S.R. returned to favour in Iraq, and several joint economic ventures were announced.

The case of Andrey Sakharov (*see* BIOGRAPHIES), dissident Soviet physicist, received much publicity in the West during the year. At the same time, however, the Kremlin recorded some success in its battle to convince defectors that life at home was better than in the West. In October Svetlana Alliluyeva, Stalin's daughter, who had defected in

TASS/SOVFOTO

Soviet Defense Minister Dmitry Ustinov (left rear) and Foreign Minister Andrey Gromyko watch as Soviet leader Konstantin Chernenko (right front) and Polish leader Wojciech Jaruzelski exchange cooperation agreements in Moscow in May.

1967, returned to the U.S.S.R. Soviet citizenship, which she had lost in 1969, was restored to her and conferred on her 13-year-old daughter, Olga. The move was surprising since Svetlana had once reportedly described the U.S.S.R. as a "prison full of pain and trauma." She exculpated herself by claiming that all her writings while she was in the West had been dictated by Western intelligence agents. A more bizarre case was that of Oleg Bitov, a Soviet journalist, who returned to Moscow in September a year after apparently defecting to the West. Back in Moscow, he claimed that he had in fact been kidnapped while in Italy by the secret service of the U.K. Two soldiers who had spent some months in the U.K. after defecting from the Soviet Army in Afghanistan decided to return to the U.S.S.R. in November. (MARTIN MCCAULEY)

YUGOSLAVIA

> A federal socialist republic, Yugoslavia is in southern Europe on the Adriatic Sea. Area: 255,804 sq km (98,766 sq mi). Pop. (1984 est.): 23,053,000. Cap.: Belgrade. Monetary unit: Yugoslav dinar, with (Oct. 29, 1984) a free rate of 185.02 dinars to U.S. $1 (223.32 dinars = £1 sterling). Presidents of the Presidium of the League of Communists in 1984, Dragoslav Markovic and, from June 26, Ali Sukrija; presidents of the Collective Presidency, Mika Spiljak and, from May 15, Veselin Djuranovic; president of the Federal Executive Council (premier), Milka Planinc.

Yugoslavia experienced serious economic difficulties in 1984 but maintained its independent position between East and West. Relations with the U.S.S.R. continued to be good except for a brief disagreement in October when Yugoslavia claimed that the Soviets were belittling the role of the Yugoslav forces in the liberation of Belgrade from the Germans in 1944. At the end of February, soon after Konstantin Chernenko became general secretary of the Communist Party of the Soviet Union, Vidoje Zarkovic, vice-president of Yugoslavia's Collective Presidency, visited Moscow and held talks with Soviet leaders.

Yugoslavia's relations with the West concentrated on economic issues. During the second half of the year the government was engaged in talks with the International Monetary Fund (IMF) about rescheduling its $20 billion debt, one-third of which was owed to Western governments, one-third to international institutions, and one-third to commercial banks. The government was also seeking a relaxation of IMF conditions, which it had found economically and politically difficult to meet. Creditors, however, wanted Yugoslavia to remain under tight IMF supervision. Toward the end of November Yugoslavia indicated that it was willing to accept the conditions on the understanding that a new IMF standby loan would be made available.

Other important diplomatic contacts in 1984 included a visit to China in May by Dragoslav Markovic, president of the Presidium of the League of Communists, and a trip to Yugoslavia in August–September by Chinese Pres. Li Xiannian (Li Hsien-nien). In July Milka Planinc became the first Yugoslav premier to visit Bulgaria since the end of World War II. Janos Kadar, the Hungarian Communist Party leader, paid a visit to Belgrade in March.

Yugoslavia's relations with Albania worsened in October when the government called off talks on scientific and cultural cooperation because of Albania's alleged unwillingness to consider special claims by the Yugoslav minority in Albania. Polemics between the two countries continued in 1984 over the situation in Kosovo, the largely Albanian-inhabited autonomous province of Serbia, and trials of Kosovo Albanians accused of "separatism" and

"irredentism" took place. Nevertheless, trade between the two countries reached $111 million, and a trade protocol signed in October envisioned an 8% increase in 1985.

A crowd estimated at more than 300,000 attended the Roman Catholic national eucharistic congress in Marija Bistrica, Croatia, on September 8–9, the largest religious gathering in Eastern Europe outside Poland in the post-1945 era. Pope John Paul II was expected to attend, but his visit was postponed at the request of the government.

The election of Veselin Djuranovic as the new president of the Collective Presidency in May was criticized in Slovenia on the grounds that, as premier during the period 1977–82, he had been responsible for causing Yugoslavia to become heavily indebted. Two senior ministerial changes were made. Raif Dizdarevic, a Bosnian Muslim, became foreign minister, and Dobroslav Culafic, a Montenegrin, was appointed minister of the interior. The appointment of Svetislav Dolasevic, a Serbian, as president of the League of Communists in Kosovo was bitterly criticized in Albania on the grounds that it represented a step backward to the period of Serbian domination in Kosovo. Under the annual system of rotation, Dragoslav Markovic was replaced as president of the Presidium of the League of Communists in June by Ali Sukrija.

During the first six months of 1984, industrial output increased by 5%, while exports grew by 4% and imports by 3%. The trade deficit in the first nine months of the year was $1.5 billion. Unemployment stood at 13%, and with real wages 7% lower than in 1983 strikes were more frequent. On September 1 the price freeze introduced a year earlier was lifted from over half the industrial products covered. In the first nine months retail prices were 67% higher than in the same period of 1983.

A new foreign investment law promulgated in November ended the profit limit for foreign partners in joint ventures with Yugoslav firms. It also waived the rule prohibiting foreign partners from holding a majority stake in such ventures. (K. F. CVIIC)

North America

CANADA

> Canada is a federal parliamentary state and member of the Commonwealth covering North America north of conterminous United States and east of Alaska. Area: 9,970,610 sq km (3,851,809 sq mi). Pop. (1984 est.): 25,150,400. Cap.: Ottawa. Monetary unit: Canadian dollar, with (Oct. 29, 1984) a free rate of Can$1.32 to U.S. $1 (Can$1.60 = £1 sterling). Queen, Elizabeth II; governors-general in 1984, Edward R. Schreyer and, from May 14, Jeanne Sauvé; prime ministers, Pierre Elliott Trudeau, John Turner from June 30, and, from September 17, Brian Mulroney.

Domestic Affairs. The long dominance of the Liberal Party in Canadian national politics was dramatically shattered in a general election held on Sept. 4, 1984. The Progressive Conservative Party, in opposition for almost 42 of the last 50 years, captured 211 of the 282 seats in the House of Commons. It was the second most decisive electoral victory in Canada's history. (The largest electoral sweep occurred in 1958 when the Conservatives under John Diefenbaker captured 208 seats in a House of 265.) The Conservatives gained a majority of the popular vote in every region of Canada, a result that had not occurred for generations. The leader of the party, Brian Mulroney (see BIOGRAPHIES), became Canada's 18th prime minister on September 17. The Conservative triumph was a stinging personal rebuke

For Pope John Paul II's appearance at a youth rally in Montreal during his Canadian pastoral visit in September, white-clad dancers formed a dove, the symbol of the Holy Spirit.
FRANCOIS LOCHON—GAMMA/LIAISON

for former prime minister Pierre Trudeau, who had resigned office on June 30 after more than 15 years in power. Although Trudeau had not run in the election, many voters expressed their dissatisfaction with the last years of his leadership.

The train of events that led to this sweeping political change began in late February when, during a walk in the winter's worst snowstorm, Trudeau reached the decision that he would leave public life. His resignation was announced on February 29, and the Liberal Party called a convention to choose a new leader for June 14–16 in Ottawa. Six members of Trudeau's Cabinet declared their candidacy, the one with the largest following being Jean Chrétien, the minister of energy. But on March 16 a former member of the Trudeau Cabinet, John Turner (*see* BIOGRAPHIES), a Toronto corporation lawyer, threw his hat into the ring. Turner had resigned the post of minister

PAUL CHIASSON—GAMMA/LIAISON

After winning leadership of the Liberal Party in June, and thus becoming prime minister-designate, John Turner (left) called on retiring leader Prime Minister Pierre Trudeau at his official residence in Ottawa.

of finance in 1975, following a disagreement with Trudeau, and had left politics. It soon became apparent that he possessed the support of most of the Trudeau ministers as well as the Liberal Party establishment. Although Chrétien campaigned vigorously across the country, Turner won the leadership on a second convention ballot on June 16. He polled 1,862 votes to Chrétien's 1,368.

Turner assumed office as 17th prime minister on June 30. He experienced difficulty in forming a Cabinet since he was determined to include Chrétien, and the latter imposed conditions upon his participation. In the end, Chrétien was named secretary of state for external affairs and deputy prime minister. Some of his supporters were also brought into the ministry. The Turner Cabinet contained 29 members, down from the 36 in Trudeau's administration. The main portfolios were held by 23 former Trudeau ministers, most of whom had backed Turner in his bid for the party leadership. Inevitably, these arrangements hurt the image of a fresh Turner team, which the new prime minister had hoped to establish.

Turner's attempt to distance himself from the unpopular Trudeau administration was fatally compromised by his promise to Trudeau to appoint 17 retiring members of Parliament to posts in the appointed Senate, the courts, or the diplomatic service. On July 9 Turner—buoyed by opinion polls showing the Liberals with an 8–10% popular lead over the Conservatives—advised the governor-general to dissolve Parliament and call a general election for September 4. The appointments were announced at this time, and the blatant patronage involved repelled many Canadians. Turner weakly defended the appointments in a television debate with the other party leaders on July 25, claiming that he had "no option" but to honour his promise to Trudeau. But Mulroney, the leader of the Conservatives, and Edward Broadbent of the New Democratic Party (NDP) relentlessly pursued the subject throughout the election campaign.

Turner's campaign through the summer was a series of disasters. It was apparent that he had been precipitate in calling the election before he had established policies for his new government. In spite of the party's claim that it was ready to fight the election, only 40 Liberals had been nominated when the election was called, compared with 240 for the Conservatives and 155 for the NDP. The Liberals had no election strategy and were saddled with an inept
(continued on page 559)

New Beginnings

BY PETER WARD

Canada began 1985 with a new government, a new spirit, and more political unity than it had enjoyed for 22 years. Progressive Conservative Party leader Brian Mulroney (*see* BIOGRAPHIES) broke several records at the polls in the September 4 election, winning 211 seats in the 282-seat House of Commons and electing members from every province in sufficient numbers to make solid regional representation around the Cabinet table possible. No Canadian government had managed that since the 1958–62 government of Conservative John Diefenbaker. No Liberal government since 1953 had included elected members from every province. (*See* CANADA.)

Shape of the New Government. Quebec was a particular challenge for Mulroney in the election, and the party's success there surprised even Conservatives. Quebec elected Conservatives to 58 of the province's 75 seats, nothing short of a Conservative miracle, since Quebec is a traditional Liberal stronghold. Quebec Conservatives had been held to no more than four seats in each of the five previous elections. In 1984 the Liberal contingent was slashed to 17 seats, and separatist Premier René Lévesque proclaimed that the province's political freedom from the federal Liberal machine had been obtained. Lévesque came close to conceding the death of the separatist movement. He at least shunted the issue to a back burner by pledging to end Quebec's boycott of federal-provincial conferences and by promising to give Canadian confederation another chance. In effect, separation of Quebec was no longer an issue. Confrontation was out; cooperation was in.

Mulroney received promises of cooperation from each of the ten provincial premiers shortly after his election victory. In turn, he pledged to consult the provincial governments, even to the extent of holding a top-level economic conference in Ottawa before the first Conservative federal budget was produced early in 1985, so that provincial concerns could be reflected in federal policy. Often in the past 15 years, federal economic strategy had been implemented with little consultation, resulting in contradictory aims from the two levels of government and the consequent ineffectiveness of budgetary measures.

A measure of former prime minister Pierre Trudeau's relations with the provincial governments was the fact that Mulroney managed to secure the active aid of seven of the ten premiers during the election campaign. He also had a measure of support from Lévesque and from British Columbia's William Bennett, plus an unexpected degree of neutrality from the New Democratic Party (NDP) government of Howard Pawley in Manitoba. The seven premiers who offered active support were all Conservative. Crucial to Mulroney's success was the support offered by Ontario's Premier William Davis, who planned to retire early in 1985. Davis had offered only token support to the

previous federal Conservative leader, Joe Clark, but for Mulroney, Davis unleashed the full might of his political machine, the most powerful in Canada. It was Davis's tacticians who constructed the federal Conservative victory, and Mulroney owed Davis for his support. That debt to Ontario, combined with the strong Conservative representation from Quebec, made western Canada nervous.

Because Quebec with its 75 seats and Ontario with its 95 can dominate Canada's Parliament, western Canada had been shut out of mainstream decision making for most of the past two decades. The West voted Conservative consistently throughout the Trudeau years. Following the 1984 Conservative landslide, concern was expressed in the four western provinces that the two central provinces of Ontario and Quebec might continue to dominate affairs under a Mulroney government. The distrust between the western and central provinces was one of the wounds in the Canadian psyche that Mulroney was intent upon healing. Throughout the campaign he promised to replace confrontation with conciliation and to restore the checks and balances of democracy.

Mandate for Change. Former prime minister Pierre Trudeau, who on Feb. 29, 1984, announced his decision to retire, had achieved his aims during 16 years of leadership largely through confrontation. He provoked extreme reactions in both western Canada and Quebec. Trudeau and Lévesque were longtime enemies who disliked each other intensely. Mulroney's conciliatory style was a total reversal of Trudeau's techniques, and change was exactly what Canadians wanted.

A Gallup Poll conducted shortly after the September 4 election showed that one-third of Canadians had voted for change and not for the policies of any particular party. The Liberals had realized that Canada wanted change. The race for the Liberal leadership resulted, on June 16, in the victory of former Liberal finance minister John Turner (*see* BIOGRAPHIES), who quit the Trudeau Cabinet

N. PONOMAREFF—PHOTOREPORTERS

Canada changed its political direction with its September elections, which gave a landslide victory to the Progressive Conservative Party, making its leader, Brian Mulroney, here with his wife acknowledging his victory on election night, Canada's new prime minister.

Peter Ward operates Ward News Services Canada in the Parliamentary Press Gallery, Ottawa.

in 1975 because of economic disagreements with the prime minister. Turner, who automatically became entitled to the prime minister's job once he won the party leadership, took power on June 30. Nine days later, against the advice of some of his strategists, he called a federal election, and the result was disaster. Some critics charged that Turner's election timing was a major reason for his defeat. Others maintained that the Canadian mood for change was so strong that Liberals would have been defeated no matter when Canadians voted. (*See* CANADA.)

The New Broom. On assuming power, Mulroney lost little time in pursuing one of his chief campaign pledges—creating a better climate between Ottawa and Washington. U.S. Pres. Ronald Reagan had complained in previous years about Canada's Foreign Investment Review Agency (FIRA) and its National Energy Program. Both would be remedied, Mulroney said. He planned to scrap FIRA not so much because it represented an actual barrier to foreign investment as because it had become a psychological block. FIRA had turned down few applications for foreign investment in recent years, but applicants had used up millions of dollars in legal fees and wasted valuable time awaiting decisions.

In mid-October former prime minister Joe Clark, appointed minister of external affairs in Mulroney's new government, met for two days with U.S. Secretary of State George Shultz in Toronto, underlining with every statement the theory that a new day of cooperative relationship was dawning for Canada and the U.S. The words were sweet music, but Shultz gave Clark the same answer on acid rain that the Reagan administration had been offering for four years—there had to be more study on the subject before billions were spent cleaning up air pollution. The scientific community might now agree that acid rain comes from air pollution and is causing billions of dollars in damage to the northeastern U.S. and eastern Canada; nevertheless, it was clear that no new relationship between Ottawa and Washington was powerful enough to bring about action on a cleanup, at least before the U.S. election in November.

The lack of concrete U.S. moves to defuse such issues as acid rain and the Garrison diversion dam was not something that greatly concerned most Canadian observers—provided there was hope of negotiation after the U.S. election. Of more immediate concern was the Canadian economy. Mulroney won his massive victory because he ran an optimistic campaign that promised positive action on unemployment, interest rates, the federal deficit, and

inflation. But few governments had ever come to power with less room for maneuver. By March 1985 the national debt had climbed to $185 billion, or slightly more than $7,500 for every Canadian, and the annual federal deficit was in excess of $35 billion. In the 1984–85 fiscal year, it cost the federal government $21 billion just to service the debt. Conservatives were blaming the Liberals for years of bad management. Liberals were challenging Conservatives to fulfill their campaign promises on job creation and better budget making—without cutting into the expensive network of social programs constructed by successive Liberal governments.

Canadians received reassurance in the speech from the throne that social services would not be dismantled by the Mulroney government, despite economic difficulties. The speech from the throne, delivered by the governor-general but written by the prime minister's most senior advisers, traditionally opens a new session of Parliament in Canada and outlines, in general terms, the intentions of the government. The document read in Ottawa on November 5, as the 33rd Parliament opened, promised action in all the areas covered during the election campaign, but—with a few exceptions—it was short on specifics.

Unemployment and the need to reduce the deficit were named as priorities for domestic policy. Increased spending on defense, adherence to Canada's NATO commitments, and closer relations with the U.S. were to be the cornerstones of foreign policy. The Mulroney government, said the speech from the throne, intends to try to recapture Canada's former reputation for constructive internationalism, beginning with an intensive search for nuclear disarmament.

Politics promised to be less combative under the Mulroney government than they had been under Trudeau. The opening of Parliament was notable for the extreme civility displayed between Mulroney, Turner, and NDP leader Ed Broadbent. They laughed, backslapped, and complimented one another. At one point Mulroney and Turner marched down the aisle of Parliament with arms around each other's shoulders. If Canadians voted for less political confrontation, that was certainly what they got.

A Gallup Poll taken after the election showed that 68% of those polled were satisfied with the result and with the overwhelming mandate given to Mulroney's Progressive Conservatives. That level of satisfaction would last only if Canada's economic woes could be repaired and if the practice of conciliation really could bring the country's fractious regions together to work for a common purpose.

(continued from page 557)

campaign organization that had to be shaken up halfway to election day. In Quebec, where the Liberals had held 74 of 75 seats, the party organization had become atrophied. There was a rift between Chrétien and the other Quebec ministers. It was clear, as the campaign progressed, that the Liberals were tired, bereft of new ideas, complacently riding on their record, and still regarded as the party of Pierre Trudeau. The opinion polls swung massively against Turner. The Conservatives emphasized the need for change and portrayed themselves as the party of reconciliation between regions and groups within Canada. With a warm personality, a resonant voice, and aided by an attractive young wife, Mulroney projected an image of reassurance and optimism. Broadbent made a strong impression in the television debates, appealing to "ordinary Canadians" and women with a list of practical policies.

The Conservatives took an early lead in the election

and held it across Canada. Although every commentator had predicted their victory, its size astonished the country. Nearly 100 Liberal seats in the House of Commons were lost, and 15 members of Turner's Cabinet went down to defeat. In the West, where the Liberals had only two MP's, they lost one of their seats, but Turner, who had courageously run in Vancouver, B.C., to show his identification with the West, succeeded in taking a seat from the Conservatives. The Liberals elected only 40 MP's and gained only 28% of the popular vote, the worst defeat in their history. Outside Quebec the party stood in third place among the national parties.

The Conservatives gained an electoral victory second only to the one in 1958. In 1984 they won 50% of the popular vote; in 1958 they had won 53%. But in 1984 they won the largest share of the popular vote in each of the ten provinces, a record for them. Their most spectacular showing was in Quebec, where they had been all but shut out for a quarter of a century. There they captured 58 of 75 seats. There were several explanations for this dramatic turnaround. It represented a personal tribute to Mulroney, who won a seat on the rugged north shore of the Gulf of St. Lawrence, where he had been born. Mulroney spoke the language of small-town Quebec and was regarded by Quebeckers as *un des nôtres,* "one of ours." He understood the ways of Quebec and had carefully selected the Conservative candidates. Perhaps the most profound reason, however, was that Quebec, sensing a change, wanted to be part of the new government in Ottawa. Previous elections had shown a potentially dangerous polarization in Canada, with the Liberals dominant in Quebec but having no representation in the West, the Conservatives strong in the West but a negligible force in Quebec. Now the Conservatives emerged as a truly national party, strong in every region, in cities as well as in rural areas.

Election Results, Sept. 4, 1984
(1980 results in parentheses)

Area	Progressive Conservatives	Liberals	New Democratic Party
Atlantic region (Newfoundland, Nova Scotia, New Brunswick, Prince Edward Island)			
32 (32)	25 (13)	7 (19)	0 (0)
Quebec			
75 (75)	58 (1)	17 (74)	0 (0)
Ontario			
95* (95)	67 (38)	14 (52)	13 (5)
West (Manitoba, Saskatchewan, Alberta, British Columbia)			
77 (77)	58 (49)	2 (2)	17 (26)
North (Northwest Territories, Yukon)			
3 (3)	3 (2)	0 (0)	0 (1)
Total			
282 (282)	211 (103)	40 (147)	30 (32)

*Includes one independent.

The NDP fared better than had been expected, capturing 19% of the popular vote and electing 30 members from Ontario and the West. This was an impressive result in the face of the Conservative sweep, especially in the West, where NDP support was considered "soft" in some ridings (districts).

Turner resigned on September 17, having led an administration for only 80 days, the shortest-serving prime minister in 20th-century Canada. Mulroney led his new government to office on the same day. With such a majority in the House, it was not surprising that the new Cabinet was a large one, comprising 40 members. There were 11 ministers each from Ontario and Quebec, 5 from the Maritimes, and 13 from the West. Sixteen of the ministers had served in the short-lived government of Joe Clark in 1979–80, and one had been a member of the last Diefenbaker administration, but 23 had had no previous experience in government. There were 19 women elected in the Conservative ranks and, of this group, 6 found their way into the Cabinet. The most important posts went to Clark, whom Mulroney had defeated for the leadership a year before (external affairs), and to others who had competed with Mulroney for the leadership: Michael Wilson (finance), John Crosbie (justice), and Sinclair Stevens (regional industrial expansion).

Mulroney faced a severe test in holding together his diverse army of MP's and giving them meaningful tasks and a sense of purpose. The new leader had made his business reputation as an industrial conciliator; it was apparent that he would need to display all his skills when the new Parliament assembled on November 5. (*See* Special Report.)

A provision of Quebec's controversial 1977 language law, which restricted access to English schools to children with at least one parent educated in English in Quebec, was struck down by the Supreme Court of Canada in a decision announced on July 26. The court held that the Quebec law violated the language guarantees in the Charter of Rights and Freedoms, part of the Canadian constitution since 1982. The charter allows children of parents educated in English or in French to have the right to English- or French-language education in any province where numbers warrant. The decision was a further setback to Quebec's attempt to control its educational system and confirmed the province's isolation in the Canadian confederation. This had been manifest since 1981, when Quebec had refused to cooperate with the federal government and the nine other provinces in a procedure for amending the constitution.

Canada gained the first woman governor-general in its history on May 14 when Jeanne Sauvé (*see* BIOGRAPHIES), a former MP from Quebec and the first woman speaker of the Commons, was sworn into the vice-regal post.

Only one province held an election in 1984. The conservative mood of the country contributed to Premier John Buchanan's landslide victory in Nova Scotia on November 6. Buchanan's Progressive Conservative Party, in office since 1978, gained 4 seats to send 42 members to the 52-seat legislature. The opposition Liberals lost their leader and elected only 6 members. The New Democratic Party won 3 seats, and there was an independent Labor Party member returned from Cape Breton Island.

The Economy. Following years of recession and recovery in 1982 and 1983, the Canadian economy regained its pre-recession peak in January 1984 and began to move ahead with confidence. The gross national product was forecast at $387 billion for 1984, an output that benefited from the strong demand for Canadian products in the U.S. The country's merchandise trade surplus for 1984 was expected to surpass $20 billion, a substantial improvement over the $17.8 billion recorded in the previous year. With 77% of all Canada's exports going to the U.S., and with automobiles and auto parts making up one-quarter of this flow, the strength of the U.S. car market was clearly of major importance to its northern neighbour.

Although helped by strong export sales to the U.S., the Canadian dollar followed a roller-coaster course during 1984. From 80 cents U.S. in March, it fell to an all-time low of 74.86 cents U.S. on July 11. In October it hovered around 75 cents U.S. Unemployment continued high despite the healthier economic environment. It was reported that 11.3% of the labour force was unemployed in October, an army of 1,400,000 Canadians. For the 15–24-year age group, the ratio rose in September to 18.4%. Yet the number of jobs in the economy was increasing at a gratifying rate. The explanation appeared to be that, as expectations of finding a job arose, people rejoined the labour force after having left it in discouragement at an earlier time. The bright spot among economic indicators was the inflation rate, which was down to 3.8% on a year-to-year basis in September, the lowest rise in consumer prices in 13 years. Interest rates remained high, with the Bank of Canada rate standing at 12.2% in October.

Finance Minister Marc Lalonde brought down what was to be his last budget on February 15. There were few surprises, except that the estimated deficit for 1984–85, at $29.6 billion, was larger than had been predicted. About $550 million of the increased deficit was to go for job creation. Public-sector wage controls, introduced in 1982, were to be phased out, thus allowing a return to collective bargaining in the public service. There were tax concessions for small businesses, but the elimination of the $100 standard medical deduction and a 1% increase in the federal sales tax (coming into effect October 1) meant a heavier burden for individual taxpayers.

The new finance minister, Michael Wilson, presented a minibudget on November 8, slashing government spending for the fiscal year beginning on April 1, 1985, by $4.2 billion, reducing unemployment insurance benefits, and giving Canadians immediate higher gasoline prices. The federal government's deficit for 1984–85 was now predicted at $34.6 billion, but Wilson promised to reduce it in the next fiscal year.

Foreign Affairs. Prime Minister Trudeau's "peace initiative," designed to return the superpowers to arms negotiations, represented the final phase in Trudeau's role as an international statesman. The attempt to inject political energy into the stalemated East-West relationship took Trudeau, from November 1983 to February 1984, to Western Europe, Japan, India, China, the U.S., the U.S.S.R., and three Eastern European countries. In a report to the Canadian Parliament on February 9, Trudeau admitted the limited effectiveness of his efforts. He said, however, that he was encouraged by signs that cold war rhetoric was being "turned down." The new Conservative external affairs minister, Joe Clark, indicated that he intended to follow in Trudeau's footsteps when he made his inaugural address before the UN on September 25. Peace and disarmament, he stated, would continue to be the priorities in Canadian foreign policy.

Visitors to Canada during 1984 included Premier Zhao Ziyang (Chao Tzu-yang) of China (January), who continued to be cool to Trudeau's proposal, made earlier in China, that there be a conference of the five nuclear powers; Pres. Miguel de la Madrid of Mexico (May), who

A deranged Canadian soldier sprayed submachine-gun fire inside the Quebec National Assembly building on May 8, killing 3 persons and wounding 13, one of whom is wheeled to an ambulance.

discussed bilateral issues; and Zehdi Terzi, the Palestine Liberation Organization's permanent representative at the UN, who made a controversial appearance before a parliamentary committee on April 5. Pope John Paul II also went to Canada for 12 days in September, his first visit as pope. Starting in Quebec, the site of the first Roman Catholic diocese in northern North America, the pontiff traveled to the Pacific coast and back to Ottawa, giving 34 sermons and speeches in a grueling tour. Canadian athletes enjoyed their best showing ever at the Olympic Games in Los Angeles in July and August. They won 43 medals, more than the country had collected in all the Olympic Games from 1948 to 1976, inclusive.

The testing of the U.S. cruise missile, which had aroused a storm of controversy in 1983, receded somewhat as an issue as the first test occurred in northern Canada on March 6. A missile strapped to a B-52 bomber, using its own navigation and terrain contour-matching equipment, guided the aircraft over a 2,400-km (1,500-mi) flight to an air weapons range on the Saskatchewan-Alberta border. A Canadian naval officer, Comdr. Marc Garneau of Quebec (see BIOGRAPHIES), became the first Canadian astronaut when he joined the crew of the space shuttle "Challenger" for an eight-day spaceflight ended on October 13. Garneau carried out tests in medicine and physics during the flight and attempted additional use of the successful Canadian-built cargo-handling arm, Canadarm.

Prime Minister Mulroney showed his determination to "refurbish" the Canadian-U.S. relationship after the Trudeau years by paying a visit to Pres. Ronald Reagan on September 25, just eight days after taking office. Mulroney spoke of the need for Canada to maintain a strong and healthy tie with the U.S. to assist his new government in its task of "economic renewal." Trade, investment, and markets, all connected with the U.S., were vital elements in creating the climate for economic growth that Mulroney desired. It was reported that there was good "chemistry" between the two leaders, who agreed to hold working meetings at least once a year. Cabinet ministers from the two countries were also to meet on a more regular basis.

A historic decision dividing the rich fishing waters of the Gulf of Maine between New England and Nova Scotia was handed down by a special panel of the International Court of Justice in The Hague, Neth., on October 12. Canada gained 1,336 square nautical miles lying near Georges Bank, about half of what it had claimed. The zone encompassed 50% of the valuable scallop-fishing grounds, a major resource for the fishermen of western Nova Scotia. The two parties in the long-standing dispute had agreed in advance to accept the panel's decision, which was rendered by a 4–1 vote. The fact that both the Canadian and U.S. judges supported the majority opinion was seen as an auspicious indication that the award would be duly implemented by the two governments. Still to be settled was an arrangement for the management of free-swimming fish stocks inhabiting the gulf. (D. M. L. FARR)

UNITED STATES

The United States of America is a federal republic composed of 50 states, 49 of which are in North America and one of which consists of the Hawaiian Islands. Area: 9,372,571 sq km (3,618,770 sq mi), including 205,856 sq km of inland water but excluding the 156,492 sq km of the Great Lakes that lie within U.S. boundaries. Pop. (1984 est.): 236,634,000. Cap.: Washington, D.C. Monetary unit: U.S. dollar, with (Oct. 29, 1984) a free rate of U.S. $1.21 to £1 sterling. President in 1984, Ronald Reagan.

Domestic Affairs. As expected, Pres. Ronald Reagan (*see* BIOGRAPHIES) swept to victory on Nov. 6, 1984, in a landslide reelection to a second term. Reagan drew 59% of the popular vote—just short of the 61% record established by Pres. Lyndon B. Johnson in 1964 and the 60% share taken by Pres. Franklin D. Roosevelt in 1936. He won all but one state, a feat matched only by Richard M. Nixon in 1972, and amassed an unprecedented total of 525 electoral votes. That left just 13 electoral votes for Walter F. Mondale (*see* BIOGRAPHIES), his Democratic opponent, who carried the District of Columbia and his home state of Minnesota. (*See* Special Report.)

A major factor in the Reagan victory was the economic recovery, which helped to create a sense of well-being and optimism that worked in the Republicans' favour. The economy boomed during the first part of the year, while inflation, which had helped bring down the Carter administration four years earlier, remained low. Despite the federal deficit, interest rates, vital to the building and construction and automobile industries, declined slightly. Toward year's end there were signs of a slowdown—or leveling off—of growth, but administration spokesmen turned even this to advantage, pointing out that it would prevent overheating of the economy and a recurrence of inflation.

The economic picture was not entirely bright. Pockets of high unemployment remained, particularly in the smokestack industries of the northeastern and north central states. Critics noted that, while unemployment had fallen, many of the new jobs being created were in the relatively low-paid service sector. Various studies reported that the number of people below the poverty level had risen, at least in part because of cutbacks in federal welfare programs. (*See* SOCIAL SECURITY AND WELFARE SERVICES.) The burgeoning federal deficit remained a worrying factor, but Mondale's suggestion that taxes would have to be raised to reduce it only contributed to his defeat. While it was good news to American tourists abroad, the strong

OWEN FRANKEN—SIPA/SPECIAL FEATURES

Before U.S. Pres. Ronald Reagan's reelection, Soviet Foreign Minister Andrey Gromyko (right), here with Reagan and U.S. Ambassador to the UN Jeane Kirkpatrick, was cool to U.S.-Soviet talks. After election day, things changed.

dollar made U.S. exports less attractive, and there were rumblings of discontent among farmers. But whether or not these were warning signs portending difficulties ahead, as some economists feared, the majority of voters answered the question "Are you better off than you were four years ago?" with a resounding "Yes." (*See* ECONOMIC AFFAIRS.)

Though public opinion surveys had correctly projected the outcome of the election from the start of the campaign, the final vote tally was deeply discouraging to Democrats. They had hoped that Mondale's selection of Rep. Geraldine A. Ferraro (*see* BIOGRAPHIES) of New York as his vice-presidential running mate—the first woman chosen to run on the presidential ticket of a major party—would persuade women voters to support him. However, the so-called Ferraro factor was neutralized early in the campaign by disclosures in the media of questionable aspects of the candidate's finances and those of her husband, John A. Zaccaro. Momentum was lost as Ferraro was forced to defend herself against the media's allegations.

The Republican Party's elation over Reagan's triumph was tempered somewhat by the GOP's lacklustre showing in congressional and gubernatorial races. The Republicans gained 14 seats in the House of Representatives (one race, in the 8th district of Indiana, was still undecided at year's end), well short of making up the 26 they had lost in the 1982 midterm elections. In the Senate, Democrats held on to 13 of the 14 seats they were defending, and three Democratic House members captured Republican seats, giving the party a net gain of two in the upper chamber. In Illinois Paul Simon narrowly defeated three-term veteran Charles H. Percy, chairman of the Foreign Relations Committee and a national figure. In Iowa Tom Harkin defeated Roger W. Jepsen, and in Tennessee Albert Gore, Jr., crushed former state senator Victor Ashe to take the seat being vacated by Howard H. Baker, Jr., the Senate majority leader, who was retiring from Congress (though not necessarily, from politics—he was widely thought to have presidential ambitions).

The 13 gubernatorial elections held on November 6 did little to reduce the Democrats' 2-to-1 advantage in governorships. Republicans won victories in North Carolina, Rhode Island, Utah, and West Virginia, where the statehouses were left vacant by departing Democratic incumbents. However, the Democrats succeeded in capturing three new seats, toppling Republican incumbents in North Dakota and Washington and picking up the seat left open by retiring GOP Gov. Richard A. Snelling in Vermont. Republicans thus scored a net gain of only one, increasing the number of governorships under their control from 15 to 16 and reducing the number of states in the Democratic column from 35 to 34.

Even before the votes were counted on November 6, Baker's decision not to seek another term had set the stage for a spirited campaign among Republican senators to succeed him as Senate majority leader. In a five-way contest, decided in a closed-door caucus on November 28, the 53-member GOP majority elected Robert Dole of Kansas by a vote of 28 to 25 over Ted Stevens of Alaska. Alan K. Simpson of Wyoming was chosen to replace Stevens as majority whip, the second-ranking party leadership post in the Senate. Both Dole and Simpson were associated with the Republican Party's moderate wing.

Dole's elevation to the post of majority leader meant that he was obliged to resign his chairmanship of the Senate Finance Committee, the body responsible for handling tax legislation in the Senate. This opened the way for GOP moderate Bob Packwood of Oregon to succeed him as

(continued on page 565)

The U.S. Elections— A Message for the Democrats

BY BRUCE L. FELKNOR

The 1984 U.S. elections set few records but bore several significant messages. At the national level, they left the Democrats in a position like that of Republicans in 1948: an endangered species. The GOP had lost five straight presidential elections in 1948. The Democrats in 1984 had lost only four out of five, but there was no national hero in sight to lead them out of the wilderness. Ronald Reagan (*see* BIOGRAPHIES) won virtually every demographic group except blacks. Men and women, young, old, and middle-aged, flocked to his banner of pride and prosperity. The Reagan campaign was crafted to make a vote against the president seem unthinkable and probably anti-American. His total was greatly swelled by Democrats tired of waiting for their party to find a direction to replace Lyndon Johnson's Great Society.

The numbers were utterly convincing. Reagan's plurality of 16,876,932 popular votes was the second largest in history, surpassed only by Richard Nixon's over George McGovern in 1972 (17,994,460). His electoral landslide of 525–13 (97.6%) was second only to Franklin Roosevelt's over Alf Landon in 1936 (523–8, or 98.5%). His margin over Democrat Walter Mondale (*see* BIOGRAPHIES) exceeded the total vote cast for Warren G. Harding in 1920. Moreover, Mondale carried only the District of Columbia (three electoral votes) by a convincing margin. He won his home state of Minnesota by a scant 3,800 votes (less than 0.2%). He came within hailing distance in nine other states, but, even if he had mustered the 1,061,000 votes needed to carry them, they would have added a mere 96 votes to his electoral tally.

Below the presidential level, however, the message was sharply different. Republicans did make inroads in state legislatures, diminishing the majority controlled by Democrats, and they won an additional governorship. (See *Developments in the States,* below.) But this left the Democrats in control of more than half of the state legislatures and two-thirds of the statehouses. Moreover, Democrats reduced Republican control in the U.S. Senate by two seats, to 53–47, and in the House of Representatives they lost only 14 seats, retaining control by 252–182 (one race was undecided at year's end). Thus the electorate's message was that at the level of local legislative districts, congressional districts, and governorships, Democrats might still be trusted. It was hardly a ringing endorsement for the party, however, because ever since Watergate political survivors had been running independent of party. The 1984 election was a vote for divided government: another helping of checks and balances, please.

An interesting aspect of the election was its predictabil-ity. In general, in win-or-lose terms, the polls were correct from beginning to end, though individual polls varied throughout the campaign on the size of the landslide. On election eve only Gallup called the actual percentages of 59–41 correctly. Other major poll takers showed the margin as low as 14 percentage points (ABC News/ *Washington Post*) and as high as 25 (*USA Today*).

Jesse Jackson and the Primaries. It is possible that the failed Democratic effort to evict Reagan from the White House will be remembered as a turning point, when the party got the voters' message and revised its approach to national government. What is certain is that the campaign was the setting for two epochal events: the first serious national candidacies of a black and a woman.

The first occurred in the primary season with Jesse Jackson's (*see* BIOGRAPHIES) candidacy for the Democratic presidential nomination. When he announced, at the end of 1983, no one believed he would win either nomination or election, but no one denied that his public stature guaranteed him equal opportunity to compete seriously for the nomination. A young activist in the civil rights ferment of the 1960s who later sought to claim the mantle of Martin Luther King, Jr., Jackson was an eloquent preacher, an exhorter of black youth to study, work, and excel, and a peripatetic thorn in the flank of the black establishment. His presence in the TV debates that punctuated the endless Democratic primary campaign was a wild card, eliciting, variously, confrontation, consternation, flamboyance, soulful rhetoric, and even homilies on civil comportment for his white rivals. His style and the novelty of the situation gave him a conspicuous advantage when television news editors snipped the day's footage for a few seconds of news from the primaries.

The questions raised by Jackson's candidacy as a Democrat and the demands he made on the party for recognition and on blacks for support supplied much of the drama of the campaign. They also led to much

J. L. ATLAN—SYGMA

The Reagan campaign was based on a euphoric mood; the president felt insulated from any questions by reporters. Apart from the debates, it was as though Mondale and the Democrats did not exist.

Bruce L. Felknor, director of yearbooks for Encyclopædia Britannica, was executive director (1956–66) of the Fair Campaign Practices Committee.

soul-searching debate within both the Democratic Party and black leadership structures. A crucial element of the Democratic constituency since the New Deal, black voters were registered in vast numbers in 1984 as a result of Jackson's candidacy and his efforts. His demands that they no longer be taken for granted by the party led to compromises in the party platform that were more rhetorical than substantive, but even these gave some Southern Republicans an opportunity for racial demagoguery that helped frustrate Democratic efforts to regain a Southern presence.

The Democratic primaries were contested—in addition to Jackson—by one former governor (Reubin Askew of Florida), two former senators (McGovern of South Dakota and Mondale), and four incumbent senators (Alan Cranston of California, John Glenn of Ohio, Gary Hart of Colorado, and Ernest Hollings of South Carolina). The pre-primary odds makers had favoured Mondale, with Glenn tagged as his most probable close rival, but Glenn ran a lacklustre campaign and foundered early. So did most of the others, but Hart, to his own surprise, came in second in the Iowa caucuses and won the New Hampshire primary. Quick to spot what seemed to be a trend, the media all but wrote off Mondale, though at this point only two states had been heard from. Mondale, no longer the front-runner, abandoned his defensive stance and picked up every IOU he could find from party leaders and backers. Borrowing a slogan from a television commercial for a hamburger chain ("Where's the beef?"), he found a way to deflate Hart's pretensions as the candidate of "new ideas" and finally slogged his way to the nomination. But it was a victory that left everyone concerned exhausted.

The primary campaign was marked by a sustained flap that began when a black journalist, Milton Coleman of the *Washington Post,* reported that Jackson had alluded to Jews as "Hymies" and New York City as "Hymietown." In the weeks before he apologized, Jackson alienated much Jewish support. Making matters worse, he was defended by the militant leader of a small Black Muslim sect, Louis Farrakhan (*see* BIOGRAPHIES), who broadcast a death threat to the reporter and a farrago of further disparagement of Jews and Judaism.

Ferraro and the Campaign. The other epochal event of the campaign climaxed the Democratic national convention. Many women had been nominated for vice-president at party conventions, but until 1984 they were named only ceremonially, to honour past service to the party. Geraldine Ferraro (*see* BIOGRAPHIES), Mondale's choice

The Mondale campaign made history by nominating a woman for vice-president. From there on at the national level, it was downhill all the way. The House seat Geraldine Ferraro held for three terms was retained by the Democrats.
LARRY DOWNING/NEWSWEEK

as his running mate, was the first to be chosen by a major party as its actual candidate. Just as John Kennedy's election in 1960 broke the taboo against a Roman Catholic president, the Ferraro nomination rewrote the unwritten rule that, for vice-president, no women need apply.

Ferraro, a three-term congresswoman from New York, had exactly as much seniority in national politics—six years—as Nixon had when he became Dwight Eisenhower's running mate in 1952. Nixon, by virtue of his central role in the Hiss-Chambers affair, had greater name recognition, but he also was encumbered by a reputation as a dirty campaigner. Not so the pert, witty Ferraro, a former assistant district attorney and a protégée of House Speaker Tip O'Neill, who had headed the party's platform committee with articulate style. Her selection by Mondale was far from mere ceremony; it was intended to galvanize a campaign moribund from the primary bloodletting.

It did, but the campaign train was derailed almost immediately by a month-long controversy over Ferraro's finances. She was the wife of a New York real estate operator, John A. Zaccaro, and an officer in a firm they owned jointly. The Mondale organization's cursory check of her background did not discover that she had refused to disclose her husband's financial information in the report required by post-Watergate House rules, claiming exemption from the requirement on the grounds that she knew nothing about his business and gained nothing from it. (The Federal Election Commission ruled against this claim after the election but levied no penalty.)

The media jumped at this chink in Ferraro's armour, and disclosures and pseudo-disclosures tumbled out, including the revelation that she and her husband were multimillionaires and some tacky innuendoes about vague family connections with the Mafia. Ferraro pledged full

Electoral vote, 1984 presidential election

Reagan 525

Mondale 13

Wash. 10
Oregon 7
Calif. 47
Nevada 4
Idaho 4
Montana 4
Utah 5
Arizona 7
Wyoming 3
Colorado 8
New Mexico 5
N. Dakota 3
S. Dakota 3
Nebraska 5
Kansas 7
Okla. 8
Texas 29
Minn. 10
Iowa 8
Mo. 11
Ark. 6
La. 10
Wis. 11
Ill. 24
Miss. 7
Mich. 20
Ind. 12
Tenn. 11
Ala. 9
Ga. 12
Ohio 23
Ky. 9
Va. 12
W. Va. 6
N.C. 13
S.C. 8
Fla. 21
Pa. 25
N.Y. 36
Vt. 3
N.H. 4
Mass. 13
R.I. 4
Conn. 8
N.J. 16
Del. 3
Md. 10
D.C. 3
Maine 4
Hawaii 4
Alaska 3

disclosure of her husband's finances, he refused, and Mondale squirmed in (public) silence. At length Zaccaro released most of his fiscal background. Ferraro held a press conference defending her position for which she got generally good marks (some reporters applauded), and the campaign at last got down to business.

Mondale never found the issue that would strike sparks. Fairness between rich and poor, the skyrocketing federal deficit (his pledge to raise taxes backfired), alleged misbehaviour by Reagan aides, Reagan's close ties with aggressive fundamentalist groups (*see* RELIGION: *Introduction*), all failed to dent the approval ratings of the man supporters called "the great communicator" and enemies called "the Teflon president" because no charges ever stuck to him. A brief upward blip in the Mondale fortunes came when, in the first of two nationally televised debates, Reagan appeared tired and confused. His inept performance brought into the open the hitherto unmentioned issue of Reagan's age (73), and for a brief interval the Democrats took heart. By the second debate, however, the president was back in command. Mondale needed a major Reagan mistake, and it did not come.

Meanwhile, the Republican campaign hardly wavered from its appointed course. Apart from the debates, the president appeared only in controlled and euphoric settings, insulated from the rude questions of the press. The campaign ran against a backdrop that was a conservative equivalent of Socialist Realist painting, filled with strong, smiling people and sturdy tractors ushering in the dawn of the golden age. It capitalized on the new mood of national pride and self-congratulation that reached a peak in the Los Angeles Olympic Games. The economic recovery helped, but even among voters who disagreed with— or were victims of—administration policies, interviewers and exit pollers found a preference for Reagan because, for them, he somehow represented leadership, patriotism, optimism, the old verities that the public, in this election year, seemed to yearn for.

Aftermath. The campaign ended as it began, with the polls predicting a runaway victory varying only in degree. Democrats began post-mortems and the search for a new direction, and for a way to win back whites, especially the young and upwardly mobile—the "yuppies" who had flocked to Hart rallies and then vanished from the Democratic scene. Republicans pondered how much of a mandate the president had received given the reduced GOP majority in the Senate and the only slightly augmented minority in the House; some wondered how to attract black voters.

Elections to Congress brought few surprises but perhaps some further messages. There were a number of conspicuously vicious campaigns, most notably in Illinois and North Carolina. In Illinois Charles H. Percy, chairman of the Senate Foreign Relations Committee, and Paul Simon, a downstate congressman, followed their media advisers into a television campaign of mutual deprecation that came off like a small-town schoolyard fight, with both squandering their reputations for restraint and level-headedness. Percy lost. In North Carolina, Republican Sen. Jesse Helms, godfather of the religious right, taxed Gov. James Hunt with every kind of godlessness and perversity, losing no opportunity to depict Hunt in the company of blacks, while Hunt adopted similar tactics to link Helms with Salvadoran death squads. The campaign, one of the most expensive in history, ended with Helms winning 52% of the vote. It probably turned most of all on one count of guilt by association that Hunt could not disprove: pro forma support for Mondale and the national Democratic campaign.

(continued from page 562)

head of that panel. The rise of Dole and Packwood in the Senate hierarchy was viewed with apprehension by conservative Republicans. Both were on record as saying that reduction of the federal budget deficit should take precedence over reshaping the federal tax code. While pragmatic Republicans such as Dole were willing to consider raising taxes as a means to combat the massive and still-growing deficit, the White House at year's end remained adamantly opposed to such a measure. A first look at the administration proposals for tax reform was provided by a 408-page Treasury Department document made public on December 3. In a series of prior "trial balloons," Treasury Department officials had maintained that about 80% of all individual taxpayers would find their tax obligations largely unchanged, possibly even lowered, as would many businesses. The proposals, to be phased in over a period of years, were said to be "neutral" in that they would neither raise nor lower total federal revenues, but their overall effect would be to shift part of the federal tax burden from individuals to corporations.

The second session of the 98th Congress, which adjourned less than a month before election day, provided the usual mixed bag of good and bad news for the party in control of the White House. Congress sent Reagan some legislation he supported, including bills to revamp the nation's bankruptcy laws, to pressure states to raise their minimum drinking age to 21, to establish a national policy for cable television franchising, and more bills to create wilderness areas than had been approved in any of the previous 20 years. Also approved were measures of special interest to women, including one that expanded pension coverage for female workers and enforced payments for child support. Substantial progress was also made in the field of health legislation. Congress cleared a bill to place stronger health warnings on cigarette packages. It also cleared a measure making low-cost generic drugs more widely available to consumers and an organ transplant bill to set up a national computer network that would match patients who needed transplants with organ donors.

Nevertheless, Reagan encountered many disappointments on Capitol Hill in 1984. He could not persuade Congress to approve his "social agenda," headed by constitutional amendments to outlaw abortion and to allow prayer in public schools. Congress also failed to approve his plan to allow tuition tax credits to parents who send their children to private schools or his enterprise zone system, designed to extend tax relief to businesses that create jobs in economically depressed areas. Moreover, Congress did not act on the president's call for constitutional amendments requiring a balanced federal budget and giving the chief executive the power to veto individual items in appropriations bills.

Possibly the emotional high point of Reagan's year, and of the nation's as well, was the staging of the 1984 summer Olympic Games in Los Angeles, beginning on July 28. The Soviet Union had announced on May 8 that it would not participate, and 14 other countries sympathetic to Moscow's reasoning soon followed suit. Albania, Iran, and Libya also were nonparticipants. Even so, a record 140 countries took part in the parade of nations during the opening ceremonies. By the end of the Games, on August 12, the U.S. had captured 174 medals (83 gold, 61 silver, 30 bronze) to lead all other countries. (*See* SPORTS AND GAMES: *Track and Field Sports:* Special Report.)

Less pleasing to the White House were controversies involving two of Reagan's close associates, Labor Secretary Raymond J. Donovan and Attorney General-designate Edwin Meese III. Donovan announced that he was temporarily relinquishing his Cabinet post after a grand jury in Bronx County, N.Y., handed down a 137-count indictment on October 1 charging him with grand larceny, offering falsified documents to the New York Transit Authority, and falsifying business records. Meese, nominated to succeed retiring Attorney General William French Smith, came under fire for irregularities in his personal finances. During hearings on his nomination before the Senate Judiciary Committee in March, questions also were raised about his commitment to civil rights and his ability to be independent of the White House. An independent counsel—formerly known as a "special prosecutor"—was later appointed to investigate the allegations. The counsel's report, issued September 20, found "no basis" for bringing charges against Meese.

Veterans of the Vietnam war had reason to feel vindicated in 1984. On May 7 a $180 million out-of-court settlement was announced in a class-action suit brought by Vietnam veterans against seven chemical companies. The veterans had claimed injuries resulting from exposure to dioxin, a powerful poison that was a by-product of Agent Orange, a herbicide used by the U.S. military to destroy vegetation used for cover by Viet Cong guerrillas. Then, on May 28, President Reagan attended solemn ceremonies honouring an "unknown" U.S. serviceman killed in the Vietnam war. The serviceman, the only member of the nation's armed forces who had died in Vietnam and had not been identified, was interred in the Tomb of the Unknown Soldier in Arlington National Cemetery with unidentified servicemen from World Wars I and II and the Korean War. Over Veterans Day weekend in November, ownership of the privately financed Vietnam Veterans Memorial in Washington, D.C., was formally transferred to the government. Frederick Hart's group statue, "Three Servicemen," had been unveiled near the memorial earlier in the week.

On February 3 the space shuttle "Challenger" began its fourth flight and the tenth mission of the National Aeronautics and Space Administration (NASA) shuttle program. The highlight of the mission came four days later, when two U.S. astronauts became the first humans to fly freely in space, unconnected to their spacecraft and propelled only by jet backpacks. The successful space walk followed several failures in the shuttle mission, including the loss of two satellites and one target balloon. Things improved when the shuttle "Discovery" made its maiden flight August 30–September 5. NASA officials were elated by the near-perfect flight, which was highlighted by the successful launching of three communications satellites from the craft's cargo bay. The flight had been postponed twice in June, the second time by an engine shutdown just seconds before the scheduled liftoff.

Another high point of the "Discovery" mission came when Charles D. Walker, the shuttle's first commercial passenger, began operating a drug-processing machine on August 31. The object of the experiment was to test the feasibility of making biological materials of a purity unattainable on Earth under conditions of gravity. The machine's automatic controls failed several times, and Walker was forced to operate it manually. The following day the crew deployed an experimental solar-powered panel in the first test of an electricity-generating system to be used in planned space stations. "Discovery's" second flight of the year, November 8–16, was even more successful. The mission included the launching of two satellites as well as the retrieval of the two commercial satellites that had been placed in faulty orbits by the "Challenger" crew

in February. It marked the first time that lost satellites had been salvaged in space. NASA flight director Jay Greene called the "Discovery" mission "the most challenging" of all the shuttle missions. (*See* SPACE EXPLORATION.)

Several court cases involving well-known public figures attracted wide media coverage in 1984. After a 22-week trial, a U.S. District Court jury in Los Angeles acquitted former auto manufacturer John Z. De Lorean of eight counts connected to an alleged plan to distribute 25 kg (55 lb) of cocaine. If he had been convicted on the charges of drug conspiracy, possession, and distribution, De Lorean could have been sentenced to as many as 67 years in prison and fined up to $185,000. Government prosecutors in the case had asserted that De Lorean participated in a $24 million plot to distribute cocaine in order to obtain money for his automobile company in Belfast, Northern Ireland, which was then in receivership. De Lorean and his attorneys insisted that his prosecution resulted from an overzealous and improper investigation by ambitious federal agents. The prosecution's case was weakened by admissions that government evidence had been altered. Videotapes that allegedly showed De Lorean taking part in negotiations for the drug deal were played repeatedly during the trial, but the jurors revealed afterward that the tapes had had little effect on their verdict. The case had implications for the legitimacy of undercover operations carried out by law enforcement agencies.

After a long series of delays, the libel suit brought by retired army Gen. William C. Westmoreland against CBS Inc. went to trial on October 11 in U.S. District Court in New York City. Westmoreland had filed suit in 1982, charging that he had been held up to "scorn, contempt and ridicule" by a CBS News television documentary, "The Uncounted Enemy: A Vietnam Deception," which was broadcast in January of that year. Among other things, the documentary implied that Westmoreland, while he was commander

AP/WIDE WORLD

A month before the election U.S. Secretary of Labor Raymond Donovan was indicted on fraud charges dating from 1978 by a Bronx, N.Y., grand jury at the urging of a tough and public-relations-wise district attorney. Donovan, the first Cabinet member to be indicted while in office, took an unpaid leave to fight the charges.

This statue of combat-weary U.S. servicemen in the Vietnam war—privately financed by the Vietnam Veterans Memorial Fund—was installed in November near the black granite commemorative wall erected in 1982 on the Mall in Washington, D.C.

DENNIS BRACK—BLACK STAR

of U.S. forces in Vietnam, had conspired with others to deceive Washington policymakers about the strength of enemy troops. Because it concerned former high-level public officials, a powerful news organization, and unanswered questions about the Vietnam war, the Westmoreland suit was widely seen as one of the most significant libel actions in U.S. history.

In another closely watched libel case, which also opened in U.S. District Court in New York late in the year, former Israeli defense minister Ariel Sharon sued *Time* magazine. At issue was an article suggesting that in 1982, when Israeli forces controlled Beirut, Sharon had participated in discussions of revenge with the family of an assassinated Lebanese Phalangist leader shortly before Phalangists massacred hundreds of Palestinians in West Beirut refugee camps. Sharon testified that *Time*'s report of the alleged discussion was "nothing but a lie." Lawyers for the magazine insisted that the article was substantially true and, in any case, was not damaging to Sharon.

Difficulties of another sort confronted Vanessa Williams, the reigning Miss America of 1984. Williams relinquished her title on July 23, after the publisher of *Penthouse* magazine disclosed that nude photographs of her would appear in the September issue. It was the first time in the 63-year history of the Miss America Pageant that a Miss America had been forced to resign. Suzette Charles, chosen as first runner-up in the contest held the previous September in Atlantic City, N.J., was immediately named as the new Miss America to serve out the remaining two months of Williams's term.

Three bombings of abortion clinics in Pensacola, Fla., on Christmas Day focused attention on what seemed to be a growing militance within the antiabortion movement. There were 24 such bombings or arson attacks during 1984. All took place when the premises were empty, so there were no casualties (though property damage was heavy), and appeared to be the work of isolated individuals or small groups. While leaders of recognized pro-life organizations deplored the violence, several expressed sympathy with the frustration of antiabortion activists over their inability to reverse the effects of *Roe* v. *Wade,* the Supreme Court decision that had legalized abortion almost 12 years earlier. The polarization over the issue was illustrated during the election campaign, when Ferraro and New York Gov. Mario Cuomo (*see* BIOGRAPHIES), both practicing Roman Catholics, were attacked for their attempts to reconcile personal opposition to abortion with their duty as public servants to enforce existing law.

Foreign Affairs. As usual, the main focus of U.S. foreign policy in 1984 was the Soviet Union. Relations between the two superpowers had cooled during the first three years of the Reagan administration, but as the president's reelection prospects approached the level of inevitability, Washington and Moscow moved cautiously to patch up their differences.

Reagan took the initiative with a major address on U.S.-Soviet relations on January 16. In it, he called for resumption of parallel sets of bilateral arms-control talks in Geneva (on strategic and intermediate nuclear forces) and multilateral negotiations in Vienna on reducing conventional forces in central Europe. The Soviet Union had refused to continue the three sets of talks in retaliation for the installation of intermediate-range cruise and Pershing II missiles in Western Europe. Moscow's response—as indicated in remarks made by Soviet Pres. Yury V. Andropov and distributed by the government news agency TASS on January 24—was wary but restrained. Andropov criticized important points of Reagan's speech and urged the U.S. to take substantive steps to improve bilateral relations. Diplomatic observers noted, however, that the tone of the exchange was notably more outgoing than had been the case in previous months.

Andropov's death on February 9 necessarily put any further improvement in U.S.-Soviet relations on hold. According to a March report in the *New York Times,* his successor, Konstantin U. Chernenko, refused to meet with Brent Scowcroft, a private White House envoy to the Kremlin. On April 8 Chernenko was quoted by TASS as saying that the U.S. was using its "sometimes peace-loving rhetoric" to mask its efforts to block arms-control agreements and continue its drive for "military superiority" over the Soviet Union. Matters seemed to take a turn for the worse on May 20, when Soviet Defense Minister Dmitry Ustinov announced that his country had increased the number of nuclear-armed submarines operating off U.S. coasts. Nevertheless, Reagan continued to make overtures to Moscow. At a news conference on June 14, he eased his conditions for holding a summit meeting with Chernenko. Two weeks later, on June 27, he said his administration was trying to broaden its contacts with the Soviet Union in a wide range of areas. The following month the two countries exchanged a series of proposals and counterproposals on preventing the militarization of outer space. (*See* MILITARY AFFAIRS: *Special Report.*)

An off-the-record joke by Reagan as he prepared for his weekly radio program on August 11 seemed at first to negate all the rocky progress toward better relations. Testing the microphone, the president said, "My fellow Americans, I'm pleased to tell you today that I've signed legislation that will outlaw Russia forever. We begin bombing in five minutes." The comments, which were recorded and later made public, elicited indignant comments from Moscow and from U.S. allies, but the episode was soon forgotten. That was demonstrated when Reagan and Soviet Foreign Minister Andrey A. Gromyko met at the White House on September 28 for three and a half hours, the president's first formal meeting with a high-level Soviet official since he took office. Shortly before, Reagan had made an address to the UN General Assembly that was notable for its conciliatory tone toward Moscow. The Reagan-Gromyko meeting set the stage for the announcement, on Thanksgiving Day, that Gromyko would meet in Geneva in January with U.S. Secretary of State George P. Shultz. The expectation was that the two leaders would explore ways to resume bilateral arms-control negotiations and other areas of mutual concern.

As U.S. relations with the Soviet Union eased somewhat, contacts with other Communist countries also improved. On August 3 the Reagan administration announced that it was lifting some of the economic sanctions levied against

Poland immediately following the imposition of martial law in that country in December 1981. The move came in reaction to the Polish government's declaration of amnesty for political prisoners on July 21. Possibly more significant in the long term was Reagan's visit to China from April 26 to May 1, his first trip to a Communist country. During the visit Reagan twice addressed the Chinese people by television, although his remarks criticizing the Soviet Union and extolling the merits of capitalism, democracy, and religion were deleted. The issue of Taiwan was discussed, but China continued to describe it as an obstacle in Sino-U.S. relations.

The always-vexing Middle East continued to trouble the White House and the State Department in 1984. The year opened with good news. U.S. Navy airman Robert O. Goodman, Jr., who had been shot down over Syrian-controlled territory in Lebanon the previous month, was freed on January 3 through the good offices of U.S. civil rights leader Jesse Jackson (*see* BIOGRAPHIES). Jackson had journeyed to Syria in order to make a dramatic personal appeal to Pres. Hafez al-Assad. After initially disapproving the Jackson mission, Reagan sent a letter to Assad thanking him and said of Jackson's feat, "You can't quarrel with success."

Not much else in the Middle East went right for the U.S. during the year. On February 7, following a rapid worsening of conditions in Beirut, Reagan ordered the U.S. contingent of the multinational peacekeeping force in Lebanon to begin withdrawing to U.S. ships offshore. The withdrawal, completed on February 26, involved about

Church Membership in the United States

Religious body	Total clergy	Inclusive membership	Religious body	Total clergy	Inclusive membership
Baptist bodies			Jews	6,500	5,728,075
American Baptist Association	...	225,000	Latter Day Saints (Mormons)		
American Baptist Churches in the U.S.A.	6,780	1,637,099	Church of Jesus Christ of Latter-day Saints	27,745	3,602,000
Baptist General Conference	1,470	128,913	Reorganized Church of Jesus Christ of L.D.S.	16,400	192,830
Baptist Missionary Association of America	3,000	234,142	Lutherans		
Conservative Baptist Association of America	...	225,000	American Lutheran Church	7,314	2,343,412
Free Will Baptists	2,867	226,422	Evangelical Lutheran Churches, The Assn. of	665	110,934
General Baptists (General Association of)	1,398	75,133	Lutheran Church in America	8,324	2,925,008
Liberty Baptist Fellowship	374	130,000	Lutheran Church—Missouri Synod	7,682	2,630,947
National Baptist Convention of America	28,574	2,668,799	Wisconsin Evangelical Lutheran Synod	1,356	414,199
National Baptist Convention, U.S.A., Inc.	27,500	5,500,000	Mennonite Church	2,957	110,294
National Primitive Baptist Convention	636	250,000	Methodists		
Primitive Baptists	...	72,000	African Methodist Episcopal Church	6,550	2,210,000
Progressive National Baptist Convention	863	521,692	African Methodist Episcopal Zion Church	6,269	1,134,179
Regular Baptist Churches, General Association of	2,045	300,839	Christian Methodist Episcopal Church	2,650	718,922
Southern Baptist Convention	61,900	14,178,051	Free Methodist Church of North America	1,733	70,657
United Free Will Baptist Church	915	100,000	United Methodist Church	36,882	9,405,164
Buddhist Churches of America	117	70,000	Wesleyan Church	2,455	107,672
Christian and Missionary Alliance	2,094	215,857	Moravian Church in America	244	54,621
Christian Congregation	1,438	101,351	North American Old Roman Catholic Church	147	62,380
Church of God (Anderson, Ind.)	3,229	182,190	Pentecostals		
Church of the Brethren	1,940	164,680	Apostolic Overcoming Holy Church of God	350	75,000
Church of the Nazarene	8,223	507,574	Assemblies of God	25,378	1,992,754
Churches of Christ—Christian Churches			Church of God	2,737	75,890
Christian Church (Disciples of Christ)	6,668	1,145,918	Church of God (Cleveland, Tenn.)	11,763	493,904
Christian Churches and Churches of Christ	...	1,043,642	Church of God in Christ	10,425	3,709,661
Churches of Christ	...	1,600,000	Church of God in Christ, International	1,600	200,000
Community Churches, International Council of	254	173,500	Church of God of Prophecy	5,358	74,384
Congregational Christian Churches, Natl. Assn. of	812	105,865	Full Gospel Fellowship of Churches and Ministers, Intl.	809	65,000
Eastern Churches			International Church of the Foursquare Gospel	4,707	164,688
American Carpatho-Russian Orthodox Greek Catholic Ch.	68	100,000	Pentecostal Church of God	1,540	89,559
Antiochian Orthodox Christian Archdiocese of N. Am.	80	280,000	Pentecostal Holiness Church, International	2,168	108,229
Apostolic Catholic Assyrian Ch. of the East, N. Am. Dioc.	57	80,000	United Pentecostal Church, International	6,659	465,000
Armenian Apostolic Church of America	33	350,000	Plymouth Brethren	500	98,000
Armenian Church of America, Diocese of the	61	450,000	Polish National Catholic Church of America	141	282,411
Bulgarian Eastern Orthodox Church	11	86,000	Presbyterians		
Coptic Orthodox Church	27	100,000	Cumberland Presbyterian Church	740	99,887
Greek Orthodox Archdiocese of N. and S. America	655	1,950,000	Presbyterian Church in America	1,451	155,988
Orthodox Church in America	531	1,000,000	Presbyterian Church (U.S.A.)	18,880	3,122,213
Russian Orth. Ch. in the U.S.A., Patriarchal Parishes	60	51,500	Reformed bodies		
Russian Orthodox Church Outside of Russia	168	55,000	Christian Reformed Church in North America	1,029	218,659
Serbian Eastern Orth. Ch. in the U.S.A. and Canada	73	97,123	Reformed Church in America	1,549	344,526
Ukrainian Orthodox Church in the U.S.A.	131	87,745	Roman Catholic Church	57,891	52,392,934
Episcopal Church	13,342	2,794,690	Salvation Army	5,159	428,046
Evangelical Covenant Church of America	863	82,943	Seventh Day Adventist Church	4,434	623,523
Evangelical Free Church of America	1,401	146,000	Triumph the Church and Kingdom of God in Christ	1,375	54,307
Friends United Meeting	597	56,371	Unitarian Universalist Association	949	169,168
Independent Fundamental Churches of America	1,366	120,446	United Church of Christ	10,095	1,701,513
Jehovah's Witnesses	None	649,697			

Table includes churches reporting a membership of 50,000 or more and represents the latest information available.
Source: National Council of Churches, *Yearbook of American and Canadian Churches, 1985.*

(CONSTANT H. JACQUET)

Protests against the Reagan administration's policy toward South Africa took place at the South African embassy in Washington, D.C., at the end of the year.

MARK REINSTEIN—UNIPHOTO

1,300 U.S. troops, most of them marines. The pullout did not end U.S. troubles in Lebanon, however. On September 20 a station wagon loaded with explosives charged through a volley of bullets and swerved through concrete-block defenses before detonating in front of the U.S. embassy annex in East Beirut, killing 14 persons. Subsequent press reports indicated that the U.S. had received prior warning of the attack, and there were charges of laxness and delay in putting the building's defenses in place. In any case, concern about foreign terrorism led to the installation of antivehicle barriers in front of the White House and other prominent government buildings in Washington. In an unrelated development in August, the U.S. and several other countries sent mine-sweeping equipment to the Red Sea to help Egypt search for mines that had damaged as many as 15 ships in the previous month. The source of the mines was never discovered.

The National Bipartisan Commission on Central America, appointed by Reagan in 1983 to make recommendations on U.S. policy in the region, made public its report January 11. It endorsed most major elements of the administration's policy, advocating an $8 billion economic aid plan and a sizable increase in military aid to El Salvador. It also implicitly supported continued aid to antigovernment rebels in Nicaragua. At a meeting with congressional leaders on February 3, the president substantially repeated his proposals. The White House initiative was set back in April, following revelations that the U.S. Central Intelligence Agency (CIA) had directed the mining of Nicaraguan ports. Congress voted April 10–12 to condemn the action, and Nicaragua took its complaint to the International Court of Justice at The Hague, Neth. The U.S. announced that it would not accept the court's jurisdiction on Central American matters for two years. (*See* Law: *International Law.*)

The White House was embarrassed by the disclosure of a manual on psychological warfare, issued by CIA operatives in Central America, which seemed to countenance such activities as assassination of government leaders. It caused

a brief furor in Congress but appeared to do little lasting political damage. Meanwhile, Daniel Ortega Saavedra, coordinator of the ruling junta in Nicaragua, charged that the Reagan administration was planning a military action against his country. He asserted that the justification for such an undertaking would be that it was a response to pleas from other Central American nations, following the pattern of the previous year's invasion of Grenada. More distressing to the White House was the vote by both houses of Congress on October 11 to continue for five months a ban on funds for Nicaraguan insurgent forces, or *contras,* largely considered right-wing, that were attempting to overthrow the Sandinista government.

Toward the end of 1984, the Reagan administration was taken by surprise by the depth and extent of public rejection of its policy toward South Africa. Protest demonstrations organized by U.S. antiapartheid organizations were held before the South African embassy in Washington, D.C., during which several members of Congress and other prominent citizens were arrested. Administration policy toward Pretoria had been one of "constructive engagement," the stated aim of which was to bring about reform of the country's repressive racial laws through open, diplomatic discussion rather than through scolding and attempted intimidation. This rationale was obviously unpersuasive in the eyes of the protesters, since the demonstrations in the nation's capital soon were repeated in other cities where South Africa had diplomatic representation. In an effort to defuse the situation, the president, in a speech delivered on December 10—International Human Rights Day—called on South Africa's white-dominated government to "reach out to its black majority" and "move toward a more just society."

After a hiatus of 116 years, the U.S. and the Vatican established full diplomatic relations on January 10. Congress had opened the way late in 1983 by repealing an 1867 law prohibiting federal funding for a Vatican embassy. The new diplomatic status was acclaimed by the U.S. Catholic Conference, which said that it "reflects the role played so effectively by the Holy See, under the leadership of Pope John Paul II and his predecessors, on behalf of peace and justice in the world." Some Protestant groups were strongly opposed to the move, however, as were Jewish groups and civil rights organizations, which cited the U.S. tradition of separation of church and state. A court challenge to the move was begun late in the year.

At the second UN International Conference on Population, held in Mexico City in August, the U.S. and the Vatican won approval for a compromise recommendation that abortion "in no case be promoted as a method of family planning." The Reagan administration had previously caused a domestic and international controversy when it announced on June 17 that it intended to cut off U.S. aid to international population programs that practiced or advocated abortion. Some Reagan aides reportedly acknowledged that the proposal was motivated by election-year politics.

In a policy directive signed in April, Reagan authorized a government-wide effort to combat international terrorism. The new policy reportedly was designed to give the government an offensive rather than defensive stance against terrorists, enabling the U.S. to launch preventive and retaliatory strikes against terrorists abroad. In practice, however, antiterrorist action continued to be inhibited by lack of solid information about who committed specific terrorist acts and who supported them.

(RICHARD L. WORSNOP)

See also *Dependent States,* below.

Developments in the States in 1984

A national economic recovery eased problems for state governments during 1984, raising revenues and allowing some jurisdictions to cut taxes and increase services. But economic improvement led to additional difficulty in the states' relationship with the federal government, prompting calls for cutbacks in aid to states as a means of easing the massive federal budget deficit. Voters in four states turned down tax-limitation initiatives, leading to declarations that the conservative tax revolt of the late 1970s was now over.

Under heavy federal pressure, states moved to reverse a decade-old trend toward a lower drinking age, and two states initiated the nation's first effective mandatory seat-belt laws for adults. The threat to state treasuries from sex discrimination complaints by state workers seemed to ease during the year. Government-run lotteries as a revenue-raising measure were approved by four more states, and the end of legal appeals threatened to make executions a common occurrence again in many states.

Forty-three states held regular legislative sessions during 1984, and 13 staged special sessions on a variety of subjects.

Party Strengths. Republicans made significant gains in 1984 state elections, picking up more than 300 seats and reducing the states in which Democrats controlled both legislative houses from 34 to 27. One state was pried away from the all-Democratic roster early in the year when Michigan voters elected two Republican senators to replace Democrats recalled from office in an antitax revolt in late 1983, thus giving control of the state Senate to the GOP. Six additional states went from all-Democratic to split control following the November elections, while the number of states in which Republicans had full legislative control remained steady at 11.

Just over half of the state legislatures had Democratic majorities in both houses. Those that did not included Arizona, Colorado, Connecticut, Idaho, Indiana, Kansas, New Hampshire, North Dakota, South Dakota, Utah, and Wyoming (where Republicans organized both houses); Alaska, Michigan, New York, Ohio, and Pennsylvania (where Democrats controlled the lower chamber and Republicans the upper body); Delaware, Minnesota, Nevada, and Vermont (where the Republicans organized the lower body and Democrats the upper chamber); Montana and New Mexico (where Democrats controlled one chamber and the other was tied); and Nebraska (a nonpartisan, one-house legislature).

Republicans picked up one governorship overall in the November balloting, establishing the prospective gubernatorial lineup for 1985 at 34 Democrats and 16 Republicans. Democrats were elected to replace Republican predecessors in North Dakota, Vermont, and Washington, but Republicans swept out Democratic administrations in North Carolina, Rhode Island, Utah, and West Virginia. At least modestly inspired by the presence of the first woman on a national ticket, women made solid gains at the polls, with 14.3% of state Senate and House seats in female hands at the year's end, up from 13.3% in 1983.

Vermont elected the nation's second current woman governor, Madeleine Kunin, a Democrat.

Government Structure, Powers. A nationwide trend aimed at trimming back the powers, staff, and authority of state legislators developed during the year, with the movement particularly strong in California. In June voters approved an initiative cutting California's legislative budget by 30%, curtailing leadership powers, and rewriting legislative rules. Measures to strip the legislature of authority to draw political district boundaries and to sharply limit contributions to political candidates also qualified for the November ballot before pro-legislature forces staged a comeback. Voters defeated both fall ballot propositions, and a judge overturned the June budget-limitation vote. Nonetheless, serious movements to curtail legislative powers were under way in six other states during the year.

Courts also protected legislative prerogatives in another important area, knocking initiatives calling for a national constitutional convention off the ballot in California and Montana. Both courts ruled that only a state legislature could petition Congress for such a convention. The judicial defeats, plus a narrow setback in the Michigan legislature, were particularly frustrating to tax-limitation groups that were seeking an amendment requiring an annual balanced federal budget.

The court battles highlighted another trend: the increased cost and complexity of so-called citizen initiatives. After expensive legal challenges, rare in the past, courts removed seven initiatives from state ballots during the year and allowed four others to proceed. Several initiative campaigns involved multimillion-dollar expenditures for direct mail and advertising, replacing the shoe-leather approach of the past.

Arkansas voters approved a change in terms for the governor and six other state officers from two to four years, but New Hampshire voters rejected a similar four-year gubernatorial term. The New Hampshire proposition was one of ten amendments set forth by a state constitutional convention held earlier in the year.

Rhode Island and Wisconsin passed state laws protecting the job security of whistle-blowers, state employees who report suspected wrongdoing by co-workers and supervisors.

New York became the fifth state to adopt an official fossil: *Eurypterus remipes,* a prehistoric crab. A survey indicated that all states had official birds, trees, and flowers and that all except Alaska had nicknames and mottoes. Nineteen had official fish, 15 had state insects, 5 had a grass, 4 a beverage, 2 a horse, and 2 a dog. Texas had an official dish (chili), Washington a dance (square), and Virginia a shell (oyster).

Government Relations. The U.S. Supreme Court gave states a rare victory in their ongoing battle with the federal government over power sharing. The high court ruled on January 23 that federal courts could not exercise supervisory authority over state officials except in matters of federal law, a decision hailed by some state authorities as important for the restoration of federalism. At the year's end, states were battling on a new front; citing relatively healthy surpluses in state treasuries nation-wide, the deficit-ridden federal administration threatened drastic cuts in state aid. State officials lobbied hard against serious cutbacks, arguing that they should not be penalized for making difficult budget decisions (raising taxes and lowering expenditures) over the past three years.

For the first time in 13 years, the Gallup polling organization found that the public believes it gets more for its tax dollar from state rather than federal government. The 1984 results found that 35% rated local government as most efficient, compared with 27% for state and 24% for federal government.

Colorado became the 12th state to ratify an obscure U.S. constitutional amendment that would prevent U.S. congressional pay raises from taking effect until an election had intervened. The amendment, which required 38 state signatures, was proposed in 1789 without a ratification deadline.

A commuter-tax feud between Oregon and Washington escalated during the year. After Oregon in 1983 increased its income tax affecting Oregon workers who lived in Washington, the Washington legislature in 1984 allowed counties in the state to levy an excise tax on workers commuting from Oregon (Washington had no income tax). Washington's attorney general also threatened a lawsuit over Oregon's taxation of commuters in an effort to force its repeal, but there was no response from Oregon.

Twelve prominent New Jersey citizens filed suit in November in an effort to reclaim the Statue of Liberty and Ellis Island from New York. Liberty and Ellis islands lie on the New Jersey side of the Hudson River, and New Jersey provides power, water, and telephone service to them, but the New Jersey governor gave away control to New York in what state citizens now believed was a coerced bargain in 1834. Tax and tourism revenue was expected to increase markedly when the Statue of Liberty refurbishment was completed in 1986.

Finances. The national economic recovery, along with higher taxes imposed over three previous years, led to a relatively healthy fiscal situation for most states during 1984. A survey by the Tax Foundation revealed that 11 states had raised taxes during the year by a modest $3.3 billion, while nine states were lowering taxes by $2.2 billion. Most of the tax hikes occurred in energy-producing states hard hit by depressed world oil prices.

Voters in four states defeated major tax-and spending-cut initiatives in fall balloting. Measures in California, Michigan, Nevada, and Oregon would have rolled back taxes and required voter approval for new levies, but a wide assortment of opponents successfully convinced voters that the measure would impinge on needed services and imperil state credit ratings. South Carolina voters approved a less drastic measure, tying state spending growth to performance of the state's economy, but Arizona and Louisiana voters rejected limitation of state appropriation growth based on increases in personal income.

Nine states adopted tax amnesty programs inspired by Massachusetts, which collected more than $65 million from 60,000 taxpayers by offering to waive penalties. State authorities estimated that between 6 and 14% of potential income tax revenue was being lost to nonfilers, evaders, and delinquents.

Under lobbying pressure from vendors, eight additional states passed prompt-pay laws, bringing to 35 the states requiring interest payments when states are tardy in paying invoices.

A state-federal task force headed by Secretary of the Treasury Donald Regan announced agreement in May on a plan to curb state taxation of worldwide profits of multinational firms. Unitary taxation, used by 12 states after Oregon repealed its law in 1984, is designed to ensure that companies pay for profit-making activity within state borders instead of ascribing the profit to lower-tax jurisdictions. In November seven state officials on the task force accused Regan of misrepresenting their views in his report, which called for an immediate switch to taxation of in-state or water's edge profits rather than worldwide profits of the multinationals.

New York experimented with an innovative labour system to save funds. After determining that many state jobs did not require full-time jobholders, the state offered employees reduced work hours in return for corresponding wage cuts. Louisiana faced financial troubles over its New Orleans world's fair; despite two state loans totaling $27.5 million, the fair declared bankruptcy.

Among measures to raise additional tax revenue, Louisiana, Maine, Oklahoma, South Carolina, Tennessee, and Texas increased sales taxes or broadened the sales tax base, and Alabama, Arizona, Louisiana, Maine, and Texas increased tobacco excise levies. Motor fuel taxes were raised in Connecticut, Louisiana, Oklahoma, Texas, and Utah. Corporate income taxes were raised in Utah and Vermont, and personal income tax rates were increased in Vermont. Alcoholic beverage taxes went up in Arizona, Louisiana, Oklahoma, and Texas.

Most states able to reduce taxes concentrated on personal income levies. Delaware, Michigan, Minnesota, Nebraska, Ohio, Rhode Island, and Wisconsin lowered personal income tax rates, and Minnesota, Michigan, and Wisconsin accelerated their planned phasing out of income tax surcharges. Corporate income taxes were lowered in Nebraska, Pennsylvania, and Wisconsin, while Georgia and Washington enacted minor sales tax decreases.

Figures compiled in 1984 revealed that state revenue from all sources totaled $357.6 billion during the 1983 fiscal year, an increase of 8.1% over the preceding 12 months. General revenue (excluding state liquor and state insurance trust revenue) totaled $290.5 billion, up 5.6%. Total state expenditures rose 7.6% to $334 billion, creating a technical surplus of $23.6 billion for the year. General expenditures, not including outlays of the liquor stores and insurance trust system, amounted to $285 billion, up 5.8% for the year. Of the general revenue, 59.1% came from the state taxes and licenses; 15.9% came from charges and miscellaneous revenue, including educational tuition; and 25% came from intergovernmental revenue (mostly from the federal government).

The largest state outlay was $107.7 billion for education, of which $36.5 billion went to state colleges and universities and $63.1 billion to local public schools. Other major outlays included $57.5 billion for public welfare, $26.4 billion for highways,

and $23.9 billion for health and public hospitals.

Ethics. John Kerr, former top aide to Pennsylvania Auditor General Al Benedict, was convicted in June on 139 counts in a scheme to sell state jobs; prosecutors said $200,000 was raised to finance Benedict's ultimately unsuccessful race for state treasurer in 1984. Nebraska Attorney General Paul Douglas was impeached and later indicted for perjury and obstruction of justice in connection with a legislative investigation into a failed industrial savings company in Lincoln. Massachusetts state Rep. Vincent J. Piro was convicted of conspiracy in November; he was accused of extorting $25,000 from a mall developer for liquor licenses. New York state Sen. Joseph Pisani was convicted on 18 felony mail-fraud and tax-evasion charges stemming from the embezzlement of $83,000 from state, campaign fund, and law firm accounts. Sam Caldwell, Georgia commissioner of labour, was convicted of fraud in April for using state employees to work on a boat he owned.

Former Oklahoma house speaker Dan Draper and onetime majority leader Joe Fitzgibbon, suspended in 1983 after being found guilty of federal vote-fraud charges, were granted a new trial by an appeals court. Two libel suits filed by Gov. William Janklow of South Dakota against a book publisher, booksellers, and *Newsweek* magazine were dismissed; the courts ruled that a book's allegations that Janklow had raped an Indian girl in 1967 were not defamatory. In Louisiana the state natural resources secretary, William Huls, resigned after newspaper reports suggested overly close ties between state officials and major oil companies. Huls, a former oilman, had fired a national accounting firm from an audit of Texaco royalty payments after the auditors suggested that Texaco had underpaid by $100 million; the auditors were rehired after Huls's resignation.

Alaska, Georgia, and Mississippi toughened state ethics rules for legislators. Illinois expanded economic disclosure requirements for state employees, and Rhode Island expanded conflict-of-interest laws.

Education. Amid national concern with declining educational standards, 12 states stepped up required student testing programs, to be followed in most instances by remedial help for those needing it. Several states also moved to upgrade minimal standards in higher education facilities. Florida joined Georgia in requiring sophomores at public universities to pass a basic academic skills test before becoming juniors.

The Colorado legislature moved to equalize school district spending through a matching-funds program. West Virginia voters approved a state constitutional amendment permitting prayer in public schools, even though such prayers had been declared violative of the federal Constitution by the U.S. Supreme Court.

Health and Welfare. Controversy over abortion continued in several states during 1984. Colorado voters approved, but Washington voters turned down, ballot initiatives to prohibit the use of public funds for abortions. A similar referendum was struck from the Arkansas ballot by judicial decree. As of 1984 a total of 35 states forbade the use of public-aid funding for abortions, but the Colorado measure was

the first such action by voter initiative.

States also struggled with rising hospital costs and with ethical and financial problems associated with organ transplantation. Arizona voters turned down five competing initiatives on hospital cost containment, two of which would have given state government broad authority over medical practices and hospital fees. Illinois established an organ transplant fund to help pay for costly operations, and Pennsylvania and Rhode Island moved to follow Massachusetts in setting up a state income tax checkoff to help fund transplants. Illinois also required hospitals to post price lists publicly and to quote charges to inquirers over the telephone.

California voters rejected a measure that would have cut the state's welfare benefits, highest in the nation, by approximately 25%. In another display of solicitude, District of Columbia voters overwhelmingly ordered the city government to provide overnight shelter for the homeless. Georgia, Louisiana, West Virginia, and Wyoming joined states establishing a right to die by rejection of artificial life-prolonging medical technology.

Montana voters approved legalization and regulation of denturism, the sale and fitting of dentures by nondentist technicians. South Carolina, stung by news reports calling it the adoption capital of the nation, approved a law making the selling of babies a felony.

Drugs. In a move that caught state lobbyists by surprise, the U.S. Congress ordered a reduction in highway construction assistance for states that failed to set 21 as the minimum drinking age by 1986. Several state officials objected that the federal move preempted legitimate state authority, and South Dakota authorities unsuccessfully moved for a court injunction to halt what they termed federal coercion. Before the federal action 30 states allowed persons under 21 to purchase at least some alcoholic beverages, but Arizona, Nebraska, Rhode Island, and Tennessee moved later in the year to a minimum age of 21, and authorities predicted that others would eventually follow suit.

The same legislation contained incentives to reward states that enacted mandatory sentencing laws for convicted drunk drivers. Arizona, Iowa, Kentucky, Maine, and Wisconsin toughened their penalties for underage drivers who drink, usually mandating an automatic license suspension.

Law and Justice. A variety of new laws to protect children were passed during the year. Rhode Island stiffened its sexual assault against minors law; New Mexico increased penalties for the use of children in pornography; and Arizona, Florida, Georgia, Minnesota, and Wisconsin tightened child abuse statutes. Florida, Illinois, Kentucky, and Washington joined Utah in establishing statewide databanks to combat the problem of missing children.

Oregon voters and the New York legislature approved the death penalty for certain crimes. But courts in New York and Massachusetts declared unconstitutional capital punishment laws in those states, leaving the jurisdictions with death penalty statutes at 38.

Indiana narrowed the use of the insanity defense, and Iowa and Nebraska shifted the burden of proof in insanity pleas to the criminal defendant. Ohio, Pennsylvania, and Wisconsin approved new crime victim assistance packages, but Oregon voters turned down a "victims' bill of rights" initiative, in part because of objections to the expanded powers that would be given to police and prosecutors.

North Dakota and Utah voters affirmed their rights to keep and bear arms. Florida, Kentucky, and Missouri upgraded dogfighting to felony status. Texas became the tenth state to curb or outlaw paramilitary training.

Prisons. The number of executions increased markedly during the year as lengthy appeals of many death row inmates were finally exhausted. Before 1984 only 11 prisoners had been executed since the U.S. Supreme Court approved resumption of capital punishment in 1976, but 21 more were put to death in state prisons during the year. One of them was convicted multiple murderer Margie Velma Barfield, who died from a lethal injection in Raleigh, N.C., on November 2, the first woman executed in the U.S. in 22 years. A key Supreme Court decision in January speeded the trend; the justices ruled that states need not conduct a complicated proportionality review of death sentences in order to ensure that the punishment was in line with other verdicts in similar cases. Even so, the pace of executions failed to keep up with death sentence verdicts, and at year's end there were 1,450 inmates on death row nationwide.

Although the nation's crime rate dropped for the fourth consecutive year, the population of state prisons continued to rise to new record levels. With court decisions ordering the release of nonthreatening mental patients, Kansas and Missouri moved to convert underutilized mental hospitals to prisons. A plan to transform a University of South Dakota campus into a prison was abandoned after citizen protests.

A survey by the Criminal Justice Institute revealed that states paid nearly $16,000 per year to house, feed, and clothe a typical prisoner. Unsurprisingly, that led to a search for alternatives to incarceration, including halfway houses, intensively supervised probation, and community work correction plans. Texas, traditionally a hard-line corrections state, illustrated the trend by appropriating $11 million over two years for restitution houses, where offenders could hold jobs to repay their victims.

Another alternative to incarceration received national attention when a South Carolina judge offered three rape convicts surgical castration and probation in place of 30-year prison sentences. The offenders chose castration, although imposition of the sentence was delayed for legal appeals. Courts in Michigan and California prescribed chemical castration through administration of the drug Depo-Provera, a sexual depressant. The Oklahoma House of Representatives approved a bill for "asexualization" of certain sex offenders, but the measure died in the state Senate.

Gambling. The popularity of state-run games of chance surged during 1984. Voters in California, Missouri, Oregon, and West Virginia approved the establishment of state lotteries, bringing to 21 the number of jurisdictions with government lottery

operations. In addition, Alabama, Minnesota, and Oklahoma scheduled the start of pari-mutuel horse-race betting. However, proposals to extend casino gambling, legal in 1984 only in Nevada and Atlantic City, N.J., did not fare well. Voters rejected legalization of casino operations in Hot Springs, Ark., and Pueblo, Colo., in part because of fears about an influx of organized crime.

Concern mounted in some states over the spread of legal gambling. New Mexico became the sixth state in which high-stakes bingo operations were being conducted on Indian reservations, outside state regulation. In Nebraska a judge ruled that communities could allow video gambling machines under authority of the state lottery law, but the state legislature finally outlawed the devices.

Environment. Maryland, Pennsylvania, and Virginia began a joint effort to clean up Chesapeake Bay in cooperation with federal authorities. A U.S. Environmental Protection Agency (EPA) study found severe nutrient enrichment and toxic contamination in much of the bay, which had damaged marine life and the seafood industry. The EPA also threatened to take over air-quality control in 34 states containing significant national park and wilderness areas unless those states submitted acceptable quality-control plans. Only two states, Alaska and Louisiana, had submitted satisfactory plans since the EPA demanded them in 1980.

Oregon and Colorado became the first states to regulate wood-burning stoves, which had become a major source of air pollution in some states. Kansas and Iowa established state "superfund" accounts to facilitate the cleanup of toxic-waste dumps. Michigan created a state conservation corps, thus becoming the eighth state to merge environmental and youth-employment concerns.

New York mounted a major assault on presumed causes of acid rain, limiting emissions of sulfur dioxide and nitrogen oxide emissions. Washington citizens voted to end the special fishing rights enjoyed by various Indian tribes, and Arkansas voters rejected a major sales tax increase that would have funded wildlife programs.

Energy. Problems with nuclear generating plants, especially over the disposal of low-level radioactive waste, continued to occupy state officials in 1984. By the year's end 37 states had ratified eight regional agreements for nuclear-waste disposal, but the nation's three existing dump sites were becoming overburdened, and no new locations were volunteered. Several states, including Illinois and New York, fearful of becoming regional waste repositories, threatened to abandon the regional approach and handle the problem internally. Voters continued to be uneasy about nuclear power. Oregon voters set a zero-emission standard for nuclear-waste dumps, and South Dakota citizens mandated voter approval before a new dump could be established. Wisconsin banned new nuclear generators, and Illinois and Oregon set up citizen utility boards to monitor power rate hikes associated with costly nuclear construction.

Equal Rights. The concept of "comparable worth"—equal pay for jobs judged similar in skills and the amount of training

demanded—seemed to lose steam during the year. A lawsuit charged that 37,000 California state employees had been discriminated against on the basis of sex, but two federal appeals courts turned down a comparable worth claim lodged by the University of Washington nursing faculty. That meant, legal experts predicted, that an estimated $800 million back-pay judgment awarded Washington state female employees in 1983 would be overturned. Although commissions in 24 states were studying the idea at the year's end, five state legislatures rejected bills mandating comparable pay during the year.

Maine voters rejected a proposal to add an equal rights amendment to the state constitution. The California governor vetoed a gay rights bill that prohibited job discrimination against homosexuals. Mississippi belatedly approved the 19th amendment to the U.S. Constitution, which in 1920 had granted women the right to vote; that left Delaware as the only state that had not ratified it. California voters approved a nonbinding advisory measure that would restrict ballot language solely to English.

Wisconsin became the first state to approve a model marital property act that establishes both spouses as full economic partners in marriage. The law formally recognizes the contributions of nonearning spouses and grants them full legal rights to one-half of all property acquired during the marriage.

Consumer Protection. New York and New Jersey approved the nation's first effective mandatory seat-belt laws for adults, starting what the federal government hoped would be a national trend. The New York law provided $50 fines for violators. U.S. Secretary of Transportation Elizabeth Dole ordered automobile manufacturers to install costly air bags on their 1986 models but offered to repeal the order if enough states passed mandatory safety-belt laws to cover two-thirds of the U.S. population by 1989. Idaho, Missouri, Texas, Utah, and Vermont joined states mandating belt restraints for children.

New Jersey, Ohio, and Massachusetts outlawed "happy hour" promotions in taverns, the selling of drinks at reduced prices during certain times of the day. Arizona, Colorado, Hawaii, Iowa, Maryland, Montana, Pennsylvania, Tennessee, Virginia, and West Virginia joined states with "lemon laws" that require manufacturers to replace chronically defective cars. Attempting to fill a regulatory void, Illinois and Pennsylvania mandated annual inspection of amusement park rides. Utah voters overturned a proposed ban on sexually explicit cable television programs.

North Carolina and Virginia deregulated intrastate telephone service, and Minnesota became the first jurisdiction allowing businesses to buy and install pay telephones. Alaska voters approved an end to state regulation of transportation, but Montana voters rejected a proposal to cancel the state's milk-price-fixing system.

The U.S. Supreme Court ruled illegal a Maryland statute prohibiting charities from spending more than 25% of their gross income on fund-raising. The court rejected claims that high solicitation costs are indicative of fraud; similar laws in 17 other states presumably were invalidated by the decision.   (DAVID C. BECKWITH)

Latin America and the Caribbean

LATIN–AMERICAN AFFAIRS

In 1984 Latin America's economic difficulties intensified, though its external indebtedness eased slightly. Elections took place in several countries, reinforcing a trend toward civilian rule that had gathered momentum since the start of the 1980s. Presidential elections held in May were won by León Febres Cordero in Ecuador, José Napoleón Duarte in El Salvador, and Nicolás Ardito Barletta in Panama (*see* BIOGRAPHIES). Pres. Jaime Lusinchi (*see* BIOGRAPHIES) took office in February, after winning Venezuela's December 1983 election, while in Uruguay presidential elections held in November 1984 were won by Julio Sanguinetti, who was to take office in March 1985. Elections to a constitutional assembly took place in Guatemala in July to prepare the way for increased democratization, and general elections were held in Nicaragua in November, with partial participation by opposition parties.

Argentina and Chile signed a treaty in Rome in November settling their long-standing dispute over the Beagle Channel. While Argentina recognized Chile's entitlement to the islands of Picton, Lennox, and Nueva in the channel, both countries recognized the so-called bioceanic principle, by which Argentina restricted its maritime claims to the Atlantic Ocean, and Chile to the Pacific Ocean. The dispute, which had brought the two countries to the brink of war in 1978, was settled through negotiations initiated by and conducted under the auspices of the Vatican. The dispute between Argentina and the U.K. over the Falkland Islands/Islas Malvinas remained unresolved, however. The U.K. adamantly refused to negotiate on the question of sovereignty over the islands.

Central America continued to be subjected to political and social disorders. There was a full-scale guerrilla war in El Salvador, although rebel groups joined with the government in tentative discussions. Widespread guerrilla activity continued in Guatemala, and incursions into Nicaragua by rebel groups were covertly backed by the U.S. Peace initiatives were under way throughout the year. The Contadora Group, formed in January 1983 by Colombia, Mexico, Panama, and Venezuela, drafted a peace treaty for the re-gion that called for a mutual reduction of arms, troops, and foreign advisers, including those from the U.S. and Cuba, and an end to external support for rebels in Nicaragua and El Salvador. The draft treaty was accepted by the Nicaraguan government. However, U.S. allies objected that the plan lacked adequate verification and control mechanisms to ensure Nicaraguan compliance. In October the foreign ministers of the Contadora countries agreed to discuss the objections with Central American governments; any changes would have to be acceptable to Nicaragua. The UN General Assembly voted to support the draft treaty late in October.

In January a report was published containing long-term recommendations for U.S. involvement in Central American development. The report was prepared by a 12-member bipartisan commission headed by Henry Kissinger, former U.S. secretary of state. Its principal recommendations were that the U.S. provide economic assistance worth $8 billion during the period 1985–89, making an effort to ensure that by 1990 a total of $24 billion was being directed to the area; and that a new agency, the Central American Development Organization, with representatives from the U.S. and Central American governments, be created to act as a channel for about one-quarter of the U.S. assistance. In a nationally televised address on May 9, U.S. Pres. Ronald Reagan pressed for Congress to accept the recommendations of the Kissinger report and called for urgent military aid to friendly governments in the region. He stated, however, that U.S. troops would not be sent into combat in Central America. In August Congress approved a $503 million aid package for the area. Military funding allocated for El Salvador was raised from $126 million in 1983 to $197 million in 1984.

The foreign ministers of 21 countries (the ten members of the European Communities [EC], along with Spain, Portugal, and nine Latin-American countries) met in San José, Costa Rica, at the end of September. It was agreed to increase EC aid to Central America from the current $30 million a year to $45 million in 1985, with the possibility of extending assistance at that annual level for an additional five years. The aid was to be devoted mainly to the development of agriculture.

Heads of government of the 13-country Caribbean Com-

UPI/BETTMANN

The Organization of American States met in Washington, D.C., on March 12 and elected João Clemente Baena Soares of Brazil its secretary-general. He stands here behind Permanent Council Chairman Francisco Posada de la Pena of Colombia, who is congratulating him after the swearing-in ceremonies on June 20.

munity (Caricom) met in Nassau, The Bahamas, in July and agreed on measures to stimulate trade among Caricom members. The accord ended two years of wrangling that had threatened the future of the 11-year-old organization. The U.S. Caribbean Basin Initiative (CBI) operated fitfully throughout the year. The CBI, which had become law in August 1983, was an integrated program of tax and trade measures, including an agreement that allowed a range of Caribbean and Central American products duty-free access to the U.S. market for 12 years. During the period January–June 1984 only 6.3% of $4.7 billion worth of imports from Caribbean Basin countries to the U.S. carried the CBI's duty-free status.

The Latin American Integration Association (LAIA), which consisted of Argentina, Bolivia, Brazil, Chile, Colombia, Ecuador, Mexico, Paraguay, Peru, Uruguay, and Venezuela, recorded modest progress in 1984. In Montevideo, Uruguay, in May the Council of Foreign Ministers, LAIA's highest decision-making body, approved an act providing for a system of preferential regional tariffs. The new arrangement meant that from July 1 products moving from one LAIA country to another were eligible for reduced import duties, ranging from 10 to 2% less than duties that applied to imports from non-LAIA countries. The size of the reduction depended on whether a member country was classified as less developed (Bolivia, Ecuador, and Paraguay), intermediately developed (Chile, Colombia, Peru, Uruguay, and Venezuela), or more developed (Argentina, Brazil, and Mexico). When duties were lower under the new system than under previous agreements made within LAIA, the new rates were to apply. In July Argentina and Uruguay signed the first agricultural agreement negotiated under the auspices of LAIA.

In December 1983 the EC signed an economic cooperation pact with the Andean Group (Bolivia, Colombia, Ecuador, Peru, and Venezuela). The purposes of the pact were to foster industrial cooperation and to develop scientific and technical exchanges. Each party granted the other most-favoured-nation treatment within the terms of the General Agreement on Tariffs and Trade.

In 1983 Latin America's economic crisis deepened and broadened with an average decline in gross domestic product of 3% and a fall of 5.3% in per capita income. In particular there were sharply reduced capital inflows and a drastic decline in domestic investment. Merchandise imports in 1983 reached $56 billion, some $40 billion down from the 1981 figure. Net financial inflows, primarily from international commercial banks, declined by more than $20 billion in 1982 and an additional $10 billion in 1983. Gross domestic investment fell in real terms by 13% from the 1982 level. The region's total external debt reached $336 billion at the end of 1983 and was estimated at about $350 billion in mid-1984.

Governments in the region became increasingly worried about the problem of foreign debt during 1984. Finance and foreign ministers of 11 countries held two major meetings on the subject. At the first, in Cartagena, Colombia, on June 21–22, Brazil, Mexico, and Colombia blocked moves sponsored by Argentina and other countries for unilateral Latin-American action to reduce outflows of debt repayments. The meeting called for concessions by international banks on interest payments and maturities in debt negotiations and for the expansion and streamlining of the role of international financial organizations. A second meeting, held at Mar del Plata, Arg., on September 13–14, produced a series of moderate proposals to solve Latin America's external debt difficulties. There were calls for direct political talks with Western creditor governments in the first half of

1985 and for an expansion of lending by the International Monetary Fund (IMF) and the World Bank.

During the year international banks reached a measure of understanding with the four largest debtor countries on their servicing commitments. Mexico was seeking to reschedule $49 billion of its $90.6 billion external debt over a 14-year period, to reach an agreement on partial repayment of $5 billion of 1983 debt and recycling of the balance, and to restructure the $20.1 billion of public-sector debt due in 1985–90. In September Venezuela negotiated similar terms with the banks involving the restructuring over 12 years of $20.7 billion of bank debt maturing between 1983 and 1988; this represented some 94% of the nation's refinanceable debt. In January the Brazilian government, the IMF, and international banks approved a package to cover Brazil's 1983–84 financing gap, including a $6.5 billion new-money loan and recycling of 1984 medium-term maturities on a debt of $89 billion at the end of 1983. Negotiations on Brazil's external financial requirements in 1985 began in November. In late December Argentina reached an agreement with the IMF that included a $1.4 billion 15-month standby facility and adoption of a wide-ranging economic austerity program. Foreign banks also agreed to provide a substantial new money loan and to reschedule about $14 billion of Argentina's foreign debt.

Among the smaller borrowers, Chile obtained new credits of $800 million to cover its 1984 foreign borrowing needs, and Ecuador arranged with creditor banks in August to reschedule $348 million of public-debt principal originally due to have been repaid in 1984. On the other hand, Peru and Bolivia defaulted on interest payments.

(ROBIN CHAPMAN)

MIDDLE AMERICA

BELIZE

A parliamentary state and member of the Commonwealth, Belize is on the Caribbean coast of Central America. Area: 22,965 sq km (8,867 sq mi). Pop. (1984 est.): 158,000. Cap.: Belmopan. Monetary unit: Belize dollar, with (Oct. 29, 1984) a free rate of BZ$2 to U.S. $1 (BZ$2.42 = £1 sterling). Queen, Elizabeth II; governor-general in 1984 Dame Minita Gordon; prime ministers, George Cadle Price and, from December 17, Manuel Esquivel.

The opposition United Democratic Party led by Manuel Esquivel won 21 of 28 seats in the House of Representatives in general elections on Dec. 14, 1984, the first since Belize became independent in 1981. The UDP victory ended the long rule of the left-of-centre People's United Party under George Cadle Price, who had served as head of government since 1961.

Stricter constraints were imposed on the flow of illegal aliens and immigrants into Belize during the year. The government called on all aliens to register, and by the end of July more than 8,000 had complied. On May 1 amnesty was granted to all aliens who lived in the country.

The Central Statistical Office reported marked improvement in the national economy ·in the first half of 1984. Total domestic exports had increased to some BZ$73.2 million from BZ$62 million during the same period of the previous year. The improvement was a result of higher export prices for agricultural commodities such as sugar, molasses, and citrus concentrate and increased garment sales to the U.S.

During the year Brazil, Japan, Israel, and Italy appointed nonresident ambassadors to Belize. Israel's move was significant because that nation previously had supported Guatemala's claim to Belize.

Minita Gordon, the governor-general, was created a dame by Queen Elizabeth II during a visit to London.

(INES T. BAPTIST)

This article updates the *Macropædia* article CENTRAL AMERICA: *Belize.*

COSTA RICA

The Central American republic of Costa Rica has coastlines on the Caribbean Sea and the Pacific Ocean. Area: 51,100 sq km (19,730 sq mi). Pop. (1984 prelim.): 2,460,200. Cap.: San José. Monetary unit: colón, with (Oct. 29, 1984) a free rate of 44.81 colones to U.S. $1 (54.09 colones = £1 sterling). President in 1984, Luis Alberto Monge Álvarez.

Costa Rica's position of neutrality in Central America came under pressure in 1984. In May the government's request for security assistance from the U.S. sparked a 20,-000-strong peace march through San José. A further strain was imposed by Costa Rica's increasingly hostile relations with Nicaragua, evidenced by a growing number of border skirmishes. In June Pres. Luis Alberto Monge Álvarez, who had been elected on a platform of unprecedented economic austerity, visited 12 European countries, seeking political and economic support, and gained promises of aid that was worth $135 million. He also arranged for meetings between Central American countries and European countries in San José in September, at which time further assistance was promised.

The economic program imposed by the International Monetary Fund (IMF) began to show results in 1983. Inflation was reduced to 10%, from almost 100% in 1982, and the exchange rate improved. However, all sectors except agriculture experienced a recession, resulting in a 1% contraction in gross domestic product, and servicing of the $4 billion foreign debt used up over 40% of foreign-exchange earnings. In August 1984 the government approved a further package of measures required by the IMF, paving the way for a new $60 million loan.   (INGRID IVERSEN)

This article updates the *Macropædia* article CENTRAL AMERICA: *Costa Rica.*

EL SALVADOR

The republic of El Salvador is situated on the Pacific coast of Central America. Area: 21,041 sq km (8,124 sq mi). Pop. (1984 est.): 5 million. Cap.: San Salvador. Monetary unit: colón, with (Oct. 29, 1984) a free rate of 2.49 colones to U.S. $1 (3 colones = £1 sterling). President of the civilian-military junta to June 1, 1984, Álvaro Alfredo Magaña Borjo; president from June 1, José Napoleón Duarte.

None of the eight candidates won an outright majority in the first round of El Salvador's presidential elections on March 25, 1984. A second round was held on May 6 between the two leading contenders, José Napoleón Duarte (*see* BIOGRAPHIES) of the Christian Democratic Party and Maj. Roberto d'Aubuisson of the Nationalist Republican Alliance (Arena). Duarte won 54% of the vote and was sworn in as president on June 1.

The guerrilla forces of the Farabundo Martí National Liberation Front (FMLN) and its political wing, the Democratic Revolutionary Front (FDR), did not participate in the elections, and they claimed to have prevented balloting in 89 constituencies under their control. Before the elections they presented a peace program that proposed the setting up of a provisional government, in which they would share power, before any elections were held, and the reorganization of the armed forces.

After Duarte's victory the guerrillas reaffirmed their commitment to their proposals. The new president offered to enter into dialogue, but not formal negotiations, with FMLN-FDR if the insurgents laid down their arms and dropped their request for changes in the structure of government. In a speech at the UN on October 8, President Duarte offered to open talks. The two sides met at La Palma, Chalatenango Province, on October 15. Each expressed optimism after the talks, but major differences remained to be discussed. Little progress was made at a second meeting on November 30. Further talks were agreed on, although no definite date was set. The two sides also agreed to allow civilian traffic on the highways during the Christmas holiday period, but beyond that the prospect was uncertain. The five-year death toll in the fighting exceeded 52,000, mostly civilians.

AP/WIDE WORLD

Five Salvadoran national guardsmen were tried—after years of delay by El Salvador's courts and because the U.S. Congress had voted to withhold military aid—and convicted of murdering four U.S. churchwomen in 1980. They were sentenced to the maximum of 30 years in prison. The officer believed to have ordered the killings was later cleared on a legal technicality.

On January 1 insurgents blew up the Cuscatlán Bridge across the Lempa River, which linked San Salvador with the eastern part of the country. More than 100 soldiers had been killed when the guerrillas took El Paraíso garrison, Chalatenango Province, two days before. On June 28, when guerrilla forces overran the Cerrón Grande hydroelectric dam and held it for ten hours, at least 120 died in the bitter fighting and damage worth $3.5 million was inflicted. Earlier in the month, the Army recaptured a number of important towns in the guerrilla-controlled province of Morazán. Having taken delivery of more U.S.-built helicopters, government forces increased the aerial bombardment of rebel-held areas. On the ground, however, the military began to adopt tactics designed to win the confidence of villagers, rather than relying on force. Massacres of 100 people in northern Chalatenango in September and 68 in Cabañas Province in July were reported.

President Duarte issued more humane codes of conduct to the Army and set up a commission to investigate alleged human rights abuses. He also disbanded the 100-strong intelligence unit of the feared Treasury Military Police. In an effort to control the activity of right-wing death squads, three colonels suspected of involvement were given diplomatic or educational posts abroad. In May five national guardsmen were found guilty of the murder of three U.S. nuns and a lay worker in December 1980 and in June were sentenced to 30 years in prison. Duarte cashiered one officer out of the Army without pension after a court let him avoid prosecution for the 1981 murder of three U.S. Agency for International Development workers. His attacks on human rights abuse and his meeting with the guerrillas incurred the displeasure of the ultraright, but it was not monolithic, since his policies encouraged the U.S. to offer greater support. In fiscal 1984 the U.S. Congress approved military aid to El Salvador worth $126 million, and in August the House of Representatives reversed an earlier decision to block $70 million in emergency funds requested by U.S. Pres. Ronald Reagan. Duarte's visits to

CLAUDE URRACA—SYGMA

Pres. José Napoléon Duarte of El Salvador addressed a crowd outside the La Palma church where he met with political and military leaders of antigovernment guerrillas in October.

the U.S. in May and July helped to soften the attitude of Democrats. However, the U.S. Court of Appeals upheld legislation that linked military aid to human rights progress. Duarte visited Western Europe in July and secured support from the West German and British governments. In August the U.K. announced the reopening of its embassy in El Salvador.   (BEN BOX)

This article updates the *Macropædia* article CENTRAL AMERICA: *El Salvador*.

GUATEMALA

A republic of Central America, Guatemala has coastlines on the Caribbean Sea and the Pacific Ocean. Area: 108,889 sq km (42,042 sq mi). Pop. (1984 est.): 7,599,000. Cap.: Guatemala City. Monetary unit: quetzal, at par with the U.S. dollar, with (Oct. 29, 1984) a free rate of 1.21 quetzales to £1 sterling. Chief of state in 1984, Gen. Oscar Humberto Mejía Victores.

When Gen. Oscar Humberto Mejía Victores assumed power in August 1983, he promised a return to "authentic" democracy in Guatemala. Elections for a constituent assembly were held on July 1, 1984, to pave the way for general elections planned for March 1985. Though the turnout was high, with over 80% of the electorate voting, polling was marred by an excessive number of spoiled and invalid votes, estimated at one-quarter of the total. Voting was compulsory under Guatemalan law, and nonvoters were fined the equivalent of two day's earnings at the legal minimum wage level. The resignation of several judges and other electoral officials in May had raised doubts about the fairness of the elections, but the government, pointing to the high turnout, claimed that they were a successful first move toward a return to democracy, and many independent observers reiterated that view.

The parties of the centre together polled one-third of the votes, the most successful single party in percentage terms being the Christian Democrats (DCG). The extreme right-wing coalition of the National Liberation Movement (MLN) and the Authentic Nationalist Centre (CAN) was pushed into third place by the centre-right Union of the National Centre (UCN). However, because the MLN-CAN coalition was most strongly represented in sparsely populated regions, while DCG and UCN received their support in the urban areas, the coalition and other right-wing parties controlled a total of 27 seats in the 88-seat assembly while winning only 23% of the votes, while the DCG and UCN won 22 seats each.

The people's desire for change was reflected in the movement away from MLN and its policy of violence in purging the country of what its propaganda termed the "communistoids." The elections were seen by some as a turning point, but others still questioned the likelihood of democratic elections taking place in 1985. Meanwhile, the Army remained in control, and a major offensive against the insurgents put a strain on the economy and the social fabric of the country., There were many deaths and a steady flow of refugees into neighbouring Mexico.

The U.S. Congress had banned all aid to Guatemala in 1983 because of continued human rights violations by the military regime. However, the ban was circumvented by the raising and transmittal of funds by private voluntary organizations. Aid from the U.S. was expected to reach $33.6 million in 1984, compared with $27.5 million in 1983. Though the U.S. had provided no military aid since 1977, the sale of helicopter parts continued. Israel and South Africa were the main suppliers of arms. The U.K. and Guatemala agreed in principle to reestablish consular

A gas distribution centre blew up in a Mexico City suburb at the end of November, killing hundreds, injuring thousands, and forcing the evacuation of more than 100,000.

SIPA/SPECIAL FEATURES

relations, severed in 1981, in order to seek a resolution of the dispute over Guatemala's territorial claim to Belize.

The economy deteriorated further, with 1983 results showing a negative growth rate. The improvement in the agricultural sector was undermined by poor world prices and low demand for its products. Exports remained depressed, and this factor, combined with capital flight and increases in debt-servicing payments, resulted in serious foreign-exchange shortages. (INGRID IVERSEN)

This article updates the *Macropædia* article CENTRAL AMERICA: *Guatemala*.

HONDURAS

A republic of Central America, Honduras has coastlines on the Caribbean Sea and the Pacific Ocean. Area: 112,088 sq km (43,277 sq mi). Pop. (1984 est.): 4,135,000. Cap.: Tegucigalpa. Monetary unit: lempira, with (Oct. 29, 1984) a par value of 2 lempiras to U.S. $1 (free rate of 2.42 lempiras = £1 sterling). President in 1984, Roberto Suazo Córdova.

Democracy in Honduras, held up by the U.S. as a model for neighbouring Central American republics, came under threat in 1984. Alleged attempts by Pres. Roberto Suazo Córdova to manipulate voting registers to suit his own Liberal Party and internal dissent in both the Liberal and the rival National parties led to postponement of the elections scheduled for November 1985. The economy, already in sharp recession, was poorly managed. Austerity measures insisted on by the International Monetary Fund were suspended in June to avert a threatened general strike.

On March 31 Gen. Gustavo Álvarez Martínez, commander in chief of the armed forces, was forced into exile by officers who resented his autocratic style of leadership and his plans to remodel the command structure. Honduras then pressed the U.S. for more aid, more control over U.S. military personnel stationed in the country, and greater involvement in the U.S. training base at Puerto Castilla. The government went so far as to announce in September that no more Salvadoran personnel could be trained by the U.S. at Puerto Castilla until Honduras and El Salvador had settled a long-standing border dispute. Relations improved in October when the U.S. signed a supplementary aid package worth $141 million. (BEN BOX)

This article updates the *Macropædia* article CENTRAL AMERICA: *Honduras*.

MEXICO

A federal republic of North America, Mexico has coastlines on the Pacific Ocean, the Gulf of Mexico, and the Caribbean Sea. Area: 1,958,201 sq km (756,065 sq mi). Pop. (1984 est.): 74,025,000. Cap.: Mexico City. Monetary unit: peso, with (Oct. 29, 1984) a free rate of 208.76 pesos to U.S. $1 (251.97 pesos = £1 sterling). President in 1984, Miguel de la Madrid Hurtado.

In his address to the nation in September 1984, Pres. Miguel de la Madrid Hurtado of Mexico said the worst effects of the economic crisis were being overcome, although recovery was only incipient. Following the introduction of austerity measures, the economy was expected to register slight growth, with manufacturing making a reasonable recovery in the first five months, after a poor performance in the early part of 1983. Inflation was subsiding and was expected to reach around 50% in 1984, compared with 80% the previous year. Good weather allowed a reduction in food imports of up to one-third. Unemployment inched downward, but austerity measures affected living standards.

Mexico asked for some $48.5 billion of loans (representing over half of the $96 billion external debt due to mature during the period 1984–90) to be refinanced for up to 14 years at lower spreads. Non-U.S. banks would also be permitted to convert up to 50% of their dollar-denominated credits to their own currencies. In return, Mexico undertook to supply commercial banks with the semiannual reports on the state of the economy supplied to the International Monetary Fund by all IMF members.

Mexican officials stated early in the year that the country would maintain an output of 2.7 million bbl a day of crude oil, but petroleum exports (which had averaged 1.5 million bbl a day) were cut by 10% in December. Together with Venezuela, Mexico continued to supply ten Caribbean Basin nations with oil, but it suspended the 6,000 bbl a day shipped to Haiti when the latter was reported to be reexporting its supplies. The government also continued to follow the pricing policy of the Organization of Petroleum Exporting Countries, though otherwise it remained independent of the cartel.

The administration carried on its campaign aimed at the "moral renovation" of public life. Legislation was introduced ending the preferential right of unions to take contracts from public-sector enterprises or firms trading with official entities and then sell or sublet the contracts to third parties, an arrangement that had permitted the petroleum workers' union, in particular, to finance its activities. Instead, the union's "share" of all drilling contracts signed by the state oil company, Petróleos Mexicanos—ostensibly used for its retirement and social benefit fund—was increased from 2 to 4%. Former union official Héctor García Hernández, known as El Trampas ("the Trickster"), was arrested in 1983 on charges of corruption. From his prison cell he persisted in his campaign against Sen. Salvador Barragán Camacho, the secretary-general of the union until December, whom he accused, together with union political adviser Joaquín Hernández Galicia, of having diverted union funds to his personal use during the period 1980–81. Arturo Durazo Moreno, the former Mexico City chief of police, was arrested in Puerto Rico by U.S. authorities and taken to Los Angeles to await extradition proceedings after he was charged with fraud and arms-traffic offenses. Extradition was also sought for Jesús Chavarría García, a former supplies manager for Petróleos Mexicanos, who was charged with fraud. He was now living in Chile.

At the end of May one of Mexico's senior investigative journalists, Manuel Buendía, was shot dead. Although no motive or responsibility could be attributed, his killing was linked in the press to the publication of a book he had written about right-wing groups and foreign intelligence activities in Mexico.

Relations with John Gavin, the U.S. ambassador to Mexico, were strained because of accusations by the ruling Partido Revolucionario Institucional (PRI) that the Republican Party in the U.S. was granting financial assistance to the opposition Partido de Acción Nacional after the latter attended the Republican convention in Dallas, Texas, in August. Gavin replied that members of the PRI had them-

CINDY KARP—BLACK STAR

Mexico's Chiapas State borders Guatemala and is the focus of immigrant pressure by refugees from guerrilla fighting there. Some 100,000 have crossed into Chiapas in recent years, sparking a Mexican removal of the refugees from border camps like this northward into Campeche, Mexico.

selves attended the earlier Democratic convention in San Francisco. He later accused Adolfo Lugo Verduzco, the president of the PRI, of making irresponsible allegations in accusing him of meddling in Mexico's internal affairs. Relations with the U.S. eased toward the end of the year when Mexico, among other countries, agreed voluntarily to limit its exports of blister copper and steel to the U.S.

Diplomatic moves within Central America continued to be handled through the Contadora Group of Mexico, Colombia, Panama, and Venezuela. Its original 21-point document of objectives, issued in 1983, was countered by proposals from Honduras, Costa Rica, and El Salvador. (See *Latin American Affairs,* above.) Strong official protests were made at the end of May when more than 50 Guatemalan refugees were murdered or abducted during incursions by armed groups thought to have crossed from Guatemala into Mexico at the Chupadero and Flor de Café refugee camps. The government proposed to relocate Guatemalan "migrants" (the Mexican authorities did not consider them refugees) in Campeche State over the next two years.

In September Hurricane Odile hit the Pacific coast, causing severe damage and flooding in vacation resorts, including Acapulco and Ixtapa-Zihuatanejo, and leaving 7,000 people homeless. At the same time, Hurricane Norbert threatened areas southwest of the port of Manzanillo. In November a series of explosions at a gas distribution centre caused a huge blaze that killed hundreds and left over 4,000 homeless in a crowded surburb of Mexico City.

(BARBARA WIJNGAARD)

NICARAGUA

A republic of Central America, Nicaragua has coastlines on the Caribbean Sea and the Pacific Ocean. Area: 127,662 sq km (49,291 sq mi). Pop. (1984 est.): 2,914,000. Cap.: Managua. Monetary unit: córdoba, with (Oct. 29, 1984) a free rate of 10.01 córdobas to U.S. $1 (12.08 córdobas = £1 sterling). Coordinator of the three-member Junta of the Government of National Reconstruction in 1984, Daniel Ortega Saavedra.

Elections were held in Nicaragua on Nov. 4, 1984, for president, vice-president, and a 96-member National Assembly. Final results showed that 67% of those eligible voted, with the Sandinista National Liberation Front winning 63% of the valid votes. Six other parties participated in the campaign. (For tabulated results, see *Political Parties,* above.) A right-wing grouping, the Nicaraguan Democratic Coordinating Board (CDN), refused to take part on the grounds that the Sandinista government, despite some relaxation of press censorship and of restrictions on open debate, failed to adequately guarantee the status of opposition parties. This caused the U.S. to denounce the elections as a "sham." After the elections all parties, including the CDN, were invited to participate in a national dialogue preparatory to writing a new constitution.

The popularity of the Sandinistas at the polls was not matched by support from abroad. At the Vatican's insistence, four Roman Catholic priests in the government promised to resign after the elections, highlighting the disagreements within the Nicaraguan church over the role of religion in the state. The Costa Rican-based Democratic Revolutionary Alliance (ARDE) rebels persisted in their attacks, despite an assassination attempt on their leader, Edén Pastora Gómez (*see* BIOGRAPHIES), scant financial resources, a split in their forces, and a border pact between Nicaragua and Costa Rica. The antigovernment *contras* based in Honduras received aid from many private sources

In November Nicaragua held the first national elections since the Sandinistas took power. Seven parties—including the Independent Liberal Party (PLI), the largest non-Sandinista party—were on the ballot.
CLAUDE URRACA—SYGMA

in the U.S. and covertly from the U.S. Central Intelligence Agency. The CIA was severely criticized in the U.S. and abroad for its involvement in the mining of Nicaraguan ports and for supplying the *contras* with a manual detailing destabilization methods. The U.S. administration failed to win the support of the House of Representatives for $21 million for the *contras* in June. In a Senate-House compromise, a further request for $28 million in October was reduced to $14 million, which would not become available until Feb. 28, 1985, and then only with the approval of both houses.

Attempts to find a peace formula for the Central American region centred on the proposals of the Contadora Group of Venezuela, Mexico, Colombia, and Panama. (See *Latin-American Affairs,* above.) Relations with the U.S. soured immediately after elections took place in both countries in early November. For a time the U.S. credited reports that Nicaragua was taking delivery of Soviet MiG fighter aircraft (later revealed as other military equipment), and Nicaragua reiterated its charge that a U.S. invasion was imminent.

The cost of defense and economic sabotage forced the government to prevent any real wage increases and to maintain rationing of many basic goods.   (BEN BOX)

This article updates the *Macropædia* article CENTRAL AMERICA: *Nicaragua.*

PANAMA

A republic of Central America, Panama lies between the Caribbean Sea and the Pacific Ocean on the Isthmus of Panama. Area: 77,082 sq km (29,762 sq mi). Pop. (1984 est.): 2,101,000. Cap.: Panama City. Monetary unit: balboa, at par with the U.S. dollar, with a free rate (Oct. 29, 1984) of 1.21 balboas to £1 sterling. Presidents in 1984, Ricardo de la Espriella, Jorge Illueca from February 13, and, from October 11, Nicolás Ardito Barletta Vallarina.

The presidential election in Panama in 1984 prompted a surge of political interest, in great part because it was the first in 16 years. Many assumed that the president, Ricárdo de la Espriella, though not eligible for election, would lead the way to a restoration of democratic government. But on February 13 he stepped down from his office, probably because of pressure from Gen. Manuel A. Noriega and the National Guard. The vice-president, Jorge Illueca, took his place. Two men quickly emerged as leading presidential candidates: 82-year-old Arnulfo Arias, veteran of 50 years of political contests, and Nicolás Ardito Barletta (*see* BIOGRAPHIES), educated in the United States and a one-time vice-president of the World Bank. Arias accused the National Guard of corruption and participation in the drug traffic. Ardito Barletta, as the candidate of the Guard, was on the defensive.

The election was held on May 6, and approximately 700,000 voters cast their ballots. The result was very close, and until May 16 the election board struggled with voter challenges and interrupted counting. On that day it proclaimed Ardito Barletta the victor with 300,748 votes to 299,035 for Arias. He was inaugurated on October 11.

The condition of Panama's economy was reflected by the new president when he referred to the "grave economic stagnation" and the "contagious desperation" of his country. He promised to increase income, eliminate waste, and make payments on debts.

During the year Panama played host to several meetings of the Contadora Group, which included Colombia, Venezuela, and Mexico as well as Panama. To promote peace in the region, members of the group sought to freeze the importation of arms and the size of armies, to reduce the number of foreign military advisers, and to deny the use of territory to aggressors. The measures proposed by the group were not always approved by the United States. Panama urged the methods of diplomacy and characterized the U.S. military action in Grenada in October 1983 as "regrettable." Disagreement was more acute over Ft.

RICARDO WATSON—PICTORIAL PARADE

In Panama's first presidential election in 16 years, Nicolás Ardito Barletta, shown here campaigning at an April rally in Panama City, won a slender victory over Arnulfo Arias.

Gulick, a U.S.-operated school for teaching military techniques. By the terms of the 1977 agreement on the status of the Canal Zone, it was to be transferred to Panama. This was not disputed, but the details were bothersome. The U.S. flag was lowered on September 21.

(ALMON R. WRIGHT)

This article updates the *Macropædia* article CENTRAL AMERICA: *Panama*.

SOUTH AMERICA

ARGENTINA

The federal republic of Argentina occupies the eastern section of the "southern cone" of South America, along the Atlantic Ocean. Area: 2,780,092 sq km (1,073,399 sq mi). Pop. (1984 est.): 30,097,000. Cap.: Buenos Aires. Monetary unit: peso, with (Oct. 29, 1984) a free rate of 110.78 pesos to U.S. $1 (133.72 pesos = £1 sterling). President in 1984, Raúl Alfonsín.

Domestic Affairs. After taking office on Dec. 10, 1983, Pres. Raúl Alfonsín moved immediately to reduce the power of the military. By removing the armed forces from their paramount position in political and economic life in Argentina, he also aimed to improve professionalism and efficiency in the three services. His first acts were to place the military-industrial complex, Fabricaciones Militares, under civilian control; to reshuffle the military high command, retiring more than 70 senior officers; and to repeal the law giving amnesty to those accused of human rights violations. Nine members of the three juntas that had governed during 1976–82 were ordered court-martialed on charges of murder and human rights abuse, while three (Gen. Leopoldo Galtieri, Brig. Basilio Lami Dozo, and Adm. Jorge Anaya) also faced court-martial for their role in the Falkland Islands/Islas Malvinas conflict of 1982. Over a dozen other senior officers were called before civilian judges on charges brought by the families of the *desaparecidos* ("disappeared persons"). Around 800 private court claims arising from human rights violations were pending.

The people of Argentina were shocked by the extent of the abuses perpetrated by the military. Because of the censorship imposed at the time, many had been unaware of the scale of the atrocities. At the beginning of 1984 mass burial sites were uncovered, one of which held 482 bodies. Exhumation of the corpses revealed that death had been violent and that in many cases hands had been chopped off to prevent identification. The military, however, remained united, solidly defending its actions during the "dirty war" against subversives in the 1970s. A commission appointed by the president and led by the writer Ernesto Sábato completed a report on 8,960 disappeared persons in September. The report gave details of a network of secret prisons and torture centres and named some 1,200 military officers allegedly implicated in the campaign of illegal repression.

Alfonsín's plan for the armed forces to judge themselves foundered when the Supreme Council of the armed forces failed to meet repeatedly postponed deadlines to complete the court-martialing. The Federal Appeals Court announced in October that the nine former junta members would be tried by civilian courts, though the accused refused to recognize the civilian courts' authority. In October Brazil agreed to the extradition of Mario Firmenich, leader of the Montoneros urban guerrilla group, to stand trial for murder and kidnapping. The extradition was significant because the government needed to demonstrate that it was bringing both sides involved in the "dirty war" to justice.

In May former president María Estela ("Isabel") Martínez de Perón returned to Argentina for three weeks to head a delegation of Peronists in talks between the government and opposition leaders. Perón's return was made possible by a congressional resolution that exonerated her from any further judicial proceedings relating to charges of corruption during her presidency (1974–76). She had been in voluntary exile in Spain since 1981, except for a brief visit in December 1983. The talks aimed to quell criticism of the government's policies and to reach broad agreement on solving economic problems, specifically the refinancing of the foreign debt and the consequent introduction of an austerity program. After two weeks of talks, 16 political parties signed a vaguely worded, 15-point accord with Alfonsín agreeing to foster social justice, economic growth, and national unity and to defend the democratic system. Perón urged trade-union leaders to cooperate with the government, but her plea fell short of telling them to end the growing wave of strikes.

Labour discontent ran high in 1984. The government

ENRIQUE SHORE—WOODFIN CAMP

This rally was held in the Plaza de Mayo in Buenos Aires to support a bill designed to make Argentine labour unions more democratic.

tried to introduce legislation providing for a secret ballot in trade-union elections, but the attempt was defeated by Peronist opposition in the Senate. Inflation soared, reaching a peak of 27.5% in September (687.8% on an annual basis), and strikes were widespread. Despite the government's pledge to increase the real value of wages by 6–8% during the year, the purchasing power of wages was being eroded as the actual rate of inflation invariably exceeded the expected rate, on which increases were based. A general strike on September 3 was only moderately successful, but individual strikes continued.

Foreign Relations. Territorial disputes involving the Beagle Channel and the Falkland Islands dominated foreign relations. In January Argentina and Chile signed a joint declaration of peace and friendship in Rome after five years of painstaking negotiations by the Vatican. The two countries then entered the final phase of negotiations, which culminated in the signing of a treaty in November, after the settlement had been approved by the Argentinian electorate. The treaty awarded Chile sovereignty of three disputed islands—Lennox, Picton, and Nueva—at the entrance to the Beagle Channel, along with from 3 to 12 nautical miles of territorial waters around them. In return, Chile lost its claim to part of the Atlantic Ocean south of Cape Horn.

In July the first diplomatic contact in two years between the U.K. and Argentina took place in Bern, Switz. However, talks aimed at normalizing trade, transport, and diplomatic relations collapsed after 24 hours when the issue of sovereignty of the Falkland Islands/Islas Malvinas was raised. Argentina then shifted the emphasis to a UN General Assembly vote on a motion that called for an early resumption of talks on the sovereignty issue under UN auspices. Despite intense lobbying by Alfonsín during a visit to France and Italy in October, Argentina failed to separate the U.K. from its European partners, and the Assembly voted for the motion by 89 votes to 9 with 54 abstentions. The government pointed to its agreement with Chile as an example of its determination to settle arguments by peaceful means. The U.K. ambassador continued to stress the right of the islanders to self-determination.

The Economy. The debt issue was paramount following the failure of the previous administration to renegotiate loans with 320 international banks and the breakdown of the agreement with the International Monetary Fund (IMF). At the end of 1983 total external debt amounted to $46.3 billion, of which the government was seeking to reschedule about $20 billion over a 15-year period. Argentina's inability to service its debts led to a buildup of arrears, and several rescue operations were launched by creditor banks. In March Brazil, Colombia, Mexico, and Venezuela made available an unprecedented $300 million emergency credit, which Argentina repaid in August. Despite the government's attempts to bring payments up to date, some of its long-overdue loans were downgraded to "substandard" by U.S. bank regulators in November.

In midyear an attempt to persuade the IMF to approve an economic program set out in a letter of intent proved abortive, and the government was forced to change some of its policies. A new economic austerity package was outlined in a memorandum of understanding with the IMF in September. The government agreed to reduce the budget deficit by cutting spending instead of by raising income taxes and to set a target of reducing inflation to 300% in the year ending September 1985. By tightening wage and price controls and credit and monetary expansion, the government succeeded in lowering the monthly rate of inflation to 19.3% in October. It was also agreed that the peso

had become overvalued again and that devaluation should at least keep pace with domestic prices. During October the daily rate of adjustment was increased to make up for previous lags, and the peso was devalued by 29.8% against the U.S. dollar. The IMF also insisted on rescheduling of Argentina's foreign debt, but in late December agreement was reached with the steering group of Argentina's creditor banks. Finally, on December 28, the IMF approved an aid package including a $1.4 billion extended credit facility.

Despite the austerity, the gross domestic product (GDP) grew by 2.8% in 1983, although this was still below the 1977 level. In the first half of 1984 GDP rose by 3.4%, with a growth of 4.8% in the manufacturing sector. After two years of sharp decline, investment fell by a further 1.9% in 1983 and by 8.8% in the first half of 1984. It was not expected to pick up in the second half because of uncertainties over the implementation of the IMF program and a general lack of confidence in the economic policies of the government. (SARAH CAMERON)

BOLIVIA

Bolivia is a landlocked republic in central South America. Area: 1,098,581 sq km (424,165 sq mi). Pop. (1984 est.): 6,253,000. Judicial cap., Sucre; administrative cap., La Paz. Monetary unit: peso, with (Oct. 29, 1984) a par value of 2,000 pesos to U.S. $1 (free rate of 2,419 pesos = £1 sterling). President in 1984, Hernán Siles Zuazo.

Events in 1984 brought no alleviation of Bolivia's political and economic troubles. In late 1983 the Cabinet had resigned en masse following a two-day general strike, organized by the Communist-led Bolivian Workers' Confederation (COB) to protest the government's failure to grant wage increases. Pres. Hernán Siles Zuazo formed a new Cabinet in January 1984, his fourth since taking office 15 months earlier. It was smaller than the previous Cabinet but similar in political complexion, despite the stated intention to form a broader coalition. The Movimiento Izquierda Revolucionaria (Movement of the Revolutionary Left), which had left the coalition in January 1983 in protest against the government's inaction in the face of economic crisis, rejoined in April 1984.

On June 30 President Siles was kidnapped in an attempt to overthrow the government. He was released after ten hours of negotiations during which his kidnappers were promised political asylum. The kidnapping appeared to be part of a coup plot involving middle-ranking army and police officers linked to the lucrative cocaine trade; over a hundred people were arrested, including two former Cabinet ministers. The coup attempt had been preceded by months of unrest in military units in Cochabamba and the eastern lowlands, the main coca-growing areas.

Bolivia experienced its fourth year of negative economic growth. Floods and drought again diminished crops, resulting in serious food shortages and a high import bill for staples. A series of strikes by tin miners reduced output, and this, combined with low world tin prices, caused export earnings to decline. Against this background, the government tried to introduce austerity measures required by the International Monetary Fund. In April the peso was devalued by 75% and gasoline and food prices were raised. These measures met strong opposition. Workers, led by the COB, staged a series of strikes, culminating in a five-day strike in May that paralyzed the country.

In response to the crisis, the government suspended repayments on its $1 billion debt to foreign banks; repayments to governments and international institutions were to be maintained by the allocation of one-quarter of ex-

Conspirators in an aborted coup attempt kidnapped Bolivian Pres. Hernán Siles Zuazo on June 30. He was released after ten hours of negotiations. President Siles is shown here with one of his captors.
UPI/BETTMANN

port earnings. Bolivia had been in technical default on its foreign loans since September 1982 and had made no interest payments since March 1984. However, this latest action made it the first Latin-American country to suspend payment officially. The move eased tension between the government and workers and allowed pay increases to be granted. However, with inflation running at an annual rate of over 1,000%, the lull was temporary, and strike action intensified later in the year. A week-long general strike ended December 4 when the government agreed to wage increases of more than 750% and a freeze on basic food prices. During an earlier general strike in November, Siles announced that elections would be held in 1985, a year early. Following the steady fall in the value of the peso, a two-tier exchange rate was introduced in August to allow a preferential rate for essential imports.

The Cabinet resigned on October 8, but most of the ministers were reappointed. Siles undertook a hunger strike October 24–29 to protest his censure by the Congress. The censure followed revelations that Siles had authorized a meeting between the head of the nation's antidrug agency and Roberto Suárez Gómez, a leading drug trafficker, at which Suárez reportedly offered a $2 million credit toward payment of the foreign debt in return for freedom to continue his operations.   (INGRID IVERSEN)

BRAZIL

Brazil is a federal republic in eastern South America on the Atlantic Ocean. Area: 8,512,000 sq km (3,286,500 sq mi). Pop. (1984 est.): 135,564,000. Cap.: Brasília. Monetary unit: cruzeiro, with (Oct. 29, 1984) a free rate of 2,543.61 cruzeiros to U.S. $1 (3,070.14 cruzeiros = £1 sterling). President in 1984, Gen. João Baptista de Oliveira Figueiredo.

Domestic Affairs. The political year in Brazil was dominated by preparations for the presidential elections and by related debate about the constitution. Throughout 1984 the administration of Pres. João Baptista de Oliveira Figueiredo, which had taken office in March 1979, pursued a policy designed to return the country to civilian rule and to bring to an end the period of military government that had begun in April 1964. President Figueiredo's successor,

who was to take office in March 1985, was to be chosen in January 1985 by an electoral college of 686 members comprising representatives of Congress and of the state assemblies. Two candidates for the presidency were officially announced in August; these were Paulo Salim Maluf, former state governor of São Paulo, representing the ruling Social Democratic Party (PDS), and Tancredo Neves, former state governor of Minas Gerais, running on behalf of the Brazilian Democratic Movement Party (PMDB) as well as various other small opposition groups and a large number of PDS dissidents who had formed a splinter group known as the Liberal Party.

Maluf favoured the maintenance in broad terms of current economic policies along with increased efforts to stimulate exports. Neves proposed the introduction of moderate measures to reflate the economy, regionally based projects to increase employment, and the renegotiation of Brazil's external debt commitments by linking payments to a proportion of export income and interest-capping. Both candidates expressed an intention to adhere as closely as possible to the domestic and external economic adjustment program agreed upon with the International Monetary Fund (IMF) in early 1983 and scheduled to extend until 1985. Both undertook to provide special development assistance for northeastern Brazil and for the housing sector. Neves promised to establish a constitutional assembly to draft a new constitution, to restore full legislative powers to Congress, and to introduce direct presidential elections.

From the beginning of the year there was an upsurge in popular support for opposition rallies at which the focus of political and economic grievances was the call for direct presidential elections. Demonstrations were organized by the opposition parties in many of the major cities, particularly São Paulo, Rio de Janeiro, and Belo Horizonte. On April 16 a rally in São Paulo was attended by as many as one million people.

In April a proposal to amend the constitution to allow direct elections was defeated in the Chamber of Deputies. However, the opposition campaign began to attract increasing support among PDS representatives in Congress, throwing the ruling party into disarray and presenting the Figueiredo administration with serious problems. On the day of the São Paulo demonstration, President Figueiredo revealed plans for a compromise that would reduce the term of the presidency from six to four years and allow direct elections in 1988. But in June the proposed amendment was withdrawn because of broadly based opposition to it within Congress and because of government fears that there might now be enough support to pass an amendment providing for direct elections in 1985. In July Vice-Pres. Aureliano Chaves joined the Liberal Party, which commanded the support of some 100 disaffected PDS deputies and provided the opposition with what was potentially a large absolute majority in the Chamber of Deputies.

A report by the UN Children's Fund underlined the devastation that six years of drought had brought to the northeast of the country. Two-thirds of the children in the area were said to be suffering from malnutrition. Heavy rains in late March ended the drought but caused severe flooding.

The Economy. The economic recession, which began in 1980, appeared to have bottomed out during 1984. Gross domestic product was expected to increase by about 1%, following a decline of 3.9% in 1983. The fall in overall industrial output slowed from 5.7% in 1983 to 5.1% in the year ended June 1984, partly as a result of a buoyant export performance. Agricultural expansion reached 4–5% as against 2.1% in 1983, thanks to good soybean, cotton, rice, and sugarcane crops and to the improved productivity of harvests in central and southern parts of the country. Growth in the service sector was patchy because of weak consumer demand and austerity in public expenditure.

The inflation rate remained a great problem. The general price index rose by 219% in the year ended in August, compared with an annual rate of 211% in 1983. The chief causes of high inflation were the indexation of wages, the depreciation of the cruzeiro, and the reductions in subsidies implemented as part of the program agreed upon with the IMF. Efforts to curb inflation were centred on tight fiscal and monetary policies and met with only limited success.

Brazil's external accounts strengthened greatly after January, when the government, international commercial banks, and the IMF signed a package to cover the country's 1983–84 financing gap. The package included a new loan worth $6.5 billion and the recycling of 1984 loan maturities on the registered medium- and long-term external debt. Arrears on interest and other payments of $2.3 billion, which had built up during 1983, were cleared by the end of March. By midyear international reserves stood at $7.9 billion. The trade balance improved from a positive one of $6.1 billion in 1983 to an accumulated surplus of $8.6 billion by the end of August, largely as a result of a 24.5% growth in exports during the first eight months of the year. This ensured that the 1984 trade surplus target of $9.1 billion would be met and, indeed, surpassed. In addition to encouraging an all-out export drive, the government severely restricted imports, although it relaxed some controls in September. The current account deficit reached $200 million during the first half of 1984 and was expected to total $2.7 billion for the whole year, well below the 1983 figure of $6.2 billion. In 1984 about one-third of Brazil's apparent energy consumption was derived from petroleum, compared with 48% in 1983. Local output was estimated at 530,000 bbl a day, as against 339,000 bbl a day in 1983. Oil imports in 1984 cost some $6.6 billion, down from $8.1 billion in 1983.   (ROBIN CHAPMAN)

CHILE

The republic of Chile extends along the Pacific coast of the "southern cone" of South America. Area: 736,905 sq km (284,520 sq mi), not including Chile's Antarctic claim. Pop. (1984 est.): 11,665,000. Cap.: Santiago. Monetary unit: peso, with (Oct. 29, 1984) a free rate of 117.23 pesos to U.S. $1 (141.50 pesos = £1 sterling). President in 1984, Maj. Gen. Augusto Pinochet Ugarte.

Protests against the military government of Pres. Augusto Pinochet Ugarte in Chile continued throughout 1984. During the first three months of the year there were some 130 bomb attacks, mainly in the major cities of Santiago, Valparaíso, and Rancagua. On April 1 a series of explosions cut off electricity supplies to two-thirds of the country; a left-wing guerrilla group, the Manuel Rodríguez Patriotic Front (FPMR), claimed responsibility. A new antiterrorist law, which came into operation on May 15, provided for tough jail sentences for terrorists and the death penalty for those guilty of terrorist murders.

On March 23 President Pinochet declared a 90-day state of emergency, which was later extended. Since a previous state of emergency expired in August 1983, a "state of threat to internal peace" had been in effect. By the end of March more than 600 arrests had been made, and Santiago was placed under curfew for two days. An order censoring four opposition newspapers was withdrawn after protests by foreign and domestic press organizations.

On April 2 the economics minister and the finance minister, both free-market advocates, were replaced. A priority of the new ministers was to reduce the high unemployment, a major contributor to the unrest. The opposition mounted days of national protest on March 27 and again in April, May, and early September. Two days of protest on October 29–30 were to include a general strike on the 30th, but several major unions declined to participate, and reports of its success varied. The October protests were preceded by a wave of bombings that caused blackouts in Santiago and several other cities.

On November 5 the Cabinet resigned to give Pinochet greater freedom to deal with the situation. Pinochet an-

For the first presidential election with civilian candidates in some 20 years—to be held in January 1985—Tancredo Neves was chosen as the Brazilian Democratic Movement Party's candidate.

nounced its reappointment with minor changes the following day, and at the same time declared a state of siege—the first in six years—to replace the state of emergency. A curfew was imposed, and tight controls were placed on the media. On November 10 and November 15 the military staged raids on poor neighbourhoods in Santiago, and over 500 persons were arrested.

The Roman Catholic Church during the year became more critical of the government's record on human rights. Figures compiled by the church and the Chilean human rights commission and published in January indicated that in 1983 there had been a fivefold increase in reported torture cases over the previous year, as well as a rise in the number of people sentenced to internal exile and a massive increase in arrests and interrogations.

At the same time, the church became more outspoken in its support for opposition groups. In January it took up the cause of four members of the left-wing Movement of the Revolutionary Left (MIR) who sought political asylum in the Vatican's diplomatic mission in Santiago. The four people were accused by the government of having been involved in the murder of the military governor of Santiago in August 1983. After a plea by Pope John Paul II, the four were granted safe conduct and left for Ecuador on April 7. In February, while President Pinochet was attending an official ceremony in the city of Punta Arenas, some 400 protesters took shelter in the cathedral when violence erupted during a demonstration. Pinochet had harsh criticism for the church, which he accused of organizing the protest and of turning young people against the government. A nadir in relations between church and state was reached in early September when, during one of the organized days of protest, a French priest was shot and killed by security forces.

Between February and September the Council of State continued its work on a draft law to legalize and regulate the operations of political parties and to prepare the country for general elections. However, disagreements within

CARRION—SYGMA

In Chile protests against the military government of Pres. Augusto Pinochet Ugarte continued throughout 1984. President Pinochet announced in September that he intended to stay in power at least until the end of his term in 1989.

the ruling junta soon became apparent. One suggestion was that elections might be moved forward from 1989, the date specified in the constitution, to 1987. The Alianza Democrática (AD), a group of five opposition parties formed in August 1983, denounced the government's draft and proposed that the laws regulating political activity should be established by a national accord of government and opposition. President Pinochet declared abruptly in September that he intended to remain in power until at least the end of his term in 1989. On October 29 he said that the legitimation of political parties was being postponed and that no elections would be held before the scheduled date.

In May a group of 24 opposition leaders filed a case with the Supreme Court of Chile accusing President Pinochet and his family of corruption. The government responded with a threat to sue the litigants for libel, while on May 25 an Appeal Court judge ruled that he did not have the constitutional authority to try the president. Soon afterward a group of lawyers, attempting to bring a related but separate case against Pinochet, alleged that the state had been defrauded of $30,000 in connection with the purchase of plots of land beside the president's home just outside Santiago. However, the case was not allowed to proceed, as the initial Appeal Court ruling was upheld.

In November Chile and Argentina signed a treaty settling the Beagle Channel dispute between the two countries. The agreement, mediated by the Vatican over a period of several years, awarded to Chile ownership of the islands in the channel that it claimed. (See *Latin-American Affairs*, above.)

In mid-September the peso was devalued from 93 to 115 to the U.S. dollar. Import duties were raised to 35% across the board to compensate for rising dollar interest rates and record low world copper prices. Inflation, which had fallen to only 12% in the 12 months to September 1984, was expected to increase again as a result of the devaluation. Finance Minister Luis Escobar Cerda announced that the adjustment would not alter his target of achieving a 4.6% growth in gross domestic product in 1984 while maintaining stability of prices. The International Monetary Fund approved the final part of a two-year, $500 million economic package for Chile on December 9. Chile had requested rescheduling of its foreign debt in 1985.

(MICHAEL WOOLLER)

COLOMBIA

A republic in northwestern South America, Colombia has coastlines on the Caribbean Sea and the Pacific Ocean. Area: 1,141,748 sq km (440,831 sq mi). Pop. (1984 est.): 28,248,000. Cap.: Bogotá. Monetary unit: peso, with (Oct. 29, 1984) a free rate of 106.19 pesos to U.S. $1 (128.17 pesos = £1 sterling). President in 1984, Belisario Betancur Cuartas.

The beginning of 1984 in Colombia was marked by a confrontation between Pres. Belisario Betancur Cuartas and the hard-line elements in his government who favoured a greater role for the Army. At a meeting of the National Security Council on January 17, Betancur made his position clear when he stated that "the armed forces are not a deliberative body, nor do they participate in politics." He also underlined his government's determination to pursue a reconciliation with its left-wing guerrilla opponents and to offer them a chance to participate in the political process. The Army argued that more effort should be put into counterinsurgency operations.

Betancur also defended his right, as head of state, to determine Colombia's foreign policy. The statement was

It was a year of drug-related murder in Colombia as cocaine traffickers and their allies tried to derail an effort by the government to crack down on drug producers and middlemen. On April 30 Minister of Justice Rodrigo Lara Bonilla, the cornerstone of the crackdown, was assassinated. President Betancur (right, behind coffin) declared a state of siege the day after the murder.

in response to public criticism by the military of his administration's attempts to restore diplomatic relations with Cuba, and of the president's leading role in the Contadora Group (Colombia, Mexico, Panama, and Venezuela), which was attempting to negotiate peace in Central America. The Army considered that Colombia's territorial claim against Nicaragua was threatened by Betancur's support for the Sandinista government there.

As a result of Betancur's warnings, Gen. Fernando Landazábal Reyes resigned as minister of defense in mid-January. A number of high-ranking officers in the Army and Air Force followed suit. Appointed new minister of defense was Gen. Gustavo Matamoros d'Acosta, until then commander in chief of the armed forces.

On April 30 Minister of Justice Rodrigo Lara Bonilla was assassinated in Bogotá. His murder was believed to be a consequence of his efforts to crack down on drug traffickers; earlier, 12 metric tons of cocaine had been seized by the authorities. His successor, Enrique Parejo González, immediately declared his commitment to carrying on Lara's fight. The day after the murder President Betancur placed the entire country under state-of-siege conditions, which had already been declared in the southwestern parts of the country in mid-March because of an upsurge in subversive activity by the opposition guerrilla groups.

The government signed a cease-fire with the nation's largest guerrilla movement, the Colombian Revolutionary Armed Forces (FARC), in March. The Marxist-Leninist, mainly peasant membership of FARC enjoyed a measure of respect because it was seen as a coherent revolutionary organization. It was not until the end of August that similar treaties were signed with the predominantly populist, middle-class M-19 movement and two other smaller guerrilla groupings. Just weeks earlier, in early August, the government's hopes of signing a cease-fire with M-19 had almost been destroyed when gunmen, believed to belong to a right-wing death squad opposed to the government's objectives, killed one of the group's founders and best-known leaders, Carlos Toledo Plata. In reprisal M-19 killed 42 people in an attack on the town of Yumbo.

In late July President Betancur dismissed Finance Minister Edgar Gutierrez for concealing the extent of the country's mounting financial problems and allowing them to continue unchecked until they reached a critical point. Gutierrez was replaced by Roberto Jungito, who estimated that the budget deficit might reach 6% of gross domestic product in 1984, mainly because of a major miscalculation

of tax receipts. Colombia faced a $1.1 billion trade deficit in 1984, while capital flight increased to about $2.5 billion in the first nine months. (MICHAEL WOOLLER)

ECUADOR

The republic of Ecuador is in western South America, on the Pacific Ocean. Area: 269,178 sq km (103,930 sq mi), including the Galápagos Islands. Pop. (1984 est.): 8 million. Cap.: Quito. Monetary unit: sucre, with (Oct. 29, 1984) an official rate of 67.26 sucres to U.S. $1 (81.18 sucres = £1 sterling) and a free rate of 110.38 sucres to U.S. $1 (133.23 sucres = £1 sterling). Presidents in 1984, Osvaldo Hurtado Larrea and, from August 10, León Febres Cordero Rivadeneira.

Political events in Ecuador were dominated by presidential elections, the first round of which took place on Jan. 29, 1984. Since none of the nine candidates secured an outright majority, a second round was held on May 6

León Febres Cordero (left) embraces Vice-Pres. Blasco Penaherrera Padilla after being sworn in as Ecuador's new president on August 10.

between the two front-runners: León Febres Cordero (*see* BIOGRAPHIES) of the Social Christian Party (PSC), who was supported by the National Reconstruction Front, a right-wing grouping whose most important members were the PSC, the Radical Liberals, the Conservatives, and the National Revolutionary Party; and Rodrigo Borja Cevallos, founder and leader of the Democratic Left (Izquierda Democrática; ID). Febres won a narrow victory, gaining 52.2% of the votes cast. A businessman representing the Guayaquil agricultural community, Febres was an advocate of free-market policies.

Elections to the single-chamber Congress coincided with the first round of the presidential poll. The results were somewhat inconclusive. (For tabulated results, see *Political Parties,* above.) The ID made significant gains, emerging as the biggest single party with 25 of the 71 seats. The major parties of the National Reconstruction Front won a total of only 16 seats, so Febres was a long way from commanding a reliable majority. The new president and Congress were sworn in on August 10.

A modest economic recovery was expected during 1984, following a severe recession the previous year. Real growth of 1.5% was forecast, after a fall of 3.3% in 1983. The foreign debt stood at $6.9 billion at the end of 1983. On August 9 Ecuador signed an agreement with creditor banks to reschedule $348 million of public-sector debt originally due to have been repaid during 1984, and on December 16 agreement was reached with the banks to reschedule approximately $4.3 billion of public-sector debt and to provide new financing amounting to more than $1 billion.

(ROBIN CHAPMAN)

GUYANA

A republic and member of the Commonwealth, Guyana is situated in northeastern South America, on the Atlantic Ocean. Area: 215,000 sq km (83,000 sq mi). Pop. (1984 est.): 923,000. Cap.: Georgetown. Monetary unit: Guyana dollar, with (Oct. 29, 1984) a free rate of G$3.79 to U.S. $1 (G$4.58 = £1 sterling). President in 1984, Forbes Burnham; prime ministers, Ptolemy Reid and, from August 16, Desmond Hoyte.

Guyana's prolonged economic stagnation, marked by acute shortages of foreign exchange and imported goods, continued throughout 1984. Food, spare parts, and other commodities were increasingly supplied by traders with access to smuggled items. Further devaluation of the Guyanese dollar, set since January at G$3.75 to the U.S. dollar, was forecast by some analysts.

In May Pres. Forbes Burnham announced a breakdown in negotiations with the International Monetary Fund, which subsequently declared Guyana ineligible for further assistance on the grounds that the government owed the IMF money it was unable to repay. Official figures put the country's external debt at $700 million. Subsequently, Burnham visited Bulgaria, China, and Cuba, while Vice-Pres. Hamilton Green went to Romania and the U.S.S.R. Barter trade was a feature of economic cooperation agreements signed during the visits.

Prime Minister Ptolemy Reid, a faithful ally of President Burnham, retired in August because of ill health. He was succeeded by Desmond Hoyte, who had been vice-president with responsibility for industrial production and agriculture. Green, widely believed to be the candidate favoured by the U.S. to succeed Burnham, was appointed first deputy prime minister. (ROD PRINCE)

This article updates the *Macropædia* article The GUIANAS: *Guyana.*

PARAGUAY

Paraguay is a landlocked republic of central South America. Area: 406,752 sq km (157,048 sq mi). Pop. (1984 est.): 3,193,000. Cap.: Asunción. Monetary unit: guaraní, with (Oct. 29, 1984) an official rate of 240.30 guaranís to U.S. $1 (290.04 guaranís = £1 sterling). President in 1984, Gen. Alfredo Stroessner.

There were signs in early 1984 that Pres. Alfredo Stroessner's government, in its 30th year of office, was permitting a small degree of liberalization. A demonstration in February by 4,000–5,000 people passed unchallenged by the authorities, and a number of prominent political exiles were allowed to return to the country. Still refused entry, however, were the Liberal leader Domingo Laín and the Christian Democrat Alfonso Resck. Then in March the daily newspaper *ABC Color,* which consistently criticized government policies and corruption, was closed indefinitely by the president.

Opponents of the regime began to work more closely together and to receive greater recognition from foreign governments, notably the U.S. and Argentina, than the government would have wished. Relations with the U.S. were not improved after four U.S. lawyers were detained, then deported, when they arrived in Asunción to study human rights issues.

Work at the Yacyretá hydroelectric project, being built jointly with Argentina, began, but haltingly. It was hoped that the new project might stimulate the economy, which had slumped after the completion of the Itaipú hydroelectric scheme. Pressure on the balance of payments, and from international agencies, eventually forced the government to devalue the guaraní from the long-maintained official rate of 126 to 240 guaranís to U.S.$1. (BEN BOX)

PERU

The republic of Peru is located in western South America, on the Pacific Ocean. Area: 1,285,215 sq km (496,224 sq mi). Pop. (1984 est.): 19,198,000. Cap.: Lima. Monetary unit: sol, with (Oct. 29, 1984) a free rate of 4,319.48 soles to U.S. $1 (5,213.61 soles = £1 sterling). President in 1984, Fernando Belaúnde Terry; prime ministers, Fernando Schwalb López Aldana to April 10, Sandro Mariátegui from April 10 to October 13, and, from October 13, Luis Pércovich Roca.

Pres. Fernando Belaúnde Terry of Peru reshuffled his Cabinet in late December 1983 following the swing away from the ruling Acción Popular (AP) party toward the left-wing Alianza Popular Revolucionaria Americana (APRA) in municipal elections held in November. The result illustrated the widespread disillusionment with the government's economic record. APRA, led by Alán García, won 34% of the votes, compared with AP's 20%.

In March Finance Minister Carlos Rodríguez Pastor was forced to resign in the face of continued criticism of his economic policies, in particular a series of measures proposed by the International Monetary Fund (IMF). When his replacement, José Benavides Muñoz, announced a policy of economic expansion in April, Prime Minister Fernando López Aldana also resigned. A new Cabinet was formed with Sandro Mariátegui as prime minister. In a further reshuffle in October, Mariátegui was replaced by Luis Pércovich Roca, interior minister in the previous Cabinet.

President Belaúnde imposed a three-day state of emergency in March when trade unionists announced a general strike. An estimated 50% of the nation's workers joined the strike, protesting against the austerity measures being

Police in Peru created a new antiguerrilla unit, heavily armed and attired in casual civilian dress. The unit was seen by police as a necessary step against the leftist guerrillas of the Sendero Luminoso (Shining Path) and others. Some sources, however, claimed that the armed forces and police were increasingly resorting to kidnappings, torture, and summary executions of civilians.

CONCHA CUBERO/THE NEW YORK TIMES

imposed on the economy to satisfy IMF requirements. At the end of May teachers and other government workers went on strike, demanding pay increases to maintain their real wages, which were being eroded by an annual inflation rate of over 100%. Determined not to bow to demands that would make it difficult to adhere to IMF targets, the president imposed a state of emergency in June, when more than 80% of Lima's civil servants went on strike, and again when a 24-hour general strike was called in November.

Sendero Luminoso (Shining Path), a Maoist guerrilla group, continued to pose a serious threat. The group was based in the region around Ayacucho, the centre of the cocaine trade, and its targets included foreign companies, the offices of political parties and government departments, and power installations. There were more than 500 deaths in the first half of 1984 from terrorist incidents and police and army reprisals, and an estimated 1,000 people were awaiting trial for terrorist offenses.

In June a guerrilla offensive was launched. The following month President Belaúnde placed the Army in overall control of the antiguerrilla operations that had previously been entrusted to the police. The discovery of mass graves, in which some of the bodies showed signs of torture, caused concern that the Army was abusing human rights in its campaign against the insurgents. Gen. Adrian Huamán Centeno, a Quechua-speaking Indian who had been in charge of the Ayacucho region since January, was removed in August. He disagreed with the policy of using the Army against the guerrillas and claimed that the root of the problem lay in years of economic neglect of the region. He was replaced by U.S.-trained Col. Wilfredo Mori Orzo.

The U.S. was funding a project that aimed at eradicating the growing of cocaine around Tingo María, some 320 km (200 mi) north of Ayacucho. However, the project had to be suspended when Sendero Luminoso stepped up attacks in the area. The president ordered an army offensive to regain control, and there were soon indications that troops had occupied much of the area.

Industrial production remained depressed, with a decline of 4% in the first quarter of 1984. There was some improvement in the fishing and mining sectors in the first half of the year, but the overall growth in gross domestic product was only 0.5%. Low world prices for commodities on which the country depended for foreign-exchange earnings made it increasingly difficult for Peru to meet debt repayments. The Club of Paris banking group agreed to reschedule $1,050,000,000 of interest and principal falling due over the 13 months beginning in June. The $1 billion debt owed to the U.S.S.R. was to be repaid through a barter agreement by which Peru would provide manufactured goods, textiles, and commodities. (INGRID IVERSEN)

SURINAME

The republic of Suriname is in northeastern South America, on the Atlantic Ocean. Area: 163,820 sq km (63,251 sq mi), not including a 17,635-km area disputed with Guyana. Pop. (1984 est.): 352,000. Cap.: Paramaribo. Monetary unit: Suriname guilder, with (Oct. 29, 1984) a par value of 1.79 Suriname guilders to U.S. $1 (free rate of 2.15 Suriname guilders = £1 sterling). Chairman of the National Military Council in 1984, Dési Bouterse; prime ministers, Errol Alibux until January 8 and, from February 3, Wim Udenhout.

Suriname's bauxite workers, on strike since December 1983 in protest against the government's proposed tax and price increases, were joined on Jan. 6, 1984, by electrical workers. On January 7 National Military Council (NMC) Chairman Dési Bouterse rescinded the increases and the following day dismissed Prime Minister Errol Alibux and his government. Agitation against the NMC continued, and the situation worsened with the temporary closing of the U.S.-owned Suralco bauxite-processing plant, which, with the Dutch-owned Billiton plant, formed the mainstay of the Surinamese economy. However, by January 22, following a poor response to a call by opposition leaders for a general strike, the bauxite workers, offered financial inducements, had voted to return to work.

On February 3 a new, interim government headed by Wim Udenhout was sworn in pending the introduction of a new constitution. On December 8 first steps toward democratization were announced; from Jan. 1, 1985, the government would be appointed by the National Assembly and not by the NMC—which, however, would retain 14 of the 31 seats in the Assembly. In preparation for the new government, Udenhout and his Cabinet on December 25 submitted their resignations, effective December 31.

In March a coup attempt against the Suriname government, planned in neighbouring French Guiana by Surinamese, mostly of Dutch nationality, was foiled when the French authorities deported them to The Netherlands, where they were allowed to go free.   (DICK BOONSTRA)

This article updates the *Macropædia* article The GUIANAS: *Suriname*.

URUGUAY

A republic of eastern South America, Uruguay lies on the Atlantic Ocean. Area: 176,215 sq km (68,037 sq mi). Pop. (1984 est.): 3,013,000. Cap.: Montevideo. Monetary unit: new peso, with (Oct. 29, 1984) a free rate of 62.20 new pesos to U.S. $1 (75.07 new pesos = £1 sterling). President in 1984, Gen. Gregorio Conrado Álvarez Armelino.

General elections on Nov. 25, 1984, returned civilian government to Uruguay for the first time since the 1973 military takeover. Inspired by the example of neighbouring Argentina, Uruguayans staged vigorous political protests, including a successful national strike on January 18, all of which prompted the government to ban public demonstrations in June. Then, as a gesture of good faith, 154 political prisoners were released on August 10. The Supreme Military Council nevertheless hinted that the elections might be scrapped if the four legalized political parties failed to accept constitutional changes giving the military at least a temporary say in government after power was handed over in March 1985.

The imprisonment of National (Blanco) Party leader Wilson Ferreira Aldunate after his triumphant homecoming from exile on June 16, 1984, represented the greatest threat to an orderly return to democracy. Ferreira's fol-

CARRION—SYGMA

It was a brief welcome for Wilson Ferreira Aldunate, the National (Blanco) Party leader who returned to Uruguay in June after 11 years in exile. He was immediately arrested and was unable to participate in the November elections.

lowers were at first determined to boycott the elections if he was not released and seemed prepared to risk exclusion from the democratic process. However, they finally selected a lawyer, Alberto Zumarán, as their candidate. Also barred from running was Gen. Liber Seregni of the leftist Broad Front, who had been released in February after nine years in prison; in his place, the Front nominated Juan José Crottogini, a 76-year-old gynecologist. These substitutions probably contributed to the victory of the Colorado Party candidate, Julio Mariá Sanguinetti, generally considered a centrist, who won about 39% of the vote to 33% for Zumarán and 21% for Crottogini. The remainder went to smaller parties or were invalid.   (PAUL MILLGATE)

VENEZUELA

A republic of northern South America, Venezuela lies on the Caribbean Sea. Area: 912,050 sq km (352,144 sq mi). Pop. (1984 est.): 15,601,000. Cap.: Caracas. Monetary unit: bolivar, with (Oct. 29, 1984) a main official rate of 12.16 bolivares to U.S. $1 (14.68 bolivares = £1 sterling). Presidents in 1984, Luis Herrera Campins and, from February 2, Jaime Lusinchi.

Jaime Lusinchi (*see* BIOGRAPHIES), clear winner in Venezuela's presidential elections held in December 1983, was sworn in on Feb. 2, 1984. His party, the social democratic Acción Democrática (AD), had also won a majority in Congress and so returned to government after five years in opposition. Major portfolios in Lusinchi's Cabinet went to Octavio Lepage Barreto (interior), Isidro Morales Paúl (foreign affairs), Manuel Azpurúa Arreaza (finance), and Luis Matos Azócar (planning).

The main problem facing the new president was the urgent need to reschedule Venezuela's $34 billion external debt. Economic stagnation and high government spending had led to a moratorium on principal repayments of public-sector debt, declared by the government in 1983. In his inaugural speech, Lusinchi reaffirmed his campaign commitment to introduce economic austerity measures that would facilitate renegotiation but would, at the same time, avoid the need for the International Monetary Fund to step in and dictate conditions that might prove unacceptable. Lusinchi's first move was to replace the presidents of the central bank and the state-owned petroleum concern, Petroleos de Venezuela S.A. (PDVSA).

A series of measures introduced in February and March had the twin objectives of stimulating the economy and cutting waste. An austerity plan aimed to cut 10% from government spending during 1984 by reorganizing or liquidating unprofitable public-sector concerns, reducing top government salaries by 10%, and controlling the expenditures of civil servants. At the same time, subsidies on gasoline and other petroleum-based products were greatly reduced. The government set a four-tier exchange rate, with the most preferential rate used for principal debt repayments and imports of food and medicine.

Because the government employed one in four members of the work force, it was unwilling to reduce the number of public servants and thus add to unemployment which already stood at 15%. In an effort to tackle unemployment, the government ordered all private-sector businesses to take on 10% more staff over the six months from March to September. Legislation introduced at the end of July aimed to set up a new system for the regulation of prices and wages that would involve representatives of organized labour and business as well as Cabinet ministers.

Municipal elections held in May suggested that support for the AD was holding up. The AD won 46% of the vote,

Venezuela's new president, Jaime Lusinchi (right), received the presidential gold chain from his predecessor, Luis Herrera Campins, on February 2 in Caracas.
CLAUDE URRACA—SYGMA

compared with 21% for the Social Christian Party (COPEI). However, a poll by the independent Caracas television station indicated that 30% of voters had abstained.

Venezuela announced in July that it was altering the terms of the 1980 San José accord whereby Venezuela, together with Mexico, supplied petroleum and soft credits on very favourable terms to nine Central American and Caribbean countries. Under the new terms, one-half of any future loan agreed to by Venezuela would be in U.S. dollars, with the remainder in bolivares; recipient countries would have to pay cash for oil deliveries; and higher interest rates would be applied to loans. Previously, all loans had been made in U.S. dollars, at an estimated cost of $137 million a year, and beneficiary countries had often asked for extra credit when they did not have the foreign exchange to pay for oil deliveries. Government officials estimated that net cumulative disbursements under the San José scheme had reached $4.3 billion by the end of 1982.

Talks between the government and Venezuela's international bank creditors began on July 23. A month later it was announced that $20.8 billion of public-sector debt falling due between 1983 and 1988 had been rescheduled over 12½ years.   (MICHAEL WOOLLER)

CARIBBEAN

ANTIGUA AND BARBUDA

A parliamentary state and member of the Commonwealth, Antigua and Barbuda comprises the islands of Antigua, Barbuda, and Redonda in the eastern Caribbean Sea. Area: 442 sq km (171 sq mi). Pop. (1984 est.): 79,000. Cap.: Saint John's. Monetary unit: East Caribbean dollar, with (Oct. 29, 1984) a free rate of EC$2.70 to U.S. $1 (EC$3.26 = £1 sterling). Queen, Elizabeth II; governor-general in 1984, Sir Wilfred E. Jacobs; prime minister, Vere Cornwall Bird.

A general election on April 17, 1984, returned the governing Antigua Labour Party to power with 16 out of the 17 seats in the House of Representatives. The party won three seats from the opposition Progressive Labour Move-

ment and in so doing took all the seats in Antigua. The other seat, representing Barbuda, was held unopposed by an independent. In his new Cabinet, Prime Minister Vere Bird retained his son Lester as deputy prime minister and foreign minister. He appointed another son, Vere Bird, Jr., minister of public utilities and communications. The government, which promised 3,000 new jobs in tourism and 1,200 in light industry, continued its search for foreign aid and investment. A 350-room hotel and condominium project was to be financed by a $46 million loan from a 13-bank consortium after the original investor, the Brazilian government, withdrew because of financial difficulties.

Lester Bird visited Nigeria in August. He announced that Nigeria would supply oil for Antigua's West Indies Oil Company refinery, which had been shut down in 1983, though he did not mention a reopening date. Increased aid from Venezuela and assistance from China in education and agriculture were also obtained.   (ROD PRINCE)

This article updates the *Macropædia* article The WEST INDIES: *Antigua and Barbuda.*

BAHAMAS, THE

A parliamentary state and member of the Commonwealth, The Bahamas comprises an archipelago of about 700 islands in the North Atlantic Ocean just southeast of the United States. Area: 13,939 sq km (5,382 sq mi). Pop. (1984 est.): 227,000. Cap.: Nassau. Monetary unit: Bahamian dollar, with (Oct. 29, 1984) a par value of B$1 to U.S. $1 (free rate of B$1.21 = £1 sterling). Queen, Elizabeth II; governor-general in 1984, Sir Gerald Cash; prime minister, Sir Lynden O. Pindling.

A crisis erupted in the Bahamian government in October 1984 over allegations of ministerial involvement in drug trafficking, the subject of inquiry by a royal commission appointed in December 1983. Minister of Youth Kendal Nottage and Minister of Agriculture George Smith, against whom allegations of corruption were made in evidence to the commission, resigned. Deputy Prime Minister Arthur Hanna, who was also accused of taking payoffs but was exonerated, resigned as well. Hanna was a major force in the movement to force the ouster of Prime Minister Sir Lynden Pindling. Soon after Hanna's resignation, Minister of Housing Hubert Ingraham and Minister of Tourism Perry Christie, who had backed Hanna, were dismissed from their positions. Pindling, who allegedly failed to disclose millions of dollars in loans and gifts from foreign businessmen, ignored demands for his resignation.

The royal commission report, issued to Parliament December 17, stated that the drug traffic had spread corruption throughout Bahamian society. The commissioners found that Pindling's spending "far exceeded" his income but could not determine whether the money was drug-related.

In the all-important tourist industry, which accounted for approximately 70% of gross domestic product, visitor arrivals were targeted at 2.2 million in 1984, compared with 1.9 million in 1983. In July the heads of government of the Caribbean Community (Caricom) countries met in Nassau for a four-day conference.   (ROD PRINCE)

This article updates the *Macropædia* article The WEST INDIES: *The Bahamas.*

BARBADOS

The parliamentary state of Barbados, a member of the Commonwealth, occupies the most easterly island in the southern Carribbean Sea. Area: 430 sq km (166 sq mi). Pop. (1984 est.): 252,000. Cap.: Bridgetown. Monetary unit: Barbados dollar, with (Oct. 29, 1984) a free rate of BDS$2 to U.S. $1 (BDS$2.42 = £1 sterling). Queen, Elizabeth II; governors-general in 1984, Sir Deighton Lisle Ward to January 9 and, from February 24, Sir Hugh Springer; prime minister, J. M. G. Adams.

A modestly inflationary budget in April 1984 heralded a more optimistic outlook for Barbados after two years of financial stringency. The 1983–86 development plan, announced in February, projected a 3.5% annual growth rate and a gradual increase in tourist arrivals to an optimum of 400,000 a year. In 1983 the figure was 328,325, an improvement over 1982. The 1984 sugar crop was expected to be below 100,000 metric tons once again. Crop diversification was to be encouraged in order to reduce the food import bill.

The government suffered a political setback in July when the ruling Barbados Labour Party (BLP) lost a by-election to the opposition Democratic Labour Party (DLP) by one vote. However, the result was declared null and void, and the BLP won the seat when the by-election was rerun on November 22.

Relations with Trinidad and Tobago had soured after the invasion of Grenada in October 1983, which Barbados supported while Trinidad and Tobago did not. However, talks at the Caribbean Community summit meeting in The Bahamas in July eased the situation.   (ROD PRINCE)

This article updates the *Macropædia* article The WEST INDIES: *Barbados*.

CUBA

The socialist republic of Cuba comprises the island of Cuba and several thousand smaller islands and cays in the Caribbean Sea. Area: 110,922 sq km (42,827 sq mi). Pop. (1984 est.): 9,945,000. Cap.: Havana. Monetary unit: peso, with (Oct. 29, 1984) a free rate of 0.88 peso to U.S. $1 (1.06 pesos = £1 sterling). President of the Councils of State and Ministers in 1984, Fidel Castro Ruz.

In the aftermath of the U.S.-led invasion of Grenada in October 1983 and in the face of the U.S. government's accompanying hard-line rhetoric, Cuba was forced during 1984 to reappraise its foreign policy. Strong demonstra-

tions of support, even verbal, for the leftist guerrillas in El Salvador and the Sandinista government in Nicaragua were notably lacking, and Cuba made it clear, much to the annoyance of the Soviet Union, that is was in no position to offer substantial tangible help to the friends of both nations in Central America.

The invasion of Grenada dealt a painful blow to Cuba's military pride, although Pres. Fidel Castro skillfully evoked a "Dunkirk spirit" in the population, claiming that the U.S. was planning direct action against Cuba. The hostility that had gripped U.S.-Cuban relations in varying degrees since the 1959 revolution was intensified by the Grenadan intervention and by the belief, widely held in the U.S., that Cuba was the sponsor of the insurgency in El Salvador.

Cuba was considering withdrawing its 25,000–30,000 troops from Angola but was unwilling to make a commitment until South Africa negotiated a withdrawal from Namibia and promised to cease supporting the rebel forces of the National Union for the Total Independence of Angola (UNITA). (*See* Africa South of the Sahara: *Angola,* above.) Furthermore, Castro was reluctant to make any foreign policy concessions that might conceivably be regarded as beneficial to the reelection campaign of U.S. Pres. Ronald Reagan.

Despite frosty bilateral relations, the U.S. and Cuba were able to negotiate an agreement to repatriate some 2,700 Cuban criminal and mentally ill refugees who had been slipped in among the boatloads fleeing Cuba for the U.S. during the great exodus from the port of Mariel in 1980. In return, the U.S. would resume issuing preference immigrant visas to Cubans, especially those with close relatives in the U.S., and would admit 3,000 former political prisoners. It was thought possible that the agreement might be the prelude to fuller talks on the normalization of travel between the two countries, despite an earlier ruling by the U.S. Supreme Court that upheld the travel restrictions imposed by the U.S. Department of State.

Castro was the only leader of a member country who did not attend the Moscow meeting of the Council for Mutual Economic Assistance (Comecon) in June. His absence was seen as a mild protest and was thought to reflect Cuba's assertion that its geographic position made a rapproche-

BRUCE TALAMON/TIME MAGAZINE

During a whirlwind tour of Central America and Cuba in June, the Rev. Jesse Jackson (left) met with Cuban Pres. Fidel Castro (right) and won the release of 22 Americans and 26 Cubans from Cuban prisons.

ment with the U.S. a necessity. However, Cuba dutifully though reluctantly toed the Soviet line and joined in the boycott of the Olympic Games in Los Angeles. The Soviet link thus was as strong as ever, and Cuba remained one of the best supported of the U.S.S.R.'s satellites.

The economy surpassed expectations with 5.2% real growth in 1983. The leading sector was construction, which expanded by 9.3%. In 1983 more than 30,000 housing units were completed. Sugar production, which continued to dominate the economy despite all the postrevolutionary attempts to diversify the productive base, consistently failed to achieve its output targets. The 1983–84 figure of 8 million metric tons was a disappointment. Although this represented a substantial improvement over the previous season's 7.2 million metric tons, Cuba seemed to be no nearer to achieving its dream of an annual output of 10 million metric tons, which would make it the world's leading producer. The harvest was affected by the perennial problems of absenteeism and shortages of willing labour; also, for the second year in succession, unseasonably heavy rain between January and March led to excessive weed growth, causing mud and foreign material to reach the grinding mills and resulting in numerous breakdowns. Excess water in the fields also produced cut cane with a lower than normal sucrose content.

Cuba was able to sell all the sugar that it produced, and much of it fetched mouth-watering prices; in 1983 the U.S.S.R. bought 3,315,000 metric tons, or 49% of total sugar exports, at an average price some six times the going free-market rate. Cuba's Comecon relationship was a source of irritation to other International Sugar Agreement (ISA) signatories; because of it Cuba had little incentive to cut back sugar production in any collective bid to shore up depressed prices. The ISA meeting in June 1984 broke up in rancour, as prices slumped to below 5 cents per pound. (The average 1983 price was 8.6 cents per pound.)

Despite the attractive prices Cuba received for its sugar and nickel under Soviet protocols, these sales were denominated in convertible rubles. Cuba relied on its ISA quota to provide the bulk of its hard Western currency needs. Toward the end of 1983 Cuba attempted to boost sugar prices with a massive speculation. Brokers acting on Cuba's behalf bought 300,000 metric tons, which were sold six months later; a similar lot was bought in early 1984. The combined operation was thought to have cost Cuba more than $100 million.

Cuba's domestic oil production increased by 37.2% in 1983 to 14,900 bbl a day, enabling $600 million worth of surplus Soviet-supplied oil to be sold on the free market. However, the U.S.S.R. was considering cutting back its supplies to Cuba because of its own production difficulties. Oil reexports helped Cuba's balance of payments, but depressed sugar prices caused a 12% slump in exports to $1.4 billion in 1983. Because of foreign-exchange shortages, Cuba was again obliged to call a moratorium on all payments of principal debt in 1984. On July 19 agreement was reached with the Paris Club to reschedule Cuba's 1984 maturities of official debt, totaling $254 million, and on July 23 commercial banks holding $113 million of debt due in 1984 also agreed to reschedule. (PAUL MILLGATE)

This article updates the *Macropædia* article The WEST INDIES: *Cuba*.

DOMINICA

An island republic within the Commonwealth, Dominica is in the eastern Caribbean Sea. Area: 750 sq km (290 sq mi). Pop. (1984 est.): 74,000. Cap.: Roseau. Monetary unit: East Caribbean dollar, with (Oct. 29, 1984) a par value of EC$2.70 to U.S. $1 (free rate of EC$3.26 = £1 sterling). President in 1984, Clarence Augustus Seignoret; prime minister, Eugenia Charles.

During 1984 Dominica continued its gradual recovery from the economic catastrophe wrought by Hurricane David in 1979. The 1983 results had shown a growth rate of 3.5%, inflation brought down to 4%, and the current account deficit held to 9.5% of gross domestic product. In July 1984 the government obtained a standby agreement with the International Monetary Fund worth $1.6 million, though Prime Minister Eugenia Charles stated that she did not intend to draw from it. Charles announced that she was negotiating for financial assistance from other, unnamed governments. During the year the U.S. provided $9.6 million for road building and undertook to finance an electrification scheme for the eastern part of the island.

Controversial legislation establishing a banana marketing corporation and a growers' association was passed by Parliament in May. Earlier, banana farmers had objected that the bills would reduce their say in the industry, and the measures had been amended. The U.S. was providing EC$4.7 million for the restructuring plan.

In municipal by-elections held in August, the opposition United Dominica Labour Party made gains at the expense of the governing Dominica Freedom Party. (ROD PRINCE)

This article updates the *Macropædia* article The WEST INDIES: *Dominica*.

DOMINICAN REPUBLIC

The Dominican Republic covers the eastern two-thirds of the Caribbean island of Hispaniola, which it shares with Haiti. Area: 48,442 sq km (18,704 sq mi). Pop. (1984 est.): 5,923,000. Cap.: Santo Domingo. Monetary unit: peso, at par with the U.S. dollar, with a free rate (Oct. 29, 1984) of 1.21 pesos to £1 sterling. President in 1984, Salvador Jorge Blanco.

In April rioting broke out in many cities in the Dominican Republic in reaction to the removal of food subsidies. The riots left at least 60 people dead in their wake.

While conducting negotiations for the second installment of a $400 million loan from the International Monetary Fund (IMF), the government of the Dominican Republic imposed harsh austerity measures that caused widespread public discontent and disorder. In April Dominicans took to the streets in many cities in reaction to the removal of food subsidies; three days of rioting left at least 60 people dead and prompted a security purge against potential "troublemakers." To placate the labour unions, which had called a 24-hour general strike on May 9, the government granted a 43% increase in the minimum wage.

The government earlier agreed to the IMF demand that import purchases and $160 million in corporate letters of credit be placed on the parallel exchange rate of three pesos to the U.S. dollar, but it refused for months to shift petroleum imports from the official rate of one peso to the U.S. dollar. When the government finally submitted in July, the Fund responded by granting an interim arrangement to allow the republic access to frozen funds from the U.S. Agency for International Development. At the root of the crisis was the collapsing value of sugar, the major export commodity. Some 90% of all export earnings were spent on petroleum imports and on servicing the $2.4 billion external debt.   (PAUL MILLGATE)

This article updates the *Macropædia* article The WEST INDIES: *Dominican Republic.*

GRENADA

A parliamentary state within the Commonwealth, Grenada (with its dependency, the Southern Grenadines) is in the eastern Caribbean Sea. Area: 345 sq km (133 sq mi). Pop. (1984 est.): 112,000. Cap.: Saint George's. Monetary unit: East Caribbean dollar, with (Oct. 29, 1984) a par value of EC$2.70 to U.S. $1 (free rate of EC$3.26 = £1 sterling). Queen, Elizabeth II; governor-general in 1984, Sir Paul Scoon; chairman of the interim advisory council to December 4, Nicholas Brathwaite; prime minister from December 4, Herbert A. Blaize.

MATTHEW NAYTHONS/TIME MAGAZINE

In Grenada a general election took place on December 3. The New National Party won overwhelmingly, and on December 4 Herbert A. Blaize was sworn in as prime minister.

The upheaval in Grenada set off by the collapse of the People's Revolutionary Government (PRG) in October 1983 continued throughout 1984. The island remained under military occupation by about 300 U.S. troops and 450 members of the Caribbean Peacekeeping Force, mainly from Jamaica and Barbados.

Three main political groupings took part in the general election on December 3: the Grenada United Labour Party, led by the former prime minister Sir Eric Gairy, who returned from exile in the U.S. in January; the New National Party, a coalition of centre-right parties supported by the U.S.; and the Maurice Bishop Patriotic Movement, led by two former PRG ministers. The New Jewel Movement (NJM) announced that it would boycott the poll. The New National Party won overwhelmingly, gaining 14 of the 15 seats in Parliament, and on December 4 Herbert A. Blaize, who had headed the Grenadan government during the 1960s, was sworn in as prime minister.

Ten members of the NJM's Central Committee, including former deputy prime minister Bernard Coard, were among 19 people committed for trial in August on charges of murdering Prime Minister Maurice Bishop and seven other people on Oct. 19, 1983. The trial opened on October 16.

The economic outlook remained uncertain. Closing of most of the previous government's economic projects led to a sharp increase in unemployment. Almost all capital allocation in the 1984–85 budget was earmarked for the international airport at Point Salines. The airport project received $19 million of a U.S. aid allocation of $57 million for 1984–85.   (ROD PRINCE)

This article updates the *Macropædia* article The WEST INDIES: *Grenada.*

HAITI

The republic of Haiti occupies the western one-third of the Caribbean island of Hispaniola, which it shares with the Dominican Republic. Area: 27,750 sq km (10,715 sq mi). Pop. (1984 est.): 5,248,000. Cap.: Port-au-Prince. Monetary unit: gourde, with (Oct. 29, 1984) a par value of 5 gourdes to U.S. $1 (free rate of 6.05 gourdes = £1 sterling). President in 1984, Jean-Claude Duvalier.

Haiti continued to maintain political stability during 1984, with Pres. Jean-Claude Duvalier further consolidating his position, though there were some signs of social discontent. Elections to renew the unicameral National Legislative Assembly were held on February 12. The 59 seats were won without exception by representatives of the pro-government party, the Conseil National d'Action Jean-Claudiste. Of the approximately 300 candidates who contested the elections, not one was from an opposition group.

Rioting on a considerable scale occurred in May in the two large towns of Gonaïves and Cap-Haïtien in the northwest. Up to ten people were killed in the disturbances, and many arrests were made. The riots reportedly were caused mainly by food shortages. The trouble in Cap-Haïtien began when slum dwellers tried to loot the food stocks of CARE, the U.S. charitable organization. Following the incidents five Cabinet ministers were dismissed.

Economic performance was hampered by poor agricultural output and a decline in tourist arrivals. Forecasts of the 1984–85 harvests for two of the country's main agricultural products, coffee and sugar, were unpromising, and exports of those commodities to the U.S. declined sharply during the first third of 1984.   (ROBIN CHAPMAN)

This article updates the *Macropædia* article The WEST INDIES: *Haiti.*

JAMAICA

A parliamentary state within the Commonwealth, Jamaica occupies an island in the Caribbean Sea. Area: 10,991 sq km (4,244 sq mi). Pop. (1984 est.): 2,295,-000. Cap.: Kingston. Monetary unit: Jamaica dollar, with (Oct. 29, 1984) a free rate of J$4.18 to U.S. $1 (J$5.05 = £1 sterling). Queen, Elizabeth II; governor-general in 1984, Florizel Glasspole; prime minister, Edward Seaga.

Jamaica's acute economic difficulties occupied most of the government's attention during 1984. After months of negotiations, an agreement with the International Monetary Fund was reached in June for assistance totaling $143.5 million on extremely stringent conditions. The agreement stipulated that the government's budget deficit should be halved within a year to 8.3% of gross domestic product. Unemployment was expected to rise from the October 1984 level of 26%.

The introduction of a unified exchange rate for the Jamaican dollar was followed by a series of devaluations, giving a rate of J$4.18 to the U.S. dollar in October. The consequent rises in the prices of imported goods and in public utility charges helped to produce an inflation rate of about 20%. Signs of labour unrest appeared in July, with strikes in the bauxite industry and public services.

Toward the end of the year the opposition People's National Party issued calls for new elections. In October Prime Minister Edward Seaga announced that the security forces had discovered a plot by a local drug dealer to kill him. (ROD PRINCE)

This article updates the *Macropædia* article The WEST INDIES: *Jamaica*.

SAINT CHRISTOPHER AND NEVIS

A parliamentary federated state and member of the Commonwealth, St. Christopher and Nevis is comprised of the islands of St. Christopher and Nevis in the eastern Caribbean Sea. Area: 261 sq km (101 sq mi). Pop. (1984 est.): 45,000. Cap.: Basseterre. Monetary unit: East Caribbean dollar, with (Oct. 29, 1984) a par value of EC$2.70 to U.S. $1 (free rate of EC$3.26 = £1 sterling). Queen, Elizabeth II; governor-general in 1984, Sir Clement Arrindell; prime minister, Kennedy A. Simmonds.

The general election held in St. Christopher and Nevis (St. Kitts-Nevis) on June 21, 1984, produced a decisive victory for the governing coalition headed by Prime Minister Kennedy Simmonds. The People's Action Movement (PAM) won six out of the eight seats on St. Kitts, while its coalition partner, the Nevis Reformation Party (NRP), won all three Nevis seats. The Labour Party retained only two seats, and its leader, Lee Moore, lost to Constance Mitchum, the country's first woman member of Parliament. Moore subsequently resigned the party leadership.

Simmonds took the ministries of finance, home affairs, and foreign affairs in the new Cabinet. Simeon Daniel, leader of the NRP and former finance minister and deputy prime minister, was appointed minister of natural resources and environment. His demotion reflected the NRP's loss of influence once the PAM gained a parliamentary majority.

The sugar industry recorded a slightly improved performance in 1984, with a harvest of 30,100 metric tons. Presenting a tax-free balanced budget in January, Daniel said the government was continuing its efforts to lessen the economy's dependence on sugar. (ROD PRINCE)

This article updates the *Macropædia* article The WEST INDIES: *Saint Christopher and Nevis*.

SAINT LUCIA

A parliamentary state and member of the Commonwealth, St. Lucia is the second largest of the Windward Islands in the eastern Caribbean Sea. Area: 616 sq km (238 sq mi). Pop. (1984 est.): 126,000. Cap.: Castries. Monetary unit: East Caribbean dollar, with (Oct. 29, 1984) a par value of EC$2.70 to U.S. $1 (free rate of EC$3.26 = £1 sterling). Queen, Elizabeth II; governor-general in 1984, Sir Allen Lewis; prime minister, John Compton.

After some years of stagnation, there were signs of improvement in St. Lucia's economy during 1984. In April, while presenting a record budget that featured a big increase in capital spending, Prime Minister John Compton claimed that unemployment had been reduced to 22%, compared with 27% two years earlier, and that inflation was down to 1.5%. The improvement was also visible in tourism, where arrivals had risen by 9% in 1983. Early in 1984 two U.S. firms set up manufacturing operations in St. Lucia.

The divided opposition presented no political challenge to the United Workers' Party government during the year. In August the St. Lucia Labour Party elected a new leader—Julian Hunte, former mayor of Castries, who had not figured in the party's recent internal disputes.

In January Compton visited Hong Kong, South Korea, and Taiwan, and in May the government established diplomatic relations with Taiwan. Agreement was reached on a $2 million line of credit, technical assistance in agriculture and fisheries, and private-sector investments in electronics and garment manufacturing. (ROD PRINCE)

This article updates the *Macropædia* article The WEST INDIES: *Saint Lucia*.

SAINT VINCENT AND THE GRENADINES

A parliamentary state within the Commonwealth, St. Vincent and the Grenadines comprises the islands of St. Vincent and the northern Grenadines in the eastern Caribbean Sea. Area: 388 sq km (150 sq mi). Pop. (1984 est.): 138,000. Cap.: Kingstown. Monetary unit: East Caribbean dollar, with (Oct. 29, 1984) a par value of EC$2.70 to U.S. $1 (EC$3.26 = £1 sterling). Queen, Elizabeth II; governor-general in 1984, Sir Sydney Gun-Munro; prime ministers, Milton Cato and, from July 30, James Fitz-Allen Mitchell.

General elections in St. Vincent and the Grenadines on July 25, 1984, produced a decisive defeat for the St. Vincent Labour Party, in office since 1974, at the hands of the New Democratic Party (NDP), which won 9 out of the 13 seats in the National Assembly. NDP leader James ("Son") Mitchell took over from Milton Cato as prime minister.

Mitchell, who had been prime minister during the period 1972–74, fought the election on a cautious left-of-centre program. He pledged the abolition of income taxes for those earning less than EC$10,000 a year and urged social reform, while emphasizing the role of the private sector in the economy. He also sought a revival in agriculture and tourism, to be based on the construction of an international airport. His campaign was strongly supported by the business community.

Among pressing problems facing Mitchell were the poor financial condition of several state enterprises and the bad reputation of the country's offshore banking sector. Despite a national debt of EC$189 million, Mitchell said in October that his government would not approach the International Monetary Fund for assistance.

(ROD PRINCE)

This article updates the *Macropædia* article The WEST INDIES: *Saint Vincent and the Grenadines*.

TRINIDAD AND TOBAGO

A republic and member of the Commonwealth, Trinidad and Tobago consists of two islands in the Caribbean Sea off the coast of Venezuela. Area: 5,128 sq km (1,980 sq mi). Pop. (1984 est.): 1,203,000, Cap.: Port-of-Spain. Monetary unit: Trinidad and Tobago dollar, with (Oct. 29, 1984) a par value of TT$2.40 to U.S. $1 (free rate of TT$2.90 = £1 sterling). President in 1984, Sir Ellis Clarke; prime minister, George Chambers.

During 1984 the government of Trinidad and Tobago pursued a policy of economic stringency, based on an austerity budget introduced in February which levied new taxes and cut public-sector subsidies. The import controls and foreign-exchange rationing that had been imposed in October 1983 remained in force. The measures produced a trade surplus of TT$133.4 million in the first half of 1984, ending two years of deficits. However, foreign-exchange reserves continued to shrink rapidly.

Oil production rose for the first time in five years, averaging 162,326 bbl a day in the first six months of 1984, 1.5% above the 1983 average. In September the government announced that it was purchasing the assets of Texaco-Trinidad Inc.'s petroleum operations for $175 million. The manufacturing sector remained sluggish. Of total exports amounting to TT$5.7 billion in 1983, non-oil manufactured goods represented only TT$122 million.

In September the four main opposition parties formed the National Alliance for Reconstruction (NAR) to fight the 1986 elections. The NAR's fortunes received a boost in November when one of the four parties, the Democratic Action Congress, won 11 out of 12 seats in elections to the Tobago House of Assembly. The remaining seat went to the governing People's National Movement. (ROD PRINCE)

This article updates the *Macropædia* article The WEST INDIES: *Trinidad and Tobago*.

Oceania

AUSTRALIA

A federal parliamentary state and member of the Commonwealth, Australia occupies the smallest continent and includes the island state of Tasmania. Area: 7,682,300 sq km (2,966,200 sq mi). Pop. (1984 est.): 15,462,000. Cap.: Canberra. Monetary unit: Australian dollar, with (Oct. 29, 1984) a free rate of $A1.19 to U.S. $1 ($A1.44 = £1 sterling). Queen, Elizabeth II; governor-general in 1984, Sir Ninian Martin Stephen; prime minister, Robert J. Hawke.

Domestic Affairs. Domestic affairs in Australia were marked by stability and economic growth in 1984. Unemployment remained a problem, but the fight against inflation began to succeed. Prime Minister Robert (Bob) Hawke towered above both political opponents and critics within his own Australian Labor Party (ALP), distancing himself from a series of state and federal political and legal corruption inquiries and bringing a sense of purpose and direction to the community. Clearly confident of his government's popularity, Hawke called general elections for December 1, almost 2½ years early. Hawke was reelected with a reduced majority in the House of Representatives and failed to gain control of the Senate. In the House, enlarged from 125 to 148 seats, the ALP, with 82 seats, held a majority of 16, compared with 25 in the previous Parliament. The Liberal Party increased its standing from 33 to 45 seats. (*See* Special Report; for tabulated results, see *Political Parties,* above.)

In 1984 Douglas Anthony retired as leader of the National Party, and in January Ian Sinclair was elected in his place. This provoked discussion of a possible amalgamation between the Liberal and National parties, since some critics of Liberal leader Andrew Peacock believed that Sinclair's reputation as a tough "head-kicker" would make him a more practical and effective opponent to Hawke. However, Peacock retained his position as leader of the opposition coalition, and Sinclair became deputy leader. During the election campaign Peacock fought hard to present a stronger personality. John Howard, deputy leader of the Liberals and a former treasurer in the administration of Malcolm Fraser, performed so well, however, that Peacock faced the strong possibility that he might lose the party leadership to Howard. Peacock's new stance was so aggressive that Hawke threatened the opposition leader with legal action if he did not tone down the language of his personal attacks.

One of the major issues that divided the ALP and the Liberal Party was immigration. Previously a bipartisan agreement had existed between the ALP and the Liberals not to criticize immigration policy. In 1984, however, the question of Asian immigration was hotly debated, and the government's policy was perceived to be to encourage Vietnamese immigration at the expense of Australia's traditional migrant pool in Europe, especially the U.K. Both parties tried to avoid charges of "racism" and to reduce the emotional level of the immigration debate.

A second serious issue dividing the parties was the problem of how to deal with the revelations about organized crime that were expected from the final report of the royal commission under Frank Costigan that was investigating the issue. Peacock claimed that the government was trying to stifle revelations about Australia's crime bosses by transferring the function of the locally based Costigan inquiry to a National Crimes Authority. He argued that the National Crimes Authority would be prevented by state and party political interests from doing its job effectively and fearlessly. In particular, he accused the government of trying to cover up any links that might exist between politics and crime. Despite his general allegations, made in the House of Representatives under parliamentary privilege, Peacock was unable to provide evidence that the prime minister was a "little crook," as he described him, or that he associated with criminals. The royal commission completed its report in October after more than four years of inquiries. Though much of the report remained confidential, its most immediate effect was to provoke controversy over allegations it contained about the highly successful businessman Kerry Packer. Packer maintained that he had committed no offense and that he had been denied natural justice by being publicly named without having the opportunity to defend himself.

The government also experienced difficulties with the new medical health plan, Medicare, introduced by Minister of Health Neal Blewett in February. The problems centred on a dispute between Blewett and specialist radiologists and pathologists working in public hospitals. Blewett insisted that the specialist doctors should sign contracts giving the minister control over their fee schedules and conditions of employment. Faced with the threat of resignations, Blewett amended the original legislation to reduce his own powers and established an independent inquiry into the specialists' claims. Blewett's new guidelines allowed salaried specialists to earn $A12,500 above their salary of $A50,000 and outside nonsalaried specialists to earn $A62,500 before being required to contribute a proportion of their earnings to hospital funds.

Hawke's Cabinet was temporarily depleted when Stewart West, minister for immigration and ethnic affairs, resigned in November 1983. West, representing the left wing of the ALP, left in protest against the government's decision to continue to mine uranium. He was reinstated in April 1984 after agreeing to accept the principle of Cabinet solidarity. However, uranium mining remained a public concern. Michael (Mick) Young, who had resigned from the Cabinet in July 1983 over his involvement in the Combe-Ivanov affair, was reinstated as special minister of state in January, though he was to face further controversy during the year. (*See* Special Report.) Hawke made a number of changes to his Cabinet at the start of his second term in December. Lionel Bowen became attorney general in place of Gareth Evans, who lost Cabinet rank when he was appointed to the post of resources and energy minister, while Kim Beazley took over the defense portfolio from Gordon Scholes. West, who moved to the Housing and Construction Ministry, and Young both remained in the Cabinet.

In April John Burke, a former British Royal Air Force technician, alleged that Aboriginals had been killed during tests of nuclear weapons carried out by the U.K. at Maralinga, South Australia, in 1963. Burke made the allegations on the eve of his own death from cancer, which he claimed he had developed as a result of being exposed to radiation during the tests. Subsequently, Aboriginals went to the U.K. to try to claim compensation for health damage resulting from the tests, and Australian scientists visited the area to monitor any residual radioactivity that remained in the desert.

Considerable interest was generated by a reassessment of Aboriginal origins. Milford Wolpoff, a paleoanthropologist at the University of Michigan, led those who argued that Australia was visited by several succeeding waves of migration beginning 45,000 years ago. The *New York Times* reported the new controversy over Aboriginal evolution in July, pointing out that fossil evidence was being lost as a result of successful pressure from Aboriginal groups to have Aboriginal remains taken from museums and buried.

Foreign Affairs. It was a difficult year for Australian foreign-policy makers. Foreign Minister William (Bill) Hayden traveled widely. His most important but least successful visit was to the U.S.S.R., where Soviet Foreign Minister Andrey Gromyko paused only briefly to discuss

foreign affairs with him and icily refused Hayden's attempt to discuss civil rights in the U.S.S.R. Relations were also often poor with Indonesia, Papua New Guinea, the Philippines, and even New Zealand.

Relations with Indonesia were damaged by the publication of an Australian defense planning document in March. The document, entitled "The Strategic Basis of Australian Defense Policy," argued that Indonesia was Australia's only serious threat and urged the government to encourage Papua New Guinea to suppress Irian Jayan (West New Guinean) rebels in an effort to reduce a potential threat to Papua New Guinea from Indonesia. The document, which, according to the *National Times,* was accepted virtually without comment by the federal Cabinet, noted that Australia should be in a position to develop nuclear weapons as quickly as any neighbour that seemed likely to do so.

Indonesian Foreign Minister Mochtar Kusumaatmadja twice attacked Australian attitudes toward Indonesia. He complained that the left wing of the ALP, by calling on the government to adopt a tougher stance on Indonesia's annexation of East Timor, was ignoring the views of Australia's silent majority on the question. Mochtar asserted that, among Australians, the majority of "students, high school kids, the general public, businessmen, and those who have been to Bali" either had no definite view or had a positive view of Indonesia. To underline the point, Indonesia canceled a proposed Australian fact-finding inspection of East Timor in retaliation against the tour of Australia undertaken by José Ramos Horta, spokesman for East Timor's Fretilin independence movement. The Indonesians also pointed out that several small turboprop aircraft had been observed making unexplained flights over East Timor. They asked the Australians to investigate the possibility that these sorties might be unauthorized spy flights by Australians gathering intelligence about troop movements in the area.

Relations between Australia and Papua New Guinea were soured in 1984 when the Australian Broadcasting Corporation (ABC) broadcast material that damaged Papua New Guinea's rapport with its most important neighbour, Indonesia. The Papua New Guinea government threatened sanctions against the ABC if it broadcast an interview with an Irian Jayan rebel leader, James Nyaro. Despite the ef-
(continued on page 598)

NEWS LTD., THE BULLETIN, SYDNEY

This blockade in Daintree National Park in northern Queensland symbolizes the controversy over the degree to which "progress"—roadbuilding in this case— may be held off to protect fragile natural resources such as the tropical rain forest.

The Hawke Phenomenon

BY A. R. G. GRIFFITHS

Robert (Bob) Hawke took office as Australia's prime minister in high spirits after a landslide election victory for the Australian Labor Party (ALP) in March 1983 that had all but destroyed the opposition Liberal (conservative) Party. Within months Hawke had established himself as the most popular prime minister in Australian history. By the first anniversary of his accession to office, public opinion polls were rating his popularity with electors at an extraordinary 73%, almost twice that of opposition leader Andrew Peacock. Hawke continued to exude confidence, looked tanned and fit, and assured the press that he felt great and that his tennis was better on his first anniversary than it had been before. But by the end of the year his party had suffered a defeat at the polls, and his personal popularity appeared to have declined considerably.

Successes. Australia profited from the first 12 months of the new administration, with an unprecedented turnaround in the economy. Hawke attributed the positive changes not only to the breaking of a drought, which led to an upturn in demand and consumption based on an agricultural boom, but also to a newly emerged optimism in the community. In his opinion the basis of Australian prosperity lay in a new mood of cooperation, and he contrasted his attitudes toward government with those of his conservative predecessor, Malcolm Fraser. Industrial harmony and economic progress went hand in hand, said Hawke, and both could be achieved if Australians agreed to be governed by consensus, not force. "The concept of consensus," said Hawke, "is something I find intellectually sensible, instinctively compelling and the natural outcome of the experiences I have had with Australians in all walks of life."

Hawke first had his idea of consensus accepted by the representatives of capital and labour at a "national economic summit" convened in April 1983, from which conservative opposition politicians were excluded. The summit accepted Hawke's vision and agreed to forgo sectional interests for the foreseeable future. In a spirit of accord, guidelines were laid down—and subsequently put into practice—in order to facilitate economic and social harmony.

The first results of the accord were encouraging. The number of strikes dropped significantly. Inflation slowed to such an extent that the Arbitration Court was confident enough to grant Australia's workers full cost-of-living increases in 1984, the judges being sure that no large increases would subsequently be justified by inflation figures in the near future. The employers, for their part, reluctantly but patriotically admitted that the country did have the capacity to pay.

By mid-1984, however, problems were occurring that an abstract commitment to consensus could not solve. Critics of Hawke pointed out that the dramatic fall in the rate of inflation had been achieved to some extent by fiddling the books, the cost of health care having been removed from the calculation of living costs on the introduction of the government's Medicare health-insurance scheme.

THE BULLETIN, SYDNEY

Robert Hawke was jubilant after his Australian Labor Party won a landslide election victory in March 1983, and shortly after taking office, he had established himself as the most popular prime minister in Australian history. It didn't last.

Unemployment rates fell slightly, but the University of Melbourne's Applied Economic and Social Research Institute predicted no long-term decline from a figure of about 10%.

The Party Conference. Crucial to the assessment of Hawke by both the general public and his party was the prime minister's standing at the biennial ALP national conference in July. Hawke went into the conference assailed on all sides. As one critic put it, he had won government, reduced inflation, created industrial harmony, broken the drought, and presided over an economic recovery, but what had he done in the last two months? Hawke was under pressure from those who wished to see his government take a hard line on uranium mining, East Timor, the readmission to the party of right-wing trade unions associated with the Roman Catholic Church, visits to Australia by nuclear-powered warships, and the presence and role of U.S. military bases on Australian soil.

On the eve of the national conference Hawke spoke to the media about his attitudes toward the impending debate within the party. He pointed out that there was a difference between the luxury of opposition and the responsibility of government. He claimed that the hallmark of his government had been its understanding of its obligations to Australia, and not simply to the ALP. During the conference itself Hawke's mastery of the party machine was evident. On all major issues his line was accepted. The conference even voted 55–44 to allow three uranium mines at Roxby Downs, Narbarlek, and Ranger to operate. Hawke wiped the floor with left-wing opponents within the ALP, and his pro-mining stand guaranteed employment in the industry for thousands and $1 billion in revenue from the Ranger mine alone over a ten-year period.

Setbacks. Not all was smooth going, however. The first rough patch came in May 1983 with revelations of a spy scandal that badly damaged Hawke's standing with the left wing of his party. In this imbroglio a former high ALP party officer, ex-federal secretary David Combe, was embarrassed after his private conversations with a Soviet diplomat, Valery Ivanov, were recorded by Australia's secret service agency. As a result of the bugged conversation, Ivanov had been expelled from Australia in April. Combe became a chief witness before a royal commission, which among other things investigated the role of one of Hawke's ministers, Mick Young (a special minister of state), who admitted leaking secret Cabinet discussions to an individual with tenuous but direct links to Ivanov. The royal commission determined that Combe had committed no offense and criticized Young for his indiscretion. Young's central position in the power structure of the ALP, however, led to his reinstatement in January 1984 after a suitable sojourn on the back benches.

Hawke was bitterly criticized by the left wing of the party for his role in the Combe-Ivanov affair. No sooner had Combe been readmitted to the party's good graces at the ALP national conference than Mick Young was in hot water again. On the second occasion the matter was small: Young had been careless in filling out a customs declaration form concerning the import of goods on behalf of his family. But ministers had to be above suspicion. Hawke set another inquiry in place, into what was called "the Paddington Bear affair" (one of the undeclared items was a toy bear), and Young was again forced to stand aside from the ministry before his eventual reinstatement some weeks later.

Hawke, however, rode out both the Combe-Ivanov and the Young storms and faced the future with undisguised confidence and optimism, determined to cash in on his popularity by holding an early general election. This he prepared for with a gentle annual budget that promised tax cuts and with a new willingness to meet the press on a weekly basis to discuss both his and Australia's problems.

Hawke's problems soon became public property. In a sensational political development the prime minister broke down and cried at a press conference during which he was being questioned about allegations made in Parliament that he was "a little crook." Hawke explained that the tears were caused by anguish at a family tragedy that had developed when his daughter was found to have become a drug addict. Although a similar outburst of emotion had knocked Edmund Muskie out of the 1972 U.S. presidential primary campaign, Australian electors overlooked the breakdown, and Hawke's great personal popularity continued. A key reason for Hawke's high approval rating was his frankness and spontaneous, uncalculating behaviour, widely thought to be typically Australian. Sometimes it was appropriate to shed tears, and the electorate widely endorsed Hawke's paternal concern.

However, when the election campaign began, it was soon obvious that approval for Hawke as a caring father did not extend to a blanket support for all his policies. The decision to hold a long election campaign of seven weeks turned out to be a bad one, as was Hawke's decision to debate on television the issues of the election with opposition leader Andrew Peacock. During the campaign the traditional conservatism of Australian voters began to reassert itself and, while the public supported Hawke's general economic policies, they were not prepared to give the ALP overall control of the Australian parliamentary system. Hawke blamed the ALP loss on a new voting system that resulted in the invalidation of a disproportionately large number of ALP votes. Postelection comment by voters, however, suggested that the setback was a protest against both the calling of an early election and Hawke's style of leadership. In fact, Hawke's conduct of the election campaign was seriously defective, and he suffered a swing against him that left him with a reduced but workable majority in the lower house and at the mercy of the Australian Democrats, who held a seven-vote balance of power, in the upper. Hawke was not able to deal adequately with critics who complained that he had deserted traditional ALP policies on uranium, nor could even he escape the traditional Australian custom of cutting the heads off the tall poppies.

A. R. G. Griffiths is a senior lecturer in history at the Flinders University of South Australia.

In early July a bomb exploded at the home of Justice Raymond Watson of the Australian Family Law Court. Justice Watson's wife was killed in this latest in a series of violent attacks directed against family court judges. Judges of the family court are responsible for decisions concerning divorce, custody, and property settlements.
NEWS LIMITED

(continued from page 595)

forts of the chairman of the ABC to show sensitivity to the Papua New Guinea government's point of view, the interview was screened. In retaliation the Papua New Guinea government decided not to grant visas to ABC news and current-affairs staff.

Relations with the Philippines were damaged by the long-protracted trial of an Australian priest, Brian Gore, on charges of murder in the Philippines. The foreign minister himself intervened on Gore's behalf. Hayden met Pres. Ferdinand Marcos of the Philippines and quoted him as saying that he wished the Gore case had never occurred, as the trial was vexatious and was creating problems between the two countries. After 12 months the prosecution and defense counsel both moved that the charges against Gore be dismissed; he was soon released and returned to Australia.

Relations between Australia and New Zealand were strained when the new Labour Party government in New Zealand declined to allow U.S. nuclear-armed or nuclear-powered warships to enter New Zealand waters. This action put the ANZUS defense alliance between Australia, New Zealand, and the U.S. at risk.

The Economy. The economy had mixed fortunes in 1984. The Australian dollar exchange rate stood up well in relation to the country's major trading partners but was severely devalued in relation to the U.S. currency. High interest rates were not sufficient to attract U.S. dollar funds into the country, since most holders of U.S. dollars preferred to keep their funds in the U.S., at least until the presidential elections had taken place there. On the positive side, the inflation rate in Australia fell to such an extent that the central wage-fixing authority was not obliged to grant any increases to wage earners beyond that made in April, when workers were granted a 4.1% wage increase based on the rise in the cost of living. In making the award the president of the Arbitration Commission, Sir John Moore, observed that it was justified not only on the grounds of cost-of-living increases but also because workers had respected an undertaking not to seek pay raises outside the arbitration system. Employers and companies soon benefited from the new prices-and-incomes accord because industry was in a position to plan longer-term strategies based on known wage costs.

Unemployment remained a problem. Good results by private enterprise and government industries, for example by Broken Hill Proprietary Limited and Trans Australia Airlines, were achieved at the cost of considerable layoffs of workers. The government airline achieved a profit turnaround and became market leader only after 1,200 employees lost their jobs. The manufacturing sector was also in difficulties, with the automobile industry in particular facing a dilemma: on the one hand the industry had to maintain its high levels of employment in order to justify the tariffs imposed by the government on its imported competitors, and on the other it had to be cost-competitive on the international scene. The government tried to resolve the dilemma by introducing a system of export credits whereby components made in Australia and exported to other countries were taken into consideration when assessing the duty on imported motor vehicles. At the same time, the government tried to force the five major car manufacturers in the country—General Motors, Ford, Toyota, Nissan, and Mitsubishi—to increase the efficiency of their activities with the object of possibly contracting to form three major companies in the near future. This aim was to be achieved by a combination of market forces, interchange of component parts, and "badge engineering," a system by which different makes would be created from similar basic vehicles by the addition of embellishing details.

Of overwhelming importance to the economy was the government's decision to hold an early election. Hawke and his treasurer, Paul Keating, framed the 1984–85 budget with an election in mind, and as a result the budget contained tax cuts. The cut that affected the most people was $A7.60 for paychecks between $A240 and $A538 a week. The government also slightly increased indexed pension and unemployment benefits. There were also new concessions for business interests. The depreciation rate of new factories was raised and, more important, companies were permitted to offset losses against other companies in the same group. Mining companies were also helped by provisions that permitted them to write off exploration expenditure.

Introducing the budget in August, Keating claimed that the government's strategy was designed to continue the economic recovery by reducing inflationary pressures and improving job prospects. The ALP maintained that its policies would overturn a history of more than a decade of economic stops and starts and of recoveries that were squandered by senseless and destructive rounds of price-and-wage increases. The government based its optimism on the projection that the climate of moderation in workers' pay claims would continue.

The budget deficit for the 1984–85 fiscal year was set at $A6,745,000,000, a reduction of $A1,216,000,000 from the previous year. Capital expenditure was expected to rise by 11% to a total of $A5,630,000,000. Spending on social security and welfare accounted for $A18,047,000,000, while $A1,252,000,000 was allocated to housing, which was singled out as a key ingredient in the government's economic policy.

Most interest was focused on a new tax on wine. A 10% sales tax was imposed on all alcoholic wines and cider. Keating explained that, in the past, beer and spirit drinkers had been discriminated against in favour of those who drank wine, which had not been taxed. Revenue from the new tax was expected to yield A$62 million in a full year. The government estimated that the new wine tax would lead to an increase in the consumption of beer and tried to head off criticism from winemakers and grape growers by holding an independent inquiry into the industry to investigate all aspects of its structure.

A more serious criticism was leveled at the budget by Peacock, who maintained that it represented a preelection sweetener and that it would inevitably be followed by a tougher blueprint for socialism should the ALP be successful in the polls. Peacock especially feared the possibility of new capital-gains taxes and claimed that the government's economic policy was particularly damaging to those under 18 and over 65.

The government reassessed its foreign-aid program and set a new target of 0.7% of national income to be given in aid, up from the current 0.5%. A report commissioned by the government recommended that the Pacific region should became the main, almost exclusive, recipient of overseas aid.   (A. R. G. GRIFFITHS)

See also *Dependent States*, below.

NEW ZEALAND

New Zealand, a parliamentary state and member of the Commonwealth in the South Pacific Ocean, consists of North and South islands and Stewart, Chatham, and other minor islands. Area: 269,057 sq km (103,883 sq mi). Pop. (1984 est.): 3,265,500. Cap.: Wellington. Monetary unit: New Zealand dollar, with (Oct. 29, 1984) a free rate of Z2.05 to U.S. $1 (Z2.48 = £1 sterling). Queen, Elizabeth II; governor-general in 1984, Sir David Stuart Beattie; prime ministers, Sir Robert David Muldoon and, from July 26, David Russell Lange.

Prime Minister Sir Robert Muldoon of New Zealand called a snap general election for July 14, 1984, five months before his government's third term was due to end. Though his National Party (Conservative) government had a narrow majority in Parliament, Sir Robert said that he could no longer rely on the support of some members in critical divisions. It had been an aggressive government, no less so during its last term when it used a wages-and-prices freeze and interest regulations to drag inflation down to 2.9% for the six months to July and legislated to make union membership voluntary.

Labour Party leader David Lange (*see* BIOGRAPHIES) campaigned on the need to eradicate bitterness from political and public life, to end big borrowing to support a deficit budget, and to arrest the rise in unemployment. His campaign received spirited support from National defectors, who had formed a New Zealand Party dedicated to reducing intervention by government in business and private lives. The outcome was a 4.5% swing to Labour, giving it a comfortable majority of 56 seats as against National's 37. (For tabulated results, see *Political Parties*, above.)

Within hours of the election, Lange was plunged into a crisis when expectations of a currency devaluation caused a run on the New Zealand dollar. Sir Robert, who remained caretaker prime minister at the time, dramatically resisted advice to devalue, and a constitutional crisis threatened. Labour's decision to devalue by 20% was finally pushed through, though it remained controversial. In his new Cabinet, Lange appointed Mike Moore to overseas trade, Roger Douglas to finance, Richard Prebble to transport and a new Pacific Islands portfolio, and David Caygill to trade and industry and national development. Geoffrey Palmer, leader of the House, attorney general, and minister of justice, was an unseen hand in many executive initiatives.

Soon after Parliament reconvened following the election, it adjourned so the House could accommodate a promised public seminar of representatives of all industries and ways

With the smile of a winner, David Lange waved to his supporters at his Auckland campaign headquarters after learning that his Labour Party had won a majority in Parliament, ousting Prime Minister Sir Robert Muldoon's government.

of life. The strategy was copied from one used successfully by the new Australian Labor Party government to settle any disputes left over from the previous administration. After three days of discussions, a 23-point communiqué was drawn up. It urged the channeling of aid to the poor and unemployed through a combination of wages, tax cuts, and government spending; restraint of claims for wage increases by others until the economy improved; widening the tax base to avoid increasing personal income tax; more careful control over government spending; special policies to deal with Maori unemployment; fiscal, monetary, and exchange-rate policies that would allow future investment to flow into sectors and industries where it could be used most effectively; and a tax system that did not penalize effort and innovation but still fairly reflected ability to pay. As a preliminary to the public conference, the government, employers, and unions agreed on a new wage-fixing system that would involve, among other things, talks on the state of the economy before each wage round.

Labour had campaigned on a policy of refusing port facilities to ships armed with nuclear weapons. Practically, the policy would affect only ships of the U.S. Navy, a partner in New Zealand's post-World War II ANZUS defense agreement with the U.S. and Australia. A Labour Party conference in September called for New Zealand to withdraw from ANZUS. The proposal had little chance of becoming government policy. Nevertheless, Lange sought to minimize any danger to relations during a visit to the U.S. to address the UN General Assembly later that month.

On November 29 Sir Robert was replaced as leader of the National Party by Jim McLay, who had been deputy leader, but said he planned to remain in Parliament. The party did nothing in the months after defeat to heal the rift with the breakaway New Zealand Party.   (JOHN A. KELLEHER)

See also *Dependent States,* below.

PACIFIC ISLAND STATES

FIJI

> A parliamentary state and member of the Commonwealth, Fiji occupies an island group in the South Pacific Ocean. Area: 18,273 sq km (7,055 sq mi). Pop. (1984 est.): 686,000. Cap.: Suva. Monetary unit: Fiji dollar, with (Oct. 29, 1984) a free rate of F$1.12 to U.S. $1 (F$1.35 = £1 sterling). Queen, Elizabeth II; governor-general in 1984, Ratu Sir Penaia Ganilau; prime minister, Ratu Sir Kamisese Mara.

In December 1983 Jai Ram Reddy, leader of the opposition, led a parliamentary walkout of his supporters after a dispute over the speaker's rulings. After Reddy subsequently resigned from Parliament, Siddiq Koya, his predecessor, returned to the opposition leadership and ended the boycott in May 1984. During a Cabinet reshuffle in January, Charles Walker, who had previously resigned as minister of finance, was reinstated as minister for primary industry.

Because of cyclones in 1982 and drought in 1983, sugarcane production in Fiji was halved in the 1983–84 season. There were hopes that the completion of the Monasavu hydroelectricity dam would allow petroleum imports to be cut in future years. Japan announced plans to conduct a fisheries survey in Fiji's exclusive economic zone.

In May Fiji was host to the African, Caribbean, and Pacific signatories to the Lomé Convention in their aid negotiations with the European Communities. The third Pacific Trade Union Conference, held in Suva in October, demanded a nuclear-free Pacific and independence for

New Caledonia. The meeting was attended by Soviet observers. In April Fiji established diplomatic relations with the U.S.S.R. but continued to refuse permission for a Soviet embassy.   (BARRIE MACDONALD)

This article updates the *Macropædia* article PACIFIC ISLANDS: *Fiji.*

KIRIBATI

> A republic in the western Pacific Ocean and member of the Commonwealth, Kiribati comprises the former Gilbert Islands, Banaba (Ocean Island), the Line Islands, and the Phoenix Islands. Area: 717 sq km (277 sq mi). Pop. (1984 est.): 62,000. Cap.: Bairiki. Monetary unit: Australian dollar, with (Oct. 29, 1984) a free rate of $A1.19 to U.S. $1 ($A1.44 = £1 sterling). President *(berititenti)* in 1984, Ieremia Tabai.

There was continuing concern about Kiribati's lack of economic resources and its dependence on aid during 1984. The best prospect for improvement lay in developing the fishing industry. License fees for Japanese vessels operating in the Kiribati exclusive economic zone increased by 50% to $A1.5 million in 1984. At the same time, Japan was providing aid for Kiribati's own fishing fleet and conducting a survey of tuna resources. In August Kiribati's study of economic development strategies for small island states was a major subject of discussion at the South Pacific Forum meeting in Tuvalu. Speaking at the Commonwealth heads of government meeting in India in November 1983, Pres. Ieremia Tabai stressed that even small, remote, and peaceful island states felt vulnerable in a troubled world in which large and powerful countries were subduing the small and weak. During the year diplomatic relations were formalized with Nauru, Tuvalu, and Tonga.

Steps were taken toward establishing a national bank in partnership with Westpac, formerly the Bank of New South Wales. An urban sewerage scheme on Tarawa, initiated after an outbreak of cholera there in 1977, was completed with assistance from Australia. An Australian government report on aid to third world countries recommended some migration from Kiribati to relieve population pressure in the islands.   (BARRIE MACDONALD)

This article updates the *Macropædia* article PACIFIC ISLANDS: *Kiribati.*

NAURU

> An island republic within the Commonwealth, Nauru lies in the Pacific Ocean about 1,900 km (1,200 mi) east of New Guinea. Area: 21 sq km (8 sq mi). Pop. (1984 est.): 8,000. Cap.: Yaren. Monetary unit: Australian dollar, with (Oct. 29, 1984) a free rate of $A1.19 to U.S. $1 ($A1.44 = £1 sterling). President in 1984, Hammer DeRoburt.

After general elections held in Nauru on Dec. 3, 1983, the new Parliament reelected Hammer DeRoburt as president by ten votes to six with two abstentions. DeRoburt, who also held the portfolios of external and internal affairs, civil aviation, public service, and island development and industry, introduced his own brand of consensus politics by including three former opponents in his Cabinet: Kenas Aroi retained the portfolio of finance and Lawrence Stephen that of health and education, while Bernard Dowiyogo, who had briefly replaced DeRoburt as president in 1976–78, was appointed to the Justice Ministry. The fifth member of the Cabinet was Buraro Detudamo, minister of works and community services and minister assisting the president.

Following the elections there was a heated debate be-

Tumultuous enthusiasm greeted Pope John Paul II when he arrived in Papua New Guinea in May. He is shown here in Port Moresby, the capital.

FRANCOIS LOCHON—GAMMA/LIAISON

tween critics of DeRoburt, many of them expatriates, who argued that he had too much influence, and those who maintained that he had secured the maximum possible benefit for his people from the tiny island's natural resources. Much of the discussion was on a personal level, taking in the president's ability as a musician as well as his right to direct Nauru's destiny.   (A. R. G. GRIFFITHS)

This article updates the *Micropædia* article NAURU.

PAPUA NEW GUINEA

A parliamentary state and member of the Commonwealth, Papua New Guinea is situated in the southwestern Pacific Ocean and comprises the eastern part of the island of New Guinea, the islands of the Bismarck, Trobriand, Woodlark, Louisiade, and D'Entrecasteaux groups, and parts of the Solomon Islands, including Bougainville. Area: 462,840 sq km (178,704 sq mi). Pop. (1984 est.): 3,228,000. Cap.: Port Moresby. Monetary unit: kina, with (Oct. 29, 1984) a free rate of 0.93 kina to U.S. $1 (1.12 kinas = £1 sterling). Queen, Elizabeth II; governor-general in 1984, Sir Kingsford Dibela; prime minister, Michael Somare.

Papua New Guinea continued to have diplomatic brushes with Indonesia during 1984. The most serious complaint followed an incident in March, when two Indonesian jet fighters strayed into Papua New Guinea's airspace. The government considered the incursion "a flagrant violation of its territorial sovereignty and a serious breach of international law." On the land border with Indonesia, clashes between the Indonesian Army and the Free West Papua Movement in Irian Jaya (West New Guinea) caused a refugee exodus into Papua New Guinea. The government had difficulty administering relief to the refugees, and tragic scenes of starvation, disease, and death in the refugee camps attracted international attention. In October the two governments signed a new border agreement that included arrangements for the safe passage of refugees wishing to return to Indonesia.

Pope John Paul II visited Papua New Guinea in May, greeting the people in their own language before being welcomed with a traditional dance. Describing Papua New Guinea as a young and vigorously developing country, he noted that the zealous efforts and personal sacrifices of missionaries there were known throughout the world. In August the prince of Wales opened the new Parliament House at a ceremony attended by leaders from more than 20 Asian and Pacific countries. The building, a gift from Australia, cost $30 million.   (A. R. G. GRIFFITHS)

This article updates the *Macropædia* article EAST INDIES: *Papua New Guinea.*

SOLOMON ISLANDS

A parliamentary state and member of the Commonwealth, the Solomon Islands comprises a 1,450-km (900-mi) chain of islands and atolls in the western Pacific Ocean. Area: 27,556 sq km (10,640 sq mi). Pop. (1984 est.): 259,000. Cap.: Honiara. Monetary unit: Solomon Islands dollar, with (Oct. 29, 1984) a free rate of SI$1.31 to U.S. $1 (SI$1.58 = £1 sterling). Queen, Elizabeth II; governor-general in 1984, Baddeley Devesi; prime ministers, Solomon Mamaloni and, from November 19, Sir Peter Kenilorea.

In general elections held in the Solomon Islands on Oct. 24, 1984, all 38 members of Parliament lost their seats. Sir Peter Kenilorea became prime minister of a coalition government consisting of his own United Party, a new group, the Solomone Ano Sagufenua, and four independents. (For tabulated results, see *Political Parties,* above.)

The future constitutional status of the country was earlier called into question when Prime Minister Solomon Mamaloni's government investigated the possibility of replacing Queen Elizabeth II as chief of state by an elected president.

In midyear the government seized a U.S. fishing vessel and fined its master. The incident provoked a ban on imports of fish from the Solomons to the U.S., which refused to acknowledge any government's proprietary claim over highly migratory species of tuna. A proposal to establish diplomatic relations at the consular level with Taiwan jeopardized plans to exchange ambassadors with China. The government announced that foreign powers would have to declare in writing that their ships and aircraft were neither nuclear armed nor nuclear powered before they would be allowed to enter the country or its territorial waters.

Pope John Paul II paid a one-day visit to the islands in May during a Pacific tour.   (BARRIE MACDONALD)

This article updates the *Macropædia* article PACIFIC ISLANDS: *Solomon Islands.*

TONGA

A monarchy and member of the Commonwealth, Tonga is an island group in the Pacific Ocean east of Fiji. Area: 747 sq km (288 sq mi). Pop. (1984 est.): 106,000. Cap.: Nukualofa. Monetary unit: pa'anga, with (Oct. 29, 1984) a free rate of 1.19 pa'anga to U.S. $1 (1.44 pa'anga = £1 sterling). King, Taufa'ahau Tupou IV; prime minister in 1984, Prince Fatafehi Tu'ipelehake.

In 1984 Tonga's economy continued to make only a slow recovery from the cyclone devastation suffered in 1982. Foreign reserves were boosted by increased remittances from Tongans overseas and also by foreign aid, but there were few signs of growth, and urban unemployment was in excess of 20%. In attempts to attract tourists, customs duties were abolished on a wide range of goods, and a major wharf extension that would allow cruise liners to berth at Nukualofa was planned.

Despite evidence that similar institutions in Western Samoa, Kiribati, and Tuvalu were having difficulty in placing their graduates, Tonga proceeded with plans to establish a training school for merchant seamen with West German assistance. After a visit to Southeast Asia and Europe by King Taufa'ahau Tupou IV, it was announced that a new interisland ship was to be built in West Germany. Japan was to undertake a survey of seabed minerals in Tonga's exclusive economic zone.

In August a group of about 80 Tongans who were supposedly attending the Olympic Games in Los Angeles were held by immigration authorities in the U.S. The tour organizer was later charged with conspiring to introduce illegal aliens into the U.S. (BARRIE MACDONALD)

This article updates the *Macropædia* article PACIFIC ISLANDS: *Tonga.*

TUVALU

A constitutional monarchy within the Commonwealth, Tuvalu comprises nine main islands and their associated islets and reefs in the western Pacific Ocean. Area: 24 sq km (9 sq mi). Pop. (1984 est.): 8,500. Cap.: Funafuti. Monetary unit: Australian dollar, with (Oct. 29, 1984) a free rate of $A1.19 to U.S. $1 ($A1.44 = £1 sterling). Queen, Elizabeth II; governor-general in 1984, Fiatau Penitala Teo; prime minister, Tomasi Puapua.

A major political wound was healed in 1984 when Tuvalu's $A500,000 investment with a U.S. property speculator, Sidney Gross, was returned. The question of the safety of the financial venture, entered into by then prime minister Toaripi Lauti in 1979, had been politically divisive. The Tuvalu Church was also reimbursed for its share in a property speculation in Texas organized through an associate of Gross; the land had been bought in the hope that it would lead to immigration opportunities.

Parliament approved legislation to establish a 200-mi exclusive economic zone, thus formalizing controls that had operated since independence. Agreements granting fishing rights to Taiwanese and South Korean vessels within the zone were renewed. It was also announced that Japan would finance and conduct a survey of Tuvalu's fisheries resources.

In August Tuvalu was host to a meeting of the 14 members of the South Pacific Forum. The Forum considered development strategies for small states and agreed to work toward a treaty establishing a nuclear-free zone in the South Pacific. France was urged to accelerate the processes by which New Caledonia was moving toward independence. The meeting also condemned illegal fishing

by U.S. vessels and the U.S. refusal to recognize controls on highly migratory species of fish. (BARRIE MACDONALD)

This article updates the *Macropædia* article PACIFIC ISLANDS: *Tuvalu.*

VANUATU

The republic of Vanuatu, a member of the Commonwealth, comprises 12 main islands and some 60 smaller ones in the southwestern Pacific Ocean. Area: 12,190 sq km (4,707 sq mi). Pop. (1984 est.): 130,700. Cap.: Vila. Monetary unit: vatu, with (Oct. 29, 1984) a free rate of 98.55 vatu to U.S. $1 (118.95 vatu = £1 sterling). President in 1984, George Sokomanu; prime minister, the Rev. Walter Lini.

After elections held in Vanuatu in November 1983, in which the Vanuaaku Party was returned with a reduced majority, it emerged during 1984 that there was some substance to claims that U.S. and perhaps French business interests opposed to the government of Prime Minister Walter Lini had helped to finance the election campaign of his rivals. Pres. George Sokomanu resigned from office in February after being convicted of failing to pay road taxes, but he was reelected for another five-year term by the electoral college the following month.

In March the U.K. agreed to contribute 142 million vatu toward a government fund that was to be used to compensate for damages caused during the rebellion on the island of Santo at the time of independence in 1980. The government was awaiting a response to its request that France provide a similar amount.

At the South Pacific Forum and elsewhere, Prime Minister Lini continued to advocate the setting up of a nuclear-free zone in the Pacific and to be the most forthright among Pacific leaders in calling on France to grant early independence to New Caledonia. In August the Asian Development Bank established its regional office in Vanuatu. Links with China were expanded during the year.

(BARRIE MACDONALD)

This article updates the *Macropædia* article PACIFIC ISLANDS: *Vanuatu.*

WESTERN SAMOA

A constitutional monarchy and member of the Commonwealth, Western Samoa occupies an island group in the South Pacific Ocean. Area: 2,831 sq km (1,093 sq mi). Pop. (1984 est.): 161,000. Cap.: Apia. Monetary unit: tala, with (Oct. 29, 1984) a free rate of 2.14 tala to U.S. $1 (2.58 tala = £1 sterling). Head of state (*O .le Ao o le Malo*) in 1984. Malietoa Tanumafili II; prime minister, Tofilau Eti.

Western Samoa continued to face serious economic difficulties during 1984. Almost half of the financing for a record budget came from foreign aid and loans. Australia, New Zealand, and Japan were the major donors. Inflation was constant at an annual rate of 20%. Over the year Western Samoa devalued its currency three times for a total devaluation of 18%. The government tried to increase revenue from import duties but was forced to abandon its plans to impose a 20% tax on Bibles and educational materials.

There was renewed controversy over higher education. Western Samoa announced its intention to withdraw from the agreement under which the agricultural college at Alafua was shared with the University of the South Pacific, based at Suva, Fiji. Instead, Western Samoa opted to use the facility as the basis for its own national university. The plan was opposed by the country's teachers.

Work began on extending the runways at the international airport at Faleolo. Australia was providing assistance for the project, which would permit larger aircraft to use the airport and thus promote tourism.

(BARRIE MACDONALD)

This article updates the *Macropædia* article PACIFIC ISLANDS: *Samoa*.

Dependent States

Although no dependent state achieved full independence during 1984, there were significant moves toward increased autonomy in several states, while developments in southern Africa held promise of a resolution of the conflict in South West Africa/Namibia. The future of Gibraltar and Hong Kong was the subject of active negotiations by the U.K. government with Spain and China, respectively.

Europe and the Atlantic. In elections held in Gibraltar on Jan. 26, 1984, the ruling Gibraltar Labour Party-Association for the Advancement of Civil Rights (GLP-AACR) retained its 8 seats in the 15-member House of Assembly. The elections were notable for the demise of the Democratic Party for British Gibraltar, which lost all six of its seats. The Gibraltar Socialist Labour Party won the remaining seven seats. Sir Joshua Hassan, leader of the GLP-AACR, was returned for his fourth term as chief officer.

During the year the British and Spanish governments moved closer to resolving their dispute over the future of Gibraltar, which had led Spain to close its border with Gibraltar in 1969. The process of implementing the 1980 Lisbon Declaration, under which the Spanish government agreed to lift border restrictions on condition that the U.K. agree to discuss Spanish proposals for the future of the colony, had been at a standstill, apart from Spain's reopening of the border to pedestrian traffic in 1982. However, the proposed accession of Spain to the European Communities (EC) by January 1986 brought a new impetus to discussions. In November 1984 the two governments agreed to implement the Lisbon Declaration by Feb. 15, 1985. While reiterating its pledge to honour the wishes of Gibraltarians, the U.K. for the first time agreed to discuss the question of its sovereignty over Gibraltar, which Spain disputed.

Greenland and the EC agreed on the terms by which Greenland was to withdraw from the EC by Jan. 1, 1985. Greenland was to be accorded Overseas Countries and Territories status by the EC, allowing its fisheries products duty-free access to EC markets, while EC fishing fleets were to be granted fishing rights in Greenland's territorial waters. However, the parliaments of several EC member states failed to ratify the agreement by the end of the year, so the date for withdrawal had to be postponed. Although Greenland's Landsting (parliament) approved the terms by 24 votes to 2 on March 10, the vote divided the ruling coalition of the Siumut (Forward Party) and the Inuit Ataqatigiit (Eskimo Movement). The latter voted against the terms because it favoured a complete break with the EC, as well as with Denmark. As a result, fresh elections were held on June 6. In the new Landsting the support of both the Siumut and the opposition Atassut (Unity Party) fell from 12 to 11 seats. The Inuit Ataqatigiit, with three seats, retained the balance of power and again chose to form a coalition with the Siumut.

In July officials of the U.K. and Argentina met in Bern, Switz., to discuss restoring trade, transport, and diplomatic relations, broken off after their conflict over the Falkland Islands/Islas Malvinas in 1982. However, the talks broke down after a day because the U.K. refused to discuss the issue of its sovereignty over the islands, which Argentina disputed. In December a British all-party House of Commons Foreign Affairs Select Committee published its report on the Falkland Islands. The report claimed that "the historical and legal evidence demonstrates such areas of uncertainty that we are unable to reach a categorical conclusion on the legal validity of the historical claims of either country [to the islands]." The report conceded that the U.K. would have to seek some sort of accommodation with Argentina, not only in view of the cost to the U.K. of its "Fortress Falklands" policy but also in order to guarantee the long-term economic prospects of the islanders themselves.

On August 3 Francis Baker succeeded John Massingham as governor of St. Helena. In April Prince Andrew attended the island's celebrations of 150 years as a British colony.

Caribbean. A snap election in Anguilla on March 9 brought the Anguilla National Alliance (ANA), led by Emile Gumbs, to power, defeating the incumbent Anguilla People's Party (APP), led by Ronald Webster. The ANA won four of the seven seats in the House of Assembly. Webster, who lost his seat, subsequently resigned as party leader. In September a visiting team from the UN Decolonization Committee held discussions with the islanders, a majority of whom stated that they did not want independence but wanted more development aid from the U.K. In

A toast to Hong Kong—British now, Chinese after 1997—was drunk by Sir Richard Evans (left), the British ambassador to China, and two members of the Chinese delegation. Evans and Chinese Deputy Foreign Minister Zhou Nan had just initialed a joint declaration on the reversion of the British crown colony to China's control after the expiration of Britain's 99-year lease.

Montserrat Chief Minister John Osborne said in a speech in June that it was time for the islanders to start thinking seriously about managing their own affairs. However, he added that he was thinking at least two years ahead. Plans to establish a casino as part of a resort development at Little Bay aroused considerable controversy. In September opposition leader Austin Bramble and his brother Howell were arrested in Florida for allegedly attempting to steal evidence relating to a lawsuit involving two competitors for the casino contract.

The Bermuda central bank warned in July that the island could face a "very real" balance of payments problem unless sharply rising salaries were matched by productivity increases. The bank estimated Bermuda's gross domestic product at $845 million, or $14,800 per capita, one of the highest in the world. Elections in the Turks and Caicos Islands on May 29 returned the Progressive National Party (PNP) to power. The PNP won eight seats to three for the opposition People's Democratic Movement. A $40 million tourist complex was to be built on Providenciales Island, with finance from Dubai. The Cayman Islands government agreed in September to hand over financial documents to U.S. narcotics investigators, and a wider law enforcement treaty was to be negotiated.

In the French overseas départements of Guadeloupe, Martinique, and French Guiana, a bombing campaign took place between April and July. Targets included police stations, public buildings, shops, and recreational facilities. The most serious incident occurred on July 24 in Guadeloupe, when four men were killed. The victims, members of the pro-independence Union Populaire pour la Libération de la Guadeloupe, appeared to have died while transporting bombs.

Dom Martina, premier of the Netherlands Antilles, resigned in September after losing his parliamentary majority. He was succeeded on September 18 by Maria Liberia-Peters, a Social Christian and the islands' first woman premier. In November Exxon announced that its oil refinery on Aruba, the island's economic mainstay, would close at the end of 1984. It had incurred losses for the year estimated at $55 million–$60 million.

In elections held on November 6 in Puerto Rico, Gov. Carlos Romero Barceló, representing the pro-statehood New Progressive Party, lost to Rafael Hernández Colón of the Popular Democratic Party, which also captured two-thirds of the seats in both houses of the Legislative Assembly. Romero, who had been governor for eight years, was accused shortly before the election of concealing the truth about the police killing of two pro-independence activists in 1978.

Africa. During 1984 some progress was made toward bringing about independence in South West Africa/Namibia. The year began with fierce fighting in southern Angola, across Namibia's northern border, as South African Defense Force (SADF) troops pursuing South West Africa People's Organization (SWAPO) guerrillas clashed with Angolan government troops. Angola and South Africa signed a cease-fire agreement in February in Lusaka, Zambia, under which South Africa agreed to carry out a phased withdrawal of its forces from southern Angola while the Angolan government undertook to curb SWAPO activities. Although implementation of the agreement progressed only slowly, the cease-fire nevertheless represented an essential first step toward securing a cessation of hostilities between the SADF and SWAPO itself. Representatives of both SWAPO and the South African government attended a conference on Namibian independence in Lusaka in May, but the meeting ended without a breakthrough.

In November Angolan Pres. José Eduardo dos Santos made an important concession when he publicly linked the withdrawal of Cuban troops from Angola with the Namibian independence process. In the past the South African government had insisted that the Cuban presence in Angola was the main obstacle in the way of its accepting UN Resolution 435, which set a schedule for achieving Namibian independence. The co-founder of SWAPO, Herman Toivo Ja Toivo (*see* BIOGRAPHIES), was released from prison by the South African authorities in March.

Morocco maintained its claim to the Western Sahara (formerly two Spanish territories), and in November it left the Organization of African Unity (OAU) in protest when the Saharan Arab Democratic Republic, Western Sahara's government-in-exile, occupied a seat at the OAU summit for the first time. Morocco extended its defensive wall in the Western Sahara during the year, while the Popular Front for the Liberation of Saguia el Hamra and Río de Oro (Polisario Front) continued its guerrilla attacks against the Moroccans. However, military support for the Polisario Front was seriously threatened when Libya, one of the Front's major backers, signed a treaty of unity with Morocco in August.

Indian Ocean. In Mayotte no date was set for a referendum to determine whether or not the inhabitants wished the island to remain a French dependency. The referendum was to have taken place by the end of 1984. Pres. Ahmed Abdallah of Comoros continued to press for reintegration of Mayotte into Comoros.

The UN supervised a referendum in the Cocos Islands on April 6 in which 231 islanders voted in favour of integration with Australia, compared with 30 who voted for free association or independence. Observers from the UN Committee on Decolonization criticized the Australian government for failing to inform islanders adequately of the choices facing them, given the high rate of illiteracy that existed in the islands. In October the High Court in Canberra ruled that the Australian government was not empowered to make a compulsory purchase of the remaining land on the islands belonging to John Clunies-Ross, the Cocos Islands' former owner.

Pacific. In an attempt to establish a working relationship with all factions in New Caledonia, Georges Lemoine, the French secretary of state for overseas départements and territories, announced an autonomy plan under which a new government was to be formed in 1984 and given greater powers of internal self-government for a five-year period. At the end of that time a referendum would decide the future political status of New Caledonia. Pro-independence groups rejected the scheme, formed a coalition Front de Libération Nationale Kanake et Socialiste, and in November established their own provisional government. In elections to the new Territorial Assembly on November 18, the main anti-independence group, the Rassemblement pour la Calédonie dans la République, won an absolute majority. Against a background of mounting violence between the Kanak (indigenous Melanesian) and the mainly French settler population, the French government announced that it would accelerate the process of self-determination and hold a referendum before 1986. However, the plan did not restore calm. In December ten members of a pro-independence group were killed by gunmen. Edgard Pisani was appointed special envoy to New Caledonia by the French government with a brief to prepare an outline settlement by early 1985.

In French Polynesia, French proposals for increased autonomy were accepted by the Territorial Assembly and implemented in September. Despite six cyclones in 1982–

Two U.S. diplomats were killed in an April bomb explosion in northern South West Africa/Namibia. They had been monitoring South African withdrawal of troops from Angola. The body of one of the diplomats is borne by South African soldiers in Johannesburg, South Africa.

AP/WIDE WORLD

83, French Polynesia, with special assistance from France, was able to restore its economy without resorting to drastic budgetary measures. After a visit in mid-May from Sir Thomas Davis, premier of the neighbouring Cook Islands, the two governments made plans to strengthen ties by holding biannual talks at both political and official levels.

In the Cook Islands, Premier Davis's majority was threatened by dissident elements within his own Democratic Party, which had returned to power in November 1983 after a brief period in opposition. Davis formed a coalition government in August with the opposition Cook Islands Party, whose leader, Geoffrey Henry, became deputy premier. In June the Cook Islands failed in its attempt to join the African, Caribbean, and Pacific group of signatories to the Lomé Convention, which established trade, aid, and development relations with the EC. In Niue, Sir Robert Rex, leader of the Niueans for 30 years, was again returned as premier. Niue's usual heavy dependence on aid was increased by continuing drought through 1983–84.

As part of its proposals for a new constitution presented in February, the government of American Samoa asked for citizenship to be defined by ancestry. The move would effectively have excluded any U.S. nationals not of American Samoan ancestry from holding political office in the territory. The proposal was withdrawn in the face of criticism from the U.S. Justice Department and from the U.S. Congress, which would have had to pass approving legislation. The new constitution also sought to protect customary political structures and systems of land tenure and to give the territory increased financial responsibility.

In the Trust Territory of the Pacific Islands, there was only slow and tortuous progress toward decolonization. Three of the four island groups—the Federated States of Micronesia, the Republic of Palau (Belau), and the Marshall Islands—were negotiating to become self-governing in free association with the U.S. The impasse over the incompatibility of Belau's "nonnuclear" constitution and U.S. military requirements continued. In September voters in a referendum endorsed a revised compact of free association by a majority of 66%; however, as had been the case in 1983, this was short of the 75% needed to revoke the ban on nuclear weapons. The draft compact of association between the U.S. and the Trust Territory governments was sent to Congress for approval by U.S. Pres. Ronald Reagan in February. However, progress was slowed by jurisdictional disagreements between congressional committees

and then by committee hearings. New findings suggested that the cost of rehabilitating Bikini Atoll, in the Marshall Islands group, the site of nuclear testing by the U.S. in the 1940s and 1950s, would total $50 million–$100 million. Plans for resettling Bikini Islanders on Maui, in Hawaii, were under consideration.

East Asia. On September 26 representatives of the U.K. and Chinese governments initialed a draft agreement providing for the future of Hong Kong after the U.K.'s lease on the New Territories, forming the bulk of Hong Kong's land mass, was due to expire in 1997. Under the agreement, Hong Kong was to become a special administrative region of China, and Hong Kong's "capitalist system and life-style" were to remain unchanged for 50 years after the lease expired. The U.K.-appointed governor was to be replaced by a chief executive, to be chosen through elections or local consultations and appointed by the Chinese government. While Hong Kong was to have autonomy in economic, financial, and monetary fields, China was to assume responsibility for defense and foreign affairs.

The draft, the result of two years of negotiations, was proclaimed by both sides as an object lesson in the peaceful settlement of differences. Advising the people of Hong Kong to accept the proposal, the British government pointed out that China was not prepared to reopen discussions, and their choice was therefore between reversion of Hong Kong to China under "legally binding international arrangements" or reversion to China without such arrangements. In Hong Kong itself reaction to the draft agreement was relatively calm. The Hong Kong Stock Exchange index recorded a modest fall, in contrast to the dramatic slumps that had occurred at intervals during the previous two years. U.K. Prime Minister Margaret Thatcher flew to China in December to sign the agreement, one week after Parliament approved it. China's National People's Congress was expected to ratify the accord by mid-1985.

In Macão new electoral laws were introduced to extend equal voting rights to all the territory's residents, some 97% of whom were Chinese. Previously, voting had been restricted mainly to the Macanese (of mixed Chinese and Portuguese descent), locally born Portuguese, and Portuguese-speaking Chinese. After the Macanese-dominated Legislative Assembly clashed with the governor, Adm. Vasco Almeida e Costa, over the new laws, the Assembly was dissolved and fresh elections took place in July and August. In the new 17-seat Assembly, made up of 6 directly elected, 6 indirectly elected, and 5 appointed deputies, there were 9 Chinese members.

(BARRIE MACDONALD; ROD PRINCE: LOUISE WATSON)

This article updates the *Macropædia* articles HONG KONG; INDIAN OCEAN ISLANDS; PACIFIC ISLANDS; SOUTHERN AFRICA: *South West Africa/Namibia;* The WEST INDIES.

Polar Regions

ANTARCTICA

Worldwide interest in Antarctica increased during 1983–84. In response to a Malaysian initiative in the UN on behalf of several third world countries, the General Assembly asked the secretary-general to prepare a comprehensive study on all aspects of Antarctica. This was the first time in the 38-year history of the UN that Antarctica had been a subject of discussion. During the year environmental groups such as Greenpeace and Friends of the Earth began to make Antarctica a special area of concern.

Discussions relating to the possible development of an international regime for the exploration and exploitation of Antarctic mineral resources continued during meetings in Bonn, West Germany, Washington, D.C., and Tokyo. Some press reports indicated that an agreement was near, but there was no official confirmation. The Antarctic Treaty nations took steps to broaden the dissemination of information by opening their consultative meetings to all nations that had acceded to the treaty and by releasing details of the discussions to the public. Within Antarctica, scientific research continued to be the purpose of national presences.

National Programs. ARGENTINA. Eight permanent bases continued to be operated, but Almirante Brown was destroyed by fire in April 1984. It had been used for 19 years. Basic research was carried on, especially in the earth and atmospheric sciences. A satellite dish antenna for telephone communications with the mainland was installed at Marambio Station on Seymour Island, and a second telecommunications link was planned for Esparanzo Station at Hope Bay.

AUSTRALIA. Research programs were continued at Casey, Mawson, and Davis bases. The government's failure to carry out an adequate research program was criticized by the Antarctic Research Policy Advisory Committee. Glaciologic traverses dominated fieldwork in the interior. One traverse, some 1,000 km (620 mi) from Casey, met a Soviet traverse en route to Vostok with the annual resupply.

BRAZIL. The Commander Ferraz summer research station (62° 05′ S, 58° 23′ W) was built on the Keller Peninsula, King George Island, in the South Shetlands, and occupied. Two ships made three scientific cruises in Antarctic waters, concentrating research on the second BIOMASS (Biological Investigational Marine Antarctic Systems and Stocks) experiment and upper atmosphere observations. Research in biology and geology was also conducted.

CHILE. Three permanent and four summer stations continued to be maintained. Plans were announced to develop a permanent colony on the Antarctic Peninsula; three children were expected to be born there during the 1984–85 winter.

FRANCE. Construction went forward on the permanent runway at Dumont d'Urville Station, despite protests from environmental groups. A more active research program was expected once the runway was completed.

INDIA. Dakshin Gangotri (72° S, 10° E), the permanent base built on the Princess Astrid Coast of Queen Maud Land, was manned by 12 scientists and technicians during the winter. A satellite link was used to maintain communications with India. Summer research programs were continued in glaciology, geology and geophysics, medicine, and microbiology.

JAPAN. The new icebreaking research ship "Shirase" brought the 25th Japanese Antarctic Research Expedition to Syowa Station. Glaciology dominated research in the interior. A traverse from Mizuho Station to the area southeast of Syowa was conducted. A temporary camp was built at the termination point; by 1988 it would become Japan's third permanent Antarctic base.

NEW ZEALAND. Major support resources were devoted to the building of a small base at Butter Point, New Harbour, for the long-term drilling program known as CIROS (Cenozoic Investigations in the Ross Sea). Sixteen scientific parties worked in the dry valleys, around Ross Island, and as far south as the Ohio Range. New Zealand was host to visiting scientists from China and Uruguay, both of which were expected to send expeditions to Antarctica in the near future.

POLAND. Arctowski, the station on King George Island, was maintained despite severe economic conditions at home. Small-scale biology programs made up the scientific effort.

SOUTH AFRICA. Fifteen men operated SANAE base during the 1984 winter.

UNITED KINGDOM. British Antarctic Survey scientists occupied the new Halley Station on the Brunt Ice Shelf in February 1984. Research in the earth sciences dominated the scientific program and included a cooperative effort with the U.S. between the Ellsworth and Thiel mountains. Biologists working in sub-Antarctic waters discovered high death rates among infant penguins, fur seals, and seabirds, presumably as a result of the disappearance of large swarms of krill, reported in early 1984.

UNITED STATES. Almost 300 scientists conducted 90 research projects, supported by 4 ships, 17 airplanes and helicopters, and almost 1,200 civilian and military support personnel. Major efforts were conducted in West Antarctica, including the start of a three-year program to determine the stability of the West Antarctic Ice Sheet. Mt. Siple, in Pine Island Bay, was visited for the first time; the visiting scientists determined that Mt. Siple is a large volcano and that existing maps had misplaced it by some 48 km (30 mi). McMurdo, Amundsen-Scott South Pole, and Palmer stations were operated over the winter, but Siple Station was closed for the winter season.

Researchers in the Allan Hills continued their success in collecting meteorites. Of the 364 recovered, one appeared to be a very rare carbonaceous chondrite type with an estimated age of 4.6 billion years. Geologically young marine fossils were found at high elevations in the Transantarctic Mountains, indicating that the East Antarctic Ice Sheet was much thicker as recently as two million years ago. In the Antarctic Peninsula area a multiuniversity team returned to Seymour Island to continue work in the rich fossil beds. After putting the research party ashore, the icebreaker "Westwind" was caught in the Larsen Ice Shelf but escaped being crushed when the winds changed. The wooden-hulled research vessel "Hero" was retired in favour of a leased Canadian-flag steel ship, "Polar Duke."

U.S.S.R. The Soviet Union continued the expansion of its Antarctic program by declaring its intent to build another winter-over station, this one on Berkner Island in the Ronne-Filchner Ice Shelf near the Weddell Sea. The site survey was conducted during the 1983–84 austral summer, with construction scheduled for 1984–85. The ice-core-

U.S. F-15 jet fighters patrol Arctic airspace in tight formation. The region had gained increasing strategic significance recently, especially since the shooting down of a South Korean commercial airliner in September 1983.

LARRY DOWNING—WOODFIN CAMP & ASSOCIATES

drilling program at Vostok continued, reaching a depth of 2,083 m (6,832 ft). The goal was to reach bedrock at about 3,700 m (12,000 ft). On July 21, 1983, a new world record low temperature, −89.2° C (−128.6° F), was recorded at Vostok. Scientists from the summer Soyuz camp at Beaver Lake in the Prince Charles Mountains discovered that Radok Lake, at 346 m (1,135 ft), is the deepest known lake in Antarctica.

WEST GERMANY. Glaciologic research was concentrated on the Filchner Ice Shelf, and biological work was conducted from the ice-strengthened research ship "Polarstern." The permanent base at Atka Bay, Georg von Neumayer Station, was relieved, and glaciologic and photogrammetric work was continued.

OTHER NATIONS. Belgium and Norway did not send expeditions to Antarctica in 1983–84. China announced the formation of the China Institute on Polar Regions, to be located in Shanghai. An Antarctic meteorology group was established in Beijing (Peking), and an oceanography group was set up in Hangzhou (Hangchow). Chinese scientists continued to work with Australian, Chilean, New Zealand, and U.S. expeditions. East German scientists continued their work in Antarctica within the Soviet Antarctic Expedition.   (PETER J. ANDERSON)

ARCTIC REGIONS

Alaska. Oil, gas, and other resource developments dominated the news in 1984. In January the Shell Oil Co. announced that exploratory wells at its Seal Island site were yielding from 600 to 5,000 bbl a day of high-quality oil. The *Anchorage Daily News* described the find of an estimated 300 million bbl of recoverable crude as the biggest for Shell since the Cook Inlet discovery in the early 1960s. In February *Alaska* magazine reported that 17 oil companies were betting billions of dollars on a major oil discovery in the Beaufort Sea off Alaska's north coast. Rights to explore the Mukluk geologic structure—where the first well drilled turned up dry in December 1983—cost $1.6 billion and, if oil was found, development could cost an additional $15 billion. In the same month, the Yukon-Pacific Corp. announced it was applying for permits to construct a 1,320-km (820-mi) pipeline to carry North Slope natural gas to Fairbanks and then on to a liquefaction plant on the Kenai Peninsula. The cost of the project was estimated at over $14 billion.

Atlantic Richfield announced a $227 million program as

its share of an estimated $750 million project to enhance recovery of oil and natural gas liquids from the Prudhoe Bay field. The project represented the first major commercial use of the vast Prudhoe Bay natural gas reserves. *Alaska from the Inside* reported that construction was to begin during the year on a number of gravel islands in Prudhoe Bay off the Sagavanirktok River delta, in water up to 4.3 m (14 ft) deep. The islands would support facilities that were expected, in four years, to produce 100,000 bbl of oil per day from the Endicott Reservoir. In August a sale of oil and gas leases in the outer continental shelf of the Beaufort Sea between Barrow and the Canadian border brought $877,131,327. The high figure was taken as a sign of continuing strong interest in Arctic offshore exploration.

In July Pres. Ronald Reagan signed into law the Arctic Research and Policy Act of 1984. The act broadly defines the Arctic to include "all U.S. and foreign territory north of the Arctic Circle . . ." and extends the benefits of the act into the Arctic Ocean, the contiguous Beaufort, Bering, and Chukchi seas, and the Aleutian chain. Among the main purposes of the legislation were the establishment of national policies, priorities, and goals for the Arctic; provision of a federal program for basic and applied research in the area; and establishment of an Arctic Research Commission to promote Arctic research and recommend research policy.

During the year Alaska natives prepared once more to negotiate ownership of the land they lived on. Ten years earlier the Alaska Native Claims Settlement Act had established 13 regional corporations to manage a $962.5 million cash settlement, plus about 16 million ha (40 million ac) of land. The natives were made shareholders in the corporations but were prohibited from selling their stock until 1991. In 1984 fears were being expressed that the natives would lose control over their lands when the prohibition lapsed. A Department of the Interior report on the status of native claims indicated that natives had realized some gains in employment and education under the act but that the corporations had a long way to go in raising the standard of living.

Canada. After three years of study and public hearings, the federal Environmental Assessment Panel, reviewing Beaufort Sea oil and gas development, concluded that development could proceed provided it was phased in gradually, carried out on a small scale, and met certain terms and conditions. It was anticipated that the earliest date for commercial shipments of oil from the region would probably be 1988. In July Indian and Northern Affairs, Canada, announced plans for a thorough review of the Polar Gas Project, a consortium that had applied to construct a natural-gas pipeline from the Mackenzie Delta to Alberta. The application requested authorization for the $3.3 billion project by the end of 1985, with construction to begin in 1987.

The first barrel of crude oil to be shipped out of the Arctic Islands by tanker was unloaded in Montreal on September 12 by Panarctic Oils Ltd. The symbolic barrel, produced from Panarctic's 1976 West Bent Horn A-02 discovery well on Cameron Island, was transported to demonstrate the company's capacity to move large quantities of Arctic crude safely by ship. In 1985, pending government approval, the company planned to ship 100,-000 bbl of crude from Cameron Island. This would be the first commercial shipment of oil from the Canadian Arctic. In October *The Economist* reported that the discovery by Gulf Oil's Canadian subsidiary at its Amauligak J-44 well in the Beaufort Sea had raised industry speculation about a possible "Alaska-scale oil field" off Canada's Arctic coast. Preliminary tests indicated that the well would have a production capacity of 13,600 bbl a day and that the total reserves of the field could reach 400 million–500 million

COURTESY, OWEN BEATTIE, UNIVERSITY OF ALBERTA, EDMONTON

John Torrington, petty officer in the British Navy, died on an ill-fated Arctic expedition led by Sir John Franklin in search of the Northwest Passage in 1845. His grave was opened 138 years later, and his body was so well preserved in the permafrost of the tundra that it permitted a virtual autopsy on tissue samples and internal organs.

bbl. It was expected that an application to build production and transportation facilities would be submitted in 1985.

There was steady, if sometimes controversial, progress on the settlement of native land claims. Early in the year two settlements were proposed between the federal government and native groups in the Northwest Territories and the Yukon, under which the native people would receive multimillion-dollar settlements and ownership of thousands of acres of land in return for abandoning aboriginal rights to their larger, historic territories. The proposals generated heated controversy among native groups because they would "extinguish" some of the very rights the natives were seeking to have entrenched in the constitution.

At the end of March the federal Cabinet approved a final agreement with the Committee for Original Peoples Entitlement (COPE). The agreement, signed in June, affected 2,500 Inuvialuit in the Western Arctic. It provided a wide range of benefits and rights including $152 million in cash over 12 years, full surface and subsurface title to approximately 11,000 sq km (4,250 sq mi) of land, and title to a further 78,000 sq km (30,000 sq mi), excluding oil, gas, and mineral rights. The agreement also covered management of wildlife harvesting, economic measures, and Inuvialuit participation on advisory boards dealing with land-use and environmental planning. In April the Cabinet approved in principle an agreement to settle the claim of 5,500 Yukon Indians, living in 12 communities. After taking inflation into account, the cash payments to the Indians could reach $540 million during the 20 years covered by the agreement. In addition, the Indians would receive something over 20,000 sq km (7,700 sq mi) of land, including subsurface rights, and would be guaranteed a role in land-use planning, environmental assessment, and wildlife management and a share of hunting, trapping, and fishing opportunities.

The Soviet North. In April Canada and the Soviet Union signed an unprecedented agreement to cooperate on their common scientific interests in the Arctic. It committed the two countries to exchange knowledge and research information in four main areas: geoscience and petroleum, the environment, building construction, and native peoples. The Canadians were especially interested in the prospect of learning first-hand about the Soviet native peoples. Previously, the Soviets had been exceedingly reluctant to give foreigners access to the 26 ethnic groups of their far north.

After years of discussion, the Soviets announced plans to redraw the map of Eurasia by diverting water that normally flows north to the Barents Sea into the Volga River, for use in irrigating farmland in the steppes and desert to the south. The initial diversion, amounting to some 13,200,-000,000 litres (3,500,000,000 gal) a day, was expected to begin in 1990 and would irrigate 5.4 million ha (13 million ac). The diversion was not expected to affect the climate, but it had been criticized inside the U.S.S.R. because areas rich in ancient monuments and cultural heritage would be flooded.

In August it was reported that the U.S.S.R. had proposed a natural-gas pipeline from western Siberia to Eastern Europe. The pipeline was seen as a means of compensating the Soviet-bloc countries for expected declines in Soviet oil shipments. Late in the year, the Soviet news agency TASS reported completion of the last segment of track on the 3,200-km (2,000-mi) Baikal-Amur railway, designed to open up development of a 1,550,000-sq km (600,000-sq mi) region of southeastern Siberia. Years of work remained before the project would be fully operational.

(KENNETH DE LA BARRE)

This article updates the *Macropædia* article The ARCTIC.

Plate 1

Flags of the Nations

Afghanistan

Albania

Algeria

Andorra*

Angola

Antigua and Barbuda

Argentina*

Australia

Austria*

*State flag shown; national flag does not carry coat of arms.

Plate 2 Flags of the Nations

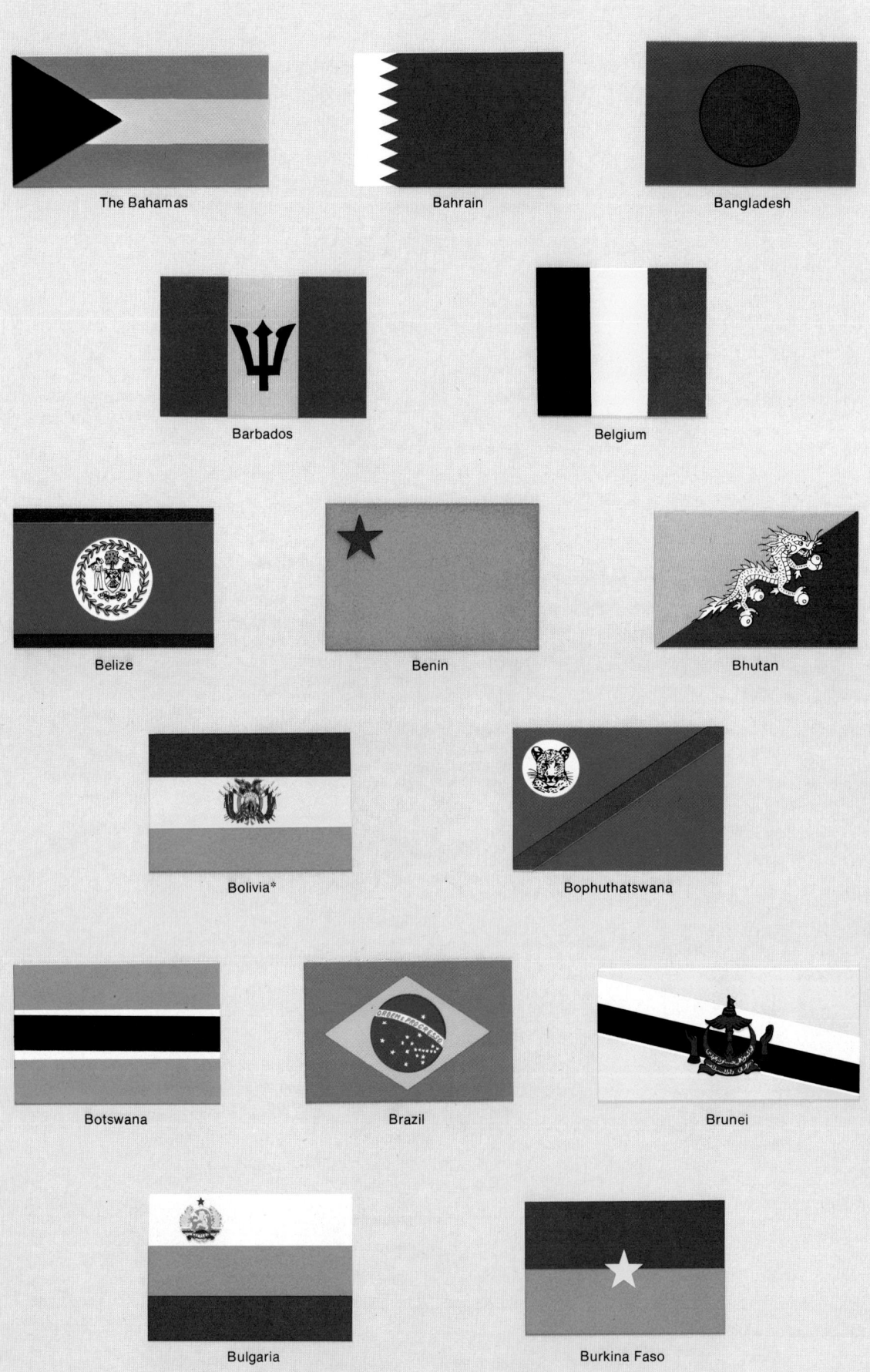

The Bahamas

Bahrain

Bangladesh

Barbados

Belgium

Belize

Benin

Bhutan

Bolivia*

Bophuthatswana

Botswana

Brazil

Brunei

Bulgaria

Burkina Faso

*State flag shown; national flag does not carry coat of arms.

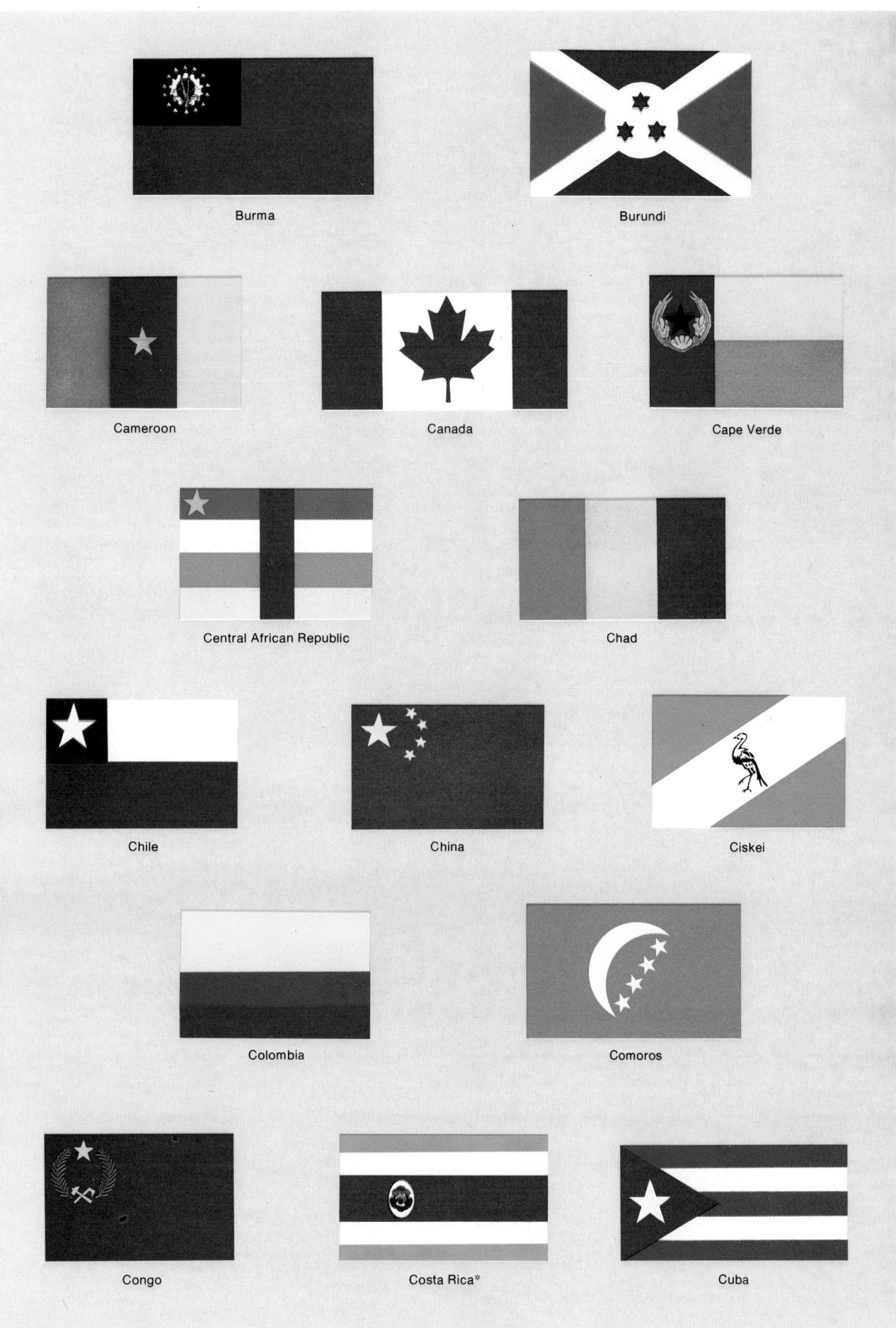

Burma

Burundi

Cameroon

Canada

Cape Verde

Central African Republic

Chad

Chile

China

Ciskei

Colombia

Comoros

Congo

Costa Rica*

Cuba

*State flag shown; national flag does not carry coat of arms.

Plate 4   Flags of the Nations

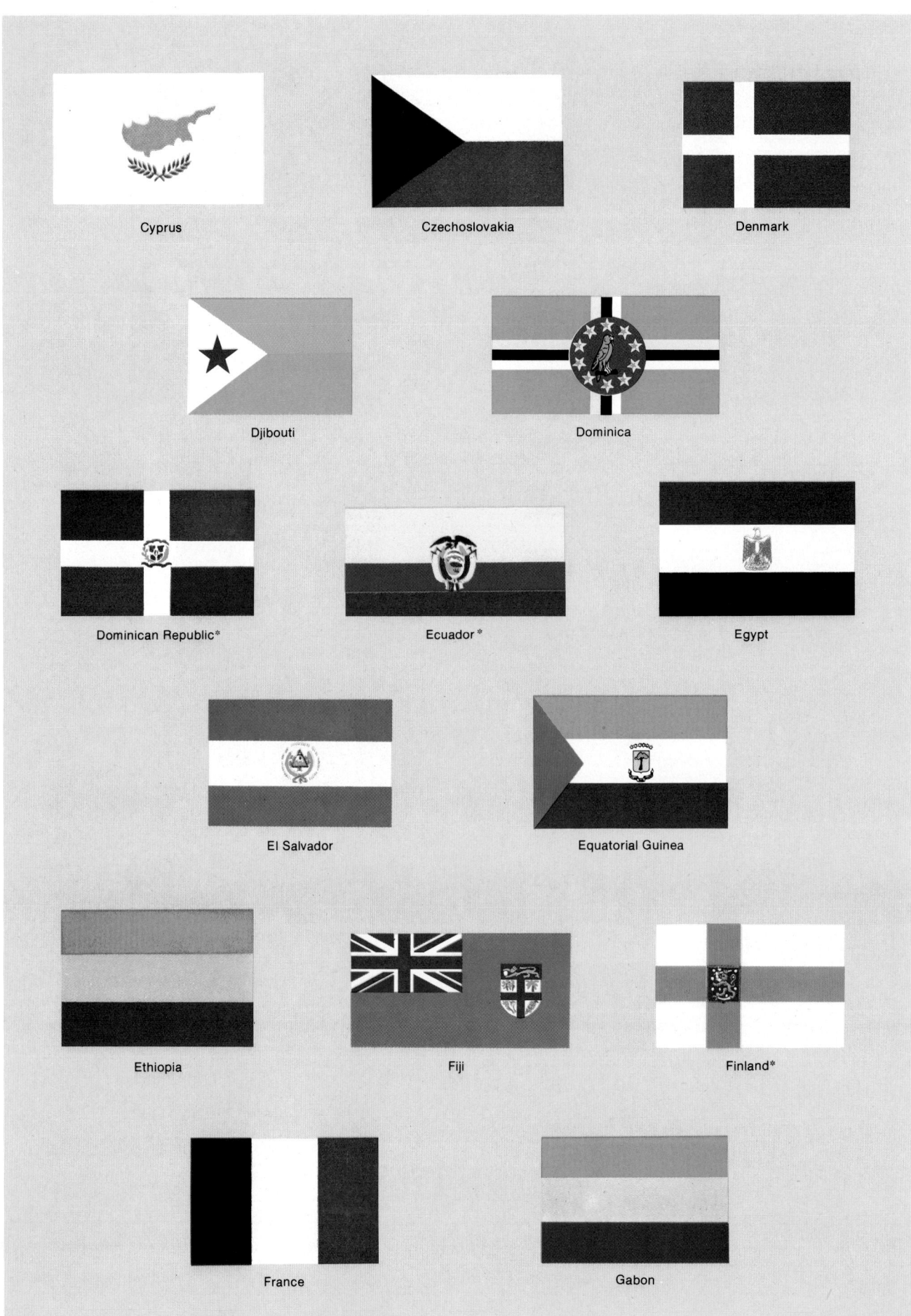

Cyprus

Czechoslovakia

Denmark

Djibouti

Dominica

Dominican Republic*

Ecuador *

Egypt

El Salvador

Equatorial Guinea

Ethiopia

Fiji

Finland*

France

Gabon

*State flag shown; national flag does not carry coat of arms.

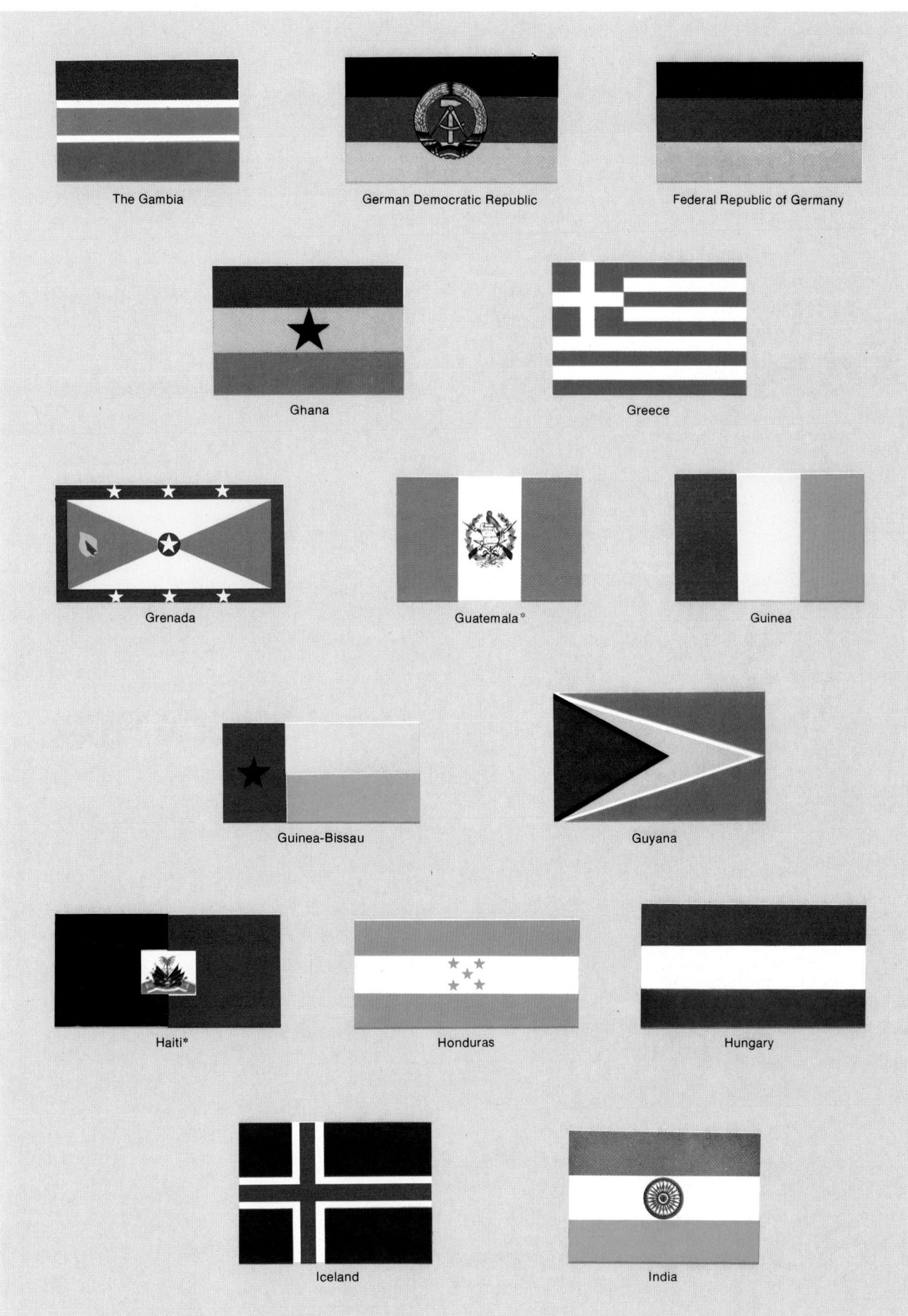

The Gambia

German Democratic Republic

Federal Republic of Germany

Ghana

Greece

Grenada

Guatemala*

Guinea

Guinea-Bissau

Guyana

Haiti*

Honduras

Hungary

Iceland

India

*State flag shown; national flag does not carry coat of arms.

Plate 6   Flags of the Nations

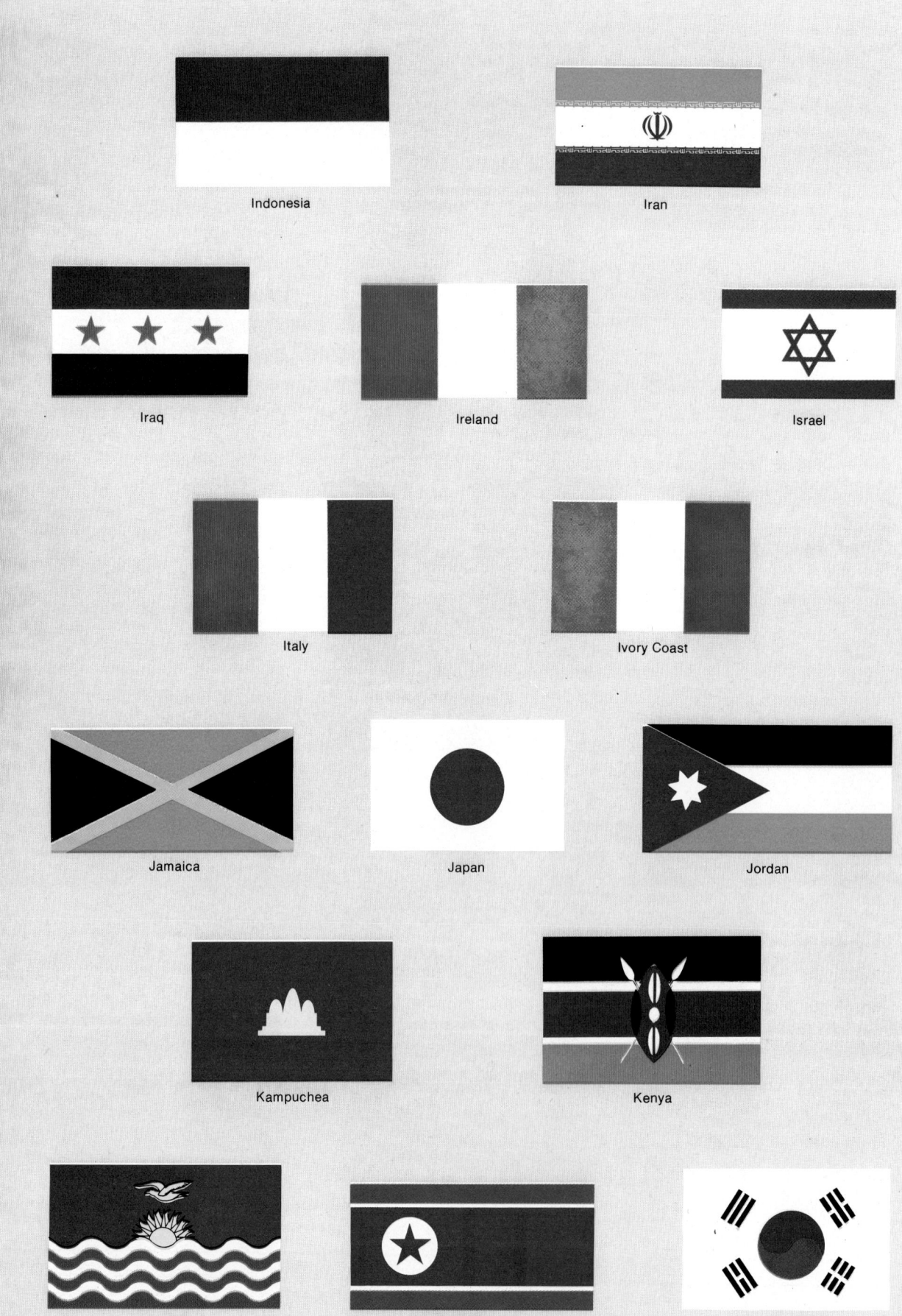

Indonesia

Iran

Iraq

Ireland

Israel

Italy

Ivory Coast

Jamaica

Japan

Jordan

Kampuchea

Kenya

Kiribati

North Korea

South Korea

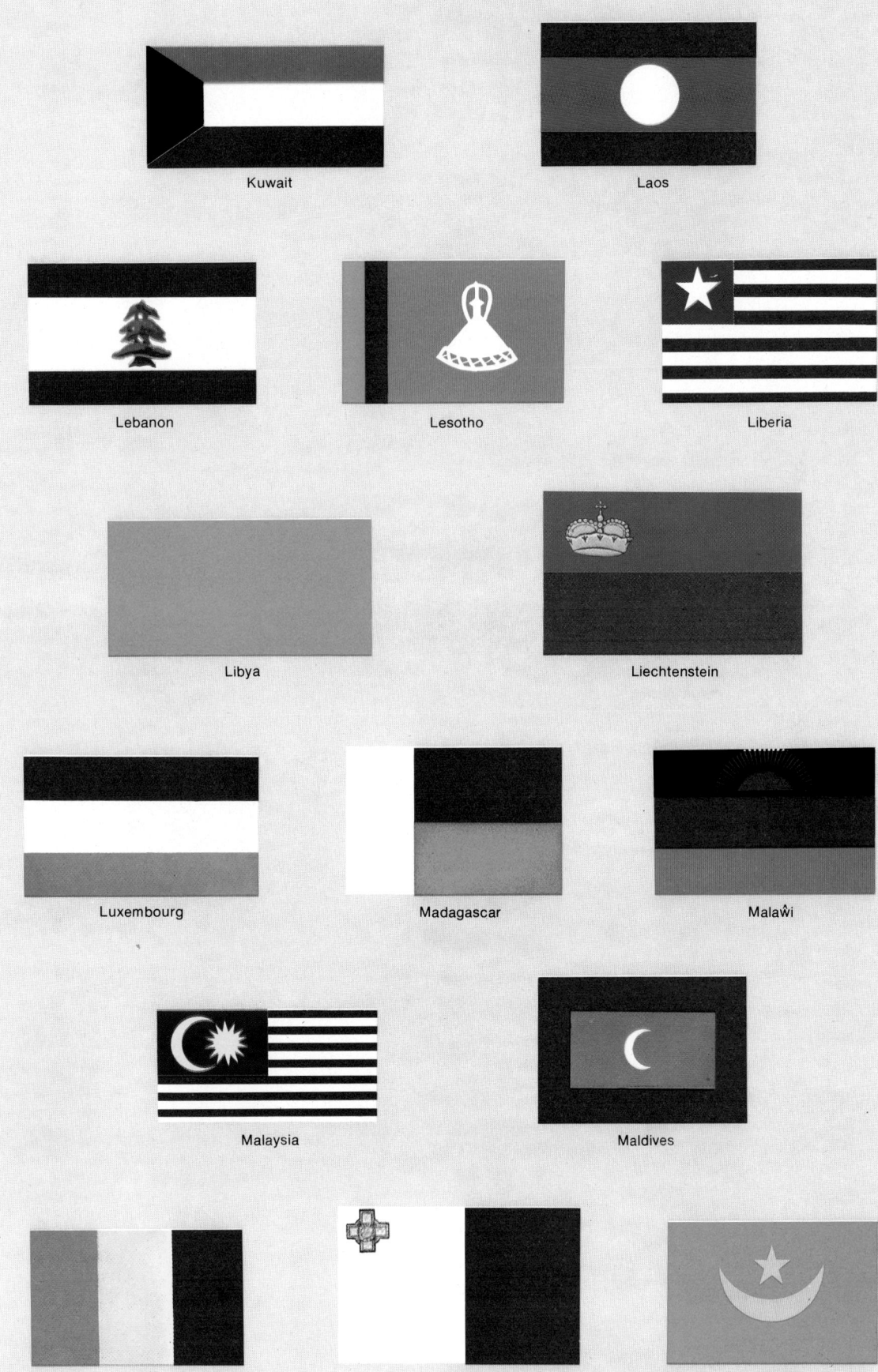

Kuwait

Laos

Lebanon

Lesotho

Liberia

Libya

Liechtenstein

Luxembourg

Madagascar

Malawi

Malaysia

Maldives

Mali

Malta

Mauritania

Plate 8   Flags of the Nations

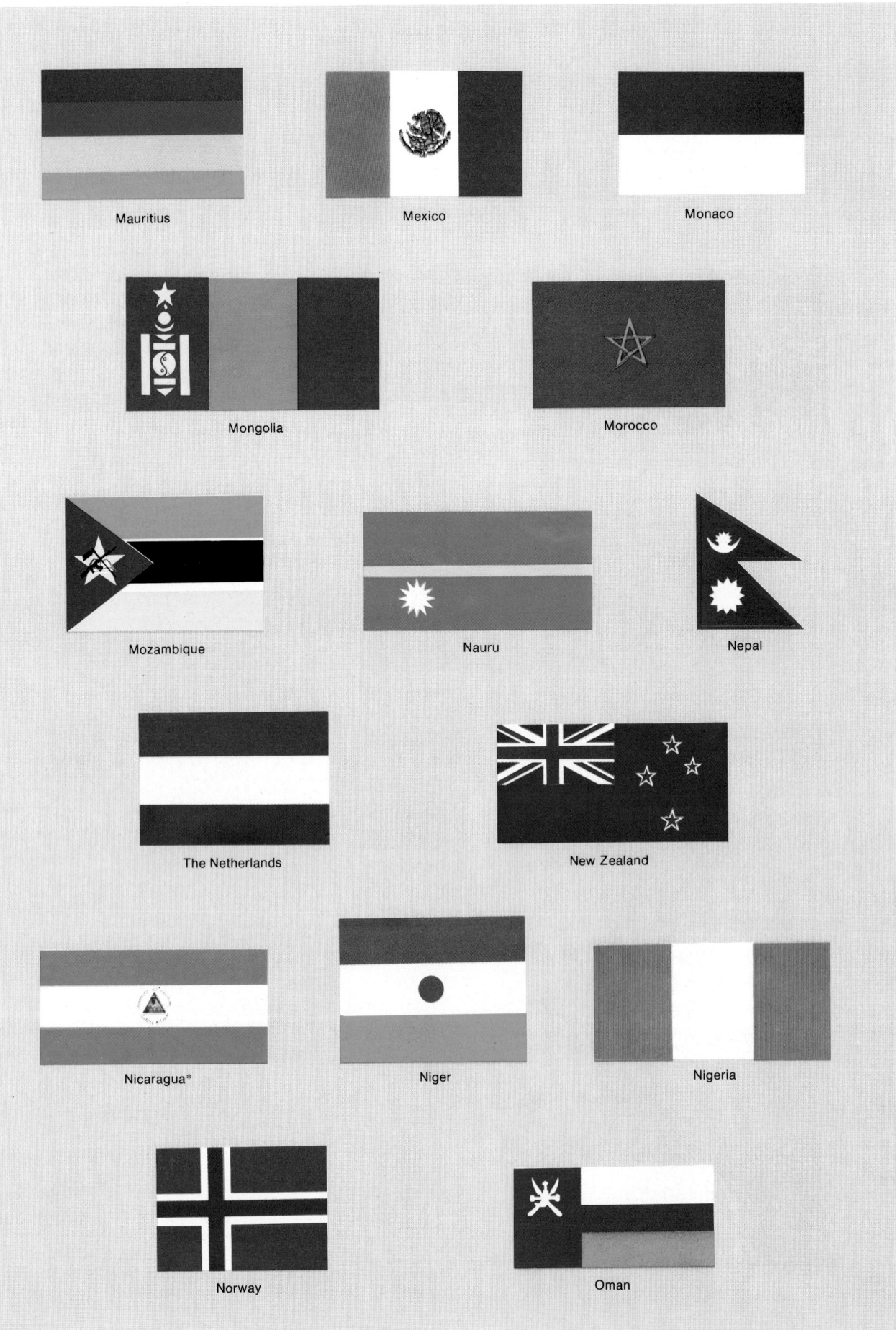

Mauritius

Mexico

Monaco

Mongolia

Morocco

Mozambique

Nauru

Nepal

The Netherlands

New Zealand

Nicaragua*

Niger

Nigeria

Norway

Oman

*State flag shown; national flag does not carry coat of arms.

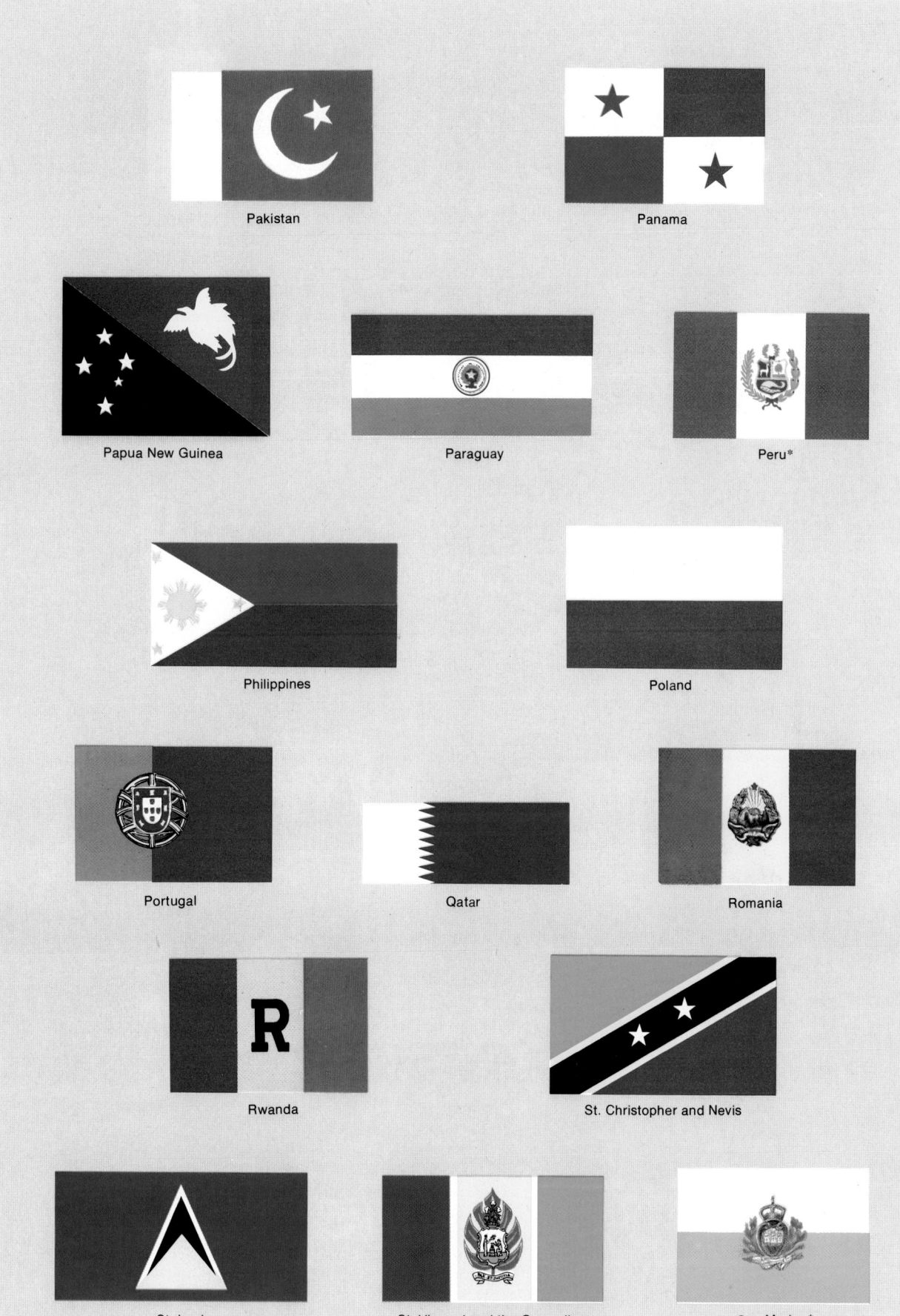

Pakistan

Panama

Papua New Guinea

Paraguay

Peru*

Philippines

Poland

Portugal

Qatar

Romania

Rwanda

St. Christopher and Nevis

St. Lucia

St. Vincent and the Grenadines

San Marino*

*State flag shown; national flag does not carry coat of arms.

Plate 10   Flags of the Nations

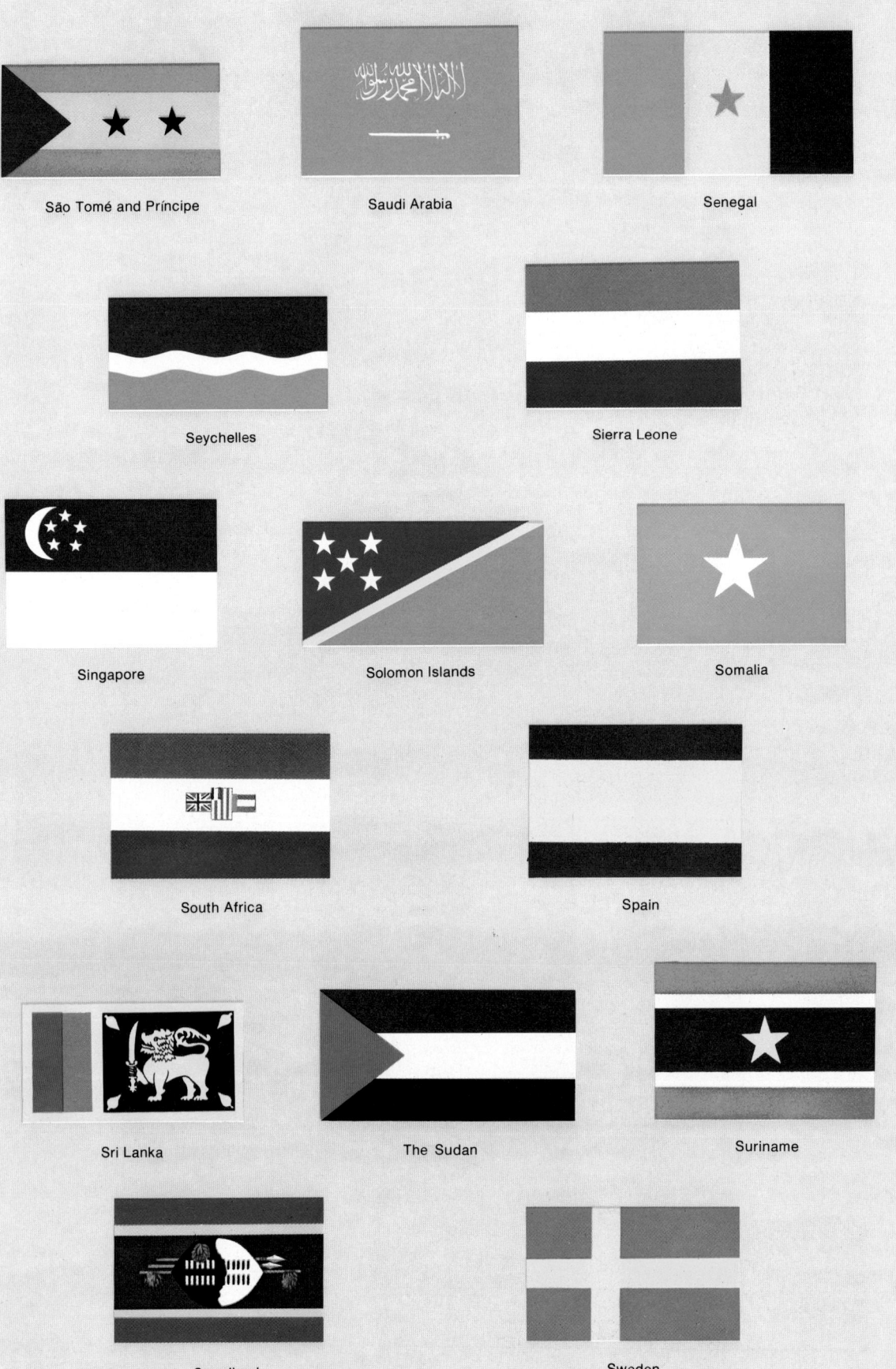

São Tomé and Príncipe

Saudi Arabia

Senegal

Seychelles

Sierra Leone

Singapore

Solomon Islands

Somalia

South Africa

Spain

Sri Lanka

The Sudan

Suriname

Swaziland

Sweden

Switzerland

Syria

Taiwan

Tanzania

Thailand

Togo

Tonga

Transkei

Trinidad and Tobago

Tunisia

Turkey

Tuvalu

Uganda

Union of Soviet Socialist Republics

United Arab Emirates

Plate 12 Flags of the Nations

United Kingdom

United States

Uruguay

Vanuatu

Vatican City

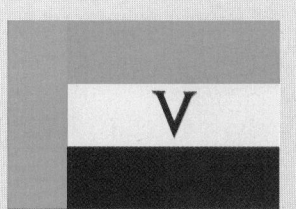

Venda

Venezuela*

Vietnam

Western Samoa

People's Democratic Republic of Yemen

Yemen Arab Republic

Yugoslavia

Zaire

Zambia

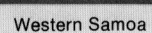

Zimbabwe

*State flag shown; national flag does not carry coat of arms.

1985
Britannica
World Data

Encyclopædia Britannica, Inc.

Chicago

Auckland/Geneva/London/Manila/Paris/Rome

Seoul/Sydney/Tokyo/Toronto

CONTENTS

621 The Nations of the World

819　Comparative National Statistics

INTRODUCTION

The third edition (1797) of the *Encyclopædia Britannica* introduced a new article on "Statistics." The article began by noting that statistics was a "word lately introduced to express a view or survey of any kingdom, county, or parish." The aggregation and analysis of numbers to describe states and their peoples, societies, and economies have not changed from that day to this, although the quantity and quality of data, and the sophistication of the analytical tools that can be brought to bear upon them, have improved by light-years. It may not have been the novelty of statistical description in 1797, however, that moved the editor of the first article on the subject to continue:

> If similar surveys (says the public-spirited editor of this work) were instituted in the other kingdoms of Europe, it might be the means of establishing, on sure foundations, the principles of that most important of all sciences, viz. political or statistical philosophy; that is, the science, which, in preference to every other, ought to be held in reverence. No science can furnish, to any mind capable of receiving useful information, so much real entertainment; none can yield such important hints, for the improvement of agriculture, for the extension of commercial industry, for regulating the conduct of individuals, or for extending the prosperity of the state; none can tend so much to promote the general happiness of the species.

W. H. Auden, on the other hand, says, "Thou shalt not sit with statisticians."

In the pages that follow, it will be evident that the compilers of this work not only sit but also sup with statisticians. And while we cannot realistically suppose that every user of the *Britannica World Data* will find "so much real entertainment" in the numbers as that public-spirited editor did, the reader will nevertheless find a body of up-to-date, internationally comparable data that define the place, fortune, and prospects of a people or country.

The *Britannica World Data* serves a number of purposes. The principal goal of its creation was to supplement the essentially subjective, impressionistic means that the authors of articles in the *Encyclopædia Britannica* must adopt to convey a sense of the enormously complex mosaic of event, circumstance, and historical process that characterizes any country. At the same time, it was intended to provide a more complete annual set of statistical portraits of the countries of the world than the previous design and format of the *Britannica Book of the Year* permitted.

Plan. The *Britannica World Data* is divided into two principal parts, the "Nations of the World" section, which comprises 197 pages of single-country statistical summaries, and the "Comparative National Statistics" section, in which comparative data for approximately 200 countries are arrayed in 23 six-page thematic tables. The country tables present the most significant statistical facts about each of the independent countries in the world and each dependency of more than 50,000 population—those, that is, large enough to have a well-developed civilian economy that can be discussed in the same terms as those of the older and larger countries. The topics covered in the country tables include political detail; the area, the population, and the capital of each first-order administrative subdivision; and the principal aggregates of demography and vital statistics, national economy, foreign trade, transportation and communication, education and health, and the military establishment. In the "Comparative National Statistics" section, these topics are developed in additional detail, with an emphasis on those aspects that best permit international comparisons.

Intent. Of the purposes referred to above for the creation of the *Britannica World Data*, the chief was to supplement articles in the *Encyclopædia Britannica* and the *Britannica Book of the Year* with a consistent set of up-to-date statistics on the major elements of each country's people, society, and economy. The need for this kind of supplement, particularly one that is updated annually, can be illustrated by a typical example: An article on a certain nation may contain the statement that "The principal crops are wheat, rice, and coffee." The statement seems clear and unambiguous, but it contains the potential for misunderstanding and for datedness the moment it is set to paper. The statement may mean simply that, in physical quantity, more wheat, rice, and coffee are produced than anything else. But perhaps, in context, the author actually meant that the value of these crops was greater: a ton of coffee is more valuable than a ton of wheat.

Whichever of these meanings was intended, the further question arises: for what period of time is this true? Was it for the latest year, a five-year average, the entire 20th century? And still further, these crops are "principal" from what perspective: the contribution they make to the net food supply of the country, to the country's balance of trade, to the efficient use of good land by large commercial landowners in preference to its inefficient use by smallholders, or to the absorption of excess manpower by relatively labour-intensive tasks when jobs cannot be created in the cities?

Timeliness is another problem, for even after the author looks away from the landscape to set a statement to paper, things continue to change: new crops supplant old, new industrial uses are found for food crops, a new export market is developed, new opportunities for jobs in the cities reduce the farm labour force and make concentration of landholdings and abandonment of labour-intensive crops a necessity. The author or editor of each article cannot explain all of this in the space available to him, but the *Britannica World Data* can at least track the major elements in this mosaic and assign values to them.

Use. The statistics in the *Britannica World Data* are compiled for what they *can* say about the subjects to which they refer, but the critical reader must also bear in mind the things the numbers *cannot* say. Researchers and editors habitually divide published sources of data into those that they consider ''primary'' and those that are ''secondary,'' and they prefer the primary on the ground that the data originate more closely to the subject (or, as is said in the case of a country, they are ''official'') and are thus thought to be more reliable. As a general principle, this trust is justified, but anyone who uses primary sources must also be aware of the limitations to which they are subject.

A national planning organization, for example, may mandate that production of wheat for year x is to be y. That quota begins as a set of assumptions: that since last year's production was z (often, in view of reporting procedures, a very shaky assumption) and that since productivity (output per unit area) of that crop (assuming some means exists to assess the planted area accurately) can continue at last year's level (weather permitting, and assuming sustained levels of input of fertilizer, machinery, manpower, etc., all often inadequately reported), area q must be planted this year to permit production of y. What then may happen is that the farmer finds that, because of excess rains and soggy ground, he can plant only three-fourths of his allotment of area q, and that, because his village's new tractor is still on the dock in the capital city, he can fully cultivate only 60% of that area, and that, because the new pesticides are available only in limited quantities, insects and mice eat 10% of his crop in the field and another 10% in storage. To fool the grain inspectors, the farmer intermixes dirt and wet wheat with his good crop to increase the bulk. The district agricultural officer, whose continuance in office depends upon meeting quotas, has very little incentive to question the initial production figures, which are then passed through the system to be aggregated at the national level with dozens, hundreds, or thousands of other defective figures. The result is a national total that is difficult as a practical matter to check and that is unlikely as a political matter to be checked.

This example illustrates a principle that obtains everywhere—that to understand the quality of any datum, one must understand why that particular item of information was collected; whether the system of classification in which it is contained is unambiguous and complete; whether the enumeration of the activity being surveyed is complete or incomplete, biased or unbiased; whether the system for reporting and publishing the data is simple or sophisticated, prompt or slow, politically, racially, or intellectually biased or as neutral and unbiased as professional statistical skills can make it.

One fundamental difficulty with international comparisons is that they usually begin with a national survey that adopts a particular set of definitions and categories, all quite appropriate to the situation of the country itself but often at variance with those used by other countries. The example below illustrates the range of definitions that various countries apply to the term urban.

Ethiopia: localities of 2,000 or more inhabitants.
The Gambia: Banjul only.
Ghana: localities of 5,000 or more inhabitants.
Liberia: localities of more than 2,000 inhabitants.
Libya: total population of Tripoli and Benghazi, plus the urban parts of Beida and Derna.
Malawi: all townships and town planning areas and all district centres.
Mali: localities of 5,000 or more inhabitants and district centres.
Mauritania: urban centres.
Mauritius: towns with proclaimed legal limits.
Morocco: 184 urban centres.
Rwanda: Kigali, the capital, administrative centres of prefectures, and important agglomerations and their surroundings.
Senegal: agglomerations of 10,000 or more inhabitants.
Seychelles: Port Victoria, the capital.
Sudan: localities of administrative and/or commercial importance or with populations of 5,000 or more inhabitants.
Swaziland: localities proclaimed as urban.

The United Nations and other international organizations have published recommendations for improving the comparability and quality of such statistics, but implementation of these recommendations is slow and often incomplete.

Similar examples could be supplied of the very different meanings assigned throughout the world for scores of terms used in the *Britannica World Data*. The purpose of this compilation, however, is both to offer a tabulation of data that are themselves sound and comparable and to edit these data in such a way as to either improve their comparability (when this can be done through our own analysis) or explain their limitations through footnotes when printing the numbers without comment would create misleading implications. Definitions of all terms as used in the "Nations of the World" section are given beginning on page 617. Terms used in the "Comparative National Statistics" section are discussed in the headnotes to the individual tables.

Quality and recency of data. The researchers and editors who compile and edit the *Encyclopædia Britannica*, *Britannica Book of the Year,* and the other publications that the *Britannica World Data* supplements must consult thousands of reference works, statistical and otherwise, to assure the continued quality, accuracy, and up-to-dateness of our publications. The "Bibliography and sources" beginning on page 958 enumerates some of the national and international sources used in compilation of the *Britannica World Data*. All of these sources are held, and updated continuously, in the statistical collections of Encyclopædia Britannica, Inc. The publications themselves are issued in some 75 languages in common use among the countries of the world, and the information contained in them is supplemented by unpublished data received in correspondence, as well as by information published by international organizations.

The holdings for a given country with a well-developed statistical and publishing program may include any of the following documents: the national statistical abstract; the most recent censuses of population; periodic reports or monographs on vital statistics, social characteristics, agriculture, mining, wholesale and retail trade, finance and economic development, foreign trade, and transportation and communication; and such distinctive works as gazetteers, national atlases, and central bank publications.

ABBREVIATIONS

Measurements

cu m	cubic metre
kg	kilogram
km	kilometre
kW	kilowatt
kW-hr	kilowatt-hour
metric ton-km	metric ton-kilometre
mi	mile
passenger-km	passenger-kilometre
passenger-mi	passenger-mile
short ton-mi	short ton-mile
sq km	square kilometre
sq m	square metre
sq mi	square mile
troy oz.	troy ounce
yr	year

Political Units and International Organizations

EEC	European Economic Community
FAO	United Nations Food and Agriculture Organization
IMF	International Monetary Fund
U.K.	United Kingdom
U.S.	United States
U.S.S.R.	Union of Soviet Socialist Republics

Months

Jan.	January
Feb.	February
Mar.	March
Apr.	April
Aug.	August
Sep.	September
Oct.	October
Nov.	November
Dec.	December

Miscellaneous

avg.	average
c.i.f.	cost, insurance, and freight
est.	estimate
excl.	excluding
f.o.b.	free on board
GDP	gross domestic product
GNP	gross national product
govt.	government
mo.	month
n.a.	not available (in text)
NMP	net material product
no.	number
pl.	plural
pos.	position
pub. admin.	public administration
SDR	Special Drawing Right
svcs.	services
teacher tr.	teacher training
transp.	transportation
voc.	vocational
...	not available (in tables)
—	none, nil, or not applicable

Currencies

$a	Argentine peso
$A	Australian dollar
AF	afghani
$b	Bolivian peso
B	Panamanian balboa
B	Thai baht
B$	Bahamian dollar
BDS$	Barbados dollar
Ber$	Bermuda dollar
BF	Belgian franc
Br$	Brunei dollar
Br	Ethiopian birr
Bs	Venezuelan bolivar
BZ$	Belize dollar
₡	Costa Rican colón
₡	Ghanaian cedi
₡	Salvadoran colón
C$	Nicaraguan cordoba
Can$	Canadian dollar
CF	Comorian franc
CFAF	CFA (Communauté financière africaine [African Financial Community]) franc
CFP fr	CFP (Comptoir Français du Pacifique [French Bank of the Pacific]) franc
Ch$	Chilean peso
Col$	Colombian peso
Cr$	cruzeiro (Brazil)
C.V. Esc	Cape Verde escudo
D	Gambian dalasi
D	Tunisian dinar
D	Vietnamese dong
DA	Algerian dinar
Db	São Tomé and Príncipe dobra
DF	Djibouti franc
Dh	U.A.E. dirham
DH	Moroccan dirham
Din	Yugoslav dinar
DKr	Danish krone
DM	Deutsche Mark (Fed. Rep. of Germany)
Dr	Greek drachma
E	lilangeni (pl. emalangeni [Swaziland])
EC$	East Caribbean dollar
EK	Equatorial Guinean ekwele
Esc	Portuguese escudo
f.	Netherlands guilder
F	French (metropolitan) franc
F$	Fiji dollar
FBu	Burundi franc
FMG	Malagasy franc
Fmk	Finnish markka
Fr	French franc (Monaco)
Ft	Hungarian forint
G	Haitian gourde
₲	Paraguayan guaraní
G$	Guyana dollar
GS	Guinean syli
HK$	Hong Kong dollar
ID	Iraqi dinar
Irf	Irish pound
IS	shekel (Israel)
ISK	Icelandic króna
J$	Jamaica dollar
JD	Jordan dinar
K	Burmese kyat
K	Papua New Guinea kina
K	Zambian kwacha
Kčs	koruna (Czechoslovakia)
KD	Kuwaiti dinar
KN	kip (Laos)
K Sh	Kenya shilling
L	Honduran lempira
£	pound sterling (United Kingdom and dependencies)
L$	Liberian dollar
£C	Cyprus pound
LD	Libyan dinar
Le	Sierra Leonean leone
LE	Egyptian pound
lei	Romanian leu (pl. lei)
LFr	Luxembourg franc
Lit	Italian lira
LL	Lebanese pound
Lm	Maltese lira
LS	Syrian pound
LSd	Sudanese pound
LT	Turkish lira
M	loti (pl. maloti [Lesotho])
M	Mark (German Dem. Rep.)
M$	ringgit (Malaysia)
Mau Rs	Mauritian rupee
Mex$	Mexican peso
MF	Mali franc
MK	Malawi kwacha
₦	Nigerian naira
NA f.	Netherlands Antillean guilder
NKr	Norwegian krone
NRs	Nepalese rupee
NT$	new Taiwan dollar
Nu	ngultrum (Bhutan)
NUr$	Uruguayan new peso
P	Philippine peso
P	Botswana pula
PG	Guinea-Bissau peso
PRs	Pakistan rupee
Ptas	Spanish peseta
Q	Guatemalan quetzal
QR	Qatar riyal
R	South African rand
RD$	Dominican peso
Rf	Maldivian rufiyaa
RF	Rwanda franc
Rls	Iranian rial
RO	rial Omani
Rp	Indonesian rupiah
Rs	Indian rupee
S	Austrian Schilling
S$	Singapore dollar
S/.	Ecuadoran sucre
S/.	Peruvian sol
Sf	Suriname guilder
SFr	Swiss franc (Liechtenstein)
SI$	Solomon Islands dollar
SKr	Swedish krona
SL Rs	Sri Lanka rupee
So. Sh.	Somali shilling
SR	Seychelles rupee
SRls	Saudi Arabian riyal
Sw F	Swiss franc
$T	pa'anga (Tonga)
Tk	Bangladesh taka
T Sh	Tanzania shilling
TT$	Trinidad and Tobago dollar
UM	Mauritanian ouguiya
U.S.$	U.S. dollar
U Sh	Uganda shilling
VT	vatu (Vanuatu)
W	Korean won
WS$	Western Samoa tala
Y	renminbi (yuan) (China)
¥	Japanese yen
YD	Yemeni dinar
YRls	Yemen rial
Z	New Zealand dollar
Z	zaire
Z$	Zimbabwe dollar

GLOSSARY

A number of terms that are used to classify and report data in the "Nations of the World" section require some explanation.

Those italicized terms that are used regularly in the country compilations to introduce specific categories of information (*e.g.,* "birth rate," "budget") appear in this glossary in italic boldface type, followed by a description of the precise kind of information being offered and how it has been edited and presented. In some instances, additional discussion is provided on aspects of data collection and classification.

All other terms are printed here in roman boldface type. Many terms have rather specific meanings in statistical reporting, and they are so defined here. Other terms have less specific application as they are used in different countries or by different reporting organizations. Any ambiguities in the application of terms used in the country compilations and any departures from the definitions given in this glossary are usually annotated or footnoted at the appropriate places.

Terms that appear in small capitals in certain definitions are themselves defined at their proper alphabetical locations.

Terms whose definitions are marked by an asterisk(*) refer to data that are supplied only in the large two-page country compilations.

access to services, a group of measures indicating level of access to public services for the general population, including electrical power, treated public water, sewage removal, and fire protection.*

age breakdown, the distribution of a given population by age, usually reported here as percentages (of total population) based on the number of persons in each 15-year age bracket. For some censuses there are substantial numbers of persons for whom age is unknown or from whom there is no response, which imparts a degree of uncertainty to the distribution.

area and population, usually the first-order administrative subdivisions of the country (such as the states of the United States), with area, capital or administrative seat, and population. Occasionally, when these subdivisions are especially numerous, a regional, political, or other scheme has been substituted.

associated state, *see* state.

autonomous, *see* self-governing.

balance of trade, the net value of all international goods trade of a country, usually excluding re-exports (goods received only for transshipment), and the percentage that this net represents of total trade.

More generally, the balance of trade, also known as merchandise account, is the difference between the value of a country's imports and the value of its exports of goods as usually recorded by customs authorities. Balance of trade refers only to the visible international trade of goods and is thus a segment of a country's balance of payments, which takes all visible and invisible trade with other countries into account. (Invisible trade refers to imports and exports of services such as transport, tourism, and insurance.) A country has a favourable balance of trade when the value of exports exceeds that of imports.

barrel (bbl), a unit of liquid measure. The barrel conventionally used for reporting crude petroleum and petroleum products is equal to 42 U.S. gallons or 159 litres. The number of barrels of crude petroleum per metric ton depends upon the specific gravity of the petroleum and ranges from 6.65 in Cuba to 8.09 in Bolivia; the world average is roughly 7.33.

birth rate, the number of live births annually per 1,000 population.

See also crude birth rate.

budget, the recurrent or annual receipts and expenditures of the central government for its activities only; does not include the revenues and expenditures of state, provincial, and other local governments unless otherwise specified. Figures for budgets are limited to ordinary recurring receipts and matching expenditures and wherever possible exclude capital expenditures, *i.e.,* funds for development and other special projects and foreign-aid grants (which nonetheless often appear as receipts on the budgets of recipient countries).

capital, the actual seat of administration and government of a political entity. When more than one capital exists, each is identified by kind; when interim arrangements exist during the creation of a new national capital, the de facto situation is described.

chief of state / head of government, as prescribed or practiced, although divergences in form and practice are considerable.

In general usage, the chief of state is the formal head of a national state. The primary responsibilities of the chief of state are usually ceremonial—convening legislatures, greeting foreign officials, hosting state dinners, and bestowing honours. The head of government is the chief executive officer of a national state who exercises actual executive powers. Thus, for example, in the United Kingdom the prime minister is the head of government while the reigning monarch is the chief of state. In some countries the two positions may be merged. Thus, in the United States the president is both chief of state and head of government.

college graduates, depending upon how a given country reports, and as noted in each particular table, either (1) the number of persons holding degrees from higher level institutions, per 100,000 population; or (2) the number of persons graduated from such institutions in the year cited, per 100,000 population.

See also educational attainment.

colony, an area annexed to, or controlled by, an independent state but not an integral part of it; a non-self-governing territory. A colony has a charter and may have a degree of self-government. A crown colony is a colony originally chartered by the British government.

commonwealth (U.S.), a self-governing political entity associated with the United States; examples are the Philippines from 1935 to 1946 and Puerto Rico since 1952.

Commonwealth, also called the Commonwealth of Nations, a loose voluntary association of states, including the United Kingdom and a number of its former dominions, colonies, and dependencies, established under the Statute of Westminster in 1931.

communications, collectively, the means available for the public transmission of information within a country. Data are provided for daily newspapers, their number and total circulation, and the per capita rate of circulation implied by that total; for radios, televisions, and telephone receivers, total numbers and rates of availability are supplied.

constitutional monarchy, *see* monarchy.

consumer price index, also known as the retail price index or the cost-of-living index, a series of index numbers assigned to the price of a selected "basket," or assortment, of basic consumer goods and services in a country or region to measure changes over time in prices paid by a typical household for those goods and services. Items included in the consumer price index are ordinarily determined by governmental surveys of typical household expenditures and are assigned weights relative to their proportion of those expenditures.

co-principality, *see* monarchy.

crude birth rate, the number of live births annually per 1,000 of midyear population. Birth rates for individual countries may be compared with the world annual average of 27.5 births per 1,000 population between 1980 and 1985.

crude death rate, the number of deaths annually per 1,000 of midyear population. Death rates for individual countries may be compared with the world annual average of 10.6 deaths per 1,000 population between 1980 and 1985.

daily caloric supply per capita, the calories equivalent to the known average daily supply of foodstuffs for human consumption in a given country divided by the population of the country. This estimated measure may differ from actual daily per capita consumption of food as a result of waste, inefficient distribution, and exploitation of sources of food not included in the known supply of foodstuffs. The daily per capita caloric intake of a country may be compared with the corresponding daily per capita caloric requirement. The latter is calculated by the Food and Agriculture Organization (FAO) of the United Nations from the age and sex distributions, average body weights, and environmental temperatures in a given country to determine the calories needed to sustain a person there at normal levels of activity and health. The daily per capita caloric requirement ranges from 2,200 to 2,400 in most Asian, African, and Latin American countries to 2,500 and more in North America and most European and Oceanian countries. The world daily per capita caloric requirement approaches 2,400.

See also food.

de facto population, for a given area, the population enumerated on the basis of those present at a particular time, including temporary visitors and excluding residents temporarily absent.

de jure population, for a given area, the population enumerated on the basis of legal residence, excluding temporary visitors and including residents temporarily absent.

deadweight tonnage, the maximum weight of cargo, fuel, fresh water, stores, and persons that may safely be carried by a ship. It is customarily measured in long tons of 2,240 pounds each, equivalent to 1.016 metric tons. Deadweight tonnage is the difference between the tonnage of a fully loaded ship and the fully unloaded tonnage of that ship.

death rate, the number of registered deaths or, where registration is incomplete, the estimated number of deaths annually per 1,000 population.

See also crude death rate.

density (of population), usually the total area of the country divided into its DE FACTO POPULATION. Special adjustment is made for inland water or other uninhabitable areas, *e.g.*, excluding the lake area of Finland, the ice area of Greenland, or the desert area of Egypt.

The crude density of population of a particular country can be compared with the world average of 93 persons per square mile (36 persons per square kilometre) in 1984.

department, a first-order civil administrative subdivision. *Overseas department* (France), an overseas subdivision of the French Republic, almost equivalent to a department of metropolitan France, with elected representation in the French Parliament.

dependency, any area outside of and under the jurisdiction of an independent state but not annexed to it.

direct taxes, taxes levied directly on firms and individuals, such as taxes on income, profits, and capital gains. The immediate incidence, or burden, of direct taxes is on the firms and individuals thus taxed; the incidence of direct taxes on firms may, however, be passed on to consumers and other economic units in the form of higher prices for goods and services, with the result that the distinction between direct and indirect taxes is not always clear. Figures given for individual countries are limited to direct taxes levied by their respective central governments unless otherwise specified.

distribution of income / wealth, the portion of national household income or wealth accruing to households or individuals comprising each respective decile (tenth) or quintile (fifth) of the total number of households or individuals.*

See also household income and expenditures.

divorce rate, the number of legal, civilly recognized divorces annually per 1,000 population.

doubling time, the number of complete years required for a country to double its population at its current rate of natural increase; it does not take into account expected demographic change during the period, such as declining birth rate or population migration.

earnings index, *see* monthly earnings index; price and earnings indexes.

economically active population, *see* persons economically active.

education, tabulation of the principal elements of the country's educational establishment, classified as far as possible according to the country's own system of primary, secondary, and higher levels (the usual age limits for these levels being identified in parentheses), with total number of schools (physical facilities) and of teachers and students (whether full- or part-time). The student–teacher ratio is calculated whenever available data permit.

educational attainment, the distribution of the adult population by the highest level of formal education attained or completed.*

See also college graduates.

emirate, *see* monarchy.

empire, *see* monarchy.

enclave, a portion of a state separated geographically from its main part and having boundaries only with some other state or states. The surrounded area is said to be an enclave with respect to the area that borders on it and an *exclave* with respect to the state of which it is a part.

ethnic / linguistic composition, ethnic, racial, or linguistic composition of a national population, reported here according to the most reliable breakdown available from national sources (when available) or external analysis (when the subject is not addressed in national sources [usually because of social or political sensitivity about the consequences of publishing such data]). For a discussion of some of the classificational problems, *see* the Languages of the world table at page 838.

exclave, *see* enclave.

exports, material goods legally leaving a country and subject to customs regulations. The total value and distribution by percentage of the major items (in preference to groups of goods) exported are given, together with the distribution of trade among major trading partners (single countries). Figures given for goods exported are free on board (FOB) unless otherwise specified. The value of goods exported and imported free on board (FOB) is calculated from the cost of production and excludes the cost of transport, which is passed on to the consumer.

external territory (Australia), *see* territory.

fabricated metal, refined metal that has been converted through processing into finer or more finished forms, such as rolled shapes from ingots.

farm, economic unit comprising an operator and the land on which agricultural operations are conducted. The legal tenure of the farm may be under the control of a person, partnership, or corporation. In the United States, a farm is such a place with annual gross sales of farm products of $1,000 or more.

federal, consisting of first-order political subdivisions that are prior to and independent of the central government in certain functions.

federal republic, *see* republic.

federation, a union of coequal political entities that retain some degree of autonomy within the union.

fertility rate, *see* general fertility rate; total fertility rate.

financial aggregates, tabulation of seven-year time series, providing the principal measures of the financial condition of a country: exchange rate of the national currency against the U.S. dollar, the pound sterling, and the International Monetary Fund's Special Drawing Rights (SDR); the amount and kind of international reserves (holdings of SDRs, gold, and foreign currencies) and reserve position of the country in the International Monetary Fund; principal economic rates and prices (central bank discount rate, government bond yields, and industrial stock [share] prices). For balance of payments, the origin in terms of component balance of trade items and balance of invisibles (net) is given.*

fish catch, the live-weight equivalent of the aquatic animals (including fish, crustaceans, mollusks, etc., but excluding whales, seals, and other aquatic mammals) caught in freshwater or marine areas by national fleets and landed in domestic or foreign harbours for commercial, industrial, or subsistence purposes.

food, total per capita supply of food (assumed to equal actual consumption since detailed data on waste, or actual consumption loss, are seldom available); summarized in calories and distributed as percentages by vegetable and animal origin.

See also daily caloric supply per capita.

form of government / political status, the structure of a country's administration provided for in normal constitutional operation, whether or not suspended by extralegal military or civil action, although such de facto administrations are identified; together with the number of members (as prescribed by the constitution) for each legislative house, named according to

its English rendering. Dependencies are classified according to the status of their political association with the administering country.

general fertility rate, the number of live births per 1,000 females of childbearing age, generally considered to be between the ages of 15 and 49 years. Stillborn births are generally excluded from the general fertility rate.

See also total fertility rate.

gross domestic product (GDP), the total value of the final goods and services produced by residents and nonresidents within a given country during a given year. The GDP excludes the value of net income earned abroad, which is included in the GROSS NATIONAL PRODUCT (GNP).

gross national product (GNP), the total and per capita value, in U.S. dollars, of final goods and services produced in a given year. GNP is equal to GROSS DOMESTIC PRODUCT plus net factor income from abroad (the latter including balance-of-goods trade and international financial transactions).

gross output in factor values, the total market value of goods and services produced in a given period in a given country, less all INDIRECT TAXES on production but including all current subsidies received in support of production activity.

gross output value in producers' prices, the total market value of goods and services produced in a given period in a given country, including all INDIRECT TAXES on production but excluding subsidies.

gross registered ton, unit of measure of the permanently enclosed volume of a ship, less certain exempted spaces such as those devoted to machinery, bunkers, crew accommodations, and so on; the gross registered tonnage of a ship is thus a rough estimation of its volumetric cargo capacity. The gross registered ton is equivalent to 100 cubic feet or 2.83 cubic metres.

gross ton, also called long ton, in British Imperial and U.S. Customary measure, 2,240 pounds, equivalent to 1.016 metric tons.

head of government, *see* chief of state / head of government.

health, total number of accredited physicians (according to Western criteria) by specialization and their ratio to the total population; similarly for hospital beds, except that psychiatric and other specialized institutional beds are excluded.

household income and expenditure, data for average household size (by number of individuals) and for average household income. Sources of income and expenditures for major items of consumption (but not for savings, investment, or insurance) are reported as percentages.

In general, household income is the amount of funds, usually measured in monetary units, received by the members (generally those 14 years old and over) of a HOUSEHOLD in a given time period. The income can be derived from wages or salaries, nonfarm or farm SELF-EMPLOYMENT, pensions, investments, rental property, public assistance, unemployment benefits, etc. The income of a household is expressed as a gross amount before deductions for taxes.

households, groups of related or unrelated individuals living in the same HOUSING UNIT, distributed by size of household. A family household is one composed principally of individuals related by blood or marriage.*

housing unit, a single room or a group of rooms occupied exclusively as separate living quarters, whose occupants do not live or eat with other occupants (if any) in the same structure. A housing unit has direct access from the outside of its building and also has exclusive kitchen facilities.

immigration, usually the number and origin of

those immigrants admitted to a nation in a legal status that would eventually permit the granting of the right to settle permanently or to acquire citizenship.*

imports, material goods legally entering a country and subject to customs regulations; excludes financial movements. The total value and distribution by percentage of the major items (in preference to groups of goods) imported are given, together with the distribution of trade among major trading partners (single countries). The value of goods imported is given free on board (FOB) unless otherwise specified; FOB is defined above under EXPORTS.

incorporated territory (U.S.), *see* territory.

independent, of a state, autonomous and controlling both its internal and external affairs.

indirect taxes, taxes levied on sales or transfers of selected intermediate goods and services, including excises, value-added taxes, and tariffs, that are ordinarily passed on to the ultimate consumers of the goods and services. Figures given for individual countries are limited to indirect taxes levied by their respective central governments unless otherwise specified.

infant mortality rate, the number of children born live who die before their first birthday per 1,000 live births. Total infant mortality includes neonatal mortality, which is deaths of children within one month of birth.

kingdom, see monarchy.

land tenure, the legal or customary arrangement by which a farmer occupies and operates a farm, or agricultural holding; also, the rights of the individual under such an arrangement.

land use, distribution by classes of vegetational cover or economic use of the land area only (excluding inland water, for example, but not marshland), reported as percentages.

leisure, the principal uses or reported preferences in the use of the individual's free time for personal recreation, rest, or self-improvement.*

life expectancy, the number of years a person born within a particular population group would be expected to live, based on actuarial calculations.

  Life expectancy at birth is usually lower than after the first year of life because of INFANT MORTALITY. Life expectancy is often used to compare the general health of populations of different countries. Life expectancy in the early 1980s ranges from low (50 years or less at birth) in some African countries to high (about 75 years) in Scandinavia.

major causes of death, the major diseases or other causes of death (accident, suicide, war), usually reported as a rate per 100,000 population.

major cities, the five (or ten*) largest cities proper whose population is at least one-tenth that of the primary city (usually the national capital).

manufacturing, mining, and construction enterprises, a detailed tabulation of the principal industries in these three sectors, showing for each industry the number of enterprises and employees, wages in that industry as a percentage of the general average wage, and the value of that industry's output in terms of value added or turnover.*

marriage rate, the number of legal, civilly recognized marriages annually per 1,000 population.

material well-being, a group of measures indicating the percentage of households or dwellings possessing certain goods or appliances, including automobiles, telephones, television receivers, refrigerators, air conditioners, and washing machines.*

merchant marine, the privately or publicly owned ships of a nation (limited to those in Lloyd's of London statistical reporting of 100 or more GROSS REGISTERED TONS) that are employed in commerce. It usually consists of oil and chemical tankers; liquefied gas, ore, and bulk carriers; and general cargo and container ships.

military expenditure, the apparent value of all identifiable military expenditure by the central government on hardware, personnel, pensions, research and development, etc., reported here as a percentage of the GNP, with a comparison to the world average.

military personnel, *see* total active duty personnel.

mobility, a measure of the rate at which individuals or households change dwellings (or remain in them), usually measured between censuses and including international as well as domestic migration.*

monarchy, a government in which the CHIEF OF STATE holds office, usually hereditarily, but sometimes electively, and for life (sometimes electively for a term). The state may be a co-principality, emirate, empire, kingdom, principality, shaykhdom, or sultanate. The powers of the monarch may range from absolute, *i.e.*, he or she both reigns and rules, through various degrees of limitation of authority, to merely nominal, as in a constitutional monarchy, in which the titular monarch reigns but others, as elected officials, rule or participate in the ruling.

monetary unit, currency in official use in a given country; name, spelling, and abbreviation in English according to International Monetary Fund recommendations or local practice; valuation usually according to commercial rates.

monthly earnings index, a series of index numbers assigned average monthly wages in selected industries in a country or region to measure changes over time in those wages. The scope of the monthly earnings index varies from country to country; the index is commonly limited to earnings in manufacturing industries. The index for each country applies to all wage earners in a designated group and ordinarily takes into account basic wages, bonuses, cost-of-living allowances, and contributions toward social security by the wage earners in question. Some countries include payments in kind. Contributions toward social security by employers are usually excluded, as are social security benefits received by wage earners.

  See also price and earnings indexes.

natural increase, also called natural growth or the balance of births and deaths, the excess of births over deaths in a population; the rate of natural increase is the difference between the CRUDE BIRTH RATE and the CRUDE DEATH RATE of a given population. Natural increase is added to the balance of migration to calculate the total growth of that population.

non-ferrous metal, metal that does not contain significant quantities of iron and its alloys; usually this term is reserved for base metals such as copper or lead.

official language(s), that (or those) prescribed for actual day-to-day conduct and publication of a country's official business. Other languages may have local protection, may be permitted in legal action (such as a trial), or may be "national languages," for the protection of which special provisions have been made, but these are not deemed official.

official name, the local official form(s) short or long, of a country's legal name(s) taken from the country's constitution or from other official documents. The English-language form is usually the protocol form in use by the country, the U.S. Department of State, and the United Nations.

official religion, generally, any religion prescribed or given special protection by the constitution or legal system of the country.

organized territory (U.S.), *see* territory.

origin of gross domestic product with labour, tabulation of the principal elements of the national economy, according to standard industrial categories, together with the distribution of the labour force (when possible the economically active population) that generates the gross domestic product.

overseas department (France), *see* department.

overseas territory (France), *see* territory.

parliamentary state, *see* state.

part of a realm, a dependent political entity with some degree of self-government and having a special status above that of a colony (*e.g.*, the prerogative of rejecting for local application any law enacted by the motherland).

passenger-miles or passenger-kilometres, carriage by public or commercial means of a single passenger a distance of one mile (or kilometre); in aggregate the total miles or kilometres traveled by all passengers in a given country via specified means of transportation. Figures given for countries ordinarily exclude passengers carried free of charge.

people's republic, *see* republic.

persons economically active, the total number of persons (above a set age for economic labour, usually 10–15 years) in all employment statuses—self-employed, wage- or salary-earning, part-time, seasonal, unemployed, etc.

  The United Nation's *Yearbook of Labour Statistics* defines the economically active population as "all persons of either sex who furnish the supply of labour for the production of economic goods and services. National practices vary between countries as regards the treatment of such groups as armed forces, inmates of institutions, persons living on reservations, persons seeking their first job, seasonal workers and persons engaged in part-time economic activities. In some countries, all or part of these groups are included among the economically active while in other countries they are treated as inactive. However, in general, the data on economically active population do not include students, women occupied solely in domestic duties, retired persons, persons living entirely on their own means, and persons wholly dependent upon others."

place of birth/national origin, if the former, numbers of native- and foreign-born population of a country by actual place of birth; if the latter, any of several classifications, including those based on origin of passport at original admission to country, on cultural heritage of family name, on self-designated (often multiple) origin of (some) ancestors, and on other systems for assigning national origin.*

population projection, the expected population in 1990 and 2000, embodying the country's own projections wherever possible. Estimate of the future size of a population is based on assumed future levels of fertility, mortality, and migration. Assumptions about these future levels are commonly made from cohort analysis, which describes a group of persons who experience a particular life event, such as birth or marriage, within the same period of time. Projections in the tables, based on estimates by the United Nations, World Bank, U.S. Department of Commerce, or the country itself, unless otherwise specified, are medium (*i.e.*, most likely) variants wherever possible.

price and earnings indexes, tabulation comparing the change in the consumer price index over a period of seven years with the change in the general labour force's earnings index for the same period. No adjustment is possible, however, for other measures of disposable income.

  See also monthly earnings index.

principality, *see* monarchy.

processed mineral, mineral that is not in its original raw form but that has undergone any of a number of physical, chemical, or metallurgical processes such as crushing, sorting, sizing, or concentrating by chemical, magnetic, electrostatic, or other treatment.

production, the physical quantity or monetary value of the output of an industry, usually tabulated here as the most important items or groups of items (depending on the available detail) of primary (extractive) and secondary (manufactured) production. When a single consistent measure of value, such as "value added," can be obtained, this is given, ranked by value; otherwise, quantity of production is given for the major groups and items.

public debt, the current outstanding debt of all periods of maturity for which the central government and its organs are obligated. For many developing countries, only figures for external public debt are available.

quality of working life, a group of measures including weekly hours of work (including overtime); rates per 100,000 for job-connected injury, illness, and mortality; coverage of labour force by insurance for injury, permanent disability, and death; work days lost to labour strikes and stoppages; and commuting patterns (length of journey to work in minutes and usual method of transportation).*

railroads, mode of transportation by self-driven or locomotive-drawn cars over fixed rails. Length of track figures given for individual countries ordinarily include the total length of all mainline and spurline running track and exclude switching sidings and yard track. Route length, when given, does not compound multiple running tracks laid on the same trackbed. Auxiliary lines traversed by ferries and motor vehicles are excluded unless otherwise specified.

religious affiliation, distribution of practicing or nominal religionists, by percentage of total population. This usually assigns to children the religion of their parents, since few sources conform to any other practice.

republic, a state with elected leaders and a centralized presidential form of government, local subdivisions being subordinate to the national government. *Federal republic* (as distinguished from a unitary republic), a republic in which power is divided between the central government and local subdivisions (*e.g.*, states, provinces, or cantons) in whom it is held to originate, the division of power being defined in a written constitution and jurisdictional disputes usually being settled in a court; sovereignty usually rests with the authority that has the power to amend the constitution. *People's republic*, in the dialectics of Communism, the first stage of development toward a communist state, the second stage being a *socialist republic. Soviet republic*, a republic governed by an elected soviet (council). *Unitary republic* (as distinguished from a federal republic), a republic in which power is held by a central authority and not derived from constituent subdivisions.

roundwood, wood obtained from removals from forests, felled or harvested (with or without bark), in various forms such as round, split, roots, stumps, etc. It can be broadly divided into two classes: softwoods, from coniferous trees, and hardwoods, from nonconiferous trees.

rural, *see* urban–rural.

self-employment, work in which income derives from direct employment in one's own business, trade, or profession, as opposed to work in which salary or wages are earned from an employer.

self-governing, of a state, in control of its internal affairs in degrees ranging from control of most internal affairs (though perhaps not of

public order or of internal security) to complete control of all internal affairs (*i.e.*, the state is autonomous) but having no control of external affairs or defense. In this list the term self-governing refers to the final state in the successive stages of increasing self-government, generally followed by independence.

service/trade enterprises, a detailed tabulation for the largest sectors of the domestic economy—services and wholesale and retail trade—as defined, surveyed, and reported by individual countries, providing: number of enterprises and employees, wages as a percentage of the general average wage, and the value of that industry's output in terms of value added or turnover.*

sex distribution, ratios, calculated as percentages, of male and female population to total population.

shaykhdom, *see* monarchy.

social deviance, a group of measures, usually reported as rates per 100,000, for principal categories of socially deviant behaviour, including crime, alcoholism, drug abuse, and suicide.*

social participation, a group of measures indicative of the degree of social engagement possessed by a particular population, including rates of participation or membership in public activities such as elections, voluntary work (or non-job-connected organizational memberships), trade unions, and religious organizations.*

social security, public programs designed to protect individuals and families from loss of income owing to unemployment, old age, sickness or disability, or death and to provide other assistance, such as medical care or other services. Such programs may include social insurance, health and welfare programs, income maintenance programs, or other modes of public aid.

socialist republic, *see* republic.

soviet republic, *see* republic.

state, an autonomous political entity; also, a first-order civil administrative subdivision, especially of a federated union. *Associated state*, an autonomous state in free association with another that conducts its external affairs and defense. *Parliamentary state*, an independent state in the COMMONWEALTH OF NATIONS that is governed by a parliament and that recognizes the British monarch as its titular head.

subsidy, financial aid or grant given by a government to a private or public enterprise deemed to be in the public interest. Subsidies may be employed for a wide range of purposes, such as to support a vital industry (*e.g.*, agriculture, steelmaking) or to keep prices of certain goods low or stable.

sultanate, *see* monarchy.

tenure, the forms and methods by which real property is held, such as by lease, by fee, or by title. Tenure of housing is the legal form of occupancy (owned, rented, or subrented) by a HOUSEHOLD of its living quarters.

territory, a noncategorized political dependency; a first-order administrative subdivision; a dependent political entity with some degree of self-government, but with fewer rights and less autonomy than a colony since there is no charter. *External territory* (Australia), a territory situated outside the area of the country. *Incorporated territory* (U.S.), a part of the United States with nonvoting representation in the Congress, but with most constitutional provisions extended to its inhabitants (*e.g.*, Alaska until 1959). *Organized territory* (U.S.), a territory for which a system of laws and a settled government have been provided by an act of the United States Congress. *Overseas territory* (France), an overseas subdivision of the French Republic with elected representation in the French Parlia-

ment, having individual statutes, laws, and internal organization adapted to local conditions. *Trust territory*, a non-self-governing former mandate of the League of Nations, administered by an independent state under trust arrangements with the United Nations, with the goal of eventual self-government. *Unincorporated territory* (U.S.), a dependency of the United States with limited self-government, whose inhabitants can claim the fundamental but not all of the procedural rights (*e.g.*, trial by jury) guaranteed by the United States Constitution.

theocracy, a state governed by hierarchs, *i.e.*, by religious leaders.

ton-miles or **ton-kilometres**, aggregate measure of freight hauled in a specified period of time, equal to tons of freight multiplied by the miles (or kilometres) each ton is transported. Figures given for individual countries indicate the aggregate ton-miles (or ton-kilometres) traveled by freight via the means of transportation indicated. Figures ordinarily exclude mail, specie, passengers' baggage, the fuel and stores of the conveyance in question, and goods carried free of charge.

total active duty personnel, full-time active duty military personnel (excluding militias and part-time, informal, or other semicivilian elements), with their distribution by percentages among the major services.

See also military expenditure.

total fertility rate, the average number of children each woman in a particular age group would have during her lifetime if she were to live to the end of her childbearing years.

See also general fertility rate.

tourism, service industry comprising activities connected with domestic and international travel for pleasure or recreation; confined here to international travel and reported as number of border crossings, or estimated expenditures by tourists of all nationalities visiting a particular country and, conversely, the estimated expenditures of that country's nationals in all countries of destination.

transport, all mechanical methods of moving persons or goods. Data reported for national establishments include: for railroads, length of track and volume of traffic for passengers and cargo (but excluding mail, etc.); for roads, length of network and numbers of passengers cars and of commercial vehicles, *i.e.*, trucks and buses (no data on traffic); for merchant marine, the number of vessels of more than 100 gross tons and their total deadweight tonnage (no data on traffic); for air transport, traffic data for passengers and cargo, and the number of airports with scheduled flights.

trust territory, *see* territory.

unincorporated territory (U.S.), *see* territory.

unitary republic, *see* republic.

urban–rural, social characteristic of local or national populations, defined by predominant economic activities, "urban" referring to a group of predominantly nonagricultural pursuits, "rural" to agricultural pursuits. The distinction is usually based on the country's own definition of urban, which may depend only upon the size (population) of a place, or upon factors like employment, density of housing, public services, etc.

value added, also called value added by manufacture, the GROSS OUTPUT VALUE of a firm or industry minus the cost of inputs—raw materials, supplies, and other inputs for which other firms are paid—required to produce it. Value added is the portion of the sales value of gross output value that is actually created by the firm or industry. Value added generally includes labour costs, administrative costs, and operating profits. The terms net output and value added are sometimes used synonymously.

The Nations of the World

Afghanistan

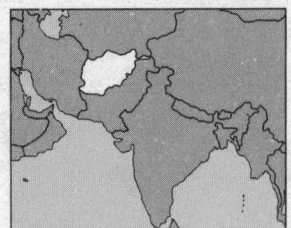

Official name: Da Afghānestān
Dimukratik Jamhuriyat (Pashto);
Dowlat-e Jumhūrī-ye Dimukrātīk-
e Afghānestān (Persian) (Democratic
Republic of Afghanistan).
Form of government: unitary
single-party republic with one
transitional legislative body
(Revolutionary Council [57])*.
Chief of state: President of the
Revolutionary Council.
Head of government: Prime Minister.
Capital: Kābul.
Official languages: Pashto; Persian.
Official religion: none.
Monetary unit: 1 afghani (AF) = 100
puls (puli); valuation (Oct. 29, 1984)
1 U.S.$ = AF82.02; 1 £ = AF99.00.

Area and population

Provinces	Capitals	area sq mi	area sq km	population 1981 estimate
Badakhshān	Feyzābād	18,302	47,403	521,000
Bādghīsāt	Qal'eh-ye Now	8,439	21,858	244,000
Baghlān	Baghlān	6,606	17,109	517,000
Balkh	Mazār-e Sharīf	4,862	12,593	610,000
Bāmīān	Bāmīān	6,724	17,414	281,000
Farāh	Farāh	18,451	47,788	245,000
Fāryāb	Meymaneh	8,602	22,279	610,000
Ghaznī	Ghaznī	9,026	23,378	676,000
Ghowr	Chaghcharān	14,929	38,666	354,000
Helmand	Lashkar Gah	23,872	61,829	542,000
Herāt	Herāt	23,674	61,315	808,000
Jowzjān	Sheberghān	9,866	25,553	616,000
Kābul	Kābul	1,770	4,585	1,518,000
Kāpīsā	Mahmūd-e 'Erāqī	722	1,871	262,000
Konarhā	Asadābād	4,046	10,479	262,000
Laghmān	Mehtar Lam	2,784	7,210	325,000
Lowgar	Pol-e 'Alam	1,796	4,652	226,000
Nangarhār	Jalālābād	2,941	7,616	782,000
Nīmrūz	Zaranj	15,968	41,356	108,000
Orūzgān	Tarīn Kowt	11,311	29,295	465,000
Paktīā	Gardēz	3,699	9,581	506,000
Paktīkā	Zareh Sharan	7,466	19,336	256,000
Parvān	Chārīkār	3,629	9,399	528,000
Qandahār	Qandahār	18,408	47,676	598,000
Qondūz	Qondūz	3,022	7,827	583,000
Samangān	Aybak	5,971	15,465	274,000
Takhār	Tāloqān	4,778	12,376	544,000
Vardak	Kowt-e 'Ashrow	3,484	9,023	301,000
Zābol	Qalāt	6,677	17,293	188,000
TOTAL		251,825	652,225	16,363,000†

Demography

Density‡ (1984): persons per sq mi 70.1, persons per sq km 27.1.
Urban–rural§ (1981): urban 15.8%; rural 84.2%.
Sex distribution§ (1981): male 51.42%; female 48.58%.
Age breakdown§ (1980): under 15, 44.5%; 15–29, 26.9%; 30–44, 15.8%; 45–59, 8.6%; 60–74, 3.6%; 75 and over, 0.6%.
Population projection: (1990) 20,618,000; (2000) 26,528,000.
Doubling time§: 27 years.
Ethnolinguistic composition (1980): Pashtun 53.3%; Tadzhik 20.1%; Uzbek 8.5%; Hazāra 8.3%; other 9.9%.
Religious affiliation (1980): Sunnī Muslim 87%; Shī'ah Muslim 12%; other 1%.
Major cities (1980): Kābul 973,000; Qandahār 185,000; Herāt 145,000; Mazār-e Sharīf 107,000.

Vital statistics

Birth rate per 1,000 population (1981): 47.0 (world avg. 29.0).
Death rate per 1,000 population (1981): 25.6 (world avg. 12.0).
Natural increase rate per 1,000 population (1981): 21.4 (world avg. 17.0).
Total fertility rate (avg. births per childbearing woman; 1981): 6.9.
Marital status of population 15 years and over (1980): married 71.9%; single 20.3%; widowed 6.3%; divorced 1.5%.
Infant mortality rate per 1,000 live births (1981): 204.8.
Life expectancy at birth (1981): male 36.4 years; female 38.5 years.
Major causes of hospitalization ‖ (1977): bacillary dysentery and amebiasis 5,247; diarrheal diseases 4,447; tuberculosis (all forms) 2,602.

National economy

Budget (1980–81). Revenue: AF34,950,900,000 (internal revenue sources 75.0%, of which natural gas revenues 32.9%; loans 20.4%; grants-in-aid 4.5%). Expenditures: AF34,950,900,000 (governmental ministries 47.3%; developmental budget 31.8%; surplus 15.9%; foreign debt service 2.9%).
Public debt (external, outstanding; 1982): U.S.$1,324,000,000.
Tourism: n.a.
Production (metric tons except as noted). Agriculture, forestry, fishing (1981–82): cereals 4,491,000, of which wheat 2,850,000, corn (maize) 798,000, rice 475,000, barley 330,000; fruits 913,000, of which grapes 500,000; livestock (number of live animals): 18,900,000 sheep (of which 4,600,000 karakul), 3,750,000 cattle, 2,900,000 goats, 1,303,000 asses, 412,000 horses. Mining and quarrying (1981): cement 95,000. Manufacturing (by production value in afghanis; 1981–82): food products 3,762,000,000; textiles (all forms)

2,770,000,000; industrial chemicals (including fertilizers) 751,000,000; printing and publishing 539,000,000. Construction: n.a. Energy production (consumption): electricity (kW-hr; 1982) 976,000,000 (976,000,000); coal (metric tons; 1982) 145,000 (145,000); petroleum products (metric tons; 1982) none (302,000); natural gas (cu m; 1982) 2,429,305,263 (129,179,400).
Gross national product (at current market prices; 1982): U.S.$3,500,000,000 (U.S.$230 per capita).

Origin of gross domestic product (current prices)

	1980–81 in value AF'000,000	% of total value	labour force	% of labour force
Agriculture and forestry	85,200	61.9	2,134,000	57.2
Manufacturing, mining, and public utilities	29,900	21.7	454,000	12.2
Construction	5,900	4.3	47,000	1.3
Trade	10,000	7.2	123,000	3.3
Transportation and communication	4,900	3.6	65,000	1.7
Education, public health, and culture	---	---	102,000	2.7
Public administration	---	---	66,000	1.8
Public services	---	---	148,000	4.0
Other	1,800	1.3	591,000	15.8
TOTAL	137,700	100.0	3,730,000§	100.0

Persons economically active (1979–80): total 3,634,600§ (27.9%); female participation in the labour force 299,500 (8.2%); unemployed 198,700 (5.5%).

Price indexes (1980 = 100)

	1977	1978	1979	1980	1981	1982	1983
Consumer price index	72.8	78.8	99.1	100.0	104.9	...	...
Monthly earnings index	...	...	...	...	...	...	...

Household size. Average household size§ (1979): 6.2.
Land use (1981): forested 2.9%; meadows and pastures 46.3%; agricultural and under permanent cultivation 12.5%; other 38.3%.

Foreign trade¶

Balance of trade (current prices)

	1976–77	1977–78	1978–79	1979–80	1980–81	1981–82
AF'000,000	+1,566	−2,014	−3,870	+3,006	+7,038	+3,637
% of total	6.2%	6.6%	11.8%	7.6%	12.2%	5.4%

Imports (1981–82): AF31,494,000,000 (vehicles 22.7%; petroleum products 18.0%; sugar 8.1%; woven fabrics of flax or ramie 7.9%; processed animal and vegetable oils 4.2%; tea 4.0%). *Major import sources:* U.S.S.R. 58.6%; Japan 12.6%; Hong Kong 4.4%; India 2.7%; West Germany 2.7%.
Exports (1981–82): AF35,131,000,000 (natural gas 39.2%; dried fruit 25.2%; carpets and rugs 10.5%; fresh fruit 7.3%; wool and hides 3.4%). *Major export destinations:* U.S.S.R. 59.4%; Pakistan 8.8%; India 6.2%.

Transport and communications

Transport. Railroads (1982): length 4 mi, 6 km. Roads (1979): total length 11,652 mi, 18,752 km (paved 15%). Vehicles (1981): passenger cars 34,200; trucks and buses 30,997. Merchant marine: none. Air transport (1982): passenger-mi 181,252,000, passenger-km 291,697,000; short ton-mi cargo 11,567,000, metric ton-km cargo 18,616,000; airports (1984) with scheduled flights 3.
Communications. Daily newspapers (1983): total number 3; total circulation 67,200; circulation per 1,000 population 3.9. Radios (1982): total number of receivers 135,000 (1 per 124 persons). Television (1982): total number of receivers 12,500 (1 per 1,340 persons). Telephones (1981): 23,700 (1 per 690 persons).

Education and health

Education (1981–82)

	schools	teachers	students	student/ teacher ratio
Primary	4,018	37,537	1,198,286	31.9
Secondary	424⁹	6,409	144,858	22.6
Vocational	42	1,053	13,201	12.5
Higher	5	1,226	12,868	10.5

College graduates per 100,000 population (students graduating; 1981): 9.6.
Literacy (1980): total population literate 1,436,000 (20.0%); males literate 1,236,000 (33.2%); females literate 200,000 (5.8%).
Health (1981): physicians 1,215 (1 per 13,467 persons); hospital beds 6,875 (1 per 2,380 persons).
Food (1978–80): daily per capita caloric intake 1,833 (vegetable products 92.0%, animal products 8.0%); 75% of FAO recommended minimum.

Military

Total active duty personnel (1982): 46,000 (army 87.0%; air force 13.0%).
Military expenditure as percent of GNP (1981): 3.0% (world 5.7%); per capita expenditure U.S.$6.

*The provisional Basic Principles of the Democratic Republic of Afghanistan, adopted in 1980, provides for the eventual election of a Grand National Assembly. †Total includes 2,615,000 nomads not distributed by province. Afghan refugees in Pakistan number upward of 2,500,000 and in Iran upward of 1,500,000. ‡Includes both settled and nomadic population. §Based on settled population only. ‖ Infectious diseases only. ¶Excluding imports and lesser exports classified as special transactions and commodities. ⁹1980–81.

Albania

Official name: Republika Popullore e Shqipërisë (People's Socialist Republic of Albania).
Form of government: unitary single-party republic with one legislative house (People's Assembly [250]).
Chief of state: President (Chairman).
Head of government: Premier (Chairman).
Capital: Tiranë.
Official language: Albanian.
Official religion: none.
Monetary unit: 1 lek (plural lekë) = 100 qindars; valuation (Oct. 29, 1984) 1 U.S.$ = 8.33 lekë; 1 £ = 10.05 lekë.

Area and population

Provinces	Capitals	area		population
		sq mi	sq km	1980 estimate
Berat	Berat	396	1,026	147,200
Dibër	Peshkopi	605	1,568	128,300
Durrës	Durrës	327	848	209,500
Elbasan	Elbasan	572	1,481	197,600
Fier	Fier	454	1,175	203,400
Gjirokastër	Gjirokastër	439	1,137	58,500
Gramsh	Gramsh	268	695	36,300
Kolonjë	Erseka	311	805	21,600
Korçë	Korçë	842	2,181	193,000
Krujë	Krujë	234	607	88,200
Kukës	Kukës	514	1,331	81,880
Lezhë	Lezhë	185	479	50,500
Librazhd	Librazhd	391	1,013	59,300
Lushnjë	Lushnjë	275	712	110,900
Mat	Burrel	397	1,028	64,260
Mirditë	Rrëshen	335	867	42,400
Përmet	Përmet	359	930	35,200
Pogradec	Pogradec	280	725	59,000
Pukë	Pukë	399	1,033	42,400
Sarandë	Sarandë	424	1,097	74,400
Shkodër	Shkodër	976	2,528	198,580
Skrapar	Çorovoda	299	775	39,800
Tepelenë	Tepelenë	315	817	43,300
Tiranë	Tiranë	478	1,238	297,700
Tropojë	Bajram	403	1,043	38,800
Vlorë	Vlorë	621	1,609	149,600
TOTAL		11,100*	28,748	2,671,620

Source: Official government figures.

Demography

Density (1984): persons per sq mi 261.8, persons per sq km 101.1.
Urban–rural (1980): urban 35.3%; rural 64.7%.
Sex distribution (1980): male 50.92%; female 49.08%.
Age breakdown (1980): under 15, 37.3%; 15–29, 28.9%; 30–44, 16.5%; 45–59, 10.2%; 60–74, 5.5%; 75 and over, 1.6%.
Population projection: (1990) 3,350,000; (2000) 4,000,000.
Doubling time: 28 years.
Ethnic composition (1980): Albanian 93.1%; Gypsy 2.5%; Greek 2.4%; other 2.0%.
Religious affiliation (1980): Muslim 20.5%; Christian 5.4%; atheist 18.7%; nonreligious 55.4%.
Major cities (1981 est.): Tiranë 220,000; Durrës 70,000; Shkodër 65,000; Elbasan 60,000; Vlorë 58,000.

Vital statistics

Birth rate per 1,000 population (1984): 26.0 (world avg. 28.0).
Death rate per 1,000 population (1984): 6.0 (world avg. 11.0).
Natural increase rate per 1,000 population (1984): 20.0 (world avg. 17.0).
Total fertility rate (avg. births per childbearing woman; 1980): 3.6.
Marriage rate per 1,000 population (1984): 9.0.
Divorce rate per 1,000 population: n.a.
Infant mortality rate: n.a.
Life expectancy at birth (1981): male 66.8 years; female 71.4 years.
Major causes of death: n.a.

National economy

Budget (1983). Revenue: 8,800,000,000 lekë (surplus from state enterprises 93.0%, other 7.0%). Expenditures: 8,750,000,000 lekë (national economy 57.5%, social and cultural services 27.4%, defense 11.5%, administration 1.6%).
Public debt: n.a.
Tourism (1982): number of tourists 6,000; receipts from visitors, n.a.; expenditures by nationals abroad, n.a.
Production (metric tons except as noted). Agriculture, forestry, fishing (1982): wheat 530,000, corn (maize) 370,000, sugar beets 330,000, potatoes 120,000, grapes 97,000, olives 53,000, oats 30,000, barley 25,000, sunflower seeds 25,000, tobacco 20,000; livestock (number of live animals) 1,170,000 sheep, 670,000 goats, 580,000 cattle, 125,000 pigs, 74,000 mules and asses, 43,000 horses; roundwood 2,330,000 cu m; fish catch 4,000. Mining and quarrying (1982): chromite ore 1,200,000; iron ore 600,000; salt 66,500; copper 16,200; nickel 5,800. Manufacturing (1980): bitumen (asphalt) 1,300,000; cement 1,000,000; distillate fuel oils 300,000; nitrogenous and phosphate fertilizers 78,000; raw sugar 35,000; paper and paperboard 17,000; olive oil 7,000;

wine 214,000 hectolitres; beer 160,000 hectolitres; cigarettes 6,100,000,000 units; cotton and woolen fabrics 60,650,000 m. Construction (1980): 1,821,-000,000 lekë. Energy production (consumption): electricity (kW-hr; 1981) 2,650,000,000 (2,050,000,000); coal (metric tons; 1982) 2,400,000 (2,400,-000); crude petroleum (barrels; 1982) 25,655,000 (25,655,000); petroleum products (metric tons; 1982) 2,665,000 (2,665,000); natural gas (cu m; 1982) 397,435,500 (397,435,000).
Gross national product (at current market prices; 1981): U.S.$2,380,000,000 (U.S.$850 per capita).

Origin of gross domestic product (current prices)

	1978			
	value	% of total value	labour force	% of labour force
Agriculture	...	37.9	557,800	50.0
Mining	...	†	†	†
Manufacturing	...	45.4	221,400	19.8
Construction	...	7.2	49,700	4.5
Trade	...	‡	38,600	3.5
Public utilities	...	†	†	†
Transportation and communication	...	‡	33,000	3.0
Finance	...	‡	§	§
Pub. admin., defense	...	‡	§	§
Services	...	‡	80,300	7.2
Other	...	9.5	134,200	12.0
TOTAL	...	100.0	1,115,000	100.0

Persons economically active (1978): total 1,115,000 (42.7%); female participation in the labour force 473,900 (42.5%); unemployed, n.a.
Price and earnings indexes: n.a.
Household income and expenditure. Average household size (1980) 4.5; average annual income per household: n.a.; sources of income: n.a.; expenditure: n.a.
Land use (1981): forested 45.3%; meadows and pastures 20.4%; agricultural and under permanent cultivation 27.4%; other 6.9%.

Foreign trade

Balance of trade (current prices)

	1978	1979	1980	1981	1982	1983
'000,000 lekë	...	100	...	...	...	...
% of total	...	5.3	...	...	...	...

Imports ‖ (1979): 900,000,000 lekë (chromite ore and concentrates, electricity, iron ore, nickel, petroleum products, copper, pyrite ore, bauxite, dolomite, chemicals, building materials [cement, marble facings], textile and leather goods, fruit and vegetables, and wine). *Major import sources:* Czechoslovakia 12.0%; Yugoslavia 12.0%; China 10.0%; Italy 8.0%; Poland 8.0%; West Germany 7.0%.
Exports ‖ (1979): 1,000,000,000 lekë (machinery and equipment, iron and steel, and consumer goods). *Major export destinations:* Czechoslovakia 11.0%; Yugoslavia 10.0%; Italy 10.0%; China 9.0%; Poland 7.0%; West Germany 7.0%.

Transport and communications

Transport. Railroads (1981): length 249 mi, 400 km; passenger-mi 181,000,-000, passenger-km 291,000,000; short ton-mi cargo 87,000,000, metric ton-km cargo 127,000,000. Roads (1981): total length 13,049 mi, 21,000 km (paved 14%). Vehicles (1970): passenger cars 3,500; trucks and buses 11,200. Merchant marine (1983): vessels (100 gross tons and over) 20; total deadweight tonnage 79,940. Air transport: passengers, n.a.; cargo, n.a.; airport (1984) with scheduled flights 1.
Communications. Daily newspapers (1981): total number 2; total circulation 145,000; circulation per 1,000 population 54.2. Radios (1983): total number of receivers 210,000 (1 per 13.3 persons). Television (1983): total number of receivers 20,500 (1 per 136.3 persons). Telephones (1966): 13,991 (1 per 152.6 persons).

Education and health

Education (1979–80)

	schools	teachers	students	student/ teacher ratio
Primary (age 7–15)	1,539	22,390	579,000	25.9
Secondary (age 16–18)	23	957	29,000	30.3
Voc., teacher tr.	242	...	114,000	...
Higher	17	1,015¶	14,695¶	...

College graduates per 100,000 population (1980): 177.0. *Literacy* (1970): total population literate 1,234,376 (75.0%).
Health (1978): physicians 3,013 (1 per 687 persons); hospital beds 17,000 (1 per 151 persons).
Food (1978–80): daily per capita caloric intake 2,837 (vegetable products 82.8%, animal products 17.2%); 118% of FAO recommended minimum requirement.

Military

Total active duty personnel (1981): 40,400 (army 74.3%; navy 7.9%; air force 17.8%). *Military expenditure as percent of GNP* (1981): 8.1% (world 5.7%); per capita expenditure U.S.$69.

*Detail does not add to total given because of rounding. †Mining and public utilities are included with manufacturing. ‡Trade, transportation, finance, public administration, defense, and services are included with other. §Finance and public administration are included with services. ‖ No figures are available for commodity breakdown since 1964. ¶1977.

Algeria

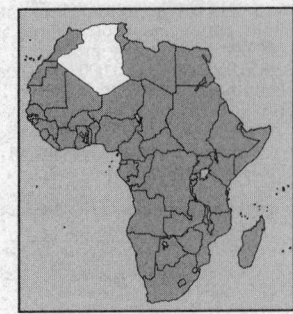

Official name: al-Jumhūrīyah
al-Jazā'irīyah ad-Dīmuqrātīyah
ash-Sha'bīyah (Arabic) (Democratic
and Popular Republic of Algeria).
Form of government: single-party
republic with one legislative house
(The National People's Assembly
[281]).
Head of state and government:
President.
Capital: Algiers.
Official languages: Arabic, French.
Official religion: Islām.
Monetary unit: 1 Algerian dinar
(DA) = 100 centimes; valuation (Oct.
29, 1984) 1 U.S.$ = DA5.11;
1 £ = DA6.17.

Area and population

Wilāyats*	Capitals	area sq mi	area sq km	population 1984 estimate
Adrar	Adrar	163,127	422,498	161,936
Alger	Algiers	303	786	2,442,303
Annaba	Annaba	1,347	3,489	650,096
Batna	Batna	5,746	14,882	691,079
Béchar	Béchar	118,147	306,000	184,069
Bejaïa	Bejaïa	1,329	3,442	659,040
Biskra	Biskra	42,366	109,728	662,778
Blida	Blida	1,430	3,704	1,126,303
Bouira	Bouira	1,744	4,517	454,805
ech-Cheliff	ech-Cheliff	3,350	8,677	1,040,563
Constantine	Constantine	1,375	3,562	809,245
Djelfa	Djelfa	8,844	22,905	403,500
Guelma	Guelma	3,330	8,624	633,733
Jijel	Jijel	1,431	3,705	604,319
Laghouat	Laghouat	43,263	112,052	391,817
Mascara	Mascara	2,257	5,846	526,644
Médéa	Médéa	3,361	8,704	575,305
Mostaganem	Mostaganem	2,712	7,024	896,767
M'sila	M'sila	7,654	19,825	540,013
Oran	Oran	703	1,820	889,800
Ouargla	Ouargla	215,921	559,234	261,760
Oum-el-Bouaghi	Oum-el-Bouaghi	3,136	8,123	464,806
Saïda	Saïda	41,227	106,777	450,594
Sétif	Sétif	3,996	10,350	1,176,673
Sidi-Bel-Abbes	Sidi-Bel-Abbes	4,497	11,648	604,773
Skikda	Skikda	1,833	4,748	597,530
Tamanrasset	Tamanrasset	214,673	556,000	62,680
Tébessa	Tébessa	6,400	16,575	439,638
Tiaret	Tiaret	9,056	23,456	731,542
Tizi-Ouzou	Tizi-Ouzou	1,450	3,756	1,028,864
Tlemcen	Tlemcen	3,585	9,284	678,025
TOTAL		919,595†	2,381,741	20,841,000

Source: Official government figures.

Demography

Density (1984): persons per sq mi 22.7, persons per sq km 8.8.
Urban–rural (1984): urban 66.6%; rural 33.4%.
Sex distribution (1984): male 49.94%; female 50.06%.
Age breakdown (1980): under 15, 47.3%; 15–29, 26.4%; 30–44, 12.8%; 45–59,
8.1%; 60–74, 4.3%; 75 and over, 1.1%.
Population projection: (1990) 25,300,000; (2000) 36,000,000.
Doubling time: 21 years.
Ethnic composition (1980): Arab 83.5%; Berber 16.1%; French 0.4%.
Religious affiliation (1980): Muslim 99.1%; Roman Catholic 0.3%; other
0.6%.
Major cities (1981): Algiers 2,200,000.

Vital statistics

Birth rate per 1,000 population (1982): 42.9‡ (world avg. 29.0); legitimate,
n.a.; illegitimate, n.a.
Death rate per 1,000 population (1982): 10.5‡ (world avg. 11.0).
Natural increase rate per 1,000 population (1982): 32.4‡ (world avg. 18.0).
Total fertility rate (avg. births per childbearing woman; 1979): 7.2.
Marriage rate per 1,000 population (1978): 6.9†.
Divorce rate per 1,000 population: n.a.
Infant mortality rate per 1,000 live births (1982): 92.9.
Life expectancy at birth (1980–85): male 56.7 years; female 58.9 years.
Major causes of death: n.a.

National economy

Budget (1981). Revenue: DA68,405,000,000 (petroleum and gas revenues
67.5%, business taxes 11.0%, customs duties 5.7%). Expenditures: DA67,-
788,250,000 (education 20.2%; housing 12.1%; defense 7.7%).
Public debt (external, outstanding; 1982): U.S.$16,794,000,000.
Tourism (1981): receipts from visitors U.S.$54,000,000; expenditures by na-
tionals abroad U.S.$430,000,000.
Production (metric tons except as noted). Agriculture, forestry, fishing (1982):
wheat 1,200,000, barley 650,000, potatoes 610,000, grapes 360,000, oranges
250,000, tomatoes 190,000, millet 50,000; livestock (number of live animals)
13,700,000 sheep, 2,760,000 goats, 1,390,000 cattle, 150,000 camels; roundwood 1,678,000 cu m; fish catch 64,500. Mining and quarrying (1982): iron
ore 3,900,000; barite 100,000; clay 58,100; zinc 12,900; sulfur 10,000; lead
3,600; copper 900; silver 110,000 troy ounces. Manufacturing (1980): ce-

ment 4,159,000; fuel oils 4,000,000; pig iron and ferro-alloys 669,000; crude
steel 345,000. Construction (1981): residential 28,000 units. Energy production (consumption): electricity (kW-hr; 1983) 8,926,000,000 (8,926,000,000);
coal (metric tons; 1982) 7,000 (757,000); crude petroleum (barrels; 1983)
233,000,000 (31,300,000); petroleum products (metric tons; 1982) 20,460,-
000 (4,737,000); natural gas (cu m; 1982) 48,000,000,000 (5,058,000,000).
Gross national product (at current market prices; 1982): U.S.$44,587,000,000
(U.S.$2,310 per capita).

Origin of gross domestic product (current prices)

	1981 in value DA'000,000	1981 % of total value	1978 labour force	1978 % of labour force
Agriculture	11,240	6.2	692,160	29.6
Mining	56,681	31.4	69,142	3.0
Manufacturing	20,101	11.1	302,054	12.9
Construction	21,113	11.7	345,816	14.8
Trade	41,268§	22.9§	183,580	7.8
Public utilities	1,867	1.0	30,265	1.3
Transportation and communication	§	§	132,420	5.7
Finance	§	§	17,769	0.8
Pub. admin., defense	19,864	11.0	88,800	3.8
Services	...	...	391,433	16.7
Other	8,400 ‖	4.7 ‖	83,532	3.6
TOTAL	180,534	100.0	2,336,971	100.0

Persons economically active (1982): total 4,505,000 (22.6%); female participation in the labour force, n.a.; unemployed, n.a .

Price and earnings indexes (1980 = 100)

	1977	1978	1979	1980	1981	1982	1983¶
Consumer Price index	69.9	81.9	91.3	100.0	114.6	122.3	124.4
Earnings index	...	...	...	...	...	...	...

Household income and expenditure. Average household size (1980) 4.9; average annual income per household: n.a.; expenditure: n.a.
Land use (1981): forested 1.8%; meadows and pastures 15.2%; agricultural
and under permanent cultivation 3.2%; other 79.8%.

Foreign trade

Balance of trade (current prices)

	1977	1978	1979	1980	1981	1982
DA'000,000	−3,175	−4,061	+6,939	+19,493	+19,836	+11,151
% of total	6.1%	7.5%	10.4%	19.4%	19.0%	10.1%

Imports (1982): DA49,384,000,000 (machines and transport equipment
39.1%, of which transport equipment 14.8%; food and food preparations
17.7%; consumer products 7.6%). *Major import sources:* France 20.9%; West
Germany 13.9%; Italy 8.8%; Spain 7.6%; Japan 7.3%; United States 7.0%.
Exports (1982): DA60,535,000,000 (mineral fuels and lubricants 98.2%, of
which petroleum 84.2%). *Major export destinations:* EEC 66.2%; United
States 17.1%; Japan 3.8%; U.S.S.R. 0.7%.

Transport and communications

Transport. Railroads (1983): route length 2,576 mi, 4,146 km; passenger-mi,
n.a., passenger-km, n.a.; short ton-mi cargo, n.a., metric ton-km cargo, n.a.
Roads (1981): total length 44,795 mi, 72,091 km (paved 54%). Vehicles
(1981): passenger cars 573,573; trucks and buses 265,577. Merchant marine
(1983): vessels (100 gross tons and over) 143; total deadweight tonnage
1,976,387. Air transport (1980): passenger-mi 1,430,000,000, passenger-km
2,300,000,000; short ton-mi cargo 8,840,000, metric ton-km cargo 12,900,-
000; airports (1984) with scheduled flights 26.
Communications. Daily newspapers (1982): total number 5; total circulation
570,000; circulation per 1,000 population 27.5. Radios (1983): total number
of receivers 3,500,000 (1 per 6 persons). Television (1983): total number
of receivers 1,325,000 (1 per 15.6 persons). Telephones (1982): 606,869 (1
per 33 persons).

Education and health

Education (1981–82)

	schools	teachers	students	1 student/ teacher ratio
Primary (age 6–11)	9,263	104,500	4,250,000	40.7
Secondary (age 12–18)	1,178	38,845♀	1,350,000	...
Voc., teacher tr.♀	71	2,292	26,218	11.4
Higher	15	8,573	100,000	11.7

College graduates per 100,000 population (students graduating; 1980): 40.
Literacy (1980): total population literate 4,342,300 (41.8%); males literate
2,771,400 (55.6%); females literate 1,570,900 (29.1%).
Health (1980): physicians 6,081 (1 per 3,046 persons); hospital beds 45,160
(1 per 410 persons).
Food (1978–80): daily per capita caloric intake 2,406 (vegetable products
85.5%, animal products 10.5%); 100% of FAO recommended minimum.

Military

Total active duty personnel (1983): 140,000 (army 85.7%; navy 5.7%; air force
8.6%). *Military expenditure as percent of GNP* (1982): 1.9% (world 6.0%);
per capita expenditure U.S.$42.

*Separate area and population figures are not available for the 16 new *wilāyat*s created in February 1984. †Detail does not add to total given because of rounding. ‡For
Algerian population only. §Transportation, communication, and finance are included
with trade. ‖ Net indirect taxes only. ¶Third quarter only. ♀1980–81.

Andorra

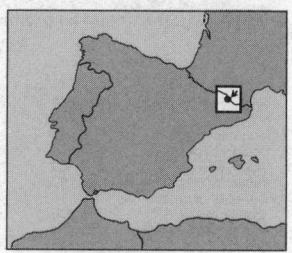

Official name: Principat d'Andorra; les Valls d'Andorra (Principality of Andorra; the Valleys of Andorra).
Form of government: co-principality with one nonpartisan legislative house (General Council of the Valleys [28]).
Chiefs of state: President of France; Bishop of Urgel, Spain.
Head of government: Syndic (Chairman) of the General Council of the Valleys.
Capital: Andorra la Vella.
Official language: Catalan.
Official religion: Roman Catholicism.
Monetary unit: There is no local currency. The French franc and Spanish peseta are both in circulation. 1 franc (F) = 100 centimes; 1 peseta (Pta) = 100 céntimos. Valuation (Oct. 29, 1984) 1 U.S.$ = F9.41, 1 £ = F11.36; 1 U.S.$ = Ptas 171.71, 1 £ = Ptas 207.25.

Area and population

Parishes	Capitals	area sq mi	area sq km	population 1982 estimate
Andorra la Vella	Andorra la Vella	23	59	14,928
Canillo	Canillo	47	121	743
Encamp	Encamp	29	74	4,194
La Massana	La Massana	24	61	2,529
Les Escaldes–Engordany	...	†	†	10,475
Ordino	Ordino	34	89	725
Sant Julià de Lòria	Sant Julià de Lòria	23	60	4,457
TOTAL		179‡	464	38,051

Source: Official government figures.

Demography

Density (1984): persons per sq mi 223.5, persons per sq km 86.2.
Urban–rural (1982): urban 66.8%; rural 33.2%.
Sex distribution (1982): male 53.74%; female 46.26%.
Age breakdown§ (1973): under 18, 31.0%; 19–50, 51.6%; 51 and over, 17.4%.
Population projection: Population change is difficult to predict because of the small population base and highly variable migration trends.
Doubling time: n.a.
Ethnic composition (1982): Spanish 58.6%; Andorran 27.1%; French 6.2%; Portuguese 3.5%; British 1.1%; other 3.5%.
Religious affiliation (1980): Roman Catholic 99.1%; Protestant 0.5%; Jewish 0.4%.
Major town (1982): Andorra la Vella 14,928.

Vital statistics

Birth rate per 1,000 population (1981): 14.8 (world avg. 30.0).
Death rate per 1,000 population (1981): 4.1 (world avg. 12.0).
Natural increase rate per 1,000 population (1981): 10.7 (world avg. 18.0).
Total fertility rate (avg. births per childbearing woman): n.a.
Marriage rate per 1,000 population (1981): 4.1.
Divorce rate per 1,000 population: n.a.
Infant mortality rate per 1,000 live births (1979): 12.0.
Life expectancy at birth: n.a.
Major causes of death: n.a.

National economy

Budget (1983). Revenue: Ptas3,719,700,000 (tax on consumer goods and gasoline *c.* 90.0%). Expenditures: Ptas3,683,400,000 (n.a.).
Public debt: n.a.
Production (metric tons except as noted). Agriculture (1981): potatoes 472, tobacco 264; livestock (number of live animals, 1982) 9,000 sheep, 1,115 cattle, 217 horses. Mining and quarrying (1982): lead and iron ore. Manufacturing (1982): ceramics, cigarettes, clothing, jewelry, textiles, and wooden furniture. Construction (1973): 10.3% residential; 89.7% nonresidential. Energy production (consumption): electricity (kW-hr; 1981) 100,000,000 (n.a.); coal, none (n.a.); petroleum, none (n.a.); natural gas, none (n.a.).
Gross national product: n.a.

Origin of gross domestic product (current prices)

	1982 value in francs	% of total value	labour force	% of labour force
Agriculture and forestry	...	...	87	0.5
Mining	...	...	386	2.2
Manufacturing	...	...	2,244	13.1
Construction	...	...	2,295	13.4
Trade	...	...	4,337	25.2
Transportation and communication	...	...	275	1.6
Finance	...	...	1,049	6.1
Pub. admin., defense	...	...	1,101	6.4
Services and hotel	...	...	4,603	26.8
Other	...	...	807	4.7
TOTAL	...	...	17,184	100.0

Persons economically active (1982): total 17,184 (45.2%); female participation in labour force, n.a.; unemployed, n.a.

Price and earnings indexes (1980 = 100) ‖

	1978	1979	1980	1981	1982	1983	1984
Consumer price index	74.8	86.5	100.0	114.6	131.0	147.0	158.4¶
Earnings index	...	...	...	...	...	...	...

Household income and expenditure: n.a.
Land use (1981): forested 23.7%; meadows and pastures 44.2%; agricultural and under permanent cultivation 4.0%; other 28.1%.
Tourism (1982): receipts from visitors, n.a.; expenditures by nationals abroad, n.a.; number of visitors, more than 6,000,000; number of hotels 235; number of hotel rooms 9,085.

Foreign trade

Balance of trade (current prices)♀

	1976	1977	1978	1979
U.S.$'000,000	−150	−204	−208	−338
% of total	92.4%	94.6%	94.9%	94.8%

Imports (1979): U.S.$347,300,000, of which from France U.S.$219,600,000, from Spain U.S.$127,700,000 (includes fuels, perfumes, clothing, and radio and television sets).
Exports (1979): U.S.$9,200,000, of which to France U.S.$5,200,000, to Spain U.S.$4,000,000 (includes wooden furniture, handicrafts, cigarettes, and cigars).

Transport and communications

Transport. Railroads: none. Roads (1981): total length 138 mi, 220 km (paved 55%). Vehicles (1982): passenger cars 26,000; trucks and buses, n.a. Merchant marine (1983): vessels (100 gross tons and over) none. Air transport (1983): none; the airport at nearby Seo de Urgel, Spain, has scheduled daily flights to Barcelona and Palma (on Majorca).
Communications. Daily newspaper (1983): total number 1; circulation, n.a. Radios (1983): total number of receivers 7,000 (1 per 5.7 persons). Television (1983): total number of receivers 4,000 (1 per 10.0 persons). Telephones (1982): 17,719 (1 per 2.1 persons).

Education and health

Education (1979–80)

	schools	teachers	students	student/ teacher ratio
Primary (age 6–12)	12	305	4,711	15.4
Secondary (age 12–18)	1	120δ	2,134	17.8
Voc., teacher tr.	8	...	...	...
Higher	...	...	...	...

College graduates per 100,000 population: n.a. *Literacy* (1981): total population literate (virtually 100%).
Health: physicians, n.a.; hospital beds, n.a.
Food: daily per capita caloric intake, n.a.

Military

Total active·duty personnel (1982): none. France and Spain provide for Andorra's defense. The city of Barcelona police and French *gendarmerie* alternate year-by-year in assisting the 32-member Andorran police force.

*Total area of Andorra per survey of 1978 is 181 sq mi (468 sq km). †Included with Andorra la Vella. ‡Detail does not add to total given because of rounding. §Andorra la Vella only. ‖ Spanish peseta. ¶First quarter only. ♀The trade value of French francs and Spanish pesetas are converted into U.S. dollars for purposes of standardization. δ1974–75.

PORTERFIELD—CHICKERING/PHOTO RESEARCHERS

Village of Pal, La Massana Parish, Andorra.

Angola

Official name: República Popular de
Angola (People's Republic of Angola).
Form of government: people's republic
with one legislative house (People's
Assembly [207]).
Head of state and government:
President.
Capital: Luanda.
Official language: Portuguese.
Official religion: none.
Monetary unit: 1 kwanza (Kw) = 100
lwei; valuation (Oct.29, 1984)
1 U.S. $ = Kw30.82; 1 £ = Kw37.20.

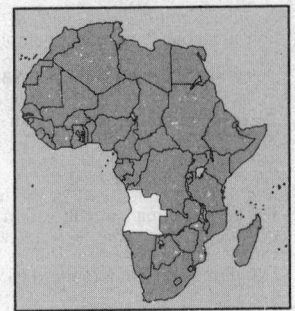

Area and population

Provinces	Capitals	area* sq mi	area* sq km	population 1970 census
Bengo†	Caxito	...	...	...
Benguela	Benguela	12,300	31,800	475,000
Bié	Kuito	27,150	70,300	650,000
Cabinda	Cabinda	2,800	7,300	81,000
Huambo	Huambo	13,250	34,300	838,000
Huíla	Lubango	28,950	75,000	492,000*
Kuando Kubango	Menongue	76,850	199,000	112,000
Kuanza Norte	Ndalatando	9,300	24,100	298,000
Kuanza Sul	Ngunza	21,500	55,700	459,000
Kunene	Ngiva	34,500	89,300	153,000*
Luanda	Luanda	13,050	33,800	561,000
Lunda Norte	Lucapa	39,750	103,000	210,000*
Lunda Sul	Saurimo	29,950	77,600	99,000*
Malanje	Malange	25,250	65,400	551,000*
Moxico	Luena	86,100	223,000	213,000
Namibe (Moçâmedes)	Namibe (Moçâmedes)	22,450	58,100	53,000
Uíge	Uíge	22,650	58,700	386,000
Zaire	Mbanza Kongo	15,500	40,100	42,000
TOTAL		481,350‡	1,246,700‡	5,673,000§

Source: Official government figures.

Demography

Density (1984): persons per sq mi 15.2, persons per sq km 5.9.
Urban–rural (1980): urban 21.0%; rural 79.0%.
Sex distribution (1980): male 49.15%; female 50.85%.
Age breakdown (1980): under 15, 43.9%; 15–29, 25.7%; 30–44, 15.9%; 45–59, 9.5%; 60–74, 4.3%; 75 and over, 0.7%.
Population projection: (1990) 8,632,000; (2000) 11,239,000.
Doubling time: 26 years.
Ethnic composition (1978): Ovimbundu 35.7%; Mbundu 22.3%; Kongo 12.6%; Luimbe 8.6%; Chokwe 8.2%; Nyaneka 4.2%; Humbe 2.5%; Ambo 2.4%; Lunda 0.9%; other 2.6%.
Religious affiliation (1980): affiliated Christian 65.7%, of which Roman Catholic 55.1%, Protestant 9.2%; nominal Christian 24.3%; tribal religionist 9.5%; other 0.5%.
Major cities (1982): Luanda 1,200,000; Namibe 100,000 ‖.

Vital statistics

Birth rate per 1,000 population (1981): 48.8 (world avg. 29.0).
Death rate per 1,000 population (1981): 22.7 (world avg. 12.0).
Natural increase rate per 1,000 population (1981): 26.1 (world avg. 17.0).
Total fertility rate (avg. births per childbearing woman; 1981): 6.5.
Marriage rate per 1,000 population: n.a.
Divorce rate per 1,000 population: n.a.
Infant mortality rate per 1,000 live births (1981): 152.1.
Life expectancy at birth (1981): male 40.6 years; female 42.9 years.
Major causes of death: n.a., however, major diseases are malaria, tuberculosis, and tetanus.

National economy

Budget (1981). Revenue: Kw93,478,000,000 (taxes 57.0%; loans 21.1%; state returns from mixed enterprises 12.6%; other 9.3%). Expenditures: Kw91,640,000,000 (economic and social development 37.5%; defense 20.2%¶; education, health, and other social services 15.1%; administration 12.9%; other 14.3%).
Public debt (external, outstanding; 1982): U.S.$553,000,000.
Tourism: n.a.
Production (metric tons except as noted). Agriculture, forestry, fishing (1982): sweet potatoes, taros, and yams 2,350,000, cassavas 1,950,000, sugarcane 420,000, bananas 280,000, corn (maize) 250,000, citrus fruits 80,000, millet 50,000, palm oil 40,000, coffee 35,000; livestock (number of live animals) 3,250,000 cattle, 945,000 goats, 440,000 pigs, 5,600,000 chickens; roundwood 8,986,000 cu m; fish catch 112,414. Mining and quarrying (1982): diamonds, of which gem quality 1,000,000 carats, industrial quality 400,000 carats; cement 300,000. Manufacturing (1981): raw sugar 50,000°; crude steel 10,000; soaps 6,000; paints 5,000; beer 1,350,000 hectolitres◊; matches 55,000 boxes; cigarettes 2,400,000,000 units◊; shirts 2,300,000 units; skirts 967,000 units; leather shoes 306,000 units. Construction: n.a. Energy production (consumption): electricity (kW-hr; 1982) 1,600,000,000 (1,600,000,000); coal (metric tons; 1982) none (minuscule); crude petroleum (barrels; 1982) 46,985,300 (8,136,300); petroleum products (metric tons; 1982) 890,000 (513,000); natural gas (cu m; 1982) 89,743,500,000 (89,743,500,000).
Gross national product (at current market prices; 1982): U.S.$7,634,000,000 (U.S. $1,032 per capita).

Origin of gross domestic product (current prices)

	1981 in value Kw'000,000	1981 % of total value	1979 labour force	1979 % of labour force
Agriculture	68,400	34.3	1,150,000	60.0
Mining	41,000	20.6		
Manufacturing	4,200	2.1		
Construction	3,300	1.7		
Trade, finance	9,500	4.8	307,000	16.0
Public utilities	700	0.3		
Transportation and communication	8,300	4.2		
Pub. admin., defense	20,400	10.2	460,000	24.0
Other	43,700	21.9		
TOTAL	199,500	100.0‡	1,917,000	100.0

Persons economically active (1981): total 1,910,000 (26.3%); female participation in the labour force 181,000 (9.5%); unemployed, n.a.
Price and earnings indexes: n.a.
Household income and expenditure. Average household size (1980) 4.8; average annual income per household: n.a.; source of income: n.a.; expenditure: n.a.
Land use (1981): forested 43.0%; meadows and pastures 23.3%; agricultural and under permanent cultivation 2.8%; other 30.9%.

Foreign trade

Balance of trade (current prices)□

	1978	1979	1980	1981	1982
Kw'000,000	+8,600	+11,400	+4,100	+3,200	+18,100
% of total	18.3%	16.9%	3.8%	3.1%	21.4%

Imports (1981): Kw49,500,000,000 (mostly purchases of military hardware, food [particularly grains], and other machinery and transport equipment). *Major import sources:* Portugal 15%; France 11%; U.S.S.R. 9%; South Africa 9%; Brazil 8%; United Kingdom 7%.
Exports (1981): Kw52,700,000,000 (crude petroleum 74%, petroleum products 10%, diamonds 10%, coffee 5%). *Major export destinations:* United States 49%; The Bahamas 15%; Spain 7%; Brazil 7%.

Transport and communications

Transport. Railroads (1981): route length 1,739 mi, 2,798 km; passenger journeys 7,620,000; cargo transported 725,000 metric tons. Roads (1975): total length 44,900 mi, 72,300 km (paved 12%). Vehicles (1982): passenger cars 75,000; trucks and buses 25,000. Merchant marine (1983): vessels (100 gross tons and over) 59; total deadweight tonnage 133,416. Air transport (1981): passenger-mi 444,607,000, passenger-km 715,527,000; short ton-mi cargo 42,221,000, metric ton-km cargo 61,642,000; airports (1984) with scheduled flights 18.
Communications. Daily newspapers (1982): total number 2; total circulation 50,000◊; circulation per 1,000 population 7.2◊. Radios (1983): total number of receivers 130,000 (1 per 54 persons). Television (1983): total number of receivers 22,000 (1 per 318 persons). Telephones (1981): 56,900 (1 per 120 persons).

Education and health

Education (1981–82)

	schools	teachers	students	student/ teacher ratio
Primary	7,026	40,027	1,258,858	31.5
Secondary	...	3,870	132,205	34.2
Voc., teacher tr.	...	...	5,206	...
Higher	1	300	3,150	10.5

College graduates: n.a. *Literacy* △(1980): total population literate 1,500,000 (about 20%); males literate† 298,000 (81.9%); females literate† 188,800 (51.2%).
Health (1980): physicians 436 (1 per 15,510 persons); hospital beds 20,700 (1 per 327 persons).
Food (1978–80): daily per capita caloric intake 2,110 (vegetable products 91.8%, animal products 8.2%); 90% of FAO recommended minimum requirement.

Military

Total active duty personnel (1983): 37,500⊕ (army 93.3%; navy 2.7%; air force 4.0%). *Military expenditure as percent of GNP* (1975): 3.6% (world 6.0%); per capita expenditure U.S.$27.

*Approximate; adjusted for postcensus boundary changes. †Area and population of Bengo province are included with Luanda province. ‡Detail does not add to total given because of rounding. §No later breakdown available; in 1984 population was estimated at 7,770,000. ‖ 1981 estimate; population (1970 census) of other important towns were: Huambo 62,000, Lobito 60,000, and Benguela 41,000. ¶According to unofficial estimates, defense consumed more than 50% of the budget in 1981. ○1980. ◊1979. □Figures for 1980–82 are approximations. ◊*O Jornal de Angola* only. △An intensive campaign was launched in 1976 aimed at eliminating illiteracy by 1985. In 1981, about 750,000 adults were enrolled in 37,000 literacy classes. †Ages 15–19 only. ⊕In 1983, about 25,000 Cuban troops and several hundred other Soviet-bloc advisers and technicians were assisting government forces.

Antigua and Barbuda

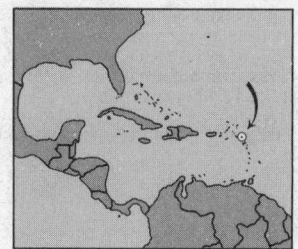

Official name: Antigua and Barbuda.
Form of government: parliamentary state with appointed Senate (17) and elected House of Representatives (17).
Chief of state: British Monarch represented by governor-general.
Head of government: Prime Minister.
Capital: Saint John's.
Official language: English.
Official religion: none.
Monetary unit: 1 East Caribbean dollar (EC$) = 100 cents; valuation (Oct. 29, 1984) 1 U.S.$ = EC$2.70; 1 £ = EC$3.26.

Area and population

Parishes	area		population
	sq mi	sq km	1982 estimate
Saint George	10.2	26.4	...
Saint John's	26.2	67.9	...
Saint Mary	25.1	65.0	...
Saint Paul	17.7	45.8	...
Saint Peter	12.8	33.2	...
Saint Phillip	16.0	41.4	...
Islands			
Barbuda	62.0	160.6	...
Redonda	0.5	1.3	*
TOTAL	170.5	441.6	77,200

Demography

Density (1984): persons per sq mi 462.0, persons per sq km 178.7.
Urban–rural (1980): urban 30.7%; rural 69.3%.
Sex distribution (1982): male 48.00%; female 52.00%.
Age breakdown: n.a.
Population projection: (1990) 81,000; (2000) 87,400.
Doubling time: 46 years.
Ethnic composition (1980): black 94.4%; mixed 3.5%; European 1.3%; other 0.8%.
Religious affiliation (1980): Anglican 44.5%; other Protestant 41.6%; Roman Catholic 10.2%; other 3.7%.
Major cities (1982 est.): Saint John's 30,000; Codrington 1,200.

Vital statistics

Birth rate per 1,000 population (1983): 16.5 (world avg. 29.0); (1981) legitimate 18.5%, illegitimate 81.5%.
Death rate per 1,000 population (1983): 6.5 (world avg. 11.0).
Natural increase rate per 1,000 population (1983): 10.0 (world avg. 18.0).
Total fertility rate (avg. births per childbearing woman; 1980): 2.6.
Marriage rate per 1,000 population (1981): 2.7.
Divorce rate per 1,000 population (1981): 0.8.
Infant mortality rate per 1,000 live births (1980): 32.0.
Life expectancy at birth (1975–80): 69.1 years.
Major causes of death per 10,000 population (1978): cerebrovascular disease 9.7; malignant neoplasms (cancers) 7.6; hypertensive diseases 3.8; diabetes mellitus 2.7.

National economy

Budget (1982). Revenue: EC$84,916,000 (indirect taxes 50.3%; import and export duties 22.5%; company income tax 12.4%; transfer payments from abroad 4.9%). Expenditure: EC$81,498,000 (salaries 56.8%; net expenditures on goods and services 22.8%; interest on public debt 8.9%; pensions and gratuities 5.8%).
Total public debt (1984): EC$47,200,000.
Tourism (1983): receipts from visitors U.S.$42,500,000; expenditures by nationals abroad, n.a.
Production (metric tons except as noted). Agriculture, forestry, fishing (1981): sweet potatoes and yams 190, mangoes 90, bananas 81, cabbage 81, pumpkins and squash 64, eggplants 47, cucumbers 46, tomatoes 42, carrots 40, corn (maize) 33, cassava 27, okras 18, seed cotton 15, milk 28,880 hectolitres; livestock (number of live animals; 1982) 9,000 sheep, 7,000 goats, 7,000 pigs, 6,000 cattle; fish catch 1,050. Mining and quarrying (1981): gravel 36,689. Manufacturing (gross value in EC$; 1981): clothing 84,410,200; mattresses 23,429,100; household appliances 6,350,000; paint and paint products 2,937,000; plastic products 1,758,000; furniture 1,464,-000; concrete 1,125,300. Construction (1981): Total building applications 919; gross value in EC$41,313,100. Energy production (consumption): electricity (kW-hr; 1982) 63,000,000 (63,000,000); petroleum products (metric tons; 1982) none (66,000); liquefied petroleum gas (metric tons; 1982) none (3,000); gases, other than natural gas (cu m; 1982) none (3,512,800).
Persons economically active (1980): total 28,378 (37.7%); female participation in the labour force 11,132 (39.2%); unemployed 5,887 (20.7%).
Household income and expenditure. Average household size (1970) 4.2; average annual income per household: n.a.; sources of income: n.a.; expenditure: n.a.

Price and earnings indexes (1980 = 100)

	1977	1978	1979	1980	1981	1982	1983
Consumer price index	68.1	72.2	84.0	100.0	111.5	116.3	118.6 ‖
Weekly earnings index	68.9	76.5	85.8	100.0	...	...	...

Gross national product (at current market prices; 1982): U.S.$128,100,000 (U.S.$1,660 per capita).

Origin of gross domestic product (current prices)

	1982		1979	
	in value EC$'000,000	% of total value	labour force	% of labour force
Agriculture	20.9	7.2	2,092	9.5
Mining	1.8	0.6	75	0.3
Manufacturing	15.2	5.2	1,539	7.0
Construction	24.4	8.4	2,476	11.2
Trade	73.6	25.3	4,867	22.1
Public utilities	10.1	3.5	319	1.4
Transportation and communication	46.9	16.1	2,596	11.8
Finance	52.8	18.1	742	3.4
Pub. admin., defense	44.0	15.1	†	†
Services	16.0	5.5	7,322‡	33.3
Other	−14.5§	−5.0§	...	...
TOTAL	291.2	100.0	22,028	100.0

Land use (1981): forested 15.9%; meadows and pastures 6.8%; agricultural and under permanent cultivation 18.1%; other 59.2%¶.

Foreign trade

Balance of trade (current prices)

EC$'000,000	1977	1978	1979	1980	1981	1982
	−82	−80	−150	−177	−232	−243
% of total	69.6%	53.9%	70.0%	51.9%	53.0%	56.8%

Imports (1981): EC$324,187,900 (machinery and transport equipment 29.6%; food and live animals 26.2%; manufactured goods, classified by materials 19.1%; miscellaneous manufactured articles 9.9%; chemicals 6.3%; beverages and tobacco 3.4%; crude materials, except fuels, 2.7%; mineral fuels, lubricants, and related materials 1.7%). *Major import sources:* United States 47.4%; United Kingdom 18.8%; Canada 5.9%; Puerto Rico 4.8%; Trinidad and Tobago 2.9%; Jamaica 1.6%; Barbados 1.5%; Guyana 1.1%.
Exports (1981): EC$92,431,600 (miscellaneous manufactured articles 52.1%; machinery and transport equipment 33.3%; manufactured goods, classified chiefly by materials 7.6%; chemicals 3.1%; beverages and tobacco 1.8%; food and live animals 1.2%). *Major export destinations:* United States 46.7%; Trinidad and Tobago 14.8%; United Kingdom 9.7%; Puerto Rico 7.7%; Barbados 6.2%; Jamaica 2.8%; Canada 1.7%.

Transport and communications

Transport. Railroads♀ (1982): 48 mi (78 km). Roads (1982): total length 237 mi, 380 km (paved 63%). Vehicles (1981): passenger cars 6,664; trucks and buses 1,209. Merchant marine (1983): vessels (100 gross tons and over) 3; total deadweight tonnage 443. Air transport (1981): passenger-mi 67,691,-000, passenger-km 108,938,000; short ton-mi cargo 68,000, metric ton-km cargo 100,000; airports (1984) with scheduled flights 1.
Communications. Daily newspapers (1983): total number 2; total circulation 5,500; circulation per 1,000 population 71. Radios (1982): total number of receivers 19,000 (1 per 4.1 persons). Television (1982): total number of receivers 16,500 (1 per 4.7 persons). Telephones (1980): 6,712 (1 per 11.0 persons).

Education and health

Education (1980)

	schools	teachers	students	student/teacher ratio
Primary (age 5–10)	44	431	10,660	24.7
Secondary (age 11–16)	18	318	4,526	14.2
Voc., teacher tr.	1	...	...	...
Higher	...	...	...	...

College graduates per 100,000 population: n.a. *Literacy* (1977): total population literate 38,800 (95%).
Health: physicians (1981) 33 (1 per 2,340 persons); hospital beds (1982) 215 (1 per 359 persons).
Food (1978–80): daily per capita caloric intake 2,141 (vegetable products 68.5%, animal products 31.5%); 88% of FAO recommended minimum requirement.

Military

Total active duty personnel: n.a. *Military expenditure as percent of GNP:* n.a.

*Uninhabited. †Public administration and defense are included with services. ‡Including unemployed. §Less imputed bank service charges. ‖ Third quarter. ¶Thin-soiled and eroded limestone. ♀Serving sugarcane plantations only.

Argentina

Official name: República Argentina.
(Argentine Republic).
Form of government: federal republic,
with two legislative houses (Senate
[46]; Chamber of Deputies [254]).
Head of state and government:
President.
Capital: Buenos Aires.
Official language: Spanish.
Official religion: Roman Catholicism.
Monetary unit: 1 new Argentine peso*
($a) = 100 centavos; valuation (Oct.
29, 1984) 1 U.S.$ = $a110.78;
1 £ = $a133.72.

Area and population

Provinces	Capitals	area sq mi	area sq km	population 1983 estimate
Buenos Aires	La Plata	118,754	307,571	11,625,000
Catamarca	San Fernando del Valle de Catamarca	38,984	100,967	221,000
Chaco	Resistencia	38,469	99,633	750,000
Chubut	Rawson	86,752	224,686	290,000
Córdoba	Córdoba	65,161	168,766	2,536,000
Corrientes	Corrientes	34,054	88,199	697,000
Entre Ríos	Paraná	30,418	78,781	946,000
Formosa	Formosa	27,825	72,066	319,000
Jujuy	San Salvador de Jujuy	20,548	53,219	449,000
La Pampa	Santa Rosa	55,382	143,440	222,000
La Rioja	La Rioja	34,626	89,680	174,000
Mendoza	Mendoza	57,462	148,827	1,277,000
Misiones	Posadas	11,506	29,801	641,000
Neuquén	Neuquén	36,324	94,078	277,000
Río Negro	Viedma	78,384	203,013	428,000
Salta	Salta	59,759	154,775	718,000
San Juan	San Juan	34,614	89,651	495,000
San Luis	San Luis	29,633	76,748	226,000
Santa Cruz	Río Gallegos	94,187	243,943	127,000
Santa Fe	Santa Fe	51,354	133,007	2,589,000
Santiago del Estero	Santiago del Estero	52,222	135,254	630,000
Tucumán	San Miguel de Tucumán	8,697	22,524	1,048,000
Other federal entities				
Distrito Federal	Buenos Aires	77	200	2,910,000
Tierra del Fuego	Ushuaia	8,210	21,263	32,000
TOTAL		1,073,399	2,780,092	29,627,000

Source: Official government figures.

Demography

Density (1984): persons per sq mi 28.0, persons per sq km 10.8.
Urban–rural (1983): urban 83.0%; rural 17.0%.
Sex distribution (1980): male 49.22%; female 50.78%.
Age breakdown (1980): under 15, 30.4%; 15–29, 23.9%; 30–44, 18.8%; 45–59, 15.1%; 60–74, 9.0%; 75 and over, 2.8%.
Population projection: (1990) 32,880,000; (2000) 37,197,000.
Doubling time: 47 years.
Ethnic composition (1983): European 98%; mestizo 2%.
Religious affiliation (1980): Roman Catholic 91.6%; other 8.4%.
Major cities (1980): Buenos Aires 2,923,000 (Greater Buenos Aires 9,766,-000); Córdoba 969,000; Rosario 876,000; La Plata 455,000.

Vital statistics

Birth rate per 1,000 population (1983): 24.6 (world avg. 29.0); legitimate 73.5%, illegitimate 26.5%†.
Death rate per 1,000 population (1983): 8.7 (world avg. 11.0).
Natural increase rate per 1,000 population (1983): 15.9 (world avg. 18.0).
Total fertility rate (avg. births per childbearing woman; 1981): 2.8.
Marriage rate per 1,000 population (1977): 7.0.
Divorce rate per 1,000 population: ‡.
Infant mortality rate per 1,000 live births (1981): 44.4.
Life expectancy at birth (1981): male 68.6 years; female 73.3 years.
Major causes of death per 100,000 population (1979): circulatory diseases 388.7; malignant neoplasms (cancers) 151.2; respiratory diseases 47.3.

National economy

Budget (1981)§. Revenue: $a9,227,500,000 ‖ (taxes on goods and services 44.0%; taxes on international trade 23.9%; social security contributions 15.8%). Expenditures: $a12,260,500,000 ‖ (social welfare 44.9%; economic services 23.8%; defense 15.2%; education 9.7%; health 1.8%).
Public debt (external, outstanding; 1982): U.S.$15,780,000,000.
Tourism (1980): receipts from visitors U.S.$344,000,000.
Production (metric tons except as noted). Agriculture, forestry, fishing (1983): sugarcane 15,794,000, wheat 12,300,000, corn (maize) 9,000,000, sorghum 8,250,000, soybeans 3,570,000, grapes 3,555,000, sunflower seed 2,300,000, potatoes 2,013,000, alfalfa 1,789,000¶, cotton (all forms) 914,000¶, linseed 670,000; livestock (number of live animals) 53,670,000 cattle, 30,000,000 sheep, 3,800,000 pigs; roundwood 10,478,000 cu m¶; fish catch 475,000¶. Mining and quarrying (1982): gold 15,272 troy oz.; silver 2,200,000 troy oz.; uranium 155. Manufacturing (by value in '000,000,000 of old $a; 1982): motor vehicles 32,296; cigarettes 20,404; steel, pig iron, and alloys 14,630; paper and paper products 13,793; steel pipes and tubes 13,668; sugar 13,-290; industrial plastics 9,630; vegetable oils 9,565; tires 9,510; cement 7,591. Construction, n.a. Energy production (consumption): electricity (kW-hr; 1982) 39,804,000,000 (39,849,000,000); coal (metric tons; 1982) 515,000

(1,189,000); crude petroleum (barrels; 1982) 181,310,000 (188,017,000); petroleum products (metric tons; 1982) 21,959,000 (19,489,000); natural gas (cu m; 1982) 10,072,000,000 (12,118,000,000).
Gross national product (at current market prices; 1981): U.S.$72,120,000,000 (U.S.$2,560 per capita).

Origin of gross domestic product (at current prices)

	1982 in value U.S.$'000,000	1982 % of total value	1980 labour force	1980 %of labour force
Agriculture	8,616	15.5	1,584,000	15.2
Mining	1,515	2.7	52,000	0.5
Manufacturing	12,434	22.3	2,189,000	21.0
Construction	3,429	6.2	917,000	8.8
Trade	7,089	12.7		
Public utilities	2,258	4.1		
Transportation and communication	6,225	11.2	5,682,000	54.5
Finance	4,751	8.5		
Pub. admin., defense	6,017	10.8		
Other	3,387	6.1		
TOTAL	55,721	100.0⁹	10,424,000	100.0

Persons economically active (1983): total 10,815,000 (38.3%); female participation in total labour force 2,860,000 (26.4%); unemployed 220,000 (5.7%).

Price and earnings indexes (1980 = 100)

	1977	1978	1979	1980	1981	1982	1983
Consumer price index	7.0	19.2	49.8	100.0	204.5	541.4	2,402.8
Monthly earnings index♂	7.6	14.8	40.1	100.0	...	...	...

Land use (1981): forested 21.9%; meadows and pastures 52.3%; agricultural and under permanent cultivation 12.9%; other 12.9%.

Foreign trade

Balance of trade (current prices)

	1977	1978	1979	1980	1981	1982	1983
U.S.$'000,000	+1,488	+2,624	+1,107	−2,528	−334	+2,288	+3,180
% of total	15.1%	25.8%	7.6%	13.6%	1.8%	17.7%	26.0%

Imports (1982): U.S.$5,337,000,000 (machinery and transport equipment 35.3%; chemicals 19.6%, of which organic chemicals 6.4%; basic manufactures 15.2%, of which iron and steel 5.9%; mineral fuels 12.8%, of which natural gas 7.1%). *Major import sources:* United States 22.1%; Brazil 12.9%; West Germany 9.0%; Japan 8.0%; Bolivia 7.4%.
Exports (1982): U.S.$7,625,000,000 (food and live animals 50.0%, of which unmilled wheat 8.9%, unmilled corn [maize] 7.7%, frozen bovine meat 6.0%, animal feed stuffs [excluding cereals] 5.8%, petroleum products 7.1%; machinery and transport equipment 6.7%; soybeans 5.6%; fixed vegetable oils 5.4%). *Major export destinations:* U.S.S.R. 20.8%; United States 13.4%; The Netherlands 7.9%; Brazil 7.4%; West Germany 4.4%.

Transport and communications

Transport. Railroads (1983): route length 21,443 mi, 34,509 km; passenger-mi 6,997,258,000□, passenger-km 11,260,995,000□; short ton-mi cargo 6,327,193,000□, metric ton-km cargo 9,237,533,000□. Roads (1978): total length 128,847 mi, 207,630 km (paved 22%). Vehicles (1981): passenger cars 3,193,892; commercial vehicles and buses 1,279,346. Merchant marine (1983): vessels (100 gross tons and over) 532; total deadweight tonnage 3,563,290. Air transport (1983): passenger-mi 3,764,834,000; passenger-km 6,058,924,000; short ton-mi cargo 131,036,000, metric ton-km cargo 191,-309,000; airports (1984) with scheduled flights 65.
Communications. Daily newspapers (1982): total number 159; total circulation 2,485,000◇; circulation per 1,000 population 85. Radios (1983): total number of receivers 10,000,000 (1 per 3.0 persons). Television (1983): total number of receivers 5,910,000 (1 per 5.0 persons). Telephones (1982): 3,041,475 (1 per 9.6 persons).

Education and health

Education (1982)

	schools	teachers	students	student/ teacher ratio
Primary (age 6–12)	20,201	206,535	4,197,372	20.3
Secondary (age 13–17)	1,942	81,026	594,167	7.3
Vocational	2,954	110,703	831,481	7.5
Higher△	1,041	53,166	550,556	10.4

College graduates† per 100,000 population (students graduating; 1980): 358.
Literacy (1980): total population literate 18,482,774 (94.9%); males literate 9,045,647 (95.6%); females literate 9,437,127 (94.4%).
Health: physicians (1979): 71,253 (1 per 390 persons); hospital beds (1973): 133,847 (1 per 188 persons).
Food (1978–80): daily per capita caloric intake 3,386 (vegetable products 67.9%; animal products 32.1%); 128% of FAO recommended minimum.

Military

Total active duty personnel (1983): 153,000 (army 65.0%; navy 24.0%; air force 11.0%). *Military expenditure as percent of GNP* (1981): 2.6% (world 5.7%); per capita expenditure: U.S.$111.

*Introduced June 1, 1983, at the rate of 1 new peso = 10,000 old pesos. †National statistics not kept since 1967. ‡Argentina has no legal provision for divorce. §Consolidated current and capital accounts. ‖ In new pesos. ¶1982. ⁹Detail does not add to total given because of rounding. ♂Skilled workers in manufacturing only. □1981. ◇Partial circulation only. △Includes teacher training. †Graduates of universities and superior schools.

Australia

Official name: Commonwealth of Australia.
Form of government: federal parliamentary state with two legislative houses (Senate [64]; House of Representatives [125]).
Chief of state: British monarch represented by the Governor General.
Head of government: Prime Minister.
Capital: Canberra.
Official language: English.
Official religion: none.
Monetary unit: 1 Australian dollar ($A) = 100 cents; valuation (October 29, 1984) 1 U.S.$ = $A1.19; 1 £ = $A1.44.

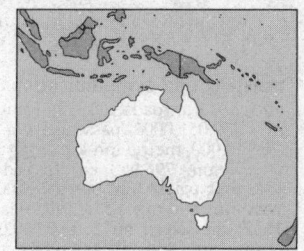

Area and population

States	Capitals	area sq mi	area sq km	population 1983 estimate
New South Wales	Sydney	309,500	801,600	5,360,400
Queensland	Brisbane	666,900	1,727,200	2,471,600
South Australia	Adelaide	379,900	984,000	1,341,500
Tasmania	Hobart	26,200	67,800	432,600
Victoria	Melbourne	87,900	227,600	4,037,600
Western Australia	Perth	975,100	2,525,500	1,364,500
Territories				
Australian Capital Territory	Canberra	900	2,400	236,600
Northern Territory	Darwin	519,800	1,346,200	133,900
TOTAL		2,966,200	7,682,300	15,378,600*

Source: Official government figures.

Demography

Density (1984): persons per sq mi 5.2, persons per sq km 2.0.
Urban–rural (1981): urban 85.7%; rural 14.3%.
Sex distribution (1981): male 49.86%; female 50.14%.
Age breakdown (1981): under 15, 25.1%; 15–29, 25.3%; 30–44, 20.5%; 45–59, 15.2%; 60–74, 10.4%; 75 and over, 3.5%.
Population projection: (1990) 16,170,000; (2000) 17,795,000.
Doubling time: 63 years.
Ethnic composition (1971): British 94.3%; Italian 1.2%; Greek 0.8%; Yugoslavian 0.5%; other 3.2%.
Religious affiliation (1981): Christian 76.4%, of which Church of England 26.1%, Roman Catholic 26.0%, Protestant 20.8% [Uniting Church 4.9%, Presbyterian 4.4%, Methodist 3.4%], Orthodox 2.9%; Muslim 0.5%; Jewish 0.4%; Buddhist 0.2%; no religion 10.8%; other 11.7%.
Major cities (1983 est.): Sydney 3,334,950; Melbourne 2,864,600; Brisbane 1,138,370; Adelaide 969,160; Perth 809,035†; Newcastle 258,972†; Canberra 255,900; Wollongong 208,651†; Hobart 128,603†; Gold Coast 154,706†.
Place of birth (1981): 78.2% native-born; 20.6% foreign-born, of which: U.K. 7.8%‡, Italy 1.9%, New Zealand 1.2%, Greece 1.0%, Yugoslavia 1.0%, East and West Germany 0.8%, The Netherlands 0.7%, Poland 0.4%, Malta 0.4%, Lebanon 0.3%; not stated 1.2%.
Mobility (1982). Population living in the same residence as in 1981: 84.0%; different residence, same state 9.4%; different states and territories 6.6%.
Households (1981). Average household size 3.1; 1 person 18.0%, 2 persons 29.2%, 3 persons 16.9%, 4 persons 19.1%, 5 persons 10.5%, 6 persons 4.1%, 7 or more persons 2.2%. Family households: 4,529,948 (97.0%), nonfamily 138,961 (3.0%).
Immigration (1982): permanent immigrants admitted 107,171, from U.K. and Ireland 32.4%, New Zealand 10.3%, Malaysia and Singapore 7.0%, E. and W. Germany 5.1%, Austria 4.5%, Thailand 3.4%, Philippines 3.4%, South Africa 3.1%, United States 2.3%, Indonesia 2.0%, Yugoslavia 1.8%. Refugee arrivals 17,522.

Vital statistics

Birth rate per 1,000 population (1982–83): 15.8 (world avg. 29.0); (1979) legitimate 88.3%; illegitimate 11.7%.
Death rate per 1,000 population (1982–83): 7.3 (world avg. 11.0).
Natural increase rate per 1,000 population (1982–83): 8.5 (world avg. 18.0).
Total fertility rate (avg. births per childbearing woman; 1982): 1.9.
Marriage rate per 1,000 population (1982): 7.7.
Divorce rate per 1,000 population (1982): 2.9.
Infant mortality rate per 1,000 live births (1982): 10.3.
Life expectancy at birth (1982): male 71.2 years; female 78.2 years.
Major causes of death per 100,000 population (1982): diseases of the circulatory system 380; malignant neoplasms (cancers) 166; diseases of the respiratory system 59; accidents, poisonings, and violence 55; diseases of the digestive system 26; endocrine, nutritional, and metabolic diseases and immunity disorders 14.

Social indicators

Educational attendance and level of qualification (1981). Percent of population over 15: not attending 83.5%, attending full-time 6.1%, attending part-time 3.8%; total with qualification 24.2%, of which trade certificate 9.4%, diploma 3.6%, bachelor's degree 2.9%, graduate diploma 0.7%, higher degree 0.5%; no qualification 64.1%; still at school 3.5%; not stated 8.2%.

Distribution of family income (1981)

income group	$A0–6,000	$A6,000–12,000	$A12,000–18,000	more than $A18,000
% of population	24.0%	25.2%	21.1%	29.7%

Quality of working life (1983). Average work week: 34.8 hours (3.7% overtime). Annual rate per 100,000 workers for: injury or accident n.a., industrial illness n.a., death n.a.. Proportion of employed persons insured for damages or income loss resulting from: injury 100%, permanent disability 100%, death 100%. Average days lost to labour stoppages per 1,000 work days (1982): 1.6. Means of transportation to work (1981): 62.2% private automobile; 13.9% public transportation; 1.3% bicycle; 5.4% foot; 17.2% other. Proportion of unemployed workers discouraged (considered by employers to be too young or too old and no vacancies in line of work) (1981): 29.5%.
Access to services (1976). Proportion of dwellings having access to: electricity 99.5%, bathroom 96.0%, flush toilet 92.2%, kitchen 97.9%, public sewer 73.4%.
Social participation. Eligible voters participating in last national election 86.8%. Population participating in voluntary work n.a. Trade union membership in total workforce 47%. Practicing religious population in total affiliated population: n.a.
Social deviance (1981). Offense rate per 100,000 population for: murder 3.3, rape 8.7, serious assault 44.8, auto theft 536.0, burglary and housebreaking 1,407.1, fraud and forgery 435.5. Incidence in general population (per 100,000) of: alcoholism n.a., drug and substance abuse (charges) 214, suicide 11.5.
Leisure (1983). Favourite leisure activities: water sports (swimming, surfing, and yachting), golfing, bowling, squash, cricket, bushwalking (hiking); all, except water sports, are often enjoyed through membership in licensed clubs; sports of increasing popularity are trail bike riding and off-road driving.
Material well-being (1983). Households possessing: automobile 100%, telephone 100%, television receiver 100%, refrigerator 99.6%, air conditioner 32.3%, washing machine 91.7%, hot water 98.7%, central heating 3.9%, swimming pool 10.1%.

National economy

Gross national product (at current market prices, seasonally adjusted annual rate; 1984‡): U.S.$174,500,000,000 (U.S.$11,258 per capita).

Origin of gross domestic product (current factor cost)

	1980–81 in value $A'000,000	1980–81 % of total value	1981 labour force	1981 % of labour force
Agriculture	7,161	6.2	379,388	6.0
Mining	5,145	4.4	88,993	1.4
Manufacturing	22,938	19.8	1,114,668	17.7
Construction	8,286	7.2	398,162	6.3
Trade	16,175	14.0	1,093,946	17.4
Public utilities	3,915	3.4	125,620	2.0
Transportation and communication	8,717	7.5	455,224	7.2
Finance§	23,177	20.0	531,413	8.5
Pub. admin., defense	5,848	5.1	353,541	5.6
Services	17,638	15.2	1,268,430	20.2
Other ‖	–3,273	–2.8	483,246¶	7.7¶
TOTAL	115,727	100.0	6,292,631	100.0

Budget (1983–84). Revenue: $A48,289,000,000 (income tax 61.2%, of which individual 51.1%, corporate 10.1%; indirect taxes 30.1%). Expenditures: $A56,955,000,000 (transfer payments to personal benefits 33.7%; states and local governments 32.7%; current expenditure 11.5%; defense 8.7%).
National debt (1984♀): $A41,913,000,000.
Tourism (1982): receipts from visitors U.S.$1,097,000,000; expenditures by nationals abroad U.S.$1,852,000,000.

Manufacturing, mining, and construction enterprises (1981–82)

	no. of establishments	no. of employees	hourly wages as a % of avg. of all wages	annual value added ($A'000,000)
Manufacturing				
Food, beverages, and tobacco	3,485	178,732	95.6	5,325
Basic metal products	548	96,114	108.4	3,080
Transport equipment	1,394	131,467	96.0	2,998
Paper, printing, and publishing	2,946	102,913	103.8	2,984
Fabricated metal products	4,509	116,332	94.7	2,860
Chemical, petroleum, and coal products	942	60,218	102.0	2,767
Wood, wood products, and furniture	4,184	80,419	...	1,770
Nonmetallic mineral products	1,777	45,957	...	1,685
Clothing and footwear	2,032	77,507	...	1,380
Textiles	655	35,945	76.2	856
Mining				
Coal	132	31,778	...	2,214
Metallic minerals	236	34,700	...	2,167
Construction⌀	51,351	246,510	103.3	3,925

Production (gross value in $A'000 except as noted). Agriculture, forestry, fishing (1982–83): livestock slaughtered—cattle 2,079,400, sheep and lambs 574,300, pigs 415,500; wool 1,765,800; wheat 1,539,300, vegetables 594,700, sugarcane 509,400, fruits 501,700, barley 299,800, grapes 220,300, cotton 160,400, sorghum 152,200, oats 115,600; livestock (number of live animals, 1983) 133,186,000 sheep, 22,471,000 cattle, 2,498,000 pigs, 45,556,000 poultry; roundwood 16,915,000 cu m□; fish catch 161,000 metric tons□.

Mining and quarrying (metric tons; 1982–83): iron ore 80,991,000; bauxite 22,865,000; refined metals, aluminum 403,917, zinc 288,250, lead 212,176, copper 172,456, tin 2,898, gold 25,784 kilograms. Manufacturing (metric tons; 1982–83): raw steel 5,306,000; cement 5,076,000; iron and steel slabs 3,583,000; super phosphate 2,986,000; sulphuric acid 1,782,000; beef and veal 1,543,700; wheat flour 1,088,000; refined sugar 701,700; lamb 280,400; mutton 249,800; pork 239,100; plaster sheets 49,879,000 sq m; textile floor coverings 33,693,000 sq m; woven cotton cloth 32,915,000 sq m; roofing tiles 14,738,000 sq m; woven woollen cloth 10,348,000 sq m; automotive gasoline 14,968,000,000 litres; furnace fuel 3,038,000,000 litres. Construction (building starts by value in $A'000; 1982–83): new dwellings 4,599,200; alterations and additions to dwellings 649,500; other buildings in private sector 2,730,500.

Retail sales and service enterprises (1979–80)

	no. of estab-lishments	no. of employees	total wages and salaries ($A'000,000)	annual turnover ($A'000,000)
Motor vehicle dealers, gasoline and tire dealers	26,516	175,995	1,319	18,203
Food stores	39,416	260,266	1,131	12,747
Department and general stores	857	99,569	717	4,254
Clothing, fabrics, and furniture stores	17,908	81,797	519	4,143
Household appliances and hardware stores	8,196	43,542	320	2,966
Restaurants, hotels and accommodations	17,702	183,310	1,022	4,670
Licensed clubs	3,243	52,297	697	1,515
Laundries and dry cleaners	1,365	12,106	91	224
Motion picture theatres	577	6,777	45	178
Hairdressers and beauty salons	2,265	12,282	78	173

Energy production (consumption): electricity (kW-hr; 1982–83) 105,933,000,-000 (105,933,000,000); coal (metric tons; 1982–83) 142,292,000 (49,271,000); crude petroleum (barrels; 1982) 137,071,000 (203,041,000); petroleum products (metric tons; 1982–83) 26,964,000 (25,369,000); natural gas (cu m; 1982) 10,256,400,000 (10,256,400,000).
Persons economically active (April 1984): total 7,160,900 (46.3%); female participation in the labour force 2,727,500 (38.1%); unemployed 678,600 (9.5%).

Price and earnings indexes (1980 = 100)

	1978	1979	1980	1981	1982	1983	1984◇
Consumer price index	83.3	90.8	100.0	109.7	121.9	134.2	138.1
Weekly earnings index	82.3	89.3	100.0	111.4	124.5	133.5	146.4

Household income and expenditure. Average household size (1981) 3.1; average annual income per household $A9,328 (U.S.$8,582); sources of income (1982–83): wages and salaries 60.5%, income from property and entrepreneurship 22.6%; current transfers from government 11.6%, supplements to wages and salaries 4.2%; expenditure (1982–83): rent 19.2%, transport and communications 19.0%, food 16.9%, household equipment and operation 10.0%, recreation and education 9.2%, clothing and footwear 6.8%.
Land use (1981): forested 13.9%; meadows and pastures 59.8%; agricultural and under permanent cultivation 5.7%; other 20.6%.

Financial aggregates

	1978	1979	1980	1981	1982	1983	1984 (9 mo.)
Exchange Rate, $A1.00 per:							
U.S. Dollar	1.14	1.12	1.14	1.15	1.02	0.90	0.84
£	0.59	0.53	0.49	0.57	0.50	0.59	0.64
SDR	0.88	0.84	0.93	0.97	0.89	0.85	0.83
International reserves (U.S.$)							
Total (excl. gold; '000,000)	2,062	1,424	1,690	1,671	6,371	8,869	7,651
SDR's ('000,000)	129	42	---	52	86	81	187
Reserve pos. in IMF ('000,000)	210	206	325	294	---	114	136
Foreign exchange ('000,000)	1,723	1,176	1,365	1,325	6,285	8,675	7,328
Gold, ('000,000 fine troy oz.)	7.79	7.93	7.93	7.93	7.93	7.93	7.93
% world reserves	0.8	0.8	0.8	0.8	0.8	0.8	0.8△
Interest and prices							
Central bank discount (%)	...	...	...	...	...	...	...
Gov't. Bond yield(%)+	9.1	9.8	11.6	14.0	15.4	14.3	13.2△
Industrial share prices (1980 = 100)	54.4	66.9	100.0	104.2	79.5	100.4	117.3△
Balance of payments (U.S.$'000,000)							
Balance of visible trade	93	2,511	1,378	−2,322	−2,614	241	...
Imports, f.o.b.	14,023	16,066	20,181	23,545	23,411	19,354	...
Exports, f.o.b.	14,116	18,577	21,559	21,223	20,797	19,595	...
Balance of invisibles	−3,805	−4,255	−4,692	−4,110	−4,771	−4,898	...
Balance of payments, current account	−4,201	−2,260	−3,668	−7,811	−7,848	−5,114	...

Foreign trade

Balance of trade (current prices)

	1977–78	1978–79	1979–80	1980–81	1981–82	1982–83
$A'000,000	+1,101	+489	+2,653	+212	−3,417	+104
% of total	4.7%	1.7%	7.6%	0.6%	8.0%	0.2%

Imports (1982–83): $A21,266,000,000 (industrial supplies 25.6%; capital goods and parts 25.5%; consumer goods 15.1%; fuels and lubricants 14.2%; transport equipment and parts 13.1%; food and beverages 4.4%). *Major import sources:* United States 21.8%; Japan 20.7%; United Kingdom 6.7%; West Germany 6.0%; Saudi Arabia 4.5%; New Zealand 3.2%.
Exports (1982–83): $A21,370,000,000 (coal, coke, and briquettes 14.4%; nonferrous ores 8.5%; wool 8.5%; meat 7.9%; iron ore 7.0%; wheat and flour 6.5%; sugar 2.6%; dairy products 1.5%). *Major export destinations:* Japan

27.1%; United States 10.1%; United Kingdom 5.3%; New Zealand 5.2%; South Korea 3.8%; Singapore 3.3%.

Transport and communications

Transport. Railroads⊙ (1982): route length 24,171 mi, 38,900 km; passenger-mi 1,359,051,000♂, passenger-km 2,187,120,000♂; short ton-mi cargo 25,-570,000,000, metric ton-km cargo 37,332,000,000. Roads (1983): total length 495,207 mi, 796,960 km (paved 39%). Vehicles (1983): passenger cars 7,322,500; trucks and buses 789,000. Merchant marine (1983): vessels (100 gross tons and over) 578; total deadweight tonnage 3,013,890. Air transport (1982): passenger-mi 15,680,900,000, passenger-km 25,236,000,000; short ton-mi cargo 434,531,000, metric ton-km cargo 634,404,000; airports (1983) with scheduled flights 443.
Communications. Daily newspapers (1979): total number 63; total circulation 4,851,000; circulation per 1,000 population 336. Radios (1983): total number of receivers 20,000,000 (1 per 0.8 person). Television (1983): total number of receivers 6,500,000 (1 per 2.4 persons). Telephones (1983): 8,266,662 (1 per 1.9 persons).

Education and health

Education (1983)

	schools	teachers	students	student/ teacher ratio
Primary (age 6–12)	8,336	94,224	1,809,035	19.2
Secondary (age 13–17)	1,572	93,273	1,206,771	12.9
Voc., teacher tr.	373	44,776	729,291	16.3
Higher	64	21,866	349,243	16.0

College graduates per 100,000 population (students graduating; 1981): 218.
Literacy (1980): 99.5%.
Health: physicians (1982) 27,500 (1 per 552 persons); hospital beds (1982) 94,137 (1 per 161 persons).
Food (1978–80): daily per capita caloric intake 3,202 (vegetable products 64.2%, animal products 35.8%); 120% of FAO recommended minimum requirement.

Military

Total active duty personnel (1983): 72,473 (army 45.3%; navy 23.7%; air force 31.0%). *Military expenditure as percent of GNP* (1982): 2.5% (world 6.0%); per capita expenditure U.S.$292.

*Detail does not add to total given because of rounding. †1981 census. ‡Includes both Northern Ireland and Republic of Ireland. §Finance includes ownership of dwellings. ‖ Less imputed bank service charges. ¶Includes other services. ⊊First quarter. ♂1978–79. □1982. ◇Second quarter. △August. +Long term only. ⊙Government railways only.

DOUGLASS BAGLIN

Koala (*Phascolarctos cinereus*).

Austria

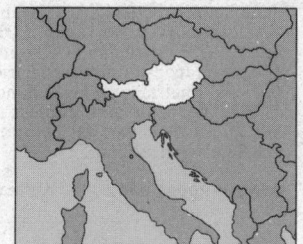

Official name: Republik Österreich (Republic of Austria).
Form of government: federal multi party republic with two legislative houses (Federal Council [63]; National Council [183]).
Chief of state: President.
Head of government: Chancellor.
Capital: Vienna.
Official language: German.
Official religion: none.
Monetary unit: 1 schilling (S) = 100 groschen; valuation (Oct. 29, 1984) 1 U.S.$ = S21.54; 1 £ = S26.00.

Area and population

States	Capitals	area sq mi	area sq km	population 1984 estimate
Burgenland	Eisenstadt	1,531	3,965	268,300
Karnten	Klagenfurt	3,681	9,534	538,700
Niederosterreich	Vienna	7,402	19,172	1,423,200
Oberosterreich	Linz	4,626	11,980	1,278,000
Salzburg	Salzburg	2,762	7,154	451,200
Steiermark	Graz	6,327	16,387	1,183,800
Tirol	Innsbruck	4,883	12,647	594,400
Vorarlberg	Bregenz	1,004	2,601	307,600
Wien	—	160	415	1,505,800
TOTAL		32,376	83,855	7,551,000

Source: Official government figures.

Demography

Density (1984): persons per sq mi 233.2, persons per sq km 90.0.
Urban–rural (1981): urban 55.1%; rural 44.9%.
Sex distribution (1984): male 47.53%; female 52.47%.
Age breakdown (1982): under 15, 19.6%; 15–29, 23.7%; 30–44, 20.4%; 45–59, 16.7%; 60–74, 13.3%; 75 and over, 6.3%.
Population projection: (1990) 7,560,000; (2000) 7,606,000.
 During the intercensal period 1971–81 the annual growth rate was 0.1%; since 1981, however, the population has been decreasing.
Ethnic composition (1978): Austrian 91.8%; German 3.1%; Slovene 0.8%; Croat 0.7%; Hungarian 0.4%; Turk 0.3%; other 2.9%.
Religious affiliation (1980): Roman Catholic 85.4%; Protestant 6.1%; nonreligious and atheist 2.7%; Eastern Orthodox 0.8%; Muslim 0.6%; other 4.4%.
Major cities (1981): Vienna 1,531,346; Graz 243,166; Linz 199,910; Salzburg 139,426; Innsbruck 117,287.

Vital statistics

Birth rate per 1,000 population (1982): 12.5 (world avg. 29.0); (1982) legitimate 82.2%, illegitimate 17.8%.
Death rate per 1,000 population (1982): 12.1 (world avg. 11.0).
Natural increase rate per 1,000 population (1982): 0.4 (world avg. 18.0).
Total fertility rate (avg. births per childbearing woman; 1980–85): 1.6.
Marriage rate per 1,000 population (1982): 6.3.
Divorce rate per 1,000 population (1982): 1.9.
Infant mortality rate per 1,000 live births (1982): 12.9.
Life expectancy at birth (1981): male 71.2 years; female 75.9 years.
Major causes of death per 100,000 population (1982): heart and circulatory disease 637.9, of which ischemic heart disease 203.2; malignant neoplasms (cancers) 243.6; accidents 61.9; diseases of the respiratory system 56.7.

National economy

Budget (1982). Revenue: S270,942,000,000 (taxes 89.4%, of which direct income 39.2%, indirect 45.8%). Expenditures: S324,722,000,000 (goods and services 24.0%; transfers 48.2%; interest on public debt 7.9%).
Tourism (1982): receipts from visitors U.S.$5,649,000,000; expenditures by nationals abroad U.S.$2,772,000,000.
Production (metric tons except as noted). Agriculture, forestry, fishing (1983): sugar beets 1,975,000, barley 1,442,000, corn (maize) 1,437,000, wheat 1,415,000, potatoes 1,015,000, grapes 518,000, wine 370,000, rye 348,000, milk 3,725,000; livestock (number of live animals) 3,981,000 pigs, 2,546,000 cattle, 15,000,000 chickens; roundwood 13,095,000*. Mining and quarrying (1982): iron ore 3,300,000†; magnesite 1,031,000; zinc 21,938†; lead 5,574†. Manufacturing (value in S'000,000; 1980) machinery 143,680, of which electrical 55,640, transport 28,580; food products 76,700; chemical products 54,990; iron and steel 54,990; textiles and apparel 45,010; petroleum products 38,870; paper and paper products 26,080. Construction (dwellings completed, 1981): residential 4,500,000 sq m; nonresidential 100,000 sq m. Energy production (consumption): electricity (kW-hr; 1982) 42,891,000,000 (38,552,000,000); coal (metric tons; 1982) 3,098,000 (6,635,-000); crude petroleum (barrels; 1982) 8,996,000 (56,236,000); petroleum products (metric tons; 1982) 7,029,000 (9,149,000); natural gas (cu m; 1982) 1,371,614,000 (4,199,919,000).
Persons economically active (1982): total 3,278,800 (43.7%); female participation in labour force 1,265,000 (38.6%); unemployed 105,350 (3.2%).

Price and earnings indexes (1980 = 100)

	1978	1979	1980	1981	1982	1983	1984 ‖
Consumer price index	90.7	94.0	100.0	106.8	112.6	116.3	122.7
Monthly earnings index	87.6	92.7	100.0	106.1	112.6	...	...

Gross national product (at current market prices; 1983): U.S.$66,745,000,000 (U.S.$8,840 per capita).

Origin of gross domestic product (current prices)

	1982 in value S'000,000	% of total value	labour force	% of labour force
Agriculture	44,150	3.9	320,000	9.7
Mining	4,850	0.4	18,000	0.5
Manufacturing	306,000	26.8	982,000	29.7
Construction	146,070	12.8	289,000	8.8
Trade	188,880	16.6	439,000	13.3
Public utilities	40,220	3.5	37,000	1.1
Transportation and communication	64,690	5.7	212,000	6.4
Finance	98,440	8.6	‡	...
Pub. admin., defense	154,630	13.6	‡	...
Services	46,020	4.0	998,000	30.2
Other	47,130	4.1	7,000	0.2
TOTAL	1,141,080	100.0	3,302,000	100.0§

Household income and expenditure. Average household size (1982) 2.8; income per household (1982) S415,980 (U.S.$24,385); sources of income (1980): wages and salaries 60.0%, social security benefits and social assistance grants 16.9%, self-employment 15.7%; expenditure (1982): food 26.8%, housing and utilities 14.9%, clothing and footwear 9.6%.
Land use (1981): forested 39.7%; meadows and pastures 24.7%; agricultural and under permanent cultivation 19.9%; other 15.7%.

Foreign trade

Balance of trade (current prices)

	1978	1979	1980	1981	1982	1983
S'000,000	−55,776	−63,609	−89,677	−82,741	−65,690	−71,200
% of total	13.7%	13.4%	16.5%	14.1%	11.0%	11.4%

Imports (1982): S332,550,600,000 (machinery and transport equipment 27.8%, of which road vehicles 8.0%; manufactured goods 18.5%, of which textile yarn 4.8%, iron and steel 2.9%; petroleum and related materials 11.2%; chemicals and related products 10.0%). *Major import sources:* West Germany 40.6%; Italy 8.6%; U.S.S.R. 5.1%; Switzerland 4.8%; France 3.9%; United States 3.8%.
Exports (1982): S266,860,400,000 (manufactured goods 35.0%, of which iron and steel 9.2%; textile yarn 6.6%; machinery and transport equipment 29.5%, of which road vehicles 4.6%; chemicals 9.0%). *Major export destinations:* West Germany 29.3%; Italy 9.1%; Switzerland 7.0%; United Kingdom 4.3%; France 4.2%.

Transport and communications

Transport. Railroads (1982): length 3,577 mi, 5,757 km; passenger-mi 4,548,-000,000, passenger-km 7,320,000,000; short ton-mi cargo 6,919,719,000, metric ton-km cargo 10,102,620,000. Roads (1982): total length 66,569 mi, 107,132 km (paved 100%). Vehicles (1982): passenger cars 2,361,071; trucks and buses 220,689. Merchant marine (1983): vessels (100 gross tons and over) 22; total deadweight tonnage 195,887. Air transport (1983): passenger-mi 805,000,000, passenger-km 1,296,000,000; short ton-mi cargo 14,600,000, metric ton-km cargo 21,300,000; airports (1984) with scheduled flights 6.
Communications. Daily newspapers (1983): total number 28; total circulation 2,362,000; circulation per 1,000 population 312¶. Radios (1983): total number of receivers 5,520,000 (1 per 1.4 persons). Televisions (1983): total number of receivers 3,180,000 (1 per 2.4 persons). Telephones (1982): 3,177,475 (1 per 2.4 persons).

Education and health

Education (1983–84)

	schools	teachers	students	student/ teacher ratio
Primary (age 6–9)	3,421	27,942	364,548	13.0
Secondary (age 10–18)	298	16,636	171,806	10.3
Voc., teacher tr.	1,228	22,850	385,571	16.9
Higher	44	10,897	143,459	13.2

College graduates per 100,000 population (students graduating; 1981): 118.
Literacy (1983): virtually 100%.
Health (1982): physicians 19,513 (1 per 388 persons); hospital beds 83,830 (1 per 90 persons).
Food (1978–80): daily per capita caloric intake 3,495 (vegetable products 59.6%, animal products 40.4%); 135% of FAO recommended minimum requirement.

Military

Total active duty personnel (1982): 50,000 (army 90.8%; navy, none; air force 9.2%). *Military expenditure as percent of GNP:* 1.2% (world 6.0%); per capita expenditure U.S.$108.

*1982. †Metal content only. ‡Finance and pub. admin. and defense are included with services. §Detail does not add to total given because of rounding. ‖July. ¶Based on weekday circulation of 23 newspapers.

Bahamas, The

Official name: The Commonwealth of the Bahamas.
Form of government: parliamentary state with two legislative houses (Senate [16]; House of Assembly [43]).
Chief of state: British Monarch represented by governor-general.
Head of government: Prime Minister.
Capital: Nassau.
Official language: English.
Official religion: none.
Monetary unit: 1 Bahamian dollar (B$) = 100 cents; valuation (Oct. 29, 1984) 1 Bahamian dollar = U.S.$1.00 = £0.83.

Area and population

Islands and Groups†	Capitals	area* sq mi	area* sq km	population 1980 census‡
Abaco, Great and Little, Mores Island and cays	Marsh Harbour	649	1,681	7,324
Acklins Island	Pompey Bay	192	497	616
Andros Island	Kemps Bay	2,300	5,957	8,397
Berry Islands	Nicolls Town	12	31	509
Biminis, North and South, Cay Lobos, and Cay Sal	Alice Town	11	28	1,432
Cat Island	Arthur's Town	150	388	2,143
Crooked Island	Colonel Hill	84	218	517
Eleuthera, Harbour Island, and Spanish Wells	Rock Sound	200	518	10,600
Exuma, Great and Little, and cays	George Town	112	290	3,672
Grand Bahama	Freeport	530	1,373	33,102
Inagua, Great and Little	Matthew Town	599	1,551	939
Long Cay		9	23	33
Long Island	Clarence Town	230	596	3,672
Mayaguana	Abraham's Bay	110	285	476
New Providence	Nassau	80	207	135,437
Ragged Island and cays	Duncan Town	14	36	146
San Salvador and Rum Cay	Cockburn Town	90	233	790
TOTAL		5,382	13,939	223,545

Source: Official government figures.

Demography

Density (1984): persons per sq mi 42.2, persons per sq km 16.3.
Urban-rural (1980): urban 54.4%; rural 45.6%.
Sex distribution (1980): male 48.77%; female 51.23%.
Age breakdown (1980): under 15, 38.1%; 15–29, 27.8%; 30–44, 17.9%; 45–59, 9.8%; 60–74, 5.1%; 75 and over, 1.3%.
Population projection§: (1990) 229,700; (2000) 251,800.
Doubling time: 75 years.
Ethnic composition (1980): black 72.3%; mixed 14.2%; white 12.9%; other 0.6%.
Religious affiliation (1980): Protestant (Baptist and Methodist) 46.6%; Roman Catholic 25.5%; Anglican 20.7%; other 7.2%.
Major cities (1980): Nassau 143,148 ‖ ; Freeport 25,423.

Vital statistics

Birth rate per 1,000 population (1980): 24.3 (world avg. 30.0); legitimate 39.7%, illegitimate 60.3%.
Death rate per 1,000 population (1980): 6.4 (world avg. 12.0).
Natural increase rate per 1,000 population (1980): 17.9 (world avg. 18.0).
Total fertility rate (avg. births per childbearing woman; 1980): 3.3.
Marriage rate per 1,000 population (1980): 6.7.
Divorce rate per 1,000 population (1980): 0.6.
Infant mortality rate per 1,000 live births (1980): 30.0.
Life expectancy at birth (1980): male 64.0 years; female 69.0 years.
Major causes of death per 100,000 population (1980): diseases of the circulatory system 181.0; malignant neoplasms (cancers) 81.9; all accidents 80.5; cerebrovascular disease 56.7; heart disease 54.8.

National economy

Budget (1983). Revenue: B$290,005,000 (customs receipts 57.8%; nontax revenue 18.1%; stamp taxes 7.1%; service taxes 5.5%; business and professional licenses 4.2%; departure tax 3.7%; property tax 3.1%; motor vehicle taxes 1.7%). Expenditures: B$314,257,000 (education 23.6%; health 15.7%; interest on the public debt 11.7%; general administration 10.2%; police 9.0%; tourism 9.0%).
Public debt (external, outstanding; 1984): U.S.$199,271,000.
Tourism (1981): receipts from visitors U.S.$639,000,000; expenditures by nationals abroad U.S.$91,000,000.
Production (metric tons except as noted). Agriculture, forestry, fishing (1982): sugarcane 227,000, tomatoes 9,000, bananas 7,000, dry onions 2,000, corn (maize) 1,000, pigeon peas 1,000; milk 3,000; livestock (number of live animals): 37,000 sheep, 18,000 pigs, 18,000 goats, 4,000 cattle, 810,000 chickens; pulpwood 100,000 cu m; fish catch 4,686; Mining and quarrying (1982): aragonite 3,049,000; salt (unrefined) 816,000; limestone 532,000¶.

Manufacturing (1982): petroleum products 6,875,000; cement 71,000¶; dressed poultry 6,000; sulfur 5,000. Construction (number of units completed; 1983): residential 832; commercial, industrial, and other 95. Energy production (consumption): electricity (kW-hr; 1982) 900,000,000 (900,000,-000); coal (metric tons; 1982) none (16,000); petroleum (barrels; 1982) none (63,038,000); petroleum products (metric tons; 1982) 6,875,000 (873,000).
Gross national product (at current market prices; 1981): U.S.$780,000,000 (U.S.$3,620 per capita).

Origin of gross domestic product (current prices of 1982)

	1982 in value B$'000,000	1982 % of total value	1979 labour force	1979 % of labour force
Agriculture	66.7	4.2	1,415	1.9
Mining	126.7	8.0	74	0.1
Manufacturing, public utilities	51.6	3.2	5,137	6.9
Construction	43.6	2.8	5,361	7.2
Trade	408.3	25.8	22,334	30.0
Transportation and communication	173.8	11.0	7,523	10.1
Finance	199.3	12.5	4,247	5.7
Pub. admin., defense	262.4	16.6	23,820	32.0
Other services	251.4	15.9	4,542	6.1
TOTAL	1,583.8	100.0	74,453	100.0

Persons economically active (1979): total 77,056 (36.8%); female participation in labour force 35,283 (45.8%); unemployed♀ 11,327 (14.3%).

Price and earnings indexes (1975 = 100)

	1978	1979	1980	1981	1982	1983	1984
Consumer price index	114.2	124.5	139.6	155.1	164.4	171.1	178.4δ
Monthly earnings index	...	...	...	...	...	...	...

Household income and expenditure. Average household size (1980) 4.3; income per household (1979) B$13,537 (U.S.$13,537); sources of income: n.a.; expenditure (1980): food 34.3%, housing 25.0%, clothing and footwear 10.1%, transportation 9.1%, health care 7.0%.
Land use (1981): forested 32.2%; meadows and pastures 0.1%; agricultural and under permanent cultivation 1.6%; other □ 66.1%.

Foreign trade

Balance of trade (current prices)◊

	1977	1978	1979	1980	1981	1982	1983
B$'000,000	−296	−368	−498	−677	−688	−591	−454
% of total	5.4%	8.0%	6.6%	6.5%	8.9%	10.7%	8.1%

Imports (1980): B$5,506,577,000 (crude oil 90.2%; food and live animals 1.2%; transportation equipment 0.7%; other 7.9%). *Major import sources:* Iran 28.2%; Nigeria 20.4%; Angola 5.4%.
Exports (1980): B$4,829,578,000 (petroleum products 95.9%; organic chemicals 1.0%; rum 0.4%; aragonite 0.1%; salt 0.1%). *Major export destinations:* United States 29.7%; West Germany 6.9%; The Netherlands 3.2%; United Kingdom 2.6%; Italy 2.0%.

Transport and communications

Transport. Railroads: none. Roads (1982): total length 2,500 mi, 4,023 km (paved 40%). Vehicles (1982): passenger cars 63,592; trucks and buses 10,-597. Merchant marine (1983): vessels (100 gross tons and over) 122; total deadweight tonnage 1,184,415. Air transport (1981): passenger-mi 72,313, passenger-km 116,373; short ton-mi cargo 6,343, metric ton-km cargo 9,261; airports (1984) with scheduled flights 22.
Communications. Daily newspapers (1983): total number 3; total circulation 35,120, circulation per 1,000 population 163. Radios (1983): total number of receivers 115,000 (1 per 1.9 persons). Televisions (1983): total number of receivers 50,000 (1 per 4.5 persons). Telephones (1982): 75,100 (1 per 3.2 persons).

Education and health

Education (1980–81)

	schools	teachers	students	student/teacher ratio
Primary (age 5–11)	190	1,768	37,399	21.2
Secondary (age 11–16)	38	1,236	23,761	19.2
Higher	1	127	4,093	32.2

Adult literacy (1979): total population literate 191,000 (93.0%).
Health (1979): physicians 198 (1 per 1,060 persons); hospital beds 908 (1 per 230 persons).
Food (1978–80): daily per capita caloric intake 2,328 (vegetable products 63.0%, animal products 37.0%); 96% of FAO recommended minimum requirement.

*Total includes land area (10 sq mi [26 sq km]) not otherwise accounted for. †The Bahamas have no first-order administrative units but are divided into 41 supervisory districts, corresponding to portions of islands or groups of islands. ‡The individual island figures are de jure, and total for the Bahamas is de facto. §Based on 1970 and 1980 de jure population. ‖ Figure refers to whole island of New Providence, which is considered as the metropolitan area of Nassau. ¶1981. ♀For New Providence and Grand Bahamas only. δMarch 1984. □Mostly swamps and mangroves. ◊Includes petroleum trade.

Bahrain

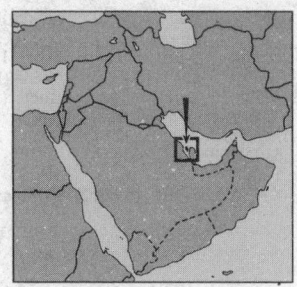

Official name: Dawlat al-Bahrain (State of Bahrain).
Form of government: monarchy (emirate) with a cabinet (17) appointed by the Emir.
Chief of state: Emir.
Head of government: Prime Minister.
Capital: Manama.
Official language: Arabic.
Official religion: Islām.
Monetary unit: 1 Bahrain dinar (BD) = 1,000 fils; valuation (Oct. 29, 1984) 1 BD = U.S.$2.63 = £2.17.

Area and population

	area		population
			1981
Regions	sq mi	sq km	census
Towns/villages			
Central	...	...	16,776
Central villages	...	...	16,776
Jidd Ḥafṣ	...	...	33,693
Jidd Ḥafṣ	...	...	7,232
Jidd Ḥafṣ villages	...	...	26,461
al-Manāmah	...	...	121,986
Manama	...	...	108,684
al-Manāmah villages	...	...	13,302
al-Muḥarraq	...	...	61,853
al-Muḥarraq	...	...	46,061
al-Muḥarraq villages	...	...	15,792
Northern	...	...	22,117
Northern villages	...	...	22,117
Rifā'	...	...	28,150
ar-Rifā'	...	...	22,408
Rifā' villages	...	...	5,742
Sitrah	...	...	22,993
Sitrah villages	...	...	22,993
Western	...	...	14,503
Western villages	...	...	14,503
Towns with special status			
al-Hadd	...	...	7,111
Madīnat 'Īsā	...	...	21,275
Islands			
Hawār and other	...	...	341
TOTAL	261.7*	677.9*	350,798

Source: Official government figures.

Demography

Density (1984): persons per sq mi 1,517, persons per sq km 585.6.
Urban–rural (1981): urban 80.7%; rural 19.3%.
Sex distribution (1981): male 58.38%; female 41.62%.
Age breakdown (1981): under 15, 32.9%; 15–29, 34.5%; 30–44, 20.0%; 45–59, 8.8%; 60–74, 3.1%; 75 and over, 0.7%.
Population projection: (1990) 423,000; (2000) 521,000.
Doubling time: 33 years.
Ethnic composition (1981): Bahraini 70.0%; non-Bahraini 30.0%.
Religious affiliation (1981): Muslim 85.0%; Christian 7.3%; other 7.7%.
Major cities (1981): Manama 108,684; al-Muḥarraq 46,061; ar-Rifā' 22,408; Madīnat 'Īsā 21,275.

Vital statistics

Birth rate per 1,000 population (1981): 32.9 (world avg. 29.0).
Death rate per 1,000 population (1981): 5.5 (world avg. 12.0).
Natural increase rate per 1,000 population (1981): 27.4 (world avg. 17.0).
Total fertility rate (avg. births per childbearing woman; 1981): 4.8.
Marriage rate per 1,000 population (1981): 7.8.
Divorce rate per 1,000 population (1981): 2.1.
Infant mortality rate per 1,000 live births (1981): 51.8.
Life expectancy at birth (1980–85): male 65.7 years; female 69.9 years.
Major causes of death per 100,000 population (1981): diseases of the circulatory system 89.8; ill-defined diseases 43.0; accidents and acts of violence 33.1; malignant neoplasms (cancers) 23.1; respiratory diseases 18.8.

National economy

Budget (1982). Revenue: BD 497,800,000 (petroleum company dividends and oil field receipts 74.8%; taxes on international trade 6.6%; social security contributions 3.8%). Expenditures: BD 473,700,000 (defense 22.3%; public utilities 15.9%; education 10.7%; housing 7.9%; health 6.9%).
Public debt (external, outstanding; 1982): U.S.$560,000,000.
Tourism (1981): receipts from visitors, n.a.; expenditures by nationals abroad U.S.$131,000,000.
Production (metric tons except as noted). Agriculture, forestry, fishing (1982): dates 40,000, tomatoes 11,000, cow's milk 6,000, onions 3,000, cabbages 1,000; livestock (number of live animals; 1982) 15,000 goats, 7,000 sheep, 6,000 cattle, 830,000 chickens. Manufacturing (1982): fuel oil 2,712,000, gasoline 2,618,000, motor spirits and aviation gasoline 2,510,000, naphtha 1,075,000, kerosine 365,000, asphalt 232,000, aluminum (unwrought) 126,-400†. Construction (number of permits issued; 1981): residential 4,611; nonresidential 1,665. Energy production (consumption): electricity (kW-hr; 1982) 1,810,000,000 (1,810,000,000); coal, none (n.a.); crude petroleum (barrels; 1983) 14,965,000 (72,374,000‡); petroleum products (metric tons; 1982) 8,520,000 (259,000); natural gas (cu m; 1983) 5,487,796,000 (2,816,151,000‡).

Gross national product (at current market prices; 1981): U.S.$3,240,000,000 (U.S.$8,960 per capita).

Origin of gross domestic product (current prices)

	1981			
	value in BD'000,000	% of total value	labour force	% of labour force
Agriculture	16.5	1.1	3,691	2.6
Mining	...	...	4,772	3.4
Manufacturing	297.7	19.3	11,354	8.0
Construction	...	...	29,208	20.5
Trade	...	...	18,493	13.0
Public utilities	...	...	2,845	2.0
Transportation and communication	...	...	13,157	9.2
Finance	...	...	4,614	3.2
Pub. admin., defense	...	...	18,084	12.7
Services	...	...	29,431	20.7
Other	1,228.8	79.6	6,735	4.7
TOTAL	1,543.0	100.0	142,384	100.0

Persons economically active (1981): total 142,384 (40.6%); female participation in the labour force 16,205 (11.4%); unemployed 4,492 (3.2%).

Price and earnings indexes (1975 = 100)

	1977	1978	1979	1980	1981	1982	1983
Consumer price index	144.3	167.0	170.8	177.4	197.5	215.0	221.4
Monthly earnings index	...	...	...	...	...	...	...

Household income and expenditure. Average household size (1981) 6.0; average annual income per household: n.a.; source of income: n.a.; expenditure: n.a.
Land Use (1981): meadows and pastures 6.5%; agricultural and under permanent cultivation 3.2%; other§ 90.3%.

Foreign trade

Balance of trade (current prices)

	1978	1979	1980	1981	1982	1983
BD'000,000	+19	+96	+173	+238	++201	+71
% of total	1.3%	5.4%	6.8%	7.9%	7.6%	3.0%

Imports (1981): BD1,397,000,000 (crude petroleum 69.2%; food and live animals 4.0%, of which fruits and vegetables 1.2%; chemicals and chemical products 4.0%; electrical machinery, apparatus, and appliances 3.2%; machinery except electrical 2.8%; transportation equipment 2.1%; furniture, fixtures, and fittings 1.8%). *Major import sources:* Saudi Arabia 60.0%; United Kingdom 5.5%; Japan 4.8%; United States 4.1%; Australia 3.3%.
Exports (1981): BD1,634,600,000 (petroleum products 89.3%; aluminum 2.4%). *Major export destinations:* United Arab Emirates 18.0%; Singapore 10.0%; Japan 8.0%; United States 9.0%.

Transport and communications

Transport. Railroads: none. Roads: n.a. Vehicles (1982): passenger cars 67,-240; trucks and buses 21,288. Merchant marine (1983): vessels (100 gross tons and over) 65; total deadweight tonnage 26,631. Air transport ‖ (1978): passenger-mi 301,015,000, passenger-km 484,437,000; short ton-mi cargo 6,595,000, metric ton-km cargo 9,629,000; airport (1984) with scheduled flights 1.
Communications. Daily newspapers (1982): total number 3; total circulation 25,000; circulation per 1,000 population 71. Radios (1983): total number of receivers 140,000 (1 per 2.5 persons). Television (1983): total number of receivers 121,000 (1 per 2.9 persons). Telephones (1982): 85,800 (1 per 4.1 persons).

Education and health

Education (1980–81)

	schools	teachers	students	student/ teacher ratio
Primary (age 6–11)	114	2,963	48,406	16.3
Secondary (age 12–17)	21	951	23,727	24.9
Voc., teacher tr.	5	233	2,846	12.2
Higher	2	159	3,650	22.9

College graduates per 100,000 population (students graduating; 1980): 26.8.
Literacy (1981): total population literate 164,176 (69.8%); males literate 112,116 (76.5%); females literate 52,060 (58.6%).
Health (1980): physicians 363 (1 per 964 persons); hospital beds 1,107 (1 per 316 persons).
Food: daily per capita caloric intake, n.a.

Military

Total active duty personnel (1983): 2,700 (army 85.2%; navy 11.1%; air force 3.7%). *Military expenditure as percent of GNP* (1982): 8.1% (world 6%); per capita expenditure U.S.$661.

*Total area includes numerous small uninhabited islands and dependencies of Bahrain. †1981. ‡1982. §Mostly sandy plains and salt marshes. ‖ International scheduled airlines only.

Bangladesh

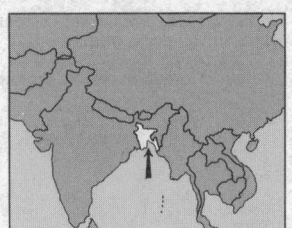

Official name: Gana Prajātantrī Bangladesh (People's Republic of Bangladesh).
Form of government: military dictatorship; constitution suspended in 1982; parliamentary elections pending for end of 1984.
Head of state and government: President (Chief Martial Law Administrator).
Capital: Dhākā (formerly Dacca).
Official language: Bengali.
Official religion: Islām.
Monetary unit: 1 Bangladesh Taka (Tk) = 100 paisa; valuation (Oct. 29, 1984) 1 U.S.$ = Tk25.50; 1 £ = Tk31.82.

Area and population

Divisions Districts	Administrative centres	area sq mi	area sq km	population 1981 census*
Chittagong	Chittagong	17,283	44,763†	22,565,000
Chittagong	Chittagong	2,786	7,216	5,476,000
Chittagong Hill Tracts	Rangamati	5,089	13,180	746,000
Comilla	Comilla	2,592	6,713	6,880,000
Noākhāli	Noākhāli	2,033	5,265	3,813,000
Sylhet	Sylhet	4,783	12,388	5,650,000
Dhākā	Dhākā	11,922	30,878	26,249,000
Dhākā	Dhākā	2,880	7,459	10,049,000
Faridpur	Faridpur	2,669	6,913	4,768,000
Jamālpur	Jamālpur	1,315	3,406	2,445,000
Mymensingh	Mymensingh	3,749	9,710	6,543,000
Tangail	Tangail	1,309	3,390	2,444,000
Khulna	Khulna	13,023	33,729†	17,150,000
Barisāl (Bakerganj)	Barisāl	2,792	7,231	4,668,000
Jessore	Jessore	2,584	6,693	4,016,000
Khulna	Khulna	4,630	11,992	4,353,000
Kushtia	Kushtia	1,342	3,476	2,273,000
Patuākhāli	Patuākhāli	1,675	4,338	1,840,000
Rājshāhi	Rājshāhi	13,370	34,628†	21,087,000
Bogra	Bogra	1,501	3,888	2,718,000
Dinājpur	Dinājpur	2,609	6,757	3,198,000
Pābna	Pābna	1,906	4,937	3,418,000
Rājshāhi	Rājshāhi	3,653	9,461	5,263,000
Rangpur	Rangpur	3,701	9,586	6,490,000
TOTAL		55,598	143,998†	87,052,000

Source: Official government figures.

Demography

Density (1984): persons per sq mi 1,740, persons per sq km 672.
Urban–rural (1981): urban 15.2%; rural 84.8%.
Sex distribution (1981): male 51.56%; female 48.44%.
Age breakdown (1981): under 15, 46.6%; 15–29, 24.5%; 30–44, 15.1%; 45–59, 8.2%; 60 and over, 5.6%.
Population projection: (1990) 108,346,000; (2000) 127,903,000.
Doubling time: 30 years.
Ethnic composition (1978): Bengali 97.6%; Bihārī 1.4%, tribal (Chakmā, Gāro, Khāsi, Santāl, etc.) 1.0%.
Religious affiliation (1982): Muslim 86.0%; Hindu 12.7%; Buddhist 0.6%; Christian 0.5%; other 0.2%.
Major cities (1981): Dhākā 3,160,200; Chittagong 1,388,500; Khulna 623,200; Nārāyanganj 298,400; Rājshāhi 171,600.

Vital statistics

Birth rate per 1,000 population (1980–85): 45.2 (world avg. 27.5).
Death rate per 1,000 population (1980–85): 17.3 (world avg. 10.6).
Natural increase rate per 1,000 population (1980–85): 27.9 (world avg. 16.9).
Total fertility rate (avg. births per childbearing woman; 1980–85): 6.3.
Marriage rate per 1,000 population: n.a.
Divorce rate per 1,000 population: n.a.
Infant mortality rate per 1,000 live births (1980–85): 133.0.
Life expectancy at birth (1980–85): male 47.5 years; female 47.0 years.
Major causes of death per 100 deaths (1976): diseases of the respiratory system 20.9; malignant neoplasms (cancers) 19.8; infectious intestinal diseases 15.5; diseases of the liver and kidney 11.4.

National economy

Budget (1983–84). Revenue: Tk33,968,000,000 (customs duties 39.2%, excise duties 16.1%, sales tax 12.8%, income taxes 9.1%, railways 5.2%, interest receipts 2.7%). Expenditures: Tk24,135,000,000 (defense 17.3%, education 13.2%, debt service 10.4%, general administration 10.2%, justice and police 9.7%, transport and communications 8.9%).
Public debt (external, outstanding; 1982): U.S.$4,417,000,000.
Tourism (1982): receipts from visitors U.S.$10,000,000; expenditures by nationals abroad‡ U.S.$23,000,000.
Production (metric tons except as noted). Agriculture, forestry, fishing (1982): paddy rice 21,000,000, sugarcane 7,136,000, potatoes 1,084,000, wheat 967,000, jute and jute-like fibres 879,000, sweet potatoes 692,000, bananas 663,000, mangoes 203,000, pineapples 159,000, tobacco leaves 51,000, tea 42,000; livestock (number of live animals; 1982) 35,070,000 cattle, 11,800,000 goats, 1,644,000 buffalo, 1,150,000 sheep, 73,000,000 chickens, 20,859,000 ducks; roundwood 10,929,000 cu m; fish catch 736,000. Mining and quarrying (1982): rock salt 180,000; limestone 45,000. Manufacturing (1982–83): jute textiles 553,000; chemical fertilizers 471,000; cement 302,-

000; iron and steel 202,000; cotton yarn and clothing 166,000; cigarettes (actual number) 14,031,000,000. Construction: n.a. Energy production (consumption): electricity (kW-hr; 1982) 3,305,000,000 (3,305,000,000); coal (metric tons; 1982) none (255,000); crude petroleum (barrels; 1982) 44,000 (9,558,000); petroleum products (metric tons; 1982) 1,104,000 (1,401,000); natural gas (cu m; 1982) 1,688,200,000 (1,688,200,000).
Gross national product (at current market prices; 1981): U.S.$12,840,000,000 (U.S.$140 per capita).

Origin of gross domestic product (current prices)

	1981 in value Tk'000,000	% of total value	labour force§	% of labour force
Agriculture	95,434	45.6	14,000,000	68.5
Mining	‖	‖	—	—
Manufacturing	15,011 ‖	7.2 ‖	1,600,000	7.8
Construction	11,301	5.4	600,000	2.9
Trade and finance	24,574	11.7	1,309,000	6.4
Public utilities	466	0.2	23,000	0.1
Transportation and communication	13,331	6.4	522,000	2.6
Pub. admin., defense	8,138	3.8	889,000	4.3
Services and other	41,231	19.7	1,507,000	7.4
TOTAL	209,485†	100.0	20,450,000	100.0

Persons economically active (1979): total 37,227,000 (35.6%); female participation in labour force 1,073,000 (2.9%); unemployed, n.a.

Price and earnings indexes (1977 = 100)

	1977	1978	1979	1980	1981	1982	1983
Consumer price index	100.0	113.1	127.5	144.2	163.4	178.5	192.9
Monthly earnings index¶	100.0	111.1	121.0	187.5	197.6	199.2	...

Household income. Average household size (1981) 5.8; income per household (1977) Tk8,672 (U.S.$564); source of income: wages and salaries 26.9%, self-employment 44.7%, transfer payments 0.2%.
Land use (1981): forested 16.4%; meadows and pastures 4.5%; agricultural and under permanent cultivation 68.2%; other 10.9%.

Foreign trade

Balance of trade (current prices)

	1978	1979	1980	1981	1982	1983
Tk'000,000	−12,352	−16,541	−24,380	−29,692	−28,528	−30,055
% of total	42.8%	44.7%	51.0%	51.2%	45.6%	45.7%

Imports (1982): Tk45,577,000,000 (machinery and transport equipment 20.1%; chemicals and chemical products 12.8%; crude and refined petroleum 11.1%; wheat 11.0%. *Major import sources:* Japan 13.0%; Saudi Arabia 9.0%; United States 8.0%; China 5.0%.
Exports (1982): Tk17,049,000,000 (jute products 50.7%; raw jute and jute cuttings 16.1%; hides, skins, and leather goods 8.7%; fish and fish preparations 8.1%; tea 6.6%). *Major export destinations:* Singapore 11.0%; United States 10.0%; Japan 6.0%; Pakistan 5.0%; United Kingdom 5.0%; U.S.S.R. 5.0%.

Transport and communications

Transport. Railroads (1981–82): route length 1,791 mi, 2,883 km; passenger-mi 3,333,000,000, passenger-km 5,364,000,000; short ton-mi cargo 578,000,-000, metric ton-km cargo 844,000,000. Roads (1980): total length 3,536 mi, 5,691 km (paved? 87%). Vehicles (1981): passenger cars 35,487; trucks and buses 20,779. Merchant marine (1983): vessels (100 gross tons and over) 237; total deadweight tonnage 514,205. Air transport (1982): passenger-mi 813,000,000, passenger-km 1,308,000,000; short ton-mi cargo 15,600,000, metric ton-km cargo 22,800,000; airports (1984) with scheduled flights 8.
Communications. Daily newspapers (1983): total number 30; total circulation 542,000; circulation per 1,000 population 5.7. Radios (1982): total number of receivers 770,000 (1 per 117 persons). Television (1982): total number of receivers 252,000 (1 per 357 persons). Telephones (1982): 122,-190 (1 per 737 persons).

Education and health

Education (1980–81)

	schools	teachers	students	student/ teacher ratio
Primary (age 5–9)	42,683	175,821	8,655,770	49.2
Secondary (age 10–16)	9,050	92,558	2,528,069	27.3
Voc., teacher tr.	120	1,890	23,382	12.4
Higher	394	14,114	328,940	23.3

College graduates per 100,000 population (students graduating; 1980): 30.
Literacy (1981): total population literate 13,600,000 (29.2%); males literate 9,560,000 (39.7%); females literate 4,040,000 (18.0%).
Health (1981): physicians 10,065 (1 per 8,510 persons); hospital beds 19,727 (1 per 4,342 persons).
Food (1978–80): daily per capita caloric intake 1,877 (vegetable products 96.4%, animal products 3.6%); 85% of FAO recommended minimum.

Military

Total active duty personnel (1983): 81,300 (army 89.8%; navy 6.5%; air force 3.7%). *Military expenditure as percent of GNP* (1982): 1.6% (world 6.0%); per capita expenditure U.S.$2.

*Preliminary. †Detail does not add to total given because of rounding. ‡1981. §Restricted to economically active persons who are specifically identified within an occupational group. ‖ Mining is included with manufacturing. ¶Skilled wage earnings in manufacturing. ?1979.

Barbados

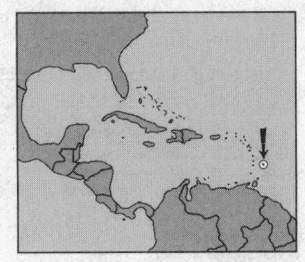

Official name: Barbados.
Form of government: parliamentary state with two legislative houses (Senate [21]; House of Assembly [27]).
Chief of state: BritishMonarch represented by governor-general.
Head of government: Prime Minister.
Capital: Bridgetown.
Official language: English.
Official religion: none.
Monetary unit: 1 Barbados dollar (BDS$) = 100 cents; valuation (Oct. 29, 1984) 1 U.S.$ = BDS$2.00; 1 £ = BDS$2.42.

Area and population

Parishes*	area sq mi	area sq km	population 1984 estimate
Christ Church	22	57	42,000
St. Andrew	14	36	7,000
St. George	17	44	17,000
St. James	12	31	17,400
St. John	13	34	10,200
St. Joseph	10	26	7,200
St. Lucy	14	36	9,000
St. Michael†	15	39	102,400
St. Peter	13	34	11,000
St. Philip	23	60	19,500
St. Thomas	13	34	11,000
TOTAL	166	431	253,700

Source: Official government figures; Britannica estimate.

Demography

Density (1984): persons per sq mi 1,526.3, persons per sq km 588.6.
Urban–rural (1980): urban 39.3%; rural 60.7%.
Sex distribution (1983): male 47.70%; female 52.30%.
Age breakdown (1980): under 15, 29.4%; 15–29, 29.9%; 30–44, 14.9%; 45–59, 11.0%; 60–74, 10.2%; 75 and over, 4.6%.
Population projection: (1990) 278,000; (2000) 320,000.
Doubling time: 65 years.
Ethnic composition (1980): Negro 91.9%; white 3.3%; mulatto 2.6%; East Indian 0.5%; other 1.7%.
Religious affiliation (1980): Anglican 39.7%; Protestant 18.2% (includes Methodist, Pentecostal, and Seventh-day Adventist); Roman Catholic 4.4%; other 37.7%.
Major cities (1980): Bridgetown 7,466.

Vital statistics

Birth rate per 1,000 population (1983): 17.8 (world avg. 29.0); (1975) legitimate 23.9%, illegitimate 76.1%.
Death rate per 1,000 population (1983): 6.9 (world avg. 11.0).
Natural increase rate per 1,000 population (1983): 10.9 (world avg. 18.0).
Total fertility rate (avg. births per childbearing woman; 1980–85): 2.0.
Marriage rate per 1,000 population (1980): 2.7.
Divorce rate per 1,000 population (1979): 0.6.
Infant mortality rate per 1,000 live births (1983): 13.5.
Life expectancy at birth (1975–80): male 67.7 years; female 71.9 years.
Major causes of death per 100,000 (1980): heart disease 236.4; cerebrovascular disease 115.4; malignant neoplasms (cancers) 128.5; diabetes mellitus 48.2.

National economy

Budget (1982–83). Revenue: BDS$495,712,000 (individual income tax 22.8%; consumption tax 16.2%; import duties 15.1%; corporate tax 13.8%). Expenditures: BDS$477,164,000 (education 21.4%; health 15.7%; economic services 15.4%, of which roads and transport 10.8%).
Public debt (external, outstanding; 1982): U.S.$229,000,000.
Production (metric tons except as noted). Agriculture, forestry, fishing (1982): sugarcane 900,000, yams 3,500, sweet potatoes 3,000, corn (maize) 2,000, cassava 1,000, eggs 1,400; livestock (number of live animals): 64,000 pigs, 20,000 cattle, 2,000 horses, 850,000 chickens. Manufacturing (1982): sugar 86,000; beer 73,000 hectolitres; rum 46,900 hectolitres; cigarettes 260,-000,000‡. Construction (new buildings authorized; 1976): residential 788; nonresidential 753. Energy production (consumption): electricity (kW-hr; 1982) 336,000,000 (356,462,000); coal, n.a. (n.a.); petroleum (barrels; 1982) 265,000 (1,398,000); natural gas (cu m; 1982) 8,800,000 (5,996,000).
Persons economically active (1982): total 112,600 (44.8%); female participation in labour force 51,100 (45.6%); unemployed 15,400 (13.7%).

Price and earnings indexes (1980 = 100)

	1979	1980	1981	1982	1983	1984
Consumer price index	90.4	100.0	118.6	130.8	137.7	140.7¶
Monthly earnings index	...	...	...	...	...	...

Household income and expenditure. Average household size: n.a.; income per household: n.a.; sources of income: n.a.; expenditure: n.a.
Tourism (1982): receipts from visitors U.S.$240,359,000; expenditures by nationals abroad U.S.$12,279,000.
Gross national product (at current market prices; 1984): U.S.$983,600,000 (U.S.$3,900 per capita).

Origin of gross domestic product (current prices)

	1982 in value BDS$'000	1982 % of total value	1983 labour force	1983 % of labour force
Agriculture	124,242	6.2	8,400	7.5
Mining	14,231	0.7	§	§
Manufacturing	219,369	10.9	15,400	13.7
Construction	128,164	6.4	9,200	8.2
Trade	397,979	19.8	25,200	22.4
Public utilities	44,695	2.2	2,100	1.9
Transportation and communication	134,783	6.7	5,900	5.2
Finance	250,145	12.4	3,700	3.3
Pub. admin., defense, and services	490,829	24.4	38,800	34.4
Other	205,795	10.2	3,900	3.5
TOTAL	2,010,232	100.0 ‖	112,600	100.0 ‖

Land use (1981): meadows and pastures 9.3%; agricultural and under permanent cultivation 76.7%; other 14.0%.

Foreign trade

Balance of trade (current prices)

	1978	1979	1980	1981	1982	1983
BDS$'000,000	−367.5	−546.8	−593.7	−760.0	−589.9	−531.6
% of total	49.6%	54.0%	46.8%	56.1%	44.2%	27.0%

Imports (1982): BDS$1,106,588,000 (machinery and transport equipment 28.6%; mineral fuels, lubricants 16.1%; food and live animals 13.8%; beverages and tobacco 1.9%). *Major import sources:* United States 38.3%; United Kingdom 9.6%; Canada 6.1%; Japan 3.4%; Guyana 0.6%.
Exports: (1982): BDS$506,162,000 (machinery and transport equipment 30.1%; food and live animals 14.9%; chemicals 7.1%; beverages and tobacco 2.3%). *Major export destinations:* United States 29.5%; United Kingdom 9.1%; Canada 2.1%; Guyana 0.4%.

Transport and communications

Transport. Railroads: none. Roads (1980): total length 960 mi, 1,546 km (paved 94%). Vehicles (1980): passenger cars 24,600; trucks and buses 5,100. Merchant marine (1983): vessels (100 gross tons and over) 34; total deadweight tonnage 142,622. Air transport (1980): passenger-mi 205,000,-000, passenger-km 330,000,000; short ton-mi cargo 342,000, metric ton-km cargo 500,000; airport (1984) with scheduled flights 1.
Communications. Daily newspapers (1983): total number 2; total circulation 39,000; circulation per 1,000 population 154.2. Radios (1983): total number of receivers 191,000 (1 per 1.3 persons). Television (1983): total number of receivers 52,000 (1 per 4.8 persons). Telephones (1982): 72,850 (1 per 3.5 persons).

Education and health

Education (1982–83)

	schools	teachers	students	student/ teacher ratio
Primary (age 4–11)	139	1,492♂♀	34,848	...
Secondary (age 12–16)	36	1,281♀	26,552	...
Vocational♀	6	...	2,343	...
Higher♀	2	317	4,033	12.7

College graduates per 100,000 population (1980): 272.4. *Literacy* (1980): total population literate 169,894 (98.0%); males literate 78,022 (98.3%); females literate 91,872 (97.7%).
Health: physicians (1979) 208 (1 per 1,230 persons); hospital beds (1976) 2,225 (1 per 110 persons).
Food (1978–80): daily per capita caloric intake 3,054 (vegetable products 70.9%, animal products 29.1%); 126% of FAO recommended minimum requirement.

Military

Total active duty personnel (1983–84): small paramilitary marine components only.

*The parishes do not have separate administrative centres. †Includes Bridgetown. ‡1981. §Manufacturing includes mining. ‖ Detail does not add to total given because of rounding. ¶First quarter. ♀1981–82. ♂Public schools only.

Belgium

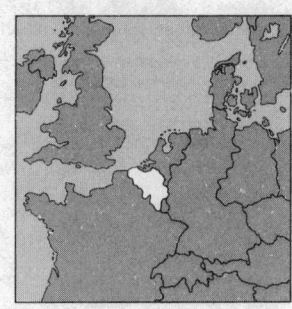

Official name: Koninkrijk België
(Dutch), Royaume de Belgique
(French) (Kingdom of Belgium).
Form of government: constitutional
monarchy with two legislative
houses (Senate [182]; House of
Representatives [212]).
Chief of state: Monarch.
Head of government: Prime Minister.
Capital: Brussels.
Official languages: Dutch, French, and
German.
Official religion: none.
Monetary unit: 1 Belgian franc
(BF) = 100 centimes; valuation (Oct.
29, 1984) 1 U.S.$ = BF62.47;
1 £ = BF74.40.

Area and population

Provinces	Capitals	area		population
		sq mi	sq km	1983 estimate
Antwerp	Antwerp	1,107	2,867	1,577,000
Brabant	Brussels	1,297	3,358	2,221,000
East Flanders	Ghent	1,151	2,982	1,332,000
Hainaut	Mons	1,462	3,787	1,292,000
Liège	Liège	1,491	3,862	996,000
Limburg	Hasselt	935	2,422	724,000
Luxembourg	Arlon	1,715	4,441	223,000
Namur	Namur	1,415	3,665	409,000
West Flanders	Brugge	1,210	3,134	1,084,000
TOTAL		11,783	30,518	9,858,000

Source: Official government figures.

Demography

Density (1984): persons per sq mi 836.7, persons per sq km 323.1.
Urban–rural (1980): urban 72.4%; rural 27.6%.
Sex distribution (1982): male 48.83%; female 51.17%.
Age breakdown (1982): under 15, 20.0%; 15–29, 23.7%; 30–44, 19.1%; 45–59,
18.6%; 60–74, 12.8%; 75 and over, 5.8%.
Population projection: (1990) 9,905,000; (2000) 9,964,000.
Doubling time: During the intercensal period 1970–81, the average growth
rate was 0.2%; since 1981, however, the population has been decreasing.
Ethnic composition (1980): Belgian 92.1%, of which Flemish 58.5%, Walloon
33.6%; German 0.6%; Italian 2.6%; Dutch 0.6%; other 4.1%.
Religious affiliation (1983): Roman Catholic 96.0%; other 4.0%.
Major cities (1983 est.): Antwerp 490,524; Ghent 236,540; Charleroi 216,144;
Liège 207,496; Brussels 137,738 (metropolitan area; 1982 est. 994,774).

Vital statistics

Birth rate per 1,000 population (1982): 12.2 (world avg. 29.0); (1981) legiti-
mate 95.5%, illegitimate 4.5%.
Death rate per 1,000 population (1982): 11.1 (world avg. 11.0).
Natural increase rate per 1,000 population (1982): 1.1 (world avg. 18.0).
Total fertility rate (avg. births per childbearing woman; 1982): 1.1.
Marriage rate per 1,000 population (1982): 6.3.
Divorce rate per 1,000 population (1982): 1.6.
Infant mortality rate per 1,000 live births (1982): 11.7.
Life expectancy at birth (1980–85): male 69.3 years; female 75.9 years.
Major causes of death per 100,000 population (1978): heart disease 287.9;
malignant neoplasms (cancers) 268.3; cerebrovascular disease 146.6.

National economy

Budget (1983). Revenue: BF1,278,230,000,000 (direct taxes 59.2%; value-
added, stamp, and similar taxes 28.4%; custom and excise duties 7.0%).
Expenditures: BF1,701,247,000,000 (government departments 44.8%; public
debt 17.7%; educational and cultural services 15.3%; pension 9.7%).
Public debt (external, outstanding; 1983): U.S.$72,674,646,000.
Tourism (1981): receipts from visitors U.S.$1,584,900,000; expenditures by
nationals abroad U.S.$2,644,100,000 .
Production (metric tons except as noted). Agriculture, forestry, fishing (1982):
wheat 1,010,000, barley 745,100, oats 133,400, corn (maize) 52,400, sugar
beets 7,430,000, potatoes 1,310,000, linseed 6,700, milk 3,809,000; livestock
(number of live animals); 5,113,400 pigs, 2,896,000 cattle, 82,500 sheep, 29,-
900 horses; roundwood 2,590,000 cu m*; fish catch 41,000. Manufacturing
(value in BF'000,000; 1980): metal products and machinery 261,500; food
products 114,300; industrial chemicals and other chemical products 88,400;
textiles and spinning and weaving products 77,100; pottery, china, glass,
and nonmetal products 36,900; furniture and fixtures 35,600; iron and steel
35,300; printing and publishing 25,200. Construction (1982): residential
16,776,000 cu m; nonresidential 17,136,000 cu m. Energy production (consumption): electricity (kW-hr; 1981) 50,755,000,000 (51,195,000,000); coal
(metric tons; 1981) 6,136,000 (15,475,000); petroleum (barrels; 1981) none
(215,126,720); natural gas (cu m; 1981) 32,692,275 (9,802,964,556).
Gross national product (at current market prices; 1983): U.S.$81,162,481,000
(U.S.$8,235 per capita).
Household income and expenditure. Average household size (1981) 2.7;
source of income: n.a; expenditure (1979): food 21.8%, housing 18.7%,
transportation 10.8%, clothing and footwear 8.1%, recreation 7.0%, other
33.6%.

Land use (1981): forested 21.2%; meadows and pastures 21.2%; agricultural
and under permanent cultivation 26.5%; other 31.1%.

Origin of gross domestic product (current prices)

	1982			
	in value BF'000,000	% of total value	labour force	% of labour force
Agriculture	94,900	2.4	125,276	2.9
Mining	20,500	0.5	27,564	0.6
Manufacturing	946,600	24.0	862,884	20.5
Construction	240,100	6.1	241,948	5.6
Trade	543,100	13.8	765,257	17.7
Public utilities	139,500	3.5	32,870	0.8
Transportation and communication	337,000	8.6	279,860	6.5
Finance	303,500	7.7	260,020	6.0
Pub. admin., defense	344,500	8.7	†	†
Services	425,300	10.8	1,132,127	26.3
Other	547,000	13.9	564,948‡	13.1
TOTAL	3,942,000	100.0	4,312,754	100.0

Persons economically active (1982): total 4,312,754 (43.8%); female participation in the labour force 1,700,664 (39.4%); unemployed 559,800 (13.8%).

Price and earnings indexes (1975 = 100)

	1978	1979	1980	1981	1982	1983	1984§
Consumer price index	122.2	127.6	136.1	146.5	159.2	171.5	179.0
Hourly earnings index	129.8	139.8	152.8	168.2	178.6	186.3	191.9

Foreign trade ‖

Balance of trade (current prices)

	1977	1978	1979	1980	1981	1982
BF'000,00C	−103,277	−115,786	−123,129	−210,448	−236,884	−247,817
% of total	3.7%	3.9%	3.6%	5.3%	5.4%	4.9%

Imports (1982): BF2,642,280,047,000 (machinery and transport equipment
21.5%; mineral fuels, lubricants, and related materials 20.6%, of which
petroleum, petroleum products, and related materials 15.9%; food and live
animals 9.9%; chemical and related products 8.9%; crude inedible materials except fuels 6.6%). *Major import sources:* West Germany 20.0%; The
Netherlands 17.6%; France 13.9%; United Kingdom 7.0%; United States
7.0%.
Exports (1982): BF2,394,463,014,000 (machinery and transport equipment
22.6%; chemicals and related products 11.8%; food and live animals 9.6%;
mineral fuels, lubricants, and related materials 8.6%; basic manufactures,
iron and steel 8.1%). *Major export destinations:* West Germany 20.4%;
France 19.4%; The Netherlands 14.2%; United Kingdom 9.7%; Japan 5.0%.

Transport and communications

Transport. Railroads (1982): length 2,442 mi, 3,930 km; passenger-mi
4,302,000,000, passenger-km 6,924,000,000; short ton-mi cargo 4,220,000,-
000, metric ton-km cargo 6,792,000,000. Roads (1982): total length 78,908
mi, 126,990 km (paved 95%). Vehicles (1982): passenger cars 3,230,951;
trucks and buses 303,815. Merchant marine (1983): vessels (100 gross
tons and over) 322; total deadweight tonnage 3,690,728. Air transport
(1983): passenger-mi 3,291,062,000, passenger-km 5,296,461,000; short ton-
mi cargo 335,032,000, metric ton-km cargo 489,138,000; airports (1984)
with scheduled flights 4.
Communications. Daily newspapers (1982): total number 38; total circulation 2,242,000¶; circulation per 1,000 population 228¶. Radios (1983):
total number of receivers 4,617,037 (1 per 2.1 persons). Televisions (1983):
total number of receivers 2,976,383 (1 per 3.3 persons). Telephones (1982):
3,818,626 (1 per 2.6 persons).

Education and health

Education (1981–82)

	schools	teachers	students	student/ teacher ratio
Primary (age 6–12)	5,035	45,130	835,586	18.0
Secondary (age 12–18)	...	...	848,903	...
Voc., teacher tr.	...	...	190,682	...
Higher	...	...	201,882	...

College graduates per 100,000 population (1980): 160. *Literacy* (1984): virtually 100.0% literate.
Health (1981): physicians 25,629 (1 per 384 persons); hospital beds 92,436
(1 per 106 persons).
Food (1978–80): daily per capita caloric intake ‖ 3,938 (vegetable products
62.1%, animal products 37.9%); 153% of FAO recommended minimum
requirement.

Military

Total active duty personnel (1983): 94,717 (army 73.6%; navy 4.8%; air force
21.6%). *Military expenditure as percent of GNP* (1982): 3.4% (world 6.0%);
per capita expenditure U.S.$354.

*1981. †Public administration included with services. ‡Includes unemployed and
persons in the armed forces. §First quarter. ‖ Includes Luxembourg. ¶1979.

Belize

Official name: Belize.
Form of government: constitutional monarchy with two legislative houses (Senate [9]; House of Representatives [19]).
Chief of state: British Monarch represented by Governor General.
Head of government: Prime Minister.
Capital: Belmopan.
Official language: English.
Official religion: none.
Monetary unit: 1 Belize dollar (BZ$) = 100 cents; valuation (Oct. 29, 1984) 1 U.S.$ = BZ$2.00*; 1 £ = BZ$2.42.

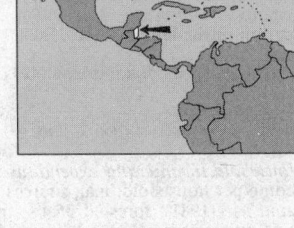

Area and population

Districts	Capitals	area sq mi	area sq km	population 1984 estimate
Belize	Belize City	1,624	4,206	51,400
Cayo	San Ignacio	2,061	5,338	26,300
Corozal	Corozal	718	1,860	26,700
Orange Walk	Orange Walk	1,829	4,737	25,700
Stann Creek	Dangriga	840	2,176	14,700
Toledo	Punta Gorda	1,795	4,649	13,000
TOTAL		8,867	22,965†	157,800

Source: Official government figures; Britannica estimate.

Demography

Density (1984): persons per sq mi 17.8, persons per sq km 6.9.
Urban–rural (1980): urban 50.0%; rural 50.0%.
Sex distribution (1982): male 50.65%; female 49.35%.
Age breakdown (1980): under 15, 46.2%; 15–29, 27.1%; 30–44, 11.8%; 45–59, 8.4%; 60–74, 4.7%; 75 and over, 1.8%.
Population projection: (1990) 175,000; (2000) 203,000.
Doubling time: 36 years.
Ethnic composition (1980): Creole 39.7%; mestizo 33.1%; Garifuna (Black Carib) 7.6%; Maya 6.8%; white 4.2%; other 8.6%.
Religious affiliation (1980): Roman Catholic 61.7%; Anglican 11.8%; Methodist 6.0%; Mennonite 3.9%; other 16.6%.
Major cities (1980): Belize City 39,770; Orange Walk 8,440; Corozal 6,900; Dangriga 6,660; Belmopan 2,940.

Vital statistics

Birth rate per 1,000 population (1981): 40.7 (world avg. 29.0); (1981) legitimate 48.0%, illegitimate 52.0%.
Death rate per 1,000 population (1981): 4.8 (world avg. 12.0).
Natural increase rate per 1,000 population (1981): 35.9 (world avg. 17.0).
Total fertility rate (avg. births per childbearing woman): n.a.
Marriage rate per 1,000 population (1982): 5.6.
Divorce rate per 1,000 population (1968): 0.1.
Infant mortality rate per 1,000 live births (1982): 21.3.
Life expectancy at birth (1970): male 65.4 years; female 69.1 years.
Major causes of death per 100,000 population (1981): perinatal mortality 46.6; pneumonia 40.0; cerebrovascular diseases 34.0; ischemic heart disease 28.7; intestinal diseases 27.3.

National economy

Production (metric tons except as noted). Agriculture, forestry, fishing (1982): sugarcane 1,113,000, oranges 44,000, grapefruits 27,000, corn (maize) 21,000, bananas 18,000, rice 8,000, coconuts 3,000, vegetables and melons 3,000, dry beans 2,000; livestock (number of live animals) 51,000 cattle, 17,000 pigs, 350,000 chickens; roundwood 117,000 cu m; fish catch 1,350. Mining and quarrying (1982): sand and gravel 521,000; marl 503,900; limestone 356,100. Manufacturing (1982): sugar 96,160; molasses 31,840; wheat flour 4,950; fertilizer 3,270; beer 30,960 hectolitres; cigarettes 56,000,000 units; garments 577,000 units; batteries 4,840 units. Construction (1977): residential 7,150 sq m, nonresidential 2,018 sq m. Energy production (consumption): electricity (kW-hr; 1982) 57,000,000 (57,000,000); coal, none (n.a.); crude petroleum, none (n.a.); petroleum products (metric tons; 1982) none (56,000);natural gas, none (n.a.).
Gross national product (at current market prices; 1982): U.S.$151,000,000 (U.S.$993.4 per capita).

Origin of gross domestic product (current prices)

	1981 in value BZ$'000	% of total value	labour force	% of labour force
Agriculture	73,600	20.7	14,000	28.6
Mining	800	0.2	...	...
Manufacturing	46,400	13.1	6,900	14.1
Construction	17,000	4.8	5,900	12.0
Trade	56,100	15.8	3,900	8.0
Public utilities	5,100	1.4	‡	‡
Transportation and communication	32,800	9.2	§	§
Finance	‖	‖	...	...
Pub. admin., defense	‖	‖	9,800	20.0
Services	‖	‖	...	...
Other	123,100	34.7	8,500	17.3
TOTAL	354,900	100.0†	49,000	100.0

Budget (1982–83 est.). Revenue: BZ$87,100,000 (current revenue BZ$86,100,000, of which import duties and excise taxes 43.3%, direct taxes 22.5%, licenses 2.1%). Expenditures: BZ$76,400,000 (wages and salaries 48.8%, goods and services 26.6%, pensions and social security 8.1%, interest 6.5%).
Public debt (external, outstanding; 1982): U.S.$51,500,000.
Tourism (1981): receipts from visitors U.S.$7,500,000; expenditures by nationals abroad, n.a.
Persons economically active (1981): total 49,000 (32.7%); female participation in the labour force, n.a.; unemployed 8,500¶ (17.3%).
Price and earnings indexes: n.a.
Household income and expenditure. Average household size (1982) 5.3; income per household: n.a.; source of income (1969): wages, salaries, self-employment 84.1%, gifts and other assistance 8.1%, rent 4.2%; expenditure: n.a.
Land use (1981): forested 44.4%; meadows and pastures 1.9%; agricultural and under permanent cultivation 2.3%; other 51.4%.

Foreign trade

Balance of trade (current prices)

	1976	1977	1978	1979	1980	1981
BZ$'000,000	−93.3	−91.2	−102.6	−142.3	−135.4	−174.4
% of total	40.6%	33.9%	31.6%	36.9%	29.2%	36.8%

Imports (1981): BZ$323,934,000 (manufactured goods 30.2%; food 24.6%; machinery and transport 17.8%; fuels 15.8%; chemicals 7.1%; crude materials 1.5%). *Major import sources:* United States 35.4%; United Kingdom 14.1%; Canada 2.1%.
Exports (1981): BZ$149,492,000 (food 82.3%, of which domestic sugar 28.5%; manufactured goods 14.9%; crude materials except fuels 2.2%; chemicals 0.4%). *Major export destinations:* United States 60.8%; United Kingdom 30.8%; Canada 0.6%.

Transport and communications

Transport. Railroads: none. Roads (1980): total length 1,600 mi, 2,576 km (paved 13%). Vehicles (1980): passenger cars, trucks, and buses 10,227. Merchant marine (1983): vessels (100 gross tons and over) 3; total deadweight tonnage 805. Scheduled international air transport (1981): passenger arrivals 30,409, passenger departures 31,958; cargo loaded 84 metric tons, cargo unloaded 1,766 metric tons; airports (1984) with scheduled flights 7.
Communications. Daily newspapers: none. Radios (1983): total number of receivers 71,000 (1 per 2.2 persons). Televisions: total number of receivers, n.a. Telephones (1982): 8,645 (1 per 17.4 persons).

Education and health

Education (1982)

	schools	teachers	students	student/ teacher ratio
Primary (age 5–14)	196	1,468	35,081	23.9
Secondary (age, n.a.)	22	352	6,289	17.9
Voc., teacher tr.	5	33	619	18.8
Higher	...	...	...	...

College graduates per 100,000 population (1970): 538. *Literacy* (1980): total population literate 64,100¶ (90%).
Health (1982): physicians 75 (1 per 2,027 persons); hospital beds 578 (1 per 263 persons).
Food (1978–80): daily per capita caloric intake 2,659 (vegetable products 73.6%, animal products 26.4%); 118% of FAO recommended minimum requirement.

Military

Total active duty personnel (early 1980s): Belize has a small infantry force♀ consisting of the former Special Force of the Belize Police and the Belize Volunteer Guard. A British garrison of 1,800 troops remains in the country.

*The Belize dollar is officially pegged to the U.S. dollar. †Detail does not add to total given because of rounding. ‡Public utilities are included with public administration and defense. §Transportation and communication is included with construction. ‖Finance, public administration, and services are included with other. ¶Estimated. ♀The infantry force is financed by Belize and the United Kingdom.

Benin

Official name: République Populaire du Bénin (People's Republic of Benin).
Form of government: unitary single-party people's republic with one legislative house (National Revolutionary Assembly [196]).
Head of state and government: President.
Capitals: Porto-Novo (official); Cotonou (de facto).
Official language: French.
Official religion: none.
Monetary unit: 1 CFA franc (CFAF) = 100 centimes; valuation (Oct. 29, 1984) 1 U.S.$ = CFAF 470.59; 1 £ = CFAF 568.00.

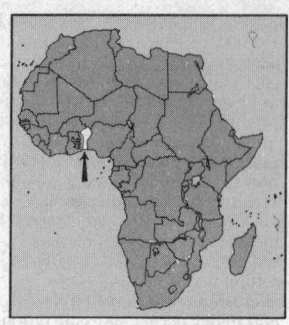

Area and population

Provinces	Capitals	area sq mi	area sq km	population 1982 estimate
Atacora	Natitingou	12,050	31,200	522,000
Atlantique	Cotonou	1,250	3,200	752,000
Borgou	Parakou	19,700	51,000	532,000
Mono	Lokossa	1,450	3,800	517,000
Ouémé	Porto-Novo	1,800	4,700	680,000
Zou	Abomey	7,200	18,700	618,000
TOTAL		43,450	112,600	3,621,000

Source: Official government figures.

Demography

Density (1982): persons per sq mi 83.3, persons per sq km 32.2.
Urban–rural (1981): urban 14.6%; rural 85.4%.
Sex distribution (1980): male 49.26%; female 50.74%.
Age breakdown (1980): under 15, 43.6%; 15–29, 25.8%; 30–44, 15.8%; 45–59, 9.2%; 60 and over, 5.6%.
Population projection: (1990) 4,861,000; (2000) 6,756,000.
Doubling time: 22 years.
Ethnic composition* (1978): Fon 59.2%; Somba 10.3%; Yoruba 10.3%; Bariba 8.9%; Fulani 5.9%; other 5.4%.
Religious affiliation (1980): traditional beliefs 61.4%; Christian 21.6%, of which Roman Catholic 17.4%, Protestant 2.2%; Muslim 15.2%; other 1.8% .
Major cities (1982 est.): Cotonou 487,000; Porto-Novo 208,000; Parakou 66,000; Abomey 54,000; Kandi 53,000.

Vital statistics

Birth rate per 1,000 population (1981): 49.0 (world avg. 29.0).
Death rate per 1,000 population (1981): 17.1 (world avg. 12.0).
Natural increase rate per 1,000 population (1981): 31.9 (world avg. 17.0).
Total fertility rate (avg. births per childbearing woman; 1981): 6.5.
Marriage rate per 1,000 population (1980–85): 12.8.
Divorce rate per 1,000 population (1980–85): 0.8.
Infant mortality rate per 1,000 live births (1981): 152.1.
Life expectancy at birth (1981): male 48.3 years; female 51.6 years.
Major causes of death per 100,000 population (1977): malaria 227.7; diseases of the respiratory system 206.5; diseases of the digestive system 200.7.

National economy

Budget (1979). Revenue: CFAF45,905,000,000 (customs duties 31.0%; grants from abroad 22.5%; taxes on income, profits, and capital gains 9.2%; taxes on goods and services 8.1%). Expenditures: CFAF42,065,000,000 (economic services 20.8%; education 20.3%; general public services 13.1%; defense 8.7%; health 5.6%).
Production (metric tons except as noted). Agriculture, forestry, fishing (1982): cassavas 650,000, corn (maize) 250,000, palm kernels 75,000, peanuts (groundnuts) 65,000, sorghum 60,000, dry beans 50,000, seed cotton 24,000; livestock (number of live animals) 970,000 sheep, 940,000 goats, 785,000 cattle, 475,000 pigs, 4,450,000 chickens; roundwood 3,879,000 cu m; fish catch 3,100†. Mining and quarrying (1982): cement 315,000. Manufacturing (1978): beer and beverages CFAF3,100,000,000; palm oil 36,000‡; cotton fibre 7,500. Construction: n.a. Energy production (consumption): electricity (kW-hr; 1982) 5,000,000 (125,000,000); coal, none (n.a.); crude petroleum (barrels; 1983) §; petroleum products (metric tons; 1982) none (90,000).
Gross national product (at current market prices; 1981): U.S.$1,140,000,000 (U.S.$320 per capita).

Origin of gross domestic product (current prices)

	1981 in value CFAF'000,000	1981 % of total value	1980 labour force	1980 % of labour force
Agriculture	100,500 ‖	38.6 ‖	726,000	46.0
Mining	...	...	...	...
Manufacturing	16,100¶	6.2¶	253,000	16.0
Construction	13,200	5.1	...	...
Trade and finance	58,200	22.4	...	...
Transportation and communication	15,700	6.0	...	...
Pub. admin., defense	26,000	10.0	...	...
Other	—	—	600,000	38.0
Net indirect taxes	30,400	11.7	—	—
TOTAL	260,100	100.0	1,579,000	100.0

Public debt (external, outstanding; 1982): U.S.$566,000,000.
Tourism (1982): receipts from visitors U.S.$10,000,000; expenditures by nationals abroad, n.a.
Persons economically active (1980): total 1,579,000 (45.4%); female participation in the labour force 715,000 (45.3%); unemployed, n.a.

Price and earnings indexes (1977 = 100)

	1978	1979	1980	1981	1982	1983	1984
Consumer price index	...	...	...	...	...	...	...
Hourly earnings index⁹	100.0	100.0	115.0	115.0	115.0	180.4	180.4⁵

Household income and expenditure. Average household size (1979) 5.4; income per household: n.a.; sources of income: n.a.
Land use (1981): forested 35.4%; meadows and pastures 4.0%; agricultural and under permanent cultivation 16.3%; other 44.3%.

Foreign trade□

Balance of trade (current prices)

	1974	1975	1976	1977	1978	1979
CFAF'000,000	−25,290	−35,109	−41,474	−55,674	−64,057	−58,327
% of total	55.2%	71.6%	65.1%	69.2%	82.5%	74.9%

Imports (1979): CFAF68,099,800,000 (fabrics 15.0%; petroleum products 10.0%; clothing 9.5%; machinery 8.6%; tobacco 8.4%; road motor vehicles 6.9%; iron and steel [all forms] 6.2%; beverages [including liquors] 5.8%). *Major import sources:* France 25.8%; The Netherlands 10.0%; United Kingdom 9.0%; India 7.3%; Japan 6.7%.
Exports (1979): CFAF9,772,900,000 (cocoa beans 30.2%; palm kernel oil 22.9%; cotton [all forms] 12.1%; cement 7.1%; palm kernel cake 4.3%). *Major export destinations:* The Netherlands 25.2%; France 20.5%; United Kingdom 13.9%; Niger 10.4%; Denmark 10.2%.

Transport and communications

Transport. Railroads (1981): route length 359 mi, 578 km; passenger-mi 116,600,000, passenger-km 187,600,000; short ton-mi cargo 120,900,000, metric ton-km cargo 176,500,000. Roads (1978): total length 4,182 mi, 6,730 km (paved 10%). Vehicles (1980): passenger cars 9,592; trucks and buses 7,025. Merchant marine (1983): vessels (100 gross tons and over) 12; total deadweight tonnage 4,880. Air transport◊ (1982): passenger-mi 137,840,000, passenger-km 221,830,000; short ton-mi cargo 15,432,000, metric ton-km cargo 22,531,000; airports (1984) with scheduled flights 3.
Communications. Daily newspapers (1983): total number 3; total circulation 12,000▲; circulation per 1,000 population 3.2. Radios (1982): total number of receivers 68,000 (1 per 53 persons). Television (1982): total number of receivers 12,800 (1 per 283 persons). Telephones (1981): 18,000 (1 per 200 persons).

Education and health

Education (1981–82)

	schools	teachers	students	student/ teacher ratio
Primary	2,480	10,381	404,297	38.9
Secondary	...	1,215†	83,207⊕	—
Vocational	...	...	4,441⊕	—
Higher	1	304	4,730	15.6

College graduates per 100,000 population (students graduating; 1979): 25.
Literacy (1980): total population literate 530,000 (27.9%); males literate 368,000 (39.8%); females literate 162,000 (16.6%).
Health: physicians (1980) 204 (1 per 17,485 persons); hospital beds (1981) 4,025 (1 per 905 persons).
Food (1978–80): daily per capita caloric intake 2,310 (vegetable products 95.6%, animal products 4.4%); 100% of FAO recommended minimum requirement.

Military

Total active duty personnel (1981): 3,100 (army 96.8%; navy, none; air force 3.2%). *Military expenditure as percent of GNP* (1981): 2.3% (world 5.7%); per capita expenditure U.S.$6.

*Includes related ethnic groups. †1981. ‡1982. §Production of offshore petroleum began in 1982, reaching a daily flow rate of 4,000 barrels in 1983. A surplus is expected for export. ‖ Includes hunting, forestry, and fishing. ¶Includes public utilities. ⁹Minimum salary of hourly employees in industrial professions. ⁵As of January 1984. □Figures do not include unaccountable re-exports of black market goods, which originate mainly in Nigeria and amounted to an estimated 90% of Benin's actual exports in 1981. ◊Cotonou airport only. ▲Circulation for government daily only. †1978. ⊕1980–81.

Bermuda

Official name: Colony of Bermuda.
Political status: colony (United Kingdom) with two legislative houses (Senate [11]; House of Assembly [40]).
Chief of state: British Monarch, represented by Governor.
Head of government: Premier.
Capital: Hamilton.
Official language: English.
Official religion: none.
Monetary unit: 1 Bermuda dollar (Ber$) = 100 cents; valuation (Oct. 29, 1984) 1 U.S.$ = Ber$1.00*; 1 £ = Ber$1.21.

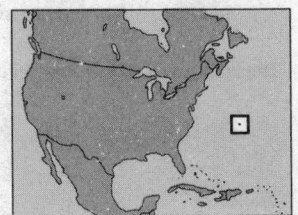

Area and population	area†		population
			1980
Municipalities	sq mi	sq km	census
Hamilton	0.3	0.8	1,617
St. George	0.5	1.3	1,647
Parishes			
Devonshire	1.9	4.9	6,843
Hamilton	2.0	5.2	3,784
Paget	2.0	5.2	4,497
Pembroke	1.8	4.7	10,443
St. Georges	1.7	4.4	2,940
Sandys	1.9	4.9	6,255
Smiths	1.9	4.9	4,463
Southampton	2.2	5.7	4,613
Warwick	2.2	5.7	6,948
TOTAL	18.5‡§	47.9‡	54,050

Source: Official government figures.

Demography

Density (1984): persons per sq mi 3,072, persons per sq km 1,186.
Urban-rural (1980): urban 100.0%; rural, none.
Sex distribution (1985): male 48.81%; female 51.19%.
Age breakdown (1985): under 15, 21.3%; 15–29, 24.6%; 30–44, 25.0%; 45–59, 16.1%; 60–74, 9.7%; 75 and over, 3.3%.
Population projection: (1990) 58,600; (2000) 62,700.
Doubling time: 100 years.
Ethnic composition (1980): black 61.3%; white 37.3%; other 1.4%.
Religious affiliation (1980): Anglican 37.3%; Roman Catholic 13.8%; African Methodist Episcopal 10.2%; Methodist 6.1%; other 32.6%.
Major cities (1980): St. George 1,647; Hamilton 1,617.

Vital statistics

Birth rate per 1,000 population (1983): 16.4 (world avg. 29.0); legitimate 70.3%, illegitimate 29.7%.
Death rate per 1,000 population (1983): 7.0 (world avg. 11.0).
Natural increase rate per 1,000 population (1983): 9.4 (world avg. 18.0).
Total fertility rate (avg. births per childbearing woman; 1975–80): 1.9.
Marriage rate per 1,000 population (1983): 12.0.
Divorce rate per 1,000 population (1982): 4.7.
Infant mortality rate per 1,000 live births (1983): 8.7.
Life expectancy at birth (1980): male 68.8 years; female 76.3 years.
Major causes of death per 10,000 population (1978): diseases of the circulatory system 33.3; malignant neoplasms (cancers) 14.0; endocrine and metabolic disorders 5.0; diseases of the respiratory system 4.3.

National economy

Budget (1983–1984). Revenue: Ber$165,498,200 (customs duties 40.4% employment tax 9.4%; hospital levy 9.4%; international companies tax 5.1%; land tax 5.0%; hotel occupancy tax 4.6%). Expenditures: Ber$165,466,400 (health and social services 21.9%; education 16.3%; public works 8.7%; police 7.9%; tourism 7.4%; marine and air services 3.4%; agriculture and fisheries 3.2%).
Public debt (external, outstanding; 1982): U.S.$279,000,000.
Tourism (1983): receipts from visitors U.S.$329,000,000; expenditures by nationals abroad, n.a.
Production (value in Ber$ except as noted). Agriculture, fishing (1982): vegetables 4,066,000, fruits 1,053,000, eggs 932,000, milk 886,000, meat 460,000, honey 160,000, flowers 55,000; livestock (number of live animals) 2,000 pigs, 1,000 cattle, 1,000 goats, 47,000 chickens; fish catch 2,200. Mining and quarrying: n.a. Manufacturing: major industries are pharmaceuticals, electronics wares, handicrafts, woodworking, small boat building, and textiles. Construction (value in Ber$; 1982): residential 18,100,000; nonresidential 27,400,000. Energy production (consumption): electricity (kW-hr; 1982) 353,000,000 (353,000,000); petroleum products (metric tons; 1982) none (130,000).
Gross national product (at current market prices; 1982–83): U.S.$787,300,000 (U.S.$14,250 per capita).
Persons economically active (1983): total 31,810 (56.6%); female participation in the labour force 14,030 (44.6%); unemployed 270 (0.8%).

Price and earnings indexes (1978 = 100)						
	1979	1980	1981	1982	1983	1984
Consumer price index	113.7	130.7	146.2	157.6	170.2	175.0
Monthly earnings index	107.2	113.5	129.2	180.7	...	...

Origin of gross domestic product (current prices)

	1983			
	in value Ber$'000	% of total value	labour force	% of labour force
Agriculture	9,739	1.2	320	1.0
Mining	...	...	‖	‖
Manufacturing	...	...	1,090	3.4
Construction	...	...	2,010	6.3
Trade	...	...	11,470	36.1
Public utilities	...	...	410	1.3
Transportation and communication	...	...	2,120	6.7
Finance	...	...	4,220	13.3
Pub. admin., defense	...	...	¶	¶
Services	...	...	9,900	31.1
Other	777,561	98.8⁹	270	0.8
TOTAL	787,300	100.0	31,810	100.0

Household income and expenditure. Average household size (1980) 2.9; income per household Ber$28,170 (U.S.$28,170); source of income (1981–82): employment 83.1%, rent 13.9%, self-employment 3.0%; expenditure◇ (1980–81): food 19.8%, housing 14.3%, clothing 8.4%, transportation 5.6%, recreation 5.6%, health 4.9%, electricity 3.8%.
Land use (1981): forested 14.7%; meadows and pastures, 0.6%; agricultural and under permanent cultivation, 4.7%; built on, wasteland, and other 80.0%.

Foreign trade

Balance of trade (current prices)						
	1978	1979	1980	1981	1982	1983
Ber$'000,000	−210.9	−233.8	−310.8	−321.9	−350.3	−355.0
% of total	−99.3%	−99.8%	−99.5%	−99.5%	−99.6%	−88.6%

Imports (1983): Ber$377,732,530 (petroleum and petroleum products 14.0%; electrical machinery, including apparatus and appliances 9.9%; clothing 7.3%; transport equipment 6.3%; meat and meat preparations 5.3%; machinery other than electric 5.0%; fruit and vegetables 3.6%). *Major import sources:* United States 56.3%; United Kingdom 8.3%; Canada 6.5%; Japan 4.8%; Denmark 1.7%; Hong Kong 1.7%.
Exports (1983): Ber$22,762,118 (drugs and medicine 58.2%, electronic supplies 5.9%, electrical supplies 4.2%, scientific supplies 4.1%, aircraft supplies 2.3%, books and papers 2.3%, liquor 1.1%). *Major export destinations:* Italy 30.7%; United States 24.9%; United Kingdom 7.5%; Canada 7.1%; The Netherlands 6.7%; Brazil 5.3%.

Transport and communications

Transport. Railroads: none. Roads (1982): total length 248 mi, 400 km (paved 100.0%). Vehicles (1982): passenger cars 15,118; trucks and buses 2,955. Merchant marine (1983): vessels (100 gross tons and over) 67; total deadweight tonnage 1,291,421. Air transport (passengers; 1982): arrivals 555,589, departures 554,993; short ton cargo handled 8,930, metric ton cargo handled 8,100; airport (1984) with scheduled flights 1.
Communications. Daily newspaper (1983): total number 1; total circulation 14,431; circulation per 1,000 population 259. Radios (1983): total number of receivers 100,000 (1 per 0.6 person). Television (1983): total number of receivers 66,000 (1 per 0.8 person). Telephones (1982): 48,958 (1 per 1.1 persons).

Education and health

Education (1983–84)				
	schools	teachers	students	student/ teacher ratio
Primary (age 5–11)	22	312	5,538	17.8
Secondary (age 11–16)	13	355	4,227	11.9
Vocational	1	55	438	8.0
Higher	1	15	551	36.7

College graduates per 10,000 population (1980): 1,487. *Literacy* (1980): total population literate 39,577 (96.9%); males literate 19,026 (96.7%); females literate 20,551 (97.0%).
Health (1983): physicians 60△ (1 per 927 persons); hospital beds 233 (1 per 239 persons).
Food (1978–80): daily per capita caloric intake 2,774 (vegetable products 58.8%, animal products 41.2%); 107% of FAO recommended requirement.

Military†

Total active duty personnel: Bermuda has a small infantry force numbering about 700.

*The Bermuda dollar is at par with the U.S. dollar. †Includes land area only. ‡Detail does not add to total given because of rounding. §Actual area is 20.6 sq mi (53.3 sq km), of which 2.3 sq mi leased to the U.S. for military bases is excluded. ‖ Mining is included with agriculture. ¶Public administration and defense are included with services. ⁹Includes all sectors except agriculture and fishing. ♂1982. □Second quarter. ◇As a percent of total consumer expenditure. △Hospital physicians only. †External defense is the responsibility of the U.K.

Bhutan

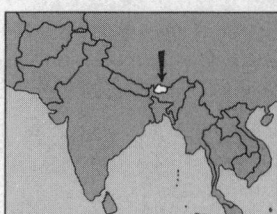

Official name: Druk-Yul (Kingdom of Bhutan).
Form of government: monarchy with one legislative house (National Assembly [150]).
Head of state and government: Monarch.
Capital: Thimphu (official); Paro (administrative and summer).
Official language: Dzongkha Bhutanese.
Official religion: Mahāyāna Buddhism.
Monetary unit: 1 Ngultrum (Nu) = 100 Indian paisa; valuation (Oct. 29, 1984) 1 U.S.$ = Nu12.10*; 1 £ = Nu14.60.

Area and population

Districts	Capitals	area		population
		sq mi	sq km	1980 estimate
Bumthang	Jakar	1,154	2,990	47,600
Chirang	Damphu	309	800	103,200
Dagana	Dagana	540	1,400	21,300
Gasa	Gasa	2,000	5,180	13,000
Gaylegphug	Gaylegphug	1,019	2,640	...
Ha	Paro	826	2,140	26,900
Kurtey	Lhuntshi	1,124	2,910	57,400
Mongar	Mongar	707	1,830	152,500
Phuntsholing	Phuntsholing	826	2,140	71,900
Punakha	Punakha	332	860	26,700
Rinphu	Paro	580	1,500	79,300
Samdrup Jongkhar	Samdrup Jongkhar	903	2,340	...
Shemgang	Shemgang	981	2,540	66,800
Shumar	Pema Gatsel	147	380	...
Tashigang	Tashigang	1,645	4,260	295,300
Thimphu	Thimphu	625	1,620	76,600
Tongsa	Tongsa	568	1,470	58,300
Wangdi Phodrang	Wangdi Phodrang	1,158	3,000	77,200
TOTAL		15,444	40,000	1,174,000

Source: Official government figures.

Demography

Density (1984): persons per sq mi 91.8, persons per sq km 35.4.
Urban-rural (1980): urban 3.9%; rural 96.1%.
Sex distribution (1980): male 51.54%; female 48.46%.
Age breakdown (1982): under 15, 39.2%; 15–29, 26.5%; 30–44, 16.3%; 45–59, 10.9%; 60–69, 4.2%; 70 and over, 2.9%.
Population projection: (1990) 1,628,000; (2000) 2,030,000.
Doubling time: 32 years.
Ethnic composition (1978): Bhutia 60.7%; Gurung 15.8%; Assamese 13.5%; other 10.0%.
Religious affiliation (1980): Buddhist 69.3%; Hindu 24.8%; Muslim 5.0%; other 0.9%.
Major cities (1982 est.): Thimphu 12,000; Phuntsholing 10,000.

Vital statistics

Birth rate per 1,000 population (1983): 39.3 (world avg. 29.0); legitimate, n.a.; illegitimate, n.a.
Death rate per 1,000 population (1983): 18.0 (world avg. 11.0).
Natural increase rate per 1,000 population (1983): 21.3 (world avg. 18.0).
Total fertility rate (avg. births per childbearing woman; 1983): 5.5.
Marriage rate per 1,000 population: n.a.
Divorce rate per 1,000 population: n.a.
Infant mortality rate per 1,000 live births (1983): 143.0.
Life expectancy at birth (1980–85): male 46.0 years; female 44.5 years.
Major causes of death: n.a.; however, malaria and tuberculosis are the major health problems.

National economy

Budget (1981–82). Revenue: Nu101,100,000 (government departments† 31.4%; excise refunds from the government of India 24.7%; excise duties 13.8%; sales tax 6.7%; royalties from forests and mines 4.8%; income tax 3.9%). Expenditures: Nu169,700,000 (economic services 38.1%, of which agriculture‡ 13.4%, communications 11.8%, tourism 4.4%; general public services 36.1%; education 16.8%; health 8.8%).
Public debt (external, outstanding): n.a.
Tourism (1981–82): receipts from visitors U.S.$1,411,400; expenditures by nationals abroad, n.a.
Production (metric tons except as noted). Agriculture, forestry, fishing (1982): rice 54,000, vegetables and melons 46,000, wheat 22,000, potatoes 14,000, corn (maize) 13,000, barley 11,000, jute 6,000, millet 5,000, tobacco 1,000; livestock (number of live animals) 312,000 cattle, 56,000 pigs, 44,000 sheep, 26,100 yaks, 22,000 goats, 21,000 horses, 187,000 chickens; roundwood 3,224,000 cu m; fish catch 1,000. Mining and quarrying: n.a.; however, some marble and slate are quarried, and gypsum and graphite are mined. Manufacturing (value in Nu; 1980–81): distillery products 47,000,000; cement 36,000,000; chemical products 19,000,000; processed food 14,000,000; forest products 3,000,000. Construction (number of buildings completed; 1977–78): residential 10; nonresidential (guest house) 1. Energy production (consumption): electricity (kW-hr; 1982) 24,000,000 (24,000,000); coal, none (n.a.); crude petroleum, none (n.a.); petroleum products (metric tons; 1982) none (1,000); natural gas, none (n.a.).

Gross national product (at current market prices; 1981): U.S.$124,402,400 (U.S.$110 per capita).

Origin of gross domestic product (current prices)

	1980–81		1981–82	
	in value Nu'000,000	% of total value	labour force	% of labour force
Agriculture	645	63.2	613,000	94.3
Mining	9	0.9	...	...
Manufacturing	33	3.2	6,000	0.9
Construction	19	1.9	...	...
Trade	29	2.8	9,000	1.4
Public utilities	3	0.3	...	...
Transportation and communication	33	3.2	...	...
Finance	15	1.5	...	...
Pub. admin., defense	107	10.5	...	...
Services	117	11.5	22,000	3.4
Other	11§	1.1	...	...
TOTAL	1,021	100.0 ‖	650,000	100.0

Persons economically active (1981–82): total 650,000 (55.9%); female participation in the labour force, n.a.; unemployed, n.a.

Price and earnings indexes (1980–81 = 100)

	1977–78	1978–79	1979–80	1980–81	1981–82
Consumer price index	71.8	80.4	91.3	100.0	110.3
Earnings index	...	...	...	...	...

Household income and expenditure. Average household size (1977): 5.0; income per household: n.a.; sources of income: n.a.; expenditure: n.a.
Land use (1981): forested 69.6%; meadows and pastures 4.6%; agricultural and under permanent cultivation 2.0%; other 23.8%.

Foreign trade¶

Balance of trade (current prices)

	1978	1979	1980	1981	1982	1983
Nu'000,000	...	...	...	...	...	−226.5
% of total	...	...	...	...	...	38.9%

Imports (1981–82): Nu404,521,000 (machinery and equipment 22.1%, petroleum products 14.2%, iron and steel products 8.1%, motor vehicles 7.3%, rice 3.9%, fabrics 3.0%, stationery and books 2.2%, wheat and wheat flour 1.6%). *Major import source:* India.
Exports (1981–82): Nu177,981,000♀ (cement 26.6%, oranges 9.6%, sawn timber 9.0%, potatoes 8.7%, talcum powder 6.1%, cardamoms 6.1%, rosin 4.0%, menthol products 2.7%). *Major export destination:* India.

Transport and communications

Transport. Railroads: none. Roads (1979): total length 1,103 mi, 1,775 km (paved 35%). Vehicles (1982): passenger cars 1,363; trucks and buses 706. Merchant marine: none. Air transport: n.a.; airport (1984) with scheduled flights 1.
Communications. Daily newspapers: noneδ. Radios (1982): total number of receivers 12,000 (1 per 97 persons). Television: total number of receivers, n.a. Telephones (1981–82): 14,638 (1 per 79 persons).

Education and health

Education (1981–82)

	schools	teachers	students	student/ teacher ratio
Primary (age 6–11)	119	797	22,288	28.0
Secondary (age 12–17)	30	520	14,546	28.0
Voc., teacher tr.	4	66	522	7.9
Higher	1	16	204	12.8

College graduates per 100,000 population (students graduating; 1980): 7.
Literacy (1977): total population literate 124,000 (18.0%); males literate 98,000 (31.0%); females literate 26,000 (9.0%).
Health (1977): physicians 52 (1 per 21,154 persons); hospital beds 526 (1 per 2,090 persons).
Food (1975–77): daily per capita caloric intake 2,058 (vegetable products 98.3%, animal products 1.7%); 89% of FAO recommended minimum requirement.

Military

Total active duty personnel: Bhutan has a small army numbering about 4,000 men.

*The Ngultrum is at par with the Indian rupee. †Includes tourism, transport service, lotteries, telephones, and posts and telegraphs. ‡Also includes irrigation, animal husbandry, and forestry. §Includes tourism only. ‖ Detail does not add to total given because of rounding. ¶Only with India. ♀Excludes Nu55,700,000 exports to countries other than India. δ A government weekly is published from Thimphu in Dzongkha, English, and Nepalese.

Bolivia

Official name: República de Bolivia (Republic of Bolivia).
Form of government: unitary, multiparty republic with two legislative houses (Chamber of Senators [27]; Chamber of Deputies [130]).
Head of state and government: President.
Capital: La Paz (administrative); Sucre (judicial).
Official languages: Spanish, Aymara, Quechua.
Official religion: Roman Catholicism.
Monetary unit: 1 Bolivian peso ($b) = 100 centavos; valuation (Oct. 29, 1984) 1 U.S.$ = $b2,000; 1 £ = $b2,414.

Area and population

Departments	Capitals	area sq mi	area sq km	population 1984 estimate
Beni	Trinidad	82,458	213,564	232,000
Chuquisaca	Sucre	19,893	51,524	454,000
Cochabamba	Cochabamba	21,479	55,631	955,000
La Paz	La Paz	51,732	133,985	2,029,000
Oruro	Oruro	20,690	53,588	403,000
Pando	Cobija	24,644	63,827	46,000
Potosi	Potosi	45,644	118,218	860,000
Santa Cruz	Santa Cruz	143,098	370,621	1,012,000
Tarija	Tarija	14,526	37,623	262,000
TOTAL		424,164	1,098,581	6,253,000

Demography

Density (1984): persons per sq mi 14.7, persons per sq km 5.7.
Urban–rural (1982): urban 45.8%; rural 54.2%.
Sex distribution (1982): male 49.36%; female 50.64%.
Age breakdown (1982): under 15, 43.0%; 15–29, 26.5%; 30–44, 15.8%; 45–59, 9.4%; 60–74, 4.4%; 75 and over, 0.9%.
Population projection: (1990) 7,314,000; (2000) 9,724,000.
Doubling time: 26 years.
Ethnic composition (1982): mestizo 31.2%; Quechua 25.4%; Aymara 16.9%; white 14.5%; other 12%.
Religious affiliation (1980): Roman Catholic 92.7; Baha'i 2.6%; other 4.7%.
Major cities (1984): La Paz 953,634; Santa Cruz 419,042; Cochabamba 304,960; Oruro 172,814; Sucre 84,505.

Vital statistics

Birth rate per 1,000 population (1980): 24.9 (world avg. 30.0).
Death rate per 1,000 population (1980): 4.8 (world avg. 12.0).
Natural increase rate per 1,000 population (1980): 20.1 (world avg. 18.0).
Total fertility rate (avg. births per childbearing woman; 1980–85): 6.2.
Marriage rate per 1,000 population (1980): 4.8.
Divorce rate per 1,000 population: n.a.
Infant mortality rate per 1,000 live births (1975–80): 138.2.
Life expectancy at birth (1980–85): male 48.6 years; female 53.0 years.
Major causes of death: n.a.

National economy

Budget (1981). Revenue: $b14,069,200,000 (internal taxes 36.1%, customs taxes 22.4%, royalties on petroleum 17.1%). Expenditures: $b24,286,000,000 (services 53.8%, public debt 12.7%, transfers and contributions 11.0%, materials and equipment 10.4%).
Public debt (external, outstanding; 1982): U.S.$3,816,559,000.
Tourism (1981): receipts from visitors U.S.$36,000,000; expenditures by nationals abroad U.S.$50,000,000.
Production (metric tons except as noted). Agriculture, forestry, fishing (1982): sugarcane 2,600,000, potatoes 900,000, bananas 160,000, oranges 85,000, rice 80,000, corn (maize) 70,000, wheat 70,000; livestock (number of live animals): 9,200,000 sheep, 4,100,000 cattle, 3,100,000 goats, 1,550,000 pigs, 790,000 asses, 410,000 horses; roundwood 1,323,000 cu m; fish catch 5,617. Mining and quarrying (metric tons of pure metal; 1982): zinc 45,667; tin 26,773; antimony 13,978; lead 12,433; iron ore 4,891; tungsten 3,195; copper 2,270; gold 1,249 kilograms. Manufacturing (gross value in $b; 1981): food and beverages 16,080,982,808, of which food 12,254,780,842; non-ferrous metals 7,606,061,069; non-metallic mineral products 1,328,121,249; metal products 1,194,120,108; wood and wood products 999,542,335; machinery and equipment 516,844,375. Construction* (1980): residential dwellings 2,075. Energy production (consumption): electricity (kW-hr; 1982) 1,702,962,000 (1,543,879,000); coal (metric tons; 1981) none (1,000); crude petroleum (barrels; 1982) 8,921,000 (7,395,970†); petroleum products (metric tons) 861,000 (1,033,000); natural gas (cu m; 1982) 5,319,000,000 (361,999,638†).
Persons economically active (1982): total 1,871,600 (31.6%); female participation in the labour force 434,030 (23.2%); unemployed, n.a.

Price and earnings indexes (1980 = 100)

	1977	1978	1979	1980	1981	1982	1983
Consumer price index	51.4	56.7	67.9	100.0	132.1	295.4	1,109.4
Monthly earnings index	...	...	...	...	...	...	...

Gross national product (at current market prices; 1982): U.S.$5,441,000,000 (U.S.$920 per capita).

Origin of gross domestic product (current prices)

	1981 in value $b'000,000	1981 % of total value	1982 labour‡ force	1982 % of labour‡ force
Agriculture	34,731	17.9	792,600	46.4
Mining	13,492	7.0	76,200	4.5
Manufacturing	27,199	14.0	155,500	9.1
Construction	9,657	5.1	56,500	3.3
Trade	48,394§	24.9§	128,800	7.5
Finance	§	§	13,300	0.8
Public utilities	2,288	1.2	7,200	0.4
Transportation and communication	17,625	9.1	94,700	5.5
Pub. admin., defense	13,647	7.0	...	...
Services	...	...	382,600	22.4
Other	26,951	13.9	...	...
TOTAL	193,984	100.0	1,707,400	100.0 ‖

Land use (1981): forested 51.8%; meadows and pastures 24.9%; agricultural and under permanent cultivation 3.1%; other 20.2%.

Foreign trade

Balance of trade (current prices)

	1977	1978	1979	1980	1981	1982
U.S.$'000,000	−31.6	+83.8	−128.5	+200.0	+169.9	+310.0
% of total	2.4%	5.2%	7.0%	10.7%	9.3%	22.9%

Imports (1982): U.S.$522,100,000 (capital goods 43.2%, of which capital goods for industry 24.3%, transport equipment 10.5%; raw materials 40.3%, of which raw materials for industry 37.2%; consumer goods 16.5%, of which nondurable consumer goods 9.8%, durable consumer goods 6.7%). *Major import sources:* United States 29.0%; Argentina 14.6%; Japan 11.0%; Brazil 10.2%; West Germany 7.3%; Chile 2.9%; Peru 2.7%.
Exports (1982): U.S.$832,000,000 (crude minerals 46.7%, of which tin metal and concentrate 31.0%; mineral fuels, lubricants, and related materials 43.5%, of which natural gas 42.5%; coffee 1.7%; wood 1.3%; sugar 0.9%). *Major export destinations:* Argentina 51.8%; United States 26.1%; The Netherlands 4.0%; West Germany 3.7%; United Kingdom 3.4%; Peru 2.6%; Belgium 2.1%; Switzerland 2.1%.

Transport and communications

Transport. Railroads: length (1982) 2,320 mi, 3,733 km; passenger-mi 299,600,000†, passenger-km 482,200,000†; short ton-mi cargo 424,990,000†, metric ton-km cargo 620,480,000†. Roads (1980): total length 24,638 mi, 39,651 km (paved 3%). Vehicles (1982): passenger cars 40,638; trucks and buses 36,051. Merchant marine (1983): vessels (100 gross tons and over) 2; total deadweight tonnage 18,934. Air transport (1983): passenger-mi 488,764,000, passenger-km 786,592,000; short ton-mi cargo 12,213,000, metric ton-km cargo 17,831,000; airports (1984) with scheduled flights 15.
Communications. Daily newspapers (1983): total number 9; total circulation 190,000; circulation per 1,000 population 32. Radios (1983 est.): total number of receivers 480,000 (1 per 12.7 persons). Television (1983): total number of receivers 386,292 (1 per 15.7 persons). Telephones (1982): 144,300 (1 per 41.0 persons).

Education and health

Education (1983)

	schools	teachers	students	student/ teacher ratio
Primary (age 6–13)	8,514	50,703	1,154,819	22.8
Secondary (age 14–17)	845	8,091	174,982	21.6
Higher	25	1,487	13,388	9.0

College graduates per 100,000 population (1980): 2.1. *Literacy* (1976): total population literate 1,706,718 (63.2%).
Health (1978): physicians 3,410 (1 per 1,433 persons); hospital beds 9,353 (1 per 523 persons).
Food (1978–80): daily per capita caloric intake 2,086 (vegetable products 83.7%, animal products 16.3%); 87% of FAO recommended minimum requirement.

Military

Total active duty personnel (1983): 27,600 (army 72.5%; navy 13.0%; air force 14.5%). *Military expenditure as percent of GNP* (1982): 1.5% (world 6.0%); per capita expenditure U.S.$16.

*National government sponsored only. †1981. ‡Employed persons only. §Finance is included with trade. ‖ Detail does not add to total given because of rounding.

Botswana

Official name: Republic of Botswana.
Form of government: multiparty
  republic with one legislative body
  (National Assembly [37]).
Head of state and government:
  President.
Capital: Gaborone.
Official language: English.
Official religion: none.
Monetary unit: 1 pula (P) = 100 thebe;
  valuation (Oct. 29, 1984)
  1 U.S.$ = P1.47; 1 £ = P1.78.

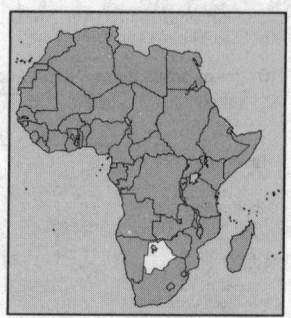

Area and population

Districts	Capitals	area sq mi	area sq km	population 1984 estimate
Central	Serowe	57,039	147,730	355,000
Ghanzi	Ghanzi	45,525	117,910	21,000
Kgalagadi	Tshabong	41,290	106,940	26,000
Kgatleng	Mochudi	3,073	7,960	49,000
Kweneng	Molepolole	13,857	35,890	128,000
North East	Masunga	1,977	5,120	40,000
North West				
Chobe	Kasane	8,031	20,800	9,000
Ngamiland	Maun	42,135	109,130	75,000
Southern	Kanye	10,992	28,470	138,000
South East	Ramotswa	687	1,780	34,000
Towns				
Francistown		27	70	36,000
Gaborone		27	71	79,000
Lobatse		25	64	22,000
Orapa		*	*	58,000
Selebi-Pikwe		20	52	33,000
TOTAL		224,706†	581,987	1,103,000

Source: Official government figures.

Demography

Density (1984): persons per sq mi 4.9, persons per sq km 1.9.
Urban–rural (1981): urban 15.9%; rural 84.1%.
Sex distribution (1981): male 47.09%; female 52.91%.
Age breakdown (1981): under 15, 56.5%; 15–29, 19.9%; 30–44, 10.2%; 45–59,
  6.6%; 60–74, 3.4%; 75 and over, 3.4%.
Population projection: (1990) 1,302,000; (2000) 1,878,000.
Doubling time: 18.6 years.
Ethnic composition (1980): Bantu 93.6%; Bushman 4.8%; European 0.7%;
  other 0.9%.
Religious affiliation (1980 est.): folk religionist 49.2%; Protestant 26.6%;
  indigenous Christian 11.8%; Roman Catholic 9.4%; other 3.0%.
Major cities (1984): Gaborone 79,000; Francistown 36,000; Selebi-Pikwe
  33,000; Serowe 29,000; Mahalapye 25,000; Molepolole 24,000.

Vital statistics

Birth rate per 1,000 population (1980–85): 50.5 (world avg. 27.5); legitimate,
  n.a.; illegitimate, n.a.
Death rate per 1,000 population (1980–85): 15.6 (world avg. 10.6).
Natural increase rate per 1,000 population (1980–85): 34.9 (world avg. 16.9).
Total fertility rate (avg. births per childbearing woman; 1980–85): 6.5.
Marriage rate per 1,000 population: n.a.
Divorce rate per 1,000 population: n.a.
Infant mortality rate per 1,000 live births (1975–80): 87.0.
Life expectancy at birth (1980): male 56.0 years; female 62.0 years.
Major causes of death (as percent of total deaths; 1977): measles 16.3%;
  heart disease 8.4%; influenza and pneumonia 7.6%; diarrheal diseases 7.5%;
  malignant neoplasms (cancers) 6.0%.

National economy

Budget (1981–82). Revenue: P275,280,000 (import duties 38.1%, income
  tax 36.6%, property income 20.4%). Expenditures: P300,130,000 (education
  21.2%, public services 20.4%, defense 8.7%, roads 8.1%, health 5.9%).
Public debt (external, outstanding; 1982): U.S.$388,000,000.
Tourism (1981): receipts from visitors U.S.$22,000,000; expenditures by na-
  tionals abroad U.S.$18,000,000.
Production (metric tons except as noted). Agriculture, forestry, fishing
  (1982): cereals 22,000 (of which sorghum 15,000, corn [maize] 5,000, millet
  2,000), pulses 18,000, sunflower seeds, roots, and tubers 7,000, peanuts
  (groundnuts) 2,000; livestock (number of live animals) 3,000,000 cattle,
  700,000 goats, 200,000 sheep, 42,000 mules and asses; roundwood 786,000
  cu m; fish catch 1,400. Mining and quarrying (1983): diamonds 10,731,-
  165 carats (P650,000,000); nickel–copper matte (metal content‡); copper
  18,375§; nickel 17,756§; cobalt 254§. Manufacturing (1980): beer 112,000
  hectolitres. Construction (1981): residential 120,200 sq m; nonresidential
  119,900 sq m. Energy production (consumption): electricity (kW-hr; 1982)
  604,408,000 (604,408,000); coal (metric tons; 1982) 414,778 (n.a.); crude
  petroleum, none (n.a.); natural gas, none (n.a.).
Persons economically active (1981): total 315,475 (33.5%); female participation in the labour force 127,158 (25.5%); unemployed, n.a .

Price and earnings indexes (1980 = 100)

	1978	1979	1980	1981	1982	1983	1984
Consumer price index	78.7	87.8	100.0	116.2	129.6	142.9	151.1δ
Earnings index	...	...	...	...	...	...	...

Gross national product (at current market prices; 1981): U.S.$830,100,000
  (U.S.$880 per capita).

Origin of gross domestic product (current prices)

	1981 in value P'000,000	1981 % of total value	1981 labour ‖ force	1981 % of labour force
Agriculture	97.0	12.2	4,800	4.9
Mining	206.0	25.9	8,100	8.3
Manufacturing	47.6	6.0	6,400	6.6
Construction	41.8	5.2	15,200	15.6
Trade	¶	¶	15,300	15.7
Public utilities	18.9	2.4	1,600	1.6
Transportation and communication	15.6	2.0	3,900	4.0
Finance	260.6¶	32.7¶	4,100	4.2
Pub. admin., defense	109.0⌀	13.7⌀	25,800	26.5
Services	⌀	⌀	12,200	12.6
TOTAL	796.5	100.0†	97,400	100.0

Household income and expenditure. Average household size (1981) 5.7;
  average annual income per household, n.a.; source of income: wages and
  salaries 67.4%, self-employment 27.7%, transfers 4.8%; expenditure (1980):
  food, beverages, and tobacco 48.2%, rent and services 12.6%.
Land use (1981): forested 1.6%; meadows and pastures 75.2%; agricultural
  and under permanent cultivation 2.3%; other 20.9%.

Foreign trade

Balance of trade (current prices)

	1978	1979	1980	1981	1982	1983
P'000,000	−109.0	−68.7	−146.1	−332.4	−264.0	−106.8
% of total	22.9%	8.8%	15.7%	33.3%	20.2%	7.1%

Imports (1982): P786,526,000 (mineral fuels 14.2%; machinery, mechanical
  appliances, and electrical equipment 13.8%; transport equipment 11.7%;
  base metals 9.3%). *Major import sources:* CCA (Common Customs Area,
  which includes Lesotho, South Africa, and Swaziland) 86.5%; Zimbabwe
  6.1%; United Kingdom 2.3%.
Exports (1982): P522,464,000 (precious and semi-precious stones 52.1%;
  live animals and animal products 17.3%; base metals 14.0%). *Major export
  destinations:* Switzerland 48.2%; United States 11.9%; United Kingdom
  11.5%; CCA 11.3%.

Transport and communications

Transport. Railroads (1982): length 439 mi, 707 km; number of passengers
  566,372; short ton-mi cargo 875,959,000, metric ton-km cargo 1,278,879,-
  000. Roads (1983): total length 4,987 mi, 8,026 km (paved 22%). Vehicles
  (1983): passenger cars 11,039; trucks and buses 20,739. Merchant marine:
  none. Air transport (1980): passenger-mi 355,000,000, passenger-km 570,-
  000,000; short ton-mi cargo 24,180,000, metric ton-km cargo 35,300,000;
  airports (1984) with scheduled flights 4.
Communications. Daily newspaper (1984): total number 1; total circulation
  18,000; circulation per 1,000 population 19.0. Radios (1983): total number
  of receivers 75,000 (1 per 13.3 persons). Television (1981): none. Telephones (1981): 7,193 (1 per 131 persons).

Education and health

Education (1983–84)

	schools	teachers	students	student/ teacher ratio
Primary (age 7–13)	518	6,753	209,345	31.0
Secondary (age 14–19)	56	1,065	22,044	20.7
Voc., teacher tr.	19	...	2,321	...
Higher	1	144□	1,232	...

College graduates per 100,000 population (students graduating; 1979): 27.
Literacy (1981): total population literate 262,000 (52.4%); males literate
  106,841 (47.7%); females literate 155,159 (56.2%).
Health (1980): physicians 111 (1 per 7,378 persons); hospital beds 2,141 (1
  per 382 persons).
Food (1978–80): daily per capita caloric intake 2,182 (vegetable products
  81.8%, animal products 18.2%); 94% of FAO recommended minimum
  requirement.

Military

Total active duty personnel (1982): 3,000 (army 95.0%; navy, none; air force
  5.0%). *Military expenditure as percent of GNP* (1982): 2.7% (world 6.0%);
  per capita expenditure U.S.$26.

---

*Area included with Central District. †Detail does not add to total given because
of rounding. ‡Approximate recoverable mine output. §1982. ‖ Excludes domestic
servants, workers employed in traditional agricultural, and other informal sector employees. ¶Trade included with finance. ⌀Services included with public administration
and defense. δFirst quarter. □1982–83.

Brazil

Official name: República Federativa do Brasil (Federative Republic of Brazil).
Form of government: multi-party federal republic (controlled by the military) with 2 legislative houses (Federal Senate [69]; Chamber of Deputies [479]).
Chief of state and government: President.
Capital: Brasília.
Official language: Portuguese.
Official religion: none.
Monetary unit: 1 Cruzeiro (Cr$) = 100 centavos; valuation (Oct. 29, 1984)
1 U.S.$ = 2,543 cruzeiros;
1 £ = 3,070 cruzeiros.

Area and population		area*		population
				1984
States	Capitals	sq mi	sq km	estimate
Acre	Rio Branco	58,915	152,589	348,000
Alagoas	Maceió	10,676	27,652	2,199,000
Amazonas	Manaus	601,928	1,558,987	1,674,000
Bahia	Salvador	216,198	559,951	10,504,000
Ceará	Fortaleza	56,686	146,817	5,785,000
Espírito Santo†	Vitória	17,605	45,597	2,239,000
Goiás	Goiânia	247,891	642,036	4,347,000
Maranhão	São Luís	125,335	324,616	4,525,000
Mato Grosso	Cuiabá	340,156	881,001	1,418,000
Mato Grosso do Sul	Campo Grande	135,347	350,548	1,562,000
Minas Gerais	Belo Horizonte	224,938	582,586	14,381,000
Pará	Belém	473,952	1,227,530	4,058,000
Paraíba	João Pessoa	21,765	56,372	2,971,000
Paraná	Curitiba	76,857	199,060	7,994,000
Pernambuco	Recife	37,946	98,281	6,661,000
Piauí	Teresina	96,886	250,934	2,378,000
Rio Grande do Norte	Natal	20,469	53,015	2,085,000
Rio Grande do Sul	Porta Alegre	103,293	267,528	8,358,000
Rio de Janeiro	Rio de Janeiro	16,720	43,305	12,502,000
Rondônia	Porto Velho	93,840	243,044	688,000
Santa Catarina	Florianópolis	36,866	95,483	4,011,000
São Paulo	São Paulo	95,491	247,320	28,820,000
Sergipe	Aracaju	8,492	21,994	1,260,000
Other federal entities				
Distrito Federal	—	2,228	5,771	1,505,000
Amapá	Macapá	53,694	139,068	207,000
Fernando de Noronha‡	Fernando de Noronha	10	25	1,000
Roraima	Boa Vista	88,844	230,104	99,000
TOTAL*		3,265,075§	8,456,508§	132,580,000

Source: Official government figures.

Demography

Density (1984): persons per sq mi 40.6, persons per sq km 15.7.
Urban–rural (1980): urban 67.6%; rural 32.4%.
Sex distribution (1980): male 49.68%; female 50.32%.
Age breakdown (1980): under 15, 38.2%; 15–29, 29.0%; 30–44, 16.6%; 45–59, 10.0%; 60–69, 3.8%; 70 and over, 2.3%; unknown 0.1%.
Population projection: (1990) 153,200,000; (2000) 187,500,000.
Doubling time: 30 years.
Ethnic composition (1980): Brazilian white 53.0%, of which Portuguese 15.0%, Italian 11.0%, Spanish 10.0%, German 3.0%, other 14.0%; mulatto 22.0%; mestizo 12.0%; black 11.0%; Japanese 0.8%; indigenous Indian 0.1%; other 1.1%.
Religious affiliation (1980): Roman Catholics 87.8%, of which Spiritist Catholics 15.7% ‖, Evangelical Catholics 9.0%¶; Protestants 4.0%; Brazilian indigenous Christians 2.1%; Afro-American Spiritists 2.0%❡; Spiritists 1.7%ŏ; nonreligious 1.0%; atheists 0.4%; Buddhists 0.3%; Jews 0.2%; other 0.5%.
Major cities (1980): São Paulo 7,033,000 (metropolitan area 12,589,000); Rio de Janeiro 5,091,000 (metropolitan area 9,014,000); Salvador 1,492,000 (metropolitan area 1,767,000); Belo Horizonte 1,442,000 (metropolitan area 2,540,000); Recife 1,184,000; Porto Alegre 1,109,000; Curitiba 844,000; Belém 758,000; Goiânia 703,000; Fortaleza 649,000.
Total number of immigrants entering Brazil (1884–1973): 5,072,000; *place of national origin:* Portugal 31.1%; Italy 30.2%; Spain 13.8%; Japan 4.9%; Germany 4.0%; Russia (Soviet Union) 2.2%; other 13.8%.
Mobility (1980). Households living in same residence as in 1970: 25.0%.
Households (1980). Average household size 4.7; 1 person 6.1%, 2 persons 13.6%, 3 persons 17.1%, 4 persons 17.8%, 5 persons 14.6%, 6 persons 10.3%, 7 or more persons 20.5%. Family households: n.a.
Immigration (1981): permanent immigrants admitted 4,303, from United Kingdom 29.2%, Japan 15.4%, Uruguay 10.1%.

Vital statistics

Birth rate per 1,000 population (1981): 30.5 (world avg. 29.0).
Death rate per 1,000 population (1981): 8.2 (world avg. 12.0).
Natural increase rate per 1,000 population (1981): 22.3 (world avg. 17.0).
Total fertility rate (avg. births per childbearing woman; 1981): 4.0.
Marriage rate per 1,000 population (1981): 7.5.
Divorce rate per 1,000 population (1981): 0.2.
Infant mortality rate per 1,000 live births (1981): 75.4.
Life expectancy at birth (1981): male 61.6 years; female 65.7 years.
Major causes of death per 100,000 population (1979): diseases of the circulatory system 181.1, of which cerebrovascular disease 59.0, diseases of

pulmonary circulation 46.6, acute myocardial infarction 34.5; infectious and parasitic diseases 74.1; malignant neoplasms (cancers) 57.1; conditions originating in the perinatal period 50.9; accidents 37.6; pneumonia 36.1; homicide and other violence 25.0.

Social indicators

Educational attainment (1980). Percent of adult population having: less than full primary education 60.2%, primary 33.6%, secondary 3.8%, 4-year higher degree 2.3%, post-graduate 0.1%.

Distribution of income (1980)									
percent of national income by decile									
1	2	3	4	5	6	7	8	9	10 (highest)
1.2	2.0	3.0	3.6	4.4	5.6	7.2	9.9	15.4	47.9

Quality of working life. Average work week: (1980): 80.6% of the labour force works 40 or more hours per week. Annual estimated rate per 100,000 insured urban workers (1982) for: injury or accident 5,500, industrial illness n.a., death 21. Proportion of labour force participating in national social insurance system: 51.8%. Average days lost to labour stoppages per 1,000 work days: n.a. Average duration of journey and method of transport to work: n.a. Rate per 1,000 workers of discouraged (unemployed no longer seeking work): n.a.
Access to services. Proportion of dwellings having access to: electricity (1980) 67.4%, of which urban dwellings having access: 88.5%, rural dwellings having access 20.5%; safe public water supply (1976) 63.0%, of which urban dwellings having access 75.0%, rural dwellings having access 46.0%; public sewage collection (1976) 21.0%, of which urban dwellings having access 34.0%, rural dwellings having access, minuscule; public fire protection n.a.
Social participation. Eligible voters participating in last national election 82.7%◻. Population participating in voluntary work n.a. Trade union membership in total workforce (1980 est.) 10–15%. Practicing religious population in total affiliated population: Most men, and in particular Portuguese-Brazilian men, attend Mass only on special occasions. They believe religion is the domain and duty of women.
Social deviance: The incidence of crime is not accurately reported. Felonies per official statistics (1978): 64,915, of which murder and bodily assault 42.0%, robbery, extortion, and fraud 39.0%, rape and pandering 4.5%, trafficking or using illegal narcotics 10.5%. Suicide (1981): 4,800; additional potential suicides 9,698.
Leisure. Favourite leisure activities: n.a.
Material well-being (1980). Households possessing: automobile 28.3%, telephone 17.5%, television receiver 73.1%, refrigerator 66.2%, air conditioner n.a., washing machine n.a.

National economy

Gross national product (at current market prices; 1982): U.S.$190,860,000,000 (U.S.$1,505 per capita).

Origin of gross domestic product (current prices at factor cost)				
	1982		1980	
	in value Cr$'000,000,000	% of total value	labour force⊕	% of labour force
Agriculture, forestry hunting, fishing	5,321	11.6	12,661,000	29.3
Mining and quarrying	366	0.8	251,300	0.6
Manufacturing	12,396	27.1	6,939,400	16.1
Construction	2,488	5.4	3,171,100	7.3
Trade	7,687	16.8	4,037,900	9.3
Public utilities	814	1.8	410,700	0.9
Transportation and communication	2,658	5.8	1,800,300	4.2
Finance and insurance	3,205	7.0	788,800	1.8
Pub. admin., defense	3,224	7.1	1,722,300	4.0
Rent and real estate	5,278	11.5	190,600	0.4
Other	2,277	5.0	11,262,300	26.0**
TOTAL	45,714	100.0§	43,235,700	100.0§

Budget (1981). Revenue: Cr$6,072,600,000,000 (tax revenue 73.5%, of which taxes on goods and services 27.2% [including excises 18.4%], social security contributions 25.4%, taxes on income, profits, and capital gains 13.0%; nontax revenue 25.5%, of which property income 21.6%). Expenditures: Cr$4,987,800,000,000 (social security and welfare 34.6%; economic services 24.1%, of which mining, manufacturing, and construction 9.3%, agriculture, forestry, fishing 7.2%; general public services 16.6%; health 7.4%; interest 7.0%; education 3.8%; defense 3.4%).
Total debt (external, outstanding; 1982): U.S.$70,712,700,000.

Manufacturing enterprises (1979)			wages	annual
	no. of enter- prises	number of labourers	of labourers as a % of avg. of all wages	value of production (Cr$'000,000)
Chemicals	3,138	130,438	141.6	244,137
Metallurgy	9,223	443,797	111.2	221,430
Food products	20,657	402,850	62.4	195,872
Mechanical products	6,928	423,667	162.5	180,618
Textile	4,451	337,682	46.0	121,247
Transport vehicle	2,560	234,733	139.9	116,988
Electrical products and communications	2,274	198,171	115.2	110,835
Combustible fuels (not metals)	9,223	260,421	75.7	98,679
Clothing and footwear	7,969	345,721	57.4	80,839
Paper and paper products	1,399	88,574	101.8	57,002
Publishing and printing	4,238	100,876	127.8	47,001
Lumber	7,360	163,556	57.2	42,720
Plastics	2,059	95,593	84.7	42,504
Pharmaceutical products	472	28,401	115.0	35,255
Furniture	4,634	122,816	70.4	31,935

Tourism (1982): receipts from visitors U.S.$1,608,000,000; expenditures by nationals abroad U.S.$1,411,000,000.

Production (metric tons except as noted). Agriculture, forestry, fishing (1981): sugarcane 155,920,000, cassava 24,520,000, corn (maize) 21,120,000, soybeans 15,010,000, oranges 9,312,000, rice 8,230,000, bananas 6,696,000, coffee 4,060,000, beans 2,340,000, wheat 2,210,000, potatoes 1,910,000, cotton 1,540,000, tomatoes 1,450,000; livestock (number of live animals)◊ 11,660,000 cattle, 9,170,000 pigs, 901,000 sheep, 312,000 goats 240,000 asses, horses, and mules; roundwood 216,463,000 cu m◊; fish catch 850,000 metric tons◊; extractive products (in Cr$) babassu palm oil 3,938,000,000, maté 3,931,000,000, rubber 2,294,000,000, carnauba palm wax 1,070,000,000, piassava fibre 829,000,000. Mining and quarrying (value of production in U.S.$, (1982 est.)△: mineral fuels 3,800,000,000, of which crude petroleum 3,139,000,000, natural gas 388,000,000, coal 273,000,000; metals 1,900,000,000, of which iron ore 982,000,000, gold 323,000,000†, bauxite 158,000,000, tin 135,000,000, manganese 131,000,000; nonmetals 1,500,000,000 of which granite 372,000,000, limestone 345,000,000, clay 173,000,000, phosphates 144,000,000, sand 105,000,000. Manufacturing (value of production in U.S.$, 1980): chemicals 33,956,000,000, metallurgical products 24,658,000,000, food products 24,541,000,000, machinery 13,961,000,000, transport vehicles 13,767,000,000, textiles 12,255,000,000, electrical appliances and products of communication 9,414,000,000, products of mineral fuels 7,282,000,000, clothing and footwear 6,273,000,000, paper and paper products 4,898,000,000, plastics 3,728,000,000, lumber 3,502,000,000, rubber goods 2,734,000,000, furniture 2,680,000,000, printed matter 2,668,000,000, pharmaceuticals 1,984,000,000. Construction (1981): residential 16,111 sq m; nonresidential 3,479 sq m.

Retail trade enterprises (1975)

	no. of enterprises	total no. of employees	annual wage as a % of all wages	annual value of sales (Cr$'000,000)
Food stores	392,122	708,262	155.8	66,144
Automotive stores	19,195	131,279	222.0	64,185
General merchandise, including food products	8,558	143,487	133.2	44,625
Combustibles and lubricating products	19,201	124,931	127.3	44,119
Hardware stores	22,239	115,183	140.2	28,299
Clothing stores	66,732	218,788	159.0	26,479
Electric and electronic machine stores	12,301	79,429	120.0	22,062
Machinery and agricultural equipment stores	4,709	42,384	113.8	20,317
Chemical and pharmaceutical stores	24,310	94,702	91.9	17,725
Textile and textile product stores	17,071	85,812	80.9	13,275
General merchandise, excluding food products	3,278	58,338	82.3	13,172
Bedding and tapestry stores	8,306	39,675	51.5	8,462
Paper products and bookstores	8,444	36,985	44.4	5,624
Beverages and tobacco stores	5,004	11,558	6.3	1,731
Rubber and plastic products	1,392	6,028	7.1	1,172

Energy production (consumption): electricity (kW-hr; 1982) 152,089,000,000 (151,721,000,000); hard coal (metric tons; 1982) 6,400,000 (10,006,000); crude petroleum (barrels; 1982) 92,330,000 (378,099,000); petroleum products (metric tons; 1982) 45,613,000 (42,416,000); natural gas (cu m; 1982) 1,359,920,000 (1,359,920,000).

Persons economically active (1982)⊙: total 47,925,851 (52.7%); female participation in labour force 16,087,515 (32.2%); unemployed n.a.

Price and earnings indexes (1980 = 100)

	1978	1979	1980	1981	1982	1983	1984
Consumer price index	35.8	54.7	100.0	205.6	407.0	984.9	2,116.4††
Earnings index‡‡	31.0	52.0	100.0	205.2	404.3	§§	...

Household income and expenditure. Average household size (1980) 4.7; average annual income per household of families having income (1981) Cr$488,124 (U.S.$5,241); sources of income: n.a.; expenditure (1974)‖ ‖: food 48.5%, household (including rent) 28.9%, clothing and footwear 4.7%, hygiene and health 4.5%, transportation 3.5%, tobacco 3.0%, recreation 0.6%, education 0.5%.

Land use (1981): forested 67.7%; meadows and pastures 19.1%; agricultural and under permanent cultivation 8.7%; other 4.5%.

Financial aggregates

	1979	1980	1981	1982	1983	1984 (9 mo.)
Exchange rate, Cr$ per:						
U.S. dollar	42.53	65.50	127.80	252.67	984.0	2,329.00
£	94.59	156.22	243.84	407.94	1,427.39	2,906.59
SDR	56.03	83.54	148.75	278.72	1,030.20	2,326.69
International reserves (U.S.$)						
Total (excl. gold; '000,000)	8,966	5,769	6,604	3,928	4,355	8,966¶¶
SDR's ('000,000)	383	384	452	♀♀	♀♀	1
Reserve pos. in IMF ('000,000)	241	344	264	287	♀♀	♀♀
Foreign exchange ('000,000)	8,342	5,042	5,888	3,641	4,355	8,965¶¶
Gold, ('000,000 fine troy oz.)	1.70	1.88	2.20	0.15	0.54	1.18
% world reserves	0.18	0.20	0.23	0.02	0.06	0.11
Interest and prices						
Central bank discount (%)	35.00	38.00	49.00δδ	...	...	...
Gov't. bond yield (%)	...	...	...	...	...	...
Industrial share prices	...	...	...	...	...	...
Balance of payments (U.S.$'000,000)						
Balance of visible trade	−2,717	−2,823	1,185	778	6,469	...
Imports, f.o.b.	17,961	22,955	22,091	19,395	15,429	...
Exports, f.o.b.	15,244	20,132	23,276	20,173	21,898	...
Balance of invisibles	−7,778	−10,152	−13,135	−17,082	−13,306	...
Balance of payments, current account	−10,478	−12,806	−11,751	−16,312	−6,837	...

Foreign trade

Balance of trade (current prices)

	1978	1979	1980	1981	1982	1983
U.S.$'000,000	−2,011	−4,560	−4,828	−786	−894	5,098
% of total	7.4%	13.0%	10.7%	1.7%	2.2%	13.2%

Imports (1982): U.S.$21,061,282,000 (crude petroleum 48.7%; chemicals 9.2%, of which organic chemicals 5.2%; nonelectrical machinery 8.6%; basic manufactures 7.0%, of which iron and steel 1.5%; electrical machinery [including switchgear and telecommunications equipment] 6.5%; cereals 4.8%, of which wheat 4.0%; transport equipment 2.1%). *Major import sources*⊡⊡: Iraq 19.2%; Saudi Arabia 15.2%; United States 15.0%; Venzuela 5.0%; Japan 4.6%; West Germany 4.4%.

Exports (1982): U.S.$20,173,041,000 (food and live animals 33.8%, of which coffee 10.6%, feeding stuff for animals [specifically, residues of vegetable oils] 8.7%, sugar and honey 2.9%, fruit [mostly orange] or vegetable juice 2.9%, frozen fresh meat 2.6%; cocoa [all forms] 2.1%, iron ore 8.8%; petroleum products 7.1%; nonelectrical machinery 6.7%; road motor vehicles 5.6%; iron and steel 5.0%; chemicals 4.5%; textile yarn and fabric 2.6%; electrical machinery 2.4%). *Major export destinations*⊡⊡: United States 20.5%; Japan 6.5%; West Germany 5.8%; The Netherlands 5.6%; Italy 4.9%; France 4.3%.

Transport and communications

Transport. Railroads (1982): route length 18,122 mi, 29,164 km; passenger-mi 8,243,000,000, passenger-km 13,266,000,000; short ton-mi cargo 53,528,000,000, metric ton-km cargo 77,815,000,000. Roads (1982): total length 877,335 mi, 1,411,936 km (paved 7%). Vehicles (1982): passenger cars 9,921,887; trucks and buses 1,144,614. Merchant marine (1983): vessels (100 gross tons and over) 698; total deadweight tonnage 9,624,845. Air transport (1982): passenger-mi 10,859,497,000, passenger-km 17,476,701,000; short ton-mi cargo 548,722,000, metric ton-km cargo 801,119,000; airports with scheduled flights (1984) 126.

Communications. Daily newspapers (1981): total number 315; total circulation 3,099,000; circulation per 1,000 population 25.2. Radios (1983): total number of receivers 17,500,000 (1 per 7.5 persons). Television (1983): total number of receivers 12,425,000 (1 per 10.6 persons). Telephones (1982): 8,536,000 (1 per 15.0 persons).

Education and health

Education (1982)

	schools	teachers	students	student/teacher ratio
Primary (age 7–14)	192,976	912,958	22,297,583	24.4
Secondary (age 15–17)	8,454	203,676	2,874,505	14.1
Higher	878	123,243	1,203,468	9.8

College graduates per 100,000 population (students graduating, 1981): 157.

Literacy (1980): total population literate 54,793,000 (74.5%); males literate 27,602,000 (76.3%); females literate 27,191,000 (72.8%).

Health (1980): physicians 70,000 (1 per 1,700 persons); hospital beds 509,104 (1 per 234 persons).

Food (1978–80): daily per capita caloric intake 2,517 (vegetable products 83.9%, animal products 16.1%); 105% of FAO recommended minimum requirement.

Military

Total active duty personnel (1982): 277,100 (army 66.0%; navy 17.7%; air force 16.3%). *Military expenditure as percent of GNP* (1981): 0.7% (world 6.0%); per capita expenditure U.S.$15.

---

*Land area only, including 1,035 sq mi (2,680 sq km) in dispute between the states of Amazonas and Pará and 1,009 sq mi (2,614 sq km) in dispute between Ceará and Piauí. Total area including inland water is 3,286,487 sq mi (8,511,965 sq km). †Includes the islands of Trinidade and Martin Vaz. ‡Includes Rocas atoll and the rocks of São Pedro and São Paulo. §Detail does not add to total given because of rounding. ‖ Spiritist Catholics are actively and regularly involved in the practice of medium religions; about 60,000,000 Roman Catholics defer to spiritist dogma and participate in organized spiritism from time to time. ¶Evangelical Catholics are persons who are officially regarded as Roman Catholic, but who are affiliated to Protestant or Brazilian indigenous churches. ♀Non-Christian followers of Afro-Brazilian syncretistic religions ("low spiritism"). δNon-Christian followers of Kardecism ("high spiritism"). ⊡1982 election for state governors, federal senators, and federal deputies. Detail cited here is based on the electoral returns for federal deputies. ◊1982. △Does not include value of production for diamonds and other gems; 1981 value of production figure for diamonds and other gems was U.S.$71,000,000. †82% of which was mined by 200,000 to 300,000 *garimpeiros* (prospectors) mostly concentrated in the states of Pará, Mato Grosso, Amazonas, and Rondônia. ⊙10 years and over. **Services account for 19.3% of total labour force. ††First two quarters only. ‡‡Based on the minimum salary paid in the city of São Paulo. With the exception of 1983, earnings indices are based on minimum salaries paid from May 1 of the year within the column to April 30 of the following year. §§May 1 through October 30, 699.8; the month of November, 1,149.4 ‖ ‖ Based on sample survey of families living in Rio de Janeiro state having an annual income of between 4,500 and 8,999 cruzeiros. ¶¶August 1984. ♀♀Less than 0.5. δδEnd of second quarter figure. ⊡⊡1982.

Brunei

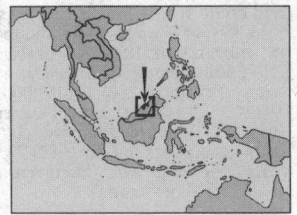

Official name: Negara Brunei
 Darussalam (State of Brunei, Abode
 of Peace).
Form of government: monarchy.
Chief of state: Sultan.
Head of government: Prime Minister.
Capital: Bandar Seri Begawan.
Official language: Malay.
Official religion: Islām.
Monetary unit: 1 Brunei dollar
 (Br$) = 100 cents; valuation (Oct. 29,
 1984) 1 U.S.$ = Br$2.15;
 1 £ = Br$2.59.

Area and population		area		population
				1982
Districts	Capitals	sq mi	sq km	estimate
Belait	Kuala Belait	1,052	2,725	52,763
Brunei and Muara	Bandar Seri Begawan	220	570	119,139
Temburong	Bangar	504	1,305	6,443
Tutong	Tutong	450	1,165	22,045
TOTAL		2,226	5,765	200,390

Source: Official government figures.

Demography

Density (1984): persons per sq mi 97.0, persons per sq km 37.5.
Urban–rural (1981): urban 59.4%; rural 40.6%.
Sex distribution (1982): male 53.39%; female 46.61%.
Age breakdown (1982): under 15, 38.1%; 15–29, 32.1%; 30–44, 17.3%; 45–
 59, 8.1%; 60–69, 2.6%; 70 and over, 1.8%.
Population projection: (1990) 272,000; (2000) 400,000.
Doubling time: 18 years.
Ethnic composition (1982): Malay 65.2%; Chinese 20.5%; Indian 3.1%; other
 11.2%.
Religious affiliation (1982): Muslim 63.4%; Buddhist 14.0%; Christian 9.7%;
 other 12.9%.
Major cities (1981): Bandar Seri Begawan 63,868; Seria 23,511; Kuala Belait
 19,281.

Vital statistics

Birth rate per 1,000 population (1982): 29.8 (world avg. 29.0); (1978) legiti-
 mate 99.3%, illegitimate 0.7%.
Death rate per 1,000 population (1982): 3.9 (world avg. 11.0).
Natural increase rate per 1,000 population (1982): 25.9 (world avg. 18.0).
Total fertility rate (avg. births per childbearing woman): n.a.
Marriage rate per 1,000 population (1982): 6.7.
Divorce rate per 1,000 population (1982): 0.6*.
Infant mortality rate per 1,000 live births (1982): 12.8.
Life expectancy at birth (1981): male 70.1 years; female 72.7 years.
Major causes of death per 100,000 population (1981): diseases of the
 circulatory system 42; accidents, poisoning, and violence 38; malignant
 neoplasms (cancers) 25; diseases of the respiratory system 11; infectious
 and parasitic diseases 7.

National economy

Budget (1984). Revenue: Br$6,500,000,000 (largely from petroleum profits).
 Expenditures: Br$2,650,000,000 (development fund 35.8%, defense 12.8%,
 public works 8.7%, education 8.2%, police 1.8%).
Public debt (external, outstanding; 1982): U.S.$10,000,000.
Tourism (1982): number of visitors 4,907.
Production (metric tons except as noted). Agriculture, forestry, fishing
 (1982): rice 10,000, vegetables and melons 4,000, roots and tubers 4,000,
 cassava 3,000, bananas 3,000, pineapples 3,000, oranges 1,000, eggs 1,900;
 livestock (number of live animals) 15,000 pigs, 14,000 buffaloes, 4,000
 cattle, 1,000 goats, 1,221,000 chickens; roundwood 294,000 cu m; fish
 catch 2,312†. Mining and quarrying (1983): other than petroleum and
 natural gas (see below), none except sand and gravel for construction.
 Manufacturing (1982): gasoline 49,400; distillate fuel oils 43,100; naphtha 3,700. Construction, n.a. Energy production (consumption): electricity
 (kW-hr; 1982) 570,000,000 (570,000,000); coal (metric tons; 1982): none
 (minuscule); crude petroleum (barrels; 1982) 59,391,000 (n.a.); petroleum
 products (metric tons; 1982) 141,000 (166,000); natural gas (cu m; 1982)
 8,882,000 (1,161,000).
Persons economically active (1981): total 70,690 (36.7%); female participation in the labour force 16,830 (23.8%); unemployed 2,560 (3.6%).

Price and earnings indexes (1977 = 100)♀							
	1976	1977	1978	1979	1980	1981	1982
Consumer price index	...	100.0	...	...	...	129.0	137.2
Monthly earnings index	92.2	100.0	113.3	114.8	133.0	143.0	...

Household income and expenditure. Average household size (1971) 5.8.;
 income per household, n.a.; source of income, n.a.; expenditure (1981)
 food 45.1%; transportation and communication 17.2%; recreation, education, and cultural services 8.9%; household furnishings 8.3%; clothing and
 footwear 6.1%; rent and utilities 5.0%.

Gross national product (at current market prices; 1981): U.S.$4,050,000,000
 (U.S.$21,005 per capita).

Origin of gross domestic product (current prices)				
	1981			
	in value Br$'000,000	% of total value	labour force	% of labour force
Agriculture	71.5‡	0.8	3,440	4.9
Mining	7,471.8‡	81.8‡	3,860	5.5
Manufacturing	‡	‡	2,780	3.9
Construction	138.2	1.5	12,650	17.9
Trade	858.8	9.4	7,360	10.4
Public utilities	−2.4	−0.0	1,960	2.8
Transportation and communication	68.0	0.7	4,530	6.4
Finance	181.8	2.0	...	...
Services	410.7§	4.5§	31,290	44.3
Other	−61.0 ‖	−0.7 ‖	2,820	4.0
TOTAL	9,137.4	100.0	70,690	100.0¶

Land use (1981): forested 78.8%; meadows and pastures 1.1%; agricultural
 and under permanent cultivation 1.7%; other 18.4%.

Foreign trade

Balance of trade (current prices)						
	1977	1978	1979	1980	1981	1982
Br$'000,000	+3,320	+3,556	+4,934	+8,622	+7,327	+6,582
% of total	70.9%	73.6%	74.1%	77.8%	74.3%	67.7%

Imports (1982)ð: Br$1,571,652,300 (industrial machinery 19.2%, iron and
 steel 10.7%, manufactured metals 10.0%, electrical machinery 7.8%, road
 motor vehicles 7.0%, cement and other building materials 2.3%). *Major import sources:* Japan 23.6%; Singapore 20.9%; United States 17.0%; United
 Kingdom 7.0%; Malaysia 3.4%.
Exports (1982)□: Br$8,153,258,100 (crude oil 56.1%, natural gas 40.2%,
 petroleum products 2.8%). *Major export destinations:* Japan 67.6%; United
 States 12.7%; Singapore 6.0%; Thailand 2.6%; The Philippines 2.0%.

Transport and communications

Transport. Railroads◇ (1982): length 7 mi, 12 km. Roads (1979): total length
 884 mi, 1,423 km (paved 52%). Vehicles (1982): passenger cars 54,441;
 trucks and buses 8,933. Merchant marine (1983): vessel (100 gross tons
 and over) 1; total deadweight tonnage 498. Air transport (1982): passenger
 arrivals 171,390, passenger departures 159,075; cargo loaded 543 metric
 tons, cargo unloaded 6,228 metric tons; airport (1984) with scheduled
 flights 1. Marine transport (1982): cargo loaded 20,320,000 metric tons,
 cargo unloaded 593,000 metric tons.
Communications. Daily newspapers (1983): none. Radios (1983): total number of receivers 50,000 (1 per 4 persons). Television (1983): total number
 of receivers 30,000 (1 per 7 persons). Telephones (1982): 21,928 (1 per 9
 persons).

Education and health

Education (1980–81)				student/
	schools	teachers	students	teacher ratio
Primary (age 5–11)	175	1,800	31,677	17.6
Secondary (age 12–20)	27	1,326	16,805	12.7
Voc., teacher tr.	6	212	1,284	6.1
Higher	1	57	143	2.5

College graduates per 100,000 population (students graduating; 1979): 62.
Literacy (1981): total population literate 92,253 (77.8%); males literate 55,-
 179 (85.2%); females literate 37,074 (69.0%).
Health (1981): physicians 97 (1 per 1,988 persons); hospital beds 630 (1
 per 306 persons).
Food (1978–80): daily per capita caloric intake 2,664 (vegetable products
 80.7%, animal products 19.3%); 119% of FAO recommended minimum
 requirement.

Military

Total active duty personnel (1984): 3,650 (army 100.0%). *Military expenditure as percent of* GNP (1980): 5.4% (world 5.6%); per capita expenditure
 U.S.$714.

*Muslim divorces only. †1981. ‡Mining includes manufacturing. §Community, so-
cial, and personal services only. ‖ Bank charges. ¶Detail does not add to total given
because of rounding. ♀For Bandar Seri Begawan only. ðIncludes re-imports. □Includes
re-exports. ◇For industrial purposes only.

Bulgaria

Official name: Narodna Republika Bŭlgaria (People's Republic of Bulgaria).
Form of government: unitary single-party republic with one legislative house (National Assembly [400]).
Chief of state: Chairman.
Head of government: Premier.
Capital: Sofia.
Official language: Bulgarian.
Official religion: none.
Monetary unit: 1 lev (leva) = 100 stotinki; valuation (Oct. 29, 1984) 1 lev = U.S.$1.08; 1 £ = 1.31 leva.

Area and population

Provinces	Capitals	area sq mi	area sq km	population 1982 estimate
Blagoevgrad	Blagoevgrad	2,496	6,464	337,615
Burgas	Burgas	2,936	7,605	435,274
Gabrovo	Gabrovo	798	2,068	177,512
Khaskovo	Khaskovo	1,547	4,008	295,996
Kŭrdzhali	Kŭrdzhali	1,552	4,020	285,538
Kyustendil	Kyustendil	1,159	3,002	198,571
Lovech	Lovech	1,594	4,128	211,398
Mikhaylovgrad	Mikhaylovgrad	1,401	3,629	233,521
Pazardzhik	Pazardzhik	1,691	4,379	322,206
Pernik	Pernik	909	2,355	175,042
Pleven	Pleven	1,685	4,364	373,358
Plovdiv	Plovdiv	2,167	5,612	753,093
Razgrad	Razgrad	1,022	2,646	193,240
Ruse	Ruse	1,002	2,595	297,466
Shumen	Shumen	1,303	3,374	251,626
Silistra	Silistra	1,104	2,859	173,943
Sliven	Sliven	1,397	3,618	235,635
Smolyan	Smolyan	1,358	3,518	174,438
Sofiya	Sofia	2,822	7,310	308,883
Stara Zagora	Stara Zagora	1,935	5,012	411,165
Tolbukhin	Tolbukhin	1,821	4,716	251,993
Tŭrgovishte	Tŭrgovishte	1,063	2,754	172,424
Varna	Varna	1,471	3,810	467,265
Veliko Tŭrnovo	Veliko Tŭrnovo	1,822	4,719	346,857
Vidin	Vidin	1,184	3,066	169,293
Vratsa	Vratsa	1,547	4,006	291,303
Yambol	Yambol	1,607	4,162	205,324
City Commune				
Sofia		430	1,113	1,155,602
TOTAL		42,823	110,912	8,905,581

Source: Official government figures.

Demography

Density (1984): persons per sq mi 209.4, persons per sq km 80.9.
Urban–rural (1983): urban 64.2%; rural 35.8%.
Sex distribution (1982): male 49.78%; female 50.22%.
Age breakdown (1982): under 15, 22.1%; 15–29, 21.1%; 30–44, 20.3%; 45–59, 20.3%; 60–74, 12.1%; 75 and over, 4.1%.
Population projection: (1990) 9,413,000; (2000) 9,698,000.
Doubling time: During the period 1970–80, the average growth rate was 0.4%; since 1980, however, the population has been decreasing.
Ethnic composition (1978): Bulgarian 89.0%; Turkish 8.4%; other 2.6%.
Religious affiliation (1982): Eastern Orthodox 26.7%; Muslim 7.5%; Protestant 0.7%; Roman Catholic 0.5%; other 0.1%; atheist 64.5%.
Major cities (1982 est.): Sofia 1,082,000*; Plovdiv 358,176; Varna 293,950; Ruse 176,013; Burgas 173,078.

Vital statistics

Birth rate per 1,000 population (1982): 13.9 (world avg. 29.0); (1980) legitimate 89.1%, illegitimate 10.9%.
Death rate per 1,000 population (1982): 11.2 (world avg. 11.0).
Natural increase rate per 1,000 population (1982): 2.7 (world avg. 18.0).
Total fertility rate (avg. births per childbearing woman; 1980): 2.2.
Marriage rate per 1,000 population (1982): 7.5.
Divorce rate per 1,000 population (1982): 1.5.
Infant mortality rate per 1,000 live births (1982): 18.2.
Life expectancy at birth (1976): male 68.7 years; female 73.9 years.
Major causes of death per 100,000 population (1981): diseases of the circulatory system 615.6; malignant neoplasms (cancers) 152.3.

National economy

Budget (1982). Revenue: 16,687,700,000 leva (turnover tax, taxes from state enterprises, and income tax 62.3%). Expenditures: 16,526,400,000 leva (national economy 52.4%; education, health, and culture 17.3%; social security 16.4%).
Public debt (external, outstanding; 1981): U.S.$2,975,000,000.
Tourism (1982): number of tourists 5,646,840; receipts from visitors U.S.$260,000,000†; expenditures by nationals abroad, n.a.
Production (metric tons except as noted). Agriculture, forestry, fishing (1982): wheat 4,913,000, corn (maize) 3,418,000, sugar beets 1,583,000, barley 1,436; livestock (number of live animals, 1983) 1,389,227 cattle, 8,719,244 sheep, 2,779,620 pigs; roundwood 3,900,000 cu m; fish catch 115,267. Mining and quarrying (1982): iron ore 1,553,000; lead 96,000; zinc 65,000; copper 63,-000; manganese 45,000. Manufacturing (1982): cement 5,614,000; pig iron

and crude steel 4,146,000; rolled steel 3,253,000; fertilizers 998,900; sulfuric acid 891,400; wood pulp and paper 511,000; cotton fabrics 364,500,000 m; rubber tires 1,561,700 units; wine 4,637,000 hectolitres. Construction (1982): residential 4,292,000 sq m. Energy production (consumption): electricity (kW-hr; 1982) 40,459,000,000 (43,106,000,000); coal (metric tons; 1982) 35,013,000; (39,162,000); crude petroleum (barrels; 1982) 2,199,000 (93,824,000); petroleum products (metric tons; 1982) 11,390,000 (13,310,-000); natural gas (cu m; 1982) 73,051,000,000 (4,560,000,000).
Gross national product (at current market prices; 1982): U.S.$26,000,000,000 (U.S.$2,920 per capita).

Origin of net material product (current prices)

	1982 in value '000,000 leva	% of total value	labour force	% of labour force
Agriculture	4,601.0	20.1	929,434	22.8
Mining	‡	‡	41,385	1.0
Manufacturing	12,237.6	53.6	1,405,981	34.5
Construction	2,207.7	9.7	348,731	8.5
Trade	1,383.6	6.0	342,381	8.4
Public utilities	‡	‡	51,424	1.3
Transp., comm.	1,795.7	7.9	303,970	7.5
Finance	§	§	21,500	0.5
Pub. admin., defense	§	§	58,011	1.4
Services	§	§	572,269	14.0
Other	623.9§	2.7§	1,285	0.0
TOTAL	22,843.5	100.0	4,076,371	100.0

Persons economically active (1982): total 4,076,371 (45.7%); female participation in the labour force 1,996,041 (49.0%); unemployed n.a.

Price and earnings indexes (1970 = 100)

	1976	1977	1978	1979	1980	1981	1982
Consumer price index	101.2	101.6	103.2	107.8	122.9	123.5	123.7
Monthly earnings index	119.3	121.8	126.6	133.1	155.6	163.7	167.7

Household income and expenditure. Average household size (1982) 3.3; income per household 5,092 leva (U.S.$5,249); sources of income: wages and salaries 62.9%, social welfare 20.0%, other 17.1%; expenditure (1981): food 36.5%, clothing and footwear 8.6%, housing 6.7%, transportation 5.4%.
Land use (1981): forested 34.8%; meadows and pastures 18.2%; agricultural and under permanent cultivation 37.7%; other 9.3%.

Foreign trade

Balance of trade (current prices)

	1977	1978	1979	1980	1981	1982
'000,000 leva	−39.7	−151.3	+303.4	+618.6	−97.6	−121.3
% of total	0.3%	1.1%	2.0%	3.5%	0.5%	0.6%

Imports (1982): 10,867,500,000 leva (fuels 46.3%; transport equipment 13.6%; chemicals 5.5%; pulp and paper 4.6%; power and electrical machinery 2.6%; agricultural machinery 2.4%). *Major import sources:* U.S.S.R. 55.9%; East Germany 5.8%; Poland 4.8%.
Exports (1982): 10,746,200,000 leva (machinery 38.1%; transport equipment 11.5%; minerals 9.7%; tobacco 7.8%; chemicals, 4.9%). *Major export destinations:* U.S.S.R. 51.6%; East Germany 5.4%; Libya 4.7%.

Transport and communications

Transport. Railroads (1983): length 4,379 mi, 7,626 km; passenger-mi 5,015,-000,000, passenger-km 8,071,000,000; short ton-mi cargo 12,518,000,000, metric ton-km cargo 18,276,000,000. Roads (1983): total length 22,431 mi, 36,100 km (paved 90%). Vehicles (1980): passenger cars 815,549; trucks and buses 130,000. Merchant marine (1983): vessels (100 gross tons and over) 197; total deadweight tonnage 1,856,342. Air transport (1983): passenger-mi 1,678,000,000, passenger-km 2,701,000,000; short ton-mi cargo 35,069,000, metric ton-km cargo 51,200,000; airports (1984) with scheduled flights 13.
Communications. Daily newspapers (1982): total number 14; total circulation 2,221,000; circulation per 1,000 population 249.4. Radios (1983): total number of receivers 2,085,000 (1 per 4.3 persons). Television (1983): total number of receivers 1,683,000 (1 per 5.3 persons). Telephones (1983): 1,513,000 (1 per 5.9 persons).

Education and health

Education (1982–83)

	schools	teachers	students	student/ teacher ratio
Primary and secondary (age 7–17)	3,510	68,409	1,165,361	17.0
Voc., teacher tr.	533	17,547	200,163	11.4
Higher	29	13,254	65,003	4.9

College graduates per 100,000 population (students graduating; 1982): 19.1.
Literacy (1980): 95%.
Health (1983): physicians 23,100 (1 per 385 persons); hospital beds 81,000 (1 per 110 persons).
Food (1978–80): daily per capita caloric intake 3,638 (vegetable products 78.9%, animal products 21.1%); 141% of FAO recommended minimum.

Military

Total active duty personnel (1983): 162,300 (army 74.0%; navy 5.2%; air force 20.8%). *Military expenditure as percent of GNP* (1982): 10.0% (world 6.0%); per capita expenditure U.S.$398.

*1983 estimate. †1980. ‡Mining and public utilities are included with manufacturing. §Finance, public administration, and services are included with other.

Burkina Faso*

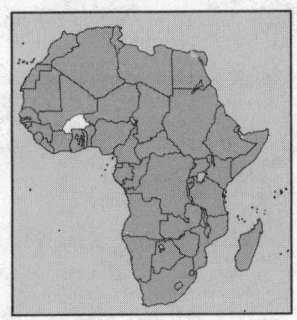

Official name: Burkina Faso
(Burkina Faso).
Form of government: military
government†.
Head of state and government:
President in conjunction with the
National Revolutionary Council.
Capital: Ouagadougou.
Official language: French.
Official religion: none.
Monetary unit: 1 CFA franc
(CFAF) = 100 centimes; valuation
(Oct. 29, 1984) 1 U.S.$ = CFAF470.6;
1 £ = CFAF568.0.

Area and population

Provinces	Capitals	area sq mi	area sq km	population 1985 estimate
Bam	Kongoussi	1,551	4,017	175,130
Bougouriba	Diébougou	2,736	7,087	213,019
Boulgou	Tenkodogo	3,722	9,639	358,617
Burkina	Koudougou	3,592	9,303	582,012
Comoé	Barfora	7,102	18,393	210,758
Ganzourgou	Zorgho	1,578	4,087	149,744
Gnagna	Bogandé	2,528	6,548	147,570
Gourma	Fada Ngourma	11,067	28,664	231,073
Houet	Bobo Dioulasso	6,360	16,472	370,847
Kénédougou	Orodara	3,207	8,307	118,603
Kossi	Nouna	5,088	13,177	244,320
Nahouri	Pô	1,484	3,843	88,287
Namentenga	Boulsa	3,545	9,182	329,751
Nouhoun	Dédougou	4,032	10,442	240,318
Oubritenga	Ouagadougou	4,315	11,175	787,011
Passoré	Yako	1,575	4,078	262,548
Poni	Gaoua	4,000	10,361	216,604
Sahel	Dori	9,081	23,519	265,428
Sanmatenga	Kaya	3,557	9,213	340,938
Sissili	Léo	5,303	13,736	144,642
Soum	Djibo	5,154	13,350	159,975
Sourou	Tougan	3,663	9,487	279,186
Tapoa	Diapaga	5,707	14,780	110,599
Yatenga	Ouahigouya	4,746	12,293	636,991
Zoundwéogo	Manga	1,099	2,847	109,960
TOTAL		105,792	274,000	6,773,931

Source: Official government figures.

Demography

Density (1985): persons per sq mi 64.0, persons per sq km 24.7.
Urban–rural (1980): urban 8.5%; rural 91.5%.
Sex distribution (1980): male 49.51%; female 50.49%.
Age breakdown (1980): under 15, 44.5%; 15–29, 26.0%; 30–44, 15.6%; 45–59, 9.1%; 60–74, 4.1%; 75 and over, 0.7%.
Population projection: (1990) 7,400,000; (2000) 8,800,000.
Doubling time: 35 years.
Ethnic composition (1978): Mossi 53.4%; Lobi 6.9%; Bobo 6.9%; Fulani 5.6%; Gurunsi 5.0%; Tuareg 4.1%; other 18.1%.
Religious affiliation (1978): tribal religionist 44.8%; Muslim 43.0%; Christian 12.2%, of which Roman Catholic 9.8%, Protestant 2.4%.
Major cities (1985): Ouagadougou 359,801; Bobo Dioulasso 202,807; Koudougou 59,644; Ouahigouya 41,595.

Vital statistics

Birth rate per 1,000 population (1981): 47.8 (world avg. 29.0); legitimate, n.a.; illegitimate, n.a.
Death rate per 1,000 population (1981): 21.5 (world avg. 12.0).
Natural increase rate per 1,000 population (1981): 26.3 (world avg. 17.0).
Total fertility rate (avg. births per childbearing woman; 1981): 6.5.
Marriage rate per 1,000 population (1982): 9.4.
Divorce rate per 1,000 population (1975): 1.3.
Infant mortality rate per 1,000 live births (1981): 208.1.
Life expectancy at birth (1981): male 43.2 years; female 45.0 years.
Major diseases (1980): bilharziasis, kwashiorkor, malaria, measles, and onchocerciasis ("river blindness").

National economy

Budget (1983). Revenue: CFAF53,608,400,000 (indirect taxes 65.8%, of which customs duties 41.9%; direct taxes 16.9%; current transfers 10.7%). *Expenditures:* CFAF57,949,600,000 (general public services 26.7%; defense 17.5%; education 16.8%; debt payment 14.2%; investment 7.2%).
Public debt (external, outstanding; 1982): U.S.$344,000,000.
Tourism (1980): receipts from visitors U.S.$7,000,000; expenditures by nationals abroad, n.a.
Production (metric tons except as noted). Agriculture, forestry, fishing (1982): sorghum 700,000, millet 420,000, sugarcane 400,000, pulses 178,000, roots and tubers (including sweet potatoes) 169,000, corn (maize) 100,000, peanuts (groundnuts) 78,000, seed cotton 62,000, rice 40,000, karite 22,000, sesame 9,000; livestock (number of live animals) 2,970,000 goats, 2,880,000 cattle, 1,970,000 sheep, 11,600,000 chickens; roundwood 7,093,000 cu m; fish catch 7,000. Mining and quarrying (1982): phosphates 3,000. Manufacturing (1982): cotton yarn 54,600; soap 11,248; bicycles and motorcycles 12,200 units; footwear 1,644,000,000 pairs; beer 692,801 hectolitres; soft drinks 142,880 hectolitres. Construction: n.a. Energy production (consumption): electricity (kW-hr; 1982) 115,000,000 (115,000,000); coal, none (n.a.);

crude petroleum, none (n.a.); petroleum products (metric tons; 1982) 140,-000 (140,000); natural gas, none (n.a.).
Gross national product (at current market prices; 1981): U.S.$1,490,000,000 (U.S.$240 per capita).

Origin of gross domestic product (factor cost at current prices)

	1981 in value CFAF'000,000	1981 % of total value	1975 labour force	1975 % of labour force
Agriculture	121,900	41.4	1,292,400	91.4
Mining	‡	‡	...	...
Manufacturing‡	34,800	11.8	45,229	3.2
Construction	10,300	3.5	3,738	0.3
Trade, finance	60,100	20.4	25,847	1.8
Public utilities	3,000	1.0	723	§
Transportation and communication	20,700	7.0	6,393	0.5
Pub. admin., defense	40,000	13.6	17,985	1.3
Services	...	...	9,709	0.7
Other	3,600	1.2	11,668	0.8
TOTAL	294,400	100.0 ‖	1,413,692	100.0

Persons economically active (1981): total 3,302,000 (52.2%); female participation in labour force 1,422,000 (46.1%); unemployed, n.a.

Price and earnings indexes (1980 = 100)

	1978	1979	1980	1981	1982	1983	1984
Consumer price index	77.5	89.1	100.0	107.6	120.5	130.6	133.4¶
Hourly earnings index	80.0	100.0	100.0	100.0	126.7	126.7	...

Household income and expenditure. Average household size (1981) 4.9; average annual income per household CFAF238,000 (U.S.$875); source of income: n.a.; expenditure: n.a.
Land use (1981): forested 26.1%; meadows and pastures 36.5%; agricultural and under permanent cultivation 9.6%; other 27.8%.

Foreign trade

Balance of trade (current prices)

	1977	1978	1979	1980	1981	1982
CFAF'000,000	−37,742	−41,475	−47,678	−56,548	−71,524	−95,599
% of total	58.1%	68.4%	67.9%	59.7%	64.2%	72.5%

Imports (1982): CFAF113,708,000,000 (machines and transport equipment 39.0%, of which transport equipment 31.8%; electrical machinery 5.8%; petroleum products 16.5%; cereals 10.2%; construction materials 4.7%; preserved dairy products 4.4%; iron and steel 3.6%). *Major import sources:* France 32.0%; Ivory Coast 12.4%; United States 6.6%; The Netherlands 4.3%; West Germany 3.7%; Japan 3.6%.
Exports (1982): CFAF18,109,000,000 (raw cotton 41.9%; karite nuts 12.8%; live animals 12.7%; karite oil 4.1%; vegetables 3.3%). *Major export destinations:* Ivory Coast 21.0%; France 14.5%; West Germany 7.4%; United Kingdom 6.6%; Japan 5.2%; Italy 4.9%.

Transport and communications

Transport. Railroads (1981)♀: length 321 mi, 517 km; passenger-mi 667,351,-000, passenger-km 1,074,000,000; short ton-mi cargo 422,000,000, metric ton-km cargo 616,000,000. Roads (1983): total length 5,395 mi, 8,684 km (paved 23%). Vehicles (1983): passenger cars 21,182; trucks and buses 6,647. Merchant marine (1983): none. Air transport (1980): passenger-mi 112,-000,000, passenger-km 180,000,000; short ton-mi cargo 12,300,000, metric ton-mi cargo 18,000,000; airports (1984) 9.
Communications. Daily newspapers (1984): total number 6; total circulation, n.a. Radios (1983): total number of receivers 116,000 (1 per 57 persons). Television (1983): total number of receivers 15,000 (1 per 438 persons). Telephones (1981): 10,625 (1 per 588 persons).

Education and health

Education (1982–83)

	schools	teachers	students	student/ teacher ratio
Primary	1,176	4,410	251,269	57.0
Secondary	69	1,290	27,618	21.4
Vocational	22	374	4,945	13.2
Higher	8	212	3,086	14.6

College graduates per 100,000 population (students graduating; 1980): 9.1.
Literacy (1975): total population literate 267,500 (9.1%); males literate 217,000 (15.1%); females literate 50,500 (3.2%).
Health: physicians (1981) 127 (1 per 49,220 persons); hospital beds (1979) 3,444 (1 per 1,755 persons).
Food (1978–80): daily per capita caloric intake 2,018 (vegetable products 95.3%, animal products 4.7%); 85% of FAO recommended minimum.

Military

Total active duty personnel (1983): 3,775 (army 98.0%; navy, none; air force 2.0%). *Military expenditure as percent of GNP* (1981): 2.6% (world 5.7%); per capita expenditure U.S.$5.

---

*Known as Upper Volta before Aug. 2, 1984. †The functions of the legislative house (National Assembly; [57]) and all political parties have been suspended since 1980. ‡Mining is included with manufacturing. §Less than 0.1%. ‖ Detail does not add to total given because of rounding. ¶April. ♀Passenger-mi and short ton-mi cargo figures are based on traffic between Abidjan (Ivory Coast) and Ouagadougou.

Burma

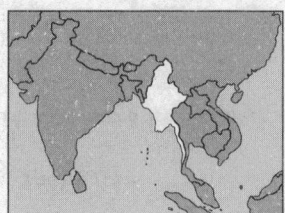

Official name: Pyeidaungzu Socialist Thammada Myanma Naingngandaw (Socialist Republic of the Union of Burma).
Form of government: single-party people's republic with one legislative house (People's Assembly [475]).
Chief of state: Chairman (President).
Head of government: Prime Minister.
Capital: Rangoon.
Official language: Burmese.
Official religion: none.
Monetary unit: 1 Burmese kyat (K) = 100 pyas; valuation (Oct. 29, 1984) 1 U.S.$ = K9.03; 1 £ = K10.90.

Area and population

Divisions	Capitals	area sq mi	area sq km	population 1983 census*
Irrawaddy	Bassein	13,567	35,139	4,991,057
Magwe	Magwe	17,305	44,820	3,241,103
Mandalay	Mandalay	14,295	37,024	4,580,923
Pegu	Pegu	15,214	39,404	3,800,240
Rangoon	Rangoon	3,927	10,170	3,973,782
Sagaing	Sagaing	36,535	94,625	3,855,991
Tenasserim	Tavoy	16,735	43,343	917,628
States				
Arakan (Rakhine)	Sittwe (Akyab)	14,200	36,778	2,045,891
Chin	Haka	13,907	36,019	368,985
Kachin	Myitkyinā	34,379	89,041	903,982
Karen	Pa-an	11,731	30,383	1,057,505
Kayah	Loi-kaw	4,530	11,733	168,355
Mon	Moulmein	4,748	12,297	1,682,041
Shan	Taunggyi	60,155	155,801	3,718,706
TOTAL		261,228	676,577	35,308,009

Source: Official government figures.

Demography

Density (1984): persons per sq mi 139.2, persons per sq km 53.8.
Urban–rural (1983): urban 23.9%; rural 76.1%.
Sex distribution (1983): male 49.59%; female 50.41%.
Age breakdown (1980): under 15, 41.2%; 15–29, 25.8%; 30–44, 16.0%; 45–59, 10.9%; 60–74, 5.2%; 75 and over, 0.9%.
Population projection: (1990) 40,500,000; (2000) 48,458,000.
Doubling time: 38 years.
Ethnic composition (1983): Burman 68.0%; Shan 6.9%; Karen 6.6%; Rakhine 4.4%; other 14.1%..
Religious affiliation (1980): Buddhist 87.2%; Christian 5.6%; Muslim 3.6%; tribal religions 1.9%; other 1.7%.
Major cities (1973): Rangoon 2,056,118†; Mandalay 417,266; Bassein 355,-588; Henzada 283,658; Pegu 254,761; Myingyan 220,129.

Vital statistics

Birth rate per 1,000 population (1982): 34.0 (world avg. 29.0).
Death rate per 1,000 population (1982): 14.0 (world avg. 11.0).
Natural increase rate per 1,000 population (1982): 20.0 (world avg. 18.0).
Total fertility rate (avg. births per childbearing woman; 1982): 4.7.
Marriage rate per 1,000 population, n.a.
Divorce rate per 1,000 population, n.a.
Infant mortality rate per 1,000 live births (1982): 105.
Life expectancy at birth (1982): male 51.4 years; female 54.5 years.
Major causes of death per 100,000 population (1978)‡: malaria 31.3§; pneumonia 15.5; heart diseases 10.1; enteritis and other diarrheal diseases 9.7; tuberculosis 9.1.

National economy

Budget (1981). Revenue: K7,572,000,000 (tax revenue 56.2%, of which general sales or turnover tax 33.6%, customs duties 14.7%; nontax revenue 40.2%, of which property income 29.3%). Expenditures: K7,046,000,000 (agriculture, forestry, and fishing 26.1%; defense 21.7%; general public services 14.2%; education 10.1%).
Public debt (external, outstanding; 1982): U.S.$1,960,100,000.
Tourism (1980): receipts from visitors U.S.$3,000,000.
Production (metric tons except as noted). Agriculture, forestry, fishing (1982): rice 14,500,000 ‖ , sugarcane 3,300,000 ‖ , peanuts (groundnuts) 568,000, corn (maize) 232,000, dry beans 216,000, sesame seed 204,000 ‖ , chick peas 157,000, potatoes 119,000, wheat 118,000, coconuts 99,000, sunflower seed 95,000 ‖ , millet 87,000 ‖ , cottonseed 74,000 ‖ , tobacco leaves 51,000, jute 39,000, natural rubber 17,000; livestock (number of live animals) 8,698,-000 cattle, 2,225,000 pigs, 1,979,000 buffaloes, 625,000 goats, 24,732,000 poultry; roundwood 18,834,000 cu m; fish catch 584,400, of which marine fishing areas 430,800. Mining and quarrying (by metal content except as noted; 1982): lead 16,050; zinc 5,382; tin 1,681; tungsten 844; silver 526,000 troy oz.; jadeite 9,682 kg. Manufacturing (1981): cement 317,-000; gasoline 245,000; nitrogenous fertilizers 60,000; soap 48,500; cotton yarn 15,590; cigarettes 2,792,000,000 units. Construction¶ (gross value in K; 1976) 5,076,000. Energy production (consumption): electricity (kW-hr; 1982) 1,715,000,000 (1,715,000,000); coal (metric tons; 1982) 49,000 (249,-000); crude petroleum (barrels; 1982) 11,084,000 (10,263,000); petroleum products (metric tons; 1982) 988,000 (989,000); natural gas (cu m; 1982) 520,256,000 (520,256,000).

Gross national product (at current market prices; 1982): U.S.$5,900,000,000 (U.S.$180 per capita).

Origin of gross domestic product (current prices)

	1981–82 in value K'000,000	% of total value	labour force	% of labour force
Agriculture	20,278	47.0	9,205,000	63.6
Mining	514	1.2	71,000	0.5
Manufacturing	4,110	9.5	1,104,000	7.7
Construction	718	1.7	208,000	1.4
Trade	11,015	25.6	1,310,000	9.1
Public utilities	169	0.4	16,000	0.1
Transportation and communication	1,576	3.7	458,000	3.1
Finance, Services	4,678⊙	10.9⊙	818,000	5.7
Other	⊙	⊙	1,272,000	8.8
TOTAL	43,058	100.0	14,462,000	100.0

Persons economically active (1981–82): total 14,462,000 (39.9%); (1981) female participation in the labour force 4,807,152 (35.5%); unemployed 672,000 (4.7%).

Price and earnings indexes (1975 = 100)

	1978	1979	1980	1981	1982	1983	1984
Consumer price index	113.7	120.1	120.8	121.2	126.4	134.8	143.0⑤
Monthly earnings index□	116.0	123.0	129.0	131.0	...	...	...

Household income and expenditure. Average household size (1980) 5.1; average annual income per household: n.a.; source of income: n.a.; expenditure (1973–74)◊: food and beverages 49.1%, clothing and footwear 15.3%, rent 10.4%, education 5.9%, fuel and power 4.0%, transport and communications 3.8%, medical care and health 2.4%, recreation 1.1%.
Land use (1981): forested 48.9%; meadows and pastures 0.5%; agricultural and under permanent cultivation 15.3%; other 35.3%.

Foreign trade

Balance of trade (current prices)

	1977	1978	1979	1980	1981	1982	1983
K'000,000	−590	−1,184	+361	+510	+761	−116	+753
% of total	15.5%	22.4%	7.6%	9.3%	12.3%	1.9%	14.9%

Imports (1982): K3,178,000,000 (△nonelectrical machinery and transport equipment 35.8%; nonspecified 34.4%; base metals and manufactures 14.0%; chemicals, fertilizers, and pharmaceuticals 8.3%). *Major import sources* (1981): Japan 39.0%; Singapore 10.8%; United States 5.3%.
Exports (1982): K3,062,000,000 (△rice and rice products 37.2%; teak 26.0%; nonspecified [including pulses] 23.4%; base metals [including semiprecious stones] 9.9%). *Major export destinations* (1981): Indonesia 15.3%; Singapore 12.0%; Japan 11.9%; Hong Kong 7.2%; Malaysia 5.1%.

Transport and communications

Transport. Railroads (1982): route length 1,949 mi, 3,137 km; passenger-mi 2,312,200,000, passenger-km 3,721,000,000; short ton-mi cargo 478,000,000, metric ton-km cargo 698,000,000. Roads (1981): total length 14,125 mi, 22,732 km (paved 11%). Vehicles (1980): passenger cars 43,300; trucks and buses 44,700. Merchant marine (1983): vessels (100 gross tons and over) 102; total deadweight tonnage 128,242. Air transport (1982): passenger-mi 123,800,000, passenger-km 199,200,000; short ton-mi cargo 823,300, metric ton-km cargo 1,202,000; airports (1984) with scheduled flights 32.
Communications. Daily newspapers (1983): total number 7; total circulation 525,000; circulation per 1,000 population 15. Radios (1983): total number of receivers 1,600,000 (1 per 22 persons). Television (1983): total number of receivers 500 (1 per 71,000 persons). Telephones (1983): 49,600 (1 per 720 persons).

Education and health

Education (1980)

	schools	teachers	students	student/ teacher ratio
Primary (age 5–9)	24,199	82,543	3,968,300	48.1
Secondary (age 10–15)	1,948	31,149	976,500	31.3
Voc., teacher tr.	76	1,281	19,700	15.4
Higher	37	4,449	143,000	32.1

College graduates per 100,000 population, n.a. *Literacy* (1980): total population literate 13,673,800 (65.9%); males literate 7,709,800 (75.9%); females literate 5,964,000 (56.3%).
Health (1981): physicians 7,321 (1 per 4,705 persons); hospital beds 29,510 (1 per 1,168 persons).
Food (1978–80): daily per capita caloric intake 2,286 (vegetable products 95.9%, animal products 4.1%); 106% of FAO recommended minimum requirement.

Military

Total active duty personnel (1983): 179,000 (army 91.1%; navy 3.9%; air force 5.0%). *Military expenditure as percent of GNP* (1982): 3.4% (world 6.0%); per capita expenditure U.S.$7.

*Preliminary. †1983 preliminary census figure for Rangoon is 2,458,712. ‡Based on incomplete tabulations. §Based on 1981 statistics. ‖ 1983. ¶Government, residential only. ⊙Other included with finance and services. ⑤June only. □Male workers in manufacturing only. ◊Rangoon only. △Percentage breakdown applies to first six months only.

Burundi

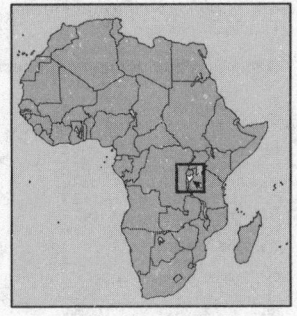

Official name: République du Burundi (French); Republika y'Uburundi (Kirundi) (Republic of Burundi).
Form of government: unitary single-party republic with one legislative house (National Assembly [65]).
Chief of state and government: President.
Capital: Bujumbura.
Official languages: French; Kirundi.
Official religion: none.
Monetary unit: 1 Burundi franc (FBu) = 100 centimes; valuation (Oct. 29, 1984) 1 U.S.$ = FBu123.00; 1 £ = FBu152.42.

Area and population

Provinces	Capitals	area sq mi	area sq km	population 1981 estimate
Bubanza	Bubanza	1,047	2,712	343,700
Bujumbura	Bujumbura	510	1,322	499,500
Bururi	Bururi	1,914	4,957	477,600
Gitega	Gitega	1,331	3,447	713,300
Muramvya	Muramvya	597	1,546	396,200
Muyinga	Muyinga	1,429	3,700	570,500
Ngozi	Ngozi	1,045	2,707	807,500
Ruyigi	Ruyigi	2,208	5,718	408,400
TOTAL		10,081	26,109	4,216,700

Source: Official government figures.

Demography

Density (1984): persons per sq mi 465.3, persons per sq km 179.7.
Urban–rural (1981): urban 2.3%; rural 97.7%.
Sex distribution (1979): male 48.31%; female 51.69%.
Age breakdown (1980): under 15, 41.9%; 15–29, 27.0%; 30–44, 16.0%; 45–59, 9.8%; 60–74, 4.5%; 75 and over, 0.8%.
Population projection: (1990) 5,516,000; (2000) 7,207,000.
Doubling time: 27 years.
Ethnic composition (1980): Hutu 83.3%; Tutsi 12.8%; Tutsi from Rwanda 1.6%; Zairian 1.2%; Twa Pygmy 1.0%; other 0.1%.
Religious affiliation (1980): affiliated Christian 79.5%, of which Roman Catholic 73.3%, Protestant 4.4%; tribal religionist 13.5%; nominal Christian 6.0%; Muslim 0.9%; other 0.1%.
Populated places (1982 est.): Bujumbura 200,000; Gitega 35,000; Ngozi 20,000.

Vital statistics

Birth rate per 1,000 population (1981): 46.3 (world avg. 29.0).
Death rate per 1,000 population (1981): 20.3 (world avg. 12.0).
Natural increase rate per 1,000 population (1981): 26.0 (world avg. 17.0).
Total fertility rate (avg. births per childbearing woman; 1981): 6.5.
Marriage rate per 1,000 population: n.a.
Divorce rate per 1,000 population: n.a.
Infant mortality rate per 1,000 live births (1981): 119.6.
Life expectancy at birth (1981): male 43.4 years; female 46.7 years.
Major causes of death: n.a.; however, major diseases are malaria and tuberculosis.

National economy

Budget (1981). Revenue: FBu16,118,000,000 (taxes 64.9%, of which beer 14.0%, customs duties 12.3%, corporate 8.1%, income 7.2%, property 6.5%; grants from abroad 27.4%). Expenditures: FBu20,956,000,000* (current expenditures only: education 22.9%, road transport 9.3%, health 5.9%, agriculture 5.0%).
Public debt (external, outstanding; 1982): U.S.$200,900,000.
Tourism (1980): receipts from visitors U.S.$2,450,000; expenditures by nationals abroad, n.a.
Production (metric tons except as noted). Agriculture, forestry, fishing (1982): yams and taros 2,312,000, cassavas 1,288,000, bananas 960,000, sweet potatoes 947,000, pulses 220,000, corn (maize) 142,000, sorghum 95,000, peanuts (groundnuts) 42,000, millet 30,000, coffee 24,000; livestock (number of live animals) 890,000 cattle, 723,000 goats, 349,000 sheep, 3,300,000 chickens; roundwood 3,435,000 cu m; fish catch 11,900. Mining and quarrying: negligible. Manufacturing (1979): cotton fibre 2,000; cigarettes 1,300,000,000 units; beer 526,000 hectolitres; carbonated beverages 96,000 hectolitres; footwear 471,000 pairs; plastic bags 64,000 kilograms; acetylene 8,000 kilograms; oxygen 44,000 cu m. Construction: n.a. Energy production (consumption): electricity (kW-hr; 1982) 2,000,000 (152,000,000); coal, none (n.a.); crude petroleum, none (n.a.); petroleum products (metric tons; 1982) none (34,000); natural gas, none (n.a.); peat† (metric tons; 1981) 6,500 (n.a.).
Gross national product (at current market prices; 1981): U.S.$990,000,000 (U.S.$230 per capita).

Price and earnings indexes (1980 = 100)

	1978	1979	1980	1981	1982	1983	1984◊
Consumer price index	66.9	91.4	100.0	107.8	118.5	128.4	138.4
Monthly earnings index	...	...	...	...	...	...	...

Origin of gross domestic product (current prices)

	1980 in value FBu'000,000	1980 % of total value	1979 labour force	1979 % of labour force
Agriculture	38,907	54.5	2,246,200	93.1
Mining	419‡	0.6‡	1,400	0.1
Manufacturing	6,715	9.4	36,700	1.5
Construction	4,373	6.1	14,700	0.6
Trade	6,099§	8.5§	20,900	0.9
Public utilities	‡	‡	1,700	0.1
Transportation and communication	1,795	2.5	6,400	0.3
Finance	§	§	1,300	0.1
Pub. admin., defense	4,201	5.9	80,700 ‖	3.3 ‖
Other	8,882	12.4	3,100	0.1
TOTAL	71,390¶	100.0¶	2,413,100	100.0¶

Persons economically active (1979): total 2,413,100 (59.9%); female participation in the labour force, n.a.; unemployed, n.a.
Household income and expenditure. Average household size (1980): 4.9; average annual income per household: n.a.; source of income: n.a.; expenditure: n.a.
Land use (1981): forested 2.4%; meadows and pastures 35.9%; agricultural and under permanent cultivation 50.9%; other 10.8%.

Foreign trade

Balance of trade (current prices)

	1978	1979	1980	1981	1982	1983
FBu'000,000	−2,600	−4,360	−9,230	−7,765	−11,381	−9,569
% of total	17.2%	18.9%	44.0%	36.5%	41.9%	38.9%

Imports (1980): FBu15,109,000,000 (basic manufactures 27.3%, of which manufactures of metal 8.0%, synthetic fibre yarn 5.3%, woven cotton fabrics 4.2%; petroleum products 15.7%; chemicals 8.0%; electrical machinery 7.6%; nonelectrical machinery 7.6%; road vehicles 7.6%; cereals and cereal preparations 7.2%). *Major import sources*δ: Iran 19.5%; Belgium-Luxembourg 15.2%; France 7.8%; Japan 7.5%; West Germany 6.9%; Kenya 6.8%.
Exports (1980): FBu5,906,000,000 (nut roasted coffee 86.8%, of which Arabica species 79.5%, Robusta species 7.1%; tea 3.6%; raw cotton 1.9%; asbestos cement 0.8%). *Major export destinations*δ: United States 43.3%; European Economic Community 38.8%; Zaire 4.1%; Japan 2.4%.

Transport and communications

Transport. Railroads: none. Roads (1981): total length 3,196 mi, 5,144 km (paved 7%). Vehicles: private motor vehicles (1981) 6,100; trucks and buses (1979) 2,400. Merchant marine (1979): vessel (100 gross tons and over) 1; total gross tonnage 385. Air transport (1981)□: passenger arrivals and departures 22,735; cargo loaded and unloaded 3,305 short tons, 2,999 metric tons; airports (1984) with scheduled flights 2.
Communications. Daily newspaper (1981): total number 1; total circulation 20,000; circulation per 1,000 population 4.6. Radios (1982): total number of receivers 152,000 (1 per 31 persons). Television: total number of receivers, n.a. Telephones (1982): 5,601 (1 per 853 persons).

Education and health

Education (1981–82)

	schools	teachers	students	student/ teacher ratio
Primary	794	5,570	207,457	37.2
Secondary	34	510	8,727	17.1
Voc., teacher tr.	45	634	9,889	15.6
Higher	1	166	1,901	11.5

College graduates per 100,000 population (students graduating; 1979): 11.
Literacy (1979): total population literate 742,000 (32.0%); males literate 463,000 (42.3%); females literate 279,000 (22.8%).
Health (1979): physicians 102 (1 per 39,494 persons); hospital beds 2,667 (1 per 1,510 persons).
Food (1978–80): daily per capita caloric intake 2,152 (vegetable products 96.9%, animal products 3.1%); 92% of FAO recommended minimum requirement.

Military

Total active duty personnel (1981): a national army of 6,500 comprised largely of Tutsi. *Military expenditure as percent of GNP* (1982): 4.7% (world 6.0%); per capita expenditure U.S.$10.

*Includes capital expenditures. †Peat is not yet popularly accepted as a fuel. It is mostly used by industries, schools, and the military. ‡Public utilities are included with mining. §Finance is included with trade. ‖ Includes personal services. ¶Detail does not add to total given because of rounding. δFirst quarter. δ1981. □Bujumbura Airport; first 6 months only.

Cameroon

Official name: République Unie du
Cameroun (French); United Republic
of Cameroon (English).
Form of government: federal republic
with one legislative house (National
Assembly [120]).
Head of state and government:
President.
Capital: Yaoundé.
Official languages: French; English.
Official religion: none.
Monetary unit: 1 CFA franc
(CFAF) = 100 centimes; valuation
(Oct. 29, 1984) 1 U.S.$ = CFAF
470.59; 1 £ = CFAF 568.00.

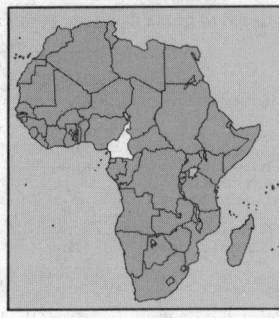

Area and population		area		population
				1981
Provinces	**Capitals**	sq mi	sq km	estimate
Centre-Sud	Yaoundé	44,760	115,940	1,714,000
Est	Bertoua	42,050	108,900	424,000
Littoral	Douala	7,810	20,220	1,125,000
Nord	Garoua	63,340	164,050	2,459,000
Nord-Ouest	Bamenda	6,680	17,300	1,073,000
Ouest	Bafoussam	5,360	13,890	1,169,000
Sud-Ouest	Buea	9,620	24,910	693,000
TOTAL		179,716*	465,458*	8,657,000

Demography

Density (1984): persons per sq mi 51.5, persons per sq km 19.9.
Urban–rural (1981): urban 33.8%; rural 66.2%.
Sex distribution (1981): male 49.87%; female 50.13%.
Age breakdown (1981): under 15, 42.8%; 15–29, 26.4%; 30–44, 16.3%; 45–59,
9.5%; 60 and over, 5.0%.
Population projection: (1990) 10,838,000; (2000) 13,937,000.
Doubling time: 28 years.
Ethnic composition (1982): Cameroon Highland Bantu 27%; Equatorial
Bantu 25%; Kirdi 15%; Fulani 9.5%; Northwestern Bantu 8%; Hausa 8%;
Baya-mbum 6%; other 1.5%.
Religious affiliation (1980): Roman Catholic 35%; Protestant 18%; animist
25%; Muslim 22%.
Major cities (1981): Douala 637,000; Yaoundé 435,900; Nkongsamba 86,900;
Maroua 81,900; Garoua 77,900.

Vital statistics

Birth rate per 1,000 population (1980–85): 42.2 (world avg. 27.5); legitimate,
n.a., illegitimate, n.a.
Death rate per 1,000 population (1980–85): 17.6 (world avg. 10.6).
Natural increase rate per 1,000 population (1980–85): 24.6 (world avg. 16.9).
Total fertility rate (avg. births per childbearing woman; 1980–85): 5.7.
Marriage rate per 1,000 population: n.a.
Divorce rate per 1,000 population: n.a.
Infant mortality rate per 1,000 live births (1978): 157.
Life expectancy at birth (1980–85): male 46.9 years; female 50.1 years.
Major causes of death per 100,000 population: n.a.

National economy

Budget (1982–83). Revenue: CFAF410,000,000,000 (direct and assimilated
taxes 49.5%, customs duties and taxes 26.9%, receipts for services 8.6%,
indirect taxes 8.1%). Expenditures: CFAF410,000,000,000 (planning and
development 23.9%, education 9.9%, state subsidies 9.2%, external public
debt 7.3%, armed forces 6.8%).
Public debt (external, outstanding; 1981): U.S.$2,034,000,000.
Production (metric tons except as noted). Agriculture, forestry, fishing (1983):
sugarcane 580,000†, coffee 115,000, cocoa 90,000, palm kernels 47,000†,
cotton lint 30,000, corn (maize) 400,000, millet 360,000, peanuts (groundnuts) 120,000†, dry beans 105,000, cassava 1,077,000†, sweet potatoes 130,-
000†, bananas 58,000, milk 46,000†, eggs 8,771†; livestock (number of live
animals; 1982) 3,338,000 cattle, 2,180,000 sheep, 1,331,000 pigs, 10,764,000
chickens; roundwood 10,291,000 cu m†; fish catch 83,061†. Mining and
quarrying (1981): limestone 35,000. Manufacturing (CFAF, gross value;
1981): beverages and tobacco 52,185,000,000; textiles and clothing 22,070,-
000,000; metal products 20,622,000,000; foods, prepared 20,000,000,000;
chemical products 17,106,000,000; construction materials 12,552,000,000.
Construction (CFAF, gross value; 1981): 12,522,000,000. Energy production
(consumption): electricity (kW-hr; 1982) 1,908,000,000 (1,908,000,000); coal
(metric tons; 1982) n.a. (minuscule†); petroleum (barrels; 1982) 34,817,500
(21,403,600); petroleum products 2,681,000 (2,795,000); natural gas (cu m;
1982) none (n.a.).
Persons economically active (1982): total 3,543,000 (40.0%); female participation in the labour force 1,329,000 (37.5%); unemployed 161,270 (4.6%).

Price and earnings indexes (1980 = 100)							
	1976	1977	1978	1979	1980	1981	1982
Consumer price index	66.5	75.9	85.4	91.0	100.0	110.6	124.2
Monthly earnings index	...	...	...	...	...	...	...

Land use (1981): forested 54.4%; meadows and pastures 17.7%; agricultural
and under permanent cultivation 14.8%; other 13.1%.

Gross national product (at current market prices; 1981): U.S.$7,078,000,000
(U.S.$820 per capita).

Origin of gross domestic product (current prices)				
	1981		1982	
	in value CFAF'000,000,000	% of total value	labour force	% of labour force
Agriculture	455.6	26.8	2,594,800	73.2
Mining	91.8	5.4	1,580	0.1
Manufacturing	140.0	8.2	159,560	4.5
Construction	78.3	4.6	62,860	1.8
Trade and finance	251.2	14.7	149,200	4.2
Public utilities	19.6	1.2	3,230	0.1
Transportation and communication	96.8	5.7	47,400	1.3
Pub. admin., defense, services, and other	569.7	33.4	524,370	14.8
TOTAL	1703.0	100.0	3,543,000	100.0

Tourism (1981): receipts from visitors U.S.$17,000,000; expenditures by na-
tionals abroad U.S.$87,000,000.

Foreign trade

Balance of trade (current prices)					
	1976	1977	1978	1979	1980	1981
CFAF'000,000,000	−23.7	−19.6	−55.5	−30.6	−47.0	−89.3
% of total	8.8%	5.4%	13.2%	6.0%	7.5%	13.0%

Imports (1981): CFAF389,000,000,000 (machinery and electrical and
non-electrical equipment 18.4%, crude mineral and energy products 17.0%,
transport equipment 12.5%, chemical products 11.6%, raw and wrought
metals 11.1%, textiles and textile products 6.2%). *Major import sources:*
France 41.0%; United States 6.4%; Japan 5.8%; West Germany 5.5%; Italy
4.6%.
Exports (1981): CFAF 299,700,000,000 (crude petroleum 38.9%, cacao 17.2%,
coffee 17.1%, logs and timber 4.8%, aluminum 2.8%, cotton 1.2%, bananas
0.5%). *Major export destinations:* United States 38.2%; France 19.6%; The
Netherlands 14.4%; West Germany 5.8%; Italy 5.0%.

Transport and communications

Transport. Railroads (1981): length 726 mi, 1,168 km; passenger-mi 173,-
000,000, passenger-km 279,000,000; short ton-mi cargo 481,000,000, metric
ton-km cargo 702,000,000. Roads (1981): total length 20,024 mi, 32,226 km
(paved 8%). Vehicles (1980): passenger cars 45,893; trucks and buses 30,887.
Merchant marine (1983): vessels (100 gross tons and over) 45; total deadweight tonnage 2,273,503. Air transport (1983): passenger-mi 345,511,000,
passenger-km 547,999,000; short ton-mi cargo 34,291,000, metric ton-km
cargo 50,064,000; airports (1983) with scheduled flights 13.
Communications. Daily newspapers (1980): total number 1; total circulation
50,000; circulation per 1,000 population 5.9. Radios (1983): total number of
receivers 780,000 (1 per 11.3 persons). Televisions: n.a. Telephones (1981):
26,000 (1 per 333 persons).

Education and health

Education (1981–82)				
	schools	teachers	students	student/ teacher ratio
Primary (age 6–14)	5,148	28,585	1,443,728	50.5
Secondary (age 15–24)	334	6,227	180,248	28.9
Voc., teacher tr.	187	2,540	61,572	24.2
Higher	13	557	11,407	20.5

College graduates per 100,000 population: n.a. *Literacy* (1980): total population literate 2,344,100 (55.2%); males literate 1,453,200 (70.2%); females
literate 890,900 (41.0%).
Health: physicians (1981) 640 (1 per 13,527 persons); hospital beds (1980)
24,541 (1 per 353 persons).
Food (1978–80): daily per capita caloric intake 2,451 (vegetable products
95.1%, animal products 4.9%); 106% of FAO recommended minimum
requirement.

Military

Total active duty personnel (1983): 7,300 (army 90.4%; navy 4.8%; air force
4.8%). *Military expenditure as percent of* GNP (1982): 1.2% (world 6.0%);
per capita expenditure U.S.$10.

*Total includes 96 sq mi (248 sq km) of water area. †1982. ‡Less than 500 metric tons.

Canada

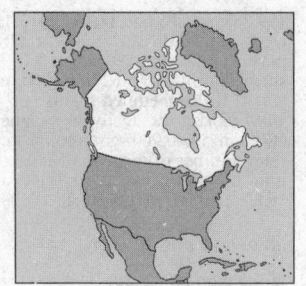

Official name: Canada.
Form of government: federal multi-party parliamentary state with two legislative houses (Senate [104]; House of Commons [282]).
Chief of state: British Monarch represented by governor-general.
Head of government: Prime Minister.
Capital: Ottawa.
Official languages: English, French.
Official religion: none.
Monetary unit: 1 Canadian dollar (Can $) = 100 cents; valuation (Oct. 29, 1984) 1 U.S.$ = Can$1.32; 1 £ = Can$1.60.

Area and population

Provinces	Capitals	area sq mi	area sq km	population 1984 estimate
Alberta	Edmonton	248,800	644,390	2,349,000
British Columbia	Victoria	358,971	929,730	2,863,000
Manitoba	Winnipeg	211,723	548,360	1,054,000
New Brunswick	Fredericton	27,834	72,090	712,000
Newfoundland	St John's	143,510	371,690	579,000
Nova Scotia	Halifax	20,402	52,840	868,000
Ontario	Toronto	344,090	891,190	8,917,000
Prince Edward Island	Charlottetown	2,185	5,660	125,000
Quebec	Quebec	523,859	1,356,790	6,540,000
Saskatchewan	Regina	220,348	570,700	1,003,000
Territories				
Northwest Territories	Yellowknife	1,271,442	3,293,020	49,000
Yukon Territory	Whitehorse	184,931	478,970	22,000
TOTAL		3,558,096*	9,215,430†	25,082,000*

Source: Official government figures.

Demography

Density (1984): persons per sq mi 7.0, persons per sq km 2.7.
Urban–rural (1981): urban 75.7%; rural 24.3%.
Sex distribution (1981): male 49.80%; female 50.20%.
Age breakdown (1981): under 15, 23.4%; 15–29, 28.9%; 30–44, 20.0%; 45–59, 15.0%; 60–74, 9.6%; 75 and over, 3.1%.
Population projection: (1990) 26,826,000; (2000) 29,028,000.
Doubling time: 58 years.
Ethnic composition (by language, 1981): English 61.2%; French 25.6%; Italian 2.2%; German 2.1%; Ukrainian 1.2%; other European 4.6%; Asiatic 2.3%; Amerindian and Inuktitut (Eskimo) 0.8%.
Religious affiliation (1981): Roman Catholic 46.5%; Protestant 41.2%; Eastern Orthodox 1.5%; Jewish 1.2%; Muslim 0.4%; Hindu 0.3%; non-religious 7.4%; other 1.5%.
Major metropolitan areas (1983 est.): Toronto 3,067,100; Montreal 2,862,300; Vancouver 1,310,600; Ottawa-Hull 737,600; Edmonton 698,600; Calgary 634,500; Winnipeg 600,700; Quebec 580,400; Hamilton 548,100; St. Catharines-Niagara 304,400.
Place of birth (1971): 84.7% native-born; 15.3% foreign-born, of which: United Kingdom 4.3%, other to European 3.5%, other 7.5%.
Mobility (1981). Population living in the same residence as in 1976: 52.4%; different residence, same province 24.9%; different province 22.7%.
Households (1981). Average household size 2.9; 1 person 20.3%, 2 persons 28.9%, 3 persons 17.5%, 4 persons 18.6%, 5 persons 9.1%, 6 persons 3.5%, 7 or more persons 2.1%. Family households: 6,324,976 (76.4%), nonfamily 1,956,555 (23.6%, of which 1-person 20.3%).
Immigration (1983): permanent immigrants admitted 88,846, from Asia 41.3%, Europe 27.2%, United States 8.2%, West Indies 8.0%, other 15.3%.

Vital statistics

Birth rate per 1,000 population (1983): 14.8 (world avg. 29.0); legitimate, 91.0%; illegitimate, 9.0%.
Death rate per 1,000 population (1983): 7.0 (world avg. 11.0).
Natural increase rate per 1,000 population (1983): 7.8 (world avg. 18.0).
Total fertility rate (avg. births per childbearing woman; 1981): 1.7.
Marriage rate per 1,000 population (1983): 7.2.
Divorce rate per 1,000 population: (1981). 2.1.
Infant mortality rate per 1,000 live births (1982): 9.6.
Life expectancy at birth (1981): male 71.5 years; female 78.7 years.
Major causes of death per 100,000 population (1978): diseases of the circulatory system 312.1; malignant neoplasms (cancers) 159.7; accidents 68.5; diseases of the respiratory system 34.4.

Social indicators

Educational attainment (1976). Percent of adult population having: no schooling 1.8%, less than full primary education 18.5%, primary 12.2%, secondary 36.6%, post secondary 30.9%; graduates by level (1984): 4-year higher degree 90,870, master's 13,675, doctorate 1,870.

Distribution of income (1977)

percent of national income by quintile

1	2	3	4	5 (highest)
3.8%	10.7%	17.9%	25.6%	42.0%

Quality of working life (1983). Average work week: 37.6 hours (6.7% ov-

ertime). Annual rate per 100,000 workers for (1978): injury, accident, or industrial illness 4,924, death 8.3. Proportion of labour force insured for damages or income loss resulting from: injury 99.0%, permanent disability 99.0%, death 99.0%. Average days lost to labour stoppages per 1,000 employee-work days: 1.9. Average duration of journey to work (1977)‡ 23 minutes (26.0% public transportation, 74.0% other). Rate per 1,000 workers of discouraged (unemployed no longer seeking work): 10.5.
Access to services (1978). Proportion of households having access to: electricity 87.2%, public water supply 98.5%§, public sewage collection 98.5%, public fire protection 90.4%.
Social participation. Eligible voters participating in last national election 69.7%. Population over 18 years of age participating in voluntary work, n.a. Trade union membership in total workforce 39.0%. Practicing religious population in total affiliated population 92.7%.
Social deviance (1978). Offense rate per 100,000 population for: murder 5.9, rape 8.5, other assault 493.5, grand and auto theft 354.0, burglary and housebreaking 1,185.9. Incidence in general population of: alcoholism 2.7%§, drug and substance abuse 0.07%‖. Rate per 100,000 population of suicide 12.8.
Leisure (1982). Favourite leisure activities: watching television 23.7 hrs/week, listening to radio 18.5 hrs/week.
Material well-being (1983). Households possessing: automobile 100.0%, telephone 100.0%, colour television receiver 86.0%, refrigerator 99.4%, air conditioner 15.3%, washing machine 59.1%.

National economy

Gross national product (at current market prices; 1984): U.S.$317,326,000,000 (U.S.$12,650 per capita).

Origin of gross domestic product (current prices)

	1982–1983 in value Can$'000,000	% of total value	labour force	% of labour force
Agriculture	13,501	3.7	519,000	4.4
Mining	19,050	5.2	157,000	1.3
Manufacturing	57,458	15.6	1,785,000	15.0
Construction	18,709	5.1	507,000	4.2
Trade	35,061	9.5	1,817,000	15.3
Public utilities	13,438	3.6	117,000	1.1
Transportation and communication	26,814	7.3	735,000	6.2
Finance	29,147	7.9	591,000	4.9
Pub. admin., defense	¶	¶	647,000	5.4
Services	154,529¶	42.1¶	3,453,000	29.0
Other	...	...	1,570,000¶	13.2
TOTAL	367,707	100.0	11,898,000	100.0

Budget (1983–84). Revenue: Can$ 58,618,000,000 (personal income tax 49.5%, indirect taxes 25.2%, corporation income tax 13.3%). Expenditures: Can$ 55,012,000,000 (education, health, and welfare 29.7%; national development 19.7%; public debt interest 18.3%; defense 8.9%).
National debt (Sept. 1984): Can$153,003,000,000.
Tourism (1982): receipts from visitors U.S.$3,020,000,000; expenditures by nationals abroad U.S.$3,950,000,000.

Manufacturing, mining, and construction enterprises (1981)

	no. of enterprises	no. of employees	hourly wages as a % of avg. of all wages	annual value added (Can$'000,000)
Manufacturing				
Food and beverages	4,492	234,077	86.6	10,354.5
Transport equipment	1,270	178,612	110.7	8,041.1
Paper and related products	758	131,024	96.9	6,965.5
Metal fabricating	5,072	158,832	101.4	6,137.7
Chemicals and chemical products	1,232	90,186	102.6	6,099.5
Primary metals	439	125,168	93.8	5,836.6
Electrical products	1,121	127,924	99.0	5,163.4
Machinery	1,620	108,531	85.0	4,690.5
Printing, publishing, and related products	4,508	107,488	91.7	4,082.5
Wood	3,394	112,570	103.5	3,442.3
Petroleum and coal products	111	26,638	133.3	2,722.9
Building materials	1,574	55,269	104.0	2,510.5
Textile	952	67,673	73.3	2,283.9
Clothing	2,125	95,850	59.8	2,148.4
Rubber and plastic	1,030	61,504	97.0	2,280.4
Furniture and fixtures	2,464	53,361	92.0	1,456.1
Tobacco products industries	25	8,744	117.9	642.7
Leather industries	415	26,207	60.8	617.9
Knitting mills	262	20,495	73.3	463.4
Mining	...	178,200	147.9	17,288.7
Construction	...	475,100	144.7	18,239.6

Production (farm cash receipts in Can$'000). Agriculture, forestry, fishing (1983): wheat 3,729,300, barley 835,200, rapeseed 726,400, corn (maize) 598,400, vegetables 436,800, floriculture 302,000, potatoes 293,700, tobacco 287,000, fruits 268,000, soybeans 249,000; livestock (number of live animals) 12,585,000 cattle, 9,857,000 pigs, 809,000 sheep, 93,262,000 poultry; roundwood 13,468,000 cu m; pelts 4,423,395 metric tons§; fish catch 1,300,000 metric tons. Mining and quarrying (value in Can$'000,000; 1982): petroleum 11,640, natural gas 7,089; coal 1,299, iron ore 1,213, copper 1,181, zinc 1,100, gold 930, uranium 815, potash 627, nickel 581, asbestos 403. Manufacturing (value added in Can$000,000; 1982): food and beverages 11,107; transportation equipment 7,546, of which motor vehicles 2,389; paper and paper products 6,079; chemicals 5,864; fabricated metal products 5,682; electrical products 5,161; primary metals 4,804; printed matter 4,272; agricultural, commercial, and industrial machinery 4,145; primary wood products (sawn and planed lumber, veneers, doors, and kitchen cabinets, excluding furniture) 2,708. Construction (1983): residential Can$8,859,200,000; nonresidential Can$5,712,100,000.

Service enterprises (1983)

	no. of enter-prises	no. of employees	weekly wage as a % of all wages	annual sales (Can$'000,000)
Retail trade				
Food stores	...	213,400	...	26,237.1
Motor vehicle dealers	...	79,800	...	17,198.0
Department stores	...	□	...	10,930.5
Service stations	...	63,700	...	10,295.4
Clothing stores	...	50,200	...	4,873.8
Pharmacies	...	52,400	...	4,294.0
Furniture and appliance stores	...	62,100	...	2,708.1
Automotive stores	...	31,500	...	2,492.9
General merchandise	...	231,700□	...	2,312.0
General stores	...		...	1,909.8
Variety stores	...	45,100	...	1,129.9
Shoe stores	...	18,400	...	1,115.2
Hardware stores	...	17,300	...	984.0
Jewelry stores	...	14,000	...	837.9

Energy production (consumption): electricity (kW-hr; 1983) 395,528,000,000 (356,095,000,000δ); coal (metric tons; 1983) 44,250,000 (41,474,000δ); crude petroleum (barrels; 1982) 461,804,000 (508,129,000δ); petroleum products (metric tons; 1983) 86,337,000 (68,396,000δ); natural gas (cu m; 1983) 95,-497,200,000 (50,104,668,000δ).
Persons economically active (July 1984): total 12,422,000 (49.5%); female participation in the labour force 4,649,000 (42.0%); unemployed 1,361,000 (11.0%).

Price and earnings indexes (1975 = 100)

	1978	1979	1980	1981	1982	1983	1984
Consumer price index	126.5	138.1	152.1	171.0	189.5	200.5	210.3◇
Monthly earnings index	130.5	141.8	156.1	174.9	192.2	204.8	...

Household income and expenditure. Average household size (1983) 2.9; average annual income per household Can$32,718△ (U.S.$26,385); sources of income: wages and salaries 65.7%, social welfare 14.8%, interest, dividends, and other investment income 12.4%, other 7.1%; expenditure (1982): food 18.0%, housing 17.1%, transportation 14.4%, clothing 6.3%, health 3.4%, education 2.8%.
Land use (1981): forested 35.4%; meadows and pastures 2.6%; agricultural and under permanent cultivation 5.0%; built-on, wasteland, and other 57.0%.

Financial aggregates

	1978	1979	1980	1981	1982	1983	1984 (10 mo.)
Exchange rate, Can$ per:							
U.S. dollar	1.19	1.17	1.19	1.19	1.23	1.24	1.32
£	2.42	2.60	2.84	2.42	2.15	1.88	1.60
SDR	1.54	1.54	1.52	1.38	1.36	1.30	1.31
International reserves (U.S.$)							
Total (excl. gold; '000,000)	3,544	2,856	3,041	3,492	3,000	3,465	2,829
SDR's ('000,000)	522	586	453	174	71	21	39
Reserve pos. in IMF ('000,000)	557	391	579	402	365	703	700
Foreign exchange ('000,000)	2,464	1,879	2,090	2,916	2,564	2,741	2,090
Gold, ('000,000 fine troy oz.)	22.13	22.18	20.98	20.46	20.26	20.17	20.17
% world reserves	2.13	2.35	2.20	2.00	2.14	2.13	2.13
Interest and prices							
Central bank discount (%)	10.75	14.00	17.26	14.66	10.05	9.96	11.71
Gov't. bond yield (%)	9.30	10.26	12.49	15.22	14.26	11.79	12.18
Industrial share prices (1980 = 100)	50.6	73.3	100.0	97.4	77.9	109.8	110.9†
Balance of payments (U.S.$'000,000)							
Balance of visible trade, of which:	4,184	4,180	8,001	6,612	14,959	14,877	...
Imports, f.o.b.	43,975	53,474	59,472	65,940	55,471	60,830	...
Exports, f.o.b.	48,159	57,654	67,473	72,552	70,431	75,706	...
Balance of invisibles	−8,517	−8,870	−9,982	−12,923	−13,961	−14,147	...
Balance of payments, current account	−4,298	−4,119	−954	−5,048	2,019	1,365	...

Foreign trade

Balance of trade (current prices)

	1978	1979	1980	1981	1982	1983
Can$'000,000,000	3.0	2.8	6.9	4.5	15.8	19.4
% of total	2.9%	2.2%	4.7%	2.8%	9.9%	11.8%

Imports (1983): Can$75,586,600,000 (machinery and transport equipment 64.0%, of which motor vehicle parts 12.3%, road motor vehicles 10.5%; food, feed, beverages, and tobacco 6.5%; crude petroleum 4.3%; nonferrous metals 2.7%; chemicals 2.2%; plastics and synthetic rubber 1.8%; textiles 1.4%). *Major import sources:* United States 71.6%; Japan 5.8%; United Kingdom 2.4%; West Germany 2.1%; Mexico 1.4%; Taiwan 1.2%; France 1.1%; Hong Kong 1.1%.
Exports (1983): Can$90,963,900,000 (road motor vehicles 15.5%; wheat 5.1%; newsprint 4.4%; lumber 4.4%; natural gas 4.3%; crude petroleum 3.8%; wood pulp 3.4%; chemicals 2.4%; aluminum 1.9%). *Major export destinations:* United States 72.9%; Japan 5.2%; United Kingdom 2.8%; Soviet Union 1.9%; China 1.8%; West Germany 1.3%; The Netherlands 1.1%; Belgium-Luxembourg 0.8%; France 0.7%; Italy 0.6%.

Transport and communications

Transport. Railroads (1983): length 74,564 mi, 120,000 km; passenger-mi 1,359,000,000, passenger-km 2,187,000,000; short ton-mi cargo 150,724,-000,000, metric ton-km cargo 220,053,000,000. Roads (1983): total length 549,462 mi, 884,249 km (paved 81%). Vehicles (1982): passenger cars 10,-199,388; trucks and buses 3,192,197. Merchant marine (1983): vessels (100 gross tons and over) 1,300; total deadweight tonnage 4,164,920. Air transport⊕ (1983): passenger-mi 17,836,000,000, passenger-km 28,704,000,000; short ton-mi cargo 627,586,000, metric ton-km cargo 916,260,000; airports (1984) with scheduled flights 60.
Communications. Daily newspapers** (1983): total number 115; total circulation 5,400,000; circulation per 1,000 population 215.3. Radios (1983): total number of receivers 28,000,000 (1 per 0.9 persons). Television (1983): total number of receivers 12,400,000 (1 per 2 persons). Telephones (1983): 16,802,000 (1 per 1.5 persons).

Education and health

Education (1982–83)

	schools	teachers	students	student/teacher ratio
Primary (age 6–12)	13,564	180,763	3,450,547	19.1
Secondary (age 13–18)	2,085	91,026	1,542,205	16.9
Higher††	262	59,020	738,900	12.0

College graduates per 100,000 population (students graduating; 1984): 412.
Literacy (1975): total population literate 16,185,000 (95.6%); males literate 8,003,000 (95.6%); females literate 8,182,000 (95.7%).
Health (1979): physicians 43,192 (1 per 546 persons); hospital beds 270,118 (1 per 110 persons).
Food (1978–80): daily per capita caloric intake 3,358 (vegetable products 58.4%, animal products 41.6%); 126% of FAO recommended minimum requirement.

Military

Total active duty personnel (1984): 82,858 (army 15.7%; navy 6.7%; air force 18.5%; not identified by service 59.2%). *Military expenditure as percent of GNP* (1982): 2.2% (world 6.0%); per capita expenditure U.S.$253.

*Detail does not add to total given because of rounding. †Land area only; freshwater area is 291,576 sq mi (755,180 sq km); total area is 3,849,672 sq mi (9,970,610 sq km). ‡Urban areas. §1976. ‖1977. ¶Public administration and defense included with services. ⊊Unemployed and not previously employed. δ1982. □Department and general stores included with general merchandise. ◇September. △Disposable personal income. †April 1984. ⊕Air Canada and CP Air only. **English and French only. ††1983–84.

Mt. Robson, 12,972 ft (3,954 m), British Columbia.

Cape Verde

Official name: República de Cabo Verde (Republic of Cape Verde).
Form of government: unitary single-party republic with one legislative house (National People's Assembly [56]).
Chief of state: President.
Head of government: Premier.
Capital: Praia.
Official language: Portuguese.
Official religion: none.
Monetary unit: 1 escudo (CV Esc) = 100 centavos; valuation (Oct. 29, 1984) 1 U.S.$ = CV Esc 80.13; 1 £ = CV Esc 96.71.

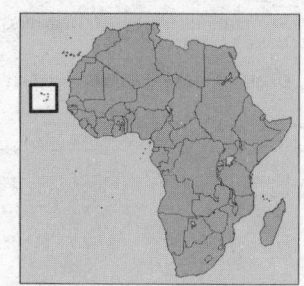

Area and population

Islands Counties	Capitals	area sq mi	area sq km	population 1980 census*
Boa Vista		239	620	3,245
Boa Vista	Sal Rei			
Brava		26	67	6,896
Brava	Nova Sintra			
Fogo		184	476	30,233
Fogo	São Filipe			
Maio		104	269	3,888
Maio	Porto Inglês			
Sal		83	216	5,851
Sal	Santa Maria			
Santiago		383	991	141,843
Praia	Praia			55,318
Santa Catarina	Assomada			39,614
Santa Cruz	Pedra Badejo			22,743
Tarrafal	Tarrafal			24,168
Santo Antão		301	779	42,613
Paúl	Pombas			7,931
Porto Novo	Porto Novo			12,998
Ribeira Grande	Ponta Sol			21,684
São Nicolau		150	388	13,314
São Nicolau	Ribeira Brava			
São Vicente		88	227	40,962
São Vicente	Mindelo			
TOTAL		1,557†	4,033	288,845

Source: Official government figures.

Demography

Density (1984): persons per sq mi 192.6, persons per sq km 74.4.
Urban–rural (1980): urban 35.1%; rural 64.9%.
Sex distribution (1980): male 46.32%; female 53.68%.
Age breakdown (1980): under 15, 46.0%; 15–29, 27.6%; 30–44, 9.1%; 45–59, 9.0%; 60–74, 6.3%; 75 and over, 2.0%.
Population projection: (1990) 319,000; (2000) 353,000.
Doubling time: 69 years.
Ethnic composition (1980): mixed 70%; black 28%; white 2%.
Religious affiliation (1982): Roman Catholic 98.0%; Protestant 2.0%.
Major cities (1980): Praia 37,676; Mindelo 36,746; São Filipe 4,370.

Vital statistics

Birth rate per 1,000 population (1980–85): 23.8 (world avg. 27.5); (1975) legitimate 55.2%, illegitimate 44.8%.
Death rate per 1,000 population (1980–85): 8.1 (world avg. 10.6).
Natural increase rate per 1,000 population (1980–85): 15.7 (world avg. 16.9).
Total fertility rate (avg. births per childbearing woman; 1980–85): 2.6.
Marriage rate per 1,000 population (1975): 5.4.
Divorce rate per 1,000 population: n.a.
Infant mortality rate per 1,000 live births (1979): 105.
Life expectancy at birth (1980–85): male 60.3 years; female 64.0 years.
Major causes of death per 100,000 population (1980): enteritis and other diarrheal diseases 85.5; heart disease 51.9; cerebrovascular disease 45.7; malignant neoplasms (cancers) 43.8; measles and other infectious parasitic diseases 34.6; pneumonia 27.2; bronchitis, emphysema, and asthma 20.4; avitaminoses and other nutritional deficiencies 14.5.

National economy

Budget (1981). Revenue: CV Esc1,076,475 (indirect taxes 52.1%, of which import duties 42.8%; direct taxes 28.7%, of which taxes from industry 8.6%; receipts from petroleum 8.2%). Expenditures: CV Esc4,896,320 (investment expenditure CV Esc3,814,320 [77.9%], of which industry and energy 28%, transportation 25%, agriculture 17%).
Public debt (external, outstanding; 1982): U.S.$60,500,000.
Tourism: n.a.
Production (metric tons except as noted). Agriculture, forestry, fishing (1982): corn (maize) 20,000, bananas 10,000, coconuts 10,000, sweet potatoes 1,000; livestock (number of live animals) 70,000 goats, 24,000 pigs, 13,000 cattle, 2,000 sheep; fish catch 10,381. Mining and quarrying (1981): Salt CV Esc7,638,000. Manufacturing (by value in CV Esc; 1981): flour 93,852, bread 54,931, canned tuna 43,342, alcoholic beverages 21,763, biscuits 12,959, cigars 8,166, soft drinks 2,540; frozen fish 1,300 metric tons. Construction (value added; 1981): CV Esc876,600,000. Energy production (consumption): electricity (kW-hr; 1982) 12,000,000 (12,000,000); coal, none

(none); crude petroleum, n.a. (n.a.); petroleum products (metric tons; 1982) n.a. (39,000); natural gas, n.a. (n.a.).
Gross national product (at current market prices; 1981): U.S.$97,400,000 (U.S.$325 per capita).

Origin of gross domestic product (current prices)

	1981 in value CV Esc'000,000	% of total value	labour force	% of labour force
Agriculture, fishing	560.0	17.6	58,000	55.8
Mining	9.0	0.3	‡	‡
Manufacturing	125.0§	3.9§	1,700	1.6
Construction	645.0	20.3	‡	‡
Public utilities	§	§	‡	‡
Pub. admin., defense	550.0	17.3	‡	‡
Trade, finance, other ‖	1,290.0	40.6	44,300	42.6
TOTAL	3,179.0	100.0	104,000	100.0

Persons economically active (1982): total 107,000 (35.4%); female participation in labour force, n.a.; unemployed, n.a.

Price and earnings indexes (1975 = 100)

	1976	1977	1978	1979	1980	1981
Consumer price index	101.2	108.3	122.7	131.2	150.4	167.7
Monthly earnings index	...	...	...	...	...	...

Household income and expenditure. Average household size (1980) 4.3; average annual income per household: n.a.; source of income: n.a.; expenditure: n.a.
Land use (1981): forested 0.2%; meadows and pastures 6.2%; agricultural and under permanent cultivation 9.9%; other 83.7%.

Foreign trade

Balance of trade (current prices)

	1977	1978	1979	1980	1981
CV Esc'000,000	−1,210	−1,833	−1,895	−2,743	−3,300
% of total	89.0%	92.4%	91.1%	99.9%	91.5%

Imports (1981): CV Esc3,451,700,000 (mineral products 18.4%, foodstuffs and beverages 13.8%, vegetable products 13.8%, machinery and electrical equipment 10.6%, transport equipment 6.7%, chemical products 5.8%, base metals 5.8%, textiles and textile products 4.6%, fats and oils 4.1%). *Major import sources:* Portugal 39.9%; The Netherlands 9.9%; United Kingdom 4.9%; the United States 4.9%.
Exports (1981): CV Esc151,479,000 (vegetable products 57.2%, animals and animal products 14.0%, textiles and textile products 9.7%, foodstuff and beverages 9.2%, mineral products 7.9%, skins and hides 0.7%). *Major export destinations:* Portugal 60.6%; Angola 9.4%; Central African Republic 4.3%; Zaire 2.0%; Guinea-Bissau 0.8%; United Kingdom 0.4%.

Transport and communications

Transport. Railroads: none. Roads (1982): total length 1,398 mi, 2,250 km (paved 29%). Vehicles (1981): passenger cars 4,000; trucks and buses 1,343. Merchant marine (1983): vessels (100 gross tons and over) 22; total deadweight tonnage 20,905. Air transport (1982)¶: passenger arrivals 21,200, passenger departures 23,106; metric tons of cargo loaded 104.7, metric tons of cargo unloaded 615.3; airports (1984) with scheduled flights 8.
Communications. Daily newspapers: none. Radios (1983): total number of receivers 46,857 (1 per 6.2 persons). Television: none. Telephones (1981): 1,739 (1 per 168 persons).

Education and health

Education (1982–83)

	schools	teachers	students	student/ teacher ratio
Primary (age 7–10)	436	1,459	50,000	34.3
Secondary (age 10–17)	16	603	10,454	17.3
Voc., teacher tr.	4	76	923	12.1

College graduates: n.a. *Literacy* (1981): total population literate 78,839 (49.3%); males literate 43,814 (55.3%); females literate 35,025 (43.4%).
Health (1980): physicians 51 (1 per 5,664 persons); hospital beds 632 (1 per 457 persons).
Food (1978–80): daily per capita caloric intake 2,756 (vegetable products 89.1%, animal products 10.9%); 117% of FAO recommended minimum requirement.

Military

Total active duty personnel (1984): 1,100 (army 90.9%; navy 6.8%; air force 2.3%). *Military expenditure as percent of GNP* (1982): 2.2% (world 6%); per capita expenditure U.S.$7.

---

*Preliminary. †Detail does not add to total given because of rounding. ‡Included with trade, finance, and other. §Public utilities included with manufacturing. ‖ Includes transportation and communication. ¶Data for Amílcar Cabral airport only.

Central African Republic

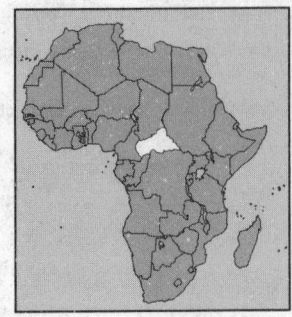

Official name: République Centrafricaine (Central African Republic).
Form of government: military dictatorship with one ruling body (Military Committee for National Recovery [23]).
Head of state and government: Chairman.
Capital: Bangui.
Official language: French.
Official religion: none.
Monetary unit: 1 CFA franc (CFAF) = 100 centimes; valuation (Oct. 29, 1984) 1 U.S.$ = CFAF470.6; 1 £ = CFAF568.0.

Area and population

Prefectures	Capitals	area sq mi	area sq km	population 1982 estimate
Bamingui-Bangoran	Ndélé	22,471	58,200	30,000
Bangui	Bangui	26	67	320,000
Basse-Kotto	Mobaye	6,797	17,604	185,000
Gribingui-Économique	Kaga-Bandoro	7,720	19,996	85,000
Haut-Mbomou	Obo	21,440	55,530	50,000
Haute-Kotto	Bria	33,456	86,650	225,000
Haute-Sangha	Berbérati	11,661	30,203	40,000
Kemo-Gribingui	Sibut	6,642	17,204	75,000
Lobaye	Mbaiki	7,427	19,235	155,000
Mbomou	Bangassou	23,610	61,150	130,000
Nana-Mambere	Bouar	10,270	26,600	190,000
Ombella-Mpoko	Bimbo	12,292	31,835	125,000
Ouaka	Bambari	19,266	49,900	205,000
Ouham	Bossangoa	19,402	50,250	260,000
Ouham-Pendé	Bozoum	12,394	32,100	240,000
Sangha-Économique	Nola	7,495	19,412	25,000
Vakaga	Birao	17,954	46,500	60,000
TOTAL		240,324*	622,436	2,400,000

Source: Official government figures; Britannica estimate.

Demography

Density (1984): persons per sq mi 10.8, persons per sq km 4.2.
Urban–rural (1981): urban 18.5%; rural 81.5%.
Sex distribution (1980): male 47.86%; female 52.14%.
Age breakdown (1981): under 15, 42.4%; 15–59, 54.1%; 60 and over, 3.5%.
Population projection: (1990) 2,965,000; (2000) 3,736,000.
Doubling time: 28 years.
Ethnic composition (1978): Banda 44.6%; Baya 14.3%; Ngbandi 10.7%; Azande 9.6%; Mbaka 4.3%; Sara 3.9%; Kare 2.5%; other 10.1%.
Religious affiliation (1980): Protestant 50.0%; Roman Catholic 33.1%; tribal 12.0%; Muslim 3.2%; Bahá'í 0.3%; other 1.4%.
Major cities (1982): Bangui 387,143; Bambari 43,618; Bouar 40,794; Berberati 38,174; Bossangoa 35,205.

Vital statistics

Birth rate per 1,000 population (1980): 35.5 (world avg. 30.0); legitimate, n.a.; illegitimate, n.a.
Death rate per 1,000 population (1980): 8.5 (world avg. 12.0).
Natural increase rate per 1,000 population (1980): 27.0 (world avg. 18.0).
Total fertility rate (avg. births per childbearing woman; 1981): 5.5.
Marriage rate per 1,000 population: n.a.
Divorce rate per 1,000 population: n.a.
Infant mortality rate per 1,000 live births (1981): 146.3.
Life expectancy at birth (1980–85): male 46.9 years; female 50.1 years.
Major causes of death per 100,000 population (1978): infectious and parasitic diseases 59.0.

National economy

Budget (1982). Revenue: CFAF29,995,000,000 (indirect taxes 52.4%, non-fiscal receipts 21.1%, direct taxes 20.3%). Expenditures: CFAF38,203,000,-000 (education and culture 13.9%, defense 8.3%, repayment of public debt 8.1%).
Public debt (external, outstanding; 1982): U.S.$222,000,000.
Tourism (1981): receipts from visitors U.S.$3,000,000; expenditures by nationals abroad, n.a.
Production (metric tons except as noted). Agriculture, forestry, fishing (1982): roots and tubers 1,255,000, cassava 1,028,000, peanuts (groundnuts) in shell 128,000, bananas 84,000, plantains 62,000, seed cotton 57,000, millet 50,000, corn (maize) 40,000, coffee 18,000, rice 16,000; livestock (number of live animals) 1,313,000 cattle, 988,000 goats, 140,000 pigs, 87,000 sheep, 1,637,000 chickens; roundwood 3,090,000 cu m; fish catch 13,000. Mining and quarrying (1983): diamonds 200,000 carats; gold 48 kg. Manufacturing (1980): footwear 473,000 pairs; motorcycles 7,000 units; bicycles 4,000 units; beer 283,000 hectolitres; soft drinks 38,000 hectolitres; woven cotton fabrics 3,000,000 sq m†; blankets 41,000 units†. Construction: n.a. Energy production (consumption): electricity (kW-hr; 1982) 68,000,000 (68,000,-000); coal, none (n.a.); crude petroleum, none (n.a.); petroleum products (metric tons; 1982) 68,000 (63,000); natural gas, none (n.a.).

Gross national product (at current market prices; 1981): U.S.$560,000,000 (U.S.$235 per capita).

Origin of gross domestic product (current prices)

	1981 in value CFAF '000,000	% of total value	labour force	% of labour force
Agriculture	69.7	36.9	1,094,000	86.8
Mining	4.1	2.2	‡	‡
Manufacturing	10.5	5.6	50,400‡	4.0
Construction	8.1 ‖	4.3	‡	‡
Trade	35.7 ‖	18.9 ‖	§	§
Public utilities	2.5	1.3	‡	‡
Transportation and communication	3.4	1.8	§	§
Finance	‖	‖	§	§
Pub. admin., defense	23.2	12.3	§	§
Services	¶	¶	100,900§	8.0§
Other	31.6¶	16.7¶	15,700	1.2
TOTAL	188.8	100.0	1,261,000	100.0

Persons economically active (1982): total 1,283,000 (53.3%); female participation in the labour force 597,700♀ (47.7%); unemployed, n.a.

Price and earnings indexes (1980 = 100)

	1977	1978	1979	1980	1981	1982	1983
Consumer price index	68.3	74.5	85.4	100.0	112.6	127.5	144.5
Earnings index	...	...	...	...	...	...	...

Household income and expenditure. Average household size (1980) 4.3; average annual income per household CFAF91,985 (U.S.$435); source of income: n.a.; expenditure: n.a.
Land use (1981): forested 63.7%; meadows and pastures 4.8%; agricultural and under permanent cultivation 3.1%; other 28.4%.

Foreign trade

Balance of trade (current prices)

	1977	1978	1979	1980	1981
CFAF'000,000	+8,260	+6,738	+5,713	+11,300	+1,595
% of total	26.0%	26.3%	20.3%	30.2%	3.9%

Imports (1980): CFAF13,084,000,000 (machinery and equipment 33.9%, food 20.9%, chemicals and plastics 12.2%, textiles 8.4%, fuels and lubricants 1.8%). *Major import sources:* France 61%; Japan 7%.
Exports (1980): CFAF24,384,000,000 (diamonds 36.3%, wood 28.8%, coffee 27.4%, cotton 7.5%). *Major export destinations:* France 52%; Belgium–Luxembourg 14%; Israel 8%; United States 5%.

Transport and communications

Transport. Railroads (1983): none. Roads (1982): total length 14,018 mi, 22,560 km (paved 1%). Vehicles (1978): passenger cars 14,200; trucks and buses 4,000. Merchant marine: vessels (100 gross tons and over) none. Air transport (1982): passenger-mi 105,804,000, passenger-km 170,276,000; short ton-mi cargo 20,677,000, metric ton-km cargo 30,188,000; airport (1984) with scheduled flights 1.
Communications. Daily newspapers: none. Radios (1980): total number of receivers 120,000 (1 per 19.7 persons). Television (1980): total number of receivers 700 (1 per 3,374 persons). Telephones (1981): 2,755 (1 per 809 persons).

Education and health

Education (1979–80)

	schoolsδ	teachersδ	students	student/ teacher ratio
Primary (age 6–11)	797	3,690	247,782	...
Secondary (age 12–18)	...	462	33,189	...
Voc., teacher tr.	...	223	3,617	...
Higher	...	279	2,094	...

College graduates per 100,000 population (1977): 4.4. *Literacy* (1980): total population literate 447,800 (38.5%); males literate 322,800 (58.8%); females literate 125,000 (20.4%).
Health: physicians (1980) 108 (1 per 21,296 persons); hospital beds (1977) 2,983 (1 per 689 persons).
Food (1978–80): daily per capita caloric intake 2,161 (vegetable products 93.2%, animal products 6.8%); 96% of FAO recommended minimum requirement.

Military

Total active duty personnel (1983): 2,300 (army 87.0%; navy, none; air force 13.0%). *Military expenditure as percent of GNP* (1982): 2.1% (world 6.0); per capita expenditure U.S.$6.

*Detail does not add to total given because of rounding. †1978. ‡Mining, construction, and public utilities are included with manufacturing. §Trade, transportation and communication, finance, and public administration and defense are included with services. ‖ Finance is included with trade. ¶Services are included with other. ♀1981. δ1977–78.

Chad

Official name: République du Tchad
 (Republic of Chad).
Form of government: military
 regime with no political parties or
 legislative bodies.
Head of state and government:
 President.
Capital: N'Djamena.
Official language: French.
Official religion: none.
Monetary unit: 1 CFA franc
 (CFAF) = 100 centimes; valuation
 (Oct. 29, 1984) 1 U.S.$ = CFAF470.59;
 1 £ = CFAF568.00.

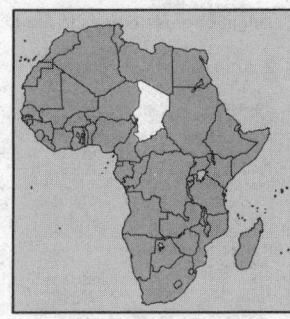

Area and population

Préfectures	Capitals	area sq mi	area sq km	population 1979 estimate
Batha	Ati	34,285	88,800	354,000
Biltine	Biltine	18,090	46,850	175,000
Borkou-Ennedi-Tibesti	Faya	231,795	600,350	88,000
Chari-Baguirmi	N'Djamena	32,010	82,910	676,000
Guéra	Mongo	22,760	58,950	207,000
Kanem	Mao	44,215	114,520	200,000
Lac	Bol	8,620	22,320	135,000
Logone Occidental	Moundou	3,355	8,695	295,000
Logone Oriental	Doba	10,825	28,035	307,000
Mayo-Kebbi	Bongor	11,625	30,105	684,000
Moyen-Chari	Sarh	17,445	45,180	524,000
Ouaddaï	Abéché	29,435	76,240	347,000
Salamat	Am Timan	24,325	63,000	107,000
Tandjilé	Laï	6,965	18,045	302,000
TOTAL		495,755*	1,284,000	4,401,000

Source: Official government figures.

Demography

Density (1984): persons per sq mi 9.8, persons per sq km 3.8.
Urban–rural (1980): urban 17.8%; rural 82.2%.
Sex distribution (1980): male 48.50%; female 51.50%.
Age breakdown (1980): under 15, 41.8%; 15–29, 26.1%; 30–44, 16.0%; 45–59,
 10.3%; 60–74, 4.9%; 75 and over, 0.9%.
Population projection: (1990) 5,558,000; (2000) 7,063,000.
Doubling time: 33 years.
Ethnic composition (1978): Sudanic Arab 30.2%; Bagirmi, Sara, and Kreish
 25.5%; Teda 7.7%; Mbum 6.8%; Masalit 6.5%; Tama 6.3%; Mubu 4.2%;
 Kanuri 2.3%; Hausa 2.2%; other 8.3%.
Religious affiliation (1980): Muslim 44.0%; Christian 33.0%, of which nom-
 inal only 15.5%, Protestant 8.8%, Roman Catholic 8.3%; traditional beliefs
 22.8%; other 0.2%.
Major cities (1979 est.): N'Djamena 303,000; Moundou 66,000; Sarh 65,000;
 Abéché 54,000; Kélo 27,000.

Vital statistics

Birth rate per 1,000 population (1981): 42.9 (world avg. 29.0); legitimate,
 n.a.; illegitimate, n.a.
Death rate per 1,000 population (1981): 21.9 (world avg. 12.0).
Natural increase rate per 1,000 population (1981): 21.0 (world avg. 17.0).
Total fertility rate (avg. births per childbearing woman; 1981): 5.5.
Marriage rate per 1,000 population: n.a.
Divorce rate per 1,000 population: n.a.
Infant mortality rate per 1,000 live births (1981): 146.3.
Life expectancy at birth (1981): male 41.5 years; female 43.9 years.
Major causes of death: n.a.

National economy

Budget† (1978). Revenue: CFAF17,084,000,000 (indirect taxes 55.9%, of
 which customs receipts 47.0%, direct taxes 21.4%). Expenditures: CFAF17,-
 084,000,000 (defense 39.0%, education 11.6%, community projects 9.5%,
 health 6.6%).
Public debt (external, outstanding; 1982): U.S.$189,400,000.
Tourism (1981): receipts from visitors U.S.$2,000,000; expenditures by na-
 tionals abroad, n.a.
Production (metric tons except as noted). Agriculture, forestry, fishing
 (1982): millet 600,000, roots and tubers 417,000, cassavas 197,000, peanuts
 (groundnuts) 118,000, cotton seed 73,000, seed cotton 72,000, rice 47,000,
 lint cotton 43,000, dry beans 42,000, sweet potatoes 39,000, mangoes 31,000,
 dates 27,000, raw sugar 20,000; livestock (number of live animals) 3,800,-
 000 cattle, 2,358,000 sheep, 2,358,000 goats, 3,330,000 chickens; roundwood
 7,944,000 cu m; fish catch 115,000. Mining and quarrying (1982): clay
 and natron. Manufacturing (1980): beef and veal 28,000; mutton and
 lamb 16,000; salted, dried, or smoked fish 20,000‡; refined sugar 17,000;
 wheat flour 4,000; woven cotton fabrics 15,600,000 metres; beer 163,000
 hectolitres; cigarettes 349,000,000 units. Construction: n.a. Energy production (consumption): electricity (kW-hr; 1982) 65,000,000 (65,000,000); coal,
 none (n.a.); crude petroleum, none (n.a.); petroleum products (metric tons;
 1982) none (67,000); natural gas, none (n.a.).
Gross national product (at current market prices; 1981): U.S.$550,000,000
 (U.S.$125 per capita).
Household income and expenditure. Average household size (1980) 3.9;

average annual income per household CFAF96,806 (U.S.$458); source of
 income: n.a.; expenditure: n.a.
Land use (1981): forested 16.3%; meadows and pastures 35.7%; agricultural
 and under permanent cultivation 2.5%; other 45.5%.

Origin of gross domestic product (current prices)

	1981 in value CFAF'000,000	% of total value	labour force	% of labour force
Agriculture	69.2	64.4	1,438,000	83.1
Mining	0.2	0.2	§	§
Manufacturing	3.9	3.6	121,000	7.0
Construction	2.3	2.1	§	§
Trade	28.5	26.6	‖	‖
Public utilities	0.9	0.8	§	§
Transportation and communication	2.5	2.3	‖	‖
Finance	¶	¶	‖	‖
Pub. admin., defense	¶	¶	171,000	9.9
Services	¶	¶		
TOTAL	107.5	100.0	1,730,000	100.0

Persons economically active (1982): total 1,771,000 (38.1%); female participation in the labour force 329,000♀ (23.2%); unemployed, n.a.

Price and earnings indexes (1970 = 100)

	1972	1973	1974	1975	1976	1977	1978δ
Consumer price index	109.3	115.3	128.3	148.4	153.3	166.2	190.9

Foreign trade□

Balance of trade (current prices)

	1977	1978	1979	1980	1981	1982
CFAF'000,000	−20,288	−26,705	+644	−534	−6,684	−16,733
% of total	27.9%	37.4%	1.7%	1.7%	12.9%	30.6%

Imports (1975): CFAF 28,325,200,000 (machinery and transport equipment
 28.8%, of which nonelectrical machinery 13.6%, road motor vehicles 7.9%,
 trucks 4.9%; basic manufactures 18.4%, of which textile yarns and fabrics 5.1%; chemicals 16.4%, of which pesticides 5.6%; petroleum products
 14.1%; raw and refined sugar 4.7%). *Major import sources:* France 40.7%;
 Nigeria 10.7%; The Netherlands 7.1%; United States 5.8%; Cameroon 5.7%.
Exports (1975): CFAF 10,103,300,000 (raw cotton 65.5%; kerosine 7.0%;
 frozen bovine meat 6.8%; salted and dried fish 3.8%). *Major export destinations* (based on incomplete statistics): Nigeria 20.4%; France 5.9%; Congo
 5.5%; Niger 4.1%.

Transport and communications

Transport. Railroads: none. Roads (1976): total length 19,092 mi, 30,725 km
 (paved 1%). Vehicles (1982): passenger cars 7,000; trucks and buses 5,000.
 Merchant marine vessels (100 gross tons and over) none. Air transport
 (1981)◇: local passenger arrivals and departures, 344; cargo loaded and
 unloaded, n.a.; airport (1984) with scheduled flights 1.
Communications. Daily newspapers (1983): total number 3; total circulation
 1,500△; circulation per 1,000 population, n.a. Radios (1983): total number
 of receivers 75,000 (1 per 63 persons). Television (1983): none. Telephones
 (1981): 900 (1 per 5,000 persons).

Education and health

Education (1976–77)

	schools	teachers	students	student/ teacher ratio
Primary (age 6–12)	783	2,610	210,882†	77.0
Secondary (age 13–19)	...	590	18,382	31.2
Voc., teacher tr.	...	...	1,198	...
Higher⊙	1	85	550	6.5

College graduates per 100,000 population (students graduating; 1976): 5.0.
Literacy (1980): total population literate 466,500 (17.8%); males literate
 459,700 (35.6%); females literate 6,800 (0.5%).
Health: physicians (1980) 94 (1 per 47,530 persons); hospital beds (1977)
 3,553 (1 per 1,185 persons).
Food (1978–80): daily per capita caloric intake 1,808 (vegetable products 92.1%, animal products 7.9%); 76% of FAO recommended minimum
 requirement.

Military

Total active duty personnel (1983): 4,200 (army 95.2%; navy, none; air force
 4.8%). *Military expenditure as percent of GNP* (1979): 4.7% (world 5.5%);
 per capita expenditure U.S.$4.

*Detail does not add to total given because of rounding. †The budget for 1983
balanced at CFAF36,000,000. ‡1979. §Mining, construction, and public utilities are
included with manufacturing. ‖ Trade, transportation and communication, finance,
public administration, and defense are included with services. ¶Finance, public administration, defense, and services are included with trade. ♀1977. δThird quarter.
□Imports CIF; exports FOB. ◇The airport at N'Djamena is underutilized because
of the political and military unrest in Chad. △Partial circulation only. †Excluding
Islâmic private education (9,453 students in 1975). ⊙1981–82.

Chile

Official name: República de Chile.
 (Republic of Chile).
Form of government: military regime.
Head of state and government:
 President (general) assisted by a four-
 member junta.
Capital: Santiago.
Official language: Spanish.
Official religion: none.
Monetary unit: 1 peso (Ch$) = 100
 centavos; valuation (Oct.29, 1984) 1
 U.S.$ = Ch$117.23; 1 £ = Ch$141.50.

Area and population

Regions	Capitals	area sq mi	area sq km	population 1982 census*
Tarapacá	Iquique	22,422	58,073	273,427
Antofagasta	Antofagasta	48,381	125,306	341,203
Atacama	Copiapó	30,219	78,268	183,071
Coquimbo	La Serena	15,308	39,647	419,178
Valparaíso	Valparaíso	6,220	16,109	1,204,693
Libertador General Bernardo O'Higgins	Rancagua	7,024	18,193	584,989
Maule	Talca	11,783	30,518	723,224
Bío-Bío	Concepción	14,218	36,824	1,516,552
Araucanía	Temuco	12,263	31,760	692,924
Los Lagos	Puerto Montt	25,904	67,090	843,430
Aisén, del General Carlos Ibáñez del Campo	Coihaique	42,085	108,999	65,478
Magallanes y de la Antártica Chilena	Punta Arenas	43,363†	112,310†	132,333†
Región Metropolitana de Santiago	Santiago	5,331	13,808	4,294,938
TOTAL		284,520†	736,905†	11,275,440‡

Demography

Density (1984): persons per sq mi 41.8, persons per sq km 16.1.
Urban–rural (1982): urban 81.0%; rural 19.0%.
Sex distribution (1982): male 48.97%; female 51.03%.
Age breakdown (1982): under 15, 31.9%; 15–29, 29.1%; 30–44, 19.1%; 45–59, 11.7%; 60–74, 6.3%; 75 and over, 1.9%.
Population projection: (1990) 13,128,000; (2000) 15,511,000.
Doubling time: 41 years.
Ethnic composition (1980): mestizo 92%; Indian (mostly Mapuche) 6%; others (mainly European) 2%.
Religious affiliation (1982 est.): Roman Catholic 79.2%; Protestant 6.0%; atheist and non-religious 2.0%; other 12.8%.
Major urban areas (1984): Greater Santiago 4,225,300; Greater Valparaíso 718,100; Greater Concepción 522,700.

Vital statistics

Birth rate per 1,000 population (1982): 23.9 (world avg. 29.0); (1980) legitimate 72.4%, illegitimate 27.6%.
Death rate per 1,000 population (1982): 6.1 (world avg. 11.0).
Natural increase rate per 1,000 population (1982): 17.8 (world avg. 18.0).
Total fertility rate (avg. births per childbearing woman; 1981): 3.0.
Marriage rate per 1,000 population (1980): 7.7.
Divorce rate per 1,000 population (1980): 0.3.
Infant mortality rate per 1,000 live births (1982): 23.6.
Life expectancy at birth (1981): male 65.4 years; female 70.1 years.
Major causes of death per 100,000 population (1980): circulatory diseases 176.8; malignant neoplasms (cancers) 102.0; respiratory diseases 63.3.

National economy

Budget (1981). Revenue: Ch$391,688,000,000§ (tax revenue 83.1%, of which taxes on goods and services 40.9%, taxes on income and profits 16.9%, social security contributions 15.3%, nontax revenue 16.9%). Expenditures: Ch$382,859,000,000 (social security and welfare 37.9%; education 14.4%; defense 12.0%; economic services 11.4%; health 6.4%).
Public debt (external, outstanding; 1982): U.S.$13,964,700,000.
Tourism: receipts from visitors (1982) U.S.$123,000,000; expenditures by nationals abroad (1981): U.S.$260,000,000.
Production (metric tons except as noted). Agriculture, forestry, fishing (1983): grapes 1,000,000, sugarbeets 963,000 ‖, potatoes 684,000, wheat 586,000, corn (maize) 512,000, apples 355,000, tomatoes 160,000, oats 146,-000; livestock (number of live animals) 6,308,000 sheep ‖ , 3,865,000 cattle, 1,260,000 pigs; roundwood 12,751,000 cu m ‖ ; fish catch 3,673,000 ‖ , of which pilchard (sardines) 1,780,000 ‖ , jack mackerel 1,495,000 ‖ . Mining and quarrying (1982): iron ore 6,470,000; copper 1,255,100; nitrates 577,000; molybdenum 20,048; iodine 2,596; silver 12,288,000 troy oz.; gold 543,-573 troy oz. Manufacturing (value added in '000,000 of Ch$; 1979): food products 30,042; nonferrous metals 25,987; beverages 9,291; textiles 9,028; paper and paper products 8,830; refining of petroleum 8,178; iron and steel 7,869; tobacco products 7,753. Construction¶ (value in '000,000 of Ch$; 1981) residential 31,957; nonresidential 10,122. Energy production (consumption): electricity (kW-hr; 1982) 11,871,000,000 (11,871,000,000); coal (metric tons; 1982) 1,025,000 (1,193,000); crude petroleum (barrels; 1982) 15,627,000 (26,127,000); petroleum products (metric tons; 1982) 3,537,000 (4,818,000); natural gas (cu m; 1982) 884,435,000 (884,435,000).
Gross national product (at current market prices; 1982): U.S.$22,061,000,000 (U.S.$1,920 per capita).

Origin of gross domestic product (current prices)

	1982 in value Ch$ '000,000	% of total value	labour force⁹	% of labour force
Agriculture	75,604	6.2	458,900	16.2
Mining	75,080	6.1	51,700	1.8
Manufacturing	240,493	19.6	356,200	12.6
Construction	61,698	5.0	80,400	2.8
Trade	226,081	18.4	489,400	17.3
Transportation and communication	57,604	4.7	173,900	6.2
Utilities	36,977	3.0	24,500	0.9
Finance	∂	∂	100,600	3.6
Pub. admin., defense, and services	∂	∂	1,086,800	38.5
Other	455,163∂	37.0∂	2,100	0.1
TOTAL	1,228,700	100.0	2,824,500	100.0

Persons economically active (1982): total 3,503,600 (30.5%); female (1981) 1,060,900 (24.7%); unemployed 679,100 (19.4%).

Price and earnings indexes (1980 = 100)

	1978	1979	1980	1981	1982	1983	1984□
Consumer price index	55.5	74.0	100.0	119.7	131.6	167.4	193.6
Monthly earnings index	46.1	68.1	100.0	130.3	142.9	162.5	192.3

Household income and expenditure. Average household size (1982) 5.1◊; income per household, n.a.; expenditure (1978): food 41.9%; housing 13.3%; transportation and communication 11.8%; recreation and education 8.2%; household goods 7.8%; clothing and footwear 7.6%.
Land use (1981): forested 20.7%; meadows and pastures 15.9%; agricultural and under permanent cultivation 7.4%; other 56.0%.

Foreign trade

Balance of trade (current prices)△

	1978	1979	1980	1981	1982	1983
U.S.$'000,000	−524	−324	−453	−2,458	+182	+1,082
% of total	9.6%	4.0%	4.6%	24.1%	2.5%	16.4%

Imports (1982): U.S.$3,528,000,000 (technical and electrical equipment 19.6%, mineral fuels [mostly crude oil, gasoline, and diesel oil] 18.5%, transport equipment 9.2%, vegetable products 8.6%, chemicals 8.4%, textiles 6.8%). *Major import sources:* United States 23.9%; Venezuela 6.8%; Brazil 6.7%; Japan 6.0%; West Germany 5.6%.
Exports (1982): U.S.$3,710,000,000 (copper 46.7%, fruits and vegetables 7.5%, fish meal 6.9%, base metals manufactures 6.6%, paper and paper products 5.9%, iron ore and concentrates 4.3%). *Major export destinations:* United States 20.9%; Japan 11.5%; West Germany 11.3%; Brazil 8.1%; United Kingdom 5.4%.

Transport and communications

Transport. Railroads (1982): route length 4,860 mi, 7,821 km; passenger-mi 933,700,000, passenger-km 1,502,700,000; short ton-mi cargo 909,000,000, metric ton-km cargo 1,327,100,000. Roads (1981): total length 48,482 mi, 78,025 km (paved 12%). Vehicles (1983) passenger cars 620,000; trucks and buses 257,000. Merchant marine (1983): vessels (100 gross tons and over) 200; total deadweight tonnage 745,899. Air transport (1981): passenger-mi 1,411,666,000, passenger-km 2,271,860,000; short ton-mi cargo 205,362,000, metric ton-km cargo 299,824,000; airports (1984) with scheduled flights 13.
Communications. Daily newspapers (1983): total number 66; total circulation 1,407,300; circulation per 1,000 population 120. Radios (1983): total number of receivers 3,250,000 (1 per 3.6 persons). Television (1983): total number of receivers 2,643,000 (1 per 4.4 persons). Telephones (1982): 595,-108 (1 per 19 persons).

Education and health

Education (1983)

	schools	teachers	students	student/ teacher ratio
Primary (age 6–13)	8,858	...	2,139,155	...
Secondary (age 14–17)	1,282	...	541,739	...
Vocational	347	...	143,689	...
Higher	24	...	125,363	...

College graduates per 100,000 population (students graduating; 1981): 177.
 Literacy (1983): total population literate 8,681,900 (95.6%); males literate 3,933,000 (95.0%)†; females literate 4,024,200 (93.8%)†.
Health (1981): physicians 10,877 (1 per 1,037 persons); hospital beds 37,547 (1 per 301 persons).
Food (1978–80): daily per capita caloric intake 2,738 (vegetable products 84.2%, animal products 15.8%); 112% of FAO recommended minimum.

Military

Total active duty personnel (1982): 97,000 (army 54.6%; navy 29.9%; air force 15.5%). *Military expenditure as percent of GNP* (1982): 4.8% (world 6.0%); per capita expenditure: U.S.$121.

*Preliminary. †Excludes 490,243 sq mi (1,269,723 sq km) of Antártica Chilena, portions of which are disputed with the United Kingdom and Argentina. ‡Includes 1,368 residents of Antártica Chilena not shown separately. §Excludes capital revenue totaling Ch$18,238,000,000 and grants totaling Ch$22,620,000,000. ‖ 1982. ¶Includes authorized private construction only. ⁹Employed persons only. ∂Other includes finance, public administration, defense, and services. □May. ◊Based on a sample survey of about two-thirds of the population. △Imports, c.i.f.; exports, f.o.b. †Calculated from the 1981 literacy rate of 94.4%.

China

Official name: Chung-hua Jen-min Kung-ho-kuo (People's Republic of China).
Form of government: single-party people's republic with one legislative house (National People's Congress [2,978*]).
Chief of state: President.
Head of government: Premier.
Capital: Peking (Beijing).
Official language: Mandarin Chinese.
Official religion: none.
Monetary unit: 1 Renminbi (yuan) (Y) = 10 jiao = 100 fen; valuation (Oct. 29, 1984) 1 U.S.$ = Y2.64; 1 £ = Y3.19.

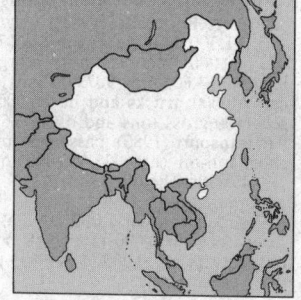

Area and population†

Provinces	Capitals	area sq mi	area sq km	population 1982 census
Anhwei (Anhui)	Ho-fei (Hefei)	54,000	139,900	49,665,724
Chekiang (Zhejiang)	Hangchow (Hangzhou)	39,300	101,800	38,884,603
Fukien (Fujian)	Foochow (Fuzhou)	47,500	123,100	25,873,259
Heilungkiang (Heilongjiang)	Harbin (Harbin)	179,000	463,600	32,665,546
Honan (Henan)	Cheng-chou (Zhengzhou)	64,500	167,000	74,422,739
Hopeh (Hebei)	Shih-chia-chuang (Shijazhuang)	78,200	202,700	53,005,875
Hunan (Hunan)	Ch'ang-sha (Changsha)	81,300	210,500	54,008,851
Hupeh (Hubei)	Wu-han (Wuhan)	72,400	187,500	47,804,150
Kansu (Gansu)	Lan-chou (Lanzhou)	141,500	366,500	19,569,261
Kiangsi (Jiangxi)	Nan-ch'ang (Nanchang)	63,600	164,800	33,184,827
Kiangsu (Jiangsu)	Nanking (Nanjing)	39,600	102,600	60,521,114
Kirin (Jilin)	Ch'ang-ch'un (Changchun)	72,200	187,000	22,560,053
Kwangtung (Guangdong)	Canton (Guangzhou)	89,300	231,400	59,299,220
Kweichow (Guizhou)	Kuei-yang (Guiyang)	67,200	174,000	28,552,997
Liaoning (Liaoning)	Shen-yang (Shenyang)	58,300	151,000	35,721,693
Shansi (Shanxi)	T'ai-yüan (Taiyuan)	60,700	157,100	25,291,389
Shantung (Shandong)	Tsinan (Jinan)	59,200	153,300	74,419,054
Shensi (Shaanxi)	Sian (Xi'an)	75,600	195,800	28,904,423
Szechwan (Sichuan)	Ch'eng-tu (Chengdu)	219,700	569,000	99,713,310
Tsinghai (Qinghai)	Hsi-ning (Xining)	278,400	721,000	3,895,706
Yunnan (Yunnan)	K'un-ming (Kunming)	168,400	436,200	32,553,817
Autonomous regions				
Inner Mongolia (Nei Monggol)	Hu-ho-hao-t'e (Hohhot)	454,600	1,177,500	19,274,279
Kwangsi Chuang (Guangxi Zhuang)	Nan-ning (Nanning)	85,100	220,400	36,420,960
Ningxia Hui (Ningsia Hui)	Yin-ch'uan (Yinchuan)	25,600	66,400	3,895,578
Sinkiang Uighur (Xinjiang Uygur)	Urumchi (Urumqi)	635,900	1,646,900	13,081,681
Tibet (Xizang)	Lhasa (Lhasa)	471,700	1,221,600	1,892,393
Municipalities				
Peking (Beijing)		6,500	16,800	9,230,687
Shanghai (Shanghai)		2,400	6,200	11,859,748
Tientsin (Tianjin)		4,400	11,300	7,764,141
TOTAL		3,696,100‡	9,572,900	1,003,937,078

Source: Official government figures.

Demography

Density (1984): persons per sq mi 290.9, persons per sq km 112.3.
Urban–rural (1985): urban 28.4%; rural 71.6%.
Sex distribution (1985): male 51.04%; female 48.96%.
Age breakdown (1982): under 15, 33.6%; 15–29, 29.1%; 30–44, 17.5%; 45–59, 12.2%; 60–74, 6.3%; 75 and over 1.3%.
Population projection: (1990) 1,127,636,000; (2000) 1,257,298,000.
Doubling time: 60 years.
Ethnic composition (1982): Han 93.3%; Chuang 1.3%; Hui 0.7%; Uighur 0.6%; Yi 0.5%; Miao 0.5%; Manchu 0.4%; Tibetan 0.4%; other 2.3%.
Religious affiliation (mid-1980s): non-religious 59.2%; Chinese folk-religionists 20.1%; atheists 12.0%; Buddhists 6.0%; Muslims 2.4%; other 0.3%.
Major cities (1982): Shanghai 6,270,000; Peking (Beijing) 5,550,000; Tientsin (Tianjin) 5,130,000; Shenyang 4,020,000; Wu-han 3,230,000; Canton (Guangzhou) 3,120,000; Chungking 2,650,000; Harbin 2,550,000; Ch'eng-tu 2,470,000; Sian 2,180,000.
Place of birth: n.a.
Mobility: n.a.
Households (1982). Average rural household size 5.5; urban household size 4.1. Family households: 220,100,755 (99.5%), collective 1,073,010 (0.5%).
Immigration: n.a.

Vital statistics

Birth rate per 1,000 population (1983): 18.6 (world avg. 29.0); legitimate, n.a.; illegitimate, n.a.
Death rate per 1,000 population (1983): 7.1 (world avg. 11.0).
Natural increase rate per 1,000 population (1983): 11.5 (world avg. 18.0).
Total fertility rate (avg. births per childbearing woman; 1980–85): 2.5.
Marriage rate per 1,000 population: n.a.
Divorce rate per 1,000 population: n.a.
Infant mortality rate per 1,000 live births (1978–79): 56.
Life expectancy at birth (1980–85): male 68.5 years; female 71.1 years.
Major causes of death per 100,000 population (1973–75): respiratory diseases 117.9; malignant tumours 77.1; trauma, toxicosis, and accidents 70.6;

diseases of the digestive system 66.8; infectious diseases 63.8; diseases of the circulatory system 62.6; infant diseases 46.4; tuberculosis 43.3; heart disease 24.9.

Social indicators

Educational attainment (1982). Percent of adult population having: primary education 39.9%, junior middle 20.0%, senior middle 7.5%, some college 0.2%, university or college 0.5%, semi-literate 31.9%.

Distribution of rural income (1980)

percent of household income by quintile				
1	2	3	4	5 (highest)
3.9%	25.8%	41.7%	18.4%	10.2%

Quality of working life (1982). Average work week: 48 hours. Annual rate per 100,000 workers for: injury or accident, n.a., industrial illness, n.a.; death, n.a. Money spent on labour insurance and collective amenities (including pensions for the retired) Y20,940,000,000§. Average days lost to labour stoppages per 1,000 work days, n.a. Average duration of journey to work, n.a. (n.a., private automobile; n.a., public transportation; n.a., bicycle; n.a., foot; n.a., other). Rate per 1,000 workers of discouraged (unemployed no longer seeking work): n.a.
Access to services (1979). Proportion of communes having access to: electricity 87.1%; safe public water supply, n.a.; public sewage collection, n.a.; public fire protection, n.a.
Social participation. Eligible voters participating in last national election, n.a. Population participating in voluntary work, n.a. Trade union membership in total workforce 62.5%. Practicing religious population in total affiliated population, n.a., of which: daily, n.a.; weekly, n.a.; monthly, n.a.; yearly, n.a.
Social deviance (1981). Smuggling: ships and boats caught (number) 1,251, captured contraband goods valued Y205,000,000; total number of criminal offenders ‖ arrested 180,086¶.
Leisure. Favourite leisure activities: n.a.
Material well-being (1982). Households possessing (number per household): clocks and watches 1.04, bicycles 0.52, radio sets 0.50, sewing machines 0.33, television sets 0.02.

National economy

Gross national product (at current market prices; 1983): U.S.$313,000,000,000 (U.S.$308 per capita).

Origin of gross domestic product (current prices)

	1981 in value Y'000,000,000	1981 % of total value	1982 labour force ('000)	1982 % of labour force
Agriculture	156.3	34.7	320,130	71.6
Mining	...	♀	...	♀
Manufacturing	190.7	42.3	59,300♀	13.3♀
Construction	15.4	3.4	13,400	3.0
Trade	27.4	6.1	18,200	4.1
Public utilities	...	...	...	...
Transp. and commun.	13.3	3.0	8,500	1.9
Finance	...	...	...	...
Pub. admin., defense	...	...	6,110	1.4
Services	...	...	16,460	3.7
Other	47.6	10.6	4,960	1.1
TOTAL	450.7	100.0§	447,060	100.0§

Budget (1983). Revenue: Y124,900,000,000 (taxes 62.1%; receipts from state enterprises 19.3%). Expenditures: Y129,300,000,000 (capital construction 29.6%; culture, education, public health 17.3%; defense 13.7%).
Public debt (total national): U.S.$n.a.
Tourism (1982): receipts from visitors U.S.$7,940,522,000; expenditures by nationals abroad U.S.$n.a.

Manufacturing and mining enterprises (1982)

	no. of enterprises	no. of employees□	annual wages as a % of avg. of all wages□	annual gross output value◇ (Y'000,000)
Manufacturing				
Chemical fibres	200			866,850
Machine-building	102,300	9,175,000	343.8	882,100
Food and oil	26,100	...	68.0	755,520
Clothing	23,000	...	101.3	495,310
Metallurgical	4,600	3,012,000	125.5	485,230
Chemical	24,300	2,815,000	100.5	412,110
Household equipment	...	...	...	342,960
Power	10,900	...	...	207,070
Leather	6,500	...	...	141,000
Canned food	600	...	...	131,540
Cement and products	12,500	...	66.9	82,280
Glass	700	...	66.9	13,750
Mining				
Ferrous metals	...	...	...	337,280
Coal	8,400	3,770,000	175.0	155,140
Petroleum extraction	22	478,000	21.1	132,310

Production (metric tons except as noted). Agriculture, forestry, fishing (1982): chestnuts 220,000,000, rice 155,111,000, sweet potatoes 120,960,000, walnuts 115,000,000, corn (maize) 64,100,000, wheat 63,003,000, palm kernels 48,000,000, sugarcane 43,000,000, potatoes 15,042,000, sorghum 8,011,000, soybeans 7,477,000, sugar beets 6,920,000, peanuts (groundnuts) 3,870,000, barley 3,700,000, cotton lint 3,300,000, tobacco 1,523,000, jute 1,300,000, tea 393,000; livestock (number of live animals) 298,526,000 pigs, 109,470,000 sheep, 78,437,000 goats, 55,058,000 cattle, 10,972,000 horses; roundwood, coniferous 105,593,000 cu m, nonconiferous 119,035,000 cu m; fish catch 4,926,683. Mining and quarrying (1982): salt 16,008,000; gypsum 3,400,000; sulphur 2,400,000; magnesite 2,000,000; barite 900,000; fluorspar 480,000; aluminum△ 360,000; copper△ 200,000; gold 1,900,000 troy ounces. Manufacturing (1983): cement 108,250,000; steel 40,020,000; chemical fertilizer 13,789,000; sugar 3,770,000; cloth 14,880,000,000 metres; wristwatches 34,-690,000 units; bicycles 27,580,000 units; sewing machines 10,870,000 units; television sets 6,840,000 units. Construction (1981): residential 78,340,000 sq m; nonresidential 47,550,000 sq m.

Service enterprises (1982)

	no. of enter-prises	no. of employees	annual wage as a % of all wages	annual gross output value◇ (Y'000,000)
Public utilities	...	...	...	...
Electrical power	8,923	786,000□	29.5□	17,672
Transport	...	...	...	...
Communication	...	...	...	...
Wholesale trade	...	...	...	...
Service trade	597,000	1,824,000	...	...
Consumer goods				
repair shops	217,000	414,000	...	...
Barber shops	83,000	264,000	...	...
Hotels	49,000	393,000	...	...
Retail trade	2,607,000	8,709,000	...	206,735†
Grocery stores	150,000	1,160,000	...	...
Department stores	122,000	1,217,000	...	...
Grain and				
oil shops	35,000	378,000	...	...
Hardware stores	20,000	202,000	...	...
Drugstores	20,000	150,000	...	...

Energy production (consumption): electricity (kW-hr; 1982) 327,680,000,000 (327,952,000,000); coal (metric tons; 1982) 660,000,000 (655,746,000); crude petroleum (barrels; 1982) 748,540,000 (641,815,000); petroleum products (metric tons; 1982) 62,440,000 (58,635,000); natural gas (cu m; 1982) 11,-906,398,400 (11,906,398,400).
Persons economically active (1982): total 474,384,000 (47.3%); female participation in the labour force⊕ 152,000,000 (32.0%); unemployed n.a.

Price and earnings indexes (1980 = 100)

	1977	1978	1979	1980	1981	1982	1983
Consumer price index	90.5	91.3	93.1	100.0	102.6	104.5	106.7
Earnings index	...	...	...	...	...	...	...

Household income and expenditure. Average household size (1982) 4.5; average annual income per household, n.a.; sources of income**: from the collective 51.9%; from household sideline production†† 38.0%; other non-borrowing incomes 10.1%; expenditure‡‡ (1983): food 59.3%, clothing 11.2%, housing 11.1%, daily expenses 10.8%.
Land use (1981): forested 13.3%; meadows and pastures 30.6%; agricultural and under permanent cultivation 10.8%; other 45.3%.

Financial aggregates

	1978	1979	1980	1981	1982	1983	1984 (10 mo.)
Exchange rate, Y per:							
U.S. dollar	1.58	1.50	1.53	1.75	1.92	1.98	2.64
£	3.21	3.33	3.65	3.33	3.10	2.87	3.21
SDR	2.06	1.97	1.95	2.03	2.12	2.07	2.63
International reserves (U.S.$)							
Total (excl. gold; '000,000)	1,557	2,154	2,545	5,048	11,339	14,853	17,302§§
SDR's ('000,000)	...	...	92	275	214	335	403
Reserve pos. in IMF ('000,000)	...	...	191	...	...	176	223
Foreign exchange	1,557	2,154	2,262	4,773	11,125	14,342	16,674§§
Gold, ('000,000 fine troy oz.)	12.8	12.8	12.8	12.7	12.7	12.7	12.75§§
% world reserves	1.2	1.4	1.5	1.3	1.3	1.3	1.3§§
Interest and prices							
Central bank discount (%)	...	...	...	...	...	...	...
Gov't. bond yield (%)	...	...	...	...	...	...	...
Industrial share prices	...	...	...	...	...	...	...
Balance of payments (Y'000,000)							
Balance of visible trade, of which:							
Imports, f.o.b.							
Exports, f.o.b.							
Balance of invisibles							
Balance of payments, current account							

Foreign trade

Balance of trade (current prices)

	1978	1979	1980	1981	1982	1983
Y'000,000	−430	−1,110	−290	+3,020	+5,664	+5,160
% of total	1.3%	2.6%	0.5%	4.3%	7.3%	6.3%

Imports (1982): Y35,769,000,000 (wheat 15.2%, rolled steel 9.1%, manufactured fertilizer 6.5%, uncombed cotton 3.7%, sugar 3.4%, logs 2.6%, synthetic fibres 2.0%, wool 1.5%, paper and paperboard 1.1%, ships 1.1%). *Major import sources:* United States 22.7%; Japan 20.6%; Hong Kong 6.9%; Canada 6.6%; West Germany 5.1%; Australia 4.8%; Romania 2.2%; Italy 1.7%.
Exports (1982): Y41,433,000,000 (crude oil 14.8%, garments 7.2%, petroleum products 6.4%, cotton cloth 3.2%, coal 1.6%, canned food 1.6%, aquatic products 1.4%, raw silk 1.3%). *Major export destinations:* Hong Kong 23.7%; Japan 22.0%; United States 8.0%; Jordan 6.0%; West Germany 3.5%; Singapore 2.9%; Brazil 1.7%; North Korea 1.3%.

Transport and communications

Transport. Railroads (1983): length 32,625 mi, 52,500 km; passenger-mi 110,191,300,000, passenger-km 177,336,000,000; short ton-mi cargo 454,-421,000,000, metric ton-km cargo 663,444,000,000. Roads (1982): total length 563,600 mi, 907,000 km (paved, n.a.). Vehicles (1982): passenger cars 70,000; trucks and buses 900,000. Merchant marine ‖ ‖ (1983): vessels (100 gross tons and over) 1,693; total deadweight tonnage 17,507,068. Air transport (1980): passenger-mi 567,000,000, passenger-km 913,000,000; short ton-mi cargo 35,600,000, metric ton-km cargo 52,000,000; airports (1984) with scheduled flights 71.
Communications. Newspapers (1982): total number 277; total circulation, n.a; circulation per 1,000 population, n.a. Radios (1983): total number of receivers 13,000,000 (1 per 78 persons). Television (1983): total number of receivers 9,700,000 (1 per 105 persons). Telephones (1982): 2,342,500 (1 per 429 persons).

Education and health

Education (1982)

	schools	teachers	students	student/teacher ratio
Primary (age 7–13)	880,516	5,505,000	139,720,000	25.4
Secondary (age 13–17)	101,649	2,871,000	45,285,000	15.8
Secondary specialized	3,076	...	1,039,000	...
Higher	715	287,000	1,154,000	4.0

College graduates per 100,000 population (students graduating, 1981): 15. *Literacy* (1982): total population literate¶¶ 605,932,447 (68.1%); males literate, n.a.; females literate, n.a.
Health (1982): physicians 1,305,000♀♀ (1 per 791 persons); hospital beds 2,280,000 (1 per 453 persons).
Food (1978–80): daily per capita caloric intake 2,472 (vegetable products 89.7%, animal products 10.3%); 105% of FAO recommended minimum requirement.

Military

Total active duty personnel (1984): 4,000,000 (army 79%; navy 8.8%; air force 12.2%). *Military expenditure as percent of GNP* (1982): 7.1% (world 6%); per capita expenditure U.S.$44.

*Number of deputies in the 6th Congress, June 1983. †Names of the provinces, autonomous regions, municipalities, and their capitals are given in Wade–Giles, followed by Pinyin spellings. ‡Includes 4,600 sq mi (11,900 sq km) not shown separately. §1983. ‖ Includes murderers, robbers, rapists, and arsonists. ¶1982. ♀Mining is included in manufacturing. ♂Detail does not add to total given because of rounding. □In state-owned industry. ◇In 1980 constant prices. △DMetal content. †Average value of sales. ⊖Estimate. **Net income per peasant. ††Includes income from farming, forestry, hunting, fishing, raising livestock and poultry, and handicrafts. ‡‡Rural families. §§9 months. ‖ ‖ Including Taiwan. ¶¶Age 6 and over. ♀♀Includes 303,000 physicians of traditional Chinese medicine.

Great Wall of China and watchtower.

Colombia

Official name: República de Colombia (Republic of Colombia).
Form of government: unitary, multiparty republic with two legislative houses (Senate [114]; House of Representatives [199]).
Head of state and government: President.
Capital: Bogotá.
Official language: Spanish.
Official religion: Roman Catholicism.
Monetary unit: 1 peso (Col$) = 100 centavos; valuation (Oct. 29, 1984) 1 U.S.$ = Col$106.19; 1 £ = Col$128.17.

Area and population

Commissariats	Capitals	area sq mi	area sq km	population 1981 estimate
Amazonas	Leticia	42,342	109,665	18,000
Guainía	San Felipe (Obando)	27,891	72,238	11,000
Guaviare	Guaviare	16,342	42,327	...
Vaupés	Mitú	25,200	65,268	37,000
Vichada	Puerto Carreño	38,703	100,242	14,000
Departments				
Antioquia	Medellín	24,561	63,612	3,936,000
Atlántico	Barranquilla	1,308	3,388	1,404,000
Bolívar	Cartagena	10,030	25,978	1,322,000
Boyacá	Tunja	8,953	23,189	1,194,000
Caldas	Manizales	3,046	7,888	772,000
Caquetá	Florencia	34,349	88,965	290,000
Cauca	Popayán	11,316	29,308	827,000
Cesar	Valledupar	8,844	22,905	781,000
Chocó	Quibdó	17,965	46,530	332,000
Córdoba	Montería	9,660	25,020	915,000
Cundinamarca	Bogotá	8,735	22,623	1,224,000
Huila	Neiva	7,680	19,890	557,000
La Guajira	Riohacha	8,049	20,848	394,000
Magdalena	Santa Marta	8,953	23,188	942,000
Meta	Villavicencio	33,064	85,635	389,000
Nariño	Pasto	12,845	33,268	1,070,000
Norte de Santander	Cúcuta	8,362	21,658	1,023,000
Quindío	Armenia	712	1,845	401,000
Risaralda	Pereira	1,598	4,140	558,000
Santander	Bucaramanga	11,790	30,537	1,477,000
Sucre	Sincelejo	4,215	10,917	523,000
Tolima	Ibagué	9,097	23,562	1,070,000
Valle	Cali	8,548	22,140	3,160,000
Intendancies				
Arauca	Arauca	9,196	23,818	82,000
Casanare	Yopal	17,236	44,640	...
Putumayo	Mocoa	9,608	24,885	79,000
San Andrés and Providencia	San Andrés	17	44	30,000
Special District				
Bogotá		613	1,587	...
TOTAL		440,831*	1,141,748	26,729,000

Source: Official government figures.

Demography

Density (1984): persons per sq mi 64.1, persons per sq km 24.7.
Urban–rural (1983): urban 65.4%; rural 34.6%.
Sex distribution (1980): male 50.11%; female 49.89%.
Age breakdown (1980): under 15, 39.4%; 15–29, 30.2%; 30–44, 15.7%; 45–59, 9.2%; 60–74, 4.6%; 75 and over, 0.9%.
Population projection: (1990) 31,820,000; (2000) 37,999,000.
Doubling time: 32 years.
Ethnic composition (1980): mestizo 47.8%; mulatto 23.0%; white 20.0%; black 6.0%; jungle Amerindian 1.6%; other 1.6%.
Religious affiliation (1983): Roman Catholic 97%; other 3%.
Major cities (1982 est.): Bogotá 4,584,000; Medellín 1,664,000; Cali 1,450,000; Barranquilla 924,000; Cartagena 470,000; Bucaramanga 441,000.

Vital statistics

Birth rate per 1,000 population (1980–85): 31.0 (world avg. 27.5); legitimate 75.2%, illegitimate 24.8%.
Death rate per 1,000 population (1980–85): 7.7 (world avg. 10.6).
Natural increase rate per 1,000 population (1980–85): 23.3 (world avg. 16.9).
Total fertility rate (avg. births per childbearing woman; 1980–85): 3.9.
Marriage rate per 1,000 population (1977): 3.5.
Infant mortality rate per 1,000 live births (1980–85): 39.5.
Life expectancy at birth (1980–85): male 61.4 years; female 66.0 years.
Major causes of death per 100,000 population (1977): diseases of the circulatory system 129.2; infectious and parasitic diseases 86.6.

National economy

Budget (1981). Revenue: Col$262,468,000,000 (taxes 81%; capital 16%). Expenditures: Col$263,862,000,000 (education 21%; public debt 12%; public works 10%; defense 8%; health 7%; police 7%; development 5%).
Public debt (external, outstanding; 1983): U.S.$6,211,000,000.
Tourism (1982): receipts from visitors U.S.$624,000,000; expenditures by nationals abroad U.S.$324,000,000.
Production (metric tons except as noted). Agriculture, forestry, fishing (1983): potatoes 2,234,000, plantains 2,220,000, cassavas 2,000,000, rice 1,791,400, sugarcane 1,320,600, bananas 1,171,000, corn (maize) 926,100,

tobacco 28,400; roundwood 16,312,000 cu m†; fish catch 49,000†; livestock (number of live animals, 1982) 24,499,000 cattle, 2,749,000 sheep. Mining and quarrying (1982): iron ore 445,434; gold 469,755 troy oz.; silver 127,244 troy oz. Manufacturing (value added in Col$'000; 1981): beverages 59,066; processed food 55,837; chemicals 47,576; textiles 38,745; metal products 15,412; transport equipment 15,285. Construction (1983)‡: residential 5,220,503 sq m; nonresidential 1,099,632 sq m. Energy production (consumption): electricity (kW–hr; 1982) 25,605,000,000 (25,575,000,000); coal (metric tons; 1982) 5,550,000 (5,227,000); crude petroleum (barrels; 1982) 51,765,000 (59,092,000); petroleum products (metric tons; 1982) 8,056,000 (7,250,000); natural gas (cu m; 1982) 4,458,180,000 (4,458,180,000).
Gross national product (at current market prices; 1983): U.S.$42,580,610,000 (U.S.$1,550 per capita).

Origin of gross domestic product (current prices)

	1982 in value Col$'000,000	1982 % of total value	1980 labour force	1980 % of labour force
Agriculture	591,782	26.4	2,412,413	28.5
Mining	44,832	2.0	49,740	0.6
Manufacturing	479,702	21.4	1,136,735	13.4
Construction	130,013	5.8	242,191	2.9
Trade and finance	363,139	16.2	1,539,843	18.1
Public utilities	49,315	2.2	44,233	0.5
Transp., comm.	170,362	7.6	352,623	4.2
Pub. admin., defense	163,637	7.3	...	...
Services	248,818	11.1	1,998,460	23.6
Other	§	§	690,762	8.2
TOTAL	2,241,600	100.0	8,467,000	100.0

Persons economically active (1980): total 8,467,000 (31.6%); female participation in labour force 2,220,000 (26.2%); unemployed 320,800 (3.8%).

Price and earnings indexes (1978 = 100)

	1977	1978	1979	1980	1981	1982	1983
Consumer price index	84.8	100.0	129.8	164.2	208.0	257.7	300.76
Monthly earnings index	76.8	100.0	132.9	170.4	221.1	284.8	...

Average household size (1981) 5.4.
Land use (1981): forested 50.5%; meadows and pastures 28.9%; agricultural and under permanent cultivation 5.4%; other 15.2%.

Foreign trade

Balance of trade (current prices)

	1978	1979	1980	1981	1982	1983
U.S.$'000,000	+166	+67	−718	−2,243	−2,383	−1,471
% of total	2.8%	10.2%	8.3%	27.5%	27.8%	19.7%

Imports (1983): U.S.$4,883,736,000 (machinery and equipment 17.1%; mineral fuels, petroleum, and petroleum products 13.0%; automobiles and other land vehicles 10.1%). *Major import sources:* United States 34.7%; EEC countries 14.4%; Venezuela, Ecuador, and Peru 13.6%; Japan 7.9%.
Exports (1983): U.S.$3,069,322,000 (coffee, tea, and spices 49.1%; combustibles, minerals, and products 13.6%; fruits and melons 4.9%). *Major export destinations:* EEC countries 37.8%; United States 28.6%; Venezuela, Ecuador, and Peru 5.9%.

Transport and communications

Transport. Railroads (1982): length 1,754 mi, 2,822 km; passenger-mi 97,920,000, passenger-km 157,587,000; short ton-mi cargo 378,813,000, metric ton-km cargo 553,057,000. Roads (1980): total length 46,438 mi, 74,735 km. Vehicles (1981): passenger cars 672,385; trucks and buses 168,096. Merchant marine (1983): vessels (100 gross tons and over) 82; total deadweight tonnage 358,869. Air transport (1982): passenger-mi 1,829,567,000, passenger-km 2,944,408,000; short ton-mi cargo 35,890,000, metric ton-km cargo 52,398,000; airports (1983) with scheduled flights 79.
Communications. Daily newspapers (1983): total number 27; total circulation 1,222,121; circulation per 1,000 population 44. Radios (1983): 3,025,000 (1 per 9 persons). Televisions (1983): 1,800,000 (1 per 15 persons). Telephones (1982): 1,747,689 (1 per 15.9 persons).

Education and health

Education (1981)

	schools	teachers	students	student/ teacher ratio
Primary	34,641	137,721	4,217,800	30.6
Secondary	...	88,103 ‖	1,891,530 ‖	21.5
Higher	70	34,844	318,293	9.1

College graduates per 100,000 population (students graduating; 1981): 107.
Literacy rate (1980): 81.0%.
Health (1977): physicians 12,720 (1 per 1,969 persons); hospital beds 40,406 (1 per 620 persons).
Food (1978–80): daily per capita caloric intake 2,473 (vegetable products 85%, animal products 15%); 107% of FAO recommended minimum.

Military

Total active duty personnel (1983): 70,200 (army 81.2%; navy 12.8%; air force 6.0%). *Military expenditure as percent of GNP* (1982): 0.8% (world 6.0%); per capita expenditure U.S.$12.

*Detail does not add to total given because of rounding. †1982. ‡Ten major cities. §Other is included with public administration and services. ‖ Includes vocational and teacher training.

Comoros*

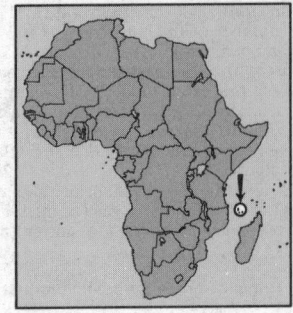

Official name: Jumhurīyat al-Qumur al-Ittihādīyah al-Islāmīyah (Arabic); République Fédéral Islamique des Comores (French) (Federal Islāmic Republic of the Comoros).
Form of government: federal Islamic republic with one legislative house (Federal Assembly [39]).
Chief of state: President.
Head of government: Prime Minister.
Capital: Moroni.
Official languages: Arabic; French.
Official religion: Islam.
Monetary unit: 1 Comorian franc (CF) = 100 centimes; valuation (Oct. 29, 1984) 1 U.S.$ = CF470.6; 1 £ = CF568.0.

Area and population

Islands†	Capitals	area		population
		sq mi	sq km	1980 census
Moili (Mohéli)	Fomboni	112	290	17,194
Ngazidja (Grande Comore)	Moroni	443	1,148	192,177
Ndzouani (Anjouan)	Mutsamudu	164	424	137,621
TOTAL		719	1,862	346,992

Source: Official government figures.

Demography

Density (1984): persons per sq mi 540.6, persons per sq km 208.8.
Urban-rural (1980): urban 33.4%; rural 66.6%.
Sex distribution (1980): male 50.14%; female 49.86%.
Age breakdown (1980): under 15, 45.1%; 15–29, 26.9%; 30–44, 15.1%; 45–59, 8.5%; 60–74, 3.6%; 75 and over, 0.8%.
Population projection: (1990) 460,900; (2000) 612,300.
Doubling time: 25 years.
Ethnic composition (1980): Comorian (a mixture of Bantu, Arab, and Malagasy peoples) 96.9%; Makua (a Bantu people from East Africa) 1.6%; French 0.4%; other 1.1%.
Religious affiliation (1980): Sunnī Muslim 99.3%; Christian 0.6%; Baha'ī 0.1%.
Major cities (1980): Moroni 20,112; Mutsamudu 12,518; Domoni 7,658; Quani 7,051; Iconi 5,770; Fomboni 5,663.

Vital statistics

Birth rate per 1,000 population (1980–85): 46.2 (world avg. 27.5).
Death rate per 1,000 population (1980–85): 18.1 (world avg. 10.6).
Natural increase rate per 1,000 population (1980–85): 28.1 (world avg. 16.9).
Total fertility rate (avg. births per childbearing woman; 1980–85): 6.7.
Marriage rate per 1,000 population: n.a.
Divorce rate per 1,000 population: n.a.
Infant mortality rate per 1,000 live births (1975–80): 97.0.
Life expectancy at birth (1980–85): male 46.4 years; female 49.7 years.
Serious illnesses (late 1970s): malaria, 30,352 clinically diagnosed cases in 1976; filariasis; tuberculosis; leprosy; kwashiorkor.

National economy

Budget (1982). Revenue: CF2,565,000,000 (indirect taxes on foreign trade 63.5%; grants 26.0%; turnover tax 5.6%; income from state enterprises 2.5%; registry and stamps 1.7%). Expenditures: CF4,062,000,000 (capital expenditures 21.0%; general administration 19.1%; defense 15.0%; education, youth, and recreation 14.7%; community expenses 5.8%; public debt payments 5.1%; public works 4.1%; infrastructure and environment 3.1%; transport and tourism 2.7%; health 2.4%).
Public debt (external, outstanding; 1982): U.S.$67,000,000.
Tourism‡ (early 1980s): fewer than 2,000 visitors annually.
Production (metric tons except as noted). Agriculture and fishing‡ (1982): roots and tubers (including sweet potatoes, taros, and yams) 120,000, cassava 88,000, coconuts 45,000, bananas 33,000, rice 14,000, corn (maize) 5,000, cloves 1,134§, vanilla 177§; livestock (number of live animals): 88,000 goats, 81,000 cattle, 8,000 sheep, 300,000 chickens; fish catch 6,000§. Mining and quarrying (1982): pozzolana; sand; gravel. Manufacturing (1983): copra 684; ylang-ylang essence 49; sawnwood 4,000 cu m ‖; other important products are cement, handicrafts, soaps, and soft drinks. Construction: n.a. Energy production (consumption): electricity (kW-hr; 1982) 10,000,000 (10,000,000); coal, none (n.a.); crude petroleum, none (n.a.); petroleum products (metric tons; 1982) none (12,000); natural gas, none (n.a.).
Persons economically active‡ (1980 est.): total 145,000 (35.9%); (1977 est.) female participation in the labour force 64,600 (35.1%); unemployed, n.a.

Price and earnings indexes (1979 = 100)

	1976	1977	1978	1979	1980	1981
Consumer price index	70.1	75.5	87.9	100.0	111.2	...
Monthly earnings index	...	...	...	...	...	...

Household income and expenditure. Average household size‡ (1980) 4.8; average annual income per household: n.a.; sources of income: n.a.; expenditure: n.a.
Gross national product (at current market prices;1982): U.S.$92,351,000 (U.S.$250 per capita).

Origin of gross domestic product (current prices)

	1982		1976‡	
	in value U.S.$'000,000	% of total value	labour force¶	% of labour force
Agriculture	41.4	44.8	3,200	26.2
Mining	—	—	—	—
Manufacturing	4.5	4.9	300	2.5
Construction	9.7	10.5	1,000	8.2
Public utilities	0.7	0.8	...	...
Transportation and communication	...	...	500	4.1
Trade	...	...	1,000	8.2
Public administration, services	36.0⁹	39.0⁹	2,200	18.0
Other	...	...	4,000	32.8
TOTAL	92.4⁵	100.0	12,200	100.0

Land use‡ (1981): forested 16.2%; meadows and pastures 35.7%; agricultural and under permanent cultivation 2.5%; other 45.6%.

Foreign trade

Balance of trade (current prices)

	1978	1979	1980	1981	1982	1983
CF'000,000	−2,230	−2,406	−4,185	−4,330	−4,291	−5,680
% of total	34.7%	24.4%	51.6%	32.5%	25.0%	27.7%

Imports (1981): CF8,791,000,000 (rice 34.4%, petroleum products 11.1%, meat 6.0%, cement 6.0%). *Major import source:* France 57.2%.
Exports (1981): CF4,461,000,000 (vanilla 48.7%, cloves 38.8%, ylang-ylang 10.2%, copra 1.8%). *Major export destination:* France 57.5%□.

Transport and communications

Transport. Railroads: none. Roads (1980): total length of paved roads 280 mi, 451 km. Vehicles (early 1980s): passenger cars, trucks and buses, 1,800. Merchant marine (1983): vessels (100 gross tons and over) 2; total deadweight tonnage 1,793. Air transport (1982): passengers, n.a.; cargo, n.a.; airports (1984) with scheduled flights 3.
Communications. Daily or weekly newspapers (1983): none. Radios (1983): total number of receivers 40,000 (1 per 9.4 persons). Television: total number of receivers, none. Telephones (1981): 3,200 (1 per 112 persons).

Education and health

Education (1980–81)

	schools	teachers	students	student/ teacher ratio
Primary (age 7–13)	236	1,292	59,709	46.2
Secondary	32	434	13,528	31.2
Voc., teacher tr.	4	27	327	12.1

College graduates: n.a. *Literacy* (1977 est.): total population literate 61,560 (20.0%).
Health: physicians, n.a.; hospital beds (1976) 555 (1 per 526 persons).
Food (1978–80): daily per capita caloric intake 2,306 (vegetable products 94.7%, animal products 5.3%); 99% of FAO recommended minimum requirement.

Military

Total armed forces◊ (1982): 11,000. *Military expenditure as percent of GNP* (1982): 1.9% (world 6.0%); per capita expenditure U.S.$5.

*Excludes Mayotte, a *collectivité territoriale* (territorial collectivity) of France, unless otherwise indicated. †Island names in Comorian Swahili and French. ‡Includes Mayotte. §1981. ‖ 1977. ¶Salaried employees only. ⁹Transportation and communication, trade, and other are included with public administration and services. ⁵Detail does not add to total given because of rounding. □Most of the remaining export trade is conducted with other members of the European Economic Community. ◊Devoted entirely to internal security duties.

FREDERICK AYER—PHOTO RESEARCHERS

Friday Mosque (Mosquée du Vendredi) and waterfront, Moroni, Grande Comore Island, Comoros.

Congo (Brazzaville)

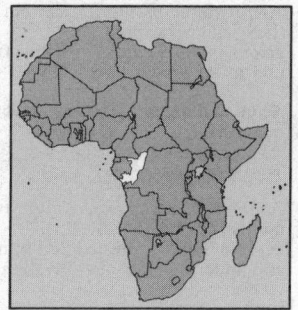

Official name: République Populaire de Congo (People's Republic of the Congo).
Form of government: military regime with one legislative body (People's National Assembly [153]).
Head of state and government: President (Chairman).
Capital: Brazzaville.
Official language: French.
Official religion: none.
Monetary unit: 1 CFA franc (CFAF) = 100 centimes; valuation (Oct. 29, 1984) 1 U.S.$ = CFAF470.60; 1 £ = CFAF568.00.

Area and population

Regions	Capitals	area sq mi	area sq km	population 1980 estimate
Bouenza	Nkayi	4,735	12,265	129,000
Cuvette	Owando	28,900	74,850	121,000
Kouilou	Pointe-Noire	5,287	13,694	76,000
Lékoumou	Sibiti	8,089	20,950	63,000
Likouala	Impfondo	25,500	66,044	32,000
Niari	Loubomo	10,016	25,942	106,000
Plateaux	Djambala	14,826	38,400	103,000
Pool	Kinkala	13,127	34,000	208,000
Sangha	Ouesso	21,544	55,800	41,000
Communes				
Brazzaville		21	55	422,000
Loubomo		*	*	31,000
Nkayi		*	*	33,000
Pointe-Noire		†	†	185,000
TOTAL		132,000‡	342,000	1,550,000

Source: Official government figures.

Demography

Density (1984): persons per sq mi 13.2, persons per sq km 5.1.
Urban–rural (1980): urban 37.3%; rural 62.7%.
Sex distribution (1980): male 49.25%; female 50.75%.
Age breakdown (1980): under 15, 43.3%; 15–29, 25.5%; 30–44, 15.9%; 45–59, 9.8%; 60–74, 4.5%; 75 and over, 1.0%.
Population projection: (1990) 2,000,000; (2000) 2,620,000.
Doubling time: 26 years.
Ethnic composition (1978): Kongo 52.3%; Teke 24.0%; Bubangui 5.2%; Kota 4.5%; Mboshi 3.4%; other 10.6%.
Religious affiliation (1980): Roman Catholic 53.9%; Protestant 24.4%; animist 19.0%; other 2.7%.
Major cities (1980): Brazzaville 422,400; Pointe-Noire 185,110; Nkayi 32,520; Loubomo 30,830.

Vital statistics

Birth rate per 1,000 population (1980–85): 44.2 (world avg. 27.5); legitimate, n.a.; illegitimate, n.a.
Death rate per 1,000 population (1980–85): 17.2 (world avg. 10.6).
Natural increase rate per 1,000 population (1980–85): 27.0 (world avg. 16.9).
Total fertility rate (avg. births per childbearing woman; 1980–85): 6.0.
Marriage rate per 1,000 population: n.a.
Divorce rate per 1,000 population: n.a.
Infant mortality rate per 1,000 live births (1980–85): 134.5.
Life expectancy at birth (1980–85): male 46.9 years; female 50.1 years.
Major causes of death: n.a.

National economy

Budget (1981). Revenue: CFAF159,900,000,000 (domestic tax on goods and services 30.5%, social security contributions 28.9%, customs duties 18.8%, income tax 13.7%, nontax revenue 5.8%). Expenditures: CFAF159,900,000,000 (social security and welfare 30.8%, education 24.6%, economic services 18.3%, health 5.1%, defense 2.6%).
Public debt (external, outstanding; 1982): U.S.$1,369,900,000.
Tourism (1982): receipts from visitors U.S.$13,000,000§; expenditures by nationals abroad U.S.$54,000,000.
Production (metric tons except as noted). Agriculture, forestry, fishing (1982): palm oil 8,664,000, palm kernels 600,000, roots and tubers 595,000, cassava 533,000, sugarcane 225,000, fruits 201,000, pineapples 104,000, plantains 35,000, vegetables 28,000, sweet potatoes 26,000, bananas 26,000, corn (maize) 15,000, peanuts (groundnuts) in shell 14,000, pulses 7,000, coffee beans 5,000, cacao beans 4,000, rice 4,000; livestock (number of live animals) 139,000 goats, 75,000 cattle, 72,000 sheep, 56,000 pigs, 1,183,000 chickens; roundwood 2,196,000 cu m; fish catch 17,934. Mining and quarrying (1982): lead 8,000; zinc 4,500 ‖; copper 149; gold 6,000 troy ounces. Manufacturing (1980): cement 39,242¶; raw sugar 20,000; palm oil 7,000; soap 4,600; wheat flour 3,000; cigarettes 706; beer 445,000 hectolitres; soft drinks 168,000 hectolitres; veneer sheets 72,000 cu m; footwear 836,000 pairs. Construction: n.a. Energy production (consumption): electricity (kW-hr; 1981) 165,000,000 (165,000,000); coal, none (n.a.); crude petroleum (barrels; 1982) 33,000,000 (3,000,000§); petroleum products (metric tons; 1981) 35,000 (127,000); natural gas (cu m; 1982) 368,000,000 (2,564,000§).
Gross national product (at current market prices; 1982): U.S.$2,079,000,000 (U.S.$1,300 per capita).

Origin of gross domestic product (current prices)

	1981 in value CFAF'000,000,000	% of total value	labour force	% of labour force
Agriculture	42.7	7.9	180,000	34.0
Mining	212.8	9.3	♀	♀
Manufacturing	34.3	6.3	♀	♀
Construction	25.1	4.6	♀	♀
Trade	60.1ᵟ	11.1ᵟ	♀	♀
Public utilities	3.5	0.6	♀	♀
Transportation and communication	43.9	8.1	♀	♀
Finance	ᵟ	ᵟ	♀	♀
Pub. admin., defense	56.3	10.4	♀	♀
Services	63.0	11.7	♀	♀
Other	...	...	350,000♀	66.0♀
TOTAL	541.7	100.0	530,000	100.0

Persons economically active (1982): total 550,000 (33.9%); female participation in the labour force 217,234□ (44.6%); unemployed, n.a .

Price and earnings indexes (1980 = 100)

	1977	1978	1979	1980	1981	1982	1983
Consumer price index	78.3	86.2	93.2	100.0	117.1	132.0	142.3
Earnings index	...	...	...	...	...	...	...

Household income and expenditure. Average household size (1980) 4.7; average annual income per household CFAF1,016,000◇ (U.S.$ 4,500); source of income: n.a.; expenditure: n.a.
Land use (1981): forested 62.5%; meadows and pastures 29.3%; agricultural and under permanent cultivation 1.9%; other 6.3%.

Foreign trade

Balance of trade (current prices)

	1977	1978	1979	1980	1981	1982
CFAF'000,000,000	−0.7	5.0	46.5	73.0	66.5	55.7
% of total	0.8%	4.4%	27.3%	23.7%	12.9%	9.5%

Imports (1982): CFAF244,600,000,000△ (machinery 17.7%; finished steel products 11.4%; electrical machinery 10.4%; petroleum products 8.3%; automobiles 7.0%; minerals, including cement 3.9%; library materials 3.2%; meat 3.2%; cotton textiles 2.6%; pharmaceutical products 2.1%). *Major import sources:* France 63.5%; Brazil 7.0%; Belgium-Luxembourg 3.1%; Japan 3.1%; The Netherlands 3.1%; United States 3.0%; Italy 2.0%.
Exports (1982): CFAF326,100,000,000 (crude petroleum 89.6%; wood and wood products 4.7%; pearls and precious stones 2.7%; petroleum products 0.8%; coffee, cocoa, and tobacco 0.7%). *Major export destinations:* United States 50.8%; Italy 21.0%; Spain 10.4%; France 10.0%; Belgium-Luxembourg 2.7%.

Transport and communications

Transport. Railroads (1981): length 497 mi, 800 km; passenger-mi 222,000,000, passenger-km 358,000,000; short ton-mi cargo 374,000,000, metric ton-km cargo 546,000,000. Roads (1982): total length 5,124 mi, 8,246 km (paved 7%). Vehicles (1980): passenger cars 20,000; trucks and buses 14,000. Merchant marine (1983): vessels (100 gross tons and over) 22; total deadweight tonnage 10,840. Air transport (1981): passenger-mi 101,387,000, passenger-km 163,167,000; short ton-mi cargo 17,943,000, metric ton-km cargo 26,197,000; airports (1984) with scheduled flights 18.
Communications. Daily newspapers (1982): total number 4; total circulation 24,000; circulation per 1,000 population 14.1. Radios (1981): total number of receivers 92,000 (1 per 18.4 persons). Television (1981): total number of receivers 3,500 (1 per 484 persons). Telephones (1982): 8,899 (1 per 180 persons).

Education and health

Education (1980–81)

	schools ‖	teachers	students	student/ teacher ratio
Primary (age 6–13)	1,310	7,186	390,276	54.3
Secondary (age 14–18)	122	3,649	168,718	46.2
Voc., teacher tr.	36	1,468	18,867	12.8
Higher ‖	1	681	6,848	10.0

College graduates per 100,000 population (students graduating; 1980): 86.0.
Literacy (1980): total population literate 375,060 (56.4%); males literate 230,740 (69.5%); females literate 144,320 (44.0%).
Health (1976): physicians 190 (1 per 7,312 persons); hospital beds 6,912 (1 per 201 persons).
Food (1978–80): daily per capita caloric intake 2,200 (vegetable products 95.0%, animal products 5.0%); 99% of FAO recommended minimum requirement.

Military

Total active duty personnel (1983): 8,700 (army 92.0%; navy 2.3%; air force 5.7%). *Military expenditure as percent of GNP* (1981): 7.6% (world 4.6%); per capita expenditure U.S.$88.

*Areas of Loubomo and Nkayi communes are included with Niari. †Area of Pointe-Noire commune is included with Kouilou. ‡Detail does not add to total given because of rounding. §1981. ‖ 1978. ¶1982. ♀Other includes all categories except agriculture. ᵟFinance is included with trade. □1974. ◇Derived from GNP. △Import figures are c.i.f. ‖ 1979–80.

Costa Rica

Official name: República de Costa Rica
(Republic of Costa Rica).
Form of government: unitary multiparty
republic with one legislative house
(Legislative Assembly [57]).
Head of state and government:
President.
Capital: San José.
Official language: Spanish.
Official religion: Roman Catholicism.
Monetary unit: 1 Costa Rican colón
Ȼ = 100 céntimos; valuation (Oct. 29,
1984) 1 U.S.$ = Ȼ44.81; 1 £ = Ȼ54.22.

Area and population

Provinces	Capitals	area sq mi	area sq km	population 1984 census
Alajuela	Alajuela	3,766	9,753	430,634
Cartago	Cartago	1,206	3,125	269,860
Guanacaste	Liberia	3,915	10,141	193,024
Heredia	Heredia	1,026	2,656	195,389
Limón	Limón	3,548	9,188	187,057
Puntarenas	Puntarenas	4,354	11,277	291,008
San José	San José	1,915	4,960	893,254
TOTAL		19,730	51,100	2,460,226

Source: Official government figures.

Demography

Density (1984): persons per sq mi 124.7, persons per sq km 48.1.
Urban–rural (1981): urban 43.9%; rural 56.1%.
Sex distribution (1984): male 50.04%; female 49.96%.
Age breakdown (1980): under 15, 37.9%; 15–29, 31.5%; 30–44, 15.8%; 45–59, 9.2%; 60–74, 4.4%; 75 and over, 1.2%.
Population projection: (1990) 2,776,000; (2000) 3,377,000.
Doubling time: 26 years.
Ethnic composition (1981): European (nearly all of Spanish descent) 86.8%; mestizo 7.0%; Chinese 1.9%; other 4.3%.
Religious affiliation (1980): Roman Catholic 96.8%; other 3.2%.
Major cities (1984): San José 245,370; Limón 59,487; Puntarenas 48,963; Alajuela 33,929; Cartago 23,884.

Vital statistics

Birth rate per 1,000 population (1981): 29.7 (world avg. 29.0).
Death rate per 1,000 population (1981): 4.3 (world avg. 12.0).
Natural increase rate per 1,000 population (1981): 25.4 (world avg. 17.0).
Total fertility rate (avg. births per childbearing woman; 1981): 3.5.
Marriage rate per 1,000 population (1982): 7.7.
Divorce rate per 1,000 population (1982): n.a.
Infant mortality rate per 1,000 live births (1981): 18.0.
Life expectancy at birth (1981): male 70.5 years; female 74.7 years.
Major causes of death per 100,000 population (1980): diseases of the circulatory system 105.2; malignant neoplasms (cancers) 67.3; accidents 42.9.

National economy

Budget (1981). Revenue: Ȼ10,198,500,000 (social security contributions 25.2%, export duties 18.4%, excises 17.6%, individual income taxes 14.6%, other 24.2%). Expenditures: Ȼ11,994,400,000 (health 29.7%, education 23.7%, roads 10.6%, social security and welfare 10.3%, defense 2.6%, other 23.1%).
Public debt (external, outstanding; 1982): U.S.$2,669,000,000.
Tourism (1982): receipts from visitors U.S.$131,000,000; expenditures by nationals abroad U.S.$36,000,000.
Production (metric tons except as noted). Agriculture, forestry, fishing (1982): sugarcane 2,500,000, bananas 1,150,000, rice 180,000, coffee 113,000, corn (maize) 90,000; livestock (number of live animals): 2,416,000 cattle, 243,000 pigs, 5,496,000 chickens; roundwood 2,627,000 cu m; fish catch 10,902. Mining and quarrying (production value in Ȼ; 1980): 66,000,000 (of which gold 16,000 troy ounces). Manufacturing (production value in Ȼ; 1980): cigarettes and beer 3,449,000,000; chemical and rubber products 1,133,000,000; textiles and leather goods 731,000,000; machinery and fabricated metal products 716,000,000; lumber and wooden products 526,000,000. Construction (1981): residential 805,000 sq m; nonresidential 1,049,000 sq m. Energy production (consumption): electricity (kW-hr; 1982) 2,500,000,000 (2,500,000,000); coal, none (n.a.); crude petroleum (barrels; 1982) none (3,309,000); petroleum products (metric tons; 1982) 416,000 (714,000); natural gas, none (n.a.).

Origin of gross domestic product (current prices)

	1982 in value Ȼ'000,000	1982 % of total value	1984 labour force†	1984 % of labour force
Agriculture	23,950	24.7	224,064	26.8
Manufacturing, mining	19,644	20.3	131,954	15.8
Construction	3,795	3.9	46,479	5.5
Trade	18,932	19.5	155,875	18.7
Public utilities	3,000	3.0	48,267*	5.8*
Transportation and communication	5,513	5.7	*	*
Services, finance, and other	22,168	22.9	228,675	27.4
TOTAL	97,002	100.0	835,314	100.0

Gross national product (at current market prices; 1982): U.S.$2,068,000,000 (U.S.$890 per capita).
Persons economically active (1984): total 835,314 (34.0%); female participation in the labour force† 183,537 (30.3%); unemployed† 76,661 (8.7%).

Price and earnings indexes (1980 = 100)

	1977	1978	1979	1980	1981	1982	1983
Consumer price index	73.1	77.5	84.7	100.0	137.1	260.6	345.6
Monthly earnings index	...	...	...	...	...	...	...

Family income and expenditure: average family size (1977) 5.02; income per family Ȼ29,318 (U.S.$3,421).
Land use (1981): forested 34.1%; meadows and pastures 41.3%; agricultural and under permanent cultivation 9.7%; other 14.9%.

Foreign trade

Balance of trade (current prices)

	1977	1978	1979	1980	1981	1982	1983
Ȼ'000,000	−788	−1,572	−2,796	−3,308	−1,755	+2,261	+3,557
% of total	5.3%	9.6%	14.9%	16.2%	3.9%	3.9%	5.2%

Imports (1981): Ȼ26,301,000,000‡ (machinery 23.4%, of which telecommunications equipment 4.0%; manufactured goods 22.4%, of which paper and paper products 5.2%, iron and steel [all forms] 4.3%; chemicals 19.6%, of which synthetic plastics and disinfectants 7.5%; crude petroleum 10.5%). *Major import sources* (1980): United States 34.5%; Japan 10.8%; Venezuela 6.8%; Guatemala 6.3%; Mexico 6.1%.
Exports (1981): Ȼ22,006,000,000‡ (coffee 23.7%; bananas 22.8%; basic manufactures 11.4%; chemical products, including medicinals 8.0%; beef 7.3%; sugar [all forms] 4.2%). *Major export destinations* (1980): United States 34.9%; Nicaragua 12.4%; West Germany 11.4%; Guatemala 6.4%; El Salvador 5.1%.

Transport and communications

Transport. Railroads (1983): route length 435 mi, 700 km; passenger-mi, n.a., passenger-km, n.a.; short ton-mi cargo, n.a., metric ton-km cargo, n.a. Roads (1981): total length 17,725 mi, 28,525 km (paved 9.0%). Vehicles (1982): passenger cars 90,000; trucks and buses 85,000. Merchant marine (1983): vessels (100 gross tons and over) 27; total deadweight tonnage 25,936. Air transport (1982): passenger-mi 388,283,000, passenger-km 624,882,000; short ton-mi cargo 14,942,000, metric ton-km cargo 21,815,000; airports (1984) with scheduled flights 8.
Communications. Daily newspapers (1983): total number 5; total circulation 182,152; circulation per 1,000 population 76. Radios (1983): total number of receivers 190,000 (1 per 12.3 persons). Television (1983): total number of receivers 450,000 (1 per 5.2 persons). Telephones (1982): 255,898 (1 per 9.3 persons).

Education and health

Education (1983)

	schools	teachers	students	student/ teacher ratio
Primary (age 5–11)	3,511	11,615§	343,800	...
Secondary (age 12–17)	242	8,213§	153,971	...
Vocational	...	...	...	...
Higher	14	...	58,942	...

Literacy (1980): total population literate 1,292,200 (93.0%); males literate 649,000 (93.2%); females literate 643,200 (92.8%).
Health: physicians (1979) 1,506 (1 per 1,477 persons); hospital beds (1980) 7,570 (1 per 295 persons).
Food (1978–80): daily per capita caloric intake 2,635 (vegetable products 81.8%, animal products 18.2%); 118% of FAO recommended minimum requirement.

Military

Military expenditure as percent of GNP: negligible; per capita expenditure: negligible. Army officially abolished in 1948. About 3,000 long-term volunteers conduct both police and paramilitary duties.

*Transport and communication is included with public utilities. †1981; employees only. ‡Based on conversion of U.S.$ (used in official government sources) into Ȼ, using the average exchange rate of 1981. Import value is *c.i.f.* (cost, insurance, and freight). §1982.

Cuba

Official name: República de Cuba
(Republic of Cuba).
Form of government: unitary socialist
republic with one legislative house
(National Assembly [481]).
Head of state and government:
President.
Capital: Havana (La Habana).
Official language: Spanish.
Official religion: none.
Monetary unit: 1 peso = 100 centavos;
valuation (Oct. 29, 1984)
1 peso = U.S.$1.14 = £0.94.

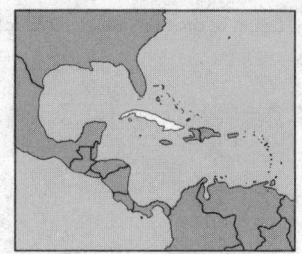

Area and population

| | | area | | population |
| | | | | 1982 |
Provinces	Capitals	sq mi	sq km	estimate
Camagüey	Camagüey	5,460	14,142	675,200
Ciego de Ávila	Ciego de Ávila	2,505	6,488	325,900
Cienfuegos	Cienfuegos	1,603	4,151	330,300
Ciudad de la Habana	Havana	286	741	1,942,300
Granma	Granma	3,265	8,457	743,300
Guantánamo	Guantánamo	2,459	6,369	468,300
Holguín	Holguín	3,440	8,910	918,000
Isla de la Juventud	—	849	2,200	59,800
La Habana	Havana	2,191	5,674	592,100
Las Tunas	Las Tunas	2,462	6,376	441,700
Matanzas	Matanzas	4,508	11,675	562,900
Pinar del Río	Pinar del Río	4,195	10,865	646,500
Sancti Spíritus	Sancti Spíritus	2,602	6,740	402,500
Santiago de Cuba	Santiago de Cuba	2,450	6,346	915,500
Villa Clara	Villa Clara	3,117	8,073	770,200
TOTAL		42,827*	110,922*	9,794,500

Source: Official government figures.

Demography

Density (1984): persons per sq mi 232.2, persons per sq km 89.7.
Urban-rural (1982): urban 69.7%; rural 30.3%.
Sex distribution (1982): male 50.49%; female 49.51%.
Age breakdown (1982): under 15, 28.3%; 15–29, 27.9%; 30–44, 19.3%; 45–59, 12.2%; 60 and over, 10.8%; unknown 1.5%.
Population projection: (1990) 10,540,000; (2000) 11,718,000.
Doubling time: 67 years.
Ethnic composition (1980): white 72%; mulatto 15%; black 12%; other 1%.
Religious affiliation (1980): non-religious 48.7%; Roman Catholic 39.6%; atheist 6.4%; Afro-American Spiritist 1.6%; Protestant 1.4%; other 2.3%.
Major cities (1981): Havana (1983) 1,951,000; Santiago de Cuba 563,455; Santa Clara 525,402; Camagüey 480,620; Holguín 456,595.

Vital statistics

Birth rate per 1,000 population (1982): 16.3 (world avg. 29.0).
Death rate per 1,000 population (1982): 5.8 (world avg. 11.0).
Natural increase rate per 1,000 population (1982): 10.5 (world avg. 18.0).
Total fertility rate (avg. births per childbearing woman; 1980–85): 1.9.
Marriage rate per 1,000 population (1982): 8.2.
Divorce rate per 1,000 population (1982): 3.1.
Infant mortality rate per 1,000 live births (1982): 17.3.
Life expectancy at birth (1980–81): male 71.9 years; female 75.4 years.
Major causes of death per 100,000 population (1978): ischemic heart disease 141.2; malignant neoplasms (cancers) 99.8; accidents 63.9; cerebrovascular disease 53.9; pneumonia 44.2.

National economy

Budget (1981). Revenue: 11,201,300,000 pesos (government sector 98.9%; taxes 0.9%). Expenditures: 11,197,400,000 pesos (production capital 41.7%; education and public health 16.5%; defense and internal security 7.5%).
Public debt (external, outstanding; 1982): U.S.$12,000,000,000†.
Production (metric tons except as noted). Agriculture, forestry, fishing (1982): sugarcane 75,000,000, citrus fruits 554,000, rice 480,000, sweet potatoes 347,000, potatoes 300,000, bananas and plantains 269,000, tobacco 45,000, coffee 21,000; livestock (number of live animals; 1982): 6,200,000 cattle, 2,000,000 pigs; forestry (pesos; 1981) 77,800,000; fish and seafood (metric tons; 1981) 98,000. Mining and quarrying (1982) nickel 35,614; chromite 27,000; copper 2,700; cobalt 1,497. Manufacturing (pesos; 1981): processed food (excluding sugar and fish) 1,619,800,000; sugar and honey 1,416,400,000; non-electrical machinery 567,600,000; textiles, leather, and clothing 514,600,000; fuels 507,900,000; chemicals 425,300,000; construction materials 369,900,000; beverages and tobacco 335,300,000. Construction (1982): number of residential apartments 30,300. Energy production (consumption): electricity (kW-hr; 1982) 10,788,000,000 (10,788,000,000); coal (metric tons; 1982) negligible (130,000); crude petroleum (barrels; 1982) 3,980,190 (46,494,190); petroleum products (metric tons; 1982) 5,730,000 (9,680,000); natural gas (cu m; 1982) 10,769,220 (10,769,220).
Gross material product‡ (at current market prices; 1980): U.S.$15,516,300,000 (U.S.$1,592 per capita).

Price and earnings indexes (1972 = 100)

	1976	1977	1978	1979	1980	1981	1982
Consumer price index	...	...	...	...	...	...	...
Monthly earnings index♀	107.9	115.0	...	118.9	120.4	136.5	141.1

Origin of global social product‡ (current prices)

| | 1982 | | | |
	in value '000,000 pesos	% of total value	labour force ‖	% of labour force ‖
"Productive"				
Agriculture, forestry	3,395	14.7	636,300	22.1
Manufacturing, mining, fishing, and public utilities	10,025	43.4	599,900	20.8
Construction	1,769	7.7	260,700	9.0
Trade	5,983	25.9	324,100	11.2
Transportation and communications	1,786	7.7	203,000	7.0
Other	120	0.5	...	...
"Non-Productive"				
Public and personal services			85,700	3.0
Science and technology			21,300	0.7
Education	not included in	357,000	12.4
Culture and art	global social	35,000	1.2
Public health	product	153,700	5.3
Other (incl. government and administration)			205,000	7.1
TOTAL	23,079§	100.0§	2,881,700	100.0§

Persons economically active¶ (1981): total 3,579,400 (36.9%); female participation in the labour force 894,900 (33.8%); unemployed 121,700 (3.4%).
Land use (1981): forested 16.2%; meadows and pastures 21.9%; agricultural and under permanent cultivation 28.0%; other 33.9%.

Foreign trade

Balance of trade (current prices)

	1977	1978	1979	1980	1981	1982
'000,000 pesos	−543.2	−133.7	−186.6	−542.2	−240.0	−597.5
% of total	8.5%	1.9%	2.6%	6.4%	2.8%	5.7%

Imports (1978): 5,537,100,000 pesos (machinery and transport equipment 31.6%; mineral fuels and lubricants 27.2%; food and live animals 14.1%; basic manufactured products 13.7%). *Major import sources:* Soviet Union 67.8%; East Germany 3.7%; Czechoslovakia 3.2%; Bulgaria 3.0%.
Exports (1982): 4,939,600,000 pesos (sugar and sugar products 77.1%; minerals and concentrates 6.2%; tobacco and tobacco products 2.1%; fish and fish preparations 2.%). *Major export destinations:* Soviet Union 76.0%; East Germany 3.3%; Bulgaria 3.2%; Czechoslovakia 2.3%.

Transport and communications

Transport. Railroads (1980): length 11,256 mi, 18,115 km; passenger-mi 1,120,000,000, passenger-km 1,802,000,000; short ton-mi cargo 1,793,200,000, metric ton-km cargo 2,885,700,000. Roads (1975): total length 18,357 mi, 29,543 km. Vehicles (1981): passenger cars 18,657; trucks and buses 28,098. Merchant marine (1983): vessels (100 gross tons and over) 418; total deadweight tonnage 1,216,721. Air transport (1980): passenger-mi 843,600,000, passenger-km 1,357,600,000; short ton-mi cargo (1981) 15,100,000, metric ton-km cargo 22,100,000; airports with scheduled flights, n.a.
Communications. Daily newspapers (1983): total number 16; total circulation 924,000; circulation per 1,000 population 95ठ. Radios (1984): total number of receivers 2,130,000 (1 per 4.6 persons). Television (1984): total number of receivers 750,000 (1 per 13 persons). Telephones (1982): 406,355 (1 per 24 persons).

Education and health

Education (1981)

	schools	teachers	students	student/ teacher ratio
Primary (age 6–11)	11,771	83,113	1,409,765	17.0
Secondary (age 12–17)	...	68,580	861,700	12.7
Voc., teacher tr.	...	17,998	195,063	10.8
Higher□	32	...	173,400	

College graduates per 100,000 population (students graduating; 1983) 205.
Literacy (1980): total population literate 6,087,000 (91.1%); males literate 3,101,000 (91.1%); females literate 2,986,000 (91.1%).
Health (1982): physicians 21,200 (1 per 462 persons); hospital beds 47,400 (1 per 206 persons).
Food (1978–80): daily per capita caloric intake 2,717 (vegetable products 77.6%, animal products 22.4%); 117% of FAO recommended minimum requirement.

Military

Total active duty personnel (1983): 153,000 (army 81.7%; navy 7.8%; air force 10.5%). *Military expenditure as percent of GNP* (1982): 5.0% (world 6.0%); per capita expenditure: U.S.$113.

*Total includes 1,434 sq mi (3,715 sq km) of islands and cays not distributed by province. †Debt to Soviet Union and Western countries only. ‡Measures of output in centrally-planned economies include only production of material goods and provision of material support services; personal and social services not contributing to material production are excluded. §Detail does not add to total given because of rounding. ‖ Civilian only. ¶State (civilian and military) and private labour force, and unemployed. ♀Industrial workers only. ठ Based on 1981 population. □1982–83.

Cyprus

Official name*: Kipriakí Demokratía
(Kípros) (Greek)/Kıbrıs Cumhuriyeti
(Turkish) (Republic of Cyprus).
Form of government: unitary multiparty
republic with a unicameral legislature
(House of Representatives [50]).
Chief of state: President.
Head of government: Minister to the
President.
Capital: Nicosia.
Official languages: Greek; Turkish.
Official religion: none.
Monetary unit†: 1 Cyprus pound
(£C) = 1,000 mils; valuation (Oct. 29,
1984) 1£C = U.S.$1.60 = £1.33.

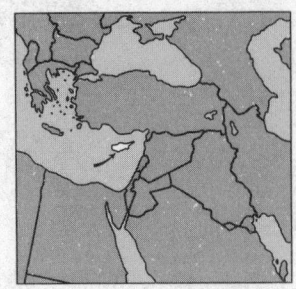

Area and population

Districts	Capitals	area		population
		sq mi	sq km	1984 estimate
Famagusta	Famagusta	766	1,984	...
Kyrenia	Kyrenia	247	640	...
Larnaca	Larnaca	433	1,121	...
Limassol	Limassol	538	1,393	...
Nicosia	Nicosia	1,049	2,717	...
Paphos	Paphos	539	1,396	...
TOTAL		3,572	9,251	657,000‡

Source: Official government figures.

Demography

Density (1984): persons per sq mi 183.9, persons per sq km 71.0.
Urban–rural (1982): urban 53.0%; rural 47.0%.
Sex distribution (1980): male 49.84%; female 50.16%.
Age breakdown (1980): under 15, 24.4%; 15–29, 28.0%; 30–44, 20.2%; 45–59,
13.4%; 60–74, 10.4%; 75 and over, 3.6%.
Population projection: (1990) 708,000; (2000) 793,000.
Doubling time: 53 years.
Ethnic composition (1980): Greek 80.7%; Turk 18.7%; other 0.6%.
Religious affiliation (1980): Greek Orthodox 76.2%; Muslim 18.7%; other
Christian 2.7%; other 2.4%.
Major cities (1982): Nicosia 123,298; Limassol 100,254; Larnaca 35,823.

Vital statistics

Birth rate per 1,000 population (1983): 22.3 (world avg. 29.0); (1980) legiti-
mate 99.4%; illegitimate 0.6%.
Death rate per 1,000 population (1983): 8.5 (world avg. 11.0).
Natural increase rate per 1,000 population (1983): 13.8 (world avg. 18.0).
Total fertility rate (avg. births per childbearing woman; 1980–85): 2.3.
Marriage rate per 1,000 population (1981): 11.2.
Divorce rate per 1,000 population (1981): 0.3.
Infant mortality rate per 1,000 live births (1982): 17.2.
Life expectancy at birth (1979–81): male 72.3 years; female 76.0 years.
Major causes of death: n.a.

National economy

Budget§ (1981). Revenue: £C191,250,000 (tax revenue 83.2%, of which import duties 19.7%; property income 9.8%). Expenditures: £C258,590,000
(general public services 16.7%; education 12.0%; defense 6.8%; health 6.7%).
Public debt (external, outstanding; 1982): U.S.$611,900,000.
Tourism ‖ (1982): receipts from visitors U.S.$292,000,000; expenditures by
nationals abroad U.S.$67,000,000.
Production (metric tons except as noted). Agriculture, forestry, fishing (1982):
potatoes 224,000, grapes 222,000, oranges 123,000, grapefruit 89,000, barley
80,000, lemons 41,000, olives 35,000, wheat 20,000; livestock (number of
live animals) 530,000 sheep, 360,000 goats, 194,000 pigs, 43,000 cattle.
Mining and quarrying¶ (1982): building stone 980,000; flotation pyrites
55,525; gypsum 28,900; asbestos 18,952; chromium ore (oxide content)
2,878. Manufacturing♀ (1982): cement 1,067,757; olive kernels 4,308; canned
vegetables 2,333; olive oil 2,567; cigarettes 3,353,112,000 units. Construc-
tion♀ (value added in £C; 1981) 111,800,000. Energy production (consumption): electricity (kW-hr; 1982) 1,444,000,000 (1,444,000,000); coal, none
(none); crude petroleum (barrels; 1982) 3,731,000 (3,753,000); petroleum
products (metric tons; 1982) 487,000 (822,000); natural gas, n.a. (n.a.).
Persons economically active (1981): total 208,100 (33.1%); female participation in the labour force 72,800 (35.0%); unemployed 3,713 (1.8%).

Price and earnings indexes (1970 = 100)

	1975	1976	1977	1978	1979	1980	1981
Consumer price index	143.1	148.5	159.6	171.3	187.5	212.9	237.5
Monthly earnings index	160.9	167.9	208.6	258.2	315.8	388.0	433.4

Household income and expenditure♀. Average household size: n.a.; average
annual income per household: n.a.; source of income: n.a.; expenditure
(1971): food and beverages 27.6%, housing 18.6%, transportation 14.2%,
clothing and footwear 11.6%, recreation 8.1%.
Land use (1981): forested 18.5%; meadows and pastures 10.1%; agricultural
and under permanent cultivation 46.8%; other 24.6%.
Gross national product♀ (at current market prices; 1982): U.S.$2,172,000,000
(U.S.$3,340 per capita).

Origin of gross domestic product♀ (current prices)

	1981			
	in value £C'000,000	% of total value	labour force	% of labour force
Agriculture	81.6	10.2	44,500	21.4
Mining	10.8	1.4	1,700	0.8
Manufacturing	147.2	18.4	38,500	18.5
Construction	106.0	13.3	18,100	8.7
Trade	172.1δ	21.6δ	19,100	9.2
Public utilities	13.0	1.6	1,500	0.7
Transportation and communication	62.2	7.8	8,300	4.0
Finance	δ	δ	4,000	1.9
Pub. admin., defense	59.4	7.4	12,100	5.8
Services	...	...	28,700	13.8
Other	145.7	18.3	31,600	15.2
TOTAL	798.0	100.0	208,100	100.0

Foreign trade□

Balance of trade (current prices)

	1978	1979	1980	1981	1982	1983
£C'000,000	−155.5	−196.9	−236.6	−251.9	−322.8	−376.6
% of total	37.9%	37.9%	38.7%	34.7%	38.4%	41.5%

Imports (1982): £C581,670,000 (machinery and transport equipment 22.6%,
petroleum and petroleum products 19.7%, cereals and cereal preparations
4.3%, iron and steel 3.9%). *Major import sources:* United Kingdom 12.7%;
Italy 10.3%; Iraq 9.1%; Japan 8.9%; West Germany 8.8%; U.S. 7.1%.
Exports (1982): £C258,830,000 (vegetables and fruit 26.7%, clothing and
accessories excluding footwear 16.1%, alcoholic beverages 5.4%, cigarettes
4.6%, machinery and transport equipment 4.1%). *Major export destinations:* United Kingdom 22.6%; Lebanon 13.5%; Saudi Arabia 10.3%; Iraq
7.6%; U.S.S.R. 5.2%; Syria 4.5%; United Arab Emirates 3.5%.

Transport and communications

Transport. Railroads: none. Roads (1983): total length 7,016 mi, 11,292 km
(paved 48%). Vehicles (1983): passenger cars 110,230; trucks and buses 38,-
919. Merchant marine (1983): vessels (100 gross tons and over) 593; total
deadweight tonnage 5,784,798. Air transport (1982): passenger-mi 531,597,-
000, passenger-km 855,525,000; short ton-mi cargo 66,347,000, metric ton-
km cargo 96,865,000; airports (1984) with scheduled flights 2.
Communications. Daily newspapers (1983): total number 12; total circulation 69,306; circulation per 1,000 population 106.5. Radios (1983): total
number of receivers 400,000 (1 per 1.6 persons). Television (1983): total
number of receivers 111,000 (1 per 5.8 persons). Telephones (1982): 86,144
(1 per 7.5 persons).

Education and health

Education (1983–84)

	schools	teachers	students	student/ teacher ratio
Primary (age 5–12)	413	2,212	46,653	21.0
Secondary (age 12–18)	89	2,606	44,071	16.9
Vocational	18	505	5,395	10.7
Higher	16	240	2,201	9.2

College graduates per 100,000 population (students graduating; 1981): 298.
Literacy (1980): total population literate 416,000 (89.0%); males literate
216,000 (93.5%); females literate 200,000 (84.5%).
Health (1983)♀: physicians 635 (1 per 1,024 persons); hospital beds 5,375 (1
per 121 persons).
Food (1978–80): daily per capita caloric intake 3,199 (vegetable products
75.7%, animal products 24.3%); 129% of FAO recommended minimum.

Military

Total active duty Greek-Cypriot personnel (1983): 10,000 (army 100.0%). *Military expenditure* (1982): U.S.$45,311,000; per capita expenditure U.S.$91.
Total active duty Turkish-Cypriot personnel (1983): 4,500. *Military expenditure* (1982): U.S.$4,980,000; per capita expenditure U.S.$33.

*In July 1974 Turkey invaded Cyprus, and an autonomous Turkish-Cypriot admin-
istration was established in the northern part of the island. On Feb. 13, 1975, the
occupied territory was declared the "Turkish Federated State of Cyprus," and a
legislative assembly comprised of 40 members was convened. Following a unilateral
declaration of independence in November 1983, the autonomous sector was renamed
the "Turkish Republic of Northern Cyprus." The state is not recognized internationally. †Monetary unit of the Turkish sector is the Turkish lira (LT); valuation (Oct.
29, 1984) 1 U.S.$ = LT416.51; 1 £ = LT502.73. ‡Population (1981) for government
controlled areas (the Greek south) was officially 209,886 (de jure). The 1982 estimated
population for the Turkish sector was given as 153,239; however, a 1984 estimate for
the entire island including Turkish immigrants, internal refugees no longer resident
in their home districts, and international immigrants, is probably about 657,000.
§Budget data are for government controlled areas only. *Budget* for the Turkish sector
(1984). Revenue: LT17,760,000,000 (local taxes 36.9%, local loans 30.8%, foreign
aid 32.3%). Expenditures: LT17,760,000,000 (personnel 39.8%, investment 25.5%, defense 6.0%). ‖ Tourism is for government controlled areas only. The Turkish sector
contains the two most popular resorts, Famagusta and Kyrenia. ¶Mining data are for
government controlled areas only. About 56% of the island's total mining and quarrying output originates in the Turkish sector. ♀Data are for government controlled
areas only; GDP for Turkish sector (1981) U.S.$237,000,000 (U.S.$1,558 per capita).
δFinance included with trade. □Foreign trade data are for government controlled
areas only. *Foreign trade* for the Turkish sector (1982). *Imports:* LT19,402,900,000.
Major import sources: Turkey 30.4%; United Kingdom 16.3%; West Germany 5.2%;
Italy 3.9%. *Exports:* LT6,371,300,000 (citrus fruit, potatoes, carobs, tobacco). *Major
export destinations:* United Kingdom 45.3%; Turkey 16.1%.

Czechoslovakia

Official name: Československá Socialistická Republika (Czechoslovak Socialist Republic).
Form of government: federal republic with two legislative houses (House of the People [200]; House of Nations [150]).
Chief of state: President.
Head of government: Premier.
Capital: Prague.
Official languages: Czech; Slovak.
Official religion: none.
Monetary unit: 1 koruna (Kčs) = 100 halura; valuation (Oct. 29, 1984) 1 U.S.$ = Kčs6.67; 1 £ = Kčs8.05.

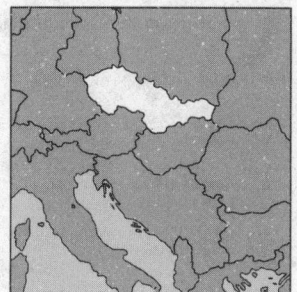

Area and population

Republics Regions	Capitals	area sq mi	area sq km	population 1983 estimate
Czech Socialist Republic	Prague			
Jihočeský	České Budějovice	4,380	11,345	693,200
Jihomoravský	Brno	5,802	15,028	2,051,700
Severočeský	Ústí nad Labem	3,015	7,810	1,173,800
Severomoravský	Ostrava	4,273	11,067	1,944,700
Středočeský	Prague	4,248	11,003	1,147,100
Východočeský	Hradec Králové	4,340	11,240	1,248,000
Západočeský	Plzeň	4,199	10,876	878,000
Slovak Socialist Republic	Bratislava			
Středoslovenský	Banská Bystrica	6,944	17,985	1,549,100
Východoslovenský	Košice	6,250	16,188	1,428,600
Západoslovenský	Bratislava	5,595	14,491	1,701,500
Capital Cities				
Prague	—	191	495	1,185,700
Bratislava	—	142	368	394,600
TOTAL		49,381*	127,896	15,396,000

Source: Official government figures.

Demography

Density (1984): persons per sq mi 309.5, persons per sq km 120.9.
Urban–rural (1983): urban 73.3%; rural 26.7%.
Sex distribution (1984): male 48.7%; female 51.3%.
Age breakdown (1984): under 15, 24.4%; 15–29, 21.7%; 30–44, 21.5%; 45–59, 16.2%; 60–74, 11.7%; 75 and over, 4.5%.
Population projection: (1990) 15,758,000; (2000) 16,278,000.
Doubling time: 250 years.
Ethnic composition (1983): Czech 63.6%; Slovak 31.0%; Hungarian 3.8%; Polish 0.5%; German 0.4%; Russian and Ukrainian 0.4%; other 0.3%.
Religious affiliation (1980): Roman Catholic 65.6%; atheist 20.1%; Czechoslovak Church 4.4%; Evangelist Church of Czech Brethren 1.4%; other 8.5%.
Major cities (1984 est.): Prague 1,187,300; Bratislava 404,900; Brno 382,300; Ostrava 324,700; Košice 216,300.

Vital statistics

Birth rate per 1,000 population (1983): 14.8 (world avg. 29.0); (1982) legitimate 94.2%, illegitimate 5.8%.
Death rate per 1,000 population (1983): 12.0 (world avg. 11.0).
Natural increase rate per 1,000 population (1983): 2.8 (world avg. 18.0).
Total fertility rate (avg. births per childbearing woman; 1982): 2.3.
Marriage rate per 1,000 population (1984): 6.6.
Divorce rate per 1,000 population (1984): 2.3.
Infant mortality rate per 1,000 live births (1983): 15.6.
Life expectancy at birth (1982): male 67.1 years; female 74.4 years.
Major causes of death per 100,000 population (1983): cerebrovascular disease 335.6; ischemic heart disease 320.1; malignant neoplasms (cancers) 232.6; bronchitis, emphysema, and asthma 98.2.

National economy

Budget (1982). Revenue: Kčs314,203,000,000 (receipts from enterprises 70.6%; taxes 13.6%). Expenditures: Kčs314,046,000,000 (education, health, social welfare, and culture 41.6%; national economy 38.1%; defense 12.0%; general administration 1.9%).
Public debt (external, outstanding, to the West; 1981): U.S.$4,620,000,000.
Tourism (1979): receipts from visitors U.S.$385,300,000; expenditures by nationals abroad U.S.$276,100,000.
Production (metric tons except as noted). Agriculture, forestry, fishing (1983): sugar beets 6,037,000, wheat 5,820,000, barley 3,600,000, potatoes 3,105,000, corn (maize) 710,000; livestock (number of live animals) 7,126,-000 pigs, 5,131,000 cattle, 47,000,000 chickens; roundwood 18,960,000 cu m†; fish catch 18,021†. Mining and quarrying (1982): iron ore 1,861,000; magnesite 672,000; copper 26,980; zinc 13,857. Manufacturing (1983): crude steel 15,024,000; cement 10,498,000; rolled steel 10,072,000; wood pulp and paper 1,597,000; sulfuric acid 1,244,000; plastic and resins 956,400; chemical fertilizers 917,000; cotton fabrics 585,321,000 m; beer 24,957,000 hectolitres; wine 1,402,000 hectolitres; television sets 415,494 units. Construction (1982): 7,702,000 sq m. Energy production (consumption): electricity (kW-hr; 1983) 76,259,000,000 (76,553,000,000†); coal (metric tons; 1983) 125,793,000 (124,007,000†); crude petroleum (barrels; 1982) 652,000 (120,622,000); petroleum products (metric tons; 1982) 13,446,000 (13,539,-000); natural gas (cu m; 1982) 583,330,000 (7,992,120,000).
Land use (1982): agricultural 40.4%; forested 35.8%; meadows and pastures 13.2%; other 10.6%.

Gross national product (at current market prices; 1982): U.S.$85,837,000,000 (U.S.$5,585 per capita).

Origin of gross domestic product (current prices)

	1982 in value Kčs'000,000	% of total value	labour force	% of labour force
Agriculture	41,639	8.4	1,061,262	13.6
Mining	‡	‡	‡	‡
Manufacturing	306,393‡	61.6‡	3,048,684‡	39.2‡
Construction	50,502	10.2	633,797	8.1
Trade	59,331	11.9	871,019	11.2
Public utilities	‡	‡	‡	‡
Transportation and communication	25,577	5.1	501,643	6.4
Finance	§	§	§	§
Pub. admin., defense	§	§	§	§
Services	11,942	2.4	1,583,267	20.3
Other	1,816§	0.4§	82,352§	1.1§
TOTAL	497,200	100.0	7,782,024	100.0*

Persons economically active (1982): total 7,782,024 (50.6%); female participation in the labour force 3,565,316 (45.8%); unemployed, n.a.

Price and earnings indexes (1970 = 100)

	1976	1977	1978	1979	1980	1981	1982
Consumer price index	101.6	103.0	104.6	108.6	111.8	112.7	...
Monthly earnings index	123.1	127.9	132.2	136.1	139.2	142.8	...

Household income and expenditure. Average household size (1982) 3.1; income per household Kčs50,360 (U.S.$8,580); sources of income: wages and salaries 59.8%, welfare 34.1%, other 6.1%; expenditure (1982): food 26.5%, clothing and footwear 26.6%, services 12.9%.

Foreign trade

Balance of trade (current prices)

	1978	1979	1980	1981	1982	1983
Kčs'000,000	−4,465	−5,604	−1,377	+1,413	+1,345	+1,105
% of total	3.4%	3.8%	0.9%	0.8%	0.7%	0.5%

Imports (1982): Kčs94,217,000,000 (machinery and transport equipment 30.8%, of which industrial machinery 8.4%, agricultural and construction machinery 8.4%, transport equipment 5.4%; crude petroleum and petroleum products 18.9%; chemicals 7.3%; food 7.1%; nonferrous metals 3.3%; iron and steel 2.2%). *Major import sources:* U.S.S.R. 43.4%; East Germany 9.5%; Poland 6.3%; Hungary 5.5%; West Germany 4.7%; Yugoslavia 4.6%; Austria 3.3%.
Exports (1982): Kčs95,562,000,000 (machinery and transport equipment 50.1%, of which industrial machinery 11.3%, road vehicles and parts 8.6%, textile and leather machinery 4.8%; iron and steel 7.1%; mineral fuels and lubricants 5.1%; footwear 3.3%). *Major export destinations:* U.S.S.R. 40.7%; East Germany 9.1%; Poland 6.2%; Hungary 5.3%; West Germany 5.1%; Yugoslavia 4.1%; Austria 3.0%; Bulgaria 2.8%.

Transport and communications

Transport. Railroads (1983): length 8,166 mi, 13,142 km; passenger-mi 11,833,000,000, passenger-km 19,043,000,000; short ton-mi cargo 45,308,-000,000, metric ton-km cargo 66,149,000,000. Roads (1983): total length 45,900 mi, 73,900 km (paved 100%). Vehicles (1982): passenger cars 2,416,205; trucks and buses 385,959. Merchant marine (1983): vessels (100 gross tons and over) 19; total deadweight tonnage 276,647. Air transport (1982): passenger-mi 1,148,000,000, passenger-km 1,847,000,000; short ton-mi cargo 32,809,000, metric ton-km cargo 47,900,000; airports (1984) with scheduled flights 14.
Communications. Daily newspapers (1983): total number 30; total circulation 4,364,822; circulation per 1,000 population 284. Radios (1983): total number of receivers 4,132,865 (1 per 3.7 persons). Television (1983): total number of receivers 4,307,748 (1 per 3.6 persons). Telephones (1983): 3,306,155 (1 per 4.6 persons).

Education and health

Education (1983–84)

	schools	teachers	students	student/ teacher ratio
Primary (age 6–14)	6,445	92,435	1,992,400	21.6
Secondary (age 15–18)	338	9,189	144,948	15.8
Voc., teacher tr.	569	16,923	290,038	17.1
Higher	36	18,406	180,995	9.8

College graduates per 100,000 population (students graduating; 1982): 536.8.
Literacy (1979): total population literate 11,518,120 (99.5%); males literate 5,529,792 (99.6%); females literate 5,988,328 (99.4%).
Health (1983): physicians 44,600 (1 per 345 persons); hospital beds 154,000 (1 per 100 persons).
Food (1978–80): daily per capita caloric intake 3,472 (vegetable products 64.8%, animal products 35.2%); 141% of FAO recommended minimum.

Military

Total active duty personnel (1983): 204,500 (army 72.4%; navy, none; air force 27.6%). *Military expenditure as percent of GNP* (1982): 5.2% (world 6.0%); per capita expenditure U.S.$467.

*Detail does not add to total given because of rounding. †1982. ‡Mining and public utilities are included with manufacturing. §Finance, public administration, and defense are included with other.

Denmark

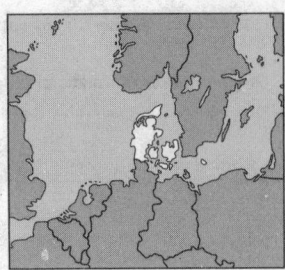

Official name: Kongeriget Danmark
(Kingdom of Denmark).
Form of government: parliamentary
state and constitutional monarchy
with one legislative house (Folketing
[179]).
Chief of state: Danish Monarch.
Head of government: Prime Minister.
Capital: Copenhagen.
Official language: Danish.
Official religion: Evangelical Lutheran.
Monetary unit: 1 krone (Dkr; plural
kroner) = 100 øre; valuation (Oct 29,
1984) 1 U.S.$ = Dkr11.06;
1 £ = Dkr13.35.

Area and population*

Counties	Capitals	area sq mi	area sq km	population 1984 estimate
Århus	Århus	1,761	4,561	579,800
Bornholm	Rønne	227	588	47,200
Frederiksborg	Hillerød	520	1,347	332,900
Fyn	Odense	1,346	3,486	453,900
København	—	202	522	616,200
Nordjylland	Ålborg	2,383	6,173	482,100
Ribe	Ribe	1,209	3,132	215,200
Ringkøbing	Ringkøbing	1,874	4,853	264,100
Roskilde	Roskilde	344	891	207,100
Sønderjylland	Åbenrå	1,517	3,930	249,800
Storstrøm	Nykøbing	1,312	3,398	257,600
Vejle	Vejle	1,157	2,997	326,700
Vestsjælland	Sorø	1,152	2,984	277,800
Viborg	Viborg	1,592	4,122	230,600
Cities				
Copenhagen (København)	—	34	88	482,900
Frederiksberg	—	3	9	88,100
TOTAL		16,633	43,081†	5,112,100†

Source: Official government figures.

Demography

Density (1984): persons per sq mi 307.3, persons per sq km 118.7.
Urban–rural (1982): urban 84.0%; rural 16.0%.
Sex distribution (1984): male 49.25%; female 50.75%.
Age breakdown (1980): under 15, 20.9%; 15–29, 22.2%; 30–44, 21.2%; 45–59,
16.3%; 60–74, 13.9%; 75 and over, 5.5%..
Population projection: (1990) 5,101,000; (2000) 5,086,000.
Doubling time: ‡.
Ethnic composition (1983): Danish 98.4%; other Scandinavian 0.4%; Turkish
0.3%; other 0.9%.
Religious affiliation (1980): Evangelical Lutheran 95.6%; Muslim 1.2%; Ro-
man Catholic 0.6%; other 2.6%.
Major cities (1983 est.): Greater Copenhagen 1,372,000; Århus 249,000;
Odense 171,000; Ålborg 155,000.

Vital statistics

Birth rate per 1,000 population (1982): 10.3 (world avg. 29.0); (1982) legiti-
mate 61.7%, illegitimate 38.3%.
Death rate per 1,000 population (1982): 10.8 (world avg. 11.0).
Natural increase rate per 1,000 population (1982): −0.5 (world avg. 18.0).
Total fertility rate (avg. births per childbearing woman; 1980–85): 1.7.
Marriage rate per 1,000 population (1982): 4.8.
Divorce rate per 1,000 population (1982): 2.9.
Infant mortality rate per 1,000 live births (1982): 8.2.
Life expectancy at birth (1981–82): male 71.4 years; female 77.4 years.
Major causes of death per 100,000 population (1982): ischemic heart disease
321.6; malignant neoplasms (cancers) 269.1; cerebrovascular disease 103.1.

National economy

Budget (1982). Revenue: Dkr243,715,000,000 (general sales tax 28.2%, ordinary income tax 24.8%, excises 12.3%, property income 9.3%, other 25.4%).
Expenditures: Dkr286,716,000,000 (current outlays 92.9%, of which income
transfers 47.0%, final consumption expenditures 45.9%).
Public debt (outstanding; 1982): U.S.$33,349,000,000.
Tourism (1982): receipts from visitors U.S.$1,306,000,000; expenditures by
nationals abroad U.S.$1,331,000,000.
Production (metric tons except as noted). Agriculture, forestry, fishing (1983):
barley 4,450,000, sugar beets 2,632,000, wheat 1,577,000, milk 5,427,000;
livestock (number of live animals) 9,289,000 pigs, 2,900,000 cattle; roundwood 3,051,000 cu m§; fish catch 1,927,000§. Manufacturing (value added
in kroner; 1981): fabricated metal products and machinery 23,690,000,000,
of which machinery 13,630,000,000; food, beverages, and tobacco 18,070,-
000,000, of which food 14,420,000,000, chemicals and chemical products
7,300,000,000; paper and printed products 6,290,000,000. Construction
(1983 ‖): residential 2,264,000 sq m; nonresidential 3,774,000 sq m. Energy
production (consumption): electricity (kW-hr; 1982) 22,068,000,000 (23,-
807,000,000); coal (metric tons; 1982) none (9,619,000); crude petroleum
(barrels; 1982) 12,360,000 (43,640,000); petroleum products (metric tons;
1982) 5,596,000 (9,647,000); natural gas (cu m; 1982) none (n.a.)
Land use (1981): forested 11.6%; meadows and pastures 5.8%; agricultural
and under permanent cultivation 62.6%; other 20.0%.
Gross national product (at current market prices; 1983): U.S.$50,444,000,000
(U.S.$9,870 per capita).

Origin of gross domestic product (current prices)

	1983 in value Dkr'000,000	% of total value	labour force	% of labour force
Agriculture	24,508	5.4	177,000	7.3
Mining	3,580	0.8	3,000	0.1
Manufacturing	86,876	19.1	503,000	20.7
Construction	27,820	6.1	157,000	6.4
Trade	60,241	13.2	320,000	13.2
Public utilities	8,754	1.9	14,000	0.6
Transportation and communication	35,791	7.9	178,000	7.4
Finance¶	75,316	16.6	156,000	6.5
Pub. admin., defense	105,570	23.2 }	886,000	36.7
Services	22,984	5.1		
Other	3,216	0.7	25,000	1.0
TOTAL	454,656♀	100.0	2,418,000†	100.0

Persons economically active (1983): total 2,730,000 (53.4%); female participation in total labour force 1,087,000 (45.0%); unemployed 312,000 (8.2%).

Price and earnings indexes (1980 = 100)

	1978	1979	1980	1981	1982	1983	1984♂
Consumer price index	81.2	89.0	100.0	111.7	123.0	131.5	139.9
Monthly earnings index	80.5	89.8	100.0	108.9	120.5	128.4	...

Household income and expenditure. Average household size (1984) 2.4; income per household (1981) Dkr133,031 (U.S.$18,161); principal source of
income (1980): wages and salaries 75.5%, pensions 12.6%, self-employment
7.6%; expenditure (1981): rent 23.8%, food and beverages 17.1%, education,
recreation, and culture 12.9%, transportation 12.5%, utilities 6.2%.

Foreign trade

Balance of trade (current prices)

	1978	1979	1980	1981	1982	1983
'000,000 kroner	−16,097	−19,478	−13,717	−10,373	−10,692	−2,223
% of total	11.0%	11.2%	6.7%	4.3%	4.0%	0.8%

Imports (1982): Dkr138,865,000,000 (mineral fuels 22.1%, of which crude
petroleum and petroleum products 17.7%, coal 3.6%; machinery and transport equipment 21.2%; manufactured goods 19.7%, of which iron and steel
5.9%; chemicals and related products 10.0%; food and live animals 9.6%).
Major import sources: West Germany 20.7%; Sweden 11.8%; United Kingdom 11.0%; The Netherlands 6.9%; United States 6.8%.
Exports (1982): Dkr128,173,000,000 (food and live animals 30.6%, of which
meat and meat preparations 14.2%, dairy products 5.5%, fish and shellfish
5.0%; machinery and transport equipment 23.6%; chemicals and related
products 8.4%). *Major export destinations:* West Germany 17.5%; United
Kingdom 14.1%; Sweden 10.9%; Norway 6.5%; United States 5.8%.

Transport and communications

Transport. Railroads (1982): length 1,529 mi, 2,461 km; passenger-mi
2,619,000,000, passenger-km 4,215,000,000; short ton-mi cargo 1,027,000,-
000, metric ton-km cargo 1,653,000,000. Roads (1982): total length 43,285
mi, 69,661 km (paved 100%). Vehicles (1982): passenger cars 1,358,238;
trucks and buses 388,071. Merchant marine (1983): vessels (100 gross
tons and over) 1,112; total deadweight tonnage 7,926,127. Air transport
(1982): passenger-mi 5,859,082,000, passenger-km 9,429,297,000; short ton-
mi cargo 80,098,000, metric ton-km cargo 116,941,000; airports (1984) with
scheduled flights 10.
Communications. Daily newspapers (1983): total number 47; total circulation 1,805,000; circulation per 1,000 population 353. Radios (1983): total
number of receivers 2,042,100 (1 per 2.5 persons). Television (1983): total number of receivers 1,886,322 (1 per 2.7 persons). Telephones (1982):
3,483,323 (1 per 1.5 persons).

Education and health

Education (1981–82)

	schools	teachers	students	student/ teacher ratio
Primary and lower secondary (age 7–14)	2,536	65,257	722,387	11.1
Upper secondary (age 15–19)	154	6,951	208,202	30.0
Teacher training	72□	...	23,232	...
Other higher	286□	...	83,437	...

College graduates per 100,000 population: n.a. *Literacy* (1983): virtually
100%.
Health (1982): physicians 7,796 (1 per 656 persons); hospital beds 39,273 (1
per 130 persons).
Food (1978–80): daily per capita caloric intake 3,502 (vegetable products
55.7%, animal products 44.3%); 136% of FAO recommended minimum.

Military

Total active duty personnel (1982): 31,200 (army 57.7%; navy 18.6%; air force
23.7%). *Military expenditure as percent of GNP* (1982): 2.6% (world 6.0%);
per capita expenditure U.S.$309.

---

*Excluding Greenland (*q.v.*) and the Faeroe Islands. †Detail does not add to total
given because of rounding. ‡Not applicable; population is declining. §1982. ‖ Completed during year. ¶Includes finance, insurance, real estate, and business services.
♀An adjusted figure of Dkr441,591,000,000 is obtained by subtracting imputed bank
service charges. ♂June, 1984. □1979–80.

Djibouti

Official name: Jumhūrīyah Jībūtī (Arabic); République de Djibouti (French) (Republic of Djibouti).
Form of government: unitary single-party republic with one legislative house (National Assembly [65]).
Chief of state: President.
Head of government: Prime Minister.
Capital: Djibouti.
Official languages: Arabic; French.
Official religion: none.
Monetary unit: 1 Djibouti Franc (DF) = 100 centimes; valuation (Oct. 29, 1984) 1 U.S.$ = DF174.00; 1 £ = DF210.00.

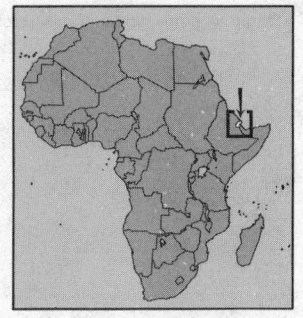

Area and population

Districts	Capitals	area* sq mi	area* sq km	population 1984 estimate
Ali-Sabieh	Ali-Sabieh	925	2,400	15,000
Dikhil	Dikhil	2,775	7,200	30,000
Djibouti	Djibouti	225	600	200,000
Obock	Obock	2,200	5,700	15,000
Tadjourah	Tadjourah	2,825	7,300	30,000
TOTAL		8,950	23,200	335,000†

Source: Official government figures; Britannica estimate.

Demography

Density (1984): persons per sq mi 37.4, persons per sq km 14.4.
Urban–rural: n.a.
Sex distribution (1980): male 49.24%; female 50.76%.
Age breakdown (1980): under 15, 42.3%; 15–24, 18.1%; 25–64, 36.2%; 65 and over, 3.4%.
Population projection: (1990) 375,000; (2000) 453,000.
Doubling time: 36 years.
Ethnic composition‡ (1978): Afar 38%; Issa 28%; Issachar and Gad 20%; Arab 5%; European 5%; other 4%.
Religious affiliation‡ (1980): Sunnī Muslim 90.5%; Roman Catholic 7.9%; other 1.6%.
Major city and towns (1982): Djibouti 200,000§; Ali-Sabieh 4,000; Tadjourah 3,500.

Vital statistics

Birth rate per 1,000 population (1980–85): 44.8 (world avg. 27.5).
Death rate per 1,000 population (1980–85): 21.1 (world avg. 10.6).
Natural increase rate per 1,000 population (1980–85): 23.7 (world avg. 16.9).
Total fertility rate (avg. births per childbearing woman; 1980–85): 6.1.
Marriage rate per 1,000 population (1982): 7.9.
Divorce rate per 1,000 population (1982): 2.3.
Infant mortality rate per 1,000 live births (1982): 63.4.
Life expectancy at birth: n.a.
Major causes of death of hospitalized patients ‖ (1977): dehydration (children only) 58; heart disease 40; tuberculosis 36; premature birth (infants only) 30.

National economy

Budget (1984). Revenue¶: DF21,854,600,000 (indirect taxes 53.1%, direct taxes 24.1%, customs duties 5.9%, excises 3.1%). Expenditures: DF21,854,-600,000 (defense 21.7%, general administration 16.2%, economic development and services 9.0%, social welfare and health 7.6%, education 6.7%, debt payment 3.1%).
Public debt (external, outstanding; 1982): U.S.$43,000,000.
Tourism: n.a.
Production (metric tons except as noted). Agriculture♀ and fishing (1982): tomatoes 278, carrots 11, pimientos 5; livestock (number of live animals) 550,000 goats, 380,000 sheep, 54,000 camels, 43,000 cattle, 7,000 asses; fish catch 299. Mining and quarrying (1982): mineral production limited to locally used construction material and evaporated salt. Manufacturing (1982): n.a. Main items produced are furniture, nonalcoholic beverages, light electromechanical goods, and mineral water. Construction (1982): residential 68,162 sq m; nonresidential 26,755 sq m. Energy production (consumption): electricity (kW-hr; 1982) 130,900,000 (130,900,000); coal, none (n.a.); crude petroleum, none (n.a.); petroleum products (metric tons; 1982) none (69,000); natural gas, none (n.a.).
Persons economically active: n.a.

Price and earnings indexes (1975 = 100)

	1977	1978	1979	1980	1981	1982	1983
Consumer price index	...	...	...	...	...	...	...
Monthly earnings indexδ	100.0	100.0	100.0	126.7	...	...	...

Household income and expenditure. Average household size☐ 1982) 5.6; average income per salaried employee DF621,086 (U.S.$3,494); source of income: n.a.; expenditure: n.a.
Land use (1981): forested 0.3%; meadows and pastures 11.1%; agricultural and under permanent cultivation ♀; other 88.6%.
Gross national product (at current market prices; 1981): U.S.$180,000,000 (U.S.$480 per capita).

Origin of gross domestic product (current prices)

	1980 in value DF'000,000	1980 % of total value	1982 labour forceδ	1982 % of labour force
Agriculture	4,800	7.1	63	0.4
Mining	—	—	—	—
Manufacturing	4,630	6.9	726	4.5
Construction	3,882	5.8	2,309	14.3
Trade, restaurants, and hotels	15,857	23.7	3,148	19.5
Public utilities	1,699	2.5	456	2.8
Transportation and communication	5,867	8.7	2,711	17.0
Finance	7,745	11.5	1,296	8.0
Pub. admin., defense	14,009	20.8	3,347	20.7
Services	866	1.3	915	5.6
Other	7,838	11.7	1,168	7.2
TOTAL	67,193	100.0	16,139	100.0

Foreign trade◊

Balance of trade (current prices)

	1977	1978	1979	1980
DF'000,000	−15,585	−25,963	−31,431	−47,474
% of total	69.8%	80.4%	88.7%	91.4%

Imports (1980): DF49,695,000,000 (special transactions, including importation of gold coins, personal effects, and military goods 31.4%; food and live animals 18.3%, of which cereals and cereal preparations 7.7%; machinery and transport equipment 13.0%, of which electrical machinery and appliances 5.6%; textiles [all forms], fabrics, yarns 5.9%; kat [a stimulant] 5.4%; tobacco 3.5%). *Major import sources:* France 50.3%; Ethiopia 6.5%; North America 5.6%; Benelux 5.2%; Japan 5.0%.
Exports (1980): DF2,221,000,000 (unspecified special transactions 44.9%; live animals [including camels] 8.6%; meat and fish [all forms] 6.7%; fruits and vegetables 6.3%; hides, skins, and leather products 6.1%). *Major export destinations:* France 65.7%; Italy 5.7%; Somalia 5.0%; Benelux 2.4%.

Transport and communications

Transport. Railroads (1982): length 66 mi, 106 km; short tons cargo 138,780, metric tons cargo 154,200△. Roads (1983): total length 1,806 mi, 2,906 km (paved 11%). Vehicles (1982): passenger cars 9,000; trucks and buses 1,500. Merchant marine (1983): vessels (100 gross tons and over) 9; total deadweight tonnage 3,256. Air transport+ (1982): passenger arrivals 70,572, passenger departures 63,318; cargo arrivals (metric tons) 7,096,000, cargo departures (metric tons) 1,758,000; airports (1984) with scheduled flights 3.
Communications. Daily newspapers: none. Radios (1982): total number of receivers 17,500 (1 per 19 persons). Television (1982): total number of receivers 11,000 (1 per 30 persons). Telephone subscribers (1982): 3,460 (1 per 97 persons).

Education and health

Education (1982–83)

	schools	teachers	students	student/ teacher ratio
Primary (age 6–14)	48	467	20,670	44.3
Secondary (age 12–20)	7	200	4,429	22.1
Voc., teacher tr.	2	83	1,065	12.8
Higher	—	—	184	

College graduates per 100,000 population: n.a. *Literacy* (c. 1980): 11.9%; 8.8% if discounting the expatriate population.
Health (1983): physicians 61 (1 per 5,492 persons); hospital beds 1,239 (1 per 270 persons).
Food: n.a.

Military

Total active duty personnel (1982): 2,700 (army 96.3%; navy 0.7%; air force 3.0%)⊕. *Military expenditure as percent of GNP:* n.a.

*Approximate figures. †Including 45,000 unaccounted, not shown separately; 13,000 refugees from Ethiopian Djibouti, out of a total of about 45,000, had returned to their homeland by May 1984. ‡Excluding refugees. §Population of district. ‖ Actual number of deaths. ¶Current revenue only. ♀In 1982 only 450 ac (200 ha) of land were cultivated. δSalaried employees only. ☐Sample survey in the city of Djibouti only. ◊The value of imports includes merchandise destined for Ethiopia and northern Somalia. The value of exports excludes reexports originating in Ethiopia or northern Somalia; in 1980 the value of reexports from Ethiopia and northern Somalia was approximately five times more significant than the value of domestic exports. △Total weight of Ethiopian exports and imports transported to and from the port of Djibouti. +City of Djibouti airport only. ⊕In 1982, 3,250 French military personnel were also stationed in Djibouti.

Dominica

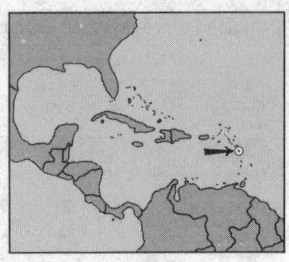

Official name: Commonwealth of
Dominica.
Form of government: multiparty
republic with one legislative house
(House of Assembly [31]).
Chief of state: President.
Head of government: Prime Minister.
Capital: Roseau.
Official language: English.
Official religion: none.
Monetary unit: 1 East Caribbean dollar
(EC$) = 100 cents; valuation (Oct. 29,
1984) 1 U.S.$ = EC$2.70*;
1 £ = EC$3.26.

Area and population	area		population
			1970
Parishes	sq mi	sq km	census
St. Andrew	69	179	11,998
St. David	49	127	6,709
St. George	21	54	20,114
St. John	23	60	5,283
St. Joseph	46	119	6,393
St. Luke	4	10	1,622
St. Mark	4	10	1,943
St. Patrick	32	83	10,085
St. Paul	26	67	4,459
St. Peter	11	29	1,696
TOTAL	290†	751†	70,302

Source: Official government figures.

Demography

Density (1984): persons per sq mi 258.5, persons per sq km 99.8.
Urban-rural (1970): urban 46.2%; rural 53.8%.
Sex distribution (1970): male 47.40%; female 52.60%.
Age breakdown (1970): under 15, 49.1%; 15–29, 21.2%; 30–44, 11.2%; 45–59,
10.0%; 60–74, 6.3%; 75 and over, 2.2%.
Population projection: (1990) 95,000; (2000) 108,000.
Doubling time: 43 years.
Ethnic composition (1970): black 79.8%; mixed 17.7%; Amerindian 1.8%;
white 0.5%; other 0.2%.
Religious affiliation (1981): Roman Catholic 91.8%; other 8.2%.
Major towns (1981): Roseau 8,346; Portsmouth 2,220.

Vital statistics

Birth rate per 1,000 population (1978): 21.4 (world avg. 30.5); (1980) legiti-
mate 35.0%; illegitimate 65.0%.
Death rate per 1,000 population (1978): 5.3 (world avg. 12.0).
Natural increase rate per 1,000 population (1978): 16.1 (world avg. 18.5).
Total fertility rate (avg. births per childbearing woman; 1978): 3.7.
Marriage rate per 1,000 population (1969): 3.3.
Divorce rate per 1,000 population: n.a.
Infant mortality rate per 1,000 live births (1978): 19.6.
Life expectancy at birth (1980–85): male 66.5 years; female 72.8 years.
Major causes of death per 10,000 population (1975): diseases of the circula-
tory system 16.1; malignant neoplasms (cancers) 7.3; accidents, poisoning,
and violence 5.2; infectious and parasitic diseases 4.6; diseases of the res-
piratory system 3.3.

National economy

Budget (1979)‡. Revenue: EC$32,410,000§ (consumption duties 20.1%; prop-
erty tax 17.2%; import duties 14.1%; income tax 13.2%; stamp taxes 10.0%;
social security funds 7.8%). Expenditures: EC$53,400,000 (general public
services 23.6%; roads 15.2%; education 10.1%; health 8.8%; agriculture,
forestry, and fishing 4.0%; community development 3.0%; defense 1.2%).
Public debt (external, outstanding): n.a.
Tourism (1981): receipts from visitors U.S.$2,000,000; expenditures by na-
tionals abroad, n.a.
Production (metric tons except as noted). Agriculture and fishing (1982):
fruits excluding melons 62,000, bananas 32,000, coconuts 19,000, lemons
and limes 13,000, sugarcane 4,000, copra 3,000, cacao 1,000, eggs 270;
livestock (number of live animals) 8,000 pigs, 6,000 goats, 4,000 cattle,
4,000 sheep, 115,000 chickens; fish catch 1,550. Mining and quarrying
(1980): pumice 110,000. Manufacturing (1981): soap 6,900. Construction:
n.a. Energy production (consumption): electricity (kW-hr; 1982) 17,000,-
000 (17,000,000); coal, none (n.a.); petroleum products (metric tons; 1982)
n.a. (12,000); natural gas, none (n.a.).
Persons economically active¶ (1980): total 27,380 (37.0%); female participation in the labour force 9,500 (34.7%); unemployed 5,750 (21.0%).

Price and earnings indexes (1980 = 100)							
	1977	1978	1979	1980	1981	1982	1983
Consumer price index	59.3	63.9	76.6	100.0	113.3	118.3	123.2
Earnings index	...	...	...	...	...	...	...

Household income and expenditure. Average household size (1960) 4.9;
average annual income per household: n.a.; source of income: n.a.; expenditure: n.a.
Gross national product (at current market prices; 1981): U.S.$60,000,000
(U.S.$810 per capita).

Origin of gross domestic product (current prices)				
	1980		1970	
	in value EC$'000,000	% of total value	labour force	% of labour force
Agriculture	56.0	30.2	7,720	39.4
Mining	1.3	0.7	6	—
Manufacturing	10.3	5.6	1,545	7.9
Construction	22.9	12.4	1,906	9.7
Trade	22.2	12.0	1,737	8.8
Public utilities	2.5	1.3	1,219	6.2
Transportation and communication	13.0	7.0	704	3.6
Finance	8.8	4.7	...	...
Pub. admin., defense	43.0	23.2	...	...
Services	1.9	1.0	4,662	23.8
Other	3.4	1.8	118	0.6
TOTAL	185.3	100.0 ‖	19,617	100.0

Land use (1981): forested 41.3%; meadows and pastures 2.7%; agricultural
and under permanent cultivation 22.7%; other 33.3%.

Foreign trade

Balance of trade (current prices)						
	1977	1978	1979	1980	1981	1982
EC$'000,000	−26.8	−33.9	−34.6	−102.4	−82.3	−62.2
% of total	29.3%	28.3%	40.5%	66.1%	44.3%	32.0%

Imports (1980): EC$128,730,000 (basic manufactures 20.3%; machinery and
transport equipment 20.1%, of which passenger motor vehicles 8.2%; food
and live animals 20.0%, of which cereals and preparations 3.6%, meat and
preparations 3.4%, dairy products 3.2%; chemicals 11.6%; mineral fuels
8.8%). *Major import sources:* United States 26.8%; CARICOM 26.8% (principally Trinidad and Tobago); United Kingdom 23.1%; Canada 4.2%.
Exports (1980): EC$26,302,000 (soap 49.9%; fruits and vegetables 35.2%, of
which bananas 30.3%, citrus fruits 4.7%). *Major export destinations:* CARI-
COM 61.5% (principally Jamaica); United Kingdom 34.7%; United States
0.9%.

Transport and communications

Transport. Railroads: none. Roads (1976): total length 749 mi, 1,205 km
(paved 38%). Vehicles (1983): motor vehicles 5,717. Merchant marine
(1983): vessels (100 gross tons and over) 3; total deadweight tonnage 1,243.
Air transport: passengers, n.a.; cargo, n.a.; airport (1984) with scheduled
flights 1.
Communications. Daily newspapers: none. Radios (1983): total number of
receivers 30,000 (1 per 2.5 persons). Television: total number of receivers,
n.a. Telephones (1979): 4,573 (1 per 15.3 persons).

Education and health

Education (1978–79)				
	schools	teachers	students	student/ teacher ratio
Primary (age 5–11)	63	423	15,220	36.0
Secondary (age 12–18)	66	299	9,814	32.8
Voc., teacher tr.	5	27	449	16.6
Higher	2	8	154	19.3

College graduates per 10,000 population (students graduating; 1980): 2. *Literacy* (1979): total population literate 31,782 (70.0%); males literate 13,984;
females literate 17,798.
Health (1983): physicians 26 (1 per 2,846 persons); hospital beds 237 (1
per 312 persons).
Food (1978–80): daily per capita caloric intake 2,196 (vegetable products
83.3%, animal products 16.7%); 91% of FAO recommended minimum
requirement.

Military

Total active duty personnel: The police force is responsible for defense.

*Since July 1976 the exchange rate has been U.S.$1.00 = EC$2.70. †Includes 5 sq mi
(13 sq km) water area not shown separately. ‡Estimated recurrent budget for 1983–84
was: revenue EC$70,456,850; expenditure EC$70,170,010. §Excludes EC$19,670,000
in grants and EC$50,000 in capital revenue. ‖ Detail does not add to total given
because of rounding. ¶Estimated.

Dominican Republic

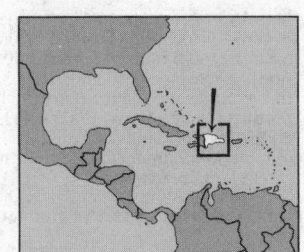

Official name: República Dominicana (Dominican Republic).
Form of government: multiparty republic with two legislative houses (Senate [27]; Chamber of Deputies [91]).
Head of state and government: President.
Capital: Santo Domingo.
Official language: Spanish.
Official religion: none.
Monetary unit: 1 Dominican peso (RD$) = 100 centavos; valuation (Oct. 29, 1984) 1 U.S.$ = RD$1.00*; 1 £ = RD$1.21.

Area and population

Provinces	Capitals	area sq mi	area sq km	population 1981 census
Azua	Azua	938	2,430	142,770
Bahoruco	Neiba	531	1,376	78,636
Barahona	Barahona	976	2,528	137,160
Dajabón	Dajabón	344	890	57,709
Duarte	San Francisco de Macorís	499	1,292	235,544
El Seibo	El Seibo	1,154	2,989	157,866
Espaillat	Moca	386	1,000	164,017
Independencia	Jimaní	719	1,861	38,768
La Altagracia	Higüey	1,191	3,084	100,112
La Estrelleta	Elías Piña	690	1,788	65,384
La Romana	La Romana	209	541	109,769
La Vega	La Vega	1,304	3,377	385,043
María Trinidad Sánchez	Nagua	506	1,310	112,629
Montecristi	Montecristi	768	1,989	83,407
Pedernales	Pedernales	373	967	17,006
Peravia	Baní	626	1,622	168,123
Puerto Plata	Puerto Plata	726	1,881	206,757
Salcedo	Salcedo	206	533	99,191
Samaná	Samaná	382	989	65,699
Sánchez Ramírez	Cotué	453	1,174	126,567
San Cristóbal	San Cristóbal	1,445	3,743	446,132
San Juan	San Juan	1,375	3,561	239,957
San Pedro de Macorís	San Pedro de Macorís	450	1,166	152,890
Santiago	Santiago de los Caballeros	1,205	3,122	550,372
Santiago Rodríguez	Sabaneta	394	1,020	55,411
Valverde	Mao	220	570	100,319
National district				
Santo Domingo	...	570	1,477	1,550,739
TOTAL		18,703†	48,442†	5,647,977

Source: Official government figures.

Demography

Density (1984): persons per sq mi 316.7, persons per sq km 122.3.
Urban–rural (1983): urban 52.4%; rural 47.6%.
Sex distribution (1981): male 50.56%; female 49.44%.
Age breakdown (1980): under 15, 44.8%; 15–29, 29.0%; 30–44, 14.1%; 45–59, 7.8%; 60–74, 3.5%; 75 and over, 0.8%.
Population projection: (1990) 7,534,000; (2000) 9,329,000.
Doubling time: 26 years.
Ethnic composition (1982): mulatto 75%; white 15%; black 10%.
Religious affiliation (1983): Roman Catholic 98%; other 2%.
Major cities (1981): Santo Domingo 1,313,170; Santiago de los Caballeros 278,640; La Romana 91,570; San Pedro de Macorís 78,560.

Vital statistics

Birth rate per 1,000 population (1983): 38.6 (world avg. 29.0); (1976) legitimate, 32.8%, illegitimate 67.2%.
Death rate per 1,000 population (1983): 8.5 (world avg. 11.0).
Natural increase rate per 1,000 population (1983): 30.1 (world avg. 18.0).
Total fertility rate (avg. births per childbearing woman; 1980): 4.2.
Marriage rate per 1,000 population (1981): 4.9.
Divorce rate per 1,000 population: (1981): 1.7.
Infant mortality rate per 1,000 live births (1983): 28.3.
Life expectancy at birth (1980–85): male 60.7 years; female 64.6 years.
Major causes of death per 100,000 population (1977): infectious and parasitic diseases 75.3; diseases of the circulatory system 65.5; diseases of the respiratory system 36.9; accidents, poisoning, and violence 34.6.

National economy

Budget (1981). Revenue: RD$998,000,000‡ (excise tax 21.5%; import duties 18.3%; income from property 17.6%; corporation profits tax 11.3%; income tax 7.3%; customs duties 4.9%). Expenditures: RD$1,174,400,000 (agriculture, forestry, and fishing 17.3%; education 13.9%; transport and communication 11.2%; health 9.7%; defense 8.9%).
Public debt (external, outstanding; 1983): U.S.$1,960,000,000.
Tourism (1980): receipts from visitors U.S.$173,000,000; expenditures by nationals abroad U.S.$166,000,000.
Production (metric tons except as noted). Agriculture, forestry, fishing (1982): sugarcane 10,544,000, fruits 1,419,000, bananas and plantains 955,000, rice 384,000, vegetables and melons 246,000, cassava 135,000, coffee 57,000, cacao 32,000, tobacco 31,000; livestock (number of live animals) 2,157,000 cattle, 385,000 goats, 8,400,000 chickens; roundwood 566,000 cu m; fish catch 1,721. Mining and quarrying (1982): bauxite 152,200; nickel ore 14,-000; silver 2,200,000 troy oz.; gold 390,000 troy oz. Manufacturing (1981): cement 960,000; bauxite 139,000§; nickel ore 19,000. Construction (1980):

residential 881,000 sq m; nonresidential 296,000 sq m. Energy production (consumption): electricity (kW-hr; 1982) 2,965,000,000 (2,965,000,000); coal (metric tons; 1982) n.a. (1,000); crude petroleum (barrels; 1982) n.a. (9,052,-550); petroleum products (metric tons; 1982) 1,176,000 (1,589,000).
Gross national product (at current market prices; 1981): U.S.$7,070,000,000 (U.S.$1,252 per capita).

Origin of gross domestic product (current prices)

	1981 in value RD$'000,000	1981 % of total value	1980 labour force	1980 % of labour force
Agriculture	1,332	18.4	661,600	41.3
Mining	272	3.8	1,600	0.1
Manufacturing	1,124	15.6	325,200	20.3
Construction	564	7.8	56,100	3.5
Trade	1,174 ‖	16.02 ‖	¶	¶
Public utilities	67	0.9	¶	¶
Transportation and communication	390	5.4	¶	¶
Finance	♀	♀	¶	¶
Pub. admin., defense	♀	♀	¶	¶
Services	♀	♀	¶	¶
Other	2,304 ‖	31.9 ‖	557,500¶	34.8¶
TOTAL	7,227	100.0	1,602,000	100.0

Persons economically active (1982): total 1,641,000 (28.2%).

Price and earnings indexes (1980 = 100)

	1978	1979	1980	1981	1982	1983	1984
Consumer price index	78.5	85.7	100.0	107.5	115.8	123.1	136.1§
Earnings index	...	...	...	...	...	...	...

Household income and expenditure. Average household size (1980) 3.8; average annual income per household (1969) RD$297.6 (U.S.$297.6); source of income: wages and salaries 41.7%, self-employment 31.8%, remittances, gifts, and other assistance 16.3%; expenditure: n.a.
Land use (1981): forested 13.1%; meadows and pastures 31.4%; agricultural and under permanent cultivation 25.5%; other 30.0%.

Foreign trade

Balance of trade (current prices)

	1978	1979	1980	1981	1982	1983
RD$'000,000	−184.2	−186.0	−463.8	−458.8	−488.1	−489.5
% of total	12.0%	9.7%	19.4%	18.8%	24.1%	23.8%

Imports (1981): RD$1,449,887,000 (petroleum and products 32.9%, chemicals 11.9%, nonelectrical machinery 8.4%, cereals and preparations 7.2%, electrical machinery 5.9%). *Major import sources:* United States and Puerto Rico 42.2%; Venezuela 16.0%; Netherlands Antilles 8.8%; Mexico 8.6%..
Exports (1981): RD$991,088,000 (sugar and honey 54.2%, iron and steel 11.2%, leaf tobacco 6.7%, chemicals 4.3%, fruits and vegetables 3.0%, bauxite 1.6%). *Major export destinations:* United States and Puerto Rico 69.1%; Venezuela 7.6%; Spain 4.8%; The Netherlands 3.0%.

Transport and communications

Transport. Railroads (1983): route length 233 mi, 375 km. Roads (1982): total length 10,788 mi, 17,362 km (paved 29%). Vehicles (1982): passenger cars 102,127; trucks and buses 66,570. Merchant marine (1983): vessels (100 gross tons and over) 35; total deadweight tonnage 58,747. Air transport (1982): passenger-mi 298,896,000, passenger-km 481,027,000; cargo, n.a.; airports (1984) with scheduled flights 3.
Communications. Daily newspapers (1983): total number 8; total circulation 398,970□. Radios (1983): total number of receivers 225,000 (1 per 26.6 persons). Television (1983): total number of receivers 388,000 (1 per 15.4 persons). Telephones (1982): 175,054 (1 per 33.2 persons).

Education and health

Education (1980–81)

	schools	teachers	students	student/ teacher ratio
Primary (age 7–12)	5,487◇	22,672	1,105,730	48.8
Secondary, voc. (age 13–18)	...	11,716	331,471	28.3
Teacher training	...	50◇	1,392△	...
Higher†	...	1,435◇	42,412△	...

College graduates per 100,000 population (students graduating; 1978): 47.
Literacy (1980): total population literate 2,329,000 (73.6%); males literate 1,161,600 (73.4%); females literate 1,167,400 (73.8%).
Health: physicians (1976) 1,215 (1 per 4,020 persons); hospital beds (1973) 12,618 (1 per 351 persons).
Food (1978–80): daily per capita caloric intake 2,133 (vegetable products 86.3%, animal products 13.7%); 94% of FAO recommended minimum.

Military

Total active duty personnel (1983): 23,000 (army 60.8%; navy 19.6%; air force 19.6%). *Military expenditure as percent of GNP* (1982): 1.4% (world 6.0%); per capita expenditure U.S.$18.

*The value of the Dominican Republic peso is at par with the U.S. dollar. †Total includes 63 sq mi (163 sq km) of surrounding islands not shown separately. ‡Includes RD$17,300,000 in grants and capital revenue. §1982. ‖ Trade excludes restaurants and hotels, which are included with other. ¶Trade, public utilities, transportation and communication, finance, public administration and defense, and services included with other. ♀Finance, public administration, defense, and services are included with other. ◇March. □Partial circulation. ◇1975–76. △1978–79. †Universities only.

Ecuador

Official name: República del Ecuador (Republic of Ecuador).
Form of government: unitary multiparty republic with one legislative house (National Chamber of Representatives [69]).
Head of state and government: President.
Capital: Quito.
Official language: Spanish.
Official religion: none.
Monetary unit: 1 Sucre (S/.) = 100 centavos; valuation (Oct. 29, 1984) 1 U.S.$ = S/.110.38; 1 £ = S/.113.23.

Area and population

Regions Provinces	Capitals	area sq mi	area sq km	population 1982 census
Coastal				
El Oro	Machala	2,281	5,908	337,818
Esmeraldas	Esmeraldas	5,854	15,162	247,311
Guayas	Guayaquil	8,256	21,382	2,047,001
Los Ríos	Babahoyo	2,459	6,370	457,065
Manabí	Portoviejo	6,990	18,105	858,780
Eastern				
Morona-Santiago	Macas	10,200	26,418	70,217
Napo	Tena	20,200	52,318	115,110
Pastaza	Puyo	11,687	30,269	31,779
Zamora-Chinchipe	Zamora	7,102	18,394	46,691
Sierra				
Azuay	Cuenca	3,124	8,092	443,044
Bolívar	Guaranda	1,599	4,142	141,566
Cañar	Azogues	1,344	3,481	174,674
Carchi	Tulcan	1,446	3,744	125,452
Chimborazo	Riobamba	2,338	6,056	320,268
Cotopaxi	Latacunga	2,007	5,198	279,765
Imbabura	Ibarra	1,921	4,976	245,745
Loja	Loja	4,429	11,472	358,952
Pichincha	Quito	6,404	16,587	1,376,831
Tungurahua	Ambato	1,201	3,110	324,286
Island territory				
Galápagos Islands	Puerto Baquerizo Moreno	3,086	7,994	6,119
TOTAL		103,930*	269,178	8,050,630†

Demography

Density (1984): persons per sq mi 81.3, persons per sq km 31.4.
Urban–rural (1982): urban 49.7%; rural 50.3%.
Sex distribution (1982): male 49.94%; female 50.06%.
Age breakdown (1982): under 15, 41.6%; 15–29, 28.3%; 30–44, 15.4%; 45–59, 8.6%; 60–74, 4.6%; 75 and over, 1.5%.
Population projection: (1990) 10,949,000; (2000) 14,596,000.
Doubling time: 22 years.
Ethnic composition (1981): Quechua 41.3%; mestizo 40.0%; white 10.0%; black 5.0%; jungle Amerindian 1.0%; other 2.7%.
Religious affiliation (1980): Roman Catholic 96.4%; Protestant 1.9%; other 1.7%.
Major cities (1982): Guayaquil 1,175,300; Quito 858,700; Cuenca 150,900; Machala 105,300; Portoviejo 101,200.

Vital statistics

Birth rate per 1,000 population: (1981) 39.6 (world avg. 29.0); legitimate 67.9%, illegitimate 32.1%.
Death rate per 1,000 population (1981): 9.2 (world avg. 12.0).
Natural increase rate per 1,000 population (1981): 30.4 (world avg. 17.0).
Total fertility rate (avg. births per childbearing woman; 1980–85): 6.0.
Marriage rate per 1,000 population (1980): 5.8.
Divorce rate per 1,000 population (1980): 0.3.
Infant mortality rate per 1,000 live births (1981): 79.8.
Life expectancy at birth (1981): male 59.8 years; female 63.6 years.
Major causes of death per 100,000 population (1979)‡: diseases of the respiratory system 127.1; infectious intestinal diseases 105.3; diseases of the circulatory system 97.0; accidents 61.9.

National economy

Budget (1983). Revenue: S/.83,739,100,000 (income from petroleum 32.9%; capital income [domestic and foreign aid] 29.1%; taxes on production and general sales 14.2%; import duties 12.2%; income tax 8.3%). Expenditures: S/.83,739,100,000 (education and culture 22.9%; interest on public debt 16.2%; defense 9.4%; health 6.6%; transport and communication 6.1%; agriculture 4.7%).
Public debt (external, outstanding; 1982): U.S.$3,943,000,000.
Tourism (1981): receipts from visitors U.S.$131,000,000; expenditures by nationals abroad U.S.$250,000,000.
Production (metric tons except as noted). Agriculture, forestry, fishing (1982): bananas 1,999,000, oranges 501,000, potatoes 416,000, rice 384,000, corn (maize) 264,000, raw sugar 254,000, cassava 240,000, pineapples 137,000, cacao 85,000, coffee 84,000, palm oil 43,000; livestock (number of live animals) 4,181,000 pigs, 3,034,000 sheep, 3,000,000 cattle, 24,927,000 chickens; roundwood 7,729,000 cu m; fish catch 636,500. Mining and quarrying (1982): limestone 1,200,000; silver 10,000 troy oz., gold 260 troy oz. Manufacturing (value in S/.'000,000; 1983): food products 19,432;

petroleum products 16,446; textiles and clothing 6,495; base metals 3,438; beverages (including liquors) 2,706. Construction (in S/.§; 1981): residential 6,645,100,000; nonresidential 2,506,700,000. Energy production (consumption): electricity (kW-hr; 1982) 3,350,000,000 (3,365,000,000); coal, none (n.a.); crude petroleum (barrels; 1982) 81,455,000 (34,949,000); petroleum products (metric tons; 1982) 4,442,000 (3,974,000); natural gas (cu m; 1982) 68,846,000 (68,846,000).
Gross national product (at current market prices; 1983): U.S.$11,873,290,000 (U.S.$1,283 per capita).

Origin of gross domestic product (current prices)

	1982 in value S/.'000,000	% of total value	labour force	% of labour force
Agriculture	45,410	11.1	786,530	33.0
Mining	51,214	12.5	7,050	0.3
Manufacturing	70,406	17.2	284,780	11.9
Construction	39,322	9.6	158,530	6.6
Trade	57,236	14.0	266,640	11.2
Public utilities	3,628	1.0	14,560	0.6
Transportation and communication	36,886	9.0	103,850	4.4
Finance	...	...	38,420	1.6
Services	...	...	614,240	25.7
Other	104,778	25.6	112,650	4.7
TOTAL	408,880	100.0	2,387,250	100.0

Persons economically active (1981): total 2,808,160 (32.5%); female participation in the labour force 750,270 (26.7%); unemployed 52,137 (1.9%).

Price and earnings indexes (1980 = 100)

	1977	1978	1979	1980	1981	1982	1983
Consumer price index	71.9	80.2	88.5	100.0	113.0	131.3	195.0
Annual earnings index ‖	61.5	66.5	75.0	100.0	111.6	...	...

Household income and expenditure. Average household size (1980) 6.0; average annual income per household: n.a.; expenditure: n.a.
Land use (1981): forested 52.2%; meadows and pastures 13.6%; agricultural and under permanent cultivation 9.5%; other 24.7%.

Foreign trade

Balance of trade (current prices)

	1978	1979	1980	1981	1982	1983
S/.'000,000	−4,375	+1,350	+7,550	+4,550	+4,864	+32,145
% of total	5.4%	1.3%	6.3%	3.7%	3.6%	19.9%

Imports (1983): S/.64,626,445,700 (chemical products 18.5%, mineral products 15.8%, industrial machinery 12.5%, food products 9.4%, transportation equipment 8.3%. *Major import sources:* United States 34.0%; Japan 9.3%; West Germany 8.7%; Brazil 5.0%; Italy 5.0%.
Exports (1983): S/.96,771,281,600 (crude petroleum 67.1%, fish products 8.2%, coffee 6.8%, bananas 6.7%, petroleum products 4.8%). *Major export destinations:* United States 56.8%; Panama 9.9%; Colombia 6.1%.

Transport and communications

Transport. Railroads (1983): route length 600 mi, 965 km; (1979) passenger-mi 42,900,000, passenger-km 69,000,000; (1979) short ton-mi cargo 19,900,000, metric ton-km cargo 29,000,000. Roads (1980): total length 20,000 mi, 32,185 km (paved 52%). Vehicles (1981): passenger cars 231,390; trucks and buses 35,744. Merchant marine (1983): vessels (100 gross tons and over) 130; total deadweight tonnage 543,756. Air transport (1980)¶: passenger-mi 534,931,000, passenger-km 860,889,000; short ton-mi cargo 28,094,000, metric ton-km cargo 41,016,000; airports (1984) with scheduled flights 13.
Communications. Daily newspapers (1983): total number 9; total circulation 554,000; circulation per 1,000 population 59.9. Radios (1983): total number of receivers 1,800,000 (1 per 5 persons). Television (1983): total number of receivers 135,000 (1 per 69 persons). Telephones (1982): 290,200 (1 per 28 persons).

Education and health

Education (1982–83)

	schools	teachers	students	student/ teacher ratio
Primary (age 4–12)	13,291	47,559	1,676,681	35.3
Secondary (age 12–18)	1,633	39,738	657,085	16.7
Voc., teacher tr.♀	374	8,487	164,089	19.3
Higher	17	11,679	274,353	23.4

College graduates per 100,000 population (students graduating; 1981): 179.
Literacy (1982): total population literate 3,945,930 (83.9%).
Health: physicians (1977) 4,660 (1 per 1,585 persons); hospital beds (1979) 14,316 (1 per 543 persons).
Food (1978–80): daily per capita caloric intake 2,092 (vegetable products 81.4%, animal products 18.6%); 91% of FAO recommended minimum.

Military

Total active duty personnel (1983): 36,800 (army 74.7%; navy 12.2%; air force 13.1%). *Military expenditure as percent of GNP* (1981): 2.3% (world 6.0%); per capita expenditure U.S.$37.

*Detail does not add to total given because of rounding. †Total includes 42,156 persons not shown separately. ‡Excludes nomadic Indian tribes. §Authorized construction only. ‖ For salaried industrial workers. ¶All scheduled and non-scheduled international traffic of Ecuatoriana airlines. ♀1981–82.

Egypt

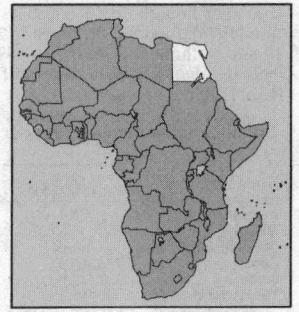

Official name: Jumhūrīyah Miṣr al-ʿArabīyah (Arab Republic of Egypt).
Form of government: republic with one legislative house (People's Assembly [392]).
Chief of state: President.
Head of government: Prime Minister.
Capital: Cairo.
Official language: Arabic.
Official religion: Islām.
Monetary unit: 1 Egyptian pound (LE) = 1,000 millièmes = 100 piastres; valuation (Oct. 29, 1984) 1 LE = U.S.$1.20 = £0.99.

Area and population

Regions Governorates	Capitals	area sq mi	area sq km	population 1983 estimate
Desert				
al-Baḥr al-Aḥmar	al-Ghurdaqah	78,643	203,685	68,000
al-Wādī al-Jadīd	al-Khārijah	145,369	376,505	106,000
Maṭrūḥ	Marsā Maṭrūḥ	81,897	212,112	156,000
Sīnāʾ	al-ʿArīsh...	23,442	60,714	164,000
Lower Egypt				
ad-Daqahlīyah	al-Manṣūrah	1,340	3,471	3,281,000
al-Buḥayrah	Damanhūr	3,911	10,130	2,976,000
al-Gharbīyah	Ṭanṭā	750	1,942	2,715,000
al-Minūfīyah	Shibīn al-Kawm	592	1,532	2,049,000
al-Qalyūbīyah	Banhā	386	1,001	2,074,000
ash-Sharqīyah	az-Zaqāzīq	1,614	4,180	3,167,000
Dumyāṭ (Damietta)	Dumyāṭ	227	589	690,000
Kafr ash-Shaykh	Kafr ash-Shaykh	1,327	3,437	1,696,000
Upper Egypt				
al-Fayyūm	al-Fayyūm	705	1,827	1,410,000
al-Jīzah	al-Jīzah	32,859	85,105	2,965,000
al-Minyā	al-Minyā	873	2,262	2,517,000
Aswān	Aswān	262	679	744,000
Asyūṭ	Asyūṭ	591	1,530	2,059,000
Banī Suwayf	Banī Suwayf	510	1,322	1,342,000
Qinā	Qinā	715	1,851	2,066,000
Sawhāj	Sawhāj	597	1,547	2,316,000
Urban				
al-Iskandarīyah (Alexandria)	—	1,034	2,679	2,708,000
al-Ismāʿīlīyah (Ismailia)	—	557	1,442	447,000
al-Qāhirah (Cairo)	—	83	214	5,881,000
as-Suways (Suez)	—	6,888	17,840	241,000
Būr-Saʿīd (Port Said)	—	28	72	364,000
TOTAL		385,202*	997,668	44,202,000

Source: Official government figures.

Demography

Density (1984): persons per sq mi 122.3, persons per sq km 47.2.
Urban–rural (1980): urban 45.4%; rural 54.6%.
Sex distribution (1982): male 50.77%; female 49.23%.
Age breakdown (1980): under 15, 39.7%; 15–29, 27.5%; 30–44, 17.0%; 45–59, 10.1%; 60–74, 4.8%; 75 and over 0.9%.
Population projection: (1990) 53,481,000; (2000) 65,200,000.
Doubling time: 28 years.
Ethnic composition (1980): Egyptian 99.7%; other 0.3%.
Religious affiliation (1980): Muslim 81.8%; Christian 17.8%; other 0.4%.
Major cities (1983): Cairo 5,881,000; Alexandria 2,708,000; al-Jīzah 1,509,600; Shubrā al-Khaymah 486,400; al-Maḥallah al-Kubrā 345,800.

Vital statistics

Birth rate per 1,000 population (1982): 37.3 (world avg. 29.0); legitimate, n.a.; illegitimate, n.a.
Death rate per 1,000 population (1982): 10.4 (world avg. 11.0).
Natural increase rate per 1,000 population (1982): 26.9 (world avg. 18.0).
Total fertility rate (avg. births per childbearing woman; 1980–85): 4.7.
Marriage rate per 1,000 population (1979): 9.4.
Divorce rate per 1,000 population (1979): 1.8.
Infant mortality rate per 1,000 live births (1978–80): 76.4.
Life expectancy at birth (1980–85): male 55.9 years; female 58.4 years.
Major causes of death per 100,000 population (1978): symptoms and ill-defined conditions 239.2; bronchitis, emphysema and asthma 50.8; pneumonia 33.2; ischemic heart disease 26.3.

National economy

Budget (1984–85). Revenue: LE12,877,000,000 (sovereign tax 59.4%; domestic savings and foreign credit 32.6%). Expenditures: LE18,277,000,000 (public-sector wages 18.0%; subsidies 11.3%; health and education 11.1%).
Public debt (external, outstanding; 1982): U.S.$14,935,200,000.
Tourism (1981): receipts from visitors U.S.$375,400,000; expenditures by nationals abroad U.S.$630,000,000.
Production (metric tons except as noted). Agriculture, forestry, fishing (1982): corn (maize) 2,709,000, tomatoes 2,500,000, rice 2,287,000, wheat 2,017,000, watermelons 1,313,000, potatoes 1,100,000, dry onions 657,000; millet 633,000, cotton (lint) 452,000, dates 393,000, grapes 309,000; livestock (number of live animals) 2,321,000 cattle, 2,447,000 buffaloes, 1,700,000 sheep, 1,542,000 goats, 1,781,000 asses, 90,000 camels, 28,208,000 chickens; roundwood 1,890,000 cu m; fish catch 137,208. Mining and quarrying (1982): iron ore 2,139,000; fire clay 975,263; crude gypsum and anhydrite 931,150. Manufacturing (1982): cement 3,627,000; sugar 600,000; cotton yarn 245,000; jute textile 31,000; steel castings 3,758; cotton textiles LE483,000,000.

Construction (value added in LE; 1980): 761,000,000. Energy production (consumption): electricity (kW-hr; 1982) 17,720,000,000 (17,720,000,000); coal (metric tons; 1982) none (1,270,000); crude petroleum (barrels; 1983) 251,850,000 (112,872,000†); petroleum products (metric tons; 1982) 15,246,000 (14,146,000); natural gas (cu m; 1983) 2,908,140,000 (1,897,434,000†).
Gross national product (at current market prices; 1983): U.S.$32,894,290,000 (U.S.$730 per capita).

Origin of gross domestic product (current prices)

	1981–82 in value LE'000,000	% of total value	labour force	% of labour force
Agriculture	3,891.5	19.8	4,247,500	36.2
Mining	‡	‡	24,500	0.2
Manufacturing	5,610.4‡	28.6‡	1,462,700	12.5
Construction	930.2	4.7	664,100	5.7
Trade	3,597.0§	18.3§	1,175,700§	10.0§
Public utilities	155.0	0.8	130,400	1.1
Transportation and communication	1,551.4	7.9	452,100	3.9
Finance	§	§	§	§
Services	3,546.7	18.1	3,396,600	29.0
Other ‖	356.6	1.8	171,300	1.5
TOTAL	19,638.8	100.0	11,724,900	100.0*

Persons economically active (1980): total 10,335,000 (24.4%); female participation in the labour force 857,800 (8.3%); unemployed 535,900 (5.2%).

Price and earnings indexes (1980 = 100)

	1977	1978	1979	1980	1981	1982	1983
Consumer price index	67.9	75.4	82.9	100.0	110.4	126.8	147.2
Earnings index	...	...	...	...	...	...	...

Household income and expenditure. Average household size (1980) 4.9; average annual income per household: n.a.; source of income: n.a.; expenditure¶ (1974–1975): food 49.7%, clothing and footwear 14.2%, housing 12.4%, transportation 5.2%, tobacco 4.9%, recreation 1.3%.
Land use (1981): meadows and pastures 0.1%; agricultural and under permanent cultivation 2.9%; built-on, wasteland, and other 97.0%.

Foreign trade

Balance of trade (current prices)

	1977	1978	1979	1980	1981	1982	1983
LE'000,000	−1,215.8	−1,952.4	−1,398.4	−1,269.8	−3,924.5	−4,170.4	−4,982.0
% of total	47.6%	58.9%	35.2%	22.9%	46.4%	48.8%	52.3%

Imports (1982): LE6,354,517,000 (cereals and preparations 14.1%; transport equipment 10.6%; chemicals 7.8%; electrical machinery 6.8%). *Major import sources:* United States 19.0%; West Germany 10.1%; Italy 7.6%; France 7.5%.
Exports (1982): LE2,184,122,000 (petroleum and petroleum products 66.2%; textile fibres 13.8%). *Major export destinations:* Italy 22.1%; Israel 14.2%; France 6.9%; Romania 5.9%; The Netherlands 5.4%.

Transport and communications

Transport. Railroads (1982): length 2,725 mi, 4,385 km; passenger-mi 11,660,000,000, passenger-km 18,765,000,000; short ton-mi cargo 1,577,000,000, metric ton-km cargo 2,302,000,000. Roads (1983): total length 18,684 mi, 30,069 km (paved 47%). Vehicles (1983): passenger cars 597,869; trucks and buses 227,224. Merchant marine (1983): vessels (100 gross tons and over) 351; total deadweight tonnage 828,048. Air transport (1982): passenger-mi 2,267,000,000, passenger-km 3,648,000,000; short ton-mi cargo 38,466,000, metric ton-km cargo 56,160,000; airports (1984) with scheduled flights 9.
Communications. Daily newspapers (1983): total number 5; total circulation 2,503,000; circulation per 1,000 population 54.6. Radios (1983): total number of receivers 8,000,000 (1 per 5.5 persons). Television (1983): total number of receivers 3,850,000 (1 per 11.5 persons). Telephones (1982): 521,625 (1 per 82.4 persons).

Education and health

Education (1981–82)

	schools	teachers♀	students	student/ teacher ratio
Primary (age 6–11)	11,761	140,146	4,748,414	...
Secondary (age 12–17)♀	2,715	78,086	2,060,100	26.4
Voc., teacher tr.♀	519	38,635	672,362	17.4
Higher	12	11,910	594,597	...

College graduates per 100,000 population (students graduating◊; 1982): 230.
Literacy (1980): total population literate 10,608,000 (41.9%); males literate 7,140,000 (56.3%); females literate 3,468,000 (27.5%).
Health (1982): physicians 92,000 (1 per 467 persons); hospital beds 86,600 (1 per 497 persons).
Food (1978–80): daily per capita caloric intake 2,950 (vegetable products 93.6%, animal products 6.4%); 118% of FAO recommended minimum.

Military

Total active duty personnel (1982): 447,000 (army 70.5%; navy 4.5%; air force 25.0%). *Military expenditure as percent of GNP* (1982): 8.2% (world 6.0%); per capita expenditure U.S.$50.

*Detail does not add to total given because of rounding. †1982. ‡Mining is included with manufacturing. §Finance is included with trade. ‖ Includes housing only. ¶Urban only. ♀1980–81. ◊University and technical graduates.

El Salvador

Official name: República de El Salvador (Republic of El Salvador).
Form of government: republic with one legislative house (Constituent Assembly [60]).
Chief of state and government: President.
Capital: San Salvador.
Official language: Spanish.
Official religion: none.
Monetary unit: 1 colón ($\mathcal{Q}$) = 100 centavos; valuation (Oct. 29, 1984) 1 U.S.\$ = 2.49; 1 £ = $\mathcal{Q}$3.01.

Area and population

Departments	Capitals	area sq mi	area sq km	population 1983 estimate
Ahuachapán	Ahuachapán	479	1,240	258,500
Cabañas	Sensuntepeque	426	1,104	191,000
Chalatenango	Chalatenango	779	2,017	248,000
Cuscatlán	Cojutepeque	292	756	215,000
La Libertad	Nueva San Salvador	638	1,653	417,200
La Paz	Zacatecoluca	472	1,224	266,100
La Unión	La Unión	801	2,074	331,900
Morazán	San Francisco (Gotera)	559	1,447	227,200
San Miguel	San Miguel	802	2,077	462,000
San Salvador	San Salvador	342	886	1,043,800
Santa Ana	Santa Ana	781	2,023	471,700
San Vicente	San Vicente	457	1,184	215,000
Sonsonate	Sonsonate	473	1,226	346,000
Usulután	Usulután	822	2,130	422,200
TOTAL		8,124	21,041	5,115,700

Source: Official government figures.

Demography

Density (1984): persons per sq mi 661.9, persons per sq km 255.5.
Urban–rural (1980): urban 39.0%; rural 61.0%.
Sex distribution (1980): male 48.98%; female 51.02%.
Age breakdown (1980): under 15, 45.2%; 15–29, 27.7%; 30–44, 14.3%; 45–59, 8.0%; 60–74, 3.8%; 75 and over, 1.0%.
Population projection: (1990) 6,330,000; (2000) 8,310,000.
Doubling time: 25 years.
Ethnic composition (late 1960s): mestizo (white and Indian) 89%; Indian 10%; white 1.0%.
Religious affiliation (1980): Roman Catholic 96.2%; Protestant 2.4%; other 1.4%.
Major cities (1983): San Salvador 445,100; Santa Ana 132,200; Mejicanos 86,500; San Miguel 86,500; Delgado 64,600.

Vital statistics

Birth rate per 1,000 population (1982): 31.4 (world avg. 29.0); (1980) legitimate 31.1%, illegitimate 68.9%.
Death rate per 1,000 population (1982): 6.7 (world avg. 11.0).
Natural increase rate per 1,000 population (1982): 24.7 (world avg. 18.0).
Total fertility rate (avg. births per childbearing woman; 1980): 5.8.
Marriage rate per 1,000 population (1982): 4.1.
Divorce rate per 1,000 population (1980): 0.4.
Infant mortality rate per 1,000 live births (1982): 42.2.
Life expectancy at birth (1981): male 61.7 years; female 65.3 years.
Major causes of death per 100,000 population (1979): ill-defined diseases 180.4; enteritis and other diarrheal diseases 76.3; accidents and acts of violence 59.3; respiratory diseases 58.8.

National economy

Budget (1982). Revenue: $\mathcal{Q}$1,109,828,000 (value-added and excise taxes 39.0%, export and import duties 25.1%, income tax 20.2%). Expenditures: $\mathcal{Q}$1,864,699,000 (general expenditures 39.1%, capital investment 9.8%, purchase of goods and services 9.0%, interest on public debt 8.6%).
Public debt (June 1983 prelim.): U.S.\$1,760,000,000.
Tourism (1982): receipts from visitors U.S.\$17,000,000; expenditures by nationals abroad, n.a.
Production (value added in $\mathcal{Q}$'000,000 except as noted). Agriculture, forestry, fishing (1982): coffee 987.3, corn 122.2, sugarcane 99.3, cotton 86.9; livestock (cattle and pigs) 270.8, chickens 109.2; forestry products 35.1; fish, principally shrimp 56.0. Manufacturing (1982): processed food 446.2; beverages 196.8; refined petroleum products 135.8; textiles 75.0; chemical products 73.8; electrical machinery 24.5; leather goods 23.4. Construction (1982): private residential 110.6; nonresidential 189.9. Energy production (consumption): electricity (kW-hr; 1982) 1,489,344 (1,289,248); coal, none (n.a.); petroleum, none (n.a.); petroleum products (metric tons; 1982) 647,-000 (601,000); natural gas, none (n.a.).
Persons economically active (1980): total 1,593,353 (35.5%); female participation in labour force 553,907 (34.8%); unemployed 27,027 (1.7%).

Price and earnings indexes (1980 = 100)

	1977	1978	1979	1980	1981	1982	1983
Consumer price index	64.9	73.5	85.2	100.0	114.8	128.3	145.1
Monthly earnings index	...	...	...	...	...	...	...

Household income and expenditure. Average household size (1978) 5.1; income per household $\mathcal{Q}$8,650 (U.S.\$3,460); source of income: n.a.; expenditure (1978): food 39.3%, housing 20.4%, transportation and communication 10.8%, clothing and footwear 9.4%, recreation 4.4%.
Gross national product (at current market prices; 1983): U.S.\$3,765,600,000 (U.S.\$740 per capita).

Origin of gross domestic product (current prices)

	1982 in value wdtbl2'000,000	1982 % of total value	1980 labour force	1980 % of labour force
Agriculture	2,027.4	22.8	636,617	40.0
Mining	13.6	0.2	4,394	0.3
Manufacturing	1,351.0	15.2	247,621	15.5
Construction	300.6	3.4	80,089	5.0
Trade	2,117.4	23.9	256,086	16.1
Public utilities	191.7	2.2	9,681	0.6
Transportation and communication	343.7	3.9	65,593	4.1
Finance	309.7	3.5	15,863	1.0
Pub. admin., defense	1,049.7	11.8	*	*
Services	1,165.7	13.1	250,158*	15.7*
Unemployed	...	...	27,027	1.7
Other	...	...	224	0.0
TOTAL	8,870.5	100.0	1,593,353	100.0

Land use (1981): forested 6.5%; meadows and pastures 29.4%; agricultural and under permanent cultivation 35.0%; other 29.1%.

Foreign trade

Balance of trade (current prices)

	1977	1978	1979	1980	1981	1982 prelim.
$\mathcal{Q}$'000,000	+108.3	−566.1	+230.6	+279.7	−469.5	−447.1
% of total	2.3%	12.4%	4.2%	5.5%	10.5%	11.3%

Imports (1982): $\mathcal{Q}$2,207,161,000 (chemical products 21.0%, of which medicinal and pharmaceutical products 5.6%, cosmetics and perfume 2.1%; crude petroleum 16.2%; food products 17.0%, of which fruits and vegetables 5.6%, wheat and wheat products 3.5%, dairy products 2.3%). *Major import sources:* United States 27.4%; Guatemala 23.8%; Mexico 9.1%; Venezuela 8.6%; West Germany 4.5%; Costa Rica 4.1%; Japan 3.1%.
Exports (1982): $\mathcal{Q}$1,760,038,000 (food products 66.2%, of which coffee 57.6%, shrimp 3.2%, refined sugar 2.3%; cotton and cotton products 8.3%; wearing apparel 3.0%). *Major export destinations:* United States 36.4%; West Germany 28.4%; Guatemala 18.7%; Japan 3.1%; Costa Rica 2.9%; Nicaragua 2.5%.

Transport and communications

Transport. Railroads (1981): length 374 mi, 602 km; passenger-mi 8,730,490, passenger-km 14,050,388; short ton-mi cargo 195,183, metric ton-km cargo 284,962. Roads (1982): total length 7,624 mi, 12,269 km (paved 14%). Vehicles (1982): passenger cars 72,547; trucks and buses 67,755. Merchant marine (1983): vessels (100 gross tons and over) 11; total deadweight tonnage 3,497. Air transport: passengers, n.a.; cargo, n.a.; airport (1984) with scheduled flights 1.
Communications. Daily newspapers (1981): total number 6; total circulation† 240,000; circulation per 1,000 population 50. Radios (1981): total number of receivers 1,600,000 (1 per 2.8 persons). Television (1981): total number of receivers 310,000 (1 per 13 persons). Telephones (1982): 86,316 (1 per 56 persons).

Education and health

Education (1981–82)

	schools	teachers	students	student/ teacher ratio
Primary	2,390	18,182	810,827	44.6
Secondary	233	5,123	74,258	14.6
Voc.	23	...	8,684	...
Higher	18	1,414	23,418	16.6

College graduates per 100,000 population (students graduated; 1980): 204.
Literacy (1978): total population literate 1,514,845 (64.2%); males literate 764,815 (68.8%); females literate 750,030 (60.1%).
Health: physicians (1980) 1,491 (1 per 3,220 persons); hospital beds (1978) 7,668 (1 per 570 persons).
Food (1978–80): daily per capita caloric intake 2,163 (vegetable products 87.1%, animal products 12.9%); 96% of FAO recommended minimum requirement.

Military

Total active duty personnel (1983): 24,650 (army 89.3%; navy 1.2%; air force 9.5%). *Military expenditure as percent of GNP* (1982): 4.1% (world 6%); per capita expenditure U.S.\$29.

*Public administration and defense included with services. †Partial circulation only.

Equatorial Guinea

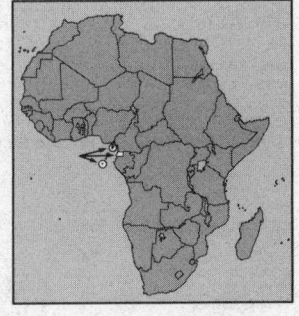

Official name: República de Guinea Ecuatorial (Republic of Equatorial Guinea).
Form of government: unitary single-party republic with one legislative house (National Assembly [41]).
Head of state and government: President.
Capital: Malabo.
Official language: Spanish.
Official religion: none.
Monetary unit: 1 ekwele (EK, plural bikwele) = 100 céntimos; valuation (Oct. 29, 1984) 1 U.S.$ = EK344.16; 1 £ = EK415.40.

Area and population	area		population
	sq mi	sq km	1983 census*
Islands			
Annobon	7	17	3,000
Bioko	779	2,017	70,000
Corisco	6	15	1,000†
Great Elobey	1	2	...
Little Elobey	0.1	0.2	...
Continent			
Rio Muni	10,038	26,000	230,000
TOTAL	10,831	28,051	304,000

Source: Official government figures.

Demography

Density (1984): persons per sq mi 28.8, persons per sq km 11.1.
Urban–rural (1980): urban 53.6%; rural 46.4%.
Sex distribution (1980): male 49.04%; female 50.96%.
Age breakdown (1980): under 15, 41.5%; 15–29, 25.8%; 30–44, 15.6%; 45–59, 10.6%; 60–74, 5.4%; 75 and over 1.1%.
Population projection: (1990) 359,000; (2000) 438,000.
Doubling time: 27 years.
Ethnic composition (1978): Fang 71.5%; Bubi 14.3%; Duala 2.9%; Ibibio 1.4%; other 9.9%.
Religious affiliation (1980): Christian 88.8%; tribal 4.6%; atheist 1.4%; Muslim 0.5%; other 0.2%; none 4.5%.
Major city (1974 est.): Malabo 25,000.

Vital statistics

Birth rate per 1,000 population (1980–85): 42.2 (world avg. 27.5); legitimate n.a.; illegitimate n.a.
Death rate per 1,000 population (1980–85): 17.6 (world avg. 10.6).
Natural increase rate per 1,000 population (1980–85): 24.6 (world avg. 16.9).
Total fertility rate (avg. births per childbearing woman; 1980–85): 5.7.
Marriage rate per 1,000 population: n.a.
Divorce rate per 1,000 population: n.a.
Infant mortality rate per 1,000 live births (1975–80): 148.5.
Life expectancy at birth (1980–85): male 46.9 years; female 50.1 years.
Major causes of death: n.a.; however, major diseases are cholera, leprosy, trypanosomiasis, and malaria.

National economy

Budget (1981). Revenue: EK2,731,000,000 (import duties 45.8%, export duties 25.6%, nontax revenue 15.7%, income tax 6.3%). Expenditures: EK2,887,000,000 (wages and salaries 65.9%, goods and services 20.4%, capital expenditure 10.6%).
Public debt (external, outstanding; 1981): U.S.$59,200,000.
Tourism: n.a.
Production (metric tons except as noted). Agriculture, forestry, fishing (1982): cassavas 53,000, sweet potatoes 34,000, bananas 16,000, cacao beans 8,000, coffee 7,000, coconuts 7,000, palm oil 4,900, palm kernels 2,700; livestock (number of live animals) 34,000 sheep, 7,000 goats, 5,000 pigs, 4,000 cattle, 160,000 chickens; roundwood 465,000 cu m; fish catch 4,000‡. Mining and quarrying: n.a.; however, iron ore, lead, zinc, and molybdenum are present in the sedimentary rocks; traces of gold, diamonds, and radioactive ores have also been located. Manufacturing (1979): sawnwood 16,000 cu m. Construction: n.a. Energy production (consumption): electricity (kW-hr; 1982) 26,000,000 (26,000,000); coal, none (n.a.); crude petroleum, none (n.a.); petroleum products (metric tons; 1982) none (21,000); natural gas, none (n.a.).
Persons economically active (1982): total 112,000 (37.3%); female participation in the labour force, n.a.; unemployed, n.a.
Price and earnings indexes: n.a.
Household income and expenditure. Average household size (1980) 4.5; average annual income per household: n.a.; source of income: n.a.; expenditure: n.a.
Land use (1981): forested 60.6%; meadows and pastures 3.7%; agricultural and under permanent cultivation 8.2%; other 27.5%.

Gross national product (at current market prices; 1981): U.S.$140,000,000 (U.S.$518 per capita).

Origin of gross domestic product (at current factor cost)				
	1979		1982	
	in value EK'000,000	% of total value	labour force	% of labour force
Agriculture	1,990	46.7	82,000	73.2
Manufacturing	220	5.2	...	...
Construction	210	4.9	...	...
Trade	430	10.1	...	...
Public utilities	20	0.5	...	...
Transportation and communication	90	2.1	...	...
Finance	30	0.7	...	...
Pub. admin., defense	1,110	26.0	...	...
Services	160	3.8	...	...
Other	...	...	30,000	26.8
TOTAL	4,260	100.0	112,000	100.0

Foreign trade

Balance of trade (current prices)					
	1978	1979	1980	1981	1982§	1983§
EK'000,000	+547.6	+351.9	−4,704.0	−5,400.0	−6,657.0	−9,326.0
% of total	18.6%	9.8%	54.8%	51.1%	27.5%	29.3%

Imports (1981): EK7,982,000,000 (food, beverages, and tobacco 24.9%; petroleum and petroleum products 22.4%; motor vehicles and machinery 17.4%; iron and steel products 12.4%; clothing 6.0%). *Major import sources:* Spain 79.9%; Cameroon 7.2%.
Exports (1981): EK2,582,000,000 (cacao 71.5%; timber 24.4%; coffee 2.8%). *Major export destinations:* Spain 86.7%; West Germany 3.5%; The Netherlands 3.2%.

Transport and communications

Transport. Railroads: none. Roads (1982): total length 1,715 mi, 2,760 km (paved 12%). Vehicles: n.a. Merchant marine (1983): vessels (100 gross tons and over) 2; total deadweight tonnage 6,700. Air transport (1980): passenger-mi 4,000,000, passenger-km 7,000,000; short ton-mi cargo 700,000, metric ton-km cargo 1,000,000; airport (1984) with scheduled flights 1.
Communications. Daily newspapers (1981): total number 2; total circulation, n.a. Radios (1982): total number of receivers 90,000 (1 per 3.3 persons). Television (1982): total number of receivers 2,000 (1 per 150 persons). Telephones (1982): 1,366 (1 per 220 persons).

Education and health

Education (1980–81)				
	schools	teachers	students	student/ teacher ratio
Primary (age 6–11)	511	647	40,110	62.0
Secondary (age 12–17), voc., teacher tr.	14	288	3,013	10.5

College graduates: n.a. *Literacy* ‖ (1980): total population literate 27,700 (83.2%); males literate 14,700 (88.5%); females literate 13,000 (77.8%).
Health (1977): physicians 5 (1 per 64,000 persons); hospital beds 3,577 (1 per 90 persons).
Food (1978–80): daily per capita caloric intake, n.a.; FAO recommended minimum requirement for the region is 2,300 calories.

Military

Total active duty personnel (1982): 1,550 (army 90.3%; navy 6.5%; air force 3.2%). *Military expenditure as percent of GNP* (1981): 1.8% (world 5.7%); per capita expenditure U.S.$9.

*Preliminary; population figures for the islands are estimated. †Includes population for Great and Little Elobey. ‡1981. §Estimated. ‖ Age 15–19 only.

Ethiopia

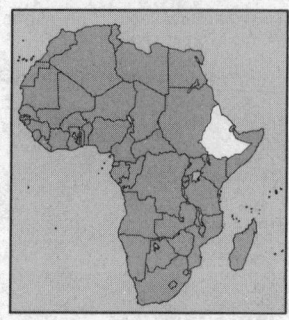

Official name: Hebretasebawit
Etiyop'iya (Socialist Ethiopia).
Form of government: socialist state
ruled by a Provisional Military
Administrative Council (PMAC).
Head of state and government:
Chairman of the PMAC and of the
Council of Ministers.
Capital: Addis Ababa.
Official language: Amharic.
Official religion: none.
Monetary unit: 1 Ethiopian Birr
(Br) = 100 cents; valuation (Oct. 29,
1984) 1 U.S.$ = Br2.07;
1 £ = Br2.50.

Area and population

Regions	Capitals	area		population 1984 census
		sq mi	sq km	
Arsi	Asela	9,500	24,600	1,662,233
Bale	Goba	49,500	128,300	1,006,491
Eritrea	Asmera	45,300	117,400	2,704,000
Gemu Gofa	Arba Minch	15,400	40,100	1,248,034
Gojam	Debre Markos	24,900	64,500	3,244,882
Gonder	Gonder	28,300	73,400	2,905,362
Hararge	Harer	98,400	254,800	4,151,706
Ilubabor	Metu	19,600	50,800	963,327
Kefa	Jima	20,500	53,000	2,450,369
Shewa	Addis Ababa	33,000	85,500	9,503,140
Sidamo	Awasa	45,100	116,700	3,790,579
Tigray	Mekele	25,400	65,700	2,409,700
Welega	Nekemte	27,000	69,800	2,369,677
Wello	Dese	30,500	79,000	3,609,918
TOTAL		472,400	1,223,600	42,019,418

Source: Official government figures.

Demography

Density (1984): persons per sq mi 88.9, persons per sq km 34.3.
Urban–rural (1984): urban 11.3%; rural 88.7%.
Sex distribution (1984): male 49.85%; female 50.15%.
Age breakdown (1980): under 15, 45.5%; 15–29, 24.4%; 30–44, 16.4%; 45–59,
8.4%; 60–64, 1.8%; 65 and over, 3.5%.
Population projection: (1990) 50,100,000; (2000) 66,600,000.
Doubling time: 24 years.
Ethnic composition (1978): Amhara 37.7%; Galla 35.3%; Tigrai 8.4%; Gurage
3.2%; other 15.4%.
Religious affiliation (1980): Ethiopian Orthodox 48.9%; Muslim 31.4%;
tribal religionist 11.4%; Protestant 3.5%; Evangelical 3.1%; Roman Catholic
0.7%; other 1.0%.
Major cities (1984): Addis Ababa 1,412,575; Asmera 275,385; Dire Dawa
98,104; Gonder 68,958; Dese 68,848.

Vital statistics

Birth rate per 1,000 population (1980–85): 49.7 (world avg. 27.5).
Death rate per 1,000 population (1980–85): 23.1 (world avg. 10.6).
Natural increase rate per 1,000 population (1980–85): 26.6 (world avg. 16.9).
Total fertility rate (avg. births per childbearing woman; 1980–85): 6.7.
Marriage rate per 1,000 population: n.a.
Divorce rate per 1,000 population: n.a.
Infant mortality rate per 1,000 live births (1975–80): 150.0.
Life expectancy at birth (1980–85): male 39.4 years; female 42.6 years.
Major causes of death (hospital inpatients only; 1977–78): infectious and
parasitic diseases 524; digestive system diseases 384; allergy, endocrine,
metabolic, nutritional, and circulatory diseases 326; respiratory diseases
216.

National economy

Budget (1982–83). Revenue: Br2,100,000,000 (income and profit taxes 28.4%;
domestic excise and sales taxes 21.4%; customs duties 9.7%, coffee export
surtax 8.5%). Expenditures (recurrent and capital): Br3,301,700,000 (capital
expenditure on economic development 33.4%, of which mining, industry,
and tourism 9.2%, agriculture 8.7%; central government 32.1%; education
9.2%).
Public debt (external, outstanding; 1982): U.S.$874,600,000.
Tourism (1981): receipts from visitors U.S.$10,000,000; expenditures by na-
tionals abroad U.S.$5,000,000.
Production (metric tons except as noted). Agriculture, forestry, fishing (1982):
sugarcane 1,480,000, sorghum 1,300,000, barley 1,150,000, corn (maize)
1,000,000, wheat 650,000, millet 200,000, niger seed (*neug*) 52,100*, sesame
seed 36,000, linseed 28,000, dry broad beans 450,000, dry peas 190,000,
chick peas 150,000, bananas 73,000, coffee 202,000, cotton 27,000; livestock
(number of live animals) 26,200,000 cattle, 23,350,000 sheep, 17,220,000
goats, 3,900,000 asses, 1,557,000 horses, 1,400,000 mules, 1,000,000 camels,
54,000,000 chickens. Mining and quarrying (1982): cement 180,000; kaolin
clay 9,000; crude gypsum and anhydrite 4,000; gold 12,000 troy ounces.
Manufacturing (gross value in Br; 1981): textiles, spinning, weaving, and
wearing apparel 386,360,000; food products 244,300,000; beverages 189,900,-
000; tobacco 54,030,000; paper and paper products, printing, and publishing
39,080,000; leather and leather products 25,650,000; industrial chemicals
and other chemical products 23,790,000. Construction (authorized; 1978):
residential 229,300 sq m; nonresidential 12,300 sq m, of which commercial

5,300 sq m. Energy production (consumption): electricity (kW-hr; 1982)
679,000 (679,000); coal n.a. (none); crude petroleum (barrels; 1982) n.a.
(4,947,750); petroleum products (metric tons; 1982) 650,000 (660,000); natural gas n.a. (n.a.).
Gross national product (at current market prices; 1982): U.S.$4,727,000,000
(U.S.$120 per capita).

Origin of gross domestic product (current prices)

	1983		1982	
	in value Br'000,000	% of total value	labour force	% of labour force
Agriculture	4,162.2	43.1	10,457,000	78.0
Mining	10.8	0.1		
Manufacturing	961.3	9.9		
Construction	333.8	3.5		
Trade	931.7	9.6		
Public utilities	59.6	0.6		
Transportation and communication	474.4	4.9	2,956,000	22.0
Finance	325.7	3.4		
Pub. admin., defense	694.4	7.2		
Services	569.6	5.9		
Other†	1,136.7	11.8		
TOTAL	9,660.2	100.0	13,413,000	100.0

Persons economically active (1982): total 13,413,000.

Price and earnings indexes (1980 = 100)

	1978	1979	1980	1981	1982	1983	1984
Consumer price index	82.5	95.7	100.0	106.1	112.4	111.6	109.1‡
Monthly earnings index	...	...	...	...	...	...	...

Land use (1981): forested 24.1%; meadows and pastures 41.2%; agricultural
and under permanent cultivation 12.7%; other 22.0%.

Foreign trade

Balance of trade (current prices)

	1977	1978	1979	1980	1981	1982
Br'000,000	−88.9	−439.9	−300.6	−614.2	−723.8	−775.6
% of total	5.8%	25.6%	14.7%	25.9%	31.0%	31.7%

Imports (1982): Br1,610,730,000 (petroleum, petroleum products 24.4%, of
which crude petroleum 22.2%; machinery, including aircraft 14.8%; road
motor vehicles 11.8%; metal manufactures 9.7%; food and live animals
chiefly for food 7.7%; chemicals and chemical products 6.0%). *Major import sources:* Soviet Union 27.1%; Italy 11.0%; West Germany 9.7%; United
States 7.7%; Japan 7.1%; United Kingdom 6.0%; Saudi Arabia 3.7%.
Exports (1982): Br835,155,000 (food and live animals chiefly for food 67.0%,
of which coffee 61.2%; pulses 4.4%; hides and skins 9.8%; kat [a narcotic
leaf] 3.9%; oilseeds 2.3%; incense 4.0%; beeswax 0.2%). *Major export destinations:* United States 20.6%; West Germany 10.4%; Saudi Arabia 6.3%;
Japan 7.4%; Italy 7.0%; Yemen 6.3%; France 5.3%; Djibouti 5.1%.

Transport and communications

Transport. Railroads§ (1983): length 485 mi, 781 km; passenger-mi 153,-
000,000 ‖, passenger-km 247,000,000 ‖ ; short ton-mi cargo 101,000,000 ‖ ,
metric ton-km cargo 148,000,000 ‖ . Roads (1982): total length 22,612 mi,
36,391 km (paved 34%). Vehicles (1982): passenger cars 43,107; trucks
and buses 17,222. Merchant marine (1983): vessels (100 gross tons and
over) 20; total deadweight tonnage 43,177. Air transport (1983): passenger-
mi 473,697,000, passenger-km 762,343,000; short ton-mi cargo 18,587,000,
metric ton-km cargo 27,136,000; airports (1984) with scheduled flights 30.
Communications. Daily newspapers (1982): total number 4; total circulation
70,000; circulation per 1,000 population 1.8. Radios (1983): total number
of receivers 2,000,000 (1 per 20.5 persons). Television (1983): total number
of receivers 36,000 (1 per 1,138 persons). Telephones (1982): 100,783 (1
per 395 persons).

Education and health

Education (1980–81)

	schools	teachers	students	student/ teacher ratio
Primary (age 7–12)	6,208	37,844	2,374,362	62.7
Secondary (age 13–18)	...	11,184	487,179	43.6
Voc., teacher tr.	...	...	...	...
Higher	...	1,137	11,822	10.4

College graduates per 100,000 population age 20 to 24 (students graduating;
1979): 163.4. *Literacy* (1980): total population literate 1,000,000 (4.8%);
males literate 950,000 (9.3%); females literate 50,000 (0.5%).
Health (1980): physicians 433 (1 per 86,859 persons); hospital beds 11,147
(1 per 3,374 persons).
Food (1978–80): daily per capita caloric intake 1,729 (vegetable products 91.4%, animal products 8.6%); 74% of FAO recommended minimum
requirement.

Military

Total active duty personnel (1983): 250,500 (army 97.6%; navy 1.0%; air force
1.4%). *Military expenditure as percent of* GNP (1982): 9.8% (world 6.0%);
per capita expenditure (1982) U.S.$12.

*1981. †Includes net indirect taxes and statistical discrepancies. ‡First quarter. §In-
cludes 62 mi (100 km) of the Chemin de Fer Djibouti-Ethiopien (CDE) in Djibouti.
‖ 1979–80.

Fiji

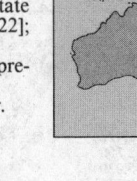

Official name: Dominion of Fiji.
Form of government: parliamentary state with two legislative houses (Senate [22]; House of Representatives [52]).
Chief of state: British Monarch represented by governor-general.
Head of government: Prime Minister.
Capital: Suva.
Official language: English.
Official religion: none.
Monetary unit: 1 Fiji dollar (F$) = 100 cents; valuation (Oct. 29, 1984) F$1.00 = U.S.$1.12 = £1.35.

Area and population		area		population
Divisions				1984
Provinces*	**Capitals**	sq mi	sq km	estimate
Central	Suva			
Naitasiri		643	1,666	86,000
Rewa		105	272	103,600
Serua-Namosi		541	1,400	18,100
Tailevu		369	955	44,800
Eastern	Levuka			
Kandavu		185	478	8,800
Lau		188	487	13,800
Lomaiviti		159	411	13,700
Rotuma		18	46	2,600
Northern	Labasa			
Mathuata		774	2,004	69,300
Mbua		532	1,379	12,800
Thakaundrove		1,087	2,816	39,100
Western	Lautoka			
Mba		1,017	2,634	192,200
Nandronga-Navosa		921	2,385	53,200
Ra		518	1,341	28,100
TOTAL		7,055†	18,274	686,000†

Source: Official government figures; Britannica estimate.

Demography

Density (1984): persons per sq mi 97.2, persons per sq km 37.5.
Urban–rural (1983): urban 45.8%; rural 54.2%.
Sex distribution (1983): male 50.53%; female 49.47%.
Age breakdown (1983): under 15, 37.2%; 15–29, 30.4%; 30–44, 17.7%; 45–59, 9.4%; 60–74, 4.1%; 75 and over, 1.2%.
Population projection: (1990) 736,000; (2000) 817,000.
Doubling time: 35 years.
Ethnic composition (1983): Indian 50.2%; Fijian 44.7%; part-European 1.6%; Rotuman 1.2%; Chinese 0.7%; European 0.7%; other 0.9%.
Religious affiliation (1980): Christian 49.7%; Hindu 40.9%; Muslim 7.8%; other 1.6%.
Major cities (1982 est.): Suva 71,000; Lautoka 26,000; Nadi 9,000; Ba 7,000; Nausori 6,000.

Vital statistics

Birth rate per 1,000 population (1982): 30.9 (world avg. 29.0); (1978) legitimate 82.7%, illegitimate 17.3%.
Death rate per 1,000 population (1982): 5.8 (world avg. 11.0).
Natural increase rate per 1,000 population (1982): 25.1 (world avg. 18.0).
Total fertility rate (avg. births per childbearing woman; 1980–85): 3.1.
Marriage rate per 1,000 population (1981): 9.7.
Divorce rate per 1,000 population (1979): 0.7.
Infant mortality rate per 1,000 live births (1982): 17.4.
Life expectancy at birth (1980–85): male 70.2 years; female 74.1 years.
Major causes of death per 100,000 population (1982): heart disease 225.1; respiratory diseases 70.3; malignant neoplasms (cancers) 25.5; infectious and parasitic diseases 30.7; endocrine and metabolic disorders 18.1.

National economy

Budget (1983). Revenue: F$286,693,000 (income tax and gift duties 45.7%; customs and port duties 34.7%). Expenditures: F$304,106,000 (education 16.7%; economic services 13.5%; health 7.2%; general public services 11.1%; defense 3.5%).
Public debt (external, outstanding; 1984): U.S.$264,738,000.
Tourism (1983): receipts from visitors U.S.$140,000,000; expenditures by nationals abroad U.S.$19,000,000.
Production (metric tons except as noted). Agriculture, forestry, fishing (1983): sugarcane 2,202,000, centrifugal sugar 487,000, coconuts 210,000, copra 24,000, paddy rice 16,000; livestock (number of live animals; 1982) 156,000 cattle, 28,000 sheep, 27,000 pigs; roundwood 167,033 cu m; fish catch 11,066. Mining and quarrying (1983): gold 1,423 kilograms; silver 401 kilograms; cement 109,900. Manufacturing (1983): refined sugar 276,000; coconut oil 16,000; soap 6,700; beer 191,000 hectolitres; paint 23,000 hectolitres. Construction (value in F$; 1983): residential 15,075,000; non-residential 5,465,000. Energy production (consumption): electricity (kW-hr; 1983) 327,000,000 (327,000,000).
Household income and expenditure. Average household size (1980) 4.1; income per household F$2,837 (U.S.$3,546); sources of income: wages and salaries 81.5%, self-employment 9.1%, other 9.4%; expenditure (1979): food 33.8%, housing 15.0%, transportation 13.9%, clothing and footwear 8.7%.
Gross national product (at current market prices; 1983): U.S.$1,017,900,000 (U.S.$1,535 per capita).

Origin of gross domestic product (constant prices of 1977)

	1983			
	in value F$'000,000	% of total value	labour force	% of labour force
Agriculture	142.1	20.9	85,059	40.6
Mining	0.6	0.1	1,171	0.6
Manufacturing	77.6	11.4	14,348	6.8
Construction	52.6	7.7	6,983	3.3
Trade	120.9	17.8	15,792	7.5
Public utilities	7.4	1.1	2,449	1.2
Transportation and communication	77.9	11.4	7,450	3.6
Finance	93.8	13.8	5,148	2.4
Pub. admin., defense, services	127.9	18.8	25,600	12.2
Other	−20.3‡	−3.0‡	45,703§	21.8§
TOTAL	680.5	100.0	209,703	100.0

Persons economically active (1983): total 209,703 (31.2%); female participation in labour force 36,279 (17.3%); unemployed 14,643 (7.0%).

Price and earnings indexes (1979 = 100)

	1979	1980	1981	1982	1983	1984
Consumer price index	100.0	114.5	127.3	136.2	145.4	152.3 ‖
Daily earnings index	100.0	109.4	119.8	129.2		

Land use (1981): forested 64.9%; agricultural and under permanent cultivation 12.9%; meadows and pastures 3.3%; other 18.9%.

Foreign trade

Balance of trade (current prices)

	1978	1979	1980	1981	1982	1983
F$'000,000	−133.5	−177.8	−153.2	−270.9	−208.0	−248.3
% of total	28.6%	29.3%	20.0%	33.5%	28.0%	33.6%

Imports (1983): F$493,206,000 (manufactured goods 28.2%; mineral fuels and related materials 23.3%; machinery and transport equipment 18.9%; food, beverages, and tobacco 16.6%; chemicals 7.9%). *Major import sources:* Australia 38.2%; Japan 16.7%; New Zealand 16.4%; United Kingdom 5.0%; Singapore 4.2%; United States 3.9%; China 2.1%; Taiwan 1.7%; Hong Kong 1.5%.
Exports (1983): F$244,902,000 (sugar 45.7%; minerals [mainly gold] 6.8%; fish 6.1%; coconut oil 4.3%; wood and by-products 4.2%; manufactured goods 3.8%; molasses 0.8%). *Major export destinations:* United Kingdom 30.9%; Australia 14.9%; Malaysia 11.7%; United States 9.8%; France 6.0%; New Zealand 6.0%.

Transport and communications

Transport. Railroads (1980): length 660 mi, 1,062 km. Roads (1982): total length 2,669 mi, 4,295 km (paved 13%). Vehicles (1983): passenger cars 27,916; trucks and buses 19,237. Merchant marine (1983): vessels (100 gross tons and over) 56; total deadweight tonnage 26,551. Air transport (1983): passenger-mi 254,634,000, passenger-km 409,795,000; short ton-mi cargo 2,212,000¶, metric ton-km cargo 3,229,000¶; airports (1984) with scheduled flights 16.
Communications. Daily newspapers (1983): total number 2; total circulation 70,278; circulation per 1,000 population 106. Radios (1983): total number of receivers 400,000 (1 per 1.6 persons). Television: none. Telephones (1983): 49,542 (1 per 13.1 persons).

Education and health

Education (1983)

	schools	teachers¶	students	student/ teacher ratio
Primary (age 5–15)	660	4,256	120,244	...
Secondary (age 16–19)	140	2,467	44,415	...
Vocational	37	314	1,028¶	3.3¶
Higher	5	...	3,947	...

College graduates per 100,000 population: n.a. *Literacy* (1976): total population literate 273,680 (79.0%); males literate 146,282 (84.0%); females literate 127,398 (74.0%).
Health (1982): physicians 325 (1 per 2,000 persons); hospital beds 1,720 (1 per 377.9 persons).
Food (1978–80): daily per capita caloric intake 2,885 (vegetable products 86.1%, animal products 13.9%); 108% of FAO recommended minimum requirement.

Military

Total active duty personnel (1983): 2,579 (army 94%; navy 6%; air force none). *Military expenditure as percent of GNP* (1982): 1.0% (world 6.0%); per capita expenditure: U.S.$22.

*The provinces are autonomous only with respect to local affairs. †Detail does not add to total given because of rounding. ‡Less imputed service charges. §Self-employed and unemployed. ‖ April. ¶1982.

Finland

Official name: Suomen Tasavalta (Finnish), Republiken Finland (Swedish) (Republic of Finland).
Form of government: multiparty parliamentary republic with one legislative house (Eduskunta [200]).
Chief of state: President.
Head of government: Prime Minister.
Capital: Helsinki.
Official languages: Finnish; Swedish.
Official religion: none.
Monetary unit: 1 markka (Fmk) = 100 penni; valuation (Oct. 29, 1984) 1 U.S.$ = Fmk6.37; 1 £ = Fmk7.68.

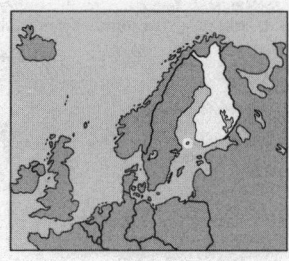

Area and population

Provinces	Capitals	land area sq mi	land area sq km	population 1984 estimate
Ahvenanmaa	Mariehamn	590	1,527	23,400
Häme	Hämeenlinna	6,568	17,010	672,700
Keski-Suomi	Jyväskylä	6,266	16,230	246,400
Kuopio	Kuopio	6,375	16,511	255,100
Kymi	Kouvola	4,163	10,783	342,300
Lappi	Rovaniemi	35,929	93,057	200,200
Mikkeli	Mikkeli	6,310	16,342	209,100
Oulu	Oulu	21,956	56,866	430,200
Pohjois-Karjala	Joensuu	6,866	17,782	177,700
Turku ja Pori	Turku	8,559	22,170	710,700
Uusimaa	Helsinki	3,822	9,898	1,165,400
Vaasa	Vaasa	10,211	26,447	442,600
TOTAL		117,615	304,623	4,875,800

Source: Official government figures.

Demography

*Density** (1984): persons per sq mi 41.5, persons per sq km 16.0.
Urban–rural (1982): urban 59.9%; rural 40.1%.
Sex distribution (1982): male 48.37%; female 51.63%.
Age breakdown (1982): under 15, 19.9%; 15–29, 24.0%; 30–44, 22.6%; 45–59, 16.8%; 60–74, 12.4%; 75 and over, 4.3%.
Population projection: (1990) 5,020,000; (2000) 5,058,000.
Growth rate: negligible.
Ethnic composition (1975): Finnish 99.8%; Lappish 0.1%; Gypsy 0.1%.
Religious affiliation (1982): Lutheran 90.1%; Orthodox 1.1%; nonaffiliated 7.9%; other 0.9%.
Major cities (1984 est.): Helsinki 484,019; Tampere 167,690; Turku 162,984; Espoo 149,695; Vantaa 140,355.

Vital statistics

Birth rate per 1,000 population (1983): 13.8 (world avg. 29.0); (1981) legitimate 86.7%, illegitimate 13.3%.
Death rate per 1,000 population (1983): 9.4 (world avg. 12.0).
Natural increase rate per 1,000 population (1983): 4.4 (world avg. 18.0).
Total fertility rate (avg. births per childbearing woman; 1981): 1.6.
Marriage rate per 1,000 population (1983): 6.1.
Divorce rate per 1,000 population (1982): 2.0.
Infant mortality rate per 1,000 live births (1982): 6.0.
Life expectancy at birth (1981): male 69.5 years; female 77.8 years.
Major causes of death per 100,000 population (1979–80): ischemic heart disease 271.6; malignant neoplasms (cancers) 187.8; cerebrovascular diseases 106.6; accidents 44.5; pneumonia 41.1; suicide and self-inflicted injuries 25.7.

National economy

Budget (1983). Revenue: Fmk65,595,000,000 (income and property 29.6%, excise tax 44.1%, import and export 2.6%). Expenditures: Fmk72,985,000,000 (education 17.1%, social security 15.1%, health 9.4%, defense 5.8%).
Public debt (external, outstanding; 1983): U.S.$1,988,000,000.
Tourism (1982): receipts from visitors U.S.$579,000,000; expenditures by nationals abroad U.S.$630,000,000.
Production (metric tons except as noted). Agriculture, forestry, fishing (1982): barley 1,599,000, oats 1,320,000, sugar beets 756,000, potatoes 601,000, milk, 2,858,000,000 litres, beef and veal 117,000; livestock (number of live animals) 1,705,100 cattle, 1,509,000 pigs, 245,500 reindeer; roundwood 39,209,000 cu m; fish catch 145,636. Mining and quarrying (1982): iron ore 862,000†; chromite 245,000; limestone 4,662,000. Manufacturing (value added in Fmk; 1982): machinery 22,352,000,000, of which transport equipment 4,248,000,000, electrical 3,372,000,000; food, processed 8,335,000,000; paper and paper products 7,486,000,000; chemical products 7,127,000,000. Construction (1982): residential 17,690,000 cu m; industrial and commercial 25,410,000 cu m. Energy production (consumption): electricity (kW-hr; 1982) 39,350,000,000 (41,686,000,000); coal (metric tons; 1982) none (2,650,000); crude petroleum (barrels; 1982) none (69,327,140); petroleum products (metric tons; 1982) 8,309,000 (9,177,000); natural gas (cu m; 1982) none (641,025,000).
Gross national product (at current market prices; 1983): U.S.$46,351,000,000 (U.S.$9,540 per capita).
Household income and expenditure. Average household size (1980): 3.0; income per household Fmk61,406 (U.S.$16,160); sources of income (1979): wages and salaries 82.2%, self-employed 13.8%, income from property 4.0%; expenditure (1981): food 28.1%, housing§ 26.1%, transportation and communications 17.1%, recreation 8.4%, clothing and footwear 5.1%.

Origin of gross domestic product (current prices)

	1982 in value Fmk'000,000	% of total value	labour force	% of labour force
Agriculture	22,010	9.4	264,000	10.7
Mining	1,105	0.5	10,000	0.4
Manufacturing	63,205	27.0	599,000	24.3
Construction	17,015	7.3	172,000	7.0
Trade	22,100	9.4	328,000	13.3
Public utilities	6,565	2.8	26,000	1.1
Transportation and communication	15,425	6.6	174,000	7.1
Finance	13,700	5.9	141,000	5.7
Pub. admin., defense	32,930	14.1	642,000	26.1
Services	9,945	4.2	...	...
Other	30,050	12.8	107,000	4.3
TOTAL	234,050	100.0	2,463,000	100.0

Persons economically active (1982): total 2,463,000 (51.0%); female participation in the labour force 1,160,000 (47.1%); unemployed 152,700 (6.2%).

Price and earnings indexes (1980 = 100)

	1978	1979	1980	1981	1982	1983	1984‡
Consumer price index	83.4	89.6	100.0	112.0	122.4	132.9	138.6
Hourly earnings index	80.0	89.0	100.0	113.0	125.0	138.0	144.0

Land use (1981): forested 76.3%; meadows and pastures 0.5%; agricultural and under permanent cultivation 7.8%; other 15.4%.

Foreign trade

Balance of trade (current prices)

	1979	1980	1981	1982	1983	1984‡
Fmk'000,000	+1,998.3	−1,410.0	+3,107.0	+1,725.0	+1,242.1	+4,137.0
% of total	2.4%	1.3%	2.6%	1.4%	0.9%	11.7%

Imports (1982): Fmk64,751,000,000 (machinery and transport equipment 28.2%, of which nonelectrical machinery 14.2%; mineral fuels 27.4%, of which crude petroleum 17.5%; chemical products 8.7%; textiles 3.9%; iron and steel 3.2%). *Major import sources:* U.S.S.R. 24.6%; West Germany 13.2%; Sweden 12.2%; United Kingdom 7.0%; United States 6.1%.
Exports (1982): Fmk63,026,000,000 (machinery and transport equipment 25.2%, of which nonelectrical 11.0%, ships and boats 7.8%; paper and paperboard 20.0%; refined petroleum products 3.7%; iron and steel 3.6%). *Major export destinations:* U.S.S.R. 26.7%; Sweden 11.9%; United Kingdom 10.8%; West Germany 9.0%; Norway 4.9%; France 3.9%.

Transport and communications

Transport. Railroads (1981): length 5,688 mi, 9,153 km; passenger-mi 2,034,444,000, passenger-km 3,274,126,000; short ton-mi cargo 5,747,151,000, metric ton-km cargo 8,390,700,000. Roads (1982): total length 46,881 mi, 75,448 km (paved 50%). Vehicles (1982): passenger cars 1,352,055; trucks and buses 182,797. Merchant marine (1983): vessels (100 gross tons and over) 339; total deadweight tonnage 3,600,996. Air transport (1982): passenger-mi 2,542,857,000, passenger-km 4,092,339,000; short ton-mi cargo 41,858,000, metric ton-km cargo 61,111,000; airports (1984) with scheduled flights 24.
Communications. Daily newspapers (1982): total number 64; total circulation 2,484,000; circulation per 1,000 population 515. Radios (1983): total number of receivers 2,515,000 (1 per 1.9 persons). Television (1983): total number of receivers 2,200,000 (1 per 2.2 persons). Telephones (1982): 2,511,306 (1 per 1.9 persons).

Education and health

Education (1982–83)

	schools	teachers	students	student/teacher ratio
Primary (age 7–12)	4,238	24,752	365,965	14.8
Secondary (age 13–19)	1,078	22,279	325,763	14.6
Voc., teacher tr.	535	14,819	106,998	7.2
Higher ‖	21	5,087	127,657	25.1

College graduates per 100,000 population (students graduating; 1980): 550.
Literacy (1982): virtually 100.0% literate.
Health (1981): physicians 9,538 (1 per 504 persons); hospital beds 74,381 (1 per 64 persons).
Food (1978–80): daily per capita caloric intake 3,127 (vegetable products 56.1%, animal products 43.9%); 121% of FAO recommended minimum requirement.

Military

Total active duty personnel (1982): 40,400 (army 86.3%; navy 6.2%; air force 7.5%). *Military expenditure as percent of GNP* (1982): 1.8% (world 6.0%); per capita expenditure U.S.$185.

*Land area only. †Metal content only. ‡First quarter. §Includes utilities, furnishings, etc. ‖ Universities only.

France

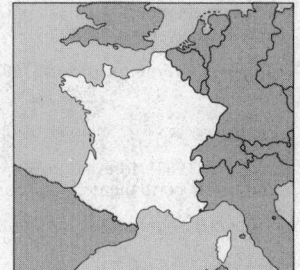

Official name: République Française (French Republic).
Form of government: republic with two legislative houses (Parliament; National Assembly [491], Senate [317]).
Chief of state: President.
Head of government: Premier.
Capital: Paris.
Official language: French.
Official religion: none.
Monetary unit: 1 Franc (F) = 100 centimes; valuation (Oct. 29, 1984) 1 U.S.$ = F9.41; 1 £ = F11.36.

Area and population

Regions Departments	Capitals	area sq mi	area sq km	population 1982 census
Alsace				
Bas-Rhin	Strasbourg	1,848	4,787	915,676
Haut-Rhin	Colmar	1,360	3,523	650,372
Aquitaine				
Dordogne	Périgueux	3,546	9,184	377,356
Gironde	Bordeaux	3,861	10,000	1,127,546
Landes	Mont-de-Marsan	3,566	9,237	297,424
Lot-et-Garonne	Agen	2,069	5,358	298,522
Pyrénées-Atlantiques	Pau	2,946	7,629	555,696
Auvergne				
Allier	Moulins	2,829	7,327	369,580
Cantal	Aurillac	2,217	5,741	162,838
Haute-Loire	Le Puy	1,917	4,965	205,895
Puy-de-Dôme	Clermont-Ferrand	3,071	7,955	594,365
Basse Normandie				
Calvados	Caen	2,137	5,536	589,559
Manche	Saint-Lô	2,296	5,947	465,948
Orne	Alen	2,355	6,100	295,472
Bretagne				
Côtes-du-Nord	Saint-Brieuc	2,656	6,878	538,869
Finistère	Quimper	2,620	6,785	828,364
Ille-et-Vilaine	Rennes	2,609	6,758	749,764
Morbihan	Vannes	2,611	6,763	590,889
Bourgogne				
Côte-d'Or	Dijon	3,384	8,765	473,548
Nièvre	Nevers	2,640	6,837	239,635
Saône-et-Loire	Mâcon	3,307	8,565	571,852
Yonne	Auxerre	2,867	7,425	311,019
Centre				
Cher	Bourges	2,791	7,228	320,174
Eure-et-Loire	Chartres	2,269	5,876	362,813
Indre	Châteauroux	2,617	6,778	243,191
Indre-et-Loire	Tours	2,364	6,124	506,097
Loiret	Orléans	2,603	6,742	535,669
Loir-et-Cher	Blois	2,438	6,314	296,220
Champagne-Ardenne				
Ardennes	Charleville-Mézières	2,015	5,219	302,338
Aube	Troyes	2,317	6,002	289,300
Haute-Marne	Chaumont	2,400	6,216	210,670
Marne	Châlons-sur-Marne	3,152	8,163	543,627
Corse				
Corse-du-Sud	Ajaccio	1,550	4,014	108,604
Haute-Corse	Bastia	1,802	4,666	131,574
Franche-Comté				
Doubs	Besançon	2,019	5,228	477,163
Haute-Saône	Vesoul	2,063	5,343	231,962
Jura	Lons-le-Saunier	1,934	5,008	242,925
Territoire de Belfort	Belfort	236	610	131,999
Haute-Normandie				
Eure	Évreux	2,318	6,004	462,323
Seine-Maritime	Rouen	2,415	6,254	1,193,039
Languedoc-Roussillon				
Aude	Carcassonne	2,406	6,232	280,686
Gard	Nîmes	2,258	5,848	530,478
Hérault	Montpellier	2,360	6,113	706,499
Lozère	Mende	1,995	5,168	74,294
Pyrénées-Orientales	Perpignan	1,578	4,086	334,557
Limousin				
Corrèze	Tulle	2,263	5,860	241,448
Creuse	Guéret	2,146	5,559	139,968
Haute-Vienne	Limoges	2,128	5,512	355,737
Lorraine				
Meurthe-et-Moselle	Nancy	2,021	5,235	716,846
Meuse	Bar-le-Duc	2,402	6,220	200,101
Moselle	Metz	2,399	6,214	1,007,189
Vosges	Épinal	2,267	5,871	395,769
Midi-Pyrénées				
Ariège	Foix	1,888	4,890	135,725
Aveyron	Rodez	3,373	8,735	278,654
Gers	Auch	2,415	6,254	174,154
Haute-Garonne	Toulouse	2,433	6,301	824,501
Haute-Pyrénées	Tarbes	1,740	4,507	227,922
Lot	Cahors	2,019	5,228	154,533
Tarn	Albi	2,220	5,751	339,345
Tarn-et-Garonne	Montauban	1,435	3,716	190,485
Nord				
Nord	Lille	2,215	5,738	2,520,526
Pas-de-Calais	Arras	2,563	6,639	1,412,413
Pays de la Loire				
Loire-Atlantique	Nantes	2,661	6,893	995,498
Maine et Loire	Angers	2,753	7,131	675,321
Mayenne	Laval	1,997	5,171	271,784
Sarthe	Le Mans	2,398	6,210	504,768
Vendée	La Roche-sur-Yon	2,595	6,721	483,027
Picardie				
Aisne	Laon	2,849	7,378	533,970
Oise	Beauvais	2,261	5,857	661,781
Somme	Amiens	2,384	6,175	544,570
Poitou-Charentes				
Charente	Angoulême	2,298	5,953	340,770
Charente-Maritime	La Rochelle	2,644	6,848	513,220
Deux-Sèvres	Niort	2,318	6,004	342,812
Vienne	Poitiers	2,697	6,985	371,428
Provence-Côte d'Azur				
Alpes-Maritimes	Nice	1,658	4,294	881,198
Alpes-de-Haute-Provence	Digne	2,681	6,944	119,068
Bouches-du-Rhône	Marseille	1,974	5,112	1,724,199
Hautes-Alpes	Gap	2,131	5,520	105,070
Var	Toulon	2,316	5,999	708,331
Vaucluse	Avignon	1,377	3,566	427,343
Île-de-France				
Essonne	Évry	699	1,811	988,000
Hauts-de-Seine	Nanterre	68	175	1,387,039
Paris	Paris	41	105	2,176,243
Seine-et-Marne	Melun	2,285	5,917	887,112
Seine-Saint-Denis	Bobigny	91	236	1,324,301
Val-de-Marne	Créteil	94	244	1,193,655
Val-d'Oise	Pontoise	482	1,249	920,598
Yvelines	Versailles	877	2,271	1,196,111
Rhône-Alpes				
Ain	Bourg-en-Bresse	2,222	5,756	418,516
Ardèche	Privas	2,132	5,523	267,970
Drôme	Valence	2,519	6,525	389,781
Haute-Savoie	Annecy	1,695	4,391	494,505
Isère	Grenoble	2,886	7,474	936,771
Loire	Saint-Étienne	1,843	4,774	739,521
Rhône	Lyon	1,241	3,215	1,445,208
Savoie	Chambéry	2,330	6,036	323,675
TOTAL		210,036	543,994	54,334,871

Source: Official government figures.

Demography

Density (1984): persons per sq mi 259.6, persons per sq km 100.2.
Urban–rural (1975): urban 73.0%; rural 27.0%.
Sex distribution (1984): male 49.12%; female 50.88%.
Age breakdown (1984): under 15, 21.0%; 15–29, 23.3%; 30–44, 21.0%; 45–59, 16.9%; 60–74, 11.9%; 75 and over, 5.9%.
Population projection: (1990) 55,600,000; (2000) 57,500,000.
Growth rate: during 1975–1982, the average growth rate was 0.4%.
Ethnic composition (1980): French 82.9%; Alsatian 2.6%; Italian 2.2%; Breton 2.0%; Algerian 1.7%; Portuguese 1.4%; Spanish 1.0%; Jewish 1.0%; Polish 0.7%; Moroccan 0.6%; Corsican 0.5%; Flemish 0.5%; Basque 0.2%; other 2.7%.
Religious affiliation (1980): Roman Catholics 76.4%; other Christian 3.7%; atheist 3.4%; Muslim 3.0%; other 13.5%.
Major cities (1982): Paris 8,706,963; Lyon 1,220,844; Marseille 1,110,511; Lille* 936,295; Bordeaux 640,012; Toulouse 541,271; Nantes 464,857; Nice 449,496; Toulon 410,393; Grenoble 392,021.
Place of national origin (1982): 90.6% French; Algerians 1.5%, Portuguese 1.4%, Moroccans 0.8%, Spanish 0.6%, Italian 0.6%, other 4.5%.
Mobility (1975). Population living in same residence as in 1968: 49.5%; different residence, same region 32.6%; different region 8.7%; different country 3.2%.
Households (1982). Average household size 2.7; 1 person 24.6%, 2 persons 28.5%, 3 persons 18.8%, 4 persons 16.1%, 5 persons 7.4%, 6 persons or more 4.6%. Family households: 14,118,940 (72.1%), non-family 5,471,460 (27.9%, of which 1-person 24.6%).
Immigration (1981): permanent immigrants admitted 34,400, from Portugal 17.8%, Spain 16.5%, Italy 11.2%.

Vital statistics

Birth rate per 1,000 population (1983): 13.8 (world avg. 29.0); (1981) legitimate, 87.3%; illegitimate, 12.7%.
Death rate per 1,000 population (1983): 10.3 (world avg. 11.0).
Natural increase rate per 1,000 population (1983): 3.5 (world avg. 18.0).
Total fertility rate (avg. births per childbearing woman; 1980–85): 1.8.
Marriage rate per 1,000 population (1983): 5.1.
Divorce rate per 1,000 population (1983): 1.9.
Infant mortality rate per 1,000 live births (1983): 8.9.
Life expectancy at birth (1982): male 70.2 years; female 78.5 years.
Major causes of death per 100,000 population (1983): all malignant neoplasms 228.7; ischemic heart disease 208.8; cerebrovascular disease 118.2.

Social indicators

Educational attainment (1974). Percent of adult employed population having: less than full primary education 36.2%, primary 30.4%, secondary 21.0%, some post secondary 7.0%, 4-year higher degree 2.4%, post-graduate 2.8%.

Distribution of income (1975)
percent of household income by quintile

1	2	3	4	5 (highest)
5.3	11.1	16.0	21.8	45.8

Quality of working life (1982). Average work week: 39.5 hours (overtime, n.a.). Annual rate per 100,000 workers for: injury or accident 27.7, industrial illness 0.5, death 0.003. Proportion of labour force insured for damages or income loss resulting from: injury n.a., permanent disability n.a., death n.a. Average days lost to labour stoppages per 1,000 workers (1980): 77.5%. Average duration of journey to work (1974) 53 minutes; method of transportation: n.a. Rate per 1,000 workers of discouraged (unemployed no longer seeking work): n.a.
Access to services (1982). Proportion of dwellings having central heating 67.5%, piped water supply 99.3%, indoor plumbing 85.0%, natural gas 48.9%.
Social participation. Eligible voters participating in last national election

65.9%. Population over 15 years of age participating in voluntary associations 28%. Trade union membership in total workforce n.a. Practicing religious population in total affiliated population n.a.%.

Social deviance. Offense rate per 100,000 population (1975) for: murder 2.8, rape 25.7, other assault, n.a., theft, including burglary and housebreaking 2,342.7. Incidence per 100,000 in general population of: alcoholism (late 1970s)† 3,500–4,000, drug and substance abuse n.a., suicide (1983) 21.8.

Leisure (1981). Favourite leisure activities: television 34%, lectures 14%, knitting 10%, conversations 10%, games 8%, walking 4%, radio 4%.

Material well-being (1982). Households possessing: automobile 72.1%, telephone 100.0%, television receiver 91.0%, refrigerator 96.1%, air conditioner 30.7%, washing machine 81.7%.

National economy

Gross national product (at current market prices; 1982): U.S.$530,632,000,-000 (U.S.$9,770 per capita).

Origin of gross domestic product (current prices)

	1982			
	in value F'000,000	% of total value	labour force	% of labour force
Agriculture	150,600	4.2	1,758,000	8.4
Mining	31,200	0.9	137,000	0.7
Manufacturing	875,300	24.7	5,172,000	24.7
Construction	229,100	6.5	1,739,000	8.3
Trade	434,900	12.2	3,421,000	16.3
Public utilities	75,600	2.1	194,000	0.9
Transp. and commun.	185,100	5.2	1,360,000	6.5
Finance	387,100	10.9	1,567,000	7.5
Other (incl. pub. admin., defense, and services)	1,180,800	33.3	5,598,00	26.7
TOTAL	3,549,700	100.0	20,946,000	100.0

Budget (1981). Revenue: F681,440,000 (taxes on business turnover 43.9%; direct taxes 39.6%). Expenditure: F639,409,000,000 (education 14.4%, defense 9.9%, health and social security 4.9%, agriculture 4.8%.).

Public debt (internal; 1983): F573,680,000,000.

Tourism (1982): receipts from visitors U.S.$6,991,000,000; expenditures by nationals abroad U.S.$5,157,000,000.

Manufacturing and mining enterprises (1981)

	no. of enterprises	no. of employees	hourly wages as a % of avg. of all wages	annual value added (F'000,000)
Food products	...	506,000	100	106,900
Transport equipment	707	661,000	109	101,700
Electrical machinery	692	478,000	101	58,600
Industrial chemicals	316	151,000	115	40,000
Metal products	3,514	271,000	110	38,500
Iron and steel	202	241,000	105	35,800
Petroleum refineries	47	32,000	120	33,300
Textiles	1,970	271,000	84	27,800
Beverages	...	53,000	100	20,600
Paper and products	658	118,000	108	19,200
Printing, publishing	1,736	202,000	120	20,100
Wearing apparel	2,216	242,000	78	17,400
Rubber products	199	105,000	99	14,700
Tobacco	...	10,000	100	8,200
Coal	5	57,000	120	9,600

Production (metric tons except as noted). Agriculture, forestry, fishing (1982): sugar beets 30,480,000, wheat 25,342,000, grapes 11,230,000, barley 10,026,000, corn (maize) 9,833,000, wine 7,966,000, potatoes 6,750,000, apples 3,016,000, oats 1,804,000 tomatoes 876,000, carrots 538,000, peaches 438,000, pears 435,000, sorghum 259,000, tobacco 40,000; timber 37,827,000 cu m; livestock (number of live animals) 186,656,000 poultry, 23,605,000, cattle, 13,121,000 sheep, 11,859,000 pigs, 1,241,000 goats, fish catch 764,-532. Mining and quarrying (1983): iron ore 15,972,000; bauxite 1,660,000; potash salts 1,651,000; zinc 62,300; lead 27,000; gold 37,000 troy ounces‡. Manufacturing (1983): cotton yarn and fabrics 344,800,000; synthetic yarn and fabrics 207,120,000; cement 24,504,000; crude steel 17,616,000; pig iron 13,752,000; paper and paperboard 7,102,000; sulfuric acid 4,240,800; rubber products 587,760. Construction (units; 1983): 332,400.

Retail trade enterprises (1980)

	no. of enterprises	no. of employees	weekly wage as a % of all wages	annual purchases (F'000,000)
Large food stores	1,844	264,639	...	144,452
Small food stores	134,083	387,537	...	100,946
butcher shops	51,994	158,019	...	34,658
Clothing stores	74,643	203,055	...	31,446
Pharmacies	19,329	95,048	...	22,191
Gas, coal, and other energy products	5,947	23,802	...	22,072
Department stores	1,464	75,374	...	20,328
Furniture stores	7,087	55,413	...	15,919
Electrical and electronics stores	11,584	53,734	...	12,871
Publishing and paper	20,546	59,771	...	9,060

Energy production (consumption): electricity (kW-hr; 1983) 277,164,000,000 (263,628,000,000); coal (metric tons; 1983) 33,396,000 (52,428,000); crude petroleum (barrels; 1982§) 12,080,000 (603,700,000); petroleum products (metric tons; 1982§) 75,273,000 (78,495,000); natural gas (cu m; 1983) 6,662,000,000 (25,276,000,000‡).

Household income and expenditure. Average household size (1980) 2.8; average annual income per household (1975) F58,480 (U.S.$13,631). Sources of income (1974): salaries 44.0%; social security 23.0%; private business 20.9%; property 8.4%; other 3.7%; expenditure (1982): food 20.1%, housing 19.4%, recreation 16.3%, health 10.4%, transportation 3.2%.

Persons economically active (1982): total 23,525,120 (43.3%); female participation in the labour force 9,645,299 (41.0%); unemployed 2,059,160 (8.8%).

Price and earnings indexes (1975 = 100)

	1978	1979	1980	1981	1982	1983	1984 ‖
Consumer price index	130.6	144.8	164.1	186.1	208.1	228.1	248.3
Hourly earnings index	145.7	164.6	189.7	218.2	251.9	280.6	319.3

Land use (1982): forested 26.6%; meadows and pastures 23.2%; agricultural and under permanent cultivation 32.1%; other 18.1%.

Financial aggregates

	1979	1980	1981	1982	1983	1984 (5 mo.)
Exchange rate, F per:						
U.S. dollar	4.25	4.23	5.43	6.57	7.62	8.42
£	9.01	9.86	11.02	11.49	11.58	11.62
SDR	5.29	5.76	6.69	7.42	8.74	8.81
International reserves (U.S.$)						
Total (excl. gold; '000,000)	17,579	27,340	22,262	16,531	19,851	21,090
SDR's ('000,000)	849	935	1,257	979	442	435
Reserve pos. in IMF ('000,000)	630	1,067	1,029	958	1,352	1,332
Foreign exchange	16,100	25,338	19,976	14,594	18,057	19,304
Gold ('000,000 fine troy oz.)	81.92	81.85	81.85	81.85	81.85	81.85
% world reserves	8.7	8.6	8.6	8.6	8.7	8.7
Interest and prices						
Central bank discount (%)	9.50	9.50	9.50	9.50	9.50	9.50
Gov't. bond yield (%)	9.48	12.99	15.66	15.56	13.61	12.76
Industrial share prices (1980 = 100)	87.2	100.0	88.1	85.4	115.4	141.0
Balance of payments (U.S.$'000,000)						
Balance of visible trade	−3,220	−13,418	−9,970	−15,784	−8,063	...
Imports, f.o.b.	97,504	120,921	110,844	107,284	97,922	...
Exports, f.o.b.	94,284	107,503	100,873	91,499	89,858	...
Balance of invisibles	12,385	13,379	9,393	8,322	7,508	...
Balance of payments, current account	5,141	−4,208	−4,809	−12,084	−4,370	...

Foreign trade

Balance of trade (current prices)

	1979	1980	1981	1982	1983	1984¶
F'000,000	−26.8	−79.4	−78.2	−125.2	−76.9	−11.88
% of total	3.0%	7.5%	6.3%	9.0%	5.0%	2.7%

Imports (1982): F758,340,000,000 (crude petroleum 17.2%, mechanical machinery 7.0%, wearing apparel 5.1%, refined petroleum 4.8%, natural gas 3.1%, paper and paper products 2.4%, coal 1.4%). *Major import sources:* West Germany 16.8%; Italy 9.6%; United States 7.9%; Belgium and Luxembourg 7.7%; Saudi Arabia 6.3%; United Kingdom 6.1%, The Netherlands 5.5%; Algeria 3.4%.

Exports (1982): F633,070,000,000 (mechanical machinery 9.9%; vegetables 6.1%; private cars 5.6%; wearing apparel 5.2%; vehicles spare parts 4.5%; dairy products 2.1%; beverages, alcohols, and tobacco 1.7%). *Major export destinations:* West Germany 14.8%; Italy 11.3%; Belgium and Luxembourg 8.6%; United Kingdom 7.2%; United States 5.7%, The Netherlands 4.6%; Spain 3.1%; Algeria 2.3%.

Transport and communications

Transport. Railroads: (1982) route length 21,493 mi, 34,590 km; (1983) passenger-mi 36,216,000,000, passenger-km 58,284,000,000; short ton-mi cargo 40,669,000,000, metric ton-km cargo 59,376,000,000. Roads (1983): total length 499,945 mi, 804,585 km (paved 92%). Vehicles (1983): passenger cars 20,600,000; trucks and buses 3,230,000. Merchant marine (1983): vessels (100 gross tons and over) 1,173; total deadweight tonnage 16,819,510. Air transport (1982): passenger-mi 23,426,044,000, passenger-km 37,700,636,000; short ton-mi cargo 3,880,710,000, metric ton-km cargo 5,665,742,000; airports (1984) with scheduled flights 60.

Communications. Daily newspapers (1983): total number 97; total circulation 11,260,792; circulation per 1,000 population 209. Radios (1983): total number of receivers 20,000,000 (1 per 2.7 persons). Television (1983): total number of receivers 19,000,000 (1 per 2.8 persons). Telephones (1982): 17,920,454 (1 per 3.0 persons).

Education and health

Education (1980–81)

	schools	teachers	students	student/ teacher ratio
Primary (age 2–10)	68,643	290,933	7,252,575	24.9
Secondary (age 11–18)	11,314	256,284	5,181,556	20.1
Voc., teacher tr.♀				
Higher	1,094	40,585	1,017,775	25.1

College graduates per 100,000 population: n.a. *Literacy* (1980): total population literate 41,112,000 (98.8%); males literate 19,933,000 (98.9%); females literate 21,179,000 (98.7%).

Health (1981): physicians 108,054 (1 per 499.4 persons); hospital bedsδ 548,-896 (1 per 98.3 persons).

Food (1978–80): daily per capita caloric intake 3,381 (vegetable products 63.8%, animal products 36.2%); 135% of FAO recommended minimum.

Military

Total active duty personnel (1982): 492,850 (army 62.3%; navy 13.6%; air force 20.1%; strategic nulcear forces 4.0%). *Military expenditure a percent of GNP* (1982): 4.2% (world 6.0%); per capita expenditure U.S.$471.

*French part only. †Estimated as per a narrowly-defined meaning of alcoholism. ‡1982. §Includes Monaco. ‖Sept. 1984. ¶Second quarter. ♀Included with secondary education. δPublic only.

French Guiana

Official name: Département de la Guyane Française (Department of French Guiana).
Political status: overseas department of France with one legislative house (General Council [16]), one representative in the French National Assembly, and one senator in the French Senate.
Chief of state: President of France.
Head of government: Commissioner.
Capital: Cayenne.
Official language: French.
Official religion: none.
Monetary unit: 1 franc (F) = 100 centimes; valuation (Oct. 29, 1984) 1 U.S.$ = F9.41; 1 £ = F11.36.

Area and population

Arrondissements	Capitals	area		population
		sq mi	sq km	1982 census
Cayenne	Cayenne	20,077	52,000	61,587
Saint-Laurent-du-Maroni	Saint-Laurent-du-Maroni	15,830	41,000	11,435
TOTAL		35,907	93,000*	73,022

Source: Official government figures.

Demography

Density (1984): persons per sq mi 2.2, persons per sq km 0.8.
Urban–rural (1982): urban 73.4%; rural 26.6%.
Sex distribution (1982): male 52.66%; female 47.34%.
Age breakdown (1982): under 16, 34.9%; 16–29, 27.2%; 30–39, 15.6%; 40–49, 9.2%; 50–59, 6.1%; 60 and over, 7.0%.
Population projection: (1990) 93,000; (2000) 125,800.
Doubling time: 23 years.
Ethnic composition (1982): Guianese (mixed) Creole 42.6%; Guiana Chinese 14.0%; French (metropolitan) 10.7%; Haitian 7.5%; French West Indian 6.6%; Bush Negro 4.7%; Brazilian 4.6%; Amerindian 4.1%; other (other West Indian, Surinamese, Hmong, and other Southeast Asian) 5.2%.
Religious affiliation (1980): Roman Catholic 87.1%; Protestant 3.9%; non-religious 2.5%; Afro-American spiritist 2.0%; animist 1.5%; Chinese folk religionist 1.3%; Muslim 1.0%; Baha'í 0.7%.
Major cities (1982): Cayenne 38,135; Kourou 6,465; Saint-Laurent-du-Maroni 5,042.

Vital statistics

Birth rate per 1,000 population (1983): 30.2 (world avg. 29.0); (1983) legitimate 21.6%; illegitimate 78.4%.
Death rate per 1,000 population (1983): 6.2 (world avg. 11.0).
Natural increase rate per 1,000 population (1983): 24.0 (world avg. 18.0).
Total fertility rate (avg. births per childbearing woman; 1975–79): 3.1.
Marriage rate per 1,000 population (1983): 3.2.
Divorce rate per 1,000 population (1983): 0.5.
Infant mortality rate per 1,000 live births (1983): 24.3.
Life expectancy at birth (1975–79): male 63.4 years; female 69.7 years.
Major causes of death per 100,000 population (1981): cardiovascular disease 119; accidents and murders 90; neoplasms (cancers), including malignant tumours 49; illnesses of the digestive system 48; infectious diseases 43.

National economy

Budget (1982). Revenue: F647,300,000 (diverse taxes 52.3%, French participation in the provision of services 31.3%, fiscal receipts 13.7%, new loans 2.3%). Expenditures: F647,600,000 (health and social assistance 56.3%, other services 28.7%, capital investments 5.2%, loans by department of infrastructure and public works 3.9%).
Public debt (external, outstanding; 1982): U.S.$18,000,000.
Tourism (1982): visitors arriving 21,600.
Production (metric tons except as noted). Agriculture, forestry, fishing (1982): sugarcane 8,769†, cassavas 8,000, dasheens 3,400‡, sweet potatoes 2,000, plantains 1,000, corn (maize) 1,000, bananas 750‡, rice 447, limes 60; livestock (number of live animals) 12,000 cattle, 10,000 pigs, 100,000 chickens, 4,000 ducks; roundwood 68,100 cu m†; fish catch, of which shrimps 3,227, other fish 1,503. Mining and quarrying (1982): gold 163 kg; stone, sand, and gravel 400,000. Manufacturing (1983): frozen shrimp 2,357§; frozen fish 279§; sawnwood and veneer sheets 29,955 cu m; finished wood products 2,092§; rum 3,407 hectolitres; other important products include wood essences, wooden boats, cement, leather goods, textiles and clothing, handicrafts, beer, and soft drinks. Construction (1983): residential 16,856 sq m; nonresidential, n.a. Energy production (consumption): electricity (kW-hr; 1983) 162,700,000 (138,100,000); coal, none (n.a.); crude petroleum, none (n.a.); petroleum products (metric tons; 1982) none (128,000); natural gas, none (n.a.); fuelwood and charcoal (cubic metres; 1981) 68,000 (68,000).
Household income and expenditure. Average household size (1982) 3.3; income per household (1980) F75,762 (U.S.$16,776); sources of income (1980): salaries 76.4%, industrial and commercial profits 12.3%, pensions and rents 3.8%, noncommercial profits 2.5%, income from stocks and bonds 1.6%, other 3.4%.
Land use (1982): forested 81.9%; meadows and pastures 0.1%; agricultural and under permanent cultivation 0.0□%; other 18.0%.

Gross national product (at current market prices; 1981): U.S.$220,000,000 (U.S.$3,143 per capita).

Origin of gross domestic product (current prices)

	1982			
	in value	% of total value	labour force	% of labour force
Agriculture	...	...	4,320	13.8
Mining	...	...	89	0.3
Manufacturing	...	...	3,609	11.6
Construction	...	...	1,953	6.3
Trade	...	...	‖	‖
Public utilities	...	...	‖	‖
Transportation and communication	...	...	1,818¶	5.8¶
Finance	...	...		
Pub. admin.	...	...		
Services	...	...	‖	‖
Other, including unemployed	...	...	19,394	62.2
TOTAL	...	...	31,183	100.0

Persons economically active (1982): total 31,183 (42.7%); female participation in the labour force 11,589 (37.2%); unemployed 4,989 (16.0%).

Price and earnings indexes (1980 = 100)

	1978	1979	1980	1981	1982	1983	1984
Consumer price index	79.7	88.9	100.0	116.5	130.3	142.4	159.2♀
Monthly earnings index	76.4	87.4	100.0	120.1	139.9	151.0	164.4♂

Foreign trade

Balance of trade (current prices)

	1978	1979	1980	1981	1982	1983
F'000,000	−828	−997	−973	−1,163	−1,431	−1,843
% of total	92.6%	87.7%	82.2%	75.2%	77.1%	75.8%

Imports (1983): F2,137,000,000 (non-specific consumer goods [including textiles and clothing] 23.3%; fuel and energy products 16.1%; food products 13.0%; construction materials 8.5%; transport vehicles used in tourism 5.1%). *Major import sources* (1982): France 51.7%; Trinidad and Tobago 19.1%; United States 8.5%; Japan 4.7%.
Exports (1983): F294,100,000 (shrimps 74.0%, wood and wood products 5.4%). *Major export destinations* (1982): United States 48.4%; France 21.0%; Japan 13.2%; Martinique 7.1%; Guadeloupe 4.2%.

Transport and communications

Transport. Railroads (1982) none. Roads (1982): total length 422 mi, 680 km (paved 75%). Vehicles (1981): passenger cars 16,789; trucks and buses 2,013. Fishing fleet (1982): vessels 9; total deadweight tonnage, n.a. Air transport (1983)◇: passenger arrivals 62,032, passenger departures 63,841; cargo loaded 1,127 metric tons, cargo unloaded 2,522 metric tons; airports (1984) with scheduled flights 8.
Communications. Daily newspaper (1983): total number 1; total circulation 16,000; circulation per 1,000 population 212. Radios (1983): total number of receivers 73,000 (1 per 1 person). Television (1983): total number of receivers 40,000 (1 per 1.8 persons). Telephones (1982): 19,627 (1 per 3.7 persons).

Education and health

Education (1981–82)

	schools	teachers△	students	student/ teacher ratio
Primary (age 6–11)	66	598	13,675	...
Secondary (age 12–18)	14	365	6,339	...
Voc., teacher tr.	5	149	1,802	...
Higher	1	...	236	—

College graduates per 100,000 population (1974): 1,520. *Literacy* (1974): total population literate 29,297 (81.5%); males literate 15,468 (81.7%); females literate 13,829 (81.2%).
Health (1981): physicians 80 (1 per 875 persons); hospital beds 907 (1 per 77 persons).
Food (1978–80): daily per capita caloric intake 2,385 (vegetable products 72.8%, animal products 27.2%); 105% of FAO recommended minimum requirement.

Military

Total active duty personnel (1982)†: 4,350 (army 92.0%; navy 3.5%; air force 4.5%).

---

*In the mid-1980s the area south of the confluence of the Maroni and Litany rivers remained disputed by French Guiana and Suriname. †1983. ‡1981. §1982. ‖ Included under other, including unemployment. ¶Includes only Kourou space centre workers. ♀June 1984. ♂July 1984. □Less than 0.01 percent. ◇Commercial traffic only at Rochambeau international airport, Cayenne. △1980–81. †Most military personnel stationed in French Guiana are from Europe. Most Guianese males fulfill their military obligations elsewhere.

French Polynesia

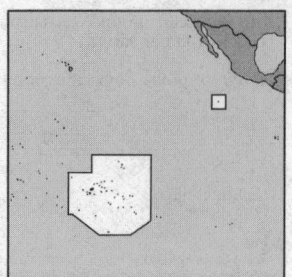

Official name: Territoire de la
Polynésie Française (Territory of
French Polynesia).
Political status: overseas territory
(France) with one legislative house
(Territorial Assembly [30]), two
representatives in the French National
Assembly, and one senator in the
French Senate.
Chief of state: President of France.
Head of government: High
Commissioner.
Capital: Papeete.
Official language: French.
Official religion: none.
Monetary unit: 1 Franc de la Comptoir
française du pacifique (CFP fr) = 100
centimes; valuation (Oct. 29, 1984)
1 U.S.$ = CFP fr165.70; 1 £ = CFP
fr200.00.

Area and population

Circumscriptions	Capitals	area* sq mi	sq km	population 1983 census
Îles Australes	Mataura	57	148	6,283
Îles Marquises	Taiohae	405	1,049	6,548
Îles sous le Vent	Uturoa	156	404	19,060
Îles Tuamotu et Gambier	Papeete	280	726	11,793
Îles du Vent	Papeete	461	1,194	123,069
TOTAL		1,359	3,521	166,753

Source: Official government figures.

Demography

*Density** (1984): persons per sq mi 126.4, persons per sq km 48.8.
Urban–rural (1977): urban 39.7%; rural 60.3%.
Sex distribution (1984): male 51.06%; female 48.94%.
Age breakdown (1984): under 15, 38.5%; 15–29, 29.7%; 30–44, 16.5%; 45–59,
10.3%; 60–74, 4.2%; 75 and over, 0.8%.
Population projection: (1990) 180,888; (2000) 211,275.
Doubling time: 35 years.
Ethnic composition (1977): Polynesian (Maori) 65.6%; mixed (demie) 17.3%;
European (other than metropolitan French) 9.1%; Chinese 4.1%; French
(metropolitan) 2.0%; other 1.9%.
Religious affiliation (1980): Roman Catholic 39.4%; Evangelical Church of
French Polynesia 29.8%; Mormon 5.1%; Polynesian indigenous Christian
2.6%; Seventh-day Adventist 1.3%; other Protestant 12.8%; other 9.0%.
Major cities (1983): Papeete 23,496; Faaa 21,927; Punaauia 12,414; Pirae
12,023; Mahina 8,954.

Vital statistics

Birth rate per 1,000 population (1983): 32.1 (world avg. 29.0); (1980) legiti-
mate 45.1%; illegitimate 54.9%.
Death rate per 1,000 population (1983): 5.9 (world avg. 11.0).
Natural increase rate per 1,000 population (1983): 26.2 (world avg. 18.0).
Total fertility rate (avg. births per childbearing woman; 1985): 3.5.
Marriage rate per 1,000 population (1980): 8.0.
Divorce rate per 1,000 population (1980): 1.2.
Infant mortality rate per 1,000 live births (1983): 22.8.
Life expectancy at birth (1980–85): male 63.5 years; female 67.8 years.
Major causes of death per 100,000 population (1970): diseases of the circu-
latory system 54.7; diarrhea, gastroenteritis, and diseases of the digestive
system 28.7; malignant neoplasms (cancers) 23.5; diseases of the respira-
tory system 17.4.

National economy

Budget (1983)†. Revenue: CFP fr73,223,172,000 (French civilian operating
budget 30.5%, French military budget 27.2%, entry and customs duties
20.3%, advances and loans 4.7%, business taxes 2.2%, tobacco taxes 1.8%,
other excise taxes 1.6%, service taxes 1.4%). Expenditures: CFP fr70,-
584,427,000 (French civilian operating expenses 24.5%, military operating
expenses 23.2%, services 9.2%, payments and refunds 7.2%, pensions 5.6%,
advances and loans 5.2%, subsidies to public and private agencies 4.3%,
payments on public debt 3.2%).
Public debt (external, outstanding; 1982): U.S.$114,000,000.
Tourism (1982): receipts from visitors U.S.$94,000,000; expenditures by na-
tionals abroad, n.a.
Production (metric tons except as noted). Agriculture, forestry, fishing (1982):
coconuts 130,000, cassava 6,000, potatoes 4,000, sugarcane 4,000, tomatoes
2,000, milk 2,000, watermelons and other melons 1,851, pineapples 1,224,
bananas 1,000, sweet potatoes 1,000, avocados and mangoes 694, taros
248, citrus fruits 157, coffee 55, vanilla 13, flowers CFP fr191,000,000; livestock (number of live animals) 34,000 pigs, 10,000 cattle, 600,000 chickens,
26,000 ducks; fish 2,244, crustaceans 22, mother-of-pearl 6, pearls 32 kg.
Mining and quarrying: none. Manufacturing (1982): shredded copra 11,-
013‡; animal feed 10,415; coconut oil 7,674‡; copra cake 3,777‡; frozen fish
2,037; monoï oil 118; dried and smoked fish 9; beer 100,000 hectolitres§;
pineapple juice 4,403 hectolitres; printed cloth 200,000 metres ‖ ; sandals
600,000 pairs ‖ ; boats and aircraft repairs CFP fr2,248,000,000§; construction materials CFP fr1,130,000,000§; handicrafts CFP fr598,000,000§; pharmaceuticals CFP fr409,000,000. Construction (buildings completed; 1983):

residential, 459; commmercial, industrial, and other, 105. Energy production (consumption): electricity (kW-hr; 1983) 172,400,000 (156,200,000);
solar power (installed) 72.6 kW.
Gross national product (at current market prices; 1981): U.S.$1,050,000,000
(U.S.$6,980 per capita).

Origin of gross domestic product (current prices)

	1980 in value CFP fr'000	% of total value	1983 labour force	% of labour force
Agriculture	4,649,000	5.3	6,667	10.8
Mining	—	—	—	—
Manufacturing	7,003,000	8.0	2,356	3.8
Construction	8,565,000	9.8	6,793	11.0
Trade	21,923,000	25.0	5,010	8.1
Public utilities	1,173,000	1.3	555	0.9
Transportation and communication	5,475,000	6.3	3,578	5.8
Finance	12,245,000	14.0	2,870	4.6
Pub. admin., defense	15,266,000	17.4	19,863	32.2
Services	11,258,000	12.9	8,080	13.1
Other, including unemployed	—	—	5,969	9.7
TOTAL	87,577,000	100.0	61,741	100.0

Persons economically active (1984): total 53,931 (33.8%); female participation in labour force 18,608 (34.5%); unemployed 942 (1.7%).

Price and earnings indexes (1980 = 100)

	1978	1979	1980	1981	1982	1983	1984¶
Consumer price index	80.3	89.8	100.0	116.7	133.6	151.9	164.4
Monthly earnings index	77.9	86.8	100.0	119.8	149.4	177.2	190.2

Household income and expenditure. Average household size (1980) 5.0;
average annual income per household (1977) CFP fr2,118,161 (U.S.$23,-
624); sources of income: salaries 46.3%, self-employment 44.5%, transfer
payments 7.2%, profit distribution 2.0%; expenditure (1977): consumption
77.5%, savings 20.1%, payments to government 1.2%, taxes 0.8%, household help salaries 0.4%.
Land use (1981): forested 31.4%; meadows and pastures 5.5%; agricultural
and under permanent cultivation 20.5%; other 42.6%.

Foreign trade

Balance of trade (current prices)

	1978	1979	1980	1981	1982	1983
CFP fr'000,000	−30,097	−34,490	−39,690	−51,982	−58,957	−70,197
% of total	83.5%	88.6%	89.5%	90.0%	90.0%	87.9%

Imports (1983): CFP fr75,017,000,000 (electrical machinery and equipment
15.5%, petroleum products 14.2%, transport equipment 14.1%, processed
foods and beverages 8.4%, metal and metal manufactures 7.6%, live animals and animal products 5.6%, chemicals and chemical products 4.8%).
Major import sources: France 45.8%; United States 15.8%; New Zealand
6.0%; Singapore 4.6%; Japan 4.3%.
Exports (1983): CFP fr4,820,000,000 (reexports 67.3%, cultured pearls 17.8%,
coconut oil 12.7%, vanilla 0.9%, mother-of-pearl 0.6%, monoï oil 0.4%).
Major export destinations: France 68.0%; Italy 14.5%; United States 7.0%;
Japan 6.5%.

Transport and communications

Transport. Railroads: none. Roads (1982): total length 460 mi, 741 km
(paved 33%). Vehicles (1975): passenger cars 16,500; trucks and buses 8,500.
Merchant marine: vessels (100 gross tons and over), n.a. Air transport
(1983): passengers landed and departed 585,400; short tons cargo landed
and shipped 7,052, metric tons cargo landed and shipped 6,397; airports
(1984) with scheduled flights 32.
Communications. Daily newspapers (1983): total number 2; total circulation
19,800; circulation per 1,000 population 127. Radios (1983): total number
of receivers 77,000 (1 per 2 persons). Television (1983): total number of receivers 25,500 (1 per 6 persons). Telephones (1982): 24,818 (1 per 6 persons).

Education and health

Education (1982–83)

	schools	teachers	students	student/ teacher ratio
Primary (age 6–10)	228	2,012	39,869	19.8
Secondary (age 11–17)	23	1,203♀	12,049	...
Voc., teacher tr.	7	♀	3,443	...
Higher	1	10δ	124δ	12.4δ

College graduates per 100,000 population (1977): 24.7. Literacy□ (1977): total population literate 81,213 (97.8%); males literate 43,553 (98.0%); females
literate 37,660 (97.6%).
Health (1980): physicians 139 (1 per 1,039 persons); hospital beds 408 (1
per 354 persons).
Food (1978–80): daily per capita caloric intake 2,659 (vegetable products
80.0%, animal products 20.0%); 100% of FAO recommended minimum.

Military

Total active duty personnel: no domestic military establishment is maintained; external security is the responsibility of France.

*Land area only; total area 1,544 sq mi (4,000 sq km). †Includes French civilian
and military budget expenditures in French Polynesia. ‡1983. §1980. ‖ 1979. ¶June
1984. ♀Vocational and teacher training teachers included with secondary. δ1981–82.
□Age 14 and over.

Gabon

Official name: République Gabonaise (Gabonese Republic).
Form of government: unitary single-party republic with one legislative house (National Assembly [93]).
Chief of state: President.
Head of government: Prime Minister.
Capital: Libreville.
Official language: French.
Official religion: none.
Monetary unit: 1 CFA franc (CFAF) = 100 centimes; valuation (Oct. 29, 1984) 1 U.S.$ = CFAF470.6; 1 £ = CFAF568.0.

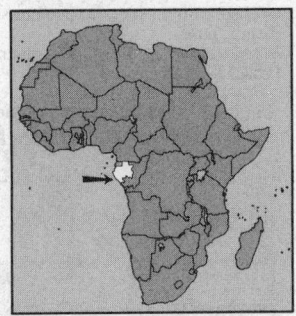

Area and population*

Provinces	Capitals	area sq mi	area sq km	population 1978 estimate
Estuaire	Libreville	8,008	20,740	359,000
Haut-Ogooué	Franceville	14,111	36,547	213,000
Moyen-Ogooué	Lambaréné	7,156	18,535	49,000
Ngounié	Mouila	14,575	37,750	118,000
Nyanga	Tchibanga	8,218	21,285	98,000
Ogooué-Ivindo	Makokou	17,790	46,075	53,000
Ogooué-Lolo	Koulamoutou	9,799	25,380	49,000
Ogooué-Maritime	Port-Gentil	8,838	22,890	194,000
Woleu-Ntem	Oyem	14,851	38,465	166,000
TOTAL		103,347†	267,667	1,300,000†

Source: Official government figures.

Demography*

Density (1983 est.): persons per sq mi 12.6, persons per sq km 4.9.
Urban–rural (1980 est.)‡: urban 35.8%; rural 64.2%.
Sex distribution (1980 est.)‡: male 49.09%; female 50.91%.
Age breakdown (1970): under 15, 35.4%; 15–29, 19.3%; 30–44, 22.2%; 45–59, 16.3%; 60–74, 6.3%; 75 and over, 0.5%.
Population projection: n.a.
Doubling time: n.a.
Ethnic composition (1980)‡: Fang 29%; Eshira 19%; Mbete 15%; Kota 11%; French 6%; other 20%.
Religious affiliation (1980)‡: Christian 94.5%, of which Roman Catholic 63.8%, Protestant 18.4%, African indigenous 12.1%; tribal religionist 2.9%; Muslim 0.8%; other 1.8%.
Major cities (1983 est.): Libreville 257,000; Port-Gentil 123,300; Franceville 38,030.

Vital statistics*

Birth rate per 1,000 population (1960–61): 35.0 (world avg. 34.8).
Death rate per 1,000 population (1960–61): 30.0 (world avg. 15.1).
Natural increase rate per 1,000 population (1960–61): 5.0 (world avg. 19.7).
Total fertility rate (avg. births per childbearing woman; 1960–61): 4.2.
Number of married persons per 1,000 adult population (1960–61): 707.
Number of divorced persons per 1,000 adult population (1960–61): 100.
Infant mortality rate per 1,000 live births (1960–61): 229.
Life expectancy at birth: n.a.
Major causes of death (1980): malaria, trypanosomiasis, and tuberculosis.

National economy

Budget (1983). Revenue: CFAF466,000,000,000 (taxes on petroleum organizations 35.4%; petroleum fees 24.1%; customs duties 17.8%; tax on organizations 5.2%; income tax 4.2%; business tax 3.9%). Expenditures: CFAF563,200,000,000 (development expenditure 42.8%, of which infrastructure 22.5%, social services 6.5%, defense 5.0%, administration and tourism 4.3%; current expenditure 31.9%; public debt 24.9%).
Public debt (external, outstanding; 1982): U.S.$1,080,000,000.
Tourism (1980): receipts from visitors U.S.$13,000,000; expenditures by nationals abroad U.S.$95,000,000.
Production (metric tons except as noted). Agriculture, forestry, fishing (1982): roots and tubers 239,000, sugarcane 140,000, cassavas 100,000, plantains 63,000, corn (maize) 10,000, peanuts (groundnuts) 9,000, bananas 8,000, cacao beans 2,460§, palm oil 1,425§, coffee 1,395§; livestock (number of live animals) 140,000 pigs, 77,000 sheep, 1,500,000 chickens; roundwood 1,390,000 cu m§; fish catch 52,638. Mining and quarrying (1983): manganese 1,800,000; uranium 1,022; gold 550 troy oz. ‖. Manufacturing (1983): cement 183,000; flour 21,500; raw sugar 15,000; beer 475,000 hectolitres; soft drinks 179,800 hectolitres; cigarettes 16,400,000 packs; textiles CFAF2,200,000,000¶. Construction: n.a. Energy production (consumption): electricity (kW-hr; 1983) 734,300,000 (628,000,000); crude petroleum (barrels; 1983) 54,787,500 (10,628,500 ‖); petroleum products (metric tons; 1983) 1,013,500 (387,500); natural gas (cu m; 1983) 82,000,000 (82,000,000); fuelwood and bagasse (cu m; 1982) 1,271,000 (1,271,000).
Persons economically active (1983): total 137,867♀; female participation in the labour force, n.a.; unemployed, n.a.

Price and earnings indexes (1980 = 100)

	1978	1979	1980	1981	1982	1983	1984
Consumer price index	82.5	89.0	100.0	108.7	126.8	137.0	143.6□
Earnings index	...	...	100.0	101.1	126.6	156.3	...

Gross national product (at current market prices; 1983): U.S.$3,071,540,000 (U.S.$2,380 per capita).

Origin of gross domestic product (factor cost at current prices):

	1983 in value CFAF'000,000	% of total value	labour force	% of labour force
Agriculture, fishing forestry	75,800	5.9	14,118♀	10.2♀
Mining	605,700	47.2	3,919	2.9
Manufacturing	57,200	4.5	4,123	3.0
Construction	93,000	7.3	13,154	9.5
Trade	105,000	8.2	3,732	2.7
Public utilities	19,500	1.5	δ	δ
Transportation and communication	50,600	4.0	δ	δ
Finance	10,000	0.8	δ	δ
Pub. admin., defense	102,600	8.0	42,678	31.0
Services	85,100	6.6	δ	δ
Other, including taxes on imports	77,500	6.0	56,143	40.7
TOTAL	1,282,000	100.0	137,867♀	100.0

Household income and expenditure. Average household size (1960–61) 3.9; average annual income per household n.a.; sources of income♀ (1983): private sector 73.4%; public sector 26.6%; expenditure: n.a.
Land use (1981): forested 77.6%; meadows and pastures 18.2%; agricultural and under permanent cultivation 1.8%; other 2.4%.

Foreign trade

Balance of trade (current prices)

	1979	1980	1981	1982	1983	1984
CFAF'000,000	+269,200	+351,000	+371,100	+252,100	+421,700	+492,600
% of total	54.3%	48.8%	45.0%	32.4%	39.4%	40.8%

Imports (1983): CFAF324,900,000,000 (machinery and mechanical equipment 23.8%; transport equipment and parts 15.1%; food, beverages, and tobacco products 12.3%; metal and metal products 10.7%; household and consumer products 5.3%; clothing and textiles 4.6%). *Major import sources* (1982): France 51.5%; United States 15.3%; Japan 6.9%; West Germany 6.1%.
Exports (1983): CFAF746,600,000,000 (crude petroleum and petroleum products 83.5%; wood 7.4%, of which okoumé and ozigo 5.5%; manganese ore and concentrate 4.2%; uranium ore and yellow cake 3.3%). *Major export destinations* (1982): France 26.0%; United States 25.0%; Brazil 13.8%; United Kingdom 4.7%; Spain 4.3%; The Netherlands 4.2%.

Transport and communications

Transport. Railroads (1984): length 210 mi, 338 km; (1983) passengers carried 106,500; short ton cargo carried 609,776, metric ton cargo carried 553,180. Roads (1983): total length 4,668 mi, 7,513 km (paved 8%). Vehicles (1982): passenger cars 16,043; trucks and buses 10,695. Merchant marine (1983): vessels (100 gross tons and over) 17; total deadweight tonnage 143,789. Air transport (1983): passengers carried 850,000; cargo carried 36,376 short tons (33,000 metric tons); airports (1984) with scheduled flights 25.
Communications. Daily newspaper (1983): total number 1; total circulation 18,000; circulation per 1,000 population 14. Radios (1983): total number of receivers 100,000 (1 per 13 persons). Television (1983): total number of receivers 20,000 (1 per 65 persons). Telephones (1982): 11,133 (1 per 108 persons).

Education and health

Education (1982–83)

	schools	teachers	students	student/ teacher ratio
Primary	901	3,781	165,559	43.8
Secondary	47	1,161	22,350	19.3
Voc., teacher tr.	29	582	10,545	18.1
Higher	1	297	2,651	8.9

College graduates per 100,000 population (1983): 65. *Literacy* (1978 est.): total population literate 800,000 (75%); males literate, n.a.; females literate, n.a.
Health (1980): physicians 265 (1 per 4,649 persons); hospital beds 4,617 (1 per 267 persons).
Food (1978–80): daily per capita caloric intake 2,844 (vegetable products 87.5%, animal products 12.5%); 122% of FAO recommended minimum requirement.

Military

Total active duty personnel (1982): 2,200 (army 68.2%; navy 9.1%; air force 22.7%), not including 600 French troops. *Military expenditure as percent of GNP* (1982): 2.7% (world 6.0%); per capita expenditure U.S.$74‡.

*Unless otherwise indicated, ratios or percentages per total population are computed per official government census or estimates only. Base years used within this table include the 1960–61 census, 448,564 (readjusted by Gabon to 650,000); 1970 census, 950,009; 1980 estimate, 1,232,000 de jure (de facto 1,110,000); 1983 estimate, 1,300,100. In 1981 the population estimates of Gabon by the Population Division of the United Nations and the World Bank were 1,090,000 and 669,000, respectively; the United Nations estimate in mid-1983 was 1,127,000. †Detail does not add to total given because of rounding. ‡Nongovernmental source. §1983. ‖1982. ¶Value added. ♀Official government figures for salaried workers only, not including traditional agricultural workers; agricultural workers (FAO estimate, 1982) totaled 423,000 (75.2% of the labour force). δPublic utilities, transportation and communication, finance, and service employees included with other. □First quarter.

The Gambia

Official name: Republic of The Gambia.
Form of government: multiparty republic with one legislative house (House of Representatives [49]).
Head of state and government: President.
Capital: Banjul.
Official language: English.
Official religion: none.
Monetary unit: 1 dalasi (D) = 100 butut; valuation (Oct. 29, 1984) 1 U.S.$ = D4.14; 1 £ = D5.00.

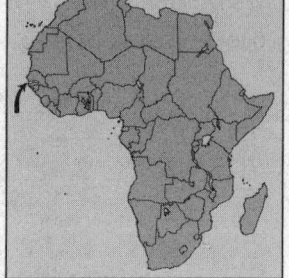

Area and population

Divisions	Capitals	area* sq mi	area* sq km	population 1983† census
Kombo Saint Mary	Kanifing	29	76	102,858
Lower River	Mansakonko	598	1,548	55,620
MacCarthy Island	Kuntaur/Georgetown	534	1,382	130,041
North Bank	Kerewan	831	2,152	111,411
Upper River	Basse	775	2,008	112,916
Western	Brikama	679	1,759	138,504
City				
Banjul		5	13	44,536
TOTAL		3,451	8,938	695,886

Source: Official government figures.

Demography

Density (1984): persons per sq mi 206.8, persons per sq km 79.9.
Urban–rural (1983): urban 21.2%; rural 78.8%.
Sex distribution (1980): male 49.42%; female 50.58%.
Age breakdown (1980): under 15, 44.3%; 15–29, 26.4%; 30–44, 15.4%; 45–59, 9.1%; 60–74, 4.0%; 75 and over, 0.7%.‡
Population projection: (1990) 831,000; (2000) 1,072,000.
Doubling time: 27 years.
Ethnic composition (1978): Malinke 44.0%; Fulani 17.5%; Wolof 12.3%; Dyola 7.0%; Soninke 7.0%; other 12.2%.
Religious affiliation (1980): Muslim 84.8%; traditional beliefs 11.0%; Roman Catholic 1.9%; Baha'i 0.9%; other 1.4%.
Major cities (1983†): Banjul 44,536; Brikama 20,208; Basse 5,612; Kau-Ur 5,338; Bansang 4,137.

Vital statistics

Birth rate per 1,000 population (1980–85): 47.5 (world avg. 27.5); legitimate, n.a.; illegitimate, n.a.
Death rate per 1,000 population (1980–85): 21.7 (world avg. 10.6).
Natural increase rate per 1,000 population (1980–85): 25.8 (world avg. 16.9).
Total fertility rate (avg. births per childbearing woman; 1980–85): 6.4.
Marriage rate per 1,000 population: n.a.
Divorce rate per 1,000 population: n.a.
Infant mortality rate per 1,000 live births (1975–80): 203.5.
Life expectancy at birth (1980–85): male 40.9 years; female 44.1 years.
Major causes of death: n.a.; however, major infectious diseases are malaria, gonococcal infections and syphilis, leprosy, chicken pox, schistosomiasis, tetanus, tuberculosis, and trypanosomiasis.

National economy

Budget (1983–84). Revenue: D157,362,000 (import and excise duties 46.6%; income tax 14.2%; export duties 4.5%). Expenditures: D271,227,000§ (public works, transport, and communications 33.9%; agriculture and natural resources 11.0%; education, sports, and culture 9.6%; health, labour, and social welfare 7.2%).
Public debt (external, outstanding; 1982): U.S.$149,300,000.
Tourism (1981): receipts from visitors U.S.$20,000,000; expenditures by nationals abroad, n.a.
Production (metric tons except as noted). Agriculture, forestry, fishing (1982): peanuts (groundnuts) in shell 130,000, rice 35,000, millet 35,000, corn (maize) 11,000, natural rubber 9,000, cassava 6,000, palm oil 2,500, palm kernels 2,000; livestock (number of live animals) 350,000 cattle, 185,000 goats, 175,000 sheep, 11,000 pigs, 300,000 chickens; roundwood 933,000 cu m; fish catch 9,704. Mining and quarrying: n.a.; however, deposits of kaolin, tin, ilmenite, zircon, and rutile are important. Manufacturing: n.a.; however, major agriculture-based industries are peanut (groundnut) and palm kernel processing for oil and cake, fish preservation (salting, drying, and smoking), and brewing of alcoholic drinks; other industries include plastics, confectionery, furniture, and toiletries. Construction: n.a. Energy production (consumption): electricity (kW-hr; 1982) 40,000,000 (40,000,-000); coal, none (n.a.); crude petroleum, none (n.a.); petroleum products (metric tons; 1982) none (52,000); natural gas, none (n.a.).
Persons economically active (1982): total 306,000 (47.8%); female participation in labour force, n.a.; unemployed, n.a.

Price and earnings indexes (1980 = 100)

	1978	1979	1980	1981	1982	1983	1984
Consumer price index	88.3	93.7	100.0	106.1	117.6	130.1	154.2¶
Earnings index	...	...	...	...	...	...	...

Household income and expenditure. Average household size (1980) 4.9;

average annual income per household: n.a., source of income: n.a.; expenditure: n.a.
Gross national product (at current market prices; 1981): U.S.$220,000,000 (U.S.$370 per capita).

Origin of gross domestic product (current prices)

	1982–83 in value D'000,000	1982–83 % of total value	1982 labour force	1982 % of labour force
Agriculture	154.1	27.2	236,000	77.1
Mining	0.5	0.1	...	...
Manufacturing	41.1	7.2	...	...
Construction	45.7	8.1	...	...
Trade	134.4	23.7	...	...
Public utilities	2.6	0.5	...	...
Transportation and communication	47.8	8.4	...	...
Finance	60.8	10.7	...	...
Public administration	79.6	14.0	...	...
Services	14.2	2.5	...	...
Other	−13.6 ‖	−2.4 ‖	70,000	22.9
TOTAL	567.2	100.0	306,000	100.0

Land use (1981): forested 21.0%; meadows and pastures 16.0%; agricultural and under permanent cultivation 27.2%; other 35.8%.

Foreign trade

Balance of trade (current prices)

	1978	1979	1980	1981	1982	1983
D'000,000	−90.9	−62.7	−129.1	−97.9	−137.1	−177.3
% of total	36.0%	22.3%	39.8%	28.5%	41.0%	41.1%

Imports (1983): D304,247,000 (food 27.6%, manufactured goods 22.8%, minerals and fuel 16.3%, machinery and transport equipment 14.0%, chemicals 6.1%, beverages and tobacco 5.4%). *Major import sources* (1982): EEC (excluding United Kingdom) 31.2%; United Kingdom 21.5%; China 11.4%; Japan 4.4%; Senegal 3.8%.
Exports (1983): D126,906,000 (shelled peanuts [groundnuts] 38.7%, peanut oil 9.9%, peanut meal 3.1%, fish and fish preparations 2.7%). *Major export destinations:* EEC (excluding United Kingdom) 40.7%; West Africa 22.1%; United Kingdom 6.2%.

Transport and communications

Transport. Railroads: none. Roads (1983): total length 1,916 mi, 3,083 km (paved 15%). Vehicles (1983): passenger cars 6,100; trucks and buses 1,030. Merchant marine (1983): vessels (100 gross tons and over) 8; total deadweight tonnage 4,243. Air transport: passengers, n.a.; cargo, n.a.; airport (1984) with scheduled flights 1.
Communications. Daily newspapers: none. Radios (1983): total number of receivers 100,000 (1 per 6.4 persons). Television: none. Telephones (1980): 3,476 (1 per 172.6 persons).

Education and health

Education (1982–83)

	schools	teachers	students	student/ teacher ratio
Primary (age 6–12)	164	2,347	53,774	22.9
Secondary (age 13–18)	23	627	11,366	18.1
Voc., teacher tr.	7	148	1,058	7.1

College graduates per 100,000 population: n.a. *Literacy* (1980): total population literate 67,700 (20.1%); males literate 47,700 (29.1%); females literate 20,000 (11.6%).
Health (1978): physicians 49 (1 per 11,632 persons); hospital beds 699 (1 per 815 persons).
Food (1978–80): daily per capita caloric intake 2,250 (vegetable products 93.2%, animal products 6.8%); 95% of FAO recommended minimum requirement.

Military

Total active duty personnel (1983): 475 (army 84.2%; navy 10.5%; air force 5.3%). *Military expenditure as percent of GNP:* n.a.

*Land area; total area is 4,017 sq mi (10,403 sq km). †Preliminary. ‡Detail does not add to total given because of rounding. §Includes D119,400,000 development expenditure. ‖ Less imputed bank charges. ¶Second quarter.

German Democratic Republic

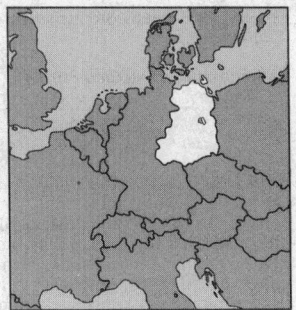

Official name: Deutsche Demokratische Republik (German Democratic Republic).
Form of government: unitary single-party republic with one legislative house (People's Chamber [500]).
Chief of state: Chairman, Council of State.
Head of government: Premier.
Capital: Berlin.
Official language: German.
Official religion: none.
Monetary unit: 1 Mark of Deutsche Demokratische Republik (M) = 100 Pfennige; valuation (Oct. 29, 1984) 1 U.S.$ = M3.06; 1 £ = M3.70.

Area and population

Districts	Capitals	area sq mi	area sq km	population 1983 estimate
Berlin, capital city	—	156	403	1,173,028
Cottbus	Cottbus	3,190	8,262	884,545
Dresden	Dresden	2,602	6,738	1,799,928
Erfurt	Erfurt	2,837	7,349	1,238,156
Frankfurt	Frankfurt	2,775	7,186	707,058
Gera	Gera	1,546	4,004	741,992
Halle	Halle	3,386	8,771	1,816,253
Karl-Marx-Stadt	Karl-Marx-Stadt	2,320	6,009	1,911,082
Leipzig	Leipzig	1,917	4,966	1,395,594
Magdeburg	Magdeburg	4,450	11,526	1,259,980
Neubrandenburg	Neubrandenburg	4,227	10,948	620,618
Potsdam	Potsdam	4,853	12,568	1,120,195
Rostock	Rostock	2,731	7,074	893,502
Schwerin	Schwerin	3,348	8,672	590,881
Suhl	Suhl	1,489	3,856	549,494
TOTAL		41,827	108,333*	16,702,306

Source: Official government figures.

Demography

Density (1984): persons per sq mi 399.1; persons per sq km 154.1.
Urban–rural (1983): urban 76.5%; rural 23.5%.
Sex distribution (1983): male 47.07%; female 52.93%.
Age breakdown (1983): under 15, 17.8%; 15–30, 25.6%; 31–45, 20.1%; 46–60, 17.7%; 61–75, 12.4%; 76 and over, 6.4%.
Population projection: (1990) 16,604,000; (2000) 16,483,000; during 1960–69 the average growth rate was 0.1%, but since 1970 the population has been decreasing.
Ethnic composition (1984 est.): German 99%; other 1%.
Religious affiliation (1983 est.): Protestant 80%; Roman Catholic 10%; atheist 10%.
Major cities (1983 est.): Berlin 1,173,000; Leipzig 557,900; Dresden 521,900; Karl-Marx-Stadt 320,000; Magdeburg 288,300; Rostock 239,400.

Vital statistics

Birth rate per 1,000 population (1983): 14.4 (world avg. 27.0); legitimate, 74%, illegitimate, 26%.
Death rate per 1,000 population (1983): 13.7 (world avg. 11.0).
Natural increase rate per 1,000 population (1983): 0.7 (world avg. 16.0).
Total fertility rate (avg. births per childbearing woman; 1980–85): 1.8.
Marriage rate per 1,000 population (1983): 7.5.
Divorce rate per 1,000 population: (1983): 3.0.
Infant mortality rate per 1,000 live births (1983): 11.4.
Life expectancy at birth (1982): male 69.0 years; female 74.8 years.
Major causes of death per 100,000 population (1983): circulatory diseases 825.0; malignant neoplasms (cancers) 212.0; pneumonia 23.0; stomach and intestinal diseases 9.0; tuberculosis 4.0.

National economy

Budget (1982). Revenue: M182,836,000,000 (revenue from nonagricultural state-owned enterprises 70.0%, social security contributions 8.8%, banking revenue 4.1%, health care contributions 4.0%). Expenditures: M182,071,-400,000 (economic subsidies and price supports 18.6%, social welfare 16.7%, health care 6.0%, education 6.0%, defense 6.0%, transfers to state governments 4.8%, cultural activities 1.0%).
Public debt (external, outstanding): n.a.
Tourism (1978): total tourist arrivals 817,618.
Production (metric tons except as noted). Agriculture, forestry, fishing (1982): potatoes 8,883,069, sugar beets 7,193,462, barley 4,054,932, wheat 2,739,298, rye 2,118,829, oats 847,635; livestock (number of live animals) 12,106,700 pigs, 5,690,100 cattle, 2,198,200 sheep, 51,356,000 chickens; commercial timber 9,600,400 cu m, firewood 747,700 cu m; fish catch 269,-867. Mining and quarrying (1982; metal content except as noted): bauxite (gross amount) 65,000; iron ore 20,000; copper ore 13,000; nickel 2,500; tin 1,700; silver 1,450,000 troy oz. Manufacturing (1982): cement 11,721,000; steel 7,169,000; fertilizer 4,669,000; pig iron 2,149,000; plastics and synthetic resins 990,000; sulfuric acid 920,000; sugar 896,000; paper 857,000; lumber 2,206,000 cu m; vacuum cleaners 1,224,000 units; radios 900,000 units; refrigerators 700,000 units; television sets 652,000 units; washing machines 485,000 units. Construction (M; 1982): residential 5,081,400,000; nonresidential 15,730,900,000. Energy production (consumption): electric-

ity (kW-hr; 1983) 104,928,000,000 (104,054,000,000†); coal (metric tons; 1983) 278,000,000 (281,425,000†); crude petroleum (barrels; 1982) 440,000 (154,333,000); petroleum products (metric tons; 1982) 18,134,000 (15,284,-000); natural gas (cu m; 1982) 8,212,000,000 (8,692,000,000).
Gross national product (at current market prices; 1982): U.S.$85,240,000,000 (U.S.$5,100 per capita).

Origin of net material product (constant 1980 prices)

	1982 in value M'000,000	% of total value	labour force	% of labour force
Agriculture	16,680	7.8	888,900	10.6
Mining, manufacturing	148,640	69.8	3,439,000	41.1
Construction	12,340	5.8	584,800	7.0
Trade	20,120	9.4	853,100	10.2
Transportation and communication	8,810	4.1	620,200	7.4
Other‡	6,510	3.1	1,981,600	23.7
TOTAL	213,100	100.0	8,367,600	100.0

Persons economically active (1982): total 8,367,000 (50.1%); female participation in the labour force 4,148,700 (49.6%); unemployed, n.a.

Price and earnings indexes (1970 = 100)

	1976	1977	1978	1979	1980	1981	1982
Consumer price index	98.4	98.2	97.8	98.4	98.6	98.9	98.9
Monthly earnings index	120.0	124.0	128.8	132.8	135.2	138.5	141.3

Household income and expenditure. Average household size (1982) 3.5; average annual income per household M30,900 (U.S.$9,000); source of income: wages and salaries 68.8%, transfer payments 30.7%; expenditure (1982): consumer goods 29.8%, food and beverages 29.2%, education 15.5%, rent and utilities 11.0%, health and social services 6.3%.
Land use (1981): forested 27.9%; meadows and pastures 11.8%; agricultural and under permanent cultivation 47.3%; other 13.0%.

Foreign trade

Balance of trade (current prices)

	1977	1978	1979	1980	1981	1982
M'000,000	−8,037	−4,544	−4,005	−5,840	+1,073	+5,353
% of total	8.8%	4.7%	3.7%	4.9%	0.8%	3.7%

Imports (1982): M69,878,300,000 (combustibles, minerals, and unfabricated metals 39.9%; machinery, equipment, and transportation equipment 32.3%; fabricated and partially fabricated industrial materials 16.3%; chemical products and other goods 7.4%).
Exports (1982): M75,231,000,000 (machinery, equipment, and transportation equipment 48.5%; combustibles, minerals and unfabricated metals 18.5%; consumer goods 14.2%; chemical products 12.7%). *Direction of total trade§:* U.S.S.R. 38.0%; Czechoslovakia 7.2%; Hungary 6.5%; Poland 5.0%; Bulgaria 3.2%; Romania 3.0%.

Transport and communications

Transport. Railroads (1983): length 8,843 mi, 14,231 km; passenger-mi 14,-048,000,000, passenger-km 22,608,000,000; short ton-mi cargo 37,595,000,-000, metric ton-km cargo 54,888,000,000. Roads (1982): total length 74,851 mi, 120,461 km (paved, 39%). Vehicles (1982): passenger cars 2,921,575; trucks and buses 281,349. Merchant marine (1983): vessels (100 gross tons and over) 416; total deadweight tonnage 1,793,102. Air transport (1982): passenger-mi 1,426,790,000, passenger-km 2,296,200,000; short ton-mi cargo 49,738,505, metric ton-km cargo 72,617,000; airports (1984) with scheduled flights 1.
Communications. Daily newspapers (1982): total number 39; total circulation 8,658,000; circulation per 1,000 population 518. Radios (1983): total number of receivers 6,440,000 (1 per 2.6 persons). Television (1983): total number of receivers 5,847,000 (1 per 2.9 persons). Telephones (1983): 3,344,263 (1 per 5.0 persons).

Education and health

Education (1982)

	schools	teachers	students	student/teacher ratio
Primary and secondary (age 6–18)	5,865	171,381	2,128,580	12.4
Vocational	973	16,640	431,047	25.9
Higher	54	...	130,442	...

College graduates per 100,000 population (students graduating; 1982): 150.
Literacy (1984): virtually 100%.
Health (1983): physicians 35,377 (1 per 472 persons); hospital beds 171,280 (1 per 98 persons).
Food (1978–80): daily per capita caloric intake 3,746 (vegetable products 62.9%, animal products 27.1%); 143% of FAO recommended minimum requirement.

Military

Total active duty personnel (1982): 166,000 (army 68.1%; navy 9.0%; air force 22.9%). *Military expenditure as percent of GNP* (1982): 6.9% (world 6.0%); per capita expenditure U.S.$267.

*Detail does not add to total given because of rounding. †1982. ‡Includes finance, services, public administration, and defense. §Separate figures are not available for import sources and export destinations. ¶Excludes more than 45,000 mi (73,000 km) of municipal roads.

Germany, Federal Republic of

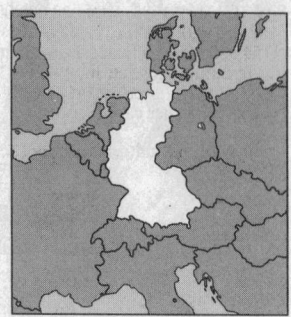

Official name: Bundesrepublik Deutschland (Federal Republic of Germany).
Form of government: federal multiparty republic with two legislative houses (Federal Council [45]; Federal Diet [520]).
Chief of state: President.
Head of government: Chancellor.
Capital: Bonn (provisional).
Official language: German.
Official religion: none.
Monetary unit: 1 Deutsche Mark (DM) = 100 Pfennige; valuation (Oct. 29, 1984) 1 U.S.$ = DM 3.06; 1 £ = DM 3.70.

Area and population

States	Capitals	area sq mi	area sq km	population 1984 estimate
Baden–Württemberg	Stuttgart	13,804	35,752	9,243,300
Bayern	Munich	27,240	70,551	10,969,500
Bremen	Bremen	156	404	676,900
Hamburg	Hamburg	292	755	1,609,500
Hessen	Wiesbaden	8,152	21,114	5,565,000
Niedersachsen	Hannover	18,311	47,426	7,248,500
Nordrhein–Westfalen	Düsseldorf	13,153	34,067	16,836,500
Rheinland–Pfalz	Mainz	7,663	19,846	3,633,500
Saarland	Saarbrücken	993	2,571	1,052,800
Schleswig–Holstein	Kiel	6,070	15,721	2,616,600
Berlin (West)*	Berlin (West)	185	480	1,854,500
TOTAL		96,019	248,687	61,306,700

Source: Official government figures.

Demography

Density (1984): persons per sq mi 638.5, persons per sq km 246.5.
Urban–rural (1980): urban 84.7%; rural 15.3%.
Sex distribution (1984): male 47.80%; female 52.20%.
Age breakdown (1983): under 15, 16.5%; 15–29, 24.0%; 30–44, 21.0%; 45–59, 18.6%; 60–74, 13.6%; 75 and over 6.3%.
Population projection: (1990) 59,622,000; (2000) 58,822,000.
Doubling time: not applicable; population is declining.
Ethnic composition (1983): German 92.5%; Turk 2.5%; Yugoslav 1.0%; Italian 0.9%; Greek 0.5%; Austrian 0.3%; Spanish 0.3%; Dutch 0.2%; other 1.8%.
Religious affiliation (1980): Christian 92.8%, of which Protestant 46.7% (including Lutheran-Reformed tradition 23.5%, Lutheran tradition 21.7%, Reformed tradition 0.7%, other 0.8%), Roman Catholic 43.8%, New Apostolic (non-Roman) Catholic 0.8%, Greek Orthodox 0.6%, other 0.9%; nonreligious 3.7%; Muslim 2.4%; atheist 0.9%; Jewish 0.1%; other 0.1%.
Major cities (1984 est.): Berlin (West) 1,854,500; Hamburg 1,609,500; Munich 1,283,500; Cologne 940,700; Bonn 291,500; (1983 est.) Essen 635,200; Frankfurt am Main 614,700; Dortmund 595,200; Düsseldorf 579,800; Stuttgart 571,100.
Place of birth: n.a.
Mobility: n.a.
Households (1982). Number of households 25,336,000; average household size 2.4; 1 person 31.3%, 2 persons 28.7%, 3 persons 17.7%, 4 persons 14.3%, 5 or more persons 8.0%. Family households: 17,406,000 (68.7%), nonfamily 7,930,000.
Immigration (1982): immigrants admitted 420,754, from Poland 14.0%, Italy 10.4%, Turkey 10.3%, Yugoslavia 5.4%, United States 5.3%, Austria 4.4%, United Kingdom 4.1%, Romania 3.7%, German Democratic Republic 3.7%.

Vital statistics

Birth rate per 1,000 population (1983): 9.7 (world avg. 29.0); legitimate, 91.5%; illegitimate, 8.5%.
Death rate per 1,000 population (1983): 11.7 (world avg. 11.0).
Natural increase rate per 1,000 population (1983): −2.0 (world avg. 18.0).
Total fertility rate (avg. births per childbearing woman; 1982): 1.4.
Marriage rate per 1,000 population (1983): 6.0.
Divorce rate per 1,000 population (1982): 1.9.
Infant mortality rate per 1,000 live births (1983): 10.2.
Life expectancy at birth (1980–82): male 70.2 years; female 76.9 years.
Major causes of death per 100,000 population (1981): diseases of the circulatory system 595.7, of which cerebrovascular disease 169.1, diseases of pulmonary circulation 151.7, acute myocardial infarction 136.5, hypertensive disease 23.1; malignant neoplasms (cancers) 257.3, of which bronchial, lung, and tracheal 40.7, stomach 28.5, colon 23.8; bronchitis, emphysema, and asthma 37.2; chronic liver disease and cirrhosis 26.9.

Social indicators

Educational attainment (1982). Percent of adult population having: less than full primary education, virtually zero; primary and secondary 34.9%, of which primary with general secondary 15.9%; some post-secondary in preparation for higher education 10.0%; completion of more advanced education 55.1%, of which trade school graduates with apprenticeship 44.7%,

skilled technicians or craftsmen 4.6%, engineers 1.9%, university graduates (all levels) 3.9%.

Distribution of income (1974)
percent of household income by quintile

1	2	3	4	5 (highest)
6.9	11.0	15.9	21.9	44.8

Quality of working life (1982). Average work week: 40.8 hours. Annual rate per 100,000 workers for: injury or accident at work 6,215, injury or accident on way to work 687, industrial illness 144, death 13.4. Proportion of labour force insured for damages or income loss resulting from: injury, virtually 100%, permanent disability, virtually 100%, death, virtually 100%. Average days lost to labour stoppages per 1,000 workers (1983): 2. Principal means of journey to work: private automobile 32.4%, public transportation 19.2%, bicycle, 6.2%, foot 37.5%, other 4.7%. Percentage of unemployed workers not eligible for unemployment benefits (1983) 27.1%.
Access to services. Proportion of dwellings having electricity 99.7%, piped water supply 99.2%, flush sewage disposal 94.2%, public fire protection, n.a.
Social participation. Eligible voters participating in last national election 89.1%. Population participating in voluntary work, n.a. Trade union membership in total workforce (1983): 27.1%. Practicing religious population in total affiliated population, n.a.
Social deviance (1982). Offense rate per 100,000 population for: murder 5.8; sexual abuse 84.3; assault and battery 129.4; larceny 5,324.9, of which, auto theft 150.7, burglary of private dwellings 185.5. Incidence per 100,000 in general population (late 1970s) of: alcoholism 2,500 to 3,000, drug and substance abuse 650, suicide 22†.
Leisure (late 1970s). Favourite leisure activities: watching television 56%, reading 30%.
Material well-being (1983). Households possessing: automobile 65%, telephone 88%, colour television receiver 73%, refrigerator 79%, air conditioner 56%‡, electric washing machine 83%.

National economy

Gross national product (at current market prices; 1983): U.S.$625,955,000,000 (U.S.$10,171 per capita).

Origin of gross domestic product (current prices)

	1982 in value DM '000,000	% of total value	labour force	% of labour force
Agriculture,	37,400	2.5	1,405,000	5.1
Mining	58,900§	3.9§	366,000	1.3
Manufacturing	508,300	33.9	8,788,000	32.0
Construction	97,100	6.5	2,009,000	7.3
Trade	152,600	10.2	4,124,000	15.0
Public utilities	§	§	237,000	0.9
Transportation and communication	92,900	6.2	1,583,000	5.7
Finance	‖	‖	1,613,000	5.9
Pub. admin., defense	‖	‖	¶	¶
Services	551,700	36.8	6,925,000	25.2
Other	—	—	437,000	1.6
TOTAL	1,498,900	100.0	27,487,000	100.0

Budget (1981). Revenue: DM 451,700,000,000 (tax revenue 95.2%, of which social security contributions from employers 25.5%, from employees 21.5%, taxes on individual wages 14.1%, value added tax on goods and services 13.2%, taxes paid by self-employed or nonemployed 8.0%, petroleum tax 4.9%, tobacco tax 2.5%; nontax revenue 4.4%, of which income from property 2.9%). Expenditures: DM 481,640,000,000 (social security and welfare 51.4%, health 18.4%, defense 9.2%, economic services 6.6%, general public services 4.1%, education 0.8%).
Total national debt (1984) DM 353,270,000,000.
Tourism (1982): receipts from visitors U.S.$5,614,000,000; expenditures by nationals abroad U.S.$16,263,000,000.

Manufacturing, mining, and construction enterprises (1982)

	no. of enterprises	no. of tradesmen and professionals	wages as a % of avg. of all wages	annual gross production value† (DM'000,000)
Chemical	1,168	579,000	122.1	143,041
Food and beverage	3,898	476,000	89.1	139,207
Road motor vehicle	1,920	793,000	111.0	136,992
Machinery (nonelectric)	4,566	991,000	104.9	132,897
Machinery and appliance (electric)	2,287	954,000	103.3	122,100
Petroleum and natural gas	56	41,000	157.1	117,272
Iron and steel	98	269,000	102.4	51,193
Calculator, computer	2,135	277,000	90.2	34,736
Mining	87	238,000	112.3	33,960
Textile	1,526	262,000	75.1	32,594
Cement, sand, and gravel	2,246	167,000	101.3	29,569
Wood and wood products	2,335	209,000	86.7	26,913
Plastics	1,669	185,000	88.2	25,809
Metalware	1,307	159,000	106.0	24,375
Construction	16,943	1,075,000	90.8	...

Production (value in DM). Agriculture, forestry, fishing (1982): agricultural products—grains 6,206,000,000, grape juice and semi-processed grape juice 2,992,000,000, sugar beets 2,598,000,000, fruit 2,444,000,000, flowers and ornamental plants 2,380,000,000, vegetables 1,017,000,000, potatoes 992,000,000, seedlings 715,000,000, edible and nonedible oils 547,000,000, hops 267,000,000; animal products—milk 16,303,000,000, pork 12,290,000,000, beef 10,309,000,000, eggs 1,882,000,000, poultry 954,000,000, veal 865,000,000; livestock (number of live animals, 1982) 22,310,000 pigs, 14,992,000 cattle, 1,108,000 sheep, 364,000 horses, 77,743,000 chickens; roundwood 27,004,000 cu m; fish catch 313,524 metric tons. Mining and quarrying (value added at factor cost in DM; 1981): all mining 13,486,000,000§; cement, sand, and gravel 8,869,000,000. Manufacturing (value added at factor cost in DM; 1981): power–generating machinery and nonelectric industrial and agricultural machinery 51,552,000,000; electrical machinery and household electrical appliances 47,594,000,000; road motor vehicles 43,329,000,000; chemicals (including medicinal products) 36,761,000,000; food and beverages 22,969,000,000; calculators and computers 12,894,000,-000; semi-processed iron and steel 12,234,000,000; textiles 10,198,000,000; furniture and other wood products 9,690,000,000; metalware 8,983,000,000; plastics 8,270,000,000; printed matter 7,689,000,000; precision and optical matter, clocks 7,444,000,000; clothing 6,633,000,000; office machines 5,088,000,000; cast metals 5,067,000,000. Construction (1981): residential 33,617,000 sq m; nonresidential 879,000,000 sq m; restoration and conversion 2,712,000,000 sq m.

Service enterprises (1982)

	no. of enter-prises	no. of employees	weekly wage as a % of all wages	annual turnover (DM '000,000)
Gas	108	23,000	...	32,795
Water	162	17,000	...	3,479
Electrical power	461	225,000	...	96,022
Transport				
air	150	35,000	...	9,160
buses, trains	5,566	147,000	...	10,427
shipping	2,053	12,000	...	...
Communication				
press†	2,043	193,000	...	22,682
film†	2,111	23,000	...	...
Mail	18,230	503,000ô	...	42,065
Hotels and restaurants□	...	670,500ô	...	38,569
Wholesale trade◊	132,000	1,239,000ô	...	...
Retail trade◊	507,000	2,282,000ô	...	...
Health services◊	88,000	318,000ô	...	...
Financial services	36,000	427,000ô	...	...

Energy production (consumption): electricity (kW-hr; 1983) 371,844,000,000 (373,669,000,000△); hard coal (metric tons; 1982) 96,318,000 (91,951,000); lignite-brown coal (metric tons; 1982) 127,352,000 (130,126,000); coke (metric tons; 1982) 26,440,000 (19,425,000); crude petroleum (barrels; 1982) 30,843,000 (572,955,000); petroleum products (metric tons; 1982) 82,155,-000 (101,401,000); natural gas (cu m; 1982) 14,880,000,000 (45,683,000,000).
Persons economically active (1982): total 27,487,000 (44.6%); female participation in the labour force 10,540,000 (38.3%); unemployed (1983) 2,263,500 (9.2%).

Price and earnings indexes (1980 = 100)

	1978	1979	1980	1981	1982	1983	1984†
Consumer price index	91.1	94.9	100.0	106.3	111.9	115.6	118.3
Hourly earnings index	88.7	93.8	100.0	105.6	110.5	114.0	116.0

Household income and expenditure. Average household size (1982) 2.4; average annual net income per household (1983) DM 30,799 (U.S.$12,062); sources of take home income (1983): wages 84.2%, self-employment 6.7%, investments 9.0%, pensions and disability payments 5.2%; expenditure (1983): food 26.1%, rent 17.3%, transportation 15.9%, household expenses 10.2%, entertainment and education 8.7%, clothing and footwear 8.1%, electricity and gas 6.7%, other 7.0%.
Land use (1981): forested 30.0%; meadows and pastures 19.3%; agricultural and under permanent cultivation 30.6%; other 20.1%.

Financial aggregates

	1978	1979	1980	1981	1982	1983	1984 (9 mo.)
Exchange rate, DM per:							
U.S. dollar	1.8280	1.7315	1.9590	2.2548	2.3765	2.7238	3.0253
£	3.7191	3.8509	4.6722	4.3022	3.8369	3.9511	3.7756
SDR	2.3815	2.2810	2.4985	2.6245	2.6215	2.8517	3.0223
International reserves (U.S.$)							
Total (excl. gold; '000,000)	48,474	52,549	48,592	43,719	44,762	42,674	40,868
SDR's ('000,000)	1,796	2,076	1,840	1,609	2,054	1,613	1,406
Reserve pos. in IMF ('000,000)	4,302	3,125	2,291	2,465	3,088	3,748	3,744
Foreign exchange	42,376	47,348	44,461	39,645	39,620	37,313	35,718
Gold, ('000,000 fine troy oz.)	118.64	95.25	95.18	95.18	95.18	95.18	95.18
% world reserves	11.44	10.09	9.99	10.00	10.05	10.06	10.96⊕
Interest and prices							
Central bank discount (%)	3.0	6.0	7.5	7.5	5.0	4.0	4.5
Gov't. bond yield (%)	6.4	7.7	8.7	10.6	9.1	8.0	7.6
Industrial share prices							
(1980 = 100)	112.3	106.8	100.0	100.4	99.0	133.5	149.4
Balance of payments ('000,000 U.S.$)							
Balance of visible trade	24.73	16.85	8.99	16.58	25.26	22.25	...
Imports, f.o.b.	112.97	148.89	176.50	154.49	143.67	140.40	...
Exports, f.o.b.	137.70	165.75	185.48	171.07	168.93	162.65	...
Balance of invisibles	−6.64	−11.39	−11.39	−10.44	−10.14	−7.79	...
Balance of payments, current account	9.23	−6.20	−15.96	−5.72	3.44	4.00	...

Foreign trade

Balance of trade (current prices)

	1978	1979	1980	1981	1982	1983
DM '000,000	+41,200	+22,429	+8,947	+27,720	+51,277	+42,089
% of total	7.8%	3.7%	1.5%	3.6%	6.4%	5.1%

Imports (1981): DM 369,179,000,000 (mineral fuels 24.3%, of which crude petroleum 13.3%, refined petroleum products 5.6%, petroleum gases 3.9%; machines and transport equipment 19.7%, of which road motor vehicles 4.3%, electrical machinery 3.3%; basic manufactures 16.1%, of which textile yarns and fabrics 3.3%, iron and steel 3.3%; miscellaneous manufactured goods 11.2%, of which clothing and accessories 4.4%). *Major import sources:* The Netherlands 12.1%; France 11.0%; United States 7.7%; Italy 7.5%; United Kingdom 7.5%; Belgium-Luxembourg 6.7%; Saudi Arabia 3.9%.
Exports (1981): DM 396,898,000,000 (machinery and transport equipment 44.8%, of which road vehicles 14.8% [including passenger motor cars 7.8% and motor vehicle parts 3.4%], general industrial machinery 6.4%, machinery specialized for particular industries 6.3%, electrical machinery 5.2%; basic manufactures 19.4%, of which iron and steel [all forms] 5.9%, metal manufactures 3.3%; chemicals 12.5%, of which organic chemicals 3.3%; miscellaneous manufactured goods 9.1%). *Major export destinations:* France 13.1%; The Netherlands 8.6%; Italy 7.9%; Belgium-Luxembourg 7.2%; United States 6.6%; United Kingdom 6.5%; Switzerland 5.2% .

Transport and communications

Transport. Railroads (1983): route length 17,607 mi, 28,335 km; passenger-mi 24,442,000,000, passenger-km 39,336,000,000; short ton-mi cargo 38,-302,000,000, metric ton-km cargo 55,920,000,000. Roads (1983): total length 302,772 mi, 487,251 km (paved 99%). Vehicles (1983): passenger cars 24,688,843; trucks and buses 1,547,714. Merchant marine (1983): vessels (100 gross tons and over) 1,769; total deadweight tonnage 10,797,478. Air transport (1983**): passenger-mi 14,199,868,000, passenger-km 22,852,517,-000; short ton-mi cargo 2,890,433,000, metric ton-km cargo 4,219,962,000; airports (1984) with scheduled flights 26.
Communications. Daily newspapers (1979): total number 380; total circulation 8,658,000; circulation per 1,000 population 141.1. Radios (1983): total number of receivers 24,300,000 (1 per 2.5 persons). Television (1983): total number of receivers 21,836,000 (1 per 2.8 persons). Telephones (1982): 30,122,023 (1 per 2.0 persons).

Education and health

Education (1982–83)

	schools	teachers	students	student/ teacher ratio
Primary (age 6–10)	...	...	2,451,788	...
Secondary (age 10–19)	23,881††	508,866††	5,604,064	...
Voc., teacher tr.	7,097	118,398	2,477,719	20.9
Higher	3,204	177,146	1,405,478	7.9

College graduates per 100,000 population (students graduating, 1979): 303.0. Literacy (1983): virtually 100%.
Health: physicians (1983) 146,221 (1 per 420 persons); hospital beds (1980) 707,710 (1 per 87 persons).
Food (1978–80): daily per capita caloric intake 3,537 (vegetable products 61.1%, animal products 38.9%); 132% of FAO recommended minimum requirement.

Military

Total active duty personnel (1982): 495,000 (army 67.8%; navy 7.3%; air force 21.4%; other 3.5%). *Military expenditure as percent of GNP* (1982): 5.8% (world 6.0%); per capita expenditure U.S.$166.

*Berlin (West) is under tripartite (France, United Kingdom, United States) jurisdiction and is only administratively a part of West Germany. †1981. ‡1979. §Public utilities included with mining. ‖ Finance and public administration and defense included with services. ¶Public administration and defense included with services. ⊕By value, about 90% anthracite and lignite. ôIncludes part time. □1980. ◊1970. △1982. †First quarter. ⊕8 months. **Lufthansa only. ††Includes primary.

Rhine shipping, with Cologne Cathedral in the background.

Ghana

Official name: Republic of Ghana.
Form of government: military
dictatorship with one ruling body
(Provisional National Defense
Council [7]).
Head of state and government:
Chairman of the Provisional National
Defense Council.
Capital: Accra.
Official language: English.
Official religion: none.
Monetary unit: 1 cedi (Ȼ) = 100
pesewas; valuation (Oct. 29, 1984)
1 U.S.$ = Ȼ38.69; 1 £ = Ȼ46.70.

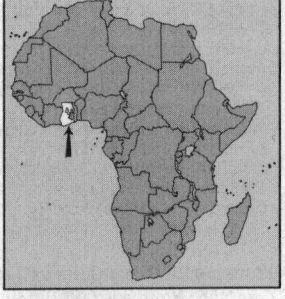

Area and population		area		population
				1984
Regions	Capitals	sq mi	sq km	census*
Ashanti	Kumasi	9,417	24,390	2,089,683
Brong-Ahafo	Sunyani	15,273	39,557	1,179,409
Central	Cape Coast	3,794	9,826	1,145,520
Eastern	Koforidua	7,713	19,977	1,679,483
Greater Accra	Accra	1,001	2,593	1,420,066
Northern	Tamale	27,175	70,383	1,162,645
Upper East	Bolgatanga	3,414	8,842	771,584
Upper West	Wa	7,134	18,477	439,161
Volta	Ho	7,943	20,572	1,201,095
Western	Sekondi-Takoradi	9,236	23,921	1,116,930
TOTAL		92,100	238,538	12,205,576

Source: Official government figures.

Demography

Density (1984): persons per sq mi 132.5, persons per sq km 51.2.
Urban–rural (1981): urban 36.6%; rural 63.4%.
Sex distribution (1980): male 49.44%; female 50.56%.
Age breakdown (1980): under 15, 46.6%; 15–64, 50.6%; 65 and over, 2.8%.
Population projection: (1990) 16,200,000; (2000) 22,350,000.
Doubling time: 23 years.
Ethno-linguistic composition (1978): Akan 52.6%; Mossi-Dagomba 15.9%; Ewe 11.8%; Ga-Adangme 7.6%; other 12.1%.
Religious affiliation (1983): Christian 43%, of which Protestant 29%. Roman Catholic 14%; traditional beliefs 38%; Muslim 12%; other 7%.
Major cities (1982 est.): Accra 1,045,400; Kumasi 436,100; Tema 345,800; Tamale 219,200; Sekondi-Takoradi 123,600.

Vital statistics

Birth rate per 1,000 population (1980–85): 48.2 (world avg. 27.5); legitimate, n.a.; illegitimate, n.a.
Death rate per 1,000 population (1980–85): 15.5 (world avg. 10.6).
Natural increase rate per 1,000 population (1980–85): 32.7 (world avg. 16.9).
Total fertility rate (avg. births per childbearing woman; 1980–85): 6.7.
Marriage rate per 1,000 population: n.a.
Divorce rate per 1,000 population: n.a.
Infant mortality rate per 1,000 live births (1975–80): 107.0.
Life expectancy at birth (1980–85): male 49.1 years; female 52.5 years.
Major causes of death per 100,000 population: n.a.; however, among the major infectious diseases are malaria, tuberculosis, leprosy, trypanosomiasis (sleeping sickness), and onchocerciasis (river blindness).

National economy

Budget (1982–83): Ȼ4,642,500,000 (income tax 31.4%; excise duties 31.1%; import duties 11.6%; sales tax 5.1%). Expenditures: Ȼ9,778,100,000 (interest on general debt 22.1%; education 18.3%; general administration 13.5%; economic services 12.4%, of which agricultural and non-mineral resources 9.8%; social security and welfare 7.6%).
Public debt (external, outstanding; 1982): U.S.$1,233,000,000.
Tourism (1980): receipts from visitors U.S.$23,000,000; expenditures by nationals abroad, n.a.
Production (metric tons except as noted). Agriculture, forestry, fishing (1983): cassava 1,729,000, yams and cocoyams 1,586,000, plantains 342,000, sugarcane 220,000†, cacao 190,000†, corn (maize) 172,000, coconuts 160,000†, peanuts (groundnuts) 110,000†, guinea corn 56,000, millet 40,000, rice 40,-000; livestock (number of live animals; 1982) 2,150,000 goats, 1,750,000 sheep, 970,000 cattle, 435,000 pigs, 12,500,000 chickens; roundwood 9,803,-000 cu m; fish catch 223,950 (of which anchovies 65,181). Mining and quarrying (1983): manganese ore and concentrate 175,300; bauxite 70,235; diamonds 336,600 carats; gold 8,606 kg. Manufacturing (1982): kerosine, diesel, and gasoline 420,000; crude petroleum 244,000; wheat flour 25,401; cocoa cakes, cocoa butter, and cocoa liquor 21,700; soap and toothpaste 4,773; beer 339,000 hectolitres; milk 76,000 hectolitres; ice cream 6,280 hectolitres; soft drinks 800,000 crates; cigarettes 1,208,000 units. Construction (1981): Ȼ1,752,600,000. Energy production (consumption): electricity (kW-hr; 1982) 4,981,000,000 (4,506,000,000); coal, none (n.a.); crude petroleum (barrels; 1983) 391,944 (7,931,100†); petroleum products (metric tons; 1982) 969,000, (639,000); natural gas, none (n.a.).
Household income and expenditure. Average household size (1978) 5.2; average annual income per household Ȼ9,600 (U.S.$ ‖); source of income: n.a.; expenditure (1978): food and beverages 36.9%, housing 14.8%, clothing and footwear 14.7%, transport and communication 6.1%, health care 2.3%.

Gross national product (at current market prices; 1981): U.S.$4,800,000,000 (U.S.$400 per capita).

Origin of gross domestic product (current prices)				
	1981			
	in value Ȼ'000,000	% of total value	labour force	% of labour force
Agriculture	39,028	50.9	2,226,000	50.0
Mining	406	0.5	...	...
Manufacturing	4,527	5.9	...	...
Construction	1,480	1.9	...	...
Trade	22,876	29.8	...	...
Public utilities	363	0.5	...	...
Transportation and communication	1,602	2.1	...	...
Finance	1,564	2.0	...	...
Pub. admin., defense	...		...	...
Services	400	0.5	...	...
Other	4,409	5.8	2,227,000	50.0
TOTAL	76,655	100.0‡	4,453,000	100.0

Persons economically active (1981): total 4,453,000 (36.9%); female participation in the labour force 1,830,000 (41.1%); unemployed, n.a.

Price and earnings indexes (1980 = 100)							
	1978	1979	1980	1981	1982	1983	1984
Consumer price index	43.2	66.6	100.0	216.5	264.8	590.1	836.8§
Earnings index	...	...	...	...	...	...	...

Land use (1981): forested 37.8%; meadows and pastures 15.1%; agricultural and under permanent cultivation 12.0%; other 35.1%.

Foreign trade

Balance of trade (current prices)					
	1977	1978	1979	1980	1981	1982
Ȼ'000,000	−27.2	−101.2	+391.1	+552.0	−117.0	+463.0
% of total	1.2%	3.1%	7.7%	8.7%	2.0%	10.7%

Imports (1979): Ȼ2,344,200,000 (chemicals 16.1%; crude petroleum 16.1%; transport equipment 15.1%, of which road motor vehicles 14.1%; nonelectrical machinery 13.9%; electrical machinery 3.8%; iron and steel 2.6%; cement 1.4%). *Major import sources:* United Kingdom 20.2%; West Germany 13.3%; Nigeria 12.9%; United States 10.7%; Japan 4.9%.
Exports (1979): Ȼ2,736,899,000 (cocoa 80.4%, of which cocoa beans 73.1%, cocoa butter and paste 7.2%; aluminum 8.3%). *Major export destinations:* U.S.S.R. 20.8%; The Netherlands 16.0%; United Kingdom 15.1%; West Germany 10.0%; Japan 9.0%; United States 7.7%.

Transport and communications

Transport. Railroads (1980): length 592 mi, 953 km; passenger-mi 285,600,-000, passenger-km 459,600,000; short ton-mi cargo 72,880,000, metric ton-km cargo 106,400,000. Roads (1983): total length paved 13,535 mi, 21,-783 km. Vehicles (1983): passenger cars 52,864; trucks and buses 24,312. Merchant marine (1983): vessels (100 gross tons and over) 135; total deadweight tonnage 296,757. Air transport (1980): passenger-mi 201,000,000, passenger-km 324,000,000; short ton-mi cargo 1,900,000, metric ton-km cargo 2,800,000; airports (1984) with scheduled flights 4.
Communications. Daily newspapers (1979): total number 5; total circulation 345,000; circulation per 1,000 population 33. Radios (1983): total number of receivers 2,000,000 (1 per 6.2 persons). Television (1983): total number of receivers 71,000 (1 per 176 persons). Telephones (1982): 70,653 (1 per 173 persons).

Education and health

Education (1982–83)				
	schools	teachers¶	students	student/ teacher ratio
Primary	...	51,129	1,574,719	30.8
Secondary	...	38,684	770,455	19.9
Voc., teacher tr.	...	...	...	...
Higher	3	...	7,953	...

College graduates per 100,000 population (students graduating; 1979): 26.
Literacy (late 1970s): total population literate 31%; males literate 43%; females literate 18%.
Health (1979): physicians 1,485 (1 per 7,630 persons); hospital beds 14,525 (1 per 780 persons).
Food (1978–80): daily per capita caloric intake 2,016 (vegetable products 94.9%, animal products 5.1%); 88% of FAO minimum recommended requirement.

Military

Total active duty personnel (1983): 12,600 (army 79.4%; navy 9.5%; air force 11.1%). *Military expenditure as percent of GNP* (1981): 0.5% (world 5.7%); per capita expenditure U.S.$11.

*Preliminary. †1982. ‡Detail does not add to total given because of rounding. §February. ‖ Unofficial exchange rate (7.5 to 9.9 times the official rate) does not allow direct conversion into other currencies. ¶Figures include untrained teachers.

Greece

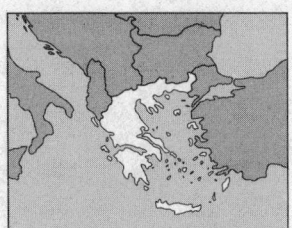

Official name: Elliniki Dimokratía
(Hellenic Republic).
Form of government: unitary multiparty
republic with one legislative house
(Greek Chamber of Deputies [300]).
Chief of state: President.
Head of government: Prime Minister.
Capital: Athens.
Official language: Greek.
Official religion: Eastern Orthodox.
Monetary unit: 1 drachma (Dr) = 100
leptae; valuation (Oct. 29, 1984)
1 U.S.$ = Dr125.60; 1 £ = Dr151.60.

Area and population*

Regions	area sq mi	area sq km	population 1981 census
Aegean Islands	3,522	9,122	428,533
Central Greece and Évvoia	9,417	24,391	1,099,841
Crete	3,219	8,336	502,165
Greater Athens	165	427	3,027,331
Ionian Islands	891	2,307	182,651
Ípiros	3,553	9,203	324,541
Macedonia	13,066	33,841	2,120,481
Pelopónnisos	8,254	21,379	1,012,528
Thessalía	5,420	14,037	695,654
Thráki	3,312	8,578	345,220
Autonomous administration			
Ayion Oros (Mt. Athos)	130	336	1,472
TOTAL	50,949	131,957	9,740,417

Source: Official government figures.

Demography

Density (1984): persons per sq mi 194.2, persons per sq km 75.0.
Urban–rural (1981): urban 58.1%; rural 41.9%.
Sex distribution (1982): male 49.16%; female 50.84%.
Age breakdown (1982): under 15, 22.0%; 15–29, 21.8%; 30–44, 19.2%; 45–59, 19.5%; 60–74, 12.4%; 75 and over, 5.1%.
Population projection: (1990) 10,533,000; (2000) 11,521,000.
Doubling time: 66 years.
Ethnic composition (1982): Greek 94.9%; Macedonian 1.8%; Turkish 0.6%; Albanian 0.6%; other 2.1%.
Religious affiliation (1982): Christian 98.1%, of which Greek Orthodox 97.6%, Roman Catholic 0.4%, Protestant 0.1%; Muslim 1.5%; other 0.4%.
Major cities (1981): Athens 885,737; Thessaloníki 406,413; Piraiévs 196,389; Pátrai 142,163; Iráklion 102,398.

Vital statistics

Birth rate per 1,000 population (1983): 13.4 (world avg. 29.0); legitimate 98.4%; illegitimate 1.6%.
Death rate per 1,000 population (1983): 9.2 (world avg. 11.0).
Natural increase rate per 1,000 population (1983): 4.2 (world avg. 18.0).
Total fertility rate (avg. births per childbearing woman; 1982): 2.3.
Marriage rate per 1,000 population (1983): 6.7.
Divorce rate per 1,000 population (1982): 0.7.
Infant mortality rate per 1,000 live births (1982): 14.3.
Life expectancy at birth (1982): male 72 years; female 76 years.
Major causes of death per 100,000 population (1983): malignant neoplasms (cancers) 178.5; cerebrovascular disease 178.2; diseases of pulmonary circulation and other forms of heart disease 117.1; ischemic heart disease 97.2.

National economy

Budget (1983)†. Revenue: Dr958,086,700,000 (indirect taxes 48.3%, direct taxes 28.0%, credit receipts from domestic and foreign sources 15.4%). Expenditures: Dr873,456,900,000 (finance 31.4%, defense 14.3%, health and social welfare 10.9%, education and culture 8.2%, agriculture 5.0%).
Public debt (external; 1982): U.S.$8,842,000,000.
Tourism (1982): receipts from visitors U.S.$1,527,000,000; expenditures by nationals abroad U.S.$231,000,000.
Production (metric tons except as noted). Agriculture, forestry, fishing (1982): wheat 2,992,000, tomatoes 1,918,000, grapes 1,617,000, olives 1,590,000, corn (maize) 1,310,000, potatoes 888,000, barley 853,000, oranges 653,000, watermelons 634,000, olive oil 351,000, sugar (raw value) 315,000, apples 257,000, onions 133,000, tobacco 115,000, cotton lint 115,000, rice 83,000, oats 81,000; livestock (number of live animals) 8,316,000 sheep, 4,623,000 goats, 1,378,000 pigs, 836,000 cattle, 223,000 asses, 97,000 horses, 36,296,-000 chickens; roundwood 2,755,000 cu m; fish catch 106,000. Mining and quarrying (1983): bauxite 198,900; iron ore 111,000. Manufacturing (1983): cement 1,177,000; sulfuric acid 82,300; aluminum 12,000; cotton yarn 9,800. Construction (cu m; 1982): residential buildings 3,095,000; nonresidential buildings 1,292,000. Energy production (consumption): electricity (kW-hr; 1982) 23,272,000,000 (23,994,000,000); coal (metric tons; 1982) 27,399,000 (27,717,000); crude petroleum (barrels; 1982) 7,513,300 (105,-156,200); petroleum products (metric tons; 1982) 13,999,000 (9,634,000); natural gas, none (n.a.).
Household income and expenditure. Average household size (1981) 3.2; income per household (1982): Dr250,420 (U.S.$3,548); sources of income (1982): wages and salaries 42.8%, property and entrepreneurship 26.1%, agriculture 16.5%, transfer payments 14.6%; expenditure (1982): foods, drinks, and tobacco 41.5%, rent 9.9%, clothing and footwear 8.9%, durable household goods 6.3%.

Gross national product (at current market prices; 1983): U.S.$34,863,000,000 (U.S.$3,545 per capita).

Origin of gross domestic product (current prices)

	1981 in value Dr'000,000	% of total value	labour force	% of labour force
Agriculture	317,500	15.6	1,084,500	29.5
Mining	30,600	1.5	19,600	0.5
Manufacturing	360,800	17.7	700,700	19.1
Construction	136,600	6.7	313,500	8.5
Trade	292,100‡	14.4‡	540,900	14.7
Public utilities	37,500	1.8	30,800	0.8
Transportation and communication	143,800	7.1	280,800	7.7
Finance	‡	‡	118,900	3.2
Pub. admin., defense	189,300	9.3	...	...
Services	§	§	509,400	13.9
Other	525,800§	25.9§	78,700 ‖	2.1 ‖
TOTAL	2,034,000	100.0	3,677,800	100.0

Persons economically active (1982): total 3,707,000 (37.9%); female participation in labour force 1,167,700 (31.4%); unemployed 215,000 (5.8%).

Price and earnings indexes (1980 = 100)

	1978	1979	1980	1981	1982	1983	1984
Consumer price index	67.3	80.1	100.0	124.5	150.8	181.5	201.0
Hourly earnings index	65.2	78.6	100.0	127.2	169.8	202.7	...

Land use (1981): forested 20.0%; meadows and pastures 40.2%; agricultural and under permanent cultivation 30.1%; other 9.7%.

Foreign trade

Balance of trade (current prices)

Dr'000,000	1978	1979	1980	1981	1982	1983
	−164.0	−212.6	−231.8	−255.8	−379.6	−453.9
% of total	39.9%	42.4%	34.4%	35.0%	40.6%	36.6%

Imports (1983): Dr846,680,000,000 (crude petroleum 24.9%; meat fresh, chilled, and frozen 5.2%; iron and steel 3.9%; passenger motor cars 2.2%; milk and cream 1.5; medicinal and pharmaceutical products 1.3%). *Major import sources:* West Germany 18.4%; Italy 9.6%; Japan 7.7%; France 7.4%; The Netherlands 7.1%; Saudi Arabia 6.5%; United Kingdom 4.4%; United States 3.7%; East Germany 2.9%.
Exports (1983): Dr392,740,000,000 (clothing 11.9%; petroleum products 6.5%; textile yarn 6.2%; olive oil 5.3%; cement, hydraulic 5.2%; concentrated tomato purée 2.4%). *Major export destinations:* West Germany 20.1%; Italy 14.1%; France 7.4%; Saudi Arabia 6.8%; United States 5.6%; United Kingdom 5.1%; The Netherlands 3.4%; East Germany 3.1%; Japan 0.6%.

Transport and communications

Transport. Railroads (1982): route length 1,540 mi, 2,479 km; passenger-mi 932,950,000, passenger-km 1,501,440,000; short ton-mi cargo 401,096,-000, metric ton-km cargo 585,590,000. Roads (1983): total length 66,047 mi, 106,292 km (paved 83%). Vehicles (1983): passenger cars 1,042,840; trucks and buses 574,782. Merchant marine (1983): vessels (100 gross tons and over) 3,169; total deadweight tonnage 65,986,213. Air transport♀ (1983): passenger-mi 3,469,932,000, passenger-km 5,584,325,000; short ton-mi cargo 46,422,000, metric ton-km cargo 67,775,000; airports (1984) with scheduled flights 22.
Communications. Daily newspapers (1979): total number 116; total circulation, n.a.; circulation per 1,000 population, n.a. Radios (1983): total number of receivers 4,000,000 (1 per 2.5 persons). Television (1983): total number of receivers 1,700,000 (1 per 5.8 persons). Telephones (1982): 2,956,663 (1 per 3.3 persons).

Education and health

Education (1981–82)

	schools	teachers	students	student/ teacher ratio
Primary (age 6–11)	...	33,974	901,209	26.5
Secondary (age 12–17)	...	32,228	671,363	20.8
Voc., teacher tr.	...	12,068	135,077	11.2
Higher	...	7,489	87,476	11.7

College graduates per 100,000 population (students graduating; 1982): 143.4.
Literacy (1982): total population literate 6,949,700 (92.5%); males literate 3,463,300 (96.6%); females literate 3,486,400 (88.5%).
Health (1982): physicians 13,040 (1 per 750 persons); hospital beds 58,438 (1 per 168 persons).
Food (1978–80): daily per capita caloric intake 3,629 (vegetable products 78.4%, animal products 21.6%); 145% of FAO recommended minimum requirement.

Military

Total active duty personnel (1983): 185,000 (army 76.8%; navy 10.5%; air force 12.7%). *Military expenditure as percent of GNP* (1982): 6.9% (world 6.0%); per capita expenditure U.S.$284.

*For reasons of fit, political subdivisions or departments (*nomoi*) are not included in the table. Regions cited are geographic entities except for Ayion Oros (Mt. Athos), which is a self-governing monastic community. †Eleven months only. ‡Finance is included with trade. §Services included with other. ‖ Includes unemployed. ¶First quarter. ♀All scheduled and nonscheduled flights of Olympic Airways only.

Greenland

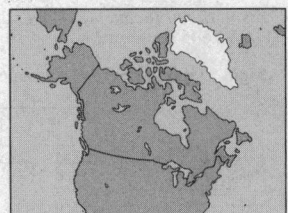

Official name: Greenland (Grønland [Danish]; Kalaallit Nunaat [Greenlandic]).
Political status: integral part of the Danish realm with a local legislative house (Landsting [26]).
Chief of state: Danish Monarch.
Heads of government: High Commissioner (for Denmark); Prime Minister (for Greenland).
Capital: Nuuk (Godthåb).
Official languages: Greenlandic; Danish.
Official religion: Lutheran Church of Greenland (Evangelical Lutheran).
Monetary unit: 1 Danish krone (DKr) = 100 øre; valuation (Oct. 29, 1984) 1 U.S.$ = DKr 11.06; 1 £ = DKr 13.35.

Area and population

Counties	Capitals	area* sq mi	sq km	population 1983 estimate
Avanersuaq (Nordgrønland)	—	41,200	106,700	795
Kitaa (Vestgrønland)	—	46,000	119,100	46,516
Tunu (Østgrønland)	—	44,800	115,900	3,263
TOTAL		131,900	341,700	51,903†

Demography

*Density** (1984): persons per sq mi 0.40, persons per sq km 0.15.
Urban–rural (1984): urban (town) 77.8%; rural (settlement) 22.2%.
Sex distribution (1983): male 54.28%; female 45.72%.
Age breakdown (1982): under 15, 27.4%; 15–29, 33.4%; 30–44, 22.1%; 45–59, 11.5%; 60–74, 4.5%; 75 and over, 1.1%.
Population projection‡: (1990) 55,300; (2000) 60,500.
Doubling time‡: 53 years.
Ethnic composition (by place of birth; 1983): born in Greenland 82.2%; born elsewhere 17.8%.
Religious affiliation (1980): Protestant 97.8%; other 2.2%.
Major towns (1983): Nuuk (Godthåb) 9,848; Sisimiut (Holsteinsborg) 4,298; Ilulissat (Jakobshavn) 3,878; Aasiaat (Egedesminde) 3,169.

Vital statistics

Birth rate per 1,000 population (1982): 20.7 (world avg. 29.0); legitimate 35.5%, illegitimate 64.5%.
Death rate per 1,000 population (1982): 8.2 (world avg. 11.0).
Natural increase rate per 1,000 population (1982): 12.5 (world avg. 18.0).
Total fertility rate (avg. births per childbearing woman; 1982): 2.3.
Marriage rate per 1,000 population (1982): 6.0.
Divorce rate per 1,000 population (1981): 2.6.
Infant mortality rate per 1,000 live births (1976–80): 37.8.
Life expectancy at birth (1976–80): male 57.2 years; female 66.6 years.
Major causes of death per 100,000 population (1982): malignant neoplasms (cancers) 161.4; accidents (not including motor vehicles) 126.4; suicide 93.3.

National economy

Budget (1981). Revenue: DKr1,660,000,000 (block grant and contributions from central Danish government 39.4%, income taxes 16.6%, reimbursements 12.9%, share of import duties 10.3%). Expenditures: DKr1,660,000,000 (education and culture 22.5%, social welfare 19.4%, construction 13.6%, administration 11.3%, welfare institutions 3.0%).
Public debt (external, outstanding): n.a.
Tourism: receipts from visitors, n.a.; expenditures by nationals abroad, n.a.
Production. Agriculture, forestry, hunting, fishing (value in DKr§; 1982): fishery products 557,697,000, of which shrimps and prawn, 299,090,000, cod 155,445,000, salmon 30,482,000; hunting products 10,248,000, of which pelts, seal meat, and blubber 7,981,000, whale meat and blubber 1,780,000; products of sheep farming 8,318,000; reindeer skins and antlers 1,617,000. Mining and quarrying (metric tons; 1981): zinc concentrates 140,000; cryolite 46,000; lead concentrates 38,000. Manufacturing (1981): principally handicrafts and food processing. Housing (1976): gross floor space of all dwellings 11,823 sq m; gross floor space of dwellings owned or rented by persons born in Greenland 8,526 sq m. Energy production (consumption): electricity (kW–hr; 1982) 175,000,000 (175,000,000); coal (metric tons; 1982 miniscule (1,000); crude petroleum, none (n.a.); petroleum products (metric tons; 1982) none (165,000); natural gas, none (n.a.).
Gross national product (at current market prices; 1981): U.S.$550,000,000 (U.S.$10,850 per capita).
Persons economically active (1976): total 21,378 (43.0%); female participation in the labour force 35.9%; unemployed, n.a.

Price and earnings indexes (January 1975 = 100)

	1978	1979	1980	1981	1982	1983	1984
Consumer price index¶	132.3	142.3	160.0	181.3	208.0	233.2	251.9
Monthly earnings index¶	131.0	141.6	158.6	175.9	203.6	228.7	247.1

Household income and expenditure. Average household size (1976) 3.9; income per taxpayer (1980) DKr60,100♀ (U.S.$10,664); sources of income: n.a.; expenditure (1977–78): food 24.6%, fuel and light 7.6%, clothing 7.4%, taxes 7.2%, beverages 6.8%, housing 5.5%, tobacco 5.3%.

Economically active population (1976)

	labour force	% of labour force
Agriculture, fishing, hunting, and sheep breeding	3,222	15.1
Mining, manufacturing	3,205	15.0
Construction	3,112	14.6
Trade	2,153	10.1
Public utilities	293	1.4
Transportation and communication	1,842	8.6
Pub. admin., education	3,233	15.1
Social and health services	2,141	10.0
Other	2,177	10.2
TOTAL	21,378	100.0 ‖

*Land use** (1981): forested 0.1%; meadows and pastures 0.7%; agricultural and under permanent cultivation, none; other (principally ice cap) 99.3%.

Foreign trade

Balance of trade (current prices)

	1977	1978	1979	1980	1981	1982
DK'000,000	−409	−421	−581	−802	−772	875
% of total	26.9%	27.3%	25.1%	27.7%	22.4%	23.4%

Imports (1981): DKr2,097,000,000 (petroleum and petroleum products 19.7%; machinery [other than transport equipment] 18.2%; transport equipment 8.3%; metal products 6.2%; beverages 4.7%; meat and meat products 3.6%). *Major import sources:* Denmark 72%; Norway 7%; United States 6%; United Kingdom 5%.
Exports (1981): DKr1,325,000,000 (shrimps and prawns 38.7%; zinc ores and concentrates 22.2%; fish 20.8%; lead ores and concentrates 7.9%; helicopters 4.0%). *Major export destinations:* Denmark 51%; France 12%; West Germany 7%; United States 7%.

Transport and communications

Transport. Railroads: none. Roads (1982): n.a. Vehicles (1983): passenger cars 1,586; trucks and buses 1,198. Merchant marine (1981): vessels (100 gross tons and over) 35; total deadweight tonnage, n.a. Air transport (1982): passenger-mi 13,939,000, passenger-km 22,433,000; short ton-mi cargoδ 229,000, metric ton-km cargoδ 335,000. Passenger conveyance within Greenland□ (1982): by ship 57,322; by aircraft 84,541.
Communications. Daily newspapers (1983): none. Radios (1982): total number of receivers 13,000 (1 per 4.0 persons). Television (1982): total number of receivers 10,000 (1 per 5.1 persons). Telephone subscribers (1982): 10,721 (1 per 4.8 persons).

Education and health

Education (1982–83)

	schools	teachers	students	student/ teacher ratio
Primary (age 6–15)	97◊	} 1,092	8,045	...
Secondary (age 15–19)	37◊		2,439△	...
Voc., teacher tr.	5◊		1,499	...

College graduates per 100,000 population (1982): n.a. *Literacy* (1979): virtually 100%.
Health (1981): physicians 54 (1 per 937 persons); hospital beds 592 (1 per 86 persons).
Food (1978–80): daily per capita caloric intake, n.a.

Military

Total active duty personnel+ (1980): 320.

---

*Ice-free area; total area of Greenland is 840,000 sq mi (2,175,600 sq km). †Includes 1,329 people not belonging to any of the 18 specific municipalities within the country. ‡Only persons born in Greenland; 1983 estimated population of this group is 42,669. §Based on both internal and external sales. ‖ Detail does not add to total given because of rounding. ¶Based on January only. ♀Average income per taxpayer born in Greenland, DKr42,800; born outside Greenland, DKr145,800. δInternational only; 1981 short ton-mi cargo (domestic only) 109,000, metric ton-km cargo 159,000. □Western Greenland only. ◊1979–80. △Does not include 182 students studying in Denmark. +Foreign troops only. Mostly air force personnel from the United States.

Grenada

Official name: State of Grenada.
Form of government: parliamentary
state with two legislative houses
(Senate [13]; House of Representatives
[15])*.
Chief of state: British Monarch,
represented by a Governor General.
Head of government: Prime Minister.
Capital: St. George's.
Official language: English.
Official religion: none.
Monetary unit: 1 East Caribbean dollar
(EC$) = 100 cents; valuation (Oct. 29,
1984) 1 U.S.$ = EC$2.70;
1 £ = EC$3.26.

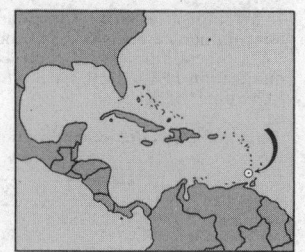

Area and population

Parishes	Capitals	area		population
		sq mi	sq km	1984 estimate
Carriacou†	Hillsborough	13	34	...
St. Andrew	Grenville	35	91	...
St. David	...	18	47	...
St. George's	St. George's	26	67	...
St. John	Gouyave	15	39	...
St. Mark	Victoria	9	23	...
St. Patrick	Sauteurs	17	44	...
TOTAL		133	345	112,000

Source: Official government figures; Britannica estimate.

Demography

Density (1984): persons per sq mi 842.1, persons per sq km 324.6.
Urban–rural (1980): urban 13.4%; rural 86.6%.
Sex distribution (1980): male 48.89%; female 51.11%.
Age breakdown (1980): under 15, 39.4%; 15–29, 31.2%; 30–44, 10.1%; 45–59, 9.2%; 60–74, 7.3%; 75 and over, 2.8%.
Population projection: (1990) n.a.; (2000) n.a.
Doubling time: n.a.
Ethnic composition (1983): black 84%; mixed 12%; East Indian 3%; white 1%.
Religious affiliation (1980): Roman Catholic 64%; Anglican 22%; Methodist 3%; other 11%.
Major cities (1980): St. George's 7,500; Gouyave 2,980.

Vital statistics

Birth rate per 1,000 population (1980): 23.6 (world avg. 30.0); (1979) legitimate, 22.5%; illegitimate, 77.5%.
Death rate per 1,000 population (1980): 6.6 (world avg. 12.0).
Natural increase rate per 1,000 population (1980): 17.0 (world avg. 18.0).
Total fertility rate (avg. births per childbearing woman): n.a.
Marriage rate per 1,000 population (1979): 3.0.
Divorce rate per 1,000 population (1979): 0.2.
Infant mortality rate per 1,000 live births (1979): 15.4.
Life expectancy at birth (1975–80): male 66.5 years; female 72.8 years.
Major causes of death per 10,000 population (1978): diseases of the circulatory system 25.5; malignant neoplasms (cancers) 6.5; diseases of the respiratory system 6.3; infectious and parasitic diseases 5.2; endocrine and metabolic disorders 3.2.

National economy

Budget (1979). Revenue: EC$56,340,000 (import duties 22.8%; export duties 13.2%; income taxes 12.4%; corporate taxes 9.4%; post office 4.2%). Expenditures: EC$57,724,000 (education 18.5%; charges on public debt 15.6%; communications, roads, and labour 15.1%; military and police 13.9%; health and housing 13.3%).
Public debt (external, outstanding; 1979): U.S.$8,040,000.
Tourism (1981): receipts from visitors U.S.$21,000,000; expenditures by nationals abroad, n.a.
Gross national product (at current market prices; 1981): U.S.$100,000,000 (U.S.$890 per capita).

Origin of gross domestic product (current prices)

	1980			
	in value EC$'000,000	% of total value	labour force	% of labour force
Agriculture	51	22.0	...	...
Mining	...	...	...	...
Manufacturing	5	2.2	...	...
Construction	17	7.3	...	...
Trade	32§	13.8§	...	...
Public utilities	3	1.3	...	...
Transportation and communication	12	5.2	...	...
Finance	§	§	...	...
Pub. admin., defense	39	16.8	...	...
Services	...	...	...	...
Other	73 ‖	31.5	...	...
TOTAL	232	100.0¶	38,000♀	100.0

Persons economically active (1980): total 38,000 (35.0%); female participation in the labour force, n.a.; unemployed, n.a.
Price and earnings indexes: n.a.

Production (metric tons except as noted). Agriculture, fishing (1982): fruits except melons 30,000, bananas 20,000, coconuts 18,000, sugarcane 10,000, cacao 2,000, nutmeg 1,500‡, mace 200‡; livestock (number of live animals) 16,000 sheep, 13,000 goats, 10,000 pigs, 9,000 cattle, 260,000 chickens; fish catch 1,800. Mining and quarrying: n.a. Manufacturing (1979): beer 16,700 hectolitres; rum 3,600 hectolitres; cigarettes 113,000 cartons; sugar 480; coconut meal 130; soap 30. Construction: n.a. Energy production (consumption): electricity (kW-hr; 1982) 25,000,000 (25,000,000); coal, none (n.a.); petroleum products (metric tons; 1982) n.a. (20,000); natural gas, none (n.a.).
Household income and expenditure. Average household size (1980) 2.9; average annual income per household: n.a.; source of income: n.a.; expenditure: n.a.
Land use (1981): forested 8.8%; meadows and pastures 8.8%; agricultural and under permanent cultivation 41.2%; other 41.2%.

Foreign trade

Balance of trade (current prices)

	1977	1978	1979	1980	1981	1982	1983
EC$'000,000	−48.5	−50.9	−60.2	−88.6	−95.4	−102.3	−99.1
% of total	38.5%	35.8%	34.2%	48.5%	48.2%	50.5%	49.2%

Imports (1982): EC$152,429,220 (food 27.5%; manufactured goods 26.4%; machinery and transport equipment 14.8%; mineral fuels, lubricants, and related materials 13.3%; chemicals 10.0%; beverages and tobacco 2.6%). *Major import sources:* United States 20.2%; Trinidad and Tobago 19.9%; United Kingdom 15.1%; Canada 5.4%; Cuba 4.4%; Barbados 3.6%.
Exports (1982): EC$50,086,800ō (food 84.0%, of which cocoa 24.9%, bananas 17.8%, nutmeg 16.2%, mace 5.0%; clothing 13.3%; furniture 1.2%). *Major export destinations:* United Kingdom 32.2%; Trinidad and Tobago 26.6%; Canada 2.4%; United States 2.4%.

Transport and communications

Transport. Railroads: none. Roads (1981): total length 534 mi, 860 km (paved 60%). Vehicles (1981): passenger cars 4,784; trucks and buses 981. Merchant marine (1983): vessels (100 gross tons and over) 3; total deadweight tonnage 577. Air transport (1980): aircraft arrivals, commercial 2,890, private 602; airports (1984) with scheduled flights 2.
Communications. Daily newspaper: none□. Radios (1983): total number of receivers 50,000 (1 per 2.2 persons). Television: total number of receivers, n.a. Telephones (1983): 5,200 (1 per 21.3 persons).

Education and health

Education (1980–81)

	schools	teachers	students	student/teacher ratio
Primary (age 5–11)	77◇	704	23,065	32.8
Secondary (age 12–18)	23◇	284	6,120	21.5
Voc., teacher tr.	4◇	35◇	484◇	13.8
Higher	1◇	43△	704△	16.4

College graduates per 10,000 population (students graduating; 1979): 14.
Literacy (1981): total population literate 49,000♀ (85.0%).
Health (1980): physicians 39 (1 per 2,800 persons); hospital beds 325 (1 per 336 persons).
Food (1978–80): daily per capita caloric intake 2,103 (vegetable products 81.9%, animal products 18.1%); 87% of FAO recommended minimum requirement.

Military

Total active duty personnel (1983): 2,180. *Military expenditure as percent of GNP* (1982): 4.2% (world 6.0%); per capita expenditure U.S.$60.

*The advisory council, a nine-member interim executive body, has been in power since November 15, 1983; elections were to be held in late 1984. †Includes Carriacou and Petit Martinique islands. ‡1980. §Finance is included with trade. ‖ Includes net indirect taxes. ¶Detail does not add to total given because of rounding. ♀Estimated. ōIncludes EC$2,338,700 in re-exports. □Two weeklies are published from St. George's. ◇1979–80. △1981–82.

Guadeloupe

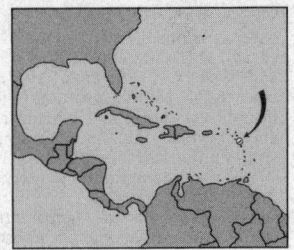

Official name: Département de la Guadeloupe (Department of Guadeloupe).
Political status: overseas department (France), with one legislative house (General Council [36]), three representatives in the French National Assembly, and two senators in the French Senate.
Chief of state: President of France.
Head of government: Commissioner.
Capital: Basse-Terre.
Official language: French.
Official religion: none.
Monetary unit: 1 Franc (F) = 100 centimes; valuation (Oct. 29, 1984) 1 U.S.$ = F9.41; 1 £ = F11.36.

Area and population

Arrondissements	Capitals	area sq mi	area sq km	population 1982 census*
Basse-Terre†	Basse-Terre	369	957	138,242
Pointe-à-Pitre‡	Pointe-à-Pitre	288	746	179,027
Saint-Martin-Saint Barthélemy	Marigot	30	77	11,131
TOTAL		687	1,780	328,400

Source: Official government figures.

Demography

Density (1984): persons per sq mi 479.5, persons per sq km 185.1.
Urban–rural (1985): urban 45.7%; rural 54.3%.
Sex distribution (1982): male 49.10%; female 50.90%.
Age breakdown (1985): under 15, 27.8%; 15–29, 32.6%; 30–44, 16.2%; 45–59, 12.9%; 60–74, 8.4%; 75 and over, 2.1%.
Population projection: (1990) 332,300; (2000) 337,300.
Growth rate: During the intercensal period 1974–82, the growth rate was 0.1%; since the mid-1980s, however,the population has been decreasing.
Ethnic composition (1980): Creole (mulatto) 77.0%; black 10.0%; Guadeloupe mestizo (French–Amerindian) 10.0%; white 2.0%; East Indian and Syrian 1.0%.
Religious affiliation (1980–82): Roman Catholic 90.6%; Protestant 5.8%; Hindu–Catholic spiritist 0.9%; Muslim 0.9%; Baha'í 0.2%; other 1.6%.
Major cities (1982*): Les Abymes 56,165; Pointe- à-Pitre 25,310; Basse-Terre 13,656.

Vital statistics

Birth rate per 1,000 population (1982): 20.2 (world avg. 29); (1980) legitimate 47.9%, illegitimate 52.1%.
Death rate per 1,000 population (1982): 6.5 (world avg. 11).
Natural increase rate per 1,000 population (1982): 13.7 (world avg. 18).
Total fertility rate (avg. births per childbearing woman; 1980–85): 2.4.
Marriage rate per 1,000 population (1982): 4.8.
Divorce rate per 1,000 population (1982): 1.3.
Infant mortality rate per 1,000 live births (1982): 15.5.
Life expectancy at birth (1980–85): male 67.8 years; female 73.0 years.
Major causes of death per 100,000 population (1977–80): cardiovascular disease 220.2; neoplasms (cancers), including malignant tumours 74.5; diseases of the digestive and intestinal systems 46.7.

National economy

Budget (1982). Revenue: F1,302,000,000 (receipts from public services 43.2%, taxes 23.1%, carried over and supplementary receipts 22.0%, new loans 6.7%). Expenditures: F1,320,000 (health and social services 41.2%, carried over and supplementary expenses 22.0%, capital investments and works 18.7%, other services 8.9%, socioeconomic assistance 5.4%).
Public debt (external, outstanding; 1982): U.S. $68,000,000.
Tourism (1982): receipts from visitors U.S.$10,112,000; expenditures by nationals abroad, n.a.
Production (metric tons except as noted). Agriculture, forestry, fishing (1982): sugarcane 613,252§, bananas 101,935§, sweet potatoes 5,000, eggplants 4,000, coconuts 3,000, cucumbers 3,000, cabbage 3,000, cassava 2,000, flowers and commercial plants 15, milk 13,000; livestock (number of live animals) 93,000 cattle, 51,000 pigs, 36,000 goats, 1,000,000 chickens; roundwood 17,000 cu m; fish catch 8,800. Mining and quarrying (1980): pumice, sand, and gravel. Manufacturing (1982): cement 222,200, raw sugar 56,504§, molasses 35,280, flour 33,070, cardboard cartons 7,000, rum 65,453 hectolitres§, sawnwood 1,000 cu m; other important products include fruit juices and processed foods, chemicals and pharmaceuticals, furniture and bedding, metal manufactured goods, glass and mirrors, rubber and plastic goods, and clothing and shoes. Construction (value in F; 1982): residential 54,000,000 (433 buildings); commercial, industrial, and other 39,500,000 (344 buildings). Energy production (consumption): electricity (kW-hr; 1983) 442,300,000 (442,300,000);petroleum products (metric tons; 1982) 206,000 (206,000); fuelwood (cubic metres; 1982) 15,000 (15,000).
Gross national product (at current market prices; 1981): U.S.$1,430,000,000 (U.S.$4,370 per capita).
Household income and expenditure. Average household size (1980) 3.7; income per household F72,898 (U.S.$16,142); source of income: salaries

76.8%, industrial and commercial benefits 9.3%, pensions and rents 4.0%, noncommercial benefits 3.9%, income from stocks and bonds 2.6%, other 3.4%; expenditure (1972): food 44.5%, housing 17.2%, transport and communication 11.8%, clothing and footwear 8.9%, health care 6.7%, recreation 5.0%, other 5.9%

Origin of gross domestic product (current prices)

	1979 in value F '000	1979 % of total value	1982 labour force	1982 % of labour force
Agriculture	385,606	7.4	12,997	10.7
Manufacturing, public utilities	348,719	6.7	7,346	6.0
Construction, quarrying	237,276	4.5	9,997	8.2
Trade	777,149	14.9	10,062	8.3
Transportation and communication	206,955	4.0	‖	‖
Finance	286,774	5.5	1,408	1.2
Public services, admin., defense	1,476,692	28.3	26,105	21.4
Services	1,307,226	25.1	13,162	10.8
Other, including unemployed	188,188	3.6	40,749	33.4
TOTAL	5,214,585	100.0	121,826	100.0

Persons economically active (1982): total 121,826 (37.1%); female 31,567 (25.9%); unemployed 29,427 (24.1%).

Price and earnings indexes (1978 = 100)

	1979	1980	1981	1982	1983	1984
Consumer price index	112.5	129.3	147.4	160.5	174.0	...
Monthly earnings index	114.3	130.9	157.1	183.1	197.6	...

Land use (1982): forested 39.8%; meadows and pastures 12.5%; agricultural and under permanent cultivation 21.6%; other 26.1%.

Foreign trade

Balance of trade (current prices)

	1978	1979	1980	1981	1982	1983
F'000,000	−1,411	−2,058	−2,628	−3,025	−3,569	−4,412
% of total	58.5%	68.1%	85.9%	74.8%	76.5%	77.9%

Imports (1983): F5,039,000,000 (consumer goods 15.8%, food 15.6%, petroleum products 14.7%, construction materials 7.6%, tourist vehicles 6.6%, textiles and clothing 6.3%, other vehicles 2.7%). *Major import sources* (1982): France 62.4%; Martinique 9.2%; United States 5.5%; Italy 3.0%; Japan 2.7%; West Germany 2.6%; Netherlands Antilles 1.9%.
Exports (1983): F627,000,000 (bananas 51.7%, sugar 14.7%, rum 7.8%). *Major export destinations* (1982): France 67.8%; Martinique 18.6%; China 3.0%; Portugal 2.8%; French Guiana 1.9%; Cuba 1.6%; Dominica 0.8%.

Transport and communications

Transport. Railroads (1982): only private, narrow-gauge railways serving sugar plantations. Roads (1982): total length 1,235 mi, 1,988 km (paved 85%). Vehicles (1981): passenger cars 87,785; trucks and buses 33,350. Merchant marine (1983): vessels (100 gross tons and over) n.a.; total deadweight tonnage, n.a. Air transport (1983): passenger arrivals 528,768¶, passenger departures 525,203¶; short tons cargo handled 11,536¶, metric tons cargo handled 11,536¶; airports (1984) with scheduled flights 7.
Communications. Daily newspaper (1983): total number 1; total circulation 20,000; circulation per 1,000 population 60.5. Radios (1983): total number of receivers 25,000 (1 per 13 persons). Television (1983): total number of receivers 5,000 (1 per 66 persons). Telephones (1982): 74,072 (1 per 4.4 persons).

Education and health

Education (1981–82)

	schools	teachers	students	student/ teacher ratio
Primary (age 6–12)	284	2,744♀	55,751	...
Secondary (age 11–17)	59	2,602♂	49,606	...
Voc., teacher tr.	22♂	381□	10,059♀	...
Higher	1	80	3,700	46.3

College graduates per 100,000 population: n.a. *Literacy* (1980): total population literate 217,900 (91.5%); males literate 106,500 (92.7%); females literate 111,400 (90.3%).
Health: physicians (1981) 370 (1 per 885 persons); hospital beds (1979) 4,261 (1 per 77 persons).
Food (1978–80): daily per capita caloric intake 2,732 (vegetable products 73.4%, animal products 26.6%); 113% of FAO recommended minimum requirement.

Military◊

*Preliminary. †Comprising Basse-Terre 364 sq mi (943 sq km) and Îles des Saints 5 sq mi (14 sq km). ‡Comprising Grand-Terre 219 sq mi (566 sq km), Marie-Galante 58 sq mi (150 sq km), La Désirade 10 sq mi (27 sq km), and the uninhabited Îles de la Petite-Terre and Tintamarre 1 sq mi (3 sq km). §1983. ‖ Transportation and communication is included with other. ¶Pointe-à-Pitre and Grand Bourg (Marie-Galante) airports only. ♀1979–80. ♂1978–79. □1975–76. ◊Defense is the responsibility of France; no domestic force is maintained.

Guam

Official name: Guam.
Political Status: self-governing organized unincorporated territory of the United States with one legislative house (21).
Chief of state: President of the United States.
Head of government: Governor.
Capital: Agana.
Official language: English.
Official religion: none.
Monetary unit: 1 United States dollar (U.S.$) = 100 cents; valuation (Oct. 29, 1984) 1 U.S.$ = £0.83.

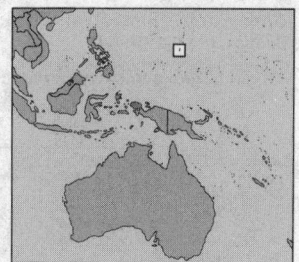

Area and population		area*		population†
Election Districts		sq mi	sq km	1980 census
Agana		1	3	896
Agana Heights		1	3	3,284
Agat		10	26	3,999
Asan		6	16	2,034
Barrigada		9	23	7,756
Chalan Pago-Ordot		6	16	3,120
Dededo		30	78	23,644
Inarajan		19	49	2,059
Mangilao		10	26	6,840
Merizo		6	16	1,663
Mongmong-Toto-Maite		2	5	5,245
Piti		7	18	2,866
Santa Rita		17	44	9,183
Sinajana		1	3	2,485
Talofofo		17	44	2,006
Tamuning		6	16	13,580
Umatac		6	16	732
Yigo		35	91	10,359
Yona		20	52	4,228
TOTAL		209	541‡	105,979

Source: Official government figures.

Demography

Density (1984): persons per sq mi 522, persons per sq km 201.
Urban–rural (1980): urban 39.5%; rural 60.5%.
Sex distribution (1980): male 52.20%; female 47.80%.
Age breakdown (1980): under 15, 34.9%; 15–29, 30.6%; 30–44, 19.4%; 45–59, 10.5%; 60–74, 3.9%; 75 and over, 0.7%.
Population projection: (1990) 118,700; (2000) 133,200.
Doubling time: 33 years.
Ethnic composition (1978): Chamorro 47.8%; white 22.0%§; Filipino 20.0%; Korean 2.9%; Micronesian 2.7%; other 4.6%.
Religious affiliation (1980): Roman Catholic 79.5%; Protestant 15.7%; other 4.8%.
Major populated places (1980): Tamuning 8,862; Apra Harbor 5,633; Andersen Air Force Base 4,892; Mangilao 4,029.

Vital statistics

Birth rate per 1,000 population (1982): 25.2 (world avg. 29.0); (1980) legitimate 80.3%, illegitimate 19.7%.
Death rate per 1,000 population (1982): 3.8 (world avg. 11.0).
Natural increase rate per 1,000 population (1982): 21.4 (world avg. 18.0).
Total fertility rate (avg. births per childbearing woman): n.a.
Marriage rate per 1,000 population (based on groom's place of residence, 1979): residents of Guam only 16.7; including military personnel and Japanese tourists, 33.1.
Divorce rate per 1,000 population (1979): 3.9.
Infant mortality rate per 1,000 live births (1980): 16.3.
Life expectancy at birth (1976–78): male 69.7 years; female 78.7 years.
Major causes of death per 100,000 population (1979): heart disease 97.1; accidents 49.0; malignant neoplasms (cancers) 44.1; cerebrovascular diseases 25.5.

National economy

Budget (1980). Revenue: U.S.$124,332,733 (local income taxes 49.1%, gross business receipts taxes 25.3%, revenues from United States agencies ‖ 14.3%, property taxes 1.8%). Expenditures: U.S.$141,752,638 (public education 39.3%, general government operations 26.8%, continuing projects 11.6%, law and public safety 10.2%).
Public debt (external, outstanding): n.a.
Tourism (1980): receipts from visitors U.S.$117,900,000; expenditures by nationals abroad, n.a.
Production (total value in U.S.$). Agriculture, forestry, fishing (1980): eggs 2,086,522, fruits and vegetables 1,725,891, pork 868,064, poultry 63,600, beef 49,400; fish catch 177,566 kilograms. Mining and quarrying (1983): sand and gravel. Manufacturing (value of gross business receipts in U.S.$; 1980): petroleum refining and related products 322,083,000; food processing 11,742,000; printing and publishing 6,039,000; industrial and medical goods and materials 412,000. Construction (value of gross business receipts in U.S.$; 1980): private sector 80,609,000; military 43,331,000. Energy production (consumption): electricity (kW-hr; 1982) 1,150,000,000 (1,150,-000,000); coal, none (n.a.); crude petroleum (barrels; 1982) none (11,700,-

000); petroleum products (metric tons; 1982) 1,407,000 (704,000); natural gas, none (n.a.).
Gross national product (at current market prices; 1981): U.S.$750,000,000 (U.S.$6,840 per capita).

Origin of gross business income (current prices)

	1980		1981	
	in value U.S.$'000,000	% of total value	salaried employees¶	% of salaried employees
Agriculture	3.7	0.3	100	0.4
Manufacturing	340.3	30.6	1,100	4.8
Construction	80.6	7.2	2,100	9.1
Trade♀	445.2	40.0	6,400	27.8
Transportation and communication	26.4	2.4	2,700	11.7
Finance	75.9	6.8	1,200	5.2
Pub. admin., defense	...	...	...	...
Services	141.6	12.7	9,400	40.9
TOTAL	1,113.8‡	100.0	23,000	100.0‡

Persons economically active (1983): total 33,860 (60.1%); female participation in the labour force 13,010 (38.4%); unemployed (1982) 3,500.

Price and earnings indexes (1978 = 100)

	1977	1978	1979	1980	1981	1982
Consumer price index	88.6	100.0	112.1	134.0	161.4	169.6
Hourly earnings index	92.7	100.0	122.1	132.2	...	...

Household income and expenditure. Average household size (1980) 4.1; average annual income per household (1978) U.S.$19,309; source of income: n.a.; expenditure (1978): housing 28.6%, food 24.1%, transportation 18.0%, clothing 10.6%, health and recreation 9.8%.
Land use (1981): forested 18.2%; meadows and pastures 14.6%; agricultural and under permanent cultivation 21.8%; other 45.4%.

Foreign trade

Balance of trade (current prices)

	1978	1979	1980
U.S.$'000	−236,227	−403,144	−483,141
% of total	76.7%	82.5%	79.8%

Imports (1979): U.S.$445,822,478 (crude petroleum 34.9%; food and live animals 12.7%; miscellaneous manufactured goods 8.1%; transportation equipment and parts 6.3%; machinery 5.5%; metal and metal manufactured goods 4.7%; beverages and tobacco 4.1%). *Major import sources:* Saudi Arabia 49.2%; United States 32.4%; Japan 7.0%; Hong Kong 2.7%.
Exports (1979): U.S.$44,408,560 (refined petroleum products 27.7%; transshipments 26.3%; miscellaneous manufactured products 18.2%; crude petroleum and natural gas 3.9%; clothing and footwear 3.4%; watches, clocks, and parts 2.7%; fish and fish products 2.1%). *Major export destinations:* Trust Territory of the Pacific 47.3%; United States 25.1%; Taiwan 15.4%.

Transport and communications

Transport. Railroads: none. Roads (1983): total length 419 mi, 674 km (paved 100%). Vehicles♂ (1980): passenger cars 39,002; trucks and buses 14,653. Merchant marine (1980): vessels (100 gross tons and over) n.a.; surface cargo loaded, unloaded, or transshipped (1980): 623,900 metric tons. Air transport (1980): passenger arrivals 291,133; passenger departures, n.a.; cargo loaded, 3,645 metric tons; cargo unloaded, 5,856 metric tons; airports (1984) with scheduled flights 1.
Communications. Daily newspaper (1982): total number 1; total circulation 18,000; circulation per 1,000 population 162.5. Radios (1983): total number of receivers 300,000 (1 per 0.4 person). Televisions (1983): total number of receivers 78,000 (1 per 1.5 persons). Telephones (1982): 14,379 (1 per 7.7 persons).

Education and health

Education (1981–82)

	schools	teachers	students	student/teacher ratio
Primary (age 5–12)	37	772	17,784	23.0
Secondary (age 13–18)	19	512	11,997	23.4
Voc., teacher tr.	1	75	1,186	15.8
Higher	2□	162	3,499	21.6

College graduates per 100,000 population (students graduating; 1980–81): 195. *Literacy:* n.a.
Health: physicians (1980) 70 (1 per 1,514 persons); hospital beds (1979) 361 (1 per 287 persons).
Food: daily per capita caloric intake, n.a.

Military

Total active duty U.S. personnel (1982): 10,800 (navy 58.4%; air force 37.0%; other 4.6%).

---

*The entire area of Guam is considered equivalent to a U.S. county for census purposes. †Includes 22,800 active duty personnel, Department of Defense employees, and dependents. ‡Detail does not add to total given because of rounding. §Primarily military. ‖ Consists largely of federal income tax. ¶Excluding 10,200 military personnel who do not contribute to gross business income. ♀Most important industry in the private sector; provided work for about 30% of the 16,700 privately employed in 1980. ♂Excluding military vehicles. □1982–83.

Guatemala

Official name: República de Guatemala (Republic of Guatemala).
Form of government: military regime.
Head of state and government:
   General pending election of a civilian president scheduled for July 1985.
Capital: Guatemala City.
Official language: Spanish.
Official religion: none.
Monetary unit: 1 Guatemalan quetzal (Q) = 100 centavos; valuation (Oct. 29, 1984) 1 U.S.$ = Q1.00*; 1 £ = Q1.21.

Area and population

Departments	Capitals	area sq mi	area sq km	population 1984 estimate
Alta Verapaz	Cobán	3,354	8,686	436,700
Baja Verapaz	Salamá	1,206	3,124	157,000
Chimaltenango	Chimaltenango	764	1,979	276,200
Chiquimula	Chiquimula	917	2,376	229,300
El Progreso	Progreso	742	1,922	98,500
Escuintla	Escuintla	1,693	4,384	394,000
Guatemala	Guatemala City	821	2,126	1,510,500
Huehuetenango	Huehuetenango	2,857	7,400	580,900
Izabal	Puerto Barrios	3,490	9,038	254,400
Jalapa	Jalapa	797	2,063	174,400
Jutiapa	Jutiapa	1,243	3,219	353,000
Petén	Ciudad Flores	13,843	35,854	186,300
Quezaltenango	Quezaltenango	753	1,951	461,400
Quiché	Santa Cruz	3,235	8,378	443,400
Retalhuleu	Retalhuleu	717	1,856	187,600
Sacatepéquez	Antigua Guatemala	180	465	141,400
San Marcos	San Marcos	1,464	3,791	590,100
Santa Rosa	Cuilapa	1,141	2,955	250,400
Sololá	Sololá	410	1,061	186,500
Suchitepéquez	Mazatenango	969	2,510	297,300
Totonicapán	Totonicapán	410	1,061	239,500
Zacapa	Zacapa	1,039	2,690	151,500
TOTAL		42,042	108,889	7,599,300†

Source: Official government figures.

Demography

Density (1984)†: persons per sq mi 180.8, persons per sq km 69.8.
Urban–rural (1981)‡: urban 34.3%; rural 65.7%.
Sex distribution (1981)‡: male 49.81%; female 50.19%.
Age breakdown (1981)‡: under 15, 44.9%; 15–29, 26.8%; 30–44, 14.8%; 45–59, 8.5%; 60–74, 3.9%; 75 and over, 1.1%.
Population projection: (1990) 8,708,000; (2000) 12,739,000.
Doubling time: 30 years.
Ethnic composition (1983): Maya 55%; mestizo 42%; white or black 3%.
Religious affiliation (1983): Roman Catholic (including nominal) *c.* 80%; Protestant *c.* 20%.
Major cities (1981)‡: Guatemala City 754,200; Quezaltenango 62,700; Escuintla 36,900; Izabal 24,200.

Vital statistics

Birth rate per 1,000 population (1983): 42.7 (world avg. 29.0).
Death rate per 1,000 population (1983): 10.5 (world avg. 11.0).
Natural increase rate per 1,000 population (1983): 32.2 (world avg. 18.0).
Total fertility rate (avg. births per childbearing woman; 1981): 5.3.
Marriage rate per 1,000 population (1980): 4.1.
Divorce rate per 1,000 population (1979): 0.2.
Infant mortality rate per 1,000 live births (1983): 64.1.
Life expectancy at birth (1981): male 57.3 years; female 60.5 years.
Major causes of death per 100,000 population (1980): typhoid and other intestinal infectious diseases 194.2; pneumonia and other respiratory diseases 151.3; birth trauma and other conditions originating in the perinatal period 125.5; homicide and injury purposely inflicted by other persons 63.0; diseases of the circulatory system 49.8.

National economy

Budget (1982). Revenue: Q1,033,100,000 (sales tax 43.0%; taxes on international trade transactions 29.5%, of which import duties 14.4%; income tax 13.8%). Expenditures: Q1,202,400,000 (social services 36.8%; general services 35.1%; economic services 19.9%).
Public debt (external, outstanding; 1983): U.S.$1,187,000,000.
Tourism: receipts from visitors U.S.$12,028,000; expenditures by nationals abroad U.S.$100,292,800.
Production (metric tons except as noted). Agriculture, forestry, fishing (1983): sugarcane 6,624,000, corn (maize) 1,046,000, bananas 675,000, coffee 154,000, tomatoes 92,000, dry beans 89,000, cottonseed 87,000, sorghum 81,000; livestock (number of live animals; 1982) 1,880,000 cattle, 835,000 pigs, 500,000 sheep, 14,500,000 chickens; roundwood 6,652,000 cu m§; fish catch 4,284§. Mining and quarrying (1981): antimony ore (metal content) 51,000; nickel ore 6,900 ‖. Manufacturing (1981): raw sugar 474,000; cheese 15,000; butter 5,000; beer 700,000 hectolitres¶; cigarettes 2,699,000,000 units ‖; cement 576,000 ‖. Construction (1980)♀: residential 128,500 sq m; nonresidential 99,700 sq m. Energy production (consumption): electricity (kW-hr; 1982) 1,640,000,000 (1,640,000,000); coal, none (n.a.); crude petroleum (barrels; 1982) 3,592,000 (7,257,000); petroleum products (metric tons; 1982) 755,000 (1,050,000); natural gas, none (n.a.).

Gross national product (at current market prices; 1982): U.S.$8,606,000,000 (U.S.$1,145 per capita).

Origin of gross domestic product (current prices of 1982)

	1982 in value Q'000	1982 % of total value	1981 labour force	1981 % of labour force
Agriculture	2,406,800	25.4	908,513	53.6
Mining	30,800	0.3	2,348	0.1
Manufacturing	1,493,900	15.7	177,494	10.5
Construction	323,600	3.4	86,191	5.1
Trade	2,493,600	26.3	147,120	8.7
Public utilities	163,200	1.7	7,714	0.5
Transportation and communication	626,700	6.6	43,255	2.5
Finance	801,800	8.5	21,159	1.2
Pub. admin., defense	555,600	5.9	¶	¶
Services	δ	δ	214,980	12.7
Other	591,500δ	6.2δ	87,137	5.1
TOTAL	9,487,500	100.0	1,695,911	100.0

Persons economically active (1981): total 1,695,911 (28.1%); female participation in the labour force 247,039 (14.6%); unemployed, n.a.

Price and earnings indexes (1980 = 100)

	1977	1978	1979	1980	1981	1982	1983
Consumer price index	75.0	81.0	90.3	100.0	111.4	111.6	115.0
Annual earnings index □	74.2	78.7	90.2	100.0	131.2	139.3	135.3

Household income and expenditure. Average household size (1980) 4.5; income per household: n.a.; source of income: n.a.; expenditure◊ (1975): food 40%, housing 19%, clothing and footwear 11%.
Land use (1981): forested 41.1%; meadows and pastures 8.0%; agricultural and under permanent cultivation 19.9%; other 31.0%.

Foreign trade

Balance of trade (current prices)

	1977	1978	1979	1980	1981	1982
Q'000,000	+73.2	−191.4	−180.3	+47.2	−241.0	−268.2
% of total	3.3%	8.1%	6.9%	1.6%	8.5%	10.7%

Imports (1982): Q1,387,963,000 (mineral fuels and lubricants 21.8%; machinery and transport equipment 21.6%; chemical products 19.4%; manufactured goods 18.7%). *Major import sources:* United States 30.7%; El Salvador 8.5%; Mexico 7.4%; Netherlands Antilles 7.1%; Venezuela 5.9%; West Germany 5.6%.
Exports (1982): Q1,119,773,000 (nonspecified 36.5%; coffee 32.0%; cotton 7.0%; bananas 5.6%; petroleum 4.1%; beans and legumes 3.3%; cardamom 2.7%). *Major export destinations:* United States 27.1%; El Salvador 17.0%; West Germany 6.9%; Japan 5.0%; Costa Rica 4.6%.

Transport and communications

Transport. Railroads (1983): route length 467 mi, 751 km. Roads (1980): total length 16,422 mi, 26,429 km (paved 11%). Vehicles (1980): passenger cars 166,900; trucks and buses 81,500. Merchant marine (1983): vessels (100 gross tons and over) 9; total deadweight tonnage 27,186. Air transport△ (1983): passenger-mi 97,225,000, passenger-km 156,469,000; short ton-mi cargo 4,306,000, metric ton-km cargo 6,287,000; airports (1984) with scheduled flights 2.
Communications. Daily newspapers (1983): total number 8; total circulation 224,500; circulation per 1,000 population 30. Radios (1983): total number of receivers 500,000 (1 per 15 persons). Television (1983): total number of receivers 202,000 (1 per 38 persons). Telephones (1982): 97,670 (1 per 77 persons).

Education and health

Education (1980)

	schools	teachers	students	student/ teacher ratio
Primary (age 7–12)	6,959	23,770	803,404	33.8
Secondary (age 13–18)+	...	9,613	156,612	16.3
Voc., teacher tr.+	...	...	...	...
Higher§	5	4,490	51,556	11.4

College graduates per 100,000 population (students graduating; 1979): 19.
Literacy (1980): total population literate 2,076,500 (51.1%); males literate 1,203,000 (58.6%); females literate 873,500 (43.5%); Maya literate 450,000 (20.0%).
Health: physicians (early 1980s) 1,250 (1 per 5,700 persons); hospital beds (1973) 12,115 (1 per 426 persons).
Food (1978–80): daily per capita caloric intake 2,064 (vegetable products 90.6%, animal products 9.4%); 94% of FAO recommended minimum.

Military

Total active duty personnel (1982): 21,560 (army 92.8%; navy 4.4%; air force 2.8%). *Military expenditure as percent of GNP* (1982): 1.7% (world 6.0%); per capita expenditure U.S.$20.

*The value of the quetzal is fixed at par with that of the U.S.$. †Based on estimated de facto population. ‡Based on final de jure census figure of 6,054,227. §1982. ‖ 1980. ¶1979. ♀Applies only to authorized private construction in Guatemala City. δOther includes Services. □Includes real annual wages and salaries paid to workers affiliated with the Guatemalan Institute of Social Security. ◊Urban families. △International scheduled traffic of Aviateca airlines. +Secondary includes vocational and teacher training.

Guinea

Official name: République de Guinée (Republic of Guinea).
Form of government: interim military regime ruling through the Military Committee for National Rectification (CMRN [25]) with an appointed government (41).
Head of state and government: President.
Capital: Conakry.
Official language: French.
Official religion: none.
Monetary unit: 1 Guinean syli (GS) = 100 cauris; valuation (Oct. 29, 1984) 1 U.S.$ = GS24.80; 1 £ = GS29.93.

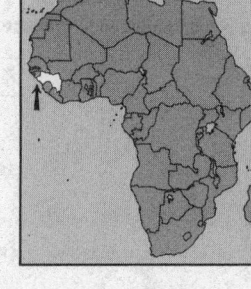

Area and population

Regions	Capitals	area* sq mi	area* sq km	population 1977 census
Beyla	Beyla	6,736	17,446	140,000
Boffa	Boffa	2,317	6,001	121,000
Boké	Boké	4,266	11,049	149,000
Conakry	Conakry	119	308	581,000
Coyah (Dubréka)	Coyah	2,191	5,675	122,000
Dabola	Dabola	3,474	8,998	75,000
Dalaba	Dalaba	2,220	5,750	110,000
Dinguiraye	Dinguiraye	2,817	7,296	109,000
Faranah	Faranah	5,057	13,098	135,000
Forécariah	Forécariah	1,785	4,623	132,000
Fria	Fria	...	...	45,000
Gaoual	Gaoual	4,439	11,497	98,000
Guéckédou	Guéckédou	1,605	4,157	173,000
Kankan	Kankan	10,610	27,480	175,000
Kérouané	Kérouané	...	...	60,000
Kindia	Kindia	3,408	8,827	186,000
Kissidougou	Kissidougou	3,424	8,868	160,000
Koubia	Koubia	...	...	70,000
Koundara	Koundara	2,000	5,180	65,000
Kouroussa	Kouroussa	6,332	16,400	102,000
Labé	Labé	2,980	7,718	170,000
Lélouma	Lélouma	...	...	105,000
Lola	Lola	...	...	100,000
Macenta	Macenta	3,362	8,708	142,000
Mali	Mali	3,419	8,855	145,000
Mamou	Mamou	2,377	6,156	133,000
Mandiana	Mandiana	...	...	90,000
Nzérékoré	Nzérékoré	3,931	10,181	187,000
Pita	Pita	1,583	4,100	175,000
Siguiri	Siguiri	9,023	23,369	140,000
Télimélé	Télimélé	3,109	8,052	170,000
Tougué	Tougué	2,316	5,998	90,000
Yomou	Yomou	...	...	72,000
TOTAL		94,900	245,790	4,527,000

Source: Official government figures.

Demography

Density (1984): persons per sq mi 58.8, persons per sq km 22.7.
Urban–rural (1980): urban 19.1%; rural 80.9%.
Sex distribution (1980): male 49.52%; female 50.48%.
Age breakdown (1980): under 15, 43.8%; 15–29, 25.5%; 30–44, 16.3%; 45–59, 9.5%; 60–74, 4.2%; 75 and over 0.7%.
Population projection: (1990) 6,072,000; (2000) 7,623,000.
Doubling time: 30 years.
Ethnic composition (1978): Mande 50.2%, of which Malinke 21.0%, Susu 11.4%; Fulani 39.9%; Kissi 5.5%; other 4.4%.
Religious affiliation (1980 est.): Muslim 69.0%; tribal religionist 29.5%; Roman Catholic 1.1%; other 0.4%.
Major cities (1983 est.): Conakry 656,000; Kankan 278,000; Labé 273,000; Nzérékoré 250,000.

Vital statistics

Birthrate per 1,000 population (1980–85): 45.7 (world avg. 27.5).
Death rate per 1,000 population (1980–85): 18.8 (world avg. 10.6).
Natural increase rate per 1,000 population (1980–85): 26.9 (world avg. 16.9).
Total fertility rate (avg. births per childbearing woman; 1980–85): 6.2.
Marriage rate per 1,000 population: n.a.
Divorce rate per 1,000 population: n.a.
Infant mortality rate per 1,000 live births (1975–80): 171.5.
Life expectancy at birth (1980–85): male 44.4 years; female 47.6 years.
Major causes of death: n.a.; however, major diseases are malaria, venereal disease, intestinal infections, influenza, measles, and schistosomiasis.

National economy

Budget (1979). Revenue: GS11,250,000,000 (no breakdown available). Expenditures: GS11,250,000,000 (current budget 60.4%; capital budget 39.6%).
Public debt (external, outstanding; 1984): U.S.$1,500,000,000.
Tourism: receipts from visitors n.a.; expenditures by nationals abroad n.a.
Production (metric tons except as noted). Agriculture, forestry, fishing (1982): roots and tubers 803,000, of which cassava 620,000, sweet potatoes 75,000; cereals 547,000, of which rice 400,000, corn (maize) 67,000; fruits 548,000, of which plantains 230,000, bananas 110,000, pineapples 18,000; vegetables and melons 385,000, sugarcane 220,000, peanuts (groundnuts) 85,000, palm kernels 35,000, pulses 32,000, coffee 15,000; milk 43,000, eggs 8,925; livestock (number of live animals) 1,850,000 cattle, 445,000 sheep,

425,000 goats, 42,000 pigs, 8,500,000 chickens; roundwood 3,634,000 cu m; fish catch 18,453. Mining and quarrying (1982): bauxite† 10,446,000; alumina 578,000; industrial diamonds 23,000 carats; gem diamonds 10,000 carats. Manufacturing (1982): palm oil 45,000; raw sugar 20,000; plywood 2,000 cu m. Construction: n.a. Energy production (consumption): electricity (kW-hr; 1982) 498,000,000 (498,000,000); petroleum products (metric tons; 1982) none (287,000).
Gross national product (at current market prices; 1981): U.S.$1,538,000,000 (U.S.$300 per capita).

Origin of gross domestic product (current prices)

	1980 in value GS'000,000	% of total value	labour force	% of labour force
Agriculture	11,600	36.6	1,908,960	82.0
Mining and related industry‡	7,900	24.9	256,080§	11.0§
Manufacturing	1,200	3.8	§	§
Construction	1,200	3.8	§	§
Public utilities	300	1.0	§	§
Services, pub. admin., defense	3,600	11.4	162,960 ‖	7.0 ‖
Transportation and communication	700	2.2	‖	‖
Trade and finance	5,200	16.4	‖	‖
TOTAL	31,700	100.0¶	2,328,000	100.0

Persons economically active (1982): total 2,328,000 (44.1%); female participation in the labour force (1981) 40.7%.
Price and earnings indexes: n.a.
Household income and expenditure. Average household size (1980) 4.7; average annual income per capita (1981) GS4,815 (U.S.$230).
Land use (1981): forested 43.0%; meadows and pastures 12.2%; agricultural and under permanent cultivation 6.4%; other 38.4%.

Foreign trade

Balance of trade (current prices)º

	1976	1977	1978	1979	1980	1981
GS'000,000	−700	+700	−400	−400	+1,000	+1,611
% of total	6.1%	6.0%	3.0%	2.7%	4.8%	9.9%

Imports (1981): GS7,349,000,000 (food; machinery and transport equipment; petroleum products; building materials; textiles). *Major import sources:* EEC; United States; Soviet Union.
Exports (1981): GS8,960,000,000 (bauxite 10,833,030 metric tons; alumina 230,169 metric tons; coffee; pineapples; bananas; palm kernels). *Major export destinations:* United States; France; West Germany; Soviet Union; Spain.

Transport and communications

Transport. Railroads (1982): route length 411 mi, 662 km. Roads (1982): total length 17,600 mi, 28,400 km (paved 5%). Vehicles (1982): passenger cars 9,948; trucks and buses 9,992. Merchant marine (1983): vessels (100 gross tons and over) 18; total deadweight tonnage 2,927. Air transport (1981): passenger-mi 21,000,000, passenger-km 34,000,000; short ton-mi cargo 2,100,000, metric ton-km cargo 3,000,000; airport (1984) with scheduled flights 1.
Communications. Daily newspaper (1979): total number 1; total circulation 20,000; circulation per 1,000 population 4. Radios (1981): total number of receivers 144,000 (1 per 36 persons). Television (1981): total number of receivers 7,000 (1 per 769 persons). Telephones (1981): 10,000 (1 per 515 persons).

Education and health

Education (1980–81)

	schools	teachers	students	student/ teacher ratio
Primary (age 7–12)	2,555	7,165	257,547	35.9
Secondary (age 13–18)	...	3,520	89,900	25.5
Voc., teacher tr.ᵟ	...	425	3,491	8.2
Higher	...	1,289	18,270	14.2

College graduates: n.a. *Literacy* (1980): total population literate 527,900 (18.7%); males literate 464,900 (33.5%); females literate 63,000 (4.4%).
Health (1980): physicians 301 (1 per 16,630 persons); hospital beds (1976) □ 7,032 (1 per 630 persons).
Food (1978–80): daily per capita caloric intake 1,934 (vegetable products 96.2%, animal products 3.8%); 84% of FAO recommended minimum requirement.

Military

Total active duty personnel (1983): 9,900 (army 85.8%; navy 6.1%; air force 8.1%). *Military expenditure as percent of* GNP (1981): 5.1% (world 5.7%); per capita expenditure U.S.$15.

*Separate area figures are not available for the newly created regions of Fria, Kérouané, Koubia, Lélouma, Lola, Mandiana, and Yomou. †Dry basis. ‡Includes alumina production. §Manufacturing, construction, and public utilities are included with mining and related industry. ‖ Transportation and communication, trade and finance are included with services, pub. admin., and defense. ¶Detail does not add to total given because of rounding. ºGoods and services through 1980; goods only for 1981. ᵟ1970. □Government hospitals only.

Guinea-Bissau

Official name: Républica da Guiné-Bissau (Republic of Guinea-Bissau).
Form of government: single-party republic with a single ruling body (Revolutionary Council [13]).
Head of state and government: President.
Capital: Bissau.
Official language: Portuguese.
Official religion: none.
Monetary unit: 1 peso (PG) = 100 centavos; valuation (Oct. 29, 1984) 1 U.S.$ = PG84.44; 1 £ = PG101.92.

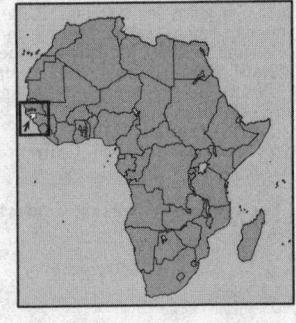

Area and population		area		population
				1979
Regions	Capitals	sq mi	sq km	census*
Bafatá	Bafatá	2,309	5,981	115,656
Bissau	Bissau	324	840	51,796
Bolama	Bolama	1,013	2,624	25,449
Cacheu	Cacheu	1,998	5,175	127,514
Gabú	Gabú	3,533	9,150	103,683
Oio	Farim	2,086	5,403	131,271
Quinara	Fulacunda	1,212	3,138	35,567
Tombali	Catió	1,443	3,736	55,088
Autonomous Sector				
Bissau		30	78	107,281
TOTAL		13,948	36,125	753,305

Source: Official government figures.

Demography

Density (1984): persons per sq mi 63.2, persons per sq km 24.4.
Urban–rural (1979): urban 14.0%; rural 86.0%.
Sex distribution (1979): male 48.22%; female 51.78%.
Age breakdown (1979): under 15, 44.3%; 15–29, 25.5%; 30–44, 15.1%; 45–59, 8.2%; 60–74, 4.7%; 75 and over, 2.2%.
Population projection: (1990) 999,000; (2000) 1,231,000.
Doubling time: 33 years.
Ethnic composition (1979): Balante 27.2%; Fulani 22.9%; Malinke 12.2%; Mandyako 10.6%; Pepel 10.0%; other 17.1%.
Religious affiliation (1983): traditional beliefs 66%; Muslim 30%; Christian 4%.
Major cities (1979): Bissau 105,273; Bafatá 13,429; Gabú 7,803; Mansôa 5,390; Catió 5,179.

Vital statistics

Birth rate per 1,000 population (1981): 40.9 (world avg. 29.0); legitimate, n.a.; illegitimate, n.a.
Death rate per 1,000 population (1981): 21.9 (world avg. 11.0).
Natural increase rate per 1,000 population (1981): 19.0 (world avg. 18.0).
Total fertility rate (avg. births per childbearing woman; 1982): 5.4.
Marriage rate per 1,000 population: n.a.
Divorce rate per 1,000 population: n.a.
Infant mortality rate per 1,000 live births (1975–80): 154.0.
Life expectancy at birth (1975–80): male 39.4 years; female 42.6 years.
Major causes of death: n.a.; however, major diseases are tuberculosis, malaria, and pneumonia.

National economy

Budget (1981). Revenue: PG1,137,000,000 (indirect taxes 49.6%; direct taxes 25.8%; duties, fines, and other penalties 3.0%). Expenditures: PG1,944,-000,000.
Public debt (external, outstanding; 1982): U.S.$127,000,000.
Tourism: n.a.
Production (metric tons except as noted). Agriculture, forestry, fishing (1982): cereals 53,000 (of which rice 30,000, millet 10,000), roots and tubers (sweet potatoes and cassavas) 40,000, peanuts (groundnuts) 30,000, coconuts 25,000, plantains 25,000, palm kernels 10,000, cashews 4,500; livestock (number of live animals) 220,000 cattle, 140,000 goats, 125,000 pigs, 420,-000 chickens; roundwood 527,000 cu m; fish catch 3,729. Manufacturing (in PG'000,000; 1982): beverages 143.7, of which beer 122.3, orange- and lemonades 16.5; clothing 14.0†; peanut oil 7.0; palm oil 2.4. Construction (1982): total buildings PG2,500,000. Energy production (consumption): electricity (kW-hr; 1982) 13,000,000 (13,000,000); coal, none (n.a.); crude petroleum (barrels; 1981) none (210,000); natural gas, none (n.a.).
Persons economically active (1979): total 198,575 (25.9%); female participation in the labour force, n.a.; unemployed 940 (0.5%).

Price and earnings indexes (1975 = 100)							
	1975	1976	1977	1978	1979	1980	1981
Consumer price index	100.0	101.5	104.5	114.1	136.6	147.4	147.4
Earnings index	...	...	...	...	...	...	...

Household income and expenditure. Average household size (1981) 4.1; average annual income per household, n.a.; source of income: n.a.; expenditure: n.a.
Land use (1981): forested 29.6%; meadows and pastures 35.4%; agricultural and under permanent cultivation 7.9%; other 27.1%.

Gross national product (at current market prices; 1981): U.S.$150,000,000 (U.S.$190 per capita).

Origin of gross domestic product (current prices)				
	1980		1979	
	in value PG'000,000	% of total value	labour force	% of labour force
Agriculture	2,499.7	52.8	157,320	79.2
Mining	‡	‡	...	...
Manufacturing	448.1‡	9.4‡	3,006	1.5
Construction	‡	‡	1,727	0.9
Trade	§	§	5,250	2.6
Public utilities	‡	‡	270	0.1
Transportation and communication	35.0	0.7	2,438	1.2
Finance	612.4§	12.9§	207	0.1
Pub. admin., defense	1,143.5 ‖	24.1 ‖	27,417	13.8
Services	...	...	‖	‖
Other	...	...	940	0.5
TOTAL	4,738.7	100.0¶	198,575	100.0¶

Foreign trade

Balance of trade (current prices)						
	1978	1979	1980	1981	1982	1983
PG'000,000	−1,308.8	−1,588.0	−1,477.6	−1,334.1	−1,500.8	−1,227.5
% of total	60.0%	62.3%	65.9%	56.0%	61.1%	63.2%

Imports (1983): PG1,585,600,000 (food and beverages 33.7%, of which cereals 22.7%; textiles and clothing 15.8%; transport equipment 12.8%; machinery and apparatus, including electrical 8.2%). *Major import sources:* Portugal 32.7%; Italy 11.0%; The Netherlands 9.9%; France 6.9%; Senegal 5.7%.
Exports (1983): PG358,100,000 (vegetables and fruits, including peanuts [groundnuts] and cashew nuts 66.1%; fish including shrimps 23.7%; cork and wood 4.5%). *Major export destinations:* Portugal 65.9%; Senegal 11.1%; Guinea 10.9%.

Transport and communications

Transport. Railroads: none. Roads (1982): total length 3,143 mi, 5,058 km (paved, n.a.). Vehicles (1981): private motor vehicles 3,807. Merchant marine (1983): vessels (100 gross tons and over) 15; total deadweight tonnage 2,523. Air transport (1980): passenger-mi 5,000,000, passenger-km 8,000,-000; short ton-mi cargo 700,000, metric ton-km cargo 1,000,000; airport (1983) with scheduled flights 1.
Communications. Daily newspaper (1984): total number 1; total circulation 6,000; circulation per 1,000 population 7.5. Radios (1981): total number of receivers 26,000 (1 per 30.8 persons). Television (1984): none. Telephones (1981): 5,000 (1 per 160 persons).

Education and health

Education (1981–82)	schools	teachers	students	student/ teacher ratio
Primary (age 7–13)	732	3,256	83,155	25.5
Secondary (age 13–18)	8	432	10,740	24.9
Voc., teacher tr.	4	96	827	8.6

College graduates per 100,000 population: n.a. *Literacy* (1980): total population literate 28.0%.
Health (1978): physicians 88 (1 per 8,250 persons); hospital beds♀ 910 (1 per 800 persons).
Food (1978–80): daily per capita caloric intake 2,357 (vegetable products 93.0%, animal products 7.0%); 102% of FAO recommended minimum requirement.

Military

Total active duty personnel (1983): 6,050 (army 94.2%; navy 4.5%; air force 1.3%). *Military expenditure as percent of GNP* (1982): 7.0% (world 6.0%); per capita expenditure U.S.$11.

*Preliminary. †Production figure for first three quarters only. ‡Mining, construction, and public utilities included with manufacturing. §Trade included with finance. ‖ Services included with public administration and defense. ¶Detail does not add to total given because of rounding. ♀Government hospitals only.

Guyana

Official name: Co-operative Republic of Guyana.
Form of government: unitary single-party republic with one legislative house (National Assembly [65]).
Chief of state: President.
Head of government: Prime Minister.
Capital: Georgetown.
Official language: English.
Official religion: none.
Monetary unit: 1 Guyana dollar (G$) = 100 cents; valuation (Oct. 29, 1984) 1 U.S.$ = G$3.79; 1 £ = G4.58.

Area and population

Regions	Capitals	area		population
		sq mi	sq km	1983 estimate
East Berbice	New Amsterdam	...	...	...
East Demerara	Enmore	...	...	...
Essequibo	Suddie	...	...	...
Essequibo Islands	Enterprise	...	...	...
Georgetown*	Georgetown	...	...	188,000
Mazaruni-Potaro	Bartica	...	...	...
North West	Mabaruma	...	...	...
Rupununi	Lethem	...	...	...
West Berbice	Fort Wellington	...	...	...
West Demerara	Vreed en Hoop	...	...	...
TOTAL		83,000†	215,000†	918,000

Source: Official government figures.

Demography

Density (1984): persons per sq mi 12.3, persons per sq km 4.7.
Urban–rural (1983): urban 28.0%; rural 72.0%.
Sex distribution (1980): male 50.06%; female 49.94%.
Age breakdown (1980): under 15, 40.2%; 15–29, 31.3%; 30–44, 13.8%; 45–59, 8.8%; 60–74, 4.8%; 75 and over, 1.1%.
Population projection: (1990) 952,000; (2000) 1,110,000.
Doubling time: 34 years.
Ethnic composition (1980): East Indian 50.8%; Black African 30.4%; other 18.8%.
Religious affiliation (1980): Hindu 34.4%; Protestant 18.0%; Roman Catholic 18.0%; Anglican 16.0%; Muslim 9.0%; other 4.6%.
Major cities (1970): Greater Georgetown 188,000‡; Linden 30,000; New Amsterdam 18,000; Corriverton 17,000.

Vital statistics

Birth rate per 1,000 population (1983): 29.0 (world avg. 29.0); legitimate, n.a.; illegitimate, n.a.
Death rate per 1,000 population (1983): 7.0 (world avg. 11.0).
Natural increase rate per 1,000 population (1983): 22.0 (world avg. 18.0).
Total fertility rate (avg. births per childbearing woman; 1980–85): 3.2.
Marriage rate per 1,000 population: n.a.
Divorce rate per 1,000 population: n.a.
Infant mortality rate per 1,000 live births (1983): 45.0.
Life expectancy at birth (1980–85): male 67.7 years; female 73.3 years.
Major causes of death per 100,000 population (1977): circulatory disease 223.6; symptoms and ill-defined conditions 90.8; infectious and parasitic diseases 83.4; respiratory diseases 65.6.

National economy

Budget (1983). Revenue: G$610,400,000 (income tax 35.0%, excise duties 34.5%, post office and miscellaneous revenue 10.5%). Expenditures: G$1,-368,200,000 (debt charges 33.3%, education 5.3%, defense 5.3%, law and order 3.4%, health 2.9%).
Public debt (external, outstanding; 1983): U.S.$702,000,000.
Tourism (1980): receipts from visitors U.S.$4,000,000; expenditures by nationals abroad: n.a.
Production (metric tons except as noted). Agriculture, forestry, fishing (1982): rice 303,000, raw sugar 288,000, plantains 21,000, coconuts 20,000, oranges 12,000, hen eggs 4,000; livestock (number of live animals) 305,000 cattle, 140,000 pigs, 116,000 sheep, 13,500,000 chickens; roundwood 201,000 cu m; fish catch 21,100. Mining and quarrying (1982): bauxite 1,159,000, alumina 73,157, gold 19,000 troy oz.§, diamonds 10,000 metric carats§. Manufacturing (1980): rum 151,300 hectolitres, cigarettes 567,000,000 units, refined sugar 242,000, stock feeds 55,000, flour 36,000, margarine 3,000. Construction: n.a. Energy production (consumption) (kW-hr; 1982) 359,000,000 (304,000,000); coal, none (n.a); crude petroleum, n.a. (n.a.); petroleum products (metric tons; 1981) none (537,000); natural gas, n.a. (n.a.).
Persons economically active (1977): total 165,031 (21.1%); female participation in labour force 42,343 (25.7%); unemployed 27,039¶.

Price and earnings indexes (1980 = 100)

	1977	1978	1979	1980	1981	1982	1983
Consumer price index	64.6	74.4	87.7	100.0	124.7	147.8	169.9
Weekly earnings index	60.8	90.0	95.2	100.0	110.0	...	...

Household income and expenditure. Average household size (1980) 5.0; average annual income per household, n.a.; sources of income (1974): wages and salaries 73.0%, transfer payments 6.3%, other 20.7%; expenditure: n.a.
Gross national product (at current market prices; 1983): U.S.$431,568,000 (U.S.$470 per capita).

Origin of gross domestic product (current prices)

	1981		1977	
	in value G$'000,000	% of total value	labour force	% of labour force
Agriculture	351	26.0	48,003	29.1
Mining	101	7.5	4,621	2.8
Manufacturing	150	11.1	30,697	18.6
Construction	110	8.1	10,332	6.2
Trade	145	10.7	17,750	10.8
Public utilities	...	...	4,096	2.5
Transportation and communication	90	6.7	7,822	4.7
Finance	64	4.7	...	...
Pub. admin., defense	276	20.4	...	...
Services	40	3.0	41,645	25.3
Other	23	1.8	65	‖
TOTAL	1,350	100.0	165,031	100.0

Land use (1981): forested 83.2%; meadows and pastures 6.2%; agricultural and under permanent cultivation 2.5%; other 8.1%.

Foreign trade

Balance of trade (current prices)

	1977	1978	1979	1980	1981	1982
G$'000,000	−70.0	+107.3	+9.9	+73.4	−262.3	−20.9
% of total	5.0%	7.7%	0.7%	3.8%	11.9%	1.4%

Imports (1982): G$744,900,000 (fuels and lubricants 38.8%, machinery and transport equipment 16.4%; food, beverages, and tobacco 7.1%; chemicals 5.4%; clothing and footwear 3.0%). *Major import sources§:* Trinidad and Tobago 33.6%; United States 24.8%; United Kingdom 15.9%; Canada 3.9%.
Exports (1982): G$724,000,000 (sugar 36.4%, calcined bauxite 25.8%, rice 8.4%, dried bauxite 8.0%; alumina 5.0%; timber 2.0%). *Major export destinations§:* United Kingdom 26.1%; United States 21.7%; Trinidad and Tobago 8.6%; Jamaica 5.5%; Canada 5.2%.

Transport and communications

Transport. Railroads: length (1980) 80 mi, 130 km; passenger-mi (1974) 2,486,000, passenger-km 4,000,000; cargo, n.a. Roads (1983): total length 3,426 mi, 5,513 km (paved 9%). Vehicles (1982): passenger cars 20,000; trucks and buses 4,610. Merchant marine (1983): vessels (100 gross tons and over) 84; total deadweight tonnage 19,633. Air transport (1982): total passengers 155,000; total cargo 3,100 metric tons; airports (1984) with scheduled flights 21.
Communications. Daily newspaper (1983): total number 1; total circulation 58,000; circulation per 1,000 population 63.2. Radios (1983): total number of receivers 300,000 (1 per 3.1 persons). Television: n.a. Telephones (1982): 28,500 (1 per 32.2 persons).

Education and health

Education (1979–80)

	schools	teachers	students	student/ teacher ratio
Primary (age 6–11)	424	6,021	164,830	27.4
Secondary (age 12–17)	87	2,513	46,595	18.5
Voc., teacher tr.	15	348	4,647	13.4
Higher	1	...	1,889	...

College graduates per 100,000 population (students graduating; 1981): 58.
Literacy (1980): total population literate 505,300 (95.5%); males literate 255,200 (97.1%); females literate 250,100 (94.0%).
Health: physicians (1980) 100♀ (1 per 8,170 persons); hospital beds (1979) 4,002 (1 per 217 persons).
Food (1978–80): daily per capita caloric intake 2,483 (vegetable products 87.7%, animal products 12.3%); 109% of FAO recommended minimum requirement.

Military

Total active duty personnel (1981): 5,000 (army 100%). *Military expenditure as percent of GNP* (1982): 4.5% (world 6.0%); per capita expenditure U.S.$26.

*Greater Georgetown. †Estimated; no dated survey available. ‡1983 estimate. §1981. ‖ Less than 0.1 percent. ¶1982. ♀Government physicians only.

Haiti

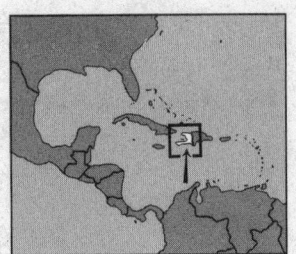

Official name: République d'Haïti (Republic of Haiti).
Form of government: republic with one legislative house (National Assembly [59]).
Head of state and government: President.
Capital: Port-au-Prince.
Official language: French.
Official religion: Roman Catholicism.
Monetary unit: 1 gourde (G) = 100 centimes; valuation (Oct. 29, 1984) 1 U.S.$ = 5.00 G; 1 £ = G6.5.

Area and population

Departements	Capitals	area sq mi	area sq km	population 1982 census
Centre	Hinche	1,389	3,597	361,470
Grande Anse	Jérémie	1,917	3,100	489,957
L'Artibonite	Gonaïves	1,890	4,895	732,932
Nord	Cap-Haïtien	840	2,175	564,002
Nord-Est	Fort-Liberté	656	1,698	189,573
Nord-Ouest	Port-de-Paix	808	2,094	293,531
Ouest	Port-au-Prince	1,774	4,595	1,551,792
Sud	Les Cayes	1,005	2,602	502,624
Sud-Est	Jacmel	802	2,077	367,911
TOTAL		10,360†	26,833	5,053,792

Source: Official government figures.

Demography

Density (1984): persons per sq mi 501.6, persons per sq km 193.7.
Urban–rural (1982): urban 20.6%; rural 79.4%.
Sex distribution (1982): male 48.48%; female 51.52%.
Age breakdown (1982): under 15, 39.2%; 15–29, 26.9%; 30–44, 15.6%; 45–59, 10.0%; 60–74, 5.4%; 75 and over, 2.9%.
Population projection: (1990) 5,655,000; (2000) 6,511,000.
Doubling time: 25 years.
Ethnic composition (1980): black 95%; mulatto 5%.
Religious affiliation (1982): Roman Catholic 80.3%; Baptist 9.7%; Pentecostal 3.6%; other 6.4%.
Major cities (1982*): Port-au-Prince 449,831; Cap-Haïtien 64,406; Pétionville 35,333; Gonaïves 34,209; Les Cayes 34,090.

Vital statistics

Birth rate per 1,000 population (1980–85): 41.3 (world avg. 27.5).
Death rate per 1,000 population (1980–85): 14.1 (world avg. 10.6).
Natural increase rate per 1,000 population (1980–85): 27.2 (world avg. 16.9).
Total fertility rate (avg. births per childbearing woman; 1980–85): 5.7.
Marriage rate per 1,000 population (1980): 0.7‡.
Divorce rate per 1,000 population (1980): 0.1‡.
Infant mortality rate per 1,000 live births (1980–85): 126.9.
Life expectancy at birth (1980): male 49.0 years; female 52.0 years.
Major causes of death: tuberculosis, typhoid fever, malaria, dermatosis, parasitic worms, ulcers, and influenza.

National economy

Budget (1982). Revenue: G1,113,000,000§ (current G1,017,400,000, of which tax revenue 91.3% [import duties 21.3%, income tax 17.9%, excise tax 14.8%]; nontax revenue 8.7%). Expenditures: G1,349,600,000 (expenditure on goods and services 59.4%).
Production (metric tons except as noted). Agriculture, forestry, fishing (1982): sugarcane 3,000,000, bananas and plantains 510,000, sweet potatoes 275,000, cassava 260,000, corn (maize) 190,000, sorghum 120,000, rice 105,000, coffee 28,000, cocoa beans 3,000; livestock (number of live animals) 1,200,000 cattle, 1,000,000 goats, 600,000 pigs; roundwood 5,129,000 cu m; fish catch 4,000. Mining and quarrying (1982 est.): aluminum (bauxite, dry equivalent) 377,000. Manufacturing (1980): cement G89,010,000; chemicals G1,126,100; wheat flour 151,000; raw sugar 55,400; essential oils, soap, and detergents 8,750; cigarettes (cartons of 200) 5,470,600; footwear 788,200 pairs. Construction: n.a. Energy production (consumption): electricity (kW-hr; 1982) 360,000,000 (360,000,000); petroleum products (metric tons; 1982) none (202,000).
Gross national product (at current market prices; 1983): U.S.$1,648,000,000 (U.S.$310 per capita).

Origin of gross domestic product (constant prices of 1976)

	1982 in value G'000,000	% of total value	labour force	% of labour force
Agriculture	1,629	31.5	1,222,859	65.4
Mining	70	1.4	19,260	1.0
Manufacturing	888	17.2	121,208	6.5
Construction	269	5.2	22,192	1.2
Trade	952	18.4	285,728	15.3
Public utilities	38	0.7	2,057	0.1
Transportation and communication	106	2.1	16,386	0.9
Finance	‖	‖	4,030	0.2
Pub. admin., defense	‖	‖	...	...
Services	...	...	124,475	6.7
Other	1,214	23.5	51,261	2.7
TOTAL	5,166	100.0	1,869,456	100.0

Public debt (external, outstanding; 1981): U.S.$463,900,000.
Tourism (1981): receipts from visitors U.S.$85,000,000; expenditures by nationals abroad U.S.$26,000,000.
Persons economically active (1982): total 2,129,658 (42.1%); female participation in the labour force 872,243 (41.0%); unemployed 260,203 (12.2%).

Price and earnings indexes (1980 = 100)

	1978	1979	1980	1981	1982	1983	1984
Consumer price index	75.1	84.9	100.0	110.9	119.0	131.2	140.4
Monthly earnings index	...	...	...	...	...	...	...

Household income and expenditure. Average household size (1980) 5.1; household expenditure (1970): food and drink 48.9%, medical care and health 8.6%, housing 7.9%, fuel and power 7.0%, household equipment and operation 4.9%, clothing and footwear 3.5%, transport and communication 2.8%, other 16.4%.
Land use (1981): forested 3.7%; meadows and pastures 18.3%; agricultural and under permanent cultivation 32.5%; other 45.5%.

Foreign trade

Balance of trade (current prices)

	1976	1977	1978	1979	1980	1981
G'000,000	−410.9	−316.8	−389.9	−433.3	−904.1	−1,531.2
% of total	−24.8%	−17.5%	−20.1%	−18.9%	−31.7%	−49.8%

Imports: (1978): G1,103,430,000 (basic manufactures 19.1%, of which textile yarn and fabric 5.9%; food and live animals 17.7%, of which cereals and preparations 7.4%, dairy products and eggs 5.0%; petroleum products 10.9%; transport equipment 10.4%; chemicals 9.1%). *Major import sources:* United States 44.6%; Netherlands Antilles 9.8%; Japan 8.8%; Canada 7.6%; West Germany 4.6%; France 3.4%.
Exports: (1978): G794,740,000 (food and live animals 48.1%, of which coffee 39.1%, cocoa 4.5%; bauxite 10.8%; toys, sporting goods 10.2%; chemicals 6.1%; electrical machinery 4.6%; cement 1.8%). *Major export destinations:* United States 58.6%; France 13.4%; Italy 7.0%; Belgium–Luxembourg 5.8%; Ireland 4.4%; The Netherlands 2.8%; Canada 1.3%.

Transport and communications

Transport. Railroads (1980): length 155 mi, 250 km. Roads (1981): total length 2,139 mi, 3,443 km (paved 17%). Vehicles (1981): passenger cars 17,377; trucks and buses 3,646. Merchant marine (1983): vessels (100 gross tons and over) 6; total deadweight tonnage 851. Air transport (1980): passenger arrivals 253,337, passenger departures 233,354; short ton-mi cargo 1,301,400, metric ton-km cargo 1,900,000; airports (1984) with scheduled flights 2.
Communications. Daily newspapers (1982): total number 4; total circulation 19,500; circulation per 1,000 population 3.8. Radios (1983): total number of receivers 120,000 (1 per 42 persons). Television (1983): total number of receivers 30,000 (1 per 169 persons). Telephones (1980): 34,900 (1 per 144 persons).

Education and health

Education (1982–83)

	schools	teachers	students	student/ teacher ratio
Primary (age 6–12)	3,241	16,986	723,041	42.6
Secondary (age 13–18)	290	5,367	117,081	21.8
Higher	11	582	3,464	6.0

College graduates per 100,000 population (students graduating; 1978): 7.
Literacy (1982): total population literate 1,066,966 (21.1%); males literate 547,318 (22.3%); females literate 519,648 (20.0%).
Health: physicians (1979) 600 (1 per 8,200 persons); hospital beds (1977) 3,900 (1 per 1,220 persons).
Food (1978–80): daily per capita caloric intake 1,882 (vegetable products 92.0%, animal products 8.0%); 83% of FAO recommended minimum requirement.

Military

Total active duty personnel (1982): 7,500 (army 93.3%; navy 4.0%; air force 2.7%). *Military expenditure as percent of GNP:* (1982): 1.6% (world 6.0%); per capita expenditure U.S.$5.

*Preliminary. †Detail does not add to total given because of rounding. ‡Registered only. §Includes G95,000,000 in grants, 8.6% of total revenue. ‖ Finance, pub. admin., defense, and services are included with other. ¶June, 1984.

Honduras

Official name: República de Honduras (Republic of Honduras).
Form of government: multiparty republic with one legislative house (National Assembly [82]).
Head of state and government: President.
Capital: Tegucigalpa.
Official language: Spanish.
Official religion: none.
Monetary unit: 1 Honduran lempira (L) = 100 centavos; valuation* (Oct. 29, 1984) 1 U.S.$ = L2.00; 1 £ = L2.42.

Area and population

Departments	Administrative centres	area sq mi	area sq km	population 1983 estimate
Atlántida	La Ceiba	1,641	4,251	242,000
Choluteca	Choluteca	1,626	4,211	290,000
Colón	Trujillo	3,427	8,875	128,000
Comayagua	Comayagua	2,006	5,196	211,000
Copán	Santa Rosa de Copán	1,237	3,203	217,000
Cortés	San Pedro Sula	1,527	3,954	624,000
El Paraíso	Yuscarán	2,787	7,218	207,000
Francisco Morazán	Tegucigalpa	3,068	7,946	736,000
Gracias a Dios	Puerto Lempira	6,421	16,630	35,000
Intibucá	La Esperanza	1,186	3,072	111,000
Islas de la Bahía	Roatán	100	261	19,000
La Paz	La Paz	900	2,331	87,000
Lempira	Gracias	1,656	4,290	175,000
Ocotepeque	Nueva Ocotepeque	649	1,680	64,000
Olancho	Juticalpa	9,402	24,351	228,000
Santa Bárbara	Santa Bárbara	1,975	5,115	287,000
Valle	Nacaome	604	1,565	126,000
Yoro	Yoro	3,065	7,939	304,000
TOTAL		43,277	112,088	4,091,000

Source: Official government figures.

Demography

Density (1984): persons per sq mi 97.8, persons per sq km 37.8.
Urban–rural (1982): urban 36.4%; rural 63.6%.
Sex distribution (1981): male 50.13%; female 49.87%.
Age breakdown (1981): under 15, 47.7%; 15–29, 26.2%; 30–44, 13.6%; 45–59, 8.1%; 60–74, 3.7%; 75 and over 0.7%.
Population projection: (1990) 5,105,000; (2000) 6,978,000.
Doubling time: 20 years.
Ethnic composition (1982): mestizo 90.0%; black (including Black Caribs) 5.0%; Indian 4.0%; white 1.0%.
Religious affiliation (1980): Roman Catholic 93.6%; Protestant 3.0%; Afro-American spiritist 0.5%; Muslim 0.3%; other 2.6%.
Major cities (1983 est.): Tegucigalpa 508,000; San Pedro Sula 363,000; El Progreso 117,000; Choluteca 84,000; La Ceiba 73,000.

Vital statistics

Birth rate per 1,000 population (1982): 43.9 (world avg. 29.0); legitimate, n.a.; illegitimate, n.a.
Death rate per 1,000 population (1982): 10.1 (world avg. 11.0).
Natural increase rate per 1,000 population (1982): 33.8 (world avg. 18.0).
Total fertility rate (avg. births per childbearing woman; 1981): 6.6.
Marriage rate per 1,000 population (1979): 4.0.
Divorce rate per 1,000 population (1979): 0.2.
Infant mortality rate per 1,000 live births (1982): 87.0.
Life expectancy at birth (1980–85): male 58.2 years; female 61.7 years.
Major causes of death n.a.; however, principal causes include diseases of early infancy, gastritis and other enteric diseases (particularly typhoid fever), pneumonia and influenza, accidents, and cardiovascular diseases.

National economy

Budget (1982). Revenue: L1,572,300,000 (taxes 45.5%, of which tax on production and internal trade 15.1%; capital revenue 51.8%; other 2.7%). Expenditures: L1,572,300,000 (consumption 54.8%, of which wages and salaries 46.5%; net allowance on loans 19.6%; capital expenditure 16.3%; other 9.3%).
Public debt (external, outstanding; 1983): U.S.$1,620,000,000.
Tourism (1981): receipts from visitors U.S.$31,000,000; expenditures by nationals abroad U.S.$128,000,000.
Production (metric tons except as noted). Agriculture, forestry, fishing (1982): sugarcane 3,200,000, bananas and plantains 1,513,000, milk 214,000, corn (maize) 175,000, African palm 96,000, coffee 82,000, dry beans 42,000, seed cotton 19,000, cotton seed 11,000; livestock (number of live animals) 2,358,000 cattle, 590,000 pigs; roundwood 5,071,000; fish catch 5,023. Mining and quarrying (1982): limestone 500,000; marble 40,000; salt 30,000; zinc ore and concentrate 26,875; lead 13,687; gold 1,711 troy ounces. Manufacturing (1982): cement 250,000; iron and steel semimanufactures 20,000; raw sugar 218,000; beef and veal 65,000; palm oil 12,500; soft drinks 15,780,000 hectolitres; beer 3,922,000 hectolitres; matches 3,023,000 units; cigarettes 2,281,000 units. Construction (value added in lempiras; 1981)†: residential 44,200,000; nonresidential 17,400,000. Energy production (consumption): electricity (kW-hr; 1982) 1,090,000,000 (1,086,000,000); coal, none (n.a.); crude petroleum (barrels; 1982), none (3,824,000); petroleum products (metric tons; 1982) 508,000 (568,000); natural gas, none (n.a.).

Gross national product (at current market prices; 1983): U.S.$2,840,000,000 (U.S.$694 per capita).

Origin of gross domestic product (current prices)

	1982 in value L'000,000	% of total value	labour force	% of labour force
Agriculture	1,381	27.5	547,900	54.1
Mining	105	2.1	3,900	0.4
Manufacturing	820	16.3	132,200	13.0
Construction	270	5.4	43,100	4.3
Trade	646	12.8	95,500	9.4
Public utilities	117	2.3	3,600	0.4
Transportation and communication	396	7.9	38,900	3.8
Finance	251	5.0	9,200	0.9
Pub. admin., defense	244	4.9		
Services	450	8.9	139,200	13.7
Other, real estate	349	6.9		
TOTAL	5,029	100.0	1,013,500	100.0

Persons economically active (1982): total 1,013,500 (28.9%); female participation in the labour force (1981) 181,749 (16.2%); unemployed (1981) 111,745 (9.9%).

Price and earnings indexes (1980 = 100)

	1977	1978	1979	1980	1981	1982	1983
Consumer price index	72.4	76.9	86.5	100.0	110.2	121.2	132.7
Monthly earnings index	...	...	...	...	...	...	...

Household income and expenditure: n.a.
Land use (1981): forested 35.6%; meadows and pastures 30.4%; agricultural and under permanent cultivation 15.8%; other 18.2%.

Foreign trade

Balance of trade (current prices)

	1977	1978	1979	1980	1981	1982
L'000,000	−20.3	−28.4	−26.9	−103.8	−114.8	−101.7
% of total	1.9%	2.2%	1.7%	5.7%	6.8%	3.7%

Imports (1982): L1,423,800,000 (mineral fuels, lubricants, and related materials 23.9%; manufactured goods 21.6%; machinery and transport equipment 19.2%; chemicals and related products 18.0%. Major import sources: United States 38.4%; Trinidad and Tobago 15.1%; Guatemala 6.7%; Japan 6.3%; Venezuela 3.8%.
Exports (1982): L1,322,100,000 (bananas 33.0%; coffee 23.2%; wood 6.7%; refrigerated meat 5.1%; shrimps and lobsters 4.4%; sugar 3.7%; lead and zinc 3.0%; silver 1.7%). Major export destinations: United States 52.8%; West Germany 9.1%; Belgium 6.1%; Japan 5.6%; Guatemala 3.7%.

Transport and communications

Transport. Railroads (1983): route length 581 mi, 935 km; passengers, n.a.; cargo, n.a. Roads (1983): total length 5,618 mi, 9,042 km (paved 22%). Vehicles (1983): passenger cars 58,920; trucks and buses 24,385. Merchant marine (1983): vessels (100 gross tons and over) 191; total deadweight tonnage 298,125. Air transport (1982): passenger-mi 168,279,000, passenger-km 270,820,000; short ton-mi cargo 25,524,000, metric ton-km cargo 37,265,000; airports (1984) with scheduled flights 4.
Communications. Daily newspapers (1983): total number 6; total circulation 236,000; circulation per 1,000 population 60. Radios (1983): total number of receivers 1,534,620 (1 per 2.7 persons). Television (1983): total number of receivers 135,024 (1 per 30 persons). Telephones (1982): 33,667 (1 per 117 persons).

Education and health

Education (1981)

	schools	teachers	students	student/teacher ratio
Primary (age 6–13)	6,264	17,378	704,612	40.5
Secondary (age 12–20)	295	3,238‡	100,743	31.1
Voc., teacher tr.	11	...	20,169	...
Higher	2	1,774	30,258	17.1

College graduates per 100,000 population (students graduating; 1980) 25.
Literacy (1980): total population literate 1,309,500 (68.6%); males literate 676,700 (71.1%); females literate 632,800 (66.2%).
Health (1982): physicians 1,440 (1 per 2,746 persons); hospital beds 5,506 (1 per 718 persons).
Food (1978–80): daily per capita caloric intake 2,175 (vegetable products 89.1%, animal products 10.9%); 96% of FAO recommended minimum requirement.

Military

Total active duty personnel (1983): 15,200 (army 88.8%; navy 3.3%; air force 7.9%). Military expenditure as percent of GNP (1979): 2.3% (world 5.5%); per capita expenditure U.S.$13.

*The Honduran lempira is officially pegged to the U.S. dollar. †Tegucigalpa, San Pedro Sular, La Ceiba only. ‡Includes teachers of vocational training.

Hong Kong

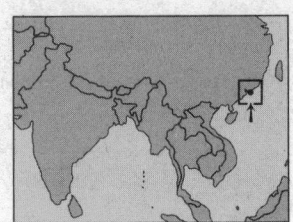

Official name: Hsiang Kang (Chinese);
Hong Kong (English).
Political status: colony (United
Kingdom) with three nominated
advisory councils (Executive Council
[15], Legislative Council [50], Urban
Council [24]).
Chief of state: British Monarch.
Head of government: Governor.
Capital: Victoria.
Official languages: Chinese; English.
Official religion: none.
Monetary unit: 1 HK dollar
(HK$) = 100 cents; valuation (Oct. 29,
1984) 1 U.S.$ = HK$7.75;
1 £ = HK$9.35.

Area and population

Districts	area* sq mi	area* sq km	population† 1981 census
Hong Kong Island	29.9	77.4	1,203,342
Kowloon	17.0	44.1	2,458,279
New Territories	353.6	915.7	1,324,939
TOTAL	400.5	1,037.2	4,986,560

Demography

Density (1984): persons per sq mi 13,188.3, persons per sq km 5,088.7.
Urban–rural (1981)‡: urban 85.9%; rural 14.1%.
Sex distribution (1981): male 52.22%; female 47.78%.
Age breakdown (1981): under 15, 24.8%; 15–29, 32.7%; 30–44, 17.7%; 45–59, 14.6%; 60–74, 8.2%; 75 and over, 2.0%.
Population projection: (1990) 6,144,530; (2000) 7,431,060.
Doubling time: 37 years.
Ethnic composition (1984): Chinese 98.6%; British 0.9%; other 0.5%.
Religious affiliation (1983): predominantly Buddhist; some Confucianist and Taoist; approximately 500,000 Christian.
Major city (1981): Victoria 590,771.

Vital statistics

Birth rate per 1,000 population (1983): 15.5 (world avg. 29.0).
Death rate per 1,000 population (1983): 5.0 (world avg. 11.0).
Natural increase rate per 1,000 population (1980–85): 10.5 (world avg. 18.0).
Total fertility rate (avg. births per childbearing woman; 1980–85): 2.2.
Marriage rate per 1,000 population (1983): 9.0.
Divorce rate per 1,000 population (1983): 0.5.
Infant mortality rate per 1,000 live births (1981): 10.0.
Life expectancy at birth (1980–85): male 73.5 years; female 78.6 years.
Major causes of death per 100,000 population (1983): diseases of circulatory system 146.7; malignant neoplasms (cancers) 137.0; diseases of respiratory system 84.6.

National economy

Budget (1983–84). Revenue: HK$32,270,000,000 (earnings and profit taxes 37.1%; income from properties and investments 18.4%; excise duties 9.3%; fees and charges 7.8%). Expenditures: HK$35,475,000,000 (education 15.2%; law and order 7.8%; medical 7.6%; housing 5.7%; social welfare 4.9%; defense 4.4%).
Public debt (external, outstanding; 1982): U.S.$267,300,000.
Production (metric tons except as noted). Agriculture, forestry, fishing (1983): vegetables 151,000, flowers 76,000, fruits and nuts 4,900, rice 2,000, milk 4,300; livestock (number of live animals) 390,000 pigs, 860 cattle; roundwood 174,000 cu m§; fish catch 180,990§. Mining and quarrying (1983): feldspar sand 51,270; feldspar 5,280; kaolin 830. Manufacturing (gross value in HK$; 1979): wearing apparel 20,584,752,000; basic metals, fabricated metal products, machinery, and equipment 16,119,014,000; textiles 15,625,257,000; electrical and electronic products 15,052,603,000; plastic products 6,535,755,000; food, beverages, and tobacco 3,529,757,000; cement 1,716,580 metric tons ‖. Construction (1982): residential 720,000 sq m; nonresidential 2,424,000 sq m. Energy production (consumption): electricity (kW-hr; 1982) 14,504,000,000 (14,232,000,000); coal (metric tons; 1982) none (1,455,000); petroleum products (metric tons; 1982) none (5,245,000); natural gas (cu m; 1983) none (151,897,000).

Origin of gross domestic product (current prices)

	1981 in value HK$'000,000	% of total value	labour force	% of labour force
Agriculture	1,122	0.7	48,273	1.9
Mining	253	0.2	1,644	—
Manufacturing	36,049	22.8	1,025,009	40.9
Construction	11,922	7.5	197,490	7.9
Trade	30,749	19.4	476,098	19.0
Public utilities	2,229	1.4	14,932	0.6
Transportation and communication	11,853	7.5	189,205	7.6
Finance	37,688	23.8	117,288	4.7
Pub. admin., defense, and services	20,995	13.3	382,350	15.3
Other	5,313¶	3.4¶	51,515º	2.0
TOTAL	158,173	100.0	2,503,804	100.0ᵟ

Gross national product (at current market prices; 1981): U.S.$26,000,000,000 (U.S.$5,100 per capita).
Persons economically active (1981): total 2,404,067 (48.2%); female participation in labour force 852,624 (35.5%); unemployed 99,737 (4.0%).

Price and earnings indexes (1973–74 = 100)

	1976	1977	1978	1979	1980	1981	1982
Consumer price index	111.2	117.7	124.7	139.2	160.8	185.5	205.2
Daily earnings index	125	138	156	180	209	244	265

Household income and expenditure. Average household size (1981) 3.9; income per household HK$3,705 (U.S.$674); sources of income: n.a.; expenditure (1979–80): food 38.3%, housing 20.1%, clothing and footwear 7.8%, transportation 6.4%, recreation 2.0%.
Tourism (1982): receipts from visitors U.S.$1,457,000,000; expenditures by nationals abroad, n.a.
Land use (1981): forested 13.0%; meadows and pastures 1.0%; agricultural and under permanent cultivation 8.0%; built-on, wasteland, and other 78.0%.

Foreign trade

Balance of trade (current prices)

	1978	1979	1980	1981	1982	1983
HK$'000,000	−9,148	−9,903	−13,408	−16,212	−15,508	−14,743
% of total	7.8%	6.1%	6.4%	6.2%	5.7%	4.4%

Imports (1983): HK$175,442,000,000 (machinery and transport equipment 22.5%, of which electrical machinery 9.3%; textile yarn and fabrics 13.7%; food and live animals 10.8%, of which vegetables and fruits 2.8%; chemicals and related products 7.3%; photographic apparatus, watches, and clocks 6.2%; petroleum and petroleum products 5.8%). *Major import sources:* China 24.4%; Japan 23.0%; United States 10.9%; Taiwan 7.1%; Singapore 6.0%.
Exports (1983): HK$160,699,000,000□ (clothing accessories and wearing apparel 24.2%; machinery and transport equipment 23.0%, of which electrical machinery 8.2%; textile yarn and fabrics 9.3%; travel goods 1.6%). *Major export destinations:* United States 32.2%; China 11.4%; United Kingdom 5.3%; West Germany 5.0%; Japan 4.4%.

Transport and communications

Transport. Railroads (1981–82): length 37 mi, 60 km; passenger journeys (1982) 373,197,000. Roads (1982): total length 756 mi, 1,217 km (paved 100%). Vehicles (1982): passenger cars 227,658; trucks and buses 77,248. Merchant marine (1983): vessels (100 gross tons and over) 294; total deadweight tonnage 7,248,268. Air transport (1982): passenger arrivals 3,661,883, passenger departures 3,777,485; airport (1983) with scheduled flights 1.
Communications. Daily newspapers (1983): total number 61; total circulation 2,441,510◊; circulation per 1,000 population, n.a. Radios (1981): total number of receivers 2,610,000 (1 per 2.0 persons). Television (1983): total number of receivers 1,163,000 (1 per 4.5 persons). Telephones (1982): 1,822,846 (1 per 2.9 persons).

Education and health

Education (1981)

	schools	teachers	students	student/ teacher ratio
Primary (age 6–11)	762	19,843	540,595	27.2
Secondary (age 12–18)	407	17,622	431,143	24.5
Voc., teacher tr.	18	...	11,393△	...
Higher	22	3,457	34,338	9.9

College graduates per 100,000 population (students graduating; 1981): 212.
Literacy (1981): total population literate 3,885,281 (77.9%); males literate 2,195,720 (84.3%); females literate 1,689,561 (70.9%).
Health (1982): physicians 4,137 (1 per 1,205 persons); hospital beds 22,690 (1 per 220 persons).
Food (1978–80): daily per capita caloric intake 2,884 (vegetable products 72.6%, animal products 27.4%); 126% of FAO recommended minimum requirement.

Military

Military expenditure as percent of GNP (1980): 0.7% (world 5.6%); per capita expenditure U.S.$56. Defense is the responsibility of the U.K. Internal security is maintained by a police force of 27,380§.

*Excludes the surface areas of reservoirs. †Excludes 13,906 transients and 20,600 Vietnamese refugees but includes 49,747 marine population. ‡Excludes 49,747 marine population. §1982. ‖ 1983. ¶Includes import duties and other adjustments. ºIncludes unclassifiable and first-time job-seekers. ◊Detail does not add to total given because of rounding. □Includes re-exports. ◊Partial circulation only. △Excludes teacher training.

Hungary

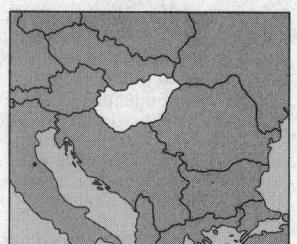

Official name: Magyar Népköztársaság
(Hungarian People's Republic).
Form of government: unitary
single-party republic with one
legislative house (National Assembly
[352]).
Chief of State: President.
Head of government: Premier.
Capital: Budapest.
Official language: Hungarian.
Official religion: none.
Monetary unit: 1 forint (Ft) = 100
fillér; valuation (Oct. 29, 1984)
1 U.S.$ = Ft50.35; 1 £ = Ft60.77.

Area and population

Counties	Capitals	area sq mi	area sq km	population 1984 estimate
Baranya	Pécs	1,732	4,487	434,000
Bács-Kiskun	Kecskemét	3,229	8,362	564,000
Békés	Békéscsaba	2,175	5,632	429,000
Borsod-Abaúj-Zemplén	Miskolc	2,798	7,248	801,000
Csongrád	Szeged	1,646	4,263	453,000
Fejér	Székesfehérvár	1,689	4,374	423,000
Győr-Sopron	Győr	1,549	4,012	430,000
Hajdú-Bihar	Debrecen	2,398	6,212	552,000
Heves	Eger	1,404	3,637	346,000
Komárom	Tatabánya	869	2,250	323,000
Nógrád	Salgótarján	982	2,544	237,000
Pest	Budapest*	2,469	6,394	983,000
Somogy	Kaposvár	2,331	6,036	357,000
Szabolcs-Szatmár	Nyíregyháza	2,293	5,938	586,000
Szolnok	Szolnok	2,165	5,608	441,000
Tolna	Szekszárd	1,430	3,704	268,000
Vas	Szombathely	1,288	3,337	283,000
Veszprém	Veszprém	1,810	4,689	389,000
Zala	Zalaegerszeg	1,461	3,784	316,000
Capital City Budapest*		203	525	2,064,000
TOTAL		35,921	93,036	10,679,000

Source: Official government figures.

Demography

Density (1984): persons per sq mi 297.2, persons per sq km 114.7.
Urban-rural (1983): urban 54.4%; rural 45.6%.
Sex distribution (1984): male 48.35%; female 51.65%.
Age breakdown (1984): under 15, 21.8%; 15–29, 20.7%; 30–49, 27.3%; 50–59, 12.3%; 60 and over, 17.9%.
Population projection: (1990) 10,920,000; (2000) 10,964,000.
During the intercensal period 1970–80, the average growth rate was 0.2%; since 1980s, however, the population has been decreasing.
Ethnic composition (1980): Magyar 98.8%; German 0.3%; other 0.9%.
Religious affiliation (1980): Christian 83.2%, of which Roman Catholic 53.9%, Protestant 21.6%; Jewish 0.9%; nonreligious 8.7%; atheist 7.2%.
Major cities (1984): Budapest 2,064,300; Miskolc 212,000; Debrecen 205,000; Szeged 176,000; Pécs 175,000; Győr 128,000.

Vital statistics

Birth rate per 1,000 population (1983): 11.9 (world avg. 29.0); (1982) legitimate 92.9%, illegitimate 7.1%.
Death rate per 1,000 population (1983): 13.9 (world avg. 11.0).
Natural increase rate per 1,000 population (1983): −2.0 (world avg. 18.0).
Total fertility rate (avg. births per childbearing woman; 1980–85): 2.1.
Marriage rate per 1,000 population (1983): 7.1.
Divorce rate per 1,000 population (1983): 2.7.
Infant mortality rate per 1,000 live births (1983): 19.0.
Life expectancy at birth (1982): male 66.1 years; female 73.7 years.
Major causes of death per 100,000 population (1983): diseases of the circulatory system 743.1; malignant neoplasms (cancers) 269.3; diseases of the respiratory system 85.1.

National economy

Budget (1984). Revenue: Ft563,200,000,000 (payments by enterprises 82.6%, personal income tax 7.2%). Expenditures: Ft566,700,000,000 (social welfare and health 26.1%, economic tasks 23.9%, interest on public debt 9.5%, education 9.2%, defense 6.0%).
Public debt (external, outstanding; 1982): U.S.$10,030,000,000 .
Tourism (1982): receipts from visitors U.S.$15,386,000,000; expenditures by nationals abroad U.S.$3,837,000.
Production (metric tons except as noted). Agriculture, forestry, fishing (1982): corn (maize) 7,959,000, wheat 5,762,000, sugar beets 5,371,000, potatoes 1,459,000, barley 871,000, sunflower seeds 582,000; livestock (number of live animals; 1983) 9,035,000 pigs, 3,180,000 sheep, 1,922,000 cattle, 45,397,000 poultry; roundwood 6,520,000 cu m; fish catch 42,042,000. Mining and quarrying (1983): bauxite 2,917,000; dolomite 1,324,000; iron ore 441,000. Manufacturing (value in Ft'000,000; 1982): chemicals 7,154,000; cement 4,369,000; crude steel 3,702,000; rolled steel 2,583,000; pig iron 2,181,000; cotton cloth 311,135,000 sq m; woolen cloth 40,973,000 sq m; buses and trucks 12,749 units. Construction (consumption) (units; 1982): residential 796; nonresidential 869. Energy production (consumption): electricity (kW-hr; 1983) 25,698,000,000 (33,345,000,000†); coal (metric tons; 1983) 25,213,000 (28,403,000†); crude petroleum (barrels; 1983) 14,629,200 (63,-

632,000†); petroleum products (metric tons; 1982) 7,384,000 (8,675,000); natural gas (cu m; 1983) 6,497,000,000 (9,956,000,000†).
Gross national product (at current market prices; 1983): U.S.$18,631,000,000 (U.S.$1,750 per capita).

Origin of net material product (current prices)

	1983 in value Ft'000,000,000	% of total value	labour force	% of labour force
Agriculture	139.9	18.8	1,082,800	21.8
Mining and and manufacturing	335.5	45.1	1,577,500	31.7
Construction	89.3	12.0	373,000	7.5
Trade	104.2	14.0	497,000	10.0
Public utilities	3.0	0.4	77,000	1.6
Transportation and communication	68.4	9.2	393,000	7.9
Services	...	...	969,200	19.5
Other	3.7‡	0.5‡	...	...
TOTAL	744.0	100.0	4,970,100	100.0

Persons economically active (1984): total 4,935,000 (46.2%); female participation in the labour force 2,243,500§ (45.1%); unemployed, n.a.

Price and earnings indexes (1970 = 100)

	1977	1978	1979	1980	1981	1982	1983
Consumer price index	125.0	130.8	142.4	155.4	162.5	173.7	185.9
Monthly earnings index	153.7	166.8	176.9	187.6	199.5	212.3	224.1

Household income and expenditure. Average household size (1983): 3.0; income per household Ft163,100 (U.S.$3,800); source of income: wages 65.5%, social income 34.5%; expenditure (1983): food 33.2%, housing 17.5%, clothing and footwear 10.0%, transportation 8.8%.
Land use (1983): forested 17.5%; meadows and pastures 13.8%; agricultural and under permanent cultivation 57.0%; other 11.7%.

Foreign trade

Balance of trade (current prices)

	1977	1978	1979	1980	1981	1982	1983
Fts'000,000,000	−238.6	−60.2	−26.8	−18.9	−14.9	−0.3	9.1
% of total	5.7%	11.1%	4.5%	3.2%	2.4%	0.1%	1.2%

Imports (1983): Ft364,963,100,000 (machinery and transport equipment 28.9%, crude petroleum and petroleum products 14.0%, chemicals and related products 13.6%, food 5.6%; textile yarn and fabrics 4.7%, iron and steel 3.0%, non-ferrous metals 2.9%, paper and paperboard 1.8%). *Major import sources:* U.S.S.R. 29.5%; West Germany 11.1%; East Germany 6.8%; Czechoslovakia 5.3%; Austria 5.0%; Poland 3.9%; Yugoslavia 3.1%.
Exports (1983): Ft374,107,900,000 (machinery and transport equipment 31.5%, of which electrical machinery and telecommunication equipment 15.0%; food 20.4%, of which meat 7.3%; chemicals 10.2%; petroleum products 6.1%; iron and steel 3.3%). *Major export destinations:* U.S.S.R. 33.5%; West Germany 7.2%; East Germany 6.1%; Czechoslovakia 5.6%; Austria 3.8%; Poland 3.7%; Italy 3.4%; Yugoslavia 3.3%.

Transport and communications

Transport. Railroads (1983): length 8,106 mi, 13,045 km; passenger-mi 6,890,000,000, passenger-km 11,104,000,000; short ton-mi cargo 15,939,000,000, metric ton-km cargo 23,271,000,000. Roads (1983): total length 18,557 mi, 29,864 km (paved 86%). Vehicles (1983): passenger cars 1,258,498; trucks and buses 153,992. Merchant marine (1983): vessels (100 gross tons and over) 21; total deadweight tonnage 112,485. Air transport (1983): passenger-mi 733,838,000, passenger-km 1,181,000,000; short ton-mi cargo 20,196,000, metric ton-km cargo 29,486,000; airports (1984) 4.
Communications. Daily newspapers (1983): total number 29; total circulation 2,842,000; circulation per 1,000 population 265.6. Radios (1980): 2,700,000 (1 per 4.0 persons). Television (1983): 2,864,000 (1 per 3.8 persons). Telephones (1984): 1,383,200 (1 per 8.0 persons).

Education and health

Education (1983–84)

	schools	teachers	students	student/ teacher ratio
Primary (age 6–13)	3,546	83,496	1,269,900	15.2
Secondary (age 14–17)	545	16,889	225,300	13.3
Vocational	269	11,090	174,800	15.8
Higher	58	14,452	62,900	4.3

College graduates per 100,000 population (1982): 389.7. *Literacy* (1982): total population literate 8,256,900 (98.9%); males literate 3,941,800 (99.3%); females literate 4,315,100 (98.5%).
Health (1984): physicians 33,035 (1 per 323.3 persons); hospital beds 99,098 (1 per 107.7 persons).
Food (1982): daily per capita caloric intake 3,226 (vegetable products 67.0%; animal products 33.0%); 134% of FAO recommended minimum.

Military

Total active duty personnel (1983): 105,000 (army 80.0%; air force 20.0%).
Military expenditure as percent of GNP (1982): 8.9% (world 6.0%); per capita expenditure U.S.$270.

*Budapest has separate county status. The area and population of the city are excluded from the larger county (Pest), which it administers. †1982. ‡Includes other material activities, balance of taxes on products and value differences, and cost of nonmaterial services. §1983.

Iceland

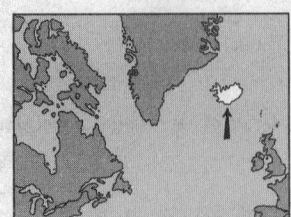

Official name: Lýdhveldidh Ísland (Republic of Iceland).
Form of government: unitary multiparty republic with two legislative houses (Upper House [20]; Lower House [40]).
Head of state and government: President.
Capital: Reykjavík.
Official language: Icelandic.
Official religion: Evangelical Lutheran.
Monetary unit: 1 króna (ISK) = 100 aurar; valuation (Oct. 29, 1984) 1 U.S.$ = 33.90 ISK; 1 £ = 40.92 ISK.

Area and population

Regions Counties*	Administrative centres	area sq mi	area sq km	population 1983 estimate
Austurland		8,683	22,490	13,100
Austur-Skaftafellssýsla	Höfn	2,347	6,080	2,300
Nordhur-Múlasýsla	Seydisfjördur	4,799	12,430	3,300
Sudhur-Múlaysýsla	Eskifjördur	1,537	3,980	7,500
Nordhurland eystra		8,370	21,680	26,100†
Eyjafjardharsýsla	Akureyri	1,602	4,150	18,900
Nordhur-Thingeyjarsýsla	Húsavík	2,077	5,380	1,700
Sudhur-Thingeyjarsýsla	Húsavík	4,691	12,150	5,500
Nordhurland vestra		4,973	12,880	10,800
Austur-Húnavatnssýsla	Blönduós	1,900	4,920	2,700
Skagafjardharsýsla	Saudárkrókur	2,077	5,380	6,500
Vestur-Húnavatnssýsla	Blönduós	996	2,580	1,600
Rekjavíkursvaedhi og				
Reykjanessvaedhi		741	1,920	140,100†
Gullbringusýsla	Keflavík	405	1,050	31,800
Kjósarsýsla	Hafnarfjördur	336	870	108,400
Sudhurland		9,649	24,990	19,800
Arnessýsla	Selfoss	3,401	8,810	10,300
Rangárvallasýsla	Hvolsvöllur	3,197	8,280	8,200
Vestur-Skaftafellssýsla	Vík	3,050	7,900	1,300
Vestfirdhir		3,676	9,520	10,500†
Austur-Bardhastran- darsýsla	Patreksfjördur	444	1,150	400
Nordhur-Isafjardharsý- sla	Isafjördur	1,181	3,060	5,200
Strandasýsla	Hólmavik	1,015	2,630	1,200
Vestur-Bardhastran- darsýsla	Patreksfjördur	598	1,550	2,000
Vestur-Isafjardharsýsla	Isafjördur	436	1,130	1,600
Vesturland		3,676	9,520	15,100
Borgarfjardharsýsla	Borgarnes	753	1,950	6,800
Dalasýsla	Budardalur	815	2,110	1,100
Mýrasýsla	Borgarnes	1,262	3,270	2,600
Snaefellsnessýsla	Stykkishólmur	846	2,190	4,600
TOTAL		**39,768**	**103,000**	**235,500†**

Source: Official government figures.

Demography

Density (1984): persons per sq mi 6.0, persons per sq km 2.3.
Urban–rural (1983): urban 88.8%; rural 11.2%.
Sex distribution (1983): male 50.39%; female 49.61%.
Age breakdown (1983): under 15, 26.7%; 15–29, 18.6%; 30–44, 9.5%; 45–59, 27.4%; 60–74, 13.5%; 75 and over, 4.3%.
Population projection: (1990) 254,900; (2000) 273,800.
Doubling time: 108 years.
Ethnic composition (1983): native Icelander 97.2%; other European 2.2%; other 0.6%.
Religious affiliation (1983): Lutheran 96.9%; other 3.1%.
Major cities (1983 est.): Reykjavík 86,092; Kópavogur 14,279; Akureyri 13,-758; Hafnarfjördur 12,460; Keflavík 6,747.

Vital statistics

Birth rate per 1,000 population (1982): 18.5 (world avg. 29.0); (1982) legitimate 55.4%, illegitimate 44.6%.
Death rate per 1,000 population (1982): 6.8 (world avg. 11.0).
Natural increase rate per 1,000 population (1982): 11.7 (world avg. 18.0).
Total fertility rate (avg. births per childbearing woman; 1982): 2.3.
Marriage rate per 1,000 population (1982): 5.6.
Divorce rate per 1,000 population (1982): 1.8.
Infant mortality rate per 1,000 live births (1982): 7.1.
Life expectancy at birth (1983): male 73.5 years; female 79.5 years.
Major causes of death per 100,000 population (1981): heart and circulatory diseases 351.4; malignant neoplasms (cancers) 158.1; pneumonia 54.2.

National economy

Budget (1983). Revenue: ISK15,100,000,000 (indirect taxes 80.8%, of which sales tax 37.1%; direct taxes 16.0%; other 3.2%). Expenditures: ISK16,598,-000,000 (social services 57.5%, of which health 10.7%; industrial services 26.8%; government operations 10.2%; other 5.5%).
Public debt (external, outstanding; 1982): U.S.$545,500,000.
Tourism (1983): receipts from visitors U.S.$58,800,000; expenditures by nationals abroad U.S.$49,000,000.
Production (gross value in ISK except as noted). Agriculture, forestry, fishing (1982): fodder crops 3,413,000 metric tons; potatoes 14,000 metric tons; milk 118,000 metric tons; livestock (number of live animals) 748,000 sheep, 64,000 cattle, 54,000 horses; cod 1,895,300,000, herring 170,400,000, lobster, shrimp, shellfish 170,200,000, capelin 7,700,000. Mining and quar-

rying (1982): diatomite 24,000 metric tons. Manufacturing (1982): fresh and frozen fish 3,856,200,000; salted fish 1,684,100,000; stockfish 1,130,600,-000; cement 124,000 metric tons; aluminum, refined 76,200 metric tons; ferrosilicon 49,100 metric tons. Construction (1980): residential 74,520,-000,000; nonresidential 64,060,000,000. Energy production (consumption): electricity (kW-hr; 1982) 3,575,000,000 (3,225,000,000); coal (metric tons; 1982) none (24,000); petroleum, none (none); petroleum products (metric tons; 1981) none (484,000); natural gas, none (none).
Gross national product (at current market prices; 1983): U.S.$2,133,600,000 (U.S.$9,060 per capita).

Origin of gross domestic product (current prices)

	1981 in value ISK'000,000	% of total value	labour force	% of labour force
Agriculture	1,002	4.7	7,738	7.3
Fishing and processing	4,095	19.2	15,264	14.4
Manufacturing	2,986	14.0	17,490	16.5
Construction	1,877	8.8	10,388	9.8
Trade	2,154	10.1	16,324‡	15.4‡
Public utilities	768	3.6		
Transportation and communication	1,792	8.4	7,526	7.1
Finance	3,029	14.2	31,270§	29.5§
Pub. admin., defense, services, and other	3,626	17.0		
TOTAL	21,330	100.0	106,000	100.0

Persons economically active (1982): total 110,000 (46.7%); female participation in the labour force 34,540 (31.4%); unemployed 660 (0.6%).

Price and earnings indexes (1975 = 100)

	1977	1978	1979	1980	1981	1982	1983
Consumer price index	172.4	248.4	361.3	558.6	864.2	1,255.2	2,334.9
Hourly wages index	178.6	274.3	391.4	593.9	906.9	1,350.0	...

Household income and expenditure. Average household size: n.a.; disposable income per person (1980): ISK 50,580 (U.S.$10,540); sources of income (1982): wages, salaries, and self-employment 80.0%, transfer payments and other 20.0%; expenditure (1973): food 25.7%, housing 17.8%, transportation 14.5%, clothing and footwear 9.2%, health 7.7%, education 0.5%, other 24.6%.
Land use (1981): forested 1.2%; meadows and pastures 22.7%; agricultural and under permanent cultivation 0.1%; other 76.0% ‖.

Foreign trade

Balance of trade (current prices)

	1978	1979	1980	1981	1982	1983
ISK'000,000	+87	+93	+153	−196	−1,885	−1,973
% of total	2.5%	1.7%	1.8%	1.5%	10.0%	5.0%

Imports (1983): ISK20,596,000,000 (machinery and transport equipment 19.2%, of which ships 2.7%; petroleum and petroleum products 14.9%; cereals and other foodstuffs 8.1%; textile yarn, fabrics, and clothing accessories 7.7%; wood and paper products, excluding furniture 5.7%). *Major import sources:* West Germany 11.8%; U.S.S.R. 10.4%; Denmark 9.7%; United Kingdom 8.8%; Sweden 8.3%; Norway 8.0%.
Exports (1983): ISK18,623,000,000 (fish and fish products 63.6%, of which frozen fish fillets 31.0%, dried, salted, and smoked fish 26.0%; aluminum, refined 10.1%; knitted garments, excluding gloves, stockings, and headgear 2.7%). *Major export destinations:* United States 28.3%; United Kingdom 11.9%; West Germany 9.7%; U.S.S.R. 7.4%; Portugal 6.1%.

Transport and communications

Transport. Railroads (1982): none. Roads (1982): total length 7,227 mi, 11,631 km (paved 6.0%). Vehicles (1982): passenger cars 94,744; trucks and buses 11,715. Merchant marine (1983): vessels (100 gross tons and over) 394; total deadweight tonnage 168,793. Air transport (1982): passenger-mi 963,900, passenger-km 1,551,200; short ton-mi cargo 12,936, metric ton-km cargo 18,886¶; airports (1984) with scheduled flights 15.
Communications. Daily newspapers (1982): total number 5; total circulation 114,000; circulation per 1,000 population 503. Radios (1982): 70,035 (1 per 3.4 persons). Television (1982): 62,634 (1 per 3.8 persons). Telephones (1982): 111,358 (1 per 2.1 persons).

Education and health

Education (1982–83)

	schools	teachers	students	student/ teacher ratio
Primary (age 7–12)	187	2,600	25,000	9.6
Secondary (age 12–19)	157	...	21,800	...
Voc., teacher tr.	44	...	4,280	...
Higher	4	280	4,780	17.1

College enrollment per 100,000 population (1982): 2,030. *Literacy* (1983): total population literate 172,570 (100.0%).
Health (1982): physicians 532 (1 per 442 persons); hospital beds 2,551 (1 per 92 persons).
Food (1978–80): daily per capita caloric intake 3,013 (vegetable products 52.5%, animal products 47.5%); 113% of FAO recommended minimum.

*Counties include county cities and towns, which are within, but administratively independent of, the counties. †Detail does not add to total given because of rounding. ‡Includes finance. §Includes public utilities. ‖ Glaciated, covered with peat bogs, or lava desert. ¶Includes Icelandair only.

India

Official name: Bharat (Hindī) (Republic of India).
Form of government: multiparty federal republic with two legislative houses (Council of States [244], House of the People [544]).
Chief of state: President.
Head of government: Prime Minister.
Capital: New Delhi.
Official languages: English, Hindī.
Official religion: none.
Monetary unit: 1 Indian rupee (Rs) = 100 paisa; valuation (Oct. 29, 1984).
1 U.S.$ = Rs12.10; 1 £ = Rs14.60.

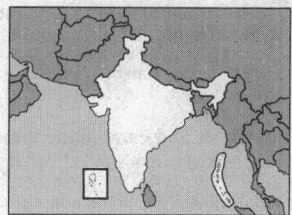

Area and population

States	Capitals	area sq mi	area sq km	population 1981 census
Andhra Pradesh	Hyderābād	106,200	275,100	53,549,673
Assam	Prāgjyotiṣapura	30,300*	78,500*	19,896,843†
Bihār	Patna	67,100	173,900	69,914,734
Gujarāt	Gāndhinagar	75,700	196,000	34,085,799
Haryāna	Chandīgarh	17,100	44,200	12,922,618
Himāchal Pradesh	Simla	21,400	55,500	4,280,818
Jammu and Kashmir‡	Srinagar	86,100*	222,900*	5,987,389
Karnātaka	Bangalore	74,100	191,800	37,135,714
Kerala	Trivandrum	15,000	38,900	25,453,680
Madhya Pradesh	Bhopāl	171,200	443,400	52,178,844
Mahārāshtra	Bombay	118,800	307,700	62,784,171
Manipur	Imphāl	8,600	22,300	1,420,953
Meghālaya	Shillong	8,600	22,400	1,335,819
Nāgāland	Kohīma	6,400	16,600	774,930
Orissa	Bhubaneswar	60,100	155,700	26,370,271
Punjab	Chandīgarh	19,500	50,400	16,788,915
Rājasthān	Jaipur	132,100	342,200	34,261,862
Sikkim	Gangtok	2,700	7,100	316,385
Tamil Nādu	Madras	50,200	130,100	48,408,077
Tripura	Agartala	4,100	10,500	2,053,058
Uttar Pradesh	Lucknow	113,700	294,400	110,862,013
West Bengal	Calcutta	34,200	88,700	54,580,647
Union Territories				
Andaman and Nicobar Islands	Port Blair	3,200	8,200	188,741
Arunāchal Pradesh	Itanagar	32,300	83,700	631,839
Chandīgarh	Chandīgarh	40	100	451,610
Dādra and Nagar Haveli	Silvassa	200	500	103,676
Delhi	Delhi	600	1,500	6,220,406
Goa, Daman, and Diu	Panaji	1,500	3,800	1,086,730
Lakshadweep	Kavaratti	40	100	40,249
Mizorām	Aizawl	8,100	21,100	493,757
Pondicherry	Pondicherry	200	500	604,471
TOTAL		1,269,400*	3,287,800*	685,184,692

Source: Official government figures.

Demography

Density (1984): persons per sq mi 582.4, persons per sq km 224.8.
Urban–rural (1981): urban 23.7%; rural 76.3%.
Sex distribution (1981): male 50.28%; female 49.72%.
Age breakdown (1980): under 15, 40.1%; 15–29, 27.8%; 30–44, 17.0%; 45–59, 10.1%; 60–74, 4.2%; 75 and over, 0.8%.
Population projection: (1990) 820,860,000; (2000) 960,611,000.
Doubling time: 33 years.
Linguistic composition (1971): Hindī 24.0%; Marāṭhī 9.0%; Bengali 8.1%; Telugu 7.9%; Tamil 7.6%; other 43.4%.
Religious affiliation (1971): Hindu 82.7%; Muslim 11.2%; Christian 2.6%; Sikh 1.9%; Buddhist 0.7%; Jain 0.5%; other 0.4%.
Major cities (1981): Calcutta 9,165,650; Bombay 8,227,332; Delhi 4,884,234§; Madras 4,276,635; Bangalore 2,913,537; Hyderābād 2,528,198; Ahmadābād 2,515,195; Kānpur 1,688,242; Pune 1,685,300; Nāgpur 1,297,977; Lucknow 1,006,538; Jaipur 1,004,669.
Place of birth: n.a.
Mobility (1971). Population living in same district as at birth: 106,000,000 (62.3%); different district, same state 36,000,000 (21.2%); different state 19,000,000 (11.2%); moved outside the country 9,000,000 (5.3%).
Households (1971). Average household size 5.3 ‖; number of rooms per household: 1 room 47.8%, 2 rooms 28.2%, 3 rooms 12.0%, 4 rooms 6.0%, 5 or more rooms 5.9%, unspecified number of rooms 0.1%. Household population 543,000,000 (99.1%), houseless population 2,000,000 (0.4%), institutional population 3,000,000 (0.5%).
Emigration (1980): persons living abroad, accepting foreign citizenship: 6,750,800, of whom Nepal 2,388,000 (35.4%), Malaysia 1,009,500 (15.0%), Mauritius 612,500 (9.1%), Sri Lanka 433,000 (6.4%), Guyana 424,100 (6.3%), Fiji 300,700 (4.5%), United Kingdom 250,000 (3.7%).

Vital statistics

Birth rate per 1,000 population (1981): 33.3 (world avg. 29.0); legitimate, n.a.; illegitimate, n.a.
Death rate per 1,000 population (1981): 12.5 (world avg. 12.0).
Natural increase rate per 1,000 population (1981): 20.8 (world avg. 17.0).
Total fertility rate (avg. births per childbearing woman; 1980–85): 4.5.
Marriage rate per 1,000 population: n.a.
Divorce rate per 1,000 population: n.a.

Infant mortality rate per 1,000 live births (1981): 117.
Life expectancy at birth (1981): male 53.9 years; female 52.9 years.
Major causes of death: no data available; however, major infectious diseases are influenza, tuberculosis, amebiasis, typhoid and paratyphoid fevers, viral hepatitis, whooping cough, measles, syphilis, chicken pox, tetanus, rabies, diphtheria, and cholera.

Social indicators

Educational attainment (1981). Percent of adult population having: primary education 31.5%, middle school 17.6%, secondary 11.6%, some post secondary 4.1%, higher degree or diploma 0.6%, post-graduate 3.9%, other 30.7%¶.

Distribution of income (1975–76)

percent of household income by quintile:

1	2	3	4	5 (highest)
7.0%	9.2%	13.9%	20.5%	49.4%

Quality of working life (1981). Average work week: 45 hours (n.a., overtime). Rate of injuries per 1,000 workers (1975): factories 50.9, railways 21.1, mines 4.7. Employees covered under Employee's State Insurance Scheme 7,200,000, number of beneficiaries 27,800,000. Average days lost to labour stoppages per 1,000 work days (1982): 1.4. Average duration of journey to work n.a. Rate per 1,000 workers of discouraged (unemployed no longer seeking work): n.a.
Access to services (1980). Proportion of villages having access to electricity 47.8%, safe public water supply (for urban population only) 98.0%♀.
Social participation. Eligible voters participating in last national election 55.5%. Trade union membership in total workforce 46.3%♂. Practicing religious population in total affiliated population n.a.
Social deviance (1973). Offense rate per 100,000 population for: murder 3.0, kidnapping and abduction 1.8, cheating 2.5, theft 66.1, robbery and housebreaking 34.9. Incidence in general population of: alcoholism n.a., drug and substance abuse n.a.□. Rate per 100,000 population of suicide 0.02♀.
Leisure (1983). Favourite leisure activities: radio 4.2%◊, cinema 3,467,500,-000△.
Material well-being (1980). Households possessing: automobile 0.7%, telephone 2.3%, television receiver 1.6%, radio 16.7%, air conditioner n.a., washing machine n.a.

National economy

Gross national product (at current market prices; 1982): U.S.$173,876,000,-000 (U.S.$249 per capita).

Origin of gross domestic product (current prices)

	1981 in value Rs'000,000,000	% of total value	labour force†	% of labour force
Agriculture	470.9	32.0	1,306,000	5.5
Mining	31.4	2.1	960,000	4.1
Manufacturing	224.7	15.3	6,318,000	26.8
Construction	62.4	4.2	1,182,000	5.0
Trade	200.3	13.6	390,000	1.7
Public utilities	24.2	1.6	735,000	3.1
Transportation and communication	76.6	5.2	2,842,000	12.1
Finance	⊕	⊕	1,019,000	4.3
Pub. admin., defense	⊕	⊕	...	...
Services	⊕	⊕	8,806,000	37.4
Other	383.0⊕**	26.0⊕	...	...
TOTAL	1,473.5	100.0	23,558,000	100.0

Budget (1983–84). Revenue: Rs206,253,500,000 (customs duties 28.5%; interest receipts 13.6%; corporate taxes 11.6%. Expenditures: Rs224,188,700,000 (defense 23.9% social and community services 6.4%; agriculture and allied services 6.3%; industry and minerals 5.8%).
National debt (1983–84): Rs647,130,000,000; public debt (external, outstanding) U.S.$20,687,000,000 .
Tourism (1982): receipts from visitors U.S.$800,000,000; expenditures by nationals abroad U.S.$220,000,000♂.

Manufacturing enterprises (1978–79)

	no. of factories	no. of employees	annual wages as a % of avg. of all wages	annual value added (Rs'000,000)
Chemicals and chem. products	4,881	426,000	154.5	12,990
Cotton textiles	7,601	1,118,000	96.8	11,550
Basic metals and alloys	5,250	549,000	141.2	9,570
Iron and steel	4,502	500,000	...	8,380
Cement	62	90,000	...	7,556
Machinery except electrical	6,387	384,000	132.1	6,640
Food products	16,310	1,132,000	42.5	6,300
Electrical machinery	2,882	285,000	150.8	5,750
Rubber, plastic, petroleum, and coal products	2,350	144,000	135.0	3,790
Paper products, printing, publishing, etc.	4,901	259,000	107.3	3,190
Nonmetallic mineral products	5,639	337,000	72.4	2,970
Wool, silk, and synthetic textiles	3,216	193,000	100.1	2,950
Beverages and tobacco prod.	8,240	392,000	37.5	2,460
Metal products	5,818	184,000	96.1	2,300
Jute, hemp, and mesta (kenaf) textiles	247	264,000	88.0	1,710

Production (metric tons except as noted). Agriculture, forestry, fishing (1982): sugarcane 183,647,000, rice 68,000,000, wheat 37,833,000, sorghum 10,-800,000, millet 9,000,000, corn (maize) 6,500,000, peanuts (groundnuts) in shell 5,700,000, cassava 5,567,000, bananas 4,724,000, chickpeas 4,567,000, coconuts 4,500,000, seed cotton 3,930,000, dry beans 2,700,000, onions 2,700,000, rapeseed 2,363,000, barley 2,012,000, cotton (lint) 1,310,000, jute 1,220,000, tea 565,000, tobacco 525,000, linseed 474,000, copra 385,000, cashew nuts 194,000; livestock (number of live animals) 182,000,000 cattle, 72,000,000 goats, 62,000,000 buffaloes, 41,700,000 sheep, 1,150,000 camels; roundwood—coniferous 8,191,000, nonconiferous 210,435,000; fish catch 2,335,150. Mining and quarrying (1983): limestone 38,208,000; iron ore 37,992,000; copper ore 3,528,000; bauxite 1,860,000; manganese ore 1,260,000; gypsum 972,000; chromite 372,000; zinc concentrates 76,000; lead concentrates 32,000. Manufacturing (1982–83): cement 23,200,000; steel ingots 11,000,000; sugar 8,200,000; fertilizer 4,404,000; jute textiles 1,300,000; aluminum 208,000; motorcycles and scooters 399,800 units; refrigerators 379,000 units; sewing machines 309,000 units; railway wagons 15,400 units; cotton cloth 9,200,000,000 metres; man-made fibre 1,368,000,000 metres; machinery Rs3,906,000,000, of which cotton textile machinery Rs3,151,000,000. Construction (number of buildings; 1981): residential 46,493; nonresidential 9,644.

Service enterprises (1978–79)

	no. of enterprises	no. of employees	annual wage as a % of all wages	annual value added (Rs'000,000)
Public utilities (waterworks, gas)	229	13,000	122.0	160
Electrical power	216	645,000	118.0	12,190
Transport equipment (including				
shipbuilding and motor vehicles)	2,528	392,000	148.0	5,920
Railways††	7,072‡‡	1,800,000	...	29,661§§
Communicationδ				
Post and telegraph	178,246 ‖‖	852,000	...	...
Film	10,782¶¶	200,000	...	5,500**
Radio and television	106ǫǫ	...	...	172δδ
Finance (banks)††	40,828▫▫	...	...	461,280◊◊
Wholesale trade△△	116,000	...	...	264
Retail trade△△	3,760,000	4,925,000	...	24,524
Tourism†	1,288,160††	...	...	7,500⊙⊕
Health services	29,300***	419,100†††	...	...
Cold storage services	413	7,000	46.6	60
Other: repair services	2,908	216,000	124.9	1,980

Energy production (consumption): electricity (kW-hr; 1982) 138,677,000,000 (138,616,000,000); coal (metric tons; 1982) 134,992,000 (132,887,000); crude petroleum (barrels; 1982) 144,650,000 (234,194,000); petroleum products (metric tons; 1982) 24,896,000 (28,434,000); natural gas (cu m; 1982) 2,272,484,910 (2,272,484,910).
Persons economically active (1982): total 271,352,000 (38.9%); female participation in the labour force, n.a.; unemployed 18,646,000 (6.9%).

Price and earnings indexes (1980 = 100)

	1978	1979	1980	1981	1982	1983	1984
Consumer price index	84.4	89.7	100.0	113.0	121.9	136.3	150.0‡‡‡
Earnings index	...	...	...	...	...	...	...

Household income and expenditure. Average household size (1980) 5.3; average annual income per household, n.a.; source of income: n.a.; expenditure (1981–82): food 56.1%, clothing and footwear 10.2%, tobacco and intoxicants 4.6%, housing 3.6%, fuel and power 3.5%, taxes 0.1%.
Land use (1981): forested 22.7%; meadows and pastures 4.0%; agricultural and under permanent cultivation 57.0%; other 16.3%.

Financial aggregates

	1978	1979	1980	1981	1982	1983	1984 (9 mo.)
Exchange rate, Rs per:							
U.S. dollar	8.19	8.13	7.86	8.66	9.46	10.10	11.82
£	15.73	17.24	18.29	17.56	16.55	15.32	14.88
SDR	10.67	10.42	10.11	10.59	10.63	10.99	11.88
International reserves (U.S.$)							
Total (excl. gold; '000,000)	6,426	7,432	6,944	4,693	4,315	4,937	5,957§§§
SDR's ('000,000)	294	489	480	545	374	110	181
Reserve pos. in IMF ('000,000)	90	213	420	384	402	510	486
Foreign exchange('000,000)	6,042	6,731	6,043	3,764	3,539	4,318	5,114§§§
Gold, ('000,000 fine troy oz.)	8.362	8.560	8.594	8.594	8.594	8.594	8.594§§§
% world reserves	0.8	0.9	0.9	0.9	0.9	0.9	0.9§§§
Interest and prices							
Central bank discount (%)	9.0	9.0	9.0	10.0	10.0	10.0	10.0
Gov't. bond yield (%)	6.4	6.5	6.7	7.2	7.6	8.0	8.7
Industrial share prices							
(1980 = 100)	81.0	92.7	100.0	122.7	120.1	126.2	136.5
Balance of payments							
(U.S.$'000,000)							
Balance of visible trade	−884	−2,222	−5,644	−5,711	...	...	...
Imports, f.o.b.	7,402	9,819	13,947	14,149	...	...	...
Exports, f.o.b.	6,518	7,597	8,303	8,437	...	...	...
Balance of invisibles							
Balance of payments,	−50	+226	+525	+7	...	...	...
current account	659	48	−1,785	−2,698	...	...	...

Foreign trade

Balance of trade (current prices)

	1979	1980	1981	1982	1983	1984 ‖‖
Rs'000,000	−16,375	−49,254	−61,599	−51,275	−48,553	−19,803
% of total	11.4%	26.7%	30.0%	22.5%	22.0%	30.6%

Imports (1981–82): Rs35,877,000,000 (petroleum oil and lubricants 38.2%, nonelectrical machinery 8.7%, iron and steel 8.4%, fertilizer 4.0%, edible oils 2.9%, chemical elements and compounds 2.9%, pearls and precious and semiprecious stones 2.5%, nonferrous metals 2.2%). *Major import sources:* United States 10.5%; Iran 9.8%; U.S.S.R. 8.5%; Japan 6.9%; West Germany 6.7%; United Kingdom 6.2%; Belgium 3.8%; Iraq 3.1%; Canada 2.2%; Kuwait 2.0%.
Exports (1981–82): Rs77,962,000,000 (handicrafts 13.3%, engineering goods

10.5%, cotton apparel 5.9%, leather and leather manufactures 4.8%, tea 4.8%, iron ore 4.4%, chemicals 4.4%, cotton fabrics 3.5%, fish and fish preparations 3.5%). *Major export destinations:* U.S.S.R. 19.3%; United States 11.3%; Japan 8.9%; United Kingdom 5.9%; West Germany 4.9%; Belgium 2.1%; The Netherlands 1.9%; France 1.9%; Kuwait 1.7%; Iran 1.4%.

Transport and communications

Transport. Railroads (1982): route length 38,046 mi, 61,230 km; passenger-mi 137,190,000,000, passenger-km 220,787,000,000; short ton-mi cargo 119,318,000,000, metric ton-km cargo 174,202,000,000. Roads (1981): total length 953,346 mi, 1,534,265 km (paved 43%). Vehicles (1982): passenger cars 907,445; trucks and buses 741,630. Merchant marine (1983): vessels (100 gross tons and over) 677; total deadweight tonnage 10,081,564. Air transport (1982): passenger-mi 8,239,000,000, passenger-km 13,260,000,000; short ton-mi cargo 305,570,000, metric ton-km cargo 446,124,000; airports (1980) with scheduled flights 62.
Communications. Daily newspapers (1981): total number 1,264; total circulation 15,255,000; circulation per 1,000 population 32.5. Radios (1983): total number of receivers 22,000,000 (1 per 32 persons). Television (1983): total number of receivers 2,095,537 (1 per 339 persons). Telephones (1982): 2,981,609 (1 per 234 persons).

Education and health

Education (1982–83)

	schools	teachers	students	student/ teacher ratio
Primary (age 5–10)	503,741	1,389,356	55,220,443	39.7
Secondary (age 10–17)	180,580	1,849,504	57,867,196	31.3
Voc., Teacher tr.	4,878	...	468,993	...
Higher¶¶¶	3,465	145,842	2,832,000	19.4

College graduates per 100,000 population (students graduating; 1978): 172. *Literacy*ǫǫǫ (1981): total population literate 237,991,932 (36.2%); males literate 158,837,215 (46.7%); females literate 79,154,717 (24.9%).
Health (1981): physicians 268,712 (1 per 2,554 persons); hospital beds 540,768 (1 per 1,269 persons).
Food (1978–80): daily per capita caloric intake 1,998 (vegetable products 95.5%, animal products 4.5%); 90% of FAO recommended minimum requirement.

Military

Total active duty personnel (1983): 1,120,000 (army 85.7%; navy 4.2%; air force 10.1%). *Military expenditure as percent of GNP* (1982): 3.5% (world 6.0%); per capita expenditure U.S.$9.

*Area data for Assam and Jammu and Kashmir are from 1971. †Estimate. ‡Area data includes 32,400 sq mi (83,800 sq km) of Pakistani-occupied Jammu and Kashmir; population data pertains to the Indian-occupied portion only. §Excludes the population of New Delhi (273,036) and Delhi Cantonment (85,166). ‖ 1980. ¶Includes uneducated persons who can read and write. ǫ1977. δ1981. ▫In 1983 India's codeine consumption (11,500 kg) was fourth highest in the world. ◊Weekly time spent. △Average annual attendance. †Employed persons only. ⊕Finance, services, and public administration and defense included with other. **Also includes indirect taxes and subsidies. ††1982. ‡‡Number of railway stations. §§Gross revenue. ‖ ‖ Number of post and telegraph offices. ¶¶Number of cinemas. ǫǫNumber of radio and television stations. δδEarnings from commercials. ▫▫Number of bank branches. ◊◊Total deposits. △△1970. ††Number of tourists. ⊙⊕Foreign exchange earned. ***Number of hospitals, dispensaries, and primary health centres. †††Number of physicians and nurses. ‡‡‡July. §§§Six months. ‖ ‖ ‖ First quarter. ¶¶¶1979–80. ǫǫǫIncludes all ages.

Tāj Mahal, mausoleum of Mumtāz Maḥal (d. 1631), Āgra, Uttar Pradesh.

Indonesia

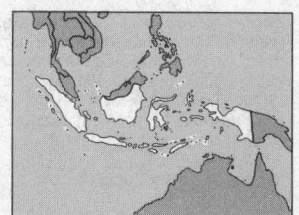

Official name: Republik Indonesia (Republic of Indonesia).
Form of government: unitary multiparty republic with two legislative houses (People's Consultative Assembly [920]; House of People's Representatives [460]).
Head of state and government: President.
Capital: Jakarta.
Official language: Bahasa Indonesia.
Official religion: none.
Monetary unit: 1 Indonesian rupiah (Rp) = 100 sen; valuation (Oct. 29, 1984) 1 U.S.$ = Rp1,061.67; 1 £ = Rp1,281.43.

Area and population

Metropolitan district	Capitals	area sq mi	area sq km	population 1980 census
Jakarta Raya	Jakarta	228	590	6,503,449
Provinces				
Bali	Denpasar	2,147	5,561	2,469,930
Bengkulu	Bengkulu	8,173	21,168	768,064
Irian Jaya	Jayapura	162,927	421,981	1,173,875
Jambi	Jambi	17,345	44,924	1,445,994
Jawa Barat	Bandung	17,876	46,300	27,453,525
Jawa Tengah	Semarang	13,207	34,206	25,372,889
Jawa Timur	Surabaya	18,503	47,922	29,188,852
Kalimantan Barat	Pontianak	56,664	146,760	2,486,068
Kalimantan Selatan	Banjarmasin	58,919	152,600	2,064,649
Kalimantan Tengah	Palangka Raya	14,541	37,660	954,353
Kalimantan Timur	Balikpapan	78,162	202,440	1,218,016
Lampung	Tanjung Karang	12,860	33,307	4,624,785
Maluku	Ambon	28,766	74,505	1,411,006
Nusa Tenggara Barat	Mataram	7,790	20,177	2,724,664
Nusa Tenggara Timur	Kupang	18,485	47,876	2,737,166
Riau	Pakan Baru	36,510	94,562	2,168,535
Sulawesi Selatan	Ujung Pandang	28,101	72,781	6,062,212
Sulawesi Tengah	Palu	26,921	69,726	1,289,635
Sulawesi Tenggara	Kendari	10,690	27,686	942,302
Sulawesi Utara	Menado	7,345	19,023	2,115,384
Sumatera Barat	Padang	19,219	49,778	3,406,816
Sumatera Selatan	Palembang	40,034	103,688	4,629,801
Sumatera Utara	Medan	27,331	70,787	8,360,894
Timor Timur	Dili	5,743	14,874	555,350
Special autonomous districts				
Aceh	Kutaraja	21,387	55,392	2,611,271
Yogyakarta	Yogyakarta	1,224	3,169	2,750,813
TOTAL		741,101*	1,919,443	147,490,298

Demography

Density (1984): persons per sq mi 221.8, persons per sq km 85.6.
Urban–rural (1980): urban 22.3%; rural 77.7%.
Sex distribution (1980): male 49.72%; female 50.28%.
Age breakdown (1980): under 15, 40.8%; 15–29, 27.0%; 30–44, 16.4%; 45–59, 10.2%; 60–74, 4.5%; 75 and over, 1.1%.
Population projection: (1990) 173,530,000; (2000) 198,687,000.
Doubling time: 40 years.
Ethnic composition (1980): Javanese 42.0%; Sundanese 13.6%; Madurese 7.0%; other 37.4%.
Religious affiliation (1980): Muslim 83.6%; Protestant 4.8%; Roman Catholic 2.7%; other 8.9%.
Major cities (1980): Jakarta 6,503,449; Surabaya 2,027,913; Bandung 1,462,637; Medan 1,378,955; Semarang 1,026,671.

Vital statistics

Birth rate per 1,000 population (1983): 30.3 (world avg. 29.0); legitimate (n.a.), illegitimate (n.a.).
Death rate per 1,000 population (1983): 12.9 (world avg. 11.0).
Natural increase rate per 1,000 population (1983): 17.4 (world avg. 18.0).
Total fertility rate (avg. births per childbearing woman; 1983): 3.8.
Marriage rate per 1,000 population (1978): 8.8.
Divorce rate per 1,000 population (1978): 1.5.
Infant mortality rate per 1,000 live births (1983): 106.0.
Life expectancy at birth (1983): male 51.4 years; female 54.2 years.
Major causes of death: n.a.; however, major diseases are tuberculosis, malaria, dysentery, cholera, and plague.

National economy

Budget (1982–83). Revenue: Rp14,358,290,000,000 (direct taxes 69.7%, of which oil companies corporation tax 56.9%; indirect taxes 13.7%; development receipts 13.5%. Expenditures: Rp14,355,920,000,000 (development expenditures 51.3%; operating expenditures 48.7%).
Public debt (external, outstanding; 1982): U.S.$184,212,100,100.
Tourism (1981): receipts from visitors U.S.$288,000,000; expenditures by nationals abroad U.S.$644,000,000.
Production (metric tons except as noted). Agriculture, forestry, fishing (1982): paddy rice 34,104,100, cassavas 12,676,000, corn (maize) 3,207,000, sweet potatoes 1,897,000, sugarcane 1,565,200, palm oil 807,400, soybeans 514,000, peanuts (groundnuts) 434,000, rubber 287,000, tea 70,200, coffee 18,200, cacao 12,300; livestock (number of live animals) 7,985,000 goats, 6,435,000 cattle, 4,196,000 sheep, 3,296,000 pigs; roundwood 128,357,000 cu

m; fish catch 2,020,000. Mining and quarrying (1982): nickel ore 1,640,922; bauxite 700,247; copper ore† 223,704; iron ore† 144,493; tin ore† 33,806; silver 3,058 kg. Manufacturing (1982): cement 7,650,000; paper 296,900; cotton yarn 121,551 bales; beer 84,924,000 litres; transportation vehicles 188,444 units. Energy production (consumption): electricity (kW-hr; 1982) 7,365,000,000 (7,365,000,000); coal (metric tons; 1982) 481,000 (273,000); crude petroleum (barrels; 1982) 483,000,000 (172,000,000); petroleum products (metric tons; 1982) 21,675,000 (20,459,000); natural gas (cu m; 1982) 16,573,000,000 (4,207,000,000).
Gross national product (at current market prices; 1982): U.S.$87,199,000,000 (U.S.$570 per capita).

Origin of gross domestic product (current prices)

	1980 in value Rp'000,000	% of total value	labour force	% of labour force
Agriculture	11,252.5	25.7	28,040,462	55.5
Mining	11,672.5	26.7	369,282	0.7
Manufacturing	3,845.5	8.8	4,360,657	8.6
Construction	2,523.8	5.8	1,573,142	3.1
Trade	6,167.5	14.1	6,611,397	13.1
Public utilities	225.1	0.5	84,684	0.2
Transportation and communication	1,706.1	3.9	1,467,771	2.9
Finance‡	2,231.6	5.1	231,935	0.5
Pub. admin., defense	3,144.6	7.2 }	7,786,558	15.4
Services and other	995.8	2.3		
TOTAL	43,765.0	100.0*	50,525,888	100.0

Persons economically active (1980): total 52,153,345 (35.4%); female 17,203,026 (33.0%); unemployed 896,101 (1.7%).

Price and earnings indexes (1980 = 100)

	1978	1979	1980	1981	1982	1983	1984§
Consumer price index	70.0	84.4	100.0	112.2	122.9	137.4	152.1§
Monthly earnings index ‖	54.1	70.2	100.0	...	...	...	...

Household income and expenditure. Average household size (1980) 4.9; income per household: n.a.; source of income: n.a.; expenditure (1978): food 60.6%, housing 13.0%, recreation 8.4%, clothing and footwear 5.7%.
Land use (1981): forested 67.2%; meadows and pastures 6.6%; agricultural and under permanent cultivation 10.8%; other 15.4%.

Foreign trade

Balance of trade (current prices)

	1977	1978	1979	1980	1981	1982
U.S.$'000,000	+4,622.3	+4,952.8	+8,387.8	+13,116.0	+11,892.4	+5,469.4
% of total	27.1%	27.0%	44.6%	37.7%	30.9%	14.0%

Imports (1982): U.S.$16,858,900,000 (machinery, transport equipment, and parts 37.1%; mineral fuels and lubricants 21.1%; basic manufactures 16.2%; chemicals 10.7%; food and live animals 6.4%). *Major import sources:* Japan 25.4%; Singapore 16.7%; United States 14.3%; West Germany 7.1%.
Exports (1982): U.S.$22,328,300,000 (petroleum and petroleum products 69.4%; natural gas 13.0%; rubber 2.7%; wood 2.5%; tin 1.7%; coffee 1.5%). *Major export destinations:* Japan 50.1%; U.S. 15.9%; Singapore 14.0%.

Transport and communications

Transport. Railroads: (1980) length 4,264 mi, 6,877 km; (1982) passenger-km 6,293,000,000; (1982) metric ton-km cargo 885,000,000. Roads (1979): total length 80,094 mi, 128,899 km (paved 45%). Vehicles (1982): passenger cars 791,019; trucks and buses 791,534. Merchant marine (1983): vessels (100 gross tons and over) 1,391; total deadweight tonnage 2,801,546. Air transport (1982): passenger-km 7,523,000,000; metric ton-km cargo 173,300,000; airports (1983) 94.
Communications. Daily newspapers (1982): total number 89; total circulation 2,603,190; circulation per 1,000 population 17.2. Radios (1983): total number of receivers 6,550,000 (1 per 23.2 persons). Television (1983): total number of receivers 3,000,000 (1 per 50.6 persons). Telephones (1982): 600,600 (1 per 252.6 persons).

Education and health

Education (1981–82)

	schools	teachers	students	student/ teacher ratio
Primary (age 7–12)	100,050	713,222	23,862,488	33.5
Secondary (age 13–18)	15,018	289,979	5,022,484	17.3
Voc., teacher tr.	2,752	65,528	810,424	12.4
Higher	50	56,322	480,981	8.5

College graduates per 100,000 population (1980): 156. *Literacy* (1980): total population literate 72.0%; males literate 80.5%; females literate 63.8%.
Health: physicians (1980) 13,000 (1 per 11,345 persons); hospital beds (1982) 101,029 (1 per 1,502 persons).
Food (1978–80): daily per capita caloric intake 2,296 (vegetable products 97.8%, animal products 2.2%); 106% of FAO recommended minimum.

Military

Total active duty personnel (1983): 281,000 (army 74.7%; navy 14.9%; air force 10.4%). *Military expenditure as percent of GNP:* (1982) 3.2%; (world 6.0%); per capita expenditure U.S.$19.

*Detail does not add to total given because of rounding. †Concentrates. ‡Includes business services. §Second quarter. ‖ Manufacturing industries only, including benefits.

Iran

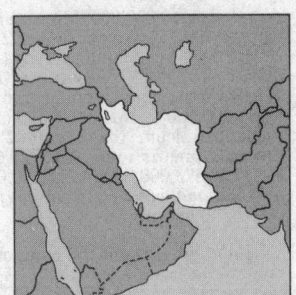

Official name: Jomhūrīyeh Islāmīyeh Īrān (Islāmic Republic of Iran).
Form of government: unitary Islāmic republic with a single legislative house (Islāmic Consultative Assembly [270]).
Chief of state: Velayat Faghih (religious leader).
Head of state: President.
Head of government: Prime Minister.
Capital: Tehrān.
Official language: Farsī (Persian).
Official religion: Islām.
Monetary unit: 1 rial (Rls) = 100 dinars; valuation (Oct. 29, 1984) 1 U.S.$ = Rls93.21; 1£ = Rls112.50.

Area and population

Provinces	Capitals	area sq mi	area sq km	population 1983–84 estimate
Azārbāijān-e Gharbī	Orūmīyeh	15,000	38,850	1,688,000
Azārbāijān-e Sharqī	Tabrīz	25,908	67,102	3,679,000
Bakhtarān	Bakhtarān	9,137	23,667	1,225,000
Boyer Aḥmad-e Kohkilūyeh	Yāsūj	5,506	14,261	292,000
Būshehr	Būshehr	10,676	27,653	428,000
Chahār Maḥāl-e Bakhtīārī	Shahr Kord	5,741	14,870	476,000
Eṣfahān	Eṣfahān	40,405	104,650	2,770,000
Fārs	Shīrāz	51,466	133,298	2,442,000
Gīlān	Rasht	5,679	14,709	1,822,000
Hamādan	Hamādan	7,638	19,784	1,253,000
Hormozgān	Bandar 'Abbās	25,818	66,870	568,000
Īlām	Īlām	7,352	19,044	266,000
Kermān	Kermān	71,997	186,472	1,317,000
Khorāsān	Mashhad	120,980	313,337	3,938,000
Khūzestān	Ahvāz	24,981	64,702	2,672,000
Kordestān	Sanandaj	9,651	24,998	923,000
Lorestān	Khorramābād	12,117	31,383	1,074,000
Markazī	Arāk	15,403	39,895	1,301,000
Māzandarān	Sārī	18,291	47,375	2,861,000
Semnān	Semnān	34,764	90,039	322,000
Sīstān-e Balūchestān	Zāhedān	70,107	181,578	829,000
Tehrān	Tehrān	7,381	19,118	7,192,000
Yazd	Yazd	24,673	63,905	424,000
Zanjān	Zanjān	14,053	36,398	1,309,000
TOTAL		634,724	1,643,958	41,071,000

Source: Official government figures.

Demography

Density (1983): persons per sq mi 65.4, persons per sq km 25.6.
Urban–rural (1980): urban 49.9%; rural 50.1%.
Sex distribution (1980): male 50.72%; female 49.28%.
Age breakdown (1981–82): under 15, 43.5%; 15–29, 28.7%; 30–44, 14.7%; 45–59, 8.7%; 60–64, 1.6%; 65 and over, 2.8%.
Population projection: (1990) 51,033,000; (2000) 64,916,000.
Doubling time: 26 years.
Ethnic composition (1976): Persian 45.0%; Indo–European 43.2%; Kurd 8.2%; Turk 2.6%; Arab 1.9%.
Religious affiliation (1980): Muslim 97.9%; Bahā'ī 0.9%; other 1.2%.
Major cities (1982 est.): Tehrān 5,734,199; Mashhad 1,119,748; Eṣfahān 926,601; Shīrāz 800,416; Ahvaz 470,927.

Vital statistics

Birth rate per 1,000 population (1981): 42.7 (world avg. 29.0).
Death rate per 1,000 population (1981): 11.0 (world avg. 11.0).
Natural increase rate per 1,000 population (1981): 31.7 (world avg. 18.0).
Total fertility rate (avg. births per childbearing woman; 1981): 6.0.
Marriage rate per 1,000 population (1980): 7.5.
Divorce rate per 1,000 population (1980): 0.6.
Infant mortality rate per 1,000 live births (1975–80): 114.8.
Life expectancy at birth (1981): male 57.1 years; female 59.0 years.
Major causes of death per 100,000 population: no data available; however, major infectious diseases are influenza, strep throat, dermatomycosis, typhoid and paratyphoid fevers, measles, malaria, brucellosis, and chicken pox.

National economy

Budget (1982–83). Revenue: Rls3,104,627,000,000 (oil and gas 47.9%, taxes 21.5%, investment 7.5%, trade and services 2.6%, other 20.5%). Expenditures: Rls2,980,000,000,000 (development 26.2%, Irani–Iraqi war 13.4%, other 60.4%).
Tourism (1982): receipts from visitors U.S.$20,000,000; expenditures by nationals abroad, n.a.
Production (metric tons except as noted). Agriculture, forestry, fishing (1982): wheat 6,500,000, rice (paddy) 1,400,000, barley 1,200,000, grapes 988,000, watermelons 967,000, potatoes 768,000, melons 521,000, sugar (raw value) 460,000, apples 460,000; livestock (number of live animals) 34,832,000 sheep, 13,847,000 goats, 8,567,000 cattle, 1,800,000 asses, 350,000 horses, 73,592,000 chickens. Mining and quarrying (1982): kaolin 110,000; barite 80,000; chromium ore (oxide content) 40,000; zinc ore 34,800. Manufacturing (value in Rls; 1980): petroleum products 116,680,000,000; textiles 93,870,000,000; transport equipment 28,200,000,000; electrical machinery 27,600,000,000; chemicals 26,200,000,000; iron and steel 25,900,000,000; processed food 65,660,000. Construction (vaule in Rls; 1979): new buildings completed 305,600,000,000, of which residential 278,100,000,000.

Energy production (consumption): electricity (kW-hr; 1981) 16,900,000 (16,900,000); coal (metric tons; 1981) 1,000,000 (1,060,000); petroleum (barrels; 1983) 876,600,000 (193,000,000); petroleum products (metric tons; 1981) 22,880,000 (17,595,000); natural gas (cu m; 1983) 17,700,000,000,000 (5,764,000,000)*.
Gross national product (at current market prices; 1977): U.S.$75,257,512,857 (U.S.$2,123 per capita).

Origin of gross domestic product (current prices):

	1976 in value Rls'000,000	% of total value	labour force	% of labour force
Agriculture	426,300	9.6	3,615,314	36.9
Mining	1,678,100	37.7	90,230	0.9
Manufacturing	490,100	11.0	1,682,188	17.2
Construction	335,800	7.5	1,202,061	12.3
Trade	527,600†	11.8†	671,735	6.9
Public utilities	34,300	0.8	61,761	0.6
Transportation and communication	150,700	3.4	433,364	4.4
Finance	†	†	100,653	1.0
Pub. admin., defense	480,000	10.8	...	...
Services	...	...	1,523,688	15.6
Other	330,100	7.4	415,061	4.2
TOTAL	4,453,000	100.0	9,796,055	100.0

Persons economically active (1976): total 9,796,055 (28.5%); female participation in labour force 1,985,728 (20.3%); unemployed, n.a.

Price and earnings indexes (1980 = 100)

	1978	1979	1980	1981	1982	1983§
Consumer price index	75.0	82.9	100.0	124.2	147.4	176.6
Monthly earnings index‡	49.9	73.8	100.0	108.9	119.7	125.4

Household income and expenditure. Average household size (1974–75) 5.2; income per household Rls298,761 (U.S.$4,235); sources of income: wages 40.8%, self-employment 28.2%, assistance 4.5%; expenditure (1974–75): food 29.2%, housing 21.7%, clothing and footwear 11.8%, transportation 8.7%, recreation 1.4%.
Land use (1981): forested 11.0%; meadows and pastures 26.9%; agricultural and under permanent cultivation 9.8%; other 52.3%.

Foreign trade

Balance of trade (current prices) ‖

	1978	1979	1980	1981	1982	1983
Rls'000,000	+330,600	+878,500	+228,200	+119,200	+587,500	+275,800
% of total	11.9%	20.6%	12.9%	6.5%	27.0%	8.9%

Imports (1981): Rls861,600,000,000 (machinery and transport equipment 28.0%, chemicals 14.5%, food and live animals 13.9%). *Major import sources:* West Germany 15.2%; Japan 9.8%; U.S.S.R. 7.6%; United Kingdom 7.3%; Switzerland 4.2%; Austria 3.3%.
Exports (1981): Rls980,800,000,000 (petroleum and petroleum products 96.3%). *Major export destinations:* West Germany 45.2%; U.S.S.R. 12.4%; Italy 8.1%; Saudi Arabia 3.6%; France 3.1%.

Transport and communications

Transport. Railroads (1983): route length 2,837 mi, 4,567 km. Roads (1981): total length 59,462 mi, 95,696 km (paved 28%). Vehicles (1981): passenger cars 1,532,269; trucks and buses 313,006. Merchant marine (1983): vessels (100 gross tons and over) 270; total deadweight tonnage 2,907,389. Air transport (1982): passenger-mi 1,532,490,000, passenger-km 2,466,308,000; short ton-mi cargo 225,464,000, metric ton-km cargo 329,172,000; airports (1984) with scheduled flights 10.
Communications. Daily newspapers (1983): total number 14; circulation, n.a. Radios (1983): total number of receivers 7,500,000 (1 per 5.4 persons). Televisions (1983): total number of receivers 2,000,000 (1 per 20.3 persons).

Education and health

Education (1982–83)

	schools	teachers	students	student/ teacher ratio
Primary (age 7–11)	44,900	250,167	5,592,808	22.4
Secondary (age 12–18)	9,312	63,611	1,717,097	26.9
Voc., teacher tr.	3,707	66,010	1,002,569	15.2
Higher	114	9,042	117,148	12.9

College graduates per 100,000 population: n.a. *Literacy* (1980): total population literate 10,980,000 (42.8%); males literate 7,163,000 (55.4%); females literate 3,817,000 (30.1%).
Health: physicians (1979) 16,234 (1 per 2,320 persons); hospital beds (1975) 51,298 (1 per 650 persons).
Food (1978–80): daily per capita caloric intake 2,912 (vegetable products 90.5%, animal products 9.5%); 121% of FAO recommended minimum.

Military

Total active duty personnel (1982): 2,000,000¶ (army 73.2%; navy 9.7%; air force 17.1%). The estimated defense expenditures for 1982–83 range from U.S.$6,900,000,000 to U.S.$13,300,000,000. Total war costs to end of 1982 were reported at about U.S.$100,000,000,000.

*1981. †Finance is included with trade. ‡Compensation paid to employees in large manufacturing establishments. §Second quarter only. ‖ Imports derived from the Direction of Trade Statistics (DOTS). ¶Includes about 1,800,000 active paramilitary.

Iraq

Official name: al-Jumhūrīyah al-ʿIrāqīyah (Republic of Iraq).
Form of government: unitary single-party republic with one legislative house (National Assembly [250]).
Head of state and government: President.
Capital: Baghdād.
Official language: Arabic.
Official religion: Islām.
Monetary unit: 1 Iraqi dinar (ID) = 20 dirhams = 1,000 fils; valuation (Oct. 29, 1984) 1 ID = U.S.$3.18; 1 ID = £2.63.

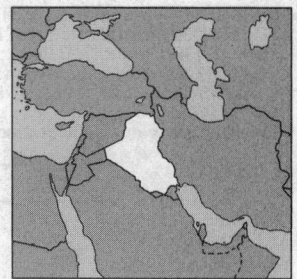

Area and population

Governorates	Capitals	area		population
		sq mi	sq km	1977 census
al-Anbār	ar-Ramādī	32,332	83,740	466,059
Bābil	al-Ḥillah	2,035	5,270	592,016
Baghdād	Baghdād	1,988	5,150	3,189,700
al-Baṣrah	al-Baṣrah	7,363	19,070	1,008,626
Dhī Qār	an-Nāṣirīyah	5,261	13,626	622,979
Diyālā	Baʿqūbah	7,452	19,301	587,754
Karbalāʾ	Karbalāʾ	22,348	57,880	269,822
Maysān	al-ʿAmārah	5,445	14,103	372,575
al-Muthannā	as-Samāwah	18,962	49,111	215,637
an-Najaf	an-Najaf	10,615	27,494	389,680
Ninawā	Mosul	13,794	35,726	1,105,671
al-Qādisiyah	ad-Dīwānīyah	3,285	8,507	423,006
Ṣalāḥ ad-Dīn	Sāmarrāʾ	11,198	29,004	363,819
at-Taʾmim	Kirkūk	3,729	9,659	495,425
Wasiṭ	al-Kūt	6,683	17,308	415,140
Kurdish Autonomous Region				
Dahūk	Dahūk	3,407	8,824	250,575
Irbīl	Irbīl	5,587	14,471	541,456
as-Sulaymānīyah	as-Sulaymānīyah	6,083	15,756	690,557
TOTAL		168,878*†	437,393*	12,000,497

Source: Official government figures.

Demography

Density (1984): persons per sq mi 88.6, persons per sq km 34.2.
Urban–rural (1980): urban 71.6%; rural 28.4%.
Sex distribution (1980): male 50.78%; female 49.22%.
Age breakdown (1980): under 15, 46.5%; 15–29, 26.4%; 30–44, 15.0%; 45–59, 8.0%; 60–74, 3.5%; 75 and over 0.6%.
Population projection: (1990) 18,136,000; (2000) 24,198,000.
Doubling time: 26 years.
Ethnic composition (1978): Arab 76.9%; Kurd 18.6%; Turkmen 1.5%; Persian 1.3%; Assyrian 0.8%; other 0.9%.
Religious affiliation (1980 est.): Muslim 95.8%, of which Shīʿī 53.5%, Sunnī 42.3%; Christian 3.5%; other 0.7%.
Major cities (1978 est.): Baghdād 3,400,000‡; Baṣrah 915,000; Mosul 900,000§; Kirkūk 500,000§.

Vital statistics

Birth rate per 1,000 population (1980–85): 45.1 (world avg. 27.5).
Death rate per 1,000 population (1980–85): 11.5 (world avg. 10.6).
Natural increase rate per 1,000 population (1980–85): 33.6 (world avg. 16.9).
Total fertility rate (avg. births per childbearing woman; 1980–85): 6.7.
Marriage rate per 1,000 population (1975–80): 11.1.
Divorce rate per 1,000 population (1975–80) 0.8.
Infant mortality rate per 1,000 live births (1975–80): 84.0.
Life expectancy at birth (1980–85): male 55.9 years; female 59.1 years.
Major causes of death per 100,000 population (1975): heart disease (except ischemic) 69.9; accidents (all types) 27.6; pneumonia 27.2; malignant neoplasms (cancers) 19.6; during the early 1980s, however, there was a high incidence of trachoma, influenza, measles, whooping cough, and tuberculosis.

National economy

Budget (1981). Revenue: ID5,025,000,000 (revenue from oil and public enterprises 88.5%, sales tax 7.7%, income tax 1.3%). Expenditures: ID5,025,000,000 (economic services 44.9%, defense 24.0%, local government 8.3%, internal security 5.2%, health 4.6%, education 2.9%).
Public debt (external, outstanding; 1978): U.S.$878,000,000.
Tourism (1981): receipts from visitors U.S.$170,000,000; expenditures by nationals abroad, n.a.
Production (metric tons except as noted). Agriculture, forestry, fishing (1982): wheat 900,000, barley 550,000, sugarcane 260,000, rice 250,000, potatoes 110,000, corn (maize) 90,000, vegetables 2,302,000, eggs 22,000,000, milk 1,125,000; livestock (number of live animals) 11,900,000 sheep, 3,800,000 goats, 3,100,000 cattle, 450,000 asses, 250,000 camels, 240,000 buffaloes, 20,000,000 poultry; roundwood 131,000 cu m; fish catch 26,219. Mining and quarrying (1982): gypsum 170,000; elemental sulfur 140,000; salt 80,000; iron and steel 25,000. Manufacturing (1980): cement 5,300,000; nitrogenous fertilizers 355,000; pig iron and crude steel 350,000; paper and paperboard 28,000; sugar 25,000‡; diesel oil 2,900,000; kerosine 811,000; jet fuels 531,000; cigarettes 7,500,000,000 units; beer 200,000 hectolitres§. Construction (1978): residential 9,800,000 sq m; nonresidential 3,068,000 sq m. Energy production (consumption): electricity (kW-hr; 1982) 6,310,000,000 (6,310,000,000) coal, n.a. (n.a.); crude petroleum (barrels; 1982) 330,950,000

(65,970,000); petroleum products (metric tons; 1982) 8,100,000 (6,160,000); natural gas (cu m; 1982) 448,717,500 (448,717,500).
Gross national product (at current market prices; 1981): U.S.$31,300,000,000 (U.S.$2,300 per capita).

Origin of gross domestic product (current factor cost)

	1976		1977	
	in value ID'000,000	% of total value	labour force	% of labour force
Agriculture	348.7	7.5	943,890	30.1
Mining	2,475.2	53.1	36,835	1.2
Manufacturing	324.5	7.0	284,395	9.1
Construction	355.1	7.6	321,696	10.3
Trade	197.8	4.3	224,104	7.1
Public utilities	22.5	0.5	23,190	0.7
Transportation and communication	217.7	4.7	177,799	5.7
Finance	75.8	1.6	31,089	1.0
Pub. admin., defense	284.9	6.1	‖	‖
Services	191.6	4.1	957,979	30.6
Other and unemployed	165.2	3.5	132,962	4.2
TOTAL	4,659.0	100.0	3,133,939	100.0

Persons economically active (1977): total 3,133,939 (26.1%); female participation in the labour force 533,931 (17.0%); unemployed 74,725 (2.4%).

Price and earnings indexes (1973 = 100)

	1974	1975	1976	1977	1978	1979	1980
Consumer price index	107.7	118.0	133.1	145.3	151.9	...	...
Yearly earnings index¶	154.4	180.4	224.4	284.7	...	...	...

Household income and expenditure. Average household size (1980) 5.8; average annual income per household, n.a.; source of income: n.a.; expenditure (1971–72): food and beverages 55.4%, housing 18.2%, clothing and footwear 10.3%, transport and communications 5.3%, medical care and health 2.4%, recreation 1.2%.
Land use (1981): forested 3.4%; meadows and pastures 9.2%; agricultural and under permanent cultivation 12.6%; built-on, wasteland, and other 74.8%.

Foreign trade

Balance of trade (current prices)

	1976	1977	1978	1979	1980	1981
ID'000,000	+1,587	+1,527	+2,022	+4,125	+3,342	+2,414
% of total	40.8%	36.6%	44.8%	48.1%	27.3%	27.9%

Imports (1978): ID1,242,668,000 (machinery other than electric 29.6%, electrical machinery 12.9%, transport equipment 11.2%, cereals 6.0%, iron and steel 5.9%, textile yarns and fabrics 5.8%). *Major import sources:* Japan 20.9%; West Germany 11.2%; United States 10.1%; France 7.0%.
Exports (1978): ID3,263,681,000 (petroleum, crude 98.1%, fruits and vegetables 0.6%, petroleum products 0.6%). *Major export destinations:* France 19.1%; Italy 17.0%; Brazil 12.0%; United Kingdom 8.6%; Japan 7.0%.

Transport and communications

Transport. Railroads (1982): length 1,265 mi, 2,035 km; passenger-mi 543,300,000♀, passenger-km 874,300,000♀; short ton-mi cargo 1,977,000,000♀, metric ton-km cargo 2,887,000,000♀. Roads (1981): total length 15,699 mi, 25,265 km (paved 65%). Vehicles (1981): passenger cars 229,530; trucks and buses 152,768. Merchant marine (1983): vessels (100 gross tons and over) 161; total deadweight tonnage 2,694,455. Air transport (1982): passenger-mi 917,000,000, passenger-km 1,476,000,000; short ton-mi cargo 37,463,000, metric ton-km cargo 54,696,000; airport (1984) with scheduled flights 1.
Communications. Daily newspapers (1981): total number 4; total circulation 262,000; circulation per 1,000 population 21. Radios (1981): total number of receivers 2,250,000 (1 per 6 persons). Television (1981): total number of receivers 700,000 (1 per 19 persons). Telephones (1978): 313,000 (1 per 39 persons).

Education and health

Education (1981)

	schools	teachers	students	student/ teacher ratio
Primary (age 6–11)	10,816	98,422	2,637,023	26.8
Secondary (age 12–17)	1,579δ	30,580	1,028,348	33.6
Voc., teacher tr.	155δ	5,245	82,307	15.7
Higher♀	62δ	6,515	102,430	15.7

College graduates per 100,000 population (students graduating; 1979): 176.
Literacy (1980): total population literate 3,044,500 (43.4%); males literate 2,233,100 (62.9%); females literate 811,400 (23.3%).
Health (1981): physicians 7,634 (1 per 1,773 persons); hospital beds 25,443 (1 per 532 persons).
Food (1978–80): daily per capita caloric intake 2,643 (vegetable products 92.2%, animal products 7.8%); 110% of FAO recommended minimum.

Military

Total active duty personnel (1983): 517,250 (army 91.8%; navy 0.8%; air force 7.4%). *Military expenditure as percent of GNP* (1982): 46.4% (world 6.0%); per capita expenditure U.S.$835.

*Includes 1,310 sq mi (3,393 sq km), half of neutral zone, shared with Saudi Arabia. †Detail does not add to total given because of rounding. ‡1981 estimate. §1979. ‖ Public administration and defense included with services. ¶Large industries only. ♀1980. δ1978–79.

Ireland

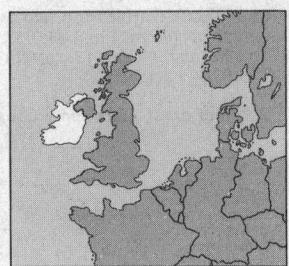

Official name: Éire; Ireland (Irish Republic).
Form of government: unitary multi-party republic with two legislative houses (Senate [60]; House of Representatives [166]).
Chief of state: President.
Head of government: Prime Minister.
Capital: Dublin.
Official languages: Irish; English.
Official religion: Roman Catholic.
Monetary unit: 1 Irish pound (IR£) = 100 new pence; valuation (Oct. 29, 1984) 1 IR£ = U.S.$1.00 = £0.83.

Area and population

Provinces Counties	area* sq mi	sq km	population 1981 census
Connacht	6,611	17,122	424,410
Galway	2,293	5,940	172,018
Leitrim	581	1,525	27,609
Mayo	2,084	5,398	114,766
Roscommon	951	2,463	54,543
Sligo	693	1,796	55,474
Leinster	7,580	19,633	1,790,521
Carlow	346	896	39,820
Dublin	356	922	1,003,164
Kildare	654	1,694	104,122
Kilkenny	796	2,062	70,806
Laoighis	664	1,719	51,171
Longford	403	1,044	31,140
Louth	318	823	88,514
Meath	902	2,336	95,419
Offaly	771	1,998	58,312
Westmeath	681	1,763	61,523
Wexford	908	2,351	99,081
Wicklow	782	2,025	87,449
Munster	9,315	24,127	998,315
Clare	1,231	3,188	87,567
Cork	2,880	7,460	402,465
Kerry	1,815	4,701	122,770
Limerick	1,037	2,686	161,661
Tipperary North Riding†	771	1,996	58,984
Tipperary South Riding†	872	2,258	76,277
Waterford	710	1,838	88,591
Ulster	3,093	8,012	230,159
Cavan	730	1,891	53,855
Donegal	1,865	4,830	125,112
Monaghan	498	1,291	51,192
TOTAL	26,600	68,894	3,443,405

Demography

Density (1981)‡: persons per sq mi 129.4, persons per sq km 50.0.
Urban–rural (1981): urban 55.6%; rural 44.4%.
Sex distribution (1981): male 50.22%; female 49.78%.
Age breakdown (1980): under 15, 30.9%; 15–29, 24.0%; 30–44, 16.1%; 45–59, 13.6%; 60–74, 11.2%; 75 and over, 4.2%.
Population projection: (1990) 3,595,000; (2000) 3,771,000.
Doubling time: 77 years.
Ethnic composition (1982): Irish 100.0%.
Religious affiliation (1983): Catholic 94.0%; Anglican 4.0%; other 2.0%.
Major cities (1981): Dublin 525,882; Cork 136,344; Limerick 60,736.

Vital statistics

Birth rate per 1,000 population (1983): 19.0 (world avg. 29.0); (1980) legitimate 95.0%, illegitimate 5.0%.
Death rate per 1,000 population (1983): 9.3 (world avg. 11.0).
Natural increase rate per 1,000 population (1983): 9.7 (world avg. 18.0).
Total fertility rate (avg. births per childbearing woman; 1980–85): 3.2.
Marriage rate per 1,000 population (1983): 5.5.
Infant mortality rate per 1,000 live births (1981): 10.6.
Life expectancy at birth (1980–85): male 70.3 years; female 75.7 years.
Major causes of death per 100,000 population (1980): heart and circulatory diseases 490.1; malignant neoplasms (cancers) 260.3; pneumonia 61.7.

National economy

Budget (1983). Revenue: IR£5,757,900,000 (value-added taxes 40.7%; income taxes 30.2%, postal services 7.5%). Expenditures: IR£6,654,600,000 (debt service 26.0%; social welfare 15.4%; health 13.7%; education 11.4%).
Public debt (external, outstanding; 1983): U.S.$8,752,900,000.
Tourism: receipts from visitors (1982) U.S.$477,000,000; expenditures by nationals abroad (1981) U.S.$511,000,000.
Production (metric tons except as noted). Agriculture, forestry, fishing (1982): sugar beets 1,550,000, barley 1,450,000, potatoes 1,050,000, wheat 320,000, oats 90,000, cow milk 5,200,000; livestock (number of live animals): 6,771,000 cattle, 3,657,000 sheep, 1,141,000 pigs, 8,100,000 chickens; roundwood 1,100,000 cu m; fish catch 179,300; total fish catch 179,300. Mining and quarrying (metric tons; 1982): gypsum 371,000; barite 265,800; lead-zinc ore 206,200. Manufacturing (gross value in IR£; 1978): dairy products 784,263,000; meat and meat products 721,036,000; industrial chemicals, including fertilizers and man-made fibres 619,268,000; textiles, including knitwear 315,154,000; nonmetallic mineral products 314,905,000; flour, sugar, and chocolate confectionery 307,620,000. Construction (1983): number of dwellings built 23,751; floor area 2,787,000 sq m§. Energy

production (consumption): electricity (kW-hr; 1982) 10,931,000,000 (10,-931,000,000); coal (metric tons; 1982) 62,000 (1,308,000); crude petroleum (barrels; 1982) none (3,511,000); petroleum products (metric tons; 1982) 470,000 (3,805,000); natural gas (cu m; 1982) 1,977,500,000 (1,976,800,000).
Gross national product (1982): U.S.$16,776,000,000 (U.S.$4,820 per capita).

Origin of gross domestic product (current prices)

	1979		1981	
	in value '000,000 IR£	% of total value	labour force	% of labour force
Agriculture	955	12.8	190,000	16.5
Mining			11,000	0.9
Manufacturing	2,669	35.8	239,000	20.8
Construction			97,000	8.4
Public utilities			14,000	1.2
Trade			162,000	14.1
Transportation and communication	2,577	34.6	68,000	5.9
Finance			43,000	3.7
Services			222,000	19.3
Other	1,249 ‖	16.8 ‖	106,000	9.2
TOTAL	7,450	100.0	1,152,000	100.0

Persons economically active (1982): total 1,283,000 (36.8%); female participation in labour force 369,500 (28.8%), unemployed 137,300 (10.7%).

Price and earnings indexes (1975 = 100)

	1978	1979	1980	1981	1982	1983	1984
Consumer price index	144.3	163.4	193.2	232.7	272.6	301.0	326.3¶
Weekly earnings index	161.5	186.0	219.8	256.5	289.5	323.3	...

Household income and expenditure. Average household size (1983) 3.9; income per household: n.a.; source of income: n.a.; expenditure (1979): food 40.6%, transportation 13.2%, clothing and footwear 8.0%, housing 6.4%, energy 5.3%, health care 2.3%, education 2.3%.
Land use (1981): forested 4.7%; meadows and pastures 70.2%; agricultural and under permanent cultivation 14.2%; other 10.9%.

Foreign trade

Balance of trade (current prices)

	1978	1979	1980	1981	1982	1983
IR£'000,000	−750	−1,365	−1,342	−1,698	−1,120	−474
% of total	11.2%	16.7%	14.3%	15.1%	9.1%	3.4%

Imports (1982): IR£6,686,000,000 (machinery, except electrical 17.1%, of which transport and transport equipment 8.4%; petroleum and petroleum products 13.1%; electrical and electronic machinery 12.9%; textile yarn, fabrics, and clothing accessories, excluding footwear 7.8%; cereals and other foodstuffs 5.7%; iron and steel 2.6%). *Major import sources:* United Kingdom 48.1%; United States 12.9%; West Germany 7.7%; France 4.6%.
Exports (1982): IR£5,591,000,000 (electrical and electronic machinery 17.2%; meat and dairy products 15.8%, of which fresh and frozen meat 8.1%; chemicals and related products 14.2%, of which organic chemicals 6.9%; textile yarn, fabrics, and clothing accessories, except footwear 6.7%; live animals 3.0%). *Major export destinations:* United Kingdom 38.8%; West Germany 9.3%; France 8.7%; United States 7.2%; The Netherlands 5.2%.

Transport and communications

Transport. Railroads (1982): route length 1,236 mi, 1,989 km; passenger-mi 514,500,000, passenger-km 828,000,000; short ton-mi cargo 427,400,000, metric ton-km cargo 624,000,000. Roads (1982): total length 57,349 mi, 92,294 km (paved 94%). Vehicles (1982): passenger cars 709,000; trucks and buses 72,034. Merchant marine (1983): vessels (100 gross tons and over) 162; total deadweight tonnage 266,296. Air transport (1982): passenger-mi 2,027,381,000, passenger-km 3,262,753,000; short ton-mi cargo 78,600,000, metric ton-km cargo 114,755,000; airports (1983) with scheduled flights 7.
Communications. Daily newspapers (1982): total number 7; total circulation 778,584; circulation per 1,000 population 224. Radios (1983): 1,315,000 receivers (1 per 2.6 persons). Television (1983): 838,000 receivers (1 per 4.1 persons). Telephones (1982): 779,000 (1 per 4.5 persons).

Education and health

Education (1980–81)

	schools	teachers	students	student/ teacher ratio
Primary (age 6–14)	3,494	20,068	568,364	28.3
Secondary (age 12–18)	822	18,457	293,809	15.9
Voc., teacher tr.	47	202	6,792	33.6
Higher	58	3,983	41,928	10.5

College graduates per 100,000 population (students graduating; 1980): 269.
Literacy (1980): total population literate 99.5%.
Health: physicians (1981) 4,443 (1 per 775 persons); hospital beds (1980) 33,028 (1 per 103 persons).
Food (1978–80): daily per capita caloric intake 3,764 (vegetable products 64.7%; animal products 35.3%); 150% of FAO recommended minimum.

Military

Total active duty personnel (1983): 15,231 (army 88.2%; navy 6.3%; air force 5.5%). *Military expenditure as percent of GNP* (1982): 2.0% (world 6.0%); per capita expenditure U.S.$97.

*Includes land area only. †The north and south ridings of Tipperary are administered separately. ‡Based on land area. §1980. ‖ Includes government services and other financial adjustments. ¶Second quarter.

Israel

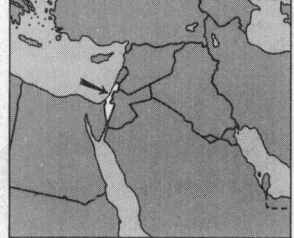

Official name: Medinat Yisra'el (Hebrew); Isrā'īl (Arabic) (State of Israel).
Form of government: multiparty republic with one legislative house (Knesset [120]).
Chief of state: President.
Head of government: Prime Minister.
Seat of government: Jerusalem.
Official languages: Hebrew; Arabic.
Official religion: none.
Monetary unit: 1 Israeli shekel (IS) = 100 new agorot; valuation (Oct. 29, 1984) 1 U.S.$ = IS502.1; 1 £ = IS607.54.

Area and population		area*		population†
Districts	**Seats of government**	**sq mi**	**sq km**	**1982 estimate**
Central	Ramle	479	1,242	808,000
Haifa	Haifa	330	854	570,000
Jerusalem	Jerusalem	215	557	457,000
Northern	Tiberias	1,347	3,490	626,000
Southern	Beersheba	5,555	14,387	486,000
Tel Aviv	Tel Aviv	66	170	1,004,000
TOTAL		7,992	20,700	3,978,000

Source: Official government figures.

Demography†

Density* (1984): persons per sq mi 539.4, persons per sq km 208.3.
Urban–rural (1982): urban 86.9%; rural 13.1%.
Sex distribution (1982): male 49.94%; female 50.06%.
Age breakdown (1982): under 15, 33.2%; 15–29, 25.4%; 30–44, 17.3%; 45–59, 12.3%; 60–74, 8.9%; 75 and over, 2.9%.
Population projection‡: (1990) 4,638,800; (2000) 5,339,600.
Doubling time: 41 years.
Ethnic composition (1980): Jewish 83.1%; Palestinian Arab 15.4%; Bedouin Arab 1.3%; other 0.2%.
Religious affiliation (1982): Jewish 83.5%; Muslim 12.9%; Christian 2.3%; Druze and other 1.3%.
Major cities (1982): Jerusalem 415,000; Tel Aviv–Yafo 329,500; Haifa 227,400; Bat Yam 132,800; Holon 132,300.

Vital statistics†

Birth rate per 1,000 population (1983): 24.1 (world avg. 29.0); (1980) legitimate 97.5%, illegitimate 2.5%.
Death rate per 1,000 population (1983): 6.8 (world avg. 17.3).
Natural increase rate per 1,000 population (1983): 17.3 (world avg. 18.0).
Total fertility rate (avg. births per childbearing woman; 1981): 3.3.
Marriage rate per 1,000 population (1983): 7.3.
Divorce rate per 1,000 population (1983): 1.2.
Infant mortality rate per 1,000 live births (1982): 13.9.
Life expectancy at birth (1981): male 72.7 years; female 75.9 years.
Major causes of death per 100,000 population (1980): heart disease 231.5; malignant neoplasms (cancers) 123.9; cerebrovascular disease 76.9.

National economy

Budget (1982–83). Revenue: IS458,891,000,000 (income tax 29.8%, foreign loans and grants 19.3%, value-added tax 12.3%). Expenditures: IS521,691,000,000 (defense 25.0%, interest 13.6%, debt repayment 12.7%, business enterprises 8.9%).
Public debt (external, outstanding; 1982): U.S.$8,982,000,000.
Tourism (1982): receipts from visitors U.S.$900,000,000; expenditures by nationals abroad U.S.$653,000,000.
Production (IS except as noted). Agriculture, forestry, fishing (value of producers' organized sales; 1983): field crops 36,401,500,000; fruits (excluding citrus and melons) 12,366,700,000; vegetables, potatoes, and melons 9,605,300,000; citrus fruits 9,270,900,000; poultry meat 13,367,900,000; eggs 4,755,700,000; milk 9,895,900,000; beef 2,177,200,000; nursery plants 2,829,300,000; plywood (cu m) 98,003; fish 1,251,900,000. Mining and quarrying (1983): phosphate rock 1,965,700 metric tons. Manufacturing (gross value; 1981): food, beverages, and tobacco 2,973,000,000; metal products 1,788,000,000; textiles and wearing apparel 1,669,900,000; chemicals and allied products, petroleum and coal products 1,605,800,000; electrical machinery 1,506,000,000; transport equipment 991,900,000. Construction (1983): residential 3,690,000 sq m; nonresidential 1,280,000 sq m. Energy production (consumption): electricity (kW-hr; 1983) 14,577,700,000 (12,555,400,000); coal (metric tons; 1983) none (1,678,000); crude petroleum (barrels; 1983) 84,000 (53,217,000); petroleum products (metric tons; 1982) 7,136,000 (6,231,000); natural gas (cu m; 1982) 70,513,000 (70,513,000).
Persons economically active (1983)§: total 1,402,400 (34.2%); female participation in the labour force 550,000 (39.2%); unemployed 63,000 (4.5%).

Price and earnings indexes (1980 = 100)							
	1978	**1979**	**1980**	**1981**	**1982**	**1983**	**1984¶**
Consumer price index	24.3	43.3	100.0	216.8	477.8	1,173.5	2,539.6
Daily earnings index	23.3	43.4	100.0	245.4	553.8	1,414.8	2,892.4

Gross national product (at current market prices; 1982): U.S.$22,209,000,000 (U.S.$5,520 per capita).

Origin of gross domestic product (current prices)				
	1982		**1983**	
	in value IS'000,000	% of total value	labour force§	% of labour force§
Agriculture	27,062	5.9	73,700	5.3
Manufacturing, mining	86,965	19.0	303,400	21.6
Construction	36,276	7.9	86,200	6.1
Public utilities	10,110	2.2	12,700	0.9
Trade, finance	59,802	13.1	296,400	21.1
Transportation and communication	30,341	6.6	87,000	6.2
Services, other	206,447	45.2	543,000	38.7
TOTAL	457,003	100.0 ‖	1,402,400	100.0 ‖

Household income and expenditure. Average urban household size (1979–80) 3.4; monthly income per household IS2,309 (U.S.$653); source of income: employed work and membership in cooperative 58.5%, other 41.5%; expenditure (1979–80): housing and its maintenance 30.1%, food 23.5%, transportation and communication 11.9%, recreation 10.0%, clothing and footwear 6.4%, miscellaneous 18.1%.
Land use (1981): forested 5.7%; meadows and pastures 40.2%; agricultural and under permanent cultivation 20.6%, of which irrigated land 9.8%; other 33.5%.

Foreign trade

Balance of trade (current prices)						
	1978	**1979**	**1980**	**1981**	**1982**	**1983**
IS'000,000	−4,631	−8,049	−16,310	−40,089	−68,787	−212,187
% of total	24.5%	24.9%	21.5%	22.9%	21.2%	26.2%

Imports (1983): IS510,904,800,000 (fuel and lubricants 18.7%; raw materials, including precious metals and chemical products 17.4%; machines and equipment 15.2%; rough diamonds 8.4%). *Major import sources:* United States 19.2%; West Germany 12.1%; United Kingdom 7.8%; Belgium 6.7%; Switzerland 6.1%.
Exports (1983): IS298,717,550,000 (polished diamonds 23.6%; chemicals 12.6%; electrical equipment 10.5%; metal products 8.6%; transport equipment 5.5%). *Major export destinations:* United States 26.0%; United Kingdom 8.1%; West Germany 7.0%; France 4.9%; Belgium 4.8%.

Transport and communications

Transport. Railroads (1982): length 514 mi, 827 km; passenger-mi 150,500,000, passenger-km 242,200,000; short ton-mi cargo 551,900,000, metric ton-km cargo 805,800,000. Roads (1982): total length 7,680 mi, 12,360 km (paved 100%). Vehicles (1982): passenger cars 459,178; trucks and buses 103,836. Merchant marine (1983): vessels (100 gross tons and over) 71; total deadweight tonnage 865,663. Air transport (1982): passenger-mi 2,984,610,000, passenger-km 4,803,133,000; short ton-mi cargo 567,845,000, metric ton-km cargo 829,038,000; airports (1982) with scheduled flights 6.
Communications. Daily newspapers (1983): total number 26; total circulation 824,850; circulation per 1,000 population 205. Radios (1983): total number of receivers 1,050,000 (1 per 3.8 persons). Television (1983): total number of receivers 600,000 (1 per 6.7 persons). Telephones (1982): 1,302,000 (1 per 3.1 persons).

Education and health

Education (1981–82)				
	schools	teachers	students	student/ teacher ratio
Primary (age 6–13)	1,820	44,980	586,829	13.0
Secondary (age 14–17)º	846	31,570	278,435	8.8
Voc., teacher tr.	46	3,207	28,258	8.8
Higher	7	8,347	60,685	7.3

College graduates per 100,000 population (students graduating; 1979): 237.1.
Literacy (1979): total population literate 2,412,200 (91.6%); males literate 1,241,900 (95.6%); females literate 1,170,300 (87.7%).
Health (1981): physicians 10,200 (1 per 387 persons); hospital beds 26,703 (1 per 149 persons).
Food (1978–80): daily per capita caloric intake 3,045 (vegetable products 77.5%, animal products 22.5%); 127% of FAO recommended minimum requirement.

Military

Total active duty personnel (1983): 172,000 (army 78.5%; navy 5.2%; air force 16.3%). *Military expenditure as percent of* GNP (1982): 25.5% (world 6.0%); per capita expenditure U.S.$1,412.

*Excludes 10,150 sq mi (26,300 sq km) of occupied territories as of January 1982. †De jure; includes East Jerusalem and about 27,000 Israeli residents living in occupied territories but excludes others, mainly Palestinians. In 1982 about 747,500 persons lived on the West Bank (officially Jordan) and 476,300 lived in the Gaza Strip (officially Egypt). ‡Based on migration balance of 5,000 per year in 1980s and nil in 1990s. §Excludes armed forces; includes occupied territories. ‖ Detail does not add to total given because of rounding. ¶First quarter. ºIncludes intermediate education age 12–14.

Italy

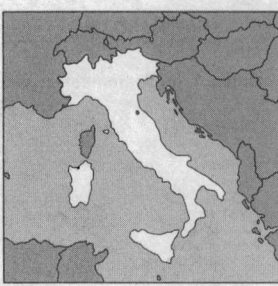

Official name: Repubblica Italiana (Italian Republic).
Form of government: republic with two legislative houses (Senate [315]; Chamber of Deputies [630]).
Chief of state: President.
Head of government: Prime Minister.
Capital: Rome.
Official language: Italian.
Official religion: Roman Catholicism.
Monetary unit: 1 Lira (Lit, plural Lire) = 100 centesimi; valuation (Oct. 29, 1984) 1 U.S.$ = Lit1,900; 1 £ = Lit2,293.

Area and population

Regions Provinces	Capitals	area sq mi	area sq km	population 1984 estimate
Abruzzi	L'Aquila	4,168	10,794	1,236,060
Chieti	Chieti	999	2,587	376,667
L'Aquila	L'Aquila	1,944	5,034	295,288
Pescara	Pescara	473	1,225	290,366
Teramo	Teramo	752	1,948	273,739
Basilicata	Potenza	3,858	9,992	614,522
Matera	Matera	1,331	3,447	205,551
Potenza	Potenza	2,527	6,545	408,971
Calabria	Catanzaro	5,823	15,080	2,098,137
Catanzaro	Catanzaro	2,026	5,247	758,035
Cosenza	Cosenza	2,568	6,650	759,463
Reggio di Calabria	Reggio di Calabria	1,229	3,183	580,639
Campania	Napoli	5,249	13,595	5,563,230
Avellino	Avellino	1,078	2,792	440,377
Benevento	Benevento	800	2,071	293,140
Caserta	Caserta	1,019	2,639	777,674
Napoli	Napoli	452	1,171	3,020,816
Salerno	Salerno	1,900	4,922	1,031,223
Emilia-Romagna	Bologna	8,542	22,123	3,952,304
Bologna	Bologna	1,429	3,702	925,113
Ferrara	Ferrara	1,016	2,632	378,391
Forlì	Forlì	1,123	2,910	604,936
Modena	Modena	1,039	2,690	596,782
Parma	Parma	1,332	3,449	398,723
Piacenza	Piacenza	1,000	2,589	276,799
Ravenna	Ravenna	718	1,859	356,485
Reggio nell'Emilia	Reggio nell'Emilia	885	2,292	415,075
Friuli-Venezia Giulia	Trieste	3,030	7,847	1,228,280
Gorizia	Gorizia	180	467	143,858
Pordenone	Pordenone	878	2,273	276,631
Trieste	Trieste	82	212	277,475
Udine	Udine	1,890	4,895	530,316
Lazio	Roma	6,642	17,203	5,056,119
Frosinone	Frosinone	1,251	3,239	470,085
Latina	Latina	869	2,251	447,771
Rieti	Rieti	1,061	2,749	144,060
Roma	Roma	2,066	5,352	3,722,053
Viterbo	Viterbo	1,395	3,612	272,150
Liguria	Genova	2,091	5,416	1,789,225
Genova	Genova	708	1,834	1,028,348
Imperia	Imperia	446	1,155	223,943
La Spezia	La Spezia	341	882	239,818
Savona	Savona	596	1,545	297,116
Lombardia	Milano	9,211	23,857	8,891,318
Bergamo	Bergamo	1,066	2,760	902,932
Brescia	Brescia	1,846	4,782	1,024,631
Como	Como	798	2,067	780,734
Cremona	Cremona	684	1,771	331,083
Mantova	Mantova	903	2,339	375,566
Milano	Milano	1,066	2,762	4,001,423
Pavia	Pavia	1,145	2,965	508,865
Sondrio	Sondrio	1,240	3,212	175,327
Varese	Varese	463	1,199	790,757
Marche	Ancona	3,743	9,694	1,420,829
Ancona	Ancona	749	1,940	436,391
Ascoli Piceno	Ascoli Piceno	806	2,087	355,231
Macerata	Macerata	1,071	2,774	293,928
Pesaro e Urbino	Pesaro	1,117	2,893	335,279
Molise	Campobasso	1,713	4,438	331,670
Campobasso	Campobasso	1,123	2,909	238,645
Isernia	Isernia	590	1,529	93,025
Piemonte	Torino	9,807	25,399	4,431,064
Alessandria	Alessandria	1,375	3,560	460,373
Asti	Asti	583	1,511	213,277
Cuneo	Cuneo	2,665	6,903	548,763
Novara	Novara	1,388	3,594	505,785
Torino	Torino	2,637	6,830	2,311,649
Vercelli	Vercelli	1,159	3,001	391,217
Puglia	Bari	7,470	19,348	3,946,871
Bari	Bari	1,980	5,129	1,488,158
Brindisi	Brindisi	710	1,838	399,573
Foggia	Foggia	2,774	7,185	691,597
Lecce	Lecce	1,065	2,759	785,528
Taranto	Taranto	941	2,437	582,015
Sardegna	Cagliari	9,301	24,090	1,617,265
Cagliari	Cagliari	2,662	6,895	744,032
Nuoro	Nuoro	2,720	7,044	276,123
Oristano	Oristano	1,016	2,631	157,145
Sassari	Sassari	2,903	7,520	439,965
Sicilia (Sicily)	Palermo	9,926	25,708	5,006,684
Agrigento	Agrigento	1,175	3,042	479,809
Caltanissetta	Caltanissetta	822	2,128	290,904
Catania	Catania	1,371	3,552	1,029,515
Enna	Enna	989	2,562	193,536
Messina	Messina	1,254	3,247	677,634
Palermo	Palermo	1,927	4,992	1,223,892
Ragusa	Ragusa	623	1,614	281,235
Siracusa	Siracusa	814	2,109	401,123
Trapani	Trapani	951	2,462	429,036
Toscana	Firenze	8,877	22,992	3,581,291
Arezzo	Arezzo	1,248	3,232	313,409
Firenze	Firenze	1,498	3,879	1,201,263
Grosseto	Grosseto	1,739	4,504	220,683
Livorno	Livorno	468	1,213	347,478
Lucca	Lucca	684	1,773	385,059
Massa-Carrara	Massa-Carrara	447	1,157	203,851
Pisa	Pisa	945	2,448	389,010
Pistoia	Pistoia	373	965	265,552
Siena	Siena	1,475	3,821	254,986
Trentino-Alto Adige	Bolzano	5,259	13,620	875,780
Bolzano-Bozen	Bolzano	2,857	7,400	432,231
Trento	Trento	2,402	6,220	443,549
Umbria	Perugia	3,265	8,456	813,507
Perugia	Perugia	2,446	6,334	586,400
Terni	Terni	819	2,122	227,107
Valle d'Aosta	Aosta	1,259	3,262	113,418
Veneto	Venezia	7,090	18,363	4,361,527
Belluno	Belluno	1,420	3,678	219,295
Padova	Padova	827	2,142	813,061
Rovigo	Rovigo	691	1,789	252,644
Treviso	Treviso	956	2,477	726,271
Venezia	Venezia	950	2,460	839,978
Verona	Verona	1,195	3,096	778,898
Vicenza	Vicenza	1,051	2,721	731,380
TOTAL		116,324	301,277	56,929,101

Source: Official government figures.

Demography

Density (1984): persons per sq mi 488.3, persons per sq km 188.5.
Urban–rural (1984): urban 71.7%; rural 28.3%.
Sex distribution (1981): male 48.71%; female 51.29%.
Age breakdown (1984): under 15, 19.6%; 15–29, 22.7%; 30–44, 19.8%; 45–59, 18.8%; 60–74, 13.5%; 75 and over 5.6%.
Population projection: (1990) 58,000,000; (2000) 59,707,000.
Growth rate: during the intercensal period 1971–81, the growth rate was 0.4%.
Ethnic composition (1980): Italian 98.1%; other 1.9%.
Religious affiliation (1980): Roman Catholic 83.2%; nonreligious 13.6%; atheist 2.6%; other 0.2%.
Major cities (1984): Rome 2,830,650; Milan 1,561,438; Naples 1,208,545; Turin 1,069,013; Genoa 746,785; Palermo 712,342; Bologna 447,971.
National origin (1980): 98.1% Italian; 1.9% foreign, of which Austrian 0.2%, French 0.2%, Slovene 0.2%, Albanian 0.1%, other 1.2%.
Mobility (1977). Population living in the same residence as in 1967: 52.0%.
Households (1982). Average household size 3.0; (1980) 1 person 13.9%, 2 persons 23.4%, 3 persons 22.6%, 4 persons 21.6%, 5 persons 11.1%, 6 or more persons 7.4%. Family households: 13,088,040 (74.3%), nonfamily 4,527,088 (25.7%, of which 1-person 13.9%).
Immigration (1982): immigrants admitted 92,423, from Europe 76.9%, of which West Germany 34.3%, Switzerland 25.7%, France 6.0%; Africa 6.0%; Latin America 5.7%; United States 5.2%; Asia 2.6%.

Vital statistics

Birth rate per 1,000 population (1983): 10.6 (world avg. 29.0); legitimate 95.4%; illegitimate 4.6%.
Death rate per 1,000 population (1983): 9.9 (world avg. 11.0).
Natural increase rate per 1,000 population (1983): 0.7 (world avg. 18.0).
Total fertility rate (avg. births per childbearing woman; 1980–85): 1.8.
Marriage rate per 1,000 population (1983): 5.3.
Divorce rate per 1,000 population: (1983): 0.3.
Infant mortality rate per 1,000 live births (1983): 12.3.
Life expectancy at birth (1977–79): male 70.6 years; female 77.2 years.
Major causes of death per 100,000 population (1982): diseases of the circulatory system 432.7; malignant neoplasms (cancers) 220.0; diseases of the respiratory system 59.1; diseases of the digestive system 52.7.

Social indicators

Educational attainment (1980). Percent of adult population having: less than full primary education 14.4%, primary 42.8%, junior secondary 27.5%, upper secondary 12.5%, 4-year higher degree 2.8%, post-graduate, n.a.

Distribution of income (1977)

percent of household income by quintile

1	2	3	4	5 (highest)
6.2	11.3	15.9	22.7	43.9

Quality of working life (1982). Average work week: 38.7 hours. Annual rate per 100,000 workers* for: injury or accident 5,928, industrial illness 405, death 66. Proportion of labour force insured for damages or income loss resulting from: injury 100%, permanent disability 100%, death 100%. Average days lost to labour stoppages per 1,000 work days: 2.8. Average duration of journey to work, n.a. Rate per 1,000 workers of discouraged (unemployed no longer seeking work): 0.9.
Access to services (1978). Proportion of dwellings having access to: electricity 99.9%, safe water supply 99.7%, toilet facilities 96.1%, bath facilities 87.0%.
Social participation (1983). Eligible voters participating in last national election 89.0%. Population participating in voluntary work, n.a. Trade union membership in total workforce (1982) 62.4%. Practicing religious population in total affiliated population (1980) 65.7%, of which weekly 28.0%.
Social deviance (1982). Offense rate per 100,000 population for: murder 13.5, rape 1.7, other assault 212.7, theft, including burglary and housebreaking 2,473.2. Incidence per 100,000 in general population of: alcoholism 2.0*, drug and substance abuse 25.1*, suicide (1983) 5.0.
Leisure (1982). Favourite leisure activities (as % of public spending on culture): cinema 35.6%, sporting events 16.3%, theatre 10.6%.

Material well-being. Rate per 1,000 of population possessing: (1982) automobile 346, telephone 360. Households possessing: (1982) T.V. 72%, refrigerator 91%†, air conditioner 9%†, washing machine 88%†.

National economy

Gross national product (at current market prices; 1983): U.S.$350,038,850,-000 (U.S.$6,170 per capita).

Origin of gross domestic product (current prices)

	1982			
	in value 000,000,000 lire	% of total value	labour force	% of labour force
Agriculture	27,328	5.8	2,506,000	11.0
Mining	16,967	3.6	672,700	3.0
Manufacturing	116,206	24.7	4,786,300	21.0
Construction	36,805	7.8	1,754,000	7.7
Trade	73,315	15.6	4,079,400	17.9
Public utilities	21,067	4.5	196,000	0.9
Transp. and commun.	29,419	6.3	1,230,200	5.4
Finance	53,681	11.4	356,100	1.6
Pub. admin., defense	64,087	13.7	3,025,000	13.3
Services	36,922	7.9	2,079,500	9.1
Other	−6,000‡	−1.3‡	2,068,000§	9.1§
TOTAL	469,797	100.0	22,753,200	100.0

Budget (1982). Revenue: 150,530,000,000,000 lire (property and income taxes 42.2%, transfer payments 21.5%, business taxes 21.3%, sales taxes 8.8%). Expenditures: 209,245,000,000,000 lire (social services 20.3%, economic aid and subsidies 13.9%, regional and local subsidies 13.9%, education and culture 10.6%, national defense 4.1%).
Public debt (external, outstanding; 1984): U.S.$271,000,000,000.
Tourism (1982): receipts from visitors U.S.$8,234,000,000; expenditures by nationals abroad U.S.$1,709,000,000.

Manufacturing, mining, and construction enterprises (1979)

	no. of enterprises	no. of employees	hourly wages as a % of avg. of all wages	annual value added (000,000,000 lire)
Industrial chemicals	1,034	263,000	120.9	7,795
Transport equipment	707	418,000	110.0	7,141
Machinery, nonelectrical	2,507	306,000	107.4	6,424
Electrical machinery	1,161	336,000	...	6,037
Iron and steel	841	244,000	117.5	5,463
Textiles	3,125	306,000	93.8	4,946
Food products	1,661	176,000	106.2	4,495
Pottery, ceramics, and glass	2,539	217,000	...	4,233
Metal products	2,494	214,000	...	3,911
Wearing apparel	1,814	181,000	86.9	2,228
Printing, publishing	805	87,000	124.1	2,121
Paper and paper products	623	67,000	119.6	1,689
Plastic products	921	74,000	105.4	1,507
Petroleum and gas	9	7,000	115.2	1,201
Nonmetal mining and quarrying	304	20,000	115.2	318
Construction ‖	326,000	1,199,013	...	31,920

Production (metric tons except as noted). Agriculture, forestry, fishing (1982): sugar beets 12,365,000, grapes 11,150,000, milk 10,600,000, wheat 8,998,000, corn (maize) 6,820,000, tomatoes 4,075,000, potatoes 2,680,000, olives 2,500,000, apples 2,200,000, oranges 1,500,000, peaches 1,400,000, pears 1,070,000, barley 1,020,000, rice 915,000, lettuce and endive 868,100; livestock (number of live animals) 9,257,000 sheep, 9,132,000 pigs, 8,534,-137 cattle, 110,192,000 chickens; fish catch 468,610; roundwood 7,990,000 cu m. Mining and quarrying (1982): limestone 56,200,000; tuff 14,897,-000 ‖; pozzolan 5,500,000; salt 4,604,000; basalt 4,200,000; alabaster and onyx 3,500,000; marble 2,100,000 ‖; serpentine 1,900,000. Manufacturing (1983): cement 39,761,766; crude steel 21,683,000; pig iron 10,512,000; chemical fertilizers 9,775,143; textiles and clothing 4,349,000; pulp and paperboard 4,257,407; plastic and resins 2,412,000; sulfuric acid 2,338,800; caustic soda 1,309,000; ceramic tiles 26,001,632 cu m¶; beer 10,319,974 hectolitres; shoes 421,751,000 pairs¶; refrigerators 3,900,268; washing machines 3,306,533; bicycles 1,978,333; televisions 1,619,000; automobiles 1,386,000. Construction (buildings completed 1982): residential 199,215; commercial, industrial, and other 22,191.

Service enterprises (1981)

	no. of enterprises	no. of employees	hourly wage as a % of all wages	annual value added (000,000,000 lire)
Public utilities	61	11,000	...	5,082
Electrical power	49	125,000	...	4,017
Transport and communication†	195,828	1,135,950	...	24,760
Communication	...	...	...	5,842
Finance	234,334	938,904	...	46,343
Wholesale and retail trade†	1,589,785	3,694,238	...	61,884
Pub. admin., services†	494,153	3,553,304	...	57,333

Energy production (consumption): electricity (kW-hr; 1983) 180,672,000,000 (191,595,000,000¶); coal (metric tons; 1983) 1,908,000 (1,957,000¶); crude petroleum (barrels; 1982) 12,923,000 (590,629,000); petroleum products (metric tons; 1983) 69,932,000 (70,273,000¶); natural gas (cu m; 1983) 14,-009,217,000 (26,207,512,000¶).
Persons economically active (1982): total 22,753,200 (40.3%); female participation in the labour force 7,711,000 (33.9%); unemployed 2,278,000♀ (9.9%).

Price and earnings indexes (1980 = 100)

	1978	1979	1980	1981	1982	1983	1984
Consumer price index	71.9	82.5	100.0	117.8	137.2	157.3	175.3◇
Monthly earnings index	68.8	82.0	100.0	123.9	145.7	168.5	185.7□

Household income and expenditure. Average household size (1982) 3.0; average annual income per household 9,978,000 lire† (U.S.$12,009); sources of income†: salaries and wages 52.9%, private enterprise 17.3%, professions 3.6%; expenditure (1982): food and beverages 28.2%, transport and communications 13.5%, utilities 6.3%, recreation and education 5.8%.
Land use (1982): forested 21.2%; meadows and pastures 17.0%; agricultural and under permanent cultivation 40.9%, other 20.9%.

Financial aggregates

	1979	1980	1981	1982	1983	1984 (Oct.)
Exchange rate, Lit per:						
U.S. dollar	830.9	856.4	1,136.8	1,352.5	1,518.8	1,880.9
£	1,762.8	1,992.2	2,305.3	2,367.6	2,304.0	2,289.8
SDR	449	521	673	711	565	619
International reserves (U.S.$)						
Total (excl. gold; '000,000)	18,197	23,140	20,134	14,090	20,105	20,373
SDR's ('000,000)	592	665	783	785	591	616
Reserve pos. in IMF ('000,000)	312	823	734	696	990	1,010
Foreign exchange ('000,000)	17,294	21,652	18,617	12,610	18,524	18,746
Gold, ('000,000 fine troy oz.)	66.71	66.67	66.67	66.67	66.67	66.67
% world reserves	7.1	7.0	7.0	7.0	7.1	7.1
Interest and prices						
Central bank discount (%)	15.00	16.50	19.00	18.00	17.00	16.50
Gov't. bond yield (%)	14.05	16.11	20.58	20.90	18.02	15.54
Industrial share prices (1980 = 100)	78.7	100.0	151.7	123.1	153.1	173.7
Balance of payments (U.S.$'000,000)						
Balance of visible trade	−990	−16,417	−10,901	−8,130	−4,390	...
Imports, f.o.b.	−72,379	−93,236	−85,803	−80,678	−75,215	...
Exports, f.o.b.	71,389	76,819	74,902	72,548	70,827	...
Balance of invisibles	6,614	5,402	1,537	1,701	2,555	...
Balance of payments, current account	5,414	−9,801	−8,604	−5,767	−641	...

Foreign trade

Balance of trade (current prices)

	1978	1979	1980	1981	1982	1983
'000,000,000 lire	1,537	−1,905	−15,716	−14,056	−16,966	−6,667
% of total	1.4%	1.4%	9.2%	6.7%	7.9%	3.0%

Imports (1982): 116,212,033,000,000 lire (crude oil 22.0, food and live animals 13.3%, chemicals and chemical products 8.6%, metal and semi-processed metal 7.7%, machinery and parts 7.1%, automobiles and spare parts 7.0%, refined petroleum products 5.9%). *Major import sources*: W. Germany 16.1%; France 12.5%; U.S. 6.8%; Saudi Arabia 5.9%; The Netherlands 4.3%; Soviet Union 4.1%.
Exports (1982): 99,246,476,000,000 lire (machinery and parts 17.3%; textiles and clothing 12.5%; refined petroleum products 7.1%; automobiles and parts 6.5%; chemicals 6.3%; food and live animals 6.0%; iron and steel products 5.6%; leather shoes 4.1%; stone and ceramic products 4.0%; silver, gold, and platinum 3.3%). *Major export destinations*: W. Germany 15.6%; France 15.2%; U.S. 7.1%; U.K. 6.3%; Switzerland 4.0%.

Transport and communications

Transport. Railroads (1983): length 12,314 mi, 19,817 km; passenger-mi 23,184,000,000, passenger-km 37,312,000,000, short ton-mi cargo 10,882,-000,000, metric ton-km cargo 15,888,000,000. Roads (1982): total length 184,538 mi, 296,986 km. Vehicles (1982): passenger cars 19,616,106; trucks and buses 1,671,706. Merchant marine (1983): vessels (100 gross tons and over) 1,609; total deadweight tonnage 16,474,699. Air transport (1983): passenger-mi 7,836,000,000, passenger-km 12,612,000,000; short ton-mi cargo 433,832,000, metric ton-km cargo 633,384,000; airports (1984) 36.
Communications. Daily newspapers (1983): total number 79; total circulation 7,044,958△; circulation per 1,000 population 124△. Radios (1983): 14,007,892 (1 per 4.1 persons). Television (1983): 13,609,892 (1 per 4.2 persons). Telephones (1982): 20,444,037 (1 per 2.8 persons).

Education and health

Education (1983–84)

	schools	teachers†	students	student/ teacher ratio
Primary (age 6–10)	28,786	276,716	4,068,324	...
Secondary (age 11–13)□	13,135	333,062	3,708,960	...
Voc., teacher tr.	4,430	199,268	1,620,659	...
Higher	71†	47,844	1,046,807	...

College graduates per 100,000 population (students graduating; 1983) 38.2.
Literacy (1971): total population literate 38,421,342 (93.9%); males literate 18,767,897 (95.3%); females literate 19,653,445 (92.7%).
Health: physicians (1981⊕) 77,805 (1 per 726.2 persons); hospital beds (1982) 515,152 (1 per 109.8 persons).
Food (1978–80): daily per capita caloric intake 3,643 (vegetable products 75.4%, animal products 24.6%); 145% of FAO recommended minimum.

Military

Total active duty personnel (1984): 375,100 (army 69.3%; navy 11.9%; air force 18.8%). *Military expenditure as percent of GNP*: (1982) 2.6% (world 6.0%); per capita expenditure U.S.$164.

*1978. †1979. ‡Imputed bank charges less indirect duties on import. §Unemployed. ‖ 1981. ¶1982. ♀1983. ♂August. □June. ◇Sept. 1984. △Data for 62 dailies only. ↑1982–83. ⊕In hospitals only.

Ivory Coast

Official name: République de Côte
  d'Ivoire (Republic of Ivory Coast).
Form of government: republic with
  one legislative house (National
  Assembly [147]).
Head of state and government:
  President.
Capital: Abidjan.
Official language: French.
Official religion: none.
Monetary unit: 1 CFA franc
  (CFAF) = 100 centimes; valuation
  (Oct. 29, 1984) 1 U.S.$ = CFAF470.6;
  1 £ = CFAF568.0.

Area and population

Departments	Capitals	area sq mi	area sq km	population 1975 census*
Abengourou	Abengourou	2,664	6,900	177,692
Abidjan	Abidjan	5,483	14,200	1,389,141
Aboisso	Aboisso	2,413	6,250	148,823
Adzopé	Adzopé	2,019	5,230	162,837
Agboville	Agboville	1,486	3,850	141,970
Biankouma	Biankouma	1,911	4,950	75,711
Bondoukou	Bondoukou	6,382	16,530	296,551
Bongouanou	Bongouanou	2,151	5,570	216,907
Bouaflé	Bouaflé	2,189	5,670	164,817
Bouaké	Bouaké	9,189	23,800	808,048
Bouna	Bouna	8,290	21,470	84,290
Boundiali	Boundiali	3,048	7,895	96,449
Dabakala	Dabakala	3,734	9,670	56,230
Daloa	Daloa	4,483	11,610	265,529
Danané	Danané	1,776	4,600	170,249
Dimbokro	Dimbokro	3,293	8,530	258,116
Divo	Divo	3,058	7,920	202,511
Ferkessedougou	Ferkessedougou	6,845	17,728	90,423
Gagnoa	Gagnoa	1,737	4,500	174,018
Guiglo	Guiglo	5,463	14,150	137,672
Issia	Issia	1,386	3,590	104,081
Katiola	Katiola	3,637	9,420	77,875
Korhogo	Korhogo	4,826	12,500	276,816
Lakota	Lakota	1,054	2,730	76,105
Man	Man	2,722	7,050	278,659
Mankono	Mankono	4,116	10,660	82,358
Odienné	Odienné	7,954	20,600	124,010
Oumé	Oumé	927	2,400	85,486
Sassandra	Sassandra	6,768	17,530	116,644
Séguéla	Séguéla	4,340	11,240	75,181
Soubré	Soubré	3,193	8,270	75,350
Tingréla	Tingréla	849	2,200	35,829
Touba	Touba	3,367	8,720	77,786
Zuénoula	Zuénoula	1,093	2,830	98,792
TOTAL		123,847†	320,763	6,702,866

Source: Official government figures.

Demography

Density (1984): persons per sq mi 77.2, persons per sq km 29.8.
Urban–rural (1980): urban 32.0%; rural 68.0%.
Sex distribution (1980): male 51.68%; female 48.32%.
Age breakdown (1980): under 15, 44.6%; 15–29, 26.6%; 30–44, 17.6%; 45–59,
  7.7%; 60–74, 3.0%; 75 and over 0.5%.
Population projection: (1990) 12,568,000; (2000) 18,847,000.
Doubling time: 16 years.
Ethnic composition (1978): Bete 19.7%; Senufo 14.4%; Baule 11.8%; Anui
  10.5%; Malinke 6.6%; Dan 5.6%; Lobi 5.3%; other 26.1%.
Religious affiliation (1980): folk religionist 43.8%; Christian 32.0%; Muslim
  24.0%; other 0.2%.
Major cities (1975): Abidjan 1,686,100‡; Bouaké 175,264; Daloa 60,837; Man
  50,288; Korhogo 45,250.

Vital statistics

Birth rate per 1,000 population (1980–85): 46.4 (world avg. 27.5); legitimate,
  n.a.; illegitimate, n.a.
Death rate per 1,000 population (1980–85): 16.4 (world avg. 10.6).
Natural increase rate per 1,000 population (1980–85): 30.0 (world avg. 16.9).
Total fertility rate (avg. births per childbearing woman; 1980–85): 6.7.
Marriage rate per 1,000 population: n.a.
Divorce rate per 1,000 population: n.a.
Infant mortality rate per 1,000 live births (1980–85): 134.5.
Life expectancy at birth (1980–85): male 46.9 years; female 50.2 years.
Major causes of death: n.a.; however, the major infectious diseases are
  malaria, dysentery, yaws, pneumonia, leprosy, and syphilis and gonorrhea.

National economy

Budget (1982). Revenue: CFAF 420,700,000,000 (indirect taxes 72.8%; direct
  taxes 22.9%). Expenditures: CFAF 420,700,000,000 (public services 56.9%).
Public debt (external, outstanding; 1982): U.S.$4,861,400.
Tourism (1981): receipts from visitors U.S.$73,000,000; expenditures by na-
  tionals abroad U.S.$239,000,000.
Production (metric tons except as noted). Agriculture, forestry, fishing
  (1982): sugarcane 2,400,000, cassava 800,000, plantains 780,000, rice 500,-
  000, cacao beans 390,000, corn (maize) 300,000, coffee 250,000, coconuts
  160,000, seed cotton 150,000, bananas 150,000; livestock (number of live
  animals) 1,320,000 sheep, 1,320,000 goats, 750,000 cattle, 385,000 pigs;

roundwood 10,619,000 cu m; fish catch 92,469. Mining and quarrying
(1982): diamonds 37,000 carats. Manufacturing (1981): cement 1,080,000;
gas oil 347,000; motor spirit 192,000; wheat flour 150,000; sugar 132,000;
palm oil 126,000; cocoa powder 70,000; conserved pineapples 66,000. Construction (CFAF; 1981) 267,000,000,000. Energy production (consumption):
electricity (kW-hr; 1982) 1,929,000,000 (1,929,000,000); coal, none (n.a.);
crude petroleum (barrels; 1982) 5,538,000 (13,783,000); petroleum products
(metric tons; 1982) 1,915,000 (1,637,000); natural gas, none (n.a.).
Gross national product (at current market prices; 1981): U.S.$10,800,000,000
(U.S.$1,320 per capita).

Origin of gross domestic product (current prices)

	1979 in value CFAF'000,000,000	% of total value	labour force	% of labour force
Agriculture	529.7	27.2	3,124,000	79.9
Mining	4.9	0.3	...	...
Manufacturing	216.4	11.1	...	...
Construction	159.6	8.2	...	...
Trade	404.1	20.8	...	...
Public utilities	23.4	1.2	...	...
Transportation and communication	142.8	7.3	...	...
Finance, services, other	463.8§	23.9§	785,000 ‖	20.1 ‖
TOTAL	1,944.7	100.0	3,909,000	100.0

Persons economically active (1982): total 4,228,000 (49.3%); female participation in the labour force, n.a.; unemployed, n.a.

Price and earnings indexes (1975 = 100)

	1978	1979	1980	1981	1982	1983	1984
Consumer price index	166.8	183.7	191.1	200.2	223.2	236.4	249.0¶
Earnings index	...	...	...	...	...	...	...

Household income and expenditure. Average household size (1980) 4.5; average annual income per household, n.a.; source of income: n.a.; expenditure
(1979): food 51.1%, housing 11.6%, clothing 8.4%.
Land use (1981): forested 29.5%; meadows and pastures 9.4%; agricultural
and under permanent cultivation 12.4%; other 48.7%.

Foreign trade

Balance of trade (current prices)

	1978	1979	1980	1981	1982	1983
CFAF'000,000,000	−1.8	+6.0	+49.5	+7.8	+36.8	+92.5
% of total	0.1%	0.6%	3.9%	0.6%	2.0%	6.1%

Imports (1981): CFAF681,464,000,000 (crude petroleum 17.4%; machinery
9.2%; cereals 7.0%; iron and steel 5.6%; electrical equipment 4.1%; paper
and paperboard 3.2%). *Major import sources:* France 29.8%; United States
6.9%; Japan 4.7%; West Germany 4.1%; Nigeria 3.6%.
Exports (1981): CFAF689,298,000,000 (cacao beans 29.0%; wood 13.7%; coffee 10.0%; petroleum products 5.8%; cocoa butter 2.9%; pineapples 2.9%).
Major export destinations: France 18.6%; The Netherlands 13.2%; United
States 11.5%; Italy 7.9%; West Germany 6.6%.

Transport and communications

Transport. Railroads (1983): length 761 mi, 1,225 km; passenger-mi 620,-
382,000, passenger-km 998,410,000; short ton-mi cargo 360,759,000, metric
ton-km cargo 526,700,000. Roads (1982): total length 28,943 mi, 46,580
km (paved 8%). Vehicles (1982): passenger cars 166,920; trucks and buses
69,500. Merchant marine (1983): vessels (100 gross tons and over) 66; total
deadweight tonnage 195,263. Air transport (1983): passenger-mi 178,682,-
000, passenger-km 287,561,000; short ton-mi cargo 37,582,000, metric ton-
km cargo 54,869,000; airports (1984) with scheduled flights 12.
Communications. Daily newspaper (1983): total number 1; total circulation
75,000; circulation per 1,000 population 8.4. Radios (1983): total number
of receivers 800,000 (1 per 11.2 persons). Television (1983): total number
of receivers 562,000 (1 per 16.0 persons). Telephones (1980): 78,370 (1
per 103 persons).

Education and health

Education (1979–80)

	schools	teachers	students	student/ teacher ratio
Primary (age 6–11)	4,419	24,441	954,190	39.0
Secondary (age 12–18)	113⁹	4,569	172,280	37.7
Voc., teacher tr.	38	650◊	44,481	...
Higher	1	475□	10,772	...

College graduates per 100,000 population: n.a. *Literacy* (1980): total population literate 1,560,000 (35.0%).
Health (1978): physicians 429 (1 per 16,795 persons); hospital beds 9,962
(1 per 723 persons).
Food (1978–80): daily per capita caloric intake 2,623 (vegetable products
93.2%, animal products 6.8%); 114% of FAO recommended minimum.

Military

Total active duty personnel (1982): 5,070 (army 78.9%; navy 9.9%; air force
11.2%). *Military expenditure as percent of GNP* (1982): 1.7% (world 6.0%);
per capita expenditure U.S.$16.

*Preliminary. †Detail does not add to total given because of rounding. ‡1981. §In-
cludes public administration and defense. ‖Includes all nonagricultural activities.
¶Second quarter. ⁹Public schools only. ◊1976–77. □1978–79.

Jamaica

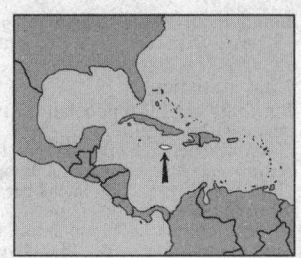

Official name: Jamaica.
Form of government:
parliamentary state with two
legislative houses (Senate [21]; House
of Representatives [60]).
Chief of state: British Monarch
represented by governor-general.
Head of government: Prime Minister.
Capital: Kingston.
Official language: English.
Official religion: none.
Monetary unit: 1 dollar (J$) = 100
cents; valuation (Oct. 29, 1984)
1 U.S.$ = J$4.18; 1 £ = J$5.05.

Area and population

Counties Parishes	Capitals	area sq mi	area sq km	population 1982 census
Cornwall				
Hanover	Lucea	174	450	60,420
Saint Elizabeth	Black River	468	1,212	132,353
Saint James	Montego Bay	230	595	127,994
Trelawny	Falmouth	338	875	65,038
Westmoreland	Savanna-la-Mar	312	807	116,163
Middlesex				
Clarendon	May Pen	462	1,196	194,885
Manchester	Mandeville	321	830	136,517
Saint Ann	Saint Anns Bay	468	1,213	132,475
Saint Catherine	Spanish Town	460	1,192	315,970
Saint Mary	Port Maria	236	611	101,442
Surrey				
Kingston	Kingston	8	22	100,637
Portland	Port Antonio	314	814	70,787
Saint Andrew	Saint Andrews	166	431	464,850
Saint Thomas	Morant Bay	287	743	76,347
TOTAL		4,244	10,991	2,095,878

Source: Official government figures.

Demography

Density (1982): persons per sq mi 493.8, persons per sq km 190.7.
Urban–rural (1981): urban 41.9%; rural 58.1%.
Sex distribution (1982): male 49.70%; female 50.30%.
Age breakdown (1982): under 15, 38.2%; 15–29, 28.3%; 30–49, 16.1%; 50–59, 6.7%; 60–64, 3.0%; 65 and over, 7.7%.
Population projection: (1990) 2,535,000; (2000) 2,872,000.
Doubling time: 43 years.
Ethnic composition (1983): African 76.3%; Afro-European 15.1%; East Indian and Afro-East Indian 3.4%; white 3.2%; Chinese and Afro-Chinese 1.2%; other 0.8%.
Religious affiliation (1983–84): Protestant 70.7%, of which Anglican 16.0%; Roman Catholic 9.6%; African Christian 8.1%; other 11.6%.
Major cities (1982): Saint Andrews 393,590; Kingston 100,637; Spanish Town 81,416; Montego Bay 59,614; May Pen 37,682.

Vital statistics

Birth rate per 1,000 population (1982): 27.6 (world avg. 29.0).
Death rate per 1,000 population (1982): 5.7 (world avg. 11.0).
Natural increase rate per 1,000 population (1982): 21.9 (world avg. 18.0).
Total fertility rate (avg. births per childbearing woman; 1981): 3.8.
Marriage rate per 1,000 population (1982): 4.5.
Divorce rate per 1,000 population (1982): 0.3.
Infant mortality rate per 1,000 live births (1982): 9.9.
Life expectancy at birth (1981): male 69.2 years; female 73.3 years.
Major causes of death per 100,000 population (1978): cerebrovascular disease 86.2; heart disease 83.3; malignant neoplasms (cancers) 80.1; pneumonia and influenza 31.7.

National economy

Budget (1981–82). Revenue: J$1,428,934,000 (customs and excise taxes 34.5%; income tax 30.1%; property, vehicle, and entertainment tax 3.8%). Expenditures: J$1,615,716,000 (public debt charges 26.3%; education 19.5%; social security and justice system 12.0; health 8.2%).
Public debt (external, outstanding; 1982): U.S.$3,415,900,000.
Tourism (1980): receipts from visitors U.S.$135,700,000; expenditures by nationals abroad U.S.$6,570,000.
Production (metric tons except as noted). Agriculture, forestry, fishing (1982): sugarcane 2,460,000, roots and tubers 227,000 (of which yams and sweet potatoes 141,000), bananas and plantains 118,000, citrus fruits 89,000, cassava and taros 70,500; livestock (number of live animals) 400,000 goats, 310,000 cattle, 265,000 pigs; roundwood 34,000 cu m; fish catch* 7,874. Mining and quarrying (1983): bauxite 7,300,000. Manufacturing (value added in J$000,000; 1981): processed food 261.4, of which alcoholic beverages 105.9; tobacco and tobacco products 114.9; chemicals and plastics 85.4; refined petroleum 80.0; textiles, wearing apparel, and footwear 39.7; wood and wood products 28.4. Construction (1978): residential 1,565,000 sq ft†. Energy production (consumption): electricity (kW-hr; 1982) 1,335,400,000 (1,335,400,000); coal, none (none); crude petroleum (barrels; 1982) none (14,200,000); petroleum products (metric tons; 1982) 846,000 (2,364,000); natural gas, none (none).
Land use (1981): forested 28.1%; meadows and pastures 18.9%; agricultural and under permanent cultivation 24.5%; other 28.5%.

Gross national product (at current market prices; 1982): U.S.$3,027,300,000 (U.S.$1,440 per capita).

Origin of gross domestic product (current prices)

	1981 in value J$'000,000	% of total value	labour force	% of labour force
Agriculture	419.6	7.9	269,200	26.3
Mining	673.6	12.7	8,800	0.9
Manufacturing	783.9	14.8	84,800	8.3
Construction	363.5	6.8	32,100§	3.1§
Trade‡	...	...	...	...
Public utilities	80.3	1.5	§	§
Transportation and communication	249.9	4.7	34,400	3.4
Finance‡	1,704.1	32.1	103,600	10.1
Pub. admin., defense	780.2	14.7	106,300	10.4
Services	...	...	118,000	11.5
Unemployed	...	...	261,500	25.6
Other	254.7	4.8	4,200	0.4
TOTAL	5,309.8	100.0	1,022,900	100.0

Persons economically active (1981): total 1,022,900 (48.8%); female participation in labour force 476,200 (46.6%); unemployed 261,500 (25.6%).

Price and earnings indexes (1980 = 100)

	1978	1979	1980	1981	1982	1983	1984
Consumer price index	60.8	78.6	100.0	112.7	120.1	130.0	150.8 ‖
Monthly earnings index	...	...	...	...	...	...	...

Household income and expenditure. Average household size (1982): 4.2; income per household (1982): J$10,180 (U.S.$5,715); sources of income (1982): wages and salaries 70.9%, self-employed 27.3%, transfers 1.8%; expenditure (1980): food 29.8%, housing 19.4%, transportation and communication 11.8%, recreation 6.0%, health care 5.4%, clothing and footwear 2.6%.

Foreign trade

Balance of trade (current prices)

J$'000,000	1977	1978	1979	1980	1981	1982
	−74.3	−187.8	−309.2	−380.2	−898.3	−1,105.4
% of total	5.0%	8.0%	9.7%	10.0%	12.2%	29.9%

Imports (1980): J$2,098,700 (crude petroleum 22.2%; cereal products 9.8%, of which wheat products 2.4%, rice products 2.1%; meat, eggs, and dairy products 3.8%; textiles 3.1%; transport equipment 3.0%; paper and paper products 2.5%; iron and steel 1.8%). *Major import sources:* United States 31.5%; Venezuela 22.4%; Netherlands Antilles 14.4%; United Kingdom 6.7%; Canada 6.0%.
Exports (1980): J$1,718,500 (aluminum oxide and hydroxide 55.7%; bauxite 20.6%; food and live animals 10.3%, of which raw sugar 5.7%, bananas 1.1%; alcoholic beverages 2.0%; petroleum products 2.0%; aircraft 1.8%). *Major export destinations:* United States 37.4%; United Kingdom 19.4%; Norway 10.9%; U.S.S.R. 5.2%; Spain 5.0%; Ghana 4.5%.

Transport and communications

Transport. Railroads (1984): length 205 mi, 330 km; passenger-mi¶ 79,308,-357, passenger-km 49,279,833; short ton-mi cargo* 88,514,000, metric ton-km cargo 129,228,000. Roads (1984): total length 6,986 mi, 11,250 km (paved 67%). Vehicles (1982): passenger cars 41,163; trucks and buses 17,-394. Merchant marine (1983): vessels (100 gross tons and over) 13; total deadweight tonnage 12,878. Air transport: passengers, n.a.; cargo, n.a.; airports (1984) with scheduled flights 2.
Communications. Daily newspapers (1981): total number 3; total circulation 200,000; circulation per 1,000 population 91. Radios (1981): total number of receivers 850,000 (1 per 2.6 persons). Television (1981): total number of receivers 180,000 (1 per 12.2 persons). Telephones (1982): 125,727 (1 per 16.7 persons).

Education and health

Education (1980–81)

	schools	teachers⁹	students	student/ teacher ratio
Primary (age 6–11)	894	9,140	364,637	39.9
Secondary (age 12–16)	694	9,520	233,723	24.6
Voc., teacher tr.	19	500	9,204	18.4
Higher	11	890	12,143	13.5

College graduates per 100,000 population (students graduating; 1980): 1,963.
Literacy (1980): total population literate 1,100,600 (88.6%); males literate 542,600 (88.2%); females literate 558,000 (89.1%).
Health (1980): physicians 716 (1 per 3,035 persons); hospital beds 6,408 (1 per 339 persons).
Food (1978–80): daily per capita caloric intake 2,570 (vegetable products 84.2%, animal products 15.8%); 114% of FAO recommended minimum requirement.

Military

Total active duty personnel (1982): 3,220 (army 93.2%; navy 4.3%; air force 2.5%). *Military expenditure as percent of GNP* (1982): 1.6% (world 6.0%); per capita expenditure U.S.$20.

*1981. †Estimated from incomplete data; public construction only. ‡Trade included with finance. §Public utilities included with construction. ‖ First quarter. ¶1978. ⁹Total number extrapolated from number of public school teachers.

Japan

Official name: Nihon (Japan).
Form of government: constitutional monarchy with two legislative houses (National Diet [252]; House of Representatives [511]).
Chief of state: Emperor.
Head of government: Prime Minister.
Capital: Tōkyō.
Official language: Japanese.
Official religion: none.
Monetary unit: 1 Yen (¥) = 100 sen; valuation (Oct. 29, 1984) 1 U.S.$ = ¥246.40; 1 £ = ¥297.40.

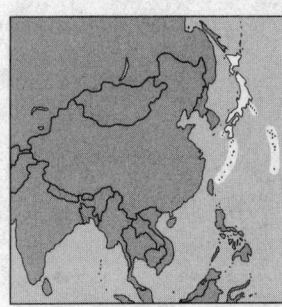

Area and population

Regions Prefectures	Capitals	area sq mi	area sq km	population 1983 estimate
Chūbu				
Aichi	Nagoya	1,981	5,132	6,356,000
Fukui	Fukui	1,617	4,189	806,000
Gifu	Gifu	4,091	10,596	2,001,000
Ishikawa	Kanazawa	1,620	4,197	1,138,000
Nagano	Nagano	5,245	13,585	2,109,000
Niigata	Niigata	4,856	12,578	2,467,000
Shizuoka	Shizuoka	3,001	7,773	3,515,000
Toyama	Toyama	1,642	4,252	1,112,000
Yamanashi	Kōfu	1,723	4,463	816,000
Chūgoku				
Hiroshima	Hiroshima	3,268	8,463	2,792,000
Okayama	Okayama	2,736	7,087	1,895,000
Shimane	Matsue	2,559	6,628	787,000
Tottori	Tottori	1,348	3,492	612,000
Yamaguchi	Yamaguchi	2,356	6,102	1,600,000
Hokkaidō				
Hokkaidō (Territory)	Sapporo	32,246	83,517	5,660,000
Kantō				
Chiba	Chiba	1,986	5,143	4,999,000
Gumma	Maebashi	2,454	6,356	1,889,000
Ibaraki	Mito	2,353	6,093	2,664,000
Kanagawa	Yokohoma	927	2,400	7,210,000
Saitama	Urawa	1,467	3,799	5,695,000
Tochigi	Utsunomiya	2,476	6,414	1,831,000
Kinki				
Hyōgo	Kōbe	3,233	8,374	5,230,000
Mie	Tsu	2,231	5,777	1,725,000
Nara	Nara	1,425	3,692	1,274,000
Shiga	Ōtsu	1,551	4,016	1,126,000
Wakayama	Wakayama	1,824	4,723	1,091,000
Kyūshū				
Fukuoka	Fukuoka	1,913	4,954	4,670,000
Kagoshima	Kagoshima	3,538	9,163	1,804,000
Kumamoto	Kumamoto	2,859	7,406	1,818,000
Miyazaki	Miyazaki	2,986	7,734	1,170,000
Nagasaki	Nagasaki	1,586	4,108	1,596,000
Ōita	Ōita	2,446	6,334	1,241,000
Saga	Saga	939	2,433	874,000
Ryukyu				
Okinawa	Naha	869	2,250	1,146,000
Shikoku				
Ehime	Matsuyama	2,228	5,770	1,518,000
Kagawa	Takamatsu	726	1,881	1,014,000
Kōchi	Kōchi	2,744	7,107	835,000
Tokushima	Tokushima	1,601	4,145	830,000
Tohoku				
Akita	Akita	4,483*	11,611*	1,255,000
Aomori	Aomori	3,713*	9,616*	1,531,000
Fukushima	Fukushima	5,322	13,783	2,059,000
Iwate	Morioka	5,899	15,278	1,430,000
Miyagi	Sendai	2,815	7,291	2,144,000
Yamagata	Yamagata	3,601	9,327	1,256,000
Metropolis				
Tōkyō†	Tōkyō	832	2,155	11,728,000
Urban prefectures				
Kyōto‡	Kyōto	1,781	4,613	2,573,000
Ōsaka‡	Ōsaka	720	1,865	8,594,000
TOTAL		145,856§	377,765§	119,483,000 ‖

Source: Official government figures.

Demography

Density (1984): persons per sq mi 822.9, persons per sq km 317.7.
Urban–rural (1980): urban 76.2%; rural 23.8%.
Sex distribution (1984): male 49.21%; female 50.79%.
Age breakdown (1984): under 15, 22.1%; 15–29, 20.6%; 30–44, 24.1%; 45–59, 19.0%; 60–69, 7.6%; 70 and over, 6.6%.
Population projection: (1990) 122,834,000; (2000) 128,119,000.
Doubling time: During the intercensal period 1975–80, the annual growth rate was 0.9%; since 1981, however, the population has been decreasing.
Ethnic composition (1984): Japanese 99.4%; other (mainly Korean) 0.6%.
Religious affiliation (1980): Shintoist 84.0%¶; Buddhist 75.0%¶; Protestant 0.5%; Roman Catholic 0.3%.
Major cities (1984 est.): Tōkyō 8,389,800; Yokohama 2,940,300; Ōsaka 2,631,000; Nagoya 2,108,400; Sapporo 1,522,100; Kyōto 1,487,000; Kōbe 1,402,000; Fukuoka 1,147,000; Kawasaki 1,077,000; Kitakyūshū 1,060,000.
Place of birth (1984): 99.4% native-born; 0.6% foreign-born (mainly Korean).
Mobility (1980). Population living in same residence as in October 1975: 68.0%; different residence, same prefecture 24.2%; different prefecture 7.8%.
Households (1980). Average household size 3.3; 1 person 15.8%, 2 persons 17.6%, 3 persons 19.0%, 4 persons 26.6%, 5 persons 11.7%, 6 persons 6.0%, 7 or more persons 3.3%. Family households 27,872,000⁹ (76.4%), nonfamily 8,625,000⁹⁵ (23.6%), of which 1-person 18.1%.

Immigration (1981): permanent immigrants admitted 1,552,296, from United States 20.0%, Taiwan 19.7%, South Korea 16.2%.

Vital statistics

Birth rate per 1,000 population (1983): 12.7 (world avg. 29.0); (1980) legitimate 99.2%, illegitimate 0.8%.
Death rate per 1,000 population (1983): 6.2 (world avg. 11.0).
Natural increase rate per 1,000 population (1983): 6.5 (world avg. 18.0).
Total fertility rate (avg. births per childbearing woman; 1982): 1.7.
Marriage rate per 1,000 population (1983): 6.4.
Divorce rate per 1,000 population (1983): 1.5.
Infant mortality rate per 1,000 live births (1983): 6.2.
Life expectancy at birth (1983): male 74.2 years; female 79.8 years.
Major causes of death per 100,000 population (1983): malignant neoplasms (cancers) 147.4; cerebrovascular diseases 122.1; heart diseases 110.7; pneumonia and bronchitis 39.1; accidents and adverse effects 24.7; senility without mention of psychosis 24.6; suicides 20.9; cirrhosis of the liver 14.1; hypertensive diseases 11.3; nephritis, nephrotic syndrome, and nephrosis 10.3.

Social indicators

Educational attainment (1980). Percent of population 15 years old and over having: less than full primary education 0.3%, primary and lower secondary 38.5%, higher secondary 38.0%, junior college and higher professional 5.7%, university and post graduate 8.0%, still in school 9.5%.

Distribution of income (1980)

percent of avg. annual household income by decile

1	2	3	4	5	6	7	8	9	10 (highest)
44.7	60.2	69.6	77.6	86.1	95.8	106.6	120.0	141.6	196.9

Quality of working life (1983). Average work week: 46.8 hours (10.7% overtime). Annual rate of industrial deaths per 100,000: n.a. Proportion of labour force insured for damages or income loss resulting from injury, permanent disability, and death 65.4% □. Average man-days lost to labour stoppages per 1,000 work days: 0.03. Average duration of journey to work: 32 minutes (26.7%◇ private automobile, 67.4%◇ public transportation, 5.5%◇ taxi, 0.4%◇ other). Rate per 1,000 workers of discouraged (unemployed no longer seeking work): n.a.
Access to services (1980). Proportion of households having access to: gas supply 63.0%, safe public water supply 91.4%, public sewage collection 89.4%.
Social participation. Eligible voters participating in last national election (June 26, 1983) 57.0%. Population over 15 years of age participating in social service activities on a voluntary basis 26.0%. Trade union membership in total work force 22.1%. Practicing religious population in total affiliated population, n.a.
Social deviance (1982). Offense rate per 100,000 population for: murder 1.5, rape 2.0, larceny and theft 1,107.0, robbery 1.9. Incidence in general population of: alcoholism, n.a.; drug and substance abuse, n.a. Rate per 100,000 population of suicide (1983) 20.9.
Leisure (1981). Favourite leisure activities: domestic travel 70.5%, learning (except school work) 45.4%, baseball and softball 20.9%, volleyball 9.8%, tennis 9.0%, golf 8.1%.
Material well-being (1983). Households possessing: automobile 62.9%, telephone virtually 100%, color television receiver virtually 100%, refrigerator virtually 100%, air conditioner 49.6%, washing machine virtually 100%.

National economy

Gross national product (at current market prices; 1984): U.S.$1,215,189,000,-000 (U.S.$10,120 per capita).

Origin of gross domestic product (current prices)

	1982 in value ¥'000,000,000	% of total value	labour force	% of labour force
Agriculture	9,099.9	3.3	5,480,000	9.5
Mining	1,226.2	0.4	100,000	0.2
Manufacturing	81,345.1	29.5	13,800,000	23.9
Construction	22,764.2	8.3	5,410,000	9.4
Trade	32,243.5	11.7	12,960,000	22.4
Public utilities	8,566.9	3.1	340,000	0.6
Transportation and communication	18,365.7	6.7	3,490,000	6.0
Finance	42,449.5	15.4	2,060,000	3.6
Pub. admin., defense	12,722.4	4.6	1,950,000	3.4
Services	46,575.0	17.0	10,650,000	18.4
Other	—	—	1,500,000△	2.6
TOTAL	264,706.7	100.0	57,740,000	100.0

Budget (1984)†. Revenue: ¥50,627,000,000,000 (income tax 27.6%, public bonds 25.0%, corporation tax 21.7%, liquor tax 4.4%). Expenditures: ¥50,-627,000,000,000 (social security 18.4%, national debt 18.1%, local finance 17.9%, public works 12.9%, education and science 9.6%, national defense 5.8%).
Public debt (1984): U.S.$496,439,471,000.
Persons economically active (1983): total 58,890,000 (49.3%); female participation in the labour force 23,250,000 (39.5%); unemployed 1,560,000 (2.6%).

Price and earnings indexes (1980 = 100)

	1978	1979	1980	1981	1982	1983	1984§§
Consumer price index	89.4	92.6	100.0	104.9	107.7	109.7	112.8
Monthly earnings index	88.8	94.1	100.0	105.3	110.0	113.8	120.5

Household income and expenditure (1983): Average household size 3.8; average annual income per household ¥4,866,204 (U.S.$20,108); sources of income: wages and salaries of household head 64.9%, wages and salaries of other household members 11.7%, other 23.4%; expenditure: food 21.6%, transportation and communication 7.7%, reading and recreation 7.0%, clothing and footwear 5.7%, fuel, light, and water 4.7%, housing 3.9%.
Tourism (1982): receipts from visitors U.S.$754,000,000; expenditures by nationals abroad U.S.$4,116,000,000.

Manufacturing, mining, and construction enterprises (1981)

	no. of enterprises	avg. no. of persons engaged⊙	monthly contract wages as a % of avg. of all contract wages**	annual value added (¥'000,000,000)
Electrical machinery	29,627	1,449,000	95.1	9,949
Nonelectrical machinery	41,722	1,155,000	109.0	9,423
Transport equipment	14,715	907,000	115.4	8,213
Food products	48,614	1,020,000	83.5	6,106
Iron and steel	7,168	422,000	124.9	5,534
Metal products	51,298	807,000	98.2	5,184
Printing and publishing	28,482	493,000	116.2	4,080
Chemical products	3,648	206,000	113.5	3,743
Textiles	47,643	766,000	73.8	3,382
Industrial chemicals	1,787	205,000	113.5	2,997
Nonmetal products	16,483	356,000	94.3	2,924
Plastic products	18,096	350,000	...	2,251
Paper and paper products	12,163	284,000	96.2	2,137
Mining	920	56,000	108.6	387
Construction	550,798	4,969,163	102.7	9,198††

Production (metric tons except as noted). Agriculture, forestry, fishing (1983): rice 10,366,000, potatoes 4,945,000, mandarin oranges 2,859,000, radishes 2,548,000, cabbages 1,568,000, Chinese cabbages 1,507,000, onions 1,170,000, cucumbers 1,048,000, apples 1,040,000, wheat 695,000; livestock (number of live animals) 10,273,000 pigs, 4,590,000 cattle, 172,451,000 hens, 134,612,000 broiler chickens; roundwood (1982) 66,305,000 cu m; fish catch 11,908,000, of which sardines 3,695,000, mackerel 805,000, tuna 358,000. Mining and quarrying (1982): limestone 168,302,000; quicklime 8,000,000; gypsum 6,363,000; dolomite 5,016,000; nitrogen 1,652,000; pyrophyllite 1,386,000; fire clay 1,332,000; sodium carbonate 1,161,000; iron ore 362,000; zinc 250,000. Manufacturing (1983): crude steel 97,179,000; semifinished steel 90,204,000; cement 80,891,000; hot-rolled steel products 77,552,000; pig iron 72,936,000; asbestos slate 66,189,000; cold-rolled steel strips 18,889,000; number of units—7,152,000 passenger cars; 3,953,000 trucks and buses; 135,754,000 motor vehicle tires; 42,929,000 motor vehicle tubes; 12,372,000 colour TV receivers, 18,217,000 videotape recorders; 35,584,000 general tape recorders; 12,849,000 35mm cameras; 116,939,000 watches; 302,678,000 fluorescent lamps. Construction (1983): residential 9,265,000 sq m; nonresidential 6,509,000 sq m.

Service enterprises (1981)

	no. of enterprises	avg. no. of persons engaged	monthly contract wages as a % of all contract wages	annual value (¥'000,000,000)
Eating and drinking services	794,758	3,123,287	79.4	31,804
Real estate	238,358	628,877	107.2	26,511
Transport and communication	160,643	3,400,845	114.0	17,412
Finance and insurance	84,136	1,711,421	110.5	12,017
Public utilities	7,034	159,631	127.2	7,386‡‡
Retail trade	1,781,075	7,395,977	86.9	...
Wholesale trade	452,317	4,378,028	99.7	...
Medical services	170,420	1,982,627	94.5	...
Educational services	82,059	1,960,885	115.2	...
Electrical power	3,880	162,574	...	...

Energy production (consumption): electricity (kW-hr; 1983) 555,510,000,000 (499,790,000,000); coal (metric tons; 1983) 17,062,000 (93,018,000); crude petroleum (barrels; 1983) 3,108,000 (1,192,856,000); petroleum products (metric tons; 1983) 158,767,000 (167,878,000); natural gas (cu m; 1983) 2,355,023,000 (25,985,000,000).
Land use (1981): forested 67.9%; meadows and pastures 1.6%; agricultural and under permanent cultivation 13.1%; other 17.4%.

Financial aggregates

	1978	1979	1980	1981	1982	1983	1984 (latest mo.)
Exchange rate, ¥ per:							
U.S. dollar	210.44	219.14	226.74	220.54	249.05	237.52	246.79
£	403.94	464.93	527.47	447.23	435.96	360.32	300.91
SDR	253.52	315.76	258.91	255.95	259.23	243.10	248.58
International reserves (U.S.$)							
Total (excl. gold; '000,000)	32,407	19,522	24,636	28,208	23,334	24,602	25,948
SDR's ('000,000)	1,372	1,688	1,738	1,934	2,091	1,935	1,918
Reserve pos. in IMF ('000,000)	2,139	1,477	1,331	1,558	2,071	2,303	2,236
Foreign exchange ('000,000)	28,896	16,357	21,567	24,716	19,172	20,364	21,794
Gold, ('000,000 fine troy oz.)	23.97	24.23	24.23	24.23	24.23	24.23	24.23
% world reserves	2.3	2.6	2.5	2.5	2.6	2.6	2.6
Interest and prices							
Central bank discount (%)	3.50	6.25	7.25	5.50	5.50	5.00	5.00
Gov't. bond yield (%)	6.09	7.69	9.22	8.66	8.06	7.42	6.63
Industrial share prices (1980 = 100)	87.6	94.9	100.0	116.3	115.8	136.5	169.8
Balance of payments (U.S.$'000,000,000)							
Balance of visible trade	25.6	1.9	2.1	20.0	18.1	31.5	4.1
Imports, f.o.b.	70.0	99.4	124.6	129.6	119.6	114.0	10.7
Exports, f.o.b.	95.6	101.2	126.7	149.5	137.7	145.5	14.8
Balance of invisibles	−8.1	−10.7	−12.9	−15.2	−11.2	−10.7	−0.9
Balance of payments, current account	17.5	−8.8	−10.8	4.8	6.9	20.8	3.2

Foreign trade

Balance of trade (current prices)

	1978	1979	1980	1981	1982	1983
¥'000,000,000	+5,429	+591	+55	+4,603	+4,473	+7,373
% of total	15.2%	1.3%	0.1%	7.4%	6.9%	11.8%

Imports (1983): ¥27,537,000,000,000 (crude petroleum 31.7%, petroleum products 4.5%, coal 3.9%, nonferrous metals 3.3%, fish and shellfish 3.1%, wood 3.1%, iron ore 2.5%, textiles 2.4%). *Major import sources:* United States 19.5%; Saudi Arabia 12.3%; Indonesia 8.2%; United Arab Emirates 6.2%; Australia 5.3%; China 4.0%; Canada 3.5%.
Exports (1983): ¥34,910,000,000,000 (motor vehicles 17.8%, iron and steel 8.7%, tape recorders 4.5%, vessels 4.1%, scientific and optical equipment 3.7%, office machines 3.5%, metal products 2.7%). *Major export destinations:* United States 29.2%; Saudi Arabia 4.5%; South Korea 4.1%; West Germany 4.0%; Hong Kong 3.6%; Taiwan 3.5%; United Kingdom 3.4%; China 3.3%.

Transport and communications

Transport. Railroads: length (1982) 16,784 mi, 27,012 km; passenger-mi (1983) 199,746,000,000, passenger-km 321,452,000,000; short ton-mi cargo (1983) 18,936,000,000, metric ton-km cargo 27,646,000,000. Roads (1983): total length 697,974 mi, 1,123,283 km (paved 53%). Vehicles (1983): passenger cars 24,283,000; trucks and buses 8,692,000. Merchant marine (1983): vessels (100 gross tons and over) 10,593; total deadweight tonnage 66,640,057. Air transport (1983): passenger-mi 36,320,000,000, passenger-km 58,449,000,000; short ton-mi cargo 1,717,000,000, metric ton-km cargo 2,506,000,000; airports (1984) with scheduled flights 72.
Communications. Daily newspapers (1982): total number 125; total circulation 68,142,000; circulation per 1,000 population 579. Radios (1983): total number of receivers 93,000,000 (1 per 1.3 persons). Television (1983): total number of receivers 30,200,000 (1 per 4 persons). Telephones (1982): 60,611,000 (1 per 2 persons).

Education and health

Education (1984)

	schools	teachers	students	student/teacher ratio
Primary (age 6–11)	25,064	468,675	11,465,108	24.4
Secondary (age 12–17)	16,474	537,557	10,721,217	19.9
Higher	1,059	131,923	2,431,708	18.4

College graduates per 100,000 population (1980): 6,108. *Literacy* (1984): total population literate 93,210,000 (100%); males literate 45,300,000 (100%); females literate 47,910,000 (100%).
Health (1982): physicians 166,212 (1 per 715 persons); hospital beds 1,402,000 (1 per 84.7 persons).
Food (1978–80): daily per capita caloric intake 2,883 (vegetable products 79.6%, animal products 20.4%); 123% of FAO recommended minimum requirement.

Military

Total active duty personnel (1984): 245,000 (army 63.3%; navy 18.0%; air force 18.7%). *Military expenditure as percent of GNP* (1982): 1.0% (world 6.0%); per capita expenditure U.S.$87.

*Excludes Lake Towada (60 sq km [23 sq mi]), which is part of both Akita and Aomori prefectures. †Part of Kantō geographical region. ‡Part of Kinki geographical region. §1983 survey; also includes Lake Towada. ‖ Detail does not add to total given because of rounding. ¶Many Japanese adhere to both Shintoism and Buddhism. ♀1983. ⊗Total comprises single persons in boarding houses and single persons in company dormitories. □This data, for 1982, pertains to establishments with 100 or more employees only. ◊Applies to passengers carried within the metropolitan areas of Tōkyō, Ōsaka, and Nagoya only. △Includes unemployed. †Initial budget. ⊕Consists of employees, proprietors, unpaid family workers, and salaried managers and directors. **1980. ††Value of construction orders received for 1980. ‡‡Includes electrical power. §§September.

Mt. Fuji (Fuji-san), Honshu Island, Japan.

Jordan*

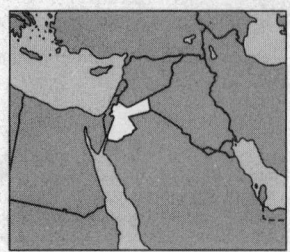

Official name: al-Mamlakah
al-Urdunnīyah al-Hāshimīyah
(al-Urdun) (Hashemite Kingdom of
Jordan).
Form of government: constitutional
monarchy with two legislative houses
(Senate [30 appointed by king]; House
of Deputies [60 elected]).
Chief of state: Monarch.
Head of government: Prime Minister.
Capital: Amman.
Official language: Arabic.
Official religion: Islām.
Monetary unit: 1 Jordan Dinar
(JD) = 1,000 fils; valuation (Oct. 29,
1984) JD1.00 = U.S.$2.47 = £2.05.

Area and population

Regions Governorates	Capitals	area sq mi	area sq km	population 1983 estimate
East Bank		34,443	89,206	2,415,200
al-Āṣimah	Amman	6,904	17,882	1,333,400
al-Balqā'	as-Salt	413	1,069	170,500
al-Karak	al-Karak	1,777	4,601	141,800
Irbid	Irbid	8,747	22,654	685,200
Ma'ān	Ma'ān	16,602	43,000	84,300
West Bank		2,175	5,633	...
al-Khalīl	Hebron	417	1,081	...
al-Quds	Jerusalem	791	2,049	...
Nābulus	Nābulus	967	2,503	...
TOTAL		36,618	94,839	2,415,200†

Source: Official government figures.

Demography

Density (1983): persons per sq mi 70.1, persons per sq km 27.1.
Urban-rural (1979): urban 59.5%; rural 40.5%.
Sex distribution (1979): male 52.27%; female 47.73%.
Age breakdown (1979): under 15, 51.8%; 15–29, 23.3%; 30–44, 13.4%; 45–59, 4.2%; 60 and over, 4.2%.
Population projection‡: (1990) 4,657,000; (2000) 6,510,000.
Doubling time: 20 years.
Ethnic composition (1982): Arab 98.0%; Circassian 1.0%; Armenian 1.0%.
Religious affiliation (1980): Sunni Muslim 93.0%; Christian 4.9%; other 2.1%.
Major cities (1983 est.): Amman 744,000; az-Zarqā 255,000; Irbid 131.200.

Vital statistics

Birth rate per 1,000 population (1980–85): 45.3 (world avg. 27.5).
Death rate per 1,000 population (1980–85): 9.1 (world avg. 10.6).
Natural increase rate per 1,000 population (1980–85): 36.2 (world avg.16.9).
Total fertility rate (avg. births per childbearing woman; 1980–85): 7.1.
Marriage rate per 1,000 population (1979): 7.2.
Divorce rate per 1,000 population (1979): 1.0.
Infant mortality rate per 1,000 live births (1981): 67.0.
Life expectancy at birth (1980–85): male 60.3 years; female 64.2 years.
Major causes of death: n.a.

National economy

Budget (1981). Revenue: JD560,970,000 (foreign grants and loans 57.5%, indirect taxes 16.8%, fees 8.7%, direct taxes 7.0%). Expenditures: JD624,520,-000 (development expenditure§ 43.1%, defense and police 25.0%, education 6.7%, health and social welfare 2.7%).
Public debt (external, outstanding; 1982): U.S.$1,709,000,000.
Tourism (1982): receipts from visitors U.S.$510,000,000; expenditures by nationals abroad U.S.$365,000,000.
Production (metric tons except as noted). Agriculture, forestry, fishing (1982): tomatoes 210,000, eggplants 63,000, watermelons 35,000, grapes 26,000, oranges 24,000, wheat 20,000, barley 20,000, olives 8,000; livestock (number of live animals) 1,000,000 sheep, 500,000 goats, 39,000 cattle, 13,000 camels ‖. Mining and quarrying (1982): phosphate ore 4,353,700; marble 400,000; gypsum ore 40,760. Manufacturing (1980): cement 913,000; steel 238,000; wheat flour 183,000; tobacco products 43,000; phosphate fertilizer 13,300. Construction (1980): residential 770,300 sq m; nonresidential 123,100 sq m. Energy production (consumption): electricity (kW-hr; 1981) 1,237,000,000 (1,237,000,000); coal, none (none); crude petroleum (barrels; 1981) none (15,971,000); petroleum products (metric tons; 1981) 2,008,000 (1,714,000); natural gas¶ (cu m; 1981) 68,897,000 (70,077,000).
Gross national product (at current market prices; 1982): U.S.$4,809,500,000 (U.S.$1,990 per capita).
Persons economically active (1980): total 529,200 (43.4%); female participation in the labour force 34,400 (6.5%); unemployed 10,600 (2.0%).

Price and earnings indexes (1975 = 100)

	1978	1979	1980	1981	1982	1983	1984
Consumer price index	136.6	156.0	173.3	194.2	200.5	210.6	216.8§
Daily earnings index□	152.7	164.7	200.0	213.3	...	...	...

Household income and expenditure. Average household size (1979) 6.4; income per household (1979) JD1,820◇ (U.S.$6,055); sources of income: n.a.; expenditure (1980): food 53.4%, housing 8.2%, clothing and footwear 8.2%, transportation 5.7%, health 3.9%, education 2.2%, other 18.4%.

Origin of gross domestic product (current prices)

	1981 in value JD'000,000	% of total value	1981 labour force	% of labour force
Agriculture	69.4	5.8	...	...
Mining	46.8	3.9	2,130	1.7
Manufacturing	145.5	12.1	19,680	15.8
Construction	104.3	8.7	2,850	2.3
Trade	212.8	17.7	6,840	5.5
Public utilities	22.8	1.9	2,480	2.0
Transportation and communication	114.7	9.6	6,950	5.6
Finance	145.8	12.2	4,830	3.9
Pub. admin., defense	191.2	15.9	♀	♀
Services	35.3	2.9	♀	♀
Other	110.5	9.3	78,430	63.2
TOTAL	1,199.1	100.0	124,190	100.0

Land use (1981): forested 1.3%; meadows and pastures 1.0%; agricultural and under permanent cultivation 14.2%; other 83.5%△.

Foreign trade

Balance of trade (current prices)

	1978	1979	1980	1981	1982	1983
JD'000,000	−319	−405	−468	−693	−756	−774
% of total	63.7%	62.6%	57.7%	58.8%	58.8%	64.7%

Imports (1981): JD935,250,000 (machinery and transportation equipment 32.1%, of which road motor vehicles 8.4%; food and live animals 16.7%, of which animals, meat, and dairy products 4.8%, cereals 3.5%; chemical and petroleum products 6.5%; textiles and clothing 4.1%). *Major import sources:* Saudi Arabia 16.6%; United States 15.8%; West Germany 11.3%; Japan 7.0%; Italy 5.8%.
Exports (1981): JD 242,640,000 (fertilizers 39.3%; fruit and vegetables 14.7%, of which tomatoes 2.7%; soap, medicine, and other chemical products 8.1%; wood products, including furniture 4.7%). *Major export destinations:* Iraq 26.2%; Saudi Arabia 8.6%; Syria 4.4%; India 4.3%; Kuwait 2.8%.

Transport and communications

Transport. Railroads (1983): route length 384 mi, 618 km. Roads (1982): total length 3,248 mi, 5,227 km (paved 100%). Vehicles (1982): passenger cars 118,852; trucks and buses 48,884. Merchant marine (1983): vessels (100 gross tons and over) 7; total deadweight tonnage 53,057. Air transport (1981): passenger-mi 2,007,888, passenger-km 3,231,382; short ton-mi cargo 76,616, metric ton-km cargo 111,857; airports (1983) with scheduled flights 2.
Communications. Daily newspapers (1981): total number 6; total circulation 126,000; circulation per 1,000 population 58.5. Radios (1982): total number of receivers 546,000 (1 per 4.4 persons). Televisions (1982): total number of receivers 201,000 (1 per 12.0 persons). Telephones (1981): 70,781 (1 per 31.4 persons).

Education and health

Education (1981–82)

	schools	teachers	students	student/ teacher ratio
Primary (age 5–13)	1,129	14,873	473,027	31.8
Secondary (age 12–17)	1,036	8,520	181,432	21.3
Voc., teacher tr.	487	6,476	86,269	13.3
Higher	46	2,075	50,210	24.2

College enrollment per 100,000 population (1980): 990. *Literacy* (1980): total population literate 357,400 (31.2%); males literate 253,670 (42.1%); females literate 103,730 (19.1%).
Health (1981): physicians 1,966 (1 per 1,130 persons); hospital beds 2,735 (1 per 813 persons).
Food (1978–80): daily per capita caloric intake 2,397 (vegetable products 84.9%, animal products 15.1%); 97% of FAO recommended minimum requirement.

Military

Total active duty personnel (1983): 72,800 (army 89.3%; navy 0.4%; air force 10.3%). *Military expenditure as percent of GNP* (1982): 21.3% (world 6.0%); per capita expenditure U.S.$298.

*Statistics exclude the West Bank, which is Jordanian territory under Israeli control. †East Bank only. ‡Includes the West Bank. §Includes development budget and other capital expenditure. ‖ 1981. ¶Includes manufactured gas. ♀Services, public administration, and defense are included with "other". ◊First quarter. □Includes persons employed in non-agricultural activities only. ◇Households involved in non-agricultural activities only. △Mostly desert.

Kampuchea

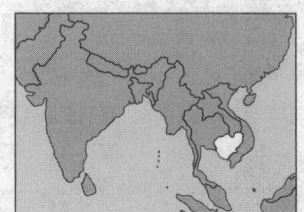

Official name: Kampuchea
 Pracheatipateyy/Sathearanakrath
 Pracheachon Kampuchea (Democratic
 Kampuchea/People's Republic of
 Kampuchea)*.
Form of government: single-party
 people's republic with one legislative
 house (National Assembly [117])†.
Chief of state: President, Council
 of State†.
Head of government: Prime Minister†.
Capital: Phnom Penh.
Official language: Khmer.
Official religion: none.
Monetary unit: 1 riel = 100 sen;
 valuation (Dec. 31, 1983)
 1 U.S.$ = 4.00 riels; 1 £ = 5.81 riels.

Area and population

Provinces	Capitals	area sq mi	area sq km	population 1971 estimate
Bătdâmbâng	Bătdâmbâng	7,407	19,184	671,000
Kâmpóng Cham	Kâmpóng Cham	3,783	9,799	999,000
Kâmpóng Chhnăng	Kâmpóng Chhnăng	2,132	5,521	333,000
Kâmpóng Spoe	Kâmpóng Spoe	2,709	7,017	374,000
Kâmpóng Thum	Kâmpóng Thum	10,657‡	27,602‡	390,000‡
Kâmpôt	Kâmpôt	2,302	5,962	414,000
Kândal	...	1,472	3,812	859,000
Kaôh Kŏng	Krŏng Kaôh Kŏng	4,309	11,161	48,000
Krâchéh	Krâchéh	4,283	11,094	154,000
Môndól Kiri	Senmonorom	5,516	14,288	18,000
Ŏtdâr Méanchey	Phumi Sâmraông	§	§	§
Poŭthisăt	Poŭthisăt	4,900	12,692	219,000
Preăh Vihéar	Phnum Tbeng Meanchey	‡	‡	‡
Prey Vêng	Prey Vêng	1,885	4,883	592,000
Rôtânôkiri	Lumphăt	4,163	10,782	60,000
Siĕmréab	Siĕmréab	6,354§	16,457§	380,000§
Stœng Trêng	Stœng Trêng	4,283	11,092	42,000
Svay Riĕng	Svay Riĕng	1,145	2,966	352,000
Takêv	Takêv	1,376	3,563	566,000
Independent Municipalities				
Bok Koŭ		0.4	1	1,000
Kâmpóng Saôm		26	68	9,000
Kêb		17	45	9,000
Phnom Penh		18	46	479,000
TOTAL		69,898 ‖	181,035 ‖	6,968,000 ‖

Source: Official government figures.

Demography

Density (1984): persons per sq mi 87.5, persons per sq km 33.8.
Urban-rural (1980): urban 13.9%; rural 86.1%.
Sex distribution (1980): male 49.96%; female 50.04%.
Age breakdown (1980): under 15, 36.5%; 15–64, 60.7%; 65 and over, 2.8%.
Population projection: (1990) 6,866,000; (2000) 8,287,000.
Doubling time: 50 years.
Ethnic composition (1982): Khmer 93%; Chinese 3%; Vietnamese 4%.
Religious affiliation (1980): Buddhist 88.4%; Muslim 2.4%; other 9.2%.
Major cities (1971 est.): Phnom Penh 500,000¶; Kâmpóng Cham 34,706;
 Kâmpóng Chhnăng 15,813; Kratié 14,765; Pursat 14,736; Svay Riĕng
 13,766.

Vital statistics

Birth rate per 1,000 population (1980–85): 38.1 (world avg. 27.5); legitimate,
 n.a., illegitimate, n.a.
Death rate per 1,000 population (1980–85): 18.9 (world avg. 11.0).
Natural increase rate per 1,000 population (1980–85): 19.2 (world avg. 16.5).
Total fertility rate (avg. births per childbearing woman; 1980–85): 4.7.
Marriage rate per 1,000 population: n.a.
Divorce rate per 1,000 population: n.a.
Infant mortality rate per 1,000 live births (1971): 157.0.
Life expectancy at birth (1980–85): male 42.0 years; female 44.9 years.
Major causes of death per 100,000 population (registered deaths only; 1966):
 tuberculosis of the respiratory system 154; all accidents other than vehicle
 accidents 111; malaria 55; pneumonia 51.

National economy

Budget (1974 est.). Revenue 23,000,000,000 old riels♀ (1971 breakdown: tax
 on income and wealth 51.0%, customs duties and excise taxes 32.6%,
 land tax 1.6%). Expenditures: 71,000,000,000 old riels♀ (1971 breakdown:
 defense 63.5%, loans and advances 3.1%).
Public debt: n.a.
Tourism (1970): receipts from visitors U.S.$1,350,000; expenditures by na-
 tionals abroad, n.a.
Production (metric tons except as noted). Agriculture, forestry, fishing
 (1982): cereals 1,610,000, rice 1,500,000, roots and tubers 172,000, cassava
 150,000, corn (maize) 110,000, sweet potatoes 16,000, beans 14,000, rubber
 600; livestock (number of live animals) 1,000,000 cattle, 410,000 buffaloes,
 225,000 pigs, 6,800,000 chickens; roundwood 5,107,000 cu m; fish catch
 84,700. Mining and quarrying (1979): salt 5,000. Manufacturing (1980):
 cement 50,000; pig meat 26,000; beef and veal 17,000; sawnwood 43,000
 cu m; plywood 2,000 cu m; cigarettes 4,100,000,000 units. Construction:

n.a. Energy production (consumption): electricity (kW-hr; 1982) 136,000,-
 000 (136,000,000); coal, n.a. (n.a.); crude petroleum, n.a. (n.a.); petroleum
 products (metric tons; 1982), n.a. (13,000); natural gas, n.a. (n.a.).
Gross national product (at current market prices; 1970): U.S.$970,000,000
 (U.S.$130 per capita).
Origin of gross domestic product: n.a.
Persons economically active (1981): total 2,612,000 (38.3%); female partici-
 pation in the labour force n.a.; unemployed n.a.

Price and earnings indexes (1970 = 100)

	1967	1968	1969	1970	1971	1972	1973
Consumer price index♂	79.5	84.1	89.4	100.0	172.0	215.2	556.1
Earnings index	...	...	...	...	...	...	...

Household income and expenditure. Average household size (1980) 5.6;
 average annual income per household: n.a.; source of income: n.a.; expenditure: n.a.
Land use (1981): forested 75.8%; meadows and pastures 3.3%; agricultural
 and under permanent cultivation 17.2%; other 3.7%.

Foreign trade

Balance of trade (current prices)

	1978	1979	1980	1981	1982	1983
U.S.$'000,000	...	...	...	−60	...	...
% of total	...	...	...	41.1%	...	...

Imports (1973): 14,200,100,000 old riels♀ □ (agricultural and food products
 54.4%; textiles 12.4%; mineral products 11.7%; pharmaceuticals 9.8%; metals and metal products 9.0%; chemicals 2.3%). *Major import sources◊:*
 Japan 17.8%; Thailand 16.5%; Hong Kong 14.9%; France 14.4%; United
 States 10.1%; Singapore 5.3%.
Exports (1973): 2,732,500,000 old riels♀ △ (rubber 93.1%; haricot beans 4.4%;
 sesame seeds 2.0%; rice 0.5%). *Major export destinations◊:* South Vietnam
 54.8%; Hong Kong 18.3%; Singapore 10.2%; Japan 4.1%; France 4.1%;
 United States 3.0%.

Transport and communications

Transport. Railroads (1981): length 403 mi, 649 km; passenger-mi 33,554,-
 000, passenger-km 54,000,000; short ton-mi cargo 6,850,000, metric ton-km
 cargo 10,000,000. Roads (1981): total length 8,296 mi, 13,351 km (paved
 20%). Vehicles (1972): passenger cars 27,200; trucks and buses 11,100. Merchant marine (1983): vessels (100 gross tons and over) 3; total deadweight
 tonnage 3,839. Air transport (1977): passenger-mi 26,098,800, passenger-
 km 42,000,000; short ton-mi cargo 274,000, metric ton-km cargo 400,000;
 airport (1983) with scheduled flights 1.
Communications. Daily newspapers (1979): total number 17; total circulation, n.a. Radios (1978): total number of receivers 171,000 (1 per 40
 persons). Television (1970): total number of receivers 50,000 (1 per 130
 persons). Telephones (1981): 7,315 (1 per 790 persons).

Education and health

Education (1982)

	schools	teachers	students	student/ teacher ratio
Primary (age 6–11)	...	...	1,430,000	...
Secondary			40,000	
Voc., teacher tr.				
Higher	...	...	1,500	...

College graduates per 100,000 population (students graduating; 1970): 3.
Literacy (1969): total population literate (age 10 and older) 54.1%.
Health (1971): physicians 438 (1 per 15,297 persons); hospital beds 7,500 (1
 per 893 persons).
Food (1978–80): daily per capita caloric intake 1,795 (vegetable products 94.6%, animal products 5.4%); 81% of FAO recommended minimum
 requirement.

Military

Total active duty personnel (1982): 30,000†. *Military expenditure as percent
 of GNP:* n.a.; per capita expenditure, n.a.

*The UN continues to seat Democratic Kampuchea (DK), whose present government
calls itself the Coalition Government of Democratic Kampuchea and is composed of
Khmer People's National Liberation Front, the DK, and the organization of Norodom
Sihanouk. The Socialist Republic of Vietnam has installed a government in Phnom
Penh that calls itself the People's Republic of Kampuchea. Vietnamese military
forces occupy and police most of the country while military forces of Democratic
Kampuchea control enclaves along the western border. †People's Republic of Kampuchea. ‡Preăh Vihéar included with Kâmpóng Thum. §Ŏtdar Méanchey included
with Siĕmréab. ‖ Detail does not add to total given because of rounding and also
province areas exclude 1,158 sq mi (3,000 sq km) of inland water, official 1981
census figure was 5,756,141. ¶1981 estimate. ♀The 1973–74 exchange rate was about
245 old riels per U.S. dollar. ♂Phnom Penh only. □In 1981 imports were estimated to
be U.S.$103,000,000. ◊1972. △In 1981 exports were estimated to be U.S.$43,000,000.
†Excludes about 175,000 Vietnamese troops and about 28,000 opposition forces of
Democratic Kampuchea.

Kenya

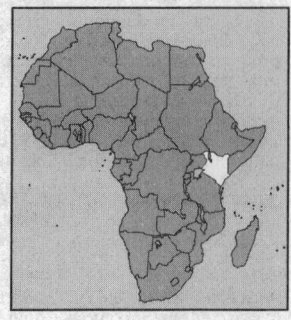

Official name: Jamhuri ya Kenya (Republic of Kenya).
Form of government: unitary single-party republic with one legislative house (National Assembly [172]).
Head of state and government: President.
Capital: Nairobi.
Official language: Swahili.
Official religion: none.
Monetary unit: 1 Kenyan shilling (K Sh) = 100 cents; valuation (Oct. 29, 1984) 1 U.S.$ = K Sh 15.22; 1 £ = K Sh 18.38.

Area and population

Provinces	Provincial headquarters	area* sq mi	area* sq km	population 1984 estimate
Central	Nyeri	5,087	13,176	2,926,200
Coast	Mombasa	32,279	83,603	1,688,000
Eastern	Embu	61,734	159,891	3,423,500
Nairobi	Nairobi	264	684	1,103,600
North Eastern	Garissa	48,997	126,902	484,700
Nyanza	Kisumu	6,240	16,162	3,508,500
Rift Valley	Nakuru	67,131	173,868	4,132,400
Western	Kakamega	3,228	8,360	2,269,400
TOTAL		224,961	582,646	19,536,300

Source: Official government figures.

Demography

Density (1984): persons per sq mi 89.7, persons per sq km 34.6.
Urban–rural (1979): urban 13%; rural 87%.
Sex distribution (1979): male 49.63%; female 50.37%.
Age breakdown (1979): under 15, 48.3%; 15–29, 26.9%; 30–44, 12.8%; 45–59, 7.1%; 60–74, 3.5%; 75 and over, 1.4%†.
Population projection: (1990) 24,831,000; (2000) 37,138,000.
Doubling time: 16.9 years.
Ethnic composition (1979): African 99.3% (Kikuyu 20.9%, Luhya 13.8%, Luo 12.8%, Kamba 11.3%, Kalenjin 10.8%); Asian 0.3%; Arab 0.1%; European 0.3%.
Religious affiliation (1980): Roman Catholic 26.4%; Protestant 19.3%; other Christian 27.3%; tribal religionist 18.9%; Muslim 6.0%; other non-Christian 2.1%.
Major cities (1983 est.): Nairobi 1,103,600‡; Mombasa 425,600‡; Kisumu 167,100; Nakuru 101,700; Machakos 92,300.

Vital statistics

Birth rate per 1,000 population (1980–85): 53.5 (world avg. 27.5).
Death rate per 1,000 population (1980–85): 12.7 (world avg. 10.6).
Natural increase rate per 1,000 population (1980–85): 40.8 (world avg. 16.9).
Total fertility rate (avg. births per childbearing woman; 1980–85): 8.1.
Infant mortality rate per 1,000 live births (1981): 84.7.
Life expectancy at birth (1980–85): male 53.7 years; female 58.2 years.
Major causes of death per 100,000 population: n.a., however, major health problems include malaria, gastroenteritis, venereal diseases, diarrhea and dysentery, trachoma, and schistosomiasis.

National economy

Budget (1983–84). Revenue: K Sh 19,337,640,000 (sales tax 31.5%; income tax 20.1%; import duties 19.1%; excise duties 8.4%). Expenditures: K Sh 25,156,020,000 (economic services 24.1%; education 16.3%; public administration 15.3%; defense 11.2%).
Public debt (external, outstanding; 1982): U.S.$2,509,000,000.
Tourism: receipts from visitors (1982) U.S.$185,000,000; expenditures by nationals abroad (1980) U.S.$33,000,000.
Production (metric tons except as noted). Agriculture, forestry, fishing (1983): sugarcane 3,107,735, corn (maize) 2,000,000, wheat 270,000, tea 112,000, coffee 88,393; livestock (number of live animals) 75,400 cattle; cypress wood (1982) 214,000 cu m; total catch of fresh water fish (1982) 70,577. Mining and quarrying (value in K Sh; 1982): soda ash 15,700,000; fluorspar 9,240,000; lime and limestone 7,820,000; corundum (ruby) 6,340,000. Manufacturing (output in K Sh; 1982) petroleum products 6,597,000,000; miscellaneous foods 5,467,980,000; metal products 2,096,540,000; grain mill products 1,869,520,000; beverages and tobacco 1,806,860,000. Construction (1982): residential 18,000 sq m; nonresidential 6,000 sq m. Energy production (consumption): electricity (kW-hr; 1982) 1,804,000,000 (2,016,000,000); coal (metric tons; 1982) none (32,000); crude petroleum (barrels; 1982) none (16,684,000); petroleum products (metric tons; 1982) 1,919,000 (1,111,000).
Persons economically active (1982): total 1,272,900 (7.4%).

Price and earnings indexes (1972 = 100) ‖

	1977	1978	1979	1980	1981	1982	1983
Consumer price index	177.7	196.0	210.1	234.5	266.9	335.4	387.2
Monthly earnings index	188.7	209.8	251.5	296.4	360.2	394.2	...

Consumer expenditure (1983) ‖ : food 40.0%; transportation 7.9%; recreation 4.5%; clothing and footwear 11.9%; housing 16.0%; miscellaneous 19.7%.

Gross national product (at current market prices; 1982): U.S.$6,089,778,000 (U.S.$355 per capita).

Origin of gross domestic product (current prices)

	1982			
	in value K Sh '000,000	% of total value	labour force	% of labour force
Agriculture	20,639.6§	35.0	272,100	21.4
Mining	115.6	0.2	3,100	0.2
Manufacturing	7,688.8	13.0	180,000	14.1
Construction	3,427.0§	5.8	61,600	4.8
Trade	6,197.2	10.5	199,200	15.6
Public utilities	1,325.4	2.2	14,000	1.1
Transportation and communication	3,282.0	5.6	57,200	4.5
Finance	6,954.4	11.8	46,400	3.6
Pub. admin., defense	8,983.6	15.2	439,300	34.7
Services, other	398.8§	0.7	...	...
TOTAL	59,012.4§	100.0	1,272,900	100.0

Land use (1981): forested 4.4%; meadows and pastures 6.6%; agricultural and under permanent cultivation 4.1%; other 84.9%.

Foreign trade

Balance of trade (current prices)

	1977	1978	1979	1980	1981	1982	1983
K Sh '000,000	−757	−5,356	−4,227	−8,987	−7,904	−6,633	−5,327
% of total	3.7%	25.3%	20.5%	30.4%	26.9%	22.6%	31.3%

Imports (1982): K Sh 18,006,100,000 (crude petroleum 33.3%; transport equipment 27.0%; machinery other than electrical 7.7%; electrical machinery 5.1%; glass and glassware 4.5%; vegetable oils and fats 2.5%; chemical oils and compounds 2.2%; wire products 2.1%). *Major import sources:* United Kingdom 15.1%; Saudi Arabia 14.9%; West Germany 8.4%; Japan 7.8%; France 3.1%; The Netherlands 2.6%.
Exports (1982): K Sh 11,372,860,000 (coffee, not roasted 26.5%; petroleum products 26.0%; tea 14.2%; building cement 3.6%; sisal fibre and tow 2.0%). *Major export destinations:* United Kingdom 12.7%; West Germany 11.0%; Uganda 10.1%; United States 6.1%; The Netherlands 5.1%.

Transport and communications

Transport. Railroads (1982): length 1,295 mi, 2,084 km; passenger-mi 464,807,200, passenger-km 748,000,000; short ton-mi cargo 1,436,354,900, metric ton-km cargo 2,097,040,000. Roads (1981): total length 33,299 mi, 53,588 km (paved 12%). Vehicles (1982): passenger cars 114,710; trucks and buses 88,203. Merchant marine (1983): vessels (100 gross tons and over) 20; total deadweight tonnage 3,266. Air transport (1983): passenger-mi 600,060,000, passenger-km 965,676,000; short ton-mi cargo 20,759,000, metric ton-km cargo 30,308,000; airports (1984) with scheduled flights 9.
Communications. Daily newspapers: total number (1983) 4; total circulation (1980) 258,859; circulation per 1,000 population (1980) 16. Radios (1983): total number of receivers 580,000 (1 per 29 persons). Television (1983): total number of receivers 75,000 (1 per 224 persons). Telephones (1982): 216,674 (1 per 76 persons).

Education and health

Education (1982)

	schools	teachers	students	student/ teacher ratio
Primary (age 5–11)	11,497	115,094	4,184,602	36.4
Secondary (age 12–17)	2,131	16,848	438,424	26.0
Voc., teacher tr.	39	1,255	20,604	16.4
Higher¶	2	...	8,967	...

College graduates per 100,000 population: (students graduating; 1980) 17.3.
Literacy (1980): total population literate 3,814,900 (47.1%); males literate 2,377,200 (60%); females literate 1,437,700 (34.8%).
Health (1982): physicians 2,151 (1 per 7,969 persons); hospital beds 29,044 (1 per 590 persons).
Food (1978–80): daily per capita caloric intake 2,055 (vegetable products 89.1%, animal products 10.9%); 89% of FAO recommended minimum requirement.

Military

Total active duty personnel (1983): 16,000 (army 81.2%; navy 4.1%; air force 14.7%). *Military expenditure as percent of GNP* (1982): 3.9% (world 6.0%); per capita expenditure U.S.$14.

*Excludes 4,336 sq mi (11,230 sq km) inland water area. †Includes age not specified. ‡1984. §Includes traditional economy. ‖ Nairobi only. ¶1981–82.

Kiribati

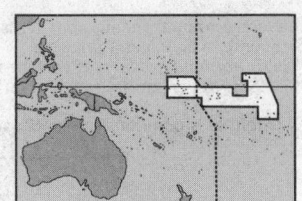

Official name: Republic of Kiribati.
Form of government: unitary republic with one legislature (House of Assembly [38]).
Head of state and government: President.
Capital: Bairiki, on Tarawa Atoll.
Official language: none.
Official religion: none.
Monetary unit: 1 Australian Dollar ($A) = 100 cents; valuation (Oct. 29, 1984) 1 U.S.$ = $A1.19; 1 £ = $A1.44.

Area and population

Island Groups Islands	Capitals	area sq mi	area sq km	population 1983 estimate
Gilberts Group	Bairiki Islet	110	285	58,000
Abaiang		7	18	3,800
Abemama		10	27	2,700
Aranuka		5	12	1,000
Arorae		4	10	1,700
Banaba		2	6	70
Beru		7	18	2,500
Butaritari		5	14	3,500
Kuria		6	16	900
Maiana		7	17	1,900
Makin		3	8	1,600
Marakei		5	14	2,600
Nikunau		7	19	2,100
Nonouti		8	20	2,700
Onotoa		6	16	2,300
Tabiteuea		15	38	4,600
Tamana		2	5	1,600
Tarawa		12	31	22,500
Line Group	Kiritimati	207	535	2,300
Northern		167	432	2,300
Kiritimati (Christmas)		150	388	1,400
Tabuaeran (Fanning)		13	34	500
Teraina (Washington)		4	10	500
Southern (Caroline, Flint, Malden, Starbuck, Vostok)		40	103	—
Phoenix Group (Birnie, Enderbury, Kanton [Canton], McKean, Manra [Sydney], Nikumaroro [Gardner], Orona [Hull], Rawaki [Phoenix])	Kanton	11	29	—
TOTAL		328	849	60,300

Source: Official government figures.

Demography

Density (1984): persons per sq mi 223.8*, persons per sq km 86.5*.
Urban–rural (1983): urban 33.2%; rural 66.8%.
Sex distribution (1978): male 49.32%; female 50.68%.
Age breakdown (1978): under 15, 41.1%; 15–29, 28.1%; 30–44, 15.0%; 45–59, 10.0%; 60–74, 4.8%; 75 and over, 1.0%.
Population projection: (1990) 68,000; (2000) 81,000.
Doubling time: 42 years.
Ethnic composition (1978): Micronesian 97.9%; Polynesian 1.5%; European, Chinese, and other 0.6%.
Religious affiliation (1978): Roman Catholic 50.4%; Kiribati Protestant (Congregational) 44.0%; Baha'i 2.1%; Seventh-day Adventist 1.6%; other 1.9%.
Major cities (1983 est.): Urban Tarawa 20,050 .

Vital statistics

Birth rate per 1,000 population (1980–85): 34.8 (world avg. 27.5); legitimate, n.a.; illegitimate, n.a.
Death rate per 1,000 population (1980–85): 7.6 (world avg. 10.6).
Natural increase rate per 1,000 population (1980–85): 27.2 (world avg. 16.9).
Total fertility rate (avg. births per childbearing woman; 1980–85): 2.4.
Marriage rate per 1,000 population (1973): 4.5.
Divorce rate per 1,000 population: n.a.
Infant mortality rate per 1,000 live births (1978): 87.
Life expectancy at birth (1978): male 50 years; female 54 years.
Major causes of death (1977†): n.a.; however, major causes of death were diarrheal diseases and pneumonia.

National economy

Budget (1982). Revenue: $A15,871,000 (external aid and income 53.3%, indirect taxes 23.8%, direct taxes 6.3%). Expenditures: $A16,956,000 (education 18.3%, communications 18.1%, home affairs 10.5%, health 10.0%, works and energy 8.3%, police 6.6%).
Public debt: n.a.
Tourism (1977): visitors 796.
Production (metric tons except as noted). Agriculture, forestry, fishing (1982): coconuts 75,000, copra 9,000, vegetables 4,000, bananas 4,000, eggs 107; livestock (number of live animals) 10,000 pigs, 191,000 chickens; fish catch 19,540, of which skipjack tuna 5,000, yellowfin tuna 3,000, emperors 2,500, snappers 2,500. Mining and quarrying (1983): none. Manufacturing (1981): copra $A2,930,000; other important products are processed fish, baked goods, clothing, boats, and handicrafts. Energy production (consumption): electricity (kW-hr; 1982) 6,000,000 (6,000,000); petroleum products (metric tons; 1982) none (9,000).

Gross national product (at current market prices; 1981): U.S.$25,942,000 (U.S.$440 per capita).

Origin of gross domestic product (current prices)

	1978 in value $A'000	% of total value	labour force	% of labour force
Agriculture	7,300	18.5	495	7.0
Mining‡	16,800	42.5	317	4.5
Manufacturing	700	1.8	183	2.6
Construction	3,100	7.9	972	13.8
Trade	2,400	6.1	913	13.0
Public utilities	600	1.5	193	2.8
Transportation and communication	1,000	2.5	691	9.8
Finance	600	1.5	32	0.5
Pub. admin., defense	4,700§	11.9§	1,016	14.4
Services	§	§	1,805	25.6
Other, including unemployed	2,300	5.8	424	6.0
TOTAL	39,500	100.0	7,041	100.0

Persons economically active (1978): total 7,041 (12.5%); female participation in labour force 1,420 (20.2%); unemployed 416 (5.9%).

Price and earnings indexes (1975 = 100)

	1976	1977	1978	1979	1980	1981	1982
Consumer price index	111.6	124.7	138.9	147.9	173.0	183.5	186.6
Monthly earnings index	...	...	...	...	...	...	...

Household income and expenditure. Average household size (1978) 6.1; income per household: n.a.; source of income: agriculture 35.9%, wages only 27.5%, wages and other 19.3%, agriculture and other 12.6%, other 4.7%; expenditure (1982): food 50.0%, tobacco and alcohol 14.0%, clothing 8.0%, transportation 8.0%, housing and household operation 7.5%.
Land use (1981): forested 2.8%; agricultural and under permanent cultivation 50.7%; other 46.5%.

Foreign trade

Balance of trade (current prices)

	1975	1976	1977	1978	1979	1980	1981
$A'000	+18,453	+8,085	+6,529	+7,281	+5,664	−14,422	−16,312
% of total	49.9%	28.7%	21.8%	20.5%	15.4%	−74.8%	−71.2%

Imports (1980): $A16,848,000 (food and food preparations, beverages, and tobacco 40.0%; machinery and transport equipment 17.2%; manufactured goods 13.6%; mineral fuels and lubricants 10.8%; miscellaneous manufactured articles 9.7%; chemicals 5.4%). *Major import sources:* Australia 57.5%; Japan 12.9%; United States 7.3%; United Kingdom 5.6%; New Zealand 5.2%; Fiji 4.8%.
Exports (1980): $A2,426,000 (copra 89.2%; fish and fish preparations 10.7%; handicrafts 0.1%). *Major export destinations:* United Kingdom 89.2%; Fiji 3.0%; Japan 1.0%; Australia 0.8%.

Transport and communications

Transport. Roads (1982): total length 398 mi, 640 km (paved, n.a.). Vehicles (1978): passenger cars and trucks 163; motorcyles 2,822. Merchant marine (1983): vessels (100 gross tons and over) 4; total deadweight tonnage 1,846. Air transport (1978): passengers carried 14,593; airports (1984) with scheduled flights 17.
Communications. Daily newspapers: none. Radios (1983): total number of receivers 58,600 (1 per 1.0 person). Television (1983): total number of receivers 11,000 (1 per 5.5 persons). Telephones (1982): 821 (1 per 73.1 persons).

Education and health

Education (1982–83)

	schools	teachers	students	student/ teacher ratio
Primary (age 6–13)	106	450	13,836	30.7
Secondary (age 14–18)	5	65	950	14.6
Voc., teacher tr.	2	14	122	8.7
Higher ‖	1	17	113	6.6

College graduates per 10,000 population (students graduating; 1980): 20.9.
Literacy (1982): total population literate 31,806 (90.0%).
Health: (1981) physicians 16 (1 per 3,750 persons); (1978) hospital beds 307 (1 per 183 persons).
Food (1978–80): daily per capita caloric intake 2,304 (vegetable products 90.4%, animal products 9.6%); 88% of FAO recommended minimum requirement.

*Density based on inhabited island areas (277 sq mi [717 sq km]). †Leading causes of death at Tungaru Central Hospital. ‡Mining of phosphates on Banaba (Ocean Island) ceased in 1979. §Public administration and defense includes services. ‖ Teachers college.

Korea, North

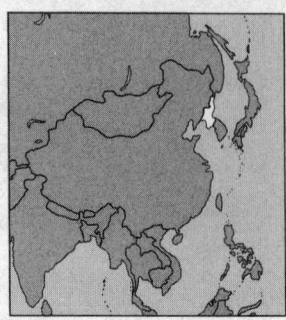

Official name: Chosŏn Minjujuŭi
In'min Konghwaguk (Democratic
People's Republic of Korea).
Form of government: unitary
single-party republic with one
legislative house (Supreme People's
Assembly [615]).
Chief of state: President.
Head of government: Premier.
Capital: P'yŏngyang.
Official language: Korean.
Official religion: none.
Monetary unit: 1 won = 100
chon; valuation (Oct. 29, 1984)
1 U.S.$ = 1.30 won; 1 £ = 1.57 won.

Area and population

Provinces	Capitals	area sq mi	area sq km	population 1984 estimate
Chagang-do	Kanggye	...	...	...
Hamgyŏng-namdo	Hamhŭng	...	...	...
Hamgyŏng-pukto	Ch'ŏngjin	...	...	...
Hwanghae-namdo	Haeju	...	...	...
Hwanghae-pukto	Sariwŏn	...	...	...
Kangwŏn-do	Wŏnsan	...	...	...
P'yŏngan-namdo	P'yŏngsan	...	...	...
P'yŏngan-pukto	Sinŭiju	...	...	...
Yanggang-do	Hyesan	...	...	...
Special cities				
Ch'ŏngjin-si	—	...	...	...
Hamhŭng-si	—	...	...	...
P'yŏngyang-si	P'yŏngyang	...	...	...
Special district				
Kaesŏng-chigu	Kaesŏng	...	...	...
TOTAL		47,077	121,929	19,630,000*

Demography

Density (1984): persons per sq mi 417.0, persons per sq km 161.0.
Urban–rural (1980): urban 59.7%; rural 40.3%.
Sex distribution (1980): male 49.44%; female 50.56%.
Age breakdown (1980): under 15, 40.0%; 15–29, 28.7%; 30–44, 15.9%; 45–59,
9.6%; 60–74, 4.7%; 75 and over, 1.1%.
Population projection: (1990) 22,443,000; (2000) 27,256,000.
Doubling time: 30 years.
Ethnic composition (1980): Korean 99.3%; Chinese, Mongolian, and Russian
0.7%.
Religious affiliation (1980): atheist or non-religious 67.9%; traditional reli-
gionists 15.6%; Ch'ŏndogyo 13.9%; Buddhist 1.7%; Christian 0.9%.
Major cities (1981 est.): P'yŏngyang 1,283,000; Hamhŭng-Hŭngnam† 775,-
000; Ch'ŏngjin 490,000; Kaesŏng 240,000; Wŏnsan 240,000.

Vital statistics

Birth rate per 1,000 population (1983): 31.0 (world avg. 29.0).
Death rate per 1,000 population (1983): 7.5 (world avg. 11.0).
Natural increase rate per 1,000 population (1983): 23.5 (world avg. 18.0).
Total fertility rate (avg. births per childbearing woman; 1980–85): 4.0.
Marriage rate per 1,000 population: n.a.
Divorce rate per 1,000 population: n.a.
Infant mortality rate per 1,000 live births (1975–80): 37.0.
Life expectancy at birth (1980–85): male 62.7 years; female 66.6 years.
Major causes of death: n.a.; however, major diseases are malignant neo-
plasms (cancers), hypertensive and heart diseases, and intestinal infections.

National economy

Budget (1984). Revenue: 26,237,000,000 won‡ (detail n.a.). Expenditures: 26,-
237,000,000‡ (national economy 59.0%§; social and cultural affairs 23.0%§;
defense 15.1%§; other 2.9%§).
Public debt (external, outstanding; 1978 est.): U.S.$2,000,000,000.
Tourism: n.a.
Production (metric tons except as noted). Agriculture, forestry, fishing (1983):
rice 5,200,000, corn (maize) 2,500,000, potatoes 1,650,000, millet 475,000,
apples 530,000, barley 420,000, soybeans 380,000; livestock (number of live
animals; 1982) 2,300,000 pigs, 970,000 cattle, 18,100,000 chickens; roundwood 6,020,000 cu m ‖; fish catch 1,550,000 ‖. Mining and quarrying
(1981): iron ore 8,000,000, crude magnesite 1,900,000; calcined magnesite
800,000; pyrites 620,000; salt 570,000; zinc 140,000¶; barite 110,000; lead
100,000¶; silver 1,550,000 troy oz.¶; gold 160,000 troy oz.¶. Manufacturing
(1981): crude steel 3,500,000; steel semimanufactures 3,300,000; pig iron
3,000,000; chemical fertilizers 920,000; cement 800,000; synthetic resin
100,000; automobiles 15,000 units; television sets 50,000 units; machine
tools 30,000 units. Construction: n.a. Energy production (consumption):
electricity (kW-hr; 1982) 40,000,000,000 (40,000,000,000); coal (metric tons;
1982) 47,000,000 (47,400,000); crude petroleum (barrels; 1982) none (14,-
700,000); petroleum products (metric tons; 1982) 2,010,000 (2,500,000);
natural gas, none (n.a.).
Persons economically active (1982): total 8,455,000 (45.1%); female participation in the labour force, n.a.; unemployed, n.a.
Price and earnings indexes: n.a.
Household income and expenditure. average household size (1980) 5.7;

average annual income per household 3,677 won (U.S.$4,275); source of
income, n.a.; expenditure, n.a.
Gross national product (at current market prices; 1982): U.S.$16,200,000,000
(U.S.$790 per capita).

Origin of gross domestic product (current prices)

	1980 in value '000,000won	% of total value	labour force	% of labour force
Agriculture	...	...	3,916,000	49.0
Mining	...	...	...	...
Manufacturing	...	...	2,637,000	33.0
Construction	...	...	...	...
Trade	...	...	♀	♀
Public utilities	...	...	...	...
Transportation and communication	...	...	...	...
Finance	...	...	...	...
Pub. admin., defense	...	...	...	...
Services	...	...	1,439,000♀	18.0♀
Other	...	...	...	...
TOTAL	...	...	7,992,000	100.0

Land use (1981): forested 74.4%; meadows and pastures 0.4%; agricultural
and under permanent cultivation 18.7%; other 6.5%.

Foreign trade

Balance of trade (current prices)

	1974	1976	1978	1979	1980	1981
'000,000 won	−601	−176	−53	+165	−256	−285
% of total	31.6%	11.5%	3.3%	6.3%	9.4%	10.3%

Imports (1981): 1,520,000,000 won (crude petroleum, machinery and equipment [including trucks], industrial chemicals, coking coal, and grain are
among the major imports). *Major import sources:* U.S.S.R. 22.0%; Japan
18.0%; China 17.0%.
Exports (1981): 1,235,000,000 won (minerals [including lead, magnesite,
and zinc], metallurgical products, agricultural products, and manufactured
goods [including machine tools] are among the major exports). *Major export destinations:* U.S.S.R. 26.0%; China 17.0%; Japan 9.0%; Saudi Arabia
9.0%; India 5.0%.

Transport and communications

Transport. Railroads (1983): length 2,720 mi, 4,380 km; passengers, n.a.;
cargo, n.a. Roads (1981): total length 12,600 mi, 20,280 km (paved 2%).
Vehicles: n.a. Merchant marine (1983): vessels (100 gross tons and over)
57; total deadweight tonnage 724,779. Air transport (1979): passenger-mi
52,200,000, passenger-km 84,000,000; short ton-mi cargo 1,370,000, metric
ton-km cargo 2,000,000; airport (1983) with scheduled flights 1.
Communications. Daily newspapers (1983): total number 10; total circulation, n.a. Radios (1983): total number of receivers 1,000,000 (1 per 19
persons). Television (1982): total number of receivers 200,000 (1 per 94
persons). Telephones: n.a.

Education and health

Education (1982)

	schools	teachers	students	student/ teacher ratio
Primary (age 5–9)	4,700δ	...	c. 2,500,000	...
Secondary (age 10–15)	...	c. 100,000□	c. 2,500,000◇	...
Voc., teacher tr.	...	...	...	...
Higher	175	9,244	200,000	21.6

College graduates per 100,000 population: n.a. *Literacy* (1979): 90%.
Health (1982): physicians 45,000 (1 per 417 persons); hospital beds 244,000
·(1 per 77 persons).
Food (1978–80): daily per capita caloric intake 2,972 (vegetable products
93.8%, animal products 6.2%); 126% of FAO recommended minimum
requirement.

Military

Total active duty personnel (1983): 784,500 (army 89.2%; navy 4.3%; air force
6.5%). *Military expenditure as percent of* GNP (1982): 21.6% (world 6.0%);
per capita expenditure U.S.$187.

*The figure provided is a UN estimate; the last official estimate, made in 1963, was
11,568,000. †Urban area. ‡Provisional. §1979. ‖ 1982. ¶By metal content. ♀Services
include trade. δ1976. □Includes primary, secondary, and vocational teachers. ◇In-
cludes vocational students.

Korea, South

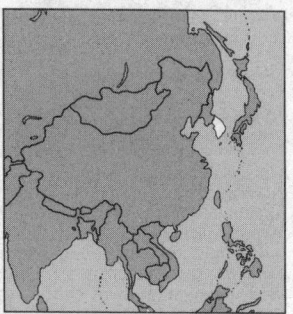

Official name: Taehan Min'guk
(Republic of Korea).
Form of government: unitary republic
with a Legislative Council for
National Security (81 members).
Chief of state: President.
Head of government: Prime Minister.
Capital: Seoul.
Official language: Korean.
Official religion: none.
Monetary unit: 1 won (W) = 100 chon;
valuation (Oct. 29, 1984)
1 U.S.$ = W824.81; 1 £ = W995.55.

Area and population

Provinces	Capitals	area sq mi	area sq km	population 1984 estimate
Cheju-do	Cheju	705	1,825	490,000
Chŏlla-namdo	Kwangju	4,706	12,189	3,908,000
Chŏlla-pukto	Chŏnju	3,109	8,051	2,355,000
Ch'ungch'ŏng-namdo	Taejŏn	3,400	8,807	3,098,000
Ch'ungch'ŏng-pukto	Ch'ŏngju	2,868	7,429	1,458,000
Kangwŏn-do	Ch'unch'ŏn'	6,523	16,894	1,866,000
Kyŏnggi-do	Inch'ŏn*	4,191	10,855	4,458,000
Kyŏngsang-namdo	Masan	4,575	11,850	3,203,000
Kyŏngsang-pukto	Taegu*	7,501	19,427	3,600,000
Special cities				
Inch'ŏn-si	Inch'ŏn	78	202	1,249,000
Pusan-si	Pusan	167	433	3,473,000
Sŏul-t'ŭkpyŏlsi	Seoul	234	605	9,416,000
Taegu-si	Taegu	176	455	2,004,000
TOTAL		38,233	99,022	40,578,000

Source: Official government figures; Britannica estimate.

Demography

Density (1984): persons per sq mi 1,061.3, persons per sq km 409.8.
Urban–rural (1983): urban 62.9%; rural 37.1%.
Sex distribution (1983): male 50.46%; female 49.54%.
Age breakdown (1981): under 15, 34.0%; 15–29, 30.0%; 30–44, 18.4%; 45–59,
11.4%; 60–74, 5.1%; 75 and over, 1.1%.
Population projection: (1990) 44,475,000; (2000) 52,849,000.
Doubling time: 44 years.
Ethnic composition (1982): Korean 99.9%; other 0.1%.
Religious affiliation (1981): Buddhist 37.4%; Protestant 25.7%; Confucian
17.5%; Roman Catholic 4.8%; Ch'ondogyo 3.6%; Wonbulgyo 3.2%; other
7.8%.
Major cities (1983): Seoul 9,204,300; Pusan 3,395,200; Taegu 1,958,800; In-
ch'ŏn 1,220,300; Kwangju 843,500.

Vital statistics

Birth rate per 1,000 population (1983): 23.2 (world avg. 29.0).
Death rate per 1,000 population (1983): 6.3 (world avg. 11.0).
Natural increase rate per 1,000 population (1983): 16.9 (world avg. 18.0).
Total fertility rate (avg. births per childbearing woman; 1980–85): 2.6.
Marriage rate per 1,000 population (1981): 3.1.
Divorce rate per 1,000 population (1981): 0.4.
Infant mortality rate per 1,000 live births (1983): 37.0.
Life expectancy at birth (1985)†: male 64.9 years; female 76.3 years.
Major causes of death per 100,000 population: n.a.

National economy

Budget (1984). Revenue: W10,966,700,000,000 (internal taxes 58.9%, custom
duties 14.4%, monopoly profits 7.7%). Expenditures: W10,386,300,000,000
(defense 33.2%, education 21.9%, economic services 16.5%, social security
6.9%, health 2.6%).
Public debt (external, outstanding; 1982): U.S.$20,061,400,000.
Tourism (1982): receipts from visitors U.S.$502,318,000; expenditures by
nationals abroad, n.a.
Production (metric tons except as noted). Agriculture, forestry, fishing
(1983): rice 5,400,000, barley and wheat 930,000, potatoes 407,000, pulse
277,000; livestock (number of live animals) 3,650,000 pigs, 1,940,000 cattle,
49,230,000 chickens; timber 1,252,000 cu m; fish catch 2,790,000. Mining
and quarrying (1983): anthracite 18,945,000; iron ore 591,000; zinc ore 113,-
890; lead ore 21,146; tungsten ore 4,132; refined silver 48,997 kilograms.
Manufacturing (1983): petroleum products 28,216,000 kilolitres; cement
21,282,000; pig iron 8,024,000; crude steel 5,062,000; urea fertilizer 737,000;
man-made fibres 394,011; cotton yarn 271,338; cotton fabrics 442,263,-
000 sq m; passenger cars 128,490 units. Construction (1983): residential
W3,300,000,000,000; nonresidential W2,380,000,000,000. Energy production (consumption): electricity (kW-hr; 1983) 48,850,000 (37,879,000‡); coal
(metric tons; 1983) 19,900,000 (21,500,000).
Household income and expenditure. Average household size (1983) 4.5; income per household W3,258,000 (U.S.$4,100); source of income: wages and
salaries 60.3%, other 39.7%; expenditure (1983): food 38.8%, housing including utilities 11.8%, education 9.9%, clothing and footwear 8.3%, health
7.5%, transportation 6.5%.
Land use (1982): forested 66.0%; agricultural and under permanent cultivation 22.0%; other 12.0%.

Gross national product (at current market prices; 1983): U.S.$73,389,000,000
(U.S.$1,850 per capita).

Origin of gross domestic product (current prices)

	1982 in value W'000,000,000	% of total value	labour force	% of labour force
Agriculture	7,906	15.8	4,623,000	30.7
Mining	703	1.4	111,000	0.7
Manufacturing	13,838	27.8	3,046,000	20.2
Construction	3,973	8.0	831,000	5.5
Trade	7,391	14.8	3,180,000	21.1
Public utilities	1,128	2.3	31,000	0.2
Transportation and communication	3,741	7.5	608,000	4.0
Finance	§	§	382,000	2.6
Pub. admin., defense	§	§	‖	‖
Services	11,171§	22.4 ‖	1,612,000 ‖	10.6 ‖
Other	...	...	656,000¶	4.4¶
TOTAL	49,851	100.0	15,080,000	100.0

Persons economically active (1983): total 15,128,000 (38.1%); female participation in total labour force 5,642,000‡ (39.1%); unemployed 613,000 (4.0%).

Price and earnings indexes (1970 = 100)

	1977	1978	1979	1980	1981	1982	1983
Consumer price index	258.7	295.9	350.1	450.7	546.7	586.4	606.2
Monthly earnings index	472	634	816	1,004	...	...	...

Foreign trade

Balance of trade (current prices)

	1978	1979	1980	1981	1982	1983
US$'000,000	−1,781	−4,396	−4,384	−3,628	−2,400	−1,970
% of total	6.5%	13.0%	11.3%	8.1%	5.4%	3.9%

Imports (1983): U.S.$26,190,000,000 (machinery and transport equipment
31.2%, mineral ores 29.2%, chemical products 14.9%, textile yarn and fabrics 5.1%). *Major import sources:* United States 25.9%; Japan 25.8%; Saudi
Arabia 8.3%; Australia 4.0%; Malaysia 3.2%; Kuwait 2.9%; West Germany
2.7%; United Kingdom 1.9%.
Exports (1983): U.S.$24,220,000,000 (textile products 25.0%, ships 15.4%,
electronic products 12.5%, iron and steel products 10.2%, footwear 5.2%).
Major export destinations: United States 31.0%; Japan 12.8%; Saudi Arabia
5.4%; Hong Kong 3.1%; West Germany 3.0%; Canada 2.4%; Kuwait 2.3%.

Transport and communications

Transport. Railroads (1984): length 3,808 mi, 6,129 km; passenger-mi 13,070,-
000,000‡, passenger-km 21,034,000,000; short ton-mi cargo 7,460,399,000‡,
metric ton-km cargo 10,892,000,000. Roads (1982): total length 31,277 mi,
50,336 km (paved 60%). Vehicles (1983): passenger cars 380,993; trucks
and buses 391,440. Merchant marine (1982): vessels (100 gross tons and
over) 1,733; total deadweight tonnage 10,429,775. Air transport (1982):
passenger-mi 7,532,987,000, passenger-km 12,123,191,000; short ton-mi
cargo 718,218,000, metric ton-km cargo 1,048,581,000; airports (1984) with
scheduled flights 3.
Communications. Daily newspapers (1983): total number 25; total circulation 6,748,100; circulation per 1,000 population 171. Radios (1981): total
number of receivers 15,000,000 (1 per 4.5 persons). Television (1984): total number of receivers 7,225,517 (1 per 5.5 persons). Telephones (1983):
5,357,499 (1 per 7.4 persons).

Education and health

Education (1983)

	schools	teachers	students	student/ teacher ratio
Primary (age 6–12)	6,500	126,163	5,257,164	41.7
Secondary (age 13–18)	3,109	97,782	3,804,556	38.9
Vocational	769	35,039	1,099,010	31.4
Higher	279	23,336	845,193	36.2

College graduates per 100,000 population (1982): 432. *Literacy* (1981): total
population literate 13,191,432 (92.7%); males literate 6,937,242 (97.5%);
females literate 6,254,190 (87.9%).
Health (1982): physicians 28,365 (1 per 1,387 persons); hospital beds 44,976
(1 per 874 persons).
Food (1978–80): daily per capita caloric intake 2,926 (vegetable products
8.0%; animal products 92.0%); 124.0% of FAO recommended minimum
requirement.

Military

Total active duty personnel (1982): 622,000 (army 86.8%; navy 7.9%; air force
5.3%). *Military expenditure as percent of GNP:* 6.9% (world 6.0%); per capita
expenditure: U.S.$132.

*During 1981–82 Inch'ŏn and Taegu also became special cities. †Official government
estimate. ‡1982. §Finance and public administration and defense are included with
services. ‖ Public administration and defense is included with services. ¶Unemployed.

Kuwait

Official name: Dawlat al-Kuwayt (State of Kuwait).
Form of government: Constitutional monarchy with a single parliamentary house (National Assembly [65]), possessing limited power.
Chief of state: Emir.
Head of government: Prime Minister.
Capital: Kuwait City.
Official language: Arabic.
Official religion: Islām.
Monetary unit: 1 Kuwaiti dinar (KD) = 1,000 fils; valuation (Oct. 29, 1984) 1 KD = U.S.$3.33 = £2.76.

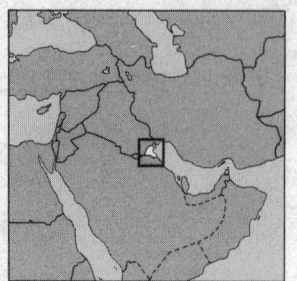

Area and population

Governorates	Capitals	area sq mi	area sq km	population 1980 census
Ahmadī	Ahmadī City	1,984	5,138	232,643
Al-Jahra	Jahra	4,372	11,324*	190,820
Capital	Kuwait City	38	98	182,266
Hawallī	Hawallī	138	358	752,223
TOTAL		6,532	16,918	1,357,952

Demography

Density (1984): persons per sq mi 273, persons per sq km 105.
Urban–rural (1980): urban 88.4%; rural 11.6%.
Sex distribution (1984): male 59.62%; female 40.38%.
Age breakdown (1980): under 15, 40.2%; 15–29, 28.2%; 30–44, 21.7%; 45–59, 7.7%; 60 and over, 2.2%.
Population projection: (1990) 2,101,000; (2000) 2,936,000.
Doubling time: 14.4 years.
Ethnic composition (1980): Kuwaiti 41.7%; other Arab 42.3%; Asian 15.0%; other 1.0%.
Religious affiliation (1980): Islāmic 91.5%; Christian 6.4%; other 2.1%.
Major cities (1980): Hawallī 152,402; Salmiya 145,991; Odailya 69,631; al-Jahrah 67,311; Kuwait City 60,525.

Vital statistics

Birth rate per 1,000 population (1980–85): 40.9 (world avg. 27.5).
Death rate per 1,000 population (1980–85): 4.1 (world avg. 10.6).
Natural increase rate per 1,000 population (1980–85): 36.9 (world avg. 16.9).
Total fertility rate (avg. births per childbearing woman; 1980–85): 6.2.
Marriage rate per 1,000 population (1979): 5.9.
Divorce rate per 1,000 population (1979): 1.3.
Infant mortality rate per 1,000 live births (1982): 22.8.
Life expectancy at birth (1980–85): male 68.0 years; female 72.9 years.
Major causes of death per 100,000 population (1981): circulatory diseases 94.7; accidents, poisonings, and violence 49.4; neoplasms (cancers) 28.1; respiratory diseases 26.3.

National economy

Budget (1983–84). Revenue: KD3,025,000,000 (oil revenue 92.2%, nontax income 4.7%, customs duties 2.8%, other 0.3%). Expenditures: KD-2,839,300,000 (economic services 45.5%, defense 14.4%, social services 11.9%, education 11.4%, other 16.8%).
Public debt: none.
Tourism (1982): receipts from visitors U.S.$198,000,000; expenditures by nationals abroad U.S.$1,306,000,000.
Production (metric tons except as noted). Agriculture, forestry, fishing (1982): milk 56,000, clover 34,072†, tomatoes 13,000, poultry meat 15,000, white radishes 3,589†, melons 3,000; livestock (number of live animals) chickens 7,200,000, sheep 500,000; fish catch 4,497. Mining and quarrying (1982): cement 1,550,000; nitrogen (N content of ammonia) 150,000; sulfur 120,000; lime 22,000. Manufacturing (1981): petroleum products 13,415,-000; concrete (cu m) 36,000; asbestos pipes 43,000; concrete pipes 21,000 units; flour 200,000; bran 35,000. Construction (cu m; 1982): residential 244,000; nonresidential 114,000. Energy production (consumption): electricity (kW-hr; 1982) 12,016,000,000 (12,016,000,000); coal, none (none); petroleum (barrels; 1982) 302,246,000 (169,181,000); natural gas (cu m; 1983) 191,000,000,000 (172,000,000,000).
Gross national product (at current market prices; 1981): U.S.$30,600,000,000 (U.S.$20,900 per capita).

Origin of gross domestic product (current prices)

	1983 in value KD'000,000	1983 % of total value	1980 labour force	1980 % of labour force
Agriculture	34	0.5	9,150	1.9
Mining (oil sector)	3,094	49.8	6,659	1.4
Manufacturing	401	6.4	41,260	8.5
Construction	289	4.6	97,099	20.0
Trade	508	8.2	58,417	12.1
Public utilities	34	0.5	8,167	1.7
Transportation and communication	191	3.1	30,153	6.2
Finance	319	5.1	12,686	2.7
Pub. admin., defense, services, and other	1,349	21.8	220,453	45.5
TOTAL	6,219	100.0	484,044	100.0

Persons economically active (1980): total 484,044 (35.6%); female participation in the labour force 62,099 (12.8%); unemployed, n.a.

Price and earnings indexes (1980 = 100)

	1977	1978	1979	1980	1981	1982	1983
Consumer price index	79.4	87.4	93.5	100.0	107.4	115.7	121.2
Monthly earnings index	...	...	...	...	...	...	...

Household income and expenditure. Average household size (1980) 6.9; annual income per household (1973)‡ KD4,246 (U.S.$12,907); source of income: wages and salaries 53.8%, self-employment 20.8%, other 25.4%; expenditure (1983): food 35.7%, housing 18.7%, transportation 15.3%, household appliances 11.0%, clothing 10.0%, other 9.3%.
Land use (1981): forested 0.1%; meadows and pastures 7.5%; agricultural and under permanent cultivation§; other, built-up, and wasteland 92.4%.

Foreign trade

Balance of trade (current prices)

	1978	1979	1980	1981	1982	1983
KD'000,000	+1,600	+3,652	+3,604	+2,585	+885	+1,204
% of total	38.8%	56.6%	50.5%	39.9%	16.8%	23.1%

Imports (1981): KD1,945,400,000 (machinery and transport equipment 41.0%, manufactured goods 23.3%, miscellaneous manufactured articles 14.9%, food and live animals 13.1%, chemicals 3.9%, crude materials except fuels 1.5%). *Major import sources:* Japan 22.7%; United States 14.0%; West Germany 12.0%; United Kingdom 7.8%; Italy 5.8%.
Exports (1981): KD4,530,400,000 (mineral fuels 87.6%, machinery and transport equipment 4.9%, manufactured goods 4.0%, miscellaneous manufactured articles 1.3%). *Major export destinations:* Japan 23.7%; Taiwan 11.5%; South Korea 8.2%; The Netherlands 6.7%; Iraq 6.3%.

Transport and communications

Transport. Railroads: none. Roads (1982): total length 940 mi, 1,513 km (paved 100%). Vehicles (1982): passenger cars 480,000; trucks and buses 171,000. Merchant marine (1983): vessels (100 gross tons and over) 235; total deadweight tonnage 4,122,000. Air transport (1982): passenger-mi 2,238,890,000, passenger-km 3,603,047,000; short ton-mi cargo 77,110,000, metric ton-km cargo 112,578,000; airport (1984) with scheduled flights 1.
Communications. Daily newspapers (1984): total number 7; total circulation 283,000; circulation per 1,000 population 208. Radios (1984): total number of receivers 710,000 (1 per 2 persons). Television (1984): total number of receivers 575,000 (1 per 2.4 persons). Telephones (1982): 232,000 (1 per 5.9 persons).

Education and health

Education (1983–84)

	schools	teachers	students	student/ teacher ratio
Primary (age 6–9)	252	8,968	165,696	18.5
Secondary (age 10–17) ‖	337	16,871	219,758	13.0
Higher	9	763	13,233	17.3

College graduates per 100,000 population (1980): 4,533. *Literacy* (1980): total population literate 829,000 (86.2%); males literate 535,000 (92.9%); females literate 295,000 (76.2%).
Health (1981): physicians 2,377 (1 per 571 persons); hospital beds 5,561 (1 per 244 persons).
Food (1978–80): daily per capita caloric intake 3,460; 144% of FAO recommended minimum requirement.

Military

Total active duty personnel (1983): 12,400 (army 80.7%; navy 4.0%; air force 15.3%). *Military expenditure as percent of GNP* (1982): 6% (world 6%); per capita expenditure (1980) U.S.$965.

*Excludes Bubian Island and Warba Island. †1980. ‡Kuwaiti households only. §Less than 0.1 percent. ‖ Includes vocational and teacher training schools.

INGEBORG LIPPMANN—PETER ARNOLD, INC.

Al-Ahmadī oilfield, Kuwait.

Laos

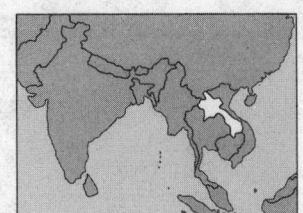

Official name: Sathalanalat
Paxathipatai Paxaxôn Lao (Lao
People's Democratic Republic).
Form of government: unitary
single-party republic with an interim
legislature (Supreme People's
Council [264]).
Chief of state: President.
Head of government: Premier.
Capital: Vientiane.
Official language: Lao.
Official religion: none.
Monetary unit: 1 kip (KN) = 100 at;
valuation (preferential rate; Oct. 29,
1984) 1 U.S.$ = KN 35.07;
1 £ = KN 42.33.

Area and population

Provinces*	Capitals	area sq mi	area sq km	population 1975 estimate
Attapu	Attapu	4,595	11,900	102,000
Borikhan	Muang Pakxan	2,395	6,200	52,000
Champasak	Champasak	1,005	2,600	107,000
Houakhong	Houayxay	4,980	12,900	146,000
Houaphan	Xam Nua	6,290	16,300	218,000
Khammouan	Khammouan	10,195	26,400	267,000
Louangphrabang	Louangphrabang	14,360	37,200	465,000
Phôngsali	Phôngsali	6,100	15,800	131,000
Saravan	Saravan	7,090	18,360	172,000
Savannakhét	Savannakhét	8,380	21,700	471,000
Sithandon	Muang Không	2,045	5,300	70,000
Vapikhamthong	Khôngxédôn	1,250	3,240	126,000
Vientiane	Vientiane	5,560	14,400	362,000
Xaignabouri	Xaignabouri	7,105	18,400	220,000
Xedon	Pakxé	2,550	6,600	151,000
Xiangkhoang	Xiangkhoang	7,530	19,500	225,000
TOTAL		91,430	236,800	3,285,000

Source: Official government figures.

Demography

Density (1984): persons per sq mi 47.2, persons per sq km 18.2.
Urban–rural (1980): urban 13.4%; rural 86.6%.
Sex distribution (1980): male 50.34%; female 49.66%.
Age breakdown (1980): under 15, 42.4%; 15–29, 26.3%; 30–44, 16.7%; 45–59,
9.7%; 60–74, 4.2%; 75 and over, 0.7%.
Population projection: (1990) 5,017,000; (2000) 6,444,000.
Doubling time: 27.4 years.
Ethnic composition (1977 est.): Lao-Lu 49%; Lao-Theng 25%; Lao-Tai 13%;
other 13%.
Religious affiliation (1980 est.): Buddhist 58%; tribal 34%; Christian 2%;
other 2%; none 4%.
Major cities (1975 est.): Vientiane 210,000†; Savannakhét 53,000; Pakxé
47,000; Louangphrabang 46,000.

Vital statistics

Birth rate per 1,000 population (1980–85): 41.5 (world avg. 27.5).
Death rate per 1,000 population (1980–85): 18.1 (world avg. 10.6).
Natural increase rate per 1,000 population (1980–85): 23.4 (world avg. 16.9).
Total fertility rate (avg. births per childbearing woman; 1980–85): 5.8.
Marriage rate per 1,000 population: n.a.
Divorce rate per 1,000 population: n.a.
Infant mortality rate per 1,000 live births (1975–80): 135.0.
Life expectancy at birth (1980–85): male 44.6 years; female 47.5 years.
Major causes of death: no data available; however, during the 1970s malaria,
influenza, dysentery, and pneumonia were among the country's major
health problems.

National economy

Budget (1981). Revenue: KN930,000,000 (private sector taxes 15.1%, state
enterprises 75.3%). Expenditures: KN2,160,000,000 (current expenditure
56.0%, capital expenditure 44.0%).
Public debt (external, outstanding; 1982): U.S.$60,000,000.
Tourism (1980): total number of tourists 28,000.
Production (metric tons except as noted). Agriculture, forestry, fishing (1982):
rice 1,184,000, pineapples 34,000, corn (maize) 33,000, onions 33,000, melons 28,000, oranges 22,000; coffee 6,000; livestock (number of live animals)
1,223,000 pigs, 897,000 buffaloes, 473,000 cattle, 5,863,000 chickens; roundwood 3,836,000 cu m; fish catch 20,000. Mining and quarrying (1982):
gypsum 13,000‡; tin 1,000. Manufacturing (1982): fuelwood 2,949,000 cu
m; industrial roundwood 227,000 cu m; sawed wood 130,000 cu m; wood-
based panels 5,000 cu m; plywood 5,000 cu m; pork 44,000; buffalo meat
44,000; beef and veal 7,000; cattle and buffalo hides 4,100; fresh goatskins
32; cigarettes 1,100,000,000 units§. Construction: n.a. Energy production
(consumption): electricity (kW-hr; 1982) 1,000,000,000 (280,000,000); coal
(metric tons; 1981) 1,000 (1,000); crude petroleum, n.a. (n.a.); petroleum
products (metric tons; 1982) none (152,000); natural gas, n.a. (n.a.).

Price and earnings indexes (1970 = 100)

	1969	1970	1971	1972	1973	1974	1975
Consumer price index	99.6	100.0	101.3	126.8	165.7	248.1	457.3
Monthly earnings index	...	...	...	...	...	...	...

Gross national product (at current market prices; 1981): U.S.$290,000,000
(U.S.$80 per capita).

Origin of gross domestic product

	1972 value in kip	1972 % of total value	1980 labour force	1980 % of labour force
Agriculture	...	24.5	...	75.0
Mining	...	0.4	...	
Manufacturing	...	11.6	...	6.0
Construction	...	1.4	...	
Trade	...	11.6	...	
Public utilities	...	1.6	...	
Transportation and communication	...	4.8	...	
Finance	...	...	...	
Pub. admin., defense	...	...	...	
Services	...	...	...	19.0
Other	...	44.1	...	
TOTAL		100.0 ‖		100.0

Persons economically active (1981): total 1,796,000 (47.1%); female participation in labour force, n.a; unemployed, n.a.
Household income and expenditure. Average household size (1980) 5.3; average annual income per household KN 3,710 (U.S.$371); source of income:
n.a.; expenditure: n.a.
Land use (1981): forested 55.9%; meadows and pastures 3.5%; agricultural
and under permanent cultivation 3.8%; other 36.8%.

Foreign trade

Balance of trade (current prices)

	1977	1978	1979	1980	1981
KN'000,000	−98	−256	−204	−580	−610
% of total	71.0%	72.7%	57.3%	67.4%	61.6%

Imports (1981): KN 800,000,000 (1974; cereals 22.1%, metals and metal manufactures 12.0%, petroleum products 11.0%, electrical machinery 10.1%,
nonelectrical machinery 8.3%, transport equipment 7.3%). *Major import
sources:* Thailand 33.6%; Singapore 17.2%; Japan 11.6%.
Exports (1981): KN 190,000,000 (1980; wood 76.5%, coffee 13.7%, furniture 9.8%). *Major export destinations:* Japan 37.4%; United States 11.0%;
Hong Kong 7.7%.

Transport and communications

Transport. Railroads: none. In 1982, however, the government announced
plans to establish railway links with Vietnam. Roads (1981): total length
6,338 mi, 10,200 km (paved 13%). Vehicles (1982): passenger cars 15,000;
trucks and buses 3,000. Merchant marine: none. Air transport (1980):
passenger-mi 4,300,000, passenger-km 7,000,000; short ton-mi cargo 700,-
000, metric ton-km cargo 1,000,000; airport (1984) with scheduled flights 1.
Communications. Daily newspapers (1983): total number 2; total circulation
12,500; circulation per 1,000 population 3.0. Radios (1983): total number of
receivers 225,000 (1 per 18.7 persons). Television: n.a. Telephones (1981):
2,353 (1 per 1,598 persons).

Education and health

Education (1980)

	schools	teachers	students	student/ teacher ratio
Primary (age 6–11)	6,339	16,109	479,291	29.8
Secondary (age 12–16)	...	4,605	90,435	19.6
Voc., teacher tr.	...	939	11,510	12.3
Higher	...	140	1,408	10.1

College graduates (students graduating; 1979): 229. *Literacy* (1980): total
population literate 878,800 (41.0%); males literate 591,100 (54.9%); females
literate 287,700 (27.0%).
Health: physicians (1981) 30 (1 per 127,000 persons); hospital beds (1983)
100,000 (1 per 42.1 persons).
Food (1978–80): daily per capita caloric intake 1,856 (vegetable products 92.0%, animal products 8.0%); 84% of FAO recommended minimum
requirement.

Military

Total active duty personnel (1983): 53,000 (army 94.3%; navy 1.9%; air force
3.8%). *Military expenditure as percent of GNP* (1980): 14.3% (world 5.6%);
per capita expenditure U.S.$6.

*The administrative division provided may have been superseded by government
reorganizations subsequent to 1975. †1981 estimate. ‡Province of Savannakhét only.
§1980. ‖ Includes services and public administration and defense.

Lebanon

Official name: al-Jumūrīyah
al-Lubnānīyah (Republic of Lebanon).
Form of government: multiparty
republic with one legislative house
(Chamber of Deputies [99]).
Chief of state: President.
Head of government: Prime Minister.
Capital: Beirut.
Official language: Arabic.
Official religion: none.
Monetary unit: 1 Lebanese pound
(LL) = 100 piastres; valuation (Oct.
29, 1984) 1 U.S.$ = LL8.00;
1 £ = LL9.65.

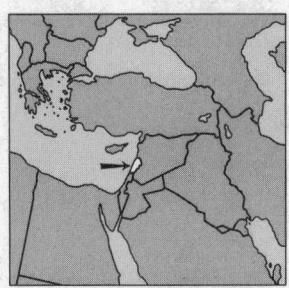

Area and population

Governorates	Capitals	area sq mi	area sq km	population 1970 estimate
Bayrūt	Bayrūt	7	18	474,870
al-Biqā'	Zaḥlah	1,653	4,280	203,520
Jabal Lubnān	B'abdā	753	1,950	833,055
al-Janūb	Ṣaydā	364	943	249,945
an-Nabaṭīyah*	...	408	1,058	...
ash-Shamāl	Ṭarābulus	765	1,981	364,935
TOTAL		3,950	10,230	2,126,325

Source: Official government figures; United Nations.

Demography

Density †(1984): persons per sq mi 784.8, persons per sq km 303.0.
Urban–rural (1980): urban 75.9%; rural 24.1%.
Sex distribution (1984): male 49.37%; female 50.63%.
Age breakdown (1984): under 15, 35.6%; 15–29, 30.4%; 30–44, 15.0%; 45–59, 11.0%; 60–74, 6.0%; 75 and over, 2.0%.
Population projection: (1990) 3,301,000; (2000) 3,992,000; in the period 1970–75 the average growth rate was 2.6%; however, since 1976 the population is decreasing from the massive emigration resulting from the civil war.
Ethnic composition (1983): Lebanese 82.6%; Palestinian 9.6%; Armenian 4.9%; Syrian, Kurd, and other 2.9%.
Religious affiliation: no official data exist subsequent to the 1932 census, when Christians (predominantly Roman Catholic) were a slight majority; it is thought that Muslims today constitute the majority but by what margin is impossible to ascertain. There is a substantial Druze minority.
Major cities (1975): Beirut 1,172,000; Tripoli 150,000‡.

Vital statistics

Birth rate per 1,000 population (1982): 29.9 (world avg. 29.0), legitimate, n.a.; illegitimate, n.a.
Death rate per 1,000 population (1982): 8.3 (world avg. 11.0).
Natural increase rate per 1,000 population (1982): 21.6 (world avg. 18.0).
Total fertility rate (avg. births per childbearing woman; 1982): 2.0.
Marriage rate per 1,000 population (1973): 7.0.
Divorce rate per 1,000 population (1973): 0.6.
Infant mortality rate per 1,000 live births (1981): 40.2.
Life expectancy at birth (1980–85): male 65.0 years; female 68.9 years.
Major causes of death (mid-1970s): heart ailments and gastrointestinal diseases, including typhoid and dysentery.

National economy

Budget (1982). Revenue: LL5,945,000,000 (no detail available). Expenditure: LL6,300,000,000 (defense 19.8%; public works 17.4%; education 15.6%; debt payment 7.6%; social welfare and health 6.2%).
Public debt (external, outstanding; 1981): U.S.$246,200,000.
Tourism: n.a.
Production (metric tons except as noted). Agriculture, forestry, fishing (1982): oranges 205,000, grapes 161,000, tomatoes 132,000, apples 130,000, potatoes 126,000, olives 75,000, lemons and limes 56,000, wheat 23,000, bananas 15,000, tobacco 4,000; livestock (number of live animals) 440,000 goats, 145,000 sheep, 54,000 cattle, 7,500,000 chickens; roundwood 486,000 cu m; fish catch 1,500. Mining and quarrying (1982): gypsum 5,000; hydraulic cement 1,500,000. Manufacturing (1974): tobacco manufactures 6,337. Construction: (1981): 5,863,000 sq m.. Energy production (consumption): electricity (kW-hr; 1982) 1,290,000,000 (1,320,000,000); coal (metric tons; 1982) n.a. (1,000); crude petroleum (barrels; 1982) n.a. (3,600); petroleum products (metric tons; 1982) 472,000 (1,097,000); natural gas, none (n.a.).
Persons economically active (1982): total 1,149,000 (44.9%); female participation in the labour force 228,700 (19.9%); unemployed 33,345 (5.8%).

Price and earnings indexes (1970 = 100)

	1970	1971	1972	1973	1974
Consumer price index	100.0	101.6	106.6	113.0	125.5
Earnings index	...	...	...	...	...

Household income and expenditure. Average household size (1980) 5.3; average annual income per household: n.a.; source of income: n.a.; expenditure: n.a.
Gross national product (at current market prices; 1983): U.S.$4,600,000,000–$5,500,000,000 (U.S.$1,636–$1,956 per capita).

Origin of gross domestic product (current prices)

	1977 in value LL'000,000	1977 % of total value	1982 labour force	1982 % of labour force
Agriculture	700	8.5	238,188	20.7
Mining	...	...	§	§
Manufacturing	1,070	13.1	223,136§	19.4§
Construction	280	3.4	71,698	6.2
Trade	2,320	28.3	203,258	17.7
Public utilities	445	5.4	8,503	0.7
Transportation and communication	630	7.7	62,161 ‖	5.4 ‖
Finance	...	...	‖	‖
Pub. admin., defense	835	10.2	¶	¶
Services	1,920	23.4	342,057¶	29.8¶
Other	...	...	...	...
TOTAL	8,200	100.0	1,149,001	100.0♀

Land use (1981): forested 7.0%; meadows and pastures 0.9%; agricultural and under permanent cultivation 34.2%; other 57.9%.

Foreign trade

Balance of trade (current prices)

	1978	1979	1980	1981	1982	1983
LL'000,000	−3,031	−5,601	−8,631	−8,906	−9,890	−12,461
% of total	40.5%	52.8%	59.1%	45.0%	48.5%	69.0%

Imports (1982): LL15,146,000,000 (consumer goods 40.0%; machinery and transport equipment 35.0%; petroleum products 20.0%). *Major import sources:* Italy 15.2%; France 10.3%; United States 9.1%; West Germany 7.6% Saudi Arabia 5.7%.
Exports (1982): LL5,256,000,000 (agricultural products 21.3%, of which vegetables 15.9%; textile products 11.3%; metal products 8.5%; precious metals, jewelry, and coins 5.0%). *Major export destinations:* Saudi Arabia 29.7%; Iraq 22.1%; Jordan 10.8%; Syria 7.4%; Kuwait 5.5%.

Transport and communications

Transport. Railroads (1982): length 258 mi, 415 km; passenger-mi 5,325,000, passenger-km 8,570,000; short ton-mi cargo 28,770,000, metric ton-km cargo 42,010,000. Roads (1982): total length 4,300 mi, 7,000 km (paved 80%). Vehicles (1982): passenger cars 460,400; trucks and buses 35,000. Merchant marine (1983): vessels (100 gross tons and over) 260; total deadweight tonnage 681,151. Air transport (1982δ): passenger-mi 224,530,000, passenger-km 361,350,000; short ton-mi cargo 30,250,000, metric ton-km cargo 44,160,000; airport (1984) with scheduled flights 1.
Communications. Daily newspapers (1983): total number 11; total circulation 252,000; circulation per 1,000 population 89.6. Radios (1983): total number of receivers 1,500,000 (1 per 1.9 persons). Television (1983): total number of receivers 450,000 (1 per 6.2 persons). Telephones (1973): 227,000 (1 per 12 persons).

Education and health

Education (1981–82)

	schools	teachers	students	student/ teacher ratio
Primary (age 5–9)	1,116	□	398,977	...
Secondary (age 10–16)	1,405	53,450□	250,028	...
Voc., teacher tr.	181	3,563	39,045	11.0
Higher	18	...	70,314	...

College graduates per 100,000 population (students graduating; 1981): 345.
Literacy (1980): total population literate 1,183,000 (73.4%); males literate 643,000 (82.6%); females literate 540,000 (64.2%).
Health (1982): physicians 3,000 (1 per 1,000 persons); hospital beds 11,400 (1 per 263 persons).
Food (1978–80): daily per capita caloric intake 2,496 (vegetable products 86.2%, animal products 13.8%); 101% of FAO recommended minimum requirement.

Military

Total active duty personnel (1982): 27,000 (army 94.4%; navy 0.9%; air force 4.7%); factional armies (1983) Lebanese forces (Maronite) 10,000–15,000, Progressive Socialist Party/Druze forces 5,000, Amal (Shī'ite) 10,000. *Military expenditure as percent of GNP* (1982): 16.5% (world 6.0%); per capita expenditure: U.S.$104.

*Created in 1975; includes the districts of Nabaṭīyah, Bint Jubayl, Marj 'Uyūn, and Ḥāṣbayya, which were formerly part of al-Janub. †The estimated population for 1984 was 3,100,000 which included 500,000 Palestinian refugees. ‡1972. §Mining included with manufacturing. ‖Finance included with transportation and communication. ¶Public administration and defense included with services. ♀Detail does not add to total given because of rounding. δData for one or more months missing. □Primary included with secondary.

Lesotho

Official name: Lesotho (Sesotho) (Kingdom of Lesotho).
Form of government: constitutional monarchy with two legislative houses (National Assembly [93]; Senate [33]).
Chief of state: King.
Head of government: Prime Minister.
Capital: Maseru.
Official languages: Sesotho; English.
Official religion: Christianity.
Monetary unit: 1 loti (plural maloti [M]) = 100 lisente; valuation (Oct. 29, 1984) 1 U.S.$ = M1.79; 1 £ = M2.16.

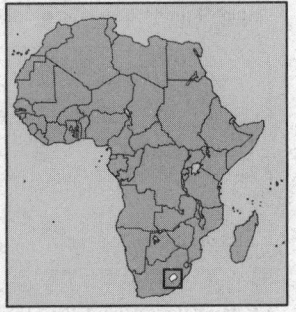

Area and population

Districts	Capitals	area sq mi	area sq km	population 1981 estimate
Berea	Teyateyaneng	858	2,222	162,400
Butha-Buthe	Butha-Buthe	682	1,767	84,800
Leribe	Hlotse	1,251	3,240	234,400
Mafeteng	Mafeteng	818	2,119	175,900
Maseru	Maseru	2,340	6,061	292,200
Mohale's Hoek	Mohale's Hoek	1,363	3,530	152,300
Mokhotlong	Mokhotlong	1,765	4,571	80,900
Qacha's Nek	Qacha's Nek	1,517	3,929	84,700
Quthing	Quthing	1,126	2,916	98,300
TOTAL		11,720	30,355	1,365,900

Source: Official government figures.

Demography

Density (1984): persons per sq mi 125.8, persons per sq km 48.6.
Urban–rural (1982): urban 17.2%; rural 82.8%.
Sex distribution (1976): male 48.27%; female 51.73%.
Age breakdown (1980): under 15, 40.9%; 15–29, 25.9%; 30–44, 15.9%; 45–59, 10.6%; 60–74, 5.5%; 75 and over, 1.2%.
Population projection: (1990) 1,643,000; (2000) 2,064,000.
Doubling time: 30 years.
Ethnic composition (1978): Sotho 99.6%; other 0.4%.
Religious affiliation (1980): Roman Catholic 43.5%; Lesotho Evangelical 29.8%; Anglican 11.5%; other Christian 8.0%; tribal 6.2%; other 1.0%.
Major City: Maseru 52,127.

Vital statistics

Birth rate per 1,000 population (1980–85): 38.6 (world avg. 27.5); legitimate, n.a.; illegitimate, n.a.
Death rate per 1,000 population (1980–85): 14.6 (world avg. 10.6).
Natural increase rate per 1,000 population (1980–85): 24.0 (world avg. 16.9).
Total fertility rate (avg. births per childbearing woman; 1980–85): 5.4.
Marriage rate per 1,000 population: n.a.
Divorce rate per 1,000 population: n.a.
Infant mortality rate per 1,000 live births (1976): 107.0.
Life expectancy at birth (1980–85): male 51.7 years; female 53.9 years.
Major causes of death: n.a.

National economy

Budget (1982–83). Revenue: M215,510,000 (customs and excise duties 55.0%). Expenditures: M269,220,000 (capital accounts 38.7%, public debt servicing 13.4%, education 9.6%, security 6.7%, health 3.1%).
Public debt (external, outstanding; 1982): U.S.$138,600,000.
Tourism (1980): number of tourists 73,128; expenditures by nationals abroad, n.a.
Production (metric tons except as noted). Agriculture, forestry, fishing (1982): corn (maize) 83,000, sorghum 26,000, wheat 14,000; livestock (number of live animals) 1,279,000 sheep, 872,000 goats, 537,000 cattle, 102,000 horses, 97,000 asses, 62,000 pigs, 814,000 poultry; round wood 293,000 cu m; Fish catch 20. Mining and quarrying (1981): diamonds 52,291 carats. Manufacturing (1983): food processing, manufacture of carpets, and handicrafts. Construction: n.a. Energy production (consumption): electricity, none (*); coal, none (n.a.); petroleum, none (n.a.); natural gas, none (n.a.).
Gross national product (at current market prices; 1982–83): U.S.$496,000,000 (U.S.$350 per capita).

Origin of gross domestic product (current prices)

	1979–80 in value M'000,000	% of total value	labour force	% of labour force
Agriculture	67.1	25.5	588,000	81.8
Mining	18.2	6.9	121,000†	18.2
Manufacturing	12.1	4.6	...	...
Construction	21.3	8.1	...	...
Trade	28.7	10.9	...	...
Public utilities	2.1	0.8	...	...
Transportation and communication	4.2	1.6	...	...
Finance	...	...	...	...
Pub. admin., defense	...	...	...	...
Services	...	...	...	...
Other	109.5	41.6	...	...
TOTAL	263.2	100.0	709,000	100.0

Persons economically active (1982): total 729,000‡ (52.1%); female participation in the labour force, n.a.; unemployed, n.a.

Price and earnings indexes (1973 = 100)

	1977	1978	1979	1980	1981	1982	1983
Consumer price index	171.2	193.4	222.3	261.9	305.2	335.9	394.5
Monthly earnings index	...	...	...	...	...	...	...

Household income and expenditure. Average household size (1979–80) 5.4; average annual average annual income per household M1,550 (U.S.$1,150); source of income: n.a.; expenditure (1973): food 34.0%, clothing 19.3%, housing 9.7%, transportation 9.5%, education 4.1%, health 1.8%.
Land use (1982): meadows and pastures 65.9%; agricultural and under permanent cultivation 9.8%; other 24.3%.

Foreign trade

Balance of trade (current prices)

	1978	1979	1980	1981	1982	1983
M'000,000	−209.0	−265.7	−315.5	−415.3	−609.5	...
% of total	79.1%	77.8%	77.7%	82.5%	87.4%	...

Imports (1979): M303,612,000 (food and live animals 22.6%, of which cereal preparations 9.2%; livestock 3.0%; clothing 10.4%; petroleum products 7.5%; motor vehicles 7.4%; textile yarn and fabrics 6.3%; chemicals and related products 5.4%; electrical machinery 4.1%; other machinery 3.0%). *Major import sources:* South Africa 97.4%; United Kingdom 0.9%; West Germany 0.6%; United States 0.2%; Japan 0.2%.
Exports (1979): M37,916,000 (diamonds 56.0%; mohair 11.4%; wool 8.9%; medical and pharmaceutical products 3.5%; clothing and footwear 3.0%; fruits and vegetables 1.0%). *Major export destinations:* Switzerland 55.6%; South Africa 34.2%; West Germany 4.1%; Belgium–Luxembourg 3.4%; United Kingdom 1.1%.

Transport and communications

Transport. Railroads (1980): length 1 mi, 2 km. Roads (1983): total length 2,538 mi, 4,085 km (paved 11%). Vehicles (1982): passenger cars 5,129; trucks and buses 11,962. Merchant marine (1982): vessels (100 gross tons and over) none. Air transport (1981): passenger-mi 8,000,000, passenger-km 13,000,000; short ton-mi cargo 70,000, metric ton-km cargo 100,000; airports (1984) with scheduled flights 11.
Communications. Daily newspapers (1983): total number 2; total circulation 42,000; circulation per 1,000 population 30. Radios (1983): total number of receivers 40,000 (1 per 35 persons). Television (1981): none. Telephones (1981): 5,916 (1 per 232 persons).

Education and health

Education (1982–83)

	schools	teachers§	students	student/ teacher ratio
Primary (age 6–11)	1,103	4,782	277,945	...
Secondary (age 12–17)	108	940	27,799	...
Voc., teacher tr.	12	121	2,054	...
Higher	1	115	1,100	...

College graduates per 100,000 population (1977): 81.0. *Literacy* (1980): total population literate 534,700 (69.9%); males literate 217,500 (57.5%); females literate 317,200 (80.0%).
Health (1980): physicians 82 (1 per 15,963 persons); hospital beds 2,224 (1 per 588.5 persons).
Food (1978–80): daily per capita caloric intake 2,442 (vegetable products 93.4%, animal products 6.6%); 107% of FAO recommended minimum requirement.

Military

Total active duty personnel (1980): 1,500 ‖. *Military expenditure as percent of GNP:* n.a.

*All electricity is imported via the South African grid. †Migrants employed in South African mines. ‡Includes 140,000 migrants employed in South African mines. §1979–80. ‖ Lesotho paramilitary force.

Liberia

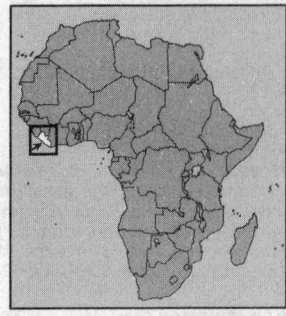

Official name: Republic of Liberia.
Form of government: military dictatorship with one ruling body (People's Redemption Council [22]).
Head of state and government: Chairman of the People's Redemption Council.
Capital: Monrovia.
Official language: English.
Official religion: none.
Monetary unit: 1 Liberian dollar (L$) = 100 cents; valuation (Oct. 29, 1984) 1 U.S.$ = L$1.00; 1 £ = L$1.21.

Area and population

Counties	Capitals	area sq mi	area sq km	population 1981 estimate
Bong	Gbarnga	3,650	9,454	230,700
Grand Bassa	Buchanan	5,075	13,144	163,400
Grand Cape Mount	Robertsport	2,250	5,827	78,600
Grand Gedeh	Zwedru	6,575	17,029	91,700
Lofa	Voinjama	7,475	19,360	219,800
Maryland	Harper	1,675	4,338	100,900
Montserrado*	Monrovia	2,550	6,605	625,300
Nimba	Sanniquellie	4,650	12,044	324,100
Sinoe	Greenville	4,350	11,266	76,600
TOTAL		38,250	99,067	1,911,100

Source: Official government figures.

Demography

Density (1984): persons per sq mi 59.4, persons per sq km 22.9.
Urban–rural (1981): urban 37.1%; rural 62.9%.
Sex distribution (1981): male 50.40%; female 49.60%.
Age breakdown (1980): under 15, 47.6%; 15–29, 25.8%; 30–44, 14.5%; 45–59, 8.0%; 60–74, 3.5%; 75 and over, 0.6%.
Population projection: (1990) 2,821,000; (2000) 4,002,000.
Doubling time: 20 years.
Ethnic composition (1982): indigenous black African, including Kpelle, Bassa, Kru, Grebo, Gola, Kissi, Krahn, and Mandingo 97.0%; Americo-Liberians, descendants of repatriated slaves 3.0%.
Religious affiliation (1980): traditional beliefs 43.5%; Christian 35.0%; Muslim 21.2%; Bahā'ī 0.3%.
Major cities (1980 est.): Monrovia 243,243; Yekepa 14,189†; Tubmanburg 14,089†; Gbarnga 10,860.

Vital statistics

Birth rate per 1,000 population (1980–85): 48.4 (world avg. 27.5).
Death rate per 1,000 population (1980–85): 12.4 (world avg. 10.6).
Natural increase rate per 1,000 population (1980–85): 36.0 (world avg. 16.9).
Total fertility rate (avg. births per childbearing woman; 1980–85): 6.9.
Marriage rate per 1,000 population: n.a.
Divorce rate per 1,000 population: n.a.
Infant mortality rate per 1,000 live births (1981): 151.5.
Life expectancy at birth (1980–85): male 54.5 years; female 56.2 years.
Major causes of death per 100,000 population‡ (1981): pregnancy 613.8; diarrheal dysentery 257.7; malaria 174.6; pneumonia 168.4; anemia 73.7; measles 49.4.

National economy

Budget (1982–83). Revenue: L$190,800,000 (income and wealth taxes 36.4%, import duties 27.6%, excise tax 13.3%, tax on foreign vessels 10.6%). Expenditures: L$269,200,000 (development expenditure 38.5%, wages and salaries 21.2%, goods and services 10.0%).
Public debt (external, outstanding; 1982): U.S.$641,200,000.
Tourism: n.a.
Production (metric tons except as noted). Agriculture, forestry, fishing (1982): cassava 320,000, paddy rice 268,000, natural rubber 82,000§, bananas 77,000, plantains 32,000, sweet potatoes 16,000, green coffee 10,000, oranges 7,000, pineapples 7,000, cocoa beans 5,000; livestock (number of live animals) 220,000 sheep, 220,000 goats, 112,000 pigs, 41,000 cattle, 2,800,000 chickens, 233,000 ducks; fuel wood 4,078,000 cu m ‖ ; fish catch 13,553. Mining and quarrying (1983): iron ore (68% metal content) 15,200,000; diamonds 336,000 metric carats§; gold 16,400 troy ounces. Manufacturing (1979): cement 185,000; palm oil 26,000; frozen fish 13,000; beverages 128,000 hectolitres. Construction: n.a. Energy production (consumption): electricity (kW-hr; 1982) 1,100,000,000 (1,100,000,000); coal, none (n.a.); crude petroleum (barrels; 1982) none (4,764,500); petroleum products (metric tons; 1982) 625,000 (508,000); natural gas, none (n.a.).
Gross national product (at current market prices; 1981): U.S.$1,010,000,000 (U.S.$520 per capita).

Price and earnings indexes (1975 = 100)

	1976	1977	1978	1979	1980	1981	1982
Consumer price index	105.6	112.2	120.4	134.4	152.9	165.5	174.3
Monthly earnings index	...	...	...	...	...	...	...

Household income and expenditure. Average household size (1980) 4.9; income per household: n.a.; source of income: n.a.; expenditure (1981): food, beverages, and tobacco (including alcohol) 40.1%, rent 14.9%, clothing 13.8%, health, personal care, services 11.4%, household goods and furniture 6.1%, fuel and light 5.0%.

Origin of gross domestic product (current factor cost):

	1981 in value L$'000,000	% of total value	1981 labour force¶	% of labour force
Agriculture	118.3	16.5	515,000	79.3
Mining	131.4	18.4	20,000	3.1
Manufacturing	290.4	40.6	11,000	1.7
Construction	♀	♀	7,500	1.2
Trade	♀	♀	32,000	4.9
Public utilities	19.1	2.7	1,500	0.2
Transportation and communication	♀	♀	12,000	1.8
Finance	♀	♀	♂	♂
Pub. admin., defense	155.8	21.8	32,000	4.9
Other services	□	□	18,500	2.9
TOTAL	715.0	100.0	649,500	100.0

Persons economically active (1981): total 1,232,387 (62.5%); female participation in the labour force 386,970 (31.4%); unemployed 93,522 (7.6%).
Land use (1981): forested 39.0%; meadows and pastures 2.5%; agricultural and under permanent cultivation 3.8%; other 54.7◊%.

Foreign trade

Balance of trade (current prices)

	1977	1978	1979	1980	1981	1982
L$'000,000	26.0	66.9	76.1	51.8	120.8	105.5
% of total	3.0%	7.1%	7.6%	5.1%	12.9%	12.4%

Imports (1981): L$477,400,000 (petroleum and petroleum products 27.1%, of which crude petroleum 21.4%; machinery and transportation equipment except electrical 22.5%, of which civil engineering equipment 7.5%, road vehicles 6.8%; cereals and cereal preparations 12.0%, of which rice 9.4%; chemical products 6.9%; electrical machinery and appliances 2.4%). *Major import sources:* United States 29.8%; West Germany 10.2%; The Netherlands 8.5%; United Kingdom 5.3%; Japan 4.7%; France 2.8%.
Exports (1981): L$529,200,000 (iron ore 61.5%; rubber 16.4%; logs and timber 6.1%; diamonds 4.4%; coffee 3.7%; cocoa 2.6%). *Major export destinations:* West Germany 25.0%; United States 23.3%; Italy 13.3%; France 9.9%; The Netherlands 5.2%; Belgium–Luxembourg 5.2%.

Transport and communications

Transport. Railroads△ (1981–82): route length 304 mi, 490 km; short ton-mi cargo 1,967,500,000†, metric ton-km cargo 2,872,500,000†. Roads (1981): total length 6,268 mi, 10,087 km (paved 7%). Vehicles (1981): passenger cars 1,632; trucks and buses 1,088. Merchant marine (1983): vessels (100 gross tons and over) 2,062; total deadweight tonnage 133,239,734. Air transport (1980): passenger-mi 10,600,000, passenger-km 17,000,000; short ton-mi cargo 68,000, metric ton-km cargo 100,000; airports (1984) with scheduled flights 8.
Communications. Daily newspapers (1979): total number 3; total circulation 11,000; circulation per 1,000 population 6. Radios (1982): total number of receivers 330,000 (1 per 5.9 persons). Television (1982): total number of receivers 35,000 (1 per 55.4 persons). Telephones (1981): 6,989 (1 per 273.4 persons).

Education and health

Education (1980)

	schools	teachers	students	student/teacher ratio
Primary (age 6–12)	1,151	9,099	227,431	25.0
Secondary (age 13–18)	275	1,146	52,301	45.6
Voc., teacher tr.	6	63	2,322	38.9
Higher	3	190	3,789	19.9

College graduates per 100,000 population (students graduating; 1981): 30⊕.
Literacy (1980): total population literate 696,010 (70.5%); males literate 290,730 (58.4%); females literate 405,280 (82.4%).
Health: physicians (1981) 227 (1 per 8,415 persons); hospital beds (1980) 2,503 (1 per 737 persons).
Food (1978–80): daily per capita caloric intake 2,474 (vegetable products 90.1%, animal products 9.9%); 107% of FAO recommended minimum requirement.

Military

Total active duty personnel (1982): 5,550 (army 88.3%; navy 7.2%; air force 4.5%). *Military expenditure as percent of GNP* (1982): 5.1% (world 6.0%); per capita expenditure U.S.$25.

*Both area and population figures for the commonwealth district of Monrovia are included with Montserrado county. †1974 census. ‡Hospital inpatient morbidity rates. §1981. ‖ 1980. ¶Employed only. ♀Construction, trade, transportation and communication, and finance are included with manufacturing. ♂Finance is included with other services. □Services are included with public administration and defense. ◊Primarily swampy lowland. △For iron ore transport only. †Refers to Liberian American-Swedish Minerals Company railroad only. ⊕University of Liberia and Cuttington University College only.

Libya

Official name: al-Jamāhīrīyah al-'Arabīyah al-Lībīyah ash-Sha'bīyah al-Ishtirākīyah (Socialist People's Libyan Arab Jamahiriya).
Form of government: socialist state with one policy-making body (General People's Congress [approx. 1,000]).
Chief of state*: Muammar al-Qaddafi.
Head of government: Secretary-general of the General People's Committee (premier).
Capital: Tripoli.
Official language: Arabic.
Official religion: Islām.
Monetary unit: 1 Libyan dinar (LD) = 1,000 dirhams; valuation (Oct. 29, 1984) 1 Libyan dinar = U.S.$3.37 = £2.79.

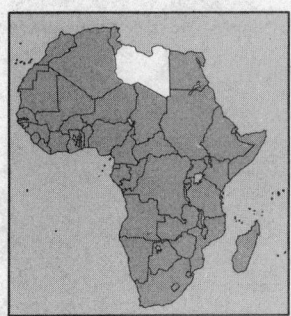

Area and population

Baladiyat	Capitals	area sq mi	area sq km	population 1981 estimate
Tubruq	Ṭubruq	...	...	71,800
Darnah	Dernah	...	...	70,500
al-Baydā'	al-Baydā'	...	...	96,300
al-Marj	al-Marj	.	...	75,000
Banghāzī	Banghāzī	...	...	367,600
Ajdābiyā	Ajdābiyā	...	...	71,000
Surt	Surt	...	...	34,900
Banī Walīd	Banī Walīd	...	...	33,800
al-Kufrah	al-Kufrah	...	...	16,200
Miṣrātah	Miṣrātah	...	...	116,900
Zlīṭan	Zlīṭan	...	...	72,200
al-Jufrah	Hūn	...	...	18,800
al-Khums	al-Khums	...	...	111,800
Tarhunah	Tarhunah	...	...	57,000
Ṭarābulus	Tripoli	...	...	858,500
al-'Azīzīyah	al-'Azīzīyah	...	...	63,800
az-Zāwiyah	az-Zāwiyah	...	...	177,500
Zuwārah	Zuwārah	...	...	129,600
Gharyān	Gharyān	...	...	86,900
Yafran	Yafran	...	...	54,700
Ghadamis	Ghadamis	...	...	30,000
Sabhā	Sabhā	...	...	49,700
ash-Shāṭi	Birāk	...	...	34,800
Awbārī	Awbārī	...	...	33,200
Marzuq	Marzuq	...	...	29,500
TOTAL		685,524	1,775,500	3,223,000†

Source: Official government figures.

Demography

Density (1984): persons per sq mi 5.1, persons per sq km 2.0.
Urban–rural (1981): urban 53.8%; rural 46.2%.
Sex distribution (1980): male 52.92%; female 47.08%.
Age breakdown (1980): under 15, 46.6%; 15–29, 25.1%; 30–44, 16.2%; 45–59, 8.3%; 60–74, 3.2%; 75 and over, 0.6%.
Population projection: (1990) 4,416,700; (2000) 6,538,800.
Doubling time: 17 years.
Ethnic composition (1982): Libyan (Berber and Arab with some Negro stock) 82.4%; foreign nationals 17.6%.
Religious affiliation (1982): Sunnī Muslim 97.0%; other 3.0%.
Major cities (1979): Tripoli 587,400; Banghāzī 267,700; Miṣrātah 52,200.

Vital statistics

Birth rate per 1,000 population (1980–85): 46.0 (world avg. 27.5).
Death rate per 1,000 population (1980–85): 11.2 (world avg. 10.6).
Natural increase rate per 1,000 population (1980–85): 34.8 (world avg. 16.9).
Total fertility rate (avg. births per childbearing woman; 1980–85): 7.2.
Marriage rate per 1,000 population (1979): 6.0.
Divorce rate per 1,000 population (1979): 1.5.
Infant mortality rate per 1,000 live births (1981): 97.5.
Life expectancy at birth (1980–85): male 56.1 years; female 59.4 years.
Major causes of death: n.a.; however, major diseases are trachoma, tuberculosis, malaria, and dysentery.

National economy

Budget (1982). Revenue and expenditure: LD3,855,000,000 (development 67.4%, administrative 32.6%).
Public debt (external, outstanding; 1982): U.S.$844,000,000.
Tourism (1981): receipts from visitors U.S.$14,000,000; expenditures by nationals abroad U.S.$645,000,000.
Production (metric tons except as noted). Agriculture, forestry, fishing (1982): tomatoes 235,000, wheat 160,000, potatoes 113,000, olives 100,000, dates 94,000, barley 71,000, oranges 40,000, grapes 16,000, peanuts (groundnuts) in shell 13,000; livestock (number of live animals) 5,600,000 sheep, 1,500,000 goats, 194,000 cattle, 135,000 camels, 60,000 asses; roundwood 630,000 cu m; fish catch 7,425. Mining and quarrying (1982): gypsum 172,400, salt 10,000. Manufacturing (gross value in LD'000,000; 1980): cement and quicklime 29; processed foods 25.4; electrical, metal, and engineering products 15.9; carpets, textiles, and leather goods 9.5; chemicals 9.4; cigarettes and cigars 8.4; sawnwood and furniture 7.2; paper and printed products 6.8; soft drinks 5.2. Construction (gross value in LD; 1977): residential 51,330,000; nonresidential 118,045,000. Energy production (consumption): electricity (kW-hr; 1982) 6,000,000,000 (6,000,000,000); coal (metric tons; 1982) none (1,000); crude petroleum (barrels; 1983) 373,830,000 (41,781,000‡); petroleum products (metric tons; 1982) 4,605,000 (5,007,000); natural gas (cu m; 1983) 2,670,290,000 (594,871,000‡).
Gross national product (at current market prices; 1981): U.S.$26,080,000,000 (U.S.$8,450 per capita).

Origin of gross domestic product (current prices)

	1980 in value LD'000,000	% of total value	labour force	% of labour force
Agriculture	160	1.5	153,000	18.8
Mining	6,608	63.6	21,500	2.6
Manufacturing	239	2.3	58,000	7.1
Construction	907	8.7	173,000	21.3
Trade	658	6.3	43,000	5.3
Public utilities	49	0.5	19,500	2.4
Transp. and commun.	351	3.4	72,000	8.9
Finance	§	§	10,000	1.2
Pub. admin., defense	542	5.2	65,000	8.0
Services	‖	‖	137,000	16.8
Other	881	8.5	61,500¶	7.6¶
TOTAL	10,395	100.0	813,500	100.0

Persons economically active (1980): total 813,500 (25.1%); female participation in the labour force 59,000 (7.3%); unemployed, n.a.

Price and earnings indexes (1975 = 100)

	1973	1974	1975	1976	1977	1978	1979
Consumer price index	85.3	91.6	100.0	105.4	112.1	145.0	137.1
Monthly earnings index	...	...	...	...	...	...	...

Household income and expenditure. Average household size (1980) 5.1; average annual income per household: n.a.; source of income: n.a.; expenditure (1977): food 37.2%, housing 32.2%, transportation 9.4%, education and recreation 8.5%, clothing 6.9%, medical care 3.3%.
Land use (1981): forested 0.3%; meadows and pastures 7.4%; agricultural and under permanent cultivation 1.2%; other 91.1%♀.

Foreign tradeδ

Balance of trade (current prices)

	1978	1979	1980	1981	1982	1983
LD'000,000	+1,794	+3,345	+4,674	+378	+1,894	+1,348
% of total	42.2%	54.1%	56.3%	4.3%	29.8%	25.9%

Imports (1981): LD2,481,422,000 (food and live animals 16.3%; transport equipment and parts 14.9%; nonelectrical machinery 13.1%; electrical machinery 10.2%; metal manufactured products 9.7%; textiles and clothing 6.2%; iron and steel 5.1%; chemicals 4.5%). *Major import sources:* Italy 30.2%; West Germany 10.5%; Japan 7.6%; United Kingdom 6.9%; France 6.3%; United States 6.3%; Spain 3.0%; Turkey 2.3%.
Exports (1981): LD4,609,851,000 (crude petroleum 99.6%; chemicals 0.4%). *Major export destinations:* United States 27.4%; Italy 23.8%; West Germany 10.3%; Spain 6.7%; Turkey 5.1%; Greece 5.0%.

Transport and communications

Transport. Railroads: none. Roads (1982): total length 12,000 mi, 19,300 km (paved 56%). Vehicles (1982): passenger cars 415.509; trucks and buses 334,405. Merchant marine (1983): vessels (100 gross tons and over) 104; total deadweight tonnage 1,604,965. Air transport□ (1981): passenger-mi 831,027,000, passenger-km 1,337,411,000; short ton-mi cargo 9,004,000, metric ton-km cargo 13,146,000; airports (1984) with scheduled flights 8.
Communications. Daily newspapers (1983): total number 1; circulation, 40,000; circulation per 1,000 population 11.9. Radios (1982): total number 165,000 (1 per 20.8 persons). Television (1982): total number 170,000 (1 per 20.1 persons). Telephones (1976): 59,000 (1 per 42.0 persons).

Education and health

Education (1981–82)

	schools	teachers	students	student/ teacher ratio
Primary (age 6–12)	2,679	39,214	718,124	18.3
Secondary (age 13–18)	1,429	23,891	286,414	12.0
Voc., teacher tr.	184	3,926	44,789	11.4
Higher	8	1,340◊	25,700	...

College graduates per 100,000 population: n.a. *Literacy* (1981): total population literate 860,000 (52.4%).
Health (1981): physicians 4,690△ (1 per 660 persons); hospital beds 15,375 (1 per 201 persons).
Food (1978–80): daily per capita caloric intake 3,418 (vegetable products 87.0%, animal products 13.0%); 145% of FAO recommended minimum.

Military

Total active duty personnel (1983): 73,000 (army 79.5%; navy 8.9%; air force 11.6%). *Military expenditure as percent of GNP* (1982): 2.8% (world 6.0%); per capita expenditure U.S.$220.

---

*No formal title exists. †Total includes about 461,000 foreign nationals (concentrated primarily at Tripoli and Banghāzī, who are excluded from the figures for the municipalities. ‡1982. §Finance is included with trade. ‖Services are included with other. ¶Including unemployed. ♀Mostly desert. δDiscrepancy between balance of trade data and import-export detailed data for 1981 resulted from incomplete coverage in two different sources. □International scheduled flights only. ◊1979–80. △Personnel in government services only.

Liechtenstein

Official name: Fürstentum Liechtenstein (Principality of Liechtenstein).
Form of government: constitutional monarchy with one legislative house (Diet [15]).
Chief of state: Grand Duke.
Head of government: Prime Minister.
Capital: Vaduz.
Official language: German.
Official religion: none.
Monetary unit: 1 Swiss franc (SFr) = 100 centimes; valuation (Oct. 29, 1984) 1 U.S.$ = SFr2.52; 1 £ = SFr3.04.

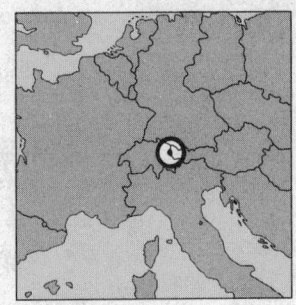

Area and population	area		population
			1984
Communes	sq mi	sq km	estimate
Balzers	7.6	19.6	3,400
Eschen	4.0	10.3	2,700
Gamprin	2.4	6.1	800
Mauren	2.9	7.5	2,600
Planken	2.1	5.3	300
Ruggell	2.9	7.4	1,200
Schaan	10.3	26.8	4,600
Schellenberg	1.4	3.5	600
Triesen	10.2	26.4	3,000
Triesenberg	11.5	29.8	2,200
Vaduz	6.7	17.3	4,900
TOTAL	62.0	160.0	26,500*

Source: Official government figures.

Demography

Density (1984): persons per sq mi 427.4, persons per sq km 165.0.
Urban–rural: n.a.
Sex distribution (1984): male 49.00%; female 51.00%.
Age breakdown (1984): under 15, 21.5%; 15–29, 27.1%; 30–44, 24.7%; 45–59, 13.5%; 60–74, 9.7%; 75 and over, 3.5%.
Population projection: (1990) 29,000; (2000) 35,000.
Doubling time: Population growth is negligible.
Ethnic composition (1984): Liechtensteiner 64.0%; Swiss 8.7%; Austrian 3.9%; other 23.4%.
Religious affiliation (1984): Roman Catholic 85.5%; Protestant 8.7%; other 5.8%.
Major cities (1984): Vaduz 4,896; Schaan 4,619.

Vital statistics

Birth rate per 1,000 population (1983): 13.2 (world avg. 29.0); (1983) legitimate 94.8%; illegitimate 5.2%.
Death rate per 1,000 population (1983): 5.7 (world avg. 11.0).
Natural increase rate per 1,000 population (1983): 7.5 (world avg. 18.0).
Total fertility rate: n.a.
Marriage rate per 1,000 population (1983): 8.7.
Divorce rate: n.a.
Infant mortality rate: no infant deaths in 1983.
Life expectancy at birth: n.a.
Major causes of death per 100,000 population (1983): malignant neoplasms (cancers) 144.0; heart disease 132.7; cerebrovascular disease 75.8.

National economy

Budget (1982). Revenue: SFr244,005,179 (taxes and interest 70.3%; post, telephone, and telegraph 21.5%). Expenditures: SFr239,290,038 (financial affairs 47.2%; education 13.4%; post, telephone, and telegraph 12.3%; social affairs 9.4%).
Public debt: none.
Tourism (1983): 79,426 visitors; expenditures by nationals abroad, n.a.
Production (metric tons except as noted). Agriculture, forestry (1982): silo corn (maize) 20,000, milk 9,841, potatoes 400, barley 280, wheat 160; livestock (number of live animals; 1983) 6,052 cattle, 3,048 pigs, 2,218 sheep; timber fellings (cu m) 19,354. Mining and quarrying: none. Manufacturing (1982): whipped cream 1,332; yogurt 59; cheese 11; wine (litres) 79,190; metal manufacturing is also important. Construction (1982): residential 164,458 cu m; nonresidential 169,523 cu m. Energy production (consumption): electricity (kW-hr; 1982) 53,350,000 (152,065,000); coal (metric tons; 1982) none (128); petroleum products (metric tons; 1982) none (35,000); natural gas (kg; 1982) none (2,271,140).
Persons economically active (1984): total 12,252 (46.2%); female participation in labour force 4,140 (33.8%); unemployed 35 (0.3%).

Price and earnings indexes (1966 = 100)							
	1976	1977	1978	1979	1980	1981	1982
Consumer price index†	166.0	168.1	169.9	176.0	183.1	195.0	206.0
Monthly earnings index	...	...	...	...	...	...	...

Household income and expenditure. Average household size (1980) 3.0; average annual income per household: n.a.; source of income: n.a.; expenditure: n.a.
Gross national product (at current market prices; 1980): U.S.$527,710,000 (U.S.$20,928 per capita).

Origin of gross domestic product				
	1984			
	in value SFr	% of total value	labour force	% of labour force
Agriculture	...	...	377	3.1
Mining	...	...	48	0.4
Manufacturing	...	...	4,278	34.9
Construction	...	...	1,050	8.6
Trade	...	...	1,643	13.4
Public utilities	...	...	113	0.9
Transportation and communication			382	3.1
Finance			686	5.6
Pub. admin., defense			582	4.8
Services			2,969	24.2
Other	...	...	124	1.0
TOTAL			12,252	100.0

Land use (1981): forested 18.7%; meadows and pastures 31.3%; agricultural and under permanent cultivation 25.0%; other 25.0%.

Foreign trade

Balance of trade (current prices)						
	1977	1978	1979	1980	1981	1982
SFr'000,000	+259.9	+235.6	+398.0	+454.6	+531.9	+523.5
% of total	33.4%	28.3%	35.3%	34.1%	38.6%	39.3%

Imports (1982): SFr403,914,000 (machinery and transport equipment 29.6%, hardware 14.2%, chemical products 6.5%, unrefined and semi-fabricated metal 4.6%). *Major import sources:* n.a..
Exports (1982): SFr927,404,000 (machinery and transport equipment 44.7%, hardware 23.1%, chemical products 7.2%). *Major export destinations:* countries of the European Economic Community 39.2%; Switzerland 23.9%; other countries of the European Free Trade Association 8.0%.

Transport and communications

Transport. Railroads (1984): length 11.5 mi, 18.5 km. Roads (1980): total length 201 mi, 323 km. Vehicles (1983): passenger cars 13,498; trucks and buses 1,488. Merchant marine: none. Air transport: none.
Communications. Daily newspapers (1984): total number 2; total circulation 14,500; circulation per 1,000 population 547. Radios (1982): total number of receivers 8,068 (1 per 3.2 persons). Television (1982): total number of receivers 7,608 (1 per 3.4 persons). Telephones (1982): 22,220 (1 per 1.2 persons).

Education and health

Education (1984–85)	schools	teachers	students	student/ teacher ratio
Primary (age 7–12)	14	97	1,793	18.5
Secondary (age 13–19)	8	141	1,805	12.8
Vocational‡	1	25	67	...

College graduates per 100,000 population: n.a. *Literacy:* 100%.
Health (1982): physicians 20 (1 per 1,307 persons); hospital beds, n.a.
Food: daily per capita caloric intake, n.a.

Military

Total active duty personnel: none. *Military expenditure as percent of* GNP: none.

*Detail does not add to total given because of rounding. †The index is for Switzerland, which is united with Liechtenstein in a customs and monetary union. ‡One evening school with part-time teachers.

Schloss (castle) Gutenberg, village of Balzers, Liechtenstein.

Luxembourg

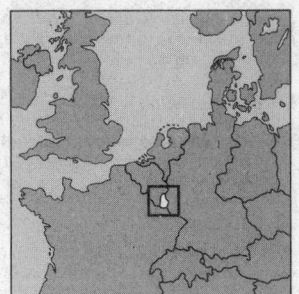

Official name: Grand-Duché
de Luxembourg (French),
Grossherzogtum Luxemburg
(German) (Grand Duchy of
Luxembourg).
Form of government: constitutional
monarchy with one legislative house
(Chamber of Deputies [59]).
Chief of state: Grand Duke.
Head of government: Prime Minister.
Capital: Luxembourg.
Official languages: French; German.
Official religion: none.
Monetary unit: 1 Luxembourg franc
(LFr., plural LFr.) = 100 centimes;
valuation (Oct. 29, 1984)
1 U.S.$ = LFr.61.81
1 £ = LFr.74.60.

Area and population	area		population
Districts Cantons	sq mi	sq km	1984 estimate
Diekirch	447	1,157	55,600
Clervaux	128	332	9,800
Diekirch	92	239	24,200
Redange	103	267	10,300
Vianden	21	54	2,600
Wiltz	102	265	8,700
Grevenmacher	203	525	39,700
Echternach	72	186	10,900
Grevenmacher	82	211	16,700
Remich	49	128	12,100
Luxembourg	349	904	278,700
Capellen	77	199	28,900
Esch	94	243	114,300
Luxembourg (Ville et Campagne)	92	238	118,100
Mersch	86	224	17,400
TOTAL	999	2,586	374,000

Source: Official government figures.

Demography

Density (1984): persons per sq mi 374.6, persons per sq km 144.6.
Urban–rural (1980): urban 78.4%; rural 21.6%.
Sex distribution (1981): male 48.78%; female 51.22%.
Age breakdown (1981): under 15, 18.5%; 15–29, 23.7%; 30–44, 21.2%; 45–59,
18.7%; 60–74, 12.8%; 75 and over, 5.1%.
Population projection: (1990) 355,000; (2000) 349,000.
During the intercensal period 1970–80, the average growth rate was 0.6%;
since 1980, however, the population has been decreasing.
Ethnic composition (1981): Luxemburger 76.3%; Italian 6.4%; Portuguese
5.6%; French 2.8%; German 2.8%; other 6.1%.
Religious affiliation (1980): Roman Catholic 93.0%; Protestant 1.2%; other
5.8%.
Major cities (1981): Luxembourg 78,924; Esch-sur-Alzette 25,142; Dudelange
14,074; Differdange 8,588.

Vital statistics

Birth rate per 1,000 population (1980–85): 10.8 (world avg. 27.5); (1982)
legitimate 96.9%, illegitimate 3.1%.
Death rate per 1,000 population (1980–85): 12.0 (world avg. 10.6).
Natural increase rate per 1,000 population (1980–85): −1.2 (world avg. 16.9).
Total fertility rate (avg. births per childbearing woman; 1980–85): 1.5.
Marriage rate per 1,000 population (1982): 5.7.
Divorce rate per 1,000 population (1982): 1.7.
Infant mortality rate per 1,000 live births (1982): 12.1.
Life expectancy at birth (1980–85): male 68.8 years; female 76.8 years.
Major causes of death per 100,000 population (1982): circulatory diseases
530.5; malignant neoplasms (cancers) 283.3.

National economy

Budget (1983). Revenue: LFr.59,263,500,000 (direct taxation 49.3%; turnover
tax, customs, and other indirect taxation 30.5). Expenditures: LFr.59,-
483,700,000 (social security 24.7%; transport and power 23.8%; education
and arts 14.7%).
Public debt (outstanding; 1983): U.S.$664,362,820.
Tourism: receipts from visitors (n.a.); expenditures by nationals abroad
(n.a.).
Production (metric tons except as noted). Agriculture, forestry, fishing
(1982): barley 69,200, oats 36,600, wheat 24,900; livestock (number of live
animals) 220,738 cattle. Mining and quarrying (1981): iron ore 429,000.
Manufacturing (1982): steel ignots and castings 3,510,000; pig iron 2,587,-
000; processed meat 19,400; wine 256,500 hectolitres. Construction (1979):
residential 466,700 sq m; nonresidential 55,500 sq m. Energy production
(consumption): electricity (kW-hr; 1982) 941,000,000 (4,093,000,000); coal
(metric tons; 1982) none (283,000); crude petroleum, none (n.a.); natural
gas (cu m; 1982) none (325,179,162).
Gross national product (at current market prices; 1981): U.S.$5,320,000,000
(U.S.$14,590 per capita).
Household income and expenditure. Average household size (1981) 2.8; income per household LFr.431,520 (U.S.$13,100); source of income: (n.a.);

expenditure (1977): food 35.0%, transportation 14.4%, housing 12.4%, clothing and footwear 8.6%, recreation 6.2%.

Origin of gross domestic product (current prices)				
	1980			
	in value LFr.'000,000	% of total value	labour force	% of labour force
Agriculture	2,656	1.6	8,500	5.3
Mining	40,994	24.9	700	0.4
Manufacturing			42,000	26.2
Construction	9,746	5.9	15,900	9.9
Trade	21,120	12.8	51,700	33.4
Public utilities	3,572	2.2	1,400	0.9
Transportation and communication	8,151	5.0	11,800	7.4
Finance	28,905	17.6	8,100	5.1
Pub. admin., defense	17,552	10.7	19,700	12.3
Services	20,473	12.4		
Other, value-added tax, import taxes	11,163	6.8	...	...
TOTAL	164,332	100.0*	159,800	100.0

Persons economically active (1981): total 150,720 (41.3%); female participation in labour force 49,956 (33.1%); unemployed 1,559 (1.0%).

Price and earnings indexes (1975 = 100)							
	1978	1979	1980	1981	1982	1983	1984
Consumer price index	120.8	126.3	134.2	145.1	158.6	172.3	180.6‡
Hourly earnings index†	132.7	138.9	149.4	156.3	...	...	...

Land use§ (1981): forested 21.4%; meadows and pastures 21.3%; agricultural
and under permanent cultivation 26.7%; other 30.6%.

Foreign trade

Balance of trade (current prices)						
	1977	1978	1979	1980	1981	1982
LFr.'000,000	−7,515	−8,652	−6,062	−12,704	−17,192	−15,868
% of total	5.4%	5.7%	3.4%	6.7%	8.8%	7.2%

Imports (1982): LFr.117,766,000,000 (machinery and transport equipment
21.9%; mineral fuels, lubricants, and related materials 20.1%; nonprecious
unworked and worked metals 10.9%; chemicals and related products 7.5%;
food, beverages, and tobacco 7.3%). *Major import sources:* Belgium 37.3%;
West Germany 34.1%; France 12.5%; The Netherlands 3.6%; United States
2.5%.
Exports (1982): LFr.101,898,000,000 (nonprecious unworked and worked
metals 47.7%; machinery and transport equipment 13.2%; plastic materials
and rubber manufactures 13.1%; textile yarn, fabrics, and related products
5.9%). *Major export destinations:* West Germany 27.9%; Belgium 17.0%;
France 16.7%; The Netherlands 6.0%; United States 5.2%.

Transport and communications

Transport. Railroads (1982): length 168 mi, 270 km; passenger-mi 193,188,-
000, passenger-km 310,907,000; short ton-mi cargo 378,122,000, metric ton-
km cargo 552,048,000. Roads (1982): total length 3,174 mi, 5,108 km (paved
99%). Vehicles (1982): passenger cars 159,580; trucks and buses 14,889.
Merchant marine: vessels (100 gross tons and over) n.a.; total deadweight
tonnage (n.a.). Air transport (1982): passenger arrivals 301,964, departures
305,211; cargo arrivals 26,287 metric tons, cargo departures 37,812 metric
tons; airport (1984) with scheduled flights 1.
Communications. Daily newspapers (1982): total number 6; total circulation
130,000; circulation per 1,000 population 355. Radios (1983): total number
of receivers 225,000 (1 per 1.6 persons). Television (1983): total number
of receivers 91,100 (1 per 4.0 persons). Telephones (1982): 228,000 (1
per 1.6 persons).

Education and health

Education (1981–82)	schools	teachers	students	student/ teacher ratio
Primary (age 6–15)	541	1,734	27,927	16.1
Secondary (age 12–18)	...	2,145 ‖¶	9,080	
Voc., teacher tr.	1	49§	152	
Higher	1	132§	232	

College graduates per 100,000 population: n.a. *Literacy* (1983): virtually
100% literate.
Health (1982): physicians 605 (1 per 604 persons); hospital beds 4,816 (1
per 76 persons).
Food (1978–80): daily per capita caloric intake§ 3,938 (vegetable products
62.1%, animal products 37.9%); 153% of FAO recommended minimum.

Military

Total active duty personnel (1983): 720 (army 100.0%,). *Military expenditure* as percent of GNP (1982): 1.0% (world 6.0%; per capita expenditure
U.S.$125.

*Detail does not add to total given because of rounding. †Manufacturing only. ‡First
quarter. §Figures for Belgium–Luxembourg. ‖ Includes full-time and part-time teachers. ¶Includes primary and secondary (secondary entered at 12 or 15 years of age).

Macau

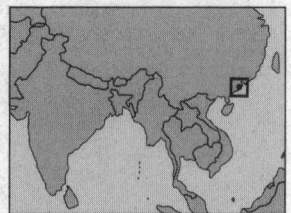

Official name: Provincia de Macau
(Province of Macau).
Political status: overseas province
(Portugal).
Head of state and government:
Governor (appointed).
Capital: Macau.
Official language: Portuguese.
Official religion: Roman Catholicism.
Monetary unit: 1 pataca* = 100 avos;
valuation (Oct. 29, 1984)
1 U.S.$ = 8.13 patacas; 1 £ = 9.83
patacas.

Area and population

Districts	Capital	area sq mi	area sq km	population 1981 census
Marine area				13,472
Islands†		3.90	10.09	10,093
Macau	Macau	2.09	5.42	238,413
TOTAL		5.99	15.51	261,680

Demography

Density (1984): persons per sq mi 43,686, persons per sq km 16,872.
Urban–rural (1981): urban 94.9%‡.
Sex distribution (1981): male 51.95%; female 48.05%.
Age breakdown (1970): under 15, 37.6%; 15–29, 28.9%; 30–44, 15.0%; 45–59, 11.3%; 60–74, 5.9%; 75 and over, 1.3%.
Population projection: (1990) 273,000; (2000) 286,000.
Doubling time: 36 years.
Ethnic composition (1970): Chinese 96.5%; Portuguese 3.0%; other 0.5%.
Religious affiliation (1970): Buddhist and Taoist 76.7%; Roman Catholic 9.4%; nonreligious 11.9%; other 2.0%.
Major city (1981): Macau 238,413.

Vital statistics

Birth rate per 1,000 population (1982): 15.4 (world avg. 29.0).
Death rate per 1,000 population (1982): 4.5 (world avg. 11.0).
Natural increase rate per 1,000 population (1982): 10.9 (world avg. 18.0).
Total fertility rate (avg. births per childbearing woman; 1980–85): 3.4.
Marriage rate per 1,000 population (1982): 5.7.
Divorce rate per 1,000 population (1982): 0.1.
Infant mortality rate per 1,000 live births (1982): 11.6.
Life expectancy at birth (1979): male 68.0 years; female 73.0 years.
Major causes of death per 100,000 population (1982): diseases of the circulatory system 124.9; malignant neoplasms (cancers) 83.4; infectious and parasitic diseases 33.1.

National economy

Budget (1982). Revenue: 661,296,000 patacas (direct taxes 31.5%, indirect taxes 20.2%, property sales 5.7%). Expenditures: 661,296,000 patacas (expenditures on financial services 31.2%, security forces 16.9%, health and social welfare 6.6%, education 5.2%).
Public debt: none.
Tourism (1982): number of tourists 4,987,303.
Production (metric tons except as noted). Fishing (1982): fish 7,545. Mining and quarrying (1982): granite 656,920. Manufacturing (1982): clothing 25,-529; knitwear 11,659; meat 9,356; furniture 2,042; wine 1,188; explosive and pyrotechnic products 732; optical materials 314; footwear 244. Construction (1982): residential 39,633 sq m; commercial 22,126 sq m; industrial 25,991 sq m; mixed use 175,257 sq m. Energy production (consumption): electricity (kW-hr; 1982) 337,000,000 (337,000,000); coal (metric tons; 1982) none (1,000); petroleum (barrels; 1981) none (2,559); petroleum products (metric tons; 1982) none (154,000); natural gas, none (n.a.).
Gross national product (at current market prices; 1980): U.S.$640,000,000 (U.S.$1,980 per capita).

Origin of gross domestic product

	1981 in value	1981 % of total value	labour force	% of labour force
Agriculture	...	...	4,332	5.7
Mining	...	...	62	0.1
Manufacturing	...	...	47,377	62.7
Construction	...	...	4,897	6.5
Trade	...	...	10,171	13.5
Public utilities	...	...	1,006	1.3
Transportation and communication	...	...	971	1.3
Pub. admin. and services	...	...	6,872	9.1
TOTAL	...	...	75,517	100.0§

Persons economically active (1981): total 75,517 (28.9%).

Price and earnings indexes (1970 = 100)

	1975	1976	1977	1978	1979	1980	1981
Consumer price index	165.3	195.6	208.3	219.3	223.5	270.4	291.4
Monthly earnings index	...	...	...	...	...	...	...

Household income and expenditure: n.a.
Land use (1979): forested 50.0%; agricultural and under permanent cultivation 4.0%; other 46.0%.

Foreign trade

Balance of trade (current prices)

'000,000	1977	1978	1979	1980	1981	1982
patacas	119.1	50.6	196.4	−38.0	−112.2	38.5
% of total	5.1%	2.0%	5.1%	−0.7%	−1.4%	0.4%

Imports (1982): 4,440,785,000 patacas (woven cotton fabrics 13.1%; machinery and electrical equipment 9.3%; man-made fabrics 7.8%; mineral fuels 5.9%; building materials 4.8%; iron and steel casting 2.8%; plastic materials 2.1%; tobacco [manufactured] 1.9%; cattle for slaughter 1.9%; paperboard 1.6%; clothing 1.5%). *Major import sources:* Hong Kong 37.6%; China 29.3%; Japan 9.4%; United States 8.1%; United Kingdom 2.3%; Portugal 0.6%.
Exports (1982): 4,479,262,000 patacas (textile and textile articles 64.7%, of which articles of apparel and clothing 35.4%, knitwear 29.3%; ceramic products 1.4%; leather manufactures 1.2%; shrimp 0.7%; optical articles 0.6%). *Major export destinations:* United States 23.5%; Hong Kong 21.0%; West Germany 12.0%; France 11.7%; United Kingdom 6.0%; Italy 4.3%; The Netherlands 2.4%; Portugal 2.0%.

Transport and communications

Transport. Railroads (1982): none. Roads (1982): total length 56 mi, 90 km (paved 100%). Vehicles (1982): passenger cars 15,606; trucks and buses 4,023. Merchant marine (1981): vessels 137; total deadweight tonnage 14,-381. Air transport: none.
Communications. Daily newspapers (1983): total number 8; circulation, n.a. Radios (1983): total number of receivers 78,000 (1 per 3.9 persons). Television (1979): total number of receivers 59,000 (1 per 5.3 persons). Telephones (1982): 15,955 (1 per 16 persons).

Education and health

Education (1982–83)

	schools	teachers	students	student/ teacher ratio
Primary (age 6–11)	62	1,023	30,134	29.5
Secondary (age 12–18)	25	590	10,876	18.4
Voc., teacher tr.	6	70	1,635	23.4
Higher	1	90	1,165	12.9

College graduates per 100,000 population (1982): none. *Literacy* (1979): total population literate 123,321 (49.5%); males literate 66,568 (52.1%); females literate 56,753 (46.9%).
Health: physicians (1982) 386 (1 per 907 persons); hospital beds (1977) 1,708 (1 per 158 persons).
Food (1978–80): daily per capita caloric intake 2,320 (vegetable products 74.2%, animal products 25.8%); 101% of FAO recommended minimum requirement.

Military

Total active duty personnel (1982): 1,800 (army 100%).

*The pataca free floats with the Hong Kong dollar and has a parity of 1 pataca equal to HK$0.93. †Comprising the islands of Coloane and Taipa. ‡5.1% of Macau's population lives on sampans and other vessels. §Detail does not add to total given because of rounding.

FRED WARD—BLACK STAR

Ruins of Saint Paul (São Paulo), Macau.

Madagascar

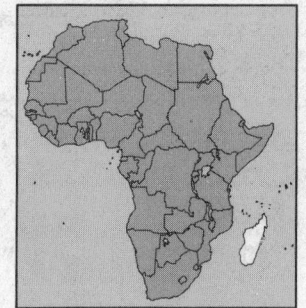

Official name: Repoblika Demokratika
Malagasy (Malagasy), République
Démocratique de Madagascar
(French) (Democratic Republic of
Madagascar).
Form of government: multiparty
republic with one legislative house
(National People's Assembly [137]).
Chief of state: President.
Head of government: Prime Minister.
Capital: Antananarivo.
Official languages: Malagasy
and French.
Official religion: none.
Monetary unit: 1 franc (FMG) = 100
centimes; valuation (Oct. 29, 1984)
1 U.S.$ = FMG630.99;
1 £ = FMG761.60.

Area and population		area		population
		sq mi	sq km	1985 estimate
Provinces	**Capitals**			
Antananarivo	Antananarivo	22,503	58,283	3,058,100
Antsiranana	Antsiranana	16,624	43,056	660,500
Fianarantsoa	Fianarantsoa	39,526	102,373	2,114,800
Mahajanga	Mahajanga	57,924	150,023	1,029,100
Toamasina	Toamasina	27,765	71,911	1,382,500
Toliary	Toliary	62,319	161,405	1,336,700
TOTAL		226,662*	587,051	9,581,700

Sources: Official government figures; Britannica estimates.

Demography

Density (1985): persons per sq mi 42.3, persons per sq km 16.3.
Urban–rural (1980): urban 18.4%; rural 81.6%.
Sex distribution (1985): male 49.25%; female 50.75%.
Age breakdown (1985): under 15, 44.2%; 15–29, 25.8%; 30–44, 15.3%; 45–59, 9.3%; 60–74, 4.5%; 75 and over, 0.9%.
Population projection: (1990) 11,222,000; (2000) 14,453,000.
Doubling time: 27 years.
Ethnic composition (1978): Malagasy 98.8%, of which Merina 25.9%, Betsimisaraka 14.6%, Betsileo 12.0%, Tsimihety 7.3%, Sakalava 6.1%; Antandroy 54.4%; Comorian 0.3%; Indian and Pakistani 0.2%; French 0.2%; other 0.5%.
Religious affiliation (1985): Christian 51.0%; traditional beliefs 47.0%; Muslim 1.7%; other 0.3%.
Major cities (1980): Antananarivo 547,139; Toamasina 95,505; Fianarantsoa 83,250; Mahajanga 80,881.

Vital statistics

Birth rate per 1,000 population (1980–85): 44.8 (world avg. 27.5); legitimate n.a., illegitimate n.a.
Death rate per 1,000 population (1980–85): 17.2 (world avg. 10.6).
Natural increase rate per 1,000 population (1980–85): 27.6 (world avg. 16.9).
Total fertility rate (avg. births per childbearing woman; 1980–85): 6.1.
Marriage rate per 1,000 population: n.a.
Divorce rate per 1,000 population: n.a.
Infant mortality rate per 1,000 live births (1981): 69.5.
Life expectancy at birth (1980–85): male 46.9 years; female 50.2 years.
Major causes of death per 100,000 population: no data available; however, the major diseases are malaria, leprosy, and tuberculosis.

National economy

Budget (1984). Revenue: FMG190,550,000,000 (indirect taxes 45%, direct taxes 30%). Expenditures: FMG248,550,000,000 (education 20.9%, defense 12.8%, health 4.8%).
Public debt (external, outstanding; 1983): U.S.$1,300,000,000.
Tourism (1981): receipts from visitors U.S.$5,000,000; expenditures by nationals abroad U.S.$38,000,000.
Production (metric tons except as noted). Agriculture, forestry, fishing (1982): rice 2,000,000, cassava 1,807,000, sweet potatoes 422,000, bananas 280,000, potatoes 271,000, sugarcane 152,000, corn (maize) 127,000, coffee 83,600, sisal 13,700, cloves 12,500, vanilla 4,500, black pepper 3,000, cacao 1,900; livestock (number of live animals) 10,150,000 cattle, 1,474,000 goats, 721,000 pigs, 633,000 sheep; roundwood 6,262,000 cu m; fish catch 48,000. Mining and quarrying (1983): chromite 42,920; graphite 13,548; mica 1,096. Manufacturing (1982): distillate fuel oils 116,740; motor spirit 76,005; cement 35,921; sugar 82,159; residual fuel oils 163,068 cu m; kerosene 46,506 cu m; beer 190,071 hectolitres. Construction (1981): residential 32,900 sq m; nonresidential 5,100 sq m. Energy production (consumption): electricity (kW-hr; 1982) 425,000,000 (425,000,000); coal (metric tons; 1982) none (13,-000); crude petroleum (barrels; 1982) none (2,720,610); petroleum products (metric tons; 1982) 351,000 (383,000); natural gas, none (n.a.).
Persons economically active (1981): total 4,353,000 (48.5%); female participation in the labour force 1,937,000 (44.5%); unemployed n.a.

Price and earnings indexes (1980 = 100)						
	1978	1979	1980	1981	1982	1983	1984†
Consumer price index	74.2	84.6	100.0	130.5	171.5	205.3	216.8
Earnings index	...	...	...	...	...	...	...

Gross national product (at current market prices; 1981): U.S.$2,960,000,000 (U.S.$330 per capita).

Origin of gross domestic product (current prices)				
	1981			
	in value FMG'000,000,000	% of total value	labour force	% of labour force
Agriculture	276.4	35.2	3,590,000	82.5
Mining	...	...	...	...
Manufacturing	113.0	14.4	...	...
Construction	...	...	...	...
Trade	...	...	...	...
Public utilities	90.0	11.5	...	...
Transportation and communication	...	...	...	...
Finance	...	...	...	...
Pub. admin., defense	...	...	...	...
Services	...	...	...	...
Other	304.6	36.8	763,000	17.5
TOTAL	784.0	100.0*	4,353,000	100.0

Household income and expenditure. Average household size (1981) 5.1; average annual income per household FMG4,485 (U.S.$1,650); source of income: n.a.; expenditure (1981): food 60.4%, housing and other 14.9%, fuel and lighting 9.1%.
Land use (1981): forested 22.9%; meadows and pastures 58.5%; agricultural and under permanent cultivation 5.2%; other 13.4%.

Foreign trade

Balance of trade							
	1977	1978	1979	1980	1981	1982	1983
FMG'000,000,000	−2.29	−12.42	−51.49	−41.99	−38.86	−56.6	−43.7
% of total	1.4%	6.6%	23.%	19.8%	18.8%	19.9%	...

Imports (1981): FMG122,584,000,000 (machinery 21.7%; mineral products 14.7%, of which petroleum 6.4%; chemical products 10.9%; metal products 10.0%; vehicles and parts 8.8%; electrical equipment 7.0%). *Major import sources:* France 38.5%; West Germany 10.3%; Italy 4.7%; United States 4.2%; The Netherlands 3.2%; Japan 3.1%; Belgium–Luxembourg 3.0%.
Exports (1981): FMG83,720,000,000 (coffee [green] 36.3%; cloves and clove oil 22.1%; rice 21.5%; vanilla 8.9%). *Major export destinations:* France 20.8%; United States 12.1%; Japan 9.2%; West Germany 6.7%; The Netherlands 3.5%; Réunion 3.0%; Italy 2.2%; United Kingdom 1.7%.

Transport and communications

Transport. Railroads (1983): route length 644 mi, 1,036 km; passenger-mi 173,861,000, passenger-km 279,802,000; short ton-mi cargo 152,507,000, metric ton-km cargo 222,657,000. Roads (1982): total length 30,843 mi, 49,637 km (paved n.a.). Vehicles (1982): passenger cars 55,000; trucks and buses 50,000. Merchant marine (1983): vessels (100 gross tons and over) 58; total deadweight tonnage 107,071. Air transport (1983): passenger-mi 239,-000,000, passenger-km 384,000,000; short ton-mi cargo 13,500,000, metric ton-km cargo 19,700,000; airports (1984) with scheduled flights 35.
Communications. Daily newspapers (1983): total number 2; total circulation n.a. Radios (1983): total number of receivers 910,000 (1 per 10.3 persons). Television (1983): total number of receivers 71,000 (1 per 132 persons). Telephones (1983): 37,100 (1 per 253 persons).

Education and health

Education (1978)				
	schools	teachers	students	student/ teacher ratio
Primary (age 6–14)	8,002	23,937	1,311,000	54.8
Secondary	...	114,468‡	5,088‡	...
Voc., teacher tr.	...	942§	10,900 ‖	...
Higher	...	557	16,226	29.1

College graduates per 100,000 population (students graduating, 1979): 14.1.
Literacy (1980): total population literate 2,826,000 (53.0%); males literate n.a.; females literate n.a.
Health: physicians (1981) 901 (1 per 9,945 persons); hospital beds (1978) 20,625 (1 per 400 persons).
Food (1978–80): daily per capita caloric intake 2,436 (vegetable products 92.8%, animal products 7.2%); 107% of FAO recommended minimum requirement.

Military

Total active duty personnel (1984): 21,100 (army 94.8%; navy 2.8%; air force 2.4%). *Military expenditure as percent of GNP* (1982): 3.0% (world 5.7%); per capita expenditure U.S.$12.

*Detail does not add to total given because of rounding. †January. ‡1976. §1973. ‖ 1979.

Malaŵi

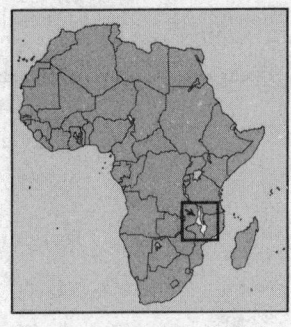

Official name: Malaŵi (Republic of Malaŵi).
Form of government: unitary single-party republic with one legislative house (National Assembly [101]).
Head of state and government: President.
Capital: Lilongwe.
Official languages: Chichewa; English.
Official religion: none.
Monetary unit: 1 Malaŵi kwacha (MK) = 100 Tambala; valuation (Oct. 29, 1984) 1 U.S.$ = MK1.53; 1 £ = MK1.85.

Area and population

Regions Districts	Capitals	area* sq mi	area* sq km	population 1977 census
Central	Lilongwe	13,742	35,592	2,143,716
Dedza	Dedza	1,399	3,624	298,190
Dowa	Dowa	1,174	3,041	247,603
Kasungu	Kasungu	3,042	7,878	194,436
Lilongwe	Lilongwe	2,378	6,159	704,117
Mchinji	Mchinji	1,296	3,356	158,833
Nkhotakota	Nkhotakota	1,644	4,259	94,370
Ntcheu	Ntcheu	1,322	3,424	226,454
Ntchisi	Ntchisi	639	1,655	87,437
Salima	Salima	848	2,196	132,276
Northern	Mzuzu	10,398	26,931	648,853
Chitipa	Chitipa	1,353	3,504	72,316
Karonga	Karonga	1,141	2,955	106,923
Mzimba	Mzimba	4,027	10,430	301,361
Nkhata Bay	Nkhata Bay	1,579	4,090	105,803
Rumphi	Rumphi	2,298	5,952	62,450
Southern	Blantyre	12,260	31,752	2,754,891
Blantyre	Blantyre	777	2,012	408,062
Chikwawa	Chikwawa	1,836	4,755	194,425
Chiradzulu	Chiradzulu	296	767	176,184
Machinga	Machinga	2,303	5,964	341,836
Mangochi	Mangochi	2,422	6,272	302,341
Mulanje	Mulanje	1,332	3,450	477,546
Mwanza	Mwanza	886	2,295	71,405
Nsanje	Nsanje	750	1,942	108,758
Thyolo	Thyolo	662	1,715	322,000
Zomba	Zomba	996	2,580	352,334
TOTAL		36,400	94,276†	5,547,460

Source: Official government figures.

Demography

*Density** (1984): persons per sq mi 187.9, persons per sq km 72.5.
Urban–rural (1980): urban 9.6%; rural 90.4%.
Sex distribution (1980): male 49.30%; female 50.70%.
Age breakdown (1980): under 15, 47.6%; 15–64, 49.9%; 65 and over, 2.5%.
Population projection: (1990) 8,634,000; (2000) 12,014,000.
Doubling time: 22 years.
Ethnic composition (1978): Maravi (including Nyanja, Chewa, Tonga, and Tumbuka) 58.2%; Lomwe 18.3%; Yao 13.2%; Ngoni 6.7%; other 3.6%.
Religious affiliation (1980): Christian 57.2%, of which Protestant 25.7%, Roman Catholic 25.0%; animist 19.0%; Muslim 16.2%; other 7.6%.
Major cities (1977): Blantyre 219,011; Lilongwe 98,718; Zomba 24,234.

Vital statistics

Birth rate per 1,000 population (1981): 56.2 (world avg. 29.0).
Death rate per 1,000 population (1981): 22.8 (world avg. 12.0).
Natural increase rate per 1,000 population (1981): 33.4 (world avg. 17.0).
Total fertility rate (avg. births per childbearing woman; 1981): 7.8.
Marriage rate per 1,000 population (1977): 7.8.
Divorce rate per 1,000 population (1977): 1.4.
Infant mortality rate per 1,000 live births (1981): 169.1.
Life expectancy at birth (1981): male 42.7 years; female 45.4 years.
Major causes of death‡ (1980): measles 1,122; pneumonia 927; avitaminosis and other nutritional deficiencies 642; diarrheal diseases 551.

National economy

Budget (1982–83). Revenue: MK286,240,000 (indirect taxes 43.3%, of which surtax 20.8%; import duties 16.1%; direct taxes 25.9%; grants and reimbursements 14.4%). Expenditures: MK408,600,000 (public debt charges 20.3%; education and health 19.8%; agriculture and natural resources 13.9%).
Public debt (external, outstanding; 1982): U.S.$691,800,000.
Tourism (1982): receipts from visitors U.S.$10,964,400; expenditures by nationals abroad, n.a.
Production (metric tons except as noted). Agriculture, forestry, fishing (1982): sugarcane 1,829,000, corn (maize) 1,415,000, peanuts (groundnuts) 180,000, sorghum 145,000, potatoes 121,000, tobacco 56,000, tea 38,000; livestock (number of live animals) 880,000 cattle, 656,000 goats; roundwood 6,252,000 cu m; fish catch 58,416. Mining and quarrying (1981): marble 116,000; cement 78,000. Manufacturing (value added in MK; 1979): cigarettes 39,100,000; beverages 32,000,000; processed food 29,500,000; textiles, nettings, and blankets 25,500,000. Construction (value in MK; 1981)§: residential 4,228,000; nonresidential 3,430,000. Energy production (consumption): electricity (kW-hr; 1983) 445,800,000 (393,300,000); coal (metric tons; 1982) none (72,000); crude petroleum, none (none); petroleum products (metric tons; 1982) none (139,000); natural gas (cu m; 1982) none (n.a.).

Gross national product (at current market prices; 1981): U.S.$1,250,000,000 (U.S.$200 per capita).

Origin of gross domestic product (current prices)

	1982 in value MK'000,000	% of total value	labour force ‖	% of labour force
Agriculture¶	518	36.7	178,100	51.7
Mining	...	...	600	0.2
Manufacturing	144	10.2	31,700	9.2
Construction	57	4.1	24,500	7.1
Trade	175	12.4	23,000	6.7
Public utilities	25	1.8	4,300	1.2
Transportation and communication	74	5.2	16,800	4.9
Finance	64	4.5	9,900	2.9
Public administration	142	10.1	—	—
Private services	49	3.5	55,400⍩	16.1
Other	162	11.5	200	...
TOTAL	1,410	100.0	344,500	100.0

Persons economically active (1977): total 2,288,351ŏ (41.4%); female participation in the labour force 1,056,539 (46.2%); unemployed 44,414 (1.9%).

Price and earnings indexes (1977 = 100)

	1977	1978	1979	1980	1981	1982	1983
Consumer price index	100.0	108.6	120.5	143.5	157.1	171.1	198.1
Monthly earnings index	100.0	116.7	122.7	143.1	161.6	180.8	...

Household income and expenditure (1979–80). Average household size□ 4.5; income per household MK1,934 (U.S.$2,419◊); source of income: wages 83.3%, household enterprise 6.0%; expenditure: food 23.7%, transportation and communication 13.7%, household equipment 9.9%, clothing and footwear 8.0%, housing 7.6%.
Land use (1981): forested 46.3%; meadows and pastures 19.6%; agricultural and under permanent cultivation 24.7%; other 9.4%.

Foreign trade

Balance of trade (current prices)

	1977	1978	1979	1980	1981	1982
MK'000	−29,434	−129,090	−143,130	−126,200	−64,455	−50,941
% of total	7.5%	29.3%	28.3%	21.5%	11.1%	8.5%

Imports (1981): MK321,900,000 (petroleum products 16.7%; fertilizers 10.6%; boilers, machinery, and mechanical appliances 9.7%; road vehicles [including parts] 6.8%; electrical machinery 6.5%; iron and steel [all forms] 4.7%; cereals 3.8%). *Major import sources:* South Africa 32.3%; United Kingdom 13.7%; West Germany 8.0%; Japan 6.1%; Zimbabwe 5.9%.
Exports (1981): MK246,000,000△ (tobacco 41.3%, sugar 27.3%, tea 12.6%, peanuts [groundnuts] 4.3%). *Major export destinations:* United States 27.8%; United Kingdom 22.6%; Zimbabwe 8.2%; West Germany 7.4%.

Transport and communications

Transport. Railroads (1982): route length 490 mi, 789 km; passenger-mi 60,413,000, passenger-km 97,225,000; short ton-mi cargo 126,917,000, metric ton-km cargo 185,295,000. Roads (1981): total length 6,693 mi, 10,772 km. Vehicles (1981): passenger cars 14,102; trucks and buses 17,247. Merchant marine (1983): vessel (100 gross tons and over) 1; total deadweight tonnage 100. Air transport (1982): passenger-mi 89,337,000, passenger-km 143,774,000; short ton-mi cargo 825,000, metric ton-km cargo 1,205,000; airports (1984) with scheduled flights 4.
Communications. Daily newspaper (1983): total number 1; total circulation 13,000; circulation per 1,000 population 2. Radios (1983): total number of receivers 500,000 (1 per 12 persons). Television (1983): total number of receivers, n.a. Telephones (1981): 15,130 (1 per 421 persons).

Education and health

Education (1980–81)

	schools	teachers	students	student/ teacher ratio
Primary	2,340	12,540	809,862	64.6
Secondary	66	834	18,006	21.6
Teacher training	5	114	2,931†	15.4
Higher	1	173	1,712	9.9

College graduates per 100,000 population (students graduating; 1980): 9.
Literacy (1980): total population literate 1,027,700 (32.7%); males literate 717,300 (46.6%); females literate 310,400 (19.3%).
Health: physicians (1981) 121 (1 per 52,644 persons); hospital beds (1980) 11,375⊕ (1 per 525 persons).
Food (1978–80): daily per capita caloric intake 2,219 (vegetable products 95.8%, animal products 4.2%); 96% of FAO recommended minimum.

Military

Total active duty personnel (1982): 4,550 (army 100%). *Military expenditure as percent of GNP* (1981): 3.0% (world 5.7%); per capita expenditure U.S.$6.

*Land area only. Total area of Malaŵi is 45,747 sq mi (118,484 sq km). †Detail does not add to total given because of rounding. ‡Reported inpatient deaths in hospitals. §New construction in the cities of Blantyre and Lilongwe only. ‖ Employed persons only. ¶Both estate and smallholder agriculture. ⍩Community, social, and personal services. ŏIncludes 1,932,122 people working in agriculture. □Based on a sample survey of the city of Blantyre. ◊Based on end of 1979 conversion factor. △Not including MK11,500,000 worth of re-exports. †Includes 1,180 vocational students. ⊕Includes primary health care centres and dispensaries.

Malaysia

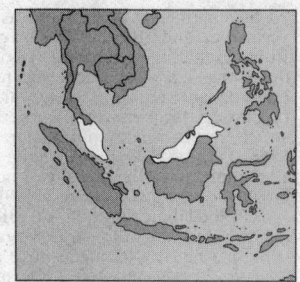

Official name: Malaysia.
Form of government: federal constitutional monarchy with two legislative houses (Senate [68]; House of Representatives [154]).
Chief of state: Yang di-Pertuan Agung.
Head of government: Prime Minister.
Capital: Kuala Lumpur.
Official language: Malay.
Official religion: Islām.
Monetary unit: 1 ringgit, or Malaysian dollar (M$) = 100 cents; valuation (Oct. 29, 1984) 1 U.S.$ = M$2.39; 1 £ = M$2.88.

Area and population

Regions States	Capitals	area sq mi	area sq km	population 1982 estimate
East Malaysia				
Sabah	Kota Kinabalu	28,460	73,711	1,313,000
Sarawak	Kuching	48,050	124,449	1,690,000
West Malaysia				
Johor	Johor Baharu	7,330	18,985	1,649,000
Kedah	Alor Setar	3,639	9,425	1,122,000
Kelantan	Kota Baharu	5,765	14,931	904,000
Melaka	Melaka	640	1,658	465,000
Negeri Sembilan	Seremban	2,565	6,646	574,000
Pahang	Kuantan	13,884	35,960	805,000
Pinang	Pinang	398	1,031	930,000
Perak	Ipoh	8,110	21,005	1,811,000
Perlis	Kangar	307	795	150,000
Selangor	Shah Alam	3,072	7,956	1,486,000
Terengganu	Kuala Terengganu	5,002	12,955	552,000
Federal Territory				
Kuala Lumpur	Kuala Lumpur	94	243	959,000
TOTAL		127,317*	329,750	14,410,000

Source: Official government figures.

Demography

Density (1984): persons per sq mi 119.7, persons per sq km 46.2.
Urban–rural (1980): urban 34.2%; rural 65.8%.
Sex distribution (1980): male 50.16%; female 49.84%.
Age breakdown (1980): under 15, 39.5%; 15–29, 29.1%; 30–44, 16.5%; 45–59, 9.2%; 60–74, 4.6%; 75 and over, 1.1%.
Population projection: (1990) 17,036,000; (2000) 20,308,000.
Doubling time: 38 years.
Ethnic composition (1980): Malay 47.1%; Chinese 31.7%; Indian 8.4%; other 12.8%.
Religious affiliation (1980): Muslim 52.9%; Buddhist 17.3%; Chinese folk-religionist 11.6%; Hindu 7.0%; Christian 6.4%; other 4.8%.
Major cities (1980): Kuala Lumpur 919,610; Ipoh 293,849; Pinang 248,241; Johor Baharu 246,395; Petaling Jaya 207,805.

Vital statistics

Birth rate per 1,000 population (1983): 28.6 (world avg. 29.0); legitimate, n.a., illegitimate, n.a.
Death rate per 1,000 population (1983): 6.4 (world avg. 11.0).
Natural increase rate per 1,000 population (1983): 22.2 (world avg. 18.0).
Total fertility rate (avg. births per childbearing woman; 1983): 3.5.
Marriage rate per 1,000 population (1979): 1.7.
Divorce rate per 1,000 population (1979): 0.02.
Infant mortality rate per 1,000 live births (1983): 40.0.
Life expectancy at birth (1983): male 65.2 years; female 69.0 years.
Major causes of death per 100,000 population (1979): diseases of the circulatory system 40.6; malignant neoplasms (cancers) 17.5; diseases of the respiratory system 11.8; infectious and parasitic diseases 9.7.

National economy

Budget (1983). Revenue: M$18,129,000,000 (indirect taxes 45.4%, direct taxes 42.7%, nontax revenue 11.9%). Expenditures: M$28,257,000,000 (economic services 28.6%, education 14.7%, public debt service 13.9%, defense 11.9%, general administration 6.7%, health 3.8%).
Public debt (external, outstanding; 1982): U.S.$7,670,700,000.
Tourism (1981): receipts from visitors U.S.$357,000,000; expenditures by nationals abroad U.S.$480,000,000.
Production (metric tons except as noted). Agriculture, forestry, fishing (1983): palm oil 3,017,900, rice 1,818,100, rubber 1,561,300, palm kernel oil 403,700, pineapples 153,000, coconut oil 72,000, cacao 65,000, peppers 23,-500; livestock (number of live animals; 1982) 2,111,000 pigs, 538,000 cattle, 328,000 goats, 181,000 buffaloes, 69,000 sheep, 53,630,000 poultry; roundwood 34,231,000 cu m; fish catch 713,300. Mining and quarrying (1983): bauxite 501,800; copper 123,400; iron ore 113,700; tin concentrates 41,400. Manufacturing (1981): cement 3,126,000†; refined sugar 462,071; chemical fertilizers 462,016; iron and steel pipes and tubes fittings 144,994; condensed milk 106,362; galvanized iron sheets 70,483; coconut oil expressed 61,685; canned pineapple 36,261; manufactured tobacco 15,115‡; footwear 28,334,000 pairs†. Construction: n.a. Energy production (consumption): electricity (kW-hr; 1983) 12,200,000,000 (9,700,000,000); coal (metric tons; 1982) none (136,000); petroleum (barrels; 1983) 144,966,000 (48,520,000†); petroleum products (metric tons; 1982) 5,852,000 (8,103,000); natural gas (cu m; 1982) 1,380,000,000, (2,256,000,000).

Gross national product (at current market prices; 1983): U.S.$29,781,000,000 (U.S.$2,010 per capita).

Origin of gross domestic product (current prices)

	1983 in value M$'000,000	% of total value	labour force	% of labour force
Agriculture	15,116	22.4	1,940,900	34.8
Mining	2,969	4.1	64,900	1.2
Manufacturing	12,079	17.9	800,300	14.3
Construction	3,779	5.6	345,600	6.2
Trade	9,110	13.5	662,100	11.9
Public utilities	1,620	2.4	56,800	1.0
Transportation and communication	5,397	8.0	241,800	4.3
Finance	5,399	8.0	50,700	0.9
Pub. admin., defense	8,975	13.3	837,100	15.0
Services	1,754‡	2.6‡	244,600	4.4
Other	1,282	1.9	...	...
Unemployed			335,200	6.0
TOTAL	67,480	100.0	5,580,000	100.0

Persons economically active (1983): total 5,580,000 (37%); female participation in the labour force, n.a.; unemployed 335,000 (6.0%).

Price and earnings indexes (1980 = 100)

	1978	1979	1980	1981	1982	1983	1984
Consumer price index	90.5	93.7	100.0	109.7	116.1	120.4	125.4§
Earnings index	...	...	...	...	...	...	...

Household income and expenditure. Average household size (1980) 5.3; average annual income per household: n.a.; source of income: n.a.; expenditure (1973): food 39.6%, transportation 15.2%, housing 10.9%, clothing 6.4%, health 2.0%, education 0.8%.
Land use (1981): forested 67.4%; meadows and pastures 0.1%; agricultural and under permanent cultivation 13.2%; other 19.3%.

Foreign trade

Balance of trade (current prices)

	1978	1979	1980	1981	1982	1983
M$'000,000	+3,428	+7,061	+4,721	+505	−865	+2,100
% of total	11.1%	17.1%	9.1%	0.9%	1.5%	3.3%

Imports (1983): M$30,700,000,000 (petroleum products 7.8%; crude petroleum 5.3%; cereals 2.7%, of which corn (maize) 1.1%, wheat 0.8%, rice 0.8%; passenger cars 2.7%). *Major import sources:* Japan 25.3%; Australia 16.1%; Singapore 14.0%; West Germany 5.2%; Saudi Arabia 4.3%.
Exports (1983): M$32,800,000,000 (crude petroleum 24.0%; sawlogs and sawn lumber 12.2%; rubber 11.2%; palm oil and palm kernel oil 10.6%; tin and concentrates 5.2%) *Major export destinations:* Singapore 22.5%; Japan 19.7%; United States 13.2%; The Netherlands 5.4%; South Korea 4.7%.

Transport and communications

Transport. Railroads (1982): length 1,666 mi, 2,681 km; passenger-mi 1,269,-000,000, passenger-km 2,042,000,000; short ton-mi cargo 762,342,000, metric ton-km cargo 1,113,000,000. Roads (1982): total length 24,084 mi, 38,759 km (paved 65%). Vehicles (1983): passenger cars 1,150,630; trucks and buses 266,340. Merchant marine (1983): vessels (100 gross tons and over) 376; total deadweight tonnage 2,075,387. Air transport (1982): passenger-mi 3,366,000,000, passenger-km 5,418,000,000; short ton-mi cargo 101,851,000, metric ton-km cargo 148,700,000; airports (1984) with scheduled flights 39.
Communications. Daily newspapers (1983): total number 40; total circulation 1,994,600; circulation per 1,000 population 133. Radios (1982): total number of receivers 2,000,000 (1 per 7.2 persons). Television (1982): total number of receivers 1,303,985 (1 per 11.1 persons). Telephones (1983): 976,500 (1 per 15.2 persons).

Education and health

Education (1983–84)

	schools	teachers	students	student/ teacher ratio
Primary (age 6–12)	6,557	83,760	2,149,014	25.6
Secondary (age 13–16)	1,171	57,329	1,264,043	22.0
Voc., teacher tr.	90	3,173	36,543	11.5
Higher	9	5,452	55,816	10.2

College graduates per 100,000 population (1981): 51.8. *Literacy* (1980): total population literate 7,133,775 (75.0%); males literate 3,913,865 (83.0%); females literate 3,213,400 (66.9%).
Health (1983): physicians 4,234 (1 per 3,510 persons); hospital beds 34,538 (1 per 430 persons).
Food (1978–80): daily per capita caloric intake 2,650 (vegetable products 87.9%, animal products 12.1%); 118% of FAO recommended minimum requirement.

Military

Total active duty personnel (1984): 124,500 (army 80.7%; navy 8.8%; air force 10.5%). *Military expenditure as percent of GNP* (1982): 8.2% (world 6.0%); per capita expenditure U.S.$141.

---

*Detail does not add to total given because of rounding. †1982. ‡Includes import duties and imputed bank service charges. §July.

Maldives

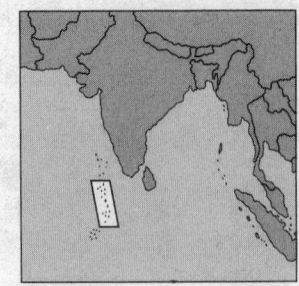

Official name: Divehi Jumhuriyya (Republic of Maldives).
Form of government: republic with one legislative house (People's Council [48]).
Head of state and government: President.
Capital: Male.
Official language: Divehi.
Official religion: Islām.
Monetary unit: 1 Maldivian Rufiyaa (Rf) = 100 laaris; valuation (Oct. 29, 1984) 1 U.S.$ = Rf7.57; 1 £ = Rf9.16.

Area and population

Administrative atolls*	Capitals	area sq mi	area sq km	population 1983 estimate
Haa-Alifu	Dhidhdhoo	...	...	9,300
Haa-Dhaalu	Nolhivaranfaru	...	...	10,700
Shaviyani	Farukolhu Funadhoo	...	...	7,000
Noonu	Manadhoo	...	...	6,800
Raa	Ugoofaaru	...	...	8,500
Baa	Eydhafushi	...	...	6,200
Lhaviyani	Naifaru	...	...	6,100
Kaafu	Male	...	...	42,200
Alifu	Mahibadhoo	...	...	6,700
Vaavu	Felidhoo	...	...	1,200
Meemu	Muli	...	...	3,400
Faafu	Magoodhoo	...	...	2,200
Dhaalu	Kudahuvadhoo	...	...	3,200
Thaa	Veymandoo	...	...	6,700
Laamu	Hithadhoo	...	...	6,600
Gaafu-Alifu	Viligili	...	...	5,400
Gaafu-Dhaalu	Thinadhoo	...	...	8,300
Gnyaviyani	Foah Mulah	...	...	4,500
Seenu	Hithadhoo	...	...	15,200
TOTAL		115	298	160,200

Source: Official government figures.

Demography

Density (1984): persons per sq mi 1,547, persons per sq km 597.
Urban–rural (1977): urban 20.7%; rural 79.3%.
Sex distribution (1977): male 52.66%; female 47.34%.
Age breakdown (1977): under 15, 44.6%; 15–29, 24.8%; 30–44, 16.4%; 45–59, 9.6%; 60 and over, 4.6%.
Population projection: (1990) 230,000; (2000) 344,000.
Doubling time: 22 years.
Ethnic composition: Sinhalese; Dravidian; Arab; Negro.
Religious affiliation: Muslim.
Major cities (1984): Male 38,000.

Vital statistics

Birth rate per 1,000 population (1982): 44.5 (world avg. 29.0).
Death rate per 1,000 population (1982): 13.3 (world avg. 11.0).
Natural increase rate per 1,000 population (1982): 31.2 (world avg. 18.0).
Total fertility rate: n.a.
Marriage rate per 1,000 population (1981): 34.6.
Divorce rate per 1,000 population (1981): 25.5.
Infant mortality rate per 1,000 live births (1982): 78.5.
Life expectancy at birth (1977 est.): male 52 years; female 49 years.
Major causes of death: n.a.; however, major diseases are cholera, diarrhea, gastroenteritis, malaria, tuberculosis, and typhoid.

National economy

Budget (1982). Revenue: Rf122,800,000† (current revenue 95,000,000, of which property taxes 30.1%, customs duties 19.2%, taxes on goods and services 10.2%, administrative fees and charges 9.5%). Expenditures: Rf142,400,000 (general public services 29.4%; social welfare 17.9%; transportation 14.3%; agriculture, forestry, and fishing 9.2%; housing and community amenities 9.1%; education 8.5%; health 5.8%).
Public debt (external, outstanding; 1982) U.S.$47,000,000.
Tourism (1981): receipts from visitors U.S.$18,300,000; expenditures by nationals abroad, n.a.
Gross national product (at current market prices; 1981): U.S.$67,000,000 (U.S.$441 per capita).

Origin of gross domestic product (current prices)

	1980 in value Rf'000,000	% of total value	labour force‡	% of labour force
Agriculture	78.6	15.7	35,900	54.9
Mining	5.6	1.1	...	...
Manufacturing	11.6	2.3	13,600	20.8
Construction	19.2	3.8	3,100	4.7
Trade	85.6	17.1	2,000	3.1
Public utilities	0.7	0.1	200	0.3
Transportation and communication	39.8	8.0	3,300	5.0
Finance	11.2	2.2	...	...
Pub. admin., defense	33.2	6.6	...	...
Services	132.1	26.4	5,300	8.1
Other	82.5	16.5	2,000	3.1
TOTAL	500.1	100.0§	65,400	100.0

Production (metric tons except as noted). Agriculture and fishing (1982): vegetables and melons 15,000; coconuts 9,000; roots and tubers 8,000; fruits, excluding melons 7,000; copra 1,000; fish catch 30,300. Mining and quarrying: n.a. Manufacturing: n.a.; however, major industries are boat building and repairing, coir yarn and mat weaving, coconut and fish processing, lacquer work, garment manufacturing, and handicrafts. Construction: n.a. Energy production (consumption): electricity (kW-hr; 1982) 8,000,000 (8,000,000); coal, none (n.a.); petroleum products (metric tons; 1982) none (6,000); natural gas, none (n.a.).
Persons economically active (1980): total 65,400 (45.1%); female participation in the labour force 25,400 (38.8%); unemployed (1977) 3,532 (5.8%).
Household income and expenditure. Average household size (1977) 6.1; income per household: n.a.; source of income: n.a.; expenditure: n.a.
Land use (1981): forested 3.3%; meadows and pastures 3.3%; agricultural and under permanent cultivation 10.0%; other 83.4%.

Foreign trade

Balance of trade (current prices)

	1976	1977	1978	1979	1980	1981
Rf'000,000	−9.8	−22.1	−35.2	−71.8	−137.8	−144.0
% of total	29.3%	44.5%	52.2%	66.6%	54.0%	52.6%

Imports (1981): Rf208,905,000 (manufactured goods 19.8%, machinery and transport equipment 18.4%, petroleum products 16.8%, rice 13.4%, sugar 5.7%, chemicals 4.3%). *Major import sources* (1979): India 25.0%; West Germany 15.0%; Japan 14.0%; Sri Lanka 11.0%; Burma 7.0%; Pakistan 7.0%.
Exports (1981): Rf64,867,500 (fresh fish 60.6%, dried fish 18.7%). *Major export destinations* (1978): Japan 56.1%; Sri Lanka 22.0%; Singapore 16.2%.

Transport and communications

Transport. Railroads: none. Roads: total length n.a. Vehicles (1981): passenger cars 254; jeeps and buses 109. Merchant marine (1983): vessels (100 gross tons and over) 39; total deadweight tonnage 267,326. Air transport (1980): passenger-mi 12,430,000, passenger-km 20,000,000; short ton-mi cargo 205,500, metric ton-km cargo 300,000; airport (1984) with scheduled flights 1.
Communications. Daily newspapers (1982): total number 2; circulation, n.a. Radios (1983): total number of receivers 11,956 (1 per 17.4 persons). Television (1983): total number of receivers 1,100 (1 per 189 persons). Telephones (1982): 1,540 (1 per 104 persons).

Education and health

Education (1983–84)

	schools	teachers	students	student/ teacher ratio
Primary (age 6–11)	65	590	42,598	72.2
Secondary (age 11–18)	4	93	841	9.0
Voc., teacher tr.	3	27	206	7.6

College graduates per 10,000 population (1981): 3.7. *Literacy* (1982): total population literate 62,365 (81.1%); males literate 31,896 (80.2%); females literate 30,469 (82.0%).
Health: physicians (1981) 9 (1 per 15,870 persons); hospital beds (1977) ‖ 40 (1 per 3,571 persons).
Food (1978–80): daily per capita caloric intake 1,781 (vegetable products 90.8%, animal products 9.2%); 81% of FAO recommended minimum requirement.

Military

Total active duty personnel: Maldives maintains one security force numbering about 700–1,000; it performs both army and police functions.

*Maldives is divided into 19 administrative districts corresponding to atoll groups; arrangement from north to south. †Includes Rf27,800,000 in grants and sales of fixed capital assets. ‡Employed persons only. §Detail does not add to total given because of rounding. ‖ In government establishments only.

GRIFFITHS—MAGNUM

Dhoni sailing craft, the Maldive Islands.

Mali

Official name: République du Mali (Republic of Mali).
Form of government: unitary single-party republic with one legislative house (National Assembly [82]).
Head of state and government: President.
Capital: Bamako.
Official language: French.
Official religion: none.
Monetary unit: 1 Mali franc (MF) = 100 centimes; valuation (Oct. 29, 1984) 1 U.S.$ = MF470.6; 1 £ = MF568.0.

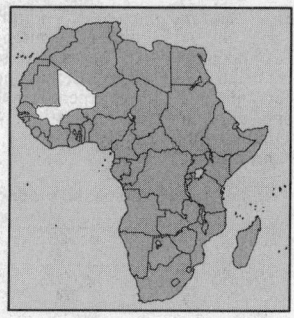

Area and population

Regions	Capitals	area sq mi	area sq km	population 1980 estimate
Gao	Gao	124,323	321,996	409,315
Kayes	Kayes	76,356	197,760	962,901
Koulikoro*	Koulikoro	29,000	75,000	1,027,183
Mopti†	Mopti	50,259	130,169	1,245,322
Ségou†	Ségou	...	...	1,195,411
Sikasso*	Sikasso	25,100	65,000	1,211,049
Tombouctou*	Tombouctou	173,700	450,000	540,887
District				
Bamako	Bamako	103	267	477,750
TOTAL		478,841	1,240,192	7,069,818

Source: Official government figures.

Demography

Density (1984): persons per sq mi 16.1, persons per sq km 6.2.
Urban–rural (1980): urban 17.4%; rural 82.6%.
Sex distribution (1980): male 48.85%; female 51.15%.
Age breakdown (1980): under 15, 44.1%; 15–29, 24.9%; 30–44, 16.0%; 45–59, 8.7%; 60–74, 4.8%; 75 and over, 1.5%.
Population projection: (1990) 8,784,000; (2000) 11,848,000.
Doubling time: 30 years.
Ethnic composition (1978): Bambara 31.8%; Fulani 12.7%; Senufo 11.9%; Malinke 9.5%; Soninke 8.7%; Songai 5.9%; Tuareg 5.6%; Dogon 4.9%; Diula 3.2%; Bobo 2.5%; other 3.3%.
Religious affiliation (1980): Muslim 80%; tribal religionist 18.1%; Christian 1.9%.
Major cities (1976): Bamako 440,000‡; Ségou 64,890; Mopti 53,885; Sikasso 47,030; Kayes 44,736.

Vital statistics

Birth rate per 1,000 population (1980–85): 49.4 (world avg. 27.5); legitimate, n.a., illegitimate, n.a.
Death rate per 1,000 population (1980–85): 22.2 (world avg. 10.6).
Natural increase rate per 1,000 population (1980–85): 27.2 (world avg. 16.9).
Total fertility rate (avg. births per childbearing woman; 1980–85): 6.7.
Marriage rate per 1,000 population: n.a.
Divorce rate per 1,000 population: n.a.
Infant mortality rate per 1,000 live births (1975–80): 160.4.
Life expectancy at birth (1980–85): male 40.6 years; female 43.8 years.
Major causes of death: no data available; however, major infectious diseases are malaria, syphilis and gonococcal infections, influenza, measles, amebiasis, and strep throat.

National economy

Budget (1983). Revenue: MF113,100,000,000 (indirect taxes 46.9%, direct taxes 16.9%, regional transfers 5.1%). Expenditures: MF95,140,000,000 (general services 86.8%, regional transfers 9.2%).
Public debt (external, outstanding; 1982): U.S.$822,000,000.
Tourism (1981): receipts from visitors U.S.$9,000,000; expenditures by nationals abroad U.S.$17,000,000.
Production (metric tons except as noted). Agriculture, forestry, fishing (1982): millet 952,000, sugarcane 225,000, peanuts (groundnuts) in shell 170,000, rice 142,000, seed cotton 125,000, corn (maize) 81,000, cottonseed 80,000, cassava 65,000, sweet potatoes 52,000, cotton lint 36,000, wheat 2,000; livestock (number of live animals) 7,000,000 goats, 6,350,000 sheep, 5,134,000 cattle, 420,000 asses, 173,000 camels, 139,000 horses, 12,500,000 chickens; roundwood 4,452,000 cu m; fish catch 90,000. Mining and quarrying (1980): salt 5,000. Manufacturing (1982): goat, mutton, and lamb 47,000; beef and veal 39,000; butter 4,355; sugar 15,000; beer 17,000 hectolitres; cement 26,000‡. Construction: n.a. Energy production (consumption): electricity (kW-hr; 1982) 110,000,000 (110,000,000); coal, none (n.a.); crude petroleum, none (n.a.); petroleum products (metric tons; 1982) none (139,000); natural gas, none (n.a.).
Persons economically active (1982): total 3,906,000 (53.2%); female participation in the labour force, n.a.; unemployed¶ 52,000 (1.3%).

Price and earnings indexes (1970 = 100)

	1977	1978	1979	1980	1981	1982	1983
Consumer price index♀	245.0	327.0	313.0	382.7	429.5	439.4	482.6
Earnings index	...	...	...	...	...	...	...

Gross national product (at current market prices; 1981): U.S.$1,340,000,000 (U.S.$190 per capita).

Origin of gross domestic product (current prices)

	1981 in value MF'000,000,000	1981 % of total value	1982 labour force	1982 % of labour force
Agriculture	252.5	41.5	3,355,300	85.9
Manufacturing	34.0	5.6	195,300	5.0
Construction	25.1	4.1	...	...
Trade	154.6	25.4	...	...
Public utilities	6.8	1.1	...	...
Transportation and communication	41.8	6.9	...	...
Pub. admin., defense	74.0	12.2	...	...
Other	19.2§	3.2§	355,400 ‖	9.1 ‖
TOTAL	608.0	100.0	3,906,000	100.0

Household income and expenditure. Average household size (1980) 5; average annual income per household, n.a.; source of income: n.a.; expenditure: n.a.
Land use (1981): forested 7.2%; meadows and pastures 24.6%; agricultural and under permanent cultivation 1.7%; other 66.5%.

Foreign trade

Balance of trade (current prices)

	1978	1979	1980	1981	1982	1983
MF'000,000,000	−42.5	−50.6	−51.3	−71.4	−122.6	−67.4
% of total	29.6%	28.7%	22.8%	29.9%	39.0%	21.0%

Imports (1982): MF218,400,000,000 (machinery, appliances, and transportation equipment 28.4%; petroleum products 20.9%; food products 18.5%, of which cereals 7.7%, sugar and honey 4.0%; chemicals and pharmaceutical products 9.2%; construction materials 9.2%). Major import sourcesδ: France 40%; West Africa 20%; Western Europe 9%; Asia 6%.
Exports (1982): MF95,800,000,000 (live animals 35.6%; raw cotton 35.6%; oil seeds, oil nuts, and oil kernels 1.8%; fish, salted, dried, or smoked 1.3%). Major export destinationsδ: France 30%; Western Europe 28%; Asia 20%; West Africa 18%.

Transport and communications

Transport. Railroads (1981): length 401 mi, 646 km; passenger-mi 195,000,000, passenger-km 314,000,000; short ton-mi cargo 93,500,000, metric ton-km cargo 136,500,000. Roads (1981): total length 8,080 mi, 13,004 km (paved 14%). Vehicles (1982): passenger cars 20,000; trucks and buses 5,000. Merchant marine: vessels (100 gross tons and over) none. Air transport (1981): passenger arrivals 68,300, passenger departures 68,622; metric ton cargo loaded 2,547, metric ton cargo unloaded 4,281; airports (1984) with scheduled flights 9.
Communications. Daily newspaper (1981): total number 1; total circulation 40,000; circulation per 1,000 population 5.7. Radios (1983): total number of receivers 102,000 (1 per 72 persons). Television: total number of receivers, n.a. Telephones (1982): 8,485 (1 per 865 persons).

Education and health

Education (1979–80)

	schools	teachers	students	student/ teacher ratio
Primary (age 5–11)	1,220	7,054	298,697	42.3
Secondary (age 12–17)	234	2,582	58,786	22.8
Voc., teacher tr.	...	700	5,939	8.5
Higher□	6	489	5,281	10.8

College graduates per 100,000 population (students graduating, 1979): 6.9.
Literacyδ (1980): total population literate 361,800 (10.1%); males literate 329,200 (18.6%); females literate 32,600 (1.8%).
Health (1980): physicians 319 (1 per 22,130 persons); hospital beds 4,056 (1 per 1,743 persons).
Food (1978–80): daily per capita caloric intake 1,996 (vegetable products 91.8%, animal products 8.2%); 85% of FAO recommended minimum requirement.

Military

Total active duty personnel (1982): 4,950 (army 92.9%; navy 0.1%; air force 6.1%). Military expenditure as percent of GNP (1982): 2.4% (world 6%); per capita expenditure U.S.$13.

*Area for Koulikoro, Sikasso, and Tombouctou regions are estimated. †Area for Ségou is included with Mopti region. ‡1980 estimate. §Other includes finance and services. ‖ Construction, trade, public utilities, transportation and communication, public administration and defense, and services are included with other. ¶Urban areas; estimated. ♀Includes food index for Bamako only. δEstimated. □1978–79.

Malta

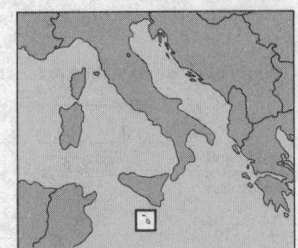

Official name: Repubblika ta' Malta (Republic of Malta).
Form of government: unitary multiparty republic with one legislative house (House of Representatives [65]).
Chief of state: President.
Head of government: Prime Minister.
Capital: Valletta.
Official languages: English; Maltese.
Official religion: Roman Catholicism.
Monetary unit: 1 Maltese lira (Lm) = 100 cents = 1,000 mils; valuation* (Oct. 29, 1984) 1 Lm = U.S.$1.60 = £1.32.

Area and population	area		population‡
Census regions†	sq mi	sq km	1983 estimate
Gozo and Comino	27	70	23,600
Inner Harbour	6	15	119,300
Northern	30	78	25,600
Outer Harbour	12	32	85,000
South Eastern	20	53	37,600
Western	27	69	37,900
TOTAL	122	317	329,400

Source: Official government figures.

Demography

Density (1984): persons per sq mi 2,673.8, persons per sq km 1,029.0.
Urban–rural (1979): urban 83.3%; rural 16.7%.
Sex distribution (1984): male 48.54%; female 51.46%.
Age breakdown (1984): under 15, 24.5%; 15–29, 23.7%; 30–44, 23.5%; 45–59, 15.3%; 60–74, 9.4%; 75 and over, 3.6%.
Population projection: (1990) 396,000; (2000) 420,000.
Doubling time: 80 years.
Ethnic composition (1980): Maltese 95.7%; British 2.1%; other 2.2%.
Religious affiliation (1980): Roman Catholic 97.3%; Anglican 1.2%; other 1.5%.
Major cities (1983 est.): Sliema 20,100; Birkirkara 17,900; Qormi 16,900; Valletta 14,000; Hamrun 14,000.

Vital statistics

Birth rate per 1,000 population (1983): 15.0 (world avg. 29.0); legitimate 99.1%, illegitimate 0.9%.
Death rate per 1,000 population (1983): 8.3 (world avg. 11.0).
Natural increase rate per 1,000 population (1983): 6.7 (world avg. 18.0).
Total fertility rate (avg. births per childbearing woman): n.a.
Marriage rate per 1,000 population (1983): 7.6.
Divorce rate per 1,000 population: n.a.
Infant mortality rate per 1,000 live births (1982): 14.9.
Life expectancy at birth (1982): male 69.6 years; female 72.9 years.
Major causes of death per 100,000 population (1982): diseases of the circulatory system 528.5; neoplasms 167.9; endocrine, nutritional, and metabolic diseases of blood and blood-forming organs 52.4; diseases of the respiratory system 44.4; diseases of the digestive system 35.6.

National economy

Budget (1983). Revenue: Lm224,523,000 (national insurance 23.4%, income tax 20.9%, customs and excise taxes 15.4%, rent 2.7%, lotteries 1.5%). Expenditures: Lm183,316,000 (national insurance benefits 26.7%, labour and social services 16.8%, health and environment 10.9%, education 9.2%).
Public debt (external, outstanding; 1982): U.S.$101,100,000.
Tourism (1982): receipts from visitors U.S.$184,336,000; expenditures by nationals abroad U.S.$57,065,000.
Production (value added in Lm except as noted). Agriculture, forestry, fishing (1981–82): tomatoes 2,629,003, potatoes 1,357,936, wheat 944,869, melons 445,158, barley 350,110, onions 205,911; livestock (number of live animals) 15,000 cattle, 5,000 pigs, 1,114,000 chickens; fish landed 1,093,000§. Mining and quarrying (1982): limestone, building blocks, coralline spalls, and sand 1,035,300; salt from sea water 3,100. Manufacturing (1982): textiles and wearing apparel 33,551,000, of which wearing apparel 29,162,000; food, beverages, and tobacco 22,082,000; metals and machinery 21,612,000, of which electrical machinery 12,003,000; paper and printing 7,130,000; cane, cork, furniture, and fixtures 6,467,000; nonmetallic minerals 3,659,000; footwear 3,199,000. Construction (1982): 17,343,800. Energy production (consumption; kW-hr; 1982) 561,000,000 (561,000,000); coal (metric tons; 1982) none (negligible); crude petroleum (barrels; 1982) none (n.a.); petroleum products (metric tons; 1982) none (376,000); natural gas (metric tons; 1982) none (n.a.).
Gross national product (at current market prices; 1982): U.S.$1,237,000,000 (U.S.$3,790 per capita).
Persons economically active (1982): total 120,843 (37.0%); female participation in the labour force♀ 30,914 (25.4%); unemployed 10,356 (8.6%).

Price and earnings indexes (1980 = 100)						
	1978	1979	1980	1981	1982	1983	1984
Consumer price index	80.6	86.4	100.0	111.5	118.0	117.0	116.5ð
Annual earnings index	...	...	100.0	108.7	120.2	...	...

Household income and expenditure. Average household size (1982): 3.6; average annual income per household (1982) Lm4,736 (U.S.$11,399); source of income (1982): wages and salaries 50.1%, social security and other assistance 13.6%, professional and unincorporated enterprises 13.6%, property income 11.0%; expenditure (1982): food and beverages 33.3%, transportation and communication 14.3%, furniture and household operations 10.0%, clothing and footwear 7.2%, recreation and education 6.4%, rent and utilities 6.1%.

Origin of gross domestic product (current prices)				
	1982		1981	
	in value Lm'000	% of total value	labour force	% of labour force
Agriculture	16,767	4.0	6,600	5.4
Manufacturing	125,024	29.9	37,800	31.0
Mining	23,546 ‖	5.6 ‖	1,300	1.1
Construction	‖	‖	4,900	4.2
Trade	63,184	15.1	14,600	11.9
Public utilities	21,958	5.3	1,200	0.9
Transportation and-communication	20,396	4.9	7,900	6.5
Finance	21,262	5.1	...	...
Pub. admin.	58,152	13.9	...	...
Services	38,415	9.2	41,900	34.4
Other	29,041	7.0	5,703¶	4.6¶
TOTAL	417,745	100.0	121,903	100.0

Land use (1981): agricultural and under permanent cultivation 43.8%; other 56.2% (infertile clay soil with underlying limestone).

Foreign trade

Balance of trade (current prices)						
	1978	1979	1980	1981	1982	1983
Lm'000,000	−67.6	−92.8	−124.9	−125.6	−123.8	−128.1
% of total	20.4%	23.4%	27.3%	26.6%	26.8%	28.9%

Imports (1983): Lm316,633,102□ (food and live animals 13.2%; yarns, fabrics, and textiles 12.5%; petroleum products and natural gas 11.7%; transportation equipment 9.8%; nonelectrical machinery 8.1%; electrical machinery 6.7%). (electrical machinery and apparatus 6.7%; fruits and nuts 2.0%; complete motor cars and cycles 2.0%; meat, fresh, chilled, or frozen 1.6%; meat, canned 1.2%; cheese curd 0.9%; animal feed 0.8%; sugar, refined 0.7%; cereals 0.4%; textile machinery 0.4%). *Major import sources:* Italy 26.8%; United Kingdom 16.9%; West Germany 16.0%; United States 11.3%; The Netherlands 3.8%; France 3.4%; Belgium 1.5%; Japan 1.4%.
Exports (1983): Lm156,748,059 (clothing and footwear 39.7%; electrical appliances and apparatus 9.8%; photographic and small mechanical goods 9.1%; printed matter 4.9%; rubber manufactures 2.9%; toys and sporting goods 2.9%; tobacco manufactures 2.8%). *Major export destinations:* West Germany 32.1%; United Kingdom 16.5%; Italy 9.9%; Belgium 4.9%; The Netherlands 4.7%; Libya 3.8%; France 2.2%; Sweden 1.9%.

Transport and communications

Transport. Railroads: none. Roads (1982): total length 808 mi, 1,300 km (paved 94%). Vehicles (1982): passenger cars 74,773; trucks and buses 17,871. Merchant marine (1983): vessels (100 gross tons and over) 147; total deadweight tonnage 1,341,915. Air transport (1982): passenger-mi 399,938,000, passenger-km 643,639,000; short ton-mi cargo 2,202,055, metric ton-km cargo 3,215,000; airport (1984) with scheduled flights 1.
Communications. Daily newspapers (1981): total number 2; circulation, n.a. Radios (1983): total number of receivers 75,000 (1 per 4.3 persons). Television (1983): total number of receivers 76,600 (1 per 4.2 persons). Telephones (1982): 60,507‡ (1 per 5.4 persons).

Education and health

Education (1982–83)	schools	teachers	students	student/teacher ratio
Primary (age 5–13)	120	1,656	33,208	20.1
Secondary (age 11–20)	67	1,828	21,986	12.0
Voc., teacher tr.	32	425	5,271	12.4
Higher	1	146	1,010	6.9

College graduates per 100,000 population (students graduating; 1980): 63.6.
Literacy (1980): total population literate 261,900 (81.6%); males literate 129,500 (83.4%); females literate 132,400 (79.7%).
Health: physicians (1975) 382 (1 per 794 persons); hospital beds (1980) 3,431 (1 per 93 persons).
Food (1978–80): daily per capita caloric intake 3,046 (vegetable products 71.8%, animal products 28.2%); 123% of FAO recommended minimum requirement.

Military

Total active duty personnel (1982): 800 (paramilitary forces). *Military expenditure as percent of GNP* (1982): 1.1% (world 6.0%); per capita expenditure U.S.$35.

*The Maltese lira is tied to the currencies of several principal trading partners. †Malta has no first-order political subdivisions. Data are collected according to census regions. ‡De jure population. §1982. ‖ Construction is included with mining. ¶Includes unemployed persons. ♀1981. ðSecond quarter. □Imports c.i.f.

Martinique

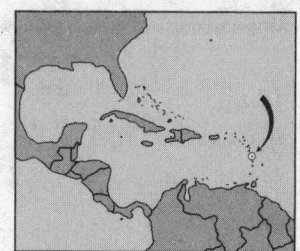

Official name: Département de la Martinique (Department of Martinique).
Political status: overseas department (France) with one legislative house (General Council [36]), three representatives in the French National Assembly, and two senators in the French Senate.
Chief of state: President of France.
Head of government: Commissioner.
Capital: Fort-de-France.
Official language: French.
Official religion: none.
Monetary unit: 1 Franc (Francs) (F, plural F) = 100 centimes; valuation (Oct. 29, 1984) 1 U.S.$ = F9.41; 1 £ = F11.36.

Area and population

Arrondissements	Capitals	area sq mi	area sq km	population 1982 census
Fort-de-France	Fort-de-France	141.0	365.1	174,854
Marin	Le Marin	154.1	399.2	78,350
La-Trinité	La Trinité	126.3	327.0	73,513
TOTAL		421.4	1,091.3	326,717

Source: Official government figures.

Demography

Density (1984): persons per sq mi 776.5, persons per sq km 299.8.
Urban–rural (1982): urban 57.1%; rural 42.9%.
Sex distribution (1982): male 48.49%; female 51.51%.
Age breakdown (1982): under 15, 28.4%; 15–29, 30.3%; 30–44, 16.2%; 45–59, 13.2%; 60–74, 8.6%; 75 and over, 3.3%.
Population projection: (1990) 328,600; (2000) 331,000.
Population growth is negligible.
Ethnic composition (1982): mulatto 90.4%; French (metropolitan) 5.1%; East Indian 1.9%; other West Indian 1.7%; Creole (Martinique white) 0.7%; other (Chinese, Vietnamese, Syrian) 0.2%.
Religious affiliation (1982): Roman Catholic 94.3%; Seventh-day Adventist 3.1%; Jehovah's Witness 0.6%; Baha'i 0.5%; other 1.5%.
Major cities (1982): Fort-de-France 97,814; Le Lamentin 26,367; Sainte-Marie 18,536; Schoelcher 18,203; Le François 14,382; La Trinité 10,079.

Vital statistics

Birth rate per 1,000 population (1983): 17.2 (world avg. 29); (1983) legitimate 39.4%; illegitimate 60.6%.
Death rate per 1,000 population (1983): 6.7 (world avg. 11).
Natural increase rate per 1,000 population (1983): 10.5 (world avg. 18).
Total fertility rate (avg. births per childbearing woman; 1980–85): 2.4.
Marriage rate per 1,000 population (1983): 4.1.
Divorce rate per 1,000 population (1983): 1.0.
Infant mortality rate per 1,000 live births (1983): 13.8.
Life expectancy at birth (1980–85): male 67.8 years; female 73.0 years.
Major causes of death per 100,000 population (1981): cardiovascular disease 217.2; neoplasms (cancers), including malignant tumours 95.1; accidents 46.6; illnesses of the nervous system 45.7.

National economy

Budget (1982). Revenue: F1,284,000,000 (French participation in provision of services 32.4%, deferred and supplementary receipts 20.2%, gasoline tax 14.8%, other taxes 9.9%, other foreign assistance 6.4%, new loans 5.8%). Expenditures: F1,284,000,000 (health and social assistance 38.7%, infrastructure and public works 22.4%, deferred and supplementary expenses 20.2%, other services 14.1%).
Tourism (1982): receipts from visitors U.S.$89,000,000; expenditures by nationals abroad, n.a.
Production (metric tons except as noted). Agriculture, forestry, fishing (1982): sugarcane 201,900, bananas 156,500, pineapples 21,100, carrots 8,000, sweet potatoes 5,000, milk 4,800, avocados 3,700, tomatoes 3,000, eggplants 2,000, mangoes 2,000, plantains 2,000, flowers 121; livestock (number of live animals) 41,300 cattle, 39,300 sheep, 22,200 pigs, 9,600 goats, 375,000 chickens, 21,000 ducks; non-coniferous roundwood 11,000 cu m; fish catch 5,500. Mining and quarrying (1980): sand and gravel for construction industry. Manufacturing (1983): refined petroleum products 649,100; cement 207,100; pineapple preserves 12,900; sugar 3,950; pineapple juice 553*; rum 104,440 hectolitres; clay bricks 5,759,000 units*; cement blocks 4,430,000 units*; other important products include furniture, clothing and textiles, metal and rubber products, industrial equipment, and precision instruments. Construction (1983): residential, 1,559 buildings completed; commercial, industrial, and other 32,779 sq m authorized. Energy production (consumption): electricity (kW-hr; 1983) 355,992,000 (355,992,000); fuelwood (metric tons; 1981) 10,000 (10,000).

Price and earnings indexes (1979 = 100)

	1977	1978	1979	1980	1981	1982	1983
Consumer price index	82.1	89.7	100.0	118.5	129.3	145.6	160.9
Monthly earnings index	77.7	87.4	100.0	114.4	137.5	158.3	179.3

Gross national product (at current market prices; 1981): U.S.$1,570,000,000 (U.S.$4,820 per capita).

Origin of gross domestic product (current prices)

	1979 in value F'000	1979 % of total value	1982 labour force	1982 % of labour force
Agriculture	424,470	7.7	9,844	7.8
Manufacturing	304,994	5.5	5,862	4.7
Construction and mining	168,476	3.0	7,832	6.2
Trade	791,826	14.3	9,864	7.8
Public utilities	108,159	2.0	1,006	0.8
Transportation and communication	201,102	3.6	5,197	4.1
Finance	262,191	4.7	2,063	1.6
Pub. admin., defense	1,739,565	31.4	29,370	23.3
Services	1,350,534	24.4	15,815	12.6
Other, including unemployed	186,747	3.4	39,134	31.1
TOTAL	5,538,064	100.0	125,987	100.0

Persons economically active (1982): total 125,987 (38.6%); female 40,443 (32.1%); unemployed 33,851 (26.9%).
Household income and expenditure. Average household size (1982) 3.8; income per household (1979) F70,009 (U.S.$17,415); source of income: salaries 74.2%, industrial and commercial profits 10.0%, pensions and rents 4.8%, income from stocks and bonds 3.9%, noncommercial profits 3.4%, other 3.7%. Expenditure (1977): services 36.2%, food 30.7%, goods for current consumption 19.8%, energy and utilities 5.7%, durable goods 4.7%, intermediate goods 2.9%.
Land use (1981): forested 41.2%; meadows and pastures 18.2%; agricultural and under permanent cultivation 19.4%; other 21.2%.

Foreign trade

Balance of trade (current prices)

	1978	1979	1980	1981	1982	1983†
F'000	-451,000	-2,303,000	-3,072,000	-3,293,000	-4,038,786	-3,457,141
% of total	24.4%	67.0%	75.7%	64.8%	88.2%	73.8%

Imports (1982): F4,663,776,000 (food and food products 22.4%, crude petroleum 17.2%, industrial equipment 12.5%, chemicals 9.6%, construction materials 6.2%, tourist vehicles 6.2%, clothing and textiles 5.8%, metal goods 5.8%, private automobiles 4.8%, spare parts 3.5%, household goods 2.5%). *Major import sources:* France 58.5%; Venezuela 10.4%; Saudi Arabia 5.7%; United States 4.0%; Italy 2.9%; West Germany 2.5%.
Exports (1982): F624,990,000 (bananas 38.6%, refined petroleum products 18.3%, rum 10.7%, pineapple preserves and juice 3.2%, cardboard cartons 3.1%). *Major export destinations:* France 59.8%; Guadeloupe 27.6%; French Guiana 3.5%; West Germany 3.3%.

Transport and communications

Transport. Railroads: none. Roads (1982): total length 1,131 mi, 1,820 km (paved 82%). Vehicles (1982): passenger cars 126,666; trucks and buses 3,498. Fishing fleet (1982): vessels (10 gross tons and over) 8. Air transport (1983): passenger arrivals 927,700, short ton cargo (loaded and unloaded) 11,667, metric ton cargo 10,584; airport (1984) with scheduled flights 1.
Communications. Daily newspaper (1983): total number 1; total circulation 30,000; circulation per 1,000 population 91.7. Radios (1983): total number of receivers 45,000 (1 per 7 persons). Television (1983): total number of receivers 42,000 (1 per 8 persons). Telephones (1982): 68,908 (1 per 5 persons).

Education and health

Education (1982–83)

	schools	teachers	students	student/ teacher ratio
Primary (age 6–11)	297	3,222‡	57,532	...
Secondary (age 12–18)	71§	3,042§	47,316 ‖	...
Vocational	12	...	2,144	...
Higher	3	77§	3,460¶	...

College graduates per 100,000 population (1982): 3,325. *Literacy♀* (1982): total population literate 206,807 (92.5%); males literate 97,538 (91.8%); females literate 109,269 (93.2%).
Health: physicians (1981) 376 (1 per 867 persons); hospital beds (1980) 4,178 (1 per 78 persons).
Food (1978–80): daily per capita caloric intake 2,806 (vegetable products 79.0%, animal products 21.0%); 116% of FAO recommended minimum requirement.

Military

No domestic military forces are maintained; France is responsible for defense.

*1982. †Through third quarter only. ‡Public school teachers only. §1979–80. ‖ 1981–82. ¶Teacher training college only; other schools had 1,475 students in 1979–80. ♀Age 16 and over.

Mauritania

Official name: al-Jumhūrīyah-al
Islāmīyah al-Mūrītānīyah (Arabic),
République Islamique de Mauritanie
(French) (Islāmic Republic of
Mauritania).
Form of government: military regime.
Head of state and government:
President assisted by Military
Committee for National Salvation.
Capital: Nouakchott.
Official languages: Arabic and French.
Official religion: Islām.
Monetary unit: 1 Mauritanian Ouguiya
(UM) = 5 khoums; valuation (Oct. 29,
1984) 1 U.S.$ = UM66.62;
1 £ = UM80.41.

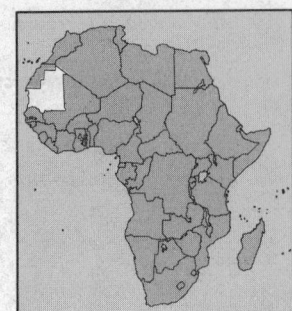

Area and population

Regions*	Capitals	area sq mi	area sq km	population 1982 estimate
Hodh ech-Chargui	Néma	70,500	182,700	235,000
Hodh el-Gharbi	'Ayoûn el-'Atroûs	20,600	53,400	154,000
el-'Açâba	Kiffa	14,100	36,600	152,000
Gorgol	Kaédi	5,200	13,600	169,000
Brakna	Aleg	12,700	33,000	171,000
Trarza	Rosso	26,200	67,800	242,000
Adrar	Atar	83,100	215,300	60,000
Dakhlet Nouadhibou	Nouadhibou	8,600	22,300	30,000
Tagant	Tidjikja	36,800	95,200	84,000
Guidimaka	Sélibaby	4,000	10,300	102,000
Tiris Zemmour	Fdérik	97,600	252,900	28,000
Inchiri	Akjoujt	18,100	46,800	23,000
District				
Nouakchott	Nouakchott	46	120	150,000
TOTAL		397,700†	1,030,020	1,600,000

Source: Official government figures.

Demography

Density (1984): persons per sq mi 4.2, persons per sq km 1.6.
Urban–rural (1981): urban 24.4%; rural 75.6%‡.
Sex distribution (1980): male 49.48%; female 50.52%.
Age breakdown (1980): under 15, 45.9%; 15–29, 26.2%; 30–44, 14.7%; 45–59,
8.7%; 60–74, 3.9%; 75 and over, 0.6%.
Population projection: (1990) 1,944,000; (2000) 2,481,000.
Doubling time: 28 years.
Ethnic composition (1980): white Moor 53%; black Moor 28%; Tukulor 8%;
Fulani 5%; Soninke 3%; other 3%.
Religious affiliation (1980): Muslim 99.4%; Christian 0.4%; other 0.2%.
Major cities (1977): Nouakchott 135,000§; Nouadhibou 22,000; Kaédi 20,-
800; Zouérate (Zouîrât) 17,500.

Vital statistics

Birth rate per 1,000 population (1981): 43.6 (world avg. 29.0); legitimate
n.a.; illegitimate n.a.
Death rate per 1,000 population (1981): 20.3 (world avg. 12.0).
Natural increase rate per 1,000 population (1981): 23.3 (world avg. 17.0).
Total fertility rate (avg. births per childbearing woman; 1981): 6.0.
Marriage rate per 1,000 population: n.a.
Divorce rate per 1,000 population: n.a.
Infant mortality rate per 1,000 live births (1981): 140.7.
Life expectancy at birth (1981): male 42.8 years; female 46.1 years.
Major causes of death: ‖ .

National economy

Budget (1982). Revenue: UM11,466,000,000 (tax revenue 69.5%, of which
taxes on international trade 42.8%, taxes on income and profits 16.6%;
capital receipts 10.1%; loans 8.7%; subsidies and grants 7.4%). Expenditures: UM11,326,000,000 (administration 56.6%, of which defense 18.1%;
education 12.4%; health and social affairs 3.6%; public debt service 12.6%;
investments 4.9%).
Public debt (external, outstanding; 1982): U.S.$1,000,700,000.
Tourism (1981): receipts from visitors U.S.$6,000,000; expenditures by na-
tionals abroad U.S.$15,000,000.
Land use (1981): forested 14.7%; meadows and pastures 38.1%; agricultural
and under permanent cultivation 0.2%; desert 47.0%.
Production (metric tons except as noted). Agriculture, forestry, fishing (1982):
millet 40,000, dates 10,000, rice 9,000, corn (maize) 6,000, peanuts (groundnuts) 4,000; livestock (number of live animals) 4,900,000 sheep, 2,650,000
goats, 1,200,000 cattle, 800,000 camels, 3,200,000 chickens; roundwood 53,-
000 cu m; fish catch 37,000 of which marine fishing areas 27,000. Mining
and quarrying (1982): iron ore (gross weight) 8,000,000; hydraulic cement
65,000; gypsum 5,000. Manufacturing (1981): fresh beef and veal 17,000;
fresh mutton and lamb 12,000; cheese 1,700. Construction (value added
in U.S.$; 1982): 60,000,000. Energy production (consumption): electricity
(kW-hr; 1982) 103,000,000 (103,000,000); coal (metric tons; 1982) none
(7,000); crude petroleum, none (n.a.); petroleum products (metric tons;
1982) none (197,000); natural gas, none (n.a.).
Gross national product (at current market prices; 1981): U.S.$710,000,000
(U.S.$460 per capita).

Origin of gross domestic product (current prices)

	1981 in value UM'000,000	% of total value	labour force	% of labour force
Agriculture	8,545	25.2	420,000	82.2
Mining	2,898	8.5	...	...
Manufacturing	2,249¶	6.6¶	...	...
Construction	2,141	6.3	...	...
Trade and finance	6,024	17.7	...	...
Public utilities	...¶	...¶	...	...
Transportation and communication	2,700	8.0	...	...
Pub. admin., defense	5,910	17.4	...	...
Services	...	...	...	...
Other	3,477	10.2	91,000	17.8
TOTAL	33,944	100.0†	511,000	100.0

Persons economically active (1982): total 524,000 (30.3%); female participation in labour force 21,973♀ (4.3%); unemployed, n.a.

Price and earnings indexes (1980 = 100)

	1977	1978	1980	1981	1982	1983
Consumer price index	77.3	82.8	90.3	100.0	119.1	134.1	135.3
Earnings index	...	...	...	...	...	...

Household income and expenditure. Average household size (1980) 5.0;
average annual income per household, n.a.; source of income: n.a.; expenditure: n.a.

Foreign trade

Balance of trade (current prices)

	1978	1979	1980	1981	1982	1983
UM'000,000	−2,670	−5,137	−4,203	−294	−2,165	+3,537
% of total	19.0%	27.6%	19.1%	1.2%	8.2%	12.4%

Imports (1980): UM13,119,000,000 (foodstuffs 33.6%, of which tea, sugar,
and rice 17.3%; fuels 11.9%; building materials 5.9%; spare parts and
tires 5.4%; vehicles 4.3%). *Major import sources:* France 31.3%; Senegal
11.4%; Spain 5.6%.
Exports (1980)δ: UM8,916,000,000 (iron ore 77.8%; fish 21.9%; gypsum 0.2%).
Major export destinations: France 27.1%; Spain 11.3%; Senegal 10.2%.

Transport and communications

Transport. Railroads (1983): route length 428 mi, 689 km; passenger-mi,
n.a., passenger-km, n.a.; short ton-mi cargo 9,891,000,000, metric ton-
km cargo 14,441,000,000□. Roads (1980): total length 4,685 mi, 7,540 km
(paved 18%). Vehicles (1980): passenger cars 11,262; trucks and buses
8,437. Merchant marine (1983): vessels (100 gross tons and over) 28; total
deadweight tonnage 5,687. Air transport (1981)◊: passenger arrivals and
departures 186,843; cargo loaded and unloaded 2,361 metric tons; airports
(1984) with scheduled flights 8.
Communications. Daily newspaper (1983): total number 1; total circulation,
n.a. Radios (1983): total number of receivers 95,000 (1 per 19 persons).
Television: total number of receivers, n.a. Telephones (1982): 3,161 (1
per 493 persons).

Education and health

Education (1980–81)

	schools	teachers	students	student/ teacher ratio
Primary (age 6–11)	599	2,183	90,530	41.5
Secondary (age 12–17)	...	646	20,248	31.3
Voc., teacher tr.	...	...	1,854	...
Higher	2	25	400	16.0

College graduates per 100,000 population (1981): 55.8△. *Literacy* (1978)
adult literacy rate: 17.0%.
Health: physicians (1977) 99 (1 per 14,350 persons); hospital beds (1979) 561
(1 per 2,653 persons).
Food (1978–80): daily per capita caloric intake 2,051 (vegetable products
72.6%, animal products 27.4%); 89% of FAO recommended minimum
requirement.

Military

Total active duty personnel (1982): 8,470 (army 94.5%; navy 3.8%; air force
1.7%). *Military expenditure as percent of GNP* (1982): 7.9% (world 6.0%);
per capita expenditure U.S.$37.

*Regions arranged geographically. †Detail does not add to total given because of
rounding. ‡The percentage of nomads in Mauritania declined from about 80% of
the total population in 1970 to about 25% of the total population in 1983. §1982
estimated population of Nouakchott was 250,000–300,000. ‖ No data available; however, malaria is endemic in the Sénégal River Valley north to Nouakchott, respiratory
diseases are the major causes of death in refugee camps, and during drought localized typhoid fever and cholera may occur in epidemic proportions. ¶Manufacturing
includes public utilities. ♀1981. δExports (1983): UM15,982,000,000 (fish 54.9%; iron
ore 45.1%). □11 months only. Principal traffic is iron ore. ◊Nouakchott and Nouadhibou airports. △ Ratio based on the total number (871) of residents graduating from
the two local institutes of higher education.

Mauritius

Official name: Mauritius.
Form of government: unitary multiparty state with one legislative house (Legislative Assembly [70]).
Chief of state: British Monarch represented by governor-general.
Head of government: Prime Minister.
Capital: Port Louis.
Official language: English.
Official religion: none.
Monetary unit: 1 Mauritian Rupee (Mau Re, plural Mau Rs) = 100 cents; valuation (1984) 1 U.S.$ = Mau Rs 15.07; 1 £ = Mau Rs 18.17.

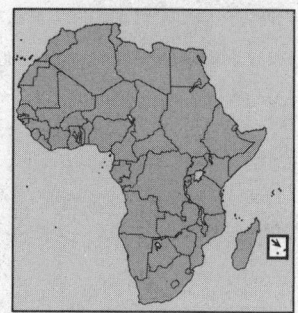

Area and population

Islands Districts	area sq mi	area sq km	population 1983 census
Mauritius	720	1,865	960,200
Black River	100	259	36,700
Flacq	115	298	107,400
Grand Port	101	262	92,300
Moka	89	230	61,300
Pamplemousses	69	179	90,200
Plaines Wilhems	78	202	301,300
Port Louis	17	44	132,200
Rivière du Rampart	57	148	80,500
Savanne	94	243	58,300
Rodrigues	40	104	33,000
Agelega	27	70	350
Saint Brandon	1	3	150
TOTAL	788	2,042*	993,700

Source: Official government figures.

Demography

Density (1984): persons per sq mi 1,280.2, persons per sq km 494.3.
Urban–rural† (1982): urban 42.5%; rural 57.5%.
Sex distribution (1983): male 48.93%; female 51.07%.
Age breakdown† (1982): under 15, 32.8%; 15–29, 32.1%; 30–44, 17.2%; 45–59, 11.0%; 60–74, 5.8%; 75 and over, 1.1%.
Population projection: (1990) 1,117,000; (2000) 1,248,000.
Doubling time: 45 years.
Ethnic composition (1982): Indian 68.0%; Creole 27.0%; Chinese 3.0%; English and French 2.0%.
Religious affiliation (1980): Hindu 46.1%; Roman Catholic 31.2%; Muslim 16.4%; Protestant 1.5%; Bahá'í 1.0%; Buddhist 0.6%; other 3.2%.
Major cities (1983 est.): Port Louis 148,040; Beau Bassin–Rose Hill 87,520; Quatre Bornes 56,676; Vacoas–Phoenix 56,011; Curepipe 57,613.

Vital statistics†

Birth rate per 1,000 population (1982): 22.4 (world avg. 29.0).
Death rate per 1,000 population (1982): 6.7 (world avg. 11.0).
Natural increase rate per 1,000 population (1982): 15.7 (world avg. 18.0).
Total fertility rate (avg. births per childbearing woman; 1981): 3.0.
Marriage rate per 1,000 population (1983): 11.2.
Divorce rate per 1,000 population (1982): 0.4.
Infant mortality rate per 1,000 live births (1982): 29.4.
Life expectancy at birth (1980–85): male 63.3 years; female 68.4 years.
Major causes of death per 100,000 population (1982): heart diseases 303.4; respiratory diseases, including pneumonia, bronchitis, emphysema, and asthma 76.4; malignant neoplasms (cancers) 53.3; injury and poisoning 42.6.

National economy

Budget (1982–83). Revenue: Mau Rs 3,908,300,000 (total from loans 22.9%, of which external 18.8%; import duties 15.9%; individual income tax 10.3%; export duties 9.5%; excise duties 7.0%). Expenditures: Mau Rs 4,916,000,000 (debt servicing 25.7%, employee compensation 23.9%, development projects 23.9%, social security transfers 5.5%, subsidy on rice and flour 4.1%).
Public debt (external, outstanding; 1982): U.S.$386,400,000.
Tourism (1982): receipts from visitors U.S.$450,000,000; expenditures by nationals abroad U.S.$145,000,000.
Gross national product (at current market prices; 1982): U.S.$1,021,000,000 (U.S.$1,075 per capita).

Origin of gross domestic product (current prices)

	1982 in value Mau Rs '000,000	% of total value	labour force	% of labour force
Agriculture	1,515	13.0	52,438	27.2
Mining	20	0.2	147	0.1
Manufacturing	1,630	14.0	38,170	19.8
Construction	610	5.2	5,568	2.9
Trade	1,315	11.3	9,115	4.7
Public utilities	240	2.0	4,451	2.3
Transportation and communication	1,145	9.8	8,085	4.2
Finance	1,730	14.8	4,669	2.4
Pub. admin., defense	1,260	10.8	63,858	33.1
Services	560	4.8		
Other	1,650	14.1	6,376	3.3
TOTAL	11,675	100.0	192,877	100.0

Production (metric tons except as noted). Agriculture, forestry, fishing (1982): sugarcane 6,582,000, tea (green leaf) 26,482, potatoes 13,500, tomatoes 9,530, bananas 6,415, peanuts (groundnuts) 1,940, corn (maize) 1,375; livestock (number of live animals; 1982) 13,431 goats, 11,323 pigs, 6,308 cattle, 2,508 sheep; roundwood 43,000,000 cu m; fish catch 4,720. Manufacturing (1982): sugar, refined 687,940; molasses 195,000; fertilizers 49,032; processed tea 4,917; soft drinks 307,885 hectolitres; beer and stout 136,774 hectolitres; rum 41,406 hectolitres; matches 179,646 boxes. Construction‡ (1982): residential 462,000 sq m; nonresidential 62,400 sq m. Energy production (consumption): electricity (kW-hr; 1982) 362,700,000 (293,100,000); coal (metric tons; 1982) none (1,000); crude petroleum, none (n.a.); petroleum products (metric tons; 1982) none (150,000); natural gas, none (n.a.).
Persons economically active (1981): total 332,000 (34.2%); female participation in the labour force 75,700 (22.8%); unemployed 60,074 (18.1%).

Price and earnings indexes (1980 = 100)

	1978	1979	1980	1981	1982	1983	1984
Consumer price index	61.5	70.4	100.0	114.5	127.5	134.7	140.0§
Monthly earnings index	72.3	79.4	100.0	117.9	129.5	...	...

Household income and expenditure. Average household size (1980) 4.6; income per household (1979) Mau Rs 15,540 (U.S.$2,430); sources of income: n.a.; expenditure: n.a.
Land use (1981): forested 31.4%; meadows and pastures 3.8%; agricultural and under permanent cultivation 57.8%; other 7.0%.

Foreign trade

Balance of trade (current prices)

	1977	1978	1979	1980	1981	1982
Mau Rs '000,000	−909	−1,089	−1,202	−1,380	−1,978	−1,060
% of total	18.2%	21.5%	19.8%	17.1%	24.8%	11.7%

Imports‖ (1981–82): Mau Rs 4,971,800,000 (food and live animals 24.0%, of which cereal and cereal preparations 11.2%, dairy products and eggs 3.6%; petroleum products 19.2%; textile yarn, cotton, and clothing accessories 8.9%; chemical products 7.4%; cement and fabricated construction material 3.9%). *Major import sources:* Bahrain 16.6%; France 9.9%; South Africa 9.2%; United Kingdom 7.9%; Australia 5.3%; United States 5.0%.
Exports (1981–82): Mau Rs 3,853,000,000 (sugar 60.0%, clothing and textiles 26.1%, molasses 2.1%, tea 1.7%, fish and fish preparations 1.7%, processed diamonds and synthetic stones 1.1%). *Major export destinations:* United Kingdom 53.2%; France 21.4%; United States 8.1%; West Germany 4.0%; Italy 2.0%; Belgium 1.6%.

Transport and communications

Transport. Railroads: none. Roads (1981): total length 1,107 mi, 1,782 km (paved 92.0%). Vehicles (1982): passenger cars 25,536; trucks and buses 17,494. Merchant marine (1983): vessels (100 gross tons and over) 28; total deadweight tonnage 5,687. Air transport (1982): passenger-mi 149,136,000, passenger-km 240,012,000; short ton-mi cargo 1,961,000, metric ton-km cargo 2,863,000; airports (1984) with scheduled flights 2.
Communications. Daily newspapers (1979): total number 8; total circulation 74,000; circulation per 1,000 population 79. Radios (1983): total number of receivers 115,000 (1 per 8.3 persons). Television (1983): total number of receivers 85,000 (1 per 11.3 persons). Telephones (1982): 45,127 (1 per 21.3 persons).

Education and health

Education (1982)

	schools	teachers	students	student/ teacher ratio
Primary (age 5–12)	262	6,420	131,594	20.5
Secondary (age 12–20)	148	3,144	76,308	24.3
Voc., teacher tr.	8	69	508	7.4
Higher	2	184	499	2.7

College graduates per 100,000 population (students graduating; 1981): 37.
Literacy (1980): total population literate 557,100 (84.6%); males literate 297,700 (90.5%); females literate 259,400 (78.8%).
Health† (1982): physicians 634 (1 per 1,514 persons); hospital beds¶ 2,862 (1 per 335 persons).
Food (1978–80): daily per capita caloric intake 2,703 (vegetable products 88.3%, animal products 11.7%); 119% of FAO recommended minimum requirement.

Military

Total active duty personnel: n.a. *Military expenditure as percent of GNP* (1982): 0.3% (world 6.0%); per capita expenditure U.S.$3.

*Detail does not add to total given because of rounding. †Island of Mauritius only. ‡Construction authorized. §First quarter. ‖ c.i.f. ¶Government hospitals only.

Mayotte

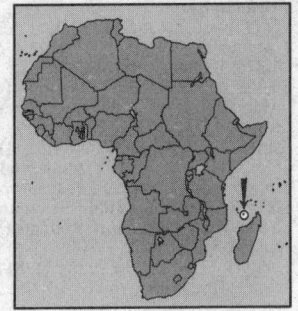

Official name: Collectivité Territoriale de Mayotte* (Territorial Collectivity of Mayotte).
Political status: overseas dependency of France with one legislative house (General Council [17]), one representative in the French National Assembly, and one senator in the French Senate.
Chief of state: President of France.
Head of government: Commissioner.
Capital: Dzaoudzi; Mamoudzou is the capital designate.
Official language: French.
Official religion: none.
Monetary unit: 1 French (metropolitan) franc (F) = 100 centimes; valuation (Oct. 29, 1984) 1 U.S.$ = F9.41; 1 £ = F11.36.

Area and population		area		population
				1978
Islands Communes	Capitals	sq mi	sq km	census
Grande Terre				
Acoua	—	4.9	12.6	1,910
Bandraboua	—	12.5	32.4	2,551
Bandrele	—	14.1	36.5	2,148
Boueni	—	5.4	14.1	2,211
Chiconi	—	3.2	8.3	2,880
Chirongui	—	10.9	28.3	2,244
Dembeni	—	15.0	38.8	1,518
Kani-Keli	—	7.9	20.5	1,962
Koungou	—	11.0	28.4	2,362
Mamoudzou	—	16.2	41.9	7,798
Mtsamboro	—	5.3	13.7	2,976
M'tsangamouji	—	8.4	21.8	2,349
Ouangani	—	7.3	19.0	1,948
Sada	—	4.3	11.2	3,228
Tsingoni	—	13.4	34.8	2,206
Petite Terre				
Dzaoudzi	—	2.6	6.7	4,256
Pamanzi	—	1.7	4.3	2,832
TOTAL		144.1	373.2†	47,379‡

Source: Official government figures.

Demography

Density (1984): persons per sq mi 395.2, persons per sq km 152.6.
Urban–rural: n.a.§
Sex distribution (1978): male 49.94%; female 50.06%.
Age breakdown (1978): under 15, 50.2%; 15–29, 23.4%; 30–44, 13.9%; 45–59, 7.0%; 60–74, 3.8%; 75 and over, 1.7%.
Population projection: (1990) 65,800; (2000) 85,000.
Doubling time: 22 years.
Ethnic composition (1980): Comorian (a mixture of Bantu, Arab, and Malagasy peoples) 97.3%; Makua (a Bantu people from East Africa) 1.6%; French 0.7%; Malagasy 0.2%; other 0.2%.
Religious affiliation (1980): Sunnī Muslim 98.8%; Christian 1.2%, of which Roman Catholic 0.9%, Protestant 0.3%.
Major towns (1978): Mamoudzou 7,798; Dzaoudzi 4,256. ‖

Vital statistics

Birth rate per 1,000 population (1978): 49.8 (world avg. 30.0); (1978) legitimate (monogamous marriage) 70.8%; legitimate (polygamous marriage) 18.4%; illegitimate 10.8%.
Death rate per 1,000 population: n.a.
Natural increase rate per 1,000 population: n.a.
Total fertility rate (avg. births per childbearing woman): n.a.
Marital status of adult population (1978): monogamous marriage 51.8%; unmarried 27.3%; polygamous marriage 11.0%; divorced 6.6%; widowed 3.3%.
Infant mortality rate per 1,000 live births: n.a.
Life expectancy at birth: n.a.
Major illnesses: malaria is a significant contagion; filariasis, formerly widespread, and leprosy are now practically nonexistent.

National economy

Budget (1982). Revenue: F144,246,000 (subsidies 30.8%, loans 13.8%, indirect taxes 11.4%, receipts from public property 10.7%, direct taxes 6.5%). Expenditures: F144,246,000 (roads 16.0%, debt service 12.7%, construction of buildings 9.9%, health 7.6%, education 6.5%, water supply 3.0%).
Public debt: n.a.
Tourism: n.a.
Production (metric tons except as noted). Agriculture and fishing (1983): mangoes 1,500, bananas 1,300, breadfruit 700, cassavas 500, citrus fruits 250, taros 200, pineapples 200, coffee 35–40¶, ylang-ylang 24,300 kilograms, vanilla 2,700 kilograms, cinnamon 650 kilograms, cloves 650 kilograms; coconut palm trees (number of producing trees) 350,000; livestock (number of live animals; 1982) 10,000–15,000 goats, 3,000–6,000 cattle, 2,000–3,000 pigs; fish catch 600–700. Mining and quarrying: minuscule. Manufacturing (1982): mostly involves processing of agricultural products for export. Construction (gross value in F'000; 1982): residential 11,050; commercial and other 32,185. Energy production (consumption): electricity (kW-hr;

1982) 5,000,000 (5,000,000); coal, none (n.a.); crude petroleum, none (n.a.); petroleum products, none (n.a.); natural gas, none (n.a.).
Gross national product (at current market prices): n.a.

Origin of gross domestic product				
	1978			
	in value	% of total value	labour force	% of labour force
Agriculture, forestry, and fishing	...	...	9,298	65.4
Mining	...	...	19	0.1
Manufacturing	...	...	833	5.9
Construction	...	...	1,361	9.6
Trade	...	...	672	4.7
Public utilities	...	...	133	0.9
Transportation and communication	...	...	287	2.0
Finance	...	...	220	1.5
Pub. admin., defense	...	...	218	1.5
Education, health	...	...	348	2.4
Other	...	...	825	5.8
TOTAL	...	...	14,214	100.0†

Persons economically active (1978): total 14,214 (30.0%); female participation in the labour force 5,333 (37.5%); unemployed, n.a.

Price and earnings indexes (1982 = 100)							
	1977	1978	1979	1980	1981	1982	1983
Consumer price index♀	...	...	...	...	...	100.0	113.3
Hourly earnings index♂	36.5	54.5	72.8	72.8	81.7	100.0	111.4

Household income and expenditure. Average household size (1978) 4.7; average annual income per household: n.a.; source of income: n.a.; expenditure: n.a.
Land use (1982): agricultural 64.3%, of which 21.4% is under permanent cultivation; other 35.7%.

Foreign trade

Balance of trade (current prices)						
	1978	1979	1980	1981	1982	1983
F'000,000	−38	−56	−69	−96	−110	−140
% of total	71.1%	76.9%	83.8%	83.9%	91.1%	90.1%

Imports (1983): F147,818,000 (food products 25.6%; mineral fuels 20.9%; machinery 10.1%; transport equipment 10.1%; metal and metal products 7.8%; chemical products 7.1%; wood and wood products 4.0%; textiles and clothing 3.7%). *Major import sources¶:* France 56.2%; Kenya 16.3%; South Africa 10.7%; Pakistan 8.0%
Exports (1983): F4,623,000 (ylang-ylang 65.8%; vanilla 17.6%; coffee 13.2%; copra 1.9%; fish products 1.0%). *Major export destination¶:* France 81.3%.

Transport and communications

Transport. Railroads: none. Roads (1982): total length 133 mi, 215 km (paved 40%). Vehicles (1982): 1,300. Merchant marine: vessels (100 gross tons and over) n.a. Air transport (1983): passenger arrivals and departures 17,235; cargo loaded and unloaded (metric tons) 466; airport (1984) with scheduled flights 1.
Communications. Daily or weekly newspapers (1981): none. Radios (1982): total number of receivers 5,000 (1 per 10.6 persons). Television: total number of receivers, n.a. Telephone subscribers (1981): 400 (1 per 130 persons).

Education and health

Education (1982–83)				
	schools	teachers	students	student/ teacher ratio
Primary	62	317	12,670	40.0
Secondary	2	48	987	20.6
Voc., teacher tr.	23	13	379	29.2
Higher	...	...	31□	

College graduates◇ (1978): 116. *Literacy* (1982): total population literate 17,600 (75%).
Health: physicians (1979) 9 (1 per 5,200 persons); hospital beds (1981) 86 (1 per 547 persons).
Food: daily per capita caloric intake, n.a.

Military

Total active duty personnel: Mayotte maintains no domestic military force; however, French military personnel of about 2,000 are in residence.

*Final status of Mayotte is not yet determined. The designation *collectivité territoriale* if of an intermediate status between overseas territory and overseas *departement.* †Detail does not add to total given because of rounding. ‡Total estimated population in 1982 was 53,000; no breakdown available. §In the late 1970s 87% of all residents of Mayotte lived in villages of less than 1,000 inhabitants. ‖ Populations cited are for villages with adjoining communes. ¶1982. ♀Based on January prices. ♂Based on pay increases for salaried employees occurring in August 1977, January 1978, February 1979, January 1981, January 1982, and April 1983. □Students are enrolled in either France or Réunion. ◇Including former matriculants who may not have graduated.

Mexico

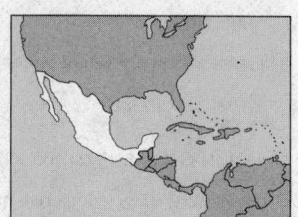

Official name: Estados Unidos
Mexicanos (United Mexican States).
Form of government: federal republic
with two legislative houses (Senate
[64] and Chamber of Deputies [400]).
Chief of state and head of government:
President.
Capital: Mexico City.
Official language: Spanish.
Official religion: None.
Monetary unit: 1 peso (Mex$) = 100
centavos; valuation (Oct. 29, 1984)
1 U.S.$ = Mex$208.76;
1 £ = Mex$251.97.

Area and population

States	Capitals	area sq mi	area sq km	population 1984 est.
Aquascalientes	Aquascalientes	2,112	5,471	615,000
Baja California Norte	Mexicali	26,997	69,921	1,327,000
Baja California Sur	La Paz	28,369	73,475	263,000
Campeche	Campeche	19,619	50,812	514,000
Coahuila	Saltillo	57,908	149,982	1,776,000
Colima	Colima	2,004	5,191	399,000
Chiapas	Tuxtla Gutiérrez	28,653	74,211	2,332,000
Chihuahua	Chihuahua	94,571	244,938	2,186,000
Durango	Durango	47,560	123,181	1,295,000
Guanajuato	Guanajuato	11,773	30,491	3,358,000
Guerrero	Chilpancingo	24,819	64,281	2,354,000
Hidalgo	Pachuca	8,036	20,813	1,714,000
Jalisco	Guadalajara	31,211	80,836	4,887,000
México	Toluca	8,245	21,355	9,840,000
Michoacán	Morelia	23,138	59,928	3,118,000
Morelos	Cuernavaca	1,911	4,950	1,121,000
Nayarit	Tepic	10,417	26,979	814,000
Nuevo León	Monterrey	25,067	64,924	2,933,000
Oaxaca	Oaxaca	36,275	93,952	2,526,000
Puebla	Puebla	13,090	33,902	3,751,000
Querétaro	Querétaro	4,420	11,449	872,000
Quintana Roo	Chetumal	19,387	50,212	324,000
San Luis Potosí	San Luis Potosí	24,351	63,068	1,860,000
Sinaloa	Culiacán	22,521	58,328	2,147,000
Sonora	Hermosillo	70,291	182,052	1,717,000
Tabasco	Villahermosa	9,756	25,267	1,208,000
Tamaulipas	Ciudad Victoria	30,650	79,384	2,148,000
Tlaxcala	Tlaxcala	1,551	4,016	622,000
Veracruz	Jalapa	27,683	71,699	6,171,000
Yucatán	Mérida	14,827	38,402	1,215,000
Zacatecas	Zacatecas	28,283	73,252	1,220,000
Federal District				
Distrito Federal	—	571	1,479	9,750,000
TOTAL		756,066	1,958,201	76,377,000

Source: Official government figures. Britannica estimate.

Demography

Density (1984): persons per sq mi 101.0, persons per sq km 39.0.
Urban–rural (1980): urban 66.3%; rural 33.7%.
Sex distribution (1980): male 49.43%; female 50.57%.
Age breakdown (1980): under 15, 43.0%; 15–29, 27.8%; 30–44, 14.9%; 45–59,
8.5%; 60 and over, 5.8%.
Population projection: (1990) 86,900,000; (2000) 106,600,000.
Doubling time: 28 years.
Ethnic composition (1981): mestizo 55.0%; Amerindian 29.0%; Mexican
white 15.0%; black 0.5%; Spanish 0.3%; other 0.2%.
Religious affiliation (1980): Roman Catholic 89.4%; Protestant (including
Evangelical) 3.6%; Jewish 0.1%; other 0.8%; none 2.9%; unspecified 3.2%.
Major cities (1980): Mexico City 9,981,000; Guadalajara 2,178,000; Mon-
terrey 1,702,000; Puebla 771,000; Ciudad Juárez 680,000; León 596,000;
Tijuana 542,000; Mexicali 495,000; Tampico 428,000.
Place of birth (1970): 99.6% native-born; 0.4% foreign-born.
Mobility (1970). Population living in the same state as in 1960: 87.2%;
different state 12.8%.
Households (1970). Average household size 4.9; 1 person 7.8%, 2 persons
14.4%, 3 persons 14.4%, 4 persons 13.4%, 5 persons 12.2%, 6 persons 11.0%,
7 or more persons 26.8%. Family households: 9,082,661 (92.2%), nonfamily
768,381 (7.8%).
Immigration (1980): permanent immigrants admitted 73,260.
Emigration (1979): legal immigrants to the United States 52,100.

Vital statistics

Birth rate per 1,000 population (1983): 32.7 (world avg. 29.0); (1978) legiti-
mate 91.0%, illegitimate 7.9%, unspecified 1.1%.
Death rate per 1,000 population (1983): 7.0 (world avg. 11.0).
Natural increase rate per 1,000 population (1983): 25.7 (world avg. 18.0).
Total fertility rate (avg. births per childbearing woman; 1980–85): 4.9.
Marriage rate per 1,000 population (1981): 7.1.
Divorce rate per 1,000 population (1980): 0.3.
Infant mortality rate per 1,000 live births (1983): 53.0.
Life expectancy at birth (1980–85): male 63.9 years; female 68.2 years.
Major causes of death per 100,000 population (1978): birth trauma* 487.5;
other causes of perinatal mortality* 458.9; obstetric causes (other than
abortion)* 93.7; heart disease 71.1; pneumonia 61.2; enteritis and other
diarrheal diseases 60.6; accidents 40.1; malignant neoplasms (cancers) 36.9.

Social indicators

Educational attainment (1980). Percent of population 15 years and over
having: no primary education 13.7%, up to 3 years of primary 19.0%, 4 to
6 years of primary 28.0%, some post-primary 26.7%, unspecified 12.6%.

Distribution of income (1977)

percent of household income by quintile

1	2	3	4	5 (highest)
2.9	7.0	12.0	20.4	57.7

Quality of working life. Average work week (1980): 46.0 hours. Annual rate
(1979) per 100,000 workers for: temporary disability 2,789, indemnification
41, death 7. Labour conflicts (1978): 39,313, involving 84,773 workers.
Labour stoppages (1978): 758, involving 14,976 workers. Average duration
of journey to work: n.a. Method of transport: n.a. Rate per 1,000 workers
of discouraged (unemployed no longer seeking work): n.a.
Access to services (1980). Proportion of dwellings having access to: electricity
74.6%, safe public water supply 71.2%, public sewage collection 49.2%. ·
Social participation. Eligible voters participating in last national election
74.9%. Population participating in voluntary work: n.a. Trade union membership in total workforce: n.a. Practicing religious population in total
affiliated population (1970): weekly 10% of urban dwellers, 25% of rural
dwellers; yearly 55% of urban dwellers, 73% of rural dwellers.
Social deviance (1975). Criminal cases tried by local authorities per 100,-
000 population for: murder 10.4, rape 3.0, other assault 31.4, theft 21.0.
Incidence per 100,000 in general population of: alcoholism n.a., drug and
substance abuse n.a.†, suicide 0.88‡.
Leisure (1979). Favourite leisure activities (attendance): cinema 40.1%,
sporting events 22.8%, live theatre 10.1%, museums or archaeological sites
5.2%, bullfights 2.2%.
Material well-being (1970). Households possessing: radio 46.3%, television
1.8%, radio and television 29.4% .

National economy

Gross national product (at current market prices; 1982): U.S.$157,940,000,-
000 (U.S.$2,165 per capita).

Origin of gross domestic product (current prices)

	1982 in value Mex$'000,000	1982 % of total value	1980 labour force	1980 % of labour force
Agriculture	817.2	8.8	5,699,971	25.8
Mining	356.5	3.8	477,017	2.2
Manufacturing	2,239.8	24.2	2,575,124	11.7
Construction	504.8	5.4	1,296,337	5.9
Trade	2,359.5	25.5	1,729,296	7.8
Public utilities	149.4	1.6	115,932	0.5
Transportation and communication	695.9	7.5	672,011	3.0
Finance	785.4	8.5	405,754	1.8
Pub. admin., defense	305.4	3.3		
Other (incl. services)	1,041.9	11.3	9,094,542	41.2
TOTAL	9,255.8	100.0§	22,066,084	100.0§

Budget (1982). Revenue: Mex$1,545,800,000,000 (income taxes 28.8%, excise
and value added taxes 24.5%, export and import duties 21.5%). Expenditures: Mex$1,907,900,000,000 (goods and services 37.3%, transfer payments
and subsidies 35.7%, interest on public debt 27.0%).
Public debt (external, outstanding; 1983): U.S.$88,557,000,000.
Tourism (1982): receipts from visitors U.S.$1,406,000,000; expenditures by
nationals abroad U.S.$788,000,000.

Manufacturing, mining, and construction enterprises (1981)

	no. of establish- ments	average no. of employees	average yearly wages in Mex$	GDP 1983 (Mex$'000,000 [prices of 1970])
Manufacturing	...	...	...	189,060
Food, beverages, and tobacco	473	94.4	208,000	53,415
Chemicals	205	41.6	297,000	36,980
Metal products	57	28.4	193,000	33,240 ‖
Machinery and transport equipment	110	45.7	276,000	‖
Textiles and apparel	135	59.8	162,000	24,765
Nonmetallic mineral products	73	21.2	304,000	10,705
Paper and printing	96	31.6	245,000	10,590
Basic metal manufactures	107	59.1	273,000	10,575
Wood and wood products	17	5.8	149,000	6,100
Other manufactures	...	...	...	2,690
Construction	...	...	...	42,195
Petroleum and coal products	14	5.3	240,000	35,355
Mining	...	...	...	11,270

Production (metric tons except as noted). Agriculture, forestry, fishing
(1983): corn (maize) 13,190,000, sorghum 4,830,000, wheat 3,491,000, raw
sugar 2,900,000, bananas 1,624,000, oranges 1,480,000, dry beans 1,427,-
000, tomatoes 1,300,000, potatoes 910,000, soybeans 880,000, rice 655,000,
lemons and limes 580,000, barley 557,000, grapes 480,000, cottonseed
315,000, coffee 240,000, cotton lint 220,000, tobacco 66,000; livestock
(number of live animals) 36,000,000 cattle, 18,000,000 pigs, 10,378,000
goats, 6,500,000 sheep, 3,233,000 asses¶, 3,130,000 mules¶, 191,000,000
chickens; roundwood 19,462,000 cu m¶; fish catch 1,506,000¶, of which
sardines 513,000¶, anchovies 248,000¶. Mining and quarrying: (metals by
metal content; 1983) iron ore 5,310,000; zinc 257,000; copper 205,000; lead
167,000; manganese 134,000; silver 61,000,000 troy oz.; gold 196,200 troy
oz.¶; (nonmetals; 1983) sulfur 1,600,000; fluorite 560,000; phosphate rock
512,000¶; barite 360,000; graphite 34,000¶. Manufacturing (value added

Mex$'000,000,000, 1980): food and beverages 222.9; machinery and transport equipment 164.6, of which transport equipment 68.4 [motor vehicles 62.2]; electrical machinery 48.6; textiles 71.9; clothing and footwear 67.3; printing and paper products 51.4; industrial chemicals 51.3; iron and steel products 47.5; furniture and wood products 39.1; rubber products 17.6; plastic products 17.3. Construction (gross value of new construction in Mex$'000,000,000, 1980): residential 205.8; nonresidential 96.1.

Service enterprises (1970)

	no. of establishments	no. of employees	weekly wage as a % of all wages	annual value added (Mex$'000,000)
Food and beverage preparation	71,524	177,399	...	3,236
Recreation and resorts	20,850	78,149	...	3,189
Food and beverage service	51,884	141,105	...	2,539
Lodging	6,708	54,509	...	2,515
Exhibitions and shows	3,550	33,323	...	2,143
Repair, excluding industries requiring parts	41,572	95,553	...	1,908
Professional services	9,522	32,058	...	1,772
Medical and social assistance	16,244	43,731	...	1,449
Educational services	5,016	43,781	...	1,355
Personal grooming and cleaning	29,708	65,060	...	1,212
Automobile repair	18,848	51,588	...	1,105
Alcoholic beverages	19,640	36,294	...	697
Mechanical repair	8,195	17,562	...	404
Shoe repair	4,532	6,737	...	73

Energy production (consumption): electricity (kW-hr; 1982) 80,589,000,000 (80,590,000,000); coal (metric tons; 1982) 8,200,000 (8,510,000); crude petroleum (barrels; 1982) 1,015,500,000 (449,900,000); petroleum products (metric tons; 1982) 55,317,000 (53,168,000); natural gas (cu m; 1982) 32,575,000,000 (29,561,000,000).
Persons economically active (1980): total 23,687,684 (35.4%); female participation in the labour force 6,585,175 (27.8%); unemployed n.a.

Price and earnings indexes (1980 = 100)

	1978	1979	1980	1981	1982	1983	1984
Consumer price index	67.0	79.1	100.0	127.9	203.3	410.4	621.3⁹
Monthly earnings index	71.0	83.0	100.0	133.0	195.3⁵		

Household income and expenditure. Average household size (1980) 4.9; average annual income per household, n.a. Source of income, n.a.; expenditure (1980): food and beverages 36.8%, housing 23.2%, clothing and footwear 11.1%, transportation and communication 10.0%, recreation and entertainment 5.5%, health and medical services 4.4%.
Land use (1981): forested 26.4%; meadows and pastures 23.6%; agricultural and under permanent cultivation 18.9%; other 31.1%.

Financial aggregates□

	1979	1980	1981	1982	1983	1984
Exchange Rate, Mex$ per:						
U.S. Dollar	22.81	22.95	24.51	56.40	120.09	161.85⁵
£	48.39	53.39	49.70	98.73	182.18	222.75⁵
SDR	29.47	29.87	28.90	62.27	128.38	167.57⁵
International reserves (U.S.$)						
Total (excl. gold; '000,000)	2,072	2,960	4,074	834	3,913	6,161⁹
SDR's ('000,000)	201	144	178	6	23	9⁵
Reserve pos. in IMF ('000,000)	—	128	187	—	95	—⁵
Foreign exchange	1,871	2,688	3,709	828	3,795	6,128⁹
Gold ('000,000 fine troy oz.)	1.98	2.06	2.26	2.07	2.31	2.36⁹
% world reserves	0.21	0.22	0.24	0.22	0.24	0.25⁹
Interest and prices						
Treasury bill rate	17.89	27.73	33.23	57.44	53.78	48.36⁵
Balance of payments (U.S.$'000,000)						
Balance of visible trade	−2,830	−2,830	−4,099	+7,646	+14,507	...
Imports, f.o.b.	12,131	18,896	24,037	14,435	7,721	...
Exports, f.o.b.	9,301	16,066	19,938	22,081	22,228	...
Balance of invisibles	−2,629	−5,332	−9,800	−13,399	−9,299	...
Balance of payments, current account	−5,459	−8,162	−13,899	−5,753	+5,208	...

Foreign trade

Balance of trade (current prices)

	1978	1979	1980	1981	1982	1983
Mex$'000,000,000	−39.8	−64.6	−64.9	−100.5	+431.2	+1,742.1
% of total	12.3%	13.2%	8.1%	9.3%	20.1%	48.4%

Imports (1983): Mex$927,200,000,000 (unprocessed agricultural products [excluding livestock] 21.0%, of which corn [maize] 8.2%, sorghum 5.6%, soybean seed 2.8%; industrial machinery 18.0%, of which metalworking equipment 3.3%; chemicals 10.6%; transportation and communication equipment 8.8%, of which maritime vessels, parts, and equipment 3.1%; manufactured food products 6.8%; electrical machinery and apparatus 5.9%; petrochemicals 4.8%; iron and steel 4.7%). *Major import sources* (1982): United States 62.5%; West Germany 6.3%; Japan 5.9%; Italy 3.0%; Spain 2.6%.
Exports (1983): Mex$2,669,300,000,000 (crude petroleum 66.6%; petroleum products 3.3%; transportation and communication equipment 3.3%, of which automobile motors 1.8%; chemicals 2.2%; coffee 2.2%; silver bars 1.8%; frozen shrimp 1.7%; natural gas 1.6%). *Major export destinations* (1982): United States 53.5%; Spain 8.6%; Japan 6.9%; France 4.4%; United Kingdom 4.3%; Israel 3.5%; Brazil 3.4%.

Transport and communications

Transport. Railroads (1982): route length 9,735 mi, 15,667 km◇; passenger-mi 3,325,401,000, passenger-km 5,351,724,000; short ton-mi cargo 26,575,861,000, metric ton-km cargo 38,800,049,000. Roads (1982): total length 133,223 mi, 214,403 km (paved 46%). Vehicles (1982): passenger cars 5,221,159; trucks and buses 1,978,327. Merchant marine (1983): vessels (100 gross tons and over) 619; total deadweight tonnage 2,148,815. Air transport (1982)△: passenger-mi 8,253,637,000, passenger-km 13,282,967,000; short ton-mi cargo 75,562,000, metric ton-km cargo 110,318,000; airports (1979) 68.
Communications. Daily newspapers (1980): total number, more than 350; total circulation, n.a.; circulation per 1,000 population, n.a. Radios (1983): total number of receivers 21,000,000 (1 per 3.4 persons). Television (1983): total number of receivers 7,550,000 (1 per 9.6 persons). Telephones (1982): 5,411,108 (1 per 13.5 persons).

Education and health

Education (1982–83)

	schools	teachers	students	student/teacher ratio
Primary (age 6–12)	77,900	415,425	15,222,916	36.6
Secondary (age 12–18)	15,509	212,183	3,990,637	18.8
Voc., teacher tr.	3,738	104,804	1,725,601	16.5
Higher	336	85,943	1,013,117	11.8

College students per 100,000 population (students graduating, 1981): 110.
Literacy (1980): total population literate 31,475,670 (83.0%); males literate 15,955,272 (86.2%); females literate 15,520,398 (79.9%).
Health (1980): physicians 53,053 (1 per 1,260 persons); hospital beds (1978) 66,093 (1 per 1,011 persons).
Food (1978–80): daily per capita caloric intake 2,803 (vegetable products 85.6%, animal products 14.4%); 120% of FAO recommended minimum requirement.

Military

Total active duty personnel (1984): 120,000 (army 78.8%; navy 16.6%; air force 4.6%). *Military expenditure as percent of GNP* (1982): 0.5% (world 6.0%); per capita expenditure (1982) U.S.$12.

*Per 100,000 live births. †Through 1982, cannabis remained the most abused drug in Mexico. ‡1980. §Detail does not add to total given because of rounding. ‖ Machinery and transport equipment included with metal products. ¶1982. ⁹First seven months only. ⁵First nine months only. □Exchange rates and treasury bill rates are expressed in period averages. International reserves are expressed in end of period rates. ◇1983. △All scheduled traffic of Mexicana and AeroMexico airlines.

Fishermen with "butterfly" nets *(tiruspetacuas)*, on Lake Pátzcuaro, Michoacán State, Mexico.

Mongolia

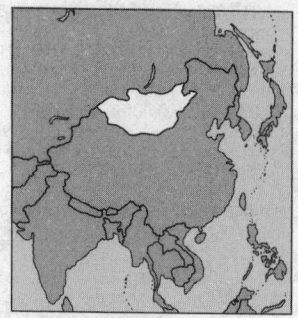

Official name: Büged Nayramdah Mongol Arad Ulas (Mongolian People's Republic).
Form of government: unitary single-party republic with one legislative house (People's Great Hural [370]).
Chief of state: Chairman.
Head of government: Premier.
Capital: Ulaanbaatar.
Official language: Khalkha Mongolian.
Official religion: none.
Monetary unit: 1 tugrik = 100 möngös; valuation (Oct 29, 1984) 1 U.S.$ = 3.78 tugriks; 1 £ = 4.56 tugriks.

Area and population

Provinces	Capitals	area sq mi	area sq km	population 1981 estimate
Arhangay	Tsetserleg	21,000	55,000	79,300
Bayanhongor	Bayanhongor	45,000	116,000	65,300
Bayan-Ölgiy	Ölgiy	18,000	46,000	74,500
Bulgan	Bulgan	19,000	49,000	43,500
Dornod	Choybalsan	47,000	122,000	61,900
Dornogovi	Saynshand	43,000	111,000	44,900
Dundgovi	Mandalgov	30,000	78,000	40,800
Dzavhan	Uliastay	32,000	82,000	81,700
Govi-Altay	Altay	55,000	142,000	58,000
Hentiy	Öndörhaan	32,000	82,000	55,600
Hovd	Hovd	29,000	76,000	64,500
Hövsgöl	Mörön	39,000	101,000	91,100
Ömnögovi	Dalandzadgad	64,000	165,000	34,100
Övörhangay	Arvayheer	24,000	63,000	86,000
Selenge	Sühbaatar	16,000	42,000	69,900
Sühbaatar	Baruun-urt	32,000	82,000	44,600
Töv	Dzuunmod	31,000	81,000	84,400
Uvs	Ulaangom	27,000	69,000	74,800
Autonomous municipalities				
Darhan	—	100	200	56,400
Erdenet	—	300	800	38,700
Ulaanbaatar	—	800	2,000	435,400
TOTAL		604,000*	1,565,000	1,685,400

Source: Official government figures.

Demography

Density (1984): persons per sq mi 2.9, persons per sq km 1.1.
Urban–rural (1983): urban 51.5%; rural 48.5%.
Sex distribution (1983): male 50.08%; female 49.92%.
Age breakdown (1980): under 15, 43.1%; 15–29, 26.1%; 30–44, 16.2%; 45–59, 9.5%; 60–74, 4.1%; 75 and over, 1.0%.
Population projection: (1990) 2,170,000; (2000) 2,686,000.
Doubling time: 26 years.
Ethnic composition (1978): Khalkha Mongol 80.5%; Kazakh 4.4%; Dörbed Mongol 2.8%; Buryat Mongol 2.2%; Dariganga Mongol 1.9%; other 8.2%.
Religious affiliation: n.a.
Major cities (1981): Ulaanbaatar 461,000†; Darhan 56,400; Erdenet 38,700.

Vital statistics

Birth rate per 1,000 population (1982): 36.6 (world avg. 29.0); legitimate, n.a.; illegitimate, n.a.
Death rate per 1,000 population (1982): 9.4 (world avg. 11.0).
Natural increase rate per 1,000 population (1982): 27.2 (world avg. 18.0).
Total fertility rate (avg. births per childbearing woman; 1982): 4.8.
Marriage rate per 1,000 population (1982): 5.3.
Divorce rate per 1,000 population (1982): 0.3.
Infant mortality rate per 1,000 live births (1982): 49.0.
Life expectancy at birth (1980–85): male 62.9 years; female 66.8 years.
Major causes of death: n.a.

National economy

Budget (1983). Revenue: 5,155,600,000 tugriks (turnover tax 65.8%, deductions from profits 20.2%, social insurance contributions 3.4%). Expenditures: 5,145,600,000 tugriks (social and cultural services 40.9%, national economy 38.9%, defense 15.9%, administration and other 4.3%).
Public debt: heavily dependent on U.S.S.R.
Tourism (1982): number of tourists 9,000; receipts from visitors, n.a.; expenditures by nationals abroad, n.a.
Production (metric tons except as noted). Agriculture and forestry (1982): wheat 440,000, potatoes 75,100, barley 63,000, oats 31,600; livestock (number of live animals; 1983) 14,955,000 sheep, 4,802,000 goats, 2,396,000 cattle, 2,028,000 horses, 39,400 pigs; roundwood 2,390,000 cu m. Mining and quarrying (1982): fluorspar 667,000. Manufacturing (1982): cement 179,000; flour 120,000; lime 90,400; meat 68,100; woolen cloth 963,500 m; leather shoes 1,750,500 pairs; sheep skins 3,510,400 units; goat skins 1,186,900 units; beer 9,408,600 hectolitres. Construction (1980): residential 183,400 sq m; nonresidential 113,300 sq m. Energy production (consumption): electricity (kW-hr; 1982) 1,518,000,000 (2,150,000,000); coal (metric tons; 1982) 4,921,000 (4,921,000); crude petroleum, none (n.a.); petroleum products (metric tons; 1982) none (660,000); natural gas, none (n.a.).
Gross national product (at current market prices; 1979): U.S.$1,244,100,000 (U.S.$780 per capita).

Origin of gross domestic product (current prices)

	1982 value	% of total value	1982 labour force	% of labour force
Agriculture	...	17.9	343,400	52.5
Mining	...	‡	‡	‡
Manufacturing	...	30.9‡	77,400‡	11.8‡
Construction	...	5.1	25,300	3.9
Trade	...	33.8	37,500	5.7
Public utilities	...	‡	15,300‡	2.3‡
Transportation and communication	...	10.5	33,500	5.1
Pub. admin., defense	...	1.8	27,000	4.1
Services	...		94,600	14.5
Other	...			
TOTAL	...	100.0	654,000	100.0*

Persons economically active (1982): total 654,000 (37.1%); female participation in the labour force 300,000 (46.0%); unemployed, n.a.
Price and earnings indexes: n.a.
Household income and expenditure. Average household size (1980) 5.0; average annual income per household: n.a.; source of income: n.a.; expenditure: n.a.
Land use (1981): forested 9.7%; meadows and pastures 78.8%; agricultural and under permanent cultivation 0.8%; other 10.7%.

Foreign trade

Balance of trade (current prices)

	1977	1978	1979	1980	1981	1982
U.S.$'000,000	−150.4	−133.7	−207.5	−138.7	−225.7	−220
% of total	23.5%	19.6%	18.5%	15.2%	20.1%	17.0%

Imports (1982): U.S.$757,000,000 (machinery and equipment 35.4%; fuels, minerals, and metals 28.7%; consumer goods 17.7%; food products 8.4%; chemical products, fertilizers, and rubber 7.1%; raw materials except food 2.7%). *Major import sources:* U.S.S.R. and socialist countries 98.6%; capitalist countries 1.4%.
Exports (1982): U.S.$537,000,000 (minerals and metals 39.1%; raw materials except food 28.0%; food [mainly canned and frozen meat] 19.6%; consumer goods 12.3%). *Major export destinations:* U.S.S.R. and socialist countries 98.4%; capitalist countries 1.6%.

Transport and communications

Transport. Railroads (1982): length 985 mi, 1,585 km; passenger-mi 217,000,000, passenger-km 350,000,000; short ton-mi cargo 2,681,000,000, metric ton-km cargo 3,914,000,000. Roads (1982): total length 29,018 mi, 46,700 km (paved 2%). Vehicles: n.a. Merchant marine: vessels (100 gross tons and over) none. Air transport (1982): passenger-mi 155,000,000, passenger-km 249,000,000; short ton-mi cargo 3,562,000, metric ton-km cargo 5,200,000; airport (1984) with scheduled flights 1.
Communications. Daily newspapers (1983): total number 2; total circulation 177,000; circulation per 1,000 population 99.7. Radios (1982): total number of receivers 180,000 (1 per 9.7 persons). Television (1982): total number of receivers 65,300 (1 per 26.8 persons). Telephones (1983): 42,900 (1 per 40.8 persons).

Education and health

Education (1982–83)

	schools	teachers	students	student/teacher ratio
Primary and secondary (age 8–18)	669	15,100	401,000	26.6
Voc., teacher tr.	37	1,100	22,900	20.8
Higher	8	1,300	21,300	16.4

College graduates per 100,000 population (1982): 219.8. *Literacy* (1980): total population literate 849,000 (89.5%); males literate 443,000 (93.4%); females literate 406,000 (85.5%).
Health (1982): physicians 3,900 (1 per 449.5 persons); hospital beds 19,200 (1 per 91.3 persons).
Food (1978–80): daily per capita caloric intake 2,711 (vegetable products 61.6%, animal products 38.4%); 112% of FAO recommended minimum requirement.

Military

Total active duty personnel (1983): 25,100 (army 99.6%; navy, none; air force 0.4%). *Military expenditure* (1982): 816,400,000 tugriks ($243,701,000); estimated foreign military assistance $600,000; per capita expenditure U.S.$138.

*Detail does not add to total given because of rounding. †1983 estimate. ‡Mining and public utilities are included with manufacturing.

Morocco

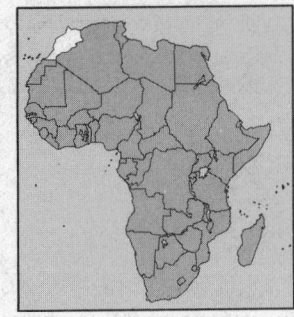

Official name: al-Mamlakah al-Maghribīyah (Kingdom of Morocco).
Form of government: constitutional monarchy with one legislative house (Chamber of Representatives [264]).
Chief of state: King.
Head of government: Prime Minister.
Capital: Rabat.
Official language: Arabic.
Official religion: Islām.
Monetary unit: 1 Moroccan dirham (DH) = 100 Moroccan francs; valuation (Oct. 29, 1984) 1 U.S.$ = DH9.32; 1 £ = DH11.25.

Area and population

Provinces	Capitals	area sq mi	area sq km	population 1981 estimate
Agadir	Agadir	6,741	17,460	985,000
Azilal	Azilal	3,880	10,050	415,000
Beni Mellal	Beni Mellal	2,732	7,075	610,900
Ben Slimane	Ben Slimane	1,066	2,760	191,300
Boulemane	Boulemane	5,558	14,395	133,600
Chaouen	Chaouen	1,680	4,350	314,400
el-Hoceima	el-Hoceima	1,371	3,550	323,100
el-Jadida	el-Jadida	2,317	6,000	734,400
el-Kelaa Sraghna	el-Kelaa Sraghna	3,888	10,070	587,100
er-Rachidia	er-Rachidia	23,006	59,585	424,900
Essaouira	Essaouira	2,446	6,335	489,400
Fès	Fès	2,085	5,400	788,100
Figuig	Figuig	21,618	55,990	113,700
Guelmim*	Guelmim	11,100	28,750	97,500
Ifrane†	Ifrane†	...	...	...
Kenitra	Kenitra	3,400	8,805	1,264,900
Khémisset	Khémisset	3,207	8,305	449,300
Khenifra	Khenifra	4,292	11,115	313,900
Khouribga	Khouribga	1,641	4,250	453,100
Laayoune‡	El Aaiún	...	...	...
Marrakech	Marrakech	5,697	14,755	1,288,400
Meknès	Meknès	3,286	8,510	823,500
Nador	Nador	2,367	6,130	646,700
Ouarzazate	Ouarzazate	17,938	46,460	612,200
Oujda	Oujda	7,992	20,700	822,000
Safi	Safi	2,813	7,285	678,300
Settat	Settat	3,764	9,750	727,300
Tangier	Tangier	461	1,195	404,800
Tan-Tan	Tan-Tan	6,678	17,295	27,900
Taounate	Taounate	2,156	5,585	591,700
Tata	Tata	10,010	25,925	111,000
Taza	Taza	5,799	15,020	652,000
Tétouan	Tétouan	2,326	6,025	723,100
Tiznit	Tiznit	2,687	6,960	353,000
Prefectures				
Casablanca		623	1,615	2,553,300
Rabat-Salé		492	1,275	941,200
TOTAL		177,117	458,730	20,646,000

Source: Official government figures.

Demography

Density (1984): persons per sq mi 130.5, persons per sq km 50.4.
Urban–rural (1982): urban 42.7%; rural 57.3%.
Sex distribution (1981): male 50.05%; female 49.95%.
Age breakdown (1981): under 15, 45.6%; 15–29, 26.8%; 30–44, 14.8%; 45–59, 8.4%; 60–74, 3.7%; 75 and over, 0.7%.
Population projection: (1990) 27,840,000; (2000) 36,509,000.
Doubling time: 24 years.
Ethnic composition (1982): Arab–Berber 99.1%; other 0.9%.
Religious affiliation (1982): Muslim 98.7%; Christian 1.1%; Jewish 0.2%.
Major cities (1982): Casablanca 2,139,204; Rabat 518,616; Fès 448,823.

Vital statistics

Birth rate per 1,000 population (1980–85): 44.1 (world avg. 27.5).
Death rate per 1,000 population (1980–85): 11.7 (world avg. 10.6).
Natural increase rate per 1,000 population (1980–85): 32.4 (world avg. 16.9).
Total fertility rate (avg. births per childbearing woman; 1980–85): 6.4.
Marriage rate per 1,000 population: n.a.
Divorce rate per 1,000 population: n.a.
Infant mortality rate per 1,000 live births (1975–80): 114.4.
Life expectancy at birth (1980–85): male 56.1 years; female 59.4 years.
Major causes of death per 100,000 population (1981)§: conjunctivitis of the newborn 819.0; measles 508.0; trachoma 108.5; bilharzia 37.8.

National economy

Budget (1983). Revenue: DH37,800,000,000 (loans 39.2%; indirect taxes 22.8%; direct taxes 15.1%; customs duties 14.0%). Expenditures: DH44,-500,000,000 (personnel 26.0%; finance 6.9%; defense 6.1%; agriculture 5.2%; education 3.8%).
Public debt (external, outstanding; 1982): U.S.$9,643,000,000.
Tourism (1981): receipts from visitors U.S.$440,100,000; expenditures by nationals abroad, n.a.
Production (metric tons except as noted). Agriculture, forestry, fishing (1982): barley 1,901,000, wheat 1,824,000, oranges 695,000, potatoes 539,-000, sugar (raw value) 395,000, dates 65,000; livestock (number of live animals) 14,900,000 sheep, 6,250,000 goats, 2,900,000 cattle; roundwood 1,667,000; fish catch 361,686. Mining and quarrying (1982): phosphates ‖

21,416,000; barite 537,900; iron 223,800; lead 148,500; manganese 94,100; copper 63,300. Manufacturing (1980): cement 3,561,160; rugs 33,637 units. Construction (value added in DH; 1982): 4,211,300,000. Energy production (consumption): electricity (kW-hr; 1982) 5,436,000,000 ‖ (5,030,000,000); coal (metric tons; 1982) 730,000 (678,000); crude petroleum (barrels; 1982) 99,000 (30,400,000); petroleum products (metric tons; 1982) 3,627,000 (3,669,000); natural gas (cu m; 1982) 92,308,000 (92,308,000).
Gross national product (at current market prices; 1981): U.S.$15,045,000,000 (U.S.$720 per capita).

Origin of gross domestic product (current prices)

	1981 in value DH'000,000	1981 % of total value	1982 labour force	1982 % of labour force
Agriculture	10,887	14.2	2,867,000	50.0
Mining	4,283	5.6	...	...
Manufacturing	13,416	17.6	...	...
Construction	5,364	7.0	...	...
Trade and finance	14,965	19.6	...	...
Public utilities	2,935	3.8	...	...
Pub. admin., defense	9,958	13.0	...	...
Other	14,637	19.2	2,870,000	50.0
TOTAL	76,445	100.0	5,737,000	100.0

Persons economically active (1981): total 5,451,000 (26.4%); female participation in the labour force 867,000 (15.9%); unemployed, n.a.

Price and earnings indexes (1975 = 100)

	1977	1978	1979	1980	1981	1982	1983
Consumer price index	122.2	134.0	145.3	158.9	178.8	197.7	209.9
Monthly earnings index	...	...	...	...	...	...	...

Household income and expenditure. Average household size (1980) 5.8; average annual income per household: n.a.; expenditure (1981): food 54.0%, transportation and communication 18.5%, housing 13.5%, clothing 8.5%.
Land use (1981): forested 11.6%; meadows and pastures 28.0%; agricultural and under permanent cultivation 18.8%; other 41.6%.

Foreign trade

Balance of trade (current prices)

	1978	1979	1980	1981	1982	1983
DH'000,000	−4,617	−4,987	−5,136	−7,406	−10,405	−8,173
% of total	26.9%	24.6%	21.0%	23.1%	29.5%	22.2%

Imports (1982): DH25,990,248,000 (crude petroleum 25.4%; industrial machinery and equipment 20.7%; food and beverages 13.4%, iron and steel products 4.8%). *Major import sources:* France 24.7%; Saudi Arabia 13.5%; United States 6.0%; U.S.S.R. 5.2%; West Germany 4.8%.
Exports (1982): DH12,439,745,000 (nonmetallic minerals, metals, and ores 33.1%; food, beverages, and tobacco 24.3%; chemicals and chemical products 16.5%; textile products and wearing apparel 8.3%). *Major export destinations:* France 24.0%; West Germany 7.9%; Spain 6.7%; Italy 6.7%; India 5.7%.

Transport and communications

Transport. Railroads (1982): route length 1,105 mi, 1,779 km; passenger-mi 854,000,000, passenger-km 1,374,000,000; short ton-mi cargo 2,638,000,000, metric ton-km cargo 3,851,000,000. Roads (1982): total length 35,778 mi, 57,577 km (paved 45%). Vehicles (1983): passenger cars 470,239; trucks and buses 232,857. Merchant marine (1983): vessels (100 gross tons and over) 218; total deadweight tonnage 587,024. Air transport (1982): passenger-mi 1,135,000,000, passenger-km 1,827,000,000; short ton-mi cargo 26,600,000, metric ton-km cargo 38,900,000; airports (1984) 14.
Communications. Daily newspapers (1982): total number 9; total circulation 282,000¶; circulation per 1,000 population 14¶. Radios (1983) 2,500,000 (1 per 8.4 persons). Television (1983): 817,000 (1 per 25.7 persons). Telephones (1982): 241,000 (1 per 87.1 persons).

Education and health

Education (1982)

	schools	teachers	students	student/ teacher ratio
Primary (age 7–12)	2,498	63,157	2,418,385	38.3
Secondary (age 14–21)	644	39,035	900,694	23.1
Voc., teacher tr.	...	...	10,300	...
Higher	19	2,558	98,513	38.5

College graduates per 100,000 population (students graduating; 1980): 31♀.
Literacy (1980): total population literate 7,655,000 (70.7%); males literate 4,459,000 (82.4%); females literate 3,196,000 (58.7%).
Health (1981): physicians 1,153 (1 per 17,906 persons); hospital beds 24,342 (1 per 848 persons).
Food (1978–80): daily per capita caloric intake 2,651 (vegetable products 93.7%, animal products 6.3%); 110% of FAO.

Military

Total active duty personnel (1984): 144,000 (army 86.8%; navy 4.2%; air force 9.0%). *Military expenditure as percent of GNP* (1982): 8.8% (world 6.0%); per capita expenditure U.S.$63.

*Excludes area and population of the portion of the province in the Moroccan-occupied Western Sahara. †Area and population included in Meknès; separate figures not available. ‡Separate figures not available for the portion of the province within pre-1976 metropolitan Morocco. §Reported cases only. ‖1983. ¶Refers to eight dailies only. ♀For universities only.

Mozambique

Official name: República Popular de Moçambique (People's Republic of Mozambique).
Form of government: people's republic with a single legislative house (People's Assembly [226]).
Chief of state and head of government: President.
Capital: Maputo.
Official language: Portuguese.
Official religion: none.
Monetary unit: 1 metical (MT, plural meticais) = 100 centavos; valuation (Oct. 29, 1984) 1 U.S.$ = MT43.73; 1 £ = MT52.78.

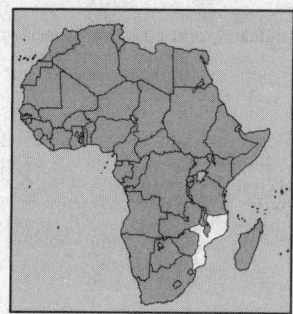

Area and population

Provinces	Capitals	area sq mi	area sq km	population 1982 estimate
Cabo Delgado	Pemba	31,900	82,600	977,600
Gaza	Xai-xai	29,200	75,700	1,030,500
Inhambane	Inhambane	26,500	68,600	1,037,500
Manica	Chimoio	23,800	61,700	666,800
Maputo	Maputo	10,000	25,800	511,500
Nampula	Nampula	31,500	81,600	2,498,800
Niassa	Lichinga	49,800	129,100	534,700
Sofala	Beira	26,300	68,000	1,107,800
Tete	Tete	38,900	100,700	864,200
Zambézia	Quelimane	40,500	105,000	2,600,200
City				
Maputo	—	200	600	785,500
TOTAL		308,600	799,400	12,615,100

Source: Official government figures.

Demography

Density (1984): persons per sq mi 42.8, persons per sq km 16.5.
Urban-rural (1980): urban 8.7%; rural 91.3%.
Sex distribution (1982): male 48.71%; female 51.29%.
Age breakdown (1980): under 15, 43.7%; 15–29, 25.2%; 30–44, 16.0%; 45–59, 9.7%; 60–74, 4.6%; 75 and over, 0.8%.
Population projection: (1990) 16,132,000; (2000) 21,713,000.
Doubling time: 25 years.
Ethnic composition (1978): Makua 52.3%; Tsonga 23.6%; Malawi 12.1%; other 12.0%..
Religious affiliation (1980): tribal religionist 47.8%; Roman Catholic 31.4%; Muslim 13.0%; Protestant 6.8%; other 1.0%.
Major cities (1982): Maputo 785,500; Nampula 126,126*; Beira 113,770*.

Vital statistics

Birth rate per 1,000 population (1980–85): 44.6 (world avg. 27.5); (1974) legitimate 73.1%, illegitimate 26.9%.
Death rate per 1,000 population (1980–85): 17.2 (world avg. 10.6).
Natural increase rate per 1,000 population (1980–85): 27.4 (world avg. 16.9).
Total fertility rate (avg. births per childbearing woman; 1980–85): 6.1.
Marriage rate per 1,000 population (1974): 0.7.
Divorce rate per 1,000 population (1973): 0.01.
Infant mortality rate per 1,000 live births (1982): 105.0.
Life expectancy at birth (1980–85): male 46.9 years; female 50.2 years.
Major causes of death per 100,000 population (1980): n.a.; however, major infectious diseases per 100,000 population are measles 227.4; pulmonary tuberculosis 55.9; viral hepatitis 19.2; leprosy 13.8; cholera 4.6; tetanus 4.5.

National economy

Budget (1981). Revenue: MT16,000,000,000. Expenditures: MT16,900,000,000 (social sector 27.8%, economic sector 22.5%, other sectors 49.7%).
Public debt (external, outstanding; 1982): U.S.$583,000,000.
Tourism: n.a.
Production (metric tons except as noted). Agriculture, forestry, fishing (1982): cassavas 2,900,000, corn (maize) 270,000, sorghum 155,000, raw sugar 130,000, peanuts 80,000, bananas 65,000, copra 50,000; livestock (number of live animals) 1,430,000 cattle, 18,000,000 chickens; roundwood (cu m) 13,566,000; fish catch 37,000. Mining and quarrying (1981): marine salt 28,000; hydraulic lime 10,000; bentonite 1,500; copper 1,000. Manufacturing (1981): cement 261,000; rock salt 86,000; feed 66,000; soap 24,000; coconut oil 23,000; hoes 489,000 units; tires 167,000 units; inner tubes 135,000 units; beer (litres) 51,100,000. Construction (1974): residential 247,000 sq m; nonresidential 121,000. Energy production (consumption): electricity (kW-hr; 1982) 3,400,000,000 (1,334,000,000); coal (metric tons; 1982) 380,000 (420,000); crude petroleum (barrels; 1982) none (3,811,600); petroleum products (metric tons; 1982) 468,000 (508,000); natural gas, none (none).
Persons economically active (1970): total 2,928,000 (35.8%); female participation in the labour force 771,000 (26.3%); unemployed 30,000 (1.0%).

Price and earnings indexes (1970 = 100)

	1971	1973	1975	1977
Consumer price index	115.7	130.6	164.2	195.5
Monthly earnings index	...	...	...	...

Household income and expenditure. Average household size (1980) 4.2; average annual income per household: n.a.; source of income: n.a.; expenditure: n.a.
Gross national product (at current market prices; 1981): U.S.$4,466,000,000 (U.S.$358 per capita).

Origin of gross domestic product (current prices)

	1981 in value MT'000,000	1981 % of total value	1980 labour force	1980 % of labour force
Agriculture	64,374	40.0	...	66.0
Mining	684	0.4	...	
Manufacturing	13,276	8.3	...	18.0
Construction	8,925	5.6	...	
Trade and finance	38,482	23.9	...	
Public utilities	2,168	1.3	...	
Transportation and communication	6,032	3.8	...	
Pub. admin., defense	12,816	8.0	...	
Services			...	16.0
Other	14,002	8.7	...	
TOTAL	160,759	100.0		100.0

Land use (1981): forested 19.6%; meadows and pastures 56.1%; agricultural and under permanent cultivation 3.9%; other 20.4%.

Foreign trade

Balance of trade (current prices)

	1976	1977	1978	1979	1980	1981
MT'000,000	−4,445	−5,735	−11,795	−10,264	−11,383	−12,668
% of total	32.5%	37.2%	52.5%	38.2%	32.5%	32.6%

Imports (1981): MT25,783,000,000 (raw materials 45.5%, consumer goods 20.5%, equipment 19.3%, spare parts 14.6%). *Major import sources* (1980): South Africa 19.8%; West Germany 14.9%; Portugal 9.6%; Iraq 9.1%; United Kingdom 7.2%.
Exports (1981): MT13,115,000,000 (cashews 16.0%, shrimps 15.5%, sugar and molasses 12.1%, tea 9.2%, cotton fibre 7.5%). *Major export destinations* (1980): United States 26.9%; Portugal 16.1%; South Africa 7.0%; United Kingdom 6.9%; The Netherlands 5.7%.

Transport and communications

Transport. Railroads: length (1983) 1,867 mi, 3,004 km; passenger-mi (1981) 354,200,000, passenger-km 570,000,000; short ton-mi cargo (1981) 1,034,000,000, metric ton-km cargo 1,509,000,000. Roads (1982): total length 16,200 mi, 26,000 km (paved, n.a.). Vehicles (1981): passenger cars 49,500; trucks and buses, n.a. Merchant marine (1983): vessels (100 gross tons and over) 97; total deadweight tonnage 41,034. Air transport (1982): passenger-mi 417,649,000, passenger-km 672,142,000; short ton-mi cargo 9,122,000, metric ton-km cargo 13,318,000; airports (1984) with scheduled flights 7.
Communications. Daily newspapers (1983): total number 2; total circulation 54,000; circulation per 1,000 population 4.2. Radios (1983): total number of receivers 275,000 (1 per 47 persons). Television (1983): total number of receivers 1,000 (1 per 13,000 persons). Telephones (1982): 56,000 (1 per 224 persons).

Education and health

Education (1981)

	schools	teachers	students	student/ teacher ratio
Primary (age 5–9)	5,709	18,751	1,376,865	73.4
Secondary (age 10–16)*	138	3,9415tr	3137,990	35.0
Voc., teacher tr.	...	1,177	18,014	15.3
Higher	...	...	1,852	

College graduates per 100,000 population (students graduating; 1980): 115.
Literacy (1980): total population literate 1,959,000 (33.2%); males literate 1,272,000 (44.4%); females literate 687,000 (22.7%).
Health (1981): physicians 365 (1 per 32,900 persons); hospital beds 12,927 (1 per 928 persons).
Food (1978–80): daily per capita caloric intake 1,891 (vegetable products 96.7%, animal products 3.3%); 81% of FAO recommended minimum requirement.

Military

Total active duty personnel (1983): 12,650 (army 87.0%; navy 5.1%; air force 7.9%). *Military expenditure as percent of* GNP (1982): 3.4% (world 6.0%); per capita expenditure U.S.$13.

* 1970. †Includes an intermediate level of education.

Nauru

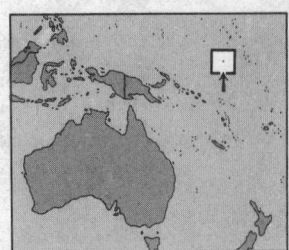

Official name: Naoero (Republic of Nauru).
Form of government: republic with one legislative house (Parliament [18]).
Head of state and government: President.
Capital: Yaren*.
Official language: Nauruan.
Official religion: none.
Monetary unit: 1 Australian dollar ($A) = 100 cents; valuation (Oct. 29, 1984) 1 U.S.$ = $A1.19; 1 £ = $A1.44.

Area and population	area		population
			1977
Districts	sq mi	sq km	census
Aiwo	0.4	1.1	439
Anabar	0.6	1.5	102
Anetan	0.4	1.0	149
Anibare	1.2	3.1	55
Baiti	0.5	1.2	254
Boe	0.2	0.5	448
Buada	1.0	2.6	334
Denigomodu	0.3	0.9	151
Ewa	0.5	1.2	235
Ijuw	0.4	1.1	52
Meneng	1.2	3.1	637
Nibok	0.6	1.6	278
Uaboe	0.3	0.8	231
Yaren	0.6	1.5	413
TOTAL	8.2	21.2	7,254†

Source: Official government figures.

Demography

Density (1984): persons per sq mi 975.6, persons per sq km 377.3.
Urban–rural (1983): urban 0.0%; rural 100.0%.
Sex distribution‡ (1977): male 52.03%; female 47.97%.
Age breakdown‡ (1977): under 20, 56.7%; 20–45, 31.0%; 45 and over, 12.3%.
Population projection: (1990) 8,000; (2000) 9,000.
Doubling time: 54 years.
Ethnic composition (1977): Nauruan 57.5%; other Pacific islander 26.1%; Chinese 8.6%; European 7.8%.
Religious affiliation (1980): Protestant 57.6%; Roman Catholic 24.0%; Confucian and Taoist 8.4%; Buddhist 1.7%; Baha'i 1.7%; none 6.6%.
Major cities: none.

Vital statistics

Birth rate per 1,000 population (1981): 24.0 (world avg. 29.0); legitimate, n.a.; illegitimate, n.a.
Death rate per 1,000 population (1981): 10.5 (world avg. 12.0).
Natural increase rate per 1,000 population (1981): 13.5 (world avg. 17.0).
Total fertility rate (avg. births per childbearing woman): n.a.
Marriage rate per 1,000 population‡ (1977): 6.3.
Divorce rate per 1,000 population‡ (1977): 0.3.
Infant mortality rate per 1,000 live births (1981): 31.2.
Life expectancy at birth‡ (1976–81): male 49.0 years; female 62.0 years.
Major causes of death per 10,000 population (1976–81): diseases of the circulatory system 10.0; malignant neoplasms (cancers) 4.3; infectious and parasitic diseases 3.8; endocrine and metabolic disorders 3.2.

National economy

Budget (1981–82). Revenue: A$109,500,000. Expenditures: A$85,600,000.
Public debt (external, outstanding): n.a.
Tourism: receipts from visitors, n.a.; expenditures by nationals abroad, n.a.
Production (metric tons except as noted). Agriculture, forestry, fishing (1982): coconuts 2,000; livestock (number of live animals) 2,000 pigs. Mining and quarrying (1982): phosphate rock 1,360,000. Manufacturing (1983): phosphate production is the only industry. Construction (1977): 65 units. Energy production (consumption): electricity (kW-hr; 1982) 26,000,000 (26,000,000); coal, none (n.a.); petroleum, none (n.a.); petroleum products (metric tons; 1982) none (41,000); natural gas, none (n.a.).
Gross national product (at current market prices; 1981): U.S.$155,400,000 (U.S.$21,400 per capita).
Origin of gross domestic product: n.a.
Persons economically active (1977): total 2,211 (30.5%); female participation in labour force, n.a.; unemployed, n.a.
Price and earnings indexes: n.a.
Household income and expenditure. Average household size (1977) 8.0; average annual income per household: n.a.; source of income: n.a.; expenditure: n.a.
Land use: n.a.

Foreign trade

Balance of trade (current prices)				
	1978	1979	1980	1981
A$'000,000	...	+66.8	...	+61.9
% of total	...	75.9%	...	67.5%

Imports (1979): A$10,600,000 (food, fuel, water, machinery for phosphate industry, and building materials). *Major import sources:* Australia 58.0%; United Kingdom, New Zealand, and Japan.
Exports (1979): A$77,400,000 (phosphate 100%). *Major export destinations:* Australia 51.0%; New Zealand 41.0%; Japan 4.0%; South Korea 3.0%.

Transport and communications

Transport. Railroads (1981): length 3 mi, 5 km. Roads (1981): total length 12 mi, 19 km (paved 100%). Vehicles (1977): passenger cars, trucks, and buses 1,761. Merchant marine (1983): vessels 8; total deadweight tonnage, n.a. Air transport: n.a.; airport (1984) with scheduled flights 1.
Communications. Daily newspapers: none. Radios (1983): total number of receivers 4,500 (1 per 1.7 persons). Television: none. Telephones (1979): 1,500 (1 per 4.8 persons).

Education and health

Education (1980)	schools	teachers	students	student/ teacher ratio
Primary (age 5–11)	9	102	1,704	16.7
Secondary (age 12–16)	1	36	339	9.4
Voc., teacher tr.	2	5	80	16.0

College graduates per 100,000 population: none. *Literacy* (1979): total population literate 99.0%.
Health (1980): physicians, n.a.; hospital beds 200 (1 per 40.0 persons).
Food (1978–80): daily per capita caloric intake 3,202 (vegetable products 64.2%, animal products 35.8%); 120% of FAO recommended minimum requirement.

Military

Total active duty personnel: none. *Military expenditure as percent of GNP:* n.a.

*Seat of government. †Total population includes 396 Nauruans unable to complete forms; also includes 564 Europeans, 626 Chinese, and 1,890 other Pacific islanders not shown separately. ‡Nauruan population only.

RENE BURRI—MAGNUM

Traditional fishing craft and conveyors for loading phosphates for export, Nauru.

DR. DONALD A. ROWLEY

Terraced fields and traditional stone farmhouse, north of Pokhara, Nepal.

Nepal

Official name: Nepāl Adhirājya
(Kingdom of Nepal).
Form of government: constitutional
monarchy with one legislative house
(National Panchayat [140]).
Chief of state: King.
Head of government: Prime Minister.
Capital: Kāthmāndu.
Official language: Nepālī.
Official religion: none.
Monetary unit: 1 Nepalese rupee
(NRs) = 100 pice; valuation (Oct. 29,
1984) 1 U.S.$ = NRs16.12;
1 £ = NRs19.46.

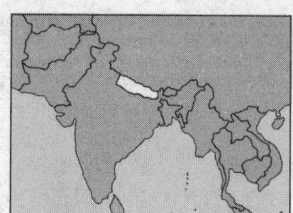

Origin of gross domestic product (current prices)

	1982		1976	
	in value NRs'000,000	% of total value	labour force	% of labour force
Agriculture	16,792	55.0	5,571,790	85.1
Mining	68	0.2	20	—
Manufacturing	1,189	3.9	42,140	0.6
Construction	2,537	8.3	4,950	0.1
Trade	1,070	3.5	282,630	4.3
Public utilities	90	0.3	1,880	—
Transportation and communication	1,992	6.5	5,720	0.1
Finance	†	†	8,250	0.1
Services	†	†	280,460	4.3
Other	6,801†	22.3†	348,300	5.3
TOTAL	30,539	100.0	6,546,140	100.0‡

Persons economically active (1976): total 6,546,140 (50.9%); female participation in the labour force 2,501,560 (38.2%); unemployed 348,300 (5.3%).

Price and earnings indexes (1980 = 100)

	1978	1979	1980	1981	1982	1983	1984
Consumer price index	84.2	87.2	100.1	111.1	124.1	139.2	139.8§
Monthly earnings index	...	...	...	...	...	...	...

Household income and expenditure. Average household size (1980) 5.3; income per household (1973–74) NRs791 (U.S.$75); source of income (1973–74) ‖: wages and salaries 39.2%, self-employment 33.6%, owner-occupied dwellings 17.5%; expenditure (1973–75) ‖: food and beverages 48.0%, housing 20.0%, clothing and footwear 8.8%, fuel and power 4.2%, recreation 3.4%, education 3.2%.
Land use (1981): forested 32.5%; meadows and pastures 13.1%; agricultural and under permanent cultivation 17.0%; other 37.4%.

Foreign trade

Balance of trade (current prices)

	1976	1977	1978	1979	1980	1981
NRs'000,000	−796	−843	−1,423	−1,588	−2,330	−2,820
% of total	25.1%	26.6%	40.5%	38.0%	50.3%	46.7%

Imports (1981): NRs4,428,200,000 (manufactured goods 28.4%, machinery and transport equipment 18.1%, food and live animals chiefly for food 13.6%, mineral fuels 13.2%, chemicals 11.9%, crude materials except fuels 2.6%). *Major import sources:* India 43.6%; Japan 24.8%; South Korea 7.5%; Singapore 4.7%; United States 4.2%; Hong Kong 2.3%.
Exports (1981): NRs1,608,600,000 (food and live animals chiefly for food 36.6%, crude materials except fuels 34.9%, manufactured goods 15.8%, animal and vegetable oils 2.3%, beverages and tobacco 1.0%). *Major export destinations:* India 23.0%; United Kingdom 12.9%; United States 8.5%; Singapore 3.8%; Japan 3.0%.

Transport and communications

Transport. Railroads (1981): length 39 mi, 63 km. Roads (1978): total length 2,858 mi, 4,600 km (paved 41%). Vehicles (1978): passenger cars 14,201; trucks and buses 9,988. Merchant marine: none. Air transport (1981): passenger-mi 70,650,000, passenger-km 113,701,000; short ton-mi cargo 938,000, metric ton-km cargo 1,369,000; airports (1984) with scheduled flights 30.
Communications. Daily newspapers (1983): total number 7; total circulation 75,000; circulation per 1,000 population 5.0. Radios (1983): total number of receivers 300,000 (1 per 50 persons). Television: total number of receivers n.a. Telephones (1979): 9,584¶.

Education and health

Education (1981–82)

	schools	teachers	students	student/teacher ratio
Primary (age 6–11)	10,340	29,134	1,142,900	39.2
Secondary (age 12–17)	4,253	17,154	558,996	32.6
Higher	10	2,918	38,450	13.2

College graduates per 100,000 population (students graduating; 1980): 3.5.
Literacy (population 6 years and over; 1981): total population literate 2,833,440 (23.3%); males literate 2,117,030 (34.0%); females literate 716,410 (12.0%).
Health (1980): physicians 536 (1 per 26,138 persons); hospital beds 2,669 (1 per 5,249 persons).
Food (1978–80): daily per capita caloric intake 1,914 (vegetable products 93.1%, animal products 6.9%); 87% of FAO recommended minimum requirement.

Military

Total active duty personnel (1983): 25,000 (army 100.0%). *Military expenditure as percent of GNP* (1982): 0.9% (world 6.0%); per capita expenditure U.S.$2.

Area and population

		area		population
Development regions Geographic regions	Capitals	sq mi	sq km	1981 census
Eastern	Dhankuta	10,987	28,456	3,708,923
Mountain				338,439
Hill				1,257,042
Tarai				2,113,442
Central	Kāthmāndu	10,583	27,410	4,909,357
Mountain				413,143
Hill				2,108,433
Tarai				2,387,781
Western	Pokhara	11,351	29,398	3,128,859
Mountain				19,951
Hill				2,150,939
Tarai				957,969
Mid-western	Surkhet	16,362	42,378	1,955,611
Mountain				242,486
Hill				1,042,365
Tarai				670,760
Far-western	Dipāyal	7,544	19,539	1,320,089
Mountain				288,877
Hill				604,336
Tarai				426,876
TOTAL		56,827	147,181	15,022,839

Source: Official government figures.

Demography

Density (1984): persons per sq mi 283.4, persons per sq km 109.4.
Urban–rural (1981): urban 6.4%; rural 93.6%.
Sex distribution (1981): male 50.32%; female 49.68%.
Age breakdown (1981): under 15, 39.7%; 15–29, 26.7%; 30–44, 17.2%; 45–59, 10.9%; 60–74, 4.6%; 75 and over, 0.9%.
Population projection: (1990) 18,500,000; (2000) 23,300,000.
Doubling time: 30 years.
Ethnic composition (1978): Nepalese 54.4%; Bihārī (including Maithilī and Bhojpurī) 18.2%; Tamang 5.8%; Newār 4.5%; Thārū 4.3%; other 12.8%.
Religious affiliation (1981): Hindu 89.5%; Buddhist 5.3%; Muslim 2.7%; Jain 0.1%; other 2.4%.
Major cities (1981): Kāthmāndu 235,160; Birātnagar 93,544; Lalitpur 79,875; Bhaktapur 48,472; Pokhara 46,642.

Vital statistics

Birth rate per 1,000 population (1983): 41.5 (world avg. 29.0).
Death rate per 1,000 population (1983): 18.2 (world avg. 11.0).
Natural increase rate per 1,000 population (1983): 23.3 (world avg. 18.0).
Total fertility rate (avg. births per childbearing woman; 1983): 6.2.
Marriage rate per 1,000 population: n.a.
Divorce rate per 1,000 population: n.a.
Infant mortality rate per 1,000 live births (1981): 146.5.
Life expectancy at birth (1975–80): male 44.0 years; female 42.5 years.
Major causes of death: n.a.; however, major diseases are cholera, malaria, tuberculosis, and typhoid.

National economy

Budget (1981). Revenue: NRs3,233,400,000* (current revenue 73.4%, of which customs duties 31.2%, sales tax 22.6%, excise duties 10.2%). Expenditures: NRs3,966,800,000 (electricity, gas, steam, and water 18.5%; agriculture, forestry, and fishing 17.8%; roads 14.0%; education 9.7%; defense 6.5%; health 3.6%).
Public debt (external, outstanding; 1982): U.S.$305,000,000.
Tourism (1982): receipts from visitors U.S.$494,000,000; expenditures by nationals abroad, n.a.
Production (metric tons except as noted). Agriculture, forestry, fishing (1982): rice 2,300,000, corn (maize) 612,000, wheat 450,000, sugarcane 380,000, potatoes 320,000, millet 122,000, jute 39,000, tobacco 5,000, milk 734,000, eggs 1,540; livestock (number of live animals) 6,950,000 cattle, 4,250,000 buffaloes, 2,520,000 goats, 360,000 pigs; roundwood 14,368,000 cu m; fish catch 4,400. Mining and quarrying (1976–77): talc 72; garnet 30; limestone 26,000 cu m. Manufacturing (value in NRs; 1976–77): husked rice 1,989,270,000; wheat flour 133,287,000; refined sugar 74,482,000; sawnwood 62,117,000; cotton fabrics 51,505,000; wooden furniture 42,105,000; bricks 20,274,000; drugs and medicines 6,961,000. Construction: n.a. Energy production (consumption): electricity (kW-hr; 1982) 198,000,000 (259,000,000); coal (metric tons; 1982) n.a. (20,000); petroleum products (metric tons; 1982) n.a. (87,000); natural gas, n.a. (n.a.).
Gross national product (at current market prices; 1981): U.S.$2,300,000,000 (U.S.$153 per capita).

*Includes NRs858,600,000 in grants. †Finance and services are included with other. ‡Detail does not add to total given because of rounding. §First quarter. ‖ For Kāthmāndu only. ¶Number of telephone lines.

The Netherlands

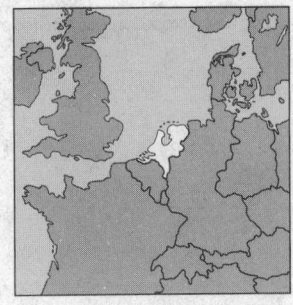

Official name: Koninkrijk der Nederlanden (Kingdom of The Netherlands).
Form of government: constitutional monarchy with two legislative houses (First Chamber [75]; Second Chamber [150]).
Chief of state: Monarch.
Head of government: Prime Minister.
Capital: The Hague.
Official language: Dutch.
Official religion: none.
Monetary unit: 1 Netherlands guilder (f.) = 100 cents; valuation (Oct. 29, 1984) 1 U.S.$ = f.3.45; 1 £ = f.4.16.

Area and population

Provinces	Capitals	area sq mi	area sq km	population 1984 estimate
Drenthe	Assen	1,025	2,654	427,300
Friesland	Leeuwarden	1,288	3,336	597,200
Gelderland	Arnhem	1,933	5,006	1,735,800
Groningen	Groningen	902	2,335	561,500
Limburg	Maastricht	838	2,170	1,083,500
Noord-Brabant	's-Hertogenbosch	1,914	4,957	2,103,000
Noord-Holland	Haarlem	1,030	2,668	2,307,400
Overijssel	Zwolle	1,471	3,811	1,042,100
Utrecht	Utrecht	514	1,332	929,400
Zeeland	Middelburg	689	1,785	355,500
Zuid-Holland	's-Gravenhage	1,122	2,907	3,139,200
Municipalities*				
Almere	—	57	148	33,000
Dronten	—	129	333	22,200
Lelystad	—	105	271	55,100
Zeewolde	—	86	223	800
TOTAL		13,103	33,936	14,394,400†

Source: Official government figures.

Demography

Density (1983): persons per sq mi 1,094.0, persons per sq km 422.4.
Urban–rural (1983): urban 88.3%; rural 11.7%.
Sex distribution (1983): male 49.53%; female 50.47%.
Age breakdown (1983): under 15, 20.9%; 15–29, 25.6%; 30–44, 21.7%; 45–59, 15.5%; 60–74, 11.5%; 75 and over, 4.8%.
Population projection: (1990) 14,973,000; (2000) 15,644,000.
During the period 1971–81 the annual growth rate was 0.4%; since 1981, however, the population has been decreasing.
Ethnic composition (by nationality; 1983): Netherlander 96.2%; Turkish 1.1%; Moroccan 0.7%; other 2.0%.
Religious affiliation (1983): Roman Catholic 36.1%; Protestant 27.2%; other 4.4%; no religion 32.3%.
Major cities (1984 est.): Amsterdam 676,400; Rotterdam 555,300; 's-Gravenhage 445,200; Utrecht 230,400; Eindhoven 192,900.

Vital statistics

Birth rate per 1,000 population (1983): 11.8 (world avg. 29.0); (1982) legitimate 94.1%, illegitimate 5.9%.
Death rate per 1,000 population (1983): 8.2 (world avg. 11.0).
Natural increase rate per 1,000 population (1983): 3.6 (world avg. 18.0).
Total fertility rate (avg. births per childbearing woman; 1982): 1.5.
Marriage rate per 1,000 population (1982): 5.8 .
Divorce rate per 1,000 population (1982): 2.2.
Infant mortality rate per 1,000 live births (1982): 8.3.
Life expectancy at birth (1981): male 72.7 years; female 79.3 years.
Major causes of death per 100,000 population (1981): malignant neoplasms (cancers) 217.8; ischemic heart disease 176.3; acute myocardial infarction 145.8; accidents 29.8.

National economy

Budget (1983 est.). Revenue: f.125,200,000,000 (income and corporate taxes 40.1%, excise and import taxes 33.5%, natural gas royalties 10.3%). Expenditures: f.158,600,000,000 (social security and public health 19.5%, education and culture 17.7%, defense 7.8%).
Public debt (1983): U.S.$61,243,000,000.
Tourism (1982): receipts from visitors U.S.$1,540,000,000; expenditures by nationals abroad U.S.$3,402,000,000.
Production (value added in f.'000,000 except as noted). Agriculture, forestry, fishing (1982): animal products 21,721, of which livestock and meat 11,097, eggs and dairy products 10,285; flower plants, bulbs, and seeds 3,532; potatoes 1,496; fish catch 360. Manufacturing (1982): foodstuffs, beverages, and tobacco products 63,800; electrical machinery 18,200; transport equipment 11,600; petroleum products 31,200; printing and publishing products 15,300. Construction (1982): residential 6,983; nonresidential 5,655. Energy production (consumption): electricity (kW-hr; 1982) 60,313,000,000 (63,177,000,000); coal (metric tons; 1982) none (7,443,000); Crude petroleum (barrels; 1983) 374,758,776 (233,600,000‡); petroleum products (metric tons; 1982) 42,909,000 (24,186,000); natural gas (cu m; 1983) 75,860,000,000 (35,885,000,000).
Land use (1981): forested 8.6%; meadows and pastures 33.9%; agricultural and under permanent cultivation 25.5%; other 32.0%.

Gross national product (at current market prices: 1983): U.S.$135,095,000,000 (U.S.$9,460 per capita).

Origin of gross domestic product (current prices)
1982

	in value f.'000,000	% of total value	labour force	% of labour force
Agriculture	13,100	4.4	275,000	4.9
Mining	§	§	8,500	0.1
Manufacturing	75,500	25.5	730,700	13.1
Construction	21,370	7.2	320,900	5.8
Trade	44,480	15.0	659,700	11.9
Public utilities	5,630	1.9	314,700	5.6
Transportation and communication	20,060	6.8	309,000	5.6
Finance	‖	‖	443,200	8.0
Pub. admin., defense	46,820	15.8	97,800	1.8
Services	83,270	28.1	1,275,500	22.9
Other	−13,870¶	−4.7¶	1,131,000	20.3
TOTAL	296,360	100.0	5,566,000	100.0

Persons economically active (1983): total 5,891,000 (41.1%); female participation in labour force 2,018,000 (34.3%); unemployed 800,600 (13.6%).

Price and earnings indexes (1970 = 100)

	1978	1979	1980	1981	1982	1983	1984♀
Consumer price index	183.0	190.0	203.1	216.7	229.6	235.9	243.3
Hourly earnings index	236.0	246.0	257.0	266.0	284.0	291.0	293.0

Household income and expenditure. Average household size (1982) 2.8; income per household (1981) f.36,200 (U.S.$14,500); sources of income: wages and salaries 42.3%, transfer payments 28.2%, self-employed 17.4%, other 12.1%; expenditure (1981): housing 31.7%, food 20.8%, health care 13.0%, transportation and communication 11.3%, recreation 9.6%, clothing and footwear 8.2%.

Foreign trade

Balance of trade (current prices)

	1978	1979	1980	1981	1982	1983
f.'000,000	−6,170.2	−7,197.7	−5,312.0	+6,773.0	+9,735.0	+11,582.0
% of total	2.8%	2.7%	1.8%	2.0%	2.8%	3.4%

Imports (1982): f.167,116,000,000 (petroleum products 23.2%; machinery and transport equipment 19.4%, of which road vehicles 4.5%, textile products 2.6%; iron and steel 2.9%). *Major import sources:* West Germany 21.4%; Belgium and Luxembourg 11.3%; United States 9.5%; United Kingdom 8.6%.
Exports (1982): f.176,851,000,000 (mineral fuels 23.9%, of which refined petroleum 14.9%, natural gas 8.1%; food and live animals 18.3%, of which eggs and dairy products 4.6%; machinery and transport equipment 16.2%). *Major export destinations:* West Germany 29.4%; Belgium and Luxembourg 14.3%; France 10.5%; United Kingdom 8.3%.

Transport and communications

Transport. Railroads (1982): length 1,837 mi, 2,956 km; passenger-mi 5,826,000,000, passenger-km 9,376,000,000; short ton-mi cargo 1,997,000,000, metric ton-km cargo 2,915,000,000. Roads (1982): total length 57,517 mi, 92,565 km (paved 100%). Vehicles (1982): passenger cars 4,650,000; trucks and buses 352,600. Merchant marine (1983): vessels (100 gross tons and over) 1,266; total deadweight tonnage 7,479,719. Air transportð (1982): passenger-mi 10,512,000,000, passenger-km 16,917,000,000; short ton-mi cargo 726,700,000, metric ton-km cargo 1,061,000,000; airports (1984) 9.
Communications. Daily newspapers (1979): total number 80; total circulation 4,553,000; circulation per 1,000 population 325. Radios (1982): total number of receivers 4,500,000 (1 per 3.2 persons). Television (1982): total number of receivers 6,189,000 (1 per 2.3 persons). Telephones (1982): 7,769,115 (1 per 1.8 persons).

Education and health

Education (1982–83)

	schools	teachers	students	student/ teacher ratio
Primary (age 6–12)	9,735	65,112	1,297,220	19.9
Secondary (age 12–18)	1,487	55,919	836,220	14.9
Voc., teacher tr.	1,902	56,210	611,490	10.9
Higher	384	29,000	295,556	10.2

College graduates per 100,000 population (students graduating; 1980): 357.1.
Literacy (1984): virtually 100% literate.
Health (1983): physicians 28,807 (1 per 498 persons); hospital beds 69,600 (1 per 206 persons).
Food (1978–80): daily per capita caloric intake 3,490 (vegetable products 60.2%, animal products 39.8%); 130% of FAO recommended minimum requirement.

Military

Total active duty personnel (1982): 102,957 (army 65.9%; navy 17.0%; air force 17.1%). *Military expenditure as percent of GNP:* (1982) 3.3 (world 6.0%); per capita expenditure U.S.$333.

*Former parts of Zuidelijke IJsselmeerpolders not yet included in any province.
†Includes about 1,300 persons having no fixed municipality of residence. ‡1982.
§Mining is included with manufacturing. ‖ Finance is included with services. ¶Less imputed bank service charge. ♀First quarter. ðTraffic and transport by KLM only.

Netherlands Antilles

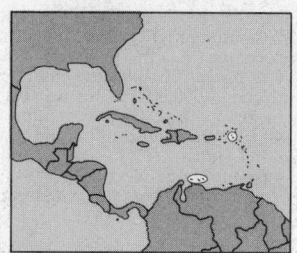

Official name: Nederlandse Antillen (Netherlands Antilles).
Political status: nonmetropolitan territory of The Netherlands with one legislative house (Parliament [22])*.
Chief of state: Dutch Monarch represented by the governor.
Head of government: Prime Minister.
Capital: Willemstad.
Official language: Dutch.
Official religion: none.
Monetary unit: 1 Netherlands Antillean guilder (NA f.) = 100 cents; valuation (Oct. 29, 1984) 1 U.S.$ = NA f.1.79; 1 £ = NA f.2.16.

Area and population

Island authorities	Capitals	area sq mi	area sq km	population 1981 census
Aruba	Oranjestad	75	193	60,312
Bonaire	Kralendijk	111	288	8,753
Curaçao	Willemstad	171	444	147,388
Windward Islands	...	26	68	15,479
Saba	The Bottom	5	13	965
Sint Eustatius or Statia	Oranjestad	8	21	1,358
Sint Maarten (Dutch part only)	Philipsburg	13	34	13,156
TOTAL		383	993	231,932

Source: Official government figures.

Demography

Density (1984): persons per sq mi 605.6, persons per sq km 236.6.
Urban–rural (1980): urban 90.0%; rural 10.0%.
Sex distribution (1981): male 48.80%; female 51.20%.
Age breakdown (1972): under 15, 38.1%; 15–29, 26.7%; 30–44, 16.6%; 45–59, 10.3%; 60–74, 6.5%; 75 and over, 1.8%.
Population projection: (1990) 241,000; (2000) 251,500.
Population growth is negligible.
Ethnic composition (1980): Antillean (Dutch/black) creole 84.0%; white 6.1% (of which Dutch 5.3%, U.S. 0.8%); other West Indian 4.9%; Suriname creole 2.9%; other 2.1%.
Religious affiliation (1980): Roman Catholic 87.2%; Protestant 9.7%; nonreligious 1.9%; Jewish 0.4%; Chinese folk religionist 0.2%; Buddhist 0.2%; other 0.4%.
Major cities (1980 est.): Willemstad (urban area) 100,000; Oranjestad (on Aruba) 20,000; Philipsburg 10,000.

Vital statistics

Birth rate per 1,000 population† (1980): 17.4 (world avg. 30.0); legitimate 60.4%; illegitimate 39.6%.
Death rate per 1,000 population† (1980): 4.9 (world avg. 12.0).
Natural increase rate per 1,000 population† (1980): 12.5 (world avg. 18.0).
Total fertility rate (avg. births per childbearing woman): n.a.
Marriage rate per 1,000 population† (1980): 5.8.
Divorce rate per 1,000 population† (1980): 2.1.
Infant mortality rate per 1,000 live births (1980):13.4‡.
Life expectancy at birth† (1974–79): male 69.8 years; female 75.7 years.
Major causes of death per 100,000 population (1973): neoplasms (cancers) 91.3; diseases of the circulatory system 86.6; accidents, poisoning, and violence 43.1.

National economy

Budget (1983). Revenue: NA f.290,000,000 (import duties 34.1%, tax sharing from Aruba and Curaçao 33.4%, excise taxes 14.1%, foreign exchange tax 5.9%, Dutch development aid 4.5%, other taxes 3.1%). Expenditures: NA f.313,000,000 (social service expenditures 62.3%, pensions 9.6%, interest on domestic debt 7.7%, transfers to Aruba and Curaçao governments 6.8%, national airline subsidy 6.7%).
Public debt (external, outstanding; 1982): U.S.$623,000,000.
Tourism (1983): receipts from visitors U.S.$320,556,000; total cruise passenger visits 216,590; total stay-over tourists 592,363.
Production (metric tons except as noted). Agriculture and fishing (1982): milk 5,000, sorghum 1,000; livestock (number of live animals) 21,000 goats, 9,000 cattle, 8,000 pigs, 8,000 sheep, 132,000 chickens; fish catch *c.* 6,000. Mining and quarrying (1981): unrefined salt (mostly from Bonaire) 399,000; limestone phosphates. Manufacturing (1982): residual fuel oil 16,000,000; gas-diesel oils 3,400,000; motor gasoline 2,600,000; jet fuels 1,500,000; lubricating oils 500,000; aviation gasoline 210,000; liquefied petroleum gas 125,000; sulfur (recovered as a by-product) 90,000§; kerosine 75,000; beer 134,000 hectolitres ‖; concrete 17,061,000 cubic metres§. Construction† (1981): residential 531 buildings; nonresidential 561 buildings. Energy production (consumption): electricity (kW-hr; 1982) 2,310,000,000 (2,310,-000,000); crude petroleum (barrels; 1982) none (188,381,000); petroleum products (metric tons; 1982) 23,910,000 (2,681,000).
Household income and expenditure. Average household size (1980) 4.5; average annual income per household: n.a.; source of income: n.a.; expenditure (1982): food 22.6%, transportation and communication 19.0%, housing 18.7%, household supplies 9.7%, clothing and footwear 8.6%, recreation and education 5.8%.

Gross national product (at current market prices; 1981): U.S.$1,190,000,000 (U.S.$4,540 per capita).

Origin of gross domestic product (current prices)
1983

	in value '000,000	% of total value¶	labour force	% of labour force
Agriculture	...	...	320	0.3
Mining	...	...	177	0.2
Manufacturing	...	...	8,428	8.8
Construction	...	...	7,029	7.3
Trade, restaurants, and hotels	...	...	21,865	22.8
Public utilities	...	...	1,697	1.7
Transportation and communication	...	...	5,876	6.1
Finance	...	...	4,941	5.1
Community, social, and personal services	...	...	30,232	31.5
Other	...	...	15,628	16.2
TOTAL	...	...	96,193	100.0

Persons economically active (1983): total 96,193 (38.0%); female participation in the labour force 38,055 (39.6%); unemployed 15,462 (16.1%).

Price and earnings indexes (1980 = 100)

	1977	1978	1979	1980	1981	1982	1983
Consumer price index	72.4	78.3	87.2	100.0	112.2	119.0	123.1♀
Earnings index	...	...	...	...	...	...	...

Land use (1981): meadows and pastures 8.3%; agricultural and under permanent cultivation, negligible; other 91.7%ᵹ.

Foreign trade

Balance of trade (current prices)

	1977	1978	1979	1980	1981	1982	1983
NA f.'000,000	−805.4	−895.3	−667.6	−1,290.3	−1,335.4	−1,088.0	−1,112.7
% of total	6.9%	7.7%	4.1%	9.9%	5.9%	5.6%	6.3%

Imports (1979): NA f.7,911,000,000 (crude petroleum 73.3%; petroleum products 10.6%, of which residual fuels 9.1%; machines and transport equipment 3.2%; food and live animals 3.1%; basic manufactures 2.6%; chemicals 1.6%; clothing 1.6%). *Major import sources*□: Venezuela 68.3%; Nigeria 5.9%; Qatar 2.9%; Ecuador 2.4%; unaccounted 17.6%.
Exports (1979): NA f.7,139,000,000 (petroleum and petroleum products 98.4%, of which residual fuels 38.2%; distillate fuels 21.0%; gasoline 15.9%; kerosine 12.4%; crude petroleum 4.0%; lubricating oils 3.6%). *Major export destinations:* U.S. 44.7%; Puerto Rico 3.9%; U.K. 3.1%; Colombia 2.8%.

Transport and communications

Transport. Railroads: none. Roads (1984): total paved length 750 mi, 1,200 km. Vehicles (1982): passenger cars 55,000; trucks and buses 8,000. Merchant marine vessels (100 gross tons and over) n.a. Air transport (1981): passenger-mi 103,787,000, passenger-km 167,030,000; short ton-mi cargo 444,000, metric ton-km cargo 648,000; airports (1984) 6.
Communications. Daily newspapers (1983): total number 6; total circulation 48,701; circulation per 1,000 population 208. Radios (1983): total number of receivers 175,000 (1 per 1.3 persons). Television (1983): total number of receivers 56,500 (1 per 4.1 persons). Telephones (1982): 72,168 (1 per 3.2 persons).

Education and health

Education (1976)

	schools	teachers	students	student/ teacher ratio
Primary (age 6–12)	148	1,898	43,966	23.2
Secondary (age 12–17)	6	138	3,084	22.3
Voc., teacher tr.	44	687	9,278	13.5
Higher◇	1	20	500	25.0

College graduates per 100,000 population (students graduating; 1973): 35.
Literacy (1980): total population literate 95.0%; males literate, n.a.; females literate, n.a.
Health (1975): physicians 164 (1 per 1,488 persons); hospital beds 2,051 (1 per 119 persons).
Food (1978–80): daily per capita caloric intake 2,618 (vegetable products 69.9%, animal products 30.1%); 108% of FAO recommended minimum requirement.

Military

Total active duty personnel (1982): A small Dutch naval contingent is stationed permanently in the Netherlands Antilles*. *Military expenditure as percent of GNP:* n.a.

*The Netherlands Antilles has administrative autonomy from The Netherlands with the exception of foreign affairs and defense. The governments of Aruba and Curaçao are partially autonomous from the central government of the Netherlands Antilles. †Aruba and Curaçao only. ‡Excluding Sint Eustatius. §1981. ‖ Excluding buildings by or for the central government. ¶In 1979 petroleum refining accounted for about 18% of the GDP, tourism about 16%, other manufacturing about 9%, construction about 5%, mining and agriculture about 1%, and other (including offshore banking activities, crude oil transshipments, and other transportation and trade) about 51%. ♀First three quarters only. ᵹMostly nonproductive dry savanna woodland in Aruba, Bonaire, and Curaçao; and mainly nonproductive tropical seasonal dry forest in the Windward Islands. □Based on crude petroleum and residual fuels trade only. ◇1982.

New Caledonia

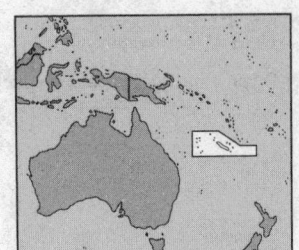

Official name: Territoire de la Nouvelle Calédonie et Dépendances (Territory of New Caledonia and Dependencies).
Political status: overseas territory (France) with one legislative house (Territorial Assembly [36]).
Chief of state: President of France.
Head of government: High Commissioner.
Capital: Nouméa.
Official language: French.
Official religion: none.
Monetary unit: 1 franc de la comptoirs français du Pacifique (CFP fr, plural CFP francs) = 100 centimes; valuation (Aug. 31, 1984)
1 U.S.$ = CFP fr166.00;
1 £ = CFP fr200.00.

Area and population		area		population
Subdivisions Communes	**Capitals**	sq mi	sq km	1983 census
Est	Poindimié	1,530*	3,962	14,704
Hienghène		413	1,069	1,729
Houaïlou		363	941	3,995
Poindimié		293	759	3,644
Ponérihouen		273	707	1,932
Pouébo		78	203	1,503
Touho		109	283	1,901
Loyauté	We (on Lifou)	765	1,981	15,510
Lifou		466	1,207	8,128
Maré		248	642	4,610
Ouvéa		51	132	2,772
Ouest	Koné	2,305	5,969	16,174
Bélep		27	69	686
Bourail		308	798	3,410
Kaala-Gomen		277	718	1,231
Koné		148	383	2,919
Koumac		212	550	1,405
Ouégoa		254	657	1,468
Pouembout		260	674	692
Poum		181	469	816
Poya		327	846	1,961
Voh		311	805	1,586
Sud	La Foa	2,616	6,776	38,868
Boulouparis		334	865	1,139
Canala		317	822	3,842
Dumbéa		98	255	5,538
Farino		19	48	253
Ile des Pins		59	152	1,287
La Foa		179	464	2,094
Moindou		124	322	378
Mont-Doré		251	649	14,164
Païta		270	700	4,834
Sarraméa		41	106	483
Thio		385	998	3,019
Yaté		539	1,395	1,387
Nouméa	Nouméa	18	46	60,112
TOTAL		7,233*	18,734	145,368

Source: Official government figures.

Demography

Density (1984): persons per sq mi 20.3, persons per sq km 7.9.
Urban–rural (1983): urban 58.5%; rural 41.5%.
Sex distribution (1983): male 51.10%; female 48.90%.
Age breakdown (1983): under 15, 36.2%; 15–29, 26.9%; 30–44, 19.5%; 45–59, 11.2%; 60–74, 5.1%; 75 and over, 1.1%.
Population projection: (1990) 151,000; (2000) 159,000.
Doubling time: 55 years.
Ethnic composition (1983): Melanesian 42.6%; European 37.1%; Wallisian 8.4%; Tahitian 3.8%; Indonesian 3.7%; Vietnamese 1.6%; other 2.8%.
Religious affiliation (1980): Roman Catholic 72.5%; Evangelical 11.6%; Muslim 4.0%; Free Church 2.1%; other Protestant 1.9%; nonreligious 4.5%.
Major cities (1983): Nouméa 60,112; Mont-Doré 14,614.

Vital statistics

Birth rate per 1,000 population (1983): 25.2 (world avg. 29.0); (1980) legitimate 57.5%, illegitimate 42.5%.
Death rate per 1,000 population (1983): 5.6 (world avg. 11.0).
Natural increase rate per 1,000 population (1983): 19.6 (world avg. 18.0).
Total fertility rate (avg. births per childbearing woman; 1980): 4.0.
Marriage rate per 1,000 population (1980): 5.6.
Divorce rate per 1,000 population (1980): 0.9.
Infant mortality rate per 1,000 live births (1983): 11.2.
Life expectancy at birth (1982): 68.6 years.
Major causes of death per 100,000 population (1978): malignant neoplasms (cancers) 35.1; perinatal mortality 24.9; cerebrovascular disease 24.2; heart disease and hypertensive disease 14.6; cranial fractures 13.9.

National economy

Budget (1983). Revenue: CFP fr29,950,000,000 (import and export taxes 31.9%, French aid 29.6%, income tax 5.9%). Expenditures: CFP fr25,950,-000,000 (personnel expenditures 41.0%, education 19.0%, debt payments 10.5%).
Public debt (external, outstanding; 1982): U.S.$184,000,000.

Tourism (1983): number of tourists 90,300.
Production (metric tons except as noted). Agriculture, forestry, fishing (1983): coconuts 14,000†, plantains 4,000†, bananas 3,000†, cereals 2,700, copra 600, coffee 250; livestock (number of live animals) 14,200 cattle, 8,800 pigs; timber 6,990,000 cu m; fish catch 5,321†. Mining and quarrying (1983): nickel ore 2,200,000; chromium ore 225,000. Manufacturing (1982): cement 48,801; ferronickel alloy and matte 35,900; milled rice 5,000; iron sheets 3,147; meat 2,930‡. Construction (units; 1983): 394. Energy production (consumption): electricity (kW-hr; 1983) 924,300,000,000 (924,300,000,000).
Gross national product (at current market prices; 1981): U.S.$1,010,000,000 (U.S.$7,100 per capita).

Origin of gross domestic product (current prices)				
	1982		**1983**	
	in value CFP fr'000,000	% of total value	labour force	% of labour force
Agriculture	1,820	1.7	9,888	22.0
Mining	13,476	12.5	2,900	6.5
Manufacturing	4,985	4.6	1,647	3.7
Construction	6,782	6.3	2,725	6.1
Trade	28,395	26.3	4,370	9.7
Public utilities	2,091	1.9	565	1.3
Transportation and communication	4,761	4.4	2,659	5.9
Finance	§	§	1,025	2.3
Pub. admin., defense	§	§	‖	‖
Services	§	§	18,922 ‖	42.2 ‖
Other, including unemployed	45,783§	42.3§	141	0.3
TOTAL	108,093	100.0	44,842	100.0

Persons economically active (1983): total 44,842 (30.8%); female participation in the labour force 16,841 (37.6%); unemployed 3,497 (7.8%).

Price and earnings indexes (1975 = 100)							
	1977	1978	1979	1980	1981	1982	1983
Consumer price index	113.9	121.3	133.4	145.8	167.9	192.6	214.5
Hourly earnings index	111.9	119.8	131.6	147.0	170.4	203.3	218.7

Household income and expenditure. Average household size (1980) 4.3; average annual income per household CFP fr1,670,000 (U.S.$20,600); source of income: salaries 71.6%, other 28.4%; expenditure (1980): food 34.7%, housing 12.0%, transport 11.8%, clothing 5.8%, education and health 5.0%.
Land use (1982): forested 73.4%; meadows and pastures 21.0%; agricultural and under permanent cultivation 0.5%; other 5.1%.

Foreign trade

Balance of trade (current prices)						
	1978	1979	1980	1981	1982	1983
CFP fr'000,000	−6,427	+10	−4,236	−7,734	−11,680	−20,872
% of total	15.5%	0.02%	6.4%	10.6%	15.4%	32.5%

Imports (1982): CFP fr43,735,000,000 (food 22.1%, petroleum products 20.5%, machinery and transport equipment 19.4%. *Major import sources:* France 33.9%; United States 14.1%; Australia 14.0%; Japan 6.1%; New Zealand 5.1%; West Germany 3.0%.
Exports (1982): CFP fr32,055,000,000 (ferronickel metal 57.7%, nickel ore and matte 32.1%, chrome ore 0.7%, other products and reexports 9.5%). *Major export destinations:* France 55.9%; Japan 30.5%; United States 5.5%.

Transport and communications

Transport. Railroads: none. Roads (1983): total length 4,427 mi, 7,125 km (paved 72%). Vehicles (1983): passenger cars 34,100; trucks and buses 1,730. Merchant marine (1981): vessels (all types and tonnages) 319. Air transport (1982): passengers arriving and departing 229,745¶; metric ton cargo loaded and unloaded 6,018; airports (1984) with scheduled flights 18.
Communications. Daily newspaper (1983): total number 1; total circulation 13,000; circulation per 1,000 population 89.7. Radios (1983): receivers 78,-000 (1 per 2 persons). Television (1983): receivers 30,000 (1 per 5 persons). Telephones (1981): 27,953 (1 per 5 persons).

Education and health

Education (1984)	schools	teachers	students	student/ teacher ratio
Primary (age 6–10)	278	1,589	33,884	21.3
Secondary (age 11–17)	41	976	12,683	13.2
Vocational	32	309	5,264	17.0
Higher	5	59	660	11.2

College graduates per 100,000 population (students graduating; 1980): 93.
Literacy (1976): total population literate 75,819 (89.4%); males literate 40,-296 (90.1%); females literate 35,523 (88.7%).
Health (1980): physicians 135 (1 per 1,007 persons); hospital beds 1,685 (1 per 83 persons).
Food (1978–80): daily per capita caloric intake 2,601 (vegetable products 78.7%, animal products 21.3%); 98% of FAO recommended minimum.

Military

New Caledonia maintains no domestic military establishment; France is responsible for external security.

*Detail does not add to total given because of rounding. †1982. ‡1983. §Finance, public administration and defense, and services included with other. ‖ Public administration and defense included with services. ¶Tontouta International Airport only.

New Zealand

Official name: Dominion of New Zealand.
Form of government: multiparty parliamentary state with one legislative house (House of Representatives [92]).
Chief of state: British Monarch, represented by the Governor-General.
Head of government: Prime Minister.
Capital: Wellington.
Official language: English.
Official religion: none.
Monetary unit: 1 New Zealand dollar (Z) = 100 cents; valuation (Oct. 29, 1984) 1 U.S.$ = Z2.05; 1£ = Z2.48.

Area and population

Statistical areas*	area		population
	sq mi	sq km	1983 estimate
North Island			
Central Auckland	2,155	5,581	863,900
East Coast	4,203	10,885	48,900
Hawke's Bay	4,359	11,289	150,200
Northland	4,885	12,653	118,300
South Auckland– Bay of Plenty	14,240	36,882	506,500
Taranaki	3,756	9,729	105,900
Wellington	10,720	27,766	585,800
South Island			
Canterbury	16,736	43,346	422,500
Marlborough	3,942	10,210	36,500
Nelson	7,316	18,948	78,200
Otago	14,237	36,873	182,000
Southland	10,990	28,464	108,100
Westland	5,976	15,477	23,200
TOTAL	103,515	268,103	3,230,000

Source: Official government figures.

Demography

Density (1984): persons per sq mi 31.5, persons per sq km 12.2.
Urban–rural (1981): urban 83.6%; rural 16.4%.
Sex distribution (1984): male 49.66%; female 50.34%.
Age breakdown (1983): under 15, 25.2%; 15–29, 26.3%; 30–44, 20.3%; 45–59, 13.8%; 60–74, 10.6%; 75 and over, 3.8%.
Population projection: (1991) 3,506,000; (2001) 3,772,000.
Doubling time: 63 years.
Ethnic composition (1981): European 85.8%; Maori 8.9%; Pacific Island Polynesian 2.8%; other and not specified 2.5%.
Religious affiliation (1981): Anglican 25.7%; Presbyterian 16.5%; Roman Catholic 14.4%; Methodist 4.7%; other 38.7%.
Major cities (1983 est.): Manukau 173,000; Christchurch 162,700; Auckland 144,100; Wellington 134,300; Hamilton 93,600.

Vital statistics

Birth rate per 1,000 population (1984): 15.7 (world avg. 28.0); legitimate 76.2%, illegitimate 23.8%.
Death rate per 1,000 population (1984): 8.1 (world avg. 11.0).
Natural increase rate per 1,000 population (1984): 7.6 (world avg. 17.0).
Total fertility rate (avg. births per childbearing woman; 1983): 2.0.
Marriage rate per 1,000 population (1983): 7.9.
Divorce rate per 1,000 population (1981): 2.2.
Infant mortality rate per 1,000 live births (1983): 12.5.
Life expectancy at birth (1983): male 70.8 years; female 76.9 years.
Major causes of death per 100,000 population (1980): ischemic heart disease 234.8; malignant neoplasms (cancers) 172.0; cerebrovascular disease 99.4; pneumonia 34.8.

National economy

Budget (1983–84). Revenue: Z10,355,000,000 (income tax 72.0%, sales tax 12.5%, customs duties 5.2%, highways tax 2.3%). Expenditures: Z17,234,500,000 (social services 23.5%, development of industry 18.2%, debt services and investment 15.2%, health 10.7%, education 9.8%).
Public debt (external, outstanding; 1982): U.S.$10,813,374,000.
Tourism (1982): receipts from visitors U.S.$226,000,000; expenditures by nationals abroad U.S.$504,000,000.
Production (value in Z except as noted). Agriculture, forestry, fishing (1981): dairy products 866,000,000, wool 846,000,000, sheep and lamb 635,000,000, cattle 587,000,000, crops and seeds 215,000,000, fruit 178,000,000, vegetables 168,000,000, poultry and eggs 127,000,000, pigs 63,000,000; roundwood (1982) 9,543,000 cu m; fish catch 86,000,000. Mining and quarrying (total turnover in Z; 1978–79): rock, sand, and gravel 48,000,000; limestone 10,000,000; salt 750,000†; clay 460,000. Manufacturing (total turnover in Z; 1978–79): food, manufactured 2,824,000,000; metal products and machinery 1,817,000,000; transport equipment 743,000,000; chemical products 726,000,000; paper and paper products 720,000,000; textiles 526,000,000. Construction (1982): residential 179,000 sq m; nonresidential 205,000 sq m. Energy production (consumption): electricity (kW-hr; 1982) 22,963,000,000 (20,104,000,000); coal (metric tons; 1982) 2,244,400 (1,665,000†); petroleum (barrels; 1982) 15,456 (17,154,411†); natural gas (cu m; 1982) 2,080,844,000 (1,126,178,361†).

Gross national product (at current market prices; 1982): U.S.$21,029,891,000 (U.S.$6,590 per capita).

Origin of gross domestic product (current prices)

	1982			
	in value Z'000,000	% of total value	labour force	% of labour force
Agriculture	2,673	9.2	146,000	10.9
Mining	260	0.9	5,000	0.4
Manufacturing	6,948	23.9	313,000	23.4
Construction	1,395	4.8	86,000	6.4
Trade	6,183	21.2	217,000	16.2
Public utilities	840	2.9	15,000	1.1
Transportation and communication	2,187	7.5	106,000	7.9
Finance	3,934	13.5	95,000	7.1
Services	5,011	17.2	299,000	22.3
Other	−314‡	−1.1	58,000	4.3
TOTAL	29,117	100.0	1,340,000	100.0

Persons economically active (1982): total 1,340,000 (42.2%); female participation in the labour force 460,000 (34.3%); unemployed 47,000 (3.5%).

Price and earnings indexes (1980 = 100)

	1978	1979	1980	1981	1982	1983	1984§
Consumer price index	75.1	85.3	100.0	115.3	134.0	143.8	146.8
Weekly earnings index	73.0	84.0	100.0	119.0	133.0	134.0	134.0

Household income and expenditure. Average household size (1981) 3.2; income per household: Z15,810 (U.S.$13,755); source of income: n.a.; expenditure (1982): housing 22.2%, food 18.7%, transportation 17.7%, household operation 15.6%, apparel 7.0%, tobacco and alcohol 4.7%.
Land use (1981): forested 26.4%; meadows and pastures 52.8%; agricultural and under permanent cultivation 1.7%; other 19.1%.

Foreign trade

Balance of trade (current prices)

	1978	1979	1980	1981	1982	1983
Z'000,000	+295	+493	+343	+478	−311	+766
% of total	4.7%	6.4%	3.4%	4.1%	2.3%	5.2%

Imports (1983): Z6,928,200,000 (machinery and electrical equipment 23.0%; mineral fuels 19.4%, of which petroleum 7.2%; chemicals 10.6%; transport equipment 9.0%, of which motor cars 3.4%; textiles, clothing, and footwear 6.6%). *Major import sources:* Australia 19.7%; United States 16.9%; Japan 16.8%; United Kingdom 9.2%; Singapore 5.7%.
Exports (1983): Z7,694,300,000 (food and live animals 51.8%, of which meat and meat preparations 24.3%, dairy products and eggs 16.8%; wool 13.2%; forest products 6.4%; chemicals 4.0%). *Major export destinations:* United States 15.2%; Japan 13.8%; United Kingdom 12.9%; Australia 12.4%; U.S.S.R. 4.5%.

Transport and communications

Transport. Railroads (1982): length 2,754 mi, 4,433 km; passenger-mi 267,000,000, passenger-km 429,000,000; short ton-mi cargo 2,227,000,000, metric ton-km cargo 3,252,000,000. Roads (1982): total length 57,870 mi, 93,133 km (paved 53%). Vehicles (1983): passenger cars 1,431,739; trucks and buses 303,020. Merchant marine (1983): vessels (100 gross tons and over) 117; total deadweight tonnage 269,949. Air transport (1982): passenger-mi 3,634,465,000, passenger-km 5,849,116,000; short ton-mi cargo 152,300,000, metric ton-km cargo 222,400,000; airports (1984) with scheduled flights 36.
Communications. Daily newspapers (1983): total number 33; total circulation 1,046,552; circulation per 1,000 population 324. Radios (1983): total number of receivers 2,780,000 (1 per 1.2 persons). Television (1983): total number of receivers 924,821 (1 per 3.5 persons). Telephones (1982): 1,875,538 (1 per 1.7 persons).

Education and health

Education (1982)

	schools	teachers	students	student/ teacher ratio
Primary (age 5–12)	2,545	21,467	486,167	22.6
Secondary (age 13–17)	411	13,044	223,501	17.1
Voc., teacher tr.	29 ‖	2,886	142,077	49.2
Higher¶	7	3,071	54,149	17.6

College graduates per 100,000 population (students graduating; 1981): 365.
Literacy (1983): total population literate 825,470 (100.0%); males literate 422,460 (100.0%); females literate 403,010 (100.0%).
Health (1982): physicians 8,565 (1 per 372 persons); hospital beds 31,030 (1 per 102.8 persons).
Food (1981): daily per capita caloric intake 3,119 (vegetable products 46.7%, animal products 53.3%); 118% of FAO recommended minimum requirement.

Military

Total active duty personnel (1982): 12,808 (army 44.3%; navy 22.3%; air force 33.4%). *Military expenditure as percent of GNP* (1982): 2.1% (world 6.0%); per capita expenditure U.S.$140.

*The statistical areas listed have no administrative significance but provide a convenient way of presenting the statistical data. †1981. ‡Includes import duties plus other indirect taxes minus imputed bank service charges. §First quarter. ‖ 1979. ¶Universities only.

Nicaragua

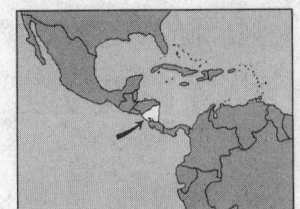

Official name: República de Nicaragua (Republic of Nicaragua).
Form of government: unitary multiparty state; with one legislative body (National Assembly [90]) elected Nov. 5, 1984 and empowered to write a new constitution.
Head of state and government: President (coordinator of the junta).
Capital: Managua.
Official language: Spanish.
Official religion: none.
Monetary unit: 1 Nicaraguan córdoba (C$) = 100 centavos; valuation (Oct. 29, 1984) 1 U.S.$ = C$10.01; 1 £ = C$12.08.

Area and population

Zones Departments	Capitals	area* sq mi	sq km	population 1981 estimate
Atlantic				
Río San Juan	San Carlos	2,876	7,448	29,000
Zelaya	Bluefields	22,816	59,094	202,000
North Central				
Boaco	Boaco	1,924	4,982	89,000
Chontales	Juigalpa	1,910	4,947	98,000
Estelí	Estelí	849	2,199	110,000
Jinotega	Jinotega	3,697	9,576	127,000
Madriz	Somoto	679	1,758	72,000
Matagalpa	Matagalpa	2,623	6,794	221,000
Nueva Segovia	Ocotal	1,290	3,341	98,000
Pacific				
Carazo	Jinotepe	398	1,032	109,000
Chinandega	Chinandega	1,800	4,662	229,000
Granada	Granada	372	964	113,000
León	León	2,021	5,234	249,000
Managua	Managua	1,403†	3,597†	820,000†
Masaya	Masaya	210	581	149,000
Rivas	Rivas	830	2,149	109,000
National District				
Distrito Nacional		†	†	†
TOTAL		45,698	118,358	2,824,000

Source: Official government figures; Britannica estimate.

Demography

Density (1984)‡: persons per sq mi 63.7, persons per sq km 24.6.
Urban–rural (1983): urban 55.3%; rural 44.7%.
Sex distribution (1980): male 48.97%; female 51.03%.
Age breakdown (1980): under 15, 47.9%; 15–29, 25.7%; 30–44, 14.2%; 45–59, 7.5%; 60–74, 3.6%; 75 and over, 1.1%.
Population projection: (1990) 3,778,000; (2000) 5,154,000.
Doubling time: 20 years.
Ethnic composition (1980): mestizo (Spanish/Indian) 68.8%; white 14.0%; black 8.0%; Zambo (black/Indian) 5.0%; Amerindian 4.0%; other 0.2%.
Religious affiliation (1980): Roman Catholic 87.8%; Protestant 8.4%; other 3.8%.
Major cities (1979 est.): Managua 552,900; León 81,647; Granada 56,232.

Vital statistics

Birth rate per 1,000 population (1980–85): 44.6 (world avg. 27.5).
Death rate per 1,000 population (1980–85): 10.6 (world avg. 10.6).
Natural increase rate per 1,000 population (1980–85): 34.0 (world avg. 16.9).
Total fertility rate (avg. births per childbearing woman; 1980–85): 6.2.
Marriage rate per 1,000 population (1975–80): 6.3.
Divorce rate per 1,000 population (1975–80): 0.3.
Infant mortality rate per 1,000 live births (1983): 75.2.
Life expectancy at birth (1982): male 56 years; female 60 years.
Major causes of death per 100,000 population (1978): heart disease 56.7; diarrheal diseases 37.3; accidents 29.8; malignant neoplasms (cancers) 12.8.

National economy

Budget (1983). Revenue: C$8,171,000,000 (sales tax 47.3%; import duties 17.7%; income tax 14.2%; property tax 4.6%). Expenditures: C$10,107,-000,000 (goods and services 47.4%; current transfers and subsidies 12.0%; interest payments 4.6%).
Public debt (external, outstanding; 1983): U.S.$2,900,000,000.
Tourism (1979): receipts from visitors U.S.$19,500,000; expenditures by nationals abroad U.S.$54,100,000.
Production (metric tons except as noted). Agriculture, forestry, fishing (1982): sugarcane 3,000,000, corn (maize) 248,000, bananas and plantains 241,000, seed cotton 190,000, other fruits and vegetables 151,000, rice 150,000, milk 124,000, sorghum 101,000, lint cotton 62,000, dry beans 60,000, coffee 57,000, cassava 27,000; livestock (number of live animals) 2,186,000 cattle, 520,000 pigs, 4,964,000 chickens; roundwood 3,237,000 cu m; fish catch 5,944. Mining and quarrying (1980): gold 2§; silver 5; salt 20,000. Manufacturing (gross value in C$'000,000; 1981): processed foods 1,433; chemical products 385; beverages 334; petroleum products 157; textiles 141; footwear and clothing 125; metal products 115. Construction (1981) ‖ : residential 45,400 sq m; nonresidential 9,200 sq m. Energy production (consumption): electricity (kW-hr; 1982) 1,045,000,000 (1,049,000,000); coal, none (n.a.);

crude petroleum (barrels; 1982) none (3,665,000); petroleum products (metric tons; 1982) 459,000 (516,000); natural gas, none (n.a.).
Gross national product (at current market prices; 1983): U.S.$3,493,700,000 (U.S.$1,140 per capita).

Origin of gross domestic product (current prices)

	1983 in value C$'000,000	1983 % of total value	1980 labour force	1980 % of labour force
Agriculture	7,335	25.8	391,963	45.4
Mining	255	0.9	6,566	0.7
Manufacturing	6,681	23.5	91,403	10.6
Construction	561	2.0	37,322	4.3
Trade	5,468	19.2	105,053	12.2
Finance	1,862	6.5	16,761	2.0
Transportation and communication	1,665	5.8	30,064	3.4
Public utilities	722	2.5	6,652	0.8
Pub. admin., defense	2,450	8.6	¶	¶
Services	♀	♀	158,789¶	18.4¶
Other	1,469♀	5.2♀	19,352	2.2
TOTAL	28,468	100.0	863,925	100.0

Persons economically active (1981): total 830,300 (29.9%); female participation in the labour force 187,600 (22.6%); unemployed 111,260 (13.4%).

Price and earnings indexes (1980 = 100)

	1977	1978	1979	1980	1981	1982	1983
Consumer price index	47.7	49.9	73.9	100.0	123.9	154.6	202.6
Hourly earnings indexð	58.8	62.0	77.7	100.0	125.1	...	...

Household income and expenditure. Average household size (1980) 6.9; average annual income per household: n.a.; source of income (1978): wages and salaries 70.8%, property and entrepreneurial income 27.6%, other 1.6%; expenditure (1981): food 34.0%, housing 24.2%, clothing and footwear 24.0%.
Land use (1982): forested 42.5%; meadows and pastures 38.7%; agricultural and under permanent cultivation 10.4%; other 8.4%.

Foreign trade

Balance of trade (current prices)

	1978	1979	1980	1981	1982	1983
C$'000,000	+742.1	+2,198.9	−3,735.4	−4,263.7	−3,697.1	−3,804.1
% of total	8.9%	26.5%	29.2%	29.4%	31.1%	36.5%

Imports (1982): C$7,794,600,000□ (machinery and transport equipment 23.2%; crude petroleum 19.3%; chemicals and chemical products 15.8%; food 9.4%). *Major import sources:* Mexico 20.0%; United States 19.0%; U.S.S.R. 5.0%; France 4.2%; Cuba 3.9%.
Exports (1982): C$4,097,500,000 (food 62.9%, of which coffee 34.8%, beef 8.5%, sugar 8.2%; chemicals and chemical products 5.2%). *Major export destinations:* United States 22.0%; West Germany 14.2%; Japan 11.5%; Costa Rica 6.7%.

Transport and communications

Transport. Railroads (1983): route length 214 mi, 344 km; (1978) passenger-mi 10,426,000, passenger-km 16,779,000; short ton-mi cargo 6,978,000, metric ton-km cargo 10,188,000. Roads (1981): total length 4,171 mi, 6,712 km (paved 10%). Vehicles (1982): passenger cars 24,887; trucks and buses 9,789. Merchant marine (1983): vessels (100 gross tons and over) 20; total deadweight tonnage 18,604. Air transport (1980): passenger-mi 47,000,000, passenger-km 76,000,000; short ton-mi cargo 3,800,000, metric ton-km cargo 5,500,000; airport (1984) with scheduled flights 1.
Communications. Daily newspapers (1983): total number 3; total circulation 150,000; circulation per 1,000 population 50. Radios (1983): total number of receivers 200,000 (1 per 15 persons). Television (1983): total number of receivers 127,000 (1 per 24 persons). Telephones (1982): 51,237 (1 per 57 persons).

Education and health

Education (1982)

	schools	teachers	students	student/teacher ratio
Primary (age 7–12)	4,976	14,105	509,240	36.1
Secondary (age 13–18)	323	...	114,868	...
Voc., teacher tr.	62	...	21,761	...
Higher	...	1,369	32,838	24.0

College graduates per 100,000 population (1980): n.a. *Literacy* (1980): total population literate 1,273,000 (87.0%).
Health: physicians (1981) 1,570 (1 per 1,800 persons); hospital beds (1980) 5,115 (1 per 517 persons).
Food (1978–80): daily per capita caloric intake 2,284 (vegetable products 81.0%, animal products 19.0%); 102% of FAO recommended minimum.

Military

Total active duty personnel (1983): 48,800 (army 96.3%; navy 0.6%; air force 3.1%). *Military expenditure as percent of GNP* (1981): 6.9% (world 5.7%); per capita expenditure U.S.$65.

*Land area only; water area 3,592 sq mi (9,304 sq km); total area 49,290 sq mi (127,662 sq km). †Distrito Nacional is included with Managua. ‡Based on land area. §Export figure. ‖ Authorized. ¶Public administration and defense included with services. ♀Services included with other. ðNonagricultural activities. □Value c.i.f.

Niger

Official name: République du Niger
(Republic of Niger).
Form of government: military
government with one advisory
body (National Development
Council*[150]).
Head of state and government:
President in conjunction with the
Supreme Military Council.
Capital: Niamey.
Official language: French.
Official religion: none.
Monetary unit: 1 CFA franc
(CFAF) = 100 centimes; valuation
(Oct. 29, 1984)
1 U.S.$ = CFAF470.6;
1 £ = CFAF568.0.

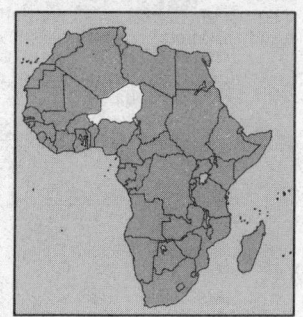

Area and population

Departments	Capitals	area sq mi	area sq km	population 1984 estimate
Agadez	Agadez	244,869	634,209	176,900
Diffa	Diffa	54,138	140,216	186,000
Dosso	Dosso	11,970	31,002	798,700
Maradi	Maradi	14,896	38,581	1,117,700
Niamey	Niamey	34,862	90,293	1,423,000
Tahoua	Tahoua	41,188	106,677	1,126,600
Zinder	Zinder	56,151	145,430	1,177,700
TOTAL		458,074	1,186,408	6,006,600

Source: Official government figures.

Demography

Density (1984): persons per sq mi 13.1, persons per sq km 5.1.
Urban–rural (1982): urban 14.0%; rural 86.0%.
Sex distribution (1981): male 49.48%; female 50.52%.
Age breakdown (1980): under 15, 46.6%; 15–29, 26.4%; 30–44, 14.4%; 45–59, 8.3%; 60–74, 3.7%; 75 and over, 0.6%.
Population projection: (1990) 7,087,000; (2000) 9,600,000.
Doubling time: 23 years.
Ethnic composition (1978): Hausa 52.1%; Zerma 14.6%; Fulani 10.0%; Kanuri 9.0%; Songhai 8.0%; Tuareg 3.0%; other 3.3%.
Religious affiliation (1980): Muslim 87.9%; tribal religionist 11.7%; Christian 0.4%.
Major cities (1983 est.): Niamey 399,100; Zinder 82,800; Maradi 65,100; Tahoua 41,900.

Vital statistics

Birth rate per 1,000 population (1981): 51.5 (world avg. 29.0).
Death rate per 1,000 population (1981): 20.7 (world avg. 12.0).
Natural increase rate per 1,000 population (1981): 30.8 (world avg. 17.0).
Total fertility rate (avg. births per childbearing woman; 1982): 7.0.
Marriage rate per 1,000 population: n.a.
Divorce rate per 1,000 population: n.a.
Infant mortality rate per 1,000 live births (1982): 132.0.
Life expectancy at birth (1981): male 43.1 years; female 46.1 years.
Major causes of death per 100,000 population (1976)†: malaria 317; measles 229; meningitis 145.

National economy

Budget (1980). Revenue: CFAF77,436,000,000 (taxes 84.5%, of which import duties 31.5%, goods and services 18.0%, corporate 16.5%; nontaxes 15.3%, of which mining royalties on uranium 5.8%). Expenditures: CFAF98,727,-000,000 (economic services 32.4%, of which roads 10.2%; general public services 19.6%; education 18.0%; health 4.1%; defense 3.8%).
Public debt (external, outstanding; 1982): U.S.$692,000,000.
Tourism (1981): receipts from visitors U.S.$3,000,000; expenditures by nationals abroad, n.a.
Production (value of production in CFAF except as noted). Agriculture, forestry, fishing (1982‡): millet 4,011,000,000, sorghum 2,105,000,000, beans 1,250,000,000, peanuts (groundnuts) 416,000,000, cotton 241,000,000, gum arabic 13,000,000; livestock (number of live animals) 7,300,000 goats, 3,350,000 cattle, 2,900,000 sheep, 460,000 asses, 410,000 camels, 270,000 horses; roundwood 3,620,000 cu m; fish catch 6,840 metric tons. Mining and quarrying (1983): uranium 92,319,000,000; cassiterite§ 208,000,000. Manufacturing (1980): cement 39,000; woven cotton fabrics 16,000,000 sq m; beer 70,000 hectolitres. Construction: n.a. Energy production (consumption): electricity (kW-hr; 1982) 62,000,000 (181,000,000); coal, none (n.a.); crude petroleum, none (n.a.); petroleum products (metric tons; 1982) none (181,000); natural gas, none (n.a.); uranium (metric tons; 1983) 3,416 (n.a.).
Persons economically active (1982): total 1,745,000 (31.0%); female participation in the labour force, n.a.; unemployed, n.a.

Price and earnings indexes (1980 = 100)

	1978	1979	1980	1981	1982	1983	1984
Consumer price index	84.5	90.7	100.0	122.9	137.2	133.8	145.8¶
Hourly earnings index	74.5	89.9	100.0	107.3	107.3	107.3	...

Gross national product (at current market prices; 1981): U.S.$1,890,000,000 (U.S.$330 per capita).

Origin of gross domestic product (factor cost at current prices)

	1981 in value CFAF'000,000	% of total value	labour force	% of labour force
Agriculture	139,800	30.1	1,481,000	87.2
Mining	76,000	16.4	...	...
Manufacturing	36,800	7.9	...	...
Construction	35,100	7.6	...	...
Trade and finance	43,100	9.3	...	...
Public utilities	1,700	0.4	...	...
Transportation and communication	21,900	4.7	...	...
Pub. admin., defense	42,500	9.1	...	...
Other	67,900	14.6	217,000	12.8
TOTAL	464,800	100.0 ‖	1,698,000	100.0

Household income and expenditure. Average household size (1980) 5.2; average annual income per household: n.a.; source of income: n.a.; expenditure (1983)♀: food and beverages 50.5%, household expenses 19.1%, clothing 7.3%.
Land use (1981): forested 2.3%; meadows and pastures 7.6%; agricultural and under permanent cultivation 2.7%; other 87.4%.

Foreign trade

Balance of trade (current prices)

	1977	1978	1979	1980	1981	1982
CFAF'000,000	−8,900	−5,200	−2,800	−5,900	−14,900	−36,000
% of total	10.1%	3.9%	1.5%	2.4%	5.4%	14.2%

Imports (1981): CFAF138,500,000,000 (machinery [all forms] 17.2%, petroleum products 14.8%, transport equipment 8.3%, rice 6.7%, cotton fabrics 5.7%, iron and steel [all forms] 4.1%, tobacco 2.4%, hydraulic cement 2.3%). *Major import sources:* France 35.9%; Nigeria 13.3%; Algeria 7.2%; Ivory Coast 4.7%; Pakistan 4.4%.
Exports (1981): CFAF123,600,000,000 (uranium 79.3%, live animals 12.2%, tobacco and cigarettes 3.3%, leather and hides 1.0%). *Major export destinations:* France 35.7%; Japan 17.7%; Nigeria 17.2%; Libya 14.9%; Spain 5.1%.

Transport and communications

Transport. Railroads (1982): none. Roads (1982): total length 11,886 mi, 19,129 km (paved 17%). Vehicles (1982): passenger cars 34,240; trucks and buses 8,761. Merchant marine: vessels (100 gross tons and over) none. Air transport (1982)ठ: passenger arrivals and departures 125,084; cargo loaded and unloaded 11,296 metric tons; airports (1984) with scheduled flights 6.
Communications. Daily newspaper (1984): total number 1; total circulation 5,000; circulation per 1,000 population 0.8. Radios (1983): total number of receivers 160,000 (1 per 38 persons). Television (1983): total number of receivers 11,000 (1 per 553 persons). Telephones (1981): 9,320 (1 per 588 persons).

Education and health

Education (1980–81)

	schools	teachers	students	student/ teacher ratio
Primary (age 7–12)	1,664	5,518	228,855	41.5
Secondary (age 13–19)	64	1,371	32,892	24.0
Voc., teacher tr.	8	120	2,351	19.6
Higher□	1	189	1,825	9.7

College graduates per 100,000 population (students graduating; 1980): 6.2.
Literacy (1980): total population literate 278,000 (9.8%); males literate 195,000 (14.0%); females literate 83,000 (5.8%).
Health: physicians (1980) 136 (1 per 38,790 persons); hospital beds (1979) 3,261 (1 per 1,641 persons).
Food (1978–80): daily per capita caloric intake 2,217 (vegetable products 92.1%, animal products 7.9%); 94% of FAO recommended minimum requirement.

Military

Total active duty personnel (1982): 2,220 (army 96.8%; air force 3.2%). *Military expenditure as percent of GNP* (1982): 0.9% (world 6.0%); per capita expenditure U.S.$2.85.

*The legislature (National Assembly) was suspended in 1974. In 1983 the National Development Council assumed the role of a constituent assembly to draft a new constitution and define the powers of a legislature. †As reported by a survey of the U.S. Mission of the Niger Health Sector Assessment. ‡Value of agricultural crop production is for 1982–83. §1981. ‖ Detail does not add to total given because of rounding. ¶Second quarter. ♀Estimated. ठNiamey airport only. □Université de Niamey.

Nigeria

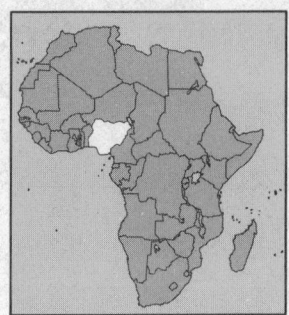

Official name: Federal Republic of Nigeria.
Form of government: military dictatorship (constitution suspended Dec. 31, 1983) with one ruling body (Supreme Military Council).
Head of state and government: Chairman (Supreme Military Council).
Capital: Lagos.
Official language: English.
Official religion: none.
Monetary unit: 1 Nigerian naira (₦) = 100 kobo; valuation (Oct. 29, 1984) 1 ₦ = U.S.$1.14 = £1.06.

Area and population

States	Capitals	area sq mi	area sq km	population 1983 estimate
Anambra	Enugu	6,824	17,675	5,880,600
Bauchi	Bauchi	24,944	64,605	3,975,200
Bendel	Benin City	13,707	35,500	4,023,700
Benue	Makurdi	17,442	45,174	3,968,200
Borno	Maiduguri	44,942	116,400	4,901,000
Cross River	Calabar	10,516	27,237	5,696,800
Gongola	Yola	35,286	91,390	4,259,700
Imo	Owerri	4,575	11,850	6,004,900
Kaduna	Kaduna	27,122	70,245	6,700,800
Kano	Kano	16,712	43,285	9,442,000
Kwara	Ilorin	25,818	66,869	2,808,200
Lagos	Lagos	1,292	3,345	2,733,500
Niger	Minna	25,111	65,037	1,933,100
Ogun	Abeokuta	6,472	16,762	2,533,900
Ondo	Akure	8,092	20,959	4,483,100
Oyo	Ibadan	14,558	37,705	8,516,700
Plateau	Jos	22,405	58,030	3,313,600
Rivers	Port-Harcourt	8,436	21,850	2,812,100
Sokoto	Sokoto	39,589	102,535	7,421,000
Federal Capital Territory		2,824	7,315	...
TOTAL		356,669*	923,768	91,408,100

Source: Official government figures.

Demography

Density (1984): persons per sq mi 265.0, persons per sq km 102.3.
Urban–rural (1980): urban 20.4%; rural 79.6%.
Sex distribution (1980): male 49.45%; female 50.55%.
Age breakdown (1980): under 15, 47.4%; 15–64, 50.2%; 65 and over, 2.4%.
Population projection: (1990) 107,954,000; (2000) 149,965,000.
Doubling time: 27 years.
Ethno-linguistic composition (1978): Hausa 21.5%; Yoruba 21.0%; Ibo 18.4%; Fulani 11.1%; other 28.0%.
Religious affiliation (1963): Muslim 47%; Christian 34%; traditional beliefs and other 19%.
Major cities (1983): Lagos 1,097,000; Ibadan 1,060,000; Ogbomosho 527,400; Kano 487,100; Oshogbo 344,500; Abeokuta 308,800; Port Harcourt 296,200.

Vital statistics

Birth rate per 1,000 population (1980–85): 49.5 (world avg. 27.5); legitimate, n.a.; illegitimate, n.a.
Death rate per 1,000 population (1980–85): 16.0 (world avg. 10.6).
Natural increase rate per 1,000 population (1980–85): 33.5 (world avg. 16.9).
Total fertility rate (avg. births per childbearing woman; 1980–85): 6.9.
Marriage rate per 1,000 population: n.a.
Divorce rate per 1,000 population: n.a.
Infant mortality rate per 1,000 live births (1975–80): 124.0.
Life expectancy at birth (1980–85): male 48.3 years; female 51.7 years.
Major causes of death per 100,000 population: n.a.; however, among the major diseases are malaria, tuberculosis, trypanosomiasis (sleeping sickness), onchocerciasis (river blindness), and leprosy.

National economy

Budget (1982). Revenue: ₦10,617,700,000 (petroleum profits tax 45.6%; mining [rents, fees, etc.] 19.0%; import duties 15.5%; export duties 6.5%; company income tax 5.2%). Expenditures: ₦12,817,300,000 (transfers 69.9%, of which to state and local governments 38.0%, development fund 24.1%; defense 5.2%; education 5.0%; health 1.2%).
Public debt (1982): U.S.$7,889,000,000.
Tourism (1981): receipts from visitors U.S.$55,000,000; expenditures by nationals abroad U.S.$774,000,000.
Production (metric tons except as noted). Agriculture, forestry, fishing (1982): roots and tubers 29,788,000 (of which cassava 11,500,000); cereals 10,238,000 (of which sorghum 3,800,000, millet 3,300,000, corn [maize] 1,650,000; rice 1,400,000); sugarcane 1,200,000; palm kernels and oil 1,050,000; peanuts (groundnuts) 600,000; cacao 150,000; livestock (number of live animals) 25,600,000 goats, 140,000,000 chickens; roundwood 102,585,000 cu m; fish catch 511,984. Mining and quarrying (1983): cassiterite ore (1,583 contained tin); limestone 1,650,000. Manufacturing (value added in producers' prices ₦'000,000; 1978): machinery and transport equipment 201.9, of which motor vehicles 41.0; chemical products 386.9, of which drugs and medicines 59.6; food products 327.1; textiles 309.3; rubber products 63.0. Construction (1978): residential ₦884,830,000; nonresidential ₦1,769,640,000. Energy production (consumption): electricity (kW-hr; 1982) 7,500,000,000 (7,381,000,000); coal (metric tons; 1982) 210,000 (210,-

000); crude petroleum (barrels; 1983) 449,000,000 (90,000,000); petroleum products (metric tons; 1982) 6,805,000 (6,805,000); natural gas (cu m; 1982) 5,128,200,000 (5,128,200,000).
Gross national product (at current market prices; 1982): U.S.$68,975,000,000 (U.S.$775 per capita).

Origin of gross domestic product (current prices)

	1982 in value ₦'000,000	% of total value	labour force	% of labour force
Agriculture	10,410.3	21.8	15,736,000	51.4
Mining	11,670.7	24.4	...	...
Manufacturing	2,647.5	5.5	...	...
Construction	4,001.6	8.4	...	...
Trade	10,593.8	22.2	...	...
Public utilities	332.6	0.7	...	...
Transportation and communication	2,583.0	5.4	...	...
Finance	†	†	...	...
Pub. admin., defense	†	†	...	...
Services	†	†	...	...
Other	5,572.9†	11.6†	14,879,000	48.6
TOTAL	47,812.3*	100.0	30,615,000	100.0

Persons economically active (1982): total 30,615,000 (34.4%); female participation in the labour force 12,185,000 (39.8%); unemployed (registered) 16,300 (0.1%).

Price and earnings indexes (1980 = 100)

	1977	1978	1979	1980	1981	1982	1983
Consumer price index	68.1	80.8	89.8	100.0	120.9	130.0	156.0
Earnings index‡	83.4	89.1	98.1	100.0	...	...	...

Household income and expenditure. Average household size (1982) 5.0; average annual income per household ₦2,600 (U.S.$3,875); source of income: n.a.; expenditure: n.a.
Land use (1981): forested 16.0%; meadows and pastures 23.0%; agricultural and under permanent cultivation 33.4%; other 27.6%.

Foreign trade

Balance of trade (current prices)

	1978	1979	1980	1981	1982	1983
₦'000,000	−1,430	+4,507	+5,091	−2,043	−3,861	−330§
% of total	9.6%	26.8%	21.9%	8.6%	18.2%	2.1%

Imports (1982): ₦12,566,000,000 (machinery and transport equipment 46.2%; manufactured goods 25.5% [important sectors include iron and steel products, textiles, paper products, and rubber products]; food and beverages ‖ 7.7%). *Major import sources:* United Kingdom 22.3%; West Germany 16.0%; United States 11.2%; Japan 11.0%; France 7.2%; The Netherlands 4.2%.
Exports (1982): ₦8,705,000,000 (crude petroleum 98.6%; other important exports include cocoa, rubber, and palm kernels). *Major export destinations:* United States 46.2%; The Netherlands 12.1%; France 10.1%; West Germany 6.6%; United Kingdom 2.3%; Ghana 1.2%.

Transport and communications

Transport. Railroads (1981): length 2,178 mi, 3,505 km; total passengers 10,092,200; short ton cargo handled 1,735,900, metric ton cargo handled 1,578,100. Roads (1980): total length 67,102 mi, 107,990 km (paved 78%). Vehicles (1980): passenger cars 262,550; trucks 90,731. Merchant marine (1983): vessels (100 gross tons and over) 169; total deadweight tonnage 638,123. Air transport (1982): passenger-mi 1,401,000,000, passenger-km 2,256,000,000; short ton-mi cargo 18,444,000,000, metric ton-km cargo 26,928,000,000; airports (1984) with scheduled flights 15.
Communications. Daily newspapers (1980): total number 15; total circulation 1,295,000; circulation per 1,000 population 15.2. Radios (1981): total number of receivers 5,820,000 (1 per 15 persons). Television (1981): total number of receivers 480,000 (1 per 180 persons). Telephones (1982): 708,390 (1 per 127 persons).

Education and health

Education (1980–81)

	schools	teachers	students	student/ teacher ratio
Primary (age 6–12)	36,683	384,201	14,022,164	36.5
Secondary (age 12–17)	4,495	69,005	2,024,024	29.3
Voc., teacher tr.	470	12,156	359,817	29.6
Higher	77	...	153,306	

College graduates per 100,000 population (students graduating; 1981): 19.5.
Literacy (1980): total population literate (34.0%).
Health (1980): physicians 8,037 (1 per 10,800 persons); hospital beds 74,901 (1 per 1,160 persons).
Food (1978–80): daily per capita caloric intake 2,337 (vegetable products 95.5%, animal products 4.5%); 99% of FAO recommended minimum requirement.

Military

Total active duty personnel (1982): 133,000 (army 90.2%; navy 3.0%; air force 6.8%). *Military expenditure as percent of GNP* (1982): 2.3% (world 6.0%); per capita expenditure U.S.$22.

*Detail does not add to total given because of rounding. †Finance, public administration, defense, and services included with other. ‡For wages earned in nonagricultural activities only. §Eleven months only (excludes December). ‖ Includes tobacco products.

Norway

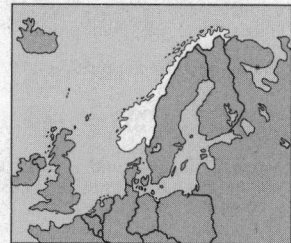

Official name: Kongeriket Norge (Kingdom of Norway).
Form of government: constitutional monarchy with one legislative house (Parliament [155]).
Chief of state: King.
Head of government: Prime Minister.
Capital: Oslo.
Official language: Norwegian.
Official religion: Evangelical Lutheran.
Monetary unit: 1 Norwegian krone (NKr, plural) = 100 oere; valuation (Oct. 29, 1984) 1 U.S.$ = NKr.8.88; 1 £ = NKr.10.72.

Area and population

Counties	Capitals	area sq mi	area sq km	population 1983 estimate
Akershus	—	1,898	4,917	376,129
Aust-Agder	Arendal	3,557	9,212	92,751
Buskerud	Drammen	5,766	14,933	217,402
Finnmark	Vardø	18,783	48,649	77,394
Hedmark	Hamar	10,575	27,388	187,784
Hordaland	Bergen	6,036	15,634	394,545
Møre og Romsdal	Molde	5,832	15,104	237,315
Nordland	Bodø	14,798	38,327	245,017
Nord-Trøndelag	Steinkjer	8,673	22,463	126,713
Oppland	Lillehammer	9,753	25,260	182,108
Oslo	Oslo	175	454	448,747
Østfold	Moss	1,615	4,183	234,751
Rogaland	Stavanger	3,529	9,141	312,576
Sogn og Fjordane	Leikanger	7,195	18,634	106,175
Sør-Trøndelag	Trondheim	7,271	18,831	246,200
Telemark	Skien	5,913	15,315	161,944
Troms	Tromsø	10,021	25,954	147,709
Vest-Agder	Kristiansand	2,811	7,280	138,745
Vestfold	Tønsberg	856	2,216	188,702
TOTAL		125,057	323,895*	4,122,707†

Source: Official government figures.

Demography

Density (1984): persons per sq mi 33.0, persons per sq km 12.8.
Urban–rural (1981): urban 70.7%; rural 29.3%.
Sex distribution (1983): male 49.49%; female 50.51%.
Age breakdown (1983): under 15, 21.5%; 15–29, 22.9%; 30–44, 19.6%; 45–59, 15.3%; 60–74, 14.6%; 75 and over, 6.1%.
Population projection: (1990) 4,225,000; (2000) 4,325,000.
Population growth is negligible.
Ethnic composition (by country of citizenship; 1983): Norway 98.5%; Denmark 0.4%; Sweden 0.2%; Finland 0.1%; other 0.8%.
Religious affiliation (1980): Lutheran 87.9%; other 3.7%; nonreligious 3.2%; unknown 5.2%.
Major cities (1983): Oslo 448,800; Bergen 207,300; Trondheim 134,700; Stavanger 92,000; Kristiansand 61,800; Drammen 50,600.

Vital statistics

Birth rate per 1,000 population (1983): 12.0 (world avg. 29.0); (1982) legitimate 82.4%, illegitimate 17.6%.
Death rate per 1,000 population (1983): 10.2 (world avg. 11.0).
Natural increase rate per 1,000 population (1983): 1.8 (world avg. 18.0).
Total fertility rate (avg. births per childbearing woman; 1982): 1.7.
Marriage rate per 1,000 population (1983): 5.2.
Divorce rate per 1,000 population (1983): 2.9.
Infant mortality rate per 1,000 live births (1982): 8.1.
Life expectancy at birth (1982): male 72.6 years; female 79.4 years.
Major causes of death per 100,000 population (1982): ischemic heart disease 265.5; malignant neoplasms (cancers) 221.8; cerebrovascular disease 128.0.

National economy

Budget (1983). Revenue: NKr165,200,000,000 (indirect taxes 34.8%, social security and pension premiums 26.9%, tax on petroleum extraction 18.6%, income and property tax 13.6%, other 6.1%). Expenditures: NKr165,200,-000,000 (social services 29.7%, church and education 8.8%, communications 8.7%, defense 7.7%, other 45.1%).
Public debt (external, outstanding; 1982): U.S.$3,372,000,000.
Tourism (1982): receipts from visitors U.S.$815,000,000; expenditures by nationals abroad U.S.$1,834,000,000.
Production (metric tons except as noted). Agriculture, forestry, fishing (1982): barley 607,000, oats 501,000, potatoes 443,000, apples 44,000; livestock (number of live animals) 1,009,000 cattle, 2,227,100 sheep, 686,100 pigs, 98,000 goats, 3,683,500 chickens; roundwood 9,502,000 cu m; fish 2,488,-000. Mining and quarrying (1983): iron ore 3,535,309; titanium 544,328; zinc 61,591; nickel 28,309; copper 26,191. Manufacturing (1983): petroleum products 6,035,561; wood pulp and paper 2,428,379; cement 1,617,914; aluminum and aluminum alloys 710,637; sulfuric acid 84,000; woolen yarn and fabric 4,221; transport equipment 5,270,000 kroner, of which ships and boats 3,990,000 kroner. Construction (1983): residential 3,739,000 sq m; nonresidential 2,776,000 sq m. Energy production (consumption): electricity (kW-hr; 1983) 106,243,000,000 (87,012,000,000‡); coal (metric tons; 1983) 477,800 (986,000‡); crude petroleum (barrels; 1983) 95,283,000 (47,-960,200‡); petroleum products (metric tons; 1982) 6,685,000 (8,062,000); natural gas (cu m; 1983) 25,610,709,000 (985,922,100‡).

Gross national product (at current market prices; 1982): U.S.$49,931,000,000 (U.S.$12,110 per capita).

Origin of gross domestic product (current prices)

	1982 in value NKr'000,000	% of total value	1982 labour force	% of labour force
Agriculture	14,915	4.1	156,000	8.0
Mining	61,412	16.9	16,000	0.8
Manufacturing	52,276	14.4	384,000	19.7
Construction	20,911	5.8	154,000	7.9
Trade	49,997	13.8	336,000	17.3
Public utilities	13,911	3.8	19,000	1.0
Transportation and communication	35,956	9.9	185,000	9.5
Finance	15,473	4.3	105,000	5.4
Pub. admin., defense, and services	94,303	26.0	589,000	30.3
Other	3,403	0.9	2,000	0.1
TOTAL	362,557	100.0*	1,946,000	100.0

Persons economically active (1983): total 1,957,000 (47.5%); female participation in the labour force 818,000 (41.8%); unemployed 62,853 (3.2%).

Price and earnings indexes (1970 = 100)

	1978	1979	1980	1981	1982	1983	1984
Consumer price index	191.4	199.2	215.7	253.2	288.0	306.7	313.4
Monthly earnings index	241.7	244.3	281.5	304.6	339.7	...	...

Household income and expenditure. Average household size (1982): 2.7; income per household NKr80,900 (U.S.$10,400); sources of income: wages and salaries 45.8%, social security 22.5%, other 31.7%; expenditure (1982): food 20.6%, housing 16.2%, transportation 15.1%, recreation 8.2%, clothing and footwear 7.8%.
Land use (1982): forested 27.0%; meadows and pastures 0.4%; agricultural and under permanent cultivation 2.7%; built up and other 69.9%.

Foreign trade

Balance of trade (current prices)

	1978	1979	1980	1981	1982	1983
NKr'000,000	−3,034	−811.7	8,070	14,578	13,489	32,816
% of total	−2.6%	−0.6%	4.6%	7.5%	6.3%	14.3%

Imports (1983): NKr98,401,000,000 (machinery and transport equipment 36.8%, of which transport equipment 16.9%, nonelectric machinery 13.8%, electrical and telecommunication equipment 6.1%; crude petroleum and petroleum products 11.2%; chemicals 6.1%; iron and steel 4.8%; metalliferous ores 3.2%; food 5.2%; clothing 4.2%). *Major import sources:* Sweden 17.1%; West Germany 15.5%; United Kingdom 11.8%; United States 9.2%.
Exports (1983): NKr131,217,000,000 (crude petroleum and petroleum products 32.1%; natural gas 19.2%; machinery and transport equipment 14.9%, of which ships and boats 7.0%; aluminum and aluminum alloys 4.4%; fish and fish preparations 4.3%). *Major export destinations:* United Kingdom 36.5%; West Germany 20.2%; Sweden 9.2%; The Netherlands 5.8%.

Transport and communications

Transport. Railroads (1983): length 2,636 mi, 4,242 km; passenger-mi 1,393,000,000, passenger-km 2,242,000,000; short ton-mi cargo 1,743,000,-000, metric ton-km cargo 2,545,000,000. Roads (1982): total length 51,252 mi, 82,482 km (paved 59%). Vehicles (1983): passenger cars 1,337,884; trucks and buses 180,608. Merchant marine (1983): vessels (100 gross tons and over) 2,340; total deadweight tonnage 33,524,485. Air transport (1982): passenger-mi 2,558,000,000, passenger-km 4,118,000,000; short ton-mi cargo 95,275,000, metric ton-km cargo 139,100,000; airports (1984) with scheduled flights 35.
Communications. Daily newspapers (1983): total number 81; total circulation 1,950,036; circulation per 1,000 population 473. Radios (1983): total number of receivers 1,500,000 (1 per 2.7 persons). Television (1983): total number of receivers 1,295,267 (1 per 3.2 persons). Telephones (1982): 2,203,649 (1 per 1.9 persons).

Education and health

Education (1981–82)

	schools	teachers	students	student/ teacher ratio
Primary (age 7–13)	3,526	30,124	586,071	19.5
Secondary (age 14–18) and vocational	967	14,992	184,334	12.3
Higher	199	6,695	39,280	5.9

College graduates per 100,000 population (students graduating; 1981): 9.1.
Literacy (1983): virtually 100% literate.
Health: physicians (1981) 8,311 (1 per 494 persons); hospital beds (1982) 27,700 (1 per 148 persons).
Food (1978–80): daily per capita caloric intake 3,288 (vegetable products 62.3%, animal products 37.7%). 123% of FAO recommended minimum.

Military

Total active duty personnel (1983): 43,170 (army 56.0%; navy 21.2%; air force 22.8%). *Military expenditure as percent of* GNP (1982): 3.1% (world avg. 6.0%); per capita expenditure U.S.$440.

*Excludes Svalbard and Jan Mayen (24,366 sq mi [63,107 sq km]). †Includes the Norwegian population of Svalbard and Jan Mayen registered as residents in municipalities on the mainland. ‡1982. §Second quarter.

Oman

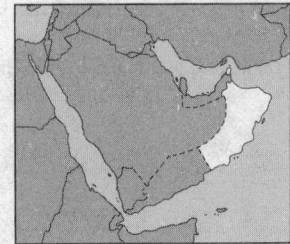

Official name: Saltanat 'Umān
(Sultanate of Oman).
Form of government: monarchy with a
consultative council (55) appointed by
the Sultan.
Chief of state: Sultan.
Head of government: Prime Minister.
Capital: Muscat.
Official language: Arabic.
Official religion: Islām.
Monetary unit: 1 rial Omani
(RO) = 1,000 baizas; valuation (Oct.
29, 1984) 1 RO = U.S.$2.90 = £2.40.

Area and population	area*		population†
			1984
Geographical areas	sq mi	sq km	estimate
al-Bāṭinah	...	...	...
al-Ḥajar al-Gharbī	...	...	...
al-Ḥajar ash-Sharqī	...	...	...
al-Jaww	...	...	...
al-Masīrah	...	...	...
ash-Sharqīyah	...	...	...
az-Ẓāhirah	...	...	...
Capital	...	...	...
Dhofar-Southern	...	...	...
Ja'lan	...	...	...
Ru'ūs al-Jibāl	...	...	...
'Umān al-Wusṭā	...	...	...
TOTAL	120,000	300,000	1,009,000

Demography

Density (1984): persons per sq mi 8.7, persons per sq km 3.4.
Urban–rural (1980): urban 7.3%; rural 92.7%.
Sex distribution (1980): male 50.61%; female 49.39%.
Age breakdown (1980): under 15, 45.2%; 15–29, 25.8%; 30–44, 15.6%; 45–59,
8.8%; 60–74, 3.9%; 75 and over, 0.7%.
Population projection: (1990) 1,218,000; (2000) 1,651,000.
Doubling time: 22.3 years.
Ethnic composition (1980): Arabic 87.0%; Baluchi 4.0%; Persian 2.3%; other
6.7%.
Religious affiliation (1980): Muslim 98.9%; Hindu 0.3%; other 0.8%.
Major city (1981 est.): Muscat 50,000.

Vital statistics

Birth rate per 1,000 population (1980–85): 47.7 (world avg. 27.5).
Death rate per 1,000 population (1980–85): 16.7 (world avg. 10.6).
Natural increase rate per 1,000 population (1980–85): 31.0 (world avg. 16.9).
Total fertility rate (avg. births per childbearing woman; 1980–85): 7.1.
Marriage rate per 1,000 population: n.a.
Divorce rate per 1,000 population: n.a.
Infant mortality rate per 1,000 live births (1978): 200.
Life expectancy at birth (1980–85): male 48.7 years; female 50.9 years.
Major causes of death per 100,000 population: n.a.

National economy

Budget (1983). Revenue: RO1,333,900,000 (oil revenue 89.0%, gas revenue
1.5%, other 9.5%). Expenditures: RO1,488,400,000 (defense 45.1%, financing of civil ministries 43.9%, other 11%).
Public debt (external, outstanding; 1982): U.S.$677,100,000.
Tourism: n.a.
Production (metric tons except as noted). Agriculture, forestry, fishing
(1982): dates 72,000, bananas 31,000, limes 13,000; livestock (number of
live animals) 250,000 goats, 150,000 cattle, 138,000 sheep, 598,000 chickens; fish catch 89,000. Mining and quarrying (1982): stone 6,220,000; sand
and gravel 1,343,000; marble 50,000. Manufacturing (1980): major products
include cement blocks and floors, furniture and other wooden products,
and processed iron parts . Construction: n.a. Energy production (consumption): electricity (kW-hr; 1983) 1,387,400,000 (1,297,700,000); coal, none
(none); crude petroleum (barrels; 1983) 141,900,000 (13,300,000); petroleum
products (metric tons; 1984) 2,400,000 (n.a.); natural gas (cu m; 1983)
2,455,070,000 (n.a.).
Gross national product (at current market prices; 1982): U.S.$6,482,050,000
(U.S.$6,007 per capita).

Origin of gross domestic product (current prices)				
	1982			
	in value RO'000,000	% of total value	labour force‡	% of labour force‡
Agriculture	46	1.9	6,583	2.9
Mining (oil sector)	1,416	57.7	3,426	1.5
Manufacturing	36	1.5	8,034	3.5
Construction	153	6.2	46,279	20.0
Trade	299	12.2	33,740	14.6
Public utilities	25	1.0	423	0.2
Transportation and communication	86	3.5	2,483	1.1
Finance	59	2.4	3,272	1.4
Pub. admin., defense	263	10.7	44,087	19.1
Services	22	0.9	8,139	3.5
Other	51	2.0	74,442	32.2
TOTAL	2,456	100.0	230,908	100.0

Persons economically active (1982): total 230,908; female participation in the
labour force, n.a.; unemployed, n.a.

Price and earnings indexes (1978 = 100)						
	1977	1978	1979	1980	1981	1982	1983
Consumer price index§	...	100.0	108.5	119.3	122.7	124.0	118.6
Monthly earnings index						

Household income and expenditure. Average household size (1980) 5.5;
average annual income per household: n.a.; source of income: n.a.; food
expenditure (1983): meat and eggs 20.6%, cereals 15.2%, fruits and nuts
12.4%, vegetables 11.9%, dairy products 10.3%, other foods 29.6%.
Land use (1981): meadows and pastures 4.7%; agricultural and under permanent cultivation 0.2%; other (mostly desert and developed area) 95.1%.

Foreign trade

Balance of trade (current prices)						
	1977	1978	1979	1980	1981	1982
RO'000,000	+245.3	+224.8	+356.9	+696.3	+831.6	+600.4
% of total	28.9%	25.6%	29.3%	36.8%	34.5%	24.5%

Imports (1982): RO926,546,000 (transport equipment 18.4%, nonelectrical
machinery 13.3%, petroleum and petroleum products 10.1%, electrical
machinery and appliances 9.5%, iron and steel 6.1%, metal manufactures
4.6%). *Major import sources:* Japan 20.7%; United Kingdom 14.4%; United
Arab Emirates 14.0%; West Germany 8.3%; United States 8.0%.
Exports (1982): RO1,526,900,000 (crude petroleum 92.3%, transport equipment ‖ 5.1%, nonelectrical machinery ‖ 0.7%, fish and fish preparations
0.2%). *Major export destinations¶:* Japan 39.8%; Singapore 21.7%; The
Netherlands 6.5%; West Germany 6.3%; United States 5.5%.

Transport and communications

Transport. Railroads: none. Roads (1982): total length 13,050 mi, 21,000 km
(paved 14%). Vehicles (1982): private vehicles 14,930; commercial vehicles
11,822. Merchant marine (1983): vessels (100 gross tons and over) 25; total
deadweight tonnage 10,917. Air transport (1982): passengers handled 973,-
000; international cargo handled 15,500 metric tons; airports (1984) with
scheduled flights 2.
Communications. Daily newspapers (1984): total number 2; total circulation,
n.a. Radios (1983): total number of receivers 250,000 (1 per 4.5 persons).
Television (1983): total number of receivers 45,000 (1 per 25.1 persons).
Telephone lines (1982): 19,600.

Education and health

Education (1982–83)	schools	teachers	students	student/ teacher ratio
Primary (age 6–11)♀	204	6,575δ	116,467	...
Secondary (age 12–17)♀□	251	...	24,115	...
Voc., teacher tr.	...	...	1,994	...
Higher	none	none	1,399◊	---

College graduates: n.a. *Literacy* (1979)△: total population literate 38%; males
literate 55%; females literate 20%.
Health (1982)†: physicians 393 (1 per 2,746 persons); hospital beds 2,041 (1
per 529 persons).
Food: daily per capita caloric intake, n.a.

Military

Total active duty personnel (1983): 23,550 (army 83.0%; navy 8.5%; air force
8.5%); foreign troops (U.K.) 660. *Military expenditure as percent of GNP*
(1982): 28.5% (world 6.0%); per capita expenditure U.S.$1,870.

*No boundaries or administrative seats have been established; hence, no breakdown
is available. †No census has ever been taken in Oman; the total provided is an
unofficial estimate. For planning purposes the Omani government uses its own 1975
estimate of 1,500,000. ‡Civil employees and non-Omani workers only. §Applies to
food and beverages in the capital area only. ‖ Reexports only. ¶Exports of crude
petroleum only. ♀Government schools only; Omani statistics for private schools do
not distinguish between primary and secondary levels. In 1982–83 there were 39
private schools with 6,284 students and 372 teachers; the student/teacher ratio was
16.0. δIncludes teachers in preparatory and secondary schools. □Includes preparatory
school for students 12–14 years old. ◊Omani students studying abroad. △Pertains to
population 6 years old and over. †Under government auspices only.

Pakistan

Official name: Islāmī Jamhūrīya–e–Pākistān (Islāmic Republic of Pakistan).
Form of government: federal republic with two legislative houses (Senate [63]; National Assembly [210]).
Chief of state: President (Chief Martial Law Administrator).
Head of government: Prime Minister.
Capital: Islāmābād.
Official language: Urdū.
Official religion: Islām.
Monetary unit: 1 Pakistan Rupee (PRs) = 100 paisa; valuation (Oct. 29, 1984) 1 U.S.$ = PRs14.42; 1 £ = PRs17.40.

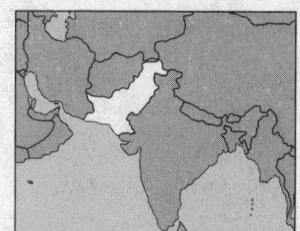

Area and population

Provinces	Capitals	area		population
		sq mi	sq km	1983 estimate
Baluchistān	Quetta	134,050	347,188	4,611,000
North–West Frontier	Peshāwar	28,773	74,522	11,658,000
Punjab	Lahore	79,284	205,345	50,460,000
Sind	Karāchi	54,407	140,913	20,312,000
Federally Administered Tribal Areas	...	10,510	27,221	2,329,000
Federal Capital Area				
Islāmābād	—	350	906	359,000
TOTAL		307,374	796,095	89,729,000

Source: Official government figures.

Demography

Density (1984): persons per sq mi 298.9, persons per sq km 115.4.
Urban–rural (1981): urban 28.3%; rural 71.7%.
Sex distribution (1981): male 52.47%; female 47.53%.
Age breakdown (1981): under 15, 45.2%; 15–29, 23.9%; 30–44, 15.0%; 45–59, 9.2%; 60–74, 5.1%; 75 and over, 1.6%.
Population projection: (1990) 105,613,000; (2000) 133,477,000.
Doubling time: 22 years.
Linguistic composition (1980): Punjābī 60%; Sindhī 12%; Pashto 7%; Urdū 6%; other 15%.
Religious affiliation (1980): Muslim 96.8%; Christian 1.8%; Hindu 1.3%; other 0.1% .
Major cities (1981): Karāchi 5,103,000; Lahore 2,922,000; Faisalābād 1,092,000; Rāwalpindi 928,000; Hyderābād 795,000.

Vital statistics

Birth rate per 1,000 population (1983): 42.3 (world avg. 29.0).
Death rate per 1,000 population (1983): 15.0 (world avg. 11.0).
Natural increase rate per 1,000 population (1983): 27.3 (world avg. 18.0).
Total fertility rate (avg. births per childbearing woman; 1983): 5.8.
Marriage rate per 1,000 population (1975–80): 10.7.
Divorce rate per 1,000 population (1975–80): 0.3.
Infant mortality rate per 1,000 live births (1983): 119.
Life expectancy at birth (1983): male 51.2 years; female 49.2 years.
Major causes of death: n.a.; however, the major diseases are tuberculosis, cancer, poliomyelitis, typhoid, dysentery, pertussis, trachoma, and malaria.

National economy

Budget (1983–84). Revenue: PRs73,232,000,000 (customs duties 30.1%, federal excise 22.4%, income from property and enterprise 14.2%, income tax and corporation tax 13.3%, sales tax 5.5%). Expenditures: PRs65,746,300,000 (defense 38.4%, general administration 5.3%, social services 3.3%, subsidies 2.9%, law and order 2.1%).
Public debt (external, outstanding; 1983): U.S.$12,399,600,000.
Tourism (1982): receipts from visitors U.S.$187,000,000; expenditures by nationals abroad U.S.$115,700,000*.
Production (metric tons except as noted). Agriculture, forestry, fishing (1983–84): sugarcane 34,502,000, wheat 11,531,000, rice 3,368,000, corn (maize) 1,008,000, cotton 65,000, tobacco 65,000; livestock (number of live animals) 28,700,000 goats, 24,200,000 sheep, 16,300,000 cattle, 12,800,000 buffaloes, 890,000 camels, 79,000,000 poultry; roundwood 18,570,000 cu m†; fish catch 337,290†. Mining and quarrying (1982–83): dolomite 100,300; fire clay 48,336; barite 20,088; feldspar 5,490; chromite 2,929; bauxite 2,772; magnesite 1,504. Manufacturing (1982–83): cement 3,938,000; chemical fertilizers 2,573,000; light steel products 614,000; chemicals 215,000; jute textiles 66,000; tea 50,000; paper 48,000; cotton textiles 316,767,000 sq m; beverages 730,097,000 bottles; cigarettes 38,199,000,000 units; bicycles 449,000 units; automobiles (manufacture/assembly) 69,000 units. Construction (value in PRs; 1980): residential 5,284,000,000; nonresidential 7,816,000,000. Energy production (consumption): electricity (kW-hr; 1982–83) 19,831,600,000 (17,779,000,000†); coal (metric tons; 1982–83) 1,544,000 (2,233,000†); crude petroleum (barrels; 1982–83) 4,132,000 (31,782,900†); petroleum products (metric tons; 1982) 3,745,000 (4,343,000†); natural gas (cu m; 1982–83) 10,006,000,000 (7,797,800,000†).
Household income and expenditure. Average household size (1981) 6.7; income per household PRs20,530 (U.S.$2,075); source of income (1971–72): wages and salaries 17.9%, self-employed 66.9%, rent 4.8%; expenditure (1971–72): food 53.3%, housing 17.4%, clothing and footwear 9.7%, transportation and communication 2.5%, recreation 0.7%.
Gross national product (at current market prices; 1983): U.S.$30,744,800,000 (U.S.$343 per capita).

Origin of gross domestic product (current prices)

	1982–83			
	in value PRs'000,000	% of total value	labour force	% of labour force
Agriculture	101,593	30.8	13,918,000	50.8
Mining	3,533	1.1	37,000	0.1
Manufacturing	54,786	16.6	3,835,000	14.0
Construction	15,392	4.7	1,303,000	4.8
Trade	51,882	15.7	2,927,000	10.7
Public utilities	7,035	2.1	196,000	0.7
Transportation and communication	24,790	7.5	1,251,000	4.5
Finance	8,160	2.5	227,000	0.9
Pub. admin., defense	24,396	7.4	‡	‡
Services	27,875	8.5	2,670,000	9.7
Other	10,359	3.1	1,043,000‡	3.8‡
TOTAL	329,801	100.0	27,407,000	100.0

Persons economically active (1982–83): total 27,407,000 (30.5%); female 1,015,596 (3.7%); unemployed 972,000 (3.5%).

Price and earnings indexes (1980 = 100)

	1978	1979	1980	1981	1982	1983	1984
Consumer price index	82.5	89.3	100.0	111.9	118.5	127.3	133.5§
Monthly earnings index	...	...	...	...	...	...	...

Land use (1981): forested 3.6%; meadows and pastures 6.4%; agricultural and under permanent cultivation 26.1%; built-on, wasteland, and other 63.9%.

Foreign trade

Balance of trade (current prices)

	1978–79	1979–80	1980–81	1981–82	1982–83	1983–84
PRs'000,000	−19,463.1	−23,519.0	−24,264.2	−33,211.6	−33,709.1	−34,556.5
% of total	36.5%	33.4%	29.3%	38.7%	32.9%	30.1%

Imports (1982–83): PRs68,150,800,000 (machinery 16.7%, transport equipment 7.9%, edible oil 5.4%, iron and steel 4.0%, fertilizers 3.1%, tea 2.5%, synthetic and art silk yarn 2.4%). *Major import sources:* Saudi Arabia 14.5%; Japan 13.2%; United States 9.6%; Kuwait 8.6%; United Kingdom 6.0%; West Germany 5.5%.
Exports (1982–83): PRs34,441,700,000 (rice 10.7%, cotton fabric 10.3%, cotton yarn 9.1%, carpets and rugs 5.6%, petroleum products 2.9%, fish and fish products 2.6%, sports goods 1.3%). *Major export destinations:* Saudi Arabia 8.8%; Iran 8.6%; Japan 8.0%; Dubai 7.0%; United States 5.8%; United Kingdom 4.8%.

Transport and communications

Transport. Railroads (1982–83): length 5,473 mi, 8,808 km; passenger-mi 11,204,000,000, passenger-km 18,031,000,000; short ton-mi cargo 5,009,000,000, metric ton-km cargo 7,313,000,000. Roads (1982): total length 57,350 mi, 92,294 km (paved 64%). Vehicles (1983): passenger cars 197,630; trucks and buses 82,709. Merchant marine (1983): vessels (100 gross tons and over) 87; total deadweight tonnage 785,023. Air transport (1982–83): passenger-mi 4,128,700,000, passenger-km 6,644,500,000; short ton-mi cargo 157,021,000, metric ton-km cargo 229,247,000; airports (1984) with scheduled flights 18.
Communications. Daily newspapers (1981): total number 109; total circulation 1,580,000; circulation per 1,000 population 18. Radios (1981): total number of receivers 6,000,000 (1 per 14 persons). Television (1982–83): total number of receivers 1,116,200 (1 per 77 persons). Telephones (1982–83): 445,000 (1 per 194 persons).

Education and health

Education (1983–84)

	schools	teachers	students	student/ teacher ratio
Primary (age 5–9)	72,093	216,200	6,201,000	28.7
Secondary (age 10–14)	10,316	139,600	2,692,000	19.3
Voc., teacher tr.	266	3,798	52,000	13.7
Higher	636	23,879	556,000	23.3

College graduates per 100,000 population (1981): 1,530. *Literacy* ‖ (1980): total population literate 15,825,000 (23.3%); males literate 11,400,000 (31.8%); females literate 4,425,000 (13.7%).
Health (1983): physicians 33,584 (1 per 2,672 persons); hospital beds 52,161 (1 per 1,720 persons).
Food (1978–80): daily per capita caloric intake 2,300 (vegetable products 89.3%, animal products 10.7%); 100% of FAO recommended minimum requirement.

Military

Total active duty personnel (1983): 478,600 (army 94.0%; navy 2.3%; air force 3.7%). *Military expenditure as percent of* GNP (1982): 6.1% (world 6.0%); per capita expenditure U.S.$23.

*1981. †1982. ‡Public administration and defense is included with other. §Second quarter. ‖ Age 5 and over.

Panama

Official name: República de Panamá (Republic of Panama).
Form of government: multiparty republic with two legislative houses (National Legislative Council [56]; National Assembly of Municipal Representatives [505]).
Head of state and government: President.
Capital: Panama City.
Official language: Spanish.
Official religion: none.
Monetary unit: 1 balboa (B) = 100 cents; valuation (Oct. 29, 1984) 1 U.S.$ = B1.00; 1 £ = B1.21.

Area and population

Provinces	Capitals	area sq mi	area sq km	population 1983 estimate
Bocas del Toro	Bocas del Toro	3,442	8,917	69,200
Chiriquí	David	3,381	8,758	331,500
Coclé	Penonomé	1,944	5,035	153,900
Colón	Colón	1,915	4,961	151,800
Darién	La Palma	6,488	16,803	34,000
Herrera	Chitré	937	2,427	95,000
Los Santos	Las Tablas	1,493	3,867	80,000
Panamá	Panamá	4,642	12,022	937,900
Veraguas	Santiago	4,280	11,086	197,800
Special territory				
Comarca de San Blas	El Porvenir	1,238	3,206	37,500
TOTAL		29,760	77,082	2,088,600

Source: Official government figures.

Demography

Density (1983): persons per sq mi 70.2, persons per sq km 27.1.
Urban-rural (1980): urban 49.3%; rural 50.7%.
Sex distribution (1980): male 50.74%; female 49.26%.
Age breakdown (1980): under 15, 39.2%; 15–29, 27.9%; 30–44, 16.4%; 45–59, 9.6%; 60–74, 5.1%; 75 and over, 1.8%.
Population projection: (1990) 2,340,000; (2000) 2,823,000.
Doubling time: 33 years.
Ethnic composition (1982): mestizo (and mulatto) 70%; white 12%; black 12%; Indian and other 6%.
Religious affiliation (1980): Roman Catholic 89.0%; Protestant 5.0%; Muslim 4.5%; Bahā'ī 1.0%; Hindu 0.3%; other 0.2%.
Major cities (1980): Panamá 386,393; San Miguelito 156,361; Colón 59,043; David 50,621.

Vital statistics

Birth rate per 1,000 population (1982): 25.5 (world avg. 29.0); (1980) legitimate 28.6%, illegitimate 71.4%.
Death rate per 1,000 population (1982): 3.8 (world avg. 11.0).
Natural increase rate per 1,000 population (1982): 21.7 (world avg. 18.0).
Total fertility rate (avg. births per childbearing woman; 1980–85): 3.6.
Marriage rate per 1,000 population (1982): 4.5.
Divorce rate per 1,000 population (1982): 0.5.
Infant mortality rate per 1,000 live births (1979): 24.9.
Life expectancy at birth (1980–85): male 68.5 years; female 73.0 years.
Major causes of death per 100,000 population (1980): heart and circulatory disease 103.7, of which myocardial infarction 25.0, ischemic disease 22.9; malignant neoplasms (cancers) 59.6; pneumonia 16.5.

National economy

Budget (1981). Revenue: B1,029,800,000 (income taxes 24.9%, social security 18.8%, value added and excise taxes 16.6%; import and export taxes 10.7%). Expenditures: B1,322,100,000 (health 13.2%, education 12.8%, social security and welfare 9.3%, housing 3.5%).
Public debt (1983): U.S.$ 3,072,200,000.
Tourism (1982): receipts from visitors U.S.$169,000,000; expenditures by nationals abroad U.S.$78,000,000.
Production (metric tons except as noted). Agriculture, forestry, fishing (1982): sugarcane 2,800,000, bananas and plantains 1,200,000, rice 150,000, corn (maize) 63,000, coffee 8,000, cacao 1,000; livestock (number of live animals) 1,683,000 cattle, 200,000 pigs; roundwood 2,047,000 cu m; fish catch 91,144. Manufacturing (value added in B; 1982): processed food 676,800,000, of which prepared meat 130,800,000, refined sugar 91,600,000; chemical products 82,800,000, of which cosmetics and perfumes 36,600,000; milled products 72,500,000; textile products 67,400,000; wood pulp and paper products 56,500,000; petroleum products 1,872,000 metric tons. Construction (value added in B; 1980): residential 78,800,000; nonresidential 56,700,000. Energy production (consumption): electricity (kW-hr; 1982) 2,700,000,000 (2,700,000,000); coal, none (n.a.); crude petroleum (barrels; 1982) none (12,937,500); petroleum products (metric tons; 1982) 1,690,000 (894,000).
Land use (1981): forested 54.5%; meadows and pastures 15.3%; agricultural and under permanent cultivation 7.6%; other 22.6%.
Gross national product (at current market prices; 1983): U.S.$4,160,300,000 (U.S.$2,280 per capita).

Origin of gross domestic product (current prices)

	1982 in value B'000,000	1982 % of total value	1980 labour force	1980 % of labour force
Agriculture	376.4	8.8	168,025	30.3
Mining	9.3	0.2	1,005	0.2
Manufacturing	397.2	9.3	57,180	10.3
Construction	380.6	8.9	32,695	5.9
Trade	679.4	15.8	71,780	13.0
Public utilities	152.6	3.6	8,260	1.5
Transportation and communication	496.5	11.6	30,460	5.5
Finance	*	*	19,940	3.6
Pub. admin., defense	*	*	17,000	3.1
Services	*	*	137,105	24.8
Other	1,795.1*	41.9*	10,190	1.8
TOTAL	4,287.1	100.0†	553,640	100.0†

Persons economically active (1980): total 553,640 (30.3%); female participation in labour force 147,400 (26.6%); unemployed 44,920 (8.1%).

Price and earnings indexes (1980 = 100)

	1978	1979	1980	1981	1982	1983	1984
Consumer price index	81.4	87.9	100.0	107.3	111.9	114.2	115.6‡
Monthly earnings index	...	...	...	...	...	...	...

Household income and expenditure. Average household size (1980) 4.6; income per household (1982) B7,620 (U.S.$7,620); sources of income (1979): wages and salaries 85.3%, transfers 9.2%, other 5.5%; expenditure (1978): food 47.3%, housing 12.7%, transportation 6.8%, health care 4.9%, clothing 4.8%.

Foreign trade

Balance of trade (current prices)

	1978	1979	1980	1981	1982	1983
B'000,000	−595.54	−889.10	−928.41	−1,224.74	−1,032.59	−945.15
% of total	50.1%	60.1%	56.3%	66.0%	57.9%	59.5%

Imports (1981): B1,540,080,000 (machinery and transport equipment 23.2%, of which passenger vehicles 3.1%; crude petroleum 23.1%; food products 7.4%, of which cereal products 2.1%, fruits and vegetables 1.9%, meat and dairy products 1.8%; iron and steel products 2.2%). *Major import sources:* United States 33.3%; Venezuela 8.8%; Mexico 8.2%; Saudi Arabia 7.9%; Japan 5.6%; Trinidad and Tobago 3.7%.
Exports (1981): B315,340,000 (food and animal products 68.3%, of which bananas 22.0%, raw sugar 16.1%, shrimps 13.5%, coffee and cocoa 4.6%; petroleum products 18.4%; clothing and leather products 1.8%). *Major export destinations:* United States 20.0%; Costa Rica 13.3%; Ecuador 9.8%; Colombia 5.4%; Nicaragua 4.8%; Chile 3.1%.

Transport and communications

Transport. Railroads (1984): length 171 mi, 275 km. Roads (1980): total length 5,351 mi, 8,612 km (paved 32%). Vehicles (1982): passenger cars 104,295; trucks and buses 35,607. Merchant marine (1983): vessels (100 gross tons and over) 5,316; total deadweight tonnage 58,318,952. Air transport (1981): passenger-mi 197,732,000, passenger-km 318,219,000; short ton-mi cargo 10,344,000§, metric ton-km cargo 15,102,000§; airports (1984) with scheduled flights 19.
Communications. Daily newspapers (1979): total number 6; total circulation 148,000; circulation per 1,000 population 79. Radios (1983): total number of receivers 290,000 (1 per 7.2 persons). Television (1983): total number of receivers 226,500 (1 per 9.2 persons). Telephones (1982): 212,992 (1 per 9.0 persons).

Education and health

Education (1981–82)

	schools	teachers	students	student/ teacher ratio
Primary (age 6–11)	2,347	12,853	333,740	26.0
Secondary (age 12–17)	197	6,502	129,203	19.9
Voc., teacher tr.	116	2,422	45,588	18.8
Higher	3	3,456	45,361	13.1

College graduates per 100,000 population (students graduating; 1981): 149.
Literacy (1980): total population literate 917,633 (84.6%); males literate 464,780 (85.2%); females literate 452,853 (84.0%).
Health: physicians (1979) 1,686 (1 per 1,060 persons); hospital beds (1977) 6,836 (1 per 259 persons).
Food (1978–80): daily per capita caloric intake 2,290 (vegetable products 82.7%, animal products 17.3%); 99% of FAO recommended minimum requirement.

Military

Total active duty personnel (1983): 2,000 (army 75.0%; navy 15.0%; air force 10.0%). *Military expenditure as percent of GNP* (1982): 0.8% (world 6.0%); per capita expenditure U.S.$16.

*Finance, public administration, defense, and services are included with other. †Detail does not add to total given because of rounding. ‡First quarter. §International scheduled service only.

Papua New Guinea

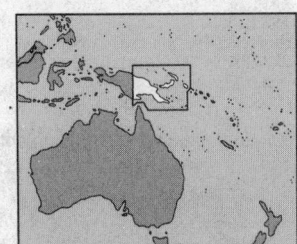

Official name: Papua New Guinea.
Form of government: unitary multiparty parliamentary state with one legislative house (National Parliament [109]).
Chief of state: British Monarch.
Head of government: Prime Minister.
Capital: Port Moresby.
Official language: English.
Official religion: none.
Monetary unit: 1 Papua New Guinea kina (K) = 100 toea; valuation (Oct. 29, 1984) 1 kina = U.S.$1.08 = £.89.

Area and population

Provinces	Administrative centres	area sq mi	area sq km	population 1984 estimate*
Central	Port Moresby	11,400	29,500	122,700
Chimbu	Kundiawa	2,350	6,100	183,600
Eastern Highlands	Goroka	4,300	11,200	296,000
East New Britain	Rabaul	6,000	15,500	138,400
East Sepik	Wewak	16,550	42,800	240,800
Enga	Wabag	4,950	12,800	174,900
Gulf	Kerema	13,300	34,500	67,600
Madang	Madang	11,200	29,000	228,700
Manus	Lorengau	800	2,100	27,500
Milne Bay	Alotau	5,400	14,000	137,900
Morobe	Lae	13,300	34,500	340,600
National Capital District	Port Moresby	100	240	133,300†
New Ireland	Kavieng	3,700	9,600	70,800
Northern	Popondetta	8,800	22,800	83,800
North Solomons	Kieta	3,600	9,300	137,600
Southern Highlands	Mendi	9,200	23,800	250,900
Western	Daru	38,350	99,300	86,200
Western Highlands	Mount Hagen	3,300	8,500	287,800
West New Britain	Kimbe	8,100	21,000	98,700
West Sepik	Vanimo	14,000	36,300	120,200
TOTAL		178,700	462,840	3,228,000†

Source: Official government figures.

Demography

Density (1984): persons per sq mi 18.2, persons per sq km 7.0.
Urban–rural (1980): urban 13.1%; rural 86.9%.
Sex distribution (1980): male 52.35%; female 47.65%.
Age breakdown (1980): under 15, 43.0%; 15–29, 25.9%; 30–44, 17.0%; 45–59, 10.4%; 60–74, 3.5%; 75 and over, 0.2%.
Population projection: (1990) 3,680,000; (2000) 4,500,000.
Doubling time: 30 years.
Ethnic composition (1978): New Guinea Papuan 83.3%; New Guinea Melanesian 15.5%; other 1.2%.
Religious affiliation (1980): Protestant 58.4%; Roman Catholic 32.8%; Anglican 5.4%; animist 2.5%; Baha'i 0.6%; other 0.3%.
Major cities (1984 est.): Port Moresby 144,300; Lae 73,400; Madang 23,700; Wewak 22,100; Goroka 20,900.

Vital statistics

Birth rate per 1,000 population (1983): 40.1 (world avg. 29.0); legitimate, n.a.; illegitimate, n.a.
Death rate per 1,000 population (1983): 13.4 (world avg. 11.0).
Natural increase rate per 1,000 population (1983): 26.7 (world avg. 18.0).
Total fertility rate (avg. births per childbearing woman; 1983): 5.9.
Marriage rate per 1,000 population: n.a.
Divorce rate per 1,000 population: n.a.
Infant mortality rate per 1,000 live births (1983): 97.0.
Life expectancy at birth (1980–85): male 53.5 years; female 53.0 years.
Major causes of death‡: pneumonia 22.6%; gastroenteritis 9.3%; accidents and violence 4.9%; tuberculosis 4.7%; malaria 4.6%.

National economy

Budget (1982). Revenue: K648,411,000 (foreign government grants 28.8%, customs and excise taxes 20.2%, personal income tax 17.3%, loans 12.6%). Expenditures: K666,760,000 (central government departments 42.4%, provincial governments 23.8%, interest payments 9.1%).
Public debt (external, outstanding; 1982): U.S.$748,000,000.
Tourism (1981): receipts from visitors U.S.$25,800,000; expenditures by nationals abroad U.S.$19,000,000.
Production (metric tons except as noted). Agriculture, forestry, fishing (1982): bananas 949,000, sweet potatoes 455,000, copra 135,000, cassava 98,000, palm oil 69,000, coffee 54,000, cocoa 31,000, tea 8,000; livestock (number of live animals) 430,000 pigs, 133,000 cattle, 16,000 goats, 1,270,000 chickens; roundwood 6,910,000 cu m; fish catch 26,932. Mining and quarrying (1982): copper 216,249; silver 1,832,010 troy oz.; gold 800,581 troy oz. Manufacturing (value added in K; 1982): food, beverages, and tobacco 117,982,000; wood and wood products 38,450,000; metals, metal products, machinery, and equipment 33,701,000. Construction (value§; 1983): residential K16,315,000; nonresidential K33,086,000. Energy production (consumption): electricity (kW-hr; 1982) 1,272,000,000 (1,272,000,000); coal, none (n.a.); crude petroleum (barrels; 1981) none (4,266,060); petroleum products (metric tons; 1982) none (601,000); natural gas, none (n.a.).

Gross national product (at current market prices; 1981): U.S.$2,408,000,000 (U.S.$787 per capita).

Origin of gross domestic product (current prices)

	in value K'000.000	% of total value	labour ‖ force	% of labour force
	1979			
Agriculture	1,412,190	84.8	35,179	20.0
Mining	¶	¶	4,301	2.4
Manufacturing	209,032	12.5	12,732	7.3
Construction	8,587	0.5	8,119	4.6
Trade	6,677	0.4	20,815	11.9
Public utilities	14,716	0.9	1,805	1.0
Transportation and communication	3,581	0.2	7,996	4.6
Pub. admin., defense	...	...	27,833	15.8
Services	10,155	0.6	56,827♀	32.4♀
Other	1,362¶	0.1¶	♀	♀
TOTAL	1,666,300	100.0	175,607	100.0

Persons economically active (1980): total 1,148,000 (38.5%); female participation in the labour force 430,000 (37.5%); unemployed, n.a. (12.8%δ).

Price and earnings indexes (1980 = 100)

	1978	1979	1980	1981	1982	1983	1984
Consumer price index	84.4	89.2	100.0	108.1	114.0	123.0	132.3□
Monthly earnings index	...	...	...	...	...	...	...

Household income and expenditure. Average household size (1980) 4.6; income per household (1975–76) K2,771 (U.S.$3,483); source of income: n.a.; expenditure: n.a.
Land use (1981): forested 71.3%; agricultural and under permanent cultivation 0.8%; meadows and pastures 0.2%; other 27.7%.

Foreign trade

Balance of trade (current prices)

	1977	1978	1979	1980	1981	1982	1983
K'000,000	+123.2	+72.1	+125.3	+7.5	−173.7	−180.8	−138.0
% of total	12.1%	7.0%	10.0%	0.5%	13.3%	13.7%	9.2%

Imports (1982): K751,667,000 (machinery and transport equipment 30.7%; manufactured goods 23.0%; mineral fuels, lubricants, and related materials 19.4%; food and live animals 18.5%). *Major import sources:* Australia 41.2%; Singapore 14.7%; Japan 14.3%; United States 8.5%; United Kingdom 4.5%; Hong Kong 2.0%.
Exports (1982): K570,855,000 (copper ore and concentrates, and gold 50.3%; coffee 13.6%; timber 8.6%; cocoa beans 5.6%; palm oil 3.8%; copra 2.3%; copra oil 2.1%). *Major export destinations:* Japan 32.9%; West Germany 25.7%; Australia 10.3%; United Kingdom 5.8%; Spain 4.6%; United States 1.9%.

Transport and communications

Transport. Railroads (1983): none. Roads (1982): total length 11,523 mi, 18,545 km (paved 6%). Vehicles (1981): passenger cars 17,730; trucks and buses 27,938. Merchant marine (1983): vessels (100 gross tons and over) 80; total deadweight tonnage 25,919. Air transport (1981): passenger-mi 332,192,000◇, passenger-km 534,611,000◇; short ton-mi cargo 6,081,000◇, metric ton-km cargo 8,878,000◇; airports (1984) with scheduled flights 134.
Communications. Daily newspaper (1983): total number 1; total circulation 27,000; circulation per 1,000 population 8.3. Radios (1983): total number of receivers 215,000 (1 per 15.2 persons). Television : n.a. Telephones (1983): 25,554 (1 per 127.5 persons).

Education and health

Education (1982)

	schools	teachers	students	student/ teacher ratio
Primary (age 7–12)	2,197	10,163	319,174	31.4
Secondary (age 13–16)	111	1,715	42,345	24.7
Voc., teacher tr.	108	633	9,074	14.3
Higher	3	644	3,954	6.1

Literacy (1980): total population literate 757,500 (42.3%); males literate 490,100 (52.4%); females literate 267,400 (31.3%).
Health: physicians (1980) 192 (1 per 16,052 persons); hospital beds (1980) 12,697 (1 per 243 persons).
Food (1978–80): daily per capita caloric intake 2,286 (vegetable products 89.8%, animal products 10.2%); 100% of FAO recommended minimum requirement.

Military

Total active duty personnel (1982): 3,775 (army 90.1%; navy 7.9%; air force 2.0%). *Military expenditure as percent of GNP* (1982): 1.5% (world 6.0%); per capita expenditure U.S.$12.

*De jure. †National Capital District includes noncitizens; 30,000 other noncitizens in the country bring the de facto total to 3,258,000. ‡By percentage of total deaths occurring in hospitals and health centres. §Urban only. ‖ Formal employees only; excludes about 85 percent of the economically active population consisting mainly of smallholder agricultural (coffee, cacao, copra, and rubber) workers and subsistence farmers, and other unskilled labourers. ¶Mining is included with other. ♀Other is included with services. δ1977; in six urban centres. □Second quarter, 1984. ◇Air Niugini.

Paraguay

Official name: República del Paraguay
(Republic of Paraguay).
Form of government: republic with
two legislative houses (Congress [30];
Chamber of Deputies [60]).
Head of state and government:
President.
Capital: Asunción.
Official language: Spanish.
Official religion: Roman Catholicism.
Monetary unit: 1 Paraguayan Guaraní
(₲) = 100 céntimos; valuation*
(Oct. 29, 1984) 1 U.S.$ = ₲240.30;
1£ = ₲290.04.

Area and population

Regions Departments	Capitals	area sq mi	area sq km	population 1982 census
Occidental		95,338	246,925	54,480
Alto Paraguay	Fuerte Olimpio	17,754	45,982	8,960
Boquerón	Dr. Pedro P. Peña	18,034	46,708	13,860
Chaco	Mayor Pablo Lagerenza	14,041	36,367	260
Nueva Asunción	General Eugenio A. Garay	17,359	44,961	220
Presidente Hayes	Pozo Colorado	28,150	72,907	31,180
Oriental		61,710	159,827	2,980,880
Alto Paraná	Puerto Presidente Stroessner	5,751	14,895	198,500
Amambay	Pedro Juan Caballero	4,994	12,933	68,730
Asunción	Asunción	45	117	457,210
Caaguazú	Coronel Oviedo	4,748	12,298	299,970
Caazapá	Caazapá	3,666	9,496	110,050
Canendiyú	Salto del Guairá	5,663	14,667	66,670
Central	Asunción	952	2,465	493,500
Concepción	Concepción	6,970	18,051	135,200
Cordillera	Caacupé	1,910	4,948	194,450
Guairá	Villarrica	1,167	3,022	143,430
Itapúa	Encarnación	6,380	16,525	264,020
Misiones	San Juan Bautista	3,690	9,556	78,270
Ñeembucú	Pilar	4,690	12,147	72,380
Paraguarí	Paraguarí	3,361	8,705	203,330
San Pedro	San Pedro	7,723	20,002	195,170
TOTAL		157,048	406,752	3,035,360

Source: Official government figures.

Demography

Density (1984): persons per sq mi 19.8, persons per sq km 7.7.
Urban–rural (1982): urban 42.8%; rural 57.2%.
Sex distribution (1982): male 50.07%; female 49.93%.
Age breakdown (1982): under 15, 41.1%; 15–29, 28.1%; 30–44, 15.4%; 45–59, 9.1%; 60–74, 4.8; 75 and over, 1.5% .
Population projection: (1990) 4,231,000; (2000) 5,405,000.
Doubling time: 23 years.
Ethnic composition (1980): mestizo (Spanish–Guaraní) 90.8%; Amerindian 3.0%; German 1.7%; other 4.5%.
Religious affiliation (1980): Roman Catholic 96.0%; Protestant 1.8%; other 2.2 %.
Major cities (1982): Asunción 457,210; San Lorenzo 74,240; Lambaré 67,180; Fernando de la Mora 66,450.

Vital statistics

Birth rate per 1,000 population (1980–85): 36.7 (world avg. 27.5); (1981)† legitimate 67.4%; illegitimate 32.6%.
Death rate per 1,000 population (1980–85): 7.6 (world avg. 10.6).
Natural increase rate per 1,000 population (1980–85): 29.1 (world avg. 16.9).
Total fertility rate (avg. births per childbearing woman; 1980–85): 4.85.
Marriage rate per 1,000 population (1981): 5.0.
Divorce rate per 1,000 population: n.a.
Infant mortality rate per 1,000 live births (1980–85): 49.0.
Life expectancy at birth (1980–85): male 62.8 years; female 67.5 years.
Major causes of death per 100,000 population (1980): diseases of the circulatory system 93.2; ill-defined conditions 79.7; enteritis and other diarrheal diseases 35.1.

National economy

Budget (1981). Revenue: ₲72,840,000,000 (domestic taxes on goods and services 16.4%, corporate taxes 15.4%, import duties 15.3%, other 52.9%). Expenditures: ₲75,619,000,000 (general public services 19.3%, social security and welfare 19.0%, economic services 19.0%, defense 13.2%, other 29.5%).
Public debt (1981): U.S.$374,650,000.
Tourism (1982): receipts from visitors U.S.$54,000,000; expenditures by nationals abroad, n.a.
Production (metric tons except as noted). Agriculture, forestry, fishing (1982): cassava 2,111,000, sugarcane 1,500,000, corn (maize) 620,000, soybeans 600,000, bananas 314,000, seed cotton 285,000, oranges 227,000, vegetables and melons 219,000, milk 177,000, sweet potatoes 119,000, lint cotton 90,000, wheat 80,000; livestock (number of live animals) 5,506,000 cattle, 1,349,000 pigs. Mining and quarrying (1982): limestone (n.a.), gypsum 10,000, kaolin 55,000. Manufacturing (1982): cotton fibre 14,954,000,000, beef for domestic consumption 11,709,000,000, soft drinks 10,816,400,000, wheat flour 5,493,700,000, sugar 4,779,000,000, vegetable oils 2,635,000,000, cotton textiles 1,805,000,000, cigarettes 1,702,300,000, Portland cement 1,534,500,000. Construction (1981)‡: residential 359,817 sq m; nonresidential 1,297,558 sq m. Energy production (consumption): electricity (kW-hr;

1982) 1,100,000,000 (1,049,000,000); coal, none (none); crude petroleum (barrels; 1982) none (1,860,309); petroleum products (metric tons; 1982) 243,000 (473,000); natural gas, none (none).
Gross national product (at current market prices; 1982): U.S.$5,833,700,000 (U.S.$1,923 per capita).

Origin of gross domestic product (current prices)

	1982 in value ₲'000,000	% of total value	labour force	% of labour force
Agriculture	190,645	25.9	600,434	44.9
Mining	3,141	0.4	11,578	0.9
Manufacturing	120,966	16.4	207,787	15.5
Construction	49,544	6.7	59,166	4.4
Trade§	196,158	26.6	120,519	9.0
Public utilities	18,120	2.5	4,362	0.3
Transportation and communication	31,107	4.2	31,384	2.3
Services ‖	127,359	17.3	239,043	17.9
Other	...	...	63,039	4.7
TOTAL	737,040	100.0	1,337,312	100.0¶

Persons economically active (1982): total 1,337,312 (44.1%); female participation in the employed labour force 224,300 (21.5%); unemployed 298,700 (9.8%).

Price and earnings indexes (1980 = 100)

	1977	1978	1979	1980	1981	1982	1983
Consumer price index	57.6	63.7	81.7	100.0	114.0	121.7	138.0
Monthly earnings index	...	...	...	...	...	...	...

Household income and expenditure: average household size (1982) 5.2.
Land use (1981): forested 51.7%; meadows and pastures 39.4%; agricultural and under permanent cultivation 4.9%; other 4.0%.

Foreign trade

Balance of trade (current prices)

	1978	1979	1980	1981	1982	1983
₲'000,000	−8,131	−17,410	−26,071	−26,532	−32,301	−29,308
% of total	11.3%	18.8%	25.0%	26.3%	25.5%	26.6%

Imports (1983): ₲69,679,000,000 (fuels and lubricants 25.1%, of which crude petroleum 12.1%, gasoline 9.0%; machines, apparatus, and engines 22.5%; iron and iron manufactures 8.3%; food, beverages, and tobacco 9.8%; transport equipment 6.2%). *Major import sources:* Brazil 28.1%; Argentina 18.7%; Algeria 13.5%; West Germany 6.9%.
Exports (1983): ₲40,371,000,000 (cotton fibres 32.9%; soybeans 31.2%; timber 6.8%; animal fodder 5.1%; tung oil 4.7%; tobacco 3.6%; cowhide 2.5%; processed meat 2.1%; sugar 1.9%). *Major export destinations:* Brazil 20.5%; The Netherlands 14.0%; West Germany 11.7%; Argentina 11.5%; United States 8.9%).

Transport and communications

Transport. Railroads (1980): length 274 mi, 441 km; passenger-mi 13,900,000, passenger-km 22,400,000; short ton-mi cargo 23,600,000, metric ton-km cargo 34,400,000. Roads (1983): total length 7,034 mi, 11,320 km (paved 19%). Vehicles (1982): passenger cars 35,000; trucks and buses 26,000. Merchant marine (1983): vessels (100 gross tons and over) 33; total deadweight tonnage 34,421. Air transport (1981): passenger-mi 163,000,000, passenger-km 263,000,000; short ton-mi cargo 2,000,000, metric ton-km cargo 2,900,000; airport (1983) with scheduled flights 1.
Communications. Daily newspapers (1983): total number 5; total circulation 158,000; circulation per 1,000 population 51. Radios (1983): total number of receivers 198,000 (1 per 16 persons). Television (1983): total number of receivers 81,000 (1 per 38 persons). Telephones (1981): 54,741 (1 per 60 persons).

Education and health

Education (1981)

	schools	teachers	students	student/ teacher ratio
Primary (age 7–12)	3,511	19,748	530,083	26.8
Secondary (age 13–18)♀	183	...	124,481	...
Higherδ	9	2,014	27,041	13.4

College graduates per 100,000 population (students graduating; 1981): 50.
Literacy (1980): total population literate 1,459,100 (85.7%); males literate 753,000 (89.6%); females literate 706,100 (81.9%).
Health: physicians (1979) 1,795 (1 per 1,710 persons); hospital beds (1981) 3,305 (1 per 989 persons).
Food (1978–80): daily per capita caloric intake 2,902 (vegetable products 80.2%, animal products 19.8%); 126% of FAO recommended minimum requirement.

Military

Total active duty personnel (1983): 16,070 (army 77.8%; navy 15.6%; air force 6.6%). *Military expenditure as percent of GNP* (1982): 1.7% (world 6%); per capita expenditure U.S.$26.

*Currency pegged to U.S.$; 1 U.S.$ = ₲160.00 for luxury goods. †Among births registered on time. ‡Permits granted, Asunción and interior towns. §Excludes restaurants and hotels. ‖ Includes finance, insurance, real estate, and other services. ¶Detail does not add to total given because of rounding. ♀Includes vocational education. δData encompass nine branches of two universities and include teacher training.

Peru

Official name: República del Perú
(Republic of Peru).
Form of government: unitary multiparty
republic with two legislative
houses (Senate [60]; Chamber of
Deputies [180]).
Head of state and government:
President.
Capital: Lima.
Official languages: Spanish; Quechua.
Official religion: Roman Catholicism.
Monetary unit: 1 Peruvian sol (S/.)
= 100 centavos; valuation (Oct. 29,
1984) 1 U.S.$ = S/.4,319;
1 £ = S/.5,214.

Area and population

Departments	Capitals	area sq mi	area sq km	population 1984 estimate
Amazonas	Chachapoyas	15,945	41,297	289,800
Ancash	Huaraz	14,158	36,669	922,900
Apurimac	Abancay	7,934	20,550	370,700
Arequipa	Arequipa	24,528	63,528	798,200
Ayacucho	Ayacucho	17,058	44,181	566,200
Cajamarca	Cajamarca	13,486	34,930	1,170,800
Cuzco	Cuzco	29,471	76,329	945,200
Huancavelica	Huancavelica	8,139	21,079	390,800
Huánuco	Huánuco	13,088	33,897	546,500
Ica	Ica	8,205	21,251	483,000
Junín	Huancayo	15,944	41,296	969,500
La Libertad	Trujillo	8,973	23,241	1,072,100
Lambayeque	Chiclayo	5,304	13,737	766,100
Lima	Lima	13,058	33,821	5,396,600
Loreto	Iquitos	146,342	379,025	513,300
Madre de Dios	Puerto Maldonado	30,271	78,403	38,700
Moquegua	Moquegua	6,065	15,709	111,600
Pasco	Cerro de Pasco	9,356	24,233	249,700
Piura	Piura	14,055	36,403	1,249,000
Puno	Puno	27,947	72,382	984,000
San Martin	Moyobamba	20,197	52,309	358,500
Tacna	Tacna	5,881	15,232	159,600
Tumbes	Tumbes	1,827	4,732	116,800
Ucayali	Pucallpa	38,931	100,831	237,300
Constitutional Province				
Callao	Callao	57	148	491,000
TOTAL		496,222*	1,285,216*	19,197,900

Source: Official government figures.

Demography

Density (1984): persons per sq mi 38.7, persons per sq km 14.9.
Urban–rural (1981): urban 64.9%; rural 35.1%.
Sex distribution (1983): male 50.38%; female 49.62%.
Age breakdown (1981†): under 15, 42.6%; 15–29, 27.6%; 30–44, 15.4%; 45–
59, 9.0%; 60–74, 4.3%; 75 and over, 1.1%.
Population projection: (1990) 23,355,000; (2000) 30,703,000.
Doubling time: 28 years.
Ethnic composition (1981): Quechua 47.1%; mestizo 32.0%; white 12.0%;
Aymara 5.4%; jungle Amerindian 1.7%; other 1.8%.
Religious affiliation (1980): Roman Catholic 95.0%; other 5.0%.
Major cities (1981): Lima 3,969,000 (metropolitan Lima 4,601,000); Are-
quipa 447,400; Callao 441,400; Trujillo 354,600.

Vital statistics

Birth rate per 1,000 population (1983): 35.4 (world avg. 29.0); (1977) legiti-
mate 57.8%, illegitimate 42.2%.
Death rate per 1,000 population (1983): 10.6 (world avg. 11.0).
Natural increase rate per 1,000 population (1983): 24.8 (world avg. 18.0).
Total fertility rate (avg. births per childbearing woman; 1983): 5.3.
Marriage rate per 1,000 population (1977): 2.3†.
Divorce rate per 1,000 population (1968): 0.2†.
Infant mortality rate per 1,000 live births (1981): 85.4.
Life expectancy at birth (1980–85): male 57.6 years; female 60.7 years.
Major causes of death per 100,000 population (1977)†‡: influenza and
pneumonia 83.7; enteritis and other diarrheal diseases 62.7; malignant
neoplasms (cancers) 32.7; heart diseases 30.9.

National economy

Budget (1983). Revenue: S/.3,732,000,000,000 (tax on external trade 27.0%,
tax on fuel 24.6%, income tax 17.4%, property tax 3.6%). Expenditures:
S/.7,626,000,000,000 (debt service 38.7%; defense and interior 25.7%; goods
and services 14.0%; investments 13.0%).
Public debt (external, outstanding; 1983): U.S.$8,317,000,000.
Tourism (1981): receipts from visitors U.S.$460,000,000; expenditures by
nationals abroad U.S.$104,000,000.
Production (metric tons except as noted). Agriculture, forestry, fishing
(1983): potatoes 1,152,900, rice 790,800, corn (maize) 594,900, raw sugar
452,000, cotton 104,400, coffee 90,900, wheat 75,100; livestock (number of
live animals; 1981) 14,750,000 sheep, 4,030,000 cattle, 2,400,000 alpacas,
2,138,000 pigs; roundwood 7,769,000 cu m§; fish catch 1,099,000. Mining and quarrying (value in U.S.$'000,000; 1983): silver 668, copper 483,
zinc 339, lead 90, iron ore 81, gold 71 ‖. Manufacturing (value added in
S/.'000,000; 1976) food, beverages, and tobacco 60,183; fabricated metals
36,992; chemicals and plastics 30,665; textiles and clothing 29,748. Con-

struction: n.a. Energy production (consumption): electricity (kW-hr; 1982)
10,400,000,000 (10,400,000,000); coal (metric tons; 1982) 55,000 (85,000);
crude petroleum (barrels; 1982) 72,344,000 (56,558,000); petroleum products (metric tons; 1982) 7,377,000 (6,104,000); natural gas (cu m; 1982)
760,256,000 (760,256,000).
Gross national product (at current market prices; 1982): U.S.$19,211,583,000
(U.S.$1,055 per capita).

Origin of gross domestic product (constant prices of 1973)

	1982 in value S/.'000,000	% of total value	labour force	% of labour force
Agriculture	64,290	12.7	2,296,100	35.9
Mining	40,750	8.1	68,100	1.1
Manufacturing	118,010	23.4	745,800	11.7
Construction	19,123	3.8	246,300	3.8
Trade	68,485	13.6	976,000	15.3
Public utilities	6,187	1.2	12,900	0.2
Transportation and communication	34,123	6.8	282,000	4.4
Finance	61,368	12.2	104,900	1.6
Services	96,279	19.1	1,245,500	19.5
Other	−3,925¶	−0.8	417,000	6.5
TOTAL	504,690	100.0*	6,394,700	100.0

Persons economically active (1982): total 6,394,700 (35.1%); female participation in labour force 1,876,100 (29.3%); unemployed 417,000 (6.5%).

Price and earnings indexes (1980 = 100)

	1977	1978	1979	1980	1981	1982	1983
Consumer price index	23.9	37.7	62.8	100.0	175.4	288.4	609.0
Monthly earnings index	...	...	...	...	...	...	...

Household income and expenditure. Average household size (1980) 4.8; income per household (1971–72) S/.51,170 (U.S.$1,322); source of income:
n.a.; expenditure (1983)♀: food, drink, and tobacco 38.1%, rent and utilities
15.6%, transportation 9.8%, recreation and education 7.4%.
Land use (1981): forested 55.2%; meadows and pastures 21.2%; agricultural
and under permanent cultivation 2.7%; other 20.9%.

Foreign trade

Balance of trade (current prices)

	1978	1979	1980	1981	1982	1983
S/.'000,000	+39,200	+429,100	+473,000	+58,600	+343,000	+531.408
% of total	6.8%	36.9%	26.7%	2.2%	8.0%	5.7%

Imports (1983): S/.4,368,268,800,000 (capital goods 32.7%, of which private
consumption 16.5%, public consumption 16.2%; food items 15.8%, of which
wheat 5.6%; other consumer goods 8.1%). *Major import sources* (1980):
U.S. 36.7%; Japan 10.4%; West Germany 8.4%.
Exports (1983): S/.4,899,676,500,000 (petroleum [all forms] 18.0%, copper
14.7%, silver 13.0%, zinc 10.2%, lead 9.7%). *Major destinations* (1980): U.S.
32.4%; Japan 8.8%; West Germany 5.5%; Italy 4.4%.

Transport and communications

Transport. Railroads (1982): route length 1,039 mi, 1,672 km; passenger-
mi 263,808,000, passenger-km 424,558,000; short ton-mi cargo 355,206,000,
metric ton-km cargo 518,591,000. Roads (1982): total length 19,999 mi,
32,185 km (paved 19%). Vehicles (1982): passenger cars 359,700; trucks and
buses 196,013. Merchant marine (1983): vessels (100 gross tons and over)
679; total deadweight tonnage 1,014,483. Air transport (1981): passenger-mi
1,090,500,000, passenger-km 1,755,000,000; short ton-mi cargo 32,629,000,
metric ton-km cargo 47,638,000; airports (1983) 22.
Communications. Daily newspapers (1983): total number 59; total circulation 2,237,600ठ; circulation per 1,000 population 120. Radios (1982): total
number of receivers 2,200,000 (1 per 8.3 persons). Television (1982): total
number of receivers 860,000 (1 per 21.2 persons). Telephones (1982): 129,-
742 (1 per 140 persons).

Education and health

Education (1981–82)

	schools	teachers	students	student/ teacher ratio
Primary (age 6–11)	25,748	116,550	3,692,273	31.7
Secondary (age 12–16)	3,289	66,874	1,429,219	21.4
Voc., teacher tr.	768	8,744	142,154	16.3
Higher	35	23,435	277,304	11.8

College graduates per 100,000 population (students graduating; 1980): 107.
Literacy (1981): total population literate 11,458,810 (78.7%); males literate
6,092,490 (84.3%); females literate 5,366,320 (73.1%).
Health (1982): physicians 14,751 (1 per 1,236 persons); hospital beds 29,991
(1 per 608 persons).
Food (1978–80): daily per capita caloric intake 2,166 (vegetable products
86.4%, animal products 13.6%); 92% of FAO recommended minimum.

Military

Total active duty personnel (1983): 135,500 (army 55.4%; navy 15.1%; air
force 29.5%). *Military expenditure as percent of GNP* (1982): 4.7% (world
6.0%); per capita expenditure U.S.$17.

*Detail does not add to total given because of rounding. †Excludes Indian jungle
population. ‡Statistics based on incomplete information. §1982. ‖ Value of exports
only. ¶Includes import duties, plus other indirect taxes, minus imputed bank service
charges. ♀Estimate for Lima metropolitan area only. ठPartial circulation.

Philippines

Official name: Republika ňg Pilipinas
(Republic of the Philippines).
Form of government: federal
parliamentary state with one
legislative house (National Assembly
[175]).
Chief of state: President.
Head of government: Prime Minister.
Capital: Manila.
Official languages: Pilipino; English.
Official religion: none.
Monetary unit: 1 Philippine peso
(₱) = 100 centavos; valuation (Oct. 29,
1984) 1 U.S.$ = ₱19.14;
1 £ = ₱23.10.

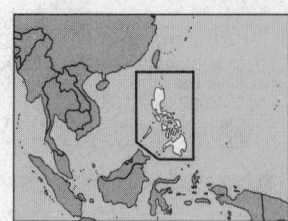

Area and population

Regions	area sq mi	area sq km	population 1984 estimate*
Bicol	6,808	17,633	3,766,000
Cagayan Valley	14,055	36,403	2,451,000
Central Luzon	7,039	18,231	5,308,000
Central Mindanao	8,994	23,293	2,451,000
Central Visayas	5,773	14,951	4,124,000
Eastern Visayas	8,275	21,432	3,031,000
Ilocos	8,328	21,568	3,783,000
National Capital Region	246	636	6,720,000
Northern Mindanao	10,937	28,328	3,117,000
Southern Mindanao	12,237	31,693	3,815,000
Southern Tagalog	18,117	46,924	6,901,000
Western Mindanao	7,214	18,685	2,770,000
Western Visayas	7,808	20,223	4,933,000
TOTAL	115,831	300,000	53,170,000

Source: Official government figures.

Demography

Density (1984): persons per sq mi 459.0, persons per sq km 177.2.
Urban–rural (1980): urban 36.2%; rural 63.8%.
Sex distribution (1984): male 50.21%; female 49.79%.
Age breakdown (1980): under 15, 41.9%; 15–29, 29.4%; 30–44, 15.4%; 45–59, 8.8%; 60–74, 3.8%; 75 and over, 0.7%.
Population projection: (1990) 60,185,000; (2000) 74,810,000.
Doubling time: 28 years.
Ethnic composition (by mother tongue; 1975): Cebuano 24.4%; Tagalog 23.8%; Ilocano 11.1%; Hiligaynon Ilongo 10.0%; Bicol 7.0%; Samar-Leyte 4.6%; Pampango 3.4%; Pangasinan 2.3%; other 13.4%.
Religious affiliation (1980): Roman Catholic 84.1%; Aglipayan (Philippine Independent Church) 6.2%; Muslim 4.3%; Protestant 3.5%; other 1.9%.
Major cities (1980): Manila 1,630,485; Quezon City 1,165,865; Davao 610,-375; Cebu 490,281; Caloocan 467,816.

Vital statistics

Birth rate per 1,000 population (1983): 32.0 (world avg. 29.0); (1980) legitimate 96.3%, illegitimate 3.7%.
Death rate per 1,000 population (1983): 6.8 (world avg. 11.0).
Natural increase rate per 1,000 population (1983): 25.2 (world avg. 18.0).
Total fertility rate (avg. births per childbearing woman; 1983): 4.2.
Marriage rate per 1,000 population (1979): 7.7.
Divorce rate per 1,000 population: n.a.
Infant mortality rate per 1,000 live births (1983): 50.0.
Life expectancy at birth (1983): male 63.0 years; female 66.5 years.
Major causes of death per 100,000 population (1977): pneumonia 106.5; tuberculosis 71.6; enteritis and other diarrheal disease 40.6; malignant neoplasms (cancers) 31.5; bronchitis 14.3.

National economy

Budget (1983). Revenue: ₱44,300,000,000 (tax revenue 86.1%, of which income tax 21.8%, import duties 20.4%, excise tax 16.7%; nontax revenue 13.9%). *Expenditures:* ₱65,000,000,000 (economic services 26.4%; education 13.3%; interest on debt 12.9%; defense 10.4%; general public services 10.0%; health 6.6%).
Public Debt (external, outstanding; 1982): U.S.$11,933,000,000.
Tourism (1981): receipts from visitors U.S.$344,000,000; expenditures by nationals abroad U.S.$127,000,000.
Production (gross value added in constant prices of 1972 in ₱'000,000). Agriculture, forestry, fishing (1981): 24,722, of which agriculture 19,216 (rice 4,249, bananas 2,378, corn 1,457, sugarcane 1,371, coconuts, including copra 1,358, livestock 1,673, poultry 1,866); forestry 1,418; fishing 4,088. Mining and quarrying (1981): 2,275, of which copper 1,497; stone, clay, and sand 278; gold 140. Manufacturing: 24,958, of which processed food 8,884; chemicals and chemical products 2,911; products of petroleum and coal 1,297; electrical machinery 1,292; textiles 1,291; footwear and wearing apparel 1,142; metal products 1,095. Construction (1979): 6,368, of which government 2,745; private 3,623. Energy production (consumption): electricity (kW-hr; 1982) 19,406,000,000 (19,406,000,000); coal (metric tons; 1982) 565,000 (509,000); petroleum (barrels; 1982) 3,441,200 (68,169,000); petroleum products (metric tons; 1982) 8,439,000 (10,149,000); natural gas, n.a. (n.a.).
Gross national product (at 1980 prices; 1983): U.S.$30,432,000,000 (U.S.$598 per capita).

Origin of gross domestic product (current prices)

	1981 in value ₱'000,000	% of total value	labour force	% of labour force
Agriculture	69,359	22.8	9,009,000	50.0
Mining	6,849	2.2	127,000	0.7
Manufacturing	75,151	24.7	1,835,000	10.2
Construction	26,238	8.6	584,000	3.2
Trade	72,377*	23.8*	2,095,000	11.6
Finance	*	*	374,000	2.1
Public utilities	3,344	1.1	66,000	0.4
Transportation and communication	19,618	6.4	755,000	4.2
Pub. admin., defense†	...	...	...	...
Services and other	31,836	10.4	3,171,000	17.6
TOTAL	304,772	100.0	18,017,000 ‖	100.0

Persons economically active (1982): total 19,085,000 (35.9%); female participation in the labour force 6,433,000‡ (35.7%); unemployed 755,000 (4.0%).

Price and earnings indexes (1980 = 100)

	1977	1978	1979	1980	1981	1982	1983
Consumer price index	66.4	71.4	84.9	100.0	113.3	125.7	139.4
Daily earnings index	87.7	91.4	96.2	100.0	...	...	...

Household income and expenditure. Average household size (1980) 5.6; income per family (1975) ₱5,840 (U.S.$777.5); source of income (1971): wages and salaries 44.8%, self employment 40.3%, owner-occupied dwellings 7.1%, pensions, social security, and related benefits 2.1%, other 5.7%; expenditure (1975): food and beverages 51.3%, housing 9.8%, clothing and other 7.9%, fuel, light, and water 4.8%, household furnishings and operations 4.4%, transport and communication 3.9%, education 3.8%, other 14.1%.
Land use (1981): forested 40.6%; meadows and pastures 3.5%; agricultural and under permanent cultivation 33.3%; other 22.6%.

Foreign trade

Balance of trade (current prices)

	1978	1979	1980	1981	1982	1983
'000,000₱	−9,805	−11,615	−14,898	−18,153	−23,090	−28,566
% of total	16.4%	14.7%	14.7%	16.9%	21.4%	20.7%

Imports (1981): ₱66,990,000,000 (crude petroleum 25.3%; nonelectrical machinery 11.1%; chemicals and related products 9.9%; electrical machinery, apparatus, and appliances 4.8%; petroleum products 4.2%; iron and steel 4.1%; motor vehicles 3.4%; cereals and cereal preparations 3.2%; textile yarns and fabrics 1.9%; dairy products 1.7%). *Major import sources:* United States 22.5%; Saudi Arabia 13.1%; Kuwait 5.2%; West Germany 4.0% .
Exports (1981): ₱44,620,000,000 (clothing 10.8%; sugar 9.9%; coconut oil 9.3%; copper concentrates 7.5%; fruits and vegetables 6.6%; gold 3.8%; wood in the rough and simply worked 3.6%; veneers and plywood 2.7%; fish 2.5%; electrical machinery, equipment, and appliances 2.1%). *Major export destinations:* United States 30.4%; Japan 21.9%; The Netherlands 5.6%; West Germany 4.2%; Hong Kong 3.9%.

Transport and communications

Transport. Railroads (1982): length (1979) 1,120 mi, 1,800 km; passenger-mi 127,000,000, passenger-km 204,000,000; short ton-mi cargo 16,439,000, metric ton-km cargo 24,000,000. Roads (1982): total length 95,952 mi, 154,-421 km (paved 13%). Vehicles (1981): passenger cars 318,085; trucks and buses 120,961. Merchant marine (1983): vessels (100 gross tons and over) 884; total deadweight tonnage 4,719,338. Air transport (1982): passenger-mi 2,990,000,000, passenger-km 4,812,000,000; short ton-mi cargo 78,225,000, metric ton-km cargo 114,206,000; airports (1983) with scheduled flights 41.
Communications. Daily newspapers (1983): total number 12; total circulation 974,000; circulation per 1,000 population 19. Radios (1983): total number of receivers 2,185,000 (1 per 23 persons). Television (1983): total number of receivers 955,000 (1 per 53 persons). Telephones (1982): 638,835 (1 per 79.4 persons).

Education and health

Education (1981–82)

	schools	teachers	students	student/ teacher ratio
Primary (age 7–12)	33,972	264,653	8,670,544	32.8
Secondary (age 13–16)	5,023	85,465	2,935,732	34.4
Voc., teacher tr.	331	...	94,588¶	...
Higher	1,038	45,893	1,226,365	26.7

College graduates per 100,000 population (students graduating; 1979): 396.
Literacy (1980): total population literate 25,139,700 (88.7%); males literate 12,772,200 (89.9%); females literate 12,367,500 (87.5%).
Health: physicians (1977) 16,123 (1 per 2,793 persons); hospital beds (1981) 88,070 (1 per 562 persons).
Food (1978–80): daily per capita caloric intake 2,315 (vegetable products 90.6%, animal products 9.4%); 102% of FAO recommended minimum.

Military

Total active duty personnel (1983): 104,800 (army 57.3%; navy 26.7%; air force 16.0%). *Military expenditure as percent of GNP* (1982): 2.5% (world 6.0%); per capita expenditure U.S.$17.

*Trade includes finance. †Distributed among other sectors. ‡1981. ‖ Detail does not add to total given because of rounding. ¶1980–81.

Poland

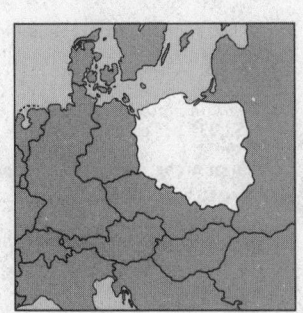

Official name: Polska Rzeczpospolita Ludowa (Polish People's Republic).
Form of government: unitary single-party republic with one legislative house (Sejm [460]).
Chief of state: President (Chairman).
Head of government: Prime Minister.
Capital: Warsaw.
Official language: Polish.
Official religion: none.
Monetary unit: 1 złoty = 100 groszy; valuation (Oct. 29, 1984)
1 U.S.$ = 125.49 złotys;
1 £ = 151.47 złotys.

Area and population

Provinces	Capitals	area sq mi	area sq km	population 1983 estimate
Biała Podlaska	Biała Podlaska	2,065	5,348	291,000
Białystok	Białystok	3,882	10,055	652,000
Bielsko	Bielsko Biala	1,430	3,703	849,000
Bydgoszcz	Bydgoszcz	3,996	10,349	1,054,000
Chełm	Chełm	1,492	3,865	234,000
Ciechanów	Ciechanów	2,456	6,362	410,000
Częstochowa	Częstochowa	2,387	6,182	755,000
Elbląg	Elbląg	2,356	6,103	451,000
Gdańsk	Gdańsk	2,855	7,394	1,360,000
Gorzów	Gorzów Wielkopolski	3,276	8,484	468,000
Jelenia Góra	Jelenia Góra	1,690	4,378	498,000
Kalisz	Kalisz	2,514	6,512	679,000
Katowice	Katowice	2,567	6,650	3,856,000
Kielce	Kielce	3,556	9,211	1,080,000
Konin	Konin	1,984	5,139	447,000
Koszalin	Koszalin	3,270	8,470	471,000
Kraków	Kraków	1,257	3,255	1,188,000
Krosno	Krosno	2,201	5,702	458,000
Legnica	Legnica	1,559	4,037	473,000
Leszno	Leszno	1,604	4,154	365,000
Łódź	Łódź	588	1,523	1,142,000
Łomża	Łomża	2,581	6,684	330,000
Lublin	Lublin	2,623	6,793	954,000
Nowy Sącz	Nowy Sącz	2,153	5,576	642,000
Olsztyn	Olsztyn	4,759	12,327	698,000
Opole	Opole	3,295	8,535	987,000
Ostrołęka	Ostrołęka	2,509	6,498	375,000
Piła	Piła	3,168	8,205	448,000
Piotrków	Piotrków Trybunalski	2,419	6,266	618,000
Płock	Płock	1,976	5,117	500,000
Poznań	Poznań	3,147	8,151	1,262,000
Przemyśl	Przemyśl	1,713	4,436	385,000
Radom	Radom	2,817	7,295	711,000
Rzeszów	Rzeszów	1,698	4,398	664,000
Siedlce	Siedlce	3,281	8,499	623,000
Sieradz	Sieradz	1,880	4,869	394,000
Skierniewice	Skierniewice	1,529	3,959	402,000
Słupsk	Słupsk	2,878	7,453	379,000
Suwałki	Suwałki	4,050	10,490	431,000
Szczecin	Szczecin	3,854	9,981	915,000
Tarnobrzeg	Tarnobrzeg	2,426	6,283	565,000
Tarnów	Tarnów	1,603	4,151	619,000
Toruń	Toruń	2,065	5,348	621,000
Wałbrzych	Wałbrzych	1,609	4,168	721,000
Warszawa	Warszawa	1,463	3,788	2,364,000
Włocławek	Włocławek	1,700	4,402	418,000
Wrocław	Wrocław	2,427	6,287	1,091,000
Zamość	Zamość	2,695	6,980	478,000
Zielona Góra	Zielona Góra	3,424	8,868	623,000
TOTAL		120,727	312,683	36,399,000

Demography

Density (1984): persons per sq mi 308.4, persons per sq km 119.1.
Urban–rural (1983): urban 59.5%; rural 40.5%.
Sex distribution (1983): male 48.82%; female 51.18%.
Age breakdown (1981): under 15, 24.6%; 15–29, 25.5%; 30–44, 19.3%; 45–59, 17.1%; 60–74, 9.7%; 75 and over, 3.8%.
Population projection: (1990) 38,967,000; (2000) 41,217,000.
Doubling time: 78 years.
Ethnic composition (1981): Polish 98.7%; Ukrainian 0.6%; other 0.7%.
Religious affiliation (1980): Roman Catholic 81%; other 19%.
Major cities (1983 est.): Warsaw 1,628,900; Łódź 845,700; Kraków 730,900.

Vital statistics

Birth rate per 1,000 population (1982): 19.4 (world avg. 29.0).
Death rate per 1,000 population (1982): 9.2 (world avg. 11.0).
Natural increase rate per 1,000 population (1982): 10.2 (world avg. 18.0).
Total fertility rate (avg. births per childbearing woman; 1982): 2.3.
Marriage rate per 1,000 population (1982): 8.7.
Divorce rate per 1,000 population (1982): 1.3.
Infant mortality rate per 1,000 live births (1982): 24.6.
Life expectancy at birth (1981): male 66.9 years; female 75.4 years.
Major causes of death per 100,000 population (1982): diseases of the circulatory system 367.0; malignant neoplasms (cancers) 169.0.

National economy

Budget (1982). Revenue: 2,345,288,000,000 złotys (tax on state enterprises 67.1%). Expenditures: 2,434,200,000,000 złotys (social insurance 12.5%; health and welfare 8.8%; education 7.9%; defense 7.2%).
Tourism (1982): receipts U.S.$65,000,000; expenditures U.S.$111,000,000.

Production (metric tons except as noted). Agriculture, forestry, fishing (1982): potatoes 31,951,000, sugar beets 15,085,000, rye 7,792,000, wheat 4,476,000, tobacco 96,000; livestock (number of live animals, 1983) 17,564,000 pigs, 11,022,000 cattle; roundwood 21,973,000 cu m; fish catch 618,200. Mining and quarrying (1982): copper ore 338,000; zinc 145,000; lead 57,495; silver 21,058 troy oz. Manufacturing (1982): crude steel 14,795,000; sausages and smoked meat 672,000; woven cotton fabrics 692,000,000 m. Construction (1982): 12,413,000 sq m. Energy production (consumption): electricity ('000,000 kW-hr, 1982) 118,000 (118,000); coal ('000 metric tons; 1982) 226,963; (190,629); crude petroleum (barrels; 1982) 1,766,530 (101,337,000); natural gas ('000,000 cu m; 1982) 5,164 (9,229).
Gross national product (at current market prices; 1982): U.S.$133,800,000,000 (U.S.$3,710 per capita).

Origin of gross domestic product (current prices)

	1982 in value '000,000 złotys	1982 % of total value	1982 labour force	1982 % of labour force
Agriculture	925.0	19.5	5,357,300	31.4
Mining	*	*	532,000	3.1
Manufacturing	2,387.6*	50.2*	4,334,900	25.4
Construction	510.0	10.7	1,223,500	7.2
Trade	655.5	13.8	1,360,800	8.0
Public utilities	*	*	148,000	0.9
Transp. and commun.	206.5	4.3	1,294,700	7.6
Finance	†	†	350,400	2.1
Services	†	†	2,344,200‡	13.7‡
Other	68.4†	1.5†	96,700	0.6
TOTAL	4,753.0	100.0	17,042,500	100.0

Persons economically active (1982): total 47.0%; females 45.4%§.

Price and earnings indexes (1975 = 100)

	1976	1977	1978	1979	1980	1981	1982
Consumer price index	104.4	109.5	118.4	126.7	138.6	168.0	337.2
Monthly earnings index	109.8	121.2	128.4	135.3	157.0	218.7	338.9

Household income and expenditure. Average size (1980) 3.0; average annual income 1,020,800 złotys (U.S.$11,600); source of income: wages 83.5%; expenditure (1980): food 38.9%, clothing 14.9%, housing 12.3%.
Land use (1982): forested 28.5%; meadows 13.3%; agricultural and under permanent cultivation 48.9%; other 9.3%.

Foreign trade

Balance of trade (current prices)

	1977	1978	1979	1980	1981	1982	1983
'000,000,000 złotys	−7.8	−6.2	−4.1	−6.4	−7.5	+82.2	+95.3
% of total	8.7%	6.5%	3.9%	5.8%	7.7%	4.5%	4.7%

Imports (1982): 868,908,000,000 złotys (machinery and transport equipment 27.0%; chemicals 14.6%; cereals and food products 14.6%; crude petroleum 12.4%; iron and steel products 10.2%). *Major import sources:* U.S.S.R. 37.8%; W. Germany 7.0%; E. Germany 6.8%; Czechoslovakia 5.8%.
Exports (1982): 951,162,000,000 złotys (machinery and transport equipment 43.8%; hard coal 12.0%; chemicals and related products 9.0%; textiles and leather articles 7.3%). *Major export destinations:* U.S.S.R. 30.1%; W. Germany 8.1%; Czechoslovakia 5.4%; E. Germany 4.7%; U.K. 3.6%.

Transport and communications

Transport. Railroads (1982): length 27,168 km; passenger-km 53,962,000,000; metric ton-km cargo 112,655,000,000. Roads (1983): total length 299,499 km (paved 62%). Vehicles (1983): passenger cars 3,178,905; trucks and buses 731,976. Merchant marine (1983): vessels (100 gross tons and over) 812; total deadweight tonnage 5,069,024. Air transport (1983): passenger-km 1,754,779,000; metric ton-km cargo 160,807,000; airports (1984) 12.
Communications (1983): Daily newspapers 42; total circulation 7,902,000; circulation per 1,000 population 217. Radios 8,875,000 (1 per 4.1 persons). Television 8,347,000 (1 per 4.4 persons). Telephones 3,648,000 (1 per 10 persons).

Education and health

Education (1982–83)

	schools	teachers	students	student/ teacher ratio
Primary (age 7–15)	14,341	244,800	4,465,300	18.2
Secondary (age 15–19)	1,171	22,800	380,800	16.7
Voc., teacher tr.	9,973	84,400	1,555,800	18.4
Higher	91	56,600	396,600	7.0

College graduates per 100,000 population (students graduating; 1982): 20.8.
Literacy (1980): total population literate 26,704,936 (98.5%).
Health (1983): physicians 67,100 (1 per 542.4 persons); hospital beds 257,000 (1 per 141.6 persons).
Food (1978–80): daily per capita caloric intake 3,545 (vegetable products 65.4%, animal products 34.6%); 135% of FAO recommended minimum.

Military

Total active duty personnel (1983): 340,000 (army 67.6%; navy 6.5%; air force 25.9%). *Military expenditure as percent of GNP* (1982): 7.2% (world 6.0%); per capita expenditure U.S.$373.

*Mining and public utilities are included with manufacturing. †Finance, public administration and defense, and services are included with other. ‡Public administration and defense are included with services. §1978.

Portugal

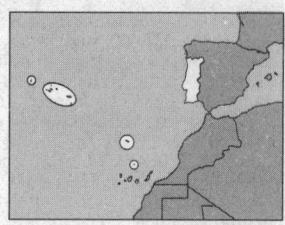

Official name: República Portuguesa
(Republic of Portugal).
Form of government: parliamentary
state with one legislative house
(Assembly of the Republic [250]).
Chief of state: President.
Head of government: Prime Minister.
Capital: Lisbon.
Official language: Portuguese.
Official religion: none.
Monetary unit: 1 Escudo (Esc) = 100
centavos; valuation (Oct. 29, 1984)
1 U.S.$ = Esc163.38; 1 £ = Esc197.20.

Area and population

		area		population
Continental Portugal				1981
Districts	Capitals	sq mi	sq km	census
Aveiro	Aveiro	1,084	2,808	619,966
Beja	Beja	3,948	10,225	184,252
Braga	Braga	1,032	2,673	709,763
Bragança	Bragança	2,551	6,608	181,375
Castelo Branco	Castelo Branco	2,577	6,675	232,967
Coimbra	Coimbra	1,524	3,947	441,001
Évora	Évora	2,854	7,393	179,241
Faro	Faro	1,915	4,960	328,605
Guarda	Guarda	2,131	5,518	205,405
Leiria	Leiria	1,357	3,515	418,942
Lisboa	Lisboa	1,066	2,761	2,085,861
Portalegre	Portalegre	2,342	6,065	142,141
Porto	Porto	925	2,395	1,561,310
Santarém	Santarém	2,605	6,747	458,229
Setúbal	Setúbal	1,955	5,064	654,312
Viana do Castelo	Viana do Costelo	871	2,255	255,395
Vila Real	Vila Real	1,671	4,328	263,972
Viseu	Viseu	1,933	5,007	421,752
Azores	Ponta Delgada	868	2,247	249,101
Corvo	...	7	17	375
Faial	...	67	173	15,563
Flores	...	55	143	4,393
Graciosa	...	24	62	5,373
Pico	...	172	446	15,224
Santa Maria	...	38	97	6,388
Sao Jorge	...	95	246	10,255
Sao Miguel	...	255	661	132,326
Terreira	...	155	402	59,204
Madeira	Funchal	306	794	259,251
Madeira	...	291	752	254,880
Porto Santo	...	16	42	4,371
TOTAL		35,516	91,985	9,852,841

Source: Official government figures.

Demography

Density (1981): persons per sq mi 277.4, persons per sq km 107.1.
Urban–rural (1980): urban 30.6%; rural 69.4%.
Sex distribution (1981): male 48.07%; female 51.93%.
Age breakdown (1981): under 15, 26.3%; 15–29, 25.0%; 30–44, 17.7%; 45–59, 16.6%; 60–74, 11.1%; 75 and over, 3.3%.
Population projection: (1990) 10,531,000; (2000) 11,154,000.
Doubling time: 115 years.
Ethnic composition (1981): Portuguese 99.7%; Spanish 0.2%; Brazilian 0.1%.
Religious affiliation (1980): Roman Catholic 94.1%; Protestant 0.8%; other 5.1%.
Major cities (1981): Lisbon 817,600; Porto 330,200.

Vital statistics

Birth rate per 1,000 population (1981): 15.7 (world avg. 29.0).
Death rate per 1,000 population (1981): 9.9 (world avg. 12.0).
Natural increase rate per 1,000 population (1981): 5.8 (world avg. 17.0).
Total fertility rate (avg. births per childbearing woman; 1980–85): 2.3.
Marriage rate per 1,000 population (1981): 7.7.
Divorce rate per 1,000 population (1979): 0.6.
Infant mortality rate per 1,000 live births (1979): 26.1.
Life expectancy at birth (1980–85): male 67.5 years; female 74.9 years.
Major causes of death per 100,000 population (1979): circulatory system diseases 407.7; tumours, including malignant neoplasms (cancers) 136.6.

National economy

Budget (1981). Revenue: Esc491,855,100,000 (capital receipts 36.3%; current receipts 52.5%, of which indirect taxes 31.1%, direct taxes 17.5%). Expenditures: Esc451,328,900,000 (finance and planning 35.2%; education and science 11.4%; social affairs 10.6%; defense 8.9%).
Public debt (external, outstanding; 1982): U.S.$9,099,500,000.
Tourism (1982): receipts from visitors U.S.$878,000,000; expenditures by nationals abroad U.S.$251,000,000.
Production (metric tons except as noted). Agriculture, forestry, fishing (1982): grapes 1,400,000, potatoes 1,100,000, wine 1,000,000, corn (maize) 464,000, wheat 445,000; livestock (number of live animals) 1,000,000 cattle, 5,200,000 sheep, 3,500,000 pigs; fish catch 253,379. Mining and quarrying†: stone, clay, and sand Esc7,567,298,000*; non-ferrous metals Esc2,936,000*. Manufacturing (gross value in Esc'000; 1981): fabric and clothing 148,-816,232; refined petroleum 105,138,574; refined oil 55,070,785; paper and paper products 47,941,164; transport equipment 34,993,560; animal feed 34,019,001. Construction (1982): residential 3,912,000 sq m; nonresidential

1,080,000 sq m. Energy production (consumption): electricity (kW-hr; 1982) 15,002,033 (19,119,000,000); coal (metric tons; 1982) 178,536 (544,000); crude petroleum (barrels: 1982) none (58,134,230); petroleum products (metric tons: 1982) 7,016,000 (7,802,000); natural gas, none (n.a.).
Gross national product (at current market prices; 1982): U.S.$22,470,000,000 (U.S.$2,234 per capita).

Origin of gross domestic product (current prices)

	1981			
	in value Esc'000	% of total value	labour force	% of labour force
Agriculture	124,400	8.5	1,045,000	23.9
Mining	...	...	21,000	0.4
Manufacturing	440,300	30.0	1,090,000	24.9
Construction	111,000	7.6	407,000	9.3
Trade	322,900	22.0	521,000	11.9
Public utilities	23,400	1.6	22,000	0.5
Transportation and communication	85,800	5.9	156,000	3.5
Finance	...	...	93,000	2.1
Pub. admin., defense	...	...		
Services	...	...	765,000	17.5
Other	357,600	24.4	261,000	6.0
TOTAL	1,465,400	100.0	4,381,000	100.0

Persons economically active (1981): total 4,366,000 (40.3%); female participation in the labour force 1,812,000 (41.5%); unemployed 355,500† (8.1%).

Price and earnings indexes (1980 = 100)

	1978	1979	1980	1981	1982	1983	1984
Consumer price index	69.3	85.7	100.0	120.0	147.3	184.3	219.6‡
Daily earnings index	71.9	82.6	100.0	121.6	148.0	172.7	...

Household income and expenditure. Average household size (1981) 3.3§; income per household: n.a.; sources of income (1976): wages 56.4%, self-employed 26.0%; expenditure (1976): food 38.4%, alcoholic beverages 8.1%, housing 4.5%.
Land use (1981): forested 39.7%; meadows and pastures 5.8%; agricultural and under permanent cultivation 38.7%; other 15.8%.

Foreign trade

Balance of trade (current prices)

	1978	1979	1980	1981	1982	1983
Esc'000,000	−123,000	−155,880	−243,870	−352,100	−422,240	−381,990
% of total	36.7%	30.7%	34.5%	40.7%	38.9%	27.5%

Imports (1983): Esc885,700,000,000 (mineral fuels, lubricants, and related materials 28.1%, of which mineral fuels 27.1%; power generating machinery and equipment 15.4%; vegetables, fruit, and cereals 10.4%; transport equipment 10.1%; chemicals and related products 8.7%). *Major import sources:* United States 14.2%; West Germany 11.3%; France 8.5%.
Exports (1983): Esc503,710,000,000 (textile yarn, fabrics, articles of apparel and clothing accessories 28.4%; power generating machinery and equipment 11.5%; processed food, beverages 8.1%; wood manufactures 7.3%; chemicals and related products 6.7%; mineral fuels, lubricants, and related materials 6.3%). *Major export destinations:* United Kingdom 14.8%; France 13.6%; West Germany 13.4%; The Netherlands 6.4%.

Transport and communications

Transport. Railroads (1981): length 2,933 mi, 4,720 km; passenger-mi 3,657,-181,000, passenger-km 5,885,673,000; short ton-mi cargo 686,826,000, metric ton-km cargo 1,002,749,000. Roads (1980): total length 32,282 mi, 51,953 km (paved 86%). Vehicles (1980): passenger cars 1,025,596; trucks and buses 79,027. Merchant marine (1983): vessels (100 gross tons and over) 357; total deadweight tonnage 1,357,681. Air transport (1983): passenger-mi 2,458,135,000, passenger-km 3,955,992,000; short ton-mi cargo 65,913,000, metric ton-km cargo 96,231,000; airports (1983) with scheduled flights 12.
Communications. Daily newspapers (1981): total number 27; total circulation 650,700; circulation per 1,000 population 66. Radios (1983): 2,155,000 (1 per 4.4 persons). Television (1983): 1,486,143 (1 per 6.4 persons). Telephones (1982): 1,455,804 (1 per 6.9 persons).

Education and health

Education (1980–81)

	schools	teachers	students	student/ teacher ratio
Primary (age 5–11)	1,707	66,001	1,186,375	18.0
Secondary (age 12–19)	313	15,294	456,003	29.8
Voc., teacher tr.	94	2,014	14,160	7.0
Higher	692	10,543	87,122	8.3

College graduates per 100,000 population (students graduating; 1981): 111.7.
Literacy (1980): total population literate 5,407,000 (80.1%); males literate 2,659,900 (86.1%); females literate 2,747,100 (75.1%).
Health: physicians (1981) 20,997 (1 per 466 persons); hospital beds (1978) 104,654 (1 per 88 persons).
Food (1978–80): daily per capita caloric intake 3,196 (vegetable products 81.4%, animal products 18.6%); 124% of FAO recommended minimum.

Military

Total active duty personnel (1983): 63,500 (army 64.5%; navy 20.5%; air force 15.0%). *Military expenditure as percent of GNP* (1982): 3.7% (world 6.0%); per capita expenditure U.S.$90.

*1981. †Continental Portugal only. ‡First quarter. §Average family size.

Puerto Rico

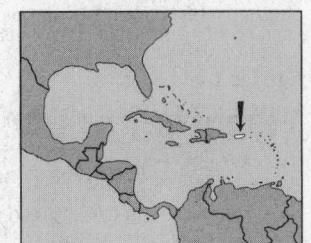

Official name: Estado Libre Asociado de Puerto Rico; Commonwealth of Puerto Rico.
Political status: self-governing commonwealth associated with the United States, having two legislative houses (Senate [27]; House of Representatives [51]).
Chief of state: President of the United States.
Head of government: Governor.
Capital: San Juan.
Official languages: Spanish; English.
Official religion: none.
Monetary unit: 1 U.S. dollar (U.S.$) = 100 cents; valuation (Oct. 29, 1984) 1 U.S.$ = 0.83 £.

Population 1980 census

Municipio*	population	Municipio*	population	Municipio*	population
Adjuntas	18,786	Fajardo	32,087	Naguabo	20,617
Aguada	31,567	Florida	7,232	Naranjito	23,633
Aguadilla	54,606	Guánica	18,799	Orocovis	19,332
Agunas Buenas	22,429	Guayama	40,183	Patillas	17,774
Aibonito	22,167	Guayanilla	21,050	Peñuelas	19,116
Añasco	23,274	Guaynabo	80,742	Ponce	189,046
Arecibo	86,766	Gurabo	23,574	Quebradillas	19,728
Arroyo	17,014	Hatillo	28,958	Rincón	11,788
Barceloneta	18,942	Hormigueros	14,030	Río Grande	34,283
Barranquitas	21,639	Humacao	46,134	Sabana Grande	20,207
Bayamón	196,206	Isabela	37,435	Salinas	26,438
Cabo Rojo	34,045	Jayuya	14,722	San Germán	32,922
Caguas	117,959	Juana Díaz	43,505	San Juan	434,849
Camuy	24,884	Juncos	25,397	San Lorenzo	32,428
Canóvanas	31,880	Lajas	21,236	San Sebastián	35,690
Carolina	165,954	Lares	26,743	Santa Isabel	19,854
Cataño	26,243	Las Marías	8,747	Toa Alta	31,910
Cayey	41,099	Las Piedras	22,412	Toa Baja	78,246
Ceiba	14,944	Loíza	20,867	Trujillo Alto	51,389
Ciales	16,211	Luquillo	14,895	Utuado	34,505
Cidra	28,365	Manatí	36,562	Vega Alta	28,696
Coamo	30,822	Maricao	6,737	Vega Baja	47,115
Comerío	18,212	Maunabo	11,813	Villalba	20,734
Corozal	28,221	Mayagüez	96,193	Vieques	7,662
Culebra	1,265	Moca	29,185	Yabucoa	31,425
Dorado	25,511	Morovis	21,142	Yauco	37,742
				TOTAL	3,196,520

Source: Official government figures.

Demography

Area: 3,515 sq mi, 9,104 sq km.
Density (1984): persons per sq mi 968.4, persons per sq km 373.9.
Urban–rural (1980): urban 66.8%; rural 33.2%.
Sex distribution (1980): male 48.7%; female 51.3%.
Age breakdown (1980): under 15, 31.6%; 15–29, 26.5%; 30–44, 18.4%; 45–59, 12.3%; 60–74, 8.3%; 75 and over, 2.9%.
Population projection: (1990) 3,680,000; (2000) 4,212,000.
Doubling time: 52 years.
Ethnic composition (1980): black 80.0%; white 20.0%.
Religious affiliation (1980): Roman Catholic 91.5%; Protestant 4.7%.
Major cities (1980): San Juan 434,849; Bayamón 196,206; Ponce 189,046; Carolina 165,954; Caguas 117,959.

Vital statistics

Birth rate per 1,000 population (1983): 19.6 (world avg. 29.0); (1980) legitimate 79.0%; illegitimate 21.0%.
Death rate per 1,000 population (1983): 6.3 (world avg. 11.0).
Natural increase rate per 1,000 population (1983): 13.3 (world avg. 18.0).
Total fertility rate (avg. births per childbearing woman; 1980–85): 2.0.
Marriage rate per 1,000 population (1980): 10.4.
Divorce rate per 1,000 population (1980): 4.8.
Infant mortality rate per 1,000 live births (1983): 16.0.
Life expectancy at birth (1980–85): male 70.8 years; female 76.9 years.
Major causes of death per 100,000 population (1980): heart disease 127.6; malignant neoplasms (cancers) 67.2; cerebrovascular disease 39.2; diabetes mellitus 28.1; conditions originating in the perinatal period 27.2; pneumonia 26.3; chronic liver disease and cirrhosis 26.2; atherosclerosis 24.9.

National economy

Budget (1982). Revenue: U.S.$4,690,000,000 (indirect business tax 28.5%; federal government grants 24.8%; personal income tax 16.2%; social insurance contributions 11.2%; corporate tax 8.8%). Expenditures: U.S.$3,909,000,000 (purchases of goods and services 67.1%, of which compensation of employees 49.5%; transfer payments to individuals 21.6%).
Public debt (outstanding; 1982): U.S.$8,041,800,000.
Tourism (1983): receipts from visitors U.S.$690,873,000; (1982) expenditures by nationals abroad U.S.$419,800,000.
Production. Agriculture, forestry, fishing (gross value in U.S.$; 1983): milk 170,621,000, coffee 58,629,000, starchy vegetables 55,482,000, fruit 27,824,000, eggs 25,729,000, sugarcane 25,344,000; livestock (number of live animals; 1982) 671,400 cattle, 118,700 pigs, 5,084,600 chickens. Manufacturing (net income in U.S.$; 1982): chemicals and allied products 2,105,700,000;

machinery and metal products 1,605,200,000; food and food products 522,700,000; apparel and other textile products 428,200,000; printing and publishing 69,100,000. Construction (gross value in U.S.$; 1983): private 323,159,000; governmental 208,491,000. Energy production (consumption): electricity (kW-hr; 1982) 11,863,000,000 (11,863,000,000); coal, none (n.a.); crude petroleum (barrels; 1982) none (38,872,700); petroleum products (metric tons; 1982) 6,024,000 (6,357,000); natural gas, none (n.a.).
Gross national product (at current market prices; 1983): U.S.$12,908,000,000 (U.S.$3,953 per capita).

Origin of gross domestic product (current prices)

	1982			
	in value U.S.$'000,000	% of total value	labour force	% of labour force
Agriculture	403	2.4	37,000	3.7
Mining	9	0.1	†	†
Manufacturing	6,556	38.6	148,000†	14.6†
Construction	280	1.6	40,000	4.0
Trade	2,602	15.3	155,000	15.3
Public utilities	593	3.5	15,000	1.5
Transp. and commun.	926	5.5	38,000	3.8
Finance	‡	‡	23,000	2.3
Pub. admin., defense	‡	‡	189,000	18.7
Services	‡	‡	145,000	14.3
Other	5,601‡	33.0‡	221,000§	21.8§
TOTAL	16,970	100.0	1,011,000	100.0

Persons economically active (1982): total 1,011,000 (31.0%); female participation in the labour force 343,000 (33.9%); unemployed 219,000 (21.7%).

Price and earnings indexes (1975 = 100)

	1977	1978	1979	1980	1981	1982	1983
Consumer price index	106.5	111.6	118.9	131.1	144.0	149.3	150.2
Monthly earnings index	118.6	131.7	144.8	157.2	172.4	...	...

Household income and expenditure. Average family size (1982) 3.7; income per family (1983): U.S.$14,430; source of income: n.a.; expenditure (1982): food, beverages, and tobacco 29.4%, housing and household operations 24.7%, transportation 16.3%, clothing 9.0%, recreation 7.2%, health 6.3.
Land use (1981): forested 20.3%; meadows and pastures 38.1%; agricultural and under permanent cultivation 15.7%; other 25.9%.

Foreign trade

Balance of trade (current prices)

	1977	1978	1979	1980	1981	1982	1983
U.S.$'000,000	−1,628	−1,788	−1,381	−1,684	−1,146	+405	+14
% of total	15.4%	15.8%	10.3%	10.8%	6.6%	2.3%	0.1%

Imports (1982): U.S.$8,167,000,000 (petroleum, natural gas, and related products 26.7%; chemicals and chemical products 7.6%; nonelectric machinery 4.9%; textile yarn, fabrics, and related products 4.8%; electrical machinery, and appliances 4.6%; meat and meat preparations 4.4%). *Major import sources:* U.S. 64.1%; Venezuela 7.3%; Neth. Antilles 3.0%.
Exports (1982): U.S.$8,888,000,000 (chemicals 25.2%; petroleum and petroleum products 14.0%; clothing and accessories 11.2%; fish and fish preparations 8.0%; electrical machinery, apparatus, and appliances 6.4%; tobacco and tobacco products 4.0%; textile yarn, fabrics, and related products 3.7%; nonelectric machinery 3.5%; sugar 2.4%). *Major export destinations:* U.S. 84.1%; Virgin Islands 2.8%; Dominican Rep. 2.5%.

Transport and communications

Transport. Railroads (1982): length 57 mi, 92 km. Roads (1982): total length 5,802 mi, 9,337 km (paved 86.0%). Vehicles (1983): passenger cars 995,067; trucks and buses 153,215. Merchant marine, n.a. Air transport (1982): aircraft departures 11,024, passenger departures 1,653,334; cargo loaded (metric tons) 52,340; airports (1984) with scheduled flights 11.
Communications. Daily newspapers (1979): total number 5; total circulation 612,000; circulation per 1,000 population 192. Radios (1982): total number of receivers 2,000,000 (1 per 1.6 persons). Television (1982): total number of receivers 810,000 (1 per 4.0 persons). Telephones (1982): 678,447 (1 per 4.8 persons).

Education and health

Education (1980–81)

	schools	teachers	students	student/teacher ratio
Primary (age 5–12)	1,618	23,154	470,089	20.3
Secondary (age 13–18)	619	13,297 ‖	337,153	25.4
Voc., teacher tr.	68	2,600	60,045	23.1
Higher	27	3,300	130,105	39.4

College graduates per 100,000 population (1980): 643¶. *Literacy* (1980): total population literate 1,924,100 (90.8%); males literate 934,400 (91.8%); females literate 989,700 (89.8%).
Health: physicians (1983) 7,146 (1 per 457 persons); hospital beds (1981) 12,198 (1 per 267 persons).

Military

Total active duty personnel: No domestic military force is maintained; the United States is responsible for defense.

*Names of administrative seats are the same as the corresponding municipio except Isabela, whose seat is Vieques. †Mining included with manufacturing. ‡Finance, services, public administration and defense are included with other. §Including unemployed. ‖ Public schools only. ¶Five years or more of college education.

Qatar

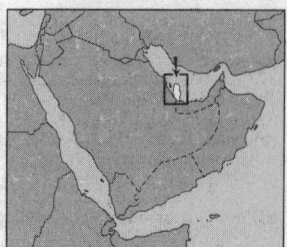

Official name: Dawlat Qaṭar (State of Qatar).
Form of government: constitutional monarchy; Islāmic law is the basis of legislation in the state.
Head of state and government: Amīr.
Capital: Doha.
Official language: Arabic.
Official religion: Islām.
Monetary unit: 1 riyal (QR) = 100 dirhams; valuation (Oct. 29, 1984) 1 U.S.$ = Qr3.65; 1 £ = Qr4.40.

Area and population	area		population
	sq mi	sq km	1984 estimate
TOTAL*	4,400	11,400	276,000

Demography

Density (1984): persons per sq mi 62.7, persons per sq km 24.2.
Urban–rural (1980): urban 86.1%; rural 13.9%.
Sex distribution (1981): male 63.62%; female 36.38%.
Age breakdown (1981): under 15, 32.3%; 15–29, 31.8%; 30–44, 25.8%; 45–59, 7.8%; 60 and over, 2.3%.
Population projection: (1990) 330,000; (2000) 425,000.
Doubling time: 19 years.
Ethnic composition (1983): South Asian 34%; Qatari 20%; other Arab 25%; Iranian 16%; other 5%.
Religious affiliation (1980): Muslim 92.4%; Christian 5.9%; Hindu 1.1%; Bahā'ī 0.2%; other 0.4%.
Major cities (1983): Doha 190,000; Musay'īd 40,000.

Vital statistics

Birth rate per 1,000 population (1983): 29.4 (world avg. 29.0); legitimate, n.a.; illegitimate, n.a.
Death rate per 1,000 population (1983): 2.2 (world avg. 11.0).
Natural increase rate per 1,000 population (1983): 27.2 (world avg. 18.0).
Total fertility rate (avg. births per childbearing woman; 1980–85): 6.8.
Marriage rate per 1,000 population: n.a.
Divorce rate per 1,000 population (1981): 5.3.
Infant mortality rate per 1,000 live births (1975–1980): 57.0.
Life expectancy at birth (1975–80): male 54.8 years; female 58.3 years.
Major causes of death: n.a.

National economy

Budget (1984–85). Revenue: QR11,970,900,000 (detail n.a.; however, crude oil provides most of the revenue). Expenditures: QR16,951,200,000 (housing and public buildings 5.9%, industry and agriculture 4.9%, electricity and water 4.3%, education 3.2%, transport and communications 3.1%, social services 1.7%, health 0.8%).
Public debt: none.
Tourism: n.a.
Production (metric tons except as noted). Agriculture, forestry, fishing (1982): tomatoes 5,000, watermelons 2,000, onions 1,000; livestock (number of live animals) 57,000 goats, 51,000 sheep, 10,000 cattle, 10,000 camels, 380,-000 chickens; fish catch 2,333. Mining and quarrying: n.a. Manufacturing (1982): urea 660,000; ammonia 530,000; ethylene 280,000; cement 255,000. Construction: n.a. Energy production (consumption): electricity (kW-hr; 1982) 2,775,000,000 (2,775,000,000); coal, none (n.a.); crude petroleum (barrels; 1983) 91,312,500 (3,122,580†); petroleum products (metric tons; 1982) 785,000 (389,000); natural gas (cu m; 1983) 2,500,000,000 (2,500,000,000).
Gross national product (at current market prices; 1979): U.S.$5,000,000,000 (U.S.$25,000 per capita).

Origin of gross domestic product (current prices)	1982		1970	
	in value QR'000,000	% of total value	labour force	% of labour force
Agriculture	...	...	2,080	4.3
Petroleum	15,235	52.8	2,225	4.6
Manufacturing, mining, public utilities	...	...	5,226	10.8
Construction	...	...	7,790	16.1
Trade	...	...	7,887	16.2
Transportation and communication	...	...	3,242	6.7
Finance	...	...	290	0.6
Pub. admin., defense	...	...	6,193	12.8
Services	...	...	13,500	27.9
Other	13,604	47.2	...	...
TOTAL	28,839	100.0	48,433	100.0

Persons economically active‡ (1981): total 111,264 (50.6%); female participation in the labour force 8,929 (8.0%); unemployed, n.a.

Price and earnings indexes (1979 = 100)	1979	1980
Consumer price index	100.0	106.8

Land use (1981): meadows and pastures 4.5%; agricultural and under permanent cultivation 0.3%; built-up, desert, and other 95.2%.

Foreign trade

Balance of trade (current prices)	1978	1979	1980	1981	1982	1983
QR'000,000	+4,403	+8,706	+15,476	+15,162	+8,377	+7,019
% of total	32.4%	44.7%	59.5%	57.7%	37.1%	39.8%

Imports (1983): QR5,299,000,000 (machinery and transport equipment 42.5%, food and live animals 11.4%, chemicals 4.8%). *Major import sources:* Japan 20.4%; United Kingdom 16.5%; United States 11.1%; West Germany 7.2%; France 5.9%; Italy 4.8%.
Exports (1983): QR12,318,000,000 (crude petroleum 91.9%). *Major export destinations:* Japan 18.3%; United Kingdom 17.7%; United States 11.3%; West Germany 6.1%; France 5.4%; Italy 5.3%.

Transport and communications

Transport. Railroads: none. Roads (1980): total length 565 mi, 909 km (paved, n.a.). Vehicles: n.a. Merchant marine (1983): vessels (100 gross tons and over) 63; total deadweight tonnage 474,126. Air transport: passengers, n.a., cargo, n.a.; airport (1984) with scheduled flights 1.
Communications. Daily newspapers (1983): total number 7; circulation, n.a. Radios (1983): total number of receivers 75,000 (1 per 3.5 persons). Television (1983): total number of receivers 110,000 (1 per 2.4 persons). Telephones (1982): 42,000 (1 per 6.6 persons).

Education and health

Education (1979–80)	schools	teachers	students	student/ teacher ratio
Primary (age 6–11)	...	2,037	28,472	14.0
Secondary (age 12–17)	...	1,475	14,360	9.7
Teacher tr.	...	26	65	2.5
Higher	...	261	2,025	7.8

College graduates per 100,000 population: n.a. *Literacy:* n.a.
Health: physicians (1978) 169 (1 per 1,180 persons); hospital beds (1980) 1,862 (1 per 118 persons).
Food: daily per capita caloric intake, n.a.

Military

Total active duty personnel (1981): 6,000 (army 83.3%; navy 11.7%; air force 5.0%). *Military expenditure as percent of GNP* (1981): 13.1% (world 5.7%); per capita expenditure U.S.$3,896.

*No administrative subdivisions exist. †1982. ‡Includes workers from abroad.

K. ARKELL—GAMMA/LIAISON

Petrochemical installation, Doha, Qatar.

Réunion

Official name: Département de la
Réunion (Department of Reunion).
Political status: overseas department
(France) with one legislative house
(General Council [36]), three
representatives in the French National
Assembly, and two senators in the
French Senate.
Chief of state: President of France.
Head of government: Commissioner.
Capital: Saint-Denis.
Official language: French.
Official religion: none.
Monetary unit: 1 Franc (Francs)
(F) = 100 centimes; valuation
(Oct. 29, 1984) 1 U.S.$ = F9.41;
1 £ = F11.36.

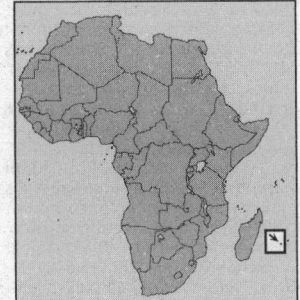

Area and population		area		population
		sq mi	sq km	1982 census
Arrondissements	**Capitals**			
Saint-Benoît	Saint-Benoît	284	736	74,312
Saint-Denis	Saint-Denis	163	423	180,647
Saint-Paul	Saint-Paul	180	467	94,378
Saint-Pierre	Saint-Pierre	339	878	166,461
TOTAL		982†	2,544†	515,798

Source: Official government figures.

Demography

Density (1982): persons per sq mi 560.1‡; persons per sq km 216.3‡.
Urban–rural (1982): urban 56.4%; rural 43.6%.
Sex distribution (1981): male 48.03%; female 51.97%.
Age breakdown (1981): under 15, 38.1%; 15–29, 29.0%; 30–39, 11.0%; 40–49, 9.0%; 50–59, 6.5%; 60 and over, 6.4%.
Population projection: (1990) 558,500; (2000) 617,000.
Doubling time: 40 years.
Ethnic composition (1980): mixed and mulatto 42.8%; East Indian 27.2%; creole (various white European) 25.7%; Chinese 4.3%.
Religious affiliation (1980): Roman Catholic 96.3%; Muslim 2.2%; Protestant 0.6%; Baha'i 0.3%; Hindu 0.2%; other 0.4%.
Major cities (1982): Saint-Denis 126,323; Saint-Pierre 90,627; Saint-Joseph 31,141; Le Port 25,377.

Vital statistics

Birth rate per 1,000 population (1983): 23.6 (world avg. 29.0); legitimate 56.5%; illegitimate 43.5%.
Death rate per 1,000 population (1983): 6.2 (world avg. 11.0).
Natural increase rate per 1,000 population (1983): 17.4 (world avg. 18.0).
Total fertility rate (avg. births per childbearing woman; 1983): 2.9.
Marriage rate per 1,000 population (1983): 6.1.
Divorce rate per 1,000 population (1983): 0.8.
Infant mortality rate per 1,000 live births (1983): 12.4.
Life expectancy at birth (1980–85): male 64.6 years; female 68.2 years.
Major causes of death per 100,000 population (1982): diseases of the circulatory system 191.7; accidents 65.7; malignant neoplasms (cancers) 53.5; diseases of the respiratory system 43.4.

National economy

Budget (1982). Revenue: F2,422,000,000 (French participation in the provision of services 47.6%, deferred and supplementary receipts 28.4%, gasoline taxes 7.4%, worldwide assistance 5.0%, new loans 4.9%). Expenditures: F2,422,000,000 (health and social services 46.8%, deferred and supplementary expenses 28.4%, infrastructure and public works 9.8%).
Tourism (1982): visitors 98,550.
Production (metric tons except as noted). Agriculture, forestry, fishing (1983): sugarcane 2,033,800, corn (maize) 11,610, bananas 4,690, potatoes 3,602, mangoes 3,462, tomatoes 3,337, onions 1,359, carrots 1,348, sweet potatoes 857, citrus fruits 978, avocados 818, tobacco 189, green vanilla 93, milk 173,800 hectolitres, eggs 36,500,000 units; livestock (number of live animals; 1982) 74,000 pigs, 45,000 goats, 22,000 cattle, 3,200,000 chickens; roundwood 33,000 cu m; fish catch 2,448. Mining and quarrying (1980): gravel and sand for cement. Manufacturing (1983): sugar 223,700; molasses 65,100; vanilla 93; geranium essence 32; khushkhus essence 19; rum 84,141 hectolitres; molasses alcohol 2,918 hectolitres; sawnwood 1,000 cu m; other important products include wooden furniture and crafts, clothing and shoes, cigarettes, beverages, fertilizers, paints, plastics and rubber goods, and iron and steel angles, shapes, and sections. Construction (buildings completed; 1983): 2,397. Energy production (consumption): electricity (kW-hr; 1983) 481,600,000 (481,600,000); fuelwood 31,000 cu m§ (31,000 cu m§); petroleum products (metric tons; 1982) none (264,000).
Household income and expenditure. Average household size (1982) 4.2; income per household F24,697 (U.S.$3,672); département-wide source of personal income: transfer payments 63.6%, wages and salaries 27.9%, self-employment 8.5%; expenditure (1976): food 33.9%, housing 18.5%, transportation 15.4%, health care 10.5%, clothing and footwear 8.8%, recreation 7.4%.
Gross national product (at current market prices; 1981): U.S.$2,050,000,000 (U.S.$3,840 per capita).

Origin of gross domestic product (current prices)				
	1980		1982	
	in value F'000,000	% of total value	labour force ‖	% of labour force
Agriculture	499	5.9	11,176	9.4
Mining	¶	¶	¶	¶
Manufacturing	802¶	9.5¶	7,369¶	6.2¶
Construction,	401	4.7	⌀	⌀
Trade	1,360	16.1	14,328	12.1
Public utilities	130	1.5	697	0.6
Transportation and communication	347	4.1	5,871	5.0
Finance	514	6.1	1,354	1.1
Pub. admin., defense	2,534	30.0	44,576	37.6
Services	1,520	18.0	14,216	12.0
Other	338	4.0	18,903⌀	16.0⌀
TOTAL	8,445	100.0†	118,490	100.0

Persons economically active (1982): total 174,107 (33.8%); female participation in the labour force 62,679 (36.0%); unemployed 54,137 (31.1%).

Price and earnings indexes (1976 = 100)							
	1977	1978	1979	1980	1981	1982	1983⌀
Consumer price index	110.5	118.2	133.6	150.4	170.7	185.7	197.8
Monthly earnings index	112.0	128.6	146.1	169.5	207.3	241.5	261.1

Land use (1982): forested 45.1%; meadows and pastures 3.5%; agricultural and under permanent cultivation 18.9%; other 32.5%.

Foreign trade

Balance of trade (current prices)					
	1978	1979	1980	1981	1982	1983
F'000,000	−2,140	−2,711	−3,368	−3,522	−4,548	−5,536
% of total	67.3%	69.5%	75.3%	76.6%	77.0%	83.9%

Imports (1983): F6,410,400,000 (consumer goods 22.3%, food and agricultural products 18.1%, intermediate goods 16.8%). *Major import sources:* France 61.9%; Bahrain 8.1%; Italy 5.1%; South Africa 4.0%; Japan 2.6%.
Exports (1983): F874,700,000 (sugar 79.5%; rum 3.4%; geranium essence 2.8%; molasses 1.3%; khushkhus essence 1.2%). *Major export destinations:* France 52.5%; Portugal 8.0%; China 6.8%; Morocco 6.2%; Italy 4.8%.

Transport and communications

Transport. Railroads□ (1982): length 382 mi, 614 km; cargo, n.a. Roads (1982): total length 1,814 mi, 2,919 km (paved 81%). Vehicles (1983): passenger cars 118,854; trucks and buses 39,046. Fishing fleet (1982): vessels (10 gross tons and over) 4; total deadweight tonnage, n.a. Air transport (1983): passenger arrivals 202,437, passenger departures 199,427; cargo loaded 2,777 metric tons, cargo unloaded 5,965 metric tons; airport (1984) with scheduled flights 1.
Communications. Daily newspapers (1982): total number 3; total circulation 57,500; circulation per 1,000 population 111. Radios (1983): total number of receivers 120,000 (1 per 4 persons). Television (1983): total number of receivers 86,142 (1 per 6 persons). Telephones (1982): 81,175 (1 per 6 persons).

Education and health

Education (1981–82)	schools	teachers	students	student/ teacher ratio
Primary (age 6–11)	513	4,963	120,580	24.3
Secondary (age 12–18)	83	4,042	66,443	16.4
Voc., teacher tr.⌀	17	599	10,058	16.8
Higher	1	74	2,420	32.7

College graduates per 100,000 population (students graduating; 1979): 111.
Literacy (1982): total population literate 343,300 (78.7%).
Health: physicians (1984) 464 (1 per 1,167 persons); hospital beds (1983) 3,849 (1 per 138 persons).
Food (1978–80): daily per capita caloric intake 2,895 (vegetable products 82.8%, animal products 17.2%); 128% of FAO recommended minimum requirement.

Military

No domestic military forces are maintained; France is responsible for defense.

*Includes 12 sq mi (32 sq km) of uninhabited islands administered as part of the département (Bassas da India, Europa, Îles Glorieuses, Juan de Nova, and Tromelin) and 3 sq mi (8 sq km) of area not included in the arrondissements. †Detail does not add to total given because of rounding. ‡Based on Réunion Island area only. §1981. ‖ Employed persons only. ¶Mining is included with manufacturing. ⌀Construction is included with other. δNine months only. □Serving sugarcane plantations only. ◊1979–80.

Romania

Official name: Republika Socialistă România (Socialist Republic of Romania).
Form of government: single-party republic with one legislative house (Grand National Assembly [369]).
Head of state and government: President.
Capital: Bucharest.
Official language: Romanian.
Official religion: none.
Monetary unit: 1 Romanian Leu (lei) = 100 bani; valuation (Oct. 29, 1984) 1 U.S.$ = 15.57 lei; 1 £ = 18.79 lei.

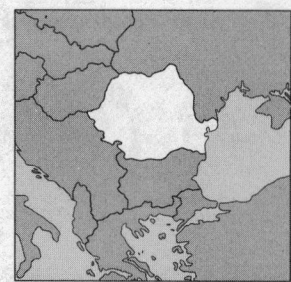

Area and population

Districts	Capitals	area sq mi	area sq km	population 1981 estimate
Alba	Alba Iulia	2,406	6,231	418,431
Arad	Arad	2,954	7,652	510,106
Argeş	Piteşti	2,626	6,801	656,800
Bacău	Bacău	2,551	6,606	694,825
Bihor	Oradea	2,909	7,535	647,016
Bistriţa-Năsăud	Bistriţa	2,048	5,305	304,228
Botoşani	Botoşani	1,917	4,965	465,318
Brăila	Brăila	1,824	4,724	392,596
Braşov	Braşov	2,066	5,351	653,553
Buzău	Buzău	2,344	6,072	519,048
Caraş-Severin	Reşita	3,283	8,503	395,061
Calaraşi	Calaraşi	1,915	4,959	337,188
Cluj	Cluj-Napoka	2,568	6,650	736,843
Constanţa	Constanţa	2,724	7,055	661,036
Covasna	Sfintu Gheorghe	1,431	3,705	218,950
Dimboviţa	Tîrgovişte	1,558	4,035	548,176
Dolj	Craiova	2,862	7,413	765,352
Galaţi	Galaţi	1,708	4,425	612,706
Giurgiu	Giurgiu	1,471	3,810	378,632
Gorj	Tîrgu Tiu	2,178	5,641	358,271
Harghita	Miercurea-Ciuc	2,552	6,610	346,141
Hunedoara	Deva	2,709	7,016	540,855
Ialomiţa	Slobozia	1,763	4,565	305,464
Iaşi	Iaşi	2,112	5,469	760,138
Maramureş	Baia Mare	2,400	6,215	522,328
Mehedinţi	Drobeta-Turnu-Severin	1,892	4,900	327,817
Mureş	Tîrgu Mureş	2,585	6,696	610,791
Neamţ	Piatra Neamţ	2,274	5,890	555,019
Olt	Slatina	2,126	5,507	530,234
Prahova	Ploieşti	1,812	4,694	847,793
Sălaj	Zalău	1,486	3,850	266,782
Satu Mare	Satu Mare	1,701	4,405	404,527
Sibiu	Sibiu	2,093	5,422	496,511
Suceava	Suceava	3,303	8,555	658,108
Teleorman	Alexandria	2,224	5,760	515,853
Timiş	Timişoara	3,356	8,692	706,724
Tulcea	Tulcea	3,255	8,430	263,304
Vaslui	Vaslui	2,045	5,297	453,159
Vîlcea	Rîmnicu Vîlcea	2,203	5,705	420,464
Vrancea	Focşani	1,878	4,863	380,490
Muncipality				
Bucharest	Bucharest	587	1,521	2,165,997
TOTAL		91,699	237,500	22,352,635

Source: Official government figures.

Demography

Density (1984): persons per sq mi 246.5, persons per sq km 95.2.
Urban–rural (1982): urban 52.2%; rural 47.8%.
Sex distribution (1982): male 49.34%; female 50.66%.
Age breakdown (1981): under 15, 27.0%; 15–29, 21.8%; 30–44, 19.3%; 45–59, 18.6%; 60–74, 10.0%; 75 and over, 3.3%.
Population projection: (1990) 23,994,000; (2000) 25,728,000.
Doubling time: 98 years.
Ethnic composition (1977): Romanian 88.1%; Hungarian 7.9%; German 1.6%; Gypsy 1.1%; other 1.3%.
Religious affiliation (1980): Romanian Orthodox 70.0%; Greek Orthodox 10.0%; Muslim 1.0%; atheist 7.0%; other 3.0%; none 9.0%.
Major cities (1981): Bucharest 1,959,000*; Braşov 320,168; Constanţa 293,866; Cluj-Napoca 289,808; Timişoara 288,237; Iaşi 279,753.

Vital statistics

Birth rate per 1,000 population (1983): 14.3 (world avg. 29.0).
Death rate per 1,000 population (1983): 9.9 (world avg. 11.0).
Natural increase rate per 1,000 population (1983): 4.4 (world avg. 18.0).
Total fertility rate (avg. births per childbearing woman; 1982): 2.4.
Marriage rate per 1,000 population (1982): 17.8.
Divorce rate per 1,000 population (1982): 1.5.
Infant mortality rate per 1,000 live births (1983): 23.9.
Life expectancy at birth (1980): male 67.5 years; female 72.3 years.
Major causes of death per 100,000 population (1982): diseases of the circulatory system 562.2; diseases of respiratory system 127.9.

National economy

Budget (1982). Revenue: 227,400,000,000 lei (benefit quotas from state economic enterprises 50.3%, income tax 14.5%, state social insurance 12.4%). Expenditures: 257,400,000,000 lei (national economy 59.6%, education 6.9%, health and social welfare 6.6%, defense 3.7%).

Public debt (external, outstanding; 1979): U.S.$1,900,000,000†.
Tourism (1982): number of tourists 7,000,000; expenditures, n.a.
Production (metric tons except as noted). Agriculture (1983): corn (maize) 10,500,000, potatoes 6,190,000, wheat 5,000,000, sugar beets 4,819,000; livestock (number of live animals, 1982) 6,082,000 cattle, 17,288,000 sheep; roundwood 20,423,000 cu m‡; fish catch 251,000. Mining and quarrying (1982): iron ore 2,400,000; bauxite 680,000; lead and zinc 88,500. Manufacturing (1983): crude steel 13,600,000; cement 13,000,000; rolled steel 9,200,000; fertilizers 2,913,000; plastics and synthetic rubber 583,836. Construction (1981): residential 5,578,000 sq m; nonresidential 3,258,000 sq m. Energy production (consumption): electricity (kW-hr; 1983) 70,200,000,000 (70,008,000,000‡); coal (metric tons; 1983) 44,500,000 (42,700,000‡); crude petroleum (barrels, 1983) 85,028,000 (165,966,000‡); natural gas (cu m; 1983) 36,100,000,000 (43,628,000,000‡).
Gross national product (at current market prices; 1981): U.S.$42,773,300,000 (lei 641,600,000,000) (U.S.$1,913 per capita).

Origin of net material product (current prices)

	1981 in value '000,000 lei	% of total value	labour force	% of labour force
Agriculture	104,547	19.7	3,039,000	29.3
Mining and manufacturing	297,722	56.1	3,748,600	36.1
Construction	40,864	7.7	797,800	7.7
Trade	32,903	6.2	619,600	6.0
Transportation and communication	35,026	6.6	740,100	7.1
Pub. admin., defense, and services	...	...	1,289,900	12.4
Other	19,638	3.7	140,500	1.4
TOTAL	530,700	100.0	10,375,500	100.0

Persons economically active (1982): total 10,469,000 (46.7%); female 45.9%.

Price and earnings indexes (1970 = 100)

	1976	1977	1978	1979	1980	1981	1982
Consumer price index	119.6	119.4	125.9	127.0	131.0	133.9	146.6
Monthly earnings index	148.5	154.7	159.0	165.1	170.0	173.2	176.9

Household income and expenditure. Average household size (1982) 3.1; income per household§ 73,470 lei (U.S.$4,900); sources of income: wages 62.6%, other 37.4%; expenditure (1980): food 62.7%, clothing 13.8%, housing 9.2%.
Land use (1982): forested 27.4%; meadows and pastures 19.3%; agricultural and under permanent cultivation 45.7%; other 7.6%.

Foreign trade

Balance of trade (current prices)

	1976	1977	1978	1979	1980	1981	1982
'000,000 lei	+210.0	−195	−3,708	−5,325	−8,043	+3,031	+25,849
% of total	0.3%	0.3%	4.9%	5.8%	7.3%	0.9%	8.7%

Imports (1981): 164,671,000,000 lei (mineral fuels 48.6%; machinery 23.6%). *Major import sources:* U.S.S.R. 18.2%; United States 7.8%; Iran 7.1%; West Germany 5.7%; East Germany 4.2%.
Exports (1981): 167,702,000,000 lei (machinery and transport equipment 29.0%; petroleum products, 27.8%; chemicals 11.4%). *Major export destinations:* U.S.S.R. 18.0%; West Germany 7.2%; United States 4.9%.

Transport and communications

Transport. Railroads (1983): length 6,913 mi, 11,125 km; passenger-km 25,578,000,000; metric ton-km cargo 62,822,000,000. Roads (1983): total length 45,586 mi, 73,364 km (paved 63%). Vehicles (1980): passenger cars 250,000; trucks and buses 130,000. Merchant marine (1983): vessels (100 gross tons and over) 379; total deadweight tonnage 3,493,047. Air transport (1983): passenger-km 2,362,000,000‡; metric ton-km cargo 39,000,000; airports (1984) 15.
Communications. Daily newspapers (1983): total number 36; total circulation 1,096,000,000; circulation per 1,000 population 48.5. Radios (1983): 3,320,000 (1 per 6.8 persons). Television (1983): 3,862,000 (1 per 5.8 persons). Telephones (1981): 2,027,000 (1 per 11.0 persons).

Education and health

Education (1981–82)

	schools	teachers	students	student/ teacher ratio
Primary (age 6–13)	14,299	157,709	3,285,073	20.8
Secondary (age 14–18)	971	47,334	1,020,789	21.6
Voc., teacher tr.	882	2,060	148,040	71.9
Higher	44	13,900	181,000	13.0

College graduates per 100,000 population (1982): 8.1. *Literacy* (1980): 95.8%.
Health (1982): physicians 36,700 (1 per 667 persons); hospital beds 209,000 (1 per 108 persons).
Food (1978–80): daily per capita caloric intake 3,396 (vegetable products 75.4%, animal products 24.6%); 128% of FAO recommended minimum.

Military

Total active duty personnel (1983): 189,500 (army 79.2%; navy 3.9%; air force 16.9%). *Military expenditure as percent of GNP* (1982): 4.6% (world 6.0%); per capita expenditure U.S.$212.

*1983 est. †To Western countries only. ‡1982. §1981.

Rwanda

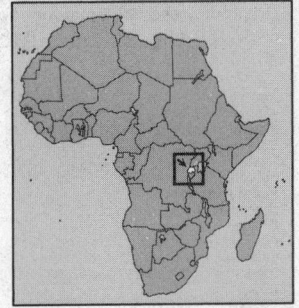

Official name: Republika y'u Rwanda (Kinyarwanda), République Rwandaise (French) (Republic of Rwanda).
Form of government: republic with one legislative house (National Development Council [70]).
Head of state and government: President.
Capital: Kigali.
Official languages: French and Kinyarwanda.
Official religion: none.
Monetary unit: 1 Rwanda franc (RF); valuation (Oct. 29, 1984) 1 U.S.$ = RF122.27; 1 £ = RF147.68.

Area and population		area		population
		sq mi	sq km	1985 estimate
Prefectures	**Capitals**			
Butare	Butare	707	1,830	637,400
Byumba	Byumba	1,925	4,987	695,300
Cyangugu	Cyangugu	859	2,226	381,500
Gikongoro	Gikongoro	846	2,192	412,400
Gisenyi	Gisenyi	925	2,395	565,200
Gitarama	Gitarama	865	2,241	720,800
Kibungo	Kibungo	1,596	4,134	502,200
Kibuye	Kibuye	510	1,320	459,000
Kigali	Kigali	1,255	3,251	1,130,000
Ruhengeri	Ruhengeri	680	1,762	582,700
TOTAL		10,169*	26,338	6,086,500

Source: Official government figures; Britannica estimate.

Demography

Density (1984): persons per sq mi 573.9, persons per sq km 221.6.
Urban-rural (1985): urban 5.1%; rural 94.9%.
Sex distribution (1985): male 49.37%; female 50.63%.
Age breakdown (1980): under 15, 46.6%; 15–29, 26.0%; 30–44, 14.4%; 45–59, 8.5%; 60–74, 3.8%; 75 and over 0.7%.
Population projection: (1990) 7,105,000; (2000) 9,845,000.
Doubling time: 22 years.
Ethnic composition (1983): Hutu 90%; Tutsi 9%; Twa 1%.
Religious affiliation (1983): Roman Catholic 56%; Protestant 12%; Muslim 9%; traditional belief systems 23%.
Major cities (1978): Kigali 117,749; Butare 21,691; Ruhengeri 16,025; Gisenyi 12,436.

Vital statistics

Birth rate per 1,000 population (1980–85): 49.4 (world avg. 27.5); legitimate, n.a.; illegitimate, n.a.
Death rate per 1,000 population (1980–85): 17.4 (world avg. 10.6).
Natural increase rate per 1,000 population (1980–85): 32.0 (world avg. 16.9).
Total fertility rate (avg. births per childbearing woman; 1980–85): 6.9.
Marriage rate per 1,000 population: n.a.
Divorce rate per 1,000 population: n.a.
Infant mortality rate per 1,000 live births (1980): 127.
Life expectancy at birth (1980–85): male 46.7 years; female 50.0 years.
Major causes of death per 100,000 population: n.a.; however, the major diseases are malaria, trypanosomiasis (sleeping sickness), pneumonia, tuberculosis, and dysentery.

National economy

Budget (1980). Revenue: RF13,805,000,000 (import and export duties 42.4%; income tax 24.7%, of which profits and capital gains 17.8%, individual 6.9%; excise taxes 19.2%). Expenditures: RF15,458,000,000 (economic services 41.4%, of which roads and waterways 12.4%; education 18.8%; defense 13.1%; health 7.5%).
Public debt (external, outstanding; 1982): U.S.$195,000,000.
Tourism (1981): receipts from visitors U.S.$4,200,000; expenditures by nationals abroad U.S.$12,000,000.
Production (metric tons except as noted). Agriculture, forestry, fishing (1982): plantains 2,158,000; roots and tubers 1,710,000, of which sweet potatoes 880,000, cassava 495,000; sugarcane 1,200,000; cereals 281,000, of which sorghum 181,000, corn (maize) 89,000; coffee 26,000; livestock (number of live animals) 653,000 cattle, 947,000 goats, 312,000 sheep, 144,000 pigs; roundwood 6,186,000 cu m; fish catch 1,210. Mining and quarrying (1983): cassiterite ore 1,526; wolframite 429; gold 40 kg†. Manufacturing (value added at producers' prices in RF'000,000; 1979): food, beverages, and tobacco products 9,029; industrial chemicals 275; textiles 162; metal products 142; printing and published materials 50; furniture and fixtures 22. Construction (1981): residential 59,600 sq m; nonresidential 34,400 sq m. Energy production (consumption): electricity (kW-hr; 1982) 163,000,000 (163,000,000); coal, none (n.a.); petroleum products (metric tons; 1982) none (63,000); natural gas (cu m; 1982) 1,100,000 (1,100,000).
Gross domestic product (at current market prices; 1982): U.S.$1,258,000,000 (U.S.$230 per capita).
Household income and expenditure: Average household size (1982) 5.2; average annual income per household RF111,630 (U.S.$1,200); sources of income (1977): salaries and wages 16.5%; self employment (profits, interest, etc.) 71.0%; transfers 9.5%; expenditure: n.a.

Origin of gross domestic product (current prices)				
	1982			
	in value RF'000,000	% of total value	labour force	% of labour force
Agriculture	52,083	44.6	2,341,000	88.6
Mining	2,507	2.1	...	...
Manufacturing	17,640	15.1	...	...
Construction	6,313	5.4	...	...
Trade	‡	‡	...	...
Public utilities	371	0.3	...	...
Transportation and communication	‡	‡	...	...
Finance	‡	‡	...	...
Pub. admin., defense	‡	‡	...	...
Services	37,972‡	32.5‡	...	...
Other	‡	‡	302,000	11.4
TOTAL	116,886	100.0	2,643,000	100.0

Persons economically active (1982): total 2,643,000 (51.7%); female participation in labour force 1,276,000 (48.3%); unemployed, n.a.

Price and earnings indexes (1980 = 100)						
	1978	1979	1980	1981	1982	1983	1984
Consumer price index	80.6	93.3	100.0	106.6	119.9	127.7	128.9§
Earnings index	...	...	...	...	...	...	...

Land use (1981): forested 10.7%; meadows and pastures 18.4%; agricultural and under permanent cultivation 39.3%; other 31.6%.

Foreign trade

Balance of trade (current prices)						
	1979	1980	1981	1982	1983	1984
RF'000,000	−6.9	−15.6	−18.6	−18.2	−18.8	−51.7§
% of total	23.9%	52.8%	55.0%	52.0%	55.3%	64.1%

Imports (1980): RF22,568,000 (transport equipment 12.8%, machinery and tools 12.8%, fuels and lubricants 12.4%, clothing 11.5%, food 9.7%, construction materials 8.7%). *Major import sources:* Belgium-Luxembourg 14.8%; Japan 11.4%; France 10.9%; Kenya 9.4%; West Germany 8.9%; Iran 8.4%.
Exports (1980): RF6,961,000 (coffee 58.6%, tea 17.2%, tin 7.9%). *Major export destinations* ‖: Kenya 13.4%¶; Belgium-Luxembourg 9.5%¶; Italy 2.3%¶; West Germany 1.7%¶.

Transport and communications

Transport. Railroads: none. Roads (1982): total length 4,910 mi, 7,900 km (paved, n.a.). Vehicles (1982): passenger cars 6,188; trucks and buses 7,168. Merchant marine: none. Air transport (1980): passenger arrivals 24,139, passenger departures 31,087; metric ton cargo loaded 18,030; metric ton cargo unloaded 11,889; airport (1984) with scheduled flights 1.
Communications. Daily newspapers: none. Radios (1983): total number of receivers 47,660 (1 per 118 persons). Television: none. Telephones (1980): 5,000 (1 per 1,030 persons).

Education and health

Education (1980–81)				
	schools	teachers	students	student/ teacher ratio
Primary (age 7–12)	1,558	13,043	743,067	57.0
Secondary (age 13–19)	...	984	12,505	12.7
Voc., teacher tr.	...	36	640	17.8
Higher⁹	...	229	1,266	6.0

College graduates per 100,000 population (students graduating, 1980): 23.9.
Literacy (1980): total population literate 1,295,900 (49.4%); males literate 798,800 (62.2%); females literate 497,100 (37.2%).
Health (1980): physicians 164 (1 per 31,510 persons); hospital beds 8,080 (1 per 640 persons).
Food (1978–80): daily per capita caloric intake 2,201 (vegetable products 98.0%, animal products 2.0%); 95% of FAO recommended minimum requirement.

Military

Total active duty personnel (1983): 5,150 (army 97.1%; navy, none; air force 2.9%). *Military expenditure as percent of GNP* (1981): 1.7% (world 5.7%); per capita expenditure U.S.$4.

*Detail does not add to total given because of rounding. †1981. ‡Trade, transportation and communication, finance, pub. admin. and defense, and other included with services. §First quarter. ‖ More than three-fifths of total exports consigned to Mombasa, Kenya, and their final destination is not known. ¶Percentages given are based on exports not consigned to Mombasa. ⁹1979.

Saint Christopher and Nevis

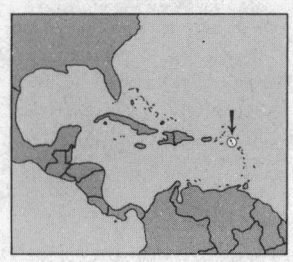

Official name: State of Saint Christopher–Nevis.
Form of government: federal parliamentary state with one legislative house (House of Assembly [13]).
Chief of state: British Monarch represented by Governor-General.
Head of government: Prime Minister.
Capital: Basseterre.
Official language: English.
Official religion: none.
Monetary unit: 1 East Caribbean dollar (ECar$) = 100 cents; valuation (Oct. 29, 1984) 1 U.S.$ = ECar$2.70; 1 £ = ECar$3.26.

Area and population

Islands Parishes	area		population 1980 census
	sq mi	sq km	
Saint Christopher	65	168	33,881
Christ Church	...	...	1,989
Saint Ann	...	...	3,145
Saint George Basseterre	...	...	14,283
Saint John	...	...	3,163
Saint Mary	...	...	3,308
Saint Paul	...	...	2,080
Saint Peter	...	...	2,497
Saint Thomas	...	...	2,255
Trinity	...	...	1,161
Nevis	36	93	9,428
Saint George	...	...	2,295
Saint James	...	...	1,691
Saint John	...	...	2,224
Saint Paul Charlestown	...	...	1,243
Saint Thomas	...	...	1,975
TOTAL	101	261	43,309

Source: Official government figures.

Demography

Density (1984): persons per sq mi 438.5, persons per sq km 169.3.
Urban–rural: n.a.
Sex distribution (1980): male 48.12%; female 51.88%.
Age breakdown (1980): under 15, 37.2%; 15–29, 30.4%; 30–44, 9.5%; 45–59, 9.4%; 60–74, 10.0%; 75 and over, 3.5%.
Population projection: (1990) 44,000; (2000) 44,000.
Doubling time: it is expected that there will be little or no population growth during the rest of the 20th century.
Ethnic composition (1970): black 95.4%; white 1.1%; mixed 3.0%; other 0.5%.
Religious affiliation (1980)*: Protestant 51.5%; Anglican 36.5%; Roman Catholic 8.2%; black indigenous 2.5%; other 1.3%.
Major towns (1980): Basseterre 14,283; Charlestown 1,243.

Vital statistics

Birth rate per 1,000 population (1982): 29.0 (world avg. 29.0); (1980) legitimate 18.6%, illegitimate 81.4%.
Death rate per 1,000 population (1982): 11.2 (world avg. 11.0).
Natural increase rate per 1,000 population (1982): 17.8 (world avg. 18.0).
Total fertility rate (avg. births per childbearing woman; 1980–85)†: 3.4.
Marriage rate per 1,000 population (1977)*: 2.6.
Divorce rate per 1,000 population (1977)*: 0.1.
Infant mortality rate per 1,000 live births (1982): 42.8.
Life expectancy at birth (1980–85)†: male 68.6 years; female 71.9 years.
Major causes of death per 100,000 population (1980): circulatory diseases 361.2; heart diseases 189.4; cerebrovascular diseases 175.5; senility without mention of psychosis 124.5; infectious and parasitic diseases 95.9.

National economy

Budget (1981). Revenue: ECar$55,363,000 (inland revenue 51.1%; customs and excises 19.7%; other 29.2%). Expenditures: ECar$58,650,000 (financial affairs 21.5%; education 15.9%; electricity, ice and cold storage 14.8%; health 10.9%).
Public debt (external, outstanding; 1980): U.S.$7,000,000.
Tourism (1981): number of visitors 39,886.
Production (metric tons except as noted). Agriculture and fishing (1982): sugarcane 368,000, raw sugar 37,000, coconuts 2,000; livestock (number of live animals) 24,000 sheep, 20,000 pigs, 15,000 goats, 8,000 cattle, 82,-000 chickens; fish catch 1,900. Mining and quarrying: n.a. Manufacturing (1980): sugar 34,400; molasses 11,300; beer and malt 13,600 hectolitres. Construction: n.a. Energy production (consumption): electricity (kW-hr; 1982) 32,000,000 (32,000,000); coal, none (n.a.); crude petroleum, none (n.a.); petroleum products (metric tons; 1982) none (21,000); natural gas, none (n.a.).
Household income and expenditure. Average household size (1980) 4.3*; average annual income per household: n.a.; source of income: n.a.; expenditure (1981): food 50.0%, housing 7.6%, clothing and footwear 7.5%, fuel and light 6.6%, household supplies 5.7%.
Gross national product (at current market prices; 1981): U.S.$50,000,000 (U.S.$1,040 per capita).

Origin of gross domestic product (current prices)

	1981		1982	
	in value ECar$'000,000	% of total value	labour force‡	% of labour force‡
Agriculture	19.7	15.6	11,600	50.9
Mining	0.3	0.2	100	0.4
Manufacturing	17.9	14.2	1,800	7.9
Construction	10.6	8.4	600	2.6
Trade	19.2	15.2	3,800	16.7
Public utilities	1.1	0.9	200	0.9
Transportation and communication	15.0	11.9	500	2.2
Finance	5.8	4.6	200	0.9
Pub. admin., defense	26.2	20.8	...	...
Services	6.6	5.2	4,000	17.5
Other	3.7	3.0	...	...
TOTAL	126.1	100.0	22,800	100.0

Persons economically active‡ (1982): total 22,800; female participation in the labour force, n.a.; unemployed, n.a.

Price and earnings indexes (January 1978 = 100)

	1978	1979	1980	1981
Consumer price index	105.7	117.0	137.9	152.3
Earnings index	...	...	...	...

Land use (1981): forested 16.7%; meadows and pastures 2.8%; agricultural and under permanent cultivation 38.9%; other 41.6%.

Foreign trade

Balance of trade (current prices)

	1976	1977	1978	1979	1980	1981
ECar$'000,000	−11.3	−18.6	−20.2	−41.2	−55.9	−63.3
% of total	10.9%	18.7%	18.3%	31.2%	30.0%	32.6%

Imports (1981): ECar$128,829,000 (machinery and transport equipment 20.5%; manufactured goods 20.1%; food 19.5%; mineral fuels, lubricants, and related materials 10.9%; chemicals 8.9%). *Major import sources:* United States 30.1%; United Kingdom 17.3%; Trinidad and Tobago 11.9%; Puerto Rico 6.7%.
Exports (1981)§: ECar$65,506,000 (food 63.4%; machinery and transport equipment 12.3%; manufactured goods 2.7%; inedible crude materials except fuels 2.0%). *Major export destinations:* United States 42.2%; United Kingdom 29.4%; Trinidad and Tobago 8.3%; Puerto Rico 6.3%.

Transport and communications

Transport. Railroads: none. Roads (1983): total length 124 mi, 200 km (paved 50%). Vehicles (1982): passenger cars 1,932; trucks and buses 407. Merchant marine (1983): vessels (100 gross tons and over) 2; total deadweight tonnage 459. Air transport: passengers, n.a.; cargo, n.a.; airports (1984) with scheduled flights 2.
Communications. Daily newspapers (1983): none. Radios (1983): total number of receivers 21,000 (1 per 2.1 persons). Television (1983): total number of receivers 20,000 (1 per 2.3 persons). Telephones (1983): 2,800 (1 per 16.1 persons).

Education and health

Education (1983–84)

	schools	teachers	students	student/ teacher ratio
Primary (age 5–12)	31	334	7,569	22.7
Secondary (age 13–17)	8	296	4,615	15.6
Voc., teacher tr.	1	18	182	10.1
Higher ‖	1	9	67	7.4

College graduates per 100,000 population: n.a. *Literacy* (1970)*: total population literate 22,484 (97.6%); males literate 9,934 (97.6%); females literate 12,550 (97.7%).
Health (1980): physicians 16 (1 per 2,706 persons); hospital beds 379 (1 per 114 persons).
Food (1978–80)*: daily per capita caloric intake 2,147 (vegetable products 77.1%, animal products 22.9%); 89% of FAO recommended minimum requirement.

Military

Total active duty personnel: the country maintains a police force and a small defense force of volunteers.

*Includes Anguilla, formerly a part of Saint Christopher–Nevis. †Applies to the area comprising Anguilla, Antigua, Bahamas, British Virgin Islands, Cayman Islands, Montserrat, Netherlands Antilles, Saint Christopher–Nevis, Turks and Caicos Islands, and United States Virgin Islands. ‡Employees only. §Includes reexports. ‖ Teachers college.

Saint Lucia

Official name: Saint Lucia.
Form of government: parliamentary
state with two legislative houses
(Senate [11]; House of Assembly [17]).
Chief of state: British Monarch
represented by the Governor-General.
Head of government: Prime Minister.
Capital: Castries.
Official language: English.
Official religion: none.
Monetary unit: 1 East Caribbean
Dollar (EC$) = 100 cents; valuation
(Oct. 29, 1984) 1 U.S.$ = EC$2.70;
1 £ = EC$3.26.

Area and population

Parishes	Capitals	area sq mi	area sq km	population 1981 census*
Anse-la-Raye	Anse-la-Raye	...	...	4,953
Babonneau		...	...	3,000
Canaries	Canaries	...	...	2,257
Castries	Castries	...	...	40,000
Choiseul	Choiseul	...	...	5,925
Dennery	Dennery	...	...	5,800
Desruisseaux	Desruisseaux	...	...	4,100
Fond St. Jacques	—	...	...	3,000
Gros Islet	Gros Islet	...	...	5,428
Laborie	Laborie	...	...	5,059
La Ressource	—	...	...	...
Marchand	—	...	...	5,000
Micoud	Micoud	...	...	...
Roseau	—	...	...	3,500
Soufrière	Soufrière	...	...	7,325
Vieux Fort	Vieux Fort	...	...	6,981
TOTAL		238	616	120,300†

Source: Official government figures.

Demography

Density (1984): persons per sq mi 521.0, persons per sq km 201.3.
Urban-rural (1982): urban 52.1%; rural 47.9%.
Sex distribution (1981): male 47.23%; female 52.77%.
Age breakdown (1981): under 15, 49.6%; 15–29, 21.3%; 30–44, 11.6%; 45–59, 9.8%; 60–74, 5.5%; 75 and over, 2.2%.
Population projection: (1990) 137,920; (2000) 160,530.
Doubling time: 45 years.
Ethnic composition (1982): black 90.3%; mixed 5.5%; East Indian 3.2%; white 0.8%; other 0.2%.
Religious affiliation (1980): Roman Catholic 90.6%; Anglican 2.4%; Seventh-day Adventist 2.1%; Afro-American Spiritist 2.1%; Evangelical Church of the West Indies 1.3%; Methodist 0.5%; Bahā'ì 0.2%; other 0.8%.
Major cities (1981): Castries 48,782; Soufrière 7,325; Vieux Fort 6,981.

Vital statistics

Birth rate per 1,000 population (1983): 31.0 (world avg. 29.0); (1980) legitimate 13.0%, illegitimate 87.0%.
Death rate per 1,000 population (1983): 6.2 (world avg. 11.0).
Natural increase rate per 1,000 population (1983): 24.8 (world avg. 18.0).
Total fertility rate (avg. births per childbearing woman; 1975–80): 5.5.
Marriage rate per 1,000 population (1981): 3.4.
Divorce rate per 1,000 population (1981): 0.2.
Infant mortality rate per 1,000 live births (1983): 26.1.
Life expectancy at birth (1980): male 67 years; female 72 years.
Major causes of death per 10,000 population (1980): diseases of the circulatory system 22.4; heart disease 12.7; cerebrovascular disease 9.1; malignant neoplasms (cancers) 8.4.

National economy

Budget (1982–83). Revenue: EC$137,280,000 (income tax 26.9%, customs duties 23.0%, aid grants 15.4%, taxes on goods and services 15.1%, nontax revenue 11.3%). Expenditures: EC$153,090,000 (current budget 76.4%, capital expenditure 23.0%, public debt repayment 0.6%).
Public debt (external, outstanding; 1983): U.S.$17,000,000.
Tourism (1982): receipts from visitors U.S.$24,475,560; expenditures by nationals abroad, n.a.
Production (metric tons except as noted). Agriculture, forestry, fishing (1982): bananas 59,000, mangoes 44,000, cacao 38,000‡, coconuts 3,500§, sweet potatoes 2,000, cassava 1,000, milk 1,000, eggs 500, ginger 142 ‖, plantains 40 ‖, nutmegs and mace 14 ‖, limes 3 ‖; other important crops include taro and parts thereof, oranges, grapefruits, breadfruit, pigeon peas, and coffee; livestock (number of live animals) 14,000 sheep, 11,000 cattle, 10,000 pigs, 10,000 goats, 200,000 chickens; fish catch 2,104, crustaceans 300. Mining and quarrying, n.a. Manufacturing (1980): copra 6,000¶; coconut oil 4,000; coconut meal 1,868 ‖; soap 300; bay rum 2,000 hectolitres; other important products include cardboard and paper products; clothing and shoes; beef and soft drinks; cigarettes; furniture and mattresses; televisions; electrical switches; iron roof sheets; excavating and levelling machinery and equipment; plastic products; industrial gases; animal feed; perfumes. Construction (plans approved, 1977): residential 339; commercial, industrial, and other 38. Energy production (consumption): electricity (kW-hr; 1982) 60,000,000 (60,000,000).

Gross national product (at current market prices; 1982): U.S.$119,259,000 (U.S.$962 per capita).

Origin of gross domestic product (current prices)

	1980 in value EC$'000,000	1980 % of total value	1981 labour force	1981 % of labour force
Agriculture	29.3	12.8	15,884⁹	32.1⁹
Mining	2.9	1.3	⁹	⁹
Manufacturing	15.4	6.7	2,166	4.4
Construction	24.5	10.7	2,527	5.1
Trade	34.1	14.9	4,332	8.8
Public utilities	4.9	2.1	δ	δ
Transportation and communication	16.4	7.1	δ	δ
Finance	35.4	15.4	δ	δ
Pub. admin., defense	36.7	16.0	δ	δ
Services, including restaurants and hotels	29.8	13.0	11,191δ	22.6δ
Other, including unemployed	...	...	13,351	27.0
TOTAL	229.4	100.0	49,451	100.0

Persons economically active (1980): total 49,451 (41.1%); female participation in labour force 27,299 (55.2%); unemployed (1983) 10,879 (22.0%).

Price and earnings indexes (1980 = 100)

	1978	1979	1980	1981	1982	1983	1984□
Consumer price index	76.5	83.7	100.0	115.1	120.4	122.2	123.7
Weekly earnings index	74.4	89.9	100.0	166.4	...	...	...

Household income and expenditure. Average household size (1978) 4.9; average annual income per household, n.a.; sources of income: n.a.; expenditure (1980): food and beverages 63.4%, housing 10.1%, clothing and footwear 8.1%, services 7.7%, utilities 5.6%, household and other expenses 5.1%.
Land use (1982): forested 13.1%; meadows and pastures 3.1%; agricultural and under permanent cultivation 53.8%; other 30.0%.

Foreign trade

Balance of trade (current prices)

	1977	1978	1979	1980	1981	1982
EC$'000,000	−99.2	−147.5	−187.2	−210.0	−234.9	−206.0
% of total	44.8%	50.5%	52.1%	45.8%	51.1%	47.8%

Imports (1980): EC$334,200,000 (petroleum products 10.0%, electrical machinery 9.5%, chemicals 8.8%, nonelectrical machinery 7.7%, transport equipment 6.6%, wood and paper products 6.5%, metal manufactured products 5.1%, meat and meat products 4.1%, cereals and cereal products 3.8%). *Major import sources:* United States 31.8%; United Kingdom 15.6%; Trinidad and Tobago 12.3%; Japan 5.7%; Canada 4.2%; Venezuela 3.7%.
Exports (1980): EC$124,200,000 (bananas 22.9%, excavating and levelling machinery 9.6%, iron sheets 9.2%, electrical switches 8.5%, beverages 6.8%, coconut oil 6.4%, clothing 6.3%, cardboard cartons 5.6%). *Major export destinations:* United States 27.6%; United Kingdom 25.1%; U.S. Virgin Islands 10.7%; Jamaica 9.2%; Trinidad and Tobago 6.1%.

Transport and communications

Transport. Railroads ◊ (1982): length 13 mi, 21 km; short ton-mi cargo n.a., metric ton-km cargo, n.a. Roads (1983): total length 792 mi, 1,275 km (paved 90%). Vehicles (1983): passenger cars 4,479; trucks and buses 1,171. Merchant marine (1983): vessels (100 gross tons and over) 8; total deadweight tonnage 5,352. Air transport (1982): passenger-mi 59,000, passenger-km 95,000; short ton-mi cargo 12,700, metric ton-km cargo 18,500; airports (1984) with scheduled flights 2.
Communications. Daily newspapers: none. Radios (1983): total number of receivers 121,000 (1 per 1 person). Television (1983): total number of receivers 90,000 (1 per 1.4 persons). Telephones (1982): 9,500 (1 per 13 persons).

Education and health

Education (1982–83)

	schools	teachers	students	student/ teacher ratio
Primary (age 5–14)	79	957△	31,785	...
Secondary (age 11–19)	12	229△	4,582	...
Voc., teacher tr.	1	25†	131	...
Higher	1	51⊖	199	...

College graduates per 100,000 population: n.a. *Literacy*** (1980): total population literate 80,735 (67.0%); males literate 36,932 (65.0%); females literate 43,803 (69.0%).
Health (1983): physicians 36 (1 per 3,444 persons); hospital beds 525 (1 per 236 persons).
Food (1978–80): daily per capita caloric intake 2,388 (vegetable products 78.1%, animal products 21.9%); 99% of FAO recommended minimum.

Military

Total active duty personnel (1983): 516 (police force 100.0%). *Military expenditure as percent of GNP:* n.a.

*Preliminary. †Total includes 17,972 persons in Micoud and La Ressource parishes for which separate figures were not available. ‡1981. §1983. ‖1977. ¶1982. ⁹Includes mining. δIncludes public utilities, transportation and communication, finance, and public administration and defense. □May. ◊Light plantation railroads only. △1980–81. †1979–80. ⊖1978–79. **All ages.

Saint Vincent and the Grenadines

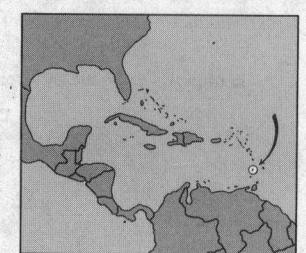

Official name: Saint Vincent and the Grenadines.
Form of government: parliamentary state with one legislative house (House of Assembly [6 senators, 13 representatives]).
Chief of state: British Monarch represented by the Governor-General.
Head of government: Prime Minister.
Capital: Kingstown.
Official language: English.
Official religion: none.
Monetary unit: 1 East Caribbean Dollar (EC$) = 100 cents; valuation (Oct. 29, 1984) 1 U.S.$ = EC$2.70; 1 £ = EC$3.26.

Area and population

Census divisions	Capitals	area sq mi	area sq km	population 1982 estimate
Barrouallie	Barrouallie	14.2	36.8	6,016
Bridgetown	Bridgetown	7.2	18.6	8,898
Calliaqua	Calliaqua	11.8	30.6	20,666
Chateaubelair	Chateaubelair	30.9	80.1	8,476
Colonarie	Colonarie	13.4	34.7	9,822
Georgetown	Georgetown	22.2	57.5	9,072
Kingstown (city)	Kingstown	1.8	4.7	24,764
Kingstown (suburbs)	Kingstown	6.0	15.5	8,930
Layou	Layou	11.1	28.7	7,459
Marriaqua		9.4	24.3	10,956
Northern Grenadines	Port Elizabeth	8.9	23.1	5,889
Sandy Bay	New Sandy Bay Village	5.3	13.7	3,601
Southern Grenadines		7.4	19.2	3,334
TOTAL		149.6	387.5	127,883

Source: Official government figures.

Demography

Density (1984): persons per sq mi 876.4, persons per sq km 338.4.
Urban–rural* (1982): urban 26.3%; rural 73.7%.
Sex distribution (1982): male 47.0%; female 53.0%.
Age breakdown (1978): under 15, 44.9%; 15–29, 29.8%; 30–44, 10.3%; 45–59, 8.2%; 60–74, 5.0%; 75 and over, 1.8%.
Population projection: (1990) 154,000; (2000) 188,000.
Doubling time: 27 years.
Ethnic composition (1981): black 65.5%; mixed 23.5%; East Indian 5.5%; white 3.5%; Carib Amerindian 2.0%.
Religious affiliation (1980): Anglican 36.0%; Roman Catholic 19.3%; Protestant Evangelicals 12.3%; Methodist 10.2%; Seventh-day Adventist 2.0%; Afro-American spiritist 2.0%; Christian Brethren 1.9%; Baptist 1.2%; Baha'i 0.8%; other 14.3%.
Major cities (1982): Kingstown 24,764; Chateaubelair, n.a.; Barrouallie, n.a.; Layou, n.a.; Georgetown, n.a.

Vital statistics

Birth rate per 1,000 population (1981): 25.7 (world avg. 29.0); legitimate, n.a.; illegitimate, n.a.
Death rate per 1,000 population (1981): 6.1 (world avg. 12.0).
Natural increase rate per 1,000 population (1981): 19.6 (world avg. 17.0).
Total fertility rate (avg. births per childbearing woman; 1978): 3.9.
Marriage rate per 1,000 population (1981): 3.2.
Divorce rate per 1,000 population (1980): 0.2.
Infant mortality rate per 1,000 live births (1981): 46.7.
Life expectancy at birth (1970): male 62.4 years; female 63.2 years.
Major causes of death per 10,000 population (1981): diseases of the circulatory system 16.4; infective and parasitic diseases 6.8; endocrine, nutritional, and metabolic diseases 6.0; neoplasms (cancers), including malignant tumours 4.0.

National economy

Budget (1981). Revenue: EC$53,016,000 (income tax 26.9%, import duties 19.5%, stamp duties 9.7%, consumption duties 9.4%, licenses 2.8%). Expenditures: EC$59,212,000 (education 19.0, public works 17.4, health 11.4, police 7.6, pensions 4.4, agriculture 2.7).
Public debt (external, outstanding; 1978–79): U.S.$7,800,000.
Tourism (1981): visitors arriving 85,242, receipts (1978) EC$89,800,000; nationals departing abroad 19,957.
Production (metric tons except as noted). Agriculture, forestry, fishing (1982): bananas 32,000, coconuts 24,000, all varieties of taro and yams 18,000, plantains 5,080†, cassava 3,000, sugarcane 2,746‡, corn (maize) 1,000, milk 1,000, arrowroot starch 997§, cacao 698, carrots 181†, peanuts (groundnuts) 1,000, ginger 124†, tobacco 100, nutmegs and mace 72†, other important crops include pigeon peas, avocados, mangoes, citrus fruits, peppers, and coffee; livestock (number of live animals) 13,000 sheep, 8,000 cattle, 6,000 pigs, 4,000 goats, 160,000 chickens; fish catch 547 marine fish. Mining and quarrying (1981): salt 50,000∥; sand and gravel 400,000 cu m; other stone 750,000 cu m. Manufacturing (1982): flour 15,400¶; copra 2,000; raw sugar 1,762; beef 1,000; rum 5,228 hectolitres†; cigarettes 20,000,000 units; other important products include cement, furniture, clothing, cardboard boxes, soft drinks, fruit juices and preserves, aluminum building elements,

solar and wind powered machinery, small boats, phonograph equipment and supplies, domestic appliances, coconut husk by-products, and animal feed. Construction (applications for permits; 1981): all types 299; 39,157 sq m. Energy production (consumption): electricity (kW-hr; 1982) 29,000,000 (29,000,000).
Gross national product (at current market prices; 1982): U.S.$77,593,000 (U.S.$618 per capita).

Origin of gross domestic product (current prices)

	1981 in value EC$'000,000	1981 % of total value	1970 labour force	1970 % of labour force
Agriculture	28.20	16.7	6,882	29.0
Mining	0.57	0.3	48	0.2
Manufacturing	18.42	10.9	1,851	7.8
Construction	21.12	12.5	2,871	12.1
Trade	21.33	12.7	2,871	12.1
Public utilities	4.44	2.6	214	0.9
Transportation and communication	24.98	14.8	1,068	4.5
Finance	23.11	13.7	♀	♀
Pub. admin., defense	29.80	17.7	♀	♀
Services	5.31	3.2	7,190♀	30.3♀
Other♂	−8.89	−5.3	736	3.1
TOTAL	168.39	100.0□	23,731	100.0

Persons economically active (1980): total 32,617◇ (30.6%); female participation in the labour force 11,242◇ (34.5%); (1984) unemployed 9,260 (25.0%).

Price and earnings indexes (1980 = 100)

	1978	1979	1980	1981	1982	1983	1984
Consumer price index	73.8	85.3	100.0	112.7	120.9	127.5	130.0△
Earnings index	...	...	...	...	...	...	...

Household income and expenditure. Average household size (1978) 5.0; average annual income per household EC$5,814 (U.S.$2,153); source of income: n.a.; expenditure (1982): food and beverages 60.5%, housing 11.1%, services 9.7%, clothing and footwear 6.9%, utilities 6.4%, household and miscellaneous expenses 5.4%.
Land use (1982): forested 41.2%; meadows and pastures 5.9%; agricultural and under permanent cultivation 50.0%; other 2.9%.

Foreign trade

Balance of trade (current prices)

	1977	1978	1979	1980	1981	1982
EC$'000,000	−55.1	−53.4	−85.2	−111.3	−91.2	−77.1
% of total	50.1%	37.6%	51.7%	56.4%	40.9%	30.6%

Imports (1981): EC$157,117,000 (food and food products 27.5%; manufactured articles 13.4%; machinery 13.0%; chemicals 11.8%; petroleum products 8.8%; textiles, clothing, and shoes 4.5%; lumber 3.9%; tobacco products 2.7%; cement 1.9%; beverages 1.7%; motor vehicles 1.6%). Major import sources: United States 32.5%; United Kingdom 17.2%; Trinidad and Tobago 13.5%; Canada 5.8%; Barbados 4.4%; Guyana 3.7%.
Exports (1981): EC$63,428,000 (bananas 42.8%, flour 13.8%, taro and parts thereof 8.7%, miscellaneous manufactured articles 7.0%, chemicals 4.5%, arrowroot 4.4%, machinery and transport equipment 3.7%, plantains 3.2%). Major export destinations: United Kingdom 45.9%; Trinidad and Tobago 23.9%; United States 6.9%; Barbados 4.8%.

Transport and communications

Transport. Railroads: none. Roads (1983): total length 633 mi, 1,019 km (paved 43%). Vehicles (1982): passenger cars 4,482; trucks and buses 1,306. Merchant marine (1983): vessels (100 gross tons and over) 44; total deadweight tonnage 80,331. Air transport (1981): passengers arriving 71,097, passengers departing 70,544; airports (1984) with scheduled flights 4.
Communications. Daily newspapers: none. Radios (1983): total number of receivers 121,000 (1 per 0.9 person). Television (1983): total number of receivers 35,000 (1 per 3.2 persons). Telephones (1982): 6,047 (1 per 18.3 persons).

Education and health

Education (1982–83)

	schools	teachers	students	student/ teacher ratio
Primary (age 5–15)	62	1,251	24,551	19.6
Secondary (age 11–19)	19	292	5,170	17.7
Voc., teacher tr.	5	48	275	5.7
Higher†	1	19	105	5.5

College graduates per 10,000 population (1979): 5.2. **Literacy** (1981): total population literate 58,804 (85.0%).
Health (1982): physicians 29 (1 per 3,818 persons); hospital beds 350 (1 per 316 persons).
Food (1978–80): daily per capita caloric intake 2,208 (vegetable products 86.9%, animal products 13.1%); 91% of FAO recommended minimum.

Military

Total active duty personnel (1983): 489 (police 100%). **Military expenditure as percent of GNP** (1981): 1.5% (world 5.7%); per capita expenditure U.S.$8.

*Based on Kingstown and Kingstown (suburbs) population. †1981. ‡1984. §1983. ∥1982. ¶1979, exports only. ♀Finance, public administration, and defense are included with services. ♂Less imputed bank service charge. □Detail does not add to total given because of rounding. ◇Projection based on 1970 census. △June only. †Teachers college.

San Marino

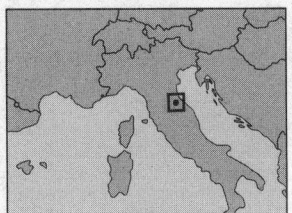

Official name: Repubblica di San Marino (Republic of San Marino).
Form of government: unitary multiparty republic with one legislative house (Great and General Council [60]).
Head of state and government: Captains-Regent (2).
Capital: San Marino.
Official language: Italian.
Official religion: none.
Monetary unit: 1 Italian lira (Lit; plural lire) = 100 centesimi; valuation (Oct. 29, 1984) 1 U.S.$ = Lit 1,900.41; 1 £ = Lit 2,293.80.

Area and population		area		population
		sq mi	sq km	1984 estimate
Castles	**Capitals**			
Acquaviva	Acquaviva	1.88	4.86	1,170
Borgo Maggiore	Borgo	6.22	16.10	9,140
Città	San Marino			
Chiesanuova	Chiesanuova	2.11	5.46	780
Domagnano	Domagnano	2.56	6.62	2,100
Faetano	Faetano	2.99	7.75	820
Fiorentino	Fiorentino	2.53	6.56	1,410
Montegiardino	Montegiardino	1.28	3.31	570
San Giovanni	San Giovanni	*	*	*
Serravalle	Serravalle	4.07	10.53	6,830
TOTAL		23.63†	61.19	22,820

Source: Official government figures; Britannica estimate.

Demography

Density (1984): persons per sq mi 965.7, persons per sq km 372.9.
Urban–rural (1981): urban 92.4%; rural 7.6%.
Sex distribution (1984): male 49.88%; female 50.12%.
Age breakdown (1984): under 15, 20.1%; 15–29, 24.7%; 30–44, 21.0%; 45–59, 17.5%; 60–74, 12.5%; 75 and over, 4.2%.
Population projection: (1990) 23,000; (2000) 25,000.
Doubling time: Population growth is negligible.
Ethnic composition (1980): Italian 99.9%; other 0.1%.
Religious affiliation (1980): Roman Catholic 95.2%; no religion 3.0%; other 1.8%.
Major cities (1982): San Marino 4,571; Serravalle 6,753; Borgo 4,213; Domagnano 1,881.

Vital statistics

Birth rate per 1,000 population (1983): 11.1 (world avg. 29.0); (1981) legitimate 96.5%, illegitimate 3.5%.
Death rate per 1,000 population (1983): 7.4 (world avg. 11.0).
Natural increase rate per 1,000 population (1983): 3.7 (world avg. 18.0).
Total fertility rate (avg. births per childbearing woman): n.a.
Marriage rate per 1,000 population (1981): 6.8.
Divorce rate per 1,000 population: n.a.
Infant mortality rate per 1,000 live births (1983): 4.1.
Life expectancy at birth (1980–85): male 70.7 years; female 76.2 years.
Major causes of death per 10,000 population (1983): diseases of the circulatory system 24.9; malignant neoplasms (cancers) 17.2; accidents 4.1.

National economy

Budget (1983). Revenue: Lit 150,638,000,000 (detail: n.a.). Expenditures: Lit 150,638,000,000 (detail: n.a.).
Production (metric tons except as noted). Agriculture, forestry, fishing (1976): wheat 1,951; barley 456; grapes 1,788. Manufacturing (1982): main products are textiles, cement, paper, leather, bricks, postage stamps, paints, and furniture. Construction (units; 1983): urban 103; rural 4; other 42. Energy production (consumption): all power is imported from Italy.

Economically active population (1984)	labour force	% of labour force
Agriculture	519	4.7
Manufacturing	3,819	34.8
Construction	887	8.1
Trade	1,481	13.5
Transportation and communication	140	1.3
Finance	146	1.3
Pub. admin., defense, services, and public utilities	3,193	29.0
Other	802	7.3
TOTAL	10,987	100.0

Persons economically active (1983): total 12,284 (57.8%); female participation in the labour force 7,183 (58.4%); unemployed 695 (5.7%).

Price and earnings indexes (1980 = 100)	1981	1982	1983
Consumer price index	139.2	150.1	165.1
Monthly earnings index	...	...	...

Tourism (1983): tourist arrivals 2,757,130.
Gross national product (at current market prices; 1980): U.S.$176,760,000 (U.S.$8,207 per capita).
Land use (1982): agricultural and under permanent cultivation 16.7%; forested 60.0%; other 23.3%.

Foreign trade

Balance of trade: n.a.
Imports (1982): manufactured goods of all kinds, oil, and gold. *Major import source:* Italy.
Exports (1982): wine, woolen goods, furniture, ceramics, building stone, and postage stamps. *Major export destination:* Italy.

Transport and communications

Transport. Railroads: none. Roads (1980): total length 137 mi, 220 km. Vehicles (1984): passenger cars 14,029; trucks and buses 550. Merchant marine: vessels (100 gross tons and over) none. Air transport: none; airports with scheduled flights, none.
Communications. Daily newspapers (1983): total number 7; total circulation 1,300‡; circulation per 1,000 population 60.9. Radios (1980): total number of receivers 8,000 (1 per 2.6 persons). Television (1981): total number of receivers 5,000 (1 per 4.2 persons). Telephones (1981): 7,685 (1 per 2.9 persons).

Education and health

Education (1982–83)	schools	teachers	students	student/ teacher ratio
Primary (age 6–10)	13	164	1,493	9.1
Secondary (age 11–18)	3	156	1,317	8.4
Voc., teacher tr.	...	...	789§	...
Higher	...	...	329§	...

College graduates per 10,000 population: n.a. *Literacy* (1982): total population literate 16,988 (97.2%); males literate 8,436 (97.8%); females literate 8,552 (96.7%).
Health: physicians (1979) 10 ‖ (1 per 2,030 persons); hospital beds (1980) 61 (1 per 338 persons).
Food (1978–80): daily per capita caloric intake 3,643 (vegetable products 75.4%, animal products 24.6%); 145% FAO recommended minimum requirement.

Military

Total active duty personnel (1983): none¶.

*Included with Borgo Maggiore and Città. †Detail does not add to total given because of rounding. ‡Circulation for 1 daily only. §In Italy. ‖ Panel physicians only. ¶Defense provided by Italy.

RAY PFORTNER—PETER ARNOLD, INC.

Panoramic view from the fort of Mt. Titano, San Marino.

São Tomé and Príncipe

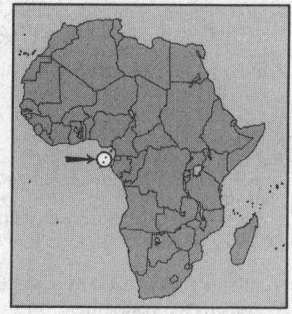

Official name: República democrática de São Tomé e Príncipe (Democratic Republic of São Tomé and Príncipe).
Form of government: republic with one legislative house (National People's Assembly [40]).
Head of state and government: President.
Capital: São Tomé.
Official language: Portuguese.
Official religion: Roman Catholicism.
Monetary unit: 1 dobra (Db) = 100 centavos; valuation (Oct. 29, 1984) 1 U.S.$ = Db45.46; 1 £ = Db54.87.

Area and population

Islands	area		population
	sq mi	sq km	1981 census
Príncipe	42	110	5,255
São Tomé	330	854	91,356
TOTAL	372	964	96,611

Source: Official government figures.

Demography

Density (1984): persons per sq mi 268.8, persons per sq km 103.7.
Urban–rural (1975): urban 15.0%; rural 85.0%.
Sex distribution (1980): male 51.57%; female 48.43%.
Age breakdown (1980): under 15, 37.3%; 15–24, 17.3%; 25–60, 38.0%; 60 and over, 7.4%.
Population projection: (1990) 114,000; (2000) 144,000.
Doubling time: 50 years.
Ethnic composition (1983): native São Toméan; Portuguese.
Religious affiliation (1980): Roman Catholic 100%.
Major city (1978): São Tomé 25,000.

Vital statistics

Birth rate per 1,000 population (1982): 38.7 (world avg. 29.0); legitimate, n.a.; illegitimate, n.a.
Death rate per 1,000 population (1982): 10.2 (world avg. 11.0).
Natural increase rate per 1,000 population (1982): 28.5 (world avg. 18.0).
Total fertility rate (avg. births per childbearing woman; 1980–85): 5.2.
Marriage rate per 1,000 population: n.a.
Divorce rate per 1,000 population: n.a.
Infant mortality rate per 1,000 live births (1982): 69.5.
Life expectancy at birth (1980–85): male 47.1 years; female 50.0 years.
Major causes of death: n.a.

National economy

Budget (1977). Revenue: Db179,600,000 (detail n.a.). Expenditures: Db454,200,000 (detail n.a.).
Public debt (external, outstanding): n.a.
Tourism: n.a.
Production (metric tons except as noted). Agriculture, forestry, fishing (1983): cacao 4,451, copra 3,727, bananas 3,641, taros 600, coconuts 228, cassava 47, coffee 17; livestock (number of live animals, 1982) 4,000 goats, 3,000 cattle, 3,000 pigs, 2,000 sheep, 1,000 asses, 123,000 poultry; roundwood 5,000 cu m*; fish catch 3,600. Mining and quarrying: none. Manufacturing (1975): bread and biscuits 1,831; palm oil 1,100*; soap 470; ice 191; limes 22; corn (maize) flour 18. Construction: n.a. Energy production (consumption): electricity (kW-hr; 1982) 14,200,000 (14,200,000); coal, none (n.a.); crude petroleum, none (n.a.); petroleum products, none (11,000); natural gas, none (n.a.).
Gross national product (at current market prices; 1982): U.S.$53,300,000 (U.S.$552 per capita).

Origin of gross domestic product (current prices)

	1981			
	in value Db'000,000	% of total value	labour force	% of labour force
Agriculture	207.3	31.3	15,077	51.3
Mining	...	...	...	...
Manufacturing	28.7	4.3	4,000†	13.6†
Construction	13.3	2.0	†	†
Trade	108.0	16.3	...	...
Public utilities	3.0	0.5	†	†
Transportation and communication	24.7	3.7	‡	‡
Finance	§	§	‡	‡
Pub. admin., defense	112.7	17.0	‡	‡
Services	§	§	‡	‡
Other	165.4§	24.9§	10,301‡	35.1‡
TOTAL	663.1	100.0	29,378	100.0

Persons economically active (1981): total 29,378 (30.4%); female participation in the labour force, n.a.; unemployed, n.a.
Price and earnings indexes: n.a.
Household income and expenditure: n.a.
Land use (1981): meadows and pastures 1.0%; agricultural and under permanent cultivation 37.5%; built-on, wasteland, and other 61.5%.

Foreign trade

Balance of trade (current prices)

	1978	1979	1980	1981	1982	1983
U.S.$'000,000	4.2	6.2	−5.2	−9.8	−8.7	−10.5
% of total	11.6%	11.8%	11.5%	34.2%	33.7%	36.8%

Imports (1975): Db288,469,000 (food products, textiles, passenger cars, and commercial vehicles). *Major import sources:* Portugal 61.2%; Angola 13.1%; The Netherlands 3.9%; France 3.3%; United Kingdom 2.2%; Mozambique 2.1%; Nigeria 1.8%.
Exports (1975): Db180,432,000 (cacao 90.3%; copra 8.7%). *Major export destinations:* The Netherlands 51.8%; Portugal 32.9%; West Germany 7.7%; Belgium-Luxembourg 2.2%; Angola 0.9%; Italy 0.9%.

Transport and communications

Transport. Railroads: none. Roads (1975): total length 178 mi, 287 km (paved 69%). Vehicles (1975): passenger cars 1,774; trucks and buses 265. Merchant marine (1983): vessels (100 gross tons and over) 2; total deadweight tonnage 992. Air transport (1975): passenger arrivals 10,050, passenger departures 9,240; short ton cargo loaded 19, unloaded 112; metric ton cargo loaded 28, unloaded 164; airport (1984) with scheduled flights 1.
Communications. Daily newspapers: none. Radios (1983): total number of receivers 25,000 (1 per 3.9 persons). Television: none. Telephones (1982): 900 (1 per 107.3 persons).

Education and health

Education (1977–78)

	schools	teachers	students	student/ teacher ratio
Primary (age 6–13)	46	527	14,162	26.9
Secondary (age 14–18)	3	111	3,145	28.3
Voc., teacher tr.	1	...	...	...
Higher	...	...	700 ‖	...

College graduates: n.a. *Literacy* (1980): total population literate (about 50%).
Health (1978): physicians 43 (1 per 2,000 persons); hospital beds 665 (1 per 129 persons).
Food (1978–80): daily per capita caloric intake 2,324 (vegetable products 90.3%, animal products 9.7%); 99% of FAO recommended minimum requirement.

Military

Total active duty personnel (1983): 1,500 Angolan troops. *Military expenditure as percent of GNP* (1980): 1.8% (world 5.6%).

*1982. †Construction and public utilities are included with manufacturing. ‡Transportation and communication, finance, public administration and defense, and services are included with other. §Finance and services are included with other. ‖ Students abroad.

Oil well near the Strait of Hormuz, Saudi Arabia.

Saudi Arabia

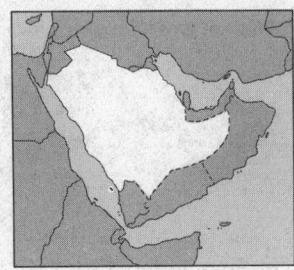

Official name: al–Mamlakah al–'Arabīyah as–Saʿūdīyah (Kingdom of Saudi Arabia).
Form of government: monarchy.
Chief of state: King.
Head of government: Prime Minister.
Capital: Riyadh.
Official language: Arabic.
Official religion: Islām.
Monetary unit: 1 Saudi riyal (SRls) = 100 halalah; valuation (Oct. 29, 1984) 1 U.S.\$ = SRls 3.53; 1 £ = SRls 4.26.

Area and population

Administrative Districts	Capitals	area sq mi	area sq km	population 1974 Census
'Asīr	Abha	...	...	682,000
al-Bāḥah	al-Bāḥah	...	...	186,000
Ḥā'il	Ḥā'il	...	...	260,000
al-Ḥudūd ash-Shamālīyah	'Ar'ar	...	...	129,000
al-Jawf	Sakākah	...	...	65,000
Jīzān	Jīzān	...	...	403,000
al-Madīnah	al-Madīnah	...	...	519,000
Makkah	Makkah	...	...	1,754,000
Najrān	Najrān	...	...	148,000
al-Qaṣīm	Buraydah	...	...	316,000
al-Qurayyāt	an-Nabk	...	...	31,000
ar-Riyāḍ	ar-Riyāḍ	...	...	1,272,000
ash-Sharqīyah	ad-Dammām	...	...	770,000
Tabūk	Tabūk	...	...	194,000
TOTAL		865,000	2,240,000	6,939,000*

Source: Official government figures.

Demography

Density (1984): persons per sq mi 12.5, persons per sq km 4.8.
Urban–rural (1980): urban 66.8%; rural 33.2%.
Sex distribution (1980): male 53.48%; female 46.52%.
Age breakdown (1980): under 15, 43.9%; 15–29, 26.9%; 30–44, 16.3%; 45–59, 8.4%; 60–74, 3.8%; 75 and over, 0.7%.
Population projection: (1990) 13,724,000; (2000) 20,327,000.
Doubling time: 17.3 years.
Ethnic composition (1974): Saudi 88.2%; North Yemeni 5.6%; South Yemeni 1.0%; other 5.2%.
Religious affiliation (1980): Muslim 98.8%; Christian 0.8%; other 0.4%.
Major cities (1974): Riyadh 1,308,000†; Jidda 1,500,000‡; Mecca 366,801; aṭ-Ṭa'if 204,857.

Vital statistics

Birth rate per 1,000 population (1980–85): 43.7 (world avg. 27.5).
Death rate per 1,000 population (1980–85): 12.6 (world avg. 10.6).
Natural increase rate per 1,000 population (1980–85): 31.1 (world avg. 16.9).
Total fertility rate: n.a.
Marriage rate per 1,000 population: n.a.
Divorce rate per 1,000 population: n.a.
Infant mortality rate per 1,000 live births (1975–80): 121.
Life expectancy at birth (1975–80): male 46.7 years; female 49.0 years.
Major causes of death: n.a.; however, major diseases are cholera, cerebrospinal meningitis, yellow fever, typhoid, tuberculosis, lung infections, and asphyxia.

National economy

Budget (1984–85). Revenue: SRls260,000,000,000 (oil 63.3%, reserves 17.7%). Expenditures: SRls260,000,000,000 (defense and security 30.7%, public administration and other government spending 14.1%, human resources development 11.7%, transport and communications 9.1%).
Public debt: none.
Tourism (1981): receipts from visitors U.S.\$1,573,000,000; expenditures by nationals abroad U.S.\$2,761,000,000.
Production (metric tons except as noted). Agriculture, forestry, fishing (1982): wheat 400,000, dates 400,000, tomatoes 210,000, sorghum 110,000, onions 60,000, grapes 60,000, barley 12,000; livestock (number of live animals) 3,500,000 sheep, 2,300,000 goats, 450,000 cattle, 160,000 camels, 110,000 asses, 7,000,000 poultry. Mining and quarrying (1982): hydraulic cement 5,263,000; lime 170,000; gypsum 91,000. Manufacturing (barrels; 1982): fuel oil 93,748,000; diesel oil 66,975,000; gasoline and naphtha 66,853,000; liquefied petroleum gas 57,243,000. Construction (value added in SRls; 1980): 42,791,000,000. Energy production (consumption): electricity (kW-hr; 1982) 25,450,000,000 (25,450,000,000); coal, n.a. (n.a.); petroleum (barrels; 1983) 1,779,498,000 (231,954,000§); petroleum products (metric tons; 1982) 36,749,000 (19,806,000); natural gas (cu m; 1983) 10,800,000,000 (1,282,050,000§).
Land use (1981): forested 0.7%; meadows and pastures 39.5%; agricultural and under permanent cultivation 0.5%; other 59.3%.
Persons economically active (1980): total 2,330,600 (27.9%).

Price and earnings indexes (1980 = 100)

	1977	1978	1979	1980	1981	1982	1983
Consumer price index	96.1	94.6	96.4	100.0	102.7	103.8	104.8
Monthly earnings index	...	...	...	...	...	...	...

Gross national product (at current market prices; 1983): U.S.\$110,560,000,000 (U.S.\$12,033 per capita).

Origin of gross domestic product (current prices)

	1982–83 in value SRls'000,000	1982–83 % of total value	1980 labour force	1980 % of labour force
Agriculture	8,725	2.1	395,100	16.9
Mining	194,659	46.6	62,100	2.7
Manufacturing	23,972	5.7	77,500	3.3
Construction	54,903	13.1	591,900	25.4
Trade	28,088	6.7	361,400	15.5
Public utilities	850	0.2	29,500	1.3
Transportation and communication	21,489	5.1	162,500	7.0
Finance	30,183	7.2	...	...
Pub. admin., defense	46,585	11.1	...	...
Services	8,408	2.0	650,600	27.9
TOTAL	417,862	100.0 ‖	2,330,600	100.0

Household income and expenditure. Average household size (1980) 5.5; income per household, n.a.; sources of income, n.a.; expenditure (1980): food 52.2%, housing 17.2%, clothing 6.6%, furniture and utensils 5.9%, transport and communication 4.5%, health care 2.1%.

Foreign trade

Balance of trade (current prices)

	1977	1978	1979	1980	1981	1982
SRls'000,000	+93.6	+59.2	+110.6	+238.9	+262.9	+120.5
% of total	47.5%	29.9%	40.4%	54.4%	52.2%	30.2%

Imports (1982): SRls139,335,000,000 (machinery, mechanical appliances, electrical equipment, and parts 25.5%; transport equipment 17.4%; textiles and textile products 5.9%; vegetable products 5.9%; live animals and animal products 3.6%; pearls, precious and semiprecious stones 2.7%). *Major import sources:* United States 21.0%; Japan 19.6%; West Germany 11.0%; United Kingdom 6.6%; Italy 6.1%; France 5.3%; South Korea 2.7%.
Exports (1982): SRls259,850,000,000 (crude petroleum 90.5%, refined petroleum 9.5%). *Major export destinations:* Japan 23.8%; France 9.0%; United States 7.8%; Singapore 5.3%; Italy 5.0%; The Netherlands 4.8%; West Germany 4.3%.

Transport and communications

Transport. Railroads (1980–81): route length 359 mi, 578 km; passenger-mi 54,378,000, passenger-km 87,514,000; short ton-mi cargo 314,000,000, metric ton-km cargo 458,400,000. Roads (1983): total length 43,268 mi, 69,634 km (paved 40%). Vehicles (1983): passenger cars 1,856,398; trucks and buses 1,704,300. Merchant marine (1983): vessels (100 gross tons and over) 435; total deadweight tonnage 9,311,863. Air transport (1983): passenger-mi 9,309,256,000, passenger-km 14,981,824,000; short ton-mi cargo 1,253,634,000, metric ton-km cargo 1,830,275,000; airports (1984) with scheduled flights 15.
Communications. Daily newspapers (1983): total number 8; total circulation 203,000; circulation per 1,000 population 23.5. Radios (1983): total number of receivers 2,700,000 (1 per 3.1 persons). Television (1983): total number of receivers 3,500,000 (1 per 2.5 persons). Telephones (1982): 463,336 (1 per 19.2 persons).

Education and health

Education (1980–81)

	schools	teachers	students	student/ teacher ratio
Primary (age 6–12)	5,744	50,010	930,436	18.6
Secondary (age 13–18)	2,052	22,730	356,747	15.7
Voc., teacher tr.	58	862	1,971	2.3
Higher	...	6,598	56,252	8.5

College graduates per 100,000 population (students graduating; 1980): 741.9.
Literacy (1980): total population literate 1,234,200 (24.6%); males literate 961,500 (34.5%); females literate 272,700 (12.2%).
Health (1981): physicians 3,576 (1 per 2,693 persons); hospital beds 14,451 (1 per 666 persons).
Food (1978–80): daily per capita caloric intake 2,889 (vegetable products 84.8%, animal products 15.2%); 119% of FAO recommended minimum requirement.

Military

Total active duty personnel (1982–83): 51,500 (army 67.9%; navy 4.9%; air force 27.2%). *Military expenditure as percent of GNP* (1982): 15.4% (world 6.0%); per capita expenditure U.S.\$2,311.

*Total includes 210,000 nomadic population. †1981 estimate. ‡1983 estimate. §1982. ‖ Detail does not add to total given because of rounding.

Senegal

Official name: République du Sénégal (Republic of Senegal).
Form of government: republic with one legislative house (National Assembly [120]).
Head of state and government: President.
Capital: Dakar
Official language: French.
Official religion: none.
Monetary unit: 1 CFA franc (CFAF) = 100 centimes; valuation* (Oct. 29, 1984) 1 U.S.$ = CFAF470.60; 1 £ = 568.0.

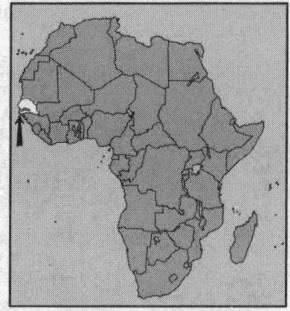

Area and population

Regions	Capitals	area sq mi	area sq km	population 1979 estimate
Cap-Vert	Dakar	212	550	1,119,000
Casamance	Ziguinchor	10,946	28,350	779,000
Diourbel	Diourbel	1,683	4,359	451,000
Fleure	Saint-Louis	17,038	44,127	575,000
Louga	Louga	11,270	29,188	444,000
Sénégal Oriental	Tambacounda	23,012	59,602	301,000
Sine-Saloum	Kaolack	9,245	23,945	1,087,000
Thiès	Thiès	2,549	6,601	752,000
TOTAL		75,955	196,722	5,508,000

Source: Official government figures.

Demography

Density (1984): persons per sq mi 83.6, persons per sq km 32.3.
Urban–rural (1980): urban 25.4%; rural 74.6%.
Sex distribution (1980): male 49.51%; female 50.49%.
Age breakdown (1980): under 15, 44.5%; 15–29, 26.0%; 30–44, 15.6%; 45–59, 9.1%; 60–74, 4.1%; 75 and over, 0.7%.
Population projection: (1990) 7,430,000; (2000) 9,747,000.
Doubling time: 26 years.
Ethnic composition (1980): Wolof 35%; Serer 16%; Fulani (Peul) 14%; Tukulor 9%; Diola (Jola) 9%; Mandingo 7%; other 10%.
Religious affiliation (1980): Muslim 91.0%; Roman Catholic 5.6%; tribal religionist 3.2%; other 0.2%.
Major cities (1979): Dakar 978,553; Thiès 126,886; Kaolack 115,679; Saint-Louis 96,594.

Vital statistics

Birth rate per 1,000 population (1980–85): 47.9 (world avg. 27.5).
Death rate per 1,000 population (1980–85): 21.1 (world avg. 10.6).
Natural increase rate per 1,000 population (1980–85): 26.8 (world avg. 16.9).
Total fertility rate (avg. births per childbearing woman; 1980–85): 6.5.
Infant mortality rate per 1,000 live births (1975–80): 152.6.
Life expectancy at birth (1980–85): male 41.8 years; female 45.0 years.
Major causes of death per 100,000 population (1978): malaria 12.7; measles 11.4.

National economy

Budget (1982–83). Revenue: CFAF151,373,000,000 (indirect taxes 68.1%; direct taxes 23.2%; stamp duties 4.7%). Expenditures: CFAF151,373,000,000 (education 22.4%; defense 11.9%; economic and financial services 5.9%; public health 5.3%)
Public debt (external, outstanding; 1982): U.S.$1,309,000,000.
Tourism (1982): receipts from visitors U.S.$62,091,000; expenditures by nationals abroad U.S.$42,225,000.
Production (metric tons except as noted). Agriculture, forestry, fishing (1982): peanuts (groundnuts) 910,000†, millet 352,000†, sugarcane 600,000, milk 104,000, paddy rice 100,000, vegetables and melons 97,000, corn (maize) 75,000, cassava 28,000; livestock (number of live animals) 2,300,000 cattle, 2,100,000 sheep, 1,050,000 goats; roundwood 3,806,000 cu m; fish catch 212,895. Mining and quarrying (1982): calcium phosphate 1,300,000†; aluminum phosphate 251,300†; salt 136,000; attapulgite 90,000. Manufacturing (1980): cement 381,000†; crude peanut (groundnut) oil 90,000; refined peanut oil 35,000; refined sugar 39,000; preserved fish 35,300; phosphatic fertilizers 28,000; soft drinks 376,000 hectolitres; beer 211,000 hectolitres; cigarettes 2,703,000,000 units; cotton fabrics 4,855,000 metres. Construction (1982)‡: residential 17,000 sq m; nonresidential 4,000 sq m. Energy production (consumption): electricity (kW-hr; 1982) 631,000,000 (631,000,000); coal, none (n.a.); petroleum (barrels; 1982) none (5,644,000); petroleum products (metric tons; 1982) 660,000 (781,000); natural gas, none (n.a.).
Land use (1981): forested 27.7%; meadows and pastures 29.7%; agricultural and under permanent cultivation 27.2%; other 15.4%.
Persons economically active (1978): total 2,068,200 (38.4%); female participation in the labour force, n.a.; unemployed (1977) 4,630.

Price and earnings indexes (1980 = 100)

	1978	1979	1980	1981	1982	1983	1984
Consumer price index	83.8	92.0	100.0	105.9	124.2	138.7	151.3
Monthly earnings index	...	...	...	...	...	...	...

Gross national product (at current market prices; 1981): U.S.$2,530,000,000 (U.S.$430 per capita).

Origin of gross domestic product (current prices)

	1980 in value CFAF'000,000,000	1980 % of total value	1979 labour force	1979 % of labour force
Agriculture	119.8	19.5	1,569,400	76.0
Mining	}			
Manufacturing	110.3	18.0	206,500§	10.0§
Public utilities	}			
Construction	35.2	5.7	...	...
Trade	145.8	23.8	...	...
Transportation and communication	39.0	6.4	...	...
Finance	}		...	...
Services	50.0	8.1	289,100	14.0
Pub. admin., defense	106.6	17.4	...	...
Other	6.8	1.1	...	...
TOTAL	613.5	100.0	2,065,000	100.0

Household income and expenditure¶. Average household size (1975) 8.6; average annual income per household CFAF1,105,800 (U.S.$5,160); source of income: wages and salaries 51.6%, remittances and gifts 17.5%, pensions, social security, and related benefits 12.5%, other 18.4%; expenditure (1979): food and tobacco 57.5%, housing, maintenance, and utilities 18.4%, clothing 11.9%, transport 5.4%, other 6.8%.

Foreign trade

Balance of trade (current prices)

	1978	1979	1980	1981	1982
CFAF'000,000,000	−85.4	−84.1	−121.5	−113.6	−163.3
% of total	33.5%	27.0%	37.6%	32.1%	34.2%

Imports (1981): CFAF233,925,000,000 (foods, beverages, and tobacco 22.7%; machines and transport equipment 21.8%, of which cereals 7.9%; basic manufactures 14.5%, of which metals and its manufactures 6.5%; crude petroleum 12.8%; chemicals and related products 9.5%). *Major import sources:* France 36.8%; United States 5.7%; West Germany 4.0%; Ivory Coast 4.0%; Algeria 3.7%.
Exports (1981): CFAF120,328,000,000 (petroleum and products 24.4%; fish and shellfish 21.5%; phosphates 13.8%; basic manufactures 9.7%; chemicals 6.1%; peanut oil and oilcake 6.0%). *Major export destinations:* France 24.9%; Ivory Coast 8.2%; Mali 7.5%; Mauritania 7.4%; United Kingdom 6.0%.

Transport and communications

Transport. Railroads (1979): length 737 mi, 1,186 km; passenger-mi 82,-600,000, passenger-km 133,000,000; short ton-mi cargo 212,000,000, metric ton-km cargo 309,000,000. Roads (1981): total length 9,134 mi, 14,700 km (paved 25%). Vehicles (1980): passenger cars 50,875; trucks and buses 27,-767. Merchant marine (1983): vessels (100 gross tons and over) 135; total deadweight tonnage 33,250. Air transport (1980): passenger-mi 110,555,000, passenger-km 177,921,000; short ton-mi cargo 12,331,000, metric ton-km cargo 18,003,000; airports (1984) with scheduled flights 11.
Communications. Daily newspapers (1983): total number 2; total circulation 43,000; circulation per 1,000 population 7.0. Radios (1983): total number of receivers 320,000 (1 per 19 persons). Television (1983): total number of receivers 50,200 (1 per 122 persons). Telephones (1979): 40,218 (1 per 137 persons).

Education and health

Education (1978–79)

	schools	teachers	students	student/ teacher ratio
Primary (age 6–11)♀	1,672	9,842	419,748	42.6
Secondaryδ (age 12–18)	187	2,064	75,265	36.5
Voc., teacher tr.□	32	1,475	9,632	6.5
Higher	9	571	10,309	18.0

College graduates per 100,000 population (1980): n.a. *Literacy* (1980): total population literate 1,274,000 (22.5%); males literate 1,755,000 (31.0%); females literate 804,000 (14.2%).
Health: physicians (1981) 449 (1 per 13,000 persons); hospital beds (1978) 7,092 (1 per 760 persons).
Food (1978–80): daily per capita caloric intake 2,389 (vegetable products 91.6%, animal products 8.4%); 100% of FAO recommended minimum requirement.

Military

Total active duty personnel (1981): 9,700 (army 87.6%; navy 7.2%; air force 5.2%). *Military expenditure as percent of GNP* (1982): 2.1% (world 6.0%); per capita expenditure U.S.$10.

*The value of the CFA franc is pegged to the French (metropolitan) franc. †1983. ‡Authorized for Dakar only. §Industry only. ‖ Second quarter. ¶Among traditional African households in Dakar. ♀1981. δIncludes middle school. □Includes professional secondary education.

Seychelles

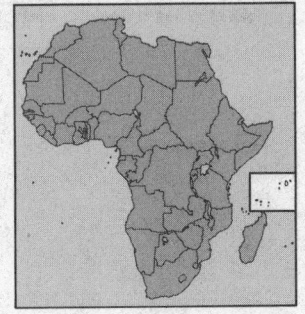

Official name: Republic of Seychelles.
Form of government: unitary
single-party republic with one
legislative house (People's Assembly
[25]).
Head of state and government:
President.
Capital: Victoria.
Official languages: English; French;
Creole.
Official religion: none.
Monetary unit: 1 Seychelles rupee
(SR) = 100 cents; valuation (Oct. 29,
1984) 1 U.S.$ = SR7.15; 1 £ = SR8.63.

Area and population

Central (granitic) group	Capitals	area sq mi	area sq km	population 1984 estimate
La Digue and satellites		6	15	2,000
Mahé and satellites	Victoria	61	158	57,400
Praslin and satellites		16	42	4,650
Silhouette		8	20	200
Other islands		2	4	50
Outer (coralline) islands		83	214	400
TOTAL		175*	453	64,700

Source: Official government figures.

Demography

Density (1984): persons per sq mi 369.9, persons per sq km 142.8.
Urban–rural (1977): urban 37.2%; rural 62.8%.
Sex distribution (1982): male 50.64%; female 49.36%.
Age breakdown (1982): under 15, 37.1%; 15–29, 30.0%; 30–44, 13.1%; 45–64,
   13.4%; 65 and over, 6.4%.
Population projection: (1990) 74,000; (2000) 87,000.
Doubling time: 32 years.
Ethnic composition (1977): Seychellois 96.9%; non-Seychellois 3.1%.
Religious affiliation (1983): Roman Catholic 96.4%; other 3.6%.
Major city (1982 est.): Victoria 57,000.

Vital statistics

Birth rate per 1,000 population (1983): 25.8 (world avg. 29.0); (1982) legiti-
   mate 33.4%, illegitimate 66.6%.
Death rate per 1,000 population (1983): 7.0 (world avg. 11.0).
Natural increase rate per 1,000 population (1983): 18.8 (world avg. 18.0).
Total fertility rate (avg. births per childbearing woman; 1982): 3.4.
Marriage rate per 1,000 population (1981): 4.8.
Divorce rate per 1,000 population: n.a.
Infant mortality rate per 1,000 live births (1983): 14.4.
Life expectancy at birth (1974–78): male 64.6 years; female 71.1 years.
Major causes of death per 10,000 population (1982): diseases of the circula-
   tory system 14.0; ill-defined conditions 14.0; malignant neoplasms (cancers)
   11.0; accidents 7.6; cerebrovascular diseases 7.0; pneumonia 6.7; abdominal
   diseases 4.2; perinatal mortality 2.0.

National economy

Budget (1982). Revenue: SR384,300,000 (import duties 33.3%, income tax
   27.0%, excise duties 6.5%, rents and royalties 5.7%, turnover tax 5.0%,
   airport landing fees 3.8%). Expenditures: SR410,000,000 (general administration 28.4%, of which defense, police, and prisons 11.8%; education
   and information 19.2%; health 10.1%; economic services 9.3%; national
   youth services 6.5%).
Public debt (external, outstanding; 1982): U.S.$36,600,000.
Tourism (1983): receipts from visitors U.S.$34,417,000; expenditures by na-
   tionals abroad, n.a.
Production (metric tons except as noted). Agriculture, forestry, fishing
   (1982): coconuts 29,000, copra 4,000, mangoes 4,000, bananas 1,000, cinnamon bark 810, tea 146†; livestock (number of live animals) 11,000
   pigs, 4,000 goats, 2,000 cattle, 134,000 chickens; forestry SR2,600,000‡; fish
   catch 3,749§. Mining and quarrying (1981†): SR400,000. Manufacturing
   (1983): beer and stout 38,700 hectolitres; soft drinks 33,700 hectolitres;
   cigarettes 51,600,000 units. Energy production (consumption): electricity
   (kW-hr; 1983) 56,700,000 (56,700,000); coal, none (n.a.); petroleum, none
   (n.a.); natural gas, none (n.a.).
Gross national product (at current market prices; 1982): U.S.$143,313,000
   (U.S.$2,225 per capita).

Origin of gross domestic product (current prices)

	1982 in value SR'000,000	% of total value	labour force ‖	% of labour force
Agriculture	55.1	5.7	1,905	10.3
Mining, manu-facturing, construction	142.8	14.8	3,945	21.4
Trade, tourism	110.0	11.4	2,086	11.3
Transportation and communication	350.3¶	36.3¶	620¶♀	3.4¶♀
Finance, services	118.7	12.3	7,205δ	39.0δ
Pub. admin., defense	188.2	19.5	δ	δ
Other	...	...	2,714	14.7
TOTAL	965.1	100.0	18,475	100.0*

Persons economically active (1980): total 29,250 (46.2%); female participation in the labour force, n.a.; unemployed 644 (2.2%).

Price and earnings indexes (1980 = 100)

	1978	1979	1980	1981	1982	1983	1984
Consumer price index	78.2	88.1	100.0	110.6	109.7	116.3	121.3□
Monthly earnings index	64.2	83.0	100.0	112.3	121.6	...	...

Household income and expenditure. Average household size (1978) 4.6; average annual income per household (1978): SR18,480 (U.S. $2,658); sources
   of income: wages and salaries 88.8%; agricultural sales 3.8%, pensions 1.9%;
   expenditure (1978): food 37.4%, beverages and tobacco 20.0%, housing
   11.3%, household goods and services 10.4%, clothing and footwear 8.9%,
   transportation 3.5%, health 1.0%.
Land use (1981): forested 18.5%; agricultural and under permanent cultivation 18.5%; built-on wasteland, and other 63.0%.

Foreign trade

Balance of trade (current prices)

	1978	1979	1980	1981	1982	1983
SR'000,000	−296.6	−396.2	−496.2	−480.7	−541.2	−456.8
% of total	58.4%	58.8%	64.7%	68.9%	73.0%	62.5%

Imports (1983): SR594,082,000 (petroleum, petroleum products, and related
   materials 24.8%; machinery and transport equipment 22.9%; chemicals and
   related products 5.6%; non-metallic mineral manufactures 4.1%; cereals
   and cereal preparations 4.0%; textile yarn, fabrics, and finished articles
   2.6%). *Major import sources:* Bahrain 14.2%; United Kingdom 13.2%; Italy
   9.8%; South Africa 9.2%; Singapore 8.4%; Japan 6.0%; France 4.7%.
Exports (1983): SR137,247,000◊ (petroleum products 72.7%△; copra 8.3%;
   frozen and fresh fish 6.7%; cinnamon bark 2.4%). *Major export destinations:* Pakistan 51.8%; Réunion 18.1%; Japan 13.9%; Algeria 3.7%; France
   2.9%; United Kingdom 1.5%.

Transport and communications

Transport. Railroads: none. Roads (1983): total length 160 mi, 257 km
   (paved 59%). Vehicles (1983): passenger cars 3,524; trucks and buses
   1,086. Merchant marine (1983): vessels (100 gross tons and over) 3; total
   deadweight tonnage 321. Air transport (1983): passenger arrivals 53,000,
   passenger departures 55,000; metric ton cargo unloaded 830, metric ton
   cargo loaded 214; airport (1984) with scheduled flights 1.
Communications. Daily newspapers (1982): total number 2; total circulation
   5,500; circulation per 1,000 population 85.4. Radios (1983): total number of
   receivers 15,000 (1 per 4.3 persons). Television (1983): total number of receivers 3,500 (1 per 18 persons). Telephones (1981): 7,105 (1 per 9 persons).

Education and health

Education (1984)

	schools	teachers	students	student/teacher ratio
Primary (age 6–14)	27	695	14,333	20.6
Secondary (age 15–17)	2	147	2,605	17.7
Voc., teacher tr.	1	143	1,284	9.0

College graduates per 10,000 population (1977): 5.7. *Literacy* (1971): total
   population literate 17,066 (57.3%); males literate 8,103 (54.9%); females
   literate 8,963 (59.6%).
Health (1983): physicians 35† (1 per 1,838 persons); hospital beds 352 (1
   per 183 persons).
Food: daily per capita caloric intake, n.a.

Military

Total active duty personnel (1982): 1,000 (army 75%; navy 15%; air force
   10%). *Military expenditure as percent of GNP* (1981): 5.6% (world 5.7%*);
   per capita expenditure U.S.$124.

*Detail does not add to total given because of rounding. †Export figures. ‡1981.
§1983. ‖ Employed persons only. ¶Includes distribution. ♀Includes tourism related
transportation. δPublic administration and defense included with finance and services. □Second quarter. ◊Includes SR112 million of reexports. △Item imported and
then reexported to international carriers. †Indicated as medical and dental officers.

Sierra Leone

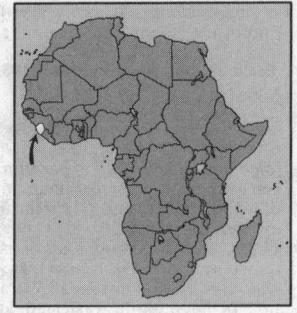

Official name: Republic of
Sierra Leone.
Form of government: a unitary
single-party republic with one
legislative house (House of
Representatives [104]).
Head of state and government:
President.
Capital: Freetown.
Official language: English.
Official religion: none.
Monetary unit: 1 leone (Le) = 100
cents; valuation (Oct. 29, 1984)
1 U.S.$ = Le2.49; 1 £ = Le3.00.

Area and population

Provinces Districts	Capitals	area sq mi	area sq km	population 1974 census
Eastern Province	Kenema	6,005	15,553	775,931
Kailahun	Kailahun	1,490	3,859	180,365
Kenema	Kenema	2,337	6,053	266,636
Kono	Sefadu	2,178	5,641	328,930
Northern Province	Makeni	13,875	35,936	1,046,158
Bombali	Makeni	3,083	7,985	233,626
Kambia	Kambia	1,200	3,108	155,341
Koinaduga	Kabala	4,680	12,121	158,626
Port Loko	Port Loko	2,208	5,719	292,244
Tonkolili	Magburaka	2,704	7,003	206,321
Southern Province	Bo	7,604	19,694	596,758
Bo	Bo	2,015	5,219	217,711
Bonthe (incl. Sherbro)	Bonthe	1,339	3,468	87,561
Moyamba	Moyamba	2,665	6,902	188,745
Pujehun	Pujehun	1,585	4,105	102,741
Western Area	Freetown	215	557	316,312
TOTAL		27,699	71,740	2,735,159

Source: Official government figures.

Demography

Density (1984): persons per sq mi 139.5, persons per sq km 53.9.
Urban–rural (1980): urban 24.5%; rural 75.5%.
Sex distribution (1980): male 49.14%; female 50.86%.
Age breakdown (1980): under 15, 43.9%; 15–29, 26.0%; 30–44, 15.3%; 45–59,
9.5%; 60–74, 4.5%; 75 and over, 0.8%.
Population projection: (1990) 4,606,000; (2000) 6,090,000.
Doubling time: 27 years.
Ethnic composition (1978): Mende 34.4%; Temne 31.3%; Kono 5.6%; Bullom
3.7%; Fulani 3.7%; Koranko 3.7%; Limba 3.7%; Kissi 2.5%; other 11.4%.
Religious affiliation (1980): traditional beliefs 51.5%; Muslim 39.4%; Protes-
tant 4.7%; Roman Catholic 2.2%; Anglican 1.2%; other 1.0%.
Major cities (1974): Freetown 500,000*; Koidu 75,846; Bo 39,371; Kenema
31,458; Makeni 26,781.

Vital statistics

Birth rate per 1,000 population (1980–85): 45.3 (world avg. 27.5); legitimate,
n.a., illegitimate, n.a.
Death rate per 1,000 population (1980–85): 17.4 (world avg. 10.6).
Natural increase rate per 1,000 population (1980–85): 27.9 (world avg. 16.9).
Total fertility rate (avg. births per childbearing woman; 1980–85): 6.1.
Marriage rate per 1,000 population: n.a.
Divorce rate per 1,000 population: n.a.
Infant mortality rate per 1,000 live births (1982): 190.
Life expectancy at birth (1980–85): male 46.7 years; female 50.0 years.
Major causes of death per 100,000 population: n.a.; however, the ma-
jor diseases are malaria, tuberculosis, leprosy, whooping cough, measles,
tetanus, and diarrhea.

National economy

Budget (1981–82). Revenue: Le182,594,000 (excise duties 23.0%, import
duties 22.1%, corporate income tax 11.9%, personal income tax 11.0%).
Expenditures: Le312,462,000 (general administration 16.5%, education and
social welfare 15.9%, construction and development 6.5%, health 5.8%).
Public debt (external, outstanding; 1982): U.S.$35,200,000.
Tourism (1981): receipts from visitors U.S.$10,000,000; expenditures by na-
tionals abroad U.S.$10,000,000.
Production (metric tons except as noted). Agriculture, forestry, fishing
(1982): rice 550,000, cassavas 97,000, palm oil 48,000, palm kernels 30,-
000, peanuts (groundnuts) 15,000, sweet potatoes 13,000, millet 11,000,
sorghum 11,000, coffee 11,000, cacao 10,000; livestock (number of live animals) 350,000 cattle, 275,000 sheep, 158,000 goats, 40,000 pigs, 4,000,000
chickens; roundwood 7,931,000 cu m†; fish catch 49,187†. Mining and
quarrying (1982): bauxite 606,000; iron ore 66,000; rutile 47,709; diamonds
210,000 carats; gold 10,033 troy ounces. Manufacturing (1982): salt 52,214;
nails 7,768; motor spirit 513,000 hectolitres; kerosene 159,000 hectolitres;
paints 4,500 hectolitres; beer and stout 62,410 hectolitres; plastic footwear
477,000 pairs; cigarettes 1,156,000 units. Energy production (consumption):
electricity (kW-hr; 1982) 236,000,000 (236,000,000); coal, none (n.a.); crude
petroleum (barrels; 1982) none (2,089,000); petroleum products (metric
tons; 1982) 256,000 (216,000); natural gas, none (n.a.).
Gross national product (at current market prices; 1982): U.S.$1,243,200,000
(U.S.$340 per capita).

Origin of gross domestic product (current prices)

	1980–81			
	in value Le'000,000	% of total value	labour force‡	% of labour force
Agriculture	373.5	27.9	5,994	8.5
Mining	114.5	8.6	5,774	8.2
Manufacturing	68.0	5.1	7,795	11.0
Construction	55.6	4.2	7,825	11.1
Trade	279.6	20.9	6,934	9.8
Public utilities	4.4	0.3	1,815	2.6
Transportation and communication	220.5	16.5	7,168	10.2
Finance	§	§	‖	‖
Pub. admin., defense	84.0	6.3	‖	‖
Services	¶	¶	27,236	38.6
Other	137.9	10.3	…	…
TOTAL	1,338.0	100.0⁹	70,541	100.0

Persons economically active (1982): total 1,353,000 (36.8%); female participation in the labour force, n.a.; registered unemployed 11,400.

Price and earnings indexes (1980 = 100)

	1978	1979	1980	1981	1982	1983	1984ᵟ
Consumer price index	74.2	90.0	100.0	123.3	161.6	274.2	372.1

Household income and expenditure. Average household size (1980) 4.9;
average annual income per household: n.a.; source of income: n.a.; expenditure (1977–78): food, beverages, and tobacco 57.5%, clothing and
footwear 13.5%, transport and communication 9.5%, furniture, furnishings,
and household equipment and operation 8.4%, rent, fuel, and power 7.1%,
recreation, entertainment, and education 4.0%.
Land use (1981): forested 28.8%; meadows and pastures 30.8%; agricultural
and under permanent cultivation 24.7%; other 15.7%.

Foreign trade

Balance of trade (current prices)

	1977	1978	1979	1980	1981	1982
Le'000,000	−66.0	−115.7	−129.9	−230.1	−205.9	−231.5
% of total	19.0%	24.8%	24.1%	34.6%	40.0%	45.8%

Imports (1982): Le368,472,000 (food 30.5%; minerals, fuels, and lubricants
22.4%; machinery and transport equipment 17.5%; manufactured goods
classified by materials 15.3%; chemicals 5.3%). *Major import sources*□:
United Kingdom 23.0%; Japan 10.0%; United States 9.0%; West Germany
8.0%.
Exports (1982): Le136,948,000 (diamonds 45.4%; cacao 13.2%; coffee 13.1%;
rutile 9.9%; bauxite 9.8%; gold 2.8%; palm kernels 1.4%). *Major export destinations*□: United Kingdom 45.0%; United States 20.0%; The Netherlands
9.0%; West Germany 8.6%.

Transport and communications

Transport. Railroads (1981): length 52 mi, 84 km. Roads (1980): total length
4,635 mi, 7,459 km (paved 16%). Vehicles (1980): passenger cars 16,009;
trucks and buses 4,826. Merchant marine (1983): vessels (100 gross tons and
over) 20; total deadweight tonnage 1,324. Air transport (1980): passenger-
mi 53,000,000, passenger-km 86,000,000; short ton-mi cargo 6,200,000,
metric ton-km cargo 9,000,000; airports (1984) with scheduled flights 7.
Communications. Daily newspaper (1982): total number 1; total circulation
10,000; circulation per 1,000 population 2.7. Radios (1982): total number
of receivers 100,000 (1 per 37 persons). Television (1982): total number
of receivers 21,500 (1 per 171 persons). Telephones (1979): 10,350 (1
per 327 persons).

Education and health

Education (1980–81)

	schools	teachers	students	student/ teacher ratio
Primary (age 5–11)	1,172	8,472	263,724	31.1
Secondary (age 12–18)	159	2,828	63,299	22.4
Voc., teacher tr.	10	301	3,007	10.0
Higher	1	270	1,809	6.7

College graduates per 100,000 population: n.a. *Literacy* (1980): total population literate 460,300 (23.6%); males literate 294,500 (31.2%); females literate
165,800 (16.5%).
Health (1981): physicians 220 (1 per 16,232 persons); hospital beds 3,752 (1
per 952 persons).
Food (1978–80): daily per capita caloric intake 2,106 (vegetable products
96.1%, animal products 3.9%); 92% of FAO recommended minimum daily
requirement.

Military

Total active duty personnel (1982): 3,100 (army 96.8%; navy 3.2%; air force,
none). *Military expenditure as percent of GNP* (1982): 1.2% (world 6.0%);
per capita expenditure U.S.$4.

*1980 estimate. †1981. ‡Employed persons only. §Finance is included with trade.
‖ Finance, public administration, and defense are included with services. ¶Services
included with other. ⁹Detail does not add to total given because of rounding. ᵟFirst
quarter. □Estimated.

Singapore

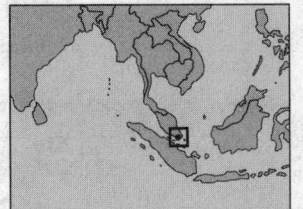

Official name: Hsin-chia-p'o
  Kung-ho-kuo (Mandarin Chinese);
  Republik Singapura (Malay) (Republic
  of Singapore).
Form of government: unitary multiparty
  republic with one legislative house
  (Parliament [75]).
Chief of state: President.
Head of government: Prime Minister.
Capital: Singapore.
Official languages: Chinese; English; `
  Malay; Tamil.
Official religion: none.
Monetary unit: 1 Singapore dollar
  (S$) = 100 cents; valuation (Oct. 29,
  1984) 1 U.S.$ = S$2.15; 1 £ = S$2.59.

Area and population	area		population
			1984
Census Areas*	sq mi	sq km	estimate
Central City Area	3	8	157,000
City Periphery	18	46	942,800
North	7	19	228,100
Northeast	4	9	301,500
West	7	18	413,200
Suburbs	49	127	754,700
East	7	19	195,000
North	13	34	309,900
West	29	74	249,800
Outlying Areas	169	437	674,600
East	46	118	301,100
North	53	137	177,500
West	70	182	196,000
TOTAL	239	618	2,529,100

Source: Official government figures; Britannica estimate.

Demography

Density (1984): persons per sq mi 10,582.0, persons per sq km 4,092.4.
Urban–rural (1983): urban 100.0%.
Sex distribution (1983): male 50.98%; female 49.02%.
Age breakdown (1983): under 15, 25.1%; 15–29, 33.6%; 30–44, 22.0%; 45–59,
  11.8%; 60–74, 5.9%; 75 and over, 1.6%.
Population projection: (1990) 2,713,000; (2000) 2,967,000.
Doubling time: 63 years.
Ethnic composition (1983): Chinese 76.6%; Malay 14.7%; Indian† 6.4%; other
  2.3%.
Religious affiliation (1980): Taoist 29.3%; Buddhist 26.7%; Muslim 16.3%;
  Christian 10.3%; Hindu 3.6%; other 0.6%; no religion 13.2%.

Vital statistics

Birth rate per 1,000 population (1983): 16.2 (world avg. 29.0).
Death rate per 1,000 population (1983): 5.3 (world avg. 11.0).
Natural increase rate per 1,000 population (1983): 10.9 (world avg. 18.0).
Total fertility rate (avg. births per childbearing woman; 1983): 1.6.
Marriage rate per 1,000 population (1983): 8.8.
Divorce rate per 1,000 population (1980): 0.7.
Infant mortality rate per 1,000 live births (1983): 9.4.
Life expectancy at birth (1980): male 68.7 years; female 74.0 years.
Major causes of death per 100,000 population (1983): diseases of the cir-
  culatory system 177.3, of which heart and hypertensive diseases 116.3;
  malignant neoplasms (cancers) 116.0; diseases of the respiratory system
  97.1, of which pneumonia 60.5; accidents, poisoning, and violence 43.4.

National economy

Budget (1983–84). Revenue: S$8,871,249,000 (income tax 34.9%; property
  tax 9.9%; import and excise duties 8.6%; motor vehicle tax 7.8%; income
  from property and financial claims 7.0%). Expenditures: S$6,882,504,000
  (defense, justice, and police 31.1%; social and community services 28.5%,
  of which education 17.3%, health 5.6%; economic services 5.7%, of which
  transport and communication 2.5%).
Public debt (external, outstanding; 1983): U.S.$317,827,000.
Tourism (1982): receipts from visitors U.S.$1,916,000,000; expenditures by
  nationals abroad U.S.$438,000,000‡.
Production (metric tons except as noted). Agriculture, fishing (1983): vegetables 35,326, fruits 8,070, sugarcane 960, tobacco 34; livestock (number
  of live animals; 1982) 1,302,000 pigs, 4,000 cattle, 3,000 goats, 2,000 buffaloes; fish catch 19,099. Mining and quarrying (value added in S$; 1983):
  granite 154,700,000. Manufacturing (value added in S$; 1983): electronic
  products and components 1,740,500,000; petroleum refining and petroleum
  products 1,422,400,000; nonelectrical machinery 887,900,000; transport
  equipment 804,800,000; fabricated metal products except machinery and
  equipment 552,500,000; paints, pharmaceuticals, and chemical products
  400,400,000; food 310,400,000. Construction (1983): residential 5,740,000
  sq m, nonresidential 2,858,000 sq m. Energy production (consumption):
  electricity (kW-hr; 1983) 8,625,900,000 (7,442,000,000‡); coal (metric tons;
  1981) none (7,000); crude petroleum (barrels; 1982) none (268,380,000);
  petroleum products (metric tons; 1982) 28,780,000 (7,617,000); natural
  gas, none (none).
Gross national product (at current market prices; 1983): U.S.$16,320,000,000
  (U.S.$6,500 per capita).

Origin of gross domestic product (current prices)

	1983			
	in value S$'000,000	% of total value	labour force ‖	% of labour force
Agriculture	344.4	1.0	11,800	1.0
Quarrying	152.7	0.4	2,400	0.2
Manufacturing	8,467.7	24.1	324,900	27.8
Construction	3,862.8	11.0	84,100	7.2
Trade	7,240.6	20.6	266,000	22.8
Public utilities	666.5	1.9	8,500	0.7
Transportation and communication	4,562.8	13.0	131,900	11.3
Finance	7,902.7	22.4	95,100	8.1
Services	4,086.7	11.6	243,300	20.8
Other	−2,115.5¶	6.0	1,600	0.1
TOTAL	35,171.4	100.0	1,169,600	100.0

Persons economically active (1983): total 1,208,500♀ (48.3%); female participation in the labour force 429,600 (35.6%); unemployed 38,900 (3.2%).

Price and earnings indexes (1980 = 100)

	1978	1979	1980	1981	1982	1983	1984δ
Consumer price index	88.7	92.2	100.0	108.3	112.4	113.8	116.9
Weekly earnings index	81.4	88.5	100.0	114.1	131.5	143.3	...

Household income and expenditure. Average household size (1980) 4.7;
  income per household: S$14,880 (U.S.$6,949); source of income: n.a.; expenditure (1982): food and beverages 25.0%, transportation and communication 13.5%, recreation and education 11.9%, clothing and footwear 8.1%,
  housing 8.0%, furniture and household equipment 7.8%, other 25.7%.
Land use (1983): forested 4.6%; agricultural and under permanent cultivation 10.4%; built-up area 47.2%; other 37.8%.

Foreign trade

Balance of trade (current prices)

	1978	1979	1980	1981	1982	1983
S$'000,000	−6,616	−7,394	−9,892	−13,957	−15,772	−13,349
% of total	−12.6%	−10.7%	−10.7%	−13.6%	−15.1%	−12.6%

Imports (1983): S$59,504,200,000 (machinery and transport equipment
  30.3%; crude petroleum 24.0%; manufactured goods and articles 20.2%;
  food 5.9%; chemicals and chemical products 5.0%; crude materials 4.4%,
  of which crude rubber 2.7%). *Major import sources:* Japan 18.0%; United
  States 15.1%; Malaysia 14.5%; China 2.9%; United Kingdom 2.8%; West
  Germany 2.7%; Hong Kong 2.1%.
Exports (1983): S$46,154,900,000 (machinery and transport equipment
  31.8%, of which office machines 10.9%, ships and boats 2.9%; petroleum
  products 27.2%; manufactured goods and articles 14.7%). *Major export destinations:* United States 18.1%; Malaysia 17.6%; Japan 9.2%; Hong Kong
  6.8%; Thailand 4.3%; Australia 2.9%; West Germany 2.3%.

Transport and communications

Transport. Railroads (1981): length 23.6 mi, 38 km. Roads (1982): total
  length 1,571 mi, 2,529 km (paved 87.0%). Vehicles (1983): passenger cars
  216,933; trucks and buses 113,075. Merchant marine (1983): vessels (100
  gross tons and over) 855; total deadweight tonnage 12,027,581. Air transport
  (1982): passenger-mi 11,315,067,000, passenger-km 18,209,870,000; short
  ton-mi cargo 504,737,000, metric ton-km cargo 736,904,000; airport (1984)
  with scheduled flights 1.
Communications. Daily newspapers (1983): total number 6; total circulation
  838,800; circulation per 1,000 population 335. Radios (1983): total number
  of receivers 490,200 (1 per 5.1 persons). Television (1983): total number
  of receivers 421,000 (1 per 5.9 persons). Telephones (1982): 771,400 (1
  per 3.2 persons).

Education and health

Education (1982)

	schools	teachers	students	student/ teacher ratio
Primary (age 6–11)	305	9,915	290,800	29.3
Secondary (age 12–17)	147	8,571	182,343	21.2
Voc., teacher tr.	16	1,060	15,610	14.7
Higher	5	2,965	30,991	10.5

College graduates per 100,000 population (students graduating; 1983): 285.
Literacy (1983): total population literate 1,788,800 (85.2%); males literate
  982,200 (92.2%); females literate 806,600 (78.1%).
Health (1983): physicians 2,361 (1 per 1,060 persons); hospital beds 9,807 (1
  per 255 persons).
Food (1978–80): daily per capita caloric intake 3,094 (vegetable products
  78.7%, animal products 21.3%); 135% of FAO recommended minimum
  requirement.

Military

Total active duty personnel (1983): 55,500 (army 81.1%; navy 8.1%; air force
  10.8%). *Military expenditure as percent of GNP* (1982): 5.6% (world 6.0%);
  per capita expenditure U.S.$355.

*The census areas have no administrative function. †Also includes Pakistani,
Bangladeshi, and Sri Lankan. ‡1981. ‖ Employed only. ¶Imputed bank service
charges minus import duties. ♀Population 10 years and older. δSecond quarter only.

Solomon Islands

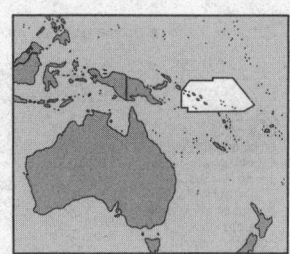

Official name: Solomon Islands.
Form of government: parliamentary
  state with one legislative house
  (National Parliament [38]).
Chief of state: British Monarch
  represented by the Governor-General.
Head of government: Prime Minister.
Capital: Honiara.
Official language: English.
Official religion: none.
Monetary unit: 1 Solomon Islands
  dollar (SI$) = 100 cents; valuation
  (Oct. 29, 1984) 1 U.S.$ = SI$1.31;
  1 £ = SI$1.58.

Area and population

Provinces	Capitals	area sq mi	area sq km	population 1981 estimate
Central Islands	Tulagi	493	1,276	16,600
Eastern Islands	Santa Cruz	358	926	12,750
Guadalcanal	Honiara	2,047	5,302	36,690
Makira/Ulawa	Kira Kira	1,231	3,188	17,380
Malaita	Auki	1,638	4,243	68,690
Santa Isabel	Buala	1,550	4,014	12,600
Western	Gizo	3,310	8,573	49,520
Municipal authority				
Honiara	Honiara	13	34	21,170
TOTAL		10,640	27,556	235,400

Source: Official government figures.

Demography

Density (1984): persons per sq mi 24.3, persons per sq km 9.4.
Urban–rural (1980): urban 25.2%; rural 74.8%.
Sex distribution (1976): male 52.23%; female 47.77%.
Age breakdown (1981): under 15, 49.0%; 15–29, 25.9%; 30–49, 17.1%; 50–59,
  4.5%; 60 and over, 3.5%.
Population projection: (1991) 330,223; (2001) 476,311.
Doubling time: 24 years.
Ethnic composition (1976): Melanesian 93.3%; Polynesian 4.0%; Micronesian
  1.4%; European 0.7%; Chinese 0.2%; other 0.4%.
Religious affiliation (1976): Church of Melanesia 34.2%; Roman Catholic
  18.7%; South Sea Evangelical Church 16.9%; United Church 11.3%;
  Seventh-day Adventist 9.7%; pagan 3.6%; Christian Fellowship Church
  2.5%; Jehovah's Witnesses 1.8%; Baha'í 0.5%; other 0.8%.
Major city (1981 est.): Honiara 21,170.

Vital statistics

Birth rate per 1,000 population (1982): 44.6 (world avg. 29.0).
Death rate per 1,000 population (1982): 11.7 (world avg. 11.0).
Natural increase rate per 1,000 population (1982): 32.9 (world avg. 18.0).
Total fertility rate (avg. births per childbearing woman; 1982): 7.3.
Marriage rate per 1,000 population: n.a.
Divorce rate per 1,000 population: n.a.
Infant mortality rate per 1,000 live births (1982): 46.
Life expectancy at birth (1982): male 54 years; female 54 years.
Major causes of death per 100,000 population: n.a.; however, major diseases
  are malaria, tuberculosis, and leprosy.

National economy

Budget* (1981). Revenue: SI$50,480,000 (recurrent revenue SI$36,059,000,
  of which income tax 26.6%, import duties 25.8%, export duties 11.3%). Expenditures: SI$50,963,000 (recurrent expenditure SI$34,667,000, of which
  administrative infrastructure 43.5%, economic infrastructure 23.7%, health
  14.3%, education 8.8%).
Public debt (external, outstanding; 1982): U.S.$16,000,000.
Tourism (1981): tourist arrivals 11,171.
Production (metric tons except as noted). Agriculture, forestry, fishing (1982):
  sweet potatoes 51,000, copra 35,000, palm oil 20,000, paddy rice 14,000,
  eggs 292; livestock (number of live animals) 40,000 pigs, 24,000 cattle,
  149,000 poultry; roundwood 512,000 cu m; fish catch 33,418. Mining and
  quarrying: n.a.; however, mining of bauxite, gold, and silver is important.
  Manufacturing: n.a.; however, major industries are palm oil, rice and saw
  milling, fish canning and freezing, soap and tobacco manufacturing, weaving, wood carving, boat building, and leather working. Construction† (gross
  value in SI$; 1980): 2,551,000. Energy production (consumption): electricity
  (kW-hr; 1982) 21,000,000 (21,000,000); coal, none (n.a.); petroleum products (metric tons; 1982) none (37,000); natural gas, none (n.a.).
Persons economically active‡ (1983): total 21,132 (8.6%); female participation in the labour force 2,860 (13.5%); unemployed, n.a.

Price and earnings indexes (1977 = 100)

	1978	1979	1980	1981	1982	1983§
Consumer price index†	106.0	115.0	130.0	151.0	171.0	177.4
Monthly earnings index ‖	109.0	109.0	117.0	128.0	...	...

Household income and expenditure. Average household size (1981) 5.4; average annual income per household (1981)¶ SI$1,776 (U.S.$2,008); source
  of income (1970)†: wages and salaries 98.8%; self-employment 0.6%; remittances, gifts, and other assistance 0.5%; expenditure (1970): food 56.9%,

housing 16.9%, clothing and footwear 5.4%, transportation 3.8%, education
2.3%, recreation 0.8%.
Gross national product (at current market prices; 1981): U.S.$150,656,000
  (U.S.$640 per capita).

Origin of gross domestic product (current prices)

	1982 in value SI$'000,000	1982 % of total value	1983 labour force‡	1983 % of labour force
Agriculture	...	...	7,022	33.2
Mining	...	...	...	...
Manufacturing	...	...	1,846	8.7
Construction	...	...	1,327	6.3
Trade	...	...	2,081	9.9
Public utilities	...	...	284	1.3
Transportation and communication	...	...	1,925	9.1
Finance	...	...	418	2.0
Pub. admin., defense	...	...	...	...
Services	...	...	6,229	29.5
Other	...	...	...	...
TOTAL	156.0	100.0	21,132	100.0

Land use (1981): forested 93.0%; meadows and pastures 1.4%; agricultural
  and under permanent cultivation 1.9%; other 3.7%.

Foreign trade

Balance of trade (current prices)

	1979	1980	1981	1982	1983	1984
SI$'000	+8,685	−748	−8,419	−874	+592	+19,714
% of total	7.9%	0.6%	6.8%	0.8%	0.4%	22.1%

Imports (1983): SI$70,632,000 (machinery and transport equipment 26.2%;
  mineral fuels and lubricants 25.3%; manufactured goods 17.8%; food 11.6%;
  chemicals 6.0%; beverages and tobacco 3.9%). *Major import sources:* Australia 33.0%; Japan 19.5%; Singapore 18.7%; New Zealand 6.9%; United
  States 4.1%; United Kingdom 3.1%.
Exports (1983): SI$71,224,000 (fish 41.0%; timber 28.1%; copra 11.8%; palm
  oil 10.9%; cocoa 3.2%; gold 0.7%). *Major export destinations:* Japan 43.5%;
  Puerto Rico 11.5%; United Kingdom 11.4%; South Korea 5.1%; Denmark
  4.5%; West Germany 4.3%.

Transport and communications

Transport. Railroads (1981): none. Roads⚲ (1980): total length 1,305 mi,
  2,100 km (paved, n.a.). Vehicles (1980): passenger cars 974; trucks and
  buses 1,287. Merchant marine (1983): vessels (100 gross tons and over) 23;
  total deadweight tonnage 3,822. Air transport (1980): passenger-mi 806,500,
  passenger-km 1,298,000; short ton-mi cargo 243, metric ton-km cargo 355;
  airports (1981) with scheduled flights 23.
Communications. Daily newspapers (1981): none. Radios (1982): total number of receivers 25,000 (1 per 9.8 persons). Television (1982): none. Telephones (1982): 2,708 (1 per 92.3 persons).

Education and health

Education (1981)

	schools	teachers	students	student/ teacher ratio
Primary (age 7–12)	383	1,199	30,316	25.3
Secondary (age 13–18)	18	299	4,262	14.3
Voc., teacher tr.	2	62	664	10.7

College graduates per 100,000 population (1981): none. *Literacy* (1976): total
  population literate 55,544 (54.1%); males literate 33,631 (62.4%); females
  literate 21,913 (44.9%).
Health (1982): physicians 38 (1 per 6,447 persons); hospital beds 1,351 (1
  per 181 persons).
Food (1978–80): daily per capita caloric intake 2,134 (vegetable products 92.1%, animal products 7.9%); 80% of FAO recommended minimum
  requirement.

Military

Total active duty personnel: no military forces are maintained, but a police
  force of about 500 provides internal security.

*Includes capital accounts. †Honiara only. ‡Employed persons only. §February only.
‖ Public service earnings. ¶Provincial centres only. ⚲Includes private roads.

Somalia

Official name: Jamhuuriyadda
Dimuqraadiga Soomaaliya (Somali
Democratic Republic).
Form of government:
military-dominated, single-party
republic with one legislative house
(People's Assembly [177]).
Head of state and government:
President.
Capital: Mogadishu.
Official languages: Somali; Arabic.
Official religion: Islām.
Monetary unit: 1 Somali shilling
(So.Sh.) = 100 cents; valuation (Oct.
29, 1984) 1 U.S.$ = So.Sh.17.03;
1 £ = So.Sh.20.56.

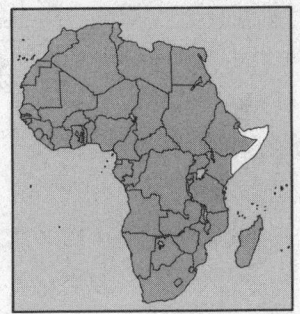

Area and population

Regions	Capitals	area sq mi	area sq km	population 1975 estimate
Bakool	Oddur	10,000	27,000	100,000
Bari	Bander Cassim	27,000	70,000	154,000
Banaadir	Mogadishu	400	1,000	380,000
Bay	Baidoa	15,000	39,000	302,000
Galguduud	Dusa Mareeb	17,000	43,000	182,000
Gedo	Garbahaarrey	12,000	32,000	212,000
Hiiraan	Beled Weyne	13,000	34,000	147,000
Jubbada Dhexe	Bu'aale	9,000	23,000	216,000
Jubbada Hoose	Chisimayu	24,000	61,000	223,000
Mudug	Galcaio	27,000	70,000	215,000
Nugaal	Garoe	19,000	50,000	87,000
Sanaag	Erigavo	21,000	54,000	145,000
Shabeellaha Dhexe	Giohar	8,000	22,000	263,000
Shabeellaha Hoose	Merca	10,000	25,000	398,000
Togdheer	Burao	16,000	41,000	258,000
Woqooyi Galbeed	Hargeysa	17,000	45,000	440,000
TOTAL		**246,000***	**637,000**	**3,722,000**

Source: Official government figures.

Demography

Density (1984): persons per sq mi 22.4, persons per sq km 8.6.
Urban–rural (1980): urban 30.2%; rural 69.8%.
Sex distribution (1980): male 45.78%; female 54.22%.
Age breakdown (1980): under 15, 43.3%; 15–29, 24.6%; 30–44, 15.4%; 45–59,
10.5%; 60–74, 5.6%; 75 and over, 0.6%.
Population projection: (1990) 5,938,000; (2000) 7,156,000.
Doubling time: 27 years.
Ethnic composition (1981): Somali 95.0%; Bantu 2.9%; Arab 1.5%; other
0.6%.
Religious affiliation (1980): Sunnī Muslim 99.8%; Christian 0.1%; other 0.1%.
Major city (1981 est.): Mogadishu 400,000.

Vital statistics

Birth rate per 1,000 population (1980–85): 48.1 (world avg. 27.5); legitimate,
n.a.; illegitimate, n.a.
Death rate per 1,000 population (1980–85): 19.1 (world avg. 10.6).
Natural increase rate per 1,000 population (1980–85): 29.0 (world avg. 16.9).
Total fertility rate (avg. births per childbearing woman; 1980–85): 6.9.
Marriage rate per 1,000 population: n.a.
Divorce rate per 1,000 population: n.a.
Infant mortality rate per 1,000 live births (1980–85): 150.0.
Life expectancy at birth (1980–85): male 41.9 years; female 45.1 years.
Major causes of death per 100,000 population: n.a.; however, major diseases
are leprosy, malaria, tetanus, and tuberculosis.

National economy

Budget (1983)†. Revenue: So.Sh.5,174,000,000 (income from government
property 51.1%, import duties 23.2%, income tax 1.0%). Expenditures:
So.Sh.4,664,200,000 (finance and central services 39.2%, defense 28.4%,
education 7.4%, foreign affairs 3.8%, transportation 3.2%, health 2.8%,
agriculture 2.1%).
Public debt (external, outstanding; 1983): U.S.$1,149,000,000.
Tourism (1981): receipts from visitors U.S.$9,000,000; expenditures by na-
tionals abroad U.S.$16,000,000.
Production (metric tons except as noted). Agriculture, forestry, fishing (1982):
sugarcane 460,000, sorghum 235,000, corn (maize) 150,000, fruits excluding melons 93,000, bananas 70,000, vegetables and melons 57,000, cassava
34,000, rice 5,000; livestock (number of live animals) 16,700,000 goats,
10,300,000 sheep, 5,600,000 camels, 4,000,000 cattle; roundwood 4,933,000
cu m; fish catch 6,580. Mining and quarrying (1979): salt 2,000. Manufacturing (1982): sugar 29,000; butter and ghee 1,630. Construction (value
added in So.Sh.; 1982): 1,687,200,000. Energy production (consumption):
electricity (kW-hr; 1982) 75,000,000 (75,000,000); coal, none (n.a.); crude
petroleum (barrels; 1982) n.a. (2,712,100); petroleum products (metric tons;
1982) 363,000 (358,000); natural gas, none (n.a.).
Household income and expenditure. Average household size (1980) 4.9;
average annual income per household: n.a.; source of income: n.a.; expenditure: n.a.
Land use (1981): forested 14.0%; meadows and pastures 46.0%; agricultural
and under permanent cultivation 1.8%; other 38.2%.

Gross national product (at current market prices; 1981): U.S.$1,240,000,000
(U.S.$330 per capita).

Origin of gross domestic product (current prices)

	1979 in value So.Sh.'000,000	1979 % of total value	1979 labour force	1979 % of labour force
Agriculture	4,269	50.4	1,177,680	84.0
Mining	30	0.3	...	...
Manufacturing	496	5.9	112,300	8.0
Construction	243	2.9	...	...
Trade	899‡	10.6‡	...	...
Public utilities	45	0.5	...	...
Transportation and communication	396	4.7	...	...
Finance	‡	‡	...	...
Pub. admin., defense	699	8.3	...	...
Services	...	...	112,020	8.0
Other	1,393	16.4	...	...
TOTAL	**8,470**	**100.0**	**1,402,000**	**100.0**

Persons economically active (1982)†: total 1,937,000 (50.1%); female participation in the labour force 581,100 (30.0%); unemployed, n.a.

Price and earnings indexes (1980 = 100)

	1977	1978	1979	1980	1981	1982	1983	1984
Consumer price index	46.1	50.7	63.0	100.0	144.4	178.5	241.4	508.5§
Earnings index	...	...	...	...	...	...	...	...

Foreign trade

Balance of trade (current prices)

	1977	1978	1979	1980	1981	1982
So.Sh.'000,000	−1,036.3	−848.0	−1,106.8	−846.3	+4.7	−14.9
% of total	56.7%	38.7%	44.2%	32.3%	0.2%	0.4%

Imports (1980): So.Sh.1,734,100,000 (food and live animals 23.8%, of which
cereals and preparations 17.4%, dairy products and eggs 2.6%; road motor
vehicles 21.1%; electrical machinery 7.5%; vegetable oil and animal fat
6.9%; cement 4.4%; iron and steel 3.3%). *Major import sources:* Italy 34.5%;
United States 9.2%; United Kingdom 7.9%; France 7.5%; Saudi Arabia
5.5%.
Exports (1980): So.Sh.887,800,000 (live animals 76.6%, of which sheep, lamb,
and goats 26.0%, bovine cattle 18.8%; fruit and vegetables 8.4%; undressed
hides, skins, and furs 5.0%; distillate fuels 4.7%). *Major export destinations:*
Saudi Arabia 69.9%; Italy 12.9%; United Arab Emirates 5.4%; Iraq 3.8%;
Yemen (Ṣanʻāʾ) 2.3%.

Transport and communications

Transport. Railroads: none. Roads (1980): total length 9,454 mi, 15,215
km (paved 15%). Vehicles (1980): passenger cars 17,200; trucks and buses
8,050. Merchant marine (1983): vessels (100 gross tons and over) 25; total
deadweight tonnage 16,727. Air transport (1982): passenger-mi 171,206,000,
passenger-km 275,530,000; short ton-mi cargo 2,881,000, metric ton-km
cargo 4,206,000; airports (1984) with scheduled flights 8.
Communications. Daily newspaper (1983): total number 1; total circulation,
n.a. Radios (1983): total number of receivers 95,000 (1 per 42 persons).
Television: total number of receivers, n.a. Telephones (1981): 4,800 (1
per 782 persons).

Education and health

Education (1981–82)

	schools	teachers	students	student/ teacher ratio
Primary (age 6–10)	...	12,007	418,935	34.9
Secondary (age 10–18) ‖	...	925	17,020	18.4
Voc., teacher tr. ‖	...	2,920	25,966	8.9
Higher¶	9	...	299	...

College graduates per 100,000 population (students graduating; 1975): 15.
Literacy (1980): total population literate 105,847 (5.2%); males literate
100,622 (10.0%); females literate 5,225 (0.5%).
Health: physicians (1980) 262 (1 per 14,290 persons); hospital beds (1978)
5,232 (1 per 714 persons).
Food (1978–80): daily per capita caloric intake 2,131 (vegetable products
63.6%, animal products 36.4%); 92% of FAO recommended minimum
requirement.

Military

Total active duty personnel (1983): 62,550 (army 95.9%; navy 0.9%; air force
3.2%). *Military expenditure as percent of GNP* (1982): 8.1% (world 6.0%);
per capita expenditure U.S.$31.

*Detail does not add to total given because of rounding. †Estimated. ‡Finance is
included with trade. §July. ‖ 1979–80. ¶1977–78.

South Africa

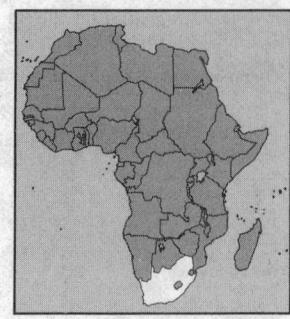

Official name: Republiek van Suid-Afrika (Afrikaans); Republic of South Africa (English).
Form of government: multiparty republic with one legislative house (House of Assembly [178]).
Chief of state: State President.
Head of government: Prime Minister.
Capitals: Pretoria (executive); Bloemfontein (judicial); Cape Town (legislative).
Official languages: Afrikaans; English.
Official religion: none.
Monetary unit: 1 rand (R) = 100 cents; valuation (Oct. 29, 1984) 1 U.S.\$ = R1.79; 1 £ = R2.16.

Area and population

Provinces	Capitals	area* sq mi	area* sq km	population 1980 census
Cape	Cape Town	247,638	641,379	5,091,000
Natal	Pietermaritzburg	35,272	91,355	2,676,000
Orange Free State	Bloemfontein	49,418	127,993	1,932,000
Transvaal	Pretoria	101,352	262,499	8,351,000
National states				
Ciskei†	Bisho	2,079	5,385	678,000
Gazankulu	Giyani	2,533	6,560	514,000
KaNgwane	Nyamasane	1,476	3,823	161,000
KwaNdebele	Siyabuswa	398	1,031	156,000
KwaZulu	Ulundi	11,642	30,153	3,422,000
Lebowa	Lebowakgomo	8,688	22,502	1,747,000
Qwaqwa	Phuthaditjhaba	194	502	158,000
TOTAL		433,680‡	1,123,226‡	24,886,000‡

Source: Official government figures.

Demography

Density (1984): persons per sq mi 70.1, persons per sq km 27.1.
Urban–rural (1980): urban 52.9%; rural 47.1%.
Sex distribution (1980)§: male 49.63%; female 50.37%.
Age breakdown (1980)§: under 15, 41.8%; 15–29, 26.2%; 30–44, 15.7%; 45–59, 9.9%; 60–74, 5.2%; 75 and over, 1.2%.
Population projection§: (1990) 31,218,000; (2000) 39,516,000.
Doubling time: 24 years.
Ethnic composition (1982): black 67.7%, of which Zulu 34.9%, North Sotho 14.4%, Xhosa 14.3%, South Sotho 10.7%, Tswana 8.3%, other 17.4%; white 18.3%; coloured 10.6%; Asian 3.4%.
Religious affiliation (1980): tribal religionist 20.4%; Afrikaans Reformed 15.5%; Roman Catholic 9.5%; Methodist 8.5%; Anglican 6.5%; other 39.6%.
Major cities (mun., 1983): Johannesburg 1,666,000; Cape Town 1,567,000; Durban 714,000; Pretoria 712,000; Port Elizabeth 560,000.

Vital statistics

Birth rate per 1,000 population (1980): 16.5 (world avg. 30.0); (1978) legitimate 75.9% ‖, illegitimate 24.1% ‖.
Death rate per 1,000 population (1980): 8.3 (world avg. 12.0).
Natural increase rate per 1,000 population (1980): 8.2 (world avg. 18.0).
Total fertility rate (avg. births per childbearing woman; 1980–85)§: 5.1.
Marriage rate per 1,000 population (1979): white 9.4.
Divorce rate per 1,000 population (1979): white 3.1.
Infant mortality rate per 1,000 live births (1980): 13.0.
Life expectancy at birth (1980–85)§: male 60.9 years; female 63.9 years.
Major causes of death per 100,000 population ‖ (1977): heart disease 215.3; malignant neoplasms (cancers) 107.3; cerebrovascular disease 90.2; pneumonia 75.2; enteritis and other diarrheal diseases 49.1.

National economy

Budget (1983–84). Revenue: R19,610,200,000 (income tax 56.3%, sales tax 20.1%, customs duty and excise tax 10.5%). Expenditures: R21,717,900,000 (provincial administration 18.9%, defense 16.3%, interest on public debt 12.2%, education 10.4%, welfare services 4.8%).
Public debt (external, outstanding; 1984): U.S.\$1,998,000,000.
Tourism (1981): visitors 709,000; nationals abroad 572,000.
Production (metric tons except as noted). Agriculture, forestry, fishing (1982): sugarcane 19,551,000, corn (maize) 8,321,000, wheat 2,339,000; livestock (number of live animals) 28,122,000 sheep, 10,162,000 cattle; forestry 15,961,000 cu m; fish catch 624,331. Mining and quarrying (1983): iron ore 16,604,900, phosphate concentrate 2,887,000, manganese ore 2,886,000, chrome 2,231,600, gold 678,000 kg, silver 173,000 kg, diamonds 10,311,400 carats. Manufacturing (value in R; 1982)¶: food 8,287,649,000; rubber products 7,116,342,000; nonelectrical machinery 4,998,518,000; chemicals 4,547,281,000; basic metal industries 3,901,157,000; electrical machinery 3,646,151,000; beverages 3,012,540,000; motor vehicles 2,446,252,000. Construction (new buildings completed; 1982): 32,232. Energy production (consumption): electricity (kW-hr; 1982)♀ 108,961,000,000 (110,977,000,000); coal (metric tons; 1982) 140,137,000 (108,000,000); petroleum (barrels; 1982)♀ none (104,086,000); petroleum products (metric tons; 1982)♀ 13,960,000 (10,792,000); natural gas, none (none).
Gross national product (at current market prices; 1983): U.S.\$75,633,191,000 (U.S.\$3,000 per capita).

Origin of gross domestic product (current prices)

	1982 in value R'000,000	1982 % of total value	1980 labour force	1980 % of labour force
Agriculture	4,504	6.2	1,299,840	15.0
Mining	10,410	14.4	820,300	9.5
Manufacturing	17,328	24.0	1,456,760	16.8
Construction	2,945	4.1	452,440	5.2
Trade	9,447	13.1	1,008,340	11.6
Public utilities	3,085	4.3	79,240	0.9
Transp. and commun.	6,578	9.1	424,040	4.9
Finance	8,243	11.4	285,840	3.3
Pub. admin., defense	7,434	10.3	...	...
Services	1,213	1.7	1,986,240	22.9
Other	1,035	1.4	852,660	9.9
TOTAL	72,222	100.0	8,665,700	100.0

Persons economically active (1979): total 9,410,000 (39.1%); female participation in the labour force 3,772,000 (40.1%); unemployed 581,000 (6.2%).

Price and earnings indexes (1980 = 100)

	1978	1979	1980	1981	1982	1983	1984
Consumer price index	77.7	87.9	100.0	115.2	132.1	148.4	168.1δ
Monthly earnings index,	76.3	85.4	100.0	122.0	142.1	...	...
white (black)	(72.5)	(82.5)	(100.0)	(120.6)	(156.6)	...	...

Household income and expenditure. Average household size (1980) 5.1; average annual income per household R8,829 (U.S.\$11,349); source of income (1982): wages and salaries 82.7%, transfer payments 4.9%; expenditure (1980): food and beverages 30.6%, transportation and communication 10.9%, clothing and footwear 8.9%, housing 8.0%, energy 7.3%.
Land use (1981): forested 3.8%; meadows and pastures 65.7%; agricultural and under permanent cultivation 11.2%; other 19.3%.

Foreign trade

Balance of trade (current prices)

	1978	1979	1980	1981	1982	1983
R'000,000	+3,989	+5,079	+5,534	−309	+843	+4,479
% of total	24.1%	20.7%	16.1%	0.8%	2.2%	12.1%

Imports (1982): R18,454,200,000 (machinery 31.9%, motor vehicles 9.8%, chemicals 8.8%, metals and metal products 4.2%, inedible raw materials 3.4%, textiles 3.0%). *Major import sources:* West Germany 19.3%; United States 19.1%; United Kingdom 15.6%; Japan 13.2%; France 5.5%.
Exports (1982): R19,297,000,000 (gold 45.7%, metal and metal products 8.3%, food excluding fruit 5.8%, diamonds 5.3%, metal ores 3.4%, machinery and transport equipment 2.6%). *Major export destinations:* Japan 14.4%; United Kingdom 11.6%; United States 10.7%; West Germany 8.3%; France 4.2%.

Transport and communications

Transport. Railroads (1982): length 14,653 mi, 23,581 km; passenger-mi 13,049,000,000, passenger-km 21,000,000,000; short ton-mi cargo 71,156,000,000, metric ton-km cargo 103,886,000,000. Roads (1982): total length 114,830 mi, 184,802 km (paved 26%). Vehicles (1983): passenger cars 2,727,202; trucks and buses 1,153,657. Merchant marine (1983): vessels 295; total deadweight tonnage 891,742. Air transport (1983): passenger-mi 5,376,251,000, passenger-km 8,652,000,000; short ton-mi cargo 266,430,000, metric ton-km cargo 388,980,000; airports (1984) with scheduled flights 36.
Communications. Daily newspapers (1982): total number 21; total circulation 1,182,046; circulation per 1,000 population 46.4. Radios (1983): 8,250,000 receivers (1 per 3.1 persons). Television (1983): 2,000,000 receivers (1 per 12.8 persons). Telephones (1982): 3,209,000 (1 per 7.9 persons).

Education and health

Education (1984)

	schools	teachers	students	student/ teacher ratio
Primary (age 6–12)	17,186□	194,066□	4,650,423	...
Secondary (age 13–17)	...	...	1,416,343	...
Voc., teacher tr.◊	63	1,460	66,081	45.3
Higher	98	15,666	273,519	17.5

College graduates (students graduating; 1977): 17,709. *Literacy*△§ (1980): total population literate 13,171,000 (79.3%); males 80.6%; females 78.0%.
Health: physicians (1983) 21,143 (1 per 1,206 persons); hospital beds (1980) 98,308 (1 per 259 persons).
Food (1978–80): daily per capita caloric intake 2,826 (vegetable products 85.3%, animal products 14.7%); 115% of FAO recommended minimum.

Military

Total active duty personnel (1984): 83,400 (army 80.8%; navy 7.2%; air force 12.0%). *Military expenditure as percent of GNP* (1982): 5.9% (world 6.0%); per capita expenditure U.S.\$34.

*The provincial totals include the national states listed except Ciskei. †According to the South African government, this state became a sovereign nation after the 1980 census. ‡Totals exclude Bophuthatswana, Transkei, and Venda, which are treated as sovereign nations by the South African government. Together these entities have an area of 34,654 sq mi (89,753 sq km) and a population of 4,814,637. §Includes Transkei, Bophuthatswana, Venda, and Ciskei. ‖ Whites, Asians, and coloureds only. ¶Value of sales. ♀Data apply to the South Africa Customs Union, which consists of South Africa, Botswana, Lesotho, South West Africa/Namibia, and Swaziland. δAugust. □Primary includes secondary. ◊ Data pertain to correspondence colleges and private vocational schools only. △UN estimate.

South West Africa/ Namibia

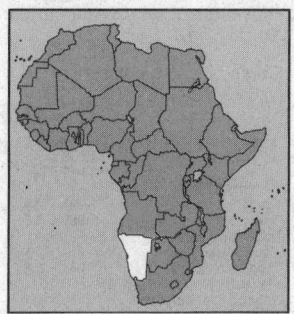

Official name: Suidwes-Afrika/Namibië (Afrikaans); South West Africa/ Namibia (English).
Political status: dependency of South Africa with one legislative house (National Assembly, dissolved Jan. 19, 1983).
Head of state and government: Administrator-General.
Capitals: Windhoek (national); Swakopmund (summer).
Official languages: Afrikaans, English.
Official religion: none.
Monetary unit: 1 South African rand (R) = 100 cents; valuation (Oct. 29, 1984) 1 U.S.$ = R1.79; 1 £ = R2.16.

Area and population*

Magisterial Districts	Capitals	area sq mi	area sq km	population 1981 census†
Bethanien	Bethanien	6,951	18,004	2,808
Gobabis	Gobabis	16,003	41,447	22,079
Grootfontein	Grootfontein	10,239	26,520	20,720
Karasburg	Karasburg	14,717	38,116	9,502
Karibib	Karibib	5,108	13,230	8,953
Keetmanshoop	Keetmanshoop	14,788	38,302	17,608
Lüderitz	Lüderitz	20,488	53,063	14,314
Maltahöhe	Maltahöhe	9,874	25,573	4,751
Mariental	Mariental	18,413	47,689	20,578
Okahandja	Okahandja	6,811	17,640	13,336
Omaruru	Omaruru	3,253	8,425	5,498
Otjiwarongo	Otjiwarongo	7,934	20,550	16,126
Outjo	Outjo	14,951	38,722	8,866
Swakopmund	Swakopmund	17,258	44,697	15,473
Tsumeb	Tsumeb	6,340	16,420	19,447
Windhoek	Windhoek	12,930	33,489	110,644
Communal Areas				
Boesmanland	Tsumkwe	7,131	18,468	2,453
Caprivi Oos	Katima Mulilo	4,453	11,533	37,923
Damaraland	Khorixas	17,977	46,560	24,214
Hereroland-Oos	Otjinene	20,058	51,949	18,918
Hereroland-Wes	Okakarara	6,371	16,500	15,411
Kaokoland	Opuwa	22,467	58,190	16,637
Kavango	Rundu	19,674	50,955	105,690
Namaland	Keetmanshoop	8,154	21,120	12,766
Owambo	Ondangwa	20,000	51,800	452,036
Rehoboth	Rehoboth	5,476	14,182	27,664
TOTAL		317,818	823,144	1,031,927

Source: Official government figures.

Demography

Density (1984): persons per sq mi 3.4; persons per sq km 1.3.
Urban–rural (1981): urban 26.0%; rural 74.0%.
Sex distribution (1981): male 49.21%; female 50.79%.
Age breakdown (1980): under 15, 44.0%; 15–29, 25.8%; 30–44, 15.6%; 45–59, 9.3%; 60–74, 4.4%; 75 and over, 0.9%.
Population projection: (1990) 1,360,000; (2000) 1,822,000.
Doubling time: 24 years.
Ethnic composition (1983): Ovambo 49.3%; Kavango 9.6%; Herero 7.3%; Damara 7.1%; white 6.8%; other 19.9%.
Religious affiliation (1981): Lutheran 51.2%, Roman Catholic 19.8%, Dutch Reformed 6.1%; Anglican 5.0%; other 17.9%.
Major cities (mun., 1983): Windhoek 104,100; Swakopmund 16,896; Tsumeb 15,760; Rundu 15,000; Rehoboth 14,000; Keetmanshoop 13,500; Otjiwarongo 10,409.

Vital statistics

Birth rate per 1,000 population (1980–85): 43.2 (world avg. 27.5); legitimate, n.a., illegitimate, n.a.
Death rate per 1,000 population (1980–85): 13.6 (world avg. 10.6).
Natural increase rate per 1,000 population (1980–85): 29.6 (world avg. 16.9).
Total fertility rate (avg. births per childbearing woman; 1980–85): 5.9.
Marriage rate per 1,000 population: n.a.
Divorce rate per 1,000 population: n.a.
Infant mortality rate per 1,000 live births (1980–85): 125.
Life expectancy at birth (1980–85): male 52.5 years; female 55.0 years.
Major causes of death per 100,000 population: no data available; however, among the major diseases are malaria, tuberculosis, and trypanosomiasis.

National economy

Budget (1983–84). Revenue: R813,000,000 (income tax and loan recoveries 35.5%, customs duties and excise taxes 30.8%, South African aid contributions 29.6%). Expenditures: R1,036,000,000.
Public debt (external, outstanding; 1983): U.S.$415,000,000.
Tourism (1981): receipts from visitors, R40,000,000; expenditures by nationals abroad, n.a.
Production (metric tons except as noted). Agriculture, forestry, fishing (1982): roots and tubers 140,000, cereals 64,000, of which corn (maize) 40,000, millet 20,000, sorghum 3,000; 2,663,000 karakul pelts§; livestock (number of live animals) 1,800,000 cattle, 5,000,000 sheep, 2,100,000 goats; fish catch 201,840, of which anchovies 83,626, mackerel 66,826. Mining

and quarrying (1982): diamonds 1,014,464 carats; salt 230,000; uranium 4,456; lead 59,121 ‖; zinc 54,500; copper 46,185 ‖; tin 3,285 ‖; vanadium 440§. Manufacturing (1984): cut gems (primarily diamonds); fur products (karakul); processed foods (fish, meats, dairy products and chocolate); textiles; carved wood products and furniture. Construction: n.a. Energy production (consumption): electricity, n.a.; capacity (1979) 311,000 KW; coal, n.a.; crude petroleum, n.a.; natural gas, n.a.
Gross national product (at current market prices; 1981): U.S.$1,160,000,000 (U.S.$1,150 per capita).

Origin of gross domestic product (current prices)

	1981 in value R'000,000	% of total value	labour force	% of labour force
Agriculture	146.5	10.2	71,402	35.0
Mining	443.0	30.9	15,515	7.6
Manufacturing	66.1	4.6	8,017	3.9
Construction	62.9	4.4	17,654	8.7
Public utilities	36.4	2.5	1,922	0.9
Trade	216.0	15.1	22,253	10.9
Transportation and communication	99.5	7.0	9,615	4.7
Finance	88.2	6.2	3,764	1.8
Services	21.1	1.5	22,417	11.0
Public administration and defense	210.6	14.7	31,079	15.2
Other	41.8	2.9	360	0.2
TOTAL	1,432.1	100.0	203,998	100.0

Persons economically active (1981): total 508,500 (49.3%); female participation in the labour force, n.a.; unemployed, n.a.

Price and earnings indexes (1975=100)¶

	1977	1978	1979	1980	1981	1982	1983
Consumer price index	...	...	...	175	200	232	260
Earnings index	...	...	...	...	...	...	...

Household income and expenditure. Average household size (1981) 4.8; average annual income per household (1980) R3,223 (U.S.$4,143); sources of income (1980): wages and salaries 80.8%, self employment 19.2%; expenditure, n.a.
Land use (1981): forested 12.7%; meadows and pastures 64.3%; agricultural and under permanent cultivation 0.8%; other 22.2%.

Foreign trade

Balance of trade (current prices)

	1975	1976	1977	1978	1979	1980
R'000,000	−59.6	−62.8	+171.9	+380.6	+384.1	+257.1
% of total	7.8%	6.9%	14.1%	29.8%	25.4%	14.4%

Imports (1980): R765,800,000 (no breakdown available). *Major import sources:* South Africa (nearly 100%).
Exports (1980): R1,022,900,000 (diamonds, uranium, copper, zinc, lead, tin, karakul pelts, fish and fish products). *Major export destinations:* South Africa, about 80%.

Transport and communications

Transport. Railroads (1981): length 1,453 mi, 2,338 km; passenger-mi, n.a., passenger-km, n.a.; short ton-mi cargo 1,300,000,000, metric ton-km cargo 1,900,000,000. Roads (1983): total length 26,011 mi, 41,860 km (paved 2,585 mi, 4,160 km). Number of registered vehicles (1974): passenger cars, trucks, and buses 71,272. Merchant marine: vessels (100 gross tons and over), none. Air transport (1977): passengers handled 177,901; cargo, n.a.; airports (1984) with scheduled flights 10.
Communications. Daily newspapers (1978): total number 4¶; total circulation, n.a. Radios (1981): total number of receivers 48,000 (1 per 21 persons). Television (1981): total number of receivers 13,400 (1 per 75 persons). Telephones (1982): 57,300 (1 per 18 persons).

Education and health

Education (1982–83)

	schools	teachers	students	student/ teacher ratio
Primary (age 6–12)	1,069	7,120	232,306	32.6
Secondary (age 13–19)	78	1,864	40,359	21.6
Voc., teacher tr.	6	81	1,200	14.8
Higher	4	137	537	3.9

College graduates per 100,000 population: n.a. *Literacy:* total population literate, about 35%; males literate, n.a.; females literate, n.a.
Health (1981): physicians 183 (1 per 5,500 persons); hospital beds 7,500 (1 per 135 persons).
Food (1978–80): daily per capita caloric intake 2,224 (vegetable products 76.3%, animal products 23.7%); 98% of FAO recommended minimum requirement.

Military

Total active duty personnel: n.a. *Military expenditure as percent of GNP:* n.a.

*Excludes area and population of Walvis Bay (part of South Africa), administered as part of South West Africa/Namibia until 1977. †Preliminary; total includes 7,512 transients not distributed by subdivision. §1978. ‖1981. ¶For Windhoek only.

Spain

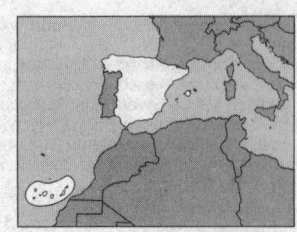

Official name: Estado Español (Spanish State).
Form of government: constitutional monarchy with two legislative houses (Senate [208]; Congress of Deputies [350]).
Chief of state: King.
Head of government: Prime Minister.
Capital: Madrid (national); San Sebastian (summer).
Official language: Spanish.
Official religion: none.
Monetary unit: 1 peseta (Pta, plural Ptas) = 100 céntimos; valuation (Oct. 29, 1984) 1 U.S.$ = Ptas171.71; 1 £ = Ptas207.25.

Area and population

Autonomous communities	Capitals	area sq mi	area sq km	population 1981 census
Andalucía	Sevilla	33,694	87,268	6,441,755
Aragón	Zaragosa	18,398	47,650	1,213,099
Asturias	Oviedo	4,079	10,565	1,127,007
Baleares	Palma de Mallorca	1,936	5,014	685,088
Canarias	Santa Cruz de Tenerife	2,796	7,242	1,444,626
Cantabria	Santander	2,042	5,289	510,816
Castilla-La Mancha	Toledo	30,591	79,230	1,628,005
Castilla León	Tordesillas	36,368	94,193	2,577,105
Cataluña	Barcelona	12,328	31,930	5,958,208
País Valenciana	Valencia	8,998	23,305	3,646,765
Extremadura	Mérida	16,063	41,602	1,050,119
Galicia	Santiago de Compostela	11,365	29,434	2,753,836
La Rioja	Logroño	1,944	5,034	253,295
Madrid	Madrid	3,087	7,995	4,726,986
Murcia	Murcia	4,370	11,317	957,903
Navarra	Pamplona	4,023	10,421	507,367
País Vasco	Vitoria	2,803	7,261	2,134,967
TOTAL SPAIN		194,885	504,750	36,616,947
Enclaves in Northern Morocco				
Ceuta	—	7.1	18.5	70,864
Melilla	—	5.4	14	58,449
Chajarinas	—	.24	.61	...
Vélez de la Gomera	—	.02	.04	...
Alhucemas	—	.004	.01	...
TOTAL		194,897.79*	504,783.16	37,746,260

Demography

Density (1984): persons per sq mi 196.9, persons per sq km 76.0.
Urban–rural (1980): urban 74.3%; rural 25.7%.
Sex distribution (1981): male 49.9%; female 50.91%.
Age breakdown (1980): under 15, 25.9%; 15–64, 63.2%; 65 and over, 10.9%.
Population projection: (1990) 40,541,000; (2000) 43,362,000.
Doubling time: 82 years.
Ethnic composition (1984): Spanish 72.8%; Catalan 16.4%; Galician 8.2%; Basque 2.3%; other 0.3%.
Religious affiliation (1980): Roman Catholic 99.0%; other 1.0%.
Major cities (1982): Madrid 3,271,834; Barcelona 1,720,998; Valencia 770,277; Sevilla 630,912.

Vital statistics

Birth rate per 1,000 population (1982): 13.4 (world avg. 29.0).
Death rate per 1,000 population (1982): 7.4 (world avg. 11.0).
Natural increase rate per 1,000 population (1982): 6.0 (world avg. 18.0).
Total fertility rate (avg. births per childbearing woman; 1982): 2.2.
Marriage rate per 1,000 population (1982): 5.0.
Infant mortality rate per 1,000 live births (1982): 9.6.
Life expectancy at birth (1980–85): male 70.7 years; female 76.2 years.
Major causes of death per 100,000 population (1979): circulatory diseases 357.0; neoplasms (cancers) 151.9; respiratory diseases 66.7.

National economy

Budget (1982). Revenue: Ptas2,836,575,000,000 (direct taxation 42.2%; consumer goods, commercial trade, and other indirect taxation 38.8%; other 19.0%). Expenditures: Ptas3,621,023,500,000 (education 24.4%; public works 11.5%; defense 10.2%; transport and communications 6.7%; other 47.2%).
Public debt (1983): U.S.$12,797,110,000.
Tourism (1982): receipts from visitors U.S.$7,126,100,000; expenditures by nationals abroad U.S.$1,007,900,000.
Production (value in local currency except as noted). Agriculture, forestry, fishing (1981): vegetables 205,833,500,000, grains 190,734,300,000, fruits excluding citrus 113,477,600,000; livestock (number of live animals; 1983) 16,731,000 sheep, 12,364,000 pigs, 4,956,000 cattle, 2,414,000 goats. Mining and quarrying (metric tons; 1983): iron ore 3,512,100; pyrites 1,059,700. Manufacturing (1981): oil and coal derived products 1,195,773,076; foods excluding beverages 645,533,087, of which fodder 205,410,172; transport equipment 641,680,334; artificial cement 145,131,115; wood products 31,607,106; natural cement, lime, and gypsum 9,457,290. Construction (1982): residential dwellings 235,019. Energy production (consumption): electricity (kW-hr; 1982) 116,760,000,000 (115,460,000,000); coal (metric tons; 1982) 39,954,000 (44,698,000); crude petroleum (barrels; 1982) 11,156,000 (325,722,000); petroleum products (metric tons; 1982) 37,252,000 (37,413,000); natural gas (cu m; 1982) 641,000 (2,051,900,000).

Gross national product (at current market prices; 1983): U.S.$156,453,000,000 (U.S.$4,105 per capita).

Origin of gross domestic product (current prices)

	1981 in value Ptas'000,000	% of total value	labour force	% of labour force
Agriculture	1,039,804	6.0	1,985,000	18.3
Mining	3,945,882	22.8	91,000	0.8
Manufacturing			2,710,500	25.1
Construction	1,227,735	7.1	948,900	8.8
Trade	2,960,006	17.1	2,174,700	20.1
Public utilities	791,923	4.6	83,400	0.8
Transportation and communication	1,231,413	7.1	645,200	6.0
Finance	826,429	4.8	406,600	3.8
Pub. admin., defense	1,708,576	9.9		
Services	2,661,733	15.4	1,773,300	16.4
Other	928,982	5.4	—	—
TOTAL	17,322,483	100.0*	10,818,700*	100.0*

Persons economically active (1982): total 13,101,100 (34.6%); female participation in the labour force 3,938,000 (30.1%); unemployed 886,000 (6.8%).

Price and earnings indexes (1975 = 100)

	1978	1979	1980	1981	1982	1983	1984†
Consumer price index	171.7	198.5	229.5	262.8	300.9	337.4	363.5
Monthly earnings index	214.1	264.1	312.7	375.5	431.8	496.2	528.5

Household income and expenditure. Average household size‡ (1981) 3.5; income per household: n.a.; source of income: n.a.; quarterly per capita expenditure (second quarter; 1982): food 43.8%, housing 9.5%, transportation 8.6%, clothing and footwear 8.4%, recreation 4.7%.
Land use (1981): forested 30.7%; meadows and pastures 21.2%; agricultural and under permanent cultivation 40.6%; other 7.5%.

Foreign trade

Balance of trade (current prices)

	1978	1979	1980	1981	1982	1983
Ptas'000,000	−429,650	−482,581	−957,466	−1,086,250	−1,207,600	−1,337,900
% of total	17.7%	16.5%	24.3%	22.3%	21.1%	19.1%

Imports (1982): Ptas2,258,000,000,000 (mineral fuels, lubricants, and related materials 39.6%; manufactured goods 32.2%, of which machinery and transport equipment 19.1%; food and food products 8.2%; chemical and chemical products 7.4%). *Major import sources:* United States 14.0%; West Germany 9.5%; Saudi Arabia 9.2%; Mexico 6.0%; United Kingdom 4.9%.
Exports (1982): Ptas3,465,600,000,000 (manufactured goods 66.3%, of which machinery and transport equipment 27.2%; food and food products 14.2%, of which fruits and vegetables 8.9%; chemical and chemical products 7.2%). *Major export destinations:* France 16.5%; West Germany 8.1%; United Kingdom 7.0%; United States 6.4%; Italy 5.7%.

Transport and communications

Transport. Railroads (1983): length 8,421 mi, 13,553 km; passenger-mi 9,378,000,000, passenger-km 15,092,000,000; short ton-mi cargo 7,260,000,000, metric ton-km cargo 10,599,000,000. Roads (1983): total length 200,170 mi, 322,143 km (paved 56%). Vehicles (1983): passenger cars 8,714,076; trucks and buses 1,604,038. Merchant marine (1983): vessels (100 gross tons and over) 2,589; total deadweight tonnage 12,788,157. Air transport (1983): passenger-mi 9,670,470,000, passenger-km 15,563,143,000; short ton-mi cargo 301,384,000; metric ton-km cargo 440,013,000; airports (1984) with scheduled flights 29.
Communications. Daily newspapers (1981): total number 100; total circulation 2,069,248§; circulation per 1,000 population 55. Radios (1983): total number of receivers 10,400,000 (1 per 3.7 persons). Television (1983): total number of receivers 11,650,000 (1 per 3.3 persons). Telephones (1982): 12,820,190 (1 per 3.0 persons).

Education and health

Education (1980–81)

	schools	teachers	students	student/teacher ratio
Primary (age 2–13)	216,653	228,307	6,788,877	29.7
Secondary (age 14–17)	2,445	66,160	1,091,197	16.5
Vocational	2,142	36,556	558,808	15.3
Higher, teacher tr.	120	40,321	649,098	16.1

College graduates per 100,000 population: n.a. *Literacy* (1980): total population literate 25,593,400 (92.8%); males literate 12,785,200 (96.3%); females literate 12,808,200 (89.6%).
Health (1982): physicians 104,759 (1 per 362 persons); hospital beds 203,819 ‖ (1 per 184 persons).
Food (1978–80): daily per capita caloric intake 3,333 (vegetable products 74.3%, animal products 25.7%); 136% of FAO recommended minimum requirement.

Military

Total active duty personnel (1983): 347,000 (army 74.9%; navy 15.6%; air force 9.5%). *Military expenditure as percent of GNP* (1982): 2.1% (world 6.0%); per capita expenditure U.S.$109.

*Detail does not add to total because of rounding. †First quarter only. ‡Family size. §Includes Sunday circulation; circulation for *El País* and *Ya* not available. ‖ Latest available 1979, includes incubators.

Sri Lanka (Ceylon)

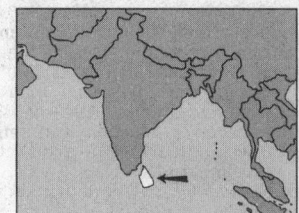

Official name: Sri Lankā Pra-
jathanthrika Samajavadi Janarajaya
(Democratic Socialist Republic of
Sri Lanka).
Form of government: unitary multiparty
republic with one legislative house
(Parliament [163]).
Chief of state: President.
Head of government: Prime Minister.
Capital: Colombo; capital designate, Sri
Jayawardenapura.
Official language: Sinhala.
Official religion: none.
Monetary unit: 1 Sri Lanka rupee
(SL Rs) = 100 cents; valuation (Oct.
29, 1984) 1 U.S.$ = SL Rs25.81;
1 £ = SL Rs31.15.

Area and population

Districts	Capitals	area sq mi	area sq km	population 1981 census*
Amparai	Amparai	1,778	4,604	388,741
Anuradhapura	Anuradhapura	2,809	7,275	587,680
Badulla	Badulla	1,090	2,822	642,622
Batticaloa	Batticaloa	1,017	2,633	330,815
Colombo	Colombo	268	695	1,697,795
Galle	Galle	652	1,689	814,264
Gampaha	Gampaha	540	1,399	1,389,269
Hambantota	Hambantota	1,013	2,623	424,083
Jaffna	Jaffna	833	2,158	831,096
Kalutara	Kalutara	624	1,615	827,298
Kandy	Kandy	833	2,158	1,126,544
Kegalle	Kegalle	642	1,663	682,538
Kurunegala	Kurunegala	1,844	4,776	1,212,590
Mannar	Mannar	778	2,014	106,991
Matale	Matale	768	1,989	357,364
Matara	Matara	481	1,247	643,947
Moneragala	Moneragala	2,188	5,666	279,811
Mullaitivu	Mullaitivu	798	2,066	77,530
Nuwara Eliya	Nuwara Eliya	555	1,437	521,853
Polonnaruwa	Polonnaruwa	1,332	3,449	263,265
Puttalam	Puttalam	1,172	3,036	493,447
Ratnapura	Ratnapura	1,251	3,239	796,169
Trincomalee	Trincomalee	1,048	2,714	256,732
Vavuniya	Vavuniya	1,021	2,645	95,920
TOTAL		25,332†	65,610†	14,848,364

Source: Official government figures.

Demography

Density (1984): persons per sq mi 622.0, persons per sq km 240.0.
Urban-rural (1981): urban 21.5%; rural 78.5%.
Sex distribution (1981): male 50.77%; female 49.23%.
Age breakdown (1981): under 15, 35.3%; 15–29, 29.6%; 30–44, 17.9%; 45–59,
10.6%; 60–74, 5.2%; 75 and over, 1.4%.
Population projection: (1991) 18,868,000; (2001) 21,786,000.
Doubling time: 42 years.
Ethnic composition (1981): Sinhalese 74.0%, of whom low-country 42.8%,
Kandyan 29.2%; Tamil 18.2%, of whom Sri Lankan 12.6%, Indian 5.6%;
Sri Lankan Moor 7.1%; other 0.7%.
Religious affiliation (1981): Buddhist 69.3%; Hindu 15.5%; Muslim 7.6%;
Christian 7.5%; other 0.1%.
Major cities (1981 prelim.): Colombo 586,000; Dehiwala–Mount Lavinia
174,000; Moratuwa 136,000; Jaffna 118,000; Kotte 102,000.

Vital statistics

Birth rate per 1,000 population (1981): 28.0 (world avg. 29.0).
Death rate per 1,000 population (1981): 6.0 (world avg. 12.0).
Natural increase rate per 1,000 population (1981): 22.0 (world avg. 17.0).
Total fertility rate (avg. births per childbearing woman; 1983): 3.3.
Marriage rate per 1,000 population (1981): 8.1.
Divorce rate per 1,000 population‡ (1981): 0.2.
Infant mortality rate per 1,000 live births (1980–85): 38.0.
Life expectancy at birth (1980–85): male 65.0 years; female 67.9 years.
Major causes of death per 100,000 population (1978): senility without men-
tion of psychosis 122.1; heart disease 57.7; accidents other than motor
accidents 33.7; enteritis and other diarrheal diseases 31.7.

National economy

Budget§ (1982). Revenue: SL Rs35,771,900,000 (current revenue SL Rs19,-
162,900,000, of which sales and turnover taxes 38.6%, import duties 18.8%,
income tax 15.4%, export duties 15.2%). Expenditures: SL Rs38,660,300,300
(current expenditure SL Rs21,164,100,000, of which administration 18.3%,
social services 15.0%, economic services 3.0%).
Public debt (external, outstanding; 1982): U.S.$1,971,300,000.
Tourism (1982): receipts from visitors U.S.$147,000,000; expenditures by
nationals abroad U.S.$79,000,000.
Production (metric tons except as noted). Agriculture, forestry, fishing
(1982): rice 2,150,000, coconuts 1,716,000, cassava 500,000, tea 190,000,
natural rubber 135,000, sweet potatoes 127,000; livestock (number of live
animals) 1,698,600 cattle, 879,200 buffaloes, 511,600 goats, 6,248,500 poultry; roundwood 8,149,000 cu m; fish catch 207,100. Mining and quarrying ‖ (1982): salt 176,400; ilmenite 68,300; asphalt 24,900; graphite 8,800.
Manufacturing ‖ (1982): cement 574,300; sugar 23,700; rolled iron 22,800;
paper 22,200; textiles 19,805,000 metres. Construction (1980): residential

285,200 sq m. Energy production (consumption): electricity (kW-hr; 1982)
2,066,000,000 (2,066,000,000); coal (metric tons; 1982) none (32,000); crude
petroleum (barrels; 1982) none (13,964,000); petroleum products (metric
tons; 1982) 1,589,000 (1,118,000).
Gross national product (at current market prices; 1982): U.S.$4,818,000,000
(U.S.$316 per capita).

Origin of gross domestic product (current producers' prices)

	1982 in value SL Rs'000,000	1982 % of total value	1980–81 labour force	1980–81 % of labour force
Agriculture	24,991	25.4	2,374,870	41.7
Mining	1,069	1.0	66,170	1.1
Manufacturing	15,866	16.1	531,065	9.4
Construction	8,740	8.9	223,750	3.9
Trade	19,645	20.0	497,855	8.8
Public utilities	1,591	1.6	18,999	0.3
Transp. and commun.	9,855	10.0	208,470	3.6
Finance	3,424	3.5	48,093	0.9
Pub. admin., defense	4,900	5.0	...	...
Community, social, and personal services	2,569	2.6	650,981	11.4
Other	5,619	5.7	1,077,693	18.9
TOTAL	98,269	100.0†	5,697,946	100.0

Persons economically active (1980–81): total 5,697,946 (38.4%); female participation in the labour force 1,561,199 (27.4%); unemployed 767,601 (13.5%).

Price and earnings indexes (1975 = 100)

	1976	1977	1978	1979	1980	1981	1982
Consumer price index¶	101.2	102.5	114.9	127.2	160.5	189.3	210.0
Daily earnings index	116.4	121.2	167.6	210.6	262.2	264.2	298.5

Household income and expenditure. Average household size (1980) 5.2;
income per household (1973) SL Rs3,936 (U.S.$611); source of income
(1973): wages 72.3%, remittances and gifts 12.5%, self-employment 6.4%,
rent 5.3%, pensions and annuities 1.5%, interest 1.3%; expenditure (1980):
food 63.4%, transportation 10.5%, housing 8.8%, clothing 7.6%, medical
care and miscellaneous goods and services 5.5%, recreation 4.2%.
Land use (1981): forested 36.8%; meadows and pastures 6.8%; agricultural
and under permanent cultivation 33.3%; other 23.1%.

Foreign trade

Balance of trade (current prices)

	1977	1978	1979	1980	1981	1982
SL Rs'000,000	+509	−1,494	−7,278	−16,007	−14,666	−20,492
% of total	4.0%	5.4%	19.2%	31.2%	26.3%	32.3%

Imports (1982): SL Rs41,946,000,000 (petroleum products 51.6%; machinery
27.6%; food and drink 8.5%; textiles and clothing 5.2%). *Major import
sources:* Japan 15.2%; Iran 11.7%; United Kingdom 6.6%; U.S. 6.3%.
Exports (1982): SL Rs21,454,000,000 (tea 30.0%; rubber 11.0%; major coconut products 4.9%, of which desiccated coconut 2.8%; precious and
semiprecious stones 3.2%). *Major export destinations:* United States 14.4%;
United Kingdom 6.6%; West Germany 5.6%; Japan 5.0%.

Transport and communications

Transport. Railroads (1982): route length 903 mi, 1,453 km; passenger-mi
1,984,100,000, passenger-km 3,194,400,000; short ton-mi cargo 147,355,000,
metric ton-km cargo 215,134,000. Roads (1981): total length 46,488 mi,
74,813 km (paved 40%). Vehicles (1982): passenger cars 131,657; trucks and
buses 101,627. Merchant marine (1983): vessels (100 gross tons and over)
68; total deadweight tonnage 586,695. Air transport (1983): passenger-mi
1,312,000,000, passenger-km 2,112,000,000; short ton-mi cargo 32,211,000;
metric ton-km cargo 47,028,000; airports (1983) 5.
Communications. Daily newspapers (1982): total number 15; total circulation 637,500; circulation per 1,000 population 32. Radios (1982): receivers
4,967,000 (1 per 3 persons). Television (1982): receivers 105,000 (1 per 141
persons). Telephones (1982): 109,900 (1 per 135 persons).

Education and health

Education (1981)

	schools	teachers	students	student/ teacher ratio
Primary (age 5–10)	9,176	131,656	2,132,596	16.2
Secondary (age 11–17)⁹	5,948	75,174	1,560,923	20.8
Voc., teacher tr.⁹	25	488	9,235	18.9
Higherᵟ□	8	1,609	10,040	6.2

College graduates per 100,000 population (students graduating; 1979): 35.
Literacy (1981): total population literate◊ 9,775,000 (86.5%); males literate
5,212,000 (90.5%); females literate 4,563,000 (82.4%).
Health (1982): physicians△ 2,035 (1 per 9,763 persons); hospital beds 42,257
(1 per 470 persons).
Food (1978–80): daily per capita caloric intake 2,251 (vegetable products
96.7%, animal products 3.3%); 101% of FAO recommended minimum.

Military

Total active duty personnel (1983): 16,560 (army 66.0%; navy 18.0%; air force
16.0%). *Military expenditure as percent of GNP* (1982): 0.5% (world 6.0%);
per capita expenditure U.S.$2.

*Preliminary. †Detail does not add to total given because of rounding. ‡Excludes
Muslim divorces. §Includes capital accounts. ‖ Public sector only. ¶Colombo only.
⁹1980. ᵟ1981–82. □Universities only. ◊Age 10 and over. △Includes only those in
department of health services.

Sudan

Official name: Jumhūrīyat as-Sūdān ad-Dīmuqrātīyah (Democratic Republic of the Sudan).
Form of government: single-party republic with one legislative house (People's Assembly [153]).
Chief of state: President*.
Head of government: Prime Minister*.
Capital: Khartoum.
Official language: Arabic.
Official religion: Islām.
Monetary unit: 1 Sudanese pound (LSd) = 100 piastres; valuation (Oct. 29, 1984) 1 U.S.\$ = LSd1.30; 1 £ = LSd1.53.

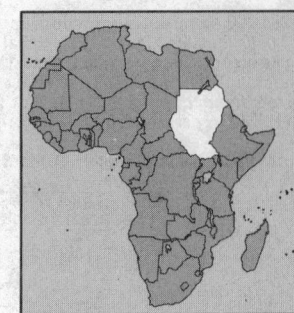

Area and population

Regions Provinces	Capitals	area sq mi	area sq km	population 1983 census
ash-Shamāliyah (Northern)	ad-Dāmir	183,800	476,040	1,083,024
an-Nīl (Nile)	ad-Dāmir	49,167	127,343	649,633
ash-Shamāliyah (Northern)	Dunqulah	134,633	348,697	433,391
al-Wastā (Central)	Wad Madanī	53,675	139,017	4,012,543
an-Nīl al-Abyaḍ (White Nile)	ad-Duwaym	16,149	41,825	933,136
al-Jazīrah (El-Gezira)	Wad Madanī	13,536	35,057	2,023,094
an-Nīl al-Azraq (Blue Nile)	ad-Damazin	23,990	62,135	1,056,313
Kurdufān (Kordofan)	al-Ubayyiḍ	146,817	380,255	3,093,294
Kurdufān al-Janūbiyah (Southern Kordofan)	Kāduqlī	61,141	158,355	1,287,525
Kurdufan ash-Shamāliyah (Northern Kordofan)	al-Ubayyiḍ	85,676	221,900	1,805,769
Dārfūr (Darfur)	al-Fāshir	196,404	508,684	3,093,699
Dārfūr al-Janūbiyah (Southern Darfur)	Nyala	62,753	162,529	1,765,752
Dārfūr ash-Shamāliyah (Northern Darfur)	al-Fāshir	133,651	346,155	1,327,947
ash-Sharqiyah (Eastern)	Kassalā	128,987	334,074	2,208,209
al-Baḥr al-Aḥmar (Red Sea)	Port Sudan	84,912	219,920	695,874
Kassalā (Kassala)	Kassalā	44,075	114,154	1,512,335
al-Istiwā'īyah (Equatoria)	Jūbā	76,436	197,969	1,406,181
al-Istiwā'īyah al Gharbiyah (Western Equatoria)	Yambio	30,398	78,732	359,056
al-Istiwā'īyah ash-Sharqiyah (Eastern Equatoria)	Jūbā	46,038	119,237	1,047,125
Bahr al-Ghazāl (Bahr el-Ghazal)‡	Wāu	77,566	200,894	2,265,510
Bahr al-Ghazāl al-Gharbiyah (Western Bahr el-Ghazal)	Raga	51,960	134,576	1,492,597
Bahr al-Ghazāl ash-Sharqiyah (Eastern Bahr el-Ghazal)	Uwayl			
al-Buḥayrāh (El Buheyrah)	Rumbek	25,606	66,318	772,913
A'ali an-Nīl (Upper Nile)	Malakāl	92,198	238,792	1,599,605
A'ali an-Nīl (Upper Nile)	Nāṣir	45,231	117,148	802,354
Junqulī (Jongley)	Bor	46,967	121,164	797,251
National Capital				
Khartūm (Khartoum)	Khartoum	10,875	28,165	1,802,299
TOTAL		966,757†	2,503,890	20,564,364

Demography

Density (1984): persons per sq mi 21.3, persons per sq km 8.2.
Urban–rural (1983): urban 30.6%; rural 69.4%.
Sex distribution (1983): male 50.98%; female 49.02%.
Age breakdown (1985): under 15, 44.6%; 15–29, 26.0%; 30–44, 15.7%; 45–59, 8.9%; 60–74, 4.0%; 75 and over, 0.8%.
Population projection: (1990) 24,949,800; (2000) 32,885,000.
Doubling time: 25 years.
Ethnic composition (1980): Sudanese Arab 46.0%; Nilotic 25.5%; Azande 5.6%; Nuba 5.6%; Beja 5.0%; other 12.3%.
Religious affiliation (1980): Sunnī Muslim 73.0%; animist 16.7%; Roman Catholic 5.6%; Anglican 2.3%; other 2.4%.
Major cities (1983): Omdurman 526,287; Khartoum 476,218; Khartoum North 341,146; Port Sudan 206,727.

Vital statistics

Birth rate per 1,000 population (1980–85): 45.3 (world avg. 27.5).
Death rate per 1,000 population (1980–85): 16.6 (world avg. 10.6).
Natural increase rate per 1,000 population (1980–85): 28.7 (world avg. 16.9).
Total fertility rate (avg. births per childbearing woman; 1980–85): 6.56.
Infant mortality rate per 1,000 live births (1981): 121.8.
Life expectancy at birth (1980–85): male 48.0 years; female 50.0 years.
Major causes of death from diseases per 100,000 population (1979)‡: pneumonia 26.4; tuberculosis 1.8; meningitis 1.3; infectious hepatitis 1.1.

National economy

Budget (1981–82). Revenue: LSd1,033,500,000 (taxes 65.1%, of which income 12.8%, excise 12.8%, import duties 37.1%; foreign capital grants 18.8%; public enterprise and finance 6.7%). Expenditures: LSd1,198,200,000 (transfers to local governments 32.3%; economic development services 23.5%, of which agriculture 8.5%; general services 18.0%; defense 9.5%.
Public debt (external, outstanding; 1982): U.S.\$5,473,000,000.
Tourism (1980–81): receipts from visitors U.S.\$5,820,000§; expenditures by nationals abroad U.S.\$75,000,000 ‖.
Production (metric tons except as noted). Agriculture, forestry, fishing (1982): sugarcane 2,529,000, sorghum 2,100,000, milk 1,513,000, peanuts (groundnuts) 800,000, seed cotton 290,000, millet 230,000, sesame seeds 200,000, lint cotton 160,000, coffee (n.a.), tobacco (n.a.); livestock (number of live animals) 19,234,000 cattle, 18,547,000 sheep, 13,174,000 goats,

2,570,000 camels; roundwood 37,073,000 cu m; fish catch 29,710. Mining and quarrying (1982): gypsum and anhydrite (crude) 28,000; salt 27,927; chromite concentrate 19,000. Manufacturing (1980): crude cottonseed and peanut (groundnut) oils 288,000¶; wheat flour 220,000; raw sugar 195,000; cement 185,000; gum arabic 38,000⁰; cotton textiles 103,000,000 sq mᵟ; motor batteries 74,000 unitsᵟ; beer 42,000 hectolitres. Construction: n.a. Energy production (consumption): electricity (kW-hr; 1982) 1,010,000,000 (1,010,000,000); crude petroleum (barrels; 1982) none (8,088,000); petroleum products (metric tons; 1982) 1,061,000 (1,124,000).
Gross national product (at current market prices; 1981): U.S.\$7,390,000,000 (U.S.\$380 per capita).

Origin of gross domestic product (current prices)

	1977–78▫ in value LSd'000,000	1977–78▫ % of total value	1976–77▫ labour force	1976–77▫ % of labour force
Agriculture	1,051.9	36.5	3,435,306	68.5
Mining	1.7	0.1	...	...
Manufacturing	215.1	7.5	185,054	4.5
Construction	118.6	4.1	92,276	1.8
Transp. and commun.	279.1	9.6	169,006	3.4
Public utilities	38.6	1.3	45,633	0.9
Trade	555.8	19.3 }	245,735	4.9
Finance				
Pub. admin., defense	621.9 }	21.6	521,560	10.4
Services			...	...
Other			320,458	5.6
TOTAL	2,882.7	100.0	5,015,028	100.0

Persons economically active (1981): total 5,973,000 (31.6%); female participation in the labour force 651,000 (10.9%); unemployed, n.a.

Price indexes (1980 = 100)

	1977	1978	1979	1980	1981	1982	1983
Consumer price index	51.0	60.8	79.8	100.0	124.6	156.6	204.5

Household income and expenditure. Average household size (1980) 5.3; average annual income per household: n.a.; source of income: n.a.; expenditure (1980)◊: food, beverages, and tobacco 66.5%, housing 12.4%, clothing 5.9%, education, health, transportation, and recreation 15.2%.
Land use (1981): forested 20.5%; meadows and pastures 23.6%; agricultural and under permanent cultivation 5.2%; desert and other 50.7%.

Foreign trade

Balance of trade (current prices)

	1978	1979	1980	1981	1982	1983
LSd'000,000	−247.2	−244.7	−516.9	−509.7	−707.1	−761.5
% of total	37.9%	34.5%	48.8%	41.7%	44.0%	32.0%

Imports (1982): LSd 1,156,404,000 (machinery 28.3%; petroleum and petroleum products 27.1%, chemicals 8.2%, sugar 5.4%). *Major import sources:* Saudi Arabia 16.2%; United Kingdom 12.0%; United States 9.6%.
Exports (1982): LSd 449,338,000 (cotton 25.1%, unmilled cereals 23.3%, sheep, lambs, and goats 12.3%). *Major export destinations:* Saudi Arabia 36.6%; Italy 7.5%; Japan 6.6%.

Transport and communications

Transport. Railroads (1981–82): route length 2,974 mi, 4,786 km; passenger-mi 714,000, passenger-km 1,149,000; short ton-mi cargo 1,096,000,000, metric ton-km cargo 1,600,000,000. Roads (1982): total length 5,604 mi, 9,018 km (paved 33%). Vehicles (1982): passenger cars 150,000; trucks and buses 22,000. Merchant marine (1982): vessels (100 gross tons and over) 22; total deadweight tonnage 124,311. Air transport (1981): passenger-mi 441,000,000, passenger-km 710,000,000; short ton-mi cargo 8,300,000, metric ton-km cargo 12,100,000; airports (1984) with scheduled flights 13.
Communications. Daily newspapers (1983): total number 3; total circulation 140,000; circulation per 1,000 population 6.8. Radios (1983): 1,400,000 (1 per 15 persons). Television (1983): 109,000 (1 per 188 persons). Telephones (1982): 68,503 (1 per 250 persons).

Education and health

Education (1979–80)

	schools	teachers	students	student/ teacher ratio
Primary (age 7–12)	5,729	41,726	1,435,127	34.4
Secondary (age 13–18)	1,477	15,078	340,238	22.6
Voc., teacher tr.	60	1,369	17,954	13.1
Higher	17	1,934	26,883	13.9

Literacy (1980): total population literate 2,507,200 (21.6%); males literate 2,131,500 (36.5%); females literate 375,700 (6.5%).
Health (1981): physicians and dentists 2,169 (1 per 8,870 persons); hospital beds 17,328 (1 per 1,110 persons).
Food (1978–80): daily per capita caloric intake 2,371 (vegetable products 88.1%, animal products 11.9%); 101% of FAO recommended minimum.

Military

Total active duty personnel (1983): 58,000 (army 91.4%; navy 3.4%; air force 5.2%). *Military expenditure as percent of GNP* (1981): 2.6% (world 4.9%); per capita expenditure U.S.\$11.

---

*The offices of president and prime minister have been held by Pres. Gaafar al-Nimeiry almost continuously since 1971. †Detail does not add to total given because of rounding. ‡Reported by hospitals and dispensaries. §Revenue of the departments of hotels and tourism. ‖ 1980. ¶1977. ⁰1981–82. ᵟ1975. ▫Year beginning July 1. ◊Low-income households.

Suriname

Official name: Republiek Suriname
(Dutch); Republic of Suriname
(English).
Form of government: military
dictatorship with one ruling body
(National Military Council [8]).
Head of state and government:
Commander-in-Chief of the
National Army .
Capital: Paramaribo.
Official languages: Dutch; English.
Official religion: none.
Monetary unit: 1 Suriname guilder
(Sf) = 100 cents; valuation (Oct. 29,
1984) 1 U.S.$ = Sf17.94; 1 £ = Sf21.65.

Area and population

Districts	Capitals	area sq mi	area sq km	population 1980 census
Brokopondo	Brokopondo	8,278	21,440	20,448
Commewijne	Nieuw Amsterdam	1,587	4,110	14,082
Coronie	Tottness	626	1,620	2,756
Marowijne	Albina	17,753	45,980	22,583
Nickerie	Nieuw Nickerie	24,946	64,610	34,598
Para	Onverwacht	378	980	14,644
Saramacca	Groningen	9,042	23,420	10,333
Suriname	...	629	1,628	164,879
Town district				
Paramaribo	Paramaribo	12	32	67,718
TOTAL		63,251	163,820	352,041

Source: Official government figures.

Demography

Density (1984): persons per sq mi 5.6, persons per sq km 2.1.
Urban–rural (1980): urban 44.8%; rural 55.2%.
Sex distribution (1980): male 49.17%; female 50.83%.
Age breakdown (1980): under 15, 39.1%; 15–65, 55.7%; 66 and over, 5.2%*.
Population projection: (1990) 361,000; (2000) 423,000.
Doubling time: population growth is negligible.
Ethnic composition (1980): Hindustani 35%; Creole 32%; Indonesian 15%;
Bush Negro 10%; other 8%.
Religious affiliation (1980): Protestant 36.6%; Roman Catholic 36.0%; Muslim 13.0%; tribal religionist 6.1%; Hindu 2.0%; other 6.3%.
Major cities (1980): Paramaribo 67,718; Nieuw Nickerie 6,078; Meerzorg 5,355; Marienburg 3,633.

Vital statistics

Birth rate per 1,000 population (1980): 28.0 (world avg. 30.0); legitimate, n.a.; illegitimate, n.a.
Death rate per 1,000 population (1980): 7.9 (world avg. 12.0).
Natural increase rate per 1,000 population (1980): 20.1 (world avg. 18.0).
Total fertility rate (avg. births per childbearing woman; 1980): 5.7.
Marriage rate per 1,000 population (1980): 6.1†.
Divorce rate per 1,000 population: n.a.
Infant mortality rate per 1,000 live births (1980): 30.4.
Life expectancy at birth (1980–85): male 66.3 years; female 71.5 years.
Major causes of death per 100,000 population (1980): diseases of the circulatory system 154.9; accidents, poisoning, and violence 72.1; malignant neoplasms (cancers) 50.6; infectious and parasitic diseases 35.1.

National economy

Budget (1976)‡. Revenue: Sf403,100,000§ (import duties 23.5%; excise tax 20.6%; corporate tax 11.1%; income tax 5.8%). Expenditures: Sf424,210,-000 (general public services 37.0%; education 15.9%; health 8.6%; mining, manufacturing, and construction 5.1%; social security 4.7%; roads 3.7%; housing 2.1%).
Public debt (external, outstanding; 1982): U.S.$15,000,000.
Tourism (1981): receipts from visitors U.S.$17,000,000; expenditures by nationals abroad U.S.$29,000,000.
Production (metric tons except as noted). Agriculture, forestry, fishing (1982): rice 280,000, sugarcane 140,000, bananas 39,000, palm kernels 25,-000, oranges 8,000, coconuts 5,000, vegetables and melons 4,000; livestock (number of live animals) 51,000 cattle, 18,000 pigs, 9,000 goats, 4,000 sheep, 1,150,000 chickens; roundwood 266,000 cu m; fish catch 6,377. Mining and quarrying (1982): bauxite 3,059,000; gravel and crushed stone 120,000; clay 100,000; gold 599 troy ounces. Manufacturing (1982): alumina 1,172,000; cement 72,000; aluminum 60,000; cattle feed 49,790 ‖ ; sawnwood 59,000 cu m; wood-based panels 26,000 cu m; plywood 20,000 cu m; shoes 383,895 pairs ‖ ; soft drinks 42,328 ‖ ; beer 13,975 ‖ ; cigarettes 402,000,000 ‖ . Construction: n.a. Energy production (consumption): electricity (kW-hr; 1982) 1,700,000 (1,700,000); hard coal (metric tons; 1982) none (1,000); crude petroleum (barrels; 1982) 124,610 (124,610); petroleum products (metric tons; 1982) none (713,000); fuelwood (cubic metres; 1982) 19,000 (19,000); bagasse (metric tons; 1982) 36,000 (36,000).
Land use (1981): forested 96.2%; meadows and pastures 0.1%; agricultural and under permanent cultivation 0.3%; other 3.4%.
Persons economically active (1982): total 83,461 (23.8%); female participation in the labour force, n.a.; (1980): unemployed 14,229 (14.6%).

Price and earnings indexes (1980 = 100)

	1978	1979	1980	1981	1982	1983	1984δ
Consumer price index	77.5	88.3	100.0	108.7	116.6	121.8	126.4
Earnings index	...	...	...	...	...	...	...

Gross national product (at current market prices; 1983): U.S.$1,271,900,000 (U.S.$3,624 per capita).

Origin of gross domestic product (current prices)

	1980 in value Sf'000,000	% of total value	labour force	% of labour force
Agriculture	165	10.1	7,600	7.8
Mining	273	16.8	5,580	5.7
Manufacturing	302	18.6	7,260	7.4
Construction	¶	¶	3,940	4.1
Trade	♀	♀	11,420	11.6
Public utilities	¶	¶	1,260	1.3
Transportation and communication	¶	¶	2,930	3.0
Finance	♀	♀	1,970	2.1
Pub. admin., defense	318	19.6	...	...
Services	568	34.9	38,040	38.9
Other	...	...	17,690	18.1
TOTAL	1,626	100.0	97,690	100.0

Household income and expenditure. Average household size (1980) 3.9; average annual income per household: n.a.; source of income: n.a.; expenditure□ (1968–69): food and drink 40.0%, household furniture and furnishings 12.3%, clothing and footwear 10.6%, transport and communications 9.5%, recreation 6.1%, fuel and power 5.5%.

Foreign trade

Balance of trade (current prices)

	1977	1978	1979	1980	1981	1982
Sf'000,000	−81.0	+11.4	+53.9	+114.4	−59.3	−49.9
% of total	6.8%	0.9%	3.5%	6.6%	3.4%	3.2%

Imports (1981): Sf905,000,000 (raw materials and semi-manufactured goods 39.0%; machinery and equipment 28.7%; refined petroleum products 19.9%). *Major import sources:* Caribbean countries 29%; United States 28%; The Netherlands 9%.
Exports (1981): Sf845,700,000 (alumina 55.9%; bauxite 13.3%; aluminum 10.3%; shrimp 7.6%; rice 7.5%; bananas 1.4%; plywood 1.2%). *Major export destinations:* United States 35%; The Netherlands 14%; Norway 13%; United Kingdom 7%.

Transport and communications

Transport. Railroads (1983): length 104 mi, 167 km; passengers, n.a.; cargo, n.a. Roads (1983): total length 19,000 mi, 30,600 km (paved 29%). Vehicles (1983): passenger cars 31,170; trucks and buses 12,850. Merchant marine (1983): vessels (100 gross tons and over) 25; total deadweight tonnage 19,187. Air transport (1980): passenger-mi 152,240,000, passenger-km 245,000,000; short ton-mi cargo 2,466,000, metric ton-km cargo 3,600,000; airports (1984) with scheduled flights 4.
Communications. Daily newspapers (1983): total number 1; total circulation 8,000; circulation per 1,000 population, 22.8. Radios (1983): total number of receivers 185,000 (1 per 2 persons). Television (1983): total number of receivers 42,500 (1 per 8.5 persons). Telephones (1982): 27,495 (1 per 13 persons).

Education and health

Education (1980–81)

	schools	teachers	students	student/ teacher ratio
Primary (age 6–12)	285	2,803	75,139	26.8
Secondary (age 13–17)	96	1,854	29,790	16.1
Voc., teacher tr.	4	148	1,275	8.6
Higher	2	155	2,353	15.2

College graduates: n.a. *Literacy* (1978): total population literate 112,000 (65.0%); males literate 44,800 (68.4%); females literate 67,200 (62.9%).
Health: physicians (1978) 214 (1 per 1,680 persons); hospital beds (1975) 2,250 (1 per 160.0 persons).
Food (1978–80): daily per capita caloric intake 2,468 (vegetable products 88.5%, animal products 11.5%); 109% of FAO recommended minimum requirement.

Military

Total active duty personnel: (1983): 5,000◊. *Military Expenditure as percent of GNP:* n.a.

*Also includes 3,654 persons (1.0%) of unknown age. †Excludes Hindu and Muslim ritual marriages. ‡1982 actual budget: revenue Sf517,000,000; expenditure Sf788,000,-000. §Includes Sf116,870,000 in capital revenue and grants. ‖1981. ¶Construction, public utilities, transportation, and communication are included with manufacturing. ♀Trade and finance are included with other. δJune 1984. □For Paramaribo and surroundings. ◊Includes all service branches.

Swaziland

Official name: Umbuso weSwatini (Kingdom of Swaziland).
Form of government: constitutional monarchy with two legislative houses (Senate [20]; House of Assembly [50]).
Chief of state: King*.
Head of government: Prime Minister.
Capitals: Mbabane (administrative); Lobamba (royal and legislative).
Official languages: siSwati; English.
Official religion: none.
Monetary unit: 1 lilangeni (plural emalangeni [E]) = 100 cents; valuation (Oct. 29, 1984) 1 U.S.$ = E1.79†; 1 £ = E2.16.

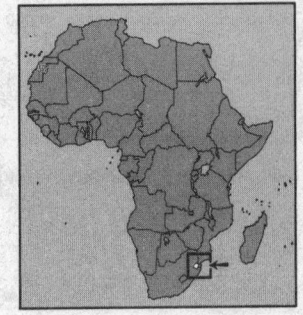

Area and population

Districts	Capitals	area sq mi	area sq km	population 1982 estimate‡
Hhohho	Mbabane	1,378	3,569	159,700
Lubombo	Siteki	2,296	5,947	121,900
Manzini	Manzini	1,571	4,068	169,200
Shiselweni	Nhlangano	1,459	3,780	134,400
TOTAL		6,704	17,364	585,200

Source: Official government figures.

Demography

Density (1984): persons per sq mi 92.9, persons per sq km 35.9.
Urban–rural (1980): urban 8.9%; rural 91.1%.
Sex distribution (1980): male 49.19%; female 50.81%.
Age breakdown (1980): under 15, 45.2%; 15–29, 26.1%; 30–44, 15.1%; 45–59, 8.8%; 60–74, 4.1%; 75 and over 0.7%.
Population projection: (1990) 754,000; (2000) 1,020,000.
Doubling time: 24 years.
Ethnic composition (1976): African 97.7%; European 1.5%; other 0.8%.
Religious affiliation (1980): Christian 77%; animist 23%.
Major cities (1982 est.): Mbabane 33,000; Manzini 14,000; Piggs Peak 3,000.

Vital statistics

Birth rate per 1,000 population (1980–85): 45.6 (world avg. 27.5); legitimate, n.a.; illegitimate, n.a.
Death rate per 1,000 population (1980–85): 17.1 (world avg. 10.6).
Natural increase rate per 1,000 population (1980–85): 28.5 (world avg. 16.9).
Total fertility rate (avg. births per childbearing woman; 1980–85): 6.5.
Marriage rate per 1,000 population: n.a.
Divorce rate per 1,000 population: n.a.
Infant mortality rate per 1,000 live births (1980–85): 140.1.
Life expectancy at birth (1980–85): male 46.8 years; female 50.0 years.
Major causes of death per 100,000 population (1970): tuberculosis of the respiratory system 29.5; gastroenteritis 18.3; malnutrition, unspecified 11.7.

National economy

Budget (1981). Revenue: E139,740,000§ (customs duties 44.8%; income tax 14.2%; corporate tax 12.9%; export duties 7.9%; property tax 4.4%). Expenditures: E163,640,000 (education 23.7%; defense 14.4%; general public services 12.8%; agriculture, forestry, fishing 11.0%; community amenities 10.4%; health 5.5%; roads 5.1%).
Public debt (external, outstanding; 1982): U.S.$204,000,000.
Tourism (1981): receipts from visitors U.S.$11,000,000; expenditures by nationals abroad U.S.$28,000,000.
Production (metric tons except as noted). Agriculture, forestry, fishing (1982): sugarcane 3,300,000, fruit excluding melons 76,000, corn (maize) 63,000, seed cotton 32,000, pineapples 28,000, lint cotton 11,000, potatoes 6,000, rice 5,000, sorghum 2,000; livestock (number of live animals) 675,000 cattle; 330,000 goats; 40,000 sheep, 22,000 pigs, 620,000 chickens; roundwood 2,223,000 cu m; fish catch 44. Mining and quarrying (1982): asbestos 30,000. Manufacturing (producers' prices in E; 1979) food products and beverages 111,246,000; wood products, furniture, fixtures 50,067,000; textiles 9,873,000; paper products 4,065,000. Construction (value in E; 1981): residential ‖ 2,144,000; nonresidential 1,417,000. Energy production (consumption): electricity, n.a. (n.a.); coal (metric tons; 1982) 90,720 (n.a.); crude petroleum, n.a. (n.a.); natural gas, n.a. (n.a.).
Persons economically active (1982): total 266,000 (45.5%); female participation in the labour force, n.a.; unemployed, n.a.

Price and earnings indexes (1980 = 100)

	1978	1979	1980	1981	1982	1983	1984
Consumer price index	72.3	84.3	100.0	120.0	133.0	155.4	160.4
Monthly earnings index	112.8	133.2	100.0	143.9	...	...	...

Household income and expenditure. Average household size (1980) 5.0; average annual income per household: n.a.; source of income: n.a.; expenditure: n.a.
Land use (1981): forested 5.8%; meadows and pastures 64.0%; agricultural and under permanent cultivation 11.0%; other 19.2%.
Gross national product (at current market prices; 1981): U.S.$480,000,000 (U.S.$850 per capita).

Origin of gross domestic product (current prices)

	1980 in value E'000,000	% of total value	labour force¶	% of labour force
Agriculture	94	20.2	29,960	39.9
Mining	14	3.0	2,590	3.4
Manufacturing	80	17.2	9,250	12.3
Construction	16	3.4	6,080	8.1
Trade	36	7.7	5,870	7.8
Public utilities	4	0.9	1,220	1.6
Transportation and communication	21	4.5	3,320	4.4
Finance	⚲	⚲	2,330	3.1
Services	⚲	⚲	14,510	19.3
Other	200⚲	43.0⚲	---	---
TOTAL	465	100.0⊡	75,130	100.0⊡

Foreign trade

Balance of trade (current prices)

E'000,000	1977	1978	1979	1980	1981	1982
	−48.5	−98.0	−162.8	−177.6	−172.7	−193.0
% of total	14.2%	22.1%	28.6%	23.7%	21.7%	22.6%

Imports (1982): E522,726,000 (machinery and transport equipment 23.1%, manufactured goods 22.1%, mineral fuels and lubricants 17.7%, food and live animals 7.5%, chemicals 6.7%). *Major import source△:* South Africa 94%.
Exports (1982): E329,710,000 (sugar 31.7%, chemicals 19.4%, wood pulp 14.1%, canned fruits 5.5%, citrus fruits 4.7%, electronic equipment 4.7%, asbestos 4.5%). *Major export destinations△:* South Africa 30%; United Kingdom 20%.

Transport and communications

Transport. Railroads (1982): route length 194 mi, 312 km; passengers, n.a.; short ton-mi cargo 94,400,000, metric ton-km cargo 137,800,000; Roads (1982): total length 1,692 mi, 2,723 km (paved 19%). Vehicles (1982): passenger cars 21,338; trucks and buses 8,376. Merchant marine: vessels (100 gross tons and over) n.a.; total deadweight tonnage, n.a. Air transport (1980): passenger-mi 18,640,000, passenger-km 30,000,000; short ton-mi cargo 685,000, metric ton-km cargo 1,000,000; airport (1984) with scheduled flights 1.
Communications. Daily newspapers (1983): total number 2; circulation, n.a. Radios (1983): total number of receivers 84,000 (1 per 7.2 persons). Television (1983): total number of receivers 6,500 (1 per 93 persons). Telephones (1982): 15,357 (1 per 38 persons).

Education and health

Education (1981)

	schools	teachers	students	student/ teacher ratio
Primary (age 6–13)	470	3,586	119,913	33.4
Secondary (age 14–18)	86	1,433	24,826	17.3
Voc., teacher tr.	3	224	1,162	5.2
Higher	1	108	979	9.1

College graduates per 100,000 population (students graduating; 1980): 146.
Literacy (1976): total population literate 107,027 (41.5%); males literate 55,865 (45.5%); females literate 51,162 (37.9%).
Health (1980): physicians 41 (1 per 13,352 persons); hospital beds 1,470 (1 per 372 persons).
Food (1978–80): daily per capita caloric intake 2,499 (vegetable products 86.4%, animal products 13.6%); 108% of FAO recommended minimum requirement.

Military

Total active duty personnel (1983): 2,657. *Military expenditure as percent of GNP* (1982): 5.5% (world 6.0%); per capita expenditure U.S.$46.

*Queen acting as Regent until successor comes of age. †The Lilangeni is at par with the South African rand. ‡De facto African population projection only. §Includes E5,050,000 in grants and capital revenue. ‖ Includes hotels, hostels, etc. ¶Employed persons only. ⚲Finance and services included with other. ⊿Imputed bank service charges. ⊡Detail does not add to total given because of rounding. ◇April. △Estimated.

Sweden

Official name: Konungariket Sverige (Kingdom of Sweden).
Form of government: constitutional monarchy and parliamentary state with one legislative house (Parliament [349]).
Chief of state: King.
Head of government: Prime Minister.
Capital: Stockholm.
Official language: Swedish.
Official religion: Lutheran.
Monetary unit: 1 Swedish krona (SKr) = 100 ore; valuation (Oct. 29, 1984) 1 U.S.$ = SKr8.72; 1 £ = SKr10.52.

Area and population

Counties	Capitals	area* sq mi	area* sq km	population 1984 estimate
Älvsborg	Vänersborg	4,400	11,395	425,500
Blekinge	Karlskrona	1,136	2,941	151,900
Gävleborg	Gävle	7,024	18,191	291,500
Göteborg och Bohus	Göteborg	1,985	5,141	709,700
Gotland	Visby	1,212	3,140	55,900
Halland	Halmstad	2,106	5,454	236,300
Jämtland	Östersund	19,273	49,916	134,900
Jönköping	Jönköping	3,839	9,944	301,000
Kalmar	Kalmar	4,311	11,166	240,100
Kopparberg	Falun	10,913	28,264	285,600
Kristianstad	Kristianstad	2,351	6,089	280,400
Kronoberg	Växjö	3,263	8,452	174,300
Malmöhus	Malmö	1,907	4,939	745,400
Norrbotten	Luleå	38,193	98,919	264,500
Örebro	Örebro	3,288	8,515	272,100
Östergötland	Linköping	4,081	10,569	392,300
Skaraborg	Mariestad	3,065	7,938	270,400
Södermanland	Nyköping	2,340	6,061	251,000
Stockholm	Stockholm	2,505	6,488	1,551,200
Uppsala	Uppsala	2,698	6,989	248,100
Värmland	Karlstad	6,788	17,582	281,200
Västerbotten	Umeå	21,390	55,401	245,300
Västernorrland	Härnösand	8,383	21,711	264,800
Västmanland	Västerås	2,433	6,302	257,000
TOTAL		158,884	411,506†	8,330,600†

Source: Official government figures.

Demography

Density (1984): persons per sq mi 52.4, persons per sq km 20.2.
Urban–rural (1980): urban 87.2%; rural 12.8%.
Sex distribution (1984): male 49.41%; female 50.59%.
Age breakdown (1983): under 15, 18.7%; 15–29, 20.7%; 30–44, 21.7%; 45–59, 16.2%; 60–74, 15.8%; 75 and over, 6.9%.
Population projection: (1990) 8,344,500; (2000) 8,328,642.
Doubling time: During the intercensal period 1975–80 the annual growth rate was 0.3%; since 1981, however, the population has been decreasing.
Ethnic composition (1983): Swedish 95.1%; Finnish 1.9%; Yugoslav 0.5%; other 2.5%.
Religious affiliation (1980): Protestant 69.9%; nonreligious or atheist 26.7%; Roman Catholic 1.3%; other 2.1%.
Major cities (1983 est.): Stockholm 649,686; Göteborg 425,875; Malmö 230,381; Uppsala 149,300; Norrköping 118,236.

Vital statistics

Birth rate per 1,000 population (1983): 11.0 (world avg. 28.0); (1982) legitimate 58.0%, illegitimate 42.0%.
Death rate per 1,000 population (1983): 10.9 (world avg. 11.0).
Natural increase rate per 1,000 population (1983): 0.1 (world avg. 17.0).
Total fertility rate (avg. births per childbearing woman; 1982): 1.6.
Marriage rate per 1,000 population (1983): 4.3.
Divorce rate per 1,000 population (1983): 2.5.
Infant mortality rate per 1,000 live births (1982): 6.8.
Life expectancy at birth (1982): male 73.4 years; female 79.4 years.
Major causes of death per 100,000 population (1981): heart disease 453.9; malignant neoplasms (cancers) 230.8; cerebrovascular disease 115.1.

National economy

Budget (1983–84). Revenue: SKr221,165,000,000 (income tax and capital gains 22.1%, value added tax 21.9%, social security contributions 21.3%, nontax revenue 10.4%). Expenditures: SKr298,177,000,000 (health and social affairs 23.6%, interest on national debt 20.3%, education and culture 11.9%, defense 7.5%).
Public debt (1984): U.S.$56,508,000,000.
Tourism (1982): receipts from visitors U.S.$1,006,050,955; expenditures by nationals abroad U.S.$1,874,363,057.
Production (metric tons except as noted). Agriculture, forestry, fishing (1982): sugar beets 2,431,000, barley 2,378,000, oats 1,663,000, wheat 1,490,000; livestock (number of live animals) 1.937,551 cattle, 2,600,587 pigs, 8,392,476 fowls and chickens; coniferous timber 22,000,000 cu m; herring and Baltic herring (1983) 129,800, industrial fish (1983) 50,500. Mining and quarrying (1983): iron ore 13,212,000; granite and gneiss 9,222,000‡. Manufacturing (1983): crude and commercial steel 8,246,000; wood pulp (excluding dissolving pulp) 6,392,000; paper and paperboard 6,350,000; cement 2,231,000; mechanical pulp 1,964,000; automobiles 281,000 vehicles.

Construction (1982): 3,759 dwellings. Energy production (consumption): electricity (kW-hr; 1983) 105,879,000,000 (110,848,000,000); coal (metric tons; 1982) 13,000 (2,468,00); crude petroleum (barrels; 1982) 102,000 (95,730,000); petroleum products (metric tons; 1982) 12,041,000 (18,289,000); natural gas, n.a. (n.a.)
Gross national product (at current market prices; 1983): U.S.$88,718,000,000 (U.S.$10,650 per capita).

Origin of gross domestic product (current prices)

	1981 in value SKr'000,000	% of total value	labour force	% of labour force
Agriculture	18,077	3.2	237,000	5.5
Mining	2,261	0.4	14,000	0.3
Manufacturing	120,672	21.2	984,000	22.7
Construction	36,948	6.5	288,000	6.6
Trade	59,209	10.4	583,000	13.5
Public utilities	15,335	2.7	37,000	0.9
Transportation and communication	34,364	6.0	293,000	6.7
Finance	66,041	11.6	282,000	6.5
Pub. admin., defense	124,972	22.0		
Services	22,373	3.9	1,508,000	34.9
Other	68,968	12.1	109,000	2.5
TOTAL	569,220	100.0	4,335,000	100.0†

Persons economically active (1983): total 4,375,000 (52.5%); female participation in labour force 2,075,000 (47.4%); unemployed 151,000 (3.5%).

Price and earnings indexes (1980 = 100)

	1978	1979	1980	1981	1982	1983	1984§
Consumer price index	82.1	87.9	100.0	112.1	121.7	132.6	142.3
Monthly earnings index	82.6	90.5	100.0	110.2	118.2	127.4	138.5

Household income and expenditure. Average household size (1980) 2.4; income per household (1981) SKr82,500 (U.S.$15,165); source of income (1981): wages and salaries 47.5%, transfer payments 21.4%, other 31.1%; expenditure (1980): food 24.2%, housing 19.1%, transportation 13.2%, recreation 9.9%, clothing and footwear 7.4%, other 26.2%.
Land use (1981): forested 64.2%; meadows and pastures 1.7%; agricultural and under permanent cultivation 7.2%; other 26.9%.

Foreign trade

Balance of trade (current prices)

	1978	1979	1980	1981	1982	1983
SKr'000,000	+5,460	−4,750	−10,700	−1,160	−5,800	+10,100
% of total	2.9%	2.0%	3.9%	0.4%	1.7%	2.5%

Imports (1983): SKr200,320,000,000 (mineral fuels, lubricants, and related materials 23.0%; nonelectrical machinery 14.6%; chemicals 9.5%; transport equipment 7.7%; electrical machinery 7.1%; food, beverages, and tobacco 6.6%; clothing and footwear 4.4%). *Major import sources:* W. Germany 17.1%; U.K. 13.9%; U.S. 8.3%; Norway 7.5%.
Exports (1983): SKr210,420,000,000 (nonelectrical machinery 17.3%; transport equipment 16.0%; paper and paperboard 9.2%; electrical machinery 7.5%; chemicals 6.1%; iron and steel 5.9%). *Major export destinations:* W. Germany 11.4%; U.K. 10.8%; Norway 10.1%; U.S. 8.8%; Denmark 8.4%.

Transport and communications

Transport. Railroads (1983): length ‖ 7,682 mi, 12,362 km; passenger-mi 4,014,000,000, passenger-km 6,460,000,000; short ton-mi cargo 10,240,000,000, metric ton-km cargo 14,951,000,000. Roads (1983): total length 80,590 mi, 129,698 km (paved 67%). Vehicles (1983): passenger cars 3,006,800; trucks and buses 215,200. Merchant marine (1983): vessels (100 gross tons and over) 674; total deadweight tonnage 5,056,492. Air transport (1983): passenger-mi 3,652,000,000, passenger-km 5,877,000,000; short ton-mi cargo 129,000,000, metric ton-km cargo 189,000,000; airports (1984) with scheduled flights 35.
Communications. Daily newspapers (1982): total number 163; total circulation 4,820,000; circulation per 1,000 population 579. Radios (1983): total, n.a. Television (1983): 3,245,000 (1 per 2.6 persons). Telephones (1982): 7,132,000 (1 per 1.2 persons).

Education and health

Education (1982)

	schools	teachers	students	student/ teacher ratio
Primary (age 7–12)	4,928¶	...	658,127	...
Secondary (age 13–18)	...	...	607,199	...
Higher	...	...	216,412	...

College graduates per 100,000 population (students graduating; 1979): 491.
Literacy (1984): virtually 100%.
Health: physicians (1981) 17,400 (1 per 478 persons); hospital beds (1980) 134,187 (1 per 62 persons).
Food (1978–80): daily per capita caloric intake 3,157 (vegetable products 57.5%, animal products 42.5%); 117% of FAO recommended minimum.

Military

Total active duty personnel (1983): 68,200 (army 71.3%; navy 14.7%; air force 14.0%). *Military expenditure as percent of GNP* (1983): 3.3% (world 6.0%); per capita expenditure U.S.$350.

*Excludes water area. †Detail does not add to total given because of rounding. ‡1981. §Second quarter. ‖1982. ¶Of whom about 1,000 pupils in compulsory education at first stage of secondary.

Switzerland

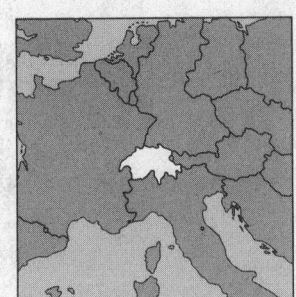

Official name: Confédération
Suisse (French); Schweizerische
Eidgenossenschaft (German);
Confederazione Svizzera (Italian)
(Swiss Confederation).
Form of government: federal republic
with two legislative houses (Council of
States [46]; National Council [200]).
Head of state and government:
President.
Capital: Bern.
Official languages: French; German;
Italian.
Official religion: none.
Monetary unit: 1 Swiss Franc
(SwF) = 100 centimes; valuation (Oct.
29, 1984) 1 U.S.$ = SwF2.52;
1 £ = SwF3.04.

Area and population

Cantons	Capitals	area sq mi	area sq km	population 1983 estimate
Aargau	Aarau	542	1,405	459,000
Appenzell Ausser-Rhoden*	Herisau	94	243	48,000
Appenzell Inner-Rhoden*	Appenzell	66	172	13,000
Basel-Landschaft*	Liestal	165	428	221,000
Basel-Stadt*	Basel	14	37	201,000
Bern	Bern	2,335	6,049	919,000
Fribourg	Fribourg	645	1,670	188,000
Genève	Geneva	109	282	356,000
Glarus	Glarus	264	684	36,000
Graubünden	Chur	2,744	7,106	171,000
Jura	Delémont	323	837	64,000
Luzern	Luzern	576	1,492	299,000
Neuchâtel	Neuchâtel	308	797	156,000
Nidwalden*	Stans	107	276	29,000
Obwalden*	Sarnen	189	491	27,000
Sankt Gallen	Sankt Gallen	778	2,014	395,000
Schaffhausen	Schaffhausen	115	298	70,000
Schwyz	Schwyz	351	908	99,000
Solothurn	Solothurn	305	791	218,000
Thurgau	Frauenfeld	391	1,013	187,000
Ticino	Bellinzona	1,085	2,811	271,000
Uri	Altdorf	416	1,076	34,000
Valais	Sion	2,018	5,226	224,000
Vaud	Lausanne	1,243	3,219	533,000
Zug	Zug	92	239	77,000
Zürich	Zürich	668	1,729	1,128,000
TOTAL		15,943	41,293	6,423,000

Source: Official government figures.

Demography

Density (1984): persons per sq mi 403.7, persons per sq km 155.9.
Urban–rural (1980): urban 57.1%; rural 42.9%.
Sex distribution (1983): male 48.71%; female 51.29%.
Age breakdown (1983): under 15, 18.5%; 15–29, 23.2%; 30–44, 22.3%; 45–59,
17.4%; 60–74, 12.8%; 75 and over, 5.8%.
Population projection: (1990) 6,493,000; (2000) 6,461,000.
Doubling time: During 1970–80, the annual growth rate was 0.2%; since the
early 1980s, however, the population has been decreasing.
Ethnic composition (1980): German 65.0%; French 18.4%; Italian 9.8%; Ro-
mansch 0.8%; other 6.0%.
Religious affiliation (1980): Roman Catholic 47.6%; Protestant 44.3%; Jewish
0.3%; other 7.8%.
Major cities (1983 est.): Zürich 364,000; Basel 180,000; Geneva 159,000;
Bern 144,000; Lausanne 127,000.

Vital statistics

Birth rate per 1,000 population (1983): 11.4 (world avg. 29.0); (1982) legiti-
mate 94.5%, illegitimate 5.5%.
Death rate per 1,000 population (1983): 9.3 (world avg. 11.0).
Natural increase rate per 1,000 population (1983): 2.1 (world avg. 18.0).
Total fertility rate (avg. births per childbearing woman; 1980–85): 1.5.
Marriage rate per 1,000 population (1983): 5.8.
Divorce rate per 1,000 population (1982): 1.8.
Infant mortality rate per 1,000 live births (1982): 7.7.
Life expectancy at birth (1980–85): male 72.1 years; female 78.1 years.
Major causes of death per 100,000 population (1982): circulatory system
diseases 393.2; malignant neoplasms 224.8; nervous system diseases 57.8.

National economy

Budget (1981). Revenue: SwF17,401,500,000 (taxes on consumption 55.6%,
of which turnover tax 30.3%, customs duties 18.6%; taxes on income
and wealth 34.9%). Expenditures: SwF17,574,700,000 (defense 21.4%; social
welfare 20.5%; communications and energy 15.9%; agriculture 8.9%).
Public debt (external, outstanding): none.
Tourism (1982): receipts from visitors U.S.$3,015,000,000; expenditures by
nationals abroad U.S.$2,216,000,000.
Production (metric tons except as noted). Agriculture, forestry, fishing
(1982): potatoes 1,050,000, sugar beets 836,000, apples 450,000, wheat 423,-
000; livestock (number of live animals) 2,093,000 pigs, 1,945,000 cattle,
5,961,000 chickens; roundwood 4,392,000 cu m; fish catch 3,859. Mining
and quarrying (1982): salt 430,000; gypsum 80,000. Manufacturing (1982):
cement 4,099,874; crude steel 950,000; salt 361,964; aluminum 75,256; tex-

tiles 30,899; woolen and blended yarn 15,467; cheese 125,000; refined sugar
113,022; chocolate 76,605. Construction (buildings completed; 1980): residential 20,806; nonresidential 8,024. Energy production (consumption)†:
electricity (kW-hr; 1982) 52,285,000,000 (41,458,000,000); coal (metric tons;
1982) none (564,000); crude petroleum (barrels; 1982) none (29,071,000);
petroleum products (metric tons; 1982) 4,128,000 (10,198,000); natural gas
(cu m; 1982) none (1,177,665,500).
Gross national product (at current market prices; 1983): U.S.$97,570,000,000
(U.S.$14,879 per capita).

Origin of gross domestic product (current prices)

	1983 in value SwF'000	1983 % of total value	1982 labour force	1982 % of labour force
Agriculture	...	...	213,600	7.0
Mining	...	...	168,600	5.6
Manufacturing	...	...	780,900	25.7
Construction	...	...	194,700	6.4
Trade	...	...	591,800	19.5
Public utilities	...	...	29,800	1.0
Transp. and commun.	...	...	188,800	6.2
Finance	...	...	141,000	4.7
Pub. admin., defense	...	...	230,000	7.6
Services	...	...	482,200	15.9
Other	...	...	11,800	0.4
TOTAL	202,700,000	100.0	3,033,200	100.0

Persons economically active (1982): total 3,033,200 (47.5%); female participation in the labour force 1,070,500 (35.3%); unemployed 6,875 (0.2%).

Price and earnings indexes (1980 = 100)

	1978	1979	1980	1981	1982	1983	1984
Consumer price index	92.8	96.1	100.0	106.5	112.5	115.9	119.3‡
Hourly earnings index	91.8	94.6	100.0	102.4	109.0	113.1	...

Household income and expenditure. Average household size (1982) 3.5; average income per household SwF61,000 (U.S.$30,045); source of income:
wages 86.0%, other 14.0%; expenditure (1982): recreation and education
12.3%, food 11.3%, transportation 9.6%, clothing and footwear 5.4%.
Land use (1981): forested 26.4%; meadows and pastures 40.5%; agricultural
and under permanent cultivation 10.3%; other 22.8%.

Foreign trade

Balance of trade (current prices)

	1977	1978	1979	1980	1981	1982
SwF'000,000	−867	−521	−4,706	−11,251	−7,272	−5,401
% of total	1.0%	6.2%	5.1%	10.2%	6.4%	4.9%

Imports (1982): SwF58,059,700,000 (road vehicles 19.1%; chemicals and
products 11.4%; refined petroleum 7.1%; articles of precious metal and
jewelry 6.9%). *Major import sources:* West Germany 29.7%; France 11.5%;
Italy 9.9%; U.S. 7.2%; U.K. 5.5%; The Netherlands 4.3%.
Exports (1982): SwF52,658,700,000 (machinery and transport equipment
32.5%, of which watches 6.6%; articles of precious metal and jewelry 8.8%;
medicinal and pharmaceutical products 8.0%; textile yarn, fabrics, and
related products 7.2%). *Major export destinations:* West Germany 18.2%;
France 9.0%; United States 7.8%; Italy 7.5%; United Kingdom 6.2%.

Transport and communications

Transport. Railroads (1983): length§ 1,777 mi, 2,860 km; passenger-mi
5,615,000,000, passenger-km 9,036,000,000; short ton-mi cargo 4,389,000,-
000, metric ton-km cargo 6,408,000,000 ‖. Roads (1983): total length 42,740
mi, 68,784 km. Vehicles (1983): passenger cars 2,520,610; trucks and buses
201,175. Merchant marine (1983): vessels (100 gross tons and over) 34; total
deadweight tonnage 478,843. Air transport (1983): passenger-mi 7,582,597,-
000, passenger-km 12,203,030,000; short ton-mi cargo 369,803,000, metric
ton-km cargo 539,903,000; airports (1984) with scheduled flights 5.
Communications. Daily newspapers (1983): total number 100; total circulation 3,889,109; circulation per 1,000 population 605. Radios (1983): receivers 2,357,541 (1 per 2.7 persons). Television (1983): receivers 2,077,809
(1 per 3.1 persons). Telephones (1982): 4,780,760 (1 per 1.3 persons).

Education and health

Education (1983–84)

	schools	teachers	students	student/ teacher ratio
Primary (age 6–11)	...	...	431,800	...
Secondary (age 11–18)	...	...	408,700	...
Voc., teacher tr.	...	...	251,400	...
Higher	...	...	95,600	...

College graduates per 100,000 population aged 20 to 24 (students graduating;
1980): 1,390. *Literacy:* virtually 100.0%.
Health (1981): physicians 7,799 (1 per 816 persons); hospital beds, n.a.
Food (1978–80): daily per capita caloric intake 3,525 (vegetable products
61.7%, animal products 38.3%); 131% of FAO recommended minimum.

Military

Total active duty personnel¶ (1983): 625,000 (army 92.8%; air force 7.2%).
Military expenditure as percent of GNP (1982): 2.0% (world 6.0%); per capita
expenditure U.S.$315.

*Demicanton; functions as a full canton and has the same legal prerogatives as a full
canton. †Figures include Liechtenstein. ‡September. §1981. ‖ Federal railway only.
¶Mobilized personnel.

Syria

Official name: al-Jumhūrīyah al-'Arabīyah as-Sūrīyah (Syrian Arab Republic).
Form of government: unitary multiparty* republic with one legislative house (People's Council [195]).
Chief of state: President.
Head of government: Prime Minister.
Capital: Damascus.
Official language: Arabic.
Official religion: none.
Monetary unit: 1 Syrian Pound (LS) = 100 piastres; valuation (Oct. 29, 1984) 1 U.S.$ = LS3.90; 1£ = LS4.71.

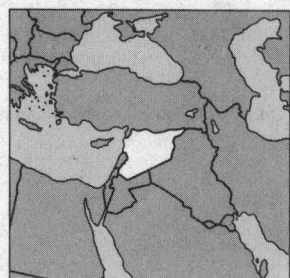

Area and population

Governorates	Capitals	area sq mi	area sq km	population 1982 estimate
al-Ḥasakah	al-Ḥasakah	9,009	23,334	668,000
al-Lādhiqīyah	Latakia	887	2,297	569,000
al-Qunayţirah	al-Qunayţirah	719	1,861	27,000
ar-Raqqah	ar-Raqqā'	7,574	19,616	358,000
as-Suwaydā'	as-Suwaydā'	2,143	5,550	204,000
Dar'ā	Dar'ā	1,440	3,730	375,000
Dayr az-Zawr	Dayr az-Zawr	12,765	33,060	419,000
Dimashq	al-Iarmouk	6,962	18,032	952,000
Ḥalab	Aleppo	7,143	18,500	1,928,000
Ḥamāh	Ḥamāh	3,430	8,883	756,000
Ḥimṣ	Homs	16,302	42,223	837,000
Idlib	Idlib	2,354	6,097	597,000
Tartous	Tartous	730	1,892	456,000
Municipality				
Dimashq	Damascus	41	105	1,129,000
TOTAL		71,498	185,180	9,295,000

Source: Official government sources.

Demography

Density (1984): persons per sq mi 138.9, persons per sq km 53.6.
Urban-rural (1981): urban 47.1%; rural 52.9%.
Sex distribution (1984): male 51.08%; female 48.92%.
Age breakdown (1981): under 15, 47.9%; 15–29, 27.3%; 30–44, 12.4%; 45–59, 7.9%; 60–74, 3.5%; 75 and over, 1.0%.
Population projection: (1990) 12,774,000; (2000) 17,085,000.
Doubling time: 19 years.
Ethnic composition (1981): Arab 88.8%; Kurdish 6.3%; other 4.9%.
Religious affiliation (1980): Muslim 89.6%; Christian 8.9%; other 1.5%.
Major cities (1984 est.): Damascus 1,178,000; Aleppo 1,109,100; Homs 406,300; Latakia 222,500; Ḥamāh 190,000.

Vital statistics

Birth rate per 1,000 population (1983): 43.6 (world avg. 29.0).
Death rate per 1,000 population (1983): 5.3 (world avg. 11.0).
Natural increase rate per 1,000 population (1983): 38.3 (world avg. 18.0).
Total fertility rate (avg. births per childbearing woman; 1980–85): 7.2.
Marriage rate per 1,000 population (1982): 8.0†.
Divorce rate per 1,000 population (1982): 0.6†.
Infant mortality rate per 1,000 live births (1980–85): 57.0.
Life expectancy at birth (1980–85): male 64.9 years; female 67.6 years.
Major causes of death per 100,000 population (1981): signs, symptoms, and other ill-defined conditions 207.3; diseases of the circulatory system 60.7; infectious and parasitic diseases 15.1.

National economy

Budget (1981). Revenue: LS21,203,000,000 (nontax revenue 42.5%, grants 30.0%, import duties 9.4%, income tax 8.7%). Expenditures: LS25,360,000,000 (national security 37.7%, economic services 30.9%, social security and welfare 8.2%, education 7.1%).
Public debt (external, outstanding; 1982): U.S.$2,676,000,000.
Tourism (1982): receipts from visitors U.S.$150,000,000; expenditures by nationals abroad, n.a.
Production (metric tons except as noted). Agriculture and fishing (1982): wheat 1,556,000, watermelons 869,000, sugar beets 860,300, tomatoes 790,000, barley 661,000, milk 599,000, olives 471,000, grapes 423,000, cotton 422,200, other melons 285,000, cucumbers 282,000, potatoes 279,000, alfalfa 206,200; livestock (number of live animals) 810,000 cattle; fish catch 3,050. Mining and quarrying (1982): phosphate 1,461,000; salt 102,000; natural asphalt 71,000; sands and gravel 15,903,000 cu m. Manufacturing (1982): cement 2,850,000; flour 887,000; sugar 183,000; ginned cotton 127,000; fertilizers 117,000; olive and vegetable oils 115,000; silk, cotton, and wool yarn and textiles 69,750; rolled iron bars 66,741; soap and detergent 64,242; tobacco 11,000; alcoholic beverages 57,000,000 litres; refrigerators 147,734 units. Construction (1981): residential 3,893,000 sq m; nonresidential 515,000 sq m. Energy production (consumption): electricity (kW-hr; 1982) 5,737,000,000 (5,737,000,000); coal (metric tons; 1982) none (5,000); crude petroleum (barrels; 1983) 60,225,000 (63,154,000‡); petroleum products (metric tons; 1982) 7,890,000 (6,214,000); natural gas (cu m; 1982) 50,513,000 (50,513,000).

Gross national product (at current market prices; 1981): U.S.$15,368,000,000 (U.S.$1,700 per capita).

Origin of gross domestic product (current prices of 1980)

	1982 in value LS'000,000	1982 % of total value	1981 labour force	1981 % of labour force
Agriculture	10,146	16.6	576,000	31.5
Mining	} 10,129	} 16.6	13,000	0.7
Manufacturing			275,000	15.0
Public utilities			17,000	0.9
Construction	3,885	6.4	203,000	11.1
Trade	16,012	26.2	185,000	10.1
Transportation and communication	4,244	7.0	114,000	6.2
Finance	3,646	6.0	...	...
Pub. admin., services	12,980	21.3	365,000	20.0
Other	...	...	80,000§	4.4§
TOTAL	61,042	100.0 ‖	1,828,000	100.0 ‖

Persons economically active (1983): total 2,112,708 (22.4%); female participation in the labour force 257,427 (12.2%); unemployed 107,322 (5.1%).

Price and earnings indexes (1980 = 100)

	1976	1977	1978	1979	1980	1981	1982
Consumer price index	68.3	76.4	80.2	84.1	100.0	118.4	135.3
Monthly earnings index	...	...	...	...	...	...	...

Average household size (1981): 6.2.
Land use (1982): steppe and pasture 44.9%; cultivable 33.5%, of which cultivated 31.3%; forested 2.6%; uncultivable 19.0%.

Foreign trade

Balance of trade (current prices)

	1978	1979	1980	1981	1982	1983
LS'000,000	−4,741	−5,590	−6,647	−9,977	−6,569	−10,281
% of total	36.3%	30.2%	28.7%	37.7%	29.2%	40.5%

Imports (1983): LS17,828,600,000 (mineral fuels and related materials 26.5%; machinery and transport equipment 25.2%; foods, beverages, and tobacco 15.5%; chemical and pharmaceutical products 14.3%; metals and metal manufactures 5.9%). *Major import sources:* Iran 26.1%; West Germany 8.5%; Belgium 7.6%; Italy 7.3%; Japan 6.7%.
Exports (1983): LS7,547,500,000 (petroleum and petroleum products 70.5%; textile, wearing apparel, and leather 20.4%; cereals and cereal preparations 5.3%; sand and stone 1.4%). *Major export destinations:* Romania 29.7%; Italy 16.1%; U.S.S.R. 10.7%; France 10.2%; Iran 5.3%.

Transport and communications

Transport. Railroads (1982): length 1,296 mi, 2,086 km; passenger-mi 256,397,000, passenger-km 412,631,000; short ton-mi cargo 485,000,000, metric ton-km cargo 708,000,000. Roads (1980): total length 11,709 mi, 18,844 km (paved 90%). Vehicles (1982): passenger cars 79,141; trucks and buses 113,440. Merchant marine (1983): vessels (100 gross tons and over) 52; total deadweight tonnage 70,305. Air transport¶ (1983): passenger-mi 690,317, passenger-km 1,110,960; short ton-mi cargo 6,363,000, metric ton-km cargo 9,290,000; airports (1982) with scheduled flights 7.
Communications. Daily newspapers (1983): total number 9; total circulation 114,400⁹; circulation per 1,000 population 79⁹. Radios (1983): total number of receivers 1,800,000 (1 per 5.2 persons). Television (1983): total number of receivers 405,000 (1 per 23.7 persons). Telephones (1982): 471,127 (1 per 19.7 persons).

Education and health

Education (1981–82)

	schools	teachers	students	student/ teacher ratio
Primary (age 6–11)	8,003	58,244	1,610,548	27.7
Secondary (age 12–18)	1,395	32,274	587,047	18.2
Voc., teacher tr.	148	5,424	46,193	8.5
Higher	24	...	119,341	...

*Literacy*δ (1983): total population literate 4,009,723 (63.3%); males literate 2,523,648 (78.4%); females literate 1,486,075 (47.7%).
Health (1982): physicians 4,633 (1 per 2,006 persons); hospital beds 10,770 (1 per 863 persons).
Food (1978–80): daily per capita caloric intake 2,863 (vegetable products 87.0%, animal products 13.0%); 115% of FAO recommended minimum requirement.

Military

Total active duty personnel (1983): 222,500 (army 76.4%; navy 1.1%; air force 22.5%). *Military expenditure as percent of GNP* (1982): 14.4% (world 6.0%); per capita expenditure U.S.$272.

*Parties other than the Communist Party form a coalition (National Progressive Front). †Syrian Arabs only. ‡1982. §First-time job seekers. ‖ Detail does not add to total given because of rounding. ¶National airline, scheduled services only. ⁹1981. δ10 years and older.

Taiwan

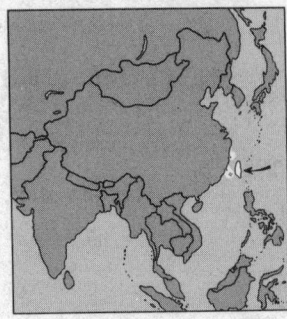

Official name: Chung-hua Min-kuo (Republic of China).
Form of government: unitary republic with a National Assembly (1,173).
Chief of state: President.
Head of government: Premier.
Capital: Taipei.
Official language: Mandarin Chinese.
Official religion: none.
Monetary unit: 1 New Taiwan dollar (NT$) = 100 cents; valuation (Oct. 29, 1984) 1 U.S.$ = NT$39.13; 1£ = NT$47.23.

Area and population

Counties	Capitals	area sq mi	area sq km	population 1984 estimate
Chang-hua	Chang-hua	415	1,074	1,204,000
Chia-i	Chia-i	706	1,829	575,000
Hsin-chu	Hsin-chu	573	1,483	366,000
Hua-lien	Hua-lien	1,787	4,629	361,000
I-lan	I-lan	825	2,137	448,000
Kao-hsiung	Feng-shan	1,078	2,793	1,058,000
Miao-li	Miao-li	703	1,820	549,000
Nan-t'ou	Nan-t'ou	1,585	4,106	533,000
P'eng-hu	Ma-kung	49	127	104,000
P'ing-tung	P'ing-tung	1,072	2,776	901,000
T'ai-chung	Feng-yuan	792	2,051	1,095,000
T'ai-nan	Hsin-ying	778	2,016	983,000
T'ai-pei	Pan-ch'iao	792	2,052	2,514,000
T'ai-tung	T'ai-tung	1,357	3,515	280,000
T'ao-yüan	T'ao-yüan	471	1,221	1,161,000
Yün-lin	Tou-liu	498	1,291	797,000
Municipalities				
Chi-lung	—	51	133	253,000
Hsin-chu	—	19	49	293,000
Kao-hsiung	—	60	156	1,262,000
Keelung	—	51	133	352,000
T'ai-chung	—	63	163	636,000
T'ai-nan	—	68	176	622,000
Taipei	—	105	272	2,388,000
TOTAL		13,900*	36,002	18,735,000

Source: Official government figures.

Demography

Density (1984): persons per sq mi 1,347.8, persons per sq km 520.4.
Urban–rural (1980): urban 70.6%; rural 29.4%.
Sex distribution (1984): male 51.99%; female 48.01%.
Age breakdown (1982): under 15, 31.2%; 15–29, 31.0%; 30–44, 17.8%; 45–59, 12.6%; 60–74, 6.1%; 75 and over, 1.3%.
Population projection: (1990) 22,358,000; (2000) 28,059,000.
Doubling time: 40 years.
Ethnic composition (1980): Taiwanese (Han Chinese) 97.0%; other 3.0%.
Religious affiliation (1980): Chinese folk religionist 48.5%; Buddhist 43.0%; Christian 7.4%; Muslim 0.5%; other 0.6%.
Major cities (1984 est.): Taipei 2,388,000; Kao-hsiung 1,262,000; T'ai-chung 636,000; T'ai-nan 622,000; Keelung 352,000; Hsin-Chu 293,000; Chi-lung 253,000.

Vital statistics

Birth rate per 1,000 population (1983): 20.6 (world avg. 29.0).
Death rate per 1,000 population (1983): 4.9 (world avg. 11.0).
Natural increase rate per 1,000 population (1983): 15.7 (world avg. 18.0).
Total fertility rate (avg. births per childbearing woman; 1983): 2.3.
Marriage rate per 1,000 population (1983): 8.5.
Divorce rate per 1,000 population (1983): 0.9.
Infant mortality rate per 1,000 live births (1983): 8.9.
Life expectancy at birth (1982): male 70.2 years; female 75.1 years.
Major causes of death per 100,000 (1980): diseases of the circulatory system 137.1; malignant neoplasms (cancers) 75.1; respiratory diseases 34.0.

National economy

Budget (1983). Revenue: NT$452,415,000,000 (taxes 88.4%, of which income taxes 19.0%, custom duties 16.2%; other 11.6%). Expenditures: NT$511,909,000,000 (general administration and defense 49.0%, education 9.2%, social welfare and health 13.4%).
Public debt (external, outstanding; 1983): U.S.$ 6,991,600,000.
Tourism (1982): receipts from visitors U.S.$953,000,000; expenditures by nationals abroad, n.a.
Production (metric tons except as noted). Agriculture, forestry, fishing (1982): sugarcane 8,274,913, vegetables 3,074,054, rice 2,482,602, corn (maize) 118,419, cassava 118,394, sweet potatoes 741,442, citrus fruits 391,281, bananas 202,942, pineapple 144,900, peanuts 82,832, tobacco 25,570, tea 24,051; livestock (number of live animals) 129,441 cattle, 5,182,487 pigs, 177,490 goats and sheep; timber 494,973 cu m; fish catch 922,520. Mining and quarrying (1982): salt 262,000; silver 15,679 kilograms; gold 2,232 kilograms. Manufacturing (1983): cement 14,808,000; crude steel 1,715,000; sulfuric acid 679,000; plastics and resins 522,000; cotton yarn 415,000; manmade fibres 743,000; paper and board 1,913,000; electronic calculators 28,787,000 units; recorders 21,737,000 units. Construction (1983): total residential and nonresidential 24,971,000 sq m. Energy production (consumption): electricity (kW-hr; 1983) 45,517,000,000 (30,848,879,000†); coal (metric tons;

1983) 2,237,000 (n.a.); petroleum (barrels; 1983) 842,767 (n.a.); natural gas (cu m; 1983) 1,237,000,000 (n.a.).
Gross national product (at current market prices; 1983): U.S.$49,754,000,000 (U.S.$2,444 per capita).

Origin of gross domestic product (current prices)

	1983 in value NT$'000,000	% of total value	1983 labour force	% of labour force
Agriculture	147,514	7.4	1,317,000	18.1
Mining	14,287	0.7	79,000	1.1
Manufacturing	793,422	39.8	2,272,000	31.3
Construction	215,814	10.8	523,000	7.2
Trade	267,777	13.4	1,229,000	16.9
Public utilities	80,721	4.1	33,000	0.4
Transportation and communication	121,865	6.1	384,000	5.3
Finance	67,220	3.4	174,000	2.4
Pub. admin., defense, and services	329,298	16.5	1,059,000	14.6
Other	−45,319	−2.3	196,000	2.7
TOTAL	1,992,599	100.0*	7,266,000	100.0

Persons economically active (1983): total 7,266,000 (38.8%); female participation in the labour force 2,509,000 (41.0%); unemployed 197,000 (2.8%).

Price and earnings indexes (1976 = 100)

	1977	1978	1979	1980	1981	1982	1983
Consumer price index	107.0	113.2	124.3	147.9	172.0	178.9	181.5
Monthly earnings index	117.8	135.8	161.0	195.4	234.9	254.2	...

Household income and expenditure. Average household size (1983) 4.5; income per household NT$36,550 (U.S.$908); expenditure (1983): food 32.8%, housing 28.9%, recreation 10.2%, clothing and footwear 6.8%, transportation 6.7%, other 14.6%.
Land use (1980): forested 55.0%; agricultural and under permanent cultivation 25.2%; other 19.8%.

Foreign trade

Balance of trade (current prices)

	1977	1978	1979	1980	1981	1982	1983
NT$'000,000	31,400	60,131	46,371	762	51,123	128,164	191,518
% of total	4.6%	6.9%	4.2%	0.1%	3.2%	8.0%	10.5%

Imports: (1983): NT$813,904,000,000 (crude petroleum, petroleum oils, and crude oils obtained from bituminous materials 20.8%; machinery, other than electrical 10.2%; electrical machinery, apparatus, and appliances 9.6%; chemicals and related products 8.3%; iron and steel 4.9%). *Major import sources:* Japan 27.5%; United States 21.8%; Saudi Arabia 9.5%; Kuwait 5.6%; Australia 3.4%; West Germany 3.4%.
Exports (1983): NT$1,005,422,000,000 (electrical machinery, apparatus, and appliances 18.2%; articles of apparel and clothing 9.9%; textile yarns and fabrics 8.4%; food 7.5%; toys and sport goods 7.0%). *Major export destinations:* United States 45.1%; Japan 9.9%; Hong Kong 6.0%; West Germany 3.4%; Saudi Arabia 3.0%; Canada 2.9%; Australia 2.5%; U.K. 2.5%.

Transport and communications

Transport. Railroads (1983): length 3,045 mi, 4,900 km; passenger-mi 5,302,191,000, passenger-km 8,533,066,000; short ton-mi cargo 1,768,000,000, metric ton-km cargo 2,581,000,000. Roads (1983): total length 10,919 mi, 17,572 km (paved 74%). Vehicles (1984): passenger cars 712,629; trucks and buses 95,096. Merchant marine (1983): vessels (100 gross tons and over) 514; total deadweight tonnage 2,879,206. Air transport (1983): passenger-mi 5,676,000,000, passenger-km 9,135,000,000; short ton-mi cargo 1,081,000,000, metric ton-km cargo 1,578,000,000; airports (1984) with scheduled flights 9.
Communications. Daily newspapers (1983): total number 26; total circulation 4,025,000; circulation per 1,000 population 215. Radios (1983): total number of receivers 5,000,000 (1 per 3.7 persons). Television (1983): total number of receivers 5,060,000 (1 per 3.6 persons). Telephones (1984): 3,641,113 (1 per 5.1 persons).

Education and health

Education (1983–84)

	schools	teachers	students	student/teacher ratio
Primary (age 6–12)	2,464	70,648	2,242,641	31.7
Secondary (age 13–18)	845	59,871	1,277,815	21.3
Vocational	202	15,002	404,549	27.0
Higher	105	19,166	395,153	20.6

College graduates per 100,000 population (1981): 20.6. *Literacy* (1982): total population literate 11,294,884 (88.9%); males literate 6,297,725 (94.9%); females literate 4,997,159 (82.9%).
Health (1982): physicians 14,381 (1 per 1,272 persons); hospital beds 53,498 (1 per 342 persons).
Food (1982): daily per capita caloric intake 2,749 (vegetable products 78.0%, animal products 22.0%); 118% of FAO recommended minimum.

Military

Total active duty personnel (1983): 451,000 (army 68.8%; navy 14.2%; air force 17.0%). *Military expenditure as percent of GNP* (1982): 7.2% (world 6.0%); per capita expenditure U.S.$198.

*Detail does not add to total given because of rounding. †By industry only.

Tanzania

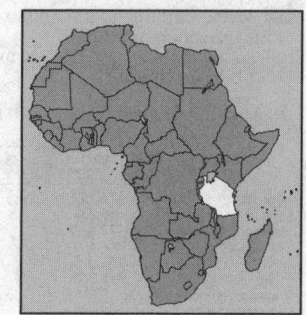

Official name: Jamhuri ya Mwungano wa Tanzania (United Republic of Tanzania).
Form of government: unitary single-party republic with one legislative house (National Assembly [239]).
Chief of state: President.
Head of government: Prime Minister.
Capital: Dar es Salaam.
Official languages: Swahili; English.
Official religion: none.
Monetary unit: 1 Tanzanian shilling (T Sh) = 100 cents; valuation (Oct. 29, 1984) 1 U.S.$ = T Sh17.92; 1 £ = T Sh21.62.

Area and population

Regions	Capitals	area sq mi	area sq km	population 1978 census*
Arusha	Arusha	33,200	86,100	928,478
Coast	Dar es Salaam	13,200	34,200	516,949
Dar es Salaam	Dar es Salaam	300	800	851,522
Dodoma	Dodoma	15,900	41,300	971,921
Iringa	Iringa	22,000	56,900	922,801
Kigoma	Kigoma	17,400	45,100	648,950
Kilimanjaro	Moshi	5,100	13,200	902,394
Lindi	Lindi	25,500	66,100	527,902
Mara	Musoma	11,400	29,500	723,295
Mbeya	Mbeya	34,800	90,100	1,080,241
Morogoro	Morogoro	28,200	73,100	939,190
Mtwara	Mtwara	6,500	16,700	771,726
Mwanza	Mwanza	14,300	37,100	1,443,418
Pemba North	Wete	400	900	106,300
Pemba South	Chake Chake }			99,570
Rukwa	Sumbawanga	18,400	47,600	451,897
Ruvuma	Songea	23,900	61,900	564,113
Shinyanga	Shinyanga	19,600	50,800	1,323,482
Singida	Singida	19,100	49,400	614,030
Tabora	Tabora	29,400	76,200	818,049
Tanga	Tanga	10,400	26,800	1,038,592
West Lake	Bukoba	15,300	39,700	1,009,379
Zanzibar North	Mkokotoni			77,424
Zanzibar South and Central	Koani }	600	1,600	52,325
Zanzibar West	Zanzibar			143,616
TOTAL		364,900	945,100	17,527,564

Source: Official government figures.

Demography

Density (1984): persons per sq mi 55.9, persons per sq km 21.6.
Urban–rural (1982): urban 13.0%; rural 87.0%.
Sex distribution (1980): male 49.49%; female 50.51%.
Age breakdown (1980): under 15, 45.9%; 15–29, 25.3%; 30–44, 14.9%; 45–59, 8.9%; 60–74, 4.2%; 75 and over, 0.8%.
Population projection: (1990) 23,646,000; (2000) 31,953,000.
Doubling time: 23 years.
Ethnic composition (1978): Nyamwezi 21.1%; Swahili 8.6%; Hehet 6.8%; Makonde 5.9%; Haya 5.9%; Chagga 5.0%; other 46.7%.
Religious affiliation (1980): Christian 44%, of which Roman Catholic 28%; Muslim 33%; traditional beliefs 23%.
Major cities (1978); Dar es Salaam 769,445; Mwanza 110,553; Tanga 103,399.

Vital statistics

Birth rate per 1,000 population (1980–85): 34.5 (world avg. 27.5).
Death rate per 1,000 population (1980–85): 10.2 (world avg. 10.6).
Natural increase rate per 1,000 population (1980–85): 24.3 (world avg. 16.9).
Total fertility rate (avg. births per childbearing woman; 1980–85): 6.5.
Marriage rate per 1,000 population (1967): 9.8.
Divorce rate per 1,000 population: n.a.
Infant mortality rate per 1,000 live births (1982): 98.0.
Life expectancy at birth (1980–85): male 51.3 years; female 54.8 years.
Major causes of death per 100,000 population: n.a., however, the major diseases are malaria, bilharziasis, tuberculosis, and sleeping sickness.

National economy

Budget (1982–83). Revenue: T Sh9,500,000,000 (sales tax 54.9%, income tax 27.4%, customs and excise tax 6.7%). Expenditures: T Sh14,144,000,000 (governmental administration 44.1%, consolidated fund services 33.2%, regional administration 22.6%).
Public debt (external, outstanding; 1982): U.S.$1,631,600,000.
Tourism (1982): receipts from visitors U.S.$15,000,000; expenditures by nationals abroad, n.a.
Production (metric tons except as noted). Agriculture, forestry, fishing (1982): cassava 4,900,000, corn (maize) 800,000, sweet potatoes 332,000, coconuts 330,000, rice 200,000, millet 150,000, seed cotton 127,000, unshelled peanuts (groundnuts) 58,000, palm kernels 9,800, chick peas 8,000; livestock (number of live animals) 13,150,000 cattle, 5,906,000 goats, 3,937,000 sheep, 25,000,000 chickens; roundwood 37,893,000 cu m; fish catch 226,000. Mining and quarrying (1982): diamonds 250,000 carats; phosphate rock 100,000; gold 917 grams†. Manufacturing (1981): cement 400,000‡; fertilizer 69,029; wheat flour 26,099; rolled steel 15,827; sisal twine and ropes 13,246; iron sheets 10,105; aluminum 4,460; textiles 85,-356,000 sq m; cigarettes 3,865,000,000 pieces; batteries 78,006,000 units;

shoes 2,444,000 pairs; blankets 1,063,000 pieces; paints 1,507,000 litres; beer 64,252,000 litres. Construction: n.a. Energy production (consumption): electricity (kW-hr; 1982) 720,000,000 (720,000,000); coal (metric tons; 1982) 1,000 (1,000); crude petroleum (barrels; 1982) none (4,118,000); petroleum products (metric tons; 1982) 519,000 (573,000); natural gas, none (n.a.).
Gross national product (at current market prices; 1982): U.S.$4,900,000,000 (U.S.$260 per capita).

Origin of gross domestic product (current prices)

	1982 in value T Sh'000,000	1982 % of total value	1980 labour force§	1980 % of labour force
Agriculture	21,722	45.4	135,490	22.3
Mining	162	0.3	5,900	0.9
Manufacturing	3,924	8.2	105,830	17.4
Construction	1,720	3.6	48,650	8.0
Trade	3,183	6.6	38,100	6.3
Public utilities	515	1.1	19,540	3.2
Transportation and communication	2,093	4.4	58,320	9.6
Finance	‖	‖	13,920	2.3
Services	14,534 ‖	30.4 ‖	181,980¶	29.9¶
TOTAL	47,853	100.0	607,730	100.0◊

Persons economically active (1982): total 7,704,000 (40.3%); female participation in the labour force 2,177,000 (29.0%)δ; unemployed, n.a.

Price and earnings indexes (1975 = 100)

	1977	1978	1979	1980	1981	1982	1983
Consumer price index	119.3	133.8	151.1	196.8	247.3	318.9	411.3
Monthly earnings index	107.2	108.8	117.2	124.7	...	...	...

Household income and expenditure. Average household size (1980) 5.1; average annual income per household, n.a.; source of income: n.a.; expenditures (1981): food 47.0%, clothing and footwear 10.8%, rent 8.6%, drinks and tobacco 7.1%, utilities 6.6%, transportation 6.4%.
Land use (1981): forested 47.4%; meadows and pastures 39.5%; agricultural and under permanent cultivation 5.9%; other 7.2%.

Foreign trade

Balance of trade (current prices)

	1977	1978	1979	1980	1981	1982
T Sh'000,000	−1,697.1	−5,127.1	−4,588.9	−6,142.2	−4,853.0	−6,414.0
% of total	16.0%	41.1%	33.8%	42.4%	34.1%	42.6%

Imports (1981): T Sh9,550,000,000 (machinery 28.9%; fuel 26.5%; transport equipment 12.4%; food, beverages, and tobacco 10.2%; metals 7.7%). *Major import sources†:* United Kingdom 17.5%; W. Germany 9.8%; Japan 8.6%; The Netherlands 6.3%; United States 6.1%; Italy 4.9%.
Exports (1981): T Sh4,697,000,000 (coffee beans 31.0%; cotton 14.7%; manufactured goods 9.8%; cloves 9.2%; cashew nuts 7.3%; sisal 6.2%; diamonds 5.4%). *Major export destinations†:* United Kingdom 17.5%; W. Germany 13.2%; Indonesia 9.9%; Italy 4.9%; The Netherlands 4.8%.

Transport and communications

Transport. Railroads (1982): length 2,218 mi, 3,569 km; passenger-mi 577,-000,000δ, passenger-km 929,000,000δ; short ton-mi cargo 475,000,000δ, metric ton-km cargo 694,000,000δ. Roads (1982): total length 33,314 mi, 53,613 km (paved 6%). Vehicles (1982): passenger cars 48,752; trucks and buses 31,930. Merchant marine (1983): vessels (100 gross tons and over) 39; total deadweight tonnage 868,076. Air transport (1982): passenger-mi 130,000,000 passenger-km 210,000,000; short ton-mi cargo 822,000, metric ton-km cargo 1,200,000; airports (1984) with scheduled flights 53.
Communications. Daily newspapers (1982): total number 3; total circulation 139,000; circulation per 1,000 population 7.0. Radios (1983): 2,000,000 (1 per 10 persons). Television (1983): 9,000 (1 per 2,193 persons). Telephones (1982): 96,521 (1 per 204 persons).

Education and health

Education (1981–82)

	schools	teachers	students	student/ teacher ratio
Primary□ (age 7–13)	9,837◊	88,370	3,512,799	39.8
Secondary (age 14–19)	145Δ	3,362	69,145	20.6
Voc., teacher tr.	34Δ	627	8,101	12.9
Higher	1Δ	719	2,984	4.2

College graduates per 100,000 population (students graduating; 1979): 4.7.
Literacy† (1978): total population literate 10,500,000 (73.5%); males literate 5,400,000 (77.7%); females literate 5,100,000 (69.6%).
Health: physicians (1980) 900 (1 per 20,590 persons); hospital beds (1977) 33,714 (1 per 501 persons).
Food (1978–80): daily per capita caloric intake 2,028 (vegetable products 90.0%, animal products 10.0%); 87% of FAO recommended minimum requirement.

Military

Total active duty personnel (1983): 40,350 (army 95.4%; navy 2.1%; air force 2.5%). *Military expenditure as percent of GNP* (1982): 5.5% (world 6.0%); per capita expenditure U.S.$16.

*Preliminary. †1980. ‡1982. §Employed persons only. ‖ Finance and public administration and defense are included with services. ¶Includes public administration and defense. ◊Detail does not add to total given because of rounding. δFor Tanzania Railways Corporation only. □Mainland only. ◊1978–79. Δ1976–77. †Age 10 and over.

Thailand

Official name: Muang Thai or Prathet Thai (Kingdom of Thailand).
Form of government: constitutional monarchy with a multiparty National Assembly (Senate [225]; House of Representatives [324]).
Chief of state: King.
Head of government: Prime Minister.
Capital: Bangkok.
Official language: Thai.
Official religion: Buddhism.
Monetary unit: 1 Thai Baht (B) = 100 stangs; valuation (Oct. 29, 1984) 1 U.S.\$ = B22.95; 1 £ = B27.70.

Area and population	area		population
	sq mi	sq km	1980 census
Regions			
Bangkok Metropolis	604	1,565	5,153,902
Central*	7,236	18,742	3,248,873
Eastern	14,481	37,507	3,419,610
Northeastern	65,195	168,854	16,087,895
Northern	65,500	169,644	9,587,517
Southern	27,303	70,715	5,823,211
Western	17,795	46,088	3,640,330
TOTAL	198,114	513,115	46,961,338

Demography

Density (1984): persons per sq mi 254.4, persons per sq km 98.2.
Urban–rural (1984): urban 17.6%; rural 82.4%.
Sex distribution (1980): male 50.30%; female 49.70%.
Age breakdown (1980): under 15, 40.2%; 15–29, 29.2%; 30–44, 16.2%; 45–59, 9.3%; 60–69, 3.2%; 70 and over, 1.9%.
Population projection: (1990) 56,860,000; (2000) 69,530,000.
Doubling time: 34 years.
Ethnic composition (1978): Thai 81.3%; Chinese 11.3%; Malay 3.8%; other 3.6%.
Religious affiliation (1980): Buddhist 95.0%; Muslim 3.8%; Christian 0.5%; other 0.7%.
Major cities (1980): Bangkok 4,967,071; Chiang Mai 101,595; Hat Yai 93,519; Khon Kaen 85,863; Nakhon Ratchasima 78,246.

Vital statistics

Birth rate per 1,000 population (1982): 22.5 (world avg. 29.0).
Death rate per 1,000 population (1982): 5.1 (world avg. 11.0).
Natural increase rate per 1,000 population (1982): 17.4 (world avg. 18.0).
Total fertility rate (avg. births per childbearing woman; 1980–85): 3.9.
Marriage rate per 1,000 population (1981): 7.2.
Divorce rate per 1,000 population (1979): 0.5.
Infant mortality rate per 1,000 live births (1982): 12.4.
Life expectancy at birth (1980–85): male 59.5 years; female 65.1 years.
Major causes of death per 100,000 population (1982): heart disease 34.1; accidents, poisonings, and violence 33.5; malignant neoplasms (cancers) 26.1; tuberculosis 11.9.

National economy

Budget (1982). Revenue: B115,980,000,000 (selective sales tax 24.3%, income tax 21.4%, business tax 19.4%, import–export duties 18.9%, other 16.0%).
Expenditures: B117,628,000,000 (social services 29.6%, defense 20.1%, economic services 18.6%, administration 11.5%, other 20.2%).
Public debt (external, outstanding; 1984): U.S.\$8,746,565,000.
Tourism (1981): receipts from visitors U.S.\$983,000,000; expenditures by nationals abroad U.S.\$257,000,000.
Production (metric tons except as noted). Agriculture, forestry, fishing (1982): sugarcane 27,000,000, tapioca root 16,000,000, rice 15,696,000, corn (maize) 4,200,000, coconuts 750,000, rubber 540,000, mung beans 275,000; livestock (number of live animals) 6,150,000 buffaloes, 4,500,000 cattle, 3,700,000 pigs, 32,000 goats, 63,264,000 chickens; roundwood 39,472,000 cu m; fish catch 1,920,000. Mining and quarrying (1982): gypsum 753,000; marl 458,000; fluorite 176,000; lead ore 44,000. Manufacturing (1982): cement 6,609,000; tin plate 62,000; detergent 53,000; cigarettes 27,000; commercial vehicles 23,000 units. Construction (value in B; 1981): residential 19,269,000,000; nonresidential 37,478,000,000.. Energy production (consumption; 1982): electricity (kW-hr; 1982) 17,220,000,000 (17,940,000,000); coal (metric tons; 1982) 1,967,000 (1,964,000); crude petroleum (barrels; 1982) 58,640 (56,441,000); petroleum products (metric tons; 1982) 7,327,000 (10,183,000); natural gas (cu m; 1982) 1,283,537,200 (1,283,537,200).
Persons economically active (1980): total 22,728,000 (48.1%); female 10,740,000 (47.3%); unemployed 204,200 (0.9%).

Price and earnings indexes (1980 = 100)							
	1978	1979	1980	1981	1982	1983	1984
Consumer price index	76.0	83.5	100.0	112.7	118.6	123.0	124.4†
Monthly earnings index	...	...	...	...	...	...	...

Household income and expenditure. Average household size (1980) 5.6; income per household B23,136 (U.S.\$1,134); source of income: wages and salaries 28.3%, nonmoney income 26.0%, other 45.7%; expenditure (1980):

food 51.7%, clothing and footwear 10.8%, transportation 10.3% ‡, housing 6.1%§, recreation 4.3%‖.
Gross national product (at current market prices; 1983): U.S.\$39,237,391,000 (U.S.\$795 per capita).

Origin of gross domestic product (current prices)				
	1982		1980	
	in value B'000,000	% of total value	labour force	% of labour force
Agriculture	177,152	20.6	15,942,700	70.1
Mining	15,703	1.8	36,600	0.2
Manufacturing	177,146	20.6	1,788,900	7.9
Construction	44,821	5.2	435,900	1.9
Trade	167,605	19.5	1,915,900	8.4
Public utilities	12,353	1.4	59,900	0.3
Transportation and communication	68,683	8.0	455,900	2.0
Finance	61,182	7.1		
Pub. admin., defense	37,032	4.3 }	1,886,800	8.3
Services	86,819	10.1		
Other	9,874	1.4	204,700	0.9
TOTAL	858,370	100.0	22,727,300	100.0

Land use (1981): forested 29.9%; meadows and pastures 0.6%; agricultural and under permanent cultivation 35.8%; other 33.7%.

Foreign trade

Balance of trade (current prices)						
	1977	1978	1979	1980	1981	1982
B'000,000	−22,979	−25,834	−37,984	−60,421	−66,025	−36,888
% of total	13.9%	13.6%	15.0%	18.5%	17.7%	10.4%

Imports (1982): B196,615,967,000 (mineral fuels and oils 29.5%, boilers and other machinery and mechanical appliances 9.9%, iron and steel 7.7%, electrical machinery 7.0%, organic chemicals 3.2%, fertilizers 1.7%, paper and paper products 1.3%). *Major import sources:* Japan 23.4%; Saudi Arabia 15.2%; West Germany 13.9%; United States 13.3%; Singapore 6.3%; Malaysia 5.2%.
Exports (1982): B159,728,166,000 (rice 14.1%, tapioca products 12.4%, sugar 8.1%, rubber 5.9%, corn (maize) 5.2%, unwrought tin 4.9%, shrimps 2.0%). *Major export destinations:* Japan 13.7%; The Netherlands 13.2%; United States 12.7%; Singapore 7.3%; Malaysia 5.2%; Hong Kong 5.0%.

Transport and communications

Transport. Railroads (1982): length 2,321 mi, 3,735 km; passenger-mi 5,874,786,000, passenger-km 9,454,570,000; short ton-mi cargo 1,625,865,000, metric ton-km cargo 2,373,719,000. Roads (1982): total length 45,000 mi, 72,000 km (paved 35%). Vehicles (1982): passenger cars 451,001; trucks and buses 63,986. Merchant marine (1983): vessels (100 gross tons and over) 219; total deadweight tonnage 868,076. Air transport (1982): passenger-mi 223,337,000, passenger-km 359,427,000; short ton-mi cargo 578,000, metric ton-km cargo 844,000; airports (1984) with scheduled flights 18.
Communications. Daily newspapers (1983): total number 21; total circulation 2,451,000; circulation per 1,000 population 48.6. Radios (1983): total number of receivers 7,200,000 (1 per 7 persons). Television (1983): total number of receivers 3,000,000 (1 per 16.8 persons). Telephones (1982): 529,106 (1 per 95.2 persons).

Education and health

Education (1980)	schools¶	teachers♀	students	student/ teacher ratio
Primary (age 7–12)	32,194	319,015	7,392,563	23.2
Secondary (age 13–18)	1,547	83,379	1,617,465	19.4
Voc., teacher tr.	417	22,385	427,302	19.1
Higherδ	...	12,483	113,351	9.1

College graduates per 100,000 population (1980): 2,300. *Literacy* (1980): total population literate 29,793,848 (89.5%); males literate 15,316,986 (93.1%); females literate 14,476,862 (86.1%).
Health (1981): physicians 6,803 (1 per 6,980 persons); hospital beds 71,858 (1 per 661 persons).
Food (1978–80): daily per capita caloric intake 2,301 (vegetable products 93.7%, animal products 6.3%); 104% of FAO recommended minimum requirement.

Military

Total active duty personnel (1983): 235,300 (army 68.0%; navy 13.7%; air force 18.3%). *Military expenditure as percent of GNP* (1982): 4.0% (world 6.0%); per capita expenditure U.S.\$32.

*Excluding Bangkok Metropolis. †Second quarter. ‡Includes communication. §Includes fuel and power. ‖ Includes education. ¶Excludes private schools that provide both primary and secondary instruction. ♀Excludes teachers in private schools with both primary and secondary instruction. δ1979.

Togo

Official name: République Togolaise (Republic of Togo).
Form of government: republic with one legislative body (People's Representatives [67]).
Head of state and government: President.
Capital: Lomé.
Official language: French.
Official religion: none.
Monetary unit: 1 CFA franc (CFAF) = 100 centimes; valuation (Oct. 29, 1984) 1 U.S.$ = CFAF470.6; 1 £ = CFAF568.0.

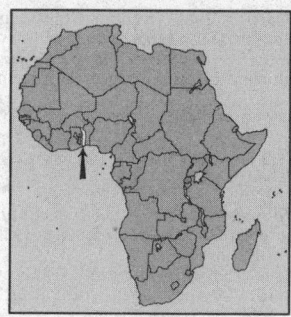

Area and population

Regions Prefectures	Capitals	area sq mi	area sq km	population 1981 census
Centrale	Sokodé			269,174
Nyala	Tchamba	*	*	44,912
Sotouboua	Sotouboua	2,892	7,490	128,617
Tchaoudjo	Sokodé	2,198	5,692	95,645
De la Kara	Kara			432,626
Assoli	Bafilo	362	938	32,444
Bassar	Bassar	2,444	6,330	118,345
Binah	Pagouda	180	465	50,077
Doufelgou	Niamtougou	432	1,120	66,120
Kéran	Kandé	653	1,692	44,762
Kozah	Kara	419	1,085	120,878
Des Plateaux	Atakpamé			561,656
Amou	Amlamé	1,692	4,382	72,951
Haho	Notsé	1,412	3,658	109,995
Kloto	Kpalimé	1,077	2,790	106,429
Ogou	Atakpamé	2,373	6,145	163,906
Wawa	Badou	†	†	108,375
Des Savanes	Dapaong			326,826
Oti	Sansanné-Mango	1,453	3,762	77,747
Tône	Dapaong	1,869	4,840	249,079
Maritime	Lomé			1,039,700
Golfe	Lomé	133	345	438,110
Lacs	Aného	275	712	140,006
Vo	Vogan	290	750	150,313
Yoto	Tabligbo	483	1,250	100,387
Zio	Tsévié	1,289	3,339	210,884
TOTAL		21,925‡	56,785	2,700,982§

Source: Official government figures.

Demography

Density (1984): persons per sq mi 134.4, persons per sq km 51.9.
Urban–rural (1981): urban 15.2%; rural 84.8%.
Sex distribution (1981): male 48.20%; female 51.80%.
Age breakdown (1980): under 15, 46.2%; 15–29, 25.8%; 30–44, 14.8%; 45–59, 8.6%; 60–74, 3.9%; 75 and over, 0.7%.
Population projection: (1990) 3,507,000; (2000) 4,688,000.
Doubling time: 24 years.
Ethnic composition (1978): Ewe 46.5%; Kabre 22.4%; Gurma 14.2%; Tem 4.2%; other African 11.7%; European 1.0%.
Religious affiliation (1980): animist 46%; Christian 37%; Muslim 17%.
Major cities (1983): Lomé 366,476; Sokodé 33,500 ‖ ; Kpalimé 25,500 ‖ .

Vital statistics

Birth rate per 1,000 population (1980–85): 47.8 (world avg. 27.5); legitimate, n.a.; illegitimate, n.a.
Death rate per 1,000 population (1980–85): 17.1 (world avg. 10.6).
Natural increase rate per 1,000 population (1980–85): 30.7 (world avg. 16.9).
Total fertility rate (avg. births per childbearing woman; 1980–85): 6.5.
Marriage rate per 1,000 population: n.a.
Divorce rate per 1,000 population: n.a.
Infant mortality rate per 1,000 live births (1980–85): 114.4.
Life expectancy at birth (1980–85): male 46.9 years; female 50.2 years.
Major illnesses per 100,000 population (1978): infectious and parasitic diseases 26,926; diseases of the respiratory system 9,296; diseases of the digestive system 8,007; accidents, poisoning, and traumas 7,172.

National economy

Budget (1980) Revenue: CFAF72,896,000,000 (corporate taxes 27.5%, import duties 22.8%, property income 11.3%, sales tax 11.1%, income tax 5.7%, export duties 4.6%). Expenditures: CFAF73,943,000,000 (housing 14.4%, education 12.6%, defense 7.0%, health 5.6%, social security and welfare 4.6%).
Public debt (external, outstanding; 1983): U.S.$805,300,000.
Tourism (1982): receipts from visitors U.S.$17,000,000; expenditures by nationals abroad U.S.$19,000,000¶.
Production (metric tons except as noted). Agriculture, forestry, fishing (1982): yams 558,000, cassava 342,000, corn (maize) 151,000, millet 134,000, vegetables 70,000, fruits 44,000, peanuts (groundnuts) 36,000, rice 29,000, cottonseed 27,024 ♀, coconuts 14,000, palm oil 13,800♀, dry beans 13,000, cacao beans 9,719♀, coffee 5,941♀, shea nuts 4,403♀; livestock (number of live animals) 835,000 sheep, 750,000 goats, 360,000 pigs, 250,000 cattle, 3,150,000 chickens; roundwood 724,000 cu m; fish catch 8,500. Mining and quarrying (1982): phosphate rock 2,100,000; salt 600,000; marble 15,087. Manufacturing (1980): cement 279,000♂; beer 385,000 hectolitres; woven cotton fabrics 20,000,000 m; footwear 1,155,000 pairs. Construction (1980): 4,000 sq m. Energy production (consumption): electricity (kW-hr; 1982)

85,000,000 (260,000,000); crude petroleum (barrels; 1982) none (2,565,000); petroleum products (metric tons; 1982) 497,000 (358,000).
Gross national product (at current market prices; 1981): U.S.$1,020,000,000 (U.S.$390 per capita).

Origin of gross domestic product (current prices)

	1981 in value CFAF'000,000	% of total value	1981 labour force	% of labour force
Agriculture	69.3	27.2	742,000	67.2
Mining	22.6	8.9	□	□
Manufacturing	16.3	6.4	□	□
Construction	11.0	4.3	□	□
Trade	52.9	20.7	□	□
Public utilities	4.1	1.6	□	□
Transp. and commun.	17.2	6.7	□	□
Finance	δ	δ	□	□
Pub. admin., defense	25.8	10.1	□	□
Services	δ	δ	□	□
Other	36.0	14.1	362,000	32.8
TOTAL	255.2	100.0	1,104,000	100.0

Persons economically active (1981): total 1,104,000 (40.8%); female participation in the labour force 448,420 ‖ (34.9%); unemployed, 25,000 ‖ (2.3%).

Price and earnings indexes (1975 = 100)

	1977	1978	1979	1980	1981	1982	1983
Consumer price index	136.7	137.3	147.6	165.9	198.5	220.6	241.4

Household income and expenditure. Average household size (1980) 5.6; average annual income per household CFAF102,000 (U.S.$452); source of income: n.a; expenditure (1972): food 56.1%, housing 13.7%, transportation 8.6%, clothing 8.5%, health 2.2%, education 0.7%.
Land use (1981): forested 31.2%; meadows and pastures 3.7%; agricultural and under permanent cultivation 26.1%; other 39.0%.

Foreign trade

Balance of trade (current prices)

	1977	1978	1979	1980	1981	1982
CFAF'000,000	−30.7	−46.7	−45.0	−61.5	−78.7	−70.1
% of total	28.2%	30.1%	24.0%	35.3%	34.5%	37.6%

Imports (1982): CFAF128,353,000,000 (cotton textiles 17.5%; food and food products 12.7%; crude petroleum 11.8%; beverages and tobacco 10.6%; machinery and mechanical equipment 6.9%; transport equipment and parts 6.2%). *Major import sources:* France 27.1%; The Netherlands 11.0%; United Kingdom 10.1%; West Germany 7.1%; Japan 6.4%; United States 4.4%.
Exports (1982): CFAF58,173,000,000 (phosphates 45.7%; clinker 14.3%; coffee 10.6%; cacao beans 9.6%; raw cotton 8.6%; cement 2.5%). *Major export destinations:* France 22.1%; The Netherlands 18.4%; Yugoslavia 9.6%; Ivory Coast 7.9%; Ghana 6.8%; West Germany 5.1%.

Transport and communications

Transport. Railroads (1981): length 321 mi, 516 km; passenger-mi 52,534,-000¶, passenger-km 84,545,000¶; short ton-mi cargo 7,152,000¶, metric ton-km cargo 10,442,000¶. Roads (1982): total length 4,638 mi, 7,464 km (paved 20%). Vehicles (1981): passenger cars 26,067; trucks and buses 13,-422. Merchant marine (1983): vessels (100 gross tons and over) 9; total deadweight tonnage 77,280. Air transport (1981): passenger-mi 121,000,000, passenger-km 194,000,000; short ton-mi cargo 14,400,000, metric ton-km cargo 21,000,000; airport (1984) with scheduled flights 1.
Communications. Daily newspapers (1983): total number 2; total circulation 10,000◊; circulation per 1,000 population, n.a. Radios (1983): total number of receivers 190,000 (1 per 15.1 persons). Television (1983): total number of receivers 8,000 (1 per 358 persons). Telephones (1981): 7,870 (1 per 340 persons).

Education and health

Education (1981–82)

	schools	teachers	students	student/ teacher ratio
Primary (age 6–11)	2,251	9,619	498,639	51.8
Secondary (age 12–18)	248	3,982	122,925	30.8
Voc., teacher tr.	22	348△	7,306	...
Higher	1	285	4,131	14.4

College graduates per 100,000 population (students graduating; 1979): 22.6.
Literacy (1980): total population literate 490,900 (35.2%); males literate 309,800 (46.1%); females literate 181,100 (46.1%).
Health (1980): physicians 132 (1 per 19,900 persons); hospital beds 3,600 (1 per 729 persons).
Food (1978–80): daily per capita caloric intake 2,106 (vegetable products 96.3%, animal products 3.7%); 92% of FAO recommended minimum.

Military

Total active duty personnel (1983): 4,330 (army 92.4%; navy 1.8%; air force 5.8%). *Military expenditure as percent of GNP* (1982): 2.1% (world 6.0%); per capita expenditure U.S.$7.

*Area included with Tchaoudjo. †Area included with Amou. ‡Detail does not add to total given because of rounding. §Total includes 71,000 persons not counted separately. ‖ 1980. ¶1979. ♀1983. δ1982. □Mining, manufacturing, construction, trade, public utilities, transport and communication, finance, public administration, defense, and services included with other. ◊For one daily only. △1979–80.

Tonga

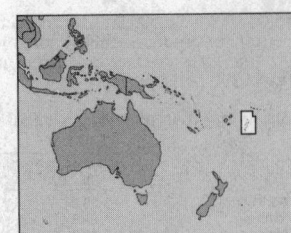

Official name: Pule'anga Tonga (Tongan); Kingdom of Tonga (English).
Form of government: constitutional monarchy with one legislative house (Legislative Assembly [24]).
Head of state and government: King.
Capital: Nukualofa.
Official languages: Tongan; English.
Official religion: none.
Monetary unit: 1 pa'anga ($T) = 100 seniti; valuation (Oct. 29, 1984) 1 U.S.$ = $T1.19*; 1 £ = $T1.44.

Area and population

Island groups	Capitals	area sq mi	area sq km	population 1981 estimate
Eua	Ohonua	33	87	4,800
Haapai	Pangai	50	129	11,700
Niuas	Hihifo	27	69	2,500
Tongatapu	Nukualofa	101	262	62,400
Vavau	Neiafu	57	148	16,400
TOTAL		288†	747†	97,800

Source: Official government figures.

Demography

Density‡ (1984): persons per sq mi 245.4, persons per sq km 152.5.
Urban–rural (1976): urban 20.3%; rural 79.7%.
Sex distribution (1983): male 51.00%, female 49.00%.
Age breakdown (1976): under 15, 44.2%; 15–29, 26.0%; 30–44, 14.7%; 45–59, 9.5%; 60–74, 4.0%; 75 and over 1.6%.
Population projection: (1990) 119,000; (2000) 140,000.
Doubling time: 30 years.
Ethnic composition (1976): Tongan 98.3%; part European 0.8%; European 0.5%; other 0.4%.
Religious affiliation (1976): Free Wesleyan 47.4%; Roman Catholic 16.1%; Free Church of Tonga 13.7%; Church of Tonga 8.9%; other 13.9%.
Major city (1983 est.): Nukualofa 20,564.

Vital statistics

Birth rate per 1,000 population (1983): 27.1 (world avg. 29.0); legitimate, n.a.; illegitimate, n.a.
Death rate per 1,000 population (1983): 3.3 (world avg. 11.0).
Natural increase rate per 1,000 population (1983): 23.8 (world avg. 18.0).
Total fertility rate (avg. births per childbearing woman): n.a.
Marriage rate per 1,000 population (1981): 6.9.
Divorce rate per 1,000 population (1981): 0.9.
Infant mortality rate per 1,000 live births (1983): 6.4.
Life expectancy at birth (1980–85): male 60.0 years; female 61.0 years.
Major causes of death: n.a.; however, major diseases are gastroenteritis, infantile diarrhea, and acute respiratory infections.

National economy

Budget (1980)§. Revenue: $T12,230,000 (import duties 31.4%; income and wealth tax 13.6%; licenses, stamp duties, registration fees 1.3%). Expenditures: $T16,275,000 (investments 37.2%; social services 22.2%; economic services 13.9%; defense 2.7%).
Public debt (external, outstanding; 1982): U.S.$16,000,000.
Production (metric tons except as noted). Agriculture and fishing (1982): coconuts 122,000, roots and tubers 95,000, sweet potatoes 81,000, copra 16,000, cassava 14,000, fruits excluding melons 10,000, vegetables and melons 6,000, lemons and limes 3,000, eggs 380; livestock (number of live animals; 1983) 90,000 pigs, 18,000 goats, 15,000 horses, 8,000 cattle, 185,000 chickens; fish catch 2,500. Mining and quarrying (1982): coral 150,000; sand 25,000. Manufacturing (value in $T; 1980): nonmetal products 493,000; beverages 409,000; metal products 332,000; furniture fixtures 281,000; wearing apparel 139,000; paper and paper products 76,000; transport equipment 57,000. Construction (value in $T; 1981): residential 2,041,400; nonresidential 5,898,600. Energy production (consumption): electricity (kW-hr; 1982) 12,000,000 (12,000,000); coal, none (n.a.); petroleum products (metric tons; 1982) n.a. (14,000); natural gas, none (n.a.).
Gross national product (at current market prices; 1981): U.S.$50,000,000 (U.S.$510 per capita).

Origin of gross domestic product (current prices)

	1982 in value $T'000,000	1982 % of total value	1976 labour force	1976 % of labour force
Agriculture	18.6	31.0	9,529	44.5
Mining	0.5	0.8	16	0.1
Manufacturing	2.6	4.3	386	1.8
Construction	2.8	4.7	1,153	5.4
Trade	8.9	14.9	825 ‖	3.8 ‖
Public utilities	0.3	0.5	114	0.5
Transportation and communication	4.6	7.7	829	3.9
Finance	¶	¶	61	0.3
Pub. admin., defense	¶	¶	º	º
Services	¶	¶	4,082º	19.0º
Other	21.6¶	36.1¶	4,440	20.7
TOTAL	59.9	100.0	21,435	100.0

Tourism (1982): receipts from visitors U.S.$3,922,000; expenditures by nationals abroad, n.a.
Persons economically active (1976): total 21,435 (23.8%); female participation in the labour force, n.a.; unemployed 2,809 (13.1%).

Price and earnings indexes (1976 = 100)

	1977	1978	1979	1980	1981	1982	1983
Consumer price index	127.9	135.4	151.9	187.3	207.2	223.9	238.8
Earnings index	...	...	...	...	...	...	...

Household income and expenditure. Average household size (1980) 6.0; average annual income per household: n.a.; source of income: n.a.; expenditure: n.a.
Land use (1981): forested 11.9%; meadows and pastures 6.0%; agricultural and under permanent cultivation 79.1%; other 3.0%.

Foreign trade

Balance of trade (current prices)

	1978	1979	1980	1981	1982	1983
$T'000,000	−17.2	−19.4	−23.0	−27.3	−37.0	−35.3
% of total	62.8%	58.7%	61.7%	63.9%	81.5%	73.6%

Imports (1982): $T41,198,000 (food and live animals 24.0%, machinery and transport equipment 14.7%, of which transport equipment 6.7%; consumer goods 14.2%; mineral fuels and lubricants 13.9%; chemicals 6.4%). *Major import sources:* New Zealand 37.1%; Australia 23.6%; United States 9.5%; Fiji 7.5%; Japan 6.1%; Singapore 6.1%; China 3.0%; Hong Kong 1.3%.
Exports (1982): $T4,185,000 (coconut oil 31.2%; vanilla beans 15.0%; metal [manufactured] products 9.3%; desiccated coconut 7.0%; watermelons 7.0%; textile products 2.5%). *Major export destinations:* Australia 45.4%; New Zealand 36.8%; United States 9.7%; Fiji 2.5%; Western Samoa 1.3%.

Transport and communications

Transport. Railroads: none. Roads (1982): total length 269 mi, 433 km (paved 60%). Vehicles (1981): passenger cars 662, commercial vehicles 1,185. Merchant marine (1983): vessels (100 gross tons and over) 19; total deadweight tonnage 20,437. Air transport: passengers, n.a.; cargo, n.a.; airport (1984) with scheduled flights 1.
Communications. Daily newspapers: none. Radios (1983): total number of receivers 65,000 (1 per 1.6 persons). Television: total number of receivers, n.a. Telephones (1982): 2,600 (1 per 38.0 persons).

Education and health

Education (1982)

	schools	teachers	students	student/ teacher ratio
Primary (age 6–10)	110	818δ	16,701	...
Secondary (age 13–18)	50	668δ	16,348	...
Voc., teacher tr.	11	...	615	...
Higher	1	...	125	...

College graduates per 100,000 population: n.a. *Literacy* (1976): total population literate 46,456 (92.8%); males literate 23,372 (92.9%); females literate 23,084 (92.8%).
Health (1979): physicians 28 (1 per 3,418 persons); hospital beds 325 (1 per 294 persons).
Food (1978–80): daily per capita caloric intake 3,221 (vegetable products 83.9%, animal products 16.1%); 121% of FAO recommended minimum requirement.

Military

Total active duty personnel: Tonga had a small defense force of about 250 in the early 1980s.

*The pa'anga is at par with the Australian dollar. †Also includes 20 sq mi (52 sq km) of uninhabited islands. ‡Density is based on land area. §Estimated budget for 1983–84: revenue $T17,373,210; expenditure $T17,357,290. ‖ Trade includes hotels and restaurants. ¶Finance, public administration, and services included with other. ºPublic administration and defense included with services. δ1978–79.

MILT & JOAN MANN

Fua'amotu village, Tongatapu Island, Tonga.

Trinidad and Tobago

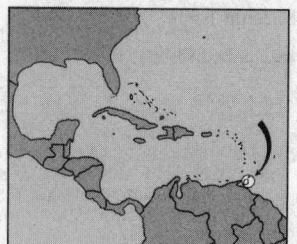

Official name: Republic of Trinidad and Tobago.
Form of government: multiparty republic with two legislative houses (Senate [31]; House of Representatives [36]).
Chief of state: President.
Head of government: Prime Minister.
Capital: Port-of-Spain.
Official language: English.
Official religion: none.
Monetary unit: 1 Trinidad and Tobago dollar (TT$) = 100 cents; valuation (Oct. 29, 1984) 1 U.S.$ = TT$2.40; 1 £ = TT$2.90.

Area and population

Counties	Capitals	area sq mi	area sq km	population 1980 census
Caroni	Chaguanas	214	554	140,200
Mayaro	Rio Claro	146	378	8,200
Nariva	Rio Claro	206	534	23,000
St. Andrew	Sangre Grande	283	733	44,900
St. David	Sangre Grande	79	205	5,100
St. George	...	354	917	388,700
St. Patrick	Siparia	261	676	123,500
Victoria	Princes Town	314	813	187,000
Municipalities				
Arima	...	4	10	11,400
Port-of-Spain	...	2	6	54,900
San Fernando	...	1	2	33,500
Ward				
Tobago	Scarborough	116	300	39,500
TOTAL		1,980	5,128	1,059,800*

Source: Official government figures.

Demography

Density (1985): persons per sq mi 632, persons per sq km 244.
Urban–rural (1980): urban 21.5%; rural 78.5%.
Sex distribution (1980): male 49.84%; female 50.16%.
Age breakdown (1980): under 15, 32.9%; 15–29, 31.9%; 30–44, 16.6%; 45–59, 11.1%; 60–74, 6.3%; 75 and over, 1.2%.
Population projection: (1990) 1,230,000; (2000) 1,376,000.
Doubling time: 37 years.
Ethnic composition (1979): Negro 43.0%; East Indian 40.0%; mixed 14.0%; other 3.0%.
Religious affiliation (1980): Christian 64.0%; Hindu 25.0%; Muslim 6.0%; other 5.0%.
Major city (1980): Port-of-Spain 54,900.

Vital statistics

Birth rate per 1,000 population (1979): 25.1 (world avg. 31.0); (1977) legitimate 56.3%, illegitimate 43.7%.
Death rate per 1,000 population (1979): 6.5 (world avg. 12.0).
Natural increase rate per 1,000 population (1979): 18.6 (world avg. 19.0).
Total fertility rate (avg. births per childbearing woman; 1979): 2.2.
Marriage rate per 1,000 population (1978): 7.4.
Divorce rate per 1,000 population (1978): 0.6.
Infant mortality rate per 1,000 live births (1979): 26.4.
Life expectancy at birth (1975–80): male 65.9 years; female 72.0 years.
Major causes of death per 100,000 population (1978): diseases of the circulatory system 244.1; malignant neoplasms (cancers) 65.3; accidents, poisoning, and violence 59.0; diseases of the respiratory system 30.9.

National economy

Budget (1982). Revenue: TT$6,788,100,000 (corporation tax 43.2%, income tax 29.9%, royalties from oil 8.0%, import duties 7.4%, taxes on goods and services 4.6%). Expenditures: TT$4,998,100,000 (education 18.6%, welfare services 17.6%, health 10.8%, justice and police 8.0%, agriculture 4.3%, transport and communication 3.5%, defense 1.5%).
Public debt (external, outstanding; 1982): U.S.$1,127,000,000.
Tourism (1981): receipts from visitors U.S.$161,000,000; expenditures by nationals abroad U.S.$167,000,000.
Production (metric tons except as noted). Agriculture, forestry, fishing (1982): sugarcane 1,000,000, coconuts 68,000, fruits except melons 63,000, vegetables and melons 34,000, rice 30,000, copra 8,000, bananas 5,000, cacao 3,000, coffee 2,000; livestock (number of live animals) 79,000 cattle, 61,000 pigs, 48,000 goats, 12,000 sheep, 8,000 buffaloes, 7,600,000 chickens; roundwood 97,000 cu m; fish catch 4,461. Mining and quarrying (cu m; 1980): gravel and sand 333,980; limestone 291,700; clay 113,800. Manufacturing (1982): fuel oils 5,811,780†; motor gasoline 2,055,220†; diesel oil 1,888,560†; fertilizer 939,700; cement 189,200; asphalt 29,700; beer 156,-650 hectolitres; edible oils 60,800 hectolitres; television sets 12,800 units; motor vehicles 10,800 units. Construction (1981): residential 43,000 sq m; nonresidential 12,000 sq m. Energy production (consumption): electricity (kW-hr; 1982) 2,260,000,000 (2,260,000,000); coal, none (none); crude petroleum (barrels; 1982) 62,901,000 (62,901,000); petroleum products (metric tons; 1982) 7,994,000 (1,687,000); natural gas (cu m; 1982) 3,192,945,500 (3,192,945,500).

Gross national product (at current market prices; 1981): U.S.$6,720,000,000 (U.S.$6,280 per capita).

Origin of gross domestic product (current prices)

	1981 in value TT$'000,000	% of total value	labour force	% of labour force
Agriculture	398	2.3	43,700	10.1
Mining	6,257	36.6	70,600‡	16.4‡
Manufacturing	1,041	6.1	‡	‡
Construction	1,512	8.8	100,600§	23.3§
Trade	1,640	9.6	78,000	18.1
Public utilities	272	1.6	§	§
Transportation and communication	1,896	11.1	33,800	7.8
Finance	1,274	7.4	...	...
Pub. admin., defense	1,827	10.7	...	...
Services	997	5.8	96,400	22.4
Other	...	...	8,300	1.9
TOTAL	17,114	100.0	431,400	100.0

Persons economically active (1981): total 431,400 (40.3%); female participation in the labour force 136,200 (31.6%); unemployed 44,900 (10.4%).

Price and earnings indexes (1980 = 100)

	1978	1979	1980	1981	1982	1983	1984
Consumer price index	74.2	85.1	100.0	114.3	127.4	148.7	174.9 ‖
Weekly earnings index	65.9	81.4	100.0	...	...	...	...

Household income and expenditure. Average household size (1980) 4.2; average annual income per household: n.a.; source of income: n.a.; expenditure (1975–76): food and drink 32.8%, clothing and footwear 15.0%, housing 13.2%, transport and communications 11.2%, household furniture and furnishings 6.0%, medical care and health 2.2%.
Land use (1981): forested 44.6%; meadows and pastures 2.2%; agricultural and under permanent cultivation 30.8%; other 22.4%.

Foreign trade

Balance of trade (current prices)

	1976	1977	1978	1979	1980	1981	1982
TT$'000,000	+567	+899	+201	+1,214	+2,158	+1,527	−1,476
% of total	5.5%	4.7%	2.1%	10.7%	12.4%	9.2%	9.0%

Imports (1982): TT$8,912,223,000 (fuels 25.2%, industrial supplies 23.6%, capital equipment 20.5%, transport equipment 10.7%). *Major import sources:* United States 35.4%; Saudi Arabia 11.6%; Indonesia 9.5%; United Kingdom 8.2%; Japan 7.2%; Canada 3.7%.
Exports (1982): TT$7,435,942,000 (petroleum products 87.9%, chemicals 5.2%, transport equipment 2.6%, food 1.7%). *Major export destinations:* United States 50.2%; The Netherlands 7.3%; Italy 4.4%; Guyana 3.6%; Suriname 3.6%; Honduras 3.1%.

Transport and communications

Transport. Railroads: none. Roads (1983): total length 5,174 mi, 8,327 km (paved 46%). Vehicles (1983): passenger cars 200,100; trucks and buses 63,220. Merchant marine (1983): vessels (100 gross tons and over) 51; total deadweight tonnage 13,776. Air transport (1980): passenger-mi 960,840,000, passenger-km 1,546,325,000; short ton-mi cargo 12,074,000, metric ton-km cargo 17,628,000; airport (1984) with scheduled flights 1.
Communications. Daily newspapers (1982): total number 6; total circulation 124,000; circulation per 1,000 population 105. Radios (1983): total number of receivers 355,000 (1 per 4 persons). Television (1983): total number of receivers 300,000 (1 per 4.7 persons). Telephones (1979): 77,639 (1 per 15 persons).

Education and health

Education (1979–80)

	schools	teachers	students	student/ teacher ratio
Primary (age 5–11)	465¶	6,443	166,763	25.9
Secondary (age 12–19)	¶	1,631⁹	84,482	...
Voc., teacher tr.	8⁹	114⁹	4,092	...
Higher	2⁹	500⁹	1,878	...

College graduates per 100,000 population (students graduating; 1977): 52.
Literacy (1980): total population literate 807,700 (96.7%); males literate 414,300 (98.2%); females literate 393,400 (95.3%).
Health: physicians (1980) 710 (1 per 1,490 persons); hospital beds (1976) 4,465 (1 per 246 persons).
Food (1978–80): daily per capita caloric intake 2,702 (vegetable products 81.0%, animal products 19.0%); 112% of FAO recommended minimum requirement.

Military

Total active duty personnel (1983): 800ð (army 62.5%; navy 31.3%; air force 6.2%). *Military expenditure as percent of GNP* (1981): 0.6% (world 5.7%); per capita expenditure U.S.$35.

*Detail does not add to total given because of rounding. †1980. ‡Manufacturing is included with mining. §Public utilities are included with construction. ‖ August only. ¶Secondary schools are included with primary schools. ⁹1975–76. ðAll services form part of the army.

Trust Territory of the Pacific Islands

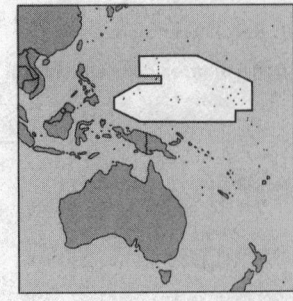

Official name: Trust Territory of the Pacific Islands.
Political status: Trust Territory (of the United Nations) under United States administration*.
Chief of state: President of the United States through the High Commissioner.
Heads of government: Marshall Islands, Micronesia, and Palau, President; Northern Mariana Islands, Governor.
Capital: Saipan.
Official language: English.
Official religion: none.
Monetary unit: 1 U.S. dollar (U.S.$) = 100 cents; valuation (Oct. 29, 1984) 1£ = U.S.$1.21.

Area and population		area		population
Island Groups				1980
Districts	Capitals	sq mi	sq km	census
Marshall Islands	Majuro	69	179	30,873
Micronesia	Kolonia	297	769	73,160
Kosrae	Kosrae	42	109	5,491
Pohnpei	Kolonia	163	422	22,081
Truk	Moen	45	116	37,488
Yap	Colonia	47	122	8,100
Northern Mariana Is.	Saipan	182	471	16,780
Palau (Belau)	Koror	178	461	12,116
TOTAL		726	1,880	132,929

Source: Official government figures.

Demography

Density (1984): persons per sq mi 199.7, persons per sq km 77.1.
Urban–rural† (1980): urban 30.3%; rural 69.7%.
Sex distribution† (1980): male 51.25%; female 48.75%.
Age breakdown† (1980): under 15, 46.8%; 15–29, 26.6%; 30–44, 12.6%; 45–59, 8.2%; 60–74, 4.6%; 75 and over, 1.2%.
Population projection: (1990) 162,000; (2000) 198,000.
Doubling time: 37 years.
Ethnic composition (1983): Micronesian 98.9%; other 1.1%.
Religious affiliation (1973): Protestant 49.2%; Roman Catholic 45.4%; other 4.2%; nonreligious and unknown 1.2%.
Major cities (1980): Saipan 14,500; Majuro 11,791; Moen 10,351; Koror 7,585; Tol 6,705.

Vital statistics

Birth rate per 1,000 population (1982): 23.7 (world avg. 29.0); legitimate, n.a.; illegitimate, n.a.
Death rate per 1,000 population (1982): 3.7 (world avg. 11.0).
Natural increase rate per 1,000 population (1982): 20.0 (world avg. 18.0).
Total fertility rate (avg. births per childbearing woman; 1980–85): 4.9.
Marriage rate per 1,000 population: n.a.
Divorce rate per 1,000 population: n.a.
Infant mortality rate per 1,000 live births (1982): 21.5.
Life expectancy at birth (1980–85): male 63.0 years; female 66.5 years.
Major causes of death per 100,000 population (1982): heart disease 32.4; cerebrovascular diseases 27.0; benign and malignant neoplasms (cancers) 24.7; pneumonia and influenza 24.7.

National economy

Budget (1981–82). Revenue: U.S.$125,100,000 (grants from U.S. 78.8%; reimbursements and other operating income 21.2%). Expenditures: U.S.$118,900,000 (education 23.8%; public works 20.1%; health 11.6%; general administration 7.6%).
Public debt: n.a.
Tourism (1979): receipts from visitors U.S.$2,400,000†; expenditures by nationals abroad, n.a.
Production (metric tons except as noted). Agriculture, forestry, fishing (1982): coconuts 205,000, copra 26,000, cassava 10,000, sweet potatoes 4,000, vegetables and melons 3,000; livestock (number of live animals) 27,000 pigs, 8,000 cattle, 4,000 goats; fish catch 5,377‡. Mining and quarrying: phosphates. Manufacturing: no data available; however, soap, shampoo, and body oil are manufactured from coconut; there is also a breadfruit flour plant; weaving and basket making are popular in several islands. Construction (1978): 103 housing units. Energy production (consumption): electricity (kW-hr; 1981) 145,000,000 (145,000,000).
Gross national product (at current market prices; 1981): U.S.$120,000,000 (U.S.$1,000 per capita).
Persons economically active (1976): total 27,711 (25.9%); female participation in the labour force n.a.; unemployed n.a.
Price and earnings indexes: n.a.
Household income and expenditure. Average household size (1980) 6.2; source of income, n.a.; expenditure, n.a.
Land use (1981): forested 22.5%; meadows and pastures 13.5%; agricultural and under permanent cultivation 33.1%; other 30.9%.

Foreign trade

Balance of trade (current prices)						
	1972–73	1973–74	1974–75	1975–76	1976–77	1977–78
U.S.$'000,000	−23.7	−24.1	−21.2	−31.4	−29.4	−20.0
% of total	81.8%	86.5%	56.9%	69.7%	58.7%	34.4%

Imports (1977–78) U.S.$39,000,000 (foodstuffs and live animals, chiefly for food 35.7%; minerals, fuels, and lubricants 13.2%; manufactured goods 12.3%; beverages and tobacco 12.0%; machinery and transport equipment 10.7%; chemicals 5.3%). *Major import sources:* United States 35.0%; Japan 25.0%; Australia 6.2%.
Exports (1977–78) U.S.$19,000,000 (coconut oil 57.0%, fish 27.0%, copra 11.0%). *Major export destinations:* United States 49.1%; European Economic Community 23.1%; American Samoa 7.2%; Guam 5.6%; Solomon Islands 4.8%.

Transport and communications

Transport. Railroads: none. Roads (1980): total length 1,000 mi, 1,600 km (paved 25%). Vehicles (1978): passenger cars 4,206; trucks and buses 2,311. Merchant marine: none. Air transport (1978): passenger-mi 187,778,000, passenger-km 302,200,000; short ton-mi cargo 3,854,000, metric ton-km cargo 5,627,000; airports (1982) with scheduled flights 9.
Communications. Daily newspapers (1983): 1; total circulation, n.a. Radios (1981): total number of receivers 30,000 (1 per 5.1 persons). Television (1981): total number of receivers 6,850 (1 per 22.5 persons). Telephones (1976): 4,317 (1 per 27.9 persons).

Education and health

Education (1982–83)				student/
	schools	teachers§	students	teacher ratio
Primary (age 6–13)	248 ‖	1,578	26,883	...
Secondary (age 14–17)	32¶	520	6,100ọ	...
Voc., teacher tr.	2	39	456	...
Higher	1	155	264	...

College graduates per 100,000 population (1978): 380. *Literacy* (1980): total population literate *c.* 120,000 (90%); males literate, n.a.; females literate, n.a.
Health (1983): physicians 30 (1 per 4,832 persons); hospital beds 528 (1 per 274 persons).
Food: daily per capita caloric intake, n.a.

Military

External security is provided by the U.S.; a missile range on Kwajalein Atoll employs 3,000 U.S. citizens and 645 Micronesians. The U.S. has a total capital investment of over U.S.$700,000,000 there.

*Separate administrative actions within the Trust Territory have, since 1978, created four new administrative entities that are to form the framework for local government upon termination of the UN trusteeship: the Commonwealth of the Northern Mariana Islands (1978); the Federated States of Micronesia (1979); the Republic of the Marshall Islands (1979); and the Republic of Palau (1981). The government of the Trust Territory has become progressively more vestigial as its functions are assumed by the governments of these four entities. Combined data are, thus, often no longer available. †Excluding the Northern Mariana Islands. ‡1980. §1978–79. ‖ 1977–78. ¶1976–77. ọ1981–82.

MILT & JOAN MANN

Tattooed Yapese making a fish trap, Federated States of Micronesia, Trust Territory of the Pacific Islands.

Tunisia

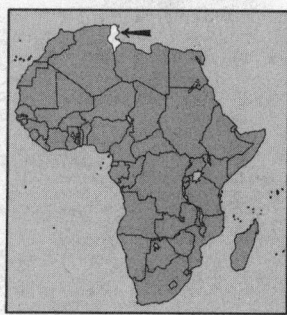

Official name: al-Jumhūrīyah at-Tūnisīyah (Republic of Tunisia).
Form of government: multiparty republic with one legislative house (National Assembly [136]).
Head of state and government: President.
Capital: Tunis.
Official language: Arabic.
Official religion: Islām.
Monetary unit: 1 dinar (D) = 1,000 millimes; valuation (Oct. 29, 1984) D1.00 = U.S.$1.20 = £0.99.

Area and population

Governorates	Capitals	area sq mi	area sq km	population 1984 census
Aryānah	Aryānah	602	1,558	374,192
Bājah	Bājah	1,374	3,558	274,706
Banzart	Banzart	1,423	3,685	394,670
Bin 'Arūs	Bin 'Arūs	294	761	246,193
Jundūbah	Jundūbah	1,198	3,102	359,429
al-Kāf	al-Kāf	1,917	4,965	247,672
Madaniyin	Madaniyin	3,316	8,588	295,889
al-Mahdīyah	al-Mahdīyah	1,145	2,966	270,435
al-Munastir	al-Munastir	393	1,019	278,478
Nābul	Nābul	1,076	2,788	461,405
Qābis	Qābis	2,770	7,175	240,016
Qafşah	Qafşah	3,471	8,990	235,723
al-Qaşrayn	al-Qaşrayn	3,114	8,066	297,959
al-Qayrawān	al-Qayrawān	2,591	6,712	421,607
Qibilī	Qibilī	8,527	22,084	95,371
Safāqis	Safāqis	2,913	7,545	577,992
Sīdī Bū Zayd	Sīdī Bū Zayd	2,700	6,994	288,528
Silyānah	Silyānah	1,788	4,631	222,038
Sūsah	Sūsah	1,012	2,621	322,491
Tatāwin	Tatāwin	15,015	38,889	100,329
Tawzar	Tawzar	1,822	4,719	67,943
Tūnis	Tūnis	134	346	774,364
Zaghwān	Zaghwān	1,069	2,768	118,743
TOTAL		59,664	154,530	6,966,173

Source: Official government figures.

Demography

Density (1984): persons per sq mi 117.2, persons per sq km 45.2.
Urban–rural (1984): urban 52.8%; rural 47.2%.
Sex distribution (1984): male 50.92%; female 49.08%.
Age breakdown (1982): under 15, 41.8%; 15–29, 27.4%; 30–44, 13.5%; 45–59, 10.6%; 60–74, 5.4%; 75 and over, 1.2%‡.
Population projection: (1990) 7,989,000; (2000) 9,856,000.
Doubling time: 28 years.
Ethnic composition (1980): Arab 97.9%; Berber 1.5%; French 0.2%; Italian 0.1%; other 0.3%.
Religious affiliation (1980): Muslim 99.4%; Christian 0.3%; Jewish 0.1%; other 0.2%.
Major cities (1984, commune): Tūnis 596,654; Safāqis 231,911; Aryānah 98,655.

Vital statistics

Birth rate per 1,000 population (1982): 32.9 (world avg. 29.0); (1974) legitimate 99.8%, illegitimate 0.2%.
Death rate per 1,000 population (1982): 7.3 (world avg. 11.0).
Natural increase rate per 1,000 population (1982): 25.6 (world avg. 18.0).
Total fertility rate: n.a.
Marriage rate per 1,000 population (1982): 14.9.
Divorce rate per 1,000 population (1982): 0.9.
Infant mortality rate per 1,000 live births (1975–80): 107.
Life expectancy at birth (1975–80): male 56.3 years; female 58.4 years.
Major causes of death per 100,000 population: n.a.; however, the major illnesses are intestinal infections, trachoma, hepatitis, tuberculosis, and syphilis.

National economy

Budget (1982). Revenue: D1,515,535,000 (indirect taxes 41.3%, investment 24.2%, direct taxes 16.1%). Expenditures: D1,792,524,000 (education 12.8%, health 5.5%, defense 4.3%, interior affairs 4.2%, agriculture 3.6%, social welfare 1.1%).
Public debt (external, outstanding; 1982): U.S.$3,177,300,000.
Tourism (1982): receipts from visitors U.S.$577,000,000; expenditures by nationals abroad U.S.$102,000,000.
Production (metric tons except as noted). Agriculture, forestry, fishing (1982): wheat 1,000,000, tomatoes 380,000, barley 300,000, watermelons 197,000, potatoes 140,000, grapes 100,000, oranges 93,000, olives 87,000, dates 52,000, cabbages 6,000; roundwood 1,738,000 cu m; fish catch 62,752; livestock (number of live animals) 4,500,000 sheep, 600,000 cattle, 800,000 goats, 173,000 camels, 14,000,000 chickens. Mining and quarrying (1982): phosphate rock 4,729,000; iron ore 274,000; lead 8,600; zinc 15,200. Manufacturing (1982): cement 1,814,900; phosphoric acid 506,200; flour 419,600; olive oil 70,000; steel 3,300; beer 357,000 hectolitres; mineral water 331,300 hectolitres; cigarettes 6,016,000,000 units. Construction (1980): number of new dwellings completed 1,978; residential 225,000 sq m. Energy production (consumption): electricity (kW-hr; 1982) 3,173,500,000 (2,381,300,000); coal

(metric tons; 1982) 7,216,000 (2,544,000); crude petroleum (barrels; 1982) 37,390,330 (10,628,500); petroleum products (metric tons; 1982) 1,262,000 (2,296,000); natural gas (cu m; 1982) 422,800,000 (93,100,000).
Gross national product (at current market prices; 1982): U.S.$7,572,000,000 (U.S.$1,125 per capita).

Origin of gross domestic product (current prices)

	1981 in value D'000,000	% of total value	labour force	% of labour force
Agriculture	557.0	15.7	537,900	32.4
Mining	513.9	14.4	16,000	0.9
Manufacturing	487.9	13.7	359,500	21.7
Construction	249.0	6.9	179,100	10.8
Trade	...		148,500	8.9
Public utilities	62.4	1.8	9,500	0.6
Transportation and communication	192.3	5.4	63,200	3.8
Finance			10,900	0.7
Pub. admin., defense	447.8	12.6	...	...
Services	...		266,500	16.1
Other	1,048.7	29.5	66,600	4.0
TOTAL	3,559.0	100.0	1,657,700	100.0*

Persons economically active (1980): total 1,609,300 (25.3%); female 359,600 (22.3%); unemployed 66,195 (4.1%).

Price and earnings indexes (1977 = 100)

	1977	1978	1979	1980	1981	1982	1983
Consumer price index	100.0	105.4	113.5	124.9	136.1	154.6	168.5
Monthly earnings index	...	...	...	...	...	...	...

Household income and expenditure. Average household size (1984): 5.5; income per household: n.a.; source of income: n.a.; expenditure (1980): food 41.7%, housing 29.0%, clothing and footwear 8.5%, recreation 7.6%, transportation 4.9%.
Land use (1981): forested 3.1%; meadows and pastures 16.4%; agricultural and under permanent cultivation 30.1%; other 50.4%.

Foreign trade

Balance of trade (current prices)

	1978	1979	1980	1981	1982	1983
D'000,000	−421.3	−430.0	−522.5	−632.9	−840.0	−845.0
% of total	31.0%	22.8%	22.4%	20.4%	26.4%	25.0%

Imports (1982): D2,008,000,000 (machinery, cars, and other transportation vehicles 4.9%; chemicals and pharmaceuticals 3.4%; textiles 3.2%; crude oil 2.5%; wheat 2.3%). *Major import sources:* France 25.9%; Italy 14.8%; West Germany 11.5%; United States 7.8%; The Netherlands 5.1%; Spain 4.1%.
Exports (1982): D1,168,000,000 (crude oil 42.2%; clothing 12.6%; phosphoric acid 5.9%; olive oil 4.9%; crude phosphates 1.9%; dates 0.7%). *Major export destinations:* United States 23.0%; France 19.3%; Italy 16.2%; West Germany 10.4%; Greece 2.7%; The Netherlands 2.4%.

Transport and communications

Transport. Railroads (1981): route length 1,251 mi, 2,013 km; passenger-mi 627,988,000, passenger-km 1,010,650,000; short ton-mi cargo 1,169,266,000, metric ton-km cargo 1,707,100,000. Roads (1982): total length 15,752 mi, 25,352 km (paved 52%). Vehicles (1982): passenger cars 141,185; trucks and buses 147,571. Merchant marine (1983): vessels (100 gross tons and over) 52; total deadweight tonnage 440,896. Air transport (1982): passenger-mi 1,486,123,000, passenger-km 2,391,688,000; short ton-mi cargo 253,769,000, metric ton-km cargo 230,216,000; airports (1984) with scheduled flights 5.
Communications. Daily newspapers (1983): total number 5; total circulation 322,000; circulation per 1,000 population 46.7. Radios (1983): total number of receivers 1,124,000 (1 per 6.1 persons). Television (1983): total number of receivers 291,000 (1 per 23.7 persons). Telephones (1981): 112,355 (1 per 58.3 persons).

Education and health

Education (1983–84)

	schools	teachers	students	student/ teacher ratio
Primary (age 6–11)	3,066	33,026	1,191,408	36.1
Secondary (age 12–18)	335	17,943	364,492	20.3
Voc., teacher tr.	...	...	...	...
Higher		4,397	35,426	8.1

College graduates per 100,000 population (students graduating; 1982): 64.1.
Literacy (1980): total population literate 1,855,017 (47.4%); males literate 1,190,891 (61.2%); females literate 664,126 (33.7%).
Health (1982): physicians 1,732 (1 per 3,883 persons); hospital beds 14,071 (1 per 478 persons).
Food (1978–80): daily per capita caloric intake 2,751 (vegetable products 91.4%, animal products 8.6%); 115% of FAO recommended minimum.

Military

Total active duty personnel (1982): 28,500 (army 80.7%; navy 12.3%; air force 7.0%). *Military expenditure as percent of GNP* (1982): 3.2% (world 6.0%); per capita expenditure U.S.$40.

*Detail does not add to 100.0% because of rounding.

Turkey

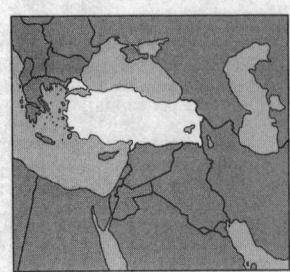

Official name: Türkiye Cumhuriyeti (Republic of Turkey).
Form of government: multiparty republic dominated by a military-controlled Presidential Council.
Chief of state: President.
Head of government: Prime Minister.
Capital: Ankara.
Official language: Turkish.
Official religion: none.
Monetary unit: 1 Turkish lira (LT) = 100 kurush; valuation (Oct. 29, 1984) 1 U.S.$ = LT 416.51; 1 £ = LT 502.73.

Area and population	area		population
	sq mi	sq km	1984 estimate
Geographical regions			
Akdeniz kıyısı	22,933	59,395	4,447,000
Batı Anadolu	29,742	77,031	3,392,000
Doğu Anadolu	68,074	176,311	6,072,000
Güneydoğu Anadolu	15,347	39,749	2,098,000
İç Anadolu	91,254	236,347	11,647,000
Karadeniz kıyısı	31,388	81,295	6,600,000
Marmara ve Ege kıyıları	32,962	85,370	9,544,000
Trakya	9,213	23,862	4,791,000
TOTAL	300,913	779,360	48,591,000

Source: Official government figures; Britannica estimate.

Demography

Density (1984): persons per sq mi 161.5, persons per sq km 62.3.
Urban–rural (1980): urban 43.9%; rural 56.1%.
Sex distribution (1980): male 50.65%; female 49.35%.
Age breakdown (1980): under 15, 38.5%; 15–29, 27.7%; 30–44, 16.0%; 45–59, 11.2%; 60–64, 1.8%; 65 and over, 4.8%*.
Population projection: (1990) 54,633,000; (2000) 67,166,000.
Doubling time: 28.5 years.
Ethnic composition (1978): Turkish 87.1%; Kurdish 9.5%; Arab 1.7%; other 1.7%.
Religious affiliation (1980): Muslim 99.2%; Eastern Orthodox 0.3%; other 0.5%.
Major cities (1980): Istanbul 2,772,708; Ankara 1,877,755; İzmir 757,854; Adana 574,515; Bursa 445,113.

Vital statistics

Birth rate per 1,000 population (1980–85): 33.6 (world avg. 27.5).
Death rate per 1,000 population (1980–85): 9.3 (world avg. 10.6).
Natural increase rate per 1,000 population (1980–85): 24.3 (world avg. 16.9).
Total fertility rate (avg. births per childbearing woman; 1980–85): 4.5.
Marriage rate per 1,000 population (1982): 3.6.
Divorce rate per 1,000 population (1982): 0.4.
Infant mortality rate per 1,000 live births (1979): 131.0.
Life expectancy at birth (1980–85): male 60.3 years; female 64.9 years.
Major causes of death per 100,000 population (1982): heart disease 85.2; birth injury and difficult labour 33.2; malignant neoplasms (cancers) 24.5; cerebrovascular disease 17.2.

National economy

Budget (1981). Revenue: LT1,480,965,000,000 (taxes on income 51.7%, taxes on goods 12.6%, taxes and fees on services 8.8%, taxes on foreign trade 7.9%). Expenditures: LT1,540,965,000,000 (finance, including intergovernmental transfers 51.8%, defense 14.8%, education 10.1%, public works 4.0%, health and welfare 2.5%).
Public debt (external, outstanding; 1982): U.S.$18,001,500,000.
Tourism (1982): receipts from visitors U.S.$370,319,000; expenditures by nationals abroad U.S.$108,917,000.
Production (metric tons except as noted). Agriculture, forestry, fishing (1982): wheat 17,500,000, sugar beets 12,732,000, barley 6,400,000, melons 4,500,000, tomatoes 3,700,000, grapes 3,650,000, potatoes 3,000,000, apples 1,600,000, corn (maize) 1,360,000, olives 1,320,000, dry onions 1,025,000; livestock (number of live animals) 49,636,000 sheep, 18,213,000 goats; firewood 8,235,000 cu m, roundwood 4,054,073 cu m; fish catch 466,044. Mining and quarrying (1982): iron 2,855,000; copper 2,700,000; boron minerals 1,399,172. Manufacturing (1982): cement 15,778,000; petroleum products 15,267,000; semifinished iron and steel products 2,801,577; crude iron 2,102,481; sugar 1,617,169; flour 1,537,163; salt 1,313,719; motor vehicles (number of units) 167,000; motor vehicle tires (number of units) 2,905,252. Construction (1982): residential 17,334,000 sq m; nonresidential 2,824,000 sq m. Energy production (consumption): electricity (kW-hr; 1982) 26,551,000,000 (28,324,000,000); coal (metric tons; 1982) 20,168,000 (21,322,000); crude petroleum (barrels; 1982) 17,166,860 (120,483,210); petroleum products (metric tons; 1982) 15,033,000 (15,084,000); natural gas, none (n.a.).
Land use (1981): forested 26.2%; meadows and pastures 12.5%; agricultural and under permanent cultivation 37.0%; other 24.3%.
Household income and expenditure‖. Average household size: n.a.; income per household (1979): LT11,880 (U.S.$385); sources of income: self-employment 46.8%, wages and salaries 38.9%, transfer grant 9.4%, other 4.9%; expenditure (1979): food 41.2%, housing 25.2%, clothing 14.8%, recre-

ation and entertainment 6.1%, transportation 5.5.%, health 3.3%, other 3.9%.
Gross national product (at current market prices; 1983): U.S.$51,036,000,000 (U.S.$1,080 per capita).

Origin of gross domestic product (market prices of 1980)

	in value LT'000,000	% of total value	labour force	% of labour force
Agriculture	925,000	21.4	10,483,000	55.1
Mining	71,200	1.6	179,000	0.9
Manufacturing	870,900	20.1	2,037,000	10.7
Construction	213,000	4.9	814,000	4.2
Trade and finance	714,600	16.5	1,408,000	7.5
Public utilities	84,600	2.0	42,000	0.2
Transportation and communication	409,200	9.5	546,000	2.9
Pub. admin., defense	377,600	8.7	†	†
Other	661,900	15.3	3,519,000†	18.5†
TOTAL	4,328,000	100.0	19,028,000	100.0

Persons economically active (1982): total 19,027,000 (41.1%); female participation in the total labour force 6,260,000 (32.9%); unemployed 3,368,000 (17.7%).

Price and earnings indexes (1975 = 100)

	1978	1979	1980	1981	1982	1983	1984
Consumer price index	216.7	343.8	722.6	986.9	1,291.2	1,664.9	2,101.3§
Daily earnings index‡	231.9	313.8	479.0	588.0	747.2	...	...

Foreign trade

Balance of trade (current prices)

	1978	1979	1980	1981	1982	1983
LT'000,000	−43,930	−80,710	−316,460	−348,540	−344,640	−566,910
% of total	28.4%	34.8%	41.7%	24.7%	15.5%	17.9%

Imports (1983): LT1,865,870,000,000 (petroleum oil, crude and crude oils obtained from bituminous minerals 35.9%; machinery except electrical 20.5%, of which transportation equipment 4.9%; chemicals and related products 12.4%, of which dyes and pharmaceuticals 9.5%; iron and steel products 8.9%). *Major import sources:* Iran 13.7%; West Germany 10.6%; Iraq 9.8%; Libya 8.6%; United States 7.5%.
Exports (1983): LT1,298,960,000,000 (cereals, livestock, and other foodstuffs 42.7%, of which fruits 9.2%; cattle, sheep, and goats 4.9%; textiles and clothing accessories 22.7%; petroleum products 4.1%; machinery and transportation equipment 4.0%). *Major export destinations:* Iran 19.0%; West Germany 14.6%; Italy 7.4%; Saudi Arabia 6.4%; Iraq 5.6%.

Transport and communications

Transport. Railroads (1982): length 5,091 mi, 8,193 km; passenger-mi 3,514,500,000, passenger-km 5,656,000,000; short ton-mi cargo 4,332,300,000, metric ton-km cargo 6,325,000,000. Roads (1980): total length 144,698 mi, 232,867 km (paved 53%). Vehicles (1980): passenger cars 812,122; trucks and buses 392,927. Merchant marine (1983): vessels (100 gross tons and over) 687; total deadweight tonnage 4,088,392. Air transport (1982): passenger-mi 1,116,473,000, passenger-km 1,796,789,000; short ton-mi cargo 115,465,000, metric ton-km cargo 168,576,000; airports (1983) with scheduled flights 21.
Communications. Daily newspapers (1979): total number 364; total circulation 3,878,000; circulation per 1,000 population 89.1. Radios (1983): total number of receivers 4,300,000 (1 per 11.0 persons). Television (1983): total number of receivers 3,610,000 (1 per 13.1 persons). Telephones (1982): 2,104,113 (1 per 22.0 persons).

Education and health

Education (1980–81)

	schools	teachers	students	student/ teacher ratio
Primary (age 5–12)	44,098	215,073	5,691,066	26.5
Secondary (age 13–18)	5,062	78,208	1,697,454	21.7
Voc., teacher tr.	1,718	33,840	503,205	14.9
Higher	331	15,502	271,138	17.5

College graduates per 100,000 population (students graduating; 1980): 71.
Literacy (1975): total population literate 14,489,917 (60.0%); males literate 9,336,607 (76.8%); females literate 5,153,310 (43.0%).
Health (1981): physicians 28,411 (1 per 1,597 persons); hospital beds 97,765 (1 per 464 persons).
Food (1978–80): daily per capita caloric intake 2,965 (vegetable products 89.8%, animal products 10.2%); 118% of FAO recommended minimum requirement.

Military

Total active duty personnel (1983): 569,000 (army 82.6%; navy 8.0%; air force 9.4%). *Military expenditure as percent of* GNP (1982): 3.7% (world 6.0%); per capita expenditure U.S.$40.

---

*Includes those of unknown age. †Includes those employed in public administration and in all community, social, and personal services. ‡Manufacturing industries only. §First quarter. ‖ Urban areas only.

Tuvalu

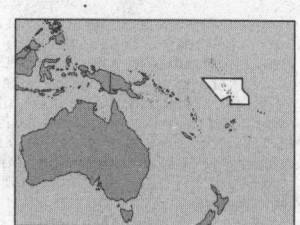

Official name: Tuvalu.
Form of government: constitutional monarchy with one legislative house (House of Assembly [12]).
Chief of state: British Monarch, represented by Governor-General.
Head of government: Prime Minister.
Capital: Funafuti Atoll.
Official language: none; Tuvaluan and English widely spoken.
Official religion: none.
Monetary unit*: 1 Tuvalu Dollar = 1 Australian Dollar ($T = $A) = 100 Tuvalu and Australian cents; valuation (Oct. 29, 1984) 1 U.S.$ = $A1.19; 1 £ = $A11.44.

Area and population

Islands	Capital	area		population 1983 estimate
		sq mi	sq km	
Funafuti	Funafuti	0.91	2.36	2,620
Nanumaga		1.00	2.59	760
Nanumea		1.38	3.57	910
Niulakita		0.16	0.41	90
Niutao		0.82	2.12	920
Nui		1.27	3.29	650
Nukufetau		1.18	3.06	740
Nukulaelae		0.64	1.66	350
Vaitupu		1.89	4.90	1,320
TOTAL		9.25	23.96	8,360

Source: Official government figures.

Demography

Density (1984): persons per sq mi 937.6, persons per sq km 362.0.
Urban-rural (1983): urban 31.3%; rural 68.7%.
Sex distribution (1979): male 46.77%; female 53.23%.
Age breakdown (1979): under 15, 33.8%; 15–29, 31.0%; 30–44, 14.3%; 45–59, 13.2%; 60–74, 6.1%; 75 and over, 1.6%.
Population projection: (1990) 11,000; (2000) 15,800.
Doubling time: 19 years.
Ethnic composition (1979): Tuvaluan (Polynesian) 91.2%; mixed (part I-Kiribati or other) 6.0%; I-Kiribati 1.3%; European and other Pacific 1.4%.
Religious affiliation (1979): Church of Tuvalu (Congregational) 96.9%; Seventh-day Adventist 1.4%; Baha'i 1.0%; Roman Catholic 0.2%; other 0.5%.
Major city (1983): Funafuti (urban) 2,620.

Vital statistics

Birth rate per 1,000 population (1982): 34.8 (world avg. 29.0).
Death rate per 1,000 population (1982): 7.6 (world avg. 11.0).
Natural increase rate per 1,000 population (1982): 27.2 (world avg. 18.0).
Total fertility rate (avg. births per childbearing woman; 1979): 2.8.
Marriage rate per 1,000 population: n.a.
Divorce rate per 1,000 population: n.a.
Infant mortality rate per 1,000 live births (1979): 42.
Life expectancy at birth (1979): male 57 years; female 60 years.
Major illnesses per 1,000 population (1981): influenza 71,729; intestinal infections 13,541; chicken pox 974; filarial infection and dracontiasis 456; tuberculosis 190.

National economy

Budget (1981). Revenue: $A5,433,141 (external aid 59.6%; philatelic sales 14.5%; customs and excise 8.5%; income tax 4.1%; other 13.3%). Expenditures: $A5,048,250 (communications and transport 28.3%; administration 19.7%; works and local government 15.5%; education 12.5%; health 6.8%; other 17.2%).
Production. Agriculture, forestry, fishing (1982): coconuts 1,000 metric tons; breadfruit, pulaka (taro), bananas, pandanus fruit, pawpaw; pigs, chickens, goats; fishing, castor-oil fish 200 metric tons. Mining and quarrying: none. Manufacturing (1982): copra 235 metric tons; handicrafts; beche-de-mer; baked goods. Construction: n.a. Energy production (consumption): electricity (kW-hr; 1981) 3,000,000 (3,000,000).
Gross national product (at current market prices; 1981): U.S.$5,000,000 (U.S.$680 per capita).

Origin of gross domestic product (current prices)

	1979			
	in value $A	% of total value	labour force	% of labour force
Agriculture	597,100	16.0	2,955	73.7
Mining	—	—	—	—
Manufacturing	37,300	1.0	62	1.5
Construction	485,200	13.0	229	5.7
Trade	1,268,900	34.0	100	2.5
Public utilities	...	...	14	0.4
Transportation and communication	149,300	4.0	111	2.8
Finance, pub. admin., and services	1,194,200	32.0	377	9.4
Other, including unemployed	—	—	162	4.0
TOTAL	3,732,000	100.0	4,010	100.0

Public debt: n.a.
Tourism (1979): number of visitors 474.
Persons economically active (1979): total 4,010 (54.6%); female 2,058 (51.4%); unemployed 162 (4.0%).

Price and earnings indexes (1978 = 100)

	1978	1979	1980	1981	1982	1983	1984
Consumer price index	100.0	104.1	117.6	129.1	...	...	...
Monthly earnings index	...	...	...	...	...	...	...

Household income and expenditure. Average household size (1979) 6.6; income per household: n.a.; households' sources of income: agriculture and other 61.2%, cash economy only 17.9%, agriculture only 14.9%, other 6.0%; expenditure: n.a.
Land use (1983): agricultural and under permanent cultivation 75%†; other 25%.

Foreign trade

Balance of trade (current prices)

	1978	1979	1980	1981	1982	1983
$A'000	−1,527	−1,594	−3,061	−2,556	−2,890	...
% of total	94.3%	75.6%	94.7%	98.6%	98.7%	...

Imports (1982): $A2,890,377 (food and live animals 22.4%, basic manufactured products 19.1%; petroleum products 16.7%; machinery and transport equipment 16.1%). *Major import sources:* Fiji 47.5%; Australia 39.7%; New Zealand 5.3%; .
Exports (1982): $A36,766 (copra 72.5%, reexported cinema films 27.5%). *Major export destinations:* n.a.

Transport and communications

Transport. Railroads: none. Roads (1983): total length 5 mi, 8 km (paved 0%). Vehicles: passenger cars, n.a.; trucks and buses, n.a. Merchant marine (1983): vessels (100 gross tons and over) 2; total deadweight tonnage 458. Air transport (1977): passenger arrivals (Funafuti) 1,443; cargo, n.a.; airport (1984) with scheduled flights 1‡.
Communications. Newspaper (1983): total number 1 (fortnightly); total circulation 250; circulation per 1,000 population 29.8. Radios (1983): total number of receivers 7,500 (1 per 1.1 persons). Television (1983): total number of receivers 1,100 (1 per 7.6 persons). Telephones (1982): 92 (1 per 88 persons).

Education and health

Education (1982–83)

	schools	teachers	students	student/ teacher ratio
Primary (age 6–14)	9	41	966	23.5
Secondary (age 12–18)	1	15	250	16.7
Vocational	8	16	354	22.1
Higher	—	—	—	—

College graduates per 100,000 population (1979): 1,000§. *Literacy* (1979): total population literate, 5,509 (95.5%); males literate 2,443 (95.5%); females literate 3,066 (95.5).
Health (1979): physicians 5 (1 per 1,470 persons); hospital beds 64‖ (1 per 102‖ persons).
Food: daily per capita caloric intake, n.a.

*The value of the Tuvalu Dollar is pegged to the value of the Australian Dollar. †Capable of supporting coconut palms, pandanus, and breadfruit. Other crops grown in trenches with specially enriched soil. ‡Six atoll lagoons have seaplane service. §Tuvaluan population only. ‖ 1977.

MILT & JOAN MANN

Boys climbing coconut palms, Funafuti atoll, Tuvalu.

Uganda

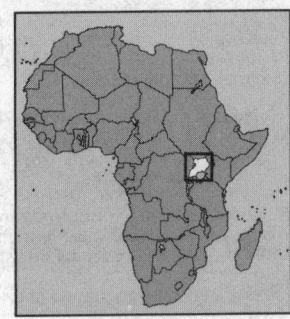

Official name: Jamhuri ya Uganda (Republic of Uganda).
Form of government: multiparty republic with one legislative house (National Assembly [156]).
Chief of state: President.
Head of government: Prime Minister.
Capital: Kampala.
Official language: English.
Official religion: none.
Monetary unit: 1 Uganda shilling (USh) = 100 cents; valuation (Oct. 29, 1984) 1 U.S.$ = USh479.3; 1 £ = USh578.5.

Area and population

Provinces Districts	Capitals	area sq mi	area sq km	population 1980 census
Busoga	Jinja	5,150	13,340	1,221,872
Iganga	Bulamogi	3,190	8,250	643,801
Jinja	Jinja	280	730	228,520
Kamuli	Namwendwa	1,680	4,360	349,551
Central	Kampala	2,420	6,270	1,117,648
Kampala	Kampala	70	190	478,895
Mpigi	Mpigi	2,350	6,080	638,753
Eastern	Mbale	8,600	22,260	2,015,530
Kapchorwa	Kaptanya	670	1,740	74,517
Kumi	Kumi	1,100	2,860	238,809
Mbale	Bunkoko	990	2,550	557,241
Soroti	Soroti	4,080	10,560	476,629
Tororo	Sukulu	1,760	4,550	668,334
Karamoja	Moroto	10,410	26,960	350,908
Kotido	Kotido	5,120	13,270	161,445
Moroto	Katikekile	5,290	13,690	189,463
Nile	Arua	6,070	15,730	811,755
Arua	Olaki	3,020	7,830	472,283
Moyo	Moyo	1,930	5,010	106,492
Nebbi	Nebbi	1,120	2,890	232,980
North Buganda	Bombo	10,430	27,010	1,554,371
Luwero	Luwero	3,550	9,200	412,474
Mubende	Bageza	3,980	10,310	510,260
Mukono	Kawuga Mukono	2,900	7,500	631,637
Northern	Gulu	16,030	41,520	1,261,364
Apac	Apac	2,510	6,500	313,333
Gulu	Bungatira	4,500	11,660	270,185
Kitgum	Labongo	6,210	16,090	307,594
Lira	Lira	2,810	7,270	370,252
South Buganda	Masaka	6,170	15,970	905,754
Masaka	Kaswa Bukoto	4,520	11,700	631,156
Rakai	Byakabanda	1,650	4,270	274,598
Southern	Mbarara	8,210	21,280	1,963,428
Bushenyi	Bumbaire	1,960	5,080	522,495
Kabale	Rubale	940	2,430	455,471
Mbarara	Kakika	4,320	11,200	687,803
Rukungiri	Kagunga	990	2,570	297,659
Western	Butebe	11,960	30,980	1,427,446
Bundibugyo	Busaru	720	1,880	112,126
Hoima	Hoima	3,120	8,080	294,221
Kabarole	Karambe	3,410	8,820	520,141
Kasese	Rukoki	1,200	3,120	277,708
Masindi	Nyangeya	3,510	9,080	223,250
TOTAL		93,100*	241,140*	12,630,076

Source: Official government figures.

Demography

Density (1984): persons per sq mi 175.4, persons per sq km 67.7.
Urban–rural (1980): urban 11.9%; rural 88.1%.
Sex distribution (1980): male 49.52%; female 50.48%.
Age breakdown (1980): under 15, 45.2%; 15–29, 25.9%; 30–44, 15.1%; 45–59, 8.9%; 60–74, 4.1%; 75 and over, 0.8%.
Population projection: (1990) 18,262,000; (2000) 25,396,000.
Doubling time: 22 years.
Ethnic composition (1978): Ganda 18.0%; Nkole 8.2%; Soga 8.2%; Turkana 8.2%; Gisu 7.4%; Chiga 7.0%; Lango 6.5%; other 36.5%.
Religious affiliation (1980): Roman Catholic 47.5%; Protestant 31.7%; Muslim 15.8%; other 5.0%.
Major cities (1980): Kampala 458,000; Jinja 45,100; Masaka 29,120; Mbale 28,039; Mbarara 23,160.

Vital statistics

Birth rate per 1,000 population (1980–85): 44.6 (world avg. 27.5).
Death rate per 1,000 population (1980–85): 12.8 (world avg. 10.6).
Natural increase rate per 1,000 population (1980–85): 31.8 (world avg. 16.9).
Total fertility rate (avg. births per childbearing woman; 1980–85): 6.1.
Infant mortality rate per 1,000 live births (1980–85): 100.5.
Life expectancy at birth (1980–85): male 53.2 years; female 56.8 years.
Major causes of death: n.a.; however, the major diseases are malaria, measles, venereal diseases, whooping cough, shigellosis (infection with dysentery), chicken pox, and leprosy.

National economy

Budget (1982). Revenue: USh21,135,000,000 (export duties 34.8%; sales tax on imported goods 22.0%; customs duties 21.0%; taxes on income and profits 9.9%; excise tax 7.4%). Expenditures: USh36,998,000,000 (general public services 37.9%; defense 19.6%; education 13.6%; agriculture, forestry, fishing 7.1%; health 4.0%).
Public debt (external, outstanding; 1982) U.S.$546,000,000.

Tourism (1981): receipts from visitors U.S.$5,000,000; expenditures by nationals abroad U.S.$20,000,000.
Production (metric tons except as noted). Agriculture, forestry, fishing (1982): cassavas 1,425,000, sugarcane 700,000, millet 528,000, sorghum 400,000, corn (maize) 293,000, coffee 155,000, peanuts (groundnuts) 90,000; livestock (number of live animals) 5,000,000 cattle, 2,165,000 goats, 1,078,-000 sheep; roundwood 25,441,000 cu m; fish catch 166,590. Mining and quarrying (1982): copper ore 2,000†. Manufacturing (1978): cement 44,000; tea 10,910; blister copper 1,300; soap and detergents 800; beer 224,500 hectolitres. Construction: n.a. Energy production (consumption): electricity (kW-hr; 1982) 668,000,000 (438,000,000); petroleum products (metric tons; 1982) none (197,000).
Gross national product (at current market prices; 1981): U.S.$2,890,000,000 (U.S.$220 per capita).

Origin of gross domestic product (current prices)

	1981 in value USh'000,000	1981 % of total value	1976 labour force	1976 % of labour force
Agriculture	353,347	68.1	78,200	21.4
Mining	145	0.0	4,100	1.1
Manufacturing	16,839	3.2	54,000	14.8
Construction	2,143	0.4	45,500	12.4
Trade	33,999	6.6	18,500	5.1
Transportation and communication	5,842	1.1	13,100	3.6
Pub. admin., defense	25,007	4.8	152,000	41.6
Other	81,489	15.7	...	...
TOTAL	518,811	100.0‡	365,400	100.0

Persons economically active§ (1982): total 5,706,000 (41.8%); female participation in the labour force 1,900,000 (33.3%); unemployed, n.a.

Price and earnings indexes (1975 = 100)

	1972	1973	1974	1975	1976	1977	1978
Consumer price index	40.0	49.8	83.2	100.0	146.6	276.3	377.1
Earnings index	...	...	...	...	...	...	...

Household size. Average household size (1980) 5.2.
Land use (1981): forested 30.1%; meadows and pastures 25.1%; agricultural and under permanent cultivation 28.8%; other 16.0%.

Foreign trade

Balance of trade (current prices)

	1975	1976	1977	1978	1979	1980
USh'000,000	+672	+1,726	+7,535	+4,848	+4,892	+1,774
% of total	21.5%	40.3%	29.0%	10.6%	32.7%	37.6%

Imports (1980): USh1,472,000,000 (machinery including agricultural machinery and transport equipment 48.4%, metals and metal products excluding iron and steel 4.6%, paper and paper products 2.2%). *Major import sources:* Kenya and Tanzania 33.8%; United Kingdom 23.3%; India 13.4%.
Exports (1980): USh3,246,000,000 (unroasted coffee 96.8%, raw cotton 1.0%). *Major export destinations:* United Kingdom 17.1%; United States 14.8%; The Netherlands 13.5%; Japan 9.5%; West Germany 3.4%.

Transport and communications

Transport. Railroads (1983): route length 788 mi, 1,268 km; passengers, n.a.; cargo, n.a. Roads (1982): total length 16,981 mi, 27,329 km (paved 11%). Vehicles (1982): passenger cars 10,633; trucks and buses 11,245. Merchant marine: vessels (100 gross tons and over) n.a. Air transport ‖ (1983): passenger-mi 88,998,000, passenger-km 143,228,000; short ton-mi cargo 26,331,000, metric ton-km cargo 38,442,000; airports (1984) with scheduled flights 7.
Communications. Daily newspapers (1983): total number 2; total circulation 25,000¶; circulation per 1,000 population, n.a. Radios (1983): total number of receivers 280,000 (1 per 49 persons). Television (1983): total number of receivers 75,000 (1 per 184 persons). Telephones (1980): 46,359 (1 per 272 persons).

Education and health

Education (1979)♀

	schools	teachers	students	student/ teacher ratio
Primary (age 6–12)	4,294	36,442	1,223,850	33.6
Secondary (age 13–18)	118	3,108	66,730	21.5
Voc., teacher tr.	48	728	12,185	16.7
Higher	4	677	6,720	9.9

College graduates per 100,000 population (students graduating; 1979): 9.8.
Literacy (1980): total population literate 3,484,600 (47.9%).
Health: (1981): physicians 611 (1 per 22,324 persons); hospital beds 19,782 (1 per 690 persons).
Food (1978–80): daily per capita caloric intake 1,862 (vegetable products 92.1%, animal products 7.9%); 80% of FAO recommended minimum.

Military

Total active duty personnel (1983): 15,000 (army 100.0%; navy, none; air force, none). *Military expenditure as percent of GNP* (1982): 0.9% (world 6.0%); per capita expenditure U.S.$7.

*Total includes 7,650 sq mi (l9,820 sq km) of inland water, mostly in Lake Victoria, not distributable by district. †Metal content. ‡Detail does not add to total given because of rounding. §Estimated. ‖ Scheduled flights only. ¶Partial circulation only. ♀State aided schools only.

Union of Soviet Socialist Republics

Official name: Soyuz Sovetskykh Sotsialisticheskikh Respublik (Sovetsky Soyuz) (Union of Soviet Socialistic Republics [Soviet Union]).
Form of government: federal people's republic with one legislative house (Supreme Soviet [1,500]).
Chief of state: President (Chairman).
Head of government: Premier (Chairman).
Capital: Moscow.
Official language: Russian.
Official religion: none.
Monetary unit: 1 ruble = 100 kopecks; valuation (Oct. 29, 1984) 1 ruble = U.S.$1.15 = £0.96.

Area and population		area*		population
				1983
Soviet Federated Socialist Republic	Capitals	sq mi	sq km	estimate
Russian S.F.S.R.	Moscow	6,592,800	17,075,400	141,012,000
Soviet Socialist Republics				
Armenian	Yerevan	11,500	29,800	3,219,000
Azerbaijan	Baku	33,400	86,600	6,399,000
Belorussian	Minsk	80,200	207,600	9,807,000
Estonian	Tallinn	17,400	45,100	1,507,000
Georgian	Tbilisi	26,900	69,700	5,134,000
Kazakh	Alma-Ata	1,049,200	2,717,300	15,452,000
Kirgiz	Frunze	76,600	198,500	3,801,000
Latvian	Riga	24,600	63,700	2,569,000
Lithuanian	Vilnius	25,200	65,200	3,506,000
Moldavian	Kishinyov	13,000	33,700	4,052,000
Tadzhik	Dushambe	55,300	143,100	4,239,000
Turkmen	Ashkhabad	188,500	488,100	3,042,000
Ukrainian	Kiev	233,100	603,700	50,461,000
Uzbek	Tashkent	172,700	447,400	17,039,000
TOTAL		8,600,400	22,274,900	271,239,000

Source: Official government figures.

Demography

Density (1984): persons per sq mi 31.8, persons per sq km 12.3.
Urban–rural (1984): urban 64.8%; rural 35.2%.
Sex distribution (1983): male 46.80%; female 53.20%.
Age breakdown (1980): under 15, 24.3%; 15–29, 26.6%; 30–44, 19.2%; 45–59, 16.9%; 60–74, 9.6%; 75 and over, 3.4%.
Population projection: (1990) 290,155,000; (2000) 310,236,000.
Doubling time: 69 years.
Ethnic composition (1979): Russian 52.4%; Ukrainian 16.2%; Uzbek 4.8%; Belorussian 3.6%; Kazakh 2.5%; Tatar 2.4%; Azerbaijani 2.1%; Armenian 1.6%; Georgian 1.4%; Moldavian 1.1%; Tadzhik 1.1%; other 10.8%.
Religious affiliation (1980): Christian 25.5%, of which Orthodox 22.5%, Protestant 1.6%, Roman Catholic 1.4%; Muslim 11.3%; Jewish 1.2%; non-religious 29.1%; atheist 22.1%; other 10.8%.
Major cities (1983 est.): Moscow 8,396,000; Leningrad 4,779,000; Kiev 2,355,000; Tashkent 1,944,000; Kharkov 1,519,000; Minsk 1,405,000; Gorky 1,382,000; Novosibirsk 1,370,000; Sverdlovsk 1,269,000; Kuybyshev 1,243,000.
Place of birth (1983): 99.9% native-born; 0.1% foreign-born.
Mobility (1979). Population living in the same residence from birth: 52.9%; 25 years and more 10.4%; 20–24 years 3.9%; 15–19 years 5.0%; 10–14 years 5.4%; 9–6 years 6.1%; 5–2 years 8.6%; less than 2 years 7.7%.
Households† (1979). Average household size 3.5; 2 persons 29.7%, 3 persons 28.8%, 4 persons 23.0%, 5 persons 9.5%, 6 persons 4.1%, 7 or more persons 4.9%. Family households population: 232,075,245 (86.9%), nonfamily population 30,360,755 (13.1%).
Emigration (1982): 2,700; (1979): 51,000.

Vital statistics

Birth rate per 1,000 population (1983): 20.1 (world avg. 29.0); legitimate, n.a., illegitimate, n.a.
Death rate per 1,000 population (1983): 10.3 (world avg. 11.0).
Natural increase rate per 1,000 population (1983): 9.8 (world avg. 18.0).
Total fertility rate (avg. births per childbearing woman; 1982): 3.1.
Marriage rate per 1,000 population (1982): 10.3.
Divorce rate per 1,000 population (1982): 3.3.
Infant mortality rate per 1,000 live births (1982): 16.3.
Life expectancy at birth (1980): male 61.9 years; female 72.0 years.
Major causes of death per 100,000 population (1982): diseases of the circulatory system 533.0, of which cardiovascular atherosclerosis 218.7, cerebrovascular disease 115.3, hypertensive heart disease 82.9, ischemic heart disease 69.2, other diseases of the circulatory system 46.9; malignant neoplasms (cancers) 144.7.

Social indicators

Educational attainment (1983). Percent of adult population having: less than full primary education 0.2%, primary 54.3%, secondary 36.9%, some post-secondary 1.3%, 4-year higher degree 6.7%, post-graduate 0.6%.
Distribution of wealth: n.a.
Quality of working life (1983). Average work week: 39.4 hours (3.0% over-

time). Annual rate per 100,000 workers for: injury or accident, n.a., industrial illness, n.a., death, n.a. Proportion of labour force insured for damages or income loss resulting from: injury 100.0%, permanent disability 100.0%, death 100.0%. Average days lost to labour stoppages per 1,000 work days, n.a. Average duration of journey to work 50 minutes (mostly by public transportation and foot). Rate per 1,000 workers of discouraged (unemployed no longer seeking work), n.a.
Access to services (1983). Proportion of dwellings having access to: electricity 100.0%, safe public water supply, n.a., public sewage collection, n.a., public fire protection, n.a.
Social participation. Eligible voters participating in last national election 99.9%. Population participating in voluntary work, n.a. Trade union membership in total workforce 100.0%. Practicing religious population in total affiliated population, n.a.
Social deviance. Offense rate per 100,000 population for: murder, n.a., rape, n.a., other assault, n.a., grand and auto theft, n.a., burglary and housebreaking, n.a. Incidence per 100,000 in general population of: alcoholism, n.a.; drug and substance abuse, n.a. Rate per 100,000 population of suicide, n.a.
Leisure (1984). Favourite leisure activities (attendance): movies 4,244,000,000, lectures 308,700,000, museums 174,800,000, library 147,117,000, concerts 141,400,000, theatre 124,900,000.
Material well-being (1983). Households possessing: automobile, n.a., telephone 27.3%, television receiver 77.6%, refrigerator 95.3%, air conditioner, none, washing machine, n.a.

National economy

Gross national product (at current market prices; 1983): U.S.$706,104,000,000 (U.S.$2,605 per capita).

Origin of gross domestic product (current prices)				
	1982			
	in value '000,000,000 rubles	% of total value	labour force	% of labour force
Agriculture	80.3	15.3	25,478,000	19.9
Mining	‡	‡	§	§
Manufacturing	266.8‡	51.0‡	39,105,000§	30.5§
Construction	51.9	9.9	11,299,000	8.8
Trade	92.8 ‖	17.7 ‖	9,863,000	7.7
Public utilities	‖	‖	4,612,000	3.6
Transportation and communication	31.6	6.0	12,337,000	9.6
Finance	♀	♀	676,000	0.5
Pub. admin., defense	♀	♀	2,591,000	2.0
Services	♀	♀	22,202,000	17.3
TOTAL	523.4	100.0¶	128,163,000	100.0¶

Budget (1982). Revenue: 353,000,000,000 rubles (share in profits of the state enterprises 29.0%; turnover tax 28.5%, income tax 6.3%). Expenditures: 343,200,000,000 rubles (national economy 57.5%, education and science 12.8%, social welfare 6.4%, defense 5.0%, health 4.7%).
Public debt: n.a.
Tourism (1982): tourist arrivals 5,000,000; tourists abroad 4,500,000.

Manufacturing, mining, and construction enterprises (1982)			
	no. of enterprises	no. of employees	monthly wages as a % of avg. of all wages	annual gross output ('000,000 rubles) 1981
Machinery and metal products	9,103	14,880,000	111.2	175,900
Food products	8,513	2,691,000	99.2	97,900
Chemicals and chemical products	1,059	1,138,000	112.8	64,400
Textiles	2,874	2,232,000	88.4	63,800
Clothing	5,149	2,272,000	88.4	31,000
Non-metallic products	3,200	2,068,000	103.8	20,500
Wood and paper	5,425	791,000	112.8	18,800
Beverages	...	376,000	95.5	16,800
Iron and steel	408	1,029,000	131.2	5,800
Tobacco	85	40,000	95.5	3,600
Leather and products	263	199,000	95.9	3,600
Glass and products	311	370,000	99.3	3,200
Building materials	3,938	...	107.1	2,200
Rubber and plastic	...	438,000	103.5	...
Petroleum and gas	1,146	1,382,000	161.1	19,800
Coal	768	1,077,000	153.9	12,000
Metal ores	1,070	191,000	153.9	12,000
Construction	...	930,000	103.3	...

Production (metric tons except as noted). Agriculture, forestry, fishing (1982): wheat 87,000,000, potatoes 83,000,000♀, sugar beets 82,000,000♀, barley 41,000,000, millet and sorghum 16,000,000, oats 14,000,000, rye 12,500,000, corn (maize) 12,000,000, raw cotton 9,284,000, flax fiber 9,200,000♀, grapes 7,300,000, sunflower 5,341,000, dry pears 5,200,000, tobacco 304,000; livestock (number of live animals, 1983) 142,182,000 sheep, 117,186,000 cattle, 76,671,000 pigs, 6,340,000 goats, 5,601,000 horses, 1,105,000,000 poultry; roundwood 298,700,000 cu m; fish catch 9,956,749. Mining and quarrying (1982): iron ore 245,000,000♀; phosphate rock 26,100,000; salt 15,500,000; potash salts 8,700,000; bauxite 4,600,000; chromium ore 3,400,000; manganese 2,780,000; asbestos 2,180,000; magnesite 2,150,000; copper 1,000,000; zinc 800,000; lead 430,000; nickel 166,000; molybdenum 1,000; tungsten 9,000; mercury 64,000 flasks; diamonds 10,900,000 carats. Manufacturing (1983): crude steel 153,000,000; cement 128,000,000; pig iron 109,000,000; rolled steel 107,000,000; mineral fertilizers 29,700,000; sulphuric acid 24,700,000; steel pipes 18,700,000; paper (excluding paperboard) 5,700,000; soda ash 4,763,000; resins and plastics 4,400,000; caustic soda 2,900,000; man-made fibres 1,400,000; metal cutting machines 2,194,000,000 rubles; reinforced concrete slabs 127,000,000 cu m; cotton fabrics 7,171,000 sq m; footwear 730,000,000 pairs♂. Construction (1983): residential 110,500,000 sq m, of which urban 109,048,000 sq m, rural 1,452,000 sq m. Energy production (consumption): electricity (kW-hr; 1983) 1,416,000,000,-

000 (1,346,000,000,000§); coal (metric tons; 1983) 716,000,000 (608,000,000); crude petroleum (barrels; 1983) 4,517,500,000 (3,302,200,000); petroleum products (metric tons; 1982) 711,585,000 (619,585,000); natural gas (cu m; 1983) 536,000,000,000 (450,000,000,000).

Service enterprises (1982)

	no. of enterprises	no. of employees	monthly wage as a % of all wages
Public utilities	...	3,751,000	78.4
Electrical power	1,433	790,000	115.7
Transport: rail	...	2,231,000	111.7
Transport: road	...	2,530,000	119.7
Transport: water	...	1,920,000	140.1
Communication	90,883	5,662,000	98.1
Finance	...	676,000	95.3
Wholesale trade	...	2,047,000	80.5
Retail trade	699,900	7,816,000	80.5
Tourism	...	...	90.4
Education	...	2,882,000	78.5
Public services and administration	...	2,591,000	90.1
Other services	276,000	22,202,000	90.1

Persons economically active (1983): total 129,100,000 (47.6%); female participation in the labour force 59,350,000 (46.0%); unemployed, n.a.

Price and earnings indexes (1975 = 100)

	1976	1977	1978	1979	1980	1981	1982
Consumer price index	100.9	101.8	103.6	105.4	109.1	110.9	112.7
Monthly earnings index	103.8	106.4	109.7	112.0	115.8	118.3	121.6

Household income and expenditure. Average household size (1982) 3.0; average annual income per household 5,316 rubles (U.S.$7,325); source of income: wages and salaries 70.6%, social welfare 23.4%, other 6.6%; expenditure (1982): food 30.7%, alcohol 17.0%, clothing 15.7%, culture 14.7%, housing 2.6%.
Land use (1982): forested 35.6%; meadows and pastures 16.7%; agricultural and under permanent cultivation 10.5%; other 37.2%.

Foreign trade

Balance of trade (current prices)

	1977	1978	1979	1980	1981	1982
'000,000,000 rubles	3.2	1.1	4.6	5.2	4.5	6.7
% of total	5.0%	1.6%	5.7%	5.5%	4.1%	5.6%

Imports (1982): 56,411,000,000 rubles (machinery and transport equipment 34.4%, cereals and food products 23.7%, raw materials 9.9%, mineral fuels and lubricants 4.6%, chemicals and related products 4.4%, textile and clothing 1.6%). *Major import sources:* East Germany 10.2%; Czechoslovakia 8.4%; Bulgaria 7.6%; Poland 7.3%; Hungary 6.6%; Japan 5.2%; Finland 5.0%; Yugoslavia 5.0%; Cuba 4.8%; United States 3.7%.
Exports (1982): 63,165,000,000 rubles (crude petroleum and petroleum products 40.2%; machinery and transport equipment 12.9%; mineral fuels and natural gas 12.3%; raw materials 7.4%; chemicals, fertilizers, and resins 3.1%; wood and paper products 2.8%). *Major export destinations:* East Germany 10.2%; Czechoslovakia 8.0%; Bulgaria 7.7%; Poland 7.6%; West Germany 6.0%; Hungary 5.9%; Cuba 5.0%; Italy 4.5%; Yugoslavia 3.9%; Finland 3.8%; France 3.6%; The Netherlands 2.5%; Romania 2.2%; Belgium 1.6%.

Transport and communications

Transport. Railroads (1983): length 89,025 mi, 143,272 km; passenger-mi 216,000,000,000, passenger-km 348,000,000,000; short ton-mi cargo 2,373,000,000,000, metric ton-km cargo 3,464,000,000,000. Roads (1983): total length 619,900 mi, 997,600 km (paved 76%). Vehicles (1980): passenger cars 8,255,000; trucks and buses 7,254,000. Merchant marine (1983): vessels (100 gross tons and over) 7,753; total deadweight tonnage 27,573,767. Air transport (1982): passenger-mi 107,000,000,000 passenger-km 173,000,000,000; short ton-mi cargo 2,075,000,000, metric ton-km cargo 3,030,000,000; airports (1980) with scheduled flights 46.
Communications. Daily newspapers (1983): total number 722; total circulation 85,108,000; circulation per 1,000 population 314. Radios (1983): total number of receivers 164,400,000 (1 per 1.6 persons). Television (1983): total number of receivers 75,000,000 (1 per 3.6 persons). Telephones (1982): 26,407,000 (1 per 10.2 persons).

Education and health

Education (1983–84)

	schools	teachers	students	student/ teacher ratio
Primary (age 6–13)	71,200	2,360,000□	35,700,000	...
Secondary (age 14–17)	59,000	□	4,714,000	...
Vocational◇	4,418	246,000	4,232,000	18.4
Higher◇	891	376,000	5,315,200	14.1

College graduates per 100,000 population (1984): 6,757. *Literacy* (1983): total population literate 200,854,000 (100%); males literate 91,103,000 (100%); females literate 109,751,000 (100%).
Health (1983): physicians 1,103,000 (1 per 248 persons); hospital beds 3,500,000 (1 per 78 persons).
Food (1978–80): daily per capita caloric intake 3,389 (vegetable products 73.7%, animal products 26.3%); 132% of FAO recommended minimum requirement.

Military

Total active duty personnel (1984): 5,115,000 (army 36.0%; command and general support troops 29.3%; paramilitary forces 13.2%; navy 9.6%; air force 7.8%; forces abroad 4.1%). *Military expenditure as percent of GNP* (1982): 15.0% (world 6.0%); per capita expenditure U.S.$95.

*Land area; the total area of the Soviet Union is 8,649,500 sq mi (22,402,200 sq km), including the White Sea (34,750 sq mi [90,000 sq km]) and the Sea of Azov (14,400 sq mi [37,300 sq km]). †Family households only. ‡Mining and public utilities included with manufacturing. §Mining is included with manufacturing. ‖ Finance, public administration, defense, and services included with trade.¶Detail does not add to total given because of rounding. ♀1983. ♂1982. □Secondary included with primary. ◇1982–83.

Work train on newly-constructed Ikabyekan-Chara section of the Baikal-Amur Mainline (Baykalo-Amurskaya Magistral) railroad, east of Lake Baikal, Buryat A.S.S.R., Soviet Union.

United Arab Emirates

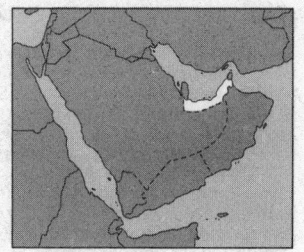

Official name: Ittiḥād al-Imārāt al-'Arabīyah (United Arab Emirates).
Form of government: monarchy; federal union of seven emirates with one legislative house (Federal National Council [40]).
Chief of state: President.
Head of government: Prime Minister.
Capital: Abu Dhabi.
Official language: Arabic.
Official religion: none.
Monetary unit: 1 U.A.E. Dirham (Dh) = 100 fils; valuation (Oct. 29, 1984) 1 U.S.$ = Dh3.64; 1 £ = Dh4.39.

Area and population

Emirates	Capitals	area sq mi	area sq km	population 1983 estimate
Abū ẕhaby	Abu Dhabi	26,000	67,340	521,000
'Ajmān	'Ajmān	100	260	44,000
Dubayy	Dubai	1,500	3,890	307,000
Al-Fujayrah	Al-Fujayrah	450	1,170	38,000
Ra's al-Khaymah	Ra's al-Khaymah	650	1,680	86,000
Ash-Shāriqah	Ash-Shāriqah	1,000	2,590	185,000
Umm al-Qaywayn	Umm al-Qaywayn	300	770	14,000
TOTAL		30,000	77,700	1,195,000

Source: Official government figures.

Demography

Density (1984): persons per sq mi 41.8, persons per sq km 16.2.
Urban–rural (1980): urban 71.8%; rural 28.2%.
Sex distribution (1980): male 68.96%; female 31.04%.
Age breakdown (1980): under 15, 30.3%; 15–29, 28.9%; 30–44, 28.3%; 45–59, 9.0%; 60–74, 2.8%; 75 and over, 0.7%.
Population projection: (1990) 1,570,000; (2000) 1,916,000.
Doubling time: 17 years.
Ethnic composition (1982): South Asian (mainly Indian, Iranian, and Pakistani) 50%; Arab 42%; other (mainly European and East Asian) 8%.
Religious affiliation (1980): Muslim 94.9%; Christian 3.8%; other 1.3%.
Major cities (1980): Dubai 266,000; Abu Dhabi 243,000; ash-Shāriqah 125,000; al 'Ayn 102,000; Ra's al-Khaymah 42,000.

Vital statistics

Birth rate per 1,000 population (1980–85): 28.8 (world avg. 27.5); legitimate, n.a.; illegitimate, n.a.
Death rate per 1,000 population (1980–85): 7.1 (world avg. 10.6).
Natural increase rate per 1,000 population (1980–85): 21.7 (world avg. 16.9).
Total fertility rate (avg. births per childbearing woman; 1980–85): 6.7.
Marriage rate per 1,000 population: n.a.
Divorce rate per 1,000 population: n.a.
Infant mortality rate per 1,000 live births (1980–84): 49.6.
Life expectancy at birth (1980–85): male 61.6 years; female 65.6 years.
Major causes of death per 100,000 population (1980): traffic accidents 57; fire accidents 6; electric shock 5; drowning 5.

National economy

*Budget** (1983). Revenue: Dh12,944,700,000 (largely oil concession receipts). Expenditures: Dh18,406,000,000 (1982; interior, justice, and defense 40.3%; education and youth 8.0%; health 7.2%; electricity and water 2.1%; agriculture and fisheries 0.6%; communications 0.5%).
Production (metric tons except as noted). Agriculture, forestry, fishing (1982): vegetables 130,000, fruits 63,000, tobacco leaves 2,000, wheat 1,000, corn (maize) 1,000, potatoes 1,000, milk 15,000, eggs 3,800; livestock (number of live animals) 400,000 goats, 140,000 sheep, 70,000 camels, 27,000 cattle, 3,000,000 chickens; fish catch 500. Mining and quarrying (1979): marble 26,000 sq m. Manufacturing (1981): petroleum gas 1,260,000; glass 844,000†; distillate fuel oils 800,000; motor gasoline 410,000; soap 153,600; kerosine 40,000; paints 10,800. Construction (1978): residential 46,100 sq m. Energy production (consumption): electricity (kW-hr; 1982) 6,010,000,000 (6,010,000,000); coal, none (n.a.); crude petroleum (barrels; 1982) 439,273,000 (8,629,200); petroleum products (metric tons; 1982) 2,879,000 (3,709,000); natural gas (cu m; 1982) 13,615,371,000 (10,626,092,000).

Origin of gross domestic product (current prices)

	1982 in value Dh'000,000	1982 % of total value	1980 labour force	1980 % of labour force
Agriculture	1,114	1.0	25,613	4.6
Mining	56,213	49.5	11,852	2.1
Manufacturing	10,158	9.0	34,876	6.3
Construction	11,015	9.7	154,978	27.8
Trade	10,483	9.2	74,332	13.3
Public utilities	1,851	1.6	10,952	2.0
Transportation and communication	5,465	4.8	42,038	7.5
Finance	‡	‡	14,946	2.7
Pub. admin., defense	‡	‡	90,921	16.3
Services	‡	‡	96,775	17.4
Other	17,304‡	15.2‡	239	—
TOTAL	113,603	100.0	557,522	100.0

Gross national product (at current market prices; 1981): U.S.$26,910,000,000 (U.S.$24,665 per capita).
Public debt (external, outstanding; 1982): U.S.$1,117,000,000.
Tourism: receipts from visitors, n.a.; expenditures by nationals abroad, n.a.
Persons economically active (1980): total 557,521 (53.5%); female participation in the labour force, n.a.; unemployed, n.a.
Price and earnings indexes: n.a.
Household income and expenditure: Average household size (1980) 3.8; average annual income per household, n.a.; source of income, n.a.; expenditure: n.a.
Land use (1981): forested —; meadows and pastures 2.4%; agricultural and under permanent cultivation 0.2%; other 97.4%.

Foreign trade

Balance of trade (current prices)

	1977	1978	1979	1980	1981	1982
Dh'000,000	+27,403	+38,885	+29,382	+25,673	+14,668	+18,187
% of total	28.4%	35.4%	31.2%	32.6%	26.1%	31.6%

Imports (1981): Dh35,417,000,000 (nonelectric machinery 16.7%; electrical machinery 9.5%; transport equipment 9.5%; food and live animals 9.1%; iron and steel 6.9%; textile yarn and fabric 5.8%; chemicals 5.1%). *Major import sources§:* Japan 21.5%; United States 11.1%; United Kingdom 9.5%; West Germany 6.6%; Italy 4.6%; Bahrain 4.1%; France 3.5%.
Exports (1981): Dh74,302,000,000 (1980 crude petroleum 88.6%; natural gas 2.7%). *Major export destinations ∥:* Japan 34.5%; United States 13.5%; France 8.0%; Netherlands Antilles 6.7%; West Germany 6.3%.

Transport and communications

Transport. Railroads: none. Roads (1981): total length 800 mi, 1,300 km (paved n.a.). Vehicles (1981): passenger cars 130,700; trucks and buses 77,600. Merchant marine (1983): vessels (100 gross tons and over) 202; total deadweight tonnage 450,327. Air transport (1983): passenger-mi 2,213,000,000, passenger-km 3,562,000,000; short ton-mi cargo 65,300,000, metric ton-km cargo 95,300,000; airports (1984) with scheduled flights 2.
Communications. Daily newspapers (1979): total number 3; total circulation 28,000; circulation per 1,000 population 31.5. Radios (1981): total number of receivers 260,000 (1 per 4 persons). Television (1981): total number of receivers 100,000 (1 per 10 persons). Telephones (1982): 240,167 (1 per 5 persons).

Education and health

Education (1982–83)

	schools	teachers	students	student/ teacher ratio
Primary (age 6–11)	244¶	6,599	115,411	17.5
Secondary (age 12–18)	68¶	4,081	45,442	11.1
Vocational♀	4¶	154	722	4.7
Higher¶	318	8,343	125,209	15.0

College graduates per 100,000 population (students graduating, 1980): 568.
Literacy (1980): total population literateŏ 550,669 (68.0%); males literate 418,792 (69.8%); females literate 131,877 (63.0%).
Health (1981): physicians 1,491 (1 per 698 persons); hospital beds 3,260 (1 per 319 persons).
Food: daily per capita caloric intake, n.a. (vegetable products, n.a., animal products, n.a.).

Military

Total active duty personnel (1983): 49,000 (army 93.8%; navy 3.1%; air force 3.1%). *Military expenditure as percent of GNP* (1982): 8.0% (world 6.0%); per capita expenditure U.S.$1,942.

*Estimated. †1978. ‡Finance, public administration, and defense are included with other. §1983. ∥ 1980. ¶1979–80. ♀Male only. ŏ10 years and over.

TOM PIX—PETER ARNOLD, INC.

Modern covered souk (market), Sharjah city, United Arab Emirates.

United Kingdom

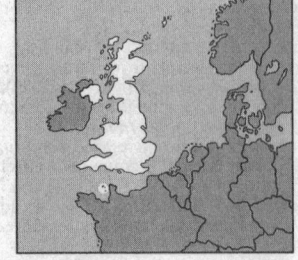

Official name: United Kingdom of Great Britain and Northern Ireland.
Form of government: constitutional monarchy with two legislative houses (House of Lords [1,195]; House of Commons [650]).
Chief of state: Sovereign.
Head of government: Prime Minister.
Capital: London.
Official language: English.
Official religion: Church of England.
Monetary unit: 1 pound sterling (£) = 100 new pence; valuation (Sept. 29, 1984) 1 £ = U.S.$1.21.

Area and population

Countries	Capitals	area sq mi	area sq km	population 1983 estimate
England	London	50,363	130,439	46,845,900
Counties				
Avon		520	1,346	935,900
Bedfordshire		477	1,235	512,900
Berkshire		486	1,259	706,900
Buckinghamshire		727	1,883	580,100
Cambridgeshire		1,316	3,409	601,400
Cheshire		899	2,329	933,200
Cleveland		225	583	564,800
Cornwall		1,376	3,564	432,200
Cumbria		2,629	6,810	483,000
Derbyshire		1,016	2,631	911,100
Devon		2,591	6,711	973,000
Dorset		1,025	2,654	609,100
Durham		941	2,436	606,800
East Sussex		693	1,795	673,800
Essex		1,418	3,672	1,491,700
Gloucestershire		1,020	2,643	506,100
Greater London*		610	1,579	6,754,500
Greater Manchester*		497	1,287	2,598,500
Hampshire		1,458	3,777	1,499,400
Hereford & Worcester		1,516	3,927	640,400
Hertfordshire		631	1,634	975,400
Humberside		1,356	3,512	854,000
Isle of Wight		147	381	119,800
Kent		1,441	3,731	1,486,300
Lancashire		1,183	3,064	1,377,600
Leicestershire		986	2,553	863,700
Lincolnshire		2,284	5,915	554,300
Merseyside*		252	652	1,500,800
Norfolk		2,073	5,368	711,300
Northamptonshire		914	2,367	538,500
Northumberland		1,943	5,032	300,200
North Yorkshire		3,208	8,309	684,700
Nottinghamshire		836	2,164	992,200
Oxfordshire		1,007	2,608	550,300
Shropshire		1,347	3,490	382,500
Somerset		1,332	3,451	435,700
South Yorkshire*		602	1,560	1,310,500
Staffordshire		1,049	2,716	1,018,000
Suffolk		1,466	3,797	612,500
Surrey		648	1,679	1,011,800
Tyne and Wear*		208	540	1,145,300
Warwickshire		765	1,981	477,800
West Midlands*		347	899	2,657,600
West Sussex		768	1,989	678,900
West Yorkshire*		787	2,039	2,059,300
Wiltshire		1,344	3,480	532,100
Northern Ireland†	Belfast	5,462	14,147	1,582,000
Scotland	Edinburgh	29,794‡	77,167	5,150,400
Regions				
Borders		1,804	4,672	101,200
Central		1,016	2,631	272,700
Dumfries and Galloway		2,459	6,370	146,200
Fife		505	1,307	342,800
Grampian		3,361	8,704	494,500
Highland		9,803	25,391	196,100
Lothian		678	1,755	744,800
Strathclyde		5,227	13,537	2,383,100
Tayside		2,893	7,493	394,900
Island areas (TOTAL)		2,049	5,307	74,100
Wales	Cardiff	8,019	20,768	2,807,800
Counties				
Clwyd		937	2,427	395,300
Dyfed		2,227	5,768	335,300
Gwent		531	1,376	439,900
Gwynedd		1,494	3,869	232,000
Mid Glamorgan		393	1,018	536,400
Powys		1,960	5,077	110,600
South Glamorgan		161	416	391,700
West Glamorgan		316	817	366,600
TOTAL		94,248	244,100	56,386,100

Source: Official government figures.

Demography

Density (1984): persons per sq mi 596.9, persons per sq km 230.5.
Urban–rural (1981): urban 89.6%; rural 10.4%.
Sex distribution (1984): male 48.60%; female 51.40%.
Age breakdown (1984): under 15, 19.5%; 15–29, 23.2%; 30–44, 19.8%; 45–59, 16.7%; 60–74, 14.6%; 75 and over, 6.2%.
Population projection: (1991) 56,912,000; (2001) 57,968,000.
Doubling time: 99 years.
Ethnic composition: n.a.
Religious affiliation§ (1983): Church of England 19.1%; Roman Catholic 8.5%; Church of Scotland 1.7%; Methodist 0.9%.

Major cities (1983 est.): Greater London 6,754,500; Birmingham 1,012,900; Glasgow 751,000; Leeds 714,000; Sheffield 542,700; Liverpool 502,500; Bradford 463,900; Manchester 457,500; Edinburgh 440,900; Bristol 399,300.
Place of birth (1981): 93.5% (50,769,700) native-born; 6.5% foreign-born, of which: Ireland 1.1%, India and Sri Lanka 0.8%, Caribbean 0.5%, African Commonwealth 0.5%, Pakistan and Bangladesh 0.4%.
Mobility. n.a.
Households (1982). Average household size 2.6; 1 person 23%, 2 persons 33%, 3 persons 17%, 4 persons 17%, 5 persons 7%, 6 or more persons 3%. Family households: 14,331,000 (73.5%), nonfamily 5,162,000 (26.5%, of which 1-person 21.8%).
Immigration (1983): permanent residents admitted 202,000, from European Community ‖ 15.3%, United States 12.9%, Australia 9.4%, African Commonwealth 8.9%, Bangladesh, India, and Sri Lanka 6.4%, Pakistan 5.9%.

Vital statistics

Birth rate per 1,000 population (Mar. 1984): 12.6 (world avg. 29.0); legitimate 83.9%; illegitimate 16.1%.
Death rate per 1,000 population (Mar. 1984): 12.8 (world avg. 11.0).
Natural increase rate per 1,000 population (Mar. 1984): −0.2 (world avg. 18.0).
Total fertility rate (avg. births per childbearing woman; June 1984): 1.7.
Marriage rate per 1,000 population (1982): 6.9.
Divorce rate per 1,000 population (1982): 2.6.
Infant mortality rate per 1,000 live births (1983): 10.2.
Life expectancy at birth (1978–80): male 70.2 years; female 76.2 years.
Major causes of death per 100,000 population (England, Wales, and Scotland; 1983): diseases of the circulatory system 574.9, of which ischemic heart disease 319.1, cerebrovascular disease 139.4, pulmonary circulation and other forms of heart diseases 60.8; malignant neoplasms (cancers) 270.9; diseases of the respiratory system 171.3, of which pneumonia and influenza 110.4; injuries and poisonings 39.9, of which motor vehicle accidents 10.4. (Northern Ireland; 1981): acute myocardial infarction without hypertension 216.3; malignant neoplasms (cancers) 187.0; cerebrovascular disease without hypertension 118.4; pneumonia 80.5; injuries and poisonings 54.7, of which motor vehicle accidents 14.6.

Social indicators

Educational attainment. n.a.

Distribution of income (1981)

percent of household income by quintile

1	2	3	4	5 (highest)
0.6	8.1	18.0	26.9	46.4

Quality of working life (1982). Average work week (hours): male 38.4, female 36.6 (male 7.7%, female 1.3% overtime). Annual rate per 100,000 workers for: injury or accident 56.9, industrial diseases 0.5, death 2.3. Proportion of labour force (employed persons) insured for damages or income loss resulting from: injury 100%, permanent disability 100%, death 100%. Average days lost to labour stoppages per 1,000 employee workdays: 0.7. Principal means of transport to work: 55% private automobile, 20.5% public transportation, 2.5% bicycle, 15% foot, 7% other. Rate per 1,000 workers of discouraged (unemployed no longer seeking work): n.a.
Access to services (1981). Proportion of households having access to: bath or shower 96%, toilet 95%, central heating 59%.
Social participation. Eligible voters participating in last national election 75.9%. Population over 16 years of age participating in voluntary work 23%. Trade union membership in total workforce 51%.
Social deviance (1982). Offense rate per 100,000 population for: theft and handling stolen goods 3,554.1, burglary 1,664.9, fraud and forgery 262.5, violence against the person 212.1, robbery 51.3, sexual offense 44.6. Incidence (per 100,000 population) of: cigarette smoking habit—males 38,000, females 33,000; notified drug addicts 7.8; suicide 7.6.
Leisure (1982). Favourite leisure activities (attendence, unless otherwise noted): cinema 60,200,000, newspapers 31,600,000 readership, football matches 21,667,000, greyhound racing 5,300,000, bingo clubs 5,700,000, motor sports 4,000,000, radio listening (average amount in hours per week) 10.
Material well-being (1981). Households possessing: automobile 61.8%, telephone 75.8%, television receiver 96.6%, refrigerator 96.1%, heating (full or partial) 60.5%, washing machine 80.7%.

National economy

Gross national product (at current market prices; 1983): U.S.$458,331,000,-000 (U.S.$8,150 per capita).

Origin of gross domestic product (current factor cost)

	1983 in value £'000,000	% of total value	labour force	% of labour force
Agriculture	5,535	2.1	349,000	1.6
Mining	¶	¶	313,000	1.5
Manufacturing	62,258¶	24.0¶	5,641,000	26.3
Construction	15,319	5.9	1,017,000	4.7
Trade	35,002	13.5	4,208,000	19.6
Public utilities and energy	29,645	11.4	608,000	2.8
Transportation and communication	18,635	7.2	1,332,000	6.2
Finance⁹	46,828	18.0	1,837,000	8.6
Pub. admin., defense	18,027	6.9	1,600,000	7.5
Services	40,436	15.6	4,562,000	21.2
Other	−11,854δ	−4.6δ	...	...
TOTAL	259,831	100.0	21,467,000	100.0

Budget (1983). Revenue: £109,834,000,000; customs and excise 28.9%, of which value added tax 14.7%; income tax 28.6%; national insurance, health, and redundancy fund 18.8%. Expenditures: £114,907,000,000 (social security benefits 27.8%; military defense 13.6%; national health service 13.1%; finance and tax collection 1.3%).
Total national debt (1983): £127,000,000,000.

Financial aggregates

	1978	1979	1980	1981	1982	1983	1984 (Oct.)
Exchange rate:							
U.S. Dollar per £	1.92	2.12	2.33	2.03	1.75	1.52	1.22
SDR's per £	1.56	1.69	1.87	1.64	1.46	1.39	1.22
International reserves (U.S.$)							
Total (excl. gold; '000,000,000)	16.03	19.74	20.65	15.24	12.40	11.34	9.27
SDR's ('000,000,000)	0.54	1.27	0.57	0.99	1.17	0.52	0.49
Reserve pos. in IMF ('000,000,000)	—	—	1.33	1.44	1.55	2.10	1.99
Foreign exchange ('000,000,000)	15.49	18.47	18.75	12.81	9.67	8.72	6.80
Gold, ('000,000 fine troy oz.)	22.83	18.25	18.84	19.03	19.01	19.01	19.03
% world reserves	2.2	1.9	2.0	2.0	2.0	2.0	2.0
Interest and prices							
Central bank discount (%)	12.50	17.00	14.00	...	...	...	...
Gov't. Bond yield (%) long term	12.47	12.99	13.79	14.74	12.88	10.81	10.69
Industrial share prices (1980 = 100)	82.4	93.6	100.0	112.8	130.7	164.9	199.8⊙
Balance of payments (U.S.$'000,000)							
Balance of visible trade,	−2,965	−7,207	+3,714	+7,756	+3,999	−812	−1,874†
Imports, f.o.b.	70,245	93,691	106,538	95,008	93,083	92,709	25,377†
Exports, f.o.b.	67,280	86,484	110,253	102,765	97,081	91,898	23,503†
Balance of invisibles	8,620	10,992	9,804	11,274	9,488	8,627	2,096†
Balance of payments, current account	2,242	−1,015	8,706	15,109	9,829	4,371	924†

Tourism (1982): receipts from visitors U.S.$5,144,000,000; expenditures by nationals abroad U.S.$5,929,000,000.

Manufacturing, mining, and construction enterprises (1981)

	no. of enterprises	no. of employees	annual wages as a % of avg. of all wages	annual gross output (£'000,000)
Manufacturing				
Food, drink, and tobacco	5,478	656,900	94.1	34,843.3
Mechanical engineering	15,343	808,000	109.1	18,601.2
Chemical	2,532	318,400	119.0	17,473.4
Electrical and elec. engineering	4,882	595,900	94.3	13,280.6
Paper and paper products; printing and publishing	12,178	483,600	123.1	12,422.1
Motor vehicles	2,061	369,500	109.9	10,164.0
Metals	1,343	238,500	123.2	9,750.7
Miscellaneous machinery and equipment	7,292	266,400	104.9	5,817.3
Aerospace equipment, mfg. and repairing	313	199,600	122.0	5,298.4
Timber and wooden furniture	11,072	216,100	96.2	5,189.9
Textile	3,122	267,300	73.6	4,917.6
Tobacco	20	33,300	123.4	4,629.8
Mining				
Extraction of mineral oil and natural gas	...	20,200	...	13,537.5
Mineral oil processing	158	23,400	150.7	12,874.5
Construction	118,899□	1,196,400	82.9	25,996.1

Production (metric tons except as noted). Agriculture, forestry, fishing (1983): wheat 10,880,000, barley 10,080,000, potatoes 6,875,000◊, turnips and rutabagas 3,655,000, corn (maize) 550,000, oats 465,000; livestock (number of live animals) 23,246,000 sheep, 13,131,000 cattle, 7,769,000 pigs, 101,973,000 poultry; roundwood 4,701,000 cu m; fish catch 911,000. Mining and quarrying (1983): iron ore 384,000; lead (refined) 322,200; aluminum (primary) 252,000; zinc (slab) 181,200; copper (primary, refined) 67,200. Manufacturing (total sales in £ million except as noted; 1983): mechanical engineering 15,830, of which boilers and process plant fabrications 1,575, mechanical lifting and handling equipment 1,177, fabricated and constructional steel-work 1,151; electrical and electronic engineering 12,981, of which basic electrical equipment 2,124, radio and electronic capital goods 2,102, telegraph and telephone apparatus 1,434; motor vehicles and parts thereof 8,623; metal goods 6,448; aerospace equipment 4,789; instrument engineering 1,880; domestic furniture 1,044; tires and tubes 627; pottery 140; woven wool and worsted fabrics 94,000,000 sq m; woven carpets 13,008,000 sq m; woven cotton cloth 254,800,000 metres; paper 2,548,000 tons; footwear 125,600,000 pairs. Construction (value in £; 1983): housing 4,849,000,000; other 3,729,000,000 (industrial 1,850,000,000; commercial 2,967,000,000).

Retail trade enterprises (1980)

	no. of enterprises	no. of employees	weekly wage as a % of all wages	annual turnover (£'000,000)
Food and grocery	38,930	568,000	...	17,201
Mixed goods (department stores)	3,307	367,000	...	8,749
News, tobacco, and confectionary	36,508	216,000	...	4,545
Electrical and music goods	7,199	71,000	...	2,388
Mail order	38	53,000	...	2,335
Furniture	10,002	70,000	...	2,200
Meat	15,095	89,000	...	2,165
Women's clothing	16,336	115,000	...	1,863
Pharmaceuticals	7,723	65,000	...	1,526
Dairy products	6,362	53,000	...	1,458
Alcoholic beverages	2,900	32,000	...	1,427
Hardware, china	10,618	60,000	...	1,332
Footwear	3,512	75,000	...	1,241
Men's clothing	4,226	51,000	...	1,157

Energy production (consumption): electricity (kW-hr; 1983) 276,204,000,000

(219,343,000,000); coal (metric tons; 1983) 119,220,000 (98,400,000); crude petroleum (barrels; 1983) 842,217,000 (530,692,000); natural gas (cu m; 1983) 33,996,600,000 (48,106,300,000).
Persons economically active (1984△): total 27,106,000 (48.2%); female participation in employment 9,265,000 (43.7%); unemployed 3,143,000 (11.6%).

Price and earnings indexes (1980 = 100)

	1978	1979	1980	1981	1982	1983	1984†
Consumer price index	74.7	84.8	100.0	111.9	121.5	127.1	133.1
Monthly earnings index	73.0	84.2	100.0	113.5	126.4	137.2	142.0

Household income and expenditure. Average household size (1983) 2.6; average annual income per household £9,550 (U.S.$14,520); sources of income: wages and salaries 61.3%, social security benefits 14.8%, rent, dividends, and interest 6.2%, income from self-employment 7.5%, private pensions, annuities etc. 7.1%, other current transfers 3.1%; expenditure (1983): food and alcohol 22.7%; housing, fuel, and power 20.5%; transport, communication, and vehicles 17.6%; services 13.1%; recreation, entertainment, and education 9.2%; household goods and services 6.9%.
Land use (1982): forested 8.8%; meadows and pastures 46.9%; agricultural and under permanent cultivation 28.9%; other 15.4%.

Foreign trade

Balance of trade (current prices)

	1978	1979	1980	1981	1982	1983
£'000,000	−4,153	−6,288	−2,409	−471	−1,420	−5,459
% of total	5.5%	7.2%	2.5%	0.5%	1.3%	4.3%

Imports (1983): £65,993,000,000 (machinery and transport equipment 30.7%, of which road vehicles 8.7%, office machines and data processing equipment 4.6%, telecommunications and sound recording equipment 2.9%; food and live animals chiefly for food 10.4%, of which vegetables and fruits 2.6%, meat and meat preparations 2.0%; petroleum, petroleum products, and related materials 8.7%; chemicals and related products 7.8%, of which organic chemicals 2.2%; textile yarn, fabrics, and related products 3.5%; nonferrous metals 3.0%; paper and paper board 2.9%; apparel and clothing accessories 2.4%). *Major import sources:* West Germany 14.6%; United States 11.3%; The Netherlands 7.7%; France 7.6%; Japan 5.1%; Italy 4.8%; Belgium-Luxembourg 4.7%; Norway 4.3%; Ireland 3.4%.
Exports (1983): £60,534,000,000 (machinery and transport equipment 30.2%, of which road vehicles 5.1%, power generating machinery and equipment 4.1%, machinery specialized for particular industries 3.9%; petroleum, petroleum products, and related materials 20.7%; chemicals and related products 11.4%, of which organic chemicals 3.2%, medicinal and pharmaceutical products 1.8%; nonmetallic mineral manufactures 3.3%; beverages and tobacco 2.5%; professional, scientific, and controlling instruments 2.4%; nonferrous metals 2.7%). *Major export destinations:* United States 13.8%; West Germany 10.0%; France 9.3%; The Netherlands 9.0%; Ireland 5.0%; Belgium-Luxembourg 4.3%; Sweden 4.0%; Italy 3.8%.

Transport and communications

Transport. Railroads** (1983): route length 10,706 mi, 17,229 km; passenger-mi†† 18,745,000,000, passenger-km†† 30,168,000,000; short ton-mi cargo 11,745,000,000, metric ton-km cargo 17,148,000,000. Roads (1982): total length 213,083 mi, 342,925 km (paved 96%). Vehicles (1982): passenger cars 16,074,735; trucks and buses 1,856,042. Merchant marine (1983): vessels (100 gross tons and over) 2,570; total deadweight tonnage 29,878,378. Air transport (1982): passenger-mi 27,313,000,000, passenger-km 43,956,000,000; short ton-mi cargo 839,414,000, metric ton-km cargo 1,225,524,000; airports (1984) with scheduled flights 128.
Communications. Daily newspapers (1980): total number 124; total circulation 22,900,000; circulation per 1,000 population 407. Radios (1983): total number of licenses 18,410,000 (1 per 3 persons). Television (1984): total number of licenses 18,702,000 (1 per 3 persons). Telephones (1983): 28,375,982 (1 per 2 persons).

Education and health

Education (1981–82)

	schools	teachers	students	student/ teacher ratio
Primary (age 5–10)	27,326	192,959	4,758,000	24.7
Secondary (age 11–19)	5,506	279,000	5,031,000	18.0
Voc., teacher tr.	787	...	254,813‡‡	...
Higher	46	33,735	785,200	23.3

College graduates per 100,000 population (students graduating; 1980): 252.
Literacy (1984): total population literate—virtually 100%.
Health (1982): physicians 28,060 (1 per 2,008 persons); hospital beds 500,000§§ (1 per 113 persons).
Food (1978–80): daily per capita caloric intake 3,315 (vegetable products 63%, animal products 37%); 132% of FAO recommended minimum requirement.

Military

Total active duty personnel (1984): 325,909 (army 49.6%; navy 21.8%; air force 28.6%). *Military expenditure as percent of GNP* (1982): 5.1% (world 6.0%); per capita expenditure U.S.$461.

*Metropolitan county. †Comprises 26 local government districts not shown separately. ‡Detail does not add to total given because of rounding. §Confirmed members only; detail does not add to 100% because of incompleteness of data. ‖Excludes Republic of Ireland. ¶Mining is included with manufacturing. ¶Finance includes ownership of dwellings. δLess imputed bank service charges. □Establishments. ◊1982. △March. †Second quarter. ⊙September. **British railways only. ††Excludes Northern Ireland. ‡‡1980–81. §§National Health Service hospitals only.

United States

Official name: United States of America.
Form of government: federal republic with two legislative houses (Senate [100] and House of Representatives [435]).
Head of state and government: President.
Capital: Washington, D.C.
Official language: English.
Official religion: none.
Monetary unit: 1 dollar (U.S.$) = 100 cents; valuation (Oct. 29, 1984)
1 U.S.$ = £0.83; 1 £ = U.S.$1.21.

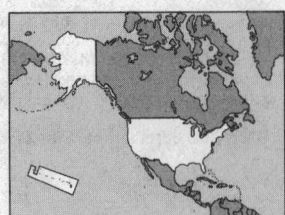

Area and population

States	Capitals	area sq mi	area sq km	population 1984 estimate
Alabama	Montgomery	51,705	133,915	3,990,000
Alaska	Juneau	591,004	1,530,693	500,000
Arizona	Phoenix	114,000	295,259	3,053,000
Arkansas	Little Rock	53,187	137,754	2,349,000
California	Sacramento	158,706	411,047	25,622,000
Colorado	Denver	104,091	269,594	3,178,000
Connecticut	Hartford	5,018	12,997	3,154,000
Delaware	Dover	2,044	5,294	613,000
Dist. of Columbia		69	179	623,000
Florida	Tallahassee	58,664	151,939	10,976,000
Georgia	Atlanta	58,910	152,576	5,837,000
Hawaii	Honolulu	6,471	16,760	1,039,000
Idaho	Boise	83,564	216,430	1,001,000
Illinois	Springfield	56,345	145,933	11,511,000
Indiana	Indianapolis	36,185	93,719	5,498,000
Iowa	Des Moines	56,275	145,752	2,910,000
Kansas	Topeka	82,277	213,096	2,438,000
Kentucky	Frankfort	40,409	104,659	3,723,000
Louisiana	Baton Rouge	47,752	123,677	4,462,000
Maine	Augusta	33,265	86,156	1,156,000
Maryland	Annapolis	10,460	27,091	4,349,000
Massachusetts	Boston	8,284	21,455	5,798,000
Michigan	Lansing	58,527	151,584	9,075,000
Minnesota	St. Paul	84,402	218,600	4,162,000
Mississippi	Jackson	47,689	123,514	2,598,000
Missouri	Jefferson City	69,697	180,514	5,008,000
Montana	Helena	147,046	380,847	824,000
Nebraska	Lincoln	77,355	200,349	1,606,000
Nevada	Carson City	110,561	286,352	911,000
New Hampshire	Concord	9,279	24,032	977,000
New Jersey	Trenton	7,787	20,168	7,515,000
New Mexico	Santa Fe	121,593	314,924	1,424,000
New York	Albany	49,108	127,189	17,735,000
North Carolina	Raleigh	52,669	136,412	6,165,000
North Dakota	Bismarck	70,702	183,117	686,000
Ohio	Columbus	41,330	107,044	10,752,000
Oklahoma	Oklahoma City	69,956	181,185	3,298,000
Oregon	Salem	97,073	251,418	2,674,000
Pennsylvania	Harrisburg	45,308	117,347	11,901,000
Rhode Island	Providence	1,212	3,139	962,000
South Carolina	Columbia	31,113	80,582	3,300,000
South Dakota	Pierre	77,116	199,730	706,000
Tennessee	Nashville	42,144	109,152	4,717,000
Texas	Austin	266,807	691,027	15,989,000
Utah	Salt Lake City	84,899	219,887	1,652,000
Vermont	Montpelier	9,614	24,900	530,000
Virginia	Richmond	40,767	105,586	5,636,000
Washington	Olympia	68,139	176,479	4,349,000
West Virginia	Charleston	24,231	62,758	1,952,000
Wisconsin	Madison	56,153	145,436	4,766,000
Wyoming	Cheyenne	97,809	253,324	511,000
TOTAL		3,618,770*	9,372,571	236,158,000*

Source: Official government figures.

Demography

Density (1984): persons per sq mi 65.3, persons per sq km 25.2.
Urban–rural (1980): urban 73.7%; rural 26.3%.
Sex distribution (1983): male 48.60%; female 51.40%.
Age breakdown (1983): under 15, 22.0%; 15–29, 26.5%; 30–44, 20.7%; 45–59, 14.5%; 60–74, 11.6%; 75 and over, 4.7%.
Population projection: (1990) 249,731,000; (2000) 267,990,000.
Doubling time: 78 years.
Ethnic composition (1980): white 83.1%; black 11.7%; American Indian 0.6%; Chinese 0.4%; Filipino 0.3%; Japanese 0.3%; Asian Indian 0.2%; Korean 0.2%; other 3.2%.
Religious affiliation (1980): Protestant 40.0%; Roman Catholic 30.0%; Jewish 3.2%; Eastern Orthodox 2.1%; nonreligious and atheist 6.9%; other 17.8%.
Major cities (1983 est.): New York 7,100,063; Los Angeles 3,158,688; Chicago 3,021,203; Houston 1,728,783; Philadelphia 1,692,364; Detroit 1,176,968; Dallas 998,827; San Diego 935,840; Phoenix 843,415; San Antonio 874,483.
Place of birth (foreign born) (1980): Mexico 2,199,221; Germany 849,384; Canada 842,859; Italy 831,922; United Kingdom 669,149; Cuba 607,814; Philippines 501,440; Poland 418,128; Soviet Union 406,022; South Korea 289,885; China 286,120; Vietnam 231,120; Japan 221,794; Portugal 211,614; Greece 210,998; India 206,087.
Mobility (1982). Population living in the same residence as in 1981: 84.2%; different residence, same county 9.9%; different county, same state 3.1%; different state 2.8%.
Households (1982). Average household size 2.7; 1 person 23.2%, 2 persons 31.7%, 3 persons 17.5%, 4 persons 15.4%, 5 persons 7.3%, 6 persons 3.0%, 7 or more persons 1.9%. Family households: 61,019,000 (73.1%), nonfamily 22,508,000 (26.9%, of which 1-person 23.2%).

Immigration (1980): permanent immigrants admitted 530,639, from Caribbean countries 13.8%, Mexico 10.7%, Vietnam 8.2%, Philippines 8.0%, South America 7.5%, Korea 6.1%, Taiwan 5.2%, India 4.3%, United Kingdom 2.9%, Laos 2.6%, Canada 2.6%, U.S.S.R. 2.0%.

Vital statistics

Birth rate per 1,000 population (1984): 15.5 (world avg. 29.0); legitimate 80.6%; illegitimate 19.4%.
Death rate per 1,000 population (1984): 8.6 (world avg. 11.0).
Natural increase rate per 1,000 population (1984): 6.9 (world avg. 18.0).
Total fertility rate (avg. births per childbearing woman; 1982): 1.9.
Marriage rate per 1,000 population (1984): 10.5.
Divorce rate per 1,000 population (1984): 4.9.
Infant mortality rate per 1,000 live births (1984): 10.6.
Life expectancy at birth (1983): male 71.6 years; female 76.3 years.
Major causes of death per 100,000 population (1984): cardiovascular diseases 411.8, of which ischemic heart diseases 228.9, other forms of heart disease 78.1, cerebrovascular diseases 66.0, atherosclerosis 10.5, other cardiovascular diseases 9.1; malignant neoplasms (cancers) 190.8; diseases of the respiratory system 53.0; accidents 39.4; diabetes mellitus 15.2; suicide 12.0; chronic liver disease and cirrhosis 11.5; nephritis and nephrosis 8.6; homicide 8.3.

Social indicators

Educational attainment (1982). Percent of adult population having: less than full primary education 8.6%, primary 7.1%, less than full secondary 13.3%, secondary 37.9%, some post-secondary 15.3%, 4-year higher degree and more 11.0%, post-graduate 6.8%.

Distribution of income (1983)

percent of national household income by quintile

1	2	3	4	5 (highest)
4.7	11.2	17.1	24.3	42.7

Quality of working life (1983). Average work week: 40.1 hours (7.5% overtime). Annual rate per 100,000 workers for: injury or accident 1,125†, death 11.0†. Proportion of labour force insured for damages or income loss resulting from: injury, permanent disability, and death 65.6%‡. Average days lost to labour stoppages per 1,000 work days: 0.7. Average duration of journey to work (1979) 22.5 minutes (85.7% private automobile, 5.9% public transportation, 1.3% bicycle or motorcycle, 3.9% foot, 2.3% work at home, 0.9% other). Rate per 1,000 workers of discouraged (unemployed no longer seeking work): n.a.
Access to services (1981). Proportion of dwellings having access to: electricity 100.0%, safe public water supply 84.0%, public sewage collection 73.6%, public fire protection, n.a.
Social participation. Eligible voters participating in last national election 59.2%. Population over 13 years of age participating in voluntary work 22.9%§. Trade union membership in total workforce 20.4% ‖. Practicing religious population in total affiliated population 49.7%, of which weekly 41.0%.
Social deviance (1983). Offense rate per 100,000 population for: murder 8.3, rape 33.7, robbery 213.8, other assault 273.3, motor vehicle theft 429.3, burglary and housebreaking 1,333.8, larceny-theft 2,866.5. Users of alcohol 68.0%¶, drug and substance 27.0%¶. Rate per 100,000 population of suicide 12.4.
Leisure (1977). Favourite leisure activities: watching television 30.0%, reading 15.0%, movies and theatre 6.0%, visiting friends 4.0%, listening to radio 4.0%, playing games 4.0%.
Material well-being (1981). Occupied dwellings with householder possessing: automobile 87.1%, telephone 92.9%, cable television 27.3%, refrigerator, n.a., air conditioner 57.1%, washing machine, n.a.

National economy

Gross national product (at current market prices; 1984): U.S.$3,701,200,000,-000 (U.S.$15,670 per capita).

Origin of gross domestic product (current prices)

	1983 in value $'000,000,000	% of total value	labour force	% of labour force
Agriculture	72.7	2.2	1,719,000	1.8
Mining	112.4	3.4	949,000	1.0
Manufacturing	685.2	21.1	18,418,000	19.0
Construction	130.7	4.0	3,920,000	4.0
Trade	536.2	16.5	20,930,000	21.6
Public utilities	99.4	3.0	875,000	0.9
Transportation and communication	207.3	6.4	4,120,000	4.2
Finance	542.5	16.7	5,627,000	5.8
Pub. admin., defense	392.1	12.0	19,448,000	20.0
Services	477.5	14.7	21,099,000	21.7
Other	0.5	...	...	...
TOTAL	3,256.5	100.0*	97,105,000	100.0

Budget (1984). Revenue: U.S.$668,404,000,000 (individual income tax 44.3%, social insurance taxes and contributions 36.1%, corporation income tax 9.6%, excise taxes 5.5%, customs duties 1.4%). Expenditures: U.S.$848,-071,000,000 (income security 32.4%, defense 28.6%, interest on debt 12.2%, health 10.7%, education 3.1%, veteran benefits and services 3.0%).
Total national debt (1984?): U.S.$1,246,600,000,000.
Tourism (1982): receipts from visitors U.S.$11,293,000,000; expenditures by nationals abroad U.S.$12,394,000,000.
Land use (1981): forested 31.2%; meadows and pastures 26.0%; agricultural and under permanent cultivation 20.9%; other 21.9%.

Manufacturing, mining, and construction enterprises (1983)

	no. of enter-prises§	no. of employees	weekly wage as a % of all wages	annual value of shipments ($'000,000)
Manufacturing				
Food and kindred products	20,720	1,622,000	117.3	286,605
Transportation equipment	8,245	1,756,000	180.1	240,496
Petroleum and coal products	2,186	195,000	210.7	191,551
Chemical and allied products	11,243	1,046,000	159.6	190,230
Machinery, except electrical	47,191	2,038,000	142.2	178,267
Electrical machinery	14,142	2,023,000	128.0	156,016
Fabricated metal products	31,557	1,373,000	136.0	120,570
Primary metals	7,134	838,000	166.8	117,904
Paper and allied products	6,115	661,000	156.0	85,135
Textile products and apparel	28,058	1,907,000	91.8	52,219
Rubber and plastic products	11,932	718,000	120.6	50,320
Instruments and related products	7,197	694,000	121.1	50,016
Stone, clay, and glass products	15,540	572,000	141.9	49,058
Tobacco products	193	68,000	135.2	15,462
Leather and products	2,581	208,000	74.6	5,230
Mining	...	...	...	112,400
Oil and gas extraction	21,501	600,000	167.4	...
Coal mining	4,226	255,200	201.0	...
Metal mining	1,014	93,800	179.5	...
Construction	40,077	3,940,000	162.0	130,700
Residential	...	1,015,000	...	...
Commercial	...	2,925,000□	...	...
Industrial	...	□	...	...

Production (metric tons except as noted). Agriculture, forestry, fishing (1983): corn (maize) 105,823,000, wheat 65,860,000, soybeans 61,970,000†, sugarcane 26,195,000†, sorghum 21,364,000†, potatoes 15,842,000†, barley 11,067,000, oats 8,995,000†, rice 4,522,000, seed cotton 6,950,000†, sunflower seeds 2,661,000†, peanuts (groundnuts) 1,561,000†, dry beans 1,123,000†, tobacco 647,000; livestock (number of live animals, 1983) 115,201,000 cattle, 53,935,000 pigs, 11,904,000 sheep, 378,509,000 poultry; roundwood 246,238,000 cu m; fish catch (1983) 2,916,538. Mining and quarrying (1983): iron ore 37,967,000; phosphate rock 37,414,000; copper 1,038,100; tin 969,000; bauxite 732,000; lead 449,000; zinc 273,000; molybdenum 35,238; nickel 2,906; silver 40,239,000 troy ounces; gold 1,447,000 troy ounces. Manufacturing (1983): crude steel 75,640,000; paper and paper products 62,722,000; wood pulp 52,537,000; cement 45,680,000; pig iron 44,217,000; sulfuric acid 36,583,000; nitrogenous and phosphate fertilizers 17,598,000; plastic and resins 12,418,000; caustic soda 9,758,000; newsprint 4,574,000; aluminum 3,353,000; synthetic rubber 1,978,280; machinery and transport equipment, except electrical U.S.$186,700,000; electrical machinery U.S.$87,800,000; tires 186,923,000 units; cotton fabric 2,427,000,000 m. Construction (1983): residential U.S.$111,729,000,000; nonresidential U.S.$60,309,000,000.

Service enterprises (1982)

	no. of enter-prises	no. of employees	weekly wage as a % of all wages	annual sales (U.S.$'000,000)
Retail trade				
Food stores	176,212	2,560,000	...	258,964
Automotive dealers	89,207	1,037,258	...	182,607
Department stores	20,070	1,523,368	...	134,369
Eating and drinking places	318,765	4,315,336	...	114,837
Gasoline service stations	116,154	604,286	...	105,374
Clothing	133,920	986,155	...	55,915
Drug stores	48,637	491,309	...	39,845
Building materials	33,869	305,259	...	35,573
Furniture	93,355	540,266	...	26,863
Liquor stores	34,071	166,160	...	20,422
Household appliances, radio and TV	67,791	348,841	...	15,237
Variety stores	10,814	155,784	...	8,818
Jewelry	22,240	130,994	...	8,240
Wholesale trade	390,160	5,259,000	...	1,144,352
Durable goods	236,893	2,964,023	...	457,713
Nondurable goods	147,676	2,024,492	...	686,639

Energy production (consumption): electricity (kW-hr; 1983) 2,310,285,000,-000 (2,163,749,000,000); coal (metric tons; 1983) 712,018,000 (667,000,000); crude petroleum (barrels; 1983) 3,170,999,000 (5,542,000,000); petroleum products (metric tons; 1983) 677,000,000 (739,000,000); natural gas (cu m; 1983) 453,921,500,000 (479,973,200,000).

Financial aggregates

	1978	1979	1980	1981	1982	1983	1984 (Oct.)
Exchange rate, U.S.$ per:							
£	2.03	2.22	2.38	1.91	1.61	1.45	1.22
SDR	1.25	1.29	1.30	1.18	1.04	1.07	0.99
International reserves (U.S.$)							
Total (excl. gold; '000,000,000)	6.98	7.78	15.60	18.92	22.81	22.63	23.47
SDR's ('000,000,000)	1.56	2.72	2.61	4.10	5.25	5.03	5.54
Reserve pos. in IMF ('000,000,000)	1.05	1.25	2.85	5.05	7.35	11.31	11.62
Foreign exchange ('000,000,000)	4.37	3.81	10.13	9.77	10.21	6.29	6.32
Gold, ('000,000 fine troy oz.)	276.41	264.60	264.32	264.11	264.03	263.39	262.80
% world reserves	26.66	28.02	27.75	27.75	27.88	27.84	27.81
Interest and prices							
Central bank discount (%)	9.50	12.00	13.00	12.00	8.50	8.50	9.00
Gov't. bond yield (%)	8.29	9.71	11.55	14.44	12.92	10.45	12.04
Industrial share prices (1980 = 100)	78.9	85.4	100.0	107.2	99.3	134.2	137.8
Balance of payments ($'000,000,000)							
Balance of visible trade	−33.98	−27.56	−25.53	−28.05	−36.47	−61.07	−24.80♀
Imports, f.o.b.	176.03	212.03	249.77	265.08	247.67	261.32	−81.11♀
Exports, f.o.b.	142.05	184.47	224.24	237.03	211.20	200.25	−56.31♀
Balance of invisibles	24.09	32.72	33.57	40.20	36.13	28.77	−9.5 ♀
Balance of payments, current account	−15.49	−0.95	0.48	4.64	−9.19	−41.58	−24.08♀

Persons economically active (1983): total 111,937,000 (47.8%); female participation in the labour force 48,692,000 (43.5%); unemployed 9,061,000 (8.1%).

Price and earnings indexes (1980 = 100)

	1978	1979	1980	1981	1982	1983	1984♀
Consumer price index	79.2	88.1	100.0	110.4	117.1	120.9	126.9
Hourly earnings index	84.9	92.1	100.0	109.9	116.9	121.5	126.3

Household income and expenditure. Average household size (1983) 2.7; average annual income per household (U.S.$27,885); sources of income: wages and salaries 60.5%, personal interest income 16.0%, other 23.5%; expenditure (1983): housing 23.9%, food 19.3%, transportation 13.6%, health 11.0%, clothing 5.9%, recreation 6.6%, education 1.5%.

Foreign trade

Balance of trade (current prices)

	1978	1979	1980	1981	1982	1983
U.S.'000,000,000	−34.0	−27.6	−25.5	−27.6	−42.6	−57.5
% of total	10.7%	7.0%	5.4%	5.6%	9.1%	12.5%

Imports (1983): U.S.$258,047,800,000 (mineral fuels and lubricants 22.5%. of which petroleum and products 20.3%; machinery 18.2%, of which electrical machinery 8.6%; transport equipment 15.2%, of which road motor vehicles and parts 13.6%; manufactured goods 13.5%; food 6.0%; chemicals 4.2%; raw materials 3.7%). *Major import sources:* Canada 20.2%; Japan 16.0%; Mexico 6.5%; West Germany 4.9%; United Kingdom 4.8%; Taiwan 3.6%; Saudi Arabia 3.0%; Nigeria 2.9%; France 2.3%; Italy 2.1%; Brazil 1.9%; Venezuela 1.9%.
Exports (1983): U.S.$200,537,700,000 (machinery 27.0%, of which electrical machinery 8.9%; transport equipment 14.1%, of which road motor vehicles and parts 7.2%; food and live animals 12.1%, of which grain and cereal 6.9%; chemicals 9.8%; crude materials, except fuels 9.3%; manufactured goods 7.4%; mineral fuels and lubricants 4.7%). *Major export destinations:* Canada 19.1%; Japan 10.9%; United Kingdom 5.3%; Mexico 4.5%; West Germany 4.3%; Saudi Arabia 4.2%; The Netherlands 4.0%; France 3.0%; South Korea 2.6%; Italy 1.9%; Egypt 1.4%; Venezuela 1.4%; U.S.S.R. 1.0%.

Transport and communications

Transport. Railroads (1981): length 184,235 mi, 296,489 km; passenger-mi 10,995,000,000, passenger-km 17,695,000,000; short ton-mi cargo 919,000,-000,000, metric ton-km cargo 1,341,717,000,000. Roads (1983): total length 3,866,296 mi, 6,222,030 km (paved 85%). Vehicles (1983): passenger cars 124,800,000; trucks and buses 35,600,000. Merchant marine (1983): vessels (100 gross tons and over) 6,437; total deadweight tonnage 29,295,016. Air transport (1983): passenger-mi 252,706,000,000, passenger-km 406,692,000,-000; short ton-mi cargo 7,279,300,000, metric ton-km cargo 10,627,620,000; airports (1983) with scheduled flights 12,562.
Communications. Daily newspapers (1983): total number 1,711; total circulation 62,487,177; circulation per 1,000 population 370.5. Radios (1983): total number of receivers 485,000,000 (1 per 0.5 persons). Television (1983): total number of receivers 143,000,000 (1 per 1.6 persons). Telephones (1984): 134,400,000 (1 per 1.7 persons).

Education and health

Education (1983–84)

	schools	teachers	students	student/teacher ratio
Primary and preprimary (age 5–12)	...	1,359,000	30,780,000	22.6
Secondary and vocational (age 14–17)	...	1,035,000	13,495,000	13.0
Higher, including teacher-training colleges	...	870,000	12,400,000	14.2

College graduates per 100,000 population (students graduating; 1980): 774.
Literacy (1980): total population literate 166,497,565 (95.5%); males literate 79,161,126 (95.7%); females literate 87,336,439 (95.3%).
Health (1982): physicians 455,723 (1 per 508 persons); hospital beds 1,359,-783 (1 per 170 persons).
Food (1978–80): daily per capita caloric intake 3,652 (vegetable products 63.6%, animal products 36.4%); 138% of FAO recommended minimum requirement.

Military

Total active duty personnel (1984): 2,135,900 (army 36.6%; navy 26.4%; air force 27.8%; marine 9.2%). *Military expenditure as percent of GNP* (1982): 6.4% (world 6.0%); per capita expenditure U.S.$845.

*Detail does not add to total given because of rounding. †1982. ‡General health insurance. §1974. ‖ 1980. ¶Used at least once. ♀Second quarter. ♂1981. □Industrial construction is included with commercial. ◊1983.

Uruguay

Official name: República Oriental del Uruguay (Oriental Republic of Uruguay).
Form of government: military government with one appointed legislative body (Council of State [35]).
Head of state and government: President*.
Capital: Montevideo.
Official language: Spanish.
Official religion: none.
Monetary unit: 1 Uruguayan new peso (NUr$) = 100 centésimos; valuation (Oct. 29, 1984) 1 U.S.$ = NUr$62.20; 1 £ = NUr$75.07.

Area and population

Departments	Capitals	area sq mi	area sq km	population 1975 census
Artigas	Artigas	4,605	11,928	57,947
Canelones	Canelones	1,751	4,536	325,594
Cerro Largo	Melo	5,270	13,648	74,027
Colonia	Colonia del Sacramento	2,358	6,106	111,832
Durazno	Durazno	4,495	11,643	55,699
Flores	Trinidad	1,986	5,144	24,745
Florida	Florida	4,022	10,417	67,129
Lavalleja	Minas	3,867	10,016	65,180
Maldonado	Maldonado	1,851	4,793	76,211
Montevideo	Montevideo	205	530	1,237,227
Paysandú	Paysandú	5,375	13,922	98,508
Rio Negro	Fray Bentos	3,584	9,282	50,123
Rivera	Rivera	3,618	9,370	82,043
Rocha	Rocha	4,074	10,551	60,258
Salto	Salto	5,468	14,163	103,074
San José	San José de Mayo	1,927	4,992	88,000
Soriano	Mercedes	3,478	9,008	80,614
Tacuarembó	Tacuarembó	5,961	15,438	84,535
Treinta y Tres	Trienta y Tres	3,679	9,529	45,683
TOTAL		68,037†	176,215†	2,788,429‡

Source: Official government figures.

Demography

Density (1984): persons per sq mi 44.3, persons per sq km 17.1.
Urban–rural (1983): urban 83.9%; rural 16.1%.
Sex distribution (1980): male 49.15%; female 50.85%.
Age breakdown (1980): under 15, 27.2%; 15–29, 23.4%; 30–44, 17.6%; 45–59, 17.1%; 60–74, 11.1%; 75 and over, 3.6%.
Population projection: (1990) 3,166,000; (2000) 3,448,000.
Doubling time: 72 years.
Ethnic composition (1980): mixed Spanish–Italian 85.9%; mestizo 3.0%; Italian 2.6%; Jewish 1.7%; mulatto 1.2%; other 5.6%.
Religious affiliation (1980): Christian 62.9%, of which Roman Catholic 59.5%; nonreligious 35.1%; Jewish 1.7%; other 0.3%.
Major city (1980 est.): Montevideo 1,261,000; other cities (1975) Salto 72,000, Paysandú 62,000, Las Piedras 54,000.

Vital statistics

Birth rate per 1,000 population (1983): 19.0 (world avg. 29.0).
Death rate per 1,000 population (1983): 8.7 (world avg. 11.0).
Natural increase rate per 1,000 population (1983): 10.3 (world avg. 18.0).
Total fertility rate (avg. births per childbearing woman; 1982): 2.6.
Marriage rate per 1,000 population (1977): 7.8.
Divorce rate per 1,000 population (1977): 1.8.
Infant mortality rate per 1,000 live births (1983): 32.0.
Life expectancy at birth (1981): male 69.1 years; female 73.8 years.
Major causes of death per 100,000 population (1978): malignant neoplasms (cancers) 208.3; ischemic heart disease 168.6; cerebrovascular disease 119.2.

National economy

Budget (1983). Revenue: NUr$29,486,400,000 (value added tax 46.9%; nontax revenue 18.4%; import duties 15.7%; income tax 11.7%; property tax 6.7%. Expenditures: NUr$36,897,300,000 (social security and welfare 66.4%; general public services 11.1%; interest on public debt 6.0%).
Public debt (external, outstanding; 1983): U.S.$2,462,000,000.
Tourism (1982): receipts from visitors U.S.$149,000,000; expenditures by nationals abroad U.S.$304,000,000.
Production (metric tons except as noted). Agriculture, forestry, fishing (1982): sugarcane 450,000, sugar beets 367,000, paddy rice 340,000, wheat 275,000, potatoes 177,000, sorghum 123,000, grapes 110,000, corn (maize) 97,000; livestock (number of live animals) 23,369,000 sheep, 10,872,000 cattle, 530,000 horses; roundwood 1,678,000 cu m; fish catch 119,000. Mining and quarrying (1982): clays 300,000; glass sand 200,000. Manufacturing (value added in NUr$; 1981): food products excluding beverages 5,218,000,000; petroleum products 4,375,000,000; beverages 2,682,000,000; textiles (not clothing, footwear, or leather products) 2,369,000,000; tobacco 1,698,000,000; transport equipment 1,199,000,000; motor vehicles 948,000,000. Construction (1981): residential 626,200 sq m; nonresidential 236,600 sq m. Energy production (consumption): electricity (kW-hr; 1982) 6,156,000,000 (6,175,000,000); coal (metric tons; 1982) none (1,000); crude

petroleum (barrels; 1982) none (12,300,000); petroleum products (metric tons; 1982) 1,583,000 (1,462,000); natural gas, none (n.a.).
Gross national product (at current market prices; 1983): U.S.$5,077,000,000 (U.S.$1,740 per capita).

Origin of gross domestic product (factor cost at current prices)

	1981 in value NUr$'000,000	% of total value	labour force	% of labour force
Agriculture	8,743	8.2	132,000	11.6
Mining	§	§	2,000	0.2
Manufacturing	27,978§	26.3§	231,000	20.3
Construction	5,617	5.3	66,000	5.8
Trade and finance	22,634	21.3	171,000 ‖	15.0 ‖
Public utilities	1,299	1.2	16,000 ‖	1.4 ‖
Transportation and communication	7,196	6.8	58,000 ‖	5.1 ‖
Pub. admin., defense	12,396	11.7	211,000 ‖¶	18.6 ‖¶
Other	20,521	19.3	250,000	22.0
TOTAL	106,384	100.0⁹	1,137,000	100.0

Persons economically active (1982): total 1,148,000 (38.7%); female participation in the labour force (1975) 311,000 (27.7%); unemployed (1982) 103,000 (9.0%).

Price and earnings indexes (1980 = 100)

	1978	1979	1980	1981	1982	1983	1984
Consumer price index	36.7	61.2	100.0	134.0	159.5	238.0	397.1⌀
Monthly earnings index□	39.9	60.8	100.0	143.6	169.9	201.0	...

Household income and expenditure. Average household size (1980) 3.5; income per household: n.a.; source of income: n.a.; expenditure: n.a.
Land use (1981): forested 3.2%; meadows and pastures 81.6%; agricultural and under permanent cultivation 11.0%; other 4.2%.

Foreign trade

Balance of trade (current prices)

	1978	1979	1980	1981	1982	1983
U.S.$'000	−23,000	−313,500	−424,900	−283,300	+14,900	+444,600
% of total	1.6%	16.6%	16.7%	10.4%	0.7%	28.1%

Imports (1982): U.S.$1,013,700,000 (mineral products 41.6%; machinery and appliances 13.4%; chemical products 10.6%; transport equipment 10.4%; synthetic plastic, resins, and rubber 4.3%; base metals and products 4.3%). *Major import sources:* United States 12.4%; Nigeria 12.1%; Brazil 11.8%; Venezuela 8.6%; Mexico 7.9%.
Exports (1982): U.S.$1,028,600,000 (textiles and textile products 28.6%; live animals and live animal products 28.4%; vegetable products 14.9%; skins and hides 13.6%; chemical products 4.2%; synthetic plastics, resins, and rubber 1.9%). *Major export destinations:* Brazil 14.3%; Argentina 10.7%; W. Germany 9.0%; U.S.S.R. 7.7%; United States 7.4%.

Transport and communications

Transport. Railroads (1982): route length 1,867 mi, 3,004 km; passenger-mi 170,000,000, passenger-km 274,000,000; short ton-mi cargo 123,000,000, metric ton-km cargo 180,000,000. Roads (1981): total length 30,952 mi, 49,813 km (paved 20%). Vehicles (1981): passenger cars 281,275; trucks and buses 49,813. Merchant marine (1983): vessels (100 gross tons and over) 88; total deadweight tonnage 330,951. Air transport (1979): passenger-mi 105,000,000, passenger-km 169,000,000; short ton-mi cargo 508,000, metric ton-km cargo 742,000; airports (1984) with scheduled flights 7.
Communications. Daily newspapers (1983): total number 23; total circulation 555,100; circulation per 1,000 population 188. Radios (1982): 1,655,000 (1 per 1.8 persons). Television (1982): 368,000 (1 per 8.1 persons). Telephones (1981): 287,140 (1 per 10.2 persons).

Education and health

Education (1981)

	schools	teachers	students	student/ teacher ratio
Primary (age 6–12)	2,543	18,017	387,150	21.5
Secondary	...	...	162,106	...
Vocational	...	...	26,017	....
Higher◊	1	4,149	36,706	8.8

College graduates per 100,000 population (students graduating; 1981): 100.
Literacy (1983): total population literate 96.3%; males literate (1975) 922,534 (93.5%); females literate (1975) 989,727 (94.4%).
Health (1981): physicians 5,600 (1 per 523 persons); hospital beds 23,000 (1 per 127 persons).
Food (1978–80): daily per capita caloric intake 2,868 (vegetable products 63.6%, animal products 36.4%); 107% of FAO recommended minimum.

Military

Total active duty personnel (1984): 29,800 (army 74.8%; navy 15.1%; air force 10.1%). *Military expenditure as percent of GNP:* (1982): 3.7% (world 6.0%); per capita expenditure U.S.$138.

*Assisted by the National Security Council. †Includes 463 sq mi (1,199 sq km) of water area not shown separately. ‡Estimated 1984 population was 3,013,000; no breakdown available. §Mining is included with manufacturing. ‖ Projection. ¶Government and social services. ⁹Detail does not add to total given because of rounding. ⌀August. □Salaried employees only. ◊Universidad de la República.

Vanuatu

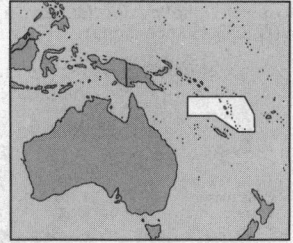

Official name: République de Vanuatu (French); Republic of Vanuatu (English).
Form of government: republic with a single legislative house (Parliament [39]).
Chief of state: President.
Head of government: Prime Minister.
Capital: Vila.
Official languages: French; English.
Official religion: none.
Monetary unit: vatu (VT); valuation (Oct. 29, 1984) 1 U.S.$ = VT98.55; 1 £ = VT118.95.

Area and population	area		population
Local Government Regions	sq mi	sq km	1985 estimate
Ambrym	340	880	7,400
Ambae/Maewo	270	700	11,600
Banks/Torres	1,640	4,250	6,200
Efate	790	2,050	25,400
Epi	195	500	2,900
Malekula	255	665	17,600
Paama/Lopevi	25	60	2,400
Pentacost	170	445	11,000
Santo/Malo	35	85	23,200
Shepherds	355	925	5,200
Taféa	630	1,630	20,700
TOTAL	4,705	12,190	133,600

Source: Official government figures; Britannica estimate.

Demography

Density (1985): persons per sq mi 28.4, persons per sq km 11.0.
Urban–rural (1979): urban 17.8%; rural 82.2%.
Sex distribution (1979): male 53.10%; female 46.90%.
*Age breakdown** (1979): under 15, 45.4%; 15–29, 27.5%; 30–44, 15.0%; 45–59, 7.7%; 60–74, 3.4%; 75 and over, 1.1%.
Population projection: (1990) 150,700; (2000) 198,700.
Doubling time: 25 years.
Ethnic composition (1979): Melanesian (Ni-Vanuatu) 93.8%; European 2.2%; other 4.0%.
Religious affiliation (1979): Christian 76.6%, of which Presbyterian 36.7%, Anglican 15.1%, Roman Catholic 14.8%, Seventh-day Adventist 6.1%; other 23.4%.
Major cities (1979): Vila (Port Vila) 9,971; Santo (Luganville) 5,183.

Vital statistics

Birth rate per 1,000 population (1978): 45† (world avg. 28.5); legitimate, n.a.; illegitimate, n.a.
Death rate per 1,000 population (1978): 17† (world avg. 11.4).
Natural increase rate per 1,000 population (1978): 28.0 (world avg. 17.1).
Total fertility rate (avg. births per childbearing woman): n.a.
Marriage rate per 1,000 population: n.a.
Divorce rate per 1,000 population: n.a.
Infant mortality rate per 1,000 live births (1979): 97.
Life expectancy at birth (1979): 56.8 years.
Major causes of death per 100,000 population: n.a.; however, major diseases are malaria, infantile diarrhea, influenza, hookworm, and tuberculosis.

National economy

Budget (1981). Revenue: VT2,372,000,000 (grant aid 37.9%, import and export duties 34.8%, nontax revenue 8.6%). Expenditures: VT2,876,000,000 (n.a.).
Public debt (external, outstanding; 1982): U.S.$4,100,000.
Tourism (1982): number of visitors 32,180.
Production (metric tons except as noted). Agriculture, forestry, fishing (1982): coconuts 250,000 (copra 35,000), cassavas and yams 30,000; livestock (number of live animals) 100,000 cattle, 69,000 pigs, 8,000 goats, 158,000 chickens; roundwood 30,000; fish catch 2,715, of which tuna 2,000. Mining and quarrying (1979‡): manganese ore 12,100 (5,000 contained metal). Manufacturing (1980): VT326,000,000 (canned meat, frozen fish, soft drinks, furniture). Construction (approvals in Vila and Santo; 1983): residential 9,160 sq m; nonresidential 19,700 sq m. Energy production (consumption): electricity (kW-hr; 1983) 21,000,000 (21,000,000); coal, none (n.a.); crude petroleum (barrels; 1981) none (110,000); petroleum products (metric tons; 1982) none (13,000); natural gas, none (n.a.).
Gross national product (at current market prices; 1980): U.S.$70,400,000 (U.S.$585 per capita).
Persons economically active (1979): total 51,163 (46.0%); female participation in labour force 22,177 (43.3%); unemployed, n.a.

Price and earnings indexes (1976 = 100)							
	¶1976	1977	1978	1979	1980	1981	1982
Consumer price index	100.0	107.3	115.1	120.7	130.7	152.6	178.6
Monthly earnings index	...	...	...	...	...	...	...

Household income and expenditure. Average household size (1980) 4.9; average annual income per household♀ VT414,000 (U.S.$2,865); source of income: n.a; expenditure: n.a.

Land use (1982): forested 1.1%; meadows and pastures 1.7%; agricultural and under permanent cultivation 6.4%; sedimentary and coral limestones and volcanic rock, and other 90.8%.

Origin of gross national product (current prices)				
	1980		1979	
	in value VT'000,000	% of total value	labour force	% of labour force
Agriculture	...	...	39,296	76.8
Mining	...	...	76	0.1
Manufacturing	480§	4.7§	990	1.9
Construction	...	...	1,103	2.2
Trade	...	...	2,178	4.3
Public utilities	...	...	61	0.1
Transportation and communication	...	...	1,323	2.6
Finance	...	...	326	0.6
Pub. admin., defense	...	...	‖	‖
Services	...	...	5,502‖	10.8‖
Other	...	...	308	0.6
TOTAL	10,170	100.0	51,163	100.0

Foreign trade

Balance of trade (current prices)						
	1977	1978	1979	1980	1981	1982
VT'000,000	−1241	−1532	−1780	−2544	−2283	−3462
% of total	17.6%	19.9%	21.5%	34.2%	28.7%	44.0%

Imports (1982): VT5,663,000,000ð (food and beverages 25.0%, of which cereal and cereal products 7.9%, of which rice 4.3%; machinery and transport equipment 15.9%, of which transport equipment 7.7%; fuels and lubricants 13.7%, of which fuels 12.6%; textile products 8.5%; beverages 4.1%, of which beer 1.5%; fish☐ 3.3%). *Major import sources:* Australia 33.8%; Japan 12.9%; New Zealand 10.6%; France 9.4%; Fiji 9.2%.
Exports (1982): VT2,201,000,000ð (copra 32.2%; frozen fish 31.2%; canned and frozen beef 8.4%; cocoa 2.6%). *Major export destinations:* Belgium 34.0%; The Netherlands 32.8%; New Caledonia 13.5%; France 12.0%; the United States imports reexported fish amounting to 25.5% of total exports.

Transport and communications

Transport. Railroads: none. Roads (1984): total length◊ 551 mi, 887 km; (paved, n.a.). Vehicles (on the islands of Espiritu Santo and Estate; 1983): passenger cars 3,087; trucks and buses 242. Merchant marine (1982): vessels (100 gross tons and over) 12; total deadweight tonnage 38,572. Air transport: passengers, n.a; cargo, n.a.; airports (1984) with scheduled flights 9.
Communications. Daily newspaper (1984): total number 1; total circulation 1,000; circulation per 1,000 population 9.0. Radios (1983): total number of receivers 15,500 (1 per 8 persons). Television: total number of receivers, none. Telephones: n.a.

Education and health

Education (1982)	schools	teachers	students	student/ teacher ratio
Primary (age 6–11)	286	1,063	23,595	22.2
Secondary (age 11–18)	9	126	2,067	16.4
Voc., teacher tr.	2	40	351	8.8
Higher	...	...	...	...

College graduates per 100,000 population: n.a. *Literacy:* n.a.
Health: physicians (1980) 20 (1 per 5,600 persons); hospitals, health centres, and clinics (1981) 112.
Food (1978–80): daily per capita caloric intake 2,477 (vegetable products 80.5%, animal products 19.5%); 93% of FAO recommended minimum requirement.

Military

Total active duty personnel: none.

*Detail does not add to total given because of rounding. †Estimate determined by the U.S. Bureau of the Census. ‡Because manganese ores are nearly exhausted, 1979 was the last year of production. §Manufacturing was estimated at about 4.7% of total income. ‖ Public administration and defense are included in services. ¶The CPI values are for the first quarter of their respective years. ♀Household income is derived from GNP value for 1980. ðIncludes value of reexports. ☐Does not include reexports. ◊Incomplete data.

Venezuela

Official name: República de Venezuela
(Republic of Venezuela).
Form of government: unitary,
multiparty republic with two
legislative houses (Senate [49];
Chamber of Deputies [200]).
Head of state and government:
President.
Capital: Caracas.
Official language: Spanish.
Official religion: none.
Monetary unit: 1 bolívar (B., pl.
Bs.) = 100 céntimos; valuation (Oct.
29, 1984) 1 U.S.$ = Bs.4.31;
1 £ = Bs.5.20.

Area and population

States	Capitals	area sq mi	area sq km	population 1985 estimate*
Anzoátegui	Barcelona	16,718	43,300	783,000
Apure	San Fernando de Apure	29,537	76,500	221,000
Aragua	Maracay	2,708	7,014	1,020,000
Barinas	Barinas	13,591	35,200	373,000
Bolívar	Ciudad Bolívar	91,892	238,000	779,000
Carabobo	Valencia	1,795	4,650	1,215,000
Cojedes	San Carlos	5,714	24,800	576,000
Falcón	Coro	9,575	14,800	153,000
Guárico	San Juan de Los Morros	5,091	64,986	450,000
Lara	Barquisimeto	7,645	19,800	1,081,000
Mérida	Mérida	4,363	11,300	525,000
Miranda	Los Teques	3,070	7,950	1,626,000
Monagas	Maturín	1,158	28,900	446,000
Nueva Esparta	La Asunción	444	1,150	225,000
Portuguesa	Guanare	5,869	15,200	486,000
Sucre	Cumaná	4,556	11,800	670,000
Táchira	San Cristóbal	4,286	11,100	755,000
Trujillo	Trujillo	2,857	7,400	496,000
Yaracuy	San Felipe	2,741	7,100	344,000
Zulia	Maracaibo	24,363	63,100	1,917,000
Other federal entities				
Amazonas	Puerto Ayacucho	67,857	175,750	73,000
Delta Amacuro	Tucupita	15,521	40,200	79,000
Dependencias Federales	—	46	120	1,000
Distrito Federal	Caracas	745	1,930	2,368,000
TOTAL		352,144	912,050	16,662,000

Source: Official government figures; Britannica estimate.

Demography

Density (1985): persons per sq mi 47.3, persons per sq km 18.3.
Urban–rural (1985): urban 85.7%; rural 14.3%.
Sex distribution (1985): male 50.00%; female 50.00%.
Age breakdown (1981): under 15, 40.5%; 15–29, 29.9%; 30–44, 15.8%; 45–59, 8.7%; 60–74, 4.0%; 75 and over, 1.1%.
Population projection: (1990) 18,895,000; (2000) 25,500,000.
Doubling time: 23 years.
Ethnic composition (1981): mestizo 69%; white 20%; black 9%; Indian 2%.
Religious affiliation (1982 est.): Roman Catholic 92.4%; other 7.6%.
Major cities (1981): Caracas 2,299,700; Maracaibo 929,000; Valencia 523,000; Barquisimeto 504,000.

Vital statistics

Birth rate per 1,000 population (1976–81): 35.1 (world avg. 29.0†); (1974) legitimate 47.0%, illegitimate 53.0%.
Death rate per 1,000 population (1976–81): 5.6 (world avg. 12.0†).
Natural increase rate per 1,000 population (1976–81): 29.5 (world avg. 17.0†).
Total fertility rate (avg. births per childbearing woman; 1980–85): 4.33.
Marriage rate per 1,000 population (1979): 7.0.
Divorce rate per 1,000 population (1979): 0.4.
Infant mortality rate per 1,000 live births (1980): 44.8.
Life expectancy at birth (1980–85): male 65.1 years; female 70.6 years.
Major causes of death per 100,000 population (1978): heart disease 82.5; malignant neoplasms (cancers) 53.4; diarrheal diseases 36.7.

National economy

Budget (1983). Revenue: Bs.72,858,000,000 (taxes and royalties on oil 55.5%, turnover tax 14.1%, other 30.4%). Expenditures: Bs.75,049,000,000 (detail n.a.).
Public debt (1984): U.S.$17,892,000,000.
Tourism (1981): receipts from visitors U.S.$251,000,000; expenditures by nationals abroad U.S.$2,349,000,000.
Production (metric tons except as noted). Agriculture, forestry, fishing (1982): sugarcane 5,025,000, rice 526,000, corn (maize) 377,000, sorghum 348,000, sesame 52,000, coffee 50,000, cotton 17,000, cacao 13,000, plantain 10,000, milk 1,382,000 litres; livestock 1,198,000 cattle. Mining and quarrying (1982): iron ore 11,680,000; gold 888 kilograms; diamonds 493,000 carats; coal 55,150; salt 455,000. Manufacturing (1982): steel 1,990,000; aluminum 273,000; cement 5,432,000; fertilizers 630,000; paper and cardboard 481,000; refined sugar 364,000; automobiles 94,000 vehicles. Construction (1981): residential 4,346,700 sq m; nonresidential 1,323,500 sq m. Energy production (consumption): electricity (kW-hr; 1982) 36,201,000,000 (30,-062,000,000); coal (metric tons; 1982) 55,150 (82,000); petroleum (barrels; 1982) 690,000,000 (143,000,000); liquefied petroleum gas (metric tons; 1982) 1,455,000 (930,000).

Gross national product (at current market prices; 1983): U.S.$64,647,000,000 (U.S.$3,880 per capita).

Origin of gross domestic product

	1981 in value Bs.'000,000§	% of total value	labour force	% of labour force
Agriculture	4,676	6.1	647,732	13.5
Mining	6,608	8.6	56,447	1.2
Manufacturing	12,012	15.7	729,381	15.2
Construction	4,480	5.8	432,003	9.0
Trade	6,762	8.8	840,200	17.5
Public utilities			50,453	1.0
Transportation and communication	19,855	25.9	329,564	6.9
Finance			212,696	4.4
Pub. admin., defense	10,584	13.8	1,205,405	25.1
Services	6,262	8.2		
Other	5,380	7.0	306,046	6.4
TOTAL	76,619	100.0‡	4,809,927	100.0‡

Persons economically active (1981): total 4,561,043 (31.8%); female 1,243,703 (17.4%); unemployed 272,400 (6.2%).

Price and earnings indexes (1975 = 100)

	1978	1979	1980	1981	1982	1983	1984 ‖
Consumer price index	124.3	139.6	169.7	197.2	216.8	229.6	255.8
Monthly earnings index	127.0	...	...	...	...	...	...

Household income and expenditure. Average household size (1981) 5.3; (1979) income per household Bs.2,897 (U.S.$512); source of income: n.a.; expenditure (1979): food 30.9%, transportation 15.9%, recreation 9.5%, clothing and footwear 6.6%, housing 6.2%.
Land use (1980): forested 39.7%; meadows and pastures 19.5%; agricultural and under permanent cultivation 4.2%; other 36.6%.

Foreign trade

Balance of trade (current prices)

	1978	1979	1980	1981	1982	1983
Bs.'000,000	−11,068	+15,655	+31,741	+30,131	+13,880	+42,273
% of total	9.7	6.8	12.3	14.6	9.7	47.1

Imports (1980): Bs.45,591,000,000 (machinery other than electrical 22.1%, of which road motor vehicles 11.6; chemicals and related products 10.5%; electrical machinery, apparatus, and equipment 9.3%; iron and steel 7.0%; cereals and cereal preparations 3.5%). *Major import sources:* United States 46.1%; Japan 8.2%; West Germany 7.0%; Canada 4.2%.
Exports (1980): Bs.82,507,000,000 (crude petroleum oils and crude oils obtained from bituminous materials 60.2%; petroleum products, refined 32.4%, of which residual fuel 22.2%). *Major export destinations:* United States 37.3%; Netherlands Antilles 21.7%; Canada 10.1%; United Kingdom 2.4%.

Transport and communications

Transport. Railroads (1979): length 278 mi, 448 km; passenger-mi 15,-386,973, passenger-km 24,762,933; short ton-mi cargo 16,960,000, metric ton-km cargo 17,545,936. Roads (1981): total length 38,805 mi, 62,449 km (paved 36.8%). Vehicles (1981): passenger cars 1,501,382; trucks and buses 795,856. Merchant marine (1983): vessels (100 gross tons and over) 244; total deadweight tonnage 1,356,987. Air transport (1982): passenger-mi 1,770,000,000, passenger-km 2,848,000,000; short ton-mi cargo 614,000, metric ton-km cargo 897,000; airports (1984) with scheduled flights 42.
Communications. Daily newspapers (1980): total number 54; total circulation 2,476,514; circulation per 1,000 population 178. Radios (1981): total number of receivers 4,750,000 (1 per 30 persons). Television (1981): total number of receivers 1,715,000 (1 per 8.3 persons). Telephones (1982): 1,337,630 (1 per 10.6 persons).

Education and health

Education (1980–81)

	schools	teachers	students	student/ teacher ratio
Primary (age 7–12)	12,788	97,045	2,591,051	26.7
Secondary (age 13–17)¶	1,754⁹	45,888⁸	958,233⁸	...
Higher	68⁹	28,052	307,133	10.9

College graduates per 100,000 population (1980): 114. *Literacy* (1978): total population literate 6,700,816 (84.9%); males literate 3,412,181 (87.2%); females literate 3,228,635 (82.6%).
Health (1978): physicians 14,771 (1 per 888 persons); hospital beds 41,386 (1 per 317 persons).
Food (1978–80): daily per capita caloric intake 2,649 (vegetable products 78.9%, animal products 21.1%); 107% of FAO recommended minimum.

Military

Total active duty personnel (1982): 40,800 (army 66.0%; navy 22.0%; air force 12.0%). *Military expenditure as percent of GNP:* 1.4% (world 4.5%); per capita expenditure U.S.$51.

*Excludes Indian jungle population estimated at 53,350 at the 1981 census. †1981.
‡Detail does not add to 100.0 because of rounding. §Prices of 1968. ‖Midyear.
¶Includes vocational and teacher training. ⁹1978–79. ⁸1979–80.

Vietnam

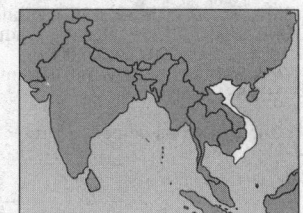

Official name: Cong Hoa Xa Hoi Chu Nghia Viet Nam (Socialist Republic of Vietnam).
Form of government: unitary single-party republic with one legislative house (National Assembly [496]).
Chief of state: President.
Head of government: Premier.
Capital: Hanoi.
Official language: Vietnamese.
Official religion: none.
Monetary unit: 1 dong (D) = 10 hao = 100 xu; valuation (Oct. 29, 1984) 1 U.S.$ = D10.42; 1 £ = D12.58.

Area and population

Provinces	Capitals	area sq mi	area sq km	population 1979 census
An Giang	Long Xuyen	1,349	3,493	1,532,362
Bac Thai	Thai Nguyen	2,521	6,530	815,105
Ben Tre	Ben Tre	859	2,225	1,041,838
Binh Tri Thien	Hue	7,081	18,340	1,901,713
Cao Bang	Cao Bang	3,261	8,445	479,823
Cuu Long	Vihn Long	1,488	3,854	1,504,215
Dac Lac	Buon Me Thoat	7,645	19,800	490,198
Dong Nai	Bien Hoa	2,926	7,578	1,304,799
Dong Thap	Cao Lamh	1,309	3,391	1,182,787
Gia Lai-Cong Tum	Cong Tum	9,860	25,536	595,906
Ha Bac	Bac Giang	1,780	4,609	1,662,671
Hai Hung	Hai Duong	986	2,555	2,145,662
Ha Nam Ninh	Nam Dinh	1,453	3,763	2,781,409
Ha Son Binh	Hanoi	2,308	5,978	1,537,190
Ha Tuyen	Ha Giang	5,219	13,518	782,453
Hau Giang	Can Tho	2,365	6,126	2,232,891
Hoang Lien Son	Lao Cai	5,734	14,852	778,217
Kien Giang	Rach Gia	2,455	6,358	994,673
Lai Chau	Lai Chau	6,586	17,068	322,077
Lam Dong	Da Lat	3,835	9,933	396,657
Lang Son	Lang Son	3,161	8,187	484,651
Long An	Tan An	1,681	4,355	957,264
Minh Hai	Bac Lieu	2,972	7,697	1,219,595
Nghe Tinh	Vinh	8,688	22,502	3,111,989
Nghia Binh	Qui Nhon	4,595	11,900	2,095,354
Phu Khanh	Nha Trang	3,785	9,804	1,188,637
Quang Nam-Da Nang	Da Nang	4,629	11,989	1,529,520
Quang Ninh	Hai Duong	2,293	5,938	750,055
Song Be	Thu Dau Mo	3,807	9,859	659,093
Son La	Son La	5,586	14,468	487,793
Tay Ninh	Ho Chi Minh City	1,556	4,030	684,006
Thai Binh	Thai Binh	577	1,495	1,506,235
Thanh Hoa	Thanh Hoa	4,300	11,138	2,532,261
Thuan Hai	Phan Thiet	4,392	11,374	938,255
Tien Giang	My Tho	918	2,377	1,264,498
Vinh Phu	Viet Tri	1,786	4,626	1,488,348
Municipalities				
Haiphong	—	585	1,515	1,279,067
Hanoi	—	826	2,139	2,570,905
Ho Chi Minh City	—	787	2,029	3,419,978
Special zone				
Vung Tau-Con Dao	—	108	279	91,610
TOTAL		**128,052**	**331,653**	**52,741,766**

Source: Official government figures.

Demography

Density (1984): persons per sq mi 455.1 persons per sq km 175.7.
Urban–rural (1979): urban 19.2%; rural 80.8%.
Sex distribution (1979): male 48.50%; female 51.50%.
Age breakdown (1980): under 15, 41.7%; 15 and over, 58.3%.
Population projection: (1990) 66,600,000; (2000) 78,980,000.
Doubling time: 29 years.
Ethnic composition (1978): Vietnamese 88.6%; Chinese 2.4%; Kho Me 1.6%; Tay 1.6%; Thai 1.4%; other 4.4%.
Religious affiliation (1980): Buddhist 55.3%; Roman Catholic 7.4%; Muslim 1.0%; other 36.3%.
Major cities (1979): Ho Chi Minh City 3,419,978; Hanoi 2,767,000*; Haiphong 1,279,067.

Vital statistics

Birth rate per 1,000 population (1983): 31.7 (world avg. 29.0); legitimate, n.a.; illegitimate, n.a.
Death rate per 1,000 population (1983): 10.9 (world avg. 11.0).
Natural increase rate per 1,000 population (1983): 20.8 (world avg. 18.0).
Total fertility rate (avg. births per childbearing woman; 1980–85): 4.3.
Marriage rate per 1,000 population: n.a.
Divorce rate per 1,000 population: n.a.
Infant mortality rate per 1,000 live births (1980): 34.7.
Life expectancy at birth (1980–85): male 54.6 years; female 58.0 years.
Major causes of death per 100,000 population (1979): diseases of the circulatory system 123.8; malignant neoplasms (cancers) 54.0; infectious and parasitic diseases 48.0.

National economy

Budget (1982). Revenue: U.S.$4,120,000,000. Expenditures: U.S.$5,560,000,-000.
Public debt (external, outstanding; 1982): U.S.$3,000,000,000.

Production (metric tons except as noted). Agriculture, forestry, fishing (1982): rice 14,169,000, sugarcane 4,400,000, cassava 2,665,000, fruits 2,643,000, vegetables 2,550,000, sweet potatoes 1,665,000, corn (maize) 487,000, coconuts 355,000; livestock (number of live animals; 1983) 10,785,000 pigs, 4,390,000 cattle, 219,000 sheep and goats, 77,200,000 poultry; roundwood 23,191,000 cu m; fish catch 800,000. Mining and quarrying (1981): phosphate rock 550,000; salt 500,000; chromite 15,000; zinc ore 6,000. Manufacturing (1982): cement 710,000; fertilizers 224,000;.sugar 222,000; paper and paperboard 52,600; crude steel 47,100; pig iron 13,600†; textiles 223,000,000 m; beer 561,000 hectolitres; tires 11,000 units; leather footwear 2,200,000 pairs†. Construction: n.a. Energy production (consumption): electricity (kW-hr; 1983) 4,370,000,000 (4,370,000,000); coal (metric tons; 1982) 6,100,-000 (6,100,000); crude petroleum, none (n.a.); petroleum products (metric tons; 1982) none (1,260,000); natural gas, none (n.a.).
Gross national product (at current market prices; 1982): U.S.$9,000,000,000 (U.S.$160 per capita).

Origin of gross domestic product (current prices)

	1982 by value	% of total value	labour force	% of labour force
Agriculture	...	...	17,578,000	69.3
Mining	...	...	‡	‡
Manufacturing	...	...	740,000‡	2.9‡
Construction	...	...	445,000	1.8
Trade	...	...	§	§
Public utilities	...	...	‡	‡
Transportation and communication	...	...	182,000	0.7
Finance	...	...	§	§
Pub. admin., defense	...	...	§	§
Services	...	...	§	§
Other	...	...	6,417,000§	25.3§
TOTAL	...	...	25,362,000	100.0

Persons economically active (1982): total 25,362,000 (45.2%); female participation in the labour force 11,538,000 (45.5%); unemployed, n.a.
Price and earnings indexes: n.a.
Household income and expenditure: n.a.
Land use (1981): forested 31.6%; meadows and pastures 15.0%; agricultural and under permanent cultivation 18.8%; other 34.6%.

Foreign trade

Balance of trade (current prices)

	1978	1979	1980	1981	1982
D'000,000	−1,476	−1,899	−1,427	−1,535	−1,834
% of total	37.4%	46.4%	38.3%	49.1%	49.4%

Imports (1980): D2,577,000,000 (fuel and raw materials 44.7%, machinery 23.2%, wheat flour and food products 17.2%). *Major import sources:* U.S.S.R. 18.3%; Japan 15.8%; India 12.9%; Singapore 6.9%; Hong Kong 6.2%.
Exports (1980): D1,150,000,000 (manufactured goods 72.8%, handicrafts 18.6%, agricultural products 8.6%). *Major export destinations:* Japan 31.0%; Hong Kong 14.1%; U.S.S.R. 11.6%; Singapore 11.4%.

Transport and communications

Transport. Railroads (1981): length 1,616 mi, 2,600 km; passenger-mi 2,830,000,000, passenger-km 4,554,000,000; short ton-mi cargo 534,000,000, metric ton-km cargo 779,000,000. Roads (1981): total length 25,594 mi, 41,190 km (paved 16%). Vehicles (1976): passenger cars 100,000; trucks and buses 200,000. Merchant marine (1983): vessels (100 gross tons and over) 114; total deadweight tonnage 389,952. Air transport (1980): passenger-mi 1,900,000, passenger-km 3,000,000; cargo, n.a.; airports (1984) with scheduled flights 3.
Communications. Daily newspapers (1983): 4; total circulation 500,000; circulation per 1,000 population 10.2. Radios (1983): 3,000,000 (1 per 18.7 persons). Television (1983): 2,000,000 (1 per 28.0 persons). Telephones (1982): 1,165,000 (1 per 48.1 persons).

Education and health

Education (1982–83)

	schools	teachers ‖	students	student/ teacher ratio
Primary (age 7–15)	12,200	383,700	11,700,000	...
Secondary (age 16–18)	¶		¶	...
Vocational	319	16,614	138,000	...
Higher	87	16,400	160,000⍥	...

College graduates per 100,000 population (1982): 529.4ᵟ. *Literacy* (1979): total population literate 28,903,500 (94.0%).
Health (1982): physicians 14,000 (1 per 4,007 persons); hospital beds 208,000 (1 per 258 persons).
Food (1978–80): daily per capita caloric intake 2,029 (vegetable products 91.7%, animal products 8.3%); 94% of FAO recommended minimum.

Military

Total active duty personnel (1984): 1,207,000 (army 97.4%; navy 1.2%; air force 1.4%). *Military expenditure as percent of GNP:* n.a. *Foreign military aid* (1982): U.S.$1,000,000,000.

*1983.   †1981.   ‡Mining and public utilities included with manufacturing.   §Trade, finance, transportation and communication, public administration, defense, and services included with other.   ‖ 1980–81.   ¶Included with primary.   ⍥5,000 Vietnamese studying in the U.S.S.R.   ᵟNumber of working specialists with higher education.

Western Samoa

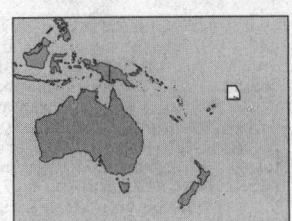

Official name: Malotuto'atasi o Samoa i Sisifo (Independent State of Western Samoa).
Form of government: constitutional monarchy with one legislative house (Legislative Assembly [47]).
Chief of state: O le Ao o le Malō.
Head of government: Prime Minister.
Capital: Apia.
Official languages: Samoan; English.
Official religion: none.
Monetary unit: 1 tala (WS$, plural tala) = 100 sene; valuation (Oct. 29, 1984) 1 U.S.$ = WS$2.14; 1 £ = WS$2.58.

Area and population	area		population
Islands Political Districts	sq mi	sq km	1981 census*
Savaii	659	1,708	43,150
Fa'aseleleaga			11,876
Gaga'emauga			3,893
Gaga'ifomauga			5,304
Lealataua			1,934
Palauli			9,234
Satupa'itea			5,391
Vaisigano			5,518
Upolu	432	1,118	113,199
A'ana			13,149
A'ana-i-Sisifo			3,363
Aiga-i-le-Tai			3,960
Aleipata			4,236
Anoama'a			7,816
Fagaloa			1,519
Falealili			4,727
Faleata			16,821
Gaga'emauga			2,750
Lefaga			3,776
Lepa and Lotofaga			3,058
Safata			6,711
Sagaga			12,253
Vaimauga			29,060
TOTAL	1,093†	2,831†	156,349

Source: Official government figures.

Demography

Density (1984): persons per sq mi 146.1, persons per sq km 56.4.
Urban–rural (1981): urban 21.2%; rural 78.8%.
Sex distribution (1981): male 51.82%; female 48.18%.
Age breakdown (1981): under 15, 44.3%; 15–29, 29.1%; 30–44, 12.2%; 45–59, 9.0%; 60–74, 3.8%; 75 and over, 1.6%.
Population projection: (1990) 166,000; (2000) 178,000.
Doubling time: 43 years.
Ethnic composition (1981): Samoan (Polynesian) 92.0%; Euronesian 7.6%; European and Chinese 0.4%.
Religious affiliation (1981): Congregational 47.3%; Roman Catholic 21.7%; Methodist 16.2%; Latter Day Saints 8.3%; Seventh-day Adventist 2.3%; other 4.2%.
Major cities (1981): Apia 33,170 .

Vital statistics

Birth rate per 1,000 population (1982): 19.1‡ (world avg. 29.0); (1978) legitimate 43.5%; illegitimate 56.5%.
Death rate per 1,000 population (1982): 2.7‡ (world avg. 11.0).
Natural increase rate per 1,000 population (1982): 16.4 (world avg. 18.0).
Total fertility rate (avg. births per childbearing woman; 1980–85): 2.7.
Marriage rate per 1,000 population (1982): 5.5‡.
Divorce rate per 1,000 population (1982): 0.29‡.
Infant mortality rate per 1,000 live births (1982): 8.6.
Life expectancy at birth (1976): male 61.0 years; female 64.3 years.
Major causes of death per 100,000 population‡ (1982): diseases of the circulatory system 49.5; diseases of the intestinal and digestive systems 26.0; diseases of the respiratory system 20.9; malignant neoplasms (cancers) 17.1.

National economy

Budget (1982). Revenue: WS$38,506,600 (customs duties 46.4%, taxes 17.5%, treasury department income 10.6%, income from public works 8.5%, postal revenue 8.1%, transport fees and licenses 3.2%). Expenditures: WS$26,-246,000 (public works 19.3%; health 17.0%; education 16.5%; treasury department 11.8%; justice, police, and prisons 7.3%).
Public debt (total, outstanding; 1982): U.S.$60,500,000.
Tourism (1982): number of visitors 32,752§; number of nationals abroad 39,141.
Production (metric tons except as noted). Agriculture, forestry, fishing (1982): coconuts 202,000, taros 41,000, bananas 22,000, papayas 11,000, mangoes 6,000, pineapples 5,000, avocados 2,000, cacao 2,000, milk 1,000; livestock (number of live animals) 27,000 cattle, 62,000 pigs, 501,000 chickens; non-coniferous roundwood 131,000 cu m; fish catch 2,400. Manufacturing (1982): coconut oil 8,037, copra 19,000, copra meal 3,924, sawnwood 21,000 cu m ‖ , veneer sheets 1,061 cu m; other important products include coconut cream, beer, cigarettes and matches, fruit juice and soft drinks, soap, furniture, textiles, handicrafts, kava, and fishing boats. Construction (per-

mits issued in WS$; 1982): residential 1,356,500; commercial, industrial, and other 3,777,500. Energy production (consumption): electricity (kW-hr; 1982) 39,000,000 (39,000,000).
Gross national product (at current market prices; 1981): U.S.$127,452,700 (U.S.$815 per capita).

Origin of gross domestic product (current prices)				
	1972		1981	
	in value WS$	% of total value	labour force	% of labour force
Agriculture	15,207,000	50.2	25,050	60.4
Mining	—	—	9	—
Manufacturing	858,900	2.8	757	1.8
Construction	1,146,800	3.8	2,279	5.5
Trade	2,861,100	9.5	1,821	4.4
Public utilities	...	...	447	1.1
Transportation and communication	666,600	2.2	1,353	3.3
Finance	1,761,800	5.8	1,305	3.1
Pub. admin., defense, government services	6,346,700	21.0	1,842	4.4
Other services	646,000	2.1	6,374	15.4
Other	769,400	2.5	269	0.6
TOTAL	30,264,300	100.0¶	41,506	100.0

Persons economically active (1981): total 41,506 (26.5%); female, n.a.; unemployed, n.a.

Price and earnings indexes (1980 = 100)							
	1978	1979	1980	1981	1982	1983	1984⁹
Consumer price index	66.2	75.2	100.0	120.5	142.6	166.0	183.2
Monthly earnings indexᵟ	71.6	91.1	100.0	115.2	...	...	...

Household income and expenditure. Average household size (1976) 5.9; income per household (1972) WS$1,518 (U.S.$2,200); source of income: wages and salaries 49.4%, self employment 22.8%, remittances, gifts, and other assistance 18.0%, land rent and royalties 8.7%, other 1.1%; expenditure: food and drink 55.1%, housing and furnishings 13.9%, clothing and footwear 11.7%, education 4.4%, tobacco 3.8%, personal care and effects 2.6%, transportation and communication 1.9%, recreation 1.8%, other 4.8%.
Land use (1981): forested 46.7%; meadows and pastures 0.3%; agricultural and under permanent cultivation 42.8%; other 10.2%.

Foreign trade

Balance of trade (current prices)						
	1978	1979	1980	1981	1982	1983
WS$'000	−27,045	−40,635	−36,902	−52,879	−43,869	−47,571
% of total	62.8%	57.9%	54.6%	72.0%	57.4%	48.2%

Imports (1982): WS$60,116,500 (food and food preparations 22.0%, machinery and transport equipment 18.2%, petroleum and petroleum products 14.4%, manufactured metal products 9.5%, miscellaneous manufactured articles 7.1%, chemicals 5.8%, animal oils and fats 3.6%). *Major import sources:* New Zealand 31.0%; Australia 21.4%; Japan 11.9%; United States 9.7%; China 7.0%; Singapore 5.7%.
Exports (1982): WS$15,548,280 (coconut oil 24.4%; copra 17.6%; taros, fruits, and vegetables 14.0%; timber 7.2%; reexports 6.6%; cocoa and shell 6.2%; coconut cream 5.6%; beer 4.2%; bananas 3.2%). *Major export destinations:* United States 28.6%; New Zealand 27.1%; Australia 9.8%; American Samoa 9.5%; Japan 7.9%; West Germany 5.8%.

Transport and communications

Transport. Railroads: none. Roads (1983): total length 289 mi, 465 km (paved 64%). Vehicles (1983): passenger cars 2,940; trucks and buses 385. Merchant marine (1983): vessels (100 gross tons and over) 4; total deadweight tonnage 5,962. Air transport (1982): passengers, n.a.; cargo, n.a.; airports (1984) with scheduled flights 3.
Communications. Daily newspapers: none. Radios (1983): total number of receivers 70,000 (1 per 2.3 persons). Television (1983): total number of receivers 2,500 (1 per 63.4 persons). Telephones (1983): 5,942 (1 per 26.7 persons).

Education and health

Education (1981–82)				
	schools	teachers	students	student/ teacher ratio
Primary (age 5–15)	162	1,460	40,475	27.7
Secondary (age 12–21)	38	495	11,839	23.9
Voc., teacher tr.	4	55	454	8.3
Higher	6	53	263	5.0

College graduates per 100,000 population: n.a. *Literacy* (1971): total population literate (age 10 and over) 93,360 (98.3%); males literate 48,146 (98.5%); females literate 45,214 (98.1%).
Health: physicians (1981) 63 (1 per 2,482 persons); hospital beds (1982) 735 (1 per 214 persons).
Food (1978–80): daily per capita caloric intake 2,289 (vegetable products 81.7%, animal products 18.3%); 100% of FAO recommended minimum requirement.

---

*Preliminary. †Includes 2 sq mi (5 sq km) of small uninhabited islands. ‡Registered only. §Excluding visitors from cruise ships. ‖ 1981. ¶Detail does not add to total given because of rounding. ⁹First quarter. ᵟGovernment employees only.

Yemen (Aden)

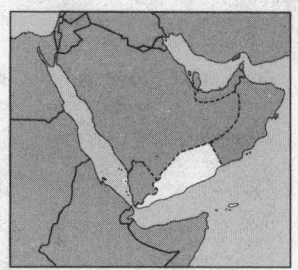

Official name: Jumhūrīyat al-Yaman ad-Dimuqrātīyah ash-Sha'bīyah (People's Democratic Republic of Yemen).
Form of government: single-party republic with one legislative house (Supreme People's Council [111]).
Head of state and government: Chairman of the Presidium of the Supreme People's Council.
Capital: Aden.
Official language: Arabic.
Official religion: none.
Monetary unit: 1 Yemeni dinar (YD) = 1,000 fils; valuation (Oct. 29, 1984) 1 YD = U.S.$2.94 = £2.43.

Area and population

Governorates	Capitals	area sq mi	area sq km	population 1973 census
Ūlá (First)	Aden	2,690	6,980	291,376
Thāniyah (Second)	Laḥij	4,930	12,760	273,611
Thālithah (Third)	Zinjibār	8,300	21,490	311,142
Rābi'ah (Fourth)	'Atāq	28,540	73,910	161,966
Khāmisah (Fifth)	al-Mukallā	32,990	85,450	450,657
Sādisah (Sixth)	al-Ghayḍah	25,620	66,350	60,876
Directorate				
Thamūd*	Thamūd	27,000	69,930	40,647
TOTAL		130,070	336,870	1,590,275

Source: Official government figures.

Demography

Density (1984): persons per sq mi 15.9, persons per sq km 6.1.
Urban–rural (1980): urban 36.9%; rural 63.1%.
Sex distribution (1980): male 49.41%; female 50.59%.
Age breakdown (1980): under 15, 46.0%; 15–29, 25.3%; 30–44, 15.1%; 45–59, 9.0%; 60–74, 3.9%; 75 and over, 0.7%.
Population projection: (1990) 2,459,000; (2000) 3,312,000.
Doubling time: 24 years.
Ethnic composition (1980): Arab 92.9%; Indo-Pakistani 2.5%; Somali 2.2%; other 2.4%.
Religious affiliation (1984): predominantly Muslim.
Major city (1981): Aden 365,000.

Vital statistics

Birth rate per 1,000 population (1980–85): 47.6 (world avg. 27.5); legitimate, n.a.; illegitimate, n.a.
Death rate per 1,000 population (1980–85): 18.9 (world avg. 10.6).
Natural increase rate per 1,000 population (1980–85): 28.7 (world avg. 16.9).
Total fertility rate (avg. births per childbearing woman; 1980–85): 6.9.
Marriage rate per 1,000 population: n.a.
Divorce rate per 1,000 population: n.a.
Infant mortality rate per 1,000 live births (1981): 142.9.
Life expectancy at birth (1980–85): male 45.3 years; female 47.7 years.
Major causes of death: n.a.; however, major infectious diseases are shigellosis (infection with dysentery), tuberculosis, influenza, malaria, measles, intestinal infections, and whooping cough.

National economy

Budget (1980–81). Revenue: YD86,020,000 (1973–74; import duties 33.5%, excise duties 14.1%, taxes on corporate income 12.7%, taxes on personal income 8.0%). Expenditures: YD96,020,000 (1973–74; defense and security 45.9%, education 16.9%, general administration 11.8%, economic services 6.8%, health 5.1%, public works and communications 4.7%).
Public debt (external, outstanding; 1982): U.S.$817,000,000.
Tourism (1981): receipts from visitors U.S.$4,000,000; expenditures by nationals abroad U.S.$10,000,000.
Production (metric tons except as noted). Agriculture, forestry, fishing (1982): millet 60,000, dates 43,000, wheat 15,000, corn (maize) 15,000, seed cotton 12,000, lint cotton 4,000, tobacco 2,000, coffee 1,000; livestock (number of live animals) 1,350,000 goats, 1,010,000 sheep, 170,000 asses, 120,000 cattle, 100,000 camels; roundwood 264,000 cu m; fish catch 69,710. Mining and quarrying (1981): salt 75,000. Manufacturing (1979): residual fuel oil 950,000; motor spirits 711,000; kerosine 410,000; distillate fuel oils 410,000; jet fuel 160,000. Construction: n.a. Energy production (consumption): electricity (kW-hr; 1982) 257,000,000 (257,000,000); coal, none (n.a.); crude petroleum (barrels; 1982) none (15,735,000); petroleum products (metric tons; 1982) 2,130,000 (1,094,000); natural gas, none (n.a.).
Persons economically active (1982)¶: total 500,000 (25.5%); female participation in the labour force 15,000 (3.0%); unemployed, n.a.

Price and earnings indexes (1980 = 100)

	1974	1975	1976	1977	1978	1979	1980
Consumer price index	63.8	71.1	73.8	77.6	79.8	90.9	100.0
Earnings index	...	...	...	...	...	...	...

Household income and expenditure. Average household size (1980) 5.5; average annual income per household: n.a.; source of income: n.a.; expenditure: n.a.

Gross national product (at current market prices; 1981): U.S.$910,000,000 (U.S.$448 per capita).

Origin of gross domestic product (current prices)

	1976 in value YD'000,000	% of total value	labour force	% of labour force
Agriculture	26.9	20.9	181,000	45.4
Mining	0.2	0.2	†	†
Manufacturing	13.8	10.7	27,000†	6.8†
Construction	10.4	8.1	28,000	7.0
Trade	19.9	15.4	30,000	7.5
Public utilities	2.0	1.6	...	...
Transportation and communication	14.6	11.3	24,000	6.0
Finance	8.4	6.5	2,000	0.5
Pub. admin., defense	21.5	16.7	...	...
Services	8.2	6.4	‡	‡
Other	3.0§	2.3	107,000‡	26.8‡
TOTAL	128.9	100.0 ‖	399,000	100.0

Land use (1981): forested 7.3%; meadows and pastures 27.3%; agricultural and under permanent cultivation 0.6%; other 64.8%.

Foreign trade

Balance of trade (current prices)

	1975	1976	1977	1978	1979	1980	1981
YD'000,000	−40.3	−65.9	−105.4	−110.7	−123.8	−258.4	−404
% of total	25.4%	35.0%	45.8%	45.4%	27.7%	32.4%	57.7%

Imports (1980): YD527,400,000 (1977; machinery and transport equipment 34.8%; food and live animals 23.4%, of which wheat and wheat flour 5.0%, rice 2.7%, refined sugar 2.4%; petroleum products 18.2%; chemicals 2.9%).
Major import sources: Kuwait 11%; Qatar 11%; United Arab Emirates 8%; Japan 6%; U.S.S.R. 6%; Saudi Arabia 6%.
Exports (1980): YD269,000,000 (petroleum products 95%). *Major export destinations:* United Arab Emirates 22%; Italy 11%; India 5%.

Transport and communications

Transport. Railroads: none. Roads (1983): total length 1,150 mi, 1,850 km (paved, n.a.). Vehicles (1980): passenger cars 16,500; commercial vehicles 16,300. Merchant marine (1983): vessels (100 gross tons and over) 36; total deadweight tonnage 14,109. Air transport (1980): passenger-mi 52,000,000, passenger-km 84,000,000; short ton-mi cargo 1,160,000, metric ton-km cargo 1,700,000; airport (1984) with scheduled flights 1.
Communications. Daily newspapers (1983): total number 3; total circulation 12,000♀. Radios (1983): total number of receivers 110,000 (1 per 19 persons). Television (1983): total number of receivers 27,000 (1 per 77.3 persons). Telephones (1981–82): 10,054 (1 per 200 persons).

Education and health

Education (1982)

	schools	teachers	students	student/ teacher ratio
Primary (age 7–12)	890	10,915	228,893	21.0
Secondary (age 13–18)	46	1,271	27,776	21.9
Voc., teacher tr.	13	173	1,556	9.0
Higherŏ	...	246	2,517	10.2

College graduates per 100,000 population (students graduating; 1980): 27.4.
Literacy (1980): total population literate 411,900 (38.9%); males literate 354,700 (66.6%); females literate 57,200 (10.9%).
Health (1980): physicians 264 (1 per 7,390 persons); hospital beds 2,900 (1 per 641 persons).
Food (1978–80): daily per capita caloric intake 2,103 (vegetable products 83.8%, animal products 16.2%); 87% of FAO recommended minimum requirement.

Military

Total active duty personnel (1983): 25,500 (army 86.3%; navy 3.9%; air force 9.8%). *Military expenditure as percent of GNP* (1980): 15.5% (world 5.6%); per capita expenditure U.S.$69.

*Thamūd is administratively part of Khāmisah governorate. †Mining is included with manufacturing. ‡Services are included with other. §Customs duties less production subsidies and interest. ‖ Detail does not add to total given because of rounding. ¶Estimated. ♀Partial circulation only. ŏ1977–78.

Yemen (Şan'ā')

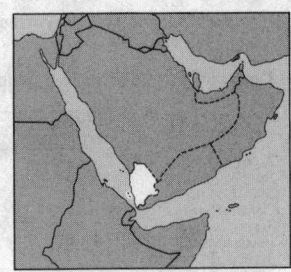

Official name: al-Jumhūrīyah al-'Arabīyah al-Yamanīyah (Yemen Arab Republic).
Form of government: military dominated single-party republic with one legislative house (Constituent People's Assembly [159]).
Head of state and government: President.
Capital: Şan'ā'.
Official language: Arabic.
Official religion: Islām.
Monetary unit: 1 Yemen Rial (YRl) = 100 fils; valuation (Oct. 29, 1984) 1 U.S.$ = YRls5.74; 1 £ = YRls6.93.

Area and population

Governorates	Capitals	area sq mi	area sq km	population 1980 estimate*
al-Baydā'	al-Baydā'	4,310	11,170	182,100
al-Hudaydah	al-Hudaydah	5,240	13,580	794,300
al-Maḥwit	al-Maḥwit	830	2,160	195,300
Dhamār	Dhamār	3,430	8,870	506,200
Ḥajjah	Ḥajjah	3,700	9,590	450,300
Ibb	Ibb	2,480	6,430	871,700
Ma'rib	Ma'rib	15,400	39,890	76,600
Şa'dah	Şa'dah	4,950	12,810	190,300
Şan'ā'	Şan'ā'	7,840	20,310	963,900
Ta'izz	Ta'izz	4,020	10,420	981,400
TOTAL		52,210†‡	135,230‡	5,212,100

Source: Official government figures.

Demography

Density (1984): persons per sq mi 122.1, persons per sq km 47.1.
Urban–rural (1980): urban 10.2%; rural 89.8%.
Sex distribution (1980): male 47.28%; female 52.72%.
Age breakdown (1980): under 15, 45.7%; 15–29, 23.2%; 30–44, 15.1%; 45–59, 10.5%; 60–74, 4.7%; 75 and over, 0.8%.
Population projection: (1990) 7,447,000; (2000) 9,828,000.
Doubling time: 26 years.
Ethnic composition (1984): Predominantly Arabs.
Religious affiliation (1980): Zaydī (Shi'a Muslim sect) 55%; Shafa'i (Sunnī Muslim sect) 40%; Ismā'īlī (Shi'a Muslim sect) 5%.
Major cities (1981): Şan'ā' 277,820; al-Ḥudaydah 126,390; Ta'izz 119,580.

Vital statistics

Birth rate per 1,000 population (1980–85): 48.5 (world avg. 27.5); legitimate n.a., illegitimate n.a.
Death rate per 1,000 population (1980–85): 21.8 (world avg. 10.6).
Natural increase rate per 1,000 population (1980–85): 26.7 (world avg. 16.9).
Total fertility rate (avg. births per childbearing woman; 1980–85): 6.8.
Marriage rate per 1,000 population: n.a.
Divorce rate per 1,000 population: n.a.
Infant mortality rate per 1,000 live births (1975–80): 170.0.
Life expectancy at birth (1980–85): male 42.7 years; female 44.8 years.
Major causes of death: n.a.; however, major infectious diseases are malaria, tuberculosis, intestinal infections, leprosy, schistosomiasis, typhoid and paratyphoid fevers, viral hepatitis, and filarial infections.

National economy

Budget (1981)§. Revenue: YRls3,282,600,000 ‖ (import duties 49.1%, income from property 13.9%, stamp tax 11.0%, excise duties 7.1%, income tax 5.2%). Expenditures: YRls6,219,900,000 (defense 32.6%, general public services 18.6%, education 14.0%, roads 6.5%, health 3.6%).
Public debt (external, outstanding; 1982): U.S.$1,406,000,000.
Tourism (1981): receipts from visitors U.S.$33,700,000; expenditures by nationals abroad U.S.$44,000,000.
Production (metric tons except as noted). Agriculture, fishing (1982): sorghum 583,000, potatoes 141,000, dates 90,000, pulses 75,000, wheat 67,000, corn (maize) 59,000, barley 53,000, tobacco 6,000, sugarcane 5,000, coffee 4,000; livestock (number of live animals) 7,500,000 goats, 3,151,000 sheep, 950,000 cattle, 740,000 asses, 107,000 camels; fish catch 22,000. Mining and quarrying (1981): salt 64,000; rock 567,000 cu m. Manufacturing (1981): cement 85,000; domestic utensils 1,600; textile fabric 3,135,000 m. Construction (1981): residential 1,196,100 sq m. Energy production (consumption): electricity (kW-hr; 1982) 230,000,000 (230,000,000); coal, none (n.a.); petroleum products (metric tons; 1982) none (506,000); natural gas, none (n.a.).
Persons economically active♀ (1982): total 1,668,000 (22.7%); female participation in the labour force 183,480 (11%); unemployed, n.a.

Price and earnings indexes (1980 = 100)

	1977	1978	1979	1980	1981	1982
Consumer price index	67.0	75.0	95.0	100.0	105.0	108.0
Earnings index	...	...	...	...	...	...

Household income and expenditure. Average household size (1980) 5.8; average annual income per household: n.a.; sources of income: n.a.; expenditure: n.a.

Gross national product (at current market prices; 1981): U.S.$3,310,000,000 (U.S.$462 per capita).

Origin of gross domestic product (current prices)

	1981 in value YRls'000,000	1981 % of total value	1975 labour force	1975 % of labour force
Agriculture	3,690	28.5	830,340	73.6
Mining	156	1.2	580	0.1
Manufacturing	770	5.9	33,920	3.0
Construction	1,140	8.8	52,640	4.7
Trade	2,263	17.5	68,980	6.1
Public utilities	89	0.7	1,510	0.1
Transportation and communication	483	3.7	24,710	2.2
Finance	¶	¶	1,980	0.2
Pub. admin., defense	¶	¶	...	...
Services	¶	¶	85,780	7.6
Other	4,358¶	33.7¶	27,330	2.4
TOTAL	12,949	100.0	1,127,770	100.0

Land use (1981): forested 8.2%; meadows and pastures 35.9%; agricultural and under permanent cultivation 14.3%; other 41.6%.

Foreign trade

Balance of trade (current prices)

	1976	1977	1978	1979	1980	1981
YRls'000,000	−1,595	−4,075	−5,062	−5,857	−8,351	−6,759
% of total	95.8%	97.6%	98.8%	97.9%	97.6%	94.0%

Imports (1980): YRls8,454,239,500 (machines and transport equipment 27.8%, of which road vehicles 11.7%, electric machinery 4.3%; food and live animals 26.1%, of which vegetables and fruits 6.4%, dairy products 5.6%, cereals and preparations 4.7%; petroleum products 7.1%; iron and steel 6.2%; chemicals 5.1%; cement 3.2%). *Major import sources:* Saudi Arabia 19.3%; Japan 12.7%; France 7.9%; West Germany 5.9%; United Kingdom 5.2%; Italy 5.0%.
Exports (1980): YRls103,130,750 (food and live animals 43.8%, of which cereals and preparations 18.5%, sugar and honey 10.0%; civil engineering equipment 16.0%; textile yarn 5.9%; road vehicles 4.0%). *Major export destinations:* Yemen (Aden) 42.4%; France 11.5%; China 9.3%; United States 8.8%; Italy 6.5%; Saudi Arabia 5.4%.

Transport and communications

Transport. Railroads: none. Roads (1983): total length 20,541 mi, 33,057 km (paved 6%). Vehicles (1983): passenger cars 99,666, trucks and buses 140,-114. Merchant marine (1983): vessels (100 gross tons and over) 10; total deadweight tonnage 1,850. Air transport (1983): passenger-mi 419,548,000, passenger-km 675,198,000; short ton-mi cargo 44,590,000, metric ton-km cargo 65,100,000; airports (1984) with scheduled flights 3.
Communications. Daily newspapers (1983): total number 2; total circulation n.a.; circulation per 1,000 population n.a. Radios (1983): total number of receivers 110,000 (1 per 68.5 persons). Television (1983): total number of receivers 27,000 (1 per 279 persons). Telephones: n.a.

Education and health

Education (1980–81)

	schools	teachers	students	student/ teacher ratio
Primary (age 7–12)	2,985	9,826	412,573	39.0
Secondary (age 13–18)	314	2,023	28,852	14.3
Voc., teacher tr.	29	196	4,023	20.5
Higher	...	58δ	4,220	...

College graduates per 100,000 population (students graduating, 1980): 7. *Literacy* (1980): total population literate 350,600 (8.3%); males literate 340,100 (15.9%); females literate 10,500 (0.5%).
Health: physicians (1981) 896 (1 per 6,629 persons); hospital beds (1983) 4,000 (1 per 1,900 persons).
Food (1978–80): daily per capita caloric intake 2,272 (vegetable products 89.4%, animal products 10.6%); 94% of FAO recommended minimum requirement.

Military

Total active duty personnel (1983): 21,550 (army 92.8%; navy 2.6%; air force 4.6%). *Military expenditure as percent of GNP* (1982): 16.8% (world 6%); per capita expenditure U.S.$72.

*Population estimate according to the Swiss Technical Co-operation Service. †Detail does not add to total given because of rounding. ‡Area shown is according to the Swiss Technical Co-Operation Service. The major part of the eastern boundary with Saudi Arabia and Yemen (Aden) is not officially defined and demarcated; however, the government of Yemen (Şan'ā') uses a higher estimate of 77,200 sq mi (200,000 sq km). §1982–83 estimated budget was: revenue YRls5,460,000; expenditure YRls8,-720,000. ‖ Also includes YRls5,600,000 in capital revenue. ¶Finance, public administration and defense, and services are included with other. ♀Estimated. δ1973–74.

Yugoslavia

Official name: Socijalistična Federativna Republika Jugoslavija (Slovenian); Socijalistička Federativna Republika Jugoslavija (Macedonian, Serbo-Croatian) (Socialist Federal Republic of Yugoslavia).
Form of government: single-party federal republic with one legislative house (Federal Assembly [88]).
Chief of state: President.
Capital: Belgrade.
Official languages: Macedonian; Serbo-Croatian; Slovenian.
Official religion: none.
Monetary unit: 1 Yugoslav dinar (Din) = 100 paras; valuation (Oct. 29, 1984) 1 U.S.$ = Din185.02; 1 £ = Din223.32.

Area and population

Socialist republics	Capitals	area sq mi	area sq km	population 1984 estimate
Bosnia and Hercegovina	Sarajevo	19,741	51,129	4,466,000
Croatia	Zagreb	21,829	56,538	4,648,000
Macedonia	Skopje	9,928	25,713	2,025,000
Montenegro	Titograd	5,333	13,812	623,000
Serbia	Belgrade	21,609	55,968	5,627,000
Slovenia	Ljubljana	7,819	20,251	1,866,000
Autonomous provinces*				
Kosovo	Priština	4,203	10,887	1,770,000
Vojvodina	Novi Sad	8,303	21,506	2,028,000
TOTAL		98,766†	255,804	23,053,000

Source: Official government figures.

Demography

Density (1984): persons per sq mi 233.4, persons per sq km 90.1.
Urban–rural (1981): urban 46.5%; rural 53.5%.
Sex distribution (1981): male 44.43%; female 55.57%.
Age breakdown (1981): under 15, 24.5%; 15–29, 25.0%; 30–44, 19.8%; 45–59, 18.3%; 60–74, 8.9%; 75 and over, 3.1%; unknown, 0.4%.
Population projection: (1990) 24,107,000; (2000) 25,653,000.
Doubling time: 87 years.
Ethnic composition (1981): Serb 36.3%; Croat 19.7%; Bosnian Muslim 8.9%; Slovenian 7.8%; Albanian 7.7%; Macedonian 6.0%; Montenegrin 2.6%; other 11.0%.
Religious affiliation (1980): Serbian Orthodox 34.6%; Roman Catholic 26.0%; Crypto-Christian 11.3%; Muslim 10.4%; other 17.7%.
Major cities (1981): Belgrade 1,470,073; Osijek 867,646; Zagreb 768,700; Niš 643,470; Skopje 506,547; Sarajevo 448,500.

Vital statistics

Birth rate per 1,000 population (1982): 16.5 (world avg. 29.0); (1981) legitimate 91.7%, illegitimate 8.3%.
Death rate per 1,000 population (1982): 8.9 (world avg. 11.0).
Natural increase rate per 1,000 population (1982): 7.6 (world avg. 18.0).
Total fertility rate (avg. births per childbearing woman; 1980–85): 2.1.
Marriage rate per 1,000 population (1982): 7.7.
Divorce rate per 1,000 population (1982): 1.0.
Infant mortality rate per 1,000 live births (1982): 29.9.
Life expectancy at birth (1981): male 67.7 years; female 73.1 years.
Major causes of death per 100,000 population (1981): diseases of the circulatory system 875.0; malignant neoplasms 273.0; accidents 128.0; diseases of the respiratory system 113.0; diseases of the digestive system 77.0.

National economy

Budget (1982). Revenue: Din349,354,000,000 (receipts from industry 38.2%, trade 18.4%, agriculture 16.0%, construction 10.1%, tourism 2.9%). Expenditures: Din386,371,000,000 (defense 26.1%, administrative services 18.8%, health and welfare 11.2%, economic development 8.0%, education 2.0%).
Public debt (external, outstanding; 1982): U.S.$10,450,800,000.
Tourism (1982): receipts from visitors U.S.$847,000,000.
Production (metric tons except as noted). Agriculture, forestry, fishing (1982): sugar beets 139,293,000, sunflower seeds 138,458,000, tobacco 61,121,000, corn (maize) 11,126,000, wheat 5,218,000, potatoes 2,636,000, grapes 1,780,-000, plums 1,028,000, apples 746,000, barley 669,000, oats 269,000, rye 84,000, rice 42,000; livestock (number of live animals; 1983) 8,370,000 pigs, 7,452,000 sheep, 5,351,000 cattle, 69,680,000 poultry; fish 40,489,000. Mining and quarrying (1982): copper ore 19,773,000; iron ore 5,106,000; lead and zinc ore 4,252,000; bauxite 3,668,000; antimony 63,000; manganese 27,000; silver (refined) 110. Manufacturing (1982): rubber 62,926,000; ceramics 19,000,000; cement 9,719,000; pig iron and crude steel 6,553,000; rolled steel 4,513,000; pulp and paper 2,881,000; fertilizers 2,321,000; fabricated metal products 2,217,000; automobile tires 9,388,000 units; radio and television receivers 641,000 units; leather 8,970,000 sq m; leather outerwear 4,955,000 sq m; cotton fabrics 372,000,000 sq m. Construction (1982): residential 9,965,000 sq m; industrial 997,000 sq m; commercial 833,000 sq m. Energy production (consumption): electricity (kW-hr; 1982) 62,324,-000,000 (54,905,000,000); coal (metric tons; 1982) 54,587,000 (56,060,000); crude petroleum (barrels; 1982) 31,812,000 (94,044,000); petroleum products (metric tons; 1982) 12,137,000 (13,196,000); natural gas (cu m; 1982) 1,789,000,000 (3,712,000,000).
Gross national product (at current market prices; 1982): U.S.$46,461,000,000 (Din2,902,890,000,000), U.S.$2,050 per capita.

Origin of gross domestic product (current prices)

	1982 in value Din'000,000	% of total value	labour force	% of labour force
Agriculture	399,203	15.5	3,638,000	36.9
Mining	57,962	2.3	197,400	2.0
Manufacturing	882,367	34.2	2,165,800	21.9
Construction	243,582	9.5	611,600	6.2
Trade	606,441	23.5	822,300	8.3
Public utilities	21,849	0.8	115,300	1.2
Transportation and communication	167,279	6.5	415,500	4.2
Finance	...	...	209,100	2.1
Pub. admin., defense, and services	188,636	7.3	1,199,200	12.2
Other	8,805‡	0.3	496,500‡§	5.0
TOTAL	2,576,124	100.0‡	9,870,700	100.0

Persons economically active (1982): total 9,870,745 (44.0%); female participation in the labour force 3,754,229 (38.0%); unemployed 942,600 ‖ (13.1%).

Price and earnings indexes (1970 = 100)

	1976	1977	1978	1979	1980	1981	1982
Consumer price index	271.0	311.5	355.9	429.2	558.7	787.4	1,041.7
Monthly earnings index	301.0	357.9	433.2	524.0	628.6	837.6	1,065.4

Household income and expenditure. Average household size (1982) 3.6; income per household Din232,600 (U.S.$3,700); source of income: wages and salaries 69.7%, welfare 15.4%, other 14.9%; expenditure (1981): food 36.5%, clothing and footwear 14.2%, transportation 11.5%, recreation 7.2%, housing 6.9%; other 23.7%.
Land use (1982): forested 36.5%; meadows and pastures 25.0%; agricultural and under permanent cultivation 30.8%; other 7.7%.

Foreign trade

Balance of trade (current prices)

	1978	1979	1980	1981	1982	1983
Din'000,000,000	−180.4	−302.0	−254.4	−180.7	−129.3	−162.2
% of total	27.6%	34.7%	25.3%	17.5%	13.1%	10.3%

Imports (1982): Din557,353,000,000 (machinery and transport equipment 27.8%, of which nonelectric machinery 16.2%, transport equipment 6.7%; mineral fuels, lubricants, and related materials 25.7%; chemicals 12.4%; iron and steel 6.0%; textile yarn and fabrics 5.5%; food products 5.0%; metalliferous ores and metal scrap 2.7%). *Major import sources:* U.S.S.R. 20.5%; West Germany 13.9%; Italy 7.7%; United States 6.3%; Czechoslovakia 4.7%; France 4.3%; Austria 3.8%; United Kingdom 3.4%.
Exports (1982): Din428,071,000,000 (machinery and transport equipment 31.1%, of which nonelectric machinery 11.2%, transport equipment 10.2%; clothing and footwear 11.6%; chemicals 10.5%; food products 9.0%; textile yarn and fabrics 5.1%; furniture 3.4%). *Major export destinations:* U.S.S.R. 33.4%; Italy 7.6%; West Germany 7.0%; Iraq 7.0%; Czechoslovakia 6.1%.

Transport and communications

Transport. Railroads (1982): length 5,834 mi, 9,389 km; passenger-mi 6,999,-700,000, passenger-km 11,265,000,000; short ton-mi cargo 17,922,000,000, metric ton-km cargo 26,166,000,000. Roads (1982): total length 71,566 mi, 115,174 km (paved 53%). Vehicles (1982): passenger cars 2,702,628; trucks and buses 237,768. Merchant marine (1983): vessels (100 gross tons and over) 479; total deadweight tonnage 3,898,464. Air transport (1982): passenger-mi 1,783,000,000, passenger-km 2,870,000,000; short ton-mi cargo 40,891,000, metric ton-km cargo 59,700,000; airports (1984) with scheduled flights 16.
Communications. Daily newspapers (1983): total number 24; total circulation 1,890,500; circulation per 1,000 population 83.6. Radios (1982): total number of receivers 4,800,000 (1 per 4.7 persons). Television (1982): total number of receivers 4,400,000 (1 per 5.1 persons). Telephones (1982): 2,542,000 (1 per 8.9 persons).

Education and health

Education (1981–82)

	schools	teachers	students	student/teacher ratio
Primary (age 7–14)	12,537	132,766	2,816,353	21.2
Secondary (age 15–18)	33,341¶	62,686	1,040,922	16.6
Higher	358	20,250	402,037	20.3

College graduates per 100,000 population (1981): 145.6. *Literacy* (1981): total population literate 16,945,900 (90.5%); males literate 8,805,400 (95.9%); females literate 8,140,500 (85.3%).
Health (1982): physicians 40,609 (1 per 550 persons); hospital beds 136,820 (1 per 163 persons).
Food (1978–80): daily per capita caloric intake 3,528 (vegetable products 76.6%, animal products 23.4%); 139% of FAO recommended minimum.

Military

Total active duty personnel (1983): 239,700 (army 79.7%; navy 5.0%; air force 15.3%). *Military expenditure as percent of GNP* (1982): 5.7% (world 6.0%); per capita expenditure U.S.$102.

---

*The autonomous provinces are administratively part of the socialist republic of Serbia. †Detail does not add to total given because of rounding. ‡Includes operation of irrigation systems, water works, and supply. §Includes private sector and noneconomic activities. ‖ March 1984. ¶Classes.

Zaire

Official name: République du Zaïre (Republic of Zaire).
Form of government: republic with one legislative house (National Legislative Council [310]).
Head of state and government: President.
Capital: Kinshasa.
Official language: French.
Official religion: none.
Monetary unit: 1 zaire (Z) = 100 makuta (singular likuta) = 10,000 sengi; valuation (Oct. 29, 1984) 1 U.S.$ = Z38.46; 1 £ = Z46.42.

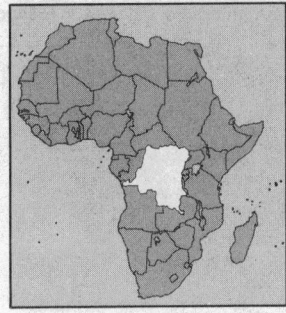

Area and population

Regions	Capitals	area sq mi	area sq km	population 1981 estimate
Bandundu	Bandundu	114,154	295,658	4,119,500
Bas-Zaire	Matadi	20,819	53,920	1,921,500
Equateur	Mbandaka	155,712	403,293	3,418,300
Haut-Zaire	Kisangani	194,302	503,239	4,541,600
Kasai Occidental	Kananga	60,605	156,967	2,935,000
Kasai Oriental	Mbuji-Mayi	64,949	168,216	2,337,000
Kivu	Bukavu	99,098	256,662	4,713,800
Shaba (Katanga)	Lubumbashi	191,879	496,965	3,823,200
Neutral City				
Kinshasa		3,848	9,965	2,338,200
TOTAL		905,365*	2,344,885	30,148,100

Source: Official government figures.

Demography

Density (1984): persons per sq mi 35.4, persons per sq km 13.7.
Urban-rural (1980): urban 34.2%; rural 65.8%.
Sex distribution (1980): male 49.22%; female 50.78%.
Age breakdown (1980): under 15, 46.2%; 15–29, 26.7%; 30–44, 15.1%; 45–59, 8.0%; 60–74, 3.4%; 75 and over, 0.6%.
Population projection: (1990) 38,081,000; (2000) 52,410,000.
Doubling time: 23 years.
Ethnic composition (1978): Benue–Kongo 85.6%, of whom Luba 18.0%, Kongo 16.2%, Mongo 13.3%, Rwanda 10.1%; Eastern Adamawa 9.5%; Chari–Nile 4.7%; other 0.2%.
Religious affiliation (1980): Roman Catholic 48.4%; Protestant 29.0%; indigenous Christian 17.1%; animist 3.4%; Muslim 1.4%; other 0.7%.
Major cities (1976): Kinshasa 2,338,200†; Kananga 704,211; Lubumbashi 451,332; Mbuji-Mayi 382,632; Kisangani 339,210.

Vital statistics

Birth rate per 1,000 population (1980–85): 46.3 (world avg. 27.5); legitimate, n.a.; illegitimate, n.a.
Death rate per 1,000 population (1980–85): 18.6 (world avg. 10.6).
Natural increase rate per 1,000 population (1980–85): 27.7 (world avg. 16.9).
Total fertility rate (avg. births per childbearing woman; 1982): 7.2.
Marriage rate per 1,000 population (1975): 7.5.
Divorce rate per 1,000 population (1975): 0.03.
Infant mortality rate per 1,000 live births (1980): 116.6.
Life expectancy at birth (1980): male 45.0 years; female 48.0 years.
Major causes of death per 100,000 population‡ (1977): measles 9.6; meningitis 1.1; influenza 0.4; whooping cough 0.3.

National economy

Budget (1984). Revenue: Z19,800,000,000 (direct and indirect taxes 84.3%, government investments 10.9%, administrative and judicial receipts 4.7%). Expenditure: Z21,600,000,000 (service of external debt 37.5%, government salaries 21.3%, service of internal debt 7.9%).
Public debt (external, outstanding; 1982): U.S.$4,086,600,000.
Tourism (1980): receipts from visitors U.S.$22,000,000; expenditures by nationals abroad, n.a.
Production (metric tons except as noted). Agriculture, forestry, fishing (1982): cassava 13,173,000, sugarcane 643,000, corn (maize) 527,000, peanuts (groundnuts) 323,000, bananas 317,000, sweet potatoes 309,000, rice 255,000, pineapples 165,000, mangoes 140,000, coffee 75,000, natural rubber 28,000; livestock (number of live animals) 2,900,000 goats, 1,266,000 cattle, 764,000 sheep, 749,000 pigs, 16,268,000 poultry; roundwood 30,391 cu m; fish catch 100,700. Mining and quarrying (1983): copper 466,728; zinc 62,535; cobalt 5,349; manganese 4,000§; tin 2,400§; silver 1,750,000 troy oz.§; gold 6. Manufacturing (1982): cement 400,000; corn (maize) flour 180,800 ‖; sulfuric acid 140,000; diamonds 9,000,000 carats, of which industrial diamonds 8,500,000 carats; woven cotton fabrics 56,218,000 sq m; beer 2,887,000 hectolitres. Construction (1978): residential 161,000 sq m; nonresidential 89,000 sq m. Energy production (consumption): electricity (kW-hr; 1982) 4,412,000,000 (4,337,000,000); coal (metric tons; 1982) 240,000 (153,000); crude petroleum (barrels; 1982) 8,385,000 (3,408,000); petroleum products (metric tons; 1982) 433,000 (880,000); natural gas, none (n.a.).
Household income and expenditure. Average household size (1982) 6.0; average annual income per household Z1,200 (U.S.$209); source of income: wages and salaries, small-scale trading; expenditure (1982): food 60%, other 40%.

Gross national product (at current market prices; 1982): U.S.$5,160,000,000 (U.S.$171 per capita).

Origin of gross domestic product (current prices)

	1981 in value Z'000,000	% of total value	labour force	% of labour force
Agriculture	7,550.0	32.0	8,975,000	73.7
Mining	3,745.6	15.9	¶	¶
Manufacturing	648.0	2.7	1,612,000¶	13.2¶
Construction	1,160.7	4.9	♀	♀
Trade	4,625.9	19.6	♀	♀
Public utilities	11.3	0.0	¶	¶
Transportation and communication	554.1	2.3	♀	♀
Finance	...	...	♀	♀
Pub. admin., defense	...	...	♀	♀
Services	4,491.5	19.0	♀	♀
Other	815.8	3.5	1,594,000♀	13.1♀
TOTAL	23,602.9	100.0*	12,181,000	100.0

Persons economically active (1982): total 12,445,000 (41.6%); female participation in the labour force, n.a.; unemployedδ.

Price and earnings indexes (1980 = 100)

	1978	1979	1980	1981	1982	1983	1984
Consumer price index	33.7	70.4	100.0	134.9	185.1	325.5	492.9□
Monthly earnings index							

Land use (1981): forested 78.2%; meadows and pastures 4.1%; agricultural and under permanent cultivation 2.8%; other 14.9%.

Foreign trade

Balance of trade (current prices)

	1978	1979	1980	1981	1982	1983
Z'000,000	+482	+1,430	+2,226	+115	+515	+5,084
% of total	29.8%	38.6%	32.3%	2.0%	8.6%	33.8%

Imports (1980): Z2,327,800,000 (consumer goods 33.3%, of which food 16.4%; energy 24.6%; primary manufactures 19.5%). Major import sources: Belgium-Luxembourg 22.0%; France 13.2%; United States 10.3%; West Germany 10.1%; Japan 6.3%; Italy 5.2%.
Exports (1980): Z4,553,800,000 (copper 54.7%; cobalt 25.4%; coffee 10.1%; diamonds 5.3%). Major export destinations: United States 36.2%; Belgium-Luxembourg 31.2%; France 6.3%; West Germany 5.4%.

Transport and communications

Transport. Railroads (1981): length 3,576 mi, 5,755 km; passenger-mi 241,869,000, passenger-km 389,250,000; short ton-mi cargo 1,214,000, metric ton-km cargo 1,772,000. Roads (1980): total length 28,435 mi, 45,760 km (paved 18%). Vehicles (1982): passenger cars 89,471; trucks and buses 16,807. Merchant marine (1982): vessels (100 gross tons and over) 34; total deadweight tonnage 133,256. Air transport (1982): passenger-mi 249,490,000, passenger-km 401,516,000; short ton-mi cargo 46,627,000, metric ton-km cargo 68,072,000; airports (1984) with scheduled flights 33.
Communications. Daily newspapers (1983): total number 4; total circulation 45,000; circulation per 1,000 population 1.5. Radios (1981): total number of receivers 2,500,000 (1 per 10.6 persons). Television (1981): total number of receivers 10,000 (1 per 2,650 persons). Telephones (1980): 30,284 (1 per 871 persons).

Education and health

Education (1978–79)

	schools◊	teachers◊	students	student/ teacher ratio
Primary (age 6–11)	7,909	132,759	3,919,395	...
Secondary (age 12–17)	2,511	42,212	611,349	...
Voc., teacher tr.	20	△	192,329◊	...
Higher	3	2,782	28,430	...

College graduates per 100,000 population (1974): 41.3. *Literacy* (1980): total population literate 9,123,500 (57.9%); males literate 5,957,200 (77.2%); females literate 3,166,300 (39.4%).
Health (1978): physicians 1,723 (1 per 16,106 persons); hospital beds 78,938 (1 per 352 persons).
Food (1978–80): daily per capita caloric intake 2,133 (vegetable products 97.2%, animal products 2.8%); 96% of FAO recommended minimum requirement.

Military

Total active duty personnel (1983): 26,000 (army 84.6%; navy 5.8%; air force 9.6%). *Military expenditure as percent of GNP* (1981): 1.4% (world 5.7%); per capita expenditure U.S.$2.

---

*Detail does not add to total given because of rounding. †1981. ‡Infectious diseases only. §1982. ‖ 1980. ¶Mining, construction, and public utilities are included with manufacturing. ♀Trade, transportation and communication, finance, administration, defense, and services are included with other. δUnemployment in Kinshasa reached 40% in 1982, in other large towns 70–80%. □May. ◊1977–78. △Included with secondary.

Zambia

Official name: Republic of Zambia.
Form of government: republic with one legislative house (National Assembly [136]).
Head of state and government: President.
Capital: Lusaka.
Official language: English.
Official religion: none.
Monetary unit: 1 Zambian kwacha (K) = 100 ngwee; valuation (Oct. 29, 1984) 1 U.S.$ = K1.99; 1 £ = K2.40.

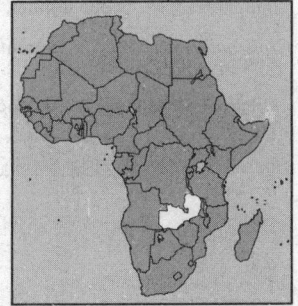

Area and population

Provinces	Capitals	area sq mi	area sq km	population 1980 census
Central	Kabwe	36,446	94,395	513,835
Copperbelt	Ndola	12,096	31,328	1,248,888
Eastern	Chipata	26,682	69,106	656,381
Luapula	Mansa	19,524	50,567	412,798
Lusaka	Lusaka	8,454	21,896	693,878
Northern	Kasama	57,076	147,826	677,894
North-Western	Solwezi	48,582	125,827	301,677
Southern	Livingstone	32,928	85,283	686,469
Western	Mongu	48,798	126,386	487,988
TOTAL		290,586	752,614	5,679,808

Source: Official government figures.

Demography

Density (1984): persons per sq mi 22.1, persons per sq km 8.5.
Urban-rural (1980): urban 43.0%; rural 57.0%.
Sex distribution (1984): male 49.48%; female 50.52%.
Age breakdown (1984): under 15, 46.5%; 15–29, 26.5%; 30–44, 14.6%; 45–59, 8.2%; 60–74, 3.6%; 75 and over 0.6%.
Population projection: (1990) 7,611,000; (2000) 10,276,000.
Doubling time: 23 years.
Ethnic composition (1978): Bemba 34.7%; Tonga 16.4%; Malawi 13.7%; Lozi 9.5%; Lunda 6.5%; Luena 5.1%; other 14.1%.
Religious affiliation (1980): Christian 72.0%, of whom Protestant 31.9%, Roman Catholic 26.2%, African Christian 8.3%; traditional beliefs 27.0%; Muslim 0.3%; other 0.7%.
Major cities (1980): Lusaka 538,469; Kitwe 314,794; Ndola 282,439; Luanshya 184,000; Mufulira 149,778; Chingola 145,869.

Vital statistics

Birth rate per 1,000 population (1980–85): 47.4 (world avg. 27.5); legitimate, n.a.; illegitimate, n.a.
Death rate per 1,000 population (1980–85): 15.4 (world avg. 10.6).
Natural increase rate per 1,000 population (1980–85): 32.0 (world avg. 16.9).
Total fertility rate (avg. births per childbearing woman; 1980–85): 6.9.
Marriage rate per 1,000 population: n.a.
Divorce rate per 1,000 population: n.a.
Infant mortality rate per 1,000 live births (1980–85): 110.6.
Life expectancy at birth (1980–85): male 49.1 years; female 52.5 years.
Major causes of death: n.a.; however, major diseases are avitaminosis and nutritional deficiencies and infectious and parasitic diseases.

National economy

Budget (1982). Revenue: K1,038,000,000 (customs duties and excise taxes 52.2%, income tax 37.9%). Expenditures: K1,501,000,000 (constitutional and statutory expenditures 42.4%, rural development 11.4%, education 6.7%, health 5.9%, police 2.7%).
Public debt (external, outstanding; 1982): U.S.$106,704,000.
Tourism (1982): receipts from visitors U.S.$59,000,000; expenditures by nationals abroad U.S.$43,000,000.
Production (metric tons except as noted). Agriculture, forestry, fishing (1982): sugarcane 1,050,000, corn (maize) 810,000, cassava 180,000, millet 60,000, sorghum 40,000, sweet potatoes 21,000, sunflower seed 20,000, pulses 13,000, peanuts (groundnuts) 9,000, lint cotton 7,000, tobacco 3,000; livestock (number of live animals) 2,250,000 cattle, 343,000 goats, 240,000 pigs, 38,000 sheep, 13,000,000 poultry; roundwood 5,707,000; fish catch 55,809. Mining and quarrying (1983): copper 575,000; zinc 42,000; lead 14,554; cobalt 2,500; gold 328 kilograms*. Manufacturing (1981): sulfuric acid 275,769; cement 262,058; nitrogen fertilizer 34,806; commercial vehicles 2,000 units. Construction (value in K; 1980): residential 90,200,000; nonresidential 92,000,000. Energy production (consumption): electricity (kW-hr; 1982) 10,584,000,000 (7,404,000,000); coal (metric tons; 1982) 612,000 (612,000); crude petroleum (barrels; 1982) none (5,074,000); petroleum products (metric tons; 1982) 1,300,000 (1,283,000); natural gas, none (none).
Persons economically active (1982): total 2,204,000 (36.6%); female participation in the labour force 451,200 (17.1%); unemployed 16,496* (0.9%).

Price and earnings indexes (1975 = 100)

	1976	1977	1978	1979	1980	1981	1982
Consumer price index	118.8	142.3	165.6	181.7	202.9	231.2	260.0
Monthly earnings index	129.7	136.6	151.5	...	200.0	...	...

Gross national product (at current market prices; 1983): U.S.$2,853,000,000 (U.S.$473 per capita).

Origin of gross domestic product (current prices)

	1982 in value K'000,000	% of total value	labour force	% of labour force
Agriculture	488	15.1	1,439,000	65.3
Mining	192	6.0	60,300	2.7
Manufacturing	589	18.3	48,100	2.2
Construction	140	4.3	42,200	1.9
Trade	432	13.4	48,200	2.2
Public utilities	66	2.0	8,100	0.4
Transportation and communication	210	6.5	25,400	1.1
Finance	†	†	25,400	1.1
Pub. admin., defense	†	†	‡	‡
Services	†	†	104,800	4.8
Other	1,104†	34.3†	402,500‡	18.3‡
TOTAL	3,221	100.0§	2,204,000	100.0

Household income and expenditure. Average household size (1981) 5.8; average annual income per household K1,041 (U.S.$908); source of income: wages and salaries 94.0%, other 6.0%; expenditure (1977): food 37.7%, housing 11.0%, clothing 8.3%, transportation 4.3%, education 2.1%, health 1.0%.
Land use (1981): forested 27.5%; meadows and pastures 47.2%; agricultural and under permanent cultivation 7.0%; other 18.3%.

Foreign trade

Balance of trade (current prices)

	1978	1979	1980	1981	1982	1983
K'000,000	+192.9	+493.3	+110.4	−171.5	+57.9	+242.7
% of total	16.3%	29.2%	6.0%	8.5%	3.0%	12.2%

Imports (1980): K870,000,000 (machinery and transport equipment 34.8%; mineral fuels, lubricants, and electricity 22.0%; basic manufactures 20.6%; chemicals 12.4%; food 4.4%). *Major import sources:* United Kingdom 22.4%; South Africa 15.7%; United States 7.0%; West Germany 6.9%; Japan 5.0%; China 0.6%.
Exports (1980): K980,400,000 (copper 86.8%; cobalt 8.2%; zinc 2.0%; lead 0.7%). *Major export destinations:* Japan 16.4%; United Kingdom 13.8%; United States 11.2%; West Germany 8.3%; China 2.9%; South Africa 0.6%.

Transport and communications

Transport. Railroads (1982): length 1,360 mi, 2,188 km; passengers 1,570,000 ‖; short ton cargo 5,946,000, metric ton cargo 5,394,000¶. Roads (1983): total length 23,135 mi, 37,232 km (paved 15.1%). Vehicles (1981): passenger cars 103,000; trucks and buses 90,000. Merchant marine: vessels (100 gross tons and over) none. Air transport (1982): passenger-mi 347,617,000, passenger-km 559,436,000; short ton-mi cargo 50,643,000, metric ton-km cargo 73,937,000; airports (1984) with scheduled flights 14.
Communications. Daily newspapers (1983): total number 2; total circulation 109,000; circulation per 1,000 population 17.5. Radios (1982): total number of receivers 200,000 (1 per 30.1 persons). Television (1982): total number of receivers 80,000 (1 per 75 persons). Telephones (1981): 61,000 (1 per 91 persons).

Education and health

Education (1981)

	schools	teachers	students	student/ teacher ratio
Primary (age 7–13)	2,854	23,100	1,068,314	46.2
Secondary (age 14–18)	135	4,650	98,862	21.2
Voc., teacher tr.	28	406	9,972	24.6
Higher	1	334	3,603	10.8

College graduates per 100,000 population (1979): 40.6. *Literacy* (1980): total population literate 2,128,500 (68.6%); males literate 1,207,300 (79.3%); females literate 921,200 (58.3%).
Health (1981): physicians 821 (1 per 7,101 persons); hospital beds 20,638 (1 per 282 persons).
Food (1978–80): daily per capita caloric intake 1,992 (vegetable products 93.6%, animal products 6.4%); 86% of FAO recommended minimum requirement.

Military

Total active duty personnel (1983): 14,300 (army 87.4%; navy, none; air force 12.6%). *Military expenditure as percent of GNP* (1980): 3.8% (world 5.6%); per capita expenditure U.S.$21.

*1981. †Finance, public administration and defense, and services are included with other. ‡Public administration and defense are included with other. §Detail does not add to total given because of rounding. ‖ 1980. ¶1979.

Zimbabwe

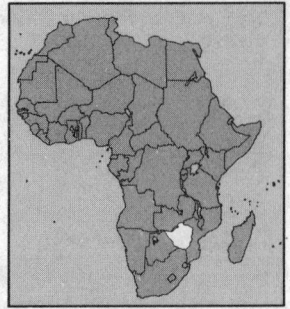

Official name: Republic of Zimbabwe.
Form of government: unitary multiparty republic with two legislative houses (Senate [40]; House of Assembly [100]).
Chief of state: President.
Head of government: Prime Minister.
Capital: Harare.
Official language: English.
Official religion: none.
Monetary unit: 1 Zimbabwe Dollar (Z$) = 100 cents; valuation (Oct. 29, 1984) 1 U.S.$ = Z$1.43; 1 £ = Z$1.72.

Area and population		area		population
		sq mi	sq km	1982 census
Provinces	**Capitals**			
Manicaland	Mutare	13,598	35,219	1,096,000
Mashonaland Central	Mount Darwin	11,383	29,482	563,000
Mashonaland East	Harare	10,353	26,813	1,491,000
Mashonaland West	Kadoma	21,520	55,737	859,000
Masvingo (Victoria)	Masvingo	21,536	55,777	1,034,000
Matabeleland North	Bulawayo	29,658	76,813	880,000
Matabeleland South	Gwanda	21,213	54,941	517,000
Midlands	Gweru	21,613	55,977	1,092,000
TOTAL		150,873*	390,759	7,532,000

Demography

Density (1984): persons per sq mi 52.7, persons per sq km 20.4.
Urban–rural (1982): urban 23.0%; rural 77.0%.
Sex distribution (1982): male 49.34%; female 50.66%.
Age breakdown (1982): under 15, 51.0%; 15–29, 26.3%; 30–44, 13.4%; 45–59, 6.5%; 60–74, 1.2%; 75 and over, 1.7%.*
Population projection: (1990) 9,200,000; (2000) 11,300,000.
Doubling time: 25 years.
Ethnolinguistic composition (1982): Shona-speaking Bantu 70.0%; Ndebele-speaking Bantu 16.0%; white 2.3%; other 11.7%.
Religious affiliation (1980): Christian 44.8%, of which Protestant (including Anglican) 17.5%, African indigenous 13.6%, Roman Catholic 11.7%; animist 40.4%; other 14.8%.
Major cities (1982): Harare 656,000; Bulawayo 414,000; Chitungwiza 173,000; Gweru 79,000; Mutare 70,000.

Vital statistics

Birth rate per 1,000 population (1981): 54.4 (world avg. 29.0).
Death rate per 1,000 population (1981): 12.7 (world avg. 12.0).
Natural increase rate per 1,000 population (1981): 41.7 (world avg. 17.0).
Total fertility rate (avg. births per childbearing woman; 1981): 8.0.
Marriage rate per 1,000 population (1981): n.a.
Divorce rate per 1,000 population (1981): n.a.
Infant mortality rate per 1,000 live births (1981): 72.4.
Life expectancy at birth (1981): male 53.3 years; female 56.8 years.
Major causes of death: †.

National economy

Budget (1983–84). Revenue: Z$2,111,000,000 (income tax 39.4%, sales tax 23.2%, customs duties 14.5%, excise tax 9.4%). Expenditures: Z$2,802,605,000 (defense 20.3%, education 20.1%, health 6.6%, police 5.9%, social security and welfare 5.2%).
Public debt (external, outstanding; 1983): U.S.$1,678,000,000.
Tourism (1982): receipts from visitors U.S.$46,000,000; expenditures by nationals abroad, n.a.
Production (value of production in Z$ except as noted). Agriculture, forestry, fishing (1983): tobacco 184,527,000; beef 110,317,000‡; cotton 83,622,000; sugar 81,775,000; corn (maize) 73,984,000; whole milk 36,584,000; wheat 27,362,000; roundwood 8,679,000 cu m§; fish catch 18,106 metric tons§. Mining and quarrying (1983): gold 193,913,000; asbestos 69,335,000; nickel 43,099,000; coal 42,172,000; copper 32,944,000; chrome 26,063,000. Manufacturing ‖ (1981–82): agricultural, mining, and industrial machinery 273,600,000; metal products, including alloys 235,800,000; cloth, canvas, and yarns 204,800,000; clothing 154,500,000; industrial chemicals 122,600,000; fertilizers and agricultural chemicals 106,800,000; fresh meat, poultry, and fish 99,200,000. Construction (1982): residential 28,600,000; nonresidential 176,000,000. Energy production (consumption): electricity (kW-hr; 1982) 4,134,000,000 (7,732,000,000); coal (metric tons; 1982) 2,769,000 (2,769,000); crude petroleum, none (none); petroleum products (metric tons; 1982) none (634,000); natural gas, none (none).
Persons economically active (1981): total 2,485,000 (32.7%); female participation in the labour force 726,000 (29.2%); unemployed n.a.

Price and earnings indexes (1977 = 100)							
	1977	1978	1979	1980	1981	1982	1983
Consumer price index	100.0	105.6	124.9	131.6	148.8	164.7	202.8
Monthly earnings index¶	100.0	109.6	123.7	151.1	187.2	226.2	...

Household income and expenditure. Average household size (1980) 5.8; income per household Z$1,689 (U.S.$2,628); source of income: n.a.; expenditure (1982): food 22.1%, clothing, footwear, and textiles 13.9%, alcohol and tobacco 10.4%, hotel accommodations and travel 8.6%, household

equipment 8.3%, public utilities, coal, and petroleum products 7.4%, other 29.3%.
Gross national product (at current market prices; 1982): U.S.$4,425,000,000 (U.S.$590 per capita).

Origin of gross domestic product (current prices)				
	1982			
	in value Z$'000,000	% of total value	labour force¶	% of labour force
Agriculture	670	15.0	274,300	26.2
Mining	243	5.4	63,700	6.1
Manufacturing	1,096	24.5	180,500	17.3
Construction	150	3.4	51,100	4.9
Trade	656	14.7	79,800	7.6
Public utilities	77	1.7	6,500	0.6
Transportation and communication	356	8.0	50,400	4.8
Finance	277	6.2	14,600	1.4
Pub. admin., defense	357	8.0	81,300	7.8
Health and education	420	9.4	90,700	8.7
Other	163	3.7	153,100♀	14.6♀
TOTAL	4,465	100.0	1,046,000	100.0

Land use (1981): forested 61.6%; meadows and pastures 12.6%; agricultural and under permanent cultivation 6.9%; other 18.9%.

Foreign trade

Balance of trade (current prices)						
	1977	1978	1979	1980	1981	1982
Z$'000,000	+162,700	+205,600	+166,400	+99,800	−46,000	−113,400
% of total	17.3%	20.3%	13.1%	5.8%	2.3%	5.5%

Imports (1982): Z$1,081,800,000 (machinery and transport equipment 40.7%; basic manufactures 14.5%, of which textile yarns and fabrics 4.2%, iron and steel 4.1%; petroleum products 14.3%; chemicals 11.6%). *Major import sources*δ: South Africa 22.1%; United Kingdom 15.0%; United States 9.6%; West Germany 8.2%; Japan 5.2%.
Exports (1982): Z$968,400,000 (tobacco 20.1%, gold 14.5%, ferro-alloys 8.0%, asbestos 6.3%, cotton 5.4%, sugar 5.4%, nickel 4.7%, corn [maize] 4.1%). *Major export destinations*☐: South Africa 17.1%; United Kingdom 9.5%; West Germany 8.0%; United States 7.9%; The Netherlands 4.5%.

Transport and communications

Transport. Railroads◇ (1983): length 2,100 mi, 3,400 km; number of passengers 2,050,000; short ton-mi cargo 5,660,000,000, metric ton-km cargo 6,289,000,000. Roads (1982): total length 105,900 mi, 170,400 km (paved 7%). Vehicles (1982): passenger cars 224,453; trucks and buses 24,246. Air transport (1982): passenger-mi 343,937,000, passenger-km 553,514,000; short ton-mi cargo 6,576,000, metric ton-km cargo 9,601,000; airports (1984) with scheduled flights 8.
Communications. Daily newspapers (1982): total number 3; total circulation 190,000; circulation per 1,000 population 25. Radios (1982): total number of receivers 200,000 (1 per 38 persons). Television (1982): total number of receivers 96,500 (1 per 78 persons). Telephones (1983): 231,260 (1 per 33 persons).

Education and health

Education (1983)	schools	teachers	students	student/ teacher ratio
Primary (age 7–13)	3,880§	49,588§	2,044,847	41.2
Secondary (age 14–19)	...	6,112§	316,438	...
Voc., teacher tr.	...	...	14,272	...
Higher	1	...	3,314	...

College graduates per 100,000 population: n.a. *Literacy* (1980): total population literate 2,774,600 (70.8%); males literate 1,507,200 (78.0%); females literate 1,267,400 (63.8%).
Health (1980): physicians 1,148 (1 per 6,411 persons); hospital beds 21,418 (1 per 344 persons).
Food (1978–80): daily per capita caloric intake 1,911 (vegetable products 91.4%, animal products 8.6%); 80% of FAO recommended minimum requirement.

Military

Total active duty personnel (1983): 41,300 (army 96.9%; air force 3.1%). *Military expenditure as percent of GNP* (1982): 6.9% (world 6.0%); per capita expenditure U.S.$52.

---

*Detail does not add to total given because of rounding. †In 1979 measles, pneumonia, diarrheal diseases, cardiac and circulatory diseases (other than common heart attacks), and cancers accounted for nearly 43% of all registered adult deaths among non-white residents. ‡First three quarters of 1983 only. §1982. ‖ By sector's sales of own products in Z$. ¶Wage-earning workers only. ♀Includes private domestic services. δDoes not include petroleum products of unknown origin valued free on rail South Africa. ☐Does not include gold sales. ◇Includes operations in Botswana.

Comparative National Statistics

Government and administrative subdivisions

This table summarizes principal facts about the governments of the countries of the world, their principal governmental authorities and organs, the topmost layers of local government comprising their chief administrative subdivisions, and the participation of their central governments in the principal intergovernmental organizations of the world.

In this table "date of independence" may refer to a variety of circumstances. In the case of the newest countries, those that attained full independence after World War II, the date given is usually just what is implied by the heading—the date when the country, within its present borders, attained full sovereignty over both its internal and external affairs. In the case of longer-established countries, the choice of a single date is somewhat more complicated: When, for example, did Switzerland become "independent"? Was it, as some authorities suggest, in 1291, the date of the formation of the Swiss Confederation?; or in 1315, with the defeat of the Habsburgs that secured independence for some of the core cantons around Luzern?; in 1499, with the acknowledgment of its status by the Holy Roman Empire through the Treaty of Basel?; or in 1638, when full recognition was granted by all the European powers through the Treaty of Westphalia? In this table 1499 has been adopted, but grounds for the other dates certainly exist. The reader interested in this subject should refer to MACROPAEDIA and MICROPAEDIA articles on national histories and relevant historical acts. In general, the date given here for any country refers either to the final act of union of a state comprised of smaller entities or to the final act of separation from a larger whole (e.g., the separation of Bangladesh from Pakistan in 1971).

The date of the current, or last, constitution is in some ways a less complicated question, but governments sometimes do not, upon taking power, either adhere to existing constitutional forms or trouble to terminate the previous document and legitimize themselves by the installation of new constitutional forms. Often, however, the desire to legitimize extra-constitutional political activity by associating it with existing forms of long precedent leads to partial or incomplete modification, suspension, or abrogation of the constitution, so that the actual day-to-day conduct of government may be entirely unrelated to the provisions of a constitution still theoretically in force. When a date in this column is given in italics, it refers to a document that has been suspended, abolished by extra-constitutional action, or modified extensively.

The characterizations adopted under "kind of government" represent a compromise between the ideal forms provided for by the constitution and the more pragmatic language that a political scientist might adopt to describe these same systems. For an explanation of the application of these terms in the Britannica World Data, see the Glossary at p. 617.

The positions denoted by the terms "chief of state" and "head of government" are usually those identified with those functions by the constitution. Very often the position of chief of state will be a largely ceremonial one, with little or no authority over the day-to-day conduct of government, although the formal assent of the office to executive or legislative action may be required by the constitution. In other cases, such as in some of the Middle Eastern monarchies, the chief of state may also be the effective head of government. In certain countries, an official of a political party or a revolutionary figure entirely outside the constitutional structure may effectively exercise the powers of both positions.

Membership in the legislative house (-s) of each country as given here includes all elected or appointed members, as well as ex officio members (those who by virtue of some other office or title are members of the body), whether voting or non-voting. The legislature of a country with a unicameral system is shown as the upper house in this table.

Principal administrative subdivisions are listed for each country down to the second level and are identified as to type. A single country may, depending on its size, complexity, and historical antecedents, have as many as five levels of administrative subordination (as does the U.S.S.R.) or it may have none at all. Each level of subordination may have several kinds of subdivisions: In the United Kingdom, for example, Greater London, 47 counties, 6 metropolitan counties (in England and Wales), and 9 regions and three island authorities (in Scotland) all coexist at a roughly comparable level of subordination to the central government. The abbreviations used to designate these kinds of subdivisions are explained on the facing page.

Finally, in the second half of the table are listed the memberships each country maintains in the principal international intergovernmental organizations of the world. This part of the table may also be utilized to provide a complete membership list for each of these organizations as of Dec. 1, 1984.

Notes for the column headings
a. As applicable, the date given may also be either that of the organization of the present form of government or the inception of the present administrative structure (federation, confederation, union, etc.).
b. Constitutions whose dates are in italic type had been wholly or substantially suspended or abolished as of late 1984.
c. For abbreviations used in this column see the list on the facing page.
d. Unicameral legislatures are also listed under this category.
e. When a legislative body has been adjourned or otherwise suspended, figures in parentheses indicate the number of members in the legislative body as provided for in the constitution. If the provision for the legislative body in the constitution has been abrogated then the space has been marked with an "X".
f. States contributing funds to or receiving aid from UNICEF in 1980.
g. Palestine is also a member.
h. Palestine Liberation Organization is also a member.

Government and administrative subdivisions

country	date of independence[a]	date of current or last constitution[b]	type of government	chief of state[c]	head of government[c]	upper house[d][e] (members)	lower house[e] (members)	first-order no.	type[c]	no.	type[c]	second-order no.	type[c]	no.	type[c]
Afghanistan	Aug. 19, 1919	*Jan. 26, 1977*	people's republic	president RC	president CM	x	x	29	pro	—	—	185	dis	—	—
Albania	Nov. 28, 1912	Dec. 27, 1976	people's republic	chairman PPA	chairman CM	250	—	26	dis	—	—	200	loc	—	—
Algeria	July 5, 1962	Nov. 19, 1976	republic	—president—		281	—	35	pro	—	—	168	dis	—	—
American Samoa	—	—	territory (U.S.)	U.S. president	governor	18	20	3	dis	2	isl	—	—	—	—
Andorra	Dec. 6, 1288	—	co-principality	co-princes (2)	syndic	28	—	7	par	—	—	—	—	—	—
Angola	Nov. 11, 1975	Nov. 11, 1975	people's republic	—president—		207	—	18	pro	—	—	139	dis	—	—
Anguilla	—	Apr. 1, 1982	territory (U.K.)	British monarch	governor	11	—	2	par	—	—	—	—	—	—
Antigua and Barbuda	Nov. 1, 1981	Nov. 1, 1981	parliamentary state	British monarch	prime minister	17	17	6	par	2	dpn	—	—	—	—
Argentina	July 9, 1816	July 9, 1853	federal republic	—president—		46	254	22	pro[3]	2	fed	367	dep	121	dis
Australia	Jan. 1, 1901	July 9, 1900	federal parl. state	British monarch	prime minister	64	125	6	sta	2	ter[4]	866	mnu	—	—
Austria	c. Oct. 30, 1918	Oct. 1, 1920	federal republic	president	chancellor	63	183	9	sta	—	—	98	dis	—	—
Bahamas, The	July 10, 1973	July 10, 1973	parliamentary state	British monarch	prime minister	16	43	—	—	—	—	41	sdt	—	—
Bahrain	Aug. 15, 1971	May 26, 1973	monarchy (emirate)	emir	prime minister	x	—	11	reg	—	—	—	—	—	—
Bangladesh	Mar. 26, 1971	*Nov. 4, 1972*	republic	—president—		(330)	—	4	div	—	—	20	dis	—	—
Barbados	Nov. 30, 1966	Nov. 30, 1966	parliamentary state	British monarch	prime minister	21	27	11	par	—	—	—	—	—	—
Belgium	Oct. 4, 1830	1831	const. monarchy	monarch	prime minister	182	212	3	reg	—	—	9	pro	—	—
Belize	Sept. 21, 1981	Sept. 21, 1981	const. monarchy	British monarch	prime minister	9	19	6	dis	—	—	—	—	—	—
Benin	Aug. 1, 1960	Nov. 1979	people's republic	—president—		196	—	6	pro	—	—	84	dis	—	—
Bermuda	—	June 8, 1968	colony (U.K.)	British monarch	premier	11	40	9	par	2	mun	—	—	—	—
Bhutan	Mar. 24, 1910	—	monarchy	—king—		150	—	4	reg	—	—	18	dis	—	—
Bolivia	Aug. 6, 1825	Feb. 1967	republic	—president—		27	130	9	dep	—	—	99	pro	—	—
Botswana	Sept. 30, 1966	Mar. 1965	republic	—president—		37	—	10	dis	5	twn	—	—	—	—
Brazil	Sept. 7, 1822	Jan. 24, 1967	federal republic	—president—		69	479	23	sta	4	ter[5]	3,963	mun	—	—
British Virgin Islands	—	June 1, 1977	colony (U.K.)	British monarch	governor	9	—	—	—	—	—	—	—	—	—
Brunei	Jan. 1, 1984	Sept. 29, 1959	monarchy (sultanate)	sultan	prime minister	21	—	4	dis	—	—	—	—	—	—
Bulgaria	Oct. 5, 1908	May 18, 1971	people's republic	chairman SC	chairman CM	400	—	28	dis	—	—	4,823	mun	—	—
Burkina Faso	Aug. 5, 1960	*Nov. 27, 1977*	republic	—president CNR—		x	—	25	pro	—	—	44	sup	—	—
Burma	Jan. 4, 1948	Jan 4, 1974	socialist republic	president	prime minister	475	—	7	sta	7	div	...	tow	—	—
Burundi	July 1, 1962	Nov. 18, 1981	republic	—president—		65	—	8	pro	—	—	18	dis	—	—
Cameroon	Jan. 1, 1960	May 20, 1972	republic	—president—		150	—	10	pro	—	—	40	dep	—	—
Canada	July 1, 1867	April 17, 1982	federal parl. state	British monarch	prime minister	104	282	10	pro	2	ter	4,740	mun	—	—
Cape Verde	July 5, 1975	Sept. 7, 1980	republic	president	premier	56	—	14	dis	—	—	31	par	—	—
Cayman Islands	—	Aug. 22, 1972	colony (U.K.)	British monarch	governor	15	—	—	—	—	—	—	—	—	—
Central African Republic	Aug. 13, 1960	*Feb. 6, 1981*	republic	—chairman CMRN—		(...)	—	17	pre	—	—	47	sup	—	—
Chad	Aug. 11, 1960	*Aug. 29, 1978*	republic	—president—		x	—	14	pre	—	—	54	sup	—	—
Chile	Sep. 18, 1810	March 11, 1981[6]	republic	—president—		12	reg	1	met	50	pro	—	—		
China	1523 BC	Dec. 4, 1982	people's republic	president	premier SC	2,978	—	24	pro[7]	5	aur	174	pre	36	aup
Christmas Island	—	—	external territory (Aust.)	Australian GG	administrator	—	—	—	—	—	—	—	—	—	—
Cocos (Keeling) Islands	—	—	external territory (Aust.)	Australian GG	administrator	—	—	—	—	—	—	—	—	—	—
Colombia	July 20, 1810	Aug. 5, 1886	republic	—president—		114	199	24	dep	9	int[8]	978	mun	—	—

International organizations, conventions

ACP	African, Caribbean, and Pacific (Lome II) convention
ASEAN	Association of South East Asian Nations
COMECON	Council for Mutual Economic Assistance
EC	The European Communities
ECOWAS	Economic Community of West African States
EEC	European Economic Community
FAO	Food and Agriculture Organization
GATT	General Agreement on Tariffs and Trade
I-ADB	Inter-American Development Bank
IAEA	International Atomic Energy Agency
IBRD	International Bank for Reconstruction and Development
ICAO	International Civil Aviation Organization
ICJ	International Court of Justice
IDB	Islamic Development Bank
ILO	International Labour Organisation
IMF	International Monetary Fund
IMO	International Maritime Organization
ITU	International Telecommunication Union
LAS	League of Arab States
NATO	North Atlantic Treaty Organization
OAS	Organization of American States
OAU	Organization of African Unity
OPEC	Organization of Petroleum Exporting Countries
SPC	South Pacific Commission
UNCTAD	United Nations Conference on Trade and Development
UNESCO	United Nations Educational Scientific and Cultural Organization
UNICEF	United Nations Children's Fund
UNIDO	United Nations Industrial Development Organization
UPU	Universal Postal Union
WHO	World Health Organization
WIPO	World Intellectual Property Organization
WMO	World Meteorological Organization
WTO	Warsaw Treaty of Friendship, Co-operation and Mutual Assistance (The Warsaw Pact)

Abbreviations used in the executive branch column

CM	Council of Ministers
CMRN	Military Committee for National Recovery
CNR	National Council of the Revolution
CS	Council of State
GG	Governor-general
GPC	General People's Committee
JGNR	Junta of the Government of National Reconstruction
NA	National Assembly
PC	Presidential Council
PMAC	Provisional Military Administrative Council
PNDC	Provisional National Defense Council
PPA	Presidium, People's Assembly
PPGH	Presidium, People's Great Hural
PRC	People's Redemption Council
PSPC	Presidium, Supreme People's Council
PSSU	Presidium, Supreme Soviet of the U.S.S.R.
RC	Revolutionary Council
SC	State Council
SMC	Supreme Military Council

Abbreviations used in the administrative subdivisions columns

add	administrative district	can	canton
apr	autonomous province	cap	capital
are	area	car	capital area
arr	arrondissement	cas	castle
ato	atoll	cen	centre
auc	autonomous community	cer	cercle
aum	autonomous municipality	chi	chiefdom
aup	autonomous prefecture	cir	circumscription
aur	autonomous region	cit	city
aus	autonomous sector	cms	commissariat
bar	barrio	cnp	constitutional province
bor	borough	coa	communal area
		cod	commonwealth district
		com	commune
		cos	communal sector
		cou	county
		dep	department (département, departamento)
		dic	district council
		dir	directorate
		dis	district
		div	division
		dpn	dependency
		emi	emirate
		fct	federal capital territory
		fed	federal district
		fet	federal territory
		gov	governorate
		iau	island authority
		igr	island group
		int	intendancy
		isl	island
		lau	local authority
		loa	local area
		loc	locality
		lod	local district
		met	metropolitan region
		mnu	municipal unit
		mua	municipal authority
		muc	municipal council
		mun	municipality
		nac	national capital
		nad	national district
		nas	national state
		nat	national territory
		par	parish
		pre	prefecture
		pro	province
		qua	quarter
		reg	region
		rep	republic
		rgy	regency

rud	rural district
rup	rural province
sdt	supervisory district
sec	sector
spc	special city
spr	sub-province
sta	state
sub	subdivision
sud	subdistrict
sup	sub-prefecture
sur	subregion
tau	territorial authority
ter	territory
twn	town (-ship)
unt	union territory
urn	urban province
urp	urban prefecture
urr	urban region
vic	village council
war	ward
zon	zone

membership in international organizations

United Nations (date of admission)	UN bodies (UNCTAD, UNICEF[f], UNIDO)	UN-related organizations (FAO, GATT, IAEA, IBRD, ICAO, ICJ, ILO, IMF, IMO, ITU, UNESCO, UPU, WHO, WIPO, WMO)	Commonwealth of Nations	regional multi-purpose (ASEAN, EC, LAS[g], OAS, OAU, SPC)	economic (ACP, COMECON, ECOWAS, EEC, I-ADB, IDB[h], OPEC)	military (NATO, WTO)	country
1946							Afghanistan
1955							Albania
1962							Algeria
							American Samoa
							Andorra
1976							Angola
							Anguilla
1981			•				Antigua and Barbuda
1945							Argentina
1945							Australia
1955							Austria
1973			•				Bahamas, The
1971							Bahrain
1974							Bangladesh
1966			•				Barbados
1945							Belgium
1981			•				Belize
1960							Benin
							Bermuda
1971			•				Bhutan
1945							Bolivia
1966			•				Botswana
1945							Brazil
			•				British Virgin Islands
							Brunei
1955							Bulgaria
1960							Burkina Faso
1948							Burma
1962							Burundi
1960							Cameroon
1945							Canada
1975							Cape Verde
							Cayman Islands
1960							Central African Republic
1960							Chad
1945							Chile
1945							China
							Christmas Island
							Cocos (Keeling) Islands
1945							Colombia

Government and administrative subdivisions (continued)

country	date of independence[a]	date of current or last constitution[b]	type of government	executive branch		legislative branch		administrative subdivisions							
				chief of state[c]	head of government[c]	upper house[de] (members)	lower house[e] (members)	first-order				second-order			
								no.	type[c]	no.	type[c]	no.	type[c]	no.	type[c]
Comoros	July 6, 1975	Oct. 1, 1978	federal Islamic republic	president	prime minister	38	—	3	isl	—	—	7	reg	—	—
Congo	Aug. 15, 1960	July 8, 1979	people's republic	president	prime minister	151	—	9	reg	—	—	45	dis	—	—
Cook Islands	—	—	territory (N.Z.)	New Zealand GG	premier	24	—	—	—	—	—	—	—	—	—
Costa Rica	Sept. 15, 1821	Nov. 9, 1949	republic	——president——		57	—	7	pro	—	—	80	can	—	—
Cuba	May 20, 1902	Feb. 24, 1976	socialist republic	——president——		499	—	14	pro	—	—	169	mun	—	—
Cyprus	Aug. 16, 1960	Aug. 16, 1960	republic	president	min. to pres.	50	—	6	dis[g]	—	—	604	mun[g]	—	—
Czechoslovakia	Oct. 28, 1918	July 11, 1960	federal socialist republic	president	prime minister	150	200	2	rep	—	—	10	reg	—	—
Denmark	c. 800	June 5, 1953	constitutional monarchy	monarch	prime minister	179	—	14	cou	—	—	277	lod	—	—
Djibouti	June 27, 1977	Feb. 10, 1981	republic	president	prime minister	65	—	5	dis	—	—	11	sud	3	arr
Dominica	Nov. 3, 1978	Nov. 3, 1978	republic	president	prime minister	31	—	10	par	—	—	27	mun	—	—
Dominican Republic	Feb. 27, 1844	Nov. 28, 1966	republic	——president——		27	120	26	pro	1	nad	97	mun	—	—
Ecuador	May 24, 1822	Aug. 10, 1979	republic	——president——		69	—	20	pro	—	—	126	can	—	—
Egypt	Feb. 28, 1922	Sept. 11, 1971	republic	president	prime minister	392	—	26	gov	—	—	...	cen	—	—
El Salvador	Jan. 30, 1841	Jan. 8, 1962	republic	——president——		60	—	14	dep	—	—	261	mun	—	—
Equatorial Guinea	July 29, 1968	Aug. 15, 1982	republic	——president——		41	—	3	reg	—	—	7	pro	—	—
Ethiopia	c. 1000 BC	July 16, 1931	socialist state	chairman of the PMAC and CM		x	—	14	reg	—	—	102	sur	—	—
Faeroe Islands	—	—	part of Danish realm	Danish monarch	commissioner	32	—	—	—	—	—	—	—	—	—
Falkland Islands	—	Nov. 21, 1977	colony (U.K.)	British monarch	civil comm.	9	—	—	—	—	—	—	—	—	—
Fiji	Oct. 10, 1970	Oct. 10, 1970	parliamentary state	British monarch	prime minister	22	52	4	div	—	—	14	pro	—	—
Finland	Dec. 6, 1917	July 17, 1919	republic	president	prime minister	200	—	12	pro	—	—	380	mun	84	twn
France	Aug. 843	Sept. 28, 1958	republic	president	premier	317	491	95	dep	—	—	325	arr	—	—
French Guiana	—	—	overseas dept. (Fr.)	French president	commissioner	16	—	2	arr	—	—	15	can	—	—
French Polynesia	—	—	overseas territory (Fr.)	French president	high comm.	30	—	5	cir	—	—	100	dic	4	muc
Gabon	Aug. 17, 1960	Feb. 21, 1961	republic	president	prime minister	93	—	9	pro	—	—	37	dep	—	—
Gambia, The	Feb. 18, 1965	April 24, 1970	republic	——president——		49	—	6	div	—	—	35	dis	—	—
Germany, East	Oct. 11, 1949	April 9, 1968	people's republic	chairman CS	chairman CM	500	—	15	cou	—	—	227	dis	—	—
Germany, West	May 5, 1955	May 22–23, 1949	federal republic	president	chancellor	45	520	10	sta	—	—	30	dis	—	—
Ghana	June 6, 1957	Sept. 24, 1979	republic	——chairman PNDC——		(...)	---	10	reg	—	—	58	dis	—	—
Gibraltar	—	Aug. 11, 1969	colony (U.K.)	British monarch	governor	18	—	—	—	—	—	—	—	—	—
Greece	Feb. 1830	June 11, 1975	republic	president	prime minister	300	—	51	dep	—	—	147	pro	—	—
Greenland	—	—	part of Danish realm	Danish monarch	high comm.	21	—	3	cou	—	—	19	com	—	—
Grenada	Feb. 7, 1974	Feb. 22, 1967	parliamentary state	British monarch	prime minister	13	15	7	par	—	—	—	—	—	—
Guadeloupe	—	—	overseas dept. (Fr.)	French president	commissioner	36	41	3	arr	—	—	34	com	—	—
Guam	—	—	territory (U.S.)	U.S. president	governor	26	—	19	dis	—	—	—	—	—	—
Guatemala	Sept. 15, 1821	Sept. 15, 1965	republic	——president——		(66)	—	22	dep	—	—	326	mun	—	—
Guinea	Oct. 2, 1958	May 14, 1982	republic	——president——		210	—	33	reg	—	—	175	arr	—	—
Guinea-Bissau	Sept. 24, 1973	Nov. 10, 1980	republic	——president——		x	—	8	reg	1	aus	45	sec	—	—
Guyana	May 26, 1966	Oct. 6, 1980	republic	president	prime minister	65	—	10	reg	—	—	98	dis	2	mun
Haiti	Jan 1, 1804	June 1964	republic	——president——		59	—	9	dep	—	—	41	arr	—	—
Honduras	Nov. 5, 1838	Jan. 20, 1982	republic	——president——		82	—	18	dep	—	—	282	mun	—	—
Hong Kong	—	—	colony (U.K.)	British monarch	governor	50	—	3	dis	—	—	18	add	—	—
Hungary	Nov. 16, 1918	Aug. 18, 1949	people's republic	president PC	premier CM	352	—	19	cou	6	cit	97	dis	—	—
Iceland	June 17, 1944	June 17, 1944	republic	president	prime minister	20	40	23	cou	—	—	224	mun	—	—
India	Aug. 15, 1947	Nov. 26, 1949	federal republic	president	prime minister	244	544	22	sta	9	unt	386	dis	29	sub
Indonesia	Aug. 17, 1945	Aug. 17, 1945	republic	——president——		460	—	24	pro	3	dis	246	rgy	—	—
Iran	Oct. 7, 1906	Oct. 1979	Islamic republic	president	prime minister	270	—	24	pro	—	—	194	cou	—	—
Iraq	Oct. 3, 1932	Sept. 22, 1968	republic	——president——		250	—	18	gov	—	—	157	dis	—	—
Ireland	Dec. 6, 1921	Dec. 29, 1937	republic	president	prime minister	60	166	27	cou	—	—	49	dis	23	twn
Israel	May 14, 1948	June 1950[11]	republic	president	prime minister	120	—	6	dis	—	—	31	mun	—	—
Italy	March 17, 1861	Dec. 22, 1947	republic	president	prime minister	315	630	20	reg	—	—	94	pro	—	—
Ivory Coast	Aug. 7, 1960	Oct. 31, 1960	republic	——president——		147	—	34	dep	—	—	162	sup	—	—
Jamaica	Aug. 6, 1962	Aug. 6, 1962	parliamentary state	British monarch	prime minister	21	60	3	cou	—	—	14	par	—	—
Japan	c. 660 BC	May 3, 1957	constitutional monarchy	emperor	prime minister	252	511	47	pre	—	—	3,256	mun	—	—
Jordan	May 25, 1946	Jan. 1, 1952	constitutional monarchy	king	prime minister	30	60	5	gov[12]	—	—	14	dis[12]	—	—
Kampuchea	Nov. 9, 1953	June 1981	people's republic	chairman CS	prime minister	117	—	19	pro	—	—	...	dis	—	—
Kenya	Dec. 12, 1963	Dec. 12, 1963	republic	——president——		172	—	7	rup	1	urn	40	rud	—	—
Kiribati	July 12, 1979	July 12, 1979	republic	——president——		38	—	7	dis	—	—	—	—	—	—
Korea, North	Sept. 9, 1948	Dec. 27, 1972	people's republic	president	premier	615	—	9	pro	4	spc[13]	152	cou	—	—
Korea, South	Aug. 15, 1948	Oct. 22, 1980	republic	president	prime minister	276	—	9	pro	4	spc	139	cou	46	cit
Kuwait	June 19, 1961	Nov. 16, 1962	const. mon. (emirate)	emir	prime minister	50	—	4	gov	—	—	...	dis	—	—
Laos	July 19, 1949	May 11, 1947	people's republic	president	premier	264	—	16	pro	—	—	...	dis	—	—
Lebanon	Nov. 26, 1941	May 23, 1926	republic	president	prime minister	99	—	5	gov	—	—	26	dis	—	—
Lesotho	Oct. 4, 1966	Oct. 4, 1966	constitutional monarchy	king	prime minister	33	60	10	dis	—	—	22	war	—	—
Liberia	July 26, 1847	July 26, 1847	republic	——chairman PRC——		x	—	9	cou	1	cod	50	chi	—	—
Libya	Dec. 24, 1951	Sept. 1, 1969	republic[14]	rev. leader	chairman GPC	1,112	—	25	mun	—	—	—	—	—	—
Liechtenstein	July 12, 1806	Oct. 5, 1921	constitutional monarchy	grand duke	prime minister	15	—	11	com	—	—	—	—	—	—
Luxembourg	May 10, 1867	Oct. 17, 1868	constitutional monarchy	grand duke	prime minister	59	—	3	dis	—	—	12	can	—	—
Macau	—	—	overseas prov. (Port.)	Port. president	governor	17	—	3	dis	—	—	5	par	2	isl
Madagascar	June 26, 1960	Dec. 21, 1975	republic	president	prime minister	137	—	6	pro	—	—	18	pre	—	—
Malawi	July 6, 1964	July 6, 1964	republic	——president——		101	—	3	reg	—	—	24	dis	—	—
Malaysia	Aug. 31, 1957	Aug. 31, 1957	fed. const. monarchy	paramount ruler	prime minister	68	154	13	sta	1	fet	126	dis	—	—
Maldives	July 26, 1965	June 4, 1964	republic	——president——		48	—	19	dis	—	—	202	isl	—	—
Mali	Sept. 22, 1960	June 19, 1979	republic	——president——		82	—	7	reg	1	dis	46	cer	—	—
Malta	Sept. 21, 1964	Sept. 21, 1964	republic	president	prime minister	65	—	—	—	—	—	—	—	—	—
Martinique	—	—	overseas dept. (Fr.)	French president	commissioner	36	41	3	arr	—	—	32	com	—	—
Mauritania	Nov. 28, 1960	May 20, 1961	republic	——president——		x	—	12	reg	1	dis	53	dep	—	—
Mauritius	March 12, 1968	March 12, 1968	parliamentary state	British monarch	prime minister	70	—	9	dis	—	—	—	—	—	—
Mayotte	—	—	terr. collectivity (Fr.)	French president	commissioner	17	—	17	com	—	—	—	—	—	—
Mexico	Sept. 16, 1810	Feb. 5, 1917	federal republic	——president——		64	400	31	sta	1	fed	2,389	mun	—	—
Monaco	Feb. 2, 1861	Dec. 17, 1962	constitutional monarchy	prince	min. of state	18	—	1	com	—	—	4	cos	—	—
Mongolia	March 13, 1921	July 6, 1960	people's republic	chairman PPGH	premier	370	—	18	pro	3	aum	331	dis	—	—
Montserrat	—	Jan. 1, 1960	colony (U.K.)	British monarch	governor	11	—	3	par	—	—	—	—	—	—
Morocco	March 2, 1956	March 10, 1972	constitutional monarchy	king	prime minister	267	—	39	pro	—	—	131	cer	—	—
Mozambique	June 25, 1975	June 25, 1975	people's republic	——president——		226	—	10	pro	—	—	94	dis	—	—
Nauru	Jan. 31, 1968	Jan. 29, 1968	republic	——president——		18	—	14	dis	—	—	—	—	—	—

membership in international organizations																																			country
United Nations (date of admission)	UN bodies			UN-related organizations															Commonwealth of Nations	regional multi-purpose						economic							military		
	UNCTAD	UNICEF	UNIDO	FAO	GATT	IAEA	IBRD	ICAO	ICJ	ILO	IMF	IMO	ITU	UNESCO	UPU	WHO	WIPO	WMO		ASEAN	EC	LASg	OAS	OAU	SPC	ACP	COMECON	ECOWAS	EEC	I-ADB	IDBh	OPEC	NATO	WTO	
1975	•	•	•		•		•			•	•			•	•	•	•	•					•			•					•				Comoros
1960	•	•	•	•	•		•			•	•		•	•	•	•	•	•					•	•		•									Congo
		•																																	Cook Islands
1945	•	•	•	•		•	•	•	•	•	•	•	•	•	•	•	•	•					•						•						Costa Rica
1945	•	•	•	•		•		•	•	•		•	•	•	•	•	•	•					•						•						Cuba
1960	•	•	•	•	•		•	•	•	•	•	•	•	•	•	•	•	•	•																Cyprus
1945	•	•	•	•	•	•		•	•	•		•	•	•	•	•	•	•								•		•				•	Czechoslovakia
1945	•	•	•	•	•	•	•	•	•	•	•	•	•	•	•	•	•	•								•			•		•	•		Denmark
1977	•	•	•	•		•		•		•	•		•	•	•	•	•	•						•		•					•			Djibouti
1978	•	•	•	•[1]		•			•	•		•	•	•	•	•	•	•					•			•					•				Dominica
1945	•	•	•	•	•	•	•	•	•	•	•	•	•	•	•	•	•	•					•						•						Dominican Republic
1945	•	•	•	•		•	•	•	•	•	•	•	•	•	•	•	•	•					•						•						Ecuador
1945	•	•	•	•	•	•	•	•	•	•	•	•	•	•	•	•	•	•				•[10]		•		•					•				Egypt
1945	•	•	•	•		•	•	•	•	•	•	•	•	•	•	•	•	•					•						•						El Salvador
1968	•	•	•	•[1]		•	•	•	•	•	•	•	•	•	•	•	•	•						•		•									Equatorial Guinea
1945	•	•	•	•		•	•	•	•	•	•		•	•	•	•	•	•						•											Ethiopia
																																			Faeroe Islands
																																			Falkland Islands
1970	•	•	•	•[1]	•	•	•	•	•	•	•	•	•	•	•	•	•	•	•					•	•										Fiji
1955	•	•	•	•	•	•	•	•	•	•	•	•	•	•	•	•	•	•											•		•		•		Finland
1945	•	•	•	•	•	•	•	•	•	•	•	•	•	•	•	•	•	•			•		•			•			•				•		France
																							•												French Guiana
																									•										French Polynesia
1960	•	•	•	•	•	•	•	•	•	•	•	•	•	•	•	•	•	•						•		•				•	•				Gabon
1965	•	•	•	•	•	•	•	•	•	•	•	•	•	•	•	•	•	•	•					•		•									Gambia, The
1973	•	•	•	•		•		•		•			•	•	•	•	•	•									•		•				•	Germany, East
1973	•	•	•	•	•	•	•	•	•	•	•	•	•	•	•	•	•	•			•								•				•		Germany, West
1957	•	•	•	•	•	•	•	•	•	•	•	•	•	•	•	•	•	•	•					•		•		•							Ghana
																				•																Gibraltar
1945	•	•	•	•	•	•	•	•	•	•	•	•	•	•	•	•	•	•			•								•		•		•		Greece
																																				Greenland
1974	•	•	•	•[1]		•	•	•	•	•	•	•	•	•	•	•	•	•	•				•			•					•				Grenada
																								•												Guadeloupe
																								•												Guam
1945	•	•	•	•	•	•	•	•	•	•	•	•	•	•	•	•	•	•					•						•						Guatemala
1958	•	•	•	•	•	•	•	•	•	•	•	•	•	•	•	•	•	•						•		•		•							Guinea
1974	•	•	•	•[1]		•	•	•	•	•	•	•	•	•	•	•	•	•	•					•		•		•							Guinea-Bissau
1966	•	•	•	•	•	•	•	•	•	•	•	•	•	•	•	•	•	•	•				•			•					•				Guyana
1945	•	•	•	•		•	•	•	•	•	•	•	•	•	•	•	•	•					•						•						Haiti
1945	•	•	•	•		•	•	•	•	•	•	•	•	•	•	•	•	•					•						•						Honduras
		•		•		•		•		•		•	•	•[2]	•	•	•	•		•																Hong Kong
1955	•	•	•	•	•	•	•	•	•	•	•	•	•	•	•	•	•	•								•		•			•		Hungary
1946	•	•	•	•	•	•	•	•	•	•	•	•	•	•	•	•	•	•											•		•		•		Iceland
1945	•	•	•	•	•	•	•	•	•	•	•	•	•	•	•	•	•	•	•																India
1950	•	•	•	•	•	•	•	•	•	•	•	•	•	•	•	•	•	•		•											•	•			Indonesia
1945	•	•	•	•	•	•	•	•	•	•	•	•	•	•	•	•	•	•				•													Iran
1945	•	•	•	•		•	•	•	•	•	•	•	•	•	•	•	•	•				•							•			•			Iraq
1955	•	•	•	•	•	•	•	•	•	•	•	•	•	•	•	•	•	•			•		•						•		•				Ireland
1949	•	•	•	•	•	•	•	•	•	•	•	•	•	•	•	•	•	•					•						•		•				Israel
1955	•	•	•	•	•	•	•	•	•	•	•	•	•	•	•	•	•	•			•								•				•		Italy
1960	•	•	•	•	•	•	•	•	•	•	•	•	•	•	•	•	•	•						•		•		•		•					Ivory Coast
1962	•	•	•	•	•	•	•	•	•	•	•	•	•	•	•	•	•	•	•				•			•				•					Jamaica
1956	•	•	•	•	•	•	•	•	•	•	•	•	•	•	•	•	•	•																	Japan
1955	•	•	•	•		•	•	•	•	•	•	•	•	•	•	•	•	•				•							•						Jordan
1955	•	•	•	•[1]				•	•	•	•		•	•	•	•	•	•																	Kampuchea
1963	•	•	•	•	•	•	•	•	•	•	•	•	•	•	•	•	•	•	•					•		•				•					Kenya
	•	•	•																•						•										Kiribati
	•	•	•	•[1]						•			•	•	•																				Korea, North
	•	•	•	•		•	•	•	•	•	•	•	•	•	•	•	•	•																	Korea, South
1963	•	•	•	•		•	•	•	•	•	•	•	•	•	•	•	•	•				•										•			Kuwait
1955	•	•	•	•				•	•	•	•		•	•	•	•	•	•																	Laos
1945	•	•	•	•		•	•	•	•	•	•	•	•	•	•	•	•	•				•													Lebanon
1966	•	•	•	•[1]		•	•	•	•	•	•	•	•	•	•	•	•	•	•					•		•				•					Lesotho
1945	•	•	•	•		•	•	•	•	•	•	•	•	•	•	•	•	•						•											Liberia
1955	•	•	•	•		•	•	•	•	•	•	•	•	•	•	•	•	•				•		•							•	•			Libya
								•		•			•	•	•	•	•	•																	Liechtenstein
1945	•	•	•	•	•	•	•	•	•	•	•	•	•	•	•	•	•	•			•								•		•		•		Luxembourg
															•																				Macau
1960	•	•	•	•	•	•	•	•	•	•	•	•	•	•	•	•	•	•						•		•				•					Madagascar
1964	•	•	•	•	•	•	•	•	•	•	•	•	•	•	•	•	•	•	•					•		•									Malawi
1957	•	•	•	•	•	•	•	•	•	•	•	•	•	•	•	•	•	•	•	•															Malaysia
1965	•	•	•	•[1]		•	•	•	•	•	•	•	•	•	•	•	•	•	•[15]							•				•					Maldives
1960	•	•	•	•	•	•	•	•	•	•	•	•	•	•	•	•	•	•						•		•		•		•					Mali
1964	•	•	•	•	•	•	•	•	•	•	•	•	•	•	•	•	•	•	•							•									Malta
														•																					Martinique
1961	•	•	•	•	•	•	•	•	•	•	•	•	•	•	•	•	•	•					•	•		•		•		•					Mauritania
1968	•	•	•	•	•	•	•	•	•	•	•	•	•	•	•	•	•	•	•					•		•				•					Mauritius
																																				Mayotte
1945	•	•	•	•		•	•	•	•	•	•	•	•	•	•	•	•	•					•						•						Mexico
														•																						Monaco
1961	•	•	•	•		•				•			•	•	•	•	•	•						•		•						•			Mongolia
																																				Montserrat
1956	•	•	•	•		•	•	•	•	•	•	•	•	•	•[2]	•	•	•				•		•											Morocco
1975	•	•	•	•				•	•	•	•	•	•	•	•	•	•	•	•[15]					•		•		•							Mozambique
							•				•		•	•	•	•	•	•						•											Nauru

Government and administrative subdivisions (continued)

country	date of independence[a]	date of current or last constitution[b]	type of government	executive branch		legislative branch		administrative subdivisions							
				chief of state[c]	head of government[c]	upper house[de] (members)	lower house[e] (members)	first-order				second-order			
								no.	type[c]	no.	type[c]	no.	type[c]	no.	type[c]
Nepal	Nov. 13, 1769	Dec. 16, 1962	constitutional monarchy	king	prime minister	140	—	14	zon	—	—	75	dis	—	—
Netherlands, The	March 30, 1814	March 29, 1814	constitutional monarchy	monarch	prime minister	75	150	11	pro	—	—	912	mun	—	—
Netherlands Antilles	—	—	integral part of Neth.	Dutch monarch	governor	22	—	4	lau	—	—	—	—	—	—
New Caledonia	—	—	overseas territory (Fr.)	French president	high comm.	36	—	5	sub	—	—	32	com	—	—
New Zealand	Sept. 26, 1907	June 30, 1852	parliamentary state	British monarch	prime minister	92	—	19	reg	—	—	231	tau	—	—
Nicaragua	April 30, 1838	*March 14, 1974*	republic	—president—		90	—	16	dep	1	nad	136	mun	—	—
Niger	Aug. 3, 1960	*Nov. 8, 1960*	republic	—president SMC—		150	—	7	dep	—	—	32	arr	—	—
Nigeria	Oct. 1, 1960	*Oct. 1, 1979*	federal republic	—chairman SMC—		x	x	19	sta	1	fet	271	loa	—	—
Niue	—	—	territory (N.Z.)	New Zealand GG	premier	14	—	14	vic	—	—	—	—	—	—
Norfolk Island	—	—	external territory (Aust.)	Australian GG	administrator	9	—	—	—	—	—	—	—	—	—
Norway	June 7, 1905	May 17, 1814	constitutional monarchy	king	prime minister	155	—	19	cou	—	—	454	mun	—	—
Oman	Dec. 20, 1951	—	monarchy (sultanate)	sultan	prime minister	55	—	41	dis	1	car	—	—	—	—
Pakistan	Aug. 14, 1947	April 10, 1973	federal Islamic republic	president	prime minister	(63)	(210)	4	pro	2	fet[16]	16	div	—	—
Panama	Nov. 3, 1903	Oct. 11, 1972	republic	—president—		56	505	9	pro	—	—	65	dis	—	—
Papua New Guinea	Sept. 16, 1975	Sept. 16, 1975	prelimentary state	British monarch	prime minister	109	—	20	pro	—	—	86	dis	—	—
Paraguay	May 14, 1811	Aug. 25, 1967	republic	—president—		30	60	20	dep	—	—	190	dis	—	—
Peru	July 28, 1821	July 28, 1980	republic	—president—		60	180	24	dep	1	cnp	152	pro	—	—
Philippines	July 4, 1946	Jan. 17, 1973	republic	president	prime minister	175	—	73	pro	—	—	1,500	mun	—	—
Pitcairn Island	—	Nov. 30, 1838	colony (U.K.)	British monarch	isl. magistrate	10	—	—	—	—	—	—	—	—	—
Poland	Nov. 10, 1918	July 22, 1952	people's republic	chairman CS	prime minister	460	—	49	pro	—	—	261	mun	—	—
Portugal	July 25, 1139	April. 2, 1976	republic	president	prime minister	250	—	18	dis	—	—	3,848	par	275	mun
Puerto Rico	July 25, 1952	July 25, 1952	commonwealth (U.S.)	—governor—		27	51	78	mun	—	—	...	bar	—	—
Qatar	Sept. 3, 1971	July 1970[17]	monarchy (emirate)	—emir—		—	—	—	—	—	—	—	—	—	—
Réunion	—	—	overseas dept. (Fr.)	French president	commissioner	36	45	4	arr	—	—	24	com	—	—
Romania	May 21, 1877	Aug. 21, 1965	socialist republic	—president—		369	—	40	cou	1	mun	2,705	com	236	cit[18]
Rwanda	July 1, 1962	Dec. 20, 1978	republic	—president—		70	—	10	pre	—	—	143	com	—	—
St. Christopher and Nevis	Sept. 19, 1983	Sept. 19, 1983	fed. parl. state	British monarch	prime minister	13	—	14	par	—	—	—	—	—	—
St. Helena and Ascension	—	Jan. 1, 1967	colony (U.K.)	British monarch	governor	15[19]	—	1	isl	2	dep	—	—	—	—
St. Lucia	Feb. 22, 1979	Feb. 22, 1979	parliamentary state	British monarch	prime minister	11	17	10	qua	—	—	—	—	—	—
St. Pierre and Miquelon	—	—	overseas dept. (Fr.)	French president	commissioner	—	—	2	com	—	—	—	—	—	—
St. Vincent	Oct. 27, 1979	Oct. 27, 1979	parliamentary state	British monarch	prime minister	19	—	5	par	—	—	13	div	—	—
San Marino	855	1205	republic	—captains-regent (2)—		60	—	9	cas	—	—	—	—	—	—
São Tomé and Príncipe	July 12, 1975	Dec. 12, 1975	republic	—president—		40	—	2	pro	—	—	12	cou	—	—
Saudi Arabia	Sept. 23, 1932	—	monarchy	king	prime minister	—	—	14	dis	—	—	—	—	—	—
Senegal	Aug. 20, 1960	March 7, 1963	republic	—president—		120	—	8	reg	—	—	27	dep	3	cir
Seychelles	June 29, 1976	March 26, 1979	republic	—president—		25	—	—	—	—	—	—	—	—	—
Sierra Leone	April 27, 1961	June 14, 1978	republic	—president—		104	—	3	pro	1	are	12	dis	—	—
Singapore	Aug. 9, 1965	June 3, 1959	republic	president	prime minister	75	—	—	—	—	—	—	—	—	—
Solomon Islands	July 7, 1978	July 7, 1978	parliamentary state	British monarch	prime minister	38	—	7	pro	1	mua	5,014	loc	—	—
Somalia	July 1, 1960	Aug. 25, 1979	republic	—president—		177	—	16	reg	—	—	—	—	—	—
South Africa	May 31, 1910	May 31, 1961	republic	state president	prime minister	178	—	4	pro	7	nas	358	mun	—	—
South West Africa/Namibia	—	—	UN territory	—	admin. general	(72)	—	16	dis	9	coa	—	—	—	—
Spain	1492	Dec. 6, 1978	constitutional monarchy	king	prime minister	208	350	17	auc	—	—	50	pro	—	—
Sri Lanka	Feb. 4, 1948	Aug. 17, 1978	republic	president	prime minister	168	—	24	dis	—	—	682	lau	—	—
Sudan, The	Jan. 1, 1956	May 8, 1973	republic	president	prime minister	153	—	8	reg	1	nac	19	pro	—	—
Suriname	Nov. 25, 1975	*Nov. 25, 1975*	republic	—commander-in-chief—		x	—	9	dis	—	—	—	—	—	—
Swaziland	Sept. 6, 1968	*Sept. 6, 1968*	monarchy	king	prime minister	20	50	4	dis	—	—	—	—	—	—
Sweden	before 836	Jan. 1, 1975	constitutional monarchy	king	prime minister	349	—	24	cou	—	—	279	mun	—	—
Switzerland	Sept. 22, 1499	May 29, 1874	federal republic	—president—		46	200	23	can[22]	—	—	177	dis	—	—
Syria	April 17, 1946	March 12, 1973	republic	president	prime minister	195	—	14	dis	1	cit	41	sud	—	—
Taiwan	Oct. 25, 1945	Oct. 25, 1947	republic	president	premier	1,173	—	16	cou	7	mun	17	cit	590	twn
Tanzania	Dec. 9, 1961	April 26, 1964	republic	president	prime minister	239	—	25	reg	—	—	105	dis	—	—
Thailand	1350	Dec. 22, 1978	constitutional monarchy	king	prime minister	225	324	73	pro	—	—	621	dis	—	—
Togo	April 27, 1960	Dec. 30, 1979	republic	—president—		67	—	5	reg	—	—	21	cir	—	—
Tokelau	—	—	territory (N.Z.)	New Zealand GG	administrator	—	—	3	ato	—	—	—	—	—	—
Tonga	June 4, 1970	1875	constitutional monarchy	king	prime minister	24	—	3	igr	—	—	...	twn	...	dis
Trinidad and Tobago	Aug. 31, 1962	Oct. 26, 1976	republic	president	prime minister	31	36	8	cou	4	mun[23]	30	war	—	—
Trust Terr. of the Pacific Is.	—	—	territory (U.S.)	U.S. president	high comm.	—	—	4	rep	—	—	—	—	—	—
Tunisia	March 20, 1956	June 1, 1959	republic	—president—		136	—	23	gov	—	—	199	dis	—	—
Turkey	Oct. 29, 1923	Nov. 7, 1982	republic	president	prime minister	400	—	67	pro	—	—	572	dis	—	—
Turks and Caicos Islands	—	Aug. 30, 1976	colony (U.K.)	British monarch	governor	17	—	—	—	—	—	—	—	—	—
Tuvalu	Oct. 1, 1978	Oct. 1, 1978	parliamentary state	British monarch	prime minister	12	—	9	isl	—	—	—	—	—	—
Uganda	Oct. 9, 1962	Sept. 8, 1967	republic	president	prime minister	156	—	10	pro	—	—	33	dis	—	—
U.S.S.R.	c. 900	Oct. 7, 1977	fed. people's republic	chairman PSSU	chairman CM	750	750	15	rep	—	—	254	are[20]	—	—
United Arab Emirates	Dec. 2, 1971	Dec. 2, 1971	federation of emirates	president	prime minister	40	—	7	emi	—	—	—	—	—	—
United Kingdom	Oct. 14, 1066	—[25]	constitutional monarchy	monarch	prime minister	1,195	650	54	cou[26]	9[26]	—	448	dis	32	bor
United States	July 4, 1776	March 4, 1789	federal republic	—president—		100	435	50	sta	1	fed	3,041	cou	—	—
Uruguay	Aug. 25, 1828	*Nov. 27, 1966*	republic	—president—		x	—	19	dep	—	—	—	—	—	—
Vanuatu	July 30, 1980	July 30, 1980	republic	president	prime minister	39	—	4	dis	—	—	11	loc	—	—
Venezuela	July 5, 1811	Jan. 1961	republic	—president—		47	200	20	sta	3	fet[5]	156	dis	—	—
Vietnam	Sept. 2, 1954	Oct. 1980	socialist republic	chairman NA	chairman SC	496	—	36	pro	4	mun[28]	391	dis	—	—
Virgin Islands (U.S.)	—	—	territory (U.S.)	U.S. president	governor	15	—	3	isl	—	—	—	—	—	—
Wallis and Futuna	—	—	overseas territory (Fr.)	French president	admin. superior	20	—	—	—	—	—	—	—	—	—
Western Sahara	—	—	—	—	—	—	—	—	—	—	—	—	—	—	—
Western Samoa	Jan. 1, 1962	Oct. 28, 1960	constitutional monarchy	monarch	prime minister	45	—	21	dis	—	—	—	—	—	—
Yemen (Aden)	Nov. 30, 1967	Nov. 30, 1970	people's republic	—chairman, PSPC—		111	—	6	gov	1	dir	—	—	—	—
Yemen (Ṣan'ā')	Dec. 1918	June 19, 1974	republic	president	prime minister	159	—	10	pro	—	—	41	spr	—	—
Yugoslavia	Dec. 1, 1918	Feb. 21, 1974	federal socialist republic	—president—		88	220	6	rep	2	apr	527	com	—	—
Zaire	June 30, 1960	Feb. 15, 1978	republic	—president—		310	—	8	reg	1	ure	37	sur	—	—
Zambia	Oct. 24, 1964	Aug. 25, 1973	republic	—president—		136	—	8	reg	1	cap	53	dis	—	—
Zimbabwe	April 18, 1980	June 1, 1979	republic	president	prime minister	40	100	8	pro	—	—	—	—	—	—

[1]Full membership pending. [2]Associate member. [3]Includes one national territory. [4]In 1978, the Commonwealth of Australia transferred most of its powers to the Government of the Northern Territory; in all fields of transferred power, the Government is similar to that of the Australian states. [5]Includes one federal district. [6]Not fully effective until 1989. [7]Includes three special municipalities. [8]Includes five commissariats. [9]Includes the Turkish Federated State of Cyprus. [10]Suspended since 1979. [11]Evolving constitution adopted by Israeli parliament. [12]Excludes the West Bank. [13]Includes one special district. [14]The full name of Libya is The Socialist People's Libyan Arab Jamahiriya. *Jamahiriya* could be translated as "the masses of the people," "the populace," or "the multitude." [15]Special member participating in functional activities but not represented at meetings of Commonwealth heads of government. [16]Includes one federal capital

membership in international organizations

United Nations (date of admission)	UN bodies			UN-related organizations															Common-wealth of Nations	regional multi-purpose						economic							military		country
	UNCTAD	UNICEF[1]	UNIDO	FAO	GATT	IAEA	IBRD	ICAO	ICJ	ILO	IMF	IMO	ITU	UNESCO	UPU	WHO	WIPO	WMO		ASEAN	EC	LASg	OAS	OAU	SPC	ACP	COMECON	ECOWAS	ECC	I-ADB	IDBh	OPEC	NATO	WTO	
1955	•	•	•	•	•	•	•	•	•	•	•	•	•	•	•	•	•	•																	Nepal
1945	•	•	•	•	•	•	•	•	•	•	•	•	•	•	•	•	•	•			•					•			•[2]	•[2]			•		Netherlands, The
														•				•																	Netherlands Antilles
																		•							•										New Caledonia
1945	•	•	•	•	•	•	•	•	•	•	•	•	•	•	•	•	•	•							•										New Zealand
1945	•	•	•	•	•	•	•	•	•	•	•	•	•	•	•	•	•	•					•							•					Nicaragua
1960	•	•	•	•	•	•	•	•	•	•	•	•	•	•	•	•	•	•						•		•		•		•					Niger
1960	•	•	•	•	•	•	•	•	•	•	•	•	•	•	•	•	•	•	•					•				•		•		•			Nigeria
																			•						•										Niue
																									•										Norfolk Island
1945	•	•	•	•	•	•	•	•	•	•	•	•	•	•	•	•	•	•															•		Norway
1971	•	•	•	•		•	•	•	•	•	•	•	•	•	•	•	•	•				•													Oman
1947	•	•	•	•	•	•	•	•	•	•	•	•	•	•	•	•	•	•														•			Pakistan
1945	•	•	•	•	•	•	•	•	•	•	•	•	•	•	•	•	•	•					•							•					Panama
1975	•	•	•	•		•	•	•	•	•	•	•	•	•	•	•	•	•	•						•	•									Papua New Guinea
1945	•	•	•	•	•	•	•	•	•	•	•	•	•	•	•	•	•	•					•							•					Paraguay
1945	•	•	•	•	•	•	•	•	•	•	•	•	•	•	•	•	•	•					•							•					Peru
1945	•	•	•	•	•	•	•	•	•	•	•	•	•	•	•	•	•	•		•										•					Philippines
																									•										Pitcairn Island
1945	•	•	•	•		•	•	•	•	•	•	•	•	•	•	•	•	•								•							•		Poland
1955	•	•	•	•	•	•	•	•	•	•	•	•	•	•	•	•	•	•			•												•		Portugal
																																			Puerto Rico
1971	•	•		•	•[1]	•	•	•	•	•	•	•	•	•	•	•	•	•				•									•	•			Qatar
																									•										Réunion
1955	•	•	•	•		•	•	•	•	•	•	•	•	•	•	•	•	•								•							•		Romania
1962	•	•	•	•			•	•	•	•	•	•	•	•	•	•	•	•						•											Rwanda
1983	•	•		•			•	•		•	•	•	•	•	•	•		•	•				•							•					St. Christopher and Nevis
																			•																St. Helena and Ascension
1979	•	•		•	•[1]		•	•		•	•	•	•	•	•	•		•	•				•						•						St. Lucia
																									•										St. Pierre and Miquelon
1980	•	•		•			•	•		•	•	•	•	•	•	•		•	•				•			•			•						St. Vincent
														•	•	•	•		•																San Marino
1975	•	•	•	•			•	•		•	•	•	•	•	•	•	•	•	•					•		•									São Tomé and Príncipe
1945	•	•	•	•		•	•	•	•	•	•	•	•	•	•	•	•	•				•										•			Saudi Arabia
1960	•	•	•	•	•	•	•	•	•	•	•	•	•	•	•	•	•	•						•		•		•		•					Senegal
1976	•	•	•	•	•[1]		•	•		•	•	•	•	•	•	•		•	•					•		•			•						Seychelles
1961	•	•	•	•	•		•	•	•	•	•	•	•	•	•	•	•	•	•					•		•		•		•					Sierra Leone
1965	•	•	•	•	•	•	•	•	•	•	•	•	•	•	•	•	•	•	•	•															Singapore
1978	•	•		•	•[1]		•	•		•	•	•	•	•	•	•		•	•						•	•			•						Solomon Islands
1960	•	•	•	•		•	•	•	•	•	•	•	•	•	•	•	•	•				•		•				•				•			Somalia
1945	•	•		•	•	•	•	•	•	•	•	•	•		•	•	•	•																	South Africa
																•	•[2]																		South West Africa/Namibia
1955	•	•	•	•	•	•	•	•	•	•	•	•	•	•	•	•	•	•			•									•			•		Spain
1955	•	•	•	•	•	•	•	•	•	•	•	•	•	•	•	•	•	•	•																Sri Lanka
1956	•	•	•	•		•	•	•	•	•	•	•	•	•	•	•	•	•				•		•											Sudan, The
1975	•	•	•	•		•	•	•		•	•	•	•	•	•	•	•	•					•			•									Suriname
1968	•	•	•	•	•[1]		•	•		•	•	•	•	•	•	•		•	•					•		•			•						Swaziland
1946	•	•	•	•	•	•	•	•	•	•	•	•	•	•	•	•	•	•												•					Sweden
				•	•	•	•	•	•	•	•	•	•	•	•	•	•	•												•					Switzerland
1945	•	•	•	•		•	•	•	•	•	•	•	•	•	•	•	•	•				•										•			Syria
																									•					•					Taiwan
1961	•	•	•	•	•		•	•		•	•	•	•	•	•	•	•	•	•					•		•				•					Tanzania
1946	•	•	•	•	•	•	•	•	•	•	•	•	•	•	•	•	•	•		•										•					Thailand
1960	•	•	•	•	•		•	•	•	•	•	•	•	•	•	•	•	•						•		•		•		•					Togo
																									•										Tokelau
	•	•		•	•[1]		•			•	•	•	•		•			•	•						•	•				•					Tonga
1962	•	•	•	•	•		•	•	•	•	•	•	•	•	•	•	•	•	•				•			•			•						Trinidad and Tobago
																									•[24]										Trust Terr. of the Pacific Is.
1956	•	•	•	•		•	•	•	•	•	•	•	•	•	•	•	•	•				•		•											Tunisia
1945	•	•	•	•	•	•	•	•	•	•	•	•	•	•	•	•	•	•											•				•		Turkey
																•	•			•																Turks and Caicos Islands
																			•						•										Tuvalu
1962	•	•	•	•			•	•		•	•	•	•	•	•	•	•	•	•					•		•				•					Uganda
1945[21]	•[21]	•[21]	•[21]		•[21]		•[21]	•[21]	•[21]	•[21]		•[21]	•[21]	•[21]	•[21]	•[21]	•[21]	•[21]									•						•		U.S.S.R.
1971	•	•		•	•[1]	•	•	•	•	•	•	•	•	•	•	•	•	•				•									•	•			United Arab Emirates
1945	•	•	•	•[27]	•	•	•	•	•	•	•	•	•	•	•	•	•	•	•							•			•		•		•		United Kingdom
1945	•	•		•	•	•	•	•	•	•	•	•	•	•	•	•	•	•					•							•	•		•		United States
1945	•	•	•	•		•	•	•	•	•	•	•	•	•	•	•	•	•					•							•					Uruguay
1981	•	•		•			•	•		•	•	•	•	•	•	•		•	•							•	•			•					Vanuatu
1945	•	•	•	•		•	•	•	•	•	•	•	•	•	•	•	•	•				•	•							•		•			Venezuela
1977	•	•	•	•			•	•		•	•	•	•	•	•	•	•	•									•								Vietnam
																									•										Virgin Islands (U.S.)
																•									•										Wallis and Futuna
																								•[29]											Western Sahara
1976	•	•		•			•	•		•	•	•	•	•	•	•		•	•					•		•									Western Samoa
1967	•	•	•	•			•	•	•	•	•	•	•	•	•	•	•	•				•		•						•					Yemen (Aden)
1947	•	•	•	•			•	•	•	•	•	•	•	•	•	•	•	•				•								•					Yemen (Şan'ā')
1945	•	•	•	•	•	•	•	•	•	•	•	•	•	•	•	•	•	•																	Yugoslavia
1960	•	•	•	•		•	•	•	•	•	•	•	•	•	•	•	•	•						•		•		•		•					Zaire
1964	•	•	•	•			•	•	•	•	•	•	•	•	•	•	•	•	•					•		•				•					Zambia
1980	•	•	•	•			•	•		•	•	•	•	•	•	•	•	•	•					•		•				•					Zimbabwe

territory. [17]Provisional constitution. [18]Includes 56 municipalities. [19]For St. Helena only; Ascension Island and Tristan da Cunha also have local councils. [20]Comprised of 20 autonomous republics, 8 autonomous regions, 10 autonomous *okrugs*, 129 *krays* and *oblasts*, and 87 cities of republic subordination. [21]Belorussian S.S.R. and Ukrainian S.S.R. are also members. [22]Includes six demicantons. [23]Includes one ward. [24]The Federated States of Micronesia, the Commonwealth of the Northern Marianas, the Marshall Islands, and the Republic of Palau each send representatives. [25]Unwritten constitution based on statutes and common law. [26]Excludes Northern Ireland and three island authorities in Scotland. [27]Including all colonies and overseas territories. [28]Includes one special zone. [29]Membership in dispute.

Area and population

This table provides the area and population for each of the countries of the world and for all political dependencies with a permanent civilian population. Only countries such as the Vatican City State, the British Indian Ocean Territory, and similar anomalous cases are omitted. The data represent the latest published and unpublished data for both the surveyed area of the countries and their populations, the latter both as of a single year (1984) to provide the best comparability and as of the most recent census to provide the fullest comparison of certain demographic measures that are not always available in estimated form between successive national censuses. The 1984 estimates represent a combination of national, United Nations (UN) or other international organization, and *Encyclopædia Britannica* estimates so as to give the best fit to available published series, to take account of unpublished information received in correspondence, and to incorporate the results of very recent censuses for which published analyses and projections based upon them are not yet available.

One principal point to bear in mind when studying these statistics is that all of them, whatever degree of precision may be implied by the exactness of the numbers, are estimates—all of varying, and some of suspect accuracy. Even a country like the United States—which has a long tradition both of census taking and of the use of the most sophisticated analytical tools in processing the data—is unable to determine within 2.5 percent its total population nationally. And that is an average underenumeration. In larger cities, where enumeration of certain populations, both legal and illegal, is most difficult, the accuracy of the enumerated count may be off considerably more than five percent. When a country like Nigeria, the most populous in Africa, does not know within 20 percent its real

population and is delayed or prevented from measuring it by political circumstances, both the amount and the margin of error are likely to increase. The editors have tried to take account of the range of variation and accuracy in published data, but many sources of inaccuracy are relatively difficult to establish a value for unless some country or agency has made a relatively conscientious effort to establish both the relative accuracy (precision) of its estimate and the absolute magnitude of the quantity it is trying to measure—for example, the number of people in Kampuchea (Cambodia) who died at the hands of the Khmer Rouge. Was it 1,000,000, 2,000,000, 3,000,000? If a figure of 2,500,000 is cited, what is its accuracy: ± 1 percent, 10 percent, 50 percent? Is the source of the figure Vietnam (potential bias on the high side to justify its invasion), China (potential bias on the low side because of its political connection with the Khmer Rouge), the United States (habitually unable to obtain or produce by analysis accurate data about Southeast Asia, complicated by political bias)?

Many similar problems exist and in endless variations: What is the extent of southern European immigration to western Europe in search of jobs? How many refugees are there from Uganda or Afghanistan in surrounding countries? How many illegal immigrants are there in the United States? How many Palestinians are there in the Middle East (they are politically inconvenient to enumerate everywhere)? How many Amerindians exist in the countries of South America (any accurate answer to that question raises the question, "Where did they go?")? How many people have died or emigrated as a result of the civil violence in Central America?

Still, much information is accurate, well founded, and updated annually. The sources of this data are censuses; national population registers

Area and population

country	area			population (latest estimate)					population (most recent census)				
	square miles	square kilo-metres	rank	total 1984	rank	density		percent annual growth rate 1980–85	census year	total	male (percent)	female (percent)	urban (percent)
						per sq mi	per sq km						
Afghanistan	251,825	652,225	40	17,650,000	42	70.1	27.1	2.6	1979	13,051,358[1]	51.4	48.6	15.1
Albania	11,100	28,748	126	2,906,000	110	261.8	101.1	2.1	1979	2,591,000	51.3	48.7	35.3
Algeria	919,595	2,381,741	10	20,841,000	37	22.7	8.8	3.1	1977	16,948,000	49.7	50.3	40.6
American Samoa	77	199	190	35,000	184	454.5	175.9	1.7	1980	32,297	50.7	49.3	17.5
Andorra	181	468	173	40,000	183	221.0	85.5	2.7	1982	38,051	53.7	46.3	66.8
Angola	481,350	1,246,700	21	8,553,000	67	17.8	6.9	2.7	1970	5,673,046	52.1	47.9	14.2
Anguilla	35	91	195	7,000	197	200.0	77.2	0.7	1974	6,519	47.4	52.6	...
Antigua and Barbuda	171	442	175	79,000	174	462.0	178.7	1.5	1970	65,525	48.0[2]	52.0[2]	30.7[2]
Argentina	1,073,399	2,780,092	8	30,097,000	29	28.0	10.8	1.6	1980	27,947,446	49.2	50.8	86.3
Australia	2,966,200	7,682,300	6	15,462,000	47	5.2	2.0	1.4	1981	15,053,600	50.1	49.9	89.0
Austria	32,376	83,855	109	7,551,000	73	233.2	90.0	0.1	1981	7,555,338	47.4	52.6	55.1
Bahamas, The	5,382	13,939	140	227,000	156	42.2	16.3	0.9	1980	223,545	48.8	51.2	54.4
Bahrain	262	678	168	409,000	140	1,561.1	603.2	4.1	1981	350,798	58.4	41.6	80.7
Bangladesh	55,598	143,998	89	96,750,000	8	1,740.2	671.9	3.1	1981	89,912,000	51.5	48.5	15.7
Barbados	166	430	176	252,000	153	1,518.1	586.1	0.3	1980	248,983	47.6	52.4	39.3[2]
Belgium	11,783	30,519	124	9,859,000	62	836.7	323.1	0.1	1981	9,848,647	48.7	51.3	72.4[2]
Belize	8,867	22,965	133	159,000	161	17.9	6.9	1.8	1980	144,857	50.6	49.4	52.0
Benin	43,475	112,600	96	3,856,000	99	88.7	34.2	3.0	1979	3,338,240	47.9	52.1	14.2
Bermuda	21	53	197	56,000	178	2,719.8	1,050.1	0.2	1980	54,050	48.9	51.1	100.0
Bhutan	15,444	40,000	121	1,417,000	125	91.8	35.4	2.2	1969	931,514	51.5[2]	48.5[2]	3.9
Bolivia	424,165	1,098,581	27	6,253,000	82	14.7	5.7	2.6	1976	4,613,486	49.1	50.9	41.7
Botswana	224,600	581,700	45	1,047,000	131	4.7	1.8	3.6	1981	941,027	47.1	52.9	15.9
Brazil	3,286,500	8,512,000	5	135,564,000	6	41.2	15.9	2.3	1980	119,098,992	49.7	50.3	67.6
British Virgin Islands	59	153	192	13,000	191	220.3	85.0	1.8	1980	12,034	51.1	49.9	12.0
Brunei	2,226	5,765	149	216,000	157	97.0	37.5	3.9	1981	192,832	53.4	46.6	59.4
Bulgaria	42,823	110,912	99	8,969,000	66	209.4	80.9	0.3	1975	8,727,771	49.9	50.1	58.0
Burkina Faso	105,900	274,200	68	6,733,000	76	63.6	24.6	2.4	1975	5,638,203	50.2	49.8	9.0
Burma	261,228	676,577	39	36,368,000	26	139.2	53.8	1.0	1983	35,313,905	49.6	50.4	24.0
Burundi	10,747	27,834	128	4,525,000	94	421.1	162.6	2.8	1979	4,111,310	48.3	51.7	2.3[2]
Cameroon	179,714	465,468	50	9,254,000	65	51.5	19.9	2.3	1976	7,663,246	49.0	51.0	28.5
Canada	3,849,672	9,970,610	2	25,082,000	31	6.5	2.5	1.1	1981	24,343,181	49.6	50.4	76.4
Cape Verde	1,557	4,033	151	300,000	149	192.7	74.4	1.0	1980	288,845	46.3	53.7	35.1
Cayman Islands	102	264	185	19,000	189	186.3	72.0	4.0	1979	17,340	48.8	51.2	100.0
Central African Republic	240,324	622,436	42	2,502,000	114	10.4	4.0	2.5	1975	2,054,610	48.0	52.0	34.6
Chad	495,755	1,284,000	20	4,880,000	92	9.8	3.8	2.1	1975	4,029,917	47.7	52.3	16.0
Chile	284,521	736,905	38	11,879,000	55	41.8	16.1	1.7	1982	11,275,440	49.0	51.0	81.0
China	3,696,100	9,572,900	3	1,075,195,000	1	290.9	112.3	1.1	1982	1,008,175,288	51.5	48.5	21.2
Christmas Island	52	135	193	3,000	201	57.7	22.2	0.3	1981	2,871	66.8	33.2	...
Cocos (Keeling) Islands	5.5	14	202	600	205	109.1	42.8	...	1981	569	53.7	46.3	...
Colombia	440,831	1,141,748	26	28,248,000	30	64.1	24.7	2.0	1973	22,915,229	48.6	51.4	63.6
Comoros	719	1,862	158	389,000	141	540.6	208.8	2.8	1980	346,992	50.1	49.9	33.4
Congo	132,047	342,000	57	1,745,000	122	13.2	5.1	2.3	1974	1,300,120	48.5	51.5	37.8
Cook Islands	91	236	189	18,000	190	197.8	76.3	1.0	1981	17,754	51.7	48.3	...
Costa Rica	19,730	51,100	116	2,444,000	115	123.9	47.8	2.3	1984	2,460,226	50.0	50.0	43.9
Cuba	42,827	110,922	98	9,945,000	59	232.2	89.7	1.0	1981	9,723,605	50.6	49.4	69.0
Cyprus	3,572	9,251	147	657,000	137	183.9	71.0	1.3	1976	612,851	50.0	50.0	53.0
Czechoslovakia	49,381	127,896	92	15,459,000	48	313.1	120.9	0.3	1980	15,283,095	48.7	51.3	65.5
Denmark	16,633	43,080	118	5,109,000	91	307.2	118.6	−0.3	1983[4]	5,116,464	49.3	50.7	83.9
Djibouti	8,950	23,200	132	335,000	144	37.4	14.4	1.9	1960–61	81,200	...	...	57.4
Dominica	290	751	166	75,000	175	258.7	99.9	0.4	1981	74,851	47.4[5]	52.6[5]	14.3[5]
Dominican Republic	18,704	48,442	117	6,102,000	84	326.2	126.0	2.7	1981	5,647,977	50.1	49.9	52.0
Ecuador	103,930	269,178	69	8,451,000	68	81.3	31.4	2.9	1982	8,050,630	49.9	50.1	49.7
Egypt	385,201	997,667	29	47,120,000	20	122.3	47.2	2.5	1976	36,626,204	50.9	49.1	43.8
El Salvador	8,124	21,041	134	5,337,000	88	661.9	255.6	2.7	1971	3,554,648	49.6	50.4	39.4
Equatorial Guinea	10,831	28,051	127	325,000	148	30.0	11.6	2.2	1983	304,000	49.0[2]	51.0[2]	53.6[2]

(cumulated annually); registration of migration, births and deaths, and so on; sample surveys to establish demographic conditions; and the like.

The statistics provided for area and population by country are ranked, and the population densities based on those values are also provided. The population densities, for purposes of comparison within this table, are calculated on the basis of total area of the country. Elsewhere the reader will find densities calculated on more specialized bases: land area for Finland (because of its many lakes), ice-free area for Greenland (most of which is ice cap), or inhabited area for Egypt (which has relatively enormous areas of uninhabitable desert). The data in this section conclude with the estimated natural growth rate for the country during the last five years, extracted mainly from UN, but also from country, sources. Both absolute area and population density are calculated for both square miles and square kilometres.

In the section containing census data, information supplied includes the census total (usually de facto, the population actually present, rather than de jure, the population legally resident, who might be anywhere); the male–female breakdown; the proportion that is urban (according to the country's own definition of the term "urban," which differs very much from country to country); and finally an analysis of the age structure of the population by 15-year age groups. This last analysis may be particularly useful in distinguishing the general type of population being recorded—young, fast-growing nations show a high proportion of people under 30 (some countries like Jordan or Mayotte have more than 50 percent of their population under 15 years), while other nations (for example Sweden, which suffered no age-group losses in World War II) exhibit quite uniform proportions among age groups.

Finally, a section is provided giving the population of each country at the end of each decade from 1930 to 2000. The data for years past represent the best available analysis of the published data by the country itself, by the demographers of the United Nations, or by the editors of Britannica. The projections for 1990 and 2000, similarly, represent the best fit of available data through the mid 1980s with projected population structure and growth rates during the next 15 years. The evidence of the last 15 years with respect to similar estimates published around 1970, however, shows how cloudy is the glass through which these numbers are read. In 1970 no respectable Western analyst would have imagined proposing that mainland China could achieve the degree of birth control that it has since then (as evidenced in the 1982 census); on the other hand, even the Chinese admit that their methods have been somewhat Draconian and that they expect some backlash in terms of higher birth rates among those who have so far postponed larger families. How much is "some" by 2000? Compound that problem with all the social, economic, political, and biological factors that can affect 200 countries' populations, and the difficulty facing the prospective compiler of such projections may be appreciated.

Specific data about the vital rates affecting the data in this table may be found in great detail in both the country statistical boxes in "The Nations of the World" section and in the table on "Vital statistics, marriage, family," beginning at page 844.

Percentages in this table for male and female population will always total 100.0, but percentages by age group may not for reasons such as nonresponse on census forms, "don't know" responses, which are common in countries with poor birth registration systems, and the like.

0–14	15–29	30–44	45–59	60–74	75 and older	1930	1940	1950	1960	1970	1980	1990 projection	2000 projection	country
44.5	26.9	15.8	8.6	3.6	0.6	...	...	8,252	9,820	12,342	15,245	20,618	26,528	Afghanistan
37.3[2]	28.9[2]	16.5[2]	10.2[2]	4.5[2]	1.6[2]	1,003	1,088	1,215	1,607	2,136	2,672	3,350	4,000	Albania
47.3[2]	26.4[2]	12.8[2]	8.1[2]	4.3[2]	1.1[2]	6,489	7,628	8,753	10,800	14,330	18,828	26,946	37,041	Algeria
40.9	28.8	16.0	9.4	4.0	0.9	10	13	19	21	27	32	38	45	American Samoa
...	...	...	...	...	...	5	5	6	8	19	31	43	61	Andorra
41.7	23.2	17.0	7.4	3.8	1.0	3,344	3,738	4,145	4,841	5,673	7,720	9,939	13,226	Angola
43.4	22.2	10.6	10.2	10.1	3.5	...	...	...	6	6	7	7	7	Anguilla
44.0	24.2	12.0	11.7	—8.0—		30	34	45	55	66	75	82	87	Antigua and Barbuda
30.4	23.9	18.8	15.1	9.0	2.8	11,896	14,169	17,150	20,611	23,788	28,237	32,880	37,197	Argentina
25.1	25.3	20.5	15.2	10.4	3.5	6,503	7,079	8,219	10,315	12,552	14,488	16,170	17,795	Australia
19.9	23.6	20.1	17.1	13.2	6.1	6,435	6,684	6,935	7,048	7,447	7,553	7,560	7,606	Austria
38.1	27.8	17.9	9.8	5.1	1.3	61	70	79	113	169	210	230	252	Bahamas, The
32.9	34.5	20.0	8.8	3.1	0.7	...	90	127	162	215	346	520	777	Bahrain
46.6	24.6	14.9	8.2	—5.7—		35,353	41,259	45,482	54,699	68,171	88,257	108,346	127,903	Bangladesh
28.9	32.3	14.2	11.2	—13.3—		159	179	209	232	235	249	257	264	Barbados
20.0	23.7	19.1	18.6	12.8	5.8	8,129	8,301	8,639	9,153	9,690	9,855	9,905	9,964	Belgium
46.2	27.1	11.8	8.4	4.7	1.8	51	56	68	90	120	145	181	226	Belize
46.1[2]	25.9[2]	14.9[2]	8.6[2]	3.9[2]	0.7[2]	1,099	1,355	1,538	1,990	2,686	3,434	4,456	5,766	Benin
22.7	27.5	22.2	15.7	9.0	2.9	28	31	37	43	53	55	59	63	Bermuda
39.2[3]	26.5[3]	16.3[3]	10.9[3]	—7.1[3]—		440	500	726	853	1,045	1,296	1,628	2,030	Bhutan
41.5	27.0	15.4	9.8	4.6	1.7	2,153	2,508	2,765	3,405	4,265	5,570	7,314	9,724	Bolivia
56.5	19.9	10.2	6.6	3.4	3.4	212	278	387	522	650	903	1,290	1,862	Botswana
39.1	28.6	16.4	10.0	—5.9—		33,718	41,525	52,901	71,539	93,139	119,099	153,200	187,500	Brazil
33.7	29.2	—36.8—				5	7	7	7	10	12	17	20	British Virgin Islands
38.5	32.7	16.4	7.9	—4.5—		30	36	48	84	129	185	272	400	Brunei
21.8	22.4	20.6	18.6	13.0	3.4	5,733	6,344	7,251	7,867	8,490	8,862	9,118	9,375	Bulgaria
47.4	21.1	16.1	9.3	—6.1—		...	...	3,584	4,350	5,412	6,138	7,780	9,787	Burkina Faso
41.2[2]	25.8[2]	16.0[2]	10.9[2]	5.2[2]	0.9[2]	14,282	16,119	18,489	22,063	26,997	33,850	40,500	48,458	Burma
42.4	29.4	13.4	8.2	4.8	1.8	...	...	2,435	2,908	3,350	4,120	5,202	6,562	Burundi
43.4	24.3	16.6	9.9	4.3	1.5	...	...	4,888	5,609	6,727	8,449	10,838	13,937	Cameroon
23.4	28.9	20.0	15.0	9.6	3.1	10,498	11,693	13,737	17,909	21,324	24,086	26,826	29,028	Canada
46.0	27.6	9.1	9.0	6.3	2.0	146	181	147	200	272	289	319	353	Cape Verde
29.1	25.8	22.1	13.1	7.3	2.6	6	7	7	8	11	18	23	27	Cayman Islands
43.5	23.5	17.1	12.4	2.7	0.8	...	...	1,311	1,500	1,793	2,329	2,835	3,491	Central African Republic
40.6	28.3	17.2	9.5	—4.4—		...	...	2,639	3,032	3,643	4,524	5,558	7,063	Chad
31.9	29.1	19.1	11.7	6.3	1.9	4,365	5,063	6,091	7,585	9,368	11,104	13,128	15,511	Chile
33.6	29.1	17.5	12.2	6.3	1.3	500,000	530,000	556,613	682,020	838,396	971,000	1,127,636	1,257,298	China
25.9	26.4	35.8	10.8	—1.1—		...	...	1	3	3	3	3	3	Christmas Island
27.4	28.3	27.2	11.2	—5.9—		...	...	1	1	1	1	1	1	Cocos (Keeling) Islands
44.1	27.3	14.9	8.5	4.1	1.0	7,280	9,097	11,268	15,321	20,884	26,056	31,820	37,999	Colombia
45.1[2]	26.9[2]	15.1[2]	8.5[2]	3.6[2]	0.8[2]	...	...	...	177	245	347	461	612	Comoros
45.6	22.2	15.5	11.3	4.7	0.7	...	...	736	933	1,182	1,537	1,945	2,460	Congo
42.7	26.6	13.7	10.4	5.2	1.3	11	13	15	18	18	18	20	22	Cook Islands
37.9	31.5	15.8	9.2	4.4	1.2	499	619	866	1,250	1,737	2,245	2,776	3,377	Costa Rica
—25.4—		17.0	12.1	—9.0—		3,837	4,566	5,752	7,019	8,565	9,670	10,540	11,718	Cuba
25.4	29.0	17.9	13.4	10.8	3.5	357	413	494	573	615	629	708	793	Cyprus
24.3	22.9	19.8	17.2	11.5	4.3	13,964	14,713	12,389	13,654	14,334	15,272	15,758	16,278	Czechoslovakia
19.4	22.7	21.6	16.0	14.0	6.0	3,542	3,832	4,271	4,581	4,929	5,123	5,061	4,940	Denmark
42.3[2]		52.1[2]		—5.6[2]—		...	...	60	78	158	310	375	453	Djibouti
49.1[5]	21.2[5]	11.2[5]	10.0[5]	6.3[5]	2.2[5]	41	45	51	60	70	74	77	81	Dominica
44.8[2]	29.0[2]	14.1[2]	7.8[2]	3.5[2]	0.8[2]	1,400	1,759	2,313	3,160	4,343	5,431	7,096	8,880	Dominican Republic
41.6	28.3	15.4	8.6	4.6	1.5	2,102	2,546	3,307	4,421	5,958	7,632	10,028	13,336	Ecuador
39.9	26.7	16.6	10.6	5.2	1.0	14,822	16,942	20,461	26,085	33,329	42,126	53,481	65,200	Egypt
46.2	25.1	15.2	8.2	4.3	1.0	1,350	1,550	1,931	2,527	3,534	4,813	6,330	8,310	El Salvador
41.5[2]	25.8[2]	15.6[2]	10.6[2]	5.4[2]	1.1[2]	...	...	211	244	291	298	359	438	Equatorial Guinea

Area and population (continued)

country	area			population (latest estimate)					population (most recent census)				
	square miles	square kilo-metres	rank	total 1984	rank	density		percent annual growth rate 1980-85	census year	total	male (percent)	female (percent)	urban (percent)
						per sq mi	per sq km						
Ethiopia	472,400	1,223,600	23	42,200,000	22	89.3	34.5	2.9	1984	42,019,418	49.9	50.1	11.3
Faeroe Islands	540	1,399	160	45,000	181	83.0	32.0	1.0	1977	41,969	52.4	47.6	87.6
Falkland Islands	4,700	12,173	142	2,000	202	0.4	0.2	-0.3	1980	1,813	55.2	44.8	55.1
Fiji	7,055	18,273	137	686,000	136	97.2	37.5	2.0	1976	588,068	50.5	49.5	37.2
Finland	130,559	338,145	58	4,880,000	92	37.4	14.4	0.5	1980	4,784,710	48.3	51.7	59.9
France	210,040	544,000	46	54,872,000	16	261.2	100.8	0.5	1982	54,334,871	49.0	51.0	77.9[2]
French Guiana	34,749	90,000	108	80,000	173	2.3	0.9	3.7	1982	73,012	52.7	47.3	73.4
French Polynesia	1,359	3,521	152	170,000	159	125.1	48.3	3.0	1983	166,753	51.1	48.9	39.7
Gabon	103,347	267,667	71	1,146,000	129	11.1	4.3	1.7	1960-61	448,564	49.1[2]	50.6[2]	35.8[2]
Gambia, The	4,127	10,689	145	725,000	135	175.7	48.3	2.6	1983	695,886	49.4[2]	50.6[2]	21.2
Germany, East	41,827	108,333	101	16,697,000	43	399.1	154.1	-0.3	1981	16,705,635	47.0	53.0	76.4
Germany, West	96,019	248,687	74	61,313,000	12	638.6	246.5	-0.1	1982[4]	61,546,101	47.8	52.2	84.7[2]
Ghana	92,098	238,533	78	12,206,000	54	132.5	51.2	3.2	1984	12,205,576	49.6[5]	50.4[5]	28.9[5]
Gibraltar	2.2	5.8	204	30,000	185	13,636.4	5,172.4	1.0	1981	26,479	52.2	47.8	...
Greece	50,949	131,957	91	9,908,000	61	194.5	75.1	0.6	1981	9,740,417	49.1	50.9	58.1
Greenland	840,000	2,175,600	13	53,000	180	0.06	0.02	1.4	1983[4]	51,903	54.4	45.6	87.7
Grenada	133	345	181	112,000	168	842.1	324.6	0.1	1970	93,858	46.2	53.8	25.3
Guadeloupe	687	1,780	159	328,000	146	477.3	184.3	0.1	1982	327,002	49.2[2]	50.8[2]	43.5[2]
Guam	209	541	171	109,000	169	521.5	201.5	1.9	1980	105,821	49.9	50.1	40.1
Guatemala	42,042	108,889	100	7,599,000	72	180.8	69.8	2.3	1981	6,043,559	49.8	50.2	34.3
Guinea	94,900	245,790	75	5,297,000	89	55.8	21.6	2.3	1977	4,527,000	49.5[2]	50.5[2]	19.1[2]
Guinea-Bissau	13,948	36,125	122	881,000	134	63.2	24.4	2.1	1979	767,739	48.2	51.8	14.0
Guyana	83,000	215,000	81	934,000	133	11.3	4.3	1.8	1970	701,885	49.7	50.3	31.9
Haiti	10,360	26,833	130	5,197,000	90	501.6	193.7	1.9	1982	5,053,792	48.5	51.5	20.6
Honduras	43,277	112,088	97	4,135,000	97	95.5	36.9	3.5	1974	2,656,948	49.5	50.5	37.5
Hong Kong	409	1,060	162	5,394,000	87	13,188.3	5,088.7	1.9	1981	5,021,066	52.2	47.8	85.9
Hungary	35,921	93,036	106	10,679,000	57	297.2	114.7	-0.0	1980	10,709,463	48.4	51.6	53.2
Iceland	39,769	103,000	102	240,000	154	6.0	2.3	0.6	1983[4]	235,537	50.4	49.6	88.8
India	1,183,041	3,064,063	7	746,000,000	2	630.6	243.5	2.0	1981	685,184,692	50.3	49.7	23.7
Indonesia	741,101	1,919,443	15	164,347,000	5	221.8	85.6	2.1	1980	147,490,298	49.7	50.3	22.3
Iran	636,000	1,648,000	17	43,088,000	21	67.7	26.1	3.1	1976	33,708,744	51.5	48.5	47.0
Iraq	169,235	438,317	53	15,000,000	50	88.6	34.2	3.3	1977	12,000,497	51.5	48.5	63.7
Ireland	27,137	70,285	113	3,575,000	102	131.7	50.9	1.2	1981	3,443,405	50.2	49.8	55.6
Israel	7,992[9]	20,700[9]	135[9]	4,179,000	95	522.9	201.9	1.9	1983	4,037,620	49.8	50.2	86.9[3]
Italy	116,324	301,278	65	56,799,000	14	488.3	188.5	0.3	1981	56,243,935	48.7	51.3	69.3[2]
Ivory Coast	123,847	320,763	63	9,671,000	63	78.1	30.1	4.0	1975	6,702,866	51.8	48.2	32.0
Jamaica	4,244	10,991	144	2,141,000	118	504.5	194.8	1.1	1982	2,095,878	49.7	50.3	31.0
Japan	145,856	377,765	56	120,020	7	822.9	317.7	0.6	1980	117,060,396	49.2	50.8	76.2
Jordan	36,659[10]	94,946[10]	105[10]	2,521,000[11]	113[11]	73.2[11]	28.3[11]	2.7	1979[11]	2,123,997	52.3	47.7	59.5
Kampuchea	69,898	181,035	84	6,118,000	83	87.5	33.4	1.9	1962	5,728,771	50.0	50.0	10.3
Kenya	224,961	582,646	44	19,536,000	39	86.8	33.5	4.0	1979	15,327,061	49.6	50.4	15.1
Kiribati	328	849	165	62,000	177	189.1	73.0	1.6	1978	56,213	49.3	50.7	32.2
Korea, North	47,077	121,929	94	19,630,000	38	417.0	161.0	2.3	[8]	—	49.4[2]	50.6[2]	59.7[2]
Korea, South	38,221	98,992	104	40,578,000	23	1,061.7	409.9	1.6	1980	37,436,315	50.1	49.9	57.3
Kuwait	6,880	17,818	138	1,715,000	123	249.3	96.3	6.6	1980	1,357,952	57.2	42.8	100.0
Laos	91,500	236,800	79	4,097,000	98	44.8	17.3	2.0	[8]	—	50.3[2]	49.7[2]	13.4[2]
Lebanon	3,950	10,230	146	2,601,000	111	658.5	254.2	-0.2	1970	2,126,325	50.8	49.2	60.1
Lesotho	11,720	30,355	125	1,474,000	124	125.8	48.5	2.4	1976	1,216,815	48.3	51.7	17.2
Liberia	38,250	99,067	103	2,160,000	116	56.5	21.8	3.2	1974	1,503,368	50.5	49.5	29.1
Libya	675,000	1,749,000	16	3,648,000	101	5.4	2.1	5.1	1973	2,249,237	53.0	47.0	59.8
Liechtenstein	62	160	191	27,000	187	435.5	168.8	0.6	1980	25,215	49.6	50.4	...
Luxembourg	999	2,586	154	366,000	142	366.4	141.5	-0.1	1981	364,602	48.8	51.2	78.4[2]
Macau	6	16	201	277,000	150	46,166.6	17,312.5	1.9	1981	261,680	51.9	48.1	97.0
Madagascar	226,662	587,051	43	9,642,000	64	42.6	16.4	2.6	1975	7,603,790	50.0	50.0	16.3
Malawi	45,747	118,484	95	6,839,000	76	145.8	56.3	3.3	1977	5,547,460	48.2	51.8	8.5
Malaysia	127,317	329,750	61	15,246,000	49	119.7	46.2	2.2	1980	13,136,109	50.2	49.8	34.2
Maldives	115	298	183	173,000	158	1,503.6	580.5	3.0	1977	142,832	52.7	47.3	20.7
Mali	478,841	1,240,192	22	7,720,000	71	16.1	6.2	2.5	1976	6,394,918	48.8	51.2	16.8
Malta	124	320	182	332,000	145	2,677.4	1,033.8	0.8	1967	314,216	47.9	52.1	94.3
Martinique	421	1,091	161	327,000	147	776.7	299.7	0.1	1982	326,717	48.5	51.5	57.1
Mauritania	398,000	1,030,700	28	1,823,000	121	4.6	1.8	2.5	1976-77	1,419,939	50.1	49.9	21.9
Mauritius	788	2,040	156	1,823,000	132	1,293.5	499.0	1.5	1983	993,700	49.1	50.9	52.2[2]
Mayotte	144	373	179	56,000	178	390.3	150.7	3.2	1978	47,246	49.9	50.1	53.3
Mexico	756,066	1,958,201	14	76,377,000	11	101.0	39.0	2.6	1980	67,382,581	49.4	50.6	66.3
Monaco	0.7	1.9	206	28,000	186	40,000.0	14,736.8	1.2	1982	27,063	45.7[12]	54.3[12]	100.0
Mongolia	604,800	1,566,500	18	1,860,000	120	3.1	1.2	2.9	1979	1,594,800	50.1	49.9	51.2
Montserrat	40	102	194	12,000	193	300.0	117.6	0.4	1980	11,606	48.1	51.9	54.1
Morocco	177,117	458,730	52	21,495,000	34	121.4	46.9	2.9	1982	20,419,555	50.0[7]	50.0[7]	42.7
Mozambique	308,650	799,400	34	13,210,000	53	42.8	16.5	2.9	1980	12,130,000	48.7	51.3	8.7[2]
Nauru	8	21	200	8,000	195	1,000.0	381.0	1.3	1977	7,254	52.1[13]	47.9[13]	...
Nepal	56,827	147,181	88	16,104,000	44	283.4	109.4	2.3	1981	15,022,839	51.2	48.8	6.4
Netherlands, The	16,027	41,509	119	14,437,000	51	900.8	347.8	0.5	1983[4]	14,339,600	49.6	50.4	88.4[3]
Netherlands Antilles	383	993	163	235,000	155	612.9	236.6	0.3	1981	231,932	48.8	51.2	...
New Caledonia	7,233	18,734	136	148,000	163	20.5	7.9	1.8	1983	145,368	51.8	48.2	58.5
New Zealand	103,515	268,103	70	3,266,000	104	31.5	12.2	0.9	1981	3,175,737	49.7	50.3	83.6
Nicaragua	49,291	127,662	93	2,914,000	109	59.1	22.8	3.8	1971	1,877,952	48.3	51.7	48.0
Niger	458,074	1,186,408	25	6,278,000	81	13.7	5.3	3.0	1977	5,098,427	49.3	50.7	11.8
Nigeria	356,669	923,768	31	94,502,000	9	265.0	102.3	3.0	1963[14]	55,670,055	50.5	49.5	16.1
Niue	100	258	187	4,000	200	40.0	15.4	...	1981	3,281	51.0	49.0	...
Norfolk Island	14	35	198	2,000	202	153.8	57.1	...	1981	2,134	49.1	50.9	...
Norway	125,057	323,895	62	4,141,000	96	33.1	12.8	0.3	1980	4,092,340	49.5	50.5	70.3
Oman	120,000	300,000	66	1,181,000	128	9.8	3.9	4.4	[8]	—	50.6[2]	49.4[2]	7.3[2]
Pakistan	307,374	796,095	35	91,880,000	10	298.9	115.4	3.1	1981	83,782,000	52.5	47.5	29.0
Panama	29,762	77,082	111	2,133,000	119	71.7	27.7	2.1	1980	1,831,399	50.7	49.3	49.3
Papua New Guinea	178,704	462,840	51	3,258,000	105	18.2	7.0	2.8	1980	3,010,727	52.3	47.7	13.1

age distribution (percent)						population (by decade, '000s)								country
0–14	15–29	30–44	45–59	60–74	75 and older	1930	1940	1950	1960	1970	1980	1990 projection	2000 projection	
45.5[2]	24.4[2]	16.4[2]	8.4[2]	—5.3[2]—		...	...	16,675	20,024	24,068	37,600	50,000	66,600	Ethiopia
26.6[6]	24.7[6]	19.5[6]	13.9[6]	11.4[6]	3.9[6]	24	27	31	35	39	41	43	45	Faeroe Islands
26.7	22.4	—50.8—				2	2	2	2	2	2	2	2	Falkland Islands
41.1	29.8	16.2	8.8	3.3	0.8	181	218	289	394	520	630	736	817	Fiji
20.2	24.4	22.1	16.8	12.4	4.1	3,449	3,698	4,009	4,430	4,606	4,778	4,955	4,964	Finland
22.0	23.5	19.6	17.3	11.6	6.0	41,150	41,300	41,736	45,684	50,770	53,710	54,970	56,252	France
34.2	29.2	19.9	9.8	5.1	1.8	30	30	27	33	49	69	99	143	French Guiana
38.5	29.7	16.5	10.3	4.2	0.8	39	50	62	84	109	151	203	273	French Polynesia
35.4[5]	19.3[5]	22.2[5]	16.3[5]	6.3[5]	0.5[5]	...	...	...	...	950	1,070	1,271	1,509	Gabon
44.3[2]	26.4[2]	15.4[2]	9.1[2]	4.0[2]	0.7[2]	211	193	232	357	458	633	891	1,256	Gambia, The
19.4	24.2	20.0	17.3	12.8	6.3	15,400	16,800	18,387	17,240	17,058	16,737	16,604	16,483	Germany, East
16.5	24.0	21.0	18.6	13.6	6.3	37,500	40,600	49,986	55,433	60,714	61,561	60,343	59,149	Germany, West
46.9[5]	24.4[5]	15.8[5]	7.5[5]	3.8[5]	1.6[5]	3,110	3,636	5,297	6,958	8,789	11,032	14,089	17,897	Ghana
21.4	22.2	22.3	17.7	12.6	3.8	16	14	23	24	26	29	33	35	Gibraltar
22.3[3]	21.8[3]	19.1[3]	19.5[3]	12.4[3]	5.2[3]	6,367	7,319	7,566	8,327	8,793	9,643	10,275	10,917	Greece
28.6	32.5	21.9	11.4	4.5	1.0	16	19	23	33	41	50	55	61	Greenland
47.1	23.0	11.6	9.4	6.6	2.2	68	71	76	90	95	111	111	142	Grenada
31.0[2]	32.5[2]	14.0[2]	12.8[2]	7.6[2]	2.1[2]	151	180	206	265	320	326	331	335	Guadeloupe
34.9	30.6	19.4	10.5	3.9	0.5	19	22	59	67	85	103	117	130	Guam
44.9	26.8	14.8	8.5	3.9	1.1	1,771	2,201	3,024	4,005	5,263	6,928	8,708	10,927	Guatemala
43.8[2]	25.5[2]	16.3[2]	9.5[2]	4.2[2]	0.7[2]	...	...	2,687	3,183	3,921	4,830	6,072	7,623	Guinea
44.3	25.5	15.1	8.2	4.7	2.2	...	341	411	520	653	810	999	1,231	Guinea-Bissau
47.1	25.1	13.4	9.0	4.4	1.0	309	344	423	560	715	817	952	1,110	Guyana
39.2	26.9	15.6	10.0	5.4	2.9	2,422	2,827	3,097	3,723	4,234	4,909	5,665	6,511	Haiti
48.1	25.8	13.9	7.8	3.6	0.9	948	1,146	1,390	1,873	2,553	3,691	5,105	6,978	Honduras
24.8	32.7	17.7	14.6	8.2	2.0	821	1,786	1,974	3,074	3,942	5,038	6,145	7,431	Hong Kong
21.8	20.7	—57.5—				8,649	9,280	9,338	9,984	10,353	10,709	10,920	10,964	Hungary
26.7	27.4	18.6	13.6	9.5	4.3	107	121	143	176	204	231	254	274	Iceland
40.1[2]	27.8[2]	17.0[2]	10.1[2]	4.2[2]	0.8[2]	278,000	317,000	352,664	427,802	543,132	682,460	820,860	960,611	India
40.8	27.0	16.4	10.2	4.5	1.1	60,750	70,500	75,449	92,701	119,467	147,490	173,530	198,687	Indonesia
44.5	25.2	14.8	10.1	3.8	1.0	12,400	14,000	16,913	21,554	28,359	38,126	51,033	64,916	Iran
48.9	24.5	12.3	8.2	4.2	1.9	...	3,745	5,180	6,847	9,356	13,072	18,136	24,198	Iraq
30.1	24.9	17.2	13.1	—14.7—		2,927	2,958	2,969	2,834	2,954	3,308	3,694	4,118	Ireland
32.6	26.4	18.0	12.3	9.4	3.1	...	...	2,114	2,958	3,878	4,639	5,440		Israel
21.7[7]	22.1[7]	20.2[7]	18.6[7]	12.5[7]	4.9[7]	40,293	43,840	46,769	50,223	53,565	56,040	58,000	59,707	Italy
44.5	27.0	16.7	7.8	2.8	1.2	2,075	2,350	2,775	3,865	5,550	8,250	12,223	18,096	Ivory Coast
36.7	29.8	12.9	10.1	3.0	7.5	1,009	1,212	1,403	1,629	1,891	2,054	2,281	2,535	Jamaica
23.5	21.5	24.2	17.9	9.8	3.1	64,450	73,075	83,200	93,419	103,720	116,782	122,834	128,119	Japan
51.8	23.3	13.4	7.3	—4.2—		...	...	1,095[11]	1,384[11]	1,795[11]	2,265[11]	2,955[11]	3,851[11]	Jordan
43.8	24.9	16.8	9.8	4.1	0.6	2,800	3,400	4,163	5,364	7,060	5,692	6,855	8,248	Kampuchea
48.3	26.9	12.8	7.1	3.5	1.4	...	...	6,018	8,115	11,225	16,670	24,831	37,138	Kenya
41.1	28.2	15.0	10.0	4.8	1.0	27	29	33	41	49	58	68	81	Kiribati
40.0[2]	28.7[2]	15.9[2]	9.7[2]	4.7[2]	1.0[2]	...	...	9,740	10,526	13,892	17,892	22,443	27,256	Korea, North
34.0	30.0	18.4	11.5	5.1	1.0	...	...	21,147	25,142	32,976	38,120	44,800	48,600	Korea, South
40.2	28.2	21.7	7.7	1.9	0.4	...	...	145	292	748	1,375	2,101	2,936	Kuwait
42.4[2]	26.3[2]	16.7[2]	9.7[2]	4.2[2]	0.7[2]	930	1,075	1,949	2,382	2,962	3,721	4,682	5,729	Laos
42.6	23.8	16.7	9.1	—7.7—		...	965	1,364	1,786	2,470	2,658	3,301	3,992	Lebanon
39.1	25.5	15.5	10.4	3.9	5.6	537	566	766	885	1,043	1,308	1,643	2,064	Lesotho
40.9	26.7	17.7	8.8	4.6	1.3	...	...	758	1,004	1,393	1,967	2,821	4,002	Liberia
44.3	22.2	15.4	8.2	4.0	1.6	800	900	1,029	1,349	1,982	2,978	4,417	6,539	Libya
23.0	26.5	24.1	14.1	9.2	3.1	10	11	14	16	21	25	29	35	Liechtenstein
18.5	23.7	21.2	18.7	12.8	5.1	297	296	296	314	339	358	355	349	Luxembourg
...	...	...	...	...	...	196	375	188	169	221	262	332	379	Macau
44.4	25.7	14.2	10.0	4.6	1.1	3,722	4,034	4,330	5,370	6,720	8,700	11,222	14,453	Madagascar
44.6	25.7	14.2	9.0	1.5	4.6	1,394	1,696	3,033	3,481	4,511	6,046	8,289	11,630	Malawi
39.5	29.1	16.5	9.2	4.6	1.1	...	...	6,187	7,908	10,466	13,436	17,036	21,269	Malaysia
44.6	24.8	16.4	9.6	—4.1—		78	81	82	106	128	154	230	344	Maldives
44.0	24.9	16.1	8.7	4.8	1.5	...	...	3,426	4,224	5,690	6,980	8,959	11,481	Mali
29.8	25.9	17.6	13.8	10.2	2.7	239	270	308	329	326	318	343	363	Malta
28.4	30.3	16.2	13.2	8.6	3.3	175	200	222	252	287	326	329	331	Martinique
45.9[2]	26.2[2]	14.7[2]	8.7[2]	3.9[2]	0.6[2]	...	...	781	970	1,245	1,634	1,944	2,481	Mauritania
32.8[3]	32.1[3]	17.1[3]	11.1[3]	5.7[3]	1.2[3]	413	428	479	662	824	959	1,117	1,248	Mauritius
50.2	23.4	13.9	7.0	3.8	1.7	...	...	...	...	...	50	66	85	Mayotte
43.0	27.8	14.9	8.5	—5.8—		16,589	19,815	26,606	36,369	50,313	67,383	91,976	115,659	Mexico
12.7[12]	17.8[12]	18.6[12]	19.9[12]	20.7[12]	10.0[12]	23	20	22	23	24	26	28	30	Monaco
43.1[2]	26.1[2]	16.3[2]	9.5[2]	4.1[2]	0.9[2]	725	750	747	931	1,248	1,663	2,208	2,930	Mongolia
31.5	27.2	13.8	10.7	—16.8—		13	15	14	12	12	11	13	15	Montserrat
45.6[7]	26.8[7]	14.8[7]	8.4[7]	3.7[7]	0.7[7]	6,980	7,750	8,953	11,640	15,126	20,296	25,500	33,900	Morocco
43.7[2]	25.2[2]	16.0[2]	9.7[2]	4.6[2]	0.8[2]	3,890	5,086	5,742	7,046	9,140	12,130	16,132	21,713	Mozambique
44.1[13]	33.1[13]	11.4[13]	8.5[13]	1.9[13]	1.0[13]	3	3	4	5	7	7	8	9	Nauru
41.4	25.5	17.4	10.0	4.7	1.0	6,250	7,000	8,000	9,180	11,232	15,020	18,500	23,300	Nepal
21.5[3]	25.6[3]	21.3[3]	15.5[3]	11.4[3]	4.7[3]	7,936	8,834	10,027	11,417	12,958	14,150	14,973	15,644	Netherlands, The
38.0	26.7	16.7	10.3	6.4	1.8	72	107	162	192	223	232	241	252	Netherlands Antilles
36.2	26.9	19.5	11.2	5.1	1.1	54	53	59	79	110	140	151	159	New Caledonia
26.7	25.9	19.1	14.3	10.5	3.5	1,491	1,636	1,908	2,372	2,820	3,148	3,489	3,745	New Zealand
48.1	25.6	14.1	7.4	3.8	1.1	700	825	1,109	1,472	1,972	2,703	3,778	5,154	Nicaragua
46.6[2]	26.4[2]	14.4[2]	8.3[2]	3.7[2]	0.6[2]	...	...	2,291	2,913	4,016	5,472	7,278	10,045	Niger
43.0	31.9	16.5	5.1	2.5	1.0	...	...	33,320	42,366	56,346	84,732	108,000	150,000	Nigeria
40.1	27.2	14.0	9.8	5.9	3.0	4	4	4	4	4	3	4	4	Niue
22.2	21.2	21.7	19.3	—15.7—		1	1	1	1	2	2	2	2	Norfolk Island
22.1	22.7	18.9	16.0	14.4	5.9	2,807	2,973	3,265	3,581	3,877	4,091	4,203	4,312	Norway
45.2[2]	25.8[2]	15.6[2]	8.8[2]	3.9[2]	0.7[2]	...	...	390	494	657	980	1,460	1,909	Oman
45.2	24.0	15.0	9.1	5.1	1.6	23,600	28,300	36,450	45,851	64,449	82,143	105,613	133,477	Pakistan
39.2	27.9	16.4	9.6	5.1	1.8	523	620	800	1,082	1,458	1,960	2,340	2,823	Panama
43.0	25.9	17.0	10.4	3.5	0.2	1,306	1.308	1,613	1,920	2,419	2,997	3,680	4,500	Papua New Guinea

Area and population (continued)

country	area			population (latest estimate)					population (most recent census)				
	square miles	square kilo- metres	rank	total 1984	rank	density		percent annual growth rate 1980-85	census year	total	male (percent)	female (percent)	urban (percent)
						per sq mi	per sq km						
Paraguay	157,048	406,752	54	3,193,000	106	20.3	7.8	2.6	1982	3,035,360	50.1	49.9	42.8
Peru	496,224	1,285,215	19	19,198,000	40	38.5	14.9	2.6	1981	17,005,210	49.7	50.3	64.9
Philippines	115,800	300,000	66	54,170,000	17	459.0	177.2	2.5	1980	48,098,460	50.2	49.8	37.2
Pitcairn Island	1.8	4.5	205	53	206	29.4	11.8	...	1981	53	54.7	45.3	—
Poland	120,727	312,683	64	37,000,000	25	306.5	118.3	0.9	1978	35,061,450	51.3	48.7	57.5
Portugal	35,516	91,985	107	10,198,000	58	287.1	110.9	1.1	1981	9,852,841	48.2	51.8	29.7
Puerto Rico	3,459	8,958	148	3,325,000	103	961.3	371.2	1.0	1980	3,196,520	48.7	51.3	66.8
Qatar	4,400	11,400	143	276,000	151	62.7	24.2	3.7	1981[15]	244,534	63.6	36.4	86.1[2]
Réunion	970	2,512	155	542,000	139	558.8	215.8	2.4	1982	515,798	48.0[7]	52.0[7]	54.9[2]
Romania	91,700	237,500	80	22,794,000	33	248.6	96.0	0.6	1977	21,559,910	49.3	50.7	48.1
Rwanda	10,169	26,338	131	5,836,000	85	573.9	221.6	3.3	1978	4,830,984	48.9	51.1	4.5
St. Christopher and Nevis	101	261	186	45,000	181	445.5	172.4	-0.3	1980	43,309	48.1	51.9	37.1
St. Helena and Ascension	159	412	177	5,500	199	44.0	17.0	1.7	1976	5,147	52.0	48.0	29.6
St. Lucia	238	616	170	124,000	167	521.4	201.3	1.5	1981	120,300	47.2	52.8	52.1[3]
St. Pierre and Miquelon	93	242	188	7,000	197	75.3	28.9	0.8	1982	6,041	49.4	50.6	...
St. Vincent and the Grenadines	150	388	178	138,000	165	922.4	356.1	2.6	1970	86,314	47.3	52.7	27.0
San Marino	24	61	196	23,000	188	965.7	372.9	0.1	1976	20,284	50.4	49.6	92.4[7]
São Tomé and Príncipe	372	964	164	100,000	172	268.8	103.7	1.4	1981	95,000	...	...	...
Saudi Arabia	865,000	2,240,000	12	10,841,000	56	12.5	4.8	4.0	1974	6,939,000	53.5[2]	46.5[2]	66.8[2]
Senegal	75,955	196,722	82	6,352,000	80	83.6	32.3	2.7	1976	4,907,507	49.5	50.5	25.4[2]
Seychelles	175	453	174	65,000	176	369.9	142.8	0.6	1977	61,898	50.4	49.6	37.1
Sierra Leone	27,699	71,740	112	3,805,000	100	137.4	53.0	2.6	1974	2,735,159	54.1	45.9	24.5[2]
Singapore	239	618	169	2,529,000	112	10,582.0	4,092.4	1.1	1980	2,413,945	51.0	49.0	100.0
Solomon Islands	10,640	27,556	129	259,000	152	24.3	9.4	3.0	1976	196,823	52.2	47.8	7.6
Somalia	246,000	637,000	41	5,505,000	86	22.4	8.6	2.6	1975	3,722,000	45.8[2]	54.2[2]	30.2[2]
South Africa	470,413	1,218,364	24	31,788,000	28	67.6	26.1	2.9	1980	27,747,359	49.6[2]	50.4[2]	49.6[2]
South West Africa/Namibia	317,818	823,144	33	1,111,000	130	3.5	1.3	3.0	1981	1,031,927	49.2	50.8	26.0
Spain	194,885	504,750	48	38,435,000	24	197.2	76.1	0.7	1981	37,746,260	49.1	50.9	74.3[2]
Sri Lanka	25,332	65,610	114	15,756,000	45	622.0	240.1	1.7	1981	14,848,364	50.8	49.2	21.5
Sudan, The	966,757	2,503,890	9	21,160,000	36	21.9	8.5	2.8	1983	20,564,364[15]	51.0[6]	49.0[6]	30.6[6]
Suriname	63,251	163,820	86	352,000	143	5.6	2.1	0.1	1980	354,860	49.5	50.5	44.8[2]
Swaziland	6,704	17,364	139	623,000	138	92.9	35.9	2.9	1976	494,534	45.6	54.4	15.2
Sweden	187,901	486,661	49	8,341,000	69	44.4	17.1	0.1	1980	8,320,582	49.5	50.5	83.1
Switzerland	15,943	41,293	120	6,436,000	78	403.7	155.9	0.4	1980	6,365,960	48.9	51.1	57.1
Syria	71,498	185,180	83	9,934,000	60	138.9	53.6	3.3	1981	9,053,000	51.1	48.9	47.1
Taiwan	13,900	36,002	123	18,735,000	41	1,347.8	520.4	1.5	1980	17,968,797	52.2	47.8	70.6[2]
Tanzania	364,886	945,050	30	21,202,000	35	58.1	22.4	3.2	1978	17,512,611	49.2	50.8	13.8
Thailand	198,115	513,115	47	50,382,000	18	254.3	98.2	2.0	1980	46,961,338	50.3	49.7	17.6
Togo	21,925	56,785	115	2,947,000	108	134.4	51.9	2.9	1981	2,700,982	48.2	51.8	15.2
Tokelau	4.7	12.2	203	2,000	202	434.8	166.7	...	1981	1,572	49.4	50.6	...
Tonga	288	747	167	106,000	170	368.1	141.9	2.1	1976	90,085	51.1	48.9	20.3
Trinidad and Tobago	1,980	5,128	150	1,203,000	127	607.6	235.6	1.9	1980	1,059,825	49.8	50.2	21.5[2]
Trust Territory of the Pacific Is.	726	1,880	157	144,000	164	198.4	76.6	2.0	1980	132,929	51.4	48.6	28.4
Tunisia	59,664	154,530	87	7,076,000	74	118.6	45.8	2.5	1984	6,966,173	50.9	49.1	52.8
Turkey	300,948	779,452	36	48,591,000	19	161.5	62.3	2.1	1980	44,736,957	51.6	48.4	43.9
Turks and Caicos Islands	193	500	172	8,000	195	41.4	16.0	1.5	1980	7,436	...	...	...
Tuvalu	9	24	199	9,000	194	971.2	375.0	0.9	1979	7,349	46.8	53.2	...
Uganda	93,104	241,139	77	14,206,000	52	152.6	58.9	2.8	1980	12,630,076	49.5	50.5	8.1
U.S.S.R.	8,649,500	22,402,200	1	273,400,000	3	31.6	12.2	1.0	1979	262,436,200	46.6	53.4	62.0
United Arab Emirates	30,000	77,700	110	1,290,000	126	43.0	16.6	4.1	1981	1,043,225	69.1	31.9	80.8
United Kingdom	94,248	244,100	76	56,236,000	15	596.7	230.4	0.5	1981	55,618,374	48.6	51.4	89.6
United States	3,618,770	9,372,571	4	236,634,000	4	65.4	25.4	0.9	1980	226,545,805	48.6	51.4	73.7
Uruguay	68,037	176,215	85	3,013,000	107	44.3	17.1	0.8	1975	2,788,429	49.0	51.0	83.0
Vanuatu	4,707	12,190	141	131,000	166	27.8	10.7	2.7	1979	111,251	53.1	46.9	17.8
Venezuela	352,144	912,050	32	15,601,000	46	44.3	17.1	3.0	1981	14,516,735	50.0	50.0	85.7
Vietnam	128,052	331,653	60	58,280,000	13	455.1	175.7	2.1	1979	52,741,766	48.5	51.5	19.2
Virgin Islands (U.S.)	136	352	180	102,000	171	750.0	289.8	1.5	1980	96,569	47.8	52.2	29.6
Wallis and Futuna	106	274	184	13,000	191	113.2	43.8	2.7	1983	12,408	50.5	49.5	...
Western Sahara	103,000	266,769	72	152,000	162	1.5	0.6	1.8	1970	76,425	...	...	...
Western Samoa	1,093	2,831	153	160,000	160	146.1	56.4	0.9	1981	156,349	51.8	48.2	21.2
Yemen (Aden)	130,066	336,870	59	2,147,000	117	16.5	6.4	2.9	1973	1,590,275	49.5	50.5	33.3
Yemen (Ṣanʿāʾ)	52,213	135,230	90	6,375,000	79	122.1	47.1	2.7	1981	8,556,974[17]	47.3[18]	52.7[18]	10.2[18]
Yugoslavia	98,766	255,804	73	23,053,000	32	233.4	90.1	0.8	1981	22,424,711	49.4	50.6	47.3
Zaire	905,365	2,344,885	11	32,084,000	27	35.4	13.7	3.0	1976	25,697,575	48.5	51.5	18.2
Zambia	290,586	752,614	37	6,443,000	77	22.2	8.6	3.0	1980	5,679,808	49.0	51.0	43.0
Zimbabwe	150,873	390,759	55	8,060,000	70	53.4	20.6	2.8	1982	7,532,000	49.3	50.7	23.0

age distribution (percent) | population (by decade, '000s)

0–14	15–29	30–44	45–59	60–74	75 and older	1930	1940	1950	1960	1970	1980	1990 projection	2000 projection	country
41.1	28.1	15.4	9.1	4.8	1.5	880	1,111	1,371	1,778	2,290	3,113	3,714	4,662	Paraguay
41.3	27.7	15.6	9.3	—6.1—		5,752	6,784	7,975	9,993	13,248	17,295	22,396	27,569	Peru
42.0	—44.1—				13.9	13,094	16,459	20,988	27,561	36,850	48,316	60,185	74,810	Philippines
32.1	13.2	18.9	13.2	9.4	13.2	—	—	—	—	—	—	—	—	Pitcairn Island
23.9	27.4	18.0	16.9	—13.3—		29,500	31,500	24,824	29,561	32,657	35,805	38,967	41,217	Poland
25.5	23.5	18.0	17.2	11.9	3.9	6,804	7,696	8,405	8,826	9,040	9,580	10,531	11,154	Portugal
31.6	26.4	18.5	12.3	8.3	2.9	1,552	1,880	2,219	2,358	2,718	3,196	3,496	3,824	Puerto Rico
32.3	31.8	25.8	7.8	—2.3—		...	...	47	59	151	237	330	425	Qatar
38.1[7]	29.0[7]	—26.5[7]—		—6.4[7]—		198	221	244	338	447	491	558	617	Réunion
25.7	23.7	19.6	17.1	10.9	3.0	14,141	15,907	16,311	18,407	20,799	22,268	23,994	25,728	Romania
46.6[2]	26.0[2]	14.4[2]	8.5[2]	3.8[2]	0.7[2]	...	...	2,189	2,740	3,679	5,114	7,105	9,845	Rwanda
37.2	30.4	9.5	9.4	10.0	3.5	38	43	49	51	46	45	44	44	St. Christopher and Nevis
34.2	27.7	16.3	10.8	8.4	2.6	4	5	5	5	5	6	6	6	St. Helena and Ascension
49.6	21.3	11.6	9.8	5.5	2.2	60	70	79	94	100	116	138	161	St. Lucia
28.7	26.0	20.4	13.1	8.6	3.2	4	4	5	5	5	6	6	6	St. Pierre and Miquelon
51.2	21.8	11.0	8.8	5.4	1.8	53	61	67	80	86	124	154	188	St. Vincent
24.4	23.0	19.9	17.4	11.4	3.9	10	10	13	15	19	21	23	25	San Marino
...	...	...	...	...	...	...	60	60	64	74	91	114	144	São Tomé and Príncipe
43.9[2]	26.9[2]	16.3[2]	8.4[2]	3.8[2]	0.7[2]	...	...	3,200	4,175	6,120	9,230	13,724	20,327	Saudi Arabia
42.5	27.3	17.2	8.6	3.7	0.1	...	...	2,600	3,076	4,267	5,661	7,430	9,747	Senegal
39.7	26.3	14.1	10.8	6.9	2.2	28	32	36	42	52	64	74	87	Seychelles
36.7	27.2	19.4	9.0	—7.6—		...	...	1,809	2,165	2,692	3,474	4,606	6,090	Sierra Leone
27.0	34.7	19.8	11.3	5.9	1.3	596	751	1,022	1,639	2,075	2,414	2,713	2,967	Singapore
47.9	24.1	14.5	8.4	3.6	1.5	94	94	104	125	163	230	330	476	Solomon Islands
43.3	24.6[2]	15.4[2]	10.5[2]	5.6[2]	0.6[2]	...	...	1,826	2,226	2,790	4,610	5,938	7,156	Somalia
41.8[2]	26.2[2]	15.7[2]	9.9[2]	5.2[2]	1.2[2]	8,541	10,353	12,458	15,925	22,460	28,610	39,018	51,320	South Africa
44.0[2]	25.8[2]	15.6[2]	9.3[2]	4.4[2]	0.9[2]	283	336	405	522	761	1,009	1,200	1,400	South West Africa/ Namibia
25.9[2]	23.6[2]	18.0[2]	17.5[2]	11.1[2]	3.9[2]	23,445	25,757	27,868	30,303	33,779	37,378	40,541	43,362	Spain
35.3	29.6	17.9	10.6	5.2	1.4	5,253	5,972	7,678	9,889	12,514	14,850	18,066	21,076	Sri Lanka
44.1[2]	26.3[2]	15.9[2]	9.0[2]	4.0[2]	0.7[2]	7,500	8,500	9,322	11,256	14,090	18,371	24,950	32,885	Sudan, The
39.3	29.5	13.8	10.0	4.5	2.8	170	193	215	247	292	352	361	423	Suriname
47.7	25.2	13.7	7.9	4.5	2.8	139	154	253	320	409	553	754	1,020	Swaziland
19.4	20.6	21.2	16.7	15.7	6.4	6,142	6,371	7,041	7,498	8,081	8,318	8,399	8,386	Sweden
19.8	23.2	21.6	17.3	12.8	5.4	4,066	4,234	4,715	5,429	6,270	6,366	6,493	6,461	Switzerland
47.9	27.3	12.4	7.9	3.5	1.0	...	2,597	3,495	4,561	6,305	8,704	12,774	17,085	Syria
32.1	32.1	16.5	12.6	5.7	1.0	4,614	5,987	7,619	10,792	14,676	17,805	20,791	24,128	Taiwan
46.2	24.9	14.4	8.5	4.5	1.5	...	...	7,892	10,073	13,273	18,580	25,407	34,814	Tanzania
38.2	29.8	16.3	10.2	—5.5—		11,838	15,296	20,010	26,392	35,745	46,455	56,860	69,530	Thailand
45.6[2]	26.1[2]	15.0[2]	8.7[2]	3.9[2]	0.7[2]	750	834	1,201	1,465	1,954	2,557	3,507	4,688	Togo
...	...	...	...	...	...	1	1	1	2	2	2	2	2	Tokelau
44.4	26.2	14.8	9.5	4.0	1.1	28	37	50	65	80	97	119	140	Tonga
32.9[2]	31.9[2]	16.6[2]	11.1[2]	6.3[2]	1.2[2]	405	510	636	843	1,027	1,060	1,230	1,376	Trinidad and Tobago
46.0	26.7	13.3	8.4	4.5	1.1	70	134	57	77	109	137	170	202	Trust Territory of the Pacific Is.
41.8[3]	27.4[3]	13.6[3]	10.6[3]	5.4[3]	1.2[3]	2,381	2,887	3,530	4,221	5,137	6,367	7,989	9,856	Tunisia
38.5	27.7	16.0	11.2	—6.6—		14,448	17,723	20,809	27,509	35,232	44,438	54,663	67,166	Turkey
...	...	...	...	...	...	5	6	6	6	6	7	9	10	Turks and Caicos Islands
33.4	31.1	14.7	13.0	—7.7—		...	...	5	5	6	7	10	12	Tuvalu
45.2[2]	25.9[2]	15.1[2]	8.9[2]	4.1[2]	0.8[2]	...	...	5,969	7,551	9,806	12,600	16,262	21,396	Uganda
24.4[2]	26.6[2]	19.1[2]	16.9[2]	9.6[2]	3.4[2]	179,000	195,000	180,075	214,335	241,700	265,493	290,155	310,236	U.S.S.R.
28.6	35.1	27.8	6.6	1.7	0.2	...	...	...	795	1,040	1,570	1,916		United Arab Emirates
21.1	22.5	19.2	17.3	14.3	5.6	46,038	48,226	50,290	52,807	55,610	56,252	56,912	57,968	United Kingdom
22.6	27.4	19.1	15.2	11.3	4.4	123,616	132,594	152,271	180,671	204,879	226,505	249,731	267,990	United States
27.0	22.6	19.2	16.9	10.8	3.5	1,734	1,974	2,194	2,531	2,824	3,036	3,166	3,448	Uruguay
45.4	27.5	15.0	7.7	3.4	1.1	...	43	52	65	86	118	151	199	Vanuatu
40.5	29.9	15.8	8.7	4.0	1.1	2,980	3,740	5,145	7,635	10,559	13,913	18,895	25,500	Venezuela
41.7[2]	26.1[2]	16.0[2]	10.4[2]	4.9[2]	0.9[2]	...	...	24,600	30,200	40,064	53,740	69,862	90,121	Vietnam
36.0	24.2	21.5	11.1	5.7	1.4	22	25	27	32	75	97	110	128	Virgin Islands (U.S.)
45.8	24.8	13.8	9.0	5.7	0.9	...	...	7	8	9	11	15	18	Wallis and Futuna
42.9	27.2	16.3	7.4	4.4	1.8	...	...	14	32	76	135	178	229	Western Sahara
44.3	29.1	12.2	9.0	3.8	1.0	45	61	82	111	143	155	166	178	Western Samoa
47.3	20.8	15.8	8.6	—6.6—		...	...	907	1,109	1,436	1,858	2,459	3,312	Yemen (Aden)
45.7[18]	23.2[18]	15.1[18]	10.5[18]	4.7[18]	0.8[18]	...	...	3,622	4,429	4,840	5,820	7,447	9,828	Yemen (Ṣan'ā')
24.5	25.0	19.8	18.3	8.3	3.5	14,360	16,425	16,346	18,402	20,371	22,328	24,107	25,653	Yugoslavia
—52.8—			—47.2—			8,764	10,370	13,055	16,151	21,368	28,291	38,081	52,410	Zaire
47.1[2]	25.8[2]	14.7[2]	8.2[2]	3.6[2]	0.6[2]	1,272	1,484	2,473	3,219	4,295	5,680	7,611	10,276	Zambia
51.0	26.3	13.4	6.5	1.2	1.6	1,100	1,461	2,276	3,538	5,308	7,500	9,200	11,300	Zimbabwe

... Not available.   — None, nil, or not applicable.   [1]Settled population only.   [2]1980 estimate.   [3]1982 estimate.   [4]Yearly register figures; not an official census.   [5]1970 census.   [6]1983 estimate. [7]1981 estimate.   [8]No census ever taken.   [9]Not including territories occupied in the June 1967 war.   [10]Including about 2,100 sq mi (5,440 sq km) occupied by Israel in the June 1967 war. [11]Excluding Israeli-occupied West Bank.   [12]1975 census.   [13]Nauruan population only.   [14]A census was taken in 1973, but the results were officially repudiated.   [15]Provisional.   [16]Sudan census excludes three southern autonomous provinces.   [17]Includes 1,395,123 nonresident Yemeni citizens living abroad.   [18]1980 estimate, based on resident population only.

National capitals

This table presents some of the principal physical and social indicators that characterize the capital cities of each of the countries of the world. Where a country has more than one capital, as does Bolivia, for example, each city so designated is shown. Only data for population and area are dated; the figures represent, so far as possible, the most recent data, published or unpublished, and include any post-census annexations.

The area and population data for "city proper" refer to the total area for inland cities, or land area for cities with a substantial fraction of water area within their city limits, and population living within those boundaries. The data for "metropolitan area" depend in part on the criteria adopted by the individual country to define the term. Metropolitan area in some countries may mean the areas immediately contiguous to the central city whose economy is dependent upon it, whether these areas are actually urban or rural in character. Ideally, a metropolitan area is defined to consist only of the contiguous urban areas, but in practice, with either pre-industrial or, sometimes, post-industrial areas, the distinction in social character or degree of economic dependency can be difficult to establish.

The data for all subsequent categories is simply "latest" because additional dates (and exceptions to them) make for excessive complexity. The data for land use, for example, may represent a different date from the population data because cities do not keep as close track of land use patterns as they do of population and thus demand for city services. "Other" in this part of the compilation may mean "none of the other four categories" or "residue of columns actually containing figures." For all categories listed after population, the data refer to the city proper unless otherwise noted.

Employment data usually refer to labour force rather than economically active population. Primary activity includes agriculture, forestry, fishing, and mining; secondary includes manufacturing, construction, and public utilities. The service, or tertiary, sector is divided into two main parts—the general service sector and the governmental activities that usually form a substantial part of national capitals' employment. The proportion of the population employed should usually not be interpreted in isolation, as a number of supplemental factors must often be taken into account.

National capitals

country	capital	population							land use (percent)				
		date of census (C) or estimate (E)	city proper			metropolitan area			built up	streets	agriculture	green	other
			population	area (sq km)	density (per sq km)	population	area (sq km)	density (per sq km)					
Afghanistan	Kabul	1982E	1,036,407	213	4,866	...	...	...	...	...	...	...	...
Albania	Tiranë	1980E	194,000	26	7,462	...	...	...	...	...	...	...	...
Algeria	Algiers	1977C	1,523,000	186	8,188	1,735,226	786	2,209	...	...	...	...	...
American Samoa	Pago Pago	1980C	3,075	...	...	—	—	—	...	...	...	...	...
Andorra	Andorra La Vella	1982C	14,928	59	253	—	—	—	...	...	...	...	...
Angola	Luanda	1984E	1,200,000	125	9,600	...	...	...	...	...	...	...	...
Anguilla	The Valley					...	...	...	...	...	...	...	...
Antigua and Barbuda	Saint John's	1979E	25,000	73	342	...	...	...	...	...	...	...	...
Argentina	Buenos Aires	1980C	2,922,829	200	14,651	9,766,030	3,880	2,517	...	...	...	...	...
Australia	Canberra	1981C	219,323	82	2,675	239,798	604	397	5.4	0.9	...	2.9	90.8
Austria	Vienna	1981C	1,531,346	415	3,690	1,984,821	3,862	514	—11.2—		34.0	18.8	36.0
Bahamas, The	Nassau	1980C		—		135,437	207	654	...	...	...	...	...
Bahrain	Manama	1981C	108,684	...	...	224,643	...	...	...	...	...	...	...
Bangladesh	Dhākā	1981C	1,850,000	259	7,143	3,458,602	...	...	...	...	...	...	...
Barbados	Bridgetown	1980C	7,466	23	325	89,450	39	2,294	...	...	...	...	...
Belgium	Brussels	1983C	137,738	33	4,174	989,877	162	6,110	...	...	5.1	...	94.9
Belize	Belmopan	1980E	4,500	33	136	...	...	...	...	...	...	...	...
Benin	Porto-Novo (official)	1982E	208,258	16	13,016	...	...	...	...	...	...	...	...
	Cotonou (de facto)	1982E	487,020	20	24,351	...	...	...	...	...	...	...	...
Bermuda	Hamilton	1981C	1,624	0.7	2,312	...	...	...	...	...	...	...	...
Bhutan	Thimphu (official)	1982E	15,000	...	...	...	...	...	...	...	...	...	...
	Paro (administrative)	1982E	3,000	...	...	...	...	...	...	...	...	...	...
Bolivia	La Paz (administrative)	1984E	953,634	120	7,947	...	...	...	...	...	...	...	...
	Sucre (judicial)	1984E	84,505	17	4,971	...	...	...	...	...	...	...	...
Botswana	Gaborone	1984E	79,000	71	1,113	...	...	...	...	...	...	...	...
Brazil	Brasilia	1980C	411,305	1,014	406	1,176,748	5,771	203.9	...	...	...	...	...
British Virgin Islands	Road Town	1980C	2,525	...	...	...	...	...	...	...	...	...	...
Brunei	Bandar Seri Begawan	1982E	51,600	13	4,000	...	570	...	...	...	...	...	...
Bulgaria	Sofia	1981E	1,070,358	167	6,409	1,149,092	1,113	1,033	...	...	...	...	...
Burkina Faso	Ouagadougou	1984E	359,801	...	...	...	...	...	...	...	...	...	...
Burma	Rangoon	1983C	2,458,000	78	31,513	...	...	...	...	...	...	...	...
Burundi	Bujumbura	1981E	165,940	62	2,676	499,530	1,322	378	...	...	...	...	...
Cameroon	Yaoundé	1981E	435,900	120	3,632	...	...	...	...	...	...	...	...
Canada	Ottawa	1981C	295,163	110	2,683	717,978	3,999	180	...	...	...	...	...
Cape Verde	Praia	1980C	37,676	...	...	...	...	...	...	...	...	...	...
Cayman Islands	George Town	1979C	2,705	...	...	15,000	197	76	...	...	...	...	...
Central African Republic	Bangui	1982E	387,100	67	5,778	...	...	...	...	...	...	...	...
Chad	N'Djamena	1979E	303,000	15	20,200	...	...	...	...	...	...	...	...
Chile	Santiago	1984E	4,225,299	422	10,013	...	...	...	...	...	...	...	...
China	Beijing	1982C	5,597,972	2,701	2,073	9,230,687	16,807	549	...	0.7	20.9	...	78.4
Christmas Island	The Settlement at Flying Fish Cove	1980E	1,200	...	...	...	...	...	...	...	...	...	...
Cocos (Keeling) Islands	West Island	1981E	242	5.0	48	...	...	...	...	...	...	...	...
Colombia	Bogotá	1979E	3,996,650	1,518	2,633	4,150,000	1,714	2,421	...	...	...	...	...
Comoros	Moroni	1980C	20,112	...	...	...	...	...	...	...	...	...	...
Congo	Brazzaville	1980E	422,400	55	7,680	...	...	...	...	...	...	...	...
Cook Islands	Rarotonga Island	1981C	9,530	26	367	...	...	...	...	...	...	...	...
Costa Rica	San José	1984C	245,370	45	5,499	652,660	220	2,967	...	...	...	...	...
Cuba	Havana	1981C	1,924,886	740	2,601	1,975,000	...	...	...	...	...	...	...
Cyprus	Nicosia	1982C	123,298	...	...	149,071	...	...	37.8	10.3	18.3	3.0	30.6
Czechoslovakia	Prague	1984E	1,187,296	496	2,394	1,249,592	779	1,604	...	...	...	...	...
Denmark	Copenhagen	1982E	645,198	121	5,332	1,377,064	986	1,397	41.8	14.7	...	9.7	33.8
Djibouti	Djibouti	1980E	200,000	...	...	...	...	...	...	...	...	...	...
Dominica	Roseau	1981C	8,300	0.8	10,375	...	7.0	...	...	...	...	...	...
Dominican Republic	Santo Domingo	1981C	1,313,200	...	...	...	1,477	...	...	...	...	...	...
Ecuador	Quito	1982C	858,736	636	1,350	...	...	...	...	...	...	...	...
Egypt	Cairo	1983E	5,881,000	214	27,481	8,500,000[4]	...	...	...	...	...	...	...
El Salvador	San Salvador	1983E	445,054	72	6,160	720,000[5]	...	...	...	...	...	...	...
Equatorial Guinea	Malabo	1974E	25,000	...	...	...	...	...	...	...	...	...	...
Ethiopia	Addis Ababa	1982E	1,408,100	240	5,867	...	...	...	...	...	...	...	...
Faeroe Islands	Thorshavn	1983E	14,183	15	925	...	...	...	...	...	...	...	...
Falkland Islands	Port Stanley	1980C	1,050	0.6	404	...	3.2	...	...	...	...	...	...
Fiji	Suva	1980E	68,178	23	2,964	133,119	103	1,292	...	...	...	...	...
Finland	Helsinki	1984E	484,019	184	2,631	934,628	2,645	353	9.2	1.1	9.5	2.8	77.4

A relatively high ratio of employed to total population may be indicative of either an older, largely working-age, population or a younger, demographically vigorous capital city that simultaneously attracts jobs, governmental or industrial, and the ambitious working-age population from the hinterlands to fill them. When these proportions are relatively low, however, they may mean a relatively healthy employment situation or one complicated by high immigration of job seekers. A very low proportion is characteristic of only the least developed national capitals and may indicate large numbers of un- or under-employed whom the government has been unable either to relocate or to employ in the capital.

Among the economic indicators enumerated, dwellings refer to occupied dwellings, wherever possible. The figure for average household size has been picked up as found; when it is unknown, it is calculated as of the date of the housing information, but such calculations are less accurate than properly defined housing census data. The data on energy consumption consist of the city's total consumption figure divided by the midyear or yearly average population figure. Water consumption data include all water delivered within the city limits, whether for human consumption, industrial use, irrigation and landscaping, agriculture, etc.

In the compilation of data for the social indicators, physician refers only to graduates of accredited medical schools and excludes "traditional" practitioners. Hospital beds include beds of whatever specialization (that is, psychiatric beds as well as general hospital beds).

To a certain extent, and particularly in the least developed countries, some indicators may appear misleadingly high, since the manpower and physical plant supporting a particular economic or social capability may be located predominantly or exclusively in the capital city. This may be simply an efficient distribution of, say, medical services to the greatest number of people at the locus within the country to which the best transportation exists, or it may represent a maldistribution of manpower and matériel feeding the capital at the expense of the hinterland. In either case, the facilities are available to the residents of the capital and represent services that other parts of the country may miss.

number employed	percent of population	primary	secondary	tertiary, nongovernment	tertiary, government	dwellings	average household size	electrical energy consumption (KW-hr per capita/yr)	water consumption (cu m per capita/yr)	population per physician	hospital beds per 1,000 population	passenger cars per 1,000 population	telephone subscribers per 1,000 population	country
...	...	...	...	...	...	...	...	...	...	1,314[1]	2.3	8.0	18.0	Afghanistan
...	...	...	...	...	...	...	...	...	...	243	15.5	...	...	Albania
359,487	20.8[2]	5.4[2]	28.4[2]	41.5[2]	24.7[2]	199,000[2]	7.4[2]	...	...	1,179[2]	2.9[2]	6.3[2]	122.3	Algeria
...	...	...	...	...	...	425	...	...	...	...	...	...	...	American Samoa
...	...	...	...	...	...	...	...	...	...	...	...	...	279.0	Andorra
...	...	...	...	...	...	...	...	399.6	44.2	2,682	6.8	110.0	40.4	Angola
...	...	...	...	...	...	...	...	...	...	...	...	...	396.0	Anguilla
...	...	...	...	...	...	...	...	...	...	...	...	...	162.0	Antigua and Barbuda
3,854,990[2]	38.9[2]	0.1[2]	34.5[2]	—65.4[2]—		918,930	3.1	1,591	294.4	141	...	194.7	316.3	Argentina
101,515	45.0	0.9	8.7	57.9	32.5	72,703	3.0	...	...	173	4.0	389.0	678.0	Australia
769,225	49.0	0.3	37.7	51.4	10.6	816,317	1.9	4,297	99.8	252	15.7	306.1	718.2	Austria
...	...	...	...	...	...	...	...	...	28.4	...	...	...	396.8	Bahamas, The
...	...	...	...	...	...	21,050	5.8	...	...	...	...	114.0	203.3	Bahrain
297,906	16.1	—	48.1	—51.9—		518,612	4.3	313	—	6,068	...	19.6	25.4	Bangladesh
...	...	...	...	...	...	...	...	...	...	...	...	...	350.7	Barbados
403,051[2]	38.7[2]	—	24.8[2]	—75.2[6]—		468,200	2.5	924	...	...	...	...	723.8	Belgium
...	...	...	...	...	...	...	...	...	...	...	...	...	232.0	Belize
...	...	...	...	...	...	22,579	8.5	...	...	...	...	...	...	Benin
...	...	...	...	...	...	63,147	7.1	...	...	...	...	...	...	
2,054	50.7	1.9	21.0	—77.1—		951	2.2	...	...	...	...	...	1,261.1	Bermuda
...	...	...	...	...	...	...	...	148	...	800	70.6	...	75.0	Bhutan
221,685	34.9	2.9	26.6	70.5	99.3	146,029	4.3	...	...	...	...	...	...	Bolivia
18,144	240	6.6	24.0	—69.4—		13,934	4.3	...	...	...	...	...	100.4	
...	...	...	...	...	...	10,717	5.6	...	...	...	...	...	...	Botswana
131,004	25.0	5.2	32.8	41.1	20.9	254,071	4.5	...	...	268	2.8	184.0	157.0	Brazil
...	...	...	...	...	...	...	...	...	...	413	13.7	...	509.0	British Virgin Islands
...	...	...	...	...	...	...	...	...	...	...	...	...	131.2	Brunei
...	...	...	...	...	...	...	...	...	...	157	...	46.4	351.0	Bulgaria
...	...	...	...	...	...	...	...	...	...	...	...	...	...	Burkina Faso
...	...	...	...	...	...	...	...	...	...	...	...	...	...	Burma
...	...	...	...	...	...	...	...	...	...	...	...	...	...	Burundi
...	...	...	...	...	...	...	...	...	...	...	...	...	...	Cameroon
...	...	...	...	...	...	121,705	2.3	...	...	...	...	...	784.6	Canada
...	...	...	...	...	...	...	...	...	...	...	...	...	...	Cape Verde
3,084[2]	35.2[2]	...	...	...	13.7[2]	2,110[2]	4.2[2]	...	...	...	...	...	326.9[2]	Cayman Islands
65,502	21.8	27.3	24.1	40.3	8.1	47,500	5.6	172	...	...	...	...	60.0	Central African Republic
...	...	...	...	...	...	...	...	...	...	...	...	...	...	Chad
1,464,500[2]	33.9[2]	4.2[2]	28.2[2]	—67.6—		930,054	4.6	2,720	...	1,988	2.9	79.1	133.1	Chile
3,417,000	62.1	3.7	48.9	41.5	5.9	...	...	995	44.0	152	5.0	3.3	...	China
...	...	...	...	...	...	...	...	...	...	...	...	...	...	Christmas Island
...	...	...	...	...	...	...	...	...	...	...	17.0	...	236.7	Cocos (Keeling) Islands
814,233	31.7	...	...	...	...	333,896	5.3	950	...	539[3]	...	31.7	107.3	Colombia
...	...	...	...	...	...	...	...	...	...	...	...	...	...	Comoros
43,098	14.4	7.4	27.5	51.8	13.3	54,296	5.5	...	...	...	...	...	...	Congo
3,487	36.6	9.9	16.7	—73.4—		1,758	5.2	...	...	...	...	...	133.2	Cook Islands
172,036[2]	34.7[2]	3.4[2]	28.8[2]	—67.8[2]—		127,129[2]	5.6[2]	...	...	...	...	...	...	Costa Rica
714,687	35.7	1.8	9.2	82.4	6.6	526,441	3.8	1,165	225.8	337	...	...	117.6	Cuba
...	...	...	...	...	...	...	...	...	...	...	...	...	393.3	Cyprus
664,942	56.2	1.3	37.4	57.0	4.3	470,004	...	...	116.7	225	...	230.5	539.2	Czechoslovakia
227,282	46.3	1.0	18.9	67.8	12.3	281,075	1.7	...	...	286	16.8	171.0	...	Denmark
...	...	...	...	...	...	...	...	484	36.2	...	4.0	...	17.0	Djibouti
3,329	33.5	...	...	...	23.3	2,388	4.2	...	...	...	...	...	132.0	Dominica
...	...	...	...	...	...	321,120[2]	4.8[2]	...	...	...	...	...	102.3	Dominican Republic
199,846	33.3	1.9	27.8	—70.3—		129,402	5.0	...	...	...	...	...	121.8	Ecuador
278,025	5.5	1.9	61.2	—36.9—		...	...	385	32.8	630	...	29.3	37.6	Egypt
...	...	...	...	...	...	301,222[6]	5.0[6]	1	...	400	...	94.2	45.2	El Salvador
...	...	...	...	...	...	...	...	...	...	...	...	...	...	Equatorial Guinea
...	...	...	...	...	...	...	...	...	...	...	...	...	48.1	Ethiopia
4,607	43.0	5.2	29.7	42.0	23.1	3,674	3.5	...	...	394.0	20.0	...	...	Faeroe Islands
574	56.3	...	...	...	...	337	3.0	...	...	...	...	...	295.0	Falkland Islands
40,128[2]	31.5[2]	4.3[2]	19.4[2]	—76.3[2]—		...	5.3	...	...	...	...	...	209.5	Fiji
244,379	50.4	...	...	...	...	218,572	2.2	...	...	...	...	...	957.7	Finland

National capitals (continued)

country	capital	date of census (C) or estimate (E)	city proper population	area (sq km)	density (per sq km)	metropolitan area population	area (sq km)	density (per sq km)	built up	streets	agriculture	green	other
France	Paris	1982C	2,176,243	105	20,726	8,706,963	2,312	3,766	50.8	19.6	—	22.5	7.1
French Guiana	Cayenne	1982C	38,135	23	1,658	47,396	2,060	23	...	...	...	...	...
French Polynesia	Papeete	1981E	23,400	24	975	...	110	...	...	...	...	...	...
Gabon	Libreville	1983E	350,000	40	8,750	...	...	...	...	...	...	...	...
Gambia, The	Banjul	1983C	44,536	12	3,642	147,394	88	1,679	...	...	...	...	...
Germany, East	East Berlin	1983E	1,173,028	403	2,911	...	...	...	...	...	0.2	0.3	99.5
Germany, West	Bonn	1984E	291,509	141	2,063	...	...	...	23.2	6.4	16.4	9.9	44.1
Ghana	Accra	1984C	...	...	...	1,420,066	781	702	...	...	...	...	...
Gibraltar	Gibraltar	1983E	31,183	5.8	5,340	—	—	—	...	...	...	...	...
Greece	Athens	1981C	885,737	39	22,711	3,027,331	428	7,073	...	...	9.9		90.1
Greenland	Godthaab	1982E	9,717	...	...				...	...	...	...	...
Grenada	Saint George's	1979E	7,500	...	...	25,000	68	368	...	...	44.5[2]	24.3[2]	31.2[2]
Guadeloupe	Basse-Terre	1982C	13,700	4.3	3,186	...	...	...	...	...	...	...	...
Guam	Agana	1980C	881	3.0	294	...	...	...	...	...	...	...	...
Guatemala	Guatemala City	1981C	749,784	184	4,075	1,100,000	2,126	517	...	...	...	...	...
Guinea	Conakry	1980E	763,000	308	2,477	...	...	...	...	...	...	...	...
Guinea-Bissau	Bissau	1979C	105,273	37.6	2,800	...	...	...	...	...	...	...	...
Guyana	Georgetown	1976E	72,049	6.5	11,084	187,056	...	...	...	...	...	...	...
Haiti	Port-au-Prince	1982C	449,831	32	14,057	763,188	80	9,540	...	...	...	...	...
Honduras	Tegucigalpa	1983C	508.044	70	7,258	441,904[7]	1,396	317[7]	...	...	...	...	...
Hong Kong	Victoria	1981C	590,771	15	39,385	4,896,560	1,068	4,585	...	...	...	...	...
Hungary	Budapest	1984E	2,064,000	525	3,931	2,600,000	...	...	...	3.9	5.9	9.3	80.9
Iceland	Reykjavik	1983E	87,309	100	873	125,747[8]	120	1,047[8]	...	...	...	...	...
India	New Delhi	1981C	301,801	437	691	5,729,283	1,039	5,514	47.5	18.6	3.2	9.5	21.2
Indonesia	Jakarta	1980C	6,503,449	590	11,023	6,700,000	637	10,518	...	...	...	...	...
Iran	Tehrān	1982E	5,734,199	615	9,324	...	...	...	...	...	...	...	...
Iraq	Baghdad	1977C	...	...	...	3,205,600	5,023	638	...	...	...	...	...
Ireland	Dublin	1981C	525,882	117	4,495	1,110,000	...	...	...	...	...	...	...
Israel	Jerusalem	1983C	428,668	107	4,006	...	...	...	...	...	...	...	...
Italy	Rome	1983E	2,830,650	1,508	1,877	...	...	...	...	...	...	...	...
Ivory Coast	Abidjan	1981E	...	...	...	1,686,100	...	...	...	...	...	...	...
Jamaica	Kingston	1982C	100,637	22	4,574	393,590	...	...	...	...	...	...	...
Japan	Tokyo	1984E	8,389,758	596	14,071	28,644,523[10]	10,626	2,696[10]	21.7	5.3	1.6	1.0	70.4
Jordan	Amman	1979C	648,587	100	6,486	...	...	...	47.1	5.9	5.9	3.5	37.6
Kampuchea	Phnom Penh	1981E	400,000	46	8,696	500,000	...	...	...	...	...	...	...
Kenya	Nairobi	1984E	1,103,554	684	1,613	...	...	...	20.7	1.0	28.1	3.4	46.8
Kiribati	Bairiki	1979C	1,956	...	...	17,921	16	1,120	...	...	...	...	...
Korea, North	Pyongyang	1981E	1,283,000	200	6,415	...	700	...	...	...	...	...	...
Korea, South	Seoul	1983E	9,204,344	611	15,064	...	...	...	52.2	6.6		0.5	40.7
Kuwait	Kuwait City	1980C	60,365	7.6	7,943	780,000	11,230	69	...	...	...	...	...
Laos	Vientiane	1981E	210,000	51	4,118	...	...	...	...	...	...	...	...
Lebanon	Beirut	1975C	...	18	...	1,172,000	67	17,493	...	...	...	...	...
Lesotho	Maseru	1980E	30,000	23	1,304	277,307	145	1,912	...	...	...	...	...
Liberia	Monrovia	1980E	243,200	90	2,702	...	...	...	...	...	...	...	...
Libya	Tripoli	1981E	858,500	...	...	...	...	...	...	...	...	...	...
Liechtenstein	Vaduz	1983E	4,900	17	288	...	...	...	...	...	...	...	...
Luxembourg	Luxembourg	1981C	78,924	52	1,518	112,000	...	...	14.0	9.8	—	76.2 —	
Macau	Macau	1981C	223,584	5.4	41,404	241,730	15.5	15,595	...	...	...	...	...
Madagascar	Antananarivo	1984E	700,000	72	9,700	900,000	1,195	753	...	...	...	...	...
Malawi	Lilongwe	1984E	172,100	218	789	...	...	...	...	...	...	...	...
Malaysia	Kuala Lumpur	1980C	919,610	244	3,777	1,250,000	...	...	...	...	...	...	...
Maldives	Male	1984E	38,000	2.8	13,571	...	...	...	...	...	...	...	...
Mali	Bamako	1980E	440,000	...	...	...	...	...	...	...	...	...	...
Malta	Valletta	1983E	14,040	0.7	19,286	...	...	...	...	...	...	...	...
Martinique	Fort-de-France	1982C	97,800	44	2,223	117,938	65	1,814	...	...	...	...	...
Mauritania	Nouakchott	1977C	135,000	...	...	...	...	...	...	...	...	...	...
Mauritius	Port Louis	1983C	132,200	43	3,074	...	...	...	34.3	3.1	9.3	9.7	43.6
Mayotte	Dzaoudzi	1978C	4,256	6.7	635	...	...	...	...	...	...	...	...
Mexico	Mexico City	1980C	8,831,079	1,479	5,971	14,400,000[4]	2,286	6,299[4]	...	...	...	...	...
Monaco	Monaco	1982C	27,063	1.9	14,244	50,000	...	...	...	...	...	...	...
Mongolia	Ulan Bator	1981E	435,400	2,000	218	...	...	...	...	...	...	...	...
Montserrat	Plymouth	1980C	1,590	1.6	994	...	...	...	...	...	...	...	...
Morocco	Rabat	1982C	518,616	...	...	865,100[5]	1,275	679[5]	...	...	...	...	...
Mozambique	Maputo	1982E	785,500	602	1,305	...	...	...	...	...	...	...	...
Nauru	Yaren	1977C	413[11]	...	...	—	—	—	...	...	...	...	...
Nepal	Kathmandu	1981C	235,200	26	9,046	195,747[12]	...	...	12.5	9.1	23.7	10.0	44.7
Netherlands, The	Amsterdam (national)	1983E	687,397	168	4,092	936,410	458	2,045	...	...	...	...	...
	Hague, The (seat of government)	1983E	449,338	65	6,913	674,546	210	3,212	56.0	1.1	16.1	24.1	2.7
Netherlands Antilles	Willemstad	1970E	50,000	...	...	...	...	...	...	...	...	...	...
New Caledonia	Nouméa	1983C	60,112	46	1,315	85,098	1,637	52	...	...	...	...	...
New Zealand	Wellington	1983E	134,300	263	511	342,500	1,637	209	...	...	...	...	...
Nicaragua	Managua	1979E	552,900	70	7,899	595,713	816	730	...	...	...	...	...
Niger	Niamey	1981E	343,600	844	407	...	...	...	...	...	...	...	...
Nigeria	Lagos	1982E	1,404,000	70	20,057	2,000,000	...	...	...	...	...	...	...
Niue	Alofi	1979C	960	—	—	—	—	—	...	...	...	...	...
Norfolk Island	Kingston	1981C	...	...	...	...	...	...	...	...	...	...	...
Norway	Oslo	1984E	447,257	454	985	725,000[7]	1,420	511[7]	...	...	...	...	...
Oman	Muscat	1981E	50,000	...	...	...	...	...	...	...	...	...	...
Pakistan	Islāmābād	1981C	201,000	65	3,092	335,000	906	370	...	...	...	...	...
Panama	Panama City	1980C	388,638	106	3,666	625,000	7,208	87	...	...	...	...	...
Papua New Guinea	Port Moresby	1984E	...	...	...	144,300	270	534	...	...	...	...	...
Paraguay	Asunción	1983E	479,647	117	4,100	645,726[7]	267	2,418[7]	...	16.2		4.2	79.6
Peru	Lima	1981C	375,957	...	...	4,600,000	3,900	1,179	...	...	...	...	...
Philippines	Manila	1983C	1,725,500	38	45,408	6,406,300	832	7,700	...	...	...	...	...
Pitcairn Island	Adamstown	1984C	60	0.1	593	—	—	—	...	...	...	...	...
Poland	Warsaw	1982E	1,628,900	485	3,359	2,341,800	3,794	617	38.1	1.7	29.9	1.3	29.0

employment: number employed	percent of population	employment by sectors (percent): primary	secondary	tertiary, nongovernment	tertiary, government	housing: dwellings	average household size	electrical energy, consumption (KW-hr per capita/yr)	water consumption (cu m per capita/yr)	population per physician	hospital beds per 1,000 population	passenger cars per 1,000 population	telephone subscribers per 1,000 population	country
1,948,982[2]	20.6[2]	0.1[2]	25.4[2]	74.4[2]	0.1[2]	1,257,414	1.7	4,310	101.2	281	...	396.9	622.5	France
10,725	32.2	5.7	22.0	—64.7—		...	...	...	...	...	...	...	336.8	French Guiana
...	...	...	...	...	...	...	...	...	...	...	...	...	274.1	French Polynesia
...	...	...	...	...	...	...	...	...	...	...	...	...	35.9	Gabon
...	...	...	...	...	...	...	...	...	...	...	...	...	20.0	Gambia, The
630,070	54.1	0.9	33.7	—65.4—		477,473	2.4	...	...	246	12.8	166.4	411.6	Germany, East
117,900	41.4	...	...	...	...	116,961	...	892	...	354	16.0	345.4	747.2	Germany, West
...	...	...	...	...	...	...	...	...	104.5[2]	...	...	...	39.2	Ghana
11,823	39.9	—	24.6	62.2	13.2	7,731	4.3	1,889	19.4[6]	1,481	...	291.3	333.2	Gibraltar
...	...	...	...	...	...	766,796[2]	5.5[2]	...	...	...	9.6[2]	163.0[2]	535.3	Greece
3,509	46.9	5.9	30.7	35.5	27.9	2,502	3.9	...	...	607	68.4	...	...	Greenland
2,436	38.6	1.8	14.0	—84.2—		1,507	4.9						990.0	Grenada
...	...	...	...	...	...	...	...	...	...	813	...	...	558.1	Guadeloupe
...	...	...	...	...	...	294	2.3							Guam
269,827	35.8	...	...	...	...	140,917	4.9						111.3	Guatemala
...	...	...	...	...	...	...	...	...	...	...	...	...	...	Guinea
23,207	21.6	12.1	11.7	41.5	34.7	19,416	5.5						25.2	Guinea-Bissau
18,951	30.0	1.0	8.2	—90.8—		14,048	4.5						120.7	Guyana
203,495[2]	28.3[2]	2.6[2]	27.2[2]	—70.2—		91,413	4.9						40.0	Haiti
100,625	32.9	...	...	...	...	50,786	5.4							Honduras
2,404,067[2]	48.2[2]	2.0[2]	41.8[2]	—56.2—		1,244,738[2]	3.9[2]	2,318[2]	101.8[2]	1,280[2]	4.3[2]	42.4[2]	277.5[2]	Hong Kong
...	...	...	...	...	...	725,000	3.9	2,663	143.5	182	...	140.1	330.7	Hungary
...	...	...	...	...	...	...	...	...	...	...	...	...	651.2	Iceland
773,988[2,9]	14.6[2,9]	0.5[2,9]	34.1[2,9]	—65.4[2,9]—		664,647	...	347	34.8	...	...	21.2	51.3	India
1,533,840	25.9	1.3	34.4	—64.3—		...	...	...	...	1,968	0.8	46.4	34.4	Indonesia
...	...	...	...	...	...	...	...	...	...	...	...	79.6	94.3	Iran
219,978	38.7	0.5	40.0	51.6	7.9	289,382	...	605.8	67.4	1,729	...	10.3	45.3	Iraq
...	...	...	...	...	...	127,042	4.3	...	...	...	...	...	322.8	Ireland
...	...	...	...	...	...	108,400	3.8	...	...	...	...	...	349.1	Israel
541,210	19.5	0.8	29.8	—69.4—		952,526	...	1,717.6	...	...	...	...	569.6	Italy
...	...	...	...	...	...	...	...	847.4	...	...	1.2	...	5.0	Ivory Coast
106,791[2]	31.5[2]	0.8[2]	17.6[2]	—81.6—		31,199	3.6	...	...	...	...	...	129.8	Jamaica
6,507,064	25.2	0.2	28.7	68.1	3.0	2,865,900	2.8	3,793	127.4	231	10.8	145.3	818.6	Japan
84,283	13.1	...	...	...	...	108,960	6.6	...	...	525	2.7	...	...	Jordan
...	...	...	...	...	...	...	...	...	...	...	...	...	...	Kampuchea
284,534	30.9	2.7	32.2	—65.1—		...	...	1,021	...	...	5.9	...	128.6	Kenya
...	...	...	...	...	...	...	...	...	...	...	...	...	164.0	Kiribati
...	...	...	...	...	...	...	...	...	...	...	...	...	...	Korea, North
...	...	...	...	...	...	892,084	...	773	50.2	1,024	...	15.6	176.9	Korea, South
87,370	11.2	2.3	39.1	—58.6—		8,617	...	...	...	...	...	...	159.9	Kuwait
...	...	...	...	...	...	...	...	...	...	...	...	...	...	Laos
...	...	...	...	...	...	...	...	...	...	...	...	...	195.0	Lebanon
...	...	...	...	...	...	...	...	...	...	6,028	2.8	7.8	...	Lesotho
...	...	...	...	...	...	...	...	...	263.9	...	...	...	35.0	Liberia
126,626	17.9	18.3	2.1	—79.6—		120,012	7.1	...	77.9	...	...	...	12.0	Libya
2,441	53.0	2.7	35.1	—62.1—		1,772	2.5	...	...	701	...	656.4	962.4	Liechtenstein
...	...	...	...	...	...	...	...	...	...	274	...	...	1,325.0	Luxembourg
47,965	19.9	0.1	98.8	—1.1—		...	...	997	48.8	...	...	...	57.8	Macau
...	...	...	...	...	...	...	...	...	...	...	...	...	...	Madagascar
29,610	30.0	...	...	...	...	22,406	4.6	...	...	...	...	...	17.5	Malawi
350,236	38.1	4.8	28.6	47.8	18.8	188,228	4.8	...	...	...	2.6	...	184.5	Malaysia
9,426	31.9	6.9	27.1	58.2	7.8	3,053	9.7	...	...	4,700	...	...	10.9	Maldives
...	...	...	...	...	...	...	...	...	...	...	...	...	...	Mali
...	...	...	...	...	...	...	...	...	...	...	...	...	608.8	Malta
31,826	32.5	0.6	5.1	—84.5—		27,341	3.6	...	...	156	...	...	...	Martinique
27,905	20.8	...	...	...	...	26,437	5.0	...	...	...	...	...	...	Mauritania
...	...	...	...	...	...	...	...	...	...	...	...	...	190.0	Mauritius
862	20.8	12.1	18.4	27.2	42.3	852	4.6	...	...	...	...	9.4	...	Mayotte
4,671,677[2]	51.6[2]	0.9[2]	34.6[2]	56.4[2]	8.1[2]	1,863,093	5.0	0.6	...	554	...	188.3	122.9	Mexico
...	...	...	...	...	...	...	...	...	...	...	...	...	607.1	Monaco
...	...	3.0	13.7	—83.3—		...	...	...	...	...	...	...	53.0	Mongolia
...	...	...	...	...	...	425	3.0	...	...	...	...	...	160.6	Montserrat
...	...	...	...	...	...	71,426	5.1	...	...	...	...	...	...	Morocco
...	...	...	...	...	...	...	...	...	...	...	...	...	...	Mozambique
...	...	...	...	...	...	58[11]	7.1[11]	...	...	...	...	...	219.0	Nauru
198,055	24.5	0.7	34.4	—64.9—		302,000	2.4	...	...	...	...	...	665.0	Nepal
125,430	23.8	1.7	28.6	—69.7—		198,730[13]	2.6[13]	...	...	...	...	...	554.3	Netherlands, The
...	...	...	...	...	...	...	...	...	...	...	...	...	...	Netherlands Antilles
21,161	21.9	0.9	19.9	—79.2—		...	...	...	...	...	...	...	402.5	New Caledonia
69,600	51.3	0.6	19.4	67.5	12.5	48,426	2.8	...	...	...	...	...	770.7	New Zealand
103,209	24.0	1.7	28.7	—69.6—		...	...	...	...	...	...	...	...	Nicaragua
...	...	...	...	...	...	...	...	...	...	...	...	...	...	Niger
216	22.7	1.4	25.9	—67.6—		...	...	...	...	...	...	...	177.5	Nigeria
...	...	...	...	...	...	...	...	...	...	...	...	...	...	Niue
...	...	...	...	...	...	...	...	...	...	...	...	...	548.3	Norfolk Island
246,245	55.3	0.3	20.9	—78.1—		222,291	2.0	...	...	204	6.4	341.7	935.6	Norway
...	...	...	...	...	...	...	...	15,678	144.5	...	134	...	...	Oman
...	...	...	...	...	...	...	...	...	...	...	...	...	34.8	Pakistan
156,435	31.6	3.4	20.0	—76.6—		...	...	...	...	...	...	...	263.9	Panama
...	...	...	...	...	...	...	...	...	...	...	...	...	165.2	Papua New Guinea
...	...	...	...	...	...	91,112	5.0	...	...	...	...	...	71.0	Paraguay
...	...	...	...	...	...	...	...	...	...	...	...	...	84.3	Peru
...	...	...	...	...	...	301,356	5.4	4,023	169.8	...	...	43.8	74.8	Philippines
...	...	...	...	...	...	...	...	...	...	...	...	...	240.0	Pitcairn Island
815,037	51.1	0.5	42.7	53.7	3.1	544,406	2.9	...	...	146	8.1[2]	163.9	293.1	Poland

National capitals   (continued)

country	capital	date of census (C) or estimate (E)	city proper population	area (sq km)	density (per sq km)	metropolitan area population	area (sq km)	density (per sq km)	built up	streets	agriculture	green	other
Portugal	Lisbon	1981C	807,167	87	9,235	1,328,966	...	...	...	...	...	...	...
Puerto Rico	San Juan	1980C	422,701	97	4,358	1,535,000	697	2,202	...	...	...	...	...
Qatar	Doha	1980E	190,000	...	...	...	...	...	...	...	...	...	...
Réunion	Saint-Denis	1982C	109,100	17	6,418	111,882[5]	143	782[5]	...	...	...	...	...
Romania	Bucharest	1982E	1,979,076	246	8,045	2,211,460	605	3,655	...	...	...	...	...
Rwanda	Kigali	1981E	156,650	...	...	...	...	...	...	...	...	...	...
St. Christopher and Nevis	Basseterre	1980C	14,700	3.0	4,900	...	3.6	...	...	...	...	...	...
St. Helena and Ascension	Jamestown	1978E	1,500	...	...	...	...	...	...	...	...	...	...
St. Lucia	Castries	1978E	4,254	0.4	10,635	47,646	6.9	6,905	...	...	...	...	...
St. Pierre and Miquelon	Saint-Pierre	1982C	5,400	26	208	...	...	...	...	...	...	...	...
St. Vincent and the Grenadines	Kingstown	1982E	24,764	4.9	5,054	...	...	...	...	...	...	...	...
San Marino	San Marino	1982E	4,571	...	...	8,784	12	732	...	...	...	...	...
São Tomé and Principe	São Tomé	1978E	25,000	...	...	...	...	...	...	...	...	...	...
Saudi Arabia	Riyadh (national)	1981E	1,308,000	...	...	...	...	...	...	...	...	...	...
	aṭ-Ṭā'if (summer)	1974C	204,857	...	...	...	...	...	...	...	...	...	...
Senegal	Dakar	1979E	978,500	...	...	1,119,119	550	2,035	...	...	...	...	...
Seychelles	Victoria	1980C	23,900	10	2,390	...	...	...	...	...	...	...	...
Sierra Leone	Freetown	1980C	500,000	13	38,462	...	557	...	...	...	...	...	...
Singapore	Singapore	1984E	2,390,800[7]	33	72,448[7]	2,529,100	618	4,092	32.9	...	19.2	...	47.9
Solomon Islands	Honiara	1981C	21,300	21	1,014	...	...	...	...	...	...	...	...
Somalia	Mogadishu	1981E	400,000	126	3,175	...	...	...	...	...	...	...	...
South Africa	Cape Town (legis.)	1980C	858,940	...	...	1,490,935	...	...	...	...	...	...	...
	Pretoria (admin.)	1980C	435,100	...	...	139,043	...	...	...	...	...	...	...
	Bloemfontein (judicial)	1980C	256,020	...	...	...	...	...	...	...	...	...	...
South West Africa/Namibia	Swakopmund(summer)	1978E	16,800	79	213	...	...	...	...	...	...	...	...
	Windhoek (national)	1983E	104,100	53	1,964	...	...	...	...	...	...	...	...
Spain	Madrid	1981C	3,188,297	607	5,253	4,515,000	1,021	4,422	55.5	5.7	24.2	1.3	13.3
Sri Lanka	Colombo	1981C	585,776	37	15,832	1,083,965	100	10,840	...	...	...	...	...
Sudan, The	Khartoum	1983C	560,000	...	...	1,800,000	...	...	...	...	...	...	...
Suriname	Paramaribo	1980C	67,718	32	2,116	150,000	...	...	...	...	...	...	...
Swaziland[15]	Mbabane (admin.)	1982E	33,000	40	825	...	...	...	...	...	...	...	...
Sweden	Stockholm	1984E	650,952	188	3,470	1,409,048	3,588	393	31.8	9.6	22.8	33.2	2.6
Switzerland	Bern	1984E	142,100	52	2,759	300,600	325	926	...	...	...	...	...
Syria	Damascus	1984E	1,202,000	118	10,186	...	...	...	...	...	...	...	...
Taiwan	Taipei	1984E	2,388,374	272	8,775	...	...	...	...	...	...	...	...
Tanzania	Dar es Salaam	1978C	769,400	88	8,743	...	...	...	...	...	...	...	...
Thailand	Bangkok	1983E	—	—	—	5,479,000	1,565	3,501	25.8	0.6	73.5	0.1	—
Togo	Lome	1980E	283,000	345	820	...	...	...	...	...	...	...	...
Tokelau	—	—	—	—	—	—	—	—	—	—	—	—	—
Tonga	Nukualofa	1980E	19,900	4.7	4,234	22,561[16]	5.9	3,824[16]	...	...	...	...	...
Trinidad and Tobago	Port-of-Spain	1980C	65,906	9.6	6,865	425,000	...	...	...	...	...	...	...
Trust Territory of the Pacific Is.	Saipan	1980C	14,549	122	119	...	...	...	...	...	...	...	...
Tunisia	Tunis	1984C	596,654	...	...	774,364	346	2,238	...	...	...	...	...
Turkey	Ankara	1979E	2,106,076	369	5,708	2,539,580	3,395	748	...	...	...	...	...
Turks and Caicos Islands	Cockburn Town	1980C	3,124	18	174	—	—	—	...	...	...	...	...
Tuvalu	Funafuti	1983E	2,620	2.4	1,092	...	...	...	...	...	...	...	...
Uganda	Kampala	1980C	458,423	...	...	478,895	194	2,469	...	...	...	...	...
U.S.S.R.	Moscow	1980E	8,202,000	879	9,438	8,396,000	...	...	...	...	...	...	...
United Arab Emirates	Abu Dhabi	1980C	243,000	...	...	...	...	...	●	...	...	...	...
United Kingdom	London	1983E	6,754,500	1,580	4,275	12,231,200	10,620	1,152	46.0	11.3	28.5	...	14.2
United States	Washington, D.C.	1982E	631,000	159	3,969	3,061,000	7,286	420	...	...	...	...	...
Uruguay	Montevideo	1980E	1,260,573	530	2,378	...	...	...	...	...	...	...	...
Vanuatu	Vila	1979C	9,971	...	...	14,598	...	...	...	...	...	...	...
Venezuela	Caracas	1981C	1,162,952	77	15,103	2,640,013	...	...	...	...	...	...	...
Vietnam	Hanoi	1981E	—	—	—	2,712,000	2,139	1,268	...	...	...	...	...
Virgin Islands (U.S.)	Charlotte Amalie	1980C	11,842	2.9	4,083	19,304	...	...	...	...	...	...	...
Wallis and Futuna	Mata Utu	1983C	815	...	...	...	...	...	...	...	...	...	...
Western Sahara	El Aaiún	1984E	90,000	...	...	...	...	...	...	...	...	...	...
Western Samoa	Apia	1981C	33,170	60	549	...	...	...	...	...	...	...	...
Yemen (Aden)	Aden	1977E	271,600	54	5,030	...	18	...	...	...	...	...	...
Yemen (Şan'ā')	Şan'ā'	1980C	277,817	13	21,371	...	...	...	...	...	...	...	...
Yugoslavia	Belgrade	1981C	936,200	184	5,088	1,400,000	3,222	435	...	...	...	...	...
Zaire	Kinshasa	1979E	—	—	—	2,242,297	9,965	225	...	...	...	...	...
Zambia	Lusaka	1980C	538,469	375	1,436	...	360	...	...	...	...	...	...
Zimbabwe	Harare	1982C	656,000	857	765	...	...	...	...	...	...	...	...

number employed	percent of population	primary	secondary	tertiary, nongovernment	tertiary, government	dwellings	average household size	electrical energy consumption (KW-hr per capita/yr)	water consumption (cu m per capita/yr)	population per physician	hospital beds per 1,000 population	passenger cars per 1,000 population	telephone subscribers per 1,000 population	country
348,193	42.1	0.5	25.4	—74.1—		...	...	...	...	...	...	...	528.3	Portugal
...	...	...	...	...		310,644	3.5	...	...	...	...	...	519.5	Puerto Rico
...	...	...	...	...		...	...	...	...	...	...	...	254.2	Qatar
...	...	...	...	...		26,087[2]	4.0[2]	...	...	...	...	...	213.1	Réunion
1,063,100	49.1	1.1	53.9	43.3	1.7	...	...	...	198.3	314[3]	...	...	241.7	Romania
...	...	...	...	...		...	...	...	...	...	...	...	32.0	Rwanda
3,946	30.9	5.2	13.2	—81.6—		3,501	3.6	...	...	...	...	...	127.0	St. Christopher and Nevis
...	...	...	...	...		...	...	...	...	...	...	...	...	St. Helena and Ascension
1,368	37.8	1.5	11.7	—86.8—		1,021	3.5	...	...	...	...	...	143.4	St. Lucia
...	...	...	...	...		...	...	...	...	...	...	...	542.4	St. Pierre and Miquelon
4,742	27.7	...	...	...	29.9	3,504	4.9	...	...	...	...	...	147.4	St. Vincent and the Grenadines
1,425	42.8	1.7	19.0	—79.3—		...	...	...	...	...	...	...	401.5	San Marino
...	...	...	...	...		...	...	...	...	...	...	...	32.0	São Tomé and Príncipe
...	...	...	...	...		101,506[14]	6.6[2,7]	...	...	...	...	...	155.5	Saudi Arabia
...	...	...	...	...		30,877[14]	6.6[2,7]	...	...	...	...	...	122.7	
...	...	...	...	...		...	...	...	...	...	...	...	40.0	Senegal
8,790	38.2	...	...	...		3,236	4.8	...	...	...	...	...	227.4	Seychelles
...	...	...	...	...		...	...	...	...	...	...	...	...	Sierra Leone
1,112,700	45.5	1.2	35.3	—63.5—		...	...	2,726	113.7	1,168.5	...	71.7	317.2	Singapore
...	...	...	...	...		3,700	5.8	...	...	...	...	32.1	114.6	Solomon Islands
...	...	...	...	...		...	...	...	...	...	...	...	...	Somalia
...	...	...	...	...		...	...	...	...	...	...	...	264.0	South Africa
...	...	...	...	...		...	...	...	...	...	...	...	356.3	
...	...	...	...	...		...	...	...	...	...	...	...	201.9	
...	...	...	...	...		...	...	...	...	...	...	...	421.2	South West Africa/Namibia
...	...	...	...	...		...	...	1,952	86.4	356	...	223.6	603.6	Spain
...	...	...	...	...		...	...	...	...	...	1.9	...	32.2	Sri Lanka
...	...	...	...	...		...	...	...	...	...	...	...	25.4	Sudan, The
...	...	...	...	...		...	...	...	...	...	...	...	254.4	Suriname
...	...	...	...	...		...	...	...	...	...	...	...	...	Swaziland
450,514	45.5	0.3	19.5	—80.2—		367,189	2.7	...	169.5	...	...	...	1,313.5	Sweden
107,508	37.5	0.6	31.2	—68.2—		18,575	3.3	4,854	155.7	356	...	316.2	952.5	Switzerland
314,961	26.9	...	...	...		199,767	5.6	...	...	1,095	...	...	123.6	Syria
838,929	37.2	...	...	...		547,657	4.1	...	...	...	...	66.7	341.2	Taiwan
...	...	...	...	...		...	...	...	...	...	...	...	40.5	Tanzania
1,937,044	41.2	5.2	27.7	—67.1—		902,940	5.1	1,311	...	1,256	...	52.3	58.8	Thailand
89,967	—	1.8	11.7	76.0	10.5	—	—	—	...	...	...	...	17.0	Togo
—	—	—	—	—		—	—	—	—	—	—	—	—	Tokelau
...	...	...	...	...		2,719	6.7	...	...	...	...	...	...	Tonga
20,084	32.0	0.7	9.0	—90.3—		15,573	4.0	...	...	...	...	...	540.0	Trinidad and Tobago
...	...	...	...	...		2,937	5.0	...	...	...	...	...	...	Trust Territory of the Pacific Is.
...	...	...	...	...		...	...	...	...	...	...	...	...	Tunisia
...	...	...	...	...		...	...	...	...	...	...	...	...	Turkey
...	...	5.0	29.5	—65.5—		546	4.2	...	...	...	...	...	...	Turks and Caicos Islands
861	40.6	1.6	39.0	—59.4—		284	...	...	...	...	...	...	46.0	Tuvalu
...	...	...	...	...		...	...	...	...	...	...	...	62.0	Uganda
...	...	—	33.2	—66.8—		...	...	...	...	107[17]	...	...	339.0	U.S.S.R.
...	...	...	...	...		...	...	...	...	...	...	...	255.3	United Arab Emirates
3,709,400	52.8	0.2	26.2	64.2	9.4	2,700,000	2.5	...	...	1,925	...	263.4	863.5	United Kingdom
349,433[18]	55.4[18]	0.1[18]	8.7[18]	—91.2[18]—		276,984	2.3	...	...	...	7.4	...	1,730.2	United States
493,400	39.9	2.1	29.2	46.1	22.6	358,143	3.1	...	...	...	...	...	151.6	Uruguay
6,448	44.2	19.1	13.0	—67.9—		3,284	4.8	...	...	...	...	...	173.0	Vanuatu
...	...	...	...	...		...	...	...	...	...	...	...	...	Venezuela
...	...	...	...	...		...	...	...	...	...	...	...	...	Vietnam
4,510	38.1	1.0	12.4	75.2	11.4	4,312	3.0	...	...	...	...	...	...	Virgin Islands (U.S.)
202	36.2	51.0	...	—49.0—		129	6.3	...	...	...	...	59.1	...	Wallis and Futuna
...	...	...	...	...		...	...	...	...	...	...	...	...	Western Sahara
...	...	...	...	...		...	...	...	...	...	...	...	163.9	Western Samoa
...	...	...	...	...		...	...	...	...	...	...	...	...	Yemen (Aden)
...	...	...	...	...		...	...	...	...	...	...	...	...	Yemen (Şan'ā')
513,912	54.9	1.2	38.1	54.1	6.6	336,800	2.8	3,473	...	...	13.3	...	203.6	Yugoslavia
...	...	...	...	...		...	...	...	...	...	...	...	...	Zaire
...	...	...	...	...		...	...	...	...	...	...	...	35.5	Zambia
...	...	...	...	...		...	...	...	...	...	...	...	...	Zimbabwe

[1]Government physicians only. [2]Data refer to metropolitan area for which population is shown. [3]Includes dentists. [4]1978 estimate. [5]1977 estimate. [6]Potable water only. [7]1980 estimate. [8]1982 estimate. [9]May include wage earners only. [10]1980 census. [11]Indigenous population only. [12]1976 estimate. [13]Privately owned dwellings only. [14]Number of families. [15]Lobamba, the royal and legislative capital, is not a city, but rather a densely populated rural area. [16]1976 census. [17]Includes dentists, pharmacists, and nurses. [18]Excludes government employees, railroad employees, and self-employed persons.

Languages of the world

This table presents the major languages and their numbers of speakers for every country of the world and selected dependencies. The major languages of each country are listed alphabetically. The estimates of the number of speakers for each country total the country population estimates listed in the Area and Population Table. These estimates are based on a wide range of official and secondary sources that vary from country to country. The language populations covered in this table fall into two broad categories: mother tongue, or first language, speakers; and ethnolinguistic populations that speak a specific language with the same or different name as the ethnic population.

For countries where mother tongue data are available from the two most recent censuses, an intercensal growth rate for each language group has been calculated and projections made to the year of the corresponding population estimate in the Area and Population Table. Where only a single census count of mother tongue, or first language, speakers is available, the percentage of the total census population represented by speakers of each mother tongue group has been applied to the relevant population

estimate in the Area and Population Table. Most countries, however, do not compile official statistics on mother tongue, or first language, speakers. For these countries, ethnolinguistic population figures have been used to calculate the percentage of the total population represented by each group and that percentage applied to the relevant population estimate in the Area and Population Table.

In most instances the number of speakers of specified languages (excluding the category of others) listed for each country totals about 90 percent of its population. In a few cases the total is less than 90 percent because of the linguistic diversity of the country. Many countries have one or more major languages with official status that are used mainly in government. Many other countries designate one or more languages as official that are not among the major languages actually spoken in the particular country. Some countries also have a lingua franca (not listed in this table as a major language) that is spoken by a large number of persons on certain occasions.

Languages of the world

Major languages by country	Number of speakers	Major languages by country	Number of speakers	Major languages by country	Number of speakers	Major languages by country	Number of speakers
Afghanistan[1]		**Austria**		**Bolivia**		**Cameroon**[1]	
Baluchi	150,000	Czech	10,000	Aymaru	410,000	Bamileke	1,768,000
Hazaragi (Persian)	1,548,000	German	7,395,000	Quechua	743,000	Duala	1,416,000
Kirgiz	37,000	Hungarian	19,000	Spanish	1,975,000	Fang (Pahouin)	1,892,000
Nuristani	111,000	Serbo-Croatian	33,000	Spanish-Aymaru	887,000	Maka	466,000
Pamir	113,000	Slovak	24,000	Spanish-Quechua	1,129,000	Mandara	542,000
Pashi	101,000	Windisch	4,000	Spanish-others	199,000	Massa	380,000
Pashto	9,116,000	Other	94,000	Others	694,000	Fulani	827,000
Tadzhik (Persian)	3,440,000					Tikar	703,000
Teymur	163,000	**Bahamas, The**		**Botswana**[1]		Other	1,512,000
Turkmen	337,000	English[2]	228,000	Setswana	959,000	*French and English are*
Uzbek	1,548,000	English Creole	5,000	Khoisan	43,000	*the official languages.*
Other	536,000	French Creole	9,000	Other	36,000	
		Other	7,000	*English is the official*		**Canada**	
Albania[1]				*language.*		English	15,337,000
Albanian	2,766,000	**Bahrain**				French	6,461,000
Greek	70,000	Arabic[2]	364,000	**Brazil**		German	551,000
Macedonian	17,000	English	7,000	Portuguese	131,315,000	Italian	556,000
Montenegrin	9,000	Persian	16,000	Other	1,327,000	Ukrainian	301,000
Romanian	17,000	Urdū	9,000			Other	1,936,000
Other	27,000	Other	13,000	**British Virgin Islands**		
				English	12,000	**Cape Verde**	
Algeria		**Bangladesh**		Other	1,000	Crioulo (Cape Verdean	
Arabic[2]	17,173,000	Bengali	98,436,000			Creole)	308,000
Berber	4,000,000	Urdū	249,000	**Brunei**[1]		Other[5]	...
French	137,000	Other	900,000	Chinese	56,000	
Other	41,000			Malay	109,000	**Cayman Islands**	
		Barbados		Other	53,000	English	21,000
American Samoa		English Creole	230,000	*Malay and English are*		Other	...
Samoan	34,000	English	20,000	*the official languages.*		
Other[3]	...	Other	2,000			**Central African Republic**[1]	
				Bulgaria[1]		Banda	684,000
Andorra		**Belgium**		Bulgarian	8,063,000	Baya	632,000
Catalan[2]	12,000	Flemish	5,627,000	Romany	64,000	Mandja	183,000
French	3,000	French	3,159,000	Turkish	780,000	Mbum	158,000
Spanish	23,000	German	69,000	Other	62,000	Sara	174,000
Other	2,000	Flemish and French (includes				Other[6]	754,000
		Flemish-French Brussels		**Burkina Faso**[1]		*French is the official*	
Angola[1]		communes)	987,000	Bobo	465,000	*language.*	
Ambo	186,000	Other	30,000	Fulani	377,000	
Herero	39,000			Grunshi (Gurunsi)	337,000	**Chad**[1]	
Kikongo (Kongo)	1,002,000	**Belize**		Lobi	465,000	Arabic	1,545,000
Kimbundu (Mbundu)	1,709,000	English[2]	88,000	Mossi	3,595,000	Maba	333,000
Lunda-Chokwe	637,000	Carib	9,000	Tuareg	276,000	Mbum	348,000
Nganguela	544,000	German	6,000	Other[21]	1,218,000	Sara	1,305,000
Nyaneka-Humbe	225,000	Spanish	44,000	*French is the official*		Tama	322,000
Umbundu (Ovimbundu)	2,800,000	Maya	8,000	*language.*		Tuburi (Toubou)	394,000
Other	628,000	Other	2,000			Other	869,000
Portuguese is the official				**Burma**[1]		*French is the official*	
language.		**Benin**[1]		Burmese	25,674,000	*language.*	
		Bariba	348,000	Chin	713,000	
Anguilla		Fon	2,315,000	Chinese	713,000	**Chile**	
English	7,000	Fulani (Peul)	231,000	Kachin	713,000	Araucanian	653,000
Other	...	Somba	403,000	Karen	3,566,000	Spanish	10,954,000
		Yoruba (Nago)	403,000	Shan	2,140,000	Other	58,000
Antigua and Barbuda		Other	210,000	Other	2,140,000	
English	76,000	*French is the official*				
Other	3,000	*language.*		**Burundi**[1]		
				Rundi	4,672,000	
Argentina		**Bermuda**		Other[4]	19,000	
Guaraní	271,000	English	52,000	*French is the official*		
Italian	813,000	Other	4,000	*language.*		
Spanish	28,803,000					
Other	210,000	**Bhutan**[1]				
		Assamese	191,000			
Australia		Bhote (Bhutias)	860,000			
English	15,276,000	Gurung	224,000			
Other (including		Other	142,000			
Aboriginal languages)	186,000	*Dzongkha (Bhutani) is*				
		the official language.				

Major languages by country	Number of speakers	Major languages by country	Number of speakers	Major languages by country	Number of speakers	Major languages by country	Number of speakers
China[1]		**Denmark**[1]		**Fiji**[1]		**Ghana**[1]	
Cantonese	53,700,000	Danish	4,946,000	Fijian	309,000	Akan	5,629,000
Chuang	6,444,000	Faeroese	41,000	Hindi	333,000	Ewe	1,885,000
Dungan	6,444,000	German	51,000	Other	35,000	Ga-Adangme	1,222,000
Hakka	42,960,000	Other	71,000			Grusi	624,000
Hsiang	47,960,000			*English and Fijian are*		Mole-Dagbani	1,664,000
Kan	26,850,000	**Djibouti**[1]		*the official languages.*		Other	1,976,000
Korean	2,148,000	Arabic	16,000			*English is the official*	
Mandarin Chinese	665,881,000	Cushitic Afar	123,000	**Finland**		*language.*	
Manchurian	4,296,000	Issachar and Gad	65,000	Finnish	4,561,000		
Miao	3,222,000	Somali Issa	91,000	Swedish	297,000	**Gibraltar**	
Min	27,924,000	Other	29,000	Other	15,000	English[2]	10,000
Minnan	26,850,000	*Arabic and French are*				Spanish	11,000
Mongolian	2,148,000	*the official languages.*		**France**[1]		Other	9,000
Tibetan	4,296,000			Alsatian	1,481,000		
Uighur	6,444,000	**Dominica**		Arabic	1,371,000	**Greece**[1]	
Wu	91,290,000	French patois	71,000	Armenian	165,000	Greek	9,535,000
Other	60,146,000	Other	3,000	Basque	165,000	Macedonian	160,000
		English is the official		Breton	1,152,000	Turkish	90,000
Christmas Island[1]		*language.*		Catalan	165,000	Other	199,000
Chinese	1,700			Flemish	274,000		
Malay	800	**Dominican Republic**		French	42,256,000	**Greenland**	
Other	200	French patois	27,000	German	219,000	Danish	5,000
		Spanish	6,211,000	Hebrew	549,000	Greenlandic	48,000
Cocos Islands		Other	10,000	Polish	329,000	Other	...
English	200			Other	3,730,000		
Malay	400	**Ecuador**				**Grenada**	
Other	...	Quechuan (and other		**French Guiana**		English	112,000
		Indian languages)	581,000	Creole	68,000	French patois	
Colombia		Spanish	7,719,000	Other	7,000	(and other)	4,000
Arawakan	180,000	Other	...				
Cariban	82,000			**French Polynesia**[1]		**Guadeloupe**	
Chibchan	184,000	**Egypt**[1]		French[2]	18,000	Creole and French	310,000
Spanish	27,739,000	Arabic	46,555,000	Tahitian	118,000	Other	16,000
Other	63,000	Other	565,000	Other	23,000		
						Guam	
Comoros		**El Salvador**		**Gabon**		Chamorro[3]	60,000
Comorian (related to		Nahuatl (and other		Bakota	54,000	English	23,000
Swahili)	455,000	Indian languages)	150,000	Eshira	241,000	Other (mostly Philippine	
Other[7]	...	Spanish	4,850,000	Fang	289,000	languages)	26,000
		Other	...	Okande	41,000		
Congo[1]				M'Béti (Bandjabi)	194,000	**Guatemala**	
Congo	785,000	**Equatorial Guinea**[1]		Other	139,000	Cakehiquel	377,000
Sanka (Gabonese Bantu)	262,000	Bubi	46,000	*French is the official*		Chorti	50,000
Teke	349,000	Duala	9,000	*language.*		Ixil	66,000
Ubangi	279,000	Fang	232,000			Kanjobal	94,000
Other[8]	70,000	Other[9]	38,000	**Gambia, The**		Kekchi	277,000
French is the official		*Spanish is the official*		Fulani	140,000	Jacaltec	43,000
language.		*language.*		Dyola (Yola)	75,000	Mam	555,000
				Malinke	246,000	Pocomcii	75,000
Cook Islands		**Ethiopia**		Wolof	109,000	Quiche	795,000
Maori	16,000	Amharic[2]	10,200,000	Soninke	65,000	Spanish	3,681,000
Other[3]	2,000	Guragigna	1,088,000	Other	79,000	Other	532,000
		Oromo (Galla)	13,600,000	*English is the official*			
Costa Rica		Tigrigna	4,800,000	*language.*		**Guinea**[1]	
Spanish	2,666,000	Other	4,312,000			Fulani (Peul)	1,674,000
Other	27,000			**Germany, East**[1]		Kissi	418,000
		Faeroe Islands		German	16,551,000	Kpelle (Guerzé)	234,000
Cuba		Faeroese	44,800	Other	167,000	Loma	195,000
Spanish	9,899,000	Other[10]	...			Malinké	1,674,000
Other	46,000			**Germany, West**[1]		SuSu	893,000
		Falkland Islands		Dutch	307,000	Other	491,000
Cyprus[1]		English	2,000	English	123,000	*French is the official*	
Greek	534,000	Other	...	French	61,000	*language.*	
Turks	124,000			German	57,578,000		
Other	4,000			Greek	369,000		
				Italian	614,000		
Czechoslovakia				Spanish	184,000		
Czech[2]	9,898,000			Turkish	1,045,000		
Slovak[2]	4,801,000			Other	1,167,000		
Other	767,000						

Languages of the world (continued)

Major languages by country	Number of speakers	Major languages by country	Number of speakers	Major languages by country	Number of speakers	Major languages by country	Number of speakers
Guinea-Bissau		**Iran**[1]		**Kenya**[1]		**Madagascar**	
Balante	225,000	Arabic	701,000	Embu	196,000	Malagasy	9,645,000
Crioulo (Portuguese		Azerbaijanian	7,011,000	Gusii	964,000	Other	...
Creole)	66,000	Armenian	307,000	Kalenjin	1,713,000	*Malagasy and French*	
Fulani	257,000	Bakhtiari	833,000	Kikuyu	3,396,000	*are the official languages.*	
Mandinga	107,000	Baluchi	833,000	Luhya	2,250,000		
Manjaco	76,000	Kurdish	3,593,000	Luo	1,953,000	**Malawi**	
Other[5]	111,000	Luri	964,000	Masai	265,000	Chichewa	3,347,000
		Persian (Fārsī)	19,719,000	Meru	910,000	Chilomwe	967,000
Guyana		Turkmen	657,000	Mijikenda	765,000	Chisena	233,000
English[2]	837,000	Other	9,202,000	Somali	107,000	Chitumbuka	607,000
Other	...			Taita	160,000	Chiyao	920,000
		Iraq		Turkana	185,000	Other	594,000
Haiti		Arabic[2]	11,958,000	Other[3]	4,676,000	*Chichewa and English*	
French[2]	515,000	Assyrian	70,000	*Swahili is the official*		*are the official languages.*	
French Creole	4,634,000	Kurdish	2,288,000	*language.*			
Others	...	Turkish	46,000			**Malaysia**	
		Turkmen	247,000	**Kiribati**		Bajau	98,000
Honduras		Other	391,000	Gilbertese (Kiribati)	61,000	Chinese	888,000
Spanish	4,052,000			Other	400	Chinese and others	504,000
Indian languages		**Ireland**		*English is the official*		Dusan	160,000
and other	83,000	English	2,753,000	*language.*		English	77,000
		Irish	822,000			English and others	171,000
Hong Kong		Other	...	**Korea, North**[1]		Iban	365,000
Chinese (Cantonese)	4,986,000			Korean	19,493,000	Iban and others	60,000
Chinese (other dialects)	332,000	**Israel**[1]		Other	137,000	Malay[2]	6,610,000
English	52,000	Arabic	706,000			Malay and others	2,349,000
Other	24,000	French	50,000	**Korea, South**[1]		Tamil	595,000
		German	55,000	Korean	40,548,000	Tamil and others	10,000
Hungary[1]		Hebrew	2,768,000	Other	41,000	Other	3,443,000
Hungarian	10,574,000	Romanian	80,000				
Other	107,000	Spanish	50,000	**Kuwait**[1]		**Maldives**	
		Yiddish	202,000	Arabic	1,377,000	Maldivian (Divehi)[2]	163,000
Iceland[1]		Other	289,000	Kurdish	176,000	Other	...
Icelandic	235,000			Persian	74,000		
Other	4,000	**Italy**[1]		Other	131,000	**Mali**[1]	
		Albanian	113,000			Bambara	2,405,000
India		French	113,000	**Laos**[1]		Dogon	371,000
Assamese	11,961,000	German	339,000	Chinese	45,000	Fulani	960,000
Bāgri	1,410,000	Italian	55,127,000	Khmu	369,000	Malinke	718,000
Bengali	59,438,000	Other	733,000	Lao[2]	2,655,000	Senufo	900,000
Bhīlī (Bhilodi)	1,669,000			Man	57,000	Soninke	658,000
Bhojpuri	19,145,000	**Ivory Coast**[1]		Miao	164,000	Other	1,550,000
Chhattisgarhī	8,935,000	Akan	3,800,000	Mon-Khmer	287,000	*French is the official*	
Dogri	1,734,000	Kru	1,523,000	Tai	344,000	*language.*	
Garhwdī	1,638,000	Malinke	1,358,000	Other[12]	176,000		
Gondī	2,067,000	Southern Mande	936,000			**Malta**[1]	
Gujarātī	34,251,000	Voltaic (including		**Lebanon**[1]		English	8,000
Hindī	205,232,000	Senufo)	1,441,000	Arabic[2]	2,367,000	Maltese	349,000
Kannaḍa	28,803,000	Other	120,000	Armenian	18,000	Other	8,000
Kashmiri	3,232,000	*French is the official*		Kurdish	13,000		
Konkani	2,033,000	*language.*		Other[11]	203,000	**Martinique**	
Kumāuni	1,649,000					Creole and French	323,000
Kurukh (Oraon)	1,655,000	**Jamaica**		**Lesotho**		Other	11,000
Lamani (Banjārī)	1,606,000	Chinese	14,000	Sesotho	1,469,000		
Maghi (Magadhi)	8,862,000	English and English		Other	5,000	**Mauritania**	
Maithilī	8,173,000	Creole	2,153,000	*Sesotho and English are*		Hassania Arabic	1,468,000
Malayālam	29,260,000	Hindi and other		*the official languages.*		Fulfulde (Poular)	312,000
Marāṭhi	55,703,000	Indian languages	38,000			Other	55,000
Mārwari	6,293,000	Spanish	4,000	**Liberia**[1]		*Arabic and French are*	
Nepālī (Gorkhālī)	1,718,000	Other	86,000	Bassa	280,000	*the official languages.*	
Oriyā	26,336,000			Gio	87,000		
Pahāri	1,695,000	**Japan**[1]		Gola	108,000	**Mauritius**	
Punjābī	18,557,000	English	17,000	Grebo and Kran	346,000	French	47,000
Rajasthani	2,796,000	Chinese	49,000	Kpelle	595,000	French patois	542,000
Santālī	4,932,000	Japanese	119,137,000	Kru	118,000	Hindī	314,000
Sindhī	1,609,000	Korean	575,000	Toma (Loma)	185,000	Tamil	35,000
Tamil	50,188,000	Other	32,000	Mano	56,000	Urdū	28,000
Telugu	59,686,000			Other	385,000	Other	52,000
Tulu	1,545,000	**Jordan**[1]		*English is the official*		*English and French*	
Urdū	38,182,000	Arabic	3,468,000	*language.*		*(for certain legislative*	
Other	28,759,000	Other	60,000			*and judicial purposes) are*	
Hindī and English are				**Libya**		*the official languages.*	
the official languages.		**Kampuchea**[1]		Arabic	3,573,000		
		Chinese	459,000	Other[13]	111,000	**Mayotte**	
Indonesia[1]		Khmer[2]	5,023,000			Comoran	54,000
Batak	4,769,000	Vietnamese	379,000	**Liechtenstein**[1]		(related to Swahili)	
Javanese	69,026,000	Other[11]	257,000	German	23,000	Other	...
Achinese	3,288,000			Other	4,000	*French is the official*	
Madurese	11,504,000					*language.*	
Bugi	4,604,000			**Luxembourg**[1]			
Sundanese	22,363,000			Flemish	5,000	**Mexico**	
Balinese	3,453,000			French	15,000	Aztec	1,273,000
Other	56,934,000			German	10,000	Mayan	724,000
Bahasa Indonesia is				Italian	23,000	Mixtec	371,000
the official language.				Luxembourgish	279,000	Otomi	352,000
				Other	34,000	Spanish	62,701,000
						Totonaco	199,000
				Macau		Zapotec	451,000
				Chinese	271,000	Other	10,737,000
				Other	6,000		
				Portuguese is the official			
				language.			

Major languages by country	Number of speakers	Major languages by country	Number of speakers	Major languages by country	Number of speakers	Major languages by country	Number of speakers
Monaco[1]		**Nigeria**		**Poland**		**Sierra Leone**[1]	
English	1,000	Annang	1,116,000	Polish	36,075,000	Kono	183,000
French	16,000	Urhobo	1,057,000	Other	925,000	Koranko	141,000
Italian	5,000	Edo	1,578,000			Limba	320,000
Monegasque	4,000	Fulani	7,908,000	**Portugal**[1]		Mende	1,176,000
Other	2,000	Hausa	19,261,000	Portuguese	10,096,000	Temne	1,134,000
		Ibibio	3,316,000	Other	102,000	Other[18]	851,000
Mongolia[1]		Ibo	15,283,000			*English is the official*	
Buryat	41,000	Ijaw	1,800,000	**Puerto Rico**		*language.*	
Dariganga	35,000	Kanuri	3,734,000	English	18,000		
Dürbet	52,000	Nupé	1,085,000	Spanish	2,082,000	**Singapore**[1]	
Kazakh	82,000	Tiv	2,304,000	Spanish and English	1,523,000	Bahasa Malaysia	372,000
Khalkha	1,497,000	Yoruba	18,711,000	Other	47,000	Chinese	1,941,000
Russian	24,000	Other	14,863,000			Tamil (and other Indian	
Other	129,000	*English is the official*		**Qatar**[1]		languages)	162,000
		language.		Arabic	226,000	Other	56,000
Montserrat				Bantu languages	30,000	*English, Malay, Mandarin*	
English	12,000	**Niue**		Persian	6,000	*Chinese, and Tamil are*	
Other	...	Niuean	4,000	Other	14,000	*the official languages.*	
		Other[3]	...				
Morocco[1]				**Réunion**		**Solomon Islands**	
Arabic[2]	16,674,000	**Norfolk Island**		Creole	531,000	Areare	10,000
Berber	5,610,000	English	2,000	Other[17]	...	Kwaio	9,000
Other[11]	158,000	Other	...	*French is the official*		Kwara'ae	17,000
				language.		Other[19]	223,000
Mozambique[1]		**Norway**[1]				*English is the official*	
Makua	7,171,000	Danish	17,000	**Romania**		*language.*	
Maravi	1,659,000	English	21,000	German	295,000		
Shona	795,000	Finnish	21,000	Hungarian	1,648,000	**Somalia**[1]	
Tsonga	3,236,000	German	8,000	Romanian	20,495,000	Somali	4,010,000
Yao	507,000	Norwegian	4,033,000	Other	356,000	Other	94,000
Other	344,000	Other	45,000			*Somali and Arabic*	
Portuguese is the official				**Rwanda**		*are the official languages*	
language.		**Oman**[1]		Kinyarwanda	6,000,000		
		Arabic	878,000	Other[4]	...	**South Africa**	
Nauru		Baluchi	40,000	*Kinyarwanda and French*		Afrikaans[2]	5,546,000
Nauruan	6,300	Persian	34,000	*are the official languages.*		English[2]	2,051,000
Other[3]	1,700	Other	59,000			Nguni	13,022,000
				St. Christopher-Nevis		Shangana-Tsonga	964,000
Nepal		**Pakistan**[1]		English	44,000	Sotho	6,856,000
Bhojpuri	1,160,000	Baluchi	2,311,000	Other	1,000	Venda	529,000
Hindi (Awadhi dialect)	448,000	Brahui	832,000			Other	2,730,000
Magar	414,000	Jatt	6,100,000	**St. Helena and Ascension**			
Maithili	1,906,000	Pashto	7,856,000	English	7,000	**South West Africa/Namibia**	
Nepali[2]	8,687,000	Punjabi	55,268,000	Other	...	Afrikaans	153,000
Newari	647,000	Sindhi	11,645,000			German	29,000
Rai	332,000	Urdū[2]	7,024,000	**St. Lucia**		East Caprivi	39,000
Tamang	796,000	Other[15]	1,385,000	English[2]	1,000	Herero	70,000
Tharu	713,000			French patois	113,000	Khoisan	185,000
Other	1,475,000	**Panama**		Hindi and Urdū	4,000	Okavango	77,000
		Cuna	45,000	Other	8,000	Ovambo	511,000
Netherlands, The[1]		Guaymi	63,000			Other	47,000
Dutch	11,752,000	Spanish	1,963,000	**St. Pierre and Miquelon**[1]			
English	289,000	Other	30,000	French	6,900	**Spain**[1]	
Flemish	1,704,000			Other	100	Basque	884,000
Frisian	404,000	**Papua New Guinea**[1]				Castilian Spanish	27,980,000
German	159,000	Papuan languages	2,706,000	**St. Vincent and the Grenadines**		Catalan	6,303,000
Other	129,000	Melanesian languages	503,000	English[2]	123,000	Galician	3,152,000
		Other[16]	39,000	Other	9,000	Other	116,000
Netherlands Antilles[1]							
Dutch	22,000	**Paraguay**		**San Marino**[1]		**Sri Lanka**	
English	15,000	Guaraní	1,395,000	Italian	22,000	English	12,000
French	13,000	Guaraní and Spanish	1,499,000	Other	...	English and Sinhalese	868,000
Papiamentu	220,000	Spanish[2]	135,000			English and Tamil	180,000
Other	8,000	Other	416,000	**São Tomé and Príncipe**[1]		English, Sinhalese,	
				Fang	92,000	and Tamil	570,000
New Caledonia[1]		**Peru**		Other	9,000	Sinhalese[2]	9,509,000
French	56,000	Aymara	561,000	*Portuguese is the official*		Sinhalese and Tamil	1,472,000
Melanesian languages	62,000	Quechuan	5,140,000	*language.*		Tamil	3,097,000
Other	30,000	Spanish	13,145,000			Other	48,000
		Other	485,000	**Saudi Arabia**[1]			
New Zealand		*Spanish and Quechuan*		Arabic	10,470,000	**Sudan, The**[1]	
English[2]	3,045,000	*are the official languages.*		Other	324,000	Arabic[2]	10,383,000
Maori	104,000					Bea	1,329,000
Other	111,000	**Philippines**		**Senegal**[1]		Dinka	2,427,000
		Bicol	3,915,000	Dyola and Mandingue	965,000	Nubian	1,703,000
Nicaragua[1]		Cebuano	13,567,000	Fulani	772,000	Nuer	1,034,000
Spanish	2,856,000	Hiligaynon	5,231,000	Serer	1,222,000	Other	4,227,000
Other (including		Ilocano	5,904,000	Tukulor	579,000		
Miskito)	58,000	Pampango	1,963,000	Wolof	2,573,000	**Suriname**	
		Pangasinan	1,201,000	Other	322,000	Creole	50,000
Niger[1]		Samar-Leyte	2,342,000	*French is the official*		Dutch	134,000
Hausa	3,375,000	Tagalog	12,365,000	*language.*		Hindi	114,000
Fulani	666,000	Other	7,998,000			Javanese	56,000
Kanuri	345,000	*Pilipino (related to Tagalog)*		**Seychelles**		Other[3]	16,000
Songhai-Zerma	1,483,000	*and English are the official*		Creole patois	69,000	*Dutch is the official*	
Other	415,000	*languages.*		Other	2,000	*language.*	
French is the official				*English and French*			
language.		**Pitcairn Island**		*are the official languages.*			
		English	53				
		Other	...				

Languages of the world (continued)

Major languages by country	Number of speakers	Major languages by country	Number of speakers	Major languages by country	Number of speakers	Major languages by country	Number of speakers
Swaziland		**Thailand**[1]		**Trust Territory of the Pacific Islands**		**Uganda**[1]	
siSwati	561,000	Chinese	5,560,000	Chamorro	14,000	Acholi	713,000
Other[20]	62,000	Khmer	708,000	Kosraean	5,000	Chiga (Kiga)	999,000
English and siSwati are the official languages.		Karen	303,000	Marshallese	32,000	Ganda (Luganda)	2,568,000
		Malay	1,920,000	Mortlockese	12,000	Gisu	1,056,000
		Thai	41,096,000	Palauan	14,000	Lango	927,000
Sweden[1]		Other	961,000	Ponapean	21,000	Nkole	1,170,000
Finnish	292,000			Trukese	34,000	Nyoro	542,000
Swedish	7,557,000	**Togo**[1]		Woleaian	2,000	Rwanda	785,000
Other	483,000	Ewe	1,279,000	Yapese	6,000	Soga	1,170,000
		Gurma	388,000	Other	4,000	Turkana	1,170,000
Switzerland[1]		Kabre	616,000	*English is the official language.*		Other[4]	3,168,000
French	1,209,000	Tem	116,000			*English is the official language.*	
German	4,281,000	Other	352,000	**Tunisia**			
Italian	595,000	*French is the official language.*		Arabic (colloquial)	4,779,000	**U.S.S.R.**[1]	
Romansh	53,000			Arabic (literary)[2]	511,000	Armenian	4,525,000
Other	340,000	**Tokelau**		Arabic (literary) and French	1,679,000	Azerbaijani	6,200,000
		Tokelauan	2,000	French	71,000	Byelorussian	9,714,000
Syria[1]		Other[3]	...	Other	36,000	Estonian	1,217,000
Arabic[2]	9,161,000					Georgian	3,771,000
Armenian	289,000	**Tonga**		**Turkey**		Kazakh	7,381,000
Kurdish	650,000	Tongan	104,000	Arabic	568,000	Kirgiz	2,215,000
Other	217,000	Other[3]	2,000	Kurdish	3,357,000	Latvian	1,446,000
				Turkish[2]	43,588,000	Lithuanian	2,963,000
Taiwan[1]		**Trinidad and Tobago**[1]		Other	806,000	Moldavian	3,134,000
South Fukien Chinese	12,835,000	English[2]	688,000			Russian[2]	142,399,000
Hakka and Hokkien Chinese	1,916,000	Hindi (and other Indian languages)	477,000	**Turks and Caicos Islands**		Tadzhik	3,429,000
Mandarin Chinese[2]	4,004,000	Other	27,000	English	8,000	Turkmenian	2,399,000
Other	402,000			Other	...	Ukrainian	43,334,000
						Uzbek	14,725,000
Tanzania[1]				**Tuvalu**		Other	25,935,000
Chaga	1,060,000			Ellice (Tuvalu)	7,600		
Haya	1,251,000			Gilbertese (Kiribati)	1,300	**United Arab Emirates**[1]	
Hehet	1,442,000			Other[3]	100	Arabic	1,146,000
Luguru	1,060,000					Other	144,000
Makondi	1,251,000						
Nyakyusa	1,145,000						
Sukuma	4,474,000						
Swahili	1,823,000						
Other	7,697,000						
Swahili and English are the official languages.							

Major languages by country	Number of speakers	Major languages by country	Number of speakers	Major languages by country	Number of speakers	Major languages by country	Number of speakers
United Kingdom		**Venezuela**		**Yugoslavia**[1]		**Zimbabwe**	
English	52,281,000	Spanish	15,190,000	Albanian	1,877,000	English	625,000
Scots-Gaelic	78,000	Other	411,000	Hungarian	412,000	Nguni	1,272,000
Welsh	522,000			Macedonian	1,387,000	Nyanja	419,000
Other	3,375,000	**Vietnam**[1]		Serbo-Croatian	15,207,000	Shona	5,716,000
		Khmer	796,000	Slovene	1,773,000	Other	36,000
United States		Muong	756,000	Other	2,341,000	*English is the official*	
Chinese	707,000	Nung	577,000			*language.*	
English	210,407,000	Tay	908,000	**Zaire**[1]			
French	1,726,000	Thai	772,000	Azande	1,962,000		
German	1,749,000	Vietnamese	48,955,000	Kongo	5,210,000		
Greek	449,000	Other	5,476,000	Luba	5,788,000		
Italian	1,773,000			Lugbara	967,000		
Japanese	378,000	**Virgin Islands (U.S.)**		Mongo	4,277,000		
Korean	307,000	English (and other)	104,000	Ngala	1,865,000		
Philippine languages	520,000	Spanish	18,000	Rundi	1,222,000		
Polish	898,000			Rwanda	3,248,000		
Portuguese	402,000	**Wallis and Futuna**		Teke	868,000		
Spanish	12,624,000	Wallisian	12,000	Other[23]	6,751,000		
Yiddish	355,000	Other	...	*French is the official*			
Other	4,118,000	*French is the official*		*language.*			
		language.					
Uruguay				**Zambia**[1]			
Spanish	2,909,000	**Western Sahara**		Bemba	2,274,000		
Other	104,000	Arabic	172,000	Lozi	623,000		
		Other[22]	...	Lunda	426,000		
Vanuatu				Luzna	334,000		
Bislama	107,000	**Western Samoa**		Malawi	898,000		
Other	23,000	English	800	Ngoni	236,000		
English and French are		Samoan	77,000	Tonga	1,075,000		
the official languages.		Samoan and English	84,000	Other[3]	688,000		
		Other	200				
		Yemen (Aden)[1]					
		Arabic	1,995,000				
		Other	152,000				
		Yemen (Ṣanʿāʾ)[1]					
		Arabic[2]	7,684,000				
		Other[3]	125,000				

[1]Figures given represent ethnolinguistic groups.   [2]Official language.   [3]English also spoken.   [4]Swahili also spoken.   [5]Portuguese also spoken.   [6]Sango is the lingua franca.   [7]French and Arabic also spoken.   [8]Lingala and Monokutuba are patois.   [9]Pidgin English and Portuguese patois also spoken.   [10]Danish is taught in the schools.   [11]French also spoken.   [12]English and French also spoken.   [13]English and Italian also spoken.   [14]Swahili is the lingua franca.   [15]English is the lingua franca.   [16]About half the population also speaks Pisin (Pidgin English); English and Hiri (Police Motu) also spoken.   [17]Gujarati and Chinese also spoken.   [18]Kiro is the lingua franca.   [19]Solomon Islands Pidgin (English) is the lingua franca.   [20]Afrikaans and Portuguese also spoken.   [21]Majority of population speak Moré (language of the Mossi); Diula is language of commerce.   [22]Spanish also spoken.   [23]Swahili, Tshiluba, Lingala, and Kikongo are national languages.

Vital statistics, marriage, family

This table provides some of the basic measures that define the rate and direction of population change within a country. Data are provided for all of the independent countries of the world and for dependencies with a sufficiently large civilian population to be compared to the larger countries.

The accuracy of these data is principally a function of the efficiency of the respective national systems for collecting information about each kind of civil event (measures like the birth or death rate being directly dependent on complete registration) and of the sophistication of the analysis that can be brought to bear upon the data so compiled. Life expectancy, for example, requires an information base to calculate but is susceptible to being calculated in different ways.

Data on birth rates, however, depend not only on the completeness of registration of births in a particular country but also on the conditions under which those data are collected: Do all births take place in a hospital? Are the births reported comparably in all parts of the country? Are the records of the births tabulated in a central location with an effort to eliminate inconsistent reporting of birth events, perinatal mortality, etc.? Similarly for death rates but with the added complication of having to identify "cause of death" in a country with, say, only one physician for every 1,000 population: too few to perform autopsies to assess accurately the cause of death after the fact and also too few to provide ongoing care at a level where records would permit inference about cause of death based on prior condition or diagnosis.

Calculating natural increase, which at its most basic is simply the difference between the birth and death rates, may be complicated by the varying degrees of completeness of these data for a given country. The total fertility rate may be understood as the average number of children that would be borne per woman if all women lived to the end of their childbearing years and bore children at each age at the average rate for that age. Calculating the fertility rate is complicated by changing age structure of the population over time, changing mortality rates among mothers, and changing medical practice at births, each improvement leading to greater numbers of live-born children and greater numbers of children who survive their first year (the basis for measurement of infant mortality, another basic limit on the growth of a population).

As indicated above, data for causes of death are not only particularly difficult to obtain, since many countries are not well equipped to collect the data, but are also difficult to assess, as their accuracy may be suspect and their meaning may be subject to varying interpretation: Take the case of a citizen of a developing country who dies of what is clearly a lung infection; but was the death complicated by chronic malnutrition, itself complicated by a parasitic infestation, these last two together so weakening the subject that he died of an infection that he might have survived had his general health been better? Similarly, in a developed country: Someone may die from what is identified in an autopsy as a cerebrovascular accident, but if that accident occurred in a vascular sys-

Vital statistics, marriage, family

country	vital rates						causes of death (rate per 100,000 population)								
	year	birth rate per 1,000 population	death rate per 1,000 population	infant mortality rate per 1,000 live births	rate of natural increase per 1,000 population	total fertility rate	year	infectious and parasitic diseases	neo-plasms (cancers)	endocrine and metabolic disorders	diseases of the nervous system	diseases of the circula-tory system	diseases of the respira-tory system	diseases of the digestive system	accidents, poisoning, and violence
Afghanistan	1983	49.4	26.9	203.0	22.5	6.9	...	...	...	...	...	...	...	...	...
Albania	1982	27.8	5.9	...	21.9	3.6	...	...	...	...	...	...	...	...	...
Algeria	1982	42.9	10.5	92.9	32.4	7.2	...	...	...	...	...	...	...	...	...
American Samoa	1983	34.4	4.2	6.8	30.2	4.9	...	...	...	...	...	...	...	...	...
Andorra	1981	14.8	4.1	...	10.7	...	...	...	...	...	...	...	...	...	...
Angola	1980–85	47.6	23.1	21.0	24.5	6.4	1973	73.2	6.5	4.9	3.6	19.2	24.6	3.6	89.0
Anguilla	1980–85	30.5	6.7	...	23.8	1.9	1977	22.2	94.4	36.1	26.4	275.0	40.3	18.1	20.8
Antigua and Barbuda	1983	15.1	4.6	11.1	10.5	1.9	1979	35.4	148.0	21.7	13.5	380.5	44.8	40.3	205.6
Argentina	1980	24.7	8.5	33.2	16.2	2.8	1980	...	...	...	...	...	...	...	...
Australia	1983	15.8	7.3	10.3	8.5	2.1	1981	2.0	160.0	11.1	...	376.0	49.0	8.6	51.0
Austria	1983	11.9	12.3	12.0	−0.4	0.8	1982	4.1	143.5	11.5	15.5	233.4	46.2	66.6	90.2
Bahamas, The	1981	25.1	5.4	22.4	19.7	2.0	1980	19.5	81.9	10.0	11.4	181.1	0.0	0.0	112.5
Bahrain	1982	30.5	6.3[10]	44.0[11]	24.2	4.6	1980	14.3	23.4	7.3	5.0	79.1	15.4	5.4	35.5
Bangladesh	1983	44.5	17.3	132.0	23.1	5.2	...	...	...	...	...	...	...	...	...
Barbados	1983	17.8	8.2	14.2	8.6	2.0	1980	16.4	79.8	49.0	...	355.3	255.7	30.1	36.1
Belgium	1983	11.9	11.3	11.3	0.6	1.6	1978	9.0	269.2	44.4	29.9	485.1	85.0	38.1	83.1
Belize	1982	38.6	4.3	21.3	34.3	...	1979	55.1	19.0	21.5	1.9	119.6	31.0	10.1	10.0
Benin	1980–85	48.5	17.3	157.0	31.2	6.7	1978	12.0	...	...	...	...	...	...	...
Bermuda	1982	14.5	6.8	9.0	5.9	...	1977	4.0	159.0	48.0	7.0	286.0	25.0	19.6	50.6
Bhutan	1983	39.3	18.0	143.0	21.3	5.5	...	...	...	...	...	...	...	...	...
Bolivia	1980	24.9	4.8	77.3	20.1	6.2	...	...	...	...	...	...	...	...	...
Botswana	1980–85	49.5	15.4	96.0	34.1	6.5	...	...	...	...	...	...	...	...	...
Brazil	1981	23.1	6.4	62.2	16.7	4.0	1979	74.1	60.7	13.7	11.5	181.1	58.3	23.7	66.1
British Virgin Islands	1982	20.7	5.9	42.6	14.8	...	1982	17.6	61.8	26.5	—	158.8	79.4	26.4	52.9
Brunei	1982	29.8	3.9	12.8	25.9	...	1981	6.7	25.4	...	...	41.5	10.4	3.1	37.8
Bulgaria	1983	13.6	11.4	16.8	2.2	2.2	1981	8.2	152.3	13.3	7.6	615.6	89.8	28.6	58.2
Burkina Faso	1980–85	47.9	21.1	...	26.8	6.5	...	...	...	...	...	...	...	...	...
Burma	1983	34.0	14.0	105.0	29.3	4.7	1978	32.6	6.3	6.1	...	14.1	19.8	1.7	7.3
Burundi	1980–85	46.8	18.4	126.6	28.4	5.9	...	...	...	...	...	...	...	...	...
Cameroon	1980–85	41.1	17.4	...	23.7	5.7	...	...	...	...	...	...	...	...	...
Canada	1983	15.1	7.1	9.1	8.0	1.8	1978	4.2	159.7	13.2	0.5	312.1	34.4	5.6	68.5
Cape Verde	1980	32.9	7.9	104.9	18.2	2.6	1980	153.7	49.6	20.6	16.5	135.8	72.3	27.7	30.1
Cayman Islands	1983	20.6	5.6	...	15.0	...	1979	18.2	60.1	52.0	...	204.6	54.1	...	102.1
Central African Republic	1980–85	42.3	17.5	154.0	24.8	5.9	...	...	...	...	...	...	...	...	...
Chad	1980–85	43.8	18.9	180.0[10]	24.9	5.9	...	...	...	...	...	...	...	...	...
Chile	1982	23.9	6.1	23.6	17.8	2.9	1980	31.1	98.5	10.3	7.6	184.5	65.5	21.7	77.5
China	1983	21.1	7.8	40.0	13.3	2.5	...	...	...	...	...	...	...	...	...
Christmas Island	1982	5.6	...	...	...	...	...	...	...	...	...	...	...	...	...
Cocos (Keeling) Islands	1981	14.4	1.8	—	12.6	...	...	...	...	...	...	...	...	...	...
Colombia	1980–85	32.2	8.2	39.5	24.0	3.9	1975	49.6	52.3	...	...	140.5	46.8	...	48.0
Comoros	1980–85	37.5	16.1	51.7	21.4	6.3	...	...	...	...	...	...	...	...	...
Congo	1980–85	42.9	17.0	134.5	25.9	6.0	...	...	...	...	...	...	...	...	...
Cook Islands	1983	23.3	6.9	29.6[9]	16.4	4.1	1981	29.2	75.6	13.7	9.3	106.4	36.1	18.9	44.8
Costa Rica	1982	30.7	3.9	19.3	26.8	3.2	1980	4.1	100.7	10.0	...	55.1	47.5	...	36.9
Cuba	1983	16.8	5.9	16.8	10.9	2.0	...	...	...	...	...	...	...	...	...
Cyprus	1983	22.3	8.5	17.2	13.8	2.3	1981	6.8	227.8	18.0	...	429.9	80.9	6.6	33.1
Czechoslovakia	1983	14.8	12.0	15.6	2.8	2.3	1982	3.8	268.7	15.5	9.0	467.1	70.5	32.2	73.6
Denmark	1983	9.9	11.2	8.2	−1.3	1.4	...	...	...	...	...	...	...	...	...
Djibouti	1970	42.0	7.6	...	34.4	...	1975	46.7	73.3	26.7	10.7	161.3	33.3	20.0	52.0
Dominica	1978	21.4	5.3	19.6	16.1	3.7	...	...	...	...	...	...	...	...	...
Dominican Republic	1980	35.5.	4.8	33.2	30.7	4.2	1977	75.3	22.8	16.6	9.0	65.5	36.9	19.6	34.6
Ecuador	1980	31.3	7.4	68.3	23.9	6.0	1979	456.1	57.7	18.0	44.3	165.9	142.1	193.8	429.9
Egypt	1982	36.9	10.3	74.2	26.6	4.7	1979	29.3	19.2	8.8	0.4	194.7	187.3	288.8	47.3
El Salvador	1982	31.4	6.7	42.2	24.7	5.6	1980	75.0	19.1	11.5	...	54.3	37.6	2.5	305.7
Equatorial Guinea	1980–85	41.1	17.4	...	23.7	5.7	...	...	...	...	...	...	...	...	...

tem that was weakened by diabetes, what was the actual cause of death? Statistics on causes of death tend to identify the most proximate cause or symptom, but often this kind of analysis is misleading for those charged with interpreting the data with a view to reordering health-care priorities for a particular country.

Expectation of life is probably the most accurate single measure of the quality of life in a given society. It summarizes in a single number all of the natural and social stresses that operate upon the individuals in that society. The number may range from as few as 45 years of life in the least developed countries to as much as 80 years for women in the most developed nations. The lost potential in the years separating those two numbers is prodigious, regardless of how the loss arises—wars and civil violence, poor public health services, or poor individual health practice in matters of nutrition, exercise, stress management, and so on.

Data on marriages and marriage rates probably are less meaningful in terms of international comparisons than some of the measures mentioned above because the number, timing, and kinds of social relationships that substitute for marriage depend on many kinds of social variables—income, degree of social control, heterogeneity of the society (race, class, language communities), or level of development of civil administration (if one must travel 100 miles to obtain a legal civil ceremony, one may forego it). Nevertheless, the data for a single country say specific things about local practice in terms of the age at which a man or woman typically marries,

and the overall rate will at least define the number of legal civil marriages, though it cannot say anything about other, less formal arrangements (here the figure for the legitimacy rate for children in the next section may identify some of the societies in which economics or social constraints may operate to limit the number of marriages that are actually confirmed on civil registers). The available data usually include both first marriages and remarriages after annulment, divorce, widowhood, or the like.

The data for families provide information about the average size of a family unit (individuals related by blood or civil register) and the average number of children under a specified age (set here to provide a consistent measure of legal minority internationally, though actual minority depends on the definition of each country). When well-defined family data are not collected as part of a country's national census or vital statistics surveys, data for households are substituted on the assumption that most households worldwide represent families in some conventional sense. In the older countries of Europe and North America increasing numbers of households are comprised of unrelated individuals (unmarried heterosexual couples, aged [or younger] groups sharing limited [often fixed] incomes for reasons of economy, or homosexual couples); such arrangements are not yet so common in the rest of the world that they represent great numbers overall. Very few census programs, even in developed countries, make adequate provision for identifying these households.

expectation of life at birth (latest year)		nuptiality, family, and family planning														country
		year	marriages								families (F), households (H)					
			total number	rate per 1,000 population	age of groom at first marriage (percent)			age of bride at first marriage (percent)			families (households)		children		legal abortions	
male	female				19 and under	20–29	30 and over	19 and under	20–29	30 and over	total ('000)	size	number under age 15	percent legitimate	number	ratio per 100 live births	
40.0	41.5	1970	6,212	0.4	...	...	...	...	...	...	H 2,110[1]	H 6.2[1]	H 2.8[1,2]	...	...	...	Afghanistan
66.5	70.9	1971	15,300	7.0	...	...	...	...	...	...		F 5.4[1]	...	...	...	...	Albania
54.4	56.3	1978	121,211[3]	6.9	...	...	...	...	...	...		H 4.9[4]	...	...	...	...	Algeria
61.0	64.3	1980	343	10.6	...	...	...	...	...	...	H 4	H 7.1	H 2.9	86.0[5]	...	...	American Samoa
...	...	1981	145	3.8	...	...	...	...	...	...			...	...	...	...	Andorra
40.0	43.0	1972	26,278	4.5	...	...	...	...	...	...	...	H 4.2[4]	...	...	...	...	Angola
68.6	71.9				...	...	...	...	...	...			...	...	...	...	Anguilla
68.6	71.9	1981	204	2.7	2.0	54.9	43.1	15.2	53.9	30.9	H 15[6]	H 4.2[6]	H 1.9[6]	22.2[7]	...	...	Antigua and Barbuda
66.8	73.2	1980	182,497[7]	6.9	...	...	...	...	...	...	H 7,104	H 3.9[8]	H 1.2	73.6	...	...	Argentina
71.0	78.1	1981	117,275[9]	7.7	4.6	85.5	9.9	23.2	72.8	4.0	F 4,140[5]	F 3.1[5]	F 0.5[5]	76.2	...	...	Australia
69.3	76.4	1980	47,428[8,9]	6.3	5.3	79.6	15.1	25.2	68.0	6.8	F 2,020[9]	F 3.7[9]	F 0.7[9]	82.2	...	...	Austria
68.6	71.9	1980	1,396	6.6	...	...	...	...	...	...	H 40[6]	H 2.4	H 1.8[6]	40.9[1]	...	...	Bahamas, The
64.0	68.0	1981	5,498	15.7	...	...	...	...	...	...	H 34[12]	H 5.5[4]	H 3.0[12]	...	...	...	Bahrain
48.5	47.5	1980			...	...	...	...	...	...		H 5.6		...	...	...	Bangladesh
68.0	73.0	1978	1,057[4]	4.2	0.6	55.9	43.5	9.0	64.6	26.4	H 59[6]	H 4.0[6]	H 1.5[6]	27.9	...	...	Barbados
69.0	75.0	1981	64,380	6.5	6.4[13]	88.8[13]	4.8[13]	30.0[13]	67.9[13]	2.1[13]	F 3,613	F 2.7	F 0.5	96.6[13]	...	...	Belgium
45.0	48.0	1982	844	5.6	...	...	...	...	...	...	H 29	H 5.3	H 2.4	48.0[14]	...	...	Belize
44.0	48.0	1980			...	...	...	...	...	...		H 4.9		...	...	...	Benin
68.8	76.3	1981	579	10.6	...	...	...	...	...	...	H 18[4]	H 2.9[4]	H 0.6[4]	66.4[9]	...	...	Bermuda
46.8	45.3	1980			...	...	...	...	...	...		H 2.6		...	...	...	Bhutan
47.0	51.0	1980	26,990	4.8	...	...	...	...	...	...	H 1,050[5]	H 4.4[5]	H 1.8[5]	80.9	...	...	Bolivia
52.0	58.0				...	...	...	...	...	...	H 140[12,15]	H 4.4[12]	H 2.0[12]	...	...	...	Botswana
60.0	64.0	1980	948,164	8.0	7.7[16]	69.4[16]	22.9[16]	35.5[16]	50.2[16]	14.3[16]	H 27,967	H 4.2	H 1.6	...	...	...	Brazil
68.6	71.9	1982	228	20.1	—	50.0	50.0	6.1	69.3	24.6	H 3[4,8]	H 3.3[4]	H 1.1[4]	44.7[17]	...	...	British Virgin Islands
...	...	1981	1,107[18]	5.8	5.2[19]	79.9[19]	14.9[19]	26.7[19]	68.6[19]	4.7[19]	H 23[12]	H 5.8[12]	H 2.5[12]	99.3[13]	...	...	Brunei
68.9	74.4	1980	66,539[14]	7.5	8.2	84.5	7.3	44.8	52.5	2.7	F 2,627[17]	F 3.3[17]	F 0.7[17]	89.1	128,500[1]	98.1[1]	Bulgaria
41.8	45.0	1980			...	...	...	...	...	...		H 5.5		...	...	...	Burkina Faso
51.4	54.5	1980			...	...	...	...	...	...		H 5.1		...	...	...	Burma
45.3	48.6	1980			...	...	...	...	...	...		H 5.8		...	...	...	Burundi
43.0	46.0	1980			...	...	...	...	...	...		H 5.5[16]		...	...	...	Cameroon
70.0	77.0	1981	188,119[9]	7.6	4.4	81.9	13.7	18.3	74.4	7.3	F 6,325	F 3.9[9]	F 1.4[20]	87.9[21]	65,100	17.5[22]	Canada
58.0	62.0	1975	1,604	5.4	...	...	...	...	...	...	F 59[4]	F 5.1[4]		44.8	...	...	Cape Verde
68.6	71.9	1981	204	11.3	...	...	...	...	...	...	H 4[1]	H 3.8[1]	H 1.1[1]	66.8[21]	...	...	Cayman Islands
38.4	45.3	1980			...	...	...	...	...	...		H 4.0[10]		...	...	...	Central African Republic
42.0	45.0	1980			...	...	...	...	...	...		H 5.6		...	...	...	Chad
63.6	70.4	1981	90,564	8.0	7.2	77.1	15.7	28.3	60.9	10.8	H 1,690[6]	H 5.0[4]	H 2.0[6]	72.4[4]	2,346[4]	1.0[4]	Chile
65.4	68.4	1982	8,395,000	8.3	...	...	...	...	...	...	H 221[23]	H 4.6		...	...	...	China
63.0	66.5	1982	19	8.5	...	...	...	...	...	...	—	H 5.8[14]	H 1.5[14]	97.1[4]	...	...	Christmas Island
63.0	66.5	1981	6	10.8	...	...	...	...	...	...	—	H 6.3[24]	H 2.6[24]	93.3[24]	2[13]	40.0[13]	Cocos (Keeling) Islands
62.7	65.9	1977	88,401	3.5	...	...	...	...	...	...	F 4,772[21]	F 5.4[21]	F 2.5[21]	75.2[4]	...	...	Colombia
46.4	49.7	1964	1,959	8.5	...	...	...	...	...	...				...	...	...	Comoros
46.9	50.1	1974	78[17]	0.1[17]	...	...	...	...	...	...	H 164	H 7.9	H 0.5	...	...	...	Congo
64.0	70.0	1982	82	4.8	...	...	...	...	...	...	H 3[14]	H 5.6[14]	H 2.4[14]	...	...	...	Cook Islands
71.0	76.0	1982	17,807[8]	7.7	...	...	...	...	...	...	F 472[21]	F 4.0[21]	F 1.7[21]	64.9[4]	...	...	Costa Rica
71.0	74.0	1982	80,363[8]	8.2	12.1[13]	64.4[13]	23.5[13]	41.8[13]	41.1[13]	17.1[13]	F 2,002[6]	F 4.4[4]	H 1.6[6]	...	...	...	Cuba
70.9	74.9	1981	7,163	11.2	1.6	81.4	17.0	19.7	71.2	9.1	H 160[21]	H 3.9[21]	H 1.1[21]	99.4[4]	...	...	Cyprus
66.8	74.0	1981	117,204[8,9]	7.6	7.0	87.8	5.2	37.4	60.4	2.2	F 4,187[4]	F 3.6[4]	F 0.9[4]	94.2	130,760	55.0	Czechoslovakia
71.4	77.4	1982	24,330	4.8	0.9	72.1	27.0	6.3	81.6	12.1	F 2,563[25]	F 2.0[25]	F 0.4[25]	66.8[4]	21,462	40.8	Denmark
...	...	1981	1,445	4.5	...	...	...	...	...	...				96.8[4]	...	...	Djibouti
66.5	72.8	1969	234	3.3	...	...	...	...	...	...	H 122[6]	H 4.9[26]	H 2.2[26]	35.0[4]	...	...	Dominica
60.7	64.6	1981	26,862	4.9	...	...	...	...	...	...	H 753[6]	H 3.8[4]	H 2.5[6]	32.8[5]	...	...	Dominican Republic
60.6	64.7	1974	48,306[4]	5.8[4]	3.9[19]	65.0[19]	31.1[19]	27.6[19]	53.0[19]	19.4[19]		H 5.0[4]		67.9[4]	...	...	Ecuador
55.9	58.4	1978	375,656	9.4	10.0	68.9	21.1	54.7	41.1	4.2	H 6,946[5]	H 5.2[5]	H 2.1[5]	...	...	...	Egypt
62.6	67.1	1980	21,260[14]	4.4	7.5[27]	62.3[27]	30.2[27]	35.9[27]	45.8[27]	18.3[27]	H 686[12]	H 5.4	H 2.4[12]	31.4	...	...	El Salvador
46.9	50.1	1966	209	0.8	...	...	...	...	...	...				...	...	...	Equatorial Guinea

Vital statistics, marriage, family (continued)

country	year	birth rate per 1,000 population	death rate per 1,000 population	infant mortality rate per 1,000 live births	rate of natural increase per 1,000 population	total fertility rate	year	infectious and parasitic diseases	neoplasms (cancers)	endocrine and metabolic disorders	diseases of the nervous system	diseases of the circulatory system	diseases of the respiratory system	diseases of the digestive system	accidents, poisoning, and violence
Ethiopia	1980–85	49.9	23.1	...	26.8	6.7	1978	39.5	3.8	24.6	2.7	5.6	16.3	28.9	15.8
Faeroe Islands	1983	15.7	7.2	7.0[9]	8.5	...	...	...	...	...	...	...	...	...	...
Falkland Islands	1981	15.0	5.0	...	10.0	...	...	...	...	...	...	...	...	...	...
Fiji	1982	30.6	5.8	17.4	24.8	3.1	1982	30.7	25.5	18.1	...	225.1	70.3	2.0	41.0
Finland	1982	13.7	9.0	6.5	4.7	1.6	1982	9.1	186.2	13.2	16.2[1]	444.0	72.9	7.8	76.5
France	1983	13.7	10.2	9.0	3.5	1.8	1982	12.7	242.8	13.0	34.1	365.3	11.2	66.4	93.2
French Guiana	1982	34.2	6.8	30.5	27.4	...	1977	43.8	76.6	43.8	4.7	212.5	21.9	46.9	94.1
French Polynesia	1981	31.9	6.5	40.9	25.4	...	...	...	...	...	...	...	...	...	...
Gabon	1980–85	33.7	19.9	121.6	13.8	4.7	...	...	...	...	...	...	...	...	...
Gambia, The	1980–85	47.5	21.7	203.5	25.8	6.4	...	...	...	...	...	...	...	...	...
Germany, East	1983	14.0	13.3	10.7	−0.7	1.8	1981	6.1	240.0	31.3	...	825.1	70.1	10.6	40.1
Germany, West	1983	9.7	11.7	10.9	−2.0	1.4	1981	7.6	275.6	23.8	20.3	595.3	65.7	60.3	67.8
Ghana	1980–85	46.7	18.7	107.3	28.0	6.7	1980	92.7	...	...	...	...	...	—	—
Gibraltar	1983	17.5	8.7	...	8.8	...									
Greece	1983	13.6	9.1	14.9	4.5	2.3	1981	8.0	176.1	32.5	17.2	392.6	62.8	35.2	49.4
Greenland	1983	19.2	8.2	39.4	11.0	2.3	1982	15.5	161.1	0.0	0.0	157.3	54.4	0.0	318.4
Grenada	1979	24.5	6.8	15.4	17.7	...	1978	51.8	65.5	31.8	19.1	255.5	62.7	29.1	20.0
Guadeloupe	1982	20.2	6.5	15.5	13.7	2.4	1979	10.0	72.5	27.6	...	220.2	13.4	3.1	96.9
Guam	1983	28.7	4.2	7.5	24.5	...	...	...	...	...	...	...	...	...	...
Guatemala	1981	41.2	7.5	64.0	33.7	5.2	1980	285.1	26.0	5.0	21.2[1]	49.9	151.3	2.1	101.0
Guinea	1980–85	44.3	18.7	83.8	25.6	6.2	...	...	...	...	...	...	...	...	...
Guinea-Bissau	1980	39.2	21.1	...	18.1	5.4	...	...	...	...	...	...	...	...	...
Guyana	1978	29.7	7.6	45.9	22.1	3.2	1978	36.9	23.0	24.0	4.7	103.3	31.2	9.8	14.3
Haiti	1980–85	41.3	14.1	126.9	27.2	5.7	...	...	...	...	...	...	...	...	...
Honduras	1981	42.1	11.8	23.0	30.3	6.5	1979	88.6	18.4	4.2	21.9	48.5	36.1	22.4	50.7
Hong Kong	1983	16.0	5.0	10.0	11.0	1.9	1983	15.2	132.5	4.2	4.0	144.8	7.8	22.8	35.9
Hungary	1983	11.9	13.9	19.0	−2.0	2.1	1982	12.8	265.4	...	...	729.6	75.8	66.8	112.0
Iceland	1982	18.5	6.5	7.7	12.1	2.3	1982	6.0	157.3	4.7	6.2	325.0	75.1	2.6	53.0
India	1983	32.9	13.2	117.0	19.7	4.3	1970[31]	3.0	...	2.1	...	...	...	...	4.6
Indonesia	1983	30.3	12.9	106.0	17.4	3.8	...	...	...	...	...	...	...	...	...
Iran	1983	39.7	10.0	100.0	29.7	5.6	1981	14.5[32]	16.7	6.0	...	84.7	20.7	1.3	73.3
Iraq	1980–85	45.1	11.5	30.6	33.6	6.6	1980	9.0	182.9	8.2	1.0	490.1	97.3	6.4	79.4
Ireland	1982	20.3	9.4	10.6	10.9	3.2	1979	10.4	147.9	10.6	...	326.6	28.2	4.7	50.1
Israel	1983	24.1	6.8	14.2	17.3	3.2	1981	5.9	214.7	...	13.2	441.1	69.0	55.5	48.8
Italy	1983	10.6	9.9	12.4	0.7	1.8	...	...	...	...	...	...	...	...	...
Ivory Coast	1980–85	45.1	16.3	132.0	28.8	6.7	1978	31.5	83.3	33.1	...	790.8	31.9	...	80.1
Jamaica	1982	27.6	5.7	16.2	21.9	3.3	1982	138.4	143.6	8.3[14]	7.6[14]	242.4	34.9	14.0	42.1
Japan	1983	12.7	5.5	6.7	7.2	1.8	...	...	...	...	...	...	...	...	...
Jordan	1980–85	45.3	9.1	36.3	36.2	7.1	...	...	...	...	...	...	...	...	...
Kampuchea	1983	45.1	19.3	157.0	25.8	5.1	...	...	...	...	...	...	...	...	...
Kenya	1979	19.2	3.1	51.4	15.2	8.1	1980	3.1	...	...	...	...	...	...	...
Kiribati	1979	23.7	15.0	42.0	8.7	2.8	...	...	...	...	...	...	...	...	...
Korea, North	1980–85	31.0	7.4	36.7	23.6	3.6	...	...	...	...	...	...	...	...	...
Korea, South	1983	17.7	5.1	34.0	12.6	2.6	1980	21.9	...	...	...	...	...	...	...
Kuwait	1982	34.7	3.2	22.8	31.5	6.1	1981	25.9	28.6	3.9	4.5	94.9	26.4	9.3	49.6
Laos	1983	40.5	15.5	121.0	25.0	5.8	...	...	...	...	...	...	...	...	...
Lebanon	1980–85	29.6	7.9	13.6	21.7	3.8	...	...	...	...	...	...	...	...	...
Lesotho	1980–85	38.6	14.6	107.0	24.0	5.4	...	...	...	...	...	...	...	...	...
Liberia	1980–85	47.9	15.3	159.2	32.6	6.9	...	...	...	...	...	...	...	...	...
Libya	1981	38.2	5.0	46.3	33.2	7.2	...	...	...	...	...	...	...	...	...
Liechtenstein	1981	14.4	6.3	6.1	8.1	1.5	1980	8.1	161.2	19.4	...	266.5	43.2	12.1	63.4
Luxembourg	1983	11.8	11.3	7.2	0.5	1.5	1981	6.8	27.5	33.2	37.8	535.1	55.1	64.9	83.6
Macau	1982	15.4	4.5	11.6	10.9	3.4	1981	46.6	92.1	11.5	0.7	158.6	42.6	30.3	37.9
Madagascar	1981	45.0	18.0	53.2	27.0	6.1	...	...	...	...	...	...	...	...	...
Malawi	1980	47.1	23.7	130.0	23.4	7.0	1980	54.2	3.9	10.6	4.4	4.9	18.3	3.2	5.1
Malaysia	1983	28.6	6.4	40.0	22.2	3.5	1979	9.7	17.5	1.4	...	40.6	11.8	2.1	23.0
Maldives	1982	44.5	13.3	78.5	31.2	...	...	...	...	...	...	...	...	...	...
Mali	1980–85	49.4	21.2	120.9	28.2	6.7	...	...	...	...	...	...	...	...	...
Malta	1983	15.0	8.3	14.1	6.7	1.9	1982	4.0	154.5	51.5	4.6	528.5	44.4	24.2	27.3
Martinique	1983	18.2	7.0	13.1	11.2	2.4	1975	19.9	0.6	7.4	11.6	154.0	24.2	2.1	44.4
Mauritania	1980–85	50.4	21.3	...	29.1	6.9	...	...	...	...	...	...	...	...	...
Mauritius	1982	22.4	6.7	30.2	15.7	3.1	1982	32.1	53.3	18.9	7.9	303.4	76.4	34.4	42.6
Mayotte							...	...	...	...	...	...	...	...	...
Mexico	1981	33.6	5.3	38.5	28.3	4.8	1978	95.7	38.5	26.9	8.2	101.4	93.0	41.1	89.8
Monaco	1983	19.6	16.6	...	3.0	...	...	...	...	...	...	...	...	...	...
Mongolia	1982	36.7	9.2	49.0	27.5	4.8	...	...	...	...	...	...	...	...	...
Montserrat	1982	22.3	9.8	...	12.5	...	...	...	...	...	...	...	...	...	...
Morocco	1980–85	44.1	11.7	...	32.4	6.4	...	...	...	...	...	...	...	...	...
Mozambique	1980–85	44.6	17.2	19.1	27.4	6.1	...	...	...	...	...	...	...	...	...
Nauru	1981	24.0	10.5	31.2	13.5	...	1976–81	37.5[38]	42.5[38]	32.5[38]	15.0[38]	100.0[38]	17.5[38]	30.0[38]	132.5[38]
Nepal	1983	41.5	18.2	143.0	22.6	6.2	...	...	...	...	...	...	...	...	...
Netherlands, The	1983	11.8	8.2	8.4	3.6	1.5	1981	4.1	225.7	13.2	15.3	367.3	50.1	29.0	41.5
Netherlands Antilles	1980	17.5	4.9	14.0	12.6	...	1973	8.5	91.3	19.2	0.9	86.6	22.6	8.1	43.1
New Caledonia	1983	25.2	5.6	11.2	19.6	...	...	...	...	...	...	...	...	...	...
New Zealand	1983	16.3	7.6	12.0	8.7	2.0	1980	5.5	174.5	17.7	15.7	415.2	96.6	13.0	65.5
Nicaragua	1980	44.1	10.5	101.7	33.6	6.2	1977	116.1	19.5	7.2	7.6	84.5	36.0	26.3	71.2
Niger	1980–85	51.7	21.4	...	30.3	7.1	...	...	...	...	...	...	...	...	...
Nigeria	1980–85	49.5	16.0	...	33.5	6.9	1979	11.6[14]	0.1	0.2	0.04	0.2	0.4	1.2	0.5
Niue	1983	30.7	7.9	—	22.8	...	...	...	...	...	...	...	...	...	...
Norfolk Island	1981	10.8	7.6	...	3.2	...	...	...	...	...	...	...	...	...	...
Norway	1983	12.0	10.2	8.1	1.8	1.7	1982	7.4	221.5	9.6	...	466.4	78.8	10.9	63.0
Oman	1980–85	47.7	16.7	...	31.0	7.1	...	...	...	...	...	...	...	...	...
Pakistan	1983	42.3	15.0	119.0	27.3	5.8	...	...	...	...	...	...	...	...	...
Panama	1982	25.5	3.8	20.1	21.7	3.6	1980	32.9	59.6	10.5	4.9	103.8	38.0	3.8	54.0
Papua New Guinea	1983	40.1	13.4	97.0	26.7	5.9	1978	22.5	2.6	26.8	5.8	22.2	27.4	3.1	4.5

expectation of life at birth (latest year)		nuptiality, family, and family planning															country
		year	marriages								families (F), households (H)						
male	female		total number	rate per 1,000 population	age of groom at first marriage (percent)			age of bride at first marriage (percent)			families (households)		children		legal abortions		
					19 and under	20–29	30 and over	19 and under	20–29	30 and over	total ('000)	size	number under age 15	percent legitimate	number	ratio per 100 live births	
39.4	42.6	1980	...	...	...	...	...	...	...	...	...	H 4.5	...	...	...	...	Ethiopia
...	...	1981	217[9]	4.9	0.0	71.4	28.6	14.6	77.8	7.6	F 14[7]	F 3.0[7]	F 0.9[7]	69.8[4]	26[17]	3.3[17]	Faeroe Islands
...	...	1980	11	...	...	...	...	...	...	...	—[28]	H 3.3[28]	H 0.9[28]	75.0	...	...	Falkland Islands
70.6	74.7	1980	6,074[9]	9.2	11.1	75.6	13.3	39.1	53.7	7.2	F 97[5]	F 6.0[5]	F 2.5[5]	82.7[13]	...	...	Fiji
69.5	77.8	1982	30,564	6.3	2.9[14]	78.2[14]	18.9[14]	12.3[14]	76.4[14]	11.3	F 1,163[17]	H 2.8[4]	F 0.9[17]	86.7[14]	14,120	22.3	Finland
70.2	78.5	1980	314,600[14]	5.8	2.3	85.0	12.7	17.8	74.7	7.5	H 13,177[17]	H 2.9[17]	H 1.0[17]	88.6	171,300	21.3	France
59.2	62.9	1982	264	3.6	...	...	...	...	...	...	H 12[29]	H 3.7[29]	H 1.4[29]	21.7	...	...	French Guiana
59.2	62.9	1976	947[28]	8.0	11.3	75.8	12.9	41.5	52.5	6.0	H 26[7]	H 5.0[4]	H 2.3[7]	45.1[4]	...	...	French Polynesia
44.4	47.6	1960	...	...	...	...	...	...	...	...	...	H 3.9	...	...	...	...	Gabon
40.9	44.1	1973	...	...	...	...	...	...	...	...	H 59	H 8.3	H 3.4	...	...	...	Gambia, The
69.0	75.0	1981	128,174	7.7	7.4	86.2	6.4	30.6	66.2	3.2	F 4,781[9]	F 3.5[9]	F 0.7[9]	77.2[4]	80,100[7]	35.0[7]	Germany, East
70.1	76.7	1981	361,272[8,9]	5.9	4.0	78.8	17.2	19.1	73.6	7.3	F 22,882[9]	F 2.7[9]	F 0.5[9]	92.4[4]	87,500	14.2	Germany, West
49.1	52.5	1970	...	...	...	...	...	...	...	...	H 1,794	H 4.9[4]	H 2.2	...	...	...	Ghana
71.4	75.5	1981	429	14.1	...	...	...	...	...	...	H 7	H 3.8	H 1.0	97.1[5]	...	...	Gibraltar
71.0	75.0	1980	72,000[8,9]	7.4	2.6	70.2	27.3	31.9	56.8	11.3	H 2,990[14]	H 3.2[14]	H 0.7[14]	98.6[1]	117	0.1	Greece
59.7	67.3	1981	312[9]	6.0	0.0	57.8	42.2	4.1	75.7	20.2	F 25[9]	F 2.1[9]	F 0.4[9]	38.4[4]	539	51.3	Greenland
66.5	72.8	1979	330	3.0	...	...	...	...	...	...	H 20[6]	H 2.9[4]	H 2.2[6]	22.5	...	...	Grenada
67.8	73.0	1980	1,577[14]	4.7	...	...	...	...	...	...	H 70[29]	H 2.7	H 1.9[29]	47.9	561	8.7	Guadeloupe
63.0	66.5	1980	1,479[14]	13.5	6.4	71.5	22.1	16.8	71.3	11.9	H 25	H 4.1	H 1.5	81.2[1]	...	...	Guam
59.7	61.8	1981	29,519[4]	4.1	...	...	...	...	...	...	H 1,185	H 5.2[21]	H 2.7	34.8[28]	...	...	Guatemala
44.4	47.6	1980	...	...	...	...	...	...	...	...	...	H 5.4	...	...	...	...	Guinea
41.9	45.1	1981	100	0.2	...	...	...	...	...	...	H 124[1]	H 6.2[1]	H 2.8[1]	11.3[4]	...	...	Guinea-Bissau
69.1	73.3	1968	2,760	4.2	...	...	...	...	...	...	H 130[6]	H 5.2[4]	H 2.5[6]	61.4[4]	...	...	Guyana
51.2	54.4	1980	3,370[30]	.0.7	...	...	...	...	...	...	H 1,131[14]	H 5.1	H 1.8[14]	...	...	...	Haiti
58.2	61.7	1979	14,414	4.0	...	...	...	...	...	...	H 463[27]	H 5.7[27]	H 2.8[27]	...	...	...	Honduras
73.0	77.8	1981	50,756	9.8	1.7[4]	71.2[4]	27.1[4]	9.8[4]	82.8[4]	7.4[4]	H 1,245	H 3.9	H 1.0	90.4[4]	10,600	12.0[22]	Hong Kong
66.0	73.4	1981	75,557[9]	7.1	9.2	83.1	7.7	38.9	56.5	4.6	F 3,028[4]	F 3.4[4]	F 0.8[4]	92.9[4]	78,400	57.3	Hungary
73.9	79.4	1980	1,303[9]	5.6[9]	4.1[18]	81.6[18]	14.3[18]	15.6[18]	78.9[18]	5.5[18]	H 49[27]	H 3.3[27]	H 1.3[27]	60.3	602[9]	13.9[9]	Iceland
57.6	57.1	1981	...	...	...	...	...	...	...	...	H 97,093[12]	H 5.6[4]	H 2.4[12]	...	385,700	1.8	India
51.4	54.2	1980	...	...	...	...	...	...	...	...	H 30,263	H 4.8	H 2.0	...	...	...	Indonesia
60.6	60.2	1980	284,647	7.5	...	...	...	...	...	...	H 6,709[5]	H 4.9[5]	H 2.2[5]	...	...	...	Iran
55.9	59.1	1977	134,062	11.1	...	...	...	...	...	...	H 1,835	H 6.5	H 3.2	...	...	...	Iraq
70.3	75.6	1979	20,582[8,9]	5.9	5.1	78.6	16.3	15.4	76.1	8.5	H 726[12]	H 4.0[4]	H 1.3[12]	95.0[4]	...	...	Ireland
72.1	75.7	1981	29,652	7.3	4.6[33]	84.6[33]	10.8[33]	28.9[33]	65.8[33]	5.3[33]	H 1,026[4]	H 3.8[4]	H 1.3[4]	97.5[4]	...	...	Israel
70.7	76.2	1982	310,938	5.5	1.9[1]	78.0[1]	20.1[1]	20.9[1]	68.8[1]	10.3[1]	F 17,615[4]	F 3.2[4]	F 0.7[4]	96.0[4]	220,300[4]	34.2[4,23]	Italy
46.9	50.2	1980	...	...	...	...	...	...	...	...	...	H 5.3[34]	...	...	...	...	Ivory Coast
69.0	73.5	1980	7,781	3.6	...	...	...	...	...	...	H 420[7]	H 3.4	H 2.0[7]	...	...	...	Jamaica
74.2	79.7	1982	781,300	6.6	0.9[14]	71.4[14]	27.7[14]	3.3[14]	87.8[14]	8.9[14]	F 22,240[25]	F 5.4[25]	F 1.2[25]	99.2[4]	598,100[4]	37.7[4,22]	Japan
56.3	59.5	1980	15,597[35]	4.8[35]	7.5[35]	76.3[35]	16.2[35]	57.7[35]	39.2[35]	3.1[35]	H 320[1]	H 5.2	H 3.4[1]	...	...	...	Jordan
42.5	45.4	1980	...	...	...	...	...	...	...	...	...	H 4.9	...	...	...	...	Kampuchea
56.3	60.0	1969	...	...	...	...	...	...	...	...	H 1,938	H 4.5[4]	H 2.7	...	...	...	Kenya
57.0	60.0	1978	291[36]	...	...	...	...	...	...	...	F 12	F 5.0	F 2.0	...	...	...	Kiribati
62.7	66.6	1980	...	...	...	...	...	...	...	...	...	H 5.0	...	...	...	...	Korea, North
65.9	62.7	1981	119,763[8]	3.1	...	...	...	...	...	...	F 7,969[4]	F 4.8[4]	F 1.6[4]	...	...	...	Korea, South
68.1	72.9	1979	7,595	5.9	...	...	...	...	...	...	H 143[17]	H 6.5[17]	H 1.6[17]	...	...	...	Kuwait
48.5	51.4	1980	...	...	...	...	...	...	...	...	...	H 4.9	...	...	...	...	Laos
65.0	68.9	1973	18,601	7.0	...	...	...	...	...	...	H 405[6]	H 4.0[4]	H 2.2[6]	...	...	...	Lebanon
51.7	53.9	1976	...	...	...	...	...	...	...	...	H 242	H 4.4	H 2.0	...	...	...	Lesotho
49.1	52.5	1971	61,896	45.5	...	...	...	...	...	...	...	H 3.9[4]	...	...	...	...	Liberia
56.1	59.4	1979	17,236	6.0	...	...	...	...	...	...	F 383[21]	F 5.4[21]	F 2.9[21]	...	...	...	Libya
68.8	76.1	1980	349	13.8	...	...	...	...	...	...	H 8	H 2.9	H 0.7	96.8	...	...	Liechtenstein
68.8	76.1	1980	2,089[9,18]	5.9	4.1[18]	85.2[18]	10.7[18]	23.2[18]	73.7[18]	3.1[18]	H 128[14]	H 2.8[14]	H 0.5[14]	94.0	...	...	Luxembourg
68.7	71.2	1982	1,527	4.2	0.0	46.1	53.9	4.3	73.7	22.0	H 50[29]	H 4.8[4]	H 1.8[29]	99.3[13]	...	...	Macau
46.9	50.2	1975	18,886[28]	2.6	...	...	...	...	...	...	H 1,709	H 4.4[4]	H 2.0	...	...	...	Madagascar
46.9	50.2	1977	...	7.8[10]	...	...	...	...	...	...	...	H 4.8[4]	...	...	...	...	Malawi
65.2	69.0	1975	23,635[37]	2.0	...	...	...	...	...	...	...	H 5.8[4]	...	...	...	...	Malaysia
...	...	1981	5,428	34.6	...	...	...	...	...	...	H 23[7]	H 6.1[7]	H 2.7[7]	...	...	...	Maldives
41.8	45.0	1980	3,075	0.4	...	...	...	...	...	...	H 1,254[5]	H 5.1[13]	...	...	...	...	Mali
69.8	74.4	1979	2,813[8,9]	8.7	2.9	78.3	18.8	16.6	72.3	11.1	H 76[29]	H 4.1[29]	H 1.2[29]	99.0[4]	...	...	Malta
69.6	72.9	1981	1,199	3.9	...	...	...	...	...	...	H 71[6]	H 2.8[4]	...	43.8	...	...	Martinique
41.8	45.0	1976	...	...	...	...	...	...	...	...	H 246	H 5.5	...	...	...	...	Mauritania
62.3	70.1	1981	10,770[8,9]	10.9	1.9	53.2	44.9	21.6	58.0	20.4	F 155[28]	F 5.3[28]	F 2.0[28]	55.4[4]	...	...	Mauritius
...	...	1978	...	...	...	...	...	...	...	...	H 10	H 4.7	H 2.3	...	...	...	Mayotte
62.0	67.0	1980	495,996	7.2	...	...	...	...	...	...	H 9,851[6]	H 5.4	H 2.3[6]	91.0[13]	...	...	Mexico
...	...	1981	190	7.3	...	...	...	...	...	...	H 10[17]	H 2.3[17]	H 0.3[17]	96.8[4]	...	...	Monaco
62.9	66.8	1981	8,500	5.0	...	...	...	...	...	...	F 311[1]	F 5.1[1]	...	...	...	...	Mongolia
68.6	71.9	1982	41	4.1	...	...	...	...	...	...	H 4[4]	H 3.1[4]	...	23.4[21]	...	...	Montserrat
56.1	59.4	1971	...	...	...	...	...	...	...	...	H 2,819	H 5.4[4]	H 2.5	...	...	...	Morocco
46.9	50.2	1974	6,037	0.7	...	...	...	...	...	...	F 1,860[6]	F 4.4[6]	F 2.0[6]	73.1	...	...	Mozambique
48.9	62.1	1966	43[21]	6.3	...	...	...	...	...	...	H 1	H 6.6	H 2.6	...	...	...	Nauru
46.8	45.3	1971	...	...	...	...	...	...	...	...	H 2,084	H 5.3[4]	H 2.2	...	...	...	Nepal
72.7	79.3	1981	83,516[9]	5.8	1.5	87.3	11.2	12.9	81.4	5.7	H 5,111	H 2.8	H 0.6	95.9[4]	19,000[39]	11.1	Netherlands, The
68.2	75.4	1975	1,570[21]	6.7	4.0	77.0	18.9	22.2	61.1	16.7	H 41[12]	H 4.5[4]	H 2.1[12]	73.4[21]	...	...	Netherlands Antilles
58.0	59.9	1980	781	5.5	4.0[7]	75.3[7]	20.7[7]	33.9[7]	56.1[7]	10.0[7]	...	H 4.3	...	...	...	...	New Caledonia
70.4	76.6	1981	23,660[9]	8.1	5.1[4]	82.8[4]	12.1[4]	23.4[4]	71.2[4]	5.4[4]	H 1,004	H 3.0	H 0.8	79.1[1]	6,800	13.3	New Zealand
55.8	59.5	1980	17,174	6.3	...	...	...	...	...	...	...	H 5.7	...	...	...	...	Nicaragua
41.8	45.0	1960	...	...	...	...	...	...	...	...	H 611[40]	H 4.4[40]	H 2.4[40]	...	...	...	Niger
48.3	51.7	1980	...	...	...	...	...	...	...	...	...	H 6.0	...	...	...	...	Nigeria
63.0	66.5	1976	12[8,9]	3.5	...	...	...	...	...	...	F 1	F 4.1	F 1.9	58.2[17]	...	...	Niue
58.0	59.9	1981	16	...	0.0	90.0	10.0	7.7	61.5	30.8	...	...	..	73.9[4]	...	...	Norfolk Island
72.5	79.2	1982	21,706	5.3	2.8[14]	81.3[14]	15.9[14]	15.1[14]	78.3[14]	6.6[14]	F 1,684[4]	F 2.4[4]	F 0.6[4]	85.5[4]	13,496	26.4	Norway
48.7	50.9	1980	...	...	...	...	...	...	...	...	...	H 4.8	...	...	...	...	Oman
51.2	49.2	1980	...	...	...	...	...	...	...	...	...	H 5.8	...	...	...	...	Pakistan
68.0	72.0	1981	9,554[41]	5.3[4]	7.5[41]	71.3[41]	21.2[41]	30.3[41]	59.3[41]	10.4[41]	F 347[4]	F 4.9[4]	...	28.6[4]	...	...	Panama
53.8	53.3	1980	...	...	...	...	...	...	...	...	...	H 5.0	...	...	...	...	Papua New Guinea

Vital statistics, marriage, family (continued)

country	vital rates						causes of death (rate per 100,000 population)								
	year	birth rate per 1,000 population	death rate per 1,000 population	infant mortality rate per 1,000 live births	rate of natural increase per 1,000 population	total fertility rate	year	infectious and parasitic diseases	neo-plasms (cancers)	endocrine and metabolic disorders	diseases of the nervous system	diseases of the circulatory system	diseases of the respiratory system	diseases of the digestive system	accidents, poisoning, and violence
Paraguay	1980–85	36.0	7.2	38.6	28.8	4.8	1980	104.7	68.6	20.1	11.1	180.8	75.0	80.3	597.0
Peru	1983	35.4	10.6	145.3	24.8	5.3	1972	104.0	35.7	...	...	33.3	164.9	...	28.2
Philippines	1983	32.0	6.8	50.0	25.2	4.2	1973	165.2	29.7	37.6	10.8	82.8	162.0	26.6	38.1
Pitcairn Island	1982	—	—	—	—	...	...	...	...	...	...	...	...	...	...
Poland	1983	19.7	9.6	19.2	10.1	2.3	1982	16.0	169.0	8.0	59.0	367.0	19.0	13.0	68.0
Portugal	1980	16.3	9.9	26.0	6.4	2.3	1979	21.6	129.1	11.9	9.5	420.7	97.8	59.1	72.8
Puerto Rico	1983	19.6	6.3	16.0	13.3	2.1[10, 11]	1980	9.6	102.4	32.1	49.3	252.8	55.9	44.8	60.6
Qatar	1980–85	30.8	9.2	...	...	6.8	...	...	...	...	...	...	...	...	...
Réunion	1983	22.7	6.0	...	12.0	5.1	...	...	...	...	...	...	...	...	...
Romania	1982	14.7	9.6	30.9	5.1	2.4	1982	10.4	126.8	6.1	12.0	562.2	127.9	16.8	70.4
Rwanda	1980	19.5	5.2	50.4	14.3	6.9	...	...	...	...	...	...	...	...	...
St. Christopher and Nevis	1982	29.0	11.2	42.8	17.8	...	1979	104.7	69.9	47.2	37.0	418.9	61.6	4.1	26.3
St. Helena and Ascension	1982	24.6	10.0	16.3	14.6	...	...	...	...	...	...	...	...	...	...
St. Lucia	1983	31.0	6.2	26.4	24.8	...	1981	46.2	31.4	25.6	19.0	219.0	45.4	34.7	32.2
St. Pierre and Miquelon	1981	18.2	8.3	9.2	9.9	...	1977	72.9	108.3	102.1	25.0	366.7	45.8	39.6	39.6
St. Vincent and the Grenadines	1980	25.3	6.0	60.2	19.3	...	...	...	...	...	...	...	...	...	...
San Marino	1983	11.0	7.1	9.5	3.9	...	1982	0.0	450.1	41.4	...	510.9	32.2	0.0	92.0
São Tomé and Príncipe	1982	38.7	10.2	69.5	28.5	...	...	...	...	...	...	...	...	...	...
Saudi Arabia	1980–85	47.6	16.4	121.1	31.2	7.1	...	...	...	...	...	...	...	...	...
Senegal	1980–85	47.9	21.1	152.6	25.7	6.5	...	...	...	...	...	...	...	...	...
Seychelles	1983	25.8	7.5	14.4	18.3	...	1980	31.6	98.0	14.2	...	200.7	90.1	25.3	80.6
Sierra Leone	1980–85	45.3	17.4	136.3	27.9	6.1	...	...	...	...	...	...	...	...	...
Singapore	1983	16.6	5.3	9.2	11.3	1.6	1982	15.7	112.1	16.1	4.8	178.4	90.6	16.1	23.2
Solomon Islands	1982	44.6	11.7	46.0	32.9	7.3	...	...	...	...	...	...	...	...	...
Somalia	1980–85	48.1	19.1	150.0	29.0	6.9	...	...	...	...	...	...	...	...	...
South Africa	1980–85	36.4	9.2	100.6	27.2	5.1	...	...	...	...	...	...	...	...	...
South West Africa/ Namibia	1980–85	42.0	13.5	125.3	28.5	5.9	...	...	...	...	...	...	...	...	...
Spain	1982	13.4	7.4	6.0	14.4	2.4	1982	14.2	153.7	20.5	11.8	361.2	67.4	42.7	43.2
Sri Lanka	1983	26.8	6.6	37.0	20.2	3.3	...	...	...	...	...	...	...	...	...
Sudan, The	1980–85	44.7	16.5	131.0	28.2	6.6	...	...	...	...	...	...	...	...	...
Suriname	1980	28.0	7.9	30.4	20.1	5.7	1980	35.1	50.6	17.0	11.6	154.9	19.8	30.6	72.1
Swaziland	1980–85	45.6	17.1	140.1	28.5	6.5	...	...	...	...	...	...	...	...	...
Sweden	1983	11.0	10.9	7.8	0.1	1.6	1981	7.3	230.7	13.0	0.0	184.4	68.9	11.7	61.4
Switzerland	1982	11.4	9.3	7.6	2.1	1.5	1981	6.8	239.7	25.1	4.9	450.7	51.5	32.9	75.0
Syria	1982	45.7	5.9	67.0	39.8	7.2	1981	15.1	8.4	5.0	4.0	60.7	13.2	4.5	20.0
Taiwan	1983	20.5	4.9	8.9	15.6	2.3	1980	...	75.1	...	...	137.1	34.0	...	74.0
Tanzania	1980–85	34.5	10.2	107.4	24.3	6.5	...	...	...	...	...	...	...	...	...
Thailand	1982	21.7	5.0	12.4	16.7	3.5	1982	7.8	26.1	...	...	34.1	21.5	17.6	33.5
Togo	1979	41.4	3.1	114.4	38.3	6.5	...	...	...	...	...	...	...	...	...
Tokelau	1982	27.7	10.3	—	17.4	4.3	...	...	...	...	...	...	...	...	...
Tonga	1982	37.9	3.5	9.0	28.9	...	...	...	...	...	...	...	...	...	...
Trinidad and Tobago	1979	25.1	6.5	26.4	18.6	2.2	1978	22.3	65.3	6.3	5.7	244.1	30.9	3.7	59.0
Trust Territory of the Pacific Is.	1982	23.7	3.7	21.5	20.0	...	1982	23.9	23.9	12.4	10.0	59.4	61.0	1.5	43.3
Tunisia	1982	32.9	5.4	39.2	27.5	4.9	1980	18.2	8.9	3.9	5.2	29.3	10.0	6.2	12.4
Turkey	1980–85	33.5	9.1	131.0	24.4	4.4	1982	15.0	24.5	22.6	1.7	106.7	18.1	4.0	8.4
Turks and Caicos Islands	1982	25.5	4.6	10.2	20.9	...	...	...	...	...	...	...	...	...	...
Tuvalu	1982	34.8	7.6	42.0	27.2	2.8	...	...	...	...	...	...	...	...	...
Uganda	1980–85	44.6	12.8	100.5	31.8	6.1	...	...	...	...	...	...	...	...	...
U.S.S.R.	1983	20.1	10.3	27.7[27]	9.8	2.4	...	...	...	...	...	...	...	...	...
United Arab Emirates	1980–85	30.5	7.3	80.9	25.2	6.8	...	...	...	...	...	...	...	...	...
United Kingdom	1983	13.0	11.9	10.2	1.1	1.6	1982	4.8	252.8	12.2	13.9	591.5	164.1	67.1	48.6
United States	1983	15.8	9.0	11.0	6.8	1.8	1982	9.3	188.1	14.3	0.5	420.5	47.9	3.3	64.2
Uruguay	1982	18.4	9.4	33.2	9.0	2.8	1976	...	207.7	...	...	373.3	32.0	...	40.3
Vanuatu	1979	45.0	20.0	...	25.0	...	...	...	...	...	...	...	...	...	...
Venezuela	1981	32.1	5.5	31.6	26.6	4.3	1979	48.0	54.0	18.2	11.1	123.8	38.4	20.0	79.5
Vietnam	1983	31.7	10.9	75.0	20.8	4.3	...	...	...	...	...	...	...	...	...
Virgin Islands (U.S.)	1978	24.8	4.8	22.5	20.0	...	1980	...	...	...	...	...	...	...	76.4
Wallis and Futuna	1978	41.1	10.6	40.5	30.5	...	...	...	...	...	...	...	...	...	...
Western Sahara	1980–85	29.0	4.5	5.3	24.5	...	...	...	...	...	...	...	...	...	...
Western Samoa	1983	31.4	8.0	42.0	23.4	6.7	...	...	...	...	...	...	...	...	...
Yemen (Aden)	1980–85	47.6	18.9	...	28.7	6.9	...	...	...	...	...	...	...	...	...
Yemen (Ṣanʿāʾ)	1980–85	48.5	21.8	...	26.7	6.8	...	...	...	...	...	...	...	...	...
Yugoslavia	1983	16.6	9.6	31.7	7.0	2.1	1982	17.4	129.4	14.4	7.0	438.5	55.7	17.8	61.0
Zaire	1980–85	44.1	16.7	...	27.4	6.1	...	...	...	...	...	...	...	...	...
Zambia	1980–85	47.4	15.4	...	32.0	6.9	...	...	...	...	...	...	...	...	...
Zimbabwe	1980–85	47.2	12.4	...	34.8	6.6	1979	7.3	152.9	7.0	1.6	310.6	64.7	6.6	102.4

expectation of life at birth (latest year) male	female	year	marriages total number	rate per 1,000 population	groom 19 and under	groom 20–29	groom 30 and over	bride 19 and under	bride 20–29	bride 30 and over	families (households) total ('000)	size	children number under age 15	percent legitimate	legal abortions number	ratio per 100 live births	country
61.9	66.4	1975	17,259[4]	5.4[4]	3.4[19]	66.4[19]	30.2[19]	36.6[19]	46.9[19]	16.5[19]	H 345[4]	H 5.4[4]	...	57.0[4]	...	...	Paraguay
56.7	59.7	1972	38,297[8]	2.3	6.2[19]	60.8[19]	33.0[19]	28.1[19]	51.4[19]	20.5[19]	H 2,772	H 4.8	...	57.8[7]	...	...	Peru
63.4	66.5	1978	360,888[1]	7.7	12.0	72.4	15.6	33.3	57.2	9.5	F 8,607[4]	F 5.6[4]	F 2.4[4]	95.2[5]	...	...	Philippines
63.0	66.5	1972	2	...	...	...	...	...	...	...	...	H 2.9[4]	...	...	...	...	Pitcairn Island
68.1	75.4	1981	315,767[8,9]	8.7	3.2	89.0	7.8	18.8	75.7	5.5	F 9,435[13]	F 3.6[13]	F 0.9[13]	95.3[4]	145,600[13]	21.9[13]	Poland
70.1	73.2	1981	75,513	7.7	8.4[13]	79.1[13]	12.5[13]	31.2[13]	58.0[13]	10.8[13]	H 3,427	H 2.9	H 0.8	91.8[1]	...	...	Portugal
69.6	76.1	1980	31,916[14]	9.8	18.1	69.9	12.0	40.3	51.6	8.1	F 563[6]	H 4.1	F 1.8[6]	79.0	...	...	Puerto Rico
59.7	63.6	1981	...	...	...	...	...	...	...	...	...	H 2.9[4]	...	...	...	...	Qatar
63.0	66.5	1981	2,814	5.6	...	...	...	...	...	...	H 83[29]	H 4.0[4]	H 2.3[31]	65.3[13]	3,838	32.5	Réunion
67.4	72.1	1981	182,973	8.2	...	...	...	...	...	...	H 5,955[24]	H 3.1[4]	...	...	404,000[1]	99.0[1,22]	Romania
46.7	50.0	1974	13,899	3.3	...	...	...	...	.	...	H 894[7]	H 6.0[4]	...	...	...	...	Rwanda
68.6	71.9	1977	172	2.6	...	...	...	...	...	...	H 116	H 4.0[6]	H 1.9[6]	18.6[4]	...	...	St. Christopher and Nevis
		1982	298[8]	5.2	...	...	...	...	...	...	H 1[5]	H 4.4[5]	H 1.6[5]	56.5[4]	...	...	St. Helena and Ascension
66.5	72.8	1981	420	3.4	...	...	...	...	...	...	H 23[13]	H 1.9[13]	...	13.0[4]	...	...	St. Lucia
65.8	71.6	1981	39	6.2	...	...	...	...	...	...	H 12[7]	H 4.0[27]	H 1.4[27]	83.0[7]	...	...	St. Pierre and Miquelon
66.5	72.8	1980	414	3.4	...	...	...	...	...	...	H 20[13]	H 5.0[13]	...	...	...	...	St. Vincent and the Grenadines
		1981	146	6.8	2.8[19]	80.8[19]	16.4[19]	19.9[19]	72.6[19]	7.5[19]	F 6[4]	F 3.2[4]	F 0.8[4]	96.5[13]	...	...	San Marino
		1982	64[8]	0.7	...	...	...	...	...	...	...	...	...	9.8[7]	...	...	São Tomé and Principe
49.2	51.5	1980	...	...	...	...	...	...	...	...	...	H 5.2	...	...	...	...	Saudi Arabia
41.8	45.0	1965	1,568	0.4	...	...	...	...	...	...	...	H 4.2[4]	...	...	...	...	Senegal
64.6	71.1	1980	356	5.6	2.4	74.9	22.6	34.3	52.9	12.8	H 13[13]	H 4.6[13]	H 1.9[13]	38.2[14]	...	...	Seychelles
46.7	50.0	1968	318	2.0	...	...	...	...	...	...	...	H 4.9[4]	...	...	...	...	Sierra Leone
68.7	74.0	1981	23,214[9]	9.4	1.0	78.3	20.7	10.9	80.5	8.6	H 510[4]	H 4.7[4]	H 1.3[4]	...	18,900	45.0	Singapore
54.0	54.0	1976	...	...	...	...	...	...	...	...	F 41	F 5.6	F 2.3	...	...	...	Solomon Islands
43.4	46.6	1980	...	...	...	...	...	...	...	...	...	H 4.9	...	...	...	...	Somalia
60.9	63.9	1977	64,979	2.4	4.2[42]	79.3[42]	16.5[42]	26.1[42]	63.7[42]	10.2[42]	F 1,403	H 4.4[4]	...	75.6	...	...	South Africa
52.5	55.0		...								...						South West Africa/Namibia
70.7	76.2	1979	199,057[14]	5.3	5.8	81.6	12.6	21.0	72.4	6.6	F 10,665[14]	F 3.5[14]	...	97.9[13]	...	...	Spain
66.2	69.2	1981	121,668	8.1	...	...	...	...	...	...	H 2,721	H 5.2	H 1.9	92.5[13]	...	...	Sri Lanka
48.0	50.0	1980	...	...	...	...	...	...	...	...	H 3,737[17]	H 5.1	...	...	...	...	Sudan, The
66.3	71.5	1980	2,371[43]	6.1	...	...	...	...	...	...	...	H 3.9	...	...	...	...	Suriname
46.8	50.0	1976	360[44]	1.0	...	...	...	...	...	...	H 87[45]	H 5.7	...	...	...	...	Swaziland
73.4	79.4	1982	37,051	4.4	1.0[14]	61.8[14]	37.2[14]	5.0[14]	74.8[14]	20.2[14]	H 3,498[4]	H 2.4[4]	H 0.5[4]	60.3[4]	32,602	35.2	Sweden
72.1	78.1	1981	35,766	5.6	0.6	75.0	24.4	7.0	80.7	12.3	H 2,459[4]	H 2.6[4]	...	95.6[1]	...	...	Switzerland
45.1	47.5	1981	86,081[46]	9.2	...	...	...	...	...	...	F 1,151[6]	H 4.2[4]	F 2.4[6]	...	...	...	Syria
69.7	74.6	1982	161,780	8.8	...	...	...	...	...	...	H 3,728[4]	H 4.8[4]	H 0.5[4]	...	...	...	Taiwan
38.9	42.1	1978	3,475[29]	9.8	...	...	...	...	...	...	H 3,435	H 3.6[4]	H 2.3	...	...	...	Tanzania
60.9	64.9	1980	341,655[14]	7.2	...	...	...	...	...	...	H 8,422	H 5.3	H 2.0	...	...	...	Thailand
34.5	37.5	1979	5,753[47]	2.3	...	...	...	...	...	...	...	H 5.0[4]	...	...	...	...	Togo
63.0	66.5	1981	128[8,9]	6.0	0.0	83.3	16.7	0.0	100.0	0.0	...	H 5.5[9]	...	...	...	...	Tokelau
60.0	61.0	1981	682	6.9	...	...	...	...	...	...	F 15[5]	F 6.1[5]	F 2.7[5]	...	...	...	Tonga
66.0	72.0	1978	8,382	7.4	3.9[19]	65.0[19]	31.1[19]	27.6[19]	53.0[19]	19.4[19]	H 193[6]	H 4.2[4]	H 2.1[6]	56.3[7]	...	...	Trinidad and Tobago
60.0	66.5	1980	...	...	...	...	...	...	...	...	H 16	H 7.0	H 4.1	...	...	...	Trust Territory of the Pacific Is.
58.4	60.7	1980	47,430	7.4	...	...	...	...	...	...	H 1,010[17]	H 4.0	...	99.8[27]	20,500	9.5	Tunisia
62.2	63.8	1980	165,743[1]	3.8	11.0[27]	72.1[27]	16.9[27]	31.3[27]	61.7[27]	7.0[27]	H 8,601	H 5.2	H 2.0	...	*		Turkey
68.6	71.9	1970	27[4]	3.9	...	...	...	...	...	...	H 1	H 4.3	H 2.0	82.4[17]	...	...	Turks and Caicos Islands
57.0	60.0	1979	...	...	...	...	...	...	...	...	H 1	H 6.8	H 2.2	...	...	...	Tuvalu
53.2	56.8	1980	...	...	...	...	...	...	...	...	...	H 5.2	...	...	...	...	Uganda
65.0	74.0	1982	2,768,000[8]	10.3	...	...	...	...	...	...	F 66,307[1]	F 3.9[1]	...	...	10,000,000[6]	230.0[6]	U.S.S.R.
59.7	63.6	1980	...	...	...	...	...	...	...	...	...	H 3.8	...	...	...	...	United Arab Emirates
70.4	76.6	1981	397,800	7.1	8.4[4]	78.5[4]	13.1[4]	26.3[4]	66.9[4]	6.8[4]	H 19,949	H 2.7[48]	H 1.7	88.5	137,600[49]	19.6	United Kingdom
70.8	78.2	1982	2,495,000[8]	10.8	11.7[14]	75.7[14]	12.6[14]	28.1[14]	64.7[14]	7.2[14]	F 61,393[25]	F 2.6[25]	F 1.0[25]	82.9[1]	1,553,900[4]	42.8[4]	United States
67.1	73.7	1981	22,671	7.7	...	...	...	...	...	...	H 797[17]	H 3.5[17]	...	75.4[13]	...	...	Uruguay
58.0	59.9		...								...						Vanuatu
64.0	69.0	1973	92,648[4,32]	6.7[4]	9.5[19]	65.1[19]	25.4[19]	39.6[19]	47.2[19]	13.2[19]	...	H 5.3[4]	...	47.6[1]	...	...	Venezuela
56.9	61.3		...								...						Vietnam
68.8	71.9	1978	1,128[50]	11.8	...	...	...	...	...	...	H 28[4]	H 3.4[4]	H 1.3[4]	65.5[17]	...	...	Virgin Islands (U.S.)
59.2	62.9	1980	56[6]	5.6	...	...	...	...	...	...	...	...	...	78.3	...	...	Wallis and Futuna
		1972	459	4.9	...	...	...	...	...	...	...	...	...	...	...	...	Western Sahara
61.0	64.3	1978	656[14]	4.2	1.5	61.8	36.7	15.1	64.8	20.1	F 20[5]	F 7.8[5]	F 3.8[5]	43.5	...	...	Western Samoa
41.1	43.0	1980	...	...	...	...	...	...	...	...	...	H 5.5	...	...	...	...	Yemen (Aden)
45.4	47.6		...								...						Yemen (San'ā)
68.0	73.2	1981	173,538	7.7	3.7[1]	84.6[1]	11.7[1]	33.1[1]	62.2[1]	4.7[1]	H 6,187	H 3.6	H 0.9	92.0[13]	288,100[17]	74.0[17]	Yugoslavia
46.9	50.1	1977	1,914	0.1	...	...	...	...	...	...	...	H 5.6[4]	...	...	...	...	Zaire
49.1	52.5	1968	...	...	...	...	...	...	...	...	H 873	H 4.6[4]	H 2.1	...	...	...	Zambia
53.7	57.3	1977	2,633[51]	...	3.2	84.1	12.7	28.7	65.8	5.5	...	H 4.5[4]	...	95.8[13]	...	...	Zimbabwe

[1]1979. [2]Excludes nomadic tribes. [3]Algerian population only. [4]1980. [5]1976. [6]1970. [7]1977. [8]Provisional. [9]1982. [10]Estimates. [11]1980–85. [12]1971. [13]1978. [14]1981. [15]Number of dwellings. [16]For all marriages in state capitals only. [17]1975. [18]For de jure population. [19]For all marriages. [20]Private households. [21]1973. [22]Per 100 unlagged births. [23]Millions of households. [24]1966. [25]1983. [26]1960. [27]1974. [28]1972. [29]1967. [30]Port-au-Prince only. [31]Reported deaths only. [32]Cities only. [33]Includes data for East Jerusalem. [34]1969. [35]Includes registered Palestinian refugees but excludes Jordanian territory under Israeli occupation since 1967. [36]1968. [37]Includes Sarawak; refers to non-Muslim civil marriages and Christian ritual marriages only. [38]Annual average for 5-year period. [39]Residents only. [40]Includes polygamous and monogamous marriages. [41]Includes former Canal Zone and excludes tribal Indian population. [42]Excludes Black population. [43]Excludes Hindu and Muslim ritual marriages. [44]1964. [45]Number of homesteads. [46]Excludes nomadic tribes. [47]African population only. [48]England and Wales only. [49]Excludes Northern Ireland. [50]Americans only. [51]Non-Africans only.

National product and accounts

The national product and accounts table furnishes a breakdown of how the aggregate income (output) of a nation is produced, distributed, and spent by its population. The per capita value of a country's production provides a good indication of the general economic well-being of its inhabitants. The several breakdowns of aggregate income or expenditure (each representing a different method of computing gross domestic product [GDP] or an element of its gross national product [GNP] provide a number of specific details about each country's economy, including national patterns of consumption, investment, and foreign trade; factor costs (prices paid for the inputs of production), such as indirect taxes, capital consumption, wage compensation, and profit; industrial origin of GDP for 10 principal industrial sectors; and the principal elements of a country's balance of payments (merchandise trade, invisibles, and tourism).

Measures of national output. The two most commonly used measures of national output (except for centrally planned economies) are GNP and GDP. Each of these measures represents an aggregate value of goods and services produced within a specific country. The GDP, the more basic of these, is a measure of the value of goods and services produced entirely within each country. It is equal to the sum of all factor costs (factor incomes) or all value added provided by the combined productive capabilities of labour and capital within each economic system. The GNP, the more comprehensive value, is composed of both domestic production and the net value added (net factor income) from transactions with other countries. When the factor income value received from other countries is greater than the value paid, a country's GNP is greater than its GDP. In theory, if all national accounts could be equilibrated, the global summation of GDP (each country's value added to the world economy), would equal the total of all GNP values.

The measured GDP or GNP value for any year is its money or nominal value. Changes in nominal values in GDP from year to year measure not only real changes in output but also inflation (deflation) rates. In order to arrive at real GDP values, nominal values are adjusted for price changes (in this table 1980 was adopted as the standard year for comparison). Real per capita U.S. dollar values were derived by adjusting for domestic price changes and by using contemporary population and exchange rate values. Real GDP per capita provides a rough measure of annual monetary income per person, but values should be compared cautiously, as they are subject to a number of distortions, notably by the existence of elements of national production that do not enter the monetary economy (e.g., food, clothing, or housing produced and consumed within families or in communal groups).

In countries with centrally planned economies such as Bulgaria, China, Cuba, Czechoslovakia, East Germany, Hungary, Laos, Mongolia, Poland, Romania, and the Soviet Union, the aggregated national income/product is generally referred to as net material product (NMP) and includes only material goods and "productive" services. The GNP values presented in this table for free market economies are not directly comparable to the official NMP measures published by the centrally planned economies. The GNP value is more comprehensive and covers a number of sectors excluded from the NMP value.

The two primary differences between GNP and NMP measures are: (1) because of different accounting practices, centrally planned economies often measure final values of products with little regard for problems of double-counting along production pathways—this can and does lead to overvaluation of NMP (when compared to GNP values), and (2) some services are not considered as adding to the wealth of a country and therefore are not counted—this results in generally undervaluing NMP. Any comparison of NMP and GNP values must be cognizant of these differences.

The origin, distribution, and spending of the national product. Even though GDP values allow a general comparison of relative economic development, more information is provided when these aggregates are broken down into their component kinds of expenditure and by their industrial sectors of origin.

There are three major expenditure components of GDP: private consumption, government spending, and gross domestic investment. While the ratio of private consumption to investment spending is generally somewhat higher in less developed countries, there is no clear distinguishing pattern of spending between poorer and richer countries. A further expenditure component is net foreign trade; value is given for both exports (a positive value) and for imports (a negative value, representing obligations to other countries). The sum of these five percentages, excluding statistical discrepancies and rounding, should be 100.0% of the GDP.

The distribution of GDP by cost components usually comprises four general categories: indirect taxes (excise or value-added taxes), consumption

National product and accounts

country	GNP, nominal 1982 ('000,000,000 national currency)	gross domestic product (GDP), 1982			GDP by type of expenditure, 1980 (percent)[a]					cost components of GDP, 1980 (percent)			
		nominal ('000,000,000 national currency)	real ('000,000,000 national currency)	real per capita (in U.S.$)	consumption		gross domestic investment	foreign trade		net indirect taxes	consumption of fixed capital	compensation of employees	net operating surplus
					private	government		exports	imports				
Afghanistan	154.3[1]	136.7[1]	104.9[1]	126[1]	...	...	...	...	...	...	...	...	...
Albania	...	...	...	...	...	...	...	...	...	...	...	...	...
Algeria	9,734.0[1]	206.3	168.7	1,850	42.3	13.7	40.5	34.0	−30.6	19.7	8.4	37.2	34.7
American Samoa	0.1[1,4]	...	...	3,777[1]	...	...	...	...	...	...	...	...	...
Andorra	...	...	...	...	...	...	...	...	...	...	...	...	...
Angola	...	...	...	470[5]	...	...	...	...	...	...	...	...	...
Anguilla	...	...	...	...	...	...	...	...	...	...	...	...	...
Antigua and Barbuda	324.0[1]	0.4	0.3	1,443	70.4	20.3	41.2	72.6	−104.6	...	...	...	...
Argentina	31,732.8[1]	60,435.2	25,125.0	4,690	62.0	14.5	25.7	6.9	−9.1	...	...	...	...
Australia	153.0	155.7	127.9	8,199	60.8	16.6	23.5	17.9	−18.8	12.3	6.6	54.5	26.6
Austria	1,134.5	1,143.0	1,005.5	7,556	55.1	17.8	28.8	39.0	−40.7	13.5	11.4	53.9	21.2
Bahamas, The	1.1[3]	1.1[3]	1.2[3]	5,189[3]	57.2[3]	13.6[3]	11.1[3]	87.8[3]	−69.8[3]	...	...	...	...
Bahrain	1,218.2[1]	...	...	8,116[1]	56.4[3]	15.6[3]	32.4[3]	107.2[3]	−111.7[3]	...	...	...	...
Bangladesh	713.8[1]	265.0	213.1	102	89.5	5.6	15.1	5.7	−16.0	...	...	...	...
Barbados	2.0	2.0	1.6	3,127	64.8	15.5	23.0	68.5	−71.9	13.9	5.9	57.4	23.6
Belgium	3,903.0	3,940.0	3,466.0	7,280	64.0	18.6	21.1	59.7	−63.4	10.4	8.8	59.0	21.8
Belize	320.0[1]	336.6	294.1	735	68.7	19.5	25.7	64.1	−78.0[7]	12.1[7]	9.4[7]	—78.5[7]—	
Benin	168.7[7]	348.7	272.2	356	93.0[3]	9.2[3]	16.8[3]	27.7[3]	−46.7[3]	9.4[7]	6.5[7]	23.1[7]	61.0[7]
Bermuda	0.8[1,4]	...	...	11,694[1]	67.3[3]	14.4[3]	9.3[3]	62.4[3]	−53.5[3]	...	...	...	...
Bhutan	...	1.0[1]	...	73[1]	...	...	...	...	...	...	...	...	...
Bolivia	348.9	398.5	116.3	448	74.6	13.6	11.0	18.9	−18.1	11.0[3]	6.1[3]	35.8[3]	46.7[3]
Botswana	0.5	0.7	0.8	703	50.8	18.8	43.2	51.9	−64.7	13.3[3]	8.8[3]	34.3[3]	43.6[3]
Brazil	48,225.0	50,815.0	13,079.0	1,957	72.2	8.8	21.1	8.6	−10.7	10.4	4.8	—84.7—	
British Virgin Islands	...	...	...	...	...	...	...	...	...	11.5[7]	[9]	52.5[7]	36.0[7,9]
Brunei	4.0[1,4]	...	...	15,743[1]	...	...	...	...	...	...	...	...	...
Bulgaria[c]	3.8	...	...	2,565	...	...	...	...	...	...	...	...	...
Burkina Faso	255.9[3]	354.6	292.1	216	94.6[3]	14.5[3]	17.9[3]	13.2[3]	−40.3[3]	7.6[3]	6.9[3]	24.3[3]	61.2[3]
Burma	47.8[1]	46.9	44.0	150	—82.3—		21.5	8.2	−12.0	9.8[7]	7.2[7]	37.8[7]	45.2[7]
Burundi	89.1[1]	99.9	84.3	195	87.8	12.6	14.4	8.3	−23.0	...	...	...	...
Cameroon	2,073.3[1]	2,037.5	1,526.3	817	...	...	...	...	...	...	...	...	...
Canada	356.6	369.7	296.7	9,806	56.2	19.5	22.7	29.3	−27.6	9.8	10.9	55.4	27.8
Cape Verde	0.1[1,4]	...	...	308[1]	...	...	...	...	...	...	...	...	...
Cayman Islands	...	...	...	...	...	...	...	...	...	...	...	...	...
Central African Republic	209.2[1]	...	...	290[1]	69.6[14]	19.1[14]	18.1[14]	19.4[14]	−26.2[14]	11.7[14]	—	23.8[14]	64.4[14]
Chad	133.1[1]	...	...	100[1]	83.4[15]	9.3[15]	18.1[15]	22.2[15]	−33.1[15]	5.5[15]	6.5[15]	13.2[15]	74.7[15]
Chile	1,123.1	1,228.7	973.8	1,368	72.1	12.4	18.0	21.2	−23.6	12.8[3]	10.5[3]	37.7[3]	39.0[3]
China[c]	511.1[1]	...	...	272[1]	...	...	...	...	...	...	...	...	...
Christmas Island	...	...	...	...	...	...	...	...	...	...	...	...	...
Cocos (Keeling) Islands	...	...	...	...	...	...	...	...	...	...	...	...	...
Colombia	2,428.2	2,458.8	1,548.4	600	68.4	7.8	23.9	16.3	−16.4	10.0	9.0	34.8	46.1

of fixed capital (depreciation), and two income categories: (a) compensation of employees (salaries, wages, etc.) and (b) net operating surplus ("profits", interests, rent, etc.).

In the more developed countries the proportion of GDP devoted to employee compensation is always larger than that to net operating surplus (and is generally more than twice as large). With few exceptions, in the poorer countries the reverse is true; employees' compensation is seldom the larger proportion.

The production of final GDP values derives from three major industrial sectors:

1. The primary sector, comprised of agricultural and mineral production (including fossil fuels), generally makes up the largest proportion (often more than half) of the total output of the less developed countries. In the more developed (industrialized) countries it seldom exceeds one-fifth of GDP.

2. The secondary sector, comprised of manufacturing, construction, utilities, transportation, and communications, while generally forming a significant proportion of GDP in the more developed economies, does not in itself offer a clear pattern for evaluating relative economic development among countries.

3. The tertiary sector, which includes all domestic service and trade industries, varies, as a proportion of GDP, fairly consistently with levels of economic development. It makes up a major component of the economies of the more developed countries, providing nearly half of GDP in many of the richer countries. Percentages in this section of the table may not add to 100.0 because the value of each industry is calculated as a percentage of the total GDP, which may contain significant adjustments that are not in fact distributable to all industries.

Average annual growth rate of real GDP. The columns show average annual growth rates of real product for the 10-year period from 1970 to 1980, as well as for the two years from 1980 to 1982. Real GDP growth rates give an overall impression of the growth in final output achieved by various countries during the years covered. The negative growth rates for real GDP during 1980–82 resulted mainly from worldwide recession.

Balance of payments (external account transactions). The external account records the sum of all economic transactions of a current nature between one country and the rest of the world. The account shows a country's net receipts from overseas, including not only the trade of goods and services but also such invisible items as interest and dividends, short- and long-term investments, tourism, transfers to or from overseas residents, etc. Each transaction gives rise either to a foreign claim for payment, recorded as a deficit (*e.g.*, from imports, capital outflows), or a foreign obligation to pay, recorded as a surplus (*e.g.*, from exports, capital inflows) or a domestic claim on another country. The deficit transaction in the balance of payment of one country is automatically accompanied by a surplus in that of others. By totaling the surplus and deficit transactions on the external current account for a country, a statement of its international economic relationships can be summarized. Values are given in U.S. dollars for comparability.

Tourist trade. Income from tourism is often a significant element in a country's economic balance. A tourist is defined as a visitor who stays at least 24 hours but not more than one year in the country visited and whose activities encompass business and/or pleasure. The receipts from foreign nationals reflect payments for goods and services from foreign currency resources by tourists in the given country. Expenditures by nationals abroad are also payments for goods and services, but in this case made by the residents of the given country as tourists abroad. Unless the classification is so important as to justify separate consideration, receipts and expenditures by excursionists—cruise passengers staying less than 24 hours—are included in the total tourist trade figures.

Although tourist trade is also a component of the invisible trade classification, the importance of tourism as a source of income for many countries—the Caribbean islands, for example—warrants a separate listing of this industry. The U.S. dollar is used as the common currency for comparability by the World Tourism Organization.

... Not available.

— None, less than 0.5 of last significant figure, or not applicable.

a. Detail may not add to 100.0 because of statistical discrepancies.

b. Detail may not add to 100.0 because of statistical discrepancies or because of adjustments to the GDP such as allowances for imputed bank service charges, import duties, and value added taxes.

c. The national production/income values and derived percentage values are based upon net material product (NMP).

origin of GDP by economic sector, 1980 (percent)[b]										aver. an. growth rate of real GDP (percent)		balance of payments, 1983 (current external transactions; '000,000 U.S.$)			tourist trade, 1982 ('000,000 U.S.$)		country
primary		secondary				tertiary				1970–1980	1980–1982	net transfers		current balance of payments	receipts from foreign nationals	expenditures by nationals abroad	
agriculture	mining	manufacturing	construction	public utilities	transp., communication	trade	financial svcs.	other svcs.	govt.			goods-merchandise	invisibles				
63.0[1]	[2]	20.2[1,2]	4.8[1]	...	3.3[1]	7.4[1]		1.3[1]	...	4.5	...	...	...	...	1[1]	...	Afghanistan
...	...	...	...	...	...	...		...	...	...	...	...	...	...	...	...	Albania
6.5[3]	28.2[3]	11.8[3]	13.4[3]	1.2[3]	4.7[3]	13.4[3]		...	...	7.0	2.2	3,226	−3,312	−86	5[1]	430[1]	Algeria
...	...	...	...	...	...	...		...	...	...	...	...	...	...	...	...	American Samoa
...	...	...	...	...	...	...		...	...	...	...	...	...	...	...	...	Andorra
34.3[1]	20.6[1]	2.1[1]	1.7[1]	0.3[1]	4.2[1]	—4.8[1]—		21.9[1]	10.2[1]	−9.2	...	...	...	...	...	...	Angola
...	...	...	...	...	...	...		...	...	...	...	...	...	...	...	...	Anguilla
6.4[5]	0.8[5]	6.1[5]	7.0[5]	3.5[5]	17.2[5]	26.9[5]	17.4[5]	5.4[5]	13.8[5]	...	3.4	−90[6]	47[6]	−43[6]	510[1]	1,471[1]	Antigua and Barbuda
8.8	1.9	25.3	8.5	2.2	7.2	16.1	14.4	15.5	...	2.2	−5.4	3,716	−6,152	−2,436	1,097	1,852	Argentina
6.8[3]	6.5[3]	20.6[3]	6.4[3]	2.9[3]	6.9[3]	13.7[3]	18.4[3]	14.5[3]	4.0[3]	3.0	2.0	103	−5,476	−5,373	1,097	1,852	Australia
4.4	0.5	28.0	8.2	3.2	5.8	16.7	11.8	3.3	12.9	3.7	0.5	−3,429	3,310	−119	5,649	2,772	Austria
4.3[7]	7.8	12.0[7,8]	22.7[7]	7.8	11.7[7]	25.6[7]	12.8[7]	16.8[7]		...	...	−557	505	−52	639[1]	91[1]	Bahamas, The
1.4[3]	25.3[3]	9.9[3]	11.0[3]	1.7[3]	11.0[3]	13.6[3]	13.8[3]	8.1[3]	4.2[3]	...	...	191	−30	161	...	131[1]	Bahrain
53.6	—	7.7	6.1	0.2	6.1	11.0	7.7	5.0	2.6	3.9	3.8	...	...	...	157[5]	16[5]	Bangladesh
8.7	0.8	11.2	4.6	1.3	5.2	29.8	9.8	3.5	13.2	...	1.1	−1,349	1,203	−146	287[1]	18.0[1]	Barbados
2.1	0.5	25.4	7.7	3.1	8.7	11.4	12.0	9.3	14.8	3.0	−0.2	−2,018	1,256	−762	1,585[1]	2,644[1]	Belgium
22.8[7]	0.3[7]	12.3[7]	6.2[7]	0.7[7]	7.2[7]	15.8[7]	7.2[7]	7.6[7]	9.6[7]	...	−0.2	...	...	...	...	...	Belize
43.7[7]	0.2[7]	6.1[7]	3.6[7]	1.0[7]	8.0[7]	21.0[7]	4.0[7]	0.2[7]	7.5[7]	3.3	...	−159[7]	63[7]	−96[7]	9	4[1]	Benin
0.5[7]	2.4[7]	4.0[7]	2.7[7]	6.0[7]	9.3[7]	31.8[7]	16.9[7]	6.0[7]	12.1[7]	...	...	...	...	...	314	...	Bermuda
63.2[1]	[2]	4.1[1,2]	1.8[1]	0.3[1]	3.3[1]	2.8[1]	1.5[1]	23.0[1]	...	2.0	...	...	...	...	...	...	Bhutan
16.4	9.8	14.0	4.1	1.0	9.2	17.8	10.0	8.7	9.9	4.8	−4.8	275	−459	−184[3]	36[1]	50[1]	Bolivia
11.9	32.4	4.5	4.2	2.1	2.0	8.6	11.0	2.2	10.2	...	...	−116	−24	−140	22[1]	18[1]	Botswana
11.0	0.4	22.5	4.9	1.0	4.3	13.6	14.3	12.6	...	8.4	6.5	6,469	−13,306	−6,837	1,608	1,411	Brazil
8.9[7]	[2]	6.0[2,7]	11.7[7]	1.7[7]	9.6[7]	26.6[7]	16.8[7]	1.2[7]	10.3[7]	...	...	...	...	...	...	...	British Virgin Islands
0.6	69.6	13.1	1.2	—	0.6	10.3	1.5	3.6	...	...	...	...	...	...	...	...	Brunei
17.0	[8]	51.0[8]	9.3	[8]	8.0	13.7		3.5[10]	...	7.1	...	...	...	...	269[1]	...	Bulgaria[c]
37.2[3]	0.1[3]	11.3[3]	3.2[3]	0.8[3]	6.2[3]	15.5[3]	5.2[3]	0.6[3]	11.5[3]	3.5	...	...	...	...	6[1]	24[1]	Burkina Faso
45.0	1.0	10.0	1.3	—	3.0	29.2	1.8	3.0	5.3	4.6	7.0	−357	9	−348	3[5]	...	Burma
50.6	0.5[11]	8.4	5.5	[11]	2.2	7.6	—3.3—			2.8	−4.8	...	...	...	—	...	Burundi
...	...	...	...	...	...	...		...	...	5.6	−4.0	83	−372	−289	...	...	Cameroon
3.9	5.6	19.5	5.2	3.1	7.2	9.9	9.6	8.7	15.4	3.9	−0.6	14,877	−13,512	1,365	2,447	3,201	Canada
17.6[1]	0.3[1]	3.9[1,12]	20.3[1]	[12]	[13]	40.6[1,13]	[13]	[13]	17.3[1]	...	...	...	...	...	...	...	Cape Verde
31.0[14]	4.1[14]	13.5[12,14]	3.9[14]	[12]	2.6[14]	20.0[14]	—5.4[14]—		13.1[14]	3.0	...	−23	−5	−28	3[1]	19[1]	Central African Republic
41.4[15]	0.2[15]	16.2[15]	1.0[15]	0.6[15]	2.4[15]	30.1[15]	5.1[15]	2.1[15]	...	−0.2	...	−21	59	38	2[1]	...	Chad
9.3[6]	8.9[6]	19.0[6]	5.1[6]	2.1[6]	5.5[6]	18.5[6]	—31.6[6]—			2.4	−4.7	−1,068	2,082	1,014	192[1]	260[1]	Chile
...	...	...	...	...	...	...		...	...	5.8	...	...	...	...	...	...	China[c]
...	...	...	...	...	...	...		...	...	...	...	...	...	...	...	...	Christmas Island
...	...	...	...	...	...	...		...	...	...	...	...	...	...	...	...	Cocos (Keeling) Islands
24.9	1.8	21.8	4.8	1.5	6.6	17.8	8.4	6.0	6.3	5.9	−1.1	−1,755	−983	−2,738	624	342	Colombia

National product and accounts (continued)

country	GNP, nominal 1982 ('000,000,000 national currency)	gross domestic product (GDP), 1982				GDP by type of expenditure, 1980 (percent)[a]						cost components of GDP, 1980 (percent)			
		nominal ('000,000,000 national currency)	real ('000,000,000 national currency)	real per capita (in U.S.$)		consumption		gross domestic invest-ment	foreign trade			net indirect taxes	consump-tion of fixed capital	compen-sation of employ-ees	net operating surplus
						private	govern-ment		exports	imports					
Comoros	0.1[4]	0.1[4]	...	250		...	...	...	...	...		...	...	...	...
Congo	487.6[1]	...	...	...		59.2[7]	22.9[7]	27.3[7]	39.6[7]	−49.3[7]		16.1	18.4	41.9	23.6
Cook Islands	0.02[1]	...	...	...		80.3[14]	32.0[14]	26.2[14]	32.4[14]	−70.6[14]		...	...	...	...
Costa Rica	59.8	57.1	21.9	200		66.6	18.2	25.2	25.9	−35.8		11.8	5.1	50.2	32.8
Cuba[c]	7.4[17]	10.6[3]	...	1,372[7, 18]		——76.6[17]——		22.4[17]	31.4[17]	−30.5[17]		...	...	...	...
Cyprus	1.0	1.0	0.8	2,300		67.0	14.5	36.3	46.3	−64.0		6.3	10.3	83.3	—
Czechoslovakia[c]	482.4[5]	...	...	...		...	...	...	...	...		...	...	...	...
Denmark	452.4	469.8	381.9	7,700		56.1	26.8	18.2	33.3	−34.4		15.3	18.7	54.8	20.7
Djibouti	32.1[1]	...	...	...		...	...	...	...	...		...	...	...	...
Dominica	0.2[1]	0.2	0.2	700		89.6	28.2	54.4	21.8	−94.0		...	...	...	...
Dominican Republic	6.9	7.9	7.0	1,220		76.5	7.6	25.7	19.2	−29.0		8.2[3]	6.0[3]	85.7[3]	—
Ecuador	377.8	408.9	313.8	700		60.1	14.1	27.9	24.4	−26.5		7.7	[9]	32.7	59.6[9]
Egypt	21.2	20.3	16.0	500		69.1[3]	16.5[3]	30.4[3]	26.1[3]	−42.1[3]		4.3[3]	[9]	28.8[3]	66.9[3, 9]
El Salvador	8.6	8.9	6.9	500		75.3	14.9	11.8	31.8	−33.9		7.5	4.0	88.4	—
Equatorial Guinea	11.4[1]	...	...	...		...	...	...	...	...		...	...	...	...
Ethiopia	9.1	9.1	8.0	100		79.9	15.2	10.0	14.2	−19.4		...	...	...	...
Faeroe Islands															
Falkland Islands															
Fiji	1.1[1]	1.2[1]	1.0	1,872		59.1	15.3	30.5	47.1	−52.0		8.1	6.3	42.4	43.2
Finland	231.5	236.7	193.4	8,327		54.7	18.6	27.5	34.3	−35.1		10.5	13.2	55.9	20.4
France	3,568.5	3,552.0	2,801.3	7,855		63.3	15.2	23.1	22.4	−24.0		12.8	11.4	55.3	20.5
French Guiana	1.2[1]	...	...	...		...	...	...	...	...		...	...	...	...
French Polynesia	100.8[1]	68.0[5]	...	6,400[5, 18]		66.5[21]	41.3[21]	30.5[21]	11.2[21]	−49.5[21]		7.5[21]	19.1[21]	52.1[21]	21.3[21]
Gabon	692.9[1]	1,184.1	882.3	3,762		36.5[7]	13.7[7]	35.0[7]	61.8[7]	−46.9[7]		18.2[3]	14.5[3]	30.0[3]	37.2[3]
Gambia, The	0.5[1]	0.5	0.4	339		...	...	...	...	...		...	...	...	...
Germany, East[c]	362.3[1]	...	...	...		——78.9——		21.1	...	...		...	...	...	...
Germany, West	1,597.7	1,602.5	1,437.2	9,598		55.2	20.4	24.8	27.0	−27.4		11.2	11.8	55.7	21.3
Ghana	58.5[1]	85.9	37.4	1,171		83.5	11.9	5.4	8.6	−9.4		5.1[7]	3.5[7]	——91.4[7]——	
Gibraltar	0.07[1]	...	...	...		...	...	...	...	...		...	...	...	...
Greece	2,576.5	2,518.0	1,672.0	2,570		61.9	15.8	27.6	20.2	−25.5		11.3	8.3	37.9	42.5
Greenland	3.9[1]	...	...	...		...	...	...	...	...		...	...	...	...
Grenada	0.3[1]	0.3	0.3	1,060		...	...	...	...	...		...	...	...	...
Guadeloupe	7.6[1]	...	...	...		83.5[7]	32.3[7]	17.5[7]	12.2[7]	−45.5[7]		12.0[7]	—	64.8[7]	23.2[7, 9]
Guam	...	...	...	...		...	...	...	...	...		...	...	...	...
Guatemala	8.6	8.7	7.7	999		79.2	7.8	15.8	22.4	−25.1		...	...	...	...
Guinea	35.3[1]	...	...	...		...	...	...	...	...		...	...	...	...
Guinea-Bissau	5.7[1]	3.8[1]	...	141[18]		...	...	...	...	...		...	...	...	...
Guyana	1.3	1.4	1.0	345		52.8	28.9	29.8	69.1	−80.6		8.3[21]	4.9[21]	49.2[21]	37.6[21]
Haiti	7.7	7.6	6.8	262		——87.4——		19.9	27.6	−35.0		8.1[21]	4.4[21]	18.6[21]	68.9[21]
Honduras	5.2	5.6	4.6	587		68.2	13.7	26.4	37.3	−45.6		10.9	5.2	——83.8——	
Hong Kong	...	136.1[1]	...	4,600[1, 18]		67.7	6.6	30.6	95.7	−100.6		...	...	...	...
Hungary[c]	696.4	847.9	758.4	1,838		61.2	10.3	30.7	——2.2——			...	...	——66.7——	
Iceland	31.2	32.6	14.5	5,056		60.6	11.6	27.1	41.9	−41.3		20.2	13.1	——66.7——	
India	1,644.0	1,644.1	1,384.2	245		68.9	10.1	24.5	7.0	−10.6		...	...	——56.8——	
Indonesia	57,675.0	59,663.0	48,521.6	497		57.2	12.7	21.7	30.5	−22.1		36.7	6.5	——56.8——	
Iran	7,304.2[1]	7,271.3[1]	6,677.0[1]	2,163		54.4	22.3	26.6	14.2	−17.6		3.4[15]	4.6[15]	——92.0[15]——	
Iraq	9.2[1]	...	...	...		——51.2[25]——		35.4[25]	57.9[25]	−44.5[25]		1.3[25]	2.6[25]	20.7[25]	75.4[25]
Ireland	11.8	12.4	8.8	3,599		63.7	20.6	28.9	53.8	−67.0		9.8	9.1	60.9	20.2
Israel	538.9	559.8	117.2	1,188		57.0	34.9	22.0	43.8	−57.8		8.8	14.3	49.3	31.7
Italy	465,790.0	465,790.0	342,417.6	4,503		61.8	16.1	24.9	25.2	−28.0		7.8	9.6	54.2	28.4
Ivory Coast	2,768.9[1]	2,493.0	2,139.9	1,144		58.8[3]	18.0[3]	28.0[3]	35.6[3]	−40.3[3]		26.9[7]	6.6[7]	32.5[7]	34.0[7]
Jamaica	5.4	5.7	4.7	1,193		67.1	21.0	15.7	49.6	−53.4		8.4	8.8	51.8	31.0
Japan	264,775.0	264,707.0	245,781.8	8,331		58.2	10.0	32.6	14.0	−14.9		6.1	13.1	54.6	25.8
Jordan	1.7	1.3	1.2	1,364		86.6	30.0	41.0	53.2	−110.8		12.3	3.2	37.3	47.2
Kampuchea	...	...	...	...		...	...	...	...	...		...	...	...	...
Kenya	65.8	68.4	50.8	365		65.8	19.6	26.8	28.3	−40.5		14.3	—	35.1	50.5
Kiribati	...	...	...	...		92.8	36.4	44.0	22.5	−95.7		4.6	4.5	30.0	60.8
Korea, North	...	...	...	...		...	...	...	...	...		...	...	...	...
Korea, South	48,088.0	48,851.0	38,317.4	1,332		65.6	11.2	30.7	33.1	−40.7		12.4	8.3	37.2	42.0
Kuwait	8.5[1]	5.7	7.0	9,749		29.5	11.5	13.2	81.4	−35.6		...	...	...	...
Laos[c]	3.2	...	...	90[18]		——109.6[3]——		18.0[3]	——27.6[3, 27]——			7.9[28]	4.5[28]	——87.5[28]——	
Lebanon	...	14.0	...	277		147.6[3]	20.1[3]	39.7[3]	22.4[3]	−129.9[3]		20.2[3]	1.9[3]	27.9[3]	50.0[3]
Lesotho	0.6[1]	0.4	0.3	277		147.6[3]	20.1[3]	39.7[3]	22.4[3]	−129.9[3]		20.2[3]	1.9[3]	27.9[3]	50.0[3]
Liberia	0.8[1]	0.8[1]	0.8[1]	237		46.9	19.9	33.3	66.9	−67.0		...	...	...	...
Libya	7.7	9.2	...	...		28.0	26.9	24.5	56.2	−35.6		3.0	4.2	26.1	66.7
Liechtenstein	...	...	...	...		...	...	...	...	...		...	...	...	...
Luxembourg	197.6[1]	191.9[1]	177.5[1]	13,096		47.7	13.4	23.1	84.7	−68.9		9.8	13.0	62.7	14.4
Macau	...	...	...	...		...	...	...	...	...		...	...	...	...
Madagascar	807.0[1]	1,045.9	617.4	318		72.3[3]	17.7[3]	22.3[3]	17.6[3]	−30.0[3]		11.6[3]	1.2[3]	——87.2[3]——	
Malawi	1.4	1.4	1.2	171		80.2	9.6	21.7	21.6	−33.2		6.5[28]	—	25.6[28]	67.9[9, 28]
Malaysia	58.2	60.6	52.2	1,557		52.4	16.8	27.2	58.0	−54.4		...	...	...	...
Maldives	0.3[1]	...	...	424[1, 18]		...	...	...	...	...		...	...	...	...
Mali	529.0[1]	...	...	145[1, 18]		71.2[29]	15.9[29]	15.2[29]	19.3[29]	−21.6[29]		9.4[29]	3.9[29]	——86.6[29]——	
Malta	0.5	0.5	0.4	2,640		64.7	16.2	24.6	91.0	−96.4		11.1	3.3	46.0	39.6
Martinique	...	...	...	...		82.8	34.3	14.9	13.8	−45.9		10.2	—	66.3	23.5
Mauritania	34.3[1]	31.7[5]	31.7[5]	480[5]		72.1	28.0	32.1	29.2	−61.4		9.4[15]	5.6[15]	26.8[15]	58.2[15]
Mauritius	11.2[1]	10.3[1]	9.0[1]	1,059[1]		76.4	12.5	22.3	53.1	−64.4		12.1	—	49.6	38.3
Mayotte	...	...	...	...		...	...	...	...	...		...	...	...	...
Mexico	8,908.2	9,255.8	4,552.8	891		62.0	10.8	28.1	12.6	−13.5		8.3	5.5	36.1	50.1
Monaco	...	...	...	...		...	...	...	...	...		...	...	...	...
Mongolia[c]	...	4.1[21]	...	...		...	...	...	...	...		...	...	...	...
Montserrat	...	...	...	...		91.0	28.5	49.1	31.2	−99.8		...	...	...	...
Morocco	89.8	88.5	71.1	57.4		66.3	20.2	22.6	19.1	−28.2		13.8	—	33.2	53.0
Mozambique	51.8[1]	...	...	...		...	...	...	...	...		...	...	...	...
Nauru	.1[1]	...	...	...		...	...	...	...	...		...	...	...	...

primary — agriculture	mining	secondary — manufacturing	construction	public utilities	transp., communication	tertiary — trade	financial svcs.	other svcs.	govt.	growth 1970–1980	1980–1982	goods-merchandise	invisibles	current balance of payments	receipts from foreign nationals	expenditures by nationals abroad	country
44.8[6]	—	4.9[6]	10.5[6]	0.8[6]	[16]	39.0[6,16]	[16]	[16]	[16]	...	...	...	...	...	...	...	Comoros
16.0	16.1	9.8	3.0	1.6	8.7	14.5	7.3	0.2	18.1	3.1	...	417	-813	-396	13[1]	54	Congo
26.4	0.2	10.9	9.2	1.9	7.2	13.7	3.2	...	...	...	...	...	...	...	...	...	Cook Islands
17.3	[2]	19.6[2]	6.4	1.8	4.3	20.0	10.7	—19.9—		5.0	-23.5	90	-288	-198	131	36	Costa Rica
14.7[6]	[8]	43.4[6,8]	7.7[6]	[8]	7.7[6]	25.9[6]	...	0.5[6]	...	0.4	...	...	...	...	...	...	Cuba[c]
10.0	1.4	16.8	13.5	1.3	7.4	17.8	10.9	...	6.7	2.2	3.2	-656	470	-186	292	67	Cyprus
7.5	[8]	65.0[8]	10.6	[8]	4.2	12.3	...	0.4[10]	...	5.1	...	...	...	...	252[1]	190.4[1]	Czechoslovakia[c]
5.4	0.8	19.1	6.1	1.9	7.9	13.2	—22.4—		23.2	2.5	1.0	236	-1,412	-1,176	1,305	1,330	Denmark
5.2	[2]	7.6[2]	5.0	2.3	8.2	25.3	10.5	—22.8—		...	...	...	...	...	2[1]	...	Djibouti
...	...	...	...	...	...	...	...	...	...	...	4.3	-19	11	-8	2[1]	...	Dominica
18.4[1]	3.8[1]	15.6[1]	7.8[1]	0.9[1]	5.4[1]	16.2[1]	—31.9—			6.6	9.4	-490	48	-442	223[1]	223[1]	Dominican Republic
12.2	20.7	8.8	7.2	0.9	9.1	13.8	—11.3—			8.8	3.5	162	-1,357	-1,195	131[1]	250[1]	Ecuador
21.2	[2]	32.4[2]	4.7	1.0	8.1	15.4	—17.2—			7.4	-5.7	-3,822	3,037	-785	375[1]	630[1]	Egypt
26.6	0.1	15.3	3.3	1.9	3.7	25.2	8.2	—15.7—		4.1	-11.3	-122[6]	-30[6]	-152[6]	7	...	El Salvador
46.7[3]	—	5.2[3]	4.9[3]	0.5[3]	2.1[3]	10.1[3]	0.7[3]	3.8[3]	26.0[3]	...	...	...	...	...	...	...	Equatorial Guinea
45.6	0.2	9.7	3.7	0.6	5.0	9.2	5.5	1.1	6.1	2.0	-2.9	-337	167	-170	11	5[1]	Ethiopia
...	...	...	...	...	...	...	...	...	...	...	...	...	...	...	...	...	Faeroe Islands
...	...	...	...	...	...	...	...	...	...	...	...	...	...	...	...	...	Falkland Islands
21.2	0.2	11.8	6.3	1.5	8.2	16.3	11.4	11.3	6.4	4.7	...	-204	135	-65	143[1]	19[1]	Fiji
8.2	0.4	25.7	6.5	3.0	7.3	10.3	12.1	4.7	13.5	3.1	1.7	223	-1,165	-942	579	630	Finland
4.2	0.8	26.2	6.6	1.7	5.5	12.0	16.6	7.9	12.8	3.5	0.7	-8,063	3,703	-4,360	6,991	5,157	France
...	...	...	...	...	...	...	...	...	...	...	...	...	...	...	...	...	French Guiana
5.3	—	8.0	9.8	1.3	6.3	25.0	14.0	12.9	17.4	...	...	...	...	...	94	...	French Polynesia
6.0[1]	53.3[1]	4.4[1,12]	4.7[1]	[12]	[16]	31.6[1,12]	[16]	[16]	[16]	...	...	1,275	-1,203	72	15[1]	104[1]	Gabon
27.2[6]	0.1[6]	7.2[6]	8.1[6]	0.5[6]	8.4[6]	23.7[6]	8.3[6]	2.5[6]	14.0[6]	...	-0.8	-84[1]	34[1]	-50[1]	20	2	Gambia, The
9.3	[8]	62.9[8]	7.0	[8]	4.9	14.4	—3.1[10]—			4.8	...	...	...	...	...	...	Germany, East[c]
2.2	[2]	36.4[2]	7.8	...	5.8	9.4	9.5	14.7	11.7	2.6	-0.7	-22,250	-18,250	4,000	5,614	16,267	Germany, West
60.7[7]	0.6[7]	8.6[7]	2.5[7]	0.4[7]	2.6[7]	13.3[7]	3.1[7]	0.8[7]	7.4[7]	-0.1	-13.6	-92	-126	-218	11	33[1]	Ghana
...	...	...	...	...	...	...	...	...	...	...	...	...	...	...	21[1]	...	Gibraltar
15.5	1.4	17.4	7.6	1.4	6.8	11.5	7.7	10.9	8.6	4.9	-1.1	-4,294	2,416	-1,878	1,527	231	Greece
...	...	...	...	...	...	...	...	...	...	...	...	...	...	...	...	...	Greenland
22.0	—	2.2	7.3	1.3	5.2	—13.8—		31.4	16.8	...	...	-46	29	-17	21[1]	...	Grenada
7.4[3]	[22]	6.7[3,12]	4.5[22]	[12]	4.0[3]	14.9[3]	5.5[3]	28.7[3]	28.3[3]	...	...	...	...	...	72[3]	...	Guadeloupe
...	...	...	...	...	...	...	...	...	...	...	...	...	...	...	...	...	Guam
25.0	0.4	16.8	3.0	1.7	6.9	27.2	7.9	4.4	5.0	5.7	0.3	36	-260	-224	87	100	Guatemala
36.6	24.9	3.8	3.8	1.0	2.2	16.4[23]	[23]	—11.4—		3.3	...	...	...	...	...	...	Guinea
52.8	[24]	9.4[24]	[24]	[24]	0.7	—12.9—		—24.1—		...	-3.4	-32	-126	-158	4[1]	11[1]	Guinea-Bissau
26.0[1]	7.5[1]	11.1[1,12]	8.1[1]	[1,12]	6.7[1]	10.7[1]	4.7[1]	3.0[1]	20.4[1]	...	...	-174	29	-145	85[1]	26[1]	Guyana
32.1	1.3	18.5	5.5	0.7	2.0	18.4	5.0	2.9	9.8	4.0	-1.1	-66	-159	-225	31[1]	128[1]	Haiti
27.1	1.6	15.2	4.3	1.4	7.6	11.4	8.4	7.8	3.1	3.6	-0.3	...	...	...	...	...	Honduras
0.9[3]	0.03[3]	26.7[3]	7.1[3]	1.2[3]	5.3[3]	21.0[3]	20.8[3]	13.8[3]	...	9.3	10.3	...	...	...	1,457	...	Hong Kong
14.3	...	48.9[8]	9.9	[8]	5.4	20.2	—1.2[13]—			5.4	2.7	878	-580	298	394	128	Hungary[c]
...	...	...	...	...	...	...	...	...	...	...	0.03	20	-77	-57	25	54	Iceland
33.2	1.4	15.9	4.3	1.4	5.2	13.2	5.7	4.5	4.3	3.6	3.8	-5,711[1]	3,013[1]	-2,698[1]	800	...	India
25.7	26.7	8.8	5.8	0.5	3.9	14.1	5.1	2.3	7.2	7.6	3.4	963	-7,301	-6,338	288[1]	664[1]	Indonesia
9.0[15]	30.7[15]	11.8[15]	9.2[15]	0.7[15]	3.8[15]	5.6[15]	11.9[15]	13.9[15]	...	2.5	3.0	8,532	-3,451[15]	5,081[15]	20	...	Iran
7.4[25]	56.9[25]	5.9[25]	2.3[25]	0.4[25]	3.9[25]	4.8[25]	3.5[25]	0.8[25]	12.8[25]	12.1	...	...	...	...	170[1]	...	Iraq
16.6[15]	3.3[15]	20.1[15]	7.6[15]	2.5[15]	6.4[15]	12.6[15]	—13.4[15]—		14.3[15]	3.5	-0.3	-1,126[6]	-741[6]	-1,867[6]	477	...	Ireland
5.4	...	25.6	10.9	2.4	7.9	13.1	26.6	3.0	...	4.1	4.8	-3,180	1,003	-2,177	900	653	Israel
6.4	...	35.2[8]	7.6	[8]	6.3	15.3	—19.0—		12.1	3.0	5.4	-4,390	3,749	-641	8,234	1,709	Italy
27.2[3]	0.3[3]	11.1[3]	8.2[3]	1.2[3]	7.3[3]	20.8[3]	—32.9[3]—			6.7	...	638	-1,643	-1,005	74[1]	239[1]	Ivory Coast
8.3	14.3	15.2	5.7	1.7	5.3	21.4	12.8	3.5	14.6	-1.1	-0.4	-442	33	-409	284[1]	14[1]	Jamaica
3.8	0.6	30.2	9.1	2.9	6.9	12.4	15.7	13.8	8.7	5.0	2.1	31,460	-10,660	20,800	754	4,116	Japan
6.7	3.9	10.3	8.7	0.8	9.9	15.9	11.9	3.5	17.9	6.9	8.1	-2,120	1,729	-391	510	365	Jordan
...	...	...	...	...	...	...	...	...	...	2.4	...	...	...	...	...	...	Kampuchea
27.9	0.2	11.4	5.2	1.8	5.0	9.7	10.7	2.9	12.6	6.5	-1.0	-312	135	-177	185	45[1]	Kenya
18.5	42.6	1.8	7.9	1.5	2.5	6.1	1.5	11.9	...	...	...	...	...	...	...	...	Kiribati
...	...	...	...	...	...	...	...	...	...	...	...	...	...	...	...	...	Korea, North
15.8	1.3	28.0	9.1	2.2	6.1	15.3	7.5	7.8	4.7	9.5	4.2	-1,700	93	-1,607	502	632	Korea, South
0.2	67.9	5.9	3.0	0.3	1.7	6.3	5.4	1.0	7.4	2.5	-15.4	4,131	453	4,584	198	1,306	Kuwait
...	...	...	...	...	...	...	...	...	...	3.3	...	...	...	...	...	...	Laos[c]
8.5[15]	[2]	13.2[2,15]	3.4[15]	5.4[15]	7.7[15]	28.3[15]	—23.4[15]—		10.2[15]	3.2	...	...	...	...	...	...	Lebanon
25.5[3]	6.9[3]	4.6[3]	8.1[3]	0.8[3]	1.6[3]	10.9[3]	7.8[3]	5.9[3]	7.9[3]	7.9	2.4	-478	464	-14	...	...	Lesotho
16.8	15.5	2.0	...	...	...	5.5	5.5	11.4	...	1.7	-14.6	52	-197	-145	...	...	Liberia
2.0	54.4	2.6	11.0	0.6	4.0	5.5	5.5	11.4	...	2.2	...	3,459	-5,140	-1,681	14[1]	645[1]	Libya
...	...	...	...	...	...	...	...	...	...	...	...	...	...	...	...	...	Liechtenstein
2.0	[2]	30.4[2]	7.2	2.6	6.0	15.6	22.4	15.5	13.0	...	7.2	...	...	...	...	...	Luxembourg
...	...	...	...	...	...	...	...	...	...	...	...	...	...	...	...	...	Macau
...	...	...	...	...	...	...	...	...	...	0.3	-10.8	-262[3]	-172[3]	-434[3]	5[1]	38[1]	Madagascar
48.7[28]	0.1[28]	9.3[28]	3.6[28]	1.1[28]	5.1[28]	11.7[28]	3.9[28]	5.2[28]	5.5[28]	6.3	8.1	28[6]	-101[6]	-73[6]	6[1]	...	Malawi
22.2	4.6	20.5	4.5	2.3	6.5	12.6	8.2	15.5	...	7.8	0.3	663	-3,510	-2,847	...	480[1]	Malaysia
15.7	1.1	2.3	3.8	0.1	8.0	17.1	2.2	6.6	16.6	...	...	...	...	...	...	...	Maldives
...	...	...	...	...	...	...	...	...	...	4.9	-6.7	-74	-30	-104	9[1]	17[1]	Mali
3.4	4.0	29.4	—4.0—		5.7	13.0	9.5	8.6	11.3	11.8	0.2	-271	269	-2	185	50[1]	Malta
...	...	...	...	...	...	...	...	...	...	...	...	...	...	...	89	...	Martinique
25.2[1]	8.5[1]	6.6[1]	6.3[1]	—	8.0[1]	—17.7[1]—		10.3[1]	17.4[1]	1.7	...	-63	-133	-196	6[1]	15[1]	Mauritania
13.1	0.2	13.5	7.1	3.1	11.1	8.2	14.8	12.3	4.4	...	3.9	-16	-7	-23	41	13	Mauritius
...	...	...	...	...	...	...	...	...	...	...	...	...	...	...	...	...	Mayotte
8.4	6.7	23.1	6.5	1.0	6.5	23.4	8.2	8.8	8.6	5.7	2.2	14,507	-9,299	5,208	1,406	788	Mexico
...	...	...	...	...	...	...	...	...	...	...	...	...	...	...	...	...	Monaco
15.4	[8]	29.3[8]	6.1	[8]	11.2	36.3	—2.0[10]—			...	...	...	...	...	...	...	Mongolia[c]
5.8	0.4	6.5	11.9	4.3	6.3	19.3	11.9	13.7	11.9	...	...	...	...	...	5[1]	...	Montserrat
18.0	4.8	17.2	6.9	3.3	4.5	14.5	2.2	—24.6—		5.6	0.5	-1,243	351	-892	440[1]	94[1]	Morocco
...	...	...	...	...	...	...	...	...	...	-2.9	...	...	...	...	...	...	Mozambique
...	...	...	...	...	...	...	...	...	...	...	...	...	...	...	...	...	Nauru

National product and accounts (continued)

country	GNP, nominal 1982 ('000,000,000 national currency)	gross domestic product (GDP), 1982 nominal ('000,000,000 national currency)	real ('000,000,000 national currency)	real per capita (in U.S.$)	GDP by type of expenditure, 1980 (percent)[a] consumption private	government	gross domestic investment	foreign trade exports	imports	cost components of GDP, 1980 (percent) net indirect taxes	consumption of fixed capital	compensation of employees	net operating surplus
Nepal	28.4[1]	30.5	24.6	118	81.6[7]	7.4[7]	17.8[7]	5.9[7]	-12.7[7]	...	...	...	...
Netherlands, The	366.7	367.4	325.1	8,297	60.8	18.1	21.5	53.1	-53.4	9.6	9.8	58.7	21.9
Netherlands Antilles	2.1[1]	...	...	...	56.4[28]	21.4[28]	33.6[28]	352.4[28]	-363.8[28]	7.8[28]	—	65.7[28]	26.4[28]
New Caledonia	97.0[1]	81.0[3]	...	...	...	...	...	...	...	5.6[3]	15.0[3]	57.5[3]	21.9[3]
New Zealand	31.2	32.1	22.3	5,066	59.9	17.1	24.1	28.9	-30.0	8.3	6.8	55.7	29.2
Nicaragua	28.3	29.6	22.8	776	84.0	18.8	15.4	23.0	-41.1	8.9[7]	4.0[7]	55.8[7]	31.3[7]
Niger	513.6[1]	66.2[1]	...	385[1, 18]	...	...	...	...	...	...	...	...	...
Nigeria	46.5	44.9	34.5	569	58.0	9.9	26.4	30.8	-25.1	1.1[15]	3.5[15]	25.8[15]	69.6[15]
Niue	—	...	...										
Norfolk Island	...	...											
Norway	350.9	362.6	286.4	10,062	47.6	18.8	27.4	47.6	-41.4	10.1	14.5	51.2	24.2
Oman	2.3	2.5	...	...	21.5	23.7	25.5	71.0	-41.7	0.5	—	—99.5—	
Pakistan	350.6	327.1	276.1	446	83.4	9.5	16.8	12.8	-22.5	10.0	5.6	84.3	
Panama	4.2	4.3	3.8	1,977	60.0	15.3	27.3	47.6	-50.2	8.7	9.4	—81.8—	
Papua New Guinea	1.7	1.8	1.6	665	60.9	24.0	25.3	43.4	-53.6	6.5	6.9	38.5	48.1
Paraguay	735.0	737.0	605.6	1,478	74.0	6.2	28.8	9.6	-18.5	6.2	10.5	34.8	48.5
Peru	13,402.0	13,813.1	4,789.2	3,542	67.9	12.9	16.1	23.5	-20.5	10.0	7.1	27.1	55.7
Philippines	336.1	340.4	270.1	627	67.0	8.0	30.5	20.4	-25.9	10.4	9.9	—79.7—	
Pitcairn Island	...												
Poland[c]	6,283.4[1]	...	...	...	—86.2—		18.8	—5.0—		...			
Portugal	1,785.8	1,884.8	1,346.5	2,682	73.8	15.4	25.1	28.1	-42.4	9.3	4.4	51.7	34.6
Puerto Rico	12.3[1]	...	...	...	83.0	17.2	16.7	57.8	-74.6	7.6	6.2	50.7	35.6
Qatar	23.8[1]	...											
Réunion	10.8[1]	...	...	...	80.8[7]	35.8[7]	17.7[7]	8.2[7]	-42.5[7]	10.7[28]	—	63.8[28]	25.4[9, 28]
Romania[c]	746.9	532.5[1]	...	...	58.5	6.1	38.3	—2.9—		...			
Rwanda	124.4[1]	134.4	115.3	227	83.3	12.5	16.1	14.4	-26.4	7.6	5.6	16.5	70.2
St. Christopher	0.1[1]	0.1	...	920[5, 18]	...	...	...	...	...	...	...	...	...
St. Helena	...												
St. Lucia	0.3[1]	0.4	0.3	820	58.2	21.0	59.7	76.9	-115.8				
St. Pierre and Miquelon	...												
St. Vincent	0.2[1]	0.2	0.2	820	78.1	23.8	39.8	66.3	-108.1	17.0[3]	7.8[3]	49.0[3]	26.3[3]
San Marino	...												
São Tomé and Príncipe	1.6[1]												
Saudi Arabia	526.6	524.7	505.5	16,496	26.5	20.1	20.7	67.0	-34.3	-0.4[7]	—	24.7[7]	75.7[7]
Senegal	687.5[1]	698.4[1]	651.0	430	76.8	24.5	18.2	24.2	-43.7	15.5[3]	6.7[3]	33.3[3]	44.4[3]
Seychelles	0.9	1.0	0.9	2,136	44.2	28.7	38.3	68.0	-79.1	...	...	...	...
Sierra Leone	1.5	1.6	1.3	363	90.7	8.4	16.2	22.9	-38.2	8.0[3]	9.4[3]	25.9[3]	56.8[3]
Singapore	31.1	32.0	28.4	5,368	53.7	10.1	45.5	—9.4—		...			
Solomon Islands	0.2[1]	...	...	...	...	...	...	...	...	9.0[15]	12.1[15]	25.4[15]	53.5[15]
Somalia	...												
South Africa	76.5	79.7	60.3	2,040	48.5	13.0	30.2	34.9	-26.6	6.6	12.6	46.6	34.2
S.W. Africa/Namibia	...												
Spain	19,471.0	19,737.0	15,066.4	3,532	69.8	11.5	21.2	15.5	-18.0[3]	4.6[3]	9.1[3]	54.6[3]	31.7[3]
Sri Lanka	97.0	100.1	76.6	244	78.0	9.7	34.1	31.0	-52.8	5.8[3]	8.8[3]	43.4[3]	40.5[3]
Sudan, The	2.9[3]	3.3[3]	4.1[3]	459[3]	80.1[3]	12.5[3]	13.3[3]	7.9[3]	-13.7[3]	10.5[15]	9.3[15]	44.3[15]	35.9[15]
Suriname	1.8[5]	1.9[5]	1.9[5]	3,125[5]	67.9	16.4	20.3	58.7	-63.2	13.6[3]	10.3[3]	45.5[3]	30.5[3]
Swaziland	0.4[1]	0.6	0.5	1,056	63.7	22.3	36.9	61.2	-84.2	17.4[25]	7.1[25]	29.4[25]	46.0[25]
Sweden	609.6	622.6	82.1	9,860	51.4	29.0	21.4	30.2	-32.0	9.3	10.9	64.0	15.8
Switzerland	205.5	196.1	81.4	12,750	63.6	12.8	27.1	36.8	-40.4	5.6	10.6	61.4	22.4
Syria	57.5[1]	72.4	61.0	1,445	66.9	23.4	25.1	18.3	-33.8	...	...	...	...
Taiwan	1,828.3	1,829.5	1,513.2	2,213	50.6	15.9	36.3	53.6	-56.4	13.3[1]	8.1[1]	50.4[1]	28.2[1]
Tanzania	47.6	47.9	3.1	162	79.3	13.5	20.8	13.6	-27.2	...	...	...	...
Thailand	834.6	858.4	31.5	650	65.4	12.3	27.8	25.1	-30.6	10.4	7.4	24.2	58.0
Togo	214.8[3]	267.7	224.2	382	65.8	14.5	36.3	37.9	-54.5	112.4[3]	6.9[3]	30.3[3]	50.2[3]
Tokelau	...												
Tonga	...	...	...	...	92.8	15.5	32.8	30.1	-71.2	13.7	4.9	—81.6—	
Trinidad and Tobago	9.8[3]	17.6	15.4	5,348	43.5	9.4	35.9	49.3	-38.2	...	...	...	...
Trust Terr. of Pacific Is.	...												
Tunisia	4.7	4.7	6.3	950	60.2	15.2	28.9	41.3	-45.7	13.8	4.2	—82.0—	
Turkey	8,736	8,578	27.6	596	68.5	13.9	25.4	5.0	-12.8	5.4	6.1	23.9	65.1
Turks and Caicos Is.	...												
Tuvalu	...												
Uganda	...	64.3[7]	...	...	—87.6—		16.5	19.0[29]	-23.1	10.1[29]	...	22.4[29]	67.4[29]
U.S.S.R.[c]	458.5	...	...	...	...	74.9	23.4	—1.7[27]—		...			
United Arab Emirates	...	108.9	102.4	34,962	17.3	10.9	28.4	77.9	-34.5	-1.5	8.2	14.6	78.7
United Kingdom	271.3	271.0	384.5	6,893	60.4	21.3	15.8	27.8	-25.2	13.9	12.0	61.0	14.0
United States	3,073.0	3,025.7	2,583.8	11,137	64.4	18.1	18.2	10.2	-11.0	7.8	13.3	62.0	16.7
Uruguay	124.9	128.4	80.5	756	76.7	12.2	17.5	14.7	-21.1	13.4	5.5	36.5	44.5
Vanuatu	—	...	...	317[1]									
Venezuela	292.6	298.3	257.9	4,077	54.9	13.1	24.8	33.2	-26.1	3.0	6.8	40.6	49.6
Vietnam	...												
Virgin Islands (U.S.)	0.7[1, 4]	...	...	6,350[1]									
Wallis and Futuna	—	...	...	924[1]									
Western Sahara	...												
Western Samoa	...												
Yemen (Aden)[c]	4.2[1]	...	...	419[1]									
Yemen (San'ā')	20.9	14.6	13.3	397	102.0	18.4	43.9	6.7	-71.0	14.2[3]	2.1[3]	22.4[3]	61.3[3]
Yugoslavia	2,200.4[1]	2,902.9	1,588.2	2,846	52.7	23.0	35.1	23.1	-33.9	...	...	...	...
Zaire	29.6	31.3	17.3	204	60.1	19.7	21.2	35.5	-36.5	8.6[15]	7.0[15]	—84.4[15]—	
Zambia	3.3	3.2	3.1	516	53.9	28.3	23.5	37.8	-43.4	6.1	14.6	47.4	31.8
Zimbabwe	4.8	5.0	3.9	489	62.1	19.3	21.7	30.0	-33.0	6.1	—	53.3	40.6[11]

origin of GDP by economic sector, 1980 (percent)[b]										aver. an. growth rate of real GDP (percent)		balance of payments, 1983 (current external transactions; '000,000 U.S.$)			tourist trade, 1982 ('000,000 U.S.$)		country
primary		secondary				tertiary				1970–1980	1980–1982	net transfers		current balance of payments	receipts from foreign nationals	expenditures by nationals abroad	
agriculture	mining	manufacturing	construction	public utilities	transp., communication	trade	financial svcs.	other svcs.	govt.			goods-merchandise	invisibles				
58.1[13]	0.1[13]	3.8[3]	7.1[3]	0.2[3]	6.2[3]	3.7[3]	8.4[3]	6.4[3]	...	2.5	1.8	−84	60	−24	38	24[1]	Nepal
4.0[7]	0.2[7,30]	23.6[7,31]	7.0[7]	2.2[7]	6.3[7]	13.3[7]	13.1[7]	10.8[7]	14.0[7]	2.9	−1.1	4,259	−578	3,681	1,540	3,402	Netherlands, The
...	...	...	...	...	...	...	...	...	...	...	...	109[5]	−114[5]	−5[5]	513[1]	63[1]	Netherlands Antilles
2.9[3]	15.9[3]	6.0[3]	10.2[3]	2.2[3]	3.4[3]	20.9[3]	15.1[3]	...	...	...	...	...	...	...[3]	...	...	New Caledonia
11.3	0.7	23.2	4.3	3.1	8.3	21.2	11.4	4.7	12.8	2.3	−0.7	182	−1,224	−1,042	226	504	New Zealand
24.7[7]	0.3[7]	21.0[7]	2.9[7]	2.0[7]	5.3[7]	23.6[7]	7.8[7]	5.1[7]	7.2[7]	0.9	...	−350	−93	−443	18[1]	...	Nicaragua
...	...	...	...	...	...	...	...	...	...	2.7	...	−69[19]	−7[19]	−76[19]	3[1]	...	Niger
...	...	...	...	...	...	...	...	...	...	6.5	−6.7	−1,691	−3,047	−4,738	55[1]	774[1]	Nigeria
																	Niue
																...	Norfolk Island
4.5	14.8	15.4	6.8	3.4	9.9	14.0	10.5	4.7	13.7	4.8	0.2	4,325	−2,121	2,204	815	1,834	Norway
2.0	68.1	1.0	6.1	0.7	2.2	5.5	——4.2——		10.3	...	...	1,564	−1,479	85	...	...	Oman
27.0	1.0	15.2	5.0	2.0	6.8	13.4	5.2	7.7	6.8	4.7	5.6	14	−2,739	−2,725	187	116[1]	Pakistan
16.4[7]	0.2[7]	14.1[7]	5.6[7]	3.6[7]	8.8[7]	17.7[7]	10.7[7]	20.0[7]	3.0[7]	4.0	2.6	−619	751	132	169	78	Panama
35.5[21]	9.0[21]	8.8[21]	5.7[21]	1.2[21]	4.9[21]	7.6[21]	5.5[21]	19.5[21]	...	2.3	−3.2	−151	−222	−373	26[1]	19[1]	Papua New Guinea
29.5	0.4	16.5	6.1	2.3	4.2	25.8	2.7	9.0	3.4	8.6	2.7	−225	−22	−247	54	...	Paraguay
8.3	14.3	27.1	2.8	0.9	5.7	17.1	7.6	7.9	8.0	3.0	−1.0	293	−1,163	−870	460[1]	104[1]	Peru
23.1	3.0	25.6	7.8	1.0	6.2	17.0	8.1	3.8	4.3	6.3	0.6	−2,482	−276	−2,758	450	127[1]	Philippines
...	...	...	...	...	...	...	...	...	...	...	...	...	...	...	...	...	Pitcairn Island
15.3	[8]	54.9[8]	9.2	[8]	7.4	10.4		——2.7[13]——		...	−6.6	...	...	...	...	...	Poland[c]
13.1[21]	0.5[21]	30.8[21]	5.2[21]	2.3[21]	6.0[21]	13.1[21]	5.8[21]	2.8[21]	10.7[21]	4.6	...	−2,400	1,395	−1,005	878	251	Portugal
2.6	0.1	34.4	2.5	3.1	6.1	17.3	12.7	7.3	13.9	...	...	...	...	...	586[1]	447[1]	Puerto Rico
0.5	66.2	3.7	6.0	0.4	1.7	6.1	6.0	0.8	9.7	...	...	...	...	...	...	...	Qatar
5.2[12]	[2]	3.1[2,15]	3.9[15]	0.9[15]	3.4[15]	34.6[15]	7.8[15]	6.7[15]	30.0[15]	...	...	...	...	...	...	...	Réunion
15.2	[2]	15.3[8]	9.3	[8]	7.0	...		——1.8[10]——		8.6	1.0	1,869	−709	1,160	...	...	Romania[c]
45.8	1.7	15.3	4.5	0.1	2.1	14.7	——3.8——		8.5	4.1	...	−74	25	−49	4[1]	12[1]	Rwanda
...	...	...	...	...	...	...	...	...	...	...	...	...	...	...	...	...	St. Christopher
...	...	...	...	...	...	...	...	...	...	...	...	...	...	...	...	...	St. Helena
12.0[15]	1.1[15]	7.1[15]	9.7[15]	2.3[15]	6.9[15]	18.0[15]	12.5[15]	4.6[15]	14.9[15]	...	2.6	−69[6]	40[6]	−29[6]	34[3]	...	St. Lucia
...	...	...	...	...	...	...	...	...	...	...	...	...	...	...	...	...	St. Pierre and Miquelon
12.5[3]	0.2[3]	9.6[3]	10.7[3]	2.0[3]	12.8[3]	9.9[3]	12.4[3]	2.7[3]	15.5[3]	...	7.1	−23	20	−3	...	...	St. Vincent
...	...	...	...	...	...	...	...	...	...	...	...	...	...	...	...	...	San Marino
...	...	...	...	...	...	...	...	...	...	...	...	...	...	...	...	...	São Tomé and Príncipe
1.2[3]	62.9[3]	4.3[3]	11.1[3]	0.1[3]	3.9[3]	4.5[3]	4.9[3]	1.4[3]	6.0[3]	10.6	4.8	11,926	−30,359	−18,433	573[1]	2,761[1]	Saudi Arabia
19.5	[8]	18.0[8]	5.7	[8]	6.4	23.8	8.1	1.1	17.4	2.5	1.3	−400[6]	—	−400[6]	62	42	Senegal
14.2[15]	0.04[15]	5.0[15]	8.9[15]	1.4[15]	12.0[15]	19.4[15]	12.1[15]	3.4[15]	15.8[15]	...	−0.1	−69	43	−26	31	11[1]	Seychelles
30.4[3]	11.3[3]	7.4[3]	3.9[3]	0.3[3]	16.0[3]	13.4[3]	7.2[3]	2.4[3]	5.8[3]	1.6	6.2	−150	−20	−170	10[1]	10[1]	Sierra Leone
1.3	0.3	29.5	6.6	2.4	12.5	24.3	16.1	4.0	6.6	8.5	9.9	−5,879	4,923	−956	1,916	438[1]	Singapore
59.0[32]	[8]	1.0[8,32]	2.2[32]	[8]	1.9[32]	7.7[32]	——7.7[32]——		13.5[32]	...	...	...	...	...	2[7]	...	Solomon Islands
...	...	...	...	...	...	...	...	...	...	3.4	...	−301	124	−177	9[1]	16[1]	Somalia
6.6	23.1	22.6	3.7	3.6	8.3	14.8	11.0	3.4	8.4	3.6	1.9	4,039	−3,719	320	...	...	South Africa
...	...	...	...	...	...	...	...	...	...	...	...	...	...	...	...	...	S.W. Africa/Nambia
8.6[15]	1.7[15]	24.6[15]	7.6[15]	2.3[15]	6.4[15]	15.8[15]	8.7[15]	9.7[15]	...	4.0	0.7	−7,387	4,907	−2,480	7,126	1,008	Spain
25.8	1.2	19.9	9.3	1.1	10.1	20.0	5.1	2.4	5.2	4.1	7.6	−664	193	−471	147	79	Sri Lanka
36.5[15]	0.1[15]	7.5[15]	4.1[15]	1.3[15]	9.7[15]	19.3[15]	6.6[15]	11.0[15]	9.3[15]	4.4	...	−189	−31	−220	6[1]	95	Sudan, The
8.8[3]	16.5[3]	6.8[3]	4.0[3]	2.0[3]	3.6[3]	14.2[3]	10.2[3]	20.4[3]	...	...	...	−35	−126	−161	17[1]	29[1]	Suriname
19.4[21]	6.3[21]	24.1[21]	2.2[21]	0.9[21]	5.6[21]	13.3[21]	6.0[21]	1.6[21]	11.3[21]	...	−8.8	92	−466	−374	11[1]	28[1]	Swaziland
3.0	0.5	21.4	6.8	2.7	5.6	10.6	11.2	4.0	21.9	1.7	−1.0	1,824	−2,821	−997	1,005	1,895	Sweden
...	...	...	...	...	...	...	...	...	...	0.4	1.4	−3,042	6,568	3,526	3,015	2,216	Switzerland
20.9	12.1	7.9	6.1	0.9	6.2	21.2	6.2	2.0	16.5	10.0	1.8	−2,224	1,409	−815	150	241[1]	Syria
8.0	[8]	45.0[8]	6.0	[8]	6.0	13.0		——21.0——		8.9	...	...	...	...	1,080[1]	988[1]	Taiwan
...	...	...	...	...	...	...	...	...	...	4.9	−13.7	−350	71	−279	21[5]	...	Tanzania
25.4	2.1	19.6	5.8	0.9	6.6	22.3	7.2	5.9	4.1	7.2	3.1	−2,852	−12	−2,864	972	267	Thailand
27.6[3]	8.3[3]	5.3[3]	7.9[3]	1.6[3]	6.1[3]	18.3[3]	5.6[3]	2.0[3]	10.8[3]	3.4	−11.0[1]	...	...	...	17	...	Togo
...	...	...	...	...	...	...	...	...	...	...	...	...	...	...	...	...	Tokelau
35.1	0.7	6.7	5.6	0.7	5.6	12.3	6.1	13.7		...	...	...	...	...	5[3]	1[1]	Tonga
2.7[7]	34.3[7]	10.5[7]	8.2[7]	1.1[7]	7.0[7]	10.4[7]	10.1[7]	1.8[7]	10.1[7]	5.1	−6.3[1]	−230	−679	−909	161[1]	...	Trinidad and Tobago
...	...	...	...	...	...	...	...	...	...	...	...	...	...	...	...	...	Trust. Terr. of Pacific Is.
14.0	11.4	11.8	6.6	1.5	5.2	13.6	3.3	8.4	10.4	7.5	4.0	−1,201	616	−585	545	59[1]	Tunisia
21.7	1.5	22.4	5.0	2.0	9.7	15.4	7.5	5.4	8.7	5.9	3.9	−2,348	603	−1,745	370	109	Turkey
...	...	...	...	...	...	...	...	...	...	...	...	...	...	...	...	...	Turks and Caicos Is.
...	...	...	...	...	...	...	...	...	...	...	...	...	...	...	...	...	Tuvalu
56.4[7]	0.2[7]	5.9[7]	1.1[7]	1.4[7]	2.3[7]	8.1[7]	10.0[7]	1.5[7]	13.0[7]	5.6	...	−49[1]	57[1]	8[1]	5[1]	20[1]	Uganda
15.0	[2]	50.9[2]	10.5	...	5.7	17.8	...	...	...	...	...	...	...	...	...	...	U.S.S.R.[c]
0.7	64.4	3.8	8.8	1.2	3.4	8.3	5.6	0.9	5.4	...	−0.3	...	...	...	...	...	United Arab Emirates
1.9	4.8	21.4	5.8	2.6	6.8	8.6	13.5	13.4	12.6	1.9	−0.5	−1,135	5,499	4,364	3,184	5,929	United Kingdom
2.6	3.6	22.6	4.7	2.5	6.5	17.0	20.7	8.1	12.6	3.0	−0.9	−61,070	19,490	−41,580	11,293	12,394	United States
8.4	1.5	23.0	4.6	1.1	5.7	...	...	...	9.0	3.5	−6.3	417	−477	−60	149.0	304.0	Uruguay
...	...	...	...	...	...	...	...	...	...	...	...	...	...	...	...	...	Vanuatu
6.0	24.0	16.4	5.7	1.2	10.0	8.1	18.7	4.0	11.4	5.0	0.5	7,876	−4,169	3,707	251[1]	2,349[1]	Venezuela
...	...	...	...	...	...	...	...	...	...	8.7	...	...	...	...	...	...	Vietnam
...	...	...	...	...	...	...	...	...	...	...	...	...	...	...	...	...	Virgin Islands (U.S.)
...	...	...	...	...	...	...	...	...	...	...	...	...	...	...	...	...	Wallis and Futuna
...	...	...	...	...	...	...	...	...	...	...	...	...	...	...	...	...	Western Sahara
...	...	...	...	...	...	...	...	...	...	...	...	−33[6]	26[6]	−7[6]	...	...	Western Samoa
...	...	...	...	...	...	...	...	...	...	9.1	...	−728	419	−309	...	...	Yemen (Aden)[c]
30.3[3]	1.1[3]	4.7[3]	8.9[3]	0.5[3]	3.1[3]	22.8[3]	10.5[3]	0.9[3]	10.9[3]	9.2	5.7	−1,766	1,207	−559	34[1]	44[1]	Yemen (Ṣan'ā')
13.3	[2]	41.3[2]	10.6	...	8.1	22.1	...	...	...	5.8	1.1	−1,231	1,506	275	1,350[1]	143[1]	Yugoslavia
26.2[15]	8.8[15]	7.2[15]	3.7[15]	0.3[15]	2.2[15]	22.0[15]	3.0[15]	13.5[15]	11.9[15]	0.1	0.3	752[5]	−422[5]	330[5]	23[1]	...	Zaire
12.7	16.1	16.8	4.1	1.6	6.0	11.8	4.8	0.7	16.4	0.7	1.4	−210	−462	−252	59	43	Zambia
13.1	7.6	23.9	2.4	2.1	6.5	13.6	5.8	13.9	8.1	1.6	6.8	84	−544	−460	33[1]	150[1]	Zimbabwe

[1]1981. [2]Manufacturing includes mining. [3]1979. [4]In $U.S. [5]1980. [6]1982. [7]1978. [8]Manufacturing includes mining and public utilities. [9]Net operating surplus includes consumption of fixed capital. [10]Activities in the material sphere not elsewhere specified. [11]Mining includes public utilities. [12]Manufacturing includes public utilities. [13]Trade includes transportation, communication, and services. [14]1970. [15]1977. [16]Trade includes transportation, communications, services, and government. [17]1974. [18]Based on nominal values. [19]1983. [20]Other services include financial services and government. [21]1976. [22]Construction includes quarrying. [23]Trade includes financial services. [24]Manufacturing includes mining, construction, and public utilities. [25]1975. [26]Other services include government. [27]Balance of trade. [28]1973. [29]1971. [30]Coal mining, crude petroleum, and natural gas excluded. [31]Coal mining, crude petroleum, and natural gas included. [32]1972.

Employment and labour

This table provides international statistical data on the size and makeup of the labour force of each of the countries of the world. The data summarized include the total economically active population of each of the independent countries and major dependencies of the world. These data are then analyzed in terms of certain major components of the active population: the proportion represented by women; the proportion of the total population of working age represented by this active population (an indication of the capacity of the national labour market to absorb the potential labour force represented by its people); the proportions assignable to the major categories of employment status (employers and self-employed, employees, unpaid family workers, and others); the proportion (and absolute numbers) of the active population in the major industrial sectors of the economy; and, finally, the change in size of the labour force, both during recent decades and as estimated by the World Bank for the present and next decades.

The first part of the table focuses on the concept of "economically active population," which the International Labour Organisation (ILO) defines as persons of all ages who are either employed or looking for work. In general, economically active population does not include students, persons occupied solely in domestic duties, retired persons, persons living entirely on their own means, and persons wholly dependent on others. Persons engaged in illegal economic activities—prostitutes, drug traders, bootleggers, black marketers, and others—also fall outside the purview of the ILO definition. Countries differ markedly in their treatment as part of the labour force of such groups as members of the armed forces, inmates of institutions, persons seeking their first job, seasonal workers, and persons engaged in part-time economic activities. Some countries include some or all of these groups among the economically active population, while other countries treat them as inactive.

The data for economically active population as a percentage of total population introduce the concept of activity rate. Developing countries usually have a lower activity rate than developed countries, in part because a relatively larger portion of most developing countries' population consists of persons who cannot work: those under 10 years of age. For the purposes of this table, working age usually begins at 14, 15, or 16 years, depending on the country involved, and ends after 64.

The distribution of data for economically active population by employment status indicates that a large percentage of economically active persons in some developing countries falls under the heading "employers, self-employed." This occurs because the countries involved have poor, largely agrarian economies in which the average worker is a farmer who tills his own small plot of land. In countries with well-developed

Employment and labour

country	year	economically active population										employed population by economic sector			
		total ('000)	percent female	as a percent of working age population	activity rate (%)			employment status (%)				agriculture, forestry, fishing		mining, quarrying	
					total	male	female	employers, self-employed	employees	unpaid family workers	other	number ('000)	% of labour force	number ('000)	% of labour force
Afghanistan	1982	3,829	...	43.8	27.9	...	...	...	...	...	...	2,195	60.6	...	...
Albania	1978	584	42.4	41.8	22.8	26.0	19.8	...	...	...	...	128	22.0	...	...
Algeria	1977	3,371	8.9	41.2	20.0	36.8	3.5	16.6	47.4	2.1	33.9	683[1]	20.3[2]	69[1]	2.0[2]
American Samoa	...	...	...	...	...	...	...	...	...	...	...	...	...	...	...
Andorra	...	...	...	...	...	...	...	...	...	...	...	...	...	...	...
Angola	1974	...	...	...	...	...	...	...	...	...	...	...	...	...	...
Anguilla	1974	1.2	...	42.1	18.1	...	...	...	...	...	...	0.1	8.5	...	...
Antigua and Barbuda	1980	28	39.2	56.0	37.7	47.8	28.5	12.3[3]	69.9[3]	0.6[3]	17.2[3]	2[4]	9.5	0.1	0.3
Argentina	1983	10,815	26.4	59.1	38.3	56.6	20.1	...	...	...	...	410	6.0	91	1.3
Australia	1982	6,691[5]	37.6[5]	69.3[5]	45.9[5]	57.4[5]	34.5[5]	13.6[5]	74.3[5]	0.9[5]	11.2[5]	410	6.0	91	1.3
Austria	1982	3,278	38.6	66.1	43.7	56.6	32.0	11.2	84.5	4.3	...	40	1.4	25	0.9
Bahamas, The	1979	77	45.8	...	36.8	41.0	32.8	13.0[6]	86.7[6]	0.3[6]	...	2	2.8	0.7	0.9
Bahrain	1982	142[5]	11.4[5]	61.7[5]	40.6[5]	61.6[5]	11.1[5]	9.5[5]	85.9[5]	0.1[5]	4.5[5]	4	2.6	0.8	0.6
Bangladesh	1981	20,523[7]	4.2[7]	...	28.7[7]	53.0[7]	2.5[7]	...	...	...	...	139	10.7	0.5	0.1
Barbados	1982	116[8]	46.0[8]	73.0[8]	45.5[8]	51.5[8]	40.0[8]	8.8	76.4	0.2	14.6	8	7.4	...	...
Belgium	1982	4,313	39.4	...	43.8	54.3	33.7	11.3	73.9	...	11.7	107	2.6	28	0.7
Belize	1970	33	18.7	58.8	27.6	44.8	10.3	25.1	66.3	3.6	5.0	11.1	34.0	—	0.1
Benin	1978	1,114	36.4	58.9	33.4	42.5	25.5	...	...	...	...	0.1	0.3	4	9.6
Bermuda	1982	31	45.2	85.1	58.2	65.4	51.3	7.7[8]	88.6[8]	0.5[8]	3.2[8]	0.2	0.7	0.1	0.3
Bhutan	1982	...	...	...	...	...	...	...	...	...	...	613	94.3	...	...
Bolivia	1982	1,872	23.2	53.3	31.6	49.2	14.5	48.9[9]	38.2[9]	9.1[9]	3.8[9]	793	46.4	76	4.5
Botswana	1981	315	40.3	63.0	33.5	42.5	25.5	...	...	...	...	5	4.9	8	8.3
Brazil	1975	43,797[8]	27.5[8]	57.9[8]	36.8[8]	53.7[8]	27.0[8]	27.0	65.3[8]	5.2[8]	2.5[8]	41[10]	0.4	93[10]	1.0
British Virgin Islands	1980	5	38.5	81.3	45.4	54.6	45.4	18.5	79.7	0.8	1.0	0.2	5.3	—	[4]
Brunei	1982	77[11]	11.9[11]	61.4[11]	38.2[11]	56.6[11]	11.2[11]	16.1[12]	79.5[12]	1.8[12]	2.6[12]	0.4[10]	1.3	6[10]	18.0
Bulgaria	1982	4,448[8]	46.8[6]	75.3[6]	51.0[6]	54.3[6]	47.6[6]	...	...	...	...	929[10]	22.8	...	...
Burkina Faso	1975	1,408	3.4	...	25.0	48.1	1.7	...	...	...	...	...	...	...	...
Burma	1982	14,462[13]	...	...	...	...	...	...	...	...	...	9,205	63.7	71	0.5
Burundi	1982	2,368[4]	53.1[4]	94.4[4]	58.8[4]	57.0[4]	60.4[4]	...	...	...	...	17[10]	40.7	0.8[10]	1.9
Cameroon	1981	3,543[14]	37.5[14]	66.7[14]	39.9[14]	50.0[14]	29.8[14]	60.2[14]	14.6[14]	18.0[14]	7.1[14]	80	20.7	11	2.9
Canada	1982	12,054[5]	40.6[5]	71.6[5]	49.5[5]	59.3[5]	39.9[5]	8.7[15]	89.6[15]	0.9[15]	0.8[15]	559	4.7	167	1.4
Cape Verde	...	...	...	...	...	...	...	...	...	...	...	...	...	...	...
Cayman Islands	1970	3	35.1	58.4	34.7	47.8	22.9	9.4	89.8	0.8	—	0.1	4.0	—	0.7
Central African Republic	1975	649	46.7	54.0	31.6	35.2	28.3	...	...	...	...	543	83.7	7	1.0
Chad	1972	1,271	23.0	...	33.5	54.3	14.7	...	...	...	...	...	...	...	...
Chile	1981	3,688	28.8	51.6	32.4	46.7	18.5	24.8	57.2	6.6	11.4	508	13.8	63	1.7
China	1982	...	...	...	...	...	...	...	...	...	...	320,130	71.6	...	...
Christmas Islands	1981	1.6	9.8	76.4	56.3	76.0	16.6	...	...	...	...	...	0.1	1.1	68.2
Cocos (Keeling) Islands	1981	0.3	29.6	69.4	50.5	63.8	31.1	...	...	...	...	0.1	21.8	...	...
Colombia	1981	8,467	26.2	48.7	31.6	50.0	15.5	...	...	...	...	47	1.2	14	0.4
Comoros	1976	...	...	...	...	...	...	...	...	...	...	3[16]	35.6[17]	...	...
Congo	...	...	...	...	...	...	...	...	...	...	...	...	...	...	...
Cook Islands	1976	5	28.5	62.4	29.7	41.4	17.4	17.3	69.0	8.8	4.8	1.2[1]	21.8[2]	—	0.2[2]
Costa Rica	1982	838	26.2	56.8	36.1	53.1	18.9	...	...	...	...	228	27.2	...	...
Cuba	1977	2,633[3]	18.3[3]	52.0[3]	30.7[3]	49.0[3]	11.5[3]	9.9[3]	88.2[3]	1.3[3]	0.6[3]	628[10]	24.1	...	...
Cyprus	1982	208	35.0	...	32.7	42.4	22.9	...	...	...	...	44	20.9	1.4	0.7
Czechoslovakia	1982	7,849[8]	46.7[8]	78.9[8]	51.4[8]	56.2[8]	46.7[8]	0.1[8]	91.2[8]	8.5[8]	0.2[8]	1,039	14.0	186	2.5
Denmark	1979	2,674[5]	44.4[5]	78.5[5]	52.1[5]	58.7[5]	45.7[5]	10.9[5]	84.7[5]	2.5[5]	2.0[5]	208	7.8	1.7	0.1
Djibouti	1982	...	...	...	...	...	...	...	...	...	...	...	...	0.1	4.9
Dominica	1970	19	37.2	66.2	30.4	40.1	21.8	24.8	73.0	2.2	—	7.7	36.4	—	—
Dominican Republic	1970	1,592[4]	26.0[4]	52.7[4]	30.2[4]	44.7[4]	15.7[4]	29.4	38.2	5.9	26.5	549[1]	44.3[2]	0.8[1]	0.1[2]
Ecuador	1981	2,808	26.7	58.1	32.5	47.2	17.5	...	...	...	...	1,337[1]	47.6[2]	9[1]	0.3[2]
Egypt	1979	11,442[8]	10.4[8]	41.2[8]	27.1[8]	47.7[8]	5.7[8]	...	...	...	...	4,002	39.9	23	0.2
El Salvador	1980	1,593	34.8	62.4	35.4	47.5	24.0	28.2	59.2	10.9	1.7	637[1]	40.0[2]	4[1]	0.2[2]
Equatorial Guinea	...	...	...	...	...	...	...	...	...	...	...	...	...	...	...
Ethiopia	1980	14,006	38.8	75.5	45.1	54.6	35.3	...	...	...	...	...	...	...	...
Faeroe Islands	1977	18	27.2	...	41.9[2]	58.2	23.9	11.1	86.3	...	2.6	3[1]	18.8[2]	0.1[1]	0.6[2]
Falkland Islands	...	...	...	...	...	...	...	...	...	...	...	...	...	...	...
Fiji	1979	176[9]	16.8[9]	...	29.9[9]	49.3[9]	10.1[9]	33.4[9]	51.5[9]	7.8[9]	7.3[9]	3	3.3	0.7	0.9
Finland	1982	2,463	47.1	74.6	51.0	55.8	46.5	9.6[8]	83.6[8]	4.7[8]	2.1[8]	254	10.5	10	0.4

economies, "employees" will usually constitute the largest portion of the economically active. Caution should be exercised when using the economically active data to make inter-country comparisons, as countries often differ in their choice of classificatory schemes, definitions, and coverage of groups and in their methods of collection and tabulation of data. Data on female labour-force activity, in particular, often lack comparability. In many developing countries, particularly those dominated by the Islāmic faith, a cultural bias favouring traditional roles for women results in the undercounting of economically active females.

The next major section of the table provides data on "employed population," which the ILO defines as all persons above a specified age who, during a specified period, were either at work or not at work but formally attached to a job. The definition includes such groups as unpaid family workers and members of the armed forces. As in the case of economically active population, however, national definitions of employment often differ from the standard international definition.

The data provided by the table for employed population calculate distribution by economic sector as a percentage of total labour force; *i.e.,* employed plus unemployed seeking work. Labour force is usually smaller than economically active population, in part because the former does not usually include nonworking-age employed and unemployed.

The table's categorization of economic sectors is based largely on the divisions listed in the International Standard Industrial Classification of All Economic Activities. The category "services, other" includes such groupings as public administration and defense, educational services, medical and dental services, motion picture and other entertainment services, domestic services, and activities not adequately defined.

Finally, regarding the section on labour-force growth, it should be recognized that for many economies changes in patterns and volume of unemployment and underemployment, in international and internal migration, or in technological development may invalidate the projections.

A large part of the data presented here is summarized from various issues of the ILO's *Yearbook of Labour Statistics.* The ILO compiles its statistics from both official publications and from information submitted directly by national authorities. The editors have supplemented and updated ILO data with statistical information from Britannica's statistical holdings of official publications and from direct correspondence with relevant authorities. The *World Development Report,* published by the World Bank, furnishes the data for the table's last section, "Average Annual Growth of Labour Force."

manufacturing, construction		electricity, gas, water		trade, hotels, restaurants		transport, communications		finance, real estate		services, other		average annual growth of labour force			country
number ('000)	% of labour force	number ('000)	% of labour force	number ('000)	% of labour force	number ('000)	% of labour force	number ('000)	% of labour force	number ('000)	% of labour force	1960–1970 (%)	1970–1981 (%)	1980–2000 (%)	
516	14.2	46.5	...	126	3.5	66	1.8	...	...	717	19.8	...	...	...	Afghanistan
271	46.5	...	...	39	6.6	33	5.7	...	...	112.7	19.3	...	...	...	Albania
607[1]	18.0[2]	30[1]	0.9[2]	214[1]	6.4[2]	132[1]	3.9[2]	18[1]	0.5[2]	1,618[1]	48.0[2]	0.5	3.6	4.7	Algeria
...	...	...	...	...	...	...	...	...	...	...	...	...	...	...	American Samoa
...	...	...	...	...	...	...	...	...	...	...	...	...	...	...	Andorra
												1.6	20	2.9	Angola
0.4	35.2	...	...	0.1	9.8	0.2	13.4	—	—	0.4	33.1	...	...	...	Anguilla
4.0[4]	18.2	0.3[4]	1.4	4.9[4]	22.1	2.6[4]	11.8	0.7[4]	3.4	7.3[4]	33.2	...	...	...	Antigua and Barbuda
...	...	...	...	...	...	...	...	...	...	...	...	...	...	...	Argentina
1,657	24.2	129	1.9	1,240	18.1	503	7.4	583	8.5	1,736	25.4	2.6	1.8	1.0	Australia
1,125	38.5	34	1.2	502	17.2	208	7.1	168	5.7	711	24.4	-0.7	0.9	0.5	Austria
8	9.5	1.2	1.4	22	26.2	4	4.8	7	8.7	26	31.0	...	...	...	Bahamas, The
45	32.1	2	1.6	20	14.0	15	10.3	7	5.0	48	33.7	...	...	...	Bahrain
478	36.9	30	2.3	78	6.0	74	5.7	...	...	497	38.3	2.1	2.9	3.0	Bangladesh
21	18.9	1.6	1.4	22	19.3	5	4.4	4	3.3	35	31.5	...	...	...	Barbados
1,110	26.6	33	0.8	694	16.6	275	6.6	254	6.1	1,115	26.7	0.3	0.7	0.3	Belgium
7.4	22.5	0.3	0.9	2.7	8.1	1.5	4.4	...	...	9.8	29.9	...	...	...	Belize
2	4.9	5	11.3	7	16.3	5	11.3	16	38.4	3	7.0	2.1	2.1	2.9	Benin
3	9.9	0.4	1.2	11	36.0	2	6.9	4	12.5	10	32.4	...	...	...	Bermuda
6	0.9	...	...	9	1.4	...	...	...	...	22	3.4	1.6	1.8	2.4	Bhutan
212	12.4	7	0.4	129	7.5	95	5.5	13	0.8	383	22.4	1.7	2.3	2.9	Bolivia
22	22.2	2	1.7	15	15.7	4	4.0	4	4.2	38	39.0	...	...	...	Botswana
5,074[10]	53.5	71[10]	0.7	1,334[10]	14.1	717[10]	7.6	404[10]	4.3	1,743[10]	18.4	2.7	1.0	3.0	Brazil
0.3	6.2	0.6	12.0	0.4	8.1	0.1	2.8	0.3	5.8	1.1	22.7	...	...	...	British Virgin Islands
14[10]	44.1	...	...	5[10]	16.2	2[10]	6.3	1.9[10]	6.1	3[10]	7.9	...	...	...	Brunei
1,755[10]	43.0	...	...	342[10]	8.4	304[10]	7.5	...	...	746[10]	18.3	0.7	0.3	0.2	Bulgaria
...	...	...	...	...	...	...	...	...	...	...	...	1.6	1.5	2.8	Burkina Faso
1,312	9.1	16	0.1	1,310	9.1	458	3.2	818	5.7	600	4.1	1.1	1.4	2.2	Burma
9[10]	20.4	0.5[10]	1.2	1.8[10]	4.2	1.4[10]	3.4	1.4[10]	3.3	10[10]	24.9	1.2	1.5	2.8	Burundi
141	36.4	20	5.1	47	12.2	19	4.9	23	5.9	41	10.6	1.3	1.5	2.8	Cameroon
2,516	21.2	127	1.1	1,839	15.5	755	6.4	601	5.1	4,016	33.8	2.5	2.0	1.0	Canada
...	...	...	...	...	...	...	...	...	...	...	...	...	...	...	Cape Verde
0.9	24.7	—	1.4	0.4	12.0	0.4	11.7	...	...	1.6	45.5	...	...	...	Cayman Islands
18	28.2	1	0.2	27	4.1	5	0.8	0.6	0.1	42	6.5	1.4	1.7	2.1	Central African Republic
...	...	...	...	...	...	...	...	...	...	...	...	1.5	1.8	2.5	Chad
686	18.6	27	0.7	621	16.8	218	5.9	117	3.2	1,031	28.0	1.4	2.0	2.2	Chile
72,700	16.3	...	...	18,200	4.1	8,500	1.9	...	...	27,530	6.2	1.7	1.8	1.6	China
0.1	3.4	—	0.6	0.1	4.1	0.1	4.5	—	1.5	0.3	17.1	...	...	...	Christmas Islands
0.1	25.7	—	2.1	—	4.6	—	5.3	—	0.2	0.1	39.8	...	...	...	Cocos (Keeling) Islands
1,087	28.4	26	0.7	837	21.8	208	5.4	242	6.3	998	26.0	3.0	3.3	2.5	Colombia
1.3[16]	14.4[17]	...	...	1[16,18]	11.1[17,18]	0.5[16]	5.6[17]	...	...	3[16]	33.3[17]	...	...	...	Comoros
...	...	...	...	...	...	...	...	...	...	...	...	1.8	2.1	3.7	Congo
0.8[1]	14.8[2]	0.1[1]	1.5[2]	0.5[1]	9.2[2]	0.4[1]	8.1[2]	—	0.7[2]	2[1]	43.7[2]	...	...	...	Cook Islands
159	19.0	...	...	131	15.6	42	5.0	...	...	200	23.9	3.5	3.9	2.8	Costa Rica
860[10]	33.0	...	...	281[10]	10.8	176[10]	6.8	...	...	663[10]	25.4	0.8	1.7	1.9	Cuba
63	29.6	1.4	0.7	37	17.1	11	4.9	8	3.6	42	19.5	...	...	...	Cyprus
3,185	42.8	66	0.9	814	10.9	500	6.7	266	3.6	1,385	18.6	0.8	0.7	0.7	Czechoslovakia
736	27.6	18	0.7	334	12.5	175	6.6	177	6.6	852	32.0	1.1	0.6	0.5	Denmark
0.5	28.3	—	2.9	0.2	12.3	—	4.2	0.5	28.4	0.3	19.0	...	...	...	Djibouti
3.4	16.2	0.2	0.9	2.7	12.9	0.7	3.3	...	...	6.4	30.3	...	...	...	Dominica
129[1]	10.4[2]	1.7[1]	0.1[2]	77[1]	6.2[2]	43[1]	3.5[2]	20[1]	1.6[2]	419[1]	33.8[2]	2.2	3.6	3.3	Dominican Republic
431[1]	15.3[2]	15[1]	0.6[2]	297[1]	10.7[2]	68[1]	2.4[2]	32[1]	1.1[2]	567[1]	20.2[2]	2.9	3.3	3.5	Ecuador
1,980	19.8	66	0.7	918	9.2	488	4.9	117	1.2	1,971	19.7	2.2	2.5	2.4	Egypt
328[1]	21.6[2]	10[1]	0.6[2]	256[1]	16.1[2]	66[1]	4.1[2]	16[1]	1.0[2]	250[1]	15.7[2]	2.6	2.8	3.5	El Salvador
...	...	...	...	...	...	...	...	...	...	...	...	...	...	...	Equatorial Guinea
...	...	...	...	...	...	...	...	...	...	...	...	2.0	1.6	3.0	Ethiopia
6[1]	31.7[2]	0.1[1]	0.8[2]	2[1]	11.9[2]	1.9[1]	11.0[2]	0.3[1]	1.9[2]	4[1]	23.3[2]	...	...	...	Faeroe Islands
...	...	...	...	...	...	...	...	...	...	...	...	...	...	...	Falkland Islands
24	30.2	2	2.9	13	16.6	8	10.0	4	5.5	24	30.4	...	...	...	Fiji
723	29.8	26	1.1	316	13.0	169	7.0	139	5.7	643	26.5	0.4	0.9	0.5	Finland

Employment and labour (continued)

country	year	economically active population — total ('000)	percent female	as a percent of working age population	activity rate (%) — total	male	female	employment status (%) — employers, self-employed	employees	unpaid family workers	other	agriculture, forestry, fishing — number ('000)	% of labour force	mining, quarrying — number ('000)	% of labour force
France	1982	23,519	39.3	65.8	43.4	53.8	33.5	15.1	76.8	...	8.1	1,758	7.7	137	0.6
French Guiana	1979	...	...	...	...	...	...	...	...	...	...	0.6[10]	4.2	0.1[10]	0.8
French Polynesia	1977	...	...	...	...	...	...	...	...	...	...	7[1]	17.2[2]	0.1[1]	0.3[2]
Gabon	1977	...	...	...	...	...	...	...	...	...	...	19[19]	13.6[20]	7[19]	4.8[20]
Gambia, The	1979	...	...	...	...	...	...	...	...	...	...	2[10]	6.8		
Germany, East	1982	8,214	46.3	81.3	48.1	56.1	41.3	...	...	...	...	339[10]	4.3	na	na
Germany, West	1980	28,335[14]	38.5[14]	66.9[14]	46.0[14]	59.1[14]	33.9[14]	8.5[14]	86.7[14]	3.2[14]	1.6[14]	1,518	5.8	330	1.3
Ghana	1979	3,332[3]	44.2[3]	...	38.3[3]	42.4[3]	34.1[3]	...	...	...	...	74[10]	15.3	24[10]	4.9
Gibraltar	1982	13[5]	27.9[5]	67.4[5]	46.2[5]	66.2[5]	26.0[5]	5.9[5]	93.8[6]	...	0.3[6]	...	...	...	...
Greece	1981	3,678	31.9	55.4	37.8	52.4	23.7	36.4	46.2	13.4	4.0	1,085[1]	29.5[2]	20[1]	0.5[2]
Greenland	1976	21	33.4		43.1	53.0	31.4	12.6	82.5	0.4	4.5	3[1]	15.1[2]	0.3[1]	1.5[2]
Grenada	1970	26	37.9	58.6	30.9	40.8	22.8	17.0	80.8	2.2	—	8.6	30.1	—	0.1
Guadeloupe	1974	108	38.5	61.6	33.3	41.8	25.1	...	...	...	...	19	17.2	—	—
Guam	1981	34[15]	38.4[15]		60.1[15]	75.5[15]	45.3[15]	...	...	...	...	0.1	0.3	na	na
Guatemala	1977	1,696[5]	14.6[5]	49.1[5]	28.0[5]	48.0[5]	8.1[5]	42.2[5]	46.9[5]	6.7[5]	4.2[5]	408	68.8	4	0.6
Guinea		...	...	...	...	...	...	...	...	...	...	...	...	...	...
Guinea-Bissau		...	...	...	...	...	...	...	...	...	...	...	...	...	...
Guyana	1977	160[3]	19.0[3]	45.6[3]	22.9[3]	37.3[3]	8.6[3]	19.8[3]	77.6[3]	2.1[3]	0.5[3]	48[1]	29.1[2]	5[1]	28[2]
Haiti	1982	2,130	41.0	63.5	42.1	51.3	33.5	67.6	18.9	11.9	1.5	1,329	65.9	1.3	—
Honduras	1982	1,167	16.3	53.5	29.5	49.2	9.7	...	...	...	...	612	51.9	3	0.3
Hong Kong	1982	2,512	35.5	69.6	49.1	61.9	35.7	10.3	83.6	1.9	4.2	na	na	0.9	—
Hungary	1982	5,069[8]	43.4[8]	72.5[8]	47.3[8]	55.3[8]	39.9[8]	2.0[8]	83.8[8]	2.0[8]	12.3[8]	1,144[10]	22.9	na	na
Iceland	1978	124	42.0	79.1	52.6	60.6	44.5	...	...	...	...	16	15.6	na	na
India	1982	180,485[12]	17.4[12]	...	32.9[12]	52.5[12]	11.9[12]	10.0[12]	17.1[12]	3.3[12]	69.6[12]	1,306[10]	5.5	961[10]	4.1
Indonesia	1977	52,153[8]	33.0[8]	59.2[8]	35.5[8]	47.9[8]	23.3[8]	39.4[11]	37.3[11]	20.8[11]	2.5[11]	29,694	61.3	171	0.4
Iran	1976	9,796	14.8	50.2	29.1	48.1	8.9	30.5	48.4	10.4	10.6	3,615[1]	36.9[2]	90[1]	0.9[2]
Iraq	1977	3,134	17.4	50.2	26.1	41.9	9.4	...	...	...	...	944[1]	30.1[2]	37[1]	1.2[2]
Ireland	1979	...	...	...	...	...	...	...	...	...	...	222	18.1	12	1.0
Israel	1982	1,367	37.0	54.4	33.9	42.8	25.1	18.8	74.7	1.6	5.0	73	5.3	na	na
Italy	1982	22,981	34.1	58.1	40.3	54.7	26.7	...	...	...	...	2,545	11.3	218	1.0
Ivory Coast	1975	2,832	32.6	...	42.2	54.9	28.5	...	...	...	...	72[10]	21.7	1.7[10]	0.5
Jamaica	1981	1,023	46.6	75.9	46.4	50.0	42.9	31.2[3]	67.1[3]	1.7[3]	—	269	26.3	9	0.9
Japan	1982	57,740	39.0	68.7	48.7	60.4	37.4	16.3	71.0	10.2	2.5	5,480	9.5	100	0.2
Jordan	1981	...	...	...	...	...	...	...	...	...	...	...	...	2[10]	1.7
Kampuchea		...	...	...	...	...	...	...	...	...	...	...	...	...	...
Kenya	1982	...	...	...	...	...	...	...	...	...	...	224	21.6	3	0.3
Kiribati	1971	...	...	...	...	...	...	...	...	...	...	0.3	6.1	0.6	12.0
Korea, North		...	...	...	...	...	...	...	...	...	...	...	...	...	...
Korea, South	1982	15,080	38.4	59.2	38.3	46.8	29.7	32.6	45.5	17.5	4.4	4,623	30.7	111	0.7
Kuwait	1980	484	12.8	60.5	35.6	54.3	10.7	10.1	89.7	0.1	...	9[1]	1.9[2]	7[1]	1.4[2]
Laos		...	...	...	...	...	...	...	...	...	...	...	...	...	...
Lebanon		...	...	...	...	...	...	...	...	...	...	...	...	...	...
Lesotho		...	...	...	...	...	...	...	...	...	...	...	...	...	...
Liberia	1979	433[7]	26.8[7]	47.4[7]	28.8[7]	41.7[7]	15.6[7]	...	...	...	5.4[7]	33[10]	26.4	10[10]	8.2
Libya	1978	541[21]	6.8[21]	48.2[21]	24.1[21]	42.3[21]	3.5[21]	23.7[21]	69.6[21]	4.2[21]	2.6[21]	148	19.1	20	2.6
Liechtenstein	1980	13	35.5	73.8	51.6	66.9	36.4	...	...	...	...	...	...	...	...
Luxembourg	1981	161[8]	29.3[8]	...	38.1[8]	...	...	13.9[3]	82.1[3]	3.2[3]	0.8[3]	8	5.0	0.3	0.2
Macau		...	...	...	...	...	...	...	...	...	...	...	...	...	...
Madagascar	1982	...	...	...	...	...	...	...	...	...	...	...	...	...	...
Malawi	1981	2,288[22]	46.2[22]	71.5[22]	41.3[22]	46.1[22]	36.8[22]	79.9[22]	17.8[22]	0.3[22]	2.0[22]	153	47.5	0.6	0.2
Malaysia[23]	1979	4,375	36.0	66.4	38.4	48.7	27.9	23.1	58.9	12.3	5.7	1,505[1]	34.4[2]	45[1]	1.0[2]
Maldives	1977	67	37.2	78.6	47.3	56.5	37.1	...	...	...	...	...	...	...	...
Mali	1976	2,266	17.0	53.2	35.4	60.2	11.8	45.8	4.1	42.5	7.5	1,862[1]	82.2[2]	8[1]	0.3[2]
Malta	1981	122	25.4		38.1	58.4	18.8	15.7	79.6	...	4.7	7[10]	5.7	1.3[10]	1.1
Martinique	1974	104	41.7	59.1	32.2	38.8	26.0	...	...	...	...	15	14.7	0.2	0.2
Mauritania		...	...	...	...	...	...	...	...	...	...	...	...	...	...
Mauritius	1982	261	19.8	54.1	31.6	50.5	12.5	10.3	73.7	0.9	15.1	57[10]	29.3	0.2[10]	—
Mayotte	1978	15.1	34.3	63.3	32.1	42.0	22.1	51.0	27.9	21.0	—	9.3	65.4	—	0.1
Mexico	1979	23,988[8]	...	60.2[8]	35.6[8]	...	...	...	...	...	...	7,886[1]	40.1[2]	289[1]	1.5[2]
Monaco		...	...	...	...	...	...	...	...	...	...	...	...	...	...
Mongolia	1980	...	...	...	...	...	...	...	...	...	...	38	11.9	...	...
Montserrat	1982	3.8[3]	34.9[3]	56.1[3]	32.8[3]	45.5[3]	21.6[3]	20.4[3]	78.0[3]	1.6[3]	—	0.5	10.0	—	0.2
Morocco	1971	3,981	15.2	48.1	26.3	44.5	8.0	33.6	37.3	18.7	10.4	1,988[1]	50.2[2]	45[1]	1.1[2]
Mozambique	1970	2,928	26.3	63.4	35.8	53.4	18.7	44.4	40.0	14.5	1.1	2,135[1]	73.4[2]	124[1]	4.3[2]
Nauru	1977	2.2	...	...	30.5	...	...	...	...	...	...	...	...	...	...
Nepal	1976	4,853[12]	29.2[12]	63.0[12]	42.0[12]	59.0[12]	24.7[12]	70.2	12.3	17.5	...	5,572	89.9	—	—
Netherlands, The	1982	5,696	33.4	59.3	39.9	53.6	26.4	9.6[5]	80.7[5]	2.0[5]	7.7[5]	248	5.0	8	0.2
Netherlands Antilles	1982	96	39.6	57.4	37.7	47.1	28.9	...	...	...	...	0.3	0.4	0.2	0.2
New Caledonia	1976	50	34.0	63.6	37.9	48.0	26.9	20.5	58.8	12.8	8.0	14[1]	26.8[2]	2[1]	4.2[2]
New Zealand	1981	1,332	34.2	65.4	42.0	55.5	28.5	12.9	81.7	0.5	4.9	142	10.8	5	0.4
Nicaragua	1980	864	21.2		32.0	51.4	13.3	...	...	...	...	4[10]	2.7	2[10]	1.6
Niger	1981	...	...	...	...	...	...	...	...	...	...	3	7.3	5	14.7
Nigeria	1982	...	...	...	...	...	...	...	...	...	...	...	...	...	...
Niue	1976	0.8	29.9	44.5	23.5	33.1	13.9	5.6	89.0	0.2	5.1	0.1	9.9	—	—
Norfolk Island	1981	1.0	43.3	80.8	46.1	53.3	39.2	...	...	...	...	—	3.0	—	0.3
Norway	1982	1,998	42.2	74.6	...	...	...	10.1	84.3	2.6	3.1	156	7.8	16	0.8
Oman		...	...	...	...	...	...	...	...	...	...	...	...	...	...
Pakistan	1982	27,407[15]	12.2[15]	52.4[15]	31.0[15]	52.3[15]	7.9[15]	43.3[15]	25.9[15]	27.3[15]	3.5[15]	13,526	52.4	36	0.1
Panama	1979	548[8]	27.7[8]	49.8[8]	30.7[8]	43.8[8]	17.2[8]	23.2[8]	63.3[8]	3.6[8]	9.9[8]	155	26.8	0.7	0.1
Papua New Guinea	1980	...	...	...	...	...	...	...	...	...	...	19	27.7	4	61
Paraguay	1982	1,111	21.3	60.8	35.1	55.3	14.9	...	...	...	...	455	43.8	3	0.3
Peru	1981	5,978	28.6	56.5	31.8	45.4	18.2	49.1	45.1	5.8	...	2,067	35.8	108	1.9
Philippines	1978	17,362	37.0	65.0	36.9	46.3	27.5	36.7[5]	42.1[5]	21.2[5]	...	8,702	50.1	67	0.4
Pitcairn Island		...	...	...	...	...	...	...	...	...	...	...	...	...	...
Poland	1982	17,962[11]	45.4[11]	73.7[11]	51.2[11]	57.4[11]	45.4[11]	13.2[11]	74.0[11]	12.1[11]	0.7[11]	5,357	31.4	532	3.1

manufacturing, construction		electricity, gas, water		trade, hotels, restaurants		transport, communications		finance, real estate		services, other		average annual growth of labour force			country
number ('000)	% of labour force	number ('000)	% of labour force	number ('000)	% of labour force	number ('000)	% of labour force	number ('000)	% of labour force	number ('000)	% of labour force	1960–1970 (%)	1970–1981 (%)	1980–2000 (%)	
6,911	30.1	194	0.8	3,421	14.9	1,360	5.9	1,567	6.8	5,598	24.4	0.7	1.1	0.7	France
2[10]	13.7	0.3[10]	2.2	1.2[10]	7.9	0.6[10]	4.3	0.9[10]	6.1	8[10]	55.0	...	...	...	French Guiana
8[1]	18.5[2]	...	...	8[1,18]	18.3[2,18]	3[1]	5.9[2]	...	...	17[1]	39.8[2]	...	...	...	French Polynesia
58[19]	41.7[20]	5[19]	3.4[20]	13[19]	9.1[20]	16[19]	11.4[20]	...	...	22[19]	16.0[20]	...	...	...	Gabon
8[10]	25.5	2[10]	7.6	5[10]	16.1	4[10]	13.8	0.5[10]	1.7	8[10]	28.5	...	...	...	Gambia, The
4,094[10]	52.2	na	na	851[10]	10.9	641[10]	8.2	na	na	1,917[10]	24.4	−0.2	0.5	0.3	Germany, East
10,767	41.1	230	0.9	3,627	13.8	1,498	5.7	1,418	5.4	5,877	22.4	0.2	0.8	0.1	Germany West
108[10]	22.5	16[10]	3.3	32[10]	6.6	19[10]	3.9	13[10]	2.6	197[10]	40.9	1.6	2.3	3.9	Ghana
5[10]	43.0	0.2[10]	1.6	2[10]	18.8	0.7[10]	6.0	0.5[10]	3.9	3[10]	23.2	...	...	...	Gibraltar
1,014[1]	27.6[2]	31[1]	0.8[2]	541[1]	14.7[2]	280[1]	7.7[2]	119[1]	3.2[2]	588[1]	16.0[2]	0.0	0.8	0.5	Greece
6[1]	27.2[2]	0.2[1]	1.2[2]	3[1]	12.5[2]	1.8[1]	8.7[2]	0.3[1]	1.6[2]	7[1]	32.2[2]	...	...	...	Greenland
6.3	21.8	0.2	0.8	2.5	8.7	1.3	4.7	...	...	9.5	33.0	...	...	...	Grenada
19	17.2	0.6	0.6	12	11.0	4	3.8	1.7	1.6	53	48.6	...	...	...	Guadeloupe
3	8.8	na	na	6	17.6	3	7.4	1.2	3.3	20	54.0	...	...	...	Guam
94	15.8	1.5	0.3	39	6.5	11	1.8	16	2.7	20	3.4	2.8	3.2	2.9	Guatemala
...	...	...	...	...	...	...	...	...	...	...	...				Guinea
															Guinea-Bissau
41[1]	24.8[2]	4[1]	2.5[2]	18[1]	10.8[2]	8[1]	4.7[2]	...	...	42[1]	25.3[2]	...	...	...	Guyana
160	7.9	1.6	0.1	362	17.9	16	0.8	4	0.2	142	7.1	0.6	1.3	2.1	Haiti
172	14.6	4	0.3	88	7.5	31	2.6	9	0.8	131	11.1	2.5	3.1	3.5	Honduras
929	43.0	12	0.5	518	23.9	88	4.0	166	7.7	356	16.5	3.3	3.7	1.2	Hong Kong
1,980[10]	39.6	na	na	492[10]	9.8	393[10]	7.9	na	na	989[10]	19.8	0.5	0.3	0.1	Hungary
37	35.7	1.1	1.1	14	13.1	8	7.7	4	3.4	24	23.1	...	...	...	Iceland
7,500[10]	31.8	735[10]	3.1	391[10]	1.7	2,842[10]	12.1	1,019[10]	4.3	8,806[10]	37.4	1.7	1.9	2.2	India
5,009	10.3	32	—	6,776	14.0	1,421	2.9	85	0.2	5,126	10.6	1.7	2.5	2.0	Indonesia
2,884[1]	29.5[2]	61[1]	0.6[2]	672[1]	6.9[2]	433[1]	4.4[2]	101[1]	1.0[2]	1,939[1]	19.8[2]	2.7	2.8	3.9	Iran
606[1]	19.3[2]	23[1]	0.7[2]	224[1]	7.2[2]	178[1]	5.7[2]	31[1]	1.0[2]	1,016[1]	32.4[2]	2.9	2.9	4.0	Iraq
343	28.0	14	1.1	187	15.2	68	5.5	37	3.0	253	20.6	0.0	1.1	1.5	Ireland
375	27.4	14	1.0	156	11.4	88	6.5	117	8.5	475	34.8	3.6	2.5	2.0	Israel
7,379	32.6	na	na	4,026	17.8	1,144	5.1	603	2.7	4,627	20.5	−0.1	0.6	0.4	Italy
101[10]	30.4	13[10]	3.9	27[10]	8.3	39[10]	11.9	7[10]	2.0	70[10]	21.3	3.6	4.3	2.9	Ivory Coast
117	11.4	na	na	104	10.1	34	3.4	na	na	229	22.3	0.4	2.2	3.3	Jamaica
19,210	33.3	340	0.6	12,960	22.4	3,490	6.0	3,490	6.0	11,320	19.6	1.9	1.3	0.8	Japan
23[10]	18.1	2[10]	2.0	7[10]	5.5	7[10]	5.6	5	3.9	78	63.2	2.8	3.1	4.3	Jordan
...	...	...	...	...	...	...	...	...	...	...	...	2.0	...	...	Kampuchea
207	20.0	14	1.3	75	7.2	53	5.1	44	4.2	419	40.3	2.7	3.2	4.2	Kenya
0.7	14.4	0.2	3.4	0.7	15.1	0.6	11.8	...	...	1.8	37.2	...	...	...	Kiribati
...	...	...	...	...	...	...	...	...	...	...	...	2.4	2.9	2.9	Korea, North
3,878	25.7	31	0.2	3,180	21.1	608	4.0	382	2.5	1,611	10.7	3.1	2.6	2.2	Korea, South
138[1]	28.5[2]	8[1]	1.7[2]	58[1]	12.1[2]	30[1]	6.2[2]	13[1]	2.7[2]	220[1]	45.5[2]	7.0	4.5	2.8	Kuwait
...	...	...	...	...	...	...	...	...	...	...	...	1.0	0.7	2.7	Laos
...	...	...	...	...	...	...	...	...	...	...	...	2.1	1.0	2.8	Lebanon
...	...	...	...	...	...	...	...	...	...	...	...	1.6	1.9	2.8	Lesotho
15[10]	12.2	1[10]	0.8	29[10]	22.6	6[10]	4.4	1.7[10]	1.4	30[10]	24.0	2.4	3.1	3.5	Liberia
212	27.3	16	2.0	48	6.1	68	8.7	9	1.2	253	32.7	3.6	3.7	3.9	Libya
...	...	...	...	...	...	...	...	...	...	...	...				Liechtenstein
58	36.0	1.4	0.9	52	32.4	11	6.7	9	5.4	20	12.5	...	...	...	Luxembourg
...	...	...	...	...	...	...	...	...	...	...	...				Macau
...	...	...	...	...	...	...	...	...	...	...	...	1.7	2.1	3.0	Madagascar
60	18.7	4	1.3	21	6.6	17	5.4	11	3.3	55	17.1	2.4	2.5	3.2	Malawi
964[1]	22.0[2]	65[1]	1.5[2]	594[1]	13.6[2]	185[1]	4.2[2]	...	...	1,017[1]	23.3[2]	2.8	2.9	3.1	Malaysia[23]
...	...	...	...	...	...	...	...	...	...	...	...				Maldives
26[1]	1.1[2]	1.2[1]	0.1[2]	45[1]	2.0[2]	12[1]	0.5[2]	0.2[1]	—	312[1]	13.8[2]	2.1	2.0	3.0	Mali
43[10]	36.7	1.2[10]	1.0	15[10]	12.6	8[10]	6.8	na	na	42[10]	36.1	...	...	...	Malta
15	14.7	0.6	0.6	13	12.2	5	4.6	1.7	1.6	54	51.4	...	...	...	Martinique
...	...	...	...	...	...	...	...	...	...	...	...	1.9	2.0	2.5	Mauritania
42[10]	21.5	4[10]	2.3	9[10]	4.6	8[10]	4.0	5[10]	2.4	70[10]	35.8	...	...	...	Mauritius
2.3	15.9	0.1	0.4	0.5	3.7	0.2	1.4	0.2	1.5	1.6	11.5	...	...	...	Mayotte
4,484[1]	22.8[2]	83[1]	0.4[2]	1,975[1]	10.1[2]	582[1]	2.9[2]	...	...	4,353[1]	22.2[2]	2.8	3.2	3.5	Mexico
...	...	...	...	...	...	...	...	...	...	...	...				Monaco
89	28.2	...	...	34	10.8	34	10.7	...	...	121	38.4	2.1	2.4	3.1	Mongolia
1.2	25.7	0.1	1.9	0.6	13.5	0.3	5.6	0.2	3.6	1.9	39.5	...	...	...	Montserrat
541[1]	13.6[2]	11[1]	0.3[2]	289[1]	7.3[2]	100[1]	2.5[2]	6[1]	0.1[2]	1,001[1]	25.1[2]	1.5	3.1	4.2	Morocco
237[1]	8.2[2]	3[1]	0.1[2]	82[1]	2.8[2]	63[1]	2.2[2]	6[1]	0.2[2]	256[1]	8.8[2]	1.8	3.3	3.1	Mozambique
...	...	...	...	...	...	...	...	...	...	...	...				Nauru
47	0.8	1.8	—	283	4.5	6	0.1	8	0.2	280	4.5	1.3	2.3	2.7	Nepal
1,380	27.7	45	0.9	871	17.5	315	6.3	463	9.3	1,654	33.2	1.6	1.4	0.7	Netherlands, The
15	19.1	1.7	2.1	22	27.1	6	7.3	5	6.1	30	37.7	...	...	...	Netherlands Antilles
10[1]	19.7[2]	0.5[1]	1.1[2]	5[1]	10.6[2]	3[1]	5.2[2]	1.1[1]	2.2[2]	15[1]	30.2[2]	...	...	...	New Caledonia
391	29.8	17	1.3	230	17.5	110	8.4	90	6.9	281	21.4	2.2	2.1	1.2	New Zealand
33[10]	25.0	3[10]	1.9	16[10]	11.9	6[10]	4.6	7[10]	5.2	63[10]	47.1	2.3	3.8	3.9	Nicaragua
15	42.7	2	6.8	3	8.8	2	6.5	3	8.4	1.7	4.8	3.0	3.0	3.4	Niger
...	...	...	...	...	...	...	...	...	...	...	...	1.8	1.7	3.5	Nigeria
0.1	6.9	—	3.3	0.1	6.0	0.1	13.1	—	0.2	0.5	60.5	...	...	...	Niue
0.1	14.8	—	0.7	0.3	27.8	0.1	7.6	—	4.8	0.4	41.1	...	...	...	Norfolk Island
537	26.9	19	1.0	336	16.8	185	9.3	105	5.3	592	29.6	0.5	0.7	0.7	Norway
...	...	...	...	...	...	...	...	...	...	...	...				Oman
4,997	19.3	190	0.7	2,846	11.0	1,215	4.7	218	0.8	2,663	10.3	1.9	2.7	3.3	Pakistan
84	14.6	6	1.1	71	12.3	29	5.0	20	3.4	162	28.0	3.4	2.4	2.6	Panama
11	16.6	0.1	—	10	15.1	14	20.3	1.9	2.7	8	11.5	1.7	1.7	1.7	Papua New Guinea
217	20.8	5	0.5	117	11.3	35	3.3	na	na	208	20.0	2.3	2.9	3.0	Paraguay
1,007	17.4	na	na	770	13.3	na	na	na	na	1,436	24.9	2.1	2.9	3.0	Peru
2,396	13.8	55	0.3	1,745	10.1	681	3.9	308	1.8	2,714	15.6	2.1	2.5	2.9	Philippines
...	...	...	...	...	...	...	...	...	...	...	...				Pitcairn Island
5,559	32.6	148	0.9	1,361	8.0	1,295	7.6	350	2.1	2,440	14.3	1.7	1.4	0.8	Poland

Employment and labour

country	year	economically active population										employed population by economic sector			
		total ('000)	percent female	as a percent of working age population	activity rate (%)			employment status (%)				agriculture, forestry, fishing		mining, quarrying	
					total	male	female	employers, self-employed	employees	unpaid family workers	other	number ('000)	% of labour force	number ('000)	% of labour force
Portugal	1981	4,366	41.5	69.0	46.0	56.8	36.2	15.8	66.8	12.9	3.8	1,028	23.9	21	0.5
Puerto Rico	1982	935[15]	33.9[15]	47.1[15]	41.6[15]	58.0[15]	26.8[15]	12.3[15]	64.3[15]	1.1[15]	22.4[15]	35	3.8	...	...
Qatar	1976	87	2.2	...	47.2	65.5	3.5					...	...	...	...
Réunion	1982	173	35.9	54.0	33.5	43.8	23.6	10.4	56.3	1.1	32.2	17	11.4	na	na
Romania	1982	10,794[22]	45.6[22]	75.6[22]	50.1[22]	55.2[22]	45.1[22]	...	...	...	...	3,025	29.0	na	na
Rwanda		...			...							...		...	
St. Christopher and Nevis	1982	13	38.2	...	29.1	38.3	20.9	12.4[3]	86.6[3]	1.1[3]	—	12[10]	50.7	0.1[10]	0.4
St. Helena and Ascension		...			...										
St. Lucia	1980	49	55.2	54.4[3]	41.1	39.0	43.0	27.3[3]	70.8[3]	2.0[3]	—	10.4	35.9	—	0.1
St. Pierre and Miquelon	1974	2	25.5	...	36.9	55.6	18.6	13.1	86.0	0.7	0.3	0.1[1]	5.9[2]	...	...
St. Vincent and the Grenadines	1970	21	35.2	52.9	27.5	37.6	18.7	16.0	82.5	1.5	—	6.1	25.6	—	0.2
San Marino		...	...	...	...	...	...					...	...	...	...
São Tomé and Príncipe		...			...										
Saudi Arabia	1976	...			...							0.4[24]	0.1[25]	20[24]	5.7[25]
Senegal	1977	1,648[21]	41.0[21]	...	42.0[21]	50.5[21]	33.8[21]					10[10]	9.3	6[10]	5.6
Seychelles	1977	39[5]	42.1[5]	...	61.1[5]	70.3[5]	51.9[5]	11.9	78.1	...	10.1	5[1]	19.5[2]	na	na
Sierra Leone	1981	...			...							6	8.3	6	7.9
Singapore	1981	1,173[14]	35.7[14]	66.5[14]	47.4[14]	60.4[14]	34.2[14]	12.6[14]	82.5[14]	2.3[14]	2.6[14]	13	1.1	1.2	0.1
Solomon Islands	1981	...			...							7	32.9	—	—
Somalia		...			...							...		...	
South Africa	1970	7,986	32.7	68.3	37.3	50.9	24.1					2,239	28.0	676	8.5
South West Africa/Namibia		...													
Spain	1981	13,344[8]	28.5[8]	...	35.7[8]	52.0[8]	20.0[8]	18.3[14]	68.2[14]	6.5[14]	7.0[14]	1,985	15.5	91	0.7
Sri Lanka	1980	5,715	28.1	...	37.3	53.1	21.2	23.7	54.4	8.4	13.5	537[10]	49.8	5[10]	0.5
Sudan, The	1973	4,443	20.8	...	29.7	46.7	12.5	59.2	25.3	9.9	5.6	2,950[1]	66.5[2]	4[1]	0.1[2]
Suriname	1980	98	...	58.2	27.5	...	...	...	...	...	...	8[1]	7.8[2]	6[1]	5.7[2]
Swaziland	1981	...			...							27[10]	33.5	3[10]	3.2
Sweden	1982	4,356	46.3	81.6	52.3	56.9	47.9	7.4	89.0	0.5	2.9	236	5.4	14	0.3
Switzerland	1980	3,099	36.3	70.9	48.7	63.4	34.6	...	...	...	0.2	218	7.2	6	0.2
Syria	1979	2,174	15.8	46.5	24.9	41.2	8.0	34.4	50.7	12.4	2.5	687	31.6	...	...
Taiwan	1983	8,553[14]	34.5[14]	67.4[14]	46.3[14]	58.3[14]	33.4[14]	22.5[14]	64.2[14]	13.3[14]	...	1,291	18.0	71	1.0
Tanzania	1980	...			...							135	22.3	6	1.0
Thailand	1980	22,728	47.3	...	48.1	50.4	45.7	31.1	21.6	46.4	0.9	15,943	70.1	37	0.2
Togo	1980	1,019	44.0	69.3	41.1	47.9	34.9	...				...		...	
Tokelau	1972	0.4	15.9	...	22.5	41.0	6.6	...				...		...	
Tonga	1976	21	15.7	43.7	23.8	39.3	7.6	32.7	33.3	13.1	20.9	9.5	51.1	—	0.1
Trinidad and Tobago	1981	431	31.6	...	59.4	81.6	37.4	14.6	80.1	3.5	1.8	43	11.0	na	na
Trust Territory of the Pacific Is.	1970	14	23.6	...	15.9	23.8	7.7	...				...		...	
Tunisia	1982	1,810[8]	20.1[8]	51.4[8]	28.4[8]	45.1[8]	11.5[8]	...				539	30.2	16	0.9
Turkey	1982	19,027[8]	33.7[8]	67.0[8]	42.5[8]	54.7[8]	29.6[8]	23.0[8]	33.5[8]	38.4[8]	5.1[8]	45[19]	2.0[20]	87[19]	3.9[20]
Turks and Caicos Islands	1970	1.6	32.9	60.9	28.5	40.3	17.8	...				0.2	14.9	—	2.7
Tuvalu	1979	4.0	51.3	54.6	56.3	58.4	54.5	...				—	4.2	—	0.1
Uganda	1970	...			...							66[27]	22.0[28]	8[27]	2.6[28]
U.S.S.R.	1978	135,424[4]	49.8[4]	...	51.7[4]	55.7[4]	48.1[4]	...	82.8[6]	...	17.2[6, 26]	25,646	20.9	...	...
United Arab Emirates	1975	297	3.4	74.9	53.1	74.2	5.8	9.0	89.3	0.2	1.5	14[1]	4.6[2]	7[1]	2.3[2]
United Kingdom	1982	26,350[8]	39.1[8]	73.5[8]	47.0[8]	58.8[8]	35.9[8]	7.0[8]	85.4[8]	...	7.5[8]	632	2.7	328	1.4
United States	1982	112,384	42.7	71.3	48.5	57.3	40.3	8.1	90.2	0.6	1.1	3,571	3.2	1,028	0.9
Uruguay	1981	...			...							4	0.7	0.5	—
Vanuatu	1979	51	43.4	88.8	46.0	49.0	42.5	...				39	76.8	0.1	0.1
Venezuela	1981	4,685[14]	26.9[14]	56.0[14]	32.0[14]	46.7[14]	17.3[14]	26.5	64.1	3.1	6.3	628	13.6	61	1.3
Vietnam[29]	1973	7,031	42.6	...	35.3	41.6	29.3	...				...		...	
Virgin Islands (U.S.)	1980	38	45.5	69.4	39.4	44.9	34.4	9.5	90.2	0.3	—	0.5	1.3	—	0.1
Wallis and Futuna	1976	3.3	35.8	65.2	36.5	46.9	26.1	42.2	18.3	39.5	—	2.7	79.2	—	—
Western Sahara		...			...							...		...	
Western Samoa	1976	38	16.7	50.2	25.2	40.5	8.7	3.8	42.0	54.1	0.1	23[1]	61.1[2]	—	—
Yemen (Aden)	1973	410	18.5	...	25.8	42.4	9.4	29.8	34.2	15.1	20.9	166[1]	40.5[2]	2[1]	0.5[2]
Yemen (Ṣan'ā')	1975	1,128	11.7	...	24.8	46.0	5.6	45.2	34.0	19.1	1.7	830[1]	73.6[2]	0.6[1]	0.1[2]
Yugoslavia	1982	9,324[11]	35.9[11]	60.6[11]	42.4[11]	55.2[11]	30.0[11]	22.6[12]	49.5[12]	21.1[12]	6.7[12]	302[30]	5.1[31]	134[30]	2.2[31]
Zaire		...										...		...	
Zambia	1981	1,824	28.2	...	31.1	45.2	17.3	...				...		...	
Zimbabwe	1982	...	...	...	...	...	...	...	...	...	...	271	26.0	64	6.1

manufacturing, construction		electricity, gas, water		trade, hotels, restaurants		transport, communications		finance, real estate		services, other		average annual growth of labour force			country
number ('000)	% of labour force	number ('000)	% of labour force	number ('000)	% of labour force	number ('000)	% of labour force	number ('000)	% of labour force	number ('000)	% of labour force	1960–1970 (%)	1970–1981 (%)	1980–2000 (%)	
1,407	32.7	22	0.5	489	11.4	152	3.5	90	2.1	733	17.1	0.4	0.6	0.9	Portugal
164	18.0	13	1.4	137	15.0	33	3.6	20	2.2	301	33.0	...	...	...	Puerto Rico
...	...	...	...	...	...	...	...	...	...	...	...	...	...	...	Qatar
19	12.2	0.7	0.5	14	9.4	6	3.9	16	10.7	45	29.9	...	...	0.7	Réunion
4,616	44.3	na	na	616	5.9	732	7.0	na	na	1,439	13.8	0.9	0.6	0.7	Romania
												2.2	3.2	3.4	Rwanda
2[10]	10.2	0.2[10]	1.1	4[10]	16.4	0.5[10]	2.1	0.2[10]	0.9	4[10]	17.5				St. Christopher and Nevis
...	...	...	...	...	...	...	...	...	...	...	...				St. Helena and Ascension
5.2	17.8	0.5	1.7	3.1	10.6	1.1	3.7	...	...	8.7	30.0				St. Lucia
0.5[1]	24.7[2]	1.4	0.8[2]	0.4[1]	18.8[2]	0.2[1]	11.1[2]	—	1.2[2]	0.8[1]	37.5[2]				St. Pierre and Miquelon
4.2	17.6	0.2	0.8	2.5	10.7	0.9	4.0	...	...	9.8	41.1				St. Vincent and the Grenadines
...	...	...	...	...	...	...	...	...	...	...	...				San Marino
...	...	...	...	...	...	...	...	...	...	...	...				São Tomé and Principe
69[24]	19.9[25]	8[24]	2.3[25]	97[24]	27.8[25]	16[24]	4.5[25]	15[24]	4.3[25]	124[24]	35.5[25]	3.3	4.4	3.5	Saudi Arabia
36[10]	33.2	5[10]	5.0	21[10]	16.7	18[10]	16.7	4[10]	3.3	8[10]	7.5	1.7	2.0	2.6	Senegal
6[1]	23.2[2]	0.2[1]	0.8[2]	4[1]	15.6[2]	2[1]	8.4[2]	0.5[1]	1.8[2]	8[1]	30.5[2]				Seychelles
17	23.3	1.8	2.5	6	8.1	7	9.8	2	2.8	27	37.4	1.5	1.9	2.8	Sierra Leone
404	35.3	7	0.6	242	21.1	127	11.1	85	7.4	233	20.3	2.8	2.7	1.3	Singapore
4	17.2	0.3	1.3	2	9.6	1.4	6.4	0.3	1.5	7	31.1				Solomon Islands
...	...	...	...	...	...	...	...	...	...	...	...				Somalia
1,470	18.4	50	0.6	716	9.0	338	4.2	190	2.4	2,306	28.9	3.0	2.9	3.2	South Africa
...	...	...	...	...	...	...	...	...	...	...	...				South West Africa/Namibia
3,659	28.6	83	0.7	2,175	17.0	645	5.0	407	3.2	1,773	13.8	0.2	1.1	0.9	Spain
278[10]	25.8	5[10]	0.5	98[10]	9.1	92[10]	8.5	37[10]	3.4	261[10]	2.4	2.1	2.0	2.2	Sri Lanka
266[1]	6.0[2]	45[1]	1.0[2]	244[1]	5.5[2]	154[1]	3.5[2]	6[1]	0.1[2]	777[1]	17.4[2]	2.0	2.7	3.1	Sudan, The
11[1]	11.5[2]	1.3[1]	1.3[2]	11[1]	11.6[2]	3[1]	3.0[2]	1.9[1]	2.1[2]	56[1]	57.0[2]				Suriname
21[10]	25.9	1.5[10]	1.8	6[10]	7.4	4[10]	5.5	3[10]	3.1	16[10]	19.5				Swaziland
1,223	28.1	40	0.9	582	13.4	300	6.9	288	6.6	1,536	35.3	1.0	0.3	0.4	Sweden
1,162	38.5	22	0.7	586	19.4	180	6.0	246	8.2	592	19.6	2.0	0.3	0.3	Switzerland
622	28.6	32	1.5	217	10.0	95	4.4	21	1.0	419	19.2	2.1	3.4	4.7	Syria
2,758	38.4	33	0.5	1,236	17.2	377	5.2	164	2.3	1,078	15.0				Taiwan
154	25.4	20	3.2	38	6.3	58	9.6	14	2.3	182	29.9	2.1	2.7	3.4	Tanzania
2,225	9.8	60	0.3	1,916	8.4	456	2.0	na	na	1,887	8.3	2.1	2.8	2.3	Thailand
...	...	...	...	...	...	...	...	...	...	...	...	2.5	1.7	3.1	Togo
...	...	...	...	...	...	...	...	...	...	...	...				Tokelau
1.5	8.3	0.1	0.6	0.8	4.4	0.8	4.5	0.1	0.3	5.7	30.7				Tonga
148	38.2	na	na	73	18.9	32	8.3	na	na	92	23.7	2.5	2.6	2.1	Trinidad and Tobago
...	...	...	...	...	...	...	...	...	...	...	...				Trust Territory of the Pacific Is
561	31.5	10	0.6	155	8.7	65	3.6	11	0.6	346	19.4	0.7	3.0	3.2	Tunisia
1,494[19]	66.0[20]	94[19]	4.1[20]	141[19]	6.2[20]	109[19]	4.8[20]	21[19]	0.9[20]	273[19]	12.1[20]	1.4	2.0	2.5	Turkey
0.4	23.3	—	1.0	0.1	9.1	0.1	5.9	...	...	0.7	42.7				Turks and Caicos Islands
0.3	31.7	—	1.6	0.1	10.9	0.1	11.9	—	1.2	0.3	38.5				Tuvalu
86[27]	28.8[28]	...	...	11[27]	3.8[28]	12[27]	4.0[28]	...	...	116[27]	38.9[28]	2.6	2.1	3.6	Uganda
47,048	38.4	...	...	9,361	7.6	11,462	9.4	604	0.5	29,033	23.7	0.7	1.2	0.6	U.S.S.R.
111[1]	37.5[2]	6[1]	2.1[2]	38[1]	12.7[2]	24[1]	8.0[2]	6[1]	2.0[2]	91[1]	30.8[2]	...	...	...	United Arab Emirates
7,344	31.6	340	1.5	4,269	18.4	1,509	6.5	1,676	7.2	7,123	30.7	0.6	0.4	0.3	United Kingdom
26,042	23.6	1,428	1.3	20,758	18.8	5,124	4.6	9,066	8.2	32,512	29.7	1.8	1.9	0.9	United States
171	31.4	7	1.3	83	15.2	37	6.7	31	5.8	175	32.1	0.8	0.2	1.1	Uruguay
2	4.1	0.1	0.1	2	4.3	1	2.6	0.3	0.6	6	11.3				Vanuatu
1,086	23.5	51	1.1	829	18.0	316	6.8	197	4.3	1,161	25.2	2.8	4.0	3.1	Venezuela
...	...	...	...	...	...	...	...	...	...	...	...	...	...	2.7	Vietnam[29]
6.8	19.1	0.6	1.8	9.0	25.3	2.8	7.9	1.9	5.3	14.0	39.2				Virgin Islands (U.S.)
0.2	5.5	—	0.1	0.1	1.5	...	1.2	—	—	0.4	12.5				Wallis and Futuna
...	...	...	...	...	...	...	...	...	...	...	...				Western Sahara
3[1]	6.7[2]	0.5[1]	1.2[2]	2[1]	6.2[2]	2[1]	5.4[2]	0.3[1]	0.9[2]	7[1]	18.5[2]				Western Samoa
30[1]	7.3[2]	3[1]	0.7[2]	26[1]	6.2[2]	13[1]	3.3[2]	0.5[1]	0.1[2]	170[1]	41.4[2]	1.7	1.8	3.6	Yemen (Aden)
86[1]	7.7[2]	1.5[1]	0.1[2]	69[1]	6.1[2]	25[1]	2.2[2]	2[1]	0.2[2]	113[1]	10.0[2]	1.6	1.8	3.4	Yemen (Ṣan'ā)
2,833[30]	47.4[31]	116[30]	1.9[31]	824[30]	13.8[31]	459[30]	7.7[31]	179[30]	3.0[31]	1,133[30]	18.9[31]	0.6	0.6	0.7	Yugoslavia
...	...	...	...	...	...	...	...	...	...	...	...	1.4	2.3	3.1	Zaire
...	...	...	...	...	...	...	...	...	...	...	...	2.1	2.3	3.2	Zambia
232	22.2	7	0.6	80	7.7	50	4.8	15	1.4	326	31.2	2.7	2.5	4.5	Zimbabwe

[1]Economically active. [2]Percent of economically active population. [3]1970. [4]1979. [5]1981. [6]1975. [7]1974. [8]1980. [9]1976. [10]Employees only. [11]1978. [12]1971. [13]Total employees. [14]1982. [15]1983. [16]Salaried employees only. [17]Percent of all salaried employees. [18]Includes banking and finance. [19]Insured workers. [20]Percent of all insured workers. [21]1973. [22]1977. [23]Peninsula only. [24]Employees in privately-owned establishments. [25]Percent of all employees in privately-owned establishments. [26]Includes communal workers and their families. [27]African employees only. [28]Percent of African employees. [29]Except for growth of labour force, all data pertain to the former Republic of South Vietnam only. [30]All persons engaged. [31]Percent of all persons engaged.

Agriculture and land use

This table provides published data on the agricultural structure of the independent countries of the world and selected dependencies. The data are taken mainly from the United Nations Food and Agriculture Organization's (FAO) *World Census of Agriculture,* supplemented from local sources in countries and dependencies not covered by the FAO. The FAO's *World Census of Agriculture* programs (the 1980 census was the fourth, and included national censuses taken during the decade 1976–85) represent a cooperative effort by FAO member countries to collect agricultural data within a general framework that permits international harmonization of concepts and definitions; transfer of technical expertise; and increased effectiveness in the collection, analysis, publication, and policy-related use of such statistics. More than 100 countries eventually participated in the 1970 round of censuses.

Although the FAO reports present a standardized series of data, and many nations have organized their data along FAO guidelines, varying standards of coverage and times of reporting make country-to-country comparisons of limited value. For example, the Soviet bloc nations, Czechoslovakia excepted, publish statistics only on state collective or cooperative farms but exclude privately held plots of land, even though in some instances these provide a significant part of agricultural output. Many other countries impose a minimum size limit for holdings covered in their census reports, and this, if not sufficiently low, can substantially undercount smaller holdings.

The classification of cropland by type is also subject to differing interpretations. Some countries classify land under permanent crops as cropland or arable land; that is, land rotated between different crops. Land under temporary crops includes land requiring replanting after each harvest, but some crops—such as asparagus, strawberries, pineapples, bananas, and sugarcane—have biennial or longer growing cycles and so are sometimes arbitrarily placed under temporary and sometimes under permanent cropland. Permanently cropped land may include trees, such as cocoa or coffee, but other trees may be grown to shade these; temporarily cropped land is sometimes simultaneously planted with permanent crops, causing confusion in classification. Many countries do not distinguish consistently between temporary and permanent meadow or pasture land, and some include grassland and meadows under cropland. Land left temporarily fallow, land subject to changing use, particularly under the shifting cultivation patterns of tropical countries, may be inconsistently classified. There is also uncertainty in classifying forest and woodlands that may have commercial potential but that are also used for grazing livestock or for recreation.

Statistics on types of farms producing commodities mainly for sale in the FAO censuses suffer from the paucity of countries reporting data precisely in the categories outlined by the FAO. The terms "mainly crops" and "mainly livestock" indicate that more than half of the for-sale production was either crops or livestock, and farms not clearly fitting either category were defined as mixed.

The land tenure statistics show a breakdown of all farms according to the rights under which the farmer holds the land. Owner-operated includes two classifications under the FAO: outright ownership in which the holder

Agriculture and land use (farms[a])

country	year of last agri- cul- tural census or survey	all farms number ('000)	size average size (hectares)	size under 1 hectare (percent)	size 1 to 9 hectares (percent)	size 10 to 49 hectares (percent)	size 50 to 199 hectares (percent)	size over 200 hectares (percent)	land use cropland area ('000 hectares)	land use cropland perma- nent[h] (percent)	land use cropland tempo- rary[i] (percent)	land use cropland temporarily fallow[j] (percent)	meadows/ pastures,[d] area ('000 hectares)	woods/ forests, area ('000 hectares)	other land,[e] area ('000 hectares)
Afghanistan	...	...	...	...	...	...	...	...	...	...	...	...	...	...	...
Albania	1979	...	...	...	...	...	...	...	...	...	...	...	...	...	...
Algeria	1973	900	6.2	36.7	46.4	15.4	1.4	0.1	5,208	4.1	65.1	30.8	122	215	...
American Samoa	1980	1.3	1.8	49.2[1]	50.8[2]				1.9				0.1		0.4
Andorra	...	...	...	...	...	...	...	...	...	...	...	...	...	...	...
Angola	1970	1,067	3.9	...	...	...	...	...	...	...	...	...	...	...	...
Anguilla	...	...	...	...	...	...	...	...	...	...	...	...	...	...	...
Antigua and Barbuda	...	...	...	...	...	...	...	...	...	...	...	...	...	...	...
Argentina	1969	538	391	18.6[5]	49.2[6]	20.0[7]	12.2[8]	—	35,600				91,714	53,223	30,318
Australia	1971	249	1,997	0.6	12.4	18.2	26.2	42.6	43,930	0.4	85.9	13.7	335,583	...	117,710
Austria	1980	303	24	2.7	48.6	33.2	14.8	0.7	1,561				1,949	3,036	780
Bahamas, The	1978	4.2	8.5	55.2[1]	30.1[9]	10.6[10]	4.1[11]	—	9.1	21.5	62.9	15.6	1.8	9.3	16
Bahrain	1974	1	4.3	19.4	71.0	9.4	0.2	—	1.6	64.5	35.5		2.1		
Bangladesh	1977	6,257	1.4	90.6[12]	9.4[13]				7,884	2.1	96.3	1.5	...	...	1,003
Barbados	...	...	...	...	...	...	...	...	...	...	...	...	...	...	...
Belgium	1970	107[14]		2.3[14]	54.7[14]	39.2[14]	3.8[14]	—	813	7.4	92.6	—	727	15	48
Belize	1974	10	23.3	...	...	...	...	...	85	13.1	81.1	5.8	37	84	27
Benin	...	...	...	...	...	...	...	...	...	...	...	...	...	...	...
Bermuda	...	...	...	...	...	...	...	...	...	...	...	...	...	...	...
Bhutan	...	...	...	...	...	...	...	...	...	...	...	...	...	...	...
Bolivia	...	...	...	...	...	...	...	...	...	...	...	...	...	...	...
Botswana	1969	48	4.8	29.7	69.8	0.5	—	—	228	—	100.0	—	...	...	...
Brazil	1980	5,168	7.2	9.2	41.3	31.5	12.7	5.3	49,185	21.3	78.7	—	...	...	...
British Virgin Islands	1981	0.3	...	...	...	...	...	...	...	...	...	...	...	...	...
Brunei	1964	6.3	5.2	94.1[15]	5.9[16]				44	8.2	21.8	—	0.1	13.1	22
Bulgaria	...	...	...	...	...	...	...	...	...	...	...	...	...	...	...
Burkina Faso	...	...	...	...	...	...	...	...	...	...	...	...	...	...	...
Burma	...	...	...	...	...	...	...	...	...	...	...	...	...	...	...
Burundi	...	...	...	...	...	...	...	...	...	...	...	...	...	...	...
Cameroon	1973	926	1.6	42.7	57.0	0.3	—	—	1,450				...	...	...
Canada	1981	318	207	1.5[1]	16.3[17]	31.1[18]	31.0[19]	20.1[20]	40,668	76.1		23.9	...	3,551	...
Cape Verde	...	...	...	...	...	...	...	...	...	...	...	...	...	...	...
Cayman Islands	...	...	...	...	...	...	...	...	...	...	...	...	...	...	...
Central African Rep.	1974	283	1.7	32.2	67.7	0.1	—	—	491	11.8	88.2		...	...	...
Chad	1973	366	2.6	19.7	79.5	0.8	—	—	962				...	...	...
Chile	1976	306	94.1	...	...	...	...	...	3,318	6.1	65.5	28.4	12,169	5,950	7,322
China	1980	55[21]	...	...	...	...	...	...	...	...	...	...	...	...	...
Christmas Island	...	...	...	...	...	...	...	...	...	...	...	...	...	...	...
Cocos (Keeling) Islands	...	...	...	...	...	...	...	...	...	...	...	...	...	...	...
Colombia	1971	1,177	26.3	22.8	50.2	18.5	6.3	2.2	7,659	30.7	27.6	41.7	17,465	...	5,870
Comoros	...	...	...	...	...	...	...	...	...	...	...	...	...	...	...
Congo	1973	143	1.4	37.3	62.7	—	—	—	196	49.5	50.5	—	...	...	...
Cook Islands	...	...	...	...	...	...	...	...	...	...	...	...	...	...	...
Costa Rica	1973	82	38.1	23.3	36.7	26.0	10.7	3.3	490.4	42.2	32.3	25.4	1,558	717	357
Cuba	...	...	...	...	...	...	...	...	...	...	...	...	...	...	...
Cyprus	...	...	...	...	...	...	...	...	...	...	...	...	...	...	...
Czechoslovakia	1970	1,472	8.1	91.1	8.0	0.3	0.1	0.5	5,259	2.1	97.9	—	1,707	4,426	483
Denmark	1982	112	25.7	29.2		59.6	11.2		2,887				...	...	...
Djibouti	...	...	...	...	...	...	...	...	...	...	...	...	...	...	...
Dominica	1980	...	...	...	...	...	...	...	41				...	...	...
Dominican Republic	1971	305	9.0	32.1	56.0	9.5	1.9	0.5	1,144	27.8	54.3	17.9	1,252	316	23
Ecuador	1974	517	15.4	27.9	49.4	16.2	5.6	0.9	2,608	32.8	51.5	15.7	2,559	2,309	479
Egypt	...	...	...	...	...	...	...	...	...	...	...	...	...	...	...
El Salvador	1971	318	4.6	56.5	37.1	5.1	1.0	0.3	652	25.1	58.6	16.3	555	168	77
Equatorial Guinea	...	...	...	...	...	...	...	...	...	...	...	...	...	...	...

has title and has the right to determine use and transfer of the land; and ownerlike possession in which the holder lacks the legal title to the land but uses it under terms of perpetual lease, hereditary tenure, or long-term leases of 30 years or more with nominal, or no, rent payment.

All agricultural statistics gathered through the FAO are subject to quality-control problems. The FAO depends upon census organizations in individual countries, and these differ greatly in the completeness and accuracy of the data that they produce. Frequently terms and definitions vary from the FAO guidelines from country to country. In countries that lack sufficient manpower, financing, or transport and communications infrastructure to permit a complete census of agriculture, a sample survey may be taken. This is a limited census of a predetermined number of carefully screened holdings. From these results, nationwide projections may be prepared, but these are often of uncertain reliability. Problems of quality control include errors or biases arising from such factors as incomplete or inaccurate lists of holdings, ambiguous or misleading questions, opinionated enumerators, respondents who inadvertently or willfully do not give accurate information, failure to record data for all parts of scattered or fragmented holdings, respondents' misunderstandings of the definitions of land use and cropping methods, or a failure to report livestock temporarily absent from the holding on public or common pasture land or in transit. While sample surveys can provide a check against such discrepancies, many statistical uncertainties remain.

Much additional information on the problems of collecting and comparing agricultural data may be found in the FAO's *World Census of Agriculture 1970: Analysis and International Comparison of the Results* and *Programme for the 1980 World Census of Agriculture,* and in the United States Department of Agriculture's *Scope and Methods of the Statistical Reporting Service.*

Measurements of area are given in hectares (1 hectare is equal to 2.4711 acres). The following notes further define the column headings:
a. All properties used wholly or partly for agricultural production. A property need not have agricultural land to be considered a farm; piggeries, hatcheries, and poultry batteries are farms because they engage in agricultural production, i.e. raise livestock and produce livestock products.
b. Farms producing mainly for cash sales.
c. Describes the arrangements under which a farm is operated.
d. Land used permanently for herbaceous forage crops.
e. All land in farms that was not included in the preceding categories.
f. Under this traditional form, land is operated by a tribe, community, village, or clan. Exploitation of the land is not systematic.
g. All forms not included in the preceding categories. Includes land operated by squatters and land operated by state farms and collectives (in socialist countries).
h. Cropland that does not need to be replanted after each harvest. Does not include wood or forest land and permanent meadows and pastures.
i. Cropland that needs to be newly sown after each harvest.
j. Cropland lying idle for a short period of time.
... Not available, or no agricultural census or survey ever taken.
— None, nil, or not applicable.

all farms				mainly commercial farms[b]							country
tenure[c]				number ('000)	mainly crops		mainly livestock		mixed (crops and livestock)		
owner-operated (percent)	rented (percent)	tribal/ communal[f] (percent)	other tenure[g] (percent)		average size (hectares)	number (percent)	average size (hectares)	number (percent)	average size (hectares)	number (percent)	
...	...	...	...	...	...	...	...	...	...	...	Afghanistan
...	—	—	100.0	...	...	...	...	...	...	...	Albania
...	...	...	...	...	...	...	...	...	...	...	Algeria
82.9[3]	13.9[3]	—	3.2[3]	0.2	...	36.8[4]	...	6.5[4]	...	55.7	American Samoa
...	...	...	...	...	...	...	...	...	...	...	Andorra
...	...	...	...	...	...	...	...	...	...	...	Angola
...	...	...	...	...	...	...	...	...	...	...	Anguilla
...	...	...	...	...	...	...	...	...	...	...	Antigua and Barbuda
...	...	...	...	...	...	...	...	...	...	...	Argentina
...	...	...	...	228	414	29.4	2,847	70.6	—	—	Australia
59.0	2.3	—	38.7	...	...	...	...	...	...	...	Austria
...	...	...	...	...	...	...	...	...	...	...	Bahamas, The
37.0	61.5	—	1.5	...	...	...	...	...	...	...	Bahrain
58.3	0.6	—	41.1	...	...	...	...	...	...	...	Bangladesh
...	...	...	...	...	...	...	...	...	...	...	Barbados
28.0	23.9	—	48.1	...	...	...	...	...	...	...	Belgium
...	...	...	...	...	...	...	...	...	...	...	Belize
...	...	...	...	...	...	...	...	...	...	...	Benin
...	...	...	...	...	...	...	...	...	...	...	Bermuda
...	...	...	...	...	...	...	...	...	...	...	Bhutan
...	...	...	...	...	...	...	...	...	...	...	Bolivia
...	...	...	...	0.4	...	...	...	...	...	...	Botswana
64.4	11.7	—	23.9	...	...	...	...	...	...	...	Brazil
...	...	...	...	...	...	...	...	...	...	...	British Virgin Islands
...	...	...	...	...	...	...	...	...	...	...	Brunei
...	...	...	...	...	...	...	...	...	...	...	Bulgaria
...	...	...	...	...	...	...	...	...	...	...	Burkina Faso
...	...	...	...	...	...	...	...	...	...	...	Burma
...	...	...	...	...	...	...	...	...	...	...	Burundi
2.4	5.2	59.5	32.9	...	...	...	...	...	...	...	Cameroon
63.3	6.2	—	30.5	259.7	281.1	48.5	195.5	49.7	389.7	1.8	Canada
...	...	...	...	...	...	...	...	...	...	...	Cape Verde
...	...	...	...	...	...	...	...	...	...	...	Cayman Islands
...	...	...	...	...	...	...	...	...	...	...	Central African Rep.
...	...	...	...	...	...	...	...	...	...	...	Chad
...	...	...	...	...	...	...	...	...	...	...	Chile
...	...	...	...	...	...	...	...	...	...	...	China
...	...	...	...	...	...	...	...	...	...	...	Christmas Island
...	...	...	...	...	...	...	...	...	...	...	Cocos (Keeling) Islands
68.7	14.2	—	17.1	...	...	...	...	...	...	...	Colombia
...	...	...	...	...	...	...	...	...	...	...	Comoros
...	...	...	...	...	...	...	...	...	...	...	Congo
...	...	...	...	...	...	...	...	...	...	...	Cook Islands
85.4	4.7	—	9.9	...	...	...	...	...	...	...	Costa Rica
...	...	...	...	...	...	...	...	...	...	...	Cuba
...	...	...	...	...	...	...	...	...	...	...	Cyprus
...	...	...	...	124	0.7	34.7	4.7	24.2	121	41.1	Czechoslovakia
...	...	...	...	...	...	...	...	...	...	...	Denmark
...	...	...	...	...	...	...	...	...	...	...	Djibouti
...	...	...	...	...	...	...	...	...	...	...	Dominica
54.7	10.1	—	35.2	...	...	...	...	...	...	...	Dominican Republic
70.3	7.7	—	22.0	298	12.6	67.8	45	12.4	43	19.8	Ecuador
...	...	...	...	...	...	...	...	...	...	...	Egypt
35.3	24.0	5.4	35.3	215	5.2	95.3	30.7	4.7	—	—	El Salvador
...	...	...	...	...	...	...	...	...	...	...	Equatorial Guinea

Agriculture and land use (farms[a]) (continued)

country	year of last agricultural census or survey	all farms number ('000)	average size (hectares)	under 1 hectare (percent)	1 to 9 hectares (percent)	10 to 49 hectares (percent)	50 to 199 hectares (percent)	over 200 hectares (percent)	cropland area ('000 hectares)	permanent (percent)	temporary (percent)	temporarily fallow (percent)	meadows/pastures area ('000 hectares)	woods/forests area ('000 hectares)	other land area ('000 hectares)
Ethiopia	...	...	...	...	...	...	...	...	...	...	...	...	...	...	...
Faeroe Islands	...	...	...	...	...	...	...	...	...	...	...	...	...	...	...
Falkland Islands	1975	4	32,586	25.0[22]	41.7[23]	33.3[24]	...	...	1,173	...	...	...	...	...	...
Fiji	1969	34	7.2	25.4	58.0	16.6	—	—	146	43.8	56.2	—	37	...	62
Finland	1980	225	57	—61.7—		37.0	1.3	—	2,463	...	...	...	144	7,455	2,738
France	1979	1,263	25.5	9.5	32.0	46.8	—11.7—		17,401	...	...	...	...	...	...
French Guiana	1982	2.2	4.1	...	...	...	...	...	...	...	...	...	...	...	...
French Polynesia	...	...	...	...	...	...	...	...	...	...	...	...	...	...	...
Gabon	1975	71	1.0	67.9	32.1	—	—	—	73	...	...	...	...	...	...
Gambia, The	...	...	...	...	...	...	...	...	...	...	...	...	...	...	...
Germany, East	1980	4,502	...	...	...	...	...	...	...	...	...	...	...	...	...
Germany, West	1971	1,075	14.2	5.3	53.7	39.0	1.9	0.1	7,537	2.1	97.9	—	5,114	1,833	752.4
Ghana	1970	805	3.2	37.8	57.0	5.2	—	—	2,574	61.4	38.6	—	...	...	...
Gibraltar	...	...	...	...	...	...	...	...	...	...	...	...	...	...	...
Greece	1978	957	3.7	23.4	70.1	6.3	—0.2—		3,265	...	...	...	199.2	12	19
Greenland	...	...	...	...	...	...	...	...	...	...	...	...	...	...	...
Grenada	...	...	...	...	...	...	...	...	...	...	...	...	...	...	...
Guadeloupe	1972	23	3.0	41	57.6	1.1	0.3	—	52.8	14.3	85.7	—	9.7	6.1	0.2
Guam	1978	2	5.8	76.3	21.5	1.7	0.5	--	5.7	...	...	...	4.8	...	1.1
Guatemala	1964	414.3	8.4	87.3[26]	10.5[27]	2.2[28]	—	—	2,123	21.5	47.9	30.6	1,451	1,152	200
Guinea	...	...	...	...	...	...	...	...	...	...	...	...	...	...	...
Guinea-Bissau	1961	87	3.0	13.4	83.2	3.4	...	...	...	...	...	...	...	...	...
Guyana	...	...	...	...	...	...	...	...	...	...	...	...	...	...	...
Haiti	1971	617	1.4	58.7	40.5	0.8	—	—	...	...	...	...	...	...	...
Honduras	1974	195	13.5	17.3	61.1	17.6	3.3	0.7	1,596	11.5	79.7	8.8	470	193.1	370.4
Hong Kong	...	...	...	...	...	...	...	...	...	...	...	...	...	...	...
Hungary	1972	803	9.3	90.8	8.8	[29]	[29]	0.3	5,431	8.8	88.9	2.3	1,235	404	406
Iceland	1967	5.1	...	...	...	...	...	...	...	...	...	...	...	...	...
India	1971	70,493	2.3	50.6	45.5	3.8	0.1	—	149,582	0.6	93.2	6.2	3,086	4,603	4,791
Indonesia	1973	14,375	1.1	70.4	29.0	0.6	—	[29]	12,678	21.6	71.1	7.3	88	197	1,205
Iran	...	...	...	...	...	...	...	...	...	...	...	...	...	...	...
Iraq	1971	591	9.7	20.2	50.7	27.5	1.3	0.3	5,000	3.0	62.4	34.6	39	10.8	682
Ireland	1970	279	20.3	2.7	37.8	52.4	7.1	—	648	0.5	99.5	—	4,147	...	855
Israel	1971	40	13.5	19.8	75.7	3.3	0.4	0.8	380	20.8	79.2	—	...	...	160
Italy	1975	2,664	8.4	18.0	67.9	12.3	1.8	—	11,739	26.3	73.7	—	4,747	3,828	2,088
Ivory Coast	1975	550	5	9.5	79.3	11.1	0.1	—	2,753	65.9	34.1	—	...	...	...
Jamaica	1969	193	3.1	58.7	39.2	1.7	0.2	0.2	249	22.2	72.2	5.6	130	81	142
Japan	1970	5,354	1.0	68.0	31.8	0.2	—	—	4,849	9.8	88.0	2.2	524	...	...
Jordan	1975	56	7	...	...	...	...	...	347	8.7	69.0	22.3	1.6	1.1	41
Kampuchea	1962	840	3.6	30.7	65.3	4.0	—	...	...	...	...	...	...	...	...
Kenya	1974	1,487	4.1	31.7	68.0	0.1	0.1	0.1	2,554	31.1	68.9	...	1,793	127	1,659
Kiribati	...	...	...	...	...	...	...	...	...	...	...	...	...	...	...
Korea (North)	...	...	...	...	...	...	...	...	...	...	...	...	...	...	...
Korea (South)	1979	2,162	1.0	68.9	31.1	—	—	—	2,207	...	...	...	...	...	...
Kuwait	1970	0.4	6.1	48.6	35.6	12.7	3.1	—	0.6	7.5	92.5	—	30	...	2
Laos	...	...	...	...	...	...	...	...	...	...	...	...	...	...	...
Lebanon	1970	143	4.3	47.7	44.5	6.5	1.2	0.1	...	...	...	...	...	...	...
Lesotho	1970	187	2.0	29.3	70.7	—	—	—	372	0.1	89.7	10.2	...	...	...
Liberia	1971	122	3.0	53.0	42.9	3.7	0.4	—	366	65.5	34.5	—	...	...	...
Libya	1974	161	13.0	*	...	...	...	...	...	...	...	...	...	...	...
Liechtenstein	1980	494	...	27.5	46.6	24.7	1.2	—	...	...	...	...	...	...	...
Luxembourg	1982	4.6	27.5	13.3	20.5	47.4	18.8	—	57	...	...	...	70	...	...
Macau	...	...	...	...	...	...	...	...	...	...	...	...	...	...	...
Madagascar	...	...	...	...	...	...	...	...	...	...	...	...	...	...	...
Malawi	1969	885	1.5	39.1	60.9	—	—	—	1,361	...	...	...	...	...	...
Malaysia	...	...	...	...	...	...	...	...	...	...	...	...	...	...	...
Maldives	1974	...	...	...	...	...	...	...	3	...	...	...	...	...	...
Mali	1980	481	4.0	19.2	73.3	7.5	—	—	...	...	...	...	...	...	...
Malta	1982	12	1.1	66.7	33.0	0.3	—	—	11.6	...	...	...	...	...	1.6
Martinique	1968	...	...	7.1	33.7	21.7	37.5	—	27	...	...	...	...	...	...
Mauritania	...	...	...	...	...	...	...	...	...	...	...	...	...	...	...
Mauritius	...	...	...	...	...	...	...	...	...	...	...	...	...	...	...
Mayotte	1982	...	...	...	...	...	...	...	8	...	...	...	...	...	...
Mexico	1970	1,020	137.1	33.5	36.1	15.9	8.1	6.4	23,138	6.3	58.1	35.6	74,499	19,858	22,373
Monaco	...	...	...	...	...	...	...	...	...	...	...	...	...	...	...
Mongolia	1980	0.3	...	...	...	...	...	...	...	...	...	...	...	...	...
Montserrat	1972	1.2	1.9	90.7[31]	9.3[32]	—	—	—	0.5	...	...	...	0.9	0.9	0.2
Morocco	1974	...	...	...	...	...	...	...	...	...	...	...	...	...	...
Mozambique	1970	1,652	3.0	...	...	...	...	...	...	...	...	...	...	...	...
Nauru	...	...	...	...	...	...	...	...	...	...	...	...	...	...	...
Nepal	1971	1,722	1.0	77.6	21.7	0.7	—	—	862	...	...	...	1,143	...	...
Netherlands, The	1982	140	14.4	10.9	38.8	47.3	3.0	—	...	...	...	...	...	...	...
Netherlands Antilles	...	...	...	...	...	...	...	...	...	...	...	...	...	...	...
New Caledonia	...	...	...	...	...	...	...	...	...	...	...	...	...	...	...
New Zealand	1982	74	287.6	—20.0—		23.0	33.5	23.5	10,132	...	...	...	4,526	963	5,642
Nicaragua	...	...	...	...	...	...	...	...	...	...	...	...	...	...	...
Niger	...	...	...	...	...	...	...	...	...	...	...	...	...	...	...
Nigeria	...	...	...	...	...	...	...	...	...	...	...	...	...	...	...
Niue	...	...	...	...	...	...	...	...	...	...	...	...	...	...	...
Norfolk Island	...	...	...	...	...	...	...	...	...	...	...	...	...	...	...
Norway	1979	125	61.8	—75.6—		23.8	—0.6—		442	...	...	...	...	6,660	41
Oman	1979	65	1.3	...	...	...	...	...	41	68.6	31.4	—	...	...	...
Pakistan	1972	3,762	5.3	13.8	75.3	10.2	0.7	—	18,455	0.9	91.9	7.2	...	50	1,409
Panama	1971	115	18.2	26.1	41.9	24.5	6.5	1.0	542	20.4	39.4	40.2	1,141	345	70
Papua New Guinea[36]	1980	0.9	445.2	—55.4—				44.6	133	97.3	2.7	—	98	...	165

| all farms | | | | mainly commercial farms[b] | | | | | | | country |
| tenure[c] | | | | number ('000) | mainly crops | | mainly livestock | | mixed (crops and livestock) | | |
owner-operated (percent)	rented (percent)	tribal/communal[f] (percent)	other tenure[g] (percent)		average size (hectares)	number (percent)	average size (hectares)	number (percent)	average size (hectares)	number (percent)	
...	...	...	...	...	...	...	...	...	...	...	Ethiopia
...	...	...	...	...	...	...	...	...	...	...	Faeroe Islands
11.1	...	...	...	...	...	...	...	...	...	...	Falkland Islands
...	...	...	...	...	...	...	...	...	...	...	Fiji
...	...	...	...	...	...	...	...	...	...	...	Finland
41.5[25]	14.6[25]	—	43.9[25]	...	...	...	...	...	...	...	France
...	...	...	...	...	...	...	...	...	...	...	French Guiana
...	...	...	...	...	...	...	...	...	...	...	French Polynesia
...	...	...	...	...	...	...	...	...	...	...	Gabon
...	...	...	...	...	...	...	...	...	...	...	Gambia, The
...	...	...	...	...	...	...	...	...	...	...	Germany, East
39.8	6.7	—	53.5	...	...	...	...	...	...	...	Germany, West
...	...	...	...	...	...	...	...	...	...	...	Ghana
...	...	...	...	...	...	...	...	...	...	...	Gibraltar
...	...	...	...	...	...	...	...	...	...	...	Greece
...	...	...	...	...	...	...	...	...	...	...	Greenland
...	...	...	...	...	...	...	...	...	...	...	Grenada
46.6	19.1	—	34.3	...	...	...	...	...	...	...	Guadeloupe
80.5	5.8	—	13.7	...	...	4	...	4	...	...	Guam
57.9	11.3	4.9	25.9	...	...	...	...	...	...	...	Guatemala
...	...	...	...	...	...	...	...	...	...	...	Guinea
...	...	...	...	...	...	...	...	...	...	...	Guinea-Bissau
...	...	...	...	...	...	...	...	...	...	...	Guyana
...	...	...	...	...	...	...	...	...	...	...	Haiti
66.2	22.6	—	11.2	...	...	...	...	...	...	...	Honduras
...	...	...	...	...	...	...	...	...	...	...	Hong Kong
...	...	...	...	...	...	...	...	...	...	...	Hungary
...	...	...	...	...	...	...	...	...	...	...	Iceland
92.0	4.0	—	4.0	...	...	...	...	...	...	...	India
74.8	3.2	—	22.0	14,374	0.9	86.8	1.3	13.2	—	—	Indonesia
...	...	...	...	...	...	...	...	...	...	...	Iran
...	...	...	...	591	10.8	88.0	1.5	11.2	7.4	0.8	Iraq
...	...	...	...	...	...	...	...	...	...	...	Ireland
...	...	...	...	...	...	...	...	...	...	...	Israel
81.5[3]	6.7[3]	—	11.8[3]	...	...	...	...	...	...	...	Italy
...	...	...	...	...	...	...	...	...	...	...	Ivory Coast
...	...	...	...	...	...	...	...	...	...	...	Jamaica
...	...	...	...	...	...	92.7	...	7.3	...	—	Japan
67.3	14.9	0.1	17.7	28	8.8	60.7	5.8	14.3	16.3	25.0	Jordan
84.0	—	—	16.0	...	...	...	...	...	...	...	Kampuchea
...	...	...	...	...	...	...	...	...	...	...	Kenya
...	...	...	...	...	...	...	...	...	...	...	Kiribati
...	...	...	...	...	...	...	...	...	...	...	Korea (North)
65.9[3]	9.5[3]	—	24.6[3]	2,092	...	98.8	...	1.2	...	—	Korea (South)
73.1	26.7	—	0.2	...	...	...	...	...	...	...	Kuwait
...	...	...	...	...	...	...	...	...	...	...	Laos
...	...	...	...	74	...	77.0	...	8.1	...	14.9	Lebanon
...	...	...	...	7.5	5.0	5.3	2.3	93.3	3.0	1.4	Lesotho
...	...	...	...	39	...	92.3	...	7.7	...	—	Liberia
...	...	...	...	...	...	...	...	...	...	...	Libya
...	...	...	...	...	...	...	...	...	...	...	Liechtenstein
...	...	...	...	...	...	...	...	...	...	...	Luxembourg
...	...	...	...	...	...	...	...	...	...	...	Macau
...	...	...	...	...	...	...	...	...	...	...	Madagascar
...	...	...	...	...	...	...	...	...	...	...	Malawi
...	...	...	...	...	...	...	...	...	...	...	Malaysia
...	...	...	...	...	...	...	...	...	...	...	Maldives
...	...	...	...	...	...	...	...	...	...	...	Mali
15.4	70.7	—	13.9	...	...	...	...	...	...	...	Malta
...	...	...	...	...	...	...	...	...	...	...	Martinique
...	...	...	...	...	...	...	...	...	...	...	Mauritania
...	...	...	...	...	...	...	...	...	...	...	Mauritius
...	...	...	...	...	...	...	...	...	...	...	Mayotte
...	...	...	...	953	99.5	66.4	229.6	25.0	165.3	8.6	Mexico
...	...	...	...	...	...	...	...	...	...	...	Monaco
...	...	...	...	...	...	...	...	...	...	...	Mongolia
...	...	...	...	...	...	...	...	...	...	...	Montserrat
...	...	...	...	...	...	...	...	...	...	...	Morocco
...	...	...	...	...	...	...	...	...	...	...	Mozambique
...	...	...	...	...	...	...	...	...	...	...	Nauru
...	...	...	...	...	...	...	...	...	...	...	Nepal
44.7[33]	15.1[33]	—	40.2[33]	...	...	...	...	...	...	...	Netherlands, The
...	...	...	...	...	...	...	...	...	...	...	Netherlands Antilles
...	...	...	...	...	...	...	...	...	...	...	New Caledonia
...	...	...	...	63.9	405	12.5	280	84.5	183	3.0	New Zealand
...	...	...	...	...	...	...	...	...	...	...	Nicaragua
...	...	...	...	...	...	...	...	...	...	...	Niger
...	...	...	...	...	...	...	...	...	...	...	Nigeria
...	...	...	...	...	...	...	...	...	...	...	Niue
...	...	...	...	...	...	...	...	...	...	...	Norfolk Island
78.8[34]	6.1[34]	—	15.1[34]	...	...	...	...	...	...	...	Norway
...	...	...	...	...	...	...	...	...	...	...	Oman
41.7	34.5	—	23.8	...	...	...	...	...	...	...	Pakistan
12.3	4.4	—	83.3[35]	22.2	...	76.6	...	22.5	...	0.9	Panama
...	...	...	...	...	...	...	...	...	...	...	Papua New Guinea[36]

Agriculture and land use (farms[a]) (continued)

country	year of last agricultural census or survey	all farms number ('000)	average size (hectares)	under 1 hectare (percent)	1 to 9 hectares (percent)	10 to 49 hectares (percent)	50 to 199 hectares (percent)	over 200 hectares (percent)	cropland area ('000 hectares)	permanent[h] (percent)	temporary[i] (percent)	temporarily fallow[i] (percent)	meadows/pastures,[d] area ('000 hectares)	woods/forests, area ('000 hectares)	other land,[e] area ('000 hectares)
Paraguay	...	...	...	...	...	...	...	...	...	...	...	...	...	...	...
Peru	1972	1,391	16.9	34.8	54.2	9.0	1.4	0.6	3,436	8.5	70.3	21.2	15,370	3,084	1,580
Philippines	1971	2,354	3.6	13.6	81.5	4.7	0.2	—	7,176	35.3	54.2	10.5	691	434	193
Pitcairn Island	...	...	...	...	...	...	...	...	...	...	...	...	...	...	...
Poland	1970	3,399	4.9	19.5	68.4	12.0	0.1	—	11,446	1.5	98.5	—	2,874	1,212	886
Portugal	1968	812	6.1	39.0	52.5	7.3	0.8	0.4	3,075	19.4	59.0	21.6	143	1,732	23
Puerto Rico	1978	32	13.8	20.3[1]	54.8[37]	24.9[38]			244	...	...	...	112	59	24
Qatar	1980	0.4	7.5	79.1[39]			20.9[40]		3.2	...	...	...	...	...	...
Réunion	1973	39	2.0	73.9	26.1	—	—	—	46	2.0	95.7	2.3	...	15	16
Romania[41]	1980	5	2,198	...	...	...	...	...	9,600	...	...	...	...	...	...
Rwanda	...	...	...	...	...	...	...	...	...	...	...	...	...	...	...
St. Christopher-Nevis	...	...	...	...	...	...	...	...	...	...	...	...	...	...	...
St. Helena & Ascension	...	...	...	...	...	...	...	...	...	...	...	...	...	...	...
St. Lucia	1974	11	2.6	69.7	27.3	2.4	0.4	0.2	17	68.5	31.5	—	3	7.7	1.6
St. Pierre and Miquelon	...	...	...	...	...	...	...	...	...	...	...	...	...	...	...
St. Vincent	...	...	...	...	...	...	...	...	...	...	...	...	...	...	...
San Marino	1975	0.9	3.5	21.3	77.6		1.1		1,056	...	...	...	1,971	0.2	...
São Tomé and Príncipe	1964	11.1		88.5	10.5	0.4	0.2	0.4	...	...	...	...	...	...	...
Saudi Arabia	1974	181	6.7	38.3	49.2	10.6	1.9	—	1,115	7.2	82.8	10.0	...	...	99
Senegal	1960	295	3.6	21.5	72.4	6.1	...	...	...	...	...	...	...	4.5	7.7
Seychelles	1960	1.1	22.4	...	...	...	...	...	13	92.4	7.6	...	...	...	...
Sierra Leone	1971	286	1.8	37.9	62.1	—	—	—	521	22.6	77.4	...	...	...	...
Singapore	1973	16	0.8	77.4	22.6	—	—	—	...	...	...	...	...	...	...
Solomon Islands	...	...	...	...	...	...	...	...	...	...	...	...	...	...	...
Somalia	...	...	...	...	...	...	...	...	...	...	...	...	...	...	...
South Africa	1976	76	1,134	...	...	...	...	...	10,212	...	...	...	68,303	1,137	6,067
S. W. Africa/Namibia	...	...	...	...	...	...	...	...	...	...	...	...	...	...	...
Spain	1972	2,571	17.8	24.6	53.2	17.6	3.4	1.2	19,507	23.4	48.5	28.1	14,104	10,665	1,426
Sri Lanka	1973	1,647	1.2	71.2	28.2	0.6	—	—	1,797	62.4	37.6	—	8	43	188
Sudan, The	...	...	...	...	...	...	...	...	...	...	...	...	...	...	...
Suriname	1969	16	5.9	21.9	72.3	5.2	0.3	0.3	38	20.6	79.4	—	8.8	...	47
Swaziland	1972	39	19.7	26.2	72.4		1.4		151	2.0	81.1	16.9	464	92	60
Sweden	1982	116	75	38.5		49.7	11.8		2,950	...	...	...	351	4,458	1,019
Switzerland	1980	125	8.7	21.6	36.5	41.0	0.9		287	...	...	...	668	...	131
Syria	1981	485	11.9	...	...	...	...	...	5,759	...	...	33.1	...	...	...
Taiwan	1970	924	1.1	98.7[41]			1.3[42]		761	...	...	...	4.8	174	41.2
Tanzania	1972	2,434	1.3	58.1	38.7	3.2	—	—	3,070	...	...	...	...	...	...
Thailand	1978	4,018	3.7	15.9	38.6[43]	45.5[44]	—	—	14,107	9.5	90.5	...	...	602	245
Togo	1970	233	1.4	54.0	46.0	—	—	—	329	10.3	89.7	...	...	...	...
Tokelau	...	...	...	...	...	...	...	...	...	...	...	...	...	...	...
Tonga	...	...	...	...	...	...	...	...	...	...	...	...	...	...	...
Trinidad and Tobago	1980	1.4	3.2	...	...	...	...	...	...	...	...	...	...	...	...
Trust Terr. of the Pac. Is.	1970	4	10.0	7.4	75.8	13.2	3.6	—	27	54.2	45.8	—	7	...	5.4
Tunisia	...	...	...	...	...	...	...	...	...	...	...	...	...	...	...
Turkey	1980	3,651	6.2	15.8	66.7	16.9	0.6	—	20,594	7.2	65.1	27.7	1,174	242	755
Turks and Caicos Is.	...	...	...	...	...	...	...	...	...	...	...	...	...	...	...
Tuvalu	...	...	...	...	...	...	...	...	...	...	...	...	...	...	...
Uganda	1964	1,171	3.9	20.7	59.8[45]		19.5[46]		2,262	29.8	70.2	—	...	...	...
U.S.S.R.[47]	1982	47.9	...	...	...	...	...	...	203,400	...	...	8.1	322,500	...	...
United Arab Emirates[48]	1980	3	2.2	...	...	...	...	...	6.4	25.6	28.4	46.0	...	0.1	...
United Kingdom	1982	261	71.9	25.9		42.8	25.7	5.6	6,986	0.9	98.3	0.8	11,294	285	217
United States	1978	2,479	168.1	34.2[50]	...	26.6[51]	24.1[52]	15.1[53]	186,705	...	...	7.4	176,744	38,403	14,866
Uruguay	1970	77	214.1	—	29.8	32.8	18.8	18.6	1,852	2.6	81.6	15.8	13,629	614	423
Vanuatu	...	...	...	...	...	...	...	...	...	...	...	...	...	...	...
Venezuela	1971	288	91.9	5.8	54.9	25.6	7.9	5.8	3,506	19.0	66.9	14.1	15,076	6,022	1,866
Vietnam	...	...	...	...	...	...	...	...	...	...	...	...	...	...	...
Virgin Islands (U.S.)	1978	0.4	26.1	24.1	53.2[55]	14.0[56]	8.7[57]		0.7	...	...	...	7.7	1	0.5
Wallis and Futuna	...	...	...	...	...	...	...	...	...	...	...	...	...	...	...
Western Sahara	...	...	...	...	...	...	...	...	...	...	...	...	...	...	...
Western Samoa	...	...	...	...	...	...	...	...	...	...	...	...	...	...	...
Yemen (Aden)	1977	4	1,248	...	...	...	...	...	47.8	...	...	...	...	...	...
Yemen (Şan'ā')	...	...	...	...	...	...	...	...	...	...	...	...	...	...	...
Yugoslavia	1969	2,600	4.8	21.5	72.7	5.8	[29]	[29]	6,582	8.5	84.7	6.8	3,285	2,025	570
Zaire	1970	2,538	2.3	41.5	58.3	0.2	[29]	[29]	4,161	7.7	92.3	...	1,187	119	430
Zambia	1971	768	3.1	50.5	47.6	1.8	[29]	0.1	133	...	...	...	357	...	448
Zimbabwe	...	...	...	...	...	...	...	...	...	...	...	...	...	...	...

tenure[c] owner-operated (percent)	rented (percent)	tribal/communal[f] (percent)	other tenure[g] (percent)	number ('000)	mainly crops average size (hectares)	number (percent)	mainly livestock average size (hectares)	number (percent)	mixed (crops and livestock) average size (hectares)	number (percent)	country
62.2	8.6	4.8	24.4	...	...	...	...	...	...	...	Paraguay
58.0	29.0	—	13.0	...	...	...	...	...	...	...	Peru
...	...	...	...	...	...	...	...	...	...	...	Pitcairn Island
79.1	5.8	—	15.1	...	...	...	...	...	...	...	Poland
64.4	17.0	—	18.6	...	...	...	...	...	...	...	Portugal
81.3	5.0	—	13.7	10.9	23.6	67.9	48.0	31.2	23.7	0.9	Puerto Rico
46.1	22.5	—	31.4	...	...	...	...	...	...	...	Qatar
...	...	...	...	...	...	...	...	...	...	...	Réunion
...	...	...	...	...	...	...	...	...	...	...	Romania[41]
...	...	...	...	...	...	...	...	...	...	...	Rwanda
...	...	...	...	...	...	...	...	...	...	...	St. Christopher-Nevis
...	...	...	...	...	...	...	...	...	...	...	St. Helena & Ascension
69.1	18.3	—	12.6	...	...	...	...	...	...	...	St. Lucia
...	...	...	...	...	...	...	...	...	...	...	St. Pierre and Miquelon
...	...	...	...	...	...	...	...	...	...	...	St. Vincent
...	...	...	...	...	...	...	...	...	...	...	San Marino
...	...	...	...	...	...	...	...	...	...	...	São Tomé and Principe
92.5	4.2	29	3.3	...	...	...	...	...	...	...	Saudi Arabia
48.8	0.5	—	50.7	...	...	...	...	...	...	...	Senegal
...	...	...	...	...	...	...	...	...	...	...	Seychelles
...	...	...	...	...	...	...	...	...	...	...	Sierra Leone
7.4	88.8	—	3.8	16	0.5	12.5	0.5	6.2	0.8	81.3	Singapore
...	...	...	...	...	...	...	...	...	...	...	Solomon Islands
...	...	...	...	...	...	...	...	...	...	...	Somalia
...	...	...	...	...	...	...	...	...	...	...	South Africa
...	...	...	...	...	...	...	...	...	...	...	S. W. Africa/Namibia
...	...	...	...	...	...	...	...	...	...	...	Spain
...	...	...	...	...	...	...	...	...	...	...	Sri Lanka
...	...	...	...	...	...	...	...	...	...	...	Sudan, The
...	...	...	...	10	11.2	50.0	3.5	20.0	6.7	30.0	Suriname
86.1	13.9	—	...	2.3	4.0	87.0	...	...	3.3	13.0	Swaziland
48.4	16.2	—	35.4	...	...	...	...	...	...	...	Sweden
...	...	...	...	...	...	...	...	...	...	...	Switzerland
...	...	...	...	...	...	...	...	...	...	...	Syria
72.9	10.7	—	16.4	...	...	...	...	...	...	...	Taiwan
...	...	...	...	...	...	...	...	...	...	...	Tanzania
...	...	...	...	...	...	...	...	...	...	...	Thailand
...	...	...	...	...	...	...	...	...	...	...	Togo
...	...	...	...	...	...	...	...	...	...	...	Tokelau
...	...	...	...	...	...	...	...	...	...	...	Tonga
...	...	...	...	...	...	...	...	...	...	...	Trinidad and Tobago
...	...	...	...	...	...	...	...	...	...	...	Trust Terr. of the Pac. Is.
90.8	1.4	—	7.8	...	...	...	...	...	...	...	Tunisia
90.6	8.4	—	1.0	...	...	...	...	...	...	...	Turkey
...	...	...	...	...	...	...	...	...	...	...	Turks and Caicos Is.
...	...	...	...	...	...	...	...	...	...	...	Tuvalu
97.4	—	—	2.6	...	...	...	...	...	...	...	Uganda
...	...	...	...	...	...	...	...	...	...	...	U.S.S.R.[47]
...	...	...	...	...	...	...	...	...	...	...	United Arab Emirates[48]
67.7[49]	32.3[49]	—	—	...	...	...	...	...	...	...	United Kingdom
58.5	12.7	—	28.8	1,662	166	45.0	246	55.0	—	—	United States
58.6	22.9	—	18.5	...	...	...	...	...	...	...	Uruguay
...	...	...	...	...	...	...	...	...	...	...	Vanuatu
60.1	5.6	—	34.3[54]	180	20	63.9	438	19.4	152	16.7	Venezuela
...	...	...	...	...	...	...	...	...	...	...	Vietnam
78.0	7.4	—	14.6	...	...	...	...	...	...	...	Virgin Islands (U.S.)
...	...	...	...	...	...	...	...	...	...	...	Wallis and Futuna
...	...	...	...	...	...	...	...	...	...	...	Western Sahara
...	...	...	...	...	...	...	...	...	...	...	Western Samoa
...	...	...	...	...	...	...	...	...	...	...	Yemen (Aden)
...	...	...	...	...	...	...	...	...	...	...	Yemen (San'ā')
...	...	...	...	...	...	...	...	...	...	...	Yugoslavia
4.3	—	95.6	0.1	...	...	...	...	...	...	...	Zaire
...	...	...	...	331	...	36.6	...	22.4	...	41.0	Zambia
...	...	...	...	...	...	...	...	...	...	...	Zimbabwe

[1]Under 1.2 hectares. [2]1.2 hectares and over. [3]1970. [4]Fewer than 100 farms. [5]Up to five hectares. [6]More than five hectares and up to 100 hectares. [7]More than 100 hectares and up to 400 hectares. [8]More than 400 hectares. [9]1.2 hectares to 4.0 hectares. [10]4.0 hectares to 12.2 hectares. [11]More than 12.2 hectares. [12]Up to three hectares. [13]More than three hectares. [14]1982. [15]Under 8.1 hectares. [16]8.1 hectares and over. [17]1.2 hectares to 27.8 hectares. [18]27.8 hectares to 96.6 hectares. [19]96.6 hectares to 307.1 hectares. [20]307.1 hectares and over. [21]State farms and communes only. [22]Up to 2,025 hectares. [23]2,025 hectares to 40,470 hectares. [24]40,470 hectares and over. [25]1971. [26]Under 7.1 hectares. [27]7.1 hectares to 45 hectares. [28]More than 45 hectares. [29]Less than 0.1 percent. [30]Less than 100 hectares. [31]Up to .40 hectare. [32]More than .40 hectare. [33]1979. [34]1969. [35]More than 70 percent of all farms are operated by squatters. [36]All data pertain to large holdings only. [37]1.2 hectares to 7.6 hectares. [38]7.6 hectares and over. [39]Seven hectares and under. [40]More than seven hectares. [41]Less than four hectares. [42]Four hectares and over. [43]One hectare to 3.1 hectares. [44]3.1 hectares and over. [45]One to five hectares. [46]Five hectares and over. [47]State enterprises and producer cooperatives only. [48]Data pertains to the emirate of Abu Dhabi only. [49]Data does not include Northern Ireland; practically all farms there are owner occupied. [50]Less than 28 hectares. [51]28 hectares to 72.5 hectares. [52]More than 72.5 hectares and less than 202 hectares. [53]202 hectares and over. [54]Squatters operate nearly 30 percent of all farms. [55]One to eight hectares. [56]Eight hectares to 40 hectares. [57]40 hectares and over.

Crops and livestock

This table provides comparative data for selected categories of agricultural production for the countries of the world. The data are taken mainly from the United Nations Food and Agricultural Organization's (FAO) annual *Production Yearbook*.

Although the FAO provides standardized guidelines upon which many nations have organized their data collection systems and methods, persistent variations in standards of coverage and reporting periods limit the value of country to country comparisons. The FAO depends largely on questionnaires supplied to each country, but where no official or semiofficial responses are returned the FAO makes estimates, using unofficial or other data. Statistics are based on calendar year periods; that is, data for any particular crop refer to the calendar year in which the harvest (or the bulk of the harvest) occurred. In countries where intensive intercropping and multiple cropping are practiced, the broader parameter of food supply availability (see *Household budgets and consumption* table) may be a better indicator by which to make intercountry comparisons of agricultural production than the more specific components of agriculture presented in this table. In spite of the oftentimes tragic food shortages in several countries in recent years, worldwide agricultural production is probably more

often under-reported than over-reported. Most countries do not report total production; for example, the Soviet bloc, excepting Czechoslovakia, publishes, initially at least, statistics only for collective or cooperative production and excludes the production of privately held plots of land that in some instances represent a significant part of total agricultural production. Some countries report only crops that are sold commercially and ignore crops produced for family or communal subsistence.

Individual categories of crop production also display some peculiarities that may cause statistical discrepancies. The FAO's cereals statistics relate to crops harvested for grain. Some countries, however, report sown or cultivated areas instead, with production statistics calculated from estimates of yield. Millet and sorghum, which in many countries are used as livestock or poultry feed, are excluded by the FAO from the cereals category, while many African nations that use them for grain report them as cereals. Fruit statistics, especially for tropical fruits, are frequently unavailable, and coverage is not uniform, with some countries reporting both commercial fruits and those consumed for subsistence. Figures on wild fruits and berries tend not to be included in national reports at all. Statistical variances also occur among data for individual varieties of fruit. Some

Crops and livestock

country	crops													
	grains				roots and tubers[a]				pulses[b]				fruits[c]		vegetables[d]	
	production ('000 metric tons)		yield (kg/hectare)		production ('000 metric tons)		yield (kg/hectare)		production ('000 metric tons)		yield (kg/hectare)		production ('000 metric tons)		production ('000 metric tons)	
	1970–80 average	1982	1970–80 average	1982	1970–80 average	1982	1970–80 average	1982	1970–80 average	1982	1970–80 average	1982	1970–80 average	1982	1970–80 average	1982
Afghanistan	4,148	4,679	1,228	1,283	248	307	12,807	13,397	56	44	1,618	1,726	666	780	700	1,008
Albania	691	1,012	1,940	2,632	115	120	6,995	7,500	17	20	318	336	129	174	337	367
Algeria	1,817	1,935	614	644	408	610	6,479	7,722	54	56	558	455	1,359	1,142	680	869
American Samoa	...	...	...	...	10	18	18,571	22,622	...	...	...	...	3	2	...	...
Andorra	...	...	...	...	...	...	...	...	...	...	...	...	...	...	...	...
Angola	503	330	722	461	1,897	2,170	12,977	14,045	65	40	547	364	433	425	213	227
Anguilla	...	...	...	...	...	...	...	...	...	...	...	...	...	...	...	...
Antigua and Barbuda	...	...	2,170	2,000	...	...	3,872	2,857	...	...	...	...	8	8	1	1
Argentina	22,626	33,609	1,983	2,407	2,312	2,329	13,046	14,927	187	230	973	1,019	6,094	6,351	2,279	2,319
Australia	17,099	13,577	1,291	835	738	923	20,305	26,876	92	213	736	796	2,014	2,140	975	1,014
Austria	3,943	4,923	3,893	4,678	1,748	24,547	24,276	1,121	4	2	2,185	2,247	1,003	1,501	588	657
Bahamas, The	...	1	1,063	1,165	...	...	3,635	4,000	1	1	1,386	1,415	7	12	7	17
Bahrain	...	...	...	...	...	...	23,655	21,429	...	...	...	1,000	35	43	20	27
Bangladesh	18,139	22,019	1,772	1,990	1,603	1,775	10,190	10,312	241	214	720	676	1,320	1,331	1,082	1,113
Barbados	1.7	2	2,692	2,500	16	10	10,337	13,467	1	1	1,216	1,231	3	3	6	9
Belgium[2]	1,962	2,175	4,357	5,545	1,510	1,500	35,955	40,872	10	6	2,897	3,128	396	414	1,048	909
Belize	21	29	1,517	2,015	16	18	17,991	18,617	1	2	615	577	56	91	4	3
Benin	314	328	665	737	1,246	1,377	7,441	6,531	33	54	394	491	54	61	98	139
Bermuda	...	...	...	...	1	1	14,389	9,571	...	...	...	...	1	1	1.5	2
Bhutan	254	110	1,178	1,094	27	20	6,695	6,776	2	3	408	443	13	19	41	46
Bolivia	541	605	1,096	1,159	1,066	1,018	6,488	6,276	16	20	869	1,031	591	618	310	302
Botswana	61	22	335	139	6	7	4,888	5,385	16	18	566	600	8	11	15	16
Brazil	26,317	34,041	1,382	1,547	29,362	27,571	12,015	11,487	2,265	3,011	518	489	15,393	20,649	3,785	4,668
British Virgin Islands	...	...	...	...	...	...	...	...	...	...	...	...	...	...	...	...
Brunei	6	10	2,002	3,333	4	4	9,071	9,066	...	...	...	...	7	9	4	4
Bulgaria	7,534	9,748	3,447	4,562	358	466	11,096	11,552	81	86	796	1,147	2,084	2,118	1,985	2,081
Burkina Faso	1,070	1,282	535	588	115	124	4,418	4,644	169	178	345	375	43	61	61	77
Burma	9,689	14,433	1,831	2,697	90	186	5,469	7,739	286	438	581	679	1,034	1,044	1,761	1,920
Burundi	396	279	1,096	973	3,298	2,312	10,912	11,328	222	220	606	720	986	1,030	135	157
Cameroon	754	966	8,846	947	2,102	2,519	3,549	3,748	83	123	563	633	1,216	1,233	314	405
Canada	37,994	54,253	2,076	2,516	2,421	2,750	21,980	24,279	135	284	1,540	1,621	682	722	1,518	1,870
Cape Verde	8	5	510	240	25	19	6,904	6,446	1	4	923	1,100	14	16	5	6
Cayman Islands	...	...	...	...	...	...	...	4,600	...	...	...	...	1	1	...	...
Central African Republic	102	106	622	571	1,097	1,255	3,820	3,283	5	6	503	500	153	171	41	46
Chad	596	683	563	537	268	417	3,818	4,590	62	64	403	469	91	98	52	59
Chile	1,682	1,507	1,857	2,322	820	849	9,935	10,822	123	200	865	1,071	1,315	1,734	1,145	1,258
China	244,196	306,229	2,167	3,303	130,984	140,624	10,185	13,831	13,839	6,858	1,044	1,244	6,648	9,687	70,441	83,116
Christmas Island	...	...	...	...	...	...	...	...	...	...	...	...	...	...	...	...
Cocos (Keeling) Islands	...	...	...	...	...	...	...	...	...	...	...	...	...	...	...	...
Colombia	2,725	3,611	2,049	2,587	3,523	4,344	10,182	11,330	123	124	606	596	3,537	4,313	1,146	1,458
Comoros	17	20	1,219	1,095	97	104	3,416	3,395	2	2	553	564	55	37	2	3
Congo	14	19	675	612	599	595	5,696	6,727	7	7	607	625	181	201	25	28
Cook Islands	...	...	...	...	12	12	31,072	31,481	...	...	...	...	14	16	2	2
Costa Rica	232	315	1,915	2,250	38	47	8,275	8,087	13	13	479	549	1,327	1,359	52	63
Cuba	516	577	1,949	2,531	740	1,170	5,652	6,965	25	27	702	757	612	1,021	382	465
Cyprus	125	101	1,184	1,811	204	226	21,140	25,730	9	8	768	1,054	436	530	122	122
Czechoslovakia	9,466	10,278	3,550	4,032	4,010	3,608	16,048	18,183	117	149	1,542	1,770	650	1,087	1,061	1,186
Denmark	7,011	8,041	3,910	4,533	855	1,236	24,988	35,314	26	15	3,233	3,356	155	148	227	202
Djibouti	...	...	...	...	...	...	...	...	...	...	...	...	...	...	...	...
Dominica	...	...	1,349	1,482	9	10	9,342	9,305	1	1	571	607	54	62	5	5
Dominican Republic	340	484	2,798	3,559	349	270	10,521	9,044	63	85	1,103	1,082	1,287	1,419	185	246
Ecuador	631	740	1,331	1,655	790	603	1,004	9,771	50	47	527	575	3,901	3,975	316	327
Egypt	7,832	7,768	3,934	3,841	1,009	1,277	17,560	16,727	345	267	2,044	1,918	2,066	2,276	6,510	7,507
El Salvador	599	651	1,461	1,713	26	32	12,915	12,702	38	37	762	755	262	266	100	101
Equatorial Guinea	...	...	...	...	79	87	2,746	2,520	...	...	...	...	15	16	...	...
Ethiopia	4,685	5,712	852	1,166	987	1,520	3,192	3,352	635	1,002	734	1,100	185	206	420	499
Faeroe Islands	...	...	...	...	1	1	14,202	13,684	...	...	...	...	...	...	...	...
Falkland Islands	...	...	...	...	...	...	...	...	...	...	...	...	...	...	...	...
Fiji	25	23	2,099	1,983	152	149	10,146	9,522	2	2	860	868	12	13	13	15
Finland	3,129	3,418	2,253	2,922	736	601	15,592	15,373	11	18	2,055	2,333	90	100	110	138

banana and plantain growers, for example, report production in terms of bunches, including the weight of the stalk; others do not. Vegetable statistics include vegetables and melons grown for human consumption only. Some countries do not make this distinction in their reports, and some exclude the production of kitchen gardens and small family plots. In Austria, France, West Germany, and Italy, such small-scale production accounts for 20 to 40 percent of total ouput.

Livestock statistics may be distorted by the timing of country reports. Ireland, for example, takes a livestock enumeration in December that is reported the following year and that appears low against data for otherwise comparable countries because of the slaughter and export of animals at the close of the grazing season. It balances this, however, with a June enumeration, when numbers tend to be high. Milk production as defined by the FAO includes whole fresh milk, excluding milk sucked by young animals but including amounts fed by farmers or ranchers to livestock. Some countries—notably Czechoslovakia, France, Hungary, Italy, and West Germany—include milk sucked by young animals in their reports. Certain countries do not distinguish between milk cows and other cattle, so that yield per cow must be estimated. Some countries do not supply egg statistics, and estimates must be generated based on the numbers of chickens and reported or assumed egg-laying rates. Some other countries report egg production by number, and this must be converted to weight, using official conversion factors; but, as eggs vary in size and weight, discrepancies may be introduced.

Metric system units used in the table may be converted to English system units as follows:

metric tons $\times$ 1.1023 = short tons
kilograms $\times$ 2.2046 = pounds
kilograms per hectare $\times$ 0.8922 = pounds per acre.

The notes that follow, keyed by references in the table headings, provide further definitional information.

a. Includes such crops as potatoes and cassava.
b. Includes beans and peas harvested for dry grain only. Does not include green beans and green peas.
c. Excludes melons.
d. Includes melons, green beans, and green peas.
e. From milk cows only.
f. From chickens only.

livestock												country
cattle		sheep		hogs		chickens		milk[e]				eggs[f]		
stock ('000 head)		stock ('000 head)		stock ('000 head)		stock ('000 head)		production ('000 metric tons)		yield (kg/animal)		production (metric tons)		
1970–80 average	1982	1970–80 average	1982	1970–80 average	1982	1970–80 average	1982	1970–80 average	1982	1970–80 average	1982	1970–80 average	1982	
3,690	3,800	20,251	20,000	...	...	15,993	20,612	439	557	474	505	14,685	18,036	Afghanistan
442	580	1,283	1,170	129	125	2,172	4,400	190	330	1,321	1,737	3,988	7,670	Albania
1,083	1,390	9,654	13,700	4	5	15,962	19,000	369	530	909	964	17,147	20,300	Algeria
...	...	...	...	8	8	36	48	...	...	...	...	32	36	American Samoa
...	1¹	...	9¹	...	...	...	...	...	...	...	...	...	...	Andorra
2,910	3,250	197	235	356	440	4,891	5,600	138	148	500	500	3,673	3,750	Angola
														Anguilla
8	6	10	9	5	7	62	70	7	6	1,165	1,000	127	145	Antigua and Barbuda
55,876	57,882	38,156	30,000	4,304	3,900	33,000	40,000	5,238	5,200	1,822	1,898	199,217	300,000	Argentina
28,576	24,554	153,046	137,982	2,507	2,373	37,835	44,761	6,541	5,199	2,694	2,888	195,911	197,000	Australia
2,527	2,530	151	194	3,551	4,010	12,950	15,656	3,240	3,600	3,149	3,700	90,252	97,500	Austria
4	4	30	37	16	18	736	810	3	3	1,000	1,000	323	360	Bahamas, The
5	6	4	7	...	...	425	830	6	6	2,804	2,850	2,018	4,300	Bahrain
27,673	35,070	941	1,150	...	...	45,425	73,000	784	1,021	250	250	29,914	49,040	Bangladesh
19	20	48	53	37	64	472	850	8	7	1,176	1,286	1,335	1,400	Barbados
3,040	3,148	102	115	4,598	5,428	34,899	28,348	3,831	4,054	3,695	3,909	231,138	184,000	Belgium²
44	51	3	3	18	17	302	350	4	4	1,014	1,035	569	670	Belize
701	785	785	970	388	475	3,300	4,450	10	13	120	120	2,323	3,204	Benin
1	1	...	...	1.4	2	75	47	1.4	2	1,664	3,043	630	470	Bermuda
241	312	39	44	54	56	129	187	13	17	361	257	125	177	Bhutan
3,081	4,100	7,756	9,200	1,180	1,550	5,992	9,200	45	73	1,286	1,404	14,944	25,000	Bolivia
2,415	3,000	336	200	14	7	552	900	86	95	350	350	493	684	Botswana
92,129	93,000	20,772	17,500	45,709	33,500	319,908	448,000	9,367	10,700	787	738	548,636	830,000	Brazil
4	3	6	8	4	3	...	...	...	...	...	...	...	...	British Virgin Islands
3	4	...	...	13	15	842	1,221	...	...	...	...	1,410	1,855	Brunei
1,577	1,807	9,964	10,726	3,176	3,844	35,056	38,765	1,515	1,991	2,310	2,834	107,310	138,163	Bulgaria
2,379	2,880	1,522	1,970	156	187	9,941	11,600	54	46	143	80	4,724	8,350	Burkina Faso
7,758	8,698	204	235	1,853	2,225	17,921	24,372	265	236	457	246	38,487	27,605	Burma
771	890	283	349	33	35	2,642	3,300	49	59	310	350	2,039	2,510	Burundi
2,662	3,338	2,020	2,180	653	1,331	9,122	10,764	50	46	276	500	6,976	8,771	Cameroon
12,955	12,520	525	505	6,954	9,261	83,931	82,811	7,843	8,100	3,664	3,582	315,364	326,000	Canada
14	13	2	2	19	24	58	65	2	2	457	600	97	130	Cape Verde
5	5	...	...	1	1	18	20	...	...	...	...	81	85	Cayman Islands
687	1,313	75	87	78	140	1,273	1,637	31	40	1,098	1,100	886	1,028	Central African Republic
3,734	3,800	2,196	2,358	6	7	2,906	3,300	161	232	239	291	2,616	3,044	Chad
3,391	3,800	5,859	6,308	980	1,190	19,583	26,000	1,003	1,140	1,300	1,500	63,114	91,800	Chile
61,169	55,058	83,115	109,470	261,676	298,526	1,127,207	873,899	4,143	5,951	591	699	3,795,814	5,005,000	China
...	...	...	...	...	...	...	...	...	...	...	...	...	...	Christmas Island
...	...	...	...	...	...	...	...	...	...	...	...	...	...	Cocos (Keeling) Islands
23,061	24,499	2,083	2,749	1,772	2,179	36,640	33,000	2,376	2,957	865	1,320	130,418	187,000	Colombia
72	81	7	8	...	...	253	300	3	3	500	500	524	572	Comoros
52	78	49	72	33	56	778	1,183	2.5	3	633	1,501	600	910	Congo
...	...	...	...	15	17	62	72	...	...	...	...	82	103	Cook Islands
1,816	2,416	2	3	206	243	4,795	5,496	274	320	1,087	1,067	15,787	17,000	Costa Rica
6,160	6,200	323	375	1,607	2,000	18,214	26,173	827	1,200	1,145	1,412	79,974	106,300	Cuba
36	43	473	530	145	194	3,517	3,600	26	50	3,251	3,133	6,083	6,741	Cyprus
4,567	5,103	886	959	6,520	7,302	40,150	45,295	5,373	5,931	2,876	3,199	219,728	251,485	Czechoslovakia
2,939	2,933	57	56	8,583	9,856	15,658	15,016	4,905	5,216	4,451	5,164	74,018	79,900	Denmark
23	43	170	380	...	...	...	...	...	...	...	...	...	...	Djibouti
4	4	3	4	8	8	92	115	1	1	1,010	1,000	235	271	Dominica
1,814	2,157	54	55	743	100	7,480	8,400	347	450	1,301	1,822	21,626	32,364	Dominican Republic
2,735	3,000	2,180	3,034	2,565	4,181	14,353	24,927	750	783	1,303	1,223	29,693	70,560	Ecuador
2,081	2,321	1,883	1,700	15	15	26,191	28,208	629	650	677	669	70,255	86,259	Egypt
1,206	1,055	4	4	438	450	5,954	5,500	247	303	939	976	29,033	32,400	El Salvador
4	4	32	34	6	5	92	160	...	...	...	...	545	136	Equatorial Guinea
25,934	26,200	21,987	23,350	18	19	51,703	54,000	543	610	190	221	70,216	74,520	Ethiopia
3	2	71	72	...	...	...	...	...	...	...	...	...	...	Faeroe Islands
9	8	635	651	...	...	5	3	1	1	1,000	1,000	...	...	Falkland Islands
156	156	129	104	24	28	671	920	46	53	1,641	1,601	1,670	2,450	Fiji
1,822	1,705	129	104	1,160	1,509	9,063	7,763	3,244	3,170	4,170	4,641	77,028	77,000	Finland

Crops and livestock (continued)

country	crops														
	grains				roots and tubers[a]				pulses[b]				fruits[c]		vegetables[d]	
	production ('000 metric tons)		yield (kg/hectare)		production ('000 metric tons)		yield (kg/hectare)		production ('000 metric tons)		yield (kg/hectare)		production ('000 metric tons)		production ('000 metric tons)	
	1970–80 average	1982	1970–80 average	1982	1970–80 average	1982	1970–80 average	1982	1970–80 average	1982	1970–80 average	1982	1970–80 average	1982	1970–80 average	1982
France	40,452	48,074	4,158	4,959	7,108	6,750	24,103	31,395	224	587	2,146	3,026	14,323	15,620	5,715	7,149
French Guiana	1	2	3,417	2,776	8	10	8,473	8,960	...	...	...	...	6	5	1	1
French Polynesia					18	17	12,837	11,370	...	...	...	...	4	4	4	7
Gabon	6	11	1,396	1,686	221	239	3,680	3,886	...	...	490	555	82	79	21	20
Gambia, The	70	86	898	1,024	7	6	3,704	3,000	3	4	216	267	4	4	7	7
Germany, East	8,542	9,967	3,517	4,081	10,429	9,800	17,862	19,419	79	81	1,502	1,626	666	858	1,172	1,264
Germany, West	21,354	24,625	4,056	4,858	11,605	7,821	28,307	29,544	59	46	2,936	3,579	4,072	6,535	1,930	2,136
Ghana	708	750	833	806	3,558	3,440	6,563	6,528	13	12	131	92	1,168	1,061	420	580
Gibraltar																
Greece	3,789	5,329	2,422	3,383	891	892	15,021	17,995	115	84	1,157	1,308	3,122	3,572	3,308	3,766
Greenland	...	...														
Grenada	...	...	831	957	4	4	5,650	5,309	1	1	1,042	1,990	27	30	3	2
Guadeloupe	...	...	1,690	1,200	38	22	9,702	8,816	...	...	393	507	143	136	20	21
Guam	...	0	1,463	1,500	1	2	14,930	13,504	...	...	...	...	2	2	1	1
Guatemala	912	1,397	1,179	1,395	50	59	3,469	3,371	83	99	643	835	769	911	237	260
Guinea	651	547	723	863	577	803	7,755	7,387	28	32	536	593	446	548	244	385
Guinea-Bissau	63	53	671	624	52	40	4,218	6,154	2	2	552	567	40	40	21	20
Guyana	238	304	2,066	3,249	25	16	6,724	6,667	1	1	639	567	42	37	8	9
Haiti	493	415	999	902	410	702	4,769	3,762	86	87	756	475	824	1,039	248	294
Honduras	394	466	1,054	1,107	33	18	4,624	3,733	43	42	535	560	1,516	1,644	74	91
Hong Kong	6	0	2,037	2,000	1		15,570	24,000	...	...	...	...	3	4	191	196
Hungary	11,948	14,245	3,867	4,820	1,588	1,504	13,421	17,015	127	127	1,073	1,598	2,316	2,569	2,054	1,749
Iceland	...	...			9	10	11,916	10,526	...	...	...	...			1	1
India	96,302	134,145	1,213	1,304	14,696	16,967	12,114	13,737	11,040	11,107	481	468	16,602	18,906	36,867	42,115
Indonesia	26,574	37,906	2,380	3,233	15,961	15,375	8,336	9,290	297	313	501	499	3,103	3,930	2,350	2,055
Iran	7,427	9,189	1,047	1,177	598	768	8,833	8,519	198	218	1,031	1,032	2,324	2,618	3,346	3,815
Iraq	2,110	1,797	995	863	56	110	12,014	15,714	43	43	811	805	1,009	1,323	1,979	2,302
Ireland	1,539	1,861	4,070	4,832	1,227	1,050	26,687	29,284	10	11	4,118	4,200	21	22	353	378
Israel	256	138	1,911	1,372	183	227	31,818	40,353	9	11	1,199	1,069	1,882	2,126	708	906
Italy	16,518	18,243	3,177	3,564	3,090	2,700	16,490	18,083	396	309	1,241	1,329	19,592	19,194	12,609	13,276
Ivory Coast	685	888	834	726	2,848	3,309	4,374	3,803	7	8	624	667	1,272	1,371	267	311
Jamaica	9	8	1,319	1,633	204	227	10,542	11,501	8	9	756	799	327	273	79	86
Japan	16,152	14,011	5,480	5,308	5,652	5,693	21,877	23,655	174	157	1,405	1,624	6,373	6,159	14,989	15,334
Jordan	119	47	530	306	9	10	11,389	16,667	13	13	487	783	60	114	330	485
Kampuchea	1,944	1,610	1,272	947	89	172	7,915	5,772	18	14	607	583	168	135	401	330
Kenya	2,484	3,050	1,404	1,697	1,235	1,341	7,652	8,055	272	250	462	446	490	621	384	440
Kiribati	...	...			10	13	8,555	8,896	...	...	...	...	4	5	4	4
Korea, North	6,974	8,765	2,810	3,925	1,605	1,900	10,495	11,875	246	260	662	788	676	939	1,970	2,390
Korea, South	8,437	8,274	4,220	5,218	2,054	1,385	16,317	17,082	47	64	807	1,032	747	1,206	6,043	9,850
Kuwait			2,122	3,235			15,343	15,000					1	1	25	33
Laos	907	1,217	1,286	1,556	64	142	8,100	11,360	14	20	1,535	2,000	80	106	161	197
Lebanon	62	31	1,144	1,254	102	127	12,178	14,828	15	10	876	958	664	747	283	402
Lesotho	205	124	864	676	5	6	14,082	15,000	12	15	586	682	11	15	13	25
Liberia	215	268	1,185	1,276	309	368	4,002	3,984	3	3	498	500	112	126	61	67
Libya	230	235	486	400	68	113	7,194	7,570	7	10	987	1,113	151	177	462	593
Liechtenstein	...	...	...	...					...	...	...	...	...	...	...	...
Luxembourg[2]	...	...	...	...	10	11	18,336	18,851	...	...	...	...	...	...	...	...
Macau					1	2	10,179	10,000	...	...	...	...	4	4	2	2
Madagascar	2,088	2,128	1,736	1,601	1,999	2,605	5,772	5,840	64	61	845	845	785	754	286	320
Malawi	1,273	1,602	1,061	1,257	195	211	4,601	4,276	124	211	629	692	205	227	184	208
Malaysia	1,916	2,071	2,660	2,837	494	553	9,426	9,551	...	...	...	...	858	873	444	506
Maldives	...	...	2,003	844	6	8	5,093	5,205	...	...	601	623	7	7	14	15
Mali	1,056	1,227	692	695	107	128	9,366	9,476	32	37	1,140	1,117	9	10	115	141
Malta	5	5	2,206	2,661	20	22	8,445	9,230	2	1	2,349	2,535	8	8	44	44
Martinique	...	...	...	...	28	25	9,134	10,739					232	148	30	32
Mauritania	52	56	330	361	7	6	1,359	1,023	20	26	361	405	15	13	5	7
Mauritius	2	2	2,904	2,807	11	14	15,945	21,808	1	1	508	650	9	8	26	27
Mayotte																
Mexico	15,961	22,826	1,708	2,489	887	1,026	12,566	13,286	1,096	1,430	604	711	6,398	7,284	3,092	3,896
Monaco	...	...			...	...										
Mongolia	375	341	806	629	44	45	8,232	7,500	1	1	369	500	3	4	22	32
Montserrat	...	...	1,000	1,000			2,491	2,567					2	2		
Morocco	4,330	4,154	946	969	289	539	11,486	14,184	376	231	734	472	1,381	1,530	1,199	1,389
Mozambique	670	495	729	531	2,595	2,962	5,244	4,812	65	50	539	400	309	308	184	185
Nauru																
Nepal	3,569	3,507	1,664	1,589	359	393	5,531	6,095	47	50	427	440	127	135	181	177
Netherlands, The	1,277	1,380	4,861	6,749	5,672	6,219	35,189	37,472	30	42	2,971	4,144	580	573	2,429	2,890
Netherlands Antilles	3	1	999	737	...	...										
New Caledonia	1	4	2,207	1,985	20	24	6,063	7,493	...	...	688	1,033	9	12	3	4
New Zealand	840	999	3,930	4,776	264	261	28,342	30,257	64	60	2,750	3,000	288	398	357	433
Nicaragua	345	499	1,153	1,414	21	29	4,131	4,090	51	60	798	750	316	345	43	47
Niger	1,296	1,719	418	405	233	195	7,680	6,338	197	305	212	209	34	38	107	145
Nigeria	8,446	10,238	671	747	27,331	29,788	9,777	9,451	865	940	204	218	2,864	3,400	2,745	3,480
Niue	...	...			1	2	3,691	2,162	...	...	...	...	1	2		
Norfolk Island																
Norway	965	1,186	3,263	3,743	595	443	22,887	21,172	...	...	2,500	...	113	125	179	208
Oman	5	3	1,260	2,895	...	...	461	...	...	...	1,463	...	79	121	8	155
Pakistan	13,903	18,150	1,399	1,670	460	565	9,931	9,642	752	480	492	372	2,106	2,259	1,907	2,012
Panama	229	213	1,311	1,291	74	77	8,002	7,817	6	7	337	504	1,169	1,302	35	41
Papua New Guinea	4	3	1,883	1,415	1,078	1,133	7,107	6,817	20	20	499	500	992	1,092	233	257
Paraguay	464	770	1,289	1,516	1,645	2,238	13,761	14,194	59	89	782	842	646	786	206	219
Peru	1,170	1,563	1,636	1,999	2,514	2,585	7,209	9,450	99	100	810	859	1,572	1,654	739	746
Philippines	9,039	11,821	1,374	1,738	2,206	3,576	5,655	7,404	41	57	615	792	4,412	6,417	1,481	2,158
Pitcairn Island																
Poland	20,099	21,166	2,162	2,594	45,069	31,951	17,917	14,671	220	222	1,170	1,337	1,620	2,641	3,947	4,354

livestock														country
cattle		sheep		hogs		chickens		milk[e]				eggs[f]		
stock ('000 head)		stock ('000 head)		stock ('000 head)		stock ('000 head)		production ('000 metric tons)		yield (kg/animal)		production (metric tons)		
1970–80 average	1982	1970–80 average	1982	1970–80 average	1982	1970–80 average	1982	1970–80 average	1982	1970–80 average	1982	1970–80 average	1982	
23,359	23,605	10,864	13,121	11,433	11,859	175,299	186,656	29,620	34,500	3,000	3,441	743,143	920,000	France
3	8	...	...	6	9	88	110	...	...	...	...	...	...	French Guiana
9	10	3	2	17	34	321	600	1.5	2	2,027	1,600	610	1,000	French Polynesia
4	6	72	77	33	140	901	1,500	...	...	255	250	494	490	Gabon
283	350	106	175	8	11	258	300	5	6	175	175	301	525	Gambia, The
5,426	5,749	1,791	2,169	10,831	12,869	46,418	54,392	7,769	8,230	3,637	3,885	278,776	343,000	Germany, East
14,399	14,992	1,000	1,108	20,829	22,310	92,966	77,743	22,429	25,550	4,084	4,692	882,440	800,000	Germany, West
935	970	1,530	1,750	356	435	11,211	12,500	8	8	55	55	10,192	15,000	Ghana
														Gibraltar
1,032	836	7,944	8,316	688	1,378	28,336	36,296	643	684	1,421	2,012	109,233	125,000	Greece
...	---	...	22				—							Greenland
6	9	10	16	13	10	247	260	1	2	800	800	814	995	Grenada
82	93	4	3	32	51	482	1,000	12	13	548	500	466	700	Guadeloupe
3	2	...	...	10	14	154	191	...	...	...	...	1,420	1,250	Guam
1,895	1,880	594	500	785	835	11,426	14,500	302	328	891	911	33,994	40,500	Guatemala
1,568	1,850	412	445	33	42	5,038	8,500	36	43	185	185	5,334	8,925	Guinea
235	220	61	60	148	125	349	420	7	7	170	170	210	324	Guinea-Bissau
271	305	106	116	115	140	9,861	13,500	14	15	762	751	3,390	4,000	Guyana
849	1,200	80	91	1,650	600	3,816	5,000	34	20	303	230	6,648	3,100	Haiti
1,794	2,358	7	5	577	590	6,636	5,061	187	214	557	623	16,130	12,026	Honduras
10	4	...	...	407	520	5,306	6,600	5	5	2,299	3,750	6,273	9,000	Hong Kong
1,932	1,945	2,382	3,137	7,581	8,296	57,344	63,629	2,115	2,740	2,849	3,610	221,908	260,000	Hungary
62	60	840	795	7	12	253	271	114	131	3,512	3,669	2,645	3,600	Iceland
180,121	182,000	40,694	41,700	7,763	10,500	131,927	150,000	9,334	13,800	487	531	748,267	835,000	India
6,398	6,435	3,513	4,196	3,506	3,296	97,404	114,000	53	82	857	1,745	67,822	116,000	Indonesia
6,639	8,567	34,415	34,832	52	58	51,967	73,592	1,233	1,705	762	784	107,074	189,240	Iran
2,329	3,100	12,985	11,900	...	...	11,983	20,000	356	1,125	633	750	15,339	22,000	Iraq
6,786	6,688	3,787	3,476	1,096	1,090	9,580	8,100	4,427	5,200	2,987	3,567	38,177	37,800	Ireland
284	273	210	270	77	103	18,093	26,218	600	729	6,033	6,958	87,225	88,224	Israel
8,729	8,904	8,325	9,632	8,808	9,132	112,110	110,192	9,771	10,600	2,724	2,910	612,896	660,000	Italy
551	750	999	1,320	233	385	7,957	15,000	5	11	59	88	4,097	9,000	Ivory Coast
280	310	6	6	223	265	3,714	4,400	50	51	1,041	1,000	13,426	16,500	Jamaica
3,823	4,485	17	19	8,075	10,040	253,599	289,925	5,473	6,750	4,646	4,633	1,875,148	2,112,000	Japan
37	39	798	1,000	...	...	10,466	26,000	9	9	940	1,000	7,706	10,500	Jordan
1,526	1,000	2	1	778	...	4,039	6,800	17	16	165	170	3,092	3,500	Kampuchea
9,244	12,000	3,783	5,500	69	90	15,085	18,000	851	900	498	450	17,460	24,000	Kenya
...	...	...	...	10	15	153	177	...	...	...	...	100	107	Kiribati
829	970	239	310	1,669	2,300	18,313	18,100	29	62	2,037	2,214	76,291	110,000	Korea, North
1,485	1,506	5	4	1,666	1,832	27,227	42,999	2,038	576	3,968	5,115	181,943	272,030	Korea, South
8	17	120	500	...	...	5,394	7,200	12	30	2,272	2,500	2,253	10,000	Kuwait
465	473	...	...	1,285	1,223	12,334	5,863	6	7	200	200	19,069	25,000	Laos
81	54	212	145	20	19	6,899	7,500	70	88	2,456	5,000	26,382	30,000	Lebanon
559	562	1,533	1,337	77	62	987	815	17	21	290	290	1,002	812	Lesotho
34	41	175	220	92	112	2,008	2,800	1	1	100	100	1,954	2,688	Liberia
153	194	3,928	5,600	...	...	3,226	7,000	24	63	775	2,032	5,423	18,750	Libya
8	9	1	2	8	8	44	45	15	18	3,197	3,310	249	250	Liechtenstein
...	...	...	...	...	...	...	...	...	...	...	...	...	...	Luxembourg[2]
...	...	...	...	...	5	347	395	...	...	...	...	480	537	Macau
9,348	10,150	620	633	618	721	13,163	15,081	31	36	700	700	10,146	11,998	Madagascar
665	880	107	78	193	186	7,768	8,448	33	37	389	460	9,769	11,045	Malawi
443	555	51	66	1,347	1,785	45,360	53,620	20	23	649	678	103,248	129,624	Malaysia
														Maldives
4,673	5,134	5,483	6,350	31	45	11,288	12,500	87	107	186	203	7,041	9,524	Mali
12	15	7	5	23	5	968	1,114	27	38	4,449	4,584	6,059	7,378	Malta
50	57	36	54	34	40	941	1,830	8	5	665	738	983	1,600	Martinique
1,735	1,200	4,213	4,900	...	...	2,807	3,200	76	86	328	350	2,283	2,890	Mauritania
52	57	3	4	5	9	891	1,700	24	25	2,462	2,500	2,198	3,200	Mauritius
														Mayotte
28,176	36,200	6,822	7,990	11,847	13,117	147,620	164,000	4,835	6,930	886	770	449,292	640,000	Mexico
														Monaco
2,286	2,376	13,702	14,714	18	35	170	200	151	170	299	304	581	1,270	Mongolia
8	9	3	3	3	3	29	32	2	2	750	750	45	48	Montserrat
3,482	2,900	15,236	14,900	11	11	20,961	24,000	529	810	571	579	58,168	78,000	Morocco
1,440	1,430	124	110	147	130	14,693	18,000	58	66	170	170	8,183	10,500	Mozambique
...	...	...	...	2	2	4	4	...	...	...	...	8	9	Nauru
6,609	6,950	2,293	2,370	323	360	20,233	22,500	207	217	501	499	13,147	15,355	Nepal
47,076	5,241	751	776	7,699	10,254	63,870	87,073	10,131	12,750	4,643	5,286	341,389	630,000	Netherlands, The
8	9	10	8	6	8	84	132	4	5	1,280	1,250	495	540	Netherlands Antilles
119	110	5	2	26	19	181	220	5	3	915	600	408	1,064	New Caledonia
9,114	8,300	59,553	74,300	532	425	5,997	6,690	6,287	6,646	2,994	3,195	56,107	50,700	New Zealand
2,568	2,186	2	3	639	520	3,807	4,964	264	124	663	687	21,879	30,000	Nicaragua
2,808	3,350	2,478	2,900	27	32	7,304	11,000	79	97	176	371	5,004	7,310	Niger
11,409	12,600	8,660	12,400	931	1,220	92,280	140,000	303	371	265	290	126,089	228,000	Nigeria
1	1	...	...	1	1	16	18	...	...	804	727	34	32	Niue
2														Norfolk Island
949	1,009	1,759	2,227	701	686	4,803	3,600	1,837	1,967	4,677	5,116	39,513	45,387	Norway
108	150	84	138	...	...	624	598	27	27	700	700	485	700	Oman
14,890	15,131	19,627	30,887	92	...	34,145	76,207	1,815	2,200	660	889	48,866	120,000	Pakistan
1,358	1,683	...	2	165	200	4,142	5,300	77	98	950	1,000	12,232	15,500	Panama
129	133	...	...	1,220	1,430	1,104	1,270	2	...	287	194	1,585	1,785	Papua New Guinea
5,259	5,506	368	430	846	1,349	9,302	13,700	120	177	726	1,909	18,051	26,000	Paraguay
4,065	3,600	15,776	14,500	1,979	2,000	29,885	39,000	867	800	1,269	1,135	47,675	65,000	Peru
1,913	1,950	30	30	8,647	7,800	51,268	58,000	14	10	1,037	909	160,128	216,000	Philippines
												...	...	Pitcairn Island
12,541	11,912	3,572	3,899	19,705	18,471	104,434	65,482	16,488	15,600	2,712	2,704	447,837	422,339	Poland

Crops and livestock (continued)

country	grains production ('000 metric tons) 1970–80 average	1982	grains yield (kg/hectare) 1970–80 average	1982	roots and tubers[a] production ('000 metric tons) 1970–80 average	1982	roots and tubers[a] yield (kg/hectare) 1970–80 average	1982	pulses[b] production ('000 metric tons) 1970–80 average	1982	pulses[b] yield (kg/hectare) 1970–80 average	1982	fruits[c] production ('000 metric tons) 1970–80 average	1982	vegetables[d] production ('000 metric tons) 1970–80 average	1982
Portugal	1,606	1,316	1,036	1,066	1,226	1,170	9,532	8,617	87	67	233	214	1,852	1,864	1,677	1,507
Puerto Rico	...	...	757	741	39	39	5,202	5,853	7	8	729	727	295	307	26	32
Qatar	...	...	2,872	2,235	...	...	9,900	10,000	...	...	...	...	2	3	28	19
Réunion	13	13	2,674	5,200	12	16	14,460	17,143	1	2	2,547	3,444	24	30	11	13
Romania	16,552	21,969	2,462	3,360	3,792	5,850	12,594	20,426	122	105	162	215	2,683	3,530	3,713	3,989
Rwanda	229	281	1,073	1,137	1,272	1,710	8,080	8,298	214	233	786	817	1,913	2,188	151	181
St. Christopher and Nevis	...	...	...	...	3	3	3,500	3,931	...	...	1,037	1,037	2	3	1	1
St. Helena and Ascension	...	...	...	...	...	...	...	...	...	...	...	...	...	...	...	...
St. Lucia	...	...	815	750	10	11	4,431	4,378	...	...	1,850	2,000	105	107	1	1
St. Pierre and Miquelon	...	...	...	...	...	...	...	...	...	...	...	...	...	...	...	...
St. Vincent and the Grenadines	...	1	2,476	3,111	19	23	7,996	7,626	...	...	864	960	39	43	...	1
San Marino	...	2[3]	...	...	...	...	...	...	...	...	...	...	...	...	...	...
São Tomé and Príncipe	...	1	1,525	1,556	11	15	11,770	13,393	...	...	...	...	3	4	2	3
Saudi Arabia	285	538	1,072	890	2	3	7,200	7,500	5	7	1,676	1,944	389	506	601	746
Senegal	674	828	599	835	111	42	4,090	3,979	20	30	359	500	63	82	76	97
Seychelles	...	...	...	...	...	...	5,828	5,000	...	...	...	...	2	2	1	1
Sierra Leone	530	586	1,334	1,359	121	131	4,043	4,018	29	34	553	612	113	133	112	166
Singapore	...	...	...	...	8	5	6,577	5,763	...	...	...	...	14	8	40	38
Solomon Islands	5	14	2,819	3,610	76	80	12,216	12,375	2	2	793	865	10	11	4	4
Somalia	204	391	487	620	32	37	10,895	10,936	6	11	336	355	122	93	52	57
South Africa	10,881	11,135	1,399	1,281	724	1,025	12,200	12,349	92	92	708	845	2,764	3,344	1,518	1,870
South West Africa/Namibia	63	64	382	397	137	140	9,022	8,750	4	4	1,185	1,143	24	25	21	20
Spain	13,731	13,118	1,864	1,792	5,578	5,142	14,529	15,282	472	320	750	682	10,712	12,147	7,965	8,739
Sri Lanka	1,496	2,190	2,137	2,519	756	679	5,990	9,756	14	24	631	640	1,234	2,180	241	330
Sudan, The	2,763	2,540	727	616	677	305	3,855	3,484	77	86	1,110	1,114	715	805	770	875
Suriname	183	280	3,741	3,993	2	4	6,501	5,000	...	...	912	875	54	52	3	4
Swaziland	102	71	1,347	1,200	14	16	3,198	3,404	1	4	492	585	103	76	11	12
Sweden	5,377	5,404	3,489	3,588	1,167	1,112	25,852	27,795	22	27	1,937	2,014	231	148	231	235
Switzerland	778	873	4,408	4,904	884	1,050	36,097	42,826	2	1	3,532	3,056	744	978	272	252
Syria	2,173	2,276	872	846	153	315	13,832	15,000	183	216	719	884	595	826	2,242	3,579
Taiwan																
Tanzania	1,448	1,450	884	684	4,321	5,386	4,934	5,168	205	224	433	435	1,923	2,079	928	1,007
Thailand	17,454	20,775	1,881	1,861	9,614	21,363	14,863	13,863	248	302	875	695	3,234	4,256	2,801	2,961
Togo	281	302	796	941	1,090	1,029	9,728	11,937	25	22	330	276	37	44	60	70
Tokelau	...	...	...	...	...	...	20,317	17,200	...	...						
Tonga	...	...	...	...	91	95	11,167	11,003	...	...	...	...	11	10	6	6
Trinidad and Tobago	21	35	2,939	3,125	21	22	11,486	11,759	4	5	1,623	1,942	64	63	28	34
Trust Territory of the Pacific Is.	...	...	1,170	1,202	11	14	8,394	8,323	...	...	600	600	3	3	3	3
Tunisia	945	1,331	649	1,024	96	140	13,732	11,667	74	115	582	882	452	474	894	1,127
Turkey	21,208	26,387	1,584	1,944	2,599	2,992	14,708	16,668	727	903	1,117	1,173	6,746	7,914	11,494	13,893
Turks and Caicos Islands																
Tuvalu																
Uganda	1,389	1,248	1,178	1,504	2,076	2,311	3,928	3,865	272	413	580	839	3,468	3,791	253	284
U.S.S.R	186,941	172,507	1,563	1,464	87,773	78,000	11,860	11,377	7,058	6,508	1,341	1,263	14,343	18,000	27,607	31,991
United Arab Emirates	...	2	...	4,719	...	1	...	14,286	...	...	...	...	30	63	58	130
United Kingdom	16,026	21,818	4,222	5,412	6,719	6,550	30,198	34,293	236	233	2,873	2,855	591	544	3,918	3,977
United States	248,663	339,350	3,743	4,409	15,631	16,506	26,968	29,409	1,100	1,356	1,467	1,598	24,846	24,863	24,471	27,319
Uruguay	911	922	1,295	1,790	204	237	5,569	6,583	5	6	841	943	275	310	149	188
Vanuatu	1	1	837	521	18	30	15,509	20,003	...	...	...	...	5	6	6	7
Venezuela	1,286	1,509	1,612	2,043	636	652	8,258	8,235	47	39	473	520	2,058	2,090	326	377
Vietnam[7]	11,294	14,307	1,204	2,342	4,508	4,997	6,405	5,152	101	133	514	723	2,071	2,856	2,335	2,719
Virgin Islands (U.S.)	...	...	...	...	...	...	...	...	...	...	...	...	...	...	...	...
Wallis and Futuna	...	...	...	...	10	10	5,950	6,273	...	...	...	...	4	5	...	...
Western Sahara	1	2	687	696	...	...	...	...	...	...	...	...	...	...	...	...
Western Samoa	1	...	1,103	...	24	41	5,774	6,983	...	...	...	...	49	55	...	...
Yemen (Aden)	101	94	1,656	1,542	1	1	4,794	3,996	...	...	...	...	75	82	102	121
Yemen (Şan'ā')	1,076	763	856	919	88	141	10,992	12,137	69	75	1,023	1,107	167	190	187	277
Yugoslavia	14,968	17,443	3,225	4,042	2,860	2,774	8,889	9,533	234	203	686	1,059	2,758	3,660	2,812	2,980
Zaire	735	837	708	765	11,397	13,755	7,410	6,909	160	141	621	543	2,407	2,461	453	515
Zambia	906	930	1,005	1,024	182	203	3,385	3,362	35	13	694	813	66	83	188	222
Zimbabwe	1,723	2,329	1,571	1,131	41	83	8,721	3,990	25	26	525	599	83	112	123	138

livestock														country
cattle		sheep		hogs		chickens		milk[e]				eggs[f]		
stock ('000 head)		stock ('000 head)		stock ('000 head)		stock ('000 head)		production ('000 metric tons)		yield (kg/animal)		production (metric tons)		
1970–80 average	1982	1970–80 average	1982	1970–80 average	1982	1970–80 average	1982	1970–80 average	1982	1970–80 average	1982	1970–80 average	1982	
1,117	1,000	4,748	5,200	2,086	3,500	15,282	17,600	605	695	2,326	2,106	48,230	61,500	Portugal
536	496	6	6	236	250	5,282	7,636	403	424	2,134	2,433	18,545	24,507	Puerto Rico
7	10	41	51	...	...	151	380	5	6	1,443	1,523	...	...	Qatar
26	22	2	3	86	74	1,996	3,200	6	6	801	573	2,318	2,350	Réunion
5,768	6,082	14,493	17,288	8,758	12,464	72,765	99,000	3,958	4,021	1,799	1,924	252,533	310,000	Romania
680	653	248	312	76	144	745	1,176	31	26	307	336	593	931	Rwanda
8	8	21	24	17	20	74	82	...	...	...	...	259	318	St. Christopher and Nevis
2	1	2	2	...	1	12	13	...	...	...	...	...	...	St. Helena and Ascension
12	11	10	14	16	10	113	200	1	1	1,664	1,429	451	500	St. Lucia
...	...	...	...	...	...	...	...	...	...	...	...	...	...	St. Pierre and Miquelon
7	8	7	13	5	6	129	160	1	2	1,299	1,300	441	574	St. Vincent and the Grenadines
...														San Marino
3	3	2	2	3	3	46	100	...	...	170	170	115	156	São Tomé and Príncipe
330	450	2,957	3,500	...	...	7,789	7,000	99	250	667	1,000	12,953	24,000	Saudi Arabia
2,468	2,300	1,571	2,100	167	150	6,915	9,000	100	85	352	370	5,355	7,200	Senegal
3	2	...	...	11	11	101	134	1	1	757	500	529	555	Seychelles
281	350	120	275	31	40	3,277	4,000	12	18	283	350	3,625	4,600	Sierra Leone
8	4	...	...	1,142	1,302	13,080	13,883	1	1	1,000	1,000	22,583	26,245	Singapore
19	24	...	...	34	40	133	149	1	1	757	600	266	292	Solomon Islands
3,413	4,000	7,183	10,300	8	10	2,433	3,084	120	163	328	354	2,058	2,480	Somalia
12,573	12,200	31,315	31,700	1,350	1,330	23,322	31,500	2,653	2,500	2,685	2,717	158,335	176,000	South Africa
2,681	1,800	4,848	5,000	31	40	432	490	68	68	484	412	162	160	South West Africa/Namibia
4,424	5,073	16,477	17,095	8,495	11,712	48,981	54,158	5,174	6,080	2,757	3,278	528,647	720,000	Spain
1,660	1,726	27	30	64	94	6,460	6,296	174	192	489	465	19,880	20,300	Sri Lanka
15,218	19,234	14,674	18,547	7	8	22,423	28,021	1,063	978	507	500	21,723	37,515	Sudan, The
38	51	3	4	16	18	761	1,150	8	7	855	1,241	2,001	2,700	Suriname
622	675	38	40	17	22	492	620	32	37	198	252	261	280	Swaziland
1,898	1,941	372	430	2,497	2,716	11,698	12,758	3,150	3,654	4,607	5,485	107,290	113,000	Sweden
1,966	1,945	350	333	2,029	2,093	6,281	5,961	3,416	3,650	3,866	4,244	41,556	42,500	Switzerland
600	870	6,620	11,000	...	1	6,824	15,000	295	580	1,136	1,487	32,781	80,000	Syria
...	128[1,4]	...	177[1,5]	...	4,826[1]	...	43,899[1]	...	50[1,6]	...	...	...	...	Taiwan
12,788	13,150	3,053	3,937	50	170	19,309	25,000	683	376	323	160	21,805	39,000	Tanzania
4,712	4,500	51	22	4,439	3,700	58,106	63,264	4	5	1,266	1,324	123,465	110,500	Thailand
223	250	736	835	260	360	2,411	3,150	3	4	100	100	1,420	3,100	Togo
...	...	...	...	1	1	3	4	...	...	...	...	5	6	Tokelau
5	11	...	...	57	80	124	175	...	...	1,500	1,505	294	376	Tonga
69	79	9	12	56	61	6,297	7,600	9	6	1,727	1,622	7,573	7,600	Trinidad and Tobago
8	8	...	...	24	27	156	178	...	...	...	...	134	153	Trust Territory of the Pacific Is.
759	600	3,830	4,500	6	4	12,841	14,000	174	257	753	1,224	22,385	41,700	Tunisia
13,806	15,981	40,359	49,598	15	11	41,927	55,928	2,895	3,700	571	581	158,146	244,922	Turkey
														Turks and Caicos Islands
														Tuvalu
4,650	5,000	954	1,078	143	260	11,806	13,400	305	350	323	350	10,598	12,000	Uganda
106,873	115,919	139,766	142,358	67,694	73,302	740,783	1,006,000	88,546	89,600	2,112	2,052	3,061,937	3,971,000	U.S.S.R
21	27	106	140	...	...	583	3,000	6	5	621	500	1,697	3,800	United Arab Emirates
13,615	13,275	28,258	33,049	8,178	8,082	129,958	123,000	14,651	16,720	4,371	5,090	831,967	750,000	United Kingdom
117,408	115,690	15,703	12,936	59,984	58,688	405,690	392,110	54,671	61,553	4,861	5,637	4,033,799	4,100,000	United States
10,124	10,872	17,049	23,369	440	430	7,129	8,300	738	818	1,503	1,543	16,731	19,000	Uruguay
97	100	...	...	63	69	129	158	2	2	198	204	191	234	Vanuatu
9,405	11,500	150	351	1,867	2,600	28,205	44,000	1,149	1,391	1,082	1,235	98,611	155,650	Venezuela
1,661	1,970	13	16	9,347	11,393	55,572	46,068	20	30	800	800	111,583	130,000	Vietnam[7]
7	8	4	5	3	6	57	66	3	3	3,776	3,434	174	200	Virgin Islands (U.S.)
...	...	...	...	7	17	...	8	...	...	...	...	...	...	Wallis and Futuna
...	...	18	20	...	...	...	...	...	...	...	...	...	...	Western Sahara
24	27	...	...	50	62	331	501	1	1	1,083	990	153	165	Western Samoa
101	120	636	1,010	...	...	1,399	1,580	6	8	403	400	1,473	1,800	Yemen (Aden)
963	950	3,375	3,151	...	...	3,132	3,500	66	64	200	200	4,828	11,300	Yemen (Şan'ā')
5,507	5,160	7,861	7,398	7,094	8,431	50,294	67,838	3,604	4,454	1,366	1,632	184,801	232,400	Yugoslavia
1,093	1,266	704	764	638	749	11,121	16,268	14	6	565	845	9,954	7,801	Zaire
1,818	2,250	41	38	157	240	10,619	13,000	60	61	300	300	14,020	17,160	Zambia
5,238	5,600	567	360	170	170	8,313	9,000	242	200	2,387	2,000	9,265	11,400	Zimbabwe

[1]1981.   [2]Belgium includes Luxembourg.   [3]1976.   [4]Includes buffaloes.   [5]Includes goats.   [6]Includes goat and sheep milk.   [7]Averages are for 1975–80 only.

Extractive industries

Extractive industries are generally defined as those industries involved in the exploitation of natural resources and include such activities as mining, fishing, forestry, and agriculture; the definition is sometimes confined to nonrenewable resources. For the purposes of this table agriculture is excluded; it is covered in tables elsewhere in *Britannica World Data*.

Extractive industries are here divided into three parts: mining, forestry, and fishing. These major headings are each divided into two main subheadings, one that treats production and one that treats foreign trade. The production sections are presented in terms of volume except for mining, and the trade sections are presented in terms of U.S. dollars. The formulation of the sections was determined by the systems of classification used in standard international sources. "Extractive," for example, may imply the production of primary products only, but because of the way national statistical information is reported the table may also include some processed and manufactured items, which are often indistinguishably associated with the extractive process (sulfur from petroleum extraction, or arsenic and antimony from silver mining). This is also the case in the trade section in mining, which includes some processed and manufactured metals and petroleum products.

Mining. In the absence of a single international standard of practice for calculating or reporting value of mineral production, single-country sources have been used to compile mining production figures. Each country has its own methods of reporting mining data, which do not always accord with the principal mineral production categories used in this table; namely, "metal," "non-metal," and "energy." The available data have therefore been manipulated to make them compatible with the requirements of the categories. Included in the "metal" category are all ferrous and non-ferrous metallic ores and concentrates; the "non-metal" group includes all non-metallic minerals except the mineral fuels; the last group,

"energy," is composed predominantly of the hydrocarbon fuels, though it may also include asphalts for construction, and so on.

Statistics regarding the value of mineral production are less readily available than those regarding the volume of minerals produced in country sources. The volume figures, however, cannot be aggregated to provide any useful measure of absolute or relative economic importance. This is because the units of production such as tons, barrels, carats, cubic metres, etc., are not truly equivalent, owing to wide differences between countries in terms of the value of the commodity and of costs for manpower, transportation, capital investment, and so on. The value of production figures (gross value of mineral output), though not always available, provide a more consistent standard to compare the relative importance of these minerals to a particular national economy. Where gross value of output was not available, value added to the gross domestic product or, occasionally, export value was substituted. Since the figures for total value of production are reported here in millions of national currency units, comparisons cannot be made from country to country because of the wide variations in the value of national monetary units. Comparisons, however, can be made as to the relative importance of each sector within a given country.

Since the value of mineral production data are obtained mostly from country sources, there is wide variation in the time periods to which the data refer. In addition, the time period for which production data are available does not always correspond with the year for which mineral trade data are available.

The Standard International Trade Classification (SITC), Revision 2, was used to determine the commodity groupings for foreign trade statistics. The total value of trade was derived by adding imports and exports of the respective SITC groups. The actual trade data for these groups is taken

Extractive industries

country	mining												forestry, 1982				
	value of minerals produced						foreign trade in minerals and concentrates						production of roundwood				
	year	total ('000,000 national currency)	by category (percent)				year	total ('000,000 U.S.$)	by category (percent)				total ('000 cubic metres)	by category (percent)			
			total	metals[a]	non-metals[b]	energy[c]			total	metals[d]	non-metals[b]	energy[e]		total	coniferous (softwood)	non-coniferous (hardwood)	others
Afghanistan	1980–81	10,724[1]	100	—	0.4	99.6	1977	117	100	7.7	20.9	71.4	6,538	100	37.5	62.5	—
Albania	...	...	...	...	...	...	...	...	...	...	...	...	2,330	100	34.2	65.8	—
Algeria	1978	34,965	100	1.7	—	98.3	1980	17,079	100	5.7	2.7	91.6	1,678	100	67.5	32.5	...
American Samoa	...	...	...	...	...	...	1979	24	100	0.7	5.2	94.1	...	...	...	...	...
Andorra	...	...	...	...	...	...	1972	6	100	45.3	22.1	32.6	...	...	...	...	...
Angola	1973	8,929[2]	100	14.5	25.9	59.6	1974	893	100	12.1	13.7	74.2	8,986	100	—	100.0	—
Anguilla	...	...	...	...	...	...	...	...	...	...	...	...	...	...	...	...	...
Antigua and Barbuda	1982	1.8[3]	100	—	100.0	—	1978	2	100	57.0	15.1	27.9	...	...	...	...	...
Argentina	1980	2,459	100	3.4	12.8	83.9	1982	2,251	100	38.6	6.8	54.6	10,478	100	7.5	62.4	30.1
Australia	1979–80	8,128	100	46.6	8.4	45.0	1982	14,786	100	42.8	7.9	49.3	16,915	100	29.0	70.0	1.0
Austria	1980	24,988	100	5.8	16.1	78.1	1982	8,229	100	38.6	20.1	41.3	13,095	100	81.6	18.4	—
Bahamas, The	1978	10[5]	...	...	...	...	1977	6,488	100	—	0.3	99.7	115	100	100.0	—	—
Bahrain	1980	1,339[6]	100	—	—	100.0	1980	5,862	100	3.8	1.0	95.2	...	...	...	...	...
Bangladesh	1975–76	154[7]	100	—	5.7	94.3	1981	552	100	41.2	34.0	24.8	31,546	100	—	100.0	—
Barbados	1979	9	100	—	100.0		1980	172	100	20.6	11.7	67.7	...	...	...	...	...
Belgium	1980	24,100	100	—	42.7	57.3	1982	37,059[8]	100	29.3	26.4	44.3	2,657[8]	100	56.6	43.4	—
Belize	1981	1	...	...	...	...	1980	33	100	7.5	10.4	82.1	122	100	4.9	95.1	—
Benin	1978	360	...	...	...	...	1977	26	100	39.9	14.0	46.1	4,083	100	—	95.2	4.8
Bermuda	1978–79	2	...	...	...	...	1981	65	100	—	15.4	84.6	...	...	...	...	...
Bhutan	1980–81	18	...	...	...	...	...	...	...	...	...	...	3,224	100	—	100.0	—
Bolivia	1980	13,298[9]	100	75.4	—	24.6	1979	751	100	81.8	2.2	16.0	1,401	100	—	94.4	5.6
Botswana	1978–79	180	...	...	...	...	[10]	...	...	...	...	...	786	100	—	100.0	—
Brazil	1981	130,488[11]	100	89.0	11.0	...	1982	17,393	100	22.2	4.7	73.1	216,463	100	16.7	69.2	14.1
British Virgin Islands	...	...	...	...	...	...	1981	2	100	13.0	20.0	67.0	...	...	...	...	...
Brunei	1982	8,247[6]	100	...	...	100.0	1982	3,898	100	2.1	0.9	97.0	294	100	—	100.0	—
Bulgaria	...	...	...	...	...	...	1974	1,201	100	59.4	5.6	35.0	4,876	100	24.3	75.2	8.5
Burkina Faso	...	...	...	...	...	...	1981	92	100	12.7	29.5	57.8	7,093	100	—	98.1	1.9
Burma	1978	540[9]	...	...	...	...	1976	50	100	51.7	22.4	25.9	18,834	100	—	100.0	—
Burundi	...	...	...	...	...	...	1982	24	100	2.1	84.1	13.8	3,435	100	0.1	98.0	1.9
Cameroon	1979–80	52,600	...	...	...	...	1982	723	100	14.6	12.3	73.1	10,291	100	—	100.0	—
Canada	1980	6,296	100	43.5	12.1	44.4	1982	29,964	100	32.9	15.1	52.0	142,322	100	90.5	9.5	—
Cape Verde	1981	7.6[12]	100	—	100.0	—	1980	11	100	9.1	32.8	58.1	...	...	...	...	...
Cayman Islands	...	...	...	...	...	...	1980	20	100	12.0	23.7	64.3	...	...	...	...	...
Central African Republic	1978	8,515	100	—	100.0	—	1980	37	100	3.2	92.9	3.9	3,090	100	—	100.0	—
Chad	1975	1,210[9]	100	—	33.9	66.1	1975	33	100	11.4	30.9	57.7	7,944	100	—	73.8	26.2
Chile	1979	124,703	...	...	...	...	1980	4,275	100	71.3	5.2	23.5	12,751	100	53.8	44.2	2.0
China	...	...	...	...	...	...	...	...	...	...	...	...	224,628[13]	100	47.0	53.0	—
Christmas Island	1982–83	31	100	—	100.0	—	...	...	...	...	...	...	...	...	...	...	...
Cocos (Keeling) Islands	...	...	...	...	...	...	...	...	...	...	...	...	...	...	...	...	...
Colombia	1981	66,515	...	...	...	...	1982	1,628	100	28.7	16.5	54.8	16,312	100	1.0	83.3	15.7
Comoros	...	...	...	...	...	...	1976	2	100	15.3	4.1	80.6	...	...	...	...	...
Congo	1978	31,937	...	...	...	...	1980	1,007	100	3.7	5.6	90.7	2,196	100	—	100.0	—
Cook Islands	...	...	...	...	...	...	1978	2	100	21.7	20.0	58.3	...	...	...	...	...
Costa Rica	1978	110	100	23.6	76.4	—	1981	365	100	24.2	16.2	59.6	2,627	100	—	96.8	3.2
Cuba	...	...	...	...	...	...	1978	1,097	100	21.0	1.4	77.6	3,193	100	—	88.9	11.1
Cyprus	1980	18	100	14.3	85.7	—	1982	441	100	14.8	20.5	64.7	87	100	89.7	3.4	6.9
Czechoslovakia	1980	27,100	100	12.2	10.2	77.6	1981	7,509	100	33.5	11.3	55.2	19,186	100	76.1	23.9	—
Denmark	1981	1,727	100	—	22.3	77.7	1982	6,880	100	24.6	13.6	61.8	3,051	100	72.0	27.8	0.2
Djibouti	...	...	...	...	...	...	1979	11	100	11.1	23.7	65.2	...	...	...	...	...
Dominica	1977	1.0	...	...	...	...	1978	4	100	10.3	42.4	47.3	...	...	...	...	...

largely from the United Nations annual *Yearbook of International Trade Statistics*. The total trade figures for mining are in millions of U.S. dollars, and percentages have been calculated for the three subgroups.

Forestry. Data for the production and trade sections of forestry are based on the United Nations annual *Yearbook of Forest Products*. Production of roundwood (all wood obtained in removals from forests) is divided into three categories: coniferous (softwoods), non-coniferous (broadleaved or hardwoods), and other. For the value of trade of total forest products, exports and imports were totaled under three categories: roundwood, sawnwood, and sleepers; wood pulp and wood-based panels; and paper and paperboard. Specific figures are given only for total production of roundwood (cubic metres) and total trade in forest products ('000 U.S.$); the other categories give percentages of the totals.

Fishing. Data for nominal (live weight) catches of fish, crustaceans, mollusks, etc., in all fishing areas (inland waters and marine areas) are taken from the United Nations annual *Yearbook of Fishery Statistics (Catches and Landings)*. Total catch figures are given in metric tons; the catches in inland waters and marine areas are given as percentages of the total catch.

Figures for trade in fishing are taken from the United Nations annual *Yearbook of Fishery Statistics (Fishery Commodities)*. Total trade figures were obtained by adding imports and exports of all fishery products. Value figures for total trade in fishing are in '000 U.S. dollars, and percentages of the total are given for two principal sub-groups.

The following notes further define the column headings:

a. Includes ferrous and non-ferrous metallic ores and scraps, such as bauxite, copper, gold (except unwrought or semi-manufactured), iron ore, lead, uranium, or zinc.

b. Includes crude fertilizers, manufactured fertilizers, inorganic chemicals, non-metallic mineral manufactures (*e.g.*, cement, bricks, glass, pottery, etc.) and pearls, precious and semiprecious stones, worked and unworked.

c. Includes hydrocarbon solids, liquids, and gases and electric current.

d. Includes metalliferous ores and metal scrap, iron and steel, and non-ferrous metals in unworked or semi-manufactured form.

e. Includes coal, coke, and briquettes; petroleum and petroleum products; natural and manufactured gas and electric power.

f. Includes coniferous and non-coniferous fuelwood and charcoal, sawlogs and veneer logs, pitprops, pulpwood and particles, chips and particles, wood residues and industrial roundwood.

g. Includes mechanical wood pulp, semi-chemical and chemical wood pulp, bleached and unbleached sulfite pulp, dissolving wood pulp and other fibre pulp; and veneer sheets, plywood, particle board, and fibreboard.

h. Includes newsprint, printing and writing paper, household and sanitary paper, wrapping and package paper and board, and other paper and paperboard.

i. Includes fish, crustaceans, or mollusks in a fresh, chilled or frozen, dried, salted or smoked state.

j. Includes products and preparations of fish, crustaceans, and mollusks; oils and fats of aquatic animal origin; and meals, soluble food supplements, and similar animal feeding stuffs.

... Not available.

— None, less than 0.05% of unit indicated, or not applicable.

1 cubic metre = 35.314667 cubic feet

1 metric ton = 1.1023 short tons

foreign trade in forest products total ('000 U.S.$)	total	roundwood, sawnwood, and sleepers[f]	wood pulp, wood-based panels[g]	paper and paper-board[h]	fishing, 1982 nominal catches total (metric tons)	total	inland waters	marine areas	foreign trade in fish total ('000 U.S.$)	total	fish, crustaceans, mollusks[i]	other[j]	country
26,613	100	—	97.0	3.0	1,500	100	100.0	—	...	...	...	...	Afghanistan
2,180	100	—	27.5	72.5	4,000	100	—	100.0	...	...	...	...	Albania
190,170	100	44.0	23.0	33.0	64,500	100	—	100.0	12,136	100	34.5	65.5	Algeria
...	...	...	...	...	430	100	—	100.0	...	...	...	...	American Samoa
...	...	...	...	...	...	...	...	...	...	...	...	...	Andorra
20,723	100	50.6	25.3	24.1	112,414	100	7.1	92.9	...	...	...	...	Angola
...	...	...	...	...	...	...	...	...	...	...	...	...	Anguilla
...	...	...	...	...	949	100	—	100.0	800[4]	100[4]	100.0[4]	...	Antigua and Barbuda
225,432	100	24.2	36.3	39.5	474,981	100	3.2	96.8	197,500	100	98.3	1.7	Argentina
1,105,218	100	38.1	13.8	48.1	161,000	100	0.8	99.2	594,360	100	74.5	25.5	Australia
1,872,940	100	40.8	19.4	39.8	4,500	100	100.0	—	75,286	100	38.9	61.1	Austria
6,018	100	61.6	25.5	12.9	4,686	100	—	100.0	9,385	100	94.1	5.9	Bahamas, The
23,222	100	31.8	49.5	18.7	6,577	100	—	100.0	2,547	100	73.3	26.7	Bahrain
10,195	100	18.9	24.5	56.6	724,800	100	80.5	19.5	45,441	100	100.0	—	Bangladesh
24,361	100	39.5	16.6	43.9	3,480	100	—	100.0	1,824	100	63.4	36.6	Barbados
2,513,274[8]	100	26.4	29.2	44.4	47,841[8]	100	—	100.0	400,153[8]	100	57.4	42.6	Belgium
3,140	100	54.2	14.2	31.6	1,400	100	3.6	96.4	3,319	100	92.8	7.2	Belize
5,643	100	7.9	6.8	85.3	23,766	100	85.0	15.0	2,716	100	100.0	—	Benin
...	...	...	...	...	2,196	100	—	100.0	5,179	100	80.9	19.1	Bermuda
501	100	100.0	—	—	1,000	100	100.0	—	...	...	...	...	Bhutan
23,915	100	40.9	6.8	52.3	5,617	100	100.0	—	6,000	100	3.3	96.7	Bolivia
1,640	100	65.9	—	34.1	1,400	100	100.0	—	...	...	...	...	Botswana
916,366	100	18.3	44.1	37.6	850,000	100	23.8	76.2	227,806	100	95.2	4.8	Brazil
...	...	...	...	...	318	100	—	100.0	...	...	...	...	British Virgin Islands
6,931	100	1.9	80.4	17.7	2,307	100	5.1	94.9	5,670	100	60.0	40.0	Brunei
164,202	100	24.8	43.2	32.0	115,607	100	13.5	86.5	44,000	100	42.1	57.9	Bulgaria
4,458	100	58.9	10.4	30.7	7,000	100	100.0	—	1,470	100	81.6	18.4	Burkina Faso
121,796	100	91.2	—	8.8	584,400	100	26.3	73.7	13,500	100	100.0	—	Burma
282	100	—	100.0	—	11,900	100	100.0	—	340	100	100.0	—	Burundi
118,799	100	76.3	14.6	9.1	83,061	100	48.2	51.8	9,926	100	78.2	21.8	Cameroon
10,033,725	100	27.8	29.9	42.3	1,389,348	100	4.2	95.8	1,581,026	100	83.4	16.6	Canada
771	100	59.1	17.6	23.3	18,381	100	—	100.0	3,150	100	52.4	47.6	Cape Verde
...	...	...	...	...	...	...	...	...	...	...	...	...	Cayman Islands
29,370	100	98.1	—	1.9	13,000	100	100.0	—	630	100	20.6	79.4	Central African Republic
1,352	100	53.6	24.5	21.9	115,000	100	100.0	—	...	...	...	...	Chad
326,162	100	30.8	55.8	13.4	3,672,997	100	—	100.0	385,973	100	22.7	77.3	Chile
1,750,169[13]	100	45.7	32.4	21.9	4,926,683[13]	100	31.7	69.3	299,660[13]	100	91.6	8.4	China
...	...	...	...	...	...	...	...	...	...	...	...	...	Christmas Island
...	...	...	...	...	...	...	...	...	...	...	...	...	Cocos (Keeling) Islands
181,955	100	2.6	18.5	78.9	71,381	100	68.6	31.4	116,944	100	30.1	69.9	Colombia
...	...	...	...	...	4,000	100	—	100.0	...	...	...	...	Comoros
47,437	100	62.9	35.8	1.3	18,934	100	5.3	94.7	22,135	100	83.1	16.9	Congo
...	...	...	...	...	830	100	—	100.0	175	100	22.9	77.1	Cook Islands
84,221	100	1.4	12.1	86.5	10,902	100	4.2	95.8	14,200	100	86.2	13.8	Costa Rica
197,712	100	44.4	17.3	38.3	195,246	100	7.0	93.0	214,230	100	91.4	8.6	Cuba
52,008	100	21.8	16.8	61.4	1,602	100	2.9	97.1	9,193	100	51.7	48.3	Cyprus
518,712	100	54.2	15.3	30.5	17,341	100	100.0	—	98,516	100	40.9	59.1	Czechoslovakia
984,745	100	27.5	23.9	48.6	1,927,117	100	1.1	98.9	1,198,670	100	70.5	29.5	Denmark
57	100	—	100.0	—	426	100	—	100.0	...	...	...	...	Djibouti
1,340	100	81.6	18.4	—	1,545	100	—	100.0	231	100	57.6	42.4	Dominica

Extractive industries (continued)

country	mining value of minerals produced					foreign trade in minerals and concentrates						forestry, 1982 production of roundwood				
	year	total ('000,000 national currency)	total	metals[a]	non-metals[b]	energy[c]	year	total ('000,000 U.S.$)	total	metals[d]	non-metals[b]	energy[e]	total ('000 cubic metres)	total	coniferous (softwood)	non-coniferous (hardwood) / others
Dominican Republic	1977	199	100	95.9	4.1	—	1982	565	100	16.3	7.9	75.8	566	100	—	100.0 —
Ecuador	1980	64,949	100	...	2.0	98.0	1978	922	100	13.7	6.9	79.4	7,729	100	—	73.7 26.3
Egypt	1977	726	100	—4.1—		95.9	1982	3,685	100	19.4	14.4	66.2	1,890	100	—	100.0 —
El Salvador	1979–80	9	100	—	100.0	—	1981	318	100	16.4	8.6	75.0	4,397	100	1.3	95.5 3.2
Equatorial Guinea	...	...	...			...	...	...				...	465	100	—	100.0 —
Ethiopia	1979–80	7	100				1982	298	100	10.0	14.6	75.4	28,720	100	6.9	89.7 3.4
Faeroe Islands	1980	0.9[9]	100	—	—	100.0	1982	60	100	7.2	11.0	81.8	...	...	...	... ...
Falkland Islands	...	...					...	...					...	...	...	... ...
Fiji	1979	14	100	85.9	14.1	—	1982	245	100	8.4	8.0	83.6	224	100	13.4	86.6 —
Finland	1981	1,596	100	55.5	44.5	—	1982	6,608	100	24.6	11.8	63.6	39,209	100	79.3	20.7 —
France	1980	40,200	100	4.0	41.0	55.0	1982	59,399	100	26.4	15.1	58.5	37,827	100	46.9	51.5 1.6
French Guiana	1983	...	100	100.0	—		1982	64	100	8.8	12.1	79.1	254	100	—	97.6 2.4
French Polynesia	...	...					1982	108	100	16.6	14.9	68.5	...	...	...	... ...
Gabon	1978	206,269[9]	100	16.6	0.1	83.3	1979	1,773	100	14.9	3.1	82.0	2,482	100	—	100.0 —
Gambia, The	...	...					1977	8	100	13.1	25.4	61.5	993	100	—	75.6 24.4
Germany, East	...	...					...	...					10,124	100	78.5	21.5 —
Germany, West	1980	33,900[15]	100	19.5	0.3	80.2	1982	79,426	100	31.6	14.2	54.2	27,004	100	69.1	30.9 —
Ghana	1977	117[15]	100	82.6	17.4	—	1979	34.9	100	35.9	11.2	52.9	9,803	100	—	100 —
Gibraltar	...	...					1980	40[16]	...				...	...	...	... ...
Greece	1980	25,947[17]	100	16.2	59.0	24.8	1982	4,973	100	19.0	14.0	67.0	2,755	100	23.6	76.4 —
Greenland	1982	408[4]	100	96.5	3.5	—	1982	118	100	44.4	6.4	49.2	...	...	...	... ...
Grenada	1976	0.1	100	...	100	...										
Guadeloupe	...	...					1981	76	100	25.5	41.6	32.9	17	100	—	100.0 —
Guam	...	...											...	...	...	... ...
Guatemala	...	...					1981	1,010	100	10.2	12.4	77.4	6,652	100	81.4	18.6 —
Guinea	...	...											3,634	100	—	100.0 —
Guinea-Bissau	...	...					1980	8	100	8.0	47.5	44.5	527	100	—	100.0 —
Guyana	1980	221	...				1979	225	100	62.6	9.3	28.1	201	100	—	100.0 —
Haiti	1980	66,728[9]	...				1979	74	100	42.9	10.5	46.6	5,494	100	8.7	81.7 9.6
Honduras	1982	105[9]	...				1981	284	100	29.7	16.9	53.4	5,071	100	45.1	54.9 —
Hong Kong	...	...					1982	5,172	100	26.2	35.4	38.4	174	100	—	10.3 89.7
Hungary	1980	60,250[18]	100	8.6	5.5	85.9	1982	4,686	100	25.4	22.9	51.7	6,469	100	6.6	92.0 1.4
Iceland	...	...					1982	300	100	31.4	19.8	48.8	...	...	...	... ...
India	1981	35,402	100	7.3	8.1	84.6	1980	10,493	100	19.3	21.6	59.1	228,316	100	3.6	92.2 4.2
Indonesia	1978	481[19]	...				1982	24,958	100	9.3	2.9	87.8	128,357	100	0.5	99.0 0.5
Iran	1982–83	1,927,800[9]	100	—8.2—		91.8	1977	27,728	100	6.1	2.6	91.3	6,709	100	—	95.0 5.0
Iraq	...	...					1976	8,747	100	5.3	1.2	93.5	131	100	—	49.6 50.4
Ireland	1978	145	100	28.7	70.3	1.0	1982	2,653	100	19.7	24.2	56.1	1,100	100	98.8	1.2 —
Israel	1977	2,246[15]	100	10.7	89.3	—	1982	4,630	100	11.2	48.6	40.2	118	100	53.4	46.6 —
Italy	1980	2,559,815	100	5.0	28.8	66.1	1982	48,185	100	20.8	12.2	67.0	7,990	100	18.5	80.6 0.9
Ivory Coast	1977	3,000[9]	...				1982	976	100	9.9	11.5	78.6	11,501	100	—	92.3 7.7
Jamaica	1980	678[9]	100	99.0	1.0	—	1981	1,382	100	59.1	3.1	37.8	43	100	41.9	30.2 27.9
Japan	1980	927,100	100	11.7	23.1	65.2	1982	100,644	100	28.4	5.8	65.8	32,819	100	64.2	35.1 0.7
Jordan	1980	59	100	—	100.0	—	1982	1,217	100	13.4	30.5	56.1	10	100	—	100.0 —
Kampuchea	...	...											5,107	100	0.1	99.9 —
Kenya	1982	3	100	—	100.0	—	1980	1,630	100	10.3	8.6	81.1	28,161	100	5.3	59.7 35.0
Kiribati	1978	17					1979	23[19]	100	1.5	87.6	10.9	...	...	...	... ...
Korea, North	...	...											6,020	100	67.6	32.4 —
Korea, South	1979	397,051[15]	100	24.7	12.6	62.7	1981	13,586	100	30.4	10.9	58.7	9,785	100	67.1	32.0 0.9
Kuwait	1983	2,542[4]	100			100	1981	15,440	100	3.7	7.8	88.5	...	...	...	... ...
Laos	...	...					1974	15	100	35.1	17.2	47.7	3,836	100	—	82.8 17.2
Lebanon	...	...					1977	568	100	24.5	52.7	22.8	486	100	6.4	68.9 24.7
Lesotho	1979–80	18[9]	100		100		[10]	...					293	100	—	100.0 —
Liberia	1981	354[4,20]	100	93.4	6.6	—	1981	510	100	66.0	8.6	25.4	4,505	100	—	60.2 39.8
Libya	1977	3,444	100	—	1.0	99.0	1981	16,296	100	2.9	1.4	95.7	630	100	—	100.0 —
Liechtenstein	...	...					...	...					...	...	...	... ...
Luxembourg	1982	421	100	—	100.0	—	...	8	...				8	...	...	... ...
Macau	1979	15[15]	100	—	100.0	—	1981	103	100	26.5	28.5	45.0	...	...	...	... ...
Madagascar	...	...					1981	140	100	21.3	24.3	54.4	6,262	100	—	100.0 —
Malawi	...	...					1980	135	100	20.3	29.4	50.3	6,252	100	1.0	98.6 0.4
Malaysia	1981	1,148[9]	...				1981	7,626	100	26.3	6.7	67.0	39,860	100	—	95.0 5.0
Maldives	1980	5.6[9]	100	—	100.0	—	1978	0.6	100	9.5	9.3	81.2	...	...	...	... ...
Mali	...	...					1979	61	100	8.3	9.4	82.3	4,452	100	—	100.0 —
Malta	1982	2[15]	100	—	100.0	—	1981	213	100	17.6	16.6	65.8	...	...	...	... ...
Martinique	...	...					1982	188	100	8.2	17.3	74.4	...	...	...	... ...
Mauritania	...	...					1972	127	100	94.2	1.5	4.3	53	100	—	100.0 —
Mauritius	1980	15[9]	...				1978	119	100	19.6	41.9	38.5	43	100	23.4	76.7 —
Mayotte	...	...					...	...					...	...	...	... ...
Mexico	1980	53,439,461	100	86.0	11.4	2.6[21]	1982	19,444	100	9.5	4.2	86.3	19,462	100	49.4	47.1 3.5
Monaco	...	...					...	...					...	...	...	... ...
Mongolia	...	...											2,390	100	92.3	7.7 —
Montserrat	1980	0.2[9]	...				1978	1	100	12.3	32.2	55.5	...	...	...	... ...
Morocco	1981	4,382	100	—97.1—		2.9	1982	2,900	100	14.1	42.4	43.5	1,667	100	14.9	63.9 21.2
Mozambique	1973	275	100	15.5	66.6	17.9[22]	1974	95	100	29.4	6.0	64.6	14,128	100	—	97.1 2.9
Nauru	1982–83	126[4]	100	...	100		...	...					...	...	...	... ...
Nepal	1979	27[9]	...				1980	79	100	11.9	37.6	50.5	14,368	100	1.0	98.3 0.7
Netherlands, The	...	...					1982	43,479	100	15.7	10.2	74.1	838	100	67.9	31.4 0.7
Netherlands Antilles	...	...					1979	7,702	100	0.2	0.2	99.6	...	...	...	... ...
New Caledonia	1979	12,902[9]	...				1982	361	100	69.7	3.3	27.0	12	100	16.7	83.3 —
New Zealand	1981	194	100	19.5	59.7	20.8[22]	1982	2,139	100	36.5	16.9	46.6	10,021	100	97.1	2.9 —
Nicaragua	1978	129,525	100	100.0	—		1982	261	100	16.0	13.3	70.7	3,291	100	18.6	81.4 —
Niger	...	...					1981	129	100	8.4	30.1	61.5	3,620	100	—	100.0 —
Nigeria	1980–81	11,614[9]	100	0.2	7.4	92.4	1979	17,119	100	4.0	3.7	92.3	83,187	100	—	91.8 8.2
Niue	...	...					...	—	...				...	...	...	... ...
Norfolk Island	...	...					...	...					...	...	...	... ...

					fishing, 1982								
foreign trade in forest products					nominal catches (fish, crusta., mollusks, etc.)				foreign trade in fish				country
total ('000 U.S.$)	by category (percent)				total (metric tons)	by location (percent)			total ('000 U.S.$)	by category (percent)			
	total	roundwood, sawnwood, and sleepers[f]	wood pulp, wood-based panels[g]	paper and paper-board[h]		total	inland waters	marine areas		total	fish, crustaceans, mollusks[i]	other[j]	
62,593	100	37.8	2.9	59.3	13,169	100	13.1	86.9	17,663	100	69.9	30.1	Dominican Republic
115,085	100	8.8	46.9	44.3	636,532	100	—	100.0	210,817	100	66.3	33.7	Ecuador
527,479	100	59.5	11.0	29.6	137,202	100	82.1	17.9	54,557	100	47.1	52.9	Egypt
43,198	100	2.1	6.3	91.6	12,897	100	5.7	94.3	23,238	100	91.4	8.6	El Salvador
2,683	100	100.0	—	—	2,500	100	—	100.0	...	...	...	...	Equatorial Guinea
5,140	100	—	37.1	62.9	3,750	100	90.7	9.3	180	100	—	100.0	Ethiopia
...	...	...	...	...	248,705	100	—	100.0	145,293	100	91.2	8.8	Faeroe Islands
					—								Falkland Islands
15,519	100	13.9	22.8	63.3	12,514	100	9.3	90.7	23,851	100	28.2	71.8	Fiji
4,617,755	100	20.3	21.6	58.1	145,636	100	22.7	77.3	100,100	100	33.8	66.2	Finland
3,864,236	100	26.4	31.6	42.0	764,532	100	—	100.0	1,328,688	100	76.0	24.0	France
4,545	100	85.4	12.2	2.4	1,450	100	—	100.0	41,118	100	98.7	1.3	French Guiana
9,757	100	39.5	32.3	28.2	2,247	100	—	100.0	4,149	100	48.2	51.8	French Polynesia
153,424	100	87.0	11.1	1.9	52,638	100	5.0	95.0	13,780	100	80.4	19.6	Gabon
133	100	9.8	90.2	—	9,704	100	11.1	88.9	3,620	100	100.0	—	Gambia, The
567,000	100	42.2	20.2	37.6	235,767	100	8.1	91.9	40,200[14]	100[14]	26.5[14]	73.5[14]	Germany, East
7,550,114	100	19.1	27.7	53.2	313,524	100	7.1	92.9	1,137,409	100	55.5	44.5	Germany, West
23,434	100	75.5	10.8	13.7	223,950	100	17.9	82.1	1,720[14]	100[14]	70.3[14]	29.7[14]	Ghana
													Gibraltar
354,765	100	38.4	15.3	46.3	106,000	100	11.8	88.2	104,869	100	65.9	34.1	Greece
...	...	...	...	...	105,830	100	—	100.0	103,664	100	66.2	33.8	Greenland
					1,801	100	—	100.0	722	100	66.8	33.2	Grenada
14,202	100	56.2	15.0	28.8	8,800	100	—	100.0	7,184	100	81.8	18.2	Guadeloupe
					129	100	7.8	92.2					Guam
74,126	100	5.5	4.7	89.8	4,284	100	16.8	83.2	12,709	100	85.9	14.5	Guatemala
3,646	100	100.0	—	—	18,453	100	5.4	94.6	3,030	100	100.0	—	Guinea
228	100	57.0	—	43.0	3,729	100	—	100.0	5,251	100	96.7	3.3	Guinea-Bissau
12,932	100	48.4	2.4	49.2	21,124	100	2.6	97.4	9,100	100	100.0	—	Guyana
4,937	100	38.6	—	61.4	4,000	100	7.5	92.5	5,127	100	94.9	5.1	Haiti
58,908	100	41.8	3.1	55.1	5,023	100	1.5	98.5	29,749	100	94.6	5.4	Honduras
636,079	100	17.5	19.8	62.7	180,981	100	4.3	95.7	686,135	100	90.8	9.2	Hong Kong
346,263	100	39.7	24.9	35.4	42,042	100	100.0	—	38,755	100	12.7	87.3	Hungary
42,993	100	40.8	24.2	35.0	788,659	100	—	100.0	510,660	100	91.3	8.7	Iceland
208,673	100	9.5	28.1	62.4	2,335,151	100	38.2	61.8	354,509	100	99.7	0.3	India
1,061,738	100	57.4	31.1	11.5	2,020,000	100	26.2	73.8	276,848	100	83.7	16.5	Indonesia
291,261	100	35.3	17.5	47.2	44,757	100	10.6	89.4	51,450	100	23.3	76.7	Iran
131,059	100	54.7	26.3	19.0	26,219	100	66.7	33.3	...	...	...	...	Iraq
339,210	100	29.1	13.3	57.6	212,198	100	—	100.0	140,676	100	78.8	21.2	Ireland
226,201	100	36.2	19.3	44.5	23,679	100	56.9	43.1	25,100	100	68.5	31.5	Israel
3,352,683	100	43.9	29.5	26.6	468,610	100	8.5	91.5	855,739[18]	100	85.3	14.7	Italy
321,576	100	88.3	6.1	5.6	92,469	100	16.2	83.8	129,107	100	62.0	38.0	Ivory Coast
96,121	100	31.4	3.6	65.0	7,874	100	1.6	98.4	21,781	100	49.5	50.5	Jamaica
7,296,204	100	73.6	13.5	12.9	10,775,131	100	2.0	98.0	4,774,296	100	83.0[i]	17.0	Japan
79,205	100	21.3	20.0	58.7	19	100	—	100.0	7,900	100	32.9	67.1	Jordan
2,058	100	4.6	3.8	91.6	58,650	100	80.1	19.9	...	100	...	...	Kampuchea
52,661	100	4.6	2.9	92.5	81,133	100	91.2	8.8	2,675	100	80.0	20.0	Kenya
					19,540	100	—	100.0	556	100	—	100.0	Kiribati
1,879	100	10.6	—	89.4	1,550,000	100	5.5	94.5	31,400[4]	100[4]	30.8[4]	69.1[4]	Korea, North
1,143,023	100	56.6	33.0	10.4	2,281,332	100	1.9	98.1	814,836	100	89.6	10.4	Korea, South
184,043	100	36.8	32.0	31.2	4,497	100	—	100.0	33,270	100	86.8	13.2	Kuwait
9,522	100	91.4	—	8.6	20,000	100	100.0	—	...	...	...	...	Laos
52,524	100	37.1	9.5	53.4	1,500	100	6.7	93.3	...	...	...	...	Lebanon
					20	100	100.0	—	2,300	100	91.3	8.7	Lesotho
46,721	100	96.6	1.6	1.8	13,553	100	29.5	70.5	6,360	100	59.4	40.6	Liberia
143,223	100	62.0	24.6	13.4	7,425	100	—	100.0	30,600	100	19.3	80.7	Libya
													Liechtenstein
8	...	...	...	...	8	...	...	...	8	...	...	...	Luxembourg
12,463	100	29.0	25.9	45.1	6,456	100	—	100.0	15,250	100	99.0	1.0	Macau
8,155	100	3.0	39.5	57.4	48,001	100	81.2	18.8	20,100	100	100.0	—	Madagascar
16,761	100	2.5	13.0	84.5	58,416	100	100.0	—	2,293	100	79.6	20.4	Malawi
2,302,757	100	86.7	6.1	7.2	682,569	100	2.4	97.6	190,650	100	52.3	47.7	Malaysia
					30,300	100	—	100.0	3,472	100	94.6	5.4	Maldives
757	100	21.5	33.0	45.5	90,000	100	100.0	—	1,175	100	81.7	18.3	Mali
30,850	100	33.7	12.2	54.1	1,197	100	—	100.0	4,030	100	42.4	57.6	Malta
14,096	100	42.3	10.8	46.9	4,684	100	—	100.0	10,649	100	90.2	9.8	Martinique
					37,000	100	27.0	73.0	128,066	100	95.7	4.3	Mauritania
8,931	100	21.1	19.6	59.3	7,288	100	0.4	99.6	21,370	100	55.8	44.2	Mauritius
													Mayotte
598,493	100	13.8	22.0	64.2	1,506,020	100	7.4	92.6	520,285	100	91.2	8.8	Mexico
...	...	...	...	...									Monaco
13,250	100	70.2	2.3	27.5	537	100	100.0	—	903	100	—	100.0	Mongolia
					120	100	—	100.0					Montserrat
179,888	100	50.4	17.8	31.8	361,686	100	0.3	99.7	154,457	100	56.7	43.3	Morocco
13,972	100	27.6	3.4	69.0	36,650	100	13.6	86.4	21,647	100	100.0	—	Mozambique
													Nauru
11,000	100	100.0	—	—	4,400	100	100.0	—	...	...	...	...	Nepal
2,781,525	100	25.1	20.6	54.3	505,476	100	0.9	99.1	813,771	100	69.8	30.2	Netherlands, The
6,560	100	31.7	24.2	44.1	1,800	100	—	100.0	...	...	...	...	Netherlands Antilles
5,716	100	47.3	31.4	21.3	2,061	100	—	100.0	3,610	100	56.4	43.6	New Caledonia
456,476	100	24.5	32.7	42.8	115,593	100	—	100.0	227,093	100	87.2	12.8	New Zealand
18,139	100	17.7	13.0	69.3	5,000	100	9.7	90.3	15,070	100	98.9	1.1	Nicaragua
285	100	18.2	20.4	61.4	6,840	100	100.0	—	408	100	51.0	49.0	Niger
230,602	100	0.3	27.7	72.0	511,984	100	36.8	63.2	307,130	100	76.2	23.8	Nigeria
					18	100	—	100.0					Niue
...	...	...	...	...					...	...	...	...	Norfolk Island

Extractive industries (continued)

country	mining — value of minerals produced						mining — foreign trade in minerals and concentrates						forestry, 1982 — production of roundwood				
	year	total ('000,000 national currency)	total	metals[a]	non-metals[b]	energy[c]	year	total ('000,000 U.S.$)	total	metals[d]	non-metals[b]	energy[e]	total ('000 cubic metres)	total	coniferous (softwood)	non-coniferous (hardwood)	others
Norway	1981	59,516	100	2.3	2.0	95.7	1982	15,452	100	21.4	6.2	72.4	9,315	100	92.3	7.7	—
Oman	1980	1,241[9]	100	...	...	100	1982	561	100	29.2	21.0	49.8	...	...	...	...	...
Pakistan	1982–83	387	100	0.1	18.5	78.9	1982	2,383	100	14.8	11.5	73.7	18,570	100	5.4	94.6	—
Panama	1980	6	100	...	100	...	1982	581	100	10.5	5.6	83.9	2,047	100	—	100.0	—
Papua New Guinea	1979	315	100	100.0	—	—	1976	331	100	79.6	2.4	18.0	6,910	100	1.4	98.6	—
Paraguay	1980	2,285	...	...	...	...	1979	159	100	9.7	10.4	79.9	6,792	100	—	85.6	14.4
Peru	1980	80,259	100	80.3	...	19.7	1982	2,247	100	59.6	5.2	35.2	7,769	100	—	99.2	0.8
Philippines	1980	12,820	100	76.3	23.3	0.4	1982	4,311	100	31.1	8.6	60.3	34,967	100	0.3	99.7	—
Pitcairn Island	...						...						...				
Poland	1980	121,500	100	5.4	19.4	75.2	1981	8,025	100	31.6	13.8	54.6	22,128	100	84.7	14.6	0.7
Portugal	1980	8,968	100	30.9	65.2	3.9	1982	3,809	100	17.4	14.3	68.3	7,792	100	64.9	35.1	...
Puerto Rico	1981–82	12[9]	...	...	...	...	...						...	...	...	...	...
Qatar	1980	19,245[9]	100	...	...	100.0	1981	5,537	100	4.4	3.9	91.7	...	...	...	...	...
Réunion	...	...	...	...	...	...	1982	157	100	13.7	21.6	64.7	33	100	—	100.0	—
Romania	...	...	...	...	...	...	1973	1,458	100	47.9	13.2	38.9	20,047	100	30.0	67.0	3.0
Rwanda	1980	2,980	...	...	...	...	1980	74	100	31.9	26.9	41.2	6,186	100	—	100.0	—
St. Christopher and Nevis	1978	0.3[9]	...	...	...	...	...						...	...	...	...	...
St. Helena and Ascension	...	...	...	...	...	...	...										
St. Lucia	1977	1.9[9]	...	...	...	...	1980	27	100	31.5	22.8	45.7	...	...	...	...	...
St. Pierre and Miquelon	...	...	...	...	...	...	1982	15	100	1.2	7.2	91.6					
St. Vincent and the Grenadines	1979	0.3[9]	...	...	...	...	1976	4	100	10.4	46.0	43.6	...	...	...	...	...
San Marino	...	...	...	...	...	...	...						...	...	...	...	...
São Tomé and Príncipe	...	...	...	...	...	...	...						5	100	—	100.0	—
Saudi Arabia	1983	165,180[4]	100	...	...	100.0	1982	82,995	100	3.6	2.0	94.4	...	...	...	...	...
Senegal	...	...	...	...	...	...	1981	699	100	4.5	18.6	76.9	3,806	100	—	85.3	14.7
Seychelles	1979	2	100	—	100.0	—	1982	37	100	6.3	11.9	81.8	...	...	...	...	...
Sierra Leone	1982	33[20]	...	...	...	...	1976	113	100	9.0	64.8	26.2	7,946	100	—	34.3	65.7
Singapore	1983	153[9]	100	...	...	100.0	1982	19,615	100	11.5	4.9	83.6	...	...	...	...	...
Solomon Islands	1980	82[9]	...	...	...	...	...						512	100	1.2	98.8	—
Somalia	...	...	...	...	...	...	1980	38	100	31.2	44.8	24.0	4,933	100	—	90.8	9.2
South Africa	1979	8,864[23]	100	76.8	10.3	12.9	1981[10]	6,522	100	43.7	35.8	20.5	15,961	100	30.2	69.8	—
South West Africa/Namibia	1981	443[9]	...	...	...	...	[10]	...					...	...	...	...	...
Spain	1979	131,000[24]	100	21.4	36.6	42.0	1982	20,637	100	21.4	10.8	67.8	14,098	100	65.8	34.2	—
Sri Lanka	1980	802[9]	...	...	...	...	1982	901	100	7.3	15.4	77.3	8,149	100	—	100.0	—
Sudan, The	1977	2[9]	...	...	...	...	1981	454	100	16.6	14.0	69.4	37,073	100	—	70.1	29.9
Suriname	1980	837	100	99.9	0.1	—	1974	175	100	67.5	6.4	26.1	266	100	—	93.2	6.8
Swaziland	1980	204	100	9.4	77.3	13.3	[10]	...					2,223	100	—	29.7	70.3
Sweden	1981	3,557	100	84.3	15.7	—	1982	14,527	100	32.6	11.1	56.3	50,704	100	83.8	16.2	—
Switzerland	...	...	...	...	...	...	1982	8,880	100	28.8	33.6	37.6	4,392	100	68.1	31.9	—
Syria	1980	6,120[9]	...	...	...	...	1980	3,412	100	13.5	6.4	80.1	37	100	21.6	78.4	—
Taiwan	1982	26,059	100	—	55.5	45.5	...						13	...	...	...	...
Tanzania	1980	246	100	...	100.0	...	1980	412	100	13.8	18.5	67.7	38,747	100	0.5	97.8	1.7
Thailand	1981	8,966[25]	100	100.0	—	—	1982	4,584	100	26.6	14.9	58.5	39,472	100	—	91.7	8.3
Togo	...	...	...	...	...	...	1981	202	100	6.1	74.4	19.5	724	100	—	100.0	—
Tokelau	...	...	...	...	...	...	...						...	...	...	...	...
Tonga	1980	0.2	...	...	...	...	1982	8	100	8.4	22.6	69.0	...	...	...	...	...
Trinidad and Tobago	1980	6,553[9,26]	100	...	2.0[26]	98.0	1982	4,087	100	5.3	5.5	89.2	97	100	—	87.6	12.9
Trust Territory of the Pacific Is.	...	...	...	...	...	...	...						...	...	...	...	...
Tunisia	1979	319[15]	100	2.6	16.0	81.4	1981	2,844	100	7.7	17.5	74.8	2,634	100	9.0	66.0	25.0
Turkey	1982	199,111	100	14.5	13.9	71.6	1982	5,951	100	18.3	11.2	70.5	21,883	100	64.1	35.9	—
Turks and Caicos Islands	...	...	...	...	...	...	...						...	...	...	...	...
Tuvalu	...	...	...	...	...	...	1981	1	100	2.1	15.2	82.7	...	...	...	...	...
Uganda	1976	43	...	...	...	...	1976	64	100	17.4	5.5	77.1	25,441	100	0.1	97.3	2.6
U.S.S.R.	1980	31,700	100	—36.6—		63.4	1980	45,663	100	29.3	6.1	64.6	358,200	100	83.4	16.6	—
United Arab Emirates	1980	70,767[9]	100	...	...	100.0	...						...	...	...	...	...
United Kingdom	1981	18,837	100	0.1	4.2	95.6	1982	52,831	100	22.2	16.1	61.7	4,701	100	74.1	25.0	0.9
United States	1982	179,457	100	3.9	7.9	88.2	1982	122,978	100	20.7	14.0	65.3	393,896	100	62.5	37.5	—
Uruguay	1980	1,450[9]	...	...	...	...	1981	678	100	10.9	11.1	78.0	1,678	100	3.0	65.2	31.8
Vanuatu	1980	8[4]	100	100.0	—	—	1982	9	100	9.6	13.5	76.9	33	100	6.0	94.0	—
Venezuela	1980	67,726	100	—2.8—		89.4	1981	18,497	100	9.6	2.0	88.4	1,678	100	100.0	—	—
Vietnam	...	...	...	...	...	...	...						23,191	100	—	99.5	0.5
Virgin Islands (U.S.)	...	...	...	...	...	...	1978	2,696	100	0.2	0.3	99.5	...	...	...	...	...
Wallis and Futuna	...	...	...	...	...	...	...						...	...	...	...	...
Western Sahara	...	...	...	...	...	...	...						...	...	...	...	...
Western Samoa	...	...	...	...	...	...	1981	16	100	9.7	14.1	76.2	131	...	...	...	...
Yemen (Aden)	...	...	...	...	...	...	...						264	100	—	—	100.0
Yemen (Şan'ā')	1979	149[9]	...	...	...	...	1980	348	100	34.9	26.8	38.3	...	...	...	...	...
Yugoslavia	1980	74,800	100	28.9	21.0	50.1	1982	6,697	100	30.4	12.4	57.2	14,583	100	32.6	67.4	—
Zaire	...	...	...	...	...	...	1978	665	100	79.9	9.2	10.9	30,391	100	—	100.0	—
Zambia	1980	1,137	100	98.5	1.5	—	1979	1,417	100	85.7	3.6	10.7	5,707	100	0.2	72.2	27.6
Zimbabwe	1982	383	100	65.5	25.1	9.4	1982	635	100	43.5	16.8	39.7	8,679	100	5.8	94.2	—

foreign trade in forest products					fishing, 1982				foreign trade in fish				country
					nominal catches (fish, crusta., mollusks, etc.)				foreign trade in fish				
total ('000 U.S.$)	by category (percent)				total (metric tons)	by location (percent)			total ('000 U.S.$)	by category (percent)			
	total	roundwood, sawnwood, and sleepers[f]	wood pulp, wood-based panels[g]	paper and paper-board[h]		total	inland waters	marine areas		total	fish, crustaceans, mollusks[i]	other[j]	
1,183,409	100	19.9	28.7	51.4	2,499,916	100	0.6	99.4	936,795	100	67.7	32.3	Norway
49,632	100	46.3	38.6	15.1	89,376	100	—	100.0	13,225	100	94.9	5.1	Oman
83,539	100	17.6	13.1	69.3	337,289	100	17.5	82.5	79,356	100	95.5	4.5	Pakistan
35,271	100	8.0	5.6	86.4	91,144	100	—	100.0	73,690	100	85.2	14.8	Panama
83,699	100	95.2	4.8		26,932	100	—	100.0	59,400	100	60.6	39.4	Papua New Guinea
45,911	100	57.9	22.7	19.4	2,700	100	100.0	—	...	...	...	...	Paraguay
62,513	100	9.5	27.3	63.2	3,451,955	100	0.4	99.6	289,413	100	5.2	94.8	Peru
453,616	100	64.7	21.7	13.6	1,787,744	100	29.6	70.4	159,487	100	35.4	64.6	Philippines
...	...	...	...	...									Pitcairn Island
697,515	100	41.1	34.1	24.8	604,896	100	3.8	96.2	151,753	100	84.5	15.5	Poland
569,639	100	36.3	42.9	20.8	253,379	100	—	100.0	261,960	100	72.6	27.4	Portugal
					2,202	100	—	100.0	...	...	...	...	Puerto Rico
2,505	100	6.4	9.8	83.8	2,333	100	—	100.0	1,356	100	67.3	32.7	Qatar
21,862	100	72.6	5.3	22.1	2,983	100	—	100.0	13,767	100	72.1	27.9	Réunion
516,810	100	50.6	25.2	24.2	235,653	100	25.2	74.8	28,700[14]	100[14]	39.7[14]	60.3[14]	Romania
400	100	—	100.0		1,210	100	100.0	—	190	100	—	100.0	Rwanda
...	...	...	...	...	1,880	100	—	100.0	610	100	80.3	19.7	St. Christopher and Nevis
...	...	...	...	...	453	100	—	100.0	53	100	100.0		St. Helena and Ascension
...	...	...	...	...	2,404	100	—	100.0	752	100	65.4	34.6	St. Lucia
...	...	...	...	...	8,713	100	—	100.0	5,854	100	94.0	6.0	St. Pierre and Miquelon
...	...	...	...	...	547	100	—	100.0	630	100	61.9	38.1	St. Vincent and the Grenadines
													San Marino
...	...	...	...	...	2,688	100	...	100.0	80	100	—	100.0	São Tomé and Principe
765,996	100	51.8	34.2	14.0	26,425	100	—	100.0	99,093	100	53.6	46.4	Saudi Arabia
27,750	100	28.2	15.8	56.0	212,895	100	—	100.0	158,881	100	73.4	26.6	Senegal
...	...	...	...	...	4,100	100	—	100.0	1,200	100	97.2	2.8	Seychelles
1,130	100	36.5	49.7	13.8	65,548	100	30.6	69.4	4,141	100	100.0	—	Sierra Leone
973,738	100	44.8	32.0	23.2	19,346	100	2.7	97.3	323,295	100	74.8	25.2	Singapore
18,279	100	96.8	3.2	—	33,418	100	—	100.0	14,943	100	79.0	21.0	Solomon Islands
5,505	100	42.0	0.8	57.2	6,580	100	—	100.0	1,040	100	80.8	19.2	Somalia
541,852	100	16.1	43.7	40.2	624,331	100	0.1	99.9	146,130	100	74.7	25.3	South Africa
					201,840	100	—	100.0	...	...	...	...	South West Africa/Namibia
1,061,134	100	27.7	27.2	45.1	1,351,025	100	2.1	97.9	818,825	100	87.3	16.3	Spain
31,226	100	2.3	14.7	83.0	211,300	100	14.2	85.8	37,617	100	77.8	22.2	Sri Lanka
17,499	100	51.7	13.0	35.3	29,710	100	96.5	3.5	910	100	35.2	64.8	Sudan, The
24,770	100	24.6	21.8	53.6	6,377	100	1.1	98.9	24,100	100	92.3	7.7	Suriname
71,759	100	23.5	76.5	—	44	100	100.0	—	...	...	...	...	Swaziland
5,084,565	100	26.1	24.7	49.2	258,980	100	3.9	96.1	350,565	100	56.2	43.8	Sweden
979,830	100	21.9	27.3	50.8	3,859	100	100.0	—	197,125	100	47.3	52.7	Switzerland
147,418	100	61.3	14.7	24.0	3,777	100	75.6	24.4	10,900	100	22.9	77.1	Syria
13					13				13				Taiwan
18,133	100	6.1	0.7	93.2	226,000	100	84.1	15.9	767	100	48.5	51.5	Tanzania
257,402	100	31.6	21.8	46.6	1,920,000	100	8.9	91.1	492,498	100	62.9	37.1	Thailand
483	100	18.8	5.2	76.0	14,530	100	24.1	75.9	4,200	100	72.4	27.6	Togo
...	...	...	...	...	—	...	...	...	...	...	...	...	Tokelau
					1,993	100	—	100.0	651	100	2.8	97.2	Tonga
99,623	100	41.9	15.2	42.9	4,461	100	—	100.0	12,155	100	64.6	35.4	Trinidad and Tobago
					5,462	100	—	100.0	807	100	84.3	15.7	Trust Territory of the Pacific Is.
75,185	100	59.6	12.4	28.0	62,752	100	—	100.0	25,419	100	97.3	2.7	Tunisia
144,233	100	17.1	29.7	53.2	514,934	100	5.1	94.9	45,518	100	49.5	50.5	Turkey
...	...	...	...	...	1,050	100	—	100.0	1,398	100	100.0	—	Turks and Caicos Islands
					200	100	—	100.0	...	...	...	...	Tuvalu
3,537	100	2.0	6.7	913	166,590	100	100.0	—	...	...	...	...	Uganda
3,458,479	100	48.4	21.7	29.9	9,956,749	100	9.1	91.9	288,679	100	62.3	37.7	U.S.S.R.
					70,075	100	—	100.0					United Arab Emirates
5,964,861	100	23.2	24.1	52.7	910,079	100	—	100.0	1,173,767	100	56.2	43.8	United Kingdom
13,802,741	100	29.7	26.4	43.9	3,988,307	100	1.8	98.2	4,209,006	100	85.0	15.0	United States
38,944	100	22.9	12.7	64.4	119,298	100	0.2	99.8	48,628	100	96.7	3.3	Uruguay
1,111	100	80.2	19.8	—	2,715	100	—	100.0	14,667	100	94.3	5.7	Vanuatu
223,673	100	17.6	28.3	54.1	213,391	100	7.0	93.0	36,231	100	42.2	57.8	Venezuela
8,669	100	68.4	1.6	30.0	1,000,000	100	20.0	80.0	45,235	100	100.0	—	Vietnam
...	...	...	...	...	634	100	—	100.0	...	...	...	...	Virgin Islands (U.S.)
...	...	...	...	...	—	...	...	...	...	...	...	...	Wallis and Futuna
...	...	...	...	...									Western Sahara
					4,020	100	—	100.0	1,211	100		100.0	Western Samoa
11,629	100	70.9	13.4	15.7	69,731	100	—	100.0	5,300	100	100.0	—	Yemen (Aden)
					22,000	100	—	100.0	5,120	100	1.6	98.4	Yemen (Ṣanʿāʾ)
760,468	100	50.2	28.3	21.5	66,841	100	39.4	60.6	103,666	100	32.6	67.4	Yugoslavia
23,244	100	44.4	33.8	21.8	100,700	100	99.3	0.7	30,500	100	32.1	67.9	Zaire
21,258	100	9.1	10.4	80.5	55,809	100	100.0	—	1,720	100	61.0	39.0	Zambia
34,757	100	26.9	24.3	48.8	18,106	100	100.0	—	1,949	100	74.6	25.4	Zimbabwe

[1]Value of sales only. [2]Diamonds, petroleum, salt, and iron ore only. [3]Prices of 1970. [4]Export value (only). [5]Includes manufacturing. [6]Exports of mineral fuels. [7]Limestone, natural gas, and china clay only. [8]Belgium includes Luxembourg. [9]Value added to gross domestic product (GDP). [10]South Africa includes Botswana, Lesotho, South West Africa/Namibia, and Swaziland. [11]Excludes energy. [12]Salt only. [13]China includes Taiwan. [14]Imports only. [15]Producers' prices. [16]Mineral fuels and lubricants only. [17]Excludes natural gas and oil. [18]Net of turnover taxes. [19]Natural gas only. [20]Diamonds, iron, and gold only. [21]Coal and coke only. [22]Coal only. [23]Sales of minerals only. [24]Excludes subsidies. [25]Tin, antimony, tungsten, and fluorite only. [26]Includes agricultural chemicals. [27]Includes coal.

Manufacturing industries

This table summarizes the activity of the manufacturing sectors of the countries of the world, providing figures for value added, number of establishments, and the distribution of value added by size of establishment (as reckoned by number of employees). The data are organized to show the relative importance of six principal sectors for each country and the concentration of activity within each sector. Although the principal intent was to provide data on the manufacturing sectors of each country individually, the data may also be compared from country to country. Here, however, some caution is advised, as some countries do not classify manufacturing activity according to the scheme outlined in the International Standard Industrial Classification (ISIC) or in accord with the UN statistical paper *International Recommendations for Industrial Statistics*, rev. 1 (1983), the principal bases for the classification of data used in this table. Similarly, they may not define "business enterprise," "establishment," or "employee" in the same way. In addition, each country may use different classes in categorizing establishments—those employing more than 10 employees, say, or more than 50—skewing the reported distribution by size of establishment.

The sectors for which data have been provided include: food, beverages, and tobacco; textiles, apparel, and leather; chemicals and related products; primary and fabricated metals, and processed minerals; machinery (except electrical) and transport equipment; electrical and electronic machinery. For each of these sectors (for which ISIC definitions are provided below), data are given for value added (or, occasionally, some other measure of value, when value added was not reported), for the number of establishments with fewer than and more than 100 employees (though it sometimes proved impossible to identify the actual distribution in a particular national survey because of its summarization in a national or international source), and, where it was known, for the proportion of the sectoral value added represented by these two groups of establishments.

The collection and publication of national manufacturing data is usually carried out by one of three methods: a full census of manufacturing (usually done every five to ten years for a given country), a periodic survey of manufacturing (usually taken at regular intervals between censuses), and the onetime sample survey (often limited in geographical, sectoral, or size-of-enterprise coverage). The full census is, naturally, the most complete, but since up to ten years may elapse between such censuses, it has often been necessary to substitute a survey of more recent date, but less complete coverage, in order to provide more timely data. For each country the initial date indicates the year of the survey.

The value added in local currency is provided for each sector so that the relative importance of that sector in a country's overall national manufacturing activity may be seen. For each sector, the value added is broken down by size of enterprise wherever possible. No effort was made here to compare these values internationally in a single currency because of inherent uncertainties with respect to accounting methods, purchasing power, national price structures and preferments, exchange rates, and so on. Such value models are maintained, however, by the United Nations Industrial Development Organization (UNIDO), and these indicate that of the aggregate world manufacturing value added in the early 1980s, a declining 64 percent was represented by the developed non-Communist countries, a growing 25 percent by the centrally-planned economies, and 11 percent by the developing countries.

The figures for numbers of establishments generally refer to each separate physical facility, regardless of the number of separately incorporated legal entities (companies, partnerships, parastatal organizations), any of

Manufacturing industries

country	year	food, beverages, and tobacco					textiles, apparel, and leather					chemicals and related products				
		value added ('000,000 local currency)	enterprises				value added ('000,000 local currency)	enterprises				value added ('000,000 local currency)	enterprises			
			1–99 employees		100 or more emp.			1–99 employees		100 or more emp.			1–99 employees		100 or more emp.	
			number	percent of value added	number	percent of value added		number	percent of value added	number	percent of value added		number	percent of value added	number	percent of value added
Afghanistan[1]	1981	3,922.0	...	...	62	...	3,291.0	...	...	63	...	2,852.0[2]	...	...	86[2]	...
Albania	...	...	...	...	...	...	...	...	...	...	...	...	...	...	...	...
Algeria[3,4]	1978	2,797.0	535	...	...	...	2,293.0	752	...	...	...	1,644.0	433	...	...	...
American Samoa	...	...	...	...	...	...	...	...	...	...	...	...	...	...	...	...
Andorra	1972	...	142	...	...	...	...	104	...	...	...	...	49	...	...	...
Angola	1973	7,585.7	...	...	...	...	1,038.4	...	...	...	...	4,226.4	...	...	...	...
Anguilla	...	...	...	...	...	...	...	...	...	...	...	...	...	...	—	—
Antigua and Barbuda	1980	...	14	100.0	...	...	...	12	100.0	...	...	5,319.0	15	100.0	...	...
Argentina[6]	1981	5,359.0	1,188	...	92	...	2,460.0	1,059	...	75	...	5,319.0	1,394	...	101	...
Australia[8,9,10]	1980	5,023.5	3,889	31.6	460	68.3	2,609.6	4,071	43.8	363	56.1	5,429.7	10,412	24.6	610	75.3
Austria[10]	1982	3,165.0	775	22.8	154	77.2	1,826.0	1,293	31.3	311	68.7	4,712.0	1,646	27.2	330	72.8
Bahamas, The	1978	8.2	...	...	...	...	0.1	...	...	...	...	17.2	...	...	...	...
Bahrain	...	...	...	...	...	...	...	...	...	...	...	...	...	...	...	...
Bangladesh[11]	1979	2,542.0	440	...	...	...	3,689.0	...	...	1,160	...	1,995.0	605	...	...	...
Barbados[12]	1979	33.2[13]	38[13]	...	...	...	17.6	...	...	22	...	14.4	50	...	...	...
Belgium[8]	1980	137,400.0	7,056	...	...	...	101,300.0[14]	4,253[14]	...	...	...	190,000.0[15]	6,403[15]	...	...	...
Belize	...	...	...	...	...	...	...	...	...	...	...	...	...	...	...	...
Benin	1978	6,148.0	...	...	...	...	1,233.0	...	...	...	...	1,206.0	...	...	...	...
Bermuda	...	...	...	...	...	...	...	...	...	...	...	...	...	...	...	...
Bhutan	1980	...	...	...	...	...	...	...	...	...	...	...	...	...	...	...
Bolivia[3]	1979	8,068.0	637	...	...	...	2,179.0	454	...	...	...	4,606.0	703	...	...	...
Botswana	1979	...	22	...	...	...	...	16	...	...	...	...	11	...	...	...
Brazil[9,12,18]	1978	147,100.0	18,806	26.3	940	58.5	116,000.0	6,769	27.4	1,302	52.8	310,000.0	16,585	37.3	1,486	50.5
British Virgin Islands	1978	—	1	100.0	—	—	—	—	—	—	—	—	2	100.0	—	—
Brunei[19]	1980	...	29	100.0	...	...	...	76	100.0	...	...	...	60	100.0	...	...
Bulgaria[20]	1981	2,120.8	...	...	277	...	1,325.5	...	...	210	...	530.2	...	...	241	...
Burkina Faso	1978	19,739.0	1	...	2	...	1,868.0	1	...	3	...	5,688.0	...	...	...	...
Burma	...	...	...	...	...	...	...	...	...	...	...	...	...	...	...	...
Burundi	...	...	...	...	...	...	...	...	...	...	...	...	...	...	...	...
Cameroon[12]	1978	29,724.0	30	...	...	...	8,280.0	14	...	...	...	7,658.0	38	...	...	...
Canada[9]	1981	10,196.2	3,962	27.0	557	62.9	5,379.5	3,270[21]	35.9[21]	601	63.7	26,484.3	12,373[21]	28.5[21]	1,124	71.5
Cape Verde	...	...	...	—	—	...	...	...	—	—	...	...	...	...	...	...
Cayman Islands	...	...	...	—	—	...	...	...	—	—	...	...	...	—	—	...
Central African Republic	1978	5,024.0	52	...	...	...	1,109.0	7	...	...	...	630.0	7	...	...	...
Chad	1975	7,420.0	...	...	...	...	6,570.0	...	...	...	...	650.0	...	...	...	...
Chile[12,22]	1979	47,446.0	6,860	...	160	...	17,319.0	4,549	...	93	...	52,760.0	5,959	...	175	...
China	1981[1]	64,023.0	55,627	...	...	...	86,825.0	...	...	17,068	...	49,134.0	41,816	...	...	...
Christmas Island	...	...	...	...	...	...	...	...	...	...	...	...	...	—	—	...
Cocos (Keeling) Islands	...	...	...	...	...	...	...	...	...	...	...	...	...	—	—	...
Colombia[12,20]	1981	124,680.2	1,374	...	...	...	59,324.2	1,663	...	...	...	130,989.3	1,648	...	...	...
Comoros	...	...	...	...	...	...	...	...	...	...	...	...	...	...	...	...
Congo[8]	1971	5,008.0	...	...	19	...	383.0[23]	34[23]	...	...	...	1,568.0	...	...	13	...
Cook Islands[24]	1978	0.9	15	...	2	...	—	—	...	—	—	...	...	...	...	...
Costa Rica[12,25]	1980	2,705.0	...	...	44	...	572.0	...	...	50	...	1,563.0	119	...	...	...
Cuba[26]	1980	2,108.2	...	...	...	...	937.0	...	...	...	...	995.5	...	...	...	...
Cyprus	1981[27]	32.9	634	...	...	...	42.9	1,897	...	...	...	29.9	1,284	...	...	...
Czechoslovakia	1981	16,080.0	...	...	118	...	22,160.0	...	...	86	...	36,430.0	...	...	138	...
Denmark	1981[8]	18,070.0	921	...	...	...	3,980.0	729	...	...	...	19,430.0	2,058	...	...	...
Djibouti	...	...	...	...	...	...	...	...	...	...	...	...	...	...	...	...
Dominica	...	...	...	...	...	...	...	...	...	...	...	...	...	...	...	...
Dominican Republic[12,28]	1980	663.5	...	...	597	...	65.7	307	...	...	...	200.1	333	...	...	...
Ecuador[12]	1979	11,014.0	614	...	...	...	3,452.0	462	...	...	...	9,054.0	681	...	...	...
Egypt[12]	1976	110.3	2,072	...	...	...	218.1	1,189	...	...	...	160.9	...	...	584	...
El Salvador[12]	1978	354.0	260	...	...	...	301.0	282	...	...	...	384.0	290	...	...	...
Equatorial Guinea	...	...	...	...	...	...	...	...	...	...	...	...	...	...	...	...

which may operate more than one facility. It was often impossible to establish from the published source material what the actual distribution of establishments by size was. A single total for a particular sector was often the only datum available. In such instances, the *average* size of these establishments was calculated (since the total number of employees in the sector was known), and the figure for number of establishments was placed in the table above or below the 100-employee cutoff accordingly. Such figures are given in italics. In the case of Algeria, for example, there were 752 establishments in the textile/apparel sector, and it would be reasonable to assume that at least one had more than 100 employees. Since the average establishment had fewer than 100 employees, however, Algeria's textile sector is shown entirely in that range.

One impediment to international comparability in terms of size of establishment is the size limit the country itself establishes as the minimum reporting unit for such surveys. For a small country it may be both feasible and desirable to survey all establishments, however small, on the grounds that they are few enough to constitute a manageable body of data for analysis, and also that if the country's manufacturers are mostly small operations, then it is precisely this group on which national planners need the most information. For larger countries, the cost to collect and analyze data for all establishments may be prohibitively high, and, moreover, interest from a development point of view may be exclusively in middle and large-scale industry, that needed to permit replacement of imported goods with domestic manufactures. In such a case the country may survey only those establishments with 50 employees or more. Thus, when the distributions of number of establishments are examined, it should be noted (and has been footnoted wherever possible) when such limits in coverage may be applicable.

In terms of the industrial groups implied by the names of the manufacturing sectors used here, the content of each sector is usually defined by the two- or three-digit level of classification in the ISIC system:

group	EB category	ISIC code (-s)	remarks
1.	Food, beverages, and tobacco	31	
2.	Textiles, apparel, and leather	32	
3.	Chemicals and related products	33	wood and furniture
		34	paper and products; printing and publishing
		35	industrial chemicals, pharmaceuticals, petroleum and products, rubber, plastics
4.	Primary and fabricated metals and processed minerals	36	pottery, china, glass
		37	iron and steel; nonferrous metals
5.	Machinery (except electrical) and transport equipment	382 + 384 minus 3825	machinery and transport equipment minus office equipment and computers
6.	Electrical and electronic machinery	383 + 3825	electrical and electronic equipment, plus office equipment and computers

It should be noted that these groups do not account for ISIC groups 385 and 390 (professional goods, and other industries, respectively).

Table columns — for each of the three sectors: **value added ('000,000 local currency)**; **enterprises** with *1–99 employees* (number; percent value of added) and *100 or more emp.* (number; percent of value added). Sectors are: **primary and fabricated metals; processed minerals**, **machinery (except elec.) and transport equipment**, **electrical and electronic machinery**.

VA (metals)	1–99 no.	1–99 %	100+ no.	100+ %	VA (mach.)	1–99 no.	1–99 %	100+ no.	100+ %	VA (elec.)	1–99 no.	1–99 %	100+ no.	100+ %	country
2	...	...	2	...	2	...	...	2	...	2	...	...	2	...	Afghanistan
...	...	...	...	...	...	...	...	...	...	...	...	...	...	...	Albania
3,870.0[5]	337[5]	...	...	...	5	5	...	...	...	5	5	...	5	...	Algeria
...	38	...	...	...	...	25	...	...	...	...	83	...	...	...	Andorra
1,644.5	...	...	...	...	453.9	...	...	...	...	169.2	...	...	...	...	Angola
...	...	...	...	...	...	...	...	...	...	...	...	...	...	...	Anguilla
2,697.0	206	...	21	—	8,809.0[7]	—	—	—	—	7	—	—	—	—	Antigua and Barbuda
5,682.0	2,245	21.0	323	78.9	6,420.8	12,484[7]	72.4[7]	866[7]	25.1[7]	1,707.0	7	7	7	7	Australia
5,093.0	692	16.0	176	84.0	2,965.0	1,460[7]	18.5[7]	461[7]	81.5[7]	1,879.0	7	7	7	7	Austria
3.3	...	...	...	...	0.2	...	...	...	...	—	—	—	—	—	Bahamas, The
...	...	...	...	...	...	...	...	...	...	...	...	...	...	...	Bahrain
1,496.0	332	...	...	...	300.0	...	...	89	...	293.0	83	...	...	...	Bangladesh
7.3	25	...	...	...	15.6[7]	...	...	16[7]	...	7	7	...	7	...	Barbados
86,300.0	5,089	...	...	...	261,500.0[7,16]	...	...	1,999[7,16]	...	7	...	...	7	...	Belgium
...	...	...	...	...	...	...	...	...	...	...	...	...	...	...	Belize
498.0	...	...	...	...	1,217.0[7]	...	...	...	...	7	...	...	...	...	Benin
...	...	...	...	...	...	...	...	...	...	...	...	...	...	...	Bermuda
...	...	...	...	...	—	—	—	—	—	—	—	—	—	—	Bhutan
7,787.0	295	...	...	...	398.0	78	...	...	...	93.0	17	...	...	...	Bolivia
...	39[17]	...	...	...	...	17	...	...	...	...	17	...	...	...	Botswana
190,300.0	9,308	23.5	1,109	76.5	189,900.0	7,765[7]	14.0[7]	1,514[7]	50.2[7]	70,000.0	7	7	7	7	Brazil
...	4	100.0	—	—	...	17	17	...	...	...	...	...	...	...	British Virgin Islands
...	70[17]	100.0[17]	—	...	...	17	17	...	...	...	17	17	—	—	Brunei
4,860.6[17]	...	...	240	...	17	...	...	363	...	17	...	...	119	...	Bulgaria
3,454.0[17]	...	...	...	...	17	...	...	...	...	17	...	...	...	...	Burkina Faso
...	...	...	...	...	...	...	...	...	...	...	...	...	...	...	Burma
...	...	...	...	...	...	...	...	...	...	...	...	...	...	...	Burundi
7,186.0	10	...	...	...	2,815.0	12	...	...	...	2,460.0	5	...	...	...	Cameroon
14,104.6	6,474	27.6	622	72.3	13,449.1	5,241	28.7	565	69.0	4,643.9	859	14.5	262	85.4	Canada
...	...	...	...	...	...	...	...	...	...	...	...	...	...	...	Cape Verde
...	...	...	...	...	...	...	...	...	...	...	...	...	...	...	Cayman Islands
193.0[17]	6[17]	...	...	...	17	17	...	...	...	17	17	...	...	...	Central African Republic
940.0	...	...	...	...	...	...	...	...	...	...	...	...	...	...	Chad
47,618.0	3,173	...	100	...	9,553.0	1,577	...	49	...	4,521.0	117	...	20	...	Chile
61,158.0	...	...	49,929	...	122,617.0[7]	104,112[7]	...	...	...	7	7	...	...	...	China
—	—	—	—	—	—	—	—	—	—	—	—	—	—	—	Christmas Island
—	—	—	—	—	—	—	—	—	—	—	—	—	—	—	Cocos (Keeling) Islands
51,200.2	1,154	...	...	...	29,052.1	555	...	...	...	13,900.7	222	...	...	...	Colombia
23	23	...	...	...	23	23	...	...	...	23	23	...	—	...	Comoros
...	—	...	...	...	—	—	...	...	...	—	...	...	—	...	Congo
—	—	...	...	...	—	—	...	...	...	—	—	...	...	...	Cook Islands
389.0	42	...	...	...	280.0	14	...	...	...	152.0	19	...	...	...	Costa Rica
1,815.4	...	...	...	...	...	...	...	...	...	...	...	...	...	...	Cuba
24.6	666	...	...	...	21.5	183	...	...	...	3.6	18	...	...	...	Cyprus
41,390.0	...	...	151	...	61,510.0	...	...	209	...	11,210.0	7	...	47	...	Czechoslovakia
9,720.0	1,185	...	...	...	13,790.0	1,079	...	...	...	4,130.0	247	...	...	...	Denmark
...	...	...	...	...	...	...	...	...	...	—	—	—	—	—	Djibouti
...	...	...	...	...	...	...	...	...	...	...	...	...	...	...	Dominica
35.0	106	...	...	...	6.5[7]	...	...	4	...	7	11	...	...	...	Dominican Republic
4,421.0	332	...	...	...	677.0	69	...	...	...	1,786.0	63	...	...	...	Ecuador
102.7	...	...	838	...	67.9	...	...	128	...	29.7	...	...	45	...	Egypt
125.0	194	...	...	...	29.0	40	...	...	...	43.0	19	...	...	...	El Salvador
...	...	...	...	...	...	...	...	...	...	...	...	...	...	...	Equatorial Guinea

Manufacturing industries (continued)

country	year	food, beverages, and tobacco value added ('000,000 local currency)	enterprises 1–99 employees number	percent of value added	100 or more emp. number	percent of value added	textiles, apparel, and leather value added ('000,000 local currency)	enterprises 1–99 employees number	percent of value added	100 or more emp. number	percent of value added	chemicals and related products value added ('000,000 local currency)	enterprises 1–99 employees number	percent of value added	100 or more emp. number	percent of value added
Ethiopia[12]	1981	488.2	...	...	153	...	251.7	...	...	77	...	37.4	...	...	127	...
Faeroe Islands	...	...	...	...	...	...	...	...	...	...	...	...	...	...	...	...
Falkland Islands	...	...	...	...	...	...	...	...	...	...	...	...	...	...	...	...
Fiji[8, 19]	1980	65.7	62	...	11	...	1.9	78	...	2	...	22.2	136	...	7	...
Finland	1981	6,239.0	1,007	...	141	...	4,315.0	752	...	186	...	23,452.0	2,015	...	432	...
France	1981	135,700.0	...	...	...	...	57,200.0	...	...	...	...	184,100.0	...	...	...	...
French Guiana	...	...	...	...	...	...	...	...	...	...	...	...	...	...	...	...
French Polynesia	...	...	...	...	...	...	...	...	...	...	...	...	...	...	...	...
Gabon	1978	6,908	145	...	...	...	1,108.0	1,482[29]	...	...	...	16,599.0	64	...	...	...
Gambia, The[12, 30]	1978	6.9	25	...	2	...	0.03	14	100.0	—	—	...	...	...	...	...
Germany, East[1]	1981	49,500.0	...	...	600	...	143,300.0[31]	...	...	1,861[31]	...	31	...	...	31	...
Germany, West	1981	57,200.0	3,551	...	1,218	...	27,110.0	5,896	...	2,078	...	122,700.0	8,989	...	2,330	...
Ghana[10, 12]	1977	485.5	24	3.6	30	96.4	161.8	56	12.8	22	87.2	435.0	90	16.0	56	84.0
Gibraltar	...	...	...	...	...	...	...	...	...	...	...	...	...	...	...	...
Greece[12]	1981	67,740.0	21,202	...	143	...	88,080.0	30,491	...	254	...	79,910.0	29,689	...	148	...
Greenland	...	...	...	...	...	...	...	...	...	...	...	...	...	...	...	...
Grenada	...	...	...	...	...	...	...	...	...	...	...	...	...	...	...	...
Guadeloupe	...	...	...	...	...	...	...	...	...	...	...	...	...	...	...	...
Guam	1982	...	...	...	...	...	...	...	...	...	...	...	...	...	...	...
Guatemala[12]	1978	298.0	626	...	...	...	77.0	436	...	...	...	253.0	671	...	...	...
Guinea	...	...	...	...	...	...	...	...	...	...	...	...	...	...	...	...
Guinea-Bissau	...	...	...	...	...	...	...	...	...	...	...	...	...	...	...	...
Guyana	1979	...	31	...	...	...	...	8	...	...	...	...	20	...	...	...
Haiti[12]	1979	192.0	471	...	...	...	114.0	155	...	...	...	61.9[33]	107	...	...	...
Honduras	1975	125.8	233	...	...	...	53.4	422	...	...	...	40.5	154	...	...	...
Hong Kong[10, 12]	1980	1,695.0	906	37.8	28	62.2	14,263.9	8,225	27.5	644	72.5	6,040.0	7,199	61.2	206	38.8
Hungary[10]	1980	21,630.0	1,977	11.5	194	88.5	21,950.0	14,483	4.8	258	95.2	41,430.0	5,229	4.2	225	95.8
Iceland[8]	1978	8,637.0	174	...	...	...	9,036	244	...	...	...	22,108.0	805	...	...	...
India[8]	1980	25,380.0	24,550	...	...	...	46,840.0	13,538	...	...	...	44,970.0	15,920	...	...	...
Indonesia[8]	1980	674,700.0	...	...	2,489	...	292,200.0	...	...	2,188	...	577,400.0	...	...	1,820	...
Iran[12]	1980	83,820.0	...	...	683	...	108,940.0	...	...	1,143	...	185,880.0	...	...	825	...
Iraq	1977	71.0	5,074	...	...	...	71.3	10,959	...	...	...	110.0	6,266	...	...	...
Ireland[8]	1978	638.2	857	...	...	...	193.3	601	...	...	...	499.8	992	...	...	...
Israel[10, 12]	1979	17,374.0	711	38.9	74	61.1	15,837.0	1,470	62.3	32	37.7	37,195.0	1,555	48.4	70	51.6
Italy[24, 34]	1980	7,144.0	4,894	...	522	...	10,385.0	157,329	...	1,777	...	20,199.0	133,028	...	1,353	...
Ivory Coast	1979	76,299.0	254	...	...	...	32,149.0	80	...	...	...	68,733.0	284	...	...	...
Jamaica[8, 35]	1980	330.9	308	...	...	...	49.4	157	...	...	...	225.7	332	...	...	...
Japan[10, 34]	1981	7,329.0[6]	86,121	47.7	1,717	52.3	7,039.0	171,049	59.4	2,275	40.6	20,282.0	170,151	50.2	3,346	49.8
Jordan[12]	1980	28.0	551	...	...	...	8.3	481	...	...	...	36.5	872	...	...	...
Kampuchea	...	...	...	...	...	...	...	...	...	...	...	...	...	...	...	...
Kenya[8, 37]	1980	126.6	...	...	103	...	29.5	...	...	77	...	71.7	...	...	152	...
Kiribati	...	...	...	...	...	...	...	...	...	...	...	...	...	...	...	...
Korea, North	...	...	...	...	...	...	...	...	...	...	...	...	...	...	...	...
Korea, South[10, 34]	1980	2,049.8	31,884	23.6	206	76.4	1,615.6	26,525	19.9	721	80.1	2,895.5	11,619	23.2	352	76.8
Kuwait[12]	1978	18.8	366	...	...	...	15.7	1,635	...	...	...	188.1	622	...	...	...
Laos	...	...	...	...	...	...	...	...	...	...	...	...	...	...	...	...
Lebanon	...	...	...	...	...	...	...	...	...	...	...	...	...	...	...	...
Lesotho	...	...	...	...	...	...	...	...	...	...	...	...	...	...	...	...
Liberia	1973	10.6	...	...	...	...	1.6	...	...	...	...	15.0	...	...	...	...
Libya[38]	1977	25.3	102	...	...	...	6.1	27	...	...	...	69.3	51	...	...	...
Liechtenstein	1975	...	43	...	1	...	...	22	...	2	...	...	69	...	2	...
Luxembourg[8]	1979	2,080.0	33	...	...	...	992.0	11	...	...	...	5,966.0	...	...	39	...
Macau[12]	1980	8.7	113	...	...	...	531.2	518	...	...	...	45.2	279	...	...	...
Madagascar	1978	10,837.0	...	...	158	...	15,317.0	...	...	55	...	6,195.0	119	...	...	...
Malawi	1979	18.6	35	...	...	...	4.9	19	...	...	...	22.1[2]	31	...	...	...
Malaysia[8]	1979	1,833.6	1,255	...	...	...	498.6	489	...	...	...	2,524.7	2,412	...	...	...
Maldives	...	...	...	...	...	...	...	...	...	...	...	...	...	...	...	...
Mali	1976	9,800.0	...	...	...	...	16,000.0	...	...	...	...	5,700.0[2]	...	...	...	...
Malta[12]	1980	16.5	393	...	...	...	40.5	242	...	...	...	21.2	606	...	...	...
Martinique	...	...	...	...	...	...	...	...	...	...	...	...	...	...	...	...
Mauritania	...	...	...	...	...	...	...	...	...	...	...	...	...	...	...	...
Mauritius[12]	1981	577.0	174	...	...	...	397.0	...	...	130	...	160.0	118	...	...	...
Mayotte	...	...	...	...	...	...	...	...	...	...	...	...	...	...	...	...
Mexico[19]	1980	237,200.0	...	...	473	...	129,000.0	...	...	135	...	277,100.0	...	...	428	...
Monaco	...	...	...	...	...	...	...	...	...	...	...	...	...	...	...	...
Mongolia	1980	53.8	...	...	...	...	311.8	...	...	...	...	313.0	...	...	...	...
Montserrat	...	...	...	...	...	...	...	...	...	...	...	...	...	...	...	...
Morocco	1980	2,744.8	...	...	...	...	1,274.8	...	...	...	...	1,597.6	...	...	...	...
Mozambique	1972	5,991.8	769	...	93	...	1,854.1	5	...	62	...	2,668.1	194	...	110	...
Nauru	...	...	...	...	...	...	...	...	...	...	...	...	...	...	...	...
Nepal	1977	3,372.1	2,770	...	35	...	74.3	109	...	10	...	154.3	339	...	12	...
Netherlands, The[8, 10]	1979	10,450.0	1,242	21.7	313	78.3	2,690.0	1,039	30.0	265	70.0	32,970.0	1,444	31.9	322	69.1
Netherlands Antilles	...	...	...	...	...	...	...	...	...	...	...	...	...	...	...	...
New Caledonia	...	...	...	...	...	...	...	...	...	...	...	...	...	...	...	...
New Zealand	1979	850.9	1,106	...	122	...	367.4	1,283	...	95	...	956.7	2,640	...	130	...
Nicaragua[12]	1980	1,870.5	...	...	83	...	294.5	...	...	47	...	1,103.8	67	...	...	...
Niger	...	...	...	...	...	...	...	...	...	...	...	...	...	...	...	...
Nigeria[11, 12]	1978	649.5	...	...	213	...	356.7	...	...	133	...	664.3	...	...	433	...
Niue	...	...	...	...	...	...	...	...	...	...	...	...	...	...	...	...
Norfolk Island	...	...	...	...	...	...	...	...	...	...	...	...	...	...	...	...
Norway[10, 12, 39]	1981	5,670.0	2,987	54.8	81	45.2	1,800.0	1,108	60.0	69	40.0	14,890.0	4,556	...	234	...
Oman	...	...	...	...	...	...	...	...	...	...	...	...	...	...	...	...
Pakistan	1975	3,505.1	311	23.1	94	76.9	2,929.7	766	12.3	222	87.7	1,729.3	490	15.9	149	84.1
Panama[10, 12]	1979	167.6	199	39.2	25	60.8	38.8	88	53.9	16	46.1	83.3	172	74.1	12	25.9
Papua New Guinea	1980	72.7	154	...	...	...	1.3	11	...	...	...	53.1	169	...	...	...

primary and fabricated metals; processed minerals					machinery (except elec.) and transport equipment					electrical and electronic machinery					country
value added ('000,000 local currency)	enterprises				value added ('000,000 local currency)	enterprises				value added ('000,000 local currency)	enterprises				
	1–99 employees		100 or more emp.			1–99 employees		100 or more emp.			1–99 employees		100 or more emp.		
	number	percent value of added	number	percent of value added		number	percent of value added	number	percent of value added		number	percent of value added	number	percent of value added	
59.7	...	...	48	...	—	—	—	—	—	0.8	3	...	...	...	Ethiopia
—	—	—	—	—	...	...	...	...	...	—	—	—	—	—	Faeroe Islands
															Falkland Islands
5.8	8	...	1	...	9.8[7]	80[7]	...	3[7]	...	...	7	...	7	...	Fiji
7,548.0	1,024	...	145	...	8,543.0	896	...	203	...	2,593.0	139	...	55	...	Finland
111,000.0	...	...	...	...	210,700.0	...	...	...	...	58,600.0	...	...	...	...	France
...	...	...	...	...	...	...	...	...	...	...	...	...	...	...	French Guiana
...	...	...	...	...	...	...	...	...	...	...	...	...	...	...	French Polynesia
14,957.0	444	...	...	...	...	...	...	...	...	...	...	...	...	...	Gabon
...	...	...	...	...	...	...	...	...	...	...	...	...	...	...	Gambia, The
31	...	...	31	...	78,200.0[32]	...	...	1,438[32]	...	32,900.0	...	...	366	...	Germany, East
88,320.0	5,375	...	1,491	...	131,150.0	6,519	...	2,756	...	54,040.0	4,941	...	2,525	...	Germany, West
246.3	13	3.7	8	96.3	27.6	35[7]	19.4[7]	19[7]	80.6[7]	13.0	7	7	7	7	Ghana
...	...	...	...	...	...	...	...	...	...	...	...	...	...	...	Gibraltar
50,330.0	19,921	...	103	...	74,740.0[7]	21,662	...	67	...	7	5,272	...	36	...	Greece
...	...	...	...	...	...	...	...	...	...	...	...	...	...	...	Greenland
...	...	...	...	...	...	...	...	...	...	...	...	...	...	...	Grenada
—	—	—	—	—	—	—	—	—	—	—	—	—	—	—	Guadeloupe
...	...	...	...	...	...	...	...	...	...	...	...	...	...	...	Guam
99.0	366	...	...	...	10.0	64	...	...	...	21.0	33	...	...	...	Guatemala
...	...	...	...	...	...	...	...	...	...	...	...	...	...	...	Guinea
...	...	...	...	...	...	...	...	...	...	...	1	...	...	...	Guinea-Bissau
...	...	...	...	...	...	...	...	...	...	...	1	...	...	...	Guyana
224.4[17]	53	...	...	...	17	52[7]	...	...	...	17	7	...	...	...	Haiti
0.8	4	...	...	...	131.9	21	...	...	...	2.4	9	...	...	...	Honduras
3,835.0	363	45.5	10	54.5	1,564.0	7,092[7]	37.5[7]	278[7]	62.5[7]	5,164.0	7	7	7	7	Hong Kong
36,780.0	300	0.2	64	99.8	20,702.0	9,418[7]	2.6[7]	312[7]	97.4[7]	21,300.0	7	7	7	7	Hungary
22,063.0[17]	2,986[17]	...	...	...	17	17	...	...	...	17	17	...	...	...	Iceland
24,310.0	16,707	...	...	...	127,080.0[7]	6,562	...	...	...	7	2,882	...	...	...	India
293,900.0	1,026	...	...	...	169,500.0	...	...	310	...	112,600.0	...	...	113	...	Indonesia
120,960.0	2,943	...	...	...	42,880.0	...	...	171	...	27,600.0	...	...	86	...	Iran
171.7[17]	7,487[17]	...	...	...	17	17	...	...	...	17	17	...	...	...	Iraq
252.4	684	...	...	...	150.3	253	...	...	...	145.0	155	...	...	...	Ireland
35,513.0	342	25.5	33	74.5	18,323.0	2,128[7]	42.7[7]	124[7]	57.3[7]	17,443.0	7	7	7	7	Israel
18,874.0	28,412	...	935	...	16,791.0	94,394[7]	...	2,239[7]	...	7,224.0	7	...	7	...	Italy
22,132.0	61	...	...	...	14,902.0[7]	227	...	...	...	7	7	...	...	...	Ivory Coast
108.3[17]	417[17]	...	...	...	17	17	...	...	...	17	17	...	...	...	Jamaica
16,162.0	43,525	29.4	1,742	70.6	16,188.0	221,526[7]	35.2[7]	6,995[7]	64.8[7]	11,397	7	7	7	7	Japan
42.9[36]	1,334[36]	...	...	...	36	36	...	...	...	0.7	4	...	...	...	Jordan
...	...	...	...	...	...	...	...	...	...	...	...	...	...	...	Kampuchea
32.6	...	...	76	...	16.8	...	...	34	...	12.9	...	...	8	...	Kenya
...	...	...	...	...	...	...	...	...	...	—	—	—	—	—	Kiribati
1,452.2	5,401	20.2	153	79.8	1,877.9[6]	10,215[7]	19.8[7]	469[7]	80.2[7]	...	7	7	7	7	Korea, North
55.6	607	...	...	...	4.5	38	...	...	...	0.3	8	...	...	...	Korea, South
...	...	...	...	...	...	...	...	...	...	...	...	...	...	...	Kuwait
...	...	...	...	...	...	...	...	...	...	...	...	...	...	...	Laos
...	...	...	...	...	...	...	...	...	...	...	...	...	...	...	Lebanon
...	...	...	...	...	...	...	...	...	...	...	...	...	...	...	Lesotho
0.5[17]	...	...	...	...	17	...	...	...	...	17	7	...	...	...	Liberia
12.5	85	...	...	...	11.5[7]	6[7]	...	...	...	7	7	...	...	...	Libya
...	96	...	1	...	...	4	...	2	...	...	29	...	2	...	Liechtenstein
21,815.0	90	...	44	...	2,435.0	22	...	25	...	483.0	7	...	...	...	Luxembourg
7.3	90	...	...	...	5.8	22	...	...	...	9.4	22	...	...	...	Macau
2,233.0	27	...	...	...	1,953.0	21	...	...	...	796.0	15	...	...	...	Madagascar
2	18	...	...	...	2	3	...	...	...	2	2	...	...	...	Malawi
827.1	820	...	...	...	541.7	559	...	...	...	843.1	209	...	...	...	Malaysia
...	...	...	...	...	...	...	...	...	...	...	...	...	...	...	Maldives
2	...	...	...	...	2	...	...	...	...	2	...	...	...	...	Mali
7.8	236	...	...	...	4.0	59	...	...	...	7.5	36	...	...	...	Malta
...	...	...	...	...	...	...	...	...	...	...	...	...	...	...	Martinique
122.0	73	...	...	...	46.0	17	...	...	...	14.0	12	...	...	...	Mauritania
...	...	...	...	...	...	...	...	...	...	...	...	...	...	...	Mauritius
...	...	...	...	...	...	...	...	...	...	...	...	...	...	...	Mayotte
160,300.0	...	...	229	...	112,000.0	...	...	47	...	52,600.0	...	...	63	...	Mexico
...	...	...	...	...	...	...	...	...	...	...	...	...	...	...	Monaco
232.2	...	...	...	...	157.0[7]	...	...	...	...	7	...	...	...	...	Mongolia
...	...	...	...	...	...	...	...	...	...	...	...	...	...	...	Montserrat
832.8	...	...	...	...	1,525.3	...	...	...	...	576.7	...	...	...	...	Morocco
1,521.5	113	...	50	...	261.9	15	...	16	...	158.7	9	...	6	...	Mozambique
...	...	...	...	...	...	...	...	...	...	...	...	...	...	...	Nauru
61.0	106	...	20	...	278.1[17]	113[7]	...	12[7]	...	7	7	...	7	...	Nepal
9,500.0	552	22.2	134	77.8	8,180.0	2,513[7]	20.3[7]	441[7]	79.7[7]	7,200.0	7	7	7	7	Netherlands, The
...	...	...	...	...	...	...	...	...	...	...	...	...	...	...	Netherlands Antilles
...	...	...	...	...	...	...	...	...	...	...	...	...	...	...	New Caledonia
1,264.5[17]	1,944	...	61	...	17	954	...	15	...	17	286	...	42	...	New Zealand
242.0	...	...	28	...	13.2	3	...	...	...	18.6	2	...	...	...	Nicaragua
...	...	...	...	...	...	...	...	...	...	...	...	...	...	...	Niger
371.1	...	...	227	...	150.9	...	...	39	...	50.3	...	...	16	...	Nigeria
...	...	...	...	...	...	...	...	...	...	...	...	...	...	...	Niue
...	...	...	...	...	...	...	...	...	...	...	...	...	...	...	Norfolk Island
9,560.0	2,051	...	124	...	10,460.0	2,009	...	151	...	3,850.0	261	16.6	48	83.4	Norway
...	...	...	...	...	...	...	...	...	...	...	...	...	...	...	Oman
983.3	492	18.9	63	81.1	1,022.1	363	27.2	43	72.8	400.8	147	13.1	41	86.9	Pakistan
47.5	58	40.0	7	60.0	2.9	917[7]	71.9[7]	6[7]	28.1[7]	2.9	7	7	7	7	Panama
57.1[17]	154[17]	...	...	...	17	17	...	...	...	17	17	...	...	...	Papua New Guinea

Manufacturing industries (continued)

country	year	food, beverages, and tobacco — value added ('000,000 local currency)	food 1–99 employees number	food 1–99 percent of value added	food 100 or more emp. number	food 100 or more emp. percent of value added	textiles, apparel, and leather — value added ('000,000 local currency)	textiles 1–99 employees number	textiles 1–99 percent of value added	textiles 100 or more emp. number	textiles 100 or more emp. percent of value added	chemicals and related products — value added ('000,000 local currency)	chemicals 1–99 employees number	chemicals 1–99 percent of value added	chemicals 100 or more emp. number	chemicals 100 or more emp. percent of value added
Paraguay	1978	16,709.3	...	...	...	...	8,476.4	...	...	...	...	17,732.3	...	...	...	...
Peru[10,12]	1980	370,700.0	6,236	19.4	82	80.6	187,800.0	8,613	33.6	106	66.4	381,600.0	7,476	42.1	148	57.9
Philippines[40]	1981	20,349.9	30,605	...	...	...	4,799.9	34,253	...	...	...	12,768.9	8,950	...	...	...
Pitcairn Island		...	...	...	...	...	...	...	...	...	...	...	...	...	...	...
Poland	1981	15,300.0	10,897	...	...	...	176,300.0	...	...	9,665	...	238,800.0	...	...	5,377	...
Portugal[10,12]	1980	37,240.0	10,825	30.6	212	69.4	61,000.0	10,387	28.6	439	71.4	83,200.0	11,067	40.9	270	59.1
Puerto Rico[9,10]	1977	607.5	292	25.7	49	74.3	443.5	336	16.3	160	83.7	1,893.3	527	39.1	74	60.9
Qatar		...	...	...	...	...	...	5	...	...	...	...	16	...	...	...
Réunion	1978	...	35	...	...	...	...	...	...	...	...	...	...	...	...	...
Romania[19]	1981	...	...	...	298	...	...	...	...	219	...	...	...	...	197	...
Rwanda	1981	9,392.7	...	...	17	...	1,258.3	...	...	3	...	722.1	...	...	17	...
St. Christopher and Nevis		...	...	...	...	...	...	...	...	...	...	...	...	...	...	...
St. Helena and Ascension		...	...	...	...	...	...	...	...	...	...	...	...	...	...	...
St. Lucia		...	...	...	...	...	...	...	...	...	...	...	...	...	...	...
St. Pierre and Miquelon		...	...	...	...	...	...	...	...	...	...	...	...	...	...	...
St. Vincent and Grenadines		...	...	...	...	...	...	...	...	...	...	...	...	...	...	...
San Marino	1984	...	34	...	...	...	...	65	...	...	...	...	64	...	...	...
São Tomé and Príncipe		...	...	...	...	...	...	...	...	...	...	...	...	...	...	...
Saudi Arabia	1972	119.1	...	...	...	...	88.6	...	...	...	...	306.3[41]	...	...	...	...
Senegal	1975	25.9	49	...	...	...	10.3	28	...	...	...	9.1	59	...	...	...
Seychelles	1980	44.3	12	...	...	...	1.6	3	...	...	...	9.4	19	...	...	...
Sierra Leone	1973–74	20.8	...	...	...	...	0.7	...	...	...	...	2.8	...	...	...	...
Singapore	1982	577.9	301	...	...	...	443.4	588	...	...	...	3,028.0	1,038	...	...	...
Solomon Islands		...	...	...	...	...	...	...	...	...	...	...	...	...	...	...
Somalia[12]	1977	110.3	68	...	...	...	60.5	75	...	...	...	61.4	37	...	...	...
South Africa[12]	1976	1,110.7	1,713	19.4	451	80.6	825.6	1,543	15.7	570	84.3	2,022.6	3,639	25.6	625	74.4
South West Africa/Namibia		...	...	...	...	...	...	...	...	...	...	...	...	...	...	...
Spain[8]	1977	201,500.0	15,503	...	...	...	213,200.0	12,160	...	...	...	462,700.0	45,502	...	...	...
Sri Lanka[8]	1980	1,638.0	...	...	144	...	681.0	628	...	...	...	1,732.0	573	...	...	...
Sudan, The	1979	362.2	...	...	...	...	229.2	...	...	...	...	147.9[2]	...	...	...	...
Suriname		...	...	...	16	...	2.2	31	...	...	...	39.0	...	...	30	...
Swaziland[12]	1980	33.3	...	...	...	...	...	...	...	...	...	...	...	...	...	...
Sweden	1981	14,726.9	766	...	152	...	3,961	707	...	84	...	44,018.3	2,938	...	466	...
Switzerland[10]	1975	6,030.0	12,680	...	152	...	3,135.0	4,750	...	198	...	11,790.0	17,255	...	311	...
Syria[12]	1980	1,116.0	6,566	...	...	...	1,886.0	14,135	...	...	...	577.0	7,500	...	...	...
Taiwan		...	...	...	...	...	...	...	...	...	...	...	...	...	...	...
Tanzania		...	...	...	...	...	...	...	...	...	...	...	...	...	...	...
Thailand[12,43]	1977	90,038.1	1,050	...	...	...	15,049.9	936	...	...	...	17,293.9	1,747	...	...	...
Togo[12]	1979	6,825.0	...	...	12	...	809.0	3	...	...	...	2,292.0	26	...	...	...
Tokelau		...	...	...	...	...	...	...	...	...	...	...	...	...	...	...
Tonga	1980	...	28	100.0	—	—	...	6	100.0	—	—	...	19	100.0	—	—
Trinidad and Tobago[44]	1980	229.3	...	...	97	...	70.5	83	...	...	...	1,463.9[2]	225	...	...	...
Trust Terr. of the Pacific Is.	1982	...	...	...	...	...	...	...	...	...	...	...	...	...	...	...
Tunisia	1981	59.2	283	35.9	35	64.1	70.9	276	26.4	124	73.6	93.4	253	26.8	49	73.2
Turkey[10,12]	1981	240,000.0	18,692	22.6	175	77.4	187,100.0	65,114	33.6	195	66.4	292,900.0	28,193	39.8	150	60.2
Turks and Caicos Islands		...	...	...	...	...	...	...	...	...	...	...	...	...	...	...
Tuvalu		...	...	...	...	...	...	...	...	...	...	...	...	...	...	...
Uganda[8,9]	1971	226.0	148	19.7	24	39.0	119.2	48	8.7	9	34.1	68.8[45]	113	61.8	21	38.0
U.S.S.R.[3]	1981	118,300.0	...	...	9,171	...	102,700.0	...	...	7,789	...	83,200.0	...	...	3,740	...
United Arab Emirates[11,46]	1981	93.8	73	...	...	...	14.3	67	...	...	...	320.9	209	...	...	...
United Kingdom[8]	1980	7,663.9	4,909	...	514	...	3,875.5	12,134	...	1,062	...	16,155.9	27,488	...	1,555	...
United States[8,47]	1980	81,459.0	22,994	24.1	3,890	75.9	47,330.0	30,578	24.8	6,204	75.2	224,543.0	120,525	29.7	9,646	70.3
Uruguay	1980	5,539.0	2,789	...	...	...	3,347.0	1,995	...	...	...	3,813.0	2,905	...	...	...
Vanuatu		...	...	...	...	...	...	...	...	...	...	...	...	...	...	...
Venezuela[47]	1979	9,292.0	2,138	25.2	161	74.8	4,091.0	1,778	44.1	132	55.9	25,572.0	2,085	34.7	191	65.3
Vietnam		...	...	...	...	...	...	...	...	...	...	...	...	...	...	...
Virgin Islands (U.S.)		...	...	...	...	...	...	...	...	...	...	...	...	...	...	...
Wallis and Futuna		...	...	...	...	...	...	...	...	...	...	...	...	...	...	...
Western Sahara		...	...	...	...	...	...	...	...	...	...	...	...	...	...	...
Western Samoa		...	...	...	...	...	...	...	...	...	...	...	...	...	...	...
Yemen (Aden)		...	...	...	...	...	...	...	...	...	...	...	...	...	...	...
Yemen (Şan'ā')	1975	...	6,884	...	...	...	...	2,601	...	...	...	...	147	...	...	...
Yugoslavia	1980	62,573.0	...	...	1,369	...	83,028.0	...	...	1,563	...	141,239.0	...	...	2,788	...
Zaire	1980	322.8	...	...	...	...	146.7	...	...	...	...	264.1[2]	...	...	...	...
Zambia[12]	1974	114.9	172	...	...	...	27.7	156	...	...	...	73.4	179	...	...	...
Zimbabwe[8]	1980	218.2	...	...	...	...	217.5	...	...	...	...	247.8	...	...	...	...

primary and fabricated metals; processed minerals					machinery (except elec.) and transport equipment					electrical and electronic machinery					country
value added ('000,000 local currency)	1–99 employees number	percent value of added	100 or more emp. number	percent of value added	value added ('000,000 local currency)	1–99 employees number	percent of value added	100 or more emp. number	percent of value added	value added ('000,000 local currency)	1–99 employees number	percent of value added	100 or more emp. number	percent of value added	
876.9	...	...	...	...	2,971.6	...	...	...	...	1,315.0	...	...	...	...	Paraguay
283,700.0	98	6.3	11	93.7	120,800.0	1,774	32.9	83	67.1	50,900.0	524	70.4	5	29.6	Peru
3,904.4	7,454	...	...	...	3,261.7	2,092	...	...	...	2,493.6	...	...	268	...	Philippines
...	...	...	...	...	—	—	...	—	...	—	...	...	—	...	Pitcairn Island
135,100.0	...	...	3,209	...	247,900.0	...	...	1,814	...	75,400.0	...	...	718	...	Poland
51,350.0	7,938	27.5	226	72.5	29,410.0	1,351	18.9	112	81.1	15,960.0	155	9.4	38	90.6	Portugal
235.5	385	35.6	24	64.4	514.4	215	51.4	21	39.4	403.1	78	17.1	53	82.9	Puerto Rico
...	...	...	...	...	...	...	...	...	...	...	...	...	...	...	Qatar
...	9	...	...	...	...	18[7]	...	...	...	...	7	...	...	...	Réunion
...	...	...	463[17]	...	...	...	...	17	...	...	...	...	17	...	Romania
476.8	...	...	10[17]	...	549.8	...	...	17	...	13.1	...	...	17	...	Rwanda
...	...	...	...	...	...	...	...	...	...	...	...	...	...	...	St. Christopher and Nevis
...	...	...	...	...	...	...	...	...	...	...	...	...	...	...	St. Helena and Ascension
—	—	—	—	—	—*	—	...	—	...	—	...	...	—	...	St. Lucia
...	...	...	...	...	...	...	...	...	...	...	...	...	...	...	St. Pierre and Miquelon
...	...	...	...	...	...	...	...	...	...	...	...	...	...	...	St. Vincent and Grenadines
...	44	...	...	...	...	24[17]	...	...	...	...	7	...	...	...	San Marino
...	...	...	...	...	...	...	...	...	...	...	7	...	...	...	São Tomé and Príncipe
288.8	...	...	...	...	104.6[7, 42]	...	...	...	...	...	7	...	...	...	Saudi Arabia
6.8	34[17]	...	...	...	...	...	17	...	...	...	...	17	...	...	Senegal
3.8	4	...	...	...	...	...	...	...	...	...	...	...	...	...	Seychelles
1.6	...	...	...	...	...	...	...	...	...	...	...	...	...	...	Sierra Leone
1,092.4	498	...	...	...	2,448.9	...	...	824	...	1,687.0	...	...	300	...	Singapore
...	...	...	...	...	—	—	...	...	...	—	...	...	...	...	Solomon Islands
15.6[17]	77[17]	...	...	...	17	17	...	...	...	17	17	...	...	...	Somalia
2,197.4	3,195	17.7	559	82.3	1,268.3	2,450	28.6	344	71.6	467.5	486	16.2	129	83.8	South Africa
...	...	...	...	...	...	...	...	...	...	...	...	...	...	...	South West Africa/Namibia
399,000.0	22,997	...	...	...	202,600.0	4,955	...	...	...	105,800.0	...	...	1,171	...	Spain
495.0	174	...	...	...	244.5	...	...	...	...	175.0	...	...	...	...	Sri Lanka
2	...	...	...	...	2	...	...	...	...	2	...	...	...	...	Sudan, The
4.4	27	...	...	...	0.5	...	...	3	...	...	...	...	...	...	Suriname
...	...	...	...	...	...	...	...	...	...	...	...	...	...	...	Swaziland
13,396.2	509	...	124	...	62,490.8[7, 42]	3,470[7, 42]	...	605[7, 42]	...	7	7	...	7	...	Sweden
8,865.0	16,233	...	301	...	15,130.0	10,268	...	590	...	...	...	...	...	...	Switzerland
695.0[17]	5,202[17]	...	...	...	17	17	...	...	...	17	17	...	...	...	Syria
...	...	...	...	...	...	...	...	...	...	...	...	...	...	...	Taiwan
...	...	...	...	...	...	...	...	...	...	...	...	...	...	...	Tanzania
12,937.3	1,044	...	...	...	13,224.1	693	...	...	...	1,086.8	133	...	...	...	Thailand
1,815.0	...	...	9	...	...	...	...	...	...	...	...	...	...	...	Togo
...	...	...	...	...	...	...	...	...	...	...	...	...	...	...	Tokelau
...	11	100.0	—	—	...	2	100.0	—	—	...	3	100.0	—	—	Tonga
2	82	...	...	...	2	277	...	...	...	2	7	...	...	...	Trinidad and Tobago
...	...	...	...	...	...	...	...	...	...	...	...	...	...	...	Trust Terr. of the Pacific Is.
196.4	30	50.3	29	49.7	...	2	...	...	...	...	...	...	...	...	Tunisia
240,300.0	4,992	9.6	106	90.3	132,500.0	57,503	41.8	199	58.2	46,000.0	...	...	...	...	Turkey
...	...	...	...	...	—	—	...	—	...	—	...	...	—	...	Turks and Caicos
...	...	...	...	...	—	—	...	—	...	—	...	...	—	...	Tuvalu
108.3	20	7.9	8	92.1	...	64	77.0	5	23.0	...	...	...	...	...	Uganda
264,200.0[17]	...	...	15,878	...	17	...	...	...	...	17	...	...	...	...	U.S.S.R.
497.0	285	...	...	...	85.4	5	...	...	...	4.0	9	...	...	...	United Arab Emirates
8,209.0	15,703	...	1,114	...	17,111.7	23,098	...	1,675	...	5,720.0	4,423	...	481	...	United Kingdom
153,639.0	52,544	23.4	6,287	76.6	216,534.0	76,365	20.1	6,751	79.9	73,150.0	12,103	9.9	2,870	90.1	United States
1,097.0	1,538	...	...	...	2,403.0	761	...	...	...	514.0	361	...	...	...	Uruguay
...	...	...	...	...	...	...	...	...	...	...	...	...	...	...	Vanuatu
9,477.0	2,063	35.0	126	65.0	5,201.0	408	26.1	65	73.9	1,184.0	163	30.5	40	69.5	Venezuela
...	...	...	...	...	...	...	...	...	...	...	...	...	...	...	Vietnam
...	...	...	...	...	...	...	...	...	...	...	...	...	...	...	Virgin Islands (U.S.)
—	—	—	—	—	—	—	—	—	—	—	—	—	—	—	Wallis and Futuna
—	—	—	—	—	—	—	—	—	—	—	—	—	—	—	Western Sahara
...	...	...	...	...	...	...	...	...	...	...	...	...	...	...	Western Samoa
...	646	...	...	...	...	782[7]	...	...	...	...	7	...	...	...	Yemen (Aden)
...	...	...	...	...	...	...	...	...	...	...	...	...	...	...	Yemen (Şan'ā')
123,303.0	...	...	1,953	...	83,015.0	...	...	1,163	...	39,428.0	...	...	482	...	Yugoslavia
2	...	...	...	...	2	...	...	...	...	2	...	...	...	...	Zaire
42.7	152	...	...	...	64.5	217	...	...	...	9.7	21	...	...	...	Zambia
166.8	...	...	...	...	134.5[32]	...	...	...	...	28.3	...	...	...	...	Zimbabwe

[1]Figures in value-added columns are gross output in value of sales. [2]Group 3 includes groups 4, 5, and 6. [3]Figures in value-added columns are gross output in producers' prices. [4]Number of enterprises figures are for 1969. [5]Group 4 includes groups 5 and 6 and mining and public utilities. [6]Value-added figures are partial data. [7]Group 5 includes group 6. [8]Value-added figures are factor values. [9]Percents may not add to 100.0 because data for certain enterprises have been withheld. [10]Percents of value added by enterprise size are for 1973. [11]Establishments with 10 or more workers. [12]Value-added figures are producers' prices. [13]Excludes sugar factories and refineries. [14]Excludes leather and products. [15]Excludes synthetic fibre industry. [16]Includes professional goods. [17]Group 4 includes groups 5 and 6. [18]Percents of value added by enterprise size and number of enterprises are for 1973. [19]Number of enterprises figures are partial data. [20]Value-added figures are for 1980. [21]Includes some enterprises with more than 100 employees. [22]Value-added figures are for establishments with 50 or more workers. [23]Group 2 includes groups 4, 5, and 6. [24]Number of enterprises figures are for 1973. [25]Value-added figures are for 1979. [26]Figures in value-added columns are net material product at constant 1975 prices. [27]Number of enterprises figures are for 1980. [28]Number of enterprises figures are for 1979. [29]Includes petrochemical, rubber, and plastics industries. [30]Number of enterprises figures are for 1974. [31]Group 2 includes groups 3 and 4. [32]Includes metal products. [33]Excludes printing and publishing. [34]Value-added figures are in billions. [35]Number of enterprises figures are for 1978. [36]Group 4 includes group 5. [37]Establishments with 50 or more workers. [38]Number of enterprises figures are for 1976. [39]Value-added figures are for establishments with 5 or more workers. [40]Number of enterprises figures are for 1979. [41]Excludes petroleum refineries. [42]Includes fabricated metal products. [43]Establishments with 20 or more workers. [44]Number of enterprises figures are for 1975. [45]Includes processed mineral products. [46]Value-added figures are for 1978. [47]Percent of value added by enterprise size and number of enterprises are for 1977.

Energy and public utilities

Public utilities are enterprises that, because they distribute certain essential goods and services, are either state owned or privately owned but operated as regulated monopolies. The goods and services provided by public utilities include electricity, natural or manufactured gas, water, and sewage disposal but may include others (*e.g.*, the distribution of geothermally heated water in Iceland).

Because most public utilities operate locally or regionally rather than nationally and because substitution for the marketed goods or services is so pervasive (wood for heating instead of natural gas, septic tanks or latrines for sewage treatment and removal, vegetable oils for electrical light) and difficult to estimate (withdrawals of well water, gathering of firewood, unrestricted discharge of sewage), most countries do not aggregate data (commercial energy supplies excepted) at a national level, except in the general terms adopted for this table: value added by utilities to the gross domestic product, total employment, and the ratio that this employment represents to the total population.

As indicated above, commercial energy supplies are the principal exceptions to this rule, since their points of production or import are few enough to permit ready monitoring. Many of the data and concepts used in this table are taken from the United Nations' *Yearbook of World Energy Statistics*.

Electricity. Total installed electrical power capacity comprises the sum of the rated power capacities of all main and auxiliary generators in a country. 'Total installed capacity' (kW) is multiplied by 8,760 hours per year to yield 'Total production capacity' (kW-hr).

Production of electricity comprises the total gross production of electricity by publicly or privately owned enterprises and also that generated by industrial establishments for their own use, but usually excludes consumption by the utility itself. Measured in 1,000,000s of kilowatt hours

(kW-hr), annual production of electricity ranges generally between 30 and 40 percent of total production capacity. The data are further analyzed by type of generation: fossil fuels, hydroelectric power, and nuclear fuel.

The great majority of the world's electrical and other energy needs are met by the burning of hydrocarbon (fossil) solids, liquids, and gases, either for thermal generation of electricity or in internal combustion engines. Many renewable and nontraditional sources of energy are being used worldwide (wood, biogenic gases and liquids, tidal and wind power, photothermal [solar] energy, and so on), but collectively these sources are still negligible in the world's total energy consumption. For this reason only hydroelectric and nuclear generation are considered here separately after fossil fuels.

Though hydroelectric power accounted for only 6 percent of the world's primary production in the early 1980s, the leading producers were some of the world's principal consuming nations: Canada, the United States, the U.S.S.R., Brazil, Japan, and Norway, which together accounted for about 60 percent of the world's production of hydroelectricity.

Nuclear generation accounted for more than 3 percent of the world's total electricity production and was being utilized by some 23 countries for commercial production. The major producers, the United States and France, accounted for 46 percent of the nuclear generation of electricity.

Trade in electrical energy refers to the transfer of generated electrical output via an international grid. Total electricity consumption (residential and nonresidential) is equal to total electricity requirements less transformation and distribution losses.

Natural gas. This term refers to any combustible gas (usually chiefly methane) of natural origin from underground sources. In the mid-1980s the natural gas reserves of Eastern Europe, the U.S.S.R., and the Middle East accounted for about two-thirds of the world total. The countries with

Energy and public utilities

country	public utilities as percent of GDP, 1982	employment in public utilities, 1982 ('000)	employment in public utilities, per 1,000 population, 1982	electricity installed capacity, 1982 ('000 kW)	production, 1982 capacity ('000,000 kW-hr)	production, 1982 amount ('000,000 kW-hr)	power source, 1982 fossil fuel (%)	power source, 1982 hydro-power (%)	power source, 1982 nuclear fuel (%)	trade, 1982 exports ('000,000 kW-hr)	trade, 1982 imports ('000,000 kW-hr)	consumption amount, 1982 ('000,000 kW-hr)	consumption per capita, 1982 (kW-hr)	consumption resi-dential, 1981 (%)	consumption non-resi-dential, 1981 (%)
Afghanistan	0.21	6.92	0.422	394	3,451	976	32.3	67.7	—	—	—	976	68	...	...
Albania	...	...	...	...	...	2,750	20.0	80.0	—	600	—	2,150	753	...	...
Algeria	1.07	30.38	1.728	2,006	17,572	7,180	96.5	3.5	—	—	...	7,180	361	24.19	75.99
American Samoa	...	...	...	32	280	72	100.0	—	...	—	...	72	2,182	...	...
Andorra	1.79	...	...	...	...	...	...	...	...	...	...	...	...	...	...
Angola	0.47	...	...	600	5,256	1,600	26.2	73.8	—	—	—	1,600	197	27.5	72.5
Anguilla	...	...	...	—	—	—	—	—	...	—	—	—	—	...	...
Antigua and Barbuda	3.5	0.310	0.5010	29	254	63	100.0	—	—	—	—	63	818	...	...
Argentina	3.87	125.67	8.417	13,480	118,084	39,804	51.1	44.2	4.7	6	51	39,849	1,367	27.4	72.6
Australia	3.47	125.8	8.417	27,543	241,276	104,890	85.7	14.3	—	—	—	104,890	6,934	30.1	69.9
Austria	3.5	37.0	4.89	14,243	124,768	42,891	28.0	72.0	—	7,464	3,125	38,552	5,144	23.1	83.4
Bahamas, The	...	1.27	4.847	350	3,066	900	100.0	—	—	—	—	900	4,186	...	...
Bahrain	1.72	2.87	7.907	655	5,738	1,810	100.0	—	—	—	—	1,810	4,763	...	...
Bangladesh	0.4	23.07	0.257	990	8,672	3,305	79.0	21.0	—	—	—	3,305	35	16.5	83.5
Barbados	2.2	2.111	8.4011	94	823	336	100.0	—	—	—	—	336	1,302	...	...
Belgium	3.5	32.9	3.34	12,046	105,522	50,693	67.0	2.1	30.9	4,327	4,826	51,192	5,187	26.3	73.7
Belize	1.47	...	...	21	184	57	100.0	—	—	—	—	57	380	...	...
Benin	1.08	4.88	1.428	15	131	5	100.0	—	—	—	120	125	34	...	...
Bermuda	...	0.411	8.2011	118	1,034	353	100.0	—	—	—	—	353	4,770	...	...
Bhutan	0.37	...	...	11	96	24	12.5	87.5	—	—	—	24	18	...	...
Bolivia	1.3	7.2	1.22	508	4,450	1,703	31.1	68.9	—	—	—	1,703	290	25.810	74.210
Botswana	2.47	1.67	1.717	14	14	14	14	14	14	14	14	14	14	...	...
Brazil	1.8	410.7	3.24	38,904	340,797	152,089	7.1	92.9	—	368	—	151,721	1,196	24.2	75.8
British Virgin Islands	1.88	...	...	5	44	20	100.0	—	—	—	—	20	1,667	...	...
Brunei	0.1	2.07	1.037	240	2,102	570	100.0	—	—	—	—	570	2,280	...	...
Bulgaria	...	51.4	5.76	9,220	80,767	40,459	65.9	7.5	26.6	1,794	4,441	43,106	4,736	...	...
Burkina Faso	1.07	0.71	0.131	...	...	115	100.0	—	—	—	—	115	18	...	...
Burma	0.4	16.0	0.45	636	5,571	1,715	39.9	60.1	—	—	—	1,715	47	...	...
Burundi	...	0.57	0.127	9	79	2	100.0	—	—	—	150	152	36	...	...
Cameroon	1.27	3.2	0.36	531	4,652	1,908	5.2	94.8	—	—	—	1,908	212	...	...
Canada	3.6	117.0	4.75	83,000	727,077	387,460	23.5	67.4	9.1	34,214	2,849	356,095	14,421	24.5	75.5
Cape Verde	...	...	...	8	70	12	100.0	—	—	—	—	12	39	...	...
Cayman Islands	...	...	...	14	123	44	100.0	—	—	—	—	44	2,444	...	...
Central African Republic	1.37	...	...	30	263	68	4.4	95.6	—	—	—	68	28	...	...
Chad	0.87	...	...	38	333	65	100.0	—	—	—	—	65	14	...	...
Chile	3.0	24.5	2.13	3,208	28,102	11,871	33.7	66.3	—	—	—	11,871	1,033	...	...
China	...	...	...	76,000	665,757	327,680	77.3	22.7	—	—	272	327,952	325	4.810	95.210
Christmas Island	...	...	...	12	105	32	100.0	—	—	—	—	32	10,667	...	...
Cocos (Keeling) Islands	...	...	...	...	...	...	...	...	...	...	...	...	...	...	...
Colombia	2.2	44.22	1.632	5,820	50,983	25,605	27.5	72.5	—	30	—	25,575	950	34.7	65.3
Comoros	0.8	...	...	4	35	10	100.0	—	—	—	—	10	24	...	...
Congo	0.67	...	...	149	1,305	185	8.6	91.4	—	—	26	211	131	...	...
Cook Islands	0.68	0.17	5.267	4	35	12	100.0	—	—	—	—	12	632	...	...
Costa Rica	3.0	...	...	657	5,755	2,500	2.8	97.2	—	—	—	2,500	1,039	...	...
Cuba	...	...	...	2,704	23,687	10,788	99.1	0.9	—	—	—	10,788	1,096	...	...
Cyprus	1.7	1.57	2.347	333	2,917	1,144	100.0	—	—	—	—	1,144	1,779	...	...
Czechoslovakia	...	65.07	4.247	18,109	158,634	74,749	87.2	5.0	7.8	6,031	7,835	76,553	4,951	11.64	88.44
Denmark	1.911	14.011	2.7411	6,768	59,287	22,068	99.9	0.1	—	2,234	3,973	23,807	4,636	29.1	70.9
Djibouti	2.57	0.5	1.34	25	219	122	100.0	—	—	—	—	122	364	...	...
Dominica	1.88	...	...	7	61	17	11.8	88.2	—	—	—	17	227	...	...

the largest proved reserves were the U.S.S.R., Iran, the United States, Algeria, and Saudi Arabia. The data for production cover, to the extent possible, gas obtained from gas fields, petroleum fields, or coal mines that is actually collected and marketed. (Much natural gas in Middle Eastern oil fields is flared [burned] because it is often not economical to capture and market it.) Manufactured gas is generally a by-product of industrial operations such as gas works, coke ovens, and blast furnaces. It is usually burned at the point of production and rarely enters the market place. Natural gas is not generally a major energy source in developing countries unless they have extensive reserves of their own, as do Bangladesh, China, and Mexico.

Crude petroleum. Crude petroleum is the liquid product obtained from oil wells; the term also includes shale oil, tar sand extract, and field or lease condensate. Production and consumption data in the table refer, so far as possible, to the same year so that the relationship between national production and consumption patterns can be clearly seen; both are given in barrels.

Proved reserves are that oil remaining underground in known fields whose existence has been "proved" by the evaluation of nearby producing wells or by seismic tests in sedimentary strata known to contain crude petroleum, and that is judged recoverable within the limits of present technology and economic conditions (prices). Proved reserves of crude petroleum are heavily concentrated in the Middle East, North America including Mexico, and the U.S.S.R. The published proved reserve figures do not necessarily reflect the true reserves of a country, because government authorities or corporations often have political or economic motives for withholding or altering such data.

The estimated exhaustion rate of petroleum reserves is an extrapolated ratio of published proved reserves to the current rate of withdrawal/pro-duction. Present world published proved reserves will last about 30 years at the present rate of withdrawal, but there are large country-to-country variations above or below the average. If the use of crude oil continues to increase at the rate that has prevailed in recent years, however, present proved reserves could be exhausted in as few as 25 years.

Coal. The term coal, as used in the table, comprises all grades of anthracite, bituminous, subbituminous, and lignite that have acquired or may in future, by reason of new technology or changed market prices, acquire an economic value. These types of coal may be differentiated according to heat content (density) and content of impurities. Most coal reserve data are based on proved recoverable reserves only, of all grades of coal. Exceptions are footnoted, with proved in-place reserves reported only when recoverable reserves are unknown. Production figures include deposits removed from both surface and underground workings as well as quantities used by the producers themselves or issued to the miners. Wastes recovered from mines or nearby preparation plants are excluded from production figures.

For data in the hydrocarbons portions of the table (natural gas, petroleum, and coal), extensive use has been made of a variety of international sources, such as those of the United Nations, the International Energy Agency (of the Organisation for Economic Cooperation and Development), and the World Energy Conference; of the resources of the U.S. Department of Energy; and of various industry surveys, such as those published by British Petroleum (BP *Statistical Review of World Energy*), the *International Petroleum Encyclopedia*, the *Oil and Gas Journal*, and the *Petroleum Economist*.

natural gas						crude petroleum					coal			country
published proved reserves, 1984 ('000,000,000 cu m)	production		consumption			reserves, 1984		produc-tion, 1983 ('000,000 barrels)	consump-tion, 1983 ('000,000	refining capacity, 1984 ('000 barrels per day)	reserves, latest ('000,000 metric tons)	pro-duction, 1982 ('000 metric tons)	con-sump-tion, 1982 ('000 metric tons)	
	natural gas, 1983 ('000,000 cu m)	manufac-tured gas, 1982 ('000,000 cu m)	amount, 1982 ('000,000 cu m)	resi-dential, 1981 (%)	non-resi-dential, 1981 (%)	published proved ('000,000 barrels)	years to exhaust proved reserves							
...	4,485	—	129	...	...	...	...	...	...	—	66	145	145	Afghanistan
613	397[4]	—	397	...	...	...	...	23[4]	23[4]	40	155.[5,6]	1,600	1,790	Albania
3,120	20,020	1,401	5,058	26.8	73.2	9,220	37	251	134[4]	137	43	7	757	Algeria
...	...	...	...	...	...	—	—	...	...	...	—	—	...	American Samoa
...	—	—	...	...	...	—	—	—	...	—	—	—	...	Andorra
44	1,971	12	90	...	...	1,770	28	64	8[4]	32	...	—	—	Angola
...	—	—	...	...	...	—	—	—	...	—	...	...	...	Anguilla
691	15,563	1,713	12,118	...	...	2,429	14	176	188[4]	678	150	515	1,189	Argentina
501	11,992	6,566	10,256	...	...	1,586	11	148	215[4]	722	59,340	134,599	81,549	Australia
15	1,201	1,245	4,200	25.7	74.3	122	14	9	70	268	65[6]	3,098	6,635	Austria
...	...	35	...	...	...	...	...	...	63	500	...	...	16	Bahamas, The
210	5,488	216	2,816	...	...	185	12	15	72[4]	250	...	...	...	Bahrain
198	1,688[4]	8	1,688	4.7	95.3	...	...	0.4[4]	9[4]	22	242	—	255	Bangladesh
...	9[4]	...	9	...	...	0.6	3	0.2	1[4]	3	...	—	—	Barbados
...	31[4]	2,535	8,093	...	...	...	...	...	156[12]	694	440[11]	6,539	15,851	Belgium
...	...	...	...	...	...	...	...	...	...	...	...	...	...	Belize
...	...	...	...	...	...	100	50	2	...	...	...	...	...	Benin
...	...	...	...	...	...	...	...	...	...	...	...	...	...	Bermuda
...	...	...	...	...	...	...	...	...	...	...	...	...	...	Bhutan
139	2,786	117	587	...	...	161	20	8	8[4]	47	...	...	1	Bolivia
76	4,027	4,920	1,360	...	...	1,800	16	115	376[4]	1,301	3,500	14	14	Botswana
...	...	...	...	...	...	...	...	...	...	...	1,113	6,400	10,006	Brazil
200	8,957	18	1,161	...	...	1,390	24	57	-3[4]	10	...	—	—	British Virgin Islands
														Brunei
...	73[4]	530	4,560	...	...	...	...	...	...	300	3,730	32,182	39,162	Bulgaria
														Burkina Faso
5	476	5	520	...	...	30	3	11	10[4]	26	2	49	249	Burma
119	...	19	...	...	...	520	12	42	21[4]	41	...	...	—	Burundi
														Cameroon
2,563	68,360	14,232	50,105	20.6	79.4	6,730	13	510	494	1,807	5,906	42,907	41,474	Canada
...	...	...	...	...	...	...	...	...	...	...	...	...	...	Cape Verde
...	...	...	...	...	...	...	...	...	...	...	...	...	...	Cayman Islands
...	...	...	...	...	...	...	...	...	...	...	4	...	...	Central African Republic
														Chad
68	4,808	872	884	...	...	748	53	14	26[4]	141	1,177	1,025	1,193	Chile
858	10,506	...	11,906	...	...	19,100	25	769	618	1,810	99,000[11]	660,000	655,746	China
...	...	...	...	...	...	...	...	...	...	...	...	...	...	Christmas Island
...	...	...	...	...	...	...	...	...	...	...	...	...	...	Cocos (Keeling) Islands
122	5,247	443	4,458	...	...	560	10	57	59[4]	211	1,035	5,550	5,227	Colombia
61	...	...	...	...	...	...	...	...	...	...	...	...	...	Comoros
	2[4]	—	2			400	11	35	—	21				Congo
...	...	9	...	...	...	...	...	...	34	17	...	...	...	Cook Islands
...	11[4]	183	11	...	...	...	...	4	42[4]	160	...	...	130	Costa Rica
														Cuba
...	...	31	...	...	...	...	...	...	12[15]	15	—	—	—	Cyprus
...	583[4]	5,630	7,992	...	...	...	...	1	111[4]	455	5,560	124,560	124,007	Czechoslovakia
82	595	254	...	...	...	324	19	17	80	174	...	—	9,619	Denmark
...	...	...	...	...	...	...	...	...	...	...	...	...	...	Djibouti
...	...	...	...	...	...	—	—	...	...	...	...	...	...	Dominica

Energy and public utilities (continued)

country	public utilities as percent of GDP, 1982	employment in public utilities, 1982 ('000)	employment in public utilities, per 1,000 population, 1982	electricity installed capacity, 1982 ('000 kW)	production, 1982 capacity ('000,000 kW-hr)	production, 1982 amount ('000,000 kW-hr)	power source, 1982 fossil fuel (%)	hydro-power (%)	nuclear fuel (%)	trade, 1982 exports ('000,000 kW-hr)	imports ('000,000 kW-hr)	consumption amount, 1982 ('000,000 kW-hr)	per capita, 1982 (kW-hr)	residential, 1981 (%)	non-residential, 1981 (%)
Dominican Republic	0.9[7]	...	...	960	8,410	2,965	98.4	1.6	—	—	—	2,965	509	...	59.8[16]
Ecuador	1.0	14.6	2.54	1,200	10,512	3,350	70.4	29.6	—	—	15	3,365	394	40.2[16]	59.8[16]
Egypt	1.0[2]	65.7[1]	1.51[7]	3,782	33,130	17,720	45.3	54.7	—	—	—	17,720	408	...	...
El Salvador	2.2	9.7[2]	2.04[2]	500	4,380	1,500	6.7	53.3	40.0[17]	—	—	1,500	295	...	...
Equatorial Guinea	...	...	...	7	61	26	92.3	7.7	—	—	—	26	71	...	...
Ethiopia	0.6[11]	...	...	319	2,794	679	29.0	71.0	—	—	—	679	20	...	...
Faeroe Islands	...	...	...	48	420	170	70.6	29.4	—	—	—	170	4,146	...	...
Falkland Islands	...	...	...	1	9	3	100.0	—	—	—	—	3	1,500	...	...
Fiji	1.0	2.0	2.99	117	1,025	331	100.0	—	—	—	—	331	508	22.6[4]	77.4[4]
Finland	2.8	26.0	5.39	11,135	97,542	39,350	26.9	32.9	40.2	1,738	4,074	41,686	8,643	18.6	81.3
France	2.1	194.0	3.58	73,984[18]	648,097[18]	265,900[18]	34.6[18]	26.7[18]	38.7[18]	13,200[18]	9,400[18]	262,100[18]	4,840[18]	23.8[18]	76.2[18]
French Guiana	...	0.3[10]	4.29[10]	34	298	138	100.0	—	—	—	—	138	2,000	...	...
French Polynesia	1.3[2]	0.6[11]	3.47[11]	69	604	290	100.0	—	—	—	—	290	1,895	...	...
Gabon	1.5[11]	4.7[16]	4.56[16]	175	1,533	530	51.9	48.1	—	—	—	530	478	...	...
Gambia, The	0.5	2.2[10]	3.79[10]	11	96	40	100.0	—	—	—	—	40	66	...	...
Germany, East	...	...	...	21,183	185,562	102,906	87.7	1.7	10.6	3,144	4,292	104,054	6,232	...	...
Germany, West	2.8[2]	237.0	3.84	85,769	751,333	366,877	77.3	5.4	17.3	13,422	20,214	373,669	6,082	23.1	76.9
Ghana	0.5[7]	15.9[10]	1.43[10]	1,060	9,286	4,981	0.8	99.2	—	475	—	4,506	369	...	...
Gibraltar	...	0.2[7]	6.67[7]	21	184	60	100.0	—	—	—	—	60	2,000	...	...
Greece	1.9	30.8[7]	3.17[7]	5,979	52,376	23,272	84.7	15.3	—	49	771	23,994	2,451	24.9	75.1
Greenland	...	0.3[19]	5.86[19]	...	701	175	100.0	—	—	—	—	175	3,302	...	...
Grenada	1.3[2]	...	...	8	70	25	100.0	—	—	—	—	25	229	...	...
Guadeloupe	0.6[10]	...	...	103	902	395	100.0	—	—	—	—	395	1,246	...	...
Guam	...	...	...	302	2,646	1,150	100.0	—	—	—	—	1,150	10,088	...	...
Guatemala	1.7	7.7[7]	1.03[7]	473	4,143	1,640	78.7	21.3	—	—	—	1,640	213	...	...
Guinea	1.0[2]	...	...	175	1,533	498	83.9	16.1	—	—	—	498	98	...	...
Guinea-Bissau	0.6[10]	0.3[10]	0.35[10]	7	61	13	100.0	—	—	—	—	13	15	...	...
Guyana	...	4.1[16]	5.06[16]	165	1,445	440	98.9	1.1	—	—	—	440	489	...	...
Haiti	0.7	2.1	0.40	126	1,104	360	30.6	69.4	—	—	—	360	59	...	...
Honduras	2.3	3.6	0.91	240	2,102	1,090	20.2	79.8	—	12	8	1,086	274	...	...
Hong Kong	1.3	14.9[7]	2.90[7]	3,475	30,441	14,504	100.0	—	—	272	—	14,232	2,697	...	...
Hungary	...	77.0[11]	7.20[11]	4,865	42,617	24,604	99.4	0.6	—	1,680	10,421	33,345	3,100	...	...
Iceland	3.6[7]	1.1[8]	4.76[8]	775	6,789	3,302	4.3	92.5	3.2[17]	—	—	3,302	14,052	20.9	79.1
India	1.6[7]	735.0[7]	1.09[7]	38,808	339,957	138,677	59.7	38.0	2.3	65	4	138,616	193	...	...
Indonesia	0.6	84.7[2]	0.56[2]	2,860	25,053	7,377	78.9	21.1	—	—	—	7,365	47	34.6	65.4
Iran	1.1[7]	61.7[19]	1.83[19]	5,300	46,428	17,500	80.0	20.0	—	—	—	17,500	424	...	...
Iraq	0.5[10]	23.2[16]	1.93[16]	1,200	10,512	6,310	90.3	9.7	—	—	—	6,310	446	28.9[16]	71.1[16]
Ireland	2.5[16]	14.0[7]	4.07[7]	3,932	34,444	10,931	89.0	11.0	—	—	—	10,931	3,144	32.6	67.4
Israel	2.2	12.7[11]	3.10[11]	3,477	30,458	13,826	100.0	—	—	201	—	13,625	3,367	26.8[10]	73.2[10]
Italy	4.5	196.0	3.46	50,023[20]	438,199[20]	184,444[20]	70.9[20]	23.9[20]	3.7[20]	3,018[20]	10,169[20]	191,595[20]	3,396[20]	20.3[20]	79.7[20]
Ivory Coast	1.7[7]	13.0[1]	1.57[1]	1,163	10,188	1,929	10.4	89.6	—	—	...	1,929	218	...	...
Jamaica	1.7	...	...	740	6,482	2,350	94.5	5.5	—	—	...	2,350	1,055	24.8	75.2
Japan	3.1	340.0	2.87	154,811	1,356,138	581,147	67.7	14.5	17.6	—	—	581,147	4,916	20.8	79.2
Jordan	1.5	2.5[7]	0.82[7]	456	3,995	1,511	100.0	—	—	—	—	1,511	483	...	...
Kampuchea	...	...	...	40	350	136	58.8	41.2	—	—	—	136	20	...	...
Kenya	2.2	14.0	0.78	556	4,871	1,804	17.2	82.8	—	—	212	2,016	111	23.1	76.9
Kiribati	1.5[8]	0.2[8]	3.22[8]	2	18	6	100.0	—	—	—	6	6	100	...	...
Korea, North	...	...	...	7,000	61,320	40,000	37.5	62.5	—	—	—	40,000	2,134	...	...
Korea, South	2.3	31.1	0.79	11,597	101,589	47,197	87.7	4.3	8.0	—	—	47,197	1,204	10.9	89.1
Kuwait	0.4	8.2[2]	5.96[2]	2,860	25,053	12,016	100.0	—	—	—	—	12,016	7,823	...	...
Laos	1.6[9]	...	...	250	2,190	1,000	5.0	95.0	—	730	10	280	68	...	...
Lebanon	5.4[16]	8.0[1]	2.89[1]	668	5,852	1,290	49.6	50.4	—	[14]	[14]	[14]	[14]	[14]	[14]
Lesotho	0.5[7]	...	...	[14]	...	...	...	...	...	...	...	...	...	...	...
Liberia	2.7[7]	1.5[7]	0.78[7]	306	2,681	1,100	72.7	27.3	—	—	—	1,100	552	...	...
Libya	0.6[7]	19.5[2]	6.57[2]	1,180	10,337	6,000	100.0	—	—	—	—	6,000	1,866	...	...
Liechtenstein	...	0.1[21]	0.38[21]	[22]	[22]	[22]	[22]	[22]	[22]	[22]	[22]	[22]	[22]	[22]	[22]
Luxembourg	2.6[7]	1.4[7]	3.85[7]	1,305	11,432	941	47.5	52.5	—	399	3,551	4,093	11,245	49.0[4]	51.0[4]
Macau	...	1.0[7]	3.05[7]	104	911	337	100.0	—	—	—	—	337	1,131	...	...
Madagascar	11.5[7]	114.9[7]	12.83[7]	100	876	432	47.2	52.8	—	—	—	425	46	...	...
Malawi	1.8	4.3	0.69	111	972	428	6.8	93.2	—	2	—	426	67	...	...
Malaysia	2.4	...	...	2,550	22,338	12,350	86.3	13.7	—	—	—	12,350	850	21.6[16]	78.4[16]
Maldives	0.2	0.2[2]	1.33[2]	2	18	8	100.0	—	—	—	—	8	49	...	...
Mali	1.1[7]	...	...	42	368	110	54.5	45.5	—	—	—	110	15	...	...
Malta	5.3	1.2[7]	3.33[7]	152	1,332	561	100.0	—	—	—	—	561	1,496	...	...
Martinique	2.0[10]	1.0	3.25	65	569	273	100.0	—	—	—	—	273	878	...	...
Mauritania	...	...	...	55	482	103	100.0	—	—	—	—	103	60	...	...
Mauritius	2.0	4.5	4.69	244	2,137	429	78.3	21.7	—	—	—	429	432	...	...
Mayotte	...	0.1[8]	2.81[8]	...	...	...	...	...	...	...	...	...	...	...	...
Mexico	1.6	82.5[10]	1.22[10]	21,574	188,987	80,589	70.0	28.4	1.6[17]	8	9	80,590	1,101	15.3	84.7
Monaco	...	...	...	[18]	[18]	[18]	[18]	[18]	[18]	[18]	[18]	[18]	[18]	[18]	[18]
Mongolia	...	15.3	8.69	450	3,942	1,850	100.0	—	—	—	400	2,250	1,282	...	...
Montserrat	...	0.1[7]	9.09[7]	4	35	12	100.0	—	—	—	—	12	1,000	...	...
Morocco	3.8[7]	...	...	1,593	13,955	6,057	75.8	24.2	—	—	—	6,057	283	26.7	73.3
Mozambique	1.3[7]	...	...	1,800	15,768	3,400	12.1	87.9	—	2,166	100	1,334	103	...	...
Nauru	...	...	...	10	88	26	100.0	—	—	—	—	26	3,714	...	...
Nepal	0.3	2.0[19]	0.15[19]	79	692	198	24.7	75.3	—	4	65	259	17	...	...
Netherlands, The	1.9	314.7	21.99	18,673	163,575	60,328	93.5	—	6.5	2,866	4,210	61,672	4,299	24.2	75.8
Netherlands Antilles	...	1.7[11]	6.53[11]	340	2,978	2,310	100.0	—	—	—	—	2,310	9,130	...	...
New Caledonia	1.9	0.6[11]	3.77[11]	381	3,338	948	57.0	43.0	—	—	—	948	6,449	...	...
New Zealand	2.9	15.0	4.75	6,842	59,936	23,957	19.8	75.6	4.6[17]	—	—	23,957	7,461	35.7	64.3
Nicaragua	3.0[7]	6.7[2]	2.44[2]	400	3,504	1,045	48.8	48.8	2.4[17]	6	10	1,049	355	...	...
Niger	0.4[7]	2.3[7]	0.42[7]	23	201	62	100.0	—	—	—	119	181	32	...	...
Nigeria	0.7	30.0[1]	0.44[1]	2,770	24,265	7,500	46.7	53.3	—	119	—	7,381	86	33.9	66.1
Niue	...	0.1[7]	37.49[7]	1	9	3	100.0	—	—	—	—	3	750	...	...
Norfolk Island	...	...	...	...	...	...	...	...	...	...	...	...	...	...	...

natural gas — published proved reserves, 1984 ('000,000,000 cu m)	production — natural gas, 1983 ('000,000 cu m)	production — manufactured gas, 1982 ('000,000 cu m)	consumption — amount, 1982 ('000,000 cu m)	consumption — residential, 1981 (%)	consumption — non-residential, 1981 (%)	crude petroleum reserves, 1984 — published proved ('000,000 barrels)	reserves, 1984 — years to exhaust proved reserves	production, 1983 ('000,000 barrels)	consumption, 1983 ('000,000 barrels)	refining capacity, 1984 ('000 barrels per day)	coal reserves, latest ('000,000 metric tons)	coal production, 1982 ('000 metric tons)	coal consumption, 1982 ('000 metric tons)	country
...	...	49	...	...	...	...	...	...	94	44	...	—	1	Dominican Republic
100	476	86	69	...	...	1,675	19	86	36[4]	84	—	...	...	Ecuador
201	2,908	309	1,897	...	...	3,450	14	252	113[4]	369	13	—	1,270	Egypt
...	...	33	...	...	...	...	...	...	5[4]	16	...	...	...	El Salvador
...	...	...	...	...	...	...	...	...	...	...	...	...	...	Equatorial Guinea
...	...	6	...	...	...	...	...	...	5[4]	15	...	—	—	Ethiopia
...	...	...	...	...	...	...	...	...	...	...	...	—	—	Faeroe Islands
...	...	...	...	...	...	...	...	...	...	...	...	...	...	Falkland Islands
...	...	...	...	...	...	...	...	...	...	...	...	—	23	Fiji
...	...	500	641	...	...	...	...	...	80	299	...	—	2,650	Finland
69[18]	8,192[18]	10,744[18]	25,276[18]	32.8	67.2	140	12	12[18]	651[18]	2,670	610	21,821[18]	47,845[18]	France
...	...	...	...	...	...	...	...	...	...	...	...	...	...	French Guiana
...	...	...	...	...	...	...	...	...	...	...	...	...	...	French Polynesia
14	136	7	154	...	...	490	9	55	10[4]	20	...	...	...	Gabon
...	...	...	...	...	...	...	...	...	...	...	...	...	...	Gambia, The
...	3,000[4]	3,666	8,692	...	...	0.4[4]	...	...	152[4]	470	25,000[6]	276,038	281,425	Germany, East
193	17,137	18,682	45,683	30.3[2]	69.7[2]	304	10	30	793	2,386	59,141	223,670	222,077	Germany, West
0.1	...	8	...	...	...	4	10	0.4	8[4]	28	...	—	2	Ghana
...	...	...	...	...	...	...	...	...	15	...	...	...	...	Gibraltar
98[4]	...	597	...	...	...	51	6	9	85	369	1,550[6]	27,399	27,717	Greece
...	...	...	...	...	...	...	...	...	...	...	...	—	1	Greenland
...	...	...	...	...	...	...	...	...	...	...	...	...	...	Grenada
...	...	25	...	...	...	...	...	...	...	...	...	...	...	Guadeloupe
...	...	2	...	...	...	...	...	...	11[4]	44	...	...	...	Guam
0.9	—	2	...	...	...	48	16	3	7[4]	16	...	...	...	Guatemala
...	...	...	...	...	...	...	...	...	...	...	...	...	...	Guinea
...	...	...	...	...	...	...	...	...	...	...	...	...	...	Guinea-Bissau
...	...	...	...	...	...	...	...	...	...	...	...	...	...	Guyana
...	...	...	...	...	...	...	...	...	...	...	135	...	...	Haiti
...	...	5	...	...	...	...	...	...	4[4]	14	21[5]	...	...	Honduras
...	...	125	...	...	...	...	...	...	...	...	...	...	1,455	Hong Kong
88	6,595[4]	1,322	9,956	...	...	...	...	15	66[4]	312	4,225	26,079	28,403	Hungary
...	...	...	...	...	...	...	...	...	4	...	...	—	25	Iceland
420	2,919	1,432	2,272	...	...	3,485	25	142	238[4]	779	14,198	134,992	132,887	India
855	13,643	266	4,207	...	...	9,100	19	472	172[4]	387	539	481	273	Indonesia
13,592	14,164	1,273	9,297	...	...	51,100	54	951	199[4]	530	193[13]	800	860	Iran
744	578	420	449	...	...	45,848	139	330	67[4]	169	...	—	—	Iraq
20	1,978[4]	102	1,977	...	...	...	...	...	31	56	55[13]	62	1,308	Ireland
0.3	374	246	71	...	...	0.8	11	0.07	59[4]	190	...	—	907	Israel
123[20]	12,745[20]	8,269[20]	26,208[20]	...	...	800	57	14[20]	604[4,20]	3,050	31[6]	1,900[20]	20,988[20]	Italy
...	...	12	...	...	...	108	12	9	14[4]	90	...	...	...	Ivory Coast
...	...	40	...	...	...	...	...	...	6[4]	36	...	—	—	Jamaica
25	2,064	47,289	25,985	61.3[2]	38.7[2]	58	19	3	1,513	5,173	1,068	17,624	96,858	Japan
...	...	99	...	...	...	...	...	...	18[4]	100	...	...	...	Jordan
...	...	...	...	...	...	...	...	...	...	...	...	—	—	Kampuchea
...	...	23	...	...	...	...	...	...	16[4]	79	...	...	32	Kenya
...	...	...	...	...	...	...	...	...	...	...	...	...	...	Kiribati
...	...	...	...	...	...	...	...	...	14[4]	42	600[13]	47,000	47,400	Korea, North
...	...	1,013	...	...	...	...	...	...	182[4]	776	116[13]	20,230	27,674	Korea, South
878	4,044	1,209	1,928	...	...	63,900	157	406	169[4]	623	...	...	...	Kuwait
...	...	...	...	...	...	...	...	...	...	...	...	...	...	Laos
...	...	12	...	...	...	...	...	...	3[4]	52	...	—	1	Lebanon
...	—	—	...	...	...	...	...	...	...	...	...	14	14	Lesotho
...	...	1	...	...	...	...	...	...	4[4]	15	...	—	—	Liberia
605	2,670	439	595	...	...	21,270	57	372	43[4]	125	...	—	1	Libya
—	—	22	22	...	...	...	...	...	...	...	...	22	22	Liechtenstein
...	...	422	325	...	...	...	...	...	12	...	...	—	283	Luxembourg
...	...	...	...	...	...	...	...	...	...	...	...	—	1	Macau
...	...	2	...	...	...	...	...	...	3[4]	16	1,075[5]	—	13	Madagascar
...	...	...	0.5	...	...	...	...	...	...	...	12	—	72	Malawi
1,359	1,291	129	1,639	...	...	3,000	22	135	49[4]	205	—	—	136	Malaysia
...	...	...	...	...	...	...	...	...	...	...	...	...	...	Maldives
...	...	...	...	...	...	...	...	...	15	...	—	—	—	Mali
—	...	—	...	...	...	...	...	...	3[4]	11	...	...	...	Malta
...	...	20	...	...	...	...	...	...	3[4]	...	...	...	...	Martinique
...	...	...	...	...	...	...	...	...	...	...	...	—	7	Mauritania
...	...	...	...	...	...	...	...	...	...	...	...	—	1	Mauritius
...	...	...	...	...	...	...	...	...	...	...	...	...	...	Mayotte
2,134	41,895	6,679	29,561	...	...	48,000	49	986	449[4]	1,269	1,584	8,200	8,510	Mexico
[18]	[18]	[18]	[18]	[18]	[18]	[18]	[18]	[18]	[18]	...	...	[18]	[18]	Monaco
...	...	...	...	...	...	...	...	—	—	...	24,000[5]	4,500	4,500	Mongolia
...	...	...	...	...	...	...	...	...	...	...	...	...	...	Montserrat
...	102	199	92	...	...	0.2	3	0.07	30[4]	74	100[5]	730	678	Morocco
14	...	9	...	...	...	...	...	...	4[4]	17	240	380	420	Mozambique
...	...	...	...	...	...	...	...	...	...	...	...	...	...	Nauru
...	...	...	...	...	...	...	...	...	3[4]	15	...	...	20	Nepal
1,417	75,858	4,844	29,344	37.7[2]	62.3[2]	309	21	15	198	1,552	240[5,13]	—	6,904	Netherlands, The
...	...	146	...	...	...	...	...	...	...	740	...	...	...	Netherlands Antilles
...	...	...	...	...	...	...	...	...	...	...	2[13]	—	65	New Caledonia
157	3,205	49	2,014	12.8	87.2	170[23]	34	5	18[4]	74	211	2,259	2,115	New Zealand
...	...	14	...	...	...	...	...	...	3[4]	15	...	...	...	Nicaragua
...	...	...	...	...	...	...	...	...	...	...	55	...	...	Niger
985	4,106	29	5,128	...	...	16,550	37	450	51[4]	247	169[6]	210	210	Nigeria
...	...	...	...	...	...	...	...	...	...	...	...	...	...	Niue
...	...	...	...	...	...	...	...	...	...	...	...	...	...	Norfolk Island

Energy and public utilities (continued)

country	public utilities as percent of GDP, 1982	employment in public utilities, 1982 ('000)	employment in public utilities, per 1,000 population, 1982	installed capacity, 1982 ('000 kW)	production, 1982 capacity ('000,000 kW-hr)	production, 1982 amount ('000,000 kW-hr)	power source, 1982 fossil fuel (%)	power source, 1982 hydro-power (%)	power source, 1982 nuclear fuel (%)	trade, 1982 exports ('000,000 kW-hr)	trade, 1982 imports ('000,000 kW-hr)	consumption amount 1982 ('000,000 kW-hr)	consumption per capita 1982 (kW-hr)	consumption residential 1981 (%)	consumption non-residential 1981 (%)
Norway	3.8	19.0	4.62	22,119	193,762	93,060	0.1	99.9	—	6,691	643	87,012	21,125	27.0	73.0
Oman	1.0	0.4	0.39	419	3,670	1,160	100.0	—	—	—	—	1,160	1,075	...	...
Pakistan	2.1	196.0	2.25	4,239	37,133	17,779	42.8	56.3	0.9	—	—	17,779	191	...	...
Panama	3.6	8.32	4.532	744	6,517	2,700	55.6	44.4	—	—	—	2,700	1,321	...	...
Papua New Guinea	1.210	0.17	0.037	328	2,873	1,266	75.8	24.2	—	—	—	1,272	372	...	...
Paraguay	2.5	4.4	1.29	370	3,241	1,100	13.6	86.4	—	51	—	1,049	311	...	...
Peru	1.2	12.9	0.71	3,400	29,784	10,400	23.1	76.9	—	—	—	10,400	571	...	...
Philippines	1.17	66.07	1.337	5,003	43,826	19,406	62.3	19.4	18.217	—	—	19,406	382	...	...
Pitcairn Island	...	...	...	...	...	...	...	...	...	...	...	...	...	...	...
Poland	...	148.0	4.09	25,988	227,654	117,580	97.8	2.2	—	5,950	4,265	115,895	3,172	17.9	82.1
Portugal	1.67	22.07	2.217	5,073	44,439	15,267	55.1	44.9	—	400	3,369	19,119	1,938	19.0	81.0
Puerto Rico	3.5	15.0	4.60	4,100	35,916	11,863	99.1	0.9	—	—	—	11,863	3,598	...	...
Qatar	0.3	...	...	695	6,088	2,775	100.0	—	—	—	—	2,775	10,278	...	...
Réunion	1.52	0.77	1.397	159	1,393	432	1.4	98.6	—	—	—	432	800	...	...
Romania	...	...	...	17,232	150,952	68,900	81.4	18.6	—	1,000	500	68,400	3,032	...	...
Rwanda	0.3	...	...	39	342	163	4.9	95.1	—	—	31	194	35	...	...
St. Christopher and Nevis	0.9	0.2	5.00	15	131	30	100.0	—	—	—	—	30	566	...	...
St. Helena and Ascension	...	...	...	...	...	2	100.0	—	—	—	—	2	400	...	...
St. Lucia	2.12	...	...	16	140	60	100.0	—	—	—	—	60	488	...	...
St. Pierre and Miquelon	...	...	...	13	114	23	100.0	—	—	—	—	23	3,833	...	...
St. Vincent and the Grenadines	2.67	...	...	10	88	29	37.9	62.1	—	—	—	29	287	...	...
San Marino	...	...	...	20	20	20	20	20	20	20	20	20	20	20	20
São Tomé and Príncipe	0.57	...	...	4	35	11	72.7	27.3	—	—	—	11	124	...	...
Saudi Arabia	0.2	29.52	3.202	7,409	64,903	25,450	100.0	—	—	—	—	25,450	2,539	95.12	4.92
Senegal	...	5.416	1.0316	165	1,445	631	100.0	—	—	—	—	631	105	...	...
Seychelles	1.3	0.216	3.3316	19	166	53	100.0	—	—	—	—	53	768	...	...
Sierra Leone	0.47	1.87	0.507	95	832	236	100.0	—	—	—	—	236	69	...	...
Singapore	1.7	8.0	3.22	2,175	19,053	7,860	100.0	—	—	—	—	7,860	3,174	...	...
Solomon Islands	...	0.311	1.0911	12	105	21	100.0	—	—	—	—	21	84	...	...
Somalia	0.510	...	...	30	263	75	100.0	—	—	—	—	75	15	...	...
South Africa	4.3	72.9	2.64	23,07414	202,12714	108,96114	99.014	1.014	—	15014	2,16614	110,97714	3,22214	...	...
South West Africa/Namibia	2.02	...	...	14	14	14	14	14	14	14	14	14	14	...	...
Spain	4.67	83.47	2.227	29,900	261,923	116,760	68.5	24.0	7.5	4,200	2,900	115,460	3,030	16.7	83.2
Sri Lanka	1.6	19.02	1.292	562	4,923	2,066	22.2	77.8	—	—	—	2,066	134	...	...
Sudan, The	2.17	45.619	2.8319	313	2,742	1,010	49.5	50.5	—	—	—	1,010	51	...	...
Suriname	2.310	1.32	3.602	400	3,504	1,700	17.6	82.4	—	—	—	1,700	4,857	...	...
Swaziland	1.37	1.47	2.477	14	14	14	14	14	14	14	14	14	18.72	81.32
Sweden	2.7	37.07	4.457	29,684	260,031	100,124	5.4	55.6	39.0	2,577	5,940	103,487	12,489	26.4	73.6
Switzerland	...	29.8	4.61	14,10022	123,51522	52,28522	1.922	70.822	27.322	19,14822	8,32122	41,45822	6,50822	24.422	75.622
Syria	0.87	17.07	1.837	1,104	9,671	4,570	42.2	57.8	—	30	...	4,540	480	...	...
Taiwan	4.111	33.011	1.7811	11,869	103,969	40,899	57.8	11.6	30.6	...	...	...	...	...	...
Tanzania	1.1	19.52	1.052	258	2,260	720	22.2	77.8	—	—	—	720	36	...	...
Thailand	1.4	59.22	1.242	4,935	43,230	17,220	81.6	18.4	—	10	730	17,940	370	22.0	78.0
Togo	1.67	...	...	35	307	85	76.5	23.5	—	—	175	260	97	...	...
Tokelau	...	...	...	...	...	...	...	...	...	...	...	...	...	...	...
Tonga	0.5	0.119	1.2719	6	53	12	100.0	—	—	—	—	12	119	...	...
Trinidad and Tobago	1.67	...	...	760	6,658	2,260	100.0	—	—	—	—	2,260	2,091	22.310	77.710
Trust Territory of the Pacific Is.	...	...	...	4.5	394	145	100.0	—	—	—	—	145	1,021	...	...
Tunisia	1.5	9.57	1.467	929	8,138	3,088	99.0	1.0	—	—	—	3,088	460	...	...
Turkey	2.5	42.02	0.932	6,638	58,149	26,551	46.6	53.4	—	—	1,773	28,324	608	12.3	87.7
Turks and Caicos Islands	...	...	...	9	79	11	100.0	—	—	—	—	11	1,375	...	...
Tuvalu	...	—	1.7010	...	...	...	...	...	...	...	...	...	...	...	...
Uganda	0.97	...	...	163	1,428	668	1.3	98.7	—	230	—	438	31	...	...
U.S.S.R.	...	4,612.0	17.08	285,492	2,500,898	1,367,100	81.3	12.8	5.9	20,000	300	1,347,400	4,980	...	...
United Arab Emirates	1.6	11.02	11.82	1,510	13,228	6,010	100.0	—	—	—	—	6,010	5,309	...	...
United Kingdom	2.8	342.011	6.1511	69,191	606,110	272,162	81.8	2.1	16.1	—	—	272,162	4,877	30.4	69.6
United States	3.011	875.011	3.7311	666,405	5,837,681	2,304,211	74.0	13.5	12.3	3,540	34,284	2,334,955	10,074	34.8	65.2
Uruguay	1.4	16.07	5.467	1,364	11,949	6,156	18.6	81.4	—	2	21	6,175	2,095	...	...
Vanuatu	...	0.110	0.5510	10	88	21	100.0	—	—	—	—	21	165	...	...
Venezuela	1.7	51.27	3.587	9,312	81,573	39,000	59.7	40.3	—	—	15	39,015	2,336	14.819	85.219
Vietnam	...	...	...	9001	7,884	4,100	61.0	39.0	—	—	—	4,100	73	...	...
Virgin Islands (U.S.)	...	...	...	275	2,409	760	100.0	—	—	—	—	760	7,600	...	...
Wallis and Futuna	...	—	0.737	...	...	...	...	...	...	...	...	...	...	...	...
Western Sahara	...	...	...	56	491	78	100.0	—	—	—	—	78	549	...	...
Western Samoa	...	0.47	2.867	13	114	39	82.1	17.9	—	—	—	39	244	...	...
Yemen (Aden)	1.619	...	...	130	1,139	257	100.0	—	—	—	—	257	131	...	...
Yemen (Şan'ā')	0.77	1.51	0.281	104	911	230	100.0	—	—	—	—	230	38	...	...
Yugoslavia	0.8	115.3	5.10	14,800	129,647	62,324	55.7	37.8	4.1	1,243	3,199	64,280	2,833	...	...
Zaire	—	...	...	1,716	15,032	4,412	1.4	98.6	—	75	—	4,337	143	...	...
Zambia	2.0	8.1	1.34	1,728	15,137	10,584	0.8	99.2	—	3,200	20	7,404	1,228	...	...
Zimbabwe	1.7	6.5	0.86	1,192	10,442	4,134	12.8	87.2	—	10	3,608	7,732	980	...	...

natural gas: published proved reserves, 1984 ('000,000,000 cu m)	production: natural gas, 1983 ('000,000 cu m)	production: manufactured gas, 1982 ('000,000 cu m)	consumption: amount, 1982 ('000,000 cu m)	consumption: residential 1981 (%)	consumption: non-residential 1981 (%)	crude petroleum reserves, 1984: published proved ('000,000 barrels)	crude petroleum reserves, 1984: years to exhaust proved reserves	production, 1983 ('000,000 barrels)	consumption, 1983 ('000,000 barrels)	refining capacity, 1984 ('000 barrels per day)	coal: reserves, latest ('000,000 metric tons)	coal: production, 1982 ('000 metric tons)	coal: consumption, 1982 ('000 metric tons)	country
1,665	24,392	693	986	...	...	7,660	35	219	57	243	18[13]	440	986	Norway
80	2,455	...	...	...	...	2,790	20	138	—	48	...	...	...	Oman
447	9,667	35	7,798	...	...	83	17	5	32[4]	126	645[6]	1,765	2,194	Pakistan
...	...	30	...	...	...	...	...	...	13[4]	100	...	...	...	Panama
...	...	...	...	...	...	...	...	...	...	...	...	...	...	Papua New Guinea
...	...	1	...	...	...	...	...	...	2[4]	8	...	...	...	Paraguay
33	951	189	760	...	...	775	12	62	56[4]	169	125[5,13]	55	85	Peru
0.4	...	176	...	...	...	16	3	5	68[4]	286	82[6]	565	569	Philippines
...	...	...	...	...	...	...	...	...	...	...	...	...	...	Pitcairn Island
108	4,286[4]	5,219	9,330	...	...	...	...	2	100[4]	385	39,000	226,963	190,629	Poland
...	...	434	...	...	...	...	...	...	69	282	38	190	544	Portugal
...	...	495	...	...	...	...	...	...	39[4]	121	—	—	—	Puerto Rico
1,756	2,478	499	5,651	...	...	3,330	34	99	3[4]	63	...	...	...	Qatar
...	...	...	...	...	...	...	...	...	...	...	...	...	...	Réunion
244	33,980	3,420	43,628	...	...	...	...	89	169[4]	617	1,150	37,900	42,700	Romania
...	1[4]	...	1	...	...	...	...	...	...	...	...	...	...	Rwanda
...	...	...	...	...	...	...	...	...	...	...	...	...	...	St. Christopher and Nevis
...	...	...	...	...	...	...	...	...	...	...	...	...	...	St. Helena and Ascension
...	...	...	...	...	...	...	...	...	...	...	...	...	...	St. Lucia
...	...	...	...	...	...	...	...	...	...	...	...	...	...	St. Pierre and Miquelon
...	...	...	...	...	...	...	...	...	...	...	...	...	...	St. Vincent and the Grenadines
[20]	[20]	[20]	[20]	...	...	[20]	...	[20]	[20]	...	...	[20]	[20]	San Marino
...	...	...	...	...	...	...	...	...	...	...	...	...	...	São Tomé and Príncipe
3,426	10,803	13,260	1,282	...	...	168,848	91	1,851	232[4]	860	...	...	...	Saudi Arabia
...	...	3.5	...	...	...	750	...	...	5[4]	18	...	...	...	Senegal
...	...	...	...	...	...	...	...	...	...	...	...	...	...	Seychelles
...	...	...	...	...	...	...	...	...	2[4]	10	...	...	...	Sierra Leone
...	...	355	...	...	...	...	...	...	268[4]	1,101	...	—	1	Singapore
...	...	...	...	...	...	...	...	...	...	...	...	...	...	Solomon Islands
...	...	...	...	...	...	...	...	...	3[4]	10	...	...	...	Somalia
11	...	3,555	...	...	...	115	...	...	...	389	25,290	137,486[14]	102,486[14]	South Africa
—	—	—	—	—	...	...	...	...	...	...	...	[14]	[14]	South West Africa/Namibia
63	340	4,115	2,052	...	...	160	7	22	347	1,493	951	39,354	44,698	Spain
...	...	12	...	...	...	...	...	...	14[4]	50	...	—	32	Sri Lanka
...	...	8	...	...	...	300	...	...	8[4]	24	...	—	...	Sudan, The
...	2[7]	...	...	...	...	—	—	...	...	...	...	...	1	Suriname
...	...	...	...	...	...	—	...	...	...	...	1,820	14	14	Swaziland
...	...	672	...	...	...	...	...	—	147	453	1	13	2,468	Sweden
...	...	276[22]	1,178[22]	...	...	...	...	...	90	137	...	—[22]	564[22]	Switzerland
37	238	152	50.5	...	...	1,490	25	60	63[4]	229	...	...	5	Syria
16	1,699	...	...	...	...	6[23]	6	1	...	515	140	...	...	Taiwan
6	...	6	...	...	...	...	...	...	4[4]	17	200	1	1	Tanzania
241	1,549	161	1,284	...	...	45	11	4	56[4]	176	103[24]	1,967	1,964	Thailand
...	...	...	...	...	...	...	...	...	3[4]	20	...	...	...	Togo
...	...	...	...	...	...	...	...	...	...	...	...	...	...	Tokelau
...	...	...	...	...	...	...	...	...	...	...	...	...	...	Tonga
371	3,004	480	3,193	...	...	630	11	58	66[4]	375	...	...	...	Trinidad and Tobago
...	...	...	...	...	...	...	...	...	...	...	...	...	...	Trust Territory of the Pacific Is.
118	476	49	469	...	...	1,820	43	42	...	34	...	—	3	Tunisia
16	787	1,596	...	...	...	370	23	16	120	472	1,914	20,168	21,322	Turkey
...	...	...	...	...	...	...	...	...	...	...	...	...	...	Turks and Caicos Islands
...	...	...	...	...	...	...	...	...	...	...	...	...	...	Tuvalu
...	...	...	...	...	...	...	...	...	...	...	...	...	...	Uganda
39,644	535,273	62,270	392,590	...	...	63,000	14	4,521	3,311	11,750	233,000	684,327	673,232	U.S.S.R.
884	5,621	1,178	10,626	...	...	32,340	47	685	9[4]	185	...	...	...	United Arab Emirates
711	39,510	7,516	46,356	52.3[4]	47.7[4]	13,150	16	825	527	2,092	45,000[13]	124,711	111,139	United Kingdom
5,607	469,522	102,876	469,114	29.9	71.1	27,300	9	3,164	5,195	15,863	223,259	756,056	639,324	United States
...	...	88	...	...	...	...	...	...	12[4]	45	...	...	1	Uruguay
...	...	...	...	...	...	...	...	...	...	...	...	...	...	Vanuatu
1,545	15,835	2,490	16,667	...	...	24,850	38	654	309[4]	1,224	140	47	82	Venezuela
...	...	...	...	...	...	...	...	...	...	...	312[5]	6,100	5,100	Vietnam
...	...	...	...	...	...	...	...	...	161[4]	600	...	—	...	Virgin Islands (U.S.)
...	...	...	...	...	...	...	...	...	...	...	...	...	...	Wallis and Futuna
...	...	...	...	...	...	...	...	...	...	...	...	...	...	Western Sahara
...	...	...	...	...	...	...	...	...	...	...	...	...	...	Western Samoa
...	...	9	...	...	...	...	...	...	...	178	1[5]	...	...	Yemen (Aden)
...	...	...	...	...	...	...	...	...	...	...	...	...	...	Yemen (San'ā')
66	1,789[4]	1,389	3,712	...	...	...	...	32[4]	96	297	16,570	54,664	56,060	Yugoslavia
1	...	1	...	...	...	110	12	9	3[4]	17	600[13]	120	153	Zaire
...	...	6	...	...	...	...	...	...	5[4]	24	24[13]	612	612	Zambia
...	...	51	...	...	...	...	...	...	...	...	734	2,769	3,045	Zimbabwe

[1]1975. [2]1980. [3]1973. [4]1982. [5]Estimated reserves in place. [6]Subbituminous and lignite only. [7]1981. [8]1978. [9]1972. [10]1979. [11]1983. [12]Belgium includes Luxembourg. [13]Bituminous and anthracite only. [14]South Africa includes Botswana, Lesotho, South West Africa/Namibia, and Swaziland. [15]Cyprus includes Gibraltar and Malta. [16]1977. [17]Geothermally generated power. [18]France includes Monaco. [19]1976. [20]Italy includes San Marino. [21]1984. [22]Switzerland includes Liechtenstein. [23]Condensate. [24]Lignite only.

Transportation

This table presents data relating to the transportation infrastructure and commercial traffic of the various countries and dependencies of the world. Most states have roads and airports, with services corresponding to their traffic levels and to the general level of economic development. Some states, however, lack railroads (usually less-developed countries with alternative means to collect or ship raw materials and often also lacking the capital to develop railroads, even where need exists). Another transportation mode, pipelines (one of the oldest means of bulk transport, if aqueducts are considered), is the least developed worldwide (see below) but, although initially created to facilitate the shipment of hydrocarbon liquids and gases exclusively, now finds increasing application for slurries of coal or other raw materials.

While the United Nations' *Statistical Yearbook* and *Monthly Bulletin of Statistics* provide much data on infrastructure and traffic and have established basic categories and classifications for transportation statistics, their coverage of countries is limited. Several commercial publications maintain substantial data bases and publishing programs for their particular areas of interest: Highway and vehicle statistics are provided by the International Road Federation's annual *Road and Motor Vehicle Statistics* and *World Road Statistics*: the International Union of Railways' *International Railway Statistics* and Jane's *World Railways* provide similar data for railways; Lloyd's *Register of Shipping Statistical Tables* summarizes the world's merchant marine; the *Official Airline Guide* and the International Civil Aviation Organization's *Digest of Statistics* have also been used to supplement and update the UN data. As many of these agencies are commercial or insurance oriented, their data tend to be more complete, accurate, and timely than those of intergovernmental organizations, which depend on periodic responses to questionnaires. All of these international sources are supplemented by national statistical sources to provide additional data. Such diversity of sources, however, imposes limitations on the comparability of the statistics from country to country because the years of coverage and the degrees of rounding may differ.

The categories adapted in the table also have special problems of comparability. Total road length is subject to wide international variation of interpretation, as "roads" can mean anything from mere tracks to highly developed highways. Each country also has individual classifications that differ according to climate, availability of road building materials, traffic patterns, and so on. "Paved roads," by contrast, is a much more tightly definable category, but the proportion of paved to total roads may be distorted by the less comparable total road statistics. Automobile, truck, and bus fleet statistics, which are usually based upon registration, are relatively accurate, though some countries round off figures, and unregistered vehicles may cause substantial undercount. There is also inconsistent classification of vehicle types; in some countries a vehicle may serve either as a truck or bus, or even as both on some occasions. Only a few countries collect and maintain commercial traffic statistics.

Transportation

country	roads and motor vehicles, about 1980								railroads (latest)					
	roads			motor vehicles			cargo		track length		traffic			
	length		paved (per-cent)	auto-mobiles	trucks and buses	persons per vehicle	short ton-mi ('000,000)	metric ton-mi ('000,000)	mi	km	passengers		cargo	
	mi	km									passen-ger-mi ('000,000)	passen-ger-km ('000,000)	short ton-mi ('000,000)	metric ton-km ('000,000)
Afghanistan	11,652	18,752	15.0	34,506	33,077	224	1,993	2,910	4	6	...	...	...	...
Albania	3,100	4,989	25.8	3,500	11,200	146	...	...	249	400	181	291	87	127
Algeria	44,795	72,091	54.0	573,573	265,577	23	1,145	1,672	2,417	3,890	1,181	1,900	1,712	2,500
American Samoa	186	300	90.3	2,781	373	10	—	—	—	—	—	—	—	—
Andorra	137	220	55.1	26,000	...	2	—	—	—	—	—	—	—	—
Angola	44,900	72,300	12.0	144,000	43,000	36	...	...	1,739	2,798	156	251	822	1,200
Anguilla	55	88	80.0	...	...	...	—	—	—	—	—	—	—	—
Antigua and Barbuda	597	960	25.0	5,619	433	12	—	—	—	—	—	—	—	—
Argentina	129,015	207,630	22.0	2,865,624	1,244,358	6	...	...	22,031	35,476	6,997	11,261	6,327	9,238
Australia	495,208	796,960	38.5	7,322,500	751,000	2	32,964	48,127	4,776	7,687	...	...	21,957	32,056
Austria	66,569	107,132	100.0	2,361,071	220,689	3	6,045	8,825	3,577	5,757	4,548	7,320	6,920	10,103
Bahamas, The	2,500	4,023	40.0	63,592	10,597	3	—	—	—	—	—	—	—	—
Bahrain	...	...	...	51,105	17,578	5	—	—	—	—	—	—	—	—
Bangladesh	3,536	5,691	86.9	35,487	20,779	1,593	...	...	1,791[2]	2,883[2]	3,330	5,359	524	765
Barbados	961	1,546	94.0	24,600	5,100	8	—	—	—	—	—	—	—	—
Belgium	78,908	126,990	95.0	3,230,951	303,815	3	11,682	17,056	2,442	3,930	4,302	6,924	4,652	6,792
Belize	1,601	2,576	13.0	——10,227——		16	...	...	—	—	—	—	—	—
Benin	4,182	6,730	10.4	9,592	7,025	215	...	...	359[2]	578[2]	117	188	121	177
Bermuda	250	400	100.0	15,118	2,955	3	...	...	—	—	—	—	—	—
Bhutan	1,103	1,775	35.0	1,363	706	655	...	...	—	—	—	—	—	—
Bolivia	24,638	39,651	3.0	40,638	36,051	77	...	...	2,320	3,733	300	482	425	620
Botswana	4,980	8,015	18.4	10,068	18,677	30	...	...	153	246	...	...	825	1,204
Brazil	877,336	1,411,936	7.0	9,921,887	1,144,614	11	142,600	208,200	14,146	22,766	7,723	12,429	58,968	86,092
British Virgin Islands	66	107	...	2,100	...	6	...	...	—	—	—	—	—	—
Brunei	884	1,423	52.3	54,441	8,933	4	...	...	12	19	...	...	...	...
Bulgaria	22,440	36,114	90.3	815,549	130,000	9	7,689	11,226	4,379	7,626	5,015	8,071	12,518	18,276
Burkina Faso	5,167	8,316	11.9	19,196	6,046	252	...	...	321	517	...	...	...	...
Burma	21,609	34,776	...	39,900	42,300	392	...	...	1,945	3,130	...	...	...	...
Burundi	3,196	5,144	7.1	6,100	2,400	470	...	...	—	—	—	—	—	—
Cameroon	39,727	63,935	3.9	45,893	30,887	114	...	...	726	1,168	173	279	481	702
Canada	576,793	928,258	...	10,199,388	3,192,197	2	29,033	42,388	55,455	89,246	1,797	2,892	156,250	228,120
Cape Verde	808	1,300	...	4,000	1,343	62	...	...	—	—	—	—	—	—
Cayman Islands	110	177	68.2	5,607	...	3	...	...	—	—	—	—	—	—
Central African Republic	14,018	22,560	1.3	14,200	4,000	132	...	...	—	—	—	—	—	—
Chad	19,092	30,725	1.0	7,636	9,668	243	...	...	—	—	—	—	—	—
Chile	48,482	78,025	12.1	505,000	230,900	15	...	...	4,690	7,548	1,007	1,620	1,183	1,728
China	553,145	890,200	...	50,000	850,000	1,050	53,400	78,000	31,000	50,000	91,528	147,300	391,240	571,200
Christmas Island	20	32	...	759	383	3	...	...	12	20	...	...	...	...
Cocos (Keeling) Islands	15	24	...	...	...	...	...	...	—	—	—	—	—	—
Colombia	46,438	74,735	...	672,385	168,096	34	11,115	16,227	1,754	2,822	98	158	379	553
Comoros	444	714	56.0	300	200	620	...	...	—	—	—	—	—	—
Congo	5,124	8,246	6.5	13,250	4,670	80	46	67	317	510	178	286	322	470
Cook Islands	116	187	18.9	1,119	251	13	...	...	—	—	—	—	—	—
Costa Rica	17,725	28,525	8.5	48,188	27,143	30	...	...	435	700	...	...	...	...
Cuba	18,357	29,543	...	18,657	28,098	209	...	...	11,256	18,115	1,120	1,802	1,977	2,886
Cyprus	6,803	10,948	48.2	104,231	32,630	5	...	...	233	375	...	...	...	...
Czechoslovakia	45,850	73,788	97.9	2,416,205	385,959	5	13,956	20,376	8,166	13,142	11,833	19,043	45,308	66,149
Denmark	43,285	69,661	100.0	1,358,238	388,071	3	8,700	12,700	1,529	2,461	2,619	4,215	1,132	1,653
Djibouti	1,737	2,795	11.4	9,000	1,500	32	...	...	66	106	...	...	...	...
Dominica	390	628	55.9	2,238	901	26	...	...	—	—	—	—	—	—
Dominican Republic	10,788	17,362	28.5	102,127	66,590	33	...	...	233	375	...	...	...	...
Ecuador	20,000	32,185	13.0	231,390	35,744	32	...	...	600[2]	965[2]	43	69	20	29
Egypt	17,405	28,010	0.5	461,277	221,018	65	1,079	1,575	2,642	4,252	11,660	18,765	1,577	2,302
El Salvador	7,624	12,270	14.0	72,547	67,755	35	...	...	374	602	9	14	...	...
Equatorial Guinea	730	1,175	...	...	...	...	...	...	14	23	...	...	...	...

Data for railway track length are based on the length of lines rather than the length of routes, which may be doubletracked. Siding tracks usually are not included, but some countries fail to separate them. The United States data include only class 1 railways, which account for about 94 percent of total track length. Passenger traffic is calculated from tickets sold to fare-paying passengers. Such statistics are subject to distortion if there are large numbers of nonpaying passengers, such as military personnel, or if season tickets are sold and not all the allowed journeys are utilized. Railway cargo traffic is calculated by weight hauled multiplied by the length of the journey. Changes in freight load during the journey should be accounted for but sometimes are not, leading to discrepancies.

Merchant fleet and tonnage statistics collected by Lloyd's registry service for vessels over 100 gross tons are quite accurate. Cargo statistics, however, reflect the port and customs requirements of each country and the reporting rules of each country's merchant marine authority, and often they are estimates based on customs declarations and the count of vessels entered and cleared. Even when these elements are reported consistently, further discrepancies may be introduced because of ballast, bunkers, ships' stores, or transshipped goods included in the data.

Airport data are based on flights reported in the commercial *Official Airline Guide* and are both reliable and current. Air traffic statistics suffer in comparability from differing characteristics of the air transportation systems from country to country; data from some countries may be two to three years behind those for a single airport.

Statistics on canals and waterways are collected from several different sources. As water levels in many rivers are subject to seasonal fluctuation, and because of differing sizes of vessels used, definitions and statistics about navigable waterways may vary considerably. Canal characteristics are usually less subject to seasonal variation but are usually incorporated with total waterway figures.

Worldwide data about pipelines are too sparse and inconsistent to permit their inclusion in the main body of the table, but for many countries they represent a sizable proportion of total freight transport within the country's borders. Accordingly, a supplemental table appears at the end of the main table to provide data on length of pipeline systems (usually for crude petroleum and product pipelines only) and their annual traffic in ton-miles and ton-kilometres.

The data on volume of products shipped by pipelines are usually only available for Europe; the statistics are gathered by the United Nations using carefully defined guidelines and questionnaires, but coverage varies. West Germany excludes internal transport of petroleum products, and Spain excludes data on pipelines of less than 50 kilometres in length. Data on natural gas, coal, and other products shipped by pipeline are too incomplete to be included.

| merchant marine | | international cargo (latest) | | air | traffic (latest) | | | | canals and inland waterways (latest) | | | | country |
fleet, 1983 (vessels over 100 gross tons)	total deadweight tonnage, 1983 ('000)	loaded metric tons ('000)	off-loaded metric tons ('000)	airports with scheduled flights, 1984	passengers passenger-mi ('000,000)	passengers passenger-km ('000,000)	cargo short ton-mi ('000,000)	cargo metric ton-km ('000,000)	length mi	length km	cargo short ton-mi ('000,000)	cargo metric ton-km ('000,000)	
—	—	—	—	3	181	292	12.7	18.6	665	1,070	...	...	Afghanistan
20	79.9	510	360	1	...	...	...	...	—	...	...	...	Albania
143	1,976.4	44,824	13,299	16	1,429	2,300	8.8	12.9	—	—	—	—	Algeria
—	—	84	329	3	...	...	...	...	—	—	—	—	American Samoa
—	—	—	—	1	...	...	...	...	—	—	—	—	Andorra
59	133.4	5,590	1,608	18	445	716	42.2	61.6	727	1,170	...	...	Angola
14	5.4	...	...	1	...	...	...	...	—	—	—	—	Anguilla
3	0.4	33	113	1	76	112	—	0.1	—	—	—	—	Antigua and Barbuda
532	3,563.3	26,496	6,600	65	3,790	6,099	522.4	762.7	6,800	11,000	19,326	28,215	Argentina
578	3,013.9	147,061	25,168	213	15,681	25,236	416.9	608.7	5,200	8,368	...	...	Australia
22	195.9	...	...	6	768	1,236	92.3	134.8	222	358	4,590	6,702	Austria
122	1,184.4	22,798	19,906	21	335	539	35.6	52.0	—	—	—	—	Bahamas, The
65	26.6	8,500	2,000	1	301[1]	484[1]	6.6[1]	9.6[1]	—	—	—	—	Bahrain
237	514.2	1,022	6,103	8	813	1,308	15.6	22.8	5,238	8,430	...	...	Bangladesh
34	142.6	211	559	1	205	330	0.3	0.5	—	—	—	—	Barbados
322	3,690.7	42,226	72,183	4	3,291	5,296	335.0	489.1	1,215	1,956	3,727	5,442	Belgium
3	0.8	170	211	7	...	...	...	...	500	800	—	—	Belize
12	4.9	110	749	3	106	170	11.9	17.3	300	500	—	—	Benin
67	1,291.4	181	525	1	...	...	...	...	—	—	—	—	Bermuda
—	—	...	...	1	...	...	...	...	—	—	—	—	Bhutan
2	18.9	...	...	15	489	787	12.2	17.8	6,200	10,000	...	...	Bolivia
—	—	—	—	4	9	15	0.7	1.0	...	...	...	...	Botswana
698	9,624.8	115,648	60,718	126	6,987	11,244	362.1	528.6	27,000	43,000	2,253[3]	3,289[3]	Brazil
30	8.5	7	44	3	...	...	...	...	—	—	...	...	British Virgin Islands
1	0.5	21,150	650	1	...	...	...	...	130	209	—	—	Brunei
197	1,856.3[4]	4,488[4]	24,750[4]	13	1,678	2,701	35.1	51.2	293	470	1,610	2,351	Bulgaria
—	—	—	—	9	120	192	12.3	18.0	—	—	—	—	Burkina Faso
102	128.2	1,176	636	32	135	218	14.4	21.0	5,000	8,000	—	—	Burma
1	0.4[5]	—	—	2	3	5	0.7	1.0	...	...	...	...	Burundi
45	58.9	888	2,844	13	346	548	34.3	50.1	1,300	2,100	...	...	Cameroon
1,300	4,164.9	125,000	49,000	211	18,291	29,436	531.9	776.5	2,342	3,769	...	...	Canada
22	20.9	119	388	8	7	12	0.7	1.0	—	—	—	—	Cape Verde
259	483.8	4,005	4,131	3	...	...	...	...	—	—	—	—	Cayman Islands
—	—	—	—	1	106	170	20.7	30.2	1,296	2,085	...	...	Central African Republic
—	—	—	—	1	144	231	20.7	30.2	1,400	2,300	...	...	Chad
200	745.9	10,704	5,256	12	1,412	2,272	205.4	299.8	1,360	2,189	5,629	8,218	Chile
1,179	8,674.6[5]	36,400	37,500	72	3,100	5,000	116.4	170.0	67,000	108,000	51,000	74,000	China
—	—	1,300	53	1	...	...	...	...	—	—	—	—	Christmas Island
—	—	—	—	1	...	...	...	...	—	—	—	—	Cocos (Keeling) Islands
82	462.6	7,921	7,585	79	2,617	4,212	143.6	209.7	8,900	14,300	...	...	Colombia
2	1.8	15	39	3	...	...	...	...	—	—	—	—	Comoros
22	10.8	6,503	820	18	128	206	12.7	18.5	2,312	3,721	...	...	Congo
—	—	7	12	6	...	...	...	...	—	—	—	—	Cook Islands
27	25.9	1,121	1,059	8	388	625	14.9	21.8	475	764	...	...	Costa Rica
418	1,216.7	2,532	2,016	13	844	1,358	15.1	22.1	149	240	...	...	Cuba
593	5,784.8	1,536	2,640	2	532	856	66.3	96.9	—	—	—	—	Cyprus
19	276.6	...	...	14	1,148	1,847	32.8	47.9	295	475	2,301	3,360	Czechoslovakia
1,112	7,926.1	8,940	29,832	10	5,859	9,429	80.1	116.9	120	190	1,164	1,700	Denmark
9	3.3	550	815	3	33	53	3.4	5.0	—	—	—	—	Djibouti
3	1.2	120	64	2	...	...	...	...	—	—	—	—	Dominica
35	58.7	1,940	2,612	3	299	481	...	...	—	—	—	—	Dominican Republic
130	543.8	5,319	2,451	13	535	861	28.1	41.0	900	1,500	—	—	Ecuador
351	828.0	95,653	102,088	10	2,267	3,648	28.2	41.2	1,900	3,000	1,709	2,495	Egypt
11	3.3	312	2,217	1	152	245	21.1	30.8	...	...	—	—	El Salvador
2	6.7	85	52	1	4	7	0.7	1.0	104	167	...	...	Equatorial Guinea

Transportation (continued)

country	roads and motor vehicles, about 1980								railroads (latest)					
	roads			motor vehicles			cargo		track length		traffic			
	length		paved (per-cent)	auto-mobiles	trucks and buses	persons per vehicle			mi	km	passengers		cargo	
	mi	km					short ton-mi ('000,000)	metric ton-mi ('000,000)			passen-ger-mi ('000,000)	passen-ger-km ('000,000)	short ton-mi ('000,000)	metric ton-mi ('000,000)
Ethiopia	22,612	36,391	34.0	43,107	17,222	543	...	...	485[6]	781[6]	153	247	101	148
Faeroe Islands	124	200	...	9,617	3,987	3	...	...	—	—	—	—	—	—
Falkland Islands	317	510	5.9	720	,177	2	...	...	—	—	—	—	—	—
Fiji	2,669	4,295	13.0	25,995	17,785	15	...	...	660	1,062	—	—	—	—
Finland	46,881	75,448	50.0	1,352,055	182,797	3	12,100	17,700	5,688	9,153	2,034	3,274	5,747	8,391
France	498,593	802,407	...	20,300,000	2,890,000	2	70,000	102,000	21,352	34,362	33,867	54,504	47,582	69,468
French Guiana	421	678	75.0	16,789	2,043	4	...	...	34	54	...	...	...	...
French Polynesia	460	741	33.0	16,500	8,500	5	...	...	—	—	—	—	—	—
Gabon	4,594	7,393	6.8	16,043	10,695	21	...	...	98	158	...	...	...	...
Gambia, The	1,916	3,083	14.0	6,445	1,604	79	...	...	—	—	—	—	—	—
Germany, East	74,844	120,449	39.4	2,677,703	515,860	5	6,454	9,423	8,833	14,215	14,369	23,124	38,697	56,496
Germany, West	301,970	485,973	99.0	24,035,907	1,535,468	2	82,912	121,050	17,678	28,450	25,695	41,352	44,721	65,292
Ghana	19,884	32,000	25.0	33,000	27,000	183	...	...	592	953	286	460	73	106
Gibraltar	31	50	100.0	8,755	872	3	...	...	—	—	—	—	—	—
Greece	67,752	109,037	73.0	1,073,411	574,782	6	...	...	1,547[2]	2,489[2]	879	1,414	202	295
Greenland	96	154	40.6	1,429	1,176	20	...	...	—	—	—	—	—	—
Grenada	534	860	60.1	4,784	981	19	...	...	—	—	—	—	—	—
Guadeloupe	1,235	1,988	85.0	87,785	33,350	3	...	...	—	—	—	—	—	—
Guam	419	674	100.0	39,002	14,653	2	...	...	—	—	—	—	—	—
Guatemala	10,736	17,278	16.5	——242,250——		30	...	...	467[2]	751[2]	...	...	...	...
Guinea	17,647	28,400	4.5	9,948	9,992	239	...	...	411	662	...	...	...	...
Guinea-Bissau	3,143	5,058	15.4	——3,807——		213	...	...	—	—	—	—	—	—
Guyana	4,741	7,630	7.0	32,521	12,926	19	...	...	50	80	...	...	...	...
Haiti	2,139	3,443	17.0	17,377	3,646	243	...	...	155	250	...	...	...	...
Honduras	5,618	9,042	22.0	58,920	24,385	47	...	...	624	1,004	...	...	...	...
Hong Kong	756	1,217	100.0	227,658	77,248	17	...	...	37	60	253	407	41	60
Hungary	54,148	87,142	54.4	1,181,655	144,072	8	7,026	10,258	8,089	13,018	8,117	13,064	15,939	23,271
Iceland	7,227	11,631	5.6	94,744	11,715	2	318	464	—	—	—	—	—	—
India	996,748	1,604,110	38.9	1,035,263	837,907	348	55,500	81,000	37,862	60,933	125,574	202,092	107,616	157,116
Indonesia	80,094	128,900	44.7	577,345	453,193	144	...	...	4,264	6,877	3,910	6,293	606	885
Iran	59,463	95,696	28.0	1,532,269	313,006	21	...	...	2,837	4,567	1,560	2,526	2,645	3,861
Iraq	15,699	25,265	65.0	229,530	152,768	37	...	...	1,792	2,884	495	797	1,544	2,254
Ireland	57,349	92,294	94.1	709,000	72,034	4	...	...	1,236[2]	1,989[2]	515	828	427	624
Israel	2,878	4,631	100.0	459,178	105,079	7	...	...	514	827	151	242	552	806
Italy	184,745	297,318	79.3	18,603,370	1,547,361	3	88,451	129,136	10,025	16,133	24,189	38,928	12,321	17,988
Ivory Coast	28,943	46,580	7.9	166,920	88,286	34	...	...	760	1,223	753	1,212	411	600
Jamaica	6,990	11,250	67.6	41,163	17,394	38	...	...	205	330	49	79	88	129
Japan	695,948	1,120,020	50.7	25,539,070	15,806,586	3	124,187	181,309	13,249	21,322	194,703	313,344	26,927	39,312
Jordan[9]	3,248	5,227	100.0	118,852	48,884	21	19,133	27,934	384[2]	618[2]	...	...	...	...
Kampuchea	8,296	13,351	19.6	...	...	...	...	...	403	649	...	...	...	...
Kenya	33,298	53,588	12.2	113,629	84,193	83	...	...	1,295	2,084	465	748	1,436	2,097
Kiribati	398	640	...	——163——		356	...	...	—	—	—	—	—	—
Korea, North	12,600	20,280	1.5	...	...	...	...	...	2,700	4,400	...	...	...	...
Korea, South	33,514	53,936	35.7	305,811	341,185	61	3,491	5,097	3,798	6,113	13,070	21,034	7,460	10,892
Kuwait	940	1,513	100.0	435,291	155,236	2	...	...	—	—	—	—	—	—
Laos	6,950	11,185	7.2	16,000	3,500	195	...	...	—	—	...	...	...	...
Lebanon	4,350	7,000	80.0	460,400	35,000	6	...	...	189	304	...	...	...	...
Lesotho	2,492	4,010	9.1	5,505	10,005	89	...	...	1	2	...	...	...	...
Liberia	3,363	5,412	5.3	1,632	1,088	749	...	...	304[2]	490[2]	—	—	1,968[10]	2,873[10]
Libya	8,771	14,116	77.0	367,400	278,900	5	...	...	—	—	—	—	—	—
Liechtenstein	200	323	...	13,498	1,488	2	...	...	12	19	...	...	...	...
Luxembourg	3,174	5,108	98.9	159,580	14,889	2	190	277	168	270	193	311	378	552
Macau	56	90	100.0	15,606	4,023	18	...	...	—	—	—	—	—	—
Madagascar	30,843	49,637	9.0	14,786	18,459	278	...	...	549	884	171	276	148	216
Malawi	6,693	10,772	18.0	14,102	17,247	195	—	—	490[2]	789[2]	60	97	127	185
Malaysia	19,542	31,450	82.0	1,050,617	244,382	11	...	...	1,666	2,681	1,269	2,042	762	1,113
Maldives	...	...	...	125[11]	45[11]	222[11]	...	...	—	—	—	—	—	—
Mali	9,755	15,699	10.6	20,047	4,670	254	...	...	398	641	97	156	90	132
Malta	808	1,300	94.1	74,773	17,871	4	...	...	—	—	—	—	—	—
Martinique	1,131	1,820	82.0	126,666	3,498	3	...	...	—	—	—	—	—	—
Mauritania	4,685	7,540	18.0	11,262	8,437	83	...	...	404	650	...	...	5,347	7,807
Mauritius	1,107	1,782	92.0	25,536	17,494	23	...	...	—	—	—	—	—	—
Mayotte	133	215	40.0	——1,300——		40	...	...	—	—	—	—	—	—
Mexico	133,019	214,073	46.0	5,221,159	1,978,327	10	...	...	8,821	14,196	3,288	5,292	28,307	41,328
Monaco	28	45	100.0	13,897	3,109	2	...	...	1	2	...	...	...	...
Mongolia	29,000	46,700	1.7	...	...	...	1,047	1,529	985	1,585	217	350	2,681	3,914
Montserrat	176	283	73.9	1,323	114	8	...	...	—	—	—	—	—	—
Morocco	35,749	57,533	46.0	447,174	208,146	33	655	956	1,105[2]	1,779[2]	708	1,140	2,669	3,896
Mozambique	16,156	26,000	30.4	49,500	...	217	...	...	1,867	3,004	354	570	1,034	1,509
Nauru	12	19	100.0	——1,761——		5	...	...	3	5	...	...	...	...
Nepal	2,858	4,600	41.3	14,201	12,638	500	984	1,437	39	63	...	...	...	...
Netherlands, The	57,492	92,525	100.0	4,650,000	353,000	3	12,150	17,738	1,837	2,956	5,826	9,376	1,997	2,915
Netherlands Antilles	590	950	31.5	19,830[12]	1,122[12]	6[12]	...	...	—	—	—	—	—	—
New Caledonia	4,428	7,127	67.0	28,000	8,580	4	...	...	—	—	—	—	—	—
New Zealand	57,873	93,137	53.0	1,431,739	303,020	2	...	...	2,754	4,433	267	429	2,227	3,252
Nicaragua	4,172	6,712	9.7	24,887	9,789	81	...	...	214[2]	344[2]	10	17	7	10
Niger	5,311[13]	8,547[13]	32.4[13]	25,844	7,275	160	...	...	—	—	—	—	—	—
Nigeria	67,102	107,990	27.8	262,550	90,731	223	...	...	2,178	3,505	488	785	666	972
Niue	142	229	53.5	264	64	12	...	...	—	—	—	—	—	—
Norfolk Island	50	80	66.0	1,802	90	1	...	...	—	—	—	—	—	—
Norway	51,804	83,371	59.0	1,337,884	180,608	3	3,515	5,132	2,636	4,242	1,393	2,242	1,743	2,545
Oman	6,297	10,134	12.5	55,299	44,869	9	...	...	—	—	—	—	—	—
Pakistan	57,351	92,297	64.0	173,042	65,366	365	...	...	5,473	8,808	11,206	18,031	5,009	7,313
Panama	5,351	8,612	31.7	90,310	30,264	15	...	...	171	275	...	...	...	...
Papua New Guinea	11,523	18,545	6.0	17,730	27,938	67	...	...	—	—	—	—	—	—

merchant marine				air							canals and inland waterways (latest)				country
fleet, 1983 (vessels over 100 gross tons)	total dead-weight tonnage, 1983 ('000)	international cargo (latest)		airports with sched-uled flights, 1984	traffic (latest)						length		cargo		
		loaded metric tons ('000)	off-loaded metric tons ('000)		passengers		cargo				mi	km	short ton-mi ('000,000)	metric ton-km ('000,000)	
					passenger-mi ('000,000)	passenger-km ('000,000)	short ton-mi ('000,000)	metric ton-km ('000,000)							
20	43.2	547	1,753	30	474	762	18.6	27.1			70	113	...	...	Ethiopia
—	—	150	300	1	...	...	...	...			—	—	—	—	Faeroe Islands
5	4.1	4	9	1	...	...	...	...			—	—	—	—	Falkland Islands
56	26.6	588	828	16	198	319	2.2	3.2			—	—	—	—	Fiji
339	3,601.0	17,844	30,912	24	1,626	2,616	35.4	51.7			3,764	6,057	3,082	4,500	Finland
1,173	16,815.5	52,248	167,868	58	23,368	37,608	1,533.9	2,293.5			8,623	13,877	4,795	7,000	France
—	—	30	276	8	...	...	...	...			2,336	3,760	...	...	French Guiana
—	—	13	387	32	...	...	...	...			—	—	—	—	French Polynesia
17	143.8	8,040	631	27	232	374	18.2	26.5			199	320	...	...	Gabon
8	4.2	130	181	1	...	...	...	...			—	—	—	—	Gambia, The
416	1,793.1	4,000	15,500	4	1,320	2,130	44.9	65.5			1,430	2,302	1,290	1,884	Germany, East
1,769	10,797.5	40,824	80,784	31	14,108	22,704	1,084.7	1,583.7			2,769	4,456	34,216	49,954	Germany, West
135	296.8	1,471	2,493	4	201	324	1.9	2.8			200	320	...	...	Ghana
48	376.6	7	270	1	...	...	...	...			—	—	—	—	Gibraltar
3,169	65,986.2	22,600	26,000	28	3,311	5,328	365.5	533.7			50	80	585	854	Greece
—	—	176	291	3	14	22	0.2	0.3			—	—	—	—	Greenland
3	0.6	160	63	2	...	...	...	...			—	—	—	—	Grenada
—	—	426	1,075	7	...	...	...	...			—	—	—	—	Guadeloupe
—	—	725	2,315	1	...	...	...	...			—	—	—	—	Guam
9	27.2	926	2,057	2	99	160	13.6	19.9			...	...	...	...	Guatemala
18	2.9	10,000	545	1	21	34	2.1	3.0			805	1,295	...	...	Guinea
15	2.5	25	219	1	5	8	0.7	1.0			—	—	—	—	Guinea-Bissau
84	19.6	2,400	910	19	4	6	0.7	1.0			3,700	6,000	...	...	Guyana
6	0.9	723	561	2	...	...	1.3	1.9			60	100	...	...	Haiti
191	298.1	1,450	1,143	4	168	271	25.5	37.3			700	1,200	...	...	Honduras
294	7,248.3[7]	11,796[7]	31,548[7]	1	...	...	...	...			—	—	—	—	Hong Kong
21	112.5			1	787	1,267	20.2	29.5			1,008	1,622	316	461	Hungary
394	168.8	502	1,358	15	964[8]	1,551[8]	12.9[8]	18.9[8]			—	—	58	84	Iceland
677	10,081.6	38,900	40,380	62	8,239	13,260	307.1	448.4			12,310	19,811	...	...	India
1,391	2,801.5	84,014	22,794	94	4,675	7,523	118.7	173.3			13,409	21,579	...	...	Indonesia
270	2,907.4	80,000	6,000	10	1,532	2,466	225.5	329.2			626	1,008	...	...	Iran
161	2,694.5	95,750	4,004	2	917	1,476	34.2	48.0			631	1,015	...	...	Iraq
162	266.3	5,000	14,500	7	2,027	3,263	78.6	114.8			454	731	...	...	Ireland
71	865.7	6,456	6,468	6	3,147	5,064	...	...			—	—	—	—	Israel
1,609	16,474.7	35,000	210,000	29	7,837	12,612	337.3	492.5			1,390	2,237	134	195	Italy
66	195.3	4,601	4,622	17	139	224	12.5	18.2			460	740	...	...	Ivory Coast
13	12.9	8,335	4,018	2	768	1,236	7.0	10.2			—	—	—	—	Jamaica
10,593	66,640.1	83,764	550,948	69	34,628	55,728	1,396.2	2,038.5			1,100	1,770	145,046	211,763	Japan
7	53.1	3,845	7,837	2	2,043	3,288	76.6	111.9			...	...	19,202	28,035	Jordan[9]
3	3.8	10	22	1	...	...	...	...			2,474	3,982	...	...	Kampuchea
20	3.3	1,078	3,064	9	602	968	72.7	106.1			...	...	...	...	Kenya
4	1.8	300	69	17	...	...	...	...			3	5	...	...	Kiribati
57	724.8	1,600	4,000	1	...	...	...	...			1,400	2,250	...	...	Korea, North
1,733	10,429.8	27,005	77,500	3	7,533	12,123	718.2	1,048.6			...	...	5,398	7,881	Korea, South
235	4,121.7	33,300	6,500	1	2,239	3,603	77.1	112.6			—	—	—	—	Kuwait
—	—	—	—	1	4	7	0.7	1.0			2,900	4,600	...	...	Laos
260	681.2	200	2,500	1	604	972	322.5	470.8			—	—	—	—	Lebanon
—	—	—	—	11	8	13	—	0.1			—	—	—	—	Lesotho
2,062	133,239.7	19,000	1,051	8	11	17	1.4	2.0			230	370	...	...	Liberia
104	1,605.0	53,530	12,680	8	831[1]	1,337[1]	9.0[1]	13.1[1]			—	—	—	—	Libya
—	—	—	—												Liechtenstein
—	—	—	—	1	159	257	15.8	23.0			23	37	...	...	Luxembourg
137	14.4	550	570	—	—	—	—	—			—	—	—	—	Macau
58	107.1	336	1,099	41	313	504	11.9	17.4			727	1,170	...	...	Madagascar
1	0.1	...	...	4	89	144	0.8	1.2			891	1,434	4	6	Malawi
376	2,075.4	36,221	22,529	39	3,366	5,418	101.9	148.7			4,534	7,296	...	...	Malaysia
39	267.3	6	45	1	12	20	0.2	0.3			—	—	—	—	Maldives
				9	60	97	0.3	0.5			1,107	1,782	18	26	Mali
147	1,341.9	360	1,536	1	400	644	2.2	3.2			...	...	...	...	Malta
—	—	373	1,053	1	...	...	...	...			...	...	...	...	Martinique
28	5.9	7,546	508	10	141	227	12.7	18.6			500	800	...	...	Mauritania
18	42.0	879	779	2	138	221	15.9	23.2			—	—	—	—	Mauritius
				1	...	...	...	...			—	—	—	—	Mayotte
619	2,148.8	71,308	13,318	43	8,254	13,284	96.7	141.2			1,900	3,000	...	...	Mexico
2	26.2	...	...	1	—	1	...	...			...	...	...	...	Monaco
—	—	66	46	1	155	249	3.6	5.2			295	474	3	4	Mongolia
1	1.0	66	46	1	...	...	...	...			—	—	—	—	Montserrat
218	587.0	20,500	10,890	15	1,135	1,827	26.6	38.9			600	1,000	—	—	Morocco
97	41.0	2,613	1,260	7	418	672	9.1	13.3			2,330	3,750	...	...	Mozambique
9	95.3	2,300	68	1	66	107	6.8	10.0			—	—	—	—	Nauru
				30	71	114	0.9	1.4			—	—	—	—	Nepal
1,287	7,479.7	75,072	228,972	9	10,512	16,917	726.7	1,061.0			2,725	4,386	4,197	6,127	Netherlands, The
—	—	46,500	50,600	4	104	167	0.4	0.6			—	—	—	—	Netherlands Antilles
—	—	—	—	18	...	...	...	...			—	—	—	—	New Caledonia
117	269.9	8,772	6,936	36	3,634	5,849	152.3	222.4			1,000	1,600	1,503	2,195	New Zealand
20	25.7	366	1,000	1	47	76	5.5	8.0			1,182	1,902	...	...	Nicaragua
				5	129	208	12.5	18.2			370	600	...	...	Niger
169	638.1	58,088	15,497	15	1,401	2,256	18.4	26.9			5,328	8,575	...	...	Nigeria
—	—	—	—	1	...	...	...	...			—	—	—	—	Niue
—	—	—	—	1	...	...	...	...			—	—	—	—	Norfolk Island
2,340	33,524.5	39,576	16,356	35	2,559	4,118	95.3	139.1			190	306	6,197	9,047	Norway
25	10.9	16,160	2,800	2	...	...	...	...			—	—	—	—	Oman
87	785.0	3,084	11,712	18	4,129	6,645	157.0	229.2			...	...	...	...	Pakistan
5,316	58,319.0	778	2,698	19	206	331	22.5	32.9			548	882	...	...	Panama
80	25.9	1,950	1,646	134	332[14]	535[14]	6.1[14]	8.9[14]			...	...	...	...	Papua New Guinea

Transportation (continued)

country	roads and motor vehicles, about 1980 roads length mi	roads length km	paved (per-cent)	motor vehicles auto-mobiles	trucks and buses	persons per vehicle	cargo short ton-mi ('000,000)	metric ton-mi ('000,000)	railroads (latest) track length mi	km	traffic passengers passen-ger-mi ('000,000)	passen-ger-km ('000,000)	cargo short ton-mi ('000,000)	metric ton-km ('000,000)
Paraguay	7,893	12,703	9.1	41,895	17,600	55	...	...	274	441	14	22	24	34
Peru	36,360	58,516	10.4	359,700	196,013	34	...	...	2,402	3,865	27	44	87	127
Philippines	95,953	154,421	12.5	318,085	485,667	62	...	...	1,120	1,800	127	204	16	24
Pitcairn Island	4	6	—	—	3	18	...	...	—	—	—	—	—	—
Poland	185,893	299,166	61.4	2,881,670	690,250	10	23,305	34,024	15,171	24,415	28,782	46,320	92,287	134,736
Portugal	32,282	51,953	86.4	1,025,596	188,091	8	...	...	2,933	4,720	3,657	5,886	687	1,003
Puerto Rico	5,802	9,337	86.0	951,404	165,517	4	...	...	57	92	...	...	...	...
Qatar	565	909	55.0	45,000	25,000	3	...	...	—	—	—	—	—	—
Réunion	1,814	2,919	81.0	108,725	36,080	4	...	...	382[16]	614[16]	—	—	—	—
Romania	45,586	73,364	47.4	250,000	130,000	58	8,077	11,792	6,913	11,125	15,893	25,578	43,029	62,822
Rwanda	4,200	6,760	7.6	6,188	8,297	364	...	...	—	—	—	—	—	—
St. Christopher and Nevis	160	256	49.1	2,329	263	19	...	...	36	58	—	—	—	...
St. Helena and Ascension	109	175	74.3	—1,124[17]—		5[17]	...	...	—	—	—	—	—	...
St. Lucia	471	758	67.1	5,302	2,210	16	...	...	—	—	—	—	—	...
St. Pierre and Miquelon	67	108	40.3	1,550	532	3	...	...	—	—	—	—	—	...
St. Vincent and the Grenadines	1,076	1,731	33.5	4,061	1,070	19	...	...	—	—	—	—	—	—
San Marino	137	220	...	14,029	550	2	...	...	—	—	—	—	—	—
São Tomé and Príncipe	179	288	69.3	1,774	265	40	...	...	—	—	—	—	—	—
Saudi Arabia	34,238	55,100	42.4	757,395	661,290	7	...	...	359[2]	578[2]	54	88	314	458
Senegal	8,634	13,895	24.8	50,875	27,767	72	375	547	737	1,186	83	133	212	309
Seychelles	316	508	...	3,520	1,056	14	...	...	—	—	—	—	—	—
Sierra Leone	4,595	7,395	15.5	16,009	4,826	167	36	53	52	84	...	...	...	...
Singapore	1,540	2,478	88.0	216,933	113,075	8	...	...	24	38	...	...	...	...
Solomon Islands	1,305	2,100	11.5	974	1,040	116	...	...	—	—	—	—	—	—
Somalia	9,454	15,215	15.0	17,200	8,050	136	...	...	—	—	—	—	—	—
South Africa	114,115	183,651	25.9	2,557,000	1,019,700	7	...	...	14,653	23,581	13,050	21,000	71,156	103,886
South West Africa/Namibia	27,304	43,942	8.5	69,000		12	...	...	1,453	2,338	...	...	...	...
Spain	200,133	322,083	56.0	8,353,944	1,533,409	4	62,659	91,480	8,433	13,572	9,136	14,703	6,961	10,163
Sri Lanka	94,711	152,423	40.0	126,256	91,519	69	...	...	903[2]	1,453[2]	1,984	3,194	147	215
Sudan, The	5,604	9,018	33.0	150,000	22,000	113	...	...	2,974	4,786	725	1,167	1,795	2,620
Suriname	5,455	8,779	25.0	26,500	11,000	9	...	...	104	167	...	...	...	...
Swaziland	1,692	2,723	19.0	13,308	5,406	29	...	...	283[2]	455[2]	...	...	...	...
Sweden	80,479	129,518	64.0	2,935,985	514,101	2	14,476	21,135	7,682	12,362	4,109	6,612	9,816	14,331
Switzerland	41,422	66,662	96.4	2,473,318	292,126	2	4,206	6,140	1,777	2,860	5,570	8,964	4,455	6,504
Syria	12,614	20,300	70.6	79,141	113,440	50	1,318	1,924	1,296	2,086	256	413	485	708
Taiwan	10,893	17,530	73.0	592,154	333,736	20	4,146	6,053	3,045	4,900	5,302	8,533	1,768	2,581
Tanzania	33,315	53,616	6.0	48,752	31,930	230	...	...	2,206	3,550	...	...	695	1,015
Thailand	44,833	72,152	34.9	451,001	535,735	49	...	...	2,320	3,735	5,875	9,455	1,626	2,374
Togo	4,638	7,464	57.0	29,447	5,132	70	...	...	275	442	48	78	3,677	5,368
Tokelau	...	...	...	...	...	...	...	...	—	—	—	—	—	—
Tonga	269	433	60.6	1,082	1,294	41	...	...	—	—	—	—	—	—
Trinidad and Tobago	3,216	5,175	46.0	180,948	49,800	5	...	...	—	—	—	—	—	—
Trust Territory of the Pacific Is.	211	339	19.9	4,206	169	31	...	...	—	—	—	—	—	—
Tunisia	15,753	25,352	52.0	141,185	147,571	23	562	820	1,251[2]	2,013[2]	628	1,011	1,169	1,707
Turkey	144,259	232,162	76.0	812,122	392,927	37	26,742	39,042	5,091	8,193	3,515	5,656	4,332	6,325
Turks and Caicos Islands	75	121	20.0	...	...	...	...	...	—	—	—	—	—	—
Tuvalu	5	8	0.0	...	...	...	...	...	—	—	—	—	—	—
Uganda	16,979	27,325	11.0	10,633	11,245	643	...	...	799	1,286	...	...	...	...
U.S.S.R.	622,000	1,001,000	74.3	8,255,000	7,254,000	17	311,000	454,000	88,736	142,806	205,800	331,200	2,353,195	3,435,600
United Arab Emirates	808	1,300	60.6	108,589	3,505	9	...	...	—	—	—	—	—	—
United Kingdom	213,084	342,925	96.4	15,267,000[18]	1,854,600[18]	3[18]	66,500[18]	97,100[18]	14,408	23,187	19,700	31,704	12,082	17,640
United States	3,851,900	6,199,000	85.0	123,461,507	34,995,004	1	541,120	790,020	215,876	826,440	10,998	17,700	919,004	1,341,720
Uruguay	30,952	49,813	20.0	281,275	49,813	9	...	...	1,867[2]	3,004[2]	170	274	123	180
Vanuatu	551	887	3.5	3,087[20]	242[20]	14[20]	...	...	—	—	—	—	—	—
Venezuela	38,804	62,449	36.8	1,501,382	795,856	6	...	...	107	173	25	40	14	20
Vietnam	25,594	41,190	15.6	100,000	200,000	155	...	...	1,620	2,600	2,830	4,554	534	779
Virgin Islands (U.S.)	532	856	...	26,500	4,200	3	...	...	—	—	—	—	—	—
Wallis and Futuna	62	100	...	...	...	...	...	...	—	—	—	—	—	—
Western Sahara	3,790	6,100	7.9	6,284	424	12	...	...	—	—	—	—	—	—
Western Samoa	289	465	64.3	3,254	410	43	...	...	—	—	—	—	—	—
Yemen (Aden)	6,521	10,495	12.9	11,900	10,500	78	...	...	—	—	—	—	—	—
Yemen (Şan'ā')	13,645	21,960	9.3	80,375	115,018	31	...	...	—	—	—	—	—	—
Yugoslavia	72,124	116,072	51.0	2,568,146	228,063	8	2,877	4,201	5,834	9,389	7,000	11,265	17,922	26,166
Zaire	90,100	145,000	1.5	89,471	16,807	281	...	...	3,576	5,755	242	389	1,214	1,772
Zambia	23,135	37,232	15.0	103,000	90,000	31	...	...	1,360	2,188	...	...	...	...
Zimbabwe	105,880	170,400	7.0	224,453	24,246	30	...	...	2,100[2]	3,400[2]	...	...	...	...

crude oil and petroleum products pipelines (latest) country	length mi	km	traffic short ton-mi ('000,000)	metric ton-km ('000,000)
Algeria	5,571	8,965	...	...
Argentina	355	571	...	...
Australia	466	750	...	...
Austria	483	777	4,087	5,967
Belgium	291	469	1,142	1,668
Bolivia	685	1,102	...	...
Brazil	224	360	...	...
Burma[21]	427	687	...	...
Canada	22,370	36,000	52,159	76,151
Chile	465	748	...	...

crude oil and petroleum products pipelines (latest) country	length mi	km	traffic short ton-mi ('000,000)	metric ton-km ('000,000)
China	1,131	1,820	...	...
Colombia	570	917	...	...
Czechoslovakia	591	951	6,607	9,646
Denmark	42	68	18	26
Ecuador	956	1,538	...	...
Egypt	844	1,358	...	...
France	3,336	5,369	19,756	28,842
Gabon	182	293	...	...
Germany, East	808	1,301	3,259	4,758
Germany, West	1,296	2,086	7,701	11,243

crude oil and petroleum products pipelines (latest) country	length mi	km	traffic short ton-mi ('000,000)	metric ton-km ('000,000)
Hungary	1,251	2,013	1,971	2,878
India	1,397	2,248	...	...
Indonesia	2,371	3,816	...	...
Iran	7,493	12,058	...	...
Iraq	2,862	4,606	...	...
Israel	350	563	...	...
Italy	1,909	3,069	7,931	11,579
Kenya	250	402	...	...
Kuwait	639	1,028	...	...
Libya	4,651	7,485	...	...

merchant marine				air						canals and inland waterways (latest)				country
fleet, 1983 (vessels over 100 gross tons)	total dead-weight tonnage, 1983 ('000)	international cargo (latest)		airports with scheduled flights, 1984	traffic (latest)					length		cargo		
		loaded metric tons ('000)	off-loaded metric tons ('000)		passengers		cargo			mi	km	short ton-mi ('000,000)	metric ton-km ('000,000)	
					passenger-mi ('000,000)	passenger-km ('000,000)	short ton-mi ('000,000)	metric ton-km ('000,000)						
33	41.4	...	...	1	163	263	2.0	2.9	1,900	3,100	...	...	Paraguay
679	1,014.5	8,292	3,199	22	502	808	28.1	41.0	5,473	8,808	...	...	Peru
884	4,719.3	12,576	18,240	41	4,578	7,368	78.2	114.2	2,000	3,219	...	...	Philippines
													Pitcairn Island
812	5,069.0	22,406[7]	15,844[7]	11	813	1,308	12.8	18.8	2,408	3,875	1,073	1,566	Poland
357	2,161.1	4,100	19,000	12	2,458	3,956	65.9	96.2	510	821	...	...	Portugal
		15	15	11	...	...	...	...	—	—	—	—	Puerto Rico
63	474.1	16,420	1,700	1	...	...	...	...	—	—	—	—	Qatar
		336	1,104	1	...	...	...	...	—	—	—	—	Réunion
379	3,493.0	10,000	22,000	15	1,468	2,362	27.0	39.0	1,031	1,659	...	...	Romania
—	—	—	—	1	...	...	...	...	—	—	—	—	Rwanda
2	0.5	36	63	2	...	...	...	...	—	—	—	—	St. Christopher and Nevis
1	2.3	1	12	1	...	...	...	...	—	—	—	—	St. Helena and Ascension
8	7.2	100	188	2	...	...	...	...	—	—	—	—	St. Lucia
—	—	7	64	1	...	...	...	...	—	—	—	—	St. Pierre and Miquelon
44	123.0	16	45	3	...	...	...	...	—	—	—	—	St. Vincent and the Grenadines
													San Marino
2	1.0	12	15	1	—	—	—	—	—	—	—	—	São Tomé and Príncipe
435	9,311.9	299,257	30,000	23	7,799	12,552	1,065.1	1,555.1	—	—	—	—	Saudi Arabia
135	33.3	1,645	1,925	11	111	178	12.3	18.0	935	1,505	...	...	Senegal
3	0.3	6	100	1	1	2	...	...	—	—	—	—	Seychelles
20	1.3	113	574	7	53	86	6.2	9.0	500	800	447	652	Sierra Leone
855	12,027.6	36,276	63,852	1	11,315	18,210	504.7	736.9	—	—	—	—	Singapore
23	3.8	299	95	2	—	1	...	...	—	—	—	—	Solomon Islands
25	16.7	250	814	8	171	276	2.9	4.2	—	—	—	—	Somalia
295	891.7	69,276	26,758	36	5,376	8,652	266.4	389.0	...	...	—	—	South Africa
				8									South West Africa/Namibia
2,589	12,788.2	40,342	94,648	29	9,670	15,563	301.4	440.0	649	1,045	19,870	29,009	Spain
68	586.7	1,680	3,192	5	896	1,442	19.9	29.1	267	430	...	...	Sri Lanka
22	124.3	916	2,642	15	441	710	8.3	12.1	3,300	5,310	...	...	Sudan, The
25	19.2	6,079	1,518	4	152	245	2.5	3.6	2,800	4,500	...	...	Suriname
				1	19	30	0.7	1.0	—	—	—	—	Swaziland
674	5,056.5	40,512	48,132	35	3,652	5,877	129.0	189.0	724	1,165	7,055	10,300	Sweden
34	478.8	...	...	5	7,583	12,203	369.8	539.9	13	21	103	150	Switzerland
52	70.3	18,500	6,000	7	690	1,111	6.4	9.3	418	672	...	...	Syria
514	2,879.2	...	...	9	5,676	9,135	1,081.0	1,578.0	...	...	—	—	Taiwan
39	71.1	1,118	2,040	53	130	210	0.8	1.2	726	1,168	...	...	Tanzania
219	868.1	16,000	15,600	18	5,354	8,616	219.9	321.0	2,500	4,000	...	...	Thailand
9	77.3	704	995	1	117	188	12.3	18.0	30	50	...	...	Togo
—	—	—	—	—	—	—	—	—	—	—	—	—	Tokelau
19	20.4	23	74	4	...	...	...	...	—	—	—	—	Tonga
51	13.8	12,798	11,094	1	954	1,536	12.1	17.6	—	—	—	—	Trinidad and Tobago
—	—	25	143	9	159	256	2.2	3.2	—	—	—	—	Trust Territory of the Pacific Is.
52	440.9	4,884	8,880	5	984	1,584	14.0	20.4	—	—	—	—	Tunisia
687	4,088.4	30,648	38,148	21	1,116	1,797	115.5	168.6	1,000	1,600	35	51	Turkey
10	3.5	3	5	5	...	...	...	...	—	—	—	—	Turks and Caicos Islands
2	0.5	...	...	1	...	...	...	...	—	—	—	—	Tuvalu
—	—	—	—	7	75	120	2.1	3.0	...	...	—	—	Uganda
7,753	27,573.8	162,000	63,000	44	52,784	84,948	2,675.4	3,906.0	87,017	140,041	129,800	189,500	U.S.S.R.
202	450.3	64,788	8,500	4	...	...	...	...	—	—	—	—	United Arab Emirates
2,570	29,878.4	129,708[18]	117,204[18]	61	27,313	43,956	1,040.7	1,519.3	713[18]	1,147[18]	70[18]	100[18]	United Kingdom
6,437	29,295.0	327,768[15]	332,424[15]	824	252,706	406,692	6,965.0	10,168.7	25,543	41,107	410,849	599,830	United States
88	331.0	570[19]	454[19]	7	105	169	0.5	0.7	1,000	1,600	...	...	Uruguay
12	38.6	67	105	9	...	...	...	...	—	—	—	—	Vanuatu
244	1,357.0	60,821	12,093	42	2,565	4,128	99.0	144.6	4,400	7,100	...	...	Venezuela
114	389.6	680	5,000	3	2	3	...	...	11,000	17,702	...	...	Vietnam
—	—	9,500	12,600	3	...	...	...	...	—	—	—	—	Virgin Islands (U.S.)
—	—	—	60	2	...	...	...	...	—	—	—	—	Wallis and Futuna
				1	...	...	...	...	—	—	—	—	Western Sahara
4	6.0	34	89	3	...	...	...	...	—	—	—	—	Western Samoa
36	14.1	3,575	4,834	1	...	...	...	...	—	—	—	—	Yemen (Aden)
10	1.9	40	2,000	5	181	291	18.5	27.0	—	—	—	—	Yemen (San'ā')
479	3,898.5	5,375	22,850	16	1,783	2,870	40.9	59.7	1,243	2,001	2,877	4,201	Yugoslavia
34	133.3	845	1,513	33	249	402	46.6	68.1	8,500	13,700	678	990	Zaire
—	—	—	—	14	348	559	50.6	73.9	1,398	2,250	...	...	Zambia
—	—	—	—	8	344	554	6.6	9.6	...	...	...	...	Zimbabwe

[1]International flights only. [2]Route length. [3]Excludes coastwise shipping. [4]Includes coastwise shipping. [5]Gross tons. [6]Includes 100 km of the Chemin de Fer Djibouti–Ethiopien (CDE) in Djibouti. [7]Includes transshipments. [8]Icelandair only. [9]East Bank only. [10]LAMCO Railroad only. [11]Male atoll only. [12]Aruba and Bonaire only. [13]National roads only. [14]Air Niugini only. [15]United States includes Puerto Rico. [16]Railroads serve sugarcane plantations only. [17]St. Helena only. [18]Excludes Northern Ireland. [19]Port of Montevideo only. [20]Espiritu Santo and Efate Islands only. [21]Pipeline from Mann to Syriam only. [22]International pipelines only.

country	crude oil and petroleum products pipelines (latest)				country	crude oil and petroleum products pipelines (latest)				country	crude oil and petroleum products pipelines (latest)			
	length		traffic			length		traffic			length		traffic	
	mi	km	short ton-mi ('000,000)	metric ton-km ('000,000)		mi	km	short ton-mi ('000,000)	metric ton-km ('000,000)		mi	km	short ton-mi ('000,000)	metric ton-km ('000,000)
Mexico	5,692	9,160	...	...	Romania	...	...	3,553	5,188	U.S.S.R.	43,900	70,800	865,221	1,263,200
Mozambique[22]	187	301	...	...	Saudi Arabia	3,840	6,180	...	...	U. Arab Emirates	1,785	2,873	...	...
Netherlands[22]	243	391	...	...	South Africa	980	1,577	...	...	United Kingdom	1,967	3,166	5,928	8,654
Nigeria	2,135	3,436	...	...	Spain	954	1,535	2,143	3,129	United States	167,800	270,000	...	...
Norway	217	350	3,923	5,727	Sudan, The	492	792	...	...	Venezuela	1,717	2,763	...	...
Oman	470	756	...	...	Switzerland	149	239	762	1,112	Yugoslavia	619	996	1,597	2,331
Pakistan	1,639	2,638	...	...	Syria	415	668	...	...	Zaire	205	330	...	...
Peru	691	1,112	...	...	Tanzania	1,060	1,706	...	...	Zimbabwe	187	255	...	...
Poland	1,227	1,975	11,162	16,296	Tunisia	670	1,078	...	...					
Qatar	295	475	...	...	Turkey	1,197	1,926	11,541	16,849					

Communications

Virtually all of the states of the world have newspapers (although only daily papers are included in this table), radio broadcast systems and telephone, post office, and telegraph facilities, and most have television and telex. The focus of this table, therefore, is on the relative density and distribution of communications services. The publication of information about the infrastructure and traffic volume of these national systems, however, runs far behind the capabilities of the systems themselves. Certain countries publish no information about themselves; others publish data analyzed according to a variety of fiscal, calendar, religious, or other years; still others, while they may have the data almost simultaneously with the end of their business year, may not publish them except in company reports of limited distribution or in national statistical summaries, and only after a delay of up to several years.

The date given for each category of information denotes that of the majority of the data in the respective columns, but within each column as much as one-quarter of the data may be from different years. The data also originate in sources of varying datedness and reliability. Data for some kinds of communications apparatus and traffic are relatively easy to track; telephones, for example, must be installed, and service is recorded. But radios may be purchased by anyone and turned on whenever desired (except in certain countries). As a result, data on distribution and use of radio and television apparatus may be collected in a variety of ways—on the basis of numbers of subscribers, periodic sample surveys, census or housing surveys, or private consumer surveys. In some cases the figures have been rounded, and the population data used in calculating the distribution statistics are usually based on midyear estimates for the respective years.

The United Nations Educational, Scientific, and Cultural Organization (UNESCO) publishes extensive data on newspapers, radio, and television in its *Yearbook* that have been collected from standardized questionnaires. The completeness and recency of its data, however, depend on the timely return of a fully completed questionnaire, and response rates depend on a variety of factors. In general, response rates for inquiries by international organizations in communications are better than in other fields because these organizations and the responsible authorities in each respective country must conduct day-to-day business and, hence, have a better ongoing relationship.

Newspaper statistics are especially difficult to collect and compare. Newspapers are founded, cease publication, merge, or change frequency of publication often. Data on circulation, sales, and readership are often incomplete, slow of aggregation at the national level, or regarded as proprietary either for private or governmental publications. In some

Communications

country	daily newspapers (latest)			radio (1983)			television (1983)			telephone (1982)		traffic ('000 calls)		
	number	total circulation ('000)	circulation per 1,000 pop.	transmitters (latest)	receivers (all types) ('000)	persons per receiver	transmitters (latest)	receivers (all types) ('000)	persons per receiver	receivers ('000)	persons per receiver	local	long-distance	international
Afghanistan	14	69	4	14	135	124.3	1	12.5	1,342	31.2	498.1	41,839	13	13
Albania	2	145	54	14	210	13.6	166	20.5	138.8	4.8	582.3			
Algeria	4	425	22	55	3,500	5.9	44	1,325	15.6	606.9	32.9	1,587,500	118,369	173,719
American Samoa	2	10	310	1	33.5	1.0	3	15.0	2.3	6.0	5.5	138	...	120[1]
Andorra	1	...	...	4	7.0	2.1	...	4	3.7	17.7	2.1	12,100	2,728	142
Angola	5	120	17	55	130	53.4	...	22	315.6	29.4	224.5			
Anguilla	—	—	—	1	2.1	3.3	—	—	—	1.2	5.8	262.8[9]	...	14.8[9]
Antigua and Barbuda	1	6	80	5	19	4.1	...	16.5	4.7	6.7	11.5	5,945[9]	...	206[9]
Argentina	133	2,682	104	202	10,000	2.9	75	5,910	5.0	3,041.5	9.3	...	...	2,316
Australia	63	4,851	336	479	20,000	0.8	312	6,500	2.3	7,684.3	2.0	5,552,136[1]	677,866[1]	10,766[1]
Austria	31	2,634	351	498	5,520	1.4	799	3,180	2.4	3,177.9	2.4	...	...	...
Bahamas, The	4	33	146	5	115	1.9	...	50	4.5	75.1	3.2	125,736	1,140	1,453
Bahrain	4	25	64	3	140	2.8	1	121	3.2	85.8	4.3	122,572	...	...
Bangladesh	53	404	4	23	770	122.9	6	252	375.6	122.2	759.9	...	...	1,268
Barbados	2	78	311	5	191	1.3	2	52	4.8	72.9	3.5	300,000	...	861
Belgium	31	2,262	230	59	4,617	2.1	49	2,976.4	3.3	3,818.6	2.6	1,427,559	1,619,240	...
Belize	2	7	41	1	71	2.1	...	...	...	8.6	17.4	—28,382—		90
Benin	1	1	0.3	7	68	53.2	2	12.8	284.9	16.2	223.5	...	...	...
Bermuda	1	13	217	6	100	0.6	...	66	0.8	49.0	1.1	41,948	...	1,751
Bhutan	1	...	...	1	12	123.2	...	...	...	14.6	80.4	...	...	...
Bolivia	14	214	39	184	480	12.3	...	386	16.1	144.3	41.0	...	...	...
Botswana	1	17	21	3	75	12.9	...	...	...	11.9	66.5	...	...	...
Brazil	328	5,094	44	962	17,500	7.2	...	12,425	10.1	8,536.0	14.6	8,643,770	708,281	6,324
British Virgin Islands	—	—	—	5	6.8	1.9	...	2.4	5.4	2.0	7.0	...	...	243[9]
Brunei	1	7	60	13	50	4.0	2	30	6.7	21.9	9.1	...	22,720	...
Bulgaria	14	2,280	234	35	2,149	4.2	339	2,000	4.5	1,225.8	7.4	...	39,400[1]	1,319[1]
Burkina Faso	1	1.5	0.2	9	116	55.3	1	15	427.7	8.6	739.5	...	...	...
Burma	7	329	10	7	700	18.9	...	...	...	42.1	859.0	...	...	...
Burundi	1	...	...	5	152	29.2	...	—	—	5.6	853.2	...	...	...
Cameroon	3	28	3	19	780	11.6	...	...	...	30.0	295.1	...	...	...
Canada	126	5,700	241	1,030	28,000	0.88	1,050	12,400	2.0	15,741.7	1.6	...	...	...
Cape Verde	...	...	...	3	46.9	6.3	...	0.5	588	1.7	193.5	921	17[1]	...
Cayman Islands	...	...	...	3	18	1.1	...	...	...	9.9	1.8	11,785	...	...
Central African Republic	1	500	0.2	4	85	28.7	...	0.2	12,200	2.8	854.6	...	...	...
Chad	4	...	...	3	75	63.7	...	...	...	6.2	712.4	...	...	...
Chile	37	945	87	109	3,250	3.5	...	2,643	4.3	595.1	18.9	...	...	1,096
China	392	12,000	19	...	13,000	79.4	...	9,700	108.6	4,355.0	223.0	...	...	...
Christmas Island	—	—	—	...	2.5	1.2	...	...	...	...	...	...	...	...
Cocos (Keeling) Islands	—	—	—	...	0.8	0.9	...	...	...	0.14	4.2	...	...	...
Colombia	38	1,273	48	...	3,025	9.0	71	1,800	14.1	1,747.7	15.5	...	...	2,330
Comoros	—	—	—	7	40.0	10.7	...	...	...	1.2	310.0	...	...	...
Congo	3	...	...	10	96	17.5	...	4.5	365	8.9	181.9	31	29	1,375
Cook Islands	1	1.9	106	2	10	1.7	...	...	...	1.7	10.0	...	...	165
Costa Rica	4	155	70	123	190	12.2	...	450	5.2	255.9	9.3	588,097	481,171	1,733
Cuba	9	891	91	143	2,130	4.6	58	750	13.1	406.4	24.1	...	77,498	1,148
Cyprus	12	67	108	6	400	1.6	5	156	4.2	128.5	5.0	396,824	16	478,521
Czechoslovakia	30	4,641	304	120	4,550	3.4	72	4,300	3.8	3,226.0	4.8	3,760,588	58,222	4,596
Denmark	49	1,876	367	49	2,042	2.5	32	1,886	2.7	3,483.3	1.5	2,051,437	1,165,357	29,031
Djibouti	...	...	...	3	17.5	10.4	...	11	27.8	4.4	69.5	...	4,015[9]	462[9]
Dominica	—	—	—	3	30	2.5	...	...	...	3.0	27.0	...	...	56[1]
Dominican Republic	7	220	42	188	225	25.5	...	388	14.9	175.1	33.2	1,514,898	5,678	2,798
Ecuador	38	400	49	...	1,800	5.0	...	135	66.7	290.2	27.8	...	...	1,038
Egypt	9	2,475	60	82	8,000	5.5	36	3,850	11.3	521.6	86.3	475,887	51,734[1]	995
El Salvador	12	334	75	75	900	5.5	...	300	16.5	86.3	58.9	368,416	64,563	...
Equatorial Guinea	2	...	...	3	90	2.9	...	2.0	130.5	2.0	190.0	...	...	...
Ethiopia	5	52	2	13	2,000	16.4	...	36	911.1	100.8	323.2	314,080	3,337	180
Faeroe Islands	...	...	...	4	16	2.8	...	...	...	20.4	2.2	...	...	...
Falkland Islands	—	—	—	2	2.5	0.8	...	16	0.1	0.6	3.4	...	...	...
Fiji	2	54	87	12	400	1.6	...	...	...	46.3	14.0	...	...	...
Finland	62	2,289	480	100	2,515	1.9	143	2,200	2.2	2,511.3	1.9	5,040,296	5,751,155	813,322

countries circulation data is virtually nonexistent. In others no daily newspaper exists.

The commercially published annual *World Radio TV Handbook* (J.M. Frost, editor) is a valuable source of information on broadcast media and has both complete and timely coverage. It depends on data received from broadcasters, but because some do not respond local correspondents and monitors are used in many countries, and some unconfirmed or unofficial data are included as estimates.

Telephone data are obtained from the American Telephone and Telegraph Communications' annual, *The World's Telephones,* supplemented by the *Telephone Engineer and Management Directory* and by *Telephony's Directory and Buyers' Guide for the Telecommunications Industry,* both annual commercial publications. These collect data by sending questionnaires to the telephone agencies of each country, and their statistics tend to be accurate and timely, but not all countries supply current data. More than one-quarter of the data are from other than the base year. Several countries also report incomplete data: the Trust Territory of the Pacific Islands excludes data on the Federated States of Micronesia; Anguilla supplies statistics only on telephone exchange lines; some Pacific island states report only radio telephones. A number of countries omit data on public coin-box telephones so that their statistics may reflect an under-

count. The figures for calls under telephone traffic represent a measure of mechanical activity rather than an enumeration of actual conversations between individuals. Depending on a country's metering system, multiple counting of a single call might occur.

Post Office statistics are collected mainly from individual country sources and the principal secondary sources enumerated in the "Bibliography and sources," beginning on page 958. Because the dates of the statistics vary so widely, it is not possible to assign specific years. Where supplied, however, the data tend to be exact, not rounded. Some countries include sub-post offices and postal offices offering limited service, so that their figures appear higher than expected.

The statistics on telegraph and telex are derived mainly from the UN-affiliated International Telecommunication Union's *Yearbook of Common Carrier Telecommunication Statistics* with a few additional statistics from country sources.

UNESCO, the diverse industry sources cited above, and scores of national statistical sources have all been used in the compilation of this table because of the incompleteness of any single source.

... Not available.

—None, nil, or not applicable.

post office (1978)			telegraph (1982)			telex (1982)				country
number	persons per office	pieces of mail handled ('000)	total traffic ('000)	national traffic ('000)	international outgoing traffic ('000)	subscriber lines	traffic ('000 minutes) total	national	international outgoing	
349	36,447	11,218	183[1]	951[1]	88[1]	73[1]	...	...	25[1]	Afghanistan
292	7,328	...	...	...	...	...	...	...	...	Albania
1,534	12,170	284,884	3,470	3,008	462	4,716	25,082	17,699	7,383	Algeria
...	...	...	...	...	...	...	...	...	...	American Samoa
...	...	...	...	...	...	...	...	...	...	Andorra
...	...	3,384[2]	198[3]	44[3]	154[3]	587[3]	...	...	1,599[3]	Angola
2	3,500	...	...	...	...	...	...	...	...	Anguilla
15	5,333	2,262[4,5,6]	17	—	17	64	...	...	110[3]	Antigua and Barbuda
...	...	739,431[7]	15,532	10,326	203	7,826	...	135,982[1]	9,372	Argentina
4,906	3,093	2,512,711[8]	5,257	4,068	1,189	38,552	56,815	45,329	11,486	Australia
2,641	2,866	2,111,378	1,349	1,079	270	21,858	102,578	71,219	31,359	Austria
8	26,250	31,598	773	283	493	446	1,163	77	1,086	Bahamas, The
...	...	21,250[4,7]	149	20	129	1,845	11,315	1,926	9,389	Bahrain
7,192	12,047	333,133	...	3,470[9]	...	461[3]	...	...	855[3]	Bangladesh
14	17,857	16,917[6]	...	...	78[3]	241[3]	...	...	478[3]	Barbados
2,309	4,269	3,359,460	1,472	1,146	326	22,835	103,538	42,062	61,477	Belgium
48	3,333	...	...	...	20[3]	41	52[1]	...	52[1]	Belize
106	26,321	11,856[2]	...	422[9]	...	153[9]	...	...	244[9]	Benin
15	3,333	...	...	...	25	407[1]	1,214[1]	...	1,214[1]	Bermuda
81	16,728	2,266[10]	...	...	...	...	...	...	...	Bhutan
458	11,572	54,609	325[9]	277[9]	48[9]	930[3]	818[9]	530[9]	541[3]	Bolivia
39	2,461	1,677[11]	255[12]	209[12]	46[12]	348	1127	760	367	Botswana
4,565	25,982	2,819,449[13]	15,667[1]	15,327[1]	340[1]	49,444	264,943	247,652	17,291	Brazil
5	2,407	...	8	—	8	393	493	...	463	British Virgin Islands
8	23,750	4,878[4,5,6]	...	...	...	231[3]	...	...	419[3]	Brunei
2,857	3,101	...	7,489	7,253	236	5,900	30,145	26,375	3,770	Bulgaria
66	90,000	2,128[2]	114[2]	65[2]	49[2]	206[3]	...	...	380[3]	Burkina Faso
1,101	28,619	85,210	1,358[9]	1,280[9]	78[9]	479	...	...	209[9]	Burma
...	...	3,953	277	97	187	851	...	...	105[1]	Burundi
150	50,207	64,248[10]	...	...	...	...	...	...	...	Cameroon
8,285	2,972	1,166,912	2,585[1]	1,423[1,14]	1,162[1,14]	49,451	...	...	14,542	Canada
...	...	3,522[15]	111	98	13	40	190	58	132	Cape Verde
...	...	2,262[15]	10	—	10	131[1]	234[1]	...	234[1]	Cayman Islands
...	...	34,525[16]	473	373	103	134[3]	...	...	353[3]	Central African Republic
...	...	938[11]	320[2]	300[2]	20[2]	60[2]	...	122[17]	188[2]	Chad
1,486	7,617	129,356[15]	3,386	3,310	76	3,538	13,022	8,724	4,298	Chile
67,000	9,649	2,849,000[8]	155,291	153,811	1,480	1,021	...	...	3,565	China
2	1,500	...	...	...	...	...	...	...	...	Christmas Island
1	700	...	...	...	...	...	...	...	...	Cocos (Keeling) Islands
...	...	209,461[16]	21,126[3]	20,889[3]	237[3]	4,823	24,221[1]	91,103[3,18]	4,994[1]	Colombia
9	38,889	1,732[15]	457	207	257	37	...	...	53	Comoros
...	...	9,818	267[9]	218[9]	49[9]	329[3]	...	...	687[3]	Congo
...	...	...	...	...	240[19]	411[9]	66[19]	111[9]	551[9]	Cook Islands
...	...	22,159[2]	279	223	56	1,385	2,693	1,219	1,402	Costa Rica
700	13,271	86,991[3,6]	15,986[9]	15,592[9]	394[9]	2,352[3]	20,519[3]	19,338[3]	1,181[3]	Cuba
69	8,985	26,867	144	87	57	2,249	4,436	1,385	3,051	Cyprus
—	—	2,216,000[15]	10,023	9,677	346	9,740[3]	...	71,181[3,18]	6,034[3]	Czechoslovakia
1,321	3,876	1,395,792[2]	462	300	162	11,342	43,451	15,681	27,770	Denmark
...	...	2,033	25	—	25	128	467	8	459	Djibouti
33	2,894	...	12	—	12	28[3]	211[1]	...	211[1]	Dominica
154	25,807	21,741[11]	...	...	...	1,758	...	...	3,272	Dominican Republic
...	...	26,521[12]	...	...	95	3,476	13,511	4,584	8,927	Ecuador
8,276	4,952	337,776	9,302	8,332	970	709	1,203	454	749	Egypt
317	14,981	25,985[4]	1,218	1,185	33	...	...	...	...	El Salvador
...	...	...	...	...	...	520	1,171	420	751	Equatorial Guinea
301	108,887	55,046[4,5]	209	177	32	...	...	...	...	Ethiopia
...	...	...	...	...	...	...	...	...	...	Faeroe Islands
...	...	233[20]	6	—	6	6	11	—	11	Falkland Islands
35	18,800	22,273[10]	134	104	30	399	931	196	735	Fiji
3,847	1,248	750,579	750	648	102	7,200	25,018	11,850	13,168	Finland

Communications (continued)

country	daily newspapers (latest)			radio (1983)			television (1983)			telephone (1982)		traffic ('000 calls)		
	number	total circulation ('000)	circulation per 1,000 pop.	transmitters (latest)	receivers (all types) ('000)	persons per receiver	transmitters (latest)	receivers (all types) ('000)	persons per receiver	receivers ('000)	persons per receiver	local	long-distance	international
France	90	11,300	210	363	20,000	2.7	2,821	19,000	2.8	29,940.3	1.8	...	...	...
French Guiana	1	1.6	25	13	40	1.8	...	9.5	7.7	19.6	3.7		—90,977—	
French Polynesia	2	13	87	6	77	2.0	...	25.5	6.0	24.8	6.2	...	1,722[1]	...
Gabon	1	18	13	16	100	8.9	...	20	44.5	11.1	120.3	...	121	1,046[1]
Gambia, The	—	—	—	3	100	6.2	...	...	...	3.5	171.8	363,265[9]	129,084[9]	...
Germany, East	39	8,658	517	120	6,410	2.6	505	5,842	2.9	3,252.0	5.1	1,303,831	686,696	11,006
Germany, West	380	20,410	333	431	24,300	2.5	3,424	21,835	2.8	30,122.0	2.0	5,508,415	8,027,617	278,583
Ghana	5	345	30	4	2,000	6.1	7	71	172.4	70.7	173.2	561	232	144
Gibraltar	1	2.2	73	3	10	3.0	...	7.1	4.2	9.9	3.0	17,471	...	317
Greece	116	962	107	55	4,000	2.4	84	1,700	5.8	2,956.7	3.3	3,456,615	...	...
Greenland	—	—	—	18	13	4.0	...	10	5.2	10.4	3.3	...	...	...
Grenada	—	—	—	3	50	2.2	...	...	...	5.6	20.0	...	...	90[1]
Guadeloupe	1	18	58	5	25	12.6	8	5.0	62.9	74.1	4.3		—292,355—	
Guam	1	25	222	5	300	0.4	2	78	1.4	14.4	7.4	...	...	...
Guatemala	9	91	13	125	500	15.4	...	202	38.1	96.7	79.6	301,044	57,974	...
Guinea	1	20	4	7	125	43.0	...	7.5	716.7	10.0	514.7	...	...	...
Guinea-Bissau	1	6	11	4	20	40.6	...	...	...	2.6	347.3	94,248	...	2,825
Guyana	3	67	77	8	300	2.8	...	...	...	28.5	33.1		—100,711—	28
Haiti	4	32	7	48	120	43.3	...	30	0.2	20.0	255.2	...	140[1]	...
Honduras	7	223	63	153	1,535	2.7	...	135	30.6	33.7	117.4	...	...	...
Hong Kong	72	1,588	300	24	2,610	2.0	4	1,163	4.5	1,822.8	2.9	...	...	...
Hungary	27	2,585	242	51	5,500	2.0	42	2,810	3.8	1,296.7	8.2	1,120,882	605,266	261,324
Iceland	6	127	557	26	70	3.3	83	62.6	3.8	111.4	2.1	468,982	1,345	59,650
India	1,087	13,033	20	160	22,000	34.1	14	2,095	358.1	2,981.6	234.1	9,870,987	169,491[1]	1,043[1]
Indonesia	89	2,603	17	201	6,550	24.3	201	3,000	53.1	600.6	252.6	4,315,920	10,213	2,142
Iran	24	484	15	120	7,500	5.4	418	2,000	20.1	1,041.9	38.8	4,826,104[1]	19,249[1]	17,440[1]
Iraq	5	325	25	26	2,200	6.4	21	535	26.2	253.3	53.5	...	...	...
Ireland	7	771	229	21	1,315	2.6	21	838	4.2	720.0	4.8	...	...	...
Israel	24	801	227	52	1,050	3.8	48	600	6.7	1,302.0	3.1	1,176	2,283	6,116
Italy	75	5,308	93	1,179	14,008	4.0	1,867	13,610	4.2	20,444.0	2.7	10,408,298	4,062,971	82,897
Ivory Coast	1	53	7	24	800	10.8	12	562	15.3	78.4	105.2	...	...	...
Jamaica	3	128	59	19	857	2.7	...	200	11.6	124.3	17.9	8,010[1]	...	...
Japan	178	65,881	569	1,008	93,000	1.3	11,439	30,200	4.1	60,349.9	2.0	...	...	14,937
Jordan	6	126	58.5	13	546	6.1	5	201	16.6	21.0	110.8	...	...	...
Kampuchea	17	...	...	6	100	58.8	...	50	117.6	7.3	787.1	...	...	...
Kenya	3	156	10	22	580	31.1	...	75	240.5	216.7	79.1	562,424	6,857	715
Kiribati	—	—	—	2	11	6.0	...	—	—	1.2	50.6	...	...	34
Korea, North	11	1,000	...	...	1,000	18.7	...	...	...	...	...	...	...	...
Korea, South	29	6,496	173	118	10,250	3.8	126	7,611	5.1	5,158.4	7.6	2,990,368	335,074	3,590,883
Kuwait	7	180	170	14	710	2.2	10	575	2.7	231.6	6.7	194,832[1]	...	4,000
Laos	3	...	...	4	225	15.8	...	...	...	2.4	1,587.5	...	...	...
Lebanon	25	281	98	10	1,500	1.7	5	450	5.8	150.4	21.5	...	...	...
Lesotho	2	42	30	4	40	35.1	...	...	...	5.9	232.9	...	...	...
Liberia	3	11	6	9	330	6.2	...	35	57.8	7.7	243.2		—16,000[1]—	...
Libya	2	...	...	20	165	20.9	13	170	20.2	102.0	23.0	...	...	...
Liechtenstein	2	12	477	...	6.7	3.9	...	6.4	4.1	21.4	1.2	7,044	12,115	4,863
Luxembourg	5	130	358	7	225	1.6	3	91.1	4.0	228.0	1.6	...	122,700	14,482
Macau	6	59	197	5	78	4.5	...	1.0	351.0	23.2	12.8	...	...	3,126
Madagascar	12	...	...	21	910	10.2	14	71	128.8	37.1	253.3	...	...	...
Malawi	2	31	5	10	500	12.5	...	...	...	15.1	421.9	...	15,777[1]	108[9]
Malaysia	44	1,796	135	47	365	40.2	38	1,152	12.7	825.3	17.4	3,057,939	15,950[1]	73,216
Maldives	2	...	...	3	12.0	13.6	2	1.1	148.2	1.5	103.3	5,677[1]	152[9]	26
Mali	1	40	5.7	14	102	72.3	...	...	...	8.5	863.8	...	92	1,578
Malta	4	...	...	3	75	4.8	4	76.6	4.7	91.0	4.0	48,117	...	5,078
Martinique	1	26	83	6	45	6.8	8	42	7.4	68.9	4.7	6,867	95,016	...
Mauritania	1	...	...	4	95	16.4	...	...	...	5.2	323.5	...	...	...
Mauritius	7	74	79	3	115	8.8	...	85	11.6	37.8	25.7	...	37,587[1]	695,375[1]
Mayotte	—	—	—	...	5.0	53.0	...	...	...	...	...	...	...	...
Mexico	268	3,994	64	680	21,000	3.5	115	7,550	9.8	5,411.1	13.5	10,713,000	461,277	27,516
Monaco	2	11	432	12	9.5	2.9	5	17.2	1.6	17.0	1.6		—69,037—	81,880
Mongolia	1	112	69	...	175	9.9	...	57	30.4	16.2	105.6	...	...	...
Montserrat	—	—	—	3	4.0	3.0	...	...	...	2.6	4.6	2,267[1]	...	503
Morocco	9	230	11.8	35	2,500	8.9	20	817	27.2	241.1	84.7	...	1,258,081	475
Mozambique	2	42	4	39	275	3.6	...	1.0	990	56.3	224.1	75,150	2,400	233
Nauru	—	—	—	1	4.0	1.8	...	...	...	1.6	5.0	1,304[9]	—	229[9]
Nepal	29	96	7.5	...	300	52.6	...	—	—	5.4	2,781.5	...	...	...
Netherlands, The	80	4,553	325	39	4,500	3.2	26	6,189	2.3	7,769.1	1.8	2,802,000	2,211,012	91,614
Netherlands Antilles	5	54	206	16	175	1.4	...	56.5	4.4	72.2	3.7	74,910	...	...
New Caledonia	1	15	109	3	78	1.9	20	30	4.9	28.0	5.0	11,961[1]	4,977[1]	13,555[1]
New Zealand	37	1,068	345	65	2,780	1.1	...	925	3.3	1,875.5	1.7	...	102,380	3,075
Nicaragua	8	170	69	87	200	13.6	...	127	21.5	51.2	51.6	...	188,717	...
Niger	1	42	4.9	19	160	36.8	...	11	535.3	8.5	629.6	...	...	...
Nigeria	15	660	11	111	5,800	14.2	28	457	180.2	708.4	125.8	...	...	23
Niue	—	—	—	1	0.9	3.0	...	—	—	0.2	14.6	...	...	...
Norfolk Island	—	—	—	1	1.2	1.7	...	0.4	5.1	1.0	2.0	...	...	...
Norway	83	1,859	456	764	1,500	2.8	1,389	1,292	3.2	1,992.1	2.1	...	...	...
Oman	2	...	...	6	250	3.5	...	45	19.2	4.5	204.2	...	...	...
Pakistan	119	1,095	14	28	1,500	61.4	13	1,000	92.1	393.0	221.7	...	117,240	1,090
Panama	6	148	79	97	290	7.0	10	226.5	9.1	213.0	9.0	625,400	...	2,279
Papua New Guinea	1	19	6	26	215	14.7	...	—	—	50.1	62.4	54,403	...	2,387
Paraguay	5	200	65	56	198	15.5	...	81	37.8	58.7	53.8	153,408[1]	2,870[1]	686[1]
Peru	59	828	51	189	2,200	8.3	...	860	21.3	129.7	134.2	...	14,438	694
Philippines	19	972	21	295	2,185	23.3	43	955	53.3	624.1	81.3	...	70,966	25,657
Pitcairn Island	—	—	—	...	...	...	...	...	...	0.02	2.2	...	...	...
Poland	44	8,433	237	...	8,875	4.1	118	8,190	4.4	3,505.7	10.3	...	996,224	3,434
Portugal	22	493	50	80	2,155	4.7	...	1,486	6.8	1,455.8	6.9	...	...	...
Puerto Rico	4	475	139	...	2,000	1.6	10	810	4.0	678.4	5.8	52,695	12,042	1,646
Qatar	1	7	33	11	75	3.4	3	110	2.3	67.5	3.8	...	...	...
Réunion	3	52	106	25	120	43	...	80	6.5	81.2	6.4		—206,276—	
Romania	35	3,998	181	71	3,250	6.9	344	3,897	5.9	2,027.0	11.1	...	...	...

post office (1978)			telegraph (1982)			telex (1982)				country
num-ber	per-sons per office	pieces of mail handled ('000)	total traffic ('000)	na-tional traffic ('000)	inter-national outgoing traffic ('000)	sub-scriber lines	traffic ('000 minutes) total	national	international outgoing	
17,114	3,153	12,693,700[2]	10,755	6,690	4,065	95,383	371,841	249,218	122,623	France
...	...	...	15	13	2	175	422	341	81	French Guiana
...	...	9,394	104	78	26	144	327	5	322	French Polynesia
...	...	13,435	...	...	...	...	...	...	...	Gabon
...	...	...	28[9]	5[9]	23[9]	67[3]	...	...	100[3]	Gambia, The
11,999	1,397	1,522,073	12,477	10,315	2,162	15,695	252,956[18]	...	...	Germany, East
18,688	3,300	13,385,260[2]	6,256	3,675	2,581	148,405	2,088,377	1,914,389	173,988	Germany, West
237	41,645	103,900	1,760[9]	1,630[9]	130[9]	172[9]	...	...	298[9]	Ghana
...	...	1,014[6]	18	—	18	153	292	3	289	Gibraltar
...	...	439,174	3,816	3,461	355	14,829	47,531	27,350	20,181	Greece
—	...	...	...	...	...	...	...	...	...	Greenland
51	2,157	...	19	—	19	25	471	...	471[1]	Grenada
44	7,500	...	50	46	4	427	894	751	143	Guadeloupe
...	...	...	...	...	...	...	...	...	...	Guam
...	...	54,301[7]	...	...	...	...	...	...	...	Guatemala
...	...	30,809[2]	329[2]	298[2]	31[2]	170[3]	...	...	193[3]	Guinea
										Guinea-Bissau
158	5,570	251,400[11]	237[7]	149[7]	88[7]	64[7]	197[7]	197	178[7]	Guyana
132	33,106	1,046,472[2]	...	...	...	...	...	...	...	Haiti
508	7,264	60,689	...	...	...	...	...	...	...	Honduras
89	58,797	332,175	1,258	12	1,246	18,863	56,151	20,495	35,656	Hong Kong
2,518	4,253	1,775,121[15]	11,467	11,032	435	9,222	...	66,992[18]	6,899	Hungary
160	1,437	23,770	549	524	25	371	...	...	996	Iceland
125,283	5,096	8,143,757	70,858[9]	60,260[9]	10,598[9]	20,397	...	204,736[18]	14,866	India
2,796	52,067	252,300	7,281	7,142	139	8,105	...	440,683[18]	3,366[17]	Indonesia
...	...	918,591[20]	...	...	190	3,125[19]	...	...	4,339[19]	Iran
400	30,825	85,566	...	844	...	1,390	6,398	419	5,979	Iraq
2,096	1,662	482,153[2,6]	439	318	121	6,500	18,867	6,603	12,264	Ireland
615	5,870	448,900[2]	712	427	285	4,250	...	22,100[18,19]	5,850[19]	Israel
13,963	4,061	5,980,035	24,749[21]	22,794[21]	1,955[21]	50,091[21]	257,431[21]	156,398[21]	101,033[21]	Italy
96	67,500	59,861[6]	581[1]	508[1]	73[1]	1,181[3]	...	...	3,149[3]	Ivory Coast
138	6,824	138,161[2]	772[9]	659[9]	113[9]	312[3]	...	...	630[3]	Jamaica
23,005	5,114	12,549,900[2]	44,696[19]	43,306[19]	1,390[19]	60,000	165,822	111,103	54,719	Japan
791	3,110	33,392	...	...	...	...	...	...	...	Jordan
...	...	10,320[15]	...	...	...	...	...	...	...	Kampuchea
711	24,121	169,630[4,5,6]	...	1,014	225[12]	1,537	2,226[1]	—	2,226[1]	Kenya
5	10,800	374[20,22]	51	38	13	...	...	...	...	Kiribati
...	...	...	...	...	...	...	...	...	...	Korea, North
2,082	18,891	807,297[2]	10,392	10,160	232	4,318[1]	...	...	11,815[1]	Korea, South
...	...	88,273[5,6]	805	82	723	3,264	11,840	3,006	8,834	Kuwait
...	...	4,496	222[2]	152[2]	72[2]	15[1]	...	...	40[1]	Laos
...	...	...	...	...	...	...	...	...	...	Lebanon
...	...	28,614	...	...	...	138[3]	...	...	35[3]	Lesotho
...	...	5,407[15]	...	...	...	...	...	...	...	Liberia
200	13,700	98,741[5]	...	...	...	...	...	...	...	Libya
...	—	11,577[13]	23	23	23	23	23	23	23	Liechtenstein
104	3,461	94,133	46	13	33	1,952	9,035	1,789	7,246	Luxembourg
...	...	3,924[7]	15	—	15	292	302	11	291	Macau
547	12,724	131,526	448[3]	403[3]	45[3]	320[3]	696[3]	162[3]	534[3]	Madagascar
223	25,381	66,598	...	150[12]	1,280[9]	351[3]	...	...	752[3]	Malawi
740	17,969	503,522[6]	10,087	758	9,329	5,866	...	...	9,201	Malaysia
...	...	5,856	299	22[9]	7[9]	753	...	...	53[3]	Maldives
85	84,235	6,245	...	...	...	...	...	...	...	Mali
16	22,500	37,366	46	—	46	628	1,573	1	1,572	Malta
44	7,273	...	49	45	4	371	868	721	147	Martinique
...	...	3,035	50	35	15	204	...	3,098[18]	492	Mauritania
92	9,891	26,448	723	5[3]	67[3]	480[3]	617[1]	—	617[1]	Mauritius
										Mayotte
13,252	5,087	1,605,316[7]	37,033	36,635	398	15,885[3]	186,932[3]	171,343[3]	15,589[3]	Mexico
—	...	...	23	13	10	555	...	...	4,415	Monaco
382	3,900	...	...	...	...	...	...	...	...	Mongolia
10	1,000	1,283[2]	8[3]	—	8[3]	25	...	...	21	Montserrat
797	25,157	192,073	1,122	962	160	4,811	3,166[17]	1,680[17]	1,486[17]	Morocco
...	...	19,519[2]	...	117[9]	45	558	...	...	1,141	Mozambique
...	...	...	7[9]	—	7[9]	10[9]	279[9]	—	279[9]	Nauru
...	...	...	359	229	130	161	...	...	218	Nepal
...	...	4,410,000	968	507	461	35,564	...	344,553[18]	33,263[17]	Netherlands, The
...	...	18,733[2]	...	...	48[1]	620[1]	1,643[1]	266[1]	1,377[1]	Netherlands Antilles
52	2,808	15,287	34	7	27	143	376	8	368	New Caledonia
1,321	2,354	695,778	14,060[19]	2,069[19]	11,991[19]	4,944[19]	16,932[19]	9,148[19]	7,784[19]	New Zealand
...	...	35,890[15]	890[1]	839[1]	51[1]	391[3]	974[3]	225[3]	749[3]	Nicaragua
52	93,461	6,445[7]	323[3]	278[3]	45[3]	278	...	...	567	Niger
1,667	49,427	1,345,620[4,6]	...	...	...	...	...	...	...	Nigeria
										Niue
1	1,800	698	...	...	...	...	...	...	...	Norfolk Island
1,992	2,068	1,152,579	699	537	162	8,607	33,343	15,582	17,761	Norway
48	19,167	...	177	10	167	950	3,251	859	2,392	Oman
11,388	7,651	619,805[2]	12,918[3]	2,930[3]	9,988[3]	7427	...	283[3,17]	1,167[3]	Pakistan
305	6,229	30,908[15]	299	257	42	1,744	...	...	2,830	Panama
83	36,145	43,520[24]	1,221[25]	41[25]	1,180[25]	1,490	2,848	1,461	1,387	Papua New Guinea
...	...	...	244[3]	196[3]	48[3]	642[3]	...	...	1,023[3]	Paraguay
...	...	...	8,846[1]	8,739[1]	107[1]	2,740	...	70,348[18]	4,829	Peru
2,038	24,303	...	16,866	16,497	369	8,637	12,929	5,186	7,743	Philippines
1	53	...	...	...	...	...	...	...	...	Pitcairn Island
8,181	4,388	2,054,620[6,7]	12,392	11,917	475	27,099	...	...	7,040	Poland
11,517	860	510,770	1,588	1,375	213	11,687	49,044	32,621	16,423	Portugal
124	24,677	...	...	...	...	...	...	...	...	Puerto Rico
10	19,000	...	...	9	...	1,068	2,612	659	1,953	Qatar
50	10,340	...	37	30	7	317	789	585	204	Réunion
5,046	4,429	,795,199[2]	5,393[9]	5,150[9]	243[9]	6,750	...	...	3,683	Romania

Communications (continued)

country	daily newspapers (latest)			radio (1983)			television (1983)			telephone (1982)				
	number	total circulation ('000)	circulation per 1,000 pop.	transmitters (latest)	receivers (all types)('000)	persons per receiver	transmitters (latest)	receivers (all types)('000)	persons per receiver	receivers ('000)	persons per receiver	traffic ('000 calls)		
												local	long-distance	international
Rwanda	1	200	0.1	8	47.7	114.5	...	—	—	5.9	838.1	...	...	...
St. Christopher and Nevis	1	1.5	22	2	21	2.1	...	20	2.2	3.3	13.6			
St. Helena and Ascension	—	—	—	1	2.0	3.5		—	—	0.7	6.7	349	117	10
St. Lucia	1	4	35	4	90	1.4	...	3.0	42.0	9.5	12.8	...		...
St. Pierre and Miquelon	—	—	—	4	1.5	4.0	3	2.9	2.1	3.2	1.2	—————12,456—————		
St. Vincent and the Grenadines	—	—	—	1	35	2.9	...	0.6	169.2	6.0	20.3	————1,074————		...
San Marino	3	1.3	65	—	6.0	3.2	...	4.0	4.8	8.7	2.5	4,213	1,725	...
São Tomé and Príncipe	—	—	—	5	25	3.5	...	—	—	0.9	95.5	87[9]	3[9]	4[9]
Saudi Arabia	12	143	19	12	2,700	3.2	6	3,500	2.5	788.6	11.3	...	...	17,102
Senegal	1	25	5	11	320	19.5	1	50.2	122.8	40.2	137.3			
Seychelles	2	3.5	56	1	15	4.3	...	0.5	136.0	7.1	9.0	10,499[1]	...	...
Sierra Leone	2	10	3	3	100	35.1	2	21.5	163.3	16.0	229.5			
Singapore	11	588	249	21	490.2	5.0	6	421	5.9	771.4	3.2	3,558,261	10,551	5,058
Solomon Islands	—	—	—	3	24	11.1		—	—	2.7	90.4			36
Somalia	1	...	...	4	95	64.5	...	...	...	4.8	781.7	...	...	...
South Africa	22	1,134	40	...	8,250	3.7	...	2,000	15.4	3,208.7	8.0	10,682,776	88,382	2,503,365
South West Africa/Namibia	3	18	20	13	48	21.9	...	13.4	78.4	57.3	18.3	257,162	4,624	43,984
Spain	105	4,710	128	442	10,400	3.7	60	11,650	3.3	12,350.1	3.1	1,113,000	...	...
Sri Lanka	22	536	128	40	3,000	5.1	1	50	306.0	109.9	138.2	1,114,560	371,520	2,100
Sudan, The	3	18	1	8	1,400	13.5	3	109	173.4	68.5	283.7	36,000	68,613	1,420
Suriname	5	32	84	16	185	1.9	...	42.5	8.5	27.5	12.9	55		
Swaziland	1	8	15	8	84	7.5	...	6.5	95.9	15.4	38.0	————90,744————		574
Sweden	114	4,378	528	336	3,327	2.5	438	3,235	2.6	6,889.0	1.2			44,721
Switzerland	88	2,501	395	215	2,358	2.7	825	2,078	3.1	4,780.8	1.3	1,249,932	4,907,855	522,252
Syria	6	104	12	...	1,800	5.4	...	405	24.1	471.1	20.0	435,000	...	...
Taiwan	31	1,750	110	...	5,000	3.6	...	5,060	3.6	3,820.2	4.8	7,496,630	10,885,394	
Tanzania	2	189	11	19	2,000	9.2	...	9.0	2,055	96.5	198.0	13,623	226,289	298
Thailand	18	1,943	42	217	7,200	6.7	...	3,000	16.1	529.1	91.6			1,127
Togo	1	7	3	11	190	15.0	4	8.0	356.3	7.9	347.7	...	31,485[1]	171[1]
Tokelau	—	—	—	...	...	...		—	—	0.003	666.7	—		
Tonga	—	—	—	1	65	1.6	...	—	—	2.6	38.0	2,840	—	—
Trinidad and Tobago	4	193	171	5	355	3.4	6	300	4.0	80.0	14.8	...	...	...
Trust Territory of the Pacific Is.	—	—	—	...	...	...	5	—	—	9.2	6.7	...	...	...
Tunisia	5	271	44	12	1,124	6.0	10	291	23.2	188.5	34.8	...	...	...
Turkey	1,115	3,880	89	39	4,300	10.8	153	3,610	12.8	2,104.1	22.0	2,339,119	85,029	27,440
Turks and Caicos Islands	—	—	—	1	4.0	2.0	...	—	—	0.9	7.5	248[1]		3[1]
Tuvalu	—	—	—	...	1.1	7.3		—	—	0.1	97.8	1		
Uganda	2	20	2	13	280	47.9	...	75	178.9	46.4	271.6	47,233[9]	138,109[9]	41[9]
U.S.S.R.	8,172	40,683	152	...	140,000	1.9	2,882	75,000	3.6	23,707.0	11.3	...	1,264,800[1]	2,280[1]
United Arab Emirates	3	110	98	17	100	10.4	10	110	9.4	240.2	4.7			
United Kingdom	120	25,221	451	487	18,410	3.0	1,643	18,554	3.0	28,470.1	2.0	17,360,000	3,446,000	131,000
United States	1,787	62,223	282	...	476,000	0.5	972	141,000	1.6	181,893.0	1.3	243,443,000	18,770,000	530,066
Uruguay	28	790	267	94	1,655	1.8	21	368	8.1	294.4	10.1	504,800		
Vanuatu	1	1	9	4	15.5	7.7	...	—	—	3.0	40.0			
Venezuela	69	2,383	176	210	5,000	2.9	42	2,000	7.2	1,377.6	10.7	...	...	8,763
Vietnam	4	500	9	39	3,000	18.6	...	525	106.3	118.0	466.6	...	...	...
Virgin Islands (U.S.)	4	19	176	5	90	1.1	3	96	1.0	48.0	2.4	90,821	...	3,315
Wallis and Futuna	—	—	—	...	...	...	...	—	—	0.15	72.8	...	...	...
Western Sahara	—	—	—	...	—	—	...	—	—	1.0	86.0	...	...	...
Western Samoa	—	—	—	6	70	2.3	...	2.5	64.0	5.9	26.8	...	...	...
Yemen (Aden)	1	20	10	6	111	18.9	...	37	57.3	10.1	192.4	...	...	...
Yemen (San'ā')	2	56	10	6	110	53.2	...	27	216.7	90.4	94.7	...	...	...
Yugoslavia	27	2,282	103	738	4,800	4.7	941	4,400	5.1	2,303.5	9.8	6,212	15,597,237	2,607,212
Zaire	6	45	2	22	500	59.5	...	12	2,480	30.3	933.7	9	9	9
Zambia	2	109	17	16	150	41.0	5	76	81.9	32.7	193.6	66	2,030	317,470
Zimbabwe	2	111	16	...	200	37.5	...	96.5	77.7	224.5	33.6	187,785[1]	439,850[1]	...

post office (1978)			telegraph (1982)			telex (1982)				country
num-ber	per-sons per office	pieces of mail handled ('000)	total traffic ('000)	na-tional traffic ('000)	inter-national outgoing traffic ('000)	sub-scriber lines	traffic ('000 minutes)			
							total	national	international outgoing	
...	...	15,964	35[3]	24[3]	11[3]	79[3]	625[3]	522[3]	103[3]	Rwanda
9	5,000	6,381	16	—	16	34[3]	47[3]	...	...	St. Christopher and Nevis
8	875	76	5	—	5	7[3]	47[3]	...	...	St. Helena and Ascension
...	...	3,679[2]	19	—	19	76	...	...	105[1]	St. Lucia
...	...	1,714[2,6]	2	1	1	33	42	29	13	St. Pierre and Miquelon
48	2,708	...	14	—	14	53[3]	44[3]	...	...	St. Vincent and the Grenadines
...	...	...	21	21	21	21	21	21	21	San Marino
...	...	334	18[12]	3[12]	15[12]	34[3]	6[3,17]	—	6[3,17]	São Tomé and Príncipe
437	21,327	223,632	3,219[7]	2,243[7]	976[7]	575[7]	...	...	3,137[7]	Saudi Arabia
74	61,486	12,961[10]	225[9]	147[9]	78[9]	737	...	...	1,614	Senegal
—	—	1,618[20]	12[19]	—	12[19]	136[19]	251[19]	54[19]	197[19]	Seychelles
137	26,343	151,584[10]	93[1]	20[1]	73[1]	224[3]	373[3]	37[3]	336[3]	Sierra Leone
72	34,333	218,389	431	6	425	12,252	40,205	14,913	25,292	Singapore
85	2,823	3,820[7]	...	...	...	737	...	...	...	Solomon Islands
...	...	...	...	...	...	...	...	...	...	Somalia
2,227	13,529	1,678,751	9,169[19]	8,763[19]	406[19]	24,724[19]	...	244,442[18,19]	14,829[19]	South Africa
81	12,914	...								South West Africa/Namibia
13,694	2,749	4,377,949	7,594	7,098	496	29,246	86,450	48,650	37,800	Spain
422	35,521	670,357	2,095	1,870	225	976	4,652	1,163	3,489	Sri Lanka
231	68,095	53,529[6]	1,453[2]	1,263[2]	190[2]	416[2]	...	...	1,038[2]	Sudan, The
...	...	...	104[9]	17[9]	87[9]	192[3]	...	...	302[3]	Suriname
55	10,000	9,316[2]	51[3]	45[3]	6[3]	242[3]	1,006[3]	359[3]	647[3]	Swaziland
1,873	4,426	2,814,649	354	135	219	15,750	...	...	28,723	Sweden
3,906	1,646	3,404,806	1,591[23]	882[23]	709[23]	34,916[23]	128,769[23]	63,929[23]	64,840[23]	Switzerland
500	18,620	35,690[15]	337	173	164	1,430	...	...	1,740	Syria
11,827	1,533	...								Taiwan
...	...	83,232[2]	1,070[3]	805[3]	265[3]	1,650[3]	...	...	1,152[3]	Tanzania
555	75,441	252,436	6,871[3]	6,684[3]	187[3]	3,070	7,425	2,314	5,111	Thailand
39	53,077	32,055	26	3	23	166	...	...	586	Togo
...	...	...								Tokelau
...	...	1,063[15,24]	85[3]	79[3]	6[3]	40[3]	...	...	63[3]	Tonga
63	18,254	50,137[10]	...	217	274[12]	265	...	...	1,026	Trinidad and Tobago
6	—	...								Trust Territory of the Pacific Is.
403	15,075	144,355	628	424	204	1,828	5,405	1,603	3,802	Tunisia
10,335	4,300	770,714[2]	12,788	12,488	300	7,265	...	45,755[26]	8,078	Turkey
...	...	...	4	2	2	15[1]	14[1]	...	14[1]	Turks and Caicos Islands
...	...	2,313[2]								Tuvalu
...	...	28,275[11]	64	59	5	419	216[17]	98[17]	118[17]	Uganda
90,723	2,951	5,925,000	541,012	540,110	902	1,446	...	...	8,458	U.S.S.R.
...	...	238,898[24]	679	51	628	6,044	18,395	6,287	12,108	United Arab Emirates
22,405	2,499	10,552,736[4,6]	2,836[19]	886[19]	1,950[19]	92,622[19]	193,263[17,19]	95,864[17,19]	97,399[17,19]	United Kingdom
30,155	7,693	91,658,971[4,6,11]	56,749[3]	50,439[3]	6,310[3]	178,567	...	...	181,742	United States
1,277	2,323	35,356[2]	1,673[3]	1,551[3]	122[3]	1,043[3]	2,909[3]	222[3]	2,687[3]	Uruguay
1	120,000	...	...	...	8	51	74[17]	6[17]	68[17]	Vanuatu
809	7,215	347,500[16]	5,148[7]	4,570[7]	578[7]	15,915	...	...	10,210	Venezuela
...	...	...	5,551[3]	4,996[3]	555[3]	...	32[3,17]	10[3,17]	22[3,17]	Vietnam
5	23,200	...								Virgin Islands (U.S.)
...	...	175	9	2	7	3	—	...	—	Wallis and Futuna
...	...	...								Western Sahara
...	...	14,589	...	...	...					Western Samoa
...	...	15,058	...	17	...	149	371	4	367	Yemen (Aden)
		7,802[15]								Yemen (Şan'ā')
3,791	6,007	842,494	12,908[3]	11,280[3]	1,628[3]	10,000[3]	...	...	13,237[3]	Yugoslavia
351	61,652	60,860[16]	234	167	67	804[1]	1,006[1]	45[1]	961[1]	Zaire
232	23,578	69,175	14,446[3,25]	11,192[3,25]	3,254[3,25]	1,292	3,519	1,690	1,829	Zambia
155	48,645	137,085	433	356	77	1,190	83,053[18]	18,918[18]	64,135[18]	Zimbabwe

[1]1980. [2]1977. [3]1981. [4]Excludes postcards. [5]Excludes printed matter. [6]Excludes small packets. [7]1976. [8]Foreign received only. [9]1979. [10]1972. [11]1975. [12]1978. [13]Foreign sent and domestic only. [14]Telegraphs to U.S. are included in national. [15]1973. [16]1974. [17]Number of calls ('000). [18]Pulses ('000). [19]1983. [20]1971. [21]Italy includes San Marino. [22]Kiribati includes Tuvalu. [23]Switzerland includes Liechtenstein. [24]Foreign received and foreign sent only. [25]Number of words ('000). [26]Number of metred units ('000).

Trade: external

The following table presents comparative data on the import and export trade of all the countries of the world. The table analyzes data for both imports and exports in two ways: (1) into a group of major commodity categories defined in accordance with the United Nations system called the Standard International Trade Classification (SITC) and (2) by the direction of trade for each country with major world trading blocs or partners. For purposes of this table, several SITC categories have been aggregated so as to accommodate the commodity groupings indicated by the column headings. These groupings are defined by the use of SITC code numbers placed beneath the column headings. The single digit numbers represent broad SITC categories; the double digit numbers represent subcategories of the single digit categories (22 is a subcategory of 2; 67 is a subcategory of 6). The SITC subdivides these categories to a finer degree of detail, but such distinctions cannot be accommodated here. Where a plus or minus sign is used before one of these SITC numbers, the SITC category or subcategory is being added to or subtracted from the aggregate implied by the total of the sections preceding to form a consistently defined commodity group for all countries. The SITC commodity aggregations used here are listed at the end of this headnote. The full SITC commodity breakdown is presented in the United Nations publication *Standard International Trade Classification Revision 2.*

The SITC was developed by the United Nations through its Statistical Commission as an outgrowth of the need for a standard system of aggregating commodities of external trade to provide international comparability of foreign trade statistics. All member nations of the United Nations are urged to use the SITC system as far as possible in reporting their external trade statistics. The United Nations Statistical Commission has defined external merchandise trade as "all goods whose movement into or out of the customs area of a country compiling the statistics adds to or subtracts from the material resources of the country." Goods passing through the country for transport only are excluded. These statistics refer only to goods and exclude purely financial transactions that are covered in the "Finance" and "National product and accounts" tables.

For purposes of comparability of data, total value of imports and exports is given here in U.S. dollars; conversions from foreign currencies are determined according to International Monetary Fund (IMF) average rates for the year for which data are supplied. The commodity categories are given in terms of percentages of the total value of the country's import or export trade (with the exclusions noted above). Value, according to the United Nations Statistical Office, is based on transaction value: for imports, the value at which the goods were purchased by the importer plus the cost of transportation and insurance to the frontier of the importing

Trade: external

country	year	imports total value U.S.$ (000,000)	all food items (0 + 1 + 22 + 4)	agricultural raw materials (2 − 22 − 27 − 28)	fuels (3)	ores and metals (27 + 28 + 67 + 68)	manufactured goods total (5 + 6 − 67 − 68 + 7 + 8)	of which, chemical products (5)	of which, machinery and equipment (7)	of which, other (6 − 67 − 68 + 8)	from European Economic Community	from United States	from Union of Soviet Socialist Republics	from all other[c]
Afghanistan	1981	551.7	15.8	—	22.5	—	61.9	2.2	27.9	31.8	...	2.6	52.7	44.7
Albania	1979	c. 219.5	...	...	...	...	...	...	...	...	86.0[1]	7.0[1]	—	7.0[1]
Algeria	1980	10,524.5	21.0	3.2	2.5	9.5	63.9	9.1	36.9	18.0	62.5	7.1	0.5	29.9
American Samoa	1980	95.1	...	...	...	...	...	...	...	...	...	73.0	...	27.0
Andorra	1980	383.3	...	...	...	...	...	...	...	...	...	...	...	...
Angola	1979	315.8	26.1	10.9	—	—	61.8	2.8	39.2	19.8	0.8[2]	92.4[2]	...	6.8[2]
Anguilla	1979	...	...	...	...	...	...	...	...	...	...	...	...	...
Antigua and Barbuda	1978	40.4	33.3	1.8	1.6	3.6	59.3	8.9	23.8	26.6	34.7	34.5	—	30.8
Argentina	1980	10,539.2	5.7	3.7	10.3	8.6	71.7	12.3	40.2	19.1	25.9	22.6	0.1	51.4
Australia	1981	23,485.2	4.6	2.4	13.6	4.3	74.0	8.5	39.3	26.1	19.3	22.8	—	57.9
Austria	1982	19,514.4	6.1	3.8	16.1	7.8	65.5	10.1	28.0	27.5	59.0[3]	4.1[3]	6.2[3]	30.7[3]
Bahamas, The	1981	5,307.1	...	...	...	...	...	...	...	...	...	9.1	...	90.9
Bahrain	1980	3,479.2	6.9	0.6	58.3	3.3	30.8	3.8	15.0	12.0	13.4	5.4	—	81.2
Bangladesh	1981	1,382.2	14.9	...	9.9	...	60.7	19.3	37.6	3.8	17.8[4]	12.5[4]	1.6[4]	68.1[4]
Barbados	1980	517.1	17.9	2.4	15.4	4.7	57.9	8.7	23.7	25.5	17.0[3]	35.0[3]	0.2[3]	47.8[3]
Belgium[5]	1982	57,213.4	12.5	2.6	20.8	9.0	53.2	9.1	21.8	22.3	61.8[3]	7.1[3]	1.6[3]	29.5[3]
Belize	1981	161.9	24.6	1.5	15.9	—	55.5	12.7	32.0	10.8	22.9	35.4	—	41.7
Benin	1978	169.7	...	...	...	...	...	...	...	...	...	...	...	...
Bermuda	1981	322.3	22.7	0.8	13.5	0.4	59.6	8.9	18.1	32.6	18.8[1]	47.7[1]	...	33.5[1]
Bhutan	1982	44.6	12.2	—	—	—	87.8	16.1	34.5	37.2	—	—	—	100.0
Bolivia	1981	825.4	19.5	1.3	1.6	23.9	53.2	—	14.9	38.3	20.3	28.5	—	51.2
Botswana	1980	379.73	15.6	...	13.1	...	...	...	...	...	—	2.9	—	97.1
Brazil	1981	24,072.5	8.8	1.1	50.5	6.0	33.5	9.4	18.4	5.7	13.6	16.3	0.1	70.0
British Virgin Islands	1980	36.0	...	...	...	...	...	...	...	...	19.4[6]	52.7[6]	...	27.9[6]
Brunei	1981	596.2	17.8	0.2	1.4	14.1	64.3	8.0	37.3	19.0	20.2[1]	20.1[1]	—	59.7[1]
Bulgaria	1982	10,964.9	——8.2——		——46.2——		45.0	6.3	33.9	4.8	11.8[3]	—	54.7[3]	33.5[3]
Burkina Faso	1981	337.5	24.7	1.7	15.6	4.2	53.8	10.5	24.4	18.9	54.5[1]	9.0[1]	0.1[1]	36.4[1]
Burma	1980	633.1	——————28.4——————				68.3	—	——68.3——		22.6[6]	5.2[6]	0.7[6]	71.5[6]
Burundi	1980	167.2	14.1	1.0	15.8	2.0	61.6	8.0	20.0	33.6	39.1[3]	4.6[3]	...	56.3[3]
Cameroon	1981	1.34	...	...	...	...	...	...	...	...	61.5	6.4	4.1	28.0
Canada	1982	54,259.1	7.7	1.9	10.1	5.5	73.0	6.6	48.0	18.4	8.1[3]	68.7[3]	—	23.2[3]
Cape Verde	1980	67.8	42.7	2.1	9.1	1.4	43.3	6.6	14.0	22.9	31.0[2]	5.0[2]	0.1[2]	63.9[2]
Cayman Islands	1980	101.0	19.1	2.9	12.7	2.7	60.5	4.8	23.8	31.9	6.0[7]	77.0[7]	...	17.0[7]
Central African Republic	1980	80.5	20.9	0.9	1.8	3.3	73.1	11.8	33.9	27.4	73.5	3.5	—	23.0
Chad	1975	110.0	14.5	1.4	14.2	4.0	65.6	16.4	28.9	20.4	58.4	5.7	0.2	35.7
Chile	1980	5,777.0	...	...	...	...	...	...	...	...	17.2[3]	21.2[3]	—	61.6[3]
China	1982	192.93	21.8	...	1.0	...	60.4	15.2	16.6	28.6	10.9	22.7	1.3	65.1
Christmas Island	1981	...	...	...	...	...	...	...	...	...	...	...	...	...
Cocos (Keeling) Islands	1981	...	...	...	...	...	...	...	...	...	...	...	...	...
Colombia	1981	5,199.1	10.2	2.6	14.0	9.3	62.8	14.0	37.4	11.4	17.3[1]	39.5[1]	0.3[1]	42.9[1]
Comoros	1976	13.1	49.1	0.2	7.3	3.1	39.9	3.5	17.6	18.8	31.8	...	...	68.2
Congo	1980	418.1	19.2	0.5	13.8	9.5	56.9	10.7	22.5	23.7	67.1[4]	6.3[4]	1.4[4]	25.2[4]
Cook Islands	1979	19.3	28.4	2.1	7.3	2.8	58.8	5.6	24.1	29.1	5.7[2]	4.7[2]	—	89.6[2]
Costa Rica	1980	1,596.4	8.8	1.5	15.4	7.0	63.1	16.8	24.1	22.2	10.5	34.5	0.1	54.9
Cuba	1981	5,977.9	——23.2——		——29.0——		47.8	7.8	32.3	7.7	2.3	...	62.3	35.4
Cyprus	1981	1,101.4	16.3	1.8	21.7	4.9	55.3	7.2	19.2	28.9	49.0	7.4	3.3	40.3
Czechoslovakia	1982	15,294.8	——14.2——		——39.1——		46.7	8.1	33.1	1.5	11.1	...	39.9	49.0
Denmark	1982	16,834.2	11.6	4.1	22.5	8.1	52.4	9.9	21.1	21.4	46.5[3]	7.3[3]	1.6[3]	44.6[3]
Djibouti	1980	191.9	——44.0——		——6.4——		43.5	4.3	19.8	19.4	64.6	2.2	0.1	33.1
Dominica	1978	28.4	34.7	1.5	5.8	1.6	56.3	12.5	16.4	27.4	32.3	17.4	—	50.3
Dominican Republic	1982	1,255.8	15.6	2.0	34.1	5.1	43.2	12.2	18.6	12.4	7.1[3]	42.2[3]	—	50.7[3]
Ecuador	1980	2,215.3	8.4	1.8	1.4	8.5	79.9	13.7	49.5	16.7	19.3[4]	38.4[4]	0.2[4]	42.1[4]
Egypt	1981	8,839.5	34.2	5.1	3.0	5.8	51.8	8.9	28.2	14.7	40.7	19.7	2.6	37.0
El Salvador	1980	975.9	17.7	1.9	17.7	5.0	57.6	19.2	13.4	25.0	9.6	25.2	...	65.2
Equatorial Guinea	1981	43.4	...	...	...	...	...	...	...	...	...	...	...	...

country (c.i.f. [cost, insurance, freight] valuation); for exports, the value at which the goods were sold by the exporter, including the cost of transportation and insurance to bring the goods onto the transporting vehicle at the frontier of the exporting country (f.o.b. [free on board] valuation).

Ideally, the data assembled here should be derived from a single source, thus providing a set of statistics based on a common value system that would permit comparative analysis. It is not possible, however, to gather the required information from a single source, although the largest part of the information presented here comes from the *United Nations Yearbook of International Trade Statistics* and from the *Handbook of International Trade,* produced by the U.N. Conference on Trade and Development. These sources, however, do not always provide the most recent data and do not cover some countries listed in this table. Data for such countries as Albania, Andorra, Botswana, China, Kampuchea, North Korea, Liechtenstein, and Vietnam and many small, nonindependent countries were obtained from other sources. In some cases information was unavailable, as noted.

... Not available.

— None, less than 0.05%, or not applicable.

a. Detail may not add to 100.0 or indicated subtotals because of exclusion of unallocated commodities or because of rounding.

b. SITC category codes:
0 - food and live animals, chiefly for food.
1 - beverages and tobacco.
2 - crude materials, inedible, except fuels.
   22 - oil seeds and oleaginous fruit.
   27 - crude fertilizers and minerals.
   28 - metalliferous ores and metal scrap.
3 - mineral fuels, lubricants, and related materials.
4 - animal and vegetable oils, fats and waxes.
5 - chemicals and related products.
6 - manufactured goods classified chiefly by material.
   67 - iron and steel.
   68 - non-ferrous metals.
7 - machinery and transport equipment.
8 - miscellaneous manufactured articles.

c. Percentages in these columns may include value of trade shown as not available (...) in any of the three preceding columns.

exports total value U.S.$ (000,000)	all food items (0+1+22+4)	agricultural raw materials (2−22−27−28)	fuels (3)	ores and metals (27+28+67+68)	manufactured goods total (5+6−67−68+7+8)	of which, chemical products (5)	of which, machinery and equipment (7)	of which, other (6−67−68+8)	to European Economic Community	to United States	to Union of Soviet Socialist Republics	to all other[c]	country
705.2	29.7	7.1	33.1	...	29.4	—	—	29.4	...	—	59.3	40.7	Afghanistan
c.243.9	...	...	...	...	...	...	...	...	77.8[1]	12.0[1]	...	10.2[1]	Albania
15,623.6	0.8	—	98.5	0.6	0.2	0.1	—	0.1	39.8	48.1	0.6	11.5	Algeria
127.1	...	...	...	...	...	...	...	...	...	99.0	...	1.0	American Samoa
16.0	...	...	...	...	...	...	...	...	...	...	...	...	Andorra
444.3	14.9	...	67.7	10.7	6.7	—	—	6.7	0.2[2]	0.8[2]	...	99.0[2]	Angola
1.6	...	...	...	...	...	...	...	...	...	10.0	...	90.0	Anguilla
4.8	17.5	5.9	—	—	76.6	9.1	3.4	64.2	7.9	27.1	—	65.0	Antigua and Barbuda
8,021.4	65.0	6.2	3.5	4.0	21.4	5.0	6.5	9.9	27.6	8.9	20.1	43.4	Argentina
21,443.0	31.1	11.3	15.3	20.6	19.0	8.0	5.5	5.5	10.3	7.3	3.2	79.2	Australia
15,689.9	4.7	5.6	1.5	12.6	75.5	9.1	28.3	38.1	52.8[3]	2.6[3]	3.1[3]	41.5[3]	Austria
1,768.9	...	...	...	...	...	...	...	...	...	67.1	—	32.9	Bahamas, The
3,794.8	0.6	—	93.6	3.0	2.8	0.1	1.4	1.3	0.5	...	—	99.5	Bahrain
495.5	5.0	17.0	—	—	78.0	...	...	...	21.4[4]	13.9[4]	8.4[4]	56.3[4]	Bangladesh
149.5	45.0	0.1	0.2	1.3	51.5	7.1	15.6	28.9	10.9[3]	37.1[3]	...	52.0[3]	Barbados
51,694.6	11.0	1.7	8.6	12.9	60.5	12.2	22.8	25.6	70.2[3]	4.3[3]	1.1[3]	24.4[3]	Belgium[5]
74.8	82.3	2.2	—	—	15.5	0.4	0.1	15.1	32.2	60.8	...	7.0	Belize
20.3	53.8	36.1	0.3	1.7	8.2	0.5	1.8	6.0	60.9	...	...	39.1	Benin
29.4	2.3	—	37.9	—	48.9	41.0	3.9	4.0	4.3[1]	12.5[1]	...	83.2[1]	Bermuda
20.3	31.4	14.4	...	0.5	29.0	9.4	—	19.7	—	—	—	100.0	Bhutan
995.3	2.2	...	...	55.9	39.4	...	...	...	...	...	3.0	97.0	Bolivia
299.6[8]	7.2	...	...	81.4	10.6	—	—	10.6	...	20.9	...	79.1	Botswana
23,292.3	41.4	3.6	5.1	13.7	34.8	4.2	18.1	12.5	25.5	17.7	2.7	54.1	Brazil
1,087	...	...	...	...	...	...	...	...	...	28.0[6]	...	72.0[6]	British Virgin Islands
4,022.3	—	...	100.0	...	—	—	—	—	—	8.6[1]	—	91.4[1]	Brunei
10,868.8	——22.9——		——12.7——		62.3	6.0	47.0	9.4	10.0[3]	...	48.4[3]	41.6[3]	Bulgaria
75.0	39.8	45.3	0.2	0.8	13.8	0.3	5.9	7.6	33.2[1]	...	...	66.8[1]	Burkina Faso
481.2	49.5	34.0	—	14.7	1.8	—	—	1.8	13.4[6]	—	0.4[6]	86.2[6]	Burma
59.1	89.1	2.8	—	0.7	1.3	—	—	1.3	22.3[3]	43.9[3]	...	33.8[3]	Burundi
1.0[4]	...	40.1	38.9	...	16.1	0.8	—	15.3	46.7	38.2	1.2	13.9	Cameroon
66,977.0	13.4	8.7	14.3	12.2	51.0	5.8	32.2	12.9	10.7[3]	63.1[3]	2.3[3]	23.9[3]	Canada
4.2	84.2	1.2	0.3	9.1	5.2	1.0	0.6	3.6	1.9[2]	—	...	98.1[2]	Cape Verde
2.6	44.1	12.1	—	—	42.7	25.4	1.2	16.2	0.5[2]	...	—	99.5[2]	Cayman Islands
111.2	31.0	42.7	—	0.2	26.2	0.1	0.1	26.0	77.0	4.3	...	18.7	Central African Republic
40.0	16.2	66.9	7.9	0.8	7.7	0.5	5.4	1.9	6.1	...	...	93.9	Chad
4,722.0	...	...	...	...	...	...	...	...	33.4[3]	15.0[3]	...	51.6[3]	Chile
223.5	13.0	...	23.8	...	55.0	5.4	5.7	43.9	9.6	8.0	1.8	80.6	China
...	...	...	...	...	...	...	...	...	...	...	...	...	Christmas Island
...	...	...	...	...	...	...	...	...	...	...	...	...	Cocos (Keeling) Islands
2,955.5	62.9	7.1	1.5	0.2	27.4	3.1	3.6	20.7	32.6[1]	27.1[1]	0.5[1]	39.8[1]	Colombia
9.3	64.1	—	5.6	—	29.5	29.5	—	—	71.1	15.2	...	13.7	Comoros
955.3	1.0	2.5	89.6	0.2	6.7	—	0.2	6.5	39.2[4]	16.9[4]	0.6[4]	43.3[4]	Congo
2.6	65.5	2.0	—	—	32.1	0.4	0.3	31.4	0.5[2]	...	—	99.5[2]	Cook Islands
1,031.5	63.7	1.3	0.6	1.7	26.7	6.8	4.2	15.6	22.6	34.9	—	42.5	Costa Rica
4,936.4	——86.7——		——12.2——		1.1	0.5	0.2	0.4	4.3	...	54.3	41.4	Cuba
559.0	32.9	0.9	5.7	4.8	55.3	2.9	6.6	45.8	28.9	...	4.3	66.8	Cyprus
15,513.0	——7.3——		——14.5——		78.2	8.2	53.2	16.8	11.6	...	37.6	50.8	Czechoslovakia
14,952.8	34.0	5.6	2.6	2.8	54.3	8.2	24.5	21.6	45.9[3]	5.2[3]	0.6[3]	48.3[3]	Denmark
12.5	——57.6——		——1.0——		38.6	0.7	17.7	20.2	74.7	...	—	25.3	Djibouti
15.7	81.7	0.1	—	0.5	17.8	16.4	—	1.4	68.1	2.7	...	29.2	Dominica
627.7	82.2	0.3	—	5.1	12.4	5.5	3.5	3.4	6.9[3]	69.1[3]	1.4[3]	22.6[3]	Dominican Republic
2,104.2	39.8	1.4	56.0	0.1	2.7	0.1	0.9	1.6	8.6[4]	33.8[4]	0.2[4]	57.4[4]	Ecuador
3,232.2	7.2	15.6	64.5	4.3	8.3	0.6	—	7.7	41.9	3.8	4.1	50.2	Egypt
720.0	46.8	12.5	2.8	3.1	34.9	5.6	2.9	26.4	14.5	29.7	0.9	54.9	El Salvador
13.7	76.0	24.0	—	—	—	—	—	...	...	...	...	...	Equatorial Guinea

Trade: external (continued)

country	year	imports total value U.S.$ (000,000)	all food items (0+1 +22+4)	agricultural raw materials (2−22 −27−28)	fuels (3)	ores and metals (27+28 +67+68)	manufactured goods total (5+6 −67−68 +7+8)	of which, chemical products (5)	of which, machinery and equipment (7)	of which, other (6−67 −68+8)	from European Economic Community	from United States	from Union of Soviet Socialist Republics	from all other[c]
Ethiopia	1980	721.4	7.8	2.7	24.7	3.8	60.4	15.1	27.9	17.4	33.0	7.7	19.3	40.0
Faeroe Islands	1982	198.0	13.7	2.0	24.8	2.6	55.6	4.5	23.3	27.8	72.9[3]	...	...	27.1[3]
Falkland Islands	1975	3.4	29.0	2.0	2.6	1.6	62.7	5.7	14.4	42.6	88.5[3]	...	...	11.5[3]
Fiji	1981	631.1	16.3	0.3	25.7	5.09	49.3	7.1	21.2	21.0	9.6[1]	6.5[1]	...	83.9[1]
Finland	1982	13,448.3	7.4	3.3	27.3	7.1	54.3	9.0	28.2	17.0	32.5[3]	7.5[3]	23.5[3]	36.5[3]
France	1981	120,278.6	10.3	3.5	28.8	7.5	49.7	8.8	21.9	19.0	45.2	8.1	2.8	43.9
French Guiana	1981	249.9	27.8	0.2	16.3	2.5	52.0	5.2	26.9	20.0	59.4	9.6	0.2	30.8
French Polynesia	1981	555.6	19.1	1.8	12.7	3.5	62.2	5.2	32.7	24.4	56.5	20.9	—	23.6
Gabon	1980	677.6	19.0	0.7	1.5	5.0	73.5	7.9	38.4	27.2	73.0	9.3	—	17.7
Gambia, The	1982	98.5	25.9	1.6	12.2	1.7	50.9	6.9	14.3	29.7	46.4	3.2	1.1	49.3
Germany, East	1982	19,432.5	—16.3—		—39.9—		43.8	7.4	32.3	4.1	19.1	...	30.2	50.7
Germany, West	1981	162,691.2	12.5	3.7	24.5	8.28	48.9	7.6	19.5	21.8	47.7	7.7	2.4	42.2
Ghana	1978	1,002.6	11.7	1.8	13.8	4.8	63.5	14.5	32.7	16.2	43.4	10.7	0.4	45.5
Gibraltar	1982	119.7	—26.1—		—31.4—		42.6	4.4	28.8	9.4	44.2	1.1	...	54.7
Greece	1981	8,780.6	11.3	4.7	22.0	6.6	55.2	9.9	28.1	17.2	50.1	5.1	3.7	41.1
Greenland	1982	274.3	19.3	1.5	21.2	2.4	54.0	3.7	24.3	26.0	83.0[3]	...	—	17.0[3]
Grenada	1980	50.2	32.9	3.7	12.8	2.3	48.3	11.0	14.0	23.3	...	...	...	...
Guadeloupe	1981	588.4	26.8	1.6	4.2	3.6	62.9	9.5	25.0	28.3	79.7	5.3	0.1	14.9
Guam	1979	445.8	43.0	4.4	—	—	49.6	2.2	9.3	38.1	...	32.4	...	67.6
Guatemala	1981	2,009.3	6.2	1.5	37.8	4.8	49.6	15.9	16.0	17.7	13.4	33.5	0.1	53.0
Guinea	1979	297.6	...	...	...	...	...	...	...	...	36.0	9.0	14.0	41.0
Guinea-Bissau	1980	44.3	30.4	0.1	6.1	—	63.3	—	25.4	37.9	23.8	0.5	7.0	68.7
Guyana	1980	426.1	—14.0—		33.1	—	52.9	—	...	...	28.8[4]	28.0[4]	—	43.2[4]
Haiti	1978	220.7	25.6	3.9	11.1	4.5	54.3	9.1	20.0	25.3	15.4	44.6	...	40.0
Honduras	1981	935.2	—8.3—		17.4		73.7	17.8	26.5	29.4	7.9	41.3	...	50.8
Hong Kong	1982	23,461.1	13.5	3.4	8.0	4.6	70.0	6.7	21.5	41.8	11.5[3]	10.4[3]	0.2[3]	77.9[3]
Hungary	1982	15,918.2	—14.9—		—29.9—		55.2	15.9	30.5	8.8	23.4[3]	...	28.6[3]	48.0[3]
Iceland	1982	941.6	10.2	2.7	15.5	4.2	67.3	9.9	27.2	30.1	44.4[3]	7.8[3]	8.0[3]	39.8[3]
India	1980	15,927.6	6.3	1.7	42.5	...	...	11.2	15.2	...	24.6[4]	10.4[4]	5.5[4]	59.5[4]
Indonesia	1981	13,008.3	11.0	3.2	13.3	11.6	60.4	13.5	35.4	11.5	15.0	13.8	0.3	70.9
Iran	1977	14,447.6	12.7	2.6	0.3	12.0	72.3	7.2	44.2	20.9	43.6	16.2	1.9	38.3
Iraq	1978	4,212.6	12.6	1.2	0.3	7.3	78.5	4.7	53.6	20.2	35.8	10.1	3.5	50.6
Ireland	1982	9,696.2	12.7	2.3	14.8	4.2	63.7	11.0	27.4	25.3	70.9[3]	11.7[3]	0.5[3]	16.9[3]
Israel	1981	7,894.1	12.4	3.1	26.0	7.0	51.2	6.8	24.2	20.1	34.5	20.6	—	44.9
Italy	1982	83,834.0	13.9	6.2	32.4	7.3	39.6	8.4	19.5	11.7	41.6[3]	6.9[3]	3.5[3]	48.0[3]
Ivory Coast	1981	2,393.1	20.3	0.6	22.0	5.7	50.4	9.2	21.5	19.7	55.3[4]	6.7[4]	0.8[4]	37.2[4]
Jamaica	1980	1,177.7	20.3	0.9	37.8	3.5	37.0	11.7	11.8	13.5	11.4	31.5	—	57.1
Japan	1982	130,318.5	12.7	7.0	50.4	9.8	19.3	5.2	6.3	7.8	5.4[3]	18.0[3]	1.1[3]	75.5[3]
Jordan	1981	3,149.1	17.0	1.4	17.4	6.0	57.8	4.8	32.5	20.6	38.4[1]	8.6[1]	0.8[1]	52.2[1]
Kampuchea	...	...	...	...	...	...	...	...	...	...	...	...	...	...
Kenya	1980	2,589.9	7.7	1.2	33.9	6.5	50.6	10.8	28.0	11.9	37.0	6.4	0.1	56.5
Kiribati	1979	17.4	40.0	1.6	14.5	2.1	41.2	5.6	16.8	18.9	8.8	4.5	...	86.7
Korea, North	...	...									...	...	...	...
Korea, South	1981	26,028.3	12.0	9.3	29.8	9.3	39.4	8.1	23.0	8.2	7.1[1]	21.9[1]	—	71.0[1]
Kuwait	1980	6,554.2	14.8	1.0	0.8	6.2	76.7	4.2	36.2	36.3	31.3	14.5	0.2	54.0
Laos	1974	64.8	31.7	0.4	11.2	6.5	50.3	6.0	25.7	18.6	17.9	4.7	—	77.4
Lebanon	1977	1,692.3	22.1	2.3	7.6	14.9	53.0	5.5	24.5	23.0	47.6	8.1	0.7	43.6
Lesotho	1979	93.6	23.1	5.8	8.4	—	62.6	5.4	14.5	42.7	1.8	0.2	...	98.0
Liberia	1981	477.4	22.3	0.4	27.1	3.1	46.6	7.0	24.7	14.8	30.3	29.4	0.2	40.1
Libya	1981	8,381.7	18.1	1.2	1.0	5.9	73.8	4.5	38.2	31.1	64.0[1]	6.3[1]	1.0[1]	28.7[1]
Liechtenstein	1981	226.2	2.2	2.3	0.4	2.1	92.9	5.3	31.1	56.4	...	...	...	...
Luxembourg	1982	2,577.4	6.4	7.6	—20.1—		65.8	7.6	24.1	34.2	91.4	2.5	...	6.1
Macau	1980	543.3	29.3	6.8	7.0	2.2	54.8	2.5	9.8	42.4	2.8	4.1	—	93.1
Madagascar	1980	676.5	8.5	2.7	14.6	7.5	66.4	12.8	34.0	19.6	59.8	3.9	0.5	35.8
Malawi	1980	440.2	7.5	1.0	15.3	7.2	68.7	12.5	33.7	22.5	33.7	3.4	...	62.9
Malaysia	1981	11,508.1	12.9	1.7	17.2	9.0	58.6	8.1	37.0	13.5	12.3	13.0	...	74.7
Maldives	1979	11.2	47.8	—	10.9	0.3	41.0	3.3	8.7	29.0	...	...	...	...
Mali	1982	332.3	18.5	—	20.9	—	60.6	9.2	28.4	23.0	54.0[8]	1.7[8]	3.6[8]	40.7[8]
Malta	1981	850.8	17.8	2.0	13.5	4.9	61.3	6.3	19.3	35.8	73.7[1]	6.1[1]	0.3[1]	19.9[1]
Martinique	1981	742.7	22.3	1.1	18.9	2.4	53.7	8.2	20.5	25.0	65.7	5.2	0.1	29.0
Mauritania	1980	285.7	33.6	...	11.9	—	40.8	—	17.7	23.1	50.6	—	—	49.4
Mauritius	1981	481.8	12.4	...	17.8	5.3	60.0	5.3	11.6	43.1	30.0	5.3	—	64.7
Mayotte	1982	17.2	—26.2—		...	18.2	40.8	7.2	17.4	16.2	56.2	...	—	43.8
Mexico	1980	19,516.9	13.7	2.0	1.5	33.0	49.8	8.6	33.0	8.2	12.5[3]	63.9[3]	0.1[3]	23.5[3]
Monaco	...	...	...	...	...	...	...	...	...	...	...	...	...	...
Mongolia	1982	688.3	—11.1—		—28.7—		60.2	7.1	35.4	17.7	...	...	...	...
Montserrat	1978	10.0	30.8	1.5	7.4	1.9	58.4	6.1	25.8	26.5	38.8	25.9	—	35.3
Morocco	1981	4,352.6	23.4	5.2	27.3	9.1	35.0	6.9	18.5	9.6	40.2[1]	7.0[1]	3.8[1]	49.0[1]
Mozambique	1977	277.7	12.9	2.6	3.7	13.9	66.7	8.1	35.6	23.0	31.5	3.8	—	64.7
Nauru	1978	12.5	...								—	—	—	100.0
Nepal	1980	226.3	4.3	0.6	17.7	4.2	70.1	7.3	32.2	30.6	11.6[4]	7.0[4]	7.8[4]	73.6[4]
Netherlands, The	1981	66,108.9	15.4	2.4	26.1	6.4	48.4	9.3	18.7	20.4	52.4	9.5	2.7	35.4
Netherlands Antilles	1977	3,114.4	4.3	0.1	83.0	0.5	12.0	2.0	4.1	5.9	5.5	7.6	—	86.9
New Caledonia	1981	408.0	20.4	0.8	28.1	3.1	47.5	5.2	19.7	22.6	41.6	7.4	—	51.0
New Zealand	1981	5,731.5	5.8	1.5	19.4	8.5	64.2	13.0	32.4	18.8	16.8	18.1	0.2	64.9
Nicaragua	1980	881.9	15.4	0.7	19.9	4.6	59.4	21.6	14.1	23.7	7.9	27.5	0.1	64.5
Niger	1981	509.7	23.5	1.3	14.8	4.0	55.5	7.0	25.8	22.6	56.0[6]	6.4[6]	...	37.6[6]
Nigeria	1981	19,581.5	—14.0—		2.7	1.6	81.7	7.4	47.9	26.4	58.8	11.0	0.2	30.0
Niue	1981	3.3	...								—	—	—	100.0
Norfolk Island	1982	11.9	10.8	2.1	10.8	0.2	76.1	28.0	23.1	25.1	...	...	...	...
Norway	1982	15,471.0	6.4	2.1	13.1	8.7	69.4	7.7	36.7	25.0	46.3[3]	9.2[3]	1.1[3]	43.4[3]
Oman	1981	2,288.2	13.5	1.2	13.1	6.0	63.0	3.5	39.1	20.5	27.5	7.8	...	64.7
Pakistan	1981	5,412.7	14.0	4.4	27.8	8.8	45.0	10.6	22.8	11.5	22.3	8.6	0.7	68.4
Panama	1981	1,539.8	9.2	0.6	28.7	4.1	57.3	10.3	23.9	23.1	6.4[1]	33.8[1]	0.1[1]	59.7[1]
Papua New Guinea	1981	505.3	18.4	1.1	21.1	...	59.4	6.0	29.9	23.5	5.8	7.5	...	86.7

| exports | | | | | | | | | direction of trade (percent) | | | | country |
total value U.S.$ (000,000)	all food items (0+1 +22+4)	agricultural raw materials (2−22 −27−28)	fuels (3)	ores and metals (27+28 +67+68)	manufactured goods total (5+6 −67−68 +7+8)	of which, chemical products (5)	of which, machinery and equipment (7)	of which, other (6−67 −68+8)	to European Economic Community	to United States	to Union of Soviet Socialist Republics	to all other[c]	
424.4	74.1	18.2	7.4	0.4	0.2	—	—	0.2	31.3	18.1	9.2	41.4	Ethiopia
149.3	94.8	3.4	—	—	1.8	—	1.2	0.6	66.7[3]	12.3[3]	...	21.0[3]	Faeroe Islands
2.6	—	99.9	—	—	—	—	—	—	100.0[3]	—	—	—	Falkland Islands
210.6	94.6	1.4	—	0.2	2.9	0.4	0.7	1.8	21.5[1]	10.5[1]	—	68.0[1]	Fiji
13,110.5	3.3	12.8	4.0	6.7	73.0	5.1	25.6	42.3	35.2[3]	3.7[3]	24.8[3]	36.3[3]	Finland
101,246.2	17.0	2.4	4.7	9.6	66.1	12.2	33.7	20.2	48.2	5.5	1.8	44.5	France
34.3	79.3	12.5	—	0.1	8.0	0.1	4.1	3.8	13.9	55.5	...	30.6	French Guiana
28.8	18.9	0.4	0.1	1.3	41.4	1.4	21.5	18.5	77.6	4.7	...	17.7	French Polynesia
826.4	0.3	6.1	49.6	25.9	18.4	1.8	0.1	16.5	37.0	21.0	—	42.0	Gabon
37.0	99.1	0.2	—	—	—	—	—	—	75.6	...	—	24.4	Gambia, The
20,920.8	——6.9——		——18.5——		74.6	11.9	48.5	14.2	13.1	0.8	38.0	48.1	Germany, East
175,284.3	5.8	1.3	4.0	8.6	78.2	12.7	45.3	20.2	46.9	6.6	1.9	44.6	Germany, West
978.6	76.7	6.3	0.6	15.1	1.1	0.1	0	1.0	50.5	17.7	10.5	21.3	Ghana
41.7	——6.8——		76.2	0.7	15.8	1.0	0.1	14.7	...	...	...	...	Gibraltar
4,249.5	26.5	1.9	9.5	14.2	47.3	5.5	4.8	37.0	43.3	8.7	1.7	46.3	Greece
170.6	60.9	0.9	—	28.5	9.6	—	8.3	1.3	76.4[3]	8.1[3]	...	15.5[3]	Greenland
16.9	92.2	—	—	—	7.8	—	0.1	7.7	...	...	...	...	Grenada
92.3	86.1	0.2	—	0.7	13.0	1.8	5.6	5.6	65.9	1.6	6.7	25.8	Guadeloupe
42.6	18.7	11.3	32.7	2.5	34.7	2.3	8.3	24.1	...	26.1	—	73.9	Guam
1,114.8	54.0	14.5	2.0	1.6	27.8	11.1	1.8	14.9	16.1	25.1	0.1	58.7	Guatemala
365.6	...	...	...	...	...	...	...	...	22.0	24.0	9.0	45.0	Guinea
9.1	97.2	1.8	...	...	1.0	0.1	0.1	0.8	18.7	...	...	81.3	Guinea-Bissau
338.9	——46.1——		...	48.5	...	...	...	...	37.6[4]	18.4[4]	—	44.0[4]	Guyana
158.9	48.4	1.8	—	10.9	36.8	6.1	4.6	26.1	34.9	58.6	...	6.5	Haiti
777.6	62.3	5.5	...	4.7	...	1.7	...	...	20.8	53.5	...	25.7	Honduras
13,664.8	1.6	0.4	0.1	0.9	96.2	1.0	17.3	78.0	18.5[3]	27.8[3]	0.1[3]	53.6[3]	Hong Kong
16,224.7	——27.6——		——13.3——		59.1	10.3	32.3	16.5	17.2[3]	...	33.4[3]	49.4[3]	Hungary
684.9	77.8	1.6	—	13.9	6.4	0.1	1.0	5.3	31.3[3]	20.8[3]	6.2[3]	41.7[3]	Iceland
8,534.3	——33.4——		0.4	5.1	61.1	3.3	...	...	28.3[4]	11.5[4]	8.6[4]	51.6[4]	India
22,260.3	5.1	8.2	79.8	3.7	3.0	0.3	0.7	2.0	4.8	18.3	0.4	76.5	Indonesia
25,943.0	0.7	0.6	97.6	0.3	0.8	0.1	0.2	0.5	0.6	0.3	0.1	98.6	Iran
11,063.9	0.6	0.2	98.6	—	0.5	0.3	0.1	0.1	0.3	...	0.1	99.6	Iraq
8,060.0	30.1	2.2	0.6	2.6	60.6	14.4	24.7	21.5	69.8[3]	6.3[3]	0.5[3]	23.4[3]	Ireland
5,664.2	12.6	4.2	—	2.8	80.4	15.4	18.6	46.5	34.5	22.3	—	43.2	Israel
73,437.6	7.4	1.0	6.8	6.6	77.7	7.3	31.4	39.0	43.1[3]	6.8[3]	1.7[3]	48.4[3]	Italy
2,535.2	64.7	17.1	7.5	0.6	9.5	1.3	2.5	5.6	63.0[4]	9.5[4]	2.7[4]	24.8[4]	Ivory Coast
942.4	13.7	0.3	1.9	22.0	62.1	58.6	0.6	2.8	20.3	37.4	5.2	37.1	Jamaica
138,584.4	1.1	0.8	0.3	12.3	84.6	4.6	56.3	23.7	12.4[3]	25.6[3]	2.1[3]	59.9[3]	Japan
509.8	23.9	0.5	3.3	36.4	35.7	6.9	2.3	26.4	3.6[1]	...	...	96.4[1]	Jordan
...	...	...	...	...	...	...	...	...	...	...	...	...	Kampuchea
1,313.4	43.8	8.1	33.4	3.0	11.6	3.1	0.6	7.9	34.3	3.3	0.3	62.1	Kenya
23.7	15.2	0.1	—	84.6	—	—	—	—	14.5	0.3	—	85.2	Kiribati
...	...	...	...	...	...	...	...	...	...	...	...	...	Korea, North
21,199.8	6.9	0.9	0.8	9.6	81.3	3.2	22.1	56.0	15.0[1]	26.4[1]	—	58.6[1]	Korea, South
20,434.6	0.5	0.1	88.8	0.4	10.1	4.6	2.7	2.9	24.7	...	—	75.3	Kuwait
11.3	2.6	81.5	—	11.8	4.1	—	—	4.1	0.3	—	...	99.7	Laos
394.3	18.3	1.8	0.1	7.3	72.5	9.6	11.5	51.4	6.7	3.4	...	89.9	Lebanon
11.7	3.3	20.8	0.1	—	75.8	3.6	1.3	71.0	9.4	0.4	...	90.2	Lesotho
523.6	7.2	23.6	0.1	66.7	1.4	0.1	1.0	0.3	64.2	23.0	0.5	12.3	Liberia
15,571.1	—	—	99.6	—	0.4	0.4	—	—	39.3[1]	35.5[1]	...	25.2[1]	Libya
476.4	0.3	—	0.3	0.1	99.3	7.3	44.5	47.5	40.5	...	—	59.5	Liechtenstein
2,230.2	3.9	2.7	——1.8——		91.6	2.6	14.3	74.6	76.8	5.2	...	18.0	Luxembourg
537.0	2.4	0.6	—	0.4	96.6	0.2	1.9	94.6	54.3	19.6	0.3	25.8	Macau
386.5	79.9	4.3	6.0	3.6	6.2	1.0	2.3	3.0	38.2	17.4	1.0	43.4	Madagascar
269.5	90.9	2.4	—	—	6.4	0.4	0.1	5.8	50.7	16.9	—	32.4	Malawi
11,733.9	16.9	27.4	26.6	9.1	19.5	0.7	12.2	6.5	12.9	8.8	—	78.3	Malaysia
2.3	92.0	8.0	—	—	—	—	—	—	0.1[2]	...	—	99.9[2]	Maldives
145.8	61.2	38.8	—	—	—	—	—	—	57.0[8]	...	0.9[8]	42.1[8]	Mali
397.4	6.0	0.5	—	0.5	93.0	0.5	14.4	78.2	73.4[1]	1.8[1]	—	24.8[1]	Malta
133.0	31.6	0.8	44.9	0.6	22.1	3.5	12.5	6.1	45.5	0.4	—	54.1	Martinique
193.9	22.0	—	—	78.0	—	—	—	—	63.7	—	—	36.3	Mauritania
290.3	61.5	...	—	—	29.6	—	0.5	29.1	87.9	5.0	—	7.1	Mauritius
0.6	——98.9——		—	—	—	—	—	—	97.3	...	—	2.7	Mayotte
15,307.5	11.9	2.3	67.3	4.0	11.0	3.4	4.2	3.4	8.5[3]	55.2[3]	—	36.3[3]	Mexico
...	...	...	...	...	...	...	...	...	...	...	...	...	Monaco
488.3	——48.0——		——39.1——		12.9	0.5	0.1	12.3	...	...	...	...	Mongolia
0.7	15.3	4.3	—	8.9	71.5	0.4	30.0	41.2	32.2	37.8	—	30.0	Montserrat
2,321.7	25.3	2.8	4.5	37.4	29.9	—	12.5	17.4	47.8[1]	1.1[1]	5.7[1]	45.4[1]	Morocco
129.0	65.9	13.9	4.4	10.8	5.0	0.8	0.5	3.7	20.1	26.9	0.1	52.9	Mozambique
88.2	—	—	—	100.0	—	—	—	—	...	...	...	100.0	Nauru
93.7	21.4	48.0	—	0.1	30.5	0.5	—	30.0	20.0[4]	11.4[4]	2.8[4]	65.8[4]	Nepal
68,757.9	21.0	3.2	23.6	6.0	45.1	15.7	15.8	13.6	71.2	3.2	0.9	24.7	Netherlands, The
2,641.0	1.1	—	96.7	0.3	2.0	1.3	0.4	0.3	6.5	49.3	—	44.2	Netherlands Antilles
342.9	0.5	0.3	—	95.0	2.4	0.1	1.7	0.5	53.7	12.7	—	33.6	New Caledonia
5,330.3	51.2	22.9	1.2	4.9	19.8	3.8	4.0	12.0	20.7	12.2	4.2	62.9	New Zealand
413.8	74.6	8.1	2.5	1.6	13.2	7.8	0.5	4.9	31.3	38.7	2.0	28.0	Nicaragua
454.8	16.3	0.8	0.9	79.8	2.1	—	0.5	1.5	73.1[6]	0.1[6]	—	26.8[6]	Niger
17,066.3	——1.1——		98.2	0.1	0.4	—	—	0.4	33.4	44.5	—	22.1	Nigeria
0.5	——70.0——		—	—	...	...	—	—	...	...	...	100.0	Niue
1.2	—	10.3	—	—	89.7	—	18.2	71.5	...	...	...	...	Norfolk Island
17,583.2	6.3	2.2	52.0	10.9	28.2	5.6	15.1	7.5	70.6[3]	3.8[3]	0.7[3]	24.9[3]	Norway
3,959.3	1.1	—	93.0	0.1	5.4	—	4.6	0.8	0.8	0.1	...	99.1	Oman
2,737.7	26.8	13.6	6.6	0.5	51.1	0.8	0.7	49.6	16.8	7.1	1.7	74.4	Pakistan
316.9	70.5	0.2	18.4	1.0	9.9	1.2	0.1	8.6	12.9[1]	49.3[1]	—	37.8[1]	Panama
382.0	——39.3——		—	51.6	1.2	—	—	1.2	27.0	3.4	...	69.6	Papua New Guinea

Trade: external (continued)

country	year	imports total value U.S.$ (000,000)	Standard International Trade Classification (SITC) categories (percent)[a][b]								direction of trade (percent)			
			all food items (0+1 +22+4)	agricultural raw materials (2−22 −27−28)	fuels (3)	ores and metals (27+28 +67+68)	manufactured goods total (5+6 −67−68 +7+8)	of which, chemical products (5)	of which, machinery and equipment (7)	of which, other (6−67 −68+8)	from European Economic Community	from United States	from Union of Soviet Socialist Republics	from all other[c]
Paraguay	1980	494.3	12.8	—	26.3	3.8	50.2	6.4	34.6	9.1	17.1[3]	9.7[3]	...	73.2[3]
Peru	1980	2,573.3	19.8	2.8	2.4	7.6	67.2	16.5	40.5	10.2	21.2	36.7	—	42.1
Philippines	1981	8,477.7	8.5	2.2	30.1	5.6	40.7	9.9	22.6	8.2	10.3	22.6	—	67.1
Pitcairn Island	...	...	...	...22.3...	...	...	...34.8...	...	...	...	...	...	...	...
Poland	1982	16,607.8					42.9	9.9	25.0	8.0	18.0[3]	2.5[3]	32.5[3]	47.0[3]
Portugal	1981	9,787.4	15.8	5.9	24.4	6.9	46.9	10.0	26.6	10.3	38.0	12.0	2.4	47.6
Puerto Rico	1981	9,363.7	19.4	10.4	—		70.2	39.1[9]	19.3[10]	11.8	...	61.2	...	38.8
Qatar	1981	1,517.7	13.9	0.9	1.0	8.5	75.6	4.8	41.6	29.2	41.6[1]	11.3[1]	0.1[1]	47.0[1]
Réunion	1981	787.0	26.2	2.3	9.8	2.9	57.0	9.6	21.9	25.6	71.6	...	...	28.4
Romania	1982	8,561.0		...12.1...		...49.5...	38.4	7.6	26.6	4.2	22.0[3]	4.9[3]	18.0[3]	55.1[3]
Rwanda	1980	241.4	9.8	...	12.4	...	45.7	—	25.6	20.1	45.2	8.3	...	46.5
St. Christopher and Nevis	1974	19.7	35.1	1.7	3.6	1.3	47.1	4.7	19.0	23.4	...	...	...	...
St. Helena and Ascension	1982	4.4	26.2	5.1	15.6	—	32.2	...	12.3	19.9	50.1	...	...	49.9
St. Lucia	1980	123.8	21.0	2.8	10.0	3.8	62.4	8.8	23.7	29.9	21.2	31.8	0.1	46.9
St. Pierre and Miquelon	1981	40.7	17.5	4.0	35.9	1.4	37.2	2.7	18.4	16.1	30.0	2.6	—	67.4
St. Vincent and the Grenadines	1981	58.2	31.9	4.4	8.8	—	54.8	11.8	14.5	28.5	20.0	32.5	...	47.5
San Marino	...	...	...	...	...	...	...	...	...	...	...	...	...	...
São Tomé and Príncipe	1977	14.8	46.0	0.5	1.9	3.0	45.7	10.1	12.8	22.8	...	...	...	...
Saudi Arabia	1981	35,041.5	14.4	1.1	0.7	7.6	76.0	3.9	40.4	31.7	33.9	21.6	—	44.5
Senegal	1981	860.9	28.3	0.9	19.0	3.6	47.7	9.5	22.4	15.8	51.9	5.7	0.3	42.1
Seychelles	1980	98.9	20.8	1.6	24.4	2.8	87.8	5.7	20.0	22.1	34.2	2.5	0.1	63.2
Sierra Leone	1981	437.4	22.1	2.8	17.3	1.7	55.4	7.4	24.6	23.4	36.5[8]	8.7[8]	1.5[8]	53.3[8]
Singapore	1982	28,167.5	7.8	3.2	33.6	5.5	48.9	5.0	28.0	15.9	9.8[3]	12.6[3]	0.2[3]	77.4[3]
Solomon Islands	1980	72.0	14.4	0.7	16.0	—	68.6	5.1	39.2	24.2	9.8	3.2	...	87.0
Somalia	1980	348.0	32.5	4.2	0.7	3.5	58.8	4.7	35.3	18.9	45.0	8.3	—	46.7
South Africa	1979	8,338.0	4.9	3.9	0.6	4.9	85.2	13.7	52.2	19.4	34.9[1]	—	...	65.1[1]
South West Africa/Namibia	...	...	...	...	...	...	...	...	...	...	...	...	...	...
Spain	1981	32,081.3	11.9	3.9	42.5	7.2	34.4	7.8	17.4	9.2	29.1	13.9	1.5	55.5
Sri Lanka	1981	1,803.8	19.4	1.6	25.0	4.8	48.9	8.3	22.8	17.8	16.3	7.2	0.1	76.4
Sudan, The	1981	1,518.7	19.3	2.1	19.1	5.0	54.1	11.9	22.0	20.2	43.4[1]	7.7[1]	...	48.9[1]
Suriname	1979	410.5	15.0	1.0	30.4	...	50.2	...	21.4	28.8	27.9	32.5	...	39.6
Swaziland	1980	595.6	7.1	0.5	16.5	—	59.0	10.5	16.5	32.0	...	...	...	...
Sweden	1982	27,533.0	7.0	1.9	24.5	7.9	58.1	9.1	27.7	21.3	48.6[3]	8.2[3]	1.8[3]	41.4[3]
Switzerland	1982	28,577.1	9.0	2.6	11.7	6.1	70.5	11.3	26.5	32.8	65.7[3]	7.5[3]	2.9[3]	23.9[3]
Syria	1982	4,014.1	13.7	3.1	37.6	0.1	45.3	8.8	15.6	20.9	35.1[1]	5.3[1]	1.1[1]	58.5[1]
Taiwan	1982	18,888.0	3.6	12.5	21.3	12.1	50.5	4.8	26.5	19.2	5.6	24.1	...	70.3
Tanzania	1980	1,211.4	13.3	0.8	21.0	5.4	59.5	10.8	35.4	13.3	46.8	6.2	0.1	46.9
Thailand	1981	10,055.0	4.4	4.0	29.8	9.6	48.2	12.2	25.9	10.1	12.8[1]	16.6[1]	0.1[1]	70.5[1]
Togo	1981	435.8	25.7	1.6	8.4	3.1	61.1	6.2	21.3	33.7	59.0[4]	3.7[4]	1.1[4]	36.2[4]
Tokelau	...	...	...	...	...	...	...	...	...	...	...	...	...	...
Tonga	1981	40.2	30.4	4.4	16.4	2.4	46.2	5.4	15.7	25.0	4.2[1]	5.8[1]	—	90.0[1]
Trinidad and Tobago	1981	3,124.6	12.9	1.7	36.6	4.2	44.4	5.2	22.4	16.8	14.3	26.1	—	59.6
Trust Territory of the Pacific Is.	1977	39.0	...	...	...	...	...	...	...	...	...	...	...	...
Tunisia	1981	3,770.9	14.3	3.1	20.5	9.4	52.5	6.7	27.2	18.7	63.8[1]	5.9[1]	0.8[1]	29.5[1]
Turkey	1981	8,864.3	2.8	1.8	44.2	9.2	42.0	14.9	22.0	5.1	27.9	6.5	1.8	63.8
Turks and Caicos Islands	1982	20.9	...	...	...	...	...	...	...	...	...	...	...	...
Tuvalu	1981	3.0	35.1	2.5	16.2	0.7	43.7	4.5	13.7	25.4	...	...	...	...
Uganda	1976	157.5	7.9	0.6	29.6	3.1	58.7	11.1	26.8	20.8	29.1[8]	...	...	70.9[8]
U.S.S.R.	1982	73,261.0		...29.0...		...14.9...	56.1	9.0	34.4	12.7	14.3[3]	3.2[3]	—	82.5[3]
United Arab Emirates	1978	5,389.0	11.2	0.9	3.7	7.3	75.9	4.3	43.9	27.8	41.3	12.0	0.1	46.6
United Kingdom	1982	99,031.7	13.8	3.8	13.0	7.2	60.6	7.6	28.4	24.6	41.1[1]	11.8[1]	1.5[1]	45.6[1]
United States	1982	253,033.1	7.9	2.2	26.6	7.4	53.6	4.3	29.2	20.1	16.1[3]	—	0.1[3]	83.8[3]
Uruguay	1981	1,633.1	6.8	3.1	31.6	4.8	53.6	10.8	32.1	10.7	17.9[1]	9.8[1]	0.2[1]	72.1[1]
Vanuatu	1980	49.8	29.5	1.9	15.8	2.2	50.5	6.3	20.6	23.6	35.5[7]	2.6[7]	—	61.9[7]
Venezuela	1981	11,811.0	16.9	2.4	0.8	7.8	72.1	10.4	43.4	18.3	19.8[1]	48.1[1]	...	32.1[1]
Vietnam	1982	838.0	...	...	...	...	...	...	...	...	...	...	...	...
Virgin Islands (U.S.)	1978	667.4	11.3	0.4	58.5	1.0	23.5	3.7	8.2	11.5	0.9	58.0	—	41.1
Wallis and Futuna	1981	6.8	31.1	...	16.9	5.5	...	...	...	...	...	...	...	...
Western Sahara	...	...	...	...	...	...	...	...	...	...	...	...	...	...
Western Samoa	1980	62.5	24.8	1.1	16.5	4.3	53.3	9.1	21.0	23.2	24.5[4]	8.7[4]	0.1[4]	66.7[4]
Yemen (Aden)	1977	544.0	16.9	1.2	46.6	1.4	33.9	2.0	22.6	9.2	18.4	...	3.2	78.4
Yemen (San'ā')	1980	1,853.0	28.4	0.2	7.2	6.7	57.1	5.1	27.7	24.3	32.7	...	0.7	66.6
Yugoslavia	1981	15,757.0	6.3	7.0	24.0	11.8	50.9	12.9	27.7	10.4	35.5	6.1	18.8	39.6
Zaire	1979	373.3	20.3	2.7	3.3	6.5	66.2	13.5	33.6	19.1	54.0[2]	...	—	46.0[2]
Zambia	1979	750.2	8.6	1.2	17.9	5.8	66.4	13.4	33.9	19.0	46.0[2]	7.8[2]	—	46.2[2]
Zimbabwe	1982	1,428.0	1.1	2.0	17.2	0.7	79.0	12.4	38.9	27.7	41.0	9.6	...	49.4

exports — total value U.S.$ (000,000)	Standard International Trade Classification (SITC) categories (percent)[a][b] — all food items (0 + 1 + 22 + 4)	agricultural raw materials (2 − 22 − 27 − 28)	fuels (3)	ores and metals (27 + 28 + 67 + 68)	manufactured goods — total (5 + 6 − 67 − 68 + 7 + 8)	of which, chemical products (5)	of which, machinery and equipment (7)	of which, other (6 − 67 − 68 + 8)	direction of trade (percent) — to European Economic Community	to United States	to Union of Soviet Socialist Republics	to all other[c]	country
310.2	35.7	57.4	—	—	4.4	4.4	—	—	20.3[3]	5.2[3]	...	74.5[3]	Paraguay
3,265.5	15.8	3.7	20.6	43.5	16.2	2.6	1.8	11.9	20.6	32.4	0.5	46.5	Peru
5,712.1	34.6	4.8	0.7	15.7	22.8	1.9	2.7	18.2	16.2	30.9	3.0	49.9	Philippines
...	...		...	...									Pitcairn Island
18,166.2	—8.8—		—27.1—		64.1	4.0	46.9	13.2	15.4[3]	4.7[3]	41.7[3]	38.2[3]	Poland
4,147.1	11.3	9.3	7.1	2.7	68.4	6.0	12.6	50.0	53.7	5.2	1.3	39.8	Portugal
6,798.6	18.3	11.2	—	—	70.5	36.5[9]	17.2[10]	16.8	...	84.5	...	15.5	Puerto Rico
3,598.0	—	—	92.0	3.2	2.0	2.0	—	—	35.3[1]	1.7[1]	...	63.0[1]	Qatar
106.9	87.6	0.1	0.2	0.3	10.9	4.8	3.0	3.0	76.6	...	6.7	16.7	Réunion
10,194.8	—14.0—		—24.1—		61.9	12.1	33.0	16.8	13.6[3]	7.8[3]	18.2[3]	60.4[3]	Romania
113.6	—72.7—			23.4	—	—	—	—	10.4	0.5	—	89.1	Rwanda
12.5	52.4	0.2	29.0	0.3	16.8	0.6	15.6	0.6	...	...	...	...	St. Christopher and Nevis
57.2	77.1	—	—	—	22.9	—	—	22.9	...	...	—	...	St. Helena and Ascension
33.7	57.0	0.7	—	—	42.3	1.2	13.5	27.6	25.6	27.6	—	46.8	St. Lucia
7.1	99.9	—	—	—	—	—	—	—	17.5	58.3	—	24.2	St. Pierre and Miquelon
23.5	82.5	0.1	—	—	17.3	4.5	3.7	9.1	46.0	6.9	—	47.1	St. Vincent and the Grenadines
...	...			...	...							...	San Marino
24.1	99.7	0.1	—	...	0.2	—	0.1	0.1	...	...	...	...	São Tomé and Príncipe
119,913.1	0.1	—	99.3[1]		0.6	0.1	0.4	0.1	34.5	13.4	—	52.1	Saudi Arabia
442.8	33.2	2.7	24.4	16.5	23.2	6.1	5.2	11.9	35.9	6.0	0.7	57.4	Senegal
5.2	90.7	2.7	—	4.4	1.8	0.3	—	1.6	12.1	0.6	—	87.3	Seychelles
207.4	30.1	0.7	...	69.1	—	—	—	—	63.7[8]	17.8[8]	—	18.5[8]	Sierra Leone
20,787.9	7.7	5.6	27.5	3.8	46.9	9.2	25.5	12.2	10.5[3]	13.2[3]	0.8[3]	75.5[3]	Singapore
71.8	70.9	26.8	—	0.1	—	—	—	—	31.7	20.5	—	47.8	Solomon Islands
132.6	86.7	7.7	4.8	—	0.5	0.1	0.1	0.3	14.1	0.1	—	85.8	Somalia
9,637.5	16.2	7.0	7.2	29.3	30.3	5.0	4.6	20.7	18.0[1]	7.0[1]	...	75.0[1]	South Africa
...													South West Africa/Namibia
20,336.5	18.5	1.9	5.0	13.1	61.5	7.5	25.4	28.6	42.9	6.7	1.8	48.6	Spain
1,007.5	47.5	17.1	12.9	0.8	21.5	1.8	0.5	10.3	19.5	14.0	2.3	64.2	Sri Lanka
500.8	58.8	35.4	4.4	0.4	0.8	—	—	0.8	31.8[1]	—	1.6[1]	66.6[1]	Sudan, The
440.4	—18.0—		—	76.8	5.2	—	—5.2—		21.1	32.6	...	46.3	Suriname
358.7	56.5	20.2	1.0	6.3	16.0	8.5	—	7.5	...	...	...	...	Swaziland
26,739.6	2.9	8.6	5.2	10.4	72.2	6.1	42.6	23.5	46.3[3]	6.1[3]	1.5[3]	46.1[3]	Sweden
25,617.7	3.5	1.0	0.1	4.0	91.3	21.2	34.7	35.3	48.5[3]	8.0[3]	0.8[3]	42.7[3]	Switzerland
2,174.1	6.1	7.3	69.6	—	10.0	1.0	1.5	8.5	63.3[1]	—	5.6[1]	31.1[1]	Syria
22,204.0	5.4	2.2	—	5.2	87.2	2.6	26.3	58.3	6.0	39.4	—	54.6	Taiwan
527.7	58.1	17.5	4.7	5.6	14.0	0.7	0.6	12.7	41.1	3.9	2.9	52.1	Tanzania
6,848.8	55.5	9.0	—	8.6	25.1	0.8	5.2	19.1	25.8[1]	12.7[1]	2.5[1]	59.0[1]	Thailand
206.4	26.1	6.4	1.3	51.5	14.6	0.2	1.4	13.0	63.6[4]	1.8[4]	0.7	33.9[4]	Togo
...	...				...				...				Tokelau
7.6	88.2	5.1	—	—	6.5	0.1	0.1	6.3	3.7[1]	13.4[1]	—	82.9[1]	Tonga
3,760.8	2.0	—	89.6	0.3	8.0	3.8	3.2	1.0	14.4	58.9	—	26.7	Trinidad and Tobago
19.0	...				...			...	...			...	Trust Territory of the Pacific Is.
2,503.7	9.2	0.7	54.0	2.8	33.2	12.8	2.3	18.2	71.7[1]	14.5[1]	0.2[1]	13.6[1]	Tunisia
4,701.9	46.0	10.0	2.3	6.1	35.6	2.1	4.4	29.0	32.0	5.7	4.1	58.2	Turkey
...	...		...	...	...		...		...			...	Turks and Caicos Islands
...													Tuvalu
351.5	89.8	6.8	0.8	2.2	0.4	—	—	0.4	31.6[8]	48.4[8]	—	20.0[8]	Uganda
82,032.5	—6.5—		—60.8—		32.7	17.9	12.9	1.9	20.8[3]	...	—	79.2[3]	U.S.S.R.
9,138.2	1.2	0.1	95.0	0.3	3.4	0.1	1.4	1.9	37.1	11.4	—	51.5	United Arab Emirates
96,542.4	7.2	1.4	20.2	5.7	62.8	11.2	33.0	18.6	42.7[1]	9.5[1]	0.9[1]	46.9[1]	United Kingdom
206,044.7	17.1	4.2	6.2	3.8	65.9	10.8	42.8	12.3	21.5[3]	—	1.0[3]	77.5[3]	United States
1,216.6	47.4	21.2	1.0	0.9	29.3	3.3	2.1	24.0	30.0[1]	7.8[1]	4.6[1]	57.6[1]	Uruguay
28.1	98.9	0.5	—	0.4	0.1	—	—	0.1	45.0[7]	28.2[7]	—	26.8[7]	Vanuatu
19,292.8	0.4	—	94.0	4.5	1.1	0.5	0.4	0.2	12.9	27.3	—	59.8	Venezuela
430.0	...	...	...	...	...	...	...	...	...	...	...	...	Vietnam
2,512.1	0.2	—	91.3	0.2	8.2	6.2	0.2	1.9	1.0	96.8	1.3	0.9	Virgin Islands (U.S.)
...													Wallis and Futuna
...													Western Sahara
17.0	92.0	5.9	—	0.2	1.9	0.5	—	1.2	41.0[4]	8.8[4]	—	50.2[4]	Western Samoa
204.7	19.9	4.2	74.6	0.9	0.4	—	0.3	0.1	1.8	—	—	98.2	Yemen (Aden)
22.6	45.0	3.9	0.1	4.4	42.6	2.8	25.1	14.7	24.6	8.8	...	66.6	Yemen (San'a')
10,928.9	10.7	4.4	2.0	7.0	75.4	12.5	28.5	34.4	23.2	3.5	33.3	40.0	Yugoslavia
549.2	18.8	2.8	0.1	73.1	3.2	0.1	1.1	2.1	72.0[2]	3.6[2]	—	24.4[2]	Zaire
1,372.0	0.4	—	1.2	97.6	0.7	0.2	0.1	0.5	47.9[2]	10.2[2]	0.3[2]	41.6[2]	Zambia
1,278.3	13.8	26.1	1.2	7.8	34.3	1.3	1.5	31.5	31.1	7.9	...	61.0	Zimbabwe

[1]1980. [2]1978. [3]1981. [4]1979. [5]Figures for Belgium include Luxembourg; the latter also appears separately. [6]1976. [7]1975. [8]1977. [9]Fuels and ores are included with chemical products. [10]Ores and metals are included with machinery and equipment.

Trade: domestic

The following table presents data relating to domestic wholesale and retail trade for the countries of the world. The compilation for the section on wholesale trade is based for the most part on establishments engaged primarily in selling goods to retailers and distributors for resale or to purchasers who buy for business and farm uses. The compilation of the retail trade section is based on businesses engaged in selling merchandise for personal or household consumption.

There being no single source or common international methodology for the compilation of data on wholesale and retail trade, nor a single current year on which to base all reports, allowances must be made for variations in the information provided for each country. Variations occur in part because of the way in which countries define wholesale and retail trade; the distinction between wholesale and retail is not clear in some countries, and data may overlap in their final reports. Variations also exist in the kind and level of detail reported. For example, countries may analyze differently the size (number of employees, sales, surface area) of establishments surveyed. The depth of analysis to which the data are subjected may also vary. Trade is affected by the degree of government involvement, which may range from total control of wholesale distribution in some socialist countries, to partial involvement in some strategic sectors, or to complete non-involvement in fully private trade sectors of capitalist countries. In many smaller countries data may be collected only by inference; for instance, in a country with inadequate resources to survey trade, the number of accounts served by one national tobacco distributor may be the sole datum on the number of that country's retail outlets.

The combined value of a country's retail and wholesale trade is presented as a percentage of its gross domestic product.

Although all sales figures are given in U.S. dollars, the comparability of dollar figures may differ considerably; for instance, the purchasing power of various national currencies in domestic transactions may bear only a distant relationship to the exchange rate of the same currency in international transactions. The price of goods may also vary, depending on the degree to which they are subject to direct subsidies and artificial cost controls such as tax, investment, or free-trade preferences by a central government seeking to influence social or economic conditions.

The data on distribution of sales by kind of consumer goods may have their origin in several different types of data or analysis: One country may aggregate sales data by kind of establishment only (this may be perfectly satisfactory in a country of small, independent outlets); another may aggregate data directly by kind of goods (most easily done in a country with well-developed statistical, tax-reporting, and commercial systems); other countries may find it impolitic to publish data that reflect the poverty of their distribution network or of their supply of consumer goods and may aggregate or publish data for only a few sectors or non-food goods, for example). For countries with only a few trading enterprises in a particular sector, detail must often be withheld to preserve the confidentiality of individual businesses.

Both the wholesale and retail sections of the table provide data in similar detail: establishments or outlets, employees, sales, and relationships among these measures; the retail section provides an additional break-

Trade: domestic

country	year	domestic trade as percentage of GDP	wholesale trade					retail trade		
			establishments[a]	employees[b]	sales[c] $'000,000	employees per establishment	sales per establishment $'000	outlets[a]	employees[b]	sales[c] $'000,000
Afghanistan	1982	7.6[1]	...	...	...	...	...	...	...	...
Albania	1978	...	...	...	...	...	...	9,254[2]	...	737.1
Algeria	1971	13.5[1,3]	2,631[4]	...	749.2[4]	...	284.7[4]	3,600	18,000	9,700.0
American Samoa		...	...	...	...	...	...	...	...	...
Andorra	1972	...	...	...	...	...	...	592	2,264	...
Angola	1973	...	5	...	...	...	...	29,138[5]	...	...
Anguilla		...	...	...	...	...	...	...	...	...
Antigua and Barbuda	1976	20.9[1,6]	11	162	...	14.7	...	233	1,209	...
Argentina	1974	16.1[7]	5	5	20,533.3[8]	5	...	708,421[5]	1,847,290[5]	21,125.1[8]
Australia	1980	14.0[1]	33,356[4]	358,811[4,9]	24,641.2[4]	10.8[4,9]	738.7[4]	110,500[10]	737,378[9,10]	43,951.6[10]
Austria	1983	16.6[1,6]	11,445[7]	59,370	32,324.2	5.6[7]	2,958.4[7]	37,148[7]	60,197	16,224.7
Bahamas, The[13]	1980	25.6[1,14]	23	1,066	143.4	46.3	6,234.8	132	4,059	353.6
Bahrain		...[10]	...	...	...	...	...	...	...	...
Bangladesh	1982	8.2	...	...	...	...	...	...	...	6,300.0[15]
Barbados	1982	22.1	...	5	...	...	...	...	17,600[1,5]	...
Belgium	1980	11.4[10]	56,791	173,700	79,497.5	3.1	1,399.8	129,627	199,800	41,049.4
Belize	1981	15.8[1]	...	...	...	...	...	[5,16]	[5,16]	...
Benin	1980	20.9[1]	5	5	...	5	...	153	4,455	...
Bermuda	1979	...	60	...	...	...	...	300	4,500	335.0
Bhutan		...	...	...	...	...	...	...	...	...
Bolivia	1976	19.9[1,6]	...	5	5	...	...	...	17,414[1,5]	...
Botswana	1979	9.8[1,15]	164	1,600	300.5	9.8	1,832.3	1,333	3,600	168.1
Brazil	1975	13.6[7,10]	52,722	117,423	49,101.8	2.2	931.3	635,812	723,461	42,523.5
British Virgin Islands	1970	27.0[1,14]	...	...	...	...	...	...	361[1]	...
Brunei	1982	9.8[1]	5	5	...	5	...	654[5]	3,403[5]	...
Bulgaria	1981	12.6[1]	...	9,000[7]	...	...	...	38,304[10]	288,588	12,698.3[10]
Burkina Faso	1979	15.5[1]	...	...	...	...	...	...	...	...
Burma	1982	24.0[10]	...	...	...	...	...	...	...	2,030.0[15]
Burundi	1980	7.6[1]	...	...	...	...	...	...	...	...
Cameroon	1980	13.5[1]	...	...	...	...	...	...	...	...
Canada	1980	9.5[1,6]	30,900[18]	316,373[18]	28,761.8[18]	10.2[18]	930.8[18]	156,518[19]	624,688[19]	70,315.1
Cape Verde		...	...	...	...	...	...	...	...	...
Cayman Islands	1972	17.0	...	86	...	...	...	...	928	...
Central African Republic	1971	13.3[10]	...	...	...	...	...	...	...	...
Chad	1977	30.1[1]	...	...	...	...	...	...	...	...
Chile	1980	18.3[29]	539	19,300	4,216.8	35.8	7,823.4	1,351	28,000[14]	1,715.9[14]
China	1982	...	41,000	762,000[9]	...	18.6	...	2,607,000[10]	8,709,000[9,10]	135,795.6[10,21]
Christmas Island	1981	...	—	5	—	—	—	5	65[5]	...
Cocos (Keeling) Islands	1981	...	...	5	...	...	...	1	13[5]	...
Colombia[22]	1970	17.8[7,10]	1,363	31,628	931.4	23.2	683.3	2,785	72,310	963.1
Comoros		...	...	...	...	...	...	...	...	...
Congo	1981	11.1[1]	...	...	...	...	...	...	...	...
Cook Islands	1976	24.0[14]	...	5	...	...	...	...	409[1,5]	...
Costa Rica	1975	17.7[1,6]	332	4,073	34.6	12.3	104.2	9,713	26,486	568.6
Cuba	1980	25.9[1,6]	...	...	10,369.4	...	...	51,733	...	8,580.6
Cyprus	1982	18.9[1]	1,518	9,767[9]	1,227.2	6.4[9]	808.4	8,186[10]	15,894[9,10]	996.8[10]
Czechoslovakia	1982	14.5[1]	...	...	...	...	...	107,861	391,200[7]	22,486.6
Denmark	1980	13.4[1,15]	5,987[3]	136,000[14]	30,174.1	22.7[14]	5,531.4[14]	52,300[3]	131,000[14]	14,537.3
Djibouti	1980	25.3[1]	...	...	...	...	...	...	...	...
Dominica	1979	7.5[10]	...	...	...	...	...	...	...	...
Dominican Republic	1979	16.2[1,15]	...	...	2,008.0	...	...	...	24,936[1,20]	827.0
Ecuador	1980	14.0[1,6]	2,450	15,591	2,805.4	6.4	1,145.1	102,981	179,847	5,922.1
Egypt	1978	12.8[1,7]	1,579	40,400	3,755.5	25.6	2,378.4	1,513	42,300	2,073.8
El Salvador[23]	1978	27.6[1,6]	344	11,047	743.3	32.1	2,160.9	1,005	17,978	616.4
Equatorial Guinea		...	...	...	...	...	...	...	...	...

down of sales by the various classifications of retail sales outlets. At the extreme left, following the year to which the data refer, the combined value of the country's wholesale and retail trade as a percentage of gross domestic product is given.

The data presented here are based on information received from a variety of direct country and international sources. The direct country sources include such items as correspondence, statistical abstracts, annual reports, and censuses of business and trade. Among the more prominent international sources are various publications of the United Nations dealing with trade and production.

The notes that follow further define the various headings.
a. The number of establishments or outlets refers to an economic unit that operates at a single physical location in one principal kind of activity, whether singly owned or part of a multiunit firm. It is not necessarily identical with a company or enterprise.
b. Number of employees refers to full-time and part-time paid workers, including salaried managers and officers; it usually excludes owner-operators.
c. Total sales includes the value of merchandise sold for cash or credit; amounts received from customers for layaway purchases; receipts from rental or leasing of vehicles, equipment, tools, instruments, etc.; receipts for delivery, installation, maintenance, repair, alteration, storage, and other services.
d. Covers outlets engaged primarily in the sale of food, such as grocery stores, meat and fish markets, and bakeries.

e. Covers outlets engaged primarily in the sale of clothing and shoes; also includes outlets that sell accessory items, such as millinery, furs, umbrellas, wigs, etc.
f. Covers outlets engaged primarily in the sale of home furnishings, including furniture, draperies, floor coverings, household appliances, and home entertainment equipment.
g. Covers outlets that primarily serve food and drink, including restaurants, lunchrooms, cafeterias, social caterers, refreshment places, contract feeders, ice cream parlors, and bars and taverns.
h. Covers outlets engaged primarily in the sale of pharmaceuticals and cosmetics.
i. Covers outlets engaged primarily in the sale of building materials, hardware, garden supplies, paint, glass, and wallpaper.
j. Covers outlets engaged primarily in the sale of motor vehicles, motorcycles, bicycles, and tires, batteries, and other automotive supplies; includes service stations.
k. Covers outlets engaged in the sale of multiple lines of merchandise, such as department stores, variety stores, and country general stores.
l. Covers miscellaneous specialized outlets such as those engaged primarily in the sale of liquors, sporting goods, books, jewelry, photographic equipment, gifts, flowers, cigars, and newspapers.

food[d]	clothing, shoes[e]	home furnishings[f]	eating, drinking[g]	drugs, pharmaceuticals[h]	building materials[i]	automobile parts[j]	general merchandise[k]	other[l]	employees per outlet[b]	sales per outlet $'000	population per outlet	country
...	...	...	...	...	...	...	...	...	...	...	...	Afghanistan
63.2				36.8					...	79.6	277.0	Albania
...	...	...	...	...	...	...	...	...	5.0	2,700.0	5,146.0	Algeria
...	...	...	...	...	...	...	...	...	...	...	...	American Samoa
...	...	...	...	...	...	...	...	...	3.8	...	38.9	Andorra
...	...	...	...	...	...	...	...	...	...	...	...	Angola
...	...	...	...	...	...	...	...	...	...	...	...	Anguilla
...	...	...	...	...	...	...	...	...	5.2	...	304.7	Antigua and Barbuda
...	...	...	...	...	...	...	...	...	2.6[5]	...	...	Argentina
32.3	10.4[11]	6.6[12]	...	...	...	32.0	10.3	8.4	6.7[9,10]	397.8[10]	131.3[10]	Australia
28.9	14.0	7.9	...	4.6		15.0	10.0	19.5	1.6[7]	470.5[7]	202.2[7]	Austria
37.0	7.8	4.4	...	2.1	8.8	12.8	4.6	22.5	30.8	2,678.8	1,590.9	Bahamas, The[13]
...	...	...	...	...	...	...	...	...	...	...	...	Bahrain
...	...	...	...	...	...	...	...	...	...	...	...	Bangladesh
...	...	...	...	...	...	...	...	...	...	...	...	Barbados
...	...	...	...	...	...	...	...	...	1.5	316.7	76.0	Belgium
...	...	...	...	...	...	...	...	...	...	...	...	Belize
...	...	...	...	...	...	...	...	...	29.1[5,16]	...	22,444.4[5]	Benin
...	...	...	...	...	...	...	...	...	15.0	1,117.0	166.7	Bermuda
...	...	...	...	...	...	...	...	...	...	...	...	Bhutan
...	...	...	...	...	...	...	...	...	...	...	...	Bolivia
...	...	...	...	...	...	...	...	...	2.7	126.1	592.6	Botswana
...	...	...	...	...	...	...	...	...	1.1	66.9	165.0	Brazil
...	...	...	...	...	...	...	...	...	...	...	...	British Virgin Islands
...	...	...	...	...	...	...	...	...	5.2[5]	...	306.4[5]	Brunei
44.4	14.7	...	...	...	1.4	...	8.4	31.1	7.5	390.0[10]	137.1[7]	Bulgaria
...	...	...	...	...	...	...	...	...	...	...	...	Burkina Faso
...	...	...	...	...	...	...	...	...	...	...	...	Burma
...	...	...	...	...	...	...	...	...	...	...	...	Burundi
...	...	...	...	...	...	...	...	...	...	...	...	Cameroon
25.6	5.5	2.4	...	3.2	0.9	29.1	16.5	16.8	4.0[19]	200.2	138.0[19]	Canada
...	...	...	...	...	...	...	...	...	...	...	...	Cape Verde
...	...	...	...	...	...	...	...	...	...	...	...	Cayman Islands
...	...	...	...	...	...	...	...	...	...	...	...	Central African Republic
...	...	...	...	...	...	...	...	...	...	...	...	Chad
20.3[20]	17.6[20]	7.8[20]	4.2[20]	4.5[20]	6.6[20]	16.9[20]	...	22.1[20]	20.8[14]	1,276.7	8,216.1	Chile
44.9	18.1	...	...	...	37.0	...	...	...	3.3	52.1	389.5[10]	China
...	...	...	...	...	...	...	...	...	...	...	574.2	Christmas Island
...	...	...	...	...	...	...	...	...	...	...	555.0	Cocos (Keeling) Islands
...	...	...	...	...	...	...	...	...	26.0	345.8	...	Colombia[22]
...	...	...	...	...	...	...	...	...	...	...	...	Comoros
...	...	...	...	...	...	...	...	...	...	...	...	Congo
...	...	...	...	...	...	...	...	...	...	...	...	Cook Islands
37.7	13.5	6.9	...	8.2	7.0	15.1	5.9	5.7	2.7	58.5	202.8	Costa Rica
33.3	...	...	29.9	3.9	...	...	...	33.0	...	165.9	188.3	Cuba
21.8	10.8	...	...	3.0	6.9	24.9	...	32.6	1.9[9,10]	121.8[13]	79.4[10]	Cyprus
47.8	15.4	5.1	2.1	3.5	2.3	7.4	...	16.4	3.7	352.1	142.5	Czechoslovakia
52.3	6.6	5.7	...	0.5	2.8	14.7	8.2	9.2	...	...	97.8	Denmark
...	...	...	...	...	...	...	...	...	...	...	...	Djibouti
...	...	...	...	...	...	...	...	...	...	...	...	Dominica
...	...	...	...	...	...	...	...	...	...	...	...	Dominican Republic
24.2	29.1	8.1	3.0	4.8	4.0	17.8	3.4	5.6	1.7	57.5	81.1	Ecuador
...	...	...	...	...	...	...	...	...	28.0	1,370.7	26,318.6	Egypt
7.8	2.8	12.3	...	3.4	12.6	38.7	16.6	5.8	17.9	613.3	...	El Salvador[23]
...	...	...	...	...	...	...	...	...	...	...	...	Equatorial Guinea

Trade: domestic (continued)

country	year	domestic trade as percentage of GDP	wholesale trade					retail trade		
			establish- ments[a]	employees[b]	sales[c] $'000,000	employees per establishment	sales per establishment $'000	outlets[a]	employees[b]	sales[c] $'000,000
Ethiopia[24]	1973	9.6[10,15]	375	3,200	...	8.5	...	7,416	17,100	201.8
Faeroe Islands	1980	11.7[1]	...	5	...	...	...	...	1,484[1,5]	...
Falkland Islands	1976	...	2	...	...	...	...	21	...	...
Fiji	1976	16.4[1,7]	184	2,340	154.6	12.7	840.5	2,245	7,620	258.0
Finland	1980	10.1[1,6]	8,248	86,164[9]	26,346.1	10.4[9]	3,194.2	36,113[10]	158,717[9,10]	25,317.7[10]
France	1980	12.3[1,6]	78,588	898,530	239,219.6	11.4	3,044.0	614,626	1,778,128	162,474.2[10,25]
French Guiana	...									
French Polynesia	1980	30.3[1]	...							
Gabon	1979	7.0	...							
Gambia, The	1979	...	...	3,300	...	...	...	...	700	...
Germany, East	1982	10.0[1]	...	...	...	...	...	...	898,500	42,667.1
Germany, West	1979	12.4[1,15]	36,318	954,600	350,356.3	26.3	9,646.9	249,466	2,155,800	206,740.1
Ghana[16]	1977	14.6[1,7]	460	1,100	114.9	2.4	249.8	2,182	5,700	236.7
Gibraltar	1981	...	...	595	...	...	...	...	1,354	...
Greece	1978	12.9[10]	25,266	91,341	...	3.6	...	160,599	287,457	...
Greenland	1981	...	...	...	80.7	...	...	...	...	91.8
Grenada	1979	16.8	...	5	...	...	...	...	2,262[5]	...
Guadeloupe	1974	18.0[1,3]	...	5	...	...	...	...	11,960[1,5,9]	...
Guam	1977	...	51	546	92.67	10.7	1,525.0	531	4,070	352.67
Guatemala	1980	26.3[6,10]	...	5	...	5	...	...	51,700[5,9]	844.5[5]
Guinea	...									
Guinea-Bissau	...									
Guyana	1980	8.6	...	...	...	...	...	147	...	109.2
Haiti	1972	18.4[1,6]	...	5	...	...	...	...	3,900[5,9]	...
Honduras	1982	12.8[10]	...	5	...	...	...	...	84,541[1,5,9]	...
Hong Kong	1981	18.4[1,6]	30,887	166,593	38,563.8	5.4	1,248.5	47,774	231,163	10,916.8
Hungary	1981	10.2[6]	128	93,000	13,121.4	726.6	102,510.9	54,860	353,000	10,879.3
Iceland[26]	1979	...	970[14]	4,500[9,14]	52,598.2[14]	4.6[9,14]	54,224.9[14]	1,610	6,830[9]	57,564.2
India	1970	13.6[1,15]	116,000	...	35.2	...	303.4	3,760,000	1,753,000	3,273.7
Indonesia	1980	14.9[6,10]	5	5	5	5	5	54,632[5]	85,400[5]	3,451.7[5]
Iran	1972	6.0[1,7]	18,210	53,522[9]	2,409.0	2.9[9]	132.3	218,132	333,106[9]	3,757.5
Iraq	1976	4.2[1]	1,532	2,700	242,675.4	1.8	158,404.3	77,766	106,800	2,471,590.8
Ireland	1977	13.0[1,14]	3,073	40,584	4,592.9	13.2	1,494.6	32,332	79,870	4,170.2
Israel	1977	13.1[1,6]	4,862	33,178	9,036.6	6.8	1,858.6	40,000	85,000	1,622.3[16]
Italy	1980	15.6[1,6]	120,366[19]	390,000[19]	...	3.2[19]	...	1,013,601	410,000[19]	116,579.0
Ivory Coast	1978	20.8[1,3]	...	...	...	...	...	50,000	...	...
Jamaica	1979	19.7[1,7]	...	...	...	...	...	...	...	878.4
Japan	1982	12.4[10,15]	428,750	4,090,000[9]	1,600,373.4	9.5[9]	3,732.6	2,258,494	8,351,000[9]	413,680.0
Jordan	1982	16.2[1]	...	...	...	...	...	...	...	...
Kampuchea	...									
Kenya[27]	1982	10.5[1]	2,161	27,351	...	12.7	...	5,219	29,068	...
Kiribati	1976	6.1[1,14]	...	...	...	...	...	35	...	6.6
Korea, North	...									
Korea, South	1979	14.8[1,6]	23,835	83,222	7,957.3	3.5	333.9	556,863	323,120	18,312.9
Kuwait	1973	9.4[1,6]	981	6,700	560.5	6.8	571.4	11,306	35,300	1,385.2
Laos	...									
Lebanon	1975	28.3[1,28]	...	5	...	...	...	...	130,000[1,5,9]	...
Lesotho	1976	10.6[1,7]	...	5	...	5	...	...	4,649[1,5]	...
Liberia	1974	10.4[1,3]	...	5	...	...	...	...	16,282[1,5]	...
Libya	1973	5.8[1,15]	1,143	4.776	...	4.2	...	26,908[10]	44,836[10]	...
Liechtenstein	1975	...	67	216	...	3.2	...	228	740	...
Luxembourg	1981	12.9[1,7]	998[3]	7,472[14]	2,285.0	7.6[14]	2,318.2[3]	3,970[3]	11,381[14]	1,587.6
Macau	...									
Madagascar	1976	13.0[20]	1,104	...	...	...	...	1,570	...	696[15]
Malawi[16]	1979	11.7[1,3]	51	17,100	458.4	335.3	8,988.2	35	4,200	145.8
Malaysia[29]	1980	13.7[1,6]	17,907	102,412	13,429.6	5.7	750.0	90,037[10]	66,214[10]	5,561.7[10]
Maldives	1981	22.3[1]	...							
Mali	...									
Malta	1979	15.1[6,10]	5	5	0.642	...	128.4	3	6,599[5,10]	0.977
Martinique	1974	17.9[1,3]	...	5	...	...	...	...	12,799[1,5,9]	...
Mauritania[16]	1971	6.0[14]	23	100	21.6	4.3	939.1	59	700	21.7
Mauritius[16]	1980	12.1[1,15]	5	5	...	5	...	143[5]	6,000[5]	...
Mayotte	...									
Mexico	1975	23.2[1,15]	11,652	130,939	5,051.4	11.2	433.5	463,612	987,089	19,120.6
Monaco	...									
Mongolia[30]	1980	...	...	...	...	...	...	4,698	24,200	1,114.7
Montserrat	1980	20.8[1,6]	...	...	...	...	...	160	200	...
Morocco	1972	14.3[1,15]	...	...	...	...	...	4,000	20,000	...
Mozambique	1970	...	...	5	...	...	...	...	64,019[1,5]	...
Nauru	...									
Nepal	1976	3.5[6,10]	...	5	...	...	...	...	282,632[1,5]	...
Netherlands, The	1980	13.8[1,6]	...	597,000	...	...	...	193,077	...	64,273.4
Netherlands Antilles	1972	...	...	5	...	...	...	...	12,764[5]	...
New Caledonia	1980	21.3[1]	...							
New Zealand	1978	21.2[1,15]	6,183	77,385[9]	9,656.1	12.5[9]	1,561.7	32,334	172,851[9]	6,931.7
Nicaragua	1980	23.6[10,14]	...	5	...	...	...	...	105,053[1,5,9]	...
Niger	1977	10.2[1]	...							
Nigeria[16]	1974	22.2[1,6]	536	38,996	6,592.1[17]	72.8	6,203.7	349	22,038	1,757.6[17]
Niue	1982	...	5	...	...	...	...	22[5]	78[28]	...
Norfolk Island	1981	...	...	5	...	...	...	...	271[5]	...
Norway	1981	13.8[1,6]	11,080	95,671[9]	29,186.2	8.6[9]	2,634.1	33,225	127,105[9]	15,729.3
Oman	1981	10.0[10]	...	...	...	...	...	...	...	830
Pakistan	1981	14.2[6,10]	...	...	...	...	...	...	...	13,636
Panama	1971	15.8[1,6]	558	10,028	445.9	18.0	799.2	6,611	25,700	433.9
Papua New Guinea	1981	8.0[17]	...	...	...	...	...	...	...	775.4

retail trade									employees per outlet	sales per outlet $'000	population per outlet	country
percent breakdown of sales												
food[d]	clothing, shoes[e]	home furnishings[f]	eating, drinking[g]	drugs, pharma-ceuticals[h]	building materials[i]	automobile parts[j]	general merchandise[k]	other[l]				
...	...	...	...	...	...	...	...	...	2.3	27.2	3,580.1	Ethiopia[24]
...	...	...	...	...	...	...	...	...	...	...	...	Faeroe Islands
											90.7	Falkland Islands
27.8	10.4	1.7	...	1.0	2.6	17.1	22.7	16.7	3.4	114.9	260.6	Fiji
39.0	9.1	1.5	...	1.8	11.1	18.1	16.0	3.4	4.4[9,10]	701.1[10]	132.3[10]	Finland
39.8	15.9	19.3	...	4.8	...	3.8[25]	...	16.4	2.9	395.5	87.4	France
...	...	...	...	...	...	...	...	...				French Guiana
...	...	...	...	...	...	...	...	...				French Polynesia
...	...	...	...	...	...	...	...	...				Gabon
...	...	...	...	...	...	...	...	...			...	Gambia, The
51.0	15.1	5.6	...	5.5	6.4	...	...	16.4	...	...	...	Germany, East
25.0	12.6	9.6	6.3	5.9	6.3	13.2	...	21.1	8.6	828.7	245.9	Germany West
...	...	...	...	...	...	...	...	...	2.6	108.5	...	Ghana[16]
...	...	...	...	...	...	...	...	...				Gibraltar
...	...	...	...	...	...	...	...	...	1.8	...	58.7	Greece
...	...	...	...	...	...	...	...	...	...	...	...	Greenland
...	...	...	...	...	...	...	...	...				Grenada
...	...	...	...	...	...	...	...	...				Guadeloupe
7.0[7]	5.9[7]	3.8[7]	20.0[7]	0.6[7]	8.3[7]	14.7[7]	16.8[7]	22.9[7]	7.7	405.3	...	Guam
...	...	...	...	...	...	...	...	...			...	Guatemala
...	...	...	...	...	...	...	...	...				Guinea
...	...	...	...	...	...	...	...	...				Guinea-Bissau
9.7	18.9	13.8	4.5	2.8	10.6	18.6	...	21.1	...	743.1	5,986.4	Guyana
...	...	...	...	...	...	...	...	...			...	Haiti
...	...	...	...	...	...	...	...	...			...	Honduras
18.4	6.8	...	19.9	...	...	...	...	55.0	4.8	228.5	109.5	Hong Kong
30.5	13.3	6.5	12.0	0.7	13.1	8.2	...	15.6	6.4	198.3	195.2	Hungary
68.7	11.3	...	...	...	...	...	...	20.0	4.2[9]	35,754.2	...	Iceland[26]
...	...	...	...	...	...	...	...	...	0.5	0.871	143.4	India
...	...	...	...	...	...	...	...	...	1.6[5]	63.2[5]	2,763.2[5]	Indonesia
...	...	...	...	...	...	...	...	...	1.5[9]	17.2	141.3	Iran
...	...	...	...	...	...	...	...	...	1.4	31,782.4	147.9	Iraq
33.7	4.6	8.9	10.5	2.6	3.0	23.9	4.7	8.2	2.5	129.0	101.1	Ireland
27.3	7.6	8.4	...	...	...	...	...	56.7	2.1	...	90.2	Israel
...	...	...	...	...	...	...	...	...	0.4[19]	115.0	56.3	Italy
...	...	...	...	...	...	...	...	...	...	...	152.2	Ivory Coast
80.5	5.8	5.3	...	...	...	...	...	8.4	...	...	...	Jamaica
27.9	9.9	8.0	8.6	2.2	...	8.7	12.3	22.3	3.7[9]	183.2	52.4	Japan
...	...	...	...	...	...	...	...	...	...	...	...	Jordan
...	...	...	...	...	...	...	...	...				Kampuchea
...	...	...	...	...	...	...	...	...	5.6	...	3,487.3	Kenya[27]
...	...	...	...	...	...	...	...	...	...	188.6	1,571.4	Kiribati
...	...	...	...	...	...	...	...	...				Korea, North
29.4	13.1	8.9	18.9	5.0	...	5.4	1.2	18.0	0.6	32.9	67.4	Korea, South
17.0	6.8	13.7	3.4	0.9	7.1	13.2	1.3	36.6	3.1	122.5	77.8	Kuwait
...	...	...	...	...	...	...	...	...				Laos
...	...	...	...	...	...	...	...	...				Lebanon
...	...	...	...	...	...	...	...	...				Lesotho
...	...	...	...	...	...	...	...	...				Liberia
...	...	...	...	...	...	...	...	...	1.7[10]	...	...	Libya
...	...	...	...	...	...	...	...	...	3.2	...	105.0	Liechtenstein
31.0	12.4	12.0	...	3.6	...	32.0	...	8.9	2.9[14]	423.7[3]	90.7[3]	Luxembourg
...	...	...	...	...	...	...	...	...	...	...	...	Macau
...	...	...	...	...	...	...	...	...			...	Madagascar
...	...	...	...	...	...	...	...	...	120.0	4,165.7	165,714.3	Malawi[16]
33.4	7.3	10.8	...	2.5	...	33.3	4.4	8.3	0.7[10]	61.8[10]	123.7[10]	Malaysia[29]
...	...	...	...	...	...	...	...	...	...	...	...	Maldives
...	...	...	...	...	...	...	...	...				Mali
...	...	...	...	...	...	...	...	...	...	325.6	...	Malta
...	...	...	...	...	...	...	...	...				Martinique
...	...	...	...	...	...	...	...	...	11.9	367.8	...	Mauritania[16]
...	...	...	...	...	...	...	...	...	42.0[5]	...	...	Mauritius[16]
...	...	...	...	...	...	...	...	...				Mayotte
17.8	7.3	5.8	...	2.8	7.3	24.5	16.6	17.9	2.1	41.2	129.7	Mexico
...	...	...	...	...	...	...	...	...	...	...	...	Monaco
...	...	...	...	...	...	...	...	...	5.2	237.3	...	Mongolia[30]
...	...	...	...	...	...	...	...	...	1.3	...	63.0	Montserrat
...	...	...	...	...	...	...	...	...	5.0	...	5,061.0	Morocco
...	...	...	...	...	...	...	...	...				Mozambique
...	...	...	...	...	...	...	...	...				Nauru
...	...	...	...	...	...	...	...	...				Nepal
...	...	...	...	...	...	...	...	...	...	332.9	73.2	Netherlands, The
...	...	...	...	...	...	...	...	...			...	Netherlands Antilles
...	...	...	...	...	...	...	...	...				New Caledonia
24.3	7.8	7.9	6.7	3.0	2.2	32.8	8.3	7.0	5.3[9]	214.4	96.5	New Zealand
...	...	...	...	...	...	...	...	...				Nicaragua
...	...	...	...	...	...	...	...	...				Niger
...	...	...	...	...	...	...	...	10.5	63.1	2,213.5	...	Nigeria[16]
...	...	...	...	...	...	...	...	...				Niue
...	...	...	...	...	...	...	...	...				Norfolk Island
35.4	9.9	7.7	...	...	...	28.3	4.6	14.1	3.8[9]	473.4	123.4	Norway
...	...	...	...	...	...	...	...	...				Oman
66.5	13.0	1.1	...	0.4	...	...	...	19.0	...	...	...	Pakistan
33.5	10.9	9.5	...	...	...	...	...	46.1	3.9	65.6	223.9	Panama
55.3[17]	8.1[17]	8.7[17]	...	...	...	...	...	27.9[17]	...	...	...	Papua New Guinea

Trade: domestic (continued)

country	year	domestic trade as percentage of GDP	wholesale trade					retail trade		
			establish-ments[a]	employees[b]	sales[c] $'000,000	employees per establishment	sales per establishment $'000	outlets[a]	employees[b]	sales[c] $'000,000
Paraguay	1977	26.6[6, 10]	...	...	...	...	...	...	91,900	1,785
Peru	1973	19.0[1, 15]	4,210	34,100	2,163.2	8.1	513.8	103,010	72,200	2,014.7
Philippines	1978	17.5[1, 15]	21,651	94,010	4,815.1	4.3	222.4	288,367	314,289	5,471.1
Pitcairn Island	1982	...	—	—	—	—	—	1		
Poland[30]	1980	13.8[1, 6]	...	120,200	38,328.3	...	...	239,388	584,800	37,463.9
Portugal	1976	22.0[1, 15]	8,732	124,519	4,834.9	14.3	553.7	84,621[10]	136,739[10]	3,902.6[10]
Puerto Rico	1977	16.2[1, 15]	2,208	28,338	4,395.2	12.8	1,990.6	36,276	109,654	4,796.2
Qatar	1980	6.1[1]	...	...	...	...	...	9,996		
Réunion	1982	17.7[1, 3]	...	5	...	...	...	...	14,328[1, 5]	...
Romania	1982	...	...	...	...	...	...	80,082	448,800	16,730.1
Rwanda	1980	14.7[1]	...	...	...	...	...	...	...	...
St. Christopher and Nevis	1978	9.6[1]	...	...	...	...	...	...	...	...
St. Helena and Ascension		...	...	...	...	...	...	...	...	...
St. Lucia	1977	18.0[1]	...	...	...	...	...	...	...	...
St. Pierre and Miquelon	1982	...	...	5	...	...	...	...	279[1, 5]	...
St. Vincent and the Grenadines	1981	10.1	...	...	...	...	...	...	...	...
San Marino		...	...	...	...	...	...	...	...	...
São Tomé and Príncipe		...	...	...	...	...	...	...	...	...
Saudi Arabia[31]	1971	4.3[1, 15]	822	2,500	...	...	3.0	35,780	18,200	...
Senegal	1979	23.2[1]	...	4,600	...	...	...	...	4,400	...
Seychelles	1980	25.3[1]	...	5	...	...	...	...	1,281[5]	...
Sierra Leone[16]	1981	13.8[1]	...	5	...	...	...	...	7,182[1, 5, 7]	...
Singapore	1981	21.9[1]	18,794	107,316	27,259.6	5.7	1,450.4	19,298	90,700	4,545.4
Solomon Islands	1980	7.7[10, 32]	...	5	...	...	...	...	1,863[5, 10]	...
Somalia		...	...	...	...	...	...	...	...	...
South Africa	1977	12.9[1, 6]	10,106	232,478	18,982.9	23.0	1,878.4	60,774[33]	406,994[33]	14,563.4
South West Africa/Namibia		...	...	...	...	...	...	...	...	...
Spain	1979	17.1[1, 15]	40,000	...	...	...	...	710,865	1,400,000	84,839
Sri Lanka	1979	17.5[1, 15]	353	27,600	...	78.2	...	1,583	67,100	...
Sudan, The	1978	18.2[10]	...	5	...	...	...	...	52,000[1, 5, 8]	...
Suriname	1979	16.4[1]	...	...	...	...	...	...	...	...
Swaziland	1980	7.1[10, 15]	35	821	...	23.5	...	385	3,298	...
Sweden	1980	10.6[1, 6]	22,726	179,100	52,939.5[3]	7.9	2,505.2[3]	54,506	233,900	36,244.7
Switzerland	1975	...	13,844	130,600	...	9.4	...	49,972	274,500	27,257.0[7]
Syria	1975	23.3[1, 6]	2,792	6,200[20]	...	2.3[20]	...	81,167	110,000[9]	4,960.0[15]
Taiwan	1982	13.4[1]	54,743	153,400	3,770.4	2.8	67.6	340,893	148,100	7,491.9
Tanzania	1973	6.7[1, 6]	...	...	...	...	...	18,300	...	2,404.0[12]
Thailand	1980	23.2[1, 6]	5,647	187,737	21,531.5	33.2	3,812.9	14,622	144,864	4,021.9
Togo	1972	20.7[1, 15]	20	1,200	94.6	60.0	4,730.0	96	1,600	28.5
Tokelau	1982	...	...	...	...	...	...	3	...	...
Tonga	1976	14.9[1, 6]	...	14	...	...	...	...	687	...
Trinidad and Tobago	1977	11.0[1, 15]	124	6,786	508.6	18.3	4,101.8	370	15,986	542.9
Trust Territory of the Pacific Is.		...	...	...	...	...	...	...	...	...
Tunisia	1973	13.1[15]	...	...	...	...	...	2,200	5,000	2,310.0[15]
Turkey	1980	16.0[10, 15]	22,790	29,607[20]	2,999.4[20]	1.3[20]	132.4[20]	284,716	62,308[20]	5,827.4[3]
Turks and Caicos Islands	1969	20.5	...	...	...	...	...	...	...	...
Tuvalu		...	...	...	...	...	...	...	...	...
Uganda	1977	6.0[17]	226	4,100	...	18.1	...	251	3,200	...
U.S.S.R.	1981	17.7[1, 6]	...	2,351,000[7]	250,606.1[7]	...	...	998,100[7]	7,471,000	397,240.3
United Arab Emirates	1981	9.2[1, 6]	...	5	...	5	...	13,906[1, 5, 28]	74,332[1, 5, 7, 9]	2,180.0
United Kingdom[31]	1982	11.0[1, 6]	100,931[34]	...	217,760.5[34]	...	2,157.5[34]	349,659[25]	2,264,000[25]	122,157.0[25]
United States	1977	16.7[1, 6]	382,837	4,397,089	1,258,400.3	11.5	3,287.0	1,855,068	13,040,082	723,134.2
Uruguay	1980	17.5[1]	...	...	...	...	...	...	...	...
Vanuatu	1973	...	19	109	...	5.7	...	284	1,179	...
Venezuela	1979	8.6[1, 6]	...	...	...	...	...	...	530,978	15,764.4
Vietnam	1977	...	...	...	...	...	...	...	...	7,894.5
Virgin Islands (U.S.)	1977	...	104	980	124.4	9.4	1,196.0	1,104	5,622	278.0
Wallis and Futuna		...	...	...	...	...	...	...	...	...
Western Sahara		...	...	...	...	...	...	...	...	...
Western Samoa	1975	9.5[1, 32]	...	11	...	...	...	...	1,708	...
Yemen (Aden)	1973	...	...	5	...	...	...	...	25,509[1, 5, 9]	...
Yemen (Ṣan'ā')	1981	17.5[1]	...	...	...	...	...	...	...	...
Yugoslavia	1980	21.7[1, 15]	1,139	145,053	32,555.1	127.4	28,582.2	78,835	335,031	28,317.1
Zaire	1971	22.0[10, 28]	...	...	...	...	...	1,232	10,800	...
Zambia	1974	13.4[1, 6]	494	15,500	977.3	31.4	1,978.3	1,636	13,700	587.1
Zimbabwe	1982	14.7[1]	...	5	...	...	...	...	79,800[1, 5]	...

retail trade												country
percent breakdown of sales									employees per outlet	sales per outlet $'000	population per outlet	
food[d]	clothing, shoes[e]	home furnishings[f]	eating, drinking[g]	drugs, pharmaceuticals[h]	building materials[i]	automobile parts[j]	general merchandise[k]	other[l]				
...	...	...	...	...	...	...	...	...	0.7	19.6	144.7	Paraguay
												Peru
24.9	13.9	9.4	...	3.0	11.8	27.9	...	9.1	1.1	19.0	158.8	Philippines
												Pitcairn Island
43.9			56.1						2.4	156.5	148.6	Poland[30]
27.5	13.1	9.1	14.6	6.9	7.8	16.2	—4.8—		1.6[10]	46.1[10]	115.1[10]	Portugal
26.8	10.4	5.6	6.4	3.9	4.0	23.9	10.0	9.0	3.0	132.2	84.4	Puerto Rico
...	...	...	...	...	...	...	...	...	...	...	25.0	Qatar
...	...	...	...	...	...	...	...	...	...	...	...	Réunion
34.6	...	18.1	...	...	...	...	...	47.3	5.6	208.9	281.7	Romania
...	...	...	...	...	...	...	...	...	...	...	...	Rwanda
...	...	...	...	...	...	...	...	...	...	...	...	St. Christopher and Nevis
...	...	...	...	...	...	...	...	...	...	...	...	St. Helena and Ascension
...	...	...	...	...	...	...	...	...	...	...	...	St. Lucia
...	...	...	...	...	...	...	...	...	...	...	...	St. Pierre and Miquelon
...	...	...	...	...	...	...	...	...	...	...	...	St. Vincent and the Grenadines
...	...	...	...	...	...	...	...	...	...	...	...	San Marino
...	...	...	...	...	...	...	...	...	...	...	...	São Tomé and Príncipe
...	...	...	...	...	...	...	...	...	0.5	...	222.8	Saudi Arabia[31]
...	...	...	...	...	...	...	...	...	...	...	...	Senegal
...	...	...	...	...	...	...	...	...	...	...	...	Seychelles
...	...	...	...	...	...	...	...	...	...	...	...	Sierra Leone[16]
1.6	20.8	10.9	9.4	1.6	1.2	20.5	26.8	7.2	4.7	235.5	126.4	Singapore
...	...	...	...	...	...	...	...	...	...	...	...	Solomon Islands
...	...	...	...	...	...	...	...	...	...	...	...	Somalia
20.5	12.5	8.2	8.9	2.9	1.5	27.5	13.4	4.7	6.7[33]	233.3[33]	439.0	South Africa
...	...	...	...	...	...	...	...	...	...	...	...	South West Africa/Namibia
...	...	...	...	...	...	...	...	...	2.0	119.3	52.3	Spain
...	...	...	...	...	...	...	...	...	42.4	...	9,140.9	Sri Lanka
...	...	...	...	...	...	...	...	...	...	...	...	Sudan, The
...	...	...	...	...	...	...	...	...	...	...	...	Suriname
...	...	...	...	...	...	...	...	...	8.6	...	...	Swaziland
...	...	...	...	...	...	...	...	...	4.3	665.0	152.5	Sweden
...	...	...	...	...	...	...	...	...	5.5	...	128.3	Switzerland
...	...	...	...	...	...	...	...	...	1.4[9]	...	111.0	Syria
75.8[15]	9.0[15]	10.8[15]	...	...	...	...	...	4.4[12]	0.4	22.0	54.1	Taiwan
...	...	...	...	...	...	...	...	...	...	...	983.0	Tanzania
2.5	2.7	7.1	2.6	1.2	10.5	56.6	5.3	11.5	9.9	275.1	3,180.1	Thailand
...	...	...	...	...	...	...	...	...	16.7	296.9	21,562.5	Togo
...	...	...	...	...	...	...	...	...	...	...	666.7	Tokelau
...	...	...	...	...	...	...	...	...	...	...	...	Tonga
18.6	...	8.5	2.7	...	10.7	28.2	15.3	15.9	43.2	1,467.2	3,027.0	Trinidad and Tobago
...	...	...	...	...	...	...	...	...	...	...	...	Trust Territory of the Pacific Is.
...	...	...	...	...	...	...	...	...	2.3	...	2,905.0	Tunisia
13.5[20]	13.5[20]	13.1[20]	...	5.1[20]	9.6[20]	23.5[20]	—21.7[20]—		0.4[20]	29.1[3]	157.8	Turkey
...	...	...	...	...	...	...	...	...	...	...	...	Turks and Caicos Islands
...	...	...	...	...	...	...	...	...	...	...	...	Tuvalu
...	...	...	...	...	...	...	...	...	12.7	...	49,203.2	Uganda
49.7	26.5	3.9	8.7	...	0.8	3.7	6.7	...	7.4[7]	410.6[7]	266.0[7]	U.S.S.R.
...	...	...	...	...	...	...	...	...	5.3[1,5,28]	...	79.5	United Arab Emirates
23.1	5.0	6.5	12.7	1.8	2.3	28.1	10.8	9.7	6.5[10,25]	349.9[10,25]	161.1[10,25]	United Kingdom[31]
21.8	4.9	4.6	8.8	3.2	5.4	28.5	13.0	9.8	7.0	389.8	118.7	United States
...	...	...	...	...	...	...	...	...	...	...	...	Uruguay
...	...	...	...	...	...	...	...	...	4.2	...	316.9	Vanuatu
65.1	10.1	7.6	...	...	...	5.0	...	12.2	...	...	...	Venezuela
...	...	...	...	...	...	...	...	...	...	...	...	Vietnam
23.1[32]	7.0[32]	4.8[32]	7.9[32]	3.8[32]	5.1[32]	12.0[32]	5.1[32]	31.2[32]	5.1	251.8	86.0	Virgin Islands (U.S.)
...	...	...	...	...	...	...	...	...	...	...	...	Wallis and Futuna
...	...	...	...	...	...	...	...	...	...	...	...	Western Sahara
...	...	...	...	...	...	...	...	...	...	...	...	Western Samoa
...	...	...	...	...	...	...	...	...	...	...	...	Yemen (Aden)
...	...	...	...	...	...	...	...	...	...	...	...	Yemen (San'ā')
33.4	11.3	...	3.4	3.0	5.4	...	...	43.5	4.2	359.2	282.9	Yugoslavia
...	...	...	...	...	...	...	...	...	8.8	...	22,963.0	Zaire
...	...	...	...	...	...	...	...	...	8.4	358.9	901.0	Zambia
...	...	...	...	...	...	...	...	...	...	...	...	Zimbabwe

[1]Includes hotels. [2]Excludes retail trade network of the agricultural cooperatives. [3]1979. [4]1969. [5]Retail trade data includes wholesale trade data. [6]1982. [7]1980. [8]1973. [9]All persons engaged (includes proprietors). [10]Excludes restaurants. [11]Includes furniture stores. [12]Includes hardware stores. [13]Data refer to New Providence Island only. [14]1978. [15]1981. [16]Data refer to larger establishments only. [17]1976. [18]1966. [19]1971. [20]1970. [21]1983. [22]Data are for 12 selected cities only. [23]Data are for 14 selected cities only. [24]Excludes Addis Ababa and Asmera. [25]Excludes motor vehicles. [26]Excludes alcohol, petroleum products, construction materials, and automobiles. [27]Retail trade data includes joint wholesale and retail trade data. [28]1977. [29]Peninsular Malaysia only, except for percentage of GDP. [30]State- and cooperative-owned establishments only. [31]Urban establishments only. [32]1972. [33]Includes hotels, construction, transportation, and communication. [34]Includes dealing.

Finance

This table presents major statistical aggregates used in the analysis of national financial structure and certain international economic relationships. It includes such data as international reserves, money supply and banking activity, central bank discount rates, and external indebtedness. The country models are broadly similar and permit the comparison of internal structure and external position at a high level of generalization.

One of the principal financial criteria of the relative economic position of a country is the size of its international reserves. International reserves as represented in this table comprise the sum of a country's holdings of Special Drawing Rights (SDR's; an unconditional credit allocation, within a quota system set by the International Monetary Fund [IMF], of currency needed by a country to maintain stability of foreign exchange transactions or markets) and its holdings of foreign exchange vis-à-vis its holdings of gold. With the exception of the developed and a few petroleum-producing countries, the SDR balances of most countries are minimal, a consequence of the common practice of using SDR's for payments toward offsetting adverse balances of trade. The fact that most countries hold the bulk of their reserves in currencies underlines the scarcity value of gold. The ratio of external debt to total reserves can not be interpreted in isolation: a low ratio, for example, may characterize the situation of a country with little need to borrow or of one with substantial debt, but also the means to repay it. Much higher ratios, on the other hand, may be manageable, despite small reserves, if a country's export earnings are also high.

The section of the table outlining banking activity and the principal monetary aggregates encompasses both central bank authorities and commercial (deposit) banks. For both, the principal component aggregates are grouped under assets and liabilities. For certain countries, the four principal aggregates under assets and liabilities do not comprise the entire total given, and the percentages shown, therefore, may add to less than 100.0 percent. The items omitted by the choice of categories are the least significant worldwide but may be important locally; they include such items as quasi-money, money seasonally adjusted, unused bank overdrafts, and so on. In the case of the central bank authority, data are also provided for the money supply of the country, in terms of both total stock and per capita supply, and for the central bank discount rate, generally the controlling interest rate for banking and commercial activity in the country.

The largest portion of assets in the case of both kinds of banks comprises claims on government and government agencies and foreign assets and holdings, though some of the latter, such as the large outstanding loans to Socialist and developing countries of the late 1970s and early 1980s, have become the chief liabilities. In the case of liabilities for central bank authorities, the chief aggregates are reserve money, foreign payments, and demand and savings deposits. Large claims on government by the central bank authorities usually indicate a government-oriented monetary policy, whereas larger claims on the private sector by commercial banks point to the predominance of the private sector in the economy of the country. Large foreign liabilities under central bank authority often imply an adverse balance-of-payments position. Similarly, large foreign liabilities

Finance

| country | international reserves, 1984[a] | | | central bank authority, 1983 | | | | | | | | | | |
| | total ('000,000 SDRs) | % foreign exchange | ratio of external debt to total reserves[b] | assets (%) | | | | money supply | | liabilities (%) | | | | central bank discount rate, 1984 |
				claims on government	claims on foreign assets	claims on banks	claims on private sector	stock ('000,000,000 national currency)	M_1 per capita	reserve money	government deposits	foreign liabilities	capital accounts	
Afghanistan	232	85.8	3.6	42.0[1,2]	55.8[1]	1.5[1]	0.8[1]	50,239[1]	2,992[1]	69.9[1]	5.6[1]	0.9[1]	12.8[1]	...
Albania	...	...	...	...	...	...	...	73,500[5]	27,683[5]	...	...	...	...	...
Algeria	1,945	89.9	5.1	18.4[1]	24.9[1]	55.9[1]	0.8[1]	112,801[1]	5,653[1]	89.9[1]	0.6[1]	0.7[1]	—	...
American Samoa	...	...	...	...	...	...	...	...	...	...	...	...	...	...
Andorra	...	...	...	...	...	...	...	...	...	...	...	...	...	...
Angola	...	...	...	...	...	...	...	...	...	...	...	...	...	...
Anguilla	...	...	...	...	...	...	...	...	...	...	...	...	...	...
Antigua and Barbuda	14	100.0	1.4	24.1	75.9	—	—	53	675	100.0	...	—	—	...
Argentina	1,959	92.2	7.3	7.3	22.8	33.2	—	37,429	1,263	50.3	—	14.6	—	...
Australia	7,936	96.5	1.5	26.2	71.9	—	1.9	18,247	1,195	60.7	—	—	—	...
Austria	4,778	84.5	0.8	9.8	64.7	25.5	—	170,400	22,498	68.8	1.8	—	—	4.2
Bahamas, The	167	100.0	1.0	14.3	85.7	—	—	174	782	54.9[6]	13.2	—	31.9	10.0
Bahrain	1,306	99.6	0.5	—	100.0	—	—	266	676	19.7	54.6	6.1	16.5	...
Bangladesh	463	99.6	23.6	38.9	25.5	27.9	—	29,562	312	45.1	—	46.4	—	10.5
Barbados	111	100.0	1.8	29.9	57.4	3.8	9.0	289	1,151	46.6	11.8	35.0	6.6	16.0
Belgium	5,789	79.3	2.3[10]	20.9	79.1	—	—	893,300	90,552	97.6	—	—	—	11.0
Belize	9	100.0	5.2	55.2	44.8	—	—	44	284	61.1	+	14.0	—	...
Benin	5	100.0	100.0	24.6	3.1	72.3	—	64,440[1]	17,799[1]	42.7	7.4	40.8	—	10.5
Bermuda	...	...	...	—	503	—	—	46[1]	825[1]	7.3[1]	3.2[1]	—	—	...
Bhutan	...	...	...	...	...	...	...	6[1,11]	51[1,11]	...	...	...	...	...
Bolivia	258	87.2	13.5	78.8	14.2	7.0	—	84,593	13,909	22.6[6]	43.1	34.3	—	61.0[10]
Botswana	425	100.0	0.7	—	100.0	—	—	144	144	27.5	41.5	—	16.3	9.0
Brazil	8,859	99.6	12.1	31.7	—	10.6	54.1	5,056,600	3,900	59.6	—	22.4	—	49.0[7]
British Virgin Islands	...	...	...	...	...	...	...	...	...	...	...	...	...	...
Brunei	...	...	...	...	...	...	...	903[7]	4,682[7]	...	...	...	...	...
Bulgaria	...	...	...	...	...	...	...	...	...	...	...	...	...	...
Burkina Faso	106	100.0	5.4	27.2	50.1	22.7	—	58,370	8,885	74.8	6.6	11.5	—	10.5
Burma	95	90.5	17.2	—	6.9	93.1	—	10,644	280	87.8	—	12.2	—	...
Burundi	25	100.0	6.7	60.2[1]	21.8[1]	10.2[1]	1.2[1]	11,146[1]	2,333[1]	45.9[1]	10.7[1]	24.9[1]	—	...
Cameroon	246	99.6	27.9	13.1	28.9	58.0	—	291,250	32,129	40.7	49.6	5.4	—	...
Canada	3,369	79.0	2.3[10]	70.2	29.8	—	—	41,880	1,681	93.9	—	—	—	10.8
Cape Verde	...	...	...	...	...	...	...	...	...	...	...	...	...	...
Cayman Islands	...	...	...	...	...	...	...	8[1]	429[1]	...	...	...	...	...
Central African Republic	53	100.0	4.8	39.3	35.1	25.6	—	43,990	17,511	57.3	2.5	27.8	—	...
Chad	27	96.3	14.3	26.2[4]	10.8[4]	63.0[4]	—	27,560[4]	6,425[4]	66.2[4]	4.0[4]	21.8[4]	—	3.0[14]
Chile	2,271	97.6	2.8	13.3	28.1	41.2	17.4	87,270	7,533	8.5	2.8	25.7	20.4	75.0[15]
China	17,825	97.5	0.3	...	...	...	...	46,730	44	...	...	...	...	...
Christmas Island	...	...	...	...	...	...	...	...	...	...	...	...	...	...
Cocos (Keeling) Islands	...	...	...	...	...	...	...	...	...	...	...	...	...	...
Colombia	865	89.6	1.5	9.8[1]	66.5[1]	14.2[1]	2.4[1]	317,110[1]	11,463[1]	58.8[1]	5.3[1]	4.9[1]	2.3[1]	27.0[10]
Comoros	...	...	...	...	...	...	...	1,454[4]	3,776[4]	...	...	...	...	5.0[16]
Congo	5	80.0	36.5	49.5	14.6	35.9	—	89,020	52,550	68.4	14.2	11.5	—	...
Cook Islands	...	...	...	...	...	...	...	...	...	...	...	...	...	...
Costa Rica	338	98.2	10.8	37.3[7]	12.9[7]	45.4[7]	—	7,764[7]	3,410[7]	25.13,6,7	4.3[7]	57.9[7]	2.1[7]	26.0
Cuba	...	...	...	...	...	...	...	223[15]	23[15]	...	...	...	...	...
Cyprus	589	97.3	1.6	19.9	73.6	6.5	—	230	343	84.8	0.9	1.1	—	6.0[7]
Czechoslovakia	...	...	...	...	...	...	...	6,252[15]	415[15]	...	...	...	...	...
Denmark	3,787	98.5	1.5[4]	59.8	28.5	1.3	10.4	117,930	23,055	12.6	70.1	—	—	7.0
Djibouti	...	...	...	...	...	...	...	...	...	...	...	...	...	...
Dominica	3	100.0	1.8	77.7	22.3	—	—	27	363	35.1	—	61.5	—	...
Dominican Republic	159	99.4	12.2	46.2	8.8	45.0	—	732[1]	126[1]	38.2[6]	—	57.5	—	...
Ecuador	591	97.6	12.2	7.7[2]	23.3	48.4	20.6	82,933	9,412	44.3[6]	17.4	12.8	5.3	8.0[1]
Egypt	802	89.4	19.5	81.7	12.2	1.2	—	9,010	197	68.7[6]	10.1	21.2	—	13.0[10]
El Salvador	160	90.0	6.3	54.8	10.5	32.8	1.9	1,402	281	31.3[6]	7.2	42.1	8.5	6.1[15]
Equatorial Guinea	...	...	...	...	...	...	...	...	...	...	...	...	...	...

among the commercial banking group may in the case of a developing country represent heavy domestic development expenditure financed by the use of foreign capital. The money supply (M_1), comprising the sum of currency in circulation and demand deposits of the domestic private sector, is an indicator of inflationary trends vis-à-vis the size of the country and the per capita M_1. The effect in terms of inflation rates over a seven-year period may be seen in the consumer price indexes provided in the "Nations of the World" section.

Because the majority of the world's countries are in the developing bloc, and because their principal financial concern is external debt and its service, data are given for outstanding external debt rather than for total public debt, which is the major concern in the developed countries. For comparability, the data are given in U.S. dollars. The volume of debt by itself does not create external payment problems. If the country's external debt service (interest payments plus principal repayment) needs can be met by a strong, dependable export market, by export of services, or, occasionally, by direct remittances from abroad (by residents working abroad and sending wages home in foreign currencies, for example), no debt problem need exist. Countries whose debt service ratio (ratio of total debt service to exports of goods and services) is relatively high must base their external borrowing policy on maintenance of domestic conditions of strict efficiency and, sometimes, austerity. The failure to adhere to

such policies may lead to eventual crises of financial liquidity, deflation, and slower growth.

Ideally, the data presented here should be obtained by utilizing a single international methodology to provide a universally comparable set of national statistics. No international or national agency, however, can collect such data for all countries because of differences, both overall and in detail, in national definitions of financial aggregates, in accounting methodology, and in the completeness with which it is possible to survey a country's economy. The greater part of the data presented in the table comes from the IMF's *International Financial Statistics* and the World Bank's *World Debt Tables*. For certain countries—such as Albania, Angola, Bulgaria, Cuba, the German Democratic Republic, Kampuchea, Poland, and the Soviet Union—and many of the smaller nations, these sources are supplemented by other recent data from national, regional, or other international sources. In a few cases the desired data are negligible or unavailable, as noted.

In general, the data refer to the latest available quarter for the year cited. Detailed percentages may not add to 100.0 because of rounding, statistical discrepancy, or nonaccounting of negligible quantities.
— None, less than 0.5 of the last significant figure, or not applicable.
... Not available.
a. Latest month.
b. Year-end 1982.

deposit money banks										external debt outstanding (disbursed only), 1982[b]							country
assets, 1983 (%)				liabilities, 1983						total ('000,000 U.S.$)	comp. (%)		debt service				
loans to govern- ment	loans to private sector	re- serves	foreign assets	deposits ('000,000,000 national currency	composition (%)						public	private	total ('000,000 U.S.$)	repayment (%)		debt service ratio	
					demand depos.	savings depos.	govt. depos.	foreign liabilities						princi- pal	inter- est		
—	33.8	16.9	49.3	12,544[3]	18.7	31.2	—	—		1,216[4]	...	...	52[4]	71.1[4]	28.7[4]	16.1[4]	Afghanistan
...	...	...	...		...	...	...	...		100[5]	...	...	...	...	...	...	Albania
5.8	87.1	0.5	6.6	116,763[6]	45.2	11.2	3.1	14.9		13,567	78.6	21.4	3,915	63.5	36.5	24.8[7]	Algeria
27.0[5, 8]	—	5.6[5]	11.2[5]	5[5]	—	—	1.5[5]	...		4	...	...	...	...	...	...	American Samoa
...	...	...	...		...	...	...	...			...	...	...	...	...	...	Andorra
...	...	...	...		...	...	...	...		928	...	...	...	...	...	...	Angola
...	...	...	...		...	...	...	...			...	...	...	...	...	...	Anguilla
17.5[2]	63.9	11.9	6.7	274[6]	13.3	60.9	—	25.8		10[7]	...	...	...	...	...	...	Antigua and Barbuda
16.0	53.7	26.1	4.1	330,152[3]	4.2	27.0	—	28.7		15,780	12.6	87.4	2,342	45.7	54.3	24.5	Argentina
26.4[2]	69.5	4.1	—	72,699	16.3	73.6	1.9	1.4		13,279	...	...	...	...	...	...	Australia
16.1	53.1	2.9	27.9	1,792,500	4.8	45.4	2.5	28.4		3,800[9]	...	...	...	...	...	...	Austria
23.8[6]	70.8	4.9	—	627[3, 6]	20.8	70.1	1.6	—		119	16.0	84.0	30	52.3	47.7	2.5	Bahamas, The
1.4	52.3	3.4	42.9	1,119[6]	17.4	52.9	3.9	14.0		741	...	...	...	...	...	...	Bahrain
40.4	46.4	6.0	4.9	70,964	22.4	48.3	4.1	1.2		4,353	96.7	3.3	111	56.6	43.4	8.3	Bangladesh
19.2	70.5	6.1	4.2	1,005	15.5	60.2	10.4	13.3		220	57.9	42.1	28	41.5	58.5	3.6	Barbados
23.2	18.1	—	58.3	5,929,900[3]	5.9	16.6	—	71.1		14,400[10]	...	...	...	...	...	...	Belgium
24.0[2]	59.8	7.3	8.9	185	11.6	55.4	5.7	23.5		52	77.7	22.3	6	61.4	38.6	6.3	Belize
—	98.7	1.3	—	125,980	42.9	11.9	14.3	—		556	54.5	45.5	46	40.1	59.9	2.2[4]	Benin
—	—	7.2[1]	—	4,283[1]	20.9[1]	67.8[1]	—	—		279	...	...	...	...	...	...	Bermuda
—	—	—	70.9[1]	434[1]	38.9[1]	29.4[1]	—	10.2[1]		6[5, 12]	...	...	...	...	...	...	Bhutan
—	66.1	31.7	2.2	141,511[6]	19.3	40.7	—	24.5		2,556	54.3	45.7	260	36.5	63.5	26.2[7]	Bolivia
—	67.0	26.5	6.5	254	42.7	42.1	—	2.8		210	83.7	16.3	13	27.6	72.4	2.1	Botswana
27.3[2]	60.9	6.0	5.8	18,714,300[6]	17.4	10.4	—	50.6		47,589	17.2	82.8	9,903	40.5	59.5	33.4[7]	Brazil
—	47.7[7]	0.5[7]	—	277[7]	4.5[7]	62.8[7]	—	—		37	...	...	...	...	...	...	British Virgin Islands
...	...	...	...	2,577	...	...	...	...		10	...	...	...	...	...	...	Brunei
...	...	...	...	8,442[5, 13]	...	...	...	...		2,792	...	...	...	...	...	...	Bulgaria
14.6	75.7	8.0	1.7	101,790	27.9	19.2	23.4	18.7		335	92.0	8.0	20	63.5	36.5	3.4[4]	Burkina Faso
90.6[2]	6.1	3.3	—	27,726[3]	3.1	14.7	—	14.8		1,960	80.6	19.4	120	56.7	43.3	22.6[5]	Burma
0.1	94.1	0.9	4.9	8,101[6]	49.8	16.5	—	5.6		201	97.7	2.3	5	61.5	38.5	...	Burundi
5.9	87.9	1.6	4.6	896,370[6]	21.3	20.5	21.8	12.9		1,912	68.5	31.5	264	54.2	45.8	10.8[7]	Cameroon
7.7[2]	71.4	2.1	18.8	257,420[3]	11.5	55.8	0.9	28.1		10,878[10]	...	...	...	...	...	...	Canada
...	...	...	...		...	...	...	...		60	...	...	2	40.0	60.0	...	Cape Verde
—	—	—	100.0[1]	120,069[1]	—	—	—	100.0[1]			...	...	...	...	...	...	Cayman Islands
—	82.2	3.0	14.3	40,340[6]	26.2	11.4	7.9	—		222	72.3	27.7	4	46.7	53.3	1.6[5]	Central African Republic
—	87.7	3.2	8.7	37,580[6]	28.9	4.9	1.9	6.1		189	83.2	16.8	—	—	100.0	3.1[15]	Chad
7.9	84.2	2.4	5.5	1,328,000[3, 6]	3.2	21.0	4.8	38.6		5,239	24.9	75.1	1,033	46.7	53.3	18.7	Chile
...	...	...	...		...	...	...	...		3,845	...	...	...	...	...	...	China
...	...	...	...		...	...	...	...			...	...	...	...	...	...	Christmas Island
...	...	...	...		...	...	...	...			...	...	...	...	...	...	Cocos (Keeling) Islands
5.1	63.6	25.4	2.1	598,200[3, 6]	30.2	32.9	—	14.3		6,210	34.8	65.2	874	49.9	50.1	17.5	Colombia
...	...	...	...		...	...	...	...		66	98.9	1.1	1	11.1	88.9	—	Comoros
7.6	87.8	2.3	2.3	173,730	24.9	12.7	18.4	17.6		1,370	45.2	54.5	273	66.3	33.7	9.5[7]	Congo
...	...	...	...		...	...	...	...			...	...	...	...	...	...	Cook Islands
25.0	49.2	19.3	4.9	24,350[3, 6]	21.5	42.6	—	9.9		2,475	44.5	55.5	136	39.4	60.6	12.5	Costa Rica
...	...	...	...		...	...	...	...		1,825	...	...	...	...	...	...	Cuba
6.6	66.8	21.9	4.7	862	14.8	59.4	2.2	15.3		841	36.0	64.0	99	35.7	64.3	7.9	Cyprus
...	...	...	...		...	...	...	...		3,500[4]	...	...	...	...	...	...	Czechoslovakia
—	65.7	0.7	33.6	215,980[6]	36.5	34.5	—	28.5		4,663[4]	...	...	...	...	...	...	Denmark
...	...	...	...		...	...	...	...		40	83.3	16.7	3	70.6	29.4	...	Djibouti
20.0	54.9	8.7	16.4	127	16.2	59.8	—	19.4		8	...	...	...	...	...	—	Dominica
18.5[2]	46.5	18.9	12.4	2,751	12.6	33.4	3.3	13.7		1,620	79.9	20.1	250	56.4	43.6	18.7	Dominican Republic
—	79.5	15.1	5.4	116,880	43.3	12.3	—	—		3,912	39.9	60.1	1,101	49.0	51.0	30.8[7]	Ecuador
13.6	41.9	21.3	18.3	19,657[3]	12.2	53.6	7.3	11.6		15,468	79.5	20.5	1,878	79.2	20.8	20.9[7]	Egypt
3.6	72.7	18.5	5.2	3,666[3, 6]	19.3	50.5	—	1.5		801	93.2	6.8	51	46.5	53.5	4.6[7]	El Salvador
...	...	...	...		...	...	...	...		10	...	...	...	...	...	...	Equatorial Guinea

Finance (continued)

country	international reserves, 1984[a]			central bank authority, 1983										
	total ('000,000 SDRs)	% foreign exchange	ratio of external debt to total reserves[b]	assets (%) claims on government	claims on foreign assets	claims on banks	claims on private sector	money supply stock ('000,000,000 national currency)	M_1 per capita	liabilities (%) reserve money	government deposits	foreign liabilities	capital accounts	central bank discount rate, 1984
Ethiopia	104	93.3	4.6	55.7	14.7	—	—	2,219	66	63.2	6.5	10.9	7.2	...
Faeroe Islands	...	...	...	...	...	...	...	...	...	...	...	...	...	...
Falkland Islands	...	...	...	...	...	...	...	...	...	...	...	...	...	...
Fiji	92	98.9	2.1	13.8[2]	86.2	—	—	142	209	61.2	9.4	—	23.9	6.6
Finland	2,699	98.3	5.8	8.2	43.8	27.5	20.5	21,403	4,421	48.5	3.5	8.8	22.6	9.5
France	25,006	88.5	0.1	2.9	64.5	32.6	—	796,000	14,647	41.3	—	4.9	—	9.5
French Guiana	...	...	...	...	...	...	...	...	...	...	...	...	...	...
French Polynesia	...	...	...	...	...	...	...	4,237[1]	26,987	...	...	...	...	...
Gabon	208	100.0	2.8	—	97.5	2.4	—	126,860	137,741	32.0	55.5	1.9	—	...
Gambia, The	5	100.0	16.9	36.4	—	59.4	—	70	100	32.6[6]	5.3	54.3	7.8	6.0[15]
Germany, East	...	...	...	...	...	...	...	3,336[15]	198[15]	...	...	...	...	...
Germany, West	44,240	92.5	1.4	11.3	53.5	35.2	—	263,200	4,281	71.4	1.2	6.9	—	4.0
Ghana	206	93.2	7.1	95.2[2]	—	3.6	—	17,116	1,280	81.1	2.3	9.4	—	14.5
Gibraltar	...	...	...	...	...	...	...	6[9]	189[9]	...	...	...	...	...
Greece	1,306	89.1	6.7	55.9	11.1	31.8	1.2	464,900	46,969	65.9	10.2	—	—	20.5
Greenland	...	...	...	...	...	...	...	...	...	...	...	...	...	...
Grenada	19	100.0	1.0	47.2	52.8	—	—	61	548	68.7	—	27.2	...	...
Guadeloupe	...	...	...	...	...	...	...	727	2,213	...	...	...	...	...
Guam	...	...	...	...	...	...	...	...	...	...	...	...	...	...
Guatemala	245	92.6	8.4	77.0[2]	14.4	6.6	—	839	131	34.2[6]	19.6	40.7	5.5	9.0[1]
Guinea	...	...	...	...	...	...	...	...	...	...	...	...	...	...
Guinea-Bissau	...	...	...	...	...	...	...	...	...	...	...	...	...	...
Guyana	4	100.0	59.9	99.1	0.9	—	—	523	554	18.0	—	51.3	6.9	14.0
Haiti	12	91.7	90.6	80.0	4.8	2.7	12.5	1,121	197	40.7	7.3	33.3	7.1	...
Honduras	126	99.2	12.3	45.5[2]	20.5	13.8	—	667	162	24.5[6]	10.5	49.5	15.5	9.0[5]
Hong Kong	...	...	...	...	...	...	...	30,326	5,707	...	...	...	...	...
Hungary	1,874	98.0	5.7	58.2[2]	10.5	31.3	—	176,230	16,493	44.2[6]	9.2	46.6	—	...
Iceland	115	99.1	5.1	22.4	31.7	45.1	0.8	3,698	15,709	47.6	19.7	17.3	—	16.5
India	6,078	95.0	4.2	73.8	14.7	2.4	—	218,180	294	70.1	5.1	10.5	9.9	10.0
Indonesia	4,863	97.8	5.7	24.4[2]	33.1	30.8	11.7	7,739,000	44,088	34.0	28.0	11.5	8.8	...
Iran	8,150[5]	97.9[5]	...	75.1[1,2]	22.7[1]	2.2[1]	—	2,962,400[1]	71,897[1]	59.4[1]	14.9[1]	0.7[1]	4.2[1]	9.0[9]
Iraq	5,759[15]	97.5[15]	...	4.5[17]	95.5[17]	—	—	755[17]	65[17]	51.1[17]	34.2[17]	—	10.2[17]	...
Ireland	2,316	99.4	0.3	19.6[1]	80.4[1]	—	—	1,900[1]	537[1]	68.6[1]	9.2[1]	—	—	12.0
Israel	2,876	98.8	3.8	41.7	50.1	8.3	—	47,000	11,453	6.7	6.9	—	—	16.0
Italy	22,428	89.6	0.3	57.2	41.4	1.4	—	205,660,000	3,650,013	59.9	—	—	—	16.0
Ivory Coast	5	60.0	1,100.8	44.9	—	53.6	—	416,000	46,790	24.3	8.2	67.3	—	10.5
Jamaica	67	100.0	13.8	94.1	5.6	—	—	914	391	16.5[6]	14.1	66.8	2.6	13.0
Japan	26,468	96.8	...	51.4	22.9	25.7	—	73,893,000	618,765	84.3[6]	15.7	—	—	5.0
Jordan	656	94.4	1.8	34.5[18]	65.5[18]	—	—	869[18]	253[18]	94.3[6,18]	5.7[18]	—	—	6.2
Kampuchea	...	...	...	...	...	...	...	58,881[19]	7,636[19]	...	...	...	...	...
Kenya	410	99.3	11.0	56.2[18]	43.8[18]	—	—	14,040[18]	786[18]	44.9[18]	—	50.3[18]	4.1[18]	11.5[9]
Kiribati	...	...	...	...	...	...	...	...	6	...	...	...	...	...
Korea, North	...	...	...	...	...	...	...	...	...	...	...	...	...	...
Korea, South	2,571	99.6	7.1	28.0[2]	18.6	53.4	—	6,783,000	164,289	41.7	7.8	10.6	—	5.0
Kuwait	5,044	98.2	0.7	—	100.0[18]	—	—	1,160[18]	702[18]	42.4[6,18]	43.6[18]	—	14.0[18]	...
Laos	...	...	...	...	...	...	...	228[5]	61[5]	...	...	...	...	...
Lebanon	1,366	76.4	0.1	30.9	66.6	0.7	1.8	12,528	3,690	68.4	25.0	—	—	12.0
Lesotho	53	100.0	2.6	14.9[18]	85.1[18]	—	—	111[18]	77[18]	75.9[18]	4.5[18]	6.5[18]	6.3[18]	...
Liberia	2	100.0	96.8	95.1	1.2	2.1	1.6	72	34	18.8[6]	7.0	64.7	9.4	...
Libya	4,102	97.0	0.5	55.3[1]	44.2[1]	—	0.5[1]	3,196[1]	933[1]	61.8[1]	22.1[1]	—	—	5.0[5]
Liechtenstein	...	...	...	...	...	...	...	...	...	...	...	...	...	...
Luxembourg	...	...	...	...	...	...	...	4,700	12,869	...	...	...	...	10.0[1]
Macau	...	...	...	...	...	...	...	...	...	...	...	...	...	...
Madagascar	44	100.0	78.8	93.6[9]	—	6.2[9]	—	138,240[9]	16,740[9]	37.1[9]	—	5.2[9]	4.3[9]	5.5[5]
Malawi	70	100.0	30.4	93.8[2]	5.9	—	—	136	20	28.2[6]	12.9	58.9	—	10.0
Malaysia	3,921	97.9	2.0	24.2	75.8	—	—	12,827	855	60.6	19.1	5.6	—	5.2[1]
Maldives	...	...	...	...	...	...	...	335	217	...	...	...	...	...
Mali	11	100.0	46.5	60.2	4.1	35.7	—	146,910	19,871	32.3	—	62.8	—	...
Malta	1,039	98.5	0.1	—	100.0[18]	—	—	315	869	74.9[18]	6.3[18]	—	—	6.5
Martinique	...	...	...	...	...	...	...	856[1]	2,605[1]	...	...	...	...	...
Mauritania	76	98.7	7.2	34.8	38.7	19.6	6.9	8,770	4,921	27.2[6]	1.2	50.1	21.5	5.0[5]
Mauritius	45	97.8	9.2	89.0[18]	10.3[18]	0.7[18]	—	1,741[18]	1,752[18]	29.9[18]	—	57.5[18]	5.5[18]	11.0
Mayotte	...	...	...	...	...	...	...	505	1,070[5]	...	...	...	...	...
Mexico	6,163	98.6	55.2	80.1	16.2	1.5	—	1,060,300	14,006	76.8	—	3.7	—	4.5[15]
Monaco	...	...	...	...	...	...	...	...	...	...	...	...	...	...
Mongolia	...	...	...	...	...	...	...	...	...	...	...	...	...	...
Montserrat	...	...	...	...	...	...	...	119	972[9]	...	...	...	...	...
Morocco	98	74.5	36.8	59.3[1]	9.7[1]	18.4[1]	12.6[1]	31,967[1]	1,438[1]	65.9[1,6]	0.9[1]	33.2[1]	—	7.0
Mozambique	...	...	...	...	...	...	...	...	...	...	...	...	...	...
Nauru	...	...	...	...	...	...	...	...	...	...	...	...	...	...
Nepal	105	95.2	1.4	62.2	35.1	1.6	0.8	4,157[1]	256[1]	55.3	20.2	6.0	—	...
Netherlands, The	11,179	86.2	...	5.4	80.8	13.8	—	77,470	5,402	51.4	6.1	—	—	5.0
Netherlands Antilles	141	86.5	15.8	26.9	72.9	—	—	477	1,930	50.6	3.9	—	14.1	...
New Caledonia	...	...	...	...	...	...	...	3,122[1]	21,680[1]	...	...	...	...	...
New Zealand	1,195	99.9	8.7	29.9[18]	31.9[18]	1.3[18]	36.9[18]	3,202[18]	999[18]	26.2[18]	37.3[18]	35.1[18]	—	13.0
Nicaragua	221[10]	98.6[10]	...	63.9	9.4	26.7	—	8,472	3,012	25.9[6]	3.2	69.0	1.9	6.0[15]
Niger	91	100.0	20.2	31.3	18.5	50.2	—	58,960	9,692	49.6	25.5	18.8	—	10.5
Nigeria	991	97.6	3.7	82.2	7.8	0.8	6.9	9,944	116	56.9	9.0	0.7	2.1	8.0[10]
Niue	...	...	...	...	...	...	...	...	...	...	...	...	...	...
Norfolk Island	...	...	...	...	...	...	...	...	...	...	...	...	...	...
Norway	8,435	99.5	1.8	24.9	72.3	2.8	—	63,590	15,413	35.9	15.8	—	—	8.0
Oman	1,222[10]	99.2[10]	0.5	2.5	97.5	—	—	267	272	37.4	46.1	—	14.8	...
Pakistan	1,114	94.2	8.8	46.7[2,18]	34.6[18]	18.7[18]	—	100,253[18]	1,136[18]	54.5[18]	9.3[18]	24.7[18]	—	10.0
Panama	112	100.0	27.8	54.5[2]	12.6	—	32.9	337	161	24.7[6]	18.7	38.8	7.9	...
Papua New Guinea	455	99.3	2.2	6.2	93.8	—	—	202	62	24.8	24.8	14.2	14.9	...

deposit money banks — assets, 1983 (%); liabilities, 1983 | **external debt outstanding (disbursed only), 1982[b]**

loans to govern-ment	loans to private sector	re-serves	foreign assets	deposits ('000,000,000 national currency)	demand depos.	savings depos.	govt. depos.	foreign liabilities	total ('000,000 U.S.$)	public	private	debt service total ('000,000 U.S.$)	princi-pal	inter-est	debt service ratio	country
56.8[2]	15.7	20.0	4.7	2,584	38.2	34.5	3.8	5.0	875	90.4	9.6	55	60.6	39.4	8.1[7]	Ethiopia
...	...	...	...		...	...	...	...	...	...	...	...	...	...	...	Faeroe Islands
									27							Falkland Islands
27.0	64.5	6.6	1.9	427	19.4	70.8	3.5	1.9	265	75.3	24.7	34	34.8	65.2	6.5	Fiji
1.7	81.3	3.6	13.4	162,873	9.8	56.4	3.3	20.4	9,170	...	...	...	...	...	...	Finland
21.0	49.3	1.0	28.9	3,128,000[6]	17.8	26.8	—	32.9	2,277[8]	...	...	...	...	...	...	France
...	...	...	...		...	...	...	...	94[5,12]							French Guiana
...	...	...	...		...	...	...	...	131[5,12]							French Polynesia
16.4	76.2	3.8	3.6	282,800[6]	29.5	30.6	14.4	9.6	871	36.9	63.1	288	66.3	33.7	12.6[7]	Gabon
24.3[2]	48.2	23.3	4.2	270	12.8	20.9	—	13.4	149	81.4	18.6	3	41.7	58.3	6.5[7]	Gambia, The
...	...	...	...	99,730[5]	—	100.0[5]	—	—	10,728							Germany, East
20.7[2]	67.1	2.8	9.4	2,023,600	8.3	31.2	8.2	7.6	260[9]							Germany, West
49.6[2]	21.4	28.3	0.7	11,278	42.3	34.1	3.3	1.9	1,115	85.1	14.9	65	58.1	41.9	6.8	Ghana
—24.1—		1.2	—	142	—74.5—		—	—	79							Gibraltar
21.3	50.5	20.9	7.3	1,758,700	6.8	63.4	—	23.4	6,783	78.9	21.1	1,184	50.3	49.7	13.3	Greece
																Greenland
30.9	57.9	3.4	7.8	133	15.0	64.2	—	18.4	9	...	...	...	...	...	...	Grenada
									171[5,12]							Guadeloupe
																Guam
2.7	80.6	13.2	3.5	2,147[6]	16.1	61.5	—	6.4	1,119	90.1	9.9	88	38.6	61.4	4.0[7]	Guatemala
...	...	...	...		...	...	...	...	1,231	84.8	15.2	79	68.9	31.1	...	Guinea
									126	80.4	19.6	2	56.0	44.0	...	Guinea-Bissau
57.3[2]	18.1	23.1	1.3	2,086	11.2	48.4	—	3.2	661	73.1	26.9	49	51.0	48.9	21.5[7]	Guyana
—	67.0	28.9	8.1	1,395[5]	23.2	66.3	—	3.6	400	81.4	18.6	16	54.1	45.9	4.2	Haiti
20.7	74.5	4.1	0.7	1,609[3,6]	22.6	52.4	—	1.9	1,385	72.4	27.6	147	34.4	65.6	12.8[7]	Honduras
—	32.4	2.6	33.7	765,768	—30.4[3]—		—	40.9	267	19.7	80.3	49	54.5	45.5	0.2	Hong Kong
48.1	30.6	19.1		491,020	2.0	34.4	—	11.7	6,739	14.3	85.7	1,786	54.8	45.2	17.0	Hungary
3.3	78.5	14.6	3.6	33,925[6]	8.6	46.4	—	24.5	747							Iceland
21.0	68.1	10.8	—	690,960	16.1	70.4	—	—	19,612	93.6	6.4	1,158	59.4	40.6	7.0[5]	India
—	68.9	7.8	23.3	18,086,000[6]	24.0	32.8	4.3	4.9	18,617	60.2	39.8	2,251	49.1	50.9	8.7[7]	Indonesia
16.8	51.4	28.4	3.4	4,183,000	32.4	52.4	—	1.2	7,367[4]	...	...	1,057[4]	62.3[4]	37.7[4]	...	Iran
61.9	13.4	14.9	9.8	1,002	18.5	31.4	39.9	—	1,074[4]	...	...	239[4]	73.1[4]	26.9[4]	...	Iraq
11.4	33.8	3.6	51.2	11,107	8.2	37.3	—	52.9	761[15]	...	...	116[15]	88.8[15]	11.2[15]	...	Ireland
17.6	50.7	1.0	30.7	1,581,700[6]	1.7	56.7	—	41.6	14,900	69.3	30.7	2,119	52.8	47.2	20.8	Israel
19.8	44.5	14.2	8.9	386,872,000	43.3	38.7	—	12.1	5,381[4]	...	...	...	...	...	...	Italy
1.5	92.3	1.0	4.0	1,108,200	22.4	18.9	6.3	16.6	4,861	29.3	70.7	975	51.2	48.8	22.9[7]	Ivory Coast
31.9	56.0	5.2	6.8	3,591	17.1	65.3	1.9	6.4	1,511	69.8	30.2	243	47.3	52.7	22.5[7]	Jamaica
14.1	79.6	1.4	4.9	326,849,000	17.1	55.7	—	7.6	—	—	—	—	—	—	—	Japan
9.3	62.9	8.5	19.3	1,579	21.5	47.2	6.2	15.6	1,686	86.9	13.1	193	68.4	31.6	6.3[7]	Jordan
...	...	...	...		...	...	...	...	1	...	...	...	...	...	...	Kampuchea
17.6[2]	73.1	6.2	3.1	21,884[3,6]	44.9	38.7	2.5	3.3	2,359	67.2	32.8	325	54.6	45.4	16.7[7]	Kenya
...	...	...	...		...	...	...	...	13[5,12]	...	...	...	...	...	...	Kiribati
...	...	...	...		...	...	...	...	627	...	...	...	...	...	...	Korea, North
5.9	73.8	9.8	10.4	40,407,000[3,6]	9.6	39.9	5.7	24.6	20,061	41.5	58.5	3,716	49.1	50.9	13.1	Korea, South
—	66.4	4.1	29.5	7,090	11.6	44.8	4.9	18.1	4,431							Kuwait
...	...	...	...		...	...	...	...	1	...	...	...	...	...	...	Laos
18.1	50.7	7.3	23.9	66,771[3]	8.9	68.1	1.1	13.1	213	62.2	37.8	64	69.9	30.1	...	Lebanon
28.3[2]	22.6	21.2	27.9	240	26.8	55.9	5.2	5.9	123	85.7	14.3	7	60.0	40.0	...	Lesotho
1.2	57.6	17.4	23.8	201	27.6	30.9	—	25.5	641	77.7	22.3	33	56.3	43.7	5.1[7]	Liberia
—	53.7	28.9	17.4	2,768[6]	54.1	23.5	9.4	6.6	3,345	...	...	...	...	...	...	Libya
...	...	...	...		...	...	...	...	1,998	...	...	...	...	...	...	Liechtenstein
—	2.2	—	97.8	5,886,000	0.9	4.5	—	88.8	...	...	...	...	...	...	...	Luxembourg
									309							Macau
9.6	80.7	2.8	6.9	138,530[6]	51.0	25.8	11.3	0.8	1,565	64.1	35.9	112	62.5	37.5	7.4[9]	Madagascar
14.8[2]	71.9	9.4	3.9	354	20.2	46.6	—	13.6	705	72.0	28.0	62	48.1	51.9	21.9	Malawi
14.1	69.6	5.2	5.1	48,526	14.1	55.4	7.0	10.7	7,671	23.1	76.9	720	33.5	66.5	3.6[7]	Malaysia
—	100.0[1]	—	—		...	...	...	...	42	95.7	4.3	2	50.0	50.0	...	Maldives
46.7[2]	44.6	1.2	7.5	217,580	26.5	5.5	—	9.6	822	98.3	1.7	8	32.1	67.9	5.7	Mali
2.0	53.1	27.1	17.8	307	9.6	78.1	—	4.0	101	99.6	0.4	4	70.7	29.3	0.4	Malta
									367[5,12]							Martinique
—	92.3	4.9	2.7	15,599[6]	36.3	12.6	0.9	30.9	1,001	89.0	11.0	40	39.8	60.2	11.8	Mauritania
29.4	57.1	9.8	3.7	4,989[6]	17.7	73.6	—	2.5	365	59.4	40.6	62	46.2	53.8	12.2	Mauritius
				2	71.2	28.8	—	—								Mayotte
21.8[2]	33.9	40.1	2.0	5,190,000[3]	10.1	62.2	—	24.3	50,412	14.1	85.9	8,964	34.3	65.7	28.2[7]	Mexico
...	...	...	...		...	...	...	...								Monaco
									6							Mongolia
—100[4]—		...	...	24	20.6[4]	79.4[4]	...	...	47							Montserrat
32.6	56.4	1.6	9.4	27,607[6]	61.2	26.5	—	1.9	9,030	54.2	45.8	1,394	55.9	44.1	31.3[7]	Morocco
									583							Mozambique
—	—	0.7	—	112,787	—19.9—		—	—	29	...	...	...	...	...	...	Nauru
31.5[2]	44.9	10.9	12.7	635	17.6	75.2	—	3.1	297	100.0	—	6	45.0	55.0	1.6[7]	Nepal
11.4[2]	48.3	—	39.9	447,210[3]	11.4	34.9	—	38.5	...	...	...	...	...	...	...	Netherlands, The
—	18.9	0.8	80.1	5,688[3,6]	4.7	12.8	—	78.5	3,295	...	...	...	...	...	...	Netherlands Antilles
...	...	...	...		...	...	...	...	154[5,12]							New Caledonia
61.0	23.6	—	15.2	36,088	6.9	15.9	—	7.3	5,549	...	...	...	...	...	...	New Zealand
—	84.6	9.9	5.5	19,980[3,6]	23.1	17.5	16.6	7.5	2,504	60.4	39.6	163	32.9	67.1	7.9[9]	Nicaragua
16.3	74.6	3.9	4.7	150,530[6]	20.4	11.1	9.8	36.4	603	64.8	35.2	110	59.1	40.9	7.3	Niger
30.8	58.4	6.5	1.2	16,948	28.5	41.8	3.6	1.7	6,085	18.8	81.2	1,339	46.1	53.9	4.7[7]	Nigeria
									4[5,12]	...	...	...	...	...	...	Niue
...	...	...	...		...	...	...	...								Norfolk Island
20.1	59.8	0.7	7.4	232,290[3]	14.5	57.9	1.2	13.4	12,396	...	...	...	...	...	...	Norway
2.0	55.9	8.0	34.0	839	15.1	48.3	14.3	11.2	677	50.5	49.5	108	72.6	27.4	2.2	Oman
29.9	59.4	6.5	4.2	149,453	34.5	40.1	2.1	3.4	9,178	95.3	4.7	539	60.5	39.5	9.3	Pakistan
0.9	7.8	—	91.3	29,016[6]	0.9	4.3	—	91.2	2,820	25.6	74.4	614	45.9	54.1	13.8	Panama
19.9	76.2	3.5	2.4	579[6]	20.9	60.1	5.1	4.9	748	35.9	64.1	94	33.1	66.9	10.2	Papua New Guinea

Finance (continued)

country	international reserves, 1984[a]			central bank authority, 1983										central bank discount rate, 1984
	total ('000,000 SDRs)	% foreign exchange	ratio of external debt to total reserves[b]	assets (%)				money supply		liabilities (%)				
				claims on government	claims on foreign assets	claims on banks	claims on private sector	stock ('000,000,000 national currency)	M₁ per capita	reserve money	government deposits	foreign liabilities	capital accounts	
Paraguay	556	99.8	1.3	19.5[2]	61.3	10.8	2.7	64,599	18,320	71.8	2.9	4.6	14.3	...
Peru	1,559	96.8	4.9	30.9[2]	53.9	15.2	—	1,998,400	104,295	51.5	10.2	31.7	6.5	44.5[10]
Philippines	278	92.4	4.9	25.9[2]	35.9	17.5	—	23,500	461	21.3	5.8	61.4	—	11.0[5]
Pitcairn Island	...	...	...	...	...	...	...			...	...	...	...	...
Poland	...	...	...	...	...	...	...	408,979[7]	11,441[7]	...	...	...	...	...
Portugal	1,539	53.9	7.4	37.1	59.9	1.5	1.5	660,540	66,001	42.2	0.8	14.6	8.5	25.0
Puerto Rico	...	...	...	...	...	...	...			...	...	...	...	...
Qatar	399	90.5	1.0	—	99.6	—	—	3,361	12,586	74.7[6]	20.3	—	5.0	...
Réunion								1,843[1]	3,572[1]				...	...
Romania	747	82.9	7.5	—	2.8	48.5	48.7	156,950	6,929	38.6	22.2	5.4	—	...
Rwanda	89	100.0	1.5	15.4[2]	59.7	18.9	1.8	12,887	2,343	54.3	14.8	15.5	—	9.0[5]
St. Christopher and Nevis	...	...	...	...	...	...	...	305	673[5]	...	...	...	...	...
St. Helena and Ascension	...	...	...	...	...	...	...			...	...	...	...	...
St. Lucia	11	100.0	0.3	52.3	47.7	—	—	53	435	78.3	—	16.8	—	...
St. Pierre and Miquelon	...	...	...	...	...	...	...	42[1]	6,957[1]	...	...	...	...	...
St. Vincent and the Grenadines	6	100.0	1.0[7]	43.7	56.3	—	—	40	296	82.4	—	14.3	—	...
San Marino	...	...	...	...	...	...	...			...	...	...	...	...
São Tomé and Príncipe	...	...	...	...	...	...	...			...	...	...	...	...
Saudi Arabia	24,483	99.3	...	—	100.0	...	—	88,170	9,585	9.6	69.1	—	—	...
Senegal	8	87.5	109.3	40.7	1.2	58.1	—	176,030	28,711	30.7	6.0	62.1	—	10.5
Seychelles	3	100.0	2.8	44.1	55.9	—	—	131	2,034	77.5	—	—	10.9	...
Sierra Leone	8	100.0	41.9	96.1	3.9	—	—	359	96	37.4	6.1	53.2	—	12.0[1]
Singapore	9,488	99.6	0.2	—	100.0	—	—	8,091	3,233	31.1	17.7	—	—	8.5[5]
Solomon Islands	56	100.0	0.4	4.4[7]	78.3[7]	—	—	14[7]	617	—	17.9[7]	21.9[7]	11.3[7]	...
Somalia	9[10]	88.9[10]	139.5	73.1[2]	5.2	21.7	—	3,706	931	27.7[6]	37.0	32.9	2.3	...
South Africa	805	66.1	21.9	25.9	57.3	16.8	—	16,588	643	42.1[6]	33.8	24.1	—	13.5
South West Africa/Namibia[9]	...	...	...	...	...	...	...			...	...	...	...	...
Spain	12,116	95.8	3.1	68.8	18.5	12.7	—	5,209,000	1,376,840	95.6[6]	4.4	—	—	8.0
Sri Lanka	448	99.6	5.5	69.2	21.6	9.2	—	14,589	932	32.6	—	36.8	—	13.0[10]
Sudan, The	17	100.0	242.8	97.3[2]	0.8	1.9	—	2,303	104	39.9[6]	16.9	42.7	0.5	...
Suriname	24	91.7	0.3	76.7	23.3	—	—	455	1,253	70.4	4.9	—	8.3	...
Swaziland	87	100.0	2.2	11.2	88.1	0.7	—	102	160	64.1[6]	12.3	16.8	6.8	...
Sweden	4,527	95.3	1.8[7]	65.6[1]	34.4[1]	—	—	94,150[1]	11,301[1]	60.4[1]	—	3.1[1]	—	8.5
Switzerland	16,321	82.1	...	6.1	83.9	10.0	—	75,300	9,038	76.3	1.9	—	—	4.0
Syria	159[10]	81.8[10]	11.3	92.9[1,2]	3.3[1]	3.8[1]	—	29,518[1]	3,132[1]	67.7[1]	19.4[1]	9.6[1]	0.5[1]	5.0[1]
Taiwan[1]				20.7[2]	19.9	—	59.4	521,901	28,275	10.3	6.7	—	—	7.8
Tanzania	13	100.0	375.7	91.2	3.6	5.2	—	18,513	937	75.5	—	20.9	—	7.5[5]
Thailand	1,698	94.9	3.8	50.7	35.3	11.4	—	76,670	1,557	35.3[6]	8.1	12.2	44.4	13.0
Togo	165	100.0	4.9	29.9	65.1	5.0	—	76,270	27,017	73.7	4.5	18.5	—	10.5
Tokelau	...	...	...	...	...	...	...			...	...	...	...	...
Tonga	...	...	...	...	...	...	...	11[5]	116[5]	...	...	...	...	...
Trinidad and Tobago	1,483	99.9	0.2	—	100.0	—	—	2,261	1,867	42.2[6]	29.5	—	28.3	7.5
Trust Territory of the Pacific Is.	...	...	...	...	...	...	...			...	...	...	...	...
Tunisia	301	97.7	5.2	4.5	31.4	64.1	—	1,502	217	59.8	20.6	1.9	14.8	7.0[10]
Turkey	1,113	88.1	14.1	53.2[2]	32.7	12.0	—	1,378,900	29,165	32.1	8.1	56.1	1.2	31.5[1]
Turks and Caicos Islands	...	...	...	...	...	...	...	1[20]	74[20]	...	...	...	...	...
Tuvalu	...	...	...	...	...	...	...			...	...	...	...	...
Uganda	13[5]	100.0[5]	35.9[5]	86.6[2]	13.4	—	—	41,629	3,012	28.6[6]	—	71.4	—	...
U.S.S.R.	...	...	...	...	...	...	...			...	...	...	...	...
United Arab Emirates	2,118	98.7	1.3	4.8[2]	83.2	12.0	—	9,124	6,640	48.4[6]	21.1	0.1	30.4	...
United Kingdom	9.863	93.2	3.1	68.4	31.6	—	—	43,000	766	68.4	—	26.3	—	12.0[7]
United States	32,432	71.6	12.1	82.9	16.7	—	—	476,600	2,034	89.6[6]	10.2	—	—	8.5
Uruguay	317	71.3	7.7	41.4	13.9	12.2	11.3	9,473	7,548	30.8	12.3	26.1	—	...
Vanuatu								1,822	14,236					...
Venezuela	9,092	95.6	1.7	15.4	82.7	1.9	—	62,276	4,119	70.1	5.9	—	12.9	13.0[1]
Vietnam	...	...	...	...	...	...	...			...	...	...	...	...
Virgin Islands (U.S.)	...	...	...	...	...	...	...			...	...	...	...	...
Wallis and Futuna	...	...	...	...	...	...	...	129[1]	13,236[1]	...	...	...	...	...
Western Sahara	...	...	...	...	...	...	...			...	...	...	...	...
Western Samoa	5	100.0	18.1					15	92					...
Yemen (Aden)	234	99.6	2.6	75.6	24.4	—	—	354	169	89.8	—	9.7	—	...
Yemen (San'ā')	323	100.0	2.4	89.5[2]	10.3	—	—	12,380	2,155	82.3	11.4	0.7	0.9	...
Yugoslavia	...	...	...	7.7	17.4	67.1	7.8	874,000	38,289	62.3	0.6	33.6	—	22.0[10]
Zaire	101	85.1	74.0	78.9	19.4	—	1.3	8,728	284	51.4[6]	8.0	30.8	4.9	...
Zambia	57	100.0	36.1	84.9	6.9	—	8.2	654	103	17.6[6]	—	82.4	—	7.5[7]
Zimbabwe	97	74.2	7.8	34.2	24.4	—	41.4	751	90	40.8[6]	—	59.2	—	4.0

deposit money banks									external debt outstanding (disbursed only), 1982b							country
assets, 1983 (%)				liabilities, 1983					total ('000,000 U.S.$)	comp. (%)		debt service				
loans to govern-ment	loans to private sector	re-serves	foreign assets	deposits ('000,000,000 national currency)	composition (%)					public	private	total ('000,000 U.S.$)	repayment (%)		debt service ratio	
					demand depos.	savings depos.	govt. depos.	foreign liabilities					princi-pal	inter-est		
—	55.7	35.7	8.6	183,784[6]	15.8	53.4	—	6.0	940	59.1	40.9	81	48.9	51.1	10.3	Paraguay
0.8	59.9	33.9	5.4	3,743,800[3]	11.9	73.8	—	5.6	6,900	45.9	54.1	1,530	64.2	35.8	36.7	Peru
13.5	68.6	3.1	12.7	175,210[6]	6.4	35.3	3.9	32.3	8,836	43.5	56.5	1,029	47.9	52.1	9.97	Philippines
...	...	...	...													Pitcairn Island
...	...	...	...	3,996,500	...	...	...	...	17,423	...	...	...	...	...	...	Poland
7.6	65.5	16.5	10.4	2,697,780[6]	15.9	46.1	3.1	29.9	9,598	26.3	73.7	1,702	46.9	53.1	17.3	Portugal
—61.4[15]	—	13.9[15]	—	7,456[15]	21.0[15]	53.1[15]	...	...								Puerto Rico
—	60.6	1.6	37.8	10,175	22.9	47.7	4.2	6.8	412	...	...	...	...	...	...	Qatar
...	...	...	...													Réunion
—	63.9	9.2	2.7	569,340[3]	9.4	21.3	22.0	—	4,400[4]	...	...	...	...	...	...	Romania
14.2[2]	61.6	6.1	18.1	17,279[6]	31.5	26.4	5.2	10.9	189	100.0	—	5	63.5	36.5	3.2	Rwanda
...	...	...	...	...	...	...	...	...	49							St. Christopher and Nevis
...	...	...	...						85,[12]	100.0						St. Helena and Ascension
7.6	75.9	2.3	14.2	265	9.5	67.8	—	16.2	2	...	...	...	...	...	...	St. Lucia
...	...	...	...						25[5,12]							St. Pierre and Miquelon
25.2[2]	55.3	3.7	15.8	179	12.1	60.8	—	18.8	97	...	...	...	...	...	...	St. Vincent and the Grenadines
...	...	...	...	...	...	...	...	...	3							San Marino
...	...	...	...													São Tomé and Príncipe
—	41.3	6.3	52.4	125,650[3]	40.9	24.2	6.1	3.8		...	...	...	...	...	...	Saudi Arabia
3.5	85.7	5.3	4.9	426,540[6]	23.6	19.3	3.2	12.9	1,328	81.4	18.6	102	37.3	62.7	13.45	Senegal
38.5[2]	46.8	7.5	7.2	294	18.2	53.8	—	—	37	82.8	17.2	1	33.3	66.7	0.47	Seychelles
32.5[2]	33.3	29.3	4.9	387	40.4	49.9	—	—	370	72.8	27.2	10	77.4	22.6	20.87	Sierra Leone
7.2	65.8	4.0	23.0	46,046	8.6	33.9	7.1	35.2	1,410	33.5	66.5	236	51.4	48.6	0.8	Singapore
—	12.0[9]	54.1[9]	—	459	27.2[9]	70.4[9]	—	—	16	100.0	—	—	—	100.0	0.1	Solomon Islands
25.1	34.1	9.1	31.8	4,846[6]	42.6	27.4	—	—	1,078	84.9	15.1	20	49.3	50.7	7.4	Somalia
8.2	85.7	3.9	2.2	35,137	39.1	44.4	—	5.6	17,036	...	...	1,442	77.0	23.0	...	South Africa
—	—	20.2	—	490	26.6	24.1	—	—	11	...	...	...	...	...	...	South West Africa/Namibia[9]
9.6	64.7	14.3	10.2	22,667,000[6]	14.7	54.7	2.4	12.9	25,819	...	...	...	...	...	...	Spain
2.9	73.7	11.2	12.2	41,962	17.5	52.9	4.0	6.8	1,964	72.3	27.7	138	49.8	50.2	8.4	Sri Lanka
2.1	49.3	29.6	19.0	2,795	41.6	23.3	0.8	5.4	5,094	74.1	25.9	79	86.3	13.7	5.07	Sudan, The
5.4	71.5	16.9	6.2	900	20.5	58.9	0.8	4.3	58	...	...	...	...	...	...	Suriname
10.1	61.5	25.7	2.7	236[6]	18.7	56.6	7.8	5.7	170	93.3	6.7	18	56.0	44.0	3.5	Swaziland
16.1	56.7	1.7	10.6	482,180[3]	11.6	57.4	21.3	—	7,136[7]	...	...	...	...	...	...	Sweden
2.3	61.3	3.9	32.5	457,370	7.9	38.3	—	25.3		...	...	...	...	...	...	Switzerland
65.1	12.9	18.7	3.3	34,584	31.5	11.5	11.9	8.2	2,616	96.7	3.3	373	75.5	24.5	10.67	Syria
29.5[2]	46.4	—	—	732,269	10.7	77.3	10.9	1.1	7,853	...	...	...	...	...	...	Taiwan
81.3[2]	7.1	2.5	8.9	23,228	49.3	32.1	3.3	2.2	1,659	92.2	7.8	53	37.5	62.5	7.15	Tanzania
13.6[2]	74.2	2.5	6.2	434,560	4.9	77.9	3.4	7.5	6,206	56.3	43.7	788	38.8	61.2	8.4	Thailand
2.5	55.9	30.4	10.5	104,360	33.0	30.4	14.6	15.5	823	68.8	41.2	38	39.1	60.9	11.95	Togo
...	...	...	...	...	...	...	...	...	15,[12]							Tokelau
...	...	...	...						2							Tonga
12.5[2]	68.8	17.5	1.2	8,171	17.1	64.7	4.1	3.2	651	38.4	61.6	100	37.2	62.8	2.97	Trinidad and Tobago
...	...	...	...						145[7]							Trust Territory of the Pacific Is.
10.4	82.3	1.8	5.5	2,849[6]	30.3	25.3	4.5	9.5	3,177	72.4	27.6	495	61.4	38.6	15.4	Tunisia
15.1[2]	58.9	17.4	5.9	3,856,000[6]	24.2	34.0	12.9	2.7	15,040	65.1	34.9	1,690	52.6	47.4	15.2	Turkey
...	...	...	...	...	...	...	...	...	1							Turks and Caicos Islands
...	...	...	...						45,[12]							Tuvalu
8.7	57.3	17.2	16.8	37,252[6]	56.1	29.4	—	3.9	587	84.8	15.2	132	84.9	15.1	6.75	Uganda
...	...	...	...						28,621	...	...	...	...	...	...	U.S.S.R.
6.4[2]	43.0	3.9	45.0	77,791	8.0	34.9	5.2	31.7	2,872	...	...	...	...	...	...	United Arab Emirates
3.9[2]	19.9	0.5	70.7	458,000[3]	6.9	15.5	—	73.1	41,025	...	...	...	...	...	...	United Kingdom
17.9[2]	65.1	2.1	14.9	1,845,700	18.0	38.9	1.3	9.2	406,400	...	...	...	...	...	...	United States
10.6[2]	64.9	10.6	13.7	121,944[3]	2.7	60.9	5.7	14.9	1,738	20.9	79.1	226	68.8	31.2	13.4	Uruguay
...	...	...	...	7,693[3]	21.6	78.4	—	—	4	95.1	4.9	1	60.0	40.0	...	Vanuatu
4.5[2]	73.1	19.0	3.4	125,719[3,6]	33.0	52.4	7.5	—	12,122	2.5	97.5	3,150	50.6	49.4	12.6	Venezuela
...	...	...	...	...	...	...	...	...	383							Vietnam
...	...	...	...	...	...	...	...	...								Virgin Islands (U.S.)
...	...	...	...						6[5,12]							Wallis and Futuna
—	—	1.5	—	14	—	—	29.0	—	60	91.9	8.1	3	58.6	41.4	7.016	Western Sahara / Western Samoa
35.3	6.0	43.9	14.8	265[6]	40.4	36.8	10.3	7.8	760	100.0	—	48	83.8	16.2	6.27	Yemen (Aden)
5.2	48.9	34.2	11.7	5,771	26.2	44.8	0.9	5.9	1,312	98.4	1.6	55	81.2	18.8	3.8	Yemen (Ṣanʿāʾ)
0.6	67.1	26.8	5.5	4,739[3,6]	13.1	43.0	—	20.9	5,625	73.3	26.7	899	42.3	57.7	4.6	Yugoslavia
3.7[2]	44.1	37.5	14.7	5,409[3,6]	73.9	9.1	2.1	5.3	4,086	69.6	30.4	137	47.6	52.4	8.915	Zaire
31.8	51.8	12.9	3.5	1,404	32.0	47.2	2.2	4.2	2,394	72.5	27.5	177	52.1	47.9	16.7	Zambia
33.9[2]	55.8	9.6	0.7	1,675	30.5	56.2	—	0.8	1,221	22.6	77.4	146	35.2	64.8	...	Zimbabwe

11982. 2Includes claims on other government agencies and local governments. 3Includes foreign currency deposits. 41978. 51980. 6Excludes negative items. 71981. 8Data pertains to Development Bank only. 91979. 101983. 11Excludes Indian rupee currency. 12Indicates official development assistance only. 13Savings deposits only. 141971. 151977. 161975. 171976. 181984. 191973. 201970.

Housing and construction

The present table summarizes data about the housing stock and the construction industries of the countries of the world. The principal focus is on the elements that are most comparable internationally: the age of the housing (by decade, so far as possible), the tenure of the householder, the principal physical amenities, the sanitary arrangements, and the amount of space both absolutely (in square metres [10.76 square feet]) and relatively (persons per room). The data on construction characterize the industry in terms of number of units, area, and the portion of the gross domestic product represented by each country's construction industry.

Because utilization of housing opportunities, economic development, patterns of internal migration (favouring, for example, apartments, or temporary, sometimes seasonal, dwellings) differ greatly from country to country, the portion of each country's housing stock for which data are compared is defined as specifically as possible. In general, the numbers refer to permanent, private dwelling units that are usually occupied year-round, whether or not actually occupied on the date of the housing census or survey.

That definition implies the exclusion of certain housing that is often part of national housing censuses: vacation homes, second homes occupied less than half the year, collective or communal dwellings, and so on. The housing unit to which the data on tenure refer may be either the individual dwelling or the household, according to the reporting practice of the country concerned.

The data are collected mostly from national housing censuses and surveys. There has been much activity in recent years under United Nations sponsorship in the field of human settlement. The UN's *Compendium of Housing Statistics* is particularly useful and may be consulted for additional, though older, detail. The UN Centre for Human Settlements in Nairobi, Kenya, collects, analyzes, and publishes data on all aspects of settlement, but a particular focus is the provision of adequate, technologically appropriate housing for the many areas of the world where it is in limited supply.

Many countries conduct a meaningful housing census only in the capital city or in the few largest cities. This choice may result from the lack of ability to collect data for the entire country or from the perception, particularly in a tropical, rural country where adequate dwellings can be built by hand, that no urgent housing problem exists. This choice may be difficult, however, as planners are usually aware that much housing

Housing and construction

country	housing stock			decade built (percent)					tenure[c] (percent)			physical amenities (percent)			
	year	dwelling units[a]	median age[b] (years)	1970 or later	1960–69	1950–59	1940–49	1939 or earlier	owned	rented	collective, vacant, other	public water[e]	indoor plumbing	electricity	central heating
Afghanistan	...	...	...	...	...	...	...	...	...	...	...	...	...	...	...
Albania	...	...	...	...	...	...	...	...	...	...	...	...	...	...	...
Algeria	1977	2,208,712[5]	...	...	23.7	...	...	...	56.7	29.4	13.9	45.8	...	49.2	...
American Samoa	1980	4,728	...	5.3	...	...	...	...	80.0[8]	20.0[8]	—	70.9[8]	...	81.9[8]	...
Andorra	...	...	...	...	...	...	...	...	...	...	...	...	...	...	...
Angola	...	...	...	...	...	...	...	...	...	...	...	...	...	...	...
Anguilla	...	...	...	...	...	...	...	...	...	...	...	...	...	...	...
Antigua and Barbuda	1970	15,405[5]	11.1	—	45.1	31.4	9.7	13.8	55.9	40.4	3.7	85.4	...	...	...
Argentina	1980	8,196,284	21.6	26.1	20.2	...	—53.7—		58.7[8]	22.8[8]	18.5[8]	47.3[9]	...	69.2[9]	...
Australia	1981	5,161,163	26.1	33.1	18.6	10.4	—37.9—		61.6	22.6	15.8	...	...	98.4[11]	...
Austria	1981	3,077,200	...	...	...	...	...	...	47.7	36.2	16.1	81.3	...	...	31.7
Bahamas, The	1963	32,035[5]	...	...	...	...	...	...	55.1	35.3	9.6	67.2	...	57.7	...
Bahrain	1981	52,810	15.2	41.2	17.1	14.5	—27.2—		60.6[11]	33.6[11]	5.8[11]	92.8[11]	...	94.0[11]	...
Bangladesh	1973	13,734,999	...	...	...	...	...	...	92.4	3.8	3.8	...	...	...	...
Barbados	1970	59,391	...	—	3.1	...	...	...	73.5	20.3	6.2	60.8	...	59.1	...
Belgium	1970	3,223,432[5]	...	—	6.9	...	...	...	53.6	41.3	5.1	91.3	...	100.00	...
Belize	1970	23,082	8.4	—	59.7	18.4	—21.9—		57.9	27.4	14.7	80.0	...	42.9[13]	...
Benin	...	...	...	...	...	...	...	...	...	...	...	...	...	...	...
Bermuda	1980	18,449[5]	31.2	15.5	16.6	—67.9—			46.9	52.0	1.1	97.3	...	...	...
Bhutan	...	...	...	...	...	...	...	...	...	...	...	...	...	...	...
Bolivia	1976	989,055[5]	...	...	47.4	...	...	...	69.3	15.1	15.6	37.9	...	33.0	...
Botswana	1971	140,315	...	...	...	...	...	...	...	...	...	...	...	...	...
Brazil	1972[14]	18,029,239	...	...	...	...	...	...	60.4[8]	19.0[8]	20.6[8]	39.3	...	53.3	...
British Virgin Islands	1970	2,445	10.0	—	49.3	15.7	—35.0—		54.4	35.3	10.3	33.3	...	13.8[9]	...
Brunei	1960	6,101	...	...	...	...	...	...	20.6	79.4	...	88.1	...	90.1	...
Bulgaria	1975	2,734,717	17.9	7.0	11.1	—34.9—		47.0	77.3	22.7	—	74.6	...	99.8	...
Burkina Faso	...	...	...	...	...	...	...	...	...	...	...	...	...	...	...
Burma	...	...	...	...	...	...	...	...	...	...	...	...	...	...	...
Burundi	1979	938,000	...	...	...	...	...	...	98.7[16]	1.1[16]	0.2[16]	11.0[16]	...	0.6[16]	...
Cameroon	1976	...	...	...	...	...	...	...	87.8	7.0	5.2	22.1	...	6.7	...
Canada	1981	8,281,530[5]	14.6	27.1	17.9	13.8	—41.2—		62.1	37.9	—	98.5[12]	...	87.0[4, 17]	90.4
Cape Verde	...	...	...	...	...	...	...	...	...	...	...	...	...	...	...
Cayman Islands	1970	2,469	16.4	—	38.2	19.6	—42.2—		72.4	17.1	10.5	45.1	...	27.2[9]	...
Central African Republic	1959–60[19]	260,650	...	...	...	...	...	...	...	...	...	...	...	...	...
Chad	...	...	...	...	...	...	...	...	...	...	...	...	...	...	...
Chile	1982	2,510,275	20.4	32.7	21.1	—46.2—			53.3[8]	26.3[8]	20.4[8]	78.4[8]	...	70.6[9]	...
China	...	...	...	...	...	...	...	...	...	...	...	...	...	...	...
Christmas Island	1980	1,944	14.0	40.6	27.2	—32.2—			0.6[6]	98.7[6]	0.7[6]	100.0[11]	...	100.0[11]	...
Cocos (Keeling) Islands	1975	140	...	...	33.3	...	...	...	0.7	99.3	—	27.9	...	100.0	...
Colombia	1973	3,448,164	20.6	—	19.2	26.2	7.9	46.7	53.5	30.7	15.8	64.2	...	58.1	...
Comoros	...	...	...	...	...	...	...	...	...	...	...	...	...	...	...
Congo	1979[20]	71,000[5]	...	...	...	...	...	...	56.2	43.0	0.8	40.7	...	11.4	...
Cook Islands	1981	3,153[5]	14.0	23.0	48.6	16.8	5.7	5.9	85.3[12]	9.4[12]	5.3[12]	88.3[12]	...	60.6[12]	...
Costa Rica	1973	315,207	...	...	36.4	...	...	...	60.3	22.9	16.8	81.0	...	68.8	...
Cuba	1981	2,364,778	...	24.4	...	...	...	...	74.7[8]	24.3[8]	1.0[8]	66.8[8]	...	70.7	...
Cyprus	1973[14]	163,730	...	...	...	...	...	...	86.3	13.7	—	95.0	...	99.0[21]	...
Czechoslovakia	1980	4,908,778[5]	...	13.7	8.5	—77.8—			50.2[8]	42.8[8]	7.0[8]	78.1[8]	...	99.7[8]	...
Denmark	1981	2,161,862	30.8	16.7	22.7	11.0	6.9	42.7	54.9	43.8	1.3	98.7[8]	...	...	87.6
Djibouti	...	...	...	...	...	...	...	...	...	...	...	...	...	...	...
Dominica	1960	14,218	...	...	...	...	...	...	...	...	...	...	...	...	...
Dominican Republic	1981	1,114,833[5]	...	—87.6—			12.4		70.5[9]	15.6[9]	13.9[9]	30.1[9]	...	20.0[9]	...
Ecuador	1974	1,251,910	...	...	31.1	...	...	...	63.7	24.0	12.3	41.8	...	40.6	...
Egypt	1976	6,985,171	...	...	...	...	...	...	...	...	...	35.1	...	45.7	...
El Salvador	1971	680,456	...	...	...	...	...	...	48.1	25.5	26.4	47.2	...	34.1	...
Equatorial Guinea	...	...	...	...	...	...	...	...	...	...	...	...	...	...	...
Ethiopia	1967[20]	150,338	...	...	...	...	...	...	28.0	56.9	15.1	74.3[22, 23]	...	58.1[22, 23]	...
Faeroe Islands	1977	11,172	...	...	22.4	...	...	...	77.8[8]	18.9[8]	3.3[8]	99.6[8]	...	98.2[8]	92.0
Falkland Islands	1972	587[5]	...	...	1.7	...	...	...	...	...	...	98.6	...	...	...
Fiji	1977[14, 22]	...	8.6	...	...	...	...	...	73.6	16.1	10.3	61.1	...	39.2	...
Finland	1980	1,838,058	22.0	25.6	20.9	17.0	7.8	28.7	61.0	20.9	18.1	89.3	...	95.6[8]	80.2

is physically inadequate to protect dwellers from the elements and that too much of the stock is disadvantageously placed in relation to tainted or disease-infested water supply or to the outfall of unprocessed sewage, or is built of materials (mud, skins, thatch, etc.) that may harbour pests or disease. In the developed countries, median age and the distribution of physical amenities provide strong indicators of the quality and availability of housing.

The data for construction industries in various countries of the world refer to new construction for the most recent year in which a broad range of countries could be surveyed. The data for construction are usually from official documents that authorize construction or that certify after construction that the structure described meets building and fire codes and the like. The figures for completed construction are naturally more reliable but are not available for many countries, necessitating the provision of authorized construction data, which are sometimes available only for the capital city.

A truer indication of the level of activity in a national construction industry is in the data for its contribution to the national gross domestic product. That figure includes civil engineering projects, such as dams,

roads, harbourworks and the like, but the relative capacity indicated usually finds its way into the domestic housing (personal, collective, and commercial) industry. The predominance within the "new residential" sector of multi-unit housing usually indicates (in a developed country) a particularly mobile society, or (in a developing country) one in which limited development resources obliges planners to concentrate available physical and manpower resources in collective projects.

a. Data refer to permanent, private dwelling units that are usually occupied year-round, whether or not occupied on the census date.
b. Data are estimates unless specifically provided by a country source.
c. Data may be either for dwellings or for households, depending on country reporting practice.
d. Data may be either for construction completed or for construction authorized, depending on country reporting practice.
e. Data may include indoor plumbing if no separate figure is given.
f. Includes non-flush systems and those with no toilet facilities.

sewage disposal (percent)			space[b]			construction industry (1981)						country
						percent of GDP	new residential[d]			new nonresidential[d]		
public sewer	septic tank	other[f]	average area (sq m)	rooms per dwelling unit	persons per room		1- or 2-unit dwellings	multi-unit dwellings	floor area ('000 sq m)	number of units	floor area ('000 sq m)	
...	...	...	...	...	...	3.1	—586[1]—		...	48	65.6[2,3]	Afghanistan
						7.2[4]	...		...	...	...	Albania
39.9	14.2	45.9	...	2.2[6]	2.8[6]	11.7	—8,256[3,7]—		...	7	...	Algeria
—67.1[8]—		32.9[8]	...	2.8[8]	2.5[8]	...	...		...	...	...	American Samoa
...	...	...	...	...	...	...	—95[3]—		91.3[3]	14[3]	47.5[3]	Andorra
...	...	...	...	...	...	1.6	—1,587[3]—		585.2[3]	210[3]	164.5[3]	Angola
...	...	...	...	...	...	...	...		...	...	...	Anguilla
—17.0—		83.0	...	3.1	...	7.3	...		...	...	...	Antigua and Barbuda
—62.2[9]—		37.8[9]	...	2.8[8]	1.4[8]	6.2[10]	—27,115[7]—		3,812[7]	7	7	Argentina
—99.0—		1.0	...	5.1	0.6	6.6[3]	101,790	34,828	20,033	18,689	12,903	Australia
63.6	30.7	5.7	76.5	2.8	1.0	8.3	22,000	1,500	4,100[7]	400	7	Austria
—28.4—		71.6	...	3.5	1.2	2.8[10]	—666[3]—		...	66[3]	...	Bahamas, The
...	...	...	...	3.0[11]	2.3[11]	11.0[3]	—1,920[3]—		...	1,556[3]	...	Bahrain
—1.3—		98.7	...	2.0	...	6.0	...		...	...	...	Bangladesh
—26.6—		73.4	...	3.8	1.0	7.2	—753[12]—		...	35[12]	...	Barbados
—62.5—		37.5	...	5.0	0.6	6.3	26,440	527	20,064[2]	5,358	21,594[2]	Belgium
—1.2—		98.8	...	2.5[9]	1.9[9]	4.8	...		...	...	...	Belize
...	...	...	...	...	...	5.1	...		...	...	...	Benin
6.7	90.0	3.3	...	3.2	0.7	...	148[4]	12[4]	20.1[4]	15[4]	15.0[4]	Bermuda
...	...	...	...	...	...	1.9	...		...	...	...	Bhutan
—14.3—		87.5	...	...	...	2.9	...		...	...	...	Bolivia
...	...	...	...	...	...	4.5	—658—		120.2	353	119.9	Botswana
—24.6—		75.4	...	4.5	1.1	4.9[3]	—84,674—		16,111	4,236	3,479	Brazil
—50.1—		49.9	...	3.2[9]	1.5[9]	11.6[4]	...		...	...	...	British Virgin Islands
—62.7—		37.3	...	2.3	2.3	2.3	—12[3]—		...	60[3]	...	Brunei
—33.2—		67.8	...	3.6	1.0	9.4[15]	9,155	1,538	5,540.6	...	...	Bulgaria
...	...	...	...	...	...	3.2	...		...	...	...	Burkina Faso
...	...	...	...	...	...	1.6	...		...	...	...	Burma
—1.6[16]—		98.4[16]	...	...	...	5.8	...		...	...	...	Burundi
—2.2—		97.8	...	4.1	1.2	4.6	—1,646[4]—		...	95[4]	...	Cameroon
—97.4[12]—		2.6[12]	...	5.7	0.6[12]	5.6	—2,097—		...	10,148	...	Canada
...	...	...	...	...	...	20.3	—132[4]—		11.9[4]	10[18]	0.4[18]	Cape Verde
—47.1—		52.9	...	4.3[9]	1.1[9]	...	...		...	...	...	Cayman Islands
...	...	...	...	1.1	3.4	4.3	—124[4]—		18.8[4]	57[4]	16.6[4]	Central African Republic
...	...	...	...	...	...	2.1	...		...	...	...	Chad
—43.6[8]—		56.4[8]	...	2.9[8]	1.4[8]	6.3	...		3,660.8	...	1,274.4	Chile
...	...	...	...	...	...	3.4	...		78,340	...	47,550	China
—66.7[11]—		33.3[11]	...	2.3[11]	1.0[11]	...	...		...	...	...	Christmas Island
—27.9—		72.1	...	3.5	1.3	...	...		...	...	...	Cocos (Keeling) Islands
—46.5—		53.5	...	3.4	1.8	5.2	10,091	4,639	5,051.7	1,070	1,122.2	Colombia
...	...	...	...	3.5	1.7	11.3[10]	...		...	...	...	Comoros
...	...	...	...	...	...	4.6	...		...	...	...	Congo
—36.7[12]—		63.3[12]	...	4.0[12]	0.7[12]	4.5[4]	...		...	...	...	Cook Islands
15.4	30.7	53.9	...	4.0	1.4	5.2	—10,473—		805	912	1,049	Costa Rica
—43.9[8]—		56.1[8]	...	3.7[8]	1.2[8]	8.0[15]	—744—		1,855.7	460	266.2	Cuba
—52.7—		47.3	...	4.4	0.9	12.8	—3,704—		...	799	...	Cyprus
—57.6[8]—		42.4[8]	60.5	2.4	0.8	10.8	21,866	3,200	...	1,004	...	Czechoslovakia
—98.6—		1.4	100.8	3.3	0.8[8]	5.4	21,152	538	3,134.0	13,819	4,014.1	Denmark
...	...	...	...	...	...	5.0[3]	—65—		40.1	31	16.1	Djibouti
...	...	...	...	...	...	5.5[4]	...		...	...	...	Dominica
—11.9[9]—		88.1[9]	...	2.7[9]	2.0[9]	7.8	2,812	214	659	506	210	Dominican Republic
—32.4—		67.6	...	2.4	2.3	8.3	7,395	2,485	1,659.3	614	757.1	Ecuador
...	...	...	...	2.8[20]	1.8	4.4[3]	...		...	...	...	Egypt
16.1	6.3	77.6	...	1.7	3.2	3.3	2,901	72	180.0	3	1.6	El Salvador
...	...	...	...	...	...	...	...		...	...	...	Equatorial Guinea
...	...	...	...	...	2.7[23]	4.3	—1,637[1]—		122.8[1]	67[1]	20.8[1]	Ethiopia
—98.1—		1.9	...	5.5	1.1	...	...		...	...	...	Faeroe Islands
—98.0—		2.0	...	7.4	0.4	...	...		...	...	...	Falkland Islands
—35.4—		64.6	...	2.0	...	8.3	—1,034—		98	172	43	Fiji
90.3	—9.7—		69.0	2.8	0.8	6.4	22,020	3,062	41,215[2]	25,059	24,701[2]	Finland

Housing and construction (continued)

country	year	dwelling units[a]	median age[b] (years)	1970 or later	1960–69	1950–59	1940–49	1939 or earlier	owned	rented	collective, vacant, other	public water[e]	indoor plumbing	electricity	central heating
France	1978[14]	18,641,000	31.0	15.4	12.7		—71.9—		46.7	43.0	10.3	97.2[13]	...	98.8[24]	53.8[13]
French Guiana	1974	15,647	...	...	23.2	...	...	...	43.4[25]	43.3[25]	13.3[25]	47.2	...	71.8	...
French Polynesia		...	...	...	...	...	...	...				...	...	...	...
Gabon	1967[20]	15,886	...	...	...	...	...	...	—87.0—		13.0[26]	...	...	50.5	...
Gambia, The		...	...	...	...	...	...	...				...	...	...	...
Germany, East	1971	5,932,945	...		8.2	...	...	...	23.0	69.3	7.7	91.9	...	100.0	...
Germany, West	1972[14]	20,966,000	...		4.1	...	...	...	33.5	66.5	—	99.2	...	99.7	...
Ghana		...	...	...	...	...	...	...				...	...	...	...
Gibraltar	1974[14]	6,308	...						4.4	95.6	—	87.0	...	...	...
Greece	1971[22]	2,544,020	...						70.6	25.1	4.3	81.3	65.0	88.3	...
Greenland	1976	11,833	10.8	22.8	46.5	18.8	—11.9—		41.9	36.2	21.9	32.8[8]	...	...	64.2
Grenada	1970	19,642	18.3	—	22.9	29.0	—48.1—		76.6	14.1	9.3	81.8	...	...	...
Guadeloupe	1974	76,752	...		8.1	...	...	...	65.9[25]	24.0[25]	10.1[25]	31.8	...	54.9	...
Guam	1980	28,091	...	44.6					40.8	47.6	11.6[26]	99.5	95.8	84.5[28]	...
Guatemala	1981	1,297,611	12.5	28.0	10.0	—	62.0		56.7[29]	12.8[29]	30.5[29]	42.3[29]	...	28.5[29]	...
Guinea		...	...	...	...	...	...	...				...	...	...	...
Guinea-Bissau	1979	123,936	...									3.7	...	3.8	...
Guyana	1970	129,720	...		15.4	...	...	...	56.8	29.8	13.4	...	...	...	...
Haiti	1982	1,130,795	...	24.1					82.9[12]	4.8[12]	12.3[12]	2.9[11]	...	4.1[11]	...
Honduras	1974	526,566	...						71.8	16.5	12.7	32.6	15.4	25.0	...
Hong Kong	1981	1,061,086	...	38.3					27.9	65.3	6.8	89.1[29]	...	...	...
Hungary	1980	3,540,000	...	11.8	10.3	10.5	—67.4—		71.4	28.4	0.2	...	64.9	98.1	...
Iceland	1960	40,000	...						70.3	—29.7—		97.9	...	94.6	...
India	1971	100,251,000	...						84.6	15.4	—	33.9	...	...	...
Indonesia	1971[30]	22,471,000	...						87.0	5.0	8.0	...	...	...	...
Iran	1976	5,331,220	...	17.5		—82.5—			71.6	16.2	12.2	48.8	41.1	48.3	...
Iraq	1956	741,000	...						83.0	12.8	4.2	20.8	...	17.1	...
Ireland	1971	705,180[5]	47.2	—	15.4	—20.1—		64.5	68.8	28.9	2.3	62.2	62.9	94.7	...
Israel	1978	925,000	...						70.6	26.5	2.9	96.5[11]	...	96.5[11]	...
Italy	1981	21,852,717	19.4	22.0	27.5[33]	19.7[34]	—30.8[35]—		50.9	44.1[11]	5.0[11]	88.3[11]	82.2[11]	99.0[11]	26.9[11]
Ivory Coast	1958[36]	...	...	...	...	...	...	...				...	...	0.7	...
Jamaica	1970	420,159[5]	...						52.1	38.8	9.1	46.0	...	...	...
Japan	1978	33,188,700[5]	13.6	35.2	31.8	17.5[34]	—15.2[35]—		60.4	39.4	0.2	92.7	...	...	...
Jordan[37]	1979	378,377[38]	...						63.0	30.0	7.0	10	...	73	4
Kampuchea		...	...	...	...	...	...	...				...	...	...	...
Kenya	1962[21]	137,000[5]	...												
Kiribati	1978	10,802	...						68.2	17.9	13.9	21.3	...	23.7	...
Korea, North		...	...	...	...	...	...	...				...	...	...	...
Korea, South	1980	5,318,880[39]	...	39.9	18.2	15.8	—26.1—		91.7[8]	5.5[8]	2.8[8]	35.2[8]	...	49.9[8]	...
Kuwait	1980	180,400	14.5	34.5	38.8	—	12.2	—	29.9[13]	53.0[13]	17.1[13]	17.6[13]	...	83.3[13]	...
Laos		...	...	...	...	...	...	...				...	...	...	...
Lebanon	1970[14]	483,908[5]	...	—	29.4	40.2[40]	—30.1[41]—		...	...	...	...	82.9	93.4	9.2
Lesotho		...	...	...	...	...	...	...				...	...	...	...
Liberia	1956[20]	...	...	...	...	...	...	...				...	...	...	...
Libya	1973	284,000[5]	...						62.5	28.0	9.5	62.0	...	72.1	...
Liechtenstein	1970	6,068	...	—	41.0	10.4	—48.6—		...	...	...	...	...	...	...
Luxembourg	1981	128,281[5]	...	18.3	7.8	11.8[42]	—62.1[43]—		59.9[8]	38.8[8]	5.3[8]	99.4[8]	...	...	72.8
Macau	1970	19,306	...	—					...	...	...	...	...	97.9	...
Madagascar		...	...	...	...	...	...	...				...	...	...	...
Malawi	1972[14,44]	46,110[5]	...						39.6	—60.4—		...	...	...	...
Malaysia	1980	2,630,854	...						66.6[8,45]	21.6[8,45]	11.8[8,45]	...	...	43.4[8,45]	...
Maldives	1977	24,906	...						—				2.5	9.8	...
Mali		...	...	...	...	...	...	...				...	...	...	...
Malta	1967	87,049	...	—	18.2[46]		—81.8[47]—		32.4	63.9	3.7	93.0	...	92.9	0.21
Martinique	1974	76,135[5]	...						64.8	—35.2—		...	40.1	45.3	...
Mauritania		...	...	...	...	...	...	...				...	...	...	...
Mauritius	1972	146,569	...		27.2[48]	15.6[49]			52.5	31.9	15.6	82.9	...	70.7	...
Mayotte	1978	10,053	...						88.1	6.2	5.7	...	...	...	...
Mexico	1980	12,216,462	...	33.2	15.4	...	—51.4—		66.8	—33.2—		...	54.9	74.5	...
Monaco	1975	12,625	28.5	—25.8—		22.7	—51.4—		...	...	...	...	...	100.0	65.2
Mongolia	1969	242,000	...						100.0			...	...	47.5	...
Montserrat	1980	3,706[5]	...	28.0	24.0		—48.0—		69.2	21.9	8.8	97.3	...	72.1	...
Morocco	1971	...	...	...	...	...	...	...				...	...	...	...
Mozambique		...	...	...	...	...	...	...				...	...	...	...
Nauru	1977	508[50]	...	11.4[50]		—88.6—			11.0[23]	80.6[23]	8.4[23]	...	...	49.2[23]	...
Nepal	1961[51]	37,122	...						75.3	10.7	14.0	47.7	...	30.2	...
Netherlands, The	1977	4,573,000[5]	20.0	24.4	24.6	—29.0[52]—		22.0[53]	...	...	...	...	...	...	53.8
Netherlands Antilles	1972	46,489	...		45.3[54]		—54.7[55]—		58.6	31.0	10.4	84.1	...	87.4	...
New Caledonia	1976	34,403	...	41.0		59.0			48.6	32.2	19.2	...	72.3	68.7	...
New Zealand	1981	1,048,035	...	16.2	19.2		—64.6—		70.8	25.3	3.9	...	...	...	...
Nicaragua	1971	330,422	...									33.2	...	40.9	...
Niger		...	...	...	...	...	...	...				...	...	...	...
Nigeria	1961[14,20]	92,900	...						8.0	80.9	11.1	...	...	81.3	...
Niue	1976	708	...						75.6	6.2	18.2	...	5.1	54.9	...
Norfolk Island	1981	845	14.8	34.7	32.5		—32.8—		53.0	35.3	11.7	...	...	49.2	...
Norway	1980	1,523,512	25.3	22.5	18.7	16.8	6.9	35.1	66.6	23.5	9.9	97.5[8]	...	...	12.8
Oman	1982	2,469	...												
Pakistan	1973[14]	10,881,017	...						80.3	6.9	12.8	16.5	...	17.9	...
Panama	1980	364,325[5]	18.0	21.7	18.1	12.8	—47.4—		70.0	21.0	9.0	75.4	...	64.8	...
Papua New Guinea	1975[21]	42,860	...						40.0	—60.0—		50.0	...	56.0	...
Paraguay	1982	580,810[5]	21.1	27.0	17.0		—56.0—		80.4	10.5	9.1	11.1[56]	11.0[56]	17.5[56]	...
Peru	1972	2,686,471	...		27.0				69.5	16.6	13.9	29.6	...	32.0	...
Philippines	1970	6,099,844	...		21.5				86.9	8.5	4.6	24.0	...	23.2	...
Pitcairn Island	1981	22	...									40.7	...	85.2	...
Poland	1978	9,528,000	...	12.9								69.0[3,5]	...	96.2[8]	44.3[3,5]
Portugal	1970	2,702,215	...						49.3	45.1	5.6	40.0	...	53.9	...
Puerto Rico	1980	968,474	20.7	26.7	19.4		—53.9—		65.7	23.9	10.4	97.1	86.6	79.8[9]	...
Qatar		...	...	...	...	...	...	...				...	...	...	...
Réunion	1974	103,962	...		21.2				57.7	...	...	32.4	...	46.7	...
Romania	1966	5,380,299	...						...	...	...	48.4	...	48.6	...

public sewer	septic tank	other[f]	average area (sq m)	rooms per dwelling unit	persons per room	percent of GDP	1- or 2-unit dwellings	multi-unit dwellings	floor area ('000 sq m)	number of units	floor area ('000 sq m)	country
73.8[13]		26.2[13]	77.0	3.5[13]	0.8[13]	6.7	249,162	8,185	…	…	25,011	France
47.6		52.4	…	2.4[22,25]	1.4[25]	…	…	…	…	…	…	French Guiana
…	…	…	…	…	…	9.8[3]	…	…	…	…	…	French Polynesia
…	…	…	…	3.0	1.3	4.7	445[13]		216.1[13]	75[13]	119.4[13]	Gabon
…	…	…	…	…	…	8.5	120[13]	76[13]	…	14[13]	…	Gambia, The
56.6		43.4	…	2.7	1.2[23]	6.3[15]	…	…	…	…	…	Germany, East
94.2		5.8	…	4.2	1.5	6.4	174,888	13,333	204,614[2]	36,084	164,233[2]	Germany, West
…	…	…	…	…	…	1.9	…	…	…	…	…	Ghana
73.0		27.0	…	3.0	1.2[8]	…	…	…	…	…	…	Gibraltar
30.0	70.0		…	3.5	0.9	6.8	37,199	5,896	31,747[2]	13,232	17,077[2]	Greece
39.0		61.0	…	2.7	1.4		…	…	36.6	…	20.0	Greenland
…	…	…	…	2.9	1.7[9]	7.3[3]	…	…	…	…	…	Grenada
34.8		65.2	…	3.0[22,25]	1.5[22,25]	4.5[1,27]	460	10	91.9	31	40.9	Guadeloupe
97.5		2.5	…	4.7	0.7	7.2[3]	…	…	…	…	…	Guam
14.9[29]		85.1[29]	…	2.4	2.2	3.7	1,008[1,7]		248.2[1,7]	[1,7]	[1,7]	Guatemala
…	…	…	…	…	…	3.8[3]	…	…	…	…	…	Guinea
…	…	…	…	…	…	2.5[1]	…	…	…	…	…	Guinea-Bissau
25.5		74.5	…	2.7	2.1	6.4	1,259[3]		…	56[3]	…	Guyana
…	…	…	…	2.2[11]	…	5.4	597[7]		…	7	…	Haiti
14.4		85.6	…	2.4	2.4[23]	4.9	1,177		156.1	121	62.0	Honduras
65.4[29]		34.6[29]	53.2[11]	3.1[29]	2.0[11]	7.2	1,123		1,255	275	1,939	Hong Kong
68.0		32.0	60.0	2.0	1.5	9.9[15]	31,619	1,621	25,964[2]	4,920	23,499[2]	Hungary
86.5		13.5	…	4.8	0.9	8.8	…	…	918.9[2,3]	…	983.2[2,3]	Iceland
…	…	…	…	2.0[22]	2.6	4.2	46,493		…	9,644	…	India
22.8		77.2	…	3.1	1.5	5.8	…	…	1,445.4[18]	…	3,768.5[18]	Indonesia
…	…	…	…	3.2	…	7.2	87,339[3,7]		15,949[3,7]	7	7	Iran
…	…	…	…	…	…	7.6[12]	88,779[4]		9,800[4]	6,535[4]	3,068[4]	Iraq
72.3		27.7	…	4.7	0.9	8.8[1]	…	…	…	…	…	Ireland
99.0[31]		1.0[31]	…	2.9	1.2	8.0[32]	574	1,727	3,710	…	1,200	Israel
95.7[11]		4.3[11]	75.0[11]	3.7[11]	0.8	8.0	22,607[1]	9,047[1]	62,800[1,2]	6,372[1]	34,300[1,2]	Italy
…	…	…	…	1.9	1.8	8.0	…	…	…	…	…	Ivory Coast
31.3		68.7	…	2.4	…	7.0	1,947[13]		…	235[13]	…	Jamaica
31.4[22,29]		68.6[22,29]	80.3	4.5	0.8	8.9	733,000	208,700	120,085	228,600	86,277	Japan
16.0	84.0		…	…	…	9.2	7,821[7]		1,705.2[7]	7	7	Jordan[37]
…	…	…	…	…	…	…	…	…	…	…	…	Kampuchea
15.5		84.5	…	1.9	2.5	5.5	1,549		…	75	…	Kenya
…	…	…	…	…	…	7.9[4]	…	…	…	…	…	Kiribati
…	…	…	…	…	…	…	…	…	…	…	…	Korea, North
…	…	…	…	3.0[8]	2.3[8]	9.1	51,644		10,308	23,380	10,537	Korea, South
…	…	…	…	3.5[8]	2.1[8]	3.9	1,317		2,148	179	666	Kuwait
…	…	…	…	…	…	…	…	…	…	…	…	Laos
…	…	…	…	…	…	3.4[18]	…	…	…	…	…	Lebanon
…	…	…	…	…	…	9.1	…	…	…	…	…	Lesotho
…	…	…	…	2.3[22]	1.7	2.9	…	…	…	…	…	Liberia
40.6		59.4	…	3.3	1.8	12.5	…	…	…	…	…	Libya
86.4		13.6	…	4.2	0.7		…	…	…	…	…	Liechtenstein
93.0		7.0[8]	86.4[8]	5.3[8]	0.6[8]	5.9[3]	1,425	105	500	45	36	Luxembourg
…	…	…	…	3.2	2.5		217		37.8	10	22.2	Macau
…	…	…	…	…	…	2.5[12]	…	…	32.9	…	5.1	Madagascar
…	…	…	…	2.1	1.7	4.1[10]	161		…	58	…	Malawi
18.6[8,45]		81.4[8,45]	…	2.3[8,45]	2.6[8,45]	5.0	…	…	…	…	…	Malaysia
2.5		96.9	…	2.3	2.7	11.8	…	…	…	…	…	Maldives
…	…	…	…	…	…	4.1	…	…	…	…	…	Mali
78.5	15.4	6.1	…	3.2	1.3	3.0[3]	2,230		…	1,585	…	Malta
…	…	…	…	3.1[25]	1.4[25]	3.0	…	…	…	…	…	Martinique
…	…	…	…	…	…	6.3	…	…	…	…	…	Mauritania
33.9		66.1	…	2.0	…	5.8	4,442[3]		458[3]	461[3]	65[3]	Mauritius
…	…	…	…	…	…		…	…	…	…	…	Mayotte
44.9	4.3	50.8	…	2.3	2.5	7.0	…	…	…	…	…	Mexico
93.4		1.6	…	2.8	…		…	…	…	…	…	Monaco
	49.3	…	…	3.5	0.9	5.1[10]	…	…	…	…	…	Mongolia
…	…	…	…	2.1	2.4	8.7	…	…	…	…	…	Montserrat
…	…	…	…	…	…	7.1	40,909		…	…	…	Morocco
…	…	…	…	…	…	5.6	145[13]		51.7[13]	20[13]	25.0[13]	Mozambique
…	…	…	…	3.6[23]	1.6[23]	…	…	…	…	…	…	Nauru
6.1		93.9	…	3.7	2.0	7.2	…	…	…	…	…	Nepal
…	…	…	…	…	…	6.6	18,343		45,218[2]	12,555	56,923[2]	Netherlands, The
…	…	…	…	3.8	1.2		531		…	561	…	Netherlands Antilles
71.9		28.1	…	3.0	1.3	5.6	317[4]	7[4]	…	31[4]	…	New Caledonia
97.1[11]		2.9[11]	…	6.0	0.5	4.4	…	…	2,488	9,188	2,371	New Zealand
19.3		80.7	…	2.2	…	3.3	987		45.4	30	9.2	Nicaragua
…	…	…	…	…	…	7.6	…	…	…	…	…	Niger
7.0		93.0	…	1.4	3.0	8.5	6,761[12]		…	3,481[12]	…	Nigeria
14.1		85.9	…	4.7	1.1		…	…	…	…	…	Niue
	93.0	7.0	…	5.8	0.4	…	…	…	…	…	…	Norfolk Island
82.6		17.4	83.5	3.9	0.9	6.0	22,198	434	3,306	2,836	1,988	Norway
…	…	…	…	…	…	5.5	708		…	106	…	Oman
3.9		96.1	…	2.0	2.8	4.3	…	…	…	…	…	Pakistan
33.2	10.5	56.3	…	2.5	4.6	7.6	734	73	259.6	71	136.9	Panama
40.0		60.0	…	…	…	4.0[1]	1,029[1,7]		…	7	…	Papua New Guinea
14.3[56]	…	…	…	2.2[56]	2.4[56]	6.6	…	…	…	…	…	Paraguay
23.2		76.8	…	2.5	1.9	3.1	…	…	…	…	…	Peru
22.6		77.4	…	2.4	2.3	8.5	23,922		2,477	5,622	2,705	Philippines
…	…	…	…	5.0	0.6		…	…	…	…	…	Pitcairn Island
55.0[3,5]		45.0[3,5]	53.9[5]	3.1	1.2	7.3[15]	45,144	3,220	64,091[2]	59,298	60,139[2]	Poland
49.1		50.9	…	4.5	0.8	7.6	20,715[3]	1,643[3]	5,383[3]	6,741[3]	1,739[3]	Portugal
87.9		12.1	…	4.8	0.8	2.1	4,631	33	2,544.2	1,030	39.2	Puerto Rico
…	…	…	…	…	…	5.7	…	…	…	…	…	Qatar
32.2		67.8	…	3.1[25]	1.6[25]	5.0[1]	…	…	…	…	…	Réunion
12.2		87.8	…	2.6	1.4	7.7[15]	…	…	14,720[2]	…	…	Romania

Housing and construction (continued)

country	housing stock			decade built (percent)					tenure[c] (percent)			physical amenities (percent)			
	year	dwelling units[a]	median age[b] (years)	1970 or later	1960–69	1950–59	1940–49	1939 or earlier	owned	rented	collective, vacant, other	public water[e]	indoor plumbing	electricity	central heating
Rwanda	...	...	...	...	...	...	...	...	...	...	...	...	...	...	...
St. Christopher and Nevis	1970	11,236	24.2	—	18.6	20.7	—60.7—		52.7	32.7	14.6	82.7	...	...	...
St. Helena and Ascension	1976	1,147	23.4	...	...	...	...	...	57.7	30.1	12.2	82.7	...	62.6	...
St. Lucia	1970	21,753	...	...	7.1	...	...	...	63.8	27.4	8.8	20.6	...	36.1	...
St. Pierre and Miquelon	1982	1,760	11.3	17.2	13.8	—	69.0	—	77.3	17.8	4.9	99.7	...	99.8	...
St. Vincent and the Grenadines	1970	16,940	...	—	...	...	...	...	74.7	16.5	7.9	25.9	...	...	...
San Marino	1979[14]	7,000	...	...	...	...	...	...	73.5	21.9	4.6	99.8	...	100.0	...
São Tomé and Príncipe	...	...	...	...	...	...	...	...	...	...	...	...	...	...	...
Saudi Arabia	...	...	...	...	...	...	...	...	...	...	...	...	...	...	...
Senegal	1955	13,000	...	...	...	...	...	...	—84.6—		15.4	94.2	...	95.9	...
Seychelles	1977	12,315[5]	...	...	...	...	...	...	43.0	—57.0—		71.4	33.1	43.2	...
Sierra Leone	...	...	...	...	...	...	...	...	...	...	...	...	...	...	...
Singapore	1980	513,224	...	36.8	—63.2—				55.0	39.6	5.4	90.6[8]	...	91.8[8]	...
Solomon Islands	1976[20]	3,211	...	...	...	...	...	...	27.4	43.0	29.6	92.7	...	79.6	...
Somalia	...	...	...	...	...	...	...	...	...	...	...	...	...	...	...
South Africa	1970	1,354,520	18.6	—	35.2	24.2	16.0	24.6	...	...	...	...	...	...	...
South West Africa/Namibia	...	...	...	...	...	...	...	...	...	...	...	...	...	...	...
Spain	1970	9,542,458	...	—	19.1	...	...	...	57.2	24.4	18.3	77.6	...	89.3[9]	...
Sri Lanka	1971	2,217,478	...	...	11.1	...	...	...	63.3	27.4	9.3	20.0	...	9.0	...
Sudan, The	1966	253,060	...	...	...	...	...	...	59.2	28.3	12.6	63.9	...	26.3	...
Suriname	1964	64,434	...	...	...	...	...	...	...	...	...	38.9	...	...	...
Swaziland	1976	86,847	...	...	...	...	...	...	...	...	...	33.5	...	...	...
Sweden	1975	3,529,820	21.7	13.0	25.4	16.8	12.1	32.6	38.9	56.0	5.1	98.7	...	...	...
Switzerland	1970	2,050,483	...	—	22.9	...	...	...	28.5	68.4	3.1	100.0[9]	...	...	...
Syria	1970	990,000	...	—	8.7	...	...	...	81.6	15.5	2.8	40.2	...	41.7	...
Taiwan	1980	3,665,122[5]	15.3	29.8[59]	42.4[60]	14.0[34]	—13.8[35]—		79.1	11.8	9.1	79.4	...	...	...
Tanzania	1967[21,22]	65,502	...	...	...	...	...	...	33.2	47.8	19.0	...	...	16.5	...
Thailand	1970	5,922,827[22]	8.9	—	53.0	25.0	—22.0—		94.6[9]	1.9[9]	3.5[9]	12.5	...	18.9	...
Togo	1958–60	22,274	...	...	...	...	...	...	...	...	...	4.1	...	10.3	...
Tokelau	1972	263	...	11.1[61]	...	...	...	...	97.7	2.3	...	2.3	...	...	...
Tonga	1976	13,908[6]	22.5	20.3[62]	20.3[63]	—6.7[64]—		52.7	85.1	2.5	12.4	61.3	...	20.9	...
Trinidad and Tobago	1975	193,186[8]	18.7	0.8[8]	33.6[8]	16.4[8]	—49.2[8]—		66.2	24.1	9.7	58.6	...	77.0	...
Trust Territory of the Pacific Is.	1980	16,261[22]	...	...	...	...	...	...	...	...	...	...	...	...	...
Tunisia	1975	1,005,670	...	...	...	...	...	...	66.4	10.5	23.1	26.4	...	34.2	...
Turkey	1975	7,123,085[22]	...	...	...	...	...	...	81.4[8]	18.5[8]	0.1[8]	35.9[8]	...	56.8	4.2
Turks and Caicos Islands	1970	1,282	25.2	1.8	28.9	10.5	—58.8—		68.8	16.5	14.7	30.7	...	15.4[9]	...
Tuvalu	...	...	...	...	...	...	...	...	...	...	...	...	...	...	...
Uganda	...	...	...	...	...	...	...	...	...	...	...	...	...	...	...
U.S.S.R.	1965	61,658,000	...	...	...	...	...	...	...	...	...	...	...	...	...
United Arab Emirates	1968	38,820	...	...	...	...	...	...	...	...	...	—30.9—		24.2	...
United Kingdom	1981[65]	21,321,894[66]	32.6	16.4	16.6	13.0	—54.0—		51.1	40.3	8.6	...	98.6[67]	...	59.0
United States	1980	86,692,823	22.7	25.9	19.4	17.3	11.3	26.1	59.7	33.0	7.3[26]	83.8	99.0	52.1[17]	68.8
Uruguay	1975	878,000	...	...	...	...	...	...	52.1	32.1	15.8	63.1	...	80.7	...
Vanuatu	1979	22,513	...	...	...	...	...	...	40.9[20]	25.7[20]	33.4[20]	...	13.7	11.7	...
Venezuela	1971	2,126,921	...	...	...	...	...	...	70.4	20.4	9.2	72.4	...	76.8	...
Vietnam	1962[68]	204,000[5]	...	...	...	...	...	...	68.4	28.0	3.6	23.7	...	71.0	...
Virgin Islands (U.S.)	1980	33,548	...	...	...	...	...	...	39.9	60.1	—	...	93.1	...	...
Wallis and Futuna	1976	1,265	...	21.0	...	...	...	...	94.4	0.6	5.0	5.8	4.7	20.7	...
Western Sahara	1974	4,000	...	...	...	...	...	...	32.2[24]	62.3[24]	5.5[24]	78.5	...	95.3	...
Western Samoa	1971	32,938[9]	...	...	...	...	...	...	93.4	2.1	4.5	9.2[69]	...	18.8[69]	...
Yemen (Aden)	...	...	...	...	...	...	...	...	...	...	...	...	...	...	...
Yemen (San'ā')	1975[70]	...	...	...	...	...	...	...	85.3	7.0	7.7	...	...	...	...
Yugoslavia	1971	5,110,000	...	...	...	...	...	...	70.7	29.3	—	42.5	...	87.9	...
Zaire	1967[20]	168,000	...	...	...	...	...	...	47.4	38.3	14.3	...	...	...	...
Zambia	1969	879,000	...	...	...	...	...	...	78.8	21.1	...	27.6	15.6	12.4	...
Zimbabwe	1969	925,581	...	...	...	...	...	...	65.1[72]	32.6[72]	2.3[72]	...	...	9.3[73]	...

sewage disposal (percent)			space[b]			construction industry (1981)						country
						percent of GDP	new residential[d]			new nonresidential[d]		
public sewer	septic tank	other[f]	average area (sq m)	rooms per dwelling unit	persons per room		1- or 2-unit dwellings	multi-unit dwellings	floor area ('000 sq m)	number of units	floor area ('000 sq m)	
			...	3.0	1.3	4.4	—297—		59.6	58	34.4	Rwanda
2.2	29.6	68.2	...			8.4				...	...	St. Christopher and Nevis
—46.9—		53.1	...	4.1	1.1		...	...	...	...	...	St. Helena and Ascension
—11.0—		89.0	...	2.7	1.7	9.7[18]	—339[18]—			46[18]		St. Lucia
97.6	—2.4—		...	4.6	0.7	...	...		...	...	...	St. Pierre and Miquelon
—13.7—		86.3	...	2.8	1.8	10.7[1]						St. Vincent and the Grenadines
—98.3—		1.7	...	4.5	0.8		—120—		...	19	...	San Marino
...	...	...	...	...	...	2.0	...	...	...	...	...	São Tomé and Principe
...	...	...	...			13.15[7]	—63,463[3,7]—			7		Saudi Arabia
...	...	...	...	2.3	1.5	6.5	—658—		148.4	28	77.0	Senegal
—33.1—		66.9	...	3.6	3.6	7.4	—4,802[7,18]—			7		Seychelles
						4.2				...	...	Sierra Leone
—63.6[8]—		36.4[8]	...	1.8[8]	2.5[8]	7.0		2,001		1,853	2,336	Singapore
—89.2—		10.8	41.8	2.3	2.0	2.2[56]	1,174[3]		...			Solomon Islands
				...	...	2.9[1]	...	...				Somalia
...	...	...	...	3.4	...	3.9[58]	24,298	442		...		South Africa
						58	...	...		...		South West Africa/Namibia
—70.6—		29.4	...	4.4		7.1	7,400[12]	15,700[12]	...	...		Spain
—6.7—		93.3	18.6[8]	1.98	3.1[8]	9.5	—2,303[3]—		285.2[3]	...	...	Sri Lanka
—2.6—		97.4	...	3.7	1.3	5.2	...	...		...		Sudan, The
19.6	—80.4—		...	2.1	1.9	4.0[1]	...	...		...		Suriname
—20.0—		80.0	...	...	...	3.9	—80—			18	...	Swaziland
—96.3—		3.7	...	3.8[8]	0.7[8]	7.5	33,970	1,192		...		Sweden
—93.3—		6.7	...	4.7	0.6		16,963[3]	3,843[3]		8,024[3]	...	Switzerland
—36.0—		64.0	...	6.4	0.4	5.7	...	...	4,006[3]	...	623[3]	Syria
—69.3—		30.7	85.8	3.7	1.5	7.5[3]	...	...		...	...	Taiwan
			...	1.2	2.1	3.9	...	...		...	...	Tanzania
—1.1—		98.9	...	1.5	...	5.3	...	...	3,872	...	4,646	Thailand
—	—	100.0	...	1.8	3.4	4.3	—153[3]—		43.2[3]	12[3]	...	Togo
—2.3—		97.7	...	...	...							Tokelau
—11.2—		88.8	...	...	...	4.5	—738[7]—		668[7]	7	7	Tonga
—32.7—		67.3	...	2.9[8]	1.7[8]	10.5	—3,504[3]—		524.3[3]	84[3]	54.4[3]	Trinidad and Tobago
												Trust Territory of the Pacific Is.
20.7	10.7	68.6	...	1.3	3.2[6]	6.0	—16,152[7]—		2,309[7]	7	7	Tunisia
...	...	...	...	2.7[8]	2.2[8]	4.6	24,944	28,313	12,141	3,975	3,329	Turkey
1.6	—98.4—		...	4.0	1.2[9]		...	...		...	...	Turks and Caicos Islands
...	...	...	...	...	...	13.0[1]	...	...		...	...	Tuvalu
...	...	...	...	...	...	0.4	—229[11]—		83.3[11]	129[11]	71.8[11]	Uganda
...	...	...	...	3.0	1.3	10.1[15]	...	...	105,000[3]	315[3]	...	U.S.S.R.
...	...	...	...	...	1.9	7.9	—792[3]—		...	...	...	United Arab Emirates
...	...	...	...	4.9[66]	0.6	5.2	...	...		...	...	United Kingdom
74.4	23.7	1.9	...	5.1	0.6	4.3	...	...	150,200	...	108,300	United States
...	...	...	...	1.7	2.1	4.6	...	...	437.6[1]	...	229.5[1]	Uruguay
...	...	...	...	...	...				14.6	...	7.7	Vanuatu
40.3	13.2	46.5	...	3.9	1.5	5.5	3,204	559	4,346.7	769	1,323.5	Venezuela
...	...	...	...				—400[29]—		212.3[29]	53[29]	59.3[29]	Vietnam
...	...	...	...	4.2	0.8		833[1]	75[1]	...	262[1]	...	Virgin Islands (U.S.)
...	...	...	...	1.8	4.0		...	...		...	...	Wallis and Futuna
...	...	...	...	4.5	1.2							Western Sahara
...	...	...	...	3.9[69]	1.5[69]	3.8[56]	—138—		...	99	...	Western Samoa
...	...	...	...									Yemen (Aden)
...	...	...	...	2.0	...	8.8	—4,418—		1,196.1	...	...	Yemen (San'ā')
...	...	...	...	2.8	1.4	10.1[71]	66,595	1,919	16,228	22,716	9,333	Yugoslavia
...	...	...	...			4.9	—908—		246	174	103	Zaire
...	...	82.3	...	1.9	2.6	3.9	...	...		...	...	Zambia
...			...	2.8	1.9	2.8	—12,407—		...	...	...	Zimbabwe

[1]1979. [2]Volume ('000 cubic metres). [3]1980. [4]1978. [5]Occupied dwellings only; may include seasonal and temporary housing. [6]1966. [7]Residential includes nonresidential. [8]1970. [9]1960. [10]1982. [11]1971. [12]1976. [13]1975. [14]Data are based on results of a sample survey of housing. [15]Percent of net material product. [16]Data refer to rugos, which usually contain two or three houses each. [17]Used for cooking only. [18]1977. [19]Data refer to households and are based on results of a demographic survey of the African population, excluding Bangui town, East Dubangi, and the nomad population. [20]Data refer to the capital city only. [21]Urban areas only. [22]Data refer to households. [23]1961. [24]1968. [25]1967. [26]Vacant dwellings only. [27]Includes quarrying. [28]Used for heating water only. [29]1973. [30]Excludes West Irian. [31]1974. [32]Percent of net domestic product. [33]1961-71. [34]1946-60. [35]1945 and earlier. [36]African households in the city of Bouaka only. [37]East Bank only. [38]Includes nonconventional housing units. [39]Includes dwelling units in buildings not intended for human habitation. [40]1947-60. [41]1946 and earlier. [42]1948-60. [43]1947 and earlier. [44]Blantyre only. [45]Peninsular Malaysia only. [46]1958-67. [47]1957 and earlier. [48]1963-72. [49]1953-62. [50]Nauruan dwellings only. [51]Data are for cities of Kāthmāndu, Lalitpur, Bhaktapur, Birātnagar, Nepālganj, and Bīrganj only. [52]1931-59. [53]1930 and earlier. [54]1960-72. [55]1959 and earlier. [56]1972. [57]1983. [58]South Africa includes South West Africa/Namibia. [59]1976 and later. [60]1961-75. [61]1965 and later. [62]1966-70. [63]1956-66. [64]1939-56. [65]Data exclude Northern Ireland. [66]Data refer to "household spaces." [67]Data include those with water closets. [68]Data refer to Saigon (Ho Chi Minh City) only. [69]European-type dwellings only. [70]Data refer to living quarters. [71]Percent of gross material product. [72]Dwellings occupied by Europeans, Asians, and Coloureds only. [73]Dwellings occupied by Africans only.

Household budgets and consumption

This table provides data on disposable income of households for both sovereign states and dependencies—how it is obtained and how it is spent. For purposes of this compilation, income comprises pre-tax monetary payments and payment in kind. The first part of the table provides data on annual average income and income by source; the second part analyzes the largest portion of income use—consumption expenditure. Such expenditure is defined as the purchase of goods and services to satisfy current wants and needs. This definition excludes income allocated for debts, savings and investments, and insurance policies. The last part of the table focuses on food, which along with housing (examined in the Housing and construction table) are the two most important objects of consumer spending. The data provided include consumption by major food groups and daily available calories per capita.

For both source of income and consumption expenditure, the primary basis of analysis for most countries is the household, an economic unit that can be as small as a single person or as large as an entire family. For some of the countries that do not compile information by household, the table provides data on personal income and personal expenditure; i.e., the income and expenditure of all the individuals composing a society's households. When no expenditure data at all is available, the table reports the weights of each major category of goods and services comprising a given country's consumer (or retail) price index (CPI). The weighting of the components of the CPI usually reflects the household spending patterns within the country, its principal urban or rural areas, or sometimes only in the country's major city.

The table's income and expenditure data furnish the reader with a general view of the levels of economic development and affluence in most countries. The table shows that in poor, agrarian countries income derives largely from self-employment (usually farming) and that in industrial countries, with well-developed systems of salaried employment and social welfare, income derives mainly from wages and salaries and transfer payments (see headnote c). The table also indicates that in developing countries food sometimes absorbs as much as 50 percent or more of disposable income. By contrast, in the larger household budgets of the developed countries, food purchases may account for only 20 to 30 percent of spending.

The reader should nevertheless exercise caution when using the data to make intercountry comparisons. All the information comes from national surveys, which often differ markedly in the use of definitions, in the coverage of economic or population groups, and in the methods of collection, classification, and tabulation of data. Further, the reference period of the data varies greatly; while a significant portion of the data is from 1979 or later, information for some countries dates from the late 1960s and the early 1970s. Finally, intercountry comparisons of annual income can be especially misleading because of the distortions introduced when converting income figures in national currency units into new totals in U.S. dollars.

The table's food consumption information includes each country's daily available calories per capita (food supply), which amounts to domestic production and imports minus exports, animal feed, and nonfood uses. For each country the table furnishes a percentage breakdown of all the major food groups that comprise food supply.

Household budgets and consumption

| country | income | | | | | | consumption expenditure | | | | | | |
| | year, type of data[a] | annual average in $U.S. | by source (percent) | | | | year, type of data[b] | by kind or end use (percent of household or personal budget) | | | | | |
			wages, salaries	self employment	transfer payments[c]	other[d]		food[e]	housing	clothing[f]	health care	energy	education
Afghanistan	1977h[1]	1,017	...	...	...	...	...	...	...	...	...	...	...
Albania			...	...	...	...		...	...	...	...	...	...
Algeria	1968h	1,052	...	...	...	...	1979c[1]	45.6	13.1	14.8	2.5	—	—
American Samoa	1976p	3,643	...	...	...	...	1979c	44.3	23.4	5.6	—	—	—
Andorra			...	...	...	...		...	...	...	...	...	...
Angola			...	...	...	...		...	...	...	...	...	...
Anguilla			...	...	...	...		...	...	...	...	...	...
Antigua and Barbuda			...	...	...	...		...	...	...	...	...	...
Argentina	1967h[2]	1,521	...	...	...	...		...	...	...	...	...	...
Australia	1982p[3]	9,157	60.5	22.6[4]	11.6	5.3	1982h	16.9	19.2	6.8	—	—	—
Austria	1982h[3]	24,385	84.5[5]	11.2	[5]	4.3	1982p	22.9	18.7[6]	10.6	4.6	[6]	—
Bahamas, The	1979h[7]	13,537	...	...	...	...	1980c[8]	34.3	25.0	10.1	7.0	—	—
Bahrain			...	...	...	...		...	...	...	...	...	...
Bangladesh	1977h	564	26.9	44.7	0.2	28.2		...	...	...	...	...	...
Barbados			...	...	...	...	1980c	58.7	9.1	6.9	5.3	—	[9]
Belgium	1974h[10]	14,644	79.4	2.9	8.2	9.5	1981p	22.2	14.8	7.3	11.2	7.3	—
Belize	1969h[1]	...	84.1	—	—	15.9		...	...	...	...	...	...
Benin			...	...	...	...		...	...	...	...	...	...
Bermuda	1981h	28,170	83.1	3.0	—	13.9	1981c	24.1	20.2	6.2	6.0	4.5	9.6
Bhutan			...	...	...	...		...	...	...	...	...	...
Bolivia			...	...	...	...	1982c	54.8	16.1	13.9	—	—	—
Botswana	1981h[3]	5,000	67.5	27.7[4]	4.8	—	1980h	48.2	12.6	—	—	—	—
Brazil	1968h[11]	1,704	...	...	...	...	1968h[11]	46.8	4.2	7.5	4.4	5.0	1.9
British Virgin Islands			...	...	...	...	1974c	38.1	17.7	8.5	—	—	—
Brunei			...	...	...	...		...	...	...	...	...	...
Bulgaria	1981h	6,086	55.9	—	27.7	16.4	1981h	42.7	7.8	10.1	1.8	—	—
Burkina Faso			...	...	...	...	1978c[1]	41.3	17.1	10.9	2.9	5.9	—
Burma			...	...	...	...	1974h[1]	49.1	10.4	15.3	2.4	4.0	5.9
Burundi			...	...	...	...		...	...	...	...	...	...
Cameroon			...	...	...	...	1981c[1]	33.6	14.6	16.3	5.0	—	[12]
Canada	1982p	10,447	66.5	5.8	14.3	13.4	1982p	18.0	17.1	6.3	3.4	4.2	2.8
Cape Verde			...	...	...	...		...	...	...	...	...	...
Cayman Islands			...	...	...	...		...	...	...	...	...	...
Central African Republic	1980h	435	...	...	...	...	1978h[1]	70.5	0.6	9.5	1.0	6.5	—
Chad	1980h	458	...	...	...	...	1976c[1]	45.3	—	3.5	11.9	5.8	—
Chile	1968h	1,435	57.9	24.3	—	17.8	1978h	41.9	13.3	7.6	—	—	[9]
China	1981h[13]	266	...	...	...	...	1983h[14]	59.3	11.1	11.2	...	...	...
Christmas Island			...	...	...	...		...	...	...	...	...	...
Cocos (Keeling) Islands			...	...	...	...		...	...	...	...	...	...
Colombia	1971h	1,563	...	...	...	...	1981h	36.8	10.7	6.8	5.8	2.2	—
Comoros	1968h	...	25.6	64.5	8.7	1.2	1974c[15]	67.8	6.1	11.6	—	—	—
Congo	1980h	4,500	...	...	...	...		...	...	...	...	...	...
Cook Islands			...	...	...	...		...	...	...	...	...	...
Costa Rica	1977h[15]	4,425	...	...	...	...		...	...	...	...	...	...
Cuba			...	...	...	...		...	...	...	...	...	...
Cyprus			...	...	...	...	1980h	26.8	5.8	8.8	1.7	2.0	1.0
Czechoslovakia	1982h[16]	3,917	75.6	0.3	10.7	13.4	1970h[16]	44.8	9.9	14.9	0.3	—	0.3
Denmark	1980h	17,684	66.3	9.1	15.7	8.9	1976h	18.9	17.8	6.4	1.2	4.3	—
Djibouti	1972h	...	51.6	36.0	10.5	1.9		...	...	...	...	...	...
Dominica			...	...	...	...		...	...	...	...	...	...
Dominican Republic	1969h[1]	3,571	41.7	31.8	1.5	25.0	1976c[1]	31.9	32.4	7.5	—	—	—
Ecuador	1980h	...	41.5	53.3	5.2	—		...	...	...	...	...	...
Egypt			...	...	...	...	1975h[15]	49.7	8.8	14.2	1.8	3.6	2.1
El Salvador	1978h	3,460	...	...	...	...	1977h	40.8	7.7[6]	9.9	3.9	[6]	1.2
Equatorial Guinea			...	...	...	...		...	...	...	...	...	...

The data for daily available calories per capita provide a general view of the nutritional adequacy of each nation's food supply. The following list, based on estimates from the United Nations Food and Agricultural Organization, indicates the regional variation in recommended daily minimum nutritional requirements caused by factors such as climatic severity and average body weight:

Developing area	Daily nutritional requirement
Africa	2,334 calories
Centrally Planned Asia	2,353 calories
Far East	2,216 calories
Latin America	2,380 calories
Near East	2,455 calories

The breakdown of diet by food groups describes the composition of a nation's diet. A typical breakdown for a low-income country shows an imbalanced diet with heavy intake of cereals, potatoes, or cassava. In the high-income countries, a relatively larger portion of total calories derives from animal products (meat, eggs, and milk).

The reader should always be aware of certain limits on the utility of this food consumption data. First, the data compiled here do not reflect the dietary differences that often exist between socioeconomic groups within a single country. Second, the data, which come from national surveys, often vary in completeness of coverage and degree of accuracy, limiting somewhat the validity of intercountry comparisons.

In compiling this table, Britannica editors rely on both numerous national reports and principal secondary sources such as the International Labour Organisation's *Household Income and Expenditure Statistics 1968–1976,* the 1977 *U.N. Compendium of Social Statistics,* the *U.N. Yearbook of National Accounts Statistics* (annual), the *European Marketing Data and Statistics 1982,* and the Food and Agricultural Organization's *Food Balance Sheets 1975–77.*

The following terms further define the column headings:
a. h = household income
  p = personal income
b. h = household expenditure
  p = personal expenditure
  c = consumer price index
c. Includes pensions, family allowances, unemployment payments, and social security and related benefits.
d. Includes interest and dividends, rents and royalties, and all other income not reported under the three preceding categories.
e. Includes alcoholic and nonalcoholic beverages. Does not include tobacco except where noted.
f. Includes footwear.
g. Usually includes expenditure on household operation.
h. Includes expenditure on cultural activities.
i. May include data not shown separately in preceding categories.
j. Includes peas, beans, and lentils.
k. Represents pure fats and oils only.
l. Consists mainly of spices, stimulants, sugars and honey, and nuts and oilseeds.

transportation, communication	furniture, utensils[g]	recreation[h]	personal effects, other[i]	daily available calories per capita	cereals	potatoes, cassavas	meat, poultry	fish	eggs, milk	fruits, vegetables[j]	fats, oils[k]	other[l]	country
...	...	...	...	1,896	81.5	1.4	3.3	—	3.6	3.7	3.1	3.4	Afghanistan
				2,657	66.4	2.6	5.2	0.1	6.2	6.5	6.4	6.6	Albania
7.3	6.9	4.3	5.5	2,372	63.4	2.2	1.7	0.2	5.7	6.4	10.6	9.8	Algeria
14.9	—	—	11.8	...	...	...	...	...	...	...	...	...	American Samoa
...	...	...	...										Andorra
...	...	...	...	2,141	35.3	33.8	3.2	0.9	1.9	7.7	7.2	10.0	Angola
...	...	...	...										Anguilla
...	...	...	...	2,064	36.0	1.4	6.3	2.6	13.8	7.0	13.6	19.3	Antigua and Barbuda
...	...	...	...	3,346	30.1	4.5	21.2	0.3	7.3	5.5	11.4	19.7	Argentina
19.0	10.0	—	28.1	3,415	24.6	2.8	21.8	0.7	12.3	4.7	9.8	23.3	Australia
15.7	7.4	4.8	15.3	3,535	21.0	3.0	17.7	0.4	11.9	5.5	18.6	21.9	Austria
9.1	—	4.4	10.1	2,317	33.9	1.7	15.9	1.6	7.9	4.8	11.4	22.8	Bahamas, The
...	...	...	...										Bahrain
...	...	...	...	1,796	85.0	1.0	0.7	1.1	1.0	2.9	3.0	4.3	Bangladesh
5.5	8.9	5.6[9]	—	3,118	27.5	5.7	12.5	1.8	7.0	4.7	11.9	28.9	Barbados
12.4	8.6	8.9	7.3	3,577	19.1	6.1	18.5	0.7	9.1	4.5	22.8	19.3	Belgium
...	...	...	...	2,504	32.2	7.5	8.2	0.3	10.6	7.7	11.1	22.4	Belize
...	...	...	...	2,246	38.2	34.1	2.5	0.8	0.5	4.5	10.9	8.5	Benin
13.8	12.8	—	2.8	2,761	21.6	2.0	18.9	4.3	10.5	8.5	11.5	22.7	Bermuda
...	...	...	...	2,028	85.2	2.4	0.4	0.1	0.6	2.1	5.3	3.9	Bhutan
—	—	—	15.2	2,070	40.0	12.9	8.1	0.2	2.1	11.1	7.4	18.2	Bolivia
—	—	—	39.2	2,186	56.5	1.0	7.3	0.2	6.7	9.6	8.0	10.7	Botswana
6.4	8.6	5.7	6.4	2,559	35.8	9.4	7.3	0.4	5.7	12.5	7.2	21.7	Brazil
10.4	16.3	—	9.0	...	...	...	...	...	...	...	...	...	British Virgin Islands
...	...	...	...	2,898	48.9	2.8	5.7	1.8	5.7	5.0	9.6	20.5	Brunei
6.3	4.8	2.9	23.6	3,578	45.9	1.4	10.0	0.6	6.2	7.3	11.3	17.3	Bulgaria
—	3.9	6.8	11.2	1,990	72.0	2.4	2.0	—	1.7	10.1	2.7	9.1	Burkina Faso
3.8	0.5	1.1	7.5	2,198	79.8	0.2	1.8	1.1	0.8	6.0	5.3	5.0	Burma
...	...	...	...	2,254	24.4	39.1	1.2	0.4	1.1	23.0	2.4	8.4	Burundi
10.5	—	5.1	14.9[12]	2,459	33.1	19.6	2.8	1.0	0.8	13.3	7.0	22.4	Cameroon
14.4	8.2	7.2	18.4	3,368	20.3	3.7	20.3	0.7	12.0	5.8	15.5	21.7	Canada
...	...	...	...	2,401	51.2	7.2	1.6	2.3	5.5	9.5	9.0	13.7	Cape Verde
...	...	...	...										Cayman Islands
4.1	0.8	1.3	5.7	2,151	15.2	50.5	4.0	0.6	0.3	6.6	6.7	16.1	Central African Republic
—	—	—	33.5	1,762	57.2	11.2	3.2	1.6	2.6	8.2	3.3	12.7	Chad
11.8	7.8	8.2[9]	9.4	2,657	51.1	3.6	7.0	0.5	6.3	5.8	8.3	17.4	Chile
—	—	—18.4—		2,386	65.5	8.6	7.6	0.5	1.1	6.5	4.1	6.1	China
...	...	...	...										Christmas Island
...	...	...	...										Cocos (Keeling) Islands
14.4	5.6	5.0	12.7	2,263	30.0	9.6	7.4	0.3	6.1	11.5	7.9	27.2	Colombia
2.3	—	6.6	5.6	2,183	34.2	29.8	1.7	1.3	1.4	16.4	3.3	11.9	Comoros
...	...	...	...	2,272	17.8	52.2	1.8	1.9	0.5	8.1	5.1	12.6	Congo
...	...	...	...										Cook Islands
...	...	...	...	2,524	34.4	1.3	4.8	0.3	9.2	11.3	11.3	27.4	Costa Rica
...	...	...	...	2,635	39.4	5.2	6.7	1.1	8.8	7.2	9.0	22.6	Cuba
22.1	10.6	5.8	15.4	3,054	40.0	2.5	13.7	0.4	7.9	9.5	10.1	15.9	Cyprus
8.9	9.5	5.8	5.6	3,457	29.5	5.8	15.9	0.5	10.5	3.3	13.2	21.3	Czechoslovakia
16.9	6.6	11.1	16.8	3,419	18.3	4.6	16.9	2.0	11.7	3.7	19.2	23.6	Denmark
...	...	...	...										Djibouti
...	...	...	...	2,105	27.8	12.4	6.9	2.1	5.5	11.1	7.9	26.3	Dominica
—	—	—	28.2	2,097	34.0	5.8	3.9	0.6	5.4	20.0	11.2	19.1	Dominican Republic
...	...	...	...	2,104	32.6	8.3	4.9	1.0	8.4	14.4	8.3	22.1	Ecuador
5.2	3.6	1.3	9.7	2,787	66.4	1.3	2.3	0.3	1.7	10.0	8.3	9.7	Egypt
11.0	12.9	3.6	9.0	2,048	56.9	0.9	2.4	0.2	5.3	8.8	8.4	17.1	El Salvador
...	...	...	...										Equatorial Guinea

Household budgets and consumption (continued)

country	income						consumption expenditure						
	year, type of data[a]	annual average in $U.S.	by source (percent)				year, type of data[b]	by kind or end use (percent of household or personal budget)					
			wages, salaries	self employment	transfer payments[c]	other[d]		food[e]	housing	clothing[f]	health care	energy	education
Ethiopia	1968h[1]	495	...	...	...	...	1982c[1,17]	57.4	—	7.8	2.1	—	—
Faeroe Islands													
Falkland Islands	1974p	3,135[18]	...	...	...	...	1970c[1]	46.0	10.0	13.0		5.0	
Fiji	1973h	3,500[19]	81.5	9.1	—	9.4	1977h	45.9[20]	10.3[6]	8.7	2.0	[6]	1.8
Finland	1979h	16,060	67.3	11.2	18.1	3.4	1981h	28.1[20]	19.0[6]	5.1	2.5	[6]	[9]
France	1980h	...	54.7	10.7	26.5	8.1	1979h	25.8	24.0	7.8	6.3	—	—
French Guiana	...	...					1977c[1]	50.0	20.0	7.0	9.0	—	—
French Polynesia	1970h	...	59.1	34.0	2.7	4.3	1970h	40.0	—	15.0	—	6.0	—
Gabon	1980h	5,489	...	...	...	...	1980c[1]	54.7[20]	13.0	17.5	1.9	—	—
Gambia, The	1968h[1]	5,589	...	...	...	...	1983c[22]	58.0	5.1	17.5	—	5.4	—
Germany, East	1981h	11,947	69.7	—	21.9	8.4	1981h	29.6	10.9[6,23]	10.8	5.8	—	—
Germany, West	1983h[24]	12,062	84.2	6.7	—	9.1	1983h	26.1	17.3	8.1		6.7	—
Ghana	1968h[25]	471	41.6	47.1		11.3	1983c	55.4[20]	6.8[6]	19.2	1.8	[6]	—
Gibraltar													
Greece	1980h[3]	...	41.7	45.9[4]	12.4	—	1983c[1]	39.8	13.3	11.9	4.9		8.2
Greenland	1980p[26]	10,664	...	...	...	...	1978h[16]	29.3	6.1	9.9	1.7	8.4	5.6
Grenada		...					1975c	67.1[19]	7.0	6.2	—	4.6	—
Guadeloupe	1970h	...	52.5	17.5	21.6	8.4	1978c	24.1	28.6	10.6	4.8	—	—
Guam	1978h	19,309	...	...	...	...							
Guatemala	1970h	1,635	...	...	...	...	1975c[15]	43.8	12.8[6]	12.6		[6]	—
Guinea	1981h	230	...	...	...	...	...	...	...	...	...	...	...
Guinea-Bissau													
Guyana	1974p	...	73.0		6.3	20.7							
Haiti	...						1970h	48.9	7.9	3.5	8.6	7.0	2.2
Honduras	1968h[15]	1,500	50.2	39.2	0.4	10.2	1975h	51.0	13.4[6]	11.3	5.9	[6]	[9]
Hong Kong	1974h[15]	4,264	...	...	...	...	1980	25.3	11.9	17.1	5.3	—	1.3
Hungary	1975h[15]	9,962	79.9	1.9	10.8	7.4	1980p	42.4	3.9	9.2	6.0	3.6	[9]
Iceland	1982p	...	—80.0—		—20.0—		1973h	25.7	17.8[6]	9.2	7.7	[6]	0.5
India	1977p	...	39.2	42.9	—	17.9	1980h	57.9	4.7	10.9	2.0	4.0	2.8
Indonesia	1969h[1]	360	42.1	41.5	2.5	13.9	1978p	65.5	13.1[6]	5.7	—	[6]	—
Iran	1975h[15]	4,312	40.8	28.2	3.7	27.3	1975h[15]	29.2	18.5	11.9	4.8	3.2	1.2
Iraq	...						1972h	55.4	7.9	10.3	2.4	4.1	—
Ireland	1973h	4,877	58.4	25.0	12.3	4.3	1979h	40.6	6.4	8.0	2.3	5.3	2.3
Israel	1981h[15]	6,011	92.4	3.7	—3.9—		1980h	29.3	24.8	5.2	3.4	3.3	1.9
Italy	1980h	...	53.4	—	18.3	28.3	1982h	28.2	11.8	9.8		6.3	—
Ivory Coast	...						1969c[27]	51.1	11.6	8.4		8.1	—
Jamaica	1982h	5,715	70.9	27.3	1.8	—	1980h	37.8	10.5	3.1	1.9	4.4	0.3
Japan	1983h	...	—94.9—			5.1	1983h[28]	26.5	4.7[23]	6.9	2.4	5.8	3.8
Jordan	1979h[29]	6,005	...	...	...	...	1980h	53.4	8.2[6]	8.2	3.9	[6]	2.2
Kampuchea	...						1970c	53.0	23.0	9.0		—	—
Kenya	1975h	443	22.4	—	—	77.6	1981c[1,30]	40.0	16.0	11.9	2.4	4.4	[9]
Kiribati	1974h	...	69.8	21.4	6.0	2.8	1974h	62.3	8.5[6]	5.5	0.1	[6]	1.2
Korea, North	...						1962p[31]	46.5	0.6	29.9	15.9[32]	3.3	—
Korea, South	1980h	...	49.6	—	5.7	44.7	1981h[15]	36.5	23.0	8.2	7.6	6.7	5.5
Kuwait	1980h[33]	12,907	...	...	...	...	1983h	35.7	18.7[6]	10.0	1.0	[6]	—
Laos													
Lebanon	1970h	...	27.9	—	3.0	69.1	1974c[1]	42.8	16.8	8.6	7.2	4.5	3.9
Lesotho	1980h	1,148	...	...	...	...	1973h[15]	34.0	9.7	19.3	1.8	4.8	4.1
Liberia	...						1981c	40.1[20]	14.9	13.8	—	5.0	—
Libya	1969h[1]	2,947	...	...	...	...	1977h	37.2	32.2[6]	6.9	3.3	[6]	[9]
Liechtenstein	1981p[34]	...	91.0	9.0	—	—							
Luxembourg	1981h	13,100	...	...	...	...	1980h	20.0	13.4	7.2	7.8	6.3	—
Macau													
Madagascar	1969h[1,35]	1,176	58.8	14.1	—	27.1	1973h	38.5	—	12.0	—	—	—
Malawi	1979h	2,419	83.3	6.0	—	11.7	1979h	23.7	7.6	8.0	—	—	—
Malaysia							1973h	39.6	10.9[6]	6.4	2.0	[6]	0.8
Maldives													
Mali													
Malta	1980h[3]	...	53.0	—	11.7	35.3	1980h	33.8	10.3[6]	8.1	5.2	[6]	[9]
Martinique	...						1980p	26.4	20.9	24.0	7.2	—	—
Mauritania	...						1973c[1]	61.0	24.0	5.2	—	—	—
Mauritius	1979h	2,073	50.0[36]	45.0[36]	5.0[36]	—	1962h	53.5	10.5	10.6	2.3	—	3.4
Mayotte													
Mexico	1968h	...	58.8	25.4	—15.8—		1980h	36.7[20]	8.7[6]	11.3	4.0	[6]	[9]
Monaco	...												
Mongolia	...						...	...	...	...	...	...	...
Montserrat													
Morocco							1973c	54.0	7.0[23]	8.5	5.5	3.0	—
Mozambique													
Nauru													
Nepal	1974h[1]	899	...	...	...	...	1974h[1]	57.4	11.4[6]	10.5	4.2	[6]	[9]
Netherlands, The	1982h	20,815	42.3	17.4	28.2	12.1	1980p	18.9	11.8	8.5	13.2	5.4	0.4
Netherlands Antilles							1982c[37]	30.2	18.1	8.4	3.8	—	1.1
New Caledonia	1980h	...	63.1	23.9	13.0	—	1969h[38]	38.3	14.5	9.0	1.8	2.9	1.3
New Zealand	1982h	14,227	...	...	...	...	1982h	22.0	22.2	7.0	1.3	8.7[39]	—
Nicaragua	1978h	...	69.9	28.6	1.5	—	1978c[1]	38.5[20]	26.7	7.3	—	—	—
Niger	...						1983c	50.5	19.1[40]	7.3	—	—	—
Nigeria	1982h	3,875	...	...	...	...							
Niue													
Norfolk Island													
Norway	1982h	10,400	45.8	—	22.5	31.7	1981p	26.8[20]	16.6[6]	8.4	5.1	[6]	[9]
Oman	...						...	...	...	...	...	...	...
Pakistan	1972h	289	17.9	66.9	0.5	14.7	1972h	53.3	7.8	9.7	2.0	5.1	1.3
Panama	1979h	...	85.3	—	9.2	5.5	1978h	47.3	12.7[6]	4.8	4.9	[6]	[9]
Papua New Guinea	1970h	1,357	72.7	2.5	—	24.8	1970h[41]	56.7	7.1	7.2	0.3	1.7	0.2

				food consumption									country
				daily available calories per capita	percent of total calories derived from								
transportation, communication	furniture, utensils[g]	recreation[h]	personal effects, other[i]		cereals	potatoes, cassavas	meat, poultry	fish	eggs, milk	fruits, vegetables[j]	fats, oils[k]	other[l]	
5.3	17.1	3.0	7.3	1,793	68.8	3.9	4.2	—	2.9	9.3	2.2	8.7	Ethiopia
...	...	...	...	3,025	31.6	5.1	13.2	6.8	7.3	3.1	15.7	17.2	Faeroe Islands
—	5.0	—	21.0	...	...	...	...	...	...	...	...	...	Falkland Islands
12.6	9.2	3.1	6.4	2,628	36.6	18.0	4.2	2.1	3.4	4.8	7.5	23.4	Fiji
17.1	7.0	8.4[9]	12.8	3,156	21.6	5.7	14.2	1.6	19.3	3.5	14.7	19.4	Finland
13.4	—	6.4	16.3	3,434	21.8	5.3	17.0	0.9	10.7	5.0	17.1	22.2	France
8.0	—	6.0	—	2,545	34.6	4.4	12.9	2.0	7.5	10.8	7.5	20.3	French Guiana
—	20.0[21]	—	19.0	2,749	35.0	10.0	8.1	2.5	5.2	4.5	13.4	21.3	French Polynesia
6.3	—	—	6.6	2,428	24.2	24.3	6.2	1.9	2.8	14.0	8.3	18.3	Gabon
—	—	—	14.0	2,326	63.4	1.6	2.9	1.2	1.3	2.4	13.1	14.1	Gambia, The
—	23.3	15.2	4.4	3,644	24.6	7.7	15.9	0.7	8.4	4.2	18.3	20.2	Germany, East
15.9	10.2	8.7	7.0	3,382	19.3	4.2	19.4	0.7	9.5	5.0	18.3	23.6	Germany, West
4.3	5.1	5.5	1.9	1,986	27.6	35.7	1.8	3.1	0.5	14.0	6.1	11.2	Ghana
...	...	...	...	...	...	...	...	...	...	...	...	...	Gibraltar
12.5	7.9	—	1.5	3,400	34.3	3.5	10.6	0.8	9.4	9.1	17.2	15.1	Greece
1.5	7.3	4.1	26.1	...	...	...	...	...	...	...	...	...	Greenland
—	7.8	—	7.3	2,175	35.5	5.7	7.2	5.0	6.1	7.7	8.6	24.2	Grenada
...	...	...	...	2,630	35.8	6.7	11.0	3.0	7.1	11.0	8.7	16.7	Guadeloupe
18.0	—	5.1	8.8	...	...	...	...	...	...	...	...	...	Guam
5.2	4.7	—	20.9	2,020	57.8	0.6	2.4	0.1	4.6	4.7	6.6	23.2	Guatemala
...	...	...	...	1,943	58.1	16.1	1.2	0.5	1.0	9.8	8.8	4.5	Guinea
...	...	...	...	2,326	57.7	8.2	3.9	0.3	2.3	6.4	12.6	8.6	Guinea-Bissau
...	...	...	...	2,501	53.1	2.2	4.8	1.6	5.2	4.6	7.5	21.0	Guyana
2.8	4.9	2.7	11.5	2,101	49.9	6.3	3.2	0.2	1.8	16.6	3.5	18.5	Haiti
3.1	6.6	5.1[9]	3.6	2,106	56.5	0.6	2.5	0.1	5.0	12.3	6.8	16.2	Honduras
9.3	12.3	6.7	10.8	2,784	39.7	1.2	19.8	2.9	4.2	5.8	12.3	14.1	Hong Kong
7.4	7.9	12.6[9]	6.8	3,520	33.2	3.6	15.2	0.3	7.4	4.8	15.3	20.2	Hungary
14.5	9.5	6.4	8.7	2,935	21.9	1.8	15.5	3.7	21.6	3.3	10.8	21.4	Iceland
8.1	2.0	0.8	6.8	1,919	65.3	2.1	0.3	0.3	3.0	10.4	7.1	11.5	India
—	3.9	—	11.8	2,118	67.2	9.7	0.9	1.0	0.3	2.2	5.8	12.9	Indonesia
8.7	8.6	1.3	12.6	2,986	64.1	1.2	3.8	—	2.8	6.4	8.4	13.3	Iran
5.3	6.2	1.2	7.2	2,155	60.6	0.5	3.9	0.2	3.6	8.8	5.9	16.5	Iraq
13.2	5.3	6.1	10.5	3,551	24.1	7.0	16.7	0.7	13.6	3.5	12.4	22.0	Ireland
10.9	8.1	5.3	7.8	3,146	34.2	2.6	9.7	0.7	11.1	8.6	14.9	18.2	Israel
13.5	8.1	5.8	16.5	3,434	36.6	2.2	11.2	0.7	8.4	7.3	15.1	18.5	Italy
—	7.3	—	13.5	2,495	34.6	28.3	3.1	1.4	2.3	10.9	8.3	11.1	Ivory Coast
14.1	2.8	4.4	20.7	2,658	33.9	9.3	6.4	1.6	4.9	8.2	11.4	24.3	Jamaica
9.4	4.1	8.6	27.8	2,946	46.6	2.2	5.6	6.1	5.1	5.3	9.6	19.5	Japan
5.7	5.9	2.9	9.6	2,107	61.8	1.6	3.7	0.3	5.2	4.1	9.1	14.2	Jordan
—	—	—	15.0	1,925	80.5	1.1	3.7	1.2	0.4	5.0	1.9	6.2	Kampuchea
7.9	8.1	4.5[9]	4.8	2,166	56.4	8.9	4.6	0.2	5.1	9.1	3.5	12.2	Kenya
4.2	17.0	0.9	0.3	...	...	...	...	...	...	...	...	...	Kiribati
—	3.8	—	5.9	2,837	69.1	5.9	2.3	2.4	0.7	8.4	1.5	9.7	Korea, North
5.0	—	1.6	5.9	2,785	72.8	3.0	2.2	1.7	1.2	4.1	2.0	13.0	Korea, South
15.3	11.0	—	19.3	...	...	...	...	...	...	...	...	...	Kuwait
...	...	...	...	1,929	83.4	1.4	5.5	0.6	1.3	4.3	1.1	2.4	Laos
5.4	2.6	1.9	6.3	2,495	52.7	2.0	3.6	0.2	3.9	8.7	8.0	20.9	Lebanon
9.5	6.9	3.1	6.8	2,245	77.7	0.4	4.4	—	1.7	3.7	1.8	10.3	Lesotho
—	6.1	—	20.1	2,421	44.1	23.3	2.3	1.7	0.8	6.3	15.9	5.6	Liberia
9.4	4.6	8.5[9]	2.5	2,985	39.3	1.4	4.5	0.6	7.5	12.1	14.9	19.7	Libya
...	...	...	...	...	...	...	...	...	...	...	...	...	Liechtenstein
15.6	10.5	3.7	15.5	...	...	...	...	...	...	...	...	...	Luxembourg
...	...	...	...	2,093	48.4	0.8	16.7	2.7	2.6	7.0	10.9	10.9	Macau
9.7	—	—	39.8	2,501	63.5	14.8	4.9	0.5	0.4	6.1	2.8	7.0	Madagascar
13.7	9.9	—	37.1	2,215	71.5	2.1	1.0	1.0	0.8	11.3	2.5	9.8	Malawi
15.2	7.3	5.4	12.4	2,613	57.6	1.5	2.9	2.7	4.0	4.1	8.8	18.4	Malaysia
...	...	...	...	1,765	42.5	6.4	0.8	12.4	—	12.5	7.7	17.7	Maldives
...	...	...	...	2,117	75.3	1.8	3.3	0.9	2.2	2.7	5.8	8.0	Mali
13.9	19.8	6.8[9]	2.1	3,205	38.5	1.3	11.4	1.0	11.1	6.1	10.8	19.8	Malta
13.7	—	7.8	—	2,673	32.8	6.7	11.3	2.5	6.5	9.8	8.5	21.9	Martinique
—	—	—	9.8	1,963	53.0	0.6	6.1	2.0	17.2	7.7	3.9	9.5	Mauritania
5.9	4.9	2.8	6.1	2,593	51.4	1.0	2.9	1.5	6.6	4.0	13.4	19.2	Mauritius
...	...	...	...	...	...	...	...	...	...	...	...	...	Mayotte
10.1	13.1	5.5[9]	10.6	2,655	50.8	0.1	5.5	—	6.7	3.7	5.6	27.6	Mexico
...	...	...	...	...	...	...	...	...	...	...	...	...	Monaco
...	...	...	...	2,576	51.9	1.6	25.7	—	5.9	—	5.4	9.5	Mongolia
...	...	...	...	...	...	...	...	...	...	...	...	...	Montserrat
7.0	3.4	1.2	10.4	2,539	66.8	—	1.9	—	1.7	3.1	10.1	16.4	Morocco
...	...	...	...	1,907	37.5	36.4	1.9	—	0.1	2.4	7.1	14.6	Mozambique
...	...	...	...	...	...	...	...	...	...	...	...	...	Nauru
2.1	—	7.9[9]	6.5	2,002	83.8	3.1	1.1	—	5.0	0.1	4.4	2.5	Nepal
11.3	10.1	10.3	10.1	3,372	18.8	4.5	17.3	0.1	12.7	1.8	19.0	15.8	Netherlands, The
12.7	8.1	7.0	10.6	2,723	34.2	2.2	13.8	1.1	9.6	5.4	11.1	22.6	Netherlands Antilles
9.5	5.8	3.9	13.0	2,594	33.3	8.5	12.4	—	5.9	6.8	11.4	21.7	New Caledonia
11.5	13.1	4.4	9.8	3,321	23.0	3.4	21.9	0.1	11.6	5.2	13.9	20.9	New Zealand
—	—	—	27.5	2,446	40.5	1.2	6.1	—	7.7	5.1	9.7	29.7	Nicaragua
—	40	—	23.1	2,138	67.1	6.6	2.7	—	3.1	1.5	3.6	15.4	Niger
...	...	...	...	2,257	42.7	29.1	1.6	0.1	1.0	3.9	10.1	11.5	Nigeria
...	...	...	...	...	...	...	...	...	...	...	...	...	Niue
...	...	...	...	...	...	...	...	...	...	...	...	...	Norfolk Island
16.0	9.0	8.1[9]	10.0	3,191	23.0	5.3	12.2	2.2	16.3	4.2	18.3	18.5	Norway
...	...	...	...	...	...	...	...	...	...	...	...	...	Oman
2.5	3.8	0.7	13.8	2,281	63.6	0.5	1.7	0.1	7.1	6.0	8.5	12.2	Pakistan
6.8	8.5	5.8[9]	9.2	2,313	45.0	3.7	8.2	0.3	5.0	10.1	9.6	18.1	Panama
6.5	5.4	3.3	11.6	2,269	15.4	34.5	6.3	1.9	0.6	26.0	4.4	10.9	Papua New Guinea

Household budgets and consumption (continued)

country	income						consumption expenditure						
	year, type of data[a]	annual average in $U.S.	by source (percent)				year, type of data[b]	by kind or end use (percent of household or personal budget)					
			wages, salaries	self employment	transfer payments[c]	other[d]		food[e]	housing	clothing[f]	health care	energy	education
Paraguay	1978h[3]	...	41.6	56.9[4]	1.5	—	1964h[1,42]	48.7	16.4	9.7	3.4	—	1.5
Peru	1972h	1,322	...	...	...	...	1980c	38.1[20]	15.6[6]	7.3	2.6	[6]	—
Philippines	1971h	575	44.8	40.3	2.1	12.8	1980h	52.8	11.3[6]	6.2	2.8	[6]	2.7
Pitcairn Island	...	...	...	...	...	...	...	...	...	...	...	...	...
Poland	1980h	11,600	83.5	—	—	16.5	1980h	38.9	12.3	14.9	3.5	2.6	[9]
Portugal	1976h[3]	...	56.4	25.9[4]	17.7	—	1974h	47.8	10.5	8.8	2.7	3.1	[9]
Puerto Rico	1982h	14,496	...	...	...	...	1982h	29.4	24.7[6]	9.0	6.3	[6]	—
Qatar	...	...	...	...	...	...	...	...	...	...	...	...	...
Réunion	1982h	3,672	27.9	8.5	63.6	—	1977h	41.1	21.6[6,40]	9.1	4.8	[6]	[9]
Romania	...	...	...	...	...	...	1980h[28]	45.6	10.8	17.5	0.9	—	5.4
Rwanda	1982h	1,200	16.5	71.0	9.5	3.0	1981c[43]	55.6[20]	7.6[44]	7.5	...	6.6	...
St. Christopher and Nevis	...	...	...	...	...	...	1973c	77.0	—	10.0	—	5.0	—
St. Helena and Ascension	...	...	...	...	...	...	1977c	63.4	10.1	8.1	—	5.6	...
St. Lucia	...	...	...	...	...	...	...	...	...	...	...	...	...
St. Pierre and Miquelon	...	...	...	...	...	...	...	...	...	...	...	...	...
St. Vincent and the Grenadines	...	...	...	...	...	...	1981c	60.5	11.1	6.9	—	6.4	—
San Marino	...	...	...	...	...	...	...	...	...	...	...	...	...
São Tomé and Príncipe	...	...	...	...	...	...	...	...	...	...	...	...	...
Saudi Arabia	...	...	...	...	...	...	1980c[15,30]	52.2	17.2[23]	6.6	2.1	1.8	1.1
Senegal	...	...	...	...	...	...	1980c	56.0	8.7	11.9	4.0	5.8	...
Seychelles	1979p[45]	2,597	...	...	...	...	1979c[1]	39.3	...	...	...	...	60.7 —
Sierra Leone	1970h	350	27.9	61.6	—	10.5	1978p	55.1[20]	7.4[6]	12.9	1.3	[6]	[9]
Singapore	1980h	7,052	...	...	...	...	1982p	31.8	10.2[6]	10.3	3.1	[6]	[9]
Solomon Islands	1981h	2,130	...	...	...	...	1982c[46]	56.5[20]	15.5[6]	5.0	—	[6]	—
Somalia	1978p[10,16]	1,167	...	...	...	...	1979c[1]	62.3[20]	15.3[23]	5.6	—	4.3	—
South Africa	1982h[3]	...	82.7	—	4.9	12.4	1980h	31.2	12.1[6]	8.9	3.7	[6]	0.1
South West Africa/Namibia	1980p	...	78.6	—	2.8	18.6	...	...	...	...	...	...	...
Spain	...	...	...	...	...	...	1975h	44.2	8.8[23]	7.7	2.6	6.1	2.2
Sri Lanka	1973h	611	72.3	11.7	2.8	13.2	1980h	58.1	7.3	6.1	1.8	2.0	0.1
Sudan, The	1968h	540	35.8	53.0	—	11.2	1975h	66.8	10.6[6]	8.4	2.1	[6]	0.1
Suriname	...	...	...	...	...	...	1969h[1]	40.0	9.5	11.0	3.6	6.9	2.6
Swaziland	...	...	...	...	...	...	1980c[47]	39.3[20]	—	10.0	8.0	6.5	...
Sweden	1981h	14,546	47.5	—	21.4	31.1	1980h	24.2	19.1	7.4	1.5	5.7	[9]
Switzerland	1982h[10,16]	30,045	86.0	—	...	14.0	1982h	15.9[19]	12.6	5.4	5.6	3.9	[9]
Syria	...	...	...	...	...	...	1972h	52.6	13.6	10.8	2.8	4.2	1.1
Taiwan	1981h	7,401	62.7	24.1	—	13.2	1983h	32.8	28.9[6]	6.8	—	[6]	[9]
Tanzania	1969h	173	33.8	59.8	—	6.4	1982c	54.3[20]	8.6[23]	10.8	4.5	6.6	0.8
Thailand	1976h	1,134[48]	28.3	...	3.9	67.8	1980h	51.7	6.1[6]	10.8	—	[6]	[9]
Togo	1980h	452	...	...	...	...	1972h	56.1	13.7[6]	8.5	2.2	[6]	0.7
Tokelau	...	...	...	...	...	...	...	...	...	...	...	...	...
Tonga	...	...	...	...	...	...	...	...	...	...	...	...	...
Trinidad and Tobago	1976h	2,288	...	...	...	...	1976h	31.4	18.0	16.1	2.5	1.9	1.7
Trust Territory of the Pacific Is.	...	...	...	...	...	...	...	...	...	...	...	...	...
Tunisia	...	...	...	...	...	...	1980h	41.8	29.0	8.5	—	—	[9]
Turkey	1979h[15]	...	38.9	46.8	9.4	4.9	1979h[15]	41.2	25.2	14.8	3.3	—	—
Turks and Caicos Islands	...	...	...	...	...	...	...	...	...	...	...	...	...
Tuvalu	1979h	...	17.9	76.1	—	6.0	...	...	...	...	...	...	...
Uganda	1964h[1,49]	242	88.3	1.8	—9.9—		1964h[1,49]	63.8	9.2	7.8	1.0	—	2.1
U.S.S.R.	1976h[50]	6,494	74.5	0.9	22.3	2.3	1976h	38.6	3.0	18.6	—	0.2	—
United Arab Emirates	...	...	...	...	...	...	...	...	...	...	...	...	...
United Kingdom	1982h	15,603	62.0	7.0	23.0	8.0	1981h	21.7	15.8	7.4	—	—	...
United States	1980h	21,063	66.0[51]	5.2[51]	13.2[51]	15.6[51]	1981c[15]	20.1	21.3	5.2	6.0	14.6	1.8
Uruguay	1980h	9,813	...	...	...	...	1975c	41.3	25.3	12.9	—	—	—
Vanuatu	...	...	...	...	...	...	1975c[52]	55.9[20]	2.2[6]	14.1	10.0[53]	[6]	[53]
Venezuela	1968h[54]	4,370	...	...	...	...	1979h	40.5[20]	5.9[6]	6.3	3.7	[6]	[9]
Vietnam	...	...	...	...	...	...	...	...	...	...	...	...	...
Virgin Islands (U.S.)	...	...	...	...	...	...	1976h[55]	25.3	24.9	5.4	—	6.5	...
Wallis and Futuna	...	...	...	...	...	...	...	...	...	...	...	...	...
Western Sahara	...	...	...	...	...	...	...	...	...	...	...	...	...
Western Samoa	1972h[15]	2,284	71.7	8.7	—	19.6	1981c	58.8	12.0[44]	4.2	—	—	—
Yemen (Aden)	...	...	...	...	...	...	...	...	...	...	...	...	...
Yemen (San'ā')	1973h[3]	...	12.2	—	13.4	74.4	...	...	...	...	...	...	...
Yugoslavia	1976h[56]	3,951	96.1	—	2.6	1.3	1979h	44.1	—	11.7	5.1	6.6	—
Zaire	1982h	209	...	...	...	...	1969h[1]	69.5	10.4	7.5	2.0	—	1.0
Zambia	1981h	908	94.0	—	—	6.0	1977h	37.7[20]	11.0	8.3	1.0	—	2.1
Zimbabwe	1980h	2,628	...	...	...	...	1977h	37.7[20]	11.0[6]	8.3	1.0	[6]	2.1

transportation, communication	furniture utensils[g]	recreation[h]	personal effects, other[i]	food consumption: daily available calories per capita	percent of total calories derived from: cereals	potatoes, cassavas	meat, poultry	fish	eggs, milk	fruits, vegetables[j]	fats, oils[k]	other[l]	country
4.5	6.2	2.3	7.3	2,878	30.4	17.6	13.1	0.1	3.4	15.7	7.2	12.5	Paraguay
9.8	7.0	7.4	12.2	2,270	42.2	10.4	4.1	1.3	4.5	9.2	9.6	18.7	Peru
3.3	7.4	1.6	11.9	2,216	60.9	6.7	4.3	3.2	1.7	5.1	4.9	13.2	Philippines
...	...	...	...	...	...	...	...	...	...	...	...	...	Pitcairn Island
6.6	—	10.0[9]	11.2	3,619	33.1	9.6	12.1	1.2	13.5	3.2	11.5	15.8	Poland
7.4	4.1	4.1[9]	11.5	3,401	37.3	6.8	10.2	1.7	4.8	7.3	16.2	15.7	Portugal
16.3	—	7.2	7.1										Puerto Rico
				3,050	48.8	0.8	10.1	0.5	7.1	11.6	7.8	13.3	Qatar
10.8	40	12.6[9]	—	2,666	49.7	1.9	8.3	1.5	4.5	7.8	12.3	14.0	Réunion
8.6	7.8	—	3.4	3,448	50.1	4.6	10.2	0.4	8.3	5.3	8.0	13.1	Romania
				2,264	18.2	28.8	1.0	—	0.6	46.0	1.1	4.3	Rwanda
4.3	9.4	—	9.0										St. Christopher and Nevis
—	8.0	—	—										St. Helena and Ascension
—	5.0	—	7.7	2,233	29.1	8.6	9.5	2.4	5.3	12.8	13.7	18.6	St. Lucia
...	...	...	...	...	...	...	...	...	...	...	...	...	St. Pierre and Miquelon
—	5.4	—	9.7	2,328	32.3	9.7	4.6	1.0	6.2	8.3	8.9	29.0	St. Vincent and the Grenadines
...	...	...	...	...	...	...	...	...	...	...	...	...	San Marino
				2,093	35.0	15.2	2.0	0.1	1.9	2.6	6.0	37.2	São Tomé and Príncipe
4.5	5.9	—	8.6	2,233	49.1	0.1	6.6	—	7.4	14.4	9.4	13.0	Saudi Arabia
5.4	1.7	0.7	5.8	2,272	62.1	3.0	3.0	2.9	2.1	1.2	11.5	14.2	Senegal
													Seychelles
9.2	8.0	3.8[9]	2.3	2,088	58.4	5.2	1.1	2.2	0.1	2.1	18.4	12.5	Sierra Leone
17.2	9.9	15.2[9]	2.3	3,074	47.5	0.1	10.1	2.5	5.4	6.1	7.8	20.5	Singapore
11.0	—	—	12.0	2,169	21.3	43.1	3.9	2.2	1.2	3.5	8.0	16.8	Solomon Islands
—	—	—	12.1	2,228	44.9	1.3	12.2	—	19.5	2.9	6.6	12.6	Somalia
18.1	8.9	5.6	10.9	2,921	55.0	1.4	7.1	0.1	5.6	2.6	6.7	11.5	South Africa
				2,183	47.7	14.5	13.8	—	4.8	1.8	10.0	7.4	South West Africa/Namibia
9.4	5.4	7.6	5.9	3,152	25.0	7.3	13.3	2.0	9.4	6.3	17.2	19.5	Spain
9.7	3.4	3.6	7.9	2,059	61.9	4.6	0.4	1.0	2.3	4.9	3.3	21.6	Sri Lanka
2.5	2.4	2.8	4.3	2,274	55.9	1.9	5.3	0.1	6.1	3.7	12.0	15.0	Sudan, The
9.5	6.8	5.8	4.3	2,270	57.0	1.0	4.4	1.4	3.4	3.3	15.2	14.3	Suriname
15.3	9.0	—	11.9	2,357	53.4	2.2	8.1	—	4.9	2.4	6.5	22.5	Swaziland
13.2	7.1	9.9[9]	11.9	3,221	19.7	4.9	16.3	1.8	15.9	4.5	15.2	21.7	Sweden
9.7	4.2	12.7[9]	30.2	3,485	21.2	3.0	17.7	0.5	17.8	5.3	16.6	17.9	Switzerland
2.8	4.6	1.4	6.1	2,685	53.8	1.1	3.3	0.1	4.1	14.6	9.7	13.3	Syria
6.7	—	10.2[9]	14.6	2,749									Taiwan
6.4	6.3	1.6	0.1	2,066	35.0	27.0	2.9	1.5	4.0	14.4	4.9	10.3	Tanzania
10.3	—	4.3[9]	16.8	2,098	68.1	3.0	2.8	2.6	1.1	6.1	2.0	14.3	Thailand
8.6	3.1	0.6	6.5	2,066	39.1	36.1	2.9	0.9	0.3	4.7	5.9	10.1	Togo
...	...	...	...	...	...	...	...	...	...	...	...	...	Tokelau
				3,090	16.5	45.4	11.7	0.9	1.5	1.3	6.4	16.3	Tonga
10.9	7.9	1.3	8.3	2,695	43.8	2.6	6.5	0.7	5.8	7.3	11.4	21.9	Trinidad and Tobago
													Trust Territory of the Pacific Is.
4.9	—	7.6[9]	8.2	2,674	53.8	1.2	3.8	0.4	4.2	8.3	16.3	12.0	Tunisia
5.5	—	6.1	3.9	2,913	55.5	3.2	3.5	0.5	3.9	10.7	9.7	13.0	Turkey
...	...	...	...	...	...	...	...	...	...	...	...	...	Turks and Caicos Islands
...	...	...	...	...	...	...	...	...	...	...	...	...	Tuvalu
2.2	5.4	0.2	8.3	2,110	27.9	14.8	2.7	1.3	2.5	27.8	2.6	20.4	Uganda
—	7.8	23.6	8.2	3,460	39.3	6.8	10.1	1.8	10.3	3.3	10.3	18.1	U.S.S.R
...	...	...	...	...	...	...	...	...	...	...	...	...	United Arab Emirates
14.9	7.5	—	32.7	3,343	20.7	4.9	14.8	0.1	13.7	3.4	16.8	25.6	United Kingdom
15.6	8.0	4.2	3.2	3,578	16.9	3.2	21.2	0.1	12.2	5.3	16.3	24.8	United States
—	—	—	20.5	2,797	31.1	3.8	22.8	—	11.0	2.5	9.8	19.0	Uruguay
9.8	8.0	[53]		2,286	31.1	12.5	14.4	6.7	3.1	4.1	8.2	19.9	Vanuatu
15.6	7.7	9.0[9]	11.3	2,522	34.0	3.6	9.6	1.1	9.0	8.0	9.0	25.7	Venezuela
				2,135	72.9	8.6	4.8	2.2	0.1	3.4	2.0	6.0	Vietnam
11.7	4.3	...	21.8	...									Virgin Islands (U.S.)
...	...	...	...	...	...	...	...	...	...	...	...	...	Wallis and Futuna
...	...	...	...	...	...	...	...	...	...	...	...	...	Western Sahara
9.0	—	—	16.0	2,097	19.6	16.2	9.1	3.1	0.1	14.2	8.0	29.7	Western Samoa
				1,975	61.6	—	2.8	4.5	3.5	9.8	8.3	9.5	Yemen (Aden)
				2,311	64.9	1.2	3.8	—	4.1	5.8	4.2	16.0	Yemen (San'ā')
12.4	9.4	3.9	6.8	3,446	48.4	3.7	8.1	—	7.2	4.7	10.8	17.1	Yugoslavia
4.5	2.7	1.0	1.4	2,305	14.3	57.7	2.0	—	—	7.8	6.8	11.4	Zaire
4.3	—	—	35.6	2,038	68.2	4.9	3.4	0.1	2.3	1.7	3.8	15.6	Zambia
4.3	12.9	—	22.7	2,576	71.9	—	6.2	—	2.1	1.0	4.4	14.4	Zimbabwe

[1]Capital city only. [2]City of Rosario only. [3]Includes non-profit institutions. [4]Includes property income. [5]Wages and salaries includes transfer payments. [6]Housing includes energy. [7]New Providence and Grand Bahama only. [8]New Providence only. [9]Recreation includes education. [10]Salaried employees only. [11]Urban households in the Federal District only. [12]Personal effects and other includes education. [13]Based on a survey of working families in Peking, Tientsin, Shanghai, and 43 other cities. Income used for living expenses only. [14]Rural families only. [15]Urban areas only. [16]Wage-earning employees only. [17]Excludes rent. [18]Includes benefits in kind. [19]Six urban areas only. [20]Includes tobacco. [21]Includes all manufactured products. [22]Low-income population in Banjul and Kombo St. Mary only. [23]Housing includes water. [24]Net income only. [25]Urban areas of eastern region only. [26]Taxpayers only. [27]African population only. [28]Workers only. [29]Nonagricultural households only. [30]Middle income population only. [31]Workers and clerical workers only. [32]Includes cultural activities. [33]Kuwaiti households only. [34]Working population only. [35]Malagasy households only. [36]1962. [37]Leeward Islands only. [38]Melanesians in the capital city only. [39]Includes automobile parts and accessories. [40]Housing includes furniture and utensils. [41]Households of civil servants in nine cities only. [42]Households with three or more wage earners only. [43]Includes Anguilla. [44]Includes household supplies. [45]Formal employees only. [46]Households with an annual income of $4,500 or less. [47]Middle- to high-income families only. [48]Includes nonmoney income. [49]Unskilled African workers only. [50]Industrial wage earners only. [51]Breakdown is for personal income. [52]Urban, low-income households only. [53]Health care includes expenditure on education and recreation. [54]City of Maracaibo only. [55]St. Thomas only. [56]Four-person households only.

Health services

The provision of health services in most countries is a large and growing sector of the national economy as well as one of the principal determinants of the quality of life.

This table summarizes the basic indicators of health manpower, hospitals and health-care utilization, mortality rates that are most indicative of general health services, external controls on health (adequacy of food supply and availability of safe drinking water), and sources and amounts of expenditure on health care. Each datum refers more or less directly to the availability or use of a particular health service in a country, and, while each may be accurate as an overall measure, each may also conceal great differences in availability of the particular service to different segments of population or regions of the country. In the United States, for example, the availability of physicians ranges from about 107 per 100,000 population in the least well-served state to more than 276 in the best-served, with a rate of 533 per 100,000 in the national capital. These disparities are even more pronounced in most other countries, unless the government has made some special effort to achieve a more even distribution of manpower and facilities. Frequently, even when trained manpower exists and facilities have been created, the country may lose these professionals via the "brain drain" to the countries in which they were trained; low levels of financial support at the national level may leave facilities underserved; or lack of good transportation may prevent those most in need from reaching the clinic or hospital that could help them.

The definitions and limits of data have been made as specific as possible in the compilation of this table. For example, despite wide variation worldwide in the nature of the qualifying or certifying process that permits an individual to represent himself as a physician, organizations such as the World Health Organization (WHO) try to institute international standards for training and qualification. International statistics presented here for persons identified as "physicians" refer to the WHO standards and exclude traditional health practitioners, whatever the local custom with regard to the designation "doctor." Statistics for health manpower in this table uniformly include all those actually working in the health service field, whether in the actual provision of services or in teaching, administration, research, or other tasks. One group of practitioners for whom this type of guideline works less well is that of midwives, whose training and qualifications vary enormously from country to country but who must be included, as they represent, after nurses, perhaps the largest and most important category of health auxiliary worldwide. The statistics here refer to those midwives working in some kind of institutional setting (a hospital, clinic, community health-care centre, or the like) and exclude rural noninstitutional midwives and traditional birth attendants.

Hospitals also differ widely worldwide in terms of staffing and services. In this tabulation, the term hospital refers generally to a permanent facility offering inpatient services and/or nursing care and staffed by at least one physician. Establishments offering only outpatient or custodial care are excluded. These statistics are broken down into data for general hospitals (those providing care in more than one specialty), specialized facilities (with care in only one specialty), local medical centres, and rural health-care centres; the last two generally refer to institutions that provide a more limited range of medical or nursing care, often less than full-time. Hospital data are further analyzed into three categories of administrative classification: public, private nonprofit, and private for profit. Although it is not possible to draw valid conclusions from these distributions about the relative extent of governmental support for health-care activities between several countries, or about the origin and nature of the subsidization of nonprofit facilities (private or governmental, national or local), a high proportion of private for profit facilities will usually mark a country with both good health services and a population with the income to command them. The situation may be less clear where national health programs

Health services

country	health personnel							hospitals									
	year	physicians	dentists	nurses	pharma-cists	midwives	popu-lation per physi-cian	year	number	kinds (%)				ownership (%)			hos-pital beds per 10,000 pop.
										gen-eral	spe-cial-ized	clinics	rural	govern-ment	private non-profit	private for profit	
Afghanistan	1981	1,215[1]	8[1]	847[1]	245[1]	687[1]	13,467	1981	344	24.1[2]	[2]	75.9	[2]	72.3	27.8	—	5
Albania	1980	3,000	900[5]	2,863[6]	532[6]	5,098[6]	890	1978	928	5.2	85.5[6]	—	9.3[6]	100.0[6]	—	—	66
Algeria	1980	5,200	1,483[9]	9,757[1,9]	1,058[9]	1,004[1,9]	3,621	1979	367	46.9	2.4	50.7	—	85.3	4.4	10.3	25
American Samoa	1981	25[1]	7[1]	22[1]	1[1]	1[1]	1,280	1981	1	100.0	—	—	—	100.0	—	—	48
Andorra	...	...	...	...	...	...	...	...	...	...	...	...	...	...	...	...	...
Angola	1980	500	...	1,069[12]	87[12]	92[12]	13,958	1972	347	15.6	12.7	30.5	41.2	66.9	29.1	4.0	31
Anguilla	1975	2	1	...	1	11	5,000	1981	5	—	—	80.0	20.0	—	—	—	...
Antigua and Barbuda	1977	29	4	...	15	160	2,414	1978	6	16.6	50.0	16.6	16.6	83.3	—	16.7	88
Argentina	1980	60,000	...	...	...	...	470	1969	2,864	50.0	19.2	30.8	—	45.2[15]	15	54.8	56
Australia	1980	26,140	6,200	70,870	5,400	5,390	559	1981	1,142[16]	...	...	...	...	67.9[16]	9.7[16]	22.4[16]	64[16]
Austria	1981	17,028	2,072	22,774	3,226	1,091	441	1981	321	41.1	57.3	1.6	—	...	...	...	100
Bahamas, The	1980	197	31	...	37	104	1,218	1980	6	16.6	50.0	16.6	16.6	83.3	—	16.7	39
Bahrain	1980	363	26	873	48	113	1,003	1980	12	33.3	33.3	—	33.3	83.3	16.7	—	30
Bangladesh	1981	10,065	248[1]	3,736	...	2,239	8,908	1981	504	19.8	6.2	18.4	45.6	92.1	7.9	—	2
Barbados	1980	200	24[9]	374[9]	...	425[9]	1,245	1980	10	30.0	20.0	—	50.0	80.0	—	20.0	84
Belgium	1981	25,629[18]	4,499	28,250	9,942	1,178	385	1981	521	54.7	45.3	—	—	35.1	64.9[19]	19	94
Belize	1981	55	9	...	...	179	3,036	1979	12	58.3	25.0	—	16.7	100.0	—	—	33[17]
Benin	1980	204	13	499	55	312	17,500	1980	131	4.6	9.9	80.9	4.6	87.8	12.2	—	14
Bermuda	1980	65	32	428	27	...	832	1981	3	33.3	66.7	—	—	...	...	...	80
Bhutan	1977	52	...	...	...	...	21,154	1977	10	...	...	...	...	...	...	...	5
Bolivia	1980	2,853	1,182[22]	1,552[22]	1,902[22]	...	1,963	1975	345	20.6	13.6	27.5	38.3	76.5	3.2	20.3	19
Botswana	1980	111	20	574	10	471	7,378	1980	53	24.5	62.3	13.2	—	84.9	15.1	—	26
Brazil	1980	106,500	15,526[9]	13,342[9]	4,206[9]	...	1,149	1979	17,079	...	...	...	...	...	...	...	40
British Virgin Islands	1978	10	2	21	2	1	1,000	1980	1	100.0	—	—	—	100.0	—	—	26
Brunei	1981	97	12	280	3	115	2,474	1981	5	80.0	—	—	20.0	80.0	20.0	—	26
Bulgaria	1981	22,088	4,984	46,396	3,804	7,894	402	1981	...	...	...	...	...	...	...	...	111
Burkina Faso	1981	127[1]	14[1]	392[1]	46[1]	208	55,858	1977	44	4.5	—	88.7	6.8	100.0	—	—	6
Burma	1981	7,321	410	6,390[1]	80[1]	1,542[1]	4,940	1981	514	59.2	2.9	—	37.9	100.0	—	—	8
Burundi	1980	100	5[9]	303[9]	20[9]	73[9]	42,040	1972	136	2.9	2.2	82.4	12.5	66.9	33.1	—	12[9]
Cameroon	1980	600	21[9]	1,134[9]	107[9]	469[9]	14,303	1981	1,003	5.8	0.5	87.5	6.2	70.1	23.5	6.4	32
Canada	1980	44,000	9,900[5]	140,000[5]	15,709[5]	...	547	1978	1,226	65.8	26.9	7.3	—	93.4	—	6.6	78
Cape Verde	1980	51[1]	3	184[1]	7[1]	91	6,353	1980	21	9.5	4.8	61.9	23.8	100.0	—	—	20
Cayman Islands	1979	16	4	14	3	14	1,062	1979	2	50.0	—	—	50.0	100.0	—	—	28
Central African Republic	1980	99	3	301	18	149	22,434	1979	85	7.1	5.9	69.4	17.6	72.9	—	27.1	17
Chad	1980	100	4[1,5]	713[1,5]	9[1,5]	391[1,5]	44,160	1978	4	100.0	—	—	—	—	—	100.0	8
Chile	1980	6,800	1,477[1,9]	2,780[1,9]	290[1,9]	...	1,616	1980	300	45.3	23.4	—	31.3	78.0	—	22.0	34
China	1981	518,089	...	525,311	22,948	70,904	1,910	1981	15,911	12.2	3.6	—	84.2	100.0	—	—	20
Christmas Island	1981	2[1]	1[1]	5[1]	1[1]	...	1,500	1981	1	...	...	...	...	...	...	...	...
Cocos (Keeling) Islands	1981	1[1]	...	3[1]	...	...	569	1981	1	...	...	...	...	...	...	...	...
Colombia	1980	13,000	4,407[6]	3,326[6]	...	...	2,004	1978	809	88.0	12.0	—	—	80.8	19.2[19]	19	17
Comoros	1978	20	1	19	2	12	16,000	1978	6	33.3	66.7	—	—	100.0	—	—	22
Congo	1980	300	2[5]	785[5]	28[5]	189[5]	5,173	1978	473	0.6	91.8	5.7	1.9	94.9	5.1	—	47
Cook Islands	1981	19	10[1]	52[1]	2[1]	8[1]	1,000	1981	8	12.5	—	—	87.5	100.0	—	—	80
Costa Rica	1980	1,600[27]	448[6,27]	1,112[6]	123[1,6]	...	1,502	1980	39	48.7	28.2	23.1[28]	—	92.3	—	7.7	34
Cuba	1980	15,247	2,953[1,9]	27,062[29]	773[1,9]	...	637	1979	305	30.5	39.7	13.4	16.4	100.0	—	—	41
Cyprus	1981	601	182	423	311	177	1,060	1981	134	3.0	86.6[30]	30	10.4	14.9	0.7	84.4	55
Czechoslovakia	1982	52,493	7,676[17]	98,575[17]	6,874[17]	6,736[17]	293	1982	39.7	57.2	37.8	5.0	—	100.0	—	—	102
Denmark	1980	11,100	4,664[5]	24,023[5]	1,364[5]	694[5]	462	1979	132	87.9	12.1	—	—	89.4	10.6	—	82
Djibouti	1981	56	6	166[1]	7	2[1]	2,196	1973	24	8.3	16.7	58.3	16.7	100.0	—	—	35
Dominica	1978	10	2	68	...	40	8,000	1973	6	16.7	33.3	—	50.0	100.0	—	—	43

have resulted in the extension of government activity into formerly private sectors, such as in the United Kingdom. The statistics referring to number of beds refer to beds that are maintained and staffed on a full-time basis for a succession of inpatients to whom care is provided.

Data on hospital utilization refer to institutions defined as above. Admission and discharge, the two principal points at which statistics may be collected, are the basis for the data on the amount and distribution of care by kind of facility. These data on numbers of patients exclude babies born during a maternal confinement but include persons who die before being discharged. The bed-occupancy and average length-of-stay statistics depend on the concept of a "patient-day," which is the annual total of daily censuses of inpatients. The bed-occupancy rate is the ratio of total patient-days to potential days based on the number of beds; the average length-of-stay rate is the ratio of total patient-days to total admissions.

Two measures that give an excellent indication of the level of ordinary health care in a country are those for infant mortality and for maternal mortality. The former refers to infants who die within a year of birth, the latter to deaths directly attributable to delivery or complications of pregnancy, childbirth, or puerperium (the period immediately following birth). Levels of nutrition and access to safe drinking water are two of the most basic measures of the physical environment in which health-care activities take place. The nutritional data are based on recommendations of the United Nations' Food and Agriculture Organization for the necessary daily intake (in calories) for a moderately active person of average size in a climate of a particular kind (fewer calories are needed in a hot climate) to remain in average good health. Excess intake in the most developed countries ranges to more than 150 percent of what is required to maintain health (the excess usually being construed to diminish, rather than raise, health). The range of deficiency is less dramatic numerically but far more critical to the countries in which deficiencies are chronic, because the

deficiency leads to overall poor health (raising health service needs and costs), to decreased productivity in nearly every area of national economic life, and to the loss of social and economic potential through early mortality. By "safe" water is meant only water that has no substantial quantitites of chemical or biological pollutants, i.e., quantities sufficient to cause "immediate" health problems.

Data on health-care financing are intended to identify the principal sources in each country, as well as to provide a general indication of the absolute amount of expenditure originating with the central government. Expenditures at the national level for social security are excluded.

The following notes further define the column headings:

... Not available.

— None, nil, or not applicable.

a. Bed-occupancy rates may exceed 100% because stays of partial days are counted as full days.

b. It has been assumed that 100% of the population in countries with developed market and centrally planned economies has access to safe water.

c. Figures refer to December 1980 for all Latin-American countries.

d. Figures larger than 20% include cost of medical benefits and exclude cost of insurance.

e. In some countries significant governmental expenditures for health-care services are made at intermediate or local levels. These expenditures may include costs for national health insurance, family-planning programs, and workmen's compensation. Per capita health-care expenditures in 1980 made by all levels of government are totaled for: Belgium $454; Canada $460; Denmark $823; India $2; Norway $721; Portugal $63; Romania $82; Spain $151; Sweden $924; Switzerland $625; the United States $383; and Yugoslavia $127.

admissions or discharges					bed occu- pancy rate[a] (%)	aver- age length of stay (days)	mortality		popu- lation with access to safe water, 1975[b,c] (%)	food supply (% of FAO require- ment) 1980	financing of health care, latest year					country
	by kinds of hospital (%)						infant mortality per 1,000 live births 1982–83	maternal mortality per 100,000 live births 1980–81			health care insurance[d]			public health expendi- tures (% of natl. budget)	public health expendi- tures per capita[e] (U.S.$)	
rate per 10,000 pop.	general	special- ized	clinics	rural							indiv. (% of earn- ings)	em- ployer (% of payroll)	govt. (% of covered earnings)			
69	58.4[3]	40.8[3]	—	0.5[3]	36.6	8	203.0	...	6	73	—	8.0[8]	8.0[8]	...	1.00[4]	Afghanistan
...							49.5[7]	...	—	110	—	8.0[8]	8.0[8]	...	25.00[4]	Albania
537	98.6[10]	1.4[10]	...	—	60.1	10	125.3	...	77	101	4.5[8]	5.5[8]	—	5.6[11]	24.20[11]	Algeria
1,578	100.0	—	—	—	46.6	5	19.0	...	...	...	...	...	...	...	...	American Samoa
...							...	...	—	...	...	...	...	...	...	Andorra
339	51.1	12.6	—	36.3	45.2	15	160.4[7]	113.4[13]	...	83	...	...	...	...	7.00[4]	Angola
...							...	...	...	...	...	...	...	...	...	Anguilla
609	...	...	...	...	77.8	14	31.5[14]	...	...	...	...	...	...	...	...	Antigua and Barbuda
...							47.2[7]	84.5[5]	66	125	3.0	4.5	—	1.7	18.40	Argentina
...							10.3	9.8	—	117	...	—	100.0	10.1	278.50	Australia
2,004	...	...	...	...	...	...	12.8	13.9	—	135	3.2	3.2	50.0	13.0	509.10	Austria
932	77.2	4.9	—	17.9	88.4	13	22.4[17]	40.9[9]	...	...	1.7[8]	7.3[8]	—	13.9	125.40	Bahamas, The
795	63.2	30.6	—	6.2	72.6	9	44.0	...	98[17]	...	...	...	...	7.6	218.20	Bahrain
...							132.0	...	53	84	...	...	...	2.2	0.30	Bangladesh
841	93.9	4.6	—	1.5	92.8	35	22.7[14]	24.1	94	...	3.0[8]	3.0[8]	—	11.2	118.80	Barbados
1,519	91.1	8.9	—	—	86.4	19	11.7	13.1[5]	...	160	1.8	3.8	27.0	1.7	103.10	Belgium
...						9	21.3	...	...	...	...	...	...	13.4	55.70	Belize
...						9	157.0[20]	...	21	103	—	0.2[21]	—	...	4.00[4]	Benin
...					74.1	9	9.0	...	...	...	...	...	...	...	...	Bermuda
...							143.0	...	...	90	...	...	...	4.5[11]	0.90[11]	Bhutan
...							138.2[7]	...	34	87	2.0	8.0	...	8.6	9.20	Bolivia
766	89.1	6.7	4.2	—	90.0[16]	10[16]	96.0[20]	...	29[17]	...	...	...	...	5.4	22.20	Botswana
...							62.2[17]	...	77	109	8.0[6,23]	8.3[6,23]	—	8.5	27.30	Brazil
532	100.0	—	—	—	46.9	8	42.6	...	...	...	...	...	...	...	...	British Virgin Islands
796	98.0	—	—	2.0	35.6	4	12.8	...	...	...	...	...	...	...	...	Brunei
2,063	...	...	...	...	83.5	16	18.9[17]	23.9	—	...	—	30.0[8]	100.0[8]	...	74.00[4]	Bulgaria
47[16]	...	...	...	...	70.3[16]	13[16]	218.8[7]	...	25	95	—	11.5[21]	—	4.9	1.39	Burkina Faso
277	77.8	12.4	—	9.8	79.0	9	105.0	...	17	113	1.0	2.0	1.0	6.4	1.50	Burma
121[24]	49.9	...	...	50.1	66.0[24]	12[24]	126.6[20]	...	2[17]	96	—	—	—	4.7	13.90	Burundi
...							114.5[7]	...	26	105	—	7.0[21,23]	—	5.1	6.40	Cameroon
1,677	93.9	6.0	0.1	...	110.0	19	9.6	6.4[5]	—	127	0.8[25]	3.0[25]	50.0[25]	6.7	156.90	Canada
279	...	...	...	...	71.7	11	104.9[14]	134.0[26]	...	...	7.0	9.0	—	...	...	Cape Verde
1,260	...	—	—	—	50.9	4	...	...	...	...	...	...	...	...	...	Cayman Islands
412	43.9	1.0	37.9	17.2	50.7	8	154.0[20]	...	16	94	—	12.0[21]	—	7.1[11]	3.40[11]	Central African Rep.
...							180.0[20]	...	26	74	—	6.0	—	4.2	1.00	Chad
962	84.9	8.3	—	5.8	73.7	10	23.6	69.9	84	114	4.0	—	—	6.9	30.90	Chile
...							40.0	...	...	107	—	3.0	—	...	7.00[4]	China
...							...	...	...	...	...	...	...	...	...	Christmas Island
...							...	...	...	...	...	...	...	...	...	Cocos (Keeling) Islands
515	88.9	11.1	—	—	57.7	7	39.5[20]	133.5[6]	56	108	2.3	4.7	...	6.9[11]	11.70[11]	Colombia
510	63.2	36.8	—	—	67.9	11	51.7[20]	...	...	...	...	...	...	3.1[11]	0.80[11]	Comoros
...							134.5[20]	...	17	94	—	0.2	—	8.1	4.80	Congo
1,238	70.7	—	—	29.3	43.5[16]	9[16]	29.6	...	...	...	...	...	...	...	...	Cook Islands
1,192	77.8	16.7	5.5[28]	28	75.7	8	18.0[17]	34.7	77	116	4.0	6.8	0.3	5.1	27.40	Costa Rica
1,221	49.4	47.0	1.1	2.5	82.1[16]	9[16]	17.3	45.2[5]	...	122	—	10.0	10.0	...	45.00[4]	Cuba
564[16]	...	...	...	...	72.1[16]	8[16]	17.2	...	92[17]	...	6.0[8]	6.0[8]	100.0[8]	6.1	60.30	Cyprus
1,833	94.0	5.1	0.9	—	83.6	14	16.2	12.9[9]	—	141	—	20.0	100.0	...	151.00[4]	Czechoslovakia
1,831	97.5	2.5	—	—	80.2	13	8.4	3.8	—	133	—	—	100.0	1.7	69.80	Denmark
...							...	...	...	...	...	...	...	5.8	21.30	Djibouti
...							19.6[5]	...	...	...	3.0	5.0	—	8.8	22.10	Dominica

Health services (continued)

country	\<health personnel\> year	physicians	dentists	nurses	pharmacists	midwives	population per physician	\<hospitals\> year	number	kinds (%) general	specialized	clinics	rural	ownership (%) government	private non-profit	private for profit	hospital beds per 10,000 pop.
Dominican Republic	1980	2,200	...	284[1,31]	...	...	2,624	1973	339	80.5	6.8	—	12.7	40.7	0.3	59.0	29
Ecuador	1980	5,000	1,370[6]	1,225[6]	...	...	1,604	1979	261	18.4	9.2	—	72.4	53.6	1.9	44.4	18
Egypt	1981	53,342	7,473	34,371	17,541	2,541	815	1981	1,521	27.7	17.6	15.9	38.8	83.6	4.1	12.3	20
El Salvador	1980	1,500	441[9]	1,562[9]	597[9]	...	3,145	1979	82	15.8	17.1	15.9	51.2	69.5	1.2	29.3	18
Equatorial Guinea	1977	5	...	10[26]	...	2[26]	50,000	1981	...	...	...	...	...	...	...	...	...
Ethiopia	1980	428	16	1,588	93	...	72,582	1980	86	32.6	18.6	—	48.8	88.4	9.3	2.3	4
Faeroe Islands	1981	64[1]	28	243[1]	8[1]	16	688	1981	3	33.3	—	—	66.7	100.0	—	—	81
Falkland Islands	1980	3	1	...	...	5	667	1981	1	...	...	...	...	...	...	...	1
Fiji	1980	284	12	1,284[1,35]	44	35	2,222	1981	27	11.1	33.3	—	55.6	92.6	7.4	—	28
Finland	1981	9,538	4,068	29,293[35]	5,079	35	503	1980	...	...	...	...	...	...	...	...	156
France	1980	104,073	30,321	245,994	36,491	9,382	516	1980	4,430	75.0	16.0	—	9.0	31.4	68.6[19]	[19]	132
French Guiana	1979	59	14	287	18	11	1,186	1979	5	20.0	—	80.0	—	20.0	80.0[19]	[19]	137
French Polynesia	1980	143	47	257[1]	20	15[1]	1,084	1980	31	6.4	—	58.1	35.5	96.8	3.2	—	63
Gabon	1980	200	20[6]	...	28[6]	...	3,960	1975	41	...	...	...	...	...	...	...	76
Gambia, The	1980	100	6[5]	157[5]	2[5]	90[5]	5,910	1978	16	18.8	12.5	—	68.7	87.5	12.5	—	12
Germany, East	1980	33,894	9,709	...	3,549	...	494	1978	570[6]	...	...	...	...	...	...	...	106
Germany, West	1980	139,431	33,240	218,164	28,674	5,566	442	1980	3,234	44.7	55.3	—	—	36.8	33.9	29.3	115
Ghana	1981	1,665	95	9,383	611	6,728	7,245	1979	329	2.7	4.9	54.7	37.7	78.4	13.1	8.5	15
Gibraltar	1982	20	5	79	13	12[6]	1,500	1977	3	...	...	...	...	...	...	...	84
Greece	1981	24,724	7,727	9,255	...	1,728	394	1981	688	30.8	45.5	10.3	13.4	29.9	3.9	66.2	62
Greenland	1980	57	25	463[35]	...	35	877	1970	18	5.6	—	—	94.4	100.0	...	...	133
Grenada	1979	34	5	259	15	107[5]	2,882	1980	6	...	...	...	...	...	...	...	53
Guadeloupe	1978	313	71	821	108	55	1,054	1978	10	60.0	30.0	—	10.0	...	...	...	70
Guam	1980	70	33	230	28	1	1,714	1979	4	25.0	75.0	—	—	...	...	...	19
Guatemala	1980	2,800	...	621[1,9]	...	...	2,543	1973	159	38.4	25.8	32.7	3.1	76.7	—	23.3	22
Guinea	1981	100[1]	2[1]	64[1]	3[1]	4[1]	8,100	1976	314	1.9	—	87.9	10.1	100.0	—	—	17
Guinea-Bissau	1980	108[1]	2[1]	56[1]	3[1]	2[1]	7,306	1981	17	11.8	—	—	88.2	100.0	—	—	19
Guyana	1980	100[1]	12[1,9]	400[1,9]	32[1,9]	546[9]	8,170	1979	55	20.0	12.7	27.3	40.0	87.3	3.6	9.1	46
Haiti	1980	900	73[1,9]	627[1,9]	6[1,9]	100[9]	5,994	1980	52	73.1	11.5	15.4	—	55.8	36.5	7.7	8
Honduras	1980	1,200	183[9]	626[9]	392[9]	...	3,180	1980	35	51.4	11.5	—	37.1	60.0	—	40.0	13
Hong Kong	1981	4,097	863[27]	5,510	388[27]	7,185	1,258	1981	70	44.3	15.7	38.6	1.4	48.6	27.1	24.3	41
Hungary	1983	32,476	3,383[37]	65,200[37]	3,441[37]	2,602[37]	329	1983	...	...	...	...	...	...	...	...	90
Iceland	1980	488	168	1,161	78	154	467	1980	46	54.3	41.4	4.3	—	...	...	...	164
India	1981	268,712[27]	8,648[27]	150,339[27]	155,621[27]	144,820[27]	2,545	1981	8,626	78.9	—	—	21.1	...	...	...	8
Indonesia	1981	15,400	2,500[9]	37,693[35]	1,800[9]	35	9,774	1978	1,169	14.7	8.3	39.4	37.6	30.2	23.0	46.8	7
Iran	1981	15,182	2,218	7,256	3,000	1,765	2,590	1981	585	...	...	...	...	67.0	13.3	19.7	16
Iraq	1981	7,634	1,387	503[1]	2,132	2,267	1,772	1981	205	56.6	25.8	—	17.6	94.6	—	5.4	19
Ireland	1981	4,443	1,029	24,390[1,35]	2,068	35	774	1980	209	33.5	37.8	1.4	27.3	63.2	21.5	15.3	97
Israel	1981	9,800	1,700	14,300[35]	2,200	35	403	1981	52	71.2	28.8	—	—	32.7	55.8	11.5	33
Italy	1981	42,150[40]	...	...	43,500[9,27]	...	1,334	1981	1,826	73.7	26.3	—	—	62.8	37.2[19]	[19]	94
Ivory Coast	1980	500	24[26]	2,748[26]	115[26]	474[26]	16,108	1975	61	13.1	3.3	—	83.6	98.4	—1.6—		13
Jamaica	1980	716	54	2,124[23]	181	485	3,061	1980	35	80.00	20.0	—	—	85.7	—14.3—		30
Japan	1981	154,578	52,369	285,378	95,319	25,538	761	1981	9,224	88.5	11.5	—	—	16.4	3.4	80.2	116
Jordan	1981	1,966	434	604	647	216	1,711	1981	35	77.1	22.9	—	—	40.0	2.9	57.1	8
Kampuchea	1971	438	71	2,786	79	478	15,909	1971	94	35.1	36.2	—	28.7	57.4	2.2	40.4	11
Kenya	1981	2,057[27]	197[27]	6,892[27]	84[27]	...	8,336	1981	483	...	...	...	...	...	...	...	16
Kiribati	1981	16[1]	2[1]	118[1]	1[1]	6[1]	3,688	1981	32	3.1	—	—	96.9	100.0	...	...	48
Korea, North	1979	40,750[43]	43	...	...	...	429[43]	1981	...	...	...	...	...	...	...	...	120
Korea, South	1981	26,875	3,947	43,605	25,311	5,115	1,441	1981	6,988	...	...	...	...	...	...	...	16
Kuwait	1981	2,133	203	6,348	322	620	686	1980	12[16]	...	...	...	...	66.7[16]	33.3[16]	...	22[16]
Laos	1980	200	1[31]	423[1]	16[1]	20[31]	17,290	1975	38	...	...	...	...	...	...	...	10
Lebanon	1980	5,000	730[9]	2,566[9]	1,002[9]	574[9]	530	1973	130	...	...	...	...	...	...	...	40
Lesotho	1980	81	3	421	5	...	16,069	1980	104	—18.3—		—81.7—		40.9[6]	59.1[6]	...	16
Liberia	1980	161	21	567	4	114	11,634	1980	85	...	...	...	...	60.0	—40.0—		13
Libya	1981	4,690[1]	314[1]	5,346[1]	420[1]	1,080[1]	660	1981	74	...	...	...	...	...	...	...	50
Liechtenstein	1981	18	7	...	...	...	1,389	1981	...	...	...	...	...	...	...	...	...
Luxembourg	1981	495	113	1,055	127	43	735	1981	25	84.0	16.0	—	—	52.0	44.0	4.0	119
Macau	1981	293	105	460	5	7[1]	1,000	1977	4	50.0	50.0	—	—	...	...	...	61
Madagascar	1981	901	52	770	87	839	9,939	1981	749	0.8	1.1	75.7	22.4	100.0	—	—	20
Malawi	1981	121	6	402[35]	11	35	52,645	1981	294	15.6	2.4	72.1	9.9	61.9	38.1	—	17
Malaysia	1980	3,981	389[6]	5,969[6]	108[6]	2,532[1,6]	3,497	1981	163[45]	20.2[45]	50.4[45]	—	29.4[45]	39.9[45]	—	60.1[45]	27[45]
Maldives	1981	8[1]	...	8[1]	2[1]	...	19,625	1977	1	100.0	—	—	—	100.0	—	—	3
Mali	1980	264[1]	15[1]	715[1]	22[1]	272[1]	26,447	1980	192	0.5	81.3	—	18.2	100.0	—	—	6
Malta	1980	400	44[26]	837[26]	293[26]	95[26]	910	1983	7	28.6	71.4	—	—	...	...	...	101
Martinique	1979	364	101	876	138	102	879	1979	17	17.6	11.9	17.6	52.9	82.3	—	17.7	136
Mauritania	1980	100	4[6]	192[6]	6[6]	19[6]	15,020	1977	12	8.3	—	—	91.7	100.0	—	—	4
Mauritius	1983	634	24[1]	1,472[1]	75	622[1]	1,569	1983	24	29.2	20.8	12.5	37.5	50.0	—50.0—		31[14]
Mayotte	1980	9	1	51	1	2	5,264	1980	2	...	...	...	...	...	...	...	16
Mexico	1980	38,000	1,879[22]	17,394[22]	112[22]	532[22]	1,773	1974	1,575	47.3	10.6	26.2	15.9	...	...	...	12
Monaco	1981	58	30	195	54	6[1]	448	1981	1	100.0	—	—	—	100.0	—	—	140
Mongolia	1981	3,881[1]	70[1]	7,097[1]	269[1]	257[1]	441	1981	1,659	2.1	5.4	71.9	20.6	100.0	—	—	111
Montserrat	1978	6	1	30	—	...	1,833	1978	1	...	...	...	...	...	...	...	52
Morocco	1981	1,153	17	3,357	125	56	17,906	1981	143	19.5	23.8	45.5	11.2	100.0	—	—	12
Mozambique	1980	309	16[1]	2,156	8[1]	...	33,883	1980	325	3.1	1.2	87.7	8.0	100.0	—	—	13
Nauru	1977	10	2[48]	...	1[48]	9[48]	700	1971	2	100.0	—	—	—	50.0	50.0	—	300
Nepal	1980	487	17[1]	438[1]	1[1]	...	28,768	1980	68	88.2	11.8	—	—	82.4	17.6	—	2
Netherlands, The	1983	28,807	6,271	34,500[5]	1,672	974	498	1983	2,051	—45.6—		—54.4—		...	...	...	101
Netherlands Antilles	1975	164	34	...	17	21	1,463	1975	...	—100.0—				...	...	...	85
New Caledonia	1981	168	49	227	...	23	851	1981	38	10.5	7.9	39.5	42.1	92.1	—	7.9	107
New Zealand	1980	4,880	1,145	15,381	2,510	19	635	1981	264[16]	...	...	...	...	40.5[16]	—	59.5[16]	72[16]
Nicaragua	1980	1,212[1]	190[1]	808[1]	...	...	2,228	1976	67	34.3	9.1	41.7	14.9	46.2	—	53.8	21
Niger	1980	100	10[5]	1,080[5]	1[5]	88[5]	55,280	1978	212	1.9	0.5	94.8	2.8	97.2	2.8	—	6
Nigeria	1980	8,037	285	27,941	2,816	27,983	9,591	1980	2,374[49]	25.2	—	74.8	—	...	...	...	7[49]
Niue	1980	2[1]	3[1]	21[1]	...	2[1]	1,500	1980	1	100.0	—	—	—	100.0	—	—	210
Norfolk Island	1981	2[1]	...	8[1]	1[1]	1[1]	1,000	1981	1	...	...	...	...	...	...	...	110

rate per 10,000 pop.	general	specialized	clinics	rural	bed occupancy rate (%)	average length of stay (days)	infant mortality per 1,000 live births 1982–83	maternal mortality per 100,000 live births 1980–81	population with access to safe water, 1975 (%)	food supply (% of FAO requirement) 1980	indiv. (% of earnings)	employer (% of payroll)	govt. (% of covered earnings)	public health expenditures (% of natl. budget)	public health expenditures per capita (U.S.$)	country
59.8[32]	73.1[32]	16.7[32]	—	10.2[32]	59.8[32]	7[32]	73.1[16]	...	40	105	2.5	7.0	2.5	9.0	16.70	Dominican Republic
470	...	...	...	...	58.0	8	86.0[7]	216.3[5]	34	88	5.0	1.0	—	8.7	20.50	Ecuador
378[16]	...	...	...	...	77.1[16]	7[16]	74.2	82.3[5]	66	117	1.0	4.0	—	3.0	5.90	Egypt
...	...	...	...	...	...	...	44.0[17]	70.6	55	99	2.5	6.3	—	8.7	11.40	El Salvador
...					...	...	148.5[7]	...	...	...	...	...	...	...	...	Equatorial Guinea
1,790	76.9	—	—	23.1	95.8	11[33]	150.0[7]	...	6[34]	76	—	—	—	4.0	1.10	Ethiopia
1,680[36]	...	...	...	...	58.0	16	7.0	...	—	...	...	...	...	...	...	Faeroe Islands
...	...	...	...	...	41.7	18	...	...	...	...	...	...	...	...	...	Falkland Islands
997	59.4	10.2	—	30.4	77.1	8	28.0	52.4[5]	35[17]	...	...	...	...	8.1	40.00	Fiji
2,060	...	...	...	...	78.5	22	6.5	3.5[9]	—	118	1.0	1.8	100.0	10.5	316.40	Finland
1,751[6]	100.0[6]	—	—	—	79.2[6]	14[6]	9.3	12.9	—	134	4.5	4.5	...	15.0	623.90	France
2,020	80.0	—	—	20.0	71.3	18	28.8[17]	...	...	...	...	...	...	...	...	French Guiana
1,283	68.4	—	3.3	28.3	60.4	11	40.9[17]	...	...	...	...	...	...	...	...	French Polynesia
488	...	...	...	...	23.6	13	121.6[20]	...	1[17]	...	—	11.0	—	...	64.00[4]	Gabon
137[16]	...	...	...	...	...	...	203.5[20]	...	12[17]	...	—	—	—	6.3	6.90	Gambia, The
1,383	...	...	...	...	74.0	21	12.3	14.7	—	144	10.0	12.5[36]	—	...	251.00	Germany, East
1,653	86.0	14.0	—	—	85.1	22	11.6	20.0	—	133	3.5	3.5	—	19.8	751.90	Germany, West
...	...	...	...	...	...	...	107.3[20]	...	35	88	5.0[8]	11.5[8]	—	7.0	10.20	Ghana
1,192	...	...	...	...	46.5	12	...	...	—	...	...	...	...	...	...	Gibraltar
1,179	63.5	30.6	5.8	0.1	69.0	13	14.3	11.4	—	147	2.3	4.5	—	8.8	99.40	Greece
2,252	24.4	—	—	75.6	76.2	16	32.4	...	...	...	...	...	...	...	...	Greenland
...	...	...	...	...	...	...	15.4[9]	...	...	...	...	...	...	15.6	18.60	Granada
1,263	93.1	5.1	—	1.8	86.4	18	26.3[17]	106.4[5]	...	...	...	...	...	...	...	Guadeloupe
640	97.6	2.4	—	—	78.8	8	11.0[17]	...	...	...	...	...	...	...	...	Guam
256[16]	...	...	...	...	...	...	65.9[14]	90.9	40	93	2.0	4.0	25.0	10.9	15.30	Guatemala
...	...	...	...	...	...	...	171.5[7]	...	10	77	—	3.2	—	...	3.00[4]	Guinea
...	...	...	...	...	...	...	154.3[7]	...	...	...	...	...	...	...	...	Guinea-Bissau
326[24]	59.8	—	—	40.2	57.5[24]	11[24]	45.9[5]	153.4[31]	15	...	4.8	7.2	—	5.7	14.50	Guyana
...	...	...	...	...	...	...	126.9[20]	...	14	96	2.0	4.0	20.0	9.8[11]	1.90[11]	Haiti
429	75.6	16.7	—	7.7	70.2	8	95.4[7]	...	24	...	2.5[8]	5.0[8]	2.5[8]	8.0	9.80	Honduras
1,320	92.8	3.6	3.6	0.02	81.9	9	10.0	8.0	...	128	—	100.0	—	...	110.00[4]	Hong Kong
1,906	...	...	...	...	80.7[17]	14	19.7	20.9	—	134	3.0	24.0	40.0	...	110.00[4]	Hungary
2,244	84.0	14.2	1.8	—	98.9	26	7.7	22.8	—	87	2.0	—	100.0	20.6[11]	758.90[11]	Iceland
...	...	...	...	...	...	...	117.0	...	16[17]	87	2.2	4.4	25.0	1.7	0.60	India
65[16]	...	...	...	...	55.1[16]	9[16]	106.0	...	12	110	2.0	5.0	2.0	2.5	2.90	Indonesia
...	...	...	...	...	...	...	100.0	...	51	81	7.0[8]	20.0[8]	3.0[8]	4.4	35.40	Iran
707	69.4	29.2	—	1.4	55.0	5	84.0[7]	...	62	111	5.0	12.0[38]	—	...	21.00[4]	Iraq
1,300[16]	...	...	...	...	...	...	10.6	17.2[5]	—	148	1.0	1.0	25.0	15.2[11]	340.40[11]	Ireland
1,568[39]	97.6	2.4	—	—	91.6[39]	7[39]	15.6[17]	5.3	—	118	0.7	5.7	—	3.5	144.90	Israel
1,740	90.6	9.4	—	—	69.1	13	12.7	17.1[5]	—	150	0.3	10.6	...	12.7	411.90	Italy
171	...	...	...	...	74.9[16,41]	11[16,41]	132.0[20]	...	19	112	—	5.5	—	3.9	15.40	Ivory Coast
6	80.8	19.1	—	—	72.0[16]	7[16]	16.2[14]	135.7	86	119	2.5	2.5	2.5	7.8	43.90	Jamaica
619	97.8	2.2	—	—	82.2	56	6.7	20.5	—	124	4.2	5.3[42]	20.0	...	378.00[4]	Japan
455	88.1	11.9	—	—	62.8	4	75.1[7]	...	61	96	—	—	—	4.1	28.50	Jordan
...	...	...	...	...	...	...	157.0	...	...	88	—	—	—	...	...	Kampuchea
...	...	...	...	...	...	...	92.0[7]	...	17	88	—	—	—	7.8	8.80	Kenya
611	49.8	—	—	51.2	50.4	14	42.0[9]	...	...	...	...	...	...	...	...	Kiribati
...	...	...	...	...	...	...	36.7[20]	...	—	126	...	...	...	...	3.00[4]	Korea, North
...	...	...	...	...	...	...	34.0	...	71	128	1.5	1.5	—	1.5	3.50	Korea, South
815[16]	...	...	...	...	...	...	22.8	14.5[9]	89	...	—	—	100.0	4.9	309.00	Kuwait
100	...	...	...	...	19.7	7	121.0	...	48[17]	97	...	...	...	...	1.00[4]	Laos
...	...	...	...	...	...	...	13.6[20]	...	92[17]	100	1.5	5.5	25.0	...	...	Lebanon
410[6]	20.8[6]	0.4[6]	6.2[6]	72.6[6]	79.6[16]	10[16]	107.0[20]	...	17	107	...	...	—	3.1[11]	6.60[11]	Lesotho
...	...	...	...	...	...	...	159.2[20]	...	20	114	—	—	—	7.6	12.80	Liberia
806	...	...	...	...	48.7	11	106.9[7]	...	100	147	1.0	1.4	1.6	...	105.00[4]	Libya
...	...	...	...	...	...	...	6.1[17]	...	...	...	...	...	...	...	...	Liechtenstein
1,615	97.8	2.2	—	—	79.7	21	7.2	24.0[9]	—	...	4.0	4.0	50.0[36]	2.2	133.60	Luxembourg
...	...	...	...	...	...	...	11.6	...	...	...	...	...	...	5.7[11,44]	17.30[11,44]	Macau
699[16]	...	...	...	...	57.9[16]	21[6]	53.2[17]	...	25	109	—	8.3	—	8.1	3.00	Madagascar
379[16]	...	...	...	...	83.8[16]	8[16]	130.0[14]	...	33	94	—	—	—	5.5	4.00	Malawi
635[46]	...	...	...	...	...	...	40.0	...	62	121	—	—	100.0	6.5	22.90	Malaysia
149	...	...	...	...	...	...	78.5	...	...	...	...	...	...	...	...	Maldives
178	54.9	37.5	—	7.6	58.8	7	120.9[20]	...	9	85	—	2.0	—	4.8	1.60	Mali
...	...	...	...	...	...	...	14.9	68.2[5]	...	...	8.3	8.3	8.3	10.0	111.00	Malta
1,841	6.0	6.0	11.3	13.7	84.2	23	23.0[17]	29.6[26]	...	...	...	...	...	...	...	Martinique
115	...	...	...	...	97.8	5	148.5[7]	...	17[17]	97	—	2.0	—	2.8	4.30	Mauritania
1,122[14]	76.4[14]	6.4[14]	0.1[14]	17.1[14]	84.5[14,32]	8[14,32]	30.2	110.4	...	...	—	—	100.0	7.0	23.40	Mauritius
...	...	...	...	...	...	...	...	...	...	...	...	...	...	...	...	Mayotte
...	...	...	...	...	...	...	38.5[18]	103.4[5]	50	121	2.3	5.6	20.0[47]	2.4	12.70	Mexico
2,837	100.0	—	—	—	82.8	15	...	...	...	...	...	...	...	...	...	Monaco
2,508	25.9	33.0	1.1	40.0	89.1	14	49.0	...	21	111	...	...	...	...	11.00[4]	Mongolia
...	...	...	...	...	...	...	...	...	...	...	...	...	...	...	...	Montserrat
225	59.0	20.3	11.8	8.9	66.4	13	114.4[7]	...	51[18]	110	0.2	0.4	—	3.4	10.40	Morocco
106[16]	...	...	...	...	70.2[16]	9[16]	119.6[7]	...	...	70	...	...	...	...	...	Mozambique
2,660	100.0	...	...	...	...	...	31.2[17]	...	...	...	—	—	100.0	...	...	Nauru
46[16]	...	...	...	...	61.5[16]	7[16]	143.0	...	9	86	—	—	—	5.1	0.90	Nepal
1,179	—97.6—		—2.4—		90.8	28	8.3	7.8	—	131	5.3	13.7	...	11.7	639.40	Netherlands, The
...	...	...	...	...	...	...	14.0[14]	...	...	...	...	...	...	7.9	42.90	Netherlands Antilles
1,468	77.9	3.0	3.2	15.9	57.6	16	21.9	...	...	...	...	...	...	...	...	New Caledonia
...	...	...	...	...	...	...	12.0	13.9	—	126	—	—	100.0	15.3	417.70	New Zealand
83[16]	100.0	...	...	...	62.0[16]	9[16]	101.7[14]	...	38	99	2.3	6.0	0.3	14.6	33.60	Nicaragua
...	...	...	...	...	...	...	151.4[7]	...	27	92	—	11.0[21]	—	4.1	3.60	Niger
2,100	100.0	—	—	—	56.7	14	140.5[7]	...	20[17]	91	6.0	6.0	—	2.4[11]	2.20[11]	Nigeria
...	...	...	...	...	...	...	...	...	...	...	...	...	...	...	...	Niue
...	...	...	...	...	...	...	...	...	...	...	...	...	...	...	...	Norfolk Island

Health services (continued)

country	health personnel							hospitals		kinds (%)				ownership (%)			hospital beds per 10,000 pop.
	year	physicians	dentists	nurses	pharmacists	midwives	population per physician	year	number	general	specialized	clinics	rural	government	private non-profit	private for profit	
Norway	1981	8,311	3,484	28,464	2,761[50]	694	493	1981	928	9.1	87.6[51]	3.3	—	68.0	32.0[19]	[19]	150
Oman	1981	605	24	1,211	65	23[1]	1,519	1981	35	37.1	2.9	11.4	48.6	100.0	—	—	20
Pakistan	1982	29,931[27]	1,018[14]	10,554[27]	1,673[14]	9,932[14]	2,911	1982	614[16]	...	...	...	...	74.0[16]	0.7[16]	25.3[16]	6
Panama	1980	1,700	250[5]	1,337[5]	157[5]	...	1,127	1978	67	...	...	...	...	79.1	—	20.9	38
Papua New Guinea	1980	192	16	1,681	9	...	16,052	1980	390	5.1	—	53.6	41.2	46.2	53.8	—	41
Paraguay	1980	1,800	855[9]	336[9]	860[9]	224[9]	1,802	1975	143	63.6	4.9	—	31.5	91.6	8.4	—	14
Peru	1980	12,432	3,687	10,065	3,457	2,171	1,430	1977	437	66.4	9.1	24.5	—	60.4	15.6	24.0	18
Philippines	1981	7,378	1,090[1]	9,644[1]	539[1]	9,470[1]	6,713	1980	1,416[16]	...	...	...	...	25.1	—	74.9	19
Pitcairn Island	1975	...	...	1[1]	...	...	...	...	...	...	...	...	...	...	...	...	...
Poland	1982	65,012	16,962	153,055	15,619	16,810	555	1982	786	82.0	13.0	5.0	—	96.2[9]	3.8[9]	—	70
Portugal	1981	20,997	462	...	5,006	...	473	1981	496	80.6	19.4	—	—	81.5[5]	18.5[5,19]	[19]	51
Puerto Rico	1980	4,057	741	7,181	1,436	199	848	1980	111	72.1	27.9	—	—	48.6	19.8	31.5	41
Qatar	1981	186[1]	24[1]	437[1]	17[1]	70[1]	1,333	1981	4	25.0	75.0	—	—	100.0	—	—	30
Réunion	1979	471	116	1,390	200	82	1,038	1977	11	36.4	18.1	—	45.5	70.0[9,52]	18.6[9,52]	11.4[9,52]	80[9]
Romania	1981	34,440[1]	7,136[1]	81,214[1,53]	6,666[1]	...	652	1981	248[16]	...	...	...	...	...	...	...	87
Rwanda	1981	182	11[1]	97[1]	8[1]	201[1]	28,071	1981	232	1.7	1.0	87.8	9.5	43.1	56.9	—	15
St. Christopher and Nevis	1980	16	5	227	1	123	4,062	1980	7	28.6	57.1	—	14.3	100.0	—	—	48
St. Helena and Ascension	1982	3	1	30[9]	...	7[9]	1,667	1982	8	12.5	12.5	75.0	—	...	...	...	110
St. Lucia	1977	40	5	112	21	66	2,800	1975	7	42.9	14.2	—	42.9	85.7	14.3	—	51
St. Pierre and Miquelon	1977	6	2	20	...	1	833	1979	2	50.0	—	—	50.0	100.0	—	—	140
St. Vincent and the Grenadines	1974	22	2	34	—	85	4,318	1972	8	12.5	50.0	—	37.5	100.0	—	—	23[16]
San Marino	...	...	...	...	...	...	...	...	...	...	...	...	...	...	...	...	83
São Tomé and Príncipe	1981	38	...	118	1	...	2,263	1978	16	12.5	—	87.5	—	...	...	...	16
Saudi Arabia	1981	3,576[1]	217[1]	6,706[1]	265[1]	—	2,606	1981	95	78.9	21.1	—	—	72.6	—	27.4	16
Senegal	1981	449	70	1,766[1]	139	326	12,942	1977	44	11.4	—	79.5	9.1	100.0	—	—	11
Seychelles	1982	40	5	169	4	131[9]	1,700	1982	7	57.1	14.3	28.6	—	100.0	—	—	46
Sierra Leone	1980	190	18	...	8	751	18,284	1980	112	0.9	7.2	58.9	33.0	76.8	15.2	8.0	11
Singapore	1981	2,219	370	5,024	374	766	1,101	1981	25	56.0	44.0	—	—	48.0	52.0[19]	[19]	41
Solomon Islands	1982	38	...	392	...	...	6,421	1982	130	6.2	—	93.8	—	...	...	...	55
Somalia	1980	299	2	1,365	...	556	12,191	1972	...	...	...	...	...	...	...	...	18
South Africa	1981	22,977[27,55]	3,056[27,55]	57,324[27,55]	5,900[27,55]	...	786[55]	1980	595[55]	...	...	...	...	40.7[55]	59.3[19,55]	[19,55]	41[55]
South West Africa/Namibia	1979	152	16	665	...	...	8,947	1979	74	...	...	...	...	38.4	14.4	47.2	...
Spain	1981	96,569	4,032	123,356	24,332[50]	4,489	390	1979	1,135	68.8	31.2	—	—	...	...	...	55
Sri Lanka	1981	1,964[1]	269[1]	7,040[1]	499[1]	3,273[1]	7,631	1981	488	5.9	30.4	20.9	42.8	...	...	...	29
Sudan, The	1981	2,169[1]	207[1]	250[1]	58[1]	376[1]	8,714	1981	160	21.9	5.6	—	72.5	...	...	...	9
Suriname	1978	214	21	660	13	88	1,729	1980	17	29.4	17.6	47.1	5.9	58.8	29.4	11.8	82
Swaziland	1980	100	7[5]	84[5]	10[5]	731[5]	5,790	1978	33	9.1	9.1	48.5	33.3	21.2	57.6	21.2	35
Sweden	1980	18,300	8,320	55,770	720	3,540	454	1980	711	13.1	85.1	—	1.8	70.6	0.7	28.7	148
Switzerland	1981	17,087	2,841	40,000[9]	1,217	1,650[9]	379	1976	474	45.1	54.9	—	—	42.0	43.8	14.2	114
Syria	1981	4,165	1,404	5,910	1,886	1,776	2,236	1981	151	19.2	80.8	—	—	25.2	2.0	72.8	11
Taiwan	1982	12,621	2,609	15,037	14,054	3,078	1,462	1981	11,161	...	...	...	...	79.6	20.4[19]	[19]	25
Tanzania	1980	900	18[5]	5,658[6]	25[6]	...	20,687	1977	2,407	5.9	—	86.6	7.5	77.3	2.8	19.9	22
Thailand	1980	6,867	1,084	10,118	2,650	8,943	6,870	1979	615	9.9	5.0	10.1	75.0	96.9	3.1	—	13
Togo	1980	139	4	773	23	263	19,417	1979	65	10.8	4.6	61.5	23.1	100.0	—	—	14
Tokelau	1981	4[1]	1[1]	13[1]	...	...	500	1981	3	...	...	...	...	100.0	—	—	200
Tonga	1981	38	9[1]	147[1]	2[1]	172[1]	2,605	1981	9	44.4	—	55.6	—	100.0	—	—	34
Trinidad and Tobago	1980	786	69	2,836[1]	...	...	1,450	1979	25	8.0	16.0	40.0	36.0	60.0	—	40.0	39
Trust Territory of the Pacific Is.	...	...	...	...	...	...	...	...	...	...	...	...	...	...	...	...	21
Tunisia	1981	1,800	330	4,919[1]	764	784[1]	3,618	1980	98	28.6	16.3	—	55.1	100.0	—	—	21
Turkey	1981	28,411	6,790	22,998	11,610	206	1,632	1981	831	52.7	12.8	—	34.5	85.1	3.5	11.4	21
Turks and Caicos Islands	1979	3	1	3	...	11	2,000	1979	7	14.3	—	85.7	—	100.0	—	—	70
Tuvalu	1981	4[1]	2[1]	...	1[1]	18[1]	1,750	1981	8	12.5	—	87.5	—	100.0	—	—	100
Uganda	1981	611	17	6,778	27	—	22,291	1981	485	15.5	1.2	83.3	—	84.5	15.5	—	15
U.S.S.R.	1982	1,034,000[45]	—	2,880,000	252,000	...	258	1982	23,400	...	...	...	...	100.0	—	—	125
United Arab Emirates	1981	1,491[1]	76[1]	907[1]	83[1]	...	511	1981	22	50.0	27.3	4.5	18.2	95.5	4.5	—	43
United Kingdom	1980	90,600	2,321[1,9]	178,270[1,9]	14,140[1,9]	21,663[1,9]	618	1981	2,501	...	...	...	...	...	...	...	83
United States	1980	430,277	126,420	1,164,000	144,260	...	526	1981	6,933	87.6	12.4	—	—	36.3[14]	50.3[14]	13.4[14]	59
Uruguay	1980	5,700	2,300[9]	15,200[9]	...	1,206[9]	506	1978	66	43.9	18.2	—	37.9	100.0	—	—	40
Vanuatu	1981	22	2	255	2	—	5,545	1980	21	14.3	—	52.4	33.3	47.6	52.4	—	65
Venezuela	1979	15,359	4,645	9,077[5]	4,063	...	880	1979	446	...	...	...	...	42.1	4.3	53.6	30
Vietnam	1981	13,517	409[1]	33,108	4,977[1]	...	4,067	1981	11,550	1.3	7.9	86.8	4.0	100.0	—	—	37
Virgin Islands (U.S.)	1974	96	...	241	...	...	833	...	...	...	...	...	...	...	...	...	...
Wallis and Futuna	1981	4[1]	1[1]	1[1]	1[1]	1[1]	2,500	1981	3	33.3	—	—	66.7	100.0	—	—	90
Western Sahara	...	...	...	...	...	...	...	...	...	...	...	...	...	...	...	...	...
Western Samoa	...	...	...	...	...	...	...	1981	16	6.3	—	—	93.7	100.0	—	—	43
Yemen (Aden)	1980	258	9	150	16	25	7,636	...	...	...	...	...	...	...	...	...	5
Yemen (Şan'ā')	1981	896[1]	26[1]	896[1]	95	87[1]	6,629	1981	28	53.6	7.1	—	39.3	89.3	10.7	...	60
Yugoslavia	1981	33,444	7,059	8,716	4,638	7,915	673	1980	425	32.5	30.3	37.2	—	...	...	...	28
Zaire	1980	1,900	54[9]	4,097[9]	414[9]	967[9]	15,065	1979	942	37.3	38.9	23.8	—	40.9	44.6	14.5	35
Zambia	1981	821	52	871	35	866	7,261	1981	636	1.9	0.4	87.3	10.4	83.8	14.5	1.7	—
Zimbabwe	1980	1,148	158	5,094	354	2,490	6,411	1980	...	...	...	...	...	...	...	...	29

rate per 10,000 pop.	general	special-ized	clinics	rural	bed occu-pancy rate [a] (%)	aver-age length of stay (days)	infant mortality per 1,000 live births 1982–83	maternal mortality per 100,000 live births 1980–81	popu-lation with access to safe water, 1975 [b,c] (%)	food supply (% of FAO require-ment) 1980	indiv. (% of earn-ings)	em-ployer (% of payroll)	govt. (% of covered earnings)	public health expendi-tures (% of natl. budget)	public health expendi-tures per capita [e] (U.S.$)	country
1,535	88.4	10.8	0.8	—	87.5	31	7.5	2.0	—	124	4.4	16.8	4.9	11.2	382.90	Norway
1,129[16]	...	...	...	...	100.0[16]	6[16]	135.2[7]	...	...	...	...	...	...	3.2	59.60	Oman
...	...	...	...	...	...	...	119.0	...	29	106	—	7.0	...	1.5	0.70	Pakistan
...	...	...	...	...	...	...	20.1	72.8	68	103	1.0	8.0	0.8	12.3	72.50	Panama
253[16]	...	...	...	...	...	...	97.0	...	20	90	...	...	...	8.7	25.20	Papua New Guinea
...	...	...	...	...	...	...	38.6[20]	159.5[5]	21	134	9.5[8]	16.5	1.5	3.7	4.50	Paraguay
416	90.9	7.8	1.3	—	88.2	14	105.0[7]	103.4[5]	51	99	2.5	5.0	...	4.5	9.20	Peru
...	...	...	...	...	...	...	50.0	125.0	43	116	1.6	5.5	...	3.5	3.70	Philippines
...	...	...	...	...	...	...	...	...	...	...	...	...	...	...	...	Pitcairn Island
1,171	95.4	4.6	...	...	84.9[9]	19[9]	20.2	11.7	—	134	—	22.0[23]	100.0	9.5	127.00[4,14]	Poland
749	86.4	13.6	—	—	88.2	...	26.0[14]	30.6[9]	—	129	8.0[8]	20.5[8]	...	4.4	22.70	Portugal
1,227	95.0	5.0	—	—	64.8	8	18.6[17]	8.2	...	...	...	...	...	24.0[11,44]	148.10[11,44]	Puerto Rico
1,328	54.3	45.7	...	...	...	...	57.0[7]	...	...	...	...	...	...	...	...	Qatar
836[16]	...	...	...	...	82.0[16]	12[16]	47.1[7]	...	...	...	...	...	...	...	...	Réunion
...	...	...	...	...	...	...	30.9	139.9	...	126	—	7.0	100.0	0.3	3.90	Romania
75[16]	...	...	...	...	80.8[16]	11[16]	111.9[7]	...	35	88	—	—	...	4.8	1.40	Rwanda
70[16]	...	...	...	...	58.9[16]	10[16]	45.7[17]	...	...	...	...	...	...	...	...	St. Christopher and Nevis
...	...	...	...	...	...	...	16.3	...	...	...	...	...	...	...	...	St. Helena and Ascension
1,289	84.6	5.8	—	9.6	74.3[16]	7[16]	24.1[17]	...	...	...	5.0	5.0	...	...	...	St. Lucia
...	...	...	...	...	41.7[16,54]	12[16,54]	9.2[17]	...	...	...	...	...	...	...	...	St. Pierre and Miquelon
649[16]	...	...	...	...	68.3[16]	9[16]	60.2[14]	...	...	...	—	—	...	11.8	17.30	St. Vincent and the Grenadines
...	...	...	...	...	...	...	9.5	...	...	...	...	...	...	...	...	San Marino
1,733	76.1	—	23.9	—	68.7	12	69.5	...	...	...	—	—	...	...	132.70[11]	São Tomé and Principe
...	...	...	...	...	...	...	121.1[20]	...	84	120	—	—	...	1.4[11]	...	Saudi Arabia
324	34.2	—	54.8	11.0	77.2	10	152.6[20]	...	37	100	3.0	3.0	...	5.9	4.20	Senegal
...	...	...	...	...	...	...	14.4	...	...	...	5.0	10.0	...	8.7	23.20	Seychelles
13[16]	...	...	...	...	77.1[16]	18[16]	136.3[20]	...	12[17]	89	...	...	...	4.1	3.50	Sierra Leone
1,091	73.4	26.6	—	...	73.0	10	9.2	4.7	100	134	—	—	100.0	6.9	69.10	Singapore
...	...	...	...	...	...	...	46.0	...	...	...	...	...	...	11.2	14.00	Solomon Islands
...	...	...	...	...	...	...	150.0[20]	...	33	83	—	—	100.0	3.5[11]	4.20[11]	Somalia
...	...	...	...	...	...	...	100.6[20]	...	—	118	—	100.0	...	1.8[11]	13.90[11]	South Africa
...	...	...	...	...	...	...	125.3[20]	...	...	...	...	...	...	...	...	South West Africa/Namibia
918	91.5	8.5	—	—	68.9	15	10.3[17]	11.5[9]	—	135	5.0	28.1	...	0.8	11.40	Spain
1,519	39.7	14.2	1.1	45.0	86.3	6	37.0	...	20	102	—	—	100.0	3.3[11]	3.80[11]	Sri Lanka
81[16]	...	...	...	...	...	...	131.0[20]	...	46	101	—	—	100.0	1.4	1.20	Sudan, The
820	83.6	2.4	8.0	6.0	41.6	15	30.4[14]	...	...	...	—	—	...	8.6	47.30	Suriname
456[16]	...	...	...	...	...	...	140.1[20]	...	...	...	—	—	...	7.2	19.70	Swaziland
1,846	89.2	9.9	—	0.9	88.5	26	6.8	8.2	—	119	—	10.5	15.0	1.9	115.10	Sweden
1,388	80.7	19.3	—	...	81.2	24	7.6[17]	6.8	—	133	73	—	—	11.7	381.10	Switzerland
240[16]	...	...	...	...	53.0[16]	5[16]	67.2[7]	...	75	117	—	—	...	0.9	4.90	Syria
...	...	...	...	...	...	...	8.9	...	...	...	1.4	5.6	3.2	...	...	Taiwan
...	...	...	...	...	...	...	107.4[20]	...	39	83	5.0[8]	5.0[8]	—	5.4	4.90	Tanzania
590	14.1	3.9	1.3	80.7	66.1	5	50.0	...	22	104	...	...	...	4.2	5.70	Thailand
...	...	...	...	...	...	...	114.7[7]	...	16	95	—	2.0	—	5.6	7.30	Togo
1,010	...	...	...	...	16.7	12	...	...	...	...	...	...	...	...	...	Tokelau
612	100.0	—	—	—	43.8	8	9.0	...	...	...	...	...	...	...	...	Tonga
865	...	...	...	...	88.6	5	26.4[9]	78.9[6]	50	113	2.8	5.6	100.0	6.4	83.90	Trinidad and Tobago
...	...	...	...	...	...	...	21.5	...	...	...	...	...	...	11.6[11]	96.60[11]	Trust Territory of the Pacific Is.
621	70.5	9.9	—	19.6	66.8	8	106.5[7]	...	70	116	5.0	15.0	—	7.1	31.20	Tunisia
406	78.3	19.1	—	2.6	44.1	9	131.0[20]	...	75	122	5.0	7.0	—	3.6	11.70	Turkey
...	...	...	...	...	...	...	24.5[14]	...	...	...	...	...	...	...	...	Turks and Caicos Islands
770[16]	...	...	...	...	52.1[16]	11[16]	42.0	...	...	...	...	...	...	...	...	Tuvalu
...	...	...	...	...	...	...	100.5[20]	...	35	83	—	...	100.0	6.1	4.30	Uganda
...	...	...	...	...	...	...	16.3	...	—	132	—	4.4	50.0	...	91.00[4]	U.S.S.R.
1,385	78.3	15.5	0.8	5.4	62.1	7	80.9[20]	...	...	...	...	...	...	7.9	319.30	United Arab Emirates
1,706	...	...	...	...	77.9	...	11.0	9.0	—	132	7.8	13.7	85.0	12.8	343.80	United Kingdom
...	...	...	...	...	...	...	11.0	9.6[5]	—	139	1.30	1.30	—	10.4	274.60	United States
378[16]	...	...	...	...	61.1[16]	10[16]	33.7[17]	55.9[5]	84	110	5.0[37]	8.0[37]	...	4.8	37.10	Uruguay
970	40.5	—	14.0	45.5	33.6	8	...	...	...	...	—	—	1.5[8]	...	...	Vanuatu
...	...	...	...	...	...	...	44.8[7]	65.1[5]	80	112	2.0[8]	4.25[8]	100.0	8.7	79.70	Venezuela
1,587	12.4	8.1	56.6	22.9	80.7	7	75.0	...	14[17]	90	—	...	...	...	1.00[4]	Vietnam
...	...	...	...	...	...	...	22.5[5]	...	...	...	...	...	...	...	...	Virgin Islands (U.S.)
2,360	86.0	—	—	14.0	42.4	6	...	...	...	...	...	...	...	...	...	Wallis and Futuna
...	...	...	...	...	...	...	...	...	...	...	...	...	...	...	...	Western Sahara
746	61.9	—	...	38.1	39.3	8	42.0	...	16[18]	...	—	...	...	...	...	Western Samoa
...	...	...	...	...	...	...	153.3[7]	...	24	84	...	...	...	5.1[11]	2.10[11]	Yemen (Aden)
83	79.8	5.9	—	14.3	81.5	19	169.6[7]	...	4	76	...	...	...	3.6	5.70	Yemen (Ṣan'ā')
1,186	80.4	13.7	5.9	—	87.3	16	29.9	17.9	—	140	8.7	8.7	...	—	—	Yugoslavia
474[16]	...	...	...	...	71.6[16]	12[16]	116.6[7]	...	16	94	—	—	...	3.0[11]	1.20[11]	Zaire
391[16]	...	...	...	...	76.0[16]	7[16]	110.5[7]	...	42	93	5.0	5.0	—	6.1	15.30	Zambia
1,043	40.1	6.1	53.8	...	67.5	7	78.8[7]	37.1[56]	...	86	...	...	...	...	10.00[4]	Zimbabwe

[1]Government employed health personnel only. [2]General hospitals include specialized and rural hospitals. [3]Percentages exclude clinics and some specialized (stomatology, mental, and leprosy) hospitals. [4]May include expenditures at the intermediate and local levels of government and/or the costs of additional services such as national health insurance and family-planning programs. [5]1978. [6]1977. [7]1975–80 estimate. [8]Includes funds for old-age retirement, incapacitating disability, work injury, and death insurance. [9]1979. [10]Percentages exclude clinics. [11]Includes expenditures at the intermediate and local levels of government. [12]1973. [13]1972. [14]1980. [15]Government hospitals include private nonprofit hospitals. [16]General hospitals only. [17]1981. [18]Includes physicians practicing dentistry. [19]Private nonprofit hospitals include private for profit hospitals. [20]1980–85 estimate. [21]Employed women only. [22]1974. [23]Excludes rural workers. [24]Excludes specialized hospitals and clinics. [25]Amounts vary within the country. [26]1975. [27]Registered personnel, not necessarily those employed in the country. [28]Clinics include rural hospitals. [29]Includes assistant nurses. [30]Specialized hospitals include clinics. [31]1976. [32]Government hospitals only. [33]Rural hospitals only. [34]Urban population only. [35]Nurses include midwives. [36]Excludes hazardous occupations such as mining. [37]1982. [38]Excludes mental hospitals. [39]Excludes oilfield operations. [40]Hospital staffs only. [41]1970. [42]Contributions for men only. [43]Physicians include dentists. [44]Includes welfare. [45]Peninsular Malaysia only. [46]Government hospitals in peninsular Malaysia only. [47]Percent of employer contributions. [48]1971. [49]General hospitals and clinics only. [50]Includes pharmaceutical assistants. [51]Includes rehabilitation centres. [52]Based on bed ownership percentage. [53]Includes medical technicians. [54]1969. [55]Excludes the black independent states. [56]European population only, 1979.

Social protection

This table summarizes the principal social protective activities of the countries of the world. Because the administrative structure, financing, manning, and scope of programmed tasks vary so greatly from country to country, the basis of the comparisons is most often either manpower or finance. The principal impediment to comparison on other bases is the great variety of administrative structures that exist for the conduct of these activities.

The provision of social security programs for specific social needs is summarized simply in terms of the existence or nonexistence of a specific benefit program because of the complexity of national programs in terms of eligibility, coverage, term, age limits, financing, payments, and so on. As in the United States, activities connected with a particular benefit may take place at more than one governmental level or through more than one agency at the same level. The data shown here are summarized from the U.S. Social Security Administration's *Social Security Programs Throughout the World*. A bullet symbol (●) indicates that a country has at least

one program within the defined area; in some cases it may have several.

Data given for social security expenditure as a percentage of total central governmental budgetary expenditure are from the International Monetary Fund's *Government Finance Statistics Yearbook*, which provides the best and most comparable analytical series on the consolidated accounts of the central governments of the world.

Data on the financing of social security programs are taken in large part from the International Labour Office's *The Cost of Social Security*, supplemented by national data sources.

Figures for manpower in police and fire services are from a variety of national sources from about 1980. The relative scarcity of international sources and data on these topics is in part a reflection of the fact that in many countries these functions are viewed as matters of merely local concern, and as they are not conducted or directly funded by the central government, they tend to be ignored in the data collection and publication programs of the central government. The manpower figures refer, for the

Social protection

country	social security					expenditures, 1980 (percent of national budget)	finances									
	programs available, 1983						year	receipts					expenditures			
	old-age invalidity, death	sickness and maternity	work injury	unemployment	family allowances			total ('000,000 natl. cur.)	insured persons (%)	employers (%)	government (%)	other (%)	total ('000,000 natl. cur.)	benefits (%)	administration (%)	other (%)
Afghanistan			●			...	...	...	...	...	...	...	...	...	...	...
Albania	●	●	●		●	...	1978	5,561.1	...	...	...	...	3,049.8	...	...	...
Algeria	●	●	●		●	...		...	...	...	...	...	...	...	...	...
American Samoa	...	...	...	...	...	...		...	...	...	...	...	...	...	...	...
Andorra	...	...	...	...	...	...		...	...	...	...	...	...	...	...	...
Angola	...	...	...	...	...	...		...	...	...	...	...	...	...	...	...
Anguilla	...	...	...	...	...	...	1976		...	...	...	...	1.9	...	...	...
Antigua and Barbuda	●	●	●		●	36.3	1977	1,487,545.7	27.3	57.2	6.8	8.7	1,282,114.5	96.7	3.3	—
Argentina	●	●	●	●	●	29.0	1977	13,568.1	12.2	11.5	73.6	2.7	12,946.9	96.2	3.5	0.3
Australia	●	●		●	●											
Austria	●	●	●	●	●	38.8	1977	170,703.0	26.4	48.6	22.5	2.5	166,851.0	95.4	3.0	1.6
Bahamas, The	●	●	●			7.4[7]	1979	25.1	...	...	...	...	9.6	...	...	...
Bahrain	●		●			1.9	1981		...	...	...	...	1,434.2[8]	...	...	...
Bangladesh	...	...	...	...	...	33[2]	1977	466.7	2.2	2.2	93.7	1.9	445.3	99.6	0.4	...
Barbados	●	●	●	●		13.6	1977	75.1	11.2	13.2	67.0	8.6	59.1	97.6	2.2	0.2
Belgium	●	●	●	●	●	41.6	1980	780,853.0	20.2	41.0	34.7	4.2	797,726.0	93.1[9]	4.8[9]	2.1[9]
Belize	●	●	●				1980	—					1.5			
Benin	●	●	●		●	...	1977	3,654.7	7.4	49.4	41.9	1.3	3,165.6	91.0	8.3	0.7
Bermuda	●		●			3.1	1981						2.3[10]			
Bhutan	...	...	...	...	...	...		...	...	...	...	...	...	...	...	...
Bolivia	●	●	●		●	5.6[7]	1977	2,198.5	28.5	47.6	11.8	12.1	1,752.1	88.5	11.5	—
Botswana			●			0.7	1981		...	...	...	...	0.8	...	...	...
Brazil	●	●	●	●	●	39.8[7]	1977	145,010.8	...	...	...	...	143,106.0	86.7	11.8	1.5
British Virgin Islands	...	...	...	...	...	...		...	...	...	...	...	...	...	...	...
Brunei	●					...	1981						2.5[9,12]			
Bulgaria	●	●	●		●	...	1977	2,609.7	—	53.7	40.2	6.1	2,506.0	94.9	0.1	5.0
Burkina Faso	●	●	●		●	4.6	1977	3,727.5	10.1	61.4	24.8	3.7	2,635.7	90.5	9.5	—
Burma	●	●	●			6.1[7]	1977	340.1	1.4	40.9	57.7	—	333.1	99.2	0.8	—
Burundi	●		●		●	3.4	1981	394.0	...	...	...	...	294.0	...	...	...
Cameroon	●		●		●	4.4	1982	33.0	...	...	...	...	18.8	...	...	...
Canada	●	●	●	●	●	32.8	1977	31,766.4	7.3	11.4	73.8	7.5	27,991.7	97.8	2.2	—
Cape Verde	●	●	●		●	...		...	...	...	...	...	...	...	...	...
Cayman Islands	...	...	...	...	...	...		...	...	...	...	...	...	...	...	...
Central African Republic	●	●	●		●	...	1981	2,009.0	...	...	...	...		...	...	...
Chad	●		●		●	1.9	1976		...	...	...	...	1,675.0	...	...	...
Chile	●	●	●	●	●	28.4[2]	1977	42,330.5	17.5	45.6	30.7	6.2	32,355.8	93.0	7.0	—
China	●	●	●			...		...	...	...	...	...	...	...	...	...
Christmas Island	...	...	...	...	...	...		...	...	...	...	...	...	...	...	...
Cocos (Keeling) Islands	...	...	...	...	...	...		...	...	...	...	...	...	...	...	...
Colombia	●	●	●		●	...	1977	32,389.1	12.3	31.3	35.0	21.4	26,358.1	90.3	5.7	4.0
Comoros	●	...	●	...	●	...		...	...	...	...	...	...	...	...	...
Congo	●	●	●		●	...	1980	5,682.0	...	...	...	...	3,957.0	...	...	...
Cook Islands	...	...	...	...	...	...		...	...	...	...	...	...	...	...	...
Costa Rica	●	●	●		●	30.8	1977	1,952.4	23.4	44.2	22.3	10.1	1,537.5	90.7	7.1	2.2
Cuba	●					...		...	...	...	...	...	...	...	...	...
Cyprus	●	●		●		14.0	1977	24.0	17.9	21.3	57.4	3.4	22.6	98.5	1.3	0.2
Czechoslovakia	●	●	●		●	...	1977	77,930.0	—	2.6	95.8	1.6	77,930.0	99.6	0.4	—
Denmark	●	●	●	●	●	41.5[2]	1977	68,320.6	1.4	5.5	91.4	1.7	66,680.2	97.4	2.6	—
Djibouti	●	●	●		●	9.2[2]	1982	1,252.0	...	...	...	...	1,138.0	...	...	...
Dominica	●	●	●			1.5[7]	1979	2.5	...	...	...	...	0.8	...	...	...
Dominican Republic	●	●	●			7.4[7]	1977	117.5	—	—	67.6	32.4	115.6	94.8	5.2	—
Ecuador	●	●	●				1981	—	...	...	...	...	530.0	...	...	...
Egypt	●	●	●	●		7.6[7]	1979		...	...	...	...	24.6	...	...	...
El Salvador	●	●	●			3.3	1977	244.6	11.0	32.6	52.8	3.6	208.6	68.3	18.6	13.1
Equatorial Guinea	...	...	...	...	...	...		...	...	...	...	...	...	...	...	...
Ethiopia			●			3.8[2]	1977	182.8	12.4	29.5	49.0	9.1	146.5	99.1	0.7	0.2
Faeroe Islands	...	...	...	...	...	...		...	...	...	...	...	...	...	...	...
Falkland Islands	...	...	...	...	...	...		...	...	...	...	...	...	...	...	...
Fiji	●		●			2.9	1977	46.0	21.3	21.9	36.6	20.2	24.0	80.8	18.4	0.8
Finland	●	●	●	●	●	27.0	1977	28,259.4	10.1	49.4	36.0	4.5	24,585.6	96.6	3.3	0.1
France	●	●	●	●	●	43.9[7]	1977	487,358.4	19.4	55.7	23.2	1.7	480,516.7	87.7	3.7	8.6
French Guiana	...	...	...	...	...	...		...	...	...	...	...	...	...	...	...
French Polynesia	...	...	...	...	...	...		...	...	...	...	...	...	...	...	...
Gabon	●	●	●		●	...	1975	6,770.0	...	...	...	...	3,790.0	...	...	...
Gambia, The			●			2.0[2]	1978	—	...	...	...	...	2.6	...	...	...

most part, to full-time, paid professional staff, excluding clerical support and volunteer staff. Firemen employed by private companies are included. Personnel in military service who perform either police or fire functions are presumed to be employed in their principal activity, military service.

The figures for military manpower refer to full-time, active-duty military service and exclude reserve, militia, paramilitary, and similar organizations. Because of the difficulties attached to the analysis of data on military manpower and budgets (data withheld on national security grounds, budgetary data specifically intended to hide actual expenditure, the complexity of long-term financing of purchases of military matériel [how much was actually spent as opposed to what was committed, offset by nonmilitary transfers, etc.]), extensive use is made of the principal international analytical tools: publications such as those of the International Institute for Strategic Studies (*The Military Balance* and *Strategic Survey*), the Stockholm International Peace Research Institute (*World Armaments and Disarmament*, SIPRI *Yearbook*), World Priorities (*World Military*

and Social Expenditures), and the U.S. Arms Control and Disarmament Agency (*World Military Expenditures and Arms Transfers*).

The data on military expenditures are from the sources identified above, as well as from the IMF's *Government Finance Statistical Yearbook* and country statistical publications.

a. A police officer is a full-time, paid, professional staff person performing internal security functions. Excluded are clerical employees, volunteers, and members of paramilitary groups.
b. A fireman is a full-time, paid, professional staff member. Excluded are clerical employees and volunteers.
c. Includes all active-duty personnel, regular and conscript, performing national security functions. Excludes reserves, paramilitary forces, border patrols, and gendarmeries.

fire and police protection, about 1980					military, defense						country
government expenditures per 1,000 population		population per police officer[a]	population per fireman[b]	fire stations per 1,000 population	personnel		expenditures				
police (U.S.$)	fire (U.S.$)				armed forces ('000)[c]	armed forces per 1,000 pop.[c]	total ('000,000 U.S.$)	per capita (U.S.$)[c]	percent of national budget	percent of GDP or GNP	
...	...	...	...	...	43	2.7	165	12	17.3[2]	2.0[2]	Afghanistan
...	...	...	...	...	53	15.7	188[3]	70[3]	11.5[4]	7.9[1]	Albania
					120	8.3	1,784[3]	92[3]	4.6	1.9	Algeria
———37,240.6———		464.0	857.0	...	—	[5]	—	—	—	—	American Samoa
...	...	1,125.0			...	...	...	...	...	...	Andorra
...	...	...	...	...	47	5.2	161[6]	27[6]	20.2[3]	...	Angola
...	...	...	...	...	—	[5]					Anguilla
...	...	...	...	...	...	...	...	...	...	...	Antigua and Barbuda
14,413.9	...	461.9	...	...	175	6.3	3,186[3]	111[3]	15.2[3]	2.8[3]	Argentina
					73	4.7	4,415	292	8.7[4]	3.1	Australia
...	...	466.3	...	...	40	6.5	808	106	2.9[3]	1.2	Austria
64.8	...	164.8	...	...	...	...	...	...	1.3[7]	...	Bahamas, The
...	...	183.3	...	...	2	5.8[3]	280	700	22.3	6.1[3]	Bahrain
462.4	...	...	...	.001	77	0.8	205	2	17.3[4]	1.3[2]	Bangladesh
...	...	...	...	...	1	3.3[2]	10[3]	33[3]	3.5[3]	0.3[1]	Barbados
...	...	585.5	...	...	8.5	9.5	3,507	354	5.4[1]	3.3	Belgium
...	...	...	...	...					4.1[1]		Belize
...	...	182.9	...	...	3	0.8	23[3]	6[3]	15.3[1]	2.2[1]	Benin
...	...	...	...	...	—	[5]	—	—	2.1[1]	—	Bermuda
...	...	...	...	...	...	3.0	...	...	...	...	Bhutan
...	...	476.9	...	...	26	4.8	100	18	22.7[3]	1.8[1]	Bolivia
...	...	...	3,439.0	...	3	3.3[1]	28	28	8.7[3]	3.5[1]	Botswana
36.2[11]	—	230.3[11]	[11]	0.2	460	2.2	1,837[3]	15[3]	3.4[3]	0.6[1]	Brazil
126.2	15.7	117.3	...	...	— 4[1]	[5]	195	837	12.8[13]	2.9[1]	British Virgin Islands Brunei
...	...	...	...	...	175	16.2	3,761	423	5.7	3.2[1]	Bulgaria
...	...	...	...	...	5	1.4	32[3]	5[3]	16.9[7]	2.6[7]	Burkina Faso
...	...	645.3	...	...	179	5.5	222	6	21.7[3]	3.7[7]	Burma
...	...	...	...	...	7	1.5	48	11	11.2[9]	2.7[2]	Burundi
...	...	1,173.1[14]	...	...	12	0.8	91	10	6.8	1.3[2]	Cameroon
...	...	358.0	...	...	82	3.4	6,139	250	8.9[4]	2.0	Canada
...	...	...	...	...	3	5.9	2	7	5.0[1]	3.4[1]	Cape Verde
33,287.0	...	110.3	317.8	...	—	[5]	—	—	—	—	Cayman Islands
...	...	...	...	...	5	1.0	14	6	8.3	1.7[1]	Central African Republic
...	...	...	...	...	9[9]	2.1[9]	18[7]	4[7]	29.0[7]	5.0[7]	Chad
...	...	375.8	...	...	116	8.4	1,391	123	12.0[3]	6.0[3]	Chile
...	...	1,363.6[15]	...	...	4,490	3.9	49,500	47	13.7[4]	8.5[1]	China
...	...	206.8	...	...	—	[5]	—	—	—	—	Christmas Island
...	...	...	...	...	—	[5]	—	—	—	—	Cocos (Keeling) Islands
2,502.7	...	418.2	...	...	70	2.5	327	12	8.0[3]	1.1[1]	Colombia
...	...	[14]	...	...	...	2.5[16]	2	5	15.0	...	Comoros
...	...	[14]	...	...	16	8.8[1, 16]	93	58	2.6[3]	4.1[1]	Congo
...	...	...	...	...	—	[5]	—	—	—	—	Cook Islands
...	...	...	...	...	4	1.7[1]	14[3]	6[3]	2.6[3]	0.6[1]	Costa Rica
...	...	150.0	...	...	230	20.8[1]	1,109	113	7.5[3]	7.5	Cuba
35,382.6[17]	...	177.7[17]	...	...	17	15.0	83	138	6.8[3]	1.4[1]	Cyprus
108,696.8	13,547.6	...	...	...	213	12.8	7,634	496	12.0	3.1[1]	Czechoslovakia
...	...	...	...	...	31	6.1	1,575	309	7.0[3]	2.0	Denmark
3,924.0[11]	—	446.1[11]	[11]	...	3	8.7	3	10	21.7[13]	...	Djibouti
...	...	...	...	...	...	...	—	3[7]	1.2[7]	...	Dominica
...	...	464.4	...	...	25	4.3	107	18	8.9[3]	1.0[2]	Dominican Republic
...	...	...	...	...	36	4.3	296[3]	36[3]	9.4[4]	1.4	Ecuador
...	...	446.7	...	...	447	10.1	2,395	54	7.4[7]	7.4[1]	Egypt
...	...	...	...	...	25	3.2	142	31	11.6	3.8	El Salvador
...	...	135.0	...	...	2	10.0[7]	4[6]	13[6]	...	4.1[7]	Equatorial Guinea
...	...	956.4	...	...	250	7.6	455	15	42.6[1]	9.7[1]	Ethiopia
63.5	...	...	...	...	—	[5]	—	—	—	—	Faeroe Islands
38,723.1	...	279.5	...	...	—	[5]	—	—	—	—	Falkland Islands
3,628.8	...	460.5	...	...	2	3.0	13	19	3.5[4]	0.5[1]	Fiji
44,499.0	4,435.6	...	...	...	36	7.7	897	187	5.8[4]	1.7	Finland
...	...	485.3	...	...	485	9.1	25,612	471	17.5	4.1	France
...	...	...	...	...	—	[5]	108[4]	706[4]	—	—	French Guiana
...	...	...	...	...	—	[5]	—	—	—	—	French Polynesia
...	...	...	...	...	6	3.3	8.8	98	6.3	1.9[7]	Gabon
...	...	812.0	...	...	—	0.0	—	—	—	—	Gambia, The

Social protection (continued)

country	old-age invalidity, death	sickness and maternity	work injury	unem- ploy- ment	family allow- ances	expendi- tures, 1980 (percent of na- tional budget)	year	receipts total ('000,000 natl. cur.)	insured persons (%)	em- ployers (%)	govern- ment (%)	other (%)	expenditures total ('000,000 natl. cur.)	benefits (%)	admin- istration (%)	other (%)
Germany, East	•	•	•	...	•	...	1977	25,075.3	23.5	26.0	50.4	0.1	25,075.3	99.6	0.4	—
Germany, West	•	•	•	•	•	48.5	1977	275,312.0	29.5	41.1	26.4	3.0	279,738.0	96.0	3.1	0.9
Ghana	•	•	•	...	•	5.2	1980						243.5	...	...	...
Gibraltar	•	•	...	•	•	...										
Greece	•	•	•	•	•	27.0[2]	1977	133,844.0	26.1	44.9	24.0	5.0	109,707.0	94.5	5.0	0.5
Greenland	...	...	...	...	...	...							...	...	...	...
Grenada	•	•	...	...	...	5.0[9]							...			
Guadeloupe	...	...	...	...	...	...										
Guam	...	...	...	...	...	...										
Guatemala	•	•	•	...	...	3.3	1977	113.2	26.1	41.1	31.7	1.1	86.3	92.5	7.2	0.3
Guinea	•	•	•	...	•	...										
Guinea-Bissau	...	...	...	...	...	...										
Guyana	•	•	•	...	...	5.5[7]	1977	48.8	21.2	29.2	31.3	18.3	24.8	81.2	18.8	—
Haiti	•	•	•	...	...	...	1977	60.5	—26.6—		69.9	3.5	52.4	92.7	7.3	—
Honduras	•	•	•	...	...	4.5										
Hong Kong	•	...	...	...	•	...	1982						374.0	...	...	...
Hungary	•	•	•	...	•	...	1977	72,520.0	16.2	46.7	36.5	0.6	72,438.0	99.1	0.9	—
Iceland	•	•	•	•	•	15.2	1977	66,790.0	5.5	14.8	62.6	17.1	52,224.0	91.6	0.9	7.5
India	•	•	•	...	...	...	1976	30,870.4	—66.1—		22.8	11.1	17,842.9	98.4	0.9	0.7
Indonesia	•	...	•	...	...	...										
Iran	•	•	•	...	•	7.2[7]	1981	151,600					139,900	...	...	...
Iraq	•	•	•	...	...	...	1977	107.8	9.9	55.6	21.9	12.6	71.0	94.0	2.4	3.6
Ireland	•	•	•	•	•	...	1977	988.3	11.4	25.3	60.8	2.5	986.9	94.6	4.6	0.8
Israel	•	•	•	•	•	19.0	1977	15,979.7	13.6	46.2		8.4	14,641.2	89.6	4.7	5.7
Italy	•	•	•	•	•	27.7	1977	36,034,000.0	13.5	61.2	21.2	4.1	39,437,000.0	89.8	6.8	3.4
Ivory Coast	•	•	•	...	•	3.1	1980	34,427.0					18,864.0	...	...	...
Jamaica	•	•	•	...	...	3.3[9]	1977	161.0	10.5	12.3	67.9	9.3	118.7	88.8	11.2	—
Japan	•	•	•	•	•	14.8[7]	1977	20,911,754.0	25.0	28.8	31.8	14.4	16,202,854.0	89.4	2.3	8.3
Jordan	•	...	•	...	...	...	1981						2.3[8]	...	...	...
Kampuchea	...	...	...	...	...	...										
Kenya	•	...	•	...	...	0.1	1977	55.9	19.6	26.5	38.1	15.8	30.9	97.2	2.8	—
Kiribati	...	...	...	...	...	...										
Korea, North	•	•	•	...	...	...										
Korea, South	•	...	•	...	...	6.4										
Kuwait	•	...	...	...	...	4.0	1981						9.1	...	...	...
Laos	...	...	...	...	...	...							...	...	...	...
Lebanon	•	...	•	...	•	...										
Lesotho	•	...	•	...	...	1.4	1977	—					0.9			
Liberia	•	...	•	...	...	...	1982	—					2.0			
Libya	•	•	•	...	...	...	1977	192.9	9.1	28.7	58.7	3.5	128.2	96.2	3.2	0.5
Liechtenstein	•	•	•	•	•	...										
Luxembourg	•	•	•	•	•	47.5	1977	27,424.2	25.6	38.8	24.8	10.8	24,614.3	96.2	3.2	0.6
Macau	...	...	...	...	...	...	1981						...	...	...	...
Madagascar	•	...	•	...	•	...	1980						...			
Malawi	...	...	...	...	...	1.5	1974	4,320								
Malaysia	•	...	•	...	...	3.4[7]	1977	1,457.8	—51.6—		22.0	26.4	705.2	92.0	2.5	5.5
Maldives	...	...	...	...	...	...	1977									
Mali	•	•	•	...	•	6.8[7]	1977	6,088.0	5.1	47.0	43.3	4.6	4,745.0	82.1	16.4	1.5
Malta	•	•	•	•	•	34.4	1977	26.9	19.4	23.4	56.5	0.7	24.2	91.8	8.2	—
Martinique	...	...	...	...	...	...										
Mauritania	•	...	•	...	•	3.8[7]	1979	426.0					423.0	...	...	...
Mauritius	•	...	•	...	•	11.6	1977	344.6	6.6	25.3	64.9	3.2	301.8	99.0	0.5	0.5
Mayotte	...	...	...	...	...	...										
Mexico	•	•	•	...	...	16.0	1981	146,480.0					173,010.0	...			
Monaco	...	...	...	...	...	...										
Mongolia	...	...	...	...	...	...							...	...	...	...
Montserrat	•	•	...	...	...	...										
Morocco	•	•	•	...	•	5.2	1977	913.4	5.3	66.3	23.8	4.6	663.5	93.8	6.2	—
Mozambique	...	...	...	...	...	...										
Nauru	•	•	...	...	•	...										
Nepal	•	...	...	...	...	0.5	1981	—					21.8			
Netherlands, The	•	•	•	•	•	36.4	1982	81,266.0	53.0	36.2	9.9	0.9	81,266.0	99.5	3.6	-3.1
Netherlands Antilles	...	...	...	...	...	11.4[7]	1979	—					29.1			
New Caledonia	...	...	...	...	...	...										
New Zealand	•	•	•	•	•	...	1977	2,691.7	3.1	5.4	89.6	1.9	2,549.5	99.4	0.4	0.2
Nicaragua	•	•	•	...	•	4.4	1977	444.5	14.8	36.3	45.5	3.4	360.1	90.0	10.0	—
Niger	•	•	•	...	•	1.7	1977	2,597.7	5.2	41.0	48.4	5.4	2,015.6	94.1	4.5	1.4
Nigeria	•	...	•	...	...	1.1[9]	1978	—					126.7			
Niue	...	...	...	...	...	...							...	...	...	...
Norfolk Island	...	...	...	...	...	...										
Norway	•	•	•	•	•	30.6[9]	1977	39,433.8	21.8	39.5	37.3	1.4	37,269.9	97.7	2.3	—
Oman	...	...	...	...	...	...	1982						...	...	...	...
Pakistan	•	•	•	...	...	...	1981	—					1,798.0			
Panama	•	•	•	...	...	10.6[7]	1977	213.3	23.8	49.7	18.3	8.2	169.4	89.1	10.9	—
Papua New Guinea	...	...	•	...	...	...	1981						0.8			
Paraguay	•	•	•	...	...	19.1[7]	1981	10,846.0					8,033.0	...			
Peru	•	•	•	...	...	0.2[7]	1981	—					2,770.0			
Philippines	•	•	•	...	...	1.4	1981	—					448.0			
Pitcairn Island	...	...	...	...	...	...										
Poland	•	•	•	...	•	...	1977	223,744.0	1.2	57.4	41.1	0.3	204,858.0	99.4	0.3	0.3
Portugal	•	•	•	•	•	26.8[6]	1976	56,704.3	21.9	67.9	7.6	2.6	51,125.8	91.7	7.5	0.8
Puerto Rico	•	•	•	•	...	...							...	...	...	...
Qatar	...	...	...	...	...	...										
Réunion	...	...	...	...	...	...										
Romania	•	•	•	...	•	10.4[7]	1977	46,098.9	—	54.1	45.9	—	41,829.0	100.0	—	—

| fire and police protection, about 1980 | | | | | military, defense | | | | | | country |
| government expenditures per 1,000 population | | population per police officer[a] | population per fireman[b] | fire stations per 1,000 population | personnel | | expenditures | | | | |
police (U.S.$)	fire (U.S.$)				armed forces ('000)[c]	armed forces per 1,000 pop.[c]	total ('000,000 U.S.$)	per capita (U.S.$)	percent of national budget	percent of GDP or GNP	
...	...	—41.9[18]—		...	233	9.8	10,236	613	6.0	5.7[1]	Germany, East
...	...	2,681.3	...	...	480	8.0	24,351	395	9.23	4.3	Germany, West
...	...	624.0	4,328.2	.002	13	1.2	141[3]	11[3]	3.7[1]	1.4[9]	Ghana
...	...	167.2	487.6	...	—	5	—	—	—	—	Gibraltar
—45,876.0—		303.3	...	...	186	21.1	2,782	284	19.2[2]	6.7	Greece
108,097.9	...				—	5	—	—			Greenland
15,202.4	...	218.4	...	...	...	...	...	...	13.9[7]	...	Grenada
...	...	...	...	...	—	5	—	—	—	—	Guadeloupe
—103,131.8—		...	...	...	—	5	—	—	—	—	Guam
...	...	673.1	...	...	17	2.4	146	19	9.9[1]	0.9	Guatemala
...	...	1,143.9	...	...	17	3.6[2]	79[3]	15[3]	...	...	Guinea
...	...	...	...	...	4	7.6	9	11	6.6[1]	6.4[1]	Guinea-Bissau
15,16	...	16	...	...	7	5.7	23	29	5.3[4]	6.9[9]	Guyana
...	...	...	...	...	8	1.3	26	5	7.7[1]	1.7[2]	Haiti
...	...	1,040.0	...	...	16	3.3	46[7]	13[7]	11.4[7]	2.3[7]	Honduras
...	9,589.0	225.2	943.6	.008	...	2.0[5]	...	...	4.4[4,5]	1.3[1,5]	Hong Kong
16	...	16	...	...	112	9.9	3,108	290	6.0[13]	2.4	Hungary
...	...	...	...	...	—	0.0	—	—	—	—	Iceland
765.9	...	820.0	...	...	1,120	1.6	6,223	9	25.2	2.6[7]	India
...	...	1,319.3	...	...	270	1.8	2,876	18	12.7[3]	2.3[3]	Indonesia
21,088.2	...	19	...	...	470	6.0	7,145	179	11.7[3]	13.7[2]	Iran
...	...	193.5	...	...	450	25.2	11,689	835	14.0[1]	9.8[2]	Iraq
58,654.0	...	358.5	...	...	21	4.4	340	97	3.0[4]	1.7[3]	Ireland
23,098.5	...	199.1	...	...	180	43.3	5,838	1,497	25.0	37.9	Israel
...	...	285.7	...	...	391	6.5	9,778	174	4.1	2.6	Italy
...	...	636.1	...	...	6	0.6	146	17	3.9[1]	1.1[2]	Ivory Coast
24,258.5	2,914.9	555.5	972.4	...	2	1.0	46	20	2.7[9]	0.9[2]	Jamaica
55,594.0	25,990.0	277.8	...	...	241	2.1	12,159	103	5.8[13]	1.0	Japan
27,536.0	...	1,976.6	...	...	65	20.9	984	298	25.0[3]	13.8[3]	Jordan
...	...	...	...	...	30	16.1	67[6]	10[6]	...	11.0[6]	Kampuchea
...	...	425.1	...	...	13	0.9	278	16	11.2[4]	4.2[7]	Kenya
...	...	...	...	...	...	...	...	...	...	...	Kiribati
...	...	441.4	...	...	710	41.8	3,500	187	15.1[13]	10.2	Korea, North
...	...	—1,509.8—	...	...	600	15.3	4,783	118	35.0	7.6	Korea, South
...	...		...	...	13	7.9	1,638	1,023	14.4[4]	4.7[1]	Kuwait
...	...	275.2	...	...	57	15.6	50[7]	15[7]	10.3[6]	...	Laos
...	...	...	...	...	23	8.7	288	111	9.0	6.6[7]	Lebanon
...	...	...	...	...	2	2.2	13[3]	9[3]	...	...	Lesotho
...	...	1,570.0	...	...	7	3.5	50	25	13.5	3.6[3]	Liberia
26,666.7	...	16	...	...	55	20.2	2,750[1]	1,171[1]	20.6[5]	2.3[1]	Libya
...	...	...	...	...	...	20	...	...	—	—	Liechtenstein
15,067.0	...	...	...	...	1	1.9	49	122	2.3[3]	1.2	Luxembourg
...	...	...	1,718.8	...	...	...	16	61	16.9	—	Macau
...	...	2,904.7	...	...	20	2.3	114	13	12.8[13]	3.0[7]	Madagascar
...	...	1,666.7	...	...	4	1.0[1]	37[3]	6[3]	8.7	1.7[7]	Malawi
...	...	292.9	...	...	100	6.7	1,613	110	11.9[4]	8.0	Malaysia
2,003.2[11]	—	157.0[11,16]	[11]	...	...	6.4[16]	...	...	...	...	Maldives
...	...	...	...	...	7	1.2	2.9	4	17.4[1]	2.5[1]	Mali
...	...	276.9	...	...	1	2.5	14	35	1.7[1]	0.5[1]	Malta
...	...	...	...	...	...	5	—	—	—	—	Martinique
...	...	1,170.0	...	...	8	4.6	59	37	18.1	8.6[3]	Mauritania
...	...	243.6	...	...	—	0.4[1]	3	3	0.9	0.5[1]	Mauritius
...	...	...	...	...	...	5	—	—	—	—	Mayotte
...	...	...	...	...	145	1.6	1,261	17	2.5[3]	0.6[3]	Mexico
...	...	...	...	...	...	...	...	...	...	...	Monaco
...	...	116.7[21]	...	...	36[1]	20.4	135[9]	90[9]	15.9[4]	12.7[1]	Mongolia
16,900.6	...	153.6	...	0.15	—	5	—	—	—	—	Montserrat
16	...	16	...	...	125	6.5	1,492	67	6.1[4]	6.3[1]	Morocco
...	...	...	...	...	20	2.2[1]	163	13	28.9[1]	3.4[1]	Mozambique
...	...	106.2	...	...	...	...	...	...	...	...	Nauru
496.7	...	1,000.0	...	...	24	1.7[1]	23	1	6.5[3]	1.1[1]	Nepal
100,727.0	...	552.7	...	...	108	7.3	4,755	333	7.8[4]	3.2	Netherlands, The
...	...	...	...	...	—	5	...	...	0.4[5,7]	—	Netherlands Antilles
...	...	...	...	...	—	5	—	—	—	—	New Caledonia
38,418.3	...	646.0	1,272.6	.08	13	4.1	543	175	5.4[3]	2.0	New Zealand
...	...	93.0[22]	...	...	75	6.2	169[3]	65[3]	11.0[1]	6.7[1]	Nicaragua
...	...	2,352.9[14]	...	...	3	1.1[1]	16	3	3.8[1]	1.0[1]	Niger
...	...	1,142.1	...	...	132	1.7	1,792	22	5.2	2.9[1]	Nigeria
22,815.9	...	274.7	...	...	—	5	—	—			Niue
37,420.2	...	620.7	...	...	—	5	—	—			Norfolk Island
78,262.0	27,931.0	...	...	...	37	10.2	1,823	445	7.7[4]	3.0	Norway
...	...	131.7	...	...	15	19.0	1,685	1,872	45.1[4]	22.3[1]	Oman
1,953.5	...	722.2	...	...	478	5.5	2,033	22	36.8	5.2	Pakistan
16	...	...	...	...	10	5.8	31	16	2.9[1]	0.8[1]	Panama
...	...	721.4	...	...	3	1.2	38	12	4.0[3]	1.4[3]	Papua New Guinea
...	...	312.5	...	...	16	5.8	96	28	13.2[3]	1.2[1]	Paraguay
...	...	508.6	...	...	164	5.8	1,078	58	25.7[4]	3.9[7]	Peru
2,423.4	...	1,027.2	...	...	155	2.2	1,033	20	10.4[4]	2.2	Philippines
...	...	...	...	...	—	5	—	—	—	—	Pitcairn Island
...	...	350.0[23]	...	...	429	8.7	13,494	373	7.2	5.4[1]	Poland
...	...	654.0[24]	...	...	68	6.6	900	90	10.8	3.4	Portugal
...	...	329.0	...	...	—	5	—	—			Puerto Rico
16	...	16	...	...	6	20.8	604[1]	3,020[1]	20.1[1]	13.6[3]	Qatar
...	...	216.7	...	...	—	4.6[5]	—	—			Réunion
...	...	...	...	...	237	8.0	4,793	213	3.7	1.6	Romania

Social protection (continued)

country	old-age invalid-ity, death	sickness and matern-ity	work injury	unem-ploy-ment	family allow-ances	expendi-tures, 1980 (percent of na-tional budget)	year	receipts total ('000,000 natl. cur.)	insured persons (%)	em-ployers (%)	govern-ment (%)	other (%)	expenditures total ('000,000 natl. cur.)	benefits (%)	admin-istration (%)	other (%)
Rwanda	•	...	•	...	...	1.9[7]	1977	593.9	24.9	41.4	25.1	8.6	191.5	88.2	11.4	0.4
St. Christopher and Nevis	...	...	...	...	...	...		...	...	...	...	...	...	...	...	...
St. Helena and Ascension						...		...					...			
St. Lucia	•	•	•	...	...	...	1982	9.1	...	...	...	...	3.1	...	...	...
St. Pierre and Miquelon	•	•	•	...	...	...										
St. Vincent and the Grenadines	•	...	•	...	...	...	1981	—					—	...		...
San Marino	...	...	...	...	...	...		...	...	...	...	...	...	...	...	...
São Tomé and Príncipe	•	...	...		...	...			...	...					...	
Saudi Arabia	•	...	•		...	...		...	...	...	...	...	...	...	...	...
Senegal	•	•	•	...	•	4.7[6]	1976	12,837.9	8.7	44.1	46.2	1.0	9,905.9	91.4	8.4	0.2
Seychelles	•	•	•			6.8[11]	1977						10.6			
Sierra Leone	•	•	•			3.7[6]	1977	10.5	——26.7——		73.3	—	10.0	100.0	—	—
Singapore	•	•	•			1.3	1977	1,601.6	32.8	39.9	9.8	17.5	719.8	98.7	1.2	0.1
Solomon Islands	•					1.2[1]		...	...	...	...	...	...	...	...	...
Somalia			•			1.7[1]	1978	—					34.2			
South Africa	•	•	•	•	•	...	1980	204.0	...				165.0	...		...
South West Africa/Namibia	...	...	...	...	...											
Spain	•	•	•	•	•	57.3[6]	1977	1,245,573.3	15.9	73.2	9.1	1.8	1,238,952.7	92.9	3.2	3.9
Sri Lanka	•	•	•			25.8[11]	1977	1,131.7	13.5	25.6	44.7	16.2	710.4	98.8	1.0	0.2
Sudan, The	•	•				0.7	1982						26.8			...
Suriname	•	...		...	...	6.9[28]	1976	—					29.1			...
Swaziland	•					...	1981	—					—			...
Sweden	•	•	•	•	•	47.1	1977	118,899.4	1.2	44.1	47.3	7.4	107,085.1	97.5	2.5	—
Switzerland	•	•	•	•	•	48.3	1977	24,722.4	36.7	22.0	32.5	8.8	23,539.9	94.1	2.5	3.4
Syria	•					8.0	1981						2,086.0			
Taiwan	•	•				...		...	...	...	...	...	...	...	...	...
Tanzania	•		•			1.1[7]	1981						163.0			
Thailand			•			2.3	1982						4,557.0			
Togo	•	•	•		•	4.6[6]	1977	3,753.0	11.3	38.7	47.2	2.8	3,570.0	84.8	12.9	2.3
Tokelau	...	...	...	...	...	...		...	...	...	...	...	...	...	...	...
Tonga																
Trinidad and Tobago	•	•	•			6.3[7]	1977	284.2	9.7	20.3	64.2	5.8	211.0	96.3	3.7	—
Trust Territory of the Pacific Is.																
Tunisia	•	•	•	•	•	7.3	1977	124.5	25.6	53.9	3.7	16.8	67.8	90.0	6.1	3.9
Turkey	•	•	•	•		2.7	1977	55,872.6	31.6	50.4	3.9	14.1	35,348.6	80.5	16.0	3.5
Turks and Caicos Islands	...	...	...	...	...	...		...	...	...	...	...	...	...	...	...
Tuvalu	...	...	...	...	...	...		...	...	...	...	...	...	...	...	...
Uganda	•	•	•			...	1982						401.0			
U.S.S.R.	•	•	•	•	•	...	1977	54,271.0	—	—	96.4	3.6	54,271.0	100.0	—	...
United Arab Emirates	...	...	...	...	...	2.5	1980						330.4			
United Kingdom	•	•	•	•	•	26.2[7]	1977	23,120.0	17.7	29.5	50.5	2.3	21,334.0	94.2	3.2	2.6
United States	•	•	•	•	•	34.1	1977	280,460.0	21.4	35.6	37.8	5.2	259,531.0	94.2	2.8	3.0
Uruguay	•	•	•	•	•	47.7	1977	2,252.1[9]	24.6	47.4	22.1	3.9	2,045.7[6]	88.6	8.9	2.5
Vanuatu	...	...	...	...	...	...		...	...	...	...	...	...	...	...	...
Venezuela	•	•	•	•		6.0	1977	6,953.3	9.2	18.4	67.8	4.6	6,226.3	94.0	6.0	—
Vietnam	•	•				...		...	...	...	...	...	...	...	...	...
Virgin Islands (U.S.)	•	•	•	•		...		...	...	...	...	...	...	...	...	...
Wallis and Futuna	...	...	...	...	...	...		...	...	...	...	...	...	...	...	...
Western Sahara	•		•			...		...	...	...	...	...	...	...	...	...
Western Samoa	•		•			...		...	...	...	...	...	...	...	...	...
Yemen (Aden)	...	...	...	...	...	...	1981	...	...	...	...	...	...	...	...	...
Yemen (Şan'ā')	•	•	•	•	•	7.7	1981	—					14,450.0	...	...	...
Yugoslavia							1981	66.4	...	...			75.2	...	...	...
Zaire	•	•	•		•	0.1	1981	...								
Zambia	•	•	•	•	•		1977	119.8	——40.7——		47.9	11.4	89.4	95.4	4.6	...
Zimbabwe						...	1981	—					87.0			

fire and police protection, about 1980					military, defense						country
government expenditures per 1,000 population		population per police officer a	population per fireman b	fire stations per 1,000 population	personnel		expenditures				
police (U.S.$)	fire (U.S.$)				armed forces ('000) c	armed forces per 1,000 pop. c	total ('000,000 U.S.$)	per capita (U.S.$)	percent of national budget	percent of GDP or GNP	
27.7[11]	...	[11]	[11]	...	5	1.0	21[3]	4[3]	13.1[1]	1.7[7]	Rwanda
8,368.9[11]	—	166.4[11]	[11]	...	...	[5]	...	...	...	...	St. Christopher and Nevis
...	...	240.3	...	...	...	...	...	...	—	...	St. Helena and Ascension
...	...	—232.2—	...	...	...	[5]	...	...	...	...	St. Lucia
...	...		...	...	—	[5]	—	...	—	—	St. Pierre and Miquelon
...	...	204.5[11]	[11]	...	...	...	...	...	6.1[3]	...	St. Vincent and the Grenadines
...	...	...	...	...	...	...	...	...	...	...	San Marino
...	...	500.0	...	...	—	0.0	—	—	2.5[1]	1.3[1]	São Tomé and Príncipe
131,140.0	...	280.0	...	...	55	5.4	24,754	2,451	30.7[13]	14.9[1]	Saudi Arabia
...	...	732.7	...	...	8	2.5[2]	59	10	11.9	2.6[1]	Senegal
...	...	142.9	2,416.7	...	1	14.7	8	119	...	...	Seychelles
...	...	782.1	...	...	2	1.2[1]	14	4	3.8[1]	1.1[1]	Sierra Leone
...	...	234.8	2,841.0	.003	50	17.0	869	348	21.7[3]	6.1[3]	Singapore
5,012.0	...	614.3	...	...	...	...	...	...	...	...	Solomon Islands
...	...	537.5[11]	[11]	...	54	10.9[1]	160	26	28.4[4]	6.9[1]	Somalia
28,460.0	...	867.1	...	...	70	2.6	3,161	105	18.7	3.5[3]	South Africa
...	...	...	...	...	...	[5]	—	—	—	—	South West Africa/Namibia
...	...	362.0[26]	...	...	353	9.1[1]	4,123	109	10.2	2.0[3]	Spain
...	...	861.6	...	...	18	1.2[1]	26	2	1.7[3]	1.0[1]	Sri Lanka
12,049.0	...	740.7	...	...	65	3.0	340	17	9.5[3]	2.2[1]	Sudan, The
...	...	...	...	...	2	2.5[1]	...	...	...	...	Suriname
21,248.6	...	609.8	...	...	2	2.2	27	45	14.4[4]	2.9[1]	Swaziland
176,110.0	...	...	...	...	70	7.7	3,878	467	7.5[4]	3.1	Sweden
135,820.0	...	...	...	...	23	3.1	2,017	315	21.4	2.1	Switzerland
...	...	1,150.0	...	...	290	23.0	2,528	269	37.7[3]	14.8[3]	Syria
...	...	...	1,036.3	...	504	25.1	3,660	198	39.4[1]	7.4[1]	Taiwan
1,953.1	...	1,333.3	...	...	53	2.1	306	15	11.2[3]	5.0[1]	Tanzania
4,262.4	...	527.8	...	...	241	4.8	1,562	31	20.1	3.9	Thailand
...	...	...	...	...	4	3.1	19	7	7.0[1]	2.5[2]	Togo
...	...	214.3	...	...	—	[5]	—	—	—	—	Tokelau
7,138.7	...	409.5	...	...	...	[29]	—	5[3]	2.7[1]	—	Tonga
...	...	284.2	...	...	2	1.7	42[3]	35[3]	1.5	0.2[9]	Trinidad and Tobago
...	...	324.2[30]	...	...	—	[5]	—	—	—	—	Trust. Territory of the Pacific Is.
...	...	337.8[25]	...	...	32	4.3	283	42	4.3	2.6[3]	Tunisia
...	...	1,571.4	...	...	638	12.3	3,375	70	14.8[3]	5.2	Turkey
20,610.9[9]	—	113.1[9]	[11]	...	—	[5]	—	—	—	—	Turks and Caicos Islands
13,068.9	...	...	...	...	—	0.0	—	—	—	—	Tuvalu
1,172.7	...	1,093.3	...	...	6	7.5	102	8	19.6	1.7[2]	Uganda
...	...	1,045.4[25]	...	...	4,400	13.7	257,000	952	48.3[1,27]	8.7[3]	U.S.S.R.
...	...	138.0	...	...	44	43.4	2,179	1,816	47.5[1]	5.8[2]	United Arab Emirates
79,280.9[31]	18,439.3[31]	400.0	1,427.6	...	322	5.9	27,368	489	13.6	5.1	United Kingdom
73,687.0	27,469.0	458.5	1,062.1	...	2,108	9.1	196,345	846	28.6[13]	7.2	United States
...	...	176.5	...	...	29	10.1	409	141	12.5	3.4[3]	Uruguay
...	...	445.0	...	...	...	...	...	...	...	...	Vanuatu
...	...	324.3	...	...	56	2.8	1,638	94	5.8	1.6	Venezuela
...	...	38.1[32]	...	...	1,200	18.4	...	...	...	10.5[1]	Vietnam
201,193.2	...	315.0	676.2	...	—	[5]	—	—	—	—	Virgin Islands (U.S.)
...	...	...	...	...	—	[5]	—	—	—	—	Wallis and Futuna
...	...	...	...	...	—	[5]	—	—	—	—	Western Sahara
6,997.1	...	...	...	...	...	...	...	...	...	—	Western Samoa
...	...	1,440.0	...	...	25	13.3	120[1]	63[1]	45.9[1]	12.8[1]	Yemen (Aden)
1,905.3	...	500.0	...	...	22	4.5	610	109	32.6[3]	8.3[1]	Yemen (Şan'ā')
...	...	...	...	...	247	11.0	2,891	128	48.6	5.0[1]	Yugoslavia
...	...	1,409.1	...	...	26	1.5[1]	71	2	12.4[1]	3.1[1]	Zaire
...	...	538.1	...	...	15	2.6[1]	113[1]	19[1]	8.6[1]	3.8[1]	Zambia
12,457.2	...	750.0	...	...	40	8.4	453	56	10.2	8.8[1]	Zimbabwe

[1]1980. [2]1978. [3]1981. [4]1983. [5]Dependency. [6]1975. [7]1979. [8]Welfare payments. [9]1977. [10]Social services. [11]Fire services are part of police function. [12]Pensions only. [13]1984. [14]Includes paramilitary forces. [15]Local patrolmen only. [16]Armed forces perform police functions. [17]Greek Cypriots only. [18]Includes civil defense personnel. [19] 340.0 in urban areas; 272.0 in rural areas. [20]Military defense is the responsibility of Switzerland. [21]Includes frontier guards. [22]Includes civilian militia. [23]Citizens militia only. [24]Public security police only. [25]MVD (internal security) only. [26]Paramilitary force. [27]Spending for defense per 1982 official government figures equals 5.0%. [28]1976. [29]Military defense is the responsibility of New Zealand. [30]Palau and Marshall Islands only. [31]England and Wales only. [32]Militia only.

Education

This table presents international data on education arranged to provide comparability among the different types of educational systems in the nations of the world. The principal data are, naturally, numbers of students, teachers, and schools, arranged by four principal levels of education—the first, or primary; the general second-level (secondary); vocational second-level; and third level (higher). These data are supplemented by some indication of each country's capability to educate children who are potentially educable in the age group usually represented at each level. At the first and second level this is given as a net enrollment ratio and at the third level by a gross enrollment ratio and an additional measure of the number of persons who have completed a course of higher education. No such ratio is provided for vocational training at the second level because of the great variation worldwide in what constitutes vocational training (electronics training in a developed country such as West Germany, for example, might be at a level that would qualify as higher education in a less developed country), in the need of countries to promote and direct students into vocational programs (to support national development), and, most particularly, in the age range of students that normally constitute a national vocational system (some will be as young as 14, having just completed a primary cycle; others will be in their mid-50s, either learning a skill for the first time or retraining to acquire a new skill). For such reasons, it is not possible to construct a good comparative measure of overall national vocational programs.

At each level of education, differences in national statistical practice, in national educational structure, and in the kind and extent of public-private mix, training and deployment of teachers, and timing of cycles of enrollment or completion of particular levels of grades all contribute to the problems of comparability between national educational systems.

Even something as basic as reporting the number of schools is not simply a matter of counting red-brick buildings with classrooms in them. Often the resources of a developing country are such that temporary facilities are all that can be afforded, while in a developed but sparsely settled country students might have to travel 50 miles a day to find a classroom with 20 students of the same age, leading to the institution of traveling teachers, radio instruction at home under the supervision of parents, or similar measures.

The number of students may conceal great variation in what each country defines as a particular educational "level." Many countries do, indeed, have a primary system comprised of grades 1 through 6 that passes its students on to some kind of post-primary education. But the age of intake, the willingness (or economic ability) of parents to send their children or to permit them to finish that level, or the need to withdraw the children seasonally for agricultural work all make even a simple enrollment figure difficult to assess in isolation. All of these difficulties are compounded when a country has instruction in more than one language, or when its educational establishment is so small that higher, sometimes even secondary, education cannot take place within the country, as is the case with a number of the developing countries or among the smaller island nations of the Pacific. Enrollment figures in this table may, therefore, include students enrolled outside the country.

All of these difficulties also limit the comparability of statistics on numbers of teachers, and there may be the further complications that many at any level must work part-time, or that the institutions in which they work may perform a mixture of functions that do not break down into the tidy categories a table of this sort requires (a business school training secretaries must teach language skills as well as typing skills; a general secondary school may have a number of educators dedicated full- or part-time to the teaching of industrial arts or athletics). Separating data for

Education

country	year	first level (primary)					general second level (secondary)[a]					vocational second level	
		schools	students[c]	teachers[d]	student/teacher ratio	net enrollment ratio	schools	students[c]	teachers[d]	student/teacher ratio	net enrollment ratio	schools	students[c]
Afghanistan	1981	4,018	1,198,286	37,537	31.9	27	318[1]	144,858	6,409	22.6	...	27[1]	12,410[2]
Albania	1980	1,559	552,651	25,980	21.3	...	...	31,384	1,029	30.5	...	...	132,482
Algeria	1983	9,864	3,241,924	99,648	32.5	81[2]	1,429	1,280,719	53,261	24.0	28[3]	71[4]	26,218[4]
American Samoa	1981	32	7,098	328[6]	...	...	7	3,319	132[6]	...	...	1[3]	45[3]
Andorra	1975	...	3,802	...	...	...	...	1,753	...	...	...	...	...
Angola	1981	7,026	1,258,858	40,027	31.5	...	182[7]	134,769	...	...	...	68[7]	2,642
Anguilla	1982	6	1,487	61	24.3	...	1	473	20	23.7	...	...	153[9]
Antigua and Barbuda	1980	44	10,660	431	24.7	...	18	4,526	318	14.2	...	1	153[9]
Argentina	1982	20,201	4,197,372	206,535	20.3	...	1,942	594,167	81,026	7.3	...	2,954	831,481
Australia	1983	8,336	1,809,035	94,224	19.2	100[5]	1,572	1,206,771	93,273	12.9	79[2]	373	729,291
Austria	1982	3,434	378,956	27,731	13.7	87[2]	2,107	571,730	58,599	9.8	...	1,170	380,376
Bahamas, The	1980	190	37,399	1,768	21.2	...	38	23,761	1,276	18.6	...	...	1,823[12]
Bahrain	1980	114	48,406	2,963	16.3	78	22	23,824	971	24.5	49	4	2,749
Bangladesh	1981	43,936	8,236,526	188,234	43.8	60	8,841[12]	2,062,722	85,801	24.0	...	...	345,166
Barbados	1983	139	34,848	...	...	100[5]	36	26,552	...	...	82[5]	6[5]	2,343[5]
Belgium	1981	4,850	821,059	45,130	18.2	97	...	432,371	...	...	83	...	239,711
Belize	1982	196	35,081	1,468	23.9	...	22	6,289	352	17.9	...	...	51[10]
Benin	1981	2,480	404,297	10,381	38.9	...	...	99,295	...	...	...	...	4,441[2]
Bermuda	1984	22	5,538	312	17.8	...	13	4,227	355	11.9	...	...	227[5]
Bhutan	1981	119	22,288	797	28.0	8[3]	32	14,667	569	25.8	...	2	401
Bolivia	1983	8,514	1,154,819	50,703	22.8	...	845	174,982	8,091	21.6	...	...	...
Botswana	1983	515	195,000[6]	6,930[6]	28.1[6]	84	45	22,440	1,307	17.2	17	23[2]	1,741[2]
Brazil	1981	201,926	22,598,254	884,257	25.6	...	7,443	2,819,182	198,097	14.2	...	...	...
British Virgin Islands	1980	24	3,604	108	33.4	...	1	791	55	14.4	...	—	—
Brunei	1981	175	31,677	1,800	17.6	...	29	17,519	1,411	12.4	...	4	570
Bulgaria	1983	777	69,997	4,925	14.2	97[5]	2,733	1,095,364	63,484	17.3	70[5]	516	193,141
Burkina Faso	1981	1,037	223,843	3,744	59.8	17	...	25,273	1,112	22.7	...	...	5,870
Burma	1978	21,999	3,841,687	80,343	47.8	65[9]	1,864	1,019,567	31,403	32.5	16[9]	58	12,548
Burundi	1982	794	207,457	5,570	37.2	18[5]	60	15,710	930[6]	...	1[5]	19	2,906
Cameroon	1982	5,148	1,443,728	28,585	50.5	75[3]	353	182,530	6,442	28.3	16[2]	168	59,290
Canada	1981	...	2,296,996	119,200[3]	...	96	...	2,340,255[14]	139,100[3, 14]	...	85	...	[14]
Cape Verde	1983	449	57,262	1,959	29.2	...	3	3,192	103	31.0	...	1	724
Cayman Islands	1983	15	2,689	77	34.9	...	1[6]	2,100	135[6]	...	...	3	132
Central African Republic	1980	825	246,174	4,130	59.6	54	...	43,101	...	...	...	...	2,723
Chad	1976	783	210,882	2,610	80.8	25	...	18,931	...	...	...	...	649
Chile	1983	8,858	2,139,155	...	...	...	2,911	1,227,167	...	...	...	347	143,689
China	1982	880,516	139,720,000	5,505,000	25.4	...	107,892	47,028,000	2,871,000	16.4	...	...	1,214,900
Christmas Island	1984	1	352	29	12.1	...	1	149	16	9.3	...	...	...
Cocos (Keeling) Islands	1984	2	125	8	15.6	...	1	22	3	7.3	...	...	...
Colombia	1981	34,641	4,217,800	137,721	30.6	...	...	1,891,530[6]	88,103[6]	21.5[6]	...	...	[6]
Comoros	1980	236	59,709	1,292	46.2	...	32	13,528	434	31.2	...	3	196
Congo	1981	1,377	406,835	6,997	58.1	...	122	171,862	3,638	47.2	...	36	18,150
Cook Islands	1984	28	2,695	163	16.5	...	8	2,551	169	15.1	...	...	...
Costa Rica	1983	3,511	343,800	...	...	92[5]	242	153,971	...	...	40[5]	...	58,942
Cuba	1981	11,771	1,409,765	83,113	17.0	97	...	861,700	68,580	12.7	61[1]	...	195,063
Cyprus	1984	413	46,653	2,212	21.1	...	89	44,071	2,606	16.9	...	18	5,395
Czechoslovakia	1984	6,445	1,992,400	92,435	21.6	...	368	160,082	10,029	16.0	...	539	274,904
Denmark	1982	2,346[2]	420,064	40,261[1]	...	...	2,787[1, 14]	498,462[14]	...	...	...	[14]	[14]
Djibouti	1981	48	18,896	382	49.5	...	9	3,877	185	21.0	...	9	1,279
Dominica	1979	63	15,220	423	36.0	...	67	9,863	305	32.3	...	4	400

students and teachers in teacher-training programs is particularly difficult, since in certain countries teacher training is defined as higher education, in others a vocational form of secondary training, and so on. For purposes of this table, all teacher training at the secondary level has been treated as general education, since both training and actual local practice usually require a variety of general academic skills. At the higher level, teacher training is assumed to be one more variety of specialization in higher education itself.

With all of the limitations to the comparability of the statistics referred to above, the student-teacher ratio does, nevertheless, provide a fairly representative measure of the true ratio of trained educators to the enrolled educable. In general, at each level of education both students and teachers have been counted on the basis of full-time enrollment or employment, or full-time equivalent when country statistics permit. At the primary and secondary levels, net enrollment ratio is the ratio of the number of children within the age group for a particular level who are actually enrolled to the total number of children in that age group ($\times$ 100). This ratio is always less than 100 and is the most accurate measure of the completeness of enrollment at that particular level. It is not always, however, the best indication of utilization of that particular level. That indication is best seen in a gross enrollment ratio, which compares total enrollment (of all ages) to the population within the normal age limits for that level. For a country with substantial adult literacy or general educational programs for which both kinds of data are available, the difference may be striking: typically, for a developing country, even one with a good net enrollment ratio of 90 to 95, the gross enrollment ratio may be 20, 25, even 30 percent higher, indicating the heavy use made by the country of facilities and teachers at that level. In this table, however, gross enrollment ratio is provided only at the third level because of the wide range of ages

that are typically represented in higher educational enrollment in any particular country.

Literacy data provided here have been compiled as far as possible from data for the population age 15 and over for the best comparability internationally, even though many countries work from different assumptions about the best way to measure literacy. The age cutoffs may be much different—as low as 6 or 8 years or as high as legal majority in the country concerned. The standards of what constitutes literacy may also differ markedly; sometimes completion of a certain number of years of school is taken to constitute literacy; elsewhere it may mean only the ability to read or write at a minimal level testable by a census taker; in other countries quite sophisticated sample studies may have been undertaken to distinguish between those who have completed a good deal of school but who may still be functionally illiterate.

Finally, the data provided for public expenditure on education are generally complete in the sense that they include data for all levels of public expenditure (national, state, local) but are incomplete for certain countries in that they do not include data for private expenditure; in some countries this fraction of the educational establishment may be of significant size. Data, however, are often not available. Occasionally data for external aid to education may be included in addition to domestic expenditure.

a. Includes teacher training at this level.
b. Latest.
c. Full-time; may include students registered in foreign schools.
d. Full-time.
e. Of all degrees; may include graduates of foreign colleges and universities.

teachers[d]	student/ teacher ratio	third level (higher)							literacy[b]				public expenditure on education (percent of GNP)[b]	country
		institutions	students[c]	teachers[d]	student/ teacher ratio	gross enrollment ratio	graduates per 10,000 among population aged 20–24[b,e]	percent of population aged 25 and over with post-secondary education[b]	over age	total (%)	male (%)	female (%)		
1,262	...	29	22,974[3]	1,448[3]	15.9[3]		36.0	3.2	15	20.0	33.2	5.8	1.8	Afghanistan
4,363	30.4	...	14,568	1,103	13.2	5.4			...	71.5	79.9	63.1	...	Albania
2,292[4]	11.4[4]	15[4]	100,000[4]	8,573[4]	11.7	4.9[2]		0.3[5]	15	41.8[2]	55.6[2]	29.1[2]	8.3[5]	Algeria
4[3]	11.2[3]	1	987	...	...	...	442.9[5]	12.6[5]	...	...	...	...	6.2[5]	American Samoa
...	...	...	...	...	...	...			...	...	...	...		Andorra
...	...	1	2,415[2]	225[2]	10.7[2]	0.4[2]			15	15.0	...	...	2.9	Angola
...	...	...	...	...	...	...			15	98.0[8]	98.2[8]	97.9[8]	...	Anguilla
18[10]	...	...	...	...	...	...		1.3		88.7	89.7	88.0	4.0	Antigua and Barbuda
110,703	7.5	1,041	550,556	53,166	10.4	24.5		4.0	15	94.9	95.5	94.4	3.9	Argentina
44,776	16.3	64	349,243	21,866	16.0	26.3[5]	583.5[5]	21.5[5]	15	99.0[11]	...	...	5.9[5]	Australia
772	18.3	43	131,580	10,870	12.1	24.0	144.5	2.6	15	99.0	...	...	6.0	Austria
92[12]	19.8[12]	1	4,093	127	32.2		69.2	3.8		90.1	90.6	89.6	9.8	Bahamas, The
213	12.9	2	1,024[13]	159	6.4	5.3	69.2	3.8	15	79.1	83.0	73.7	3.0	Bahrain
540[2]	...	396	240,181[2]	12,428[2]	19.3[2]	3.0[2]	20.9	0.9	15	25.8	37.3	13.2	1.7	Bangladesh
...	...	2[5]	4,033[5]	317[5]	12.7[5]	13.6[2]		3.0[5]	15	99.3[5]	99.3[5]	99.3[5]	7.1[5]	Barbados
...	...		196,153[2]	...	...	26.1	507.2	7.2		99.0	...	...	6.1	Belgium
6[6]	8.5[6]	5	619	33	18.8			1.4	...	91.2	91.2	91.2	...	Belize
...	...	...	3,003[3]	...	...	1.0[3]	35.3		...	27.9	39.8	16.6	3.9	Benin
52[5]	4.4[5]	1	575[5]	63[5]	9.1[5]		218.2[5]	7.4[5]	15	98.4[11]	97.9[11]	98.9[11]	3.3[5]	Bermuda
49	8.2	1	204	16	12.8	0.3				...	...	...		Bhutan
...	...	25	13,388	1,487	9.0		31.3[5]	5.0[5]	15	63.2[10]	75.8[10]	51.4[10]	3.6[5]	Bolivia
227[2]	7.7[2]	1	1,022	144	7.1			0.6	15	52.4	47.7	56.2	7.7	Botswana
...	...	882	1,354,000[2]	...	...	11.9	117.9	4.3	15	77.2	78.9	75.6	3.2	Brazil
—	—	—	—	—	—			5.4	15	98.3	98.1	98.5	4.7	British Virgin Islands
127	4.5	1	436[3]	51[3]	8.5[3]		51.2	3.1	15	77.8	85.2	69.0	2.4	Brunei
16,992	11.4	46	72,025	13,809	5.2	15.3[5]	430.6	5.2	8	94.5	...	...	6.5	Bulgaria
272	21.6	...	1,643[2]	140[2]	11.7[2]		2.8		15	9.0	14.7	3.3	2.7	Burkina Faso
1,000	12.5	19	52,137	3,167	16.5	4.2	83.1		15	65.9	75.9	56.3	1.6	Burma
214	13.6	5	2,068	...	...	0.5[2]	16.6		15	34.0	42.3	22.8	3.0	Burundi
2,325	25.5	13	11,407	557	20.5	1.6[2]	38.7	0.3	15	55.2	70.2	41.0	3.9	Cameroon
14	...	235[1]	924,445	44,464	20.8	37.0	694.5	30.9	14	99.5	...	...	7.7	Canada
103	7.0	3	199	36	5.5		38.7		15	49.3	59.2	40.8	7.5	Cape Verde
...	...	3	1,348	...	...			2.9[2]	15	97.5[2]	97.5[2]	97.6[2]	...	Cayman Islands
113	24.1	...	2,450	303	8.1	1.3[5]	5.3		15	33.0	48.3	19.2	3.6	Central African Republic
...	...	...	758	62	12.2	0.2				6.3	12.1	0.6	2.4	Chad
10,736[1]	...	24	125,363	...	...	12.8[5]	155.4[5]	3.8[5]	12	95.6	...	...	5.4[5]	Chile
127,300	9.0	715	1,154,000	287,000	4.0	1.3[11]	497.0		12	77.1	...	...	5.7	China
...	...	...	...	...	...				15	40.0	35.7	50.0	...	Christmas Island
...	...	...	...	...	...					...	...	...		Cocos (Keeling) Islands
6	6	70	318,293	34,844	9.1	12.0	91.1	3.3	15	86.3	87.0	85.7	2.6	Colombia
18	10.9	—	430	—	—	—				59.0	66.1	51.7	...	Comoros
1,261	14.4	1	7,255[2]	292[2]	24.8[2]	5.6			15	62.3	75.1	50.6	6.8	Congo
...	...	...	360[4]	41.2[4]	8.8[4]			2.1[4]		91.8[4]	92.1[4]	91.4[4]	...	Cook Islands
2,206[5]	...	14[4]	60,990[2]	...	...		214.8[5]	25.8[5]	15	93.0[2]	93.2[2]	92.8[2]	7.8[5]	Costa Rica
17,998	10.8	28	151,733[2]	10,680[2]	14.2[2]	19.5[2]	271.2		15	95.4	95.7	95.1	15.7	Cuba
505	10.7	16	2,201	240	9.2		73.3[4]	1.4[4]	15	93.1[2]	97.9[2]	88.4[2]	3.9[4]	Cyprus
16,083	17.1	36	180,995	18,406	9.8	17.8[5]	237.7[5]	6.0[5]	15	99.5[3]	99.6[3]	99.4[3]	5.2[5]	Czechoslovakia
...	...	358	81,352	...	...	284.4	28.6[2]	480.9	15	...	...	...	7.0	Denmark
88	14.5	...	150	...	...		251.9			...	...	...	5.2	Djibouti
21	19.0	2	154	8	19.2	...		1.1	15	94.1	94.0	94.2	...	Dominica

Education (continued)

country	year	first level (primary)					general second level (secondary)[a]					vocational second level	
		schools	students[c]	teachers[d]	student/teacher ratio	net enrollment ratio	schools	students[c]	teachers[d]	student/teacher ratio	net enrollment ratio	schools	students[c]
Dominican Republic	1981	4,606[2]	1,149,805	...	...	86[1]	1,633	355,685	...	...	...	...	23,692
Ecuador	1983	13,291	1,676,681	47,559	35.3		1,633	657,085	39,738	16.5	...	...	...
Egypt	1980	11,630	4,662,816	167,821	27.8		2,793	2,295,259	87,512	26.2	...	441	633,909
El Salvador	1982	2,390	810,827	18,182	44.6	56[5]	233	74,258	5,123	14.5	...	23	8,684
Equatorial Guinea	1973	559	35,977	630	57.1	...	...	4,153[12]	136	30.5[7]	...	...	370[12]
Ethiopia	1981	6,208	2,374,362	37,844	62.7	...	...	432,207[2]	10,202[2]	42.4[2]	...	...	6,020[11]
Faeroe Islands	1982	53	5,716	...	...	...	...	3,004	...	...	...	—	—
Falkland Islands	1980	...	223	15	14.9	...	...	90	11	8.2	...	—	—
Fiji	1982	662	116,719	4,256	27.4	...	138	44,664	2,467	18.1	...	36	1,028
Finland	1983	4,238	365,965	24,752	14.8	...	1,078	325,763	22,279	14.6	...	535	106,998
France	1981	68,643	7,252,575	290,933	24.9	100	11,314	5,181,566	256,284	20.2	...	2,332	799,209
French Guiana	1982	66	13,675	613[2]		...	14	6,339	341[2]	...	...	5	1,802
French Polynesia	1982	227	39,115	2,012	19.4	...	24	11,258	998	11.3	...	7	3,050
Gabon	1980	864	155,081	3,441	45.1	...	64[3]	23,876	1,215	19.7	...	10[3]	5,530
Gambia, The	1983	164	53,774	2,347	22.9	49[4]	1	202	42	4.8	...	6	856
Germany, East	1981	5,127	2,106,463	170,115[15]	...	...	1,056	46,133	[15]	...	...	541	459,485[2]
Germany, West	1981	...	4,776,000	...	...	...	23,776	5,950,897	451,894	13.2	...	5,350	610,400
Ghana	1979	7,611[1]	1,295,525	48,397[1]	...	...	...	592,333[1]	30,711[1]	19.3[1]	...	...	22,451
Gibraltar	1983	9	2,916	93	31.4	...	2	1,749	190	9.2	...	1	50
Greece	1982	9,400	891,488	37,947	23.5	96[3]	2,291	669,812	33,613	19.9	74[3]	766	108,212
Greenland	1983	92[14]	10,613[14]	1,092[14]	9.7[14]	...	[14]	[14]	[14]	[14]	...	...	1,454
Grenada	1980	77	24,106	814	29.6	...	25	6,948	304	22.9	...	2	384
Guadeloupe	1979	241	54,703	2,744	19.9	...	...	38,768	2,602[1, 10]	...	...	...	10,059
Guam	1982	37	17,784	772	23.0	...	19	11,997	512	23.4	...	1	1,186
Guatemala	1980	6,959	803,404	23,770	33.8	56	...	126,844	8,604[1, 10]	...	...	...	29,768
Guinea	1980	2,555	257,547	7,165	35.9	...	...	98,337	3,520[15]	...	...	...	2,776
Guinea-Bissau	1981	732	83,155	3,256	25.5	87	...	11,051	482	22.9	4[2]	...	290
Guyana	1980	425	130,832	3,909	33.5	88[1]	...	75,335	4,236	17.8	...	...	...
Haiti	1983	3,241	723,041	16,986	42.6	40[5]	292	117,081	5,367	21.8	...	481[4]	4,549[4]
Honduras	1983	6,264	704,612	19,270	36.6	76[2]	307[14, 5]	123,245[14, 5]	3,406[14, 5]	36.2[14, 5]	...	[14]	[14]
Hong Kong	1983	769	540,022	19,285	28.0	96[5]	421[14]	151,428[14]	16,925[14]	8.9[14]	61[5]	[14]	[14]
Hungary	1981	3,604	1,213,465	78,053	15.4	97	...	98,436	6,888	14.3	...	...	119,752
Iceland	1983	187	25,000	2,600	9.6	...	161	21,800	...	...	...	40	4,100
India	1980	485,538	72,687,840	1,345,076	54.0	...	156,055	29,337,454	1,731,978	16.9	...	...	...
Indonesia	1981	110,050	23,862,488	713,222	33.5	99	15,721	5,256,117	307,376	17.1	...	2,049	576,791
Iran	1983	44,900	5,592,808	250,167	22.4	...	9,312	1,717,097	63,611	27.0	...	822	144,946
Iraq	1981	10,816	2,637,023	98,422	26.8	...	1,625	1,053,816	31,499	33.5	49	109	56,839
Ireland	1981	3,494	568,364	20,068	28.3	91[2]	822	293,809	18,457	15.9	80[2]	47	6,792
Israel	1981	1,591	641,668	42,068	15.3	...	651	181,094	14,434	12.5	...	376	82,173
Italy	1983	29,214	4,204,272	276,716	15.2	...	12,983	3,697,330	355,818	10.4	...	4,607	1,635,345
Ivory Coast	1979	4,419	954,190	24,441	39.0	...	127	174,366	4,601	37.9	...	...	...
Jamaica	1981	894	364,637	8,676[6]		93[2]	695	234,023	9,108[6]		56[2]	18	8,904
Japan	1984	25,064	11,465,108	468,675	24.5	100[5]	16,474	10,721,217	537,557	19.9	92[5]	...	...
Jordan	1981	1,149	467,696	14,891	31.4	92	1,333	263,950	12,668	20.8	...	...	17,242
Kampuchea	1983	4,000	1,600,000	43,000	37.2	...	...	87,400	...	...	...	...	1,140
Kenya	1980	10,255	3,930,991	102,489	38.4	...	...	422,752	16,648	25.4	...	...	8,575
Kiribati	1982	106	13,836	450	30.7	...	5	950	65	14.6	...	2	...
Korea, North	1976	4,700	2,561,674	...	...	...	...	...	...	...	...	...	...
Korea, South	1983	6,500	5,257,164	126,163	41.7	100[5]	3,893	4,752,097	128,950	36.9	77[5]	643	897,637
Kuwait	1983	238	160,788	8,676	18.5	78[5]	321	210,974	17,340	12.2	67[3]	...	421[2]
Laos	1980	6,339	479,291	16,109	29.8	96	46	88,433	4,316	20.5	17	18	2,002
Lebanon	1980	1,168	405,402	22,646	17.9	...	257	275,788	21,736	12.7	...	...	31,203
Lesotho	1979	1,080	235,604	4,782	49.3	67	...	21,406	940	22.8	12	...	1,682[1]
Liberia	1980	1,651	227,431	9,099	25.0	...	...	51,666	1,129	45.8	...	...	2,322
Libya	1980	2,607	662,843	36,591	18.1	...	...	280,189	22,815	12.3	...	...	16,008
Liechtenstein	1983	14	1,806	97	18.6	...	8	1,848	96	19.2	...	1	78
Luxembourg	1982	541	27,927	1,734	16.1	...	53[14]	21,783[14]	2,407[14, 19]		...	...	[14]
Macau	1980	41	33,334	732	45.5	...	40	13,034	619	21.1	...	15	2,261
Madagascar	1978	8,002	1,311,000	23,937	54.8	...	...	131,836[12, 20]	5,088[12, 20]	25.9[12, 20]	...	...	9,097[2]
Malawi	1980	2,340	809,862	12,540	64.6	43	...	19,760	887[3]		...	...	1,208[12]
Malaysia	1983	6,518	2,120,050	81,664	26.0	...	1,071	1,191,588	54,702	21.8	...	34	17,916
Maldives	1984	65	19,428	590	32.9	...	5	956	102	9.4	...	2	91
Mali	1979	...	298,831	7,214	41.4	...	...	73,136[1]	3,125[1]	23.4[1]	...	...	5,008[12]
Malta	1979	92	32,448	1,567	20.7	95	74	23,045	1,751	13.2	70	24	4,628
Martinique	1983	296[2]	57,532	3,222	17.9	...	283	38,778[2]	3,040[2, 14]		...	12	9,854[2]
Mauritania	1980	599	90,530	2,183	41.5	...	...	20,248	646	31.3	...	...	1,004
Mauritius	1981	262	131,594	6,420	20.5	89	148	76,308	3,144	24.3	33[12]	7	508
Mayotte	1983	62	12,670	317	40.0	...	3	1,004	53	18.9	...	3	362
Mexico	1983	77,900	15,222,916	415,425	36.4	...	16,031	4,180,804	225,449	18.5	...	3,216	1,535,434
Monaco	1981	6	1,347	...	...	...	2	1,314	...	...	...	1	751
Mongolia	1979	118	141,306	4,482	31.5	98	...	224,275	9,351	24.0	84	...	12,915
Montserrat	1981	15	1,725	86	20.0	...	...	871	32[2]		...	...	59
Morocco	1981	2,767	2,309,696	63,675	36.3	55	...	879,641	43,455	20.2	...	...	16,102
Mozambique	1981	5,709	1,376,865	18,751	73.4	32	138	137,990	3,946	35.0	5	...	13,778
Nauru	1983	3	1,700	...	...	...	2	400	...	...	...	1	60
Nepal	1981	10,340	1,142,900	29,134	39.2	...	4,253	558,996	17,154	32.6	...	...	16,815[10]
Netherlands, The	1983	9,735	1,297,220	65,112	19.9	92[5]	1,536	844,289	57,129	14.8	...	1,853	603,421
Netherlands Antilles	1976	148	43,966	1,898	23.2	...	6	3,084	138	22.3	...	44	9,278
New Caledonia	1982	268	26,513	1,305	20.3	...	35[2]	11,212	803	14.0	...	12[2]	4,382
New Zealand	1982	2,341	486,167	21,876[23]	22.2	98	411	223,501	13,044[23]	17.1	...	...	43,540[23]
Nicaragua	1982	4,976	509,240	14,105	36.1	75[5]	333	118,647	...	...	23[2]	52	17,982
Niger	1978	1,471	187,251	...	...	...	...	26,842	930	28.9	3	...	354
Nigeria	1980	36,683	14,022,164	384,201	36.5	...	4,806	2,309,921	77,881	29.7	...	159	73,920
Niue	1983	7	522	33	15.8	...	1	366	28	13.1	...	1	2[24]
Norfolk Island	1984	2	309	16	19.3	...	...	...	...	...	...	...	...

teachers[d]	student/ teacher ratio	institutions	students[c]	teachers[d]	student/ teacher ratio	gross enroll- ment ratio	graduates per 10,000 among population aged 20–24[b,e]	percent of population aged 25 and over with post- secondary education[b]	over age	total (%)	male (%)	female (%)	public expenditure on education (percent of GNP)[b]	country
...	...	...	42,412	...	...	...	55.0	1.9	15	67.2	68.8	65.7	2.0	Dominican Republic
...	...	17	274,353	11,679	23.5	35.0[4]	...	3.2[4]	10	85.5[4]	88.3[4]	82.9[4]	5.8[4]	Ecuador
34,487	18.3	12	528,751	22,507[3]	...	14.7	...	3.4	10	43.8	58.1	29.1	4.4	Egypt
...	...	18	23,418	1,414	16.6	3.9[2]	49.7[5]	1.9[5]	15	64.2[1]	68.8[1]	60.1[1]	4.0[5]	El Salvador
29[12]	12.8[12]	...	1,140[5]	68[5]	16.8[5]	3.6[5]	14.7	...	...	20.0	...	...	...	Equatorial Guinea
603[11]	10.0[11]	...	16,137[4]	1,353[4]	11.9[4]	0.5	...	...	15	15.0	...	...	3.7	Ethiopia
—	—	10	1,313[5]	...	...	...	...	...	15	100.0	100.0	100.0	...	Faeroe Islands
—	—								15	98.0			...	Falkland Islands
314	3.3	5	3,859	...	...	6.3[5]	49.5	3.3	15	79.0	84.0	74.0	4.9	Fiji
14,819	7.2	212[1]	127,657	5,087	25.1	30.7[2]	689.6[5]	11.9[5]	15	100.0[4]	100.0[4]	100.0[4]	5.9[5]	Finland
45,364	17.6	1,094	1,017,775	40,585	25.1	25.5	384.9	...	7	99.5	...	...	5.0	France
142[2]	...	1	236	...	...	...	...	1.1[2]	15	81.5[8]	81.7[8]	81.2[8]	...	French Guiana
...	...	...	124[2]	10[2]	12.4[2]	...	21.3	...	14	97.8	98.0	97.6	...	French Polynesia
372	14.9	3[3]	1,247	235	5.3	3.7[3]	...	...	15	63.0	71.9	54.6	3.1	Gabon
106	8.1	1[4]	291[4]	38[4]	7.7[4]	...	31.9[4]	0.2[4]	15	20.1[2]	29.1[2]	11.6[2]	3.3[4]	Gambia, The
16,355[2]	28.0[2]	290	404,618	40,835	9.9	30.4	784.8	8.5	15	100.0	100.0	100.0	4.2	Germany, East
35,798	17.0	3,147	1,223,221	171,708	17.1	...	426.6	4.3	15	...	...	...	4.6	Germany, West
1,101[1]	...	...	9,745	...	...	1.0	...	0.4	15	43.2	52.7	33.8	2.0	Ghana
20	2.5	—	—	—	—	...	...	...	...	...	...	...	...	Gibraltar
5,828	18.6	166	124,694	11,310	11.0	16.9[3]	371.2[5]	3.9[5]	14	92.6[16]	96.7[16]	88.9[16]	2.3[5]	Greece
—	—	—	—	—	—	—	...	...	15	100.0	100.0	100.0	...	Greenland
28	13.7	2	700	137	5.1	...	...	1.0	15	97.8	98.0	97.6	7.3	Grenada
10	...	...	...	...	...	...	...	0.8	...	...	...	...	...	Guadeloupe
75	15.8	1	2,496	162	15.4	...	...	21.5	...	...	...	...	11.8	Guam
10	...	...	47,555[3]	...	...	...	20.3	1.2	15	46.0	53.6	38.5	1.8	Guatemala
...	...	...	18,270	1,289	14.2	5.1[1]	...	...	...	18.7	33.5	4.4	4.2	Guinea
29[2]	...	...	...	...	...	...	...	...	...	18.9	24.6	13.4	4.4	Guinea-Bissau
...	...	...	2,491[3]	496[1]	...	3.2	130.6	1.0	15	91.6	94.3	89.0	9.8	Guyana
1,157[4]	3.9	12[4]	3,769[4]	632[4]	6.0	1.1[1]	6.9[4]	0.3[4]	15	34.7[4]	37.1[4]	32.5[4]	1.5[4]	Haiti
14	14	3	27,925[5]	1,606[5]	17.4[5]	8.2[2]	24.7	1.0	10	59.5	60.7	58.4	3.5	Honduras
14	14	23	32,697	3,222	10.1	10.1	115.7	7.1	15	77.3	90.1	64.1	3.0	Hong Kong
...	...	57	102,564	13,843	7.4	13.6	320.9	7.0	15	98.9	99.3	98.5	6.0	Hungary
...	...	4	4,780	280	17.1	19.3[5]	...	3.7	15	100.0	100.0	100.0	4.2	Iceland
...	...	6,784[1]	4,456,198[1]	231,233[1]	19.3[1]	7.5[1]	123.4	1.1	15	36.2	46.7	24.9	3.0	India
48,131	12.0	50	480,981	56,322	8.5	3.3	33.2	3.5	10	72.0	80.5	63.8	2.2	Indonesia
17,638	8.2	114	117,148	9,042	13.0	4.9[9]	158.0[5]	...	15	42.7[5]	54.7[5]	29.9[5]	8.5[5]	Iran
4,326	13.1	62	102,430[2]	6,515[2]	15.7[2]	9.0[2]	201.4	...	15	24.2	35.5	12.8	3.2	Iraq
202	33.6	58	41,928	3,983	10.5	21.3[2]	296.0	4.6	15	99.9	99.9	99.9	7.0	Ireland
8,596	9.6	...	88,786[3]	...	...	...	271.4	20.1[17]	14	93.3	96.2	90.5	8.3	Israel
176,512	9.3	71	1,022,282	47,844	21.4	27.1[2]	215.7[4]	2.6[4]	15	93.9[18]	95.3[18]	92.7[18]	4.6[4]	Italy
...	...	2	19,633	...	...	2.9[2]	98.0	1.1	15	35.0	44.8	24.0	8.4	Ivory Coast
438[6]	...	11	12,143	837[6]	...	6.4	74.4	1.1	15	96.1	95.6	96.5	7.1	Jamaica
...	...	1,059	2,431,708	131,923	18.4	...	742.0[5]	14.3	15	100.0	100.0	100.0	5.8[5]	Japan
871	19.8	31	36,549	...	...	...	433.8	0.8	15	67.6	81.0	54.3	6.3	Jordan
...	...	...	586	...	...	...	...	...	15	48.0	...	...	...	Kampuchea
433	19.8	...	12,797	...	...	1.0	74.4	...	15	47.1	60.0	34.8	6.1	Kenya
37	...	...	741[1]	...	...	...	...	...	...	...	...	...	...	Kiribati
...	...	...	...	...	...	...	...	...	...	...	...	...	3.4	Korea, North
29,328	30.6	428	1,075,969	30,049	35.8	17.5[5]	257.0[5]	8.9[5]	15	92.7[5]	97.5[5]	87.9[5]	3.4[5]	Korea, South
85[2]	5.0[2]	2	15,725[5]	1,110[5]	14.2[5]	14.1[5]	282.5	12.5	15	67.5	72.8	60.3	2.1	Kuwait
289	6.9	1	1,408	140	10.1	0.4	...	...	15	43.6	51.3	35.7	...	Laos
2,956[3]	...	12	70,314	...	...	28.3	...	3.1	15	76.5	85.4	67.7	3.0	Lebanon
...	...	9	1,682	...	...	...	15.2	0.1	15	69.0	57.5	80.0	2.7	Lesotho
...	...	2	3,789[5]	...	...	2.3[3]	19.3	1.0	15	25.4	42.2	9.3	6.1	Liberia
1,508	10.6	3	15,267[3]	...	...	6.4[3]	...	1.0	15	58.1	75.5	39.2	3.9	Libya
...	...	—	—	—	—	—	...	...	15	100.0	100.0	100.0	...	Liechtenstein
14	14	2	384	181[19]	...	2.8	...	...	15	98.0	...	...	6.6	Luxembourg
67	33.7	—	—	—	—	—	...	1.4	...	...	...	...	...	Macau
...	...	1	33,449[5]	557[1]	...	3.0	20.7	...	15	34.0	40.8	27.0	4.9	Madagascar
89[12]	13.6[12]	2	1,722	173	10.0	0.3	7.4	0.2	15	49.9	64.3	37.2	2.2	Malawi
1,611	11.1	9	56,521	5,131	11.0	4.6[5]	...	...	10	75.0	83.0	67.0	6.8	Malaysia[9]
18	5.1	...	...	...	...	...	...	0.4[4]	15	81.1[4]	80.2[4]	82.0[4]	0.6[4]	Maldives
...	...	9	5,281	489	10.8	0.9	9.8	0.2	15	9.4	13.5	5.7	4.6	Mali
478	9.7	2	1,065	153	7.0	6.2[2]	83.7	2.4	15	84.7	87.4	82.3	2.9	Malta
14	...	2	1,475[2]	772	19.2[2]	...	...	0.8	15	94.0	94.6	93.4	...	Martinique
...	...	...	...	...	...	...	...	...	6	17.4	...	...	5.0	Mauritania
69	7.4	2	901	192	4.7	...	48.9	1.2	15	79.0	86.0	72.3	6.1	Mauritius
8	45.2	—	31	—	—	...	...	...	16	75.0	...	...	...	Mayotte
91,538	16.8	336	1,013,117	85,943	11.8	14.6[5]	108.5[5]	2.6[5]	15	82.0[2]	86.2[2]	79.9[2]	3.9[5]	Mexico
...	...	...	...	...	...	...	...	6.8	...	...	...	...	...	Monaco
864	14.9	...	11,826	1,033	11.4	8.5	...	...	...	95.4	...	...	7.0	Mongolia
5	11.8	...	...	...	...	...	...	0.5	15	...	...	...	...	Montserrat
...	...	6[2,21]	80,345[21]	2,558[21]	31.4[21]	6.2	26.2	...	15	21.4	33.6	9.8	6.0	Morocco
907	15.1	...	1,852	...	...	0.2	1.1	...	15	33.2	44.4	22.7	0.6	Mozambique
—	—	...	...	...	...	...	...	...	...	99.0	...	...	...	Nauru
513[10]	32.8[10]	10	38,450	2,918	13.2	3.1	107.0	0.1	6	23.3	34.0	12.0	2.0	Nepal
55,000	10.9	384	295,556	29,000	10.2	31.1[4]	342.0[4]	7.2[4]	15	100.0[22]	100.0[22]	100.0[22]	8.4[4]	Netherlands, The
687	13.5	1	500	20	25.0	...	...	...	14	89.4	90.1	88.7	...	Netherlands Antilles
408	10.7	4[2]	421[5]	725	5.8[5]	...	95.3	2.0	14	91.0	...	...	...	New Caledonia
2,625[22]	...	15	58,652	3,626[21]	16.2	26.2	443.9	20.1	15	100.0	100.0	100.0	5.4	New Zealand
...	...	4	32,838	1,369	24.0	12.3	28.4	...	15	87.0	...	...	3.2	Nicaragua
31	11.4	...	1,435[2]	224[2]	6.4[2]	0.3[2]	...	...	15	9.8	14.0	5.8	4.3	Niger
3,280	22.5	77	153,306	...	...	2.3	...	...	15	34.0	45.6	23.0	3.8	Nigeria
1[19]	...	...	...	—	—	...	...	1.9	15	85.0	...	...	...	Niue
...	...	...	...	...	...	...	...	...	15	100.0[5]	100.0[5]	100.0[5]	...	Norfolk Island

Education (continued)

country	year	first level (primary)					general second level (secondary)[a]					vocational second level	
		schools	students[c]	teachers[d]	student/ teacher ratio	net enrollment ratio	schools	students[c]	teachers[d]	student/ teacher ratio	net enrollment ratio	schools	students[c]
Norway	1982	3,526	383,599	30,124	12.7	99[3]	...	279,960	...	...	82[1]	967	86,025
Oman	1982	269	116,591	4,399	26.5	...	...	25,954	1,828	14.2	...	...	443
Pakistan	1980	59,819	7,039,000	148,000	47.6	...	8,989	2,621,225	115,277[3]	...	...	...	25,745
Panama	1982	2,347	336,740	12,853	26.2	93	197	129,203	6,502	19.9	...	115	44,364
Papua New Guinea	1982	2,197	319,174	10,163	31.4	...	111	42,345	1,715	24.7	...	99	7,222
Paraguay	1979	...	504,377	...	...	86	745	96,559[1]	...	...	...	...	4,567
Peru	1982	25,748	3,692,273	116,550	31.7	85	3,289	1,429,219	66,874	21.4	...	768	142,154
Philippines	1980	30,595	8,033,642	264,241	30.4	92	2,445	2,928,525	85,779	34.1	...		
Pitcairn Island	1984	1	15	1	15.0	...	1	1	1	1.0	...		
Poland	1983	14,341	4,465,300	244,800	18.2	98[4]	1,171	380,800	32,800	16.7	...	9,973	1,555,800
Portugal	1981	1,707	1,186,375	66,001	18.0	...	313	156,003	15,294	29.8	...	94	14,160
Puerto Rico	1981	1,618	470,089	23,154	20.3	...	619	337,153	13,297	25.4	...	68	60,045
Qatar	1981	100	32,618	2,303	14.2	92	...	16,696	1,668	10.0	...	...	462
Réunion	1982	513	120,580	4,626	29.9	...	83	65,622	2,559[2]	...	...	17	10,058[2]
Romania	1982	14,299	3,285,073	157,709	20.8	...	971	135,376	8,909	15.2	...	903	1,027,373
Rwanda	1981	1,558	743,067	13,043	57.0	68	...	4,156	...	...	2	...	3,225
St. Christopher and Nevis	1984	31	7,569	334	22.7	...	7	4,433	278	15.9	...	1	182
St. Helena and Ascension	1982	8	647	35	18.5	...	4	604	32	18.9	...	1	38
St. Lucia	1983	79	31,785	957[5]	...	...	12	4,582	229[5]	...	...	1	131
St. Pierre and Miquelon	1983	5	661	59	11.2	...	3	531	56	9.5	...	2	217
St. Vincent and the Grenadines	1983	62	24,551	1,251	19.6	...	14	3,721	244	15.3	...	5	1,449
San Marino	1983	13	1,493	164	9.1	...	3	1,317	156	8.4	...	—	729[23]
São Tomé and Príncipe	1978	46	14,162	527	26.9	...	3	3,145	111	28.3	...	1	...
Saudi Arabia	1982	6,287	998,307	55,015	18.1	51[5]	2,364	390,092	25,163	15.5	...	186	27,444
Senegal	1981	1,795	452,679	10,586	42.8	39	...	93,001	3,574[3]	...	...	...	10,820
Seychelles	1983	27	14,456	681	21.2	...	3[14]	3,577[14]	239[14]	15.0[14]	...	14	14
Sierra Leone	1981	1,172	263,724	8,472	31.1	...	159	60,285	2,828	21.3	...	4	931
Singapore	1983	305	290,800	9,915	29.3	96[5]	147	182,343	8,571	21.2	58[3]	16	15,610
Solomon Islands	1981	370	28,870	1,148	25.1	...	16	3,663	220	16.6	...	1	367
Somalia	1982	1,425	183,793	8,265	22.2	22[2]	51	33,212	1,350	24.6	6[2]	26	9,274
South Africa	1984	17,186[15]	4,650,423	194,066	...	...	[15]	1,416,343	...	...	...	63[27]	66,081[21]
South West Africa/Namibia	1983	1,069	232,306	7,120	32.6	...	78	40,359	1,864	21.6	...	6	1,200
Spain	1981	216,653	6,788,877[29]	228,307	29.7	100[2]	2,445	1,091,197	66,160	16.5	74[2]	2,142	558,808
Sri Lanka	1981	9,176	2,132,596	131,656	16.2	...	5,948[2]	1,293,213	75,174[2]	...	...	...	4,778[10]
Sudan, The	1981	6,176	1,524,381	46,437	32.8	...	...	409,802	17,843	23.0	...	...	17,130
Suriname	1981	285	75,139	2,803	26.8	...	100	31,065	2,002	15.5	...	...	4,394[1]
Swaziland	1981	470	119,913	3,586	33.4	86	87	25,450	1,592	16.0	...	1	538
Sweden	1982	4,922	662,581	40,747	16.3	...	...	443,355	...	...	...	526	163,405
Switzerland	1984	...	431,800	...	...	...	...	408,700	...	...	...	...	251,400
Syria	1983	8,195	1,683,802	62,042	27.1	89[5]	1,466	629,263	35,251	17.9	44[5]	164	60,818
Taiwan	1983	2,430	2,216,855	69,592	31.8	...	823	1,263,064	58,292	21.7	...	202	393,022
Tanzania	1982	9,837[3]	3,512,799	88,370	39.8	72[5]	145[9]	69,145	3,862	20.6	...	34[9]	8,101
Thailand	1980	32,194	7,370,846	304,400	24.2	...	2,297	1,578,609	...	...	...	309	297,114
Togo	1981	2,251	498,639	9,619	51.8	74	...	123,299	4,020	30.7	...	...	6,932
Tokelau	1982	...	426	27	15.8	...	...	80[3]	6[3]	13.3[3]	...	...	197[3]
Tonga	1981	110	17,364	695	25.0	...	51[3]	15,942	700	22.8	...	6[3]	624
Trinidad and Tobago	1980	465	166,763	6,443	25.9	...	186	82,482	1,631	50.6	...	2	11,487
Trust Territory of the Pacific Is.	1983	249[2]	26,883	1,578[3]	...	...	32[9]	6,100[4]	520[3]	...	...	2	456
Tunisia	1983	2,937	1,142,060	30,186	37.8	86[5]	305	332,319	16,227	20.5	27[5]	...	83,546[5]
Turkey	1981	45,842	5,859,711	212,795	27.6	...	...	1,779,618	81,155	21.9	...	1,718	514,719
Turks and Caicos Islands	1983	16	1,352	80[2]	...	...	3	671	47[2]	...	...	—	—
Tuvalu	1983	9	966	41	23.6	100[4]	1	250	15	16.7	...	8	354
Uganda	1981	4,276	1,421,615	38,422	37.0	...	199	78,727	4,150	19.0	...	...	16,201
U.S.S.R.	1984	71,200	35,700,000	2,360,000[15]	...	...	59,000	4,714,000	...	...	...	4,418[16]	4,232,000[16]
United Arab Emirates	1983	244[2]	115,411	6,599[6]	...	100[5]	68[2]	45,442	4,081[6]	...	...	4[5]	2,652
United Kingdom	1982	27,326	4,758,000	192,959	24.7	96[2]	5,506	5,031,000	279,000	18.0	...	787	254,813[30]
United States	1984	...	30,780,000	1,359,000	22.6	...	...	13,495,000[14]	1,035,000[14]	13.0	...	...	14
Uruguay	1981	2,543	387,150	18,017	21.5	...	284	162,106	...	...	...	...	26,017
Vanuatu	1982	286	23,595	1,063	22.2	...	9	2,067	126	16.4	...	2	351
Venezuela	1981	12,788	2,591,051	97,045	26.7	83	1,447	798,946	...	...	...	...	43,000
Vietnam	1980	...	7,887,439	204,104	38.6	98	...	3,846,737	148,973	25.8	...	...	...
Virgin Islands (U.S.)	1983	50	19,022	1,035	18.4	...	13	13,576	909	14.9	...	2	600
Wallis and Futuna	1978	...	5,348	171	31.2	...	...	277	9	30.8	...	—	—
Western Sahara	...	...	...	...	...	...	...	...	...	...	...	...	...
Western Samoa	1982	162	40,475	1,460	27.7	...	38	11,839	495	23.9	...	3	211
Yemen (Aden)	1982	890	228,893	10,915	21.0	...	46	27,776	1,271	21.9	...	13	1,556
Yemen (Şan'ā')	1981	2,985	412,573	9,826	39.0	...	314	28,852	2,023	14.3	...	29	4,023
Yugoslavia	1981	12,537	1,446,228	60,264	24.0	79	...	1,798,375	...	...	...	...	612,457
Zaire	1978	...	3,919,395	...	...	...	...	611,349	...	...	...	...	70,342
Zambia	1981	2,854	1,068,314	23,100	46.2	...	135	98,862	4,650	21.2	...	28	9,972
Zimbabwe	1983	3,880[4]	2,044,847	49,588	...	100[4]	...	316,438	6,112[5]	...	...	...	14,272

teachers[d]	student/ teacher ratio	third level (higher)							literacy[b]				public expenditure on education (percent of GNP)[b]	country
		institutions	students[c]	teachers[d]	student/ teacher ratio	gross enroll-ment ratio	graduates per 10,000 among population aged 20–24[b,e]	percent of population aged 25 and over with post-secondary education[b]	over age	total (%)	male (%)	female (%)		
14,992	5.7	199	60,981	5,560	11.0	25.6[2]	755.5	9.1	15	100.0	100.0	100.0	9.0	Norway
43	10.3	...	...	...	...	...	...	...	...	...	...	...	2.3	Oman
...	...	554	153,536	6,239[1]	...	...	120.8	3.4	15	20.7	29.6	10.3	1.8	Pakistan
2,379	18.6	3	45,361	3,456	13.1	27.4	37.7	4.2	15	87.1	87.1	87.2	4.9	Panama
513	14.1	2	3,547	591	6.0	...	21.5	...	15	42.3	52.4	31.3	4.7	Papua New Guinea
...	...	4	20,812	...	...	...	...	2.1	15	80.1	85.1	75.5	1.3	Paraguay
8,744	16.2	35	277,304	23,435	11.8	19.0	37.5	4.5	15	72.5	83.3	61.8	3.7	Peru
...	...	...	1,276,016	43,770	29.2	26.1	368.1	11.9	15	83.4	84.6	82.2	1.6	Philippines
...	...	...	...	...	...	...	...	...	15	96.5	93.1	100.0	...	Pitcairn Island
84,400	18.4	91	396,600	56,600	7.0	16.5[5]	425.5[5]	5.7[5]	15	98.5[2]	98.9[2]	98.1[2]	3.4[5]	Poland
2,014	7.0	692	87,122	10,543	8.3	11.3[1]	179.0[1]	12.1[1]	15	80.1[2]	86.1[2]	75.1[2]	4.5[1]	Portugal
1,522	39.5	27	129,708[3]	...	...	...	480.6	12.1	15	87.8	89.2	86.6	8.2	Puerto Rico
87	5.3	...	2,981	198	15.1	12.2	...	...	...	...	...	...	3.4	Qatar
599[3]	...	1	2,201	62[2]	...	...	...	...	15	81.6[2]	82.3[2]	80.6[2]	...	Réunion
39,382	26.1	44	190,903	14,354	13.3	11.2	215.4	4.6	15	95.8[2]	97.3[2]	94.3[2]	3.1	Romania
...	...	4	1,243[2]	...	...	...	...	...	15	49.7	61.0	39.0	2.7	Rwanda
18	10.1	1	67	9	7.4	...	...	...	15	97.6[16]	97.6[16]	97.7[16]	6.5[16]	St. Christopher and Nevis
4	9.5	...	36	9	4.0	...	...	...	15	97.1	96.8	97.5	...	St. Helena and Ascension
25[2]	...	1	199	51[3]	...	...	...	1.0[2]	15	81.7[2]	80.8[2]	82.4[2]	6.8[2]	St. Lucia
40	5.4	—	—	—	—	...	...	7.5	15	99.5	99.5	99.5	...	St. Pierre and Miquelon
48	30.2	1	105	19	5.5	...	...	...	15	85.0	...	...	5.5[5]	St. Vincent and the Grenadines
...	...	...	329[25]	...	...	...	...	2.4	15	97.2	97.8	96.7	5.9	San Marino
...	...	—	111[26]	—	...	...	...	...	15	10.0[2]	...	...	...	São Tomé and Príncipe
3,174	8.6	17	63,563	6,906	9.2	7.8[5]	...	...	15	24.6[5]	34.5[5]	12.2[5]	6.4[5]	Saudi Arabia
...	...	...	13,560	684	19.8	2.8[2]	55.4	0.1	6	47.7	60.4	32.3	4.6	Senegal
14	14	...	194	28	6.9	...	36.8	2.6	15	62.0	...	...	5.9	Seychelles
89	10.5	7	3,885	482	8.1	...	20.5	...	15	15.0	13.4	17.0	3.9	Sierra Leone
1,060	14.7	5	30,991	2,965	10.5	8.1[2]	173.9[4]	3.4[4]	10	84.2	92.1	78.1	3.8[4]	Singapore
37	9.9	...	...	...	...	...	...	1.6	15	54.1	62.4	44.9	4.1	Solomon Islands
549	16.9	9[3]	2,899[3]	324[12]	...	0.1[1]	...	...	15	5.2[2]	10.0[2]	0.5[2]	1.8[2]	Somalia
1,460[27]	45.3[27]	98	273,519	15,666	17.5	...	...	3.7[16]	15	79.3[28]	80.6[28]	78.0[28]	4.3[16]	South Africa
81	14.8	4	537	137	3.9	...	...	...	15	50.0[4]	...	...	...	South West Africa/Namibia
36,556	15.3	120	649,098	40,321	16.1	23.2[2]	251.9	3.7	15	92.8	95.5	89.5	2.1	Spain
1,239[10]	3.9[10]	...	42,694[2]	4,818[2]	8.9[2]	3.1	25.7	2.3	15	86.5	90.5	82.4	3.0	Sri Lanka
846	20.2	17	33,309	6,479[3]	...	2.0	24.3	...	10	31.0	45.0	18.0	4.8	Sudan, The
249[1]	17.6[1]	2	2,353	155	15.2	...	...	86.1	15	65.0	68.4	62.9	8.3	Suriname
65	8.3	1	979	108	9.1	...	86.1	...	15	56.0	57.9	54.5	6.9	Swaziland
...	...	...	205,431	...	...	36.8	728.1	15.4	15	100.0	100.0	100.0	9.5	Sweden
...	...	...	95,600	...	...	18.4[4]	177.7[4]	2.9[4]	15	99.9[4]	...	...	5.0[4]	Switzerland
6,410	9.5	24[4]	115,229	1,332[12]	...	18.3[5]	130.0[4]	1.3[4]	10	65.7	80.0	50.8	4.3[4]	Syria
14,442	27.2	105	375,696	18,258	20.6	...	...	...	15	88.9[4]	94.9[4]	82.9[4]	3.4[4]	Taiwan
627	12.9	1[9]	2,984	719	4.2	0.3[3]	...	...	10	73.5[1]	77.7[1]	69.6[1]	5.7[1]	Tanzania
12,680[5]	...	...	911,166	35,731	25.5	19.9	67.5	1.1	10	81.8	88.9	74.9	3.6	Thailand
...	...	2	4,475	...	...	1.9	32.6	0.1	14	15.9	26.9	7.1	6.2	Togo
12[3]	16.4[3]	—	—	—	—	...	...	...	15	99.8	99.8	99.8	...	Tokelau
...	...	...	128[3]	26[3]	4.9[3]	...	...	...	15	99.6	99.7	99.5	4.9	Tonga
...	...	1	1,878	...	...	4.6	51.5	1.2	15	92.3	94.8	89.9	3.4	Trinidad and Tobago
39[3]	...	1	264	155[3]	...	...	...	...	15	90.0[2]	...	...	...	Trust Territory of the Pacific Is.
...	...	...	34,077	4,105	8.3	5.1[5]	81.7[5]	1.2[5]	15	47.4[2]	61.2[2]	33.7[2]	3.9[5]	Tunisia
35,521	14.5	331	236,605	20,917[2]	...	5.2	178.8	2.2	6	60.2	77.2	43.1	2.7	Turkey
—	—	—	100[5,26]	—	—	—	—	5.0[2]	15	86.7[1]	85.0[1]	88.0[1]	...	Turks and Caicos Islands
16	22.1	...	...	...	...	...	...	...	15	95.5	95.5	95.5	...	Tuvalu
...	...	4	6,912	...	...	...	...	0.1	15	52.5	64.6	40.5	0.7	Uganda
246,000[16]	18.4[16]	891[16]	5,315,200[16]	376,000[16]	14.1[16]	...	...	7.2[5]	15	100.0[16]	100.0[16]	100.0[16]	7.0[5]	U.S.S.R.
344	7.7	...	2,519[5]	208[2]	...	12.1[5]	...	6.0[5]	15	68.6	71.0	61.0	1.5[5]	United Arab Emirates
...	...	46	785,200	33,735	23.3	20.1[2]	517.3[2]	11.0[2]	15	99.9[22]	...	...	5.4[2]	United Kingdom
...[14]	...	...	12,400,000	870,000	14.2	58.0[2]	843.5[2]	31.1[2]	15	95.5	95.7	95.3	6.9[2]	United States
...	...	1	48,234[14]	...	...	20.4	101.7	6.3	15	90.2	90.7	90.4	2.3	Uruguay
40	8.8	...	...	...	...	...	...	...	...	...	...	...	...	Vanuatu
...	...	68	307,133	28,052[2]	...	...	115.1	2.6	15	76.5	79.7	73.4	5.2	Venezuela
...	...	...	114,701	17,242	6.6	2.5	...	...	15	64.5	...	...	3.5	Vietnam
20	30.0	...	1,990[3]	...	...	...	...	17.6	15	...	...	...	12.3	Virgin Islands (U.S.)
—	—	...	—	—	—	...	...	...	...	...	...	...	...	Wallis and Futuna
...	...	...	...	...	...	...	...	...	...	...	...	...	...	Western Sahara
38	5.6	5	85	6	14.2	...	...	4.5	10	97.0	...	...	...	Western Samoa
173	9.0	...	3,469[5]	386[2]	...	...	38.1[5]	...	15	38.9	66.6	10.9	5.9[5]	Yemen (Aden)
196	20.5	...	4,519[2]	157[2]	28.8	1.2[2]	38.1[2]	...	15	8.3[2]	15.9[2]	0.5[2]	4.9[2]	Yemen (Şan'ā')
...	...	349	411,995	24,449[2]	...	21.7	291.1	3.9	15	83.8	91.9	75.7	6.0	Yugoslavia
...	...	36	26,700	...	...	1.1	...	...	15	55.1	73.6	36.7	6.0	Zaire
406	24.6	1	3,603	334	10.8	...	10.3[2]	0.6[2]	15	68.6[2]	79.3[2]	58.3[2]	5.1[2]	Zambia
...	...	1	3,314	...	...	...	...	0.6[4]	15	70.8[2]	78.0[2]	63.8[2]	4.3[4]	Zimbabwe

[1]1978. [2]1980. [3]1979. [4]1982. [5]1981. [6]Public schools only. [7]1972. [8]1974. [9]1977. [10]1976. [11]1970. [12]1975. [13]Excludes 2,626 Bahraini students registered abroad. [14]General second level includes vocational second level. [15]First level includes second level. [16]1983. [17]Jewish population only; figure for non-Jewish population is 8.8. [18]1971. [19]Includes part-time teachers. [20]Excludes teacher training at this level. [21]Universities only. [22]1984. [23]Full-time teacher equivalents. [24]Includes part-time students. [25]Sanmarinese students registered in Italy. [26]Students registered abroad. [27]Private and correspondence schools only. [28]1980; includes Bophuthatswana, Ciskei, Transkei, and Venda. [29]Ages 2 through 13. [30]Excluding Northern Ireland.

Cultural institutions

Measurement of cultural activity in statistical terms is highly problematic: What is the significance of an extraordinarily good stage production that is seen by 450 people and never filmed, as opposed, say, to a good but unmemorable made-for-television film that is seen in 22,000,000 households? Box-office records and viewership surveys can provide the raw numbers; marketing specialists can, by direct and indirect methods, even provide some measure of the emotional impact of the two performances. But how does one gauge the importance of each production in its particular medium, or the importance of those media with respect to each other, or the place of each production in theatrical history? Of libraries, how does the value of a good public library with 200,000 volumes in open stacks, serving a city of 100,000 people, compare to that of a good university library of 1,000,000 volumes used by only 6,000 students and faculty, but used very intensively?

Such questions are largely beyond the scope of compilations of the sort provided by the table below. For the most part, it is possible only to tabulate facilities, holdings, seating capacities, participation, tickets sold, and so on. And even when these figures are recalculated on a per capita basis, the apparent differences among countries will often be more a function of each country's statistical reporting system than a reflection of actual differences among the cultural habits and preferences of the peoples of the respective countries.

Some kinds of data can not be given at all. The data on expenditures for cultural activities by governments, for example, tend to exaggerate differences. Some countries support no cultural activities at any level of government; others may directly subsidize or support them; some offer tax incentives; while still others employ artists directly within the government as teachers, performers, scholars, archivists, and so on. Most national data on manpower in cultural activities are collected on the basis of the predominant source of the individual's income, rather than on his or her aspirations or avocations, part-time paid or unpaid activities, or other less convenient measures of activity.

In sum, cultural activities cannot be measured meaningfully at the national level in terms other than those of public facilities, performance, and attendance. But even these should not be compared without an understanding of their inherent limitations. Data on libraries are for public libraries only and exclude other types of collections, such as national, school and university, private, professional, business, and governmental, even though these may play a very significant role locally or nationally. The category "public" was thought to provide the most representative set of figures for this activity. Data for "volumes" may reflect either actual holdings or an estimate based on length of occupied shelving. A large part of the data presented were obtained in a 1981 survey by UNESCO, and they refer to a wide range of years. Throughout the table, data given in Roman type are from 1980 or later; in italic, earlier than 1980.

Figures for book production generally include all works published in separate bindings except advertising works, timetables, telephone directories, price lists, catalogs of businesses or exhibitions, musical scores, maps, atlases, and the like. The figures include government publications, school texts, theses, offprints, series works, and illustrated works, even

Cultural institutions

country	public libraries				book production				cinema				number of long films produced
	number	volumes ('000)	registered borrowers ('000)	loans per 1,000 population	number of titles		number of copies		annual attendance (all cinemas)		fixed cinemas		
					books	pamphlets	books ('000)	pamphlets ('000)	number ('000,000)	per 1,000 population	number	seating capacity ('000)	
Afghanistan	38	230	...	...	415	...	5,981	...	4.9	302	34	19	5
Albania	3,631	5,712	...	...	892	151	5,389	1,211	...	...	95	29	14
Algeria	...	...	...	...	234	41	...	...	23.5	1,200	272	138	2
American Samoa	...	...	...	...	98	1	33	1	0.2	7,400	5	2	...
Andorra	...	...	...	...	...	...	...	...	0.2	6,900	5	2	...
Angola	19	...	...	...	33	24	239	191	5.9	900	55	34	1
Anguilla	...	...	...	...	---	3[1]	---	1[1]	...	...	...	...	...
Antigua and Barbuda	...	...	...	...	...	...	...	...	...	...	...	...	...
Argentina	1,528	9,532	4,201	367	4,251[2]	2	14,190[2]	2	5.6	200	1,010[3]	530	27
Australia	940[4]	15,007[4]	...	...	5,586	2,270	...	...	...	...	564[3]	...	43
Austria	2,124[6]	6,054	...	1,636	5,223	991	...	...	18.0	2,400	481	146	11
Bahamas, The	25	95	...	...	...	...	...	...	...	...	13	6	...
Bahrain	1	140	50	78	...	...	...	...	1.3	3,800	313	...	...
Bangladesh	...	...	...	...	542	...	...	...	...	...	194[3]	103	...
Barbados	1	174	...	1,922	38	178	...	...	1.2	4,800	...	...	...
Belgium	2,351	24,140	...	4,266	9,736[2]	2	...	...	21.7	2,200	500	...	9
Belize	1	101	...	...	...	...	...	...	...	...	...	...	...
Benin	...	...	...	...	13	---	18	---	1.0	300	43	4	...
Bermuda	1	140	3	...	...	...	...	...	0.2	4,200	2	1	...
Bhutan	...	...	...	...	...	...	...	...	...	...	12	5	...
Bolivia	...	...	...	...	414	182	...	...	30.9	5,700	209	160	1
Botswana	1	108	30	48	70	27	35	33	0.8	1,200	13	1	...
Brazil	2,332	12,665	...	...	12,880	5,222	186,750	132,586	215.1	1,900	3,156	1,733	90
British Virgin Islands	1	29	6	1,825	3[11]	...	1[11]	...	39.6[12]	3,300	1	0.4	...
Brunei	1	97	6	228	61	1	222	3	2.8	14,700	9	8	6
Bulgaria	5,808	48,930	2,282	3,945	4,168	868	53,911	6,897	94.2	10,400	3,006	715	42
Burkina Faso	...	...	...	...	4	---	...	...	3.8	2,000	12	14	...
Burma	...	...	...	...	...	...	...	...	...	...	175[3]	136	66
Burundi	...	...	...	...	...	...	...	...	0.4	100	7	3	...
Cameroon	...	...	...	...	22	...	94	...	...	...	52	29	1
Canada	791	45,602	...	5,301	19,063[2]	2	...	...	100.5	4,200	1,016[3]	6	32
Cape Verde	...	...	...	...	...	...	...	...	...	...	...	...	...
Cayman Islands	1	6	2	2,365	5	---	...	...	...	...	4	1	...
Central African Republic	...	...	...	...	...	...	...	...	...	...	...	...	...
Chad	...	...	...	...	...	...	...	...	25.2	6,000	13	12	...
Chile	161	581	...	382	640	278	3,660	435	14.7	1,300	172	110	...
China	1,889	...	...	...	22,920[2]	2	4,829,270[2]	2	18,250	18,100	...	...	112
Christmas Island	1	12	3	7,950	...	...	...	...	...	...	...	...	...
Cocos (Keeling) Islands	1	...	...	...	...	...	...	...	...	...	...	...	...
Colombia	...	...	...	...	4,176	1,316	19,766	2,880	64.1	2,400	391	...	2
Comoros	2	8	...	...	...	...	...	...	...	...	...	...	...
Congo	7	55	34	62	9	118	285	1,471	...	...	...	...	...
Cook Islands	1	15	3	1,060	...	...	...	...	...	...	...	...	...
Costa Rica	18	...	...	...	71	...	110	...	...	...	...	...	...
Cuba	195	2,719	...	439	1,504	715	45,392	2,935	89.3	9,200	513	268	5
Cyprus	...	236	...	226	180[14]	957[14]	290[14]	1,936[14]	...	...	...	...	...
Czechoslovakia	10,157	50,490	2,626	5,983	8,972	1,521	72,595	17,171	81.2	5,300	2,971	861	48
Denmark	247	30,739	...	15,417	5,560	3,003	...	...	16.4	3,200	471	103	13
Djibouti	1	11	...	64	...	...	...	...	0.6	5,200	4	6	...
Dominica	1	15	4	595	...	...	...	...	...	...	...	...	...
Dominican Republic	68	...	533	120	...	...	3,017	1,320	7.0	1,500	833[3]	47	...
Ecuador	...	...	...	...	...	...	...	...	...	...	...	...	...
Egypt	223	1,329	6	...	1,503	177	46,620	6,380	47.9	1,200	229	200	90
El Salvador	...	...	...	...	59	85	...	...	...	...	...	...	...
Equatorial Guinea	...	...	...	...	...	...	...	...	0.5	1,600	10	5	...

those consisting principally of illustration. Figures refer to works actually published during the year of survey, usually by a registered publisher, and deposited for copyright. A book is defined as a work of 49 or more pages, a pamphlet a work of from 5 to 48 pages. A work published simultaneously in more than one country is counted as published in each, since each is usually a separate edition.

Statistics on cinema attendance may originate from a variety of screening facilities—permanent buildings, mobile facilities, and educational or drive-in facilities—although only commercial exhibitions are tabulated for attendance. Seating capacity is given for fixed facilities only, although commercial screenings in many countries may take place in any of the kinds of facilities mentioned above, for some of which seating capacity calculated in terms of permanent seats may not be a relevant measure. The data on long (or feature) films may refer to prints with a length of from 1,000 to 3,000 metres, according to the reporting practices of various countries, but some consensus exists among reporting countries for a standard length (for classificational purposes) of 2,000 metres.

Museum data also derive in large part from UNESCO surveys, which are now conducted only every three years because of the slow pace of change in the field. Comparability is very limited internationally because of the wide range of facilities, public services, research capabilities, and collections that may be identified as museums by various countries. The data may include nature or conservation facilities, archaeological or ethnographic sites, zoos, aquariums, botanical gardens, scientific or observational facilities such as planetariums, and so on. The more conventional categories of art, history, natural history, science, and local institutions are naturally included. There may be some overlap in attendance figures with the conservation data because of national organizational structure.

Sporting events tend to assume great local importance as focuses of national or local identity, pride, and aspiration, but they tend also to be poorly recorded unless the attendance is taxed. Data given refer, so far as possible, to all indoor or outdoor public sports facilities, whether or not they are also used for commercial sports events. Data on participation include all sports or physical fitness activities participated in by the general population.

In the performing arts, each country (when such data are collected at all) usually reports on the familiar Western performance modes—music, theatre, opera, musical theatre, dance—but also on other types of live performances, including traditional, ceremonial, seasonal, festival, or holiday observances as well as such entertainments as circus, puppet and shadow theatre, and the like. Data on both performances and attendance refer to amateur and professional performances.

Data on nature conservation facilities and patronage of them generally refer to facilities operated by the national conservation authority (though in many countries, particularly those with federal systems, authority may be lodged below the national government). The data usually must include all types of facilities operated by the relevant authority, sometimes including sites of historical, ethnological, archaeological, and related interest. The possibility exists of duplication of attendance data for museums, therefore; this possibility should be borne in mind when the data are compared.

museums			sporting events			performing arts			nature preservation		country
number	annual attendance ('000)	annual attendance per 1,000 population	number of public facilities	annual participation ('000)	annual participation per 1,000 population	number of performances	annual attendance ('000)	annual attendance per 1,000 population	number of facilities	annual attendance ('000)	
7	10	0.6	...	...	...	...	...	...	5	...	Afghanistan
78	...	...	3,288	500	187	...	1,650	644	4	...	Albania
32	260	...	...	...	...	...	...	...	2	...	Algeria
1	52	1,677	...	...	...	...	...	...	...	...	American Samoa
4	52	1,733	...	...	...	14	6	190	...	...	Andorra
...	...	...	...	...	...	...	...	...	13	...	Angola
...	...	...	...	...	...	...	...	...	...	...	Anguilla
3	...	...	...	...	...	...	...	...	2	...	Antigua and Barbuda
327	5,653[4]	...	...	...	...	330	4,136[5]	159[5]	32	639[4]	Argentina
15	5,279[4]	...	...	...	...	...	...	...	417	...	Australia
99	6,177	823	...	816	108	...	...	...	20	...	Austria
7	...	...	...	...	...	...	...	...	4	...	Bahamas, The
3	4	14	...	...	...	...	...	...	...	...	Bahrain
...	...	...	...	...	...	...	...	...	3	...	Bangladesh
1	12	47	...	...	...	8[4,7]	...	...	2	...	Barbados
137[8]	4,586[8]	...	386	...	...	...	...	...	1	...	Belgium
5	9	64	...	...	...	...	...	...	9	...	Belize
39	109	39	...	...	...	...	...	...	...	...	Benin
...	...	...	...	...	...	49[4]	18[4]	---	2[10]	...	Bermuda
1	16	13	...	...	...	...	...	...	1	...	Bhutan
...	...	...	...	...	...	500[5]	123[5]	22[5]	12	...	Bolivia
2	52	66	...	...	...	297	...	...	9	...	Botswana
409	10,730[4]	...	...	...	...	1,563	...	...	42	...	Brazil
1	1	77	...	...	...	3[7]	4[7]	333[7]	6	...	British Virgin Islands
3	159	746	2	...	...	78[7]	9[7]	41[7]	...	...	Brunei
193	15,745	1,788	...	871,149	96	15,795[5]	6,448[5]	732[5]	33	...	Bulgaria
...	...	...	...	...	...	...	...	...	12	...	Burkina Faso
...	...	...	...	...	...	...	...	...	5	...	Burma
2	110	24	...	...	...	4[4,7]	77[7]	19[7]	...	...	Burundi
12	4,641	563	...	...	...	44	39	5	18	...	Cameroon
940	39,112[4]	...	...	31,800[13]	1,376[13]	14,882[4,5]	5,307[4,5]	---	83	15,713[4]	Canada
...	...	...	...	...	...	...	...	...	...	...	Cape Verde
...	...	...	...	...	...	...	...	...	...	...	Cayman Islands
65	1	0.4	...	...	...	...	...	...	14	...	Central African Republic
...	...	...	...	...	...	120[4]	...	...	3	...	Chad
69	198[4]	...	...	...	...	811[4,5]	299[4,5]	---	31	...	Chile
...	...	...	...	...	...	...	...	...	52	...	China
...	...	...	...	...	...	...	...	...	1	0.4	Christmas Island
...	...	...	...	...	...	...	...	...	1	...	Cocos (Keeling) Islands
74	1,542[4]	...	...	...	...	159[5]	91[5]	3[5]	33	60	Colombia
...	...	...	...	...	...	...	...	...	...	...	Comoros
4	6	4	...	...	...	74[4]	...	...	11	...	Congo
1	6	324	...	...	...	...	...	...	...	...	Cook Islands
...	...	...	...	...	...	347[4,5]	50[4,5]	...	19	90	Costa Rica
58	1,725	177	8,947	3,211	328	...	...	...	5	...	Cuba
26	95	153	...	...	...	793[5]	206[5]	332[5]	1	...	Cyprus
246	12,855	847	20,880	1,881	123	35,648	29,367	1,934	28	...	Czechoslovakia
282	9,622[4]	...	...	...	...	4,203[4,5]	1,654[4,5]	...	12	...	Denmark
...	...	...	...	2.5	8	...	...	...	...	...	Djibouti
...	...	...	...	...	...	...	...	...	1	...	Dominica
...	...	...	...	...	...	41[5]	74[5]	14[5]	5	...	Dominican Republic
...	...	...	...	...	...	148[5]	2[4,5]	...	11	6[15]	Ecuador
54	6,659	179	...	...	...	...	...	...	7	...	Egypt
20[4]	1,333[9]	...	...	...	...	...	...	...	...	...	El Salvador
...	...	...	...	...	...	21[5]	16[5]	47[5]	...	...	Equatorial Guinea

Cultural institutions (continued)

country	public libraries number	volumes ('000)	registered borrowers ('000)	loans per 1,000 population	number of titles books	pamphlets	number of copies books ('000)	pamphlets ('000)	cinema annual attendance (all cinemas) number ('000,000)	per 1,000 population	fixed cinemas number	seating capacity ('000)	number of long films produced
Ethiopia	...	...	...	...	150	...	993	66	...	...	40	36	...
Faeroe Islands	12	108	...	2,854	...	...	...	...	0.3	7,100	9	1	...
Falkland Islands	...	...	33	...	...	...	...	...	21.0[12]	10,500	2	0.5	...
Fiji	9	91	33	517	84	26	239	44	0.3	500	50	40	...
Finland	464	23,350	1,842	...	5,837	2,390	...	...	10.1	2,100	363	95	10
France	1,028	50,470	4,917	1,672	25,190	12,118	...	...	188.9	3,500	4,695	1,363	231
French Guiana	1	18,669	1	229	1	---	2	---	...	...	...	...	...
French Polynesia	1	18	...	...	56	16	92	10	0.5	4,000	6	3	...
Gabon	...	...	...	...	...	...	...	...	1.1	2,100	...	...	...
Gambia, The	1	67	...	86	21	60	9	...	...	...	...	...	...
Germany, East	7,271	45,795	4,817	5,536	5,235	744	113,605	27,542	77.0	4,600	2,182	348	16
Germany, West	14,284[6]	62,200	...	2,745	49,056	7,512	...	...	141.8	2,300	3,530	892	76
Ghana	7	929	70	77	105	104	163	91	4.4	400	7	16	1
Gibraltar	2	19	6	2,686	...	...	...	...	0.2	7,500	4	2	...
Greece	...	...	...	...	3,618	430	...	...	55.2	5,900	...	...	33
Greenland	1	93	...	...	...	...	...	...	...	...	...	...	...
Grenada	1	15	1	...	2	8	2	9	1.3	12,500	6	4	...
Guadeloupe	1	90	15	4,062	...	...	...	...	0.8	2,650	...	...	...
Guam	...	...	...	...	12	...	0.3	...	...	...	...	...	...
Guatemala	1	27	...	...	350	224	69	...	9.9	1,400	126[3]	85	...
Guinea	...	...	...	...	...	...	...	...	...	...	...	...	...
Guinea-Bissau	...	...	...	...	...	...	...	...	...	...	...	...	...
Guyana	...	...	...	...	18	62	...	...	13.3	14,700	50	40	4
Haiti	...	...	...	...	...	...	...	...	6.2	1,300	19[3]	3	...
Honduras	...	...	...	...	...	...	...	...	...	...	...	...	...
Hong Kong	1	1,030	851	808	3,695	1,156	24,560	11,034	58.8	12,000	83[3]	99	112
Hungary	2,241	40,769	2,242	4,872	7,910	900	94,455	8,622	67.4	6,300	3,439	544	25
Iceland	251	1,033	...	...	575	226	...	...	2.6	11,400	47[3]	...	...
India	...	...	...	...	11,062	500	...	...	4,650.0	6,800	6,991[3]	4,195	737
Indonesia	30	460	2,768	...	1,233	603	...	...	147.4	1,000	1,320	852	71
Iran	385	2,161	...	8	2,657	---	...	...	165.1	4,200	410[3]	264	68
Iraq	24	195	...	...	948	256	...	...	...	...	84	65	3
Ireland	31[21]	7,399[21]	71[21]	4,928[21]	510	205	...	...	18.0	5,800	142	...	2
Israel	...	...	...	...	1,956	481	14,887[2]	2	24.4	6,600	214	152	12
Italy	...	...	...	...	11,854	1,603	145,119	10,624	213.7	3,800	7,726	...	143
Ivory Coast	1	25	2	3	23	6	945	620	7.1	900	72	42	2
Jamaica	1	1,108	615	1,130	...	18	...	280	6.4	3,000	...	...	...
Japan	891	58,786	6,521	1,003	42,217	...	664,254	...	152.9	1,300	2,298	918	332
Jordan	1	70	1	6	...	...	...	...	10.5	4,900	41	20	...
Kampuchea	...	...	...	...	...	...	...	...	...	...	...	...	...
Kenya	3	150	...	...	168	64	...	...	8.6	600	40	20	...
Kiribati	...	...	...	...	...	...	...	...	...	...	...	...	...
Korea, North	...	...	...	...	...	...	...	...	...	...	...	...	...
Korea, South	120	1,742	...	...	24,739	1,008	75,312	3,692	42.6	1,100	423	244	87
Kuwait	1	281	...	55	5	---	325	34	3.7	2,500	12[3]	15	...
Laos	...	...	...	...	...	...	...	...	...	...	...	...	...
Lebanon	...	...	...	...	...	...	...	...	...	...	...	...	6
Lesotho	...	...	...	...	...	...	...	...	...	...	...	...	...
Liberia	...	...	...	...	...	...	...	...	1.4	800	13	9	...
Libya	...	...	...	...	48[12]	2	2,405[2]	2	10.9	3,500	49	22	2
Liechtenstein	1	...	9	1,030	...	...	...	...	...	...	...	...	...
Luxembourg	...	...	...	...	269	111	...	...	1.1	3,000	...	...	...
Macau	...	...	...	...	...	...	...	...	2.3	9,300	...	...	...
Madagascar	28	...	69	...	196	88	216	230	2.9	400	...	...	...
Malawi	1[21]	91[21]	20[21]	51[21]	39	40	...	...	4.5	900	4	2	...
Malaysia	18[21]	2,419[21]	400[21]	...	1,300	1,056	5,651	2,404	34.0	2,700	425	...	12
Maldives	...	...	...	...	3	---	...	...	...	...	...	...	...
Mali	...	...	...	...	4	2	4	4	...	...	...	...	...
Malta	1	153	35	1,582	96	36	...	...	2.1	5,700	31	21	...
Martinique	...	...	...	...	3	18	10	33	1.1	3,450	...	...	...
Mauritania	...	...	...	...	20	20	...	...	...	...	19	8	...
Mauritius	...	...	...	...	55	29	136	26	6.0	6,200	47	47	...
Mayotte	...	...	...	...	...	...	...	...	...	...	...	...	...
Mexico	485	2,102	3,574	...	2,954	26	...	...	249.3	3,700	2,701	...	88
Monaco	1	130	...	...	76[2]	2	453[2]	2	0.1	3,800	3	1	...
Mongolia	...	...	...	...	...	...	...	...	15.3	8.9	21[3]	...	...
Montserrat	...	...	...	...	...	...	...	...	...	...	...	...	...
Morocco	...	...	...	...	...	...	...	...	36.7	2,000	227	147	...
Mozambique	...	...	...	...	76	...	2,789	...	3.2	400	...	...	...
Nauru	...	...	...	...	...	...	...	...	...	...	...	...	...
Nepal	...	...	...	...	43	---	70	---	...	...	...	...	...
Netherlands, The	475[21]	30,722[21]	4,008[21]	11,490[21]	13,939	...	...	...	28.4	2,000	551	154	11
Netherlands Antilles	1	100	10	934	28	24	...	...	...	...	...	...	...
New Caledonia	1	34	...	...	12	8	4	2	0.9	6,900	17	4	...
New Zealand	209	6,077	1,151	9,455	1,240	1,259	...	...	15.0	5,100	172	103	9
Nicaragua	...	...	...	...	...	...	...	...	4.7	1,900	127	74	1
Niger	...	...	...	...	4[26]	1[26]	8[26]	1[26]	...	...	...	...	...
Nigeria	18	481	206	2	1,416	900	...	...	30.0	300	...	...	15
Niue	1	6	...	...	...	...	...	...	...	...	120	...	...
Norfolk Island	1	5	...	6,033	---	1	---	1	10[12]	5,000	1	0.1	...
Norway	454	14,037	1,059	3,959	4,238	1,340	...	...	16.4	4,000	456	134	10
Oman	...	...	...	...	...	...	...	...	0.9	1,100	12	1	...
Pakistan	...	...	...	...	1,279	...	...	...	175.6	2,200	630	305	120
Panama	18	26	...	32	114	57	75	71	7.1	4,800	...	...	...
Papua New Guinea	...	...	...	...	...	...	...	...	...	...	...	...	...
Paraguay	...	...	...	...	...	...	...	...	...	...	...	...	...
Peru	520	4,102	...	114	655	112	...	...	33.8	1,900	425[3]	...	2
Philippines	449[6]	1,012	469	102	421	10	2,087[28]	1,031[28]	315.5	7,500	716	570	143
Pitcairn Island	...	...	...	...	...	...	...	...	...	...	...	...	...
Poland	9,315	94,538	7,388	4,162	8,136	2,299	102,047	31,805	100.5	2,800	1,831	493	41

museums			sporting events			performing arts			nature preservation		country
number	annual attendance ('000)	annual attendance per 1,000 population	number of public facilities	annual participation ('000)	annual participation per 1,000 population	number of performances	annual attendance ('000)	annual attendance per 1,000 population	number of facilities	annual attendance ('000)	
...	...	...	...	...	...	253	224	7	16	...	Ethiopia
...	...	...	...	...	...	...	...	...	...	...	Faeroe Islands
1	...	40	...	...	...	...	...	...	2	...	Falkland Islands
1	25	...	...	...	...	255	57	90	15	...	Fiji
623	4,112[4]	...	...	...	...	10,378[5]	2,658[5]	558[5]	...	...	Finland
1,434[4]	11,000[4]	...	...	9,494	...	28,554[4]	...	...	29	...	France
1	12	192	...	10	140	...	...	...	3	...	French Guiana
...	...	...	...	...	...	33[5]	14[5]	99[5]	1	...	French Polynesia
...	...	...	...	...	...	...	...	...	6	...	Gabon
...	...	...	...	...	...	...	...	...	1	...	Gambia, The
642	30,700	1,838	19,485	3,324	199	75,138	26,612	1,593	2	...	Germany, East
805[17]	35,300[17]	573[17]	...	15,523	...	51,300[5]	21,400[5]	349[5]	35	3,000[18]	Germany, West
4	69	6	...	...	...	3,672	653	61	8	...	Ghana
1	16	500	...	...	...	39[7]	15[7]	453[7]	...	...	Gibraltar
138	10,430	1,072	...	...	...	14,760	5,230	563	15	...	Greece
...	...	...	...	...	...	...	...	...	2	...	Greenland
1	1	112	...	...	...	...	...	...	1	...	Grenada
5	31[4]	...	...	49	149	92	44	133	...	...	Guadeloupe
...	...	...	...	...	...	...	...	...	...	...	Guam
13	853	121	...	...	...	123[4,5]	65[4,5]	...	8	40[19]	Guatemala
20	...	...	...	...	...	...	...	...	4	...	Guinea
...	...	...	...	...	...	...	...	...	...	...	Guinea-Bissau
2	235	296	...	...	...	...	...	...	1	...	Guyana
6	91[4]	...	...	...	...	...	...	...	6	...	Haiti
5	49	15	...	...	...	...	...	...	6	...	Honduras
16	565[4]	...	...	...	...	758	419	93	...	...	Hong Kong
464	16,819[4]	...	3,265	295[20]	28[20]	11,732[5]	6,054[5]	566[5]	12	...	Hungary
...	...	...	...	...	...	...	...	...	22	...	Iceland
...	...	...	...	...	...	...	...	...	206	...	India
127	4,964[4]	...	...	...	...	4,600	2,800	19	86	...	Indonesia
44	1,963[4]	...	...	...	...	845[5]	...	...	36	...	Iran
15	664	52	...	...	...	743[5]	228[4,5]	19[5]	...	...	Iraq
49	824[4]	...	...	...	...	10,260[4,5]	...	...	5	...	Ireland
80	8,433	2,286	...	...	...	...	...	...	5	...	Israel
1,275	44,395[4]	...	45,494	...	...	64,238[5]	18,055[5]	318[5]	13	...	Italy
...	...	...	...	...	...	...	...	...	11	...	Ivory Coast
5	44[4]	...	...	...	...	839[22]	1,143[22]	543[22]	...	...	Jamaica
1,503	92,741[4]	...	219,000[23]	...	...	39,768[5]	...	...	55	173,530	Japan
6	59	20	...	...	...	64	180	84	3	5	Jordan
...	...	...	...	...	...	...	...	...	1	...	Kampuchea
...	...	...	...	...	...	...	...	...	43	...	Kenya
11	312	23	...	...	...	...	...	...	...	...	Kiribati
...	...	...	...	...	...	237	...	...	...	...	Korea, North
61	8,363[4]	...	...	...	...	1,973[5]	262[4,5]	...	11	...	Korea, South
3[9]	259[9]	204[9]	...	...	...	196[7]	...	...	...	...	Kuwait
...	...	...	...	...	...	...	...	...	...	...	Laos
...	...	...	...	...	...	...	...	...	...	...	Lebanon
1	...	...	...	...	...	...	...	...	1	...	Lesotho
...	...	...	...	...	...	...	...	...	...	...	Liberia
26	50	16	...	...	...	439	160	51	2	...	Libya
...	...	...	...	...	...	...	...	...	...	...	Liechtenstein
14	225	630	...	12	462	46[7]	...	...	...	...	Luxembourg
...	...	...	119	5.3	19	...	...	...	...	...	Macau
8	142[4]	...	...	...	...	140[7]	607	77	13	...	Madagascar
2	10	0.3	...	...	...	...	...	...	9	5[4]	Malawi
228	3,561[4]	...	...	...	...	1,303	312	25	18	13[24]	Malaysia
1	1,194	8,234	...	...	...	...	...	...	...	...	Maldives
...	...	...	...	...	...	...	...	...	8	...	Mali
22	712[4]	...	...	...	...	...	...	...	3	...	Malta
...	...	...	...	32	99	...	...	...	...	...	Martinique
...	...	...	...	...	...	...	...	...	2	...	Mauritania
3	220	234	...	...	...	...	...	...	3	...	Mauritius
...	...	...	...	...	...	...	...	...	...	...	Mayotte
230	11,845[4]	...	...	...	...	11,574[5]	4,165[5]	62[5]	30	...	Mexico
4	1,552[25]	62,080[25]	...	...	...	31	13	504	...	...	Monaco
...	...	...	...	...	...	...	...	...	3	...	Mongolia
...	...	...	...	...	...	167	47	364[7]	...	...	Montserrat
...	...	...	...	...	...	...	...	...	3	...	Morocco
...	...	...	...	...	...	...	...	...	10	...	Mozambique
...	...	...	...	...	...	...	...	...	...	...	Nauru
...	...	...	...	...	...	33[5]	...	...	9	...	Nepal
410	12,794	918	24,479	...	...	17,957[5]	4,106[5]	293[5]	21	...	Netherlands, The
...	...	...	...	...	...	...	...	...	3	...	Netherlands Antilles
1	30	219	...	...	...	46[4]	...	...	4	...	New Caledonia
110	371[4]	...	...	...	...	2,287[4,5]	515[4,5]	...	100	...	New Zealand
...	...	...	...	...	...	...	...	...	2	...	Nicaragua
5	650	130	...	...	...	...	...	...	3	...	Niger
...	...	...	...	...	...	89[5,27]	32[5,27]	...	6	...	Nigeria
...	...	...	...	...	...	...	...	...	...	...	Niue
1	20	10,000	...	...	...	7	2	1,000	...	...	Norfolk Island
195	4,573[4]	---	...	1,457	350	4,357[5]	1,147[5]	282[5]	32	...	Norway
...	...	...	...	...	...	...	...	...	2	...	Oman
10	561	7	...	...	...	...	48[5]	1[5]	11	...	Pakistan
...	...	...	...	...	...	55	...	...	8	...	Panama
2	100	32	...	...	...	122	265	91	5	...	Papua New Guinea
...	...	...	...	...	...	...	...	...	6	...	Paraguay
37	832	48	...	...	...	2,388	...	...	21	...	Peru
79	76[4]	...	...	...	...	217[4]	130[4]	...	9	...	Philippines
...	...	...	...	...	...	...	...	...	...	...	Pitcairn Island
417	21,067	601	...	278[29]	8[29]	34,646[5]	13,654[5]	390[5]	23	...	Poland

Cultural institutions (continued)

| country | public libraries | | | | book production | | | | cinema | | | | number of long films produced |
	number	volumes ('000)	registered borrowers ('000)	loans per 1,000 population	number of titles: books	number of titles: pamphlets	number of copies: books ('000)	number of copies: pamphlets ('000)	annual attendance (all cinemas): number ('000,000)	annual attendance: per 1,000 population	fixed cinemas: number	fixed cinemas: seating capacity ('000)	
Portugal	109	6,562	2,521	476	9,139[2]	2	227,020[2]	2	27.3	2,723	423	222	7
Puerto Rico	...	...	...	...	...	...	...	...	...	...	...	...	...
Qatar	6	...	1	26	316	21	2,100	105	0.7	3,200	4	4	...
Réunion	...	...	...	...	50	16	...	...	...	...	...	...	1
Romania	6,303	61,095	3,841	1,909	5,583	1,659	77,964	8,907	208.9	9,300	5,549	251[30]	31
Rwanda	...	...	...	...	...	...	...	...	0.5	100	12	4	1
St. Christopher and Nevis	...	...	...	...	---	1	...	1	...	...	...	...	...
St. Helena and Ascension	1	14	...	...	...	...	...	...	52.8[12]	8,800	...	...	...
St. Lucia	1	46	...	...	5	11	15	18	...	...	2	1	...
St. Pierre and Miquelon	3	15	...	...	...	...	...	...	...	...	...	...	...
St. Vincent and the Grenadines	...	...	...	...	...	...	...	...	...	...	...	...	...
San Marino	1	1	...	...	14	1	...	...	0.1	5,600	6	3	...
São Tomé and Principe	...	...	...	...	...	...	...	...	...	...	...	...	...
Saudi Arabia	8	...	...	...	207	11	...	...	...	...	...	...	...
Senegal	1	3	...	...	64	---	287	---	3.6	700	60	...	...
Seychelles	1	25	9	1,748	2	31	6[2]	2	0.8	13,600	2	1	...
Sierra Leone	11	392	...	...	17	44	9	12	...	...	...	...	...
Singapore	1	800	...	...	1,164[32]	619[32]	4,829[32]	3,519[32]	37.1	15,200	73	74	2
Solomon Islands	...	...	...	...	...	...	...	...	0.1	300	2	1	4
Somalia	...	...	...	...	...	...	...	...	8.0	2,300	...	...	...
South Africa	...	...	...	...	...	...	...	...	...	...	...	...	...
South West Africa/Namibia	...	...	...	...	...	...	...	...	31.2	1,200	...	...	...
Spain	1,396[4]	11,730[4]	1,308[4]	168[4]	20,126	4,443	178,920	46,038	173.2	4,600	3,970	2,608	137
Sri Lanka	381	727	178	...	825	1,527	5,628	6,725	63.9	4,300	357	202	42
Sudan, The	...	...	...	...	138[26]	---	12,905[33]	...	3.8	200	56	108	1
Suriname	2	268	54	2,056	...	...	...	...	...	...	...	...	...
Swaziland	...	...	...	...	...	...	...	...	...	...	...	...	...
Sweden	408	39,031	...	9,304	7,490	1,092	...	...	22.5	2,700	1,239[3]	...	19
Switzerland	...	3,690	...	1,369	10,544[2]	2	...	...	20.7	3,200	477	160	17
Syria	...	...	...	...	95	---	310	---	14.6	1,600	92	53	2
Taiwan	...	...	...	...	...	...	...	...	140.0	7,900	...	...	...
Tanzania	1	404	10	9	368	144	...	...	3.7	200	34	15	...
Thailand	526	586	...	...	4,003	495	...	...	71.0	1,700	376	267	55
Togo	...	...	...	...	...	...	...	...	...	...	...	...	...
Tokelau	1	2	...	...	...	...	...	...	...	...	...	...	...
Tonga	...	...	...	...	33	287	0.4	6	0.1	1,000	3	2	...
Trinidad and Tobago	1	68	1	122	101	85	47	80	...	...	72	57	...
Trust Territory of the Pacific Is.	...	16	...	...	93	40	...	...	...	...	52	...	...
Tunisia	75	875	53	175	172[26]	---	6,000[26]	---	9.1	1,500	82	41	3
Turkey	363	5,044	502	47	4,793[2]	2	...	...	63.3	1,400	938	506	65
Turks and Caicos Islands	1	7	...	1,047	...	...	...	...	...	...	3	1	...
Tuvalu	...	...	...	...	...	...	...	...	...	...	...	...	...
Uganda	1	73	157	32	...	...	...	...	2.5	200	173[3]	10	...
U.S.S.R.	165,190	2,281,872	180,502	3,455	55,972	34,674	1,471,988	620,715	4,310.0	16,100	...	...	153
United Arab Emirates	...	...	...	...	6	...	35	---	7.2	10,300	74	29	...
United Kingdom	160	131,338	...	11,393	39,589	3,383	...	...	84.3	1,500	1,541	622	41
United States	8,456	439,486	...	4,525	72,382	4,594	...	...	1,057.1	4,600	14,732	6,900	226
Uruguay	...	...	...	...	415	422	...	...	6.1	2,100	120	80	2
Vanuatu	1	12	1	...	...	...	...	...	0.1	1,000	3	1	...
Venezuela	23	977	66	171	3,596	604	1,194	...	67.3	4,700	535	...	7
Vietnam	316	4,879	...	...	1,495[2]	2	37,117[2]	2	315.0	5,700	210	178	15
Virgin Islands (U.S)	...	...	...	...	...	...	...	...	...	...	...	...	...
Wallis and Futuna	...	...	...	...	...	...	...	...	...	...	...	...	...
Western Sahara	...	...	...	...	...	...	...	...	...	...	...	...	...
Western Samoa	1	36	...	...	79	156	39	43	0.5	3,200	6	6	...
Yemen (Aden)	...	...	...	...	...	...	...	...	5.8	3,100	21	21	...
Yemen (Ṣan'ā')	...	...	...	...	...	...	...	...	13.0	2,500	35	28	...
Yugoslavia	2,101	24,123	4,368	...	8,835	2,253	52,458	12,662	78.7	3,500	1,189	427	31
Zaire	8	6	9	1	194	37	654	---	...	...	...	...	...
Zambia	4	...	18	27	8	---	235	---	5.1	1,000	12	4	...
Zimbabwe	...	...	...	...	402[2]	2	...	...	...	...	...	...	...

museums			sporting events			performing arts			nature preservation		country
number	annual atten-dance ('000)	annual atten-dance per 1,000 population	number of public facilities	annual particip-ation ('000)	annual particip-ation per 1,000 population	number of per-formances	annual atten-dance ('000)	annual attendance per 1,000 population	number of facilities	annual atten-dance ('000)	
122	2,790	278	...	...	...	4,555[4,5]	1,581[4,5]	158	9	...	Portugal
...	...	...	1,800	...	...	...	...	...	4	...	Puerto Rico
1	60	299	...	...	...	4[4,7]	1[4,7]	...	...	...	Qatar
3	111	227	...	...	...	...	...	...	...	...	Réunion
429	16,190	733	14,200	4,000	177	23,235[5]	8,274[5]	377[5]	5	...	Romania
4	12[4]	...	...	...	...	317	58[7]	127	2	...	Rwanda
...	...	...	...	...	...	...	...	...	...	...	St. Christopher and Nevis
...	...	...	...	...	...	17	17	171[7]	...	...	St. Helena and Ascension
1	7	54	...	...	...	...	...	...	1	...	St. Lucia
1	4	667	...	...	...	...	...	...	...	...	St. Pierre and Miquelon
...	...	...	...	...	...	...	...	...	...	...	St. Vincent and the Grenadines
11	741[25]	35,286[25]	...	...	...	26[5]	10[5]	457[5]	...	...	San Marino
...	...	...	...	...	...	...	...	...	...	...	São Tomé and Príncipe
1	37	5	...	...	...	897	907	117	1	...	Saudi Arabia
4	55	10	...	...	...	122[5]	52[5]	95	15	6[31]	Senegal
1	8	127	...	...	...	6[7]	3[7]	97[7]	1	...	Seychelles
19	178[4]	...	...	...	...	...	...	...	...	...	Sierra Leone
10	4,282	1,812	152	...	...	523	645	273	1	...	Singapore
1	29	146	...	...	...	37	17	57	...	...	Solomon Islands
1	...	...	...	...	...	...	...	...	1	...	Somalia
...	...	...	...	...	...	...	...	...	49	600[4]	South Africa
...	...	...	...	...	...	...	...	...	11	...	South West Africa/Namibia
610	13,897	370	...	...	...	18,862	6,702	178	14	...	Spain
15	1,476	107	...	...	...	1,008	600[7]	41[7]	35	...	Sri Lanka
5	157	9	...	...	...	...	...	...	17	...	Sudan, The
...	...	...	...	...	...	...	...	...	9	...	Suriname
...	...	...	...	...	...	...	...	...	5	...	Swaziland
267	15,505[4]	...	...	...	...	20,684	3,957	477	37	8[34]	Sweden
...	...	...	1,818	2,323	366	25,735	5,811	918	11	200[35]	Switzerland
27	509[4]	...	...	...	...	411[5]	165[5]	205	3	...	Syria
...	...	...	20	...	...	...	...	...	...	...	Taiwan
61	127[4]	...	...	...	...	21	15	1	20	...	Tanzania
119	1,103[4]	...	...	...	...	...	...	...	60	100[36]	Thailand
1	48	21	...	...	...	...	...	...	7	...	Togo
...	...	...	...	...	...	...	...	...	...	...	Tokelau
...	...	...	...	...	...	...	...	...	5	...	Tonga
3	104[4]	...	...	...	...	49[4,7]	...	...	10	...	Trinidad and Tobago
5	...	...	...	...	...	...	...	...	...	...	Trust Territory of the Pacific Is.
25	981[4]	...	...	...	...	598	164	257	12	...	Tunisia
9	5,196	120	...	344[29]	7[29]	1,952[5]	604[5]	14[5]	14	...	Turkey
...	...	...	...	...	...	...	...	...	...	...	Turks and Caicos Islands
...	...	...	...	...	...	37	17	100[7]	...	...	Tuvalu
...	...	...	...	...	...	...	...	...	17	...	Uganda
1,686	178,857[4]	...	3,693[16]	84,500	313	304,100[4,5]	160,822[5]	609[5]	149	...	U.S.S.R.
3	244[4]	...	...	...	...	12	36	40	...	...	United Arab Emirates
...	...	...	...	...	...	1,840[4,5]	2,168[4,5]	...	72	950[4]	United Kingdom
4,609	352,736	1,588	...	...	...	...	...	...	252	329,000	United States
59	...	...	...	...	...	3,097[5]	...	...	9	285[4]	Uruguay
...	...	...	...	...	...	...	...	...	...	...	Vanuatu
133	...	...	...	...	...	372	206	16	35	2,290[4]	Venezuela
9	1,918	36	...	...	...	1,313[5]	1,493[5]	31[5]	...	...	Vietnam
10	995[4]	...	...	...	...	...	...	...	4	...	Virgin Islands (U.S.)
...	...	...	...	...	...	...	...	...	...	...	Wallis and Futuna
...	...	...	...	...	...	...	...	...	...	...	Western Sahara
...	...	...	...	...	...	97	27	117	2	...	Western Samoa
...	...	...	...	...	...	...	...	...	...	...	Yemen (Aden)
...	...	...	...	...	...	...	...	...	...	...	Yemen (Șan'ā')
397	13,597	616	...	1,589	70	18,506	4,906	222	30	...	Yugoslavia
4	6[4]	...	...	...	...	40	5	0.2	12	...	Zaire
71	171[4]	...	...	...	...	...	...	...	18	...	Zambia
...	...	...	...	...	...	...	...	...	25	...	Zimbabwe

[1]Anguilla includes St. Christopher and Nevis. [2]Books includes pamphlets. [3]35-millimetre and over only. [4]Partial data. [5]Professional only. [6]Library service points. [7]Amateur only. [8]Ministry of Flemish Culture museums only. [9]National museums only. [10]Coral reef preserves only. [11]Government publications only. [12]Attendance in 1,000's. [13]Physical fitness and amateur athletics only. [14]Excludes some Turkish language publications. [15]Galapagos National Park only. [16]Stadiums only. [17]Museums with a yearly attendance 20,000 or more only. [18]Lüneburger Heide only. [19]Tikal National Park only. [20]Registered players only. [21]Public libraries financed by public authorities only. [22]All amateur performances plus professional pantomime only. [23]Includes private facilities. [24]Bako and Kinabalu National parks only. [25]Visitors are mostly foreign tourists. [26]School texts only. [27]Performances at the National Theatre of Lagos only. [28]Books received in the national library only. [29]Active sportsmen only. [30]16-millimetre cinemas only. [31]Nikolo-Koba National Park only. [32]Does not include government publications. [33]School textbooks and children's books only. [34]Padjelanta and Sarek National Parks only. [35]Swiss National Park only. [36]Khao Yai National Park only.

BIBLIOGRAPHY AND SOURCES

The following list indicates the principal sources used in the compilation of *Britannica World Data*. It is by no means a complete list, either for international or for national sources, but is indicative only of the range of materials to which reference has been made in preparing this compilation. For example, in addition to the kinds of works cited below, reference has also been made to the constitutions of each country, to the publications of its central or commercial banks, to unpublished information received in correspondence from the countries, and to other more specialized sources.

International Statistical Sources

Africana Publishing Co. Africa Contemporary Record (annual).
AT&T. *The World's Telephones* (annual).
Billboard Ltd. *World Radio TV Handbook* (annual).
British Petroleum. *BP Statistical Review of World Energy* (annual).
Council for Mutual Economic Assistance (Comecon). *Statisticheasky Yezhegodnik Stran-Chlenov Soveta Ekonomicheskoy Vzaimopomoshchi* (Statistical Yearbook of the Council for Mutual Economic Assistance [annual]).
Europa Publications Ltd. *Africa South of the Sahara* (annual); *The Europa Year Book* (2 vol.); *The Far East and Australasia* (annual); *The Middle East and North Africa* (annual).
European Communities. *ACP: Statistical Yearbook; Basic Statistics* (annual).
Food and Agriculture Organization. *Food Balance Sheets* (irreg.); *Production Yearbook; Trade Yearbook; World Census of Agriculture* (decennial); *Yearbook of Fishery Statistics; Yearbook of Forest Products.*
Gulf Publishing Co. *World Pipelines* (1983).
Her Majesty's Stationery Office. *Yearbook of the Commonwealth.*
Inter-American Development Bank. *Economic and Social Progress in Latin America* (annual).
Inter-Parliamentary Union. *World Directory of Parliaments* (annual).
International Air Transport Association. *World Air Transport Statistics* (annual).
International Bank for Reconstruction and Development/The World Bank. *World Bank Atlas* (annual); *World Debt Tables* (annual); *World Development Report* (annual); *World Tables* (2 vol. [irreg.]).
International Civil Aviation Organization. *Civil Aviation Statistics of the World* (annual); *Digest of Statistics.*
International Institute for Strategic Studies. *Strategic Survey* (annual).
International Labour Organization. *Household Income and Expenditure Statistics* (irreg.); *Year Book of Labour Statistics.*
International Monetary Fund. *Exchange Arrangements and Exchange Restrictions* (annual); *Government Finance Statistics Yearbook; International Financial Statistics* (monthly, with supplements and yearbook).
International Road Federation. *Road and Motor Vehicle Statistics* (annual); *World Road Statistics* (annual).
Jane's Publishing Co. *Jane's World Railways* (annual).
Lloyd's Register of Shipping. *Lloyd's Register of Shipping: Statistical Tables* (annual).
Longman Group Ltd. *Keesing's Contemporary Archives* (monthly).
Macmillan Press Ltd. *The Statesman's Year-Book.*
Middle East Economic Digest Ltd. *Africa Economic Digest* (semi-monthly); *Middle East Economic Digest* (semi-monthly).
Mining Journal. *Mining Annual Review.*

Nordic Council. *Yearbook of Nordic Statistics.*
Official Airline Guides, Inc. *Official Airline Guide* (monthly).
Organization for Economic Cooperation and Development. *Economic Surveys* (annual); *External Debt of Developing Countries* (annual); *National Accounts of Developing Countries* (irreg.).
Oxford University Press. *World Christian Encyclopedia* (David B. Barrett, ed. [1982]).
Pacific Publications. *Pacific Islands Year Book* (irreg.).
PennWell Publishing Co. *International Petroleum Encyclopedia* (annual).
René Moreux et Cie. *Marchés tropicaux & Méditerranéens* (semi-monthly).
Société Africaine d'Edition. *L'Année politique et économique Africaine.*
South Pacific Commission. *Key Economic Indicators* (occasional); *South Pacific Economies: Statistical Summary* (biennial).
Tokyo Metropolitan Government. *Statistics of World Large Cities* (annual).
United Nations (UN). *Compendium of Social Statistics* (irreg.); *Demographic Indicators of Countries, 1980 Assessment; Demographic Yearbook; Energy Balances 1977–1980 and Electricity Profiles 1976–1981 for Selected Developing Countries and Areas; Growth of World Industry* (2 vol. [annual]); *Monthly Bulletin of Statistics; Population Studies* (irreg.); *Population and Vital Statistics Report* (quarterly); *Statistical Yearbook; Supplement to the Statistical Yearbook and the Monthly Bulletin of Statistics* (quinquennial); *Yearbook of Construction Statistics; Yearbook of Industrial Statistics* (2 vol.); *Yearbook of International Trade Statistics* (2 vol.); *Yearbook of National Accounts Statistics* (2 vol.); *Yearbook of World Energy Statistics; World Housing Survey* (1974).
UN: Conference on Trade and Development. *Handbook of International Trade and Development Statistics* (annual).
UN: Economic Commission for Africa. *African Statistical Yearbook; Demographic and Related Socio-Economic Data Sheets for ECA Member States* (1982); *Survey of Economic and Social Conditions in Africa* (irreg.).
UN: Economic Commission for Europe. *Annual Bulletin of Housing and Building Statistics for Europe; Annual Bulletin of Transport Statistics for Europe.*
UN: Economic Commission for Latin America. *Economic Survey of Latin America* (annual); *Statistical Yearbook for Latin America.*
UN: Economic Commission for Western Asia. *Population Bulletin* (irreg.); *The Population Situation in the ECWA Region* (irreg.).
UN: Economic and Social Commission for Asia and the Pacific. *Foreign Trade Statistics of Asia and the Pacific* (annual); *Statistical Indicators for Asia and the Pacific* (quarterly); *Statistical Yearbook for Asia and the Pacific.*
UN: Educational, Scientific, and Cultural Organization. *Statistical Yearbook; Estimates and Projections of Illiteracy* (1978).
United States: Central Intelligence Agency, *The World Factbook* (annual); Dept. of Commerce, *Foreign Economic Trends* (irreg.), *Overseas Business Reports* (annual), *World Population* (annual); Dept. of Energy, *International Energy Annual;* Dept. of Health and Human Services, *Social Security Programs Throughout the World* (biennial); Dept. of Interior, *Minerals Yearbook* (3 vol.); Dept. of State, *Background Notes* (irreg.).
West India Committee and FT International. *The Caribbean Handbook, 1983/84.*
World Health Organization. *World Health Statistics* (annual.)
World Priorities. *World Military and Social Expenditures* (Ruth Leger Sivard, ed. [annual]).
World Tourism Organization. *World Tourism Statistics* (annual).

National Statistical Sources

Afghanistan. *Area Handbook for Afghanistan* (1973); *Economic and Social Indicators* (triennial); *First Seven-Year Economic and Social Development Plan, 1355–1361 (March 1976–March 1983); Preliminary Results of the First Afghan Population Census, 1979; Review of the General Socio-economic Situation in the Democratic Republic of Afghanistan During 1358 (21 March 1979–20 March 1980); Statistical Year Book.*
Albania. *Area Handbook for Albania* (1971); *Directives of the 8th Congress of the PLA for the 7th Five-Year Plan (1981–85) of Economic and Cultural Development of the PSR of Albania; An Outline of the People's Socialist Republic of Albania* (1978); *Portrait of Albania* (1982); *Vjetari statistikor R P SH* (Statistical Yearbook of the People's Republic of Albania [annual]); *35 Years of Socialist Albania* (1981).
Algeria. *Algeria: A Country Study* (1979); *Annuaire statistique* (Statistical Yearbook); *Recensement général de la population et de l'habitat, 1977.*
American Samoa. *Annual Report of the Governor of American Samoa to the Secretary of the Department of the Interior; Population of American Samoa* (ESCAP; Country Monograph Series No. 7.1 [1979]); *1980 Census of Population and Housing* (U.S.); *1980 Statistical Bulletin.*
Angola. *Angola: A Country Study* (1979); *Anuário Estatístico; Recenseamento Geral da População, 1960; Situação Economica e Financeira de Angola* (annual).
Antigua. *Statistical Yearbook.*
Argentina. *Anuario estadístico de la República Argentina; Area Handbook for Argentina* (1974); *Boletín estadístico trimestral* (quarterly); *Censo nacional agropecuario, 1969; Censo nacional de población y vivienda, 1980; Comercio exterior* (annual); *Encuesta permanente de hogares* (irreg.); *Indicadores industriales* (annual); *Índice de precios al consumidor y salarios industriales* (monthly); *Relevamiento estadístico de la economía Argentina, 1900–1980* (1982).
Australia. *Census of Retail Establishments and Selected Service Establishments* (1979–80); *Integrated Economic Censuses and Surveys* (1980–81); *Manufacturing Establishments: Details of Operations by Industry Class* (annual); *Monthly Summary of Statistics, Australia; National Income and Expenditure* (annual); *Overseas Trade* (annual); *Social Indicators* (irreg.); *Yearbook of the Commonwealth of Australia; 1981 Census of Population and Housing.*
Austria. *Area Handbook for Austria* (1976); *Der Aussenhandel Österreichs* (Austrian Foreign Trade [quarterly]); *Österreichisches Jahrbuch* (annual); *Österreichs Volkseinkommen* (Austrian National Income); *Sozialstatistische Daten 1970–1980; Statistisches Handbuch* (annual); *Volkserzählung, 1981.*
Bahamas, The. *External Trade Statistics, Report* (annual); *Household Expenditure in The Bahamas, 1973; Industrial Production Statistics* (annual); *National Accounts of The Bahamas, 1973–1979; Quarterly Statistical Summary; Social Statistics Report* (annual); *Statistical Abstract* (annual); *Vital Statistics Report* (annual); *Wholesale and Retail Trade Report* (annual); *1980 Census of Population and Housing.*
Bahrain. *Statistical Abstract* (annual); *1981 Census of Bahrain.*
Bangladesh. *Area Handbook for Bangladesh* (1975); *Bangladesh Population Census, 1981; Monthly Statistical Bulletin of Bangladesh; Population of Bangladesh* (ESCAP; Country Monograph Series No. 8 [1981]); *Statistical Pocketbook of Bangladesh* (annual); *Statistical Yearbook of Bangladesh.*
Barbados. *Barbados Economic Report, 1980; Monthly Digest of Statistics; Report on the Census of Production, 1981.*

Belgium. *Annuaire statistique de la Belgique; Area Handbook for Belgium* (1974); *Bulletin du commerce extérieur* (annual); *Bulletin de statistique* (monthly); *Chiffres officiels de la population de droit, par commune; Recensement général de l'agriculture, 1970; Recensement de la population et des logements au 1er mars 1981; Statistiques demographiques* (quarterly); *1970; Recensement de l'industrie et du commerce.*

Belize. *Abstract of Statistics* (annual); *Belize Economic Report* (1984); *Development Plan (1977–1979).*

Benin. *Annuaire statistique; Recensement général de la population et de l'habitation* (1972).

Bermuda. *Bermuda Digest of Statistics* (annual); *The Economic Structure and National Accounts of Bermuda* (annual); *Report of the Customs Imports and Exports* (annual); *Report of the Population Census, 1980; Report of the Registrar General* (annual).

Bhutan. *Development in a Himalayan Kingdom* (A World Bank Country Study [1983]).

Bolivia. *Area Handbook for Bolivia* (1974); *Bolivia en cifras, 1980; Censo Nacional de población y vivienda de 1976; Resumen estadístico, 1982.*

Botswana. *1981 Population and Housing Census; Statistical Abstract* (annual).

Brazil. *Anuário Econômico: Fiscal; Anuário de Estatística Agraria; Anuário Estatístico do Brasil; Area Handbook for Brazil* (1971); *Foreign Trade of Brazil* (annual); *Indicadores Sociais* (1979); *IX Recenseamento Geral do Brasil, 1980.*

British Virgin Islands. *Census of the British Virgin Islands, 12th May 1980 (Provisional); Statistical Abstract* (irreg.); *Trade Report* (1978–1980).

Brunei. *Annual Report; Brunei Statistical Yearbook; Report on the Census of Population, 1971.*

Bulgaria. *Area Handbook for Bulgaria* (1974); *Prebroyavane—1975: resultati, perspektivi* (Census of Population—1975: Results, Perspectives); *Statisticheskii yezhgodnik* (Statistical Yearbook).

Burkina Faso (Upper Volta). *La Population de la Haute-Volta au recensement de décembre 1975.*

Burma. *Burma: A Country Study* (1983); *Census of Burma: 1973 Advance Release and Some Preliminary Analysis; Statistical Abstract, 1976.*

Burundi. *Annuaire statistique; Recensement général de la population, 16–30 août 1979.*

Cameroon. *Area Handbook for the United Republic of Cameroon* (1974); *Note annuelle de statistique; Recensement général de la population et de l'habitat d'avril 1976; Tableaux économiques du Cameroun* (1983).

Canada. *Canada Year Book* (biennial); *Canadian Statistical Review* (monthly); *Census of Agriculture, 1981; National Income and Expenditure Accounts* (quarterly); *1981 Census of Canada.*

Cape Verde. *Boletim Trimestral de Estatística* (quarterly).

Central African Republic. *Annuaire statistique; Recensement général de la population de décembre 1975.*

Chad. *Annuaire statistique.*

Chile. *Agricultura y pesca* (annual); *Anuario de minería; Area Handbook for Chile* (1969); *Chile XV censo nacional de población y de vivienda, 21 de abril 1982; Compendio estadístico* (annual); *Cuentas nacionales de Chile, 1960–1980; Informativo estadístico* (quarterly); *Informe social* (quarterly); *Plan nacional indicativo de desarrollo* (quinquennial).

China, People's Republic of. *Almanac of China's Economy, 1981: With Economic Statistics for 1949–1980; China: A Country Study* (1981); *China Official Annual Report; China Official Yearbook; China Socialist Development* (A World Bank Country Study; 3 vol. [1983]); *Preliminary Results of the 1982 Census in China; Statistical Yearbook of China; Yearbook of the Encyclopedia of China.*

Christmas Island. *Annual Report; Census of Population and Housing, 30 June 1981.*

Cocos (Keeling) Islands. *Annual Report; Census of Population and Housing, 30 June 1981.*

Colombia. *Boletín mensual de estadística* (monthly); *The Colombian Economy* (1982); *Colombia estadística* (annual); *Cuentas nacionales de Colombia, 1970–1981; Industria manufacturera* (annual); *XIV Censo nacional de población y III de vivienda, octubre 24 de 1973.*

Comoros. *The Comoros: Problems and Prospects of a Small Island Economy* (A World Bank Country Study [1979]); *Recensement de la population des Comores, 1966.*

Congo, People's Republic of the. *Annuaire statistique; Area Handbook for the People's Republic of the Congo (Brazzaville)* (1971); *Recensement général de la population de 1974.*

Cook Islands. *Cook Islands Census of Population and Dwellings, 1981; Cook Islands Quarterly Statistical Bulletin.*

Costa Rica. *Anuario estadístico; Area Handbook for Costa Rica* (1970); *Censos Nacionales de 1973; Evolución socioeconómica de Costa Rica, 1950–1980; Plan nacional de desarrollo 1979–1982: "Gregorio José Ramírez"; IV Censo de manufactura, 1975.*

Cuba. *Anuario estadístico; Area Handbook for Cuba* (1976); *Censo de población y viviendas, 1981; Compendio estadístico de Cuba* (annual).

Cyprus. *Census of Industrial Production* (annual); *Economic Report* (annual); *Statistical Abstract* (annual); *Statistics of Imports and Exports* (annual).

Czechoslovakia. *Czechoslovakia: A Country Study* (1981); *Statistická ročenka Československé Socialistické Republiky* (Statistical Yearbook of the Czechoslovak Socialist Republic); *Sčítání lidu, domů a bytů 1980* (Census of Population).

Denmark. *Denmarks vareindførsel og-udførsel, 1982* (External Trade of Denmark by Commodities and Countries); *Folke- og boligtaellingen, 1981* (Population and Housing Census); *Statistisk årbog* (Statistical Yearbook).

Djibouti. *Annuaire statistique de Djibouti.*

Dominican Republic. *Area Handbook for the Dominican Republic* (1973); *República Dominicana en cifras* (annual); *VI Censo nacional de población y vivienda, 1981.*

Ecuador. *Censo agropecuario, 1974; Encuesta anual de manufactura y minería; Serie estadística* (quinquennial); *IV Censo de población: III de vivienda resultados anticipados por muestreo* (1982).

Egypt. *Census of Population and Housing, 1976; Egypt: A Country Study* (1982).

El Salvador. *Anuario estadístico; Area Handbook for El Salvador* (1971); *Censos económicos, 1979 (Manufactura diversa; Agroindustrias; Comercio y servicios; Electricidad, construcción, transporte comercial); El Salvador en cifras* (annual).

Ethiopia. *Ethiopia: A Country Study* (1980); *Statistical Abstract* (annual).

Fiji. *Census of Industrial Production* (annual); *Current Economic Statistics* (quarterly); *Overseas Trade of Fiji* (annual); *Report on the Census of the Population, 1976.*

Finland. *Annual Statistics of Agriculture; Economic Survey* (annual); *Population and Housing Census, 1980; Statistical Yearbook of Finland.*

France. *Annuaire statistique de la France; Les Comptes de l'industrie* (1981); *Données sociales* (1982); *Le Mouvement économique en France, 1949–1979; Recensement général de la population de 1982: Métropole.*

French Guiana. *Annuaire statistique de la Guyane; Bulletin trimestriel de statistique; Recensement général de la population en 1974: Départements d'outre-mer, Guyane.*

French Polynesia. *Annuaire statistique; Bilan statistique de l'année, 1981; Comptes économiques* (quadrennial); *Résultats du recensement de la population de la Polynésie Française, 29 avril 1977; Te avei'a: Bulletin d'information statistique* (quarterly).

Gabon. *Situation économique, financière et sociale de la République Gabonaise* (1980).

Germany, East. *Statistisches Jahrbuch der Deutschen Demokratischen Republik.*

Germany, West. *Area Handbook for Germany* (1981); *Statistisches Jahrbuch für die Bundesrepublik Deutschland; Volkszählung vom 27 Mai 1970* (Census of Population).

Ghana. *Economic Survey* (biennial); *Ghana: An Official Handbook* (1977); *Industrial Statistics* (biennial); *Population Census, 1970.*

Gibraltar. *Abstract of Statistics* (annual); *Census of Gibraltar, 1981.*

Greece. *Recensement des industries manufacturières: Artisanat, du commerce et autres services* (1978); *Recensement de la population et des habitations, 1981; Statistical Yearbook of Greece.*

Greenland. *Grønland* (annual); *Grønlands befolkning* (Greenland Population [annual]).

Grenada. *Abstract of Statistics* (annual); *Annual Digest of Trade Statistics.*

Guadeloupe. *Annuaire statistique de la Guadeloupe; Comptes économiques* (quinquennial).

Guam. *Annual Economic Review; Annual Report to the Secretary of the Interior; Census of Agriculture* (quinquennial); *1980 Census of Population and Housing.*

Guatemala. *Anuario estadístico; Censos nacionales, 1981: IX de población—IV de habitación; Guatemala: A Country Study* (1983).

Guinea, Republic of. *Area Handbook for Guinea* (1975); *Population et développement en République Populaire Revolutionnaire de Guinée* (1980).

Guinea-Bissau. *Boletim Trimestral de Estatística; Recenseamento Geral da População e da Habitação, 16 de Abril de 1979.*

Guyana. *Annual Statistical Abstract; Area Handbook for Guyana* (1969).

Haiti. *Bulletin trimestriel de statistique; Guide économique de la République d'Haiti* (1977); *Haiti: A Country Profile* (1981); *Résultats préliminaires du recensement général (Septembre 1982).*

Honduras. *Anuario estadístico; Censo nacional agropecuario, 1974; Comercio externo* (annual); *Honduras: A Country Profile* (1981); *Honduras en cifras, 1980–1982.*

Hong Kong. *Annual Digest of Statistics; Hong Kong* (annual); *Hong Kong 1981 Census; Hong Kong in Figures* (annual); *Hong Kong Social and Economic Trends* (irreg.); *1978 Survey of Industrial Production.*

Hungary. *Statisztikai évkönyv* (Statistical Yearbook); *1980, Évi népszámlálás* (Census of Population).

Iceland. *Tölfraedihandbók* (Statistical Abstract of Iceland [irreg.]); *Verslunarskýrslur* (External Trade [annual]).

India. *Census of India, 1981; Economic Survey* (annual); *India: A Reference Annual; National Accounts Statistics, 1970–71, 1978–79; Statistical Abstract* (annual).

Indonesia. *Agricultural Census, 1973; Indikator ekonomi* (monthly); *Indonesia: An Official Handbook* (1984); *Sensus penduduk Indonesia, 1980* (Census of Population); *Statistical Yearbook of Indonesia.*

Iran. *General Census of Population and Housing, November 1976; Iran: A Country Study* (1978); *Statistical Yearbook of Iran.*

Iraq. *Iraq: A Country Study* (1979); *Statistical Abstract* (annual).

Ireland. *Census of Population of Ireland, 1981; National Income and Expenditure* (annual); *Statistical Abstract* (annual).

Israel. *Foreign Trade Statistics* (quarterly); *Israel: A Country Study* (1979); *Statistical Abstract* (annual).

Italy. *Annuario di statistica agraria; Annuario di statistica forestale; Annuario di statistiche demografiche; Annuario di statistiche industriali; Annuario statistico dell'istruzione; Annuario statistico Italiano; Statistiche sociali* (1981); *12 Censimento general della popolazione, 1981.*

Ivory Coast. *Annuaire statistique; La Côte d'Ivoire en chiffres* (annual); *L'Économie Ivoirienne* (annual).

Jamaica. *Area Handbook for Jamaica* (1976); *Economic and Social Survey* (annual); *Statistical Abstract* (annual); *Statistical Yearbook of Jamaica.*

Japan. *Establishment Census of Japan, 1981; Japan: A Country Study* (1983); *Japan Statistical Yearbook; Statistical Indicators on Social Life* (annual); *Statistics on Japanese Industries, 1980; 1980 Population Census of Japan.*

Jordan. *Census 1979; Family Expenditure Survey* (1980); *Jordan: A Country Study* (1979); *National Accounts* (irreg.); *Statistical Yearbook.*

Kenya. *Economic Survey* (annual); *Kenya Statistical Digest* (quarterly); *Statistical Abstract* (annual).

Kiribati. *National Development Plan, 1979–1982; Report on the 1978 Census of Population and Housing.*

Korea (South). *Korea Statistical Yearbook; Social Indicators in Korea* (1981); *South Korea: A Country Study* (1982); *The 5th Five-Year Economic and Development Plan, 1982–1986; 1980 Population and Housing Census.*

Kuwait. *Agricultural Statistics* (annual); *Economic Report* (annual); *General Census of Population and Housing, 1980; Statistical Abstract* (annual).

Lesotho. *Annual Statistical Bulletin; 1976 Population Census Report.*

Liberia. *Area Handbook for Liberia* (1972); *Economic Survey* (annual); *1974 Census of Population and Housing.*

Libya. *External Trade Statistics* (annual); *The Five-Year Development Plan 1981–85; Libya Population Census, 1973; Statistical Abstract for Libya* (annual).

Liechtenstein. *Statistisches Jahrbuch; Volkszählung, 2 Dezember 1980* (Census of Population).

Luxembourg. *Annuaire statistique; Bulletin du STATEC* (monthly); *Recensement général de la* *population du 31 mars 1981.*

Macau. *Anuário Estatístico; Comercio Externo* (annual); *Inquerito Industrial* (annual).

Madagascar. *Recensement général de la population et des habitats, 1975; Situation économique* (annual).

Malaŵi. *Area Handbook for Malawi* (1975); *Malawi: Facts for Visitors* (1973); *Malawi Population Census, 1977; Malawi Statistical Yearbook.*

Malaysia. *Fourth Malaysia Plan, 1981–1985; Malaysia: A Country Profile* (1979); *Malaysian Annual Statistical Bulletin; 1980 Population and Housing Census.*

Maldives. *Population and Housing Census, 1977; Statistical Yearbook.*

Mali. *Annuaire statistique du Mali; Recensement de la population, 1–16 décembre 1976.*

Malta. *Annual Abstract of Statistics; Census of Agriculture* (annual); *Census of Industrial Production* (annual); *Census of Production* (annual); *Malta Trade Statistics* (quarterly).

Martinique. *Annuaire statistique de la Martinique; Bulletin de statistique* (quarterly); *Comptes économiques de la Martinique* (irreg.); *Recensement de la population dans les départements d'outre-mer, 9 mars 1982—Martinique.*

Mauritania. *Area Handbook for Mauritania* (1972).

Mauritius. *Bi-annual Digest of Statistics; 1980–1982 Two-Year Plan for Economic and Social Development.*

Mayotte. *Recensement général de la population, 1978.*

Mexico. *Anuario estadístico; X Censo general de población y vivienda, 1980.*

Mongolia. *Mongolia in Figures, 1981* (irreg.); *National Economy of the MPR, 1921–81* (1981).

Montserrat. *Caribbean Population Census, May 12, 1980; Statistical Digest* (annual).

Morocco. *Annuaire statistique du Maroc; Economic and Social Development Report, 1981; Morocco: A Country Study* (1978); *La Situation économique du Maroc* (annual).

Mozambique. *Anuário Estatístico; Area Handbook for Mozambique* (1977); *Informação Estatística* (1980); *Moçambique Informação Estatística* (annual); *IV Recenseamento Geral da População, 1970.*

Nepal. *Census of Manufacturing Establishments, 1976–1977; Population of Nepal* (ESCAP; Country Monograph Series No. 6 [1980]); *The Sixth Plan (1980–85); Statistical Pocket Book* (irreg.).

Netherlands, The. *Landbouwcijfers* (Agricultural Data [annual]); *Maandstatistiek van de buitenlandse handel per goederensoort* (Foreign Trade by Goods [annual]); *Statistical Yearbook of the Netherlands; 14e Algemene volkstelling, 28 februari 1971* (14th General Population Census).

Netherlands Antilles. *Statistisch jaarboek* (Statistical Yearbook).

New Caledonia. *Annuaire statistique; Enquête socio-économique, 1980–1981; Recensement général de la population, 1976; La Situation démographique en 1980.*

New Zealand. *New Zealand Census of Population and Dwellings, 1981; New Zealand Official Yearbook.*

Nicaragua. *Anuario estadístico; Area Handbook for Nicaragua* (1970); *Censos nacionales, 1971.*

Niger. *Annuaire statistique; Données de base* (1979).

Nigeria. *Annual Abstract of Statistics; Fourth National Development Plan* (1981); *Nigeria: A Country Study* (1981).

Niue. *Abstract of Statistics* (annual); *Census of Population and Housing, 1976; Niue National Development Plan, 1980–1985.*

Norfolk Island. *Annual Report; Census of Population and Housing, 30 June 1981.*

Norway. *Folke- og boligtelling 1980* (Population and Housing Census); *Industristatistikk* (annual); *Statistisk årsbok* (Statistical Yearbook).

Oman. *Statistical Year Book; The Second Five-Year Plan of Development, 1981–1985.*

Pakistan. *Economic Survey* (annual); *Pakistan Year Book; Pakistan Statistical Yearbook; Population Census of Pakistan, 1981; Some Socio-Economic Trends* (annual); *10 Years of Pakistan in Statistics, 1972–82* (1983).

Panama. *Indicadores económicos y sociales* (annual); *Octavo censo de población: Cuarto censo de vivienda, 11 de mayo de 1980; Panama en cifras* (annual); *Situacion económica: Comercio exterior* (annual); *Situacion económica: Cuentas nacionales* (annual); *Situacion económica: Industria* (annual); *Situacion social: Estadísticas del trabajo* (annual).

Papua New Guinea. *Abstract of Statistics* (quarterly); *National Accounts Statistics — Statistical Bulletin* (quarterly); *Papua New Guinea: Selected Development Issues* (A World Bank Country Study [1982]); *Population of Papua New Guinea (ESCAP;* Country Monograph Series No. 7.2 [1982]); *Rural Industries* (annual); *Summary of Statistics* (annual); *1980 National Population Census.*

Paraguay. *Anuario estadístico del Paraguay; Censo nacional de población y vivienda, 1982.*

Peru. *Censos nacionales: VIII de población: III de vivienda, 12 de julio de 1981; Compendio estadístico* (1982); *Informe estadístico* (annual); *Peru: A Country Study* (1980).

Philippines. *Philippine Statistical Yearbook; Philippine Yearbook; 1980 Census of Population.*

Poland. *Narodowy spis powszechny z dnia 7 XII 1978 r.* (Census of Population); *Poland: A Country Study* (1984); *Rocznik statystyczny* (Statistical Yearbook).

Portugal. *Anuário Estatístico; Estatística Agrícolas* (annual); *Estatísticas do Comercio Externo* (annual); *Estatísticas Demograficas* (annual); *Estatísticas Industriais* (annual); *Estatísticas Monetarias e Financeiras* (annual); *Estatísticas da Saúde* (annual); *Recenseamento Agricola, 1979; XII Recenseamento Geral da População: II Recenseamento Geral da Habitação, 1981.*

Puerto Rico. *Anuario estadístico; Compendio estadísticas sociales* (annual); *Informe económico al gobernador* (Economic Report to the Governor [annual]); *1980 Census of Population* (U.S.).

Qatar. *Economic Survey of Qatar* (annual).

Réunion. *Annuaire statistique de la Réunion; Comptes économiques de la Réunion* (irreg.); *Recensement général de la population en 1974: Départements d'outre-mer—Réunion.*

Romania. *Anuarul statistic al Republicii Socialiste România; Recensămîntul populaţiei şi al locuinţelor, din 5 ianuarie 1977; Romania Yearbook.*

St. Christopher and Nevis. *Annual Digest of Statistics.*

St. Lucia. *Annual Statistical Digest.*

St. Pierre and Miquelon. *Résultats du recensement de la population dans les départements d'outremer, 9 mars 1982.*

St. Vincent and the Grenadines. *Digest of Statistics* (annual).

San Marino. *Annuario statistico, 1972–1980; 3 Censimento generale dell agricoltura* (1977); *5 Censimento generale della popolazione* (1979).

Saudi Arabia. *The Statistical Indicator* (annual); *Statistical Summary* (Saudi Arabian Monetary Agency [annual]); Statistical Year Book.

Senegal. *Le Sénégal en chiffres* (annual); *Situation économique* (annual).

Seychelles. *National Development Plan, 1982–86; Statistical Abstract* (annual); *1977 Census Report.*

Singapore. *Census of Population, 1980; Economic and Social Statistics, 1960–1982; Economic Survey of Singapore* (annual); *Report on the Census of Industrial Production, 1981; Report on the Household Expenditure Survey, 1977–78; Report on the Survey of Services, 1980; Singapore Yearbook; Yearbook of Statistics Singapore.*

Solomon Islands. *Statistical Yearbook.*

Somalia. *Statistical Abstract* (annual).

South Africa. *South Africa: Official Yearbook of the Republic of South Africa; South African Statistics* (biennial).

Spain. *Anuario estadístico; Censo de población de 1981.*

Sri Lanka. *Census of Population and Housing, 1981; Census of Agriculture, 1973; Report on the Survey on Manufacturing Industries, 1979; Sri Lanka Year Book; Statistical Pocketbook of the Democratic Socialist Republic of Sri Lanka* (annual).

Swaziland. *Annual Statistical Bulletin; Report on the 1976 Swaziland Population Census.*

Sweden. *Folk- och bostadsräkningen, 1980* (Population and Housing Census); *Jorbruksstatistisk årsbok* (Yearbook of Agricultural Statistics); *Statistisk årsbok för Sverige* (Statistical Abstract of Sweden [annual]).

Switzerland. *Recensement fédéral de la population, 1980; Statistisches Jahrbuch* (Statistical Yearbook).

Syria. *Census of Agriculture, 1981; General Census of Housing and Inhabitants, 1981; Statistical Abstract* (annual).

Taiwan. *Industry of Free China* (monthly); *Social Indicators of the Republic of China* (1981); *Statistical Abstract* (annual); *Statistical Yearbook of the Republic of China; Taiwan Statistical Data Book* (annual); *Yearbook of Labor Statistics; 1980 Census of Population and Housing.*

Tanzania. *Tanzania Statistical Abstract* (annual); *1978 Population Census.*

Thailand. *Census of Business Trade or Services* (1980); *Foreign Trade Statistics* (monthly); *Report of the 1978 Industrial Census; Report of the Labor Force Survey: Whole Kingdom* (quarterly); *Statistical Handbook of Thailand* (annual); *Statistical Yearbook; 1980 Population and Housing Census.*

Togo. *Annuaire statistique; Plan de développement économique & social, 1981–1985; Recensement général de la population, 1970.*

Tokelau. *Census of Population, 1981; Report of the Administrator of Tokelau for the Year Ended: 31 March 19*** (annual).

Trinidad and Tobago. *Population Census, 1980; Trinidad and Tobago Statistical Pocket Digest* (annual).

Trust Territory of the Pacific Islands. *Report of the Trusteeship Council to the Security Council on the Trust Territory of the Pacific Islands* (annual); *Report to the United Nations* (annual).

Tunisia. *Annuaire statistique de la Tunisie; Recensement général de la population et des logements, 30 mars 1984.*

Turkey. *Diş Ticaret İstatistikleri* (Annual Foreign Trade Statistics); *Genel Sanayi ve İşyerleri Sayımı* (Census of Industry and Business Establishments [1980]); *Genel Nüfus Sayımı, 12. 10. 1980* (Census of Population); *Genel Tarım Sayımı, 1980* (Census of Agriculture); *Iç Tikaret İstatistikleri* (Internal Trade Statistics [annual]); *İnşaat İstatistikleri* (Construction Statistics [annual]); *Türkiye İstatistik Yilliği* (Statistical Yearbook of Turkey); *Tarımsal Yapi ve Üretim* (Agricultural Structure and Production [annual]).

Tuvalu. *Abstract of Statistics* (annual); *Census of the Population, 1979.*

Union of Soviet Socialist Republics. *Narodnoye Khozyaystvo SSSR* (National Economy of the U.S.S.R. [annual]).

United Arab Emirates. *Statistical Yearbook.*

United Kingdom. *Agricultural Statistics United Kingdom* (annual); *Annual Abstract of Statistics; Britain: An Official Handbook* (annual); *National Income and Expenditure* (annual); *Census 1981; Overseas Trade Statistics of the United Kingdom* (annual); *Report on the Census of Production: Summary Tables* (annual).

United States. *Agricultural Statistics* (annual); *Annual Energy Review; Current Population Reports* (series P-20, P-23, P-25, P-26, P-27, P-28, P-60); *Digest of Education Statistics* (annual); *Minerals Yearbook* (3 vol. [annual]); *National Transportation Statistics* (annual); *Statistical Abstract* (annual); *U.S. Exports: SIC-Based Products* (annual); *U.S. Imports: SIC-Based Products)* (annual); *Vital and Health Statistics* (series 1–20); *1977 Census of Construction Industries; 1977 Census of Manufacturing; 1977 Census of Mineral Industries; 1977 Census of Retail Trade; 1977 Census of Wholesale Trade; 1978 Census of Agriculture; 1980 Census of Population and Housing.*

Vanuatu. *Overseas Trade* (annual); *Recensement de la population, 1979; Statistical Indicators* (quarterly).

Venezuela. *Anuario estadístico; Censo agropecuario, 1971; Encuesta de hogares por muestreo* (annual); *Encuesta industrial* (annual); *IX Censo general de población y vivienda, 20 de octubre 1981.*

Virgin Islands of the United States. *Annual Report; 1980 Census of Population* (U.S.).

Western Samoa. *Annual Statistical Abstract; Census of Population and Housing, 1976.*

Yemen Arab Republic. *The Housing and Population Census, February 1975; Statistical Year Book.*

Yugoslavia. *Popis stanovištva i stanova od 31. marta 1981* (Census of Population and Housing as of March 31, 1981); *Statistički godišnjak Jugoslavije* (Statistical Yearbook of Yugoslavia); *Yugoslavia: A Country Study* (1982).

Zaire. *Annuaire statistique; Plan Mobutu: Programme de relance économique, 1979–1981 (Fiches des projects; Transport; Education et santé)* (3 vol.).

Zambia. *Census of Industrial Production, 1974; Household Budget Survey, 1974–1975; Monthly Digest of Statistics; Third National Development Plan, 1979–83; Zambia in Figures* (1980); *1980 Census of Population and Housing.*

Zimbabwe. *Quarterly Digest of Statistics.*

CONTRIBUTORS

Aarsdal, Stener. Journalist, *Børsen* (Denmark's Business Daily), Copenhagen.
WORLD AFFAIRS: *Denmark*

Adams, Andrew M. Free-lance Foreign Correspondent; Editor and Publisher, *Sumo World* magazine.
SPORTS AND GAMES: *Martial Arts; Wrestling (in part)*

Agrella, Joseph C. Correspondent, *Blood-Horse* magazine; former Turf Editor, *Chicago Sun-Times.*
SPORTS AND GAMES: *Horse Racing (in part)*

Allaby, Michael. Free-lance Writer and Lecturer. Author of *Who Will Eat?.*
ENVIRONMENT *(in part)*

Allan, J. A. Senior Lecturer in Geography, School of Oriental and African Studies, University of London.
WORLD AFFAIRS: *Libya*

Alston, Rex. Broadcaster and Journalist. Author of *Watching Cricket.*
SPORTS AND GAMES: *Cricket*

Amedeo, Michael. Research Editor, Britannica World Data.
BIOGRAPHIES *(in part)*

Anastaplo, George. Professor of Law, Loyola University, Chicago. Author of *The Constitutionalist* and others.
Revised *Macropædia* article: CENSORSHIP

Anderson, Peter J. Assistant Director, Institute of Polar Studies, Ohio State University, Columbus.
WORLD AFFAIRS: *Antarctica*

Archibald, John J. Feature Writer, *St. Louis Post-Dispatch;* Adjunct Professor, Lindenwood Colleges, St. Charles, Mo.
SPORTS AND GAMES: *Bowling (in part)*

Arnold, Guy. Free-lance Writer. Author of *Modern Nigeria; Aid in Africa.*
BIOGRAPHIES *(in part);* WORLD AFFAIRS: *Botswana; Burundi; Cape Verde; Equatorial Guinea; Gambia, The; Ghana; Guinea-Bissau; Lesotho; Liberia; Maldives; Mauritius; Nigeria; Rwanda; São Tomé and Príncipe; Seychelles; Sierra Leone; Swaziland*

Arnold, Mavis. Free-lance Journalist, Dublin.
WORLD AFFAIRS: *Ireland*

Arrington, Leonard J. Formerly Church Historian, Church of Jesus Christ of Latter-day Saints.
RELIGION: *Church of Jesus Christ of Latter-day Saints*

Ayton, Cyril J. Editor, *Motorcycle Sport,* London
SPORTS AND GAMES: *Motorcycling*

Baptist, Ines T. Administrative Assistant, Encyclopædia Britannica, Special Projects.
WORLD AFFAIRS: *Belize*

Barford, Michael F. Editor and Director, *World Tobacco,* London.
CONSUMER AFFAIRS: Sidebar; INDUSTRIAL REVIEW: *Tobacco*

Bargad, Warren. Milton D. Ratner Professor of Hebrew Literature and Dean, Spertus College of Judaica, Chicago.
LITERATURE: *Hebrew*

Barrett, Paul A. Managing Editor, *TV World* magazine, London.
TELEVISION AND RADIO *(in part)*

Bass, Howard. Journalist and Broadcaster. Editor, *Winter Sports,* 1948–69.
BIOGRAPHIES *(in part);* SPORTS AND GAMES: *Ice Hockey (in part); Winter Sports; Winter Sports:* Special Report

Bayliss, David. Director of Planning, London Regional Transport. Co-author of *Developing Patterns of Urbanization.*
TRANSPORTATION *(in part)*

Beattie, Roger A. Secretariat Member, International Social Security Association, Geneva.

SOCIAL SECURITY AND WELFARE SERVICES *(in part)*

Beckwith, David C. National Correspondent, *Time* magazine, Washington, D.C.
WORLD AFFAIRS: *United States:* Developments in the States in 1984

Berenson, Louis S. President, Berenson Pari-Mutuel, Inc.
SPORTS AND GAMES: *Jai-Alai*

Bergerre, Max. Vatican Affairs Correspondent, *La Vie Catholique,* Paris.
WORLD AFFAIRS: *Vatican City State*

Berkovitch, Israel. Free-lance Writer. Author of *Coal on the Switchback.*
ENERGY: *Coal*

Berman, Brenda E. Assistant Editor, *Encyclopædia Britannica.*
BIOGRAPHIES *(in part)*

Beyer, Reginald Ian. Deputy Curator, Royal Botanic Gardens, Kew, England.
BOTANICAL GARDENS AND ZOOS: *Botanical Gardens*

Bickelhaupt, David L. Professor of Insurance and Finance, College of Administrative Science, Ohio State University, Columbus.
INDUSTRIAL REVIEW: *Insurance*

Bilefield, Lionel. Technical Journalist.
INDUSTRIAL REVIEW: *Paints and Varnishes*

Bird, Thomas E. Assistant Director, Yiddish Program, Queens College, City University of New York.
LITERATURE: *Yiddish (in part)*

Bliebtreu, Hermann K. Professor of Anthropology, University of Arizona.
ANTHROPOLOGY

Boddy, William C. Editor, *Motor Sport.* Full Member, Guild of Motoring Writers.
SPORTS AND GAMES: *Automobile Racing (in part)*

Boden, Edward. Editor, *The Veterinary Record.*
HEALTH AND DISEASE: *Veterinary Medicine*

Bolt, Peter H. Secretary, British Committee, World Methodist Council.
RELIGION: *Methodist Churches*

Boltz, C. L. Free-lance Industrial Writer, London
ENERGY: *Electricity*

Boonstra, Dick. Assistant Professor, Department of Political Science, Free University, Amsterdam.
WORLD AFFAIRS: *Netherlands, The; Suriname*

Booth, John Nicholls. Lecturer and Writer. Author of *The Quest for Preaching Power.*
RELIGION: *Unitarian (Universalist) Churches*

Boswall, Jeffery. Producer of Sound and Television Programs, BBC Natural History Unit, Bristol, England.
LIFE SCIENCES: *Ornithology*

Box, Ben. Free-lance Writer and Researcher on Latin America and Iberia.
WORLD AFFAIRS: *El Salvador; Honduras; Nicaragua; Paraguay*

Boye, Roger. Coin columnist, *Chicago Tribune.*
PHILATELY AND NUMISMATICS: *Coins*

Bradsher, Henry S. Foreign Affairs Writer.
WORLD AFFAIRS: *Philippines*

Braidwood, Robert J. Professor Emeritus of Old World Prehistory, Oriental Institute and Department of Anthropology, University of Chicago. Author of *Prehistoric Men.*
ARCHAEOLOGY: *Eastern Hemisphere*

Brazee, Rutlage J. Geophysical Consultant.
EARTH SCIENCES: *Geophysics*

Brecher, Kenneth. Professor of Astronomy and Physics, Boston University. Co-author and co-editor of *Astronomy of the Ancients.*
ASTRONOMY

Burdin, Joel L. Professor of Educational Administration, Ohio University, Athens, Ohio.
EDUCATION *(in part)*

Burke, Donald P. Executive Editor, *Chemical Week,* New York City.
INDUSTRIAL REVIEW: *Chemicals*

Burks, Ardath W. Emeritus Professor of Asian Studies, Rutgers University, New Brunswick, N.J.
WORLD AFFAIRS: *Japan*

Buss, Robin. Lecturer in French, Woolwich College of Further Education, London. Author of *Vigny's Chatterton.*
BIOGRAPHIES *(in part);* LITERATURE: *French (in part)*

Butler, Frank. Former Sports Editor, *News of the World,* London. Author of *A History of Boxing in Britain.*
SPORTS AND GAMES: *Boxing; Boxing:* Sidebar

Cameron, Sarah. Economist, Group Economics Department, Lloyds Bank PLC, London.
WORLD AFFAIRS: *Argentina*

Campbell, Alexander Johns. Latin American Economist, Lloyds Bank Group Economics Department.
BIOGRAPHIES *(in part)*

Carter, Robert W. Free-lance Journalist, London.
SPORTS AND GAMES: *Horse Racing (in part)*

Cassidy, Richard J. Senior Public Relations Officer, British Gas Corporation.
ENERGY: *Natural Gas*

Chapman, Kenneth F. Former Editor, *Stamp Collecting* and *Philatelic Magazine.*
PHILATELY AND NUMISMATICS: *Stamps*

Chapman, Robin. Senior Economist, Group Economics Department, Lloyds Bank PLC, London.
WORLD AFFAIRS: *Brazil; Ecuador; Haiti; Latin-American Affairs*

Chappell, Duncan. Professor and Chairman, Department of Criminology, Simon Fraser University, Vancouver, B.C.
CRIME, LAW ENFORCEMENT, AND PENOLOGY: *Crime; Law Enforcement*

Chuprinin, Sergey. Journalist, Novosti Press Agency, Moscow.
LITERATURE: *Russian (in part)*

Clarke, R. O. Writer on Industrial Relations, Paris.
LABOUR–MANAGEMENT RELATIONS

Cleveland, William A. Editor, Britannica World Data and *Britannica Atlas.*
MINING AND METALLURGY: *Mining*

Cogle, T. C. J. Editor, *Electrical Review,* London.
INDUSTRIAL REVIEW: *Electrical*

Comba, Aldo. Executive Secretary, Department of Cooperation and Witness, World Alliance of Reformed Churches.
RELIGION: *Reformed, Presbyterian, and Congregational Churches*

Coppock, Charles Dennis. Vice-President, English Lacrosse Union.
SPORTS AND GAMES: *Lacrosse (in part)*

Costin, Stanley H. British Correspondent, *Herrenjournal International,* and others.
FASHION AND DRESS *(in part)*

Crater, Rufus W. Senior Editorial Consultant, *Broadcasting,* New York City.
TELEVISION AND RADIO *(in part)*

Cross, Colin J. Editor, *The Polo Times;* U.K. Chairman, European Polo Academy.
SPORTS AND GAMES: *Polo*

Crossland, Norman. Former Bonn Correspondent, *The Economist,* London.
BIOGRAPHIES *(in part);* WORLD AFFAIRS: *German Democratic Republic; Germany, Federal Republic of*

Cviic, K. F. East European Specialist, *The Economist,* London.
WORLD AFFAIRS: *Yugoslavia*

David, Tudor. Managing Editor, *Education,* London.
EDUCATION *(in part)*

Davies, C. R. M. Research Lecturer in Criminology and Penology, University of Liverpool, England.
CRIME, LAW ENFORCEMENT, AND PENOLOGY: *Prisons and Penology*

Davis, Donald A. Editor, *Drug & Cosmetic Industry* and *Cosmetic Insider's Report,* New York City.
INDUSTRIAL REVIEW: *Pharmaceuticals*

Davis, Kenneth C. Free-lance Writer. Author of *Two-Bit Culture.*
PUBLISHING: *Books (in part)*

Deam, John B. Technical Director, National Machine Tool Builders Association, McLean, Va.
INDUSTRIAL REVIEW: *Machinery and Machine Tools*

Decraene, Philippe. Head, Center for Advanced Studies on Modern Africa and Asia, Paris.
BIOGRAPHIES *(in part);* WORLD AFFAIRS: *Benin; Burkina Faso; Cameroon; Central African Republic; Chad; Comoros; Congo; Djibouti; Gabon; Guinea; Ivory Coast; Madagascar; Mali; Mauritania; Niger; Senegal; Togo; Tunisia*

de la Barre, Kenneth. Director, Katimavik, Montreal.
WORLD AFFAIRS: *Arctic Regions*

Denselow, Robin. Rock Music Critic, *The Guardian,* London; Current Affairs Producer, BBC Television.
MUSIC: *Popular*

De Puy, Norman R. Minister, First Baptist Church, Newton Centre, Mass.; Columnist, *American Baptist* magazine.
RELIGION: *Baptist Churches*

Deshayes-Creuilly, Marie-Jose. Head of Documentation Service, International Vine and Wine Office, Paris.
INDUSTRIAL REVIEW: *Beverages (in part)*

Dirnbacher, Elfriede. Austrian Civil Servant.
WORLD AFFAIRS: *Austria*

Dorris, Thomas Hartley. Editor, Ecumenical Press Service, Geneva.
RELIGION: *Lutheran Communion*

Duveen, Denis Ian. Consultant to the cosmetics industry in Brazil.
Revised *Macropædia* article: LAVOISIER

EIU. The Economist Intelligence Unit, London.
ECONOMIC AFFAIRS: *World Economy*

Eli, C. R. Former Executive Director, U.S. Badminton Association.
SPORTS AND GAMES: *Badminton*

Engels, Jan R. Editor, *Vooruitgang* (Bimonthly of the Centre Paul Hymans).
WORLD AFFAIRS: *Belgium*

Ewart, W. D. Marine Consultant, London. Author of *Bunkers;* and others.
INDUSTRIAL REVIEW: *Shipbuilding;* TRANSPORTATION *(in part)*

Farr, D. M. L. Professor of History and Director, Paterson Centre for International Programs, Carleton University, Ottawa.
WORLD AFFAIRS: *Canada*

Faust, Joan Lee. Garden Editor, *New York Times.*
GARDENING *(in part)*

Felknor, Bruce L. Director of Yearbooks, Encyclopædia Britannica; former Director, Fair Campaign Practices Committee.
WORLD AFFAIRS: *United States:* Special Report

Fendell, Robert J. Auto Editor, *Science & Mechanics.* Author of *The New Era Car Book and Auto Survival Guide.*
SPORTS AND GAMES: *Automobile Racing (in part)*

Ferrier, R. W. Group Historian, The British

Petroleum Company PLC, London.
ENERGY: *Petroleum*

Fiddick, Peter. Media Editor, *The Guardian,* London.
PUBLISHING: *Newspapers (in part); Magazines (in part)*

Fields, Donald. Helsinki Correspondent, BBC, *The Guardian,* and *The Sunday Times,* London.
WORLD AFFAIRS: *Finland*

Firth, David. Editor, *The Friend,* London; formerly Editor, *Quaker Monthly,* London.
RELIGION: *Religious Society of Friends*

Fisher, David. Civil Engineer, Freeman Fox & Partners, London.
ENGINEERING PROJECTS: *Bridges*

Flanagan, Jack C. Travel Counselor.
SPORTS AND GAMES: *Surfing*

Frady, William Ensign, III. Editor, *Water Polo Scoreboard,* Newport Beach, Calif.
SPORTS AND GAMES: *Water Polo*

Franklin, Harold. Editor, *English Bridge Quarterly.* Bridge Correspondent, *Yorkshire Post.*
SPORTS AND GAMES: *Contract Bridge*

Franz, Frederick W. President, Watch Tower Bible and Tract Society of Pennsylvania.
RELIGION: *Jehovah's Witnesses*

Freed, Alison. Information Officer, Glass Manufacturers Federation, London.
INDUSTRIAL REVIEW: *Glass*

Fridovich, Irwin. James B. Duke Professor of Biochemistry, Duke University Medical Center, Durham, N.C.
LIFE SCIENCES: *Molecular Biology (in part)*

Friedly, Robert Louis. Vice President for Communication, Christian Church (Disciples of Christ), Indianapolis, Ind.
RELIGION: *Christian Church (Disciples of Christ)*

Friskin, Sydney E. Hockey Correspondent, *The Times,* London.
SPORTS AND GAMES: *Field Hockey*

Frost, David. Rugby Union Correspondent, *The Guardian,* London.
SPORTS AND GAMES: *Football (in part)*

Gaddum, Anthony H. Chairman, H. T. Gaddum and Company Ltd., Silk Merchants, Macclesfield, Cheshire, England.
INDUSTRIAL REVIEW: *Textiles (in part)*

Ganado, Albert. Lawyer, Malta.
WORLD AFFAIRS: *Malta*

Ganguly, Dilip. Special Correspondent, South Asian Bureau, Agence France Presse, New Delhi, India.
WORLD AFFAIRS: *Afghanistan; Bangladesh; Bhutan; Burma; Nepal; Pakistan; Sri Lanka*

Garrad, Rob. Director of Information Services, International Headquarters, Salvation Army.
RELIGION: *Salvation Army*

Gastil, Raymond Duncan. Director, Comparative Survey of Freedom, Freedom House, New York City.
HUMAN RIGHTS

Geyer, Georgie Anne. Syndicated Columnist, Universal Press Syndicate. Author of *The New Latins; Buying the Night Flight.*
FEATURE ARTICLE: *Our Disintegrating World: The Menace of Global Anarchy*

Gibbons, J. Whitfield. Research Ecologist, Savannah River Ecology Laboratory, Aiken, South Carolina.
LIFE SCIENCES: *Zoology*

Gillespie, Hugh M. Director of Communications, International Road Federation, Washington, D.C.
ENGINEERING PROJECTS: *Roads*

Gjester, Fay. Oslo Correspondent, *Financial Times,* London.
WORLD AFFAIRS: *Norway*

Goldsmith, Arthur. Editorial Director, *Popular Photography,* New York City.
PHOTOGRAPHY

Golombek, Harry. British Chess Champion,

1947, 1949, and 1955. Chess Correspondent, *The Times,* London.
SPORTS AND GAMES: *Chess*

Goodwin, Noël. Associate Editor (to 1983) and Contributor, *Dance & Dancers.* Author of *A Ballet for Scotland.*
BIOGRAPHIES *(in part);* DANCE *(in part)*

Goodwin, Robert E. Managing Director, Billiard and Bowling Institute of America.
SPORTS AND GAMES: *Billiard Games (in part)*

Gottfried, Martin. Drama Critic, New York City. Author of *A Theater Divided; Opening Nights; Broadway Musicals.*
THEATRE *(in part)*

Gould, Donald W. Medical Writer and Broadcaster, U.K.
HEALTH AND DISEASE: *Overview (in part); Mental Health*

Griffiths, A. R. G. Senior Lecturer in History, Flinders University of South Australia. Author of *Contemporary Australia.*
WORLD AFFAIRS: *Australia; Australia:* Special Report; *Nauru; Papua New Guinea*

Grossman, Joel W. Archaeologist.
ARCHAEOLOGY: *Western Hemisphere*

Grove, Bob. Projects Officer, Richmond Fellowship for Mental Welfare and Rehabilitation, London.
HEALTH AND DISEASE: Special Report *(in part)*

Hall, Richard. Deputy Director, York Archaeological Trust. Author of *Jorvik Viking Age York; The Viking Dig.*
ARCHAEOLOGY: Special Report

Hallgren, Richard E. Assistant Administrator for Weather Services, National Oceanic and Atmospheric Administration.
EARTH SCIENCES: *Meteorology*

Hardman, Thomas C. Consulting Editor, *The Water Skier,* American Water Ski Association.
SPORTS AND GAMES: *Water Skiing*

Harper, Nick. Music Journalist and Writer, *International Music Guide.*
MUSIC: *Classical*

Hasegawa, Ryusaku. Editor, TBS-Britannica Co., Ltd., Tokyo.
SPORTS AND GAMES: *Baseball (in part)*

Havard-Williams, P. Professor and Head, Department of Library and Information Studies, Loughborough University, Leicestershire, England.
LIBRARIES *(in part)*

Hawkland, William D. Chancellor and Professor of Law, Louisiana State University, Baton Rouge.
LAW: *Court Decisions*

Hebblethwaite, Peter. Vatican Affairs Writer, *National Catholic Reporter,* Kansas City, Mo.
RELIGION: *Roman Catholic Church*

Hendershott, Myrl C. Professor of Oceanography, Scripps Institution of Oceanography, La Jolla, Calif.
EARTH SCIENCES: *Oceanography*

Herman, Robin Cathy. Free-lance Journalist.
SPORTS AND GAMES: *Ice Hockey (in part)*

Hess, Marvin G. Executive Vice-President, National Wrestling Coaches Association, Salt Lake City, Utah.
SPORTS AND GAMES: *Wrestling (in part)*

Higgins, Fitzgerald. Editor and Reviewer.
LITERATURE: *United States*

Hindin, Harvey J. Vice-President, Hi-Tech Editorial, Inc., Dix Hills, N.Y.
INDUSTRIAL REVIEW: *Telecommunications*

Hope, Thomas W. President, Hope Reports, Inc., Rochester, N.Y.
MOTION PICTURES *(in part)*

Hotz, Louis. Former Editorial Writer, *Johannesburg (S.Af.) Star.* Co-author, *The Jews in South Africa: A History.*
WORLD AFFAIRS: *South Africa*

Howkins, John. Director, International Institute of Communications, London. Author of *Understanding Television.*
TELEVISION AND RADIO *(in part)*

Hunnings, Neville March. Editorial Director, European Law Centre Ltd., London. Editor, *Common Market Law Reports.*
LAW: *International Law*

Ingham, Kenneth. Professor of History, University of Bristol, England. Author of *Reformers in India.*
WORLD AFFAIRS: *Angola; Kenya; Malawi; Mozambique; Sudan; Tanzania; Uganda; Zaire; Zambia; Zimbabwe*

Iversen, Ingrid. Economist, Group Economics Department, Lloyds Bank PLC, London.
WORLD AFFAIRS: *Bolivia; Costa Rica; Guatemala; Peru*

Jacquet, Constant H. Staff Associate, National Council of Churches. Editor of *Yearbook of American and Canadian Churches.*
WORLD AFFAIRS: *United States (table)*

Jardine, Adrian. Company Director. Member, Guild of Yachting Writers.
SPORTS AND GAMES: *Sailing*

Jaspert, W. Pincus. Technical and Editorial Consultant. Author of *State of the Art.* Editor, *Encyclopaedia of Type Faces.*
INDUSTRIAL REVIEW: *Printing*

Jenkins, Peter. Policy Editor and Political Columnist, *The Guardian,* London.
BIOGRAPHIES *(in part);* WORLD AFFAIRS: *United Kingdom*

Joffé, George. Journalist and Writer on North African Affairs.
WORLD AFFAIRS: *Algeria; Morocco*

Jones, C. M. Consultant, *World Bowls* and *Tennis.* Author of *Winning Bowls.*
SPORTS AND GAMES: *Lawn Bowls*

Jones, D. A. N. Novelist and Critic. Author of *Parade in Paris; Never Had It so Good.*
LITERATURE: *Introduction; United Kingdom*

Jones, Handel H. President, Custom MOS Arrays, Milpitas, Calif.
INDUSTRIAL REVIEW: *Microelectronics*

Jones, W. Glyn. Professor of Scandinavian Studies, University of Newcastle upon Tyne, England.
LITERATURE: *Danish*

Joseph, Lou. Senior Science Writer, Hill and Knowlton, Chicago.
HEALTH AND DISEASE: *Dentistry*

Justin, Karen. Assistant Editor, Encyclopædia Britannica, Yearbooks.
BIOGRAPHIES *(in part)*

Kapur, Rajiv. Senior Field Affairs Officer, UN High Commissioner for Refugees (UNHCR), Geneva.
WORLD AFFAIRS: *India:* Sidebar

Katz, William A. Professor, School of Library Science, State University of New York, Albany.
PUBLISHING: *Magazines (in part)*

Kelleher, John A. Group Relations Editor, INL (newspapers), Wellington, N.Z.
BIOGRAPHIES *(in part);* WORLD AFFAIRS: *New Zealand*

Kellman, Jerold L. President, Gabriel House, Inc., Skokie, Ill. Author of *The First One Hundred Years.*
BIOGRAPHIES *(in part);* LABOUR–MANAGEMENT RELATIONS: Special Report

Kennedy, Richard M. Agricultural Economist, International Economics Division of the Economic Research Service, U.S. Department of Agriculture.
AGRICULTURE AND FOOD SUPPLIES *(in part)*

Kent, Livija. Associate Professor, Botany Department, University of Massachusetts.
LIFE SCIENCES: *Botany*

Kilian, Michael D. Washington Columnist, *Chicago Tribune.* Author of *Airwords.*
SPORTS AND GAMES: *Aerial Sports*

Killheffer, John V. Associate Editor, *Encyclopædia Britannica.*
NOBEL PRIZES *(in part)*

Kimche, Jon. Formerly Editor, *New Middle East; Afro-Asian Affairs,* London. Author of *Spying for Peace; Unfought War.*

BIOGRAPHIES *(in part);* WORLD AFFAIRS: *Israel*

Kind, Joshua B. Professor of Art History, Northern Illinois University, De Kalb. Author of *Rouault; Geometry as Abstract Art.*
MUSEUMS *(in part)*

Kitagawa, Joseph M. Professor of History of Religions, Divinity School, University of Chicago. Author of *Religions of the East.*
RELIGION: *Buddhism*

Knecht, Jean. Formerly Assistant Foreign Editor, *Le Monde,* Paris.
BIOGRAPHIES *(in part);* WORLD AFFAIRS: *France*

Knox, Richard A. Technical Author; formerly Editor, *Nuclear Engineering International,* London.
INDUSTRIAL REVIEW: *Nuclear Industry*

Kolata, Gina. Writer, *Science* magazine, Washington, D.C. Co-author of *The High Blood Pressure Book.*
HEALTH AND DISEASE: *Overview (in part)*

Kriegsman, Sali Ann. Dance Writer and Consultant. Washington, D.C.; Correspondent, *Ballet News.*
DANCE *(in part)*

Kushnick, Louis. Lecturer, Department of American Studies, University of Manchester, England.
POPULATIONS AND POPULATION MOVEMENTS: *International Migration;* RACE RELATIONS

Laberis, William E. Managing Editor, *Computerworld.*
INFORMATION PROCESSING AND INFORMATION SYSTEMS

Lamb, Kevin M. Sportswriter, *Chicago Sun-Times.*
BIOGRAPHIES *(in part);* SPORTS AND GAMES: *Football (in part)*

Laqueur, Walter. Director, Institute of Contemporary History and Wiener Library, London. Author of *Europe Since Hitler;* others.
WORLD AFFAIRS: *Introduction*

Larson, Roy. Religion Editor, *Chicago Sun-Times.*
RELIGION: *Introduction*

Laurance, Jeremy. Health and Social Services Correspondent, *New Society,* London.
CRIME, LAW ENFORCEMENT, AND PENOLOGY: Special Report

Leaper, Eric. Executive Director, National Organization for River Sports, Colorado Springs, Colo.
SPORTS AND GAMES: *River Sports*

Legum, Colin. Associate Editor (1947–81), *The Observer;* Editor, *Africa Contemporary Record,* London; and others.
BIOGRAPHIES *(in part);* WORLD AFFAIRS: *African Affairs; African Affairs:* Special Report

Lennox-Kerr, Peter. Editor, *High Performance Textiles;* European Editor, *Textile World.* Author of *The World Fibres Book.*
INDUSTRIAL REVIEW: *Textiles (in part)*

Leve, Charles S. Associate Publisher and Editor, *National Racquetball* magazine.
SPORTS AND GAMES: *Racquetball*

Litsky, Frank. Sportswriter, *New York Times.*
SPORTS AND GAMES: *Archery*

Littell, Franklin H. Professor of Religion, Temple University, Philadelphia, Pa. Author of *Macmillan Atlas History of Christianity.*
RELIGION: *World Church Membership*

Logan, Robert G. Sportswriter, *Chicago Tribune.* Author of *The Bulls and Chicago—A Stormy Affair.*
SPORTS AND GAMES: *Basketball (in part)*

Luling, Virginia R. Social Anthropologist.
WORLD AFFAIRS: *Somalia*

Lunde, Anders S. Consultant; Adjunct Professor, Department of Biostatistics, University of North Carolina.
POPULATIONS AND POPULATION MOVEMENTS: *Demography*

McCauley, Martin. Lecturer in Russian and Soviet Institutions, School of Slavonic and East European Studies, University of London.

WORLD AFFAIRS: *Union of Soviet Socialist Republics*

Macdonald, Barrie. Reader in History, Massey University, Palmerston North, N.Z.
WORLD AFFAIRS: *Dependent States (in part); Fiji; Kiribati; Solomon Islands; Tonga; Tuvalu; Vanuatu; Western Samoa*

MacDonald, Trevor J. Manager, International Affairs, British Steel Corporation.
INDUSTRIAL REVIEW: *Iron and Steel.*

MacGregor-Morris, Pamela. Equestrian Correspondent, *Horse and Hound,* London.
SPORTS AND GAMES: *Show Jumping*

McKelvie, Roy. Rackets and Real Tennis Correspondent, *The Times,* London.
SPORTS AND GAMES: *Rackets; Real Tennis*

McLachlan, Keith S. Senior Lecturer, School of Oriental and African Studies, University of London.
WORLD AFFAIRS: *Iran*

Mallett, H. M. F. Editor, *Wool Record Weekly Market Report,* Bradford, England.
INDUSTRIAL REVIEW: *Textiles (in part)*

Mango, Andrew. Orientalist and Broadcaster.
BIOGRAPHIES *(in part);* WORLD AFFAIRS: *Turkey*

Marty, Martin E. Fairfax M. Cone Distinguished Service Professor of the History of Modern Christianity, University of Chicago.
RELIGION: Special Report

Mateja, James L. Auto Editor and Financial Reporter, *Chicago Tribune.*
INDUSTRIAL REVIEW: *Automobiles*

Matthíasson, Björn. Economist, Central Bank of Iceland.
WORLD AFFAIRS: *Iceland*

Mazie, David M. Associate of Carl T. Rowan, syndicated columnist. Free-lance Writer.
SOCIAL SECURITY AND WELFARE SERVICES *(in part)*

Mazze, Edward Mark. Dean and Professor of Marketing, School of Business Administration, Temple University, Philadelphia.
CONSUMER AFFAIRS *(in part);* INDUSTRIAL REVIEW: *Advertising*

Mermel, T. W. Consultant; formerly Chairman, Committee on World Register of Dams.
ENGINEERING PROJECTS: *Dams; Dams table*

Meyendorff, John. Professor of Church History and Patristics, St. Vladimir's Orthodox Theological Seminary; Professor of History, Fordham University, New York City.
RELIGION: *The Orthodox Church; Eastern Non-Chalcedonian Churches*

Miles, Peter W. University of Adelaide, Australia.
LIFE SCIENCES: *Entomology*

Miller, William P., Jr. Deputy Director and Curator, Jamaica Arts Center.
MUSEUMS: Sidebar

Millgate, Paul. Economist, Group Economics Department, Lloyds Bank PLC, London.
WORLD AFFAIRS: *Cuba; Dominican Republic; Uruguay*

Millikin, Sandra. Architectural Historian.
ARCHITECTURE; ART EXHIBITIONS AND ART SALES: *Art Exhibitions;* BIOGRAPHIES *(in part);* MUSEUMS *(in part)*

Modiano, Mario. Athens Correspondent, *The Times,* London
WORLD AFFAIRS: *Greece*

Monaco, Albert M., Jr. Executive Director, United States Volleyball Association, Colorado Springs, Colo.
SPORTS AND GAMES: *Volleyball*

Moore, John E. Hydrologist, Reston, Va.
EARTH SCIENCES: Hydrology

Morgenstern, Dan M. Director, Institute of Jazz Studies, Rutgers, The State University of New Jersey. Author of *Jazz People.*
MUSIC: *Jazz*

Morris, Jacqui M. Editor, *Oryx* magazine.
ENVIRONMENT *(in part)*

Morrison, Donald. Senior Editor, *Time* magazine.

PUBLISHING: *Newspapers (in part)*
Mortimer, Molly. Commonwealth Correspondent, *The Spectator,* London. Author of *Trusteeship in Practice; Kenya.*
WORLD AFFAIRS: *Commonwealth of Nations*
Mosey, Chris. Associate Editor, *Sweden Now,* Stockholm; Swedish Correspondent, *The Observer, Daily Mail,* and *The Times.*
WORLD AFFAIRS: *Sweden*
Muck, Terry Charles. Editor, *Leadership* magazine, Carol Stream, Ill.
SPORTS AND GAMES: *Handball*
Napier, Elspeth. Editor of publications of the Royal Horticultural Society.
GARDENING *(in part)*
Naylor, Ernest. Lloyd Roberts Professor of Zoology, University College of North Wales, Bangor.
LIFE SCIENCES: *Marine Biology*
Neill, John. Consultant, Submerged Combustion Ltd. Author of Climbers' Club Guides; and others.
SPORTS AND GAMES: *Mountaineering*
Nelson, Bert. Editor, *Track and Field News.* Author of *Olympic Track and Field.*
SPORTS AND GAMES: *Track and Field Sports*
Nelson, Susan K. Free-lance Journalist, Editor, and Broadcast Correspondent.
BIOGRAPHIES *(in part)*
Netschert, Bruce C. Vice-President, National Economic Research Associates, Inc., Washington, D.C.
ENERGY: *World Summary*
Neusner, Jacob. University Professor, Brown University, Providence, R.I. Author of *Judaism, The Evidence of the Mishnah.*
RELIGION: *Judaism*
Noblett, Geoffrey J. Tunneling Division Manager, Tarmac Construction International, Wolverhampton, England.
ENGINEERING PROJECTS: *Tunnels*
Noel, H. S. Consulting Editor, *World Fishing,* England
AGRICULTURE AND FOOD SUPPLIES: *Fisheries*
Norman, Geraldine. Saleroom Correspondent, *The Times,* London. Author of *The Sale of Works of Art.*
ART EXHIBITIONS AND ART SALES: *Art Sales*
Oates, David A. Assistant Copy Editor, Encyclopædia Britannica.
BIOGRAPHIES *(in part)*
Oberman, Bonnie. Free-lance Writer and Editor.
BIOGRAPHIES *(in part);* NOBEL PRIZES *(in part)*
O'Donoghue, Michael. Curator, Science Reference Library, London; Lecturer in Gemmology, City of London Polytechnic.
INDUSTRIAL REVIEW: *Gemstones*
O'Dwyer, Thomas. Director, Levant Bureau; Writer on East Mediterranean Affairs, Nicosia, Cyprus.
WORLD AFFAIRS: *Cyprus*
O'Keeffe, Margaret-Louise. Retired Press Officer, All England Women's Lacrosse Association.
SPORTS AND GAMES: *Lacrosse (in part)*
Olney, P. J. Curator of Birds and Reptiles, Zoological Society of London. Editor, *International Zoo Yearbook.*
BOTANICAL GARDENS AND ZOOS: *Zoos*
Osborne, Keith. Editor, *Rowing,* 1961–63. Author of *Boat Racing in Britain, 1715–1975.*
SPORTS AND GAMES: *Rowing*
Osterbind, Carter C. Associate, Gerontology Center, and Professor Emeritus of Economics, University of Florida.
INDUSTRIAL REVIEW: *Building and Construction*
Page, Campbell. Southern European Correspondent, *The Guardian,* London.
BIOGRAPHIES *(in part);* WORLD AFFAIRS: *Italy*
Palmer, John. Former European Editor, *The Guardian,* London.
WORLD AFFAIRS: *Western European Affairs; Western European Affairs:* Sidebar

Palmer, S. B. Reader, Department of Applied Physics, University of Hull, England.
PHYSICS
Parker, Sandy. Publisher of weekly international newsletter on fur industry; Co-publisher, *Fur World.*
INDUSTRIAL REVIEW: *Furs*
Paul, Charles Robert, Jr. Special Assistant to the Executive Director, U.S. Olympic Committee, Colorado Springs.
SPORTS AND GAMES: *Gymnastics; Weight Lifting*
Penfold, Robin C. Free-lance Writer in industrial topics. Editor, *Shell Polymers.* Author of *A Journalist's Guide to Plastics.*
INDUSTRIAL REVIEW: *Plastics*
Pertile, Lino. Reader in Italian, University of Sussex, England.
LITERATURE: *Italian*
Petherick, Karin. Reader in Swedish, University of London.
LITERATURE: Swedish
Pfeffer, Irving. Attorney. Author of *The Financing of Small Business; Perspectives on Insurance.*
ECONOMIC AFFAIRS: *Stock Exchanges (in part)*
Pierson, Donald C. Sportswriter, *Chicago Tribune.* Author of *Renaldo Nehemiah: The Bionic Hurdler.*
SPORTS AND GAMES: *Track and Field Sports:* Special Report
Pinfold, Geoffrey M. Director, NCL Consulting Engineers, London. Author of *Reinforced Concrete Chimneys and Towers.*
ENGINEERING PROJECTS: *Buildings*
Plotnik, Arthur. Editor, *American Libraries* magazine, American Library Association.
LIBRARIES *(in part)*
Polin, Thomas Hon Wing. Assistant Managing Editor, *Asiaweek,* Hong Kong.
BIOGRAPHIES *(in part);* WORLD AFFAIRS: *Brunei; Indonesia; Kampuchea; Korea; Laos; Malaysia; Singapore; Southeast Asian Affairs; Thailand; Vietnam*
Pollack, Jonathan D. Senior Staff Member, Political Science Department, Rand Corporation, Santa Monica, Calif.
WORLD AFFAIRS: *China; Taiwan*
Poppeliers, John. Chief, Section for Operations and Training, Cultural Heritage Division, UNESCO, Paris.
HISTORIC PRESERVATION
Post, Avery D. President, United Church of Christ, New York City.
RELIGION: *United Church of Christ*
Prasad, H. Y. Sharada. Information Adviser to the Prime Minister, New Delhi, India.
WORLD AFFAIRS: *India*
Prince, Rod. Journalist specializing in Caribbean matters.
WORLD AFFAIRS: *Antigua and Barbuda; Bahamas, The; Barbados; Dependent States (in part); Dominica; Grenada; Guyana; Jamaica; Saint Christopher and Nevis; Saint Lucia; Saint Vincent and the Grenadines; Trinidad and Tobago*
Ranger, Robin. Associate Professor, Defense and Strategic Studies, School of International Relations, University of Southern California.
MILITARY AFFAIRS; MILITARY AFFAIRS: Special Report
Rauch, Robert. Deputy Editor, Encyclopædia Britannica.
MUSIC: Sidebar
Ray, G. F. Senior Research Fellow, National Institute of Economic and Social Research, London.
INDUSTRIAL REVIEW: *Introduction*
Read, Anthony A. Director, Book Development Council, London.
PUBLISHING: *Books (in part)*
Rebelo, L. S. Reader, Department of Portuguese Studies, King's College, University of London.
LITERATURE: *Portuguese (in part)*

Reed, Dwight C. President, National Soft Drink Association, Washington, D.C.
INDUSTRIAL REVIEW: *Beverages (in part)*
Reid, J. H. Reader in German, University of Nottingham, England. Co-editor of *Renaissance and Modern Studies.*
LITERATURE: *German*
Ripley, Michael D. Senior Public Relations Officer, Brewers' Society, U.K.; formerly Editor, *Brewing Review.*
INDUSTRIAL REVIEW: *Beverages (in part)*
Robinson, David. Film Critic, *The Times,* London. Author of *A History of World Cinema.*
BIOGRAPHIES *(in part);* MOTION PICTURES *(in part)*
Roderick, John. Formerly Special Correspondent, Associated Press, Tokyo, and an expert on Chinese and Japanese affairs.
BIOGRAPHIES *(in part)*
Saeki, Shoichi. Professor of Literature, Chuo University, Tokyo. Author of *In Search of Japanese Ego.*
LITERATURE: *Japanese*
Saint-Amour, Robert. Professor, Department of Literary Studies, University of Quebec at Montreal.
LITERATURE: *French (in part)*
Sanders, Thomas H. B., Jr. Associate Professor of Metallurgy, Purdue University, West Lafayette, Ind.
MINING AND METALLURGY: *Metallurgy*
Sarahete, Yrjö. General Secretary, Fédération Internationale des Quilleurs, Helsinki.
SPORTS AND GAMES: *Bowling (in part)*
Sarmiento, Sergio. Editor-in-Chief, Spanish-language publications, Encyclopædia Britannica Publishers, Inc.
SPORTS AND GAMES: *Baseball (in part); Football (in part)*
Schneider, Stephen H. Head, Visitors Program, and Deputy Director, Advanced Study Program, National Center for Atmospheric Research, Boulder, Colo.
FEATURE ARTICLE: *Nuclear Winter: Its Discovery and Implications*
Schoenfield, Albert. Formerly Publisher, *Swimming World;* Vice-Chairman, U.S. Olympic Swimming Committee.
SPORTS AND GAMES: *Swimming*
Schöpflin, George. Lecturer in East European Political Institutions, London School of Economics and School of Slavonic and East European Studies, University of London.
WORLD AFFAIRS: *Czechoslovakia; Eastern European Affairs*
Schulman, Elias. Adjunct Professor, Queens College, City University of New York. Author of *Soviet-Yiddish Literature.*
LITERATURE: *Yiddish (in part)*
Seabury, Paul. Professor of Political Science, University of California, Berkeley.
BIBLIOGRAPHY: RECENT BOOKS *(in part);* WORLD AFFAIRS: *United Nations:* Special Report
Sears, Robert N. Editor, National Rifle Association, Washington, D.C.
SPORTS AND GAMES: *Shooting*
Shackleford, Peter. Chief of Studies, World Tourism Organization, Madrid.
INDUSTRIAL REVIEW: *Tourism*
Sharpe, Mitchell R. Science Writer; Historian, Alabama Space and Rocket Center, Huntsville. Author of *The Rocket Team.*
SPACE EXPLORATION
Shaw, T. R. Advisory Editor, *International Journal of Speleology.* Author of *History of Cave Science.*
SPORTS AND GAMES: *Spelunking*
Shelley, Andrew. Competitions Manager, Squash Rackets Association, U.K.
SPORTS AND GAMES: *Squash Rackets*
Shepherd, Melinda. Copy Editor, Encyclopædia Britannica.
BIOGRAPHIES *(in part)*

Simpson, Noel. Managing Director, Sydney Bloodstock Proprietary Ltd., Sydney.
SPORTS AND GAMES: *Horse Racing (in part)*
Smith, Donald. Editor, *Rubber World* magazine, Akron, Ohio.
INDUSTRIAL REVIEW: *Rubber*
Smith, Iola Lloyd. Free-lance Journalist; formerly Press Officer, BBC Wales.
EDUCATION: Special Report
Smith, Reuben W. Dean, Graduate School, and Professor of History, University of the Pacific, Stockton, Calif.
RELIGION: *Islam*
Smogorzewski, K. M. Writer on contemporary history. Founder and Editor, *Free Europe*, London.
BIOGRAPHIES *(in part)*; WORLD AFFAIRS: *Albania; Andorra; Bulgaria; Hungary; Liechtenstein; Luxembourg; Monaco; Mongolia; Poland; Political Parties; Romania; San Marino*
Spelman, Robert A. President, Home Furnishings Services, Washington, D.C.
INDUSTRIAL REVIEW: *Furniture*
Spittle, Hilary R. Publications Editor, American Power Boat Association.
SPORTS AND GAMES: *Motorboating*
Staerk, Melanie. Former Executive Editor, *Swiss Review of World Affairs*.
WORLD AFFAIRS: *Switzerland*
Steen, Lynn Arthur. Professor of Mathematics, St. Olaf College, Northfield, Minn. Author of *Mathematics Today*.
MATHEMATICS
Stern, Irwin. Assistant Professor of Portuguese, Columbia University, New York City.
LITERATURE: *Portuguese (in part)*
Støverud, Torbjørn. Honorary Research Fellow, University College, London.
LITERATURE: *Norwegian*
Strauss, Michael. Ski, Sports, and Feature Writer, *New York Times* (retired) and *Palm Beach Daily News*.
SPORTS AND GAMES: *Fencing*
Stuewer, Roger H. Professor of the History of Science and Technology, University of Minnesota, Minneapolis.
Revised *Macropædia* article: PLANCK
Sullivan, H. Patrick. Dean of the College and Professor of Religion, Vassar College, Poughkeepsie, N.Y.
RELIGION: *Hinduism*
Sweetinburgh, Thelma. Fashion Writer, Paris.
FASHION AND DRESS *(in part)*
Swift, Richard N. Professor Emeritus of Politics, New York University, New York City.
WORLD AFFAIRS: *United Nations*
Synan, Vinson. Assistant General Superintendent, Pentecostal Holiness Church. Author of *The Old Time Power*.
RELIGION: *Pentecostal Churches*
Taggart, Charles Johnson. Free-lance Writer.
BIOGRAPHIES *(in part)*
Taishoff, Lawrence B. President, Broadcasting Publications, Inc., and Publisher, *Broadcasting* magazine and others.
TELEVISION AND RADIO *(in part)*
Talbot, Nathan A. Manager, Committees on Publication, The First Church of Christ, Scientist, Boston.
RELIGION: *Church of Christ, Scientist*
Talbott, John A. Professor of Psychiatry, Cornell University Medical College, Ithaca, N.Y. Author of *Death of the Asylum*.
HEALTH AND DISEASE: Special Report *(in part)*
Tallan, Norman M. Chief, Metals and Ceramics Division, Materials Laboratory, Wright-Patterson Air Force Base, Dayton, Ohio.
INDUSTRIAL REVIEW: *Ceramics*
Teitz, Michael B. Professor of City and Regional Planning, University of California, Berkeley.
BIBLIOGRAPHY: RECENT BOOKS *(in part)*
Theiner, George. Editor, *Index on Censor-*

ship, London. Co-author of *The Kill Dog;* editor of *New Writing in Czechoslovakia.*
LITERATURE: *Eastern European; Russian (in part)*
Thomas, Theodore V. Free-lance Journalist and Press Consultant. Editor (1961–79), *British Toys and Hobbies.*
INDUSTRIAL REVIEW: *Games and Toys*
Tingay, Lance. Formerly Lawn Tennis Correspondent, *Daily Telegraph,* London. Author of *100 Years of Wimbledon.*
SPORTS AND GAMES: *Tennis*
Trigg, Robert H. Assistant Vice-President, Economic Research, New York Stock Exchange.
ECONOMIC AFFAIRS: *Stock Exchanges (in part)*
Trilling, Ossia. Co-editor and Contributor, *International Theatre.* Contributor, BBC, the *Financial Times,* London.
BIOGRAPHIES *(in part)*; THEATRE *(in part)*
UNHCR. The Office of the United Nations High Commissioner for Refugees.
POPULATIONS AND POPULATION MOVEMENTS: *Refugees*
Utt, Roger L. Assistant Professor of Spanish, Department of Romance Languages and Literatures, University of Chicago.
LITERATURE: *Spanish (in part)*
Vale, Norman K. Retired Director of News Services, The United Church of Canada.
RELIGION: *The United Church of Canada*
Van Doren, John. Executive Editor, *Great Ideas Today,* Encyclopædia Britannica, Inc.
BIBLIOGRAPHY: RECENT BOOKS *(in part)*
Verdi, Robert William. Sportswriter, *Chicago Tribune.*
SPORTS AND GAMES: *Baseball (in part)*
Vermeer, Ruth. Development Officer, International Organization of Consumer Unions, The Hague, Neth.
CONSUMER AFFAIRS *(in part)*
Vint, Arthur Kingsley. Counselor, International Table Tennis Federation, Hastings, East Sussex, England.
SPORTS AND GAMES: *Table Tennis*
Ward, Peter. Owner and Operator, Ward News Service, Ottawa; Parliamentary Reporter and Commentator.
WORLD AFFAIRS: *Canada:* Special Report
Warner, Antony C. Editor, *Drinks Marketing,* London.
INDUSTRIAL REVIEW: *Beverages (in part)*
Watson, Louise. Staff Editor, Encyclopædia Britannica, London.
BIOGRAPHIES *(in part)*; SPORTS AND GAMES: *Billiard Games (in part)*; WORLD AFFAIRS: *Dependent States (in part)*
Way, Diane Lois. Free-lance Historical Researcher.
BIOGRAPHIES *(in part)*
Webster, Robert E. Professor of Biochemistry, Duke University Medical Center.
LIFE SCIENCES: *Molecular Biology (in part)*
Weinthal, John R. Automotive Writer.
INDUSTRIAL REVIEW: *Automobiles (in part)*
Welsh, Melvin D. Administrator, English Basket Ball Association; Editor (1971–78), *Basketball Magazine.*
SPORTS AND GAMES: *Basketball (in part)*
Weston, Burns H. Bessie Dutton Murray Distinguished Professor of Law, University of Iowa, Iowa City.
Revised *Macropædia* article: HUMAN RIGHTS
Whelan, John. Publisher and Special Reports Publisher, *Middle East Economic Digest,* London.
BIOGRAPHIES *(in part)*; WORLD AFFAIRS: *Bahrain; Egypt; Iraq; Jordan; Kuwait; Lebanon; Middle Eastern and North African Affairs; Oman; Qatar; Saudi Arabia; Syria; United Arab Emirates; Yemen, People's Democratic Republic of; Yemen Arab Republic*
Wijngaard, Barbara. Economist, Group Economics Department, Lloyds Bank PLC, London.

WORLD AFFAIRS: *Mexico*
Wildavsky, Aaron. Professor, Political Science Department, Graduate School of Public Policy, and Survey Research Center, University of California, Berkeley.
BIBLIOGRAPHY: RECENT BOOKS *(in part)*
Wilkinson, Gordon. Information Consultant and Senior Editor, *The Analytical Instrument Industry Report.*
CHEMISTRY; INDUSTRIAL REVIEW: *Wood Products*
Wilkinson, John R. Sportswriter, East Midland Provincial Newspapers Ltd., U.K.
SPORTS AND GAMES: *Cycling*
Williams, L. Pearce. John Stambaugh Professor of the History of Science, Cornell University, Ithaca, N.Y.
Revised *Macropædia* article: FARADAY
Williams, Michael E. J. Golf Correspondent, *Daily Telegraph,* London.
SPORTS AND GAMES: *Golf*
Williams, Raymond L. Associate Professor of Spanish, Washington University, St. Louis, Mo.
LITERATURE: *Spanish (/in part)*
Williamson, Trevor. Chief Sports Subeditor, *Daily Telegraph,* London.
FOOTBALL: *Association Football (in part)*
Wilson, Michael. Consultant Editor, Jane's Publishing Co. Ltd.
INDUSTRIAL REVIEW: *Aerospace*
Witte, Randall E. Associate Editor, *The Western Horseman* magazine, Colorado Springs, Colo.
SPORTS AND GAMES: *Rodeo*
Wood, Kenneth H. Retired Editor, *Adventist Review;* President, and Chairman of Trustees, Ellen G. White Estate, Inc.
RELIGION: *Seventh-day Adventist Church*
Woods, Elizabeth. Writer. Author of *The Yellow Volkswagen; Gone; Men;* others.
LITERATURE: *English (in part)*
Woollen, Anthony. Editor (1959–79), *Food Manufacture,* London. Editor, *Food Industries Manual* (20th ed.).
AGRICULTURE AND FOOD SUPPLIES: *Food Processing*
Wooler, Michael. Economist, Group Economics Department, Lloyds Bank PLC, London.
BIOGRAPHIES *(in part)*; WORLD AFFAIRS: *Chile; Colombia; Portugal; Spain; Venezuela*
Woolley, David. Air Transport Editor, *Interavia,* London.
TRANSPORTATION *(in part)*
Worsnop, Richard L. Associate Editor, Editorial Research Reports, Washington, D.C.
WORLD AFFAIRS: *United States*
Wright, Almon R. Retired Senior Historian, U.S. Department of State.
WORLD AFFAIRS: *Panama*
Wright, Robin B. Beirut Correspondent, *The Sunday Times,* London.
WORLD AFFAIRS: *Middle Eastern and North African Affairs:* Sidebar
Wyllie, Peter John. Chairman, Division of Geological and Planetary Sciences, California Institute of Technology.
EARTH SCIENCES: *Geology and Geochemistry*
Yang, Winston L. Y. Professor of Chinese Studies, Department of Asian Studies, Seton Hall University, South Orange, N.J.
BIOGRAPHIES *(in part)*; LITERATURE: *Chinese*
Young, M. Norvel. Chancellor, Pepperdine University, Malibu, Calif. Author of *Preachers of Today.*
RELIGION: *Churches of Christ*
Young, Susan. News Editor, *Church Times,* London.
BIOGRAPHIES *(in part)*; RELIGION: *Anglican Communion*
Yuenger, James L. Director of News and Information, University of Chicago.
BIOGRAPHIES *(in part)*

Index

This index covers both *Britannica Book of the Year* (cumulative for six years) and *Britannica World Data*.

Entries in black type are titles of articles in the *Book of the Year*; an accompanying page number in light type shows where the article appears in this volume. Numbers in black type indicate the years in which such an article appears. For example, "Archaeology 84–80" indicates that the article "Archaeology" appeared every year from 1980 through 1984, and may be found in alphabetical order in each of those editions. References to article titles that appeared in previous years also appear with title and year in black type.

Indented entries in light type that follow black type article titles refer by page number to other places in the text where the subject of the article is discussed. Light type entries that are not indented refer by page number to subjects that are not themselves the titles of articles. Names of people covered in biographies and obituaries are listed as references to the sections **"Biographies"** and **"Obituaries"** within the article "People of the Year"; in those sections names appear in alphabetical order. References to illustrations are by page number, and are preceded by the abbreviation "il."

The index uses word-by-word alphabetization (treating a word as one or more characters separated by a space from the next word). Names beginning with "Mc" and "Mac" are alphabetized as "Mac"; "St." is treated as "Saint."

Tables of international statistics in *Britannica World Data* are indexed by topic and page number. Data about individual countries are referred to under the name of the country; for example under Argentina, "see also WORLD DATA." There the nations are arranged in alphabetical order.

Enke / France 973

Enke, Karin
winter sports 430
Entomology 297
botanical research 300
Environment 243. *See* **Environment 84–80**
acid rain 235
Eastern European devastation 547
rain forests and man's encroachment (special report) **82**
state protection programs 572
toxic waste (special report) **84**
U.S. housing market (special report) **80**
Environment, Department of (U.K.)
derelict land report 246
Environmental Assessment Panel (Can. agency)
Beaufort Sea oil development 607
Environmental Protection Agency (EPA)
acid rain research 244
Chesapeake Bay contamination study 572
fuel efficient cars 268
hydrological studies 201
Enzyme
molecular biology research 302
Epidermal growth factor
cancer role 254
Epinephrine
molecular biology mechanism 301
EPLF (Eritrean People's Liberation Front, Eth.) 465
Equal Employment Opportunity Commission v. *Shell Oil Co.*
employment discrimination 292
Equatorial Guinea 464. *See* **Equatorial Guinea 84–80**
see also WORLD DATA
Equestrian Sports 84–80. *See* Horse racing; Show jumping **85**
Erbium
low-temperature physics 346
Eriez Magnetics 329
Erim, Nihat: *see* **Obituaries 81**
Eritrea, Eth. (reg.)
African affairs 456
agriculture and food supplies problems 150
Eritrean People's Liberation Front (EPLF, Eth.) 465
Erlich, Simcha: *see* **Obituaries 84**
Ershad, Hossain Mohammad: *see* **Biographies 83**
Bangladeshi politics 507
ESA (European Space Agency)
space exploration 370
Espie, Stan
lawn bowls 407
Espriella, Ricardo de la
Panamanian politics 579
Estonian Soviet Socialist Republic, U.S.S.R.
internal Soviet politics 554
E.T. (Emerging Technologies)
military affairs 323
ETA (Euzkadi ta Azkatasuna, Sp. pol. group) 540
Etchebaster, Pierre: *see* **Obituaries 81**
Ethiopia 464. *See* **Ethiopia 84–80**
African affairs 456
agriculture and food supplies 150
anthropological findings 164
Djiboutian relations 463
famine
Church of Christ relief efforts 359
consequences 457
human rights 263
legal decisions 293
Ethylene
Japanese use 271
rubber industry 280
Etzel, Ed
shooting sports 413
Euler-Chelpin, Ulf Svante von: *see* **Obituaries 84**
Eurobond
economic affairs 219
Europa Carton (co., W.Ger.)
food processing 162
European affairs
race relations 355
refugees 350
winter storms 202
European Communities (EC) 521
agriculture and food supplies 150
aid to Seychelles 473
anti-air pollution directives 234
British budget contribution 545
common agricultural policy 522
common fisheries policy 160
Golf Cooperation Council relations 481
IBM investigation 285
international relations
Latin-American affairs 573
Portugal 539
Saudi Arabia 495
Spain 541
product safety conference 183
sulfur dioxide emissions study 245
U.S. iron and steel agreement 275
European Council of Chemical Manufacturers Federation (CEFIC) 271
European Investment Bank
Ghana 466
European Laboratory for Particle Physics (CERN)
research 345
European Ministerial Conference on the Environment
protection of bodies of water 245
European Molecular Biology Laboratory (Heidelberg, W.Ger.)
entomological research 297
European Parliament
Green Party election 248
Western European affairs 522
European Space Agency (ESA)
comet probe 199
space exploration 370
European Unity 84–80. *See* **Eastern European Affairs 85**. *See* **Western European Affairs 85**
Euphausia superba (krill)
ocean habitation 299
Euwe, Max: *see* **Obituaries 82**
Euzkadi ta Azkatasuna (ETA, Span. pol. group) 540
Evans, Bill (William John Evans): *see* **Obituaries 81**
Evans, Charles: *see* **Obituaries 80**
Evans, Gareth
Australian politics 595
Evans, Harold Matthew: *see* **Biographies 82**
Evans, Sir Richard
Hong Kong-British relations i!. 603
Evans of Hungershall, Benjamin Ifor Evans, Baron: *see* **Obituaries 83**
Evaton, S.Af. 474
"Every Picture Tells a Story"
motion pictures 332
Evren, Kenan
Turkey politics 497
Ewing, Patrick
basketball 382
"Example" (play)
theatre in education 229
Exchange and payments, international
economic affairs 217
national products and accounts (table) 850
Exclusive economic zone (EEZ)
fishing 159
mining 328
Exercise
heart disease dangers 254
Exeter, David George Brownlow Cecil, 6th Marquess: *see* **Obituaries 82**
Extinction (biol.)
astronomical cause of dinosaur demise 176
catastrophism 198
Exxon Shipping Co. (U.S. co.)
shipbuilding 281
Eyadema, Gnassingbe
Togolese affairs 478

F

Fabbri, Diego: *see* **Obituaries 81**
Fabius, Laurent: *see* **Biographies 85**
Cabinet appointment 526
job skill training 225
Fabre-Luce, Alfred: *see* **Obituaries 84**
Fabricaciones Militares (Arg. co.)
reform 580
"Factory" (play)
theatre in education 230
Fagerholm, Karl-August: *see* **Obituaries 85**
Fahd ibn ʿAbd al-ʿAziz al-Saud: *see* **Biographies 83**
Saudi oil production 495
Faiz, Faiz Ahmad: *see* **Obituaries 85**
Falkland Islands 603
Anglo-Argentine relations 581
Argentine court martials 580
Latin American affairs 573
Fall, Ibrahima 472
Fallaci, Oriana: *see* **Biographies 81**
Falwell, Rev. Jerry: *see* **Biographies 81**
religion and politics 357
Family
world vital statistics (table) 844
"Family Game"
motion pictures 335
Famine
African affairs 457, il. 458
Churches of Christ relief efforts 359
Ethiopia 464
UN concern 448
Fang Yi: *see* **Biographies 80**
"Fanny and Alexander"
motion pictures 332
FAO: *see* Food and Agriculture Organization, UN
Farabundo Martí National Liberation Front (FMLN, pol. group, El Sal.) 575
Farago, Ladislas: *see* **Obituaries 81**
FARC (Colombian Revolutionary Armed Forces, guerrilla group)
Colombian government treaty 585
Fargiss, Joe
show jumping il. 414
Farming: *see* Agriculture and Food Supplies
Farnsworth, Scott 415
Farrakhan, Louis: *see* **Biographies 85**
Islam in the U.S. 366, il. 367
Jackson controversy 564
Jewish slurs 357
Farrell, Edelmiro J.: *see* **Obituaries 81**
Farrell, James Gordon: *see* **Obituaries 80**
Farrell, James Thomas: *see* **Obituaries 80**
Fashion and Dress 250. *See* **Fashion and Dress 84–80**
Fassbinder, Rainer Warner: *see* **Obituaries 83**
Fauconnier, Yvon 413
Fava, Giuseppe
death 536
"Favoris de la Lune, Les"
motion pictures 334
Fawzi, Mahmoud: *see* **Obituaries 82**
FBI (Federal Bureau of Investigation)
espionage arrest 188
FCC: *see* Federal Communications Commission
FDA (Food and Drug Administration)
generic drug approval 279
FDR (Democratic Revolutionary Front, El Sal.) 575
Feather star
oceanographic research 299
Febres, Cordero, León: *see* **Biographies 85**
Ecuadorian election 586, il. 585
Federal Bureau of Investigation (FBI)
espionage arrest 188
Federal Communications Commission (FCC)
broadcasting 265
station ownership 435
Federal Executive Council (Nig.) 471
Federal Reserve Board
economic affairs 206
Federal Trade Commission (FTC)
used car regulations 183
Fédération Aéronautique Internationale 375
Fédération Internationale de Basketball Amateur 383
Federation of Nature and National Parks
acid rain deaths 244
Fedorchuk, Vitaly: *see* **Biographies 83**
Feigenbaum, Clive H.
securities 342
Feldman, Marty: *see* **Obituaries 83**
Felici, Pericle Cardinal: *see* **Obituaries 83**
"Femtionde frälsaren, Den" (Jersild)
Swedish literature 311
Fencing 392
Fenton, Clyde Cornwall: *see* **Obituaries 83**
"Ferment in Central America" (Calvert) **81**
Ferencsik, Janos: *see* **Obituaries 85**
Fernandez, Royes: *see* **Obituaries 81**
Fernández-Miranda y Hevia, Torcuato: *see* **Obituaries 81**
Ferranti, Sir Vincent Ziani de: *see* **Obituaries 81**
Ferrari, Maxime
Seychelles politics 473
Ferraro, Geraldine Anne: *see* **Biographies 85**
abortion controversy 362
election defeat 562, 564, il.
religion and politics 357
Ferras, Christian: *see* **Obituaries 83**
Ferreira Aldunate, Wilson
Uruguayan politics 588
Fertility rates: *see* Demography
"Festival of Love" ("Ustav")
motion pictures 335
FGD (flue gas desulfurization)
sulfur emission reductions 234
Fianna Fail (pol. party, Ire.) 533
Fiat (It. co.)
auto sales 267
Fibre optics
analytical instruments 181
ceramics industry 270, il. 274
Fiedler, Arthur: *see* **Obituaries 80**
Field Hockey 393. *See* **Field Hockey and Lacrosse 84–80**
Fielding, Joy: *see* **Biographies 84**
Fields, Dame Gracie: *see* **Obituaries 80**
Fignon, Laurent 391
Figure skating 427, 428
Figueiredo, João Baptista de Oliveira
Brazilian politics 582
Fiji 600. *See* **Fiji 84–80**
see also WORLD DATA
Film (photo.)
photographic innovations 343
"Financial Times" (news.)
stock exchanges 222
"Finding the Centre" (Naipaul)
English literature 305
Fine Gael (pol. party, Ire.) 533
Finland 526. *See* **Finland 84–80**
Soviet defections 554
see also WORLD DATA
Finletter, Thomas Knight: *see* **Obituaries 81**
Finnbogadóttir, Vigdís: *see* **Biographies 81**
Icelandic politics 533
Finney, Albert: *see* **Biographies 85**
FIRA (Foreign Investment Review Agency, Can.)
Canadian-U.S. relations 559
Fire
Indonesian forest damage 246
Firmenich, Mario
extradition to Argentina 580
First, Ruth: *see* **Obituaries 83**
Firyubin, Nikolay Pavlovich: *see* **Obituaries 84**
Fish
marine biology research 299
Fisheries 159. *See* **Fisheries 84–80**
world extractive industries (table) 874
Fishing Products International
fishing industry problems 160
Fisk, James Brown: *see* **Obituaries 82**
Fit to Fight (horse)
horse racing il. 403
FitzGerald, Garret: *see* **Biographies 82**
British-Irish relations 545
Irish politics 533
Fitzgibbon, Robert Louis Constantine Lee-Dillon: *see* **Obituaries 84**
Fitzmaurice, Sir Gerald Gray: *see* **Obituaries 83**
Fitzsimmons, Frank Edward: *see* **Obituaries 82**
Five Nations Tournament 395
Fix, Paul: *see* **Obituaries 84**
Fixx, James Fuller: *see* **Obituaries 85**
death from overexertion 254
Flatt, Lester Raymond: *see* **Obituaries 80**
Flat-water racing 410
"Flaubert's Parrot" (Barnes)
English literature 304
Fletcher, Harvey: *see* **Obituaries 82**
Fletcher, James
U.S. strategic defense system study 321
Flick (W.Ger. co.)
scandal 529
Flight or fight response (biol.)
epinephrine mechanism research 301
Float, Jeff 416
Floods
hydrology 201
Korean devastation 504
"Flourishing, Worldwide, Deadly: The Open Market in Arms" (Kaldor) **84**
Flue gas desulfurization (FGD)
sulfur emission reductions 234
Flutie, Doug 398
FMLN (Farabundo Martí National Liberation Front, pol. group, El Sal.) 575
"FMR" (U.S. mag.)
new publications 353
Focke, Henrich Karl Johann: *see* **Obituaries 80**
Fogarty, Anne Whitney: *see* **Obituaries 81**
"Folding Image, The: Screens by Western Artists of the 19th and 20th Centuries" (art exhibit) 174
Follows, Sir Denis: *see* **Obituaries 84**
Fomalhaut (star)
astronomical observations 177
Fonda, Henry Jaynes: *see* **Obituaries 83**
Fontanet, Joseph: *see* **Obituaries 81**
Fontanne, Lynn (Lillie Louise Fontanne): *see* **Obituaries 84**
Food: *see* Agriculture and Food Supplies
Food Act 1984 (U.K.) 161
Food and Agriculture Organization, UN (FAO)
agriculture and food supplies 150
aid to African nations
São Tomé and Príncipe 472
report on African famines 457
Rome conference on fishing 161
Food and Drug Administration (FDA)
Bendectin controversy 258
generic drug approval 279
Food Labelling Regulations 1984 (U.K.) 161
Food Processing 161. *See* **Food Processing 84–80**
unsanitary conditions in Poland 547
Food Research Association (FRA, U.K.) 163
Foot, Michael: *see* **Biographies 81**
Football 396. *See* **Football 84–80**
advertising revenue 265
broadcasting rights 437
college scandals (special report) **82**
Ford Motors (U.S. auto co.)
management bonus controversy 267
FOREGE (data base)
food processing use 163
"Foreign Affairs" (Lurie)
American literature 305
Foreign Investment Review Agency (FIRA, Can.)
Canadian-U.S. relations 559
Foreman, Carl: *see* **Obituaries 85**
Forest Fires
Indonesian environmental damage 246
wood industry protection 284
Forestry
chemical damage 245
world extractive industries (table) 874
Forlani, Arnaldo: *see* **Biographies 81**
Forman, Milos
motion pictures 332
Forssmann, Werner: *see* **Obituaries 80**
Ft. Gulick (mil. school, Panama)
Cuban-U.S. relations 579
"Fort Saganne"
motion pictures 333
Fortas, Abe: *see* **Obituaries 83**
Forum for a New Ireland
British-Irish relations 545
Foster, Harold R.: *see* **Obituaries 83**
Foster, Norman Robert: *see* **Biographies 84**
Foucault, Michel Paul: *see* **Obituaries 85**
Fouché, Jacobus Johannes: *see* **Obituaries 81**
"Foundation for Survival" (Khindaria) **81**
Fountain House, N.Y., N.Y.
mental patient care 256
Fountain Place, Dallas, Tex.
architectural design 171
Fowler, David
acid rain report 245
Fox, Carol: *see* **Obituaries 82**
Fox, Terrence ("Terry") Stanley: *see* **Obituaries 82.** *See* **Biographies 81**
Fox, Virgil Keel: *see* **Obituaries 81**
Foy, Eddie, Jr.: *see* **Obituaries 84**
FP-25 (Popular Forces of April 25, guerrilla group, Port.) 539
FPMR (Manuel Rodríguez Patriotic Front, guerrilla group, Chile) 583
FRA (Food Research Association, U.K.) 163
Fraga Iribarne, Manuel 541
France 526. *See* **France 84–80**
African affairs 456

Now there's a way to identify all your fine books with flair and style. As part of our continuing service to you, Britannica Home Library Service, Inc. is proud to be able to offer you the fine quality item shown on the next page.

Booklovers will love the heavy-duty personalized embosser. Now you can personalize all your fine books with the mark of distinction, just the way all the fine libraries of the world do.

To order this item, please type or print your name, address and zip code on a plain sheet of paper. (Note special instructions for ordering the embosser). Please send a check or money order only (your money will be refunded in full if you are not delighted) for the full amount of purchase, including postage and handling, to:

Britannica Home Library Service, Inc.
Attn: Yearbook Department
Post Office Box 6137
Chicago, Illinois 60680

(Please make remittance payable to: Britannica Home Library Service, Inc.)

IN THE BRITANNICA TRADITION OF QUALITY...

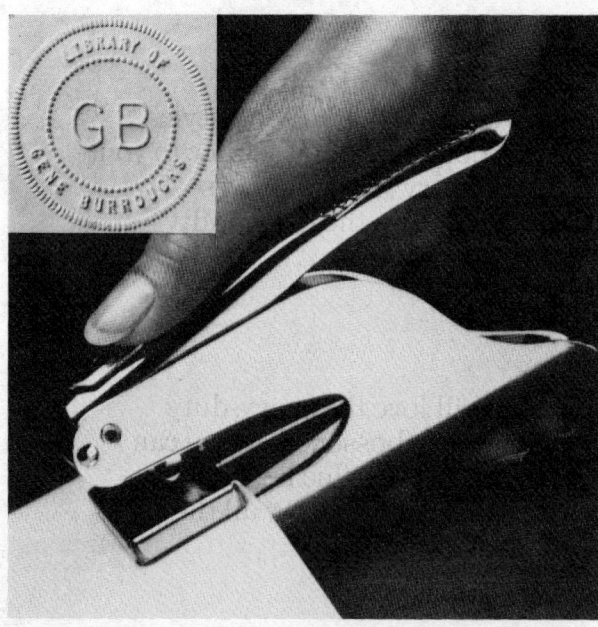

PERSONAL EMBOSSER

A mark of distinction for your fine books. A book embosser just like the ones used in libraries. The 1½″ seal imprints "Library of _____" (with the name of your choice) and up to three centered initials. Please type or print clearly BOTH full name (up to 26 letters including spaces between names) and up to three initials.
Please allow six weeks for delivery.

Just **$20.00**

plus $2.00 shipping and handling

This offer available only in the United States.
Illinois residents please add sales tax

Britannica Home Library Service, Inc.